The Archaeological Periods of Palestine

PERIOD	Wright	Dever	Mazar	Meyers
Paleolithic	100,000-8000			Upper Paleolithic 43,000-18,000
Mesolithic	8000-5500	12000-7500		Epipaleolithic (Mesolithic) 18,000-8500
Neolithic	5500-4000	7500-4000	[illegible]	[illegible]ottery A) [illegible]200 [illegible]ottery B) [illegible]000 [illegible]ry A) 6000-5000 [illegible]ry B) 5000-4500
Chalcolithic	4000-3300	4000-3150	4300-3300	Early 4500-3800 Late (Proto-Urban) 3800-3400
Early Bronze	3000-2100	I 3150-2850 II 2850-2650 III 2650-2350 IV/IIIA 2350-2200	I 3300-3050 II-III 3050-2300 IV/MB I 2300-2000	IA-B 3400-3100 II 3100-2650 III 2650-2300 IVA-C (Intermediate EB-MB, MB I) 2300-2000
Middle Bronze	2000-1500	I 2200-2000 IIA 2000-1750 IIB 1750-1550	IIA 2000-1800/1750 IIB-C 1800/1750-1550	I (IIA) 2000-1800 II (IIB) 1800-1650 III (IIC) 1650-1500
Late Bronze	1500-1200	I 1550-1400 IIA 1400-1300 IIB 1300-1200	1550-1400 IIA-B 1400-1200	IA 1500-1450 IB 1450-1400 IIA 1400-1300 IIB 1300-1200
Early Iron/ Iron I	1200-1000	IA 1200-1150 IB 1150-1000	IA 1200-1150 IB 1150-1000	IA 1200-1125 IB 1125-1000 IC (IIA) 1000-925
Iron II	1000-600	IIA 1000-900 IIB 900-800 IIC 800-586	IIA 1000-925 IIB 925-720 IIC 720-586	IIA (IIB) 925-722 IIB (IIC) 722-586
Iron III	600-330			(Neo-Babylonian) 586-520
Persian		586-332		Early 520-450 Late 450-332
Hellenistic	333-63	I 332-152 II (Hasmonean) 152-37		Early 332-200 Late 200-63
Roman	63 B.C.E.-325 C.E.	I (Herodian) 37 B.C.E.-70 C.E. II, III 70-324		Early 63 B.C.E.-135 C.E. Middle 135-250 Late 250-363
Byzantine		324-640		Early 363-460 Late 460-638
Early Arab		640-1099		638-1099
Crusader		1099-1291		Crusader/Ayyubid 1099-1291
Mamluk		1291-1516		Late Arab 1291-1516
Ottoman				1516-1917

G. E. Wright, *Biblical Archaeology* (Philadelphia, 1957); S. Paul and W. G. Dever, eds., *Biblical Archaeology* (Jerusalem, 1974); A. Mazar, *Archaeology of the Land of the Bible* (New York, 1990); E. M. Meyers, ed., *The Oxford Encyclopedia of Archaeology in the Near East* (Oxford, 1997)

EERDMANS
DICTIONARY *of the* BIBLE

EERDMANS DICTIONARY

William B. Eerdmans Publishing Company

...of the BIBLE

David Noel Freedman
Editor-in-Chief

Allen C. Myers
Associate Editor

Astrid B. Beck
Managing Editor

...Rapids, Michigan / Cambridge, U.K.

Published 2000 by Wm. B. Eerdmans Publishing Co.
255 Jefferson Ave. S.E., Grand Rapids, Michigan 49503 /
P.O. Box 163, Cambridge CB3 9PU U.K.
www.eerdmans.com

Printed in the United States of America

05 04 03 02 01 00 7 6 5 4 3 2 1

Library of Congress Cataloging-in-Publication Data

Eerdmans dictionary of the Bible / David Noel Freedman, editor-in-chief;
Allen C. Myers, associate editor; Astrid B. Beck, managing editor.
p. cm.
Includes bibliographical references.
ISBN 0-8028-2400-5 (hardcover: alk. paper)
1. Bible — Dictionaries. I. Title: Dictionary of the Bible.
II. Freedman, David Noel, 1922- III. Myers, Allen C., 1945-
IV. Beck, Astrid B.
BS440.E44 2000
220.3 — dc21 00-056124

Contents

GRAND

List of Maps

Consulting Editors

David E. Aune
Professor of New Testament
and Early Christianity
University of Notre Dame
Notre Dame, IN

Bruce C. Birch
Professor of Old Testament
Wesley Theological Seminary
Washington, DC

John J. Collins
Holmes Professor of Old Testament
Yale University Divinity School
New Haven, CT

William G. Dever
Professor of Near Eastern Archaeology
and Anthropology
University of Arizona
Tucson, AZ

Everett Ferguson
Professor Emeritus of Bible
Abilene Christian University
Abilene, TX

Victor Paul Furnish
University Distinguished Professor
of New Testament
Perkins School of Theology,
Southern Methodist University
Dallas, TX

Carol Meyers
Professor of Religion
Duke University
Durham, NC

J. Maxwell Miller
Professor of Old Testament
Candler School of Theology,
Emory University
Curator, Fernbank Museum
of Natural History
Atlanta, GA

James C. Moyer
Professor of Religious Studies,
Head, Department of Religious Studies
Southwest Missouri State University
Springfield, MO

Jack M. Sasson
Mary Jane Wirthen Professor
of Judaic and Biblical Studies
The Divinity School,
Vanderbilt University
Nashville, TN

Marion L. Soards
Professor of New Testament Studies
Louisville Presbyterian
Theological Seminary
Louisville, KY

James C. VanderKam
Professor of Hebrew Scriptures
University of Notre Dame
Notre Dame, IN

Contributors

Susan Ackerman, Associate Professor of Religion, Dartmouth College, Hanover, NH
James R. Adair, Jr., Director, ATLA Center for Electronic Texts in Religion, American Theological Library Association, Chicago, IL
Sujey Adarve-Valdes, Graduate Student,Wheaton College, Wheaton, IL
Martin C. Albl, Presentation College, Aberdeen, SD
Dale C. Allison, Jr., Associate Professor of New Testament and Early Christianity, Pittsburgh Theological Seminary, Pittsburgh, PA
Gary A. Anderson, Professor of Old Testament, Harvard Divinity School, Cambridge, MA
Robert T. Anderson, Professor of Religious Studies, Michigan State University, Lansing, MI
Stephen J. Andrews, Associate Professor of Old Testament and Hebrew, Southeastern Baptist Theological Seminary, Wake Forest, NC
Victoria Andrews, Graduate Student, Union Theological Seminary, New York, NY
Deborah Ann Appler, Assistant Professor of Hebrew Bible, Moravian Theological Seminary, Bethlehem, PA
Gary P. Arbino, Assistant Professor of Old Testament, Golden Gate Baptist Theological Seminary, Mill Valley, CA
Kenneth J. Archer, Adjunct Instructor, Ashland Theological Seminary, Ashland, OH
Melissa L. Archer, Instructor of New Testament and Greek, Ashland Theological Seminary, Ashland, OH
Randal A. Argall, Assistant Professor of Religion, Jamestown College, Jamestown, ND
Richard S. Ascough, Assistant Professor of New Testament, Queen's Theological College, Kingston, ON
Paul S. Ash, Ph.D. Candidate, Emory University, Atlanta, GA
Rodney Ashlock, Ph.D. Student, Baylor University, Waco, TX
Kenneth Atkinson, Instructor of Religion, Temple University, Philadelphia, PA
Melissa M. Aubin, Assistant Professor of Religion, Florida State University, Tallahassee, FL
Hector Avalos, Assistant Professor of Religious Studies; Chair, Latino Studies Program, Iowa State University, Ames, IA
Alan J. Avery-Peck, Kraft-Hiatt Professor in Judaic Studies, College of the Holy Cross, Worcester, MA
Lloyd R. Bailey, Visiting Professor of Religion, Methodist College, Fayetteville, NC
Martha Jean Mugg Bailey, Graduate Student, Claremont Graduate University, Claremont, CA
Randall C. Bailey, Andrew H. Mellon Professor of Hebrew Bible, Interdenominational Theological Center, Atlanta, GA
Samuel E. Balentine, Professor of Old Testament, Baptist Theological Seminary at Richmond, Richmond, VA
Andrew H. Bartelt, Chairman, Department of Exegetical Theology; Dean of Administration, Concordia Theological Seminary, St. Louis, MO
Alicia Batten, Instructor in Theology, University of St. Thomas, St. Paul, MN
Mary Ann Beavis, Assistant Professor of Religious Studies, St. Thomas More College, University of Saskatchewan, Saskatoon, SK

Lyn M. Bechtel, Drew Theological School, Madison, NJ
David R. Beck, Assistant Professor of New Testament and Greek, Southeastern Baptist Theological Seminary, Wake Forest, NC
Bob Becking, Professor, Faculty of Theology, University of Utrecht, Utrecht, Netherlands
Alice Ogden Bellis, Assistant Professor of Old Testament Language and Literature, Howard University School of Divinity, Washington, DC
Don C. Benjamin, Executive Director, Kino Institute of Theology, Phoenix, AZ
Jon L. Berquist, Academic Editor, Chalice Press, St. Louis, MO
Allan R. Bevere, Associate Minister, Mentor United Methodist Church; Adjunct Professor, Ashland Theological Seminary, Mentor, OH
Arnold Gottfried Betz, Visiting Assistant Professor of Hebrew and Old Testament, The University of the South School of Theology, Sewanee, TN
Julye Bidmead, Ph.D. Candidate, Vanderbilt University, Nashville, TN
Gerald M. Bilkes, Ph.D. Candidate, Princeton Theological Seminary, Princeton, NJ
Ira Birdwhistell, Assistant Professor of Religion, Georgetown College, Georgetown, KY
Lawrence Boadt, President, Paulist Press, New York, NY
Gabriele Boccaccini, Associate Professor of Second Temple Judaism and Early Rabbinic Literature, The University of Michigan, Ann Arbor, MI
Walter R. Bodine, Research Affiliate, Babylonian Collection, Yale University, New Haven, CT
Karla G. Bohmbach, Assistant Professor of Religion, Susquehanna University, Susquehanna, PA
Oded Borowski, Associate Professor of Biblical Archaeology and Hebrew, Emory University, Atlanta, GA
Hendrik L. Bosman, Professor, Faculty of Theology, University of Stellenbosch, Matieland, South Africa
Steven C. Bouma-Prediger, Associate Professor of Religion, Hope College, Holland, MI
Barbara E. Bowe, Associate Professor of Biblical Studies, Catholic Theological Union, Chicago, IL
Mary Petrina Boyd, Ph.D. Candidate, Union Theological Seminary in Virginia, Kent, WA
Laurie J. Braaten, Associate Professor of Old Testament, Eastern Nazarene College, Quincy, MA
Christian M. M. Brady, Director, Jewish Studies, Tulane University, New Orleans, LA
Monica L. W. Brady, University of Notre Dame, Notre Dame, IN
Robin Gallaher Branch, Ph.D. Candidate, University of Texas at Austin, Austin, TX
Joachim Braun, Professor of Musicology, Bar-Ilan University, Ramat-gan, Israel
H. Alan Brehm, Assistant Professor of New Testament, Southwestern Baptist Theological Seminary, Fort Worth, TX
James E. Brenneman, Episcopal Theological School at Claremont, South Pasadena, CA
B. Keith Brewer, Ph.D. Candidate, Drew University, Madison, NJ
Carl Bridges, Professor of New Testament, Johnson Bible College, Knoxville, TN
Thomas V. Brisco, Associate Professor of Biblical Backgrounds and Archaeology, Southwestern Baptist Theological Seminary, Fort Worth, TX
Ann Graham Brock, Ph.D. Candidate, Harvard University, Cambridge, MA
James A. Brooks, Professor of New Testament, Bethel Theological Seminary, St. Paul, MN
Alexandra R. Brown, Visitng Associate Professor of Religious Studies, Wake Forest University School of Divinity, Winston-Salem, NC
Walter E. Brown, Professor of Old Testament and Hebrew, New Orleans Baptist Theological Seminary, New Orleans, LA
William P. Brown, Associate Professor of Old Testament, Union Theological Seminary in Virginia, Richmond, VA
Daniel C. Browning, Jr., Associate Professor of Religion, William Carey College, Hattiesburg, MS
Gordon Brubacher, Associate Professor of Biblical Studies and Archaeology, Doane College, Crete, NE
Alan Ray Buescher, Adjunct Teacher, Southwestern Baptist Theological Seminary, Fort Worth, TX
Roger Bullard, Barton College, Wilson, NC
Gary M. Burge, Professor of New Testament, Wheaton College, Wheaton, IL
Theodore W. Burgh, The University of Arizona, Tucson, AZ
Aaron A. Burke, Ph.D. Student, University of Chicago, Chicago, IL
Joel Burnett, Assistant Professor of Religion, Gardner-Webb University, Boiling Springs, NC
Keith A. Burton, Oakwood College, Huntsville, AL
Rick W. Byargeon, J. Wash Watts Associate Professor of Old Testament and Hebrew, New Orleans Baptist Theological Seminary, New Orleans, LA
Ryan Byrne, Ph.D. Student, The Johns Hopkins University, Baltimore, MD
Jane M. Cahill, Archaeologist, The City of David Excavations, Hebrew University, Jerusalem, Israel
Michael Cahill, Professor of Biblical Studies, Duquesne University, Pittsburgh, PA
Chris Caldwell, Ph.D. Student, Baylor University, Waco, TX

Dexter E. Callender, Jr., Assistant Professor of Religious Studies, University of Miami, Coral Gables, FL
A. B. Caneday, Associate Professor of Biblical Studies, Northwestern College, St. Paul, MN
Greg Carey, Assistant Professor of New Testament, Lancaster Theological Seminary, Lancaster, PA
Timothy B. Cargal, University Lecturer in Philosophy and Religion, Western Kentucky University, Bowling Green, KY
David M. Carr, Professor of Hebrew Bible, Methodist Theological School in Ohio, Delaware, OH
Henry L. Carrigan, Jr., Editorial Director, Trinity Press International, Harrisburg, PA
John T. Carroll, Associate Professor of New Testament, Union Theological Seminary in Virginia, Richmond, VA
Warren Carter, Associate Professor of New Testament, Saint Paul School of Theology, Kansas City, MO
Thomas Scott Caulley, Professor of New Testament Studies, Manhattan Christian College, Manhattan, KS
J. Bradley Chance, Professor of Religion, William Jewell College, Liberty, MO
Benjamin C. Chapman, Psychologist, Fallsview Psychiatric Hospital, Cuyahoga Falls, OH
Mark W. Chavalas, Associate Professor of History, University of Wisconsin-La Crosse, La Crosse, WI
Emily Cheney, University Lecturer, Western Kentucky University, Bowling Green, KY
Randall D. Chesnutt, Professor of Religion, Pepperdine University, Malibu, CA
Mark A. Christian, Adjunct Professor of Religion, Belmont University, Nashville, TN
David Cleaver-Bartholomew, First Congregational Church of Chelsea (U.C.C.), Chelsea, MI
Ann Coble, Assistant Professor of Christian Education and Religion, Westminster College, New Wilmington, PA
R. Dennis Cole, Professor of Biblical Archaeology, New Orleans Baptist Theological Seminary, New Orleans, LA
Matthew S. Collins, Program Area Director, Society of Biblical Literature, Atlanta, GA
Michael B. Compton, Lecturer, Mary Washington College, Richmond, VA
F. Connolly-Weinert, Associate Professor of Biblical Studies, St. John's University, Jamaica, NY
Stephen L. Cook, Assistant Professor of Old Testament, Virginia Theological Seminary, Alexandria, VA
Robert B. Coote, Professor of Old Testament, San Francisco Theological Seminary, Graduate Theological Union, San Anselmo, CA
Joseph A. Coray, Ministry Center, Loyola University Chicago, Chicago, IL
L. Wm. Countryman, Professor of New Testament, The Church Divinity School of the Pacific, Berkeley, CA
Steven L. Cox, Assistant Professor of New Testament and Greek, Mid-America Baptist Theological Seminary, Germantown, TN
Sidnie White Crawford, Associate Professor of Hebrew Bible; Chair, Classics Department, University of Nebraska, Lincoln, NE
James L. Crenshaw, Robert L. Flowers Professor of Old Testament, Duke University, Durham, NC
Bruce C. Cresson, Professor of Religion, Baylor University, Waco, TX
Bennie R. Crockett, Jr., Professor of Religion and Philosophy, William Carey College, Hattiesburg, MS
Vaughn CroweTipton, Pastor, Northwest Baptist Church, Ardmore, OK
Peter T. Daniels, New York, NY
Peter H. Davids, On-Site Study Director/ Counselor and Spiritual Director, Schloss Mittersill Study Centre, Mittersill, Austria
Stevan Davies, Professor of Religious Studies, College Misericordia, Dallas, PA
Casey W. Davis, Chaplain, Roberts Wesleyan College, Rochester, NY
Thomas W. Davis, Senior Project Manager, R. Christopher Goodwin & Associates, Inc., Frederick, MD
Lisa W. Davison, Assistant Professor of Old Testament, Lexington Theological Seminary, Lexington, KY
Peggy L. Day, Associate Professor of Religious Studies, The University of Winnipeg, Winnipeg, MB
Nancy L. deClaissé-Walford, Assistant Professor of Hebrew Bible and Biblical Languages, McAfee School of Theology, Mercer University, Atlanta, GA
Robert Delsnyder, Ph.D. Candidate, Wycliffe College, Toronto, ON
Carol J. Dempsey, O.P., Assistant Professor of Biblical Studies and Theology, University of Portland, Portland, OR
Robert A. Derrenbacker, Jr., Ph.D. Candidate, Wycliffe College/Toronto School of Theology, Toronto, ON
David A. deSilva, Assistant Professor of New Testament, Ashland Theological Seminary, Ashland, OH
LaMoine F. DeVries, Assistant Professor of Religious Studies, Southwest Missouri State University, Springfield, MO
Meindert Dijkstra, Utrecht University Faculty of Theology, Utrecht, Netherlands
F. W. Dobbs-Allsopp, Assistant Professor of Semitics, Yale University, New Haven, CT
William R. Domeris, Senior Lecturer, Department of Religious Studies, University of the Witwatersrand, Johannesburg, South Africa

John R. Donahue, S.J., Professor of New Testament, Jesuit School of Theology at Berkeley, Berkeley, CA
David A. Dorman, Assistant to the President, Fuller Theological Seminary, Pasadena, CA
David A. Dorsey, Professor of Old Testament, Evangelical School of Theology, Myerstown, PA
Thomas B. Dozeman, Professor of Old Testament, United Theological Seminary, Dayton, OH
Philip R. Drey, Andrews University, Berrien Springs, MI
Mark Dubis, Lecturer in Biblical Languages, George W. Truett Theological Seminary, Baylor University, Waco, TX
Patricia Dutcher-Walls, Assistant Professor of Hebrew Scripture and Old Testament, Knox College, Toronto, ON
Keith L. Eades, Assistant Professor of Christian Studies, California Baptist College, Riverside, CA
Jennie R. Ebeling, Ph.D. Candidate, The University of Arizona, Tucson, AZ
Terry W. Eddinger, Assistant Professor of Old Testament, Houston Graduate School of Theology, High Point, NC
Bart D. Ehrman, Associate Professor of Religious Studies, University of North Carolina at Chapel Hill, Chapel Hill, NC
Dale Ellenburg, Assistant Professor of New Testament and Greek, Mid-America Baptist Theological Seminary, Germantown, TN
J. Harold Ellens, Research Scholar, Institute for Antiquity and Christianity, Claremont Graduate University, The University of Michigan, Farmington Hills, MI
Susan (Elli) Elliott, Pastor, Zion United Church of Christ, Sterling, CO
Geoff Emberling, Assistant Curator, Department of Ancient Near Eastern Art, The Metropolitan Museum of Art, New York, NY
John C. Endres, S.J., Associate Professor of Sacred Scripture (Old Testament), Jesuit School of Theology at Berkeley, Berkeley, CA
Archie W. England, Adjunct Assistant Professor of Old Testament, Mid-America Baptist Theological Seminary, Germantown, TN
Tamara Cohn Eskenazi, Professor of Bible, Hebrew Union College–Jewish Institute of Religion, Los Angeles, CA
A. Joseph Everson, Professor of Religion, California Lutheran University, Thousand Oaks, CA
Mark R. Fairchild, Associate Professor of Bible and Religion, Huntington College, Huntington, IN
Kathleen A. Farmer, Professor of Old Testament, United Theological Seminary, Dayton, OH
Fearghus O. Fearghail, D.SS., St. Kieran's College, Kilkenny, Ireland
Alysia Anne Fischer, The University of Arizona, Tucson, AZ
John T. Fitzgerald, Associate Professor of Religious Studies, University of Miami, Coral Gables, FL
James W. Flanagan, Hallinan Professor of Religion, Case Western Reserve University, Cleveland, OH
John D. Fortner, Associate Professor of Hebrew Bible and the Ancient Near East, Harding University, Searcy, AR
John Fotopoulos, Loyola University Chicago, Chicago, IL
Donald Fowler, Pastor, Cedar Heights Baptist Church, Cedar Falls, IA
James Francis, Senior Lecturer in Religious Studies, University of Sunderland, Sunderland, United Kingdom
Terence E. Fretheim, Professor of Old Testament, Luther Seminary, St. Paul, MN
Lisbeth S. Fried, Graduate Student, Department of Hebrew and Judaic Studies, New York University, New York, NY
Michael J. Fuller, Professor of Anthropology, St. Louis Community College at Florissant Valley, St. Louis, MO
Russell T. Fuller, Assistant Professor of Old Testament Interpretation, Southern Baptist Theological Seminary, Louisville, KY
Pamela Gaber, Director, Temple Emmanuel Religious School, Tucson, AZ
Dennis Gaertner, Professor of New Testament, Johnson Bible College, Knoxville, TN
Julie Galambush, Assistant Professor of Religion, The College of William and Mary, Williamsburg, VA
Aaron M. Gale, Research Assistant, John Carroll University, University Heights, OH
Jack J. Garland, Jr., Baylor University, Waco, TX
Linda Oaks Garrett, Adjunct Instructor in English, Jefferson State Community College, Birmingham, AL
Beverly Roberts Gaventa, Helen H. P. Manson Professor of New Testament Literature and Exegesis, Princeton Theological Seminary, Princeton, NJ
Conrad Gempf, Senior Lecturer, Centre for Undergraduate and Postgraduate Theological Research, London Bible College, Middlesex, England
Bruce W. Gentry, Pastor, Payneville Baptist Church, Payneville, KY
Jeffrey C. Geoghagen, University of California, San Diego, La Jolla, CA
Jeffrey B. Gibson, Lecturer in Humanities, Harry S Truman College, Chicago, IL
Florence Morgan Gillman, Associate Professor of Biblical Studies, University of San Diego, San Diego, CA

John L. Gillman, Lecturer in Religious Studies, San Diego State University, San Diego, CA
Beth Glazier-McDonald, Associate Professor of Religion, Centre College, Danville, KY
W. Edward Glenny, Professor of New Testament; Director of Postgraduate Studies, Central Baptist Theological Seminary, Minneapolis, MN
Roger Good, Ph.D. Candidate, University of California, Los Angeles, Los Angeles, CA
William R. Goodman, Jr., Professor of Religious Studies, Lynchburg College, Lynchburg, VA
Stephen Goranson, Visiting Assistant Professor of Religious Studies, University of North Carolina at Wilmington, Wilmington, NC
Frank H. Gorman, Jr., T. W. Phillips Chair of Religious Studies, Bethany College, Bethany, WV
Ronald L. Gorny, Oriental Institute, The University of Chicago, Chicago, IL
Hemchand Gossai, Assistant Professor of Religion, Culver-Stockton College, Canton, MO
Lester L. Grabbe, Head of Theology, The University of Hull, Hull, United Kingdom
Gene B. Gragg, Professor, Oriental Institute, The University of Chicago, Chicago, IL
M. Patrick Graham, Margaret A. Pitts Associate Professor of Theological Bibliography; Director, Pitts Theology Library, Emory University, Atlanta, GA
Sandra L. Gravett, Assistant Professor of Philosophy and Religion, Appalachian State University, Boone, NC
Barbara Green, O.P., Professor of Biblical Studies, Dominican School of Philosophy and Theology, Graduate Theological Union, Berkeley, CA
Joel B. Green, Professor of New Testament Interpretation, Asbury Theological Seminary, Wilmore, KY
D. Larry Gregg, Associate Professor of Religion and Philosophy, Gardner-Webb University, Boiling Springs, NC
Zeljko Gregor, Andrews University, Berrien Springs, MI
F. V. Griefenhagen, Professor of Religious Studies, Luther College, University of Regina, Regina, SK
Sheila Marie Dugger Griffith, The University of Virginia, Charlottesville, VA
Michael A. Grisanti, Associate Professor of Old Testament, Central Baptist Theological Seminary, Minneapolis, MN
Daniel Grossberg, Associate Professor of Judaic Studies and Religious Studies, The University at Albany, State University of New York, Albany, NY
Jennifer L. Groves, Director, Archaeological Publications, Andrews University, Berrien Springs, MI
Mayer I. Gruber, Associate Professor of Biblical Studies, Ben-Gurion University of the Negev, Beersheva, Israel
Michael D. Guinan, O.F.M., Professor of Old Testament and Semitic Languages, Franciscan School of Theology, Berkeley, CA
Judith M. Gundry-Volf, Associate Professor of New Testament, Yale Divinity School, New Haven, CT
Charles J. Guth, Professor of New Testament, Prairie Graduate School, Calgary, AB
Darrell D. Gwaltney, Jr., Assistant Professor of Religion and Literature, Palm Beach Atlantic College, West Palm Beach, FL
Robert D. Haak, Associate Professor of Old Testament, Augustana College, Rock Island, IL
Donald A. Hagner, George Eldon Ladd Professor of New Testament, Fuller Theological Seminary, Pasadena, CA
John F. Hall, Professor of Classics and Ancient History, Brigham Young University, Provo, UT
Kevin D. Hall, Assistant Professor of Religion, Oklahoma Baptist University, Shawnee, OK
Baruch Halpern, Chair in Jewish Studies; Professor of Ancient History, Classics, and Ancient Mediterranean Studies and Religious Studies; Director, Jewish Studies, The Pennsylvania State University, University Park, PA
Mark W. Hamilton, Ph.D. Candidate, Harvard University, Cambridge, MA
John S. Hammett, Assistant Professor of Systematic Theology, Southeastern Baptist Theological Seminary, Wake Forest, NC
Philip C. Hammond, Emeritus Professor of Anthropology, University of Utah, Fountain Hills, AZ
A. Perry Hancock, Assistant Professor of Christian Education, New Orleans Baptist Theological Seminary, New Orleans, LA
Lowell K. Handy, Senior Lecturer, Loyola University Chicago, Chicago, IL
James W. Hardin, Visiting Research Assistant, Cobb Institute of Archaeology, Mississippi State University, Mississippi State, MS
Philip A. Harland, University of Toronto, Toronto, ON
J. Albert Harrill, Assistant Professor of Religious Studies, DePaul University, Chicago, IL
Daniel J. Harrington, S.J., Professor of New Testament, Weston Jesuit School of Theology, Cambridge, MA
E. Lynne Harris, Assistant Professor, University of Illinois at Chicago, Chicago, IL
John L. Harris, Assistant Professor of Religion, East Texas Baptist University, Marshall, TX
Roy A. Harrisville, Professor of New Testament, Luther Seminary, St. Paul, MN
Stanley Harstine, Baylor University, Waco, TX
Patrick J. Hartin, Associate Professor of

Religious Studies, Gonzaga University, Spokane, WA
Paul Anthony Hartog, Teaching Fellow, Loyola University Chicago, Chicago, IL
John D. Harvey, Associate Professor of New Testament, Columbia Biblical Seminary and Graduate School of Missions, Columbia, SC
John E. Harvey, Wycliffe College, University of Toronto, Toronto, ON
Frank M. Hasel, Dozent for Systematic Theology and Biblical Interpretation, Seminar Schloss Bogenhofen, Bogenhofen, Austria
Michael G. Hasel, Associate Professor of Near Eastern Studies and Archaeology, Southern Adventist University, Collegedale, TN
Alan J. Hauser, Professor of Old Testament, Appalachian State University, Boone, NC
L. Daniel Hawk, Associate Professor of Old Testament and Hebrew, Ashland Theological Seminary, Ashland, OH
David M. Hay, Joseph E. McCabe Professor of Religion, Coe College, Cedar Rapids, IA
J. Daniel Hays, Assistant Professor of Religion, Ouachita Baptist University, Arkadelphia, AR
Charles W. Hedrick, Professor of Religious Studies, Southwest Missouri State University, Springfield, MO
Ronald S. Hendel, Associate Professor of Religious Studies, Southern Methodist University, Dallas, TX
Richard A. Henshaw, Professor Emeritus, Colgate Rochester Divinity School, Rochester, NY
Gary A. Herion, Associate Professor of Religious Studies, Hartwick College, Oneonta, NY
Richard S. Hess, Professor of Old Testament, Denver Seminary, Denver, CO
Theodore Hiebert, Professor of Old Testament, McCormick Theological Seminary, Chicago, IL
Michael D. Hildenbrand, University of California, Berkeley, Berkeley, CA
Charles E. Hill, Associate Professor of New Testament, Reformed Theological Seminary, Maitland, FL
T. R. Hobbs, Professor of Old Testament, Internantional Baptist Theological Seminary, Prague, Czech Republic
Kenneth G. Hoglund, Associate Professor of Religion, Wake Forest University, Winston-Salem, NC
Robert L. Hohlfelder, Professor of History, University of Colorado, Boulder, CO
Eric Holleyman, Pastor, Meadowbrook Baptist Church, Waco, TX
Steven W. Holloway, Lecturer, St. Xavier University, Chicago, IL
Tawny L. Holm, Department of Religious Studies, DePauw University, Greencastle, IN
Kenneth G. Holum, Professor of History, University of Maryland, College Park, MD
Michael M. Homan, Ph.D. Student, University of California, San Diego, La Jolla, CA
Paul K. Hooker, Pastor, Rock Spring Presbyterian Church, Atlanta, GA
David C. Hopkins, Professor of Hebrew Bible, Wesley Theological Seminary, Washington, DC
Denise Dombkowski Hopkins, Professor of Hebrew Bible, Wesley Theological Seminary, Washington, DC
Leslie J. Hoppe, O.F.M., Professor of Old Testament Studies, Catholic Theological Union, Chicago, IL
Edwin C. Hostetter, Instructor, Ecumenical Institute of Theology, Baltimore, MD
H. Wayne House, Academic Dean, Professor of Theology, Michigan Theological Seminary, Plymouth, MI
George Howard, Professor of Religion, University of Georgia, Athens, GA
David B. Howell, Assistant Professor of Religion, Carson-Newman College, Jefferson City, TN
Cheryl Lynn Hubbard, Doctoral Candidate, Union Theological Seminary in Virginia, Richmond, VA
Moyer Hubbard, Assistant Professor of New Testament, Talbot School of Theology, La Mirada, CA
John R. Huddlestun, Associate Professor of Religious Studies, College of Charleston, Charleston, SC
Alice Hunt Hudiburg, Ph.D. Student, Vanderbilt University, Nashville, TN
Douglas S. Huffman, Assistant Professor of Bible, Northwestern College, St. Paul, MN
Ronald V. Huggins, Spokane, WA
Bradford Scott Hummel, Southwestern Baptist Theological Seminary, Fort Worth, TX
Michael L. Humphries, Assistant Professor of Classical Literature, Southern Illinois University, Carbondale, IL
Brian P. Irwin, Ph.D. Candidate, Wycliffe College, University of Toronto, Toronto, ON
Glenna S. Jackson, Assistant Professor, Department of Religion and Philosophy, Otterbein College, Westerville, OH
Paul F. Jacobs, Professor of Philosophy and Religion, Mississippi State University, Mississippi State, MS
Clayton N. Jefford, Associate Professor of Sacred Scripture, St. Meinrad School of Theology, St. Meinrad, IN
T. J. Jenney, Pastor/Director of Campus Ministry, University Church at Purdue, West Lafayette, IN
Timothy P. Jenney, Professor of Biblical Studies, North Central University, Minneapolis, MN
Joseph E. Jensen, The Catholic University of America, Washington, DC
Alexander H. Joffe, Assistant Professor of

Anthropology and Jewish Studies, The Pennsylvania State University, University Park, PA

Richard Warren Johnson, Ph.D. Candidate, New Orleans Baptist Theological Seminary, New Orleans, LA

Marc A. Jolley, Assistant Publisher, Mercer University Press, Macon, GA

Barry A. Jones, Assistant Professor of Religion, Mars Hill College, Mars Hill, NC

F. Stanley Jones, Associate Professor of Religious Studies, Calilfornia State University, Long Beach, Long Beach, CA

Gregory Jordan, President; Professor of Bible and Religion, King College, Bristol, TN

Donald Juel, Richard J. Dearborn Professor of New Testament Theology, Princeton Theological Seminary, Princeton, NJ

Felix Just, S.J., Assistant Professor of Theological Studies, Loyola Marymount University, Los Angeles, CA

Isaac Kalimi, Seminar for Jewish Studies, The University of Oldenburg, Jerusalem, Israel

John Kaltner, Assistant Professor of Religious Studies, Rhodes College, Memphis, TN

Joel S. Kaminsky, Assistant Professor, Department of Religion and Biblical Literature, Smith College, Northampton, MA

John Kampen, Vice President, Dean of Academic Affairs, Bluffton College, Bluffton, OH

Seán Kealy, C.S.Sp., Professor of Scripture, Duquesne University, Pittsburgh, PA

Howard Clark Kee, Senior Research Fellow, University of Pennsylvania, Haverford, PA

James A. Kelhoffer, Ph.D. Candidate, The University of Chicago, Chicago, IL

Sharon R. Keller, Visiting Assistant Professor of Hebrew Bible, Hebrew Union College–Jewish Institute of Religion, New York, NY

Mark Kiley, Associate Professor of Theology and Religious Studies, St. John's University, Staten Island, NY

Hyun Chul (Paul) Kim, Ph.D. Candidate, Claremont Graduate University, Claremont, CA

Greg A. King, Associate Professor of Biblical Studies, Pacific Union College, Angwin, CA

Cheryl A. Kirk-Duggan; Director, Center for Women and Religion; Assistant Professor of Theology and Womanist Studies, Graduate Theological Union, Berkeley, CA

Paul J. Kissling, Professor of Old Testament, Great Lakes Christian College, Lansing, MI

Shmuel Klatzkin, Rabbi, Hillel Academy, Dayton, OH

Ralph W. Klein, Dean and Professor of Old Testament, Lutheran School of Theology at Chicago, Chicago, IL

Lee E. Klosinski, Director of Education, AIDS Project Los Angeles, Los Angeles, CA

Robin J. DeWitt Knauth, Harvard University, Cambridge, MA

Gary N. Knoppers, Head, Classics and Ancient Mediterranean Civilizations, The Pennsylvania State University, University Park, PA

Craig R. Koester, Associate Professor of New Testament, Luther Seminary, St. Paul, MN

Lynne Alcott Kogel, Instructor, Ecumenical Theological Seminary, Detroit, MI

Wade Kotter, Assistant Professor of Library Science, Weber State University, Ogden, UT

Charles R. Krahmalkov, Professor of Ancient and Biblical Languages, The University of Michigan, Ann Arbor, MI

Mark S. Krause, Academic Dean; Professor of New Testament, Puget Sound Christian College, Edmonds, WA

Siegfried Kreuzer, Professor of Old Testament and Biblical Archaeology, Kirchliche Hochschule/School of Theology Wuppertal-Barmen, Wuppertal, Germany

Jeffrey K. Kuan, Assistant Professor of Old Testament, Pacific School of Religion, Berkeley, CA

William S. Kurz, S.J., Professor of New Testament, Marquette University, Milwaukee, WI

Øystein S. LaBianca, Professor of Anthropology; Associate Director, Institute of Archaeology, Andrews University, Berrien Springs, MI

Samuel Lamerson, Assistant Professor of New Testament, Knox Theological Seminary, Fort Lauderdale, FL

Jeffrey S. Lamp, Pastor, First United Methodist Church, Spiro, OK

Jane S. Lancaster, Ph.D. Candidate, Southern Methodist University, Dallas, TX

Francis Landy, Professor of Comparative Studies, University of Alberta, Edmonton, AB

Christopher Scott Langston, Associate Professor of Religion, Principia College, Elsah, IL

Scott M. Langston, Adjunct in Old Testament and Hebrew, Southwestern Baptist Theological Seminary, Fort Worth, TX

Stuart Lasine, Associate Professor of Religion; Coordinator, Master of Arts in Liberal Studies Program, Wichita State University, Wichita, KS

David Paul Latoundji, Instructor of Bible, Nyack College, Nyack, NY

Betty P. Lawson, Freelance Writer, Wake Forest, NC

Gene J. Lawson, The Divinity School, Vanderbilt University, Nashville, TN

J. Gregory Lawson, Assistant Professor of Christian Education, Southeastern Baptist Theological Seminary, Wake Forest, NC

Nancy Lee, Visiting Fulbright Lecturer, Josip J. Strossmayer University, Osijek, Croatia
Timothy A. Lenchak, S.V.D., Biblical Coordinator, Society of the Divine Word, Rome, Italy; Director, Dei Verbum Biblical Pastoral Program, Nemi, Italy
Dale F. Leschert, Independent Scholar, New Westminster, BC
Amy-Jill Levine, E. Rhodes and Leona B. Carpenter Professor of New Testament Studies, The Divinity School, Vanderbilt University, Nashville, TN
Thomas E. Levy, Professor of Anthropology and Judaic Studies, University of California, San Diego, La Jolla, CA
Theodore J. Lewis, Associate Professor of Hebrew Bible and Ancient Near Eastern Studies, University of Georgia, Athens, GA
Gary W. Light, Pastor, Winfree Memorial Baptist Church, Midlothian, VA
Tod Linafelt, Assistant Professor of Biblical Studies, Georgetown University, Washington, DC
C. Shaun Longstreet, University of Notre Dame, Notre Dame, IN
Douglas Low, Associate Professor of Religious Studies, Oakland City University, Oakland City, IN
Jenny Manasco Lowery, Columbus, IN
Joe E. Lunceford, Professor of Religion, Georgetown College, Georgetown, KY
Marilyn J. Lundberg, Associate Editor, *Maarav* (Western Academic Press), Rolling Hills Estates, CA
John M. Lundquist, Susan and Douglas Dillon Chief Librarian of the Oriental Division, The New York Public Library, New York, NY
Ramón Luzárraga, Department of Theology, Marquette University, Milwaukee, WI
Larry L. Lyke, Assistant Professor of Hebrew Bible, Yale Divinity School, New Haven, CT
P. Kyle McCarter, Jr., William Foxwell Albright Professor of Biblical and Ancient Near Eastern Studies, The Johns Hopkins University, Baltimore, MD
L. David McClister, Instructor in Biblical Studies, Florida College, Temple Terrace, FL
Clifford Mark McCormick, Hebrew Instructor, University of North Carolina at Chapel Hill, Chapel Hill, NC
Jeff H. McCrory, Jr., The National Presbyterian Church, Washington, DC
Katharine A. Mackay, Ph.D. Student, The University of Arizona, Tucson, AZ
Steven L. McKenzie, Associate Professor of Old Testament, Rhodes College, Memphis, TN
John L. McLaughlin, Assistant Professor, Department of Theology and Religious Studies, Wheeling Jesuit University, Wheeling, WV
Tim McLay, St. Stephen's University, St. Stephen, NB
Iain S. Maclean, Senior Lecturer in Religion and Philosophy, Roanoke College, Salem, VA
Jennifer K. Berenson Maclean, Assistant Professor of Religion, Roanoke College, Salem, VA
John A. McLean, President, Michigan Theological Seminary, Plymouth, MI
Allan J. McNicol, Professor of New Testament, Institute for Christian Studies, Austin, TX
Patricia A. MacNicoll, Ph.D. Candidate, Union Theological Seminary in Virginia, Richmond, VA
John McRay, Professor of New Testament and Archaeology, Wheaton College Graduate School, Wheaton, IL
Dennis R. Magary, Associate Professor of Old Testament and Semitic Languages, Trinity Evangelical Divinity School, Deerfield, IL
F. Rachel Magdalene, Iliff School of Theology/ University of Denver, Denver, CO
Jodi Magness, Assistant Professor of Classical and Near Eastern Archaeology, Tufts University, Medford, MA
David C. Maltsberger, Director, Capilano Seminary Extension Centre, North Vancouver, BC
Sara R. Mandell, Professor of Religious Studies, University of South Florida, Tampa, FL
Dale W. Manor, Associate Professor of Bible and Archaeology, Harding University, Searcy, AR
Joel Marcus, Lecturer in Biblical Studies, University of Glasgow, Glasgow, Scotland
W. Harold Mare, Professor of New Testament, Covenant Theological Seminary, St. Louis, MO
Claude F. Mariottini, Professor of Old Testament, Northern Baptist Theological Seminary, Lombard, IL
W. Creighton Marlowe, Associate Professor of Old Testament Studies, Tyndale Theological Seminary, Badhoevedorp, Netherlands
Rick R. Marrs, Professor of Religion, Pepperdine University, Malibu, CA
Eric F. Mason, Ph.D. Candidate, University of Notre Dame, Notre Dame, IN
Steve Mason, Professor of Classics and Religious Studies, York University, North York, ON
Frank J. Matera, Professor of New Testament, The Catholic University of America, Washington, DC
William D. Matherly, Ph.D. Candidate, University of Notre Dame, Crossville, TN
David Lertis Matson, Assistant Professor of Biblical Studies, Milligan College, Milligan College, TN
Christopher R. Matthews, Weston Jesuit School of Theology, Cambridge, MA
Victor H. Matthews, Professor of Religious Studies, Southwest Missouri State University, Springfield, MO
Gerald L. Mattingly, Professor of Biblical Studies, Johnson Bible College, Knoxville, TN

Laura B. Mazow, Ph.D. Candidate, The University of Arizona, Tucson, AZ
Richard E. Menninger, Assistant Professor of Mathematics and Religion, Ottawa University, Ottawa, KS
David Merling, Associate Professor of Archaeology and History of Antiquities; Associate Director/Curator, Institute of Archaeology, Andrews University, Berrien Springs, MI
Marvin Meyer, Professor of Religion, Chapman University, Orange, CA
Tony S. L. Michael, Instructor, Centre for the Study of Religion, University of Toronto, Toronto, ON
Piotr Michalowski, George G. Cameron Professor of Ancient Near Eastern Languages and Civilizations, The University of Michigan, Ann Arbor, MI
Robert D. Miller, II, Assistant Professor of Scripture, Mt. St. Mary Seminary, Emmitsburg, MD
Stephen R. Miller, Professor of Old Testament and Hebrew, Mid-America Baptist Theological Seminary, Germantown, TN
Watson E. Mills, Professor of New Testament Studies, Mercer University, Macon, GA
Paul Mirecki, Associate Professor of Religious Studies, University of Kansas, Lawrence, KS
Alan C. Mitchell, Associate Professor of Biblical Studies, Georgetown University, Washington, DC
Gregory Mobley, Assistant Professor of Old Testament, Andover Newton Theological School, Newton Centre, MA
Andrea Lorenzo Molinari, Marquette University, Milwaukee, WI
Megan Bishop Moore, Ph.D. Student, Emory University, Atlanta, GA
Donn F. Morgan, Professor of Old Testament, The Church Divinity School of the Pacific, Berkeley, CA
R. David Moseman, Ph.D. Candidate, Baylor University, Waco, TX
Paul K. Moser, Professor of Philosophy, Loyola University Chicago, Chicago, IL
Harold R. Mosley, Assistant Professor of Old Testament and Hebrew, New Orleans Baptist Theological Seminary, New Orleans, LA
Alden A. Mosshammer, Professor of History, University of California, San Diego, La Jolla, CA
Mark E. Moulton, Graduate Student, Wheaton College Graduate School, Wheaton, IL
Robert L. Mowery, Archivist and Special Collections Librarian, Illinois Wesleyan University, Bloomington, IL
James R. Mueller, Associate Professor of Religion, University of Florida, Gainesville, FL
Kenneth D. Mulzac, Assistant Professor of Old Testament Interpretation, Oakwood College, Huntsville, AL
Phillip B. Munoa, III, Associate Professor of Religion, Hope College, Holland, MI
Roland E. Murphy, O. Carm., George Washington Ivey Emeritus Professor of Biblical Studies, Duke University, Washington, DC
Richard F. Muth, Fuller E. Callaway Professor of Economics, Emory University, Atlanta, GA
Edward P. Myers, Professor of Bible and Christian Doctrine, Harding University College of Bible and Religion, Searcy, AR
Daniel S. Mynatt, Assistant Professor of Religion, Anderson College, Anderson, SC
Beth Alpert Nakhai, Lecturer, Department of Near Eastern Studies and Committee on Judaic Studies, The University of Arizona, Tucson, AZ
Mark D. Nanos, St. Mary's College, University of St. Andrews, Fife, Scotland
Kathleen S. Nash, Associate Professor of Religious Studies, LeMoyne College, Syracuse, NY
Scott Nash, Assistant Professor of Christianity, Mercer University, Macon, GA
Peter K. Nelson, Assistant Professor of New Testament, Trinity Evangelical Divinity School, Deerfield, IL
Richard D. Nelson, Kraft Professor of Biblical Studies, Lutheran Theological Seminary at Gettysburg, Gettysburg, PA
Russell Nelson, Associate Professor of Religious Studies, Concordia University College of Alberta, Edmonton, AB
William B. Nelson, Jr., Associate Professor of Old Testament, Westmont College, Santa Barbara, CA
Friedbert Ninow, Eau Claire Seventh Day Adventist Church, Berrien Springs, MI
W. E. Nunnally, Associate Professor of Early Judaism and Christian Origins, Central Bible College, Springfield, MO
Richard W. Nysse, Professor of Old Testament, Luther Seminary, St. Paul, MN
Douglas E. Oakman, Associate Professor of Religion, Pacific Lutheran University, Tacoma, WA
J. Randall O'Brien, Associate Professor of Religion, Baylor University, Waco, TX
Michael Patrick O'Connor, Associate Professor of Semitics, Catholic University of America, Washington, DC
Margaret S. Odell, Assistant Professor of Religion, St. Olaf College, Northfield, MN
J. P. J. Olivier, Professor of Old Testament, University of Stellenbosch, Stellenbosch, South Africa
Ben C. Ollenburger, Professor of Biblical Theology, Associated Mennonite Biblical Seminary, Elkhart, IN
Dennis T. Olson, Associate Professor of Old Testament, Princeton Theological Seminary, Princeton, NJ

Steven M. Ortiz, Ph.D. Student, The University of Arizona, Tucson, AZ
Carroll D. Osburn, Art Carmichael Distinguished Professor of New Testament Studies, Abilene Christian University, Abilene, TX
Carolyn Osiek, Professor of New Testament, Catholic Theological Union, Chicago, IL
Richard E. Oster, Jr., Harding Graduate School of Religion, Memphis, TN
Thomas W. Overholt, Professor of Religious Studies, University of Wisconsin–Stevens Point, Stevens Point, WI
David I. Owen, Professor of Near Eastern Studies, Cornell University, Ithaca, NY
J. Edward Owens, Assistant Professor of Biblical Studies, St. John's Seminary, Camarillo, CA
Jim Oxford, Jr., Ph.D. Candidate, Baylor University, Waco, TX
James H. Pace, Professor of Religious Studies, Elon College, Elon College, NC
Wesley T. Paddock, Associate Professor of Old Testament, Manhattan Christian College, Manhattan, KS
Kim Paffenroth, Teaching Fellow, Core Humanities Seminar, Villanova University, Villanova, PA
Aaron W. Park, Ph.D. Candidate, Claremont Graduate University, Claremont, CA
Dale Patrick, Professor of Bible, Drake University, Des Moines, IA
Brian Peckham, Associate Professor of Old Testament and Hebrew, Regis College, University of Toronto, Toronto, ON
Richard I. Pervo, Professor of New Testament and Patristics, Seabury-Western Theological Seminary, Evanston, IL
Mark Anthony Phelps, Instructor, Ozarks Technical Community College, Springfield, MO
John J. Pilch, Professorial Lecturer in Theology, Georgetown University, Washington, DC
Wayne T. Pitard, Associate Professor of Hebrew Bible, University of Illinois, Urbana, IL
J. Curtis Pope, Professor of Biblical Studies, Florida College, Temple Terrace, FL
Stanley E. Porter, Professor of Theology, Roehampton Institute London, London, United Kingdom
D. T. Potts, E. C. Hall Professor of Middle Eastern Archaeology, University of Sydney, Sydney, Australia
Donald R. Potts, Chairman, Department of Religion, East Texas Baptist University, Marshall, TX
Mark Allan Powell, Robert and Phyllis Leatherman Professor of New Testament Studies, Trinity Lutheran Seminary, Columbus, OH
Terrence Prendergast, S.J., Archbishop of Halifax, Halifax, NS
Carolyn Pressler, Associate Professor of Old Testament, United Theological Seminary of the Twin Cities, New Brighton, MN
James J. H. Price, Professor of Religious Studies, Lynchburg College, Lynchburg, VA
J. Randall Price, Professor of Old Testament, Faith Theological Seminary, Tacoma, WA
William H. C. Propp, Assistant Professor of History, University of California, San Diego, La Jolla, CA
Paul R. Raabe, Professor of Old Testament, Concordia Theological Seminary, St. Louis, MO
Anson F. Rainey, Professor of Ancient Near Eastern Cultures and Semitic Linguistics, Tel Aviv University, Tel Aviv, Israel
Troy K. Rappold, Graduate Assistant, Cincinnati Bible College and Seminary, Cincinnati, OH
Ilona N. Rashkow, Associate Professor of Comparative Literature and Women's Studies, State University of New York at Stony Brook, Stony Brook, NY
Charles A. Ray, Jr., Associate Professor of New Testament and Greek, New Orleans Baptist Theological Seminary, New Orleans, LA
Paul J. Ray, Jr., Assistant to the Curator, Horn Archaeological Museum, Andrews University, Berrien Springs, MI
Paul L. Redditt, Professor of Old Testament, Georgetown College, Georgetown, KY
Jonathan L. Reed, Associate Professor of Religion, University of La Verne; Director, Brethren Colleges Abroad, Marburg, Germany
Stephen Alan Reed, Assistant Professor of Religion and Philosophy, Jamestown College, Jamestown, ND
Stephen Breck Reid, Associate Professor of Old Testament Studies, Austin Presbyterian Theological Seminary, Austin, TX
David Rensberger, Associate Professor of Old Testament, Interdenominational Theological Center, Atlanta, GA
James L. Resseguie, Dean and Professor of New Testament, Winebrenner Theological Seminary, Findlay, OH
John Reumann, Ministerium of Pennsylvania Professor of New Testament and Greek (Emeritus), Lutheran Theological Seminary at Philadelphia, Philadelphia, PA
Earl J. Richard, Professor of New Testament Studies, Loyola University, New Orleans, LA
Peter Richardson, Professor of Christian Origins, University College, University of Toronto, Toronto, ON
C. Mack Roark, Ruth Dickinson Professor of Bible, Oklahoma Baptist University, Shawnee, OK
Calvin J. Roetzel, Arnold Lowe Professor of

Religious Studies, Macalester College, St. Paul, MN
Jeffrey S. Rogers, Dana Assistant Professor of Religion, Furman University, Greenville, SC
Chris A. Rollston, Post-Doctoral Research and Teaching Appointee, The Johns Hopkins University, Baltimore, MD
C. Gilbert Romero, Campus Chaplain, California State University at Los Angeles, Los Angeles, CA
Mark F. Rooker, Associate Professor of Old Testament and Hebrew, Southeastern Baptist Theological Seminary, Wake Forest, NC
Edmon L. Rowell, Jr., Senior Editor, Mercer University Press, Macon, GA
Nicole Jeanne Ruane, Graduate Student, Union Theological Seminary, New York, NY
Michael L. Ruffin, Assistant Professor, School of Religion, Belmont University, Nashville, TN
Ronald H. Sack, Professor of History, North Carolina State University, Raleigh, NC
Katharine Doob Sakenfeld, William Albright Eisenberger Professor of Old Testament Literature and Exegesis, Princeton Theological Seminary, Princeton, NJ
Anthony J. Saldarini, Professor of Theology, Boston College, Chestnut Hill, MA
E. P. Sanders, Arts and Sciences Professor, Duke University, Durham, NC
Stanley P. Saunders, Assistant Professor of New Testament, Columbia Theological Seminary, Decatur, GA
Linda S. Schearing, Assistant Professor of Religious Studies, Gonzaga University, Spokane, WA
Donald G. Schley, Associate Professor, Colorado Technical University, Colorado Springs, CO
Brian B. Schmidt, Assistant Professor of Ancient West Asian Cultures, The University of Michigan, Ann Arbor, MI
Tammi J. Schneider, Assistant Professor of Religion, Claremont Graduate University, Claremont, CA
William Schniedewind, Assistant Professor of Biblical Studies and Northwest Semitic Languages, University of California, Los Angeles, Los Angeles, CA
William R. Scott, Director, BIBAL Press, North Richland Hills, TX
David Ralph Seely, Associate Professor of Ancient Scripture, Brigham Young University, Provo, UT
Jo Ann H. Seely, Provo, UT
Timothy W. Seid, Pastor, Smith Neck Friends Meeting House, South Dartmouth, MA
Donald Senior, Professor of New Testament, Catholic Theological Union, Chicago, IL
Charles S. Shaw, Pastor, Mount Zion United Methodist Church, Central, SC
William H. Shea, Research Associate, Biblical Research Institute, Silver Spring, MD
Steven M. Sheeley, Associate Professor of Religion, Shorter College, Rome, GA
Gerald T. Sheppard, Professor of Old Testament Literature and Exegesis, Emmanuel College of Victoria University in the University of Toronto, Toronto, ON
Stephen J. Shoemaker, Visiting Assistant Professor of Religion, Florida State University, Tallahassee, FL
Gary Steven Shogren, Professor of New Testament, Seminario ESEPA, San José, Costa Rica
Ronald A. Simkins, Associate Professor of Theology, Near Eastern Languages and Civilizations, Creighton University, Omaha, NE
Lawrence A. Sinclair, Pershing E. MacAllister Professor, Carroll College, Waukesha, WI
Thomas B. Slater, Assistant Professor of Religion, University of Georgia, Athens, GA
Barry D. Smith, Associate Professor of Religious Studies, Atlantic Baptist University, Moncton, NB
Dennis E. Smith, Associate Professor of New Testament, Phillips Theological Seminary, Enid, OK
James V. Smith, Ph.D. Student, Loyola University Chicago, Chicago, IL
Mark S. Smith, Professor of Theology, St. Joseph's University, Philadelphia, PA
Richard Smith, Lecturer, Claremont Graduate University, Claremont, CA
Robert Harry Smith, Professor of New Testament, Pacific Lutheran Theological Seminary, Berkeley, CA
Robert W. Smith, Associate Professor of History, Florida Christian College, Kissimmee, FL
Daniel L. Smith-Christopher, Associate Professor of Theological Studies (Old Testament), Loyola Marymount University, Los Angeles, CA
Will Soll, Associate Professor of Biblical Studies, Aquinas Institute of Theology, St. Louis, MO
Irving Alan Sparks, Professor of Religious Studies, San Diego State University, San Diego, CA
Kenton Lane Sparks, Scholar in Residence, Providence Baptist Church, Raleigh, NC
Michael Spence, Nashville, TN
F. Scott Spencer, Associate Professor of Religion, Wingate University, Wingate, NC
John R. Spencer, Associate Professor of Religious Studies, John Carroll University, University Heights, OH
Richard A. Spencer, Associate Professor of Philosophy and Religion, Appalachian State University, Boone, NC
Joe M. Sprinkle, Assistant Professor of Old Testament, Toccoa Falls College, Toccoa Falls, GA
Jeffrey L. Staley, Adjunct Professor of New Testament, Pacific Lutheran University, Tacoma, WA
Cecil P. Staton, Jr., Professor, College of Liberal Arts, Mercer University, Macon, GA

Richard A. Stephenson, Professor of Planning, East Carolina University, Greenville, NC
Perry L. Stepp, Pastor, DeSoto Christian Church, DeSoto, TX
Gerald L. Stevens, Associate Professor of New Testament and Greek, New Orleans Baptist Theological Seminary, New Orleans, LA
Jeanne Stevenson-Moessner, Assistant Professor of Pastoral Theology and Christian Formation, University of Dubuque Theological Seminary, Dubuque, IA
Robert R. Stieglitz, Associate Professor of Ancient Mediterranean Civilizations, Rutgers University, Newark, Newark, NJ
Robert E. Stone, II, Ann Arbor, MI
Laurence Hull Stookey, Hugh Latimer Elderdice Professor of Preaching and Worship, Wesley Theological Seminary, Washington, DC
Mark L. Strauss, Assistant Professor of New Testament, Bethel Theological Seminary, West Campus, San Diego, CA
Brent A. Strawn, Assistant Professor of Biblical Studies, Asbury Theological Seminary, Wilmore, KY
John T. Strong, Lecturer in Religious Studies, Southwest Missouri State University, Springfield, MO
L. Thomas Strong, III, Assistant Professor of New Testament Greek; Chair, Department of Theological Studies, New Orleans Baptist Theological Seminary, New Orleans, LA
Louis Stulman, Distinguished Professor of Hebrew Bible, Winebrenner Theological Seminary; Professor of Religion, University of Findlay, Findlay, OH
Jerry L. Sumney, Associate Professor of Biblical Studies, Lexington Theological Seminary, Lexington, KY
Jesper Svartvik, Doctoral Student, Lund University, Lund, Sweden
Hans Svebakken, Ph.D. Student, Loyola University Chicago, Chicago, IL
Dennis M. Swanson, Head Librarian, The Master's Seminary, Sun Valley, CA
Marvin A. Sweeney, Professor of Hebrew Bible, School of Theology at Claremont; Professor of Religion, Claremont Graduate University, Claremont, CA
Ron E. Tappy, G. Albert Shoemaker Chair of Bible and Archaeology; Director, Kelso Bible Lands Museum, Pittsburgh Theological Seminary, Pittsburgh, PA
Lynn Tatum, Lecturer in Religion, Baylor University, Waco, TX
Michelle Ellis Taylor, Ph.D. Student, Brandeis University, Waltham, MA
Lucille M. Thibodeau, P.M., President, Rivier College, Nashua, NH
Matthew A. Thomas, Ph.D. Student, Claremont Graduate University, Claremont, CA
James W. Thompson, Professor of New Testament, Abilene Christian University, Abilene, TX
Mark A. Throntveit, Professor of Old Testament, Luther Seminary, St. Paul, MN
Bonnie Thurston, Associate Professor of New Testament, Pittsburgh Theological Seminary, Pittsburgh, PA
Patrick A. Tiller, Assistant Professor of New Testament, Harvard Divinity School, Cambridge, MA
Philip L. Tite, Graduate Student, Wilfrid Laurier University, Waterloo, ON
Anthony J. Tomasino, Lecturer, University of Chicago, Chicago, IL
Michelle Tooley, Assistant Professor of Religion, Belmont University, Nashville, TN
Warren C. Trenchard, Professor of New Testament and Early Christian Literature; Senior Assistant to the President, La Sierra University, Riverside, CA
Allison A. Trites, John Payzant Distinguished Professor of Biblical Studies, Acadia Divinity College, Wolfville, NS
Jeffrey T. Tucker, Nashville, TN
W. Dennis Tucker, Jr., Assistant Professor of Religion, Ouachita Baptist University, Arkadelphia, AR
Christopher Tuckett, Rylands Professor of Biblical Criticism and Exegesis, University of Manchester, Manchester, United Kingdom
David L. Turner, Visiting Professor of New Testament, Grand Rapids Baptist Seminary, Grand Rapids, MI
Eugene Ulrich, Professor of Hebrew Scriptures, University of Notre Dame, Notre Dame, IN
J. A. Vadnais, Ph.D. Candidate, New Orleans Baptist Theological Seminary, New Orleans, LA
Jorge L. Valdes, Ph.D. Student, Loyola University Chicago, Chicago, IL
David M. Valeta, Ph.D. Candidate, University of Denver/Iliff School of Theology, Denver, CO
Donald R. Vance, Assistant Professor of Biblical Languages and Literature, Oral Roberts University, Tulsa, OK
David Vanderhooft, Assistant Professor of Theology, Boston College, Chestnut Hill, MA
Leanne Van Dyk, Associate Professor of Reformed Theology, Western Theological Seminary, Holland, MI
Miles V. Van Pelt, Lecturer in Greek, Gordon College, Wenham, MA
Robert E. Van Voorst, Professor of New Testament, Western Theological Seminary, Holland, MI
John S. Vassar, Baylor University, Waco, TX
Pauline A. Viviano, Associate Professor of Theology, Loyola University Chicago, Chicago, IL
Ralph W. Vunderink, Adjunct Professor, Aquinas College, Grand Rapids, MI
Larry L. Walker, Professor of Old Testament

and Semitic Languages, Mid-America Baptist Theological Seminary, Memphis, TN
Carey Walsh, Assistant Professor of Hebrew Bible, Rhodes College, Memphis, TN
Duane F. Watson, Associate Professor of New Testament Studies; Chair, Department of Religion and Philosophy, Malone College, Canton, OH
JoAnn Ford Watson, H. R. Gill Chair Professor of Theology; Chair, Department of Church History, Theology, and Philosophy, Ashland Theological Seminary, Ashland, OH
Judith Romney Wegner, Visiting Associate Professor of Religious Studies, Connecticut College, New London, CT
Rodney A. Werline, Assistant Professor of Hebrew Bible and Early Judaism, Emmanuel School of Religion, Johnson City, TN
Jim West, Adjunct Professor of Bible, Quartz Hill School of Theology, Petros, TN
Marsha C. White, Lecturer, Andover Newton Theological School, Newton Centre, MA
Pete F. Wilbanks, Pastor, Osyka Baptist Church, Osyka, MS
Joel F. Williams, Associate Professor of Bible, Columbia International University, Columbia, SC
Tyler F. Williams, Instructor in Old Testament, North American Baptist College/Edmonton Baptist Seminary, Edmonton, AB
Wendell Willis, Associate Professor of Bible, Abilene Christian University, Abilene, TX
J. Christian Wilson, Professor of Religious Studies, Elon College, Elon College, NC
Kevin A. Wilson, Ph.D. Student, The Johns Hopkins University, Baltimore, MD
Donald H. Wimmer, Professor of Religious Studies, Seton Hall University, South Orange, NJ
Joseph F. Wimmer, S.T.D., Assistant Professor of Biblical Studies, Washington Theological Union, Washington, DC
John D. Wineland, Associate Professor of History, Kentucky Christian College, Grayson, KY
Willard W. Winter, Professor of Biblical Studies, Cincinnati Bible College and Seminary, Cincinnati, OH
Gregory A. Wolfe, Adjunct Professor, New Orleans Baptist Theological Seminary, New Orleans, LA
Lisa Michelle Wolfe, Ph.D. Candidate, Garrett Evangelical Theological School, Evanston, IL
R. Glenn Wooden, Assistant Professor of Biblical Languages, Acadia Divinity College, Wolfville, NS
Robert B. Wright, Professor of Hebrew Bible, Temple University, Philadelphia, PA
Frank D. Wulf, Ph.D. Candidate, Columbia University/Union Theological Seminary, New York, NY
Stephen Von Wyrick, Professor of Religion, University of Mary Hardin-Baylor, Belton, TX
Seung Ai Yang, Assistant Professor of New Testament, Jesuit School of Theology at Berkeley, Berkeley, CA
Charles Yeboah, Ph.D. Student, Loyola University Chicago, Chicago, IL
Kent L. Yinger, Program Director, Center for Advanced Theological Studies, Fuller Theological Seminary, Pasadena, CA
Christine Roy Yoder, Instructor in Old Testament, Columbia Theological Seminary, Decatur, GA
K. Lawson Younger, Jr., Professor of Old Testament, Semitic Languages, and Ancient Near Eastern History, Trinity International University Divinity School, Deerfield, IL
Randall W. Younker, Assistant Professor of Old Testament and Biblical Archaeology, Director, Institute of Archaeology, Andrews University, Berrien Springs, MI
Frank J. Yurco, Egyptologist and Research Associate, Field Museum of Natural History, Chicago, IL
Juris Zarins, Professor of Anthropology, Southwest Missouri State University, Springfield, MO
Mark Ziese, Associate Professor of Old Testament, Cincinnati Bible Seminary, Cincinnati, OH
Jeffrey R. Zorn, Visiting Assistant Professor of Near Eastern Studies, Cornell University, Ithaca, NY

Preface

Two terms in the title of this volume require some comment (i.e., definition or explanation and elaboration): "Bible" and "Dictionary." "Bible" refers to the Christian Bible, as commonly used in places where the great majority of the people have some affiliation with the Christian Church, and includes both the Old and New Testaments. The OT for Protestants is the same as the Hebrew Scriptures acknowledged by the Jewish community as sacred Scripture. Catholic Christians also accept the Apocrypha or Deuterocanonicals as part of the OT. All of the above are treated in this Dictionary, as well as the NT, which is accepted as canonical Scripture by practically all Christian groups.

As for the second term, Bible dictionaries generally come in two sizes: multivolume like the classic *Hastings' Dictionary of the Bible* (ultimately in five volumes), the more recent *Interpreter's Dictionary of the Bible* (originally in four volumes with a supplement added later), and the current *Anchor Bible Dictionary* (in six volumes); and one-volume dictionaries, like the familiar *Eerdmans Bible Dictionary*, of which the present volume represents not merely a new edition but in essence a fresh beginning. It would have been better to use different labels for different products, as the two kinds of dictionary differ markedly in conception, approach, function, and utility. The former are more like encyclopedias (a better term) and make a larger claim, namely, to provide important and useful information about the Bible in its world, and to cover the subject matter in sufficient depth and breadth to enable both the general reader and the specialist to satisfy their needs and interests on a given text or topic without recourse to other sources. That is a large order indeed, and even the most extensive dictionaries strain to meet such a standard (hence they provide ample bibliographies for further study and research).

On the other hand, a one-volume Bible dictionary is intended to be a rapid-response reference work. While it should cover the same territory as the larger work, and contain approximately the same number of entries, everything from definitions to descriptions and discussions will be scaled down proportionately, to fit the more restricted format. Briefly put, it should be comprehensive but not exhaustive. It should supply sufficient factual information about books and persons, places and events, define words and longer expressions, and thereby fulfill the basic purpose of any dictionary: to explain. Beyond that basic service, it should provide the necessary and valuable leads to further elaboration and enlightenment, so that the interested reader can pursue the topic in a larger, more detailed reference work or in books and articles devoted to that subject.

More specifically, a modern Bible dictionary should provide sufficient factual data to define and explain all the distinctive terms and expressions found in the Bible. In addition, it should reflect the present state of scholarly research in this field, including not only the standard and long-established results of serious scholarship, but also more recent trends and developments in as fair-minded and nonpartisan a way as possible.

While the realization of such a goal may be regarded as beyond the reach of fallible human beings, the attempt is nevertheless justified, and different means and routes can be used to reach or approximate it. One way is to choose a paragon of unassailable virtue, whose balanced judgment and equable sensibility are unchallenged, as an editor to write all the articles and edit the whole work. This has been tried in years past, but in today's world of the Bible that is asking too much of any one person. An alternative procedure is to compile a long list of contributors, who represent and reflect a wide spectrum of views and positions relating to the Bible, and ask them to use their expertise to write about what they know best in the best way that they know. While the results will hardly be uniform and may not produce a smooth surface, the admixture will faithfully reflect the present state of studies and a full spectrum of scholarly attitudes and opinions about the central issues along with more peripheral ones.

Therefore, we make no claim to either unanimity or uniformity in the treatment of the varied and numerous topics of the Bible. But we have attempted to cover most if not all of the items likely to arise and concerning which readers will seek information and guidance. We have assembled a worthy list of contributors, whose chief common attribute is that they are serious scholars who have earned the respect of their colleagues in our field of study, and who have something of material value to offer.

We give special credit to our Associate Editor, Allen C. Myers, my former student at the University of Michigan, who has accomplished Herculean editorial work in fashioning a scholarly and approachable volume from the many and sundry pieces. His is a daunting and unenviable task. Those of us who are editors know and recognize his devoted work and countless hours to bring this project to fruition.

In presenting this work to the public, we have tried earnestly to provide useful and helpful information to maintain the high standards and the validity, integrity, and established value achieved by earlier editions of this reference work. We are following in the footsteps of proven leaders and standing on the shoulders of giants.

David Noel Freedman
Editor-in-Chief

Introduction

The *Eerdmans Dictionary of the Bible* is intended as a tool for practical Bible use, reflecting recent discoveries and the breadth of current biblical scholarship, including insights from critical analysis of literary, historical, archaeological, sociological, and other methodological issues. Approximately 5000 entries identify all persons and places named in the Bible, as well as cultural, natural, geographical, and literary phenomena — matters that Bible students at all levels may encounter in reading or discussion. Articles explaining and interpreting important focuses of biblical theology, text and transmission, Near Eastern archaeology, extrabiblical writings, and pertinent ecclesiastical traditions have been incorporated in an effort to make this the most comprehensive one-volume Bible dictionary available.

The publishers have selected as editors and contributors a host of first-rank authorities in the field. Authors represent a range of critical and theological stances and reflect the growing place of interdisciplinary interests in biblical scholarship. Contributors have been charged to remain sensitive to the broad spectrum of interpretation, presenting objectively divergent perspectives and featuring inclusive bibliographies. The editors and consulting editors have sought to identify not only pertinent persons, places, and other phenomena but also the significant issues facing biblical scholarship and related fields. To this end, they have enlisted nearly 600 leading scholars and matched them with topics related to their areas of specialization. Unsigned articles have been written by the editors.

Although the initial intent was merely to revise and update the 1987 edition of the *Eerdmans Bible Dictionary*, the publishers were encouraged by pre-eminent biblical scholar David Noel Freedman to build upon the expertise gained in producing that volume and to develop in essence an entirely new reference work that would represent the vast strides made in biblical scholarship in recent decades. The volume at hand is testimony to Professor Freedman's wisdom and vision, as well as his international reputation as a giant in the field of biblical studies and editor par excellence. We are indebted to his great devotion to biblical studies and desire to communicate the fruits of scholarship, and have benefitted immeasurably not only from his ability to marshall the current giants of the field but also from his enthusiasm for identifying and mentoring the next generation of scholars.

How To Use the *Eerdmans Dictionary of the Bible*

Articles appear in alphabetical order according to the following scheme. Compound words involving a hyphen or space (e.g., Beer-sheba; El

Elyon) are treated as a solid word. For main words followed by a comma (e.g., Isaiah, Book of) alphabetization is restricted to the word preceding the comma, as are titles including parenthetical matter (e.g., Worship [New Testament]). If the same name represents persons, places, deities, etc., separate articles are provided. When an article name designates more than one person or place, multiple entries are arranged in order of the first occurrence of the term, following the English canon, and not necessarily chronologically.

To accommodate best the nuances of English Bible translations, this edition is based on the New Revised Standard Bible, with attention to alternate readings in other versions where appropriate. Biblical citations follow the NRSV versification; variant versification for the MT or LXX follows in parentheses, e.g., "Num. 16:36-50(MT 17:1-15)." Parallel accounts are indicated by the equal sign (e.g., 2 Sam. 22:2-51 = Ps. 18:1-50) or simply by "par." (e.g., Matt. 17:1-8 par.).

Rather than attempt to devise an artificial, anglicized pronunciation for the names of persons and places, the editors have provided in the headings of articles transliterations of the Hebrew, Aramaic, or Greek forms of the names, thus approximating the original pronunciations (see the table of Transliteration and Pronunciation, front and back endsheets). Likewise, in most instances no attempt has been made to conjure a "meaning" for biblical names. Variant forms of names, including alternate spellings occurring in the NRSV and secondary names or readings of persons and places, are listed in article headings following the transliteration/pronunciation (e.g., "[also JERIMOTH]"). Technical sigla for Dead Sea and Nag Hammadi texts are indicated in the headings of those articles.

On many issues of interpretation there is currently no scholarly consensus, and the field of biblical studies reflects a pluralism of methodologies and assumptions bolstered simultaneously by increased specialization and by an appreciation for insights gained from interdisciplinary study, not to mention a massive explosion of data. In their attempts to resolve issues of continuing research, it is therefore understandable that authors will vary in their applications of texts and material evidence. Concerted effort has been made to provide balanced discussions reflecting different viewpoints (cf., e.g., the articles CONQUEST: BIBLICAL NARRATIVE and SETTLEMENT: ARCHAEOLOGY). While effort has been made to standardize such matters as spelling and citation, it has not always been possible — or perhaps even desirable — to resolve variant interpretations of dating and geographical location. Readers may on occasion wish to compare related articles for alternate chronologies and identifications. Both B.C./A.D. and B.C.E./C.E. are used with dates, following the preference of individual authors.

Modern names of historical and archaeological sites are indicated by both the standard Arabic and Modern Hebrew forms where appropriate. Further identification includes the six- to ten-digit map reference numbers keyed to the grid system used by professional archaeologists in locating sites in Israel and Jordan. The first three digits (or in some cases four or five digits preceding the period) indicate the north-south axis and the final three digits (or those following the period) specify the east-west axis. (See further, map of archaeological sites in the map section at the back of the book.)

Bibliographies provide the reader opportunity to investigate further reports of current research as well as more comprehensive and detailed treatments of subject matter. Effort has been made to indicate the most recent editions and English translations. Illustrations (charts, photos, and line drawings), as well as the color map section, have been carefully selected to significantly complement the text and further enhance understanding of the subject matter.

Acknowledgments

A project of this dimension would have been impossible without the contribution of many individuals. Particularly deserving of our appreciation are Editorial Associates Julye M. Bidmead and Bruce E. Willoughby, whose careful attention to detail in checking references and information and skillful finessing of text and format have helped to produce a reference aid that is both accurate and readable. In addition to the recommendations of the Consulting Editors, invaluable service in identifying and enlisting contributors in a variety of specializations has been provided by Oded Borowski, Kathleen Farmer, Alysia Anne Fischer, Peter Machinist, Dale W. Manor, Gerald L. Mattingly, Michael P. O'Connor, Lynn Tatum, and Randall W. Younker.

Our colleagues at Wm. B. Eerdmans Publishing Company have undergirded this project with skill and dedication throughout. Special thanks are due to Alix Kayayan, who developed the computer database without which the coordination of authors, assignments, and the editorial and production processes would have been nigh unmanageable; Donald M. Prus, for overseeing a team of keyboardists and ingeniously tackling myriad typographical concerns; T. A. Straayer, computer editor extraordinaire; and Klaas Wolterstorff, for developing a design and guiding the Dictionary through the press. In particular, we are grateful for the unflagging support of Wm. B. Eerdmans, Jr., who through the years has demonstrated unparalleled commitment to serious and responsible biblical scholarship and a fascination for and dedication to the marketplace of ideas.

In the course of preparing this volume it has become abundantly clear that, in addition to being authorities in their respective fields of specialization, biblical scholars are nonetheless mortal, subject to the trials and turmoils of human existence. Their perseverance, for some in the face of serious personal and familial illness and tragedy, is testimony to their commitment not only to scholarship but to the very truths which this volume seeks to illuminate.

THE EDITORS

Abbreviations

AARAcad	American Academy of Religion Academy Series
AASOR	Annual of the American Schools of Oriental Research
AB	Anchor Bible
ABD	*The Anchor Bible Dictionary*, ed. D. N. Freedman
ADAJ	*Annual of the Department of Antiquities of Jordan*
AGJU	Arbeiten zur Geschichte des antiken Judentums und des Urchristentums
AJA	*American Journal of Archaeology*
AJBA	*Australian Journal of Biblical Archaeology*
AJSL	*American Journal of Semitic Languages and Literature*
AJP	*American Journal of Philology*
Akk.	Akkadian
ALGHJ	Arbeiten zur Literatur und Geschichte des hellenistischen Judentums
AnBib	Analecta biblica
ANEP	*The Ancient Near East in Pictures*, ed. J. B. Pritchard
ANET	*Ancient Near Eastern Texts*, ed. J. B. Pritchard
AnOr	Analecta orientalia
ANRW	*Aufstieg und Niedergang der römischen Welt*, ed. H. Temporini and W. Haase
AOAT	Alter Orient und Altes Testament
AOS	American Oriental Series
Arab.	Arabic
ARAB	*Ancient Records of Assyria and Babylonia*, ed. D. D. Luckenbill
Aram.	Aramaic
ARM	Archives royales de Mari
ASOR	American Schools of Oriental Research
ASORDS	ASOR Dissertation Series
ASORMS	ASOR Monograph Series
Assyr.	Assyrian
ASTI	*Annual of the Swedish Theological Institute*
ASV	American Standard Version
AUM	Andrews University Monograph
AUSS	*Andrews University Seminary Studies*
BA	*Biblical Archaeologist*
Bab.	Babylonian
BAR	*The BA Reader*
BARev	*Biblical Archaeology Review*
BASOR	*Bulletin of the American Schools of Oriental Research*
BBR	*Bulletin for Biblical Research*
B.C.E.	Before the Common/Christian Era (= B.C.)
BETL	Bibliotheca ephemeridum theologicarum lovaniensium
BHK	*Biblia Hebraica*, ed. R. Kittel
BHQ	*Biblia Hebraica Quinta*
BHS	*Biblia Hebraica Stuttgartensia*

BIBAL	Berkeley Institute of Biblical Archaeology and Literature
Bibl	*Biblica*
BibOr	*Biblica et Orientalia*
BibRev	*Bible Review*
BIOSCS	*Bulletin of the International Organization for Septuagint and Cognate Studies*
BJRL	*Bulletin of the John Rylands Library*
BJS	*Brown Judaic Studies*
BLS	Bible and Literature
BN	*Biblische Notizien*
BNTC	Black's New Testament Commentaries
BR	*Biblical Research*
BSac	*Bibliotheca Sacra*
BTB	*Biblical Theology Bulletin*
BWANT	Beiträge zur Wissenschaft vom Alten und Neuen Testament
BZAW	*Beihefte zur ZAW*
BZNW	*Beihefte zur ZNW*
CAH	*Cambridge Ancient History*
CANE	*Civilizations of the Ancient Near East,* ed. J. M. Sasson
CBC	Cambridge Bible Commentary
CBQ	*Catholic Biblical Quarterly*
CBQMS	*CBQ* Monograph Series
C.E.	Common/Christian Era (= A.D.)
CIJ	*Corpus inscriptionum judaicarum*
CIL	*Corpus inscriptionum latinarum*
Comm.	Commentary
ConBNT	Coniectanea biblica, New Testament
ConBOT	Coniectanea biblica, Old Testament
Cowley	A. E. Cowley, *Aramaic Papyri of the Fifth Century*
CRINT	Compendia rerum iudaicarum ad novum testamentum
d.	died
DDD	*Dictionary of Deities and Demons in the Bible,* ed. K. van der Toorn, B. Becking, and P. W. van der Horst, rev. ed.
diss.	dissertation
DMOA	Documenta et monumenta orientis antiqui
DS	Dissertation series
EA	Tell el-Amarna tablets
EDNT	*Exegetical Dictionary of the New Testament,* ed. H. Balz and G. Schneider
Egyp.	Egyptian
Elam.	Elamite
EncJud	*Encyclopaedia Judaica* (1971-72)
EPRO	Etudes préliminaires aux religions orientales dans l'empire Romain
ERE	*Encyclopaedia of Religion and Ethics,* ed. J. Hastings
ErIsr	*Eretz-Israel*
EvQ	*Evangelical Quarterly*
ExpTim	*Expository Times*
FOTL	Forms of the Old Testament Literature
FRLANT	Forschungen zur Religion und Literatur des Alten und Neuen Testaments
Ger.	German
Gk.	Greek
GN	Place name
HAR	*Hebrew Annual Review*
HBT	*Horizons in Biblical Theology*
HDR	Harvard Dissertations in Religion
Heb.	Hebrew
Herm	Hermeneia
HO	Handbuch der Orientalistik
HR	*History of Religions*
HSM	Harvard Semitic Monographs
HSS	Harvard Semitic Studies
HTR	*Harvard Theological Review*
HTS	Harvard Theological Studies
HUCA	*Hebrew Union College Annual*
HUCM	*Hebrew Union College Monographs*
ICC	International Critical Commentary
IDB	*Interpreter's Dictionary of the Bible,* ed. G. A. Buttrick; *Sup,* ed. K. Crim
IEJ	*Israel Exploration Journal*
Int	*Interpretation*
IOS	*Israel Oriental Society*
IRT	Issues in Religion and Theology
ITC	International Theological Commentary
ISBE	*International Standard Bible Encyclopedia,* ed. G. W. Bromiley
JAAR	*Journal of the American Academy of Religion*

JAC	*Jahrbuch für Antike und Christentum*
JANES	*Journal of the Ancient Near Eastern Society*
JAOS	*Journal of the American Oriental Society*
JB	Jerusalem Bible
JBL	*Journal of Biblical Literature*
JBLMS	*JBL* Monograph Series
JCS	*Journal of Cuneiform Studies*
JEA	*Journal of Egyptian Archaeology*
JESHO	*Journal of Economic and Social History of the Orient*
JFSR	*Journal of Feminist Studies in Religion*
JIES	*Journal of Indo-european Studies*
JJS	*Journal of Jewish Studies*
JNES	*Journal of Near Eastern Studies*
JNSL	*Journal of Northwest Semitic Languages*
JPS	Jewish Publication Society
JQR	*Jewish Quarterly Review*
JRAS	*Journal of the Royal Asiatic Society*
JSJ	*Journal for the Study of Judaism*
JSNT	*Journal for the Study of the New Testament*
JSOT	*Journal for the Study of the Old Testament*
JSP	*Journal for the Study of the Pseudepigrapha*
JTS	*Journal of Theological Studies*
K	Kethibh
KAH	*Keilschrifttexte aus Assur historischen Inhalts*
KAI	*Kanaanäische und aramäische Inschriften*, ed. H. Donner and W. Röllig
KJV	King James Version
KTU	*Die keilalphabetischen Texte aus Ugarit*, ed. M. Dietrich, O. Loretz, and J. Sanmartín
Lat.	Latin
LXX	Septuagint
MAL	Middle Assyrian Laws
mg	margin
MHeb.	Modern Hebrew
MT	Masoretic Text
NAB	New American Bible
NASB	New American Standard Bible
NCBC	New Century Bible Commentary
NEAEHL	*The New Encyclopedia of Archaeological Excavations in the Holy Land*, ed. E. Stern
NEB	New English Bible
NHMS	Nag Hammadi and Manichaean Studies
NHS	Nag Hammadi Studies
NIB	*The New Interpreter's Bible*, ed. L. Keck et al.
NIBC	New International Biblical Commentary
NICNT	New International Commentary on the New Testament
NICOT	New International Commentary on the Old Testament
NIDNTT	*New International Dictionary of New Testament Theology*, ed. C. Brown
NIGTC	New International Greek Testament Commentary
NIV	New International Version
NJB	New Jerusalem Bible
NJBC	*The New Jerome Biblical Commentary*, ed. R. E. Brown, J. A. Fitzmyer, and R. E. Murphy
NJPSV	New Jewish Publication Society Version
NKJV	New King James Version
NLT	New Living Translation
NovT	*Novum Testamentum*
NRSV	New Revised Standard Version
NT	New Testament
NTOA	Novum Testamentum et orbis antiquus
NTS	*New Testament Studies*
OBO	Orbis biblicus et orientalis
OBT	Overtures to Biblical Theology
OE	Old English
OEANE	*Oxford Encyclopedia of Archaeology in the Near East*, ed. E. M. Meyers
OG	Old Greek
OGIS	*Orientis Graecae Inscriptiones Selectae*, ed. W. Dittenberger
OIP	Oriental Institute Publications
OLZ	*Orientalische Literaturzeitung*
O. Pers.	Old Persian
Or	*Orientalia*
OrSuec	*Orientalia suecana*
OSA	Old South Arabian
OT	Old Testament
OTG	Old Testament Guides
OTL	Old Testament Library

OTP	*The Old Testament Pseudepigrapha,* ed. J. H. Charlesworth
OTS	Old Testament Studies
OuTS	Oudtestamentische studien
PEF	Palestine Exploration Fund
PEQ	*Palestine Exploration Quarterly*
PGM	*Papyri graecae magicae,* ed. K. Preisendanz
Phoen.	Phoenician
PTMS	Princeton Theological Monograph Series
PW	*Real-Encyclopädie der classischen Altertumswissenschaft,* ed. A. Pauly-G. Wissowa
Q	Qere
RB	*Revue biblique*
REB	Revised English Bible
ResQ	*Restoration Quarterly*
RevExp	*Review and Expositor*
RS	Ras Shamra text
RSO	*Revista degli studi orientali*
RSV	Revised Standard Version
SAOC	Studies in Ancient Oriental Civilization
SBLABS	Society of Biblical Literature Archaeology and Biblical Studies
SBLDS	Society of Biblical Literature Dissertation Series
SBLEJL	Society of Biblical Literature Early Judaism and Its Literature
SBLMasS	Society of Biblical Literature Masoretic Studies
SBLMS	Society of Biblical Literature Monograph Series
SBLRBS	Society of Biblical Literature Resources for Biblical Study
SBLSBS	Society of Biblical Literature Sources for Biblical Study
SBLSCS	Society of Biblical Literature Septuagint and Cognate Studies
SBLSP	Society of Biblical Literature Seminar Papers
SBLSS	Society of Biblical Literature Semeia Studies
SBLWAW	Society of Biblical Literature Writings of the Ancient World
SBT	*Studies in Biblical Theology*
ScrHier	Scripta Hierosolymitana
SEÅ	*Svensk exegetisk årsbok*
Sem.	Semitic
SHANE	Studies in the History of the Ancient Near East
SJLA	Studies in Judaism in Late Antiquity
SJOT	*Scandinavian Journal of the Old Testament*
SJT	*Scottish Journal of Theology*
SNTSMS	Society for New Testament Studies Monograph Series
Sond	Sonderreihe
SOTSMS	Society for Old Testament Studies Monograph Series
SPB	Studia postbiblica
SR	*Studies in Religion/Sciences religieuses*
SSN	Studia semitica neerlandica
STDJ	Studies on the Texts of the Desert of Judah
Sum.	Sumerian
Sup	Supplement
SVTP	Studia in Veteris Testamenti Pseudepigrapha
Syr.	Syriac
TBT	*The Bible Today*
TD	*Theology Digest*
TDNT	*Theological Dictionary of the New Testament,* ed. G. Kittel and G. Friedrich
TDOT	*Theological Dictionary of the Old Testament,* ed. G. J. Botterweck, H. Ringgren, and H.-J. Fabry
TEV	Today's English Version
Tg.	Targum
TGUOS	*Transactions of the Glasgow University Oriental Society*
TNTC	Tyndale New Testament Commentaries
TOTC	Tyndale Old Testament Commentaries
TS	*Theological Studies*
TynBul	*Tyndale Bulletin*
UBS	United Bible Societies
UF	*Ugarit-Forschungen*
Ugar.	Ugaritic
USQR	*Union Seminary Quarterly Review*
UT	C. H. Gordon, *Ugaritic Textbook*
UUÅ	Uppsala universitetsårsskrift
VC	*Vigiliae christianae*
VT	*Vetus Testamentum*
VTSup	Supplements to *VT*
Vulg.	Vulgate
WBC	Word Biblical Commentary
WTJ	*Westminster Theological Journal*

WUNT	*Wissenschaftliche Untersuchungen zum Neuen Testament*
WVDOG	Wissenschaftliche Veroffentlichungen der Deutschen Orientgesellschaft
ZA	*Zeitschrift für Assyriologie*
ZÄS	*Zeitschrift für ägyptische Sprache und Altertumskunde*
ZAW	*Zeitschrift für die alttestamentliche Wissenschaft*
ZDMG	*Zeitschrift der deutschen morgenländischen Gesellschaft*
ZDPV	*Zeitschrift des deutschen Palästina-Vereins*
ZNW	*Zeitschrift für die neutestamentliche Wissenschaft*

Biblical Books

Old Testament

Gen.	Genesis
Exod.	Exodus
Lev.	Leviticus
Num.	Numbers
Deut.	Deuteronomy
Josh.	Joshua
Judg.	Judges
1–2 Sam.	1–2 Samuel
1–2 Kgs.	1–2 Kings
1–2 Chr.	1–2 Chronicles
Ezra	Ezra
Neh.	Nehemiah
Esth.	Esther
Job	Job
Ps. (Pss.)	Psalms
Prov.	Proverbs
Eccl.	Ecclesiastes
Cant.	Song of Solomon
Isa.	Isaiah
Jer.	Jeremiah
Ezek.	Ezekiel
Dan.	Daniel
Hos.	Hosea
Joel	Joel
Amos	Amos
Obad.	Obadiah
Jonah	Jonah
Mic.	Micah
Nah.	Nahum
Hab.	Habakkuk
Zeph.	Zephaniah
Hag.	Haggai
Zech.	Zechariah
Mal.	Malachi

Apocrypha/Deuterocanonicals

Tob.	Tobit
Jdt.	Judith
Add. Esth.	Additions to Esther
Wis.	Wisdom of Solomon
Sir.	Sirach
Bar.	Baruch
Ep. Jer.	Epistle of Jeremiah
Pr. Azar.	Prayer of Azariah
Sus.	Susanna
Bel	Bel and the Dragon
1–2–3–4 Macc.	1–2–3–4 Maccabees
1–2 Esdr.	1–2 Esdras
Pr. Man.	Prayer of Manasseh

New Testament

Matt.	Matthew
Mark	Mark
Luke	Luke
John	John
Acts	Acts
Rom.	Romans
1–2 Cor.	1–2 Corinthians
Gal.	Galatians
Eph.	Ephesians
Phil.	Philippians
Col.	Colossians
1–2 Thess.	1–2 Thessalonians
1–2 Tim.	1–2 Timothy
Tit.	Titus
Phlm.	Philemon
Heb.	Hebrews
Jas.	James
1–2 Pet.	1–2 Peter
1–2–3 John	1–2–3 John
Jude	Jude
Rev.	Revelation

Ancient Works

Pseudepigraphal Books

Adam and Eve	Books of Adam and Eve
Apoc. Abr.	Apocalypse of Abraham
2–3 Apoc. Bar.	2–3 Apocalypse of Baruch
Apoc. Elijah	Apocalypse of Elijah
Apoc. Mos.	Apocalypse of Moses
As. Mos.	Assumption of Moses
Asc. Isa.	Ascension of Isaiah
1–2–3 En.	1–2–3 Enoch
Ep. Arist.	Epistle of Aristeas
Gk. Apoc. Ezra	Greek Apocalypse of Ezra

Hist. Rech.	History of the Rechabites
Jub.	Jubilees
Mart. Isa.	Martyrdom of Isaiah
Odes Sol.	Odes of Solomon
Pss. Sol.	Psalms of Solomon
Sib. Or.	Sibylline Oracles
T. 12 Patr.	Testaments of the Twelve Patriarchs
T. Benj.	Testament of Benjamin

Dead Sea Scrolls

CD	Damascus Document (Zadokite Fragment)
1QapGen	Genesis Apocryphon
1QH	Thanksgiving Hymns (*Hôdayôt*)
1QIsa[a,b]	Isaiah Scroll, first and second copies
1QM	War Scroll (*Milḥāmâ*)
1QpHab	Pesher on Habakkuk
1QS	Manual of Discipline/Rule of the Community (*Serek hayyaḥad*)
3Q15/3QInv	Copper Scroll
4QDibHam	Words of the Luminaries
4QMess ar	Aramaic "Messianic" text
4QpNah	Pesher on Nahum
4QpPs37	Pesher on Psalm 37
4QSam	Samuel text
4QTob	Tobit text
4QXII	Minor Prophets text
11QMelch	Melchizedek text
11QT	Temple Scroll
8Ḥev XII gr	Greek Minor Prophets text from Naḥal Ḥever

Rabbinic Texts

ʿAbod. Zar.	*ʿAboda Zara*
ʾAbot. R. Nat.	*ʾAbot de Rabbi Nathan*
ʿArak.	*ʿArakin*
b.	Babylonian Talmud
B. Bat.	*Baba Batra*
Bek.	*Bekorot*
Ber.	*Berakot*
Bik.	*Bikkurim*
B. Meṣ	*Baba Meṣiʿa*
B. Qam.	*Baba Qamma*
Dem.	*Demai*
ʿEd.	*ʿEduyyot*
ʿErub.	*ʿErubin*
Giṭ.	*Giṭṭin*
Ḥag.	*Ḥagiga*
Ḥal.	*Ḥalla*
Hor.	*Horayot*
Ḥul.	*Ḥullin*
Ker.	*Keritot*
Ketub.	*Ketubot*
Kil.	*Kilʾayim*
m.	Mishnah
Maʿ*as.*	*Maʿaserot*
Mak.	*Makkot*
Makš.	*Makširin*
Meg.	*Megilla*
Meʿil.	*Meʿila*
Menaḥ	*Menaḥot*
Mid.	*Middot*
Midr.	Midrash
Miqw.	*Miqwaʾot*
Moʿed Qaṭ.	*Moʿed Qaṭan*
Ned.	*Nedarim*
Neg.	*Negaʿim*
Nez.	*Neziqin*
Nid.	*Niddah*
Ohol.	*Oholot*
ʿOr.	*ʿOrla*
Pesaḥ	*Pesaḥim*
Qidd.	*Qiddušin*
Qod.	*Qodašin*
Gen. Rab. (etc.)	*Genesis Rabbah*
Roš Haš.	*Roš Haššana*
Šabb.	*Šabbat*
Sanh.	*Sanhedrin*
Šeb.	*Šebiʿit*
Šebu.	*Šebuʿot*
Šeqal.	*Šeqalim*
Sop.	*Soperim*
Sukk.	*Sukka*
t.	Tosepta
Taʿan.	*Taʿanit*
Tem.	*Temura*
Ter.	*Terumot*
Tg. Ps.-J.	*Targum Pseudo-Jonathan*
Tohar.	*Toharot*
T. Yom	*Tebul Yom*
ʿUq.	*ʿUqṣin*
y.	Jerusalem Talmud
Yad.	*Yadayim*
Yebam.	*Yebamot*
Zebaḥ.	*Zebaḥim*
Zer.	*Zeraʿim*

Early Christian Writings

Acts Pil.	Acts of Pilate
Apoc. Pet.	Apocalypse of Peter
Apost. Const.	Apostolic Constitutions
Augustine	
Civ. Dei	*De civitate Dei (City of God)*
Barn.	Barnabas
Basil (the Great)	
Epp.	*Epistles*
1–2 Clem.	1–2 Clement

Clement of Alexandria
Ecl. proph. — *Eclogae ex scriptoris prophetics*
Exhort. — *Exhortation to the Greeks (Protrepticus)*
Misc. — *Miscellanies (Stromateis)*
Did. — Didache
Epiphanius
Adv. haer. — *Adversus lxxx haereses (Panarion)*
Eusebius *HE* — *Historia ecclesiastica*
Onom. — *Onomasticon*
Praep. ev. — *Praeparatio evangelica*
Vita Const. — *Life of Constantine*
Gos. Thom. — Gospel of Thomas
Hermas *Vis.* — *Visions*
Hippolytus *Ref.* — *Refutation of All Heresies*
Ignatius of Antioch *Eph.* — *Epistle to the Ephesians*
Magn. — *Epistle to the Magnesians*
Phld. — *Epistle to the Philadelphians*
Polyc. — *Epistle to Polycarp*
Rom. — *Epistle to the Romans*
Smyrn. — *Epistle to the Smyrnaeans*
Trall. — *Epistle to the Trallians*
Irenaeus
Adv, haer. — *Adversus omnes haereses*
Jerome *Ep.* — *Epistulae*
Justin Martyr
Apol. — *Apologia*
Dial. — *Dialogus contra Tryphonem*
Lactantius
Div. inst. — *Divinae institutiones*
Mart. Pol. — Martyrdom of Polycarp
Origen *Comm. in Jn.* — *Commentary on John*
Contra Cels. — *Contra Celsum*
De prin. — *De principiis*
Ex. mart. — *Exhortation to Martyrdom*
Hom. Luke — *Homilies on Luke*
Polycarp of Smyrna *Phil.* — *Epistle to the Philippians*
Prot. Jas. — Protevangelium of James
Tertullian
Ad Mart. — *Ad Martyras*
Adv. Marc. — *Adversus Marcionem*
Apol. — *Apologeticus*
De bapt. — *De baptismo*
De fuga — *De fuga in persecutione*
De praescr. haer. — *De praescriptione haereticorum*
Vincent of Lérins
Common. — *Commonitorium*

Other Ancient Works

Aeschylus *Supp.* — *The Suppliants*
Aristophanes
Plut. — *Plutus*
Athenaeus *Deip.* — *Deipnosophists*
M. Aurelius
Med. — *Meditations*
Cicero *De leg.* — *De legibus*
Ep. ad Fam. — *Epistulae ad familiares*
Tusc. disp. — *Tusculanae disputationes*
Verr. — *In Verrem*
Curtius Rufus
Hist. Alex. — *Historiae Alexandri Magni*
Dio Cassius *Hist.* — *Roman History*
Diodorus Siculus
Hist. — *Library of History*
Dionysius of Halicarnassus
Rom. arch. — *Roman Archaeology*
Euripides *Alc.* — *Alcestis*
Iph. A. — *Iphigenia in Aulis*
Iph. T. — *Iphigenia in Tauris*
Tro. — *Trojan Women*
Herodotus *Hist.* — *History*
Hesiod *Theog.* — *Theogony*
Homer *Od.* — *Odyssey*
Josephus *Ag. Ap.* — *Against Apion (Contra Apionem)*
Ant. — *Antiquities of the Jews*
BJ — *Bellum Judaicum (The Jewish War)*
Vita — *Life*
Livy *Urb. cond.* — *Ab urbe condita*
Ovid *Metam.* — *Metamorphoses*
Pausanias
Descr. Gr. — *Description of Greece*
Philo *Apol. Jud.* — *Apologia pro Iudaeis*
Flacc. — *Contra Flaccum*
Heres — *Quis rerum divinarum heres*
Leg. — *De legatione ad Gaium*
Quod omn. — *Quod omnis probus liber sit*
Somn. — *De somniis*
Spec. leg. — *De specialibus legibus*
Philostratus
Vit. Ap. — *Life of Apollonius of Tyana*
Photius *Bibl.* — *Bibliotheca (Myriobiblion)*
Plato *Symp.* — *Symposium*
Pliny (the Elder)
Nat. hist. — *Naturalis historia*
Pliny (the Younger) *Ep.* — *Epistulae*
Plutarch *Cic.* — *Cicero*
Quaest. conv. — *Quaestiones convivales*
Vita Caes. — *Life of Caesar*
Polybius *Hist.* — *Histories*
Pseudo-Philo
LAB — *Liber antiquitatum biblicarum (Biblical Antiquities)*
Ptolemy *Geog.* — *Geography*

Quintilian	
Inst. orat.	*De institutione oratoria*
Seneca *Dial.*	*Dialogues*
Ep.	*Ad Lucilium epistulae morales*
Strabo *Geog.*	*Geography*
Suetonius *Claud.*	*Life of Claudius*
Tacitus *Ann.*	*Annales ab excessu divi Augusti*
Hist.	*Histories*
Varro	
De ling. lat.	*De lingua latina*
Velleius Paterculus *Hist. rom.*	*Historia romana*
Xenophon *Anab.*	*Anabasis*
Laced.	*Lacedaemoniorum republica (Constitution of Sparta)*

A

A
A symbol used to designate the Codex Alexandrinus.

AARON (Heb. *'ahărōn*)
A descendant of Levi and brother of Moses (Exod. 6:20; Num. 26:59; 1 Chr. 6:3[MT 5:22]), a co-leader with Moses and their sister Miriam leading the Israelites out of Egypt through the wilderness (Mic. 6:4; Exod. 4:10-16; 7:1-25), and Israel's first high priest and ancestor of the priestly family of Aaronite priests (Exod. 28:1-2; Num. 18:1-7).

High Priest (Exodus-Numbers and Chronicles)

Aaron and his descendants are repeatedly featured as central figures and the predominant priests of Israel's cult in Exodus-Numbers and 1–2 Chronicles. Approximately 85 percent of the total number (346) of references to Aaron in the Bible are concentrated in the pentateuchal books of Exodus, Leviticus, and Numbers. There, particularly in the so-called Priestly portions of the Pentateuch, Aaron and his sons are the exalted high priests who oversee Israel's sacrifices and cult centered in the ark and tabernacle (Exod. 27–30). The Aaronites are in charge of the Urim and Thummim, the sacred lots for determining Yahweh's will (Exod. 28:30; Lev. 8:5-9; Num. 27:21). Aaron and his sons are the only priests authorized to preside at various rituals and offerings (Lev. 6–8). The actual ordination ceremony for Aaron and his sons is narrated in Lev. 8–9. Lev. 21 lists a series of regulations designed to maintain the holiness of the Aaronite priesthood. Aaron is a descendant of the priestly tribe of Levi (Exod. 6:16-25), but Aaron and his sons represent a special clan among the Levites who alone are authorized to come near and officiate at rituals associated with the tent of meeting (Num. 3:5-10). Aaron and his sons are assigned the duty of blessing the Israelites in the form of the so-called Aaronic benediction in Num. 6:22-27. The priestly predominance of Aaron over other Levites is emphasized in the revolt of Korah, Dathan, and Abiram in Num. 16, the budding of Aaron's rod in Num. 17, and the classification of priestly responsibilities among the Aaronites and other Levites in Num. 18.

The postexilic book of 1-2 Chronicles reflects an exalted view of the Aaronite priesthood similar to that found in the Priestly tradition of the Pentateuch. Aaron and his descendants make offerings and atonement at "the most holy place" (1 Chr. 6:49[34]). The Aaronite priests are "set apart" from other Levites for the most sacred duties of temple worship in burning incense, ministering, and blessing (1 Chr. 23–24; cf. 2 Chr. 26:16-21).

Elsewhere in the Old Testament

Allusions to Aaron or Aaronite priests are very rare or absent in other sections of the OT such as the Deuteronomistic history or the prophetic books. Even the exilic book of Ezekiel, which devotes significant attention to matters of priests and temple worship, never mentions Aaron or the Aaronites. Instead, Ezekiel designates another priestly group, the Zadokites, as the true high priests who receive assistance from the Levites (Ezek. 40:46; 44:15; 48:11). 1–2 Samuel and 1–2 Kings likewise rarely mention the Aaronite priesthood and instead focus on the Levites and the Zadokites as priests during Israel's monarchy (e.g., 1 Kgs. 2:27). Thus, the Aaronic priesthood apparently played little role in much of the preexilic and exilic literature (Deuteronomistic history, Ezekiel). However, the figure of Aaron and the Aaronite priesthood apparently emerged as the preeminent priestly group in the Second Temple or postexilic period in charge of worship and rituals in the Jerusalem temple.

Negative and Nonpriestly Portrayals

Sections of the Pentateuch that scholars often date as earlier than the exilic Priestly traditions tend to portray Aaron in a nonpriestly role as a co-leader with Moses (Exod. 4:27-31; 11:10; 12:31; 16:33-34). These earlier traditions in the Pentateuch also portray Aaron negatively in opposition or rebellion against Moses or Yahweh (Exod. 32, the idolatry of the golden calf; Num. 12, the rebellion of Aaron and Miriam against Moses; Num. 20, the unfaithfulness of Moses and Aaron in hitting the rock). The one prophetic reference to Aaron in Mic. 6:4 lists Aaron as simply a co-leader of the Israelites in the wilderness along with Moses and Miriam.

New Testament

Aaron's priesthood diminishes in importance in light of the atoning significance of Jesus' death and resurrection in the NT. Acts 7:40 recalls Aaron's idolatrous involvement with the golden calf. The book of Hebrews recognizes Aaron's legitimate role as high priest (Heb. 5:4), and yet it affirms Christ as now the greater high priest who arose "according to the order of Melchizedek" (cf. Gen. 14:17-24) rather than "according to the order of Aaron" (Heb. 7:11).

Character: A Summary

The present form of the biblical text balances Aaron's prominence as leader and priest with an awareness of the potential for disobedience among all leaders, even a high priest like Aaron (Exod. 32:1-6, 25; Lev. 10:1-3; Num. 12:1-16; 20:1-13). In the end, both the high priest Aaron and the incomparable prophet and leader Moses are condemned to die outside the Promised Land of Canaan (Num. 20:12, 22-29; Deut. 34:1-12). Aaron, like many leaders and prominent figures in the Bible, is humanly flawed, but he remained at the same time an effective agent for the blessing and saving work of God among God's people.

Bibliography. A. Cody, *A History of Old Testament Priesthood.* AnBib 35 (Rome, 1969); W. Horbury, "The Aaronic Priesthood in the Epistle to the Hebrews," *JSNT* 19 (1983): 43-71; R. D. Nelson, *Raising Up a Faithful Priest: Community and Priesthood in Biblical Theology* (Louisville, 1993); L. Sabourin, *Priesthood: A Comparative Study.* Studies in the History of Religions 25 (Leiden, 1973).

Dennis T. Olson

AB (Heb. *'aḇ*)
The fifth month of the Hebrew sacred calendar (July/Aug.); this postexilic name was borrowed by the Jews from the Babylonian Abu. In this month the grapes and figs are harvested and on the seventh day a great fast commemorates the destruction of Jerusalem by Nebuchadnezzar (587/586 B.C.E.).

ABADDON (Heb. *'ăḇaddôn*)
The "place of destruction," from the verb *'āḇaḏ,* "to perish" or "to fail." In its five occurrences in the OT (Ps. 88:11[MT 12]; Job 26:6; 28:22; 31:12; Prov. 15:11), it is a synonym of "Sheol."

In the NT Gk. *Abaddṓn* is the name of an angel that rules over the deadly swarm of locusts, which the visionary sees as plaguing humanity, and over hell itself (Rev. 9:11). The basis of this "personification" seems to trace back to Job 28:22, where Abaddon speaks, along with "death." Jim West

ABAGTHA (Heb. *'ăḇagṯā'*)
One of the seven eunuchs of King Ahasuerus (Xerxes I, ca. 480 B.C.E.) who served as his chamberlains (Esth. 1:10). The name is probably of Middle Iranian origin (perhaps "gift of good fortune").

ABANA (Heb. *'ăḇānâ*)
A river, along with the Pharpar River to the south, that feeds the vast Ghouta oasis wherein Damascus is located. The modern name of the river is Barada; its source is in a large pool high in the Anti-Lebanon Mountains (usually identified with Mt. Amana; cf. Cant. 4:8). The river descends eastward down the mountain, flows through Damascus, and disappears into a marshy lake E of the city. The Abana and the Pharpar are largely responsible for the fertility for which the region of Damascus is famous; they provide a hedge against the encroachment of the eastern desert.

Naaman, the commander of the Aramean forces, compares the Abana (Q Amana) and the Pharpar to the Jordan River in which Elisha told him to wash seven times to cure his leprosy (2 Kgs. 5:12). Ronald A. Simkins

ABARIM (Heb. *'ăḇārîm*)
A mountain range E of the Dead Sea and opposite the Judean wilderness, overlooking the Jordan Valley. The name probably reflects the ancient eastern orientation: one would go to the Abarim (i.e., "the regions beyond") on a journey eastward to Transjordan.

Since the Israelites approached Canaan from the east, they had to pass through the Abarim. They camped in its highlands and descended from them to the plains of Moab (Num. 33:47-48). From Mt. Nebo, one of the peaks of the Abarim, Moses viewed the Promised Land (Deut. 32:49).

Jeremiah gives the Abarim the same geographical significance as Lebanon and Bashan (22:20), suggesting that the Abarim were seen as encompassing a large geographical territory. There is some indication that at times the name Abarim referred to mountains S of Moab (Num. 33:44), although no boundaries for the Abarim are given.

David Merling

ABBA (Gk. *abbá*)
A term used to address God. All three NT occurrences are followed by the nominative translation "(the) Father." Mark claims that Jesus addressed God as "Abba Father" in Gethsemane (14:36), but both Matthew (26:39, 42) and Luke (22:42) omit the word Abba. Paul asserted that the Spirit cries "Abba Father" in the hearts of believers (Gal. 4:6) and that believers cry "Abba Father" in the Spirit of adoption (Rom. 8:15).

Although the formula "Abba (the) Father" treats Abba as an emphatic state form, Abba functions as a vocative in the NT. Some translations therefore punctuate this formula as "Abba! Father!"

Since both young children and grown children addressed their fathers as "Abba," this word must be translated as "father" and not as "daddy." Abba cannot be defined as a mere babbling sound voiced by little children. Most scholars assume that Abba is Aramaic, though Hebrew cannot be excluded.

Bibliography. J. Jeremias, *The Prayers of Jesus.* SBT 2/6 (Naperville, 1967), 11-65; J. Barr, "'Abbā Isn't 'Daddy,'" *JTS* N.S. 39 (1988): 28-47; M. R. D'Angelo, "*Abba* and 'Father,'" *JBL* 111 (1992): 611-30.

ROBERT L. MOWERY

ABDA (Heb. *ʿaḇdāʾ*) (also OBADIAH)

1. The father of Adoniram, one of Solomon's officials (1 Kgs. 4:6).

2. A Levite, the son of Shammua, who settled after the Exile in Jerusalem (Neh. 11:17). At 1 Chr. 9:16 his name is given as Obadiah the son of Shemaiah.

ABDEEL (Heb. *ʿaḇdĕʾēl*)
The father of Shelemiah, one of Jehoiakim's courtiers (Jer. 36:26).

ABDI (Heb. *ʿaḇdî*)

1. A Levite of the family of Merari. He was the grandfather of Ethan, a temple singer during the days of David (1 Chr. 6:44[MT 29]).

2. The father of the Levite Kish, a contemporary of King Hezekiah (2 Chr. 29:12).

3. An Israelite who had to divorce his foreign wife during the ministry of Ezra (Ezra 10:26; 1 Esdr. 9:27).

ABDIEL (Heb. *ʿaḇdîʾēl*)
A Gadite who dwelled in Gilead or in Bashan. He was the father of the chief Ahi (1 Chr. 5:15).

ABDON (Heb. *ʿaḇdôn*) **(PERSON)**
(also ACHBOR)

1. The son of Hillel the Pirathonite, one of the so-called minor judges (Judg. 12:13-15). The comment that he had 40 sons and 30 grandsons who rode on 70 donkeys is perhaps an indication of his wealth. He was buried at Pirathon in "the hill country of the Amalekites," territory allotted to the tribe of Ephraim.

2. The son of Shashak, listed among the descendants of Benjamin (1 Chr. 8:23).

3. The firstborn son of Jeiel; Saul's great uncle (1 Chr. 9:36). The genealogy also appears in 1 Chr. 8:29-38 with some textual variations.

4. The son of Micah; one of the emissaries King Josiah sent to Huldah the prophetess after Hilkiah's discovery of the book of the law (2 Chr. 34:20). In the parallel passage in 2 Kgs. 22:12 this person is called Achbor (**2**) the son of Micaiah.

JAMES R. ADAIR

ABDON (Heb. *ʿaḇdôn*) **(PLACE)**
A levitical city in the tribal territory of Asher (Josh. 21:30; 1 Chr. 6:74) assigned to the family of Gershom. It is probably Khirbet ʿAbdeh, today a ruin ca. 17 km. (10 mi.) NNE of Acco. At Josh. 19:28 Ebron should perhaps be rendered Abdon.

ABEDNEGO (Heb. *ʿăḇēḏ nĕḡô*)
One of the four young Israelite men taken into the court of the Babylonian king Nebuchadnezzar (Dan. 1:7). His Hebrew name, Azariah, was changed to Abednego by Nebuchadnezzar's chief eunuch, Ashpenaz. The name appears to be a perversion of the Akkadian name *Arad-nabû,* "servant of Nabû" (Nebuchadnezzar's personal god). Changing the names of people in order to change their futures was a common practice throughout the ancient Near East.

The adventures of the four young men in the Babylonian court are recorded in Dan. 1–3. They remain faithful to their religious traditions and dietary laws by living on vegetables and water, and therefore are given knowledge and wisdom by God. Daniel is made the ruler over the whole province of Babylon while the other three are made administrators in the kingdom (2:48-49). After refusing to worship a golden image set up by Nebuchadnezzar the men are thrown into a fiery furnace. They are saved by a messenger of God for their faithfulness, and blessed and honored by Nebuchadnezzar (3:12-30).

1 Macc. 2:59 lists Azariah, Hanaiah, and Mishael among those faithful to God.

NANCY L. DECLAISSÉ-WALFORD

ABEL (Heb. *heḇel*) **(PERSON)**
The second son of Adam and Eve; a "keeper of sheep" (Gen. 4:2).

See CAIN AND ABEL.

ABEL (Heb. *ʾāḇēl*) **(PLACE)**
Abel of Beth-maacah, perhaps a cult center renowned for its wisdom, to which Joab was referred for counsel (2 Sam. 20:18).

See ABEL-BETH-MAACAH.

ABEL-BETH-MAACAH (Heb. *ʾāḇēl bêṯ-maʿăḵâ*)
A city cited in biblical and other ancient Near Eastern texts, best identified with modern Tell Abil al-Qamḥ ("Meadow of the Wheat"; 204296). The latter is an imposing mound of 10 ha. (25 a.) on the northern border of Israel near Metulla, near a major waterfall of the Jordan River tributaries, at the juncture of the Huleh Valley and the Beqaʿ Valley in Lebanon. The site is mentioned in the 19th/18th-century B.C. Egyptian Brussels Execration Texts (no. 47); in the list of sites of Thutmose III's first Asiatic military campaign ca. 1468 (probably no. 92; *ʾu-bil*); and possibly in the 14th-century Amarna Letters (no. 256; *yuabilîma*).

Several biblical references suggest that Abel-beth-maacah (also called Abel-mayim) was originally part of the holdings of the well-known Jordanian family of Maʿacah, later allotted to the tribe of Dan as "a mother in Israel," i.e., probably a cult center (cf. 2 Sam. 20:14-22). According to 1 Kgs. 15:20 (= 2 Chr. 16:4) Abel-beth-maacah was captured by Ben-hadad I of Damascus ca. 829. Both biblical texts (2 Kgs. 15:29) and possibly Assyrian texts *(a-b-il[ak-kal])* show that Abel-beth-maacah was taken by Tiglath-pileser III ca. 733/732.

The site has never been excavated, but surface surveys by William G. Dever in 1973 produced evidence of occupation throughout nearly all of the Early, Middle, and Late Bronze Ages, with especially strong walls and a glacis of MB, as well as occupation in the Iron I-II, Persian, Hellenistic, Roman, Byzantine, and later periods. The scant archaeological evidence confirms that Abel-beth-maacah's superb stratigraphic location, abundant material resources, and strong defenses made it no doubt as important as nearby Hazor and Dan in most periods. Perched astride the historic borders of Israel, Aramea, and Phoenicia, Abel-beth-Maacah was indeed the "northern gateway" of ancient Israel.

Bibliography. W. G. Dever, "'Abel-Beth-Maʿacah: 'Northern Gateway of Ancient Israel,'" in *The Archaeology of Jordan and Other Studies,* ed. L. T. Geraty and L. G. Herr (Berrien Springs, 1986), 207-22; J. Kaplan, "The Identification of Abel-Beth-Maachah and Janoah," *IEJ* 28 (1978): 157-60; H. Tadmor, "The Southern Border of Aram," *IEJ* 12 (1962): 119-22. WILLIAM G. DEVER

ABEL-KERAMIM (Heb. *'āḇēl kĕrāmîm*)
A city in Ammon, to which Jephthah pursued the Ammonites (Judg. 11:33; Heb. "pasture of the vineyards"). It has been identified variously with modern Naʿūr (228142), ca. 14 km. (9 mi.) from Amman; Tell el-ʿUmeiri (234142), 10 km. (6 mi.) S of Amman; and Tell Saḥāb (245142), 12 km. (7.5 mi.) SE of Amman.

ABEL-MEHOLAH (Heb. *'āḇēl mĕḥôlâ*)
The home town of Elisha (1 Kgs. 19:16). According to Judg. 7:22 Gideon chased the Midianites "toward Zererah" (Zarethan), as far as "the border of Abel-meholah"(cf. 1 Kgs. 7:46). There he crossed the Jordan (Judg. 8:4), so Abel-meholah may have been a territory or town near the Jordan. 1 Kgs. 4:12 mentions Abel-meholah as part of the territory ruled by an administrator named Baana, noting that Abel-meholah lay "below Jezreel," and listing Zarethan and Beth-shean as nearby cities.

Scholars have offered numerous suggestions as to its location, including Tell Abû Sifri, near the junction of the Wadi el-Helway and the Wadi Maliḥ (which may preserve the name Meholah), S of Beth-shean but some distance from the Jordan, and Tell Abû Sûs (203197), ca. 15 km. (11 mi.) S of Beth-shean and closer to the Jordan. Of the two, the latter is more likely.

The term "Meholathite" (1 Sam. 18:19; 2 Sam. 21:8) apparently referred to a resident of Abel-meholah. PAUL L. REDDITT

ABEL-MIZRAIM (Heb. *'āḇēl miṣrayim*)
A name given to Atad, a place along the Jordan where Joseph, accompanied by Egyptian dignitaries, mourned for his deceased father Jacob (Gen. 50:11). The name is a play on Heb. *'āḇal* ("mourn") and *'ēḇel* ("mourning rites"). On the basis of Gen. 50:10-11 ("beyond the Jordan," the "inhabitants of the land") and v. 13 ("carried into the land"), some scholars have judged its location to be in Transjordan, N of the Dead Sea.

See ATAD.

ABEL-SHITTIM (Heb. *'āḇēl haššiṭṭîm*)
A place of encampment for the Israelites at the end of the wilderness wanderings (Num. 33:49). It is probably the same as Shittim, located E of the Jordan, in Moab.

ABGAR (Gk. *Abgaros*)
Common title of kings of Edessa, the capital of Osrhoene, a small kingdom at the northern bend of the Euphrates River (modern Turkey). Eusebius (*HE* 1.13) reports that the archives of Edessa contained copies of correspondence between Abgar Ukkama (Abgar V "the Black") and Jesus in which Abgar requests that Jesus come to Edessa to heal him. The story is widely regarded as apocryphal, the result of historical revisionism sometime after Abgar IX (ca. 179-214 C.E.) converted to Christianity.

CHARLES GUTH

ABI (Heb. *'ăḇî*) (also ABIJAH)
The wife of Ahaz and mother of Hezekiah (2 Kgs. 18:2). The name is a shortened form of Abijah (**5**) (2 Chr. 29:1).

ABI-ALBON (Heb. *'ăḇî-ʿălĕḇôn*) (also ABIEL)
One of David's 30 Champions (2 Sam. 23:31); called Abiel (**2**) the Arbathite at 1 Chr. 11:32 (cf. LXX *Abiēl*). He may have been an inhabitant of Beth-arabah.

ABIASAPH (Heb. *'ăḇî'āsāp̄*) (also EBIASAPH)
A Levite of the family of Korah and contemporary of Phinehas the grandson of Aaron (Exod. 6:24-25). At 1 Chr. 6:23; 9:19 he is called Ebiasaph. The Asaph of 1 Chr. 26:1 may be an abbreviated form (LXX B *Abia-Saphar*).

ABIATHAR (Heb. *'eḇyāṯār*)
A descendant of Ithamar (and Eli; 1 Sam. 22:20-23), who eventually served as high priest during David's reign.

Abiathar served as a priest at Nob with his father Ahimelech. When Saul massacred Abiathar's fellow priests, including his father, Abiathar fled to join David, bringing with him the ephod (1 Sam. 22:20-22; 23:6, 9). He served David and functioned as David's chief priest in the pre-Hebron and Hebron years. His exact function during their wilderness flight from Saul remains unclear.

Following Absalom's rebellion against David (2 Sam. 15:1-12), Zadok acted as high priest and directed the relocation of the ark, while Abiathar directed the offering of various sacrifices until all the refugees had left Jerusalem (v. 24). However, David commanded both men to return to Jerusalem with the ark and serve as his "listening posts" (15:25-29; cf. 17:15-16). Throughout the remainder of David's reign, Abiathar served as one of David's counselors (1 Chr. 27:34).

Solomon expelled Abiathar from his priestly office after Abiathar supported Adonijah as king (1 Kgs. 1–2). This represented the prophesied end of Eli's line of the priesthood. Solomon exiled Abiathar and his descendants to Anathoth and revoked his priestly privileges (1 Kgs. 1:19, 25; 2:22, 26, 35). Some have suggested that Jeremiah, who descended from a priestly family in Anathoth, may have been a descendant of Abiathar.

In a listing of David's officials, Zadok is mentioned as the priestly counterpart of Ahimelech, the son of Abiathar (2 Sam. 8:17; cf. 1 Chr. 24:3, 6, 31), but in most instances Zadok and Abiathar serve as counterparts. Thus, several scholars suggest that the names of Ahimelech and Abiathar are here reversed (cf. Syr.). Others contend that Abiathar named his son after Ahimelech. In any case, during most of this period Zadok and Abiathar shared the priestly duties.

Bibliography. P. McCarter, *2 Samuel.* AB 9 (Garden City, 1984); E. H. Merrill, *Kingdom of Priests: A History of Old Testament Israel* (Grand Rapids, 1987).

MICHAEL A. GRISANTI

ABIB (Heb. *'āḇîḇ*)
The original name of the first Hebrew month, mentioned in connection with the Feast of the Unleavened Bread or the Passover (Mar./Apr.); after the Exile it was called Nisan (Neh. 2:1; Esth. 3:7). Its designation "month of the ears" (Heb. *ḥōḏeš hā'āḇîḇ*, "month of young ear of barley [or 'other grain']"; e.g., Exod. 13:4) may point to the new moon nearest to, or preceding, the growth of barley.

ABIDA (Heb. *'ăḇîḏā'*)
A descendant of Abraham and Keturah through Midian, their fourth son (Gen. 25:4 = 1 Chr. 1:33).

ABIDAN (Heb. *'ăḇîḏān*)
The son of Gideoni; "leader" of the tribe of Benjamin during the wilderness wanderings (Num. 2:22; 10:24). Abidan assisted Moses at the taking of the census (Num. 1:11) and made his offering on the ninth day of the dedication of the tabernacle (7:60, 65).

ABIEL (Heb. *'ăḇî'ēl*) (also ABI-ALBON)

1. A Benjaminite, the father of Kish and Ner. Also the grandfather of King Saul and Abner, the commander of Saul's army (1 Sam. 9:1; 14:51).

2. An Arbathite warrior (1 Chr. 11:32) and a member of David's heroes known as the "Thirty." In 2 Sam. 23:31 he is called Abi-albon.

KENNETH ATKINSON

ABIEZER (Heb. *'ăḇî'ezer*) (also IEZER)

1. A descendant of Manasseh (1 Chr. 7:18). At Num. 26:30 an abbreviated form of his name occurs (Iezer). The Abiezrites were given a district in the tribal territory of Manasseh W of the Jordan (Josh. 17:2) which included the city of Ophrah. Gideon was an Abiezrite (Judg. 6:11; cf. v. 34).

2. One of David's Champions, the commander of the ninth division of his army (2 Sam. 23:37 = 1 Chr. 11:28; 27:12). He was from Anathoth in Benjamin.

ABIGAIL (Heb. *'ăḇîgayil, 'ăḇîgal*)

1. Wife of Nabal, then David (1 Sam. 25), and mother of David's second-born son, named variously Chileab (2 Sam. 3:3), Daniel (1 Chr. 3:1), or Daluiah (2 Sam. 3:3 LXX). Abigail accompanied David on his visit to King Achish at Gath (1 Sam. 27:3) and was later taken hostage during an Amalekite raid on David's fortress at Ziklag (30:5). After her rescue, she went with David to Hebron (2 Sam. 2:2), where she bore him a child (2 Sam. 3:3 = 1 Chr. 3:1). Of the five references to Abigail outside 1 Sam. 25, all but one (1 Chr. 3:1) refer to her as Nabal's widow. In each she is closely linked to another of David's wives, Ahinoam.

Recent literary treatments of Abigail's characterization present her as a "model wife and modest woman" (Adele Berlin) and a "woman of 'good sense'" (Athalya Brenner). A different approach emphasizes Abigail's prophetic words in 1 Sam. 25:28-31 and presents her as "God's chosen prophet-intermediary," a more subversive character than normally realized (Alice Bach).

2. Sister of David (1 Chr. 2:16) and Zeruiah (2 Sam. 17:25), and mother of Amasa (2 Sam. 17:25; 1 Chr. 2:17). She was the daughter of either Jesse (1 Chr. 2:16) or Nahash (2 Sam. 17:25) and the wife of either Ithra the Israelite (2 Sam. 17:25) or Jether the Ishmaelite (1 Chr. 2:17) or Jezreelite (1 Chr. 2:17 LXX). Some scholars suggest that Ithra/Jether was Nabal's real identity, and thus there was only one Abigail — David's sister, who later became his wife.

Bibliography. A. Bach, "The Pleasure of Her Text," in *The Pleasure of Her Text* (Philadelphia, 1990), 25-44; A. Berlin, *Poetics and Interpretation of Biblical Narratives* (Sheffield, 1983); A. Brenner, *The Israelite Woman: Social Role and Literary Type in Biblical Narrative* (Sheffield, 1985); J. D. Levenson and B. Halpern, "The Political Import of David's Marriages," *JBL* 99 (1980): 507-18.

LINDA S. SCHEARING

ABIHAIL (Heb. *'ăḇîḥayil*)

1. A Levite of the family of Merari; the father of Zuriel (Num. 3:35).

2. The wife of Abishur of the family of Judah (1 Chr. 2:29).

3. A man from the tribe of Gad; the father of seven sons (1 Chr. 5:14).

4. The daughter of David's brother Eliab and wife of David's son Jerimoth. Their daughter Mahalath became the wife of King Rehoboam of Judah (2 Chr. 11:18).

5. The father of Queen Esther and uncle of Mordecai (Esth. 2:15; 9:29).

ABIHU (Heb. *'ăḇîhû'*)
An Israelite priest of the wilderness period. The Priestly genealogy lists Abihu, Nadab, Eleazar, and Ithamar as sons of Aaron, born to him by Elisheba (Exod. 6:23; Num. 26:60; 1 Chr. 6:3[MT 5:29]; cf. Exod. 28:1). Abihu and Nadab met their demise for offering Yahweh "strange fire" (Heb. *'ēš zārâ*, a crux; Lev. 10:1-2). The P narrative here emphasizes the responsibility of the Aaronic priests and explains

the dominance of the descendants of Eleazar, Abihu's younger brother, in the Jerusalem cult (Num. 3:2, 4; 1 Chr. 24:1, 2). In contrast to P, the E strand celebrates the priestly heterogeneity that Nadab and Abihu represent with its story of their participation in the covenant ratification on Mt. Horeb (Exod. 24:1, 9).

Bibliography. J. C. H. Laughlin, "The 'Strange Fire' of Nadab and Abihu," *JBL* 95 (1976): 559-65.

STEPHEN L. COOK

ABIHUD (Heb. *'ăḇîhûḏ*)
The third son of Bela, the son of Benjamin (1 Chr. 8:3). Some scholars emend the text to read Heb. *'ăḇî 'ēhûḏ*, "the father of Ehud." Others consider it a variant of Abiud (cf. LXX *Abioud*).

ABIJAH (Heb. *'ăḇîyâ*) (also ABI, ABIJAM)

1. The second son of Samuel, who served (together with his brother, Joel) as a judge in Beersheba and was corrupted by duplicity (1 Sam. 8:2-3; 1 Chr. 6:13[MT 28]).

2. The son of Jeroboam I, king of Israel. When he fell ill, he sent his wife in disguise to the prophet Ahijah at Shiloh; the ruse failed, and Abijah died in Tirzah in accordance with the prophecy (1 Kgs. 14:1-18; cf. LXX 3 Kgdms. 12:24g-n).

3. King of Judah (ca. 913–911 B.C.E.), son of Rehoboam and Maacah (Micaiah, 2 Chr. 13:2), daughter of Absalom's daughter Tamar and Uriel. The MT of 2 Chronicles reads Abijah (*'ăḇîyâ*), while the MT of 1 Kings reads Abijam (*'ăḇîyām*); LXX *Abiou.* Abijah went to war (probably a border conflict) with King Jeroboam I of Israel (1 Kgs. 15:7b; 2 Chr. 13:3, 13-19). Although the Deuteronomistic historian thought negatively of Abijah's religious activity (1 Kgs. 15:3-5, in peculiar Deuteronomistic phrasing), the Chronicler describes him as a pious king. Therefore, according to the Chronicler, Abijah won his war against Rehoboam (2 Chr. 13:15-19). Abijah also succeeded in his personal life: he had 14 wives, 16 daughters, and 22 sons (2 Chr. 13:21). The speech in 2 Chr. 13:4-12, which was ascribed to Abijah, contains the main theological concepts of the Chronicler.

4. The head of the eighth division of priests (1 Chr. 24:10). According to Luke 1:5 Zechariah, the father of John the Baptist, belonged to this division.

5. The wife of Ahaz and mother of Hezekiah, king of Judah (2 Chr. 29:1). She is called Abi (LXX *Abou*) in 2 Kgs. 18:2.

6. The wife of Hezron (1 Chr. 2:24 MT). Abijah does not appear in the Syriac Version, and some commentators regard it as a gloss (cf. RSV).

7. The son of Becher from the tribe of Benjamin (1 Chr. 7:6, 8; LXX reads "Zamria").

8. A priest who signed ("set his seal upon") the renewed covenant of the community in the time of Nehemiah (Neh. 10:8[7]; cf. 12:4, 17).

9. A priest who returned from Babylonia with Zerubbabel and Joshua (Neh. 12:1-4) and was head of a priestly group (v. 7).

The name Abijah also occurs on a seal preserved on ostracons (e.g., from Samaria and Arad).

Bibliography. I. Kalimi, *The Books of Chronicles: A Classified Bibliography* (Jerusalem, 1990), 173-74, nos. 1691-1705.

ISAAC KALIMI

ABIJAM (Heb. *'ăḇîyām*)
A variation of the name of King Abijah of Judah (esp. MT 1 Kings).

ABILA (Gk. *Abila*)
A city located on the Wadi Quailibah, 12 Roman mi. E of Gadara (modern Umm Qeis), and ca. 4 km. (2.5 mi.) S of the Yarmuk River. Abila (231231) measures ca. 1 km. (.6 mi.) north-south and .5 km. (.3 mi.) east-west in area. It consists of two tells (Tell Abila in the north, and Umm el-'Amad in the south), a civic center in a depression in between, fertile agricultural fields all around, and a spring at the base of the south tell.

Abila, as a Decapolis city founded probably by Alexander the Great's Hellenistic successors (according to the coin tradition; Abila had the toponym Seleucia), was captured by the Seleucid king Antiochus III, by the Hasmonean king Alexander Jannaeus, and by Pompey. Pliny (*Nat. hist.* 5.74) calls it a tetrarchy/kingdom, and Ptolemy (*Geog.* 5.7.22), a Decapolis city. Abila also carried the titles Coele-Syria, "independent," and "sovereign."

Abila's archaeological history (from 3500 B.C. to A.D. 1500) reveals settlement remains from Early Bronze to Islamic times. The city follows the classical town plan of main streets at right angles. Excavated remains include basilicas, a bath-nymphaeum complex (north), a theater cavea complex (south), a church, and a forum or villa complex. A city wall of Hellenistic-Roman (and possibly Iron Age) date surrounded the Tell Abila acropolis. An extensive necropolis extends all around the site, consisting largely of Late Hellenistic and Roman and Byzantine tomb complexes.

Bibliography. W. H. Mare, "Abila," *NEAEHL* 1:1-3; Mare et al., Preliminary reports in *The Near East Archaeological Society Bulletin* (Chicago, 1981-1996).

W. HAROLD MARE

ABILENE (Gk. *Abilēnē*)
A region in the eastern part of the Anti-Lebanon range. Its capital, Abila, was ca. 27 km. (17 mi.) NW of Damascus. In NT times Lysanias was the tetrarch of this district (Luke 3:1). After Lysanias' death the tetrarchy was granted to Agrippa I (37 C.E.) and later to Agrippa II (53).

ABIMAEL (Heb. *'ăḇîmā'ēl*)
One of the sons of Joktan (Gen. 10:28; 1 Chr. 1:22); progenitor of a South Arabian tribe.

ABIMELECH (Heb. *'ăḇîmeleḵ*)

1. The king of Gerar who, believing Sarah to be Abraham's sister, took her for his own spouse (Gen. 20:2) until God revealed to him that she was Abraham's wife and death would be the result of his molesting her. Abimelech also appears in a similar story involving Rebekah and Isaac (Gen. 26:1-16), where he warns others not to molest Rebekah or they will be put to death, suggesting he learned from the first episode. In this latter tale he is called "Abimelech of the Philistines," which can only be an anachronism reflecting a story told well after the events were supposed to have taken place.

2. The son of Gideon (Jerubbaal) and his concubine in Shechem (Judg. 8:31). His story (Judg. 9) is told to demonstrate the dangers of kingship, the divine preference for individually selected rulers, and the futility of trust in gods other than Yahweh. His name, "My father is king," may be a literary device; otherwise it would suggest that Gideon saw himself as a king and so named this son to reflect that status, or perhaps it was a throne name taken after seizing power to legitimate his own claim to the throne. The name Abi-melek was relatively common in ancient Syria-Palestine.

Seeking the kingship which by inheritance should have belonged to his 70 half-brothers by Gideon's official wives, Abimelech, with the urging of the citizens of Shechem and the aid of personnel from the temple of Baal-berith ("Baal of the Covenant"), assassinated all but one of his brothers; Jothan, the youngest, managed to escape (a standard plot motif). The populace of Shechem declared Abimelech king in succession to his father, who had been a popular judge. He set up his capital outside Shechem, finally at Arumah (Judg. 9:31, 41), which may explain the ensuing revolt by Shechem. He reigned for three years.

Jothan declared that the duplicity of the Shechemites and of Abimelech would be returned upon them. This was accomplished when Shechem declared Gaal son of Ebed, a newcomer to town, its king in place of Abimelech. In the resultant battle Abimelech and his ally in the city, Zebul, defeated Shechem, overrunning the lower city and then burning the inner city with a thousand of its citizens inside. The temple of El-berith, to which the populace had fled, was no protection, for all were slain and the city's ruins sown with salt to guarantee its continued destruction.

From there Abimelech moved on Thebez and attempted the same tactic, only here a woman in the city's fortress dropped a millstone on his head. Knowing he was to die, he asked his attendant to slay him so that no one would say a woman had killed him, but this only insured that it would be remembered (2 Sam. 11:21).

3. In the heading of Ps. 34, a ruler before whom David feigned insanity in order to escape. The story to which this line alludes appears to concern Achish king of Gath (1 Sam. 21:10–22:1), but may possibly refer to another incident where David used the same ruse with a different ruler otherwise not recorded. Less likely, it has been argued that Achish and Abimelech were two different names for the same ruler.

4. One of David's two chief priests, the son of Abiathar (1 Chr. 18:16 MT). While some translations retain the Hebrew form of the name, most translators assume a scribal error and read Ahimelech son of Abiathar with 2 Sam. 8:17; 1 Chr. 24:6.

Bibliography. J. P. Fokkelman, "Structural Remarks on Judges 9 and 19," in *"Sha'arei Talmon,"* ed. M. Fishbane and E. Tov (Winona Lake, 1992), 33-45; B. Halpern, "The Rise of Abimeleck Ben-Jerubbaal," *HAR* 2 (1978): 79-100.

Lowell K. Handy

ABINADAB (Heb. *'ăḇînāḏāḇ*)

1. The father of Eleazer. 1 Sam. 7:1 reports that men from Kiriath-jearim moved the ark from Beth-shemesh to the "house of Abinadab" where the newly consecrated son of Abinadab, Eleazar, took responsibility for the ark. Abinadab was also the father of Uzzah and possibly Ahio (2 Sam. 6:3, 4; 1 Chr. 13:7), if Heb. *'aḥyô* is a personal name and not a reference to Eleazar, "his brother." Eleazar's consecration, the 20-year possession of the ark, and the ambiguous Hebrew term *bêṯ* suggest that the "house of Abinadab" refers to a temple.

2. Jesse's second son (1 Sam. 16:8; 1 Chr. 2:13), who served in Saul's army against the Philistines at Elah where David killed Goliath (1 Sam. 17:13).

3. The fourth son of Saul (1 Chr. 8:33; 9:39), who died with his brothers Jonathan and Malchishua on Mt. Gilboa (1 Sam. 31:2; 1 Chr. 10:2). 1 Sam. 14:49 omits Abinadab in Saul's genealogy.

William D. Matherly

ABINOAM (Heb. *'ăḇînō'am*)

The father of Barak of the tribe of Naphtali (Judg. 4:6, 12; 5:1, 12).

ABIRAM (Heb. *'ăḇîrām*)

1. The son of Eliab, a Reubenite (Num. 16:1). Abiram, along with his brother Dathan, his cousin On, and Korah, organized an uprising in the wilderness against Moses and Aaron. They were joined by 250 leaders of the congregation of Israel (Num. 16:1-35). The conspirators, motivated by envy, accused Moses of self-exaltation and challenged his interpretation of who was holy before God.

When Moses asked for Abiram and Dathan to appear before him, they refused, complaining that Moses had failed to bring the people into a land of fields and vineyards. Abiram, Dathan, Korah, and all of their families and possessions, except for the sons of Korah, were then swallowed alive by the earth (16:31-33). The leaders of the congregation who had joined the uprising were consumed by the Lord's fire (16:35; 26:9; Deut. 11:6; Ps. 106:17).

2. The firstborn son of Hiel, the Bethelite (1 Kgs. 16:34). Abiram died during the reign of Ahab because his father laid the foundations for the rebuilding of Jericho in direct violation of the curse spoken by Joshua after the conquest of Jericho (Josh. 6:26). Some scholars suggest that his death was intended as a foundation sacrifice.

Alan Ray Buescher

ABISHAG (Heb. *'ăḇîšaḡ*)

The Shunammite virgin who attended to the aged King David (1 Kgs. 1:4, 15). That David had no sexual relations with Abishag is sometimes interpreted as an indication of the king's inability to govern. The Talmud, however, notes that David did not make Abishag his wife because he refused to exceed the legal number of wives — 18 — allowed to a king (*Sanh.* 22a).

Later, Abishag became a political pawn in the succession struggle between David's sons. After Solomon was declared king and David had died, Adonijah asked for Abishag's hand in marriage (1 Kgs. 2:17). Solomon interpreted Adonijah's request as an attempt to overthrow the throne and ordered his execution (1 Kgs. 2:22-25).

In Jewish lore Abishag is seen in her later years as the Shunammite who gives hospitality to Elisha the prophet (2 Kgs. 4:8-37).

Robin Gallaher Branch

ABISHAI (Heb. *'ăḇîšay*)
One of the three sons of Zeruiah, David's sister, who served with David when he fled Saul's court (1 Sam. 22:1-2). Abishai held the special position of commander of David's elite warriors — the *šālîšîm* (2 Sam. 23:18-19) — among whom he was also the most renowned. One vignette credits Abishai with saving David's life during the Philistine wars (2 Sam. 21:16-17). Within David's administration, Abishai appears as a kind of second-in-command of the army, and he is typical of David's inner circle of advisors with his combination of loyalty to, yet independence from, the king.

Abishai is conspicuously absent from the intrigue surrounding the struggle between Solomon and Adonijah for the throne (1 Kgs. 1–2), and indeed he may have died sometime before it began. Benaiah ben Jehoiada appears here as the leader of David's warrior elite.

Abishai and his brother Joab also provide a key foil for the text's explication of David's personality. The record implicates Abishai in Joab's revenge slaying of Abner the son of Ner (2 Sam. 3:30), and it lumps him with Joab in David's condemnation of "the sons of Zeruiah" as ruthless men of blood (3:39; 16:10). While David appears to renounce violence toward his enemies (1 Sam. 26:6-12; 2 Sam. 16:9-14), Abishai and Joab appear as the proverbial violent men, whose ruthless deeds will overtake them. At the same time the writer appreciates — and clearly reveals — the irony in David's condemnation of the very men upon whose shoulders his kingdom's security clearly rests.

Bibliography. D. G. Schley, "Joab and David: Ties of Blood and Power," in *History and Interpretation,* ed. M. P. Graham, W. P. Brown, and J. K. Kuan (Sheffield, 1993), 90-105.

Donald G. Schley

ABISHALOM (Heb. *'ăḇîšālôm*)
An alternate rendering of the name Absalom (1 Kgs. 15:2, 10).

ABISHUA (Heb. *'ăḇîšûaʿ*)
1. The son of the high priest Phinehas (1 Chr. 6:4[MT 5:30]) and great-grandson of Aaron (6:50[35]). According to Ezra 7:5 he was an ancestor of Ezra the scribe.

2. A Benjaminite, one of the sons of Bela, and grandson of Benjamin (1 Chr. 8:4).

ABISHUR (Heb. *'ăḇîšûr*)
A Judahite of the family of Hezron; a son of Shammai and brother of Nadab. He married Abihail and became the father of two sons (1 Chr. 2:28-29).

ABITAL (Heb. *'ăḇîṭāl*)
One of David's wives and mother of his fifth son Shephatiah (2 Sam. 3:4 = 1 Chr. 3:3).

ABITUB (Heb. *'ăḇîṭûḇ*)
One of the two sons of Shamaraim and his first wife Hushin (1 Chr. 8:11).

ABIUD (Gk. *Abioúd*)
The son of Zerubbabel, according to Matthew's genealogy of Jesus (Matt. 1:13).

ABNER (Heb. *'ăḇnēr*)
Saul's uncle and the commander of his army (1 Sam. 14:50). Abner apparently had at least one son, a certain Jaasiel, who led the tribe of Benjamin during David's reign (1 Chr. 27:21).

While Saul ruled Israel, Abner may have served as Saul's personal bodyguard. David once chastised Abner for failing to protect Saul while they slept (1 Sam. 26:13-25). After Saul's death, Abner instigated the accession of Saul's son Ishbaal to the throne of Israel and spearheaded the transfer of the capital from Gibeah to Mahanaim in Transjordan (2 Sam. 2:8, 12). During Ishbaal's short reign of two years, Abner apparently still served as commander of the army, but he seems to have had much more power. When the leadership of Ishbaal was failing, Abner sought to take over by acquiring one of Saul's concubines, Rizpah (access to the royal harem indicated one's rightful claim to the throne). When confronted by Ishbaal about his machinations, Abner defected to David. Abner's motivations are uncertain, but perhaps he believed he had a greater chance to gain the throne of Israel by allying with David. He also might have expected to replace Joab as commander of David's army.

After visiting David in Hebron to arrange David's accession to the throne of Israel, Abner was murdered by Joab to avenge the death of his brother Asahel, whom Abner had killed, purportedly in self-defense following the skirmish at Gibeon (2 Sam. 2:18-28). Joab's secondary motivation may have been the threat that Abner posed to Joab's position in David's army. Although the text does not implicate David in Abner's murder, some scholars believe that he may have ordered it since 2 Samuel tries so hard to say otherwise.

Paul S. Ash

ABRAHAM (Heb. *'aḇrāhām*)
The son of Terah, husband of Sarah, father of Ishmael and Isaac, and grandfather of Jacob. He is the common patriarch of the three "Abrahamic" religions: Jews trace their ancestry to Abraham through his son Isaac and his grandson Jacob-

Israel, Muslims trace theirs through his son Ishmael, and Christians claim descent from Abraham through faith (Gal. 3:6-7, 29).

The biblical story of Abraham describes his divine selection as the ancestor of Israel and sets in motion the long process by which his descendants eventually become a populous nation in a land of their own. At the beginning Abraham is living with his wife Sarah and his nephew Lot in the Mesopotamian city of Haran. Yahweh commands him to leave his ancestral home and move to a new land, where his descendants will be divinely blessed and grow into a great nation (Gen. 12:1-3). This promise cannot be fulfilled within Abraham's own lifetime, but its realization is foreshadowed in the ensuing events, as Abraham and Sarah take up residence in the land promised to them, and Isaac, the son from whom the nation will descend, is born.

The great patriarch first appears as "Abram" (*'aḇrām,* Gen. 11:26), but eventually God changes his name to *'aḇrāhām* (17:5). The two forms probably originated as dialectal variants — the longer form, with internal *-h-*, corresponds to a pattern especially common in Aramaic; the meaning in either form was "the Father is exalted," the God of Abraham being praised as divine father of kinsmen. Even so, the author of Gen. 17, in which Abram is promised a multitude of offspring, gives a thematic interpretation of the new name as "the father of a multitude (*'aḇ-hămôn*) of nations." This chapter contains the formal articulation of the Priestly (P) version of the covenant between God and Abraham's descendants, and the change of name is an indication of the change of status that occurs when the covenant is established, signifying a new identity in relation to the name-giver (cf. 2 Kgs. 23:34). The name of Abram's wife is also changed — from Sarai to Sarah (Gen. 17:15) — and his grandson's name will be changed from Jacob to Israel (17:15; 32:28[MT 29]).

It is difficult to say whether the traditional stories about Abraham were based on the life of a historical individual and, if so, exactly when the historical Abraham might have lived. The biblical writers regarded him as a figure of the distant past, living many generations before the establishment of Israel as a political entity, and modern scholars have attempted to identify a pre-Israelite context into which the stories might fit. Following a nonurban period at the end of the 3rd millennium B.C., there were two centuries of gradual resettlement in Mesopotamia, Syria, and Palestine (Middle Bronze I or IIA), followed by an age of increased population and cultural expansion characterized by the development of large urban centers (MB II or IIB). Since Abraham and his family are presented as nomads, even after arriving in Canaan, historians have attempted to associate the travels of Abraham and his family with the movements of peoples during the settlement period of MB I, or to understand their activities in terms of our knowledge of nomadic peoples living alongside the great cities of MB II.

The earliest surviving reference to Abraham may be in a 10th-century Egyptian text, which refers to a place in the Negeb called "the Fortress of Abraham," listed among places conquered by the 22nd-Dynasty king Sheshonq (Shishak) in his incursion into Palestine during the reign of Rehoboam (cf. 1 Kgs. 14:25-26; 2 Chr. 12:2-12). If the Abraham for whom this fortress was named is the biblical patriarch, then the Abraham tradition was well established in the Negeb by the 10th century. This would be consistent with the geographical setting of the biblical narrative, in which Abraham has strong ties to the Negeb — especially to Beer-sheba, where Isaac is born and raised — and to other southern locations, most notably Hebron, near which Abraham's family had its principal residence at the "oaks of Mamre" (Gen. 13:18; 14:13; 18:1). These geographical associations are sometimes taken as an indication that the Abraham tradition originated in the south, but they are more likely the result of a southern orientation of the tradition that developed after the settlement of the Negeb in the 11th century and, more especially, after the establishment of the Davidic dynasty with its strong associations with Hebron, the traditional capital of the tribe of Judah. Indeed, there are some indications that Abraham's earliest geographical associations were not with Hebron but with the original Israelite homeland in the hill country north of Jerusalem. Whether the Abraham tradition originated in the south or the north, however, in the present form of the tradition Abraham is not a regional figure but a patriarch of the entire land. This is perhaps shown most clearly by the places of worship he is said to have founded, which range across the heartland of ancient Israel, north and south. He builds an altar to Yahweh at Shechem in the central Samarian hills (Gen. 12:6-7), another north of Jerusalem at a point between Bethel and Ai (v. 8), and a third at Hebron in the southern Judean hills (13:18). At Beer-sheba in the northern Negeb he plants a sacred tree (21:33).

As the founder of these shrines, Abraham initiates the process by which the worship of Yahweh is established throughout Canaan. He also engages in a number of other foundational activities — territorial negotiations, land purchases, even military expeditions — which determine and clarify the relationships of his family to the neighboring peoples. These are the actions of a founding patriarch, whose deeds define the social roles and ethnic consciousness of his descendants. The most important vehicle of this social and ethnic definition is the elaborate genealogy in which Abraham is introduced and which he extends by the marriages he makes and the children he begets. His family background is documented primarily in Gen. 11:10-32, a continuation of the genealogy of Noah's eldest son Shem, begun in 10:21-31. Shem was "the father of all the children of Eber" (10:21), i.e., the Hebrews, who in biblical tradition are contrasted with the Canaanites and other indigenous peoples of the Promised Land. Abraham himself was the eldest of the three sons of Terah (Gen. 11:26), during whose lifetime the family is said to have moved from Ur, in southern Mesopotamia, to Haran on the Balikh River in northwestern Mesopotamia. In the time of the biblical writers Haran was a major caravan city, from which travelers could cross the Euphrates and proceed south via the oasis of Tadmor (Palmyra) to Damascus, picking up the King's Highway and continuing, east of the Jordan, to Canaan and points farther south. This is evidently the route that Abraham's family was believed to have taken, and the family ties to Haran, and ultimately to Ur, reflect the Israelite belief that their earliest ancestral connections were with the peoples of Transeuphrates, not with the indigenous peoples of Canaan. Thus the names of Abraham's immediate ascendants (Gen. 11:22-26; 1 Chr. 1:26-27) correspond to the names of cities in the vicinity of Haran: Serug, the name of Abraham's great-grandfather, was the name of a city situated between Haran and the Euphrates; Nahor, the name of both Abraham's grandfather and one of his two brothers, was the name of a city (Nakhur) located SE of Haran on the upper Balikh; and Terah was the name of a city (Til-[sha]-Turakhi) in the Balikh River basin. The name of Abraham's other brother Haran (*hārān*) is similar but not identical to the name of the city of Haran (*ḥārān*) itself.

The names of the descendants of the three sons of Terah — Abraham, Nahor, and Haran — correspond to the names of the peoples recognized by the biblical writers as belonging to Israel's larger kinship group. Nahor's sons bear the names of the 12 tribes of the Arameans. Eight of these were located in the Syrian Desert, the Aramean homeland (Gen. 22:20-23), while the remaining four eventually expanded westward into Syria (v. 24). Haran's son Lot was the father of Moab and Ben-ammi, the eponymous ancestors of the Transjordanian Ammonites and Moabites (Gen. 19:37-38), who are therefore known in biblical tradition as "the children of Lot" (Deut. 2:9, 19; Ps. 83:8[9]). By attributing their patrimony to Abraham's nephew, the tradition accorded them a junior kinship to Israel, and by presenting the circumstances of their conception as an incestuous union between Lot and his daughters (Gen. 19:30-38), the tradition cast a shadow over their lineage, especially in contrast to the auspicious circumstances of the birth of Israel's ancestor, Isaac.

Abraham's own descendants fall into three groups: those descended from Ishmael (Ishmaelites or Arabs), those descended from Isaac (Edomites and Israelites), and those descended from the various sons of Keturah (a collateral line of Arabs). Their relative status in Israelite tradition is reflected in the status of their mothers. Isaac was the son of Abraham's wife Sarah and the father of Jacob-Israel, whose 12 sons were the ancestors of the 12 tribes who eventually would inherit the land promised to Abraham in Canaan. As shown by the "Edomite Genesis" of Gen. 36, Esau-Edom, Isaac's other son, was the eponymous ancestor of the Edomites, whom Israelite tradition divided into three groups descended from Esau's three wives. Abraham's other sons were the sons of concubines, Hagar and Keturah, and he sent them away "to the east" (Gen. 25:6), i.e., to Arabia. Thus the 12 sons of Ishmael, the son of Hagar, bear the names of 12 peoples of northern Arabia (Gen. 25:13-15; 1 Chr. 1:29-31), who inhabited the Syrian Desert east and southeast of Gilead. These were the Hagrite or Hagarene tribes (1 Chr. 5:10, 19-20; cf. Ps. 83:6[7]; Bar. 3:23); most of their names are those of tribes mentioned in biblical or extrabiblical sources. The names of Keturah's sons (Gen. 25:2; 1 Chr. 1:32) are more difficult to explain than those of Hagar, but in general they too seem to correspond to the names of Arabian groups and places.

Taken altogether, therefore, the genealogical traditions associated with Abraham identify Israel within three kinship groups of progressively narrowing boundaries and increasing affinity. The most general group is that of the Semites or descendants of Shem and, more particularly, the descendants of Eber or Hebrews. The next group comprises the Terachic peoples — the descendants of the three sons of Abraham's father, Terah. These include the Arameans and the Transjordanian peoples of Ammon and Moab. The narrowest group is that of the Abrahamic peoples, descendants of Abraham himself. They include the Ishmaelites or northern Arabian tribes, the Edomites, and the Israelites themselves.

The most striking characteristic of Abraham's portrayal in the Genesis narrative — and for which he is most admired in later tradition — is his passive obedience to the divine directives he receives. At the beginning of his story he is told to leave his homeland behind and travel "to the land that I will show you," a place about which he knows nothing. That he seems to accept this summons without question or hesitation may be a consequence of the literary economy of the narrative, but in postbiblical interpretation his passive acceptance has been seen as a paradigm of the unquestioning obedience that arises from trust in God. This is all the more true of the story of the "binding" (*ʿăqēḏâ)* of Isaac, told near the end of the Abraham narrative (Gen. 22:1-19). After Isaac is born and the divine promise of progeny, which had been jeopardized by Abraham's old age and Sarah's barrenness, seems on the way to fulfillment, God tests Abraham by instructing him to take Isaac to "one of the mountains that I shall show you" and sacrifice him there as a burnt offering. Again Abraham obeys without hesitation and is at the point of putting his son to death when God intervenes and substitutes a ram for the offering. Principally on the basis of this remarkable story, Abraham came to be regarded as a paragon of faith or trust in God for Jews and Christians — and also for Muslims, in whose tradition it is Ishmael, rather than Isaac, whose sacrifice is demanded.

P. KYLE MCCARTER, JR.

ABRAHAM, APOCALYPSE OF

A 1st- to mid-2nd century C.E. Jewish apocalypse, probably composed in a Semitic language, but extant only in Slavonic. Although the work may not be composite, most scholars identify two major parts and several possible interpolations.

1. Chs.1-8 are a late, humorous story about the conversion of Abraham from idolatry after he reflects on the nature of idols and prays that he might know the Creator, who then appears in a theophany.
2. Chs. 9-32, the original apocalypse, are a midrash on Gen. 15:9-17. God instructs the angel Iaoel *(YHWH 'l)* to help Abraham offer sacrifices on Horeb, where Abraham encounters the fallen angel Azazel. Iaoel then takes Abraham on an otherworldly journey and shows him a vision of God, God's throne and attendants (cf. Ezek. 1, 10), the various heavens, the earth and the abyss, and a picture depicting all of human history (cf. 1 En. 1-36).

Bibliography. R. Rubinkiewicz, "Apocalypse of Abraham," *OTP* 1 (Garden City, 1983): 681-705; G. Vermes, "Jewish Literature Composed in Hebrew or Aramaic," in E. Schürer, *The History of the Jewish People in the Age of Jesus Christ (175 B.C.–A.D. 135)*, rev. ed., 3/1 (Edinburgh, 1986): 288-92.

R. GLENN WOODEN

ABRAHAM, TESTAMENT OF

A pseudepigraphal book in which Abraham learns from the archangel Michael that the time has come for his death. Abraham, however, refuses to die, using his privileged position as the friend of God to forestall the inevitable. The story thus departs from an anticipated deathbed gathering (a testament) to become apocalyptic in nature as Abraham tours the inhabited world and journeys to the scene of the judgment. The principal theme is that God is compassionate and patient with sinners, desiring that all repent and live. At the end of the story, God sends the angel Death, who takes Abraham's soul by trickery.

The text exists in a long (Recension A) and short (Recension B) form. The original Jewish text was probably written in a semitizing Greek in Egypt ca. 100 C.E.

Bibliography. E. P. Sanders, "Testament of Abraham," *OTP* 1:871-902.

PAUL S. ASH

ABRAM (Heb. *'aḇrām*)

The original name of Abraham.

ABRON (Gk. *Abrōna*)

A brook along which Holofernes destroyed all the fortified towns (Jdt. 2:24; cf. Codex Sinaiticus *Chebrōn*, Vulg. *Mambre*). Some scholars identify it with the Ḫabur River.

ABRONAH (Heb. *'aḇrōnâ*)

A place where the Israelites encamped during their wilderness wanderings (Num. 33:34-35). It is an oasis, possibly 'Ain Defiyeh/'Ein Avrona, ca. 15 km. (9 mi.) N of Ezion-geber.

ABSALOM (Heb. *'aḇšālōm;* Gk. *Apsalōmos, Abessalōm*) (also ABISHALOM)

1. The third son of David, born to Maacah, daughter of Talmai king of Geshur (2 Sam. 3:3 = 1 Chr. 3:2); presumably an ancestor of Maacah the wife of Rehoboam and mother of Abijam (1 Kgs. 15:2, Abishalom). Absalom plays a major role in narratives reporting the punishment prophesied by Nathan for David's crimes of adultery and murder (2 Sam. 12:11-12). David suffered many of the promised consequences for his crimes through the actions of a son portrayed as a negative image of himself: handsome (1 Sam. 16:12; 2 Sam. 14:25), charismatic (3:36; 15:1-6), and cunning in dealing with enemies (ch. 13; 1 Kgs. 2:5-6).

Absalom planned and ordered the murder of Amnon in retaliation for the rape of Tamar and fled to exile in Geshur, his grandfather's city (2 Sam. 13). Soon after his return and reconciliation with David, orchestrated by Joab (2 Sam. 14), Absalom attempted to wrest control of the kingdom from his father. When people seeking justice arrived in Jerusalem, he assured them of their case's merit and bemoaned his lack of a position that would allow him to help. He embraced and kissed those who came to bow before him (2 Sam. 15:1-6). On the pretext of fulfilling a vow, he traveled to Hebron, where David had been crowned king, and sent agents throughout the kingdom to announce his coronation at the sound of trumpet signals. News of Absalom's rebellion spread quickly, and David was forced to flee for refuge to Mahanaim, the city E of the Jordan River where Saul's general, Abner, had failed to continue Saul's dynasty through Ishbaal. Hushai, the priests Zadok and Abiathar, and the priest's sons remained in Jerusalem as David's agents. After entering Jerusalem, Absalom demonstrated his claim to the throne by taking 10 of David's concubines. His decision to wait as Hushai advised, rather than immediately pursue and kill David as Ahithophel counseled, sealed his doom. David's followers were ready and defeated Absalom's forces. While riding a mule, Absalom's head was caught in an oak. He was killed by Joab, and his body thrown into a pit in the forest and covered with a heap of stones.

Bibliography. C. Conroy, *Absalom Absalom! Narrative and Language in 2 Samuel 13–20.* AnBib 81 (Rome, 1978); J. P. Fokkelman, *Narrative Art and Poetry in the Books of Samuel,* 1: *King David* (Assen, 1991); R. Polzin, *David and the Deuteronomist: 2 Samuel* (Bloomington, 1993); R. N. Whybray, *The Succession Narrative.* SBT, 2nd ser. 9 (Naperville, 1968).

2. One of two messengers said to be involved in negotiations between Judas Maccabeus and Lysias, the governor of Coele-Syria and Phoenicia (2 Macc. 11:17); possibly the same as the father of Mattathias (1 Macc. 11:70) and Jonathan (13:11), commanders in the Maccabean army.

KEITH L. EADES

ABYSS

Although in English translations of the OT "abyss" is rarely used (cf. Gen. 1:2 NEB, NAB), Gk. *ábyssos* ("primal ocean" or "world of the dead") appears frequently in the LXX as a translation of Heb. *tĕhôm,* "waters of the deep." *Tĕhôm,* treated as a proper name, derives from the same Semitic root as

Tiamat, the goddess in Enuma Elish, the Babylonian creation story. However, it does not appear to be personified in the OT and refers variously to the creation event (Gen. 1:2; Job 38:16; Ps. 33:7), to blessings and fertility (Gen. 49:25; Deut. 8:7; Ps. 78:15), and to destruction (Gen. 7:11; 8:2; Ezek. 26:19; Amos 7:4). It is also associated with the Reed Sea (Exod. 15:5; Isa. 51:10; Ps. 106:9).

When "abyss" is not used to translate *tĕhôm,* "the deep" is often employed (cf. Gen. 1:2 NJPSV, RSV, NRSV).

Usually translated "abyss" in the NT, it refers to the place of the dead (Rom. 10:7) and is synonymous with hell or Hades. It more frequently refers to the place where the forces of evil dwell (e.g., Luke 8:31; Rev. 9:1, 2). JOHN R. SPENCER

ACACIA

A native Mediterranean tree, of which there are five species. Most grow in the Judean desert, the Negeb, and Sinai, while one type *(Acacia raddiana)* is found in the central and northern parts of Israel. The acacia (Heb. *šiṭṭîm*) is a hardy tree, able to withstand the extreme climatic conditions of the desert. Acacia is used for fuel, construction, and shade. The trunk, branches, and leaves also provide food for a variety of animals. Although some types of acacia are shrublike, 4-5 m. (13-16 ft.) in height, others have central trunks and can reach heights of 12-15 m. (40-50 ft.). Acacia wood was used prominently in construction of the tabernacle, ark, and other sacred objects (Exod. 25-27, 30, 35-38).

Bibliography. N. Hareuveni, *Tree and Shrub in Our Biblical Heritage* (Kiryat Ono, 1984); Y. Waisel and A. Alon, *Trees of the Land of Israel* (Tel Aviv, 1980). ALAN RAY BUESCHER

ACCAD (Heb. *'akkaḏ;* Akk. *a-ga-dé*) (also AKKAD)

A city in northern Babylonia listed with Babel and Erech as a part of Nimrod's kingdom in the land of Shinar (Gen. 10:10); also called Agade, Akkad. Accad was founded as the capital city of the empire established by Sargon I (ca. 2330-2274 B.C.). The Akkadian Empire included all Mesopotamia, parts of Anatolia, and northern Syria, as far as the Mediterranean coast. With the shift of the political center of Mesopotamia from Sumer to Accad, the Semitic Akkadian language, culture, and military art superseded that of the Sumerians. Sargon's grandson Naram-sin destroyed the great palace of Ebla ca. 2250. Accad was destroyed by the Gutians ca. 2150 and never rebuilt.

The location of the city remains uncertain. Some locate it near Babylon and others near Sippor, possibly Tell Der or Tell Sesubar. Even after the destruction of the city, the name Akkad designated the northern region of Babylonia, and "Akkad and Sumer" was used as late as the Persian period to refer to all of Babylonia. BRADFORD SCOTT HUMMEL

ACCO (Heb. *'akkô*)

A Levantine coastal city identified with modern Tell el-Fukhkhâr/Tel Acco (1585.2585), a 200-dunam tell some 700 m. (2300 ft.) inland. Its importance as a major economic and political center may be attributed to its location at the junction of both maritime and overland trade routes connecting the coast with Galilee, the Jordan Valley as well as Transjordan and Syria. Originally a Canaanite center, Acco is mentioned as an unconquered city at the time of the Conquest (Judg. 1:31) as well as a harbor city in the time of Paul (Acts 21:7). The Hellenistic-Roman city was called Ptolemais, located between the harbor and the tell. During the Crusade period it was known as St. Jean D'Acre or Acre, and subsequently it was called Akka by its Arab conquerors.

Archaeological evidence and the occurrence of the name in ancient texts sources indicate that it was continually inhabited over a period of four millennia. During the Iron Age Acco was settled by the Philistines; indications of metal-working and Mycenean pottery confirm this link with the Mediterranean islands. Soon afterward it became an important Phoenician maritime and trading center, as shown by the underwater excavations in the harbor. In Area B numerous examples of household utensils, figurines, and jewelry testify to its role as a major trading center between the Phoenician coastal cities and the mainland. Due to the Assyrian westward expansion by Tiglath-pileser III tribute was exacted from the Phoenician cities that later joined the rebellion of Hezekiah, the result of which was the disastrous invasions by Sennacherib in 701 B.C. Assurbanipal boasts that he killed those inhabitants of Acco who were not submissive, hanging their corpses on poles which he placed around the city, and deported the others (*ANET,* 300). From 530 onward Acco was a strategic base for the Persian military operations against Egypt. As a city with *polis* status Acco became an important link in international trade between the Hellenistic world and the Nabateans, controlling access to the mainland of Palestine. Under Ptolemaic rule its name changed to Ptolemais. During the Maccabean wars the Seleucids used it as a center from which the Jews were persecuted. Pompey conquered the city in 63 B.C. and enlarged its territory. As Colonia Claudia Ptolemais it served as a center for the military, industry, and trade during Roman and Byzantine times. Acco is also famous because of Napoleon's defeat there in 1799.

Bibliography. M. Dothan, et al., "Acco," *NEAEHL* 1:16-31; E. Linder, "The Harbor of Akko Excavations (1973-75 Seasons)," *International Conference of Underwater Archaeology* (Philadelphia, 1975). J. P. J. OLIVIER

ACHAEMENID (also ACHAEMENIAN)

Designation of the royal house of Persia, from Cyrus II (559-530 B.C.E.) onward (from Pers. *Hakhāmanish,* perhaps "friendly in nature," eponymous ancestor of the dynasty; Gk. *Achaimenēs*). It was Cyrus who permitted the Jewish exiles to take back to Jerusalem the "vessels of the house of the Lord" (Ezra 1:7). The vast and varied resources of the empire made Achaemenian (or Achaemenid) art possible.

ACHAIA (Gk. *Achaía*)
Home of the Achaeans, as Homer called the Greeks who attacked Troy, the dominant people in the northern Peloponnesian Peninsula of Greece during the Mycenaean period. When Rome began to threaten Greece, city states of the northern Peloponnese (Achaia proper), led by Corinth, formed the Achaean League to resist. When the Romans defeated the league and destroyed Corinth, Achaia became a Roman province attached to Macedonia but recognized as distinct.

In 27 B.C.E. Augustus designated all the Peloponnese and the mainland south of a line running roughly from the Eubian Gulf west to Actium as the new senatorial province of Achaia. Corinth became its capital. Northern Greece largely formed the province of Macedonia. The Romans also frequently referred in a general way to all of Greece as Achaia.

The letters of Paul and Acts follow the Roman provincial designations and refer to southern Greece as Achaia and northern Greece as Macedonia. Paul most often used Achaia to indicate specifically Corinth and its surrounding territory (cf. Acts 18:12, 27; Rom. 15:26; 1 Cor. 16:15; 2 Cor. 1:1; 9:2; 11:10; 1 Thess. 1:7-8). SCOTT NASH

ACHAICUS (Gk. *Achaïkós*)
A Christian (Gk. "a person from Achaia") from Corinth whom the Corinthian church sent to Paul in Ephesus (1 Cor. 16:17).

ACHAN (Heb. *ʿāḵān*)
A Judahite, son of Carmi, son of Zabdi, son of Zerah who misappropriated some of the goods which were to be utterly dedicated to God after the conquest and destruction of Jericho (Josh. 7:1). Immediately afterward Israel loses its next battle against Ai and deduces that God is angry with them. Joshua prays to God, who responds that this battle loss occurred because someone violated the rules concerning the banned goods of Jericho. God instructs Joshua to cast lots to determine who violated the rules of war. When lots are cast on the following day Achan is determined the guilty party. He is confronted and confesses to having improperly taken a variety of goods and having buried them under his tent. When the goods are indeed discovered, Achan, his whole family, and all his possessions are brought up to the Valley of Achor (a wordplay on Achan) where they are burned and stoned (Josh. 7:25-26). JOEL S. KAMINSKY

ACHBOR (Heb. *ʿaḵbôr*) (also ABDON)

1. The father of the Edomite king Baal-hanan (Gen. 36:38-39 = 1 Chr. 1:49).

2. The son of Micaiah; a court official of King Josiah sent to consult the prophetess Huldah (2 Kgs. 22:12, 14). At 2 Chr. 34:20 he is called Abdon (**4**) the son of Micah. According to Jer. 26:22; 36:12 he was the father of Elnathan.

ACHIM (Gk. *Achím*)
A postexilic ancestor of Jesus (Matt. 1:14).

ACHIOR (Gk. *Achiōr*)
An Ammonite commander under the Assyrian general Holofernes who attempted to dissuade his commander from attacking the Israelites (Jdt. 5:5-21). Holofernes' officers disregarded Achior's "deuteronomistic" interpretation of history and instead threatened him with death (Jdt. 5:22-23). Judith, however, saved his life by beheading Holofernes. Seeing the hand of God in this act, Achior accepted circumcision (one of the few Ammonites to do so) and became a loyal member of the house of Israel (Jdt. 14:10).

ACHISH (Heb. *ʾāḵîš*)
The king of Philistine Gath during the time of David (1 Sam. 21–29) and early in Solomon's reign (1 Kgs. 2:39). Despite the two different patronyms, Maoch (1 Sam. 27:2) and Maacah (1 Kgs. 2:39), this is the same individual.

When David was fleeing from Saul, he twice took refuge with Achish. On the first occasion, David feigned insanity to avoid harm (1 Sam. 21:12-13[MT 13-14]) and quickly left Achish. On the second, Achish received David and, at the latter's request, gave David and his followers the city of Ziklag as a fief (1 Sam. 27:1-6). David quickly gained favor with Achish, who used him and his band as his bodyguards. In preparation for a battle with Saul, the Philistine kings gathered at Aphek (1 Sam. 29). David and his band wished to participate in the battle, but, despite Achish's efforts, the other kings insisted that David leave. Shortly afterward, David became king of Judah and left Achish's service. According to the biblical record, at least 40 years later Achish still ruled Gath (1 Kgs. 2:39-40). PAUL S. ASH

ACHOR (Heb. *ʿāḵôr*)
A valley on the Judah-Benjamine border (Josh. 15:7) where the Israelites stoned Achan and his family because of his unfaithfulness, which precipitated the defeat of the Israelites at Ai (7:11, 12, 20-21). Achor means "trouble," which may derive from Achan's plight (Josh. 7:25).

The exact location of this valley is problematic, though scholars have identified it with the modern el-Buqeiʿah.

Two 8th-century prophets cited Achor as a promise for the chosen ones. While Achor was the valley of "trouble," eschatologically it will become a resting place "for herds to lie down" (Isa. 65:10) and a "door of hope" (Hos. 2:15).

Bibliography. F. M. Cross and J. T. Milik, "Explorations in the Judaean Buqêʿah," *BASOR* 142 (1956): 5-17; L. E. Stager, "Farming in the Judean Desert during the Iron Age," *BASOR* 221 (1976): 145-58. DAVID MERLING

ACHSAH (Heb. *ʿaḵsâ*).
The only daughter of Caleb (1 Chr. 2:49), who promised her in marriage to anyone who would capture the city of Debir, known as Kirjath-sepher. Othniel, Caleb's nephew, took the town and was married to Achsah. Her dowry was a portion of the

Negeb, and later she convinced Caleb to give her as a wedding gift the upper and lower springs near Hebron (Josh. 15:16-19; Judg. 1:11-15).

CAROL J. DEMPSEY

ACHSHAPH (Heb. *'akšāp̱*)
A border settlement apportioned to the tribe of Asher (Josh 19:25). The Canaanite king of the city aligned himself with Jabin of Hazor to oppose the Israelite advance and was subsequently defeated (Josh. 11:1; 12:20). The city is mentioned in the Egyptian Execration Texts and later in the Papyrus Anatasi I (13th century B.C.). Achshaph was among the cities conquered by Pharaoh Thutmose III. A letter among the Amarna Tablets describes the king of Achshaph as sending 50 chariots to aid the king of Jerusalem. The ruins of the city may be Khirbet el-Harbaj/Tel Regev (158240) in the southern Acco Plain.

DAVID C. MALTSBERGER

ACHZIB (Heb. *'aḵzîḇ*)

1. A town in the Shephelah, belonging to the tribe of Judah (Josh. 15:44). A variant name of the town might be Chezib, where Judah's Canaanite wife bore Shelah, his third son (Gen. 38:5). Eusebius (*Onom.* 172) identified the town with Chasbi, near Adullam. Scholars largely accept this identification, which corresponds with the modern Tell el-Beiḍā/Ḥorvat Lavnin (145116), 5 km. (3 mi.) W of Adullam. The prophet Micah plays on its name, declaring that the houses of Achzib will be a deception (*'aḵzāḇ*) to the kings of Israel (Mic. 1:14).

2. An important city in antiquity located on the Mediterranean coast, along the Via Maris, ca. 14 km. (9 mi.) N of Acco. Until 1948 the tell was the site of the modern village of ez-Zib (1598.2727). The presence of the village precluded excavation of the mound, other than four extensive cemeteries, until the 1963-64 excavations by Moshe W. Prausnitz. Excavations have indicated that Achzib was occupied from the Middle Bronze Age to the Muslim period. During the Israelite period the city was assigned to the tribe of Asher (Josh. 19:29), but the biblical text claims that the tribe was unsuccessful in driving out its Canaanite inhabitants (Judg. 1:31). During MB the city was separated from the mainland by a deep fosse, joining the Wadi Qarn/Naḥal Keziv to the north with the bay to the south, turning the city into an island. The city reached its largest size during the Iron Age, extending east beyond the fosse, until it was conquered by Sennacherib during his third campaign in 701 B.C.E.

RONALD A. SIMKINS

ACRE
A unit of measurement (Heb. *ṣemeḏ*, "yoke") designating the amount of land which a team of oxen can plow in one day, which varied with agricultural methods (1 Sam. 14:14; Isa. 5:10).

ACROSTIC
A poetic form in which the initial letters or signs of each line, couplet, or stanza, when read in succession, spell out a name, sentence, alphabet, or some alphabetic pattern. Acrostics are known from many historical periods and literary traditions, the oldest coming from ancient Mesopotamia. The OT contains a number of partial and complete alphabetic acrostics (Nah. 1; Pss. 9–10, 25, 34, 111, 112, 119, 145; Prov. 31:10-31; Lam. 1, 2, 3, 4). These acrostics spell out the Hebrew alphabet with the initial letters of each line (Pss. 111, 112), couplet (Lam. 3), or stanza (Lam. 1, 2, 4).

Scholars have posited that acrostics are used in the OT as either pedagogic devices or mnemonic aids, that they were associated with magical powers, or that they simply signified a sense of completeness. Whatever the plausibility of these theories, the acrostic is fundamentally a poetic form, and it functions in ways analogous to other poetic forms (e.g., the sonnet or sestina in English poetic tradition), such as providing an aesthetic constraint on the poet's composition and presenting a formal pattern of repetition, which may be manipulated to achieve various effects, including to build in coherence and dynamism and to signal closure. Form is central to poetry in general, and the acrostic represents an important formal device in Hebrew poetry.

F. W. DOBBS-ALLSOPP

ACTS, APOCRYPHAL
Works describing the deeds of various apostles, partly inspired by but often in some tension with the book of Acts that became canonical. Composition of these works continued until the 6th century C.E. Extracts from them have remained in liturgical use. These acts, together with writings about the infancy or the passion of Jesus, attest to early Christian interest in extended accounts about the founders of Christianity. Building upon the Gospel type of narrative, they also reflect engagement with a broader literary culture, including philosophical biographies and popular novels. Theologically, the apocryphal acts represent developments of the "radical" Jesus tradition embedded in Q and the Gospel of Thomas, for their heroes are typically homeless itinerants who preach messages of renunciation and other-worldliness. Their narrative geographical horizon extends from Spain to India (not to mention heaven and hell). Readers of these books could find both uplifting messages and entertaining stories.

Five "major" compositions emerged in the period ca. 150-ca. 225: Acts of Andrew, John, Paul, Peter, and Thomas. Mutual imitation and contamination complicate the task of establishing literary relations among them. These acts have suffered from both popularity and condemnation. Because of the former, they underwent repeated expansion or abbreviation, as well as editing toward conformity with orthodox taste. Use by Manicheans and others judged heretical led to their eventual suppression. As a result, none of these acts survives in its original form, and only one is complete. Despite their general similarities, the various acts display a substantial variety of content and message.

The Acts of Andrew, possibly written in Alexandria, probably near the beginning of the 3rd century, presents a radical message influenced by Greek philosophy. The equally radical Acts of John, which may also be from Egypt and date to ca. 200, continues "heretical" trends opposed in 1–3 John. Subsequent editing thrust this work into the realm of Valentinian Gnosticism. The Acts of Paul, composed in 2nd-century Asia Minor, stands closest to the canonical work and was relatively unobjectionable to Catholic Christians. One section, the famous Acts of Thecla, survived through use in her cult. The extant portions of the Acts of Peter, also written in Asia Minor during the 2nd century, portray a less vagrant and less countercultural community leader, although fragments indicate that at some stage this book, like other apocryphal acts, highly honored celibacy. The beginnings of none of these four acts survive, but their climactic descriptions of the apostles' deaths are both well attested and highly edited. Matters are quite different with regard to the Acts of Thomas, evidently composed in Syriac in the region of Edessa during the first quarter of the 3rd century. This complete work exhibits considerable literary and theological depth. Its message, although not classically gnostic, was quite adaptable to gnostic views.

The numerous "minor" acts, featuring such figures as Barnabas, Titus, and Bartholomew, as well as later texts about the more famous apostles, tend to be orthodox in theology and ecclesiological in orientation. An exception is the Acts of Philip. Much hagiography (saints' lives) owes a large debt to the acts genre.

These texts have been the subject of vigorous attention in recent decades, yielding new editions, translations, and a number of specialist investigations. This activity reflects academic shifts toward an appreciation of pluralism and minority voices as well as the attraction of cultural studies. The apocryphal acts are important because they do attest to the diversity of early Christian thought in its popular expression and to the acient fascination with the extraordinary lives and deeds of holy persons. Their impact upon Christian art and literature remained prominent throughout the Middle Ages, and beyond.

Bibliography. J. K. Elliott, ed., *The Apocryphal New Testament,* rev. ed. (Oxford, 1993), 229-523; R. I. Pervo, "The Ancient Novel Becomes Christian," in *The Novel in the Ancient World,* ed. G. Schmeling. *Mnemosyne* Sup. 159 (Leiden, 1996), 685-711; W. Schneemelcher and R. McL. Wilson, eds., *New Testament Apocrypha,* rev. ed., 2 (Louisville, 1992), 75-482. RICHARD I. PERVO

ACTS OF THE APOSTLES

The fifth book of the NT. Composed by the author of the Gospel of Luke, the book of Acts represents the earliest attempt by a Christian writer to present a connected account of significant events in the life of the early Church from Easter to the death of Paul. Beginning with Irenaeus' *Adversus haereses* but especially with Eusebius' *Ecclesiastical History,* all succeeding attempts at the reconstruction of the earliest history of Christianity up to the modern age were profoundly determined by Acts. Notwithstanding the confidence placed in Luke's work by those chroniclers who followed him, attention to the narrative of Acts makes it clear that Luke, in line with the practices of his contemporaries, subordinated historical information to his literary project in order to present a portrait of the early Church's growth marked by ecclesiastical unity and Spirit-driven momentum.

The basic plot of Acts may be sketched as follows. Starting with the ascension of Jesus, the narrative first portrays the life and dynamic growth of the primitive community in Jerusalem under the leadership of Peter and the apostles up through the martyrdom of Stephen (Acts 1–7). The persecution ensuing upon Stephen's death drives the Church (except the apostles) into a more extensive mission outside Jerusalem characterized by overtures to non-Jews (ch. 8). These initial intimations of a gentile mission introduce the conversion of Saul/Paul (ch. 9), who will be the vital force behind the accomplishment of this mission. That these developments are legitimate and represent the purpose of God is brought home by the Cornelius episode of 10:1–11:18. Next the early missionary endeavors of Barnabas and Paul from their base in Syrian Antioch are narrated (11:19–14:28), along with an excursus featuring Peter (ch. 12), culminating in the decisive recognition of the law-free gentile mission by the Apostolic Council (ch. 15). Then the Pauline mission proper is detailed (15:36–21:26) in travelogue fashion (featuring Philippi, Thessalonica, Athens, Corinth, Ephesus, Miletus, Caesarea, Jerusalem) through numerous vivid scenes. Finally, Paul's imprisonment and trials in Jerusalem and Caesarea (featuring his interaction with numerous Roman officials) and his transfer to the Empire's capital are documented (21:27–28:31), ending with the encouraging image of Paul preaching and teaching, unhindered, in Rome.

Most scholars assume that the author of Luke and Acts was a Gentile Christian, although indications in both books support the supposition that the Lukan community included a contingent of Jewish Christians. That this individual should be identified following tradition as Luke, a companion of Paul, however, is problematic. In the undisputed Pauline Letters, Luke is mentioned only at Phlm. 24; the references at Col. 4:14; 2 Tim. 4:11 derive from Philemon and the Pauline tradition, respectively. Irenaeus (ca. 180 C.E.) understood the "we" passages (16:10-17; 20:5-15; 21:1-18; 27:1–28:16) as proof that Luke was Paul's inseparable collaborator. But the interpretation of these curious 1st person plural passages admits of other explanations that require no first-hand knowledge of Paul on the part of the author. Further, while it is clear simply from the amount of the narrative dedicated to Paul that the author admired him greatly, the resulting account seemingly reveals a profound misapprehension of Paul's work and theology as known to us through Paul's own Letters. Accordingly, when Paul preaches in Acts, his emphases (as well as the literary style of his speeches) are strikingly similar to

Central shrine of the temple of Augustus at Pisidian Antioch, a city visited by Paul on several occasions
(Phoenix Data Systems, Neal and Joel Bierling)

those featured in Peter's speeches, suggesting that in both the reader in fact encounters Luke's theology. Acts appears to be the product of a time when Paul's passionate struggles on behalf of Gentile Christians were a thing of the past. The overwhelming success of the gentile mission left Luke with the rather different concern of addressing Christian contemporaries who had become overly complacent about their Jewish origins.

While certainty on the date of composition for Acts may not be achieved, the preceding considerations indicate that it is reasonable to place it sometime after Luke's Gospel, which may be dated ca. 80-85 C.E. As far as Luke's geographical location is concerned, there are barely enough indications for speculation. Ancient tradition placed him in Antioch. His genuine concern with Paul and the Pauline tradition, even if deemed idiosyncratic when measured against the undisputed Pauline Letters, perhaps indicates his attachment to one of the principal areas of the Pauline mission around the Aegean, but this is only conjecture.

An exceptional issue with regard to the manuscript tradition of Acts is its existence in two major text types or "versions," the Alexandrian and the Western. Codex Bezae (D) intensifies the special features of the latter text type by expanding christological titles, sharpening a hostile attitude toward Jews, employing more reverential speech, smoothing over literary seams, and making other "improvements." Most scholars consider the Western version to be a secondary revision and expansion of the Alexandrian text.

Luke offers no guidance concerning the origins of his information for the narrative presented in Acts. While Luke probably utilized some sources for his account, his constant stylistic revision of the same renders their recovery unlikely (if we had only Luke's Gospel, could we reconstruct Mark?). While scholars have advanced a variety of hypothetical sources, all such suggestions are problematic. One recurrent proposal is that the biblical flavor of chs. 1–12 derives from an underlying Aramaic source. But nothing prevents the conclusion that Luke composed the narrative of the early period in an "archaic" style similar to the fashioning of the birth narratives in Luke 1–2. Another perennial idea is that an itinerary or diary of some kind provided Luke with information on Paul's missionary travels; a variant of this suggestion supposes that Luke himself was the scribe for the "we" passages of this diary. Apart from the problems inherent in the itinerary or diary hypothesis, various literary explanations serve to account for the "we" passages (e.g., a device, attested since Homer, for making a narrative more vivid). We may suppose that Luke's historical work proceeded in a manner not unlike that of his contemporaries. Without predecessors for his second book, Luke relied on a mixture of tradition and composition to portray the successful expansion of the early Christian mission throughout the Roman Empire under the direction of the Spirit according to the purpose of God.

One place where Luke's narrative designs become particularly clear is in the speeches that he has provided for the characters in the narrative. In line with the general practice of Hellenistic histori-

ACTS OF THE APOSTLES

ans, these speeches, which amount to nearly one third of the total text, may be regarded as the literary creations of Luke, inserted into the narrative to instruct and please the reader. Rather than preserving the particularity of the rhetoric of the various ancient Christian speakers, these speeches share the same literary style and consequently serve Luke's goal of demonstrating the substantial unity of the earliest Christian preaching, even as they embody Luke's own interpretation of the "events" surrounding the emergence of the Church.

Regardless of one's judgment concerning the reliability of Acts as a historical chronicle, the book certainly may be taken as an expression of early Christian theology. Luke's notion of salvation history in three epochs (Israel, Jesus, the Church) underlies his portrait of the Church as a historical entity with its own particular time. Moreover, the time of the earliest Church is distinguished by its own unique image (fostered by the employment of an archaic biblical Greek style) in contrast to the Church of Luke's own day. The peculiar and unrepeatable structures of the early community are accounted for by the presence of the apostles and eyewitnesses. Luke's concern within this portrait to highlight the continuity between Israel and the Church is expressed by the continued observance of Jewish practices in the early period in contrast to the situation implied for Luke's own day. The gap between Luke's generation and the primitive time is bridged by the endorsement of the gentile mission in the deliberations of the Apostolic Council and the promulgation of the Apostolic Decree (15:20, 29; 21:25). The latter pronouncement may have continued to function practically in the case of Luke's own community by ensuring the existence of the conditions necessary to make table fellowship between Jewish and Gentile Christians possible. Key among the factors promoting continuity within the Church itself throughout the narrative are the descriptions of the Church's proclamation and teaching about Jesus and the constancy of the presence of the Spirit as the prime mover at the crucial junctures of early ecclesiastical history (e.g., 8:29; 10:19; 16:6-7).

Acts is more theocentric than christocentric. It is God who occupies the dominant place. The notion of the preexistence of Jesus is absent and an air of "subordinationism" is present. Jesus is described as a man whom God legitimated by mighty works, wonders, and signs (2:22). The view of Christ's death as atoning occurs only once in an expression taken over from the tradition (20:28). The focal salvation event is the resurrection, which signifies the great turning point of history. Since God has offered the Resurrection as "proof" (17:31), there is no longer any excuse for rejecting the Christian message.

Paul's image had already undergone revision by Luke's day and Luke did not hesitate to introduce his own conceptions. Owing to his salvation-historical schematization, Luke was obligated to portray Paul as subject to the law. Further, in Luke's depiction Paul cannot establish the freedom of Gentile Christians from the law through theological argument (hence Paul's Letters, even if known, are of little practical value to Luke). Instead this freedom is given its historical and ecclesiastical foundation in the conversion of the gentile Cornelius (in which Peter plays the main role!) and the decision of the Apostolic Council, respectively. Discrepancies between the Lukan Paul and the Paul of the Epistles have long been observed. Thus according to Luke, Paul was a great miracle worker, an outstanding orator, not generally known as an apostle, and persecuted for teaching about the resurrection. By contrast Paul, in his Letters, stressed his weakness (2 Cor. 12:10), confessed that he was no master speaker (10:10), insisted vehemently on his credentials as an apostle (e.g., Gal. 2:1-10), and found trouble everywhere on account of his proclamation of a law-free gospel. All of these contradictions are explained when it is recognized that Acts preserves a picture of Paul from a time several decades after his death. Paul's role in Acts is thus dictated not only by his biography but also by the needs of Luke's theology; strictly historical concerns are not in view.

For Luke the Church's relation to Israel is both clear and problematic. While the Church must stand in continuity with the ancient people of God, it encounters unbelief among Jews and therefore turns to the Gentiles. But the law-free mission to the Gentiles threatened to break the continuity of salvation history. One of Luke's major concerns in Acts is to address this problem by showing that the primitive Christians held fast to their Jewish faith until they were impelled by no less than the intervention of God to welcome Gentiles into the Church. This is the fundamental motivation behind the multiple elaborations of the Cornelius episode (10:1-48; 11:1-18; 15:7-9) and the thrice-told story of Paul's conversion (9:1-19; 22:4-16; 26:9-18). That Luke depicts the acceptance on the part of Gentile Christians of certain basic OT requirements as spelled out by the Apostolic Decree is the natural correlative to Luke's fundamental concern with salvation-historical continuity, as are Paul's routine visits to the synagogue and his Jewish life-style.

Luke's portrayal of Christianity's close ties to Judaism also bolsters his appeal to Roman officials not to concern themselves with "internal theological disputes." In Luke's portrayal Roman notables express interest in Christianity (13:12; 19:31) or at least indicate that it poses no danger to the state (18:15; 19:37; 23:29; 25:25; 26:32). In this way Luke can affirm the nonsubversive nature of the Church, possibly in an effort to convince Roman citizens of his own day that nothing stood in the way of their membership in the Christian community.

Luke's purpose in writing Acts cannot be limited to any one factor. Without doubt his general aim was to encourage the Christian community to have confidence in its future by looking at its past. This was accomplished by skillfully employing a genre that allowed for a captivating narrative comprised of a succession of both entertaining and didactic lessons. As stressed above, Luke devoted considerable energy toward clarifying the Church's relationship to both Jews and Romans. Finally, for Christians of a later period who needed to know something about Paul, perhaps Acts served to offer a rehabilitation and domestication of this dangerous figure, who will be found soon enough at the root of various "heretical" impulses in the 2nd century.

See Luke, Gospel of; Paul.

Bibliography. P. F. Esler, *Community and Gospel in Luke/Acts.* SNTSMS 57 (Cambridge, 1987); E. Haenchen, *The Acts of the Apostles* (Philadelphia, 1971); J. Jervell, *The Theology of the Acts of the Apostles* (Cambridge, 1996); R. I. Pervo, *Profit with Delight: The Literary Genre of the Acts of the Apostles* (Philadelphia, 1987); B. W. Winter, ed., *The Book of Acts in Its First Century Setting.* 6 vols. (Grand Rapids, 1993–); B. Witherington, ed., *History, Literature, and Society in the Book of Acts* (Cambridge, 1996). Christopher R. Matthews

ADADAH (Heb. *ʿaḏʿāḏâ*)
A city in southern Judah (Josh. 15:22). The name should probably be read Ararah (Heb. *ʿarʿārâ*) and be identified with modern ʿArʿarah (148062), ca. 19 km. (12 mi.) SE of Beer-sheba, according to some the site of Aroer (1 Sam. 30:28).

ADAD-NIRARI (Akk. *Adad-nirari*)

1. Adad-nirari I (1307-1275 B.C.) was successful in expanding Assyria west across the Euphrates River. He conquered the Mitanni protectorate of Hanigalbat.

2. Adad-nirari II (911-891) consolidated the holdings of his predecessors and campaigned against the Arameans west of the Ḫabur River. He also fought on the Babylonian frontier, an action that resulted in a peaceful coexistence between the two states for the remainder of the 9th century.

3. Adad-nirari III (810-783), son of the legendary Semiramus, inherited a state weakened by civil war. Nevertheless, he had some moderate success in Babylonia and claims in his annals to have destroyed a coalition centered at Damascus, which he captured. Among those listed as his vassal kings are Joash of Israel (Akk. *Ia-a-su māt Sa-me-ri-na-a*), who had not been part of the Damascene coalition. Adad-nirari III may have been the "deliverer" of Israel mentioned in 2 Kgs. 13:5. Another enemy of the Syrian coalition, Zakkur of Hamath, claims to have repelled a siege from Ben-hadad of Damascus, probably benefiting from Adad-nirari III's presence in the region.

Bibliography. A. K. Grayson, *Assyrian Rulers of the Early First Millennium B.C. (1114-859 B.C.)* (Toronto, 1991); A. R. Millard and H. Tadmor, "Adad-Nirari III in Syria," *Iraq* 25 (1973): 57-64.

Mark W. Chavalas

ADAH (Heb. *ʿāḏâ*)

1. One of the two wives of Lamech the Cainite. She was the mother of Jabal and Jubal (Gen. 4:19-21, 23).

2. A wife of Esau. She was the daughter of Elon the Hittite and mother of Eliphaz (Gen. 36:2, 4).

ADAIAH (Heb. *ʿăḏāyâ, ʿăḏāyāhû*)

1. A man from Boskath, and the maternal grandfather of King Josiah (2 Kgs. 22:1).

2. A Levite of the family of Gershom (1 Chr. 6:41[MT 26]).

3. A Benjaminite, one of the sons of Shimei (1 Chr. 8:21).

4. A priest and the son of Jeroham, of the family of Malchijah (1 Chr. 9:12 = Neh. 11:12).

5-6. Descendants of Bani and of Binnui who had to send away their foreign wives (Ezra 10:29, 39).

7. A Judahite, the son of Joiarib (Neh. 11:5).

8. The father of Maaseiah; one of the "commanders of hundreds" upon whom Jehoiada the priest relied in his rebellion against Queen Athaliah (2 Chr. 23:1).

ADALIA (Heb. *ʾăḏalyāʾ*)
One of the 10 sons of Haman the Agagite (Esth. 9:8; cf. Pers. *ādārya*, "honorable").

ADAM (Heb. *ʾāḏām*) **(PERSON)**
Heb. *ʾāḏām* means "human" and can be used either collectively ("humankind") or individually ("a human"). When used in contrast to a word for woman or female, it can also indicate a specifically male human. In Gen. 1–5 the word is used to refer to the first human, Adam. This word is used in contexts that play upon all of the different senses of the word — collective, individual, gender nonspecific, and male.

The word Adam is used collectively in the creation of humans in Gen. 1:27, later alluded to in 5:1-2, where Adam ("human") is defined as "male and female." When Adam is created a second time in 2:7 (from a different source) there is the sense that this is an individual male human, since it is from him that the woman is later formed (2:22). Yet the language of sexuality and gender distinction is not used explicitly until the woman is created (2:23-24), indicating that sex and gender is not an emphasis of the identity of Adam until this time. Therefore Adam before the creation of woman is in a sense "not yet" specifically male, and can be seen as both an individual and a collective human. Hence not only Adam but all humans are born from the soil and God's vivifying breath, and God's remark that "it is not good for Adam to be alone" pertains to all humans ("it is not good for humans to be alone").

The interplay between the individual Adam and the collective "humankind" is essential to the nature of Adam in the garden of Eden. The first couple's motivations, fears, and punishments all echo those of humanity generally. In the rich but ambiguous meanings of the story, there is a sense that all "humans" recapitulate the drama of the first "humans" in moral, sexual, and spiritual terms. All humans partake of the dangerous fruit of knowledge at some point in their development, involving both gain and loss, and all humans are doomed to die.

The multiple and ambiguous meanings of the story reflect the complexity of the human condition.

A recurring motif in Gen. 1–8 is the bond between Adam and the earth (*'ăḏāmâ*). Adam is made from the soil of the earth, and it is from this *'ăḏāmâ* that Adam gets his name (2:7). In the curses pronounced by God the earth is cursed because of Adam (3:17), and Adam will return to the earth from which he was taken (3:19). The earth is an essential part of Adam, the "earthly" component of his identity, yet Adam is estranged from the earth because of disobedience. It is not entirely clear how this pertains to Adam as a representation of humankind generally, but a sense of our divided identity as both earthly and separated from nature seems to be implied. When God lifts the curse on the earth at the end of the Flood (8:21), it seems that God signals his reconciliation to the divided nature of humankind.

In postbiblical traditions the character of Adam is depicted in varying ways. The Life of Adam and Eve depicts the couple after their expulsion repenting for their sins, and as a reward for repentance Adam is taken up to the heavenly paradise. Adam's restoration to paradise is depicted as a foreshadowing of the restoration of all the righteous to paradise at the end of time. In Paul's writings the coming of Christ is the solution to Adam's sin, and through Christ the righteous will be restored to the heavenly paradise in a state of glory. In the Dead Sea Scrolls and rabbinic writings Adam is glorious and superhuman before his exile from Eden, but is diminished in stature when exiled. According to some Jewish mystical traditions, the original glory of Adam can be regained through mystical contemplation of God's eternal essences. In Augustine's reinterpretation of Pauline theology, Adam's sin is transmitted by sexual relations (specifically by semen) to each subsequent generation, with the sole exception of Christ, who was conceived without sin. RONALD S. HENDEL

ADAM (Heb. *'ăḏām*) **(PLACE)**

A city in Transjordan ca. 30 km. (19 mi.) N of the spot where the Israelites crossed the Jordan opposite Jericho (Josh. 3:16). The site is modern Tell ed-Dâmiyeh (201167), ca. 2 km. (1.2 mi.) S of the mouth of the Jabbok River.

ADAM, BOOKS OF

Various pseudepigraphal, rabbinic, and gnostic documents which expound upon the biblical narrative of Adam and Eve (Gen. 1–4). Of the many books attributed to Adam, the most important and probably the oldest are the Greek Apocalypse of Moses and the Latin Life of Adam and Eve. These documents are Jewish in thought and contain similar overlapping information, while retaining unique traditions. Their literary relationship has been difficult to determine. The documents were probably translated from Hebrew original(s) before 400 C.E. The documents are narrated in midrashic form and concentrate upon the events following Adam and Eve's expulsion from the earthly paradise, with special attention given to the nature and consequences of sin; the fallen angel Satan; God, who is to be feared and looked to for mercy; the resurrection of the dead which will restore what was lost at the fall. Significantly, sacrifice is not set forth as expiatory nor is there a concern for messianic expectation. Other Adam literature includes the Cave of Treasures, the Combat of Adam and Eve, the Testament of Adam, and the Apocalypse of Adam, a Jewish gnostic document found in the Nag Hammadi library. KENNETH J. ARCHER

ADAMAH (Heb. *'ăḏāmâ*)

A city in the territory of Naphtali (Josh. 19:36), possibly to be identified with Ḥajar ed-Damm, ca. 4 km. (2.5 mi.) NW of where the Jordan River empties into the Sea of Galilee.

ADAMI-NEKEB (Heb. *'ăḏāmî hanneqeḇ*)

A village in the Lower Galilee, apportioned to the tribe of Naphtali (Josh. 19:33). Meaning "Red Earth Pass," the village can be likely associated with modern Tel Adami/Khirbet et-Tell/ed-Dâmiyeh (193239), just W of the Sea of Galilee. Constructed on a low ridge 160 m. (524 ft.) above sea level, the settlement was built along a small streambed (Naḥal Adami). Villagers likely drew their living from pastoring herds along the nearby slopes and limited farming. DAVID C. MALTSBERGER

ADAR (Heb. *'ăḏār*)

The twelfth month of the Hebrew year (Feb.-March; Ezra 6:15), during which the feast of Purim was celebrated (Esth. 9:17, 19, 21; cf. Akk. *adaru*). In the Babylonian intercalary year, which usually fell every second or third year, a thirteenth month was added which was called "second Adar."

ADASA (Gk. *Adasa*)

The location of Judas Maccabeus' defeat of the Syrian general Nicanor in 161 B.C. (1 Macc. 7:40-45). Josephus locates the town 4 km. (2.5 mi.) SE from Beth-horon (*Ant.* 12.10.5) on the main highway to Jerusalem. Some identify the site with the modern Khirbet 'Adâseh, ca. halfway between Beth-horon and Jerusalem. DENNIS M. SWANSON

ADBEEL (Heb. *'ăḏbe'ēl*)

The third son of Ishmael (Gen. 25:13 = 1 Chr. 1:29). The inscriptions of the Assyrian king Tiglath-pileser III mention a North Arabian tribe, Idiba'ilu, which dwelt near the border of Egypt.

ADDAN (Heb. *'addān*) **(PERSON)**

A leader of Jews who returned from exile at Tel-melah and Tel-harsha (1 Esdr. 5:36). The NRSV reads the name from Gk. *charaathallan kai allar*, "Charaathalan and Allar" (LXX Codex Vaticanus).

ADDAN (PLACE) (also ADDON)

A city in Babylonia, as yet unidentified. The returning exiles who lived there could not prove their ancestry (Ezra 2:59 = Neh. 7:61, "Addon").

ADDAR (Heb. *'addār*) **(PERSON)**
A son of Bela the Benjaminite (1 Chr. 8:3), probably the same person as Ard (Gen. 46:21).

ADDAR (Heb. *'addār*) **(PLACE)**
A city along Judah's southern border (Josh. 15:3), W of the wilderness of Zin. In the parallel account in Num. 34:4 its name is combined with that of Hezron to read Hazar-addar.

ADDI (Gk. *Addí*)
1. The leader of a clan of Israelites who returned from exile and who had married foreign women (1 Esdr. 9:31).
2. According to Luke's genealogy, a preexilic ancestor of Jesus (Luke 3:28).

ADDON (Heb. *'addôn*)
Alternate form of the place name Addan (Neh. 7:61).

ADIDA (Gk. *Adida*)
A Judean town which Simon Maccabeus fortified (1 Macc. 12:38) and where he encamped against Trypho (13:13). It is probably the same as Harim (Ezra 2:32)/Hadid (Neh. 7:37).

ADIEL (Heb. *'ăḏî'ēl*)
1. A leader of the tribe of Simeon (1 Chr. 4:36).
2. A priest, the son of Jahzerah and father of Maasai (1 Chr. 9:12).
3. The father of Azmaveth, who was put in charge of David's treasuries (1 Chr. 27:25).

ADIN (Heb. *'āḏîn*)
The father and ancestor of a number of Jews returning from exile (454 at Ezra 2:15; 655 at Neh. 7:20). At Neh. 10:16(MT 17) he is one of the family heads who sealed the renewed covenant.

ADINA (Heb. *'ăḏînā'*)
One of David's mighty men, the son of Shiza of the tribe of Reuben (1 Chr. 11:42).

ADINO (Heb. *'ăḏînô*)
Older versions (e.g., KJV, NASB) have rendered 2 Sam. 23:8 as "Joshebasshebeth . . . he was called Adino the Eznite *('ăḏînô hā'eṣî)*," but most modern scholars and translations emend the text in light of 1 Chr. 11:11 to read "Joshebasshebeth . . . wielded his spear *(ye'ddnô hā'eṣnô)*." This reading is also found in some LXX manuscripts.
CHRISTIAN M. M. BRADY

ADITHAIM (Heb. *'ăḏîṯayim*)
A city in the inheritance of the tribe of Judah (Josh. 15:36), one of 14 towns mentioned together as existing in the lowland foothills of Judah. The exact location of this city is unknown. AARON M. GALE

ADLAI (Heb. *'aḏlay*)
The father of Shaphat, who tended David's herds in the valleys (1 Chr. 27:29).

ADMAH (Heb. *'aḏmâ*)
A city of the plain, situated in the valley of Siddim at the southern end of the Dead Sea, mentioned in the description of the boundaries of the Canaanites (Gen. 10:19). Its king Shinab, at first allied with Chedorlaomer (Gen. 14:2), joined the kings of Sodom, Gomorrah, and Zeboiim in a revolt against their sovereign (v. 8). Although not named in the story of the volcanic destruction of Sodom and Gomorrah (Gen. 19:24-29), Admah and Zeboiim together symbolize total devastation which can result from evil and unrepentance (Deut. 29:23[MT 22]; Hos. 11:8). RICHARD A. SPENCER

ADMATHA (Heb. *'aḏmāṯā'*)
One of the seven princes in the kingdom of the Medes and Persians under King Ahasuerus (Esth. 1:14). These legal advisors (mentioned also at Ezra 7:14) shared the actual power of government (cf. Esth. 1:13-21).

ADMIN (Gk. *Admín*)
An ancestor of Jesus who lived prior to the time of King David (Luke 3:33).

ADNA (Heb. *'aḏnā'*)
1. A son of Pahath-moab; one of those ordered to send away his foreign wife (Ezra 10:30).
2. A priest of the family of Harim who returned with Zerubbabel from exile (Neh. 12:15).

ADNAH (Heb. *'aḏnāḥ, 'aḏnâ*)
1. A "chief of thousands" from the tribe of Manasseh who deserted Saul and came to aid David at Ziklag (1 Chr. 12:20[MT 21]).
2. A high officer, perhaps commander, under King Jehoshaphat (2 Chr. 17:14). He was of the tribe of Judah.

ADONAI (Heb. *'ăḏōnāy*)
A divine name, generally translated "the Lord" or "my Lord." In the late postexilic period it became a substitute for the unspeakable name of God. The Masoretes wrote the vowels of this name with the consonants of the name Yahweh (*YHWH*), indicating to the reader that it was to be pronounced "Adonay"; later Christian translators read the combination as "Jehovah."

ADONI-BEZEK (Heb. *'ăḏōnî-ḇezeq*)
The king of Bezek, a town in southern Palestine. He was defeated by the forces of Judah, who severely mutilated him because of the cruel treatment he himself had inflicted on 70 other kings (Judg. 1:4-7). His own troops returned him to Jerusalem, where he died. Some scholars identify him with Adoni-zedek, king of Jerusalem at the time of the Conquest (cf. Josh. 10:1-3).

ADONIJAH (Heb. *'ăḏōnîyâ, 'ăḏōnîyāhû*)
1. David's fourth son, born in Hebron to his wife Haggith (2 Sam. 3:4 = 1 Chr. 3:2).
David's choice of this name, one of the earliest Israelite couplings of *'āḏôn*, "lord," with a theo-

phoric element, may represent his ambition to adopt — or adapt himself to — the Canaanite royal traditions of Judea and Jerusalem, seeing himself as the legitimate heir to the royal Canaanite line in Jerusalem.

In keeping with the Canaanite dynastic tradition, Adonijah, the king's eldest living son, on seeing his father's enfeebled state, formed a party within the royal court to advance his claim on the throne. This consisted of Joab, commander of the army (his brother Abishai was probably dead by this time), and Abiathar, son of Ahimelech, the priest of Nob who had survived the massacre by Saul to join David. Adonijah's aspirations were cut short by the stronger party of Solomon, which comprised Bathsheba, Zadok, Nathan the prophet, Benaiah ben Jehoiada, by this time commander of the bodyguard and the Cherethites and Pelethites, and perhaps even the "champions" (cf. 1 Kgs. 1:5-53). These, with the cooperation of the senile and impotent David, anointed Solomon in Adonijah's stead.

Though Solomon initially spared his elder brother's life, Adonijah's obeisance appears to have been largely political and for the moment. His true intentions were revealed by his request to Solomon to have Abishag the Shunammite, the now departed David's beautiful — and still virgin — wife, as his own. Solomon sagaciously recognized in this request his brother's attempt to assume his late father's royal virility by taking the young wife his late father had been unable to impregnate. Consequently, Solomon ordered Benaiah to kill Adonijah, along with Joab. Thus Adonijah became the last of David's sons to die in the long and bloody struggle over their father's throne. D. G. Schley

2. A Levite among those who taught the Law throughout the cities of postexilic Judah (2 Chr. 17:8).

3. An "associate" of the Levites who signed the covenant with Nehemiah (Neh. 10:16[MT 17]).

ADONIKAM (Heb. *'ăḏōnîqām*)
The head of a family of returning exiles (Ezra 2:13 = Neh. 7:18). He may be the same as the Adonijah mentioned at Neh. 10:16(MT 17).

ADONIRAM (Heb. *'ăḏōnîrām*) (also ADORAM, HADORAM)
The son of Abda; taskmaster over the forced labor under David, Solomon, and Rehoboam (1 Kgs. 4:6; 5:14). He is also called Adoram (2 Sam. 20:24; 1 Kgs. 12:18) and Hadoram (2 Chr. 10:18). Rehoboam sent him to the dissatisfied tribes of Israel, probably to negotiate with them, but to no avail; the people stoned him to death.

ADONI-ZEDEK (Heb. *'ăḏōnî-ṣeḏeq*)
An Amorite king of Jerusalem. Adoni-zedek organized a coalition of four other Amorite kings to attack Gibeon because its inhabitants made peace with Joshua (Josh. 10:1-26). Following the coalition's defeat by Joshua, the five kings were discovered hiding in a cave. Joshua had them put to death and hung their bodies on trees until sunset, and then buried them in the same cave. The name means either "my Lord is righteous" or "my Lord is Zedek." The theory that Adoni-zedek is identical with Adoni-bezek of Judg. 1 is unlikely.

Kenneth Atkinson

ADOPTION
The legal transfer of a person from a family or slavery into another family, thereby improving the situation of the adopter and adoptee. The NT uses adoption imagery to depict the relationship between believers and God. Paul assumed that the image was first applied to God's relationship with Israel (Rom. 9:4).

Adoption Formulas

Adoption in the ancient Near East was transacted before witnesses by the adopter declaring, "You are my son/daughter [henceforth 'child']," "He/she/PN is my child," or "I called him/her/PN my child." The child may respond with "You are my father/mother." The same formulas were used to "legitimize" children fathered through secondary wives such as concubines or slaves. A negative counterpart to these formulas disowned and disinherited a child or, from the child's side, repudiated the parents. The act of adoption was described as "make/take/designate/establish as a son." The parents were obligated to raise the children by providing a trade and inheritance; children were required to obey the parent. Disobedient children were punished, disinherited, and sometimes sold back into slavery. Occasionally adopters would reverse this decision and readopt the disowned child.

Adoption and Adoption Imagery

Most OT "adoptions" are really legitimizations (e.g., Gen. 30:3-5) or intergenerational transferences of inheritance (e.g., 48:5-6). The examples closest to adoption include: Pharaoh's daughter who, motivated solely by compassion, "took" Moses "as her son" (Exod. 2:10); Mordecai who "took" (NRSV "adopted") his orphaned cousin Esther "as his own daughter" (Esth. 2:7; cf. v. 15).

Yahweh's relationship with his people is sometimes couched in adoption imagery. Abraham's election reflects adoption customs: "Yahweh, the God of heaven, . . . took me from my father's house and from the land of my birth, and . . . spoke to me and swore to me, 'To your offspring I will give this land'" (Gen. 24:7). "Israel is my son, my firstborn" (Exod. 4:22) is an adoption formula, including the declaration of inheritance status. Israel's redemption from Egypt is framed in adoption formulas in Exod. 6:6b-7: "I will free you from the burdens of the Egyptians and deliver you from slavery to them . . . I will take (REB 'adopt') you as my people, and I will be your God." Hos.11:1-7 reads like an adoption repudiation contract, "When Israel was a child I loved him, since Egypt I called him 'my son'" (v. 1). Yahweh adopted Israel out of Egyptian slavery, yet because Israel spurned Yahweh's fatherly care (Hos 11:2-4) Yahweh will punish his disobedient son and send him back into slavery (i.e., Egypt and Assyria, vv. 5-7; cf. 1:9b, "You are not my people and I am not yours," NRSV mg). But Yahweh's compassion moves him to restore the relationship and take back his disowned son (Hos. 11:8-9; cf. 1:10[MT 2:1]; 2:23[25]). In Jer. 3:19 Yahweh's plan to adopt Israel and grant him an inheritance was frustrated because of the son's disobedience.

The Davidic king was declared Yahweh's son by adoption (2 Sam. 7:14) in a public installation ceremony during which Yahweh's decree is announced, "You are my son; today I have begotten you" (Ps. 2:7). The king responds "you are my Father, my God, and the Rock of my salvation!" (Ps. 89:26[27]). As God's son he bears responsibility for the wellbeing of God's people and their land (Ps. 72:2-7). God also appoints him as firstborn of kings (Ps. 89:27[28]), in whom the commission given to the ancestors is fulfilled, that "all nations be blessed in him" (Ps. 72:17; cf. Gen. 12:2-3). When this divine decree was applied to Jesus (Mark 1:11; 9:7) his role as Davidic Messiah was emphasized, not his adoption.

Paul declares that believers are delivered from slavery and become children ("sons") of God by being incorporated into Christ, God's son, through the work of the Holy Spirit (Gal. 3:26; Rom. 8:14-16). The children of God are delivered from slavery to sin and death (Rom. 6), the law's condemnation and the flesh (7:4–8:14), and elemental spirits (Gal. 4:8-9). The Spirit enables them to acknowledge their adoption through the cry, "Abba! Father!" (Rom. 8:14-15; Gal. 4:5-6). But the adoption is not complete until the full revelation of God's new creation. In the present suffering they await their final glorious bodily adoption as joint heirs with Christ, "the firstborn within a large family," into whose image they are being transformed (Rom. 8:18-29; Gal. 6:15; cf. 2 Cor. 5:17). Rev. 21:7 uses the adoption formula to make a related point: "Those who conquer will inherit these things, and I will be their God and they will be my children."

The incorporation of the Gentiles into the heritage of Israel, now manifested in the redemption of Christ, is God's work of adoption (Eph. 1:5ff.; cf. 2:11-22). Likewise, Hosea's adoption formulas are used to connote God's inclusion of the Gentiles into his final work of mercy revealed in Christ (Rom. 9:25; 1 Pet. 2:10).

Bibliography. L. J. Braaten, *Parent-Child Imagery in Hosea* (diss., Boston University, 1987); S. M. Paul, "Adoption Formulae: A Study of Cuneiform and Biblical Legal Clauses," *Maarav* 2 (1979-80): 173-85; J. H. Tigay, "Adoption: Alleged Cases of Adoption in the Bible," *EncJud* 2:298-301.

LAURIE J. BRAATEN

ADORAIM (Heb. *'ăḏôrayim*) (also ADORA)
A city in Judah which was fortified by Rehoboam (2 Chr. 11:19), later called Adora (Gk. *Adṓra*; 1 Macc. 13:20). It has been identified with modern Dûrā (152101), 8 km. (5 mi.) WSW of Hebron.

ADORAM (Heb. *'ăḏôrām*) (also HADORAM)
The son of Abda; taskmaster over the forced labor under David, Solomon, and Rehoboam (2 Sam. 20:24; 1 Kgs. 12:18). Rehoboam sent him to reconcile with the dissatisfied tribes of Israel, but they stoned him to death. At 2 Chr. 10:18 he is called Hadoram.

ADRAMMELECH (Heb. *'aḏrammelek*)
(DEITY)
A god worshipped by the Sepharvaim (2 Kgs. 17:31), a people brought by Sargon II into Samaria after its destruction in 722 B.C. Little is known about this god, who is not mentioned in any Babylonian or Assyrian writings. According to 2 Kgs. 17:31 the Sepharvaim "burned their sons to" Adrammelech, probably a magical or dedicatory rite, rather than a sacrifice, to be compared with the phrase "to pass through the fire" (v. 17; 21:6) and contrasted with burnt offerings to Baal (Jer. 19:5). The name is West Semitic and may mean "the glorious one is king."   MICHAEL D. HILDENBRAND

ADRAMMELECH (Heb. *'aḏrammelek*)
(PERSON)
One of the two sons of Sennacherib of Assyria who, with his brother, murdered his father and escaped to the land of Ararat (2 Kgs. 19:36-37 = Isa. 37:37-38). Variant forms of the name are found in the works of Abydenus and Polyhistorus.

ADRAMYTTIUM (Gk. *Adramýtteion*)
A seaport in Mysia, on the west coast of Asia Minor. On his fourth journey the Apostle Paul traveled from Caesarea to Myra in Lycia on a ship from Adramyttium (Acts 27:1-6) before transferring to a ship bound for Rome. After its plunder by Turkish pirates ca. 1100 C.E., the port was abandoned; a new settlement (modern Edremit) lies further inland.

ADRIA (Gk. *Adrías*)
Part of the Mediterranean Sea S of Italy and Greece and between Crete and Malta, now called the Ionian Sea. Here the ship carrying Paul and other prisoners was drifting before landing on Malta (Acts 27:27).

ADRIEL (Heb. *'aḏrî'ēl*)
The son of Barzillai the Meholathite to whom Saul gave his daughter Merab as wife, even though he had already promised her to David (1 Sam. 18:19; according to MT 2 Sam. 21:8 the younger daughter, Michal). Later David gave Adriel's five sons into the hands of the Gibeonites as a payment for bloodguilt of Saul (2 Sam. 21:8).

ADULLAM (Heb. *'ăḏullām*)
A town in the Shephelah of Judah (Josh. 15:35). Although unexcavated, it is commonly identified with Tell esh-Sheikj Madhkûr/Ḥorvat 'Adullam (150117), 8 km (5 mi.) S of Beth-shemesh. Located in the southern portion of the valley of Elah, Adullam, along with the site of Socoh, guarded one of the routes from the coastal plain to the Judean

highlands. It is one of the westernmost fortified towns along the boundary of Judah.

In the story of Judah and Tamar, Judah's friend Hirah is identified as an Adullamite (Gen. 38:1, 12, 20). The king of Adullam is listed among those whom Joshua and the Israelites defeated (Josh. 12:15). David took refuge from Saul in the cave of Adullam after fleeing from Gath (1 Sam. 22:1-2). David's "mighty men" assembled here; three of them ran from the cave and entered Philistine territory to get water from the well of Bethlehem for their leader (2 Sam. 23:13-17). 1 Chr. 11:15 records that the three men met David at "the rock" (Heb. *haṣṣūr*) at the cave of Adullam, a description consistent with the stronghold character of the cave; in 2 Samuel the men went down to the cave at the beginning of "harvest" (*qāṣîr*), a substitution based on the text's confusing syntax.

Adullam is included among the list of cities that Rehoboam fortified (2 Chr. 11:7) and is variously ascribed to the time of Hezekiah and Josiah. The prophet Micah (Mic. 1:15), a contemporary of Hezekiah, included it in his lamentation over the cities of Judah. Adullam was one of the cities reinhabited by the exiles returning from Babylon (Neh. 11:30). During the Hellenistic period, Judas Maccabeus and his men rested there after a battle with the governor of Idumea (2 Macc. 12:38).

Remains of a Late Roman/Byzantine public building have been identified at the site.

Bibliography. Y. Aharoni, *The Land of the Bible*, 2nd ed. (Philadelphia, 1979); V. Fritz, "The 'List of Rehoboam's Fortresses' in 2 Chr. 11:5-12: A Document from the Time of Josiah," *ErIsr* 15 (1981): 46*-53*; Z. Ilan, "Ancient Synagogues Survey: Judean Shephelah," *Excavations and Surveys in Israel* 7-8 (1988/89): 5-6; N. Na'aman, "Hezekiah's Fortified Cities and the *LMLK* Stamps," *BASOR* 261 (1986): 5-21; "The Kingdom of Judah under Josiah," *Tel Aviv* 18 (1991): 3-71; A. F. Rainey, "The Biblical Shephelah of Judah," *BASOR* 251 (1983): 1-22.

JENNIFER L. GROVES

ADULTERESS

According to covenant law, a married or formally pledged (Heb. *'rś*) woman who was adjudged to have willingly had intercourse with any male other than her (future) husband (Deut. 22:13-27). Female slaves, however, because they were legally powerless to decline sexual relations with their owners, were not held responsible if they had intercourse with their owners while pledged or perhaps married to someone else (Lev. 19:20-22).

Lev. 20:10; Deut. 22:22 clearly prescribe death as the punishment for both an adulterer and an adulteress (*nō'āpeṯ*). The seeming clarity of this pronouncement is called into question by texts that envision alternative punishments (e.g., Lev. 18:20, 24-29; Num. 5:11-31; 2 Sam. 11–12; Prov. 6:24-35). Some scholars maintain that the texts differ because they date from different historical periods and thus witness to changes over time. Others draw a distinction between the punishment exacted of those caught in the act of committing adultery as opposed to those adjudged guilty either through legal proceedings or by ritual ordeal. It has also been suggested that royalty was exempt from the law. Finally, on the basis of comparative ancient Near Eastern evidence, it has been argued that texts such as Lev. 20:10; Deut. 22:22 specify not the requisite punishment but rather the maximum, and presume as common knowledge in the culture of the time that compensation was an alternative to exacting revenge.

In several prophetical books (e.g., Jer. 2–3; Ezek. 16; 23; Hos. 1–4) and Lamentations, adultery is employed as a metaphor for breach of covenant. In Ezek. 16, e.g., Jerusalem is personified as Yahweh's wife whose "adulterous" behavior consists of giving worship to deities other than Yahweh and of inappropriate political alliances with foreign nations. The language of the former offense, which describes illicit worship in metaphorical terms as an act of sexual infidelity, has been understood as evidence for so-called "sacred" or "ritual" prostitution, allegedly a component of "fertility rites" associated with the worship of foreign deities. This interpretation has been recently and convincingly challenged as a mistaking of figurative and polemical language for social reality. Indeed, generally speaking, texts that portray metaphorical as opposed to literal adulteresses must be analyzed very carefully before using them as potential evidence for reconstructing social practices pertaining to literal adultery and adulteresses. Extreme caution is necessary because of the danger of mistakenly attributing to the vehicle, or figurative language, of the metaphor (adultery) features properly associated with the tenor, or principal subject, of the metaphor (breach of covenant).

Bibliography. P. Bird, "'To Play the Harlot': An Inquiry into an Old Testament Metaphor," in *Gender and Difference in Ancient Israel*, ed. P. L. Day (Minneapolis, 1989), 75-94; M. Fishbane, "Accusations of Adultery: A Study of Law and Scribal Practice in Numbers 5:11-31," *HUCA* 45 (1974): 25-45; J. Galambush, *Jerusalem in the Book of Ezekiel: The City as Yahweh's Wife*. SBLDS 130 (Atlanta, 1922); J. Hackett, "Can a Sexist Model Liberate Us? Ancient Near Eastern 'Fertility' Goddesses," *JFSR* 5 (1989): 65-76; R. Westbrook, "Adultery in Ancient Near Eastern Law," *RB* 97 (1990): 542-80.

PEGGY L. DAY

ADULTERY

In the ancient Near East and the OT (Lev. 18:20; 20:10; Deut. 22:22) adultery meant consensual sexual intercourse by a married woman with a man other than her husband. However, intercourse between a married man and another woman was not considered adultery unless she was married. The betrothed woman is also bound to fidelity, but leniency is shown to a married or betrothed man (Exod. 22:16-17[MT 15-16]; Deut. 22:28-29; Prov. 5:15-20; Mal. 2:14-15).

Some scholars distinguish between the ancient Near Eastern laws, where adultery was a private wrong against the husband, who could prosecute an offender, and the biblical laws, where adultery was an offense against God, with mandatory prosecution and a sentence of death, or, in some cases, atonement through a sin offering (Lev. 19:20-21). Others argue that biblical and ancient Near Eastern laws agree that adultery was an offense against the husband, with prosecution at his discretion (Prov. 6:32-35).

Mistaken paternity and its effect on family inheritance, as well as protection of the husband's economic interest, were the primary reasons why adultery was a sin and included in the Decalogue (Exod. 20:14; Deut. 5:18). Adultery was also used as a metaphor for Israel's idolatrous and immoral behavior (e.g., Jer. 3:6-13; 23:9-15; Ezek. 16:30-43; Isa. 57:3-13).

Bibliography. H. McKeating, "Sanctions against Adultery in Ancient Israelite Society," *JSOT* 11 (1979): 57-72; R. Westbrook, "Adultery in Ancient Near Eastern Law," *RB* 97 (1990): 542-80.

HENDRIK L. BOSMAN

ADUMMIM (Heb. *ʾăḏummîm*)
A mountain pass (NRSV "ascent") on the northern boundary of Judah (Josh. 15:7) and southern boundary of Benjamin (18:17). The modern name, Talʿat ed-Damm ("the ascent of blood"), refers to the red limestone rock at the site (Heb. "red rocks"). The pass is near Khan el-Aḥmar, which according to tradition was the site of the Inn of the Good Samaritan on the road from Jerusalem to Jericho (cf. Luke 10:34-35).

ADVOCATE
See PARACLETE.

AENEAS (Gk. *Ainéas*)
A man from Lydda who had been bedridden for eight years before Peter healed him of his paralysis (Acts 9:33-35).

AENON (Gk. *Ainṓn*)
A place near Salim where John the Baptist was baptizing during the early part of Jesus' ministry (John 3:23). Although this place of abundant water (from Heb. *ʿênayim,* "double spring") has not yet been identified, Eusebius (*Onom.* 40.1-4) locates it ca. 12 km. (7 mi.) S of Beth-shan, perhaps near modern Umm el-ʿAmdân.

AFRICA
Although the Bible does not mention Africa by name, various North African places and peoples figure prominently in the events and imagery of both the OT and NT.

Most frequently mentioned is Egypt. From the time of the patriarchs to the time of the apostles, Egypt possessed an abundant grain resource which was sought by nations throughout the eastern Mediterranean (e.g., Gen. 41:50–42:25). The Exodus from Egypt, arguably the most important event in Jewish history (Exod. 3:1–20:21), became a significant theological resource (e.g., Amos 5:25; Isa. 40:3). Egypt was also a place of refuge for dissident or dispersed Jews (e.g., 2 Macc. 1:1-9; Matt. 2:13-15, 19-20). Egypt and Israel also shared in the wisdom tradition of the ancient Near East (cf. Prov. 22:17–24:34 and the Egyptian Instruction of Amenemope). Finally, politics linked Egypt and Israel (e.g., 1 Kgs. 11:1; cf. Nah. 3:8-9).

Cush (Heb. lit., "black") is mentioned often in the OT. Due to Greek and Roman influences, some translate "Ethiopia." Other ancient writings refer to Cush as "Nubia." In the Bible Cush referred to lands south of Egypt. Biblical writers often linked Egypt and Cush, suggesting that they associated them in some way (e.g., Isa. 45:14; Ezek. 30:4-9; Ps. 68:31 [MT 32]). As with Egypt, Cush was also a place of refuge (Zeph. 3:10).

The NT mentions Egyptians, Cyrenians, Libyans, and Cushites/Ethiopians (e.g., Mark 15:21; Acts 2:10; 11:20-21;18:24). Acts 8:26-39 records the baptism of a high-ranking Ethiopian official by the Apostle Philip.

Recently, African-American biblical scholarship has challenged traditional Eurocentric exegesis of African peoples in the Bible as not reflecting more neutral biblical perspectives and in effect "de-Africanizing" the Bible. Rather, Africans were highly regarded and often used as positive examples by biblical writers.

Bibliography. D. Adamo, *Africa and Africans in the Old Testament* (San Francisco, 1997); R. A. Bennett, Jr., "Africa and the Biblical Period," *HTR* 64 (1971): 483-500; C. H. Felder, *Troubling Biblical Waters: Race, Class, and Family* (Maryknoll, 1989), 5-48; ed., *Stony the Road We Trod* (Minneapolis, 1991), 127-84.

THOMAS B. SLATER

AFTERLIFE, AFTERDEATH
Western, or more specifically, Judeo-Christian, preoccupation with humanity's physical fate or destiny beyond death has provided the impetus underlying much of the modern study of death and afterlife in ancient Israel. Unfortunately, Judeo-Christian notions regarding the material aspects of life beyond the grave have dominated Western treatments of other cultures to the neglect of other aspects often present in the primary data themselves. In those rare cases where the evidence from a given culture has resisted a Judeo-Christian reinterpretation, that cultural tradition has been characteristically deemed "primitive," whether in terms of its "inferior intellectual merit" or its "deficient religious virtue." This tendency also perpetuates early modern Eurocentric intellectual assumptions concerning the evolution of cultures and religions wherein ancient and foreign cultures were characterized as primitive, and so were thought to uphold primitive religious beliefs and observe archaic religious practices. Among the primitive elements detected in the traditions of the OT and in the archaeological record were those practices and beliefs associated with death cults and ancestor cults which, as typically defined by early moderns, presupposed a morbid fear of and superstition regarding ghosts. More generally, early moderns typically viewed this fear and its attendant cult as providing the original

impetus underlying the development of religious modes of thought by early humanoids.

The consensus of earlier studies underscores the fact that the world of ancient Israel was very different from that of later Judaism and Christianity, and this pertains also to their respective beliefs and rituals associated with death and the afterlife. Disparity in scholarly opinion now arises over more minor questions such as whether transformations in afterlife beliefs took place early or late in the history of Israelite/Jewish religious history; whether the catalysts for such transformations were internal or foreign influences; and if foreign, from the local region or further afield: Egyptian, Mesopotamian, or Persian.

For the longest time the consensus was that preexilic Israel had no afterlife beliefs worthy of note, at least not in the sense that later Jews and Christians eventually came to conceptualize the matter: a blessed, material, physical existence for the pious (and conversely a perpetual horrid experience for the wicked). The following will consider what constituted a fulfilling life and an "acceptable" death in ancient Mediterranean West Asia and ancient Israel in particular.

Abode of the Dead

In the OT various Hebrew terms like *šĕ'ôl* ("Sheol"), *māweṯ* ("death"), *'ereṣ* ("earth"), *šaḥaṯ* ("pit"), *bôr* ("pit"), and *'ăḇaddôn* ("place of destruction") could refer to the netherworld or abode of the dead. Some of these terms are further qualified by *taḥtît* or its various forms signifying "the lowest parts." Sheol most often designates the netherly regions, although it has few, if any, cognates in the ancient Near East, making its etymological origins all the more obscure. Of course, even if we were able to uncover its full etymological history, it would not necessarily clarify the significance or function of Sheol.

Like its Near Eastern counterparts, the netherworld in ancient Israelite tradition is typically portrayed as a place to which one must descend. It is dark, dusty, and a place of silence. It can be connected with the waters of chaos over which one typically traveled to enter the netherworld. Sheol is described as possessing bars, gates, ropes, and snares, all of which suggest the unlikelihood of completely escaping from the netherworld — at least not in the full capacity one possessed before death — and approximates what we know to be the case in Mesopotamian tradition wherein the netherworld is depicted as the "land of no return" (to the land of the living in one's former full capacity). The netherworld also overlapped with the various OT terms for "grave," suggesting that the grave was regarded as incorporated into the larger realm of Sheol. One could enter Sheol from one's grave, indicating that it could function as an entryway to the netherworld. In poetic contexts, the netherworld is personified as having an insatiable appetite by which it swallows up everything. It can grasp one with such relentless force that it never releases its victim. These elements convey something of the permanence and pervasiveness of death in early Israelite society.

Inhabitants of the Netherworld

Those who inhabit the netherworld in ancient Israel are called *mēṯîm* ("dead ones") and *rĕp̄ā'îm* ("weak ones"; cf. esp. Ps. 88:11[MT 12]; Isa. 26:14). The term "rephaim" (or *rp'm*) is used in two 6th-century Phoenician texts to denote simply the dead (KAI 13.7-8; 14.8-9). The ghosts of the dead are repeatedly designated as "the knowing ones" *(yiddĕ'ōnîm)* and "the ones who return" *('ōḇôṯ)* in rather late biblical texts when the practice of necromancy is also taken up for the first time as an adaptation from Mesopotamia. In Isa. 19:3 they are called the *'iṭṭîm* ("ghosts"), probably the Hebrew equivalent of Akk. *eṭemmu*. It is often claimed that the dead could be referred to as "gods" (*'ĕlōhîm*) based on a questionable translation of the Deuteronomistic text 1 Sam. 28:13-14 and the dubious assumption that ghosts and gods were equated in Mesopotamian and Israelite tradition. Although some Akkadian texts appear to depict two classes of otherworldly beings, the family or personal gods *('ilu)* and the ghosts of deceased relatives *(eṭemmu)*, their exact connection remains elusive.

Heb. *mēṯîm* ("dead") and *'ĕlōhîm* ("gods") likewise occur in close proximity in Isa. 8:19, which in turn has led to their erroneous equation. The two terms more likely refer to two distinct groups of otherworldly beings; the chthonic gods summoned to assist in the retrieval of a conjured ghost and the ghost itself attested in Mesopotamian necromantic traditions. With these considerations in mind, an alternative translation of 1 Sam. 28:13-14, a 6th-century composition concerned with necromancy, is possible. In the first half of King Saul's inquiry the woman refers to the appearance of the gods from the netherworld ("chthonic gods [*'ĕlōhîm*] coming up from the earth") that were typically invoked in Mesopotamian necromantic rituals for their ability to assist in the retrieval of particular ghosts. In the second part she refers to the ghost of Samuel that the gods have brought up for the woman of Endor to consult. The "gods" here are not to be equated with Samuel's ghost as a reference to its divine status (= the deified dead). Rather, the text preserves an echo of the two groups of otherworldly beings that typically participated in necromantic rituals.

The term *rĕp̄ā'îm* ("Rephaim") appears in two contexts in the OT, in the narrative texts of the Pentateuch and Deuteronomistic history as giants and as representatives of the autochthonous populations of Palestine/Israel, and in the prophetic and poetic texts as the weakened dead. The similarity in form has led to speculation of some organic connection between the two uses. Like their Ugaritic counterparts the *rp'im qdmym* ("the ancient Rephaim"), the biblical Rephaim of the netherworld are powerless (in biblical tradition they have been democratized to include the commoner as well as the elite). Nowhere are they identified as superhuman, warrior heroes of hoary antiquity, whether living or dead as often assumed. The Rephaim of the narratives, however, do take on mythic and heroic dimensions as the most ancient inhabitants of Palestine, and in this respect find their analogues in the *rp'um* traditions at Ugarit. In *KTU* 1.161 the Ugaritic *rp'um* (unqualified by *qdmym*) represent a living warrior and nobility elite who adopted that designation as a means of identifying themselves with the mythic or heroic traditions regarding the Rp'um and Ditanu. Any supposed connection between the two biblical Rephaim traditions, the heroic traditions of the narratives and the postmortem traditions of the poetic and prophetic texts, remains enigmatic. Nowhere are the Rephaim attributed supernatural postmortem powers, although such powers are not disparaged. The biblical polemic against the Rephaim traditions is restricted to their mythic, heroic stature as living inhabitants of the land of Canaan or *yĕlîḏê hārāpâ* ("descendants of the Weak One").

Transformations in Late Israelite Traditions

Following the Babylonian Exile of 586/7 B.C.E., significant transformations took place vis-à-vis Israelite/Jewish beliefs about death and the afterlife. These have been explained as the result of a combination of factors, foreign religious influence — Persian, Greek or otherwise — social and individual crises, and the inadequacy of conventional constructs of theodicy.

The resurrection of the body becomes a pervading expression of a blessed afterlife in Second Temple Judaism. Dan. 12:2, composed following the persecution of the Jews in 165, is generally recognized as indicative of this concept. Other passages have been cited as examples of the existence of this belief in earlier Israelite tradition (e.g., Ezek. 37; Isa. 26:19; 53), but opinion is divided as to whether these passages presume a belief in bodily resurrection or whether they employ "dying-and-rising-god" or fecundity imagery to refer metaphorically to the historical restoration of the nation. Most likely these passages informed developments that eventuated in the belief given clear expression later in Dan. 12. Furthermore, they might very well have derived their impetus from the dying-and-rising-god imagery in a much earlier text, Hos. 13–14, which in turn might indicate dependence upon older Canaanite imagery. These factors coupled with the possible influence of Persian religion, particularly the Zoroastrian belief in bodily resurrection during the postexilic period, might have culminated in the later Jewish belief in bodily resurrection as expressed in Dan. 12 and other Jewish apocalyptic sources.

Notions about ascension and immortality also find their way into Jewish traditions and texts in this period, from roughly the 6th century onward. Passages like Gen. 5:24 — a late Priestly text — and 2 Kgs. 2:1-12 — a Deuteronomistic production — preserve traditions concerning the bodily ascension to heaven without passing through death, as in the cases of such heroic figures as Enoch and Elijah. Enoch shows a number of amazing parallels with figures known from Mesopotamian sources — Enmeduranki, an antediluvian king, and Utnapishtim, a flood hero — who were either directly admitted into the presence of the gods or translated bodily into heaven. While notions of immortality were possibly afloat in various periods of Israelite religious history, only with the passage of time were certain forms selected for fuller elaboration and development.

Second Temple Jewish wisdom literature preserves elements of the immortality of the soul as a reward for the righteous. Works like 4 Maccabees, Jubilees, and 1 Enoch all point in this direction. The Wisdom of Solomon (ca. 100 B.C.E.) repeatedly addresses the topic of immortality (Wis. 1:15; 3:4; 4:1; 8:17; 15:3) while never explicitly taking up the topic of resurrection; some see a strong influence from Greek Platonic philosophy here. The immortality of the soul has also been identified in two postexilic wisdom Psalms, Pss. 49 and 73. Ps. 49:16 ("God will redeem my life from the clutches of Sheol") poses a direct contrast to vv. 8-10, where it is claimed that no one can redeem himself so as to live forever and never see the grave; God should be viewed here as attributed that power which no one can exercise for himself: the power to bestow immortal life.

Summary

The evidence indicates that prior to the Exile the Israelites, like many of their ancient Near Eastern neighbors, placed primary, if not sole, emphasis on the perpetuation of the memory of the family dead and on making the best of life on this side of the grave. Both commoner and elite went to some length to insure that the family name epitomized by the multigenerational graves containing the bones of family dead and located on family land would never be neglected, let alone forgotten. By regularly performing various communal and public rituals the names and memories of deceased kin were preserved from oblivion. The associated words and deeds comprised what has been described by anthropologists as the commemoration of the dead. Worship, veneration, or morbid fear of the dead had no necessary part in this complex of rites as so long assumed. The idea that the ancient Israelites observed a longstanding death or ancestor cult as conventionally understood (to include the worship or veneration of the dead) simply has no basis. It was founded upon outmoded anthropological assumptions, cultural biases, and questionable or forced interpretation of texts. What the ancient Israelite did fear was the dreaded "death after death" — the possibility that the memory of his name and the recollection of his deeds accomplished while living might be forever forgotten by his descendants, his community, or, in the case of the royalty, even his nation.

To be sure, there apparently existed the belief that in the case of neglect, one might expect the angry reprisal of the deceased's ghost, but this hardly necessitated or presumed that the living should worship or venerate the dead. Rather, it demanded persistence in caring and feeding of the dead as part of their commemoration and, should negligence have taken place, the initiation of rites to ward off or appease the ghost — i.e., exorcistic rituals might be enacted (unfortunately, the primary data on this score for ancient Israel are lacking). Furthermore, only in the latter stages of preexilic Israelite religion was the practice of necromancy introduced, which explains its occasional mention in late texts of the Holiness code, wisdom traditions, and later prophetic and Deuteronomistic additions. The mention of necromancy (e.g., Deut. 18:11; 1 Sam. 28:3-25; 2 Kgs. 21:6; 23:24; Isa. 8:19; 19:3; 29:4) finds impetus in the adaptation of Mesopotamian necromancy in Iron Age pluralistic Israelite religion. Now the otherwise feeble ghosts possessed the power that comes with knowledge concerning the future. This practice was outlawed in later Deuteronomistic and related biblical traditions by artificially attributing to it a "Canaanite" origin as a polemical strategy aimed at disparaging competing Israelite religious practices and avoiding the consternation of their Mesopotamian overlords.

A handful of other texts have been identified as pertaining to death and ancestor cult practices, but these concern mourning and so contribute nothing to the question as to whether or not the ancient Israelites observed death and ancestor rites. Deut. 14:1; 26:14 refer not to death or ancestor cult practices, but to mourning rites of tonsure and gashing and the prohibition against using the tithe as a gift of consolation for those in mourning. Similarly, Amos 6:7; Jer. 16:5 mention the *marzēaḥ*, which concerns an association organized for the purpose of advancing economic transactions among the upper echelons of society. In the exceptional instance this association might also seek to acknowledge the death of one of its members, and some attendants might indulge themselves to the point of inebriation during such a funerary ritual. However, the *marzēaḥ* has nothing to do with death and ancestor cults and only an occasional connection with funerary concerns.

Conclusion

All indications are that the dead of ancient Mediterranean West Asia and ancient Israel were perceived as weak and frail, and their material persistence beyond this life was characterized at best by a shadowy and silent existence and at worst by neglect on the part of the living. In Mesopotamian tradition, such neglect might result in the ghost's maleficence requiring exorcistic rituals to counter such behavior. Similarly, the ghosts of those who died an untimely or violent death might require ritual forms of control on the part of the living. Nonetheless, in Mediterranean West Asian sources such ghostly malevolence remains unattested. To be sure, there are instances wherein demons of various and sundry sorts must be averted by ritual means, but incantations and the like that were directed specifically toward hostile ghosts of the human dead are nowhere to be found in the archaeological, epigraphic, or literary sources (cf. the Arslan Tash incantations and some recently discovered Ugaritic incantations). Indeed, the evidence suggests that what occupied a more central place in the thought and action of ancient Israelites as they contemplated their prospects beyond the grave was the concern to perpetuate the memory of the deceased in the minds of the living. This coupled with an emphasis on making the best of life on this side of the grave — a long and healthy life span; sufficient material resources; many children, relatives, and friends; minimal pain and suffering — presented one with the prospect of obtaining a significant measure of fulfillment in this life.

Bibliography. J. Day, "The Development of Belief in Life after Death in Ancient Israel," in *After the Exile,* ed. J. Barton and D. J. Reimer (Macon, 1996), 231-57; B. B. Schmidt, *Israel's Beneficent Dead: Ancestor Cult and Necromancy in Ancient Israelite Religion and Tradition,* rev. ed. (Winona Lake, 1996).

Brian B. Schmidt

AGAG (Heb. *'ăgag*) **(PERSON)**

Name of two Amalekite kings (Num. 24:7; LXX "Gog"; 1 Sam. 15:8-9, 20, 32-33), or possibly a dynastic name for all their kings. In 1 Sam. 15 Saul's refusal finally to kill Agag, for Amalek's cruelty to Israel at the Exodus (Exod. 17:8-16; Deut. 25:17-19), results in Yahweh's and Samuel's decision to reject Saul as king. Samuel himself kills Agag.

Balaam predicts the future king(s) of Israel will be higher than the exalted king Agag (Num. 24:7). The LXX interpreting messianically reads, "he will rule over many nations; and his realm will be exalted as Gog. . ." Paul J. Kissling

AGAGITE (Heb. *'ăgagî*)

A gentilic associated with Haman, the enemy of the Jews (Esth. 3:1, 10; 8:3, 5; 9:24; cf. LXX), referring either to the Amalekite king Agag, whom Saul was commanded to kill (1 Sam. 15:2-3), or to the Amalekite nation, Israel's foe since the wilderness wanderings (Deut. 25:17-19).

AGAPE (Gk. *agápē*)

Of the several Greek words that mean "love," by far the most common in the NT is the *agápē* family. While Christians did not create the word (it is common in the LXX, rare in classical writings), they did make it a defining word for Christian life and teaching. Within the NT the verb form is more frequent. The use of *agápē* is most prominent in the writings of John (ca. one third of the total uses).

The Synoptic Gospels contain an account of Jesus' affirmation of the "Great Commandment" as the love of God and of one's neighbor (Mark 12:30-31; Matt. 22:38-39; Luke 10:27). The Gospel of John, which lacks this story, has even greater emphasis upon love in Jesus' teaching, for "God is love" (1 John 4:8). John stresses love as the indissoluble link between Jesus and God (John 15:9, 10; 1 John 3:16), Jesus and his people (John 13:1, 34), the believer and God (1 John 3:17), and among believers (John 13:34-35; 1 John 3:10-18).

Paul primarily uses the noun form to show

God's love for humanity "while we were still sinners" (Rom. 5:8). Paul describes God as the "God of love and peace" (2 Cor. 13:11), and the self-sacrifice of Christ as the real definition of "love." Rarely does Paul speak of the believer's love for God (1 Cor. 2:9; Rom. 8:28); his more common motif is "faith." However, love is one of the key realities of Christian life (with faith and hope, 1 Cor. 13:13).

Bibliography. V. P. Furnish, *The Love Command in the New Testament* (Nashville, 1972); W. Klassen, *Love of Enemies.* OBT 15 (Philadelphia, 1984).

WENDELL WILLIS

AGATE.

See CHALCEDONY.

AGE

A long, indefinite period (Heb. *ʿôlām*) that may proceed from the past to the present ("from antiquity") or extends into the future ("for ever [and ever]"). The extent of time is relative to context, but when it concerns God, who is eternal, it may be absolute (Ps. 90:2). The LXX customarily translates *ʿôlām* as Gk. *aiṓn,* with little change in meaning.

In 1st-century apocalyptic Judaism there was widespread expectation of a new age (4 Ezra 6:7-10; 7:112-113; 2 En. 65:7-8), which became the basis for the Judeo-Christian division of world history into two ages (Matt. 12:32; Eph. 1:21): the present under the rule of Satan and characterized by evil (2 Cor. 4:4; Gal. 1:4), and the one to come (Luke 18:30; John 17:3). The NT holds the conviction that the age to come has already appeared in Jesus Christ (1 Cor. 10:11; Heb. 6:5; 9:26), and will be fully manifested in his Second Coming.

DALE F. LESCHERT

AGEE (Heb. *ʾāgēʾ*)

A Hararite and father of Shammah, one of David's champions (2 Sam. 23:11).

AGRAPHA (Gk. *ágrapha*)

A technical term (lit., "unwritten [things]") referring to sayings of Jesus not recorded in the four canonical Gospels. Sayings attributed to Jesus elsewhere in the NT (e.g., Acts 20:35; 1 Cor. 11:24-25) are sometimes considered agrapha; however, the term is usually reserved for extracanonical sayings. The agrapha are located in various sources, such as ancient manuscripts of the NT (e.g., Codex Bezae [D] at Luke 6:5), apocryphal texts (e.g., Gospel of Thomas, Gospel of Philip), papyrus fragments (e.g., Oxyrhynchus Papyri), the writings of the church fathers, the Talmud, and Islamic texts. A limited number of agrapha (esp. some in the Gospel of Thomas) might be authentic sayings of Jesus, but the agrapha are more indicative of how the Jesus tradition was developed and appropriated to suit the needs of diverse communities.

Bibliography. J. Jeremias, *Unknown Sayings of Jesus,* 2nd ed. (London, 1964); W. D. Stroker, *Extracanonical Sayings of Jesus* (Atlanta, 1988).

JEFFREY T. TUCKER

AGRICULTURE

Along with herding, one of the two main components of Israelite economy. Israelite agriculturalists probably learned their skills from the Canaanites, the former inhabitants of the land. While agriculture was practiced throughout the country, its nature changed depending on particular environmental conditions characteristic of each region. The lack of suitable lands in the hill country was resolved by forest clearing and the introduction of terracing, a method which artificially created leveled areas suitable for the cultivation of field crops and orchards. The scarcity of water in arid zones was met with the practice of runoff farming which utilized catchment of rain waters and their diversion to agricultural plots.

Unlike Egypt or Mesopotamia, irrigation of agricultural plots was not commonly practiced in biblical Israel due to the lack of water sources and the nature of the terrain (cf. Deut. 11:10-11: "For the land which you are crossing over to occupy is a land of hills and valleys, watered by rain from the sky").

The most common field crops were cereals *(dāgān)* which included wheat *(ḥiṭṭâ),* barley *(śĕʿōrâ),* and millet. Legumes, although cultivated by the Israelite farmer, probably were not as common as cereals since not all species are mentioned in the Bible and most are better known from archaeological samples. Species cultivated in the Israelite period include broad bean *(pôl),* lentil *(ʿăḏāšîm),* bitter vetch, chick-pea, pea, and fenugreek. Other field crops included flax *(pištâ)* and sesame.

An important branch of Israelite agriculture was the growing of fruit trees. The most common was the grapevine *(gep̱en),* respectively followed by the olive *(zayiṯ),* pomegranate *(rimmôn),* date palm *(tāmār),* and sycamore *(šiqmîm).* Other fruit trees include *tappûăḥ* (possibly quince or apricot), *bāḵāʾ* (possibly black mulberry), and carob. Other trees cultivated for their fruit were those bearing nuts, which included the almond *(šāqēḏ),* pistachio (possibly *boṭnîm*), and walnut *(ʾĕg̱ôz).*

Not much is known about the cultivation of vegetables, a dietary element which was not highly regarded (Prov. 15:17). However, several biblical references indicate that gardening was practiced in close proximity to the home, in urban areas, and by the nobility (1 Kgs. 21:2; 2 Kgs. 21:18, 26). Only once are vegetables enumerated, when the Israelites in the desert crave meat, fish, and "the cucumbers *(qiššuʾîm),* the melons *(ʾăḇaṭṭiḥîm),* the leeks[?] *(ḥāṣîr),* the onions *(bĕṣālîm),* and the garlic *(šûmîm)*" (Num. 11:5). Cucumbers were cultivated in large patches and required guarding against theft (Isa. 1:8) and damage by birds (Jer. 10:5).

One form of gardening was the cultivation of herbs and spices, which included cumin *(kammōn),* black cumin *(qeṣaḥ)* and coriander *(gaḏ),* all of which are mentioned in the Bible.

Agriculture is a seasonal occupation, and all chores are predetermined by the time of year and the prevailing climate. Although several of the

Workers reap and winnow grain (below) while scribes register the harvest (above). Wall painting from the tomb of Menna, scribe of the fields of the lord of the two lands of Upper and Lower Egypt (15th century B.C.E.) (Courtesy of the Oriental Institute of the University of Chicago)

agricultural seasons and chores are mentioned in the Bible, the best source for the agricultural cycle is the so-called Gezer Calendar, an inscription discovered at Tell Gezer in 1908. The document opens with "two months of ingathering (of olives)" (mid-August to mid-October) followed by "two months of sowing (cereals)" (mid-October to mid-December) and "two months of late sowing (of legumes and vegetables)" (mid-December to mid-February). This was followed by "a month of hoeing weeds (for hay)" (mid-February to mid-March). Others read this entry as "a month of hoeing flax." Then come "a month of harvesting barley" (mid-March at the spring equinox to mid-April) and "a month of harvesting (wheat) and measuring (grain)" (mid-April to mid-May; the last word has several suggested readings). The listing ends with "two months of grape harvesting" (mid-May to mid-July) and "a month of (ingathering) summer fruit" (mid-July to mid-August). Analysis of the Gezer Calendar shows that the three pilgrimage festivals (Passover/Pesaḥ, Weeks/Šāḇu'ôṯ, Booths/Sukkôṯ), which started as agricultural celebrations, occur in accordance with its seasonal divisions.

Agricultural chores required special implements. Plowing, which was done for the purpose of sowing, was carried out with a wooden plow *(maḥărēšâ)* having a metal tip, and drafted by cattle (oxen, cows) or donkeys. This activity took place in the autumn after the first rains. A related tool was the goad (*malmāḏ* or *dārḇān*), which had at one end an iron tip set in a wooden shaft for prodding the animals, and a flat, shovel-like butt at the other end for removing the mud off the plow-tip. Other chores were done with other tools such as sickle (*maggāl* or *ḥermēš*) for harvesting, threshing sledge *(môrag)* or wheel-thresher *('ôpan 'ăgālâ)*, and winnowing fork *(mizreh)* and sieves (*kĕḇārâ* and *nāp̄â*). Tilling the soil in the orchards and gardens was done with a hoe *(ma'dēr)* and another digging implement *('ēṯ)*. A tool that was developed especially for work in the vineyard was a pruning knife *(mazmērâ)*, which was used also for harvesting grapes *(zāmîr)*.

Good yield was assured by restoration of soil fertility and by guarding against pests and diseases. The former employed several methods including fertilizing with animal manure *(dōmen)* and ashes (*'ēp̄er* and *dešen*), and green manuring (using legumes for the enrichment of the soil with nitrogen). All these methods were used in combination with crop rotation, which included fallowing. As for pests (locust, mice, worms) and diseases, little more could have been done under the prevalent circumstances than simply maintaining good agricultural practices. Pests and diseases were considered a punishment from Yahweh for not observing the Covenant. Thus, adhering to the terms of the Covenant was believed to prevent the infliction of pests and diseases. In the event of such an occurrence, prayer and repentance were considered to be helpful.

A good agricultural year was one which yielded an abundance of produce. The prophet Amos expresses it best: "The time is surely coming, says the Lord, when the one who plows shall overtake the one who reaps, and the treader of grapes the one who sows the seed" (Amos 9:13). To use and consume the produce, it had to be processed and stored. After its threshing and winnowing, clean grain *(bar)* was stored generally near the house in private storage pits and in large silos owned by the public sector (government, temple). For immediate use, dry produce was kept in wide-mouth jars. While cereals were mostly ground for flour and used for making bread, legumes were consumed as pottage or porridge *(nāzîḏ)*. Legumes were stored mostly in storage jars. Storage jars were used also for keeping dried fruit (figs, dates, raisins), wine, and olive oil. The production of the latter two required special installations such as the *yeqeḇ* and *gaṯ* for wine-making and the olive press for making oil. The most efficient olive press in the Israelite period was the beam press. Oil was used not just as food, but also for lighting and as an element in cosmetics. Other fruit products included fresh juice, jams, and syrups.

Surplus produce was used to pay taxes, as illustrated by the Samaria Ostraca. Some of the surplus was offered as sacrifices in local shrines and in the national temples, and a certain amount was bartered in exchange for supplies. Not only private individuals were engaged in agriculture, but also royalty and the nobility, as exemplified by King Uzziah (2 Chr. 26:10).

See HERDING.

Bibliography. O. Borowski, *Agriculture in Iron Age Israel* (Winona Lake, 1987). ODED BOROWSKI

AGRIPPA (Gk. *Agríppas*)

See HEROD (Family) 16, 18.

AGUR (Heb. *'āḡûr*)

An author or collector of proverbs (Prov. 30:1); the son of Jakeh of Massa. He was probably a compatriot of Lemuel the king of Massa (Prov. 31:1).

AHAB (Heb. *'aḥ'āḇ*)

1. King of Israel (ca. 875-854 B.C.E.) and successor to his father Omri, who arranged a marriage between Ahab and Jezebel, daughter of King Ethbaal of Tyre, to secure good relations between Phoenicia and Israel. Ahab's 70 sons in Samaria were murdered by Jehu in his coup (2 Kgs. 10), and his daughter (or sister) Athaliah reigned in Judah (843-837) until her murder. A nemesis to the prophet Elijah, Ahab is considered by the Deuteronomistic historian to be the most evil king in Israel (1 Kgs. 16:30, 33; 21:25; Mic. 6:16) and is compared to the evil Manasseh of Judah (2 Kgs. 21:3). Yet, there appear to be inconsistencies between the biblical text and archaeological data.

Biblical Account

The text assumes that Ahab's evil actions create the drought and famine that ravage Israel and lead to Elijah's prophetic activities (1 Kgs. 16:29–22:40; 2 Chr. 18, 21). Ahab's foremost sin is his collusion with Jezebel in promoting the worship of Baal in Israel alongside the worship of Yahweh. Ahab builds a house of worship and altar in Samaria for this Canaanite god (1 Kgs. 16:32), erects a sacred pole for the Canaanite goddess Asherah (v. 33) while allowing Jezebel to dine with 450 prophets of Baal and 400 prophets of Asherah (18:19). Yet Ahab's allegiance to Yahweh is evident as he battles in the name of Yahweh (1 Kgs. 20, 22), places Obadiah (Heb. "servant of Yahweh") in charge of his palace, gives his children Yahweh names, and heeds the words of the prophets Micaiah (1 Kgs. 22) and Elijah. Under Elijah's orders he gathers Baal's prophets for the test on Mt. Carmel (1 Kgs. 18) and later dons sackcloth at the words of judgment Elijah brings him (21:17-29). According to the Deuteronomist, Ahab does wrong only because he is "urged on by his wife Jezebel" (1 Kgs. 21:25), strongly illustrated in the story of Naboth's vineyard.

Naboth's vineyard (1 Kgs. 21) raises issues of royal power and prerogative in ancient Israel. Naboth represents the old tribal ethos that insists that land stay in the tribe (Lev. 25:23; Num. 36:5-9), whereas Ahab represents the new state administration that is more despotic. Ahab wants Naboth's vineyard (cf. Isa. 5, a symbol of Israel), situated next to his palace, for a vegetable garden (symbolic of fertility). His request to purchase this land is refused by Naboth because it must stay in Naboth's family as his inheritance. Defeated, Ahab returns home to his sympathetic wife, Jezebel, who devises a plan to secure the vineyard by having Naboth falsely accused of treason, whereby Ahab orders his death and confiscates the property. However, according to 2 Kgs. 9, which scholars suggest reflects an older version of the vineyard account, not only is Ahab solely responsible for Naboth's death (vv. 25-26), he also kills Naboth's sons. In punishment God promises to obliterate Ahab's line and to allow dogs to eat both him and Jezebel (1 Kgs. 21:20-24). Ahab repents and his punishment is deferred to his sons. Nevertheless, Ahab's blood is lapped up by dogs and bathed in by prostitutes (22:38), not in Jezreel as prophesied, but in Ramoth-gilead where Ahab and King Jehoshaphat of Judah join forces against the Arameans.

The text recognizes but downplays Ahab's strong leadership abilities. It is noted that he reigns for 22 years, builds and fortifies cities, maintains peaceful borders through marriage alliances (Athaliah to Jehoram of Judah, Ahab to Jezsebel of Phoenicia), and forms treaties with such rulers as Ben-hadad (1 Kgs. 20) and Jehoshaphat (ch. 22). In fact, the Chronicler records that Jehoshaphat pays tribute to Ahab and Israel (2 Chr. 18). Even an image of the valiant leader is painted as Ahab, bleeding profusely and dying, begs to be propped up in his carriage to provide encouragement to his troops as they fight the enemy. Nevertheless, the text portrays an even stronger image of Ahab as a weak leader. After returning victorious from battle (this scene neglects to mention Ahab's name), Ahab is resentful and sullen because the prophet condemns him for not offering Ben-hadad for destruction under the rules of the ban (*ḥērem;* 1 Kgs. 20). He whines and refuses to eat when unable to buy Naboth's vineyard, and he allows Jezebel to rule in his stead. It is this image of Ahab as the "henpecked husband" ruled by Jezebel that dominates the biblical story. Historical data, however, create a more prestigious image of Ahab.

Historical Account

Many historians consider Ahab's building programs to be as impressive as those of Herod and Solomon. Archaeological data suggest that Ahab fortified the cities of Dor, Megiddo, Hazor, Jezreel, Dan, and 'En-gev by building casement walls. In addition, he is considered responsible for the intricate water systems at Megiddo and Hazor that protected those cities' water supplies from Assyrian threat. Urban centers doubled under Ahab's rule, perhaps because of his willingness to balance both Canaanite and Israelite interests. The sophisticated Phoenician material culture discovered in Israel attests to the close relationship between these two cultures, especially as it disappears after the demise of the Omride dynasty. The Monolith inscription of Assyrian King Shalmaneser III records the battle of Qarqar where a coalition of kings, including Ahab, rose up against the Assyrian. Although Assyria won, neither Hamath (Hama) nor Damascus was taken. Ahab provided the greatest number of resources with his 2000 chariots and 10 thousand soldiers. In addition, the 9th-century Moabite stone (Mesha Stela) indicates that Omri (or "the land of the house of Omri" — perhaps Ahab) controlled Moab for many years. Clearly, historical evidence suggests that Ahab was a strong, politically savvy king.

Rabbinical Sources

Many rabbinical sources stress Ahab's military prowess and hold both Ahab and Manasseh to higher principles because of their greatness that was diverted to doing evil. Rabbi Johanan argues that Ahab is worthy of 22 years of power because he revered the Torah's 22 letters and supported the sages. The Zohar argues that it was acceptable for Ahab to take Naboth's property but not to execute him. Others suggest that Ahab was Naboth's relative and heir, so entitled to the property (*Sanh.* 48b).

2. Son of Kolaiah (Jer. 29:21-23) who, with Zedekiah son of Maaseiah, is accused by the prophet Jeremiah of falsely prophesying and committing adultery. He and Zedekiah predicted an early return from exile, inciting riots and chaos in Babylon which led to their execution by King Nebuchadnezzar of Babylon.

Deborah A. Appler

AHARAH (Heb. *'aḥĕraḥ*)
The third son of Benjamin (1 Chr. 8:1).

AHARHEL (Heb. *'ăḥarḥēl*)
The son of Harum of the tribe of Judah (1 Chr. 4:8).

AHASBAI (Heb. *'ăḥasbay*)
The father of Eliphelet, one of David's champions (2 Sam. 23:34). He may have been an inhabitant of Abel-beth-maacah (2 Sam. 20:14) or of Maacah in Syria (10:6).

AHASUERUS (Heb. *'ăḥašwērôš*; Gk. *'Assouēros*)
1. In all probability, the biblical name for Xerxes I (Pers. *khshayârshâ*), king of Persia 486-465 B.C.E., son and successor of Darius I. Under his father he was satrap over Babylon (498-486). Upon his accession he recaptured Egypt (484), which had revolted late in the reign of Darius I. In 480 Xerxes moved against the Greeks, to whom his father Darius had lost the battle of Marathon (490). He initially won a major battle at Thermopylae (480), but lost at Salamis (480) and Mycale (479), and decisively at Eurymedon (466). He implemented a tax structure which put non-Persians at a disadvantage. Ahasuerus is mentioned in Ezra 4:6 as the ruler when "the people of the land" leveled an unspecified accusation against the community in Jerusalem. According to the book of Esther, he first approved anti-Semitic measures (Esth. 3:12-14); subsequently, through the crucial mediation of his Jewish wife Esther, he permitted forceful resistance by the Jews against any organized assault (8:10-14).

2. Ahasuerus the Mede. Referred to in Dan. 9:1, he is otherwise unknown and considered problematic.

3. According to some versions of Tob. 14:15, along with Nebuchadnezzar a destroyer of Nineveh. The reference poses historical problems.

Gerald M. Bilkes

AHAVA (Heb. *'ahăwā'*)
A river or canal in Babylon; possibly also the name of a town or settlement associated with it. Ezra mentions Ahava as the site at which he gathered the exiles who were to return to Jerusalem and proclaimed a preparatory fast before the journey (Ezra 8:15, 21, 31).

Attempts to locate Ahava are complicated by the limited data for reconstructing the route of Ezra's return, and by the abundance of textual variants for the name in the relevant manuscripts (MT, LXX, Ethiopic). While the exact locations are unknown and several sites have been proposed, most are within a 200 km. (125 mi.) radius of Babylon.

Monica L. W. Brady

AHAZ (Heb. *'āḥāz*)
A shortened form of such names as Ahaziah and Jehoahaz ("Yahweh has grasped"). The latter appears in an Assyrian text of Tiglath-pileser III (Akk. *iaúhazi*) as the name of the Judean king (*ANET*, 282-84).

1. King of Judah in the 8th century B.C.E. At age 20 Ahaz succeeded his father Jotham and ruled over Judah for 16 years (ca. 742-727). The Deuteronomists portray Ahaz entirely in negative light in 2 Kgs. 16, censuring him with a standard evaluative formula, "He did not do what was right in the sight of the Lord his God," and comparing his wickedness with the Israelite kings, "he walked in the ways of the kings of Israel" (2 Kgs. 16:2-3). Ahaz is accused of religious apostasy (2 Kgs. 16:4), having built a new altar in the Jerusalem temple modeled after the Damascus altar (vv. 10-16), as well as making a political alliance with the Assyrian king Tiglath-pileser III (vv. 7-9). Clearly, the intent of the Deuteronomists to paint Ahaz in such a negative light is to draw a sharp contrast with his successor, Hezekiah, who according to the Deuteronomists "did what was right in the sight of the Lord" (2 Kgs. 18:3), carried out a religious reform by removing the high places, breaking down the pillars, and cutting down the sacred poles (v. 4). Moreover, Hezekiah "rebelled against the king of Assyria and would not serve him" (2 Kgs. 18:7), thus breaking the alliance established by Ahaz.

The Chronicler's presentation of Ahaz is even more negative than the Deuteronomists'. Scholars generally agree that the Chronicler reworked material from the Kings account to fit the writer's own theological perspective. While the Chronicler's overall condemnation of Ahaz is quite similar to that of the Deuteronomists, the interpretation of the events is not. First, in describing the invasion of Aram-Damascus and Israel on Judah (the so-called Syro-Ephraimite War), the Deuteronomists only note that they did not conquer Judah; but the Chronicler elaborates on the defeat of Ahaz, vis-à-vis the exile of Judeans to Damascus, a great slaughter inflicted by Pekah, and the removal of captives and booty to Samaria (2 Chr. 28:5-15). Second, Ahaz' appeal to Tiglath-pileser for help is set in the context of the Syro-Ephraimitic crisis in the Kings account, resulting in Tiglath-pileser's defeat of Aram-Damascus. The Chronicler, however, set that appeal in the context of attacks by the Edomites and the Philistines. According to the Chronicler, Tiglath-pileser attacks Ahaz instead of coming to his aid. Third, for the Deuteronomists, Ahaz' religious apostasy began with his visit to Damascus to meet Tiglath-pileser; for the Chronicler, Ahaz' apostasy came "in the time of his distress," where instead of repenting "he became yet more faithless to the Lord" and "sacrificed to the gods of Damascus" (2 Chr. 28:22-23). Evidently, the theological intent of the Chronicler is to show that Ahaz' religious sins made him the worst king in the history of Judah and as a result Yahweh punished him by handing him into the hands of his enemies. Yet, Ahaz did not repent but turned to the gods of his enemies.

An event of important significance during the reign of Ahaz is the Syro-Ephraimite War, which most scholars date to ca. 734. This crisis is related to a broader anti-Assyrian movement, headed by Rezin of Aram-Damascus, in the southwestern part of the Assyrian Empire. The attack on Jerusalem by Rezin and Pekah of Israel probably came about as a result of Ahaz' refusal to join the coalition. Isaiah indicated that the siege of Jerusalem was aimed at replacing Ahaz with a certain "son of Tabeel" (Isa. 7:6). This attempt was probably made to ensure Judah's participation in the alliance. Isaiah, however, encouraged Ahaz to remain firm in his policy of neutrality (Isa. 7:3-4).

2. A great-great-grandson of Saul, named in the Benjaminite genealogical lists in 1 Chr. 8:35-36; 9:41-42.

Bibliography. P. R. Ackroyd, "Historians and Prophets," *SEÅ* 33 (1968): 18-54; "The Biblical Interpretation of the Reigns of Ahaz and Hezekiah," in *In the Shelter of Elyon,* ed. W. B. Barrick and J. R. Spencer, JSOTSup 31 (Sheffield, 1984), 247-59; S. A. Irvine, *Isaiah, Ahaz, and the Syro-Ephraimitic Crisis.* SBLDS 123 (Atlanta, 1990). JEFFREY K. KUAN

AHAZIAH (Heb. *'ăḥazyâ, 'ăḥazyāhû*)

1. King of Judah, who succeeded his father Jehoram (Joram) at the age of 22 and reigned one year (843/842 B.C.E.). Ahaziah's mother was Athaliah, making him the grandson of Ahab and Jezebel (2 Kgs. 8:25-27). The statement in Chronicles that Ahaziah began to reign at the age of 42 must be incorrect, because his father was only 40 when he died (2 Chr 21:20–22:2). Because of his relationship to the northern kingdom, Ahaziah was considered a wicked king (2 Kgs. 8:27). He allied with Jehoram (Joram) of Israel, participating with him in battles against the Syrian king Hazael. While Jehoram was recovering in Jezreel from wounds sustained in a battle with the Syrians, Ahaziah came to visit him (2 Kgs. 8:28, 29). After Elisha anointed Jehu as the next king of Israel (2 Kgs. 9:1-13), Jehu traveled to Jezreel and there he killed Jehoram and fatally wounded Ahaziah as well; Ahaziah was taken to Megiddo where he died (2 Kgs. 9:17-29). Jehu then continued his purge by killing various relatives of Ahaziah as well (2 Kgs. 10:13, 14; cf. the sequence of events in 2 Chr. 22:7-9). In keeping with his doctrine of retribution, the Chronicler attributes Ahaziah's death to his association with Jehoram of Israel (2 Chr. 22:7a).

An Aramaic inscription, fragments of which were discovered at Tel Dan in 1993 and 1994, was apparently commissioned by Hazael; in it he claims to have killed [Jeho]ram king of Israel and [Ahaz]iah king of Judah. The biblical and epigraphic data seem to be in conflict, but there is biblical evidence of some sort of alliance between Hazael and Jehu (1 Kgs. 19:17).

Following Ahaziah's death, Athaliah killed the remaining members of the royal family in Judah and actually assumed the throne herself. Ahaziah's sister Jehosheba was able to save one of Ahaziah's sons, Jehoash (Joash). Seven years later Athaliah was deposed and killed, and Jehoash was crowned king (2 Kgs. 11:1-21; 2 Chr. 22:10–23:21).

2. Son and successor of King Ahab of Israel; he reigned ca. two years (850-849; 1 Kgs. 22:40, 51). The Deuteronomistic editor criticized Ahaziah for his aberrant religious practices, particularly his worship of Baal (1 Kgs. 22:53). According to the Chronicler, Ahaziah of Israel and Jehoshaphat of Judah jointly produced several ships at Ezion-geber. Jehoshaphat's collaboration with Ahaziah aroused the ire of Eliezer son of Dodavahu, who correctly prophesied that the ships would be destroyed (2 Chr. 20:35-37). Though the parallel pericope in Kings affirms that the ships were destroyed, it denies that Jehoshaphat collaborated with Ahaziah in building them (1 Kgs. 22:48, 49).

According to a narrative in the Elijah cycle, Ahaziah fell through the lattice in his upper chamber and was seriously injured. He sent messengers to "Baal-zebub," the god of Ekron, to learn whether or not he would recover. Intercepted and rebuked by Elijah, these messengers were told that Ahaziah would not recover. After finally consenting to appear before the king, Elijah rebuked Ahaziah for attempting to consult a deity other than Yahweh and again stated that the king would not recover. Ahaziah was succeeded as king of Israel by his brother Jehoram (2 Kgs. 1:2-18).

Bibliography. A. Biran and J. Naveh, "The Tel Dan Inscription: A New Fragment," *IEJ* 45 (1995): 1-18; M. Cogan and H. Tadmor, *II Kings.* AB 11 (Garden City, 1988); J. M. Miller and J. H. Hayes, *A History of Ancient Israel and Judah* (Philadelphia, 1986).

CHRIS A. ROLLSTON

AHBAN (Heb. *'aḥbān)*
The son of Abishur and Abihail and the brother of Molid, of the tribe of Judah (1 Chr. 2:29).

AHER (Heb. *'aḥēr)*
A Benjaminite, the father of Hushim (1 Chr. 7:12).

AHI (Heb. *'ăḥî)*
The son of Abdiel of the tribe of Gad, who dwelt in Bashan (1 Chr. 5:15). The name may be a contraction of Ahijah. At 1 Chr. 7:34 the Hebrew word should probably be taken as an epithet ("my brother"; cf. RSV, NJB) rather than as a personal name.

AHIAH (Heb. *'ăḥîyâ)*
One who put his seal to the renewed covenant under Nehemiah (Neh. 10:26[MT 27]).

AHIAM (Heb. *'ăḥî'ām)*
One of David's champions. He was the son of the Hararite Sharar (2 Sam. 23:33) or more likely Sachar (2 Chr. 11:35; cf. LXX for both).

AHIAN (Heb. *'aḥyān)*
The son of Shemida of the tribe of Manasseh (1 Chr. 7:19).

AHIEZER (Heb. *'ăḥî'ezer)*
1. The son of Ammishaddai. He was a representative from the tribe of Dan during the wilderness wanderings, assisting Moses in the census of the Israelites (Num. 1:12; 2:35) and offering a sacrifice at the dedication of the altar (7:66-72).
2. A kinsman of Saul, a chief of the Benjaminites from Gibeah, who defected to David at Ziklag (1 Chr. 12:3).

AHIHUD (Heb. *'ăḥîhûḏ, 'ăḥîhuḏ)*
1. The son of Shelomi. He was a leader of the tribe of Asher appointed to assist Moses in the division of Canaan (Num. 34:27).
2. A descendant of Ehud, head of a Benjaminite ancestral house (1 Chr. 8:7).

AHIJAH (Heb. *'ăḥîyâ)*
1. Son of Ahitub and great-grandson of Eli. Ahijah was a priest in Shiloh who served with Saul's army as the wearer of the ephod (1 Sam. 14:3). He was responsible for the ark of the covenant, then housed at Kiriath-jearim (1 Sam. 14:18-19).
2. A prophet from Shiloh. Ahijah tore his garment into 12 pieces before Jeroboam, Solomon's overseer of compulsory labor of the house of Joseph, symbolizing the coming division of the kingdom (1 Kgs. 11:29-31; 12:15; 2 Chr. 10:15). In addition to predicting Jeroboam's accession to the throne of the northern kingdom, Ahijah later foretold the death of Jeroboam's son (1 Kgs. 14:2-18; 15:29-30).
3. Son of Shisha; a secretary under Solomon (1 Kgs. 4:3).
4. Father of Baasha, king of Israel; member of the tribe of Issachar (1 Kgs. 15:27, 33; 21:22; 2 Kgs. 9:9).
5. Son of Jerahmeel; member of the tribe of Judah (1 Chr. 2:25).
6. Son of Ehud, a Benjaminite, who was carried into captivity (1 Chr. 8:7).
7. A Pelonite; one of David's mighty men (1 Chr. 11:36).
8. A Levite in charge of the temple treasury under King David (1 Chr. 26:20).

KENNETH ATKINSON

AHIKAM (Heb. *'ăḥîqām)*
The son of Shaphan (2 Kgs. 22:12) and father of Gedaliah (25:22). He was one of the officials of King Josiah sent to the prophetess Huldah to inquire of the Lord (2 Kgs. 22:14; 2 Chr. 34:20). Afterward he protected Jeremiah against Jehoiakim and his followers (Jer. 26:24).

AHIKAR, AHIQAR (Gk. *Achiacharos)*
A legendary sage and advisor at the Assyrian court, perhaps modeled on a historical figure. Books ascribed to or about Ahiqar were very widespread in Mediterranean antiquity. The earliest extant version of such a book comes from Aramaic papyri dated ca. 420 B.C.E., although its composition is generally dated a century or two earlier.

The text is in two parts. The first tells the story of Ahiqar, a respected sage and counselor who, childless in old age, adopts his nephew Nadin as his son and successor at court. Nadin, however, plots Ahiqar's disgrace and death by forging documents that make him appear guilty of treason. The plot, however, ultimately fails and recoils on Nadin's head.

The second part consists of sayings ascribed to Ahiqar that bear a general similarity to the Wisdom literature of the OT, especially the book of Proverbs (e.g., Ahiqar 7:96: "My son, do not curse the day until you have seen the night"). One bit of spare-the-rod-spoil-the-child advice is close enough to Prov. 23:13-14 to foster speculation that the two may have had a common source.

While this text was found at the Jewish colony of Elephantine, the Ahiqar who appears in the text is an Assyrian in nationality and religion. However, as the story circulated in Jewish and (later) Christian circles, references to "the gods" were replaced with references to "God" or "the Lord," and Ahiqar was given a Jewish pedigree. On the basis of such a version, the book of Tobit brought Ahiqar into Tobit's family as his nephew, the son of Hanael (Tob. 1:21). The connection serves to locate Tobit more plausibly in the court affairs of Assyria, and Ahiqar's nephew (referred to as Nadab) provides a contrast to the filial behavior of Tobias and Sarah (Tob. 11:18).

WILL SOLL

AHILUD (Heb. *'ăḥîlûḏ*)
The father of Jehoshaphat, who was recorder during the reigns of David and Solomon (2 Sam. 8:16; 20:24; 1 Kgs. 4:3). He may also have been the father of Baana, one of the 12 officers of Solomon (1 Kgs. 4:12).

AHIMAAZ (Heb. *'ăḥîma'aṣ*)
1. The father of Saul's wife Ahinoam (1 Sam. 14:50).
2. The son of Zadok the priest. Along with Jonathan, the son of Abiathar, he kept David informed of the progress of Absalom's rebellion (2 Sam. 15:27, 36; 17:20). When Absalom died, Ahimaaz insisted on personally relaying the news to the king (2 Sam. 18:19-30).
3. One of Solomon's commissary officers, assigned to Naphtali (1 Kgs. 4:15). He was married to Basemath, a daughter of Solomon. Some scholars suggest that the name indicates the father of an officer, whose name has been omitted from the account, and that he may therefore be the same as **2** above.

AHIMAN (Heb. *'ăḥîman*)
1. One of the descendants of Anak, the "giants" who inhabited pre-Israelite Palestine (Num. 13:22). Along with his brothers Sheshai and Talmai, he was driven from Hebron by Caleb (Josh. 15:14; Judg. 1:10).
2. A Levite, one of the four gatekeepers of the postexilic temple (1 Chr. 9:17-18).

AHIMELECH (Heb. *'ăḥîmeleḵ*)
1. The son of Ahitub of the house of Eli (1 Sam. 22:9) and the father of Abiathar (30:7). He was high priest during the reign of Saul at Nob (21:1[MT 2]), the chief sanctuary of Yahweh after the fall of Shiloh.

Ahimelech aided David during his flight from Saul (1 Sam. 21:1-9[2-10]). Saul then had Ahimelech and the other priests of Nob killed, thereby fulfilling the prophecy against the house of Eli (2:31-36). The incident is referred to in the superscription of Ps. 52 and by Jesus (Matt. 12:1-4; Mark 2:23-28; Luke 6:1-5).
2. A Hittite companion and friend of David when David was hiding from Saul in the wilderness (1 Sam. 26:6).
3. The son of Abiathar and grandson of Ahimelech (**1**; 2 Sam. 8:17; 1 Chr. 24:6), who held a priestly position with Zadok during David's reign (18:16; 24:31). NANCY L. DECLAISSÉ-WALFORD

AHIMOTH (Heb. *'ăḥîmôṯ*)
A Levite of the family of Kohath, the second son of Levi (1 Chr. 6:25[MT 10]); an ancestor of Elkanah the father of Samuel.

AHINADAB (Heb. *'ăḥînāḏāḇ*)
The son of Iddo. One of Solomon's 12 officers, he was in charge of the territory of Mahanaim (1 Kgs. 4:14).

AHINOAM (Heb. *'ăḥînō'am*)
1. Daughter of Ahimaaz (origin unknown) and wife of King Saul (1 Sam. 14:50). Ahinoam is the only wife named in connection with Saul and is possibly the mother of his seven children (1 Sam. 14:49-50; 1 Chr. 8:33-40; 9:39-44; but cf. 2 Sam. 12:8).
2. Jezreelite wife of David and mother of his firstborn son, Amnon. After her marriage to David (1 Sam. 25:43), she accompanied him on his visit to the Philistine king Achish (27:3). Later taken hostage in an Amalekite raid on Ziklag (30:5), Ahinoam was subsequently rescued and accompanied David to Hebron (2 Sam. 2:2), where he was crowned king of Judah. All references to Ahinoam place her in close literary proximity to another of David's wives, Abigail.

This Ahinoam and **1** above may be the same person; cf. Nathan's comment to David, "I gave you . . . your master's wives" (2 Sam. 12:8).

Bibliography. J. D. Levinson and B. Halpern, "The Political Import of David's Marriages," *JBL* 99 (1980): 507-18. LINDA S. SCHEARING

AHIO (Heb. *'aḥyô*)
1. A son of Abinadab, at whose house the ark was temporarily kept. When he and his brother Uzzah drove the ark on a cart en route to Jerusalem (2 Sam. 6:3-4; 1 Chr. 13:7), they came as far as the threshing floor of Nacon (2 Sam. 6:6).
2. A son of Beriah of the tribe of Benjamin (1 Chr. 8:14). On the basis of the LXX some translators prefer to read "his brother."
3. A Benjaminite, descendant of Jeiel and Maacah (1 Chr. 8:30-31); a brother of Kish, the father of Saul (9:35, 37).

AHIRA (Heb. *'ăḥîra'*)
The son of Enan of the tribe of Naphtali, assigned to assist Moses in the census (Num. 1:15). Num. 7:78-83 describes his offering on behalf of the tribe.

AHIRAM (Heb. *'ăḥîrām*)
The third son of Benjamin and ancestor of the Ahiramites (Num. 26:38). He may be the same person as Aher (1 Chr. 7:12) or Aharah (8:1).

AHISAMACH (Heb. *'ăḥîsāmāḵ*)
A Danite, the father of Oholiab (Exod. 31:6; 35:34; 38:23).

AHISHAHAR (Heb. *'ăḥîšaḥar*)
A Benjaminite warrior, one of the sons of Bilhan of the family of Jediael (1 Chr. 7:10-11).

AHISHAR (Heb. *'ăḥîšār*)
A high official under King Solomon, in charge of the palace (1 Kgs. 4:6).

AHITHOPHEL (Heb. *'ăḥîṯōp̄el*)
A man from the town of Giloh in the hill country of Judah. Serving as David's counselor (1 Chr. 27:33), his wisdom was highly esteemed as prophetic words from God (2 Sam. 16:23).

Dissatisfaction with David's later reign ran deep, and when David's son Absalom rebelled, Ahithophel (lit., "brother of foolishness" [?]) joined the rebel cause and became the mastermind behind the revolution (2 Sam. 15:12ff.). After occupying Jerusalem, Ahithophel counseled Absalom to defile David's harem, thus taking token possession of the kingdom, and to pursue David before his forces could consolidate (2 Sam. 16:20–17:4). His admonition to seek David was thwarted by Hushai, one of David's loyal followers and a spy, who urged delay (2 Sam. 17:5-14). His guidance being rejected and seeing that Absalom's revolt was doomed to failure, Ahithophel committed suicide by hanging (2 Sam. 17:23).

Some believe Ahithophel to have been the grandfather of Bathsheba, for she is mentioned in 2 Sam. 11:3 as the daughter of Eliam, who according to 23:34 was the son of Ahithophel. It seems improbable that Ahithophel was old enough to have a married granddaughter at the time of David's great sin. It also seems unlikely that Ahithophel would conspire against the interests of his granddaughter and her son. It is easier to believe that there were two men in Israel named Eliam. However, this would perhaps explain Ahithophel's defection, having its roots in David's murdering of his grandson by marriage and the sexual corrupting of his granddaughter Bathsheba. JOHN L. HARRIS

AHITUB (Heb. *'ăḥîṭûḇ;* Gk. *Achitōb*)

1. One of the two sons of Phinehas and grandson of Eli; the father of Ahijah (1 Sam. 14:3) and Ahimelech (22:9).

2. The son of Amariah and father of Zadok the priest (2 Sam. 8:17; 1 Chr. 6:7-8[MT 5:33-34]; cf. 1 Esdr. 8:2; 2 Esdr. 1:1); grandfather of Zadok (1 Chr. 9:11; Neh. 11:11).

3. The son of another Amariah and grandfather of another priest named Zadok (1 Chr. 6:11-12).

4. An ancestor of Judith; son of Elijah and father of Raphain (Jdt. 8:1).

AHLAB (Heb. *'aḥlāḇ*)

A coastal town in the tribal inheritance of Asher, N of Tyre. Asher was unable to expel the Canaanite residents of the city and was forced to assimilate with the people living in the land (Judg. 1:31). It is probably the same as Mahalab (Josh. 19:29), located at modern Khirbet el-Maḥâlib (172303) S of the Litani River, which fell to the Assyrian forces of Sennacherib in 701 B.C. DAVID C. MALTSBERGER

AHLAI (Heb. *'aḥlay*)

1. The daughter ("sons" at 1 Chr. 2:31 means "descendants") of Sheshan of the tribe of Judah. Because her father had no male heirs, he gave her in marriage to his Egyptian slave Jarha (1 Chr. 34-35); they were the parents of Attai.

2. The father of Zabad, one of David's champions (1 Chr. 11:41).

AHOAH (Heb. *'ăḥôaḥ*)

The son of Bela, the firstborn of Benjamin (1 Chr. 8:4). The name should probably be read Ahijah, due to probable dittography with 1 Chr. 8:7 (which gives the primary sons as Naaman, Ahijah, and Gera). The Greek, Syriac, and Aramaic versions support the alternate reading (LXX *Achia*).

NANCY L. DECLAISSÉ-WALFORD

AHOHI (Heb. *'ăḥôḥî*)

The father of Dodo and grandfather of Eleazar, one of David's champions (2 Sam. 23:9).

AHOHITE (Heb. *'ăḥôḥî*)

A patronymic or gentilic name given to three of David's champions: Dodo (1 Chr. 11:12; cf. 2 Sam. 23:9), Zalmon (23:28), and Ilai (1 Chr. 11:29; perhaps the same as Zalmon).

AHUMAI (Heb. *'ăḥûmay*)

The son of Jahath of the tribe of Judah (1 Chr. 4:2).

AHUZZAM (Heb. *'ăḥuzzām*)

A son of Ashhur and Naarah of the tribe of Judah (1 Chr. 4:6).

AHUZZATH (Heb. *'ăḥuzzaṯ*)

A "friend" (a technical term meaning "adviser") of the Philistine king Abimelech. He and Phicol accompanied their sovereign, who wished to make a covenant with Isaac (Gen. 26:26).

AHZAI (Heb. *'aḥzay*)

A priest at the time of Ezra; the father of Azarel and grandson of Immer (Neh. 11:13). He may be the same as Jahzerah at 1 Chr. 9:12.

AI (Heb. *hā'ay*)

One of the major sites conquered during the Israelite conquest of Canaan. According to the account in Joshua, the Israelites conquered Ai during the second military campaign (Josh. 8) following an earlier abortive attempt (ch. 7).

While the location of biblical Ai has been subject to debate, it has been generally identified with et-Tell (1747.1472), ca. 3-4 km. (2-2.5 mi.) E of Bethel. The site was initially investigated by John Garstang, who conducted soundings at the site in 1928. From 1933 to 1935 Judith Marquet-Krause directed the Rothschild expedition, which discovered ruins of both an Early Bronze city and an Iron Age I village. The most extensive excavations were conducted by Joseph Callaway from 1964 to 1972. The purpose of the Callaway excavations was to clarify the chronology of the Iron I village.

The excavations of Marquet-Krause and Callaway found that the site of et-Tell was occupied during two major periods — the Early Bronze Age (ca. 3100-2350 B.C.E.) and Iron I (ca. 1220-1050), with an 1100-year gap in occupation between.

During EB the site grew from a small village to a sizable city of ca. 11 ha. (27 a.), one of the major urban centers of Palestine. Archaeological evidence

Excavated area at et-Tell, including the Early Bronze Age temple and citadel (lower center) and the Iron Age village (upper center) (J. A. Callaway)

indicates that a small unwalled village was established at the site ca. 3100. The village underwent a major transition beginning ca. 3000 with the arrival of newcomers from North Syria and Anatolia who increased the size of the site and fortified it with a city wall. Ca. 2850 the defense system of the city was enhanced as the width of the wall was increased. Ca. 2700 the site experienced a radical change as the city was destroyed and rebuilt either by the Egyptians or under Egyptian influence. The new city was equipped with both a large rectangular temple and new earthen reservoir. The temple was constructed of field stones and designed with a row of pillars down the center, and the building techniques reflect Egyptian influence. The large reservoir, lined with stones, had a capacity of ca. 1.9 million l. (500 thousand gal.) of water. In spite of its massive fortification wall, however, the history of the EB city came to an end ca. 2350 as the city was destroyed.

After being unoccupied for nearly 1100 years, the site was inhabited once again ca. 1220. The new settlement, built on the ruins of the EB city, was a small Iron I village of only 1.2 ha. (3 a.). The Iron Age village was established by newcomers from the north, perhaps Hittites from Anatolia and North Syria. This was an unwalled agricultural űṛşşǫ̋ṟ̌ with cobblestone streets. The houses, commonly referred to as pillar buildings or pillar houses, were designed with stone pillars or piers that apparently served as roof supports. The inhabitants of the Iron Age village engaged in farming using terrace farming or agricultural techniques, agricultural methods designed especially for the terrain of the area. The water supply was provided by cisterns hewed in the bedrock. Lined with plaster, some of these limestone cisterns were located in the rooms of houses.

Ca. 1125 the second Iron Age village was established at Ai by yet another new population wave. The newcomers who adopted and adapted the facilities of the former inhabitants expanded the size of the village and continued to use the pillar-building architectural design of the preceding era. One of the most notable changes was the construction of numerous silo granaries, grain storage facilities that were built on the cobblestone streets. The granaries reflect the strong agriculturally-based economy of the community and the continued usage of the terrace farming techniques that had been adopted from the village's earlier population.

The Iron Age village also featured a sanctuary designed with a stone bench. Among the artifacts discovered in the sanctuary were small animal figurines and a large pottery offering stand or incense altar decorated with windows and lions' paws.

On the basis of the archaeological evidence, Callaway identified the second Iron I village with the Israelites, thus dating the conquest of Ai to ca. 1125.

Bibliography. J. A. Callaway, "Ai," *NEAEHL,* 1:39-45.

LaMoine F. De Vries

AIAH (Heb. *ʾayyâ*)

1. The son of Zibeon and brother of Anah; one of the chiefs of the Horites (Gen. 36:24; 1 Chr. 1:40).

2. The father of Rizpah, Saul's concubine (2 Sam. 3:7). His two sons were given to the Gibeonites to compensate for Saul's evil dealings with them (2 Sam. 21:8-11).

AIATH (Heb. *ʿayyāṯ*)
Alternate form of Ai (Isa. 10:28).

AIJA (Heb. *ʿayyâ*)
A town in Judah resettled after the Exile (Neh. 11:31). It may be the same as Ayyah.

AIJALON (Heb. *ʾayyālôn*)

1. A levitical city located in the original tribal area of Dan (Josh. 19:42; 21:24). When the Danites were unable to expel the Amorites (Judg. 1:34-35), they left the Shephelah and moved to northern Palestine. Eventually, Aijalon was incorporated into the kingdom of Judah. Aijalon was one of the cities which Rehoboam fortified (2 Chr. 11:5-10). It was one of the cities taken by the Philistines in the 8th century B.C. (2 Chr. 28:16-18).

Edward Robinson identified Aijalon with modern Yâlō (152138), based on descriptions by Jerome and Eusebius. Later William F. Albright distinguished a second Aijalon at Tell Qoqa, just E of Yâlō, representing the fortress of Yâlō as well as earlier occupation. No excavations have been made at either site, but sherds as early as the Late Bronze Age have been found at both.

2. The burial place of Elon the judge, located in the territory of Zebulun (Judg. 12:12).

SCOTT M. LANGSTON

AIN (Heb. *ʿayin*)

1. A town on the eastern border of the Promised Land, W of Riblah (Num. 34:11) and N of the Sea of Chinnereth (Galilee). If the Hebrew ("spring") represents a place name, its location is uncertain. Proposed locations are Khirbet Dufneh (209292) or Khirbet ʿAyûn (212236).

2. A city in Judah, listed before Rimmon at Josh. 15:32; 1 Chr. 4:32; probably the same as En-rimmon (e.g., Josh. 19:7; Neh. 11:29).

3. A levitical city given to the descendants of Aaron (Josh. 21:16). It may be the same as **2** above.

AIN FESHKA
A brackish spring ca. 2 km. (1.3 mi.) W of the Dead Sea and 12 km. (7.5 mi.) S of Jericho. It was in nearby caves that the Dead Sea Scrolls were discovered.

AIN KAREM (Heb. *ʿân kerem*)
A village 8 km. (5 mi.) W of Jerusalem, known as the traditional home of Zechariah and Elizabeth and the birthplace of John the Baptist (cf. Luke 1:57-66). Consequently, Ain Karem ("spring of the vineyard") is also identified as the place where Mary visits her relative Elizabeth and where the birth of Jesus is foretold (cf. Luke 1:39-56).

ROBERT A. DERRENBACKER, JR.

ʿAJJUL, TELL EL-
A site (0934.0976) located 9 km. (6 mi.) SW of Gaza. The first major excavations were undertaken by Sir William Flinders Petrie between 1930 and 1934, who identified the site as ancient Gaza. William F. Albright thought the site was Beth-eglayim. Aharon Kempinski challenged that identification, believing it to be the Hyksos city of Sharuhen. The site has yielded three general city occupations, five "palace"/fortress phases, and numerous tomb groups.

Occupation first began on the site in the Early Bronze IV period with cemeteries to the east and west of the mound which yielded pottery. The "courtyard" cemetery was found within the courtyard of the palace, and predates the first building phase on the mound. All of these tombs fall into the Middle Bronze I period, with some yielding scarabs of Late Middle Kingdom date, documenting the Egyptian influence at the site.

A great fosse runs around three sides of the tell. It was not built up, like the typical MB glacis, but was cut out of the sandstone of the hill itself. The removed blocks were used as foundation material for the palace complex. A mudbrick wall was built along the fosse in a later period, but may rest on MB foundations.

Covering ca. 2000 sq. m. (2392 sq. yds.), Palace I was built in a square with side chambers around a central courtyard. Placed on top of some of the tombs in the courtyard cemetery, Palace I was founded in the MB II period, after 1780 B.C. This palace was contemporary with the first level of occupation in the city (City III). A rich tomb probably of a Hyksos noble contained horses and chariot remains. The ceramic data indicate that this level was destroyed in the 16th century.

Palace II was built on top of Palace I in a different style, and much smaller. Judging from the variety of Cypriot ceramic imports, the Palace II/City II phases may have lasted until 1400 or Late Bronze IB. Palace III is a very different building from the previous palace, built of "black brick" with very thick walls and probably two stories high. Albright considered it an Egyptian fortress on the Zile-Gaza Road. The final phase of Palace III and City I goes into the 14th century. Palace IV, slightly altered in size, probably dates to LB IIB (13th century). The "governor's tomb," a very rich burial at the foot of the tell, yielded a scarab of Ramses II and a massive seal ring of Tutankhamen, documenting an official Egyptian presence on the site. The final palace, Palace V, cannot be accurately dated but may date to the Early Iron Age.

ʿAjjul is one of the richest sites in Palestine, best known for the artistic quality of its smaller finds. Using cloisonne and granulation, the ʿAjjul jewelers created magnificent gold bracelets, earrings, torques, pendants, and hair ornaments. The goldwork is contemporary with the other great art medium, bichrome-ware pottery. Known as ʿAjjul painter ware, this ceramic or its influence reached as far afield as Cyprus, Cilicia, and North Syria and flourished for ca. 60-75 years from 1550 to the early 15th century. Possibly the most attractive pottery produced in Palestine, its designs featured geometric patterns, fish, and birds painted in red and black.

Bibliography. O. Tufnell and A. Kempenski, "ʿAjjul, Tell el-," *NEAEHL* 1:49-53.

Thomas W. Davis

AKAN (Heb. *ʿăqān*) (also JAAKAN)
One of the sons of Ezer the Horite, of the family of Esau (Gen. 36:27). At 1 Chr. 1:42 he is called Jaakan.

AKELDAMA (Gk. *Akeldamách*)
The place Judas purchased with the money he received for betraying Jesus (Acts 1:18-19). Judas later suffered a fatal fall on his property, his blood spilling out onto the field, thus the name "Field of Blood" (transliterated from Aram. *ḥăqēl dĕmaʾ*). This account is often harmonized with that in Matt. 27:3-10, which also mentions a "Field of Blood" concerning Judas. In Matthew's account, however, Judas hangs himself (Matt. 27:5), the "potter's field" is bought by the high priests after Judas' death (v. 7), and the "blood" in its name refers to the "innocent blood" of Jesus (vv. 4, 6, 8). The two accounts are probably best seen as independent variants of an aetiological legend; the two authors adapted their versions of the story in quite different ways. The traditional site of Akeldama is in the Hinnom Valley S of Jerusalem, an area associated with idolatry and child sacrifice in the OT (2 Kgs. 23:10; Jer. 7:30-34; 19:1-13).

Bibliography. P. Benoit, "The Death of Judas," in *Jesus and the Gospel,* 1 (New York, 1973): 189-207; J. Finegan, *The Archaeology of the New Testament,* rev. ed. (Princeton, 1992), 245-46.

Kim Paffenroth

AKHENATEN (Egyp. *ʾkh-n-ỉtn*)
Egyptian king of the 18th Dynasty noted primarily for his religious reforms. The second son of Amenhotep III and his great wife Tiye, Akhenaten came to the throne upon his father's sudden death and ruled for 17 years (1379-1362 B.C.). Akhenaten's principal wife was Nefertiti, who played a prominent role at the court. A lesser wife, Kiya, and six daughters also are known from reliefs.

Ascending the throne as Amenhotep (Amenophis) IV, the new king initially resided in Thebes, where his father reigned in his later years, and completed work on two pylons at Karnak begun by Amenhotep III. However, Akhenaten early evidenced a singular preference for a solar deity — the Aten — symbolized by a sun disk with hands extending downward. Akhenaten built four temples to the Aten at Thebes, one of which, the Gempaaten, served as a locale for an unusual *sed* festival in the king's third year. During this period Akhenaten systematically eliminated the names of traditional gods from reliefs and instituted a revolutionary art style to depict himself and the royal family. The king appears with a long neck and nose, a gaunt face, prominent breasts, and large buttocks. Whether these features realistically portray the king's features, perhaps indicating a genetic disorder, or whether the style was intended to set the king apart from normal human experience remains debated. But the Amarna style challenged the traditional Egyptian conventions of art.

Akhenaten moved his official residence in year 5 from Thebes to a site he personally selected to honor the Aten. The new capital, Akhetaten ("horizon which the sun disk has chosen") was replete with temples for the Aten, ceremonial and personal palaces for the king, quarters for artisans and workers, and tombs for high governmental officials. The king's tomb was prepared in a remote wadi E of the city. Today known as Tell el-Amarna, Akhetaten served as Egypt's capital for 12 years and has yielded a cache of royal correspondence written in Akkadian. The Amarna Letters provide vivid detail of the southern Levant in the 14th century.

The Amarna tombs contain the "Hymn to the Aten," a poetic piece extolling the Aten as creator and sustainer of the universe. Scholars have noted similarities between this hymn and Ps. 104. Akhenaten is closely linked to the Aten in the hymn, appearing as the earthly counterpart to the great sun disk — giver of life and provider of *maat.* Whether or not Akhenaten's sweeping innovations should be described as monotheism, henotheism, or some other term again is debatable. But Akhenaten's break with traditional Egyptian religion marked him as a heretic in later generations.

Bibliography. C. Aldred, *Akhenaten, King of Egypt* (New York, 1988); B. J. Kemp, *Ancient Egypt* (New York, 1989); D. B. Redford, *Akhenaten, The Heretic King* (Princeton, 1984). Thomas V. Brisco

AKHETATEN (Egyp. *ʾkht-ʾitn*)
The capital city of the revolutionary Pharaoh Akhenaten (Amenhotep IV, ca. 1363-1347 B.C.E.), modern Tell el-Amarna, 322 km. (200 mi.) S of Cairo on the east bank of the Nile.

See Amarna.

AKIBA
The leading teacher of the rabbinic tradition for the first three decades of the 2nd century C.E. In his zealous defense of Scripture, Akiba developed a hermeneutic in which every word, letter, and critical mark demanded interpretation. For Akiba there were no superfluous words, or even letters, in Scripture. This approach served as the operating methodology for much of the midrash that would follow in the rabbinic tradition. Akiba was also credited with having arranged the oral Torah in a systematic fashion based upon subject matter.

Akiba died a martyr's death. In 132 C.E. Simon bar Kokhba, whose followers projected onto him messianic expectations, led a revolt against Emperor Trajan and the Roman government. Akiba's support of Bar Kokhba and his refusal to abandon

the public teaching of the Torah led to his untimely death at the hands of the Roman government.
W. Dennis Tucker, Jr.

AKKAD
See Accad.

AKKADIAN
Often a general term for the dialects of the ancient Semitic language spoken in and around Mesopotamia and attested in documents from as early as ca. 2350 B.C.E. to the 1st century C.E. More precisely used, Akkadian designates the earliest historical phase of East Semitic which appears in texts from ca. 2350 until ca. 1950. This phase is referred to as Old Akkadian. The majority of these texts come from the dynasty founded by Sargon of Akkad.

Thereafter varied dialects of Akkadian may be distinguished. A northern dialect within Mesopotamia was at home in the land of Assyria. While language change does not occur in neatly demarcated periods, the development of Assyrian may be broadly traced as follows. Old Assyrian is attested from ca. 1950-1750, primarily in texts from the Assyrian merchant colonies in Anatolia. Middle Assyrian comes from ca. 1530-1000, and Neo-Assyrian from ca. 1000-612. During this latter period Assyrian was increasingly influenced by Aramaic because of the expansion of the Assyrian Empire. It was in this time that Assyria reached the height of its power and in the 8th century conquered the northern kingdom of Israel and led the people of the 10 northern tribes into captivity.

A southern dialect of Akkadian within Mesopotamia appears first as Old Babylonian from ca. 2000-1600, best known from the law collection of Hammurabi. Regional subdialects may be distinguished, and an elevated form of the language known as the hymnic-epic dialect became the medium for literary compositions. Following the Kassite invasion of Babylonia, Middle Babylonian (ca. 1600-1100) emerged and during the second half of the 2nd millennium became the lingua franca of international diplomacy in the ancient Near East. In the same period Standard Babylonian (Ger. *Jungbabylonisch*), resembling the older hymnic-epic dialect, became the literary language. Neo-Babylonian (ca. 1100-539), like Neo-Assyrian, reflects the growing linguistic influence of Aramaic, which during this period in turn replaced Akkadian in international diplomacy. It was the Neo-Babylonian Empire that conquered Judah in the 6th century while Nebuchadnezzar was king of Babylon. Late Babylonian (ca. 539 B.C.E.–75 C.E.) was increasingly aramaicized and represents the final attempt of the remaining priestly class to preserve their ancient traditions, as Aramaic and then Greek became the dominant means of communication.

Several introductory grammars, a standard descriptive grammar, three syllabaries, and two multivolume dictionaries are now available, or near completion, putting the study of Akkadian on a sound basis. It is, alongside Eblaite, one of the earliest attested Semitic languages and the most extensively documented of all languages of the ancient Near East.
Walter R. Bodine

AKKUB (Heb. *ʿaqqûḇ*)
1. A son of Elioenai of the royal line of David (1 Chr. 3:24).

2. The head of a levitical family of gatekeepers in the postexilic temple (1 Chr. 9:17; Ezra 2:42 = Neh. 7:45; 11:19; 12:25).

3. The chief of a family of postexilic temple servants (Ezra 2:45).

4. A Levite who expounded the words of the Law which Ezra read before the assembled people (Neh. 8:7).

AKRABATTENE (Gk. *Akrabattḗnē*)
A fortress on the border between Judah and Idumea, near the ascent of Akrabbim, where Judas Maccabeus defeated the Idumeans (1 Macc. 5:3).

AKRABBIM (Heb. *ʿaqrabbîm*)
A mountain pass ("Scorpion Pass") on the southern border of Canaan (Num. 34:4; Josh. 15:3; Judg. 1:36), which some scholars identify with Naqb eṣ-Ṣafā. In this region Judas Maccabeus defeated the Idumeans (1 Macc. 5:3).

ALABASTER
A firm, very fine-grained, variety of gypsum, used for statuary and as an indoor decorative stone, especially for carved ornamental vases and figures. It is translucent, and usually white, but may be shaded or tinted with other light-colored tones. The biblical terms translated alabaster (Heb. *šayiš*; Gk. *alábastron*) may also refer to marble, although alabaster probably entered Israel from Egypt much earlier than marble was imported from the Greek world. In 1 Chr. 29:2 David includes alabaster among the building materials he has gathered for the temple. The Song of Solomon uses a related term, *šēš*, when describing the bridegroom's legs as alabaster pillars or columns (Cant. 5:15). The Gospels relate the story of a woman who anoints Jesus' feet with a costly perfume, which is carried in an alabaster box or vial (Matt. 26:7; Mark 14:3; Luke 7:37).
Martha Jean Mugg Bailey

ALALAKH (Akk. *alalaḫ*)
Tell ʿAṭachana (ʿAṭšan), a mound in northwest Syria (in the modern Turkish province of Hatay) near the mouth of the Orontes River. It was first excavated in 1937 by British archaeologist Sir Leonard Woolley. Tablets discovered in the second season confirmed that the site was the ancient trading city of Alalakh, which flourished during the Middle and Late Bronze Ages (ca. 2400-1200 B.C.E.). Alalakh was at various times a vassal of Ebla, Ur III, Yamḫad, Mitanni, and Hatti. It was apparently destroyed by the Sea Peoples.

Seventeen levels of settlement were discovered during the eight seasons of excavation, with royal archives found in Levels IV and VII. The archives consisted of more than 500 clay tablets, mostly in

Akkadian. The majority of the tablets were lists (e.g., censuses, inventories, rations), but contracts and deeds were also found. The texts portray a stratified society, with 'Apiru included among the lower class. The large Hurrian sector of the population in stratum VII becomes the predominant group by stratum IV. In addition to the texts, a 104-line inscription on a statue of King Idrimi offers important historical information about the period.

Bibliography. D. J. Wiseman, *The Alalakh Tablets* (New York, 1953); C. L. Woolley, *Alalakh: An Account at Tell Atchana in the Hatay, 1937-1949* (Oxford, 1955). JAMES R. ADAIR

ALAMOTH (Heb. *'ălāmôṯ*)
An obscure term that likely refers to a name of a melody, or perhaps a musical instrument or cultic procedure (Ps. 46 superscription[MT 1]; 48:14[MT 15] with emendation; 1 Chr. 15:20; and possibly in the superscription to Ps. 9 [1]). Some relate it to *'almâ*, "young woman," and suggest it denotes singing in the style of a young girl, i.e., as a soprano. Most modern versions read "according to alamoth" (Ps. 46 NRSV, NIV; cf. NJPSV).

TYLER F. WILLIAMS

ALCIMUS (Gk. *Alkimos*)
A high priest in Jerusalem (161-159 B.C.E.), appointed by the Seleucid king Demetrius I Soter (1 Macc. 7; 2 Macc. 14). He had previously served as high priest (2 Macc. 14:3), evidence which supports the claim of Josephus that he initially was appointed by Antiochus V Eupator in 162 to succeed Menelaus (*Ant.* 12.385).

Alcimus is implicated in a plot that resulted in the death of 60 Hasideans (1 Macc. 7:12-16). The sources blame him for the atrocities of Nicanor, the Greek general commissioned to put down the Jewish revolt, and the subsequent campaigns of Bacchides (1 Macc. 9:1-53). The death of Alcimus is explained as punishment for his attempt to tear down the wall of the inner court of the sanctuary (1 Macc. 9:54-57). JOHN KAMPEN

ALEMA (Gk. *Alema*)
A town in Gilead, burned by Judas Maccabeus after having liberated its Jewish captives (1 Macc. 5:26, 35). The Greek preposition *en* in v. 35 suggests that Alema was a district in which the preceding five towns were located (NRSV "Maapha"). It may be the same as Helam.

ALEMETH (Heb. *'ālemeṯ*) **(PERSON)**

1. A son of Becher of the tribe of Benjamin (1 Chr. 7:8).

2. A descendant of Saul; son of Jehoaddag (1 Chr. 8:36) or Jarah (9:42).

ALEMETH (Heb. *'ālemeṯ*) **(PLACE)**
(also ALMON)
A city of refuge in the tribal territory of Benjamin (1 Chr. 6:60), also called Almon.

ALEPH
The first letter of the Hebrew alphabet, representing the glottal stop (transliterated '). The Hebrew character (א) designates Codex Sinaiticus, a 4th-century C.E. Greek manuscript of the Bible.

ALEXANDER (Gk. *Aléxandros*)

1. Alexander III of Macedon; son of Philip II of Macedon and Olympias. Alexander's triumphant march across the ancient Near East was the catalyst which resulted in the cultural synthesis called Hellenism.

Alexander was born in 356 B.C.E. and died 32 years later in 323 of exhaustion, war wounds, disease, and drunkenness, after marching his troops from Greece across Asia Minor, Palestine, Egypt, the Near East, Mesopotamia, and all the way to the Indus River. In doing so he conquered a larger geographic area than had ever before been dominated by a single personality. Along the way he revolutionized warfare, founded cities, and planted pockets of Greek culture destined to forever change the shape and self-understanding of the ancient world. Such accomplishments led to the epithet "the Great."

Alexander's early life appears to have been dominated by his mother, a strong woman with an ambition for her son which rivaled that of her husband. Philip II succeeded in exerting domination over the mountainous reaches of northern Greece, and having consolidated his position, extended his influence over the southern regions of the peninsula. It is hardly surprising that young Alexander inherited ambition, energy, and determination from two such strong-willed progenitors. Under the tutorial influence of Aristotle, from 342 to 340, Alexander drank deeply from the well of Greek culture and never lost his love for Homer's *Iliad*. He seems to have shared both with Aristotle and his father a vision of Greek domination of the world.

In 340 the 14-year-old Alexander served as his father's regent and commanded the left wing of the Macedonian army at the battle of Chaeronea. Following his father's assassination in 336, Alexander ascended the throne at age 20. After eliminating all potential rivals and consolidating his political alliances with his father's most important generals, Antipater and Parmenion, Alexander proceeded to exert his dominance over the rest of Greece. He quickly became the titular leader of the League of Corinth, established by his father in 337, and launched an all-out attack on the declining Persian Empire.

In 334 Alexander led a combined force of approximately 40 thousand troops across the narrow strip of water separating Greece from Asia Minor. In the battles of Granicus (334) and Issus (333) he routed the Persian army, led by King Darius himself. Alexander quickly marched his troops into Syria, southward across Palestine, conquering Egypt in 331. The teetering Persian Empire sought one last time to impede his advance, but was shattered forever at Gaugamela in 331. Having overcome the last significant impediment to his progress, Alexander and his army advanced swiftly across Mesopotamia, the remains of the Persian Empire, and on to the Indus River. There his exhausted troops refused to go farther, having been on the march for eight years, leaving Alexander's dream of conquering India unfulfilled. Upon his untimely death in 323, Alexander's empire was divided among his most powerful generals, resulting in the emergence of the Seleucid Empire in Syria and the rule of the Ptolemies in Egypt. Both of these dynastic successors to Alexander exerted significant influence upon the life, culture, and religious consciousness of Judaism in the 3rd and 2nd centuries B.C.E.

Alexander is mentioned explicitly in 1 Macc. 1:1-8; 6:2. More ambiguous references seem to be indicated in Dan. 7; 11:3-4. There is some debate regarding whether Zech. 9:1-8 refers to Alexander's conquest of Palestine. The Koran lists Alexander among the prophets who preceded Mohammed, and the Talmud refers to Alexander's treatment of the Jews during the siege of Tyre.

It is difficult to overestimate the influence of Alexander's career upon the ancient world. Among the more important contributions one might list: (1) The vision of a civilization dominating culture provided a model for the later western empire builders including Julius Caesar and the Roman emperors. It could be argued that Alexander was the first great conqueror produced by Europe; prior to his time the great military leaders were the product of the empires of Mesopotamia, Egypt, and Iran-Iraq. (2) The revolutionizing of the art of warfare. Alexander streamlined his armies and eliminated excessive baggage trains and noncombatants. He made extensive use of cavalry and kept his army mobile by leaving the wounded behind. They were ordered to remain where they were to found Greek-style settlements (*pólis*) and intermarry with the local population. The result was the planting of pockets of Greek culture across Palestine-Syria, the Egyptian Delta, the Arabian Peninsula, and Mesopotamia. (3) The spread of Greek language and culture across the ancient Near East. This linguistic innovation resulted in the emergence of Koine Greek as the *lingua franca* of the ancient world enabling communication, commerce, and the exchange of ideas. Koine was destined to become the language of the NT and early Christianity. (4) The founding of cities which would become great intellectual centers such as Alexandria in Egypt. It was in Alexandria that the OT would be translated into Greek (the LXX) by Jewish scholars there. (5) The breaking down of barriers between eastern and western cultures, resulting in the rise of Hellenism. Following Alexander's conquest the tendency toward syncretism in language, culture, religion, and political institutions greatly increased.

There also appears to have been a dark underside to the personality and character of Alexander. When Philip's assassination in 336 followed so suddenly upon his divorce of Olympias, some suspected that the young Alexander and his mother played a role in Philip's death. Ancient sources report that Olympias fostered Alexander's consciousness of a special relationship with the gods. Later he would claim descent from Heracles and to be the son of Zeus-Ammon. His contact with the Persian culture led to a growing orientalism in his behavior. He seems to have been particularly attracted to the Persian practice of *proskynēsis* or prostration before the divine ruler. Some have suspected that only Alexander's death kept him from declaring his own divinity. The last years saw him living a life of debauchery which contributed indirectly, if not directly, to his death. D. Larry Gregg

2. Alexander Balas of Smyrna. Claiming to be the son of the Seleucid ruler Antiochus IV Epiphanes, he challenged the rule of Demetrius I, who himself had seized the throne from Antiochus V in 162 B.C.E. His claim is accepted by Maccabees (1 Macc. 10:1) and Josephus (*Ant.* 13.2.1 [35]), but doubted by other ancient authorities and most modern scholars. Balas was supported by powerful enemies of Demetrius I, including Ptolemy VI Philometor of Egypt; even the Roman senate approved his claim (Polybius *Hist.* 33.18).

Seeking allies against Balas' threat, Demetrius sought to win over his former enemy Jonathan Maccabeus. Balas, however, outbid Demetrius by offering Jonathan the office of high priest of the Jews together with other royal honors. Balas eventually defeated and killed Demetrius (150) and married the daughter of Ptolemy. He proved to be an unpopular and weak ruler, however, and was soon challenged by Demetrius' son (later Demetrius II). Although supported by Jonathan, Balas was decisively defeated outside Antioch in 145 by the combined forces of Demetrius and Ptolemy, who had turned against his former son-in-law. Balas fled to Arabia, only to be murdered by assassins there.

3. Alexander Janneus, Hasmonean king and high priest of Judea (103-76), successor to his brother Aristobulus. Janneus' reign was marked by continuous warfare. He aggressively expanded his kingdom by attacking the Idumeans, the Greek coastal cities, and Transjordan.

Janneus' internal enemies considered him unworthy of the high priesthood. When a crowd pelted him with citrons while he officiated at the Feast of Tabernacles, Janneus responded by massacring 6000 people. Open rebellion broke out in 94 B.C.E.; during the ensuing six-year civil war 50 thousand Jews were killed. Janneus' opponents appealed to the Seleucid Demetrius III to intervene; he initially defeated Janneus, but was eventually driven out. In revenge, Janneus crucified 800 opponents, feasting with his concubines while the opponents' wives and children were killed before their eyes (Josephus *Ant.* 13.13.5–14.2 [372-80]; *BJ* 1.4.4-6 [90-98]). The Qumran pesher on Nahum alludes to these events, calling Janneus "the angry lion" who "hanged living men from the tree." Scholarly claims that the Pharisees led opposition to Janneus and theories that some opponents formed part of the Qumran community are controversial. Janneus' excessive drinking helped lead to his death in 76 B.C.E.

4. A son of Simon of Cyrene and brother of Rufus (Mark 15:21). Mark apparently assumes that the two sons are known to his readers; the references are omitted in Matthew and Luke. A 1st-century C.E. ossuary inscription from a tomb in the Kidron Valley, possibly owned by a Cyrenian family, reads "Alexander, son of Simon"; though intriguing, it cannot be positively linked with Mark's Alexander.

5. A member of the high priestly family who questioned Peter and John after their arrest (Acts 4:6).

6. A Jew of Ephesus who attempted unsuccessfully to speak to an unruly crowd gathered to protest Paul's preaching (Acts 19:33-34).

7. One who, with Hymenaeus, "shipwrecked" his faith and was "turned over to Satan" (1 Tim. 1:19-20). Perhaps the same Hymenaeus claimed that the resurrection was already past (2 Tim. 2:17-18); Alexander may have taught this as well.

8. A coppersmith who "did great harm" to the author of 2 Timothy and opposed his teaching (2 Tim. 4:14-15). He may be the same Alexander mentioned in 1 Tim. 1:19-20.

See HEROD (Family) 7.

Bibliography. N. Avigad, "A Depository of Inscribed Ossuaries in the Kidron Valley," *IEJ* 12 (1962): 1-12; L. L. Grabbe, *Judaism from Cyrus to Hadrian,* 1: *The Persian and Greek Periods* (Minneapolis, 1992); E. Schürer, *The History of the Jewish People in the Age of Jesus Christ (175 B.C.–A.D. 135),* rev. ed., 1 (Edinburgh, 1973). MARTIN ALBL

ALEXANDRA (Gk. *Aléxandra*)

1. Alexandra Salome, Hasmonean queen of Judea (76-67 B.C.E.), also known in Hebrew as Shelamzion (or Salome, a Greek diminutive of the Hebrew). The wife of Alexander Janneus (103-76), she may also have been the widow of Judah Aristobulus I (104-3), though this is uncertain (compare Josephus *Ant.* 13.320 with *BJ* 1.85); if so, her marriage to Janneus may have been a levirate marriage. Nothing is known of her family. She appointed her elder son, Hyrcanus II, as high priest (*Ant.* 20.242; 15.179); he acted as regent during her illness, though her younger son, Aristobulus II, seized the opportunity to consolidate his position. Alexandra's reign, remembered for her piety in the rabbinic literature in glowing terms (*Lev.Rab.* 35.10; *b. Taʿan.* 23a; *Sipra* 110b), was characterized by the ascendancy of the Pharisees (*BJ* 1.108-114; *Ant.* 13.408-415). Josephus evaluates her reign in two contradictory ways: in *Ant.* 13.430-32 she is power-hungry, absolutist, and responsible for the rivalry between Hyrcanus and Aristobulus; in *BJ* she is kind, intensely religious, a skilled administrator, though under the domination of Pharisees. She strengthened Judea and kept it at peace, unlike the reigns of her husband and her sons. Apparently she is mentioned — alongside Hyrcanus and Aemilius Scaurus — in several Dead Sea calendrical fragments (4Q322, 323, 324a, b).

2. Alexandra, daughter of Hyrcanus II and mother of Mariamme I (wife of Herod); friend of Cleopatra VII of Egypt (*Ant.* 15.42, 62-63). Much of the dissension in Herod's household swirled around her. She pressured Herod to appoint her son as high priest, though he was extremely young for the position, and was devastated by his early death. When she schemed to gain control of Judea during Herod's illness, following his execution of Mariamme (29 B.C.E.), Herod executed her (ca. 28; *Ant.* 15.247-252).

3. Alexandra, daughter of Aristobulus and granddaughter of Mariamme I, married first to Philippion of Chalcis, who was murdered by his father Ptolemy Mennaeus of Chalcis, so that the latter could marry Alexandra (*BJ* 1.85-86; *Ant.* 14.126).

4. Alexandra, daughter of Phasael and Salampsio, granddaughter of Herod and Mariamme I, married to Timius of Cyprus and childless (*Ant.* 18.131).

Bibliography. P. Richardson, *Herod, King of the Jews and Friend of the Romans* (Columbia, S.C., 1996), 74-78; M. O. Wise, *Thunder in Gemini* (Sheffield, 1994) ch. 5. PETER RICHARDSON

ALEXANDRIA (Gk. *Alexandria*)

A seaport on the Mediterranean Sea, in the Western Delta at the mouth of a branch of the Nile River. The site is ca. 210 km. (130 mi.) N of Cairo, set on a slight elevation between Lake Mareotis on the south and the Sea on the north and west. This location was selected by Alexander the Great himself, who gave instructions to Cleomenes of Naukratis to arrange the finances and construction, while Deinocrates of Rhodes was commissioned to create a city plan. On 7 April 311 B.C.E. Alexandria was founded and Ceomenes became its first governor. Of all the cities and monuments built by Alexander or in his name, this proved to be the most durable and productive.

Alexandria has always been particularly well situated for sea-going commerce, featuring a peninsula known since Greco-Roman times as Cape Lochias which with the mainland shoreline forms a large bay and harbor protected by the island of Pharos. Here stood the Pharos lighthouse, one of the seven wonders of the ancient world (cf. Strabo *Geog.* 17). Since Greco-Roman times the site has sunk 4 m. (13 ft.) in elevation, modifying the shoreline and submerging many features of the ancient city, including the harbor itself, and parts of the Jewish quarter and the palaces of the nobility.

When Alexander died in 323, Ptolemy I Soter, one of his three senior military commanders, took over the southeastern part of the empire, establishing a family dynasty which ruled Egypt from Alexandria until 80 B.C.E. Under the Ptolemies Alexandria flourished as the capital of Egypt and as an intellectual, political, and economic center. As such it became the cultural and educational heart of the Hellenistic world.

In 306 B.C.E. Ptolemy established the library of Alexandria in honor of Alexander, whose body he had brought from Babylon and buried in his capital. The library achieved great fame under such librarians, research scholars, and scientists as Demetrios of Phaleron (235-283), Zenodotus of Ephesus (325-260), Apollonius of Rhodes (305-240), Callimachus of Cyrene (305-ca. 235), and Eratosthenes of Cyrene (275-195). It was actually a university center for research, teaching, and writing in science, the arts, literature, history, linguistics, and the humanities in general. The scholars and the acquisition of every possible book in the world were supported by generous stipends or allocations from the royal treasury. Demetrios collected 250 thousand books, and by the time of Julius Caesar's visit the library could boast more than 1 million volumes, in addition to a large collection of archaeological and historical artifacts and scientific instruments.

The philosophy and science for which the library has been famous since its founding was Aristotelian rational empiricism. Ca. 100-150 C.E. the stability of the Mediterranean world was greatly disturbed by the expansion of the Roman Empire, and the speculative idealism of Platonism gained influence. Religious and transcendental philosophy was in the ascendancy, mystery religions flourished, and the great research center of Alexandria shifted from the natural and social sciences toward religious speculation. Middle Platonism came to dominate Hellenistic culture. Philo Judaeus (30 B.C.E.–50 C.E.) became the most remembered scholar in Alexandria at the time of Christ. Two centuries later Neo-Platonism competed with Christian speculative theology for dominance. Plotinus (203-ca. 270), Porphyry (ca. 234-305), Olympius (350-391), and Hypatia (350-415) are prominent Neo-Platonists. The Christian perspective was represented by the Catechetical School of Clement (150-215) and Origen (185-253) and by such prelates as Theophilus (ca. 350-435) and Cyril (ca. 375-444).

Alexandria is thought to have played an important role in the rise of Christianity, influenced by the Apostle Mark, for whom the central cathedral is named. The speculative allegorical theology of the Alexandrian theologians proved to be the definitive influence that shaped orthodox Christian doctrine in the Ecumenical Councils from Nicea (325) to Chalcedon (451). After Chalcedon secular or pagan Neo-Platonism declined, and Alexandrian Christianity absorbed its essential tenets to create the Alexandrian school of Christian Neo-Platonism, an important influence on Western civilization.

In 47 B.C.E. Julius Caesar fought a naval battle in the bay at Alexandria, during which some 50 thousand volumes from the library were destroyed in a warehouse fire. In 391 C.E. Theophilus destroyed the pagan cohorts of Olympius and another who were barricaded in the public extension library in the Serapeum, destroying the pagans and another 50 thousand volumes. During the Arab conquest the city and the library were sacked in 641-642.

Philo's prominence in Alexandria at the time of Christ symbolizes the significance of the Jewish community in the life of the city. Alexander is reported to have settled a large number of Jews there at the outset. The translation of the Hebrew Bible into Greek, the LXX, was completed there sometime between 150 and 50 B.C.E. Philo says the community had grown to one million by his time. A number of repressions by Imperial Rome and subsequently by the Christian archbishops reduced the community to virtual extinction by 150 B.C.E. It resurged by the 4th century but was eliminated by Cyril of Alexandria in 415, the same year in which he had the pagan philosopher Hypatia murdered.

Bibliography. J. H. Ellens, *The Ancient Library of Alexandria and Early Christian Theological Development.* Occasional Paper 27 (Claremont, 1993-95); B. A. Pearson, "Earliest Christianity in Egypt," in *The Roots of Egyptian Christianity,* ed. Pearson and J. E. Goehring. Studies in Antiquity and Christianity 1 (Philadelphia, 1986), 132-59.

J. HAROLD ELLENS

ALGUM, ALMUG

Algum (Heb. *'algûmîm;* 2 Chr. 2:8; 9:10-11) and almug (*'almuggîm;* 1 Kgs. 10:11-12) are considered to be the same wood, red saunders or red sandalwood (*Pterocarpus santolinus* L. f.). Red sandalwood is heavy, hard, and close-grained and would have been suitable for the supports and instruments Solomon had made from algum. It also carries a pleasant scent.

Red sandalwood is native to India and East Asia, one of many possible locations for Ophir. Though 2 Chr. 2:8 reports that Solomon requested algum from Lebanon, 9:10-11 says that it was brought from Ophir. MEGAN BISHOP MOORE

ALIAH (Heb. *'alyâ*)

An Edomite tribal chief (1 Chr. 1:51).

See ALVAH.

ALIAN (Heb. *'alyān*)

A son or clan of Seir (1 Chr. 1:40).

See ALVAN.

ALIEN

See SOJOURNER.

ALLAMMELECH (Heb. *'alammelek̲*)

A town in the territory of Asher (Josh. 19:26). Although the site has not been identified, the name is preserved in that of Wadi el-Melek, which drains into the brook Kishon near Mt. Carmel.

ALLEGORY

A narrative which uses symbolic figures and actions to suggest hidden meanings behind the literal words of the text. It is similar to riddle and parable genres, which use figurative language and images to convey a truth hidden behind the literal meaning of the words. The word "allegory" originated in the Greek world and was used most frequently by authors who wished to retain the truths of traditional worldviews when ancient traditions were being challenged by new knowledge. The Homeric stories of the gods were interpreted allegorically by later

Greeks who wished to "demythologize" the tales of the capricious and immoral deities of Olympus and make them more intellectually meaningful and ethically acceptable to a people whose worldview was becoming more scientific and sophisticated. The word "allegory" itself was first used in Hellenistic times by Stoics and Cynics seeking to counter the attacks on the Olympian pantheon which had been made by Xenophanes, Pythagoras, and Plato.

In Hellenistic Judaism ca. the middle of the 2nd century B.C.E. Aristobulus of Alexandria used an allegorical interpretation of the OT extensively as he sought to reconcile the Hebrew Scriptures with Greek culture. Philo of Alexandria became the Jewish theologian who used the allegorical interpretation the most extensively and was able to maintain a balance between the allegorical and literal reading of the Law. An allegorical interpretation of the OT was employed in Palestinian Judaism, although their concerns, unlike the allegorists of Alexandria, were not so much with questions of cosmology and psychology. The allegorical interpretation of the Song of Solomon by the scribes in Palestine allowed this extraordinary work to be accepted and later added to the canon.

OT Scripture is not treated allegorically in an extensive way in the Synoptic Gospels or in John, although some biblical scholars consider the interpretation of the parable of the sower (Mark 4:13-20) an allegorization of the parable by the early Church or possibly by Jesus himself. Some find an allegorical interpretation of the parable of the tares (Matt. 13:36-43) and the parable of the seine-net (vv. 47-50).

Paul also uses allegory in 1 Cor. 5:6-8 in addressing the problem of church discipline in the matter of morality, with the leaven of the Exodus tradition representing malice and evil; Christ is designated "our paschal lamb." In 1 Cor. 9:3-10 the muzzled ox treading out grain (Deut. 25:4) represents the "thresher" of the Church who hopes for a "share in the crop." In 1 Cor. 10:1-11 baptism and the celebration of the Lord's Supper are compared to the Exodus and wilderness experiences of the Israelites, "written down to instruct us, on whom the ends of the ages have come" (v. 11).

In Gal. 4:21-31 Paul allegorizes the stories about Hagar and Sarah to show that those who depend on the law instead of faith in the promise of God will lose their inheritance. Paul's use of allegory is similar to that of Philo of Alexandria but closer to the interpretation followed by Palestinian Jews. In relating the Hebrew Scriptures to his times and experiences he prefers to use fulfillment exegesis, being convinced that the Christ event now enables believers to see the true meaning of the Scripture.

In the writings of the early church fathers (e.g., Justin Martyr, Clement, Origen, Irenaeus, Tertullian) the allegorical interpretation of Scripture became very common.

Bibliography. F. Büchsel, "allēgoréō," *TDNT* 2:260-63; J. Jeremias, *The Parables of Jesus*, 3rd ed. (London, 1972). WILLIAM R. GOODMAN, JR.

ALLON (Heb. *'allôn*)
A Simeonite, the son of Jedaiah and a descendant of Shemaiah (1 Chr. 4:37).

ALLON-BACUTH (Heb. *'allôn bāḵûṯ*)
The place (lit., "oak of weeping") near Bethel where Deborah the nurse of Rebekah was buried (Gen. 35:8). This site could be the same as the "palm tree of Deborah" where the prophetess/judge later judged Israel (Judg. 4:5). WILLARD W. WINTER

ALMIGHTY
An epithet of God (Heb. *šadday*), derived from the patriarchal deity El Shaddai (cf. LXX Gk. *pantokrátōr*). The name is similar in meaning to epithets of the Amorite Amurru *(bēl šadē)*, Canaanite Hadad *(ba'al ṣapōn)*, and Hurrian El *('il paban-ḫi-wi-ni)* and may have been associated with theophanies of Yahweh in mountain storms (e.g., Exod. 19:16-19). The name occurs in both early and archaizing poetry (e.g., Num. 24:4, 16; Ps. 68:14[MT 15]; 91:1), in passages ascribed to the Priestly source (e.g., Exod. 6:2-3), and in Ezekiel (Ezek. 1:24) and the dialogue portions of Job (31 times).

ALMODAD (Heb. *'almôḏāḏ*)
The first of the 13 sons of Joktan; the grandson of Eber. He was the ancestor of a South Arabian tribe (Gen. 10:26; 1 Chr. 1:20).

ALMON (Heb. *'almôn*) (also ALEMETH)
A city from the tribe of Benjamin (Josh. 21:18) given to the descendants of the priest Aaron as one of the 48 levitical cities (cf. Josh. 21:1-42; 1 Chr. 6:54-81). The variant Alemeth appears in 1 Chr. 6:60(MT 45). Almon is probably identified with modern Khirbet 'Almît (176136), located 8 km. (5 mi.) NE of Jerusalem. JOHN R. SPENCER

ALMOND
The almond tree, *Amygdalus communis* L., derives its Hebrew name *(šāqēḏ)* from the verb "to wake" or "to watch." In a play on words, the Lord shows Jeremiah an almond branch as a sign that he is watching and about to act (Jer. 1:11).

Three species of almond tree are found in Palestine; two wild species, *Prunus amygdalus* and *Amygdalus communis*, have bitter and inedible fruit, while the third, domesticated species, *Prunus dulcis*, has an edible nut and produces a mild almond oil. The almond tree bears light pink blossoms in February (cf. Eccl. 12:5, which compares them to the white hair of old age). Golden, almond-blossom-shaped cups adorned the lampstand in the tabernacle (Exod. 25:33-34; 37:19-20), and Aaron's staff sprouted almond blossoms and nuts, designating him as head of the priestly lineage (Num. 17:8[MT 23]). Almond nuts were among the delicacies Jacob sent to Joseph in Egypt (Gen. 43:11). Heb. *lûz* also refers to the almond tree (Gen. 30:37), and is the former name of Bethel.

MEGAN BISHOP MOORE/RANDALL W. YOUNKER

ALMON-DIBLATHAIM
(Heb. *ʿalmōn diḇlāṯayim*)
One of Israel's encampments during the wilderness wanderings (Num. 33:46, 47). It is also mentioned on the stela of King Mesha of Moab (line 30), who revolted against Israelite rule in the 9th century B.C.E. The site was evidently still in Moabite hands in the 6th century (Jer. 48:22; called Beth-diblathaim, "House of the Two Fig Cakes"). Its location is unknown, although it may be identified with Deleilât esh-Sherqîyeh (228116) or Deleilât el-Gharbiyeh. ROBERT DELSNYDER

ALMS
Gifts to the poor. Almsgiving is a pervasive part of the biblical tradition and is practiced to maintain community harmony. In the OT, caring for the poor is associated with living a just life, and kindness to the poor is viewed as the basis for a happy life (Prov. 14:21). Isaiah emphasizes giving to the poor as a prerequisite for hearing the voice of GDDDdod. Almsgiving must involve facing the poor with whom one lives, and sharing one's food and one's home; it is not simply the giving of financial resources. Care for the poor must also include the three-year tithing of the produce of the land (Deut. 14:28-29) and the leaving behind of grain in the field (24:19-22).

Almsgiving is not to be performed for public praise and self-exaltation; it is to be known only by God (Matt. 6:1-4). Caring for the poor is part of the criteria for finally judging whether one has lived a righteous life (Matt. 25:31-46). As recorded in Acts 6; 2 Cor. 8–9, the early Church was deeply concerned about the welfare of the poor.
HEMCHAND GOSSAI

ALMUG
See ALGUM, ALMUG.

ALOES
Succulents of the Liliaceae family. Aloes are identified primarily with subtropical assemblages of the Eritreo-Sudanian province to be found in East Africa and extending into Southern Arabia. A solitary plant, it is stemless with a distinctive rosette pattern of thick leaves. It is an African genus with more than 180 species, 20 species of which are to be found in Arabia. In Omani Dhofar only two species are commonly attested. *Aloe Dhufarensis* is a well-known medicinal plant used for a variety of ailments. These are treated primarily from the dried aloe juice. Four major species are known from Yemen; again although used for medicinal purposes, some have an aromatic purpose. *Aloe Barbadensis* has been scientifically analyzed and found to contain an antibiotic (barbaloin) active in fighting tuberculosis. *Aloe Barbadensis* has been equated with the widespread *Aloe Vera.*

In the biblical context (Cant. 4:14; Prov. 7:17) the alternating use of male or female plural endings for the plant suggests a nonfamiliarity with the product, and its inclusion with myrrh and frankincense and cinnamon suggests an exotic foreign product. Aloes are also mentioned in the NT (John 19:39) in connection with the burial rites of Christ. The aloe plants mentioned by Classical sources are clearly identified with southwest Arabia, prominently with the island of Socotra. Special fields in the region were constructed to grow dragon's blood, frankincense, myrrh, and aloes.

Bibliography. S. A. Ghazanfar, *Handbook of Arabian Medicinal Plants* (Boca Raton, 1994); A. G. Miller and M. Morris, *Plants of Dhofar* (Muscat, 1988). JURIS ZARINS

ALPHA AND OMEGA
The first and last characters of the Greek alphabet. The statement "I am the alpha and omega" is attributed to God (Rev. 1:8; 21:6) and to Jesus (22:13), explained as "the beginning and the end" (21:6; 22:13) and "the first and the last" (1:17; 2:8; 22:13). Likely all three phrases allude to Isa. 44:6; 48:12, where Yahweh asserts his eternal transcendent greatness. "The alpha and the omega" designate Jesus Christ as the creator and the climax of the universe (cf. Rom. 11:36; Eph. 1:10).

Bibliography. A. König, *The Eclipse of Christ in Eschatology* (Grand Rapids, 1989), 23-31.
A. B. CANEDAY

ALPHABET
See WRITING.

ALPHAEUS (Gk. *Halphaíos*)
1. The father of the Apostle James (Matt. 10:3; Mark 3:18; Luke 6:15; Acts 1:13). He is probably the same person as Clopas, the husband of Mary and father of James and Joseph (John 19:25; cf. Matt. 27:56; Mark 15:40), although this identification rests more on tradition than on any actual evidence.
2. The father of Levi the tax collector (Mark 2:14; cf. Matt. 9:9).

ALTAR

Biblical Evidence

Heb. *mizbēaḥ*, "altar," is derived from the root *zbḥ*, "slaughter." Interestingly, one thing which seems *not* to have been done on biblical altars was slaughtering. When animals were offered, their visceral and messy slaughter took place near, but not upon, altars. The altars upon which substantive offerings were made commonly stood in temple courtyards, and it was the courtyard itself which provided the venue for animal slaughter.

In the ancient Near Eastern world at large, the preparation and offering of food to the gods had much to do with the concept of deities as suprahuman beings with human bodily needs. Food and drink were offered to keep them content and thus positively disposed toward their worshippers. Worship at the Israelite altar, deriving as it did from Canaanite precedents, surely included that traditional sense of attending to the needs of the Divine. More significant, however, was the Israelite under-

Four-horned altar from Beer-sheba, reconstructed. The stones were reused in walls of the Iron II storehouse, perhaps following Hezekiah's cultic reform (Phoenix Data Systems, Neal and Joel Bierling)

standing that the altar was a place at which one could invoke — and encounter — God.

For early Israel, altars were often associated with spontaneous worship. When the flood waters receded, Noah built an altar for animal offering, and the soothing odor of the burnt offering appeased Yahweh (Gen. 8:20-21). Abraham, Isaac, and Jacob constructed altars to mark places at which Yahweh appeared to them (Gen. 12:7; 22:9-13; 35:1, 7) and to assist in invoking their God (Gen. 12:8; 13:4; 26:25). This practice continued into the period of the judges (Gideon, Judg. 6:24). Jacob and Moses built altars as part of the place-naming ceremonies, thereby consecrating places of unusual importance (Gen. 33:20; 35:7; Exod. 17:15-16). These many forms of altar construction seem appropriate, in the absence of a centralized sanctuary with a permanent altar.

In the wilderness, Israel was given specific instruction about altar construction (Exod. 20:24-26; Deut. 27:5-7). While elsewhere in the ancient Near East an altar might have stood before a statue of a god, for Israel all statues of gods were proscribed (Exod. 20:23). Altars for animal offerings could be made of earth (Exod. 20:24) or unhewn stones (v. 25) and, to preserve modesty, could not include steps (v. 26). These simple altars, undoubtedly the same type made by Israel's patriarchs, were used in rituals invoking Yahweh's name and blessing (Exod. 20:24).

In combination with sacred pillars *(maṣṣēḇâ),* altars were places of covenant-making between Israel and God (Exod. 24:4-8; Josh. 8:30-35) or among Israelite tribes (Josh. 22:26-29). At Mt. Ebal, Joshua built an unhewn stone altar as part of a covenant ceremony binding the 12 tribes and Yahweh (Josh. 8:30-31). During the period of the judges and pre-temple monarchy, altars provided a venue from which to rule (Samuel, 1 Sam. 7:17) and a means of protecting Israel from sin (Saul, 1 Sam. 14:31-35) or undeserved punishment (David, 2 Sam. 24:10-25).

Additionally, altars were places of refuge, providing sanctuary to the fearful or falsely accused (1 Kgs. 1:50-53). Those justly accused could not be saved by clinging to the altar (Exod. 21:14; 1 Kgs. 2:28-34), nor could they swear falsely by them (1 Kgs. 8:31-32).

Descriptions of the portable tabernacle altar used by Israelites during their wilderness wanderings indicate a complicated and carefully crafted object, the construction (Exod. 27:1-8; 37:25–38:7) and use (29:10-26, 36-42; Lev. 1–7) of which was subject to detailed regulation. Through proper observance of the priestly rules, holiness would be attained and Yahweh would dwell among the people of Israel (Exod. 29:37, 42-46). Here, too, regulations concerning modesty prevailed (Exod. 28:42-43). The priestly altar was used not only for animal offerings, but for grain offerings (Lev. 14:20; Num. 5:25) and blood rituals (Exod. 24:6; 29:12; Lev. 1:11; 4:18, 34; 5:9).

The late composition of this Priestly material clarifies the sharp dichotomy between the simple stone altars of the pre-Mosaic period and of the era of the Conquest and judges, and the unusually ornate styling of the tabernacle altar. The authors of the Priestly text may have imagined such ritual objects being carried through the wilderness, but the witness of archaeology and of texts written closer to the era in question (non-Priestly passages in the Torah and Writings) demonstrates that this was not the case.

Rather, it was not until the monarchical period that ornate religious objects were incorporated into Israelite worship. The impulse toward elaboration seems to have come from the Solomonic desire for the trappings of royalty, including a magnificent temple-palace complex. Because of a lack of natural resources and of Israelite workers competent to build the requisite buildings and craft the desired objects, Solomon relied upon Phoenician materials and craftsmen (1 Kgs. 5:1-11[MT 15-25]; 7:13-14).

As part of this grand design, Solomon ordered the construction and installation of a cedar altar overlaid with gold, to be placed by the inner shrine *(dĕḇîr)* of the newly constructed Jerusalem temple (1 Kgs. 6:20-22). It may have been this same altar before which Solomon made his prayer to God for Israel (1 Kgs. 8:22, 54). However, the much larger bronze altar upon which Solomon and the subsequent kings of Judah publicly sacrificed was situated out-of-doors (1 Kgs. 8:62-64).

Some two centuries later, a second outdoor altar was added to the temple. Ahaz ordered a new one, with steps, built in the fashion of the Assyrian-style altar in Damascus. It was used for priests' offerings. The bronze altar from Solomon's time was displaced from its original position, and was now used exclusively by the king (2 Kgs. 16:10-15).

Despite the biblical vision of cultic centralization subsequent to the construction of the Jerusalem temple, both textual and archaeological evidence support the popularity of altars in alternate locations. Eventually they become the symbol of Israelite wrongdoing and of the trespasses of the kings (Manasseh, 2 Kgs. 21:3-5; Josianic reforms, 23:12). As part of his effort to legitimize worship in the northern nation of Israel, Jeroboam constructed an altar at Bethel (1 Kgs. 12:32-33). This altar was later condemned as non-Yahwistic (2 Kgs. 23:15; Amos 3:14), but overall the legitimacy of multiple altars to Yahweh during the monarchical period is clear (1 Kgs. 18:30-39; 19:10, 14).

Altars were part of the legitimate religious praxis of non-Israelites as well (Balaam, Num. 23:28-30; the prophets of Baal, 1 Kgs. 18:25-27). For the prophets and Deuteronomists, they were part of the Canaanite cultic assemblage (together with sacred pillars [*maṣṣēḇâ*] and poles [*'ăšērâ*] which had to be eradicated from the Israelite midst (Exod. 34:13; Deut. 7:5; 12:3; Judg. 2:2; 6:25-32; 1 Kgs. 16:32; 18:26; 2 Kgs. 11:18).

Prophetic descriptions of altars reflect the social milieu in which they developed. Some share the above-mentioned perspective on altars, depicting nontemple altars as places of Israelite transgression (Jer. 11:12-13; 17:1-3; Hos. 4:19; 8:11; Amos 2:8). Ezekiel's priestly vision of the restored temple includes an elaborate altar, overseen by the Zadokite priesthood. Regulations for offerings there are detailed (Ezek. 40:46-47; 43:13-27).

Archaeological Evidence

The Canaanite tradition of making offerings on stone altars dates back at least to the Chalcolithic period sanctuary at En-gedi.

The Megiddo sacred area contained a series of Early Bronze Age altars, beginning with EB I. From EB III, the circular altar 4017, constructed of unhewn stones, 8 m. (26 ft.) in diameter and 1.4 m. (4.6 ft.) high, was mounted by seven steps and surrounded by a temenos wall. Animal bones and broken pieces of pottery lay around it. Somewhat later, temples 4040, 5269 and 5192 were built nearby, and included plastered mudbrick altars on their rear walls.

At Middle Bronze II Shechem a plastered stone altar stood against the rear wall of temple 7300, surrounded by pottery and animal bones. Elsewhere on the site, a series of brick altars, measuring nearly 4 m. (13 ft.) sq. was found in the courtyard of the MB IIC fortress temple 1B. In the LB IIB fortress temple 2, a hewn stone altar 5.2 m. (17 ft.) long lay over its remains.

At Hazor the inner courtyard of the Late Bronze I temple H contained a large rectangular platform and two smaller stone altars, as well as ashes and animal bones. From LB II, several nicely carved stone altars were found within the temple's inner shrine. At the same time, a huge stone altar stood in Area F, an open-air cultic place. Carved into its surface were two depressions linked by a narrow channel, which led into the nearby drainage system.

Throughout the Late Bronze Age, a plaster-covered stepped altar was located along the back wall of the Tel Mevorakh sanctuary (1441.2156). Numerous offerings were found on and near it. Similar altars, with artifacts on and around them and ashes and animal bones in their vicinity, were found in the contemporary Lachish fosse temples.

An Early Iron Age altar made of a single large rectangular stone was found within an enclosure at the Bull site, a hilltop in biblical Manasseh. In front of it, offerings lay on a surface of flat-lying stones.

Two sanctuaries were part of Solomonic-era Megiddo. A large horned altar stood in the courtyard of the building 2081 sanctuary. Smaller stone offering stands and altars, horned and otherwise, were also part of its cultic assemblage. Similar stone offering tables and altars, surrounded by ashes and animal bones, once stood at several locations in the building 338 sanctuary. If a large altar once stood in its courtyard, it has long since disappeared.

The Dan sacred precinct in Area T was constructed by Jeroboam I in the late 10th century B.C.E. An interior courtyard contained a 7.5 × 5 m. (24.5 × 16.5 ft.) altar constructed of basalt boulders covered by large travertine blocks. Cultic objects lay on the cobbled pavement surrounding the altar. The once-destroyed Dan sacred precinct was restored during the 8th-century rule of Jeroboam II. A beautifully constructed altar reached by staircases on two sides was surrounded by a large enclosure wall. A horn from a stone altar which originally stood 3 m. (10 ft.) high was found nearby, as was a smaller four-horned altar. A 1.03 m. (3.3 ft.) sq. limestone altar was uncovered in one small room. Shovels, a scoop, and ashes containing animal bones lay nearby, and two small stone altars stood near one wall.

Large stone altars were found at Divided Monarchy Arad and Beer-sheba. At Beer-sheba the 1.5 m. (5 ft.) sq. altar had been dismantled, its blocks reused, and so its original setting is unknown. It resembles the courtyard altars from Dan and Megiddo, as well as the smaller incense altars which became increasingly popular in this period. At the Judean fortress at Arad, a large square altar of unhewn stones stood in the sanctuary courtyard. It was topped with a flint slab grooved by plastered channels. The entrance to the sanctuary was flanked by two small stone incense altars.

Bibliography. Y. Aharoni, "Megiddo," *NEAEHL* 3:1003-12; A. Biran, *Biblical Dan* (Jerusalem, 1994); S. Gitin, "Incense Altars from Ekron, Israel and Judah," *ErIsr* 20 (1989): 52*-67*; A. Mazar, "The 'Bull Site' — An Iron Age I Open Cult Place," *BASOR* 247 (1982): 27-42; O. Tufnell, C. H. Inge, and L. Harding, *Lachish II (Tell el Duweir): The Fosse Temple* (Oxford, 1940); G. E. Wright, *Shechem: The Biography of a Biblical City* (New York, 1965); Y. Yadin and A. Ben-Tor, "Hazor," *NEAEHL* 2:594-606.

Beth Alpert Nakhai

ALUSH (Heb. *'ālûš*)
A place where the Israelites encamped between Dophkah and Rephidim (Num. 33:13-14), possibly modern Wadi el-'Eshsh.

ALVAH (Heb. *'alwâ*) (also ALIAH)
An Edomite chieftain and a descendant of Esau (Gen. 36:40). At 1 Chr. 1:51 he is called Aliah. He may be the same as Alvan.

ALVAN (Heb. *'alwān*) (also ALIAN)
The first son of Shobal the Horite and ancestor of a clan (Gen. 36:23). He is also called Alian (1 Chr. 1:40).

AMAD (Heb. *'am'āḏ*)
A border town of the territory of Asher near Mt. Carmel (Josh. 19:26). Its precise location is unknown.

AMAL (Heb. *'āmāl*)
One of the sons of Helem; head of an Asherite family (1 Chr. 7:35).

AMALEK (Heb. *'ămālēq*), **AMALEKITES** (*'ămālēqî*)
A nomadic (or seminomadic) people, descendants of Amalek, a grandson of Esau (Gen. 36:11-12). The Amalekites are not specifically mentioned outside the Bible, which points to their origin in Edom (cf. Gen. 36:15-16) and identifies them as traditional enemies of the Hebrews. Gen. 14:7 mentions Chedorlaomer's victory over the "country of the Amalekites," an anachronism which must be explained as an editorial insertion. In Num. 24:20, in what may be understood as the only positive reference to Amalek in the Bible, Balaam refers to the Amalekites as a very ancient people.

While they came out of Edom, their nomadic lifestyle led to a widespread distribution, mostly along the fringe of southern Canaan's agricultural zone (e.g., Num. 13:29; Judg. 12:15; 1 Sam. 15:7; 30:1-2). The Amalekites ranged across a large territory, from the western Sinai to Arabia, and made extensive use of camels (Judg. 6:5; 7:12). Because of their distribution and mobility, Amalek came into frequent contact with the Hebrews, from the wilderness wandering until the reign of David. All OT references to contacts between the Amalekites and the Israelites describe hostile interaction; the same holds true for Israel's encounters with most of the nomadic peoples who inhabited regions beyond prime agricultural lands.

The Amalekite-Israelite hostility began while the Hebrews were in Sinai, with an unprovoked attack by Amalek (Exod. 17:8-16; Deut. 25:17-18; cf. 1 Sam. 15:2-3). Although Israel defeated the Amalekites (Exod. 17:13), a long period of unbroken warfare ensued. When the Israelites attempted to enter southern Canaan, they were blocked by the Canaanites and Amalekites (Num. 14:44-45; Deut. 1:44). Later, the Moabite king Eglon hired Ammonites and Amalekites to attack the Hebrews, and the raiders from Transjordan captured "the city of palms" (Judg. 3:12-14). In the days of Gideon, Amalek invaded areas as far west and north as the region of Gaza and the valley of Jezreel (Judg. 6:3-5, 33), joining forces with the Midianites and "people of the East" and attacking on camels (Judg. 6:5; 7:12).

The accounts of 1–2 Samuel are most important for understanding the clash between Israel and Amalek, especially the demise of the latter. In the first reference to a Hebrew attack on the Amalekites, 1 Sam. 15 describes Saul's move against "the city of Amalek," which was probably more of a camp than a city. Although Saul won this battle, he failed to execute the "ban" (Heb. *ḥērem*) against Agag and the Amalekite booty; Samuel identified Saul's spiritual transgression and killed Agag, the Amalekite king (1 Sam. 15:8-9, 20, 32-33). Agag was probably a traditional name or title for an Amalekite king — or tribal chief (cf. Num. 24:7).

David continued the hostility with Amalek, who took advantage of David's absence and looted his base at Ziklag. David was able to locate this raiding party, defeat them, and recover his possessions (1 Sam. 27:8-9; 30:1-25). David learned that Saul had been killed by an Amalekite, probably a mercenary in the Philistine army (2 Sam. 1:1-10). Subsequently, David broke the Amalekite threat (2 Sam. 8:12; 1 Chr. 18:11). Apparently the Amalekites — along with other nomadic groups — were referred to thereafter with the collective term "Arab(s)."

While considerable knowledge about nomadic peoples has been recovered through archaeological research, no specific artifacts or sites are linked to

Amalek with any certainty. It is possible that some of the fortified settlements in the Negeb highlands — and even Tel Masos (near Beer-sheba) — have Amalekite connections.

Bibliography. D. Edelman, "Saul's Battle Against Amaleq (1 Sam. 15)," *JSOT* 35 (1986): 71-84; I. Eph'al, *The Ancient Arabs* (Leiden, 1982).

GERALD L. MATTINGLY

AMAM (Heb. *'ămām)*
An unidentified town in the Shephelah, allotted to Judah (Josh. 15:26). It may have been near Beer-sheba.

AMANA (Heb. *'ămānâ)*
A mountain peak (Cant. 4:8) in the Anti-Lebanon range, near the River Amana.

AMARIAH (Heb. *'ămaryâ)*

1. The second son of Hebron, cousin of Moses and Aaron, listed in the genealogy of the tribe of Levi (1 Chr. 23:19; 24:23).

2. A priest, descendant of Eleazar and Phinehas (1 Chr. 6:7, 52[MT 5:33; 6:37]).

3. The son of Azariah who served as a priest in Solomon's temple (1 Chr. 6:10-11[5:37]).

4. A high priest in the Jerusalem temple during the time of King Jehoshaphat of Judah (2 Chr. 19:11).

5. A levitical priest in the time of King Hezekiah of Judah (2 Chr. 31:15).

6. The son of Hezekiah and the father of Gedaliah, who was the prophet Zephaniah's grandfather (Zeph. 1:1).

7. A priest, son of Azariah and one of the ancestors of Ezra the scribe (Ezra 7:3).

8. A man of the family of Azzur, who had married a foreign woman in the time of Ezra (Ezra 10:42).

9. One of the priests who signed as a witness to the community commitments during the time of Nehemiah (Neh. 10:3[4]).

10. "The son of Amariah," listed in Neh. 11:4 among those who inhabited Jerusalem in the days of Nehemiah.

The name appears also on several seals (e.g., from Kiriath-jearim) and inscriptions such as the Gibeon jar handle inscription and others found at Kuntillet 'Ajrud/Ḥorvat Teman.

ISAAC KALIMI

AMARNA
Tell el-Amarna, located half-way between Memphis and Thebes on the East bank of the Nile, for which are named an age and a cultural or religious "revolution." This city of between 20 and 50 thousand inhabitants was constructed on virgin territory according to the plans of Pharaoh Amenophis IV (Akhenaten). Begun in the fifth year of this 14th-century B.C.E. monarch's reign, the site was inhabited for only a generation, after which it was abandoned. Its unique history allows it to be studied as one of the most important representatives of ancient urbanism. The king and his royal family resided in the northern part of the city and preserved

Akhenaten and Nefertiti present offerings to the sun-god Aten. Limestone relief on balustrade at Tell el-Amarna (18th Dynasty); now in Cairo Museum (Photograph courtesy of The Metropolitan Museum of Art)

their own food supply. The many private houses appear to have all been occupied by professionals with titles. Their own servants and the other laborers must have lived with them or perhaps adjacent to the larger houses. The professionals' houses are uniform in design, whether larger or smaller in size, and reflect a common identity wherein the great divide economically is between the king and his family, on the one hand, and everyone else, on the other. Some of the officials worked in a collection of small offices beside the royal house. In one of these was found the collection of cuneiform documents known as the Amarna Letters.

Akhenaten named the site Akhetaten, or "Horizon of the Aten (the disk of the sun)," reflecting the change of perspective that his reign brought to Egypt. By moving away from the religious center of Thebes (where already at the beginning of his reign he had added a cult center to the Aten at the temple of Karnak), Akhenaten broke away from traditional Egyptian religion with its worship of a variety of deities in many natural forms. In place of this complexity, Akhenaten introduced the worship of the Aten sun-disk, symbolizing the giver of all life. Akhenaten and his family received that life and mediated it to all Egypt. In the art of the period the royal family is portrayed as a unique group who alone receive the rays of the Aten disk and who appear together as a loving family. The distinctive elongation of the crania and pelvic areas in portrayals of the royal family may reflect a surrealistic artistic attempt to interpret their distinctive roles as royal intermediaries of the divine rather than indicate some genetic disease. Drawings of Akhenaten and his family, always females, enhanced the pharaoh's status and suggest to the modern viewer that despite the Amarna cultural "revolution" Akhenaten's self-perception did not differ from that of other New Kingdom pharaohs.

Although Akhenaten has often been viewed as an authentic precursor of Israel's distinctive monotheistic religion, more nuanced perspectives see in him an example of intellectual trends in Mesopotamia as well as Egypt during the 14th, 13th, and 12th centuries. Oher divinities continued to be tolerated and worshipped in Egypt, and the Hymn to the Sun and other textual sources for Amarna theology appear to borrow at length from earlier hymns and prayers to other deities. Atenism arose and disappeared with Akhenaten and his immediate family. It survived in no aspect of the religion or culture of Egypt, and the whole incident appears to have been forgotten in the succeeding generations who abandoned the site and returned to Thebes and the temple to Amon-Re at Karnak.

Bibliography. B. J. Kemp, *Ancient Egypt: Anatomy of a Civilization* (London, 1989).

RICHARD S. HESS

AMARNA LETTERS

A collection of international correspondence dating from the middle of the 14th century B.C.E. and discovered at the ancient capital of Amarna in Egypt. These texts form the bulk of the 380 separate cuneiform documents that first came to the attention of the scholarly world at the end of the 19th century. They form a partial archive of the pharaohs of Egypt and exemplify their international relations at this time. The texts are of particular interest for what they reveal concerning the social world of Syria-Palestine, the language of this region, and broader political history of the Late Bronze Age. At this time the Egyptian New Kingdom claimed Palestine and areas to the north including all of modern Lebanon and some of Syria. The correspondence from city leaders and Egyptian administrators of this region reveals a world of many small towns and city-states, each rivalling its neighbors for power and military support from the pharaoh. All leaders claimed subservience to the pharaoh, but the correspondence indicates that the town leaders were seeking their own political advantage and used every opportunity to decry their neighbors as Ḫabiru or disloyal to the crown. Rather than bearing witness to a deteriorating political situation, this correspondence more likely reflects the pharaoh's efforts to play off the political and military strengths of each city-state against the other and thereby minimize the military force required to maintain Egyptian sovereignty over this region. The social world of this period has been compared with that later portrayed in the book of the Judges, in which each locality was left to struggle for its own survival.

The surviving texts record the careers of certain leaders and their families as they rise in power until the pharaoh decides they have become a threat to the political balance. This was the case of Labaya, the leader of Shechem, who seems to have gained several cities and interfered with the activities of other independent cities (e.g., Gezer). He was apparently granted his wish to visit Pharaoh, but died or was killed before reaching Egypt. Farther to the north, the kingdom of Amurru was led by a certain Azira, who became involved in dubious politics and was recalled to Egypt. Eventually he and his kingdom allied with the enemy Hittites. On the coast, Rib-addi of Byblos wrote dozens of letters to the pharaoh expecting him to intervene and rescue Rib-addi from various troubles with local enemies. In the end we read of a coup within Byblos, with Rib-addi locked out of his city.

Although most of the Amarna correspondence is written in Akkadian cuneiform, the lingua franca of the ancient Near East at this time, it is clear that letters from scribes in the cities of Palestine and adjacent regions betray local dialects in their vocabulary, morphology, syntax, and other grammatical features. In some cases West Semitic terms are placed alongside their Akkadian equivalents with an indication that they are glosses to explain the meanings of these words. In other letters they appear as part of the text with no indication that the scribes were aware they were writing anything other than the official language of correspondence. Linguists have identified various grammatical and stylistic forms as West Semitic, such as the *waw*-consecutive as a narrative tense, 1st common singular suffixed verbal forms, and rhetorical forms of expression that resemble later Biblical Hebrew. These include the threefold repetition of phrases and ideas, the use of chiasm, and parallelism techniques common in the Psalms and other forms of biblical poetry and prose. Texts from places such as Jerusalem and Shechem, as well as Tyre and Byblos, attest to a "Canaanite" language present in 14th-century Syria-Palestine.

The ethnic constitution of the leadership in Palestine during the Amarna Age is one of West Semitic leaders along the coast, but inland the presence of leaders with northern (Hittite and Hurrian) names occurs. Thus Jerusalem has a leader whose name contains the Hurrian goddess Hebat. This influence from Anatolia and northern Syria, perhaps also reflected in some of the population groups and individuals mentioned in Joshua, Judges and 1–2 Samuel, is an example of the international world in which the Amarna texts were written. Political messages from the kings of Babylonia, Assyria, Mitanni, the Hittites, and Alashiya (Cyprus) found their way to the pharaoh's court. Each of these describes concerns for trade, whether maintaining trade routes in light of the threats of bandits and murderers, providing inventories of a vast array of luxury goods delivered to the Egyptian court in trade (officially as a "gift"), or simply seeking rights of passage through the intermediate lands and kingdoms. Here are represented an elite "club" of the most powerful nations of the age and their concerns to acquire precious goods for their own prestige. The Amarna Letters are a unique collection of documents that attest to similar trade and political concerns as were reflected later in the Israelite monarchies and decried by the prophets.

Bibliography. R. S. Hess, *Amarna Personal Names.* ASORDS 9 (Winona Lake, 1993); W. L. Moran, *The Amarna Letters* (Baltimore, 1992).

Richard S. Hess

AMASA (Heb. *'ămāśā'*)

1. Kinsman of David (2 Sam. 19:13[MT 14]) and son of either Ithra the Israelite (2 Sam. 17:25) or Jether the Ishmaelite (1 Chr. 2:17). During his rebellion against David, Absalom appointed Amasa as army commander (2 Sam. 17:25). After Absalom's defeat, David appointed Amasa as his army commander in place of Joab (2 Sam. 19:14). Shortly thereafter, David instructed Amasa to gather the men of Judah within three days to quell an uprising, but Amasa took longer than ordered and was replaced (2 Sam. 20:1-6). Later, when Joab met Amasa near the great stone in Gibeon, he stabbed him (2 Sam. 20: 7-10), just as he had done to Abner (3:27). Because the soldiers stopped to see the slain Amasa, his corpse was removed from the road (2 Sam. 20:12). Joab then resumed his role as army commander until he was slain by Benaiah for murdering Abner and Amasa (1 Kgs. 2:5, 32).

Amasa may be the same individual as Amasai (*'ămāśay*), the "chief of the thirty," who pledged allegiance to David while he was in Ziklag (1 Chr. 12:18[19]).

2. The son of Hadlai, an Ephraimite (2 Chr. 28:12). After the Israelites under Pekah captured 200 thousand Judahites in the reign of Ahaz of Judah, the prophet Oded told the Israelite army that subjugating the Judahites would only add to their offenses against the Lord. Amasa and other Ephraimite men therefore brought the captives to their kinsmen at Jericho (2 Chr. 28:8-15).

John E. Harvey

AMASAI (Heb. *'ămāśay*)

1. A Levite, the son of Elkanah, and an ancestor of Samuel (1 Chr. 6:25, 35[MT 10, 20]).

2. Chief of David's Thirty who came to him at Ziklag (1 Chr. 12:18[19]). He is perhaps the same as Amasa, the son of Abigail and Ithra.

3. One of the priests who blew the trumpet when the ark was returned to Jerusalem (1 Chr. 15:24).

4. The father of Mahath; a contemporary of King Hezekiah (2 Chr. 29:12). Although often identified with **1** above, this Amasai lived much later.

AMASHSAI (Heb. *'ămaššay*)

A priest living in Jerusalem during the time of Nehemiah. He was the son of Azarel (Neh. 11:13), and possibly identical to Maasai (1 Chr. 9:12).

AMASIAH (Heb. *'ămasyâ*)

The son of Zichri of Judah. One who volunteered for service, he was commander over 200 thousand soldiers (perhaps 200 units; 2 Chr. 17:16).

AMAW (Heb. *'ammô*)

The homeland of Balaam, W of the Euphrates (Num. 22:5). Its capital was Emar, ca. 80 km. (50 mi.) S of Carchemish and SW of Balaam's city, Pethor (Akk. Pitru). According to the Idrimi inscription, some two centuries earlier (ca. 1450 B.C.E.) Amaw was under the control of Alalakh.

AMAZIAH (Heb. *'ămaṣyâ, 'ămaṣyāhû*)

1. A Simeonite, the father of Joshah (1 Chr. 4:34).

2. A Levite of the family of Merair, who was the son of Hilkiah and the father of Hashabiah (1 Chr. 6:45[MT 30]). He was among those appointed over the song service "before the tabernacle of the tent of meeting" (1 Chr. 6:31-32[16-17]).

3. A priest at the Israelite royal sanctuary at Bethel during the reign of Jeroboam II. He reported to the king that Amos had prophesied Jeroboam's death and Israel's exile, a message that the nation could not long tolerate. Amaziah commanded Amos to return to Judah and never again prophesy at Bethel. The prophet responded by predicting disaster for Amaziah, his wife, and his children (Amos 7:10-17).

4. King of Judah, son of Joash and Jehoaddin/Jehoaddan. He assumed the throne at age 25 and reportedly continued for 29 years in the first half of the 8th century. Since it is difficult to fit Amaziah's 29 years and his son Azariah/Uzziah's 52-year reign into this period, some have suggested that the two were co-regents for part of their reigns. Amaziah's rule is described in 2 Kgs. 14:1-20, which is apparently derived from the royal archives of Judah, and in 2 Chr. 25:1-28, which is essentially a reworking of the account in 2 Kings.

2 Kings characterizes Amaziah generally in a positive light and notes that he showed restraint in the punishment of his father's assassins and waged a successful war against Edom in which he captured Sela and renamed it Jokthe-el (2 Kgs. 14:1-7). Unfortunately, Amaziah then challenged Jehoash/Joash and Israel to meet his forces in battle, and when the Israelite king attempted to dissuade him by means of an artful fable, he refused to listen. Consequently, Judah's army was defeated in battle at Beth-shemesh and Amaziah captured, Jerusalem's walls reduced by a span of 400 cubits, the temple and royal treasury plundered, and hostages taken to Samaria (2 Kgs. 14:8-14). It may be assumed that Amaziah returned to the throne, ultimately surviving Jehoash by 15 years, and later he was slain by conspirators who had pursued him to Lachish (2 Kgs. 14:17-20).

Chronicles agrees with the contours of the account in 2 Kings but supplements it greatly. As for the war with Edom, e.g., Chronicles explains that Amaziah set out to fight Edom with 300 thousand troops of his own and a force of 100 thousand Israelite mercenaries, to whom he had paid 100 talents. A prophet condemned the hiring of the Israelite troops and persuaded Amaziah to send them home. Judah conquered Edom and destroyed 20 thousand of their soldiers, rather than the 10 thousand of 2 Kings (2 Chr. 25:5-13). Moreover, Chronicles reports two additional items that relate to the subsequent war with Israel. First, the Israelite mercenaries attacked and plundered Judean cities "from Samaria to Beth-horon," because they had been dismissed from the Edomite campaign by Amaziah (2 Chr. 25:13). This attack by Israelites may be regarded as the motive for Amaziah's subsequent challenge of Israel to war. Second, Amaziah returned from his campaign against Edom with Edomite gods, and he worshipped them. When a prophet condemned his behavior, Amaziah threatened him with death, and consequently the prophet announced that God would destroy the king (2 Chr. 25:14-16). Therefore, when Amaziah challenged Joash to battle, and Joash attempted to dissuade him, Chronicles explains that the Judean king failed to heed the warning, because God intended to destroy him for his sin (2 Chr. 25:20). Although Amaziah escaped this battle with his life, Chronicles reports that the final conspiracy against Amaziah was the consequence of the king's sin (2 Chr. 25:27).

The main features of Amaziah's reign that are found in 2 Kings have been accepted by historians, but this has not been the case with the additions in Chronicles, since the size of the military forces seems excessive, and the reports about the Edomite gods and prophetic interactions with Amaziah may have been fabricated by Chronicles in order to explain the disasters of the king's reign.

Bibliography. M. P. Graham, "Aspects of the Structure and Rhetoric of 2 Chronicles 25," in *History and Interpretation,* ed. Graham et al. JSOT Sup 173 (Sheffield, 1993), 78-89. M. PATRICK GRAHAM

AMBER

A yellowish to brownish translucent fossil resin (Heb. *ḥašmal*) used for making ornamental objects (Ezek. 1:4, 27; 8:2). The LXX reads Gk. *ḗlektron* and the Vulg. has Lat. *electrum,* an alloy containing four parts gold and one part silver. Others, on the basis of Akk. *ešmaru* (from Elam. *ilmasu,* "inlay" or "bronze"), translate "gleaming bronze" (RSV).

AMEN (Heb. *'āmēn;* Gk. *amḗn*)

Transliteration of a Hebrew root implying truth, veracity, steadfastness. In both the OT and NT it accompanies weighty statements such as royal or divine pronouncements. The woman accused of adultery under the Mosaic law was to respond to the procedure for ascertaining her guilt with a double "Amen" (Num. 5:22). As the curses of the law were read to the Israelites, they were to respond with "Amen" (Deut. 27:15-26). Benaiah used the word to indicate divine affirmation of David's choice of Solomon to succeed him as king (1 Kgs. 1:36). As David brought the ark of the covenant into Jerusalem, the people responded to a lengthy song of praise to God with "Amen" (1 Chr. 16:36). In the Psalms a double "amen" is appended to prayers of blessing to the Lord (Ps. 41:13; 72:19; 89:52). Jeremiah uses this term to express his wish that Hananiah's false prophecy might become true (Jer. 28:6). In all except two of the above passages (Jer. 28:6; 1 Chr. 16:36) the LXX has *génoito,* "let it become," for *'āmēn.*

NT usage closely follows that of the OT. Gk. *amḗn* is appended to prayers, weighty pronouncements, or doxologies (e.g., Matt. 6:13; Mark 16:20; Luke 24:53; John 21:25). In two passages Jesus is referred to as our *amḗn* (2 Cor. 1:20; Rev. 3:14). The NT also contains numerous examples where *amḗn* is translated "truly" or "verily" (e.g., Matt. 5:18; Mark 3:28; Luke 4:24; John 1:51).

JOE E. LUNCEFORD

AMENEMOPE, INSTRUCTION OF

An Egyptian didactic text dated to the late 12th century B.C.E. The only complete copy is preserved on a 6th-century papyrus. Framed as the words of Amenemope to his youngest son, these instructions for well-being and proper conduct are divided into a prologue and 30 numbered chapters, the last of which functions as an epilogue. The dominant concern is to distinguish the ideal person ("the truly silent") who is honest, modest and respectful, disciplined, quiet, kind to others and concerned for the disadvantaged, from the quick-tempered and deceitful "heated one." Emphasis is placed upon honesty in personal and business interactions, satisfaction with minimal material possessions and advocacy on behalf of the poor. Close structural and thematic parallels between Amenemope and the book of Proverbs, particularly the "Words of the Wise" in Prov. 22:17–24:22, have prompted scholarly debate as to the nature of the literary relationship. Although some have argued either for the priority of Proverbs or for the derivation of both texts from a common Egyptian or Semitic original, the consensus is that Amenemope had priority and served as a model for Proverbs' collection of "30 sayings" (Prov. 22:20).

Bibliography. G. E. Bryce, *A Legacy of Wisdom* (Lewisburg, Pa., 1979); M. Lichtheim, *Ancient Egyptian Literature* (Berkeley, 1976), 2:146-63.

CHRISTINE ROY YODER

AMETHYST

A transparent purple or reddish stone prized for beads, seals, and amulets. Recent English translations read "amethyst" for Heb. *'aḥlāmâ,* an engraved stone on the high priest's breastpiece (Exod. 28:19; 39:12). The LXX has *améthystos* for *'aḥlāmâ,* and adds it to the list of stones describing Tyre's king (Ezek. 28:13). It designates a course in the foundation of the city wall in the new Jerusalem

(Rev. 21:20). Some translations read "crystal" or "jasper" for these Hebrew and Greek terms.

JOSEPH E. JENSEN

AMI (Heb. *'āmî*) (also AMON)
An ancestor of a family of "Solomon's servants" (Ezra 2:57). He is called Amon at Neh. 7:59.

AMITTAI (Heb. *'ămittay*)
The father of the prophet Jonah, from Gath-hepher in the territory of Zebulun (2 Kgs. 14:25; Jon. 1:1).

AMMAH (Heb. *'ammâ*)
A hill near Giah, "on the way to the wilderness of Gibeon" (2 Sam. 2:24), where Abner made a truce with Joab his pursuer (vv. 26-28).

AMMI (Heb. *'ammî*)
A name ("My People") given to Israel symbolizing divine acceptance (Hos. 2:1[MT 3]), in contrast to Lo-ammi ("Not My People," 1:9), which signified divine rejection of God's people.

AMMIEL (Heb. *'ammî'ēl*)

1. The son of Gemalli, of the tribe of Dan. He was one of the 12 men sent to spy out Canaan (Num. 13:12).

2. The father of Machir, a Manassehite from Lo-debar (2 Sam. 9:4; 17:27).

3. The father of Uriah's wife Bathshua/Bathsheba who later became the wife of David (1 Chr. 3:5). As the result of a transposition of the consonants, the name appears at 2 Sam. 11:3 as Eliam.

4. The sixth son of Obed-edom; a gatekeeper in the temple (1 Chr. 26:5).

AMMIHUD (Heb. *'ammîhuḏ*)

1. The father of Elishama of Ephraim (Num. 1:10; 2:18; 7:48, 53; 10:22); an ancestor of Joshua (1 Chr. 7:26).

2. The father of Shemuel, who represented the tribe of Simeon in the division of the land of Canaan (Num. 34:20).

3. The father of Pedahel of the tribe of Naphtali, who assisted in the division of the land (Num. 34:28).

4. The father of King Talmai of Geshur (2 Sam. 13:37; MT *'ammîḥûr*).

5. One of the returning exiles; the son of Omri of the family of Perez son of Judah, and father of Uthai (1 Chr. 9:4).

AMMINADAB (Heb. *'ammînāḏāḇ;* Gk. *Aminadáb*)

1. A leader of the tribe of Judah whose lineage is traced through Ruth down to David (Ruth 4:19-20; Matt. 1:4). He was the son of Ram (Ruth 4:19; called Admin in Luke 3:33), father of Nahshon (Num. 1:7; 2:3) and of Elisheba, the wife of Aaron (Exod. 6:23).

2. A Levite, son of Kohath and father of Korah (1 Chr. 6:22[MT 7]; LXX "Izhar"; cf. Exod. 6:18).

3. A chief of the levitical family of Uzziel, descendant of Kohath (1 Chr. 15:10-11). He was among the Levites who transferred the ark from the house of Obed-edom to Jerusalem.

4. The father of Esther, according to the LXX (Esth. 2:15; 9:29), though the MT names Abihail as her father.

5. The king of Beth-ammon (Akk. *Ammin-adbi*), who gave tribute to Assurbanipal (*ANET,* 294a). It is not impossible that he is identical with the same name which occurs on a 7th-century B.C.E. seal.

ISAAC KALIMI/GREGORY A. WOLFE

AMMISHADDAI (Heb. *'ammîšadday*)
The father of Ahiezer of the tribe of Dan (Num. 1:12; 2:25; 7:66, 71; 10:25).

AMMIZABAD (Heb. *'ammîzāḇāḏ*)
The son of Benaiah, one of David's Thirty. He served as commander of the division for the third month (1 Chr. 27:6).

AMMON (Heb. *'ammôn*),
AMMONITES (*'ammônîm*)
A sedentary people living east of the Jordan at the headwaters of the river Jabbok, known also from the annals of Sennacherib (*ANET,* 279), Tiglath-pileser III (282), and Assurbanipal (294). Although distinctively Ammonite material culture might not be clearly distinguishable before the Iron Age, the Ammonites as a people emerged, arguably, in the Middle Bronze Age around Rabbah (Rabbath-ammon), perhaps when the Ammonite populace overpowered the Rephaim, a rival ethnic group (cf. LXX Deut. 2:21). Ammonite culture reached its florescence in wealth, power, and influence during the 9th-6th centuries B.C. Relevant excavated sites include the Amman citadel, Tell Safut, Tell Siran, Tell Jawa (South), Khilda, Khirbet el-Hajjar, Meqabelein, Rujm el-Malfuf, Tell el-Mazar, Tell Sahab, Tell el-'Umeiri, and Umm ad-Dananir.

Geographical boundaries and political/military influence of the Ammonite kingdom doubtlessly varied from time to time. From the original area limited more or less to the broader environs of Rabbah itself, Ammonites are said to control the entire space between Wadi Môjib (Arnon) and Wadi Zerqa (Jabbok), from the eastern desert to the Jordan River. Ammonite rule was frequently eclipsed by premonarchic tribal settlements and, later, by Israelite and Judahite kings.

Ammonites enter the biblical scene in an alliance with Amalekites to help the Moabite king Eglon defeat Israel (Judg. 3:12-14). The following 18-year subjugation was construed as punishment for Israel's abandoning the relationship with God in preferring to worship the Baals and Astartes of their neighbors (Judg. 10:6-18). The Ammonites were defeated by Jephthah (Judg. 11:33), slaughtered by Saul (1 Sam. 11:11), and forced to pay tribute to David (2 Sam. 8:12), who finally conquered them. Subsequently, the Ammonite Naamah married Solomon and presented him with Rehoboam, a future king of Judah (1 Kgs. 14:21, 31). Israelite animosity toward the Ammonite (and Moabite) is forcefully stated: none "may ever be admitted to the assembly of the Lord," nor any descendants of theirs "even to the tenth generation" (Deut. 23:3[MT 4]).

Ammonite religion was of the nature/fertility sort typical of polytheism everywhere in antiquity. The male deity Baal and his female counterparts Astoreth/Astarte/Asherah coming together ritually ensured the fertility and well-being of both people and land. As Israelites accepted these beliefs and practices, the scribes and prophets denounced them. Milcom was the main Ammonite god. His precious gold crown David stole for himself. Solomon's Ammonite wife persuaded the king not simply to build a temple to Milcom, but even to abandon Yahweh for the worship of her native Ammonite god. Milcom's counterpart is represented in the form of terra-cotta female fertility figurines found in many Iron Age excavations. Ammonite religious culture, being foreign to Israelite faith, is what makes them enemies without regard to changing political-military situations.

By the time the northern and southern kingdoms collapsed, Ammonites ceased to be a common enemy to Israel and Judah. The population of lower Gilead in all likelihood had already been comprised both of Ammonite and Israelite tribes and families who were by no means always at odds with each other. During the Exile, and especially after the destruction of the Jerusalem temple, many Jews sought refuge among the Ammonites east of the Jordan (Jer. 40:11).

Perhaps it is the Priestly writer, concerned with genealogies, who puts the Ammonites in a better light. Origin narratives of eponymous ancestry link them with Abraham through Lot (Gen. 19:38). Ammonite ancestry was conceived (literarily if not also literally) in a union between Lot and, unbeknown to Lot, Lot's daughter. As with etiologies generally, the interest is not in biology but in conveying a value, in this case a positive relationship between Israelites and Ammonites due to an ancestral bond (Gen. 11:27). Lot migrates with Abraham (Gen. 12:4-5); Abraham later rescues Lot (14:12-16). Lot's younger daughter names her son Ben-ammon, "The son of my kinsman," making clear that all Ammonites are relatives of all Israelites.

One can easily see a parallel between Israelite incursions into Late Iron Rabbath-ammon and ancient Israelite invasions under Moses. The author of Deut. 2, in prohibiting Moses from invading LB Ammonite territory, gives the reason why Iron Age Judahites should not encroach on their host country: the Lord had given it to the descendants of Lot (v. 19). In the worldview of antiquity, lands belong to gods. Presenting its origins as a measure of Yahweh's own dispensation conveys Israel's recognition of the legitimacy of the Ammonite kingdom, its very existence deriving ultimately from an act of Yahweh. A plausible occasion to affirm this value would have been in the face of a common enemy: Babylon.

While it may be correct to speak of the end of an effective and distinct Ammonite kingdom shortly after Late Iron, it is erroneous to think of them as simply absorbed into the local population soon after. Ammonite strength continued. Worldwide conquests by the Persians and Greeks overshadowed but did not necessarily lessen the regional significance of the Ammonites, who lasted clearly into the Hellenistic period. The region became important again with significant Hellenistic influxes, but it was still in its own cultural continuum under the Ptolemies. Ptolemy II renamed Ammon Philadelphia and it eventually became a key city of the Decapolis. Ammonite power and influence continued at least until defeat by Judas Maccabeus in the 2nd century (1 Macc. 5:6).

DONALD H. WIMMER

AMNON (Heb. *'amnôn, 'amnōn*)

1. The firstborn son of David and Ahinoam of Jezreel (2 Sam. 3:2 = 1 Chr. 3:1). His story illustrates the judgment announced by Nathan for David's crimes of adultery and murder (2 Sam. 12:11-12). Amnon's obsessive desire for his beautiful half-sister Tamar distressed him. Acting on the advice of his cousin Jonadab, Amnon feigned illness and asked David to send Tamar to visit and prepare food for him. When Tamar brought the food into his room, he seized her and urged her to submit to his desire. She recoiled and pleaded that he speak to their father about marriage, but Amnon refused to listen. He raped her and then ordered her out of his house. When she pleaded that he not add to the wrong he had already done to her, Amnon ordered her thrown into the street. Unable to console his sister, Absalom sought revenge when two years later he invited the king and princes to celebrate the shearing of his flocks at Baal-hazor. David was not willing to go, perhaps suspicious of Absalom's request that Amnon be allowed to attend, but finally allowed all the princes to attend Absalom's feast. When Amnon was under the influence of the wine, Absalom ordered his servants to kill him, revenge he had contemplated since Amnon's rape of Tamar.

2. A son of Shimon, descendant of Judah (1 Chr. 4:20).

KEITH L. EADES

AMOK (Heb. *'āmôq*)
One of the priests and heads of families returning with Zerubbabel from exile (Neh. 12:7); an ancestor of Eber, a priest in the days of the high priest Joiakim (v. 20).

AMON (Heb. *'āmôn*) **(DEITY)**
The Egyptian god of the wind (Jer. 46:25). As Amon-Re he was the supreme god of the New Kingdom.

AMON (Heb. *'āmôn*) **(PERSON)** (also AMI)

1. King of Judah, son of Manasseh and grandson of Hezekiah, and father of Josiah. His reign was brief, lasting only two years (643-642 B.C.; 2 Kgs. 21:19-26; 2 Chr. 33:21-25).

Amon succeeded to the throne following the death of Manasseh. Only 22 at his accession (2 Kgs. 21:19), he must have been among the youngest of

Manasseh's sons. His mother was Meshullemeth, daughter of Haruz. Amon receives the common negative evaluation given by the Deuteronomistic editors (2 Kgs. 21:20). He was assassinated by his "servants" (probably officials in the royal administration) in the palace, but motives for the assassination are missing. Most likely, given Amon's apparent continuation of Manasseh's policy of submission to the Assyrians, is that his assassins may have hoped to revitalize hopes for Judean independence; if so, it was a futile effort doomed to failure. The text of 2 Kgs. 21:24 is clear that the "people of the land," probably the landed aristocracy, saw to it that Amon was replaced with his eight-year-old son Josiah, during whose minority the policy of submission continued. Another possibility is that Amon was slain by people desiring a restoration of the religious reforms initiated by Hezekiah late in the 8th century and abandoned by Manasseh early in the 7th. Also possible is that Amon was killed by other members of the royal family in a scramble for the throne. In the end, nothing conclusive can be said regarding the circumstances or motives of Amon's slaying, and the final verdict is that of the Deuteronomistic editor who condemns him for his failure to reverse the wrongs of his father.

2. An official (NRSV "governor") of the city of Samaria (1 Kgs. 22:26 = 2 Chr. 19:25). Amon appears in the narrative concerning the prophecy of Micaiah as one of two persons charged with imprisoning and guarding the prophet during the king's absence at Ramoth-gilead.

3. A person listed among those who returned from exile in Babylon under Zerubbabel and Jeshua (Neh. 7:59). In the parallel text in Ezra 2:57 the name is listed with an alternate spelling, Ami (Heb. *'āmî*).

Bibliography. M. Cogan and H. Tadmor, *II Kings.* AB 11 (Garden City, 1988), 275-76; A. Malamat, "The Historical Background of the Assassination of Amon," *IEJ* 3 (1953): 26-29.

PAUL K. HOOKER

AMORITES (Heb. *'ĕmōrî*)

An ethno-lingustic term used to render Sum. *mar-tu* and Akk. *amurrû.* The designation is imprecise, as the word Amorite was used differently in different times and places. Although attested earlier, the word made its first significant appearance during the time of the Akkad kings (2334-2154 B.C.E.), who described Jebel Bishri, in Syria, as the Amorite mountain. This does not mean that this is their homeland or only place of residence; a century later Gudea would describe two such "Amorite mountains," Jebel Bishri and Jebel Hamrin, NE of Sumer. In the earlier Ebla texts from 3rd-millennium Syria there is no trace of Amorites or of the language. A place by the name *mar-tu* is mentioned, but that is all, and therefore one must conclude that the Amorites entered the region sometime after 2400. During the time of the Ur III dynasty (2112-2004) in Mesopotamia Amorites appear for the first time in numbers. People in a wide variety of trades and occupations were identified as "Amorites" in administrative texts, but not all of them bore Amorite names. Conversely, others with Amorite names are not described as belonging to any ethnic group. The majority of these people are already integrated into Mesopotamian society. Other sources, including later copies of royal letters of the Ur III kings, describe a different situation: hostile Amorites on the northeastern borders of the empire, who continually threatened the stability of the state. More precisely, they were identified as belonging to the Tidnum clan, and a line of fortifications had to be built against them that spanned the Euphrates and Tigris rivers and ran into the Diyala region. During the reign of the last Ur III kings these Amorites, who staged their raids from the valleys in the eastern mountains, overran much of the northern part of Sumer and were a strong factor in the eventual fall of the empire. The successor states that emerged from the turmoil were governed by Amorite chiefs, who did not hide their origins and often used such titles as "Amorite chieftain" or "king of the Amnanum tribe" as part of their titulature. By the 19th century the dynasties ruling Mesopotamian cities such as Isin, Larsa, Uruk, and Babylon were of Amorite descent.

The situation was somewhat different in Syria and northern Mesopotamia. Only a handful of personal names are known from Ur III sources; most of them are linguistically closer to the old Eblaite language than to Amorite. By the time of Zimri-lim, king of Mari (18th century), all the cities and villages from the Mediterranean coast to the Zagros Mountains, down to the Persian Gulf, were in the hands of Amorite dynasties, bordered by Hurrians to the north and other language groups in Iran. No one is specifically designated by the generic term Amorite, although more specific tribal designations are well attested. In addition to the settled population, we now have textual evidence of an Amorite nomadic population, viewed in ancient sources differently from the settled folk, and designated with a special Amorite term, *hanâ.* There is abundant evidence of the tribal organization of the Amorites, which encompassed both the settled and transhumant population groups. The tribal structure was fluid, and one cannot transfer information from one period and place to another. In Syria during the 18th century the various clans were subsumed under two larger groups, the Yamina (Benê-Yamina) and the Sim'al (Benê-Sim'al), the "sons of the Left (North)" and "of the Right (South)." The former were found primarily in the Ḫabur region, while the latter were settled and grazed in the area around Mari.

Amorite, classified as West Semitic, was one of at least three Semitic linguistic stocks that were used during the 2nd millennium, together with varieties of Akkadian and a different set of dialects, possibly related to Akkadian, that were the descendants of 3rd-millennium Eblaite. Unlike the other two, it was never written, and Amorite speakers chose to write exclusively in Akkadian. The language is therefore known from personal names, loanwords in contemporary Akkadian, as well as

AMOS, BOOK OF

survivals in later Babylonian literary language. The history of the Amorites and of the Amorite language is difficult to trace after the 16th century. The words *mar-tu* and *amurrû* continued to be used in a variety of ways in texts, and a kingdom of Amurru existed in western Syria, but it is unclear what connection, if any, this has with the Amorites of earlier times.

Bibliography. G. Buccellati, "Amorites," *OEANE,* 1:107-11; R. M. Whiting, "Amorite Tribes and Nations of Second-Millennium Western Asia," *CANE,* 2:1231-42.

PIOTR MICHALOWSKI

AMOS (Heb. *ʿāmôs*), **BOOK OF**

A compilation of speeches, sayings, and vision reports attributed to the career of an 8th-century B.C.E. prophetic figure. It is the earliest of the OT books that contain the messages of individual prophets, preserved in antiquity as part of the Book of the Twelve Minor Prophets.

Amos the Prophet

According to the scant information within the book itself, which is the only available historical source, the prophet Amos was a resident of the southern kingdom of Judah who prophesied in the northern kingdom of Israel during the middle part of the 8th century. Amos is identified as a resident of Tekoa, a village 10 km. (6 mi.) S of Jerusalem, on the boundary of the Judean wilderness. Amos 1:1 describes him as a *nōqēḏ* ("shepherd"), while in 7:14 Amos refers to himself as a *bôqēr* ("herdsman") and a "tender of sycamore fig trees." This combination of vocational terms suggests that Amos was either a seasonal worker of varied skills or possibly a person of some means who owned sheep, cattle, and land sufficient to raise sycamore figs as cattle fodder. Although Amos engaged self-consciously in the activity of prophesying, he explicitly denied the vocation of a *nāḇîʾ* (7:14), a professional prophet supported by a cultic or royal shrine. He was at effort to show that he prophesied only by divine compulsion under extraordinary circumstances (3:8; 7:15). That Amos' message portrayed contemporary religious institutions as corrupt perhaps explains why a nonspecialist such as Amos was compelled to perform the prophetic role of a religious intermediary.

Historical Setting

Amos 1:1 places his activity during the reigns of Jeroboam II in Israel (786-746) and Uzziah in Judah (783-742). These two monarchs were able to exploit a period of relative weakness among the regional superpowers of Egypt and Assyria, thereby securing political stability and territorial expansion. Control of the intercontinental trade route passing through the Transjordan region fueled economic prosperity and bureaucratic expansion of Jeroboam's monarchic government. Excavations of Jeroboam's capital city of Samaria have yielded archaeological evidence of urban population growth and the development of an economic elite possessing large houses furnished with imported luxury items. The accelerated redistribution of land, economic resources, and social authority from a kinship- and land-based society to the centralized bureaucracy of an expanding state created much of the social upheaval that provides the setting for Amos' message. Amos is portrayed as Yahweh's spokesperson for those who were disenfranchised as a result of rapid social change.

Amos 1:1 dates Amos' prophesying to "two years before the earthquake." His message employed earthquake imagery (8:8; 9:1, 5, 9) to describe Yahweh's impending judgment of Israel. An earthquake during the reign of Uzziah was apparently severe enough to be remembered some three centuries later in Zech. 14:4-5. Archaeological evidence from the northern Israelite city of Hazor indicates a severe earthquake occurred during the mid-8th century. Amos also uses the image of a solar eclipse (8:9) to describe divine judgment. Two solar eclipses can be dated within Amos' presumed lifetime (784 and 763). Amos' message perhaps owes its preservation to the perception among some of his hearers that he had identified a connection between cosmic disturbances of heaven and earth and the social upheaval of 8th-century Israel.

Contents

The superscription in 1:1 very briefly describes the book as "the words of Amos . . . which he saw concerning Israel," indicating the visionary and revelatory nature of Amos' message. Amos 1:2 functions as a thesis for the entire book. The angry roar of an enraged Yahweh from his universal throne in Jerusalem signals distress and destruction encompassing the entire created order, and demonstrates the cosmic dimension of Israel's social and moral offenses.

Chs. 1 and 2 contain a unified speech comprised of seven highly stylized oracles of judgment against Israel's neighboring states, concluding with Judah and followed by an eighth, extended oracle of judgment against Israel itself. Each oracle begins with the formula "Thus says Yahweh, 'For three transgressions of ———, and for four, I will not revoke the punishment,'" followed by a general description of the nation's offense and a declaration of punishment. The rhetorical effect of the first seven oracles is to emphasize the concluding judgment against Israel itself. Unlike the general accusations against their neighbors, Israel's crimes are spelled out in a list of seven offenses that are violations of Israel's covenant traditions. In a reversal of Israel's sacred traditions of election and salvation that is characteristic of Amos' message, Israel's salvation history does not exempt them from judgment, but instead intensifies their punishment because of their unique relationship and responsibility to Yahweh (3:1-2).

Chs. 3–6 employ a variety of rhetorical devices and speech forms to describe Israel's sins and to announce Yahweh's judgment. The rhetorical versatility of this section includes the use of riddles (3:3-8; 6:12), a parable (3:12), a taunt (4:1), satire (4:4-5), doxologies (4:13; 5:8-9), a funeral lament (5:1-2), and woe oracles (5:18; 6:1; 6:4). Amos' denunciation of Israel is based upon the irony of increasing social and economic exploitation, on the one hand, and a heightened degree of religious activity, on the other. Israel's prosperity is described in references to "winter houses," "summer houses," "houses of ivory," "great houses" (3:15), and "houses of hewn stones" (5:11), where the wealthy live in leisure and indulgence (6:4-6) at the expense of the disenfranchised poor (4:1; 5:10-12). Their myriad religious practices are declared to be abhorrent to Yahweh (5:21-24) because they serve to insulate the wealthy from the plight of the poor and to mitigate the demands of conscience. Amos satirizes Israel's religious observances as activity that actually increases their transgression (4:4-5). Though they love to bring sacrifices, tithes, and freewill offerings, Israel's copious religious acts do not demonstrate that they had "returned" to Yahweh (4:6, 8, 9, 10, 11). Military conquest (3:11) and exile (5:27; 6:7) describe the judgment to be visited upon Israel.

Chs. 7–9 contain a series of reports of five visions of impending doom for Israel. In the first two visions (7:1-6), Amos is shown threatening images of judgment, first by locust plague and then fire. After each vision, Amos intercedes for Israel and Yahweh reverses the decision of judgment. The third vision of a plumb line (7:7-9), however, is followed by a declaration of judgment, with no intercession and no revocation of punishment.

The vision reports are interrupted in 7:10-17 by a narrative of Amos' confrontation with Amaziah, priest of the royal shrine at Bethel. The purpose of this narrative, which depicts the intractability of Israel's religious establishment, is to explain why Yahweh's announced judgment will not again be reversed. Yahweh's irrevocable judgment is restated in the fourth vision (8:1-3) by means of a wordplay in Hebrew. The vision of a basket of summer fruit *(qāyiṣ)* is interpreted to mean that the end *(qēṣ)* has come to Israel.

In the fifth vision, Amos sees Yahweh standing by the altar of the temple pronouncing utter and complete destruction for the people and the land in language evocative of an earthquake. The vision is followed by an oracle (9:2-4) describing the comprehensive scope of Yahweh's destruction and by a final doxology (9:5-6) that affirms the justice of the omnipotent deity who executes such judgment.

The final section of the book (9:7-15) softens the oracles of doom in the preceding sections by limiting the extent of Israel's destruction. Amos 9:8 states that Yahweh will not utterly destroy "the house of Jacob." Amos 9:9-10 uses the metaphor of a sieve, by which the sinners of Israel are sifted out through judgment while a remnant remains. Amos 9:11-15 is the most hopeful passage in the book, with its promise of a time of restoration and salvation for the people of Israel at some undetermined future date. This final passage is at such variance with the doom of the rest of the book that many conclude that it was a late addition. The cosmology of the book of Amos, however, suggests that if divine judgment is a corrective to corporate injustice, then the expected result would be a restored harmony once judgment is completed. The promised restoration of Amos 9:11-15, whatever its origin and however stark its contrast with the rest of the book, is nevertheless compatible with the cosmic dimension of Amos' message.

Composition

In addition to 9:11-15, other passages such as the three doxologies, certain references to Judah, and some of the oracles against the nations have also been questioned as late additions to an "original" collection of Amos material. Although numerous reconstructions of the various literary layers of composition of the book have been proposed, each proposal is based upon a subjective view of what "earlier" forms of the book must have been like. Recent studies have sought to demonstrate how the entire content of the book may be understood within the 8th-century historical context of the prophet Amos, or as the coherent work of an editor not far removed from Amos' historical situation. Whether or not one accepts all of the book of Amos as a product of the 8th century, the book in its present form presents a consistency of message and a coherence of thought from the diverse sayings and speech forms preserved within it. The echoes of the prophet Amos' overriding message of a created order established upon the foundation of social justice continues to inspire readers and reformers across the millennia.

Bibliography. F. I. Andersen and D. N. Freedman, *Amos.* AB 24A (New York, 1989); J. H. Hayes, *Amos, The Eighth-Century Prophet* (Nashville, 1988); S. M. Paul, *Amos.* Herm (Minneapolis, 1991); M. Polley, *Amos and the Davidic Empire* (Oxford, 1989).

BARRY A. JONES

AMOZ (Heb. *'āmôṣ*)
The father of the prophet Isaiah (2 Kgs. 19:2; Isa. 1:1). Tradition calls him the brother of King Amaziah of Judah and uncle of King Uzziah.

AMPHIPOLIS (Gk. *Amphípolis*)
A Macedonian city on the North Aegean coast, ca. 4–5 km. (2.5–3 mi.) inland from the port city of Eion and ca. 50 km. (31 mi.) WSW from Philippi along the Via Egnatia. It takes its name ("around-city") from the Strymon River, which curved around the terraced city on three sides. Founded by Thracians and colonized by Athenians (437 B.C.E.), it eventually fell to the Romans (168), who made it the capital of the first district of Macedonia.

Luke indicates that Paul and Silas passed through Amphipolis on their way from Philippi to Thessalonica (Acts 17:1). RICHARD S. ASCOUGH

AMPLIATUS (Gk. *Ampliátos*)
A member of the Christian community at Rome whom Paul calls affectionately "my beloved in the Lord" (Rom. 16:8; some Greek MSS read Amplias).

AMRAM (Heb. *'amrām*)
1. The grandson of Levi (Exod. 6:16-18) and son (or "descendant") of Kohath; husband of

Jochebed, his father's sister (Exod. 6:20; 1 Chr. 6:2-3[MT 5:28-29]). Amram's clan, the Amramites, included his three famous children: Moses, Miriam, and Aaron (Num. 26:59). As part of the tribe of Levi, the Amramites were assigned duties associated with the cult center of Israel (Num. 3:27), including the treasury (1 Chr. 26:23-24). The name appears often in genealogical lists.

2. The son of Bani. A postexilic resident of Jerusalem, he divorced his non-Judean wife during the reforms of Ezra (Ezra 10:34).

J. Randall O'Brien

AMRAPHEL (Heb. *'amrāpel*)
King of Shinar and one of the four kings from the East who joined together under Chedorlaomer, king of Elam, to attack the five kings in the Dead Sea Valley (Gen. 14:1, 9). This coalition plundered Sodom and Gomorrah before taking Abraham's nephew Lot captive. Abraham gathered together a force that defeated the coalition and rescued Lot and the other captives.

Shinar, where Amraphel resided, was later identified in the OT with Babylon (Isa. 11:11; Dan. 1:2; Zech. 5:11), while the Targums and 1QapGen 21:23 rendered it as Babel. Amraphel was once identified with the Babylonian king Hammurabi, under the assumption that Amraphel reflected an inaccurate Hebrew rendering of a variant of the cuneiform name. If correct, this would historically situate Abraham between 1728 and 1686 B.C.E. No documentation, however, exists that Hammurabi ever campaigned in Palestine. Others use the Akkadian "Chedorlaomer texts," the so-called Spartoli Tablets, to equate Amraphel with Marduk-apaliddina II (Merodach-baladan), chief of the Chaldean tribe of Bît-yakin, who twice seized the Babylonian throne from Assyria (722-710 and 703). These theories remain philogically unconvincing, although the geographical details and possible Akkadian influences support the basic credibility of the narrative. Most likely, Amraphel was a member of a coalition of minor figures, whom Abraham could rout with no more than 318 warriors.

Bibliography. M. C. Astour, "Political and Cosmic Symbolism in Genesis 14 and in its Babylonian Sources," in *Biblical Motifs*, ed. A. Altmann (Cambridge, Mass., 1966), 65-112. Kenneth Atkinson

AMULET
Charms worn to provide supernatural protection against sickness, accidents, curses, and evil spirits, and to assure physical and material well-being. Amulets were made from semiprecious stones, gems, beads, precious metals, and perishable materials, and many were inscribed with religious symbols or magical incantations (cf. Zech. 14:20; Rev. 2:17). Miniature images of gods or goddesses were also used as amulets (cf. Gen. 35:4). Amulets were pervasive throughout the ancient Near East, and numerous examples have been discovered: sun disks, crescent moons, ankhs, and Astarte figurines. Isaiah condemns the wearing of amulets and similar magical paraphernalia (Isa. 3:18-21; cf. Exod. 32:3-4; Judg. 8:21, 26; 2 Macc. 12:40).

Paul Anthony Hartog

AMZI (Heb. *'amṣî*)
1. A Levite of the family of Merari; the son of Bani and an ancestor of Ethan (1 Chr. 6:46[MT 31]).

2. A priest, the son of Zechariah and an ancestor of Adaiah (Neh. 11:12).

ANAB (Heb. *'ănaḇ*)
One of the cities in the hill country of Judah where Joshua defeated the Anakim (Josh. 11:21; 15:50). It has been identified with Khirbet 'Anâb eṣ-Ṣeghîreh (145091), ca. 5 km. (3 mi.) W of Debir.

ANAH (Heb. *'ănâ*)
1. The son of Zibeon the Horite; father of Oholibamah the wife of Esau (Gen. 36:2, 14, 18; 1 Chr. 1:40). According to Gen. 36:24 he discovered the hot springs in the wilderness.

2. The fourth son of Seir the Horite (Gen. 36:20, 29; 1 Chr. 1:38, 41). Textual difficulties make the relationship between Anah **1** and **2** highly uncertain.

ANAHARATH (Heb. *'ănāḥărāṯ*)
A city in the valley of Jezreel assigned to Issachar (Josh. 19:19). Listed among the towns captured by Thutmose III, it has been identified with Tell el-Mukharkhash/Tel Rekhesh (194228), 7 km. (4 mi.) SE of Mt. Tabor.

ANAIAH (Heb. *'ănāyâ*)
1. One of the six men (probably priests) who stood at Ezra's right hand when he read to the people from the book of the law (Neh. 8:4).

2. A chief who, on behalf of his people, set his seal to the renewed covenant under Nehemiah (Neh. 10:22[MT 23]). He may be the same as **1** above.

ANAK (Heb. *'ănāq*)
The son of Arba and ancestor of Ahiman, Sheshai, and Talmai (Num. 13:22; Josh. 15:13-14; 21:11; Judg. 1:20). The name is also taken as a tribal designation equivalent to the Anakim, regarded as the descendants of Anak.

ANAKIM (Heb. *'ănāqîm*)
Descendants of Anak (Num. 13:22) who lived in the southern part of Canaan, especially in the city of Hebron. The original name of Hebron was Kiriath-arba, named after its founder Arba, the forefather of Anak (Josh. 15:13) and the greatest of the Anakim (14:15).

Descendants of the Nephilim (Num. 13:32-33), the Anakim were a tall people (cf. Heb. *'ănāq*, "long-necked" or "giant"), to whom were compared the Rephaim in Ammon (whom the Ammonites called Zamzummites; Deut. 2:20-21) and the Emim in Moab (v. 10). Anakim may be a generic term used in the OT to describe the imposing height of all the original inhabitants of Canaan, rather than a proper name for a particular nation or tribe (cf. Amos 2:9). When Moses sent the 12 spies to explore the land of Canaan, 10 of them brought back a pessimistic report, declaring that they were terrified by the size of the inhabitants of Canaan (Num. 13:32-33).

Despite their size, the Anakim were conquered by Joshua and driven from the land. Only a small remnant survived, finding refuge in the Philistine cities of Gaza, Gath, and Ashdod (Josh. 11:21-22). When Caleb conquered Hebron, the stronghold of the Anakim, he drove out their three clans, Ahiman, Sheshai, and Talmai (Num. 13:22; Josh. 15:14).

CLAUDE F. MARIOTTINI

ANAMIM (Heb. *ʿănāmîm*)
Descendants of Egypt (Gen. 10:13; 1 Chr. 1:11), variously considered to be the Kenemites (of the Knmt oasis W of Egypt), Cyrenians, or inhabitants of the Nile Delta.

ANAMMELECH (Heb. *ʿănammeleḵ*)
A Sepharvite deity to whom children were sacrificed (2 Kgs. 17:31). Identification is uncertain, possibly the Mesopotamian Anu or Syrian Anath.

ANAN (Heb. *ʿānān*)
One of the chiefs setting his seal to the renewed covenant under Nehemiah (Neh. 10:26).

ANANI (Heb. *ʿănānî*)
One of the seven sons of Elioenai, a postexilic descendant of David (1 Chr. 3:24).

ANANIAH (Heb. *ʿănanyâ*) **(PERSON)**
The father of Maaseiah, whose son Azariah assisted in rebuilding the walls of Jerusalem (Neh. 3:23).

ANANIAH (Heb. *ʿănanyâ*) **(PLACE)**
A town which the Benjaminites resettled after the Exile (Neh. 11:32), perhaps el-ʿAzarîyeh (biblical Bethany; 174131), ca. 3 km. (2 mi.) E of Jerusalem.

ANANIAS (Gk. *Hananías*)

1. A member of the early Christian community in Jerusalem, the husband of Sapphira (Acts 5:1-10). Ananias and his wife held back some of the proceeds of the sale of their land, giving to the community only a portion. Peter interprets this as lying to the apostolic leadership, the Holy Spirit, and God. Consequently, both Ananias and Sapphira died, apparently as enactment of God's judgment. The exact nature of their sin is not made clear (e.g., the text does not say whether they explicitly claimed to be giving the entire proceeds of the sale). Confirmation from 1 Cor. 5:1-8 that such serious pronouncements were occasionally made against sinful community members allows for the possibility that the Ananias story is rooted in early Jerusalem community traditions and may have a historical kernel.

2. A disciple in Damascus who played a role in the call/conversion of Saul/Paul (Acts 9:10-18; 22:12-16). Ananias receives a vision to go to Saul, now blind in Damascus, and lay hands on him that he might receive his sight. Ananias protests, given Saul's reputation as a persecutor of the Church. Through the recounting of the vision to Ananias, the reader learns that Saul is to be God's instrument to bring God's name before Jews and Gentiles (Acts 9:15). Paul's account of this event, through his speech of Acts 22, essentially complements Acts 9. It seems unlikely that Luke would have made up this character, given the negative association of the name with other characters in Acts.

3. The 21st Jewish high priest, appointed by Herod Agrippa II, and ruling ca. 47-58 C.E. He was killed by Jewish rebels in 66 for pro-Roman leanings. Ananias appears in Acts as the priest before whom Paul was brought (Acts 23:2-5) and who personally supervised the case against Paul before the Roman governor Felix (24:1).

Bibliography. G. Lüdemann, *Early Christianity According to the Traditions in Acts* (Minneapolis, 1989).

J. BRADLEY CHANCE

ANAT (Heb. *ʿănāṯ*)
A Northwest Semitic goddess of war. Anat is portrayed unambiguously in the Ugaritic texts wielding bow and sword against both human and supernatural enemies, and is even described as joyously wading through the blood of slain warriors. Scholars agree that she plays a supportive role in her brother Baal's quest for a palace and the kingship that a royal residence implies. The consensus view that Anat is portrayed at Ugarit as a sexually active "fertility-goddess" and consort of her brother Baal has been recently challenged. The challengers claim that no text unambiguously refers to Anat having intercourse or bearing children, and impugn the notion that all female deities are sexually active and reproductive fertility goddesses.

Anat the goddess is nowhere clearly mentioned in the OT, though her name may appear as a component of the proper name Shamgar ben Anath (e.g., Judg. 3:31) and the place name Beth-anath (Josh. 19:38; Judg. 1:33). On the basis of conjectural emendation, proposals have been made to read a reference to the goddess in Exod. 32:18; Hos. 14:8(MT 9). Several scholars have suggested that the "Queen of Heaven" in Jer. 7:18; 44:17 is Anat, and one has understood Job 31:1 as referring to Anat by the Hebrew equivalent of her Ugaritic epithet *btlt* ("virgin"). Allusions to Anat have been proposed for Judg. 5; Cant. 7. Discovery of an Anat temple in Beth-shan suggests that mentioned at 1 Sam. 31:10.

Bibliography. P. L. Day, "Anat," *DDD*, 36-43; N. H. Walls, *The Goddess Anat in Ugaritic Myth*. SBLDS 135 (Atlanta, 1992).

PEGGY L. DAY

ANATH (Heb. *ʿănāṯ*)
The father of the judge Shamgar (Judg. 3:31; 5:6).

ANATHEMA
The recipient or object of a curse. Gk. *anáthema* and its cognate verb *anathematízō* ("to put under a curse") are used in the LXX to translate words from

Procession of the Twelve Gods, attendant in the New Year's festival in honor of the storm-god of Ḫattuša. Chamber B of the Hittite sanctuary at Yazilikaya (Association HATTI, Université de Paris-I, Sorbonne)

the Hebrew root *ḥrm,* which identified objects completely devoted to God and, notably, the Canaanite cities that were under Israelite ban. Several times in the NT the words refer to oaths (Mark 14:71; Acts 23:12, 14, 21).

In Paul's writings *anáthema* means "curse." God is normally the implied subject of the cursing, making the term synonymous with damnation (Rom. 9:3; 1 Cor. 16:22; Gal. 1:8, 9). Paul uses other curse language for those who seek to be justified by the Law (Gal. 3:10, 13), and he remarks that no one speaking by the Spirit (i.e., charismatic utterance) can say "Jesus is anathema," the opposite of which is the confession "Jesus is Lord" (1 Cor. 12:3).

GARY S. SHOGREN

ANATHOTH (Heb. *ʿănāṯôṯ*)

A levitical city in the tribal territory of Benjamin. Abiathar, David's priest, owned some fields there and was banished to the city by Solomon (1 Kgs. 2:26-27). Two of David's elite warriors, Abiezer (2 Sam. 23:29) and Jehu (1 Chr. 12:3), were from Anathoth. The prophet Jeremiah came from Anathoth (Jer. 1:1; 29:27) and owned a field there (32:7-9); ironically, some of Jeremiah's fiercest opposition came from the people of Anathoth (11:21-23). After the Babylonian Exile, people from this city were among the first to return to Judah (Ezra 2:23).

The location of Anathoth has not been identified conclusively. Two sites have been suggested, one near modern Anata (175135; 5 km. [3 mi.] NE of Jerusalem) and the other immediately S of Anata at Râs el-Kharrûbeh (174135). Soundings at the latter site have yielded small quantities of sherds from the Iron through the Roman periods. Some scholars believe the site shifted from Râs el-Kharrûbeh during the Iron Age to Anata during the Hellenistic and Roman periods. Recently, Khirbet Deir es-Sidd has been suggested as a third possibility; soundings from the site indicate a settlement during the late 7th and early 6th centuries B.C.

Bibliography. Y. Nadelman, "The Identification of Anathoth and the Soundings at Khirbet Deir es-Sidd," *IEJ* 44 (1994): 62-74. SCOTT M. LANGSTON

ANATOLIA

See ASIA MINOR.

ANATOLIAN CULTS

The religious life of Anatolia reflects diverse cultural influences over the course of several thousand years. From as early as the 7th millennium B.C.E., bulls' heads and a Mother Goddess featured prominently in domestic shrines at Çatal Höyük. Tablets from the 3rd millennium begin the historical record and show interactions between Old Assyrian trading colonies and local Anatolian rulers. The subsequent Hittite civilization dominated most of the peninsula for the 2nd millennium. The Hittites left huge rock sculptures of their deities, including a gallery of 63 deities in the natural rock shrine at Yazilikaya, their national sanctuary near their capital (Ḫattuša/Boghazköy) E of Ankara.

In the middle of the 1st millennium, smaller kingdoms dominated territories within the peninsula. In the mountainous east, Urartian culture flourished (ca. 900-600). The short-lived Phrygian Empire rose in the west, succeeded by the Lydian Empire centered at Sardis. Lydian culture, which shows more affinity with Greek culture, was at its height under the Mermnad dynasty (ca. 700-550) before giving way to the Persian Achaemenian Empire. Persian domination in Anatolia (546-334) left its legacy in the worship of deities such as the moon-god Mên and the goddess Anaietis (Anahita) and in religious groups which persisted well into the Christian era. A Persian family held the important priesthood of Artemis at Ephesus until the 4th century C.E. In addition, Lycians, Pisidians, Pamphylians, Carians, Lycaonians, Cilicians, and Cappadocians each represent distinct cultures in their respective ethnic territories.

In the Hellenistic era, the presence of Greek settlers and their deities expanded from western Asia Minor into the Anatolian interior. Worship of deities such as Zeus, Apollo, Leto, and Artemis, however, also reflects the application of Greek names to traditional Anatolian deities like Apollo Lairbenos. Greek and Anatolian religion should be seen as overlapping entities which mutually influenced one another.

Jewish settlements in the interior of Asia Minor were known as early as the 3rd century B.C.E. when Antiochus III resettled 2000 Jewish families from Babylonia into Lydia and Phrygia. A sizable synagogue at Sardis attests to their prominence there, and evidence remains of their importance in other locations. Scholars differ on the significance of inscriptions naming *Theos Hypsistos* (Highest God) for Jewish influence in Anatolia.

The Galatians crossed from Europe into Anatolia in 278 B.C.E. as a mass migration of hundreds of thousands of marauding Celts. They maintained their tribal organization and were a dominant presence in the interior even after they were contained by Attalus I of Pergamum. Galatians adopted many religious practices of the territories they occupied and found their way into major positions in the temple state at Pessinus.

Under Roman domination the process of Hellenization expanded, and the Roman imperial cult became another major feature of Anatolian religious life. The emperors were incorporated into the Anatolian pattern of monarchical deities. Emperor worship added impressive sanctuaries to Anatolian cities and a Roman style of public religious activity, including games, banquets, and food distributions.

Worship of the Mother of the Gods *(Mḗtēr Theṓn)* was a consistent feature of Anatolian religion. Her later Hellenized portrayals, seated between two lions, bear striking iconographic similarity to a terracotta of the goddess between two felines discovered at Çatal Höyük. In modern sources she is often called Cybele, and one of her earlier names was Kubaba. In the Greco-Roman era, in addition to *Mḗtēr Theṓn,* she was known as Agdistis or by a local place name. Usually she was named for a local mountain, such as the Mētēr Dindymene for Mount Dindymus overlooking her temple state at Pessinus. The Mḗtēr Sipylene was also a huge image of the goddess carved into Mt. Sipylus probably during the Hittite era. Similar huge rock-cut figures survive from the Phrygians. The Mother of the Gods was served by self-castrated functionaries called *galli.* Her male companion, also castrated, was Attis, and the priest-king of her temple state was called the Attis. In Cappadocia in eastern Anatolia, the Mother of the Gods gave way to the goddess Mâ (Bellona).

Forms of cult organization and worship reflect a variety of influences, including Greek and Roman forms. Several features characterize the distinctive religious ethos of Anatolia, including temple-states ruled by priest-kings and inhabited by sacred slaves *(hierodouloi).* In addition to Pessinus were the large temple-states of Mâ, Anaeitis, the Venasian Zeus, Mên, and others. Temple-states frequently functioned as commercial centers on the trade routes and had large land holdings.

Many Anatolians perceived their deities as powerful monarchical figures who administered justice at all levels of community life. Confession inscriptions from Phrygia and Lydia recount offenders' experiences of punishment by these "enforcer" deities. Having been punished by the deity, they inscribed a stela to confess and to commemorate the deity's power as a form of recompense. Abundant curses invoke divine punishment upon potential offenders, especially as protection for graves and tombstones. Victims also placed written curses in temples to plead their case and to invoke divine action against culprits. Angels and scepters also played a role in this divine judicial system. This "judicial" ethos is seen in the names of such distinctively Anatolian deities as the divine pair Holy and Just *(Hosios* and *Dikaios),* portrayed with scales and scepter, and the goddess Dikaiosynē.

Anatolian worship included enthusiastic forms associated with divine possession. The *galli* of the Mother of the Gods were known for their frenzied possession by her in their act of self-castration and subsequent bloody performances of self-punishment, but orgiastic forms of worship were not confined to them. In the Christian era, such ecstatic forms are also reflected in the Montanist movement.

The Anatolian context is significant for NT writings, including Acts, Galatians, Colossians, 1 Peter, and Revelation; and other early Christian writings, including Ignatius of Antioch, the Martyrdom of Polycarp, and the Cappadocian Fathers.

Bibliography. E. Akurgal, *Ancient Civilizations and Ruins of Turkey,* 4th ed. (Istanbul, 1978); S. Mitchell, *Anatolia: Land, Men, and Gods in Asia Minor,* 2 vols. (Oxford, 1993); S. R. F. Price, *Rituals and Power: The Roman Imperial Cult in Asia Minor* (Cambridge, 1984); L. Robert, *Opera Minora Selecta,* 5 vols. (Amsterdam, 1969-1989).

SUSAN (ELLI) ELLIOTT

ANCESTOR

Founder of a family or people. Descendants viewed themselves as expressions of immediate or distant ancestors, and ancestors were considered present in the institutions and traditions of the family. The term used for "ancestor" (Heb. *'āḇ*) is the word for "father," translated "patriarch" in some passages and versions.

Israel participated in its salvation and calling through God's gracious action toward Abraham, Isaac, and Jacob. Yahweh was "God of the ancestors" (Deut. 1:11), and through them Israel was promised land (1:8; Gen. 28:13), many descendants (Deut. 13:17), and a blessing (Gen. 12:3). Because of his covenant oath with the ancestors, Yahweh delivered Israel from Egypt (Deut. 7:8; Exod. 2:24-25; 6:2-9) and would continue to be merciful toward them (Deut. 4:31). However, continued fulfillment of the promises rested on Israel's obedience to the Sinai covenant (Deut. 29:1[MT 28:69]–30:20). The exilic prophet appealed to the ancestors to inspire hope for God's future deliverance (Isa. 51:1-3).

The NT affirms that the story of salvation culminating with God's act in Christ had its beginning in the promises and election of the ancestors (Luke 1:46-55; Acts 13:15-41; Rom. 9; Gal. 3:15-16). Paul states that through the mystery of God's mercy, the election of Israel through the ancestors would not be revoked (Rom. 11:11-35).

Bibliography. C. Barth, "God Chose the Fathers of Israel," in *God with Us* (Grand Rapids, 1991), 38-55; C. Westermann, *The Promises to the Fathers: Studies in the Patriarchal Narratives* (Philadelphia, 1980). LAURIE J. BRAATEN

ANCIENT OF DAYS

Aram. *'attîq yômîn* appears in the "throne vision" of Dan. 7:9-14, after the initial appearance of the four great beasts who rise from the sea (cf. 7:22). Such a term in reference to God, presumably the referent here, is unprecedented in the Hebrew texts, although associations with "Everlasting Father" in Isa. 9:6b have been suggested. The most likely source of the imagery is Canaanite myth, since El, the head of the heavenly pantheon, is referred to as *'abu šanima* ("father of years") and often portrayed on a throne with heavenly attendants (cf. Isa. 6). The association of El with age generally ("grey beard") is also notable in Canaanite mythology. The context of the phrase, occurring in proximity to "One like a Son of Man," which draws clearly on Baal imagery, further supports this association.

Bibliography. M. Pope, *El in the Ugaritic Texts.* VTSup 2 (Leiden, 1955).

DANIEL L. SMITH-CHRISTOPHER

ANDREW (Gk. *Andréas*)

One of the 12 apostles, always among the first four so named (Matt. 10:2; Mark 3:18; Luke 6:14; cf. Acts 1:13). Andrew is the brother of Simon Peter (Matt. 4:18; Mark 1:16; Luke 6:14; John 1:40), and the son of John (Matt. 16:17; John 1:42).

The first two Gospels identify Andrew and Peter as fishermen who plied their trade in the region around the Sea of Galilee (Matt. 4:18; Mark 1:16), and both relate that Andrew lived with Peter and his family in Capernaum (Mark 1:29). Andrew is one of four apostles who questioned Jesus about the destruction of the temple and who received special instruction (Mark 13), and he is present later in Jerusalem with the other apostles awaiting the promise of the Spirit (Acts 1:12-14).

John's Gospel depicts Andrew as one of John the Baptist's disciples who, upon hearing John proclaim that Jesus is "the Lamb of God," tells Peter that Jesus is "the Messiah" and brings him to Jesus (John 1:35-42). One of four of Jesus' disciples from Bethsaida (John 1:43-51), Andrew is the one who directs Jesus' attention to the boy with loaves and fishes (6:8) and who, along with Philip, informs Jesus that a group of Greeks wishes to see him (12:20-22).

Andrew appears in several apocryphal acts (e.g., Acts of Andrew). According to tradition, Andrew preached in Scythia and was crucified in Achaia. The patron saint of Scotland and Russia, his feast date is Nov. 30.

Bibliography. K. R. Brooks, ed., *Andreas, and the Fates of the Apostles* (Oxford, 1961); P. M. Peterson, *Andrew, Brother of Simon Peter.* NovTSup 1 (Leiden, 1958). JEFFREY T. TUCKER

ANDREW, ACTS OF

One of several apocryphal books (ca. mid-2nd century) of the acts of various individual apostles. It is first mentioned by Eusebius (*HE* 3.25.26), who regarded it as heretical. No complete manuscript survives, but it can be pieced together in large part and Gregory of Tours' *Liber de Miraculis* (6th century) contains an extensive summary. Originally written in Greek, parts and fragments are extant in Greek, Latin, Coptic, and Armenian. No discernible sources or authentic historical traditions lie behind the text. It appears to be an entirely fictional creation for the inspiration, edification, and entertainment of its 2nd-century Christian audience. The book's value lies in its reflection of the thinking of one strand of Christianity at that time.

The story tells of how, after the ascension of Jesus, the apostle Andrew, brother of Peter, embarks on missionary journeys throughout Asia Minor and Macedonia. He performs miracles, healings, and demon exorcisms and raises the dead. He encounters trouble in Patrae when he heals and subsequently converts Maximilla, wife of the proconsul Aegeates, and also converts the proconsul's brother, Stratocles. Maximilla then chooses a life of celibacy, to the horror of her husband. Aegeates takes revenge by having Andrew crucified. Andrew preaches from the cross for three days, exhorting his audience to celibacy and disdain for the things of this world. Aegeates finally decides to release Andrew, but Andrew declines. He condemns Aegeates and then dies. Aegeates later commits suicide.

The Acts of Andrew displays remarkably little Christian theology, and Andrew says little about Christ. Although some scholars have seen affinities with Gnosticism, Neo-Platonism, or Stoicism, the work shows no consistent philosophical position.

Bibliography. J.-M. Prieur and W. Schneemelcher, "The Acts of Andrew," in *New Testament Apocrypha,* ed. E. Hennecke-W. Schneemelcher, rev. ed. (Louisville, 1991), 2:101-151.

J. CHRISTIAN WILSON

ANDRONICUS (Gk. *Andrónikos*)

1. A deputy under Antiochus IV Epiphanes (2 Macc. 4:31-38). According to 2 Maccabees he was bribed by Menelaus and subsequently encouraged to murder Onias in retaliation for exposing the crime; for this Antiochus ordered his execution. Other sources indicate Antiochus IV had him killed to cover up Andronicus' murder of Seleucus IV's son Antiochus (Diodorus Siculus *Hist.* 30.7.2-3).

2. Commander of the garrison at Gerizim under Antiochus IV Epiphanes (2 Macc. 5:23; cf. v. 22, "governor").

3. A Jewish Christian, perhaps originally from the Jewish community at Tarsus, and fellow prisoner with Paul. Of those to whom the apostle sends his greetings, Andronicus and Junias are called "prominent among the apostles" (Rom. 16:7).

ANEM (Heb. *ʿānēm*) (also EN-GANNIM)
A levitical city in the tribal territory of Issachar, given to the Gershomites (1 Chr. 6:73[MT 58]). At Josh. 19:21; 21:29 it is called En-gannim, which may be identified with modern Jenîn (178207) or Khirbet Beit Jann (196235). For topographical reasons the site is more likely ʿOlam (197230), 11 km. (7 mi.) E of Mt. Tabor, or Khirbet ʿAnim (202231), 3 km. (2 mi.) NE of ʿOlam.

ANER (Heb. *ʿānēr*) **(PERSON)**
An Amorite who, with his brothers Mamre and Eshkol, aided Abraham in his battle against the four eastern kings (Gen. 14:13, 24). Like the names of the brothers, Aner may be a geographical designation.

ANER (Heb. *ʿānēr*) **(PLACE)**
A city in the half-tribe of Manasseh (1 Chr. 6:70[MT 55]), assigned to the clan of the Kohathites as a levitical city. In a second list of levitical cities in Josh. 21:25 Aner is replaced by Taanach. On the basis of this and scribal error, most scholars agree the cities are one and the same. TROY K. RAPPOLD

ANGEL
A spiritual being, primarily a messenger (Heb. *mal'āḵ;* Gk. *ángelos*) for God (e.g., Gen. 16:7, 9; Exod. 3:2; Num. 22:22-35). Other designations include "sons of God" (Job 1:6; Ps. 29:1), "holy ones" (e.g., Ps. 89:7; Dan. 8:13, and "watchers" (Dan. 4:13, 17, 23[MT 10, 14, 20]). Sometimes "heavenly hosts" or "hosts of heaven" also refer to angels (1 Kgs. 22:19 = 2 Chr. 18:18; Ps. 148:2; Neh. 9:6). Heb. *mal'āḵ* is also used for human prophets (2 Chr. 36:15-16; Isa. 44:26; Hag. 1:13), priests (Mal. 2:7), and the winds (Ps. 104:4); Gk. *ángelos* may also refer to human messengers (Luke 9:52; Mark 1:2 par.).

Angels are a part of the creation of God, created either in the beginning or sometime before the foundation of the earth (Ps. 148:2-5; Neh. 9:6; Col. 1:15-17). They are of a higher order than humans (Heb. 2:7) and are greater in power and might (2 Pet. 2:11; cf. 2 Kgs. 19:35). However, they are not to be worshipped by humans (Col. 2:18; Rev. 22:8-9). Angels are not omniscient as is God, for they do not know the time of the coming of Christ (Matt. 24:36; cf. 1 Pet. 1:12). Neither are they omnipresent, for they are said to go from place to place (Dan. 9:21-23). Angels are spirit beings (Heb. 1:14). They do not die, nor do they marry (Luke 20:36; Mark 12:25). While the number of the angels is never definitely given, they are said to be innumerable (Dan. 7:10; Heb. 12:22; Rev. 5:11).

Angels may be wicked (2 Pet. 2:4; Jude 6; cf. Rev. 12:7) or good. Good angels seem to operate in conjunction with the work of the Holy Spirit in bringing God's message to mankind. Should an angel bring another message, he would bear the curse of God (Gal. 1:8-9). Satan can still come as an angel of light, and his ministers as ministers of righteousness, in deceiving and powerful ways (2 Cor. 11:14-15). The phrase "thrones or dominions or rulers or powers" may refer to angels (Col. 1:16).

Angels have a part to play in God's order in heaven, and archangels have certain responsibilities over other angels of their order (1 Thess. 4:16; cf. Rev. 12:7). Righteous angels perform the work of God (Ps. 103:20). They effect the vengeance and wrath of God upon the disobedient, as is seen in the scourge of Israel (2 Sam. 24:16); upon Balaam (Num. 22:31); and when Jesus shall come again with his mighty angels to take vengeance on those that do not know God or obey the gospel (2 Thess. 1:7-10).

Righteous angels administer God's message to mankind in giving the law of Moses (Gal. 3:19; Heb. 2:2) and appear as humans in the revelation of God's messages to the patriarchs (Gen. 18:1–19:5). One should show hospitality to strangers, for some may have "entertained angels without knowing it" (Heb. 13:2). Angels announce the birth of Jesus to Mary (Luke 1:26-28) and in multitudes sing at his birth (2:8-15). They minister to Jesus after his temptation (Matt. 4:11) and appear at his resurrection and ascension (28:1-7; Acts 1:11). Angels are now subject to Christ and will administer his mission when he comes again (1 Pet. 3:22; 1 Thess. 4:16; Matt. 25:31).

Angels work in the destiny of nations for the good of God's people. Good angels withstand Satan while the word of God is being preached to the king of Persia (Zech. 3:1). They work in the protection of the righteous and encamp about them that fear the Lord (Ps. 34:7[8]), and they deliver God's people from their enemies (2 Kgs. 6:15-17). Angels deliver Peter from prison and reassure Paul in the great storm at sea (Acts 12:7; 27:23). They are given charge to keep the righteous in all their ways, and are ministering spirits to those who are heirs of salvation (Ps. 91:11; Heb. 1:14). Angels represent individuals before the throne of God (Matt. 18:10; cf. Dan. 12:1), and if heavenly angels are meant in Rev. 2–3, then they are given specific assignments to congregations of the Church.

Angels are active in the prayers of the righteous, and such prayers avail much before God (Dan.

9:21-23). Angels are in some way involved in assemblies of worship (cf. 1 Cor. 11:10). They rejoice over every sinner that repents (Luke 15:10), and assist in transporting the redeemed into the paradise of God (16:22).

Bibliography. H. Bietenhard, "Angel, Messenger," *NIDNTT* 1:101-3. EDWARD P. MYERS

ANGLE, THE
A location on the wall of Jerusalem where King Uzziah constructed a tower to strengthen the defenses (2 Chr. 26:9). The Angle (Heb. *hammiqṣôaʿ*) is also mentioned as part of the repairs to the walls of Jerusalem ordered by Nehemiah (Neh. 3:19-20, 24-25). It may have been located along the eastern wall, since in Neh. 3 it is listed with the Water Gate, the Wall of Ophel, and the East Gate.

Bibliography. G. Auld and M. L. Steiner, *Jerusalem,* 1: *From the Bronze Age to the Maccabees* (Macon, 1996), 16-18, 39-40; W. H. Mare, *The Archaeology of the Jerusalem Area* (Grand Rapids, 1987), 119-37. DAVID M. VALETA

ANIAM (Heb. *ʾănîʿam*)
A son of Shemida of the tribe of Manasseh (1 Chr. 7:19).

ANIM (Heb. *ʿānîm*)
A border city in the hill country of Judah (Josh. 15:50). It is called Ḫawina in the Amarna Letters. According to Eusebius (*Onom.* 26.9) it was 9 Roman mi. S of Hebron; it is possibly to be identified with Khirbet Ghuwein et-Taḥtā (156084), 20 km. (12.5 mi.) S of Hebron.

ANIMALS
Almost all commentators caution that it is virtually impossible to have 100 percent certainty when identifying Hebrew animal terms with modern scientific species. Today's fauna is not identical to that of the past; also, many of the Hebrew terms appear as isolated names which appear only one or two times in the Bible in texts which give no real hint as to the habitat or characteristics of the named animal; finally, the names for a given animal sometimes changed through time or the same animal is given a different name by neighboring peoples who speak a similar, but not identical dialect or language. In spite of the problems, however, modern scholars have arrived at a general consensus for the identity of most of the animal terms found in the Bible. They have done this by combining etymology, comparative languages, examination of the context of the text, and study of present-day fauna, as well as the fauna in the archaeological record.

Mammals

At least 128 species of wild mammals have been identified in modern Israel so far. These include a large number of small mammals (e.g., rodents, bats), as well as marine mammals. In addition to the wild mammals, at least 10 species of domesticated mammals live in Israel. These include the dog, cat, pig, sheep, goats, cattle, oxen, donkeys, horses, and camels.

The OT provides at least 60 words which have been identified as pertaining to mammals in either a generic or specific sense. Of these, eight have been applied to the horse family; six to large cattle; 14 to small cattle; 14 to carnivores; seven to rodents; one to the monkey; and one generic term referring to large animals. Nine terms are applied to other miscellaneous mammals.

Grouping these terms according to whether the mammals were wild or domesticated, it appears that at least 30 terms refer to wild mammals, while the rest are domestic. The wild mammals can be divided into three groups: large herbivores, large carnivores, and small mammals. The herbivores include the wild ox (aurochs), wild ass or onager, wild goat, gazelle, ibex, fallow deer, roebuck, addax(?), and wild swine. The carnivores include the bear, fox, wolf, hyena, jackal, panther, and lion. Small mammals include rodents, mouse, hare, hyrax, bat, and possibly the porcupine. One term, *qôp̱,* refers to the monkey, which, although probably kept as exotic pets, were nevertheless wild.

The Bible's domestic mammals can also be divided into several groups: camel, horse family (horses, asses, mules), large cattle, and small cattle (sheep and goats). The dog family should probably also be included here, although wild dogs were undoubtedly also plentiful. Of the domestic animals, sheep and goats played the most significant role in the lives of biblical peoples since they provided meat, milk, cheese, skin and wool or goats hair. Not surprisingly, their bones provide the greatest quantity of faunal remains at an archaeological site.

Amphibians

Because Palestine is mostly an arid region, there are few amphibian species. Herpetologists have identified seven species of amphibians currently living in the region — three frogs, two toads, a salamander, and a newt.

The best-known reference to an amphibian in the OT appears in the account of the second Egyptian plague (Ex. 8:1-15), generally understood to be a plague of frogs (*ṣĕp̱ardēaʿ;* cf. Ps. 78:45; 105:30). Frogs also appear in the plague of Rev. 16:13 (Gk. *bátrachos*). Since the plagues occurred in Egypt, the type of frog involved should be identified with one of the local species, either the common *Rana esculanta* (green frog) or *Rana punctata* (spotted frog).

Reptiles

While amphibians are rare, reptiles are plentiful in Palestine. At least 126 species have been identified in modern times. These include the lizard, snake, and turtle families.

The most plentiful group of reptiles is the lizards, of which there are at least 40 species. At least seven Hebrew words have been rendered as lizard by various translators, mostly from the list of unclean foods in Lev. 11:29-30, although probably only three or four words actually refer to lizards and even here there is no certainty. Heb. *lĕṭāâ* appears to be a general term for lizard, although some have equated it with the plentiful Syrian green lizard. Other common or well-known members of the lizard family that might be referred to in the Bible include the gecko (*'ănāqâ* [?]), the skink (*ḥōmeṭ* [?]), the dab lizard (a spiny-tailed hardun also known as the land crocodile, possibly Heb *ṣāḇ*), and the monitor (*kōaḥ* [?]).

There are presently some 35 species of snake in Palestine, eight of which are poisonous. Ten Hebrew and four Greek words have been translated as either serpent, viper, or adder. The contexts suggest that the Bible writers were only concerned with the poisonous snakes.

Correlating the Hebrew and Greek terms with specific species is difficult. Heb. *peṯen* probably refers to the Egyptian cobra. The *śārāp* is probably a general term for desert vipers, of which there are four species in Palestine. The one mostly likely to be identified with the fiery serpent is the carpet viper, which has been numerous and highly poisonous.

Although there do not appear to have been any references to turtles in the Bible (the KJV has mistranslated Lev. 11:29), there are, nevertheless, currently 12 members of the turtle family in Palestine. In addition to seven species or sub-species of sea turtles, there are several species of freshwater turtles and land-dwelling tortoises. The better-known members of Palestine's turtle family include the softshelled turtle (*Trionyx triunguis*), the striped-necked terrapin or pond turtle (*Mauremys caspica rivulata* [*Clemys caspica*]), and the common or spur-thighed tortoise (*Testudo graeca terrestris*).

Some important reptile species no longer live in Palestine. The Nile crocodile (*Crocodylus niloticus*) ranged from the Nile River to the rivers along the coast of Palestine until the last century. Indeed, the Zerqa River, which flows into the Mediterranean near Caesarea, was known as the Crocodile River. However, crocodiles have since been entirely eliminated from the region north of the Aswan Dam in Egypt.

RANDALL W. YOUNKER

ANNA (Gk. *Hánna*)

1. The wife of Tobit and mother of Tobias (Tob. 1:9, 20). She exemplifies the good wife and dutiful mother.

2. An elderly widow of the tribe of Asher who devoutly served daily at the temple and was there at the presentation of the infant Jesus (Luke 2:36-38). She, like Simeon, recognized the Messiah and proclaimed redemption to all in Jerusalem. She is the only woman in the NT who is given the title of prophetess.

3. Mother of Mary and grandmother of Jesus in NT apocryphal writings (esp. the Protevangelium of James). Anna was barren and received the news of her child from angelic messengers. She promised to dedicate the child to God, and took Mary to the temple at the age of three.

JO ANN H. SEELY

ANNAS (Gk. *Hánnas*)

High priest appointed by Quirinius, the governor of Syria, who served 6-15 C.E. (Josephus *Ant.* 18.2.1-2 [26-27]). Five of his sons and his son-in-law Caiaphas became high priests. Although Jesus' arrest, trial, and execution occurred during Caiaphas' priesthood, Annas is designated as high priest in Luke 3:2 (along with Caiaphas); Acts 4:6 (without Caiaphas). In John 18:13-14 Caiaphas is clearly identified as the high priest in power; however, the account implies that Annas is the high priest who first interrogated Jesus. These references to Annas as high priest reflect the power and influence that high priests continued to exert after their deposition (*b. Pesaḥ.* 57a). The desire of the Fourth Evangelist to focus on the role of the Romans in Jesus' arrest and trial may account for the longer account of Annas' inquiry (John 18:19-24) and the cursory treatment of Caiaphas' interrogation (vv. 24, 28).

EMILY CHENEY

ANNO DOMINI

Reckoning from the birth of Jesus, the dating of years "A.D." (Lat. "in the year of the Lord") and the concept of a "Christian era" resulted from the Easter cycle developed in the 6th century by the Scythian monk Dionysius Exiguus. Rather than the year 753 A.U.C. ("from the founding of the city" of Rome) upon which the system is based, the birth of Jesus is now believed to have occurred somewhat earlier, probably ca. 7 to 6 B.C.E.

ANNUNCIATION

The event when the angel Gabriel informs Mary that she will bear a son named Jesus, who will reign over Israel forever (Luke 1:26-38; cf. Matt. 1:18-25, in which an angel informs Joseph; Prot. Jas. 10-12). This annunciation parallels the prophecy of John the Baptist's birth (Luke 1:8-25) and appears to draw upon OT accounts (Gen. 18:1-15; Judg. 13:2-7).

In addition to an announcement, miraculous events surrounding the births of prominent persons were also conventional in Hellenistic literature (e.g., Diogenes Laertius *Lives* 3.1-2; Flavius Philostratus *Life of Apollonius of Tyana* 1.4-6).

GREG CAREY

ANOINT

To apply an oil or ointment to either a person or a thing. People were variously anointed for either cosmetic (Ruth 3:3; cf. Luke 7:46) or medicinal purposes (Isa. 1:6; Luke 10:34; cf. John 9:6, 11) or as part of the embalming process (Mark 16:1; cf. Matt. 26:12). In each of these cases the act was essentially mundane, although cosmetic anointings were usually associated with joyous occasions and so were not performed during periods of mourning (Dan. 10:2-3) or fasting (cf. Jesus' advice contrary to custom at Matt. 6:16-18).

Actual physical anointings, almost always with oil, could also carry important symbolic meanings. Most important in the biblical traditions was anointing with oil so as to set apart, or consecrate, an object or person to God (Exod. 30:25-29). The anointing of a stone pillar signified that the place where it was erected was sacred (Gen. 28:16-18). Similarly, the tabernacle and its furnishings and implements were anointed with oil to set them apart from common, profane uses to a holy and sacred function (Lev. 8:10; Num. 7:1). The anointing of Aaron (Exod. 29:7; Lev. 8:12) and subsequent high priests of Israel (Lev. 21:10) is probably to be understood as serving the same consecratory purpose.

In the case of the anointing of kings and prophets, however, the symbolism of the physical act seems to have gone beyond simply setting the person apart from others. In such cases the anointing also served to convey power and ability to perform the function for which one was being anointed. It further designated that the person had been chosen by God (1 Sam. 9:16), and so kings in particular could be referred to as "the Lord's anointed" (24:6). Although there are numerous references to the actual anointing of Israel's kings (1 Sam. 10:1; 16:3; 1 Kgs. 1:39; 2 Kgs. 9:6; 11:12), there is only a single reference to a literal anointing of a prophet (1 Kgs. 19:16).

Nevertheless, prophets did think of their commissioning as a kind of anointing by God, even if it were more metaphorical than physical. This metaphorical anointing could be associated with receiving the divine Spirit as a form of empowerment for the prophetic task (Isa. 61:1). It was this notion that was most explicitly linked to Jesus as God's anointed (Gk. *Christós*, "Christ"; Heb. *māšîaḥ*, "Messiah") in the NT (Luke 4:18-21; Acts 10:38). Such anointing was not, however, unique to Jesus; Paul claimed for himself and other Christians an anointing by God through the reception of the Holy Spirit (2 Cor. 1:21-22). Although the NT alludes to various contemporary beliefs about an "anointed" or messianic redeemer who would bring political deliverance, it generally distinguishes its convictions about Jesus from these popular beliefs. TIMOTHY B. CARGAL

ANT

Most likely the ants (Heb. *nĕmālâ*) mentioned in Prov. 6:6-8; 30:25 are harvester ants *(Messor Semirufus)*, the most frequent species in Israel today. Storing food during the harvest for use during the wintertime, the ant embodied two great virtues, diligence and wisdom. Actually, the ants either enter a state of dormancy when it is cold or continue working all year around. Obviously, the ants' endless carrying of grains, leaves, and matter to their ant-heaps must have been the grounds for the proverbial sayings.

Rabbinical literature discusses the damage caused by ants and even describes a kind of biological control. If soil were brought from one ant-heap to another, the two groups of ants would destroy each other (*Mo'ed Qaṭ.* 6b) because each colony has its own distinct smell. JESPER SVARTVIK

ANTELOPE

A fast, horned ruminant (Heb. *tĕ'ô*), listed as a clean animal, thus suitable for eating (Deut. 14:5). The Bible distinguishes various species, including the gazelle, ibex, and oryx. Due to its speed, hunting an antelope required the use of a net or some other trap (cf. Isa. 51:20; Israel's defeat by God's wrath is likened to an antelope caught in a net). LISA M. WOLFE

ANTHOTHIJAH (Heb. *'anĕṯōṯîyâ*)

A Benjaminite, one of the sons of Shashak (1 Chr. 8:24).

ANTHROPOLOGY

See HUMANITY.

ANTHROPOMORPHISM

The attribution of human characteristics to God, specifically the conceptualization of God as having aspects of the human (Gk. *ánthrōpos*) form (Gk. *morphḗ*), but not human emotions (such as love or anger), called anthropopathism. Anthropomorphic language is interspersed throughout the Bible, but it is more prevalent in the OT (esp. the Pentateuch and Psalms) than in the NT. Figurative descriptions of God as having human features include references to God's face (Ps. 34:16[MT 17]), eyes (2 Chr. 16:9), lips (Prov. 16:27), mouth (Isa. 1:20), ears (Jas. 5:4), hands (Exod. 15:17), finger (Luke 11:20), arm (John 12:38), and foot (Lam. 1:15). Other anthropomorphic imagery implies human characteristics. God is depicted as walking in the garden (Gen. 3:8) and smelling sacrifices (8:21). While other ancient religions imagined their deities as actually being animal or human in form — or as a hybrid of animal and human characteristics, as in Egypt — the ancient Jewish religious traditions reflected in Scripture refrained from such. Although Gen. 1:27 provides an apparent rationale for anthropomorphic imagery, the inherent danger is that such figurative language, employed to express how humans have experienced a transcendent God, is mistaken for literal language, particularly with respect to God's gender. Jesus' many references to God as "Father" can best be understood against the backdrop of Israel's anthropomorphic descriptions of God. The supreme anthropomorphism is the NT claim that God entered human flesh in the figure of Jesus of Nazareth. JEFFREY T. TUCKER

ANTICHRIST

"Antichrist" and "antichrists" appear in the Bible only in 1 John 2:18, 22; 4:3; 2 John 7 and are unknown elsewhere in Christian literature before Polycarp in the 2nd century C.E. Yet by the beginning of the 3rd century (e.g., Hippolytus) the expectation of an eschatological Antichrist had become highly developed in Christian theology and has ever remained a topic of intrinsic interest to many Christians. Attempts to identify an individual Antichrist have a long but dismal history.

It is clear that John applied the plural antichrists to those former members of the Christian congregation who had recently departed from the flock (1 John 2:19) under a mantle of false teaching and practice. But because John says very little about the singular Antichrist, the biblical antecedents for this figure are in some dispute.

Many scholars distinguish two major biblical traditions which involve eschatological figures opposed to God and his purposes, one which warns of a political or military persecutor and one of a deceptive influence. For instance, in his Olivet discourse, Jesus spoke both of the appearance of Daniel's abomination of desolation (Dan. 9:27; 11:31; 12:11; Matt. 24:15 par.) and of the coming of false prophets and false Christs who would deceive, if it were possible, even the elect (Matt. 24:24 par.). Daniel's "little horn" (Dan. 7:8, 20, 24) seems to presage a figure Paul calls the "lawless one" (2 Thess. 2:3-10), a persecuting foe with self-deifying pretensions. Daniel's dire expectations of the future are recast again in Rev. 13 as a dreadful beast to arise from the sea, incorporating many of the characteristics of the four beasts of Dan. 7:3-8. But John goes on to describe another Antichrist figure, a second beast, who rises from the land and supports the first beast in his diabolical attacks on the godly. This Earth Beast has the special characteristics of a false prophet (so named in Rev. 16:13; 19:20; 20:10) who deceives with his blasphemous lies. It is not agreed to what extent John's Antichrist represents only one of these strands or a combination, though from John's limited description in 1 and 2 John, his Antichrist figure has more in common with the deceiver/false prophet image, for it is associated with a denial of the truth about Jesus Christ (1 John 2:22; 4:1-3; 2 John 7).

Bibliography. G. C. Jenks, *The Origins and Early Development of the Antichrist Myth.* BZNW 59 (Berlin, 1991); C. E. Hill, "Antichrist from the Tribe of Dan," *JTS* N.S. 46 (1995): 99-117.

CHARLES E. HILL

ANTIGONUS (Gk. *Antígonus*)

1. One of Alexander the Great's generals, among the first of the Diadochi. Satrap in Phrygia during Alexander's life, he began extending his power throughout the East in 316 B.C.E. He claimed the crown in 306, thus designating himself Alexander's successor. Attacked by a coalition of the other Diadochi, he was killed in battle in 302.

2. Son of the Hasmonean ruler John Hyrcanus. When Antigonus' brother Aristobulus I became high priest (104), Aristobulus imprisoned his mother and other brothers, but Antigonus was allowed to remain free. Accused of plotting his brother's assassination, Aristobulus was executed (Josephus *Ant.* 13.303-317; *BJ* 1.80-84).

3. Antigonus II, king and high priest of Judea (40-37 B.C.E.); son of Aristobulus II, who had seized the throne from his brother Hyrcanus II in 67. The Romans restored Hyrcanus to the high priesthood, and took Aristobulus and Antigonus captive to Rome in 63 (Josephus *Ant.* 14.5-79; *BJ* 1.116-158). In 56 they escaped, and Aristobulus attempted to retake the throne. Though Aristobulus was recaptured, Antigonus was released (*Ant.* 14.92-95; *BJ* 1.171-74). In 40, after his father's death, Antigonus overthrew Hyrcanus with Parthian aid. He mutilated the old priest's ears (according to *BJ* 1.270, with his own teeth) so as to disqualify him from ever holding the priesthood again. The Roman senate, however, conferred kingship on Herod, and Antigonus was eventually removed from the throne. He was beheaded in 37 B.C.E. (*Ant.* 15.2; *BJ* 1.357).

ANTHONY J. TOMASINO

ANTI-LEBANON (Gk. *Antilibános*)

A mountain range E of the Lebanon Mountains, extending from Kadesh (Syria) to Dan (Jdt. 1:7). Separated from Lebanon by the Beqaʿ Valley, the range's highest peak is Mt. Hermon (cf. Deut. 3:9, Senir).

ANTIOCH (Gk. *Antiócheia*)

1. Antioch toward Pisidia. A city in the southern part of the Roman province called Galatia, in the central part of modern Turkey. More precisely it was actually located in Phrygia, a district in southern Galatia bordering on the northern boundary of the district of Pisidia. The boundaries of both districts are indefinite. The 1st-century geographer Strabo placed it in Phrygia on the south side of a mountain ridge facing Pisidia. Thus, he called it "Antioch near Pisidia" or "Antioch toward Pisidia" (*Geog.* 12.8.14). This agrees with the best manuscripts of Acts 13:14, which have "Pisidian Antioch" (NIV) rather than "Antioch of Pisidia" as in other translations.

Bypassing Perga, Paul went directly to Antioch on his first visit to Asia Minor (Acts 13:13-14). He probably visited it again on his second journey (Acts 16:6) and may have passed through it again on his third journey (18:23). The city was at the peak of its importance when Paul was there, functioning as the center of both civil and military administration in southern Galatia, with roads leading from there to the various colonies. In 25 B.C. the emperor Augustus had refounded the city as a Roman colony and populated it with veterans from the legions. Emperor worship flourished here, enhanced by a number of buildings connected with the imperial cult. Most of the construction in Antioch was done under the emperors Tiberius and Claudius. Tiberius was the principal builder of the temple of Augustus which stood in the center of the city. Two other temples stood near this one dedicated to pagan worship, one of which an excavator of Antioch has described as among the great hilltop sacred sites of southwestern Anatolia.

2. Antioch of Syria. The largest and most important of 16 cities in the ancient world that were named after the Syrian emperor Antiochus. His son, Seleucus I Nicator, founder of the Seleucid Empire, built it and named it in his honor. It was located 80 km. (50 mi.) S of the point where the peninsula of Asia Minor curves south into the Eastern Mediterranean seaboard of Syria-Palestine and at the foot of Mt. Silpius on the Orontes River, which gave it access to the Mediterranean port city of Seleucia.

The population of the city in the mid-1st century A.D. may have reached 300 thousand, though estimates run as low as 100 thousand. The larger figure is suggested by the 1st-century geographer Strabo (*Geog.* 16.2.5), who said it was not much smaller than Alexandria in Egypt. That city had more than 300 thousand freemen in the mid-1st century B.C. (Diodorus Siculus *Hist.* 17.52).

Antioch had a large, wealthy Jewish population in the 1st century (Josephus *BJ* 7:43). These Jews endowed beautifully decorated synagogues, and "constantly attracted to their religious ceremonies multitudes of Greeks" (*BJ* 7.45). The first mention of Antioch in the NT is in reference to a proselyte to the Jewish faith from this city, one Nicolaus, who accepted Christ and was subsequently appointed as one of seven men to oversee the needs of Hellenist widows in Jerusalem in the early days of the Church (Acts 6:5).

Missionary work was done by people who fled the persecutions in Jerusalem and soon after arriving in Antioch "spoke to the Greeks also" (Acts 11:20). These "Greeks" were probably "Godfearers," Gentiles who were frequently attracted to Jewish monotheism (e.g., Acts 10:22). This missionary activity resulted in "a great number" (Acts 11:21) of gentile conversions and prompted the church in Jerusalem to send Barnabas to Antioch to monitor the progress. Barnabas, impressed by the large number of converts and probably aware of Paul's commission to preach to Gentiles (Acts 26:17), brought him from Tarsus to work in Antioch.

For a year, they worked together in this gentile center (Acts 11:26) which subsequently became the sponsoring church for his missionary journeys to the gentile world (13:3; 15:40; 18:22-23). The term "Christian" ("follower of the Messiah") was first applied to the disciples of Jesus in this predominantly Gentile Christian city (Acts 11:26).

Eusebius records a tradition in the 4th century that the first bishop of Antioch was Peter (*HE* 3.36.2) who was succeeded by Evodius and then by the well-known martyr Ignatius of Antioch, who died in the reign of Trajan (ca. 108; *HE* 3.22).

One of the most remarkable events in the history of the early Church relating to ethnic distinctions occurred in Antioch. When Peter visited Paul on one occasion, these two most influential leaders in the 1st-century Church argued in the presence of the whole Church about Peter's vacillation on requirements of gentile converts. Paul accused Peter of acting "insincerely" (Gk. "hypocritically"). In this highly dramatic situation, Paul "opposed him to his face because he stood condemned" (Gal. 2:11), rebuking this chief of Apostles "before them all" (v. 14).

Antioch was undoubtedly the most important city after Jerusalem in the early expansion of the Church. After the Jerusalem conference ended, the decisions reached by the conference were immediately sent to Antioch in a letter which was taken by two "leading men among the brethren," Silas and Judas, indicating the importance of Antioch in the eyes of the Jerusalem church. Paul and Barnabas accompanied them (Acts 15:22).

Because the modern city Antakya stands on the site of ancient Antioch, little archaeological excavation has been conducted there. Much of our information about the city must therefore be derived from ancient writers, most significantly Strabo, Evagrius, Procopius, Libanius, the emperor Julian, John Chrysostom, and especially the *Chronicle* of John Malalas. A number of prominent people contributed to the building projects in Antioch, among them the Hellenistic rulers Seleucus I (311-281 B.C.) and Antiochus Epiphanes (175-164) and the Roman rulers Pompey, Julius Caesar, Augustus Caesar, Tiberius Caesar, Caligula, and Claudius.

Antioch was built on the Hippodamian grid of a typical Hellenistic city with streets laid out in city blocks 112 m. × 58 m. (367 ft. × 190 ft.). Herod the Great built a colonnaded street, which ran the full length of the city, north to south, and cut Antioch in half (Josephus *BJ* 1.425; *Ant.* 16.148). Tiberius is credited with the construction of monumental gates at each main intersection of the city's streets.

The city was surrounded by a wall and contained many important buildings including a palace and a circus, both begun in 67 B.C. Starting in 47 B.C. Julius Caesar constructed a theater, an amphitheater, bathhouses, an aqueduct, and a Kaisareion, perhaps the oldest basilica in the east, for use by the cult of Rome. It carried his name and contained a statue of himself. He also rebuilt the Pantheon temple.

Part of the rebuilding was prompted by two earthquakes which hit Antioch in the time of Paul, one in A.D. 37, at the beginning of the reign of Caligula (37-41), and the second during the reign of Claudius (41-54). The latter quake also damaged Ephesus, Smyrna, and other cities of Asia Minor.

The "Silver Chalice of Antioch," purportedly discovered here in 1910 and thought by some to be the cup used by Christ at the Last Supper, has been dated by authorities from the 2nd to the 6th century.

JOHN MCRAY

ANTIOCHUS (Gk. *Antíochos*)
The events described in 1–2 Maccabees and Daniel take place against the background of Seleucid history in the 2nd century B.C.E. The sequence of Seleucid rulers (with their approximate regnal years) is: Antiochus III (223-187), Seleucus IV Philopator (187-175), Antiochus IV Epiphanes (175-164), Antiochus V Eupator (164-162), Demetrius I Soter (162-150), Alexander I Balas (150-145), Demetrius II Nicator (145-139), Antiochus VI (and Trypho) (145-142), and Antiochus VII Sidetes (138-129). A genealogical chart can help to clarify the relationships among these rulers.

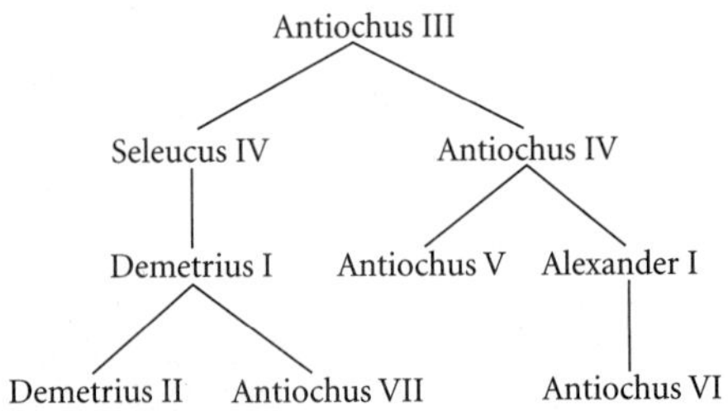

1. Antiochus III. Under his rule Judea as part of Coele-Syria came under Seleucid rather than Ptolemaic (Egyptian) control after his victory at Panium in 200 B.C.E. But his defeats by the Romans at Thermopylae (191) and Magnesia (190) and his surrender at Apamea (188) checked his imperial expansion. He died in Elam in 187 while plundering the temple of Bel.

2. Antiochus IV Epiphanes; the most famous and important Antiochus for biblical studies. The son of Antiochus III, he was sent as a hostage to Rome after the battle of Magnesia and remained there until 176. After spending some time in Athens, he learned that his brother Seleucus IV had been assassinated, and so he traveled to Antioch in Syria and claimed the Seleucid throne for himself in 175.

Antiochus IV invaded Egypt in 170 and again in 168. He was forced to withdraw from Egypt by the Roman general Popillius Laenas or be counted an enemy of Rome. On his return from Egypt he plundered the Jerusalem temple (perhaps twice, or only in 168). With the encouragement of a group of Jewish "progressives" (1 Macc.1:11-15), Antiochus IV either cooperated in or promoted a program that established Greek institutions in Jerusalem (the gymnasium, etc.), decreed new laws in place of the Torah, and brought a new order of worship to the Jerusalem temple. Described in Jewish sources as the "desolating sacrilege" or "abomination of desolation" (cf. Dan. 11:31; 12:11; 1 Macc. 1:54; Matt. 24:15; Mark 13:14), the new cult involved the worship of the "Lord of heaven" — most likely the Semitic deity Baal Shamin who was probably regarded as the equivalent of the Israelite creator and master of heaven and earth.

The extent and purpose of Antiochus IV's involvement in Jewish affairs between 168 and 164 remain disputed. His activities are attributed to personal arrogance in 1 Maccabees, while Daniel and 2 Maccabees regard them as part of God's discipline before Israel's eschatological and/or historical vindication. Modern scholars explain his actions in other ways: promoting the cultural program of hellenization, carrying out a religious persecution, intervening in a Jewish civil war, developing the eastern equivalent of the nascent Roman Empire, or raising money to pay his soldiers by putting the Jewish high priesthood up for bid and robbing the Jerusalem temple and its treasury. A combination of several of these motives seems likely.

According to 1 Maccabees, Jewish resistance to the program of Antiochus IV and his Jewish collaborators coalesced around the Maccabee or Hasmonean family led first by a priest of Modein named Mattathias (1 Macc. 2) and then by his sons Judas, Jonathan, and Simon in turn. By early 164 Antiochus IV gave conditional amnesty to the Jewish rebels and ended the religious persecution and the edict against observing the Torah. This coincided with Antiochus IV's campaign to strengthen the eastern part of his empire. The ancient sources give conflicting accounts of his death (Dan. 11:40-45; 1 Macc. 6:1-16; 2 Macc. 1:13-17; 9:1-28). He most likely died of some disease at Tabae in Persia (Polybius *Hist.* 31.9) in late 164 — around the time of Judas Maccabeus' purification and rededication of the Jerusalem temple.

The fact that his son and successor Antiochus V was called Eupator ("of a good father") suggests that Antiochus IV was respected. He was the first Seleucid king to be designated *theós* ("god") on his coinage, a practice that probably increased Jewish opposition to him. Polybius described him as charming but erratic (and so the pun *epimanḗs* ["mad"] on *epiphanḗs* ["(god) manifest"]) and as a student and patron of local religious customs (not a religious persecutor as the Jewish texts suggest).

3. Antiochus V, made king in 164 at nine years of age, with Lysias as his prime minister (2 Macc. 10:11). They were prevented from seizing back Jerusalem mainly because they had to return to Antioch and fight off a rebellion by Philip, a courtier who claimed that Antiochus IV had promised him guardianship and power (1 Macc. 6:14-17, 55-63; 2 Macc. 13:23). In late 162 or early 161 Antiochus V and Lysias were executed under Demetrius I, the son of Seleucus IV (1 Macc. 7:1-4; 2 Macc. 14:1-2).

4. Antiochus VI, the son of Alexander Balas, whose own claim to be the son of Antiochus IV (cf. 1 Macc. 10:1) was disputed even in antiquity. Antiochus VI was crowned king in early 144 through the efforts of Trypho, who became the real ruler (11:54-59) and succeeded in capturing Jonathan Maccabeus (12:39-53). Trypho went so far as to assassinate Antiochus VI in 142 and to claim the kingship for himself (13:31-32).

5. Antiochus VII. A son of Demetrius I (1 Macc. 15:1, 10), he claimed the Seleucid throne in 138. He renewed the attempt to gain greater control over Jerusalem and other parts of the land of Israel (15:38–16:10), but his major interest was expanding the Seleucid Empire against the Parthians. He died in 129, either in battle or by suicide after being defeated by the Parthian army under Phraates.

Bibliography. E. Bickerman, *The God of the Maccabees.* SJLA 32 (Leiden, 1979); M. Hengel, *Judaism and Hellenism* (Philadelphia, 1974); O. Mørkholm, *Antiochus IV of Syria* (Copenhagen, 1966); E. Schürer, *The History of the Jewish People in the Age of Jesus Christ (175 B.C.-A.D. 135),* rev. ed. (Edinburgh, 1973-1987); V. Tcherikover, *Hellenistic Civilization and the Jews* (Philadelphia, 1959).

DANIEL J. HARRINGTON, S.J.

ANTIPAS (Gk. *Antipás*)

1. Herod Antipas, son of Herod the Great and Malthace. He was the tetrarch of Galilee who had John the Baptist imprisoned and beheaded (Matt. 14:1-11 = Mark 6:14-28) and who mocked Jesus at his trial (Luke 23:7-11).

See HEROD (Family) **11.**

2. A Christian at Pergamum who was martyred on account of his faith (Rev. 2:12).

ANTIPATER (Gk. *Antipátros*)

1. Son of Jason, one of two delegates sent by the Hasmonean Jonathan to Rome and Sparta (Josephus *Ant.* 13.169; 1 Macc. 12:16; 14:22) to negotiate — apparently successfully — renewals of treaties with Judea.

2. Idumean noble (ca. 100-43 B.C.E.), son of Antipas and father of Herod.

See HEROD (Family) **1.**

3. Eldest son of Herod and his first wife Doris.

See HEROD (Family) **6.** PETER RICHARDSON

ANTIPATRIS (Gk. *Antipatrís*)

The city rebuilt by Herod the Great in 9 B.C.E. on the site of Aphek (**1**), renamed after his father Antipater. Located at modern Râs el-ʿAin/Tel Afeq (143168) on the coastal plain, it was perhaps a control point and way station between Caesarea Maritima and Jerusalem. Antipatris is mentioned in Acts 23:31 as the place of an overnight stop by Paul when taken under guard from Jerusalem to Caesarea during the procuratorship of Felix.

BRUCE C. CRESSON

ANTI-SEMITISM AND THE NEW TESTAMENT

It is a tragic fact that a number of NT texts have been used to promote anti-Semitism through the history of the Church down to and including the modern era. These texts have been ripped out of their original framework and historical contexts; they have been absolutized and repeatedly used to demonize the Jewish people; they have been employed to justify the persecution of Jews in the last 2000 years, culminating in the murder of 6 million Jews in the Nazi Holocaust.

A few of the more notorious examples may be noted here. The Gospel of Matthew, which is full of polemic against the Jews, records the crowd that calls for the crucifixion of Jesus crying out, "His blood be on us and on our children" (Matt. 27:25). The bitter words against "the Jews" in the Fourth Gospel come to their climax in the statement: "You are from your father the devil" (John 8:44). Commenting on the suffering of the Christians of Thessalonica, Paul says that the churches of Judea also suffered from "the Jews, who killed both the Lord Jesus and the prophets, and drove us out; they displease God and oppose everyone by hindering us from speaking to the Gentiles so that they may be saved. Thus they have constantly been filling up the measure of their sins; but God's wrath has overtaken them at last" (1 Thess. 2:14-16). In the letter to the church in Smyrna, John the Seer writes: "I know the slander on the part of those who say that they are Jews and are not, but are a synagogue of Satan" (Rev. 2:9; cf. 3:9).

In addition to the theme of the responsibility for the death of Jesus — the crime later described as "deicide" — many passages are concerned with judgment upon the Jews for their unbelief in the message of the gospel. Often heavily rhetorical language can be used of the Pharisees in particular: e.g., "hypocrites," "child(ren) of hell," "blind fools," "blind guides," "brood of vipers" (Matt. 23). Another key element is the theme of the displacement of Israel by the Church: e.g., "the kingdom of God will be taken away from you and given to a people that produces the fruits of the kingdom" (Matt. 21:43); "Let it be known to you [Jews] then that this salvation of God has been sent to the Gentiles; they will listen" (Acts 28:28, following a quotation of Isa. 6:9-10, applied to the Jews who do not believe in the gospel); "Many will come from east and west and will eat with Abraham and Isaac and Jacob in the kingdom of heaven, while the heirs of the kingdom will be thrown into the outer darkness, where there will be weeping and gnashing of teeth" (Matt. 8:11-12).

It is a great irony that these words, written by Jews, should be used to justify anti-Semitism. Jesus himself was a Jew, and the author of the Fourth Gospel states that "salvation is from the Jews" (John 4:22). All of the first Christians were themselves Jews and moreover regarded their faith as not alien to, but the culmination of, the hope of Israel (cf. Acts 28:20). The fact is that the vitriolic language reflects an intramural debate, with Jews arguing against Jews, Christian Jews against the Jews of the synagogue. This type of blistering language is reminiscent of that used by the OT prophets in their criticism of Israel. The harshness of the polemic furthermore reflects the conventions of ancient rhetoric.

Clearly it is wrong to regard this material as anti-Semitic (i.e., involving racial prejudice), and even the word anti-Judaism is not adequate, although to be sure there is polemic against Judaism in the NT. Because the material in question is timebound and historically conditioned, the following mitigating factors must be kept in mind: (1) the exceptionally harsh criticism of the Jews in the NT reflects not merely intramural argument but hostility resulting from the Jewish persecution of Christian Jews; (2) much of the NT polemic is directed against the leadership rather than the people as a whole; (3) to apply any of this material to Jews or Judaism of the present is to be guilty not merely of anachronism, but of a grave misunderstanding and misuse of it. Even if the NT puts the responsibility for the death of Jesus upon the Jews, that generation (and their children) have long since passed from the scene and so it makes no sense to put the blame on modern Jews. Of course, Christians who are theologically aware will realize that the real responsibility for the death of Jesus falls upon themselves as much as upon the Jews.

Given the history of the tragic abuse of this material, Christians must now regard themselves as under permanent obligation to go out of their way to emphasize what these passages do *not* mean. Christianity and anti-Semitism are mutually exclusive.

DONALD A. HAGNER

ANTONIA (Gk. *Antōnia*), **FORTRESS OF**

A large fortress built by Herod the Great on the northwest corner of the Temple Mount. The Antonia replaced an earlier fortress (Neh. 2:8; 7:2) that Herod removed during leveling excavations, replacing it with a more impressive structure named in honor of his patron Mark Antony. The Antonia, therefore, must have been built sometime prior to Antony's defeat in 31 B.C. and served as Herod's quarters in Jerusalem until the building of a new palace in the western quarter of the city.

The Antonia was located on an elevated rocky platform (45 × 120 m. [148 × 394 ft.]) now occupied by the Omariyyeh school; deep moats and natural escarpments protected it on all sides. According to Josephus (*BJ* 5.238-47), the Antonia had four towers at the corners and four turrets that dominated the temple courts below. The fortress contained baths, porticos, courtyards, and other conveniences suitable to royal visitors but sufficient to accommodate a Roman cohort normally stationed there (cf. Acts 21:27-37). The Antonia was linked to the temple precincts by two stairways leading down to the porticos of the temple enclosure and by a tunnel (*Ant.* 15.424). The Struthion pool on the northwest side of the Antonia supplied water to the fortress.

Whether or not the Antonia was the location of the trial of Jesus before Pilate is debated. The Roman procurators could also have stayed at either Herod's palace or the Hasmonean palace, both located in the upper city. THOMAS V. BRISCO

ANUB (Heb. *ʿānûḇ*)
A Judahite, son of Koz (1 Chr. 4:8).

APELLES (Gk. *Apellḗs*)
A person "approved in Christ," who is greeted by Paul (Rom. 16:10).

APHEK (Heb. *ʾăp̄ēq*)
1. A major city of antiquity, located at modern Ras el-ʾAyin (143168) just above abundant springs which give rise to the Yarkon River. Its importance is related not only to the water source (exceeded in volume only by the sources of the Jordan), but to the fact that it controlled the Via Maris, forced inland by the swamps created by the Yarkon between the springs and the Mediterranean Sea, and thus passing through the narrow valley between the springs and the beginning of the central hill ridge just east of the site.

Aphek is mentioned in the Egyptian Execration Texts and in topographical lists of both Thutmose III and Amenhotep II. It is mentioned in the stories of Joshua's conquests and of the Hebrew-Philistine conflict in the time of Eli and Samuel. The Hellenistic city located here was known as Pegae, and when Herod the Great rebuilt the city in the 1st century B.C.E. it was renamed Antipatris.

An archaeological survey of the site was made in 1923 by William F. Albright, and limited early excavations were conducted by J. Ory in 1935-36 and Abraham Eitan in 1961. A major campaign by a consortium of Israeli and American schools and organizations from 1972-1985 was directed by Moshe Kochavi and Pirhiya Beck of Tel Aviv University. This excavation produced both important finds and evidence of an extensive occupational history of the site beginning in Early Bronze I (3100), although an earlier Chalcolithic pit and scattered sherds were uncovered. Remains were documented from EB II, MB II A and B, LB I and II, Iron I and II, Persian (just off the tell proper), Hellenistic, Roman, Byzantine, Umayyad, and Ottoman periods. Archaeologically the most impressive materials are from MB IIA-B (areas A and X) with clear sequential stratification within the period identified, and from the LB occupation (area X). Kochavi has identified 11 documents from the LB period — Egyptian, Hittite, Akkadian, Sumerian, and Canaanite — including a letter from Ugarit (in Akkadian).

References to Aphek (of the Sharon) are found in Josh. 12:18 (one of the cities whose king was defeated by Joshua); 1 Sam. 4 (city from which the Philistines engaged the Hebrews from Ebenezer in battle; the victorious Philistines captured the ark of the covenant); 1 Sam. 29:1 (the gathering place from which the Philistines launched their battle against Saul at Mt. Gilboa).

Bibliography. A. Eitan, P. Beck, and M. Kochavi, "Aphek," *NEAEHL* 1:62-72. BRUCE C. CRESSON

2. A northern Canaanite town bordering the land of the Amorites (Josh. 13:4) and traditionally identified with Afqā (231382), 37 km. (23 mi.) NE of Beirut.

3. A town alloted to the tribe of Asher in the vicinity of Achzib, Ummah, and Rehob (Josh. 19:29-30; Judg. 1:31). Most scholars identify this Aphek with Tell Kurdâneh, 9 km. (5.6 mi.) SE of Acco. Others identify it with Tell Kabri (164268), 4 km. (2.5 mi.) E of Nahariya.

4 A town in the Golan from which Ben-hadad launched an assault against the Israelites, and to which he fled after defeat by Ahab (1 Kgs. 20:26-30). It is probably the Aphek mentioned in Elisha's prediction of Joash's defeat of the Arameans (2 Kgs. 13:17). Traditionally identified with Afiq in the Naḥal ʿEn Gev Valley, the town is now identified with ʿEn Gev/Khirbet el-ʿÂsheq (210243).

RONALD A. SIMKINS

APHEKAH (Heb. *ʾăp̄ēqâ*)
A city in the hill country of Judah, near Beth-tappuah (Josh. 15:53). Its precise location remains unknown; suggested sites include Khirbet el-Ḥadab (155098), Khirbet Kana'an (157102), and Khirbet Marajim (152099).

APHIAH (Heb. *ʾăp̄îaḥ*)
A Benjaminite, the father of Becorath and ancestor of King Saul (1 Sam. 9:1).

APHIK (Heb. *ʾăp̄iq*)
Alternate form of Aphek **3,** a city in the territory of Asher (Judg. 1:31).

APHORISM
One of several terms for short, pithy, popular wisdom sayings. As the expression of the insights of an individual, it can be distinguished from the proverb, which is generally an unattributed expression of collective wisdom. Its authority thus depends on

the prestige of that individual. In this sense the aphorism is closely related to the *chreia,* though the *chreia* generally is more explicit in its biographical interest.

Aphorisms represent one of Jesus' characteristic modes of speech, and therefore are of special interest for historical Jesus research. While wisdom sayings typically function to support traditional values and worldviews, the aphorisms of Jesus often reflect his radical challenges to the accepted wisdom of the day (Luke 12:37; Mark 8:35 par.; 10:31 par.; Luke 9:60; Matt. 8:22).

Aphorisms are found in many forms. In the Gospels they include beatitudes (Matt. 5:3-12; Luke 6:20-23; Gos. Thom. 54, 68–69), conditional sayings (Mark 3:24-25 par.), admonitions (Luke 12:22 par.), synonymous parallelism (Mark 4:22; John 13:16), antithetical parallelism (Mark 2:17 par.; Luke 6:45), and reciprocal statements (Luke 6:37-38; 12:8-9; Matt. 10:32-33; cf. 1 Clem. 13:2).

Aphorisms are neither spoken nor transmitted in isolation. The aphorisms of Jesus were gathered into thematic collections (Matt. 7:7-11 = Luke 11:9-13, asking; Matt. 7:1-5, judging; Luke 11:42-48; Matt. 23:13-36, woes) and used to form the conclusion to "pronouncement" stories (Mark 2:17; 12:17). Recent scholars have argued that NT writers expanded aphorisms or *chreiai* into larger narratives by use of standard rules found in the *progymnasmata* (basic rhetorical handbooks).

As Jesus' aphorisms were originally delivered and transmitted orally, the attempt to recover the exact phrasing (*ipsissima verba*) is dubious. It is more fruitful to speak of a stable structure (*ipsissima structura*) from which changes could be made. John Dominic Crossan makes the important distinction between performancial and hermeneutical variation. Performancial variation involves changes (expansions, contractions, conversion, substitution, transposition) which do not affect the basic sense of the aphorism. This would have been a natural characteristic of Jesus' teaching as he spoke to different audiences; compare "But many who are first will be last, and the last will be first" (Matt. 19:30) to "So the last will be first, and the first will be last" (20:16). The version in Gos. Thom. 4, however, is a hermeneutical variation, since it provides a distinct interpretation: "For many who are first will become last, and they will become one and the same."

Bibliography. D. E. Aune, "Oral Tradition and the Aphorisms of Jesus," in *Jesus and the Oral Gospel Tradition,* ed. H. Wansbrough. JSNTSup 64 (Sheffield, 1991), 211-65; J. D. Crossan, *In Fragments: The Aphorisms of Jesus* (San Francisco, 1983); V. K. Robbins, "The Chreia," in *Greco-Roman Literature and the New Testament,* ed. D. E. Aune. SBLSBS 21 (Atlanta, 1988), 1-23. MARTIN C. ALBL

APOCALYPSE

A genre of writings (Gk. *apokálypsis,* "revelation, disclosure") which concerns visions or prophecies of the end times or the age to come.

See APOCALYPTIC.

APOCALYPTIC

An adjective used to describe a broad category of phenomena linked by a similar worldview. It is part of a constellation of terms (apocalypticism, apocalyptic eschatology) derived from the literary genre apocalypse.

The genre name "apocalypse" derives from Gk. *apokálypsis* ("revelation" or "disclosure"), which occurs in the opening line of the NT book of Revelation. This book, the parade example of an apocalypse in early Christian literature, gives its name to the entire genre. The genre itself may be defined as "a genre of revelatory literature with a narrative framework, in which a revelation is mediated by an otherworldly being to a human recipient, disclosing a transcendent reality which is both temporal, insofar as it envisages eschatological salvation, and spatial, insofar as it involves another, supernatural world" (Collins, *Apocalypse,* 9). Apocalypses are characterized by the presence of vision, symbolism, a human seer and an otherworldly mediator, an otherworldly journey, an emphasis on events in the cosmic rather than human realm, an increased interest in angels and demons, the notion of the transcendence of God, and pseudonymity. Given this definition, there is only one example of a true apocalypse in the OT, Dan. 7–12, while the Christian NT's only apocalypse is the book of Revelation (which is exceptional for not being pseudonymous).

The genre, however, was more widespread than the canonical examples. Apocalypse as a genre flourished between 250 B.C.E. and 250 C.E., giving many more examples to the literature, such as 1 Enoch, 4 Ezra, and 2 Baruch. However, the antecedents of apocalyptic literature can be found much earlier, in the prophetic and wisdom traditions of ancient Israel, and the mythologies of the ancient Near East. Apocalyptic literature draws on prophecy, in which the message of God concerning a particular historical situation is conveyed to a human recipient through an aural or visual experience, through its emphasis on vision, the special revelation given to the human recipient, and the use of historical events to disclose God's hidden plan. Late prophetic texts which contain incipient characteristics of the apocalypse include Ezek. 1–3 and Zech. 1–6. The antecedents of the apocalypse in the wisdom tradition can be seen particularly in the speculative material of books such as 1 Enoch, where in the Book of the Heavenly Luminaries Enoch is taken on an otherworldly journey and is shown the secrets of the heavenly realm (cf. Job 37–38). Finally, the influence of ancient Near Eastern mythology, especially the literatures of Babylon and Persia, can be discerned in the type of symbols used throughout apocalyptic literature, e.g., the sea as a symbol of chaos (Dan. 7:2-3; Rev. 13:1).

The genre "apocalypse" lends its name to a broad range of phenomena loosely organized under the rubric "apocalyptic." The reasons for the rise of this type of literature and its associated phenomena in the Second Temple period are not fully understood, but there seems to be a strong connection with some crisis, bringing about a sense of social, political, or religious powerlessness, either of a community or an individual. Sometimes the crisis is clear to the later reader, such as the persecution of the Jews by Antiochus IV Epiphanes, reflected in Dan. 7–12, or the destruction of the Second Temple by the Romans in 70 C.E., reflected in 4 Ezra or 2 Baruch. However, sometimes the precipitating crisis is not at all evident, and may have been of importance only to the original author. This is the case for large portions of the Enoch literature.

This sense of crisis and impending doom explains the appearance of a phenomenon known as apocalyptic eschatology, in which the apocalyptic worldview is applied to events surrounding the end of the world, usually thought of as rapidly approaching. Apocalyptic eschatology declares that the adverse conditions of the present world, brought about by the precipitating crisis, will end in judgment for the wicked and vindication for the righteous, both from the hand of God. The judgment of the present world usually includes its destruction, followed by a new and glorified existence for the righteous. A cogent example of this is found in Rev. 20–21, in which a judgment, the "Great White Throne" judgment, of all the dead occurs, following which the damned are thrown into the lake of fire. After this judgment, the seer recounts:

> Then I saw a new heaven and a new earth; for the first heaven and the first earth had passed away, and the sea was no more. And I saw the holy city, the new Jerusalem, coming down out of heaven from God, prepared as a bride adorned for her husband. (21:1–2)

Apocalyptic eschatology is part of the movement known as apocalypticism, a term used to describe a worldview or symbolic universe whose characteristics have been extrapolated from the apocalypses. Whole communities, not simply individuals, may have a worldview best described as apocalyptic, with a tendency towards believing that history is moving toward a crisis, that the eschaton will come about soon (within the lifetime of the community or believer), and placing an emphasis on the community's possession of a revelation which gives it special (and sometimes secret) knowledge about the present age. Two communities from the Second Temple period which have been described as apocalyptic are the Qumran community and the early Christians. Although the Qumran community evidently did not produce any apocalypses as such, its literature is permeated with apocalypticism. For example, the *pesherim,* a type of biblical interpretation unique to the community, use the biblical prophets and psalms to interpret contemporary events in the sect's existence as part of the unfolding of the eschatological drama. The War Scroll (1QM), a description of the battles of the eschatological age, assumes that humans and angels fight together in the army of God, and it is only the decisive intervention of God in the final battle which brings about the defeat of Belial's army.

It has long been recognized that at least parts of

The beast from the sea and the beast with lamb's horns (Rev. 13:1-13) (Woodcut by Albrecht Dürer, 1498)

the early Christian community were apocalyptic in outlook. The Gospel of Mark understands the coming of Jesus as the dawn of the eschatological age, and the Gospel closes with the expectation of the imminent return of Jesus in glory (Mark 16:6-7). The Apostle Paul likewise expects the return of the risen Jesus in his lifetime, with the subsequent resurrection of the dead (1 Thess. 4:13–5:11). Also, Paul hints in 2 Corinthians of an otherworldly journey during which he was caught up "to the third heaven" (2 Cor. 12:1-4). Apocalypses also occur in the mystical tradition of later Judaism, e.g., 3 Enoch (Sefer Hekalot), indicating perhaps the persistence of apocalyptic thought into the rabbinic period.

Bibliography. J. H. Charlesworth, ed., *OTP,* 1: *Apocalyptic Literature and Testaments* (Garden City, 1983); J. J. Collins, *The Apocalyptic Imagination,* 2nd ed. (Grand Rapids. 1998); *The Scepter and the Star: The Messiahs of the Dead Sea Scrolls and Other Ancient Literature* (New York, 1996); Collins, ed., *Apocalypse: The Morphology of a Genre. Semeia* 14 (1979); P. D. Hanson, *The Dawn of Apocalyptic,* rev. ed. (Philadelphia, 1979).

SIDNIE WHITE CRAWFORD

APOCRYPHA

The term "Apocrypha," from the Greek for "hidden" or "obscure" (*apó* + *krýptein,* "to hide away"), refers to a collection of 15 books deemed canonical by Roman Catholics and Eastern Orthodox but not by Jews or Protestants. The reason Jerome (d. 420) and Cyril of Jerusalem (d. 386) first applied the name to the collection remains unknown; only

4 Ezra (2 Esdras) suggests a sequestered volume (12:37-38; 14:4-6, 42-46). Perhaps originally the title indicated books kept from public readings because of heretical views; perhaps it referred to writings hidden from those lacking wisdom.

The labels "OT" or "Jewish" are often added to "Apocrypha" to distinguish this collection from the "Christian" or "NT Apocrypha." The current Roman Catholic term for the collection, "Deuterocanonical," indicates not secondary status but that the volumes become canonical at a later date compared to the "Protocanonical" (Hebrew) "OT." The Eastern Church, also using "Deuterocanonical," reserves "Apocrypha" for those noncanonical works also called "Pseudepigrapha."

The 15 books most often identified as comprising the Apocrypha include texts attributed to past worthies (Baruch and the Epistle of Jeremiah usually incorporated within it; Prayer of Manasseh; 1 Esdras/3 Ezra; 2 Esdras/4 Ezra), novels (Judith), folktales (Tobit), histories (1, 2 Maccabees), wisdom literature (Ben Sirach/Ecclesiasticus, Wisdom of Solomon), and supplements to Hebrew biblical texts (Additions to/Rest of the Book of Esther; Additions to Daniel). With the exception of 4 Ezra, the texts exist in their earliest complete forms only in Greek; in copies of the LXX, they are interspersed with the Greek translations of the Hebrew texts rather than gathered separately. Fourth Ezra appears first in the Old Latin translations of the LXX, and through this connection it gains its place in the Apocrypha.

Both Greek and Slavonic Orthodox Churches expand the Apocrypha to include 3 Maccabees and Ps. 151, although these texts are sometimes seen as having lesser authority. 3 Maccabees appears in various LXX manuscripts as well as in the Peshitta and most American Bibles. Ps. 151 appears in Sinaiticus, most Greek manuscripts of the Psalter, and in the Syriac. Finally, 4 Maccabees, present in some major Greek manuscripts, holds no canonical status although it has influenced Orthodox thought and practices and appears as an appendix in Greek Orthodox Bibles. These three texts, together with the other 15, are today printed in the Apocrypha of the ecumenically targeted RSV and NRSV.

The books themselves are difficult to locate according to date, provenance, and original language. They range from the end of the 3rd century B.C.E. to the 1st century C.E., with 4 Ezra, the only apocalypse in the collection, post-dating the destruction of the Jerusalem temple in 70 C.E. Some scholars insist that save for 2 Maccabees and the Wisdom of Solomon, all were composed in Israel and in either Hebrew or Aramaic; others argue for Greek and Diaspora (especially Alexandrian) origins. The discovery at Masada of fragments of Ben Sirach in Hebrew and at Qumran not only of Ben Sirach but also of Tobit in both Hebrew and Aramaic and the Epistle of Jeremiah in Greek has not resolved the debates on language or provenance.

These books were authored by Jews, but whether Jewish communities ever held them to be divinely inspired remains an open question. Likely the Greek versions and the relatively late date of the works influenced the decision-making process. The NT, itself substantially written by Jews, contains no direct citations from the Apocrypha; however, arguments for the influence of Ben Sirach on Matthew, the Wisdom of Solomon on Paul and the Epistle to the Hebrews, and Maccabees on the Gospel of John are plausible.

Several other early Jewish sources show cognizance of apocryphal works. Josephus knows the Additions to Esther; rabbinic writings cite Ben Sirach 16 times; the celebration of Hanukkah depends on events recounted in 1 and 2 Maccabees, although the books' militaristic tenor did not commend them to rabbinic interests. The Maccabean martyred mother and her seven sons appear in the Talmud as well as Lamentations Rabbah.

Similar familiarity is displayed by patristic writers: Clement of Rome quotes the Wisdom of Solomon, Judith, and the Additions to Esther; Polycarp cites Tobit; 2 Maccabees appears in the Shepherd of Hermas, and the Apostolic Constitutions further note that Baruch is read in Jewish worship; the Muratorian fragment includes the Wisdom of Solomon as a NT volume.

The Eastern Churches, dependent upon the LXX rather than Hebrew scrolls, recognized the Apocrypha as authoritative. Although the Synod of Constantinople (1642), following earlier proclamations from the Synod of Laodicea (360) and others, regarded the books as noncanonical but worthy of reading, the Synod of Jerusalem (1672), in its self-definition of orthodoxy prompted by Protestant challenges, specifically acknowledged Ben Sirach, the Wisdom of Solomon, Judith, and Tobit as canonical.

Jerome — following the Hebrew rather than the LXX for his Latin version, the Vulgate (382) — translates only the Additions to Esther and Daniel, and, upon the request of two bishops, Tobit and Judith; these works he noted as absent from the Hebrew Scriptures. For Jerome, apocryphal texts had didactic value (e.g., he approved of Judith because it valorized a celibate widow) but not doctrinal significance. As the Western Church copied Bibles, it added the apocryphal texts, such as 4 Ezra, preserved in the Old Latin to the Vulgate, but it dropped Jerome's notation; thus the Apocrypha became included as sacred Scripture. The Council of Trent (1546) reasserted the canonicity of all the volumes for Roman Catholicism save 1–2 Esdras and the Prayer of Manasseh; even these works appear as an appendix to the 1592 Vulgate. The First Vatican council (1870) confirmed Trent's decision.

Yet Jerome's view was never lost. Wycliff's Bible (1382), translated from the Vulgate, cites Jerome in its decision to list the Apocrypha (minus 4 Ezra) as lacking authority. Luther — influenced by Jerome, the "Treatise on the Difference between Our Version [the Vulgate] and the Hebrew Truth" by the Jewish convert to Christianity Nicholas of Lyra (d. 1340), growing cultural preference for the authority of antiquity, and perhaps by Catholic citations of the Apocrypha in support of purgatory (2 Macc.

12:43-45) and merit earned by works (e.g., 2 Esdr. 8:33) — collected the Apocrypha into a section at the back of his 1534 OT and stated that the books, while edifying, were not sacred. The Geneva Bible (1599) actually omitted them entirely (this may have been unintended; the volumes appear in the Table of Contents); the third article in Calvinism's Westminster Confession (1646-1648) compares the books to secular works.

The early 17th century also witnessed the printing of the KJV without the Apocrypha. Although the Church of England included the volumes in its Bibles and readings from them in its lectionaries, the Thirty-Nine Articles (1562, 1571) deny use of the works in determining doctrine (Art. 6). In 1827 the British and Foreign Bible Society refused support for sister organizations in Europe which printed Bibles containing the Apocrypha; soon thereafter the American Bible Society began printing Bibles without the Apocrypha. Making this shorter text more popular was its decreased cost.

From the mid-20th century, as ecumenism gained popularity and as scholars recognized the Apocrypha's value for reconstructing Jewish history both in its own right and as background to Christian origins, the volumes have been reintroduced to Jewish and Protestant readers. Modern translations, such as the RSV, NRSV, and TEV, frequently contain the Apocrypha.

Historically, the Apocrypha provides substantial information about Hellenistic and early Roman Judaism. 1-2 Maccabees offer conflicting comments about the Hasmonean dynasty and the relationship between piety and politics; the Additions to Esther and Daniel as well as 2 Maccabees and Tobit emphasize resistance to assimilation, particularly in the Diaspora, through dietary regulations and endogamy; Ben Sirach reflects Hellenistic-Mediterranean views of honor and shame and the attendant concern for control over women; and the Wisdom of Solomon, influenced by Greek philosophy, develops the concept of Sophia as the manifestation of the divine. Liturgical concerns along with a deepening focus on personal piety are demonstrated not only by Ps. 151 and the invocations of Manasseh, Azariah, and the Three Young Men, but also by the prayers attributed to Tobit and his daughter-in-law Sarah, Judith, and Susanna.

Compared to the Hebrew Bible, the Apocrypha shows an increasing interest in sustained female characters, folktale motifs (Tobit), and the novel as being entertaining as well as instructive (Judith); Susanna is possibly the first detective story. Compared to the Pseudepigrapha and the latter books of the Hebrew Bible, the Apocrypha is noticeably lacking in apocalyptic and, especially, prophetic materials; this absence may be explained by the view that classical prophecy ended with Ezra or even the sense that the collection of prophets was complete.

Informative about Church and Synagogue concerns, the apocryphal works themselves influenced painting, music, and drama; Chaucer and Shakespeare, Milton and Longfellow, Handel and Anton Rubinstein, Rembrandt and Artemesia Gentileschi all draw upon apocryphal books. Even Columbus argued from 2 Esdr. 6:42 that the passage from Europe westward to Asia should take only a few days.

Bibliography. N. R. M. de Lange, *Apocrypha: Jewish Literature of the Hellenistic Age* (New York, 1978); B. M. Metzger, *An Introduction to the Apocrypha* (Oxford, 1977); S. Meurer, ed., *The Apocrypha in Ecumenical Perspective.* UBS Mon 6 (New York, 1992); H. H. Rowley, *The Origin and Significance of the Apocrypha,* rev. ed. (London, 1967); M. E. Stone, ed., *Jewish Writings of the Second Temple Period.* CRINT 2/2 (Philadelphia, 1984).

AMY-JILL LEVINE

APOCRYPHA, EARLY CHRISTIAN

The terms "OT" and "NT Apocrypha" (from Gk. *apókryphos,* "to be hidden or concealed," subsequently "esoteric") designate a diverse collection of writings outside the two canons featuring biblical figures or events. This bifurcation is problematic when, e.g., a Christian reworking of an OT or Jewish pseudepigraphical narrative does not fit well into either category. Early Christian Apocrypha is a better designation than NT Apocrypha because, although these texts employ figures from the NT, they do not necessarily hold a close connection to the NT theologically and may well have been written before the canon was formed. This amorphous corpus with no internal homogeneity entails a wide range of genres including gospels, agrapha, apocalypses, epistles, treatises, and acts. Attempting to categorize texts into these genres, however, is also problematic because they often do not fit neatly into one classification or another. Some combine several genres or present one genre in the form of another, such as a revelation discourse in the form of an epistle. Indeed, no pure forms exist because texts often build upon smaller literary units, such as hymns, creeds, poems, liturgical formulas, and parenetic material.

The apocryphal Gospels often include words and traditions about Jesus, as well as narratives concerning his birth, childhood, teachings, or Passion. This literature has preserved such well-known traditions as the animals by the manger, the birth in the cave, childhood miracles, and the descent of Christ into hell. Also portrayed are the actions and words of Jesus' disciples and family members, such as in the Gospel of Peter, the Gospel of Mary, and the Gospel of Thomas. The texts discovered at Nag Hammadi in 1945 opened up a large treasure chest of materials providing almost 50 previously unknown texts, some of which are apocryphal. Other discoveries of ancient manuscripts in monasteries and libraries in the 20th century and even recent decades indicate that studies of these texts carry much potential for future research projects. Among these finds are papyrus fragments bearing sayings of the Lord (agrapha), which even if not historically reliable reveal a great deal about the communities that preserved them. Such early Christian saying traditions as the Gospel of Thomas and the Dialogue of the Savior appear to have imbedded within them rather early oral traditions. Similar to the way in which Luke, Matthew, and Tatian bring together sources to produce a harmony, so too do certain apocryphal texts, such as the Gospel of the Ebionites, which harmonized several traditions and sources at a time when writers were freer to do so because the Gospels were not yet canonized.

The apocalypses incorporate revelations, visions, epiphanies, or postresurrection appearances to the disciples. These texts are often extant only in fragments, while others are known by name only and have yet to be found. They have preserved exhortations to repentance and, through pictorial language, portrayals of the last judgment and of heaven and hell (Apocalypse of Paul). The pseudepigraphical epistles often complement or correct doctrine and are not that much unlike the production of Deutero-Pauline epistles. Among the pseudepigraphical epistles are Paul's Epistle to the Laodiceans (Col. 4:16) and the third Epistle to the Corinthians (Acts of Paul). Other significant epistles include the correspondence between Christ and Abgar and between Paul and Seneca.

Some of the most well-known apocryphal texts are the Acts, such as the Acts of Paul and Thecla, of Peter, of Thomas, of John, of Andrew, and of Philip. The first five of these were ascribed by Photius to a certain Leucius Charinus, although clearly according to style and content they were not authored by the same person. These texts often present a truncated biography of an apostle, usually beginning with the reception of his or her mission and including his or her speeches, travels, and/or miracles. Often the final sections of the Acts describe the martyrdoms of the apostles, which must have had tremendous inspirational value in times of persecution. Many of the apocryphal texts focus upon certain apostles or claim to have been written by them, thus invoking his or her authority as the receiver, transmitter, and guarantor of that particular message. In the production of these Acts eventually a development occurs from featuring one apostle to portraying two working in tandem in their missions. Another transition occurs in the 4th and 5th centuries when apocryphal literature develops into hagiographical material such that they are sometimes difficult to distinguish. These Acts and other stories present traditions concerning the nativity and life of Mary the Mother, the inverse crucifixion of Peter, and the missionary activities of certain female disciples, such as Mary Magdalene (Acts of Philip), Thecla (Acts of Paul and Thecla), and Maximilla (Acts of Andrew). Because these texts depict such well-known but unusual narratives and were virtually the only sources for physical descriptions of the apostles (reliable or not), they are essential for understanding motifs in Christian iconography from late Hellenistic times through the Medieval period.

Because the early Christian communities did not value the same texts, this literature holds significance for scholars for shedding light upon the diverse interests in an ever-expanding Christianity. Although often presenting novelistic and imaginative elements, these texts also preserve historical kernels essential to reconstructing early Christian thought and theologies. The traditions surrounding certain apostles in some cases stem from the very origins of Christianity. With a plurality of recipients, some of the communities valuing these texts highly (e.g., Montanists, Manichaeans, or Priscillianists) were eventually marginalized by what came to be known as dominant Christianity. Filled with legends, unusual miracles, and even talking animals, these texts nevertheless offer insights into the religious, social, and cultural worlds of early Christianity, particularly the folk religion of the masses during apostolic times. They parallel, supplement, or perhaps even predate some of the information that the canonical literature presents, apparently with a variety of purposes ranging from entertainment to propaganda, from polemic or apologetic material to instruction and encouragement during persecution or even martyrdom.

The issues of dates, provenance, and authorship are often difficult or impossible to solve. Some of the texts could have been written as early as the 1st century, the largest portion in the 2nd and 3rd centuries, with some (e.g., Pistis Sophia) stemming anywhere from the 3rd to the 5th centuries. It is difficult to set a chronological limit to the range of dates for apocryphal literature because such literature continued to be produced, revised, and redacted for centuries with no clear-cut century in which it ceased to be created. Texts such as the Didache, the Epistle of Barnabas, and the Shepherd of Hermas were written early enough to have been considered for inclusion in the canon. In fact, Codex Sinaiticus, the oldest extant codex of the NT, includes both the Epistle of Barnabas and the Shepherd of Hermas in its collection. One cannot, therefore, readily generalize negatively about the reception of these texts as they were sometimes read as Scripture in the liturgical assemblies of some of the early Christian churches and still read even in the Middle Ages. Often the titles of the texts have been lost and have only been supplied by later commentators; some texts were written anonymously or pseudepigraphically.

Partly because of theology and partly because of this pseudepigraphical nature of the texts, some early church writers portrayed these texts as spurious, thus clouding them with the suspicion of heresy. Although the numerous patristic references prove how widespread they were, these references also contributed to their being viewed as inferior to what became their canonical counterparts. The broad geographical existence of these texts points to the extent of their popularity as they appear either in the original or in translation in Greek, Syriac, Coptic, Latin, Arabic, Georgian, Armenian, Slavic, Gaelic, and Ethiopic. Determining the language of the original text or reconstructing fragmentary evidence is sometimes quite difficult. For example, both the Acts of Paul and the Acts of Peter contain the "*Quo vadis?*" scene of Peter's encounter with Christ on the Appian Way, signaling that part of the ongoing challenge of these texts is determining the extent of their intertextuality or interdependence, as well as determining fissures between source material and redaction. These questions in addition to the issues of oral transmission and performances, gender studies, the complexity of manuscript evidence, and textual reconstruction provide fertile areas for future research. For that purpose critical editions with translations and notes are increasingly more available. Sources include Richard A. Lipsius and Max Bonnet for *Acta apostolorum apocrypha* (Leipzig, 1891–). English translations exist in Edgar Hennecke-Wilhelm Schneemelcher, *New Testament Apocrypha* (Philadelphia, 1963-65; 2nd ed., Louisville, 1991-92); James K. Elliot, *The Apocryphal New Testament,* rev. ed. (Oxford, 1993); and a forthcoming four-volume project from Polebridge Press. An international group of scholars, led by François Bovon and Pierre Geoltrain, called the Association pour l'étude de la littérature apocryphe chrétienne, has dedicated itself to intensive research in this field, thus helping to overcome years of scholarly neglect of these vital and rich sources of early Christian traditions.

Bibliography. J. H. Charlesworth, ed., *The New Testament Apocrypha and Pseudepigrapha* (Chicago, 1987); J. M. Robinson, ed., *The Nag Hammadi Library,* 3rd ed. (San Francisco, 1988); D. M. Scholer, *Nag Hammadi Bibliography.* NHS 1 (Leiden, 1971).

ANN GRAHAM BROCK

APOLLONIA (Gk. *Apollōnía*)
A Macedonian town S of Lake Bolbe, positioned on the Via Egnatia ca. 43 km. (27 mi.) WSW of Amphipolis and ca. 50 km. (31 mi.) E of Thessalonica. Paul and Silas passed through Apollonia on their way from Philippi to Thessalonica (Acts 17:1).

Several other towns bore this name, the most famous being the terminal point of the Via Egnatia in Illyricum.

RICHARD S. ASCOUGH

APOLLONIUS (Gk. *Apollṓnios*)

1. Son of Tharseas (or perhaps "of Tarsus"), governor of Coele-Syria and Phoenicia during the reign of Seleucus IV. According to 2 Macc. 3:4-7 he plotted with a Jew named Simon and Seleucus to plunder the treasuries of the temple in Jerusalem. Apollonius sent his chief minister Heliodorus to carry out the order, but Heliodorus was thwarted by a divine apparition.

2. Son of Menestheus, governor of Coele-Syria and Phoenicia during the reigns of Seleucus IV and Antiochus IV, perhaps identical with **1** above. According to 2 Macc. 4:21 he was sent to Egypt by Antiochus to attend the coronation of Ptolemy VI Philometor, and brought back news that Egypt had become hostile toward Antiochus.

3. General of the Mysian mercenary soldiers in the service of Antiochus IV Epiphanes. According to 2 Macc. 5:24-26; 1 Macc. 1:29-32 Apollonius was sent to Jerusalem with orders to plunder the city. Pretending to come in peace, he attacked and massacred the Jews on the sabbath day. He probably should be identified with the general Apollonius who came with a large army from Samaria in order to put down the Maccabean Revolt (1 Macc. 3:10-12). In the ensuing battle, Apollonius was defeated and lost his sword to the rebel leader Judas.

4. Son of Gennaeus, one of the local governors (Gk. *stratēgós)* who, after the rebels had made peace with Antiochus V (164 B.C.E.), "refused to allow the Jews to live in peace" and incited renewed military confrontations (2 Macc. 12:2).

5. Governor of Coele-Syria, appointed by the Seleucid monarch Demetrius II (147). Josephus identifies him as the son of **1** above (*Ant.* 13.86-102). According to 1 Macc. 10:69-87 Apollonius challenged the Hasmonaean high priest Jonathan to battle, since Jonathan supported Demetrius' rival Alexander Balas for the Seleucid throne. Jonathan responded by taking the city of Joppa from Apollonius' garrison. Apollonius attempted to lure Jonathan into an ambush, but Jonathan put him to flight. Apollonius and his troops fled to Ashdod, where they took refuge in the temple of Dagon. Jonathan burned the temple to the ground and plundered the city.

Bibliography. J. C. Dancy, *A Commentary on 1 Maccabees* (Oxford, 1954); J. Goldstein, *I Maccabees.* AB (New York, 1976); E. Schürer, *A History of the Jewish People in the Age of Jesus Christ,* rev. ed., 4 vols. (Edinburgh, 1973-1987).

ANTHONY J. TOMASINO

APOLLOS (Gk. *Apollṓs*)
An Alexandrian Jew, best known for his connection to the situation addressed by Paul in 1 Corinthians. Some Corinthians esteem him as their teacher (1 Cor. 1:12; 3:4), and Paul describes him as a coworker in the "field" of God (3:5-9) and fellow servant of Christ (3:22; 4:6). However, he is not present in Corinth when Paul writes, and he balks at Paul's suggestion to return there (16:12).

Acts 18:24-28 contains the only biographical information about Apollos. Having a thorough knowledge of Scripture and great oratorical fervor, he learned the "way of the Lord," taught accurately about Jesus, and received the baptism of John. He spoke boldly in the synagogue in Ephesus and was recognized by Priscilla and Aquila, who invited him to their home and instructed him more adequately in the gospel. Apollos then went to Achaia with encouragement and letters of recommendation from some Ephesian believers. In Corinth he greatly helped believers and vigorously refuted Jews in public debate, proving from the Scriptures that Jesus was the Christ.

This sketch has fueled speculation concerning the problems addressed by Paul in 1 Corinthians. The designation of Apollos as *anḗr lógios* ("an eloquent man," Acts 18:24) suggests that the root problem is an overvaluation of Greco-Roman rhetoric, though his Alexandrian heritage is advanced to suggest that he was a Philonic philosopher practiced in techniques of Alexandrian exegesis. This has led to suggestions that gnostic, Hellenistic-Jewish wisdom, or excessive pneumatic tendencies lay behind the divisions in Corinth. Paul does not blame Apollos for the difficulties in Corinth and depicts him as a valued partner in his ministry. The fault lies with those Corinthians who are divisive.

Bibliography. A. D. Litfin, *St. Paul's Theology of Proclamation.* SNTSMS 79 (Cambridge, 1994).

JEFFREY S. LAMP

APOLLYON (Gk. *Apollýōn*)
Greek translation of Heb. *'ăḇaddôn.* The word, meaning "destroyer," occurs only once in the NT and refers to the "angel of the bottomless pit" (Rev. 9:11). The LXX translates the Hebrew term into Greek as *apṓleia.* In Greek literature the god of destruction and pestilence is often connected with this word.

JIM WEST

APOSTASY
The act of "standing away," "rebellion," or "separation" (Gk. *apostasía,* perhaps derived from *aphístēmi,* "to stand away from," "rebel," "separate," or "fall away from"). A related term is *apostatḗs,* "a rebel" or "apostate" (cf. textual variation on Jas. 2:11).

In the LXX these terms refer to various kinds of relational separation, including political separation and rebellion (e.g., 2 Chr. 21:8; Tob. 1:4; 2 Macc. 5:8; 1 Esdr. 2:23) or religious abandonment, rebellion, or separation from God or the covenant (e.g., Deut. 32:15; Josh. 22:18-19, 22; 2 Chr. 33:19; Isa. 30:1; Jer. 2:19; 1 Macc. 2:19).

Acts 21:21 refers to the view of some Jerusalem Christians that Paul taught a rejection of Moses' law. The noun also appears as an apocalyptic reference to a rebellion at the end of the age (2 Thess. 2:3). Two specific theological uses of the verb that are problematic are a warning to avoid having an evil heart that "turns away from the living God" (Heb. 3:12), which recalls the historical analogy of the ancient Israelites' rebellion against God (Num. 14:26-45; Ps. 95:7-11), and a reference to those who "renounce the faith" in the latter days (1 Tim. 4:1). Similar uses of the verb appear in Luke 8:13; Acts 15:38; 19:9; Rev. 3:8.

According to Heb. 6:6 *(parapesóntas),* some individuals "commit apostasy" (RSV) or "have fallen away" (NRSV). This may imply the denial of the faith during persecution.

BENNIE R. CROCKETT, JR.

APOSTLE
"One sent out," generally to proclaim a message. NT use is continuous with the OT idea of a special messenger from God (cf. 2 Kgs. 2:2; 2 Sam. 24:13). The term has a variety of specific senses in the NT, but "special messenger, particularly from God" best captures the dominant sense.

According to Mark 3:14-15 Jesus "appointed twelve, whom he also named apostles, to be with him, and to be sent out to proclaim the message, and to have authority to cast out demons" (cf. Matt. 10:1-4; Luke 6:13-16). The 12 apostles, along with other disciples, were sent by Jesus to proclaim the same message he himself proclaimed: "The time is fulfilled, and the kingdom of God has come near; repent, and believe in the good news" (Mark 1:15; cf. 6:7-13; Luke 9:1-6, 60). According to Matt. 10:2-4 the Twelve were Simon, also known as Peter, and his brother Andrew; James, son of Zebedee, and his brother John; Philip and Bartholomew; Thomas and Matthew the tax collector; James, son of Alphaeus, and Thaddaeus; Simon the Cananaean, and Judas Iscariot, who betrayed Jesus (cf. Luke 6:14-16; John 1:40-51; Acts 1:13; see Acts 1:15-26 for the successor to Judas).

Initially, Jesus sent the Twelve "to the lost sheep of the house of Israel," rather than to the Gentiles or the Samaritans (Matt. 10:5-6; cf. 15:24). The relevance of the Twelve to the house of Israel becomes explicit in Matt. 19:28, where Jesus remarks to his disciples: "Truly I tell you, at the renewal of all things, when the Son of Man is seated on the throne of his glory, you who have followed me will also sit on twelve thrones, judging the twelve tribes of Israel." The Twelve thus represent Jesus' mission to bring renewal to all of Israel, through his inauguration of the kingdom of God (cf. Rev. 21:12-14).

The apostles were present at key junctures in Jesus' mission, including the feeding of the five thousand (Mark 6:30-44), the Last Supper (Luke 22:14), and Gethsemane (Mark 14:32-43). Peter and the two sons of Zebedee were also present at the transfiguration of Jesus (Mark 9:2-8), and Jesus asked them in particular to accompany him at Gethsemane (14:33). Even so, those three show no special understanding of or fidelity to Jesus (cf. Mark 10:35-41; 14:66-72; Luke 9:33). In Matt. 26:31 the apostles are portrayed as being scattered at the arrest of Jesus (cf. Mark 14:27), and John 20:19 depicts them as hiding together in fear as a result of the arrest and crucifixion of Jesus. Nonetheless, all four Gospels represent the apostles as witnesses to the resurrected Jesus (Mark 14:28; 16:7; Matt. 26:32; 28:16; Luke 24:36-53; John 20:19-29; 21:1-14; cf. Acts 1:1-3; 1 Cor. 15:5). Luke depicts the apostles as receiving the power of God's Spirit to proclaim a message of repentance and forgiveness through Jesus to all nations (Luke 24:46-48; Acts 1:4-8; 2:1-13; cf. John 20:19-23; Matt. 28:16-20).

The NT does not restrict the term "apostle" to the Twelve selected by Jesus. In Heb. 3:1 Jesus himself is called "the apostle and high priest of our confession"; this fits with Jesus' references to himself as the one "sent" by God (Matt. 15:24; Mark 9:37; Luke 9:48; John 3:17, 34; cf. Luke 10:22; Matt. 11:27). In Gal. 1:19 Paul implies that James, the brother of Jesus, was an apostle (cf. 1 Cor. 9:5), and in 1 Cor. 15:9 Paul refers to himself as an apostle (cf. 9:1; 2 Cor. 11:5; Gal. 1:1). In Acts 14:14 Luke refers to Barnabas and Paul as apostles, and in Rom. 16:7 Paul implies that Andronicus and Junias were apostles at Rome. (Perhaps the latter were husband and wife.)

Paul distinguished true from false apostles (2 Cor. 11:13; cf. Rev. 2:2), and he acknowledged "signs of a true apostle," apparently including "signs and wonders and mighty works" (2 Cor. 12:12). Paul may also have thought of his having seen the risen Jesus as sufficient for his being an apostle (1 Cor. 9:1). At any rate, some people in

Corinth and Galatia had challenged Paul's apostleship (cf. Gal. 2:8), perhaps on the ground that he had not followed the pre-resurrection Jesus. Paul insisted that he was an apostle through Jesus Christ and God the Father, not through human means (Gal. 1:1). In the Pauline tradition, apostles were apparently not just prophets (Eph. 4:11); still, this tradition could speak of apostles and prophets as the foundation of the household of God.

Bibliography. F. H. Agnew, "The Origin of the NT Apostle-Concept," *JBL* 105 (1986): 75-96; R. E. Brown, "The Twelve and the Apostolate," *NJBC*, 1377-81. PAUL K. MOSER

APOSTLES, EPISTLE OF THE

A mid-2nd century C.E. text, probably of Egyptian origin, that represents an attempt by the "orthodox" Church to use the revelation dialogue, a genre typically used by Gnostics, to combat gnosticism. Written as a letter from the disciples to the universal Church, the text includes a miracle catena (Ep. Apost. 5), a detailed resurrection appearance (9-12), and passages addressing various points of Christian theology. The text came to light in 1895 with the discovery of major portions of a Coptic translation. Latin fragments and a complete Ethiopic translation were found later.

Bibliography. C. Detlef and G. Müller, "Epistula Apostolorum," in *New Testament Apocrypha*, ed. W. Schneemelcher and R. McL. Wilson, rev. ed. 1 (Philadelphia, 1991): 249-84; J. V. Hills, *Tradition and Composition in the Epistula Apostolorum*. HDR 24 (Minneapolis, 1990). ANDREA LORENZO MOLINARI

APOSTOLIC COUNCIL

A gathering in Jerusalem (also called the Jerusalem Council) of representatives from the church in Syrian Antioch (including Paul and Barnabas) together with certain apostles and the elders of the parent church in Jerusalem, to respond to the claim of some Jewish Christians that gentile converts needed to be circumcised in order to be saved (Acts 15:1-35).

Peter is the first to speak in the assembly, and the force of his comments is strongly against insisting on circumcision as a requirement for the salvation of Gentiles (Acts 15:7-11). He reminds the Council of his experience with Cornelius, a gentile God-fearer who, together with family and friends, came to faith and received the Holy Spirit quite apart from the rite of circumcision (cf. Acts 10:1–11:18). For Peter this is compelling evidence that God looks upon the heart of Jew and Gentile alike (Acts 15:8-9); faith and not external distinctives is the one path to salvation (vv. 9-11). Next Paul and Barnabas speak of the signs and wonders God did as they ministered among Gentiles, again appealing to divine activity which wins Gentiles to the gospel as evidence that circumcision is not required for salvation.

James (probably the "half-brother" of Jesus; cf. Mark 6:3) is convinced especially by Peter's testimony, and sees biblical support for God's openness to and interest in the Gentiles (Acts 15:13-21; cf. Amos 9:11-12). James then delivers a decision which is welcomed by the apostles, the elders, and the whole Church (Acts 15:19-22): Gentiles need not be circumcised to be saved, but they are called upon to accept certain expressions of Jewish lawkeeping to promote harmony and morality within their mixed congregation (vv. 20, 29). Luke indicates that this decision is joyously accepted by the Antioch church (Acts 15:31). The fact that Jewish distinctives are not erased and OT law is not set aside no doubt makes it possible for (at least most) circumcision advocates to accept this decision (cf. Acts 21:18-26).

The question is often raised as to the possible convergence of the Jerusalem Council and the account of Paul's visit to Jerusalem in Gal. 2:1-10. In favor of these passages as recounting a single historical occasion are Paul's association with Barnabas and a concern about circumcision in both accounts. Arguments for the Galatians account as describing a visit to Jerusalem prior to the Council, however, are noteworthy. The two visits of Paul to Jerusalem described in Galatians (Gal. 1:18-19; 2:1-10) correspond to two visits mentioned by Luke in Acts prior to the Council (Acts 9:26-30; 11:30). Most importantly, if Paul were aware of the decision of the Apostolic Council prior to writing Galatians, we might well expect him to appeal to that decision in order to enhance his arguments against the "agitators" in Galatia who advocate circumcision for gentile converts (cf. Gal. 5:2, 6, 11-12; 6:12-13, 15), but he does not.

The importance of the Apostolic Council in the life of the early Church is very great. A precedent is created for handling matters of conflict and theological controversy in a civil, reasoned, Spirit-led manner, and a vital foundation of Christian theology is expressed: salvation is by grace through faith, not through human works (Acts 15:11).

Bibliography. R. N. Longenecker, *Galatians*. WBC 41 (Waco, 1990), lxxiii-lxxxiii; I. H. Marshall, *The Acts of the Apostles*. TNTC (1980, repr. Grand Rapids, 1996), 242-56. PETER K. NELSON

APOSTOLIC FATHERS

A collection of early Christian writings held to have been written by disciples or close associates of the apostles. Usually included in the Apostolic Fathers are the Didache, 1 Clement, 2 Clement, Barnabas, the letters of Ignatius, the letter(s) of Polycarp to the Philippians, the Shepherd of Hermas, and the writings of Papias. Sometimes included are the Martyrdom of Polycarp, a work better classified with the early martyr literature, and the Epistle to Diognetus, which belongs with the apologetical literature.

The description of certain individuals who were not apostles as "apostolic" goes back to the ancient Church (e.g., Mart. Pol. 1.2), but the modern designation of an actual group of writings as Apostolic Fathers derives from the 17th century. A collection of five of these authors was published in 1672 by Jean Baptiste Cotelier, and the term "Apostolic Fathers" was applied by William Wake in 1693 to his translation of 1 Clement, Polycarp, Ignatius, Martyrdom of Ignatius, Martydom of Polycarp, Barnabas, Hermas, and 2 Clement.

The name was based on the presumed connection of some of the authors with the apostles, a presumption now regarded as unlikely in most cases. The justification for keeping these works together as a distinctive body of literature is that they form the earliest noncanonical Christian writings not belonging to another classification and not associated with later heretical developments. Their dates fall between the latter part of the 1st century (Didache [?], 1 Clement) to the middle of the 2nd century (Hermas [?]). As with the NT authors but unlike the apologists, the Apostolic Fathers were writing to and for Christians.

These writings were highly regarded in the early Church, and some hovered on the boundary of canonicity; e.g., the biblical Codex Sinaiticus (4th century) included Barnabas and the Shepherd, and Codex Alexandrinus (5th century) included 1 and 2 Clement. The works of Clement and Ignatius in many respects represent characteristics that emerged in Western and Eastern Christianity respectively. They have been the most influential of the Apostolic Fathers, although through much of history this influence came about pseudonymously through expansions to Ignatius' letters and false ascriptions of other works to Clement.

The grouping together of the Apostolic Fathers is in many respects arbitrary. They overlap in date the later NT writings (e.g. Revelation) and the early NT apocrypha and pseudepigrapha (Gospel of Thomas, Gospel of Peter; Barnabas is perhaps pseudonymous), as well as the early apologists (Quadratus, Aristides) and acts of the martyrs (Mart. Pol., Acts of Justin). They represent a variety of literary types: church order (Didache); letter (Ignatius, Polycarp); letter treatise (1 Clement; Barnabas); sermon (2 Clement); apocalypse (Hermas); and perhaps commentary (Papias). They show the geographical spread of Christianity: Rome (Hermas, 1 Clement, the latter addressed to Corinth), Smyrna (Polycarp, addressed to Philippi), Antioch (Ignatius, addressed to cities in Asia), Syria (Didache [?]), and Alexandria (Barnabas [?]). They reflect the various religio-cultural influences at work in early Christianity: e.g., the compiler of the Didache lives in the atmosphere of Judaism, but Ignatius is a Hellenist and sees Christ as replacing the Jewish heritage.

Each of the Apostolic Fathers represents some of the distinctive concerns of Christians of the third generation: matters of instruction of new converts, worship, and church organization (Didache); internal unity (1 Clement); Christian living (2 Clement; Polycarp); the related matter of involvement in the affairs of the world and availability of repentance for post-baptismal sins (Hermas); the relation to Jews and the place of the OT (Barnabas); false teaching and how to meet its threat (Ignatius); and eschatological expectation (Papias). For the most part they addressed the practical needs of Christian communities and not speculative theology.

For all their diversity in personality and concerns, the Apostolic Fathers exhibit some general characteristics. They were earnest and pious individuals struggling to preserve the apostolic teachings in the early years after the living apostolic presence was removed. Not great creative thinkers themselves, they did apply originality to certain traditional Christian materials. They sought to be faithful to the fundamental Christian affirmation of the one God, salvation in his Son Jesus Christ, and the Holy Spirit dwelling in the visible Church of believers, whose unity they sought to maintain against various threats. Although each used Scripture in his own way, there are manifold citations of the Bible (especially the OT) and a common commitment to its authority as interpreted in the light of the coming of Christ. They were all very concerned with the Christian life-style in relation to the surrounding world. They are often accused of representing a falling away from the Pauline doctrines of grace and faith, but this charge derives from a one-sided understanding of Paul and fails to take into account the situations in which the respective Apostolic Fathers wrote. For the most part, they assumed the basis of salvation and addressed its consequences in the lives of believers. They are confessedly inferior to the apostolic writings in spiritual insight and inspiration, but this does not diminish the significance of their testimony to Christian life and thought at a crucial time in the Church's history.

Bibliography. E. J. Goodspeed, *Index Patristicus* (1907, repr. Peabody, 1993); R. M. Grant, ed., *The Apostolic Fathers,* vol. 1 (New York, 1964); C. N. Jefford, *Reading the Apostolic Fathers* (Peabody, 1996); J. B. Lightfoot, *The Apostolic Fathers,* 2nd ed. (Grand Rapids, 1992); Oxford Society of Historical Theology, *The New Testament in the Apostolic Fathers* (Oxford, 1905). EVERETT FERGUSON

APPAIM (Heb. *'appayim)*
A son of Nadab and father of Ishi; a descendant of Jerahmeel of Judah (1 Chr. 2:30-31).

APPHIA (Gk. *Apphía)*
A woman to whom Paul's Epistle to Philemon was addressed (Phlm. 2). She is designated "sister," often taken as indication that she was Philemon's wife, but perhaps indicating primarily her position of respect in the community (Gk. "the sister").

APPHUS (Gk. *Apphoús)*
Nickname of Jonathan (**16**), the youngest son of Matthias (1 Macc. 2:5) and successor of Judas Maccabeus.

APPIAN WAY (Lat. *Via Appia)*
The second oldest Roman highway, begun by Appius Claudius in 312 B.C. and eventually stretching 579 km. (360 mi.) from Rome to Brundisium (modern Brindisi) on the Adriatic coast. With an average width of 5.5 m. (18 ft.), there was space for

two wagons to pass. It was the prime route for all land travel between Rome and Greece and points east. Though not explicitly mentioned, this was the road Paul took en route to Rome, a fact confirmed by the mention of the "Forum of Appius" and "Three Taverns" (Acts 28:15). From Puteoli, he would have traveled 32 km. (20 mi.) to Capua, where he could catch the Via Appia and in five or six days traverse the remaining 212 km. (132 mi.) to Rome. KENT L. YINGER

APPLE
A fruit tree (Heb. *tappûaḥ*), *Malus sylvestris* Mill., known to have been cultivated in Egypt and Syria in biblical times (cf. Arab. *tufaʿḥ*). Carbonized remains of the fruit have been found in 9th-century B.C.E. debris from Kadesh-barnea. Some scholars, however, contend that the "apples of gold" (Prov. 25:11) were the apricot (*Prunus armeniaca* L.) or a citrus fruit. Tradition has established the apple as the fruit of the tree of knowledge (Gen. 2); however, nothing in the narrative suggests this identification.

This cultivated tree (Joel 1:12) bears refreshing fruit (Cant. 2:5), which has a pleasant smell (7:8). Since a mother in labor sits under a *tappûaḥ* tree, it presumably provided adequate shade (Cant. 8:5).

The term also occurs in place names (e.g., Beth-tappuah, Josh. 15:33) and the proper name Tappuah (1 Chr. 2:43).

MEGAN BISHOP MOORE/RANDALL W. YOUNKER

AQUEDUCT
An elevated structure, often supported by series of arches, on which an open channel brought water to cities and dry areas. The three pools of Solomon, ca. 21 km. (13 mi.) S of Jerusalem, were connected with the capital by means of two aqueducts; built by Herod the Great (37-4 B.C.E.), they were later repaired by Pontius Pilate (Josephus *Ant.* 18.3.2[60]).

AQUILA (Gk. *Akýlas*)

1. The husband of Priscilla/Prisca and associate of Paul. A native of Pontus, but later a resident of Rome, Aquila met Paul in Corinth after he, Priscilla, and other Jews had been expelled from Rome by Claudius (Acts 18:2-3). Many scholars associate this expulsion with Suetonius' statement that the emperor expelled Jews from Rome due to the instigation of *Chrestus* (*Claud.* 25.4), which may be a reference to the preaching of Jesus *Christos.* Later Aquila moved to Ephesus, where his home was used as a house church (Acts 18:26; 1 Cor. 16:19). According to Acts, he and Priscilla instructed Apollos "more accurately" regarding the Way (Acts 18:26), though some scholars believe this to be "pro-Pauline" propaganda from Luke, who knew Apollos to be a rival of Paul's in Corinth (cf. 1 Cor. 1:12; 3:4-9). Later Aquila moved back to Rome, again opening his home to the church (Rom. 16:3-5). Some have concluded that, as a tentmaker, able to move with relative frequency and own a home large enough for church gatherings, he was a man of some means.

2. A translator of Hebrew Scriptures into Greek during the first quarter of the 2nd century C.E. A native of Sinope in Pontus, he was first converted to Christianity, then Judaism. He studied under Rabbi Akiba. Aquila's translation was very literal and was sanctioned by the synagogue as an alternative to the LXX, which was increasingly becoming the Christians' Bible. His translation exists today only in fragments. Both Jerome and Origen employed this translation, with Origen including it in his Hexapla. Some have identified Aquila with Onqelos, the compiler of the Targum of the Pentateuch, but there is no consensus on this.

Bibliography. S. Jellicoe, *The Septuagint and Modern Study* (1968, repr. Winona Lake, 1993), 76-83. J. BRADLEY CHANCE

AR (Heb. *ʿār*)
A site near the northern Moabite border, situated at the Arnon River (Num. 21:15, 28; Deut. 2:18). The name ("city") may also refer to the Moabite territory in general (Deut. 2:9, 29). Ar and Kir together refer either to the two principal sites of Moab or to Moabite cities in general (Isa. 15:1). Ar has been identified with ancient Rabbath-moab / Areopolis (modern Rabbah) and recently with Khirbet el-Bālūʿ (244855), which better fits the geographical conditions described in Num. 21:15.

Bibliography. J. M. Miller, "The Israelite Journey through (around) Moab and Moabite Toponymy," *JBL* 108 (1989): 577-95; U. Worshech and F. Ninow, "Preliminary Report on the Third Campaign at the Ancient Site of el-Baluʿ in 1991," *ADAJ* 38 (1994): 195-203. FRIEDBERT NINOW

ARA (Heb. *'ărā'*)
A son of Jether, of the tribe of Asher (1 Chr. 7:38).

ARAB (Heb. *'ărāḇ*)
A city in the hill country of Judah, SW of Hebron (Josh. 15:52); possibly the birthplace of Paarai "the Arbite" (2 Sam. 23:35). The site has been identified as modern er-Râbiyeh (153093), E of Dumah (Deir ed-Dômeh).

ARABAH (Heb. *ʿărāḇâ*)
A term translated in some contexts as "desert," "plain," or "wilderness." Its meanings are derived from a specific place known as "the Arabah," distinguished from general contexts by the presence of the definite article (Josh. 11:16), which included three major regions within the Great Rift Valley. First is the Jordan Valley, which descends southward along the Jordan River from the southern end of the Sea of Chinnereth to the Dead Sea below sea level (Deut. 3:17). In reference to this area, the term is translated "plains," as in "the plains of Jericho" (Josh. 4:13) and opposite them "the plains of Moab" (Num. 33:49). The second region includes the Dead Sea and its surrounding lowlands. The third stretch southward ascends at first rapidly from the Dead Sea and then descends very gradually to sea level at the Gulf of Elath. Mention of this third region is associated with the "Arabah road," which refers to various roads running along north-south lines up

from Ezion-Geber (2 Sam. 4:7). As a land formation, the Arabah created a distinct border between the land of Israel and its enemies to the east, Ammon, Moab, and Edom.

Particular characteristics typify the ecology and climate of each of these three divisions of the Arabah. Although rainfall is essentially consistent for each, the Jordan Valley is the most lush along the river and particularly at its southern end, where springs abound on the plains of Jericho. In stark contrast, a desert climate characterizes the region from the Dead Sea south. Its variations both in geography and climate probably contributed to its association with and occasional translation as "jungle" or "thicket" (Jer. 49:19), "desert" (Isa. 35:6), and "plain" (2 Kgs. 25:4-5). As a diverse landscape, it would have provided excellent places for refuge, as in the case of David's flight from Saul into the wilderness of Maon (1 Sam. 23:24) and Zedekiah's attempt to escape the Chaldeans (Jer. 39:4).

AARON A. BURKE

ARABAH, WADI (Heb. *naḥal hā'ărāḇâ*)
A stream representing Israel's southern boundary in Amos' oracle of doom (Amos 6:14). If identified with the brook Zered (Wadi el-Ḥesā), its crossing by the Israelites marked the end of their wilderness wanderings (Num. 21:12; Deut. 2:13-14). It may be the same as the Wadi of the Willows (Isa. 15:7).

ARABIA
A term used to refer to an area at times encompassing the north Syrian desert (cf. Paul's detour "into Arabia" after his revelation, Gal. 1:17), at times the Sinai (the location of Mt. Sinai in "Arabia," Gal. 4:25), and anomalously to gloss Saba in LXX Ps. 72:10, 15. Biblical Arabia was certainly not construed as the entirety of the Arabian Peninsula, but may be likened to an upright parallelogram extending from the oasis of Dedan in the southwest, across to the Jawf oasis at the southern end of the Wadi Sirhan, up into the Syrian desert, across to the borders of Palestine and the Negeb, and down through the Hijaz. In this respect it was not dissimilar to the much later Roman province of Arabia. As for the inhabitants of Arabia, both the biblical and extrabiblical sources, especially the Neo-Assyrian and Neo-Babylonian records, make it clear that Arabia was populated by a variety of groups and contained sedentary communities living in cities and towns as well as agriculturalists and pastoralists.

A number of the North Arabian toponyms and ethnonyms attested in Neo-Assyrian sources can be identified with names mentioned in the OT as well. Thus, the people of Massa' (*^{uru}Mas'ayya*) who brought tribute to Tiglath-pileser III are identical with the OT Massa (Gen. 25:14; 1 Chr. 1:30), listed as a son of Ishmael and hailing from a town not far from Tema, as shown by the reference to a war against Massa' (*ms*[']) in an inscription from Jabal Ghunaym. Tema, an important oasis settlement on the route from Dedan to Dumah (Gen. 25:14), itself appears in both Neo-Assyrian and Neo-Babylonian sources (*^{uru}Temayya*), as well as in the list of the sons of Ishmael (Gen. 25:15; 1 Chr. 1:30; cf. Job 6:19; Isa. 21:14; Jer. 25:23). The homeland of the "princes of Kedar" (Ezek. 27:21) appears in Neo-Assyrian sources as *^{kur}Qid-ri, ^{kur}Qi-id-ri, ^{kur}Qí-id-ri, ^{kur}Qa-da-ri;* it is clear that the center of this region was Dumah (Gen. 25:14; Akk. *^{uru}A-du-um-ma-tu, ^{uru}A-du-mu-u, ^{uru}A-du-mu-tu*) in the Jawf oasis of modern northern Saudi Arabia, although Kedarite tribes ranged more widely from the borders of Mesopotamia to the fringes of Palestine. The Idiba'ilu (*^{lú}Idiba'ilayya*) are the Abdeel, one of the sons of Ishmael (Gen. 25:13; 1 Chr. 1:29) and, according to LXX Gen. 25:3, a son of Dedan. The Hajappa (*^{uru}Hayappâyya*) can be identified with Ephah (Gen. 25:4; 1 Chr. 1:33), a son of Midian, and sometimes identified with the site of Ruwwafa in northwestern Saudi Arabia. The inclusion of Sabaeans (*^{lú}Saba'ayya*) among the peoples from the North Arabian desert who brought tribute to Assyria suggests the existence of a northern Saba or, at the very least, of Sabaean tribes in North Arabia as well as in the south.

The OT refers variously to *'ărab/'ărāb* (Jer. 25:24; Ezek. 27:21; 2 Chr. 9:14; Isa. 21:13) or *'arḇiyyîm/'arḇî'îm/'arḇîm* (2 Chr. 17:11; 21:16; 22:1; 26:7; Neh. 4:7[MT 4:1]), i.e. "Arabs." It has been customary either to identify these as some sort of bedouin, nomads, pastoralists, tent-dwellers, or camel-breeders, or to derive the terms from *'ărāḇâ*, meaning "steppe" or "desert." Other scholars point to a number of cases (e.g., Jer. 25:24; 2 Chr. 9:14 compared with the par. 1 Kgs. 10:15) where a phrase like "all the kings of *'ereḇ* that dwell in the desert" is opposed to "all the kings of *'ărāḇ*." The Hebrew root *'ereḇ*, meaning "mixture," seems thus to be used to gloss *'ăraḇ*, a term for the North Arabian desert dwellers, whether sedentary or mobile, used also in Neo-Assyrian accounts of campaigns against Arabia (*^{kur}Arb-a-a, ^{kur}Ara/i/ub-, ^{mat}Aribi*) and the Arabs (*^{lú}Arba-a-a, ^{lú}Arab-*), and when speaking of the tribute brought to Assyria by tribes from this region. The "mixed" nature of the *'ăraḇ* may explain why they are not mentioned in the OT genealogies. It is important to remember, however, that these "Arabs" were not confined to Arabia, but appear everywhere from the Fertile Crescent to Mesopotamia.

The importance of Arabia for the inhabitants of Israel undoubtedly lay less in the wealth of its herds (cf. the 7700 rams and 7700 male goats brought by the Arabians to Jehoshaphat, 2 Chr. 17:11; cf. Ezek. 27:21) than in the wealth (e.g., gold and silver, 2 Chr. 9:14) derived from its position astride the route which linked the frankincense-bearing and trading states of South Arabia, such as Saba, and the Mediterranean world. Furthermore, it is difficult to comprehend the preoccupation of successive Neo-Assyrian monarchs, and the extended campaign in the region by Nabonidus, if it were only for the pastoral and agricultural produce of the area, all of which was available in Assyria and Babylonia. High-quality frankincense, on the other hand, was a monopoly of South Arabia, and even if other sources existed (e.g., Somalia, India) these generally produced an inferior quality.

That "Arabia" was never unified politically is patently clear from the Neo-Assyrian sources, for even if several Arabian queens are mentioned there, nothing suggests that any of them ruled over a unified country identifiable as "Arabia." Similarly, when the Bible refers to "all the kings of Arabia" (e.g., 2 Chr. 9:14; cf. Peshitta *malkē ʿarbāyē;* Vulg. *reges Arabiae*) these should probably be understood in the sense of numerous petty sheikhs, each based in one of the towns of Arabia and enjoying the allegiance of a relatively small and geographically circumscribed population. The decentralized nature of biblical Arabia accounts for the multitude of ethnonyms which can be assigned to the area, and the absence of a "king of all the Arabs," a title never attested in the Bible, confirms that "Arabia" never had a political meaning.

Bibliography. G. W. Bowersock, *Roman Arabia* (Cambridge, Mass., 1983); I. Ephʿal, *The Ancient Arabs* (Leiden, 1982); J. Retsö, "The Earliest Arabs," *Orientalia Suecana* 38/39 (1989-1990): 131-39; R. Zadok, "Arabians in Mesopotamia during the Late-Assyrian, Chaldean, Achaemenian and Hellenistic Periods," *ZDMG* 131 (1981): 42-84; "On Early Arabians in the Fertile Crescent," *Tel Aviv* 17 (1990): 223-31. D. T. Potts

ARAD (Heb. *ʿărad̲*) **(PERSON)**
A son of Beriah and descendant of Benjamin (1 Chr. 8:15).

ARAD (Heb. *ʿărād̲*) **(PLACE)**
A city in the Negeb desert region. In the account of the entry of the Israelites into the region, the "King of Arad" is mentioned as fighting against Israel (Num. 21:1-3). After an initial defeat the Israelites were victorious and "destroyed them and their cities"; the place was named Hormah, or "destruction" (cf. Num. 33:40). In Josh. 12:14 Arad appears in a list of kings defeated by Joshua. Judg. 1:16 reports that Kenites joined Judahites in settling near Arad.

The list of cities conquered by Shishak of Egypt (960 B.C.E.) includes "the citadels of Arad the Great and Arad of the house of YRHM" — either the house of Yeroham or Jerahmiel. Archaeological evidence does not clarify the identifications of these Arads.

Tel ʿArad (162075), 30 km. (19 mi.) E of Beersheba and 32 km. (20 mi.) S of Hebron, has retained the ancient name. It is a large site with a smaller but pronounced citadel mound. The lower city was excavated between 1964 and 1982 by Ruth Amiran. Unfortified settlements are attested from the Chalcolithic period to 2950 (EB I). The city walls fortifying the site date to EB II, and enclose an area of 10 ha. (25 a.). Public and private buildings including a palace and temples have been identified, as has a well-built water reservoir. The city suffered a major destruction ca. 2800, but occupation continued until ca. 2650. The demise of Canaanite Arad is probably to be attributed to declining rainfall in the area, and perhaps as well to political unrest throughout the Near East.

Excavation of the citadel by Yohanan Aharoni shows a gap of ca. 1500 years from the abandonment of the EB city to the building of a settlement in the citadel area ca. 1200. Six successive Iron III strata followed in the shape of a rectangular fortress. A temple or cult center with a holy of holies has been identified here. Aharoni suggests that stratum XI was destroyed by Shishak. Also on the citadel was an unfortified Persian settlement, followed by Hellenistic and Roman forts. The site is notable for having produced more ostraca — mostly Hebrew but some Aramaic — than any other archaeological site in the ancient biblical world.

Bibliography. M. Aharoni, R. Amiran, and O. Ilan, "Arad," *NEAEHL* 1: 75-87; Y. Aharoni, *Arad Inscriptions* (Jerusalem, 1981); R. Amiran, *Early Arad* (Jerusalem, 1978). Bruce C. Cresson

ARAH (Heb. *ʾāraḥ*)

1. The oldest son of Ulla of the tribe of Asher (1 Chr. 7:39).

2. An Israelite whose descendants (775, according to Ezra 2:5; 652 at Neh. 7:10) returned from the Exile at the time of Zerubbabel. He is probably the same as the Arah mentioned at Neh. 6:18, whose son Shecaniah was the father-in-law of Tobiah the Ammonite.

ARAM (Heb. *ʾărām*) **(PERSON)**

1. One of the sons of Shem and grandson of Noah; eponymous ancestor of the Arameans (Gen. 10:22-23; 1 Chr. 1:17).

2. The son of Kemuel and grandson of Abraham's brother Nahor (Gen. 22:20-21).

3. A son of Shemer of the tribe of Asher (1 Chr. 7:34).

4. An ancestor of Jesus (Matt. 1:3-4; Gk. *Arám*), often rendered "Ram" in English versions (cf. Luke 3:33; NRSV "Arni").

ARAM (Heb. *ʾărām*) **(PLACE)**
The territory of the Arameans, comprising the area from the Ḫabur triangle in the East, to the middle Euphrates region, through most of Syria, and south to the Beqaʿ Valley, Damascus, and the Golan Heights. In some occurrences Aram refers to this area in general or at least to large parts of it (most clearly in 1 Kgs. 10:29 = 2 Chr. 1:17, where Solomon trades with the kings of Aram), but at other times to specific components (e.g., Judg. 10:6). In Amos 9:7 it is a general designation for the people of the region.

Use of the term corresponds to the fact that Aram never became a large unified state, but rather consisted of various entities. Only in the late 9th century B.C.E., under the leadership of Hazael, did Aram-Damascus dominate most of Assyria and even rival that power. The regional division of Aram is reflected in the compound names designating the area, the main city, or the local dynasty:

Paddan-aram: Region along the road (Akk. *paddanu*) through the Ḫabur triangle, to Haran at the Balikh River, and on to the Euphrates.

Aram-naharaim: Western part of Paddan-aram (cf. Gen. 24:10) and areas along the great bend of the Euphrates (cf. Deut. 23:4[MT 5]; Judg. 3:8). In Num. 23:7; Judg. 3:10; Hos. 12:12(13) the general term Aram designates this area.

Most states of these two regions were named after the ruling dynasty or the capital, e.g., Gozan (2 Kgs. 17:6; 19:12), Haran (cf. Gen. 11:31; 29:4), Pethor (cf. Num. 22:5; Deut. 23:4[5]); Bit-Adini (cf. 2 Kgs. 19:12; Amos 1:5).

Aram-zobah, also called Aram-beth-rehob (after the founding dynasty): Comprising the Beqaʿ Valley of Lebanon, stretching partly along the Orontes, down to Hamath, and into the Anti-Lebanon Mountains, possibly also to the Euphrates (cf. 2 Sam. 8:3, 9). In the 10th century Aram-zobah became part of Aram-Damascus, but the name Zobah is still found in Assyrian lists from ca. 700 as the name of an Assyrian province in the Beqaʿ.

Aram-Damascus: According to 1 Kgs. 11:23-24, some time after David's defeat of Aram-zobah, Rezon seized power at Damascus. Damascus thus became Aramean much as Jerusalem had become Israelite through David. Aram-Damascus became the most powerful state in southern Syria. In the 9th and 8th centuries it initiated and led coalitions against Assyria. In the last third of the 9th and into the early 8th century, Aram-Damascus fought and captured parts of Israel, notably the Golan Heights (cf. 2 Kgs. 10:32-33 and the Tell Dan inscription). Under the reign of Hazael (ca. 842-800) Aram-Damascus became an empire dominating large parts of Syria and Palestine. Hazael even crossed the Euphrates to attack Assyria. Assyria recaptured Damascus in 732. Aram-Damascus represents the Aramean power in the OT, where it is often simply called Aram.

Aram-maacah and **Geshur:** Small states in Transjordan, between Mt. Hermon and the Yarmouk River, mentioned only in the OT. Aram-maacah sided with Aram-zobah against David (2 Sam. 10:6, 8). Geshur was apparently S of Aram-maacah. Maacah, daughter of Geshur's king Talmai, married David and was the mother of Absalom (2 Sam. 3:3; cf. 13:37-38). The Aramean character of Aram-maacah and Geshur is disputed, but in 2 Sam. 15:8 Geshur is explicitly called a part of Aram.

The Aramean state of Sam'al/Ya'udi, modern Zinjirli in southeastern Turkey, ca. 100 km. (62 mi.) W of the bend of the Euphrates, has yielded important documents but is not mentioned in the OT.

Bibliography. S. C. Layton, "Old Aramaic Inscriptions," *BA* 51 (1988): 172-89; P. E. Dion, "Syro-Palestinian Resistance to Shalmaneser III in the Light of New Documents," *ZAW* 107 (1995): 482-89; N. Na'aman, "Hazael of 'Amqi and Hadadezer of Beth-rehob," *UF* 27 (1995): 381-94.

Siegfried Kreuzer

ARAMAIC (Heb. *'ărāmîṯ*)

A Northwest Semitic language closely related to Hebrew. Well attested in multiple dialects and extremely long-lived (modern Aramaic dialects are spoken to this day in parts of the Middle East and elsewhere), its importance for biblical studies cannot be overemphasized. Portions of the OT (Dan. 2:4–7:28; Ezra 4:8–6:8; 7:12-26; Jer. 10:11; Gen. 31:47 [two words only]), and individual words and phrases in the NT are preserved in an Aramaic original. Aramaic was the successor to Akkadian as the international language of communication and diplomacy in the ancient Near East for much of the latter half of the 1st millennium B.C.E., and was a major spoken language during the emergence of Christianity and rabbinic Judaism. As such it had a marked influence on late Biblical and Rabbinic Hebrew. Two of the major ancient translations of the OT are composed in Aramaic — the Syriac Peshiṭta and the Jewish Targums, as are significant portions of both the Babylonian and Palestinian Talmuds and the entire literary corpus of Syriac Christianity. Lastly, Aramaic textual sources preserve a wealth of invaluable comparative material from all historical periods that touch on a wide range of subjects, such as linguistics, history, literature, epistolography, religion, international relations, and legal theory and practices.

For classificatory purposes, Aramaic may be divided into five principal phases or periods.

Old Aramaic

This is the earliest phase of Aramaic, the lower limit of which is conventionally marked by the fall of the Neo-Assyrian Empire (ca. 612). Relatively few inscriptions, written on stone or on other imperishable materials, have survived from this period. But this scarcity of written remains belies the true importance of Aramaic in this period, as it was eventually adopted as the international language of diplomacy (cf. 2 Kgs. 18:26). Linguistically, many of the features which come to characterize later Aramaic dialects are only just emerging in this early phase of the language. However, four innovative linguistic features have been identified which are shared by the early inscriptions and by all succeeding Aramaic dialects: 1) change of vocalic **ℵn* to **r* in words such as *br* "son" (cf. Heb. *bēn*, Ugar. *bn*, Phoen. *bn;* cf. also the words for "daughter" and "two" in later dialects); 2) leveling through of the ending *-*nā* for the 1st person plural; 3) creation of the causative-reflexive stem **hittaqtal;* and 4) complete loss of the niphal stem. These shared innovations constitute Aramaic as a genetic sub-branch of Northwest Semitic, alongside Ugaritic and Canaanite. In addition, the Proto-Semitic phonemic inventory remains basically in place in this early phase, though, owing to the use of the 22-letter Canaanite alphabet, some graphemes stand for more than one phoneme: *q* = *q* and *ḏ*; *z* = *z* and *ḏ*; *š* = *š*, *ś*, and *ṯ*; *ṣ* = *ṣ* and *ṯ̣* [=*ẓ*]; *ḥ* = *ḥ* and *ḫ*; ʿ = ʿ and *ġ*. Otherwise, the Aramaic of this phase is marked by a general lack of standardization and by dialectical diversity. Among the earliest inscriptions are the bilingual Akkadian-Aramaic stela from Tell Fakhariya and the Tell Dan stela, both of which date from the mid-9th century. The latter with its reference to the "House of David" *(bytdwd)* provides the first extrabiblical reference to the Davidic dynasty.

Other notable Old Aramaic inscriptions include the Zakur inscription, a stela whose content strongly resembles that of the biblical Psalms of Thanksgiving, the Sefire Treaty, which is a good source for West Semitic curses, and the Hadad and Panammu inscriptions, which represent a very idiosyncratic Old Aramaic dialect utilized by the kings of ancient Sam'al (modern Zinjirli).

Official Aramaic

This phase of Aramaic, which ends ca. 200, represents a form of the language which is highly standardized and strikingly homogenized. It is in this period that the inventory of features which comes to characterize all later Aramaic dialects is stabilized. Such features include the series of phoneme mergers which differentiates the consonantal inventory of Official Aramaic and later dialects from that of Old Aramaic (*ḍ* > ʿ; *ḏ* > *d*; *ṯ* > *t*; *ṯ̣* [= *ẓ*] > *ṭ*; *ḫ* > *ḥ*; *ǵ* > ʿ), the feminine plural jussive from *yiqtĕlān*, the peal infinitive form *miqtal*, the feminine plural nominal ending *-ān*, and the realization of the category of definiteness as the suffixal ending *-āʾ*. The name Official Aramaic (or Imperial Aramaic) arises because this dialect is used throughout the Neo-Babylonian and, most especially, the Persian empires. The textual remains from this period are scattered across a large geographical region (Egypt, Arabia, Palestine, Syria, Mesopotamia, Asia Minor, Armenia, and the Indus Valley) and represent a wide spectrum of genres (letters, legal contracts and deeds, literary texts, incantations, monumental inscriptions), which suggests that what has survived must represent only a fraction of what originally existed. The greatest number of textual finds come from Egypt, where the dry climate is very conducive to the preservation of papyrus and leather, and by far the most significant of the Egyptian finds is the archive from the Jewish military colony at Elephantine. It consists chiefly of letters, various kinds of legal documents, and fragments of literary texts. The Aramaic material from the book of Ezra probably dates from this period as well.

Middle Aramaic

This period dates roughly from ca. 200 B.C.E. to 200 C.E. and represents a phase of the language in which the standardized dialect begins to break down into recognizable regional dialects, a development influenced, no doubt, by the replacement of Aramaic by Greek as the administrative language of the Near East during the Hellenistic and Roman periods. Major epigraphic finds come from Palmyra, the Arab kingdom of Petra (Nabatean), Hatra, and Qumran. The Palmyrene texts are an especially rich source for onomastica and information about the *marzēaḥ* celebration. At Qumran most of the nonsectarian extrabiblical texts are in Aramaic, including the Genesis Apocryphon and the Targum of Job. The Aramaic portions of the book of Daniel come from this period, as do the isolated Aramaic words and phrases in the Greek texts of Josephus and the NT and the legal formulas found in early rabbinic sources. Some of the Targums (Onkelos and Jonathan) and the Aramaic material in Demotic script preserved in Papyrus Amherst 63 may date from this period as well.

Late Aramaic

This phase dates roughly from 200 C.E. to the beginning of the Islamic conquest (ca. 700) and represents the most abundantly attested corpora of literature and inscriptions in Aramaic. Late Aramaic may be divided into three main branches: 1) a Western (Palestinian) branch, consisting of Jewish Palestinian Aramaic (including the dialects of the Palestinian Talmud and Targums), Christian Palestinian Aramaic, and Samaritan Aramaic; 2) an Eastern (Babylonian) branch, consisting of the Aramaic of the Babylonian Talmud and Mandaic, the language of a non-Christian gnostic sect from southern Babylonia; and 3) literary Syriac, consisting of the liturgical literature of Syriac Christianity. Syriac is the best-attested Aramaic dialect. In the Eastern dialects, the imperfect verb forms are marked by a prefixed *l-*, while in Syriac the same form is marked by a prefixed *n-*. Both contrast with the prefixed *y-* of earlier dialects. Other linguistic features characteristic of Late Aramaic have been noted as well, including a decline in the absolute and construct states of the noun, increase in the use of the possessive pronoun *dil-*, replacement of internal passives with prefixed *ʾt-* forms, and heavy Greek influence.

Modern Aramaic

Several (Neo-)Aramaic dialects are spoken today. These include Ma'lula (a town NE of Damascus), Turoyo and Mlaḥso (spoken in southeastern Turkey), Neo-Syriac (originally spoken in parts of Kurdistan, but now widely scattered), and Neo-Mandaic (spoken in southern Iraq and western Iran).

Bibliography. K. Beyer, *The Aramaic Language: Its Distribution and Subdivisions* (Göttingen, 1986); J. A. Fitzmyer, "The Phases of the Aramaic Language," *A Wandering Aramean* (Missoula, 1979), 57-84; repr. *The Semitic Background of the New Testament* (Grand Rapids, 1997), 57-84; J. Huehnergard, "Remarks on the Classification of the Northwest Semitic Languages," in *The Balaam Texts from Deir 'Alla Re-Evaluated*, ed. J. Hoftijzer and G. van der Kooij (Leiden, 1991), 282-93; E. Y. Kutscher, "Aramaic," in *Hebrew and Aramaic Studies*, ed. Kutscher et al. (Jerusalem, 1977), 90-155.

F. W. DOBBS-ALLSOPP

ARAMEANS (Heb. *ʾărammîm*)
The designation for a large number of peoples who spoke related dialects of the West Semitic language known as Aramaic. The Aramean peoples flourished from the late 2nd millennium B.C.E. in Syria, and spread southeastward into Mesopotamia and southwestward into central and southern Syria during the early 1st millennium. The Aramean states of Zobah, Damascus, Beth-rehob, Geshur, and Maacah in southern Syria played important roles in the history of biblical Israel. While they

never coalesced into a single large political or cultural entity, the Arameans played an important part in Near Eastern history.

The Israelites felt a close cultural relationship with the Arameans and described it in the traditions preserved in the book of Genesis. In Gen. 22:21 Aram, the eponymous ancestor of the Arameans, is described as the grandson of Nahor, Abraham's brother, while in the Table of Nations in Gen. 10:22 Aram is said to be one of the sons of Shem. In Gen. 25:20; 31:20 Abraham's relatives Bethuel and Laban are called Arameans, and Jacob himself is called a "wandering Aramean" in Deut. 26:5. These traditions of family relationships must be seen in the context of general belief expressed in Genesis that Israel was related by blood to most of the Semitic-speaking peoples around them (with the exception of the Canaanites). They do not provide us with significant historical insight into the complex origins of the various ethnic groups in Syria-Palestine.

The Arameans are presumably the descendants of the Amorite peoples who lived in Syria during the first half of the 2nd millennium. But the earliest clear references to people called Arameans only occur in Assyrian texts from the late 12th and early 11th centuries. Tiglath-pileser I fought a series of battles at that time with Aramean tribes along the course of the Middle Euphrates River in the Mt. Bishri region of Syria. By the late 11th and early 10th centuries, several Aramean states had emerged in Upper Mesopotamia and in Syria, including Bir-zamani, Bīt-bahiani, Bīt-ḫalupe, and Laqu on the Tigris and Ḫabur Rivers, Bīt-adini along the Great Bend of the Euphrates River, Yahan (later called Bīt-agusi) W of Bīt-adini, and Sam'al, a small city-state known because of the large number of inscriptions found at the site. Hamath, in central Syria, apparently had a mixed population of Arameans and Anatolians. In southern Syria two other Aramean states, Aram-zobah and Aram-Damascus, became important political powers, the former in the 10th century, the latter in the 9th and 8th centuries. A number of Aramean tribes also migrated southward into Mesopotamia in the late 2nd millennium.

Israel came into conflict with Aram-zobah during David's reign in the late 11th or early 10th century. When Zobah, apparently the dominant political power in the region at the time, intervened in a conflict between Ammon and Israel, David's army fought them to a stalemate (2 Sam. 10:15-19 = 1 Chr. 19:16-19). Meeting again at the site of Helam, Israel defeated the army of Zobah and brought many of the latter's allies into Israel's orbit. A third battle described in 2 Sam. 8 may be a variant version of the battle of Helam, but is more likely an account of a final battle between the two states in which Zobah was decisively defeated. It never again played a major role in Syro-Palestinian history.

By the early 9th century Aram-Damascus had emerged as a formidable power, attacking northern Israel during the reign of Baasha (1 Kgs. 15:16-22) and leading a 12-state coalition (including Israel under Ahab) against the invasion of northern Syria by Shalmaneser III of Assyria in 853 (cf. the inscriptions of Shalmaneser in *ANET,* 278-81). In three confrontations with Shalmaneser (853, 848, 843), Hadadezer of Aram-Damascus and the coalition held back the Assyrian army. Shortly thereafter (ca. 842/841) Hazael, a usurper, seized the throne in Damascus (cf. 2 Kgs. 8:7-15) and the coalition collapsed. Hazael was forced to fight alone against Shalmaneser III three additional times (841, 838, 837), but was never fully defeated. After Shalmaneser turned his attention elsewhere, Hazael proceeded to create an empire around Damascus, dominating virtually all the states south of Damascus, including Israel and Judah (2 Kgs. 10:32-33; 12:17-18). For ca. 40 years Damascus was at the peak of its power.

The tables were turned, however, early in the 8th century, when Hazael's son Bir-hadad lost the empire his father had created. Israel regained its independence in a series of battles during the reign of King Joash (2 Kgs. 13:22-25) and actually dominated Damascus for a while during the reign of Jeroboam II (14:28). Eventually Damascus, like the other states of Syria, was annexed into the Assyrian Empire and lost its status as an independent state.

The Arameans' primary cultural contribution to ancient Near Eastern civilization was its language and script. Aramaic came to be the predominant language of Syria early in the 1st millennium, but it spread from there across the Near East. The Assyrian policy of deporting large portions of the population of rebellious states led to a large number of Arameans living in Assyria itself. By the mid-8th century the Aramaic language was extensively used in Assyria, and by the 6th century it was the predominate language in Mesopotamia. Aramaic became the official *lingua franca* of the Persian Empire, and by Hellenistic times the language and script had replaced most of the local languages and scripts of Syria-Palestine, including Hebrew. Aramaic translations of the biblical text (the Targums) were made and used beside the original Hebrew texts. Aramaic was probably the primary language of Jesus of Nazareth, and, as Syriac, continued to be used by portions of the Eastern Church for centuries.

Bibliography. J. A. Brinkman, *A Political History of Post-Kassite Babylonia, 1158-722 B.C.* AnOr 43 (Rome, 1968); J. C. Greenfield, "Aramaic Studies and the Bible," *VTSup* 32 (1981): 110-30; "Aspects of Aramean Religion," in *Ancient Israelite Religion,* ed. P. D. Miller, P. D. Hanson, and S. D. McBride (Philadelphia, 1987), 67-78; J. D. Hawkins, "The Neo-Hittite States in Syria and Anatolia," *CAH*² 3/1:372-441; W. T. Pitard, *Ancient Damascus* (Winona Lake, 1987); "Arameans," in *Peoples of the Old Testament World,* ed. A. J. Hoerth, G. L. Mattingly, and E. M. Yamauchi (Grand Rapids, 1994), 207-30.

WAYNE T. PITARD

ARAM-MAACAH (Heb. *'ărām ma'ăḵâ*)
An alternate name for the Aramean kingdom Maacah (1 Chr. 19:6).

ARAM-NAHARAIM (Heb. *'ăram nahărāyim*)
The geographical area located around the great bend of the Euphrates River in northern Syria. Egyptian texts from the last half of the 2nd millennium B.C.E. refer to this land as *Nḫrn,* and the Amarna Letters as *na-aḫ-rí-ma* and *na-rí-ma.* The exact boundaries of the land cannot be determined, but it included territory on both banks of the Euphrates, as well as cities such as Harran, Nahor, Pethor, and Tunip.

Following the LXX, the term is frequently translated "Mesopotamia" in English versions. In Gen. 24:10 it refers to the homeland of Abraham's family. Both Balaam, the son of Beor (Deut. 23:4), and King Cushan-rishathaim, who was the first to oppress Israel in the time of the Judges (Judg. 3:8), were natives of Aram-naharaim. David fought mercenary troops from the area hired by Hanun and the Ammonites (1 Chr. 19:6; cf. Ps. 60 superscription[MT 1]).

Bibliography. J. J. Finkelstein, "'Mesopotamia,'" *JNES* 21 (1962): 73-92; R. T. O'Callaghan, *Aram Naharaim.* AnOr 26 (Rome, 1948).

STEPHEN J. ANDREWS

ARAM-ZOBAH (Heb. *'ăram ṣôḇâ*)
An alternate designation of Zobah (superscription to Ps. 60[MT 1]), a powerful Aramean state defeated by David.

ARAN (Heb. *'ărān*)
The younger son of Dishan the Horite; eponymous ancestor of an Edomite clan (Gen. 36:28; 1 Chr. 1:42).

'ARAQ EL-EMIR
A site (221147) located on the Wadi eṣ-Ṣîr. It was occupied, with some gaps, from the Early Bronze Age to the Byzantine period, and is probably biblical Ramath-mizpeh (Josh. 13:26). Remains exist of Qaṣr el-'Abd, "Fortress of the Servant," identified as Tyros and built by the Tobiad Hyrcanus (2nd century B.C.), a descendant of Tobiah (Neh. 2:10; cf. Ezra 2:60; Josephus *Ant.* 12.4.1[229-35]). Two 5th-4th century Aramaic inscriptions of a Tobiah were found nearby. Gk. *týros* (from Heb. *ṣôr,* "rock") is preserved in the name of the wadi.

Bibliography. P. W. Lapp–N. L. Lapp, "'Iraq el-Emir," *NEAEHL* 2:646-49. PAUL J. RAY, JR.

ARARAT (Heb. *'ărāraṭ*)
Biblical name for a country (Assyrian Urartu) in eastern Asia Minor near Lake Van, encompassing parts of Turkey, Armenia, Iran, and Iraq. The territory gained prominence as a major political entity during the 9th century B.C.E. Urartu blocked Assyria's northern advances, and major campaigns into Urartian territory were undertaken by Assyrian rulers Shalmaneser III (859-824) and Sargon II (722-705). Urartu eventually succumbed to the Medes, who destroyed the region in 585. The territory was later incorporated into the Persian Empire.

Following the murder of their father, the sons of Sennacherib fled to the "land of Ararat" (2 Kgs. 19:37 = Isa. 37:38). In Jeremiah's oracle against Babylon the kingdom of Ararat is summoned by God, along with neighboring nations (Jer. 51:27).

Gen. 8:4 records that Noah's ark came to rest upon the "mountains of Ararat." Early tradition sought to identify a specific peak as the location of Noah's ark. Josephus quotes the 3rd-century Babylonian priest Berossus that portions of the ark had been discovered in Armenia, at the mountain of the Gordyaeans (*Ant.* 1.93). The modern identification of Mt. Ararat with Aǵri Daǵ, a mountain in eastern Turkey, rests upon a late postbiblical tradition.

KENNETH ATKINSON

ARATUS (Gk. *Arétos*)
A 3rd-century B.C.E. Stoic poet from Soli in Cilicia. In his speech on the Areopagus Paul quotes from Aratus' poem *Phaenomena* (Acts 17:28).

ARAUNAH (Heb. *'ărawnâ*) (also ORNAN)
A Jebusite inhabitant of Jerusalem who offered his threshing floor to David as a site for sacrifice in a time of plague against Israel and Jerusalem (2 Sam. 24:16-25; 1 Chr. 21:15-28). In Chronicles he is called Ornan. David insisted on a legal purchase of the threshing floor for 50 shekels of silver (2 Sam. 24:24; cf. 600 shekels of gold, 1 Chr. 21:25). In obedience to Gad the seer, David erected an altar here on which he made offerings, thus bringing an end to a three-day plague imposed by the Lord due to David's census. The Chronicler identifies the location of the threshing floor as Mt. Moriah and the site of the future temple of Solomon (1 Chr. 22:1; 2 Chr. 3:1).

The name may be related to Hurrian *iwirne,* "ruler," and thus represent a title rather than a personal name (cf. the use of the definite article with Araunah, 2 Sam. 24:16, and the association of the title "king," v. 23 MT). JOHN D. FORTNER

ARBA (Heb. *'arba'*)
The father of Anak (Josh. 15:13; 21:11), regarded as the greatest of the Anakim (14:15).

See KIRIATH-ARBA.

ARBATHITE (Heb. *hā'arḇāṯî*)
A resident of Beth-arabah, a city on the border between Judah and Benjamin. This gentilic is associated with Abi-albon/Abiel, one of David's champions (2 Sam. 23:31; 1 Chr. 11:32).

ARBATTA (Gk. *Arbátta*)
A region whose Jewish inhabitants Simon Maccabeus led safely to Jerusalem after defeating the Syrian troops in Galilee (1 Macc. 5:23). Josephus calls the place the toparchy of Narbata, which was a retreat for the Jews of Caesarea during the Jewish War of 66-70 C.E. (*BJ* 2.14.5; 18.10). It is located ca. 16 km. (10 mi.) S of Mt. Carmel, W of Samaria. RICHARD A. SPENCER

ARBELA (Gk. *Arbēla*)
A village in lower Galilee probably to be identified with Khirbet Irbid/Arbel (1955.2467) on the south-

eastern side of Wadi Hamam. The site faces a precipitous cliff with numerous strategically important caves which were favorite hideouts of refugees, rebels, and brigands. Josephus reports that the Seleucid armies besieged and captured many Jews who had fled there (*Ant.* 12.11.1; cf. 1 Macc. 9:2) and that Herod had great difficulty dislodging bandits from the caves (*Ant.* 14.15.4-5; *BJ* 1.16.2-5). Josephus himself had the caves fortified in preparation for the First Jewish Revolt (*BJ* 2.20.6; *Vita* 37) and held an important conference of Galilean Jews in the village (*Vita* 60). RANDALL D. CHESNUTT

ARBITE (Heb. *hāʾarbî*)
An epithet given to Paarai (2 Sam. 23:35), referring either to his father or the city of his residency (cf. Arab, Josh. 15:52).

ARCHAEOLOGY AND THE BIBLE

With the beginning of a new millennium the field of biblical archaeology finds itself striving to achieve a social archaeology of Syria-Palestine which moves away from the particular events mentioned in textual data, to the explanation of the more general processes responsible for cultural change. For years biblical archaeologists have been loath to experiment with theoretical perspectives that took them far from the confines of the biblical text. This is because the Bible was the primary lens through which all archaeological data had to be scrutinized. Until recently biblical archaeology was the epitome of a historical discipline obsessed with the particular events and peoples mentioned in the text. However, some schools of historical thought have also been influenced by the social sciences that place greater emphasis on the general and long term of historical processes rather than specific short-term events.

Geography, especially historical geography, has played a key role in the archaeology of the Holy Land since the early 19th century. Interdisciplinary approaches are particularly appropriate for archaeology, which by definition deals with an expansive amount of data — both material culture and textual. It is important to conceptualize long-term factors, such as those concerning physical geography, which work together to structure history, the "enabling and constraining" factors which created opportunities for societies to develop and change in Palestine.

Geographic Setting

The evolution of societies in Palestine, from the beginning more than 1.5 million years ago, has been shaped by its geographic location, which in turn has created a unique climate, topography, hydrology, and other natural resources. For all its mention in the Bible and contemporary media, the Holy Land (a less politically charged term than Israel, Jordan, Palestine, Autonomous Palestinian territories) is a very small place — generally most of the southern Levant. The Holy Land is only 410 km. (256 mi.) long from the Lebanon border to the Gulf of Eilat/Aqaba. It is ca. 80 km. (50 mi.) wide from the Jordan River to the Mediterranean. When Jordan is included, the width of the region is ca. 325 km. (225 mi.). The borders of ancient Israel, "from Dan to Beersheba," coincide with the Mediterranean and semi-arid zones where permanent settlement is facilitated by adequate rainfall for farming. The Mediterranean and semi-arid zone in Jordan forms a narrow strip running north-south which is only some 40 km. (25 mi.) wide. Taking together the fertile land of the Mediterranean zone and the semi-arid zones of the Negeb and Transjordan, the region includes some 20,000 sq. km. (7725 sq. mi.) — an area nearly the size of New Jersey.

The Holy Land's location on the land bridge connecting two major continents, Africa and Asia, has determined its role in the history of the ancient Near East. This unique location placed Palestine on the periphery of the great ancient powers in Egypt and Mesopotamia. There were no great civilizations that evolved in Palestine, but in many respects the legacy of the Bible that evolved in this peripheral area has outlasted anything that Egypt and Mesopotamia produced. Palestine lacked the great rivers such as the Nile, Tigris, and Euphrates, which provided important sources of water for highly productive farming systems that evolved in the Near East at the beginning of the Bronze Age. More than any other region in the ancient Near East, Palestine was always directly or indirectly connected with other parts of the Near East and eastern Mediterranean.

Biblical Archaeology

In the world of international academic archaeology, until recently little was heard about the archaeology of Israel and Jordan except sensational discoveries such as the Dead Sea Scrolls. Archaeology in this part of the eastern Mediterranean has been dominated by an obsession to find material proof of the events and peoples mentioned in the Bible and to verify or contradict aspects of the biblical texts. It has been "historical particular" in view. An important corrective is the French Annales school's emphasis on how societies and their respective economies change in relation to different scales of time. Developed as an alternative paradigm for European history, their stress on the dialectic between three different time scales which influence change makes it particularly appropriate for archaeology. The temporal scales include the "long term," which represents the unchanging or slowly changing conditions of physical geography and how humans respond to them. The long-term forces focus on the natural environment with geological, climatic, and geomorphological constraints and oscillations. This is followed by "middle-term" temporal dimensions, which relate to faster changing social and economic processes characterized by cycles of socio-political, agrarian, and demographic change. Finally, there are "short-term" processes, which are fast-paced events in history.

This paradigm posits a move away from the study of the unique and particular to achieve wider insights of human history. It explicitly calls for in-

 ARCHAEOLOGY AND THE BIBLE

Mudbrick walls in Area C at Tel Rehov/Tell es-Sarem, looking west. An important Iron Age site, this portion of the lower city shows three strata of occupation (10th-9th centuries B.C.E.)
(Photo by John Camp, Tel Rehov Expedition)

terdisciplinary research with all the disciplines concerned with human society, seeking to adapt data and concepts for the study of history from a wide range of fields including economics, linguistics, sociology, anthropology, psychology, and the natural sciences. One advantage is the notion that different historical processes operate at different temporal levels. Often, Syro-Palestinian archaeologists have worked according to the notion that archaeologists recover the remains of a once-living community, stopped at a particular point in time. In fact, archaeologists rarely encounter "instantaneous occurrences" fossilized in archaeological deposits. Instead, the archaeological record is usually a compound of repeated activities carried out in the same place through time, with little evidence of the individual. Thus the problem of the perception of time by archaeologists lies at the heart of recent efforts to make Syro-Palestinian archaeology a "secular" discipline removed from the historical particularism which until recently characterized biblical archaeology.

Both the "long" and "middle term" are beyond the perception of past individuals. They act as "structures" which form constraining and enabling frameworks for human life, both communal and individual. Concentration on these structures of time make the "long" and "middle term" of particular importance to archaeological researchers where the individual frequently escapes recognition in the archaeological record. These multiple, hierarchical time scales represent aspects of a continuum and provide archaeology with a heuristic tool for conceptualizing time and change in prehistoric, protohistoric, and historic societies.

Dissatisfaction with its contempt for history and its science-based quest for timeless "laws of cultural behavior" led most archaeologists working in Israel and Jordan virtually to ignore the "new" or "processual" archaeology, which developed in the U.S. in the late 1960s through 1980s. This school has since evolved to an attempt to integrate the cognitive and symbolic dimensions of ancient culture with environmental factors and to explore the role of ideology as an active organizational force. Perhaps most important is its stress on interdisciplinary projects involving specialists in archaeolozoology, archaeolobotany, geology, physical anthropology, archaeology, epigraphy, and other fields.

Examination of the more general aspects of a society, such as the domestic dimensions of ancient cultures, including religion, can illuminate the dynamic nature of ancient societies. The renewed concern with history advocated by "postprocessual" European and American archaeology demands reconsideration of how to integrate the vast quantities of accumulated archaeological and ethnohistorical data into more synthetic views of the past. For example, in his studies of Canaanite and early Israelite religion, which combine textual and archaeological data, William G. Dever has shown how Israelite religion, which the OT proclaims as supposedly Yahwistic, was somewhat more syncretistic than previously assumed.

Foundations: Politics, Prestige, and Power

From the outset, as late as 1800, the Bible stood unchallenged at the center of intellectual and religious life throughout Europe and America. With the advent of 19th-century "scientific consciousness," its literal accuracy was challenged. The growth of biblical archaeology was an effort to defend the "truth" of the Bible and develop a new understanding of the roots of its birthplace. In many respects this still characterizes the hidden agenda of many biblical archaeologists.

Perhaps the main catalyst for Western interest in the Holy Land was the political agendas of the

ARCHAEOLOGY AND THE BIBLE

19th-century European superpowers. By the end of the 18th century when the Ottoman Empire based in Turkey still held sway over much of the Middle East, including Palestine, the world was on the eve of change. Since the mid-1500s, the Ottoman Turks controlled a huge empire that incorporated not only the Middle East but also North Africa and Eastern Europe. With the weakening of this empire, Western European powers made plans to take over the Ottoman territory, especially those areas critical to ensuring smooth operation of the European "world system."

As the shore of the eastern Mediterranean was the Ottomans' weakest link, both the French and British were interested in controlling the Isthmus of Suez and thus the trade routes from India and the Far East to Europe. In addition to siege equipment and heavy artillery, Napoleon commissioned an elite corps of scientists, engineers, naturalists, orientalists, and antiquarians to survey every facet of contemporary Egypt and propose the best means for its restoration. Thus, Napoleon was instrumental in promoting the nascent discipline of archaeology and European interest in the ancient Near East. One of the most important discoveries during the Napoleonic expedition was the Rosetta Stone, which eventually served as the key to understanding Egyptian hieroglyphics. For the first time it was possible to roughly date archaeological materials in Palestine by comparing them with securely dated objects from Egypt. This was to form the cornerstone for a methodology used by later scholars to date the different layers of mounds in Palestine by the association of local materials with Egyptian imports.

Some of the early explorers who contributed to the European goal of gaining control of Ottoman territory in conjunction with research in antiquities included Johan Lewis Burckhard, who in 1812 discovered the ruins of Petra. Other adventurers included the dilettante Lady Hester Lucy Stanhope, who, informed of a marvelous treasure buried beneath the mound of Ashkelon, uncovered a headless statue of a Roman emperor, reputed to be the first archaeological artifact discovered in Palestine.

Beginning of Scientific Exploration

The beginning of scientific archaeological research in Palestine can be traced to Edward Robinson in the early 19th century. Unlike previous explorers to Palestine, Robinson was uniquely qualified to study the ancient sites based on his knowledge of biblical history and Biblical Hebrew. By 1838 he and Eli Smith were able to identify more than 100 major sites mentioned in the Bible, partly because Smith was fluent in Arabic and many of the villages retain traces of the ancient Hebrew names (e.g., Gezer/Tell Jezer).

However, archaeology was Robinson's weakest tool, on account of his own lack of experience in a field that itself was still unsophisticated. Robinson seems not to have understood even the nature of a tell, taking the thousands of ancient mounds scattered across the landscape to be natural formations and thus failing to recognize such important sites as Lachish and Jericho. Nevertheless, he pioneered the discipline of historical geography that is still an important facet of biblical archaeology research.

Early National Agendas

As a result of his travels and publications, especially *Biblical Researches in Palestine* (1841), Robinson revolutionized biblical research. In response, the British established the Palestine Exploration Fund, which sponsored several of the great geographical surveys of western Palestine and Transjordan as well as excavations at a number of major sites.

On the basis of Robinson and Smith's pioneering work in the historical geography of the Holy Land, the PEF in 1865-66 sent Charles W. Wilson, an officer of the Royal Engineers, to oversee the first scientific mapping of Jerusalem. Wilson discovered an arch leading to the temple mount which still bears his name, but when he experienced numerous technical problems with the survey the PEF dispatched another explorer, Charles Warren, whose mission ostensibly was to plan a modern sewer system for Jerusalem. Warren made a series of intricate shafts through the thick refuse layers of the Old City, effectively cutting through the town's stratigraphy, resulting in a complete lack of accurate dates with which to evaluate such discoveries as the subterranean cisterns associated with the Haram ash-Sharif, the entrance to the Herodian temple, and other finds. Perhaps the most ambitious project carried out under the auspices of the PEF was the 19th-century survey of Lieutenants Charles R. Conder and H. H. Kitchener, who later helped "conquer" the Sudan. Between 1872-1878 the two carried out a much more sophisticated geographical survey than that of Robinson, recording 10 thousand sites covering 15,500 sq. km. (6000 sq. mi.) and publishing seven volumes with remarkably accurate large-scale topographic maps of the Holy Land.

Some 10 years later an American, Navy Lt. William F. Lynch, conducted the first scientific survey of the Dead Sea, producing numerous maps, drawings, and reports on the flora, fauna, and geology of the region. A fundamentalist thinker, Lynch believed the Dead Sea valley to echo the biblical descriptions, and he sought to find the biblical Sodom and Gomorrah.

The French explorer Charles Clermont-Ganneau. who began working under the auspices of the PEF in 1873, is associated with several outstanding discoveries which serve as benchmarks for Syro-Palestinian archaeology. Included are the Gezer boundary marker bearing the Canaanite name of the site, a 1st-century B.C.E. Greek inscription warning Gentiles not to enter the temple court, and the Moabite Stone.

The eve of World War I saw the beginnings of systematic and controlled archaeological excavations in Palestine. Prior to the 1890s, the PEF had concentrated most of its work within the boundaries of the Old City of Jerusalem. In 1890 they embarked on a major excavation in the Negeb, an area close to the Sinai Peninsula with access to the strategic Isthmus of Suez, in hope of providing the first scientific evidence for the rise of biblical civilization. For this task they chose the British Egyptologist Sir William Flinders Petrie, who became the first biblical archaeologist to understand the significance of tells as artificial mounds made up of superimposed debris which represent different ancient civilizations. This he learned from Heinrich Schliemann, excavator of Homeric Troy, who demonstrated how, through observing stratigraphy, changes in material culture could be ordered in sequence, with the earliest material at the bottom and the latest at the top. Working in Egypt from 1880, Petrie developed the scientific method of pottery dating, so that a detailed chronology could be devised based on stylistic changes in common Egyptian ceramic forms. It was the prospect of linking his Egyptian chronology with that of neighboring southern Palestine that led Petrie to accept the offer to direct the first systematic excavations in the Holy Land. On the basis of a survey of sites in southern Palestine, Petrie chose Tell el-Ḥesi for his pioneer excavations in 1890. Methodically recording and dating archaeological materials, Petrie introduced a truly scientific method of replicating observations and interpretations. In six weeks of excavations at Tell el-Ḥesi he discovered 11 successive towns dating back to the Middle Bronze Age. Using Egyptian artifacts found in each layer as chronological anchors, he was able to date objectively local pottery and other remains. While this relative dating would be honed and clarified by later scholars, Petrie moved Palestinian archaeology out of the realm of purely biblical studies and helped to fit Palestinian antiquities into the cultural context of the entire Middle East.

Honing Excavation Methods

When Petrie returned to work in Egypt, the PEF chose an American, Frederick J. Bliss, as his successor at Tell el-Ḥesi from 1891-1894. There he excavated a giant, wedge-shaped trench now referred to as "Bliss' Cut." Although many British scholars castigate him for digging almost one third of the mound and using artificial "layers" cut arbitrarily through the site, Americans consider Bliss an excellent stratigrapher who refined Petrie's concepts. In 1892 he discovered the first cuneiform tablet found in Palestine, contemporary with those from Tell el-Amarna and mentioning Lachish. From 1894-1897 Bliss continued Warren's work at Jerusalem. He then joined R. A. S. Macalister in the first regional archaeological project, excavating four major tells in the Shephelah: Tell eṣ-Ṣafi/Tel Ẓafit, Tell Zakariyeh/Tel Azekah, Tell el-Judeideh, and Tell Ṣandaḥanna. This was the first time a complete sequence, spanning from the Bronze Age to the Crusader period, was uncovered.

The Rise of Biblical City Excavations

To help establish a significant British presence in the archaeology of the region, the PEF initiated a major long-term project led by Macalister, who in 1902-8 dug at Tell Jezer/el-Jazari (Gezer). Despite his great potential, Macalister's Gezer excavations reflect some of the worst practices of the time. He worked his way across the mound, digging a single trench some 12 m. (40 ft.) wide, reaching bedrock, then digging another behind it and filling the first with the back-dirt. There was no control over stratigraphy, and the interrelation between artifacts and layers was ignored. Yet despite these faults, Macalister's three-volume *The Excavation of Gezer* (1912) endures as one of the major contributions to this early phase of excavation in Palestine.

Volunteers at Tel Miqne/Ekron excavation measuring the locations of distinctive features in the balk while making a section drawing (Phoenix Data Systems, Neal and Joel Bierling)

A Permanent American Presence

By 1900 the Americans also desired to play a decisive role in the exploration of Palestine, and so formed the American Schools of Oriental Research, a consortium of universities interested in the archaeology, biblical history, and anthropology of the Holy Land, headquartered in Jerusalem (now the W. F. Albright Institute of Archaeological Research). Although American institutions had excavated elsewhere in the Middle East, they lacked experience in Palestine. Determined to conduct excavations on a scale comparable to British and Austrian efforts, they enlisted the renowned American Egyptologist George Andrew Reisner under the sponsorship of the new Harvard Semitic Museum to direct their first major campaign at Sebaste

ARCHAEOLOGY AND THE BIBLE

(Samaria). The dual role of the site as capital of the northern Israelite kingdom and the later city rebuilt by Herod the Great made it especially appealing. The fantastic palaces and public buildings built by Omri and his son Ahab would make the site one of the most important excavations in the country.

Reisner's greatest contribution to Syro-Palestinian archaeology was the introduction of the "debris-layer" technique of digging, which consists of separating the occupation layers of superimposed strata while carefully mapping the location of important artifacts. Reisner combined this method with a detailed recording system, including photo records, a daily written report or diary, maps, architectural plans, find-spots, and a registry of finds. Reisner's impact was diminished by the outbreak of World War I, which delayed publication of his report until 1924.

Lawrence and Musil

Prior to World War I the only region in western Palestine the PEF had yet to investigate was the Negeb desert in the south, adjacent to the strategic Suez Canal. For this they enlisted two young archaeologists, C. Leonard Woolley, excavator of the Mesopotamian city of Ur, and T. E. Lawrence, later known as Lawrence of Arabia for his role in the Arab revolt against the Ottomans. Because of the obvious significance of the region should hostilities break out between Britain and the Ottoman Empire, Lawrence was to use his archaeological research as a cover for military reconnaissance. Woolley and Lawrence's primary research was in the arid central Negeb desert, where they recorded such impressive Nabatean sites as Oboda (ʿAvdat), Sobata (Shivta), and Elusa (Ḥaluẓa).

Of much greater significance to scholarship and early exploration is the lesser known Czech orientalist Alois Musil (1868-1944). Musil is known to Western anthropologists for his seminal study, *The Manners and Customs of the Rwala Bedouin* (1928), still the standard ethnography of the North Arabian Bedouin. In addition to this ethnographic work, he published *Arabia Petraea* (1917-18), a series of reports on his topographical-cultural surveys of the Negeb, Transjordan, and Arabia that are still reliable. Musil was instrumental in recording hundreds of archaeological sites, inscriptions, and monuments, including many of the "desert castles" in Jordan dating to the early Islamic period.

Orientalist Tradition Par Excellence

The American scholar William F. Albright represents what may be regarded as the "Golden Age of Biblical Archaeology" (1925-1948). For almost 50 years after his first visit to Palestine in 1919, Albright produced an amazing corpus of writings touching on history, archaeology, ancient Near Eastern studies, epigraphy, and more that helped link the general disciplines of archaeology and biblical research. In the years before Albright, the archaeology of Palestine played little or no part in the biblical/historical controversies generated by Julius Wellhausen and the school of higher criticism. Albright became the most important archaeological player in the debate by enlisting new data, primarily from texts found in excavations in other Near Eastern countries. He used the broadest definition of "biblical archaeology," encompassing all lands mentioned in the Bible and thus coextensive with the "cradle of civilization." For Albright, excavations in every part of this broad region shed light, directly or indirectly, on the Bible.

During this period, the public, particularly in the English-speaking world, became fascinated with how archaeology could authenticate or "prove" the earliest history of Israel. By examining the internal evidence of the biblical text, German biblical scholars such as Albrecht Alt and Martin Noth tried to identify the "originating" historical events that were the source of OT narratives. Albright too was involved in the quest for ancient Israel, but he employed the external (nonbiblical) evidence provided by archaeology in Palestine and neighboring lands rather than the history of tradition in the Bible alone. As an "orientalist" he aimed at placing Israel and its traditions within those of the greater ancient Near East by examining the Bible in the light of ancient Near Eastern textual data and material culture.

Albright's training was in Assyriology and historical/biblical studies rooted in German scholarship. As a self-taught archaeologist, he quickly linked this field with historical geography. During his formative years in Palestine he developed not as a biblical archaeologist but rather a cultural historian, seeking to transform biblical archaeology into the history of the Eastern Mediterranean, understanding biblical literature as belonging to an environment of cultures.

The power of Albright's intellect as reflected in his prolific writings had an enormous impact on scholarly discourse from the early 1920s until his death in 1971. Surprisingly, he had little archaeological field experience. His reputation as an archaeologist is based on his important excavations at Tell Beit Mirsim, a small tell in the southern Shephelah. His analysis of the pottery and stratigraphy from the site clarified the chronology of the MB, LB, and Iron Ages — those periods most closely linked with the OT — and represents one of the pillars on which relative archaeological dating in Palestine rests. Albright's command of so many disciplines gave his voice an authority which few questioned during his lifetime. His expertise in such diverse fields as Akkadian, Hebrew, the OT, Near Eastern studies, history, religion, historical geography, and archaeology provided a model for the first generation of Israeli scholars of what should constitute a thorough grounding in biblical archaeology.

Rise of "Biblical Archaeology"

Another prominent orientalist was Roland de Vaux, O.P., a master of ancient Near Eastern history, the OT, and the archaeology of Syro-Palestine. In addition to writing lasting histories of ancient Israel,

ARCHAEOLOGY AND THE BIBLE

de Vaux excavated (1946-1960) the northern Tell el-Farʿah (identified as the site of Tirzah, capital of the northern kingdom before Omri transferred the capital to Samaria) and Khirbet Qumran. However, if scholars such as Albright, Musil, and de Vaux are distinguished by their breadth, a number of Albright's students went on to narrow biblical archaeology into a parochial field aimed at "proving" the Bible.

Perhaps more than any other, Nelson Glueck represents the archetypal "Biblical Archaeologist." His view of archaeology in the Holy Land focused more narrowly on two sets of data — the Bible and surface surveys of sites in eastern and western Palestine. Nevertheless, Glueck's contribution to the field, particularly the study of settlement patterns, cannot be minimized. From 1932 to 1947 he undertook a series of incredible one-man archaeological surveys in Transjordan, mostly in the regions of Ammon, Edom, and Moab, traveling on foot, by camel, or horseback, mapping, collecting pottery sherds, and photographing sites. He constructed maps of settlement distributions, period by period, based on characteristic types of pottery collected on the surface. Denied access to Jordan following the establishment of the state of Israel, Glueck conducted a series of similar surveys in the Negeb desert. However, Glueck had relatively little experience as an excavator, working only two significant sites, the Nabatean temple at Khirbet et-Tannur (1937) and Tell el-Kheleifeh (1938-1940), which he accepted as Solomon's port city Ezion-geber and which he dated to the 10th-5th centuries. Glueck also identified a large building complex containing thick deposits of ash, soot, and evidence of fire as a sophisticated copper smelting installation. Later research has shown the earliest pottery remains to be no earlier than the 8th century, nor do the remains indicate metalworking at the site. Rather, this represents an overly subjective application of archaeology for biblical research.

Another student of Albright, George Ernest Wright, went on to carry the mantle of "Biblical Archaeology" from the early 1950s to the 1970s. Although his early work was rooted in archaeology, having written an important thesis offering the first systematic pottery typology for Palestine (1937), Wright's greater interest in theology characterized his later career and made significant impact on American scholars' understanding of Palestinian archaeology. For Wright, the role of archaeology was to expose the historical basis of the Judeo-Christian faith and to demonstrate how revelation had come through history. To this end, he founded the journal *Biblical Archaeologist,* in part to raise popular support for archaeology in Syro-Palestine. Wright's greatest contribution as an excavator was his work at Shechem (Tell Balâtah), regarded as a watershed in American archaeology for introducing a pedagogic method of field school and data recording that influenced a generation of American archaeologists and subsequently Israeli scholars as well.

Towards a Secular Archaeology

British archaeology in Palestine never had the strong links to theology that characterized the post-Albright period of research among American scholars. Beginning in the late 1920s, British archaeology became linked to prehistory with the work of Dorothy Garrod at the Stone Age cave site of Wadi Mughara in the Carmel Mountains. From 1920-26 John Garstang served as the founding director of the British Mandatory Department of Antiquities of Palestine. In 1930-36 he carried out major excavations at Jericho, where he delved into problems related to the Exodus and revealed the existence of Pre-pottery Neolithic cultures in the Levant. A major contribution was Kathleen M. Kenyon's use of the "debris-layer" method of excavation employed in Britain by Sir Mortimer Wheeler.

Growing dissatisfaction with the theological orientation of "Biblical Archaeology" can be seen in a number of Wright's students. Like many of them a member of the Tell Balâtah excavation team, Paul W. Lapp focused on the ceramic typology of the later periods (200 B.C.E.–70 C.E.). Based on well-stratified sites, his detailed study presented the most complete ceramic corpus then possible and represented a significant breakthrough. Before he died at age 39, he had carried out major field projects spanning a wide range of sites including Bab edh-Dhraʿ (EB), ʿAraq el-Emir (Hellenistic), Taanach (Canaanite), and the Wadi ed-Daliyeh caves (containing Aramaic documents dating to ca. 375-335). Lapp also introduced the practice of preparing daily top plans, plotting on a three-dimensional map the exact location of each artifact discovered that day.

Emergence of Israeli Archaeology

The emergence and development of the state of Israel has had a profound effect on the archaeology of the Holy Land. In many respects, the sheer number of researchers and extensive local infrastructure will have significant implications for the future of the field. While the history of the Jewish people, particularly of the First and Second Temple periods, has provided considerable motivation for research, interpretation and analysis have been far from dogmatic. Many of the younger scholars concerned with the Bronze and Iron ages are proponents of the broader views of Syro-Palestinian archaeology linked to interpretive frameworks such as cultural ecology.

The roots of Israeli archaeology go back to the beginnings of the Zionist movement and the founding of the Jewish Palestine Exploration Society in 1914. Among the pioneers of archaeology in Israel were Nahman Avigad, Michael Avi-Yonah, Ruth Amiran, Immanuel Ben-Dor, Avraham Biran, Benjamin Mazar, E. L. Sukenik, and Shmuel Yeivin. Most were trained abroad in ancient Near Eastern languages, biblical studies, and classics, and they learned to excavate through foreign expeditions in their country in the 1920s and 1930s.

ARCHAEOLOGY AND THE BIBLE

In these early years the limited number of excavations carried out by Jewish Palestinian scholars were at sites related to the Bible and ancient Jewish history: the Philistine sites of ʿAfulah (Jezreel Valley) and Nahariya (Sharon coast) by Moshe Dothan and Tell Qasile by Mazar; the 2nd-4th-century village of Beth Sheʿarim by Mazar, Pesah Bar-Adon, Imanuel Dunayevsky, Moshe Jaffe, and Jacob Kaplan; and the synagogue at Beth Alpha by Sukenik and Avigad.

What catapulted young Israeli archaeological scholarship onto equal footing with American and European efforts was Yigael Yadin's work at Hazor initiated in 1955. This large-scale excavation of a key biblical site shaped Israeli field archaeology by making its major focus periods related to the OT. Yadin's excavations of Hazor were modelled as a training ground for a whole generation of Israeli archaeologists. His scholarship was rooted in a literal interpretation of the Bible with clear links to the archaeological record. However, Yadin's knowledge of ancient Near Eastern history and culture made his views more synthetic than those of Glueck or Wright. His work at Masada in the 1960s dove-tailed with the aspirations of a young nation searching for its roots.

Yadin selected Hazor, which is referred to several times in extrabiblical sources, because of its central role in the history of ancient Israel. He followed the Reisner-Fisher method of excavation, which involved the careful exposure of large areas to trace the architectural plan and urban development of the site, in many respects foreshadowing the methodology of scholars now interested in social archaeology. Yadin's approach engendered a debate between the Israeli school of archaeology, which concentrated on large aerial exposures, and the American method, which focused on smaller areas with tighter stratigraphic control. This often acrimonious debate in the 1970s was generated because Americans were re-excavating large sites such as Gezer, Ai, and Tell el-Ḥesi, with the aim of "correcting" the errors of earlier scholars.

In Israel, a rivalry developed focusing not on the philosophy of how one should do archaeology, but rather on historical interpretation. On the basis of his excavations at Hazor, Yadin argued that Israelite settlement began only after the destruction of Hazor as described in Josh. 11:10-14. Yohanan Aharoni's survey of the Upper Galilee, however, showed many unwalled Iron Age settlements in a relatively inhospitable area which had been almost uninhabited in the LB Age. These data flew in the face of Yadin's strict interpretation of the Bible and supported the views of Alt, who argued against the literal conquest depicted in Joshua. In many respects, this clash stifled collaboration among Israeli scholars, the effect of which is felt even today.

Ruth Amiran, of the newly founded Israel Museum, introduced a systemization of Palestinian pottery based on both typology and chronology in her classic *Ancient Pottery of the Holy Land* (1963). Her excavation of an EB town at Tel Arad in the northern Negeb is remarkable for the picture it provides of one of the earliest walled towns in the southern Levant.

Israeli scholars have assembled significant collections for comparative studies in archaeology. Naomi Porat and Yuval Goren have an extensive petrographic slide collection of pottery from the southern Levant at the Geological Survey of Israel and Tel Aviv University. Patricia Smith, Baruch Arensburg, and Israel Hershkovitz have amassed large collections of human remains spanning the full range of prehistoric and historic periods. Mordechai Kislev at Bar Ilan University has a copious collection of macrobotanical materials from archaeological sites in the Levant, and Eitan Tchernov has built a comprehensive collection of archaeozoological and recent fauna remains at the Hebrew University in Jerusalem. These collections serve as important reference points for specialists associated with archaeological fieldwork in the southern Levant.

Israeli scholars have played a central role in revitalizing debate concerning the processes of Israelite settlement in Canaan. The discourse focuses on four general models of settlement: a literal interpretation of a military conquest as portrayed in the book of Joshua; a more peaceful "infiltration" as seen in Judges; a "peasant revolt"; and a symbiosis model. The Israeli contribution has been spearheaded by comprehensive archaeological field surveys by Israel Finkelstein, Adam Zertal, Ram Gophna, and others. This huge settlement pattern database has made it possible to evaluate carefully these and other models with hard empirical data previously unavailable, providing an additional source of extrabiblical data to examine the historicity of the biblical accounts. Finally, there have been a number of large-scale excavations at sites including Acco, Aphek, Beth-shean, Dan, Megiddo, Tel Qasile, Tel Mevorakh, Tel Seraʿ, and Yoqneʿam which provide additional data for testing archaeological models.

Revisionist Scholarship

Since the later 1970s scholars using the methodology of literary criticism and critical theory (developed by the German "Frankfurt School," an approach emphasizing that all historical knowledge is biased by the political views of the investigator) have viewed the Bible as pure literature lacking any historical fact. By "deconstructing" the text much as literary scholars tease apart great works of literature, they contend that the editing of the OT was completed no earlier than the 2nd-1st centuries B.C.E. and that David, Solomon, and other biblical figures are merely a part of Israelite foundation myths. If correct, these views have profound effect on interpretation of the archaeological record, especially for the Iron Age when such important events as the Israelite settlement, the formation of the state, and other social processes are dated. The political agenda of the revisionists themselves is of issue, as in Philip R. Davies' book *In Search of Ancient Israel* (1992), which charges that biblical scholars and archaeologists have created a fictitious early (13th century–586) history of the Israelites in the land.

In deconstructing ancient Israel, these scholars go to great lengths to explain away many of the benchmarks of Syro-Palestinian archaeology. For example, they deny any connection between the people called "Israel" in the Merneptah stela (ca. 1208) and the Israel of David and Solomon. They further reject the validity of source-critical analysis in demonstrating older materials such as the Song of Deborah as being embedded in the Bible or extrabiblical materials. Some revisionists claim that the Siloam inscription commemorating completion of Hezekiah's tunnel does not date to the late 8th century, as universally accepted by epigraphers, but rather to the 2nd century, which ignores the evidence of syntax and lexicography. Other minimalists have gone so far as to label the "House of David" inscription discovered at Tell Dan a forgery planted by the excavator and to claim that, likewise, a 7th-century Philistine inscription discovered at Ekron is a forgery promulgated by archaeologists. Like denials of the Holocaust, these revisionist claims are in danger of being accepted by an ill-informed public, obligating objective scholars to confront and expose these falsehoods.

Recent Developments

The influence of the Annales approach to historiography has much to do with biblical archaeology's need to integrate historical data with archaeology yet work with the constraints of the textual and material culture data to produce a social history of the Holy Land. The result is a move away from the historical-particularist orientation of the field which had crystallized with Wright and Glueck. As noted, the search for a political history of Israel, with its emphasis on confirming events associated with personalities mentioned in the Bible, had been dominated in the United States by Protestant scholars steeped in the Bible and in Israel by scholars brought up on the OT and influenced by the teachings of Albright. During the 1960s professional archaeologists in the U.S. increasingly regarded biblical archaeologists as unscientific amateurs.

In 1975 William G. Dever first proposed a new secular Syro-Palestinian archaeology, dissociated entirely from what he saw as a theologically-driven, deterministic biblical archaeology. The "new archaeology" that had come to dominate other branches of archaeology in the 1960s was viewed as an explicitly scientific approach for which history was of little consequence, and Dever demonstrated value in focusing on environment, economy, and social issues.

A less outspoken critic of the traditional biblical archaeology, Lawrence E. Stager has carefully blended concepts drawn from anthropology and sociology, as well as ecology, ethnoarchaeology, biblical studies, and ancient history to interpret traditional source materials provided by the OT and "dirt" archaeology. In reconstructing the social organization of the Israelite household, he melds biblical accounts with the hard archaeological facts of settlement plans to show how the extended Israelite family lived in antiquity. Elsewhere he looks at the early phase of Israelite settlement to determine why not all the tribes answered Deborah's call to battle in Judg. 4-5. By studying the local ecology of where the various tribes lived, the archaeology of these areas, and biblical data concerning variations in economy among the tribes, Stager provides innovative insights into the social dynamics of early Israel. Similarly, he uses this broader perspective to examine the processes of Philistine settlement as well as how an "archaeology of destruction" (i.e., the Babylonian conquest of Philistia) can be established at the site of Ashkelon.

See POTTERY.

Bibliography. W. F. Albright, *The Archaeology of Palestine and the Bible* (Cambridge, Mass., 1932); W. G. Dever, "The Contribution of Archaeology to the Study of Canaanite and Early Israelite Religion," in *Ancient Israelite Religion,* ed. P. D. Miller, P. D. Hanson, and S. D. McBride (Philadelphia, 1987), 209-47; P. J. King, *American Archaeology in the Mideast* (Philadelphia, 1985); T. E. Levy, ed., *The Archaeology of Society in the Holy Land,* 2nd ed. (London, 1998); A. Mazar, *Archaeology of the Land of the Bible, 10,000–586 B.C.E.* (New York, 1990); P. R. S. Moorey, *A Century of Biblical Archaeology* (Louisville, 1991); N. A. Silberman, *Digging for God and Country: Exploration, Archaeology, and the Secret Struggle for the Holy Land, 1799-1917* (1982, repr. New York, 1990); L. E. Stager, "The Archaeology of the Family in Ancient Israel," *BASOR* 260 (1985): 1-35.

THOMAS E. LEVY

ARCHANGEL

"Chief" or "first angel" (Gk. *archángelos*). From the postexilic period the term referred to an angel who headed a particular group of angels. The number of archangels varies, from seven (Tob. 12:15; 2 Esdr. 5:20), to four (1 En. 87:2-3; 88:1), to three (90:31). Michael (Jude 9; Dan. 10:13; 12:1; 1 En. 9:1; 10:11), Gabriel (Dan. 8:16; 1 En. 9:1; 20:7; 40:9), Raphael (Tob. 3:17; 12:14; 1 En. 10:4; 40:9), and Uriel (9:1; 19:1; 20:2) are special archangels who served as mediators between God and humans. Archangels will be heard at the second coming of Christ (1 Thess. 4:16).

EDWARD P. MYERS

ARCHELAUS (Gk. *Archélaos*)

Son of Herod the Great who inherited Judea, Idumea, and Samaria at his father's death. He was designated by his father to receive the title of king. The Jewish historian Josephus is ambiguous on this, saying at one point that he did receive the title, but at another seeming to say that it was promised only after a period of probation (*Ant.* 17.195; cf. *BJ* 2.93). His only mention in the NT is Matt. 2:22, which states that Mary and Joseph were afraid to live in Judea with the infant Jesus because Archelaus was ruling there.

JOE E. LUNCEFORD

ARCHIPPUS (Gk. *Árchippos*)

A member of the Colossian church whom Paul greets and reminds to be faithful to his ministry

(Col. 4:17). Archippus ("master of the horse") is also referred to as Paul's "fellow soldier" (Gk. *sustratiōtēs*, Phlm. 2), implying that they had previously served together. He was a member of Philemon's household, perhaps a son or brother, and may have been the owner of Onesimus the slave (Phlm. 8-20). If the phrase "received in the Lord" is technical language for the beginnings of ordination, then Archippus may have been a deacon at Colossae. BONNIE THURSTON

ARCHITE (Heb. *hā'arkî*)
A member of a Benjaminite clan near Bethel. The gentilic is applied to Hushai, David's friend and adviser (2 Sam. 15:32). According to Josh. 16:2 the clan's territory was at Ataroth (perhaps Ataroth-adder).

ARCHITECTURE
Architecture, as the art or science of building, addresses the physical, ideological, social, and creative needs of humanity through the design of functional structures. Over the centuries of human existence, mankind has claimed the right to express, in personal and monumental venues, these needs within the limits of available materials. Textual and archaeological records in the ancient Near East attest to the monuments left through the course of millennia in the "cradle of civilization."

Materials and Construction

The building materials available in Palestine were limited to the natural occurrence of local limestone and basalt, woods, and earth used in forming mudbrick. Biblical references to the use of these materials are abundant and accurately reflect local construction techniques.

Quarried limestone was the most common building material, especially in the coastal regions and central hill country, while basalt was used in the north, particularly in the Jordan Valley and the Galilee. Large rough and unhewn stones were used as foundation and walls, with chinking stones placed in cracks, and uneven areas before the walls were covered in mud or plaster. It was not until the Late Bronze Age that ashlar masonry was introduced for fine building, as is evident at several of the palaces and temples at Hazor and the LB gate at Megiddo. These orthostats in northern Palestine reflect a strong Anatolian influence. During later periods ashlar masonry was further developed and used throughout Palestine, especially during the period of the Israelite monarchy and later (1 Kgs. 5:18). Stone continued to be a major construction material through Hellenistic and Roman times.

Timber was employed extensively (Josh. 17:15, 18) in the construction of roofing beams (1 Kgs. 6:9), wall reinforcement (6:36; Ezra 5:8; 6:4) and for interior columns made of wood (1 Kgs. 7:2) or stone. Local woods used in construction included the date palm, juniper, oak, olive, pine, poplar, and walnut. The well-known cedar of Lebanon was imported from the north and shipped to Palestine and Egypt, where it was prized as one of the finest lumbers (2 Sam. 5:11; 1 Kgs. 5:8-9; 7:2).

Sun-baked mudbrick was used throughout the Near East as a versatile material in constructing fortifications, domestic, cultic, and administrative buildings. It was once thought that the arch was introduced in the Persian period, but two arched gates made of mudbrick have been found at Tell Dan and Ashkelon dating to MB. The mudbrick was easily molded in forms and sun-baked, sometimes adding straw as a temper that would accelerate drying and coherence. The mudbrick was laid and mortared with mud or bitumen (Gen. 11:3). The walls were then finished with either a mud or plaster coat on the surface. Maintenance would be required on a regular basis to prevent decay. The combined use of these materials in different buildings and architectural design varied throughout the history of ancient Palestine.

General Survey

Palestine, as a land bridge between the empires of Egypt, Anatolia, and Mesopotamia, was at the crossroads of ancient civilizations. From the beginning of urbanization in EB II-III (3000-2400 B.C.) and especially during MB II-III (1850-1550) the city-states of Palestine reflected the strong influences of Syria and Mesopotamia, a factor that continued into LB accompanied by the increasing impact of Egypt on architecture and material culture. With the collapse of Bronze Age civilization over an extended period from about 1250 to 1150, architectural changes began to take hold as several ethnic groups such as the Israelites and Philistines began to extend their settlement. Throughout the following centuries powerful forces from Assyria, Persia, Greece, and Rome would play an interactive role with indigenous cultures in architectural development.

Fortifications. The construction of fortifications provided protection against marauding animals and attacking military forces. The development of the fortified city indicated permanent settlement as a population became attached to a certain region and felt that its land must be defended. Defensive structures included ramparts and glacis, walls, and gates.

The rampart and glacis were introduced during EB II and continue during urban periods until they appear again at Iron Age sites. The rampart was a built-up mound of earth that surrounded the city and served as the base for massive city walls. Some thought that it was constructed as a defense against the battering ram, but it also prevented erosion and the sapping of city walls. The glacis was the outer facing of the rampart or mound *(tell)* made of beaten earth, lime plaster, brick, or stone. It appears at the Iron II sites of Beer-sheba, Lachish, Tel Malḥata (Tell el-Milḥ), Tell en-Naṣbeh, and Gezer.

The construction of the Iron Age city wall took on several forms. In Iron I few fortified cities other than the Philistine pentapolis existed along the southern coastal plain. Excavations at Ashkelon, Tel Miqne-Ekron, and Ashdod revealed major mud-

Iron Age storehouse with two rows of monolithic pillars flanking the center aisle; Omride dynasty (ca. 875 B.C.E.), Hazor (W. S. LaSor)

brick walls and towers dating to the 12th and 11th centuries. Other cities were surrounded by a simple belt of houses, the outer walls serving for defense. Examples of this defensive system up to the United Monarchy appear at Beth-shemesh, Gezer, Megiddo, Tell en-Naṣbeh, and Lachish. During and after the Monarchy, when administration became centralized, fortifications were further developed. During the 10th through 8th centuries casemate walls were constructed at Hazor, Tell Beit Mirsim, Samaria, and ʿEn Gev. These casemate walls consisted of two parallel walls with the space between them divided by partition walls into small rooms that either functioned for storage or were filled with earth for reinforcement and support of upper courses. The offset-inset wall is found at Gezer and Megiddo, and massive walls built of stone are also evident at Tell en-Naṣbeh, Hazor, Tel Batash-Timnah, Jerusalem, and Tel Malḥata.

Life at the city gate figured in important institutions in ancient Palestine. The "square at the gate of the city" (2 Chr. 32:6) was an area for drawing up agreements before witnesses, a seat for the elders, prophets, and judges of the city. At the gates of Megiddo (stratum V-A) and Dan possible "high places" were found (2 Kgs. 23:8) that correspond to the biblical descriptions.

The Iron Age gate developed in a succinct manner. During the 10th century the three-entry gateway of the Late Bronze Age was expanded to four entries with six chambers. It was flanked on either side with massive towers about two stories high, which were open and accessible during the Iron Age. This four-entry gateway has been attributed to Solomon, who is said to have rebuilt the walls of Jerusalem, Hazor, Megiddo, and Gezer (1 Kgs. 9:15), the latter cities revealing gates of this design together with fine ashlar masonry. Although there is discussion concerning the dating of these gates to Solomon, the ashlar masonry specifically mentioned in connection with his building activities (1 Kgs. 5:15-17[MT 29-31]; 7:9-10) is cited in its favor.

During the 9th century gates with three entries became prominent at sites like Tell en-Naṣbeh, Beersheba, Megiddo, and Tel Dan/Tell el-Qadi. Other simple two-entry gates provided an essential framework at several Iron II sites.

Domestic Buildings. A new type of house was introduced at the beginning of the Iron Age. Due to its initial discovery in the hill country, the three- and four-room house was often associated ethnically with the Israelites. The building was typically designed in an oblong, rectangular shape. The broad room, the largest space, was at the back with the three front rooms built at right angles to the broad room. A row of pillars divided the front rooms creating a type of courtyard. The building may also have had a second story at least over part of the ground floor. The size of the four-room house seems to indicate that it was occupied by nuclear families.

The origin of the four-room house is thought by some to be a new innovation of the Iron Age, while others point to LB predecessors. The earliest true four-room house is found at sites such as Giloh (late 13th century), Tel Masos, and ʿIzbet Ṣarṭah. It became most common during the 12th century throughout the central hill country. Iron II administrative cities like Megiddo, Lachish, Hazor, and Tell en-Naṣbeh demonstrate careful architectural planning and a proliferation of four-room houses

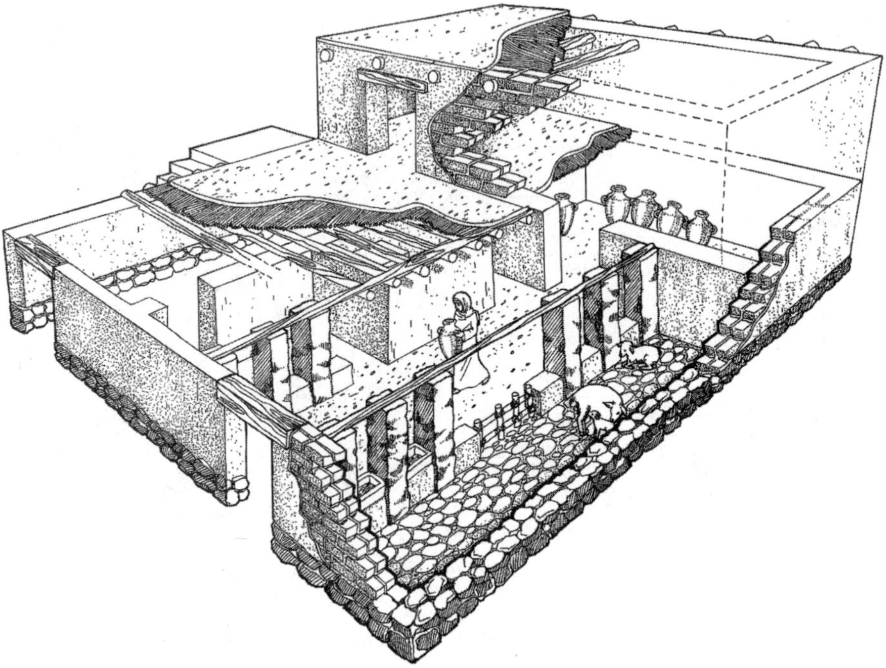

Artist's reconstruction of the Israelite "four-room house" (Giselle S. Hasel)

in domestic areas. Thus this form became increasingly popular during the Iron Age in settlements and cities occupied by Israelites and Philistines (e.g., Tell Qasile, Tel Serʿ/Tell esh-Shariʿa).

Cultic Buildings. Known only from its elaborate biblical description (1 Kgs. 6; 2 Chr. 3:1-10; Ezek. 40–43), the temple of Solomon is perhaps the best-known cultic building. It was a rectangular, long-room building with an entrance on its eastern side. Its exterior dimensions were ca. 25 × 20 m. (82 × 65 ft.), its wall ca. 2.5–6 m. (8–20 ft.) thick. Two ornamental pillars framed the entrance. The interior was divided into two compartments, the holy and the most holy. The interior floors were laid with pine, while the walls and roof were lined with cedar. The most holy place was also overlaid with gold through the aid of Phoenician craftsmen. The temple served the Israelite community until its destruction by the Babylonians in 586.

Other cultic buildings in Iron II are known from Tell Dan, Arad, and Tel Miqne-Ekron. A large podium found at Tel Dan was interpreted as a cultic high place *(bāmâ)*. Its several phases span the 10th through early 9th centuries. The outline of the perfectly square structure is built of fine ashlar masonry with an earth and basalt fill. Within its boundaries foundation walls seemed to have supported a massive superstructure.

At Arad a series of rooms within a fortress were identified as a sanctuary because of the tripartite structure, large sacrificial altar, and smaller altars within the inner chambers. Two shallow bowls were found inscribed with an abbreviated formula that might be interpreted as "sanctified for priests."

A massive Assyrian temple has been uncovered at Tel Miqne-Ekron dating to the 7th century. A dedicatory inscription mentions that Padi son of Achsi dedicated the temple to a goddess and adds considerable light to cultic practices during this period.

Administrative Buildings. Administrative buildings can be classified under palaces or large patrician houses and pillared buildings during the Late Bronze through Iron Ages.

The "governor's" residency was a development of the terminal phase of the Late Bronze Age. This type of building is said to have strong Egyptian and Syrian influences. These were square buildings made of mudbrick walls, with a central courtyard surrounded by smaller rooms. It is thought that they served local governors in ruling over Palestine in the south and along the major highways leading north. Most of these residences at such sites as Beth-shean (Tell el-Ḥuṣn), Pella, Tell Jemmeh, Tell el-Ḥesi, Tell es-Saʿidiyeh, Tel Seraʿ/Tell esh-Shariʿa, and Tell el-Farʿah (South) were destroyed during the LB/Iron Age transition (ca. 1200) but others survived or were built in Iron I (Tel Masos).

The biblical narratives provide vivid descriptions of David's and Solomon's palaces (2 Sam. 5:11; 7:7; 1 Chr. 17:1; 2 Chr. 2:3[2]; 1 Kgs. 7:1-12). Like the temple, they were erected through the skills of Phoenician craftsmen, but archaeological excavations have yet to locate them. Other palaces found at sites like Megiddo (Buildings 1723 and 6000) and Gezer ("Palace 10,000") indicate construction in the Syrian *bit ilani* tradition. These palaces were designed as two elongated halls with the longitudinal axis parallel to the facade. The first hall was a portico with a stairway leading up to the entrance. Another staircase within led to a second story. The long inner hall was the throne room. Other palaces at Ramat Raḥel, Lachish, Hazor, and Samaria indicate additional architectural developments which differed from earlier Canaanite and later Assyrian influences. Biblical references to the use of cedar beams in construction (1 Kgs. 6:36; 7:12) are supported by archaeological evidence at these sites, where gaps are found between ashlar courses. Fragments of wall paintings were found at Ramat Raḥel.

Numerous sites experienced Assyrian influence during the 8th and 7th centuries as the Assyrian Empire expanded and administrative centers were established in Palestine. Assyrian "open-court buildings" are found at Hazor (Building 3002), Megiddo (Buildings 1052, 1369, and 1853), Gezer, Tell Jemmeh/Tel Reʿim, Tel Serʿ/Tell esh-Shariʿa, and Buseirah.

Pillared buildings are another important architectural feature of the Iron Age. The rectangular structures, divided by pillars into three narrow halls, are thought to have served a public function at Hazor, Tell Abu Hawam, Megiddo, Tell Qasile, Tell el-Ḥesi, Beer-sheba, Tel Malḥata, and Tell Masos. The function of these buildings as stables, storehouses, barracks, or marketplaces remains an issue of debate.

Later Developments. Influences from the Hellenistic and Roman cultures were increasingly felt throughout the region. The Romans established no fewer than 30 cities in Palestine; one of the most impressive building programs was initiated by Herod the Great (37-4 B.C.). Cities such as Caesarea Maritima, the rebuilding of Jerusalem, Beth-shean, Pella, and Banias (Caesarea Philippi) indicate careful planning for aqueducts, cisterns, temples, amphitheaters, hippodromes, bathhouses, and palaces placed in conjunctive relationship to fountains and statues, thus creating a magnificent atmosphere of power and culture. Despite this impressive show, the construction of synagogues, the temple in Jerusalem, and other edifices attest to the persistence and indomitable nature of the social, ideological, and creative elements still inherent in the local cultures and their ancient heritage.

See also HOUSE; TEMPLE.

Bibliography. A. Biran, ed., *Temples and High Places in Biblical Times* (Jerusalem, 1981); W. G. Dever, "Palaces and Temples in Canaan and Ancient Israel," *CANE,* 1:605-14; V. Fritz, *The City in Ancient Israel* (Sheffield, 1995); A. Kempinski and R. Reich, eds., *The Architecture of Ancient Israel* (Jerusalem, 1992); G. Leick, *A Dictionary of Ancient Near Eastern Architecture* (New York, 1988); Y. Shiloh, "The Casemate Wall, the Four-Room House, and Early Planning in the Israelite City," *BASOR* 268 (1987): 3-15; L. E. Stager, "The Archaeology of the Family in Ancient Israel," *BASOR* 260 (1985): 1-35.

MICHAEL G. HASEL

ARD (Heb. *'ard*) (also ADDAR)

A descendant of Benjamin and the son of Bela, listed among ancestral clan leaders who accompanied Jacob to Egypt (Gen. 46:21; Num. 26:40). At 1 Chr. 8:3 he is called Addar.

ARDON (Heb. *'ardôn*)

The third son of Caleb and Azubah of the tribe of Judah (1 Chr. 2:18).

ARELI (Heb. *'ar'ēlî*)

A son of Gad and grandson of Jacob (Gen. 46:16; Num. 26:17).

AREOPAGITE (Gk. *Areopagítēs*)

A member of the prestigious Athenian council which held its sessions at or near the Areopagus. Dionysius, one of Paul's converts, was an Areopagite (Acts 17:34).

AREOPAGUS (Gk. *Áreios págos*) (also MARS HILL)

A rocky hill ca. 115 m. (377 ft.) high, near the Acropolis and Agora in Athens, whose name was derived from the Greek god of war Ares (also called Mars Hill after the Roman Mars). Areopagus also refers to the council that once met on the above-named hill. (This council retained the name even after moving its meeting to the Royal Stoa.) The Areopagus' authority vacillated throughout time, but during the Roman era it was responsible for various educational and philosophical/religious concerns as well as legal matters such as forgery and standards of measurement.

Epicurean and Stoic philosophers brought Paul to the Areopagus for a hearing after he debated with Jews and God-fearers in the synagogue and Agora (Acts 17:16-21). Scholars are divided as to which use of Areopagus Acts refers. Paul spoke as a skilled debater, and even though he did not convince the multitude, some Athenians did believe in Christ (Acts 17:22-34).

Bibliography. F. F. Bruce, *The Book of the Acts,* rev. ed. NICNT (Grand Rapids, 1988); H. J. Cadbury, *The Book of Acts in History* (London, 1955); F. Stagg, *The Book of Acts: The Early Struggle for an Unhindered Gospel* (Nashville, 1956).

STEVEN L. COX

ARETAS (Gk. *Harétas*)

1. Aretas I, the first Nabatean ruler named in ancient literature. According to 2 Macc. 5:8 the Jewish high priest Jason somehow ran afoul of Aretas when he fled from Jerusalem to Nabatea in 168 B.C.E. Here, Aretas is called *týrannos,* which may indicate that the Nabatean rulers were not yet called kings. After the outbreak of the Maccabean Revolt, the Nabatean leaders are depicted as sympathizing with the revolutionaries (1 Macc. 5:25; 9:35).

2. Aretas II (ca. 100 B.C.E.), who promised to aid the city of Gaza when it was besieged by the

Hasmonaean monarch Alexander Janneus (Josephus *Ant.* 13.356-364). However, his help came too late, and the city was overthrown. Josephus describes Aretas II as a "very illustrious person," indicative of the growing power of the Nabatean kingdom.

3. Aretas III (ca. 87-62 B.C.E.), who, according to Josephus, gained control over Damascus and Coele-Syria. He invaded Judea and defeated Alexander Janneus in battle, but settled on terms and returned to his own land (*Ant.* 13.392; *BJ* 1.103). In 65 Aretas III supported Hyrcanus II in his struggle against Aristobulus II, besieging Aristobulus in Jerusalem, but he was ordered to withdraw by the Roman general Scaurus. During his retreat, Aretas was attacked and overcome by Aristobulus (*Ant.* 14.14-33; *BJ* 1.123-130).

4. Aretas IV (9 B.C.E.–40 C.E.), originally called Aeneas. He provided the Romans with troops for their campaigns against the Jews during the rebellions that followed Herod the Great's death (4 B.C.E.; *Ant.* 17.287; *BJ* 2.68). Later in his reign (ca. 36 C.E.) Aretas IV became angry with Herod Antipas, the Jewish tetrarch, when Herod divorced Aretas' daughter to marry Herodias. The resulting ill will was exacerbated by border disputes, and Aretas and Herod went to battle, with Aretas emerging victorious. Although reprimanded by the Roman emperor Tiberius, Aretas suffered no repercussions from the incident. Not long after, the Apostle Paul also ran afoul of Aretas IV. In 2 Cor. 11:32-33, Paul tells of how the governor of Damascus, under King Aretas, had guarded the city in order to capture Paul, but he had escaped in a basket lowered out of a window. The story reveals that Damascus was still under Nabatean control, even though it was within the Roman province of Coele-Syria.

Bibliography. G. W. Bowersock, *Roman Arabia* (Cambridge, Mass., 1983); A. Kasher, *Jews, Idumeans, and Ancient Arabs* (Tübingen, 1988); E. Schürer, *A History of the Jewish People in the Age of Jesus Christ (175 B.C.-A.D. 135)*, rev. ed. (Edinburgh, 1973-1987).

ANTHONY J. TOMASINO

ARGOB (Heb. *'argōḇ*) **(PERSON)**
A person connected with the slaying of Pekahiah (2 Kgs. 15:25 NRSV); omitted in some translations. Some scholars regard Argob and Arieh as place names (cf. 2 Kgs. 15:29).

ARGOB (Heb. *'argōḇ*) **(PLACE)**
A region with 60 fortified cities and numerous villages in Bashan, the kingdom of Og (Deut. 3:4, 13-14). It was conquered by Israel and allotted to the tribe of Manasseh. Jair renamed it Havvoth-jair (Deut. 3:14). It is included in the discussion of Solomon's sixth administrative district and seems to be contrasted with "the villages of Jair" in Gilead (1 Kgs. 4:13). Clearly E of the Jordan River and the Sea of Chinnereth, Argob's precise location is unknown.

Argob also appears in 2 Kgs. 15:25, where, along with Arieh, it has been understood as either a reference to a person (cf. LXX, NRSV, NIV) or a place name transposed from v. 29 (cf. RSV mg).

ERIC F. MASON

ARIDAI (Heb. *'ărîḏay*)
One of the 10 sons of Haman slain by the Jews (Esth. 9:9).

ARIDATHA (Heb. *'ărîḏāṯā'*)
One of the 10 sons of Haman the Agagite (Esth. 9:8).

ARIEH (Heb. *'aryēh*)
Along with Argob, either a victim of or a conspirator in the massacre at the royal palace at Samaria (2 Kgs. 15:25 NRSV). Some versions (e.g., RSV, NJB) omit the names because of textual difficulties; according to the RSV mg they should be included with the names of places captured by Tiglath-pileser III (2 Kgs. 15:29).

ARIEL (Heb. *'ărî'el*) **(PERSON)**

1. A member of the delegation sent by Ezra the scribe to obtain ministers for the temple (Ezra 8:16; cf. 1 Esdr. 8:43, "Iduel").

2, 3. Two Moabites (RSV "two ariels of Moab"; NJB "two formidable Moabites") killed by Benaiah, one of David's champions (NRSV 2 Sam. 23:20 = 1 Chr. 11:22).

ARIEL (Heb. *'ărî'el*) **(PLACE)**
A cryptic name designating Jerusalem (Isa. 29:1-2, 7) in an oracle concerning both the siege and preservation of the city. The Hebrew term may here designate the hearth of an altar (cf. 1QIsa[a]; Ezek. 43:15-16).

ARIMATHEA (Gk. *Arimathaía*)
A place mentioned by each of the Gospels as the hometown of a rich man named Joseph. Granted permission to take the body of Jesus from the cross, he prepared it for burial and placed it in his own tomb (Matt. 27:57; Mark 15:43; Luke 23:50; John 19:38). Referred to as a "Jewish town" by Luke (Luke 23:50), it has been identified with both Ramathain and Rentis, ca. 24 km. (15 mi.) and 32 km. (20 mi.) respectively E of Jaffa. Later tradition (Eusebius and Jerome) identifies Arimathea as the birthplace of Samuel, called Ramah in 1 Sam. 1:19.

JOHN GILLMAN

ARIOCH (Heb. *'aryōḵ*)

1. King of Ellasar (Gen. 14:1, 9), who together with Amraphel, Chedorlaomer, and Tidal fought five other kings in the valley of Siddim. Arioch is perhaps identical with Arriwuk, a son of Zimrilim and contemporary of Hammurabi, known from the Mari archives, or the Ariukki of the Nuzi documents.

2. Captain of Nebuchadnezzar's bodyguards (Dan. 2:14-15, 24-25), commissioned by the king to execute all wise men in Babylon since they could not interpret Nebuchadnezzar's dream.

3. King of the Chaldeans (Jdt. 1:6), otherwise unidentified. The Greek text here is corrupt.

JESPER SVARTVIK

ARISAI (Heb. *'ărîsay*)
One of the 10 sons of Haman the Agagite who were killed by the Jews (Esth. 9:9).

ARISTARCHUS (Gk. *Arístarchos*)
A Jewish Christian whom Paul calls a "fellow worker" (Phlm. 24) and "fellow prisoner" (Col. 4:10; Gk. *sunaichmálōtos,* lit., "prisoner of war," but probably used metaphorically). A native of Thessalonica, Aristarchus worked with Paul in Asia and was with him when the crowd rioted in Ephesus (Acts 19:29). He was Paul's traveling companion from Troas to Asia (Acts 20:4, 6) and later to Rome (27:2; Phlm. 24). Both travel references in Acts occur in "we" passages, and it has been suggested that Aristarchus could only have traveled with Paul as his slave. Since Aristarchus was associated with the area and known in proconsular Asia, Philemon's community would have special concern for him. Possibly 2 Cor. 8:18-19 refers to him as "the brother" who traveled with Paul, since *sunékdēmos,* "traveling companion," is used only there and in Acts 19:29, which clearly refers to Aristarchus.

BONNIE THURSTON

ARISTEAS (Gk. *Aristaíos*), **LETTER OF**
Purported to be an epistle from Aristeas, a member of Ptolemy II Philadelphus' court, to his brother Philocrates, this pseudepigraphon tells a story of the translation of the Hebrew Bible into Greek (the LXX). Aristeas describes how Ptolemy II (285-247 B.C.E.) came to make a formal request to the high priest in Jerusalem, asking him to provide 72 translators (six from each of the 12 tribes) who would undertake the creation of a Greek version of the Jewish Law (the Pentateuch). Included in this section of the letter are a catalog of the gifts sent by the Egyptian king to the high priest, the librarian's report to the king about the Jewish Scriptures, the full "texts" of the king's request and the high priest's affirmative reply, and substantial descriptions of the Jerusalem temple and Palestine. When the translators arrive in Alexandria, the king prepares a seven-day-long banquet. During the banquet, the description of which takes up nearly one third of the book, the king questions each of the visitors about their god and religion. A brief description of the successful translation of the Law into Greek concludes the work.

The letter probably was written in Egypt, perhaps Alexandria, during the latter half of the 2nd century. Its purpose is twofold: 1) to offer an extended "apology" for Judaism and the Jewish Law; and 2) to defend the complete adequacy of the Greek translation of the Law for religious purposes. As the story came to be usurped, transmitted, and altered by Christians in the defense of their use of the LXX over against the Hebrew Bible, this second theme has come to dominate the reading of the text. However, given the extended reflections on Jewish Law, the temple, Palestine, and the wise counsel of the translators, it seems clear that the primary purpose was to promote a better understanding of Judaism in an Egyptian environment.

Bibliography. R. J. H. Shutt, "Letter of Aristeas," *OTP* 2 (Garden City, 1985): 7-34; J. R. Bartlett, *The Jews in the Hellenistic World* (Cambridge, 1985).

JAMES R. MUELLER

ARISTION (Gk. *Aristíōn*)
A 1st-century Christian known to Papias, a primary authority for traditions about the Lord. Aristion and John, characterized as "the Lord's disciples" analogously with various of the 12 apostles, are said to have conveyed information to Papias "as the word of a living and surviving voice" (Eusebius *HE* 3.39.4). Presumably the text indicates that Aristion and John personally knew Jesus, although they were not members of the Twelve. Some read the same data as implying the two were disciples not of Jesus but of some of the Twelve.

Aristion ought not to be equated with Ariston of Pella, whom Eusebius knew had written about the Bar Kokhba Revolt (*HE* 4.6.4), in spite of the identification of the two made by Maximus the Confessor. However, an identification of the Aristion known to Papias, which is widely assumed to be accurate, is that found in a 10th-century Armenian manuscript ascription of the authorship of Mark 16:9-20 (the "longer ending" of Mark) to "the presbyter Aristion." To assume this is the same person known to Papias is not, however, necessarily to assume he indeed wrote the verses in question.

FLORENCE M. GILLMAN

ARISTOBULUS (Gk. *Aristóboulos*)

1. Aristobulus I, the eldest son of John Hyrcanus; also called Judas *(Yehuda).* According to Josephus he was the first of that dynasty to claim the title of king. While Hyrcanus had transferred authority over the realm to his wife, Aristobulus seized the throne, imprisoning and starving his mother to death. He also imprisoned three of his brothers in this effort and then murdered his brother Antigonus, with whom he initially had shared power. He held the positions of high priest and king for only one year, from 104 to 103 B.C.E. Some scholars attribute the coins bearing the inscription "Judah the High Priest . . ." to him.

2. Aristobulus II, the younger son of Alexander Janneus and Salome Alexandra. Upon the death of Alexander Janneus, Alexandra appointed their eldest son Hyrcanus II as high priest while she assumed the crown. She held this post for nine years (76-66 B.C.E.). When she became ill, Aristobulus II proclaimed himself king. She died before she could challenge his claim. Aristobulus forced Hyrcanus to relinquish his claim to the throne and the high priesthood. Aligned with Antipater, the father of Herod the Great, Hyrcanus II enlisted the support of Aretas, the Nabatean king at Petra, to besiege his brother in the temple. This siege was lifted through the intervention of the Roman general Scaurus, sent by Pompey. After Pompey began to encounter the resistance of Aristobulus, he gradually was led to change his opinion and placed Aristobulus under arrest. With the aid of Hyrcanus Pompey captured Jerusalem and occupied the temple in 63 B.C.E. Aristobulus and his family were taken as captives to Rome. He escaped to raise a force in Judea once again and was again returned to Rome a captive. Aristobulus was liberated by Caesar in 49 B.C.E., but was poisoned before he could reach Judea. JOHN KAMPEN

3. A person in Rome, to whose family Paul sent greetings (Rom. 16:10). Some scholars identify him as the grandson of Herod the Great and brother of Herod Agrippa I.

See HEROD (Family) 7.

ARK OF NOAH

According to Gen. 6:1-8, the Deity decided to destroy the human race by means of a great flood, excepting only the family of the righteous Noah. The latter's means of escape was to be a great boat ("ark"), the dimensions of which are precisely given (6:14-16).

Discussion of the craft, by the church fathers and modern conservatives, has concerned whether its dimensions were adequate to accommodate the immense number of animal passengers for a year-long voyage ("of every living thing . . . two of every kind," Gen. 6:19). It has also been claimed that remnants of the ark survive to the present on a mountain in the Near East. The "adequacy" problem has arisen from interpreters' failure to realize that ancient persons described events from primeval time with fantastic imagery and symbolic numbers.

In the parallel Mesopotamian account, the hero (named Utnapishtim) escaped the Deluge by building a boat whose dimensions are 120 cubits on each side. Since measurement at the time involved decimal-place notation in base-60 (whereas the modern system uses base-10), the boat not only followed a divine blueprint but was of near magical and "ideal" dimensions: a cube of 60 × 2 cubits per side. Thus it could not fail to ride out the waters of the Flood!

Noah's boat is assigned the dimensions 300 × 50 × 30 cubits (roughly 127 × 23 × 14 m. [450 × 75 × 45 ft.]). Otherwise put, it is 60 × 5 cubits long, 60/2 cubits high, and has a volume of $(60^3 \times 2) + (60^2 \times 5)$ cubic cubits. Such dimensions are meant to signify an ideal construction of divine origin. Thus, for interpreters to have literalized the figures is not only to misunderstand the nature and intent of the text, but also to generate futile discission about the ark's capacity. Other accounts of primeval time utilize "ideal" enumeration, including the length of life of pre-Flood generations (cf. Gen. 7:11; Deut 34:7). It is clear that these numbers are symbolic, else the writers would not have allowed the contradiction with Gen. 6:3.

Modern claims that remnants of the ark yet survive are based upon contradictory accounts, supposed photographs and documents that have vanished or are of questionable origin, misidentified geological formations, and misinterpretation of satellite imagery. At least nine locations have been proposed for the ark's landing place, ranging from Asia Minor to Afghanistan. Several have produced "ark wood," claimed to have been reliably dated to an age of 5000 years (roughly the time of Noah according to biblical chronology). However, none of the tests is scientifically creditable, and the wood instead seems to belong to the 7th century C.E.

The commonly proposed landing site, the spectacular mountain Ağri Dağ (Masis, "Mt. Ararat") in Armenia (Turkey), was so identified only after the 13th century C.E. Early Christian and Jewish claims centered instead on Mt. Qardu (now called Jabal Judi).

Bibliography. L. R. Bailey, *Noah* (Columbia, S.C., 1989), ch. 4; *Genesis, Creation, and Creationism* (New York, 1993), Appendix VII.

LLOYD R. BAILEY

ARK OF THE COVENANT

The chest of acacia wood that contained the two tablets of the Ten Commandments and, according to the NT (Heb. 9:4), Aaron's budding rod (Num. 17:1-11[MT 16-26]) and a golden urn filled with manna (Exod. 16:33-34); also called "the ark of God," "the ark of the Lord," and "the ark of testimony." The shape of the ark was rectangular, measuring 2.5 × 1.5 × 1.5 cubits, or roughly 114 cm. × 69 cm. × 69 cm. (45 in. × 27 in. × 27 in.). It was suspended on poles that passed through rings on its sides and by which it could be carried (Exod. 25:10-22; 37:1-9).

Many scholars agree that the oldest textual source that mentions the ark is the so-called Song of the Ark in Num. 10:35-36. If so, then from the time of our earliest attestations the ark was presumed to represent God's presence in the cult and, in fact, was virtually synonymous with the deity. Thus, according to the Song, whenever the ark was lifted up to lead the Israelites forward in their wanderings in the wilderness, Moses said, "Arise, O Lord"; similarly, whenever the ark was set down in a new camp, Moses said, "Return, O Lord." This simultaneity of ark and deity is also indicated in what is usually considered to be the fullest and most archaic name of the ark, "the ark of the covenant of the Lord of Hosts who is enthroned upon the cherubim" (1 Sam. 4:5; cf. 2 Sam. 6:2). What seems to be imagined here is a throne whereby the deity sits invisibly above the ark, on the outstretched wings of cherubim, with the ark itself serving as God's footstool. This image of a cherub throne with footstool is frequently found in West Semitic art, and biblical texts explicitly refer to the ark as a footstool (1 Chr. 28:2; Ps. 99:5; 132:7; Lam. 2:1) and describe cherub wings unfolded above the ark after it is housed in Solomon's temple (1 Kgs. 6:23-28; 8:6-7).

The Song of the Ark and the old liturgical name associating the ark with the Lord of Hosts also both stress that God is associated with the ark as a warrior deity and that the ark itself functions for the Israelites as a palladium or shield. In the Song of the Ark Moses follows his command to the ark to

"Arise, O Lord" with an exhortation that God's enemies should then scatter and the deity's foes flee. In the liturgical name "the ark of the covenant of the Lord of Hosts who is enthroned upon the cherubim," the "hosts" are most likely the "heavenly hosts," the cosmic army that fights on God's behalf to ensure an Israelite victory in battle (e.g., Judg. 5:20, "the stars fought from heaven"). This understanding of the ark's military function also illuminates narratives such as Josh. 6:1-21, where the city of Jericho falls to the Israelites after the warriors circumambulate its walls for seven days, blowing trumpets and carrying the ark. The same military motif is present in the Ark narrative of 1 Sam. 4–6, where the ark is brought from its then shrine in Shiloh to be present as the Israelites go to war against the Philistines.

The military efficacy of the ark in the Ark narrative, however, is initially called into question, as the ark is captured by the Philistines and taken by them to the temple of the god Dagon in Ashdod (1 Sam. 5:1-2). Yet this failure of the ark to bring about an immediate military victory on earth is just prologue to an ultimate recounting of the military superiority of the ark in the cosmic realm. During the ark's sojourn in Ashdod, the cult statue of Dagon and, by implication, Dagon himself is destroyed; the citizens of Ashdod are struck by plague, as eventually are the people throughout Philistia. The Philistines have no recourse but to return the ark to Israel, who thus become the "victors" in this battle without a sword being raised.

As the ark moves from place to place as part of Israel's military campaigns and as a part of the people's general settlement in the land, it is most commonly described as being housed in a tent (although there are some indications of an actual shrine in Shiloh). Scholars have often compared the *qubbāh,* a portable tent shrine of pre-Islamic Arabs which contained two stones and which was used during times of battle and also for divination (cf. Judg. 20:27-28). Eventually, however, the ark ended up permanently in Jerusalem, in the innermost chamber of the temple. The story of how it got there is found in 2 Sam. 6 and also in Ps. 132, one of the very few explicit mentions of the ark outside the Pentateuch and the historical books (cf. otherwise only Jer. 3:16). According to the Samuel and Psalms materials, the ark disappeared after being returned to the Israelites by the Philistines; e.g., between the end of the Ark narrative in 1 Sam. 7:1-2 and 2 Sam. 6, it is mentioned only once (1 Sam. 14:18), and this reference is often assumed to be textual error. The reasons for the ark's oblivion at this point are unclear; we can only presume that, for whatever reasons, it was not regarded as important by Saul, the ruler whose monarchy is established beginning in 1 Sam. 8.

Whatever the cause of its temporary oblivion, 2 Sam. 6; Ps. 132 are both quite clear that the ark reemerges in Israelite religion when Saul's successor David sought to establish it as the cult symbol of his newly-captured capital of Jerusalem. Consistent with older tradition, David housed the ark in Jerusalem in a tent. The building of a temple and the enshrining of the ark in its holy of holies are left to David's son Solomon. Yet even in Solomon's temple, there is a nod to custom, as 1 Kgs. 8:4 seems to indicate that the older tent abode is erected over the ark in the holy of holies.

With Solomon, the ark's story ends rather abruptly. Jewish tradition and most scholars presume that it remained in the temple for almost 400 years, until the destruction of Jerusalem by the Babylonians in 586 B.C.E., yet it is not mentioned in the list of spoils the Babylonians took from the temple (2 Kgs. 25:13-17). Perhaps this indicates that the ark was taken from Jerusalem already in the late 10th century, as part of the military campaigns undertaken by Pharaoh Shishak during the reign of Solomon's son Rehoboam. Or perhaps the ark's fate after Solomon remains unknown because its chroniclers found it of little interest. Certainly in the book of Deuteronomy, whose authors also provide our primary accounts of the post-Solomonic monarchy, the ark is of much less significance than it is in, e.g., the Priestly traditions of Exod. 25:1–31:11; 35:1–40:38.

Bibliography. F. M. Cross. "The Priestly Tabernacle," in *BA Reader* 1, ed. G. E. Wright and D. N. Freedman (Garden City, 1961), 201-28; *Canaanite Myth and Hebrew Epic* (Cambridge, Mass., 1973); R. E. Friedman, "The Tabernacle in the Temple," *BA* 43 (1980): 241-48; P. D. Miller and J. J. M. Roberts, *The Hand of the Lord: A Reassessment of the "Ark Narrative" of 1 Samuel* (Baltimore, 1977); C. L. Seow, *Myth, Drama, and the Politics of David's Dance.* HSM 44 (Atlanta, 1989); R. de Vaux, *Ancient Israel* (1961, repr. Grand Rapids, 1997); M. H. Woudstra, *The Ark of the Covenant from Conquest to Kingship* (Philadelphia, 1965).

SUSAN ACKERMAN

ARKITE (Heb. *ʿarqî*)

An inhabitant of the town of Arqat, modern Tell ʿArqah (250436), ca. 18 km. (11 mi.) N of Tripoli. At Gen. 10:17; 1 Chr. 1:15 the Arkites are mentioned among the descendants of Canaan. In the Amarna Letters the town is called Irqata; in Roman times it was known as Caesarea Libani. Arkantu, mentioned by Thutmose III, may be the same place.

ARMAGEDDON (Gk. *Harmagedōn*)

The "place" where the forces of evil are to assemble for one final onslaught against the forces of God (Rev. 16:16; NRSV "Harmagedon"). The Greek name transliterates Heb. *har magedōn* (lit., "mountain of Magedon"), which many scholars believe should be read *har mĕgiddôn,* "mountain of Megiddo."

The city of Megiddo was strategic militarily because it guarded the north-south passageway through the Carmel mountain range. The region was the locus of many ancient battles (e.g., Judg. 5:19; 2 Kgs. 23:29-30 = 2 Chr. 35:22-24). Although there is no evidence of a mountain in Palestine that was ever called either Magedon or Megiddo, Mt. Carmel is a prominent peak ca. 8 km. (5 mi.) NE of

Megiddo. This may well have been the association that the author of Revelation intended his readers to make. The appropriateness of Mt. Carmel as a symbol for the defeat of evil lies in the fact that it was the location of Elijah's defeat of the prophets of Baal (1 Kgs. 18:22-40). No actual battle is described in Revelation, however; for the author, the battle in principle had already been won through the death and resurrection of Jesus. JOE E. LUNCEFORD

ARMLET

A band worn on the arm. According to 2 Sam. 1:10, King Saul wore an armlet (Heb. *'eṣ'āḏâ),* perhaps as an insignia of office. At Isa. 3:20 *haṣṣĕ'āḏôṯ* probably designates jewelry for a woman's arm (NRSV "armlets"; NIV "ankle chains"). Among the articles brought by Moses' chief officers as an atonement offering from the captured booty were "armlets and bracelets" (Heb. *'eṣ'āḏâ wĕṣāmîḏ;* Num. 31:50), distinguishing jewelry worn on the upper arm and the wrist. Gold ornaments (Num. 31:50; 2 Sam. 1:10; cf. Gen. 24:22) are rare among archaeological finds from biblical times in Palestine, but iron, copper, and bronze are common. Carvings from ancient Egypt and Mesopotamia often show male and female figures wearing ornaments on their upper arms, sometimes together with other ornaments on their wrists (cf. *ANEP).* JOSEPH E. JENSEN

ARMONI (Heb. *'armōnî)*

One of the two sons of Saul and Rizpah whom David handed over to the Gibeonites, along with five other of Saul's descendants, as payment for the former king's bloodguilt (2 Sam. 21:8).

ARMY

The Israelite army developed through four successive stages: semi-nomadic bands, peasants' militia, professional heavy infantry, and classic ancient Near Eastern chariot army. Despite these differentiations, the ideal remained an early one: the whole armed people, or every male "who drew the sword" (Judg. 8:10; 20:2). This idealized picture is concretized in the literature, both early and late, and receives special expression in 1 Chr. 27, where David's champions are made into officers over 12 monthly levies of 24 thousand men each. Such a portrayal, however, can hardly be accurate in light of other ancient armies. Thus the great conqueror Sargon of Akkad considered it significant that he could maintain a standing army of 5400, garrisoned and provisioned in palace. According to the historian Thucydides, the 5th-century Athenian expedition against Syracuse included 4000 native Athenian hoplites, 300 horse soldiers, and perhaps 45 thousand more troops from Athens' allies. This was the largest Greek army ever assembled up to that time. The Israelites under Ahab contributed 10 thousand foot soldiers and 2000 chariots to the western alliance at Qarqar. This battle marked the zenith of Israelite military power, and resulted in the defeat of the great Assyrian army. The actualities of Israel's army accord much more closely to these figures, and its history is correspondingly richer.

Semi-nomadic Origins

The army of Israel had its antecedents in the bands of Habiru marauders who appeared out of the Near Eastern steppe during the 3rd millennium B.C.E. These bands, led by clan chieftains such as Abraham and Esau, often disrupted settled life (as depicted in the Amarna texts), though they sometimes hired themselves out to, or worked with, local rulers (cf. Gen. 14).

Peasants' Militia

During the sojourn in Egypt, and after the initial settlement in Canaan, the Israelite army became a kind of peasant militia; this army forms the backdrop to Joshua and Judges. Though the term "every man who drew the sword" is applied to this era, swords were rare and expensive. According to 1 Sam. 13:19-22 the Philistines were able to embargo the sale of swords to the Israelites at the outset of Saul's reign. More common were the weapons of the poor: light javelins for throwing, bows and arrows, slings, and clubs or maces made from animal bones. Judg. 20:16 mentions an especially skillful cadre of Benjaminite slingers. Samson is said to have slain 1000 Philistines with the jawbone of an ass; more common were maces made from the thigh bone of an ox or steer.

Facing the often superior numbers and arms of their more urbanized opponents, the Israelites relied on strategem and ambush to achieve victory, or they resorted to guerrilla warfare. Organization of this national militia was around local tribal chieftains and their respective bands. Overall command in any battle seems to have fallen to the charismatic leader of the moment, or the one in whose territory the conflict lay (cf. Deborah, Barak, and Gideon).

Professional Heavy Infantry

The later period of the judges witnessed the emergence of local strongmen surrounded by bands of freebooters or ruffians. These bands lived from the spoils of raiding, as in the case of Jephthah's men, or from direct pay, as in the case of Abimelech of Shechem. In an apparent development on these bands, Israel's first king, Saul, built a corps of ca. 400 retainers to meet the trained troops of the Philistines. Faced with Philistine military superiority, Saul's private army would have improved its arms the same way guerrilla units have always done: by stripping the slain of their arms. Indeed, that Saul built and armed such a professional force is ample testimony to his military success. These troops had among them other smaller distinctions, such as the bodyguard (*mišma'aṯ;* 1 Sam. 22:14) and the *rāṣîm* ("runners"), a category which appears at later stages of Israel's history as well (1 Sam. 22:17; 2 Kgs. 10:25). These men provided their own arms from the spoils of battle. Weapons consisted of the typical, double-edged, Iron Age sword, used for stabbing or thrusting; heavy spears which could be wielded or thrust, or cast a short distance; and bows and arrows. Armor included shields, helms, and other items, such as greaves and breastplates. Saul's men comprised a small, highly mobile force ideally suited to fighting in the hill country of Israel. Given the melee tactics of the day, such a corps could serve as a strengthening core for the always unsteady militia, or they — or a group of them — could be concentrated at a single point of the enemy line to force a breach. Saul's death at Mt. Gilboa seems to have come about when the Israelite levies fled before the Philistine chariots, leaving Saul and his men to retreat up the mountain for a last stand.

David began his career as a professional soldier (*'îš milḥāmâ*) in the service of Saul (1 Sam. 16:18), from which position he rose to command a mercenary troop. Driven from Saul's court out of jealousy over his battlefield successes, David formed his own mercenary band of ca. 400 men, based on disaffected Israelite and Judean elements and his own family members (1 Sam. 22:1-2). To these he added over time foreign mercenaries, the 600 men of Gath under his friend Ittai, and the Cherethites and Pelethites. These forces probably never numbered more than 2000 or 3000, but they stood by David through thick and thin, and secured his throne against a succession of bloody popular revolts. Like Saul's army, David's consisted of smaller elite divisions: the *šālîšîm*, or "three-ers," a group of between 30 and 50 elite warriors who probably fought as special three-man squads; the term may have originated as a designation for three-man chariot teams (driver, archer, shield-bearer) in the ancient Egyptian army (cf. Exod. 14:7; 15:4). Besides the *šālîšîm* were the *gibbôrîm*, or "heroes"; the *mišma'aṯ*, or "bodyguard"; and the foreign contingents mentioned above. David appears to have had little use for chariotry, as he hamstrung most horses captured in battle (2 Sam. 8:3-4). Instead, he built a force similar to Saul's, though greater in number, and used it successfully in the hill country of Israel and the Transjordan. It is important to note that David's private army, unlike Saul's, comprised large numbers of foreigners: men whose primary loyalty was to David, and not to Israel.

Organization of the infantry was carried out along the lines of tens (squads), fifties (platoons), hundreds (companies), and thousands (battalions), as elsewhere in the ancient Orient. The units of thousands probably had their antecedents in the units by which the ancient Semitic tribes organized themselves (Judg. 6:15; 1 Sam. 10:19). Such structure and organization were probably helpful in regularizing the levies, to a degree, and for use in siege warfare, where large numbers of infantry were necessary, and where these had to be committed to battle in a disciplined and ordered fashion.

Overall command had fallen since the time of Saul to a commander-in-chief. Saul appointed his uncle, Abner, to this position; in David's army the position was successfully held by David's ruthless but courageous nephew, Joab. Nevertheless, the king was always the titular head of the army, and if he wanted to maintain his throne, he often had to be its active battlefield leader. This status derived from the ancient role of the king as the warrior-chieftain of his people. Kings who relinquished military power often faced revolts led by members of their own houses. The revolts in David's later reign may be attributed, in part, to the fact that he had long since relinquished military command to the sons of Zeruiah. The coups by Zimri, Omri, and Jehu indicate that the position of commander-in-chief could become its own political power base, from which a militarily weak or inactive king might be deposed.

Classic Ancient Near Eastern Chariot Army

David's son and successor Solomon transformed the army into a chariot army, with its concomitant expenses: professional trainers and drivers (*pārāšîm;* 2 Sam. 8:4; 1 Kgs. 10:26), and the upkeep required of thousands of horses. Whether the new emphasis on chariotry led to the creation of the kind of warrior nobility (*maryannu*) in Israel on which the chariot corps depended elsewhere in the Near East is an open question. The cost of the horses, and their training, could only be borne by such a class, in the absence of onerous taxes exacted by the crown for such purposes. The successful revolts against Solomon in both Edom and Aram-zobah are testimony to the ineffectiveness of chariotry in that hilly country, and the secession of the 10 northern tribes under Rehoboam provides further evidence of the weakness of chariotry in holding this territory. Chariotry could be massed wheel-to-wheel across vast plains, such as the Jezreel, and used to face the great powers of the Near East, as was successfully done at Qarqar in 853. Chariots served as mobile firing platforms for archers, and as shock weapons to stampede and crush the massed infantry. If the infantry broke and ran before a chariot charge, they were run down and run over. Assyrian texts describe the iron-ribbed chariot wheels splattered with blood and feces, and Mesopotamian and Egyptian reliefs depict the severed heads and limbs of those caught under the hooves and wheels. Cavalry was almost nonexistent. The later Assyrians pioneered its use, and Alexander the Great commanded an outstanding cavalry corps. Still, the much later introduction of the stirrup was necessary for the cavalry to come into its own.

As the battle at Qarqar demonstrates, the development of the chariot did not make the use of infantry obsolete. Indeed, infantry were required in support of the chariotry, and remained important in siegecraft, where chariots had little use. In the later chapters of Kings we still read of the elite infantry designations in use since the time of David and Saul: the *rāṣîm* and the *šālîšîm,* both of which played an important role in Jehu's revolt (2 Kgs. 10:25).

Bibliography. D. G. Schley, "Joab and David: Ties of Blood and Power," in *History and Interpretation,* ed. M. P. Graham, W. P. Brown, and J. K. Kuan (Sheffield, 1993), 90-105; "The *Šālîšîm:* Officers or Special Three-man Squads?" *VT* 40 (1990): 321-26; "Soldier," *ISBE* 4 (Grand Rapids, 1988): 564-65; W. von Soden, *The Ancient Orient* (Grand Rapids, 1994), 82-86.

Donald G. Schley

ARNAN (Heb. *'arnān*)
A descendant of Zerubbabel; son of Rephaiah (1 Chr. 3:21).

ARNI (Gk. *Arní*)
An ancestor of Jesus (Luke 3:33). At Matt. 1:3-4 the name is given as Aram (often rendered "Ram," following the lists of David's descendants at Ruth 4:19 and Judah's descendants at 1 Chr. 2:9-10).

ARNON (Heb. *'arnôn*)
One of Transjordan's four major perennial streams. The Arnon's source is near el-Lejjun, 16 km. (10 mi.) NE of Kerak, from which it transects the Moabite Plateau (modern Wadi Môjib) to the northwest for 24 km. (15 mi.) and then turns west where it flows for another 24 km. (15 mi.) into the Great Rift Valley, finally emptying into the eastern side of the Dead Sea at Ras el-Ghor. The great gorge that the stream has cut through the millennia (which varies from 3 km. [2 mi.] to 5 km. [3 mi.] wide and 390 m. [1300 ft.] to 690 m. [2300 ft.] deep) has served as a natural and political boundary throughout history (e.g., Num. 21:13; Deut. 3:8, 16; Josh. 13:16). RANDALL W. YOUNKER

AROD (Heb. *'ărôḏ*) (also ARODI)
The sixth son of Gad (Num. 26:17). At Gen. 46:16 he is called Arodi.

AROER (Heb. *'ărô'ēr*)
1. "Aroer on the Arnon," a town marking the southern border of Sihon of Heshbon's Amorite kingdom (Deut. 2:36; Josh. 12:2; Judg. 11:26). It was allotted to the Reubenites (Josh. 13:16), although it was the Gadites who rebuilt and occupied it (Num. 32:34). According to the Mesha inscription (l. 26), Mesha of Moab (ca. 830 B.C.E.) later took the city from the Israelites and fortified it. It temporarily fell under the rule of Hazael of Damascus (2 Kgs. 10:33) but was apparently reacquired by Moab shortly thereafter (Jer. 48:19).

Aroer on the Arnon is confidently identified with 'Arâ'ir (228097), ca. 5 km. (3 mi.) S of Dibon, E of the old Roman road. Excavations exposed six occupational levels from ca. 2250 B.C.E. to the 3rd century C.E., with an occupational gap during the Middle Bronze Age. A fortress was established on the site during the Late Bronze and Iron Ages.

2. A town in Gilead near the border of Gad and "opposite" or "in front of" Rabbah (probably Rabbath-ammon; Josh. 13:25; Judg. 11:33). Es-Sweiwina, W of Amman, has been suggested as a possible identification.

3. A town in the vicinity of Damascus (Isa. 17:2a). The LXX does not read a place name (cf. NRSV), and no such town near Damascus has been identified.

4. A settlement W of the Jordan (1 Sam. 30:28). The site may be 'Ar'arah (148062) in the Negeb, ca. 19 km. (12 mi.) SE of Beer-sheba, although excavations there have revealed no occupation prior to the 7th century B.C.E. A better candidate may be Tell Esdar (1475.0645), 2.5 km. (1.5 mi.) N of 'Ar'arah, where some 10th-9th century remains have been found. RANDALL W. YOUNKER

AROERITE (Heb. *hā'ărō'ērî*)
Gentilic associated with Hothan, the father of two of David's Champions, apparently designating a native of Aroer **1** (1 Chr. 11:44).

ARPACHSHAD (Heb. *'arpaḵšaḏ;* Gk. *Arphaxád*).
A son of Shem (Gen. 10:24; 11:10-13; 1 Chr. 1:17-18, 24; cf. Luke 3:36). The name seems to be non-Semitic, and debate continues over the identity of the nation for which he was progenitor, with conjectures based on either the first or last half of his name being derived variously from Chaldean, Assyrian, or Hurrian. W. CREIGHTON MARLOWE

ARPAD (Heb. *'arpāḏ;* Akk. *arpadda*)
An Aramaean city (Tell Rifa'at) ca. 30 km. (18.6 mi.) N of Aleppo in northwestern Syria. Arpad's territory occupied the steppe between the Orontes and Euphrates rivers. Strategic in its location, it led the north Syrian struggle against the westward advance of the Assyrians during the 9th and 8th centuries B.C.E. Although a treaty was reached between Assyria and Arpad in 754, by 740 the city fell to Tiglath-pileser III. In biblical literature Arpad is always linked with its southern neighbor, Hamath (2 Kgs. 18:34 = Isa. 36:19; Isa. 10:9; Jer. 49:23).
GARY P. ARBINO

ARPHAXAD (Gk. *Arphaxád*)
1. An unknown king of the Medes who was killed by Nebuchadnezzar (Jdt. 1:1-15).

2. An ancestor of Jesus in Luke's genealogy (Luke 3:36).

ARROW
See BOW AND ARROW.

ARSACES (Gk. *Arsakēs*)
A Parthian military leader, who in the mid-3rd century B.C.E. rebelled against Seleucus II and established a dynasty that continued until the 3rd century C.E. Arsaces became the name that all Parthian kings adopted. Parthia gained official independence from Antiochus III, who was unable to defeat a coalition in which Parthia participated. Antiochus IV also suffered defeat at the hands of Arsaces VI (Mithradates I). After Antiochus IV's death, Mithradates conquered Media and Mesopotamia. In 161 Demetrius I took Media from the Parthians after his victory over Timarchus. In 141 his son Demetrius II marched east where he met the expanding Parthian Empire still under the rule of Arsaces Mithradates I. Mithradates' commanders defeated and captured Demetrius and brought him to their king (1 Macc. 14:1-3). Mithradates, however, treated Demetrius II well, and later Demetrius married his sister. RODNEY A. WERLINE

ARTAXERXES (Heb. *'artaḥšastā';* Gk. *Artaxerxēs*)
A common name among Persian kings of the Achaemenid dynasty. Artaxerxes is mentioned as

the Persian king who commissioned the missions of Ezra and Nehemiah (Ezra 7:1-28; Neh. 2:1-8). On the basis of extrabiblical references to his antagonists Sanballat and Geshem (cf. Neh. 6:1), Nehemiah's missions are almost certainly to be placed during the reign of Artaxerxes I (445 and 433 B.C.E.; Neh. 2:1; 13:6-7). There is less agreement concerning Ezra, though increasingly scholars are inclined to date his mission also to the time of Artaxerxes I (458; Ezra 7:7).

1. Artaxerxes I Longimanus (465-424). Son and successor to Xerxes I, Artaxerxes I first faced rebellion by Egypt, which was crushed in 455 by Megabyzus, satrap of "Beyond the River" (*ʿAbar Naharâ*). In 448 Megabyzus revolted and was removed from office. Some have seen this as the background to Nehemiah's mission. Otherwise, Artaxerxes' reign unfolded quite peacefully.

2. Artaxerxes II Mnemon (404-359). Son and successor to Darius II, his claim to the throne was challenged in battle by Cyrus the Younger, as narrated in Xenophon's *Anabasis.* Cyrus' defeat (401) and the later routing of the Spartans at Cnidus (394) returned control over the West to Artaxerxes. The hegemony he sustained throughout his lengthy reign was largely due to the rivalries between the various Greek city-states and likewise between satraps.

GERALD M. BILKES

ARTEMAS (Gk. *Artemás*)
A companion of Paul whom the apostle hoped to send to Crete in order to permit Titus to join Paul at Nicopolis (Tit. 3:12).

ARTEMIS (Gk. *Ártemis*)
The patron deity of Ephesus. Artemis Ephesia — a local manifestation of the Greek goddess Artemis and the Roman Diana — is a form of the native Anatolian Mother Goddess, a fertility and lunar deity known for her protection of new life, especially animals and women in childbirth. Ephesus claimed to be the place of her birth, feted twice annually, in the month-long spring artemisia, which involved athletic, theatrical, and musical celebrations as well as banquets and assemblies, and a late summer or fall event reenacting the birth as part of a mystery cult. In these celebrations, sacred images of Artemis were carried in procession from the Artemisium, the temple, into the city and then back to the sanctuary. Songs and acclamations of the crowds, similar to "Great is Artemis of the Ephesians!" (Acts 19:28, 34), were sung during the processions. These festivals attracted thousands of visitors and were the city's primary economic industry. The tradition in Acts 19:35 that her cult image had "fallen from heaven" suggests that the original statue had been carved from a meteor, although no other literary references to that claim survive.

The center of the cult of Artemis was in Ephesus, where her image was minted on silver coins and the statuettes carried in civic processions. Conversions to Christianity certainly would have curtailed donations to the Artemisium, would have had a detrimental influence on the cult worship of the goddess, and would have been seen as a threat to the temple's ancillary economic activity. Thus, Demetrius, probably a member of the temple board, saw Christianity as a direct threat to the religion and economy of the city, and he incited the silversmiths to riot over this intrusion of the Way (Acts 19:23-41).

JOSEPH A. CORAY

ARUBBOTH (Heb. *ʾărubbôṯ*) (also ARBATTA)
A town in Solomon's third district, where Benhesed was to gather a supply of food for the king one month out of the year (1 Kgs. 4:10). Khirbet el-Hamam (163201) on the southern edge of the Dothan Valley is a likely candidate for the location. Nearby Arrabeh (169201) preserves the ancient name. At 1 Macc. 5:23 it is called Arbatta (cf. Narbata in the Roman period).

ARUMAH (Heb. *ʾărûmâ*)
A town in Ephraim where Abimelech, son of Gideon, resided (Judg 9:41), and identified with modern Khirbet el-ʿOrmah (180172), ca. 8 km. (5 mi.) S of Shechem. It may also appear in Judg. 9:31, although the text there is problematic. The MT reads *bĕṯormâ,* which appears to be the Hebrew prep. *bĕ* followed by an otherwise unattested noun. Scholars who accept this reading derive *tormâ* from the root *rmh,* "to deceive" (cf. KJV "privily"; NIV "under cover"). Others, including the NRSV, read *tormâ* as simply a corrupt form of Arumah.

WADE R. KOTTER

ARVAD (Heb. *ʾarwaḏ;* Gk. *Arados*)
The northernmost of the Phoenician city-states, occupying a small island (modern Ruad; 229473) just off the Syrian coast ca. 85 km. (53 mi.) S of Ugarit. In the Table of Nations its inhabitants are included among the Canaanites (Gen. 10:18; 1 Chr. 1:16). The Amarna Letters indicate that the navy of Arvad (Akk. *Ar-ma-da-a*) was the main military force used by a confederation of northern cities against the southern cities of Byblos, Sidon, and Tyre. Arvad's navy impressed Tiglath-pileser I of Assyria, who recounted his sail on board an Arvadite ship.

Assyrian annals record that Arvad hosted Assurnasirpal II, presumably as part of trade relations with Assyria. However, with the imperalistic advance of Shalmaneser III, Arvad joined the North Syrian coalition against Assyria at the battle of Qarqar in 853. Subsequently Arvad became a vassal of Assyria. Nebuchadnezzar captured Arvad and other coastal cities, taking their kings captive to Babylon. Arvad's continued prowess on the sea is echoed in Ezekiel's oracle against Tyre (Ezek. 27:8). The Persians granted autonomy to the Phoenician cities, but by 333 Arvad surrendered to Alexander the Great, who used her navy to besiege Tyre. By the mid-2nd century the city was once again important enough to receive a proclamation declaring the alliance between Rome and Simon Maccabee (1 Macc. 15:23).

GARY P. ARBINO

ARZA (Heb. *'arṣā'*)
A steward of the household of King Elah of Israel in whose home the king, while intoxicated, was murdered by Zimri (1 Kgs. 16:9).

ASA (Heb. *'āsā'*)

1. The grandson of Rehoboam and the third king to rule the southern kingdom of Judah after the division of the monarchy. According to 1 Kgs. 15:10 he ruled 41 years (ca. 913-873 B.C.E.). His (grand)mother Maacah served as queen mother, whose chief function was senior counselor to the king and others. Maacah took a leadership role in the Jerusalem cult, and when Asa reformed it he deposed Maacah for erecting an image for Asherah.

It was his efforts at reforming worship in Jerusalem that won Asa the praise of the author of 1 Kgs. 15. He removed the male prostitutes associated with fertility rites and destroyed the images that his predecessors had placed in Jerusalem. The images included Maacah's Asherah, which Asa cut down and burned at the Wadi Kidron. In addition, he offered to God votive gifts made of silver and gold and new utensils for worship.

According to 1 Kgs. 15:16 Asa and Baasha, king of Israel, fought a border war throughout their reigns. At one point during their war, Baasha "built Ramah" (1 Kgs. 15:17), which perhaps meant that he rebuilt or fortified Ramah of Benjamin (modern er-Ram), which lay 8 km. (5 mi.) N of Jerusalem on the road by which the Assyrians advanced against that city (Isa. 10:29). Asa offered Ben-hadad of Damascus a hefty "present" of silver and gold to break his alliance with Baasha and attack Israel. When Ben-hadad attacked the northern cities Ijon, Dan, Abel-beth-maacah, Chinneroth, and "all Naphtali," Baasha was forced to move north to Tirzah to stop Ben-hadad's advance. Asa seized the opportunity to order his people to go to Ramah and remove the building materials to use in fortifying Geba of Benjamin and Mizpah, thus establishing them as his northern border.

2 Chr. 14:1(MT 13:23)–16:14 expands this account of Asa's reign by means of a narrative (14:9-13[8-12]) of an invasion by Zerah the "Cushite" (Ethiopian) and speeches by Azariah son of Oded (15:2-7) and the seer Hanani (16:7-10). The invasion was reported as evidence that divine might would overcome military might. In the aftermath of the defeat of Zerah, Israel is said to have attacked the cities around Gerar and owners of livestock, which perhaps should be understood as further evidence of God's protection of Asa as reward for obedience. The speeches appear to have been composed by the Chronicler, the first to indicate divine approval of Asa's reforms, the second to indicate disapproval of Asa's reliance on human rather than divine protection. That motif carries over into 2 Chr. 16:12, where the Chronicler condemns Asa again for relying on physicians rather than God for healing from his fatal disease of the feet, the nature of which is obscure.

2. A Levite whose son Berechiah was among the first to receive back his family possessions after the Exile (1 Chr. 9:16).

Bibliography. N.-E. A. Andreasen, "The Role of the Queen Mother in Israelite Society," *CBQ* 45 (1983): 179-94.

PAUL L. REDDITT

ASAHEL (Heb. *'ăśâ'ēl*)

1. One of the sons of Zeruiah, David's sister. He and his brothers, Joab and Abishai, were among David's retainers from his period of exile from the court of Saul. Although Joab and Abishai served long tenures as commanders in David's army, Asahel was killed during the extended war between the house of David and the house of Saul (2 Sam. 2:18-32).

Despite his early death, Asahel is included in the list of David's *šālîšîm* (2 Sam. 23:24 = 1 Chr. 11:26), an elite corps of warriors who may have fought in squads of three. Asahel's inclusion here suggests that the list of these warriors goes back to the inception of David's monarchy. His presence here further implies that the list is cumulative over time, a fact that strengthens the likelihood that the reference here is to the *šālîšîm,* not to the *šělôšîm* (the "Thirty"). The presence of Asahel's name in the list of David's commanders of monthly levies of 24 thousand men each (1 Chr. 27:7) provides evidence that this list is a later, idealized construct.

2. One of a group of six Levites sent by King Jehoshaphat into the villages of Judah to teach the Book of the Law (2 Chr. 17:7-8).

3. A Levite who assisted in collecting tithes and devoted offerings in the temple during Hezekiah's centralization of the cultus (2 Chr. 31:11-13).

4. The father of Jonathan, one of the exiles at the time of Ezra. This Jonathan, along with Jahzeiah the son of Tikvah, stood against Ezra's efforts to have the exiles put away their foreign wives and children (Ezra 10:15).

5. A son of Ezora, who dismissed his foreign wife following Ezra's action (1 Esdr. 9:34).

DONALD G. SCHLEY

ASAIAH (Heb. *'ăśāyâ*)

1. The royal "servant" among those dignitaries sent to the prophetess Huldah to inquire of the Lord concerning the book of the law found in the temple (2 Kgs. 22:12-14 = 2 Chr. 34:20).

2. A leader of the tribe of Simeon who participated in the extermination of the Meunim (1 Chr. 4:36).

3. A head of a Merarite levitical family appointed by David to move the ark to Jerusalem (1 Chr. 6:30[MT 15]; 15:6, 11).

4. The firstborn of the Shilonites returning from the exile (1 Chr. 9:5). In a parallel list he is called Maaseiah the son of Baruch (Neh. 11:5).

ASAPH (Heb. *'āsāp̱*)

1. The father of Joah, state recorder or "herald" for King Hezekiah (2 Kgs. 18:18, 37 = Isa. 36:3, 22) and one of three officials who met with the Assyrians during the siege of Jerusalem.

2. Son of Berechiah the Levite; eponymous ancestor of one of the prominent guilds of singers and musicians. Asaph, together with Heman and Jeduthun, was put in charge of "the service of the song" by David (1 Chr. 6:39[MT 24]; cf. 25:1; 2 Chr. 5:12). He was appointed by David as "the chief" minister before the ark of the Lord in Jerusalem (1 Chr. 16:4-5; cf. 25:5, where Heman is preeminent), and is referred to once as "the seer" (Heb. *ḥōzeh;* 2 Chr. 29:30). The "sons of Asaph" are said to have "prophesied under the direction of the king" during David's reign (1 Chr. 25:1-2), and later descendants took prominence as a guild of temple singers in postexilic times (Ezra 2:41 [= Neh. 7:44; 1 Esdr. 5:27]; Neh. 11:22). The superscriptions of 12 psalms are annotated "of Asaph" (Pss. 50, 73-83), which likely indicates that they were composed in the style or tradition of Asaph. Suggestions that the psalms are of northern Israelite origins or belong to the "Ephraimite tradition" are appealing but speculative.

Bibliography. M. J. Buss, "The Psalms of Asaph and Korah," *JBL* 82 (1963): 382-92; H. P. Nasuti, *Tradition History and the Psalms of Asaph.* SBLDS 88 (Atlanta, 1988).

3. "The sons of Asaph," one of the divisions of gatekeepers in the second temple (1 Chr. 26:1). Heb. *'ebyāsāp̄* should be read as Abiasaph.

4. The keeper of King Artaxerxes' forest or park (Neh. 2:8). He was asked by the king to send timber for the rebuilding of the temple and city walls. TYLER F. WILLIAMS

ASAREL (Heb. *'ăśar'ēl*)

A son of Jehallelel of the tribe of Judah (1 Chr. 4:16).

ASCENSION

An ascent to heaven. Biblical and extrabiblical literature include many references to figures who went up to heaven. In the OT living figures ascend. Enoch is assumed to have ascended to heaven. He is described as one who "walked with God" and "was no more, because God took him" (Gen. 5:24). Elijah is explicitly described as ascending into heaven by means of a "chariot of fire and horses of fire" (2 Kgs. 2:11).

Extrabiblical Literature

Jewish literature describes descending and ascending angels and human figures who ascend and remain in heaven. The angel Raphael ascends to heaven in the presence of Tobit and his son Tobias (Tob. 12:20). Joseph and Aseneth describes an angel's ascent to heaven in a chariot in the presence of Aseneth (Jos. As. 17:7-8). 4 Ezra refers to men who have been taken up and have not tasted death (4 Ezra 4:26). Several versions of 4 Ezra add a concluding verse to ch. 14 describing how Ezra was caught up to the place of those like him. 2 Baruch suggests the future ascension of Baruch when it teaches that he will be preserved until the "end of times" (2 Bar. 13:3; 25:1). The Testament of Moses has been taken to teach that Moses ascended to heaven after his death, but the passage teaching this (T. Mos. 10:12) is questionable. The mystical texts of 1–3 Enoch build upon Gen. 5:24 by describing Enoch's heavenly ascent, experiences, and eventual glorification as the angel Metatron. Enoch's transformation into an angel may be based upon the teaching of Dan. 12:3 that the righteous will shine "like the stars," since stars are identified with angels (Job 38:7).

Several other Jewish texts feature human figures who ascend and return. Some texts leave it unclear whether the ascent is physical or revelatory (mystical). 3 Baruch describes Baruch's ascent under an angel's guidance and learning of heavenly secrets (3 Bar. 2-17). In the Testament of Levi Levi ascends to God's throne and learns mysteries that he is to declare to others. 4Q491 appears to preserve the claim of the Teacher of Righteousness (or one of his adoring followers) that he has ascended to a heavenly throne. Other Qumran materials imply ascension when they describe Qumran members communing with the angels (1QH 6:13; 3:20; 11:10; 2:10; 1QS 2:5-10). The Apocalypse of Abraham and Testament of Abraham describe how Abraham ascended to heaven under angelic guidance, learned heavenly secrets, and saw God's throne (Apoc. Abr. 18:1ff.). The Testament of Isaac describes Isaac's ascent and journey to God's throne. 3 Enoch describes Rabbi Ishmael's ascent to heaven, where he sees God's throne, is led on a tour by Metatron, and learns heavenly secrets.

These ascending and descending accounts may be based upon the Jewish tradition that Moses ascended to heaven when he received the Law (Orphica, a fragmentary version of 3 En. 15b). Philo adds the idea of Moses being deified when he entered God's presence (*Life of Moses* 2.290-91). The rabbinic story of the four rabbis who entered paradise (heaven?) preserved in *b. Ḥag.* 14b illustrates how Jews in Amoraic times continued their interest in heavenly ascents and were warned about taking mystical ascents into heaven. Mystical ascents to heaven and the required techniques were a major element of what came to be known as Merkabah ("Chariot") and Hekalot ("Thrones") mysticism.

One text refers to a heavenly ascension that appears to follow a resurrection. The Testament of Job presumes the resurrection of Job's children and teaches their heavenly ascension and glorification (T. Job 38:11–40:3); at the end of its account Job dies and his soul ascends to heaven in a chariot (52:10). The ascension of the soul after death in the Testament of Job is found elsewhere (T. Abr. 20:9-12; T. Isaac 7:1; Hist. Rech. 14:2-5).

Jesus

The ascension of Jesus is the most prominent ascension in the Bible and refers to the final departure of the risen Jesus from his followers. This event is described in Acts as an ascent to heaven following Jesus' resurrection from the dead (Acts 1:9-11). Luke contains a description of Jesus' ascension, but the reading is suspect (Luke 24:51). Luke does refer to Jesus' ascension as a geographical marker in his account of Jesus' ministry (Luke 9:51). Acts' description of Jesus' ascension on a cloud (Acts 1:9) alludes to Dan. 7:13, where the "one like a son of man" comes with the "clouds of heaven" before the "Ancient of Days." Mark and Matthew both preserve Jesus' prediction that he will return on the clouds of heaven (Mark 14:62 = Matt. 26:64). The inference is that the cloud of ascension will be the means of Jesus' return. Revelation continues this association of Jesus with clouds (Rev. 1:7) and describes "one like a son of man" (Jesus?) on a white cloud in heaven (14:14).

Acts further presents Jesus' ascension as an exaltation to the right hand of God (Acts 2:33), an allusion to Ps. 110:1 ("sit at my right hand"), and as an act of empowerment by which Jesus dispenses the Spirit and is recognized as "both Lord and Messiah" (Acts 2:33, 38). This portrayal is in keeping with the early Christian tradition that Jesus would be seated at God's right hand (Mark 14:62 par.). Acts 2:34-35 explicitly connects Jesus' ascension to a messianic interpretation of Ps. 110 which predicts the Messiah's enthronement over his enemies. Jesus' ascension and glorification in Acts is thus similar to the Enoch ascension traditions, Moses' enthronement in Ezekiel the Tragedian (2nd century B.C.E.), the enthronement claim of 4Q491, and Rabbi Akiba's belief in the enthronement of the Messiah (*b. Ḥag.* 14a).

Other NT writings either refer to Jesus' ascension as a future event or assume its occurrence. In John Jesus refers to his future ascension (John 3:13; 6:62; 20:17), and the ascension is alluded to on numerous occasions (7:33; 8:14, 21; 13:3; 14:2-3, 28; 16:5, 10, 28). John's references to ascension are used to teach Jesus' heavenly origin and his special relationship to God the Father. He is the one who descended from heaven and then ascended to heaven. This theme calls to mind Tobit and Joseph and Aseneth, where heavenly beings descend only to ascend (return) to their heavenly abode.

The Epistles and Revelation share Acts' view that Jesus' ascension resulted in enthronement at God's side and empowerment (Eph. 1:20-21; Rev. 1:12-20; 3:21; cf. 1 Pet. 3:22). Paul associates Jesus' ascension with the Passion events (Rom. 8:34; 1 Tim. 3:16 preserves what appears to be an early Christian hymn that alludes to Jesus' ascension in connection with other events from his life). The description in Phil. 2:9-10 of Jesus' exaltation by means of being given a name above every name and being paid homage alludes to his ascension-glorification (cf. 3 En. 10:1; 12:5; 14:1-5).

Hebrews refers to Jesus' ascension in the context of Jesus' role as a heavenly priest who ascended in order to enter the heavenly temple and make purification for human sin (Heb. 1:3; 4:14; 6:19-20; 9:11-12). In later Jewish tradition Metatron is not a priest offering sacrifice like Jesus, but he is appointed to liturgical service and is stationed in heaven in order to "serve the throne of glory day by day" (3 En. 7:1).

Other Ascensions in the NT

Both Paul and the John of Revelation are depicted as undertaking heavenly ascensions. Their ascensions have several parallels with 1st-century C.E. mystical Jewish texts such as the Apocalypse of Abraham and Testament of Abraham, which describe Abraham's heavenly ascent and return, and with 4Q491. In 2 Cor. 12:2-4 Paul describes his heavenly ascent where he learns heavenly secrets that he must not divulge. Rev. 4:1–16:21 depicts John's heavenly ascent, during which he sees God's throne and learns heavenly secrets (some of which he must not reveal). These accounts illustrate that early Christianity shared in the Jewish mystical interest in heavenly ascents.

In John 14:2-3 Jesus refers to his followers' heavenly ascension when he says that he will come again (descend) and take them to the heavenly dwelling places that he will prepare for them. Like Jesus, Metatron, the ascended and exalted Enoch, was in charge of the heavenly palace and its stores (3 En. 11:6). Paul also refers to the future ascension of Jesus' followers and connects it with the familiar cloud motif (1 Thess. 4:17). Paul's description of the believers' future transformation appears to be in connection with the ascension-glorification interest associated with Jesus and early Judaism (1 Cor. 15:51-57; Phil. 3:21). Revelation describes the future ascension of two martyred witnesses in a cloud (Rev. 11:12), calling to mind Acts' description of Jesus' ascension on a cloud (Acts 1:9).

Bibliography. M. G. Abegg Jr., "Who Ascended to Heaven? 4Q491, 4Q427, and the Teacher of Righteousness," in *Eschatology, Messianism, and the Dead Sea Scrolls,* ed. C. A. Evans and P. W. Flint (Grand Rapids, 1997), 61-73; M. Dean-Otting, *Heavenly Journeys: A Study of the Motif in Hellenistic Jewish Literature.* Judentum und Umwelt (Frankfurt, 1984); J. E. Fossum, *The Image of the Invisible God: Essays on the Influence of Jewish Mysticism on Early Christology.* NTOA 30 (Göttingen, 1995); M. Himmelfarb, *Ascent to Heaven in Jewish and Christian Apocalypses* (Oxford, 1993); C. R. A. Morray-Jones, "Paradise Revisited (2 Cor 12:1-12): The Jewish Mystical Background of Paul's Apostolate, Part 1: The Jewish Sources," *HTR* 86 (1993): 177-217; "Part 2: Paul's Heavenly Ascent and Its Significance," *HTR* 86 (1993): 265-92; A. F. Segal, "The Risen Christ and the Angelic Mediator Figures in Light of Qumran," in *Jesus and the Dead Sea Scrolls,* ed. J. H. Charlesworth (New York, 1992), 302-28; J. D. Tabor, *Things Unutterable: Paul's Ascent to Paradise in Its Greco-Roman, Judaic, and Early Christian Contexts* (Lanham, 1986).

PHILLIP MUNOA

ASCENT

A rising grade, including that of a road or stairway (e.g., 2 Chr. 32:33; Neh. 3:19; 12:37). Heb. *maʿălеh* often refers to a mountain pass (so NIV) because it was believed to constitute entrance to a mountain range. Important ascents include those of Akrabbim ("Scorpion Pass"; Num. 34:4; Josh. 15:3; Judg. 1:36) and Adummim (Josh. 15:7; 18:17).

At 2 Sam. 15:30 the ascent of the Mount of Olives simply means the western slope of the mountain, which David and his entourage climbed as they went east from Jerusalem. Conversely, it was on the "descent" of the same mountain that Jesus was coming down toward the city (Luke 19:37).

ASCENTS, SONGS OF
A collection of 15 psalms (Pss. 120-134) of various types united by the Hebrew superscript *šîr hamma'ălôṯ*, "the song of the ascents" (*šîr lamma'ălôṯ* in Ps. 121). Four interpretations of the superscript have been suggested. (1) Origen and Augustine understood it as referring mystically to the ascent of the soul to God. (2) Theodoret considered it as an identification of the historical songs sung by returning exiles (cf. Ezra 2:1; 7:9). (3) Some early modern scholars suggested that the title refers to the formal steplike climactic parallelism of the psalms themselves. (4) Most have argued that the songs were cultic and sung in conjunction with approaching the temple (cf. *b. Mid.* 2.5; *b. Sukk.* 51b).

Recent studies, focusing less on the superscript and more on the character of the songs themselves, have concluded either that these songs were votive offerings brought to the temple by pilgrims, and subsequently incorporated into a song- or prayerbook by cultic officials, or that they represent a "pilgrim psalter" created to encourage northern Israelites during the Persian period to make pilgrimage to the Jerusalem temple.

Bibliography. L. D. Crow, *The Songs of Ascents (Psalms 120–134)*. SBLDS 148 (Atlanta, 1996).

TYLER F. WILLIAMS

ASCETICISM
Initially referring to physical exercise, training, or practice, asceticism (from Gk. *áskēsis*) assumed religious significance in the Hellenistic period, indicating activities of the mind, soul, and will. As a religious term, ascetic purity was often viewed as a condition for approaching the gods, for fulfilling a divine commission, or for surviving a historical crisis. Although the Hebrew religion embraced the world, it also denied it at important moments. Fasting for discrete periods was practiced at the Feast of Purim (Esth. 9:31), on the Day of Atonement (Lev. 16:29-31; 23:26-32), and during periods of penance (1 Sam. 7:6) or mourning (2 Sam. 1:12; 3:35; Dan. 9:3; 10:3). Participation in the sacrificial cult (Lev. 10:9) and the assumption of the Nazarite vow (Num. 6:2) both required at least temporary abstinence from wine and sex. Rechabites vowed to have no part in the planting or cultivation of vineyards or the production and consumption of wine (Jer. 35:7). Sexual intercourse was also forbidden in preparation for divine revelation (Exod. 19:15), for fighting a holy war (2 Sam. 11:13), and for priestly service at the altar.

These ascetic acts of self-denial served a multitude of functions. Sexual abstinence practiced in the priestly Qumran community was thought to place one in the company of angels, and offered a means for reentering a lost primordial world. Abstention from sexual commitments, Paul believed, prepared one to remain faithful in the eschatological crisis (1 Cor. 7:32-35). Luke suggests that sexual asceticism ritualized a realized eschatology that bestowed angelic status on believers (Luke 20:34-36), a viewpoint shared by Corinthian enthusiasts (1 Cor. 7). This piety enabled one to transcend the physical limits so uncompromisingly set for all humanity by focusing on the eschaton. This asceticism, however, unlike that of the Cynic philosophers, had strong traditional ties to the normative Jewish and early Christian culture. Where the Cynics saw asceticism as an attempt to break free of the shackles of the normative culture, Jewish and Christian asceticism offered a means of intensifying devotion, of engaging in acts of self-denial to offer oneself unreservedly to God's tasks, and of participating in the sacred story of Israel.

CALVIN J. ROETZEL

ASENATH (Heb. *'āsĕnaṯ*) (also ASENETH)
The Egyptian daughter of Potiphera, priest of On (Heliopolis). Given to Joseph as a wife by Pharaoh as part of his reward for interpreting Pharaoh's dream (Gen. 41:45), Asenath was also the mother of Manasseh and Ephraim (Gen. 41:50-52; 46:20). The name, which means "she belongs to Neith (an Egyptian goddess)," was common during the Middle Kingdom and First Intermediate period. An apocryphal Jewish story, written in Greek around the turn of the Common Era, Joseph and Aseneth explains how the patriarch Joseph could marry the daughter of an Egyptian priest. In the story, Asenath converts to the religion of Israel before she marries Joseph and becomes the prototype for all future proselytes of Judaism.

NANCY L. DECLAISSÉ-WALFORD

ASHAN (Heb. *'āšān*)
A town in the Shephelah initially allocated to Judah (Josh. 15:42), but because the area was too large for them to conquer subsequently reassigned to Simeon (19:7-9). It was eventually given to Aaron's sons as a city of refuge (1 Chr. 6:57, 59[MT 42, 44]). Some read "Ashan" for "Ain" at Josh. 21:16, a similar list of levitical cities, but the relationship between the two names is unclear in other comparable city lists. Bor-ashan ("well of Ashan") in 1 Sam. 30:30 may be the same site. Ashan has been associated with Khirbet 'Asan, ca. 8 km. (5 mi.) NW of Beer-sheba.

LAURA B. MAZOW

ASHARELAH (Heb. *'ăśar'ēlâ*) (also JESHARELAH)
One of the sons of Asaph who with others prophesied with lyres, harps, and cymbals (1 Chr. 25:1-2; called Jesharelah in v. 14).

ASHBEL (Heb. *'ašbēl*) (also JEDIAEL)
Either the second (1 Chr. 8:1) or the third (Gen. 46:21) son of Benjamin. At 1 Chr. 7:6 the name is rendered Jediael (Heb. "known to God"), perhaps to avoid alleged pagan connotations in the name Ashbel (cf. Ishbaal, "man of Baal").

ASHDOD (Heb. *'ašdôḏ*)
One of the five principal Philistine cities. The an-

cient city is identified with modern Ashdod/Esdûd (118129), 15 km. (9 mi.) N of Ashkelon and ca. 4 km. (2.5 mi.) inland from the Mediterranean Sea.

Ashdod was part of the tribal territory of Judah (Josh. 15:46-47), although it remained in Philistine control. The city is listed as one of the few cities where the Anakim were settled during the Israelite settlement (Josh. 11:22). The Ark narrative records that the Philistines placed the ark of God in the temple of Dagon at Ashdod, where they received tumors from God (1 Sam. 5:5-6). Ashdod is not mentioned again until King Uzziah of Judah conquered the city and built cities in the "territory of Ashdod" (2 Chr. 26:6). In 713 B.C. Azuri the king of Ashdod revolted against Assyria, and Sargon II conquered the city, placing Ahimetu on the throne. From this point on the city became a vassal of Assyria. According to Herodotus, during the Assyrian king Ashurbanipal's reign Ashdod withstood an Egyptian siege for 29 years before it was conquered by Psamtik I. After Nebuchadnezar's conquest of the region, Ashdod and its territory became a Babylonian province. During this period Ashdod is mentioned several times in the oracles of the prophets (Jer. 25:20; Amos 1:8; 3:9; Zeph. 2:4; Zech. 9:6).

Ashdod (Gk. *Ázōtos*) is mentioned in various sources from the Persian to the Roman periods (Jdt 2:28; 10:77-78; 3:34; 16:10; Josephus *Ant.* 5:87; 5:128; 13:395; *BJ* 1.156, 165-66; 4.130). Judas Maccabeus captured it (1 Macc. 5:68), and his successor, Jonathan, burned it (10:84; 16:10). Philip the Evangelist passed through the city en route to Caesarea after his encounter with the Ethiopian eunuch (Acts 8:40).

Extensive excavations of the ancient site by Moshe Dothan between 1962 and 1970 have revealed a fairly complete picture of the site. The tell consists of an acropolis of ca. 8 ha. (20 a.) with a lower city of at least 40 ha. (100 a.). Tell Ashdod has been continually occupied from the Middle Bronze Age to the Byzantine period. Excavations have exposed 23 strata. A large fortification system consisting of a rampart and gate complex was built during the 17th century (MB III). During the Late Bronze Age (1500-1200) the city continued to prosper under Egyptian dominance, evidenced by the excavation of an Egyptian stronghold palace with various Egyptian artifacts and imported vessels from the Aegean. This city was destroyed and settled by the Philistines, who built a potter's workshop and new residential quarters. It continued to grow and expand in Iron Age I (1200-1000) until it was destroyed at the beginning of the 10th century. It was rebuilt and expanded in the lower city, probably as immigrants from the inner-coastal Philistine cities moved due to the strong Israelite state under David and Solomon. Subsequent occupation and destruction phases are most likely due to campaigns by Uzziah, Assyria, and Egypt. The site was continuously occupied on a much smaller scale from the Persian to the Byzantine periods, with the most notable building activity during the time of Herod. STEVEN M. ORTIZ

ASHER (Heb. *'āšēr*)

1. A god, the male counterpart of Asherah, or a variant of Ashar, a divine name element that occurs in Old Akkadian and Amorite names.

2. The eighth son of Jacob by Zilpah, the handmaiden of Jacob's wife Leah, and the eponymous ancestor of one of the 12 tribes (Gen. 30:12-13). When Leah believed herself past childbearing age, she gave Zilpah to her husband Jacob as a concubine. Asher was the second son born to Zilpah in Paddan-aram, where Jacob was working as a herdsman for Laban, his father-in-law. Asher is always mentioned after his full brother Gad in the lists of Jacob's descendants (Gen. 35:26; 46:17; Exod. 1:4; 1 Chr. 2:2).

3. A fertile tribal territory located in the western Galilee highland, with the tribes of Naphtali to its east and Zebulun to its southeast (Gen. 49:20; Deut. 33:24; Josh. 19:24-31). Because the western portion of Asher adjoined the Phoenician coast, it maintained close contact with the coastal state of Tyre. During the Conquest, the tribe failed to drive out the Canaanites and instead lived peacefully among them (Judg. 1:31). Asher was criticized in the Song of Deborah for not participating in the battle against Jabin, the Canaanite king of Hazor (Judg. 5:17). Asher later responded to Gideon's call to fight the Midianites in the Plain of Jezreel (Judg. 6:35; 7:23). The tribe is recorded as supporting the kingship of Ishbaal (Ish-bosheth) following Saul's death (2 Sam. 2:9; read "Asherites").

Asher became one of Solomon's 12 administrative districts (1 Kgs. 4:16). The northern portion of Asher, the "land of Cabul," was later relinquished by Solomon to Hiram of Tyre as payment for timber and gold used in the construction of the Jerusalem temple (1 Kgs. 9:10-14). Inhabitants of Asher are listed as responding to Hezekiah's invitation to celebrate Passover in Jerusalem (2 Chr. 30:11).

The NT lists Anna as a member of the tribe of Asher (Luke 2:36). In Rev. 7:6 Asher is among those tribes who are sealed.

Bibliography. Y. Aharoni, *The Land of the Bible*, 2nd ed. (Philadelphia, 1979), 257-58; N. Na'aman, *Borders and Districts in Biblical Historiography* (Jerusalem, 1986), 40-62. KENNETH ATKINSON

ASHERAH (Heb. *'ăšērâ*)

The Hebrew name of an Amorite or Canaanite goddess and the cult object dedicated to her. A complete distinction between the deity and the sacred poles erected in her honor is not always possible in the OT (cf. Judg. 3:7).

Asherah may have been the same as Ašratum, the consort of Amurru, one of the chief deities mentioned in an early Babylonian list of gods; in the Amarna Letters her name appears in the personal name Abdi-aširta ("Servant of Asherah"). The Ras Shamra texts portray her (Ugar. *'aṯrt*) as the spouse of the supreme god El (sometimes called Elat, "goddess") and the mother of 70 children, including Baal (perhaps also a consort); she is also called "Lady Asherah of the sea." In the Baal cycle she intercedes with El to provide a palace for

Baal. Asherah was the mother goddess, to be distinguished from Astarte, the Canaanite fertility goddess. Centers of worship were located throughout the ancient Near East, particularly Phoenicia. Manifestations of Asherah worship have been identified in Egyptian, Hittite, Philistine, and Arabic texts.

Heb. *'ăšērâ* refers not only to the goddess but also to the consecrated poles, called either Asherah (e.g., Deut. 16:21; Judg. 6:25, 28) or Asherim (e.g., Exod. 34:13; Deut. 7:5; 12:3), which represented the deity. At first they may have been living trees (cf. Deut. 16:21; possibly a sacred grove), but in later usage were wooden poles, perhaps stylized to represent a tree (cf. 2 Kgs. 17:10). These poles may also have been carved images of the goddess. Remains of what are believed to be such poles, including those discovered among Bronze Age finds at Shechem, consist mainly of postholes in which the rotted timber has left a differently colored soil.

In ancient Israel worship of Asherah is attested at local shrines during the period of the judges (Judg. 3:7-8). Both Jeroboam I of Israel (1 Kgs. 14:15) and Rehoboam of Judah (v. 23), sons and successors of Solomon, fostered Asherah worship in their respective kingdoms. When King Ahab married the Phoenician princess Jezebel, worship of Asherah was strongly promoted in the northern kingdom, together with the worship of Baal. The prophet Elijah counted some 400 of her prophets (and 450 of Baal) eating at Jezebel's table (no doubt supported by the queen; 1 Kgs. 18:19). Israel's devotion to Asherah is cited as a cause for its deportation to Assyria (2 Kgs. 17:10, 16).

Allegiance to the Asherah cult was proscribed (Exod. 34:13-14; Deut. 7:5), and various attempts were made to eradicate the practice (e.g., Gideon, Judg. 6:25-30). Maacah the queen mother had placed an "image" of Asherah in Judah which her grandson Asa destroyed in the Wadi Kidron (1 Kgs. 15:13; cf. 2 Chr. 15:16). King Josiah of Judah burned the "vessels" and the woven "hangings" of Asherah (2 Kgs. 23:4, 7; 2 Chr. 34:3, 7) which his predecessor Manasseh had erected in the temple at Jerusalem (2 Kgs. 21:7; cf. 2 Chr. 33:3, 19); earlier reforms were carried out by Jehoshaphat (2 Chr. 19:3) and Hezekiah (2 Kgs. 18:4). Prophetic judgments include references to continued devotion to the "sacred poles" (Isa. 27:9; Jer. 17:1ff.; Mic. 5:14).

Inscriptions found at Kuntillet ʿAjrud and Khirbet el-Qom mention "Yahweh and his *'ăšērâ*." Many scholars interpret this as indication of the goddess Asherah as consort of Yahweh (on the order of Baal and Asherah), but the term probably indicates the cult symbol or, less likely, a cella or chapel.

Bibliography. T. Binger, *Asherah: Goddesses in Ugarit, Israel and the Old Testament.* JSOTSup 212 (Sheffield, 1994); J. Day, "Asherah in the Hebrew Bible and Northwest Semitic Literature," *JBL* 105 (1986): 385-408; B. Margalit, "The Meaning and Significance of Asherah," *VT* 40 (1990): 264-97; Z. Meshel, "Did Yahweh Have a Consort?" *BARev* 5 (1979): 24-35; S. A. Wiggins, *A Reassessment of 'Asherah.'* AOAT 235 (Neukirchen-Vluyn, 1993); N. Wyatt, "Asherah," *DDD*, 99-105.

ALLEN C. MYERS

ASHES

A means to denote humiliation, sorrow, worthlessness, or purification. As a symbol of humility, ashes often were coupled with other items. When Abraham approached Yahweh, he referred to himself as dust and ashes (Gen. 18:27). Similarly, Daniel fasted and dressed himself in sackcloth and ashes (Dan. 9:3; cf. Matt. 11:21). In the apocryphal Additions to Esther (14:2), Esther put ashes and dung on her head as a sign of humility. Ashes commonly were used to express grief. Jeremiah encouraged the nation to mourn over the coming destruction by rolling in ashes (Jer. 6:26; cf. Job 2:8). Comparing something to ashes suggested the worthlessness of the object (Job 13:12) or its destruction (Ezek. 28:18; Job 30:19). However, the ashes that were produced by burning a red heifer were used to bring about purification (Num. 19:9-10; cf. Heb. 9:13).

SCOTT M. LANGSTON

ASHHUR (Heb. *'ašḥûr*)

The son of Hezron and Abijah, born following Hezron's death (so NRSV, following MT). According to the RSV (following MT) he was the son of Caleb and Ephrathah the wife of Hezron. Ashhur became the "father" or founder of Tekoa (1 Chr. 2:24).

ASHIMA (Heb. *'ăšîmā'*)

A deity brought by Aramean settlers from Hamath to Samaria (2 Kgs. 17:30). He is mentioned in an inscription from Teima. A relationship with Phoenician Ešmun and Elephantine Ešem-bethel or with Heb. *'āšām* ("guilt") is improbable, though Amos 8:14 may contain a pun on this name (*'ašmaṯ šomĕrôn*, "the shame of Samaria"). A connection with the ancient Semitic cattle-god *Iṯm* (identified at Ugarit with Mesopotamian Sumuqan) is possible.

MEINDERT DIJKSTRA

ASHKELON (Heb. *'ašqĕlôn*)

A large seaport of ancient Palestine, one of the cities of Philistia. The name, possibly related to Heb. *šql*, "to weigh," could refer to the city's economic role ("Place of Weights"?).

Located on the southern coast of Israel, Ashkelon (107119) occupied a strategic position along the coastal highway, the Via Maris ("Way of the Sea"). A national park outside modern Ashkelon, 16 km. (10 mi.) N of Gaza, 64 km. (40 mi.) S of Tel Aviv, marks the site of the ancient city. Populated successively from at least ca. 3000 B.C.E. until 1270 C.E. by Canaanites, Philistines, Phoenicians, Jews, Greeks, Romans, Byzantine Christians, Muslims, and Crusaders, Ashkelon witnessed and participated in the parade of oriental and occidental history.

In the Bible Ashkelon is listed as one of the five major Philistine cities, the Philistine Pentapolis (Josh. 13:3; 1 Sam. 6:17). According to Judg. 1:18 Judah took but could not hold Ashkelon. At Ashkelon Samson killed and stripped the corpses of 30 men in order to make good on a wager (Judg. 14:12, 19). In his elegy for Absalom and Saul David refers to

Ashkelon (2 Sam. 1:20). The majority of biblical references to Ashkelon are in prophetic oracles against Philistia (e.g., Jer. 25:20).

The Philistine era in Ashkelon began in the early 12th century. Nearly 600 years later, in 604, it ended when the Babylonian king Nebuchadnezzar conquered the city and took its elite into exile (Jer. 47:5); 20 years later a similar fate befell Jerusalem.

For centuries pilgrims, adventurers, and archaeologists have visited, plundered, and studied Ashkelon, where Roman columns and Fatimid ramparts still stand. Among the finds of the current excavation, led by Lawrence E. Stager, is a small silver-plated statue of a bull calf, dating from the 16th century. This physical evidence for the use of bovine iconography in Canaanite religion sheds light on the background of a number of biblical passages which mention the cultic use of bull or calf images (Exod. 32; 1 Kgs. 12:28; Hos. 8:5).

Throughout its history, Ashkelon's status as the major port of the southern Palestinian coast lent the city a cosmopolitan and diverse character. Ashkelon was famous in antiquity for its sweet onions; the word "scallion" comes from the Latin name of the city.

Bibliography. L. E. Stager, "Ashkelon," *NEAEHL* 1:103-12; *Ashkelon Discovered: From Canaanites and Philistines to Romans and Moslems* (Washington, 1991).

GREGORY MOBLEY

ASHKENAZ (Heb. *'aškĕnaz*)
The eldest of the three sons of Gomer, the son of Japheth (Gen. 10:3; 1 Chr. 1:6), and the name of a kingdom (Jer. 51:27). Most likely it was the Scythian kingdom (cf. Assyr. *Iš-ku-za*). Its connection to the Cimmerian invasions (Herodotus *Hist.* 4.11) accounts for its relation to Gomer.

Allying themselves with the Mannai, the Scythians revolted against Assyria (7th century B.C.E.) but were afterward conquered by the Medes and the Persians. In 538 they provided contingents of troops for the Persian attack against Babylon.

ASHNAH (Heb. *'ašnâ*)

1. A city in the Shephelah (lowlands) of Judah, mentioned in connection with Eshtaol and Zorah (Josh. 15:33). The modern village of Aslin, E of Azekah, and Khirbet Wadi Allin, SE of Beth-shemesh, are possible locations.

2. A city in the Shephelah of Judah, further south than **1** above (Josh. 15:43). The site may be modern Idna (148107), 10 km. (6 mi.) E of Lachish.

ASHPENAZ (Heb. *'ašpĕnaz*)
The chief of Nebuchadnezzar's eunuchs, charged with recruiting Jewish nobility among the captives for the king's service (Dan. 1:3-4).

ASHTAROTH (Heb. *'aštārôṯ*) **(DEITY)**
Plural form of the name of the Canaanite goddess Ashtart (NRSV "Astarte"). It appears in the OT in the phrase "the Baalim and the Ashtaroth" (Judg. 10:6; 1 Sam. 7:4; 12:10), where it denotes either various local manifestations of Ashtart or, more likely, goddesses in general. The latter sense is implied in 1 Sam. 7:3, where "the Ashtaroth" is added as the feminine equivalent of "foreign (male) gods" (Heb. *'ĕlōhê hannēḵār*). Ashtaroth can be understood as a singular divine name in two instances: Judg. 2:13, where it parallels sing. Baal, and 1 Sam. 31:10, which refers to "the temple of Ashtart," "a temple of goddesses," or "a temple of a goddess."

See ASHTORETH. JOEL BURNETT

ASHTAROTH (Heb. *'aštārôṯ*) **(PLACE)**
A city in Bashan, a dwelling place (along with Edrei) of the Amorite king Og, who attempted to impede the progress of the Israelites on their way to Canaan (Deut. 1:4; Josh. 12:4). After Og's defeat, the town was allotted to the half-tribe of Manasseh (Josh. 13:31) and became a levitical city of the Gershomites (1 Chr. 6:71[MT 56]).

The name (the plural form of the Canaanite fertility goddess Ashtoreth) is mentioned in variant forms in several ancient inscriptions including the Egyptian Execration Texts (19th century B.C.), records of Thutmose III (1504-1450), Amarna Letters, Ugaritic texts, and a relief of Tiglath-pileser III (745-727).

The place is probably to be identified with Tell 'Ashtarah (243244), ca. 5 km. (3 mi.) S of Sheikh Sa'd, usually identified with Ashteroth-karnaim (Gen. 14:5), and ca. 32 km. (20 mi.) E of the Sea of Galilee. The site has occupational evidence from the Early Bronze Age through Iron I.

PAUL J. RAY, JR.

ASHTERATHITE (Heb. *hā'aštĕrāṯî*)
A native of Ashtaroth, a gentilic applied to Uzzia, one of David's "mighty men" (1 Chr. 11:44).

ASHTEROTH-KARNAIM
(Heb. *'aštĕrôṯ qarnayim*)
The place where Chedorlaomer and his allies defeated the Rephaim (Gen. 14:5).

Because of the similarity of the names and because Og, king of Bashan, was among the last of the Rephaim (Deut. 3:11; Josh. 12:4; 13:12), Ashteroth-karnaim may be the same as Ashtaroth in Bashan (Deut. 1:4; Josh. 9:10; 13:31; modern Tell 'Aštarah in southern Syria; 243244). More likely, however, the asyndetic combination Ashteroth-karnaim ("the two-horned [goddess] Astarte"; cf. Deut. 1:4 MT) indicates that the site was located near Karnaim (1 Macc. 5:26; Amos 6:13), modern Tell Sheikh Ṣa'd/Tel Ṣa'd (247249). BRENT A. STRAWN

ASHTORETH (Heb. *'aštōreṯ*;
Phoen. *'štrt;* Ugar. *'ṯtrt*)
A form of the name of the Canaanite goddess Ashtart in the OT (NRSV "Astarte"). It is a deliberate parody of the name, employing the vowels of Heb. *bōšeṯ*, "shame." Ashtart is the West Semitic counterpart to Akkadian Ishtar and Sumerian Inanna in her aspect as a goddess of war and (probably) of sexuality. That Canaanite Ashtart was, like Ishtar and Inanna, a Venus deity, as the Greek tradition reflects, is likely; as the evening star she would

have shared that role with the god Ashtar, who appears as the morning star and from whose name the feminine form Ashtart is derived.

Though playing a subdued role in Ugaritic myth, Ashtart's bellicose character is reflected in a formulaic curse which summons her to smash an enemy's skull (*KTU* 1.2 I 7-8; 1.16 VI 54-57). While discussion of Ashtart's identity as a love-goddess has sometimes overstepped the evidence, in the Keret Epic she (along with Anath) is mentioned as a standard for feminine beauty (*KTU* 1.14 III 41-44). Ashtart's special relationship to Baal, perhaps as consort, is reflected in her epithet used in the above-mentioned curse formula (and in the Phoenician inscription of Eshmunazar), "name-of-Baal" (*šm bʿl*, alternatively understood as "heavens-of-Baal"), an epithet which denotes her role as the hypostatized presence of Baal (cf. "the name" of Yahweh in the OT; e.g., Exod. 20:24; Deut. 12:5; 2 Sam. 7:13).

The connection between Ashtart and Baal is reflected in texts from Egypt, where worship of the Semitic goddess was widespread. In the 12th-century B.C.E. text Horus and Seth, Ashtart and Anath, who are closely associated in Egypt as they are at Ugarit, are given as wives to Seth, the Egyptian god identified with Baal. A 13th-century magical text describing how Seth "opened the wombs" of Anath and Ashtart, "the two great goddesses who were pregnant but did not bear," may be understood as evidence for Ashtart as a goddess of sexual love but militates against a fertility aspect; the extent to which this theme in the Egyptian text preserves an element of myth original to Semitic Ashtart is uncertain. The same can be said of the fragmentary Astarte papyrus (*ANET,* 17-18), in which the goddess, as the daughter of Ptah, is given as a bride to the Sea. In Egypt Ashtart is decisively portrayed as a war-goddess, often depicted in art as riding horseback and brandishing weapons.

In Phoenician sources Ashtart is the patron goddess of both Tyre and Sidon and consort to Baal in each city. In the 6th-century inscription of Tabnit of Sidon (*KAI* 13), the king identifies himself and his father before him as "priest of Ashtart" and invokes her name in a curse. Tabnit's son Eshmunazar calls his mother "priestess of Ashtart" and claims to have constructed temples for the god Eshmun, for Baal-of-Sidon, and for Ashtart-name-of-Baal (*KAI* 14). Eshmunazar locates the temple of Ashtart in a sacral area of Sidon called "The Highest Heaven" (1.17).

Exported by the Phoenicians, the worship of Ashtart thrived throughout the Mediterranean, as indicated by the goddess' name in numerous personal names and in inscriptions from Carthage, Spain (both 8th century), and Italy (6th century, where she is equated with Etruscan Uni-Juno). By the mid-1st millennium Ashtart had assumed the goddess Asherah's role as maritime deity and had absorbed aspects of Anath, with whom she was later combined as the goddess Atargatis. During the Hellenistic and Roman periods Ashtart is identified with Aphrodite and Venus. In Greece Phoenician Astarte is known as a goddess of love and fertility.

According to 1 Kgs. 11:5, 33 worship of "Ashtoreth deity of the Sidonians" was given official sanction in Israel due to one or more of Solomon's foreign wives. Josiah is lauded for dismantling and "defiling" the cult places of Astarte and other foreign deities (2 Kgs. 23:13-14). The Philistines' placement of Saul's armor in a temple called *bêṯ ʿaštārôṯ* in 1 Sam. 31:10 possibly implies the deity's martial character. However, as *ʿaštārôṯ* here is not necessarily the name of a specific goddess, it is not certain with which deity the temple, located either in the Philistine plain or in Beth-shan, is to be associated (cf. 1 Chr. 10:10). It is unknown whether Ashtart played a central role in the religion of the Philistines, whose chief god was Dagon. The identity of "the queen of heaven" in Jer. 7:18; 44:17-25 is debated. Though New Kingdom Egyptian sources refer to Ashtart as "Lady of Heaven," this epithet was also applied to Anath and Asherah. However, evidence from 1st-millennium Phoenician and Punic personal names and the fact that the temple of Ashtart of Sidon was located in an area called "the Highest Heaven" (inscription of Eshmunazar) weigh in favor of Ashtart being the goddess in question. The fertility aspect of Ashtart is reflected indirectly in a term related to the productivity of the flock (Heb. *ʿaštěrōṯ ṣō'neāk;* Deut. 7:13; 28:4, 18, 51). Vestiges of pre-settlement period worship of Ashtart are preserved in the toponyms Ashtaroth (Josh. 12:4; 1 Chr. 6:71[MT 56]), Ashteroth-karnaim (Gen. 14:5), and Beeshterah (Josh. 21:27).

See ASHTAROTH.

Bibliography. F. M. Cross, *Canaanite Myth and Hebrew Epic* (Cambridge, Mass., 1973); S. M. Olyan, "Some Observations Concerning the Identity of the Queen of Heaven," *UF* 19 (1987): 161-74; J. B. Pritchard, *Palestinian Figurines in Relation to Certain Goddesses Known Through Literature.* AOS 24 (Philadelphia, 1943).

JOEL BURNETT

ASHUR

See ASSUR.

ASHURITES (Heb. *hā'ăšûrî*)

A people located between Gilead and Jezreel, ruled briefly by Ishbaal/Ishbosheth the son of Saul (2 Sam. 2:9). They are probably Asherites (rather than "Assyrians"), since "Asher" is the collective name for the tribes of Asher, Zebulun, and Naphtali.

ASHVATH (Heb. *ʿašwāṯ*)

One of the sons of Japhlet, a descendant of Asher (1 Chr. 7:33).

ASH WEDNESDAY

The first day of Lent, 40 weekdays (six and a half weeks, not counting Sundays) before Easter. The name comes from the imposition of ashes on the heads of worshippers, symbolizing penitence and mourning.

ASIA (Gk. *Asía*)
Designation of both the continent and the Roman province of Asia. The ancient Greeks used the term for lands bordering the eastern part of the Mediterranean Sea. The region extended in the north to the Tanais River and the Sea of Azov above the Black Sea, in the west to the Aegean Sea, in the south to parts of Africa, and in the east to the Indian Ocean. The Greeks considered Asia Minor to be a peninsula of Asia jutting out into the Mediterranean. With the death in 133 B.C.E. of Attalus III, the last king of Pergamum, much of Asia Minor was bequeathed to the Romans, who made it into a province in 129. The province suffered under unscrupulous and greedy leaders and finally joined with Mithridates VI, the king of Pontus, in revolt against Rome (88-84), which ended in their defeat by Sulla and the reorganization of the province.

In the NT, the province of Asia is mentioned mainly as a region of Paul's missionary activity (Acts 13:1–16:10; 19:1-41). Paul wrote letters to Colossae and Ephesus (the capital city where he ministered for two years, Acts 19:10). Believers in Asia are mentioned in the letters (1 Cor. 16:19; 2 Cor. 1:8; 2 Tim. 1:15; 1 Pet. 1:1). The most notable mention of Asia in the NT is John's letters to the seven churches of Asia (Ephesus, Smyrna, Pergamum, Thyatira, Sardis, Philadelphia, and Laodicea, listed in the order one would come to them during a visit), which symbolically represent all the churches in Asia Minor (Rev. 1:4–3:22).

RICHARD A. SPENCER

ASIA MINOR
A term used to describe the Anatolian peninsula bounded by the Black Sea on the north, the Aegean Sea on the west, and the Mediterranean Sea on the south. This region of ca. 518,000 sq. km. (200,000 sq. mi.) — three quarters the size of Texas — today constitutes the western two thirds of Asiatic Turkey. The central part of the peninsula consists of a high arid plateau (ca. 1219 m. [4000 ft.] above sea level) surrounded by mountains, most notably the Pontic range in the north and the Taurus Mountains along the Mediterranean coast.

During the OT period, Asia Minor's strategic location as a land bridge between Mesopotamia and Europe created the circumstances that allowed the Hittite culture to flourish. However, this geographic position also made it the battlefield between colliding cultures as seen in the Trojan War, the Persian War, and the conflicts between Alexander's successors.

Asia Minor's major biblical significance, however, lies in its important role in the spread of Christianity in the NT. The Apostle Paul was born in Tarsus in southeastern Asia Minor, and much of his evangelistic work was focused on the peninsula. On Paul's third missionary journey he invested three years in Ephesus, making it the hub of his entire mission. Timothy also worked with the Ephesian church (1 Tim. 1:3) between Paul's Roman imprisonments, and John may have lived there after the destruction of Jerusalem. Asia Minor continued to be a dominant arena for Christian labor after the apostolic period, as is evident by the four ecumenical councils held at Nicea (I and II), Ephesus, and Chalcedon.

Bibliography. E. Akurgal, *Ancient Civilizations and Ruins of Turkey,* 8th ed. (Istanbul, 1993); E. C. Blake and A. G. Edmonds, *Biblical Sites in Turkey,* 4th ed. (Istanbul, 1990).

JESSE CURTIS POPE

ASIARCH (Gk. *asiárchēs*)
Title of deputies of the assembly of Asia (Gk. *koinón Asías*), which met regularly in Ephesus, the capital of the Roman province of Asia Minor. Holding the office for a fixed term, the Asiarchs were often from leading families of major cities. They frequently were benefactors of the city's public celebrations and participated in civic and provincial government and the cult of the emperors. Asiarchs may have held temple titles, acting as leaders in local deity worship. Some of the Asiarchs are described as friends of Paul, who seek to protect him from a rioting crowd (Acts 19:31).

JOSEPH CORAY

ASIEL (Heb. *ʿăśîʾēl;* Gk. *Asiḗl*)
1. The father of Seraiah and great-grandfather of Jehu. He was one of the Simeonite chiefs who sought land in Gedor (1 Chr. 4:35).

2. An ancestor of Tobit, of the tribe of Naphtali (Tob. 1:1).

3. A scribe who copied the books dictated by Ezra (2 Esdr. 14:24).

ASMODEUS (Gk. *Asmodaíos*)
A demon in the book of Tobit who kills Sarah's husbands on her wedding night. According to one Greek recension of Tobit, Asmodeus is motivated by jealousy (4QTob^{a} 6:15, "because he loves her"), but he could also be acting simply out of malice. In the Testament of Solomon (1st-3rd century C.E.), Asmodeus says, "I am always hatching plots against newlyweds; I mar the beauty of virgins and cause their hearts to grow cold" (T. Sol. 5:7). Following the angel Raphael's instructions, Tobias causes Asmodeus to flee to Egypt, where he is bound by Raphael.

A derivation for the name Asmodeus from the Persian Aeshma Daeva, the demon of violence and wrath, was once thought to be virtually certain. However, the Asmodeus of the book of Tobit lacks Aeshma's cosmic proportions. Moreover, the philological evidence is ambiguous, and an alternative Hebrew derivation from *šmd,* "to destroy," has found increasing favor. But even if the name is not Persian, Asmodeus was probably regarded as a "local" demon active in Persia and Mesopotamia (cf. T. Sol. 5:10).

WILL SOLL

ASNAH (Heb. *ʾasnâ*)
The head of a family of temple servants returning from Exile with Zerubbabel (Ezra 2:50).

ASPATHA (Heb. *ʾaspāṯāʾ*)
One of the 10 sons of Haman killed by the Jews (Esth. 9:7).

ASRIEL (Heb. *'aśrî'ēl*)
A descendant of Manasseh (Num. 26:31; Josh. 17:2). According to 1 Chr. 7:14 his mother was an Aramean concubine.

ASS
An animal of the genus *Equus,* which includes the wild ass (*Equus africanus, asinus, hemionus*) and its descendant the domesticated donkey. The most frequent Hebrew term for "ass" is *ḥămôr,* which refers to the male domesticated animal and relates to a Semitic root meaning reddish (though the ass is often gray or white, not red) and has possible Semitic connections to stubbornness. Another common term is *'ātôn,* which designates the female domesticated ass or donkey. Occasionally *'ayir* is used, meaning a colt or young ass, which contains the linguistic sense of burden-bearing. "Wild ass" comes most frequently from Heb. *pere',* but the OT also mentions *'ārôḏ* and *'ărāḏ,* the onager (a wild Asian ass). The NT term is Gk. *ónos,* related to *ónasthai* ("to be useful"). Gk. *hypozýgion (hypó + zygós)* invokes the position of the animal "under" its "yoke." Gk. *onárion* refers particularly to a young ass.

The ass was a beast of burden, bearing supplies (Gen. 44:13; Josh. 9:4) such as food (Gen. 42:26; 1 Sam. 16:20), riches (Isa. 30:6), a corpse (1 Kgs. 13:29), and even a chariot (Isa. 21:7). The ass was used as transportation (e.g., Exod. 4:20; 1 Sam. 25:20), often with a saddle (Gen. 22:3; 1 Kgs. 13:13). The ass was a valued posession (Exod. 20:17; 21:33; Deut. 22:3; cf. Gen. 43:18; Num. 31:28-35; Josh. 7:24). It was a worthy gift (Gen. 12:16; 32:15), counted as a blessing (24:35; Job 1:3; 42:12), and used to trade for food (Gen. 47:17). Since the ass is considered unclean (Lev. 11:3; Deut. 14:3-6; but cf. 2 Kgs. 6:25), its firstborn must be redeemed by substitution (Exod. 13:13; 34:20).

The ass plays prominently in some biblical narratives. In the tale of Balaam (Num. 22:21-33) a she-ass (*'ātôn*) is anthropomorphized, speaking and heroic (through her purposeful stubbornness) in saving Balaam from the wrath of God, consequently leading him back to faithfulness. The jawbone of an ass is used to slay 1000 men in Samson's self-protective rampage against the Philistines (Judg. 15:14-20). Saul's search for his father's lost asses leads to "the seer" Samuel, who anoints Saul the next king (1 Sam. 9:1-27). In 1 Kgs. 13:13-29 a lion and ass stand together over the body of a "man of God" who was punished with death for participating in an illegitimate cultic act.

The prophecy of the Messiah riding on an ass (Zech. 9:9) is repeated in Matthew's account of Jesus' entry into Jerusalem (Matt. 21:2, 5-6), which conjures a bizarre image of Jesus side-saddled on an ass and ass' colt. There is significance to a messianic king riding on an ass as it was not an animal used in war but for work. Nonetheless, the ass was also noted as a sign of prestige (Judg. 5:10; 2 Sam. 16:2) and riches (Gen. 30:43; 32:5).

Finally, when challenged about working on the sabbath, Jesus refers to caring for an ass or pulling it from danger (Luke 13:15; 14:5).

Bibliography. G. Savran, "Beastly Speech," *JSOT* 64 (1994): 33-55. LISA MICHELLE WOLFE

ASSASSINS
A Jewish revolutionary group (Gk. *sikárioi,* from Lat. *sicarii,* "dagger carriers") that arose during the procuratorship of Felix (52-60 C.E.; Josephus *Ant.* 18.23-25; 20.160-72; cf. *BJ* 2.261-63). Named for short daggers (Lat. *sica*) they concealed under their clothing, they assassinated their enemies in broad daylight, especially during festivals when they could escape in the crowd (*BJ* 2.252-60, 425-29; *Ant.* 20.185-88; cf. 20.204-10). The Assassins promoted liberty and equality and were against human rule of any kind (even Jewish). Their relationship to the Zealots is debated. Paul was mistaken for an Egyptian leader of the group (Acts 21:38).
DOUGLAS S. HUFFMAN

ASSEMBLY
See CONGREGATION.

ASSHUR (Heb. *'aššûr*) **(PERSON)**
One of the sons of Shem; eponymous ancestor of the Assyrians (Gen. 10:22; 1 Chr. 1:17).

ASSHUR (Heb. *'aššûr*) **(PLACE)**
1. Assur, a major city in Assyria and at one point its capital (Ezek. 27:23).
2. Another name for Assyria (Num. 24:22, 24).

ASSHURIM (Heb. *'aššûrîm*)
A tribe descended from Jokshan and ultimately from Abraham and Keturah, about which little more is known (Gen. 25:3). While some commentators suppose them to be related to the Assyrians (perhaps on the basis of Gen. 25:18), they are probably an Arabian clan.

ASSIR (Heb. *'assîr*)
1. A son of Korah of the tribe of Levi (Exod. 6:24; 1 Chr. 6:22[MT 7]).
2. The son of Ebiasaph (1 Chr. 6:23[8]) and grandson of Korah (v. 37[22]).

ASSOCIATIONS, VOLUNTARY
A group of men and/or women organized on the basis of freely chosen membership for a common purpose. In antiquity such associations were popular from the 5th century B.C.E. until the late Roman Empire, despite various attempts to suppress them. Thousands of associations are attested through inscriptions and, in the case of Egypt, papyri. These inscriptions most often record the association's membership list, decrees, or statutes, although they might also record the founding of the group. These groups were relatively small, with membership generally between 10 and 100. Among the members themselves it is not uncommon to find citizens and noncitizens, masters and slaves, and men and women, rich and poor, all gathered together in a single association (cf. Gal. 3:28).

Three broad categories of associations can be distinguished. Funerary associations insured a proper burial in exchange for entrance fees and/or regular dues. Religious associations focused on the worship of a particular deity or deities through cultic acts and special festival days. Professional associations were formed by traders or artisans living in a particular locale. There is no consistency in terminology for the associations, and many titles were used including *thíasoi, collegia, ekklēsía, synagōgé,* and *koiná.* Almost all associations worshipped one or more patron deities and performed cultic acts, and most met together for social occasions such as banquets or drinking parties. Such social and religious events were funded by human patrons, who received various honors in exchange for their benefaction.

The internal organization of an association included the designation of various officials and functionaries. For the most part this replicated the civic structure. However, there is little consistency among various groups in the terminology used for these officials.

Associations are generally considered to have been popular because they offered a person a sense of belonging at a time when the traditional kinship and civic groups were being broken apart. Through membership a number of social networks could be established and charity was available to those who fell on hard times. Membership in a group also allowed for the attainment of honor and prestige which was otherwise not available to the majority of persons.

The most obvious NT reference to a voluntary association is the account at Acts 19:23-40 of the uproar caused by the silversmiths at Ephesus. Voluntary associations have also been used by a number of scholars as an analogy for understanding early Pauline community formation and social relationships, particularly the Corinthian church.

Bibliography. R. S. Ascough, *What Are They Saying About the Formation of Pauline Churches?* (New York, 1998); J. S. Kloppenborg and S. G. Wilson, eds., *Voluntary Associations in the Greco-Roman World* (London, 1996).

RICHARD S. ASCOUGH

ASSOS (Gk. *Ássos*)
A strategic city on the Gulf of Adramyttium, on the east coast of the Aegean Sea, in Mysia. The city's defenses included natural and artificial terraced cliffs that rose 215 m. (700 ft.) above sea level, complemented by a wall 3.2 km. (2 mi.) long and 19.8 m. (65 ft.) high. Various public buildings (including a gymnasium, treasury, baths, a marketplace, and theater) stood on the terraces. Assos (modern Behramköy) housed a Doric temple to Athena and was the headquarters of Platonic philosophers, including Aristotle. The Stoic Cleanthes was born in this city.

Assos was a part of the realm of the Pergamenian kings and later a port of Asia. Paul traveled from Troas to Assos on a coastal road as Luke and others rounded Cape Lectum by sea (Acts 20:13-14). STEVEN L. COX

ASSUMPTION OF MOSES
See MOSES, TESTAMENT OF.

ASSUMPTION OF THE VIRGIN
Over 50 apocrypha and homilies from before the 10th century record in nine ancient languages either the Virgin's dormition ("falling asleep") and bodily assumption ("being taken up") into heaven or her dormition without an assumption. There is, however, no reliable evidence of either doctrine before the late 5th century, at which point several witnesses, including the earliest apocryphon and homily, attest belief in the "rival" doctrines of bodily assumption and dormition without assumption, respectively. The real flowering of this tradition occurs primarily in the 6th century, during which time there is a proliferation of narratives revising the earlier texts and purging them of heterodoxy. The story's main events take place in Jerusalem (with the occasional inclusion of a trip to Bethlehem), and include the miraculous reunion of the Apostles and the return of Christ to receive his mother's soul as it leaves her body. Only certain texts continue with an account of the Virgin's resurrection and assumption, but all are characterized by a hostility to Judaism and frequent attacks on the Jewish leaders who, among other things, attempt to burn the Virgin's body. A countertradition locating the end of the Virgin's life in Ephesus develops at a later time, primarily in the medieval Syriac church.

Bibliography. W. J. Burghardt, *The Testimony of the Patristic Age Concerning Mary's Death* (Westminster, Md., 1957). STEPHEN J. SHOEMAKER

ASSUR (Heb. *'aššûr;* Akk. *aššur*) **(DEITY)**
The Assyrian national deity and head of the pantheon; principally a god of war, kingship, and royal ideology. His name is identified with the city, and from it the names Assyria and the Assyrians derive. Assur may have been a local tribal deity with no original position or lineage in the Mesopotamian pantheon. He assimilated the characteristics of Enlil, a prominent deity in the early Mesopotamian pantheon, sometime during the 2nd millennium B.C.E. Assur became the "lord of the universe" and "the father of the gods." Along with his consort Ninlil, who was also the wife of Enlil, he resided in the E-kur temple in Assur. When the Assyrian king Sennacherib destroyed Babylon (ca. 689) he replaced the Babylonian cult of Marduk with his deity Assur.

Assur is identified as An-šar in Enuma Elish, the Mesopotamian creation epic, and in the Assyrian version of this myth Assur displaces Marduk as the triumphant hero who slays Tiamat. The bronze doors of Sennecherib's New Year's temple in Assur depict scenes from this battle. Additionally, Assur assumed the essential role played by Marduk in the Akîtu, the annual New Year's festival in which the king proclaimed obedience and loyalty to Assur and the citizens of the land. The Assyrian kings were thus considered not only the administrative leaders of the state, but also acted as high priests in Assur's cult. The earliest reference to Assur appears in the Old Assyrian cuneiform texts of Cappadocia, a major trading colony, dating to ca. 2000. Assur, as a deity, is not mentioned in the OT; however, the name does appear as a component in the theophoric name of the Assyrian king, Assurbanipal ("Assur is the creator of the heir").

JULYE BIDMEAD

ASSUR (Heb. *'aššûr;* Akk. *aššur*) **(PLACE)**
The chief city of Assyria for most of that nation's history. The city (modern Qal'at Sherqat) was in the heartland of Assyria, along the west bank of the Tigris River, in the fertile region of northern Iraq N of the Lesser Zab tributary and the Jebel Hamrin range. Along with Nineveh and Erbil, Assur formed a triangle of Assyrian towns.

Although little is known about its prehistoric period, Assur was an established city by the early 3rd millennium B.C. when it was a major religious center with various public buildings, including a temple dedicated to the goddess Ishtar. After 2300 Assur became part of the Semitic Akkadian Empire, as evidenced by an inscription of the Akkadian king Manishtushu found at the site.

The name Assur has presented problems to scholars as it was not only the name of the city, but also of the chief deity (often spelled "Ashur" to distinguish it from the city). By 2100 Assur was a vassal town of the Third Dynasty of Ur, as evidenced by numerous building inscriptions of "viceroys of Assur" who wrote in the Old Assyrian dialect of Akkadian.

In the early 2nd millennium Assur appears to have been a substantial city-state with fortified city walls and commercial interests in distant areas, most notably the trading post at Kanesh in central Anatolia. According to the Assyrian King List and other texts (from Mari and Tell Leilan), the Amorite chieftain Šamši-adad I (ca. 1814-1781) conquered Assur and made it part of his far-reaching empire. Little is known of Assur's fate for the next few centuries. It was apparently under control of the Mitanni state for about a century until the reign of Assuruballit I (1365-1330), when the city became the center of a large polity. The Assyrian king Tukulti-ninurta I (1244-1208) transferred royal power across the Tigris to a brand new city, Kar-tukulti-ninurta, which did not survive for long. Assur reclaimed its title of chief city soon thereafter and continued until the reign of Assurnasirpal II (884-859), who moved to nearby Kalhu. Assur, however, continued as the main religious center of the Assyrian Empire until the city was destroyed in 614.

Bibliography. H. W. F. Saggs, *The Might That Was Assyria* (1984, repr. New York, 1991).

MARK W. CHAVALAS

ASSURBANIPAL (Akk. *Aššur-bāni-apli*)
The last of the great Assyrian kings (668-627 B.C.E.). Esarhaddon appointed his son Assurbanipal heir apparent during his reign, probably as a result of the trauma experienced upon his own succession. The Assyrian vassals swore their loyalty to Assurbanipal as king of Assyria, and to his brother Šamaš-šum-ukin, who occupied the throne of Babylon during Esarhaddon's reign. Consequently, upon Esarhaddon's death Assurbanipal did not have to begin his reign quelling revolts as other Assyrian kings did, and thus could continue his father's attempt to control Egypt.

Assurbanipal gathered auxiliary troops from the Mediterranean coast and managed to enter Thebes, the capital of Upper Egypt. The distance between Assyria and Egypt was too great for direct Assyrian management, so local rulers subject to Assyria were placed in control. Revolts erupted shortly thereafter, prompting Assurbanipal to utterly destroy Thebes. The uprising in Egypt caused Tyre and Arvad to revolt; both island cities were reduced to famine before they surrendered. Assurbanipal then became deeply involved with Elam, at which time Egypt was reinforced with Ionian and Carian troops as recorded by the Greek historian Herodotus. Assurbanipal eventually killed the Elamite ruler Te'umman and brought his head back.to Nineveh, as depicted on his wall relief. It was just after this that Šamaš-šum-ukin tired of his secondary status in Babylon and led a revolt. It took three years to quell, ending only when the Babylonian king set fire to his own palace and died in the flames. Assurbanipal took the throne of Babylon under the name Kandalanu. No extant records describe the last 12 years of his reign.

Assurbanipal is the only Assyrian ruler who claims literacy, and his library at Nineveh, discovered by Hormuzd Rassam in 1852, was one of the keys which unlocked the language and history of the Akkadian civilizations. The library includes letters, contracts, economic and historical inscriptions, literary, religious, and scientific texts.

TAMMI J. SCHNEIDER

ASSURNASIRPAL (Akk. *Aššur-naṣir-apli*)
Assurnasirpal II (883-859 B.C.E.), often considered the "classic" "Neo-Assyrian" monarch. He inherited a stable and expanding kingdom from his father, Tukulti-ninurta II, and then undertook 10 major military campaigns throughout western Asia. He reached as far as the Mediterranean in the west, and was the first Assyrian king to enter the new Phoenician, Neo-Hittite, and Aramean kingdoms, from whom he received little resistance and much tribute. He moved the capital of Assyria from the ancient and religious city of Assur to a new city which he built at Calah (Nimrud). Assurnasirpal's massive palace was the first adorned with monumental stone reliefs depicting his accomplishments. His Banquet stela preserves the guest list, menu, and festivities that inaugurated the new palace and city. Assurnasirpal's inscriptions are filled with flamboyant self-aggrandizement, vivid details of his military successes, and descriptions of the punishment of his enemies.

TAMMI J. SCHNEIDER

ASSYRIA
A political and geographic designation for a major ancient Mesopotamian civilization. The geograph-

Human-headed, winged bull, one of two which flanked the principal entrance to the throne room of the palace of Sargon II at Dur-Sharrukin/Khorsabad (721-705 B.C.E.)
(Photo by Jean M. Grant; courtesy of the Oriental Institute of the University of Chicago)

ical extent of the political entity varied due to the political status of Assyria in any period. Located in what is now northern Iraq, Assyria is commonly referred to as the land along the "middle Tigris."

The early history of Assyria is tied into the political configurations of Babylonia until the rise of Assur-uballit I (reigned 1365-1330 B.C.E.). The Middle Assyrian (1274-1077) and Neo-Assyrian periods (911-612) are sometimes referred to as "empires." Since they use different criteria (language, politics, art historical considerations), not all scholars agree on the exact dates of the Middle and Neo-Assyrian periods.

The first historical references to Assyria date to the Sargonic period (2334-2193). Assyria at this time was a series of autonomous cities. A bronze mask of King Sargon of Akkad (reigned 2334-2279) discovered in the Ishtar temple of Nineveh testifies to the Sargonic presence in Assyria. Nineveh is linked to Maništusu (reigned 2269-2255), Sargon's grandson, through an inscription of Šamši-adad (reigned 1813-1781) claiming that he restored a temple in Nineveh originally built by Maništusu. A copper spear-head belonging to Maništusu describes the ruler of Assur as the servant of Maništusu.

In the following Ur III period the various cities of Assyria were treated differently by the Ur III administration. For example, on a stone plaque discovered in Assur Zarriqum claims to be the governor of Assur and servant of the Ur III king Amar-sin (reigned 2046-2038). While Assur was a peripheral state governed by a royal appointee, economic texts from Nineveh show it to be a vassal state.

The Old Assyrian period is known from texts discovered at the site of Karum Kanesh (Kultepe) in Turkey, a town inhabited by a colony of Assyrian merchants who conducted business in Anatolia. The tablets attest to trade in tin (needed for bronze) and textiles.

Šamši-adad I is the best-known ruler of the Old Assyrian period. He was one of the Semitic-speaking Amorites who entered Mesopotamia, dominating the political situation in the first half of the 2nd millennium. He captured the city of Ekallatum and then took control of Assur. Šamši-adad I claims de-

Tiglath-pileser III (747-727 B.C.E.) standing in his war chariot with a driver and "third man" or "captain" who holds an umbrella. Gypsum relief from palace at Nimrud (Copyright British Museum)

scent from nomads, but portrayed himself as a legitimate ruler of Assur, carrying out construction in that city. More information about him comes from an archive at Mari, where Šamši-adad I established his son Yasmaḫ-adad on the throne. Much of the correspondence between father and son has been excavated. The reign of Šamši-adad I was one of relative stability and prosperity. Upon his death Hammurabi of Babylon conquered most of the areas formerly controlled by Šamši-adad.

Unity amongst the city-states of Assyria collapsed, and the following period is often called a "dark age" in Assyria because of the paucity of evidence. The Assyrian King List provides names of rulers only of the city of Assur. Many of the cities which make up "Assyria" fell under the control of the kingdom of Mitanni.

Assur-uballit I (reigned 1363-1328) marks the rise to power of the political entity of Assyria. He was the first to call himself "King of Assyria." Assur-uballit I addresses the Egyptian king as an equal in two letters from Amarna, indicating his status as a major figure in the international scene. His daughter was married to the king of Babylon, and his grandson eventually inherited the Babylonian throne. When the grandson was killed during a rebellion, Assur-uballit I deposed the usurper and placed his own choice on the throne.

The following three kings maintained Assyria's status as an international power. During the reigns of Enlil-nirari, Arik-den-ilu, and Adad-nirari Assyria's boundaries expanded, though they lost control of Babylonia. Expansion brought wealth into Assyria, laying the groundwork for the Middle Assyrian "Empire." Shalmaneser I (reigned 1274-1245) continued to campaign, and claims defeat of the Hittites, Arameans, and the army of Mitanni.

Tukulti-ninurta I (reigned 1244-1208) continued to fight the Hittites, and was the first to carry out mass deportations. He came into conflict with Babylon, plundered the city, tore down its walls, and brought the statue of its god Marduk to Assyria. For this deed he was the only Assyrian to have a historical epic composed in his honor. However, in other circles the destruction of Babylon was considered an offense to the gods, and Tukulti-ninurta I was assassinated in his palace in the new city he founded across the river from Assur.

Following Tukulti-ninurta I's assassination Assyria fell into a decline (1132-1076) coinciding with the movements and destructions ending the Late Bronze Age in the eastern Mediterranean and with the collapse of Kassite Babylonia. Assyria did not suffer as severely as the surrounding areas, so under Assur-reš-iši I (reigned 1133-1116) Assyria again became powerful. Assur-reš-iši I restored peace and prosperity to the region by recapturing and strengthening borders and rebuilding fortresses. With the kingdom secure Tiglath-pileser I (reigned 1114-1076) expanded Assyria. Conflict with Babylonia did not result in much gain, but Tiglath-pileser I's success in battle against the Mushku and the Arameans brought wealth to Assyria, ushering in a period of prosperity. As a result there were significant building operations in many Assyrian cities. Two sets of laws were compiled at this time, one a collection of palace edicts of various kings and the other a collection of laws concerned with the status (which was particularly poor at this time) of women in Assyria.

Following the death of Tiglath-pileser I, Assyria entered a period of decline, probably as a result of inadequate administration over the newly conquered lands. Assur-dan II (reigned 934-912) restored the internal stability of Assyria and was the first to campaign abroad since Tiglath-pileser I. Adad-nirari II (reigned 911-891) continued the work of his father, conducting even more extensive military expeditions. The Arameans were his chief concern, and after continued campaigning Adad-nirari could finally undertake a "show of strength" offense emulated by his son and successor Tukulti-ninurta II (reigned 890-884). He was also the first to establish storage depots, the beginning of Assyria's provincial system.

Assurnasirpal II (reigned 883-859), the son of Tukulti-ninurta I, was one of the most famous Assyrian kings. He continued to campaign, but on a scale even greater than his predecessors. He was the first to come into contact with the Aramean and Phoenician cities of the west and claims to have reached the Mediterranean. Assurnasirpal II established regular tribute for the conquered territories. This great wealth was used to build a new city Calah (Nimrud), which served as the capital of Assyria for the following reign. The palace reliefs depict campaigns and other exploits and became a hallmark of the Neo-Assyrian period. Assurnasirpal II used gory terminology, apparently revelling in cruelty, to describe his exploits.

Shalmaneser III (reigned 858-824) inherited the throne and continued to rule from Calah. He campaigned yearly for 31 years, continuing to expand the borders of Assyria. In the west he met coalitions of city-states including Hadadezer of Damascus and Ahab of Israel, culminating in the battle of Qarqar. Later in his reign "Jehu, son of Omri," who supplanted the Omride dynasty in Israel, paid tribute, a scene depicted on Shalmaneser III's famous Black Obelisk. He also helped the king of Babylon, Marduk-zakir-šumi, regain the throne from his brother Marduk-bel-usate. Shalmaneser III's *turtanu* (second-in-command) Dayan-assur led the last five military campaigns in his reign. Possibly as a result of the redistribution of power one of Shalmaneser's sons led a rebellion with the support of such cities as Assur and Nineveh. Shalmaneser III died during that rebellion. His son Šamši-adad V (reigned 823-811) managed to win the throne, but Assyria now entered a period of decline, while her neighbor and enemy Urartu gained ascendancy.

Adad-nirari III (reigned 810-783) inherited a weakened kingdom. He campaigned primarily against Babylonia with marginal success. Better known is Adad-nirari III's mother, Sammuramat, known in later traditions as Semiramis. She may have played a significant role in her son's reign since he was young when he ascended the throne; this led to her legendary status in writings among the Arameans, Greeks, and Persians. The following king Shalmaneser IV (reigned 782-773) was so weak that his *turtanu* Šamši-ilu claimed victories over Urartu without mentioning the king's name. Assur-dan III (reigned 772-755) and Assur-nirari V (reigned 754-745) did little while Urartu prospered.

Tiglath-pileser III (reigned 747-727), probably the younger brother of Adad-nirari III and not the designated heir to the throne, was the architect of the last great stage of Assyrian domination. He first chased Urartu out of Assyrian territory and then invaded Urartu itself. After his defeat of Arpad, many of the southern and western states brought voluntary submission and tribute. Tiglath-pileser III led his army through Syria and Phoenicia to southern Palestine, eventually capturing Gaza, where he created a trading center. After protracted problems with Babylonia he himself took the Babylonian throne under the name Pulu (biblical Pul, 2 Kgs. 15:19-20). He carried out a reorganization and improvement of the army and provincial administration using mass deportations as standard policy.

Little is known of Shalmaneser V (reigned 726-722) other than that he laid siege on Samaria after King Hoshea of Israel revolted. Sargon II (reigned 721-705) probably usurped the throne and began the Sargonid line that included the rest of the Assyrian kings. He claimed the capture, destruction, and deportation of Samaria's citizens. His reign began with rebellions which he had to quell at home, and only then could he turn to the problem in Samaria. Sargon continued on to Gaza, where he defeated an Egyptian army and subdued Philistia. Sargon built a new capital NE of Nineveh at Khorsabad called Dur-šarrukin ("Sargon's fortress"), which was abandoned almost as soon as it was inhabited.

Sennacherib (704-681) was raised in the "house of succession" and thus was prepared to follow his father Sargon II. Most of his time was engaged with revolts in the west and Babylonia. His annals record his campaigns to fight the rebellious towns of Sidon, Ashkelon, and Judah and the inhabitants of Ekron, who went so far as to hand their king Padi over to Hezekiah of Jerusalem. Sennacherib's destruction of Lachish is depicted on wall reliefs decorating his palace. While he waged war in the area, Sennacherib never captured Jerusalem. At the end of this campaign Sennacherib planned though never implemented an invasion of Egypt. He built a new palace in Nineveh, reinvigorating the ancient city. Babylonia regularly rebelled, eventually leading Sennacherib to destroy Babylon. He was later murdered by his sons.

Esarhaddon (reigned 680-669) came to the throne amidst the violence of his father's murder. The troublesome beginning greatly affected Esarhaddon, who reversed his father's Babylonian policy and sought appeasement, in large part through a rebuilding campaign. Despite the appearance that he was constantly ill and in fear of the gods, Esarhaddon conquered as far as the capital of Memphis in Egypt. It was on a campaign to quell rebellion in Egypt that he died. His mother Naqi'a exercised more authority than any previous woman, at times writing royal inscriptions and also building a palace at Nineveh. Her power continued into the reign of her grandson Assurbanipal.

Because of the difficulties Esarhaddon faced gaining the throne, he took steps in his lifetime to secure a smooth transition. He placed his son Assurbanipal (reigned 668-627) on the throne of Assyria and his son Šamaš-šum-ukin on the throne of Babylonia, and made all the vassals in the empire swear an oath of loyalty to both. The transition worked smoothly. Assurbanipal gathered 22 kings and began his invasion of Egypt. So far from Assyria, Assurbanipal had to appoint Egyptians to rule in his stead. Later rebellions demanded his return, at which time Assurbanipal destroyed Thebes. When Egypt revolted a third time Assurbanipal was so busy with problems in Elam that he could not regain Egypt. After 17 years Assurbanipal's brother Šamaš-šum-ukin tired of his secondary status in Babylonia and revolted. Assurbanipal responded by marching against his brother. After three years of perpetual battle, Šamaš-šum-ukin set fire to his palace and died in the flames. Assurbanipal then took the throne of Babylon under the name Kandalanu.

There is no record of the last 12 years of Assurbanipal's reign. It appears that civil strife and military setbacks weakened Assyria to a point from which it could not recover. A fight for the throne following Assurbanipal's death further weakened Assyria, so that in 614 the city of Assur was destroyed by the Medes. By 612 Nineveh, Nimrud, and Assur were all in ruins. A small force held out in Haran until 609, at which point the Neo-Babylonian "Empire" encompassed all the land formerly under Neo-Assyrian control.

Bibliography. A. L. Oppenheim, *Ancient Mesopotamia,* 2nd ed. (Chicago, 1977); G. Roux, *Ancient Iraq,* 3rd ed. (Baltimore, 1992); H. W. F. Saggs, *The Might That Was Assyria* (1984; repr. New York, 1991).

TAMMI J. SCHNEIDER

ASTARTE (Gk. *Astarte*)

See ASHTORETH.

ASTROLOGER

Mesopotamian and Egyptian stargazers practiced what moderns would call both astronomy and astrology, and their skill was sophisticated enough to allow accurate predictions of eclipses and construction of calendars. The Neo-Assyrian monarchs (743-612 B.C.E.) in particular were eager patrons of astrologers throughout their empire, and much of their extensive correspondence survives. Priests correlated celestial omens with other types, especially those from the reading of sheep entrails, all for the benefit of their rulers in an effort to predict and control the future.

Biblical texts are aware of the importance of astrology in Mesopotamia (Isa. 47:13; Jer. 10:2 call the practice the "way of the Gentiles," Heb. *derek̠ haggôyim*) and predict that its practitioners will share in the disaster awaiting their societies. While no direct evidence of Israelite astrology survives, the Bible does not explicitly repudiate the craft, and lists of forbidden divinatory practices conspicuously omit reference to it (Lev. 19:26-28; Deut. 18:9-13; Zech. 10:1-2; cf. Isa. 3:3). Second Temple texts perpetuate this ambivalence, e.g., by including Daniel among the astrologers (albeit as their superior; Dan. 2:27; 4:7, 10[MT 4, 7]; 5:7, 11) and tracing Abraham's discovery of God partly to astrology (Jub. 12:16). The magi of Matt. 2 are Iranian priests whose astrology leads them to Jesus.

Bibliography. S. Parpola, *Letters from Assyrian Scholars to the Kings Esarhaddon and Assurbanipal.* AOAT 5/1 (Neukirchen-Vluyn, 1970).

MARK W. HAMILTON

ASTROLOGY

Belief that the celestial bodies, especially the moon, sun, planets, and stars (in Greek collectively called "stars"), influence the sublunar world.

Astrology, properly speaking, arose in the Hellenistic sphere and period. Babylonians viewed the stars as only indicators of the will of the gods, not as in themselves the causes of events. This ancient Babylonian tradition (2nd millennium B.C.E.), which influenced Greece, Egypt, the Near East, and India, is called celestial *omina* ("omens") rather than astrology. As it has survived in later astrological works, however, it is sometimes termed natural astrology.

Astrology proper can be divided into four varieties: genethlialogical (one's horoscope at birth), catarchic (position of the stars at the beginning of an action), interrogatory (horoscope when a question is presented), and general (effects on groups, nations, or the world).

Astrology proper is too late to have influenced the ancient Hebrew tradition. The nature and degree of elements of ancient Near Eastern astral religion (esp. sun worship; cf. 2 Kgs. 17:16; 21:3-5; 23:11; Jer. 8:2; Ezek. 8:16) in Israelite religion are disputed. There is little evidence of the tradition of celestial omens (cf. Isa. 47:13-14).

Jewish materials combining omens and Hellenistic astrology are witnessed for the intertestamental period. Writings from Qumran and the Cairo Geniza are shedding new light on the extent and nature of ancient Jewish astrology (4Q186, 4Q318, Cambridge Geniza MS T-S H 11.51), to which Hellenistic Jewish communities such as the one in Alexandria surely contributed. These discoveries add further credence to ancient references to Jewish astrological treatises under names such as Seth, Abraham, Solomon, and Ezra. They also support the supposition of an originally Jewish nature for such treatises preserved in Greek, Latin, Syriac, and Arabic.

The general validity of astrology was confirmed in rabbinic tradition, though here it was debated whether the Jews themselves were under the influence of the stars (*b. Šabb.* 156a-b). Archaeological evidence, such as zodiacs in synagogues, points toward more widespread astrological traditions than previously supposed.

It is often thought that ancient Christianity strictly rejected astrology. Did. 3:4 does instruct not to be an interpreter of omens or an astrologer. Moral and scientific arguments against astrology developed in the Greco-Roman tradition, as well as a Jewish tradition that fallen angels taught humankind astrology, were adopted by the Christian heresiologists. Still, there is clear evidence for Christian astrology from the early period (astrological basis for sabbath observance and catarchic astrology in the book of Elchasai, 116-17 C.E.; genethlialogy in Bardaisan, beginning of 3rd century; Mani).

In the NT, Paul's remark in Gal. 4:10 about a tendency to observe days, months, seasons, and years seems equally to condemn astrological reasonings. The group of Christian opponents combatted in Col. 2:8-23 are likely to have recognized astral powers (cf. Jude 8). Astral and astrological imagery pervades Revelation (e.g., Rev. 11:12-13; 12:1), though here the power of the stars is never recognized. Such imagery is also widely witnessed among the "Gnostics," who variously used astrological calculations.

The value of astrology is praised by the author of the source of Pseudo-Clementine *Recognitions* 1.27-71 (ca. 200), who, in line with a Jewish tradition, glorifies Abraham as the pre-eminent astrologer. Also influenced by Jewish (and Hellenistic sectarian) precedent, other Christians believed that the stars have power over everyone but Christians (Clement of Alexandria *Excerpts from Theodotus* 74.2–78.1; Pseudo-Clementine *Recognitions* 9.31.1). Others, such as Origen, affirmed that the stars are indicators of divine will but that the signs are intelligible only to angels.

The star of Bethlehem (Matt. 2:1-12) was a bone of contention already in ancient Christianity. In origin the star doubtless belongs in the tradition of the omen (similar to the darkness at the death of Jesus, Mark 15:33; Luke 23:44-45), connected perhaps with an OT prophecy (Num. 24:17). The power of astrology crystallized in Christian tradition through celebration of December 25, the birthday of the sun (king of stars), as Christmas.

Bibliography. J. H. Charlesworth, "Jewish Astrology in the Talmud, Pseudepigrapha, the Dead Sea Scrolls, and Early Palestinian Synagogues," *HTR* 70 (1977): 183-200; F. Cumont, *Astrology and Religion among the Greeks and Romans* (1912; repr. New York, 1960); D. Pingree, "Astrology," *Dictionary of the History of Ideas,* ed. P. P. Wiener (New York, 1973), 1:118-26.

F. STANLEY JONES

ASTRONOMY

An ancient science which attempts to discover the laws governing the celestial bodies. It is known that calendars, based upon astronomical observations, were developed by the Egyptians and Mesopotamians as early as the 3rd millennium B.C. Astronomy was ardently studied by the early Babylonians, who blended their astral observations with their polytheism, resulting in astrology. Babylonian ziggurats, such as the tower of Babel, were structures probably used for the observation of the heavenly bodies. Hebrew astronomy was undoubtedly influenced by the Babylonians. However, as a whole the Babylonian astrological practices had little impact upon Israel.

The Hebrew literature does demonstrate some familiarity with astronomical observations. Job 9:9 refers to observations of the constellations. Similarly, the prophets Isaiah (13:10) and Amos (5:8) knew of such constellations.

In Amos 5:26 the prophet recalls Israel's recalcitrance by following astral deities (probably Saturn and Jupiter). Moreover, a common sin during the Monarchy was the problem of worshipping the host of heaven. While these practices were more the exception than the norm, they do indicate the degree to which astronomy influenced Israelite life.

Astronomical catastrophes were a common feature in Jewish apocalyptic writings as well as in eschatological passages of the Bible. Isa. 13:10 asserts that the day of the Lord would be beckoned by a darkening of the sun, moon, and stars. Joel (2:10; 3:15[MT 4:15]), Mark (13:24-25), 2 Peter (3:10) and Revelation (8:10) likewise claim that celestial calamities would accompany the day of the Lord.

Matthew's birth narrative includes a visit by the Magi (astrologers from the east) who witnessed an astronomical phenomenon and interpreted this as a sign of a new king. This has often been explained as either a comet, a supernova, or a convergence of planets. Matthew simply explains it as a star and provides no additional detail. MARK R. FAIRCHILD

ASYNCRITUS (Gk. *Asýnkritos*)

A Roman Christian to whom Paul sends his greetings (Rom. 16:14).

ATAD (Heb. *'āṭāḏ*)

A place "beyond the Jordan" where Jacob's burial procession stopped for seven days to mourn (Gen. 50:10-11). The phrase *gōren hā'āṭāḏ* is usually translated "the threshing floor of (the) Atad," but it could also be translated "the threshing floor of thorns," suggesting that Atad may not be a proper name. When local Canaanites saw the mourning (Gen. 50:11), they renamed the place Abel-mizraim ("mourning of the Egyptians").

The location and identification of Atad is unknown. It should be located in Transjordan, but the 6th-century A.D. Madeba Map provides information that an Alon-atad is located near Beth-agla (modern Deir Ḥajlah; 197136) between Jericho and the Dead Sea, which is the wrong side of the Jordan River. It is uncertain why Joseph's party would have taken the longer route around the southern end of the Dead Sea.

Bibliography. W. H. Shea, "The Burial of Jacob," *Archaeology and Biblical Research* 5 (1992): 33-44.

ZELJKO GREGOR

ATARAH (Heb. *ʿăṭārâ*)
The second wife of Jerahmeel; mother of Onam (1 Chr. 2:26).

ATARGATIS (Gk. *Atargatis*)
A Syrian goddess probably a composite of the Canaanite goddesses Astart, Anat, and Asherah. Her images usually depict her riding or flanked by lions; her consort, Hadad, is enthroned on or flanked by bulls. She is connected to fish and sacred ponds, both of which appear in her imagery and near her temples. Lucian *(De Syria Dea)* identifies Atargatis with Hera and Hadad with Zeus. In his campaign against neighboring nations, Judas Maccabeus burned a temple of Atargatis in the Gileadite town of Carnain (1 Macc. 5:43-44; 2 Macc. 12:26; called Ashteroth-karnaim in Gen. 14:5).
RODNEY A. WERLINE

ATAROTH (Heb. *ʿăṭārôṯ*)
1. A town in Transjordan taken by the Israelites from Sihon the Amorite (Num. 32:3) and allotted to the tribe of Gad, who rebuilt it (Num. 32:34; Mesha Stela l. 10). Mesha, the Moabite king, later took it from the Gadites (Mesha l. 11) after the death of Ahab. It has been identified with Khirbet ʿAṭṭārûs (213109), ca. 13 km. (8 mi.) NW of Dibon.
2. A town on the border of Ephraim and Benjamin (Josh. 16:2), probably the same place as Ataroth-addar (Josh. 16:5; 18:13).
3. A town in Ephraim (Josh. 16:7) in the Jordan Valley, possibly identified with Tell Sheikh edh-Dhiab.
4. A place in Judah (1 Chr. 2:54) which has not been identified. However, it is possible to read Atroth-beth-joab ("the crowns of the house of Joab") as an appositive to Bethlehem and the Netophathites.
PAUL J. RAY, JR.

ATAROTH-ADDAR (Heb. *ʿăṭārôṯ ʾaddār*)
A Benjaminite town, on the border between the territory of Ephraim (Josh. 16:2, 5) to the north and Benjamin (18:13) to the south. The city may be identified with Khirbet Raddana (1695.1468), just N of modern Ramallah, or with the modern village of ʿAṭṭara, located at the southern foot of Tell en-Naṣbeh (Mizpah; 179143), ca. 12 km. (8 mi.) NW of Jerusalem.

Bibliography. W. F. Albright, Review of P. F.-M. Abel, *Géographie de la Palestine* 2, *JBL* 58 (1939): 177-87; J. A. Callaway, "Raddana, Khirbet," *NEAEHL* 4:1253-54; J. R. Zorn, "Naṣbeh, Tell en-," *NEAEHL* 3:1098-1102.
JOHN R. SPENCER

ATER (Heb. *ʾāṭēr*)
1. The ancestor of a family that returned from Exile under Zerubbabel (Ezra 2:16 = Neh. 7:21).
2. A Levite, the head of a family of gatekeepers returning to Jerusalem with Zerubbabel (Ezra 2:42 = Neh. 7:45).
3. An Israelite chief who set his seal on the renewed covenant under Nehemiah (Neh. 10:17[MT 18]).

ATHACH (Heb. *ʿăṯāḵ*)
One of the towns in Judah to which David sent victory spoils from his defeat of the Amalekites (1 Sam. 30:30). It is probably the same as Ether mentioned in Josh. 15:42; 19:7. STEVEN M. ORTIZ

ATHAIAH (Heb. *ʿăṯāyâ*)
A Judahite, the son of Uzziah, who resided in Jerusalem after the Exile (Neh. 11:4).

ATHALIAH (Heb. *ʿăṯalyâ, ʿăṯalyāhû*)
Queen of Judah (ca. 842-837 B.C.E.). Her lineage is uncertain; identified as the daughter of Ahab and his wife (possibly Queen Jezebel). Some scholars say she may have been Omri's daughter and therefore Ahab's sister (2 Kgs. 8:18; 2 Chr. 22:2). Her name is the oldest documented use of a female name with the theophoric component "Yahweh."

Athaliah married Jehoram, crown prince of Judah and son of Jehoshaphat. While it may have been a good move politically because it joined the houses of Judah and Israel, the marriage was disastrous spiritually for Judah. When Jehoram was 32, he succeeded to the throne and Athaliah became queen. Jehoram's first action was to murder all his brothers and other princes (2 Chr. 21:4). Athaliah may have supported or even more likely instigated these deeds.

Athaliah introduced the worship of Baal Melqart in Jerusalem during her husband's reign (2 Kgs. 8:16-18). Like her mother Jezebel, she was fanatically devoted to Baal Melqart. The Chronicler holds her responsible for her son Ahaziah's godlessness (2 Chr. 22:3), reporting that her sons broke into the temple of God and used its sacred objects for Baal (24:7).

Jehoram died fighting the Edomites (2 Kgs. 8:24), and their son Ahaziah became king, reigning for one year (v. 26). Ahaziah went to Jezreel to visit Joram, Ahab's son. Jehu of Israel met the two kings there, killing Joram and mortally wounding Ahaziah, who then died at Megiddo (2 Kgs. 9:27). Athaliah was now a very powerful queen mother and widow; only her relatives — some of them her grandchildren — stood between her and the throne. Ambition and fanaticism spurred Athaliah to massacre the royal household, thereby almost eradicating the Davidic dynasty (2 Kgs. 11:1). Ahaziah's infant son Joash and his nurse were hidden and saved by Jehosheba, Joash's aunt (2 Kgs. 11:2 = 2 Chr. 22:11).

Believing all contenders to the throne were dead, Athaliah had herself proclaimed sovereign. For six years Jehoiada the priest and his wife Jehosheba concealed Joash. In the seventh year, Jehoiada instigated a carefully planned revolution by the priests and military. He brought Joash, who was well protected with armed guards, out of the temple. The lad was presented a copy of the covenant, anointed, and acclaimed king (2 Kgs. 11:12). When Athaliah heard the shouting, she rushed to the temple. Taking in the situation immediately, she tore her robes and cried out, "Treason! Treason!"

Temple of Olympian Zeus built in the 2nd century B.C.E. beneath the Acropolis. Originally surrounded by more than 100 Corinthian columns, this was the largest temple in Greece (Philip Gendreau, N.Y.)

— ironically and appropriately the only words she utters in the account (2 Chr. 23:13).

Athaliah was summarily led out to the Horse Gate and killed (2 Kgs. 11:15-16; 2 Chr. 23:15). After her death cult worship was purified, the temple of Baal destroyed, and its priest executed (2 Kgs. 11:18 = 2 Chr. 23:17).

2. The son of Jeroham and chief of a prominent Benjaminite family dwelling in Jerusalem (1 Chr. 8:26).

3. The father of Jeshaiah, who returned from Babylon along with Ezra and 70 men. He was a member of the family of Elam (Ezra 8:7). 1 Esdr. 8:33 gives his name as Gotholiah.

ROBIN GALLAHER BRANCH

ATHARIM (Heb. *hāʾătārîm*)
A place (so NRSV), possibly a road, where the Israelites were attacked by the king of Arad (Num. 21:1). LXX and Vulg. read "spies."

ATHBASH
A cryptographic system whereby letters equidistant from the middle of the alphabet represent each other. Thus the first letter of the consonantal Hebrew alphabet (*aleph*) is exchanged for the last (*tau*), the second letter (*beth*) for the second to last (*shin*), and so on. The Hebrew system's name represents its first two exchanges (*aleph-tau, beth-shin = athbash*).

In the OT the code has been uncovered three times in Jeremiah. In 25:26; 51:41 Babylon (*bbl*) is called "Sheshak" (*ššk*). In 51:1 Chaldea (*kśdym*) is represented by "Leb-qamai," a phrase meaning "the midst (lit., 'heart') of them that rise up against me" (*lb-qmy*).

NICOLE J. RUANE

ATHENS (Gk. *Athḗnai*)
The most famous of all Greek cities, named for the Greek goddess of wisdom, Athena. Athens imparted to the Western world influential and lasting ideas about art, philosophy, and politics. While occupation on the slopes of the Acropolis, the rocky mass that is Athens' most prominent natural feature, dates to Neolithic times, Athens held secondary status throughout the Mycenean period (1600-1200 B.C.E.) and emerged as a significant city only during the 8th century, when it began to dominate the whole region of Attica. Athens apparently resisted the Dorian invasion of Greece ca. 1200 and remained relatively stable and isolated during the Dark Ages (1200-750), though it may have played prominently in the Ionian immigration of Greeks to Asia Minor (11th and 10th centuries).

In the 7th century Athens began its move from monarchy toward democracy with periodic interruptions by tyrants. Early on, official power was divided among appointed rulers, with a council of nobles (the Areopagus) exercising advisory and appointive roles and a larger assembly of citizens gradually gaining more power. The 6th century saw a series of aristocrats, beginning with Solon (ca. 594), initiating constitutional reforms that led to a form of democratic government. Early in the 5th century Athens led Greek resistance to the Persian attempts to conquer Greece, first with the defeat of the Persian army at Marathon (490) and then in the defeat of the Persian navy at Salamis (480).

The demise of the Persian threat led to internal Greek conflict, largely caused by Athenian visions of empire and dominance of other Greek city-states through its navy and commerce. Under Pericles, Athens attained its zenith politically and economically, as well as culturally in architecture, literature, and drama. Increased rivalry between Athens and Sparta erupted in the Peloponnesian War (431-404). Though defeated by Sparta, Athens quickly rebounded as a maritime power and enjoyed its greatest era of influence in philosophy and oratory in the early 4th century.

The role of Athens as a political power gave way to Macedonia under Philip II later in the 4th century. Macedonian control of Athens, along with the rest of Greece, was sealed by Philip's victory over Theban and Athenian forces at Chaeronea in Boeotia in 338. Philip's son Alexander the Great, who had been tutored by Aristotle, extended Macedonian dominance, and with it many aspects of Athenian culture, throughout the eastern Mediterranean and beyond. At Alexander's death (323), Athens revolted against the Macedonians but was subdued by Alexander's general Antipater, who replaced the Athenian democracy with an oligarchy. Antigonus Gonatas, the founder of the Antigonid dynasty governing the Macedonian Greek portions of Alexander's empire, made Athens his cultural and religious capital (276). The Athenian yearning for freedom led to a disastrous revolt under Chremonides (267-262). The Macedonian period ended for Athens when Rome eventually defeated the last of the Antigonid rulers and divided Macedonia into four Roman provinces (168).

Athens was spared the devastation that Rome inflicted on many Greek cities during the Second (200-197) and Third (171-168) Macedonian Wars because it sided with Rome. In 88, however, Athenian nationalism led to rebellion against Rome and support of Mithridates of Pontus. The Roman general Sulla overcame Athenian resistance following his defeat of Mithridates but limited his vengeance against the city. Athens also received pardon from Julius Caesar for siding with Pompey (49-48) and from Antony and Octavian for supporting Brutus (44-42). Octavian levied only minor penalties against the city for its support of his rival Antony (31).

Under Roman rule, regional political power resided in rebuilt Corinth (44), the capital of the Roman province of Achaia. Athens continued to flourish, however, as a center of culture, with Roman nobility sending their sons there to study in its philosophical schools. Some of its artistic treasures were confiscated by Caligula and Nero, but the Roman emperors generally treated the city with great deference.

Athens is mentioned in the Bible only in connection with the Apostle Paul. Acts 17:15-34 recounts Paul preaching in Athens. He argued in the synagogue with the Jews and preached in the agora (Acts 17:17), where he encountered Epicurean and Stoic philosophers (v. 18). Epicureanism and Stoicism had been centered in Athens since the late 4th century B.C.E., as had the older Academy of Plato (a student of the famous Athenian philosopher Socrates) and the Lyceum of Plato's one-time student, Aristotle. Paul then delivered his famous sermon about the "unknown god" in the middle of the Areopagus (possibly the council chamber N of the rocky hill called the Areopagus and not the hill itself; Acts 17:22-31). He also stayed in Athens while sending Timothy to encourage the Christians in Thessalonica (1 Thess. 3:1).

Athens flourished in the 2nd century C.E. due to generous Roman patronage under Hadrian and the Antonine emperors. The agora suffered extensive damage in the Herulian (Gothic) invasion of 267, resulting in an Athenian loss of confidence in Roman protection and a reduction in the area inhabited. Under early Byzantine rule Athens declined in importance. It continued to be a center of philosophical education, however, until the Edict of Justinian (529) closed its schools. By that time, many of its famous monuments had been converted into Christian structures.

Bibliography. R. Barber, *Greece,* 5th ed. (New York, 1988); M. Grant, *The Rise of the Greeks* (New York, 1987); R. Meiggs, *The Athenian Empire* (Oxford, 1972).

SCOTT NASH

ATHLAI (Heb. *ʿaṯlay*)
An Israelite of the family of Bebai. He was one of the returned exiles requested to send away his foreign wife (Ezra 10:28).

ATONEMENT
Reconciliation between estranged parties, bringing them into agreement. The focus is the universal problem of sin, which humankind is unable to solve, and which disrupted the perfect harmony between God and creation, causing separation (Isa. 59:2) and death (Rom. 5:12; 6:23). Atonement, therefore, is God's way of bridging the gap and giving life (Heb. *kpr,* "to cover," "cancel," "purge," "purify," "decontaminate"; Gk. *katallagḗ,* "reconciliation").

Atonement is described in the Hebrew cultus as sacrifice, substitution, mediation, and judgment. Consecration of priests required sacrifice of a bull as a "sin offering for atonement" (Exod. 29:36). Daily sacrifices (the *tāmîḏ*) were offered for the forgiveness of sin (Lev. 4:20). The repentant sinner "slaughtered the sin offering" (Lev. 4:29). On the Day of Atonement a goat was slain (Lev. 16:9). Hence, atonement necessitated the death of a victim.

Lev. 17:11-14 expresses the basic idea of substitution: "It is the blood that makes atonement [for one's life] . . . For the life of every creature is its blood." The sacrificial blood represents a life that was given in place of, or on behalf of, the penitent one who presented the offering to God. The blood of the animal substituted for the sinner's blood (i.e., life).

The technical term *kipper* means "to atone by

offering a substitute." Forty-nine usages in Leviticus alone attest that this verb is associated with removal of sin (e.g., Lev. 1:4; 4:20; 8:15). It denotes a vicarious sacrifice, the innocent life given for the guilty life.

The sinner confessed his sins by placing his hands on the head of the animal, then slaying it, effectively transferring his guilt to the sacrifice. The priest then placed the blood on the horns of the altar of burnt offering. It was not until the blood was mediated by the priest (i.e., placed on the altar) that the sinner received forgiveness and reconciliation (Lev. 4:35b). Therefore, the priest stood as a mediating agent between God and the penitent.

On the Day of Atonement, generally understood as a day of judgment, a fast was prescribed as the people conducted intense self-examination. The high priest entered the holy of holies with the blood of the sin offering to make atonement for the people and the sanctuary. Another goat (Azazel, "scapegoat") was banished to perish in the wilderness, symbolizing the complete eradication of sin from the camp (Lev. 16).

Although in the NT reconciliation terminology occurs specifically only in Rom. 5:10-11; 2 Cor. 5:18-20, the concept is vigorously attested, in that the OT metaphors meet their inexorable fulfillment in Christ. The Cross presents Christ putting "away sin by sacrifice of himself" (Heb. 9:26; cf. v. 22). He is "the Lamb of God who takes away the sin of the world" (John 1:29, 36), the "paschal lamb" (1 Cor. 5:7). As the Passover commemorated God's deliverance of his people from Egyptian bondage, so Jesus' sacrifice delivers people from the slavery of sin (cf. Eph. 5:2; 1 Pet. 1:18-19). The book of Hebrews highlights Christ's perfect sacrifice for sin and espouses the superiority of his blood over animal blood (Heb. 9:13-14). This was the ideal, complete, all-encompassing sacrifice, accomplishing what the OT sacrifices could not, "one sacrifice for sins for all time" (Heb. 10:12).

Christ's sacrifice is understood in terms of expiation (Gk. *hilastḗrion;* Rom. 3:25), the canceling of guilt and cleansing of sin. The Bible does not subscribe to the pagan view of appeasing the wrath of a capricious deity. Rather, propitiation is orderly here, in that Christ's death effected the means by which God chose to manifest his "wrath" against sin, but averts it from the sinner, thereby being consistent with his holy character and still making it possible for repentant sinners to receive salvation.

Christ's death was vicarious: "Christ died for our sins" (1 Cor. 15:3); he was "offered once to bear the sins of many" (Heb. 9:28). He "bore our sins in his body" (1 Pet. 2:24) and died "the righteous for the unrighteous" (3:18). He is the "ransom" (*lýtron*), the price paid by one person to secure the freedom of another. Prisoners of war and slaves were freed in this manner. Hence, Christ's mission statement, "to give his life as a ransom 'instead of' (or 'in the place of') many" (Mark 10:45), underscores the voluntary substitutionary nature of his sacrifice (cf. Matt. 26:28; 1 Cor. 6:20; 1 Tim. 2:6; Tit. 2:14). Compare the Suffering Servant "who was wounded for our sins" (Isa. 53:5); as the *ʾāšām,* "guilt offering" (v. 10), he is the redemptive self-oblation.

Hebrews underscores Christ's high-priestly mediatorial role, which is to "make expiation (NRSV 'make a sacrifice of atonement') for the sins of the people" (Heb. 2:17). Seated at the place of authority, he is a minister in the sanctuary (8:1-12), offering the merits of "his own blood" (9:12), "in the presence of God on our behalf" (v. 24). As the only one who is truly human and divine, he could mediate (i.e., interpose) between parties as the equal friend of each, especially to effect reconciliation. Indeed, "there is one God; there is also one mediator between God and humankind, Christ Jesus, himself human, who gave himself a ransom for all" (1 Tim. 2:5-6).

The final assize will bring complete resolution to the problem of sin. Evil will be totally eradicated (Matt. 25:41; Rev. 20). God and his people will dwell together in perfect and eternal harmony, united in Christ (Eph. 1:9-10; Rev. 21-22). The chasm will have been bridged.

Bibliography. R. Letham, *The Work of Christ* (Downers Grove, 1993); L. Morris, *The Atonement* (Downers Grove, 1983); *The Apostolic Preaching of the Cross,* 3rd ed. (Grand Rapids, 1965); A. Rodriguez, *Substitution in the Hebrew Cultus* (Berrien Springs, 1982); J. R. W. Stott, *The Cross of Christ* (Downers Grove, 1986). KENNETH D. MULZAC

ATONEMENT, DAY OF

The day (Heb. *yôm kippur*) marking the sober climax in a 10-day cycle at the beginning of the Jewish new year (Heb. *rōʾš haššānâ*). It is a day of introspection, self-evaluation, and prayer rooted deeply in Israel's imagination and history.

Already in Scripture, this day represented a composite of still earlier ritual practices known outside Israel, but uniquely combined in Israel's worship for profound effect. The classical text Lev. 16 blends the ceremony of purifying the sanctuary with that of the scapegoat ritual, restricting both to performance on the tenth day of the seventh month, Tishri (16:29-34; 23:27-28).

Throughout the year were well-established rituals to beg pardon for one's known and unknown sins (Lev. 4:1–5:13). However, the sacred ritual space — including the sanctuary, tent of meeting, and altars — as well as the sacramental role of the priesthood itself all became contaminated by the contagion of sins not accounted for by the various ongoing liturgies and sacrifices. Even the people as a whole suffered the effects of sins unaccounted for and wrongs unforgiven that piled on defilement needing entreaty. So once a year, the only time he could do so, the high priest would enter the most holy place where the ark of the covenant was located to purify the sacred spaces, the priestly station, and the whole congregation, literally from the inside out.

A fast was called to underscore the seriousness of the day. The high priest removed his ornamental garments, bathed, and put on white linen. He then sacrificed a bull as a sin offering for himself and the other priests, saving the blood for the rite of purification. Afterward, he entered the most holy place, carrying with him a censer of hot coals and some incense to create a haze which would shroud the ark's sacred lid (the "mercy seat") lest he see it (or God?) and die. Once inside, he sprinkled the blood upon and in front of the ark's covering to effect removal of any sin residue due to priestly offense in the previous year. He then repeated this ritual using one of two goats donated by the congregation and chosen by lot to atone for the sin residue of the people. In effect, the blood served as a detergent removing impurities from the sanctuary and the tent of meeting. He then took some blood from each of the slain animals and cleansed the altar outside of any sinful contamination (cf. Lev. 16; 23:26-32; Exod. 30:10; Num. 29:7-11). With the sacred spaces and priestly office purified, the impurities ritually removed now required official deposition. The priest turned to the scapegoat ritual as the means to that end.

To understand the significance of animal sacrifice and the scapegoat ritual, anthropological studies have recently shown how deeply rooted in primeval time such sacred ceremonies lie. The emergence of human culture depended in large measure on the discovery that reciprocal violence between brothers (e.g., Cain and Abel) and clans and tribal groups that threatened human coexistence could be offset by ritual murder. If the violence inherent in survival of the fittest could be unanimously redirected on a common enemy within the clan, a sense of community ("us against them") could be restored. Sacrificing a victim seemed to stop the cycle of retaliation and renew the peace. The scapegoat mentality became sacralized as a means of regulating endemic reciprocal violence through vicarious sacrifice. Fortunately for Israel (and others), Yahweh required that the sacral lynching of a human victim be replaced with a surrogate victim in the form of a goat (or other animals). In Scripture, esp. Lev. 1 and 16, pouring the collective sins gathered up by the cleansing rituals of the high priest upon the scapegoat and sending it burdened by sin into the wilderness served to reconcile human community to God and to each other. Doing this every year was not only a theologically important rite, it was a social necessity. The Day of Atonement rituals profoundly respond to psychological and socio-political needs that subsequent atonement theories, focusing as they do so often on dogmatic (i.e., certain "orthodox" doctrinal) interpretations, have not yet fully appreciated.

After the scapegoat carried with it the systemic, structural, and personal sins of the people into the wilderness, the high priest once again bathed and clothed himself in his usual garb. He then offered one more sacrifice, a burnt offering of the skin, flesh, and entrails of the goat and bull outside the now consecrated camp. The atonement of the people was complete for one more year. Communal and personal shalom was restored.

The Day of Atonement would become the annual high point in early Jewish spiritual renewal and remains so to this day. NT writers with equal prophetic imagination would see in the death of Jesus the combined rituals of blood cleansing and the scapegoat mechanism writ large and permanently secured (Heb. 6–9).

Bibliography. R. Girard, *Things Hidden Since the Foundation of the World* (Stanford, 1987); L. L. Grabbe, "The Scapegoat Tradition: A Study In Early Jewish Interpretation," *JSJ* 18 (1987): 152-67; J. Milgrom, *Leviticus 1-16.* AB 3 (New York, 1991); D. P. Wright, *The Disposal of Impurity: Elimination Rites in the Bible and in Hittite and Mesopotamian Literature.* SBLDS 101 (Atlanta, 1987).

JAMES E. BRENNEMAN

ATROTH-BETH-JOAB (Heb. *ʿaṭrôṯ bêṯ yôʾāḇ*)
One of several towns in Judah mentioned in the genealogy of Salma, son of Hur, a descendent of Judah (1 Chr. 2:54). If these towns are listed in geographical order, then Atroth-beth-joab is to be located between Netophah (possibly Khirbet Bedd Fālûḥ [171119], SE of Bethlehem) and Manahath (probably el-Mâlḥah/Manaḥat [167128], NW of Bethlehem). This would place Atroth-beth-joab near the edge of the Judean wilderness, although its modern location has not yet been identified.

WADE R. KOTTER

ATROTH-SHOPHAN (Heb. *ʿaṭrōṯ šôpān*)
A city rebuilt by the tribe of Gad in Transjordan (Num. 32:35). While the LXX lacks the word *ʿaṭrōṯ*, the Vulg. adds *et* (and) between the two, thus creating two different places, Atroth and Shophan. Although Jebel ʿAṭṭarus has been proposed as the site, its location is far from certain. ZELJKO GREGOR

ATTAI (Heb. *ʿattay*)
1. A son of the Egyptian slave Jarha by Sheshan's daughter. He became the father of Nathan (1 Chr. 2:35-36).

2. A Gadite warrior who went over to David at Ziklag (1 Chr. 12:11[MT 12]).

3. A son of Rehoboam and his favorite wife Maacah (2 Chr. 11:20).

ATTALIA (Gk. *Attáleia*)
A port city (modern Antalya) lies on the southwestern corner of Asia Minor on the Mediterranean Sea, ca. 36.5 m. (120 ft.) above the mouth of the Catarrhactes River. The city, founded by and named after Attalus II Philadelphus of Pergamum (159-138 B.C.E.), was located on a trade route between Macedonia and Syria and Egypt. It was the harbor for Perga, capital of the province of Pamphylia. Paul and Barnabas passed through Attalia as they returned to Antioch (Acts 14:25).

Remnants of Hellenistic defenses are evident in the existing city walls. These walls, complemented with towers, extended to an outer harbor, which the Attalians could close by stretching a chain across the entrance. A triple gate, built by Hadrian (117-138 C.E.), and an aqueduct also survive.

STEVEN L. COX

AUDIENCE HALL

A room (Gk. *akroatḗrion,* "place of hearing") in Herod Agrippa's praetorium at Caesarea where criminal cases were decided. It was here that Paul faced not only Festus the Roman procurator and his five tribunes but also King Agrippa and Bernice, after having appealed to Caesar (Acts 25:23).

AUGUSTAN COHORT

See COHORT.

AUGUSTUS (Gk. *Augoústos)*

Augustus Caesar, the first emperor at Rome. Born 19 September 63 B.C.E., Gaius Octavius was the grandson of Julius Caesar's sister Julia. For almost a century Rome had endured the chaos of a series of civil conflicts and war between powerful factions of nobles, each vying for ultimate and lasting power in an archaic and dying Roman Republic. By 46 B.C.E. Julius Caesar, arguably the Republic's greatest military figure, had consolidated military and political power, soon to be named head of the Roman state for life. An emperor in all but name, Caesar was assassinated on the Ides of March 44 B.C.E. Caesar's will named Octavius his heir and posthumously adopted son (now called Gaius Julius Caesar Octavianus, after taking his adoptive father's name with the cognomen "Octavian" denoting his original family name). In the 13 years of chaos which followed Caesar's death Octavian gradually expanded his own political influence and military resources, finally to defeat Marc Antony and Cleopatra in 31 at the Battle of Actium and thus emerge as sole ruler of Rome's empire, expanded by his own conquest and annexation of Egypt.

Octavian reorganized the outmoded Roman government to maintain supremacy for himself and his followers, masking what was in effect the sovereignty of an emperor with the constitutional trappings of the old republican system. In this manner the politically adroit Octavian avoided Caesar's insensitivity to the Roman penchant against outward forms of monarchy. He was merely known as *princeps* (lit., "first citizen") and his government is identified by history as the Principate. For thus "restoring the Republic" Octavian was honored with yet another change in nomenclature — henceforth to be known as Imperator Augustus Caesar. The names were personal (lit., "he who rules, the ever increasing Caesar") but all three later became titles for the ruler of Rome.

The long 45-year reign of Augustus is considered Rome's golden age. Augustus' legions guarded the long frontiers of the vast empire maintaining *Pax Augusta,* the Augustan peace. Peace brought prosperity, and prosperity nourished the arts. Great achievements in literature remain even today as a witness of the times. Less enduring were the physical monuments erected by Augustus as he transformed the city of brick into a city of marble. The princeps' own popularity seemed without bound. An adoring populace named him "father of his country" and "second founder of Rome." In the provinces, Augustus insisted on just administration, with the result that the whole empire benefited from his rule, with many provincials striving to win the coveted appellation of Roman citizen and quite willing to pay Augustus the unrequested honor of a living divinity in their temples.

Augustus outlived his friend, son-in-law, and heir, Marcus Agrippa, and also his grandsons and heirs, Gaius and Lucius Caesar, so that nearing death he had only his stepson Tiberius to whom he could entrust Rome and its empire. With Augustus' death in 14 C.E. the Principate came to an end; Tiberius had no hesitation about openly calling himself emperor. Though the "Empire" derived from the Principate, Augustus' achievement is nevertheless recognized as revitalizing Rome and so permitting the continuation of its civilizing and unifying force for half a millennium to come.

Bibliography. K. Galinsky, *Augustan Culture* (Princeton, 1996); F. Millar, *The Emperor in the Roman World, 31 B.C.–A.D. 337* (1977, repr. Princeton, 1992); R. Syme, *The Roman Revolution* (1939, repr. Oxford, 1960).

JOHN F. HALL

AVARAN (Gk. *Auaran)*

Alternate name of Eleazar (**8**), son of Matthias (1 Macc. 2:5), who killed an elephant in battle at Beth-zechariah (6:43-46).

AVEN (Heb. *'āwen)*

1. An abbreviation of Beth-aven, the pejorative nickname ("House of Wickedness") of the town and sanctuary of Bethel ("House of God"; Hos. 10:8; cf. Jer. 4:15). Amos first coined the derogatory pun (Amos 5:5), and Hosea embraced it (Hos. 4:15; 10:5).

2. A derisive epithet for an Aramaean valley, probably between the Lebanon and Anti-Lebanon mountains (Amos 1:5).

3. A city which the MT vocalizes as "Aven" (*'wn,* Ezek. 30:17), probably indicting the metropolis's celebrated sun worship. The city is probably the Egyptian city On (Heliopolis; cf. Gen. 41:45, 50; 46:20).

STEPHEN L. COOK

AVENGER OF BLOOD

A male member of a murder victim's family, obligated to find and kill the person who had taken the life of his family member. The obligation existed whether the person was killed with intent or by accident. The underlying principle can be seen in the translation of Heb. *gō'ēl.* Usually translated "redeemer," a more accurate meaning might be "restorer." Killing was considered the inappropriate taking of blood belonging to the group, which the avenger (*gō'ēl haddām*) was responsible to win back by killing the one who shed the blood.

The practice of blood vengeance, found throughout the ancient Near East and in many parts of the world to this day, is connected to an awareness of group or tribal identity: the harm done to one member is harm done to the entire group. It usually arises in noncentralized societies and is intended to be a safeguard and deterrent in the absence of a formalized justice system.

Three of the four passages which mention the avenger of blood are connected to the provision for cities of refuge: Num. 35:9-34; Deut. 19:1-13; Josh. 20:1-9 (cf. Exod. 21:12-14; Deut. 4:41-43). The practice underlies the narrative of the woman of Tekoa before David (2 Sam. 14:5-11).

The establishment of cities of refuge can be seen as an effort to limit and control blood vengeance, based upon a distinction between killing with malice (murder) and killing by accident or without intention. The cities of refuge were to be set aside as places to which an unintentional killer could flee from the avenger of blood, who otherwise could execute the killer without penalty. If a slayer sought asylum in one of these cities, some kind of judicial body within the city (the texts are ambiguous) was empowered to determine guilt or innocence. If the death was determined to be accidental, the slayer was given asylum until the death of the high priest, at which time he was free to return to his own home. If found guilty, the murderer was to be turned over to the avenger of blood for execution.

Bibliography. D. Patrick, *Old Testament Law* (Atlanta, 1985); R. de Vaux, *Ancient Israel* (1961, repr. Grand Rapids, 1997). MARILYN J. LUNDBERG

AVITH (Heb. *ʿăwîṯ*)
A city of Edom and the home of King Hadad, whose father Bedad had defeated the Midianites (Gen. 36:35; 1 Chr. 1:46). A possible location is Khirbet el-Jiththeh, between Maʿân and el-Basṭa.

AVVA (Heb. *ʿawwā*)
A city in Assyria or Syria, possibly the same as Ivvah, from which Shalmaneser V took colonists, resettling them in the cities of Samaria whose Israelite inhabitants he had deported to Assyria (2 Kgs. 17:24; 722 B.C.E.).

AVVIM (Heb. *ʿawwîm*)

1. The inhabitants of the region later called the Philistine Plain, near Gaza, before the Philistines ("Caphtorim") destroyed them and settled in the area (Deut. 2:23). Some were apparently displaced to the south (cf. Josh. 13:3).

2. A city within the territory of the tribe of Benjamin (Josh. 18:23), probably between Bethel and Parah. The form of the word is gentilic and may not represent a geographical name. The place could then be identical with Ai, but there is no scholarly consensus on this. WILLARD W. WINTER

AYYAH (Heb. *ʾayyâ*)
A town settled by the Benjaminites returning from the Exile in Babylon (1 Chr. 7:28). The LXX reads "Gaza," which would be distinct from Gaza in Philistia. Ayyah may be the same as Aija at Neh. 11:31. Some identify it with a site near Ai or with Ai itself (Ezra 2:28). WILLARD W. WINTER

AZAL (Heb. *ʾāṣāl*)
Azal (KJV, NRSV) or Azel (NAS, NIV) means "noble" and possibly refers to an unidentified location near Jerusalem (Zech. 14:5). Other translations render the word as a preposition, "the side of it" (RSV), or a noun, "the other side" (TEV).

BETTY P. LAWSON

AZALIAH (Heb. *ʾăṣalyāhû*)
The son of Meshullam and father of Shaphan the secretary, mentioned in connection with the discovery of the book of the Law (2 Kgs. 22:3).

AZANIAH (Heb. *ʾăzanyâ*)
The father of Jeshua the Levite, who set his seal to the renewed covenant made under Nehemiah (Neh. 10:9[MT 10]).

AZAREL (Heb. *ʿăzarʾēl*) (also UZZIEL)

1. A Korahite who went over to David at Ziklag (1 Chr. 12:6[MT 7]).

2. A levitical singer during the days of David (1 Chr. 25:18). He is called Uzziel in 1 Chr. 25:4.

3. The son of Jeroham; leader of the tribe of Dan under David (1 Chr. 27:22).

4. An Israelite descendant of Binnui who had to send away his foreign wife during the administration of Ezra (Ezra 10:41).

5. The son of Ahzai, a descendant of Immer, and the father of Amashsai (Neh. 11:13).

6. A postexilic priest among those who played on musical instruments at the dedication of the walls of Jerusalem (Neh. 12:36). He is probably the same as **5** above.

AZARIAH (Heb. *ʿăzaryâ, ʿăzaryāhû*)

1. High priest under Solomon; a son of the priest Zadok (1 Kgs. 4:2).

2. A son of Nathan who was in charge of the "officials" (perhaps soldiers garrisoned at the palace or perhaps deputies) under Solomon (1 Kgs. 4:5).

3. The given name of King Uzziah (2 Kgs. 15:13; 2 Chr. 26:1-23). The son of Amaziah and Jecoliah, he became king of Judah at the age of 16 (2 Kgs. 14:21; 1 Chr. 3:12) and is said to have ruled 52 years (2 Kgs. 15:1-2). His reign is sometimes thought to be limited to 783-742 B.C.E., and very likely involved co-regency with his son Jotham and perhaps his father Amaziah as well.

4. The great-grandson of Judah through Zerah (one of the sons of Judah by his daughter-in-law Tamar) and Ethan (1 Chr. 2:8).

5. A distant descendant of Judah through Perez, Hezron, and Jerahmeel (1 Chr. 2:38-39).

6. A descendant of Aaron and grandson of Zadok (1 Chr. 6:9[5:35]).

7. A priest in Solomon's temple (1 Chr. 6:10[5:36]), grandson of **6** above.

8. A priest, father of Hilkiah and son of Seraiah (1 Chr. 6:13[5:39]).

9. A man of the Kohathite division of Levites, whose descendant Heman the singer ministered in the temple in the time of David (1 Chr. 6:36[21].

10. A priest and chief officer of the temple,

listed among the earliest settlers in Judah after the Exile (1 Chr. 9:11).

11. A prophet, the son of Oded, who urged Asa to pursue cultic reform (2 Chr. 15:1-7).

12. The name of two sons of King Jehoshaphat of Judah, murdered when their brother Jehoram ascended the throne (2 Chr. 21:2).

13-14. Two military officers, Azariah son of Jeroham and Azariah son of Oded, who assisted the high priest Jehoiada in the revolt against Athaliah (2 Chr. 23:1).

15. A priest, who along with 80 other priests, prevented King Uzziah from offering a sacrifice on the incense altar in the temple (2 Chr. 26:17, 20, in a narrative explaining why the king contracted leprosy).

16. An Ephraimite, numbered among the chiefs who opposed the bringing of Judahite captives into the city of Samaria (2 Chr. 28:12).

17-18. Two Levites, father of the Kohathite Joel and son of the Merarite Jehallelel, among those who assisted Hezekiah with the cleansing of the temple (2 Chr. 29:12).

19. The chief priest under Hezekiah (2 Chr. 31:10).

20. The grandfather of Ezra (Ezra 7:1).

21. The father of Amariah, another ancestor of Ezra (Ezra 7:3).

22. One of the persons who repaired the wall of Jerusalem next to his own house (Neh. 3:23-24), and a leader who participated in its dedication (12:33).

23. One of the leaders of the people who returned from Babylon to Judah under Zerubbabel (Neh. 7:7). Ezra 2:2 gives instead the name Seraiah. Both names appear as the names of priests who signed a document for Ezra promising to obey the law, to refrain from business on the sabbath, pay the temple taxes, and prevent their daughters from marrying foreigners (Neh. 10:2[3]).

24. One of the men who interpreted for the people the law read by Ezra (Neh. 8:7).

25. One of two men who, after the fall of Jerusalem in 586, led a group of Judahites to Egypt, taking Jeremiah and Baruch with them (Jer. 43:2).

26. The Hebrew name of Abednego, one of the three friends of Daniel in Babylon (Dan. 1:6-7, 11, 19; 2:17).

PAUL L. REDDITT

AZARIAH, PRAYER OF

See DANIEL, ADDITIONS TO.

AZAZ (Heb. *ʿāzāz*)
A Reubenite, the son of Shema and father of Bela (1 Chr. 5:8).

AZAZEL (Heb. *ʿăzāʾzēl*)
The male goat upon which all of the transgressions and sins of the people of Israel are laid on the Day of Atonement (Yom Kippur). The goat is then sent out into the wilderness (Lev. 16:8, 10, 21-22, 26).

There are four views regarding the original meaning of this designation: (1) a combination of *ʿz*, "goat," and *ʾzl*, "to go, go away," which can be rendered "scapegoat" (NIV, NASB); (2) "entire removal," which accords with the stated purpose for both the goat itself (v. 21) and the day in general (v. 34); (3) the place to which the goat departs; and (4) a desert demon or the devil himself (cf. 1 En. 8:1 and passim). The desert or wilderness is frequently described by both the OT and NT as the abode of evil spirits (Isa. 34:13; Matt. 12:43 = Luke 11:24; Rev. 18:2).

Bibliography. E. L. Feinberg, "The Scapegoat of Leviticus Sixteen," *BSac* 115 (1958): 320-31; L. L. Grabbe, "The Scapegoat Tradition: A Study in Early Jewish Interpretation," *JSJ* 18 (1987): 152-67; H. Tawil, "ʿAzazel the Prince of the Steepe: A Comparative Study," *ZAW* 92 (1980): 43-59.

MILES V. VAN PELT

AZAZIAH (Heb. *ʿăzazyāhû*)

1. A Levite who played the lyre when the ark of the covenant was brought to Jerusalem (1 Chr. 15:21).

2. An Ephraimite, the father of Hoshea (1 Chr. 27:20).

3. An overseer of the temple during the reign of King Hezekiah (2 Chr. 31:13).

AZBUK (Heb. *ʿazbûq*)
The father of a certain Nehemiah, one of those who worked on the restoration of the walls and gates of Jerusalem (Neh. 3:16).

AZEKAH (Heb. *ʿăzēqâ*)
A city of the Shephelah of Judah (Josh. 15:35). The five Amorite kings Joshua defeated at Gibeon fled as far as Azekah (Josh. 10:10-11). The Philistines camped between Azekah and Socoh in the prelude to the David-Goliath battle (1 Sam. 17:1), illustrating the strategic importance of the city in the border region between Judah and Philistia. It appears among the places fortified by Rehoboam (2 Chr. 11:9).

Azekah is confidently identified with Tell Zakariya (143123), a triangular, flat-topped mound atop a prominent ridge 117 m. (384 ft.) above the valley of Elah (cf. 1 Sam. 17:2). A cuneiform text attributed to Sennacherib's 701 B.C.E. invasion of Judah boasts of taking "the city of Azekah, his [Hezekiah's] stronghold . . . located on a mountain ridge, like pointed iron(?) daggers without number reaching high to heaven." Despite its apparent destruction by Assyria, Azekah's strategic importance continued until the end of the Monarchy. During the 587 invasion of Babylon Jeremiah named Azekah and Lachish as the last remaining fortified cities of Judah (Jer. 34:7). In a contemporary ostracon letter, a field commander writes to his superior at Lachish, "we are watching for the signals of Lachish . . . for we cannot see Azekah."

Judeans returning from exile settled in Azekah (Neh. 11:30), and occupation continued through the Second Temple period. Eusebius (*Onom.* 18:10) locates Azekah between Eleutheropolis (Beth Guvrin) and Jerusalem. The 6th-century C.E. Madeba Map pictures a settlement Bethzachar and a shrine for "for St. Zechariah" on the Jerusalem-Eleutheropolis road; adjacent to these features appears an unnamed village on a distinct mountain, probably a depiction of Azekah to which the name Tell Zakariya was transferred.

Excavating Tell Zakariya for the Palestine Exploration Fund in 1898-99, Frederick J. Bliss and R. A. S. Macalister discovered a rectangular fortress at the summit and separate defensive towers at the edge of the mound, perhaps originating with Rehoboam and continuing in several phases to the Roman period. One phase contained jar handles impressed with seals of winged scarabs and the word *lmlk* ("belonging to the king") known to date to the period of Hezekiah and Sennacherib's invasion in 701. Various finds suggest the settlement of the mound, with interruptions, from ca. 1500 to the Byzantine period.

Bibliography. E. Stern, "Azekah," *NEAEHL* 1:123-24.

Daniel C. Browning, Jr.

AZEL (Heb. *'āṣēl)*
A descendant of Saul and Jonathan, and father of six sons (1 Chr. 8:37-38; 9:43-44).

AZGAD (Heb. *'azgāḏ)*
The ancestor of a number of Israelite exiles, of whom some returned under Zerubbabel (Ezra 2:12 = Neh. 7:17) and some under Ezra (Ezra 8:12). He may be the Azgad of Neh. 10:15(MT 16) who set his seal to the renewed covenant under Nehemiah.

AZIEL (Heb. *'ăzî'ēl)*
One of the Levites who played the harp as the ark was brought to Jerusalem (1 Chr. 15:20). He is probably the same as the Jaaziel of 1 Chr. 15:18.

AZIZA (Heb. *'ăzîzā')*
An Israelite of the lineage of Zattu, compelled by Ezra to divorce his foreign wife (Ezra 10:27).

AZMAVETH (Heb. *'azmāweṯ)* **(PERSON)**

1. One of David's Champions (2 Sam. 23:31 = 1 Chr. 11:33), from Bahurim.

2. A Benjaminite whose two sons joined David at Ziklag (1 Chr. 12:3).

3. A person in charge of the treasuries in the palace of David (1 Chr. 27:25).

4. One of the sons of Jehoaddah; a descendant of Saul (1 Chr. 8:36; at 9:42 his father is named Jarah).

AZMAVETH (Heb. *'azmāweṯ)* **(PLACE)**
(also BETH-AZMAVETH)
A town in the hill country of Judah, to which 42 members of the clan returned from exile with Zerubbabel (Ezra 2:24). The town provided singers for the dedication of the rebuilt walls of Jerusalem (Neh. 12:29). In Neh. 7:28 it is called Beth-azmaveth. The site is identified as modern Ḥizmeh (175138), ca. 8 km. (5 mi.) NNE of Jerusalem.

Bibliography. W. F. Albright, "Alemeth and Azmaveth," *Excavations and Results at Tell el-Fûl (Gibeah of Saul).* AASOR 4 (New Haven, 1924): 156-57; J. Simons, *The Geographical and Topographical Texts of the Old Testament* (Leiden, 1959).

Dennis M. Swanson

AZMON (Heb. *'aṣmôn)*
A location in the wilderness of Zin that was part of the southern border of the land of Israel (Num. 34:4-5), and the southern border of Judah's tribal allotment (Josh. 15:4). The probable location is 'Ain Muweiliḥ (085010), E of 'Ain el-Qudeirat (Kadesh-barnea).

Pete F. Wilbanks

AZNOTH-TABOR (Heb. *'aznôṯ tāḇôr)*
A town N of Mt. Tabor which marked the western boundary of the territory of Naphtali (Josh. 19:34). Khirbet Umm-Jubeil (186237), 4 km. (2.5 mi.) N of the mountain, has been suggested as the site, based on the reported discovery of Late Bronze pottery; recent Israeli surveys have identified only Iron II and later period materials at the site.

Thomas W. Davis

AZOR (Gk. *Azṓr)*
A postexilic ancestor of Joseph and Jesus according to Matthew's genealogy (Matt. 1:13-14).

AZOTUS (Gk. *Ázōtus)*
Greek name of Ashdod.

AZRIEL (Heb. *'azrî'ēl)*

1. The head of a family from the tribe of Manasseh living in Transjordan (1 Chr. 5:24).

2. The father of Jerimoth, a chief in the tribe of Naphtali during the days of David (1 Chr. 27:19).

3. The father of Seraiah, the courtier of King Jehoiakim, during the prophetic ministry of Jeremiah (Jer. 36:26).

AZRIKAM (Heb. *'azrîqām)*

1. A son of Neariah, a descendant of Zerubbabel and David (1 Chr. 3:23).

2. A Benjaminite, son of Azel and descendant of Jonathan (1 Chr. 8:38; 9:44).

3. A Levite, the son of Hashabiah and father of Hasshub (1 Chr. 9:14 = Neh. 11:15).

4. The commander of the palace at the time of Ahaz. He was murdered along with Maaseiah and Elkanah by the Ephraimite Zichri (2 Chr. 28:7).

AZUBAH (Heb. *'ăzûḇâ)*

1. The daughter of Shilhi and mother of King Jehoshaphat (1 Kgs. 22:42 = 2 Chr. 20:31).

2. One of the wives of Caleb, the son of Hezron, and mother of three sons (1 Chr. 2:18-19).

AZZAN (Heb. *'azzān)*
The father of Paltiel, a chief of the tribe of Issachar (Num. 34:26).

AZZUR (Heb. *'azzûr)*

1. An Israelite who, as a representative of the people, put his seal on the new covenant when Nehemiah was governor (Neh. 10:17[MT 18]).

2. The father of the false prophet Hananiah of Gibeon (Jer. 28:1).

3. The father of Jaazaniah, a contemporary of Ezekiel (Ezek. 11:1).

B

B
A designation of the 4th-century-C.E. Greek Codex Vaticanus.

BAAL (Heb. *ba'al*) **DEITY**
The Canaanite storm- and fertility-god. As an epithet for various West Semitic deities, especially Hadad, the name means "lord," designating a legal state of ownership or social superiority. With the obvious exception of Yahweh, Baal is the most significant deity in the OT.

In a land dependent upon rain-fed agriculture, the storm-god is the most significant deity in the culture. Baal does serve as the most powerful god of the Canaanite pantheon, though his progenitor El is its head. Further, the cult plays a major role in the daily and ritual lives of societal members, given the paramount need for rain and its continuous impact upon the population.

Various derived epithets and functions of this deity are attested. An extension of the concept of rain is that of fertility. Baal is represented iconographically by a bull, underscoring the fructative powers of the god. Ugaritic myths record at length the struggle of Baal against his nemesis, Mot ("death"). Baal alone among the pantheon is powerful enough to engage Mot, as these two antithetical powers collide mythologically. Baal's descent into Mot (who swallows him) is representative of the agricultural cycle, as life in a dry-summer subtropical climate entails months of aridity, theologically understood as the absence of the rain-god.

The power inherent in a thunderstorm lends itself to association with warring prowess. Baal is the warrior par excellence in Ugaritic literature. His defeat of the forces of chaos, represented by the god Yamm ("sea"), saved order in the divine realm. The king of a society which revered him was to imitate Baal in this aspect, to protect mundane society from the forces of chaos (as were virtually all ancient Near Eastern kings, imitating their respective warrior gods who defeated forces of chaos). Iconographically, Baal is represented as a warrior clutching lightning as a weapon.

A number of elements of the Baal cult are attested in the OT. Ecstatic prophets are depicted in the confrontation of Elijah with 400 prophets of Baal at Mt. Carmel (1 Kgs. 18; cf. also the Egyptian work Wen-amon). The cutting mentioned in the ritual (1 Kgs. 18:28) was probably related to the cult of the dead, as the death of Baal is equated with drought. Baal's association with this cult is implied in the biblical prohibition against cutting the hair or body in mourning (Lev. 19:28; Deut. 14:1; cf. Jer. 16:6; 41:5; 47:5; Hos.7:14).

Baalistic cultic practices deeply affected Israelite and Judahite society on two levels. First, a number of liturgical themes, images, and phrases were adapted by the Israelites. Although actual worship of Baal was completely forbidden, there was naturally theological overlap between Yahweh and deities of other pantheons. That Yahweh and Baal are both pictured as storm-deities (Job 38; Ps. 29) is expected in similar ecological niches, with similar epithets. Both are warriors who "ride the clouds" (Ps. 18:10[MT 11] = 2 Sam. 22:11; Ps. 77:18[19]). The two share common enemies, Leviathan (e.g., Job 3:8; 41:1[40:25]; Ps. 74:14; Isa. 27:1), Tannin (e.g., Job 7:12; Ps. 74:13; Isa. 51:9; Ezek. 29:3), and Yamm (Ps. 89:9). The latter examples best exemplify the Israelite demythologization of the events, as the mythic battle of Baal and Yamm is reduced in an act of creation. Order is a part of creation for the Israelites, as the universe was created and controlled by Yahweh from void to completion. His enemies in the OT are mortals, who reject him or try to thwart his plans in the mundane realm.

Second, the syncretistic tendencies of the Israelites generally focus upon the Baal cult. Again, the rationale for the association stems from the overlapping theological functions within the same ecological niche. These practices begin with the wilderness narrative of events at Baal-peor (Num. 25; the orgiastic nature of Baal worship, not unusual among fertility deities, is probably reflected in Hos.

4:14; 1 Kgs. 14:24; 2 Kgs. 23:6-7). The cycles of foreign political oppression in Judges center upon worship of this deity (e.g., Judg. 2:11, 13). Indeed, Gideon is nearly killed by the village men for destroying the altar of Baal and its accompanying Asherah pole (Judg. 6:25-32; the association of Asherah with Baal in the OT may flesh out a fragmentary myth, in which this goddess, the consort of El, seems to be trying to seduce Baal). The degree of syncretism is underscored by the townspeople's decision to allow Baal to deal with Gideon (hence the folk etymology of his name, Jerubaal). This syncretistic practice plagued the Israelites to the exile (Jer. 2:8). It may be reflected in Baal names, although *ba'al* may simply be interpreted as an epithet of Yahweh. The substitution of *bōšeṯ* ("shame") for the Baal element in names is a theological statement by later biblical editors (e.g., 2 Sam. 2:10).

Baal worship was also sponsored by the monarchies of Israel and Judah. Ahab built a temple for Baal (1 Kgs. 16:31-33), and indeed worshipped him (22:53), doubtless spurred on by his Tyrian wife Jezebel. The cultic structure, including the priesthood and temple, was eradicated in Jehu's bloody coup (2 Kgs. 10:18-27). Official sanction of Baal worship in Judah was credited to Manasseh (2 Kgs. 21:3). Josiah's reform completely eradicated Baal worship from the land during his reign (2 Kgs. 23:4-5). However, the practice persisted among the masses. It was blamed for Yahweh's implementation of the covenant curses, in retribution for Israel's infidelity (cf. Deut. 30:15-20).

MARK ANTHONY PHELPS

BAAL (Heb. *ba'al*) **(PERSON)**

1. A Reubenite and descendant of Joel who lived before the deportation of the 10 northern tribes (1 Chr. 5:5).

2. A Benjaminite, the fourth son of Jeiel, a Gibeonite ancestor of Saul (1 Chr. 8:30; 9:36).

BAAL (Heb. *ba'al*) **(PLACE)**

A city in the tribal territory of Simeon (1 Chr. 4:33), identical with Balaath-beer.

BAALAH (Heb. *ba'ălâ*)

1. Another name for Kiriath-jearim (Josh. 15:9).

2. A mountain on the boundary of the tribal territory of Judah, between Ekron and Jabneel (Josh. 15:11).

3. A city in the southern part of Judah (Josh. 15:29), perhaps the same as Balah (Josh. 19:3) or Bilhah (1 Chr. 4:29). It is presumably Tulul el-Medhbah near Khirbet el-Meshash/Tel Masos (between Beer-sheba and the Dead Sea).

BAALATH (Heb. *ba'ălāṯ*)

A city originally located in the tribal territory of Dan (Josh. 19:44) and later fortified by Solomon (1 Kgs. 9:18; 2 Chr. 8:6). It is perhaps identical with Mt. Baalah (Josh. 15:9). The site has been identified as el-Maghâr (129138).

BAALATH-BEER (Heb. *ba'ălaṯ bĕ'ēr*)

A city apportioned by Joshua to the tribe of Simeon following the conquest of Canaan (Josh. 19:8). It is equated with Ramah of the Negeb. Its later identification with the city Baal (1 Chr. 4:33) may indicate Baalath-beer's cultic affiliation (the name means "lady of the well"). The city may also be identical to Bealoth (Josh. 15:24).

RYAN BYRNE

BAALBEK

A town situated near the source of the Orontes River, on the eastern edge of the fertile Beqa'a Valley. Baalbek was named Heliopolis by the Greeks after the classical sun-deity, who was identified with Baal during the Hellenistic period. The Semitic name indicates an earlier occupation or shrine, but no evidence for pre-Hellenistic occupation has been found.

The city was the cultic center of the so-called Heliopolitan triad: Jupiter (Zeus) Heliopolitanus, Mercury (Hermes), and Venus (Aphrodite). Their syncretic Semitic counterparts were Baal with Jupiter and Atargatis with Venus; the local equivalent of Mercury remains problematic. One of the city's temples is depicted on late 2nd/early 3rd-century A.D. coins.

The visible architectural remains date to the Roman period and include a major temple complex with a large staircase and ceremonial gateway leading through a hexagonal court into a vast courtyard. Pools of water flanked a central altar. West of the courtyard was the Jupiter temple, placed on a rectangular platform that raised it above the surrounding buildings. South of the Jupiter temple is the so-called temple of Bacchus, although it may have been dedicated to Venus. Late in the 4th century a Christian basilica replaced the central altar, and a mosque was placed west of the temple of Bacchus after the Arab conquest. Not far from the acropolis is a quarry where stone for the temples was prepared.

THOMAS W. DAVIS

BAAL-BERITH (Heb. *ba'al bĕrîṯ*)

The name or title of a deity worshipped by the Israelites after Gideon's death (Judg. 8:33) whose temple was at Shechem (9:4). Baal could be the Canaanite deity Hadad, known from Ugaritic and biblical texts, or the phrase could also be a title, "Lord or Master of the Covenant," applied to another deity. In Judg. 9:46 the name El-berith (found also in RS 24.278) appears, which if equated could mean that El was the "lord of the covenant" or conversely that Baal was the "god of the covenant." While many scholars equate the two temples and see the titles as referring to the same deity, some see separate sites for the two events recorded in Judg. 9.

The significance of the covenant and its deity or deities for the Shechemites cannot be determined by the context of Judg. 8–9. However, the covenant tradition of Shechem for Israel is important in Josh. 8; 24; Judg. 9; and 1 Kgs. 12. Shechem became the site of the fall festival of covenant renewal for Israel.

Bibliography. E. F. Campbell, "Shechem: Tell Balatah," *NEAEHL* 4:1345-54; F. M. Cross, *Ca-*

naanite Myth and Hebrew Epic (Cambridge, Mass., 1973). RUSSELL D. NELSON

BAALE-JUDAH (Heb. *ba'ălê yĕhûḏâ*)
"Baal of Judah," the city where the ark of the covenant was taken after its return from Philistia (2 Sam. 6:2).

See KIRIATH-JEARIM.

BAAL-GAD (Heb. *ba'al gāḏ*)
A Canaanite town marking the northern boundary of Joshua's conquests (Josh. 11:17; 12:7; 13:5). The king list in Josh. 12 implicitly includes Baal-gad within the territory of Og, king of Bashan. The town is located "below Mt. Hermon" and may have occupied the site of modern Banias. Permanent water sources are by their nature sacred sites, and the name of the town may reflect the permanent spring at Banias (2112.2949). THOMAS W. DAVIS

BAAL-HAMON (Heb. *ba'al hāmôn*)
An unknown place where Solomon had a vineyard (Cant. 8:11). According to some commentators, "vineyard" refers to the royal harem; thus the name could be a covert allusion to Jerusalem.

BAAL-HANAN (Heb. *ba'al ḥānān*)

1. A son of Achbor; the seventh king of Edom (Gen. 36:38 = 1 Chr. 1:49).

2. Overseer of the olive and sycamore trees in the Shephelah during the reign of David (1 Chr. 27:28).

BAAL-HAZOR (Heb. *ba'al ḥāṣôr*)
A mountain where Absalom, the son of King David, held a sheepshearing celebration, at which he had his brother Amnon murdered for raping his half-sister Tamar (2 Sam. 13:23). At the foot of the mountain may have been a settlement with the same name. The location is generally held to be Jebel 'Aṣûr (177153), situated some 1032 m. (3386 ft.) above the sea, 7 km. (4.5 mi.) NE of Bethel. WILLARD W. WINTER

BAAL-HERMON (Heb. *ba'al ḥermôn*)
A place in the Lebanon Mountains occupied by the Hivites (Judg. 3:3) and assigned to the half-tribe of Manasseh (1 Chr. 5:23). It is likely a Hivite town or shrine on the slopes or in the foothills of the Hermon massif. Although the site of Baal-hermon has not been identified, nearly two dozen ancient cult sites are known from the Hermon area dating from the Hellenistic and Roman periods, indicating that the local populace considered Mt. Hermon a sacred area. Like most of the higher mountains in Palestine, Mt. Hermon probably was the seat of a local deity. THOMAS W. DAVIS

BAALIS (Heb. *ba'ălîs*)
An Ammonite king during the ministry of Jeremiah (Jer. 40:14). He sent Ishmael the son of Nethaniah to murder the governor Gedaliah in order to bring about the downfall of Judah and to enlarge his own kingdom.

BAAL-MEON (Heb. *ba'al mĕ'ôn*)
A town (modern Ma'în, 219120) known variously as Baal-meon (Num. 32:38), Beon (32:3), Beth-baal-meon (Josh. 13:17), or Beth-meon (Jer. 48:23), located 14.5 km. (9 mi.) E of the Dead Sea. Part of Moses' gift to the tribes of Reuben and Gad in return for military services against Sihon the Amorite, Baal-meon was rebuilt or fortified by the Reubenites (Num. 32:38). It fell into Moabite hands in the 9th century B.C.E. in the revolt led by King Mesha, who claims in his stela (the Mesha inscription, l. 9) that he built a reservoir at Baal-meon. ROBERT DELSNYDER

BAAL-PEOR

See BETH-PEOR; PEOR.

BAAL-PERAZIM (Heb. *ba'al pĕrāṣîm*)
The location of David's victory over the Philistine army after he was established as king over the entire nation (2 Sam. 5:20 = 1 Chr. 14:11). Although not precisely located, the site is most likely above the valley of Rephaim, SW of Jerusalem (cf. Mt. Perazim in Isa. 28:21, an apparent allusion to David's victory). The high ground there afforded David the tactical advantage in his battle with the Philistines in the valley below. After his victory David gave the site its name, which means "Lord of Breaches" or "Divine Outburst." DENNIS M. SWANSON

BAAL-SHALISHAH (Heb. *ba'al šālîšâ*)
A village in the hill country of Ephraim (1 Sam. 9:4), the home of a man who gave Elisha the "bread of the first fruits" (2 Kgs. 4:42). The site may be modern Khirbet Sirisya (151168), SW of Shechem. Kefr Thilth (154174), 5.5 km. (3.5 mi.) to the north, preserves the ancient name.

BAAL-TAMAR (Heb. *ba'al tāmār*)
A town near Gibeah where Israel ambushed the Benjaminites (Judg. 20:33-36). Its location and modern identification are unclear. The biblical text suggests a location near Gibeah, in the Benjaminite teritory N of Jerusalem. Some scholars have identified Baal-tamar with the "palm of Deborah," slightly farther north in Ephraim (Judg. 4:5); others, with the biblical town of Tamar (Ezek. 47:19; 48:28) and the Roman town of Tamara (Meẓad Ḥaẓeva, 1734.0242; or Meẓad Ṭamar, 1731.0485) in the Arabah. JOHN R. SPENCER

BAAL-ZEBUB (Heb. *ba'al zĕḇûḇ*)
God of the Philistine city Ekron. The Israelite king Ahaziah consulted Baal-zebub about recovering from a fall, whereupon Elijah announced Ahaziah's death (2 Kgs. 1:2, 3, 6, 16).

The name suggests a Semitic deity adopted after the Philistines settled in Canaan, although the etymology has been disputed. Whether *ba'al* means "lord, master, husband" or refers to the Canaanite storm-god depends on the interpretation of *zĕḇûḇ* ("flies"). The simple meaning "lord of flies" suggests, by extension, control over disease.

This parallels the epithet of Zeus the healer, Gk. *apomuios* ("averter of flies"), and may be supported by Ras Ibn Hani 78.20, in which Baal drives out "demon-flies" *(dbbm)* from a sick person. However, Ahaziah suffers injury, not disease, casting doubt on Baal-zebub's connection with disease. It is more likely that the name was originally *ba'al-zĕḇûl* (cf. Beelzebul in the NT). Although *zĕḇûl* alone can mean "lofty, exalted place" (thus "lord of heaven"), the fixed phrase *zbl b'l* ("prince Baal") at Ugarit supports taking Baal-zebul as a local manifestation of the storm-god Baal. Baal-zebub would thus be a derogatory pun on the original name.

John L. McLaughlin

BAAL-ZEPHON (Heb. *ba'al ṣĕp̱ôn*)
"Lord of the North," another name for Baal, the Canaanite storm-god. Baal-zephon has been compared to the Greek Zeus-casius; both were patrons of ships and sailors.

Baal-zephon probably refers to a city which had a temple dedicated to the god, and most likely a seaport. In the biblical narrative Baal-zephon is placed in the eastern Delta near Migdol and Pi-hahiroth (Exod. 14:2, 9; Num. 33:7). Otto Eissfeldt located Baal-zephon at Mahammediyeh, at the western end of Lake Sirbonis (Lake Bardawil) E of the Bay of Pelusium (cf. Herodotus *Hist.* 2.6; 3.5). Strabo (*Geog.* 16.2.28, 32-33) mentions a temple to Jupiter-casius (Zeus-casius) midway along the strip of land between Lake Sirbonis and the Mediterranean Sea at Ras Qaṣrun. Scholars who follow Eissfeldt's northern route for the Exodus identify this site as Baal-zephon. William F. Albright offered an alternative, Tahpanhes (modern Tell Defneh in the eastern Delta), which according to ancient tradition had a temple to Baal-zephon.

The biblical reference to the site may be a later addition to indicate the location of Pi-hahiroth and Migdol.

Bibliography. W. F. Albright, "Baal-zephon," *Festschrift Alfred Bertholet* (Tubingen, 1950), 1-14; J. Baines and J. Malik, *Atlas of Ancient Egypt* (New York, 1980); O. Eissfeldt, *Baal Zaphon, Zeus Kasios und der Durchzug der Israeliten durchs Meer* (Haale, 1932).

Lawrence A. Sinclair

BAANA (Heb. *ba'ănā'*)

1. A son of Ahilud (1 Kgs. 4:12); Solomon's overseer in the southern part of the valley of Jezreel, from Megiddo to the Jordan.

2. A son of Hushai and overseer of Asher and Bealoth during the reign of Solomon (1 Kgs. 4:16). His father was probably David's counselor (2 Sam. 15:32-37; 16:15–17:4).

3. The father of Zadok, who helped repair the walls of Jerusalem (Neh. 3:4). He may be the same as Baanah **3** at either Ezra 2:2 = Neh. 7:7 or Neh. 10:27(MT 28).

BAANAH (Heb. *ba'ănâ*)

1. A son of Rimmon who, with his brother Rechab, murdered Saul's son Ishbosheth and brought his severed head to David (2 Sam. 4:2-12), in an apparent attempt to remove any perceived threat to David's succession to the throne of Israel. David's response was typical of the respect he showed Saul's house (cf. 2 Sam. 1:11-16; 3:28-29); he ordered the execution of the brothers and a proper burial for Ishbosheth.

2. The father of Heleb, one of David's "mighty men" (2 Sam. 23:29 = 1 Chr. 11:30).

3. The last among the 10 (or 11, Neh. 7:7) "leaders" (so 1 Esdr. 5:8) who returned from the Babylonian exile with Zerubbabel (Ezra 2:2). He is perhaps to be equated with the Baanah who was among those who set their seals to the covenant to keep the law (Neh. 10:27[MT 28]).

C. Mack Roark

BAARA (Heb. *ba'ărā'*)
A wife of the Benjaminite Shaharaim (1 Chr. 8:8).

BAASEIAH (Heb. *ba'ăśēyâ*)
A son of Malchijah and ancestor of Asaph the musician (1 Chr. 6:40[MT 25]).

BAASHA (Heb. *ba'šā'*)
The son of Ahijah from the tribe of Issachar; the third king of the northern kingdom who established its second dynasty. He ruled from Tirzah, NE of Shechem, for 24 years (ca. 900-877 B.C.). Baasha assassinated the Israelite king Nadab while Israel besieged the city of Gibbethon (1 Kgs. 15:27-28; cf. vv. 29-30). This battle indicates the continued instability of the tribal territories even though a king ruled the northern kingdom. Following the coup, Baasha exterminated the house of Jeroboam I, a fate also to befall his own house (1 Kgs. 16:11). Apparently the extermination of the two houses was so thorough that later generations still remembered the brutality of the events (2 Kgs. 9:9).

Baasha and King Asa of Judah were hostile toward one another throughout their reigns (1 Kgs. 15:16). Baasha blockaded Judah by fortifying Ramah, 8 km. (5 mi.) N of Jerusalem, and controlling all passage through the region (1 Kgs. 15:17; 2 Chr. 16:1). Asa constructed fortifications to defend his territory against Baasha (Jer. 41:9), but this proved insufficient against the superior force of Baasha. Asa then formed an alliance with Ben-hadad of Syria by paying the Syrian king with funds from the Jerusalem temple. Ben-hadad proceeded to attack Baasha from the north, thus forcing the Israelite king to withdraw from Ramah and to abandon his southern fortifications (1 Kgs. 15:21; 2 Chr. 16:5). Baasha lost much of his northern territory to the Syrians. At the same time, Asa removed the fortifications at Ramah that had been used by Baasha and pushed Judah's territorial claim north to Mizpah.

Baasha ruled under the scrutiny of the prophet Jehu ben Hanani. Elah, Baasha's son, succeeded his father upon Baasha's apparently peaceful death. The biblical record condemns Baasha for "walking in the way of Jeroboam" (1 Kgs. 15:34), even though Baasha was the Lord's instrument for punishing the house of Jeroboam (v. 29). Stephen Von Wyrick

BABEL (Heb. *bāḇel*), **TOWER OF**
A "city and a tower" at the center of a clash of divine and human wills portrayed in Gen. 11:1-9. Babel (Gen. 11:9) means "gate of God" (Akk. *bab-ilu*). The biblical writer, however, opts for a play on the sound of the word and explains the name by using the Hebrew verb "to mix" (*bālal*): Babel is the place where Yahweh "mixed up" the language of all the earth.

Although popular interpretation has focused on the "tower," this word never appears in the text by itself, only in the expression "a city and a tower," a figure of speech known as hendiadys in which two nouns joined by "and" express a single idea: "a city with a tower" or "a towering city." The biblical text speaks explicitly of "the city" that "was called Babel" (Gen. 11:8-9).

The story is notable for its apparent familiarity with Babylonian building techniques and technical terminology in building inscriptions. Kiln-baked bricks were used for the outer layers of monumental architecture, and hot bitumen was employed as mortar (Gen. 11:3). Extant Babylonian building inscriptions frequently contain the standard phrase, "with bitumen and baked brick" (cf. "asphalt and bricks" in proverb 44, *ANET,* 425). In addition, "a tower with its top in the heavens" (Gen. 11:4) is quite similar to frequently attested expressions of the same idea, as in the date formula for the 36th year of Hammurabi, in which it is reported "he built the temple tower . . . whose top is sky-high" (*ANET,* 270; cf. also the description of the Canaanite cities in Deut. 1:28; 9:1). Finally, the idea of securing a "name" for oneself through great building projects such as temples and cities is a common royal ambition.

The tower image in view in the biblical text is almost certainly the Mesopotamian ziggurat, an imposing "stair-tower," usually of seven levels with a temple on its ground floor and a chapel-sanctuary at its peak. The famed temple of Marduk in Babylon, Etemenanki, was ca. 90 m. (300 ft.) tall. According to Babylonian religious conception, the temple stair-tower was the place where heaven and earth meet (the same idea is reflected in Gen. 28:17, where Jacob dreams of a staircase or ladder that is designated "the gate of heaven").

Commentators have variously identified the "sin" at Babel. In traditional Jewish interpretation, it is humankind's refusal to obey the command to fill the earth (Gen. 1:28). Others have seen the building project as yet another human attempt "to be like gods" (Gen. 3:5, 22), or as an effort to secure the future apart from God. Arrogance and pride or, variously, distrust and fear (even fear of diversity) have been proposed. Read in the light of the great city-building tradition of Mesopotamia on which it clearly draws and the call of Abraham which follows in Gen. 12, the story of Babel is a critique of the urban cultic center and an affirmation of the name and the blessing that Yahweh intends "through the wandering of an obedient people" (Patrick D. Miller, 243).

Bibliography. P. D. Miller, "Eridu, Dunnu, and Babel: A Study in Comparative Mythology," *HAR* 9 (1985): 227-51; N. Sarna, *Understanding Genesis* (New York, 1966). JEFFREY S. ROGERS

BABYLON (Sum. KÁ.DINGIR.RA;
Akk. *bāb-ilim;* Heb. *bāḇel;* Gk. *Babylṓn*)
An enormously important city in antiquity ("gate of the god"), situated on the Euphrates River SW of Baghdad.

Babylon's earliest history is obscure because of the lack of written sources and the virtual obliteration of the earliest archaeological levels, but during the Ur III period (ca. 21st century B.C.E.) it was the capital of a province and the seat of a local governor. It became the preeminent political and cultural center in southern Mesopotamia during the 19th and 18th centuries under the Amorite rulers of its First Dynasty, the most illustrious of whom was Hammurabi (1792-1750). During the last quarter of his reign, Hammurabi transformed the city into the center of what may guardedly be called an extraterritorial state which controlled most of southern Mesopotamia (Akkad in the north and Sumer in the south) and, however briefly, territory in the middle Euphrates region (Mari) and Assyria. The kings of Hammurabi's dynasty lavished extensive resources on fortifying and beautifying the city, and its cultural and religious preeminence waxed. Thereafter, Babylon remained the psychological if not always the actual center of political and religious life in southern Mesopotamia. Babylon's extraterritorial influence under the First Dynasty was short-lived.

Already during the reign of Samsu-iluna, Hammurabi's successor, the southern region adjacent to the Persian Gulf, the Sea-Land, asserted its independence; subsequently, the territory under Babylon's control quickly diminished. The rising Hittite state under Mursilis I sacked Babylon just after 1600, ending the First Dynasty. For the next five and a half centuries, the non-native Kassites ruled Babylon. The period is relatively unknown because of the paucity of sources. From the end of the Kassite period until the ascendance of the northern Mesopotamian Assyrian state in the 1st millennium, a series of unremarkable dynasties ruled Babylon. The most notable monarch in the series was perhaps Nebuchadnezzar I (1125-1104), during whose reign the cult statue of the god Marduk was recovered from exile in Elam, and the great epic poem Enuma Elish, which celebrates Marduk's rise to preeminence in the pantheon, was codified. Marduk had become the supreme deity in the pantheon, patron of the city and of its kings. The erudite topographical text known as TIN-TIR=Babylon, which celebrates the theological and cosmological preeminence of the city may also date to this period.

During much of Assyria's dominance of the Near East in the 1st millennium, Babylon remained a thorn in the side of its northern neighbor. For the most part, the Assyrians respected the cultural and religious prominence of the city, even when they

Western towers of the Ishtar gate with reliefs of animals. Constructed by Nebuchadnezzar II (605-562 B.C.E.), the gate led to the sacred processional street
(Courtesy of the Oriental Institute of the University of Chicago)

ruled it, although there were exceptions, as when Sennacherib completely destroyed the city in 689 because of its persistent recalcitrance. Babylon's greatest period of prosperity and power came under the Neo-Babylonian dynasty founded by Nabopolassar. The city became the capital of an imperial state that spanned much of the Near East under the rule of his son, Nebuchadnezzar II (605-562). The Neo-Babylonian kings undertook massive building projects, and Nebuchadnezzar, partly to mimic the accomplishments of Hammurabi, sought to make Babylon the economic and administrative center of the world, a project in which he achieved some measure of success.

Excavations at Babylon were conducted between 1899 and 1917 by the Deutsche Orientgesellschaft under the direction of Robert Koldewey. Partly because the high water table obliterated earlier remains, and partly because of the sheer extent of Neo-Babylonian building projects, most of the excavation results illuminate the city in its imperial phase during the mid-6th century and later. The city was approximately rectangular in shape, bisected by the Euphrates. Two massive defensive walls and a moat surrounded it. Along with two enormous palace complexes, Babylon was home to a host of temples large and small. Undoubtedly the most important was the Esagil ("House whose head is high"), Marduk's temple complex. Just to the north of the temple was the ziggurat of Marduk, Etemenanki ("House, foundation platform of heaven and underworld"), a seven-level staged tower with a small chapel on top. Another prominent feature of the city was the Processional Street that paralleled the river in the eastern half of the city: it led to the monumental Ishtar Gate which was decorated with glazed bricks depicting lions and dragons.

Babylon figures prominently in the OT, especially in historical and prophetic texts from the imperial era, and Nebuchadnezzar, who was responsible for the final sack of Jerusalem in 587, understandably was an object of scorn. One of the most famous narratives concerning Babylon, however, is the Tower of Babel story in Gen. 11:1-9. All humanity, sharing one language, settles in the Plain of Shinar (a name for southern Mesopotamia) and determines to build a monumental tower to secure lasting repute. God confuses *(bālal)* their language to frustrate the plan, and the site is subsequently named Babel *(bāḇel)*. Scholars have long thought that the tower may be a reflex of the Etemenanki, the ziggurat of Marduk. Some have protested that the description of "the tower whose head is in the heavens" (Gen. 11:4) better reflects the ceremonial name of the Esagil temple, but note Nebuchadnezzar's claim: "I determined to raise the head of Etemenanki to rival the heavens" (Weissbach, 46, no. 3:22-26). Babylon's reputation as a magnificent if decadent imperial city outlasted the Neo-Babylonian dynasty, as can be seen in the court tales of Daniel (e.g., Dan. 4:30); much later, the early Christians assigned the opprobrious name of Babylon to imperial Rome (Rev. 14:8; 18:1-24).

Bibliography. A. R. George, *Babylonian Topographical Texts.* Orientalia Lovaniensia Analecta 40 (Leuven, 1992); J. Oates, *Babylon,* rev ed. (London, 1986); F. H. Weissbach, *Das Hauptheiligum des Marduk in Babylon, Esagila und Etemenanki.* WVDOG 59 (1938, repr. Osnabrück, 1967).

David Vanderhooft

BABYLONIA

Geography

The land known to the Greeks as Babylonia is synonymous with the southern portion of present-day Iraq. In Gen. 10:10 it is simply referred to as the "land of Shinar" and was the center of the kingdom of Nimrod. Extending roughly from Baghdad south to the Persian Gulf, it is characterized by rich alluvial soil deposited by the Tigris and Euphrates rivers as they flow south from their sources in the highlands of Asia Minor. Described by the historians of the 2nd century B.C.E. as lower Mesopotamia ("the land between the rivers"), Babylonia is quite dry, receiving less than 10 cm. (4 in.) of annual precipitation. Therefore, civilization as we define it could thrive only when irrigation methods were developed and employed. Essential irrigation could be accomplished because of the annual flood. Beginning in March-April, the waters of the Tigris and Euphrates began to rise, reaching their highest levels in late spring when they overflowed their banks in the lower reaches. Thus planting could be done only in the fall, since the land was inundated when crops are normally grown. The harvest took place in the following spring.

The annual inundation was not always reliable, and a shortfall in the flood waters could easily combine with other factors to transform Babylonia into a land of turbulence. Although the Tigris-Euphrates Valley, without irrigation, was generally inhospitable, no geographical barriers (including the Zagros Mountains and the Syrian Desert) prevented invasion of Babylonia by numerous ethnic groups. Thus, while Egypt was largely isolated from the outside world for many centuries, Mesopotamia as a whole, and Babylonia in particular, witnessed repeated migration, conquest, and reconquest. The resulting turbulence largely prevented the creation of a strong, unified nation. Such conditions inhibited the breakdown of localism and ensured instability from the time of the first appearance of urban centers to the fall of Babylon in 539.

Prehistoric Settlements

Our present archaeological evidence indicates that Babylonia was inhabited at least as early as the 6th millennium. Excavations have yielded the remains of both small and sizeable settlements, indicating a knowledge of irrigation techniques that eventually led to the establishment of major urban centers in historic times. Sites from Tell es-Sawwan to Tell al-Ubaid reveal a sedentary existence and the development of a variety of domestic dwellings, granaries, and religious structures (including the prototype of the standard Babylonian temple). Although there were most assuredly local variations in pottery styles and painted designs, diversity in house plan or general settlement pattern does not preclude the existence of one "culture" with underlying common traits. Nevertheless, the issue of the ethnicity of the inhabitants of Babylonia prior to the appearance of written records probably will not be resolved to everyone's satisfaction.

Third Millennium; Beginning of History

The closing decades of the 4th millennium witnessed the invention of writing and the appearance of the first historical records. Although the original purpose of cuneiform writing is still a subject for considerable debate, it likely was developed in Babylonia to meet the needs of a bureaucratic state. Its invention can be traced to the Sumerians, who first appeared ca. 3200 and settled in the southern half of Babylonia (called Sumer in Gen. 10). While their origins are still unknown, it is widely held that they were indigenous to Babylonia. They lived in more or less independent city-states that were considered to be individual estates of gods or goddesses cared for and governed by human agents known as *en* ("lord") or *ensi* ("steward") operating out of temple complexes. According to the Sumerian King List, these theocracies vied with each other for control of not only water rights but (in time) for the whole of Sumer itself. In the Early Dynastic period (2900-2350), cities such as Uruk, Kish, and Ur waged war with one another. At times of common crisis, several of these city-states banded together under a common leader called a *lugal* ("great man") until conditions improved enough to allow communities to resume their independent existence. Finally, ca. 2400, the ensi of Umma, Lugal-zagesi, defeated his neighbor, Lagash, and subsequently laid claim to both the city of Uruk and to kingship of all of Sumer.

After ruling for 25 years, Lugal-zagesi's forces succumbed to the armies of Sargon, leader of a Semitic people known as Akkadians. The Semites first appear in texts near Nippur in Babylonia and in northern Syria near Ebla (Tell Mardikh) ca. 2600. Quite possibly these Semites arrived even earlier, because the date of the Ebla material is still hotly disputed. Trade between the Sumerians and the Eblaite inhabitants of Syria was apparently already an established fact by the mid-3rd millennium. By contrast, the Akkadians were eastern Semites who originally came from the Arabian desert and established a common capital from which all of southern Mesopotamia was ruled. Sargon I founded the Akkadian kingdom and ruled from Agade, located somewhere in northern Babylonia (called Akkad in Gen. 10). Sargon's grandson Naram-sin not only conquered Syria and destroyed the city of Ebla, but also claimed to be divine. His Sumerian subjects considered this to be sacrilegious, and when Naram-sin's kingdom was overrun by the barbaric Guti from the Zagros Mountains, they devised a religious explanation for the conquest that emphasized Naram-sin's claim to divinity as a reason for his defeat.

The Sumerians witnessed one final period of revival, the so-called Neo-Sumerian period (2100-1925), also commonly called the Ur III period. It began when Utu-hegal of Uruk and Ur-nammu of Ur overthrew the Guti and established Ur as the common capital of a Sumerian kingdom. Under Utu-hegal's guidance, temples and ziggurats were built in southern Babylonia, weights and measures (as well as the lunar calendar) were standardized, and the first written law code in Western history was promulgated. It was in this period that the Gilgamesh stories were probably written (after being handed down orally from previous generations).

The Ur III period ended due to a combination of factors, First, a prolonged drought forced the last king of the Ur dynasty, Ibbi-sin (1950-1925), to buy grain in northern Mesopotamia at virtually any price. Second, the Elamites from Iran sacked and burned Ur and carried Ibbi-sin into captivity. Finally, another group of Semites, the Amurru (OT Amorites; lit., "people of the West"), invaded Mesopotamia from the Syrian Desert and occupied the territory the Sumerians had developed.

Black marble boundary stone of Merodach-baladan (721-710 B.C.E.) granting land to an official. Above are emblems of four deities who sanction the grant (Staatliche Museen, Berlin)

Age of Hammurabi; Coming of the Indo-europeans

Although unflatteringly labeled by some as nomads who "ate raw meat and lived in tents," the Amorites were an important Semitic group that preserved the culture and writing system of their predecessors. They were family and tribally oriented, with individual patriarchs, or tribal sheikhs, often leading them against both non-Semitic peoples and other Amorites. By 1800 they were firmly entrenched in Babylonia, and had carved it into a number of geographical areas owing allegiance to a particular tribal leader with headquarters in what amounted to a provincial capital. The city-state continued to exist only in theory, and property became decreasingly associated with temples and increasingly with private citizens.

Amorite civilization is generally divided into two phases. The first, commonly called the Isin-Larsa period (2000-1800), denotes the dominance of two urban centers, Isin and Larsa, whose "kings" vied with each other (and Amorite Assyria) for power. Toward the end of this period, the dynamic Šamši-adad (1813-1784) virtually reduced the cities of Assur, Ekallatum, and Mari to subservience through conquest, and his sons Ishme-dagan and Yasmaḫ-adad succeeded him in control of Assur and Mari, respectively. Their joint control of Assyria, however, was short-lived, as was the independence of the cities of Isin and Larsa in Sumer and Akkad.

The second phase of Amorite domination was the Old Babylonian period (1800-1600) which witnessed the rise of the city of Babylon and its ruler, Hammurabi (Hammurapi, 1792-1750). Over a period of 30 years, Hammurabi very carefully and deliberately played one Amorite kingdom against another, ferreting out weaknesses in his adversaries. With consummate skill he conquered Assur and Mari and by 1763 reduced Isin and Larsa to submission. By 1760 the whole of Mesopotamia was effectively united under the dynamic leadership of one man, and the military, cultural, legal, and administrative achievements associated with his reign amply justify the designation of the last two centuries of Amorite civilization as the "Age of Hammurabi." Without question, one of the most important events of Hammurabi's reign was the promulgation of a lengthy written code of laws.

The Old Babylonian period ended when Babylonia was invaded by a group known as Indo-europeans. Coming originally from the steppe north of the Caucasus Mountains, they split into two groups. The first, known simply as western Indo-europeans, migrated into Anatolia (modern Turkey), the Balkan Peninsula, and western Europe. The second group, the Indo-aryans, settled in Mesopotamia, Iran, and the Indus Valley. The earliest of these Indo-europeans, the Hittites, settled in the Halys River basin in Anatolia, conquered the native Ḫatti folk living there, and established a small kingdom centered around the capital city of Ḫattuša (modern Boghazköy). In 1595 the Hittite king Mursili I conducted a daring raid into Babylonia, sacking and burning Babylon, destroying Marduk's temple, and taking the statue of Marduk back to Syria. He thus ended the dynasty of Hammurabi.

A group known as the Kassites came to the fore after Babylon's destruction. Evidence presently available suggests the Kassites were Indo-aryans who worshipped such gods as Shuriya, Buriya, and Marut, all found in the Hindu Rig Veda. The Kassites rebuilt Babylon and flourished in southern Mesopotamia from 1600 to 1200. They avoided prolonged war with their northern and western neighbors, flourishing into the 12th century, when they were conquered by the Elamites.

First Millennium

Although the history of Babylonia in the early 1st millennium is still largely shrouded in mystery, the Elamites, Assyrians, Arameans, and Chaldeans played prominent roles in the period. Like their contemporaries, the Phoenicians, the Arameans were western Semites who worshipped a pantheon of gods and used a writing system that was originally derived from Egyptian hieroglyphics. However, the similarities end there. Many scholars still view the Arameans as semi-nomads who were forced to migrate as a result of the turbulence caused by the movement of the Sea Peoples in the eastern Mediterranean in the 13th century. By the 12th century they began to make their unsettling presence felt in Babylonia. The Assyrian kings Tiglath-pileser I and Assur-bel-kala had to conduct many campaigns against them, and written sources indicate that by the end of the 10th century they were firmly entrenched in the area surrounding Damascus and in Mesopotamia as well. By this time they were certainly urbanized, and traded (by donkey and camel caravan) with both the Hebrews and Assyria. Genesis (25:20; 29:1-8), 1 Samuel (14:47), 2 Samuel (8:3), and 1 Kings (10:29; 11:23-25; 15:16-21) are replete with accounts of both peaceful and hostile encounters with the Arameans during the early years of the Hebrew monarchy. Ezek. 23:23; Jer. 50:21 indicate that they were initially disruptive in Babylonia in general and in Babylon in particular. Although they do not appear to have had long-term political influence, the fact that the Arameans could never really unify under one ruler meant that they were a constant source of trouble.

The Chaldeans (Kaldu) appear in southern Babylonia as early as the beginning of the 9th century. Their place of origin and ethnicity present problems. The Greeks used the term "Chaldean" to denote particular tribes of Kaldu who eventually overthrew the powerful Assyrian Empire and established their capital at Babylon. While some persist in identifying the Chaldeans as Arameans, there is no direct evidence in the cuneiform sources to support this. What little evidence does survive suggests that they were an ethnic group separate and distinct from the Arameans, and that they were grouped into as few as five tribes. In any event, the Kaldu tribes already possessed the extreme southern part of Babylonia by the second half of the 9th century and (like the Kassites earlier) had adopted the worship of the supreme god Marduk. Northward expansion put them in direct conflict with Aramean tribes collectively called Aramu. Their supreme god was Sin, a god whose worship was centered at Ur in the south and Harran in the north. In 729 Tiglath-pileser III, the Assyrian king who conquered Israel, ended Babylon's independence. He received tribute from the elusive Marduk-apla-iddina (Merodach-baladan in 2 Kgs. 20:12; Isa. 39:1), who was sheikh of the important Chaldean tribe of Bit-yakin and a contemporary of King Hezekiah. It was he who brought Chaldean and Aramean tribes together in opposition to Assyrian expansion in southern Babylonia. The Assyrian kings Sargon II (722-705) and Sennacherib (705-681) were unable to capture him, and under his leadership both Chaldean and Aramean tribes constituted a formidable threat to the stability of the Assyrian Empire, not only in Babylonia, but in Elam, Arabia, and Judah as well. Sennacherib eventually destroyed Babylon (694), which lay in ruins until his son and successor Esarhaddon (681-669) ordered it rebuilt. The next two monarchs, Assurbanipal and his brother Šamaš-šum-ukin, partitioned the whole of Mesopotamia into two kingdoms, north and south, owing their allegiance to different sovereigns. But after a revolt in 652, Babylonia once again became a part of the Assyrian Empire, and remained so for the next 25 years.

Finally, however, the immense size and internal weakness of Assyria took their toll. In 626 the Kaldu sheikh Nabopolassar led an uprising and declared himself "king of Babylon." Both Nabopolassar and the Assyrian king Assur-etil-ilani (likely the predecessor of the Sin-šarra-iškun known to the Babylonians) claimed authority over Babylonia. Nabopolassar allied himself with the powerful Medes of northern Iran and their king Uvakshatra, known to the Greek writers as Cyaxeres. The two monarchs united forces and prepared to engage the Assyrians and their Egyptian allies. Pockets of resistance to the Chaldeans now developed in Babylonia (in Uruk and Nippur), but Nabopolassar was able to overcome them, and by 612 Nineveh itself was taken. Cyaxeres retreated to his homeland, and Nabopolassar's forces defeated the Assyrians in a last stand at Carchemish in 605. With the defeat of Assyrian king Assur-uballit II, the Assyrian Empire passed into history.

Nabopolassar died in his hour of triumph, and his throne passed to his son, Nabû-kudurri-usur (OT Nebuchadnezzar). With the independent Chaldean dynasty now firmly in control, Nebuchadnezzar made Babylon the headquarters of an imperial administrative bureaucracy. During his 43-year reign (605-562), he surrounded the capital city with no less than five fortification walls of baked and glazed brick along with several palaces which served as his royal residences. Under his guidance Marduk of Babylon was again supreme. His temple, the Esagila, and the ziggurat Etemenanki (the infamous Tower of Babel) were restored, and Babylon became the showplace of the Western world.

Nebuchadnezzar campaigned in Syria and Palestine and in 597 laid siege to Jerusalem. Judah was reduced to the status of tributary and, according to Jeremiah, 2 Kings, and 2 Chronicles, was reduced to rubble in 586, when the Babylonian monarch destroyed the temple of Solomon and deported the

Hebrews into captivity. Jehoiachin of Judah was imprisoned in Babylonia until Nebuchadnezzar's son and successor, Amel-marduk (Evil-merodach in 2 Kgs. 25:27; Jer. 52:31) set him free. The Hebrews remained in captivity for the duration of the Chaldean dynasty.

Nebuchadnezzar is very prominent in the book of Daniel, which records stories of the king's madness. These accounts no doubt reflect an attempt by the Hebrew writer to associate Nebuchadnezzar with the deeds of the last king of the Chaldean dynasty, Nabonidus (555-539). Probably of Syrian origin, Nabonidus not only introduced the worship of Sin of Harran to the capital city, but he also was absent from Babylon for several years while undertaking a campaign to the oasis of Tema in Arabia. It was during his absence that his son Bel-šarra-usur (Belshazzar in Dan. 5) ruled as coregent. Shortly after his return to Babylonia, Nabonidus had to deal with the Persians, an Indo-aryan people originally associated with the province of Parsa in southwest Iran. Under the leadership of their king Cyrus II (549-529), they took Babylon in 539, probably through a combination of force and the betrayal of the governor of Babylon, Gubarru (Gobryas in classical sources). Nabonidus was sent into exile, and the Hebrews were allowed to return to Palestine (Ezra 6). The Persians continued to rule Babylonia as a part of their empire until 331, when they were conquered by Alexander the Great.

The history of Babylonia is one of numerous and diverse cultures. Nevertheless, from the time of the emergence of Hammurabi to the fall of Babylon itself, there is evidence of continued respect for the achievements of previous centuries. Sumerian polytheism persisted, even though Marduk was worshipped as "king of the gods" in Babylon during Amorite, Kassite, and Chaldean times. Sumerian literature was translated into Akkadian, and as a result of the efforts of scribes in Amorite and Kassite times, the exploits of such heroes as Gilgamesh were preserved for posterity. Great respect was shown for the cult centers of city-state deities, and monarchs such as Nabonidus prided themselves on their restoration of "ancient" sanctuaries. The achievements of the civilizations of Babylonia (including writing, mathematics, and astrology) were largely preserved by the Greeks, through whom they became a part of the legacy of antiquity.

Bibliography. A. K. Grayson, *Assyrian and Babylonian Chronicles* (Locust Valley, 1975); J. Oates, *Babylon* (London, 1979); A. L. Oppenheim, *Ancient Mesopotamia,* 2nd ed. (Chicago, 1977); G. Roux, *Ancient Iraq,* 3rd ed. (Baltimore, 1992); H. W. F. Saggs, *The Greatness That Was Babylon,* rev. ed. (London, 1988); D. J. Wiseman, *Nebuchadrezzar and Babylon* (Oxford, 1985). RONALD H. SACK

BACA (Heb. *bāḵāʾ*), **VALLEY OF**

A valley apparently containing trees (Heb. "balsam[?]") which exuded resin or gum (the Hebrew term may be related to *bāḵâ,* "weep," hence "weeping trees"). This valley, of unknown identification, apparently was an arid region through which pilgrims passed en route to Jerusalem (Ps. 84:6[MT 7]).

BACCHIDES (Gk. *Bakchidēs*)

A Syrian official whom Demetrius I Soter sent to Jerusalem as general of an army in 162 B.C.E. He installed Alcimus as high priest, gave him control of Judea, and returned to the king, leaving behind a protective force. Bacchides returned to Jerusalem in 161/0 when he defeated and killed Judas Maccabeus. Subsequently unable to defeat Jonathan and Simon, he strengthened a number of fortresses and towns as a counter measure before leaving. He returned again in 158, but was still unable to defeat Jonathan, so he made peace (1 Macc. 7:8-20; 9:1-73; Josephus *Ant.* 12.10.1-3; 11.1-2; 13.1.1-6).

Bibliography. H. A. Kennedy, "The First Period: From Antiochus Epiphanes to the Capture of Jerusalem by Pompey," in E. Schürer, *The History of the Jewish People in the Age of Jesus Christ (175 B.C.–A.D. 135),* rev. ed. (Edinburgh, 1973), 1:169, 173-76. R. GLENN WOODEN

BAG

Most bags in the Bible are of three kinds: a pouch or purse (usually Heb. *kîs;* Gk. *ballántion*), a traveler's bag (Gk. *pḗra*), or a large sack (Heb. *ʾamtaḥaṯ*). Heb. *śaq* usually refers to the material, i.e., sackcloth.

People in both the OT and NT might carry money in a purse (Prov. 1:14; Luke 10:4) and grain in sacks (Gen. 42–44). God warns traders in the OT not to have false weights in their bags or pouches (Deut. 25:13; Prov. 16:11; Mic. 6:11). In his fight with the giant, the young David puts five slingstones in his shepherd's bag (Heb. *kĕlî;* 1 Sam. 17:40). Judith smuggles Holofernes' head out of the Assyrian camp in her provision bag (Jdt. 10:5; 13:9-10, 15).

When Jesus sends out the Twelve (Matt. 10:10 = Mark 6:8; Luke 9:3) and the Seventy(-two) (Luke 10:4), he tells them not to take a bag along. Later he tells them to take one (Luke 22:35-36). Some scholars reject the "beggar's bag" interpretation (as in TEV) and conclude that the bag was simply a piece of luggage.

Jesus uses the money bag or purse (*ballántion*) figuratively when he urges the "little flock" to give to the poor and thereby acquire "purses that will never wear out" (Luke 12:32-34). CARL BRIDGES

BAGOAS (Gk. *Bagōas*)

The eunuch in charge of the personal affairs of the Assyrian general Holofernes (Jdt. 12:11). He was instructed to invite Judith to the general's banquet and later discovered her murder of Holofernes (Jdt. 14:14-18).

BAHURIM (Heb. *baḥûrîm*)

A town (modern Khirbet Ibqeʿdan) located on the north side of the road leading from Jerusalem to Jericho, E of the Mount of Olives.

Bahurim figures prominently in the Davidic history. It is the home of Shimei, who abused and cursed David as he was fleeing from Absalom

(2 Sam. 16:5; 19:16; 1 Kgs. 2:8), and the location where Abner compelled Paltiel to leave his wife Michal, Saul's daughter, as she was being returned to David (2 Sam. 3:16). Azmaveth, one of David's elite military guard, was from Bahurim (2 Sam. 23:31; 1 Chr. 11:33 [MT "Bahurum"]).

DENNIS M. SWANSON

BAKBAKKAR (Heb. *baqbaqqar*)
A Levite who returned from the Exile and was chosen by lot to dwell at Jerusalem (1 Chr. 9:15).

BAKBUK (Heb. *baqbûq*)
A temple servant whose descendants returned from the Exile with Zerubbabel (Ezra 2:51 = Neh. 7:53).

BAKBUKIAH (Heb. *baqbuqyâ*)
A Levite (Neh. 11:17) and descendant of Asaph the musician. One of the returning exiles designated by lot to live at Jerusalem, he was a gatekeeper and the leader of a group of temple singers (Neh. 12:9, 25).

BAKERS' STREET
A street in Jerusalem (Heb. *ḥûṣ hā'ōp̄îm*), apparently the place where members of the bakers' guild were concentrated (Jer. 37:21). Because Heb. *ḥûṣ* has the more general meaning of "the out-of-doors" or "the ground between the houses," "bakers' quarter" would be a better translation.

BALAAM (Heb. *bil'ām*)
A prophet referred to in the OT and NT as well as in an 8th-century B.C.E. plaster inscription from Tell Deir ʿAllā in Jordan; the book of Numbers contains the most extensive material. Balaam is first introduced in the biblical material when the Israelites approach the land of Canaan, after their defeat of Sihon and Og (Num. 21:21-35). His homeland was in Pethor (Num. 22:5; Deut. 23:4), sometimes identified with Pitru on the Upper Euphrates. Balak, king of Transjordanian Moab, having witnessed Israel's rout of the Amorites, sent messengers to Balaam requesting that he curse the Israelites (Num. 22:1-6). After the messengers arrived with "fees for divination" (cf. Josh. 13:22), Balaam told them that he must first consult Yahweh, an intriguing statement for a non-Israelite. Balaam refused to go to Moab with these messengers, but received permission from God to go with the second group (Num. 22:7-21). After an unusual incident involving Balaam's donkey and an angel of Yahweh (22:22-35), Balaam arrived in Moab. Although Balak desired that Israel be cursed, Balaam stated that he must speak that which he was permitted to by God (22:36-39). After sacrifices were offered, Balaam sought Yahweh and received a divine message (23:1-6). Much to the chagrin of Balak, Balaam blessed Israel in his first oracle (23:7-12). Balak convinced Balaam to attempt again to curse Israel, but his second oracle was also a blessing (23:13-26). Two more blessing oracles were subsequently pronounced by Balaam, the final one predicting that Israel would rule over the Transjordanian kingdoms, including Moab (24:1-25).

Although the archaic (mostly JE) Balaam traditions in Num. 22-24 are rather positive, there are later negative traditions about him. For example, there was apparently a tradition that Balaam was actually willing to curse the Israelites, but was prevented from doing so by Yahweh (Deut. 23:3-6; Josh. 24:9-10; Neh. 13:1-2), something which differs with the statements in Num. 22-24. Num. 25:1-15 is a combined narrative, one component referring to incidents involving Israelite men and Moabite women (vv. 1-5) and a second to incidents involving an Israelite man and a Midianite woman (vv. 6-15). Num. 31 is aware of this combined narrative; it suggests that Balaam was instrumental in the initiation of the apostasy (v. 16 P) and states that he was killed along with various Midianites (v. 8). Furthermore, the NT references to Balaam are all negative, viewing him as a prototype of false teachers in the NT period (2 Pet. 2:15; Jude 11; Rev. 2:14).

Two major fragment groups of a plaster inscription were excavated at Tell Deir ʿAllā in 1967, designated Combination I and Combination II. The latter is particularly fragmentary and enigmatic. On the basis of the script as well as the archaeological context, the plaster texts are dated ca. 700. The language of the inscription has both Aramaic and Canaanite features, therefore scholars are divided as to its precise linguistic classification. As for parallels between the biblical and epigraphic material, Combination I specifically mentions "Balaam son *(br)* of Beor," a "seer of the gods" who had a night vision in which the *Šaddayyīn* conveyed the "future" to him. The fact that the name and patronymic are identical is certainly striking and indicates that both the biblical and epigraphic traditions relate to the same individual. Moreover, in both texts, nocturnal dialogues with god(s) occur (Combination I, line 1; Num. 22:8, 19) and the root *ḥzh*, "see(r)," is also used of Balaam in both texts (Combination II, line 1; Num. 24:4). Finally, the reference to *Šaddayyīn* ("Gods of the Mountain") is the linguistic equivalent of *Šadday* ("God of the Mountain" or "God Almighty"), found in a biblical oracle of Balaam (Num. 24:4). The similarities between the biblical and epigraphic data demonstrate that both draw upon a similar tradition about the same figure, but there are far more differences than similarities, revealing the distinctiveness of each tradition.

Bibliography. F. H. Cryer, *Divination in Ancient Israel and Its Near Eastern Environment.* JSOTSup 142 (Sheffield, 1994); J. A. Hackett, *The Balaam Text from Deir ʿAllā.* HSM 31 (Chico, 1984); W. C. Kaiser, Jr., "Balaam Son of Beor in Light of Deir ʿAllā and Scripture," in *Go to the Land I Will Show You,* ed. J. Coleson and V. Matthews (Winona Lake, 1996), 95-106; P. K. McCarter, Jr., "The Balaam Texts from Deir ʿAllā: The First Combination," *BASOR* 239 (1980): 49-60; G. L. Mattingly, "Moabites," in *Peoples of the Old Testament World,* ed. A. J. Hoerth, Mattingly, and E. M. Yamauchi (Grand Rapids,

1994), 317-33; M. S. Moore, *The Balaam Traditions*. SBLDS 113 (Atlanta, 1990). CHRIS A. ROLLSTON

BALADAN (Heb. *bal'ăḏān*)
The father of Merodach-baladan, king of Babylon and contemporary of King Hezekiah of Judah (2 Kgs. 20:12 = Isa. 39:1).

BALAH (Heb. *bālâ*) (also BAALAH; BILHAH)
A city in the southern part of Palestine, assigned to Simeon (Josh. 19:3). It is also called Bilhah (1 Chr. 4:29) and Baalah (Josh. 15:29).

BALAK (Heb. *bālāq;* Gk. *Balák*)
The son of Zippor and king of Moab. He was overcome with fear after the Israelites defeated the Amorites and so summoned Balaam in order to curse them (Num. 22–24). His futile attempts to seduce the people into idolatry and immorality were legendary (Judg. 11:25; Mic. 6:5; Rev. 2:14).

BALANCES
Although modern coinage had developed in the Eastern Mediterranean by the 7th century B.C.E., coins were not widely circulated in the ancient Near East during OT days. Silver and gold, which were used as media of exchange, were weighed on balances (Jer. 32:10). Weights of stone or metal marked with their weights were used to ascertain the amount of gold or silver placed on the other side of the balance.

Balance weights from the 7th century unearthed at Timnah (Tel Baṭash/Tell el-Baṭâshī) are made of stone. These round stones have flat bases, and consist of two types of weight measurements: the pim and the shekel. The three-pim stones discovered weigh 7.72, 7.88, and 8.02 gm. A two-shekel weight weighs 22.78 gm., a four-shekel weight weighs 43 gm., and two eight-shekel weights weigh 91.2 gm. and 91.16 gm.. Thus, the weights varied slightly.

Coins were widely used by NT times, but money was still sometimes weighed (Matt. 26:15). Balances are mentioned in the NT only in Rev. 6:5.

Dishonest merchants could easily use weights that were heavier than the amount etched on them. In this way, the merchant could collect more gold or silver than the purchaser thought he was paying. This dishonest practice was thoroughly condemned in the OT (cf. Lev. 19:36; also Prov. 11:1; 16:11; 20:23; Ezek. 45:10; Hos. 12:7[MT 8]; Amos 8:5; Mic. 6:11). Balances are used figuratively in the Bible to indicate a person's integrity, worthless vanity, or moral bankruptcy (Job 31:6; Ps. 62:9[10]; Dan. 5:27).

Bibliography. A. R. Burns, *Money and Monetary Policy in Early Times* (1927, repr. New York, 1965); M. I. Finley, *The Ancient Economy,* 2nd ed. (Berkeley, 1985); G. L. Kelm and M. Amihai, *Timnah* (Winona Lake, 1995).

ALAN RAY BUESCHER

BALD(NESS)
The biblical vocabulary of baldness refers to several phenomena. Natural hair loss from the head (*qaraḥ*) or the forehead (*gibbēaḥ*) is found in males. Hair loss associated with disease processes and self-inflicted baldness are found in both genders.

Baldness may be an ordinary condition (Lev. 13:40-41) or may result from carrying burdens on the head (Ezek. 29:18). Elisha reacted badly when a crowd of youngsters shouted at him, "Go on, Baldy" (2 Kgs. 2:23).

If a certain type of sore is found in bald spots, "leprosy" may exist, and the sufferer must be examined (Lev. 13:43-44; cf. v. 55).

Intentional self-inflicted baldness, associated with mourning, is an ordinary practice in Israel in Jeremiah's time (Jer. 16:6). Such baldness is among the appropriate responses to national disasters, both in Israel (Isa. 22:12; Ezek. 7:18; Amos 8:10; Mic. 1:16; among women only, Isa. 3:24) and elsewhere (Isa. 15:2; Jer. 47:5; 48:37; Ezek. 27:31). However, such baldness is prohibited in the Torah: both to priests (Lev. 21:5; cf. Ezek. 44:20) and to all Israel (Deut. 14:1). Related mourning practices include cutting off or shortening the beard (Lev. 19:27; Isa. 15:2) and cutting the flesh (Lev. 19:28; 1 Kgs. 18:28; Jer. 16:6). VICTORIA ANDREWS/M. O'CONNOR

BALM
A resinous plant exudate obtained through incisions in the bark (Heb. *ṣᵉrî/ṣŏrî*). The Ishmaelites trade it with Egypt (Gen. 37:25), and Joseph receives it as a gift from Jacob (43:11). It also appears in a list of Judean exports to Tyre (Ezek. 27:17). While these references highlight the commercial value of balm as a perfuming oil, the references in Jeremiah (Jer. 8:22; 46:11; 51:8) highlight its medicinal value and its association with Gilead. Gilead apparently was famous for both its physicians and, especially, the healing properties of the unguent, whose aroma perhaps counteracted the odor of infected wounds (Jer. 8:22).

Suggested identifications for "balm" include storax, balsam, and mastic, but none of these plants is indigenous to Palestine. Its association with Gilead may reflect the commercial importance of that region in trade. Recent excavations in the Judean desert (Tel Goren/Tell el-Jurn; 187097) have unearthed a possible production center for perfume (identified as balm). RICK R. MARRS

BALSAM
A shrub (*Balsamodendrium Opolbalsamum*) which yields a spice favored as a fragrance (Heb. *bōśem;* Cant. 5:1, 13; cf. Exod. 35:28). Heb. *bāḵā'* (2 Sam. 5:23-24; 1 Chr. 14:14-15) probably indicates the mastic tree (*Pistacia lentiscus* L.), which is more of a shrub than a tree and secretes a milky sap. A prominent shrub in the Judean hill country, its many branches and hard leaves provide a suitable place of protection or concealment.

BAMOTH (Heb. *bāmôṯ*), **BAMOTH-BAAL** (*bāmôṯ-ba'al*)
A place where the Israelites halted N of the Arnon (Num. 21:19-20). Bamoth is perhaps the same as Bamoth-baal, where Balak king of Moab assigned

Balaam to curse Israel (Num. 22:41). Bamoth-baal was one of many cities given to Reuben, as well as being numbered with the towns around Heshbon (Josh. 13:17). Bamoth-baal may also correspond to Beth-bamoth of the Mesha stela, a place Mesha was credited with rebuilding. The precise location of Bamoth-baal is unknown, but it probably was situated on the western edge of the Transjordanian plateau in the area of Mt. Nebo. Although archaeological evidence has not been found, some scholars equate it with Khirbet el-Quweiqiyeh, which matches the geographical references found in the Bible. PHILIP R. DREY

BAN

Heb. *ḥērem* is not employed in a consistent manner within the OT. It sometimes appears as a voluntary practice undertaken by the Israelites (Lev. 27:28; Num. 21:2) and other times seems to be commanded by God (Deut. 20:17; Josh. 6:17-18). In general, there are many more occurrences in which God orders the ban as opposed to instances in which it is done as part of a vow. The voluntary idea of the ban occurs primarily in texts of priestly origin (Lev. 27:21, 28; Num. 18:14; Ezek. 44:29). In Deuteronomy and the Deuteronomistic history the ban never appears as a vow and often, although not always, it is explicitly ordered by God (Deut. 7:2; 13:15[MT 16]; Josh. 10:40; 11:14, 20; 1 Sam. 15:2-3). On some occasions one is allowed to keep parts of the booty (Josh. 8:2), and at other times everything is to be destroyed (Deut. 13:15-17[16-18]; 1 Sam. 15:3). It is possible that this practice changed over time, or perhaps different texts represent this institution in different ways.

Thus Josh. 6–7 refers to a ban in which everything was to be killed, destroyed, or dedicated to God. But at least two instances in Deuteronomy allow one to plunder the livestock and booty of a nation that has been put to the ban (Deut. 2:34-35; 3:6-7). Interestingly, after the misfortune resulting from Achan's misappropriation of the banned goods in Josh. 7, the ban is reduced in ch. 8 and the people now permitted to keep the booty and the livestock (vv. 2, 27). This instance along with 1 Sam. 15 may suggest that the total ban was difficult to implement and that the more moderate versions developed out of the necessity to reward the troops.

Often the language surrounding the concept of the ban indicates that the object is consecrated or dedicated in an almost sacrificial manner (Lev. 27:28-29; Deut. 13:16[17]). A further sacral property of such banned goods is their apparent ability to transfer their dedicated status to those who misappropriate them (Deut. 7:26; Josh. 6:18). This is the most likely explanation for why Joshua executes Achan's whole family and all his livestock as well (Josh. 7).

Analogues to the idea of the ban appear in other ancient Near Eastern cultures. Such parallels strongly suggest that this practice did occur in certain periods and should not be viewed as a fictional concept invented by biblical writers who were romanticizing about the glorious past. The single closest analogue to the way in which the ban functions in the OT can be in the 9th-century Mesha Stone. Line 17 uses the root *ḥrm* to describe the Moabite king's killing and utterly dedicating a whole city to his god.

A similar usage is employed in 2 Kgs. 19:11. Here the Assyrian king Sennacherib instructs his official to tell Hezekiah: "You have heard what the kings of Assyria have done to all the lands, destroying them utterly." Whether the Assyrian delegation actually used the verb *ḥrm* cannot be known for sure, but the fact that much of ancient warfare was understood explicitly as fighting either to protect or expand various gods' territories certainly makes this a possibility.

Akk. *asakku*, found in texts from Mari, carries a similar connotation. The person who ate the *asakku* became contaminated by it and, originally, would have been killed for this offense. This taboo may have originated elsewhere, but it does occur in military contexts as well. Although it is clear that the notion of *asakku* sheds some light on the biblical notion of ban, it is also certain that it is not an exact analogue because the *asakku* can belong to a king and even a soldier, as well as a god.

Bibliography. M. Fretz, "Herem in the Old Testament," in *Essays on War and Peace: Bible and Early Church*, ed. W. M. Swartley (Elkhart, 1986), 7-44, 67-95; J. S. Kaminsky, *Corporate Responsibility in the Hebrew Bible.* JSOTSup 196 (Sheffield, 1995); S. Niditch, *War in the Hebrew Bible* (Oxford, 1993); P. D. Stern, *The Biblical Ḥerem.* Brown Judaic Studies 211 (Atlanta, 1991). JOEL S. KAMINSKY

BANI (Heb. *bānî*)

Perhaps an abbreviated form of Benaiah; however, since both names appear in the same lists, it is not likely that they are identical.

1. A Gadite who was a lesser member of David's elite warrior group known as the "Thirty" (2 Sam. 23:36). The parallel account reads "Hagri" (1 Chr. 11:38).

2. A Levite in the ancestral line of Ethan, who served in the time of David (1 Chr. 6:46[MT 31]).

3. A Judahite who was a son of Perez (1 Chr. 9:4).

4. A family of whom 642 members returned to Jerusalem from the Babylonian Exile (Ezra 2:10). Several members who had married foreign women were among those who promised to put away their foreign wives (Ezra 10:29, 34). A parallel list reads Binnui (**3**) for Bani (Neh. 7:15), but some scholars think that the names represent two distinct families.

5. The father of Rehum, who was closely involved with the revival work of Ezra. He directed a group of Levites who repaired part of the wall of Jerusalem in the time of Nehemiah (Neh. 3:17). Bani was also among those who stood with Ezra as the scribe read the law to the people (Neh. 8:7-8; cf. 9:4). Ezra would read a paragraph or two and other men would explain, expound, and possibly translate into Aramaic the text as it was read. It is not clear if they took turns doing this or if each man had a smaller group to which he presented the material.

Bani could also be the father of Uzzi, the overseer of the 284 Levites chosen by lot to move into Jerusalem to occupy the city and work at the temple (Neh. 11:22). Originally the family of Bani had been singers in the house of God in the time of David.

6. One who set his seal to the renewed covenant under Nehemiah (Neh. 10:15[16]).

WESLEY PADDOCK

BANNER

A flag, emblem, carved image, or streamer attached to a pole. Heb. *nēs* is connected with military endeavors. It is thus a banner under which individuals gather for battle (Isa. 5:26; Jer. 50:2; 51:12, 27) or celebrate victory (Exod. 17:15; Isa. 11:12). It can also describe an incident that serves as a warning from God (Num. 26:10), and it can be a metaphor of safety for those who trust in God (Ps. 60:4 MT 6). Heb. *degel* also has military connotations (Ps. 20:5[6]; Cant. 6:4, 10) but is used predominantly to refer to a banner that identified the location of particular tribes as they were camped around Mt. Sinai (Num. 2, 10). It can also describe affection for one's lover (Cant. 2:4).

No one knows what these banners looked like. Some scholars speculate that the tribes had totem animals (cf. Gen. 49), which might have adorned the banners. Indeed, stone carvings and literary texts indicate that other nations (Egypt, Babylon, Assyria, Persia, and Rome) used banners adorned with animals such as an eagle (the official standard of Rome), wolf, lion, or serpent. In other instances, one finds the image of the national god on the standard (e.g., the Assyrian god Assur drawing a bow).

RICK W. BYARGEON

BANQUET

See MARZEAH; MEALS.

BAPTISM

Ritual cleansings of the body were well established in Torah (e.g., Exod. 29:4; 30:17-21; 40:30-33; Lev. 17:15-16; Deut. 21:6), as throughout the ancient Near East. Naaman was told to wash seven times in the Jordan to be healed (2 Kgs. 5:10). Later, lustration played a central role at Qumran. Footwashing was used by Jesus as an example of his humility and of the need for submission and servanthood by his followers (John 13:2-20).

Prior to the NT period, a ritual cleansing was instituted for the purification of gentile converts to Judaism. If this was the antecedent to NT baptism, John the Baptizer assumed an altered meaning by which this earlier practice became a sign of repentance for Jews themselves. There are indications that later the Church found another crucial alteration in meaning for its own use of baptism. Had Christian baptism and John's baptism been viewed as identical, the report in Acts 19:3-5 would be inexplicable. Nor is this distinction peculiar to Luke's theology. According to Matthew, John was puzzled that Jesus should come to him for baptism, since repentance seemed to have no applicability to Jesus (Matt. 3:13-17). Within that narrative may lie the key to the distinction; Jesus requests baptism apparently not simply in order to identify himself with sinners but primarily "to fulfill all righteousness."

"To fulfill" can be translated "to bring to completion or perfection." Jesus' own baptism is thus an identifying sign about Jesus himself. He is the one who completes the intention of God, who brings to perfection all that God has envisioned since creation. Christian baptism is thus less a negation (in token of renunciation) than an affirmation of being incorporated into Christ, who is the perfection of all God wills, and thus of being granted new life as a gift.

This motif of bringing to completion all that God intends makes sense of otherwise obscure allusions in the narratives of Jesus' baptism. The Synoptics (Matt. 3:13-17; Mark 1:9-11; Luke 3:21-22) mention water and a voice, together with the descent of the Spirit — all reminiscent of God's spirit hovering over the waters and speaking creation into existence in Gen. 1:1-5. Thus Jesus at his baptism is identified as the one who fulfills the old creation by instituting the new creation. Jesus, by going into the wilderness for 40 days, is portrayed as the new Moses and the new Elijah (Exod. 24:18; 1 Kgs. 19:8). Similarly the figure of the dove further identifies him as the new Noah (Gen. 8:8-12), thus intensifying the motif of the new creation. To be baptized as a Christian is to receive and to be received into the whole sacred story in its fulfillment — a profound gift of the Holy Spirit, whose activity in baptism is so frequently asserted throughout the NT.

The precise sequence of water baptism, reception of the Spirit, and the associated laying on of hands is not clear, however. In Acts these come in a variety of orders (water, hands, Spirit: in 19:5-6 the use of hands is immediate; in 8:14-17 the laying on of hands is deferred and done by others; hands, Spirit, water: 9:17-19; Spirit, water, without mention of hands: 10:44–11:18). What is asserted overall by Luke, however, is that through baptism the presence and work of the Risen Lord (which is what the Spirit makes real to Christians) is shared within community (thus the importance of the laying on of hands). This gift is seen by Luke not as static transmission but as dynamic interaction — a perspective shared by Johannine teaching (John 3:1-8; 1 John 5:6-8). The importance of baptism to the ancient Church is attested by the evangelical status accorded the rite in Matt. 28:19.

Paul's alleged indifference to baptism in 1 Cor. 1:14-17 refers only to the person of the administrator: Whether one is baptized by Paul, Peter, or Apollos means nothing; one is to be centered on Christ into whom he or she is baptized. This sometimes distorted passage must be interpreted in light of Paul's clear affirmation of baptism as incorporation into the death and resurrection of Christ (Rom. 6:1-11) and as the putting on of Christ like a garment, thereby receiving a new identity beside which all of the usual distinctions dissolve (Gal. 3:27-29). Paul's more puzzling comment about Israel being "baptized into Moses in the cloud and in the sea" (1 Cor. 10:2) actually is quite illuminating once one resists the temptation to suppose the apostle is referring to some literal rite. Paul is suggesting that as a fragmented band of refugees found a new identity in the Exodus and its aftermath in the covenant at Sinai, so those who are baptized into Christ thereby find a new identity through their covenant with God.

So also with Peter's comparison of baptism to salvation on the ark: both events bespeak a newness given by the grace of God by which humanity is rescued from destruction. In Heb. 6:2-4; 10:32 "enlightenment" alludes to baptism; and the ancient Church when instructing catechumens liberally used John 9, Jesus' healing of the man blind from birth.

The matter of the mode of baptism in the NT is much less clear than usually supposed. The baptism of 3000 in Jerusalem on the day of Pentecost (Acts 2:41), a city without a river, casts doubt on the usual assumption that all NT baptisms were by immersion. Indeed, it can be questioned whether the NT proves immersion was used at all (though almost certainly it was). Ancient iconography persistently shows Jesus standing in water to his waist (hence the going down and the coming up of the Synoptics and of the story of the eunuch in Acts 8:36-38, as well as the need for abundant water in John 3:23), with the Baptizer pouring water over Jesus' head. When churches began to build baptisteries, some were deep enough to stand in but not broad enough to lie down in — a strange fact if immersion was the invariable mode handed down from the apostles. Rom. 6:4 may refer to mode as well as meaning; but that is not certain; it could also refer to timing, if baptism in Rome during Paul's time was administered primarily at Easter, as certainly it was there in subsequent centuries..

The argument that Gk. *baptízō* means immersion assumes that a given word can have only one meaning — as if use of the term "the Lord's Supper" today must necessarily mean an ample meal served only in the evening. If the word for baptism can mean nothing except immersion, the references from Peter and Paul make no sense, since neither in the great Deluge nor in the escape through the sea were people covered with water. Certainly the use of the word in Luke 11:38 does not imply a full bath.

Similarly, neither can the baptism of infants in the apostolic period be proved or disproved by Scripture. That there must have been infants included in the household baptisms (Acts 16:31; 18:8; 1 Cor. 1:16) is pure conjecture; the assertion that no infants could possibly have been so involved is equally the result of speculation, particularly in light of the traditional incorporation of infant males into the covenant through circumcision.

Both the mode of baptism and the age at which it may be administered must be resolved through systematic and ecclesiological theology, not by an appeal to the mandate of Scripture. Although churches differ on these matters, all agree that baptism is incorporation into Christ's community of the new creation by the grace of the Spirit. While not all churches recognize the baptism of every other church, this agreement as to essential meaning at least points toward the emphasis on unity in relation to baptism expounded in Eph. 4:5.

Bibliography. G. R. Beasley-Murray, *Baptism in the New Testament* (Grand Rapids, 1962); J. Daniélou, *The Bible and the Liturgy* (Notre Dame, 1956); W. F. Flemington, *The New Testament Doctrine of Baptism* (London, 1948); K. McDonnell, *The Baptism of Jesus in the Jordan* (Collegeville, 1996); L. H. Stookey, *Baptism* (Nashville, 1983).

LAURENCE HULL STOOKEY

BAR

A beam used to lock the gates of cities (Heb. *bĕrîaḥ;* e.g., Deut. 3:5; Judg. 16:3; Neh. 3:3, 13-15; Ps. 147:13), the doors of houses (2 Sam. 13:17), and prisons (Ps. 107:16 par. "doors"); according to Josephus (*BJ* 4.4.6 [298]) the doors of the temple were locked in the same manner. Such bars, usually wooden beams though sometimes made from iron (Isa. 45:2) or bronze (1 Kgs. 4:13), were inserted into holes in the doorposts on the inner side of the door or gate and were held in place by means of pegs. Another type of bar could be drawn into a locked position from the outside by hand or with a strap; opening such locked doors required a key (Judg. 3:25).

A city with gates and bars was considered safe. Obversely, a city that lost its bars was viewed as fallen (e.g., Amos 1:5). Metaphorically bars refer to the domain of the underworld (Heb. *bāḏ,* Job 17:16) or of the sea (38:10). At Lev. 26:13 "the bars of your yoke" *(môṭâ)* symbolize oppression.

BARABBAS (Gk. *Barabbás*)

The "notorious prisoner" (Matt. 27:16) whom Pilate released to the crowd at Passover instead of Jesus. He is also described as a bandit (Gk. *lēstḗs;* John 18:40) and one imprisoned with the rebels who had committed murder during an insurrection (Mark 15:7; cf. Luke 23:19, 25). All four Gospels indicate that Pilate wanted to set Jesus free, but the crowd insisted on Barabbas. While there is no extrabiblical evidence for the custom of releasing prisoners at Passover, similar practices existed at festivals in other ancient cultures.

Some manuscripts of Matt 27:16-17 give Barabbas' name as Jesus Barabbas. While this seems to be the preferred reading, which some scribes probably omitted out of reverence for Jesus Christ, several questions remain. Did Matthew invent the common name *Iēsoús* to create a contrast between Jesus Barabbas and Jesus who is called the Christ? Or was he following at this point a source not used by Mark? If so, did someone in Matthew's source tradition invent the name? Because we cannot answer these questions with certainty, it is impossible to know whether Barabbas was actually named Jesus.

WARREN C. TRENCHARD

BARACHEL (Heb. *bārak̲'ēl*)
The father of Job's friend Elihu, from Buz in eastern Arabia (Job 32:2, 6).

BARACHIAH (Gk. *Barachías*)
The father of Zechariah (Matt. 23:35), here confused with the Zechariah who was murdered in the temple (2 Chr. 24:20-23). Some scholars identify him with Berechiah **7** (cf. Zech. 1:1).

BARAK (Heb. *bārāq*)
An Israelite military leader (Judg. 4:6-22; 5:1-12, 15), the son of Abinoam from Kedesh in Naphtali. Barak ("lightning") had a secondary role in the battle between the Israelite militia and the Canaanite army of King Jabin of Hazor and his general Sisera, as recorded in both prose (Judg. 4) and poetic (ch. 5) accounts. Barak accepted the commission of the prophet Deborah contingent upon her accompanying his troops (4:8). This has often erroneously been interpreted as cowardice; however, it was not unusual to seek assurance of divine support from a prophet or priest before entering battle. Even though Barak led the Israelite tribal militia in a battle which they won, the prose version emphasizes that it was divine intervention (4:15), as well as the actions of two women, Deborah (vv. 8-9) and Jael (vv. 12-22), which were decisive. In the poetic account Deborah and Barak are complementary partners, acting within their respective spheres as prophet and warrior (5:12).

The catalogue of heroes in Heb. 11:32 lists Barak (and omits Deborah). In extrabiblical sources, Barak has a larger role in the battle: according to Josephus (*Ant.* 5), he slew Jabin and razed Hazor; according to Pseudo-Philo (*LAB* 31.9), Barak beheads Sisera and sends the head to the Canaanite general's mother. GREGORY MOBLEY

BARBARIAN
A person not of Greek culture or language (Gk. *bárbaros*). Originally an onomatopoeic term denoting stammering or unintelligible sounds ("bar bar"), it was used in the LXX, Philo, Josephus, and NT to distinguish "uncivilized" hellenized persons, often but not necessarily with a derogatory connotation.

In the NT the non-hellenized inhabitants of Malta, twice called *bárbaroi* (Acts 28:2, 4; NRSV "natives") without derogatory connotations, are praised for their "unusual kindness," and Paul uses the term with its original linguistic connotation (1 Cor. 14:11; NRSV "foreigner"). Paul also uses "barbarians" as an antonym to "Greeks," with the two groups together constituting the "Gentiles," who are distinguished from the "Jews" (Rom. 1:14). However, "Greeks" could be used as an inclusive term for all non-Jews (e.g., Rom. 1:16; 2:9), forming a contrast (Jew-Greek) comparable to that used by Greeks (Greek-barbarian). Perhaps three ethnic categories are also intended (Jew/circumcised, Greek/uncircumcised, barbarian [including Scythian]) along with two social categories (slave/Scythian, free) in Col. 3:11. ERIC F. MASON

BAREFOOT
Although Israelites usually wore shoes (sandals) for the prevention of disease and foot problems, at certain times they went barefoot. The state of being barefoot symbolized poverty. At times being shoeless also implied capture (2 Chr. 28:15). When self-imposed it expresses mourning (e.g., Ezek. 24:17, 23), shame (Isa. 20:2-4; 2 Sam. 15:30), and reverence for the holy (Exod. 3:5; Josh. 5:15; Acts 7:33). Removing one's shoe served to confirm a land acquisition (Ps. 60:8 = 108:9). In Ruth 4:7-8 the redeemer cedes his right of redemption to Boaz by removing his shoe. The sandal of a man refusing to do his levirate duties is forcibly removed by his deceased brother's wife, thereby marking him as a person of shame (Deut. 25:9-10).

The choice of poverty may be a part of Christian discipleship. In Luke 10:4 the Seventy disciples are told to go without shoes as an expression of their vulnerability and dependence on God. However, the Twelve disciples are permitted to have sandals (Mark 6:9). Both passages may imply that shoes were a necessity for people in ancient Judah. NICOLE J. RUANE

BARIAH (Heb. *bārîaḥ*)
A son of Shemaiah, a postexilic descendant of David (1 Chr. 3:22).

BARIS (Gk. *Baris*)
A Hasmonean designation for fortifications (Heb. *birâ*). Baris was the formal name of John Hyrcanus' palace, built ca. 138 B.C. It was erected on the site of an earlier fortress (Neh. 2:8; 7:2), primarily to protect the vulnerable north side of Jerusalem from invaders. Adjacent to the temple, it quickly became a focus for the uneasy relations of royal and priestly parties. For instance, on high holy days the priests had to apply to Baris for access to their vestments (Josephus *Ant.* 15.11.4). When Herod rebuilt it as the Antonia Fortress, it retained this religio-political importance. DAVID A. DORMAN

BAR-JESUS (Gk. *Bariēsoús*)
A Jewish magician (Acts 13:6, 8).
See ELYMAS.

BAR-JONA (Gk. *Bariōnás*)
Simon Peter's patronymic (Matt. 16:17; cf. Heb. *bar yônâ,* "son of Jonah"). At John 1:42; 21:15-17 the disciple is called "son of John." It is not clear if two different names are indicated or a single Hebrew name is rendered into Greek in two different ways.

BAR KOKHBA (Aram. *bar kôk̲bā'*)
Title given by his supporters to Simon bar Kosiba, leader of the Second Jewish Revolt (132-135 C.E.). Most frequently used in early Christian writings, this epithet sometimes appears in rabbinic texts. According to rabbinic tradition, Bar Kokhba ("son of the star") was a pun on Bar Kosiba's name, coined by Rabbi Akiba in allusion to Num. 24:17, "A star shall arise from Jacob, and a scepter shall go forth from Israel" (*y. Ta'an.* 68d). Rabbinic litera-

ture interpreted this passage as a messianic prophecy, so the title implied that bar Kosiba was the Messiah. His detractors, however, concocted a similar pun, calling him Bar Koziba, "son of the lie," which he is usually called in rabbinic literature.

According to rabbinic tradition, he was of Davidic descent, the nephew of a certain Rabbi Eleazar of Modein. Tradition depicts Bar Kosiba as a man of great strength and impetuosity. He was acclaimed messiah by Rabbi Akiba, but other rabbis opposed his aspirations. Texts discovered at the Wadi Muraba'at, including some of Bar Kosiba's personal correspondence, have revealed his actual name and also indicate that he did indeed use the messianic title "prince of Israel." They also show him to have been illiterate, dependent on others to write his letters.

The causes of the Bar Kokhba revolt are uncertain and probably complex. According to the 3rd-century Roman historian Dio Cassius, the Jews revolted on hearing rumors that the emperor Hadrian planned to convert Jerusalem into a Roman colony. Another Roman source attributes the revolt to Hadrian's attempt to ban "mutilation of the genitals," which would have meant a ban on circumcision. Eusebius seems to have attributed the revolt to simple messianic fervor. The course of the war, however, reveals that the Jews were well prepared to fight, and did not spontaneously erupt into violence as they had in the First Revolt. By virtue of their preparations, the Jewish forces inflicted heavy damage on the Roman legions before being subdued in 135. Bar Kosiba was killed in the siege of Bethar, near Jerusalem, the last remaining center of Jewish resistance.

Bibliography. E. Schürer, *The History of the Jewish People in the Age of Jesus Christ (175 B.C.-A.D. 135)*, rev. ed. (Edinburgh, 1973-1987); Y. Yadin, *Bar-Kokhba* (New York, 1971).

ANTHONY J. TOMASINO

BARKOS (Heb. *barqôs*)
The head of a family of temple servants who returned from exile with Zerubbabel (Ezra 2:53 = Neh. 7:55).

BARLEY
A winter grain (*Hordeum;* Heb. *śĕʿōrâ*) planted from late October through December. Its growing season is shorter than that of wheat, and its harvest commences in April, coinciding with the festival of *Pesaḥ/maṣṣôṯ* (Passover). Barley is much more resistant than wheat to harsh environmental conditions; thus its cultivation can be extended into regions where wheat cultivation is unsuccessful because of low precipitation or poor soils. These characteristics placed barley on the list of the seven crops and fruit trees with which biblical Israel was blessed (Deut. 8:8). Barley, which was domesticated with other cereals in the early Neolithic period, is divided into three species: six-row barley (*H. vulgare* L. emend.), two-row barley (*H. disticon* L.), and irregular barley (*H. irregulare* Åberg and Weibe).

Barley can be eaten raw (2 Kgs. 4:42) or parched (2 Sam. 17:28). It can be ground to flour (*qemaḥ śĕʿōrîm;* Num. 5:15) for bread (Judg. 7:13) and other baked goods (Ezek. 4:12). It was used to make porridge (Ezek. 4:9) and to produce beer (*šēḵār;* Isa. 29:9).

Bibliography. O. Borowski, *Agriculture in Iron Age Israel* (Winona Lake, 1987); J. M. Renfrew, *Palaeoethnobotany* (New York, 1973).

ODED BOROWSKI

BARNABAS (Gk. *Barnabás*)
Joseph, a highly-reputed apostle active in (perhaps founder of) gentile mission as senior partner to Saul/Paul. He was a diaspora Levite from Cyprus who sold a field and donated the proceeds to the apostles for the community-of-goods experiment in Jerusalem (Acts 4:36-37). The apostles nicknamed him Barnabas (according to Luke, "son of encouragement"); since the name probably means "son of Nebo" (a Syrian god), it may be a pre-Christian name from the Hellenistic Diaspora. Eusebius claims he was one of the Seventy (*HE* 1.12).

Paul implies that Barnabas is an apostle and has no wife (1 Cor. 9:1-7; cf. Acts 14:14). It cannot be known if Barnabas participated in the temple cult, but his role in Jerusalem made him a natural advocate for Saul who, after his conversion, wanted an introduction to the apostles (Acts 9:27). After Christianity had spread outside Palestine, Barnabas was sent to Antioch as a leader; needing help, he brought Saul from Tarsus to assist him (Acts 11:19-26). Because of their roles in Antioch and Syria/Cilicia, they were delegated to carry a famine-relief contribution to Jerusalem (Acts 11:27-30).

Barnabas and Saul, with John Mark (Barnabas' cousin; Col. 4:10), toured through Cyprus, with Paul still the junior partner; after Mark left them Paul began to take first place (Acts 13:13, 43, 46, 50) as they worked in Pamphylia, Lycaonia, and Pisidia. According to Luke, they used synagogues as bases and were especially successful among "Godfearers" and "proselytes." Gentiles in Lystra were so impressed that they addressed Barnabas as Zeus and Paul as Hermes (Acts 14:8-18), implying Barnabas' continued seniority.

On returning to their base at Antioch they reported on Gentile response to the Christian message (Acts 14:24-28). This led to debates over circumcision with "some from Judea," first in Antioch and then in Jerusalem (Acts 15:1-21). In Jerusalem Barnabas again took first place, no doubt because of his stature; the council's decision was sent to Christians in Antioch, Syria, and Cilicia (Acts 15:22-29).

This Acts tradition is both supported by and in tension with Paul's account in Gal. 2:1-15. Barnabas and Paul parted company soon after returning to Antioch, though the reasons given are radically different: in Acts over John Mark, in Galatians over table matters (Acts 15:30-41; Gal. 2:11-14). Paul was ambivalent to Barnabas: hostile in Gal. 2:13, friendly in 1 Cor. 9:6, neutral in Gal. 2:1, 9. It is impossible to describe Barnabas' theological views.

The Acts and Epistle of Barnabas do not stem from him. Some argue that Barnabas wrote Hebrews.

Bibliography. R. E. Brown and J. P. Meier, *Antioch and Rome* (New York, 1983); A. von Harnack, *Mission and Expansion of Christianity* (New York, 1961), 58-59; G. Lüdemann, *Opposition to Paul in Jewish Christianity* (Minneapolis, 1989); L. H. Martin, "Gods or Ambassadors of God? Barnabas and Paul in Lystra," *NTS* 41 (1995): 152-56; J. H. Schütz, *Paul and the Anatomy of Apostolic Authority* (Cambridge, 1975). PETER RICHARDSON

BARNABAS, ACTS OF

A 5th- or 6th-century C.E. legendary account in Greek, purporting to be written by John Mark. It recounts Barnabas' travels with Paul (both are apostles) and his martyrdom in a hippodrome, having been taken from a synagogue.

PETER RICHARDSON

BARNABAS, EPISTLE OF

An anonymous Christian writing from 70-135 C.E., with some epistolary features but better understood as a homily. It was included in some NT texts (Sinaiticus), presumably because of Barnabas' stature as an apostle.

A Syrian-Palestinian provenance is increasingly suggested, based on various allusions (Ep. Barn. 4:10; 9:6) and proto-rabbinic associations (7:6, 8, 10; 8:1), though a majority have located it in Egypt because of exegetical affinities with Alexandria. Asia Minor has also been proposed. Its date follows from the interpretation of 16:1-5; 4:4-5, as well as from whether the author used canonical documents. A majority date it sometime near the Second Revolt (132-135), though the late 90s seems more likely, while a few date it to the 70s.

The book has no specific address. It is addressed to both "sons and daughters" (1:1), the only early Christian work to do so, though this emphasis disappears. The Church's relationship to Judaism was a controversial issue for the community, probably mixed Jewish- and Gentile-Christian. The author was a Gentile Christian, perhaps previously a God-fearer or proselyte. The author knew Judaism well and perceived it as a threat, feeling compelled to counter its attractions. The traditional attribution to the Barnabas of Acts and Paul cannot be correct.

The work, which makes extensive use of earlier traditions, comprises a homily (2–16) and a "two-ways" document (18–20) — the latter probably sharing a common source with Did. 1–5 — held together by an introduction, transitional passage, and conclusion (1, 17, 21) with some epistolary elements. It is part of a developing Christian exegetical tradition in its dependence upon OT Scripture, mostly the LXX, though it is more than a pastiche of unrelated traditions. The homily-like material in 2–16 is chiastic in structure: sacrifice/temple (1:8–2:10; 16), fasting/sabbath (3:1–4:6a; 15), covenant (4:6b–6:19; 13–14), atonement (7–8; 12), circumcision/baptism (9–10; 11).

A typological-allegorical interpretation of Scripture dominates the epistle, serving a high christology (with no interest in the historical Jesus) and a strong ethical concern, against the background of an imminent eschatology and a strong conviction that Israel's role in God's scheme has become passé. Christians have knowledge *(gnōsis)* of past, present, and future. Much of Barnabas' significance lies in the convictions it has embraced (eighth-day observance, baptism, atoning death of Jesus, Lord's Supper) and those it has firmly rejected (fasting and food laws, sabbath, circumcision, sacrifice, temple). Barnabas warns against being "shipwrecked by proselytism to their law" (3:6), while standing generally within a halakhic tradition (2:6; 5:9); the covenant cannot be "both theirs and ours; it is ours" (4:6). There is little evidence of familiarity with canonical NT texts, but there are similarities with Matthean traditions. Barnabas is part of the development (Matthew, Hebrews, Melito) stressing differentiation from Judaism that led ultimately in an anti-Judaic direction.

Bibliography. L. W. Barnard, "The 'Epistle of Barnabas' and Its Contemporary Setting," *ANRW* II.27,1 (Berlin, 1993): 159-207; J. C. Paget, *The Epistle of Barnabas.* WUNT 2/64 (Tübingen, 1993); P. Richardson and M. B. Shukster, "Barnabas, Nerva, and the Yavnean Rabbis," *JTS* N.S. 34 (1983): 31-55; S. G. Wilson, *Related Strangers: Jews and Christians 70-170 C.E.* (Philadelphia, 1995), ch. 4.

PETER RICHARDSON

BARSABBAS (Gk. *Barsabbas*)

1. Surname of Joseph (cf. Aram. *bar-šeḇāʾ*, "son of the sabbath"), also surnamed Justus (Lat. "the just one"). Lots were cast to determine whether he or Matthias would replace Judas Iscariot as an apostle (Acts 1:23).

2. Surname of Judas, who was sent with Silas to assist Paul and Barnabas at Antioch (Acts 15:22). Like Silas, he was a prophet (Acts 15:32).

BARTHOLOMEW (Gk. *Bartholomaíos*)

One of Jesus' original 12 disciples according to the Synoptic Gospels and Acts. Some scholars identify him with the Nathanael of John 1:45-46 whom Philip brought to Jesus. The reasons are: (1) Bartholomew is paired with Philip in all three Synoptic lists. (2) The name (from Aram. *bar tōlmay*, "son of Talmai") appears to be incomplete without a personal name preceding it. (3) Bartholomew is never mentioned in John, nor is Nathanael mentioned in the Synoptics. Pending further evidence, however, this identification is speculative.

A tradition mentioned by Eusebius associates Bartholomew with missionary work in India. Another tradition places him as a missionary in the region of the Bosporus. Eusebius also states that Bartholomew left a copy of Matthew's Gospel in the Hebrew language. If such a writing ever existed, no manuscript of it has survived. The whole tradition is questionable, at best. JOE E. LUNCEFORD

BARTHOLOMEW, GOSPEL OF

An apocryphal Gospel mentioned in Jerome's commentary on Matthew (Jerome reports also that

Bartholomew preached to the Indians and died at Albanopolis in Armenia). It was condemned in the Gelasian decree, referred to in the works of Epiphanius the Monk, and may be quoted in the Pseudo-Dionysian writings. None of this Gospel has survived, though some associate it with the extant Greek, Latin, and Slavonic Questions of Bartholomew.

Bibliography. J. K. Elliott, "The Questions of Bartholomew and the Book of the Resurrection of Jesus Christ by Bartholomew the Apostle," *The Apocryphal New Testament* (Oxford, 1993), 652-72.

RICHARD A. SPENCER

BARTHOLOMEW THE APOSTLE, BOOK OF

An apocryphal writing from the 5th or 6th century, existing only in several Coptic manuscripts of the medieval period. Also known as the Book of the Resurrection of Jesus Christ, by Bartholomew the Apostle, the work includes, in haphazard order, stories about the risen Christ and his descent into hell to redeem, among others, Adam. "Doubting" Thomas appears, along with his son Siophanes, whom Thomas raises from the dead in a faraway country before his own encounter with the resurrected Jesus. The narrator, Bartholomew, commands his son, who first hears these stories, to protect them with great care from heretics and unbelievers. IRA BIRDWHISTELL

BARTIMAEUS (Gk. *Bartimaíos*)

The blind beggar who calls out, "Son of David, have mercy on me," and whose sight Jesus restores after leaving Jericho (Mark 10:46-52). Bartimaeus is not a proper name but an identification, "son of Timaeus."

The Bartimaeus story concludes the central section of Mark's Gospel (Mark 8:22–10:52), which begins with Jesus' encounter at Bethsaida with another blind individual (8:22-26). Both pericopes not only concern the restoration of physical sight but also are highly symbolic of the ideal disciple. Bartimaeus comes to see and believe in Jesus, but he also "followed him on the way" to Jerusalem and the cross (Mark 10:52).

The Markan Bartimaeus narrative is paralleled with minor differences in Matt. 20:29-34 (*two* blind men) and Luke 18:35-43 (as Jesus *enters* Jericho), but these Evangelists do not identify the blind person(s).

Bibliography. P. J. Achtemeier, "'And He Followed Him': Miracles and Discipleship in Mark 10:46-52," *Semeia* 11 (1978): 115-45.

FELIX JUST, S.J.

BARUCH (Heb. *bārûḵ*)

1. The son of Zabbai. He assisted in the reconstruction of the temple walls under the leadership of Nehemiah (Neh. 3:20).

2. One of the 80 leaders who ratified the covenant of Nehemiah (Neh. 10:6). As one of the 22 signatories of priestly descent, Baruch agreed to strict Torah observance and abstinence from exogamous contacts with the "peoples of the land."

3. The son of Colhozeh, listed in a census of Judean repatriates (Neh. 11:5). His son Maaseiah was one of the chiefs of the province who volunteered to live in Jerusalem.

4. The son of Neriah, and grandson of Maaseiah. Baruch ("one who is blessed") is presented in the book of Jeremiah as a close companion and scribe of the prophet (Jer. 36:26, 32). He is a prominent character in chs. 32, 36, 43, 45.

During the siege of Jerusalem by the Babylonians in early 587 B.C.E. Baruch participated in a business transaction between Jeremiah and Hanamel, Jeremiah's cousin (Jer. 32:12-15). The transaction involved the purchase of familial land for the purpose of preventing the loss of family property. Jeremiah entrusted the deeds of purchase to Baruch, who was instructed to place them in an "earthenware jar, in order that they may last for a long time" (Jer. 32:14). As a symbolic act, the transaction serves to illustrate that Judah would survive the present tragedy and be rebuilt and reconfigured as a new-yet-old community — beyond exile and dislocation.

In the fourth year of Jehoiakim — a year that signals danger and the dismantling of Judah's social and symbolic structures — Baruch writes on a scroll all of Jeremiah's oracles dated from the "days of Josiah" to the present (Jer. 36:1-8). Jeremiah's scribe then reads the scroll in the temple on a holy day, since the prophet himself is barred from entrance. Baruch's reading creates considerable "alarm" among court officials, who ask Baruch to repeat the scroll's contents in their presence. After the scroll is reread before the royal officials, Jehudi then reads it to King Jehoiakim, who systematically destroys it. Following the destruction of the scroll, Jeremiah dictates another scroll to Baruch with additional material of like substance (Jer. 36:32).

Some scholars discern in Jeremiah's dictation of scrolls to Baruch important clues for understanding the origins of the book of Jeremiah. Among those who hold such a view, there exists little consensus as to the content of these *Urtexts.* Other scholars, however, argue that the genre and *Tendenz* of Jer. 36 preclude judgments regarding the historical development of the book. For the latter, the pericope is more theological and didactic than historical or referential.

The remaining references to Baruch in Jeremiah "foreground" his obedience and faithfulness (cf. the exemplary behavior of Ethiopian Ebed-melech in Jer. 38:7-13; 39:15-18) in contrast to the rebellion and obduracy of the nation, which is on its way to destruction. In ch. 45 Baruch is promised his life amid a crumbling world. Notwithstanding this promise, Baruch, like Jeremiah, must suffer profoundly as a result of his vocation (Jer. 45:1-5) and eventually must face the same fate as the Judean nation: dislocation and exile to a faraway land (43:1-7).

Although Baruch is a relatively minor figure in the book of Jeremiah, Second Temple constructions transform him into an independent and principal character. Thus, while Baruch is denied the prominence he so much desired during his lifetime (Jer. 45:5), he is ironically immortalized in later Jewish literature, as 2 Baruch, which foretells his assumption.

Bibliography. W. Brueggemann, "The 'Baruch Connection': Reflections on Jer 43:1-7," *JBL* 113 (1994): 405-20; R. P. Carroll, *Jeremiah*. OTL (Philadelphia, 1986); W. L. Holladay, *Jeremiah 1*. Herm (Philadelphia, 1986); *Jeremiah 2*. Herm (Minneapolis, 1989).

LOUIS STULMAN

BARUCH, BOOK OF

A five-chapter pseudepigraphic work attributed to Baruch, the highly placed Jerusalem scribe who appears in the book of Jeremiah (Jer. 32, 36, 43, 45). It is preserved in the Greek LXX, where it immediately follows the book of Jeremiah. Bar. 1:1–3:8 and perhaps the whole book were translated from a Hebrew original. It is recognized as canonical by Roman Catholics and the Orthodox communities, but classified among the Apocrypha by the Jewish and Protestant communities because it is not part of the Hebrew Bible.

Baruch may be divided into four uneven parts, the first two of which are prose and the second two poetry: narrative introduction (1:1-14); prayer of confession and repentance (1:15–3:8); wisdom poem of admonition and exhortation (3:9–4:4); poem of consolation and encouragement (4:5–5:9). Though each of the parts of Baruch has a distinctive style and themes, the author has linked the parts with words, themes, and traditions so that their different outlooks and rhetorical purposes work together to form a rhetorical and literary unity which moves from suffering and repentance for sin (1:15–3:8) to devotion to wisdom and obedience to God's commands (3:9-4:4) and concludes with encouragement to endurance and the promise of divine intervention (4:5–5:9).

Baruch draws upon and is part of the traditions of Israel as they developed from the Babylonian Exile through the Second Temple period: cf. 1:15–3:8 with Dan. 9, Jeremiah, and Deuteronomy; 3:9–4:4 with Job 28 and the Wisdom tradition; and 4:5–5:9 with Isa. 40–66. The confession and prayer of repentance, which addresses God with the liturgically proper title "Lord," is similar to many Second Temple prayers such as Ezra 9:6-15; Neh. 1:5-11; 9:5-37; Dan. 9; the Prayer of Azariah (Dan. 3:3-22 LXX); and the Words of the Luminaries (4QDibHam^{a-c}). The wisdom poem identifies true wisdom with the biblical law (Torah) and wise behavior with obedience to God's commandments, as do other 2nd-century books (e.g., Sir. 24). Contrary to many sectarian polemical texts, such as those found at Qumran, Baruch does not distinguish between those Jews who are faithful to a certain way of keeping the law and those who are unfaithful. The author invites all Jews to acknowledge the nation's sinfulness, repent, obey the commandments, and hope for divine assistance in a restored nation. The author has produced a middle-of-the-road, traditional theology for Israel to adhere to under all circumstances. Baruch's very generality and lack of originality, for which it has often been criticized, made it attractive and available to Jews of every inclination. It seems to have been especially useful to Jews in the Greek-speaking Diaspora since it survived in Greek.

The book of Baruch is extremely difficult to date because it provides no certain allusions to events contemporary with the author(s) and is couched in traditional language that has a "timeless" quality. Modern commentators do not place the composition of Baruch in the Babylonian period assigned it by the narrative frame, but somewhere in the Greco-Roman period from 300 B.C.E. to 135 C.E., and within that time the Maccabean crisis in 167-164 B.C.E. has found favor recently. Though Bar. 1:15–2:18 is literally related to Dan. 9:4-19 as is Bar. 5:5-9 to Pss. Sol. 11, the evidence for dependence and dates is ambiguous. The internal atmosphere of the book and allusions to its time of composition are vague and contradictory.

The book of Baruch as a whole is oriented toward Jerusalem and probably originated there. The goal of the prayers and exhortations is the restoration of Jerusalem and its people. The author(s) knew thoroughly the biblical and Second Temple traditions and supported worship at the temple, the holiness of Jerusalem, the restoration of Israel, and obedience to the Torah. The author(s) may have been teachers or officials in Jerusalem, part of a learned circle devoted to the study and promotion of the traditions of Israel. In the swirl of conflicts, dangers, and changes in the Hellenistic period Baruch probably sought to influence the outlooks, commitments, and policies of the Jerusalem leadership and people by encouraging adherence to the traditional Deuteronomic theology, the wisdom of Israel articulated in the Torah, and the commandments as a guide for life. ANTHONY J. SALDARINI

BARUCH, SECOND (SYRIAC APOCALYPSE OF)

A Jewish pseudepigraphon in which Baruch, the scribe of the prophet of Jeremiah, is the recipient of revelation concerning the Babylonian destruction of Jerusalem and the temple in 587 B.C.E. The author of the text is actually writing after the Roman destruction of Jerusalem in 70 C.E. and uses the earlier tragedy to bring theological focus to the disaster of his own time.

The main issue addressed by Baruch's many questions, laments, prayers, and visions, is whether or not the disaster means that the promises of God to Israel have failed. Baruch gradually comes to understand, and subsequently teaches the people, that they have not failed.

The centerpiece of the book consists of three visions and dialogues in which God reveals, with increasing detail, how the promises will be fulfilled (2 Bar. 22-30, 36-43, 53-74). In sum, there will be a universal distress upon the earth, the Messiah will appear, judgment will take place, the dead will be raised, the wicked will go to their torment, and the righteous will inherit a renewed earth. It is curious that the restoration of the temple has no place in these central visions, for earlier in the book the earth was commanded to open and hide the temple vessels until the end time when it would be ordered to restore them (6:6-9).

After each of these visions and dialogues, Baruch offers messages of consolation which grow in their effectiveness as the visions and dialogues grow more elaborate. The people should not be so sad at what has happened, for a greater distress is coming with the shaking of the entire creation. They should persevere in the fear of God, obey the Torah and its teachers, trust in God's mercy, and hope for good in the future.

A concluding epistle (chs. 78-87), written to the nine and a half tribes of the earlier Assyrian captivity, serves as a reprise of the major themes of the apocalypse, although it fails to mention any end time role for the Messiah and even appears to eliminate the idea that the temple vessels will be restored (80:2). Clearly the role of Torah has more controlling influence over the thought of this author than does the role of Messiah or temple.

The post-70 C.E. date of the text is suggested by textual clues, such as the prophecy of two destructions of the temple in ch. 32. However, pre-70 traditional material is almost certainly employed by the author. The book was probably originally written in Hebrew in Palestine. It is extant in its entirety only in Syriac translation, though a significant fragment does exist in Greek.

Bibliography. A. F. J. Klijn, "2 (Syriac Apocalypse of) Baruch," *OTP* 1 (Garden City, 1983): 615-52. RANDAL A. ARGALL

BARUCH, THIRD (GREEK APOCALYPSE OF)
A pseudepigraphon in which an angel is sent to console Baruch, who is weeping over the destruction of Jerusalem. The angel seems to offer consolation by way of distraction as he reveals "the mysteries of God" (3 Bar. 1:8). The angel takes Baruch on a guided tour to five heavens (chs. 2-16). At the end, the angel returns Baruch to the earth where Baruch praises God (ch. 17).

In the first three heavens one finds some novel interpretations of the tower of Babel, the garden of Eden, the Flood, and the movements of the sun and moon. In the fourth heaven Baruch sees the souls of the righteous. The angel Michael descends to the fifth heaven in order to collect the virtues of the righteous. The good works are put in a huge bowl by other angels, and Michael carries the bowl to God. Michael returns with blessings for the righteous and curses for those who do evil.

The message of the book is that God remains in control of the world and does reward the righteous and punish the wicked. Jerusalem and the temple have been destroyed, but the angel Michael carries out a priestly service when he offers the virtues of the righteous at the heavenly altar.

The text is extant in Greek and Slavonic. While originally written in Greek, the content of some chapters appears to be more reliably preserved in the Slavonic version. The text is probably Jewish, with some Christian interpolations. The place and date of composition are uncertain, although many scholars favor a date in the 2nd century C.E.

Bibliography. H. E. Gaylord, Jr., "3 (Greek Apocalypse of) Baruch," *OTP* 1 (Garden City, 1983): 653-79. RANDAL A. ARGALL

BARZILLAI (Heb. *barzillay*)

1. A Gileadite of Rogelim who brought food and supplies to David and his followers at Mahanaim during Absalom's rebellion (2 Sam. 17:27-29). David offered Barzillai a permanent residence in Jerusalem as a member of the royal court, but he declined the offer because of his advanced age and asked that his son Chimham go in his place. David blessed Barzillai before proceeding to Jerusalem (2 Sam. 19:31-40), and prior to his death instructed Solomon to favor Barzillai's sons with a place at the king's table (1 Kgs. 2:7).

2. A Meholathite whose son Adriel married Saul's daughter Merab (2 Sam. 21:8).

3. A priest who married one of the daughters of Barzillai the Gileadite (likely **1** above). He adopted the name Barzillai as his own (Ezra 2:61 = Neh. 7:63; cf. 1 Esdr. 5:38). His sons were among those excluded from the priesthood as unclean, failing to provide evidence of their priestly genealogy (Ezra 2:59-63 = Neh. 7:61-65). It is suggested that Barzillai jeopardized his priestly status by adopting the name of a nonpriestly family.

KENNETH ATKINSON

BASEMATH (Heb. *bāśĕmaṯ*)

1. One of Esau's wives and mother of Reuel (Gen. 36:4, 13, 17). At Gen. 26:34 she is called a daughter of Elon the Hittite, whereas at 36:3 she is said to be Ishmael's daughter (at 36:2 Adah is called the daughter of Elon the Hittite). At Gen. 28:9 Mahalath is the name given the daughter of Ishmael married to Esau.

2. The daughter of Solomon and wife of Ahimaaz, Solomon's officer in Naphtali (1 Kgs. 4:15).

BASHAN (Heb. *bāšān*)
Although its precise boundaries changed through time, the Bashan generally refers to the sloping, fertile plateau of northern Jordan, located E of the ancient Lake Huleh, the Sea of Galilee, and the Upper Jordan Valley. Its elevation varies from 850-500 m. (2800-1650 ft.) above sea level. When its maximum extent is considered, the Bashan's northern limit was the present al-Wa'arah, a rocky desert 24 km. (15 mi.) SW of Damascus, while its southern limit was S of the Yarmuk River (which bisects the Bashan) at the point where the northern foothills of Gilead begin to emerge from the plateau, ca. 8 km. (5 mi.) S of the present Irbid-Mafraq highway.

Decomposed volcanics made the soil of the northern Bashan extremely fertile for both natural flora and agriculture. Thus, in biblical times the region was famous for its cattle, timber, and agriculture (Jer. 50:19; Mic. 7:14; Nah. 1:4; Isa. 2:13; Ezek. 27:6; Deut. 32:14; Ps. 22:12[MT 13]; Amos 4:1).

During OT times, it appears the Bashan was divided into at least four subregions which correspond fairly closely with the natural topography: (1) the land of Geshur, corresponding to the northern portion of the present Golan Heights, NE of Galilee; (2) the land of Maacah, equivalent to the Golan Heights immediately E and SE of the Galilee; (3) the Argob district in northeast Bashan; (4) Havvoth-jair, S of the Yarmuk River (Num. 32:41; Josh. 12: 4, 5; 13:30).

According to the OT, the original inhabitants of Bashan were called the Rephaim. The half-tribe of Manasseh took possession of the region, however, after defeating King Og in the battle of Edrei (Num. 21:33-35; Deut. 3:1-11; Josh. 13:7, 8, 12). Bashan technically remained within the territory of the northern kingdom after the secession, but it constantly changed hands during numerous conflicts with Damascus (1 Kgs. 22:3; 2 Kgs. 8:28; 10:32, 33; 14:25). Tiglath-pileser III finally made Bashan into an Assyrian dependency after his conquest of Damascus (2 Kgs. 15:29).

During the Greco-Roman period the Bashan was divided into three districts: (1) the Gaulanitis (which combined the former territories of Geshur and Maacah; (2) Batanea, which, although it preserves the ancient name of Bashan, actually refers only to northeastern Bashan (OT Argob) — specifically, the area sandwiched between the Gaulanitis to the west and the Jebel Druze to the east; (3) the Gadarene Plateau (southern Bashan), S of the Yarmuk. The region's major cities during this period included Seleucia, Hippos, Gamala, Decapolis, Abila, and Dion. The Bashan was in Nabataean hands in the 2nd century B.C.E., until it came under the control of Herod the Great. It was then ruled by his son Philip and finally by Agrippa II, its last Jewish ruler. RANDALL W. YOUNKER

BASILIDES, GOSPEL OF

A lost Gospel attested by Origen (*Hom. Luke* 1.5.5-7) as composed by Basilides, a Christian poet-philosopher active in Alexandria ca. 132-135, whose movement continued there into the 4th century, and whose eclectic, wide-ranging writings, including some of the earliest commentaries on the NT, survive only in fragments.

Bibliography. H.-C. Puech, "The Gospel of Basilides," in *New Testament Apocrypha*, ed. W. Schneemelcher and R. McL. Wilson, rev. ed., 1 (Louisville, 1991): 397-99; B. Layton, *The Gnostic Scriptures* (Garden City, 1987), 417-44.

IRVING ALAN SPARKS

BASIN

A shallow open vessel, represented by various Hebrew words. Heb. *'ăgarṭāl* is probably a basket (Ezra 1:9), while *'aggān* indicates a bowl (Exod. 24:6). Heb. *mizrāq* (< *zāraq*, "sprinkle") is a deep bowl into which was poured the blood of the slaughtered animals to be sprinkled on the sides of the altar of burnt offering (Exod. 29:15; cf. 38:3). Heb. *kiyyôr nĕḥōšeṯ* designates the "bronze laver" (so RSV) situated between the tent of meeting and the altar used for ceremonial washings (Exod. 30:17-21; cf. 1 Kgs. 7:38-39; 2 Chr. 4:6).

The vessel (Gk. *niptḗr*, from *níptō*, "wash off") in which Jesus washed his disciples' feet (John 13:5) may have been a kind of basin, though normally the Jews washed their feet by pouring water over them.

See LAVER.

BASKET

In biblical cultures, people used baskets for carrying burdens and storing materials. Baskets existed in various sizes, some with handles or lids. Biblical texts use various Hebrew words to refer to baskets. The *sal* carried food (Gen. 40:16; Judg. 6:19; Exod. 29:3). The *ṭene'* held food offerings (Deut. 26:2). The *kĕlûḇ* was a loosely woven basket (Amos 8:1; cf. Jer. 5:27 "birdcage"). Heb. *dûḏ* refers to different types of containers: cooking pots (Job 41:20[MT 12]), baskets for carrying burdens (Ps. 81:6[7]) or the heads of slaughtered enemies (2 Kgs. 10:7). Infant Moses was placed in a *tēḇâ*, a sealed papyrus box (Exod. 2:3, 5; *tēḇâ* refers to Noah's ark in Gen. 6:14–9:18).

The NT mentions two types of baskets. After the feeding of the 5000, the disciples gathered 12 baskets (Gk. *kóphinoi*) of leftovers (Matt. 14:20 = Mark 6:43; Luke 9:17; John 6:13). After the feeding of the 4000, they gathered leftovers in seven *spyrídes* (Matt. 15:37 = Mark 8:8, 20). The Evangelists maintain a distinction between the terms (Matt. 16:9-10; Mark 8:19-20). Further, Paul escaped Damascus by being let over the wall in a *spyrís* (Acts 9:25; in 2 Cor. 11:33 Paul describes this basket as a *sargánē*, a large hamper). Thus the *spyrís* was likely a large basket, while the *kóphinos* was smaller. PERRY L. STEPP

BASTARD

A person of dubious status (Heb. *mamzēr*, "mixed"). Whether the term denotes the offspring of an unmarried woman or the offspring of mixed parentage (one gentile parent) is unclear. A "bastard" cannot enter into the assembly of the Lord, even to the 10th generation of descendants (Deut. 23:2). Zech. 9:6 denounces the "mongrel" (NRSV) people of Philistine Ashdod.

A lack of discipline signifies illegitimacy (Heb. 12:8), since a father reproves only a son whom he loves (Prov. 3:12). Gk. *nóthos* appears also in Wis. 4:3 regarding the lack of endurance of the "illegitimate" offspring of the ungodly. SCOTT NASH

BAT

A common Palestinian mammal (Heb. *'ăṭallēp*), living in the caves of the Jordan Valley and the hill country (Isa. 2:20), sometimes by the hundreds. Usually they are insect-eating animals except for the flying dog of Egypt (*Rousettus egyptiacus*), which feeds on the fruit of sycamore trees. Bats have a large wingspan of 90-95 cm. (36-38 in.). The bat was regarded as an unclean animal (Lev. 11:19; Deut. 14:18).

BATANEA (Gk. *Batanea*)
The name of Bashan in the Greco-Roman period; one of the four divisions of Herod the Great's kingdom.

BATH
A liquid measure (Heb. *baṯ*). According to Ezek. 45:11, 14 it was one tenth of a homer and thus the equivalent of the ephah, a dry measure. Excavations at Lachish have uncovered a broken jar, dated to the 8th century B.C.E., inscribed *bt (lmlk)*, "(royal) bath"; the volume of this jar is 22 l. (5.8 gal.).

BATHING
The washing in water of the entire body, as opposed to simply the hands, face, or feet (Heb. *rāḥaṣ*; Gk. *loúō*).

It was in the course of bathing in the Nile River that Pharaoh's daughter discovered baby Moses in a basket (Exod. 2:5). Moses is said to have "bathed [Aaron and his sons] in water" in the course of inducting them into the priesthood (Lev. 8:6). According to Ezek. 16:4 it was customary to bathe newborn infants before diapering them. Lev. 14:8 refers to bathing in water as part of the extensive rites for removing the impurity of a person who had been diagnosed by a priest as having recovered from leprosy; 2 Kgs. 5:10 reports that Elisha prescribed bathing in the Jordan seven times as a cure for leprosy. John 5:2-8 contrasts the healing power of the pool of Bethesda with that of Jesus, who heals without water. It was customary for mourners not to bathe and to mark the end of a period of mourning by bathing, anointing themselves and putting on fresh clothing (2 Sam. 12:20). Women would bathe and put on cosmetics and fresh clothing and/or jewelry before enticing a man to have sex with them (Ruth 3:3; Ezek. 23:40). 2 Sam. 11:2-4 reports that David saw Bathsheba, the wife of Uriah the Hittite, bathing, which was a rite for purification following the end of her menses. According to Lev. 15:16; Deut. 23:10-11 emission of semen defiles a man; having bathed, he becomes pure again at nightfall (cf. 1 Sam. 20:26; 21:5[MT 6]).

While Exod. 2:5; 2 Kgs. 5:10-13 refer to bathing in natural bodies of water, 2 Sam. 11 refers to bathing in a pool presumably filled by rain water located atop the roof of Bathsheba's house. Judith repeatedly purifies herself in a natural spring (Jdt. 12:7). The virtuous Susanna attempted, unsuccessfully, to keep wicked men from ravishing her while she was taking a bath in a locked orchard (Sus. 17-27).

Noting that most of the references to bathing in the OT are found in the laws of purity and sacrifice in Exod. 29, 40; Lev. 14–17; Num. 19, all assigned to the postexilic era, many scholars contend that except for the wealthy most Iron Age Israelites rarely took baths. Parallels in Hittite and Assyrian texts notwithstanding, many scholars have been reluctant to accept that Leviticus' prescription of bathing as purification from defilement resulting from genital discharges (Lev. 15:18-33) was known in the preexilic period, reasoning that had it been part of preexilic law, which Jesus came to fulfill and not abrogate (Matt. 5:17), neither Jesus nor Christianity would have made light of the pentateuchal purity laws (Mark 7:15; 1 Cor. 6:11).

Archaeological testimony to bathing in Iron Age Israel includes a 9th-century bathtub found at Tel Dan, 6th-century wash basins found in the guestrooms at Tell Beit Mirsim, cisterns lined with lime plaster found in typical Israelite private dwellings from the beginning of the Iron Age, and the 8th-century pottery figure of a woman bathing in a shallow bowl (perhaps a bidet?) from er-Ras cemetery at ez-Zib.

Bibliography. A. Biran, *Biblical Dan* (Jerusalem, 1994); E. Neufeld, "Hygiene Conditions in Ancient Israel (Iron Age)," *BA* 34 (1971): 42-66; R. de Vaux, *Ancient Israel* (1961, repr. Grand Rapids, 1997).

MAYER I. GRUBER

BATH-RABBIM (Heb. *baṯ-rabbîm*)
A gate in the city of Heshbon (Cant. 7:4[MT 5]), facing Rabbah.

BATHSHEBA (Heb. *baṯ-šeḇaʿ*)
(also BATH-SHUA)
Initially the wife of Uriah the Hittite (2 Sam. 11:3), one of David's elite warriors (23:39). The story of David and Bathsheba (2 Sam. 11:1–12:25) begins with Uriah in the field while David remains in Jerusalem. Spying Bathsheba from his roof, David has her brought to him, even though inquiries disclose that she is Uriah's wife. When she becomes pregnant, David attempts to conceal his adultery by bringing Uriah back and encouraging him to visit his wife. When this fails he orders Uriah killed, and quickly marries Bathsheba so the child will appear legitimate (11:26-27a). Convicted of adultery and murder, David repents and the death sentence is transferred to his son (12:13-23). David is then guiltless and his marriage to Bathsheba is lawful, so the next child is legitimate (12:24). This is Solomon, and the narrative concludes with an anticipation of his future kingship (12:24b-25).

The David and Bathsheba story is therefore about David's crime, punishment, and repentance and Solomon's birth. Bathsheba is present only when necessary to advance the plot. She lacks characterization, merely functioning as Uriah's wife, the object of David's adultery, David's wife, and Solomon's mother.

Bathsheba next appears in the narrative of Solomon's succession to David's throne (1 Kgs. 1–2), first as co-conspirator with Nathan (1:11-31), then as queen mother mediating Adonijah's request for Abishag (2:13-22). Nathan and Bathsheba plot to convince an aging David that he had sworn to Bathsheba that Solomon would succeed him (1:11-27). Due to David's faulty memory the scheme works, and David has Solomon made king instead of Adonijah (1:28-40). The story acknowledges an actual palace coup while asserting the legality of Solomon's kingship (cf. Gen. 27). It also plays on Bathsheba's name ("daughter of oath" or "daughter of seven"), since David's oath appears seven times (1 Kgs. 1:13, 17, 20, 24, 27, 30, 35; cf. Gen. 21:25-31).

Bathsheba's mediation of Adonijah's request

and its fatal outcome (1 Kgs. 2:13-25) turn on the ambiguity of Abishag's status. She comes to the court as David's consort, but he never has relations with her (1:1-4). Bathsheba apparently does not consider Abishag one of the harem, so she mediates the request to Solomon (2:18-21). Solomon, however, needs a pretext to eliminate his rival (1:52), so he interprets the request as an arrogation of royal privilege (2:22-25; cf. 2 Sam. 16:20-22).

Solomon's historian added 2 Sam. 10–12; 1 Kgs. 1–2 to an existing court history of Saul and David in order to legitimate Solomon's succession. The scenes anticipate Solomon's rise, contrast David's weakness with Solomon's resolve, and enlist Bathsheba's aid in establishing her son's throne.

At 1 Chr. 3:5 she is called Bath-shua.

Bibliography. A. Berlin, "Characterization in Biblical Narrative: David's Wives," *JSOT* 23 (1982): 69-85; P. K. McCarter, *II Samuel.* AB 9 (Garden City, 1984). MARSHA WHITE

BATH-SHUA (Heb. *bat-šûaʿ*)

1. The Canaanite wife of Judah and the mother of his sons Er, Onan, and Shelah (1 Chr. 2:3). Her designation as the "daughter of Shua" (Gen. 38:2) suggests that "Bath-shua" does not represent a proper name.

2. An alternate form of Bathsheba, the daughter of Ammiel, wife of David, and mother of Shimea, Shobab, Nathan, and Solomon (1 Chr. 3:5).

BATTERING RAM

An instrument used in siege warfare to break through city walls. It consisted of a heavy ram suspended from a framework that was used for protection by the machine's wielders from stones and arrows thrown by the city's defenders. The entire engine was usually propelled by four or six wheels and was built of wood. Its earliest form comes from Assyria, and it was known to be an effective siege weapon of the Babylonians (Ezek. 21:22; 26:9).

Scholars believe that the fortification systems of the Bronze and Iron Age cities in Palestine were built with the battering ram in mind. In the Middle Bronze Age, when the battering ram was making its first appearance in Palestine, a complex system of thick city walls, earthen ramparts, and sophisticated gateways is common. In Ezek. 4:2 the prophet is told to make a model of sieged Jerusalem with battering rams standing against its walls. Babylonian reliefs portraying the siege of Lachish clearly show battering rams attacking the vulnerable parts of the city. JENNIE R. EBELING

BAVVAI (Heb. *bawway*)

The son of Henadad, the "ruler of half the district of Keilah" (Neh. 3:18). He was one of those Levites who aided in the restoration of the walls of Jerusalem under Nehemiah (Neh. 3:18). He may be the same as Binnui (Neh. 3:24; so NRSV).

BAZLITH, BAZLUTH (Heb. *baṣlîṯ, baṣlûṯ*)

A temple servant whose descendants returned from Exile under Zerubbabel (Neh. 7:54). In the parallel list the name is spelled "Bazluth" (Ezra 2:52).

BDELLIUM

Apparently a thick, yellowish resin or gum (Heb. *bĕḏōlaḥ*). The gum was derived from trees in Assyria, Babylonia, India, and Media and was valued as a sweet spice or a fragrant gum. The term is associated with gold and onyx as products of the land of Havilah (Gen. 2:12), perhaps denoting its value. In Num. 11:7 manna is likened to bdellium, alluding to its yellowish color. L. THOMAS STRONG III

BEALIAH (Heb. *bĕʿalyâ*)

A Benjaminite warrior who joined David at Ziklag (1 Chr. 12:5[MT 6]).

BEALOTH (Heb. *bĕʿālôṯ*)

1. A city in the Negeb of Judah (Josh. 15:24), probably the same as Baalath-beer (19:8).

2. A place in the territory of Asher (1 Kgs. 4:16; cf. LXX Gk. *Baalōth*).

BEAM

Eight Hebrew, one Aramaic, and two Greek words are translated variously as "beam," "plank," "timber," "pillar," "rafter," and "board." The most common occurrences of these terms in the OT are in the context of building construction, especially of Solomon's temple (1 Kgs. 6:6, 9, 36; 7:6). The roofs of most Israelite houses were constructed with support beams made of dressed or undressed wood and then finished with mud and plaster (Ezra 6:11; Hab. 2:11); no such roofs have survived to the present. In Ps. 104:3 God is said to have laid the beams for the upper rooms of his heavenly dwelling. "Beam" is used metaphorically for the large wooden bar of a weaver's loom to describe the width of the spearhead of Israel's enemies (1 Sam. 17:7; 2 Sam. 21:19; 1 Chr. 11:23).

In the NT, Jesus spoke of the beam or plank in the eye of the hypocrite (Matt. 7:3-5), and shipwrecked travelers were saved by taking hold of planks as they floated to shore (Acts 27:44).

DONALD FOWLER

BEAN

The broad bean, *Vicia faba* L, sown in winter and ripe in summer. The plants grow up to 1 m. (3 ft.) tall and have fragrant white blossoms. Remains of *Vicia faba* have been found at several Bronze and Iron Age sites in Israel.

David and his troops eat beans (Heb. *pôl*) at Mahanaim during Absalom's revolt (2 Sam. 17:28). God instructs Ezekiel to make bread from "wheat and barley, beans and lentils, millet and spelt" in preparation for the siege of Jerusalem (Ezek. 4:9). Ground beans are often used by the poor as a filler in bread. MEGAN BISHOP MOORE

BEARD

Hair grown on the lower half of the face, usually excluding the mustache. Beards worn during ancient periods were viewed with great reverence and often symbolized strength and virility. In some cultures, such as ancient Babylon, important oaths were sworn upon beards. In contrast, Egyptians generally wore little to no hair on their bodies, but some pharaohs wore false beards to define their position. To further illustrate the beard's importance, Queen Hatshepsut (ca. 1500 B.C.) is depicted in sculptured portraits wearing a false beard.

The beard was also paramount in ancient Israel. It was considered a sign of humiliation for an adult male not to have a beard (2 Sam. 10:4-5). However, men often shaved their beards during periods of mourning (Jer. 41:5).

Beards varied in shapes and styles in ancient Near East. Intricate designs, curls, and patterns defined the style of beards worn by the Assyrians, Babylonians, and Sumerians. Sculptures from each of these cultures depict beards extending to the mid or upper chest. Depending upon the culture, the end of the beard may have been round, flat, or pointed.

Bibliography. W. Cooper, *Hair, Sex, Society, and Symbolism* (New York, 1971); M. Roaf, *Cultural Atlas of Mesopotamia and the Ancient Near East* (New York, 1990). THEODORE W. BURGH

BEAST

Unspecified creatures from the animal kingdom. Heb. *ḥayyâ* (cf. Aram. *ḥêwâ*) and *bĕhēmâ* most often refer to mammals and are often used as collective terms for an assortment of animals. Heb. *ḥayyâ* frequently refers to wild animals, while *bĕhēmâ* is more commonly applied to domesticated animals, most often cattle.

Though a metaphorical use of the concept was not prevalent elsewhere in the OT, Daniel used Aram. *ḥêwâ* for the world powers which were hostile to Israel (Dan. 7:1-12); the emerging world rulers were seen to possess the attributes of wild beasts. This metaphor became the dominant use of beast (Gk. *thēríon*) in the NT.

The book of Revelation uses "beast" 37 times to refer to the enemies of the Church. A beast rises from the abyss (Rev. 11:7), another from the sea (13:1), another from the earth (v. 11), and another is described as a scarlet beast upon which an adulterous woman is sitting (17:3). The preeminent beast of Revelation emerges to become the antichrist who opposes and persecutes the Church and thwarts the will of God until the final battle with Christ (19:20).

This metaphorical use of beast is expanded in other NT passages. Tit. 1:12 comments derogatorily that people of Crete are liars, evil beasts, and lazy gluttons. In 1 Cor. 15:32 Paul states that he fought with wild beasts in Ephesus (Gk. *thēriomachéō*).

MARK R. FAIRCHILD

BEATITUDES

A literary form best known from the nine plural "Blessed are" statements which begin Matthew's Sermon on the Mount (Matt. 5:3-12; cf. the four in Luke's Sermon on the Plain, Luke 6:20-23). These statements are examples of a common form known as macarisms (from Gk. *makários*, "blessed" or "happy," which frequently introduces the statement) found in Egyptian, Greek, and Hebrew literature. The form seems to have belonged to liturgical contexts but appears for didactic purposes in literary material. It was used to provide a brief summary of essential doctrine. Often it assured and instructed about destiny in the afterlife or about divine justice, but in a way that has clear implications for present ethics and morality. Collections of beatitudes are also common at the beginning of literary works, as with the Sermon on the Mount.

In Jewish literature, beatitudes are most common in worship and wisdom traditions (e.g., Ps. 1:1-2; 32:1, 2; 33:12; 41:1; 106:3; 119:1, 2; Prov. 8:32, 34; Eccl. 10:17; Sir. 14:1, 2, 20; 25:8, 9; 34:17; 48:11; Wis. 3:13). They name a situation or action in which they declare God's blessing or favor is experienced. Implicitly they exhort others to manifest this way of life or experience this situation. For those who do not, the blessing functions as condemnation.

Beatitudes also appear in apocalyptic literature (Dan. 12:12; 1 En. 58:2; 81:4; 82:4; 2 En. 42:6-14; 52:1-15). In a situation of crisis, the seer reveals the imminent reversal God is to bring about. Beatitudes tend to declare God's judgment on the present, and/or promise God's anticipated, favorable verdicts in the future. As such they require a way of life now that is based on and consonant with God's righteous verdict. Beatitudes belonging to both the wisdom (Rom. 14:22) and apocalyptic traditions (Rev. 19:9; 20:6; 22:7) appear in the approximately 40 beatitudes in the NT.

The nine beatitudes at the beginning of the Sermon on the Mount have provoked much discussion. Scholars have debated their origins. The most common view sees three of the first four beatitudes, the blessings on the poor, the mourning, and the hungering (Matt. 5:3, 4, 6; cf. Luke 6:20-21), deriving in at least some form from Jesus. They exemplify Jesus' concerns with the poor and maintain a tension between present experience and future blessing, which many see as reflective of a tension evident throughout Jesus' ministry. Some scholars also claim on the grounds of multiple attestation that a fourth beatitude originates from Jesus, the blessing in 5:11-12 on suffering (cf. Luke 6:22-23).

On this view, these four beatitudes were present (in some form) in the collection of Jesus' sayings known as Q (ca. 50s C.E.). This collection was probably expanded in the time before the Gospel was written (before the 80s) by the addition of four beatitudes to a form of Q known to Matthew's community. Several of these beatitudes (Matt. 5:5, the meek; 5:8, the pure in heart) were probably formed by taking over beatitudes found in the Psalms (Ps. 37:11; 24:4). The writer of Matthew's Gospel takes the collection of eight and makes further redactional changes, perhaps on the basis of Isa. 61, and perhaps adds the beatitude found in 5:10.

Hans Dieter Betz, however, argues that the Beatitudes were by the 50s already part of the Sermon on the Mount, which had been composed to instruct Jewish Christians about being disciples of Jesus. Matthew took over the whole sermon from his version of Q and inserted it into the Gospel without changes.

There has also been considerable debate about how to interpret Matthew's beatitudes. Do they promise eschatological rewards for the virtuous who manifest these characteristics in their lives, or do they proclaim God's reversals for those who find themselves in these unfortunate circumstances? Are the Beatitudes ethicized "entrance requirements" exhorting readers to a way of life by which they might enter God's reign? Or are they "eschatological blessings" announced on those who already encounter God's reign in part? Or is it possible to read them in one consistent way? To "mourn" in Matt. 5:4 does not necessarily seem to be a virtue, while to be a "peacemaker" is not a situation that needs reversing.

Some have argued convincingly that the Beatitudes fall into three stanzas of 5:3-6, 7-10, 11-12. Each stanza has 36 words; the first and second end with a reference to "righteousness" (5:6, 10), and the first evidences alliteration of the letter *p*, in Greek and English ("the poor in spirit, the plaintive, the powerless, and those who pine for righteousness"; so David E. Garland). The first stanza underlines situations which God reverses, circumstances in which people are open to God's saving activity. The second stanza shows qualities of a way of life created by God's saving presence. The third addresses a consequence for the community's life. One advantage of this approach is that it recognizes some connection between the Beatitudes and the Gospel of which they are a part. In Matt. 4:17-25 Jesus has demonstrated the presence of the reign of God in his healing and preaching among the afflicted crowds. The beatitudes of 5:3-6 elaborate the experience of 4:23-25, while 5:7-12 delineate further consequences of that present and future blessing.

Bibliography. H. D. Betz, *The Sermon on the Mount.* Herm (Minneapolis, 1995), 91-153; W. Carter, *What Are They Saying About Matthew's Sermon on the Mount?* (New York, 1994), 12-25, 82-84; W. D. Davies and D. Allison, *The Gospel According to Saint Matthew.* ICC (Edinburgh, 1988), 1:429-69; D. E. Garland, *Reading Matthew* (New York, 1993); R. Guelich, *The Sermon on the Mount* (Waco, 1982), 62-118; M. A. Powell, *God with Us* (Minneapolis, 1995), 119-40.

WARREN CARTER

BEBAI (Heb. *bēḇay*)

1. An Israelite whose descendants returned from the Exile, some of them under Zerubbabel (Ezra 2:11 = Neh. 7:16) and some under Ezra (Ezra 8:11).

2. An Israelite, one of the chiefs of the people who set his seal to the renewed covenant under Nehemiah (Neh. 10:15[MT 16]).

BECHER (Heb. *beḵer*), **BECHERITES** (*baḵrî*)
The second son of Benjamin, according to two Benjaminite genealogies (Gen. 46:21; 1 Chr. 7:6), and the father of Zemirah, Joash, Eliezer, Elioenai, Omri, Jeremoth, Abijah, Anathoth, and Alemeth (1 Chr. 7:8). Two other Benjaminite genealogies, however, omit Becher, listing Ashbel as Benjamin's second son (Num. 26:38; 1 Chr. 8:1). In Gen. 46:21 Ashbel is listed as Benjamin's third son after Becher, but he is not listed in the genealogy of 1 Chr. 7:6. This is only one among many inconsistencies with the Benjaminite genealogies.

Becher is also listed in one genealogy as Ephraim's second son (Num. 26:35), but this name is omitted in the LXX and may have been misplaced from the Benjaminite genealogy that follows it. Elsewhere, Ephraim's second son is Bered (1 Chr. 7:20), a name that could have been confused for Becher. The geographical proximity of Benjamin and Ephraim might also have led to confusion over the ancestry of the Becherite clan.

RONALD A. SIMKINS

BECORATH (Heb. *bĕḵôraṯ*)
A Benjaminite, son of Aphiah and ancestor of King Saul (1 Sam. 9:1).

BED
The two most prominent Hebrew words for bed are *miškāḇ*, "place of lying, couch," and *miṭṭâ*, "place of reclining" or "couch." The NT counterparts are Gk. *krábattos,* more often rendered "mat" or "pallet" in modern translations, and *klínē*, "bed, couch."

Most beds were portable. Archaeological excavations at Jericho found simple woven mats as the normal bedding, though one wooden bed had string lacing. In a seminomadic society, portability was required. For the very poorest, their garments or cloaks served as beds, prompting the prohibition against keeping a cloak as security for a loan (Exod. 22:26-27). Most NT occurrences are in healing narratives, where the lame are brought to Jesus lying on their beds and leave carrying them.

Wealthier people had more substantial beds. The prophet Amos criticized the ostentatious beds inlaid with ivory (Amos 6:4) owned by some in his day, and King Ahasuerus of Persia displayed his splendor in "couches of gold and silver" (Esth. 1:6). Between the extremes of wealth and poverty are beds consisting of mattresses on raised platforms, or wooden beds with short legs (cf. 1 Sam. 19:15; 28:23). Lamps could be placed under these beds (Mark 4:21 = Luke 8:16).

The bed was used not only as a place of rest, but also as a place one went to await death (Gen. 48:2; 49:33). It was thus used as a figurative expression for death (Job 17:13; Ps. 139:8). The righteous meditate (Ps. 4:4[MT 5]; 63:6[7]) and sing to God (Ps. 149:5) on beds, while the wicked plot wickedness on their beds (Ps. 36:4[5]). The sluggard stays lazily in bed (Prov. 26:14), while he should be up doing nobler things (Ps. 132:3).

The bed is also used euphemistically for sexual relations. Reuben lay with his father's concubine, and thus defiled his father's bed (Gen. 49:4; 1 Chr. 5:1). In the only occurrence of bed in the NT Epistles, believers are admonished to keep the marriage bed undefiled (Heb. 13:4). With similar meaning the bed is used in the context of Israel's unfaithfulness to God (Isa. 57:7-8; Ezek. 23:17).

JOHN S. HAMMETT

BEDAD (Heb. *bĕḏaḏ*)
The father of Hadad, king of Edom (Gen. 36:35; 1 Chr. 1:46).

BEDAN (Heb. *bĕḏān*)
1. The son of Ulam of the tribe of Manasseh (1 Chr. 7:17). His grandmother, Manasseh's concubine, was an Aramean (1 Chr. 7:14).
2. Possibly a judge of Israel (1 Sam. 12:11). His name appears only here and is not mentioned in the book of Judges. CAROL J. DEMPSEY

BEDEIAH (Heb. *bēḏĕyâ*)
A postexilic Israelite who was compelled to send away his foreign wife (Ezra 10:35).

BEE
Heb. *dĕḇôrâ* probably refers to the banded bee *(Apis fasciatta)*. Bees are known for their propensity to get angry and sting when stirred up. The bee is a symbol of pursuit of Israel by the Amorites (Deut. 1:44), of the psalmist by his enemies (Ps. 118:12), and of God's people by God (Isa. 7:18). Bees are more commonly associated with the prized commodity they provide — honey, yet only in Judg. 14:8 are bees and honey mentioned together. Beekeeping is attested from earliest times in Egypt and Palestine, but apparently was not practiced in Mesopotamia until ca. the 8th century B.C.E.

Strangely enough, bee honey is permitted as food according to Jewish tradition, although the bee is not. The modern domestication of bees dates to 1880, in Israel largely the species *Apis ligustica*.

See HONEY.

RANDALL W. YOUNKER/JESPER SVARTVIK

BEELIADA (Heb. *bĕʿelyāḏāʿ*)
A son of David born in Jerusalem (1 Chr. 14:7). The name ("Baal knows") was changed to Eliada ("God knows") at 2 Sam. 5:16; 1 Chr. 3:8.

BEELZEBUL (Gk. *Beelzeboúl*)
The Greek rendering of Baal-zebul, corrupted into Baal-zebub in the OT. In the Synoptic Gospels Jesus is accused of performing exorcisms by the power of Beelzebul, "the ruler of the demons" (Matt. 12:24 = Mark 3:22 = Luke 11:15), and in Matt. 10:25 Jesus' opponents identify him with Beelzebul. In the NT Beelzebul is equated with Satan, not only by implication through the title "ruler of the demons" but explicitly in Mark 3:23. Peggy L. Day explains the connection through a wordplay on *bĕʿēl dîḇāḇāʾ* (the Aramaic equivalent of *baʿal zĕḇûḇ*, the corrupted form of *baʿal zĕḇûl*) and *bĕʿel dĕḇāḇāʾ* (Aram. "enemy").

See BAAL-ZEBUB.

Bibliography. P. L. Day, *An Adversary in Heaven:* śāṭān *in the Hebrew Bible*. HSM 43 (Atlanta, 1988). JOHN L. MCLAUGHLIN

BEER (Heb. *bĕʾēr*)
1. A camp place ("well") in Transjordan used by Israelites before they marched to Mattanah (Num. 21:16), associated with the well dug by princes and nobles celebrated in the Song of the Well (v. 18). Most scholars agree that the site should be found in northeastern Moab in the Wadi eth-Themed, where adequate water for a large number of people can easily be attained close to the surface. This is probably the same place as Beer-elim (Isa. 15:8).

Bibliography. N. Glueck, *Exploration in Eastern Palestine, I*. AASOR 14 (Baltimore, 1933-34): 1-113; A. H. Van Zyl, *The Moabites* (Leiden, 1960).

ZELJKO GREGOR

2. The place to which Jotham fled from his brother Abimelech (Judg. 9:21). It is perhaps to be identified with el-Bireh, E of Mt. Tabor.

BEERA (Heb. *bĕʾērāʾ*)
A son of Zophah of the tribe of Asher (1 Chr. 7:37).

BEERAH (Heb. *bĕʾērâ*)
The son of Baal; a chieftain of the tribe of Reuben who was deported to Assyria by Tiglath-pileser III (1 Chr. 5:6).

BEER-ELIM (Heb. *bĕʾēr ʾēlîm*)
A place in Moab (Isa. 15:8; "well of the terebinths"), probably the same as Beer **1**, where the Israelites encamped during the wilderness wanderings (Num. 21:16). It has been identified with the Wadi eth-Themed.

BEERI (Heb. *bĕʾērî*)
1. The Hittite father of Esau's wife Judith (Gen. 26:34).
2. The father of the prophet Hosea (Hos. 1:1).

BEER-LAHAI-ROI (Heb. *bĕʾēr laḥay rōʾî*)
A well on the road to Shur, in the vicinity of Kadesh-barnea and Bered. Here ("well of the Living One who sees me"; cf. Vulg.) Hagar met the angel of the Lord as she rested during her flight from Sarai (Gen. 16:7-14). Later, Isaac lived near this well (Gen. 24:62; 25:11).

BEEROTH (Heb. *bĕʾērôṯ*)
One of four cities of the Hivites that covenanted peace with Joshua (Josh. 9:17) and were incorporated into Benjamin (18:25-28; cf. 2 Sam. 4:2-3). Ishbosheth's assassins, Bannah and Rechab (1 Sam. 4:2-3), came from Beeroth, as did Nahari, Joab's armor-bearer (23:37 = 1 Chr. 11:39).

Eusebius spoke of a Beeroth that was contemporary with him and was "under Gideon" in OT times (*Onom.* 48.9-10). His description of the location of the village suggests an identification with el-Jib (167139) NW of Jerusalem on the road from Jerusalem to Nicopolis (Emmaus; cf. Jerome's translation of *Onom.* 49.8-9: Neapolis). Other possible locations include the ancient city at Tell-en-Naṣbeh (170143) or el-Bîreh (170146), which appears ca. 11

Residential quarter in the western part of Tell Beer-sheba (Iron II, late 8th century B.C.E.). A royal administrative center, the city was inhabited by civil service elite, with ordinary citizens dwelling in surrounding villages and farms (Phoenix Data Systems, Neal and Joel Bierling)

km. (7 mi.) up the road that leads north out of Jerusalem via el-Jib. Perhaps Eusebius' description of Beeroth in relation to the seventh milestone meant that it could be accessed or sighted from that point on the main road. MARK E. MOULTON

BEEROTH BENE-JAAKAN (Heb. *bĕʾērōṯ bĕnê-yaʿăqān*) (also BENE-JAAKAN)
The "Wells of the sons of Jaakan," a place near Edom where the Israelites encamped during the wilderness wanderings (Deut. 10:6). In Num. 33:31-32 it is called simply Bene-jaakan. Jaakan, listed as a descendant of Esau (1 Chr. 1:42), was eponymous ancestor of an Edomite clan. Modern Birein (095031), 11 km. (7 mi.) N of Kadesh-barnea, may be the site. PETE F. WILBANKS

BEER-SHEBA (Heb. *bĕʾēr šeḇaʿ*)
A major city in the Negeb. Beer-sheba, meaning either "well of an oath" (Gen. 21:25-31) or "well of seven" (26:26-35), is mentioned prominently in OT accounts from the patriarchs in Genesis to resettlement after the Exile.

Beer-sheba is often used to indicate the southern extent of the land: e.g., from Dan, in the north, to Beer-sheba, in the south (e.g., Judg. 20:1; 2 Sam. 24:2). In the assignment of tribal territories Beer-sheba went to Simeon, but Simeon's territory was assimilated into Judah. Beer-sheba was often considered the "capital of the Negeb." Brief references include the appointment of Samuel's sons as judges in Beer-sheba (1 Sam. 8:2); Elijah passing through Beer-sheba when fleeing from Jezebel (1 Kgs. 19:3); its high place destroyed by Josiah (2 Kgs. 23:8); Amos condemning the worship at Beer-sheba (Amos 5:5; 8:14); its reoccupation by returning exiles (Neh. 11:27).

The identification of the site of the well of Abraham and Isaac is not certain. Some contend for a well in modern Beer-sheba (Bir es-Sebaʿ; 130072), others for a well found at Tell es-Sebaʿ/Tell Beer Shevaʿ (134072) to the east. References to the city in the stories from Israel's period of occupation and control of the land are almost certainly to the city excavated at Tell es-Sebaʿ under the direction of Yohanan Aharoni from 1969 to 1976. The city was occupied in the Iron Age probably beginning in the 12th century B.C.E. The first fortified settlement was built ca. 1000 and continued until ca. 700, perhaps destroyed by Sennacherib.

Large areas of the tell were excavated, revealing public and private buildings, defensive walls, and, in more recent excavations, a water supply system. Aharoni identified, among many other finds, a stone horned altar — the stones of which were dismantled and in a secondary context. The tell was unoccupied for ca. 300 years, then reveals evidences of occupation in the Persian, Hellenistic, Roman, and Early Arab periods.

Bibliography. Z. Herzog, *Beer-sheba 2* (Tel Aviv, 1984); J. Perrot, et al., "Beersheba," *NEAEHL* 1:161-73. BRUCE C. CRESSON

BE-ESHTERAH (Heb. *bĕʿeštĕrâ*) (also ASHTAROTH)
A city (also called Ashtaroth) located in land owned by Manasseh and given to the levitical clans (Josh. 21:27; 1 Chr. 6:71[MT 56]). It has been identified with Tell ʿAshtarah (243244) on the King's Highway. In the 1920s William F. Albright uncovered pottery dating from the Early Bronze to Iron Ages. PHILIP R. DREY

BEGGAR
Several Hebrew terms are translated "beggar," most frequently *ʿānāw*. Greek distinguishes "beggar" (*ptōchós*), one who lives at subsistence level (the vast majority of the populace), from "poor person"

(*pénēs*), a dependent, destitute person; in the NT *ptōchós* is usually translated "poor [person]." Greco-Roman culture had no ethical or religious ideal of assistance to beggars. Biblical tradition, however, frequently portrays the destitute as under the special protection of God, due to their helplessness and dependency. Conversely, the rich and powerful are often depicted as wicked oppressors of the poor. The Gospels give two vivid depictions of beggars: the assertive and demanding Bartimaeus, a blind man sitting at the outskirts of Jericho (Mark 10:46-52), and Lazarus, a starving beggar "covered with sores," lying at a rich man's gate (Luke 16:19-31). Jesus' teaching singles out beggars as "blessed" (Matt. 5:3; Luke 6:20).

MARY ANN BEAVIS

BEHEMOTH (Heb. *behēmôṯ*)
Lit., a "great beast." The term represents the plural of majesty (plural of the Hebrew noun "beast, cattle," accompanied by singular verbs), implying a single beast (Job 40:15). The traditional identification of Behemoth has been the hippopotamus. In Egyptian religion the king, in the role of the god Horus, hunted the hippopotamus, which symbolized Seth, god of chaos, killer of Horus' father Osiris. After winning the battle, Horus assumed the Egyptian throne and established order.

Since the discovery of the Ugaritic texts which identify Leviathan (Job 41:1) as a mythic character, the identification of Behemoth as a hippopotamus has been questioned. Several postbiblical texts confirm the mythological character of both beasts (1 En. 60:7-9; 2 Esdr. 6:49-52). These texts suggest that Behemoth, like Leviathan in Ugaritic myths, had a prototype in pre-Israelite mythology, perhaps understood as a primeval monster, a mythical symbol of chaos.

PATRICIA A. MACNICOLL

BEKA
A weight equal to half (Heb. *beqaʿ*) a shekel or ca. 5.712 g. (.2 oz.), the amount of silver assessed of all male Israelites for the construction of the tabernacle (Exod. 38:26).

BEL (Heb. *bēl;* Akk. *bēlu[m]*)
An Akkadian common noun meaning "master," "ruler," "lord," or "owner"; the cognate of West Semitic *baʿl.* In Akkadian the term was widely used to refer to the king or to specify various officials (e.g., *bēl pīḫati,* "governor"). Together with the proper name of any deity, *bēlu* could be used as an appellative in deferential address: e.g., *bēlu Šamaš,* "lord Šamaš," or *Marduk bēliya,* "Marduk, my lord." The honorific title "lord" was used independently from quite early on for one of several gods: Enlil originally, and then Marduk. In Babylonia, it became an ubiquitous title of Marduk, the patron deity of the state and of the city Babylon (cf. Enuma Elish).

In the OT Bel occurs always as a name or title for Marduk (Isa. 46:1; Jer. 50:2; 51:44). All three of the texts in which it occurs date to the middle of the 6th century B.C.E., during or immediately after the Neo-Babylonian imperial era (605-539). In Isa. 46:1, Bel is paired with Nebo, the Mesopotamian god Nabû; Marduk and Nabû were the principal deities of the Babylonian state. Isa. 46:1-2 describes them in procession together departing helplessly from Babylon into exile, probably a satirical reinterpretation of their usual ritual procession during the Babylonian New Year, or *akītu*-festival. Jer. 50:2b reads: "Babylon is taken, Bel is put to shame, Merodach is dismayed." Here the use of *bēl* as a name for Marduk is explicit. In Jer. 51:44 Yahweh declares: "I will punish Bel in Babylon." It is difficult to determine whether the anti-Babylon oracles in Jer. 50-51 date to a period before or after the fall of Babylon to the Persian king Cyrus in 539. Clearly the prophet assumed that Yahweh would (or had?) rescue(d) his people from Babylon and its titular god, Marduk/Bel. Bel is encountered again later in the apocryphal story of Bel and the Dragon.

Numerous names in the Bible and West Semitic epigraphs are compounded with *baʿl.* In the Bible, however, only one name for certain is compounded with the East Semitic *bēl:* Belshazzar (spelled variously: Aram. *bēlšaʾṣṣar* in Dan. 5; *bēlʾšaṣṣar* in 7:1; 8:1); the Akkadian form is *Bēl-šarra-uṣur,* "Bel (i.e., Marduk) protect the king." Belshazzar was crown prince and son of Nabonidus, the last king of the Babylonian Empire.

DAVID VANDERHOOFT

BEL AND THE DRAGON
See DANIEL, ADDITIONS TO.

BELA (Heb. *belaʿ*) **(PERSON)**
1. The son of Beor and king of Edom who reigned from the city of Dinhabah (Gen. 36:32-33 = 1 Chr. 1:43-44).

2. The eldest son of Benjamin (Gen. 46:21; 1 Chr. 7:6; 8:1). His descendants were the Belaites.

3. The son of Azaz and herdsman ruler of the tribe of Reuben who owned a large amount of territory in the land of Gilead (1 Chr. 5:8-9).

BELA (Heb. *belaʿ*) **(PLACE)**
The original name of Zoar, one of the "cities of the valley" of Siddim (Gen. 14:3), probably located on the southeastern bank of the Dead Sea.

BELIAL (Heb. *beliyyaʿal;* Gk. *Beliár*)
In ancient Hebrew literature, the possessive "(of) *beliyyaʿal*" (e.g., Deut. 13:13[MT 14]; Judg. 19:22) provides an evil connotation to people or things (lit., "sons of *beliyyaʿal*"). Although the etymology of the word remains uncertain, from the parallelism with Mot and Sheol in 2 Sam. 22:5-6 = Ps. 18:4-5(5-6) scholars recognize an original mythological background. However, the actual biblical context and the Greek translation of the LXX always gave to the word the generic meaning of wickedness.

In the late Hellenistic-Roman period, some Jewish groups (including the early Christians), in line with the theology of the Book of the Watchers (1 En. 1–36), claimed belief in the angelic origin of evil. At a certain point, these groups took the term Belial as one of the names of the chief demon —

the devil. We do not know exactly when this phenomenon first occurred. The two references in the book of Jubilees (mid-2nd century B.C.E.) are still ambiguous and could be more properly translated as "spirit of wickedness" (Jub. 1:20) and "sons of wickedness" (15:33), similar to the biblical usage of the term as a common name. It is in the Qumran literature that Belial first appears unambiguously and repeatedly as a proper name (e.g., 1QH, 1QS, 1QM). The Damascus Document is thus probably the earliest extant literary evidence of this usage (CD 4:13, 15; 5:8). No specific theology of the role and function of the devil seems to be attached to the devil's denomination as Belial (or its variant Beliar). The name was used by ideologically diverse documents, notably the Testaments of the Twelve Patriarchs, the Lives of the Prophets (Liv. Pro. 4:6, 20; 17:2), the Sibylline Oracles (Sib. Or. 2:167; 3:63, 73), the Martyrdom and Ascension of Isaiah (e.g., Mart. Isa. 1:8, 9; 2:4), and 2 Cor. 6:15.

After the 1st century C.E., both rabbinic and Christian traditions would occasionally retain the name Belial as part of their common heritage. The name, however, never regained its former popularity.

Bibliography. P. Sacchi, *Jewish Apocalyptic and Its History*. JSP Sup 20 (Sheffield, 1997); J. A. Emerton, "Sheol and the Sons of Belial," *VT* 37 (1987): 214-17.

GABRIELE BOCCACCINI

BELL

A gold object (Heb. *pa'ămôn*, "clapper") fastened to the robes of the high priest, which acted as a warning of his movements in the sanctuary (Exod. 28:33-35; 39:25-26). At Zech. 14:20 it is prophesied that the tinkling ornamental "bells of the horses" (Heb. *mĕṣillôṯ*) would bear the same inscription as the turban of the high priest: "Holy to the Lord" (cf. Exod. 28:36; 39:30); in the eschatological age, even the most profane things would be taken up into the service of God.

BELMAIN (Gk. *Belmaín*)

(also BALBAIM, BALAMON)

A village in Palestine where the Jews erected fortifications in their struggle against Holofernes (Jdt. 4:4). If Bethulia is another name for Shechem, Belmain may have been located in the vicinity of Dothan, ca. 14 km. (9 mi.) N of Samaria (cf. Jdt. 7:3, Balbaim; 8:3, Balamon).

BELOVED DISCIPLE

A mysterious, unnamed figure in the Fourth Gospel. He appears explicitly only in the Gospel's second half (John 13-21) and serves as a witness to all the major events of Jesus' final week: the supper, trial, crucifixion, empty tomb, and resurrection. His first appearance is at Jesus' final meal, where he reclines next to the Lord and is prompted by Peter to ask personal questions about Jesus' betrayer (13:23-25). He also appears at the cross, standing with Jesus' mother while the other disciples have disappeared (19:26), receiving a commission to take Mary into his own home (v. 27). At the tomb, he outruns Peter (20:1-10) and believes even though Peter enters the tomb first. Later when the disciples are fishing in Galilee and Jesus calls from the shore, this disciple alone recognizes Jesus (21:7); and while Peter races to the shore, the Beloved Disciple labors to bring in the net of fish.

Some scholars believe that other indirect references may likewise identify the shadow of this disciple elsewhere in the Gospel. An anonymous disciple is with Andrew in John 1:35-42. In 18:15 he is with Peter at Jesus' interrogation and is known by the high priest. At the cross he is an eyewitness to the death of Jesus (19:35). Above all, 21:24 describes him as the source of the Gospel's testimonies to the life of Jesus.

Leading suggestions for the identity of this mysterious literary figure include Lazarus, the only person whom the Gospel says Jesus loved (John 11:3, 11, 36; compare 11:25-26 and 21:20-23). Another suggestion is John Mark (Acts 12:12), who is associated with Peter (1 Pet. 5:13) and may have been confused with John in antiquity. The traditional identification is John the son of Zebedee. John was one of the Twelve, and the Beloved Disciple attended Jesus' final meal. John often appears with Peter in the Synoptic tradition, thus the rivalry here with Peter. The Fourth Gospel is curiously silent about John, who appears in the Synoptics as a major figure. A number of postapostolic writers (e.g., Irenaeus and Polycarp) claim that John is the Beloved Disciple, the author of the Fourth Gospel.

Today greater interest focuses on the literary or symbolic role played by the Beloved Disciple in the theological framework of the Fourth Gospel. Some have claimed that he is the ideal disciple, offered as a model of discipleship — a person who believes without physical evidence. Others have described him as an ideal witness, who believes and testifies before the world what God has done in Christ. Some critics have even thought that he symbolically represented the charismatic Johannine church competing with the growing, formal, Petrine communities. More recently scholars have suggested that this was an unknown Christian who played a revelatory role, mediating divine truth to the community (much like the anonymous Teacher of Righteousness at Qumran). These scholars compare the Beloved Disciple with the promised Spirit-Paraclete, whose attributes may have been the same as those of the disciple.

There must, however, be a historical figure behind this name. His historical activity as the trustworthy source of eyewitness tradition demands that some person served the Johannine community as its inspiration and its link to Jesus. He is a model of faith and discipleship — but also an anchor to history and the founder of the Johannine community.

Bibliography. R. E. Brown, *The Community of the Beloved Disciple* (New York, 1979); G. M. Burge, *Interpreting the Gospel of John* (Grand Rapids, 1992), 37-54; J. Charlesworth, *The Beloved Disciple* (Valley Forge, 1995); V. Eller, *The Beloved Disciple:*

His Name, His Story, His Thought (Grand Rapids, 1987); M. de Jonge, "The Beloved Disciple and the Date of the Gospel of John," in *Text and Interpretation,* ed. E. Best and R. McL. Wilson (Cambridge, 1979), 99-114; J. N. Sanders, "Who Was the Disciple Whom Jesus Loved?" in *Studies in the Fourth Gospel,* ed. F. Cross (London, 1957), 72-82.

GARY M. BURGE

BELSHAZZAR (Heb. *bēlšaʾṣṣar;* Akk. *bēl-šar-uṣur*)
The ruler of Babylon during the time of Daniel. According to the Bible, he was killed when the city was captured by the Medes and Persians in 539 B.C. (Dan. 5:30).

Belshazzar ruled in place of his father Nabonidus (556-539), who was in Arabia for an extended period of time. Nabonidus had entrusted the army and kingship to his son, who was apparently considered co-regent, a unique situation in Mesopotamian history. Belshazzar, however, was never called king, nor did he take part in the New Year Festival. His tenure in Babylon lasted until the 14th year of his father's reign (ca. 543), which may have been when Nabonidus returned.

A number of legal texts, contracts, and letters describe Belshazzar as crown prince and delineate his duties as co-ruler, including overseeing the temple estates of Uruk and Sippar and leasing out temple land. According to the Nabonidus Chronicle, Belshazzar was a grandson of Nebuchadnezzar II (cf. Bar. 1:11-12), but this may have been an attempt to justify his father's reign, since Nabonidus was not part of the royal family.

The book of Daniel may have dated events to Belshazzar's rule (cf. Dan. 7:1; 8:1), although cuneiform texts reckoned them by the reign of his father. Belshazzar's bizarre banquet (Dan. 5) does not appear in extrabiblical sources, and there is no hint that the kingdom was about to fall. His name abruptly disappears from records in 543. He may have been captured in Babylon in 539 or defeated by the Persian Cyrus while commanding the Babylonian forces at Opis.

Belshazzar is also mentioned by the Greek historian Herodotus (*Hist.* 1.188) and Josephus *(Ant.* 10.254).

Bibliography. R. P. Dougherty, *Nabonidus and Belshazzar.* Yale Oriental Series 15 (New Haven, 1929); A. K. Grayson, *Assyrian and Babylonian Chronicles* (Locust Valley, 1975).

MARK W. CHAVALAS

BELTESHAZZAR (Heb. *bēlṭĕšaʾṣṣar*)
The Babylonian name (Akk. *balāṭsu-uṣur,* "protect his life") given to Daniel during his captivity in Babylon (Dan. 1:7; 2:26; 4:8-9). At Dan. 4:8 Nebuchadnezzar interprets the name as derived from the Babylonian deity Bel, but this is probably a popular etymology. LXX, Vulg. read "Balthasar," which in Roman Catholic tradition became the name of one of the three wise men from the East who visited the infant Jesus.

BEN
Used as a prefix, a term designating a relationship or condition (Heb. *bēn,* "son of"; pl. *bĕnê*). Most often it indicates a direct male descendant, but it can also designate a member of a tribe or people ("sons of Israel," Gen. 42:5), national or geographical origin ("son of Jabesh," 2 Kgs. 15:10), or social or professional class ("sons of the prophets," e.g., 1 Kgs. 20:35; 2 Kgs. 2:3). "Sons of God" can refer to believing, godly persons (Gen. 6:2; Hos. 1:10) or angels (Job 1:6; 2:1; 38:7).

BEN-ABINADAB (Heb. *ben-ʾăḇînāḏāḇ*)
An administrator of the Naphath-dor region supplying royal provision one month per year. He married Solomon's daughter Taphath (1 Kgs. 4:11).

WILLIAM D. MATHERLY

BENAIAH (Heb. *bĕnāyâ, bĕnāyāhû*)
1. The son of Jehoiada the priest, from the southern Judean town of Kabzeel, commander over the army under Solomon. Benaiah came to prominence under David as commander of Cherethites (Cretans) and Pelethites (Philistines), the mercenary troops of David's bodyguard (2 Sam. 8:18; 20:23; 1 Chr. 18:17). Benaiah's deeds were renowned among David's Thirty, although he was not part of the Three (2 Sam. 23:20-23 = 1 Chr. 11:22-25). At the end of David's life he sided with Solomon over against Adonijah, and secured Solomon's position on the throne (1 Kgs. 1:36-38). At Solomon's bidding, Benaiah killed Adonijah (1 Kgs. 2:25), Joab (vv. 29-34), and Shimei (v. 46). Solomon rewarded Benaiah by placing him over all the army instead of Joab (1 Kgs. 2:35).

The Chronicler adds that Benaiah was commander over the Davidic militia of 24 thousand which served during the third month, but also suggests that he gave charge of the militia to his son Ammizabad (1 Chr. 27:5-6). Another son, Jehoiada, succeeded Ahithophel as David's counselor (1 Chr. 27:34).

2. An Ephraimite from Pirathon; one of David's Thirty (2 Sam. 23:30 = 1 Chr. 11:31). He was given charge of the Davidic militia of 24 thousand that served during the eleventh month (1 Chr. 27:14).

3. One of several Simeonite chiefs who migrated to the region of Gedor during the reign of King Hezekiah (1 Chr. 4:36).

4. A Levite musician who was appointed at David's command to play the harp before the ark (1 Chr. 15:18, 20; 16:5). He is probably the grandfather of the Levite Jahaziel, who prophesied during the reign of Jehoshaphat (2 Chr. 20:14).

5. One of the priests appointed by David to blow the trumpet before the ark (1 Chr. 15:24; 16:6).

6. A Levite who assisted in overseeing the contributions to the temple during the reign of Hezekiah (2 Chr. 31:13).

7-10. Four Israelites who divorced their foreign wives during the time of Ezra. They were descendants of Parosh, Pahath-moab, Bani, and Nebo, respectively (Ezra 10:25, 30, 35, 43).

11. The father of Pelatiah, a lay official whose death was part of Ezekiel's vision (Ezek. 11:1, 13).

RONALD A. SIMKINS

BEN-AMMI (Heb. *ben-ʿammî*)
The eponymous ancestor of the Ammonites, portrayed as the offspring of the incestuous relationship between Lot and his younger daughter (Gen. 19:38).

BEN-DEKER (Heb. *ben-deqer*)
The officer over Solomon's second administrative district, which included Makaz and Beth-shemesh (1 Kgs. 4:9).

BENE-BERAK (Heb. *bĕnê-ḇĕraq*)
A city in the tribal inheritance of Dan (Josh. 19:45), located on the coastal plain. The site has been identified as modern Kheirîyah/Ibn Ibrâq (133160), 4 km. (2.5. mi.) S of Bene-barak, a suburb of Tel Aviv which preserves the biblical name.

BENEDICTUS
Zechariah's canticle (Luke 1:68-79), proclaimed at the birth of his son John the Baptist, and named for the first word in the Latin version. Like Mary's Magnificat, it is a prophetic hymn of praise to God for his visit and his genuine covenant kindness (cf. Psalms; Isa. 9; Mal. 4; 1QM 14:4-5). The hymn (esp. vv. 76-77) gives a Christian interpretation of John as precursor, although it says nothing about his work as baptizer or his death. Salvation is from (unspecified) enemies who hate (Neh. 9:27; Ps. 106:9-10) and means "freedom from fear to serve" (v. 74), forgiveness of sins (v. 77), and peace (v. 79).

SEÁN KEALY, C.S.SP.

BENE-JAAKAN (Heb. *bĕnê yaʿăqān*)
(also BEEROTH BENE-JAAKAN)
An Israelite encampment during the wilderness journey, located near the land of Edom (Num. 33:31-32). In Deut. 10:6 it is called Beeroth Bene-jaakan.

PETE F. WILBANKS

BEN-GEBER (Heb. *ben-geḇer*)
The officer over Solomon's sixth administrative district, which encompassed northern Gilead and Argob (1 Kgs. 4:13).

BEN-HADAD (Heb. *ben-hăḏaḏ*)
Likely a throne name taken by the king of Damascus (Aram. *Bir-hadad*). Although scholars debate as to precisely how many rulers bore this name in the Bible and in epigraphic evidence preserved in Akkadian and Aramaic, probably three kings are attested.

1. Ben-hadad I (ca. 885-865 B.C.E.), the son of Tabrimmon and grandson of Hezion (1 Kgs. 15:18); a contemporary of Kings Baasha of Israel and Asa of Judah. Asa called on Ben-hadad I to aid him by attacking northern Israel while Baasha was restricting access to Jerusalem through border fortifications (1 Kgs. 15:16-22 = 2 Chr. 16:1-6). The plan worked for Asa, as Ben-hadad took the towns of "Ijon, Dan, Abel-beth-maachah, and all Chinneroth, with all the land of Naphtali" (1 Kgs. 15:20). This acquisition gave Damascus control over the trade route to southern Phoenicia. By the reign of Ahab (875-853) the region was back in Israelite hands.

2. Ben-hadad II (ca. 865-842), either a son or grandson of Ben-hadad I. A contemporary of King Ahab of Israel, Ben-hadad II is known for his failed siege of Samaria, followed the next spring by his catastrophic loss at Aphek (1 Kgs. 20). He fought alongside Ahab against the Assyrian king Shalmaneser III at Qarqar (853), but Ahab died in battle against the forces of his former ally at Ramoth-gilead (1 Kgs. 22:29-36). Ben-hadad II was later murdered by the usurper Hazael, whom Ben-hadad had sent to inquire of Elisha about his recovery from an illness (2 Kgs. 8:7-15).

3. Ben-hadad III (reigned from ca. 806), the son of the usurper Hazael. Hazael had been the most powerful of the kings of Damascus, but his son suffered a series of defeats which reduced greatly his inherited kingdom. He was defeated three times by Joash, who freed Israel from vassaldom to Damascus (2 Kgs. 13:25). According to the Zakkur stela, Ben-hadad III was unsuccessful in a siege of Hazrak, a city of the kingdom of Hamath. Further, the Assyrian king Adadnirari III attacked Damascus, forcing the city's surrender by its king Mar'i (identified as Ben-hadad III) and payment of tribute in 796.

The ambiguity in numbering the attested Ben-hadads stems in part from the Melqart stela. The king of Aram (a title which a number of cities could claim, not only Damascus) commissioning the stela is Ben-hadad. His patronym is broken, and its reconstruction is a matter of debate. Frank Moore Cross is the strongest proponent of identifying this patronym with the Hadadezer of the Assyrian annals, who is usually regarded as Ben-hadad II. Thus, the Ben-hadad of the inscription would be reckoned Ben-hadad III, and the son of Hazael would then be Ben-hadad IV.

Further confusion arises from the identity of the Hadadezer of the Assyrian annals. He is identified as Ben-hadad II by most scholars, on the strength of the appearance of the biblical references denoting the leader of Damascus during this same period. This gives rise to the notion of the usage of this name as a throne name, assumed by all rulers of the city.

MARK ANTHONY PHELPS

BEN-HAIL (Heb. *ben-ḥayil*)
A prince of the tribe of Judah, whom King Jehoshaphat sent (with others) through the cities of the southern kingdom in order to instruct the people in the Law (2 Chr. 17:7).

BEN-HANAN (Heb. *ben-ḥānān*)
A Judahite, one of the four sons of Shimon (1 Chr. 4:20).

BEN-HESED (Heb. *ben-ḥeseḏ*)
Solomon's officer over the third administrative district, which included Socoh and the entire land of Hepher. He resided at Arubboth (1 Kgs. 4:10).

BEN-HINNOM, VALLEY OF
See GEHENNA; HINNOM, VALLEY OF.

BEN-HUR (Heb. *ben-ḥûr*)
An officer appointed by Solomon over the hill country of Ephraim, the first administrative district (1 Kgs. 4:8).

BENINU (Heb. *bĕnînû*)
A Levite who set his seal to the renewed covenant under Nehemiah (Neh. 10:13[MT 14]).

BENJAMIN (Heb. *binyāmîn*)
1. One of Jacob's 12 sons; also the territory and tribe which bore his name. Benjamin was the youngest child of Jacob, one of two children (along with Joseph) born to Jacob and Rachel (Gen. 34:16-19). Rachel died during childbirth, naming the child Benoni, "son of my sorrow." Jacob renamed him Benjamin, "son of the right/south" (or "son of my good fortune": Rachel's "sorrow" became Jacob's "good fortune"?). Indeed, Benjamin was Jacob's darling (Gen. 44:20), and Joseph counted on this in order to lure Jacob and clan to Egypt (ch. 42).

The territory of Benjamin was located in the southern Judean highlands. Its unstable northern border was near Bethel; its southern border, around Jerusalem. To the east Benjamin extended to the Jordan; to the west, to the Shephelah. Since Benjamin lay between Judah, the preeminent southern tribe, and Ephraim, the preeminent northern tribe, its location was strategic. The geographic orientation of its name ("son of the south") probably results from Benjamin's location S of the Joseph tribe, Ephraim. One expression of Benjamin's strategic importance is that two different biblical books, Genesis on a family level and Judges on a tribal level, end with stories about restoring an estranged Benjamin to a larger group.

Related, perhaps, to the strategic location of Benjamin was the tribe's violent history. Called a "rapacious wolf" (Gen. 49:27), Benjamin produced many warriors: the judge Ehud, assassin of Eglon, king of Moab (Judg. 3:15-23); the 700 elite troops mentioned in Judg. 20:20 (like Ehud, these warriors were "left-handed"); Saul; the assassins Baanah and Rechab (2 Sam. 4:2); and, among David's warriors, Ittai (23:29). Benjaminites from Gibeah raped and brutalized the wife of a Levite (Judg. 19), sparking a civil war between Benjamin and the other tribes (ch. 20); the Benjaminites were decimated and the surviving males resorted to bride-capture in order to maintain their lineage (ch. 21). Another notable Benjaminite was Jeremiah (Jer. 1:1).

Despite ancient connections with the house of Joseph (Ps. 80:2[MT 3]) and support for a favorite son, Saul, earlier (2 Sam. 2:9; 16:5-8), Benjamin sided with Judah following the split of the monarchy (1 Kgs. 12:21). For the rest of the monarchic period and into the postexilic period, Benjamin, along with Judah, made up the nation of Judah and later the Persian province of Yehud (Neh. 11:4).

Paul (Saul) was a Benjaminite (Rom. 11:1), namesake of the tribal ancestor mentioned by the apostle in a sermon in Antioch (Acts 13:21).

Bibliography. B. Halpern, *The First Historians: The Hebrew Bible and History* (1988, repr. University Park, Pa., 1996), 40-43. GREGORY MOBLEY

2. A son of Bilhan, a Benjaminite (1 Chr. 7:10). An Israelite of the family of Harim who had taken a foreign wife (Ezra 10:32). He may be the same person who worked on the restoration of the walls of Jerusalem and took part in their restoration (Neh. 3:23; 12:34).

BENO (Heb. *bĕnô*)
The son of Jaaziah, a Levite (1 Chr. 24:26-27). The Hebrew term may simply be rendered "his son" (cf. LXX) rather than a proper name.

BEN-ONI (Heb. *ben-'ônî*)
A name (Heb. "son of my sorrow") given by Rachel to her younger son. Jacob, however, changed it to Benjamin ("son of the right hand"; Gen. 35:18).

BEN-ZOHETH (Heb. *ben-zôḥēṯ*)
A son of Ishi of the tribe of Judah (1 Chr. 4:20). The name may also be interpreted to mean that he is the son of Zoheth and grandson of Ishi.

BEON (Heb. *bĕʿōn*)
A town in the territory of Reuben (Num. 32:3).
See BAAL-MEON.

BEOR (Heb. *bĕʿôr*)
1. The father of Bela, the first king of Edom (Gen. 36:32; 1 Chr. 1:43).
2. The father of the seer Balaam (e.g., Num. 22:5; cf. 2 Pet. 2:15, Gk. *Bosór,* following Vaticanus).

BERA (Heb. *beraʿ*)
The king of Sodom, defeated when Chedorlaomer invaded the valley of Siddim (Gen. 14:2).

BERACAH (Heb. *bĕrāḵâ*)
A Benjaminite warrior who defected to David at Ziklag (1 Chr. 12:3).

BERACAH (Heb. *bĕrāḵâ*), **VALLEY OF**
A place ("valley of blessing") where Jehoshaphat gathered his soldiers to bless God after various peoples of the Transjordan invaded his land, but then slaughtered each other (2 Chr. 20:1-30). The location may be el-Baqʿah (170116), NW of Khirbet et-Tuqu, well-situated near the ridge road between Bethlehem and En-gedi. The valley near Bethlehem where Khirbet Bereikut (164117) lies is another possible location. Since *bĕrēḵâ* means "water pool," the modern name probably reveals a traditional association with the larger, well-watered Wadi el-Arrub just south of there. In any case, the site is not far from Tekoa (2 Chr. 20:20). Joel 3:2, 12(MT 4:2,

12) may allude to the Beracah in his prophecy about an apocalyptic "valley of Jehoshaphat."

MARK E. MOULTON

BERAIAH (Heb. *bĕrāʾyâ*)
A son of Shimei and descendant of Shaharaim of the tribe of Benjamin (1 Chr. 8:21).

BEREA (Gk. *Berea*)
A place near Jerusalem, perhaps on the Nablus-Jerusalem road 16 km. (10 mi.) N of the city. Berea served as a stopping point for the forces of Bacchides and Alcimus (1 Macc. 9:4), who arrived there with 20 thousand foot soldiers and 2000 cavalry. Two other possible locations are el-Bîreh and Bir ez-Zait, ca. 13 km. (8 mi.) N of Jerusalem.

AARON M. GALE

BERECHIAH (Heb. *berekyâ, berekyāhû*)
1. The fifth son of Zerubbabel listed among David's postexilic descendants (1 Chr. 3:20).

2. The father of the levitical musician Asaph (1 Chr. 6:39[MT 24]; 15:17).

3. The son of Asa; a Levite listed with those first returning to Jerusalem after the Exile (1 Chr. 9:16). The almost parallel list in Neh. 11:3-10 omits Berechiah.

4. A gatekeeper for the ark during David's reign (1 Chr. 15:23).

5. The son of Meshillemoth, an Ephraimite chief who successfully objected to capturing Judahite slaves after the Israelite invasion during Ahaz' reign (2 Chr. 28:12).

6. The son of Meshezabel and father of Meshullam (Neh. 3:4, 30).

7. The son of Iddo and father of the prophet Zechariah (Zech. 1:1, 7). Ezra 5:1; 6:14; Neh. 12:16 identify Iddo as Zechariah's father.

WILLIAM D. MATHERLY

BERED (Heb. *bered*) **(PERSON)**
The son of Shutelah and grandson of Ephraim (1 Chr. 7:20).

BERED (Heb. *bered*) **(PLACE)**
A site near the well of Beer-lahai-roi, associated with Hagar's flight (Gen. 16:14). Beer-lahai-roi was purportedly located between Bered and Kadesh, although the exact geographical relationship between the latter two sites is uncertain. Targumic traditions suggest Bered is to be sought either N or NE of Kadesh.

RYAN BYRNE

BERI (Heb. *bērî*)
A son of Zophah of the tribe of Asher (1 Chr. 7:36).

BERIAH (Heb. *bĕrîʿâ*), **BERIITES** (Heb. *habbĕrîʿî*)
1. A son of Asher and father of Heber and Malchiel (Gen. 46:17; 1 Chr. 7:30-31). He was the eponymous ancestor of the Beriites (Num. 26:44).

2. A son of Ephraim, born after his other sons had been murdered by the men of Gath (1 Chr. 7:23). Heb. *bĕrāʿâ* ("evil) in this verse may represent a popular etymology.

3. A Benjaminite, son of Elpaal and father of nine sons (1 Chr. 8:14). The inhabitants of Aijalon were descendants of Beriah and his brother Shema (1 Chr. 8:13).

4. A son of the Levite Shimei, of the line of Gershom. Because they were few in number, his sons and those of his brother Jeush were counted as one family (1 Chr. 23:10-11).

BERNICE (Gk. *Berníkē*) (also BERENICE)
Julia Bernice (born 28 C.E.), the oldest of Agrippa I's daughters and thus a great-granddaughter of Herod the Great (Josephus *Ant.* 18.132; 19.354). Bernice first married Marcus Julius Alexander who died in 41. She was then married to her uncle Herod, king of Chalcis (*Ant.* 19.276-77; 20.104; *BJ* 2:217-21). After Herod died in 48 she lived with her brother Agrippa II. Visiting Festus in Caesarea ca. 59 they heard Paul give a defense of his faith (Acts 25:13–26:32). To squelch rumors of incest (Juvenal *Satires* 6.156-60), Bernice convinced Polemo king of Cilicia to undergo Jewish circumcision and marry her in 63, but she soon left him, returning to Agrippa (*Ant.* 20.145-47).

At the beginning of the Jewish War in 66 C.E., and with some risk to personal safety, Bernice and Agrippa stood for Jewish peace. She pled in vain with procurator Gessius Florus on behalf of the Jews he was slaughtering (*BJ* 2.310-14, 405-6, 425-29). Like Agrippa, Bernice soon sided with Rome and helped finance Vespasian's rise to emperor (Tacitus *Hist.* 2.81). She became the mistress of Titus, Vespasian's son, and moved to Rome (ca. 75), expecting to be his wife (Dio Cassius *Hist.* 65.15). But when Titus became emperor in 79 he reluctantly dismissed Bernice from Rome in an attempt to improve his reputation (Suetonius *Titus* 7). Sometime before Titus' death in 81 Bernice returned to Rome without damaging his public image (Dio Cassius *Hist.* 66.18). Bernice is often referred to as "queen" (e.g., *BJ* 2.312; *Vita* 119, 180-81; Suetonius *Titus* 7; Tacitus *Hist.* 2.2; Quintilian *Inst. orat.* 4.1).

Bernice (also Berenice; Lat. *Veronica*) was a common Herodian name.

Bibliography. D. C. Braund, "Berenice in Rome," *Historia* 33 (1984): 120-23; J. A. Crook, "Titus and Berenice," *AJP* 72 (1951): 162-75; R. Jordan, *Berenice* (New York, 1974); G. H. Macurdy, "Julia Berenice," *AJP* 56 (1935): 246-53; R. D. Sullivan, "The Dynasty of Judaea in the First Century," *ANRW* II.8,310-12

DOUGLAS S. HUFFMAN

BEROEA (Gk. *Béroia, Bérroia*)
1. A Macedonian city in the foothills of Mt. Bermion, 80 km. (50 mi.) W of Thessalonica. The Via Egnatia passed by several kilometers to the north. Under the Romans it became the headquarters of the Macedonian confederation *(koinón)* and was the seat of the imperial cult. In the 1st century C.E. it was a populous and prosperous city.

Paul and Silas fled from Thessalonica to Beroea,

where they successfully converted a number of people (Acts 17:10-14). Paul fled once again when Jewish leaders arrived from Thessalonica and incited the crowds against him. Silas and Timothy remained at Beroea and rejoined Paul later at Corinth. Sopater, a companion of Paul, is said to have been from Beroea (Acts 20:4).

2. The Hellenistic name of Aleppo in northern Syria, where Menelaus was executed (2 Macc. 13:1-8).

Richard S. Ascough

BEROTHAH (Heb. *bērôṯâ*)
A city on the northern boundary of the ideal Israel (Ezek. 47:16). It may be the same as Berothai.

BEROTHAI (Heb. *bērôṯay*)
A city of Hadadezer, king of Syria, from which David took much bronze (2 Sam. 8:8). It is probably to be identified with the modern village of Bereitân (257372), 13 km. (8 mi.) S of Baalbek. It may be the same as Berothah in Ezek. 47:16. The parallel passage 1 Chr. 18:8 reads Cun instead.

BERYL
A blue or green stone found on the Sinai Peninsula. Recent translations read "beryl" for Heb. *taršîš* (LXX *chrysólithos*), something flashing or bright (Ezek. 1:16; 10:9; Dan. 10:6), an engraved stone on the high priest's breastpiece (Exod. 28:17-20; 39:10-13), and a stone adorning the king of Tyre (Ezek. 28:13). It is also used for *bāreqeṯ* (LXX *smáragdos*) and *šōham* (LXX *bērýllion*). Gk. *bḗryllos* designates a course in the foundation of the city wall of the new Jerusalem (Rev. 21:20). Some translations read "chrysolite," "emerald," "malachite," "onyx," or "topaz" for these Hebrew and Greek terms.

Joseph E. Jensen

BESAI (Heb. *bēsay*)
The head of a family of temple servants who returned from Exile under Zerubbabel (Ezra 2:49 = Neh. 7:52).

BESODEIAH (Heb. *bĕsôḏyâ*)
The father of Meshullam, who assisted in repairing the Old Gate at Jerusalem in the time of Nehemiah (Neh. 3:6).

BESOR (Heb. *bĕśôr*), **WADI**
A brook where David left 200 weary men while he and the remaining 400 crossed in pursuit of the Amalekites (1 Sam. 30:9-10). The Amalekites had earlier raided cities of the Negeb, including Ziklag. The Wadi Besor (Wadi Shallaleh/Ghazzeh, Naḥal Besor) is one of two major wadis of the western Negeb. The Besor is the natural western drainage of the Negeb hills and the Beer-sheba basin out to the Mediterranean Sea. Several important ancient centers are located along this water source, including Tell el-Ajjul, Tell Jemmeh, and Tell el-Far'ah.

Steven M. Ortiz

BETAH (Heb. *beṭaḥ*)
A city of Hadadezer from which David seized much bronze (2 Sam. 8:8). The name is probably to be read "Tibhath" (cf. 1 Chr. 18:8).

BETEN (Heb. *beṭen*)
A city in Asher (Josh. 19:25). Eusebius identifies "Batnai" with Bethbeten (near Ptolemais or Acco), suggesting identification of the site with modern Khirbet Ibṭin/Ḥorvat Ivṭan (160241), 4 km. (2.5 mi.) ENE of Mt. Carmel.

BETH (Heb. *bêṯ*; Gk. *bēth, baith, beth*)
Heb. "house," frequently employed to designate a family or social grouping. The term is commonly the first component of such compound proper names as Bethel ("house of God"), Beth-shean, and Beth-shemesh ("house of the son").

BETHABARA (Gk. *Bēthabará*)
A place where John was baptizing E of the Jordan River (e.g., John 1:28 KJV; the Madeba Map places it W of the river). The oldest and most accurate manuscripts, however, indicate the name as Bethany **2.**

BETH-ANATH (Heb. *bêṯ-ʿănaṯ*)
A Canaanite city ("house of [the goddess] Anath") assigned to Naphtali (Josh. 19:38). The inhabitants were not expelled, but were compelled by the Israelites to do forced labor (Judg. 1:33). Named on the lists of several Egyptian pharaohs, it may be identified with modern Ṣafed el-Baṭṭîkh (190289), ca. 24 km. (15 mi.) ESE of Tyre.

BETH-ANOTH (Heb. *bêṯ-ʿănôṯ*)
A town mentioned only as part of the inheritance of the tribe of Judah (Josh. 15:59). Its location may be somewhere in the hill country of Judah, perhaps the village of Beit ʿAnûn (162107), 5 km. (3 mi.) NE of Hebron.

Aaron M. Gale

BETHANY (Gk. *Bēthanía*)
1. A village probably on the lower slope of an eastern ridge of the Mount of Olives, ca. 3 km. (2 mi.) E of Jerusalem. The Latin name *Lazarium*, traceable to the 4th century C.E. and used of both the village and an early church built on the traditional site of Lazarus' tomb, is probably reflected in the current Arabic name of the village, el-Azariyeh (174131). The name Bethany may derive from Heb. *bêṯ ʿănanyâ*, "house of the poor/afflicted." The Benjaminite village near Jerusalem referred to in Neh. 11:32 as Ananiah may be the same place. Artifacts and tombs excavated in a nearby area attest to settlement as early as 1500 B.C.E., and pottery finds in the immediate vicinity indicate that Bethany was continually occupied from the 6th century on.

The NT identifies Bethany as the home of Mary, Martha, and Lazarus. Jesus visited Bethany six days before the Passover and was anointed there by Mary (John 12:1-8). He was also anointed there by an unnamed woman in the house of Simon the Leper (Matt. 26:6; Mark 14:3), and his ascension was near there (Luke 24:50).

Pilgrims have visited the traditional crypt of

Lazarus in Bethany since at least the 4th century C.E. Excavations in the early 1950s uncovered evidence of four churches, the earliest dating to the late 4th century.

2. "Bethany beyond the Jordan," the place where John the Baptist baptized (John 1:28). The location of this Bethany is unknown, but it seems to be a city on the west side of the river (cf. Jdt. 1:9).

Bibliography. W. H. Mare, *The Archaeology of the Jerusalem Area* (Grand Rapids, 1987); S. J. Saller, *Excavations at Bethany (1949-1953)* (Jerusalem, 1957). SCOTT NASH

BETH-ARABAH (Heb. *bêṯ-hāʿărāḇâ*)
A city on the border between Judah and Benjamin (although the border between the two tribes is listed as passing north of the settlement; Josh. 15:6; 18:18). It is alternatively listed as both a Judahite (Josh. 15:61) and a Benjaminite (18:22) town, suggesting it may have changed hands. Beth-arabah has been identified with ʿAin el-Gharabeh (197139), ca. 4.8 km. (3 mi.) SE of Jericho, on the north bank of Wadi Qelt. LAURA B. MAZOW

BETH-ARBEL (Heb. *bêṯ ʾarbēʾl*)
A city whose location remains unknown. It is commonly associated with Arbela of Transjordan (modern Irbid), although another Arbela exists W of the Sea of Galilee (1 Macc. 9:2). Hosea cites Shalman's destruction of Beth-arbel to illustrate what awaited Israel (Hos. 10:14-15).
PHILIP R. DREY

BETH-ASHBEA (Heb. *bêṯ ʾašbēaʿ*)
The residence of the "house of linen workers," a guild tracing its origins to (or under the leadership of) Shelah the son of Judah (1 Chr. 4:21). Located in the Shephelah of Judah, neither the town nor the people are mentioned elsewhere in the Bible.

BETH-AVEN (Heb. *bêṯ ʾāwen*)
A Benjaminite city situated near Ai and Bethel (Josh. 7:2; 18:12); according to 1 Sam. 13:5; 13:23, a city W of Michmash near Bethel. In Hosea Beth-aven ("house of wickedness") becomes a pejorative name for Bethel (Hos. 4:15; 5:8; 10:5), because the golden calves made by Jeroboam I were worshipped there (1 Kgs. 13:28-29). Gilgal and Bethel were cities with national shrines (Amos 4:4; 5:5; Hos. 10:15; 12:4[MT 5]). Bethel and Beth-aven were two distinct cities in early Israelite history, although the identification of the latter remains uncertain. AARON W. PARK

BETH-AZMAVETH (Heb. *bêṯ-ʿazmāweṯ*)
An alternate form of Azmaveth (Neh. 7:28).

BETH-BAAL-MEON (Heb. *bêṯ baʿal mĕʿôn*)
An alternative name for Baal-meon (Josh. 13:17).

BETH-BARAH (Heb. *bêṯ bārâ*)
The place where Gideon rallied the tribe of Ephraim to cut off the fleeing Midianites (Judg. 7:24). There they captured and executed the Midianite leaders Oreb and Zeeb, and brought their heads to Gideon (Judg. 7:25). Since there has been no identification of Beth-barah, some have suggested emending the text to read "the fords of the Jordan (*hyrdn mʿbrwt*). JOHN A. MCLEAN

BETHBASI (Gk. *Baithbasi*)
A place in the wilderness SE of Jerusalem which Jonathan and Simon Maccabeus defended against Bacchides (1 Macc. 9:62, 64).

BETH-BIRI (Heb. *bêṯ-birʾî*)
A town in which the sons of Simeon lived (1 Chr. 4:31). Most scholars suggest Beth-biri is the same as Beth-lebaoth, allocated to Judah (Josh. 15:32) but later reassigned to Simeon (19:6). Jebel el-Biri, 32 km. (20 mi.) SW of Beer-sheba, may preserve the name. LAURA B. MAZOW

BETH-CAR (Heb. *bêṯ-kār*)
An elevated place SW of Mizpah, beyond which the Israelites pursued the Philistines (1 Sam. 7:11). Its precise location is unknown, although some have proposed its identification with ʿAin Kârim.

BETH-DAGON (Heb. *bêṯ-dāgôn*)

1. A town included in the list of the tribal inheritance of Judah (Josh. 15:20-62). Although the tell's exact location is uncertain, its association with cities such as Libnah, Mareshah, and Lachish (Josh. 15:41) places it within the Shephelah, or coastal lowlands of Judah. References to Beth-dagon occur in Assyrian texts *(Bit-Dagannu),* the Taylor Prism, and the texts of Rameses III *(Bet dgn).*

2. A town on the southern border of the tribal inheritance of Asher in the northern kingdom (Josh. 19:27). It has been associated with the modern site below Mt. Carmel, Jelamet el-Atiqa.
AARON A. BURKE

BETH-DIBLATHAIM (Heb. *bêṯ diḇlāṯāyim*)
A town named in Jeremiah's oracle against Moab (Jer. 48:22). It may be the same as Almon-diblathaim (Num. 33:46), a resting place during the Exodus. The town is mentioned along with Medeba and Baal-meon in the 9th-century Moabite Stone.

BETH-EDEN (Heb. *bêṯ ʿeḏen;* Akk. *Bīt-adini*)
The Hebrew name of an Aramean state located to the east of the great bend of the Euphrates River in modern Syria. Beth-eden was made part of the Assyrian Empire in 856 B.C.E. (2 Kgs. 19:12 = Isa. 37:12). During the first half of the 8th century a powerful Assyrian general, Šamši-ilu, set up a western Assyrian Empire based in Beth-eden with himself as monarch (Amos 1:5). The connection between Beth-eden, known as Paddan-aram (the ancestral home of Abraham) in Genesis, and the "garden of Eden" remains uncertain.
GARY P. ARBINO

BETH-EKED (Heb. *bêṯ-ʿēqeḏ*)
A place on the road from Jezreel to Samaria, perhaps to be identified with modern Beit Qad

(208192), ca. 5 km. (3 mi.) E of Jenîn. According to Eusebius it is Bethacath, 24 km. (15 mi.) from Legio in the plain. It was here that Jehu met and killed the kinsmen of King Ahaziah (2 Kgs. 10:12, 14).

BETHEL (Heb. *bêṯ-'ēl*) **(DEITY)**
A deity attested for the first time in a 7th-century B.C.E. treaty of Esarhaddon, though certainly venerated in earlier periods. Despite many possibilities, few references to this god in the Bible have been convincing. The most likely are the textually corrupt Zech. 7:2, in the personal name *Bêt-'ēl-śar-'eṣer* ("May Bethel protect the prince"), and Jer. 48:13, where Bethel is parallel to the Moabite deity Chemosh. Yet even these instances are uncertain. The first could be elliptical (cf. NRSV) or a circumlocution for God; the second, despite the parallelism, may still be a topographical designation.

Outside the Bible, the clearest references to Bethel are in the Elephantine papyri and Philo of Byblos, who cites the 6th-century B.C.E. Phoenician historian Sanchuniathon's report that Bethel (Baitylus) was a sibling of Elus (Kronos, El), Dagon, and Atlas, all of whom were sons of Uranus and Ge.

Bibliography. J. P. Hyatt, "The Deity Bethel and the Old Testament," *JAOS* 59 (1939): 81-98; W. Röllig, "Bethel," *DDD*, 173-75.

BRENT A. STRAWN

BETHEL (Heb. *bêṯ-'ēl*) **(PLACE)**
1. An important city ("house of God") strategically located at a crossroads 19 km. (12 mi.) N of Jerusalem at the border of Ephraim/Benjamin (for the source of that ambiguity compare Josh. 18:22 and Judg. 1:22) and Judah. Only the city of Jerusalem is mentioned more frequently in the OT. It is not cited in the NT.

Abraham pitched his tent E of Bethel (Gen. 12:8) before going to Egypt and settled in Bethel for a time upon his return (13:3). The "God of Bethel" spoke to Jacob while he was still in Haran (Gen. 31:13). Later Jacob was commanded to go to Bethel and build an altar (Gen. 35:1), which he did (v. 6). The latter episode also refers to the site by the earlier names Luz and El-bethel. Deborah, a nurse of Rebekah, is buried under an oak near Bethel (Gen. 35:8), and the more famous Deborah judged Israel at a site between Bethel and Rama (Judg. 4:5). The ark of the covenant was brought to Bethel (perhaps implied in Judg. 20:18 and confirmed in 20:27). It was at Bethel that the people of Israel gathered to inquire of the Lord who should be first to fight Benjamin to avenge the rape and murder of a Judean concubine (Judg. 20:18). Bethel was the first stop on Elijah's last journey before being taken up in the fiery chariot (2 Kgs. 2:3), and it was at Bethel that his successor Elisha expressed his anger at the children who called him an old bald head (v. 23). Jeroboam, the first king of the northern kingdom of Israel, established an Israelite sanctuary there (1 Kgs. 12:25-33) which the unnamed prophet from Judah (1 Kgs. 13) and Amos condemned. Finally, the city was destroyed by Joshua (2 Kgs. 23:15-20).

Excavations at modern Beitîn (172148) by William F. Albright and James L. Kelso imply a continuous occupation from ca. 2200 B.C.E. until Byzantine times. It was thoroughly burnt in the late 13th century (Late Bronze Age), but quickly rebuilt and prospered until the early Persian period. Bethel was only a small village following the Exile, but was rebuilt by Bacchides in the 2nd century B.C.E.

Some maintain that Bethel was primarily a sanctuary rather than a city. Albright, among others, sought ties with a West Semitic deity of the same name mentioned in the Elephantine papyri and possibly in the Ugaritic texts of Ras Shamra.

See AI.

Bibliography. W. F. Albright, *From the Stone Age to Christianity* (New York, 1957); D. Livingston, "One Last Word on Bethel and Ai," *BARev* 15/1 (1989): 11.

2. A town in the Negeb of Judah mentioned in lists of towns in 1 Sam. 30:27; Josh. 19:4 (Bethul); 1 Chr. 4:30 (Bethuel). ROBERT T. ANDERSON

BETH-EMEK (Heb. *bêṯ hā'ēmeq*)
A city on the border of the territory allotted to the tribe of Asher (Josh. 19:27). Though it is described as located between the valley of Iphtah-el to the south and the city of Cabul to the north, archaeologists have generally identified it with Tel Mīmâs (164263), NW of Cabul (modern Kabul) and NE of Acco. Others have suggested an identification with Khirbet Mudawer Tamra (169250), S of Kabul.

ERIC F. MASON

BETHER (Gk. *Baithēr;* Heb. *beṯer*)
A town in the region allocated to Judah (Josh. 15:59 LXX) near Jersualem. The site has been identified as Khirbet el-Yahudi (162126), just SW of Mittar (where the ancient name is retained), 11 km. (7 mi.) SW of Jerusalem. Bether (perhaps "house of the mountain") is also noted in Cant. 2:17, but the usage is likely descriptive as opposed to a proper name; in either case it adds nothing to the identity of the site. Bether is most notable as the location of the final capital of the Bar Kokhba Rebellion (Second Jewish Revolt), A.D. 132-135. In 135 the Roman general Hadrian took the city and massacred the rebels, ending the revolt. The site name has had varied spellings (Bettar, Bittir, and Beithther) throughout history from Iron Age I to the Roman era.

Bibliography. W. D. Carroll, "Bittir and Its Archaeological Remains," *AASOR* 5 (1923-24): 77-104; J. Simons, *The Geographical and Topographical Texts of the Old Testament* (Leiden, 1959); D. Ussishkin, "Archeological Soundings at Betar, Bar Kochba's Last Stronghold," *Tel Aviv* 20 (1993): 66-97.

DENNIS M. SWANSON

BETHESDA (Gk. *Bēthesdá*)
A pool located in Jerusalem "by the Sheep Gate" (John 5:2; possibly "the Sheep Pool"). According to John 5:1-9 many sick and physically impaired people congregated in this pool's five porticoes, and here Jesus healed a man who had been "ill" for 38

years (but not totally "paralyzed"; cf. v. 7b). Archaeological excavations beside the present church of St. Anne just N of the Temple Mount have partially uncovered the remains of a large double pool dating to pre-Christian times which is almost certainly that mentioned in John 5, but the exact location of the "five porticoes" is still debated. Therapeutic traditions continued at this site in the 2nd century and beyond through a shrine dedicated to the Roman healing-god Asclepius.

Most English Bibles read Bethesda, but there are significant variations in the Greek texts of John 5:2. Some erroneously read Bethsaida (cf. John 1:44). Others have Bethzatha (Aram. "place of olives"), which some scholars argue was the original reading (NRSV, UBS[4]), but this is probably just a variant of Bezetha, the newest section of Jerusalem in the 1st century (Josephus *BJ* 2.15.5 [328]; 5.5.2 [148-52]). Most NT manuscripts read Bethesda, meaning either "house or mercy" (Aram. *bêṯ ḥesdā'*) or "place of flowing water" (Aram. *bêṯ 'esdā'*). The latter interpretation is supported by the 1st-century Copper scroll from Qumran, in which *bet 'esdatayim* (a dual form) apparently refers to a double pool near the Jerusalem temple (3Q15 11:12). Thus, the textual confusion may stem from differing Greek transliterations of similar Aramaic names, Bethesda referring to the pool itself and Beth-zatha to its location.

Bibliography. J. Jeremias, *The Rediscovery of Bethesda* (Louisville, 1966); D. J. Wieand, "John V.2 and the Pool of Bethesda," *NTS* 12 (1966): 392-404.

FELIX JUST, S.J.

BETH-EZEL (Heb. *bêṯ hā'ēṣel*)
A city in southern Judah, perhaps to be identified with modern Deir el-ʿAṣel, ca. 16 km. (10 mi.) SW of Hebron. The prophet Micah cites it in a wordplay on Heb. *'āṣal,* "to withdraw, withhold" (Mic. 1:11).

BETH-GADER (Heb. *bêṯ-gāḏēr*)
A "son" of Hareph in the genealogy of the Judahite Hur (1 Chr. 2:51). The name, like others in this list, is probably a place name.

See GEDOR (Place) 1.

BETH-GAMUL (Heb. *bêṯ gāmûl*)
A city in Moab against which Jeremiah pronounced judgment (Jer. 48:23). It is probably to be identified with Khirbet el-Jumeil (235099), ca. 13 km. (8 mi.) E of Dibon.

BETH-GILGAL (Heb. *bêṯ haggilgāl*)
A town in Judah apparently settled by temple singers who participated in the dedication of the rebuilt walls of Jerusalem in the time of Nehemiah (Neh. 12:29). Although it has been identified with both the Gilgal of Benjamin, E of Jericho (Josh. 4:19), and that of Judah (15:7), its location remains uncertain.

BETH-HACCHEREM (Heb. *bêṯ-hakkerem*)
A town 4 km. (2.58 mi.) S of Jerusalem, most recently identified with Ramat Raḥel (1708.1275). It was noted as the site of a "fire signal station," where signal messages to and from Jerusalem and surrounding towns and military sites would be relayed (Jer. 6:1). During the Persian period it was the site of the administrative headquarters for the district of Judah S of Jerusalem (Neh. 3:14).

Several other locations have been offered as possible sites, most notably the village of ʿAin Kârim (6.5 km. [4 mi.] W of Jerusalem). There are ruins on Jebel ʿAli, overlooking this village, which could have been a signal station, but this location conflicts with the geographic reference of Jeremiah. Qumran documents (3Q15 [3QInv]; 1QapGen) indicate a site of the same name in the King's Valley (2 Sam. 18:18), but this location cannot be reconciled with the references of Jeremiah or Nehemiah. The most convincing evidence points to Ramat Raḥel, which most closely fits the OT and other sources.

Bibliography. Y. Aharoni, "The Citadel of Ramat Rahel," *Archaeology* 18 (1965): 15-25; M. Avi-Yonah, *The Holy Land,* rev. ed. (Grand Rapids, 1977); N. Glueck, *Explorations in Eastern Palestine IV.* AASOR 25-28 (New Haven, 1951).

DENNIS M. SWANSON

BETH-HAGGAN (Heb. *bêṯ-haggān*)
A town to which King Ahaziah fled from Jehu (2 Kgs. 9:27). It is located at modern Jenîn (178207)), ca. 10 km. (6 mi.) S of Jezreel near Ibleam.

BETH-HARAM (Heb. *bêṯ hārām*)
(also BETH-HARAN)
A city of Gad, located at the Jordan River opposite Jericho (Josh. 13:27); called Beth-haran at Num. 32:36. Herod the Great changed its name to Livias; Herod Antipas called it Julias in honor of Augustus' wife. It has been identified with modern Tell Iktanû (214136) on the southern side of Wadi er-Rameh.

BETH-HOGLAH (Heb. *bêṯ-ḥoglâ*)
A settlement marking the tribal border of Benjamin and Judah (Josh. 15:6; 18:19), listed as a possession of Benjamin (18:21). Beth-hoglah is presently identified on geographic and linguistic grounds with modern ʿDier Hajlah, near ʿAin Hajlah (197136).

RYAN BYRNE

BETH-HORON (Heb. *bēṯ-ḥôrôn*)
A levitical city in the tribal territory of Ephraim (Josh. 21:22; 1 Chr. 6:68). The name means "house of Horon" (perhaps a Canaanite deity). Twin cities are indicated: Lower Beth-horon was assigned to Ephraim (Josh. 16:3), while Upper Beth-horon was on the border between Ephraim and Benjamin (v. 5; 18:13-14). The Chronicler attributes their construction to Sheerah, granddaughter of Ephraim (1 Chr. 7:24). Both cities were situated on the "ascent [or descent] of Beth-horon," down which Joshua chased Amorites fleeing their defeat at Gibeon (Josh. 10:10-11). Their location on the slope leading to the hill country from the coastal plain made the cities strategically important and

Traditional Shepherds' Field at Bethlehem. In the distance is Tell Herodium (Allen C. Myers)

vulnerable to attack. Upper Beth-horon has been identified with Beit ʿUr el-Fōqā' (160143) and Lower Beth-horon with Beit ʿUr et-Taḥta (158144).

During the reign of Saul, Philistine raiders attacked Beth-horon (1 Sam. 13:18). Solomon rebuilt Lower Beth-horon (1 Kgs. 9:17; the Chronicler names both cities, calling them "fortified cities, with walls, gates, and bars"; 2 Chr. 8:5-6). The Egyptian pharaoh Shishak names Beth-horon in his list of places conquered in Palestine, recorded on the temple to Amun at Karnak. Later Beth-horon was attacked by renegade Judean mercenaries who rampaged from Samaria to Beth-horon (2 Chr. 25:13). The area remained strategically important in the intertestamental period. Judas Maccabeus won a victory there (1 Macc. 3:16, 24). The Syrians used Beth-horon as a camp (1 Macc. 7:39) and later refortified the site (9:50).

Daniel C. Browning, Jr.

BETH-JESHIMOTH (Heb. *bêṯ hayěšîmôṯ*)
One of the final stopping places of the Israelites at the end of their 40 years wanderings (Num 33:49). The town, identified with Tell el-ʿAẓeimeh (208132), was along an ancient road ("the way of Beth-Jeshimoth"; Josh. 12:3) which later became the Jericho-Livias-Esbus route connecting to Trajan's Via Nova. The town was allotted to the tribe of Reuben (Josh. 13:20), but was later taken over by the Moabites (Ezek. 25:9). In the Roman period, a town known as Besimoth (Khirbet es-Suweimeh), preserving the ancient name, was located nearby.

Bibliography. N. Glueck, "Some Ancient Towns in the Plains of Moab," *BASOR* 91 (1943): 7-26.

Paul J. Ray, Jr.

BETH-LE-APHRAH (Heb. *bêṯ lěʿaprâ*)
A small town in Judah ("house of vigor" or "house of the fawn"). The prophet Micah made a wordplay in his prophecy of doom against the southern kingdom by mockingly referring to the city as a "house of dust" (Mic. 1:10). Located E of Lachich and S of Jerusalem, the settlement may have been plundered by the Assyrian king Sennacherib during his invasion of Judah in 701 B.C. The ruin of the town can be identified with eṭ-Ṭaiyibeh (153107), NW of Hebron.

David C. Maltsberger

BETH-LEBAOTH (Heb. *bêṯ lěḇā'ôṯ*)
(also BETH-BIRI)
A town assigned to Simeon, located in the Negeb region of Judah (Josh. 19:6). At 1 Chr. 4:31 it is called Beth-biri.

BETHLEHEM (Heb. *bêṯ leḥem, bêṯ halaḥmî;* Gk. *Bēthleém*)
A city name originally derived from Heb. "*bayiṯ*, "house," denoting a cultic site, and the name of a pair of ancient Mesopotamian agricultural deities, Lahmu and Lahamu, listed early in the cosmogony of the *Enuma Elish.*

1. A village in the tribal territory of Zebulun (Josh. 19:15). It was likely the hometown of the judge Ibzan (Judg. 12:8, 10). The name survives in modern Beit Laḥm, 11 km. (7 mi.) NW of Nazareth.

2. Bethlehem of Judah, located 8 km. (5 mi.) SSW of Jerusalem, at an elevation of ca. 762 m. (2500 ft.), and just E of the Hebron road which runs along the ridge of the Judean hill country. The earliest mention of the city may be in the 14th-century B.C.E. Amarna Tablets (*ANET,* 489, n. 21) in which Jerusalem's governor Abdi-heba suggests that Bit

Lahmi (or *Bit-ilu Nin.urta*) has fallen into the hands of the marauding ʿApiru people.

The origin of the city is unknown, and the site is first mentioned as Ephrath, and parenthetically Bethlehem, just north of which Rachel died after giving birth to Benjamin (Gen. 35:19; 48:7). The city is not mentioned in the Hebrew text of the tribal allocation list for Judah in Josh. 15:1-63, though the LXX includes the city in the ninth district of Judah. Salma, a grandson of Caleb through Ephrath, is called the "father of Bethlehem" in 1 Chr. 2:51. Surface survey of a mound immediately to the east of the Church of the Nativity yielded Bronze and Iron Age remains, but no stratigraphic excavation has yet been carried out in the modern city.

Israelite inhabitants in Bethlehem are known from the time of the judges. Though the city was not allocated to the Levites, a young Levite from Bethlehem served as priest to Micah in the hill country of Ephraim (Judg. 17:7). It was the home of the concubine of an Ephraimite Levite whose slaughter precipitated civil war against the tribe of Benjamin, leading to the near annihilation of the tribe (Judg. 19–20). Bethlehem was home to Elimelech and Naomi, and here Ruth met Boaz, who as kinsman-redeemer purchased the field of her deceased husband. Hence Bethlehem was the hometown of David, their descendant through Obed and Jesse.

The city rose to prominence after Samuel anointed David as the second king of Israel (1 Sam. 16:1-13). The Philistines established a military outpost in Bethlehem in the days of Saul (2 Sam. 23:13-17) while David was assembling his band of warriors. Later Rehoboam fortified Bethlehem and 14 other Judahite cities as a defensive network around Jerusalem (2 Chr. 11:5-6). Listed among the returnees from Babylonian Exile under Zerubbabel are 123 men of Bethlehem (Ezra 2:21; Neh. 7:26 cites 188 combined from Bethlehem and Netophah).

Micah's prophecy concerning the messianic king (Mic. 5:2[MT 1]) was familiar to the religious leaders of Jerusalem whom Herod summoned when the Magi sought knowledge concerning the birth of the king (Matt. 2:1-8). Matthew records that Herod then ordered the killing of all male children two years old and under in Bethlehem (Matt. 2:13-18).

Jesus was born in Bethlehem ca. 6 B.C.E., and Christians of the early 2nd century C.E. revered a certain limestone cave as the site of the birth of the Messiah (Justin Martyr *Dial.* 78). A sacred grove at the site was dedicated to Adonis (Tammuz) in the time of Hadrian, following his suppression of the Bar Kokhba Revolt of 132-135. Jews were expelled from Bethlehem and Jerusalem in the district of Aelia Capitolina, and numerous Jewish and Christian holy sites were desecrated. Tertullian confirms the absence of Jews in Bethlehem, and the 2nd-century Protevangelium of James (Prot. Jas. 18:1; 19:2) refers to the cave as that which Joseph found for the birth of Jesus. Origen, who traveled throughout Palestine from ca. 215, spoke of the manger of Jesus (*Contra Cels.* 1.51)

With the support of Helena, mother of Constantine the Great, the construction of the first Church of the Nativity commenced over the traditional cave of Jesus' birth (Eusebius *Vita Const.* 3.25-32, 51-53). According to the Bordeaux Pilgrim (ca. 333) the "basilica" was constructed "at the grotto which had been the scene of the Savior's birth" (Eusebius 3.43). The sanctuary was dedicated on 31 May 339. Jerome resided in one of the nearby caves from 385 to 420, during which he prepared the Vulgate translation.

Bibliography. M. Avi-Yonah, "Bethlehem," *NEAEHL* 1:203-10; J. Finegan, *The Archaeology of the New Testament*, 2nd ed. (Princeton, 1992), 22-43.

R. DENNIS COLE

BETH-MAACAH (Heb. *bêṯ-maʿăḵâ*)
Alternate name of Abel-beth-maacah (2 Sam. 20:14-15).

BETH-MARCABOTH (Heb. *bêṯ hammarkāḇōṯ*)
A city apportioned to the tribe of Simeon following the conquest of Canaan (Josh. 19:5; 1 Chr. 4:31). The similarity of the parallel list in Judah's allotment (Josh. 15:31-32) may reflect Simeon's territorial assimilation with Judah, and suggests that Beth-marcaboth may be identified with Madmannah.

RYAN BYRNE

BETH-MEON (Heb. *bêṯ măʿôn*)
Alternate name of Baal-meon (Jer. 48:23).

BETH-MILLO (Heb. *bêṯ millôʾ*)
A fortress in the region of Shechem (Judg. 9:6-20), possibly associated with the tower fortress that was burned down by Abimelech and his forces (vv. 46-49). From the meaning of *millôʾ* (Heb. *mlʾ*, "to fill"), it may also be identified with the foundation of the upper city of Shechem.

JOHN A. MCLEAN

BETH-NIMRAH (Heb. *bêṯ nimrâ*)
(also NIMRAH)
A city in the inheritance of Gad (Num. 32:36; Josh. 13:27), called Nimrah at Num. 32:3. According to Eusebius (*Onom.* 44.17) it lay 8 km. (5 mi.) N of Livias (Beth-haram). The name is preserved in Tell Nimrîn (located on the Wadi Nimrîn in the Transjordan, opposite Jericho), but the oldest settlement of Beth-nimrah (during the Bronze Age) lay in nearby Tell el-Bleibil (210146).

BETH-PAZZEZ (Heb. *bêṯ paṣṣēṣ*)
A town in the territory of Issachar (Josh. 19:21). The location is not known, although some would place it at Kerm el-Ḥadîteh (196232), E of Mt. Tabor.

BETH-PELET (Heb. *bêṯ peleṭ*)
A city inherited by the tribe of Judah. Although its exact location is unknown, it may be in the extreme south of Judah near the border of Edom (Josh. 15:27). It was one of the cities inhabited after the Exile (Neh. 11:26).

AARON M. GALE

BETH-PEOR (Heb. *bêṯ peʿôr*)
A site in NW Moab that served as a cult center for the worship of Baal-peor, a deity who resided on Mt. Peor. It was located across a valley below Mt. Peor, opposite Moses' unspecified burial place (Deut 34:1-6). It eventually fell within the territory assigned to the tribe of Reuben (Josh. 13:20).

In the *Onomasticon* Eusebius located Beth-peor (Bethphogor) opposite Jericho, 9.6 km. (6 mi.) above Livias and 11 km. (7 mi.) from Esbus, a location that corresponds almost perfectly with Khirbet el-Maḥaṭṭa (= Khirbet esh-Sheik Jayil) on the Mushaqqar ridge, just N of Jebel en-Nebu, an identification that most modern scholars have endorsed. Oswald Henke, however, believes the identification of this site "migrated" during Roman times and prefers to identify OT Beth-peor with Khirbet ʿAyûn Mûsā (220131), a site at which Iron I pottery has been found (the earliest sherds at Khirbet el-Maḥaṭṭa were Iron II/Persian). None of the arguments for any of the identifications, however, can presently be considered conclusive.

Randall W. Younker

BETHPHAGE (Gk. *Bēthphagḗ*)
A village on the Mount of Olives near Bethany. The name means "the house of unripe or early figs." The Gospels name Bethphage as the starting point of Jesus' triumphal entry into Jerusalem (Luke 19:29; Mark 11:1; Matt. 21:1). In Talmudic literature Bethphage (Beth Pagi) marked the eastern limits of Jerusalem.

The Franciscan Chapel at Bethphage, from which the modern Palm Sunday ceremony commences, must be very near the location of the ancient village. Scattered finds (tombs, cisterns, a winepress) in the area indicate occupation dating from the 2nd century B.C. to the 8th century A.D.

Thomas V. Brisco

BETH-RAPHA (Heb. *bêṯ rāpā'*)
A son of Eshton of the tribe of Judah (1 Chr. 4:12), probably a clan or place name.

BETH-REHOB (Heb. *bêṯ rěḥôḇ*)
A place in southern Syria, near the city of Dan (Judg. 18:28). During David's campaign against the Ammonites, the Ammonites hired 20 thousand Syrian foot soldiers from Beth-rehob (2 Sam. 10:6). It does not appear in the parallel passage (1 Chr. 19:6-7), possibly because the Chronicler focuses on the hiring of chariots and charioteers and Beth-rehob only had foot soldiers. This may suggest that Beth-rehob refers to an upland area of the upper Golan and portions of Upper Galilee near the foothills of Mt. Hermon, where chariots could not be used. It may also refer to the entire Anti-Lebanon range.

Thomas W. Davis

BETHSAIDA (Gk. *Bēthsaïdá*)
A city located 3 km. (1.7 mi.) NNE of the mouth of the Jordan River on the Sea of Galilee. It was home to the apostles Peter, Andrew, and Philip (John 1:44; 12:21). The abundance of game and fish inhabiting the nearby plains and waters is responsible for the name Bethsaida, which means "house of the hunter/fisherman."

Josephus reports that sometime before 2 B.C.E. under the tetrarch Philip Herod, Bethsaida's status increased to that of a *polis* and was renamed Bethsaida Julias after the Emperor Augustus' daughter (*Ant.* 18.2.1). Philip is also said to be entombed at Bethsaida (*Ant.* 18.4.6).

Several miracles in Jesus' ministry are reported to have occurred at or near Bethsaida, such as the feeding of 5000 (Mark 6:30-44), Jesus' walking on water (6:45-52), and the healing of a blind man (8:22-26). Nevertheless, the inhabitants of Bethsaida appear to remain largely unmoved by these wonders, as the city is cursed by Jesus along with Chorazin for not heeding his message (Matt. 11:21-22).

Excavations on the mound of Bethsaida, modern et-Tell (208255), began in 1987 and have unearthed many remains dating from Iron II to the early Roman period, including several fishing implements such as anchors, hooks, and net weights.

Bibliography. R. Arav and R. Freund, eds., *Bethsaida* (Kirksville, Mo., 1995).

Michael M. Homan

BETH-SHAN (Heb. *bêṯ-šan*),
BETH-SHEAN (*bêṯ-šě'ān*)
A site at the junction of the Jezreel and Jordan Valleys (1977.2124) which stands sentinel over the east-west and north-south trade routes that pass through the valleys. The region is fertile with water available from the Ḥarod River which flows north of the site. The summit of Tel Beth-shean/Tell el-Ḥuṣn covers ca. 4 ha. (10 a.) and stands imposingly 80 m. (260 ft.) above the river. Access to the summit is via a saddle of land on the northwest corner where an ancient gate has been located. Otherwise, the slopes of the tell are a daunting 30° incline. The physical characteristics of the site may have contributed to its name, "house of quiet/rest."

The first biblical references to the site narrate Israel's inability to conquer it (Josh. 17:11; Judg. 1:27). Apparently the Philistines controlled Beth-shean for some time because they impaled the bodies of Saul and his sons on the city's temple wall (1 Sam. 31:12). Eventually the city came under Israelite control and appears as part of the Solomonic administrative districts (1 Kgs. 4:12).

Extrabiblical references to the site include Thutmose III's annals and the Amarna tablets. Stelae at Beth-shean indicate Egyptian presence during the reigns of Seti I, Ramses II, and Ramses III.

During Hellenistic and Roman times, the site was known as Scythopolis (or Nysa Scythopolis; cf. 2 Macc. 12:29) and was part of the Decapolis (cf. Matt. 4:25; Mark 5:20; 7:31).

Excavations at Beth-shean began under the auspices of the University of Pennsylvania (1921-33) under the directorships of C. S. Fisher, Alan Rowe, and Gerald FitzGerald. The Israelis have excavated the tell and surrounding areas since 1961, directed

Tell of Beth-shean, with Roman Scythopolis below (Phoenix Data Systems, Neal and Joel Bierling)

by Gideon Foerster, Yoram Tsafrir, Yigael Yadin, Shulamit Geva, Amihai Mazar, and Gaby Mazor.

Until Roman times, most settlements were on the mound. Remains from the Pottery Neolithic B period along with some from the Chalcolithic have come to light (strata XVIII-XVII; the Chalcolithic has been fairly well represented in remains at the foot of the tell). Oval buildings, multi-room structures, and intersecting streets represent the Early Bronze Age (XVI-XI). The distinctive EB III Khirbet Kerak ware appears in abundance.

With only some evidence of tombs from MB IIA, the site appears to have been unoccupied until MB IIB. But even with its resettlement, the unusual feature of the MB IIB period is the lack of fortifications, which were so prevalent at other MB sites.

During the Late Bronze Age, Beth-shean grew, and excavations have uncovered a sequence of temples each built over the remains of the former. Stratum IX preserves the remains of a complex temple enclosure built over the remains of an earlier one and oriented on an east-west axis. Various altars and cult rooms were found and Egyptian remains have connected the stratum with Thutmose III (ca. 1450 B.C.). Few remains of stratum VIII have been found, but the next stratum (VII) had another temple oriented north-south which likely was built during the hegemony of Ramses II (ca. 1270). This temple preserved characteristic Egyptian motifs, and the residents recovered from an earlier period a stela of Seti I and placed it in the temple.

The temple continues in stratum VI, but with some modification. Egyptian presence is further indicated by the numerous Egyptian-style paraphernalia including several cartouches and a basalt statue of Ramses III. The stratum ended with extensive conflagration, which was likely caused by an invasion of the Sea Peoples.

The stratigraphy of stratum V is confused, but to this period probably belonged a pair of temples which were oriented to the east. These likely were the temples where the bodies of Saul and his sons were impaled as trophies of war (1 Sam. 31:10; 1 Chr. 10:10). Numerous ceramic cultic vessels with molded serpents, animals, and human figures came from these temples as well as stelae of Seti I, Ramses II, and a statue of Ramses III. The stratum ended by fire, perhaps as a result of David's capture of the site. Afterward the city became part of Solomon's administrative districts (1 Kgs. 4:12), and the temple areas seem to have been converted to administrative quarters.

The next stratum had remains of buildings similar to the stables/storehouses of other Israelite towns (e.g., Megiddo, Beer-sheba). The stratum was destroyed by fire, likely by the Assyrian invasion under Tiglath-pileser III (ca. 732). The site was re-occupied with the construction of poorly built buildings, but this settlement apparently ended during the first half of the 7th century.

See SCYTHOPOLIS.

Bibliography. G. Foerster, "Beth-shean at the Foot of the Mound," *NEAEHL* 1:223-35; Foerster, et al., "The Bet She'an Excavation Project (1989-1991)," *Excavations and Surveys in Israel* 11 (1993): 1-60; F. W. James, *The Iron Age at Beth Shan* (Philadelphia, 1966); A. Mazar, "Beth-shean," *NEAEHL* 1:214-23; A. Rowe, *The Four Canaanite Temples of Beth Shan* 1 (Philadelphia, 1940); Y. Yadin and S. Geva, *Investigations at Beth Shean: The Early Iron Age Strata.* Qedem 3 (Jerusalem, 1986).

DALE W. MANOR

BETH-SHEMESH (Heb. *bêṯ šemeš*)

1. A city (lit., "house of the sun") occupying a small rise near the juncture of the Sorek Valley and the fosse along the western base of the hill country formed by the Wadi Ghurab and Wadi en-Najil. The city was apportioned to the tribe of Dan, but never conquered and occupied (Judg. 1:33). During the Solomonic period it was assigned to the second district (1 Kgs. 4:9). Amaziah and Joash battled in the region, and for a time the city fell under Philistine control during the reign of Ahaz (2 Kgs. 14:11; 2 Chr. 28:18).

Excavations of the 8 ha. (7 a.) Tel Beth Shemesh/Tell er-Rumeileh (1477.1286), W of ʿAin Shems, revealed six strata dating from the Early Bronze through Persian and Hellenistic periods. Excavators consider the Late Bronze city the most prosperous. Only scant remains of the earliest level survive. During the Hyksos period (Middle Bronze II), a wall with a Syrian-style gate and two towers enclosed the entire site.

A complete wall surrounded the LB city, with large towers set into it at intervals. This was a unique fortification style for the period as the Egyptian overlords of Canaan seldom allowed cities to construct strong defenses. The city's strategic position along the edge of the hill country required strong defenses to prevent access to the Shephelah by invaders coming down from the hills. The settlement could have defended itself successfully against invaders as an independent city-state outside Egyptian control. Remains of domestic structures reveal courtyards paved with white plaster and numerous storage bins. A furnace for smelting ore was found not far from the domestic installations. A cuneiform Ugaritic tablet and a Canaanite alphabetic ostracon were discovered nearby. A series of silos and cisterns served for wheat and water storage. Other remains include an open air sanctuary facing the setting sun and two plaques featuring the goddess Astarte.

The Iron Age city was smaller than its predecessor. Residents simply repaired the older LB wall, dwelling in typical courtyard-type houses. During Iron II (10th-8th centuries) a casemate wall surrounded the city, abutted by four-room houses. The destruction of stratum II is attributed to the Babylonian invasion in 586.

2. A village near the border of Issachar and Naphtali, S of the Sea of Galilee (Josh. 19:22). The ancient site is most likely associated with modern Khirbet Sheikh esh-Shamsāwî (199232).

3. A settlement assigned to Naphtali (Josh. 19:38), but unconquered by Israel during the period of conquest and settlement (Judg. 1:33). Located slightly north and to the west of Hazor (possibly Khirbet Tell er-Ruweisī [181271]), the site is mentioned in the later Egyptian Execration Texts (19th century B.C.E.).

4. MT name for Egyptian On (Jer. 43:13 KJV; cf. LXX *Hēlíou póleōs*).

Bibliography. E. Grant, "Beth Shemesh, 1928," *AASOR* 9 (1929); *Ain Shems Excavations* 1–3 (Haverford, Pa., 1931-34); Grant and G. E. Wright, 4–5 (1938-39); W. H. Shea, "A Potential Biblical Connection for the Beth-shemesh Ostracon," *AUSS* 25 (1987): 257-66.

DAVID C. MALTSBERGER

BETH-SHITTAH (Heb. *bêṯ haššiṭṭâ*)

A place mentioned in the account of the battle between the Gideonites and the Midianites (Judg. 7:22), most likely to be identified with modern Shutta on the northern side of the Jezreel Valley, E of the fountain of Harod (ʿAin Jālûd; 184217).

BETH-TAPPUAH (Heb. *bêṯ-tappûaḥ*)

A city in the hill country of Judah (Josh. 15:53). The name is preserved in modern Taffûḥ (154105), 5.5 km. (3.5 mi.) WNW of Hebron.

BETH-TOGARMAH (Heb. *bêṯ tôgarmâ*)

A place N of Israel, likely in modern Armenia, where the descendants of Togarmah lived (cf. Akk. Til-garimmu). In Ezekiel's oracle against Tyre Beth-togarmah ("house of Togarmah") exchanges horses and mules for merchandise (Ezek. 27:14). Ezek. 38:6 lists it as an ally of Gog. According to the Table of Nations (Gen. 10:3; 1 Chr. 1:6) Togarmah was one of the three sons of Gomer, a descendant of Noah's son Japheth.

H. WAYNE HOUSE

BETHUEL (Heb. *bĕṯû'ēl*) **(PERSON)**

The youngest son of Abraham's brother Nahor and Milcah (Gen. 22:22), also called "the Aramean" (25:20; 28:5).

BETHUEL (Heb. *bĕṯû'ēl*)
(PLACE) (also BETHUL)

A town where Simeon's descendants lived (1 Chr. 4:30). At Josh. 19:4 the name is spelled Bethul. In a comparable list of southern Judean towns, Chesil appears in its place (Josh. 15:30). Its location near Hormah and Ziklag suggests it may be the same as Bethel at 1 Sam. 30:27. The location is uncertain but proposed identifications include Khirbet er-Ras and Khirbet al-Qaryatein, near Beer-sheba.

LAURA B. MAZOW

BETHULIA (Gk. *Baithuloua*)

A city in Samaria in which events of the book of Judith are set. Its existence is uncertain and its location unknown, but Judith does provide some geographical information. Bethulia is N of Jerusalem (Jdt. 11:19), facing "Esdraelon opposite the plain near Dothan," near Betomesthaim (4:6), in the "hill country of Samaria," above springs which supplied the city's water (6:11-12; 7:12-13).

Variant spellings for Bethulia have raised the possibility that it is not an actual city name but a pseudonym (for Bethel, "house of God"). Its meaning may also be derived from *bêṯ ʿălîyâ*, "house of ascents," which may refer to a city of the Samaritan hill country such as Shechem. Scholars also argue that city names in Judith are symbolic literary elements, and thus the siege of Bethulia can be equated with the rape of Dinah (Jdt. 9; cf. Heb. *btwlh*, "virgin").

MONICA L. W. BRADY

BETH-ZAITH (Gk. *Bēthzaíth, Bēzéth*)

The place to which Bacchides withdrew and where he slaughtered many of the Jews who had deserted him (1 Macc. 7:19; cf. Heb. *bêṯ zayiṯ*, "house of olive"). It has been identified with Khirbet Beit Zita (161114), ca. 6 km. (4 mi.) N of Beth-zur; a nearby cistern is said to be the great pit into which the general threw the murdered Jews.

BETHZATHA (Gk. *Bēthzathá*)
The name used by the NRSV and found in a few ancient manuscripts for the pool more commonly called Bethesda (John 5:2). FELIX JUST, S.J.

BETH-ZECHARIAH (Gk. *Baithzacharía*)
The place where Judas Maccabeus defended himself against Antiochus V Eupator, who had marched against Beth-zur (1 Macc. 6:32-33; cf. Josephus *Ant.* 12.9.4). It is identified with Khirbet Beit Zekâriā (161118), 10 km. (6 mi.) NE of Beth-zur.

BETH-ZUR (Heb. *bêṯ-ṣûr*)
A town in the southern hill country of Judah (Josh. 15:58) which may have been of Calebite origin (1 Chr 2:45). It is said to have been fortified by Rehoboam (2 Chr 11:7) and was apparently the center of an administrative district in the postexilic period (Neh. 3:16). Judas Maccabeus defeated Lysias near Beth-zur in 165 B.C. (1 Macc. 4:29). Lysias returned in 163 and took Beth-zur by siege (1 Macc. 6:31, 49), leaving behind a small garrison. Bacchides rebuilt the fortifications in 160 (1 Macc. 9:52), and it remained in Seleucid hands until Simon recaptured the city in 145 (11:65-66).

The name of the town apparently survives in the small site of Khirbet Burj eṣ-Ṣur, 20 km. (12 mi.) S of Jerusalem. Since this site dates to the Arab and Byzantine periods, most scholars accept the claim that ancient Beth-zur is to be identified with the larger ruins of Khirbet eṭ-Ṭubeiqah (1590.1108) only 500 m. (.5 mi.) from the smaller, more recent site. Two excavation seasons in 1931 and 1957 exposed extensive remains dating from the Middle Bronze Age through the Second Temple period. These excavations discovered that the Iron Age settlement at the site was unfortified, despite its being included in the list of towns fortified by Rehoboam. The fit between the archaeological and the historical evidence is much better for the period of the Maccabean Revolt.

Bibliography. R. W. Funk, "Beth-Zur," *NEAEHL* 1:259-61; O. R. Sellers, et al., *The 1957 Excavations at Beth-Zur.* AASOR 38 (New Haven, 1968).

WADE R. KOTTER

BETONIM (Heb. *bĕṭōnîm*)
A Transjordanian city given by Moses to the tribe of Gad (Josh. 13:26). Eusebius (*Onom.* 48.11; 49.10) referred to Betonim as Botnia (Gk. *Botanei*), identified with Khirbet Baṭneh (217154) or Batana SW of eṣ-Ṣalṭ. The Heshbon to Ramath-Mizpeh to Betonim line may have delineated the boundary between Reuben and Gad. PHILIP R. DREY

BEULAH (Heb. *bĕʿûlâ*)
A symbolic name given to Israel, designating its future prosperity (Isa. 62:4 MT). Instead of being forsaken and desolate, Israel will be "married" (NRSV; lit., "possessed") and its numerous inhabitants will remove the present reproach of its widowhood.

BEYOND THE JORDAN
A geographical term (Heb. *ʿēḇer hayyardēn*) designating either the region W (e.g., Gen. 50:10-11, Jacob's burial place) or (usually) E (e.g., Judg. 5:17, Gad; Matt. 4:25, Gk. *péran*) of the river Jordan, depending on the writer's viewpoint.

BEYOND THE RIVER
1. The area E of the Euphrates (2 Sam. 10:16; 1 Kgs. 14:15; Isa. 7:20; 1 Chr. 19:16); also translated "beyond the Euphrates" (NRSV).

2. The area W of the Euphrates (1 Kgs. 4:24[MT 5:4]); also translated in various places as "west of the Euphrates" (NRSV, NIV), "Trans-Euphrates" (NIV), and "the province beyond the river" (NRSV). As early as the 8th century, Akk. *ebir nāri* ("beyond the river") was used to refer to the Syria-Palestine region. During or after the reign of Xerxes this became a satrapy by that name.

Bibliography. M. W. Stolper, "The Governor of Babylon and Across-the-River in 486 B.C.," *JNES* 48 (1989): 283-305.

3. The district of Haran from which the patriarchs came (Josh. 24:2-15). Narratively these have an eastward perspective; geographically and politically they are Mesopotamian. R. GLENN WOODEN

BEZAI (Heb. *bēṣay*)
The head of a family that returned from Exile under Zerubbabel (Ezra 2:17 = Neh. 7:23). One of their representatives set his seal to the renewed covenant (Neh. 10:18[MT 19]).

BEZALEL (Heb. *bĕṣal'ēl*)
1. A Judahite, descendant of Caleb through Hur and Ephrath (1 Chr. 2:20). A skilled artisan (Exod. 35:30–36:3), he and Oholiab were chosen to construct the tabernacle and its furnishings (Exod. 31:1-11; 38:22; 2 Chr. 1:5) as well as the ark of the covenant (Exod. 37:1).

2. A returned exile from the family of Pahath-moab who was compelled to divorce his foreign wife (Ezra 10:30).

BEZEK (Heb. *bezeq*)
1. The town where the tribes of Judah and Simeon defeated Adoni-bezek and his army (Judg. 1:1-7). Its location is unknown. Most scholars equate this city with the Bezek NE of Shechem (**2** below), but others would place it somewhere S of Shechem, probably closer to Jerusalem

2. A town where Saul mustered his troops for battle (1 Sam. 11:8-11). Most scholars identify the site as modern Khirbet Ibzik (187197), ca. 20 km. (12.4 mi.) NE of Shechem in the territory of Manasseh. However, excavations have failed to find traces of occupation prior to the late Iron Age and recent archaeological evidence suggests that the nearby Iron Age site of Khirbet Salhab (185195) was its original location. WADE R. KOTTER

BEZER (Heb. *beṣer*) **(PERSON)**
A son of Zophah of the tribe of Asher (1 Chr. 7:37).

BEZER (Heb. *beṣer*) **(PLACE)**
A city in Transjordan's wilderness in the territory of Reuben (Deut. 4:43). It was assigned to the Levites and designated a city of refuge (Josh. 20:8; 21:36). According to the Mesha Stone (l. 27), it was reconquered and fortified by the Moabite king Mesha.

The location and identity of ancient Bezer is uncertain. Umm el-'Amad (235132), 12 km. (7.5 mi.) NE of Madaba, and Tell Jalul, 5 km.(3.1 mi.) E of Madaba, have been proposed.

RANDALL W. YOUNKER

BIBLE
Neither Jews nor Christians originally called their Scriptures "the Bible" (lit., "the Book"). Jews often used words signifying "the Scrolls," and Christians did call their Scriptures "the Books" (lit., "the codices"). In the early centuries, the Christian Bible appeared almost exclusively in the form of codex fascicles, each containing either one of the larger books (e.g., Isaiah) or a collection of smaller books (Paul's Letters), so the Scriptures physically corresponded to Lat. *biblia,* "the books" (cf. Jerome: *bibliotheca,* lit., "the library"). The term derives from *bublos* or *bublion,* loanwords from Egyptian, denoting originally the stalk and, then, the inner pitch of the papyrus plant from which scrolls were commonly made.

In both the Hebrew of Jewish Scripture and its oldest Greek translations, one of the most common technical names for Scripture is "the Scrolls." In Dan. 9:2 Daniel interprets the book of Jeremiah which he finds "in the Scrolls" (cf. 1 Macc. 12:9; 2 Clem. 14:2). Without the definite article the Hebrew noun can be used generically for "literature" other than the Bible.

The NT itself lacks the Greek plural, *tá biblía,* as a name for Scripture, though this term does occur for nonbiblical collections (John 21:25; Acts 19:19; 2 Tim. 4:13; Rev. 20:12). The technical counterpart is *haí graphaí,* "the writings." The singular Greek terms, *bíblos* or *biblíon,* occur in reference only to portions of Scripture, such as a single scroll (e.g., "the book of Moses," Mark 12:26; "the book of Isaiah," Luke 3:4), a "book" within a larger single scroll (e.g., "the book [Joel] of the prophets," Acts 7:42), or even a "book" that becomes part of the NT itself (e.g., John 20:30).

The earliest references to a parchment codex used for literary purpose (Lat. *membrana*) date from the last two decades of the 1st century C.E. A Greek transliteration of this term occurs in 2 Tim. 4:13, when Paul asks Carpus to bring from Troas his cloak and "also the scrolls (*tá biblía*), especially the parchment codices (*tás membránas*)." Assuming Pauline authorship, this reference might be the earliest known reference to literary codices.

What was signified by this reference to "codices" remains a mystery, while "the scrolls" could easily suggest books of Jewish Scripture, copies of Paul's letters, or some other literature. Perhaps Paul edited and published a first edition of his own letters. *Membránas* could refer to ephemeral notes of Paul, some other unknown resources, or copies of a codex literary collection that Paul himself had published or a late letter editorially attributed to Paul.

Jewish Scripture

Heb. *tôrâ* can signify teaching, instruction, and law. It may indicate normative teaching by a priest or later rabbi (Jer. 18:18), a written collection of prophetic oracles (Isa. 8:16), parts of the book of Deuteronomy or other smaller collections of laws, the first five books (Josh. 1:7-8), or all of Jewish Scripture (cf. Dan. 9:10). Much later the term could refer to the revealed subject matter of both Written Torah (Scripture) and the Oral Torah (Mishnah and Talmud).

Since the 19th century, most scholars have identified "the book of the Torah" mentioned in 2 Kgs. 22-23 with at least the core of the present book of Deuteronomy (perhaps chs. 12–26 and 28) (cf. Athanasius, Jerome, Chrysostom). Most modern scholars have argued that behind the partly fictive depiction of events in 2 Kings lies evidence pointing to a real historical moment associated with the editing and first public reading of the book of Deuteronomy. However, the parallel account in 2 Chr. 34–35 presents these same reforms by Josiah in his 11th year (627), prior to the discovery of "the book of the Torah." The extensive citations from the Pentateuch in Chronicles also may imply that the editors probably considered this to be the pentateuchal Torah rather than just the book of Deuteronomy.

The five-book scroll of the Torah, first published and read ca. the middle of the 5th century by Ezra (Neh. 8), constitutes the earliest reliable instance of a scroll being regarded as a part of a Jewish Bible. The Torah scroll of Ezra seems to be a combination of different traditions, only partially harmonized, from different groups of exiled Judeans identified in this period as "Jews" who have been allowed to return to their land and to rebuild their temple and religious life together. (Only after this period do we begin to see evidence of "commentaries" on Jewish Scripture, with a distinction between "biblical text" and "comment.")

According to Josh. 1:7-8 Joshua commanded the people to "meditate day and night" on "this scroll of the Torah" (cf. Ps. 1:2-3). As part of a prebiblical "Deuteronomistic history," the "scroll" in question would have been Deuteronomy. But with later editing by the time of Ezra, when Deuteronomy became part of the Pentateuch, "this scroll" clearly refers back to the preceding five-book Torah of Moses.

The term "the Torah" serves the double purpose of labeling a uniquely biblical genre of literature — the five-book Torah (Deut. 1:5; 31:24) — and of naming the revelatory subject matter of that same literature, which by later extension is also the subject matter of the whole of Jewish Scripture. This Torah may be described as "secret things," which

God alone can make known to Israel (29:29[MT 28]; cf. 30:11-14). God reveals the Torah through Moses, who is a "prophet" *par excellence* (cf. 34:10). (Later Jewish tradition generalized this idea for other books of Scripture so that even Solomon is called a "prophet" in the Targums to describe his role as a writer of Scripture. Here is a specialized concept of prophetic inspiration for the books of Scripture.) The Torah is heard in a present and future tense in that it is ever addressed "to us and to our children forever" (29:29[28]; cf. 4:9-10; 6;2, 7; esp. 31:13), speaking directly to later generations rather than simply describing or recalling certain past events. The Torah is not expressed in a heavenly language but is "written" in human words on a scroll (cf. Exod. 17:14; 24:4; 34:27; Num. 33:2; Deut. 28:58, 61; 29:20, 21, 27[19, 20, 26]; 31:9, 22).

The written human words of the Bible convey revelation only when they are heard as a perpetual "witness" or "testimony" to the Torah (Deut. 31:26; cf. 32;46) i.e., when the testimony of the text and its subject matter can be heard together. In this sense, "testimony" is a mode of discourse peculiar to Scripture, analogous to but not reducible to legal statements at a trial, eyewitness statements, or final statements attendant to the reading of wills. This testimony is spoken by a prophet and bears witness to something only God can make known. The older theological language of "inspiration" (2 Tim. 3:16) sought to secure this difference on the side of the human language of the Bible, while the conception of "revelation" has been used to mark the difference in terms of the subject matter from which the testimony lives and finds its only claim to validity.

This testimony of the Torah is preserved as a written "covenant" (Deut. 31:26) between God and Israel. It delineates their identity as a people, their terms of possessing and governing a particular land, and other mutual obligations of God and Israel to each other. Beyond its essential narratives, we might best describe this covenant as a peculiar set of rules governing behavior (mundane as well as holy) and the proper construction of holy spaces, holy implements, and ritual procedures.

The difference between the laws given in Exodus and those of Deuteronomy has been explained by the claim that Moses delivered the Torah to the first generation of the Exodus but in Deuteronomy he "interpreted the Torah" (Deut. 1:5) to the next generation after the first rebellious generation had died. So, the necessity of interpreting Scripture from generation to generation is built into the structure of Jewish Scripture itself.

Within the Bible itself Moses is not called "an author," but is, more accurately, the only person named as "writing" it and may therefore be called its "designated writer" or even its "author."

The link between various named persons and books of Jewish Scripture has stimulated an endless preoccupation with the "lives" of these biblical figures, whether named explicitly as writers or not (e.g., Jonah, Ruth, Esther). These considerations must inform whatever criteria we apply in judging the integrity of a biblical book on the basis of its naming a principal, dominant, or authoritative "writer." Any modern effort to do justice to "writers" and scribes of Scripture must take into account this legacy of ponderable differences, so that only after empathetic imagination of a world foreign to our own might we venture in the vernacular of our own day an intelligible history of the same things across time.

The precise list of books and the determination of the official text of the Hebrew Bible became a particularly important issue with the dawn of rabbinic Judaism after the destruction of the temple in 70 C.E. and the Second Jewish War of 132-135. Though most of the books belonging to Jewish Scripture had been recognized by some Jewish groups as early as 180 B.C.E. (cf. Sirach), Jewish Scripture among the rabbis in the 2nd century might best be seen as an inclusive, critical mass of books corresponding to the greatest breadth of the Jewish community. That relatively comprehensive collection could be secondarily debated, leading to official lists, continued debates over certain books, refined efforts to arrange the order of biblical books, and an effort to establish an official text. It would be more accurate historically to say that Jews felt that God through Scripture had chosen them, than to say that members of their leadership ever thought they chose the books of Scripture.

The decision about the specific text of Jewish Scripture appears again more as a reaction to recognition of a Scripture than an effort to create it. From evidence of Qumran manuscripts and from old Greek translations, we see the existence in earlier periods of various textual traditions, sometimes with substantial differences. We may call "proto-Masoretic" the official text of Scripture accepted by rabbis in the 2nd century. Though it has precedents in texts that can be traced back into the preceding centuries, it also anticipates the real Masoretes of the 6th century C.E. who help to refine textual details, adding vowels, accents, and other notations.

Christian Bible

We have no evidence of a Christian Bible until the 2nd century C.E., in the same period when leaders of rabbinic Judaism officially published the scrolls of Jewish Scripture and began to codify the Mishnah. Rabbinic Judaism and postapostolic Christianity began to consolidate their own identities and sharply distinguish themselves from one another.

The Christian Bible is not the product of a triumphant Church in the West. While the Christian Bible implies a clear distinction between Jews and Christians, it also admits its direct dependence on Jewish Scripture. Christians did not need a handbook on prayer in the NT because they already had a sufficient one, the book of Psalms, which served that function for both church and synagogue. Yet, Christians traditionally interpreted the Psalms as a testimony to the gospel and read, in a manner entirely foreign to Jewish midrash, parts of the lament psalms as "messianic." In general, Christians sought to read Jewish Scripture, unlike rabbinic interpreters, in the light of the NT, but they also used "the OT" to supplement and to shed light on the NT.

The textual fragments of the Christian Bible that have survived suggest that it was published ca. 150 in the form of codex fascicles. Each codex contained a portion of Scripture, probably one for the Gospels, for Acts and the General Epistles, for Paul's Letters, and for the book of Revelation. The OT was entirely in Greek, dependent on selected (e.g., Theodotion for Daniel) and improved copies of earlier Jewish Old Greek translations of Hebrew originals. This may actually be the first published "LXX," meaning a complete collection of Greek translations of Jewish Scripture in a single publication series. We have no evidence that a complete collection of Old Greek scrolls ever played the same role as did the Greek OT within the Christian Bible.

According to Irenaeus, Bishop of Lyons, this Christian Bible ought to prevail against Marcion's version which treated Jewish Scripture as an inferior revelation and contained only a single "Gospel" — an edition of Luke expunged of its "Judaizing" elements — together with the "Apostle," a collection of 10 letters of Paul. This first Christian Bible appears to be a comprehensive, ecumenically generous, collection of books. Subsequently, scholars and church leaders would debate whether certain books truly deserved this status and seek to determine a more precise list, order, or text for the Bible. Similar to the case in Jewish Scripture, the publication of a critical mass of books seems to have gained circulation prior to more nuanced decisions, including agreement on whether the text of the OT ought to conform to the Hebrew of Jewish Scripture or simply rely on the earliest official Greek publication of the Christian Bible.

Christians knew what would characterize a Christian Bible because the notion of a scriptural corpus had already been accepted for several centuries among Jews. "The Gospel" indicates both a uniquely biblical genre of books (the four Gospels) and the subject matter of revelation for all of Christian Scripture, including the OT. Christians retained the Torah by incorporating it in various ways as interpreted and fulfilled by the Gospel or as playing more limited roles, such as a law (*nómos*) that serves as a preparation for hearing the gospel. Christian Scripture guaranteed access to the revealed gospel which had been "the Word" with God from the beginning (John 1:1-5) and belongs as well to the end of time.

The Jewish understanding of Scripture as prophetic testimony to the Torah is conspicuous when NT writers cite Jewish Scripture as a revealed "testimony" (e.g., Acts 13:22; cf. Heb. 2:6). Related statements about the nature of Christian Scripture occur in the editorial note at the end of the Gospel of John (ch. 21) and in the mention of the impending deaths of Peter in 2 Peter and of Paul in 2 Timothy. 2 Tim. 1:8 seems to assume that this testimony now belongs to a "standard" (v. 13) manifest in Scripture itself (3:14-17).

2 Tim. 3:15 clearly seems to refer to the OT, but the assurance in v. 16 that "All Scripture is inspired by God" may well reflect circumstances of the 2nd century when this Christian Scripture will be used in refutation of Marcion's gospel, as well as the proposals of others. Peter seems to anticipate the Christian Bible by referring readers to "your apostles," citing Paul as an "apostle" and Paul's own letters as a prime example. What Peter appears to describe is the transition from the prebiblical teaching of Jesus and his disciples to a biblical form of apostolic teaching, on a par with Jewish Scripture.

In sum, the Christian view of "all Scripture" as prophetic or apostolic "testimonies" to God's revelation of the Gospel plays a major role in the late editing of the NT books and finds its precedent in a Jewish understanding of Jewish Scripture. Both Jews and Christians realized from ancient times that the Bible is at most a testimony to a revelation that exists before, within, and beyond the words of the Bible. Only in this light can we understand the logic behind both midrash in Jewish rabbinic interpretation and the conception of a normative "literal sense" of Scripture as advocated by Christians. For Christians, both Torah and Gospel address them through the human witnesses of Scripture from God's side, so that the best of Christian confessions can likewise be at most a testimony to the mystery of God's revelation rather than entirely capture it in human words.

Bibliography. D. M. Carr, "Canonization in the Context of Community," in *A Gift of God in Due Season,* ed. R. D Weis and D. M. Carr. JSOTSup. 225 (Sheffield, 1996), 22-64; B. S. Childs, *Biblical Theology of the Old and New Testaments* (Minneapolis, 1992); H. Y. Gamble, *Books and Readers in the Early Church* (New Haven, 1995); G. T. Sheppard, "Biblical Interpretation After Gadamer," *PNEUMA* 16 (1994): 121-41; *The Future of the Bible as Scripture in the Church* (Toronto, 1990); W. C. Smith, *What Is Scripture?* (Minneapolis, 1993); D. Trobisch, *Paul's Letter Collection* (Minneapolis, 1994).

GERALD T. SHEPPARD

BIBLE TRANSLATIONS

"If every man's humour were followed, there would be no end of translating." Thus spoke Richard Bancroft, bishop of London, at the Hampton Court conference of 1604, where the proposal was first put forward for a new version of Scripture which would become the King James Version. However, everyone's humor cannot be followed. Translating the Bible is an ambitious and expensive undertaking. No fresh translation or revision of an existing translation can be justified without a clear and distinct purpose.

There are two factors that demand new versions or revisions from time to time: advances in biblical scholarship and linguistic change. Two additional factors make new versions at least desirable in the judgments of many: confessional translation and specific audiences. These four factors are by no means mutually exclusive, and a new version may meet more than one of these needs. In addition, occasional individuals accomplish the *tour de force* of translating the Bible, or at least the NT, on their own, often for no other reason than the simple challenge and the love of Scripture. In addition, theory and practice shift from time to time, and translations produced for any of the above reasons and by any group or individual will generally reflect some theory governing the practice of translation.

Advances in biblical scholarship

This is one of the reasons put forward by the translators of the KJV for their work, and it is one of the factors which require new versions or revisions to appear from time to time. These advances in scholarship are generally three in number.

Textual

Textual criticism, the scholarly attempt to arrive at a Hebrew or Greek text close to the form in which it left the hands of the original writers, was in its infancy at the time of the KJV, with scholars having access to the readings of few manuscripts and little critical means of evaluating different readings. During the 19th century especially a plethora of ancient manuscripts were discovered. By the end of that century so much more was known about the original text of the Bible, particularly of the NT, that a new version was needed that would translate a more accurate text. In the United States this need was met by the American Standard Version (a revision of the KJV) in 1901, as well as other translations appearing about the same time, such as the version by James Moffatt (1913-1924). Both were far more accurate than the KJV in presenting the real text of the Bible, but the ASV in particular made little effort to modernize the English. While the KJV had an archaic ring, at least charming and at most compelling, the ASV sounded simply peculiar. While the ASV, and to some extent Moffatt, was much used for several decades as a text in college and seminary classes, where accuracy was more important than effective style, the KJV continued to dominate liturgical use. The ASV was itself revised in 1952 as the Revised Standard Version. Even in that last half-century a significant amount of textual knowledge had become available, enabling the RSV to improve significantly over its immediate predecessor.

Today progress in textual criticism lies less in the discovery of new manuscripts than in new means of evaluating textual evidence. Future translations and revisions will benefit from this, as study of minuscules and lectionaries progresses, and as more data are available for computerized study. In the modern period it has never been necessary for translators to work directly from manuscripts; they have always had access to textual evidence through systems of footnoting in their printed Hebrew or Greek texts. Just as readers must rely on the work of the translators, translators must rely on the work of the textual critics, although translators are free to make their own textual decisions.

Lexicographical

The KJV preface admitted that the translators were forced to guess at the meaning of many seldom-used words, particularly in the OT. Since then knowledge of the Hebrew and Greek vocabularies has been greatly enlarged by the discovery of literary sources other than biblical. In the case of the OT, these sources have not necessarily even been in Hebrew, but in closely related languages. Study of similar roots in related languages (e.g., Arabic, Ugaritic) have enabled scholars to come to more informed opinions about the meaning of earlier unknown words; in many cases, there were unexpected meanings for well-known words. All modern versions of the OT have profited from this study, although none took it to greater lengths than the New English Bible (1970), which was widely faulted for too quickly adopting meanings that were still speculative. Much of this was corrected when the NEB was revised as the Revised English Bible (REB) in 1989.

In the NT, the discovery of many papyri, usually of a completely nonbiblical nature, made possible the understanding of the Greek vocabulary in ways not previously recorded in scholars' lexicons. All recent versions rely on such work.

Literary

Since ca. 1960 literary studies have begun to impact translation theory and practice. The RSV (1952) had relegated to the footnotes Mark 16:9-20 and John 7:53–8:11 on the textual grounds that these passages did not constitute part of the original text of the two Gospels. The second edition of the RSV (1977) restored these passages to the text, not on textual grounds, but on literary or canonical grounds. What constitutes canonicity if not continued use by the Church for centuries? The recognition that different genres of writing (e.g., poetry, prophecy, saga, proverbs, short story, history) may call for different approaches to translating manifested itself in the Today's English Version (1976). We may expect these studies to affect translation much more in the future, in interesting ways.

Linguistic change

Even if our knowledge of the Bible were static, language is always fluid through time. Many parts of the KJV are now unintelligible. More dangerously, many parts are now understood in a way never intended by authors or translators, since the meaning of English words has so changed (e.g., "mansions" in John 14:2), as to some extent have the structures of English grammar. The great fault of the ASV was that it largely ignored contemporary English style in its effort to preserve the KJV text. This was addressed by the RSV, which provided not only a more accurate text but also a more modern form of English. It met with a great deal more success than its predecessor. But even the RSV was cautious. In the 1950s it was the usual style for people, even teenagers, to pray in the archaic conjugations and pronouns ("Thou dost . . ."), and the RSV left speech addressed to God in that style. In later decades that style vanished, even in some of the most formal liturgical situations, and the New Revised Standard Version (1989) eliminated archaic language altogether. This was never even considered by the TEV or the theologically conservative New International Version (1973-1978).

The most striking linguistic change in recent years has been the move to gender inclusive language. By the last decade of the 20th century some usages (e.g., avoidance of generic "man" or use of the masculine pronoun to refer to any person) had become well enough accepted that substantial revisions were made in existing versions incorporating such adjustment. Among these were the NRSV (1989; highly successfully), TEV (1993; fairly successfully), and REB (1989, less successfully). None of these went so far as to refrain from referring to God in masculine terms. In 1995 a revision of the NRSV NT and Psalms was published as an Inclusive Version, which went to great pains to avoid masculine references to God (e.g., Father, King) or even to the exalted Christ (though not to the earthly Jesus).

Linguistic change is unpredictable, and translators try to avoid slang and even colloquialisms, since many of these usages quickly become obsolete. It seems best to aim for an audience 25-35 years old, people whose speech is no longer marked by evanescent teenage slang, but which has not yet become fossilized.

Confessional translations

Occasionally new translations are made, or less frequently revisions, by members of a particular religious community. The results may be highly tendentious and useful only for that community (e.g., The New World Translation of the Watchtower Society [1951-1960]) or of broad ecumenical appeal (e.g., the New Jerusalem Bible [Roman Catholic, 1990]). Even the KJV may be said to be confessional. Intended to serve the needs of the Church of England (and no one else), it actually came to serve the needs of the high-church constituency against the interests of the Puritans.

When the RSV appeared in 1952 it was the first viable challenge ever to the sway of the KJV, and it was roundly condemned by many conservative church people. Much of the venom against it was politically inspired, since it was published during the height of the McCarthy anti-communist scare (some pointed out that the first edition had a red cover). Evangelical scholarship was weak at this time; for those who wanted an alternative to the "liberal" RSV, none better was available than the Berkeley Version (1949, 1959), theologically innocuous but rather odd in some ways. With the reemergence of theological strength among evangelicals in the latter part of the century, the NIV was produced to serve this community. It is a textually and translationally responsible version that became the best-selling English version in the United States. Its translational approach is fairly traditional, really not much different from the RSV, but it offered an alternative for conservative Christians still distrustful of the RSV's background. Kenneth Taylor opened new ground for evangelicals with his "paraphrase" called the Living Bible (1971), freely reading his "rigid evangelical position" into the text with a breezy style marked by admirable turns of phrase. So successful was this that conservative scholarship was organized to produce a true translation inspired by Taylor's stylistic approach: the New Living Translation (1996).

It is natural that English-speaking Jews would want a version translated by Jews. The first widely used Jewish version was that of the (American) Jewish Publication Society (1917). A more successful translation has been the New Jewish Publication Society Version (1962-1985). Either of these, but especially the latter, can be used helpfully and without qualms by Christian readers.

For English-speaking Roman Catholics, the Douai-Rheims version (1582-1610, heavily revised 1750) long served as the standard version. In the 20th century the Catholic faithful were attracted to Protestant versions which had received the Church's imprimatur (e.g., RSV, TEV) before modern Catholic versions became available. Translations by Catholic scholars now in wide use are the New American Bible (1970; partially revised 1986, 1991) and the New Jerusalem Bible, a revision of the Jerusalem Bible of 1966. Many Protestants use these versions without hesitation.

Specific audiences

Most of the major translations of Scripture have been addressed to as broad an audience as possible, but some individuals and groups have sponsored versions addressed to the needs of special groups. In a sense, confessional translations are so directed; the Baptist scholars who produced the Improved Version (1912) had little expectation of its being used beyond Baptist circles. But transconfessional groups can be identified and targeted. The primary audience of the TEV was people who had learned English as a second language; it was written in "common English," defined as English used with comfort by the highly-educated native speaker and with understanding by the poorly educated. The New Living Translation is intended for Christians of very conservative theological bent. The translations included in the Anchor Bible commentary series are intended for scholars.

Occasionally portions of the Bible are presented in the current slang of some group, such as teenagers or gang members. These have little permanent interest. One of the few to elicit wide attention was Clarence Jordan's Cottonpatch Version, a clever transculturation into the language and life of the American South of 1968-1973. Today it throws light on the culture of the era to which it spoke.

Individual translations

Major translations of the Bible are virtually always the product of committee labors. (Six committees, totaling almost 50 people, translated the KJV.) Occasionally, however, individuals have translated a good portion if not the whole Bible. As early as 382 Jerome undertook the translation of the Bible into the Latin Vulgate (at least largely his work) at the request of Pope Damasus. More recently Helen Barrett Montgomery translated the NT (Centenary New Testament, 1924), sponsored by the American Baptist Publication Society. Robert G. Bratcher translated the NT of Today's English Version (1966) for the American Bible Society. Others have seen a particular need or just a challenge. The first translation of the whole Bible in English was done largely by John Wyclif (ca. 1382). Several portions of the Bible were published from 1947 by J. B. Phillips, seeking at first a form he could use with people huddled underground escaping the air war over London. Ronald Knox, a Roman Catholic priest in England, translated the entire Bible from Latin (1945-1949) into a highly idiosyncratic English style. In 1995 Everett Fox published an English version of the Torah, seeking to convey the atmosphere of the ancient Hebrew while being compellingly readable.

Translation theory

Translations may be located anywhere between the two poles of formal equivalence (literal) and dynamic equivalence (free). A strictly literal translation would be largely unintelligible, but traditional translations, such as KJV, RSV, and NIV, have tended to translate sentence structures and figures of speech literally. These are usually perceived as intelligible and often normal, if sometimes a bit unusual for English. Dynamic equivalence (NEB, TEV) makes little if any attempt to preserve original sentence structure, but seeks to state the meaning of the text in natural contemporary idiom. Original metaphors may be retained if their meaning is clear to a contemporary readership. Today it seems clear that both types of translations have their place. Formal equivalence versions are convenient for academic study, dynamic equivalence for private reading. Both are used in public worship.

The current scene exhibits conflicting tendencies. The RSV was rendered more dynamic in the NRSV, while the NEB became less so in its revision as the REB. If the NIV serves the evangelical community well as a formal equivalence translation, perhaps the NLT will serve for a dynamic equivalence version.

Bibliography. L. R. Bailey, ed., *The Word of God: A Guide to English Versions of the Bible* (Atlanta, 1982); E. S. Frerichs, ed., *The Bible and Bibles in America* (Atlanta, 1988); S. Kubo and W. F. Specht, *So Many Versions? Twentieth Century English Versions of the Bible,* rev. ed (Grand Rapids, 1983); J. P. Lewis, *The English Bible from KJV to NIV,* 2nd ed. (Grand Rapids, 1991); H. M. Orlinsky and R. G. Bratcher, *A History of Bible Translation and the North American Contribution* (Atlanta, 1991); A. C. Partridge, *English Biblical Translation* (London, 1973).

ROGER A. BULLARD

BIBLICAL CRITICISM

Biblical criticism is a child of the Enlightenment, an era when it was believed that every human endeavor must appear before the bar of reason and be judged according to its relation to universal truth. Inevitably, the OT and NT were made to appear.

The purposes for which biblical criticism were used were many and varied. For example, the French prelate Richard Simon (d. 1712) subjected the Bible to critical scrutiny in order to prove that it was not a sufficient rule for faith. The great Jewish philosopher and lens-grinder Benedict Spinoza (d. 1677) applied the critical method to distinguish whatever in the Bible gave rise to dogma, thus to persecution, and whatever in it could be recognized as eternally valid and thus could end religious conflict. Due to his rigorous examination in the *Tractatus,* Spinoza has been celebrated as the "father" of modern biblical criticism. Johan Salomo Semler (d. 1791), early Protestant biblical critic, applied the discipline to the question of the biblical canon — chiefly in order to detach the OT from the NT, and the orientalist Hermann Samuel Reimarus (d. 1768) used it to distinguish the "system" of Jesus from that of his disciples, intent on fraud.

Initially, the word "criticism" lacked negative connotation. The German term *Kritik,* for which it served as translation, simply denoted a discrete method of investigation. But owing to the largely negative results at which its advocates arrived, it came to be associated with an attack on the sacred Scriptures, and thus identified as an enemy of faith, an identification still made by some. Others, then as now, have insisted that biblical criticism could be made to serve the ends of faith. In the United States, biblical criticism actually made its advent at the hands of people of faith. Moses Stuart of Andover (d. 1852), representative of the evangelicalism of Jonathan Edwards, was early attracted to German critical scholars, whose works he proceeded to master and interpret for his American readers. Stuart's approach to the OT and NT earned him the title of "father of biblical science in America."

If biblical criticism in the 17th and 18th centuries served the ends of the Enlightenment, i.e., to lift out the "universal truths of reason" from the merely historical or "accidental," in the 19th century it engaged in historical "excavation." Through advances in archaeology and the deciphering of ancient texts, scholars encountered witnesses to the biblical texts previously unknown, which greatly facilitated approximating those texts to their originals or autographs. The German pietist Johan Albrecht Bengel (d. 1752) proceeded to group the witnesses into "families," a practice continued by Brooke Foss Westcott (d. 1901) and F. J. Anthony Hort (d. 1892) in England. This "lower" or textual criticism came to be distinguished from the "higher criticism" with its questions touching sources, structures, and religious-historical contexts of the biblical writings. While the more wary restricted themselves to the lower criticism, ultimately the restriction could not guarantee security. The so-called Textus Receptus ("received text") which had dominated since the 16th century, and on which the orthodox had based their doctrine of verbal inspiration, now fell from favor. The result was elimination of neutrality from the pursuit of the lower criticism.

In the first half of the 19th century, the greatest strides in biblical criticism were made by OT scholars, chiefly in the search for sources underlying the Pentateuch. Following the suspicion of Jewish tradition toward Moses' authorship of the Pentateuch, the French scholar Jean Astruc (d. 1766) elaborated the theory that the patriarch combined two main sources in his composition of Genesis, the one using the divine name Elohim, and the other the name Jehovah. Building on Astruc's theory, OT scholars arrived at the so-called documentary or Graf-Kuenen-Wellhausen hypothesis, named for its three principal proponents, Karl Heinrich Graf (d. 1869) and Julius Wellhausen (d. 1918) of Germany and Abraham Kuenen (d. 1891) of Holland. According to this theory the final editor of the Pentateuch combined four sources (the Jahvist/Yahwist, Elohist, Deuteronomist, and the Priestly source, hence: JEDP).

Influenced by their OT colleagues, NT scholars advanced to the problem of the similarity and dissimilarity between the first three Gospels, the "Synoptic problem." If the Pentateuch resembled a weave of sources distinguished either by their use of the divine names or by their legal or cultic character, the relationship between the NT Gospels urged an analogous source theory. Earlier opting for a single written source (Gotthold Ephraim Lessing, d. 1781) or fragments of the Jesus tradition (Friedrich Schleiermacher, d. 1834) behind all four Gospels, scholars came to settle for the theory of literary dependence among the first three (J. K. L. Gieseler, d. 1854), assigning the Fourth Gospel a separate place. According to this "multiple source hypothesis," Mark's Gospel was prior and furnished Matthew and Luke with their outline. Matthew and Luke then supplemented what they had gleaned from Mark with a second Synoptic source dubbed "Q" (i.e., Ger. *Quelle*, "source"). In addition, Mark's two co-evangelists included material peculiar to each (e.g., in Matthew the visit of the Magi, in Luke the parables of the lost sheep, lost coin, and two sons).

In the latter half of the 19th century, biblical critics turned in earnest to the question of the Bible's religious-historical context, and the History of Religions School *(Religionsgeschichtliche Schule)* was born. For example, the OT scholar Herman Gunkel (d. 1932) attempted to demonstrate the Genesis Creation story's dependence on Babylonian myth, purged of its polytheistic aspects, while Richard Reitzenstein (d. 1931) asserted the influence of Gnosticism on the NT Christology. Others insisted that Judaism alone furnished the background for understanding the two testaments, and a division among scholars ensued which has persisted to the present. The influence of the History of Religions School has been mixed. Reitzenstein's idea of a gnostic, pre-Christian "Redeemed Redeemer" as sitting for the NT portrait of the Christ has not endured in face of new evidence or of improvements in the techniques of reading the old evidence. But Gunkel's study on the Spirit in both testaments as directly contrary to the romantic identification of the Spirit with human consciousness remains axiomatic.

The greatest and best known among biblical critics of the 19th century was Ferdinand Christian Baur (d. 1860) of Tübingen, Germany. Baur, attracted to G. F. W. Hegel's tracing of the development of the "Absolute Spirit" toward self-realization, set the literature of the NT within the context of a conflict and its final resolution between two parties, the one reflected in the Gospel of Matthew, with its allegedly Jewish, particularistic, and nomistic understanding of the gospel, and the other represented by the "genuine" Pauline epistles (1–2 Corinthians, Galatians, and Romans) with their universalistic, law-free gospel. Baur's assessment of each NT book as reflecting the various stages of this conflict and its resolution has been discarded or corrected, but his insistence on interpreting the NT in its historical context has remained a principal rule of interpretation.

Prior to World War I biblical research consisted largely of "source criticism." From the Astrucs, Grafs, Kuenens, and Wellhausens, to the Lessings, Schleiermachers, and Gieselers, and the hundreds between and following affirming or denying, scholars concentrated on questions respecting literary origins. Now, attention was given the shape of the biblical text prior to its assuming written form, and on its reflecting the "situation-in-life" *(Sitz im Leben)* of the community in which it had made its home. The name of the new method was "form criticism."

In a famous 1938 essay ("Das formgeschichtliche Problem des Hexateuchs"), Gerhard von Rad of Heidelberg (d. 1971) attempted to demonstrate that the first six books of the OT rested upon "historical credos" or rehearsals of the saving deeds of God which had taken on stereotyped, "canonical" form to give shape and content to Israel's worship. Von Rad went on to fix the times and places in which these creeds originated. Those which reflected the promise of the land had their origin where the question of its possession was acute, at Gilgal near Jericho, in the time of Samuel and Saul; those which reflected the giving of the law had their "situation-in-life" at Shechem, during the coalition of the 12 tribes.

The principal pioneers in NT form criticism were Karl Ludwig Schmidt (d. 1956), Martin Dibelius (d. 1947), and Rudolf Bultmann (d. 1976). Schmidt and Dibelius cautiously proceeded with the isolating of individual units of the Gospel tradition, presumably husbanded in the oral period for preaching purposes, while Bultmann believed the method enabled him to determine the genuineness or nongenuineness of a given unit of the tradition. In *The History of Synoptic Tradition,* he concluded that the entire Jesus tradition had undergone revision before being committed to writing, having taken on accretions in analogy with the evolution

BIBLICAL CRITICISM

of traditions in nonbiblical circles. Conservative scholars registered alarm, adhering strictly to the "safer" source criticism, or contented themselves with the purely phenomenological task, classifying the various units of the gospel tradition. In the United States, Benjamin Wisner Bacon's (d. 1932) *The Beginnings of Gospel Story* (1909) anticipated form-critical analysis on the continent, and gave stimulus to the "social environment research" of the University of Chicago.

Close on the heels of form criticism followed redaction criticism, which concentrated on the question of authorial intent. If form criticism inquired after the "life" of a text prior to its assuming written form, redaction criticism inquired after the life of that text once it had come into an author's hands. Redaction criticism also had its precursors. In their work on the Gospels, Bacon, Wellhausen, and William Wrede (d. 1906) had already wrestled with the question of the degree to which an author's theological perspective affected his arrangement of the traditional material. And, as was also the case with form criticism, the method was honed and sharpened to a point its forebears may not have recognized.

Partner to every stage in the evolution of biblical criticism has been "The Quest of the Historical Jesus." In fact, inquiry into the life and career of Jesus of Nazareth as an object apart from faith has often served the critic as ultimate goal. In the 18th century, Reimarus believed that his method uncovered a purpose of Jesus antithetical to that of his disciples, and which they vainly intended to obscure, as witness the massive contradictions in the Gospels. In the early 19th century, David Friedrich Strauss (d. 1874) of Tübingen attempted to peel away from the story of Jesus the layers of myth and legend derived from Judaism and Hellenistic thought. Critics of the later 19th century heralded Markan priority and "Q" as the two great pillars on which to base an authentic life of Jesus. This confidence later shattered on the realization that each Gospel was written from a discrete theological perspective which made distinguishing the message of Jesus from that of his community impossible. In a celebrated review, Albert Schweitzer (d. 1965) declared this "first," 19th-century quest of the historical Jesus bankrupt, and concluded with a line whole generations have committed to memory:

> He comes to us as One unknown, without a name, as of old, by the lake-side, He came to those men who knew Him not. He speaks to us the same word: "Follow thou me!" and sets us to the tasks which He has to fulfil for our time. *(The Quest of the Historical Jesus)*

The 20th century has witnessed a resumption of life-of-Jesus research. Bultmann's investigation of the development of Gospel tradition had led him to outlaw the Quest and to give priority to the proclamation or *kerygma* of the primitive community, devoid of any material link to the historical Jesus. The result was revolt from all sides. Ernst Käsemann (1906-) fired the first volley with his 1954 essay, "The Problem of the Historical Jesus." He insisted that skepticism need not have the last word; that, e.g., the Sermon on the Mount reflected a clear and unequivocal reflection of the historical Jesus' consciousness of himself and his mission. Käsemann's essay was followed by a host of others. A "second" quest came into being which would occupy scholars in North America and abroad for more than 30 years. More recently, a "third" quest of the historical Jesus has come into vogue. Less disciplined than the "first" or "second" in terms of the use of accepted tools, it is more radical in its distancing the historical Jesus from the proclamation of the Christian community.

The 1950s formed the high-water mark of confidence in historical method. From that time scholars began to reflect malaise over the conflicting and at times absurd results to which biblical criticism had led, thus over the total absence of consensus in even the least arguable matters, and called for radical revision or even abandonment of traditional methods.

The consequences for text (lower) criticism have been the least dramatic, however irritating to persons schooled in traditional methods. For example, the grouping of texts into families has been abandoned in favor of the "local-genealogical" method. Once it has established the variety of witnesses to a given text or passage, this method subjects each witness to scrutiny, line by line, sentence by sentence, to determine which witness might have given birth to the other.

The result for the earlier labelled higher criticism has been a congeries of methods, intent on supplementing or replacing methods of the past. The "structuralist" method is concerned with the "synchronic" as opposed to the "diachronic" aspects of the text. Occupied with the logic of an entire narrative rather than of a given sentence, it inquires into *how* an author appears in his text and sets his readers into it. The "oral history" method treats the move from "orality" to textuality as sacrificing a "metaphysics of presence," and inquires into the social and psychological upheaval such a move reflects. Another reading convention pays exclusive attention to the text, rejecting all exclusive criticism and attention to an author's goal as an "intentional fallacy." A related method denies to words any referents beyond themselves, concerning itself solely with the intratextual relations of words, with whatever meaning may be gleaned from observing the connection between signifiers, exclusive of what they signify. "Reader-response criticism" describes the relation of the text to the reader, rejecting the text's autonomy in favor of its dependence upon the reader's participation. According to some, reading not merely discovers the meaning of a text but actually creates it, to the effect that the reader or interpreter constitutes the text. Not to be ignored is the "feminist" reading, which examines the biblical text for reflecting or inhibiting women's lives and concerns. In contrast with earlier periods, much of contemporary biblical criticism takes its lead from a community of scholars outside the theological disciplines. In the United States, names of humanities scholars appear with regularity in essays, monographs, and volumes dealing with biblical criticism and interpretation. In fact, a considerable amount of contemporary biblical criticism is Anglo-American in character, since criticism in Europe still gives large room to traditional methods.

Bibliography. K. and B. Aland, *The Text of the New Testament,* 2nd ed. (Grand Rapids, 1989); H. Conzelmann and A. Lindemann, *Interpreting the New Testament* (Peabody, 1988); R. A. Harrisville and W. Sundberg, *The Bible in Modern Culture* (Grand Rapids, 1995). ROY A. HARRISVILLE

BICHRI (Heb. *biḵrî*), **BICHRITES** (*habbiḵrîm*)
The father of Sheba, the Benjaminite who rebelled against David (2 Sam. 20:1-22). The name probably designates a member of the line of Becher (Gen. 46:21; 1 Chr. 7:6, 8; cf. 2 Sam. 20:14, "Bichrites").

BIDKAR (Heb. *biḏqar*)
Jehu's military aide at the murder of King Joram of Israel (2 Kgs. 9:25).

BIGTHA (Heb. *bigṯā'*)
One of the seven eunuchs or chamberlains of the Persian king Ahasuerus (Esth. 1:10; cf. O. Pers. *Bagadāna, Bagadāta,* "gift of God").

BIGTHAN (Heb. *bigĕṯān*), **BIGTHANA** (*bigĕṯānā'*)
A eunuch and courtier of King Ahasuerus who with his fellow courtier Teresh conspired against the king (Esth. 2:21; cf. Pers. *Bagadāna,* "gift of God"). Upon discovering their plot, Mordecai convinced his cousin Queen Esther to inform the king, who then ordered the men's execution (Esth. 6:2; cf. O. Pers. *Bagadāta,* "god given").

BIGVAI (Heb. *bigway*)

1. A leader of the postexilic community who returned from Exile with Zerubbabel (Ezra 2:2 = Neh. 7:7; cf. 1 Esdr. 5:8). This is possibly the same person who later sealed Ezra's covenant to keep the law (Neh. 10:16[MT 17]). In the Elephantine Papyri (30.1; 32.1) the name Bagohi (Aram. *bgwhy*) appears, referring to a governor of Judah (410-407 B.C.E.).

2. A large family group ("sons of Bigvai") who returned to Palestine with Zerubbabel after the Exile (Ezra 2:14, 2056 members; Neh. 7:19, 2067; 1 Esdr. 5:14, 2066). It is also the name of a smaller family group (70 members) who returned later with Ezra, led by Uthai and Zakkur (Ezra 8:14; cf. 1 Esdr. 8:40, Uthai son of Istalcurus).
MONICA L. W. BRADY

BILDAD (Heb. *bildaḏ*)
The Shuhite, one of Job's three friends whose intent is consolation (Job 2:11) but who becomes a miserable comforter (16:2). The name Bildad appears nowhere else in the OT, nor does Shuha appear as a place name, but it has been linked with Shuah, Abraham's son by Keturah, who lived in an eastern country (Gen. 25:2, 6; 1 Chr. 1:32). Scholars speculate Edomite connections.

In the first two dialogue cycles in the book of Job, the friends offer speeches of approximately equal length, to which Job responds in turn. Bildad is the second speaker in each cycle. In the first cycle Bildad's argument begins and ends with retributive justice (Job 8:1-7, 20-22). His tone is uncompromising, but hopeful: because God's justice is sure, if Job will make supplication to God and live uprightly, God will restore Job to his rightful place. Bildad appeals to the tradition of the ancestors (8:8-10) by quoting a parable of two plants and applying it to Job's circumstances (8:11-19). Bildad's condemning speech in the second cycle (ch. 18) focuses on the fate of the wicked, a common sapiential theme, moving from the wicked man's life-long experience of terror (vv. 7-15) to his death. The wicked sink into total obscurity, leaving no memory, name, or offspring (vv. 17-19). The third cycle departs from the preceding pattern: there is no speech from Zophar, and Bildad's speech is shortened (ch. 25). Scholars argue disruption of the third cycle; there are various suggestions for reconstruction of the text, but no textual evidence supports them. In his final speech, Bildad argues that no one can be righteous before God (25:4): if even the moon and stars are impure in God's sight, mortals must be also (vv. 4-5). Ultimately, Bildad's words are refuted by God (42:7).

Bibliography. D. J. A. Clines, *Job 1-20.* WBC 17 (Waco, 1989); N. C. Habel, *The Book of Job.* OTL (Philadelphia, 1985); J. G. Janzen, *Job.* Interpretation (Atlanta, 1985). PATRICIA A. MACNICOLL

BILEAM (Heb. *bil'ām*)
A city in the western portion of the half tribe of Manasseh, assigned as a levitical city of the Kohathite clan (1 Chr. 6:70[MT 55]). The name is most likely a variant form of Ibleam (Josh. 17:11; Judg. 1:27). TROY K. RAPPOLD

BILGAH (Heb. *bilgâ*)

1. The head of a priestly family, the fifteenth of the divisions in service at the time of David (1 Chr. 24:14).

2. The leader of a family of priests who returned from the Exile with Zerubbabel (Neh. 12:5, 18).

BILGAI (Heb. *bilgay*)
A priest among those who set their seals to the renewed covenant under Nehemiah (Neh. 10:8[MT 9]). He is probably the same as Bilgah **2.**

BILHAH (Heb. *bilhâ*) **(PERSON)**
A female servant of Rachel, who gave her to Jacob as a concubine (Gen. 30:3); mother of Dan and Naphtali (vv. 5-8; cf. 1 Chr. 7:13). After Rachel had given birth to Benjamin on her deathbed, Jacob's oldest son Reuben committed incest with Bilhah (Gen. 35:22; cf. 49:4).

BILHAH (Heb. *bilhâ*) **(PLACE)**
(also BAALAH, BALAH)
A town in southern Judah (1 Chr. 4:29), also called Balah (Josh. 19:3) and Baalah (15:29). The site has not been identified.

BILHAN (Heb. *bilhān*)

1. A son of the Horite Ezer and descendant of Seir (Gen. 36:27; 1 Chr. 1:42), ancestor of an Edomite clan.

2. A Benjaminite, the son of Jediael and father of seven sons (1 Chr. 7:10).

BILSHAN (Heb. *bilšān*)
A prominent Israelite who returned from the Exile with Zerubbabel (Ezra 2:2 = Neh. 7:7 = 1 Esdr. 5:8; LXX Gk. *Beelsarus*).

BIMHAL (Heb. *bimhāl*)
A son of Japhlet and descendant of Asher (1 Chr. 7:33).

BINDING AND LOOSING
Jesus entrusted the keys of the kingdom of heaven and the power of "binding and loosing" to Simon Peter after the apostle's declaration that Jesus was the Messiah (Matt. 16:16-19). Later, Jesus gave the disciples (the Twelve in Matthew) similar authority to regulate disciplinary matters in the Church (Matt. 18:18), and when he returns he will have the power to "open and shut" (Rev. 3:7).

Linking keys with the power to bind and loose establishes Peter, the proclaimer of Christ, as an authority without equal. Whereas former teachers had shut people out of the kingdom (Matt. 23:13), the apostolic preaching caused people to accept the gospel and enter the kingdom or refuse it and be excluded.

In the OT, keys also symbolized divinely ordained responsibility and authority (Isa. 22:15-25; Job 38:31). Terms such as "to forgive" and "to retain" sins in the risen Jesus' mandate to his disciples lead some to interpret "to bind and loose" as authority to forgive sins (cf. John 20:22-23).

Bibliography. G. Bornkamm, "The Authority to 'Bind' and 'Loose' in the Church in Matthew's Gospel," in *The Interpretation of Matthew,* ed. G. Stanton (Philadelphia, 1983), 101-14.

TERRENCE PRENDERGAST, S.J.

BINEA (Heb. *bin'ā'*)
A Benjaminite, the son of Moza and a descendant of Saul (1 Chr. 8:37; 9:43).

BINNUI (Heb. *binnûy*) (also BANI)

1. One of the sons of Pahath-moab who was compelled to divorce his foreign wife (Ezra 10:30).

2. The father of 13 sons who were forced to divorce their foreign wives (Ezra 10:38).

3. The head of a family whose descendants returned from exile with Zerubbabel (Neh. 7:15). He is called Bani (**4**) at Ezra 2:10.

4. A postexilic Levite and contemporary of Zerubbabel (Neh. 12:8), probably the son of Henadad who took part in the rebuilding of the walls of Jerusalem and set his seal to the renewed covenant under Nehemiah (3:24; 10:9[MT 10]). According to Ezra 8:33 he was the father of Noadiah the Levite. This person may have been the same as Bavvai (Neh. 3:18).

BIRDS
Palestine's unique geographic position as a land bridge connecting Europe, Africa, and Asia, along with the confluence of a number of environmental zones (ocean, lakes, streams, mountains, valleys, deserts) within a small geographic area, has resulted in an unusually rich assemblage of bird species. Not only do numerous species of birds make their home in Palestine — ca. 150 species are permanent residents who breed in the land — the land bridge serves as a major flyway for numerous migrating species, providing seasonal homes for these countless visitors. Indeed, in recent years at least 380 distinct species have been identified in Israel, while some 374 species of birds have been recorded for Jordan (not surprisingly, the species lists for the neighboring countries largely overlap).

The OT contains at least 60 distinctive Hebrew words in some 203 passages which refer to birds in either a generic or a specific sense. The NT contains 9 different Greek words for birds dispersed among 47 NT passages, although 8 of these words appear to refer to kinds of birds or bird terms already known from the Hebrew text, meaning that the NT adds only one additional type of bird not already known from the OT. Similarly, the Apocrypha contains 11 words for birds which are spread throughout some 43 passages but, again, only one of these words is not included in either the OT or NT. Thus, together, the OT, NT, and Apocrypha contain at least 62 terms relating to birds in a general or specific sense.

Identification

Unfortunately, precise correlation of these Hebrew, Aramaic, Greek, and Latin bird terms with modern scientific species is not always possible. Sometimes simply not enough information is provided to be precise about which species of bird is indicated. Also, a number of the Hebrew and Greek words are simply generic terms for birds, such as Heb. *'ôp* ("birds"), *gôzāl* ("young bird"), and *ṣippôr* ("small song birds"). Nevertheless, careful study of the meaning of the ancient aviary words themselves, along with the textual contexts and an understanding of the present bird population and their ecological niches, has provided ornithologists with a fairly good idea of which species are referred to in many if not most of these biblical texts.

In antiquity, of course, biblical writers did not classify birds according to our modern taxonomic system. They did, however, depict the different ways in which humans relate to birds, thus implicitly creating a number of broad categories. These categories included birds for food, birds for offerings, and birds of abomination — i.e., birds not suitable for the first two categories.

Birds of the Bible

Common Name	Hebrew/Greek	Principal References	Scientific Name
bee-eater	*šālāḵ*	Lev. 11:17; Deut. 14:17	*Merops apiaster*
bittern	*qippōḏ*	Isa. 14:23; 34:11; Zeph. 2:14	*Ixobrychus minutus; Botaurus stellaris*
bustard	*baṯ (hay)ya'ănnâ*	Lev. 11:16; Deut. 14:15; Job 30:29; Isa. 13:21; 34:13	*Otis tarda?*
buzzard (see vulture)			
chicken	*órnis, aléktōr*	Matt. 26:34, 74-75	*Gallus domesticus*
cock, hen	*śeḵwî, zarzîr*	Job 38:36; Prov. 30:31	*Gallus domesticus*
cormorant	*šālāḵ*	Lev. 11:17; Deut. 14:17	*Phalacrocorax carbo*
crane	*'āḡûr, sîs, sûs*	Isa. 38:14; Jer. 8:7	*Megalornis grus*
crow	*'ōrēḇ; kórax*	Gen. 8:7; Lev. 11:15; Deut. 14:14; Luke 12:24	*Corvus cornix*
dove	*yônâ, gôzāl*	see concordance	*Streptopelia sp.; Columba sp.*
eagle	*nešer?; aetós*	Exod. 19:4; Matt. 24:28; Luke 17:37; Rev. 4:7; 8:13; 12:14	*Aquila sp.*
falcon	*rā'â, dāyâ*	Deut. 14:13; Lev. 11:14	*Falco sp.*
goose	*barburîm*	1 Kgs. 4:23(5:2)	*Branta sp.*
griffon-vulture	*nešer*	Mic. 1:16	*Gyps fulvus*
hawk	*nēṣ*	Lev. 11:16; Deut. 14:15; Job 39:26	*Accipiter sp.*
hen	*órnis*	Matt. 23:37	*Gallus domesticus*
heron	*'ănāp̱ā*	Lev. 11:19; Deut. 14:18	*Ardea sp.*
hoopoe	*dûḵîp̱aṯ*	Lev. 11:19; Deut. 14:18	*Upupa epops*
ibis	*tinšemeṯ*	Lev. 11:18; Deut. 14:16	*Threskiornis aethiopica*
kite	*rā'â*	Deut. 14:13	*Milvus sp.*
osprey	*'ozniyâ*	Lev. 11:13; Deut. 14:12	*Pandion halietus*
ostrich	*rĕnānîm, baṯ hayya'ănâ*	Job 39:13	*Struthio camelus*
owl, barn	*yanšûp̱*	Lev. 11:17; Deut. 14:16; Isa. 34:11	*Tyto alba*
owl, eagle	*qippōz*	Isa. 34:15	*Bubo bubo*
owl, little	*kôs*	Lev. 11:17; Deut. 14:16; Ps. 102:6(7)	*Athene noctua*
owl, screech	*lîlîṯ*	Isa. 34:14	*Otus scops*
owl, short-eared	*taḥmās*	Lev. 11:16; Deut. 14:15	*Asio flammeus*
partridge	*qōrē'*	1 Sam. 26:20; Jer. 17:11	*Caccabis chukaar; Ammoperdix heyi*
pelican	*qā'aṯ*	Lev. 11:18; Deut. 14:17; Isa. 34:11; Zeph. 2:14	*Pelicanus onocrotalus*
quail	*śĕlāw*	Exod. 16:13; Num. 11:31-32; Ps. 105:40	*Coturnix coturnix*
raven (see crow)			
sparrow	*ṣippôr; strouthíon*	Matt. 10:29-31; Luke 12:6	*Passer domesticus; P. sp.*
stork	*ḥăsîḏâ*	Lev. 11:19; Deut. 14:18; Job 39:13; Ps. 104:17; Jer. 8:7	*Ciconia alba; C. nigra*
swallow	*dĕrôr*	Ps. 84:3[4]; Prov. 26:2	*Hirundo rustica*
swift	*sîs, sûs*	Jer. 8:7; Isa. 38:14	*Apus sp.; Cypselus apus*
tern (or gull)	*šaḥap*	Lev. 11:16; Deut. 14:15	*Sterna fluviatilis* or *Larus sp.*
turtledove	*tôr*	Lev. 5:7	*Streptopelia turtur*
vulture, bearded	*peres*	Lev. 11:13; Deut. 14:12	*Gypaetus barbatus*
vulture, Egyptian	*rāḥām, rāḥāmâ*	Lev. 11:18; Deut. 14:17	*Neophron percnopterus*

Domesticated Birds

A number of birds were domesticated and kept for both pets and food. They included the *yônâ* (dove/pigeon), *tôr* (turtledove), *barburîm* (geese and ducks), *qōrē'* (partridge), *śĕlāw* (quail), *dĕrôr* (swallow), and *sîs* (swift). Sometime ca. 1400 B.C.E. domestic chickens (probably Heb. *tuhoṯ* and/or *seḵwî*) were introduced to Palestine.

Some scholars have thought that the raising of doves became a major industry during the Hellenistic and later periods. The major evidence in support of this idea is the appearance of columbaria, installations consisting of dove-sized squarish niches usually cut into cave walls, throughout Palestine. *Columbarium* actually is Latin for dovecote (Lat. *columba*, "dove"; the scientific name for the dove family is *Columbidae*). Unfortunately, in the absence of any positive evidence, the actual purpose of the columbaria is still quite debatable. Other suggested uses of the niches included storage chambers for human ashes and beehives.

Birds for Offerings

An important category of birds was that used for sacrificial offerings. Birds could be used as substitute animals for special burnt offerings (Lev. 5:7-10) and various expiatory and purification offerings (Num. 6:10; Lev. 5:7, 11-12; 12:6-8; 14:10, 19-22, 30-31; 15:13-15, 29-30). The substitution of birds for animals was generally determined by social and economic status of the individuals making the offering (Lev. 5:7, 11; 12:8; 14:22, 30).

A number of Hebrew words are used for the birds that were considered suitable or were used for the sacrifices. These include *'ôp* (any bird), *tôr* (dove/pigeon), *bĕnî-yônâ* (turtledove), *gôzāl* (turtledove or any young bird), and *ṣippŏrîm* (any small bird). In the NT, *trygṓn* and *nossós*, referring to the turtledove or any young perching bird, are used.

Birds of Abomination

One of the striking features of the kinds of birds mentioned in the Bible is the large number of birds of prey, carrion birds, and scavengers. This is not really surprising in view of the fact that these birds make up a large portion of the indigenous and migratory bird population of Israel, Jordan, and Syria, due to various geographic, environmental, and ecological factors. Since these birds tend to "find their own food in gutter and dung heap, gulping down filth and rotting flesh and the foulest carrion and excrement" or rodents and other creatures that carry disease, humans have understandably tended to avoid using these birds for food. For this reason it is not surprising that at least 20 of these predatory or scavenger birds are included in the Pentateuch's two lists of unclean animals (Lev. 11:13-19; Deut. 14:11-18). The birds in these lists can be divided into five groups: (1) those with soaring wings; (2) birds with swooping wings; (3) flightless birds (ostrich); (4) silent-winged birds (owls); (5) and birds with white wings trimmed in black. The logic behind this grouping is that these flight characteristics are the most obvious ones that ancient ornithologists would have been able to observe without the aid of binoculars. Biblical birds of prey include the raven/crow, bearded vulture, and a variety of hawks, eagles, falcons, owls, and gulls.

RANDALL W. YOUNKER

BIRSHA (Heb. *birša'*)

The king of Gomorrah during the time of Abraham (Gen. 14:2), defeated after his rebellion against Chedorlaomer (vv. 8, 10).

BIRTH, NEW

See REGENERATION.

BIRTH PANGS

Birth pains are an inescapable fundament of human existence. Gen. 3:16 specifically mentions them as part of the curse on humankind, alongside death and the necessity of toil. Although there is an obvious connection between the horror of labor pain and the joy of a birth, the biblical texts often use the pain imagery by itself.

Birth pangs are an intense and perilous form of pain. Rachel's death while giving birth to Benjamin is described with realism in Gen. 35:16-18. The pain and peril are also clear in Jer. 4:31; 30:12-15, where the pain is a figure for God's judgment. Significantly in 1 En. 62:4-6 the mechanics of childbirth are mentioned, but the birth itself is not; no figurative child is to be born to the kings and governors who are under judgment; the intense pain is all they have. This is so even in some NT passages (e.g., 1 Thess. 5:3; cf. Mark 13:17 par.). We must not read birth into passages that do not contain it.

Birth pangs are a helpless pain. The prophets in particular describe the opponents of God as laboring women (e.g., Jer. 48:41; 49:22, 24; 50:41-43; Isa. 13:6-8; 26:17-18; 42:14; Ps. 48:4-6[MT 5-7]; cf. 1 QH 5). These are not hopeful passages, but images of pain, ineffectuality, and humiliation (cf. Jer. 6:24; 13:21; 22:23; 30:6). This may be the background of Rom. 8, featuring not only birth pains but frustration and the mixed metaphor of adoption. In Gal. 4:19 it is Paul who feels the birth pangs until Christ is "formed in you," an ironic expression of his helplessness.

Birth pangs can, however, be a productive pain. Some passages make explicit what others omit. In John 16:20-22 the pain is not denied but subsumed under the joy. There seems to be precedent for seeing an apocalyptic pattern of judgment and restoration in labor pains and childbirth (Isa. 66:6-9; Mic. 4:10; 5:3-4[2-3]; and explicitly in 1 QH 3; *b. Sanh.* 97-98; cf. Rev. 12:1-6).

Finally, birth pangs are a pain that must run their course: a period of time rather than a point. Thus in Mic. 4:9-10 with 5:3(2) this era before the figurative birth seems the focus rather than the predicted birth itself (so also rabbinic discussions of the "birth pains of the Messiah"; *b. Sanh.* 97-98; *Ketub.* 111a; *Šabb.* 118). In addition, there is a sense of inexorable process. Once begun, there is no escape; it must run to completion. The onset of birth pangs are not yet the end, but the beginning of the process that must surely lead to the end (4 Ezra 16:37-39; Mark 13 par.; cf. 4 Ezra 4:40-42; Acts 2:24).

Birth pangs are found through the whole sweep of the canon, from Genesis to Revelation. But by Revelation, the dominant image has been turned around. Once, the terrible appearance of Yahweh renders his enemies like women in labor. In Rev. 12, however, it is the Enemy who parades with ferocity while Salvation arrives through the humility of birth pangs and childbirth.

See MESSIANIC WOES.

Bibliography. D. C. Allison, Jr., *The End of the Ages Has Come* (Philadelphia, 1985); G. Bertram, "ōdín, ōdínō," *TDNT* 9:667-74; C. Gempf, "The Imagery of Birth Pangs in the New Testament," *TynBul* 45 (1994): 119-35.

CONRAD GEMPF

BIRTHRIGHT

The right of the firstborn son of the mother of the household to be its heir. This heir received twice the property as did the others (Deut. 21:17; MAL B:1).

Four generations made up a household (Heb. *bêṯ 'āḇ*): the father of the household and his brothers; his father and uncles; his sons; and his grandsons (Lev. 18:6-18). Households were patrilineal: members received social status from the father; only he designated heirs. Some designated "heirs" or "firstborn" (Heb. *ben*) by birthright, others by achievement. Using birthright reduced competition between the mothers and sons of the household. In the stories of Isaac and Rebekah (Gen. 27:1-45) and the Code of Hammurabi, however, achievement designates a more competent heir than the birthright male, which helped the Hebrews survive in an unstable world.

Bibliography. V. H. Matthews and D. C. Benjamin, *Social World of Ancient Israel, 1250-587 B.C.E.* (Peabody, 1993), 7-21, 110-20.

DON C. BENJAMIN

BIRZAITH (Heb. *birzāwiṯ*)

The son of Malchiel and grandson of Beriah, a descendant of Asher (1 Chr. 7:31). The name may designate a place, probably Khirbet Bir Zeit, 21 km. (13 mi.) N of Jerusalem.

BISHLAM (Heb. *bišlām*)

One of the Persian officials who sent a letter to King Artaxerxes I objecting to the building activities at Jerusalem (Ezra 4:7). Bishlam may be an Aramaic term meaning "son of peace" (cf. LXX *en eirḗnē*, "in peace"; but cf. 1 Esdr. 2:16).

BISHOP

A high office in early Church ministry and governance. It is not clear when the word (Gk. *epískopos*), as used in early Christian circles, passed from the generic meaning "overseer" or "guardian" to the specific meaning "bishop." The former meaning is likely in Acts 20:28, where Paul is said to have described the elders of the church at Ephesus (v. 17) as *epískopoi* of the flock, appointed by the Holy Spirit (cf. the association of elders, flock, and exercising guardianship [from the verb *episkopéō*] in 1 Pet. 5:1-2). The pastoral connection is also found in 1 Pet. 2:25, where Jesus is described as the Shepherd and *epískopos* of our souls. For a similar generic meaning of the related word *episkopḗ* ("position of overseer"), cf. Acts 1:20 (citing Ps. 109:8 LXX).

The meaning "bishop" seems probable in Phil. 1:1, where Paul addresses *epískopoi* along with deacons. By the time of the Pastoral Epistles, the tradition of aspiring to the office of bishop *(episkopḗ)* was well established and approved (1 Tim. 3:1). Congregations received counsel on the types of persons suited for the office (1 Tim. 3:2-7; Tit. 1:7-9). The characteristics included exemplary personal, domestic, and organizational traits. While it is clear that bishops at that time were distinct from deacons, their relationship to elders is more uncertain. Both 1 Timothy and Titus include material about elders that complements (1 Tim. 5:17-22) and overlaps (Tit. 1:5-6) their discussions of bishops. The latter may be a superior subset of the former or may be appointed by them (possibly suggested in 1 Tim. 4:14), or the two may be different titles for the same office. Certainly, by the time of Ignatius (early 2nd century) the two positions were distinct.

WARREN C. TRENCHARD

BITHIAH (Heb. *bityâ*)

A daughter of the Egyptian pharaoh, wife of the Judahite Mered (1 Chr. 4:17[MT 18]). Her name (Heb. "daughter of Yahweh") suggests that she was a follower of Yahwism.

BITHYNIA (Gk. *Bithynía*)

A mountainous region in northern Asia Minor, located on the Black (Euxine) Sea. The Hellenistic kingdom of Bithynia was bequeathed to Rome by King Nicomedes IV (74 B.C.E.) and, joined with the region to its east, became the Roman province of Bithynia-Pontus (ca. 63). Prusa, one of its major cities, was the home of the philosopher Dio Chrysostom, whose writings provide an important glimpse of 1st-century civic life in the province. A Jewish synagogue is attested at Nicomedia by the 2nd or 3rd century.

The Christian communities of Bithynia and Pontus are among those addressed in 1 Peter, and the correspondence between Pliny the Younger (the Roman governor) and emperor Trajan reveals that Christians were evident enough to warrant the negative reaction of local inhabitants (Pliny *Ep.* 10.96-97; ca. 110 C.E.). Paul and his companions were prevented from entering Bithynia by "the Spirit of Jesus" (Acts 16:7).

Bibliography. C. P. Jones, *The Roman World of Dio Chrysostom* (Princeton, 1978); D. Magie, *Roman Rule in Asia Minor* (1950, repr. New York, 1975).

PHILIP A. HARLAND

BITTER HERBS

So the Israelites might recall the bitterness of their slavery in Egypt, God prescribed that Israelites eat bitter herbs (Heb. *mĕrōrîm*) along with lamb and unleavened bread at the Passover (Exod. 12:8; Num. 9:11). Many bitter-tasting herbs grow in Lower Egypt, including dandelions, cumin, fenugreek, endive, watercress, and sorrel. The rabbis suggested five plants as suitable for eating as the *mĕrōrîm,* two of which can be positively identified as lettuce and chicory (*Pesaḥ.* 2:6). Radishes, lettuce, and horseradish may represent the bitter herbs at the modern Passover seder. MEGAN BISHOP MOORE

BITTER LAKES

Two connected lakes, the Great and Little Bitter Lakes, between the northernmost tip of the Gulf of Suez and the Mediterranean Sea. While enslaved in Egypt, the Israelites lived W of the Bitter Lakes in the land of Goshen. During the Exodus, the Israelites either entered the Sinai Peninsula S of the lakes or N of the lakes, traveling along the eastern shore toward Mt. Sinai. PETE F. WILBANKS

BITUMEN

A term used to describe all hydrocarbons that are soluble in carbon disulfide, including gases, easily mobile liquids, viscous liquids, and solids. In the natural environment bitumen is a dark-colored, comparatively hard, nonvolatile substance. Its nonmineral constituents are fusible and largely soluble in carbon disulfide. Originally the term was used for native mineral pitch, tar, asphalt, or slime, but now it is applied to any of the flammable viscid, liquid, or solid hydrocarbon mixtures, soluble in carbon disulfide. Pitch is a thick viscous substance obtained by boiling down tar, while slime is a cement made of bitumen or asphalt. Actual bitumen is not mentioned in the Bible. Slime was used as mortar to assure buoyancy for Moses' basket (Exod. 2:3; Heb. *ḥēmār*) and to build Babel (Gen. 11:3), and pitch was used for Noah's ark (Gen. 6:14) and for sealing roofs, conduits, and aqueducts.

RICHARD A. STEPHENSON

BIZIOTHIAH (Heb. *bizyôṯyâ*)

According to the MT, a town near Beer-sheba (Josh. 15:28). However, the text should read Heb. *bĕnôṯeyhā* ("her daughters," i.e., surrounding places; cf. LXX and Neh. 11:27).

BIZTHA (Heb. *bizzĕṯāʾ*)

One of the seven eunuchs who served as chamberlains for the Persian king Ahasuerus (Esth. 1:10).

BLASPHEMY

The act of cursing or slandering the name of God. It is not only an act committed against God (Exod. 22:28[MT 27]) but also an act of slandering, abusing, or reviling other people or groups (Rom. 3:8; 1 Cor. 4:13; 1 Pet. 4:4). Blasphemy also appears in Assyrian legal texts (cf. Dan. 3:29).

Generally, OT laws emphasize the personal responsibility of the individual who commits blasphemy, and thus it is the blasphemer, not his or her family, who incurs punishment for the sin (Lev. 24:10-16). Since one person's blasphemy can pollute the entire community, punishment administered by the community itself functions to "purge the evil from from [its] midst" (Deut. 17:7). Nehemiah, however, accuses all of Israel of committing "great provocations (blasphemies)" (Heb. *neʾāṣâ*) when they made and worshipped a molten calf during their wanderings in the wilderness (Neh. 9:18).

Jesus' opponents accuse him of blasphemy on several occasions (e.g., Matt. 9:3). At his trial, the Sanhedrin publicly accuse Jesus of "uttering blasphemy" and recommend the death sentence for him (Matt. 26:65-66 = Mark 14:64). Jewish authorities accuse many of Jesus' followers of blasphemy and put them to death by stoning (Acts 6:11; cf. John 10:31-39). Before his conversion Paul "blasphemed and persecuted and insulted Christ" (1 Tim. 1:13) and reviled Christians (Acts 26:11). After his conversion, Paul admonishes Christians to "put no obstacle in anyone's way" (2 Cor. 6:3), to avoid the sin of blasphemy.

In Matthew and Mark, Jesus teaches that blasphemy against the Holy Spirit is an eternal sin. Matt. 12:31-32 reports that while "people will be forgiven for every sin and blasphemy. . . whoever speaks against the Holy Spirit will not be forgiven, either in this age or in the age to come." Mark 3:29 cautions that "whoever blasphemes against the Holy Spirit. . . is guilty of an eternal sin."

HENRY L. CARRIGAN, JR.

BLASTUS (Gk. *Blástos*)

Chamberlain of King Herod Agrippa I (Acts 12:20). In their dispute with the king, the people of Tyre and Sidon "persuaded" (probably bribed) Blastus to use his influence as keeper of the royal bedchamber to secure them an audience with the king.

BLEMISH

A physical defect, prohibited on priests who serve at the altar and on animals offered on the altar (Lev. 21:17-21; 22:19-25). Blemished priests were allowed to provide other services in the sanctuary except that which involved sacrifices at the altar, and animals with limited defects could be offered as freewill offerings (Lev. 22:23). Neither the blemished priest nor the blemished animal was considered impure, since blemished priests were allowed to eat most of the offerings (Lev. 21:22) that only pure priests could eat, and blemished animals were not forbidden as food. "Without blemish" denotes the absence of general physical (Cant. 4:7; 2 Sam. 14:25) and moral (Job 11:15; 31:7) defect.

In the same way that OT sacrifices were required to be without physical blemish, so too was Christ without moral blemish as the sacrificial lamb of God (Heb. 9:14; 1 Pet. 1:19). Believers are to live their lives without moral blemish (Phil. 2:15), a characteristic they should have in the divine judgment (2 Pet. 3:14). In contrast, false teachers, by reason of their immoral behavior, are blemishes among the people of God (2 Pet. 2:13).

MICHAEL D. HILDENBRAND

BLESS, BLESSING

The Hebrew root *brk* bears a number of unrelated etymological meanings: the verbal and nominal forms of "bless"; the verbal and nominal forms of "kneel"; and a noun, "pool, pond, basin." Even within the semantic range "bless," *brk* can mean to bestow goodness or favor or to greet, congratulate, thank, make peace, worship, or praise. The qal passive participle *bārûḵ,* meaning "blessed," occurs most often in the formula "blessed be . . ." In seven occurrences, *bāraḵ* is used for "curse" (e.g., Ps. 10:3); because such curses are directed against God, most scholars attribute them to scribal emendation in spite of the lack of textual evidence.

Brk is most often a relational marker, signifying the existence of some sacral, legal, or social relationship. God, angels, and humanity may bless; God, humanity, animals, and inanimate objects can be blessed. Precisely what is conveyed by the act of blessing differs depending upon both its grantor and grantee. Foremost, however, blessing is a performative utterance, or speech act, that brings good upon someone or something in contrast to cursing, which is maleficent to its recipient.

God repeatedly blesses individuals (Job 42:12), groups (cf. Exod. 32:29), and nations (Jer. 4:2), particularly Israel (Deut. 26:15), in accordance with a divine-human covenantal relationship. This idea is emphasized in the Deuteronomistic history and the Prophets through God's conveying of blessings for covenantal obedience, as opposed to curses for covenantal breach (Deut. 27–28). Such blessings and curses would serve to enforce the provision of the law (Josh. 8:34). It is probable that the Hebrew writers modeled this covenant relationship on ancient Near Eastern suzerainty treaties. It should be noted that there is wide disagreement among scholars regarding the extent to which divine blessing has to do with salvation history rather than nature and creation as established in the primeval history. The benefactions of God are diverse and include vitality, health, longevity, fertility, land, prosperity, honor, victory, and power. God also blesses creatures (Gen. 1:22; Deut. 28:4) and inanimate objects, such as land (Deut. 26:15), dwellings (Prov. 3:33), crops (Deut. 7:13), bread and water (Exod. 23:25), work (Deut. 28:8), and the sabbath (Gen. 2:3), usually for the benefit of humanity.

Humans may also bless. While early 20th-century scholarship suggested that blessings in the ancient world held a power independent of God, the most recent scholarship concludes that God is the original source of all human blessings (Num. 6:22-27; 23:20). First, humans may bless others in their role as intermediaries for God, e.g., family heads (Gen. 9:1), leaders (Exod. 39:43), kings (2 Sam. 6:18 = 1 Chr. 16:2), prophets (Num. 23:11), priests (1 Sam. 2:20), or disciples (Acts 3:26). Such blessings may hold legal or sacral significance. A deathbed blessing from the family head serves as an irrevocable bequest of property (Gen. 27–28, 48–49). A blessing may also hold the legal status of a peace treaty when offered by a king or other in authority (2 Kgs. 18:31 = Isa. 36:16). Priests are especially important for their liturgical function (Num. 6:24-26).

Second, a human may seek to invoke divine blessing upon another, which might be offered by anyone in the more mundane affairs of life in greeting (Gen. 47:7), in parting (Gen. 24:60), between host and guest (1 Sam. 25:14), in friendship (2 Sam. 21:3), as congratulations (1 Chr. 18:10), in gratitude (Neh. 11:2), or in homage (2 Sam. 14:22). One might also bless oneself (Deut. 29:19[MT 18]). In all such cases, the blessing denotes the presence of a relationship between the giver and the receiver that is grounded in the divine-human relationship.

Third, humans sometimes bless things. This is another aspect of the invocation of God's favor upon humanity, which arises upon use of a blessed object. The consecration of articles of sacrifice is perhaps the most significant example of this category (1 Sam. 9:13).

Finally, humans and angels may bless God (Ps. 134:1-2; 103:20). Scholars disagree concerning the significance of this type of blessing: can it signify the bestowal of favor or goodness upon God? The answer depends not only upon one's view of ancient Israelite theology, but also upon one's anthropological view of the ancient Israelites regarding the magical power of the speech act itself. Later scholarship suggests that most likely *brk* here denotes only the acts of worship, praise, or thanksgiving (Ps. 115:17-18).

The English word "blessed" may additionally be used to translate Heb. *'ašrê* (or *'ōšer,* Gen. 30:13), which might also be rendered "happy." This word is most frequently found in the blessing formula found in Psalms and Proverbs: "blessed are those . . ." The NT equivalent is Gk. *makários,* found most notably in the Beatitudes (Matt. 5).

In the NT the blessings of Jesus take on considerable importance. Jesus blesses (Gk. *eulogéō*) the elements of the Lord's Supper (Matt. 26:26-28), and accordingly Paul calls the communion wine the cup of blessing (1 Cor. 10:16). Jesus also blesses the loaves of the feeding miracles (Matt.14:19), as well as the disciples themselves (Luke 24:50-51). The blessing on those who curse and revile the followers of the Lord is another significant theme (Luke 6:28). In Paul's writings "blessed" takes on additional meaning in that God is called blessed in the sense of being holy (Rom. 1:25).

Bibliography. C. W. Mitchell, *The Meaning of BRK "To Bless" in the Old Testament.* SBLDS 95 (Atlanta, 1987); R. Westbrook, "Undivided Inheritance," in *Property and the Family in Biblical Law.* JSOT Sup 113 (Sheffield, 1991), 188-41; C. Westermann, *Blessing in the Bible and the Life of the Church.* OBT (Philadelphia, 1978).

F. Rachel Magdalene

BLIGHT

An injury to standing crops and vegetation caused by the scorching heat of the dreaded east wind. Its relationship to mildew (e.g., 1 Kgs. 8:37 = 2 Chr. 6:28) could indicate a disease brought on by a fungus (*Ustilago carbo),* the spores of which were carried by the wind. At Deut. 28:22; Amos 4:9; Hag. 2:17 it comes as divine punishment.

BLINDNESS

One of the most frequently mentioned ailments in the Bible and the ancient Near East. Causes of blindness in ancient Israel included congenital defects (John 9:1), physical trauma (Judg. 16:21), and probably a wide variety of infections. Although modern societies and the Talmud recognize degrees of blindness, the usual Hebrew word for a blind person (*ʿiwwēr*) seems to refer to total blindness (e.g., Deut. 28:29). The corresponding Greek word used in the NT is *typhlós* (e.g., Mark 8:22).

Ancient Israel had ambivalent attitudes toward the blind. The OT records laws prohibiting obstacles that might injure the blind (Lev. 19:14; Deut. 27:18). But blindness was one of the curses that God could bring on the disobedient (Deut. 28:29), and some passages indicate that the blind were undesirable elements that were not allowed in the temple (2 Sam. 5:8). Lev. 21:18 prohibits the blind from serving as priests. It also was improper to offer blind animals for sacrifice (Mal. 1:8).

The community responsible for the texts at Qumran seems to expand the prohibitions against the blind. Thus, the Temple Scroll (11QT 45:12-13) prohibits the entrance of blind persons into Jerusalem for their entire life because blindness was seen as a form of impurity which could defile the sacred city.

The policies in Leviticus and Qumran texts, if actually implemented, would have created a group of second-class citizens with little access to important religious and social institutions. Although the healing of the blind was to be a sign of the coming of the Messiah (Isa. 29:18; 35:5; Matt. 11:2-6), the efforts of Jesus and other disciples to heal and minister to the blind (Matt. 9:27-31; 12:22) also may be seen as a critique of health care practices reflected in Leviticus and Qumran.

Scholars also note the literary uses of blindness and blind persons in many biblical stories. For example, Ahijah retains his perceptive prophetic powers even though he is physically blind (1 Kgs. 14:4-5). The message seems to be that God's spoken message is so clear that it need not depend on vision (cf. 1 Sam. 9:9, which notes that prophets were formerly called "seers"). Throughout the Bible, blindness also is often used as a symbol of unbelief (Isa. 43:8), ignorance (Isa. 42:16; 56:10), and other moral inadequacies (2 Pet. 1:9). HECTOR AVALOS

BLOOD

Blood is significant both as a biblical term and as a theological concept. Both Heb. *dām* and Gk. *haíma* are used in a theological sense to designate the life principle in humankind and animals. From the earliest of times blood has been associated with mystery because it was recognized as a symbol of life long before scientifically proved to be vital to the existence of life. The phrase "flesh and blood" refers to the perishable nature of humans, and it is always connected with a loss of life or a sacrifice for life (clearly stated in Lev. 17:11).

In the OT blood is regarded as sacred, expressing three major concerns about the use of blood. The focus is on the prohibition of murder. The first actual reference to blood is in Gen. 4:10, where God confronts Cain for shedding Abel's blood in murder. While customary law allowed blood vengeance (Gen. 9:6), provision is made for avoiding unlimited blood feuds (Deut. 19:6-13). The faithful appeal to God to avenge the blood of his servants (Ps. 79:10), and God promises that he himself would bring about that vengeance on shed blood (Isa. 63:1-6).

A second concern is the dietary prohibition of blood. As early as Gen. 9:4, Noah is instructed, "Only, you shall not eat flesh with its life, that is, its blood."

Third, the OT is concerned with the use of blood in the expression of worship. The covenant between Yahweh and his people was sealed by a blood rite (Exod. 24:3-8). In all animal sacrifices blood was the essential element, poured on the altar (Lev. 1:5). With the Passover observance, the blood was placed on the lintel and the doorposts (Exod. 12:7). On the Day of Atonement, the high priest entered the holy of holies and sprinkled blood on the mercy seat (Lev. 16:15). Sacrificial blood also had a consecratory value in the consecration of priests (Exod. 29:20). The rite of circumcision was also a form of blood ceremony (Gen. 17:10-11).

The NT puts an end to the bloody sacrifices of OT worship, and it abrogates the legal dispositions relating to blood vengeance. Both of these changes are brought about by the "precious blood" of Christ (Heb. 9:11-12; 1 Pet. 1:17-19). Everything in the drama of Jesus' passion focuses on blood. At the Last Supper, Jesus presents the cup by saying, "This is my blood of the covenant" (Matt. 26:28). Judas betrays "innocent blood" (Matt. 27:4). Pilate washes his hands "of this man's blood" (Matt. 27:24). By Christ's shed blood, believers are justified (Rom. 5:9) and sanctified (Heb. 10:29; 13:12).

DONALD R. POTTS

BLOOD, FIELD OF

See AKELDAMA.

BLOOD, FLOW OF

Bleeding from a woman's reproductive organs, usually from menstruation, menorrhagia, or some form of uterine hemorrhage. Like other bodily discharges, a woman's bleeding caused ritual uncleanness. Menstruation made a woman unclean for seven days (Lev. 15:19-24). During that time her impurity is transmitted to anyone or anything she touches, and thus sexual intercourse with a menstruant was prohibited (Lev. 18:19; 20:18; cf. Ezek. 22:10b). A woman suffering from irregular or prolonged bleeding was considered unclean until seven days after the bleeding ceased (Lev. 15:25-30; cf. Num. 5:21).

Jesus' healing of a woman whose bleeding had

lasted 12 years (Mark 5:25-34; Luke 8:43-48; Matt. 9:20-22) is to be understood in light of the above. When she touched Jesus' garment, he should have become unclean or she should have been destroyed (cf. Lev. 15:31; 2 Sam. 6:6-7). Instead, the power of his holiness cleansed her. FRANK D. WULF

BLOODGUILT
Guilt incurred from the unjustified killing of an animal or human. Specific infractions include failing to bring a slaughtered animal to the tabernacle for sacrifice (Lev. 17:4) and the "deliberate murder" of a thief who breaks in after sunrise (Exod. 22:3; in contrast to v. 2[MT 1], the "accidental homicide" whereby the owner of the house slays a thief breaking in at night). Other crimes incurring bloodguilt might include negligence leading to accidental death (Deut. 22:8; Ezek. 33:6-9) and blood vengeance carried out within a city of refuge (Deut. 19:10). Such infractions could be expiated only with the blood of the one accountable, and the guilty party bears full responsibility for the blood shed in carrying out his or her execution (Josh. 2:19; 2 Sam. 1:16; 1 Kgs. 2:37; Ezek. 18:13). David avoids bloodguilt by not taking vengeance on Nabal and thus usurping divine authority (1 Sam. 25:26, 33).

BOANERGES (Gk. *Boanērgés*)
A surname (from Aramaic, possibly Heb. *bĕnê regeš*, "sons of unrest," or *bĕnê rēḡez*, "sons of thunder") given by Jesus to James and John, the sons of Zebedee (Mark 3:17). The name would appropriately reflect their rather forceful behavior at a later stage of Jesus' ministry (Mark 10:35-39; cf. Luke 9:54).

BOAZ (Heb. *bōʿaz*)
1. A wealthy relative of the family of Elimelech and Naomi, owner of fields near Bethlehem. Boaz is portrayed as the protector of Naomi's foreign daughter-in-law Ruth, by ordering the workers of his fields not to harass her and to leave extra grain for her (Ruth 2:15-16); by instructing her in the preservation of her reputation (3:14); by publicly persuading Naomi's next-of-kin to relinquish his right to purchase land belonging to Elimelech (4:7-10); and by acquiring Ruth as his wife and fathering Oded, the grandfather of David (vv. 17, 22).

Bibliography. D. N. Fewell and D. M. Gunn, *Compromising Redemption: Relating Characters in the Book of Ruth* (Louisville, 1990); J. M. Sasson, *Ruth*, 2nd ed. (Sheffield, 1989).

2. The name of a pillar set in front of Solomon's temple (1 Kgs. 7:21; 2 Chr. 3:17). The meaning of this naming and its function is disputed.
ALICE H. HUDIBURG

BOCHERU (Heb. *bōḵĕrû*)
A Benjaminite, one of Azel's sons and a descendant of Jonathan and Saul (1 Chr. 8:38; 9:44).

BOCHIM (Heb. *bōḵîm*)
A place ("Weepers") W of the Jordan River where the Israelites wept for their disobedience in breaking their covenant with the Lord (Judg. 2:4-5). The site is unknown but was probably near Gilgal, in the hill country west of Jericho. Bochim has been associated with Bethel, where an early tradition (Gen. 35:8) names a burial place Allon-bacuth ("Oak of Weeping"; cf. Judg. 20:23, 26; 21:2).
LAURA B. MAZOW

BODY
Semitic thought made no clear distinction between the physical and spiritual or psychological aspects of human existence, hence the OT contains no word which connotes "body" in the modern understanding of the term. Heb. *bāśār*, "flesh," which designates basically the whole exterior being of a person (e.g., Lev. 13:3; Ps. 109:24) as distinguished from specific parts (skin, bones, blood; cf. Lam. 3:4; Ezek. 37:6, 8), refers generally to the whole living creature and can be used interchangeably with *nep̄eš*, "soul." In the OT the term refers collectively to people (Isa. 40:5), both living (Exod. 30:32) and dead (Ps. 79:2), and to all living creatures, including animals (Gen. 6:19). It can also designate flesh for food — animal flesh as food for people (Num. 11:4) and human flesh as food for animals (1 Sam. 17:44).

The NT distinguishes more clearly between "body" (Gk. *sṓma*) and "flesh" (*sárx*). Although both can refer to the external aspect, *sṓma* carries a more wholistic connotation (cf. Matt. 5:29). It refers to living humans (Matt. 6:22), dead humans (Mark 15:43), resurrected humans (Rom. 8:11), and beasts (Heb. 13:11), as well as celestial bodies (1 Cor. 15:40). Greater distinction is made between the physical nature of humans and the spiritual or soul (Matt. 10:28; 1 Thess. 5:23; cf. 2 Cor. 12:2-3). As the organ of generation, the body should not be used for sexual immorality (1 Cor. 6:13, 16) because in sex it belongs to another (7:4).

"Body" has special meaning with reference to Christ. His crucified body is God's way of reconciling sinful mankind with himself (Col. 1:22). As a result of this salvation, Christians become the body of Christ in the community of faith (1 Cor. 12:27). As the body of Christ, each member of this community needs the others and all belong together (Rom. 12:5). Through observance of the Lord's Supper, the Christian community celebrates "a sharing in the body of Christ" (1 Cor. 10:16). Likewise, the body of Christ is built up into a Church through its "work of ministry" (Eph. 4:12). Christ is not only the Savior of the body of believers, but also the head of the Church which is his body (Eph. 5:23).

Bibliography. N. P. Bratsiotis, "bāśār," *TDOT* 2:317-32. DONALD R. POTTS

BODY OF CHRIST
Metaphor for the community of Christians. The "body of Christ" derives from the words of Jesus at the Last Supper when he offered the bread to be shared as "my body which is for you" (1 Cor. 11:24; Luke 22:19). Here "body" (Gk. *sṓma*) refers to the ongoing personal presence of Christ within the community. In the sharing of the Lord's Supper, the

gathered community celebrates the presence of the risen Christ in their midst "until he comes" (1 Cor. 11:26). No other term or metaphor can convey as adequately as *sṓma* the corporate reality that Paul defines as "the body of Christ."

Paul uses *sṓma* to refer to both the individuality — it is as "body" that we will be resurrected and transformed at the end of time to be like Christ's "glorious body" (Phil. 3:21) — and the corporateness of human existence, but it is union with God "in Christ" that marks the corporateness of Christian existence. Just as the Hebrew Scriptures had spoken of Israel as a "corporate personality," so too, for Paul, the "body" retains this essentially corporate character. Paul uses the metaphor to counteract the divisive effects of the factionalism present at Corinth but expands its meaning in extraordinary ways (1 Cor. 12:12-31), affirming his conviction about the "body" of the risen Christ and identifying this body with the Christian community (v. 27) made up of "many members" (v. 12). Baptism marks the believer's entrance into this body, and sharing in a common spirit is its distinctive character. To share the "Lord's supper" (1 Cor. 11:17-34) without "discerning the body" is to disregard the presence of the Lord in the community and therefore to bring judgment upon oneself. "Discerning the body" is nothing other than recognizing in the community the body of Christ. Authentic existence for a Christian, therefore, is lived only as a member of the one body, who is Christ (Rom. 12:5).

The analogy of the human body as image for the social body was ubiquitous in antiquity (in classical texts, cf. M. Aurelius *Med.* 7.13; Livy *Urb. cond.* 2.32).

Barbara E. Bowe

BOHAN (Heb. *bōhan*)
A son or descendant of Reuben, after whom a monument (perhaps a rock; cf. Heb. *bōhen,* "thumb") was named. This stone served as a boundary marker between the tribes of Judah and Benjamin (Josh. 15:6; 18:17).

BOOK
The earliest form of the book in biblical times was the scroll (Heb. *mĕgillâ*), a document made either from papyrus or leather. The use of papyrus scrolls can be traced to ca. 3200 B.C. in Egypt, and the Israelites likely imported such scrolls for their own writing. After the Exile and by the time of the Dead Sea Scrolls, leather was the favored material for scrolls.

Recent evidence offers glimpses into the production of leather scrolls in the Qumran community. The scribes in the community used scrolls of skin and specially made inks to produce their texts. For these scribes, the materials themselves, the inks and the leather of the scrolls, contained so much power that they ensured the sanctity of the texts themselves. Scribes were required by community rules to use leather for biblical scrolls, but nonbiblical writings have been found on papyrus scrolls. In addition, papyrus scrolls of biblical writings were forbidden by the rabbis: "If it was written with caustic, red dye, or copperas, or on paper (papyrus), of diftera, he had not fulfilled his obligation, but only if it was written in Assyrian writing, on parchment, and with ink."

One of the great advances of Christianity is the production of the codex book. By the 2nd century A.D., parchment leaves were folded and sewn together, and often bound within a cover, to give the appearance of today's book. While the earliest codices may have been produced by using single-leaf papyrus sheets, later codices were actually multilayered sheets of parchment sewn to one another. The earliest known single-leaf papyrus codices were produced in Egypt but were not discovered until the 20th century at Nag Hammadi. The earliest known multi-layered parchment codices — Codex Sinaiticus, Codex Alexandrinus, and Codex Vaticanus — provide the major textual foundations for the NT writings. By the time of Constantine, the book was the standard form of writing.

In the OT and NT the term "book" (Heb. *sēper;* Gk. *biblíon*) sometimes refers to a genealogy (Gen. 5:1; Matt. 1:1), royal chronicles (Esth. 6:1), or a law book (Deut. 28:61; Josh. 1:8). Throughout the OT, various "books" are reported to provide the basis of certain biblical accounts. These include the Book of the War of the Lord (Num. 21:14), the Book of Jashar (Josh. 10:13; 2 Sam. 1:18), the Book of the Acts of Solomon (1 Kgs. 11:41), the Book of the Chronicles of the Kings of Israel (14:19; 15:31; 2 Kgs. 10:34), the Book of the Chronicles of the Kings of Judah (1 Kgs. 14:29; 15:7; 2 Kgs. 8:23), the Book of the Kings of Israel (1 Chr. 9:1; 2 Chr. 20:34), the Book of the Kings of Israel and Judah (27:7; 35:27), the Book of the Kings of Judah and Israel (16:11; 25:26), and the Book of Chronicles (Neh. 12:23). The Bible also mentions various divinely authored books: the book of remembrance (Mal. 3:16), the book of truth (Dan. 10:21), and the book of life (Phil. 4:3; Rev. 3:5; 13:8; 20:12, 15). In the NT the phrase "the books" (Gk. *tá biblía*) refers not to the entire Bible but to the books of the OT.

Bibliography. H. Y. Gamble, *Books and Readers in the Early Church* (New Haven, 1995); J. L. Sharpe III and K. Van Kampen, eds., *The Bible as Book: The Manuscript Tradition* (London, 1998).

Henry L. Carrigan, Jr.

BOOK OF LIFE
The mundane task of bookkeeping in the ancient Near East often found a parallel in the divine realm. The idea of divine scribal activity appears several times throughout both the OT and NT and is frequently mentioned in pseudepigraphal writings (cf. Exod. 32:32-33; Ps. 139:16; Isa. 65:6; Mal. 3:16; Jub. 30:19-23; 1 En. 47:3; Rev. 13:8). The Book of Life appears to be a heavenly book in which the names of the righteous are inscribed. The psalmist prays that his adversaries be blotted out of the book of life and that they not be written with the names of the righteous (Ps. 69:28[MT 29]; cf. Rev. 3:5; 21:27).

In addition to the Book of Life, other books appear in the literature. A book of destruction corresponds to the book of life (cf. 1 En. 81:1-4; Jub.

30:22; T. Levi 5:4), and other books record the deeds or events of life. These seem to be the basis for the last judgment, where "the court sat in judgment and the books were opened" (Dan. 7:10) and "the dead were judged according to their works, as recorded in the books" (Rev. 20:12). Similar usages are found also in the pseudepigraphal and apocryphal writings (cf. 2 Esdr. 6:20; 2 Apoc. Bar. 24:1; Asc. Isa. 9:22; 1 Clem. 45:8). W. DENNIS TUCKER, JR.

BOOK OF THE TWELVE

An ancient designation for the OT Minor Prophets that refers to the scribal practice of preserving these 12 prophetic writings on a single scroll. In antiquity, these individual writings were preserved, referenced, reckoned, and received into the canon as a single book.

Ancient Evidence

Evidence for the bibliographic unity of the Minor Prophets includes ancient manuscripts, literary references, and lists of canonical books. The oldest reference to the Book of the Twelve is from the early 2nd century B.C.E. in the Wisdom of Jesus ben Sira. Following references to the prophets Isaiah, Jeremiah, and Ezekiel, Sir. 49:10 speaks of "the Twelve Prophets" as a collective group. The literary evidence from Sirach is supported by manuscript evidence from Qumran. Fragments of seven different scrolls of the Twelve have been discovered. The oldest manuscript, 4QXII[a], has been dated to the middle of the 2nd century and contains parts of the books of Zechariah, Malachi, and Jonah. Partial remains of a scroll of the Twelve in Greek have also been discovered near Qumran and are dated to the middle of the 1st century B.C.E. Ancient manuscripts of the Greek translation of the Twelve contain superscriptions that number the prophetic books from 1 to 12. In the NT the Book of the Twelve is cited in the book of Acts as "the book of the prophets" (Acts 7:42). All of the ancient listings of the Jewish/OT canon and all of the medieval Hebrew manuscripts of the Minor Prophets treat these writings as a single book.

History of the Collection

A lengthy chronological gap separates the earliest, 8th-century materials within the Twelve from the time of the latest of those writings, composed ca. 450 or perhaps even later. Another lengthy span separates the writing of the latest books within the collection from the oldest explicit reference to the Book of the Twelve, ca. 200 B.C.E. Therefore, descriptions of the formation of the book can only claim greater or lesser degrees of likelihood. Nevertheless, some conclusions about its development have a relatively high degree of probability.

For example, there is some evidence of earlier collections prior to the final 12-book collection. The superscriptions of the books of Hosea, Amos, and Micah (Hos. 1:1, Amos 1:1, Mic. 1:1) suggest an ancient compilation of these three books, the purpose of which was to apply the lessons of the Assyrian destruction of Samaria, threatened in Hosea and Amos, to the political situation of Judah and Jerusalem as described by Micah. The sequence of this presumed early collection is preserved in the manuscripts of the LXX Book of the Twelve. The germ of the final collection of the Twelve is likely to be found in this early compilation. The latest book to be added to the Book of the Twelve was probably Jonah, which is formally at great variance with the rest of the collection. The oldest manuscript of the Twelve, 4QXII[a], places Jonah after Malachi at the end of the collection. Jonah also has differing positions in the Greek and Hebrew arrangements of the Twelve.

Literary Unity

The ancient and consistent practice of preserving the Minor Prophets as a single book has raised the question of whether the individual writings within this scroll possess any degree of literary unity. The possibility of unity seems quite unlikely at first glance, given the great chronological and thematic diversity of the individual books. Nevertheless, various unifying features have been identified within the collection.

The reference to the Twelve in Sir. 49:10 states that as a group the 12 prophets "comforted the people . . . with confident hope," which is perhaps a reference to the fact that many of the individual books within the Twelve conclude with a hopeful prediction of restoration and salvation. Another unifying element, beyond the theme of future restoration, is the implied historical narrative that underlies the collection. Israel and Judah's experiences at the hands of Assyria provide historical background for the books of Hosea, Amos, and Micah. The fall of Assyria and the rise of Babylon provide background for Nahum, Habakkuk, and Zephaniah. The restoration of Judah under the Persian Empire informs the books of Haggai, Zechariah, and Malachi and partially accounts for the numerous similarities between these three books.

Some of the books among the Twelve appear to be united by verbal cross references at the beginning and ending sections of each book. For example, the references to Edom in Amos 9:12; Obad. 1 help to explain their otherwise inexplicable sequence in Hebrew manuscripts of the Twelve. Likewise, the books of Joel and Amos share highly repetitive language in the opening and closing sections of each book (cf. Joel 3:16 [MT 4:16] and Amos 1:2; also Joel 3:18 [4:18] and Amos 9:14). Similarities such as these, which span the boundaries of individual books, have sparked attempts to identify certain passages throughout the book as the work of editorial hands who unified the collection by inserting similar material at various places. Although such unifying editorial additions are possible, there is no concrete evidence of previous forms of the book by which to judge the proposals of editorial additions.

A primary unifying feature of the Book of the Twelve was the theological belief of ancient religious communities that the words of the various prophets were ultimately the unified word of Israel's God. This belief underlay the preservation and common transmission of the Minor Prophets and is the same theological presupposition that allowed ancient Israelite, Jewish, and Christian communities to treat the formally and chronologically diverse words of Israel's Scriptures as a unified, canonical tradition.

Bibliography. B. A. Jones, *The Formation of the Book of the Twelve.* SBLDS 149 (Atlanta, 1995); J. D. Nogalski, *Literary Precursors to the Book of the Twelve.* BZAW 217 (Berlin, 1993); *Redactional Processes in the Book of the Twelve.* BZAW 218 (Berlin, 1993). BARRY A. JONES

BOOTHS, FEAST OF

See TABERNACLES, FEAST OF.

BORASHAN (Heb. *bôr-ʿāšān*)

A place ("cistern" or "well of Ashan") in the south of Judah to which David sent part of the spoils of his victory over the Amalekites (1 Sam. 30:30). It is perhaps the same as Ashan.

BOSOM

The word "bosom" is used in reference to both God and humankind, male and female. The bosom in its metaphorical and literal usages is the location of both intimacy and vulnerability.

In the OT and NT the bosom is foremost an intimate place. It is a source of nurture for a suckling child (Ruth 4:16), of comfort (Luke 16:22, Abraham's bosom), protection (Isa. 40:11, the bosom of God like that of a shepherd, carrying the lambs of Zion), honor (49:22), and physical warmth (1 Kgs. 1:2, Abishag in the bosom of David). It is where the grieving widow of Zarephath holds her dead son (1 Kgs. 17:19) as God holds a living One: Jesus in the bosom of God the Father (John 1:18).

The bosom is also a sign of intimate relationship. Thus "the wife of your bosom" or "the husband of your bosom" (Deut. 28:54, 56) or a ewe lamb in the poor man's bosom (2 Sam. 12:3) or a bosom friend (Ps. 41:9[MT 10]) implies the most intense connections and communion.

The bosom is a repository of emotions: grief (Ps. 35:13), taunts (79:12), insults (89:50[51]), passion (Prov. 6:27), bribery (21:14), anger (Eccl. 7:9), hidden iniquity (Job 31:33), and retaliation (Ps. 74:11). It is also a treasury of wisdom (Job 23:12). Finally, the bosom is a locus of sexual arousal and passion (Ezek. 23:3, 8, 21).

JEANNE STEVENSON-MOESSNER

BOSOR (Gk. *Bosór*) **(PERSON)**

According to 2 Pet. 2:15, the father of Balaam. Elsewhere he is called Beor (**2**).

BOSOR (Gk. *Bosór*) **(PLACE)**

A city in Gilead captured by Judas Maccabeus (1 Macc. 5:25, 36). It has been identified with Buṣr el-Ḥarîri, on the southern edge of el-Lejā.

BOUNDARY (Heb. *gĕḇûl*)

In the Deuteronomistic perspective, boundary making is associated with the sacral apportionment of the land of Israel (cf. Joshua, where Heb. *gĕḇûl*, "boundary," "territory," is used primarily of land allotment and tenure). Land division was predicated on lineage categories, proceeding from distribution among the tribes, to distribution among kin-groups, and then to distribution among extended families. The resulting assignments of land were to be permanent inheritances. Accordingly, one must not move a neighbor's boundary marker (Deut. 19:14; 27:17; Prov. 22:28; 23:10). Prophets decried a blatant disregard of such laws, as Israel's emerging state systems outpaced and eroded its older lineage-based understandings of land boundaries (e.g., 1 Kgs. 21:17-19; Mic. 2:1-5; cf. Hos. 5:10).

In priestly traditions, boundary making is further associated with demarcating the holiness of cultic areas. These traditions stress the temple mount as sacred space (Ezek. 43:12). Early texts such as Exod. 19:12, 23 establish this principle, but it is reemphasized in Ezekiel's ideal arrangements for the temple. In Ezekiel new tribal borders and definite gradations of holiness surround and protect the temple.

The function of boundaries in establishing sacred space is related to their role in biblical cosmogony. The demarcation of a cultic center and the organization of the rest of life around it archetypically symbolize the structure of the created universe. Thus the temple on Mt. Zion forms the nexus of the cosmos — the organizing center that emerged when God first differentiated the elements of the world (e.g., Ps. 74:12-17; 104:5-9; Jer. 5:22). This primeval boundary making is extended to include God's demarcation of the nations (Deut. 32:8; Acts 17:26). STEPHEN L. COOK

BOW AND ARROW

Archaeological finds have provided a relatively accurate description of the development of the bow (Heb. *qešeṯ*). The earliest bows were made from one piece of wood, which could be up to 1.7 m. (5.5 ft.) long, and strung with animal sinew. Later bows were shorter and made from bonded strips of wood and animal horn.

Rock carvings of the upper Paleolithic period attest to the bow's use in prehistoric times as a device for hunting and defense. It was one of the earliest weapons of war. With the introduction of the composite bow in Akkad in the 23rd century B.C., the bow became the preeminent long-range weapon. This development increased the effective range from 10 m. (100 yds.) to 40 m. (400 yds.) It was directly responsible for the organization of the first archery units and the development of the coat of mail. With the introduction of mail, the bow could be deployed among cavalry (cf. 2 Kgs. 9:24).

Local enemies of Israel also employed the bow. It was the Philistine archers who seem to have turned the tide of the battle in which King Saul was killed (1 Sam. 31:3). Likewise a Syrian archer was responsible for the death of King Ahab (1 Kgs. 22:35). Within Israel use of the bow developed along similar lines. The number of archers present in the Lachish relief, the number of arrowheads uncovered, and the frequency of attestation in the OT all suggest that use of the bow was widespread in Israel. Units of archers were found among Israelite troops (1 Chr. 5:18; 8:40; Ps. 78:9; cf. Gen. 49:24).

Because the bow was a common sight in ancient Israel, the term is frequently used figuratively — to mean battle-ready (Ps. 7:12[MT 13]; 11:2; Jer. 46:9; 50:14, 29; 51:3; "to bend the bow" refers not to the act of shooting, but to stringing the bow in preparation for battle), to refer to invincible forces (Isa. 21:15), the judgment of God (Ps. 7:13[14]; Hos. 1:5; Jer. 49:35), divinely imposed peace (Ps. 46:9[10]; 76:3[4]; Hos. 2:18[20]; Ezek. 39:9), wickedness (Ps. 78:57; Hos. 7:16), defeat (1 Sam. 2:4), and victory (2 Kgs. 13:15-17).

Heb. *ḥēṣ* ("arrow") is derived from the root "to divide." Egyptian artifacts show that the shaft of the arrow was normally 76 cm. (30 in.) in length and was made of a hollow reed with three sets of feathers on one end. As further confirmation, the Nuzi tablets use the same word for both "reed" and "arrow shaft." The blade was made of stone, copper, bronze, or iron, the composition changing with each technological advance. Impetus for these changes was provided by the ever-increasing effectiveness of body armor. The Bible (Gen. 27:3; Isa. 22:6; Jer. 5:16; Lam. 3:13) and archaeology indicate that arrows were stored in leather quivers. The Nuzi and Amarna tablets and Assyrian reliefs indicate that quivers could hold 20 to 50 arrows.

The arrow was such an effective weapon of destruction that it became a popular metaphor. The arrow could refer to God's judgment (Deut. 32:23, 42; Ps. 7:13[14]; 45:5[6]; 64:7[8]; Ezek. 5:16; 39:3), severe afflictions (Job 6:4; Ps. 38:2[3]), injurious speech (Ps. 64:3-4[4-5]; Jer. 9:8; Prov. 25:18), numerical strength (Ps. 127:4-5), lightning (18:14[15] [= 2 Sam. 22:15]; 77:17-18[18-19]; 144:6; Hab. 3:11), divinely imposed peace (Ps. 76:3[4]), sudden danger (91:5), and possibly Satan's trials and temptations (Eph. 6:16).

Bibliography. R. Gonen, *Weapons of the Ancient World* (Minneapolis, 1976); T. R. Hobbs, *A Time for War.* OTS 3 (Wilmington, 1989); Y. Yadin, *The Art of Warfare in Biblical Lands,* 2 vols. (Jerusalem, 1963).

W. E. NUNNALLY

BOZEZ (Heb. *bôṣēṣ*)

One of two rocky crags flanking the mountain pass near Michmash (1 Sam. 14:4), on the north side of the Wadi eṣ-Ṣuweinît ca. 11 km. (7 mi.) NNE of Jerusalem. The other crag, to the south of the gorge opposite Geba, was called Seneh.

BOZKATH (Heb. *boṣqaṯ*)

A town in the Shephelah of Judah, part of that tribe's inheritance and the home of Josiah's mother Jedidah (2 Kgs. 22:1). Although F.-M. Abel linked Bozkath with ed-Dawa'ime, 15 km. (9 mi.) SE of Lachish, his identification is not widely accepted. Bozkath was included within the same district as Lachish and Eglon (Josh. 15:39).

JENNIFER L. GROVES

BOZRAH (Heb. *boṣrâ;* Gk. *Bosorra*)

1. The capital of Edom, modern Buseirah (208018) W of the King's Highway in Jordan. Situated close to both valuable copper mines and the border with Judah, Bozrah's position was one of great strategic significance. Presumably owing to prior confrontations, various OT prophets predicted Bozrah's doom at the hands of God's vengeance (Isa. 34:6; 63:1; Jer. 49:13; Amos 1:12). Excavations at Buseirah have uncovered occupation strata dating approximately no earlier than the 8th century B.C.E. The upper city has yielded large public buildings, monumental architecture, impressive casemate defenses, and a possible temple complex. The bearing of the chronological findings on the Edomite king lists (Gen. 36:31; 1 Chr. 1:44) remains a matter of dispute among scholars.

Bibliography. C.-M. Bennett, "Excavations at Buseirah, Southern Jordan, 1971," *Levant* 5 (1973): 1-11.

2. A city listed among Moabite settlements in a polemic prophesying doom and destruction (Jer. 48:24). Bozrah may refer to *bṣr* in the Moabite Stone or Bezer, the city of refuge (Deut. 4:43; Josh. 20:8; 21:36). Despite many possible locations, a compelling archaeological identification for Bozrah remains undetermined.

3. A city in Gilead conquered by Judas Maccabeus (1 Macc. 5:26-28), identified with modern Buṣra aš-Šām. The Nabateans informed Judas that many Jews were being held captive at Bozrah. He promptly marched to their aid, slaughtered their captors and sacked the town. Trajan renamed the Nabatean town Noba Trajana Bostra during his Arabian reorganization of 105 C.E., making it the provincial capital.

RYAN BYRNE

BRACELET

A decorative object worn on the wrist or lower arm of both men and women. Bracelets in biblical times were most often made of copper and bronze, but silver, gold, iron, and later glass were also used. Bracelets were formed into various designs: flat or rounded simple rings, intertwined wires, or solid or perforated rings. Some were open-ended with animal finials. Beads and pendants made of metal, glass, faience, stone, shell, bone, and ivory were strung together and also worn on the wrist. Bracelets were considered items not only of beauty, but also of value since they were donated to the tent of meeting (Num. 31:50) and were given as gifts to Rebekah in the hopes of securing her marriage to Isaac (Gen. 24:22). They have been found on the arms of skeletons in ancient graves.

KATHARINE A. MACKAY

BRANCH

The translation of various Hebrew and Greek words, referring several times to actual branches such as those used to construct booths at a feast (Lev. 23:40) or branches used in festal processions (Ps. 118:27; Matt. 21:8). However, "branch" often bears figurative significance. Waving palm branches symbolized celebration before the Lord, and palm branches strewn in the road symbolized reception of the king (Matt. 21:8). The image of an olive tree (Hos. 14:6; Rom. 11:16-24), a cedar (Ezek. 17:23), or a vine and its branches (Ps. 80:11[MT 12]; Nah. 2:2; John 15:1-8) portrays Israel as barren or exiled and as restored and planted in the land (Ezek. 31:6; Matt. 13:32). Israel's Messiah (Isa. 4:2; 11:1) is also referred to as the "righteous Branch" that sprouts from David's royal line (Jer. 23:5; 33:15). When Israelites returned to the land from exile and began to rebuild the temple, Zechariah prophesied that one called "the Branch" would function as both priest and king (Zech. 3:8; 6:12); he would rebuild the temple of the Lord in the time of restoration. A. B. CANEDAY

BREAD

A major part of the diet in the ancient Near East, from the earliest times. Heb. *leḥem* refers to food products made from grains such as wheat or barley. Grain is ground into meal and flour, water and other ingredients are added, and some means of cooking is used to produce gruel, porridge, leavened and unleavened bread, cakes or wafers. Barley is used for cakes and gruel, whereas wheat flour can be used for leavened bread.

Bread was a staple and provided daily nourishment (Sir. 29:21). Bread and water made up the whole meal of the poor and prisoners (2 Kgs. 6:22) and part of the meal for the wealthy. Bread occurs in lists of travel provisions (2 Sam. 16:1) and food supplies (1 Sam. 25:18).

Heb. *leḥem* may be used in a general sense as "food," for people and animals (Ps. 147:9). Goats' milk is "food" for the family and servants of the goatherd (Prov. 27:27). During the wilderness wanderings, the Israelites experienced the miraculous gift of manna which was called "bread from heaven" (Neh. 9:15) or "bread of angels" (Ps. 78:25). God's blessing was essential so that food would grow (Ps. 65:9-13[MT 10-14]). People should pray for sufficient bread for each day (Prov. 30:8-9).

Bread was used for offerings and sacrifices. Offerings were called food for God (Lev. 21:6) although this is understood figuratively since God does not need food (Ps. 50:12-13). Unleavened bread was used for cereal offerings. While part or all of the bread might be burnt, sometimes part of it was eaten by the priests.

Bread can be used figuratively. If people had sorrow for nourishment they had "bread of tears" (Ps. 80:5[6]). "Bread of wickedness" (Prov. 4:17) refers to gaining nourishment by improper means. Eating "bread of idleness" means being lazy (Prov. 31:27). Lady Wisdom invites people to eat her bread (Prov. 9:5), which is didactic nourishment. Lady Folly invites people to eat "bread in secret," referring to sexual indulgence (Prov. 9:17).

Gk. *ártos* can refer to leavened or unleavened bread. Bread is part of a meal (Mark 6:44) and is taken as provisions for journeys (v. 8). Believers should not be anxious about bread, because God will provide it for them (2 Cor. 9:10). They should pray for daily bread (Matt. 6:11).

The Jewish practice of saying grace before a meal includes taking a loaf of bread, giving thanks, breaking it, and distributing it (Matt. 14:19). To "break bread" could designate a common meal (Acts 2:46) or the Eucharist, which included bread as an element (1 Cor. 11:23-26).

Bread can refer to spiritual nourishment. Jesus is called the "bread of life" (John 6:35) and the "bread that came down from heaven" (v. 41). In Luke 14:15 a blessing is pronounced upon the one who will eat bread in the kingdom of God.

Bibliography. J. Behm, "ártos," *TDNT* 1:477-78; W. Dommershausen and H.-J. Fabry, "leḥem," *TDOT* 7:521-29. STEPHEN ALAN REED

BREAD OF THE PRESENCE

Loaves of bread placed in the sanctuary on a golden table, before Yahweh. Its name derives from the fact that the bread is in the presence of God and is, therefore, holy. The bread of the presence is described in most detail by Priestly writers in Exod. 25:23-30; Lev. 24:5-9 in conjunction with the building of the tabernacle. Exod. 25:23-30 focuses on the golden table upon which the bread is placed. Lev. 24:5-9 describes the bread itself. The bread of the presence consists of 12 loaves, placed in two rows of six each. Each is made with two tenths of an ephah of flour. The bread of the presence functioned like a grain offering which was sprinkled with frankincense. Aaron would replace the loaves with new ones on a weekly basis. The bread of the presence symbolizes the eternal covenant between God and Israel. Its location in the sanctuary just in front of the holy of holies indicates the holy status of the bread. In view of its sacred character, once the bread was removed it had to be eaten by priests within the confines of the sanctuary.

The bread of the presence is mentioned sporadically in other parts of the Bible. 1 Kgs. 7:48 places the bread of the presence in the temple of Solomon. A number of references also occur in Chronicles (1 Chr. 9:32; 23:29; 28:16; 2 Chr. 2:4[MT 3]; 13:11; 29:18). 1 Macc. 1:22; 4:49 describe how Antiochus Epiphanes carried off the golden table used for the bread of the presence in 170 B.C.E. and how it was later replaced by Simon Maccabeus. 1 Sam. 21:4-6[5-7] depicts an incident when David and his men ate the bread of the presence at the sanctuary of Nob, while fleeing from Saul. The story emphasizes that David and his men were in a state of holiness because they had refrained from sexual intercourse. Thus their eating of the bread did not defile its holy status even though they were not priests. This story is mentioned in the Synoptic Gospels (Mark 2:26 par.) in a teaching of Jesus as a illustration of why it is lawful to pick grain on the sabbath.

Bibliography. M. Haran, *Temples and Temple-Service in Ancient Israel* (1978, repr. Winona Lake, 1985). THOMAS B. DOZEMAN

BREAST

The word "breast" in the OT and NT is most commonly used in its anatomical, literal sense for both animals and humankind. In Exodus, Leviticus, and

Numbers, the breasts of animals such as rams are used as wave offerings before the Lord (e.g., Lev. 8:29). The breast is a place for the sucking (Job 3:12), weaning (Isa. 28:9), safety (Ps. 2:9[MT 10]), and quieting (131:2) of a child. Sexual and sensual arousal comes from the breasts as objects of desire (Cant. 4:5; Ezek. 23:3; Hos. 2:2). The breasts are recipients of beating and tearing as in great desolation (Ezek. 23:34) or remorse (Luke 18:13).

Although the nursing breasts are usually depicted as female breasts or those of female animals, twice they are utilized metaphorically: the nursing breasts of kings (Isa. 60:16) and Jerusalem's consoling breasts (66:11). While full breasts are a blessing and indicate ripe maidenhood, dry breasts are a curse (Hos. 9:14).

Nearness to the breast of Jesus signifies a place of honor for the disciples (John 13:23 RSV). Whereas the word "bosom" is used more often in a figurative sense, "breast" is more commonly found in Scripture in its literal usage.

Jeanne Stevenson-Moessner

BREASTPIECE

A 23 × 23 cm. (9 × 9 in.) square bag made of multicolored fabrics. To it were attached 12 stones, each engraved with the name of one of the 12 tribes. The breastpiece (Heb. *ḥōšen*) was connected to the high priest's ephod (tunic) by golden rings attached to its corners. Cords of gold and blue were tied to the rings, and the other ends were attached near the waistband and shoulder straps (Exod. 28:15-28; 39:8-21).

The breastpiece (*ḥōšen mišpāṭ*, "breastpiece of judgment") functioned as a container for the Urim and Thummim (Exod. 28:30; Lev. 8:8), identified the high priest as the intercessor for a united Israel, and served as a "memorial" or "reminder," borne "over/upon the heart" (Exod. 28:29-30).

The term does not occur in the NT, and it should not be confused with the breastplate (Heb. *śiryān*), which was part of a soldier's armor.

W. E. Nunnally

BRICK

One of the most common building materials in the ancient Near East. In Mesopotamia kiln-fired bricks were common (as in the Tower of Babel account, Gen. 11:3); sun-dried bricks were used in Egypt and Palestine until the Roman period. In the hills of Palestine, where it was abundant, stone was used for foundations and mudbrick for the superstructure; in Egypt stone was used to build temples and royal monuments.

Excavations have shown that mudbrick was used extensively from as early as the Neolithic Period. At Neolithic Jericho handshaped "hog-back" bricks were common, followed by "bun" bricks, and later rectangular mold-made bricks in the Early Bronze Age. Mudbrick was used to build monumental city walls, private dwellings, and public buildings like temples.

The making of bricks has been an important occupation from prehistoric times to present-day Egypt. Egyptian wall paintings depicting the making of bricks are known from as early as Old Kingdom times; these paintings show the soaking of the clay, the mixing of the clay with straw or other materials, and the shaping of the bricks either by hand or in a wooden mold. Some Egyptian bricks were stamped with the pharaoh's name, although more numerous examples of stamped bricks have been found in Babylonia.

Jennie R. Ebeling

BRIDE OF CHRIST

An ecclesial metaphor whereby Jesus is presented as the bridegroom for his followers (Mark 2:19-20), and the wedding feast appears as a recurring image for the gathered community at the end time. The precise phrase "bride of Christ" to designate the Church never occurs. Paul is the first to describe the Church as a bride ("For I promised you in marriage to one husband, to present you as a chaste virgin to Christ"; 2 Cor. 11:2), and the author of Ephesians uses this same image to explain the relationship between Christ and the Church (Eph. 5:21-33). The author of Revelation refers to both the Church (Rev. 19:7) and the heavenly city of Jerusalem (21:2, 9) as a bride.

Bridal imagery in the OT and NT connotes the intimacy and mutual fidelity between God/Christ and God's people. It also signals the care and protection required of the bridegroom toward the bride. The bridal metaphor underscores her dependence on and obligation to show reverence toward her spouse, in accordance with the demands of gender relationships in "honor and shame" cultures. Israel's infidelity, or "harlotry" (Hos. 2), constitutes the most developed form of this marital metaphor in the OT.

Barbara E. Bowe

BRIDEGROOM OF BLOOD

An epithet in Exod. 4:24-26, arguably the most enigmatic passage in the Pentateuch. It has been seen variously as the etiology of infant circumcision in Israel; a symbolic, ritually correct, (re)circumcision of Moses; or even the expiation of Moses' bloodguilt after killing the Egyptian.

Moses returns to Egypt according to God's instructions and brings with him his wife Zipporah and his sons. Somewhere along the way, while they are encamped for the night, the Lord seeks to kill "him" (Moses or either of his sons; the pronoun is ambiguous). At this point Zipporah uses a flint to circumcise her "son," touches the foreskin to "his legs/feet" (the common euphemism for genitals), and then pronounces the mysterious phrase, "you are a bridegroom of blood unto me," whereupon God recants.

Some translations add Moses' name as the one touched with the foreskin; most commentaries also view him as the object of God's attack, and many see him as the recipient of Zipporah's words. Others see Zipporah touching and speaking directly to her son. All that is evident is that Zipporah's decisive actions avert God's attack.

The unanswerable questions surrounding this passage are manifold, and go beyond the identification of the pronominal antecedents and Zipporah's obscure formulaic pronouncement. What is God's almost demonic motivation, and why would he seek the life of either Moses or his son? Why did circumcision stay the hand of God? How did Zipporah know what to do? Why would Zipporah touch anyone with the foreskin? What does "bridegroom of blood" mean, and why is it repeated twice? Proposed answers range from the psychological (there was no actual attack; rather, Moses suffered from a serious depression, or it was all a dream), to the comparative (Zipporah performed a Midianite rite on her son to avert an attack from a pagan deity). In any event, after this episode, Moses is able to continue safely on his mission to free the children of Israel from bondage in Egypt.

SHARON R. KELLER

BRIMSTONE
Probably burning sulphur (cf. Lat. *ignis et sulphur* for Gk. *púr kaí theíon*). Except for Job 18:15, all biblical references to brimstone are coupled with fire. Sodom and Gomorrah were destroyed by fire and brimstone (Gen. 19:24). The Psalmist uses fire and brimstone as a metaphor for God's judgment upon the wicked (Ps. 11:6). The lake which burns with fire and brimstone is the final destiny of the devil, the beast, the false prophet (Rev. 19:20; 20:10), death, hades (20:14), and all people whose names are not written in the book of life (21:8).

JOE E. LUNCEFORD

BRONZE
A yellowish-brown metal alloy composed primarily of copper. Metallurgists use the term to designate copper/tin alloys of less than 11 percent tin. In ancient texts and among contemporary scholars "bronze" includes items made of copper and alloys with arsenic, antimony, lead, or silver and not just tin. In the KJV the term "brass" is used uniformly, since the term which specifies copper/zinc alloys today was used of all cuprous alloys in 1611 A.D.

Alloyed copper is used to manufacture products that are superior to those made of pure copper. Bronze alloys provide production advantages of being more fusible, requiring less annealing, and being more fluid in casting. The finished bronze products are harder, less susceptible to oxidation, and can be burnished to shine. The ratio of copper and alloying ingredients can be varied in accordance with the desired purpose of the product. Bronze is hardened but also becomes more brittle with increased proportions of tin. Tin content of ca. 20 percent, e.g., contributes a sonorous quality that is desirable in cymbals, but that would not meet the flexibility requirements for a sword. Most bronze in the ancient Near East has a tin content of 5-10 percent. This bronze hardened by hammering is as hard as 5.5 on the Mohs' scale, almost twice as hard as copper. Bronze widely replaced copper since it was a superior material for tools and weapons that needed to remain rigid or to sustain sharp edges. Bronze was the chief utilitarian metal until iron technology supplanted it.

The craft of metalworking is identified in the Bible as originating with Tubal-cain (Gen. 4:22), who is eponymously recognized as the "father of metallurgy." The early application of hammer and fire was basic to all subsequent metallurgy. Artifactual evidence points towards work in copper taking place in Upper Mesopotamia by the 6th millennium B.C. Alloys of copper, particularly arsenical copper, are widely evidenced in the 4th millennium, with the best-known examples being the horde of mace heads and crowns found at Naḥal Mishmar. This "bronze" was almost exclusively the type utilized in the 3rd millennium. Tin bronze became dominant in the 2nd millennium.

In the Bible bronze technology was widely known, and is evidenced in the assemblage of artifacts from the last half of the 2nd millennium and the initial part of the 1st. Hammering, raising, chasing, and casting are seen in the manufacture of items for the exterior of both the tabernacle and the temple (Exod. 27; 1 Kgs. 7). Copper alloys are relatively valued in taxonomic lists (Num. 31:22) as less than gold and silver, which were used inside religious structures. Bronze was used for the manufacture of extensively utilized ritual objects such as bowls, lavers, altars, and musical instruments (1 Chr. 15:19); military supplies such as armor, spears, swords and arrowheads (1 Sam. 17:5-7; 2 Chr. 12:10; Job 20:24); and domestic hardware such as doors and closing mechanisms (Ps. 107:16; 1 Kgs. 4:13). Not highlighted in the Bible but evidenced in physical remains are a wide assortment of tools and personal items that extend beyond awls (Deut. 15:17) and hand mirrors (Exod. 30:17).

Bibliography. B. Rothenberg, ed., *The Ancient Metallurgy of Copper* (London, 1990).

ROBERT WAYNE SMITH

BRONZE LAVER
A basin (so NRSV) located in the court between the tent of meeting and the burnt-offering altar, in which the priests were to wash their hands before sacrificing on the altar (Exod. 30:17-21). This object, made from bronze mirrors donated by "the women who served at the entrance of the tent of meeting" (Exod. 38:8), consisted of a stand with a bronze base (30:18). In Solomon's temple the bronze laver was replaced by the molten sea (1 Kgs. 7:23-26; 2 Chr. 4:2-5; cf. 2 Kgs. 25:13; 1 Chr. 18:8, "bronze sea").

BRONZE SEA
See SEA, MOLTEN.

BROOK
A small stream of water. In the seasonal climate of Palestine the stream beds tend to gush with rainfall runoff during the winter rains but dry up during the summer drought (1 Kgs. 17:1-7; Job 6:15-17). Perennial streams such as the Jordan River and its major tributaries are the exception to the general rule, but these streams pale in comparison with the Nile, Tigris, or Euphrates. More often stream beds become dry gulches during the summer, and sur-

vival becomes much more difficult. Thus Heb. *naḥal,* as well as Arab. *wadi,* can refer to a perennial stream or river, a temporary rainy season torrent (Judg. 5:21), or merely a valley or dry stream bed during drought (Num. 13:23; Deut. 2:13; 2 Sam. 15:23).

Metaphorically, the torrent of the rainy season illustrates the prophetic demand for pervasive justice (Amos 5:24), the blessing prophesied to come to Jerusalem (Isa. 66:12), or the wise words from the mouth of the righteous (Prov. 18:4). The problem involved in traversing the "pride" of the Jordan (either the dense vegetation along it which harbored dangerous animals or its agitated turbulent waters) fittingly pictures Israel's difficulties and dangers (Jer. 12:5; cf. 47:2). A brook at drought stage serves as an apt picture of Job's fickle friends (Job 6:15-20). The ephemeral nature of brooks must be understood if one is to appreciate the suitableness of the comparison of the deer's panting for water with the psalmist's panting for God (Ps. 42:1-2[MT 2-3]). DAVID L. TURNER

BROTHER

A designation for social relationships, sometimes familial, sometimes political. Cain and Abel are familial brothers, but the term (Heb. *'āḥ/'aḥîm*) also relates to their economic roles as farmer and shepherd within agrarian society (Gen. 4). The story of Esau and Jacob is one of family, but it also establishes the political dominance of Israel over Edom.

Biblical storytellers used the language and structure of family to weave together the disparate elements that constituted Israel. The Israelite God was both king and father of this heterogeneous nation. The tribes within the nation related themselves to this God as sons to a father, subjects to a ruler; and the covenant arrangement bound the tribes to each other through clearly defined obligations and responsibilities as brother to brother.

In narratives, brotherly relationships are often contentious as male siblings compete for divine approval (Gen. 4), paternal blessing (Gen. 27), and succession (1 Kgs. 1–2). Joseph's brothers, jealous because he is Jacob's favorite, plot to kill their arrogant sibling (Gen. 37), and Amnon rapes his half-sister Tamar, while her brother Absalom exploits her anguish to remove his brother as a rival (2 Sam. 13). Yet brothers sometimes band together against common enemies, as Dinah's brothers did (Gen. 34), or willingly support their sibling, as Jonathan did with David (1 Sam. 18, 20).

In the NT, doing the will of the Father in heaven makes one a brother or sister to Jesus of Nazareth (Mark 3:35) and to other members of the Christian community. KATHLEEN S. NASH

BROTHERS OF THE LORD

The four Gospels refer to "brothers" (Gk. *adelphoí*) of Jesus. While John (2:12; 7:3-10) never names them, Mark 6:3 (= Matt. 13:54-56) identifies them as "James and Joses (Joseph) and Judas and Simon" and indicates that Jesus had more than one sister. The Gospels also agree that none of his brothers believed in him during his lifetime (Mark 3:31-35 = Matt. 12:46-50 = Luke 8:19-20; John 7:3-10). Luke-Acts, however, adds that Jesus' brothers were present in the upper room after his ascension (Acts 1:14, 16), and Paul passes on the tradition that Jesus personally appeared to his brother James (1 Cor. 15:7), who quickly became a leader in the early Church (Acts 12:17; 15:13; 21:18; Gal. 1:19; 2:9). The books of James and Jude can be attributed to Jesus' brothers. Later tradition reports that after James was martyred (ca. 61 A.D.), Simon took over as leader of the Jerusalem church.

Jerome suggested that the Greek term be interpreted in the above contexts as "relatives," and he suggested that these men are cousins of Jesus, sons of Mary, wife of Clopas (Jesus' aunt; John 19:25), who is identified with "Mary the mother of James (and Joseph)" (Mark 16:1 = Matt. 27:56 = Luke 24:10). This interpretation would preserve the perpetual virginity of Mary the mother of Jesus. Before this view arose, however, and since the Reformation, scholars argued that the most natural meaning of the Greek term is "brothers," which makes the best sense of Mark 6:3; Acts 1:14. According to this understanding, after the birth of Jesus Mary had other children by Joseph.

Bibliography. R. Bauckham, *Jude and the Relatives of Jesus in the Early Church* (Edinburgh, 1990).

PETER H. DAVIDS

BUKKI (Heb. *buqqî*)

1. A leader of the tribe of Dan; one of those chosen to assist in dividing the Promised Land of Canaan (Num. 34:22).

2. A Levite, the son of Abishua and descendant of Aaron (1 Chr. 6:5, 51[MT 5:31; 6:36), and an ancestor of Ezra the scribe (Ezra 7:4).

BUKKIAH (Heb. *buqqîyāhû*)

A son of Heman and leader of the sixth division of levitical singers (1 Chr. 25:4, 13).

BUL (Heb. *bûl*)

The eighth month of the Israelite calendar (Oct.-Nov.; 1 Kgs. 6:38). Also known as the month of rain, it is the month for the sowing of wheat and barley and for the harvesting of olives (in northern Galilee) and winter figs. After the Exile the Hebrews adopted its Babylonian name, Marheshvan.

BULL

An adult male bovine. The bull is a very common figure in the religions of the ancient Near East. In Egypt the Apis bull, a personification of the Nile, was the sacred animal of Osiris. A bull with a sun disk and ankh between its horns, similar to bulls found in Egypt, has been discovered in Tyre. This could suggest Egyptian influence in the use of the bull in Syria-Palestine. The Bull of Heaven appears in Mesopotamian mythology as a vehicle for the gods' judgment. In Canaanite religious practice the bull was often used as a symbol for either Baal or El. In Hazor a pair of bulls has been found with feet on their backs, interpreted as a representation of Baal.

Similar depictions exist of Adad, often seen as a Mesopotamian representation of Baal.

The main role of the bull in Israelite worship was as an object of sacrifice, offered at occasions such as festivals (i.e., Passover, Sukkoth) or as purification offerings (Lev. 4, 16; cf. Heb. 9:13; 10:4). Sometimes the reason for the sacrifice is left unspecified (i.e., Ezra 6:9).

Israelite and ancient Near Eastern usage of bull imagery collided in a pair of incidents involving bulls. Exod. 32:4 reports the fashioning of golden calves, or bulls, by Aaron at the request of the people. 1 Kgs. 12:28 reports the establishment of golden bulls by Jeroboam at Bethel and Dan.

The Bull (Heb. *'āḇîr* or "Mighty One") of Jacob is an epithet for God (Gen. 49:24; Ps. 132:2, 5; Isa. 49:26; 60:16). Twelve bulls supported the bronze sea at the Jerusalem temple (1 Kgs. 7:25).

MATTHEW A. THOMAS

BULRUSH

See PAPYRUS; REED, RUSH.

BUNAH (Heb. *bûnâ*)

A Judahite, son of Jerahmeel (1 Chr. 2:25).

BUNNI (Heb. *bunnî, bûnnî*)

1. A postexilic Levite among those who took the lead in the public confession (Neh. 9:4).

2. An Israelite who set his seal to the renewed covenant under Nehemiah (Neh. 10:15[MT 16]).

3. A Levite, ancestor of the postexilic Shemaiah (Neh. 11:15).

BURIAL

Terms for burial in the Bible may refer to the burial preparation process, the interment of the body, or the place of burial. Biblical texts tend to be brief descriptions of burial practices rather than lengthy prescriptions of burial rites. Among most peoples of the ancient Near East, burial was an especially sacred act; a disturbance or desecration of the burial place was considered a heinous act. Even in times of war, conquering armies allowed for the proper disposition of the dead.

Locations

In the OT era people were buried in natural caves, rock-hewn tombs, shaft tombs, rock cairns, or cemeteries. Families of higher economic stature procured facilities for the proper disposal of themselves and their ancestors (cf. Gen. 23:3-20). Numerous Middle and Late Bronze Age examples have been excavated at sites such as Jericho, Gibeon, Tell en-Naṣbeh, and Hazor, which provide undistinguishable Canaanite parallels to the biblical practice. In these multiple usage facilities, the previously buried bodily remnants were moved to the rear of the cave-tomb, and the new corpse was laid in the primary position. Each was accompanied by grave goods necessary for proper treatment of the body or for some perceived use in the hereafter.

Only Rachel among the early matriarchs was not buried at Machpelah due to her untimely death in giving birth to Benjamin. Instead Jacob entombed her just north of Ephrath along the journey to Kiriath-arba, and memorialized the site with a stone pillar (Gen. 35:19-20). This description may reflect the rock cairn known among nomadic groups during the Bronze Ages, where the body is interred within or beneath a mound of stones. Others were buried adjacent to distinctive landmarks, as was Rebekah's nurse Deborah under an oak below Bethel (Gen. 35:8) and the cremated bodies of Saul and his sons in Jabesh-gilead under a tamarisk tree (1 Sam. 31:11-13).

In the era of the judges (Iron I), burial sites were often markers to establish or safeguard a claim to tribal territory. Family burials for multi-generational use within those tribal regions seem normative (e.g., Judg. 8:32; 16:31). The bones of Joseph were brought from Egypt in the Exodus and buried near Shechem, in the plot of ground purchased by Jacob from Hamor (Gen. 33:19-20; Josh. 24:32), and Joshua was buried "in his own inheritance" at Timnath-serah in the hill country of Ephraim (Josh. 24:30).

During the Israelite monarchy (Iron II), the kings of Judah and Israel generally were buried in royal tombs in the capital city or ancestral burial sites. The Judahite kings from David to Ahaz were buried in the ancestral royal tombs in the city of David (e.g., 1 Kgs. 2:10; 11:43). Manasseh and Amon were buried in the garden of Uzza (2 Kgs. 21:18, 26). The Omrides were buried at Samaria (e.g., 1 Kgs. 16:28; 2 Kgs. 10:35; 13:13).

After the fall of the northern kingdom, Assyrian bathtub coffins and jar burials were introduced. But rock-hewn bench tombs continued to be utilized by prominent families in Jerusalem. Examples have been excavated at St. Etienne and the Ecole Biblique in the northern part of the city, along the scarp of the Hinnom Valley and its vicinity, and along the Kidron in Silwan opposite the Ophel. The latter contained an inscription naming the owner, possibly Shebna (Isa. 22:15-16), and pronouncing a curse upon any intruder. In many of these tombs a charnel pit for collecting the bones of earlier deceased family members was hewn in a special chamber or beneath the benches upon which the most recent corpse was laid. The burials of the poor were probably in accessible natural caves or in simple cemeteries, resulting in poor preservation. As in the Bronze Age, infant children were occasionally buried beneath the floor of the house.

During the Persian and Hellenistic periods shaft tombs and pit graves were common in Judea. The shaft tombs consisted of a vertical or sloping entry into the burial chamber, some of which contained perpendicular niches *(kokhim)* for placement of individual corpses. Examples of Greek and Phoenician shaft tombs are common along the coastal plain and the western edge of the Shephelah, at sites such as Achzib, Dor, Gezer, Lachish, and Mareshah. Shallow pit graves were common along the lower classes of Palestine.

In the intertestamental and NT eras several new

Dolmen at Khirbet Umm el-Ghozlan near Wadi el-Yabis, E of the Jordan River. Prominent from the Chalcolithic through Early Bronze I periods, some tombs in the area were reused into the Roman and Byzantine periods and later (Jonathan Mabry/Gaetano Palumbo, the Wadi el-Yabis Project)

types of burial are found. Some of the very wealthy had tombs of the arcosolia type, with elaborate memorial structures built adjacent to the entry or above it. Well-known examples include Jason's tomb in southwestern Jerusalem and the so-called tombs of Absalom and Zechariah in the Kidron Valley. A second tomb type was the loculi, with a large central chamber and branching niches (*kokhim*) on three sides. The entryway to some tombs of the Herodian era, as with that of Jesus of Nazareth, were guarded by a rolling stone (1.2-1.5 m. [4-5 ft.] in diameter) set in a subterranean slot. Examples have been found in Jerusalem along the western slopes of the northern extension of the Hinnom Valley, and at the so-called Tombs of the Kings, N of the Damascus Gate.

Many bodies were also placed in large stone sarcophagi ("flesh eaters"), often inscribed with the identity of the individual or etched with symbolic faunal, floral, or geometric designs. Excellent examples have been excavated at Beth-shearim, Kedesh in Galilee, Jerusalem, and the region of Tsefat. Wooden coffins, which were deposited in rock-hewn loculi, have been uncovered around Jericho. Those of women and children often contained grave goods such as bowls, beads, and leather sandals. Later secondary burial in ossuaries (bone depositories) was utilized; after the decay of the body in the loculus, the bones were placed in a carved stone box for safekeeping.

Rites and Practices

Several descriptive phrases are used in the Bible to describe the death and burial of leading individuals. In Genesis the patriarchs generally "died and were gathered (or 'removed,' Heb. *'āsap̄*) to [their] fathers" (e.g., 25:8; 35;29; 49:33). In Kings and Chronicles the common formula describing the burial process for the kings of Israel and Judah was "X lay (*šāḵaḇ*) with his fathers, and they buried him in Y," Y denoting a place such as the city of David, Samaria, or a specially prepared tomb (e.g., 2 Kgs. 10:35; 2 Chr. 16:13-14; 1 Kgs. 2:10; 11:43; 14:31). The rare exceptions to the common practice include the desecration of the bodies of despised individuals such as Jezebel (2 Kgs. 9:37).

Preservation of the body and the person's identity by embalming, an Egyptian practice which involved treating the body with special fluids and wrappings for 70 days or more, is described only for Jacob and Joseph (Gen. 50:2-3, 26). Joseph's body was subsequently placed in a coffin, a rare practice until the Second Temple period. People were buried as soon as possible after death, a practice afforded even criminals and dead bodies discovered along the road or in a field (Deut. 21:1-9, 22–23; 1 Kgs. 13:24-30).

The inclusion of accompanying grave goods is interpreted as provision of needs for the afterlife, symbolic of such need, or indicative of the life and status of the individual. Pottery wares such as bowls, cooking pots, juglets, vases, and jewelry are among the examples uncovered, and an increasing number of metal objects such as bowls, mirrors, and bracelets from the Persian period on have been found.

The NT descriptions of burials include the treatment of the body with spices and incense for

7), murder (v. 8), perjury (vv. 9-10), and vengeance (vv. 23-24).

Before Alexander the Great brought Hellenism into the world of the Bible in 333 B.C.E., neither theologies of original sin nor etiologies about class conflict appear in ancient Near Eastern traditions. Like the Enuma Elish stories from Mesopotamia and the stories of Anubis and Bata from Egypt, the stories of Cain and Abel and those of Adam and Eve (Gen. 2:4b–4:2) were creation stories about how humans learned to bear children, farm, build cities, make tents, herd livestock, play music, work metal, administer justice, and trade.

When the stories open, Cain and Abel are ratifying covenants for seed to plant and animals to breed. "An offering of the fruit of the ground" and "... the firstlings of his flock, their fat portions" are standard biblical expressions for the sacrifices of farmers and herders. "Their fat portions" (v. 4) does not privilege the sacrifice of Abel over that of Cain. All sacrifices must be the best or "fat" portions.

Translations reading ". . . and the Lord had regard for Abel . . . but for Cain . . . he had no regard" (Gen. 4:4)" invite a painful theology portraying Yahweh as capricious. A better reading would be ". . . and the land had regard for Abel . . . but for Cain . . . the land had no regard." "Land" and "Yahweh" here are synonymous, just as in Cain's appeal later: ". . . today you have driven me away from the land, and I shall be hidden from your face" (v. 14). Even though both offer acceptable sacrifices, the land produces enough for Abel's flocks, but not enough for Cain's crops.

The sin lurking at the door (Gen. 4:7) is not the temptation to murder Abel. When harvests come in, humans easily accept fertility as a blessing; but when harvests fail, they are tempted to see their fertility as a curse. The stories remind humans that despite the temptation to forgo creativity and remain sterile, they should not let the labor which creativity requires discourage them from farming.

When Cain's grain sacrifice does not bring a good year, he sacrifices Abel. In the Enuma Elish stories, Nintu-mami uses the blood of Wei-la to moisten the clay she will use to create the first humans. Here Cain moistens soil with the blood of Abel to bring it to life. The sacrifice of Abel also alters the status of the household of Cain. By sacrificing the herder whose livestock are its insurance against starvation when crops fail, Cain places his household in complete dependence upon Yahweh for its survival.

Yahweh intervenes, not to punish Cain like a judge but rather, like a midwife, to prepare him to face the labor which human creativity demands. Yahweh teaches Cain that he will survive in the land of Nod (Heb. *nôḏ*) by foraging (*nwʿ*) and scavenging (*nwd*) to supplement farming. Cain will farm, but not without difficulty. Labor, Yahweh teaches, is life, not a life sentence.

Cain protests. Hunters kill human scavengers like animal predators. Yahweh concedes. Cain must continue to scavenge, but the apotropaic mark or tattoo on Cain warns hunters that he is under divine protection.

Cain's wife delivers a child named Enoch, whose child Irad founds Eridu, the first city built before the Flood according to the Sumerian King List. The fertility in childbearing and city-building are paralleled by giving both the same name. The delivery of a child and the building of a city describe the spread of life. Like the seven great teachers (Akk. *apkallu*) in Mesopotamian traditions, the household of Cain endows humanity with all the skills of civilization. Cain is the first teacher, followed by Enoch, Irad, Mahujael, Methushael, Lamech, and Jabal, Jubal, and Tubal-cain.

Read as an ancient Near Eastern creation story, the stories of Cain and Abel teach that the laying down of human life is part of the discovery of how to create life. Mortality enters the world either through the self-sacrifice of Adam and Eve or through the sacrifice of Abel by Cain. As painful as mortality can be, it is also the key to human creativity. Without death, there is no life. These biblical traditions encourage human beings to embrace the fertility of farming and childbearing which makes them the image of Yahweh. To give life to the land or to another human, Adam, Eve, Cain, and Abel each must lay down their lives in different ways.

Bibliography. J. D. Levenson, *The Death and Resurrection of the Beloved Son* (New Haven, 1993); S. Niditch, *Underdogs and Tricksters* (San Francisco, 1987); J. G. Williams, *The Bible, Violence and the Sacred* (Valley Forge, 1995). DON C. BENJAMIN

CAINAN (Gk. *Kaïnám*)

1. According to Luke's genealogy of Jesus, the son of Arphaxad (Luke 3:36; cf. LXX Gen. 10:24; 11:12).

2. Another name for Kenan, in Luke's genealogy (Luke 3:37; cf. Gen. 5:9-14; 1 Chr. 1:2).

CAKE

Various food products made from wheat or barley meal, figs or raisins, and shaped or molded into a compact form. Water, oil, and spices might be added to dough which was formed into ring, disk, heart, and flat shapes. Several Hebrew terms are used to denote cakes. "Wafer" is used to render Heb. *ṣappîḥiṯ*, a thin cake made of honey (Exod. 16:31). Cakes for cereal offerings could be baked in an oven, in a pan, or on a griddle (Lev. 2:4-7).

Grain cakes were part of a meal offered to guests (Gen. 18:6). Cakes of figs were used for gifts (1 Sam. 25:18) and as travel provisions (1 Chr. 12:40). Unleavened cakes made with oil were used during the ordination offering of well-being (Exod. 29:2, 23) and for grain offerings (Lev. 2:4). Some Israelites made cakes for the queen of heaven which were marked with or shaped in her image (Jer. 44:19). STEPHEN ALAN REED

CALAH (Heb. *kālaḥ;* Akk. *kalḫu*)

The capital of the Assyrian Empire during much of the Iron Age; located at modern Nimrûd near the confluence of the Tigris and Zab rivers, ca. 35 km.

(22 mi.) S of Nineveh (Tell Kuyunjik). The city was located on the banks of the Tigris. Excavations revealed that the city was inhabited from the early 3rd millennium B.C.E. onward. It is first mentioned in written documents of the 13th century. From the slight evidence from the late Middle Assyrian period it can be inferred that Kalḫu functioned as a provincial capital in that period. In the early 9th century Assurnasirpal II rebuilt and extended the city to make it the capital of the Neo-Assyrian Empire, with a number of palaces and temples. Kalḫu was located in an agricultural area in the Assyrian heartland. As a political and religious center the city also was a scribal center that housed its own library. The city functioned as the place where the army was assembled before campaigns, even after Sargon II moved the capital to Dur-sharruken. In the final years of Esarhaddon Kalḫu again functioned as a capital for a short time.

No deportation of Israelites to Kalḫu is mentioned in Assyrian inscriptions. Israelite personal names in Neo-Assyrian inscriptions, however, give evidence that after the conquest of Samaria Israelites were brought to Calah to function in the Assyrian army.

Calah is identified as one of the cities built by the heroic hunter Nimrod after he moved from Babel to Assur (Gen. 10:11-12). The Table of Nations does not supply trustworthy historical information on primeval history, but seems to reflect relations from the Neo-Assyrian Empire at its summit.

Bibliography. B. Becking, *The Fall of Samaria.* Studies in the History of the Ancient Near East 2 (Leiden, 1992), 73-87; M. E. L. Mallowan, *Nimrud and Its Remains* (London, 1966). BOB BECKING

CALAMUS

An item of trade produced from an aromatic reed (Heb. *qāneh;* Cant. 4:14; cf. Ezek. 27:19).

See SWEET CANE.

CALCOL (Heb. *kalkōl*)

1. The grandson of Judah by his daughter-in-law Tamar and their son Zerah (1 Chr. 2:6).

2. One of the sons of Mahol, which was probably the name of a guild of musicians. 1 Kgs. 4:31(MT 5:11) compares Solomon favorably to Calcol, one of the four wisest men of his day.

PAUL L. REDDITT

CALEB (Heb. *kālēḇ*)

1. The third son of Hezron; brother of Jehrahmeel and Ram. In the genealogies of the Israelite tribes the descendants of Caleb are members of the family of Hezron, the clan of Perez, and the tribe of Judah (1 Chr. 2:9 [NRSV "Chelubai"], 18, 42). Although his genealogy in 1 Chr. 2:18-24; 2:42-55 is not intelligible, it is clear that his descendants were the leaders of important Judean clans for whom the towns of Hebron, Tappuah, Bethlehem, Kiriath-jearim, and others were named.

2. The son of Jephunneh, Kenizzite (Num. 13:6; 32:12), and father-in-law of Othniel, one of the first judges of Israel (Josh. 15:17). Originally an Edomite clan (Gen. 36:15, Kenaz) that settled in southern Palestine, the Kenizzites are listed among the people of Canaan who are to be dispossessed by the descendants of Abraham (15:19). The Calebites appear in 1 Sam. 25:3 as a group distinct from the tribe of Judah. Many scholars believe that the Calebites were a Kenizzite clan which was incorporated into the tribe of Judah during the reign of David. When Moses requested each tribe to designate a man to explore the land of Canaan, Caleb was selected because he was one of the leaders of Judah (Num. 13:3). He was sent as one of the 12 spies to scout the land of Canaan and bring a report to the people of Israel. While the other 10 spies brought a pessimistic report, Caleb and Joshua encouraged the people to trust in Yahweh and take possession of the land. Because of their faithfulness, Caleb and Joshua were allowed to enter the land and take part in the conquest of Canaan (Num. 13:1–14:10; Josh. 14:6; 13-14).

When Moses appointed a group of people responsible for distributing the land of Canaan, Caleb was selected to represent the tribe of Judah (Num. 34:19). He was 85 years old when he finished conquering the land assigned to his clan (Josh. 14:7, 10). Caleb received as his inheritance the city of Hebron, formally known as Kiriath-arba from which he expelled the three leaders of the Anakim (Josh. 14:13-15; 15:14). As a reward for Othniel's conquest of Kiriath-sepher (Debir), Caleb gave his daughter Acsah in marriage (Josh. 15:15-19); since the text is not clear, it is not certain whether Othniel was Caleb's brother or nephew. The land occupied by Caleb and his descendants was known as the Negeb of Caleb (1 Sam. 30:14). Its location is unknown, but it was probably situated S of Hebron, the area where Nabal, a descendant of Caleb, lived (1 Sam. 25:3). CLAUDE F. MARIOTTINI

CALEB-EPHRATHAH (Heb. *kālēḇ 'eprāṯâ*)

The place where Hezron, the father of Caleb, died (1 Chr. 2:24). The location of the place is unknown. If the Hebrew text is correct, Caleb-ephrathah should be located in the land of Goshen, since Hezron entered Egypt with his father Perez and his grandfather Judah (Gen. 46:8-12). If the location of Caleb-ephrathah is to be found in Canaan, then it would be near Hebron, where Caleb settled after he came from Egypt. The LXX reading of 1 Chr. 2:24, "Caleb came to Ephrathah," is preferable because Caleb-ephrathah appears nowhere else in the OT as the name of a city (cf. RSV "went in to Ephrathah," i.e., a wife of Hezron). CLAUDE F. MARIOTTINI

CALENDAR

See YEAR.

CALIGULA (Lat. *Caligula*)

Gaius Julius Caesar Germanicus. Born 31 August 12 C.E. at Antium, ca. 40 km. (25 mi.) S of Rome, to Germanicus, nephew of Tiberius, he was nicknamed Caligula ("Bootkins") by mutinous Rhine legionaries in 14. Although Tiberius had his mother and two brothers killed for conspiracy, the emperor befriended Gaius and named him his successor. Gaius succeeded Tiberius in 37 with support from the praetorian guard, the senate, and the people.

Caligula's favor ended soon after. Beset by illness, he ruled despotically, instituting treason trials against senators and the praetorian guard and executing supporters and foes alike. His inclination toward extravagent spectacle and dress brought disfavor, as did confiscations and extortions. In 39 he dismissed the consuls and banished or executed members of his family for conspiracy. His campaigns in Britain and Germany failed. Upon return to Rome in 40, Caligula assumed trappings of the imperial cult popular in the east but disliked in Rome. He built a temple to himself on the Palatine and extorted large sums from citizens to be his priests, and he ordered that the Jerusalem temple be converted to an imperial shrine. After Caligula was assassinated on 24 January 41, his name was removed from official records and his statues destroyed.

Bibliography. A. A. Barrett, *Caligula: The Corruption of Power* (New Haven, 1990); C. Scarre, *Chronicle of the Roman Emperors* (London, 1995).

SCOTT NASH

CALL, CALLING

The verb (Heb. *qārā'*; Gk. *kaléō*) used to describe "naming" (Gen. 3:20; Luke 1:60) or to refer to the act of prayer, where persons "call to" or "call on" God (Ps. 145:18; Rom. 10:13). In addition, the idea of a "call" or "calling" in the sense of a (divine) commission or vocation is also present in both the OT and NT.

In the OT call narratives occur frequently with prophets (Isa. 6:1-13; Jer. 1:1-10; Ezek. 1:1-28) as well as others (e.g., Moses; Exod. 3:1–4:17). Interestingly, a consistent feature of OT call narratives is the reluctance of the person called (e.g., Moses, Exod. 4:10-13; Gideon, Judg. 6:15). Calls can also be extended to the entire community: Israel is to be a kingdom of priests (Exod. 19:6); the larger Israelite community in exile receives a commission to be God's servant (Isa. 49:3-6).

In the NT individuals and the larger community receive calls. In the Gospels call narratives occur with the disciples (e.g., Mark 1:16-20; 2:13-14). A consistent feature of the NT call narratives is that successful "calls" have two elements: first, Jesus takes the initiative; second, there is unqualified and immediate acceptance. The Gospels record a set of unsuccessful call stories, where in each case one or both of the above criteria are not fulfilled (Luke 9:57-62). In the Epistles to be a member of the Christian community is to have received a divine calling (Eph. 1:18; Phil. 3:14). GREGORY MOBLEY

CALNEH (Heb. *kalnēh*) (also CALNO)

A city in the north of Aram-naharaim (Amos 6:2). Situated at the northern end of the Orontes, this area became a center for resisting Assyrian advance in the 8th century B.C.E. Tiglath-pileser III attacked the Urartian coalition in 743, then moved against the Neo-Hittite state of Unqi, whose capital Kullania (Calneh) was taken in 738 (recorded in Amos 6:2 as a precursor to Israel's judgment). Royal inscriptions of Tiglath-pileser III show that Samaria, Damascus, and Tyre paid tribute to Assyria in 738 (*ANET*, 282-84).

The reference to Calneh in Amos 6:2 (and Isa. 10:9, where it is called Calno) helps to establish a relative chronology between Calneh's defeat in 738 and prophetic utterances after this event.

Gen. 10:10 (MT) lists Calneh as a city founded by Nimrod, presumably in southern Mesopotamia. The Hebrew text is presumed to be corrupt (cf. NRSV "and all of them," reading *wĕkullānâ*).

AARON W. PARK

CALNO (Heb. *kalnô*) (also CALNEH)

A north Syrian city captured by Tiglath-pileser III in 738 B.C.E. (Isa. 10:9). The location of Calno, called Kullanî in Assyrian inscriptions, has been identified with Kullan Köy, ca. 13 km. (8 mi.) NW of Aleppo. This former capital of the state of Unqi is called Calneh in Amos 6:2.

HYUN CHUL PAUL KIM

CALVARY

Latin translation of Golgotha (Vulg. *calvaria* for Gk. *kraníon*, "skull," Matt. 27:33 par.).

CAMBYSES (Pers. *Kanbujia, Kambujet*)

1. Cambyses I, Persian king of Anshan (ca. 600-559 B.C.E.) and a vassal of Astyages, king of the Median Empire. He married a daughter of Astyages named Mandane, by whom he fathered Cyrus II ("the Great"), founder of the Achaemenid Empire.

2. Cambyses II, successor to his father Cyrus II as king of the Achaemenid Empire (529-522). Babylonian sources depict him as overseeing affairs in Babylonia during Cyrus' administration, but he made a name for himself by carrying out his father's unfulfilled ambition to add Egypt to the empire when he conquered Memphis in 525 and founded the 27th Dynasty of Egypt. His military and administrative exploits there were quite successful (reaching south at least beyond the first cataract of the Nile and west past Cyrene), though it appears that his even grander plans for conquests to the south and west in Africa were foiled by difficulties in sustaining the lengthy supply lines necessary to sustain his armies. According to an Aramaic papyrus from Elephantine in southern Egypt, the Jewish temple there avoided destruction during Cambyses' campaign, although many Egyptian temples apparently were not as fortunate.

The circumstances of the end of Cambyses' life in Syria in 522 are uncertain. Persian sources suggest either suicide or an accident (so also Herodotus). With no clear heir to the throne (and a rebellion already under way, led either by Cambyses' brother Bardiya or an imposter, Gaumata ["Pseudo-Smerdis"], posing as him), Persian government was thrown into a state of disarray that was only eventually quelled by Darius, who seized the Persian throne in 521 and set about quelling rebellions in many places throughout the empire. In this context of dissension and instability following the death of Cambyses, the prophets Haggai and Zechariah raised expectations in Jerusalem of a return of royal power to the descendants of David, in particular to Zerubbabel who at the time was serving as governor of Judah under Persian oversight (Hag. 2:20-23; Zech. 4:6-10; 6:11-13). However, Darius and his army passed through Palestine in 519 en route to Egypt, and the renascent Judean nationalism appears to have subsided quickly.

Bibliography. J. L. Berquist, *Judaism in Persia's Shadow* (Minneapolis, 1996); J. Boardman et al., eds., *CAH*², 4: *Persia, Greece, and the Western Mediterranean* c. *525 to 479* B.C. (Cambridge, 1988).

JEFFREY S. ROGERS

CAMEL

Either of two species of camel (Heb. *gāmāl;* Gk. *kámēlos*): the dromedary, one-hump camel, native to Arabia; and the Bactrian, two-hump camel, named for its origin in central Asia. The dromedary is the one normally referred to in Scripture, though Isa. 21:7 may refer to the Bactrian camel, which had spread to Assyria by 1100 B.C.E.

Abraham is given camels by the pharaoh of Egypt (Gen. 12:16). Camels also figure in the story of Abraham's servant sent to search for a wife for Isaac (Gen. 24). More often, however, camels are owned by non-Israelites: the Egyptians (Exod. 9:3), Midianites (Judg. 6:5; 7:12), Amalekites (1 Sam. 15:3; 27:9; 30:17), the queen of Sheba (1 Kgs. 10:2), the king of Syria (2 Kgs. 8:9), and others. Camels were used during the reign of David (1 Chr. 12:40) and were brought back to Palestine by those returning from exile (Ezra 2:67), but they remained much more extensively used in lands to the south and east of Palestine, where their physiological features made them uniquely adapted to life at the desert's edge.

The Mosaic law forbade eating the meat of the camel (Lev. 11:4), but since better milk and meat were available from other domestic animals, this was no great hardship. Moreover, camels tended to be ill-tempered, intractable, and at times dangerous, and so other animals were preferred by the Hebrews.

The camel's hide was used by the Jewish people for leather, and the thick coat of hair the camel shed every spring was woven into rough cloth, such as that worn by John the Baptist (Matt. 3:4 = Mark 1:6), possibly as a symbol of his prophetic status (cf. Zech. 13:4; 2 Kgs. 1:8).

In Matt. 23:24 straining at a gnat (Aram. *qalmā'*) and swallowing a camel *(gamlā')* produces a play on words in Aramaic. Jesus comments that it is easier "for a camel to go through the eye of a needle than for a rich man to enter the kingdom of God" (Matt. 19:24 = Mark 10:25; Luke 18:25). The suggestion that Gk. *kámēlon* ("camel") should be read *kámilon* ("cable") lacks any serious basis and is disregarded by most scholars.

Bibliography. F. E. Zeuner, *A History of Domesticated Animals* (New York, 1963).

JOHN S. HAMMETT

CAMP

A temporary gathering or settlement, often situated near water (e.g., Exod. 15:27; Josh. 11:5). Temporary military settlements frequently encamped on plains or hills or near valleys (e.g., Judg. 6:33; 1 Sam. 17:2), and leaders often took up strategic positions at the edge or entrance of camps to safeguard the settlement (e.g., Exod. 32:26; 33:7; Num. 3:38; Judg. 7:13).

In the Pentateuch "camp" (usually Heb. *maḥăneh*) describes the manner in which the Israelites, organized by divisions and standards (Num. 1:52), journeyed across the desert from Egypt to Canaan. This desert camp included a tent of meeting, where Moses met with Yahweh (Exod. 33:7-8) and the Israelites brought sacrifices (Lev. 1:3). The tent may have been located outside the camp itself (Exod. 33:7) or in the center, surrounded by the Levites (Num. 1:53). Descriptions of the desert camp may be anachronistic; a festival assembly, perhaps the Feast of Booths, may have influenced the depiction of the camp.

Writings of the Second Temple period contain numerous references to military camps (e.g., Jdt. 6:11; 1 Macc. 2:32; 1QM 1:3; 1QH 2:25). In addition to military references, Qumran texts also use "camp" to describe a community separated from the world and living under specific rules of purity (e.g., CD 7:6; 9:11).

In the NT Jesus' suffering outside the "gate" is compared to the high priest burning the bodies of sacrificed animals outside the "camp" (Gk. *parembolḗ;* Heb. 13:11-12); Christians should join Jesus "outside the camp" and share in his plight (v. 13). In Rev. 20:9 "camp" describes the gathering of God's people.

JACK J. GARLAND, JR.

CANA (Gk. *Kaná*)

A village in the Galilee. The only NT references to Cana are in the Gospel of John, which uses the phrase "Cana of the Galilee" (John 2:1; 4:46; 21:2); the latter verse states that Jesus' disciple Nathanael came from Cana. The exact location of Cana (to be distinguished from Kanah in Josh. 16:8; 19:28) is uncertain. Two churches at the traditional site in the modern village of Kafr Kana commemorate Jesus' miracle of turning water into wine there (John 2:1-11). Kafr Kana, 6 km. (4 mi.) N of Nazareth, was easily accessible by Byzantine and Crusader pilgrims traveling off the main road from Sepphoris to Tiberias. However, the more likely site is Khirbet Qânā (178247; the name is etymologically closer), 13 km. (8 mi.) N of Nazareth along the plain of Asochis (perhaps connected in Josephus *Vita* 14; 41). No excavations have been carried out at this site.

JONATHAN L. REED

CANAAN (Heb. *kĕnaʿan*) (PERSON)

A son of Ham and grandson of Noah (Gen. 9:18, 22); according to 1 Chr. 1:8 Ham's youngest son. He became the ancestor of the people later called the Canaanites (Gen. 10:15-19).

For the impropriety of Ham's seeing the "nakedness" of Noah (Gen. 9:22-24), Noah cursed Ca-

CANAAN, CANAANITES

naan to be the "lowest of slaves" (Gen. 9:25) to his brothers. This curse, which applies more to his descendants than to Canaan himself, does not imply the slavery of a particular race (as some have held); rather, it suggests the inferior position of the Canaanites before the Conquest relative to the important role played by their neighbors, the Egyptians and the inhabitants of Mesopotamia.

See HAM (PERSON).

CANAAN (Heb. *kĕnaʿan*),
CANAANITES (*kĕnaʿanî*)

Name

The origin of the name Canaan and Canaanite is obscure. The obvious Semitic root seems to be **knʿ* which appears in Hebrew and Aramaic in secondary verbal stems, meaning "to bow down." The unaccented suffix *-an* is not common in Semitic. The older view that it represented the name of a blue colored cloth (cf. Nuzi *kinaḫḫu*) has been challenged. Nevertheless, cuneiform sources, especially the Amarna Letters, often speak of *Kinaḫḫi, Kinaḫni* as an orthography for Canaan. The use of *ḫ*-signs is simply a graphic means to represent the guttural *ʿayin* to which the final *-n* is often assimilated. A few LXX passages translate Canaan or Canaanites as *phoiníkōn* (Josh. 5:12; Job 40:25[MT 30]) or *phoiníkēs* (Exod. 16:35; Josh. 5:1). An eponymous ancestor *Chnā* is cited by Sanchuniaton and explained by Philo of Byblos as the first to bear the title *Phoinikos,* "Phoenician."

Land

Biblical Sources

There are two border descriptions for the geographical entity known as the land of Canaan (Heb. *ʾereṣ kĕnāʿan,* Num. 34:1-12; Ezek. 47:15-20; 48:1-28). The southern border is identical with that assigned to the tribal inheritance of Judah (Josh. 15:1-4); it begins at the southern end of the Dead Sea and reaches the Mediterranean shore at the "Brook of Egypt" (*naḥal miṣrayim* = Wadi el-ʿArîsh; cf. the inscriptions of Esarhaddon, 7th century B.C.). The midway point is marked by Kadesh(-barnea) located near ʿAin Qudeis. It is doubtful whether this southern border was in effect during the Late Bronze Age as it finds no echo in the Egyptian sources that deal with northern Sinai.

The northern border has two crucial anchor points: *lĕḇôʾ ḥâmaṯ* ("the entrance to Hamath") is surely modern Lebweh located on the watershed between the Litani and Orontes rivers in the Lebanese Beqaʿ Valley. The other site is Zedad, modern Ṣadâd N of Damascus. The border swings around to the east encompassing the entire Damascene district including the Bashan area and it touches the eastern shore of the Chinnereth (Sea of Galilee). The Jordan River is the eastern boundary (cf. the controversy in Josh. 22 about the relation of the Transjordanian tribes to Israel even though they lived outside of Canaan).

The Ezekiel passages show that this northern boundary for Canaan was recognized in the 6th century. It must reflect the actual southern boundary of the kingdom of Hamath in the Iron Age. The difference between the area actually occupied by a population associated with Israel and the geographical territory of Canaan is expressed in the "land that remains" (Josh. 13:1-6).

The reference to the zone occupied by the Canaanites (Gen. 10:19) only makes use of major geographical centers, e.g., Sidon (from which the Canaanite border was always much farther north) and Gaza (where the Canaanite border was always much farther south). There is no justification in this passage for identifying the Brook of Egypt with the Wadi Ghazzeh.

Nonbiblical Sources

Unfortunately, the famous peace treaty between Rameses II and Hattusili III does not have a border description defining the spheres under political control of the respective parties. There is reason to believe, however, that it would resemble in detail the biblical boundary description of Num. 34:7-9. A number of Bronze Age references point in this direction.

The earliest allusion to Canaanites is from a Mari text (A.3552) which is the report of a general known to be operating in the vicinity of Qatanum, where he has come to a standoff with some *ḫabbātum u Kinaḫnu* ("Raiders and Canaanites") who are located at a place called Rāḫiṣu (cf. Rôǵiṣu, topographical list of Thutmose III, no. 79; also Amarna texts).

The renegade prince Idrimi refers in his autobiography to the town of Ammiya in the land of Canaan, most likely modern Amyûn in the hills above Byblos. After he seized the throne of Alalakh, on the northern bend of the Orontes, Canaanites were present, but listed as foreigners.

Likewise, Ugaritic texts record "Yaʿilu, a Canaanite" (*KTU*² 496:7) just as they record an Egyptian or a Hittite or an Assyrian. Furthermore, a fragmentary report of a lawsuit found at Ugarit (RS 20.182 A + B) mentions the "sons of Ugarit" and the "sons of Canaan" as the disputants. Ugarit and its kingdom were not part of Canaan and its people were not considered Canaanites.

An epistle from Alashia (probably on Cyprus) makes specific reference to "the province of Canaan" (EA 36:15). The king of the Mitanni Empire sent an ambassador with a letter of introduction to "the kings of the land of Canaan" (EA 30:1).

The use of *knʿn* as a synonym for *Phoiníkē* on Beirut coins from the Hellenistic period shows that Laodicea in Canaan (Beirut) was distinguished from its more famous namesake farther north (11 km. [6.8 mi.] S of Ugarit).

People

Biblical Sources

It is not possible to define an ethnic group as the "Canaanites," but a social entity recognized in the Bible as the "inhabitants of Canaan" (Exod. 15:15) is distinct from the Philistines and the Transjordanian Edomites and Moabites. The coalition of rulers at the battle of Deborah and Barak consists of the "kings of Canaan" (Judg. 5:19). The Canaanites are often listed and sometimes contrasted with other peoples such as the Amorites (Deut. 1:7; Josh. 5:1) or Perizzites (Gen. 34:30). In Gen. 15:19-21 the Canaanites appear among a long list of peoples, thus demonstrating that the geographical entity included in that promise to Abraham ("from the river of Egypt to the great river, the river Euphrates," Gen. 15:18) was much larger than the land of Canaan. A number of these lists (Num. 13:29; Deut. 1:7; Josh. 5:1; 13:3; 17:15-18; Judg. 1:1-36) place the Canaanites on the coastal plain and the inland Jezreel and Jordan valleys.

A number of cities and populations are listed in Gen. 10:16-18 which are said to be part of the Canaanite people: Sidon (the most prominent city-state of Phoenicia during the late Israelite and Persian period), Heth (the neo-Hittites, actually speakers of Aramaic by the 9th century), and a group of pre-Israelite peoples: Jebusites, Amorites, Girgashites, and Hivites. In 2 Sam. 24:7 the "cities of the Hivites and Canaanites" are evidently those towns not conquered in the initial settlement process (Judg. 1). Other city populations in Gen. 10:17-18 (cf. extrabiblical references to ʿArqat, Siyannu, Arwad, Sumur, and Hamath on the Orontes) were all in extreme northern Phoenicia, some just outside the northern biblical boundary of Canaan.

One context uses the term Canaanites as an epithet for merchants (Isa. 23:8; cf. Prov. 31:24; Zech. 14:21; Ezek. 16:29; 17:4; Hos. 12:7[8]; Zeph. 1:11; which reflect the role of the Phoenicians, the Iron Age Canaanites, in Mediterranean commerce).

Nonbiblical Sources

The list of booty from Thutmose III's first campaign as sole ruler mentions "640 Canaanites," but no other national or ethnic groups are listed, only social groups (e.g., *ma-r-ya-na,* "chariot warriors" [noblemen]). The *Ki-na-ʿ-nu* are paralleled by the "Hurrians," here residents in the southern Levant, and the Nuǵassians, residents of central Syria. Actually, the Canaanites in the first list correspond to the Hurrians in the second. So the Egyptian knew the Canaanites as one among several national/ethnic groups in the Levant.

Culture and Religion

The most detailed picture of ancient Canaanite religious beliefs is found in Philo of Byblos' *Phoenician History,* preserved only in Eusebius' *Preparation for the Gospel* and Porphyry's *Against the Christians.* This ancient work probably is based partly on original Phoenician traditions from Tyre and Byblos and perhaps Sidon. There are a cosmogony and the history of Kronos (whom Philo equates with El), who eventually overcomes Ouranos his father. Both the sources of Philo and those of Hesiod seem to go back to earlier Near Eastern traditions such as the Hittite Kumarbi myth. The texts speak of a cosmological creation from chaos and of the rule of Kronos on earth. There are some striking points of contact with the biblical cosmogony in Gen. 1-2 and also mythological contacts with the literary myths and legends found at Ugarit. It is usually assumed in scholarly literature today that the Ugaritic materials, including the stories of various members of the pantheon, reflect "Canaanite" religion. However, geographically and politically (also ethnically) Ugarit was not a Canaanite city.

To reconstruct a clear picture of Canaanite religion is virtually impossible. Each of the coastal cities of Phoenicia as well as non-Phoenician Ugarit must have had their own distinct versions of the great religious myths, theogonies, and cosmogonies. Some features, like child sacrifice (attested mainly in late sources and in Punic [Carthage] archaeology), were known to the neighboring peoples, but the ideology of that practice is not recorded in any ancient Phoenician or Classical texts. That Baal and Asherah were the leading deities is obvious from the many biblical denunciations of their worship, but there is no record of the mythology or ideology attached to them.

The biblical view of Canaanite religious practices is thoroughly negative. A frequent theme is inclinations of Israel to adopt the practices of the peoples among whom they were living in Canaan (Judg. 3:1-6). They are frequently exhorted to "put away the foreign gods and the Ashteroth from among you" (1 Sam. 7:3). The northern kingdom was destroyed because "they went after false idols and became false; they followed the nations that were around them" (2 Kgs. 17:15; cf. Amos). Solomon also fostered the worship of the deities from the neighboring peoples (1 Kgs. 11:4-8). The reign of Manasseh was the most notorious for its adoption of foreign cult practices (2 Kgs. 21:2-9; 2 Chr. 33:2-9). Such a polemical attitude hardly permitted any biblical writer the opportunity to give an objective appraisal of Canaanite or other neighboring religion.

Phoenician inscriptions and some Greco-Roman sources furnish the names of various deities: e.g., "The Lady of Byblos," "Baal of Heaven," Melqart (at Tyre), Ashmun (at Sidon). But beyond some mythical themes preserved in Greek sources, there is no real access to religious texts.

Various temples excavated in Middle and Late Bronze contexts in Palestine (e.g., Hazor, Megiddo, Shechem, Beth-shean) show some general features in common: outer courtyard, vestibule, main chamber and inner room, niche or platform for the deity's image. However, they seldom have the same orientation to the compass, and types of altars associated with them (if found at all) are not uniformly placed.

Household worship may be implied by cult figurines and other similar artifacts, but their use is still disputed. They most likely have to do with fertility and childbirth.

Artistic forms in ceramics, ivory carving, and metalwork are basically the same in Canaan as in North Syria (including Ugarit). There really is no distinctive "Canaanite" art with features that set it apart from the entire eastern Mediterranean littoral (and Cyprus). Ivory carving and glyptic art do show considerable adoption of Egyptian forms and themes, but this is typical of the entire area, not just objects found in Canaan.

Language

The most legitimate claim to the title Canaanite goes to what modern scholars call Phoenician. Phoenician spread beyond the traditional borders of Canaan; it was adopted by kingdoms in Cilicia and northern Syria, by Phoenician colonies on Cyprus and the northern shores of Africa (Punic in Graeco-Roman times) and Malta. However, the close affinities of ancient Hebrew show that it too was a dialect of the same family. The Amarna Letters from Canaanite scribes were composed in a strange mixed Akkadian/West Semitic dialect. Since this hybrid language is confined to the area known from the geographical texts as Canaan, the West Semitic linguistic features can legitimately be called "Canaanite."

Ugaritic is usually called a Canaanite dialect, but in spite of many isoglosses (and also syntactic and literary expressions and phrases) there are strong similarities to some dialects of Aramaic. The short, so-called Phoenician alphabet of only 22 characters was known sporadically at Ugarit (in contrast to the native alphabet with many more consonants), but only as an intrusion, an import.

Bibliography. M. C. Astour, "The Origin of the Terms 'Canaan,' 'Phoenician,' and 'Purple,'" *JNES* 24 (1965): 346-50; N. P. Lemche, *The Canaanites and Their Land.* JSOTSup 110 (Sheffield, 1991); B. Mazar (Maisler), "Canaan and the Canaanites," *BASOR* 102 (1946): 7-12; *The Early Biblical Period* (Jerusalem, 1980); A. F. Rainey, *Canaanite in the Amarna Tablets,* 4 vols. HO 25 (Leiden, 1996); "Unruly Elements in Late Bronze Canaanite Society," in *Pomegranates and Golden Bells,* ed. D. P. Wright, D. N. Freedman, and A. Hurvitz (Winona Lake, 1995), 481-96; "Who Is a Canaanite? A Review of the Textual Evidence," *BASOR* 304 (1996): 1-15; K. N. Schoville, "Canaanites and Amorites," in *Peoples of the Old Testament World,* ed. A. J. Hoerth, G. L. Mattingly, and E. M. Yamauchi (Grand Rapids, 1994), 157-82; M. S. Smith, "Myth and Mythmaking in Canaan and Ancient Israel," *CANE* 3:2031-41.

ANSON F. RAINEY

CANANAEAN (Gk. *Kananaíos*)

An epithet of Simon (7), a disciple of Jesus (Matt. 10:4 = Mark 3:18), apparently a transliteration of Aram. *qan'ān,* "zealot." At Luke 6:15; Acts 1:13 he is called Simon the Zealot.

CANDACE (Gk. *kandákē*)

An Ethiopic title for the queen and queen mother. The Candace mentioned in Acts 8:27 is not identified by a personal name. Philip baptized her treasurer, an Ethiopian eunuch who came to Jerusalem to worship. According to Bion of Soli (*Aethiopica* 1, ca. 2nd century B.C.E.), the Candace was the head of the government in the Nubian kingdom of Meroe (located in modern Sudan). The title Candace is also attested in several classical sources (cf. Strabo *Geog.* 17.1.54; Dio Cassius *Hist.* 54.5.4-5; Pliny *Nat. hist.* 6.35.186; Pseudo-Callistus 3.18).

JO ANN H. SEELY

CANNEH (Heb. *kannēh*)

A Mesopotamian city that maintained trade relations with Tyre (Ezek. 27:23). Older attempts to identify it with Calneh (Amos 6:2) have been discredited.

CANON OF THE OLD TESTAMENT

A Christian term for the religious writings of ancient Israel held as sacred by Judaism and Christianity. The name "Old Testament" reflects the Christian movement's self-understanding as the fulfillment of Jeremiah's prophecy (Jer. 31:31) of a new covenant (Lat. *testamentum*) between God and Israel. Judaism uses a variety of designations for its sacred writings, including: (1) "scripture," from Heb. *miqrā',* "that which is read aloud;" (2) "Tanak," an acronym created from the names of the three traditional divisions of the Hebrew Scriptures, Torah (Law), Nebi'im (Prophets), and Kethubim (Writings); and (3) "Torah," after the section of the Scriptures that is most important for Jewish practice.

The development of the OT canon is a result of the interaction between two distinct but inseparable meanings of the term "canon." "Canon" is derived from Semitic *qāneh,* "reed," and takes its meaning metaphorically from the use of such objects as measuring devices. When applied to a literary collection, canon in its strictest sense refers to a fixed list of texts possessing an exclusive status relative to other writings. On the basis of such a definition, one might assume that the OT canon possessed a uniform shape and a precise date of origin. However, evidence for its history provides neither a clearly identifiable date of origin nor a single, universally accepted description of its contents. Under these circumstances, a broader definition is required. Canon in its broader sense is the normative functioning of given texts within social groups, without regard to the fixed content or exclusive status of the texts in use. By this definition, the texts of the OT were employed as a fluid, functional "canon-in-the-making" for many years prior to their ultimate definition as a fixed and exclusive collection.

Evidence for a Fixed Canon

Hebrew manuscripts and rabbinic listings of the definitive books of the Jewish Scriptures include 24 books arranged in a tripartite division of Torah, Prophets, and Writings. The numbering of the books reflects the number of individual scrolls used to record each book in antiquity.

The earliest reference to a fixed collection of Jewish Scriptures is found in the writings of the historian Josephus (*Ag. Ap.* 1.8, ca. 90 B.C.E.). According to Josephus, the 22 sacred books of the Jewish Scriptures were written during Israel's classical period of prophetic inspiration, from the time of Moses to the period of Judean restoration in the mid-5th century. Although the contents of the Scriptures are described in three sections, these sections are not identical to the tripartite rabbinic division. Josephus' canon consisted of: (1) the five books of Moses; (2) 13 prophetic books, including not only the eight books of the rabbinic "Prophets" section, but also Job, Daniel, Chronicles, Ezra-Nehemiah, and Esther; and (3) the four books of Psalms, Proverbs, Ecclesiastes, and the Song of Songs. The difference between the 22 books in Josephus' list and the 24 in the rabbinic lists is usually explained by counting Ruth with Judges and Lamentations with Jeremiah. The number 22 is identical to the number of letters in the Hebrew alphabet, symbolizing the completeness of the collection. The tradition of counting the books as 24 is attested in 4 Ezra 14:45, a passage roughly contemporaneous with Josephus.

Attempts to trace the history of a fixed collection of Scriptures to a time earlier than Josephus are frustrated by a complex set of findings. The LXX, the ancient translation of the Jewish Scriptures from Hebrew into Greek, provides earlier chronological evidence for the history of the OT canon, but not without complicating that history a great deal. Except for the Torah, the LXX preserves the books in a different order, based loosely on chronology and literary typology, and with a variety of textual divergences from existing Hebrew manuscripts. The most significant difference is that the Greek translation included several writings not included in the Hebrew canon. Additional texts found in the LXX but not in Hebrew manuscripts and lists include 1-2 Esdras, Judith, Tobit, 1-2 Maccabees, Wisdom of Solomon, Sirach, and Baruch, as well as numerous additions to individual books.

The Greek translation of the Jewish Scriptures owes its preservation to the Christian movement. The Greek Bible was the Scripture of the early Church, a fact reflected not only in the numerous citations of the LXX found in the NT, but also in the acceptance of most of the books of the Greek Bible into the canon of the early Church, books that have been retained until the present time in the canon of the Roman Catholic and Orthodox Christian Churches. Although Protestant Christianity accepts as canonical only those books of the Jewish Scriptures preserved in Hebrew, the Protestant OT still follows the order of the LXX and not the Hebrew Bible. Until the 19th century, even printed editions of the Protestant Bible included the deuterocanonical books of the Catholic and Orthodox OT, which are designated as "Apocrypha" by Protestant Christianity.

The best explanation of the difference between the number and order of books in the rabbinic Jewish canon and that of the LXX manuscripts and the early Church is that, apart from the five books of the Torah, the limits and divisions of the Jewish Scriptures were not fully defined at the time of the translation into Greek, between the 3rd and the 1st centuries B.C.E. The manuscript discoveries from the Dead Sea region, especially Qumran, support this conclusion. The Jewish sect living at Qumran preserved and esteemed religious writings beyond those of the subsequent Hebrew canon, such as the pseudonymous books of Jubilees and Enoch, as well as texts unique to the Qumran community. The overall picture that the LXX and Qumran manuscripts yield is that prior to the 1st century C.E. the 24 books of the Hebrew canon were preserved, translated, employed, and esteemed as Scripture, but, apart from the Torah, they did not possess an exclusive status nor a uniform shape. Based upon the available evidence, prior to the last half of the 1st century C.E., the Jewish Scriptures consisted of the Torah, a loosely defined group of writings referred to as "the Prophets," and an undefined group of miscellaneous writings.

Process of Canonization

Although identifying the mid-to-late 1st century C.E. as the date of the earliest explicitly limited collection of Jewish Scriptures satisfies the strict definition of canon as a fixed collection of exclusive status, such a description excludes extensive evidence for the authoritative usage of most of the OT at times much earlier than this minimal date of origin. Some argue that the present form of portions of biblical material may be traced back directly to the historical figure of Moses. Most would agree that, at the very least, material preserved in Deut. 12–26 is directly related to the scroll of law promulgated by King Josiah of Judah in the 7th century (2 Kgs. 22:8–23:25). A great portion of the Jewish Scriptures took their present shape in the 6th century during the Babylonian Exile, so that by the time Ezra the scribe came to Jerusalem from Babylon in the mid-5th century "with the Law of his God in his hand" (Ezra 7:14), much of the subsequent OT canon was circulating in roughly its present form.

The difference between the relatively late emergence of the exclusive status of the OT canon and the great antiquity of the normative usage of the OT writings demonstrates the necessity of expanding the definition of canon to include the more general concept of a text's function as a normative standard of evaluation. In the functional stage of canon formation, the status of a canonical work is implicitly assumed in its usage. Further, the canonical function of a work is contingent upon the situation in which it is used and is therefore subject to change given the exigencies of the moment. The fixed, definitive OT canon is the final, reflective stage of a lengthy and complex process during which the biblical texts continued to function normatively over an extended series of circumstances. Due to the implicit and somewhat random nature of the continuous normative use of the canonical books, the process of the canon's development is best described in a theoretical, rather than objective, manner.

The initial stage in the formation of the OT canon was the written preservation of its contents. For much of the OT material, however, this stage of the process is shrouded in mystery. The current written form of most OT books is the result of a process of collection or compilation of material existing in a previous form, whether oral or written, that cannot be recreated with great certainty.

In order to continue the process that leads to canonization, the written material required some form of publication or official sanction within a community. The account given in 2 Kgs. 23 of Josiah's promulgation of the Deuteronomic law code provides a rare glimpse of the kind of official publication that was necessary for the survival of biblical literature, despite the silence of the biblical record regarding such official sanctions.

The fact that ancient Near Eastern texts outside the Bible have survived only as archaeological discoveries shows that official publication and sanction alone do not guarantee continuous canonical status. Published texts must be reproduced textually, an effort not to be underestimated in a predominantly oral culture. Economic factors related to training scribes, procuring and preparing writing materials, reproducing lengthy texts by hand, storing the texts and the copies, and repeating the copying process required a highly motivated interest group. The preserved texts must have met some pressing need of the preserving community, whether for self-understanding or community governance, in order to justify such expense in terms of labor and materials. Israel's understanding of its traditions as divine revelation, whether as priestly instruction *(tôrâ)* or as prophetic word *(dāḇār)*, reflects the explicit religious value of the preserved traditions. References to ancient books no longer extant, such as the Book of the Wars of the Lord (Num. 21:14) and the Book of Jashar (Josh. 10:13; 2 Sam. 1:18), suggest that only a fraction of Israelite literature was esteemed valuable enough by succeeding generations to receive continuous reproduction.

Beyond physical reproduction, textual transmission by succeeding generations required various degrees of actualizing interpretation in order to appropriate older texts to new situations. Often such interpretation took the form of editorial alteration of the text itself, a process that is demonstrable for the OT by comparing the texts of various ancient manuscripts. Other contemporizing interpretations circulated independently of the biblical text in the form of oral tradition. The description in Neh. 8 of Ezra reading the Torah of Moses while the Levites "interpret and give the sense" provides a clear example of the role of interpretation in the transmission of valued texts.

If a text survives long enough due to continued actualization and also the continued survival of the interpreting community, then it achieves added significance not only for its content but also for its "timeless" character. The text is afforded a "classical" status relative to other literature because of its antiquity and durability. Such a phenomenon would explain the proliferation of pseudonymous writings during the 3rd and 2nd centuries. Eventually, a level of "critical" study emerges in order to distinguish classical literature from other imitative, archaizing works. The emerging boundaries between a classic text and a secondary text are illustrated by comparing the book of Daniel, which is included in the canon perhaps because of its exilic narrative setting, and the book of Sirach, which, although highly esteemed by both Judaism and Christianity, nevertheless is excluded from the Jewish canon because of its self-conscious and explicit origin in the 2nd century B.C.E. By the time of Josephus, the canon was defined to exclude not only texts written later than the time of Ezra and Nehemiah, but also those texts claiming to have been written earlier than Moses.

Study and reflection upon classical texts increases the status of those texts and provides the intellectual context for a defined canon. After the number of canonical works is determined, the text, arrangement, and classification of the contents develop a degree of standardization. It is theoretically possible that a text might be removed or added to the canon at this late stage, but such changes are extremely unlikely. The latter, reflective stages of the canonical process possess a self-perpetuating tendency.

Canon and Interpretation

The concept of the OT canon as a distinct stage in the history of the biblical text has received increased attention in recent scholarship. In addition to the various other stages of development of biblical texts, the final, "canonical" form of the text has become a topic of renewed investigation. Study of texts in their canonical form presumes that the text has undergone a genre transformation from a prior literary category to the distinct category of normative Scripture and may be productively interpreted as such.

Bibliography. J. Barr, *Holy Scripture: Canon, Authority, Criticism* (Philadelphia, 1983); J. Barton, *Oracles of God* (London, 1986); B. S. Childs, *Introduction to the Old Testament as Scripture* (Philadelphia, 1979); D. N. Freedman, *The Unity of the Hebrew Bible* (Ann Arbor, 1991); J. A. Sanders, *From Sacred Story to Sacred Text* (Philadelphia, 1987); B. H. Smith, *Contingencies of Value: Alternative Perspectives for Critical Theory* (Cambridge, Mass., 1988).

BARRY A. JONES

CANON OF THE NEW TESTAMENT

One cannot discuss the issue of the NT canon today without acknowledging a diversity of evaluations on the part of scholars who approach it from diverse starting points. The following account assumes the permanent validity of the traditional NT canon but is written in dialogue with other views, particularly those which, from the historical evidence, would question its legitimacy.

Prophetic Foundation of the Gospel

The germ of a NT canon can be regarded as implicit in the consummation of redemption which we know as the incarnation, death, resurrection, and ascension of Jesus. This is already postulated in the OT, in places such as Jer. 31:31-34, which predicts a new covenant between God and his people. The author of Hebrews, who explicitly appropriates Jeremiah's prophecy, utilizes other OT texts as well which stress the incompleteness or temporary nature of the old covenant modes and point forward to something better to be realized in Christ (Heb. 7:17, 20; 8:8-13; 10:5-10, 16-18). It was a fundamental conviction of the early Church that the OT Scriptures themselves anticipated a greater redemption, and an addendum of divine revelation cannot be seen as an unnatural consequence of the realized prophetic hope once it came. In the words of Jesus in Luke 24:47 it is seen that not only "the Christ event" but even the mission and message of Jesus' first followers were predicted by the prophets: "thus it is written. . .that repentance and forgiveness of sins is to be proclaimed in his name to all nations, beginning from Jerusalem." Isaiah had foretold a light to the nations (Isa. 49:6); a new law and word of the Lord was to break forth from Jerusalem (Isa. 2:4-5 = Mic. 4:1- 3). The prophets predicted not only a Messiah, but a message to accompany him (Rom. 1:1-2; 15:16-22; Isa. 66:18-21). Therefore, inasmuch as the eventual NT canon is the crystallization of the message of the original apostolic mission, it has its authorization in principle in the OT Scriptures themselves.

Authorization and Message of the Apostles

This authorization receives it highest validation in Jesus, as can be observed in two ways. First, the original apostolic mission was grounded in a special commission from Jesus. As his representatives the apostles stand and speak for Jesus (Matt. 10:40; cf. John 13:20; 20:21). Alongside him they constitute the foundation of the Church (Matt. 16:18; Gal. 2:9; Eph. 2:20; Rev. 21:14). They are uniquely endowed for their work by the Holy Spirit (Matt. 10:18-20; Mark 13:11; Acts 1:8; John 14:26; 15:26, 27; 16:13, 15). The concept of the "witness" in 1 Peter and Luke-Acts and the "eye-witness" appeal of John 1:1-3 correspond to this. The unique authority of the apostles, set apart from that of the continuing offices in the Church, is plainly observed in early, nonapostolic writers (1 Clem. 44:1-4; Ignatius *Rom.* 4.3; *Magn.* 6.1; *Trall.* 7.1; 12.2; Polycarp *Phil.* 3.2; 6.3).

Second, the mission of the apostles is presented in the NT as the mission of Jesus himself. In Isa. 49:6 the commission to bright light to the Gentiles belongs to the Messiah. But the mission of Paul is the mission of Jesus (Rom. 15:18-20), so Isaiah's prophecy relates directly to Paul's own calling (Acts 13:47). Throughout the book of Acts the apostles' work in evangelizing the nations is represented as the work of the ascended Christ (2:33; 14:3), and their preaching is the word of the Lord (6:7; 12:24; 19:20). The form of the gospel message was given by the Lord himself (Gal. 1:12) and by the Lord through his apostles (1 Cor. 11:23; 15:8; 2 Pet. 3:2). Jesus will bring his "other sheep," and they will heed his voice (John 10:16), but that voice they can hear only through his chosen apostles (17:18, 20). The apostolic testimony will be the means to transport sinners from unbelief to faith (John 20:31).

From the NT point of view, then, the apostolic mission is uniquely the mission of Jesus himself and is part and parcel of his own redemptive work as predicted by the prophets.

Consciousness of Apostolic Authority

It is often asserted that the 1st-century Church had only the OT, and some words of Jesus orally transmitted, as its authority. Yet in the writings of the NT it is often perceptible that the authors regarded their teachings as the Word of God (1 Thess. 2:13) in no way inferior, and in important respects superior, to the Word of God they knew as the Law, Prophets, and Writings (1 Pet. 1:10-12; Tit. 1:3; Heb. 1:1-2). Nor did this evaluation of the divine sanction of their message disappear when that message was committed to writing. Paul equates his written word by letter with his spoken word (2 Thess. 2:15; 3:14), and his spoken word of instruction and proclamation with the Word of God (1 Thess. 2:13; 2 Thess. 3:1, 6, 14; cf. 1 Cor. 14:37). In Eph. 3:4 Paul anticipates that his readers will recognize his insight into the mystery of Christ not only by hearing him but by reading his epistle. That Paul perceived his epistolary activity, though addressed to many particular concerns of individual churches, as having more than merely local validity is seen in his instructions to exchange letters (Col. 4:16) and probably in the character of Ephesians, which seems to have been sent as a circular letter to several churches initially. The collecting and publishing of Paul's letters, at any rate, mark a time when they were perceived as valid for the entire Church, and likely as perpetually valid. There is now good evidence from the contemporary practice of letter publishing and from the stability of the Pauline corpus in the manuscript tradition for believing that it was Paul himself who first collected and published an edition of his letters for distribution among the churches. A collection of Paul's letters is generally available in the congregations and known as Scripture at least by the time of 2 Pet. 3:16. And throughout the NT one discerns the deliberate construction of a legacy, a deposit, a body of teaching to be left to succeeding generations (1 Cor. 11:2; 15:1-8; 1 Tim. 6:20; 2 Tim. 1:14; 2:2; Luke 1:1-3; 2 Pet. 1:12-15; 1 John 1:1-4; Jude 3, 17; Rev. 1:3; 22:18-19).

Extent of the NT Canon

The authorization of a new installment of revelation implicit in the redemption accomplished by Jesus did not of course mark out beforehand the precise number or identity of the documents which would eventually embody that revelation. From the theological point of view, canonicity, or scriptural status, is first of all a divine judgment, though its human echo be imperfect and not immediately unanimous.

It would be the end of the 4th century (Athanasius' 39th Festal Letter, 369; the councils of Hippo Regius, 393, and Carthage, 397) before the churches

CANON OF THE NEW TESTAMENT

of East and West could concur on the full 27 books which since that time have been commonly confessed in all major branches of Christendom (portions of the Syriac and Ethiopian churches never did conform completely to the rest). Yet it has been widely recognized that by the end of the 2nd century a "core canon" of 20 or more books was generally acknowledged throughout the churches. This has been strenuously challenged, however, by scholars who maintain that the Church was unconcerned with canonicity, or the boundaries of its collections of scriptural literature, until the 4th century.

It is true that in the period of the Apostolic Fathers (ca. 90-140) the apostolic Gospels and Letters are cited along with some occasional oral traditions of Jesus' words — both used matter-of-factly, as if accepted by all Christians. Oral tradition already growing less reliable, however, the Church even at this time was depending with increasing exclusivity upon its written deposit.

Some have held that the continued production of apostolic pseudepigrapha in some circles in the early centuries demonstrates the openness of the Church to receiving new books. But the preponderant use of the names of apostles for such works shows instead where authority in the Church was perceived by all to lie. Serapion of Antioch (fl. 180s) is often cited for his willingness to accept the Gospel of Peter as a scriptural document. However, it was not a matter of scriptural status, but of fitness for edificatory reading, as can be seen from his words, "we receive Peter and the other apostles as Christ, but the writings which falsely bear their names we reject, as men of experience, knowing that such were not handed down to us" (Eusebius *HE* 6.12.3-6). Serapion, like others of his generation, did not conceive of the Church as authorized to choose the documents it pleased, but as bound to use and preserve what had been delivered to it.

It is customary to speak of "criteria" such as apostolicity, catholicity, use by the majority of churches, and orthodoxy, as used by the churches of the 2nd through 4th centuries in determining their canonical documents. Whereas these did function negatively to exclude certain books, we do not, however, read of others finding acceptance because they "passed" the tests. Such books simply functioned as they had from the beginning, as authoritative documents handed down to the Church by its apostles and prophets. Most were indeed believed to have been authored by apostles, but "apostolicity" extended also to works by the apostles' immediate co-workers involved with them in the original apostolic mission. By the end of the 2nd century, when church leaders began to reckon with the problem of differing collections, there could have been no serious question about the reception of the bulk of the books (four Gospels, Acts, 13 or 14 Pauline Epistles, 1 Peter, 1 John), and these "agreed" books set the stage, in terms of apostolic orthodoxy, for the acceptance of the rest. Whatever "criteria" might have been employed were scarcely relevant for any but Hebrews, James, 2 Peter, 2 and 3 John, Jude, and Revelation.

Of those books about which some controversy existed, Hebrews and Revelation suffered subsequently after an early recognition. In the case of Hebrews, which was used by Clement of Rome in the 1st century, the uncertainties concerned authorship, with residual doubts about a perceived penitential rigorism (Heb. 6:4-6). With Revelation, conversely, the initial attacks in the 3rd century were based on an alleged support for Montanism and then chiliasm, prompting further questions about authorship. These problems prevented unanimity in the 2nd and 3rd centuries as Hebrews was doubted in the West, and Revelation in the East even through the 4th century. Eusebius relates that besides Hebrews and Revelation, 2 Peter, 2 and 3 John, Jude, and James, though "known to most," were disputed by some (Eusebius *HE* 3.25.3). We read of no theological objections to these five short epistles; the doubts concerned authorship and were due in great part to a lack of citation in earlier writers (*HE* 2.23.25). All these books were known and used by the church in Alexandria in the 2nd and 3rd centuries, until Revelation was temporarily eclipsed.

Despite the impression sometimes given, there are only a handful of documents outside the traditional 27 which might have enjoyed temporary, local prestige approaching that of the others. Surveying the Church's history at the beginning of the 4th century, Eusebius (*HE* 3.25) lists five such works which he judges must be considered spurious: the Acts of Paul, Shepherd of Hermas, Apocalypse of Peter, Letter of Barnabas, and Teachings of the Apostles. In addition 1 Clement should perhaps be mentioned. The first of these was known to Tertullian, who says it was written recently by an Asian presbyter out of the love for Paul, though it got him defrocked (*De bapt.* 17).

The Shepherd of Hermas was cited sparingly but quite favorably by Irenaeus, Clement of Alexandria, and Origen. Though he rejects it, Eusebius tells us it was "read publicly" in many churches (*HE* 3.3.6). It was specifically excluded, however, by the Muratorian Fragment, the earliest surviving NT canon list, from ca. the end of the 2nd century, as neither apostolic nor prophetic, and late. It was sharply criticized by Tertullian, who also relates that both orthodox and Montanist councils had by then rejected it (*De pudicitia* 10).

Clement of Alexandria cited the Apocalypse of Peter, as if by Peter, though he was not followed in this by Origen. The Muratorian Fragment says it is accepted by the Church, "although some of us do not want it to be read in the church." It is absent from the 4th-century canon lists.

The Letter of Barnabas was also used by Clement of Alexandria, though this was predicated on the mistaken notion that it was written by the companion of Paul and was therefore quasi-apostolic. Origen also regarded it highly, though he did not write any commentary or homily on it. Neither Irenaeus nor Tertullian seems to know it, and it was practically unknown in the West.

The Didache, a church manual not later than the early 2nd century, was also cited favorably by both Clement and Origen. It is not mentioned by the Muratorian Fragment or evidently used by other early Fathers, though its "two ways" doctrine may be the source of the same teaching in Barnabas. It is listed by Athanasius as a catechetical document, but not canonical.

The epistle of the Roman church to the Corinthians, commonly known as 1 Clement, was universally beloved, though clearly placed by Irenaeus in a category with Polycarp's epistles, and not with the apostles. It is absent from the Muratorian Fragment and from all but the most eccentric of the 4th-century canon lists (the Apostolic Canons).

Current attempts to promote the 2nd-century Gospel of Thomas do so in the face of the unified aversion of the patristic sources. Hippolytus (ca. 235) says a book of this name belonged to the Naassene Gnostics (*Ref.* 5.7.20). Origen criticized it as spurious (*Hom. Lk.* 1), and Eusebius advised that it be "shunned as altogether wicked and impious" (*HE* 3.25.6).

Athanasius' Festal Letter of 369 is probably the first extant list of the present 27 books and them alone, though there is one disputed text in Origen. From the end of the 4th century there is virtual unanimity among East and West on the NT canon. Luther launched a well-known attack on the Epistle of James, and to a lesser extent Jude, 2 Peter, and Revelation, but not even his most devoted successors followed suit. Calvin saw no conflict in these books with the doctrine of justification by faith, found nothing in them unworthy of apostles, and accepted their self-testimony and the testimony of the early Church. The Protestant churches have confirmed this judgment, adding their voices to the confession of Orthdoxy and Roman Catholicism.

Bibliography. H. Y. Gamble, *The New Testament Canon* (Minneapolis, 1985); G. M. Hahneman, *The Muratorian Fragment and the Development of the Canon* (Oxford, 1992); C. E. Hill, "The Debate over the Muratorian Fragment and the Development of the Canon," *WTJ* 57 (1995): 437-52; B. M. Metzger, *The Canon of the New Testament* (Oxford, 1987); H. N. Ridderbos, *Redemptive History and the New Testament Scriptures,* 2nd ed. (Phillipsburg, N.J., 1988); D. Trobisch, *Paul's Letter Collection* (Minneapolis, 1994). CHARLES E. HILL

CANTICLES

See SONG OF SOLOMON.

CAPERNAUM (Heb. *kĕp̄ar naḥum*; Gk. *Kapharnaoúm*)

A city on the northwestern shore of the Sea of Galilee, identified with modern Tell Ḥum (Talḥum). Located just to the west of where the Jordan empties into the Sea of Galilee, Capernaum was a border town separating Herod Antipas' and Herod Philip's territory during Jesus' ministry. No texts prior to the 1st century C.E. mention Capernaum, and it is doubtful that the Nahum in its name refers to the OT prophet. Josephus twice anecdotally mentions Capernaum without giving it any political or cultural significance: he once fell off his horse near there, and he (perhaps incorrectly) identified the "Springs of Heptapegon" as the "Springs of Capernaum" (*Vita* 403; *BJ* 3.520). Later rabbinic literature notes Capernaum's association with the *minim,* an unorthodox Jewish group (which some simply assume to be Jewish-Christians; cf. Qoh. Rab. 1.8).

Archaeological excavations fill the void left in literary texts for Capernaum. More than a century of excavations have unearthed some walls and sherds from the Bronze Age, but the most significant remains date to the Roman, Byzantine, and Islamic periods. The most imposing structures are the 4th-century synagogue and the 5th-century octagonal church. The synagogue is one of the largest in Israel; its white limestone facades stood in stark contrast to the black basalt houses that encircled it. Of interest because of parallel names in the NT is an Aramaic inscription on a column from the Byzantine period that reads "Alphaeus, son of Zebedee, son of John, made this column; may he be blessed (*CIJ,* 982-83). Whether a basalt floor underneath this synagogue represents a 1st-century synagogue or not is disputed. The 5th-century octagonal church known as St. Peter's House was rebuilt on a 4th-century house church. Christian graffiti makes it likely that this was the site mentioned by the 4th-century pilgrim Egeria as the "house of the prince of the apostles." One speculates that the remains under this structure, the so-called *insula sacra* which was built in the 1st century B.C.E. and occupied in the 1st century C.E., were associated with Peter (Mark 1:29-31). Recent excavations have also uncovered a small bathhouse, analogous to those used by Roman soldiers stationed along Rome's borders. The obvious link to the Capernaum centurion mentioned in the NT is undermined by the bathhouse's likely date to the late 1st or 2nd century (Matt. 8:5-13 = Luke 7:1-10).

More significant than these later structures for understanding the life of Jesus has been the picture of 1st-century Capernaum that the excavations paint: crudely made basalt houses reinforced with mud and dung and covered with thatched roofs (cf. Mark 2:1-12). Houses consisted of rooms and animal pens centered around a central beaten earth courtyard. The unpaved roads, the crudely made harbor, and the lack of public Graeco-Roman architectural features renders the Gospel's use of Gk. *pólis* hardly appropriate in its proper technical sense (Matt. 9:1; Luke 4:31). With a population of no more than 1500, it was a large village that profited from fishing, as the many fishhooks found there indicate. A 1st-century boat salvaged by archaeologists at nearby Kibbutz Ginnosar provides a good illustration of the type of small boat used by Galilean fishermen. A Roman milestone dating to the early 2nd century confirms that a major road led through Capernaum towards Syria, and Matthew's traditional identification as a tax collector can perhaps more precisely be tied to border tolls (Matt. 9:9).

Ruins of the 4th-century C.E. synagogue at Capernaum, a basilica with gabled roof. Its richly ornamented architectural details are unique among the synagogues of Palestine
(Consulate General of Israel in New York)

The Gospels indicate that Jesus' ministry centered around Capernaum, and it would not be inaccurate to label it his base of operations. Matt. 4:13 states that Jesus left Nazareth for Capernaum, and Mark 2:1 describes Jesus as being "at home" there. The Gospels record several miracles as having occurred in Capernaum, including the healing of a paralytic who was lowered through an opening in the roof where Jesus was preaching (Mark 2:1-12) and the exorcism of an unclean spirit from a man in the synagogue (1:23-28). Five of the disciples were chosen in or near Capernaum: Peter and Andrew were from Capernaum and were called to follow Jesus near there (Mark 1:16, 29), James and John were fishing nearby when they were called (1:21), and Matthew's toll booth was apparently stationed there (Matt 9:9-13). Jesus' unique relationship with Capernaum is perhaps nowhere more apparent than in the vehement woe against Capernaum for its refusal to respond to his teachings (Matt. 11:23).

Bibliography. S. Loffreda, *A Visit to Capharnaum* (Jerusalem, 1972); Loffreda and V. Tzaferis, "Capernaum," *NEAEHL* 1:291-96; J. L. Reed, *The Population of Capernaum.* Institute for Antiquity and Christianity Occasional Paper 24 (Claremont, 1993); J. E. Taylor, *Christians and the Holy Places* (Oxford, 1993).

JONATHAN L. REED

CAPHAR-SALAMA (Gk. *Chapharsalama*)
A place near which the Syrian general Nicanor was ambushed, losing 500 soldiers in battle (1 Macc. 7:31-32). Some scholars identify it with Khirbet Selmah (167140) near ej-Jîb, ca. 10 km. (6 mi.) NW of Jerusalem.

CAPHTOR (Heb. *kaptôr*)
The seventh "child" of Mizraim (Egypt) (Gen. 10:13-14 = 1 Chr. 1:11-12). Deut. 2:23 reports that the Caphtorim displaced the Avvim along the Palestinian coast as far as Gaza. Caphtor is, according to Jer. 47:4; Amos 9:7, the place of origin of the Philistines. The parenthetical note in Gen. 10:14, however, indicates that the Casluhim, not the Caphtorim, are the ancestors of the Philistines, but many scholars suggest that the note be transposed to the end of the verse.

The name Caphtor is traditionally associated with the island of Crete. Texts from Mari and Ugarit mention a place called Kaptara, described as beyond the Upper Sea and within the sphere of influence of Sargon of Akkad. Egyptian documents frequently mention a place called Keftíu; since Egypt had extensive commercial relations with Crete after 2200 B.C.E., identifying Keftíu with Crete would account for the many references. Caphtor has also been identified with coastal areas of Asia Minor or Syria. (The LXX translates Caphtor as Cappadocia in Amos 9:7.) Crete, however, seems to be the most probable location.

Little archaeological or literary connections can be made between the Philistines and Crete/Caphtor. The Philistines may have "stopped over" in Caphtor in their journeys from some other homeland, or Caphtor may have become, by the 2nd millennium, a name for the entire Aegean area.

Bibliography. Y. Aharoni, *The Land of the Bible*, 2nd ed. (Philadelphia, 1979); G. A. Rendsburg, "Gen 10:13-14: An Authentic Hebrew Tradition Concerning the Origin of the Philistines," *JNSL* 13 (1987): 89-96. NANCY L. DECLAISSÉ-WALFORD

CAPPADOCIA (Gk. *Kappadokía*)

A rough, mountainous district in east central Asia Minor. Located N of Cilicia and the Tarsus Mountains, E of Phrygia and Galatia, and W of the Euphrates River, Cappadocia was renowned for raising horses, growing wheat, and producing wines. Because of its strategic mountain pass overlooks, it was often the object of foreign conquest, making it difficult to locate its shifting borders in antiquity. From 1700 until 1400 B.C.E., Cappadocia was a center of Hittite culture, known for its art of smelting iron and for its silver mines.

Originally the district included all the northeast territory of Asia Minor, but the northern part was segregated (probably under the Persians) and came to be known as Cappadocia on the Pontus (later, simply Pontus) and the southern region was called Great Cappadocia. Unlike the coastal regions of Asia Minor which came under strong Greek influence, this region deep within the rugged Anatolian territory perpetuated its Persian tendencies until the Romans made an alliance with King Ariarathes (164; cf. 1 Macc. 15:22). Mark Antony gave Cappadocia to Archelaus to rule as king (36 B.C.E.), a concession perpetuated by Augustus. When Tiberius succeeded Augustus, he called Archelaus to Rome and stripped him of his crown (14 C.E.). Cappadocia became a Roman province (17), administered as 10 districts since there were so few towns in the province.

Cappadocians were present at Pentecost (Acts 2:9), and were among the addressees of 1 Pet. 1:1. Their district was not visited by Paul, possibly because of its difficult geographical setting. Cappadocia became famous for the 4th-century theologians it produced: Basil (later of Caesarea), Gregory of Nazianzus, and Gregory of Nyssa.

RICHARD A. SPENCER

CAPTAIN

Usually a person of military rank (Heb. *śār*). The title is further qualified by the officer's specific responsibilities (e.g., Gen. 37:36; 2 Kgs. 1:9; 1 Sam. 22:7; Exod. 18:21). Heb. *śar ṣĕḇā'*, lit., "captain of the host" (2 Kgs. 5:1), is usually translated "commander in chief."

In the NT Gk. *stratēgós* is restricted to the Lukan material and is used often in its simplest sense as "captain" (Luke 22:4; NRSV "officer"), but also as "captain of the temple" (Luke 22:52; Acts 4:1; 5:24), i.e., a sanctuary guard. The plural is used of civic officials (NRSV "magistrates") in Acts (16:20, 22, 35, 36, 38).

The term *śār* is also found in the Mejad µashavyahu inscription, in an Arad letter, on two early seals, and in graffiti from Kuntilet 'Ajrud. Here, too, it is used in a military context. The seals and graffiti refer to a "captain of the city," probably the commander of a garrison town (cf. 2 Chr. 11:11, 18-23).

T. R. HOBBS

CAPTAIN OF THE TEMPLE

The priestly officer who presided over the temple guard and was subject to the high priest (Jer. 20:1; 1 Chr. 9:11; 2 Chr. 31:13; Neh. 11:11). The military aspect of the temple, for which the captain of the temple (Heb. *nāg̱îḏ*) was responsible, included policing, managing the gates, keeping sentry posts (Josephus *BJ* 6.5.3), and guarding the temple treasuries. The term, often translated as "chief officer," "supervisor," or "in charge," was also used in administrative contexts (e.g., 1 Kgs. 4:7).

In the NT the term (Gk. *stratēgós toú hieroú*) appears in Acts (4:1; 5:24; 26) and Luke (22:4, 52; the plural forms most likely indicate subordinates of the captain). Josephus notes that Ananus, the captain of the temple, was arrested with Ananias the high priest and sent to Claudius Caesar in Rome (*Ant.* 20.6.2).

BRUCE W. GENTRY

CAPTIVES

A term encompassing a range of meanings, including prisoner of war, slave, debtor, suspected criminal, deportee, exile, oppressed, and prisoner in a figurative sense. These categories must be understood in the circumstances of biblical times. The "prisoner" of the modern penal system is not found in the Bible. Thus, biblical texts dealing with liberty for captives (e.g., Luke 4:18) cannot be simplistically applied to today's society, where different principles of crime and punishment prevail.

In biblical times suspected criminals were held in what today would be termed "remand prisons" until trial and sentencing. Imprisonment was a transition to either physical punishment (e.g., flogging), death, slavery, or deportation and exile. Prisoners of war were treated the same. Imprisonment simply as a punishment was not known. Occasionally, persons suspected of subversive activities were held in prison to curb their activities and influence. Imprisonment of debtors in biblical times is best understood in the sense of hostage holding to force relatives and friends to honor the debts. The term "captives" was used of the "exiles," referring to those Israelites deported and living among foreigners such as Babylonians. In this case there is a suggestion of religious persecution: The Israelites are seen as suffering for their faith. Yet, in the eyes of the imperial authorities the deportation was political. Likewise in NT times, individuals such as Paul are viewed as imprisoned because they proclaimed Christ, while in the eyes of the civil authorities their offense was viewed as a disturbance of the peace.

With the possible exception of the debtor, the strictly biblical connotation of "captive" is that of an oppressed innocent. Today, the closest analogy is perhaps to be found in the case of refugees, displaced persons, prisoners of war, those persecuted for religious reasons, and prisoners of conscience.

MICHAEL CAHILL

CAPTIVITY

See EXILE.

CARAVAN

A traveling group with pack animals loaded with goods and merchandise. For countries lacking either the skill or ability to conduct commerce via sea travel, caravan trade was vital for economic well-being. The geographic position of Israel between three continents made it a center of overland commerce. As travel in the ancient Near East was a dangerous and difficult affair due to weather, wild animals, and roving bands of robbers, caravans provided an advantage of safety in numbers. Caravans were almost exclusively operated by governmental authorities. The king or clan leader could afford to provide an armed escort, maintain fortresses at strategic points along the way (e.g., Solomon's fortification at Arad), and guard the vital oasis water supplies. Only a very few "private" caravans are recorded in the history, though individuals and family groups were welcome to travel with a caravan. Caravans normally traveled at night to avoid the heat of the day and to reduce the likelihood of attack. Many caravans were remarkably large and could move substantial quantities of goods. Donkeys, mules and camels were the pack animals most often utilized, although by 1900 B.C. the stronger mules had replaced donkeys in most caravans. While donkeys or mules could carry larger loads and were simpler to manage, camels had the advantage of speed and the ability to travel longer distances between oases. The average caravan numbered 100-300 animals; however, one record testifies to a caravan of 3000 donkeys. On another occasion 170 camels transported 30 tons of merchandise from Damascus to Mecca.

The Bible records several notable caravans: Abraham's travels from Ur of the Chaldeans to Canaan (Gen. 12); the caravan of traders to whom Joseph was sold (Gen. 37:25); the queen of Sheba's visit to Solomon (1 Kgs. 10:1-2); and the night escape of Joseph, Mary, and Jesus from Bethlehem to Egypt (Matt. 2:14).

DENNIS M. SWANSON

CARBUNCLE

A deep red stone found on the Sinai Peninsula. The NAB reads "carbuncle" for Heb. *'eqdaḥ*, the material of idealized Zion's gates (Isa. 54:12). Other translations include "crystal," "beryl," "firestone," and "red granite." Some previous translations used "carbuncle" for *bāreqeṯ*, an engraved stone on the high priest's breastpiece (Exod. 28:17; 39:10) and a stone adorning the king of Tyre (Ezek. 28:13), where LXX *smáragdos*, "emerald," suggests a green-colored stone. Recent translations translate "emerald" or "feldspar."

JOSEPH E. JENSEN

CARCHEMISH (Heb. *karkĕmîš*)

A city in Syria located near the border of Turkey, ca. 100 km. (62 mi.) N of Aleppo. The city is well attested in the OT and Eblaite, Akkadian, Ugaritic, and Egyptian texts. Early digs by the British Museum in 1879 and 1911-1920 reveal a number of artifacts and a bit of architecture from the Neo-Hittite period.

Inhabited from Chalcolithic times, the site is near the prime ford of the upper Euphrates River. Thus the city was continually occupied, to take financial advantage of this natural geographic feature. The presence of the ford also made the site subject to frequent attacks, as most regional powers aspired to have access to the material wealth generated by the city. It enjoyed independence as reflected in the texts from Ebla, Mari, Emar, and Ugarit. Carchemish was subsumed by Mitanni (15th century B.C.E.), conquered by the Egyptian pharaoh Thutmose III (1504-1450), and ruled by the powerful Hittite king Šuppiluliuma I (ca. 1340). Beginning with his son Piyassili, five generations of Šuppiluliuma I's descendants ruled Carchemish as Hittite rule there outlived the Hittite Empire (which collapsed ca. 1200). The city dominated the political scene in Syria as a Hittite provincial capital. Hittite cultural influence likewise survived (hence the term Neo-Hittite), as statuary from the Iron Age betrays Hittite style. The city was incorporated into the Assyrian Empire in 717 by Sargon II, with its elite classes deported (cf. Isa. 10:9). The most significant event surrounding the city was the final destruction of the remnant of Assyrian forces with their Egyptian allies at the hand of Nebuchadnezzar's Babylonian forces in 605 (Jer. 46:2-12; 1 Esdr. 1:25). It was Judah's king Josiah's ill-advised attempt to prevent the Egyptian pharaoh Neco II from uniting with the Assyrians which cost him his life (2 Chr. 35:20-24).

MARK ANTHONY PHELPS

CARIA (Gk. *Karia*)

A region in southwest Asia Minor, bounded by Lydia on the north, Phrygia on the east, Lycia on the south, the Aegean Sea on the west, and the Mediterranean Sea on the southwest. The population of the coastal cities was Greek and the population of the interior would have considered themselves indigenous and related to the Lydians and Mysians. Controlled by the Persians and then after Alexander the Great by the island of Rhodes, Caria received its independence from the Romans. According to 1 Macc. 15:23 Rome wrote Caria and other countries declaring support for Simon's rule over the Jewish state. In 129 B.C.E. the region was incorporated into the Roman province of Asia.

Besides the major cities of Halicarnassus and Cnidus (Acts 27:7), Miletus was in Caria (Acts 20:15-17; 2 Tim. 4:20). Caria itself is not named in Acts since it was part of the province of Asia at the time of Paul's journeys. Ignatius of Antioch, on his journey to Rome and martyrdom, sent a letter to Tralles in Caria. Inscriptions, synagogue remains, and other evidence indicate that Caria had a significant Jewish population. DOUGLAS LOW

CARITES (Heb. *kārî*)
Bodyguards who helped Jehoiada the high priest protect the Jerusalem temple during the crowning of young Joash (2 Kgs. 11:4, 19). They may have performed a function similar to that of the Cherethites. Some scholars associate them with Caria, a region which supplied mercenaries to Egypt.

CARKAS (Heb. *karkas*)
One of the eunuchs serving as chamberlain to the Persian king Ahasuerus (Esth. 1:10).

CARMEL (Heb. *karmel*)
1. A wooded mountain range along the northern coast of Israel that runs northwest from the plain of Esdraelon to the Mediterranean coast near the modern city of Haifa, where its headland (Mt. Carmel or Jebel Kurmul) forms the harbor and the bay of Acre. The range separates the coastal plain of Acco to the north from the plains of Sharon and Philistia in the south. The average height of the mountain range is 457 m. (1500 ft.), with its highest point near Isfiya (530 m. [1742 ft.]). Because of Carmel's height and location near the coast, the temperatures during the summer are mild, and annual rainfall averages 91 cm. (36 in.). These factors gave rise to abundant vegetation, which explains why this region was called Carmel or "orchard."

The most memorable biblical event tied to this area revolved around the issue of fertility and divinity. According to 1 Kgs. 18 Elijah challenged the prophets of Baal and Asherah on Carmel. It was here that Yahweh demonstrated to the people of Israel that Baal was not the true God, by consuming the water-logged offering with fire/lightning and then sending what Baal could not, rain. The fire and rain were convincing proof of God's sovereignty to a people who had been practicing a syncretic religion.

2. A town in the Judean wilderness (cf. Josh. 15:55) that can be identified with modern el-Kirmil (162092), a village ca. 13 km. (8 mi.) SE of Hebron. It was in this area that Saul erected a monument in honor of his victory over the Amalekites (1 Sam. 15:12). In addition, the story of David and Abigail took place in this vicinity (1 Sam. 25; cf. 27:3). Carmel was part of a western line of fortifications protecting the highways of the area and the economic stability of the region, which focused primarily on animal breeding.

Bibliography. O. Borowski, "The Carmel-Formidable Barrier and Wedge into the Sea," *BibRev* 6/5 (1990): 46-52. RICK W. BYARGEON

CARMI (Heb. *karmî*) (also ACHAR)
1. The youngest son of Reuben, who accompanied the other sons of Jacob to Egypt (Gen. 46:9; Exod. 6:14; 1 Chr. 5:3; cf. Num. 26:6).

2. A Judahite and the father of Achan (Josh. 7:1, 18; called "Achar" at 1 Chr. 2:7).

3. A possible alternate name for Caleb at 1 Chr. 2:18.

CARMITES (Heb. *karmî*)
A Reubenite clan whose ancestor was Carmi **1** (Num. 26:6).

CARNAIM (Gk. *Karnaim*)
A city in Gilead whose inhabitants had been taken captive (1 Macc. 5:26; 2 Macc. 12:21, 26), identified with modern Tell Sheikh Ṣaʿd/Tel Ṣaʿd (247249), 5 km. (3 mi.) NE of Tell ʿAštarah. It may be the same as Ashteroth-karnaim.

CARNELIAN
A deep brown or red stone prized for carving and engraving. NJPSV, NAB, and NRSV read "carnelian" for Heb. *ʾōḏem* (LXX *sárdion*), an engraved stone on the high priest's breastpiece (Exod. 28:17; 39:10) and a stone adorning the king of Tyre (Ezek. 28:13). In the NT the NAB, NIV, NRSV, and REB read "carnelian" for Gk. *sárdion*, describing God's appearance (Rev. 4:3) and a course in the foundation of the city wall of the new Jerusalem (21:20). Other translations of these Hebrew and Greek terms include "ruby," "sard," "sardin," and "sardius." JOSEPH E. JENSEN

CAROB
A leguminous tree (*Ceratonia siliquia*), thought to be the *kerátion* of Luke 15:16 (cf. Matt. 3:4). It produces pods, the pea-like seeds of which are edible. The tree is sometimes called St. John's bread because tradition holds that he ate these pods. RANDALL W. YOUNKER

CARPENTER
The skill of carpentry was not fully developed in OT Israel. Perhaps because of their nomadic background, the Israelites depended on the more highly skilled artisans from Tyre in the construction of the temple and palaces under David and Solomon. King Hiram sent carpenters (Heb. *ḥārāš ʿēṣ*, "worker in wood") for these projects (2 Sam. 5:11; 1 Chr. 14:1). Later, when the temple needed repairs, Jehoash and Josiah were able to find native carpenters for the renovation projects (2 Kgs. 12:11; 22:6). However, the Babylonian Captivity depleted Jerusalem of these skilled carpenters, along with other artisans and wealthy citizens (Jer. 24:1). In Zerubbabel's time carpenters were imported from Phoenicia for the construction of the temple (Ezra 3:7).

Carpenters' tools included the compass, pencil, plane, saw, hammer, ax, adz, chisel, plumb line, drill, file, and square (Isa. 44:13; Amos 7:7-8). Joints could be formed with the use of dowels and nails. Mortised, dovetailed, and mitered joints were common. Artwork from tombs, especially in Egypt, illustrates the use of these tools and techniques. In some cities, carpenters may have formed guilds

(1 Chr. 4:14), and they also used their skills to carve idols (Isa. 40:20; Jer. 10:3).

In the NT carpentry included the construction of yokes, plows, threshing boards, benches, beds, boxes, coffins, boats, and houses. Larger construction projects, such as those sponsored by the Herods, may have provided employment for carpenters *(téktōn)* such as Joseph and Jesus (Matt. 13:55; Mark 6:3). The addition of a room to Palestinian homes was common and in some cases might require the help of a carpenter.

Bibliography. H. Hodges, *Technology in the Ancient World* (New York, 1980); S. Safrai and M. Stern, eds., *The Jewish People in the First Century*, 2 vols. (Assen, 1974-76). DENNIS GAERTNER

CARPUS (Gk. *Kárpos*)
An associate of the Apostle Paul (perhaps his host) residing at Troas, in whose care Paul had entrusted his books and parchments (2 Tim. 4:13). While in prison awaiting his execution, Paul asked that these materials be returned to him. The cloak cited here (Gk. *phailónēs*) may have been a case in which books could be placed for protection.

CARSHENA (Heb. *karšĕnāʾ*)
One of the seven princes of the Medes and Persians called to advise King Ahasuerus (Esth. 1:14).

CART
A wheeled vehicle drawn by horses (Isa. 28:28) or cows (1 Sam. 6:7) that is used to transport people or goods. Carts were most often employed for agricultural work (Isa. 28:27; Amos 12:13), but one was used to carry the ark of the covenant (1 Sam. 6:7; 2 Sam. 6:3 = 1 Chr. 13:7). The ropes that pull a cart are used as an analogy for the way in which one pulls sin behind him (Isa. 5:18), while a laden cart is a symbol for punishment given by God for Israel's transgressions (Amos 2:13).

Nonbiblical sources suggest that carts with four disc wheels were used in battle, but this type of vehicle has been found only in agricultural or mythological contexts. A cart's weight and lack of maneuverability would not allow for outstanding performance on the battlefield, nor would the rough terrain in the land of Israel be suitable for it. The two-wheeled chariot was clearly used in military contexts. Information gleaned from wall and vase paintings, reliefs, actual chariots, the context of horse skeletons, and literary descriptions suggests that the cart seems to have been accessible to all, while the chariot was the prerogative of the elite in the ancient world. KATHARINE A. MACKAY

CASIPHIA (Heb. *kāsipyāʾ*)
An unidentified place in Babylonia ("place of silversmiths[?]"), not far from the river Ahava (Ezra 8:17). It was to this village that Ezra sent a delegation asking Iddo, its leading resident, for "ministers for the house of our God."

CASLUHIM (Heb. *kasluḥîm*)
Descendants of Egypt the son of Ham (Gen. 10:6, 14; 1 Chr. 1:8, 12), called ancestors of the Philistines. Some scholars relate these people to the inhabitants of the region near Mt. Cassius, E of the Nile Delta.

See CAPHTOR.

CASSIA
A tree (*Cinnamomum cassia* Blume) whose bark peels off and produces a fragrant oil when distilled (Ps. 45:8[MT 9]). Similar to cinnamon, it is often used as a less precious substitute for that spice. Cassia (Heb. *qiddâ, qĕṣîʿâ*) is native to the Far East, and its products were brought to the ancient Near East via the "Silk Road." Cassia oil was included in the mixture Moses made to anoint the ark of the covenant and the tent of meeting (Exod. 30:24). Ezekiel mentions it as a product traded in Tyre (Ezek. 27:19). Job's second daughter was named Keziah (*qĕṣîʿâ*, Job 42:14). MEGAN BISHOP MOORE

CATHOLIC LETTERS
The seven NT letters of James, 1–2 Peter, 1–2–3 John, and Jude. Gk. *katholikós*, "catholic" or "general," denotes a letter sent to a number of churches spread out geographically or to the Church universal (almost in the sense of an encyclical). Such a letter is distinct from one sent to local churches in a community or to individuals (as were the letters of Paul). Although 2 John addresses a local congregation and 3 John addresses an individual, these letters were so closely associated with 1 John that they were included along with it within the Catholic Letters.

The designation Catholic Letters can be traced back to the late 2nd century C.E. to Apollonius (Eusebius *HE* 5.18.5) and was applied to a general letter, canonical or not. For example, Origen calls the Epistle of Barnabas a catholic epistle because it is not addressed to any one congregation (*Contra Cels.* 1.63). Thus, at first "Catholic Letters" did not denote the authority or canonical status of these seven letters as if to distinguish them as orthodox rather than heretical. Neither did the designation suggest universal recognition of their authority, for while they were called "catholic" their inclusion in the canon was being disputed. However, by the 4th century the designation was used to specify these seven as a collection (*HE* 2.23.24-25), probably in order to distinguish them from the Pauline collection. As the seven letters were canonized, "catholic" began to denote their authoritative and canonical status, something reflected in their occasional designation as "canonical epistles" *(epistolae canonicae)*.

Bibliography. B. M. Metzger, *The Canon of the New Testament* (Oxford, 1987); R. W. Wall and E. E. Lemcio, *The New Testament as Canon.* JSNTSup 76 (Sheffield, 1992), 161-83. DUANE F. WATSON

CATTLE
Together with sheep and goats, he- and she-asses, servants, camels, and tents, large cattle (bulls, oxen, cows) were always considered a measure of wealth (Gen. 12:16; 13:5). Cattle (Heb. *bāqār*) were first

domesticated for their milk, meat, hide, bone, and dung, and only later did they become draft animals. Cattle do not produce fibers for spinning and weaving. During biblical times, cattle were raised primarily for traction and their milk and dung, and secondarily for meat, hide, and other by-products available only after the animals are killed. Once cattle are judged to be too old for work as draft animals, they may provide meat and other by-products.

Cattle are not given to wandering like sheep and goats; thus their presence in the zooarchaeological record usually indicates a more settled environment, that of an agrarian village or town. Cattle need more attention than other ruminants and do best under stable conditions. In pre-industrial Palestine three native types probably were very close to those extant in the biblical period. The most common and adapted breed is the small, furry Arab cow. It is very lean, with a brown to black or black-white body and poorly developed musculature and udders. It weighs ca. 260 kg. (575 lb.) and gives 400-700 l. (105-185 gal.) of milk per year during a four-five month period when the calf is present. The bulls and oxen may be twice as large as the cow. This is a working animal whose meat is of very poor quality. It is adapted to semi-arid conditions; like a goat, it is easily satisfied and fairly resistant to diseases.

The second breed is the Beirut cow, which is actually a better-bred form of the Arab cow. Its yellow-brown to brown body is larger and weighs 230-350 kg. (507-770 lb.). It yields 1500-2000 l. (395-530 gal.) per year during a period of seven-eight months when the calf is present. Selected cows may give up to 4000 l. (1055 gal.) of milk under favorable conditions. This breed is relatively resistant to diseases, but requires supplementary feed. Its predecessor may have been the cow used in the red heifer ritual (Num. 19:2).

The best milk-producing native cow is the Damascus cow, which is native to Syria and is identical in appearance to the Egyptian cow-goddess Hathor. This reddish to dark brown cow has a smooth hide and weighs 380-500 kg. (835-1100 lb.). It is raised only where water for growing feed is available. Its yield is 3000 l. (795 gal.) of milk per year during a period of seven-eight months when the calf is present. Good cows may produce as much as 5000 l. (1325 gal.). This breed is not fit for any work, requires good nutrition, and is not resistant to climatic changes and diseases. The reference to "the cows of Bashan" in Amos 4:1 is probably to this breed because they are big, fat, and do not work.

Large herds of cattle needed large tracts of land for grazing, as alluded to in the stories about the conflict between Abraham's and Lot's herds (Gen. 13) and Jacob's family in the land of Goshen (Gen. 45:10; 47:6a). During the Israelite monarchy the king became owner of large herds of cattle. Under David, special overseers were appointed for the *bāqār* (1 Chr. 27:29). The cattle were probably used as track animals on royal lands, and for their by-products.

Young calves were considered a culinary delicacy and were prepared for special meals (Gen. 18:6-8). Calves, specially selected for fattening (*ʿēgel-marbēq*), were served on particular occasions (1 Sam. 28:24). Young calves were also considered choice animals for sacrifice (Lev. 9:2; 16:3; Num. 7).

The bull was the symbol of power and fertility. In several ancient Near Eastern cultures, the bull was the symbol of various gods, a fact which must have influenced Israelite iconography and was expressed verbally and iconographically (Exod. 32), as with the bronze bull statuette from the Bull Site in the hill-country of Samaria. Sometimes the Bible uses the bull as a symbol for Yahweh (Heb. *ʾāḇîr;* Gen. 49:24; Isa. 49:26; 1:24).

The female is mentioned significantly fewer times and mostly metaphorically (Gen. 41). Hos. 4:16 compares Israel to a stubborn cow, and Amos 4:1 ridicules northern Israelite women as "Bashan cows." However, cows were harnessed for work (1 Sam. 6), and when the red heifer was selected, she was supposed to be "without blemish or defect, one which has never borne a yoke" (Num. 19:2).

See Sheep; Goat.

Bibliography. F. S. Bodenheimer, *Animal Life in Palestine* (Jerusalem, 1935). Oded Borowski

CAUDA (Gk. *Kaúda*)

A small island, now called Gaudos, ca. 37 km. (23 mi.) S of Crete, mentioned in connection with the sudden gale that hit the ship carrying Paul and other prisoners to Rome (Acts 27:16; NRSV mg. "Clauda"). By taking shelter to the lee side (south) of the island, the crew was able to survive the tempest (Acts 27:17-19).

CAULKERS

Tradesmen (Heb. *maḥăzîqê biḏqēḵ,* "those who strengthen your breach") skilled in repairing large leaks in marine vessels (Ezek. 27:9, 27). The task would have involved the use of bitumen or pitch (cf. Gen. 6:14). More precisely, these workers were ships' carpenters, a trade centered at Gebal (Byblos; cf. 1 Kgs. 5:18). Ezek. 27 is a lamentation over "the good ship Tyre," a major Phoenician maritime center.

CAVE

A natural hollow on the side of a hill. Early humans used caves for shelter, protection, and residence, and some of the earliest expressions of human art have been found in caves, such as in France and Spain. Caves have also had mythological associations, symbolically representing the realms of birth and death, birthplaces for deities, and entrances (birth wombs) from one world into another. Some uses of caves in the biblical texts include:

(1) A burial place. Abraham bought the cave at Machpelah as a burial site for Sarah (Gen. 23:10), and according to Matthew (Matt. 27:60) Jesus was buried in a cave (cf. John 11:38).

(2) A hiding place. Five Amorite kings hid in a cave at Makkedah, where they were eventually killed and subsequently buried (Josh. 10:16-27).

David hid in the cave of Adullam (1 Sam. 22:1-2), and from there he formed his band of followers. He also used an incident within a cave to spare Saul's life, thereby indicating his support of the Lord's anointed (1 Sam. 24:1-16). Obadiah, vizier of King Ahab, saved a number of prophets from Queen Jezebel by placing them in caves (1 Kgs. 18:3-4), and caves became a hiding place from "the terror of the Lord" (Isa. 2:19-22).

(3) A place of revelation. Elijah hears the words of Yahweh in a cave at Mt. Horeb (Sinai), where God told him to anoint royal and prophetic successors (1 Kgs. 19:9-18).

Bibliography. R. Stenuit, *Caves and the Marvelous World Beneath Us* (South Brunswick, N.J., 1966). C. Gilbert Romero

CEDAR

The celebrated cedars of Lebanon are large, coniferous, evergreen mountain trees (*Cedrus libani* Loud). These cedars (Heb. *'erez*) were aptly named, as they did not grow in Israel. As young trees, cedars are cone-shaped, but as they age, the branches spread and flatten. Cedars of Lebanon grow up to 28 m. (90 ft.) tall and may live 3000 years. Many more cedar forests were in Lebanon in biblical times than exist there today. The wood of the tree was a popular commodity used in building. It carries a pleasant fragrance and resists insects.

The Bible records several instances of cedars of Lebanon used in construction, the best known being Solomon's temple. Solomon contracted with King Hiram of Tyre to bring great quantities of cedar and other wood to build the temple in Jerusalem (1 Kgs. 5; 2 Chr. 2). Cedar was used extensively in the structure, from the supports and pillars to the paneling and carved woodwork. In addition to the temple, houses of the rich were also made of cedar. David lived in a house of cedar (2 Sam. 7:2 = 1 Chr. 17:1), and Ezekiel mentions cedar that is used in construction (Ezek. 27:5).

The Bible also contains many references to the great height and strength of cedar trees. Amos prophesies that the might of the Amorites "was like the height of cedars" (Amos 2:9), and Ezekiel compares Assyria's power to a cedar of Lebanon (Ezek. 31:3-9). The psalmist compares the growth of the righteous to that of the cedars of Lebanon (Ps. 92:12[MT 13]), and Zechariah uses the image of destroyed and fallen cedars and other trees to show how devastating God's judgment will be (Zech. 11:1-2).

Cedar wood is also associated with cleansing. Cedar, along with hyssop and blood, is prescribed in cleansing rituals in Lev. 14.

Megan Bishop Moore

CELIBACY

Abstention from marriage in fulfillment of a vow. Celibacy as depicted in the NT has both Jewish and Hellenistic parentage.

The OT speaks of Nazarite vows taken for life (Judg. 13:5, 7; 16:17). The prophetic task laid on Jeremiah expressly forbade marriage (Jer. 16:1-2). Philo reports that, in order to remain in perpetual readiness for divine revelation after Sinai, Moses never again "knew" his wife Zipporah (*Life of Moses* 11.68-69). According to Jubilees, Adam and Eve were chaste in the garden until the time of their expulsion (3:34-35; 4:1), and not until the first Jubilee after their expulsion (49 years) did they have sexual intercourse and children.

As a symbol for Jerusalem, entry into the holy place and participation in the holy cult at Qumran required abiding sexual purity or celibacy. Likewise, within the popular Hellenistic philosophical currents of the last two centuries B.C.E. celibacy functioned as a precondition for entering sacred space, an escape from a destitute world, preparation for communion with the gods, and a foundation for a life of virtue. Any literate Jew in touch with the major philosophical movements of the time would have been influenced by this rich body of tradition and practice.

Early Christian celibacy shared many of these tendencies. Luke 20:34-36 reflects an early Christian belief that celibacy offered a foretaste of the eschaton, and 1 Cor. 7 bases Paul's celibacy on the impending eschatological crisis.

See Asceticism. Calvin J. Roetzel

CENCHREAE (Gk. *Kenchreaí*)

A Greek seaport located in Achaia on the Saronic Gulf, ca. 11 km. (5 mi.) E of Corinth and ca. 4 km. (2.5 mi.) S of Isthmia. It served as the eastern port of Corinth both in the classical Greek period and in the Roman period. Since the port faced toward the eastern Mediterranean, it is natural that Paul, Aquila, and Priscilla would have departed from it on their journey to Syria (Acts 18:18). Paul's letter to the Romans (Rom. 16:1-2) mentions the Christian woman Phoebe and the congregation she helped support at Cenchreae.

Richard E. Oster, Jr.

CENDEBEUS (Gk. *Kendebaios, Cendebaeus, Kendebaeus*)

A Syrian officer who was defeated by John Hyrcanus. When Antiochus VII claimed the Syrian throne, he pursued the usurper Tryphon, and in his absence he appointed Cendebeus commander-in-chief of the "coastal country" with instructions "to make war" on the Judeans (1 Macc. 15:38-39). Under Simon Maccabeus' sons Judas and John, the Judeans battled the Syrians near Modein. The Syrians fled, and John pursued them to Kedron, where 2000 fell and their fortifications were destroyed (16:1-10). Edmon L. Rowell, Jr.

CENSER

A small container for carrying hot coals, used in the service of the tabernacle (Exod. 25:38; 27:3; Lev. 16:12). The censer held live coals onto which incense was placed, creating a thick smoke and probably a pleasing smell. Heb. *maḥtâ* is also glossed as "tray," "pan," and "firepan," terms which describe functions related to the lampstand, the altar, and the offering of incense. Walter E. Brown

CENSUS
An official enumeration of a group or groups of people. The census is well attested in the ancient Near East, including Egypt, Mari, Ugarit, and Assyria. The ancient census, however, was unlike a modern one in its lack of completeness. Seldom was an entire nation counted or data collected on age, sex, income, or occupation. The nearest parallel is the "Assyrian Doomsday Book," which enumerated and ordered people by age and sex, including information on land size and such. This census, however, was restricted to the province of Haran in north Syria.

Exod. 30:11-16 makes the census of the Israelites a fixed part of the Law. In addition, the Bible reports a formal census on three occasions. According to Num. 1, shortly after the Exodus the fighting men were counted; 603,550 is most likely an exaggerated figure deriving from either embellished tradition or a later period of Israel's history. This number excludes Levites, women, and children. According to Num. 26, a census of the Israelites was taken prior to their entrance into Canaan. On this occasion, the males over 20 years of age numbered 601,730. Besides counting the men eligible for military service (Num. 1:3), these two censuses established the maintenance of the tabernacle and emphasized the Levites' exempt status (1:48-53). Further, the census in Num. 26 would determine the size of land grants for the tribes (vv. 52-56).

As recorded in 2 Sam. 24, David sent Joab out to count the males who could fight in the army. Again, the figure is exaggerated: 800 thousand men of Israel and 500 thousand of Judah (2 Sam. 24:9). Because of this census, Yahweh sent a plague against Israel and killed 70 thousand people. The reason for the plague is uncertain. Possibly, the census implied military conscription and violated the rules of holy war, subverting Yahweh's prerogative to lead the army, or perhaps a taboo against numbering the people existed. Most likely, however, cultic concerns were at root. According to Exod. 30:11-15, as part of the census the Israelites had to give a half-shekel as a ransom specifically to avoid a plague. In addition, evidence was found at Mari that a ritual cleansing was required before a census. Therefore, David most likely violated either the half-shekel purity law or another cultic demand, causing the plague.

The NT mentions a census taken during the reign of Augustus requiring the registration of all individuals in the Roman Empire (Luke 2:1). Beginning with Augustus, the Roman administration regularly conducted a census of the provinces to determine the degree of taxation. In Egypt it appears to have been conducted every 14 years. According to Luke, because of this census Joseph and Mary went to Bethlehem where Jesus was born.

PAUL S. ASH

CENTER OF THE LAND
An epithet for the holy temples of the Samaritans and the Israelites, on Mt. Gerizim and Mt. Zion respectively, which each group considered its sacred place as the earth's (spiritual) "center" (Heb. *ṭabbûr hā'āreṣ;* Judg. 9:37; Ezek. 38:12). The LXX translation "navel" (Gk. *omphalós;* cf. Lat. *umbilicus*) suggests a connection with ancient Near Eastern mythology wherein the temple serves as the bond between heaven and earth. This motif either came through the Ugaritic literature via Canaanite mythology of the cosmic mountain (i.e., Mt. Zion) or was attached to the biblical text through the LXX translation during the Hellenistic period. However, Jewish talmudic and midrashic literature understood the expression to mean that Jerusalem was the point from which the world was created (*b. Yoma* 54b; Tanhuma *Kedoshim* 10).

Bibliography. E. Burrows, "Some Cosmological Patterns in Babylonian Religion," in *The Labyrinth: Further Studies in the Relation between Myth and Ritual in the Ancient World,* ed. S. H. Hooke (London, 1935), 43-70; S. Terrien, "The Omphalos Myth and Hebrew Religion," *VT* 20 (1970): 315-38; A. J. Wensinck, "The Ideas of the Western Semites Concerning the Navel of the Earth," in *Studies of A. J. Wensinck* (New York, 1978), 43-70.

J. RANDALL PRICE

CENTURION
The rank designated for the commander of a Roman *centuria,* a subdivision of a cohort. At full strength the *centuria* would constitute 80 soldiers (not the hundred that the name implies).

The centurion (Gk. *hekatontárchēs*) was the highest-ranking noncommissioned officer in both the Roman army and the auxiliary cohorts. In a legion the senior centurion of the first cohort was designated *primus pilus;* a position he would hold for a single year, after which he was promoted out of the centurion class. In auxiliary cohorts centurions were ranked in six levels, with the senior centurion second in command after the *chiliarch* or commander. The centurion was the backbone of the Roman military organization, the professional soldiers of the empire (cf. Polybius *Hist.* 6.24). Centurions are mentioned several times in the Gospels and Acts, always in a positive manner, and two are mentioned by name: Cornelius (Acts 10:1-8) and Julius (27:1-6). Although not counted among the aristocracy in Roman society, centurions were Roman citizens and often became affluent and important in local affairs (cf. Luke 7:2-5; Acts 10:2). Jesus extolled a centurion's faith (Matt. 8:5-13).

Bibliography. T. R. S. Broughton, "The Roman Army," in *The Beginnings of Christianity,* ed. F. J. Foakes-Jackson and K. Lake (London, 1933), 5:427-45; B. Dobson, "The Significance of the Centurion and the 'Primpilaris' in the Roman Army and Administration," *ANRW* II.1, 392-434.

DENNIS M. SWANSON

CEPHAS (Gk. *Kēphás*)
Nickname or surname given the Apostle Peter (from Aram. *kêp̄ā',* "rock").

See PETER.

CEREAL OFFERING

Also translated "grain offering" (and, misleadingly, KJV "meat offering"). Heb. *minḥâ* means "gift" or "tribute" and often refers to payments to suzerains which are obligated by vassal treaties; as Israel's Lord, God also received a *minḥâ*. The religious concept *minḥâ* might have once included animal sacrifices as well as grain offerings. In Gen. 4:4 Abel's offering of the firstlings of his flock is called a *minḥâ*, and in 1 Sam. 2:17 Eli's sons' demand for a larger portion of sacrificial meat is said to show contempt for God's *minḥâ*. However, all other biblical evidence of the cultic use of this word clearly refers to offerings of cereal, and there is no reliable basis upon which to assume that *minḥâ* as cereal offering is a late or postexilic linguistic development — the preexilic Phoenician equivalent also referred to cereal offerings. Regardless of its actual etymology, this word undoubtedly brought to mind thoughts of the covenant with God. It is not insignificant that Lev. 2:13 warns that the salt of the Lord's covenant should never be omitted from the cereal offering.

Three types of cultic *minḥâ* are attested: (1) cereal offerings accompanying burnt offerings, (2) cereal offerings in lieu of burnt offerings, and (3) offerings of the firstfruits of grain and its products. Those of the third type are either *minḥaṯ bikkûrîm*, firstfruits of the harvest (crushed, parched grain from new ears), a portion of which was burned, or *rē'šîṯ*, the firsts of processed products, which were never burned. Presumably, the firstfruits offerings would apply to any grain, though one most often thinks of the barley harvest and the grain offering associated with the Festival of Weeks. The independent and accompanying cereal offerings were to be of wheat flour, which as twice as expensive as barley flour (2 Kgs. 7:16), but within reach of the common person's budget. Offered uncooked, it was to be accompanied by frankincense, a fairly expensive spice. As an alternative, it could be offered without the frankincense if it were cooked in any of four different ways (Lev. 2:4-7). The cereal offering was always unleavened, mixed with oil, and offered with salt. The prescriptions for the sin offering (Lev. 5:7, 11) make it clear that the cereal offering was an acceptable substitute for a burnt offering if the person making the offering could not afford even a pair of birds. The cereal offering is thus often called the offering of the poor and was common as such throughout the ancient Near East.

Because it could substitute for the burnt offerings, the cereal offering served the same wide range of purposes and occasions as did the burnt offerings. Unlike the burnt offerings, however, only a token portion of the priestly cereal offering was burnt. The rest was contributed to the priests. Non-Priestly sources (e.g., 2 Kgs. 16:15) suggest that the cereal offering was completely burnt. However, it is likely that divergent practices were common. One might infer this from the account of Eli's sons (1 Sam. 2) and from 2 Kgs. 23:9, which points out that the priests of the high places "ate unleavened bread (i.e., their share of cereal offerings) among their kindred." Cereal offerings, even in the postexilic period, could be offered at locations where burnt offerings would have been unthinkable (e.g., Elephantine). After the destruction of Solomon's temple, devout worshippers continued to leave cereal offerings at the temple site, even though no altar remained (Jer. 41:5). Cereal offerings were common in other ancient Near Eastern religions, and were even to be found in Judah in connection with worship of the queen of heaven (Jer. 44:19).

Bibliography. J. Milgrom, *Leviticus 1–16*. AB 3 (New York, 1991), 177-202. WILLIAM R. SCOTT

CEREMONIAL LAW

Law regarding primarily the major religious observances and cultic practices.

See LAW.

CERINTHUS (Gk. *Kērinthos*)

A Gnostic who taught an adoptionist Christology and held that Jesus was the natural son of Joseph and Mary. Living near the end of the 1st century C.E., Cerinthus is a prime example of the tendency toward syncretism in the religious life of the Hellenistic world as he brought Jewish millenarianism, early Ebionite and Egyptian Gnosticism, and a lurid imagination to bear on his understanding of the nature of Jesus of Nazareth. Further, he seems to have held that matter is essentially evil; like Marcion, that the God of the OT was an angel or demiurge who created the natural order; that the supreme God was ultimately unknowable; and that following the second advent, Jesus would reign over a lavish and sensual earthly kingdom.

D. LARRY GREGG

CHALCEDONY

A variety of quartz with a microscopic crystalline structure, occurring in many color variations. The agate form is colored with alternating bands, irregular clouds, or mosslike structures, usually of opal. When referring to gems, the term chalcedony is used for the light blue-gray variety of such quartz. The breastpiece of judgment of the high priest is decorated with 12 stones, set in gold and each engraved with the name of one of the 12 tribes. The middle stone in the third of four rows is Heb. *šeḇô*, most often translated "agate" (Exod. 28:19; 39:12). In Rev. 21:19 the third of the 12 foundation stones for the Jerusalem which comes down out of heaven is chalcedony (Gk. *chalkēdṓn*).

MARTHA JEAN MUGG BAILEY

CHALDEA

The region in southern Babylonia bordering on the Persian Gulf. After a Chaldean dynasty came to power over all of Babylonia in 626 B.C.E., the term Chaldea (Akk. *Kaldû;* Heb. *kaśdîm*) became synonymous with "Babylonia."

Land and People

This marshy region between the Tigris and Euphrates rivers bordering on the Gulf was called the "Sea-Lands" by the Assyrians and Babylonians in the 2nd millennium B.C.E., but in the 1st millennium "Land of the Chaldeans," after the tribes that lived there. The Greek name (*gḗ Chaldaíōn, Chaldaí, Chaldaíoi*) follows Akk. *Kaldû*, but the Hebrew (*kaśdîm, ʾereṣ kaśdîm;* cf. Aram. *kaśdāy*) does not. While there is no satisfactory explanation for this, the one most frequently suggested is that the Hebrew form reflects an earlier Akkadian **kašdu*. (The Hebrew *ś* would thus represent Akkadian *š* prior to the assimilation of *š* to *l* before *d*, as commonly occurs in later Akkadian). However, this postulated form **kašdu* remains unattested in cuneiform texts.

The Chaldeans were part of a heterogeneous and politically-fragmented Babylonian population that also included Aramean tribal groups and the native inhabitants of traditionally semi-independent cities. There were three major Chaldean tribes: Bīt-Dakkūri, Bīt-Amukāni, and Bīt-Yakīn, and two minor, Bīt-Šaʾalli and Bīt-Šilāni. The Bīt-Dakkūri and the Bīt-Amukāni lived along the central and lower Euphrates, the former settling south of Borsippa and the latter just above Uruk, while the Bīt-Yakīn were active along the Persian Gulf itself, from Ur to the marshlands that stretched eastward to Elam. The designation of Abraham's home as "Ur of the Chaldeans" (Gen. 11:28, 31; 15:7; Acts 7:4) reflects this latter association.

In the Bible the term "Chaldean" is used in two senses. In most contexts it occurs as a synonym for "Babylonian"; however, in Daniel it is a technical term for practitioners of traditional Babylonian sciences, i.e., astrologers, magicians, and diviners (Dan. 2:2, 4).

History

There are two major periods of Chaldean history: the first during which Babylonia and its diverse peoples were overshadowed by the Neo-Assyrian Empire; the second after the breakdown of the Neo-Assyrian Empire in which Babylonia was united under a Chaldean dynasty.

Assyrians first encountered the Chaldean tribes as they tried to stabilize trade routes to the south during the early 1st millennium. However, whenever the Assyrians left the south alone for any substantial length of time the Chaldean tribes rivaled other Babylonians for control of Babylonia; each of the three major Chaldean tribes was able to put a king on the throne during the first half of the 8th century.

Probably the greatest Chaldean of this earlier period of Chaldean history was Marduk-apla-iddina II (biblical Merodach-baladan) of the Bīt-yakīn. He fought with the Assyrians during the reigns of Tiglath-pileser III, Sargon II, and Sennacherib, and was able to take power in Babylon at least twice during the latter half of the 8th century. Merodach-baladan took refuge in Elam more than once, and the Elamites often lent their support against the Assyrians. In Isa. 39:1-8 = 2 Kgs. 20:12-19 Merodach-baladan is said to have sent an embassy to Hezekiah to request Judah's aid against the Assyrians as well; this was perhaps occasioned by a general spirit of revolt throughout the Assyrian Empire after the death of Sargon II.

The second period of Chaldean history begins after the death of Assurbanipal of Assyria. The Chaldeans under Nabopolassar were able to revolt successfully and capture Babylon in 626. Nabopolassar then allied with the Medes to overthrow the Assyrian Empire; the great Assyrian city of Assur fell in 614 and Nineveh, the capital, in 612. Nabopolassar's son, Nabû-kudurri-uṣur II (Nebuchadnezzar, 605-562) campaigned westward into Syria and Palestine and defeated the Egyptians, Babylonia's rivals for control of that region, at Charchemish in 605.

Nebuchadnezzar is most noted in the Bible for bringing about the end of the kingdom of Judah (2 Kgs. 24–25; 2 Chr. 36). In 605 during Nebuchadnezzar's western campaign, Jehoiakim of Judah initially submitted to Nebuchadnezzar. Judah later defected to the Egyptians, and Nebuchadnezzar was provoked to attack Jerusalem in 597, taking Jehoiakim's successor, Jehoiachin, and other leading citizens back with him to Babylon. Nebuchadnezzar then placed Mattaniah (throne name Zedekiah) on the throne of Judah, but Judah rebelled under his rule too. Jerusalem was finally sacked by the Babylonians in 587, and even more Judahites were taken into exile.

Nebuchadnezzar was a powerful and successful ruler who rebuilt Babylon and brought political and economic prosperity to Babylonia. After his death, the empire declined. Nebuchadnezzar's son Amêl-marduk (Evil-merodach, 2 Kgs. 25:27-30), and his successors, Neriglissar (Nergal-sharezer, Jer. 39:3) and Labāši-marduk, reigned only a few years between them. Nabonidus (556-539), with his son Belshazzar as co-regent, restored some stability, but could not prevent Babylon's eventual fall to the Persians under Cyrus the Great in 539.

Bibliography. J. A. Brinkman, *A Political History of Post-Kassite Babylonia, 1158-722* B.C. AnOr 43 (Rome 1968); *Prelude to Empire: Babylonian Society and Politics, 747-626* B.C. Occasional Publications of the Babylonian Fund 7 (Philadelphia, 1984); J. Oates, *Babylon,* rev. ed. (London, 1986); H. W. F. Saggs, *Babylonians* (London, 1995); *The Greatness That Was Babylon,* rev. ed. (London, 1988).

TAWNY L. HOLM

CHAMPIONS

Translation of Heb. *gibbôr,* "hero," or *gibbôr hayîl,* "valiant hero" (RSV awkwardly "mighty man," "mighty man of valor"). In the age of melee combat between massed bodies of infantry, before the onset of massed heavy chariotry, individuals of larger stature and greater martial prowess could by themselves force breaches in the enemy line. Such heroes were especially terrifying to more lightly armed troops and peasants' militia, as illustrated by the terror of the Israelites before Goliath (1 Sam. 17:4-11). The best literary presentation of these champions and their skills is still to be found in Homer's *Iliad,* where Ajax, Achilles, and Diomedes singly and at various times force breaches in the Trojan line.

Sometimes these warriors would challenge another of the opposing side to single combat, with both sides looking on.

Goliath, Ishbe-benob, Saph, and a fourth, unnamed champion are listed in 2 Sam. 21:15-22 as Philistine champions. The improper use of the term "giants" gives a fairy-tale cast to these stories, but the listing of Goliath's height in the Qumran texts as "four cubits and a span" — 1.98 m. (6 ft. 6 in.) — offers a more realistic impression. David countered with his own champions, listed under the title the *šĕlōšîm* (the "thirty") in 2 Sam. 23:8-39.

DONALD G. SCHLEY

CHAOS

A state of confusion, emptiness, or disorder. Chaos existed before God brought order to the universe during creation. In a parallel creation epic, the Babylonian Enuma Elish, the sea-goddess Tiamat represents the unbounded chaos and power of the ocean. Marduk defeats her in a heroic struggle and then cuts her body into pieces, thus creating the orderly boundaries of the physical world. Echoes of the Babylonian epic can be found in the book of Genesis, where the "earth was without form (Heb. *tōhû*) and void, and darkness was upon the face of the deep *(tĕhôm)*" (Gen. 1:2).

Isaiah and Jeremiah often predict desolation and chaos as God's punishment for the nations: The Lord "will lay waste the earth and make it desolate," and Babylon will become "the city of chaos," desolate and broken down (Isa. 24:1-12). So too Edom shall be laid waste "from generation to generation" when God uses his "plummet of chaos" (Isa. 34:10-11; cf. Jer. 49:7-22). Jeremiah directs his prophecy at Judah but urges all the nations to return to the ways of God or else the earth will be returned to its primeval state of "waste and void" (Jer. 4:23-28). In a passage where he prophesies that all nations will bow to Israel's God, Isaiah stresses God's omnipotence by declaring that God "did not create [the earth] a chaos, but formed it to be inhabited" (Isa. 45:18).

HENRY L. CARRIGAN, JR.

CHARIOT

A wheeled vehicle that served a variety of functions over a long history, including ordinary transportation, hunting, royal and religious processions, and warfare. Its design was altered and improved through the centuries. By the time that chariot races were held in major cities of the Roman Empire, this vehicle — in one form or another — had been used for more than three millennia. The chariot is best known for its role in war, as a mobile fighting platform (for two or three riders) in conflicts fought on broad, flat battlefields. Information about the chariot's evolution comes from a variety of sources — texts, art, and archaeological remains, i.e., the remains of actual chariots (in Egypt).

The earliest chariots were built in Mesopotamia during the latter part of the 4th millennium B.C.; these early models were heavy, four-wheeled, and sometimes pulled by teams of onagers. By the 1st millennium the chariot had passed through almost every conceivable variation in design and construction. Information on the Neo-Assyrian chariot is not equal to what is known about the Egyptian vehicle, since so many examples of the latter have survived in Egyptian tombs. While chariots were used by other ancient Near Eastern armies (e.g., in Anatolia, Syria, Israel), the Late Bronze Age Egyptian and Iron Age Assyrian war chariots were superior to their competitors, and tremendous effort (research and development) was invested to improve the war chariot. Changes in the design and construction of chariots resulted when armies returned from battles, as in the great chariot engagement at Kedesh-on-the-Orontes, in 1286.

Chariots served as symbols of power and prestige, as when the Egyptian pharaoh gave Joseph a chariot (Gen. 41:43; cf. 46:29; 50:9; 2 Sam. 15:1; 1 Kgs. 1:5). In the account of Philip and the Ethiopian eunuch, the status of the latter is indicated by his use of a chariot for transportation (Acts 8:26-40). Egyptian kings were portrayed in chariots to indicate their military prowess, and some of these chariots were buried with them in royal tombs.

The Hebrews felt overwhelmed when facing the Egyptian chariotry at the Red Sea (Exod. 14:6-7, 17-18; 15:4, 19). These were the sleek, lightweight chariots known from New Kingdom art and similar to the examples from Egyptian tombs, including six recovered from the tomb of Tutankhamen. Later, the Canaanites (Josh. 11:4-9; 17:16; Judg. 1:19; 4:3, 13) and Philistines (1 Sam. 13:5) used chariots against the Hebrews. Samuel warned the Hebrews who asked for a king that this step to nationhood would require them to give up sons to man chariots in time of war (1 Sam. 8:11-17).

David captured chariots in his war with the Arameans (2 Sam. 8:4); this was easier than Israel's building their own, since the production of chariots required considerable expertise. Solomon gave considerable attention to the development of chariot forces (1 Kgs. 4:26; 9:19, 22; 10:26, 29); the attempt to identify archaeologically Solomon's facilities for horses and chariots remains controversial. Chariots remained in use for later Hebrew kings (1 Kgs. 22:34-38; 2 Kgs. 9:21-25; 2 Chr. 35:24); Ahab contributed a chariot force to the coalition that met Shalmaneser III at Qarqar in 853. Jer. 51:21 refers to Cyrus as God's weapon who would "shatter chariot and charioteer." The only portrayal of an Israelite chariot is found on Sennacherib's wall relief that documents his attack on Lachish in 701.

Bibliography. M. A. Littauer and J. H. Crouwel, *Chariots and Related Equipment from the Tomb of Tut'ankhamun* (Oxford, 1985); *Wheeled Vehicles and Ridden Animals in the Ancient Near East.* HO 7, 1/2, B/1 (Leiden, 1979); Y. Yadin, *The Art of Warfare in Biblical Lands* (Jerusalem, 1963).

GERALD L. MATTINGLY

CHEBAR (Heb. *kĕḇār)*

A Mesopotamian canal besides whose banks Ezekiel received his inaugural vision (Ezek. 1:1–3:27) as well as a number of other prophetic oracles (10:15, 20, 22; 43:3). In antiquity its course left the

Euphrates N of Sippar and ran southeast ca. 300 km. (186 mi.) through the Nippur region before rejoining the Euphrates S of ancient Uruk. The Chebar (Akk. *ka-ba-ru*) is also mentioned in several cuneiform documents of the 5th century B.C.E. from Nippur.

Bibliography. R. Zadok, "The Nippur Region during the Late Assyrian, Chaldaean and Achaemenian Periods, Chiefly According to Written Sources," *IOS* 8 (1978): 266-332.

STEPHEN J. ANDREWS

CHEDORLAOMER (Heb. *kĕḏor-lāʿōmer*)
The king of Elam mentioned in Gen. 14 who allied with the kings of Shinar, Ellasar, and Goiim against Sodom and Gomorrah and their allies. After serving Chedorlaomer for 12 years, the cities rebelled and Chedorlaomer retaliated, capturing both and taking their people, including Lot, as booty. Abraham with only 318 men surprised them in a night raid, freeing the captives and chasing the four kings out of the territory.

The four kings represent the major powers of the four quarters of the world in the ancient Near East: Chedorlaomer of Elam (East), Amraphel of Shinar (Babylon, South), Anrioch of Ellasar (Assur, North) and Tidal of Goiim (Hittites, West). While no battle or alliance of these kings is known, it fits the context of Gen. 10–12 well, where Yahweh promises a new nation is to be formed and established from Abraham's descendants (Gen. 12:1-4). The area from which Chedorlaomer is driven by Abraham is a foreshadowing of the boundaries of the Davidic kingdom.

The name Chedorlaomer is seen as an Elamite name consisting of two elements, Kudur/Kutir, "son," and Lagamar, an Elamite deity. No known Elamite king, however, bears that name. An alternative suggestion is that Chedorlaomer is a misreading of the name Ku.Ku.Ku.(Ku).Mal = Kutir-Nuḫḫunte III (12th century) in the so-called Chedorlaomer texts, published by T. G. Pinches in 1894. The four kings of these texts who destroy Babylon and are repaid for their crimes by Marduk may be the model for the writer of Gen. 14 for all kings who would invade Israel.

Bibliography. M. C. Astour, "Political and Cosmic Symbolism in Genesis 14 and in Its Babylonian Sources," in *Biblical Motifs,* ed. A. Altmann (Cambridge, Mass., 1966), 65-112.

RUSSELL NELSON

CHEEK
The portion of the burnt offering of an ox or sheep reserved for the priest's sustenance, along with the shoulder and stomach (Deut. 18:3; NRSV "jowls"; Heb. *lĕḥî raqqâ*). A woman's cheeks, whose softness was a mark of beauty, were often perfumed and bedecked with ornaments, perhaps beads or fringe (Cant. 1:10; 5:13). Perhaps because it was regarded as the seat of modesty (cf. Cant. 4:3; 6:7), people in the ancient Near East considered it a particular affront to touch or strike a person on the cheek (1 Kgs. 22:24; Ps. 3:7; cf. Matt. 5:39 = Luke 6:29; Gk. *siagṓn*).

CHELAL (Heb. *kĕlāl*)
A descendant of the Israelite Pahath-moab who had to send away his foreign wife when the covenant to abandon mixed marriages was made (Ezra 10:30).

CHELUB (Heb. *kĕlûḇ*)

1. A Judahite, the brother of Shuhah and father of Mehir (1 Chr. 4:11).

2. The father of Ezri, an overseer of the field workers of King David (1 Chr. 27:26).

CHELUBAI (Heb. *kĕlûḇāy*)
A descendant of Hezron of Judah (1 Chr. 2:9), a variant form of the name Caleb at 1 Chr. 2:18, 42.

CHELUHI (Heb. *kĕlûhî*)
A son of the Israelite Bani who was compelled to send away his foreign wife (Ezra 10:35 **K**).

CHEMOSH (Heb. *kĕmôš*)
The national god of Moab. Chemosh was known and worshipped elsewhere, especially in northern Syria (Ebla, Ugarit). The 9th-century stela of Mesha, king of Moab, provides most of our knowledge concerning Chemosh. The ideology expressed there is similar to Israelite religious notions: e.g., Chemosh is angry with his land, allowing it to come under foreign (Israelite) control, but later delivers it (ll. 5, 9; cf. 2 Kgs. 3:27). He was apparently militaristic (later associated with the Roman god Ares) and chthonic in nature. The name Chemosh may mean something like "conqueror" or "subduer."

Biblical evidence regarding Chemosh adds little to the nonbiblical data. Moab is the "people of Chemosh" (Num. 21:29; Jer. 48:46). Solomon built a high place to Chemosh (1 Kgs. 11:7; cf. Mesha stela ll. 3-4) which Josiah later defiled (2 Kgs. 23:13). The worship of Chemosh is one of the reasons for the division of the kingdom (1 Kgs. 11:33). Jeremiah proclaims judgment against Moab and Chemosh (Jer. 48:7, 13, 46). Various attempts have been to explain the reference in Judg. 11:24 to Chemosh as the god of the Ammonites, but without satisfaction.

Bibliography. H.-P. Müller, "Chemosh," *DDD,* 186-89.

BRENT A. STRAWN

CHENAANAH (Heb. *kĕnaʿănâ*)

1. The father of Zedekiah, a false prophet during the reign of Ahab (1 Kgs. 22:11, 24 = 2 Chr. 18:10, 23).

2. A son of Bilhan and grandson of Benjamin, a "mighty warrior" (1 Chr. 7:10).

CHENANI (Heb. *kĕnānî*)
A Levite in the days of Nehemiah, among those reading from the Law and voicing confession (Neh. 9:4).

CHENANIAH (Heb. *kĕnanyāhû, kĕnanyâ*)

1. A chief of the Levites and temple singers who participated in the ceremony bringing the ark from the house of Obed-edom to the city of David (1 Chr. 15:22, 27).

2. A Levite, appointed with his sons to perform the "outside duties" of officials and judges (1 Chr. 26:29; cf. Neh. 11:16).

CHEPHAR-AMMONI (Heb. *kĕp̱ar hāʿammōnāy*)
A town (Heb. "village of the Ammonites") assigned to the tribe of Benjamin (Josh. 18:24). Khirbet Kefr ʿAnā (173153), ca. 5 km. (3 mi.) N of Bethel, has been suggested as the site, but the identification is not widely accepted.

CHEPHIRAH (Heb. *kĕp̱îrâ*)
One of the four Hivite cities that had made a covenant of peace with Joshua and the elders of Israel, thus escaping annihilation (Josh. 9:17). After the Exile the Israelites repopulated Chephirah, along with Kiriath-jearim and Beeroth (Ezra 2:25; Neh. 7:29). The city has been identified with modern Khirbet el-Kefîreh (160137), ca. 8 km. (5 mi.) WSW of el-Jîb (Gibeon).

CHERAN (Heb. *kĕrān*)
The fourth son of the Horite Dishon, head of a clan dwelling in the land of Seir (Gen. 36:26; 1 Chr. 1:41).

CHERETHITES (Heb. *kĕrēṯî, kĕrēṯîm*)
A mercenary group along with the Pelethites who served as David's bodyguards. David most likely encountered these warrior guilds when he "lived in the country of the Philistines" (1 Sam. 27:11). Although it is generally agreed that the Cherethites were of Aegean origin and lived on the Mediterranean coast SE of Philistia, there is not enough evidence to prove conclusively their exact derivation. They possibly had been settled earlier by the Egyptians as Cretan mercenaries (cf. LXX Ezek. 25:16; Gk. *Krḗtes*) to be a northern buffer-outpost. Ezek. 25:16; Zeph. 2:5 hold the Cherethites and Philistines in parallel and, along with 1 Sam. 30:14, are the only references where the Cherethites are not listed in compound with the Pelethites.

The Cherethites are listed in both of David's administrative lists (2 Sam. 8:18; 20:23) under the leadership of Benaiah. Benaiah is also listed as the general of Solomon's army in the list of 1 Kgs. 4:2-6, and there is no separate reference for the Cherethites and Pelethites. These fighters owed their utmost allegiance to David and followed him in retreat out of Jerusalem during the revolt of Absalom (2 Sam. 15:18) and were instrumental in putting down the revolt of Sheba (20:7).

Bruce W. Gentry

CHERITH (Heb. *kĕrîṯ*), **BROOK**
A stream E of the Jordan River, where Elijah sought refuge from Ahab and Jezebel (1 Kgs. 17:3-7). Some scholars equate Cherith with the Wadi Qelt, above Jericho W of the Jordan, but this location contradicts biblical evidence (1 Kgs. 17:3). The Wadi el-Yubis is currently the accepted location. Situated in northern Gilead, it corresponds to 1 Kgs. 17:1 where Elijah is described as "the Tishbite, of Tishbe of Gilead."

Philip R. Drey

CHERUB (Heb. *kĕrûḇ*) **(PLACE)**
An unidentified location in Babylonia, from which exiles returned to Jerusalem. According to Ezra 2:59 = Neh. 7:61 these exiles were unable to prove their Israelite descent. In 1 Esdr. 5:36 Cherub appears with Addan and Immer as the names of leaders who returned to Jerusalem from Tel-melach and Tel-harsha.

Jorge L. Valdes

CHERUB (Heb. *kĕrûḇ*),
CHERUBIM (*kĕrûḇîm*)
Mythological winged creatures, borrowed by the Israelites from ancient Near Eastern traditions. The Hebrew term is likely related to Akk. *kāribu* or *karūbu* ("intercessor") or *karibi, kurībi, karibāti* ("gatekeepers"), the latter referring to the colossal mythological creatures which flanked the entrances of Mesopotamian palaces and temples.

The only uniformity among the many examples known from ancient Near Eastern art is that cherubim were winged creatures. Statues and reliefs depicting various types of cherubim have been found at many Near Eastern sites, including Aleppo, Carchemish, and Byblos; carved ivory depictions of cherubim have been found at Samaria and Nimrud. Many examples of colossal winged bulls and other beasts are known from Babylonian and Assyrian palaces and temples.

In Gen. 3:24 the Lord places cherubim with flaming swords over the way to the tree of life in the garden of Eden. In 1 Sam. 22:11 = Ps. 18:10(MT 11) the Lord is depicted as riding on a cherub as he flies through the heavens. Cherubim also flank or support God's throne (Ps. 80:1[2]; 99:1; 2 Kgs. 19:15 = Isa. 37:16). Ezekiel envisions cherubim as four-winged and four-faced "living creatures" accompanied by whirling wheels (Ezek. 1:4-28; 10:1-22); in his vision, the cherubim support the platform on which the Lord is enthroned.

The Lord commands Moses to set two gold-covered wooden images of cherubim on top of the mercy seat covering the ark of the covenant (Exod. 25:18-20; 37:6-9; Num. 7:89; 1 Sam. 4:4); it was from between these creatures that the Lord would speak to Moses and reveal his plans for Israel. Pictures of cherubim were woven in the fabric of the veil and curtains of the tabernacle (Exod. 26:1, 31). Later, in the Jerusalem temple, images of cherubim were carved into the walls (1 Kgs. 6:29), woven into the veil (2 Chr. 3:14), and carved into the panels of the 10 stands of the bronze lavers (1 Kgs. 7:29, 36). Two enormous cherubim made of olivewood and overlaid in gold were placed in the holy of holies (1 Kgs. 6:23-28; 8:6-7), covering the ark of the covenant and virtually filling the small room. Cherubim were the guardians of the Lord's invisible resting place on earth, the mercy seat above the ark of the covenant in the Jerusalem temple.

In Ezek. 28:14 the king of Tyre is guarded by a cherub, which banishes him on account of his transgressions (v. 16; cf. Gen. 3:24).

Jennie R. Ebeling

CHESALON (Heb. *kĕsālôn*)
A city on the northern boundary of Judah (Josh. 15:10), identified with Keslā (154132), ca. 20 km. (12 mi.) W of Jerusalem.

CHESED (Heb. *keśeḏ*)
The fourth son of Nahor and Milcah (Gen. 22:22) and nephew of Abraham. The name of his clan may be related to the Chaldeans (cf. Heb. *kaśdîm*).

CHESIL (Heb. *kĕsîl*)
A town within the southern part of Judah's inheritance (Josh. 15:30). In comparable lists of southern Judean towns, Chesil is replaced with Bethul (Josh. 19:4) and Bethuel (1 Chr. 4:30). Contextually, it is placed between Eltolad and Hormah, which would suggest a location E of Beer-sheba.

LAURA B. MAZOW

CHESTER BEATTY PAPYRI
Greek biblical manuscripts acquired by Sir Alfred Chester Beatty in 1931 and housed in the Chester Beatty Library and Gallery of Oriental Art in Dublin, Ireland. They are the most important collection of manuscripts on papyrus because of their number (11) and their early date (2nd-4th centuries).

The papyri are most valuable for their contribution to the textual criticism of the Greek Bible. Papyrus X (𝔓967) is one of only three major witnesses to the Old Greek of Daniel. The collection also includes witnesses to Genesis, Isaiah, Ezekiel, Esther, and Revelation.

In addition to textual criticism, the papyri are also valuable because they were in the form of the codex, which shows that the codex came into use very early; they employ contractions for names such as God, Jesus, Christ, and Spirit; and they preserve alternative orders of biblical books or chapters within books. In papyrus X, Dan. 7–8 follows ch. 4; in papyrus I, the order of the Gospels is Matthew, John, Luke, and Mark; and in papyrus II, the order of NT books is Romans, Hebrews, Corinthians, Ephesians, Galatians, Philippians, Colossians, and 1 Thessalonians.

Bibliography. F. G. Kenyon, *The Chester Beatty Biblical Papyri,* 7 vols. (London, 1933-1958).

TIM MCLAY

CHESULLOTH (Heb. *kĕsûllōṯ*)
A city in Issachar (Josh. 19:18), identified with modern Iksâl (180232), 5 km. (3 mi.) SE of Nazareth. The name is a variant form of Chisloth-tabor.

CHEZIB (Heb. *kĕzîḇ*)
A town in southern Canaan where the daughter of the Canaanite Shua gave birth to Shelah, Judah's third son (Gen. 38:5). Chezib has been firmly identified with ancient Achzib in Judah (modern Tell el-Beida; 145116) near Adullam (cf. Eusebius *Onom.* 172, *Chasbi*).

CHRISTIAN M. M. BRADY

CHIDON (Heb. *kîḏōn*)
The threshing floor where Uzzah was struck dead for touching the ark of the covenant (1 Chr. 13:9). The passage does not indicate if Chidon is the name, the site, or the owner of the threshing floor. The name Nacon is used in the parallel passage (2 Sam. 6:6). After Uzzah's death, David renamed the place Perez-uzzah, meaning "outbreak against Uzzah" (2 Sam. 6:8 = 1 Chr. 13:11).

BETTY P. LAWSON

CHIEF PRIESTS
A collective term (Gk. *archiereís*) designating the aristocracy of the Jerusalem priesthood (e.g., Matt. 2:4; Mark 11:18, 27).

See PRIESTHOOD, ISRAELITE.

CHILDREN, CHILDHOOD
Children were an important part of ancient society. The vocabulary associated with childhood reflects an awareness of the child in its social setting, but that is not related to any understanding of the precise stages of a child's development (e.g., Mark 5:42 links together two quite different life stages). Children were essentially valued for their economic potential (Matt. 22:23-28) and as prospective care for adults in old age (although infant mortality was quite high and the life span of the majority of people was considerably shorter than today).

The life of the child was formed and oriented within the household under the ultimate authority of the paterfamilias, who might (Luke 11:7) or might not (in the case of the children of slaves) be the father. Children were generally left to be reared up to the age of about seven by the mother and other women; thereafter, while daughters continued to learn a domestic role, sons were socialized into the adult male environment. The value of obedience was especially emphasized (cf. Deut. 21:18-21; Sir. 3:2-16; Matt. 21:28-31; Rom. 1:30; 1 Tim. 3:4; 5:8), and since that was not thought to arise naturally, parents were exhorted to watchful discipline (Prov. 3:11-12; Heb. 12:7-11). Such discipline could be severe (Sir. 30:1-13). Nevertheless, social practices in the rearing of children reflect parents' sorrow at the death of children, and in both the Domestic Codes and the teaching of Jesus' kindness to children is clearly advocated (Matt. 7:9-11; Col. 3:21; cf. 2 Cor. 12:14; 1 Thess. 2:7; Isa. 66:12b-13; 4 Macc. 15:4).

The metaphorical understanding of childhood as a perspective for discipleship reflects the role and status of children expressed negatively as childishness, the child as an object lesson in what to avoid (1 Cor. 13:11-12; Eph. 4:14; cf. *m. 'Abot* 3:11). Given that children were viewed essentially as adults in the making, it was frequently the case that children were thought of as weak in mind, i.e., deficient in rationality. This may be further reinforced by imagery related to dietary distinctions (1 Cor. 3:1-2; Heb. 5:12-14; 1 Pet. 2:2).

Paul describes the Jewish teacher as "a guide to the blind, a light to those who are in darkness, a corrector of the foolish, a teacher of children" (Rom. 2:19-20). The corollary to this, where the image of the child has a positive meaning, lies in the praise of the schoolchild, one who can be emulated by adults as a learner. Indeed, the relationship between teacher and pupil can be defined in terms of parent and child (John 21:5; Gal. 4:19; 1 Thess. 2:11; 1 John 2:1), and discipleship may be described as filial obedience and trust (Ps. 131). While there is no emphasis on the innocence of the child (although the Gospel of Thomas establishes a link with sexual innocence), childhood may be associated with paradisal fulfillment (Isa. 11:6-9), and intuitive spontaneity may be thought to provide insight into the divine purpose (Matt. 21:15-16; cf. Ps. 8:1-2[MT 2-3]; Matt. 11:25-26 = Luke 10:21). In the ancient world the exposure of unwanted children was common (cf. Ezek. 16:5), but in Judaism children were considered to be under divine protection (Exod. 1:15–2:10; Matt. 18:10).

In the Synoptic Gospels especially, a particular significance attaches to Jesus' teaching both in terms of his welcome to children and the metaphorical significance of childhood. Two passages relate to the reception of children: the incident of the child in the midst at Mark 9:36-37 (cf. Matt. 18:2, 4-5; Luke 9:47-48) and the blessing of children at Mark 10:13-16 (cf. Matt. 19:13-15; Luke 18:15-17). In the first story, set against the background of the low social status of children, the child is welcomed and serves as an object lesson for the disciples. Moreover, the child in its own right is also declared to be an envoy of the Kingdom since it is the nature of God to care for the least. In the second story Jesus gladly welcomes and blesses the children who are brought to him (echoing the blessing by Jacob at Gen. 48) and declares that they are fully part of God's covenant. Both stories express Jesus' understanding of God's free grace bestowed on all without reference to status or merit (and thus they recall Israel's own experience as a child: Deut. 7:7-8; Hos. 11:1-4; Ezek. 16:3-7, 22). But within the Markan story of the blessing of the children there is introduced another saying about receiving the Kingdom "as a child" (Mark 10:15 par.; cf. Matt. 18:3). This should probably be understood as receiving "in a childlike manner" (as in Mark 9:37). Childhood thus now becomes a metaphor for the believer's own attitude of faith. For Mark and Luke this expresses itself as a glad and wholehearted acceptance of the Kingdom as a gift, while in Matthew (18:4) there is an emphasis on humility in the recognition of need and dependency.

Two further object lessons involving children are to be found at Matt. 11:16-19 par. (the parable of the children's game in the marketplace) and Matt. 21:15-16 (the children's voices in the temple). In the former it is not the case that Jesus is critical of the children since guesswork is part of the game. The game is a visual reference to the predicament of the present generation which has failed to understand the missions of John and Jesus. The other incident (cf. Ps. 8:2[3]) returns to a familiar theme that it is the children who are ranked with the marginal (Matt. 21:14) who display true wisdom (cf. 11:25).

In general Jesus' welcome of children and his consistently nonpejorative metaphorical understanding of childhood are noteworthy. It would be remarkable enough for an adult to think that he had anything to learn from a child, other than the zeal of the schoolchild, but Jesus welcomes children in their own right. Moreover, in contrast to the prevailing imagery of childhood as immaturity he makes of childhood a metaphor for faith. Jesus' teaching concerning children represents a sharp reevaluation of the social value of honor. It advocates the requirement to adopt the way of a child both in ready trust and in identifying with the least and the dispossessed as the way of the Kingdom. It may be this call to a change of outlook (Matt. 18:3) which influences the Fourth Gospel to relate discipleship to new birth (John 3:3-6). Birthing imagery is also descriptive of the coming of the messianic age (John 16:21; Rom. 8:22; 1 Thess. 5:3; Rev. 12:2; cf. Isa. 26:17-18; 66:7-9).

The theme of childhood also helped to shape Christology in the Gospels. It undoubtedly contributes to the wider portrait of Jesus himself as child of God, obedient through the whole of his ministry to the will of his Father. It also informs the Infancy narratives of Matthew and Luke (cf. Luke 2:49-52). In the Fourth Gospel a distinction is made whereby Jesus alone is consistently referred to as the Son of God while the believers are the children of God.

The teaching of children was part of the mission of the early Church, perhaps though not exclusively associated with the influence of women in the household (e.g., 2 Tim. 1:5; cf. Acts 16:1; 1 Cor. 7:14). But Jesus' own teaching about childhood, given within a domestic setting (Mark 9:33; 10:10), undoubtedly continued to influence the Church in its awareness of the care of children, and of all who might be described as "little ones" irrespective of age (Matt. 18:5; Luke 9:48; Barn. 19; cf. Luke 22:26).

Bibliography. W. Barclay, *Educational Ideals in the Ancient World* (1959, repr. Grand Rapids, 1974); E. Best, "Mark 10:13-16: The Child as Model Recipient," in *Disciples and Discipleship* (Edinburgh, 1986), 80-97; J. Francis, "Children and Childhood in the New Testament," in *The Family in Theological Perspective,* ed. S. C. Barton (Edinburgh, 1996), 65-85; H.-R. Weber, *Jesus and the Children* (Atlanta, 1979); T. Wiedemann, *Adults and Children in the Roman Empire* (New Haven, 1989).

JAMES FRANCIS

CHILEAB (Heb. *kil'āḇ*)
The second of David's sons, born in Hebron, the firstborn of David and Abigail, the widow of Nabal of Carmel (2 Sam. 3:2-3). He is called Daniel in the MT of 1 Chr. 3:1 (cf. Josephus *Ant.* 7.21, *Daniēlos*) and Dalouia in the LXX of 2 Sam. 3:3. Based upon these different spellings, it is conjectured that Chileab's actual name was either Daniel or Daluiah.

KENNETH ATKINSON

CHILION (Heb. *kilyôn*)
The younger son of Elimelech and Naomi, and the husband of Orpah (Ruth 1:2-4). Chilion, like his brother Mahlon, died early, leaving his wife a widow (Ruth 1:5).

CHILMAD (Heb. *kilmaḏ*)
A unknown place or region which traded with Tyre (Ezek. 27:23). Some scholars identify Chilmad with the city of Kullimeri in northern Mesopotamia (emending *klmd* to *klmr*) and others identify it with the entire country of Media (emending *klmd* to *kl mdy*).

CHIMHAM (Heb. *kimhām*)
A son (so 1 Kgs. 2:7; "servant" at 2 Sam. 19:37[MT 38]) of Barzillai the Gileadite, who declined David's reward for his aid to the king during Absalom's rebellion, asking that he instead favor the lad (vv. 34-37[35-38]). David took Chimham with him to Jerusalem (2 Sam. 19:40[41]), where he provided for his physical needs; it is possible that the king gave him a grant of land near Bethlehem, later called Geruth Chimham (Jer. 41:17).

CHINNERETH (Heb. *kinnereṯ*)
1. A large freshwater lake in northern Israel known by several names: Chinnereth (Num 34:11; Deut. 3:17; Josh. 13:27), Chinneroth (Josh. 11:2; 12:3), the Sea of Gennesaret (Mark 6:53; Luke 5:1), the Sea of Galilee (Matt. 15:29; Mark 1:16), and Lake Tiberias (John 6:1; 21:1). The name of the sea may have been derived from Heb. *kinnôr,* which means "harp," resembling the shape of the lake.

2. A city (Heb. *kinnāreṯ*) located on the northwestern side of the Sea of Chinnereth. It was one of the fortified cities in the tribal allotment of Naphtali (Josh. 19:35). The city is mentioned in Thutmose III's list of conquered cities during his campaign (ca. 1468 B.C.). The site is identified with modern Tell el-ʿOreimeh/Tel Chinnereth (2008.2529).

3. The territory around the city (Chinneroth; Heb. *kinĕrôṯ*) and the lake conquered by Ben-hadad from King Baasha of Israel (1 Kgs. 15:20). In the NT it is known as the land of Gennesaret (Matt. 14:34).

BRADFORD SCOTT HUMMEL

CHIOS (Gk. *Chíos*)
An island in the Aegean Sea, ca. 19 km. (12 mi.) W of Smyrna (Izmir). At the end of his third missionary journey Paul and his companions sailed from Mitylene past Chios before arriving at Samos the next day (Acts 20:15).

CHISLEV (Heb. *kislēw*)
The ninth month of the Hebrew calendar (Nov./Dec.; Zech. 7:1). On the 25th day of Chislev the Jews celebrated the Feast of the Renewal of the temple ("festival of the Dedication"; John 10:22).

CHISLON (Heb. *kislôn*)
A Benjaminite, the father of Elidad (Num. 34:21).

CHISLOTH-TABOR (Heb. *kislôṯ tāḇōr*)
A town on the southern border of Zebulun (Josh. 19:12). Modern Iksâl (180232), ca. 5 km. (3 mi.) SE of Nazareth, preserves the ancient name. Although most scholars identify the two, the qualifying term "Tabor" (a mountain on the borders of Issachar, Zebulun, and Naphtali) may distinguish this town from Chesulloth in Issachar (Josh. 19:18).

CHITLISH (Heb. *kiṯlîš*)
A town in the tribal allotment of Judah (Josh. 15:40), situated in the Lachish district in the southwest Shephelah. The precise location is unknown, but recent suggestion puts it in the Naḥal Adorayim basin, possibly at Khirbet el-Baqar (13006.10427). Chitlish may be the Kentisha conquered by Thutmose III and the *k-n-ti-sa* on an ostracon from Lachish. STEVEN M. ORTIZ

CHLOE (Gk. *Chlóē*)
A wealthy business woman whose people brought to Paul in Ephesus news of division within the Corinthian church (1 Cor. 1:11). Chloe's people (lit., "those of Chloe") were either her family members, business associates, slaves, or free employees. Whether she resided in Corinth and sent others to conduct business in Ephesus or vice versa is unclear. Chloe's people were undoubtedly Christian, but Chloe may not have been, although Paul's designation "those of Chloe" is typical of how he refers to Christian households (cf. Rom. 16:10-11). Chloe may have been the leader of a household church.

JOANN FORD WATSON

CHOIRMASTER
Fifty-five Psalm headings and Hab. 3:19 refer to the "choirmaster" (Heb. *mĕnaṣṣēaḥ*). The verbal form (Ezek. 3:8; 1 Chr. 23:4; 2 Chr. 2:1) means "to lead," or "to be at the head"; in 1 Chr. 15:21 the verb probably means "to make music." Undoubtedly, music had a prominent place in the religious worship of Israel (1 Chr. 15:16-24), and most likely the choirmaster led the community in the praise of God through music. W. DENNIS TUCKER, JR.

CHORAZIN (Gk. *Chorazín*)
A town in Upper Galilee rebuked by Jesus for its lack of repentance, even though the town had witnessed his miracles (Matt. 11:21; Luke 10:13). Rabbinic sources describe Chorazin as a medium-sized town with a distinctive wheat production (*b. Menaḥ.* 85a). The city prospered in the 2nd century A.D. when the region expanded with refugees from the Bar Kokhba Rebellion.

Khirbet Karâzeh (2031.2575), ca. 3 km. (2 mi.) NW of Capernaum, was first identified as Chorazin in the middle of the 19th century by C. W. M. Van de Velde. A 4th-century A.D. synagogue was uncovered there in 1926. The Israel Department of Antiquities and Museums conducted excavations there in 1962-65 and restoration work in 1982-86.

Bibliography. Z. Yeivin, "Ancient Chorazin Comes Back to Life," *BARev* 13/5 (1987): 22-36.

STEPHEN J. ANDREWS

CHRIST
Gk. *Christós*, lit., "the Anointed One," a translation of Heb. /Aram. "the Messiah." The term is related to the verb "to anoint, to smear." As with its Hebrew counterpart, "Christ" can be used adjecti-

The Transfiguration, **Duccio di Buoninsegna (1311; National Gallery, London). Christ stands before the apostles Peter, John, and James and flanked by the prophets Moses and Elijah** (Art Resource, N.Y.)

vally ("the anointed priest"; e.g., Lev. 4:5, 16) but is most common as a noun. As a title, "the Christ" makes sense only in Jewish and Christian literature where the ancient (biblical) practice of anointing with oil as part of ritual installation to office is in view. The term presumes not only a biblical context but a history of interpretation, since the form — a noun and a definite article, without modifiers — is unattested in the Greek LXX as well as in the Hebrew Bible.

Pauline Letters

The term appears in the NT most frequently in the Pauline letters (more than 200 times in the undisputed letters alone). In the vast majority of instances, "Christ" appears in nontitular form. It can appear with the proper name Jesus ("Jesus Christ," "Christ Jesus," "the Lord Jesus Christ"), or alone, in anarthrous form ("Christ died for our sins," "in Christ," "baptized into Christ"), where the reference is clearly to the one Christ, Jesus. Only once in the Pauline corpus does "the Christ" refer clearly to a figure from Jewish tradition, without necessarily being a reference to Jesus ("to them [the Israelites] belong the patriarchs, and from them, according to the flesh, comes the Christ . . ."; Rom. 9:5).

While the title never appears as a predicate nominative ("Jesus is the Christ"), the data in Paul's letters represent an advanced stage in a developing christological tradition, presupposing an initial Hebrew/Aramaic confession, "Jesus is the Messiah." It is possible to read Paul's letters without knowing much about "Christ" other than that it is some honorific designation that appears next to Jesus' name. The meaning of the term is provided by statements about the Christ, Jesus. As Nils A. Dahl has shown, however, a more careful reading of Paul's letters indicates the degree to which Paul presumes a whole history of christological tradition, including a complex and sophisticated "messianic exegesis" of Israel's Scriptures. Knowing something about Israel's messianic tradition is thus important for understanding Paul's use of the term.

Striking is how greatly Paul's "christological" statements differ from traditional Jewish messianism. Apart from a few passages like Rom. 2:16; 1 Cor. 15:24-28 that refer to judging and ruling, identifying Jesus as "Christ" has less to do with a royal office than with suffering, humiliation, and death (e.g., 1 Cor. 1:22-24; 15:3-4). Paul can speak in more traditional terms, e.g., about the Davidic descent of Jesus the Christ, but even in these instances it is Jesus' death and vindication that are the focus of his "office" (Rom. 1:2-4)

While "Son of God" is a more comprehensive term, its place in messianic oracles like 2 Sam. 7:14; Ps. 2:7, where God addresses the king as "Son," is an important feature of the title. To be the promised Christ is part of what it means to be "the Son of God."

While not explicitly developed in the extant letters, Jesus' identity as "Christ" is central to Paul's theology. While Jesus may be called "Son of God" and "Lord," terms with currency in gentile as well as Jewish religious tradition, as "Christ" Jesus belongs to Israel (Rom. 9:5). It is not surprising, therefore, that Paul should find large-scale Jewish opposition to his preaching a serious theological as well as personal problem. At stake are God's promises to Israel. Rom. 9–11 are crucial to Paul's understanding of the gospel as well as of his mission.

That Jesus is the promised Christ is likewise central to Paul's reflection on gentile freedom from adherence to the law of Moses. His argument in Gal. 3 about gentile participation in the heritage of Abraham includes actual citations and allusions to a host of texts, some of which were part of messianic tradition (2 Sam. 7:10-14; Gen. 49:10). At the center of his own argument is the image of the crucified Christ who died "on a tree" and thus under the curse of God's law (Gal. 3:13; quoting Deut. 21:23). That Gentiles are exempted from obligation to the law of Moses is bound up with Jesus' death as Christ — and his vindication by God in the Resurrection. Gal. 3 in particular affords a glimpse of a whole tradition of "messianic exegesis" which Paul both presupposes and develops further.

It is significant that at precisely the point where Paul's theological and pastoral reflection are most distant from Jewish tradition (Romans and Galatians) he makes the most extensive use of learned scriptural argument paralleling that of school traditions within Judaism. While knowledge of Jewish messianic tradition is crucial for understanding Paul's argument, what stands out is the novelty of Paul's conclusions — something even Paul's colleagues within the Church found subversive and dangerous.

Gospels

In the Gospels "Christ" is used far less frequently than in Paul's letters (Matthew, 17 times; Mark, 7; Luke, 12 [Acts, 28]; John, 18). As in the Epistles, "Christ" can be used with Jesus' name (e.g., Mark 1:1). However, the use of "the Christ" as a title is more common ("where the Christ was to be born," Matt. 2:4; "You are the Christ," Mark 8:29; "the Christ is David's son," 12:35; "Let the Christ, the King of Israel, come down from the cross now," 15:32); "but these are written so that you may believe that Jesus is the Christ, the Son of God . . .," John 20:31). Only in Luke-Acts does the term appear occasionally in its more biblical form ("the Lord's Christ," Luke 2:26; "the Christ of God," 9:20; "his Christ," Acts 3:18). In all instances, readers are expected to know what the term means: it has to do with a royal office.

There are a few exceptions, as in Luke 4:17-19, where Jesus is "anointed" to preach good news to the poor, more clearly a prophetic than a royal office. Elsewhere in Luke-Acts, however, the content of Jesus' office as "a savior who is Christ the Lord" is provided by royal tradition: he is the "Son of the Most High" who will sit "on the throne of his ancestor David"; he will "reign over the house of Jacob forever, and of his kingdom there will be no end" (Luke 1:32-33). He is the one whom God has made "both Lord and Christ" by raising him from the dead and seating him at the right hand (Acts 2:34, quoting Ps. 110:1). Passages like Luke 4 are best understood as filling out what it means to be "the Christ" by means of creative interpretation of the Scriptures.

The term is notably uncommon within the Gospel accounts of Jesus' ministry. In the Synoptic Gospels, it is the demons who from the outset know who Jesus is. Yet according to Mark and Matthew, the demons do not recognize Jesus as "Messiah" but as "the Son of God" (though "Son of God" is clearly a title associated with the royal office, as in Ps. 2:7; 2 Sam. 7:14). The common people recognize Jesus as a prophetic figure: John the Baptist, Elijah, or one of the prophets (Mark 8:28 par.). In the Gospel narratives, the only person to call Jesus "the Christ" is Peter — an insight that in Matthew Jesus characterizes as possible only through inspiration ("flesh and blood has not revealed this to you but my Father in heaven"; Matt. 16:16-17). The "confession" of Jesus as the Christ is followed by the first of Jesus' predictions of his impending rejection, death, and resurrection (Matt. 16:21-23; Mark 8:31-33). Peter's reaction — his "rebuke" of Jesus — indicates that "Christ" and cross do not belong together.

In all the Gospels, "Christ" appears most frequently, with related royal imagery, in the Passion Narratives: Jesus is arrested, tried, mocked, and executed as king. The royal office is expressed differently by various groups in the story. The chief priests use the language of the tradition in referring to Jesus as "the Christ," "the Christ of God," or "the Christ the King of Israel." Romans, appropriate to their gentile status, refer to Jesus as "the King of the Jews," using "Jews" instead of "Israel" and viewing the title exclusively as a political claim. Jesus is most frequently identified as "the Christ" (= King) at that point in the story where he looks least like the promised Messiah.

Even apart from knowledge of Jewish biblical tradition, the Gospel stories highlight the strangeness of the term when applied to Jesus in this context. To the Jewish authorities, calling Jesus "the Christ" is blasphemous and absurd (Mark 14:63-65). He is taunted as he hangs on the cross: "Let the Christ, the King of Israel, come down from the cross now, so that we may see and believe" (Mark 15:32). He does not, which means to the Jewish authorities that he is simply another pretender. The claim to be the Christ, which makes Jesus guilty of sedition in Caesar's empire, is no less absurd to the Romans, who treat Jesus to a mock investiture. They put a robe on him, make a crown, and salute him: "Hail, King of the Jews" (Mark 15:17-19). From the perspective of the characters, therefore — the religious and political authorities — there is something grossly inappropriate about calling Jesus "the Christ."

From the readers' perspective, the charges and taunts are ironic. Readers are told at various points that Jesus is the Christ; his vindication by God in his resurrection is foreshadowed throughout the Gospel narratives. That Jesus' enemies are the ones to dress him as king and to announce his identity to the world is a literary expression of Paul's insistence that God has chosen to reveal wisdom through foolishness (1 Cor. 1).

What it means to call Jesus "the Christ" is thus bound tightly to his trial, death, and resurrection. Thus there is in the Gospels and Paul a subversive element, an acknowledgment that Jesus' "messianic" career is a surprise, a scandal, a critical moment that demands a reappraisal of the whole biblical witness. It is appropriate that those who are not persuaded should find such a confession at odds with Israel's biblical heritage. And while believers in Jesus began an effort to understand the OT witness in light of his cross and resurrection — eventually remaking the notion of "the Christ" through a radical reconfiguring of messianic tradition — the scandal of a "crucified Christ" still remains.

To understand what it means that Jesus is "the Christ" in the NT is aided by knowledge of Jewish messianic tradition. The language derives from the Scriptures of Israel and the history of their exposition in postbiblical times. The specifics of NT tradition, however, are bound to the particulars of the career of Jesus of Nazareth. Only in view of those particulars, especially the accounts of Jesus' trial and death, is it possible to understand the dramatic shift in meaning of "the Messiah" as it is used of Jesus of Nazareth.

Beyond the New Testament

Jewish and Christian tradition developed in different directions from a common heritage. For the later rabbis, the Messiah-King remained one of the important figures in visions and dreams of the future. For followers of Jesus, "Christ" became largely a second name of Jesus, though significant enough to serve as the basis for a new self-designation that would distinguish those heirs of Israel's heritage who confessed Jesus from those who did not. By the end of the 2nd century, "Christian" came to designate a worshipper of Israel's God who believed in Jesus the Christ, to be distinguished from "Jew."

The later tradition of the Church took up the task of making sense theologically and christologically in a gentile setting. The confession of Jesus as "Christ" was presupposed but was largely insignificant for the dogmatic tradition and trinitarian developments. Even by the middle of the 2nd century, the issue of Jesus' identity as "Christ" was important for authors like Justin Martyr almost exclusively in the context of scriptural interpretation. More important were to be biblical images like the "Logos," the "Lord," and "the Son" and his relationship to the Father.

Yet while the NT begins the process of reflecting on the new rules for speaking about God as the one who raised Jesus from the dead and is now revealed in Jesus, Jesus remains "the Christ" — rooted in the tradition of Israel — whose identity is tied most closely to his death and vindication as "the King of the Jews."

See MESSIAH.

Bibliography. J. H. Charlesworth, ed., *The Messiah: Developments in Earliest Judaism and Christianity* (Minneapolis, 1992); N. A. Dahl, *Jesus the Christ: The Historical Origins of Christological Doctrine* (Minneapolis, 1991); D. Juel, *Messianic Exegesis: Christological Interpretation of the Old Testament in Earliest Christianity* (Minneapolis, 1988); G. Vermes, *Jesus the Jew* (1973, repr. Philadelphia, 1981).

DONALD JUEL

CHRIST AND ABGAR

One of the more intriguing legends of the early Church involving King Abgar of Edessa's correspondence with Jesus as recorded by Eusebius and the Teachings of Addai. Abgar tells Jesus that he had heard of his miraculous cures, and had concluded that Jesus must be either God or the Son of God, and then requests that Jesus come to Edessa to heal him of his "suffering." The letter concludes with an offer of safe haven since Abgar also knew of the Jews' persecution of Jesus. Jesus' letter in response praises Abgar's faith but declines the invitation. Jesus does, however, promise to send a disciple to heal Abgar and to preach the gospel after his Ascension. The Teaching of Addai differs from Eusebius' account in that Jesus sends an oral reply, along with a portrait of himself, instead of a letter. Although the Abgar legend circulated widely in the early and medieval Church (Jesus' letter was used as a charm to ward off evil), most modern interpreters concur with Rome's 6th-century determination that the letters were spurious.

Bibliography. S. H. Moffett, *A History of Christianity in Asia,* 2nd ed. (Maryknoll, 1998); S. Runciman, "Some Remarks on the Image of Edessa," *Cambridge Historical Journal* 3 (1929-1932): 238-52; H. C. Youtie, "A Gothenberg Papyrus and the Letter to Abgar," *HTR* 23 (1930): 299-302; "Gothenberg Papyrus 21 and the Coptic Version of the Letter to Abgar," *HTR* 24 (1931): 61-65.

CHARLES GUTH

CHRISTIAN

A term (Gk. *christianós*) found in the Bible only in Acts 11:26; 26:28; 1 Pet. 4:16. Among both Latin and Greek writers, it was common to add the suffix *-ianus* (Latin) or *-ianos* (Greek) to the proper name of one considered to be the leader of a group. According to Acts 11:26 it was non-Christian Antiochenes of Syria who first applied the name to followers of Jesus. This indicates that they were known by outsiders as persons who followed one known as *Christós,* and it implies that from a relatively early period people recognized something distinctively non-Jewish about the movement (since it is unlikely that Gentiles would have known the Jewish significance of the word *christós,* "messiah"). It was not until the early 2nd century that Christians began with some regularity to employ the term as a self-designation (e.g., Ignatius and the Didache). J. BRADLEY CHANCE

CHRISTMAS

From OE *Cristes Mæsse.* Not knowing the date of Christ's birth, the early Church sought one by combining calendrical speculations with the exegesis of biblical numbers. Several dates were suggested, including Mar. 25, Apr. 2, May 20, Nov. 8, Dec. 25, and Jan. 6. The earliest evidence, the *Depositio martyrum,* has the Feast of the Nativity being celebrated on Dec. 25 by the year 336 in Rome. Within a century this date was almost universally accepted.

Dec. 25 marked, in the Julian calendar, the winter solstice (the beginning of the victory of light over darkness after the year's longest night) and, after 274, the feast of the birthday of *Sol Invictus* (the "invincible sun"), patron deity of the emperor. The association between Jesus and the sun occurred early and naturally; Jesus rose on Sunday (the "Lord's Day"). As early as Clement of Alexandria (d. 216) Jesus was being identified with the "Sun of Righteousness" (Vulg. *Sol Iustitiae*) of Mal. 4:2(MT 3:20) (*Exhort.* 11). A related early tradition identified Mar. 25, the "Sunday" of creation week, as the date of Christ's conception (nine months before Dec. 25!). It was only natural that after Constantine had abandoned the patronage of *Sol Invictus* in 324, *Sol Iustitiae,* the light of the world, should supersede him.

Bibliography. O. Cullmann, "The Origin of Christmas," *The Early Church* (Philadelphia, 1956), 17-36; A. T. Kraabel, "The Roots of Christmas," *Dialog* 21 (1982): 274-80; K. Lake, "Christmas," *ERE* 3 (New York, 1958): 601-8. RONALD V. HUGGINS

CHRISTOLOGY

In the broadest sense, Christology attempts to answer the question Jesus poses to his disciples in Mark 8:27-29: "Who do people say that I am?" In a narrower sense, Christology is a study of the titles the early Church ascribed to the historical Jesus insofar as those titles (e.g., Son of Man, Christ, Son of God, Messiah, Teacher) reflect Jesus' own self-understanding. Still more narrowly, Christology refers to the theological doctrine concerning the person and nature of Christ and the extent to which the humanity and divinity are united in his person. While the NT writings raise questions about the identity of Christ, explicit christological statements do not appear until well into the 1st century when the early Church is striving for self-definition and orthodoxy.

Even though the creeds of the 4th and 5th centuries are the earliest documents to define the union of Christ's humanity and divinity, early christological confessions in the NT identify God's divine nature with Christ's human nature, particularly in the act of creation. Paul declares that "there is one God, the Father, from whom are all things and for whom we exist, and one Lord, Jesus Christ, through whom are all things and through whom we exist" (1 Cor. 8:6). In Col. 1:15-20 Christ is "the image of the invisible God . . . in him all things were created . . . in him all the fullness of God was pleased to dwell." Heb. 1:10 proclaims that Christ not only created the earth but also that "the heavens are the work of his hands." Even the early Christian writer and martyr Polycarp boldly testifies that God is the "Father of Jesus Christ," i.e., God's activity is known only through Christ's activity.

Such early christological confessions enabled the early Church to demonstrate its distinctive self-identity to Jewish and Hellenistic religious movements of the 1st century. As the Church grew, however, there were great debates between various Christian parties about the person and nature of Christ.

Within the 1st century the Docetists considered Christ's humanity and suffering to be apparent rather than real. For the Docetists, who believed that the body was evil, God could not have entered into a corrupt human body. Some Docetists claimed that Jesus escaped death, and Judas Iscariot or Simon of Cyrene took his place on the cross. In contrast, the Ebionites denied Jesus' divinity, claiming that he was the human son of Joseph and Mary upon whom God bestowed divine power at his baptism.

In the 4th century a presbyter named Arius argued that there were not two natures present in Christ. He went on to deny that Christ is truly God. At the Council of Nicea in 325 Athanasius and a number of other bishops condemned Arius' ideas and declared that Jesus was fully divine and equal with the Father. Later in the 4th century Apollinarius, bishop of Laodicea, argued that the deity of Christ was so dominant that Christ's divine nature replaced his human nature. In 381 the Council of Constantinople ratified the work of the Council of Nicea and declared that Christ was fully human and fully divine. During the 5th century Nestorius, an Antiochene monk, claimed that there were two distinct persons, one human and one divine, in Christ. Nestorius also asserted that the title ascribed to the Virgin Mary, "Theotokos," or God-bearer, contradicted the full humanity of Christ. The Council of Ephesus (431) condemned Nestorius and affirmed the Nicene formula of Christ's full humanity and divinity. Nearly 20 years later Eutychus, the head of a monastery at Constantinople, maintained that Christ had two natures "before the Incarnation" but Christ had only one nature "after the Incarnation." The Council of Chalcedon (451) condemned the heresies of Nestorius and Eutychus and established what has become the orthodox christological formula by declaring that there is "one . . . Christ . . . in two natures, without confusion, without change, without division, without separation."

Although the Chalcedonian definition has dominated Christian theological self-understanding for centuries, new currents in biblical criticism continue to raise important questions about the ways that the NT writings portray Jesus' self-understanding as well as the early Church's understanding of Jesus. Focusing on the picture of Jesus in Q and extracanonical sources, John Dominic Crossan, Leif Vaage, Burton Mack, Gregory Riley, and the Jesus Seminar have challenged the portrait of Jesus as an apocalyptic prophet (Son of Man) ushering in the imminent kingdom of God. In these writings, Jesus is less messianic Son of God than a Mediterranean Jewish peasant (Crossan) who identifies with the marginalized sectors of Palestinian society and who espouses wise moral sayings (Mack) in the fashion of a Cynic philosopher (Vaage). Such debates demonstrate the centrality of Christology to the Christian faith as well as its dynamic nature.

Bibliography. O. Cullmann, *Christology of the New Testament,* rev. ed. (Philadelphia, 1964).

HENRY L. CARRIGAN, JR.

CHRONICLE

A record or list of events. The genre of chronicle (Heb. *sēp̱er diḇrê hayyāmîm*) should not be equated with 1–2 Chronicles, which are histories that utilize various sources and genres, including chronicles. A chronicle lists events without any necessary connection or coherence and therefore does not constitute a history in itself. Chronicles were usually maintained by the palace or temple to record significant events with precise dates in chronological sequence. Chronicles typically included brief, highly stylized reports of military campaigns, building projects, hunting exploits, and royal donations. Chronicles may be as specific as daybooks, precisely dated daily records of activity in the palace, or as general as summaries of the principal deeds of the kings.

The biblical historians cite various chronicles such as the chronicles (NRSV "Annals") of the Kings of Judah (i.e., 1 Kgs. 14:29; 15:7, 23), the chronicles of the Kings of Israel (14:19; 15:31), the books of the Kings of Israel and Judah (1 Chr. 9:1; 2 Chr. 16:11), the book of the Acts of Solomon (1 Kgs. 11:41), the chronicles of King David (1 Chr. 27:24), the chronicles of Samuel, Nathan, and Gad (29:29), the chronicles of Shemaiah the Prophet and of Iddo the Seer (2 Chr. 12:15), the chronicles of the Kings of Media and Persia (Esth. 10:2), and other various chronicles (Neh. 12:23; Esth. 2:23; 6:1).

The genre of chronicles used by the biblical historians was common throughout the ancient Near East. Numerous Mesopotamian and Egyptian chronicles are extant or known in ancient references, such as the Weidner Chronicle, the Babylonian date lists, and the Assyrian eponym lists.

Bibliography. A. K. Grayson, *Assyrian and Babylonian Chronicles.* Texts from Cuneiform Sources 5 (Locust Valley, N.Y., 1975); B. Halpern, *The First Historians* (1988, repr. University Park, Pa., 1996); J. Van Seters, *In Search of History* (New Haven, 1983).

BRADFORD SCOTT HUMMEL

CHRONICLER'S HISTORY

The history beginning with the books of Chronicles and ending with Ezra-Nehemiah. Since Chronicles ends with Cyrus' decree allowing the exiled Jews to return home and rebuild the temple and Ezra begins with the same, it has been assumed that these books form part of a greater whole, a unity best explained as the work of a single author or editor. In positing a common authorship for Chronicles, Ezra, and Nehemiah, commentators have also cited similar interests in genealogies, the primacy of Jerusalem, the temple, sacrifice, and the relations between priests and Levites. Seen in this perspective, the Chronicler's history covers an enormous historical span, beginning with the first person (Adam) and ending with the second term of Nehemiah's governorship.

However, in recent decades the consensus about authorship has unravelled. Some scholars, led by Sara Japhet and H. G. M. Williamson, distinguish between the Chronicler's history, understood simply as Chronicles, and Ezra-Nehemiah. Seen in this perspective, the Chronicler's history begins with the first person (Adam) and ends with the Babylonian exile and Cyrus' summons to return home (2 Chr. 36:21-23). In spite of the growing popularity of the theory of separate authorship, some (e.g., Joseph Blenkinsopp) trenchantly defend common authorship. Others (e.g., Thomas Willi) believe that the Chronicler wrote Chronicles and Ezra-Nehemiah at two different times in his life.

The debate about authorship has involved at least five major issues. (1) Scholars debate whether the LXX book of 1 Esdras, which begins with Josiah's reign, continues with the return, and ends with the Feast of Tabernacles (cf. Neh. 8), bears witness to an original unity of Chronicles, Ezra, and Nehemiah or represents a secondary adaptation of the same. (2) Commentators disagree whether the style and characteristic language of Chronicles and Ezra-Nehemiah are similar or different. (3) Some scholars view the doublet in 2 Chr. 36:22-23; Ezra 1:1-3a as evidence for common authorship, while others view it as a secondary seam, artificially linking the two books. (4) Some commentators think that Chronicles betrays a fundamentally different, more conciliatory and open ideology from the more restricted and restricting perspective of Ezra and Nehemiah. But others (e.g., Gary N. Knoppers) think that some of the differences between the theology of Chronicles and Ezra-Nehemiah have been too sharply drawn or that some of these differences can be attributed to different subject matter (the preexilic monarchy vs. postexilic Yehud). (5) Some scholars discern different compositional techniques in Ezra-Nehemiah from those manifest in Chronicles. The authors of Ezra and Nehemiah call attention to sources, such as royal decrees and letters, while the author of Chronicles is said to integrate his sources into his narrative. Similarly, Ezra-Nehemiah evinces a consistent typology: project, opposition, and eventual success, but this dialectical view of history in which one problem (rebuilding Jerusalem's temple) after another (rebuilding Jerusalem's walls) is engaged and surmounted is said to be uncharacteristic of Chronicles.

Debate on these five issues has led to inconclusive results. To complicate matters further, it is by no means to be assumed that Ezra and Nehemiah stem from the same author. A close reading of Ezra-Nehemiah suggests that the compositional history of this work was complex. Given the diversity of perspectives in Chronicles, Ezra, and Nehemiah, it is not surprising that some scholars (e.g., Karl-Friedrich Pohlmann, David Noel Freedman, Frank M. Cross) have advanced theories of two or more redactions in the Chronicler's history. These authors affirm connections between Chronicles, Ezra, and Nehemiah, but suggest that more than one individual is responsible for all three works.

What conclusions can be drawn from this ongoing debate? New theories of authorship bear on interpretation. Scholars who hold either to separate authorship or to multiple editions no longer interpret Chronicles with primary reliance upon Ezra-Nehemiah. Because Chronicles is no longer being viewed as inseparable from Ezra-Nehemiah, its characteristic concerns are no longer forced into the mold of Ezra or Nehemiah. Such distinctions have led to a variety of fresh interpretations of both Chronicles and Ezra-Nehemiah.

Bibliography. J. Blenkinsopp, *Ezra-Nehemiah.* OTL (Philadelphia, 1988); F. M. Cross, "A Reconstruction of the Judean Restoration," *JBL* 94 (1975): 4-18; D. N. Freedman, "The Chronicler's Purpose," *CBQ* 23 (1961): 432-42; S. Japhet, "The Supposed Common Authorship of Chronicles and Ezra-Nehemiah Investigated Anew," *VT* 18 (1968): 330-71; G. N. Knoppers, "'Yhwh Is Not with Israel': Alliances as a *Topos* in Chronicles," *CBQ* 58 (1996): 601-26; H. G. M. Williamson, *Ezra, Nehemiah.* WBC 16 (Waco, 1985).

GARY N. KNOPPERS

CHRONICLES, BOOKS OF

Like many other biblical books, Chronicles is anonymous and untitled. The name ascribed to the book by the early rabbis, "the book of the events of the days" *(sēp̄er dib̠rê hayyāmîm),* indicates that they viewed Chronicles as a book about past events — a history. The name given in the LXX, *Paralipomena,* "the things left out," testifies to another early understanding: Chronicles records the events left out of earlier biblical history. But it was Jerome's description of the book as a "chronicle," a summary of divine history, that has proved most influential in the history of Christian interpretation.

Composition, Date, and Sources

By the time the Chronicler wrote in the postexilic period, much of the literature that we associate with the OT was already written. The author draws extensively upon this rich literary tradition. His dependence upon Genesis is evident in the genealogies (1 Chr. 1-9), and his dependence upon Samuel and Kings is obvious in his narration of the Monarchy (1 Chr. 10–2 Chr. 36). The Chronicler's indebtedness to antecedent literature is not confined, however, to his selective reuse of Genesis, Samuel, and Kings. Parallels with or citations from Joshua, Isaiah, Jeremiah, Ezekiel, the Psalms, and Ruth all appear in Chronicles. Scholars generally agree that the Chronicler also had access to extrabiblical sources, but the nature and extent of these sources are disputed.

Within the postexilic period Chronicles is very hard to date. There are no specific references, no absolute synchronisms, and no extrabiblical citations that could definitively situate the book within a given decade or century. Indeed, a range of more than 350 years (from the late 6th to the mid-2nd century B.C.E.) has been suggested. Although an absolute date cannot be assigned, one past the late 3rd century is unlikely. First, one must allow time for Chronicles or Chronicles-Ezra-Nehemiah to be brought to Egypt and translated into at least two different works (1 Esdras and *Paralipomena*). Second, *Paralipomena* is cited by Eupolemos, a Jewish-Hellenistic writer, in the 2nd century (Eusebius *Praep. ev.* 9.30-34).

Scholars disagree about the compositional history of Chronicles. Some believe that the book underwent a priestly, levitical, or deuteronomistic redaction. Arguments for disunity fail, however, to come to grips with the distinctive features of the Chronicler's compositional technique: his indebtedness to a variety of earlier biblical traditions, his adroitness in quoting and synthesizing originally disparate passages in the Deuteronomic and Priestly writings, and his ability to negotiate different ideological perspectives. There is no question that one encounters both pro-priestly and pro-levitical passages in Chronicles. But rather than proving that Chronicles underwent major redactions, it is more likely that these texts evince one author's concern to mediate historically different perspectives within the context of the postexilic age.

Structure and Major Themes

Chronicles has two major sections: the genealogies of 1 Chr. 1-9 and the history of the Monarchy (1 Chr. 10–2 Chr. 36). The first section, which forms the introduction to the work, includes brief genealogies for other peoples to whom Israel (Jacob) is related (1 Chr. 1), but focuses upon the identity and location of Israel's 12 tribes. The very scope and structure of the Chronicler's genealogical system underscore the indivisibility of Israel. Yet, Judah, Levi, and Benjamin receive the most extensive genealogies. The Chronicler both creates a comprehensive portrait of his people and underscores the crucial roles played by these three tribes. The list of those in the restored community (1 Chr. 9) calls attention to the continuity between postexilic society and the Israel of ages past. Population shifts, war, political turmoil, natural disaster, and exile are part of shifting history, but God's relationship with his people endures.

The Chronicler's coverage of the Monarchy proceeds according to a fundamentally historical outline. After briefly addressing and condemning the reign of Saul (1 Chr. 10), the Chronicler devotes extensive attention to the highly successful rise and reign of David (1 Chr. 11–29) and the glorious tenure of Solomon (2 Chr. 1–9). The rest of the book engages the emergence, continuation, and fall of the kingdom of Judah. By placing David and Solomon's achievements at the center of Israelite history, the author underscores the Davidic dynasty's centrality to Israelite life.

In Chronicles, David's ascent to power is a politician's dream. Whereas in Samuel the unification of Judah (2 Sam. 2:4) and Israel (5:1-10) under David's command is a long, arduous, and highly-contested process, in Chronicles representatives from all over Israel come to David to anoint him, acclaim him king, and pledge support (1 Chr. 11–12). David's first public act as king is to bring the ark of the covenant to Jerusalem. This passion for proper worship, a consistent feature of David's reign, culminates in his bequeathing to Solomon a generous endowment and detailed plans for building the Jerusalem temple (1 Chr. 22, 28–29). David also devotes great attention to Jerusalem, the Lord's chosen city (2 Chr. 6:34, 38; 12:13; 33:7), the respective responsibilities of priests and Levites (1 Chr. 15; 23–24), and to matters of song and music (1 Chr. 16:7-36; 25).

But David is more than a patron of worship, the priesthood, and music. He is also an astute leader and military genius. The support David receives and the counsel he seeks from all quarters consolidate Israel's national solidarity, while David's extraordinary success against Israel's neighbors ensures complete control over the land (1 Chr. 11–12; 14; 18–20). His bequeathing a national administration (1 Chr. 23–27) to his divinely chosen son and successor ensures a smooth transfer of power to Solomon and contributes to the latter's success. Indeed, at the end of David's reign all Israel, including the rest of David's sons, acclaims the accession of Solomon (1 Chr. 29:20-25; cf. 2 Sam. 9–20; 1 Kgs. 1–2).

Like David, Solomon receives widespread popular support at the beginning of his reign. He too is an avid patron of worship. Much of Solomon's reign is, in fact, dedicated to religious matters. At the inception of his reign, all Israel accompanies Solomon in journeying to the tent of the meeting at Gibeon (2 Chr. 1:2-5). In accordance with divine wishes, Solomon prepares for and supervises the construction of the long-awaited Jerusalem temple. All antecedent religious shrines, such as the tent of the meeting and the ark of the covenant, enjoy sacred but provisional status. The establishment of the temple under Solomon represents the culmination of disparate cultic traditions.

The value of the temple for all Israelites, repeatedly emphasized during the dedication ceremonies, is especially apparent in Solomon's prayer (2 Chr. 6:19-39; cf. 1 Kgs. 8:28-49). In praying toward the temple in times of trouble, Israelites can find divine compassion, forgiveness, and restitution. In his reply to Solomon's petitions, God affirms that should the people respond to calamity by humbling themselves, praying, seeking God, or returning to God, God will "hear from heaven, forgive their sins, and heal their land" (2 Chr. 7:14). The Chronicler's interest in the temple's national importance is not limited to his record of the United Monarchy. When later monarchs, such as Rehoboam (2 Chr. 12:1-12), Abijah (13:2-18), Asa (14:9-15[MT 8-14]), Jehoshaphat (18:28-34; 20:5-30), Hezekiah (30:13-21; 32:16-26), and Manasseh (33:10-13), respond to adversity according to Solomon's petitions, God intervenes and restores them. Conversely, when either king or people neglect the temple, Israel suffers.

In Chronicles the national solidarity that characterizes Solomon's accession and temple dedication continues throughout his reign (cf. 1 Kgs. 11). There is no hint of tension between northern tribes and southern tribes until the division. This idyllic picture of inter-tribal harmony has been upheld as a sign of the breadth of the Chronicler's vision, but this vision also has an edge. Because the Chronicler's portrayal of the united kingdom is so uniformly positive, it effectively impugns any person or group who would violate it. Having portrayed the establishment of Israel's normative political and cultic institutions in the time of David and Solomon, the Chronicler never reneges on their pertinence to all Israelites.

Following the death of Solomon and the accession of his son Rehoboam, the 10 northern tribes secede from southern rule (1 Kgs. 12:1-20; 2 Chr. 11:1-17). Whereas the author of Kings follows the course of both northern and southern kingdoms, the Chronicler concentrates upon the tribes of Judah, Benjamin, and Levi, who make up the kingdom of Judah (2 Chr. 11). Largely blaming mostly Jeroboam and his entourage for the division, the Chronicler sees both the political and the cultic separation of Israel as an affront against God (2 Chr. 13:4-12). Unlike the Deuteronomist (1 Kgs. 11:11-13, 29-38; 14:9), the Chronicler views the Davidic promises as permanently valid for all 12 Israelite tribes. Hence, the Chronicler passes over the independent history of the separatist kingdom Jeroboam founded. Nevertheless, the author shows a sustained interest in (northern) Israelite history by recording virtually every incident between north and south mentioned in Kings, as well as a number of other contacts. The Chronicler's coverage of the dual monarchies is, therefore, broadly consistent with the pattern he established in the genealogies. Israel continues to encompass all 12 tribes, but Judah, Benjamin, and Levi perpetuate the normative institutions established during the United Monarchy.

The Judahite monarchy is characterized by both achievements and failures. The writer consistently documents the achievements of Judah's best kings — Abijah (2 Chr. 13), Asa (chs. 14–15), Jehoshaphat (chs. 17; 19), Hezekiah (chs. 29–31), and Josiah (ch.

34) — instituting reforms, reuniting the people, and recovering lost territories. Major regressions occur in the reigns of Ahaz (2 Chr. 28) and Manasseh (33:1-9). Yet, consistent with the Chronicler's understanding of divine mercy, Manasseh repents and enjoys a significant recovery (33:10-19).

During the Judahite monarchy prophets play a major role in society. Whereas the Deuteronomist portrays very few active prophets in the southern kingdom until after the fall of the northern kingdom (2 Kgs. 17), the Chronicler portrays many. In Chronicles, prophecy represents an independent institution that checks royal and popular regression. Even some of Judah's better kings, such as Jehoshaphat, succumb to military, commercial, and cultic compromise (2 Chr. 18:1–19:3; 20:35-37). As a divinely ordained institution, prophets limit the excess and abuse of power, sanctioning wars (20:14-17) or refusing to do so (18:4-27), praising humility (12:5-8) or lambasting arrogance (16:7-10), encouraging reforms (15:1-7) or assailing idolatry (25:15-16). Trust in God is even equated with trust in his prophets (20:20). In commentary on the defeat and exile of Judah, the author states that although Yahweh sent a steady supply of prophets to stir the people and priestly leaders to reform, their warnings went unheeded (36:14-16).

Both Kings and Chronicles end with the Babylonian Exile, but the ending of Chronicles offers a clearer hope for the future. In the final verses of his work, the Chronicler presents the decree of Cyrus commending the return of the Babylonian deportees to Judah (2 Chr. 36:22-23). In this manner, Chronicles contains and relativizes the tremendous tragedy of the Babylonian deportations. As the beginning of Chronicles introduces the people of Israel and charts their emergence in the land, the ending anticipates their return.

Bibliography. S. Japhet, *I and II Chronicles*. OTL (Louisville, 1993); H. G. M. Williamson, *1 and 2 Chronicles*. NCBC (Grand Rapids, 1982); *Israel in the Book of Chronicles* (Cambridge, 1977).

Gary N. Knoppers

CHRONOLOGY OF THE OLD TESTAMENT

The OT contains an extensive set of chronological data which have been used to orient the history recited in time. Beginning at the end of the OT period we possess quite precise figures for the chronology of the Persian and Babylonian periods. The chronology present there probably does not vary by more than plus or minus one year. By the time one reaches the time of David at the beginning of the 1st millennium B.C.E. that variation is probably still limited to less than a decade.

The chronology for the biblical events of the 2nd millennium is based upon more variables; thus there is more flexibility to the possible times when those events occurred. The grand scheme of OT chronology worked out here places the three landmark personalities of Abraham ca. 2000, David ca. 1000, and Ezra ca. 450, providing dates for events that spanned over 1500 years.

Special Issues in Biblical Chronology

Intercalation

Virtually all Semitic calendars of Western Asia operated upon the basis of the lunar month, which is approximately 29.5 days. However, lunar months yield a year that is more than 10 days short of a solar year, the time that it takes for the earth to make a complete revolution. In order to keep the lunar calendar in alignment with the solar year, which determined the agricultural year, adjustment had to be made by adding an extra month about every third year. The postexilic community of Judah may have followed the Babylonian pattern of intercalation, which they could have brought back from exile. At most the difference involved here is one month, which is not significant.

Spring or Fall Calendars

Moses is credited with introducing a spring-to-spring calendar for the religious year (Exod. 12:2). This applied to the first Passover and then subsequently to the religious festivals that followed throughout the year (Lev. 23). The matter was complicated later, however, by the addition of a fall new year *(rōʾš haššānâ)*, which has been designated the civil year.

It appears that the spring new year was used for the civil year in the northern kingdom and the fall new year was used for the regnal year rather consistently in the southern kingdom, although some would reverse this application. Calculating the regnal years of kings, there may be a difference of up to six months, depending on if the king ascended to the throne after the spring new year or after the fall new year.

Accession and Nonaccession Year Reckoning

The ancients employed two systems to deal with the rest of the regnal year after the old king died. In nonaccession year reckoning, the first regnal year of the new king began immediately, so there was an excess of regnal years in contrast to calendar years. There was no accession period (year 0 of the new king). This was the system used in Egypt and, possibly, for some periods in the northern kingdom of Israel.

In accession year reckoning, the rest of the calendar year after the old king died was not counted, but was reckoned as year 0. The first full regnal year of the new king began at the next new year, either in the spring or the fall, whichever was in use at the time. This system kept the number of regnal years and the number of calendar years even. This system was used in Assyria and Babylonia, and also regularly in the southern kingdom of Judah. The difference that these two systems presented could involve as little as a few days or more than months.

Coregency

The practice of two living kings or co-kings on the throne at one time was an Egyptian custom as early as the 12th dynasty (ca. 2000 B.C.E.). There may have been coregencies in Judah near Egypt, but probably

Cylinder recording Cyrus' bloodless capture of Babylon (536 B.C.E.), his restoration of captives' temples, and the return of prisoners to their own lands (Copyright British Museum)

none of significance in the northern kingdom. It seems probable that there were some coregencies during the divided monarchy, following the precedent of David and Solomon. When Adonijah sought to supplant David, the aging king put Solomon on the throne (1 Kgs. 1). Thus there were two kings or coregents on the throne of the United Kingdom; David was the senior king and Solomon the junior king. Coregency was apparently adopted in times of war or when the older king was physically disabled.

Use of the LXX

In a fair number of cases the Hebrew and the LXX give a different number of years for a particular king. When taken together these variants offer a different chronological system. Probably the LXX is expansionistic (cf. Exod. 12:40).

Relative and Absolute Chronology

The OT contains a massive amount of chronological data, but almost all of it is in relative terms. For the Divided Monarchy, e.g., the dates are given in terms of the lengths of reign and synchronisms with the opposite kingdom. That gives a relative dating of king A to king B, but it does not give an absolute date B.C.E. for either of them.

Thus there needs to be a synchronism external to both kingdoms which provides an even better system of connecting these relative dates to absolute dates B.C.E. For the period of the Divided Monarchy, this is supplied by records from Assyria and Babylonia. These include king lists, eponym lists which name every year, and year-by-year entries in the royal annals or chronicles, all of which can be calibrated astronomically and mathematically by the records of eclipses, which can be dated in absolute terms by modern astronomers. Unfortunately, external synchronisms between the Bible and the ancient Near East have not yet turned up for the 2nd millennium and earlier.

OT History

From these theoretical considerations we turn to the actual chronology of the OT. Most chronologies begin at the beginning and work their way through the course of OT history to its end. The approach taken here is somewhat the reverse for the reason that the historian works from the well known to the less known.

Persian Period

Extrabiblical chronology for the postexilic period comes from various sources dating the Persian kings: cuneiform contract tablets, the Greek Olympiads, an eclipse text that mentions the death of Xerxes, and a Seleucid-period king list.

Several biblical books contain dated material from this period, which began in 539 with the fall of Babylon (Dan. 5). Cyrus' decree for the return of the Jews is dated in his first regnal year in Babylonia (2 Chr. 36:22; Ezra 1:1), 538. Darius I came to the throne in 522. In 520 the prophets Haggai and Zechariah urged the rebuilding of the temple, which was completed early in 515. Esther provides chronological data from the reign of Xerxes (biblical Ahasuerus, Esth. 1:3-4; 2:16; 3:7, 12, 13; 8:9, 12; 9:1-21). The second return of the Jews from exile led by Ezra himself following a decree by Artaxerxes I reached Jerusalem probably in the summer of 457, if Ezra was using a Jewish fall calendar (Ezra 7:7-8; cf. Neh. 1:1). Nehemiah records that he was sent back to Judah by Artaxerxes in his 20th year (Neh. 1:1; 2:1) and served as governor of Judah for 12 years (5:14), 444-432.

Neo-Babylonian Period

The chronology of the Neo-Babylonian kingdom is well established through extensive dates from contract tablets and the chronicles of Nabopolassar, Nebuchadnezzar II, and Nabonidus, and calibrated through an eclipse text from year 37 of Nebuchadnezzar. The period begins with Nebuchadnezzar coming to the throne in 605 and ends with the Persian conquest of Babylon in 539.

For biblical purposes this period may be extended back to 609, the year King Josiah died in battle with the Egyptian Necho II at Carchemish (2 Kgs. 23:29). The chronology of the last four kings of Judah after the death of Josiah follows a pattern:

Jehoahaz reigned three months (2 Kgs. 23:31)
Jehoiakim reigned eleven years (2 Kgs. 23:36)
Jehoiachin reigned three months (2 Kgs. 24:8)
Zedekiah reigned eleven years (2 Kgs. 24:18)

Correlations with Nebuchadnezzar's chronicle indicate that Jehoiakim ruled until the end of 598, and Jehoiachin surrendered to Nebuchadnezzar on 2 Adar 597. Zedekiah reigned until 587 if a spring calendar was used in Judah at this time or 586 if a fall calendar was used. Assuming the fall calendar, Jerusalem held out against Nebuchadnezzar for three years instead of two years. Nebuchadnezzar's siege of the city began early in 589 and ended in the summer of either 587 or 586.

Not only did the writers of 2 Kings and Jeremiah know the chronology of the kings of Judah well, they also knew that of the reign of Nebuchadnezzar. They double dated the last years of Judah to Jehoiachin and Zedekiah, and to Nebuchadnezzar (2 Kgs. 24:12; 25:2, 8).

Later Years of Judah

Most of the dates in this period are uncomplicated and straightforward, but its beginning with the reign of Hezekiah is one of the most difficult of problems in biblical chronology. This problem stems from the fact that the accession of Hezekiah appears to be dated in two different ways, each connected with a different event in which the Assyrians were involved. Hezekiah's "first" accession is dated in the third year of Hoshea, the last king of the northern kingdom (2 Kgs. 18:1). This would appear to date Hezekiah's accession to 728 and the siege of Samaria to 724-722. But another major Assyrian incursion in the west, which can be correlated directly with Sennacherib's third campaign in 701, is dated only in the 14th year of Hezekiah, not his 27th or 28th year. This is clarified by assuming a coregency, whereby Hezekiah's father Ahaz appointed his son as coregent in 728 and Hezekiah's sole reign began in 715 when Ahaz died.

The dates for the kings of Judah after that kingdom stood alone after the fall of Samaria can be tabulated as follows:

Hezekiah — 728-686
  coregent with Ahaz — 728-715
  coregent with Manasseh — 696-686
Manasseh — 696-642
  coregent with Hezekiah — 696-686
Amon — 642-640
Josiah — 640-609

Later Years of the Divided Monarchy

The year 841 provides a convenient turning point in the chronology of Israel and Judah because the kings of both kingdoms were executed and a new king and queen (a female regent) took over those kingdoms.

This period is one of the most complicated in all of biblical chronology because of an excess of years in relative chronology of Israel and Judah in relation to the number of calendar years in absolute chronology derived from synchronisms with Assyria. Minor adjustments made for spring and fall calendars and accession and nonaccession practices can account for a few of these.

All of the kings of Judah in this period were coregents (although the parallel reigns of Athaliah and Joash were only a quasi-coregency). For Israel, where coregency does not appear to have been practiced, the solution lies in scribal errors or adjustments. Both the reigns of Jeroboam and Pekah appear to be inaccurate by precisely a decade.

The external synchronisms available from Assyrian sources include: (1) Shalmaneser III's reception of tribute from Jehu (841), (2) the payment of tribute by Jehoash of Israel to Adad-nirari III (probably 796), (3) the payment of tribute by Menahem to Tiglath-pileser III (probably ca. 742-740), (4) the payment of tribute by Pekah to the same Assyrian king (732), (5) the conquest of Samaria by Shalmaneser in 722, and (6) the reconquest of Samaria by Sargon after a revolt in 720.

Early Years of the Divided Monarchy

The Hebrew monarchy was divided into the kingdoms of Israel and Judah shortly after the death of Solomon in 932. This date is determined by working backward through the list of successive kings. Since the first of both kingdoms dated their regnal years from Solomon's death, it makes a useful boundary for the beginning of this period. The relatively simultaneous deaths of kings Joram and Ahaziah in 841 mark a convenient ending point for this period. The only external synchronism of significance in this period is the contact between Ahab and Shalmaneser III at the Battle of Qarqar in 853.

The date of Ahab's death is disputed. The reference from Shalmaneser's annals indicates he was alive during the summer of 853. The question is whether he died later that same year or the next.

There are three coregencies in the southern kingdom in this period. The most obvious is that between Jehoram and Jehoshaphat, since the accession of Joram of Israel is double dated in terms of both of their reigns (2 Kgs. 1:17; 3:1). Jehoshaphat also had been coregent with his father Asa. Ahaziah may have been appointed as a coregent when his father Jehoram fell ill (cf. 2 Kgs. 8:25; 9:29).

United Monarchy

The dates of two of the three kings of the United Monarchy are relatively straightforward. The official regnal years of Rehoboam and Jeroboam begin in 931, placing the death of Solomon in the preceding year, 932. 1 Kgs. 11:42 indicates that his reign lasted 40 years. Given the detailed nature of court records by that time, this figure can be taken at face value.

The reign of David is also dated at 40 years.

Since this figure is broken down into seven years of rule at Hebron and 33 years in Jerusalem, the specificity of those figures should be accepted (1 Kgs. 2:11). We are given no specific indication as to how long the short-lived coregency between David and Solomon lasted and whether it was included or excluded from the totals of their regnal years. One might estimate it could have lasted from six months to two years (cf. 1 Kgs. 2:39, 46).

The length of Saul's reign is more problematic. Part of a date formula for his reign in 1 Sam. 13:1 appears to have been lost in the transmission of the text. The number "[20 and] two years" is a common estimate here, but other combinations are possible. The reference in Acts 13:21 to Saul's reign as lasting 40 years appears to be a schematized method of dealing with this gap by projecting the 40-year reigns of David and Solomon back into the time of Saul.

The dates for the kings for the United Monarchy can be outlined as follows:

Saul — (2)2 years, 1034(?)-1012
David — 40 years, 1012-972
Solomon — 40 years, 972-932

Period of the Judges

The book of Judges is replete with an extensive amount of chronological data. Approximately two dozen chronological statements are almost evenly divided between statements about the length of periods of oppression by Israel's enemies and that of periods of peace or rest initiated by Israel's liberating judges. At first glance these data would appear to provide an extensive chronology of the judges.

However, there are no synchronisms external to Israel with which to quantify the internal data. Israel's enemies in the book of Judges, with only one exception, are local enemies and not the great powers of the ancient Near East. Also, some of the oppressions were contemporary. Judg. 10:7 states that Israel was oppressed by the Philistines (in the west) and the Ammonites (in the east) during the same period of 18 years. How many more of the oppressions elsewhere in Judges were contemporaneous is not easy to determine because of lack of specific data. This question can be extended to ask how many of the oppressions in some parts of Israel were contemporaneous with periods of peace led by the judges in other parts. For example, not all tribes answered the call to arms given by Deborah and Barak (Judg. 4-5). Likewise, the oppression of Moab in Judg. 3 seems mainly to have been a northern tribe exercise.

Once the date of the Exodus has been fixed, the dates in Judges can be prorated out, since the lower limits of this period with Samuel and Saul can be fixed with reasonable approximation. Fixing the date of the Exodus, however, is not an easy process. There is, however, one more longer-range datum in Judges that may assist with that task. Jephthah's claim (Judg. 11:26) that the Israelites had settled in Ammonite territory 300 years before provides a round figure that is not precise, but it still is useful. If Jephthah's date is estimated at ca. 1100, then the initial settlement was ca. 1400. This is consistent with one of the lines of chronology that provide dates for the Exodus.

Date of the Exodus

The Exodus from Egypt was identified as a landmark event in the formation of ancient Israel as a people who covenanted with their God at Sinai. First, however, came the deliverance. Since the pharaoh of the Exodus is not named in the book of Exodus, more indirect means must be applied to determine the date of that event. This has led to four main solutions:

1. Late 16th century. This is consistent with Josephus' use of the Egyptian historian Manetho in synchronizing the departure of the Israelites with the defeat and expulsion of the Hyksos. It is universally rejected by modern scholars.
2. Mid-15th century. This date is based upon the chronological statement in 1 Kgs. 6:1 that Solomon began to build the temple in his 4th year, 480 years after the Exodus. A minority of scholars, mostly conservative, have adhered to this date.
3. 13th Century. This view is based upon three main points: (1) The name of Rameses for one of the store cities built by the Israelites in Egypt (Exod. 1:11) from which they left at the time of their departure (12:37). Rameses II was a famous and important king who ruled Egypt for more than half a century, covering the first half of the 13th century. He built up his northern capital of Per-rameses in the area of Avaris, the former Hyksos capital. The identification of this city with the biblical city is the first cornerstone of this theory. (2) What was thought to be a "wave of destructions" caused by the Israelites at strategic biblical sites in Canaan. More careful study has determined that this was a much more complex and irregular phenomenon. (3) Merneptha's stela (ca. 1200), which names Israel as a people who were settled in Canaan by the time it was written.
4. 12th Century. As the consensus about the wave of destructions in Canaan in the late 13th century crumbled, people looked elsewhere, both earlier and later, for the Exodus and the subsequent settlement. Rather specific archaeological evidence for the settlement of Israel appears in the 12th century, in the form of many small village settlements spread over the land with mainly Israelite features.

While a majority of scholars probably now lean towards the 12th century for the date of the Exodus, a significant minority leans back to the 15th century.

Sojourn

An estimate for the length of time that the Israelites spent in Egypt depends upon two main factors. (1) The genealogical statement in Exod. 6 gives the two generations that went into Egypt

(Levi and Kohath) and the two generations at the end of the sojourn (Amram and Moses). If this is a complete genealogical list, then the sojourn should have been a relatively short period of time. If, however, there is a gap in the middle of that genealogy, then the sojourn could have been considerably longer. (2) Exod. 12:40 states that the Israelites were in Egypt 430 years. A 13th-Dynasty Egyptian papyrus from the late 18th century favors the longer chronology for the sojourn. This is a list of female household slaves, a number of whom bear Semitic names, some rather distinctively Israelite. If these were descendants of Jacob and his sons, they would have to have come to Egypt during the 12th Dynasty, not the 15th (Hyksos) Dynasty as the short chronology for the sojourn would indicate.

Thus far archaeological evidence illuminating this period has been minimal. The question remains open until further evidence is discovered which bears upon the question.

Patriarchs

According to Gen. 47:7, 28, Jacob was 130 years old when he came to live in Egypt. He was born when Isaac was 60 years old (2:26). Abraham came to Canaan when he was 75 years old (12:4), and Isaac was born to him when he was 100 (21:5). These ages look inordinately high to moderns, but the historian should at least work with these figures as hypothetical.

In general terms, biblical chronology places the date for the entry of Abraham into Canaan at ca. 2000, with a margin of error of plus or minus a century. There has been considerable debate about which archaeological period should be identified as the time of the patriarchs. Those who favor Early Bronze IV note the seminomadic experience of Abraham. Those who favor Middle Bronze II A note the number of settled cities in these narratives.

Bibliography. D. N. Freedman and E. F. Campbell, "The Chronology of Israel and the Ancient Near East," in *The Bible and the Ancient Near East,* ed. G. E. Wright (1961, repr. Winona Lake, 1979), 203-28; G. Galil, *The Chronology of the Kings of Israel and Judah* (Leiden, 1996); J. H. Hayes and P. K. Hooker, *A New Chronology for the Kings of Israel and Judah* (Atlanta, 1988); S. H. Horn, "The Chronology of King Hezekiah's Reign," *AUSS* 2 (1964): 40-52; N. Na'aman, "Historical and Chronological Notes on the Kingdoms of Israel and Judah in the Eighth Century B.C.," *VT* 36 (1986): 71-92; R. A. Parker and W. H. Dubberstein, *Babylonian Chronology 626 B.C.–A.D. 75* (Providence, 1956); W. H. Shea, "Exodus, Date of the," *ISBE* 2 (Grand Rapids, 1982): 230-38; "Menaham and Tiglath-Pileser III," *JNES* 37 (1978): 43-49; E. R. Thiele, *The Mysterious Numbers of the Hebrew Kings,* rev ed. (Grand Rapids, 1994); *A Chronology of the Hebrew Kings* (Grand Rapids, 1977); D. J. Wiseman, *Chronicles of Chaldean Kings (626-556 B.C.)* (London, 1961).

WILLIAM H. SHEA

CHRONOLOGY OF THE NEW TESTAMENT

NT chronology can be divided into discussion of Jesus and of the apostolic period, including especially Paul. All study of NT chronology, however, is complicated by several factors: the NT authors were not concerned with the same kind of date-keeping as moderns are; means of calculating time were different in the ancient world; and, most importantly, there are few firmly established dates around which to create a chronology.

Jesus' Life

The issues regarding the life of Jesus are: his birth, the beginning of his ministry, its duration, and his death.

Birth

Discussion of the birth of Jesus revolves around three major events: the death of Herod the Great, the Lukan census, and the visit of the magi.

Death of Herod. Matt. 2:1; Luke 1:5 state that Jesus was born during Herod's reign over Judea, and Matt. 2:15, 19-20 that Herod died while Jesus was a baby. Josephus states that Herod died 34 years after putting Antigonus to death in 37 B.C. and 37 years after being appointed king by the Romans in 40 B.C. (ca. 4 B.C.), although some recent scholars argue for a date of 4/3 B.C. for Herod's death; *Ant.* 17.190-91; *BJ* 1.665), that there was an eclipse of the moon the year Herod died (12 or 13 March 4 B.C.; *Ant.* 17.167), and that the Passover occurred soon after his son Archelaus became king (17 April 4 B.C.; *Ant.* 17.213; *BJ* 2.10). Thus Jesus was born before April 4 B.C., not in the year 0. In the 6th century A.D. a mistake in calculating dates was made by Dionysius Exiguus, which has not been corrected.

Census. Luke 2:1-5 states that a census was taken by the Emperor Augustus before Jesus was born, and that Jesus' parents traveled to Bethlehem to enroll in their hometown. However, no Roman historian mentions a census ca. 4 B.C. In Luke 2 the census is reported in relation to the governorship of Quirinius, who became governor of Syria after A.D. 6 and took a census then (*Ant.* 17.355; 18.356). Many, if not most, scholars hold that Luke erred in his chronology, by either incorrectly identifying the governor of Syria as Quirinius, giving Quirinius the wrong title, or introducing an earlier census that never occurred.

Several factors must be considered before Luke's account is dismissed. First, the Romans undertook censuses throughout their empire. In Roman Egypt, it is well established that from A.D. 33/34 until 257/258 censuses were taken at 14-year intervals. Recently discussed evidence, however, indicates that during the reign of Augustus censuses were taken at seven-year intervals, and can be established with indirect and direct evidence for 11/10, 4/3 B.C., A.D. 4/5, and 11/12. Second, in light of the turmoil at the close of Herod's reign (*Ant.* 16.300-404; *BJ* 1.516-51), including what he perceived as threats to his power by his sons and strained relations with Rome and the fact that he was a client king who ruled only because of Roman favor, it may well be that the Egyptian census of 4/3 B.C. was extended to Judea or one like it performed there, and this is the one referred to in Luke 2:1. Third, the edict of Vibius Maximus in A.D. 104 (P. Lond. III 904.18-27), that all people return to their homes for the census, indicates the plausibility of the trip to Bethlehem recorded in the Gospels. Finally, the Greek grammar of Luke 2:2 has been interpreted that this was "the previous census, before Quirinius was governor of Syria." Luke may be using Quirinius' governorship and census as a reference point, since Quirinius' census in A.D. 6, when Judea became part of Syria, was traumatic for the Jews — it marked the end of even the pretense of self-rule. This evidence supports a date of ca. 4 B.C. for Jesus' birth.

Magi. Various proposals have been made regarding the "star" that magi or astrologers followed in search of Jesus (Matt. 2:1-12). Halley's comet, which can be seen every 76 years, would have been visible in the sky in 12/11 B.C., but this date is too early. Some posit a form of spectacular exploding star (supernova) ca. 5/4 B.C., but there is no firm evidence. The astronomer Johannes Kepler in 1606 calculated that there had been a conjunction of the planets of Mars, Jupiter, and Saturn in 7 B.C., something that only happens every 805 years. Astrology was widespread in the ancient Near East, with special events often seen to accompany the birth of significant people (e.g., Alexander the Great). However, the story of the magi adds little to establishing the date of Jesus' birth.

The evidence points to a date of Jesus' birth ca. 5/4 B.C. The traditional date of 25 December (6 January for the Eastern Church) is based upon the influence of later Roman paganism on Christianity, and cannot be relied upon.

Ministry

The beginning of Jesus' ministry revolves around that of John the Baptist, statements in the Gospels about Jesus' age, and the building of the temple. The story of Jesus' visit to the temple when he was 12 (Luke 2:41-45) provides no evidence for establishing a precise chronology.

John the Baptist. Luke 3:1-2 purports to date the beginning of John's ministry precisely to the 15th year of the Emperor Tiberius. However, this may not be as precise as first appears. If the Julian calendar is used, the date would be A.D. 29; if the regnal years beginning with Tiberius' own regency are used (most likely), the date would be 28/29; if the regnal years beginning with Tiberius' co-rule with Augustus are used (11/12), it would be 25/26 (although his co-rule is disputed by historians, and does not appear to have been used for dating events to his reign). (This assumes that Luke knew how to calculate dates according to these methods and was interested in doing so.) For most, the last date would be too early, although for some the first two are too late. There is no indication in the NT regarding the amount of time between the beginning of John's ministry and Jesus' being baptized by him, but the two probably occurred ca. 28/29.

Jesus' Age. Luke 3:23 says that Jesus was "about 30 years of age" when he began his ministry. The word translated "about" indicates that "30" is an approximate term. Although some have proposed that 30 is used here for theological reasons or to indicate an age of spiritual maturity, such proposals are probably at best secondary to this serving as an approximating temporal indicator. By reckoning from the date of Jesus' birth, he would have begun his ministry ca. 27 (the date could be later due to the length of time being imprecise).

The Temple. According to John 2:13–3:21 Jesus visits Jerusalem at Passover. He is told that it had taken 46 years to build the temple (it was still under construction, and never completely finished before the Romans destroyed it in 70). According to Josephus (*Ant.* 15.380), Herod's rebuilding of the temple began in the 18th year of his reign (in *BJ* 1.401 Josephus dates it to the 15th year). This was the same year that Augustus arrived in Syria (*Ant.* 15.354), which has been calculated to 20 B.C. (Dio Cassius *Hist.* 54.7.4). Herod's 18th year would thus have been 20/19 B.C., and 46 years from beginning the temple would be A.D. 28. Jesus probably began his ministry, therefore, ca. 28, at the age of ca. 31.

The duration of Jesus' ministry is one of the most controversial aspects in establishing the chronology of his life, especially since the Synoptic Gospels and John seem to be at odds. The Synoptics mention one Passover (Matt. 26:17; Mark 14:1; Luke 22:1), while John mentions three (John 2:13, 23; 6:4; 11:55). As a result, proposals for the length of Jesus' ministry range from one to four years. Many of the church fathers held to a one-year ministry (some viewing John 2:13; 11:55 as indicating the beginning and ending of Jesus' ministry with Passovers). Others argue for a three- to four-year ministry based on John, some even advocating an unmentioned fourth Passover between 2:13 and 6:4. Although many have criticized the reliability of John's chronology because of his theological tendencies, it is too extreme to explain every reference to Passover in theological terms. Most likely Jesus had a three-year ministry.

Death

The death of Jesus involves consideration of the day and year of that event.

Day. Determining the day of Jesus' death again apparently brings the Synoptic Gospels and John into conflict. All agree that Jesus was crucified on a Friday (Matt. 27:62; Mark 15:42; Luke 23:54; John 19:31, 42), before the beginning of the sabbath (and that he was resurrected on the third day, Sunday), and that it was the time of the Passover. The Synoptics portray Jesus as eating the Last Supper as a Passover-like meal with his disciples the night before he was crucified (Matt. 26:17-35; Mark 14:12-25; Luke 22:7-38), although there is some ambiguity that they may consider the day of Unleavened Bread as the day before the Passover (Matt. 27:62; Mark 14:12; Luke 23:54). In the Synoptics, Jesus' arrest, trial, and crucifixion apparently took place on Passover (15 Nisan), the day before the sabbath.

John, however, portrays Jesus as eating the Last Supper on the day before the Passover (John 19:14, 16), or the day of Preparation (14 Nisan), the same day on which he was killed and also the day before the sabbath. There have been many attempts to reconcile this apparent discrepancy. Some have posited that Mark (subsequently followed by Matthew and Luke) erred in linking the Last Supper with the Passover meal. Others suggest a private pre-Passover meal celebrated by Jesus and his disciples or that the Passover was celebrated on several successive days because of the large numbers of animals to be slaughtered. Some contend that various calendars were involved, according to region or religious association. Qumran may have followed a solar as opposed to a lunar calendar followed by other Jews, but there is no evidence that Jesus and his followers followed the Qumran calendar. Some suggest that the parameters of a day were calculated differently: from sunrise to sunrise (the Synoptics: Galileans and Pharisees) or from evening to evening (John: Judeans and Sadducees). Those who wish to harmonize the Gospel accounts frequently favor this last proposal. There is no scholarly consensus on this, but many scholars contend, on the basis of John and possible ambiguity in the Synoptics, that Jesus was crucified on Friday 14 Nisan.

Year. The year of Jesus' death is determined by two factors: when 14 Nisan falls on a Friday, and when the people involved in Jesus' death were in office. These people include Pilate, prefect of Judea, 26-36 (Matt. 27:2-26; Mark 15:1-15; Luke 23:1-25; John 18:28–19:16; Acts 3:13; 4:27; 13:28; *Ant.* 18.89); Herod Antipas, tetrarch of Galilee and Perea, 4 B.C.–A.D. 39 (Luke 23:6-12; *Ant.* 18.240-56; 19:351); and Caiaphas, high priest, 18-37 (Matt. 26:3, 57; John 11:49-53; 18:13-14; *Ant.* 18.35, 90-95). Within the rule of Pilate, 27, 30, 33 and 36 seem to be theoretical possibilities for 14 Nisan falling on a Friday. According to the reckoning above, however, 27 is too early and 36 too late. Most scholars, especially those who argue for a shorter ministry of Jesus, believe that Jesus was killed in 30. Scholars who argue for a longer ministry tend to believe that he died in 33.

Apostolic Period, Including Paul

Reconstructing the apostolic period involves examination of three major bodies of evidence: the book of Acts, Paul's letters, and extrabiblical people and events. Since Acts may well have been written by someone closely associated with the early Christian missionary movement, and in light of the fact that Paul's letters were not written with historical chronology in mind, the distinction often made between Acts as a secondary source and Paul's letters as primary sources is clearly overdrawn. All of the available data must be judiciously weighed.

Acts

The book of Acts provides the following sequentially-listed information regarding the chronology of the early Church, especially with reference to Paul: the stoning of Stephen, at which Paul is a "young man" (Acts 7:58; possibly indicating birth in A.D. 5 to 15); Paul's conversion, stay in Damascus, and dramatic escape (9:1-25; cf. 22:4-5; 26:12); first trip to Jerusalem, and then to Tarsus and Antioch (9:26-30; 11:25-26); second trip to Jerusalem, bringing famine relief from Antioch (11:27-30; 12:25); first missionary journey (13:1–14:28); third trip to Jerusalem, for the apostolic council (15:1-35); second missionary journey (15:35–18:22; some put the events of 18:18–19:20 together, although Antioch seems in Acts to mark a point of termination and beginning for the Pauline journeys); third missionary journey (18:23–21:16); final (fourth or fifth) trip to Jerusalem (21:17–23:10); imprisonment for two years in Caesarea (23:12–26:32); and journey to Rome and imprisonment there (27:1–28:31).

It is extremely difficult to establish the amounts of time that each stage of the chronology took, since Acts has only infrequent references to amounts of time (11:26; 14:3, 28; 18:11; 19:8, 10, 22; 20:3; 24:27; 28:30).

Epistles

Paul's letters, esp. Gal. 1–2, provide the following chronology (the relationship of these events as compiled from the individual letters is subject to difference of opinion by scholars): Paul's conversion (Gal. 1:12-16); stay in Arabia and return to Damascus (v. 17); first trip to Jerusalem (vv. 18-20); stay in Syria and Cilicia (vv. 21-24); second trip to Jerusalem to confer with Peter (2:1-10); incident at Antioch with Peter (vv. 11-14; perhaps before the second trip to Jerusalem); hints of a first Macedonian and Achaian/Greek missionary journey (1 Thess. 1:8; 3:1; cf. Phil. 4:15-16); stay in Ephesus (2 Cor. 1:8-11), before going to Troas and to Macedonia (1 Cor. 16:8-9; 2 Cor. 2:12-13); and clear reference to what was probably a later Macedonian (Philippian) and Achaian/Greek missionary journey (1 Cor. 16:1-9; 2 Cor. 8-9; Rom. 15:19-32).

Apart from the two references in Galatians (Gal. 1:18; 2:1), the Pauline letters contain no specific temporal indicators. The above list offers a probable arrangement of the events, although the first missionary journey may have occurred before the second trip to Jerusalem, since 1 Thessalonians does not mention the Jerusalem visit. This is unlikely, however, on the basis of the sequencing of Gal. 1–2.

Extrabiblical References

Extrabiblical points of chronological reference attest to eight events with possible bearing on NT chronology. All have debatable interpretations.

1. In 2 Cor. 11:32-33 Paul mentions that the ethnarch of King Aretas was guarding Damascus. Critical questions include dispute over the date of Aretas' death (between 38 and 40), the date at which Aretas took control of Damascus (possibly as late as 37, the accession of Caligula), and whether this passage even requires that Aretas was in control of Damascus. The reference may indicate that

Paul's escape took place between 37 and 38-40, or simply before 38-40.

2. Acts 11:28 says that a prophet named Agabus foretold a great famine during the reign of Claudius (41-54). Possible dates range from 45, 46, 48 to after 51. Some dispute that there was a famine at all, certainly a world-wide one (Suetonius *Claudius* 18; Tacitus *Ann.* 12.43). Further difficulty in dating the second Jerusalem trip is that the prophecy may have been given well in advance of the famine itself.

3. Acts 12:20-30 records the death of Herod Agrippa I in 44 (cf. *Ant.* 19.343-52). Acts places this between the story of Peter in vv. 1-19 and the summary statement of v. 24 and resumption of Paul's story in v. 25. It is difficult to establish the exact chronological relation of these events, although it is likely that the sequence is correct, and that the first missionary journey took place after Herod Agrippa's death.

4. Acts 13:7 says that Sergius Paulus was proconsul of Cyprus. Several inscriptions link such a person with Cyprus, but they are ambiguous with regard to reference and date.

5. Acts 18:2 refers to Claudius' having commanded all the Jews to leave Rome. Suetonius (25.4) refers to the expulsion of Jews who were causing disturbances at the instigation of a Chrestus (it is unclear that this is a reference to Christ), but no date is given. The traditional date of this event — still widely held in scholarly circles — is 49, following the 5th-century church historian Orosius (7.6.15), who dates it to the 9th year of Claudius' reign. According to Dio Cassius (60.6.6), expulsion of the Jews was not possible during Jewish uprisings in 41 because of their large numbers, but this alternative date has been championed of late due to the questionable reliability of Orosius' information and the possibility that the expulsion involved only some but not all Jews. The implications for establishing chronology are significant. The earlier date suggests an early date for Paul's first visit to Corinth, even if he did not arrive right after Priscilla and Aquila. This would also require a second visit to Corinth when Gallio was proconsul, possibly either just before or after the Jerusalem council. Acts 18 provides some evidence of conflation because v. 8 refers to Crispus and v. 17 to Sosthenes as ruler of the synagogue. The later date, which suggests that Acts 18 records a single visit to Corinth during the time of Gallio, is still more likely.

6. Acts 18:12 refers to Gallio as proconsul of Achaia, before whom Paul was dragged by the Jews. The well-known Gallio inscription (fragmentary and in several major sections) found at Delphi is an edict by Claudius referring to Gallio as proconsul. On the basis of this and other inscriptions that establish its date, as well as the fact that proconsuls usually served one-year terms, it is possible to date Gallio's term of office to 51/52. Paul appears to have been in Corinth by 51 or 52, whether or not this was his first visit.

7. In Acts 23:2; 24:1 Paul appears in the presence of Ananias the high priest. Appointed in 47, Ananias was sent to Rome in 52 as the result of a dispute between the Jews and Samaritans, but was probably restored to power when Claudius ruled in favor of the Jews, and continued in that office until replaced, probably in 59 (*Ant.* 20.128-36; *BJ* 2.241-44).

8. Acts 23:24–26:32 places Paul in the custody of the Roman procurators Felix and Festus. He was in Felix' custody for two years (24:27) before Festus took office. According to Acts, within days after his arrival Festus went to Jerusalem and was persuaded to put Paul on trial, but Paul appealed to Caesar. A few days later King Herod Agrippa II visited Caesarea, and during his stay Paul appeared before him. It is difficult to establish the dates of the procuratorships of Felix and Festus. According to Josephus, Felix took up his post in 52 or 53 (*BJ* 2.247; *Ant.* 20.137). There is dispute over when his term came to an end; many biblical scholars argue for a date ca. 55, but classical scholars prefer a later date. The early date is based on the notion that Pallas, the wealthy and highly influential treasurer of Claudius (Suetonius 28) fell out of favor with Nero in 55 and must have immediately lost his power, and thereby authority to keep his brother Felix in office. However, there is clear evidence (Tacitus *Ann.* 13-14) that Pallas retained much power, until he was poisoned by Nero in 62 (cf. *BJ* 2.250-70). The later date for Festus' succeeding Felix, however, is still disputed. Estimates range from 56, on the basis of the Latin translation of Eusebius' *Chronicle* (2.155), to 58 to 61. A very plausible date is 59.

Synthesis of a Pauline Chronology

On the basis of the evidence above, several plausible scenarios of a Pauline chronology can be developed. Perhaps most noteworthy, those from Acts and the Pauline letters have a surprisingly high degree of harmony. The bibliography below provides alternative timelines, but the following is a plausible suggestion. Not all of the data fit equally well, as the disputed items mentioned above indicate. Any chronology of the NT is subject to numerous limitations.

One must first decide when Paul was converted. A.D. 33 or 34 is likely, with the result that he stayed three years in Arabia and Damascus, before first visiting Jerusalem in 37. After ca. 10 more years (Gal. 2:1 marks 14 years after his conversion), Paul made his famine visit to Jerusalem (probably to be equated with Gal. 2:1-10). The first missionary journey was then from 47 to 48, and the Jerusalem council of Acts 15 in 49. This order, following Acts, is not incompatible with the Pauline chronology. The second missionary journey (first Macedonian and Achaian/Greek visit) lasted from 49 to 52, and the third (second Macedonian and Achaian/Greek visit) from 53 to 57. Paul was arrested in Jerusalem and imprisoned in Caesarea from 57 to 59. In 59 he was sent to Rome, where he was imprisoned until 62, and may well have died there.

At this point, Acts includes nothing further of a Pauline chronology. On the basis of a possible placement of the Pastoral Epistles within the Pauline chronology, it has been posited that Paul was released in 62, traveled for two years in the Mediterranean, possibly went west to Spain, and then was arrested and killed in Rome in 64 or 65 under Nero.

Bibliography. L. C. A. Alexander, "Chronology of Paul," in *Dictionary of Paul and His Letters,* ed. G. F. Hawthorne and R. P. Martin (Downers Grove, 1993), 115-23; R. S. Bagnall and B. W. Frier, *The Demography of Roman Egypt* (Cambridge, 1994); H. W. Hoehner, "Chronology," in *Dictionary of Jesus and the Gospels,* ed. J. B. Green and S. McKnight (Downers Grove, 1992), 118-22; R. Jewett, *A Chronology of Paul's Life* (Philadelphia, 1979); A. Kushnir-Stein, "Another Look at Josephus' Evidence for the Date of Herod's Death," *Scripta Classica Israelica* 14 (1995): 73-86; G. Lüdemann, *Paul, Apostle to the Gentiles* (Philadelphia, 1984); L. McDonald and S. E. Porter, *Early Christianity and Its Sacred Literature* (Peabody, 2000); G. Ogg, *The Chronology of the Life of Paul* (London, 1968); B. W. R. Pearson, "The Lukan Censuses, Revisited," *CBQ* 61 (1999): 262-82; R. Riesner, *Paul's Early Period* (Grand Rapids, 1998). Stanley E. Porter

CHRYSOLITE

A clear green stone, also called peridot. Some versions (NAB, NIV, NJPVS) translate Heb. *taršîš* (Gk. *chrysólithos*) as "chrysolite," something flashing or bright (Ezek. 1:16; 10:9), an engraved stone on the high priest's breastpiece (Exod. 28:17-20; 39:10-13), and a stone adorning the king of Tyre (Ezek. 28:13). "Chrysolite" is also used for Gk. *chrysólithos,* a course in the foundation of the wall of the New Jerusalem (Rev. 21:20).

Other terms translated "chrysolite" include Heb. *piṭḏâ* (Gk. *topázion,* "topaz"). Some translations render "beryl," "gold quartz," "onyx," or "topaz" for these terms. Joseph E. Jensen

CHRYSOPRASE

An apple-green variety of chalcedony, valued as a gem in Egypt, and the tenth precious stone in the foundation of the walls of the New Jerusalem (Rev. 21:20; Gk. *chrysóprasos*).

CHURCH

The common English translation of Gk. *ekklēsía.* At the time of the composition of the NT it was widely used to refer to gatherings of people in some kind of assembly. In the Greek version of the OT *ekklēsía* was used for the people of God (Israel) gathered together for an important purpose (Judg. 20:2; 1 Chr. 29:1; cf. Acts 7:38). In the NT it refers mainly to the people of God gathered in the name of Jesus or the God of Jesus Christ (Eph. 3:21; 5:23; 1 Thess. 1:1; 1 Cor. 10:32).

The NT understands "church" to refer to the visible expression of the gathered followers of Jesus Christ who have been grafted into a community created by God, under the banner of Jesus Christ, embodying in an anticipatory way the life and values of the new creation. As such the Church stands in direct continuity with the historic people of God (Israel); but as an eschatological community of the last days, marked off by its acknowledgment of Jesus as Lord and Messiah, there are discontinuities as well.

Beginnings of the Church

This tension between continuity and discontinuity with the people of God in history, precipitated by the coming of Jesus, is a fundamental factor in assessing when the Church actually began. It is a foundational presupposition of the Bible that Israel is the people of God (Lev. 26:12). Nevertheless, from a Christian perspective it is unarguable that something essentially new emerged with the coming of Jesus.

At the center of Jesus' mission was the announcement that Israel was at the edge of a new era when God was about to fulfill his promises and inaugurate his kingship. Jesus viewed himself as an ambassador for this announcement. He called around him an inner circle of followers (the Twelve) who assisted in this proclamation and who constituted the nucleus of the community (Matt. 10:1-42; Mark 3:13-19; 6:7-13; Luke 9:1-6, 10). This new community anticipated the special fellowship of the new era by dining together in celebrative meals (cf. Luke 14:1-24; 22:14-23). At these meals, and throughout his teaching, Jesus employed images such as harvest, banquet, and new wine to describe the salvation of the new era. As part of Jesus' table fellowship, traditional social distinctions created by observance of the rites of purity were abandoned; and the return of the lost was joyously celebrated as a paradigm of the anticipated repentance and restoration of Israel (Luke 15:1-32; 19:1-10; Mark 2:18-20).

Matt. 16:16-19 incorporates the historical reality of Jesus' giving the name *kêpā'/Pétros,* "the Rock," to Simon and investing it with special significance (cf. John 1:42). In the confession of Jesus as the "Messiah, the Son of the living God," Peter becomes a foundation rock of the new community of the end times. This new messianic community would have to survive a terrible ordeal (the messianic woes), which would probably involve the destruction of the Jerusalem temple (Matt. 24:2 par.). The old sanctuary would be replaced by a new sanctuary: the messianic community (Matt. 26:61 par.). In keeping with the previously spoken word of Jesus, this new sanctuary or Church would be inaugurated by Peter (Matt. 16:19).

Upon the death of Jesus, after the disciples returned to faith and the Holy Spirit fell upon the fledgling, but still frightened messianic community in Jerusalem, Peter became the instrument who furnished the word as to how humans may become part of the new messianic community and participate in the salvation brought by Jesus (Acts 2:14-42). When that day ended with the repentance and baptism of several thousand, it could be verified that the community of the end time, the Church, had been inaugurated. Jesus announced the Church and the Holy Spirit inaugurated it.

Expansion in the NT Era

Jerusalem and Judea

Luke and other Greek-speaking believers use *ekklēsía* to describe the earliest Christian community in Jerusalem after the Resurrection (Acts 5:11; 8:1). This was far more than an alternative to *synagōgḗ*, the usual term for a gathering of Torah-observant Jews. The Church as a living community viewed itself as the restored tabernacle of David (Acts 15:15-16; cf. Amos 9:11-12). The Twelve were the guiding forces directing this truly apostolic community (Matt. 19:28; Luke 22:29-30; Acts 2:42; 6:2, 6). These apostles saw Jerusalem as the central place where God would bring to fruition his eschatological plans instituted with the Resurrection (Acts 1:8). Living in vital anticipation of the culmination of these eschatological events, this community attended to the most mundane tasks of life with great fervor (2:43-47). By the end of the first generation, the Church was a substantial force in the life of Jerusalem (2:41; 4:4; 6:7).

Beyond Judea

According to Acts, the messianic community began to emerge quickly throughout the Roman province of greater Syria. Most agree that Paul's call near Damascus took place within five years of Jesus' death. Paul immediately associated with other believers there and apparently worked with churches near Damascus and east of the Jordan (Gal. 1:17). The connection between the "mother" church at Jerusalem and similar churches among the Jews in greater Syria and throughout the Jewish Diaspora is still an unsettled issue. However, each local assembly seemed to perceive itself as the visible expression of the gathered community in any given place that owed ultimate loyalty to Jesus as Lord and Savior (cf. 1 Thess. 1:1; 1 Cor. 1:2; Gal. 1:2, 22; 2 Cor. 8:1). Even the reference in Acts 9:31 to the church in Judea, Galilee, and Samaria probably refers to collections of Christians meeting in different assemblies somewhat analogous with the structure of the Jewish synagogues.

A major missionary thrust was carried out by the Hellenists, a minority of Greek-speaking Jewish Christians in the church at Jerusalem. In developing their own understanding of faith in Jesus, they quickly drew the antagonism of the authorities (Acts 6:8-15; 7:54–8:3). From this group emerged Stephen, Saul (Paul), Barnabas, Philip, and Silas. The planting and rapid growth of the church in Antioch is attributable to the Hellenists. Their worship and manner of life quickly became so distinctive from other groups within Diaspora Judaism that they were identified separately as "Christians" (Acts 11:26). Part of that distinctiveness involved the open welcoming of Gentiles to be part of the people of God through faith in Jesus as Messiah without first embracing the badges of Judaism (circumcision, dietary and sabbath observance). This not only precipitated Antioch's sponsorship of the great mission to the Gentiles but also caused problems in the relationship with the church in Jerusalem, which were resolved at an ecumenical meeting in Jerusalem ca. 48-49 (Acts 15:1-35; cf. Gal. 2:1-21).

Mission to the Gentiles

The latter half of the 1st century saw steady growth of the churches around the Mediterranean basin, especially among the Gentiles. The NT highlights the mission of Paul. But others, many of whom will forever remain unknown and who engaged in ordinary pursuits, also spread the word.

With the emergence of churches throughout the wider Greco-Roman world, the question of the relationship of these overwhelmingly gentile churches to the Jewish Christian brethren in Judea remained a burning issue. Paul was sensitive to this matter and sought to promote unity in the Church by collecting voluntary contributions from the gentile churches he had founded for the poor in Jerusalem (1 Cor. 16:1; 2 Cor. 8:1-5). Besides the political function of melding together the gentile and Jewish segments of the Church, there is evidence that Paul understood this as signalling the arrival of the messianic era (Isa. 60:4-7; Rom. 15:25-31).

Besides the consolidation of the churches founded by Paul, many other churches planted around the Mediterranean conceived of themselves as closely connected with major figures in early Christianity such as Peter (1 Pet. 1:1) and John (Rev. 2–3; 3 John 9, 10). By the end of the apostolic period the Church, although primarily still a number of small and struggling assemblies, had become a distinguishable entity in much of the Roman Empire (Col. 1:6).

Features of the Church

Organization in Ministry

Paul argued that each local congregation can be described as the working parts of a body (1 Cor. 12:12-31). God has arranged to distribute gifts (charismata) for the orderly working of the body (1 Cor. 12:27-31; Rom. 12:5-8; cf. Eph. 4:4-16). There is no absolute dichotomy between spirit and structure in the NT; rather, the spirit provided differing structures for the early Christian communities in keeping with the needs of particular situations. Thus, the Jerusalem church began under the direct guidance of the Twelve, who provided guidance and teaching (Acts 6:1-6; cf. Eph. 2:20). Later, a combination of apostles and elders became responsible for the leadership (Acts 15:2-23).

The situation in the Pauline churches was even more diverse. Paul urges submission to leaders of the home churches who "supervise" the members (1 Thess. 5:12; Rom. 12:8; cf. Heb. 13:7). Generally leadership in the Pauline churches became vested in senior men of the congregation who manifested a record of stability and holy living. Various terms that seem to be practically synonymous, such as elders (Acts 20:17; James 5:14) and overseers (Acts 20:28), describe their duties. Also, deacons (both women and men) usually assisted the leadership (Rom. 16:1; 1 Tim. 3:8-12). Evangelists were ordained to proclaim the word (Acts 21:8; Eph. 4:11; 2 Tim. 4:5). Finally, 1 Tim. 5:9-15 identifies widows as a specific group who rendered practical service.

Similar diversity of leadership was apparent in other churches not founded by Paul.

Despite the considerable influence of some centers (e.g., Jerusalem), the basic organization and ministry of the NT Church seem to have been centered in the local congregation. Yet, even though spread over a vast geographical area and having insignificant social standing, an amazing sense of solidarity and unity existed (cf. 1 Pet. 2:17; 1 Cor. 1:2). Early Christians viewed the Church not only as a gathered community in a local sense but as a spiritual unity of the total complement of believers (Col. 1:18, 24; Eph. 1:22). It was truly the vanguard of the new age.

Role of the Assembly

The understanding of worship was radically reoriented by the coming of Jesus. Essential to worship in the Greco-Roman world were (1) a temple or house of the god (2) a sacrifice made to appease the god; (3) an altar where the sacrifice is placed; (4) a priest designated to offer the sacrifice and mediate between the human and the god. All of this was obliterated by the death of Jesus who, for his followers, ended all sacrificial systems with his once-and-for-all sacrifice (Heb. 9:24-28). Christ is the Christian's high priest in the heavenly sanctuary (7:25-28). His sacrifice is the Christian's altar (13:10). In place of animal sacrifices, religious ecstasy, or even spiritual communion, the follower of Jesus offered as worship a committed life (Rom. 12:1-2).

Nevertheless, this did not vitiate the need of Jesus' followers to participate in communal life (Heb. 10:24-25). In these assemblies, which usually took place in the homes of believers, the distinction between earthly and heavenly was blurred, and an ordered world was created and represented in word and action whereby the followers of Jesus "drew near" to God. In an anticipatory sense, the believers joined the heavenly assembly in giving praise to God through Christ (12:22-23; cf. 10:1-22).

An assembly would usually take place on the first day of the week (the Lord's day), when Jesus first appeared to his disciples (cf. 1 Cor. 16:2; Rev. 1:10). Central to the assembly was a gathering around a table for a main meal (1 Cor. 11:17-33). Through participation in the bread and the cup covenant loyalties were renewed. According to 1 Cor. 14:1-40 a wide range of prayer, praise, and charismatic activity such as speaking in tongues and prophetic utterances also took place. Paul's emphasis on the need for decency and order (v. 40), and that all things ought to contribute to the spiritual growth of the Church, suggests that the central function of the assembly was not only to usher the believer into the divine world but also to build up him or her in the faith (1 Cor. 14:26).

The Hope of the Church

Central to the faith of the apostolic Church was the conviction that Jesus would return and bring to fulfillment the eschatological events inaugurated with his first coming (Acts 1:6-8; 1 John 2:28). The Aramaic word *maranatha,* "O Lord, come," was not only a shout of acclamation in early Christian assemblies associated with prophetic speech but also an anticipation of the Lord's return at the end of the age (1 Cor. 16:22; cf. Rev. 6:10-11; 22:20). The Church existed to tell the story of God's faithfulness to his creation; but the culmination of that faithfulness was considered to be Jesus' returning as the glorified Lord, vindicating the righteous through resurrection (1 Thess. 4:13-17; 1 Cor. 15:50-58) and judging the wicked (John 5:29). This was the reality that sustained the daily life of the Church through the apostolic period.

Awareness of this dominant reality explains two major concerns of the Church at the end of the apostolic period: the danger of apostasy and the need for holy living. The early canonical writers from Matthew to Revelation made strong appeals to believers to remain faithful to their commitment (Matt. 13:36-43, 47-50; 24:36–25:30; 2 Pet. 2:21; Heb. 6:4-8). There was an equal call to remain loyal to the content of the apostolic faith (Jude 3; 2 Thess. 2:15) and follow a Christian lifestyle in positive holy living (1 Pet. 1:15-16; 4:2). Thus, although the apostolic Church as a "remembering community" naturally focused on the past with respect to living under the impact of the coming of Christ, there was also a strong emphasis on the need to persist in the hope that God's eschatological purposes would be brought to completion in the near future. At this time, the kingdom would be given up to God (1 Cor. 15:24-25). Framed by a consciousness of these two comings, the apostolic Church lived in hope.

Bibliography. R. Banks, *Paul's Idea of Community,* rev. ed. (Peabody, 1994); E. Ferguson, *The Church of Christ* (Grand Rapids, 1996); K. Giles, *What on Earth Is the Church?* (Downer's Grove, 1995); H. Küng, *The Church* (New York, 1968); G. Lohfink, *Jesus and Community* (Philadelphia, 1984); P. S. Minear, *Images of the Church in the New Testament* (Philadelphia, 1960).

Allan J. McNicol

CHURCH FATHERS

Those persons whose views the Church considered to be foundational for the development of early Christian orthodoxy and spirituality. The time of the Fathers is classically divided into three periods: the foundational years (until the Council of Nicaea [325]); the formational period (until the Council of Chalcedon [451]); and the decline of the patristic era (in the Latin Church, until the death of Gregory the Great [604] or perhaps Isidore of Seville [636]; in the Greek Church, until the death of John of Damascus [749]). Viewed as founders of the mainline ecclesiastical tradition, the category of Fathers includes apostles, bishops, martyrs, apologists, heresiologists, theologians, and historians.

The meaning of the term Fathers has changed in nuance over the centuries. In antiquity the designation indicated a teacher in relationship to a student — a father to a son. Drawing from traditional Hellenistic culture, early Christians identified the teachers of Christian belief as Fathers, the spiritual teachers of the faith (1 Cor. 4:15; Mart. Pol. 12.2; Irenaeus *Adv. haer.* 4.41.2; Clement of Alexandria *Misc.* 1.1.2–2.1). The apostles were naturally included in this category, since they served as the instructors of specific Christian communities. By the 2nd century, bishops assumed the title because of their function as pastors of individual churches and as successors to the apostles (1 Clem. 62.2; Eusebius *HE* 5.4.2). During the theological controversies of the 4th and 5th centuries, the term was applied to those bishops whose teachings specifically conformed to the teachings of the orthodox faith (cf. Basil *Ep.* 140.2), especially as that faith later came to be defined by ecumenical councils (Ephesus [431] canon 7). Subsequent Christians eventually employed the term as a way to identify certain revered authors of the tradition in distinction from ecclesiastical writers in general. Vincent of Lérins (*Common.* 63, 66) represents a 5th-century movement to separate the designation of Father from the position of bishop altogether, thereby to remove any specific apostolic distinction for use of the term. Certain published lists of Fathers evolved by the 6th century, as illustrated by the Decretum Gelasianum, which identifies the Fathers according to their association with the Latin Church.

By modern criteria, the designation of Fathers of the Church is determined according to four primary criteria: orthodoxy of teaching and doctrine; holiness of lifestyle; confirmation by ecclesiastical authority; and antiquity. The title of Father is strictly an ecclesiastical concern. Those whom the Church considers as worthy to be listed among the Fathers have typically provided a solid witness to scriptural norms and the Christian tradition as sources for faith. Their work and lives are viewed a worthy testimony to these realities.

Because the Fathers are considered to reflect the foundations of early Christian faith, determination of membership among the Fathers often elicits fierce controversy. As a result, different lists of Fathers have evolved. The Latin Church naturally has chosen to revere certain figures whose theology represents Western orthodoxy: Ambrose, Jerome, Augustine, Gregory the Great. The Greek Church tends to give greater weight to those who are more sympathetic to Eastern thought: Basil the Great, Gregory of Nazianzus, Athanasius, John Chrysostom. Of course, the Latin and Greek Churches include a majority of the same names and have given consideration to the theological, sociological, and historical circumstances which affected the teachings of candidates during their times. Despite the extent of their theological contributions, however, certain teachers remain the focus of controversy either because of their break with the Catholic Church or because of their unique doctrinal positions: Tatian, Tertullian, Clement of Alexandria, Origen, Theodore of Mopsuestia.

Some of the Fathers have been further identified as Doctors of the Church, a title often given to ecclesiastical authors who have revealed special marks of Church teaching. Persons who lived after the patristic period usually receive this title as a mark that they have demonstrated theological contributions in agreement with the teachings of the Fathers. Included are theologians such as Albert the Great, Thomas Aquinas, Bonaventure, and John of the Cross.

The authority of the Fathers is based upon their support of the tradition. The teaching of any specific Father which diverges from the tradition bears no particular weight unless approved by a general council. The Church accepts the unanimous agreement of the Fathers with respect to scriptural exegesis as faith without error. The balance of their combined teachings in theology and doctrine, especially when the Fathers are taken in relation to one another, is given specific consideration in matters of modern ecclesiasical debate.

Bibliography. F. L. Cross, *The Early Christian Fathers* (London, 1960); G. L. Prestige, *Fathers and Heretics* (London, 1940); M. Wiles, *The Christian Fathers,* 2nd ed. (Oxford, 1982).

Clayton N. Jefford

CHUZA (Gk. *Chouzás*)

An "official" (NRSV "steward") of Herod Antipas. His precise office is unclear (cf. Matt. 20:8; Gal. 4:2). Chuza's wife Joanna was among Jesus' followers (Luke 8:3), suggesting that Jesus' message reached even the aristocracy. Joanna's presence among Jesus' followers has led to speculations that either Chuza had died before she began following Jesus, or that he himself was also a convert; neither is suggested by the text. Chuza may have been a Nabatean, as the name Chuza has been found in Nabatean and Syrian inscriptions.

Kim Paffenroth

CILICIA (Gk. *Kilikía*)

A country in southern Anatolia, the southeastern coast of Asia Minor. Cilicia has two distinct geographical regions, the rugged western coastlands (Cilicia Aspera) and the fertile plain in the east (Cilicia Campestris). It is ringed with mountains, on the west by its own mountains separating it from Pamphylia, on the north by the Taurus range separating it from Cappadocia and Lycaonia, and on the east by the Amanus range separating it from Syria. In antiquity Cilicia offered the main trade route between Syria and the central sections of Asia Minor.

The Cilicians claimed that their land was founded by Cilix, the son of Agenor, who accompanied his brothers Cadmus and Phoenix in search of their sister Europa, but who settled in their fertile plain. Because of its strategic location for trade, Cilicia was invaded successively by Hittites, Mycenaean Greeks, Assyrians, Persians (under whom the Cilicians had a degree of autonomy as a satrapy), Alexander the Great, the Seleucid kings, and finally the Romans who made it into a province in 102 B.C.E. In 67 B.C.E. Pompey stamped out piracy which flourished in the rugged coastlands (which were unmanageable and not added to the province until the reign of Vespasian, 69-79 C.E.). In 51-50 B.C.E. Cicero reluctantly tried as governor to correct numerous previous administrative problems. In 36 B.C.E. Mark Antony gave Cyprus and the rugged western coastlands to Cleopatra as a gift. Under Roman rulers the region was at times linked to Syria for governing purposes.

In the NT Cilicia is best known as the home country of Paul (Acts 21:39; 22:3; 23:34) and a stop on his missionary journeys through Asia Minor (15:41; Gal. 1:21). RICHARD A. SPENCER

CINNAMON

A member of the laurel family. The cinnamon tree (*Cinnamomum zeylanicum* Nees) is evergreen and grows up to 9 m. (30 ft.) tall. The fruit of the cinnamon tree (Heb. *qinnāmôn;* Gk. *kinnámōmon*) provides a fragrant oil when pressed. The distilled bark also produces oil of lesser quality. Quills of the bark and the ground inner rind of the bark are used for sweetening food. It is likely that in biblical times cinnamon was imported from the tropical Far East via the Silk Road.

In ancient times, cinnamon oil was valued as a precious perfume. It was an ingredient in the sacred oil Moses made to anoint the ark of the covenant and the tent of meeting (Exod. 30:23). The "strange" woman of Proverbs perfumed her bed with cinnamon (Prov. 7:17). In the Song of Solomon and Revelation cinnamon appears as a luxury item (Cant. 4:14; Rev. 18:13).

MEGAN BISHOP MOORE

CIRCUMCISION

The removal of the foreskin from the penis. While practiced by some ancient Near Eastern peoples for various reasons and in specific ways, circumcision had a unique place in the worship and practice of the people of Israel.

According to Genesis circumcision was first practiced by the patriarchs and involved all males of the household, including slaves; even resident aliens had to be circumcised in order to observe the Passover (Gen. 34:13-24). Normally male infants were circumcised when eight days old (Gen. 17:12; Lev. 12:3). Circumcision became the most critical distinguishing mark separating the Israelites from surrounding peoples. It was a requirement of God's covenant (Gen. 17:9-14), along with sabbath observance and food laws. By the time of the Maccabees circumcision was intimately bound up with Israel's identity as the covenant people of God (1 Macc. 1:14-15, 60-61; 2 Macc. 6:10). It was the most significant boundary marker which distinguished Jew from Gentile, those within the covenant from those outside.

Conquered peoples were circumcised so the inhabitants could be viewed as part of Israel (1 Macc. 2:46; Josephus *Ant.* 13.257-58, 318). By the time of Second Temple Judaism the terms "circumcision" and "Jew" were virtually synonymous. Even though circumcision was practiced by other peoples of the time (e.g., the Egyptians), Greco-Roman sources highlight the practice as a distinguishing mark of Judaism (e.g., Tacitus *Hist.* 5.5.2).

All this should not be misunderstood to mean that only the outward practice of circumcision was important for keeping the covenant. Circumcision and obedience to the entire covenant went hand in hand. The transformation of one's heart was of such essential importance that without it circumcision was of no value (Deut. 10:16; 30:6; Jer. 4:4; 9:25[MT 24]). A fine distinction between inward and outward cannot be maintained in Judaism; those who are the people of God must live as the people of God.

In the NT the issue of circumcision comes to the surface in the late 40s C.E. with the council of Jerusalem (Acts 15:1-29; cf. Gal. 2:1-10). Why it does not appear to be an important issue earlier in the Church is difficult to say.

The discussion of circumcision in the NT finds its focus in the Pauline corpus. In Galatians Paul insists that circumcision not be required of gentile believers. This was for Paul's opponents nothing less than the abandonment of a necessary requirement for the covenant which was so inextricably bound up with Israel's national identity. For Paul's opponents one could not abandon circumcision, the sign of God's covenant with Abraham, and remain faithful to the covenant. Paul argues quite forcefully in Galatians that the Gentiles belong to the people of God by virtue of their faith in Christ. They need not identify themselves as Jews by adopting the badges of the covenant so identified with ethnic Israel. According to Paul the Cross is the way one enters into the covenant, becoming a member of the people of God (cf. Col. 2:11). Thus Paul can accuse his opponents of diminishing the Cross in their desire to retain circumcision (Gal. 5:11; 6:12-15). For Paul there could be no importance placed on circumcision nor uncircumcision, Jew nor Gentile, in Christ Jesus.

Bibliography. J. M. G. Barclay, *Obeying the Truth: Paul's Ethics in Galatians* (Minneapolis, 1991); S. J. D. Cohen, "Crossing the Boundary and Becoming a Jew," *HTR* 82 (1989): 13-33; J. Collins, "A Symbol of Otherness: Circumcision and Salvation in the First Century," in *"To See Ourselves as Others See Us": Christians, Jews, "Others" in Late Antiquity,* ed. J. Neusner and E. Frerichs (Chico, 1985), 163-86; J. D. G. Dunn, *The Partings of the Ways: Between Christianity and Judaism and Their Significance for the Character of Christianity* (Philadelphia, 1991), 28-29, 124-27; J. Nolland, "Uncircumcised Proselytes?" *JSJ* 12 (1981): 173-94; F. Thielman, *Paul and the Law* (Downers Grove, 1994), 119-44. ALLAN R. BEVERE

CISTERN

Subterranean receptacles to collect and store the runoff water from seasonal rains. They are distinguished from open water storage facilities, which are more appropriately called pools or reservoirs, and from wells, which tap the water of underground aquifers.

The typical bottle-shaped cistern with a narrow

neck expanding into a larger storage area dates to the 4th millennium B.C.E. The interior was often lined with plaster. A raised circular stone collar was erected around the mouth of the cistern, and a heavy removable stone covered it to reduce evaporation and keep out debris. Cisterns located in wadi beds were filled by seasonal floods, while hillside cisterns received runoff channeled to them from the watershed. Marks on cistern collars indicate that water was drawn directly from them into skin or pottery containers on ropes. Cisterns varied in shape and size. Private, household cisterns tended to be small and bottle-shaped, while those serving whole communities, such as Arad and Masada, were large, rectangular enclosures, often with steps leading to the water level. Frequently caves in hillsides were enlarged and used as cisterns.

The Bible refers to cisterns (Heb. *bôr*) in passages describing wealth and the bounty of the land (Deut. 6:11; 2 Kgs. 18:31 = Isa. 36:16; 2 Chr. 26:10). They are not subject to ritual impurity (Lev. 11:36). The Israelites hid from the Philistines in cisterns (1 Sam. 13:6), Jeremiah was imprisoned in one (Jer. 38:1-13), and a cistern became the grave of those slain by Ishmael in his revolt against Gedaliah (41:7-9). Cisterns are used figuratively as symbols for rejection of God (Jer. 2:13), the judgment of God (14:3), and mortality (Eccl. 12:6).

JAMES H. PACE

CITADEL

The fortified portion of a city or a palace. It was in such quarters of the king's house (palace) at Samaria that Pekah killed Azariah, king of Judah (2 Kgs. 15:25), and at Tirzah where Zimri commited suicide (1 Kgs. 16:18). 1 Macc. 13:50 describes Simon's liberating the Jerusalem citadel from enemy hands and "cleansing the citadel from its pollution." According to Josephus the Hasmonean kings renamed it the Baris (*Ant.* 18.91). Rebuilt by Herod the Great and named the Tower of Antonia, it fell to the Romans in 70 C.E. Some scholars think that the house of the Philippian jailer was situated in Philippi's citadel (Acts 16:34). Ps. 48:3, 13(MT 4, 14) celebrates the security of Jerusalem, praising God for having "shown himself a sure defense."

HENRY L. CARRIGAN, JR.

CITIES OF REFUGE

Mosaic law calls for the establishment of a place, or places, of asylum, to which one who kills accidentally or without malice may flee to escape from the avenger of blood. Exod. 21:13 mentions only "a place to which he may flee," but Num. 35:9-34; Deut. 4:41-43; 19:1-13; Josh. 20:1-9 all speak of the setting aside of specific cities (Heb. *ʿārê miqlāṭ*) for such a purpose.

The establishment of cities of refuge can be seen as an effort to limit and control the practice of blood vengeance. In ancient Israel, as elsewhere in the ancient Near East, blood vengeance was accepted as a means of dealing with the shedding of blood outside the context of war. If a family member was killed, it was the responsibiltiy of the *gô'ēl haddām,* "avenger of blood," a male relative, to find and kill the person who had taken the life of the family member, whether the killing had been intentional or not.

The provision for places of asylum to which an accidental killer may go, however, combines the awareness of a distinction between killing with malice (murder) and killing by accident or without intention, with prohibitions against the shedding of innocent blood.

In Num. 35 the establishment of six cities of refuge from among the levitical cities is commanded, three beyond the Jordan and three in the land of Canaan. The cities were intended for anyone who killed a person without intent (cf. Num. 35:22-28). If an unintentional killer sought refuge in one of the cities, the "congregation" was to rescue the person from the avenger of blood and restore him to the city of refuge, where he had to stay until the death of the high priest.

The Numbers passage makes very clear that those guilty of murder, i.e., intentional killing, or killing with malice, had to be put to death and could in no case get off through payment of a ransom. Neither could the accidental killer return to his own city by payment of ransom. The intent in both cases seems to be to avoid polluting the land, since "blood pollutes the land" (Num. 35:33), apparently even blood shed without intent.

Josh. 20 is similar to Num. 35, but in addition calls for a trial (Josh. 20:6), and names the six cities of refuge (vv. 7-8): Kedesh in Galilee, in the hill country of Naphtali; Shechem in the hill country of Ephraim; Kiriath-arba (Hebron) in the hill country of Judah; Bezer in the wilderness within the territory of Reuben; Ramoth in Gilead from the tribe of Gad; and Golan in Bashan from Manasseh.

In Deut. 4:41-43 only the three cities beyond the Jordan are named. The setting apart of the remaining three is dealt with in Deut. 19:1-13, although those three are not named. Deuteronomy also allows for establishing three additional cities if the borders of the land are enlarged.

The intent in Deuteronomy seems to be different than in Numbers. There the purpose of asylum seem to be to prevent the killer (even if accidental) from polluting the land by keeping him within a circumscribed space. In Deuteronomy the cities are there to prevent the spilling of innocent blood, namely that of the accidental killer (Deut. 19:6, 10).

Bibliography. D. Patrick, *Old Testament Law* (Atlanta, 1985); R. de Vaux, *Ancient Israel* (1961, repr. Grand Rapids, 1997). MARILYN J. LUNDBERG

CITIES OF THE VALLEY

Five cities (also called "cities of the plain") — Sodom, Gomorrah, Admah, Zeboiim, and Bela (or Zoar) — in the region of the valley of the Jordan River and the Dead Sea, at Gen. 14:3, 8, 10 called the valley of Siddim. The kings of these cities (Heb. *ʿārê hakkikkār*) rebelled against Chedorlaomer of Elam, prompting the battle recorded in Gen. 14. Except for Zoar, the cities were destroyed by Yahweh because of their corruption (Gen. 19:24-29).

CITIZENSHIP

In biblical usage, a term signifying the community where one is a member. Throughout the Bible, individuals are portrayed holding citizenship in three types of community. The first type is citizenship within a concrete geographic entity. In Acts 21:39 Paul declares his being a "citizen of Tarsus . . . no mean city," accenting the identification of his home city with some civic pride. The second type is a group that shares a special, temporal status that transcends geography. While preaching in Philippi and again later in Jerusalem, Paul twice reveals his Roman citizenship to the authorities who arrested him (Acts 16:37; 22:25). He did so to claim the rights only those who held citizenship enjoyed throughout the Roman Empire. The third type is a group united with God as a local church. Paul proclaims to the Philippians that they already hold citizenship in heaven (Phil. 3:20). He sees not just a physical group of persons who hold faith in Jesus Christ, but a community who collectively hold the eschatological quality of Christian faith: hope in Christ's return, when they will be glorified. The letter to the Ephesians portrays the believers there as citizens of God's "household" (Eph. 2:19); once alienated from God by sin, their faith in Christ makes them citizens of a special community where God's Spirit dwells.

The portrayal in Acts of Paul's exercising his rights as a citizen of Rome is the most explicit demonstration of citizenship in the Bible. Roman citizenship was a political status granted only to free males throughout the empire. He who held it enjoyed explicit legal rights, and implicit privileges extended due to holding this status. The explicit rights of Roman citizenship were protection from unjust punishments (cf. Acts 16:37; 22:25), appeal of one's judicial case to Caesar (25:9-11), and the right to vote in Roman elections. (Some freedmen, upon receiving Roman citizenship, did not gain this right.) The first two rights held the most relevance for Roman citizens outside Italy. (A citizen had to be physically present in the city of Rome itself to cast his vote.) Paul used his rights to ensure that he continued to preach the gospel throughout the empire. His citizenship gave him a status before the local authority, whereby he could defend himself against the legal challenges leveled by opponents attempting to obstruct his evangelizing activity (e.g., Acts 17:22-23). Sometimes, Paul did not need to open his mouth, the charges being simply dismissed for not violating Roman law (e.g., Acts 18:14-15).

Later, when imprisoned by Roman authority, Paul had certain privileges extended to him due to his holding citizenship. He could receive visitors (Acts 23:17; 28:30), make pastoral visits as he did while on Malta (28:8), and order a Roman centurion to do his bidding (23:17). Most important was his privilege to preach the gospel without restriction, even as a prisoner of Caesar in the heart of the empire (Acts 28:30).

Bibliography. A. Berger, *An Encyclopedic Dictionary of Roman Law* (Philadelphia, 1953); M. Black, "Paul and Roman Law in Acts," *ResQ* 24 (1981): 209-18; P. van Minnen, "Paul the Roman Citizen," *JSNT* 56 (1994): 43-52; J. J. O'Rourke, "Roman Law and the Early Church," in *The Catacombs and the Colosseum: The Roman Empire as the Setting of Primitive Christianity*, ed. S. Benko and O'Rourke (Valley Forge, 1971), 165-86; J. Richardson, *Roman Provincial Administration, 227* B.C. *to* A.D. *117* (London, 1976); A. N. Sherwin-White, *Roman Society and Roman Law in the New Testament* (Oxford, 1963).

RAMÓN LUZÁRRAGA

CITY

Two kinds of cities appear in the world of the Bible, one ancient Near Eastern (Heb. *ʿîr*), the other Hellenistic (Gk. *pólis*). The peoples of Syria-Palestine established ancient Near Eastern cities like Jericho and Megiddo as early as 3000 B.C.E. Hebrew cities in this tradition have been excavated at Dan, Hazor, Lachish, Arad, and Beersheba. After conquering Syria-Palestine in 333, Alexander the Great of Macedonia established its first Hellenistic cities. The cities of Samaria (Gk. *Sebastos*) and Caesarea Maritima built by Herod (73-4 B.C.E.) follow this tradition, as do Jerusalem, Jerash, and Beth-shean.

Ancient Near Eastern and Hellenistic cities have been defined both by architectural design and economic structure. Architecturally, a city is a settlement where people live physically close together around a complex of monumental buildings surrounded by a wall. Economically, a city or state is a centralized system for producing and distributing goods and services. This centralized system is also called a "surplus economy," because it produces more basic goods and services than its own people need to survive. This surplus is used to trade with other cities for luxuries.

Farmers and herders make up less than 50 percent of a city's population. The remaining households specialize in skills like writing and in the manufacture of trade goods like wine at Gibeon or dyed textiles at Debir. Cities controlled not only land used for farms and pastures, but trade routes as well. The first known written documents deal with the administration of cities.

The sanctuary is the primary architectural expression of a city's authority to feed its people. Here priests tax herds and harvests as sacrifices, which are processed, stored, and redistributed. The palace with its wall and gate is the primary architectural expression of a city's authority to protect its people. Here monarchs resolve disputes between households, trade with their covenant partners, and command their soldiers. The style and arrangement of these buildings in an ancient Near Eastern city varied. Most Hellenistic cities were laid out according to the plan of Hippodamus of Miletus described in the *Politics* of Aristotle (2.1267b-1268a). The land of a Hellenistic city was surveyed in rectangles divided by a main street (Lat. *cardo*) running north-south and a main street *(decimanus)* running east-west. These streets intersected at the geographical center of the city where the market (Gk. *agorá*) or forum was located. It was surrounded by a walk

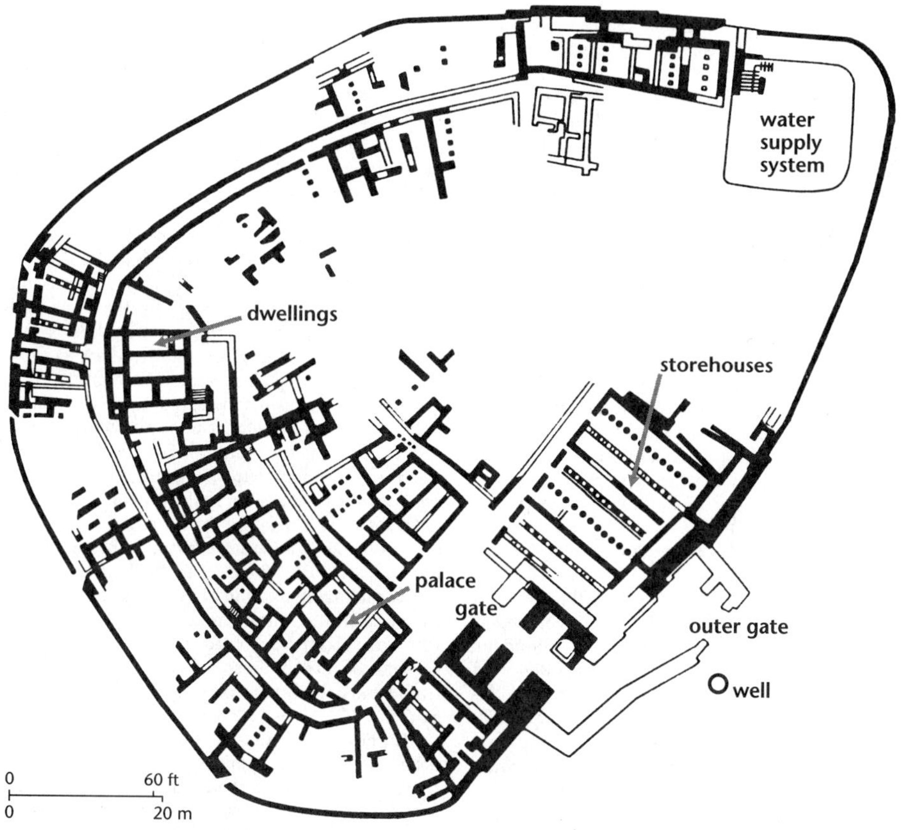

City plan of Iron Age II Beer-sheba (stratum II, 8th century B.C.E.) (following Ze'ev Herzog)

(stoá) lined with columns supporting a roof. Temples, a meeting hall *(bouleutḗrion)*, a banquet hall *(prytaneîon)*, theaters, gymnasium, stadium, and palaces were placed in predetermined positions on this Hippodamian grid.

Some traditions of ancient Israel and early Christianity in the Bible challenge the economic systems which cities support. Jericho and Ai are placed under interdict (Josh. 5:13–6:27). Bethel is sentenced for breach of the covenant between Yahweh and Israel (Amos 7:10-17). Sodom (Gen. 19), Jerusalem (Isa. 5:1-7; Jer. 34–35; Ezek. 16), and Samaria (Amos 4) are indicted for social injustice. The cities of Jerusalem and Rome martyr Jesus and Paul. This prejudice, which considers ancient Israel and early Christianity to be a nomadic or village way of life which cities threaten to destroy, is ancient and ingrained. For example, the Yahwists, whose traditions (J) are the backbone of the books of the Pentateuch, lived in the city of Jerusalem. Nonetheless, their traditions deny cities were ever a proper home for the Hebrews. For the Yahwists, the Creator gives the Adam a garden, not a city (Gen. 2:4-17). Cities are the homes of murderers like Cain (Gen. 4:3–5:32), of braggarts like the citizens of Babel (11:1-9), and of savages like the people of Sodom (19:1-38). The Yahwists' story is the exodus of Abraham from the cities of Mesopotamia (Gen. 11:27–25:18), the exodus of Moses from the cities of Egypt (Exod. 1:7–13:16), and the victory of Joshua over the cities of Canaan (Josh. 1:1–Judg. 21:25). They portray the Hebrews as a people who either abandon cities or destroy them.

Nonetheless, the traditions of ancient Israel and early Christianity in the Bible also endorse the economics which cities support. Bethel is the first land deeded to the Hebrews by Yahweh (Gen. 11:27–13:18; 28:10-22) and the setting of the ark stories (1 Sam. 4–6; 2 Sam. 6). Jerusalem is celebrated as the dwelling place of Yahweh (Ezek. 40–48; Rev. 21:1–22:7). Some of the most significant words and deeds of Jesus and Paul take place in the cities of Caesarea Philippi, the Decapolis, Jerusalem, Caesarea Maritima, Antioch, and Rome. In the traditions of the Exodus, the Settlement, the Monarchy, and the Exile, cities play an important positive role in Israel's understanding of itself and of Yahweh. At times, the Hebrews were migrant, itinerant, or pastoral, but they were always going somewhere. Even when the Hebrews were without land, they were never without a promise of land, and the core of this land, with which their destiny is so closely tied, is the city. Not only were cities fit places for the people of Yahweh to dwell, but the city was a fit symbol of Yahweh.

Anthropologists and sociologists today continue to provide evidence that a dichotomy between the values and the lifestyle of people living in cities and people living in the country appears only after the industrial revolution in western Europe. In the world of the Bible, cities and villages were two parts of a single economy. Cities depended upon farmer's and herders to provide them with goods to maintain themselves and to provide a surplus. Cities protected the farmer's crops, offered farmers homes and markets for their harvests, and provided the benefits of other skills, such as metal work, pottery making, and weaving, which farmers and herders no longer had time to practice. There may have been divisions between rich and poor, between the powerful and the powerless, between military and civilian, between governing and governed, but there was no dichotomy between people who lived in cities and those who lived in villages.

Bibliography. D. C. Benjamin, *Deuteronomy and City Life* (Lanham, Md., 1983); F. Frick, *The City in Ancient Israel.* SBLDS 36 (Chico, 1977); V. Fritz and P. R. Davies, eds., *The Origins of the Ancient Israelite States.* JSOT Sup 227 (Sheffield, 1996); Z. Herzog, "Social Organization as Reflected by the Bronze and Iron Age Cities of Israel," *Comparative Studies in the Development of Complex Societies* 2 (London, 1986); J. E. Stambaugh and D. L. Balch, *The New Testament in Its Social Environment.* Library of Early Christianity 2 (Philadelphia, 1986).

DON C. BENJAMIN

CITY (NEW TESTAMENT)

Cities played an important role in the social, cultural, and religious world of the Roman Empire, anecdotally illustrated in the Latin root for civilization (*civitas,* "city"). Jesus' ministry took place on the outskirts of cities in and around the Galilee, Paul's travels and letter-writing occurred in an urban context, and the city is a key theological concept in several NT books.

Even though the term *pólis* occurs more than 150 times in the NT, the Greek concept of a democratic, self-governing city-state had given way to the reality of Roman administrative needs. Rome ruled its empire through cities and distinguished between a bewildering variety (e.g., *civitas, colonia, municipium*). In the East, Rome integrated the local elites and rulers into a network of cities to tax efficiently its empire, and even created confederations of cities, such as the Decapolis, to facilitate its defense. Cities did have larger populations than towns or villages, but were primarily recognizable by distinctive architectural features and patterns. Roman period cities adopted several architectural features from the Greek *pólis* and provided amenities necessary for what the Romans thought of as civilized life: an *agora,* a *basilica* used as a court or administrative building, an *odeon,* an aqueduct, public baths, *nymphaea,* and temples. The architectural arrangement tended towards regularized orthogonal grids, often by artificially subduing topographical limitations and challenges. Facades of fresco, marble, or plaster, coupled with ingeniously executed colonnades created vistas that focused on monuments of Roman rule, such as a temple, an emperor's status, or the *basilica.* The social position of the wealthy was visually reinforced in seating in theaters or amphitheaters or in inscriptions declaring their munificence.

In its socio-political structure, the city's elites competed with one another for prestige by sponsoring building projects, their maintenance, and public festivals, made possible by the rents and taxes they collected from the countryside. In varying degrees, individual cities numbered few wealthy residents but many poor, some of whom had migrated after being dispossessed from their land only to become dependent upon distribution and beneficence of the elites. Aside from the few wealthy, some merchants, artisans, soldiers, and public workers, a city's population comprised primarily slaves, day laborers, the chronically poor, and indigents. Trade routes through the larger cities, and especially those near the Mediterranean coast, facilitated mobility and brought together various cultural, ethnic, and religious groups — who often clashed. Such social turmoil, and the discontent of the poorest substratum, were both feared and harshly controlled by Roman-appointed rulers.

Numerous cities in Palestine had already been urbanized in the Hellenistic sense in the first few centuries B.C.E. Herod the Great's rule (37-4 B.C.E.) as a client king of Rome was characterized by enormous architectural and urban activity — he founded Caesarea Maritima as the most modern and beautiful port city in the Levant, and Jerusalem and Sebaste-Samaria were transformed with Roman urban architecture. Herod Antipas, who inherited Galilee from his father's kingdom, built the cities of Sepphoris and Tiberias as his capitals — albeit on a smaller and less ostentatious scale — and he apparently avoided overt signs of paganism, such as statues or pagan temples, and his coins remained aniconic. Although no evidence indicates that Jesus visited these cities during his ministry, certainly they had an impact on the Galilee by realigning trade patterns and funneling profits from the countryside's agricultural produce as taxes for Antipas and Rome. The Gospel writers' proclivity for the term *pólis* — they even bestow this title on the villages of Nazareth (Matt. 2:23) and Capernaum (Matt. 9:1 and Luke 4:31) — is indicative of the imprecision with which the designation was used or perhaps even their unawareness of these sites.

While Jesus' ministry took place in Jewish Galilean village culture on the fringe of second-rate urban centers, Paul was fully immersed in the urban life of the Greco-Roman world. His hometown of Tarsus was a major port city, and the cities most identified with his missionary travels — Antioch, Corinth, Ephesus — count among the largest and most cosmopolitan of the time. Their social, religious, and cultural diversity and complexity leave their mark on Paul's letters and in Acts; Paul typically made contact with these cities' Jewish communities, and from there sought to expand to include Gentiles. The latter part of the book of Acts can even be read as the various city officials' attempts to deal with the political strife and social upheaval accompanying Paul's missions. The demographics of the Pauline communities were primarily lower-class, though some upper-class slave owners (e.g., Philemon) were included, and a mix of Jews and Gentiles with various ethnic heritages. Paul's visits to Palestine were confined primarily to the large port city of Caesarea and to Jerusalem (Acts 21–26).

The city of Jerusalem itself plays a theological role in the Gospels, Acts, and the Apocalypse. Twice Matthew explicitly calls it "the holy city" (Matt. 4:5; 27:53), and Luke presents Jerusalem as a kind of *axis mundi,* the Christian navel of the world. Jesus steadily moves towards Jerusalem in Luke's Gospel culminating in his inevitable crucifixion which must take place there, according to Luke 13:30-33. In the geographical schema of Acts, Christianity spreads from Jerusalem . . . to the ends of the earth. The crisis of the destruction of the Jerusalem temple reverberated among early Christians as well, and its devastating consequences can best be seen in the predictions found in Mark 13. The apocalyptic vision of John foresees a new Jerusalem which will supersede the fallen Babylon/Rome (Rev. 21).

Bibliography. M. Finley, *The Ancient Economy* (Berkeley, 1973); W. Meeks. *The First Urban Christians: The Social World of the Apostle Paul* (New Haven, 1983).

JONATHAN L. REED

CITY OF CHAOS

An epithet (Heb. *qiryaṯ-tōhû*) for a city of sinners (Isa. 24:10), most commonly assumed to be Jerusalem but possibly Babylon, Samaria, Tyre, or a symbolic city of evil.

CITY OF MOAB

A site vaguely noted in the narrative of Balaam and Balak (Num. 22:36; NRSV "Ir-Moab"; NIV "the Moabite town"). It is described as on the Arnon border, on the (northern) boundary of Balak's territory. Given the current evidence, any attempt to link a specific place name with the town that held such important status in Balak's day must remain speculative. Nevertheless, if "the city of Moab" is identified as "Ar of Moab" (Num. 21:28; Isa. 15:1), a number of possibilities exist — e.g., Rabbah (ancient Ar/Areopolis/Rabbath-moab), Karak (Kir/Kir-hareseth), Khirbet el-Misnaʿ (NE of Rabbah), Khirbet el-Medeineh (in the northeast region of Moab), and Khirbet el-Bālūʿ (NE of Qasr). All of these sites are located S of Wadi el-Môjib (Arnon), but most are too far from this canyon to be regarded as near Moab's border. Scholars have often identified "the city of Moab" with Ar (Num. 21:15; Deut. 2:18), but Khirbet el-Bālūʿ is the most likely option because of its location, size, and history of occupation (i.e., evidence of Late Bronze and Iron Age settlement).

Bibliography. J. M. Miller, "The Israelite Journey through (around) Moab and Moabite Toponymy," *JBL* 108 (1989): 577-95.

GERALD L. MATTINGLY

CITY OF PALM TREES

Another name for Jericho or for the surrounding valley, famous for its many palm trees (Deut. 34:3; 2 Chr. 28:15). It was the residence of the Kenites (Judg. 1:16) and, after his conquest, of King Eglon (3:13). According to ancient historians, it took five hours to travel through the palm groves by way of intersecting waterways.

CITY OF SALT

A city in Judah (Josh. 15:62; Heb. *ʿîr hammelaḥ*), located in the wilderness between Nibshan and En-gedi. Some scholars suggest identification with Khirbet Qumrân (193127) on the basis of the remains of buildings from Iron Age II (900-600 B.C.E.).

CITY OF THE SUN

A city located in the Egyptian Delta NE of modern Cairo It served as one of the important spiritual and religious centers of ancient Egypt, housing temples to the gods Re-Harachte and Atum. Their cults were characterized as cosmological, and its Heaven Feast was well known.

Potiphera, the father of Joseph's wife Asenath, was a priest of On (Gen. 41:45). The LXX (Exod. 1:11b) adds "and On, this is, Heliopolis" after Pithom and Raamses, as the third city that the Israelites built for Pharaoh. It is unlikely that these cities were located far from Goshen; therefore the originality of LXX here is doubtful. Most probably, Josephus' (*Ant.* 2.188) mention that Jacob's family settled in Heliopolis is based on the LXX. In Ezek. 30:17 the young men of Awen ("iniquity," a wordplay with the name On, symbolizing all Egypt) will fall by the sword and will go into captivity. In Isa. 19:18 the city is called *ʿîr haheres,* "the city of destruction," a play on the name "*ʿîr haḥeres*" (so 1QIsa[a] and many MSS), which is *ʿîr hašemeš* ("the city of sun"; cf. Tg. Jonathan and Vulg.; also Job 9:7; Jer. 43:13). However, according to this verse "the City of the Sun" will be one of the five Egyptian cities whose inhabitants will speak Hebrew and worship Yahweh.

ISAAC KALIMI

CITY OF WATERS

Another name for Rabbah **2** (2 Sam. 12:27; NRSV "water city").

CLAUDIA (Gk. *Klaudía*)

A Christian woman living at Rome, among those who sent greetings to Timothy via Paul (2 Tim. 4:21). According to later tradition she was the wife of the Pudens and the mother of the Linus mentioned in the same verse, or the wife of Linus.

CLAUDIUS
The fourth emperor of Rome. Tiberius Claudius Drusus was step-grandson and grandnephew of Augustus and grandson of Mark Antony. Born 1 August 10 B.C.E., Claudius survived the political murders of Sejanus during the reign of his uncle, the emperor Tiberius, but on account of physical disabilities he was not considered a candidate for the throne as were his brother and nephews. Upon the assassination of his nephew, the emperor Gaius (Caligula), Claudius was found hiding in the palace by rampaging praetorian guards who proclaimed the stunned Claudius emperor.

Claudius' reign (41-54 C.E.) demonstrated excellent management, particularly in the provinces, perhaps not unexpected of one who had spent most of his life as a historian of Rome's past. For the first time provincial leaders were admitted to the Senate at Rome. Claudius established a government bureaucracy to further facilitate efficient and fair administration of the provinces. He engaged in several building projects that improved Rome's supply of water and grain, including his successful construction of Rome's harbor at Ostia. He successfully centralized the power of the emperor, but his reliance on the counsel of freedmen and his apparent manipulation by his wives tarnished his reputation. Although early in his reign, perhaps due to the influence of his boyhood friend, Herod Agrippa, Claudius had enacted an edict protecting the religious freedom of Jews throughout the empire, he later ordered the expulsion of Jews from Rome because of their frequent rioting at the instigation of "Chrestus."

During Claudius' reign Britain and Thrace were added to the empire after their conquest by Claudius' generals. His only son was named Britannicus in honor of Britain's subjugation. Claudius' fourth wife was his niece Agrippina, who arranged the murder of first Claudius and then Britannicus, to obtain and ensure the throne for her son by a previous marriage, Nero.

Bibliography. B. Levick, *Claudius* (New Haven, 1990).

JOHN F. HALL/SCOTT NASH

CLAUDIUS LYSIAS (Gk. *Klaúdios Lysías*)
The tribune or chiliarch (commander of 1000 troops) of the Roman cohort stationed at the Fortress of Antonia in Jerusalem. Lysias was not a Roman by birth: his cognomen is Greek and his Roman citizenship came at a high price (Acts 22:28). He probably took the Latin name Claudius when he received his citizenship.

Lysias placed Paul under protective custody after Paul provoked a riot in the temple (Acts 21:27-36). Learning that Paul was not a terrorist (cf. Josephus *BJ* 2.261-63), Lysias allowed him to speak (Acts 21:37-40). When Paul nearly provoked a second riot, Lysias took him to the fortress, where Paul escaped scourging by revealing his Roman citizenship (Acts 22:1-29). After Paul appeared before the Sanhedrin the next day, Lysias learned of a plot against Paul's life and sent him by night under heavy guard to Caesarea, along with a letter to Felix, the governor of Caesarea, explaining the circumstances (Acts 23:26-30). Luke's narrative presents the Romans — as elsewhere in Acts — as fair-minded and just in their dealings with Paul.

MARK L. STRAUSS

CLEAN AND UNCLEAN
That which is clean or pure is in its proper place, whereas that which is unclean or impure is disgustingly out of place. The clean is limited by its opposite, the unclean, for dirt automatically pollutes or contaminates what is clean. In order to restore something or someone to a state of purity, the dirt must be removed.

Clean and unclean are defined by particular cultures, which determine the proper places for people and things. Realities that do not fit a culture's categories provoke anxiety and discomfort. Purity rules attempt to avoid discomfort and maintain wholeness or completeness in a society by defining what belongs (the clean) and what does not (the unclean). Impurity is especially dangerous when it is associated with death and when it threatens to gain access to the body.

In the Bible the concept of clean and unclean is not identical to the modern notion of sanitary and unsanitary. Impurity can be physical, ritual, or moral. Uncleanness is especially opposed to holiness, and so OT laws attempted to separate the unclean from the holy. The Priestly writings were especially concerned with such laws, for it was the responsibility of the priest to distinguish between the holy and the profane, between the clean and the unclean. Priests were also obligated to teach Israel the laws of purity in order to avoid offending God's holiness (Lev. 10:10-11; Ezek. 22:26; 44:23).

Ancient Israel's purity laws were concerned with the nation's relationship with God. Since the holy and the unclean were incompatible, it was necessary for the sacred to be protected from pollution. This was especially true for the sanctuary, the altar, and those who ministered in sacred places. Since the priests crossed the boundaries from the profane to the sacred in the performance of their duties, it was important that they avoid impurity.

Uncleanness was considered to be infectious or contagious, for it could be incurred through contact with an unclean person or thing. Three forms of uncleanness were especially powerful and contagious (Num. 5:2): *ṣāra'aṯ*, bodily discharges, and corpses. Each type of impurity had some connection with death.

Heb. *ṣāra'aṯ* is usually translated "leprosy," although most scholars today deny that it is identical with Hansen's disease. This "scale disease" was probably psoriasis or a fungal infection. It could even attack clothing and houses (Lev. 13:47-59). Since the victim's body appeared to be wasting away, the disease was seen as a punishment from God (Num. 12:10-15). Those with *ṣāra'aṯ* were separated from the community as the dead were separated from the living (Lev. 13:45-46).

Bodily discharges, especially from sexual organs, were also considered to be strong pollutants

(Lev. 15:1-33). The Bible says little about the necessary functions of urinating and defecating (Deut. 23:12-14). But vaginal blood and semen symbolized life, and their loss seemed to represent death. Childbirth, too, was dangerous: not only were bodily fluids lost, but the boundary between life and death was breached.

Contact with animal and especially human corpses also brought uncleanness (Num. 19:11-22). Priests (Lev. 10:6-7; 21:1-4; Ezek. 44:25-26) and Nazirites (Num. 6:6-7), because of their holy status, had to avoid contact with the dead. A high priest could not even approach the corpse of his own father or mother (Lev. 21:11).

Purity laws also regulated other areas of life where boundaries could become blurred. Mixtures, whether of cloth, agricultural practices, or animal breeding, were forbidden (Lev. 19:19; Deut. 22:9-11). Adultery, incest, bestiality, and homosexuality were also seen as crossing boundaries and thus were prohibited (Lev. 18:6-23; 20:10-21). Foreign lands were automatically unclean (Josh. 22:19; Amos 7:17).

Since uncleanness was contagious, it had to be removed by rituals. Contact with uncleanness normally required simple acts of bathing, washing one's clothes, and waiting until evening. More dangerous pollution, such as menstrual blood or a corpse, required seven days of waiting and even sprinkling with special water (Lev. 15:19-24; Num. 19:11-13). The uncleanness associated with *ṣāraʿaṯ*, irregular bodily discharges, and childbirth necessitated ritual actions by a priest (Lev. 12:1-8; 14:1-57; 15:1-15, 25-30). Since uncleanness was opposed to holiness, it had a vague connection with sin and guilt. All impurity was potentially damaging to the sanctuary (Lev. 15:31). The altar and sanctuary had to be regularly purified from the effects of uncleanness and sin (Lev. 4:1-35; 16:14-16).

Food could also be clean or unclean. Israelites were absolutely forbidden to "eat" blood with their meat, since blood was associated with life and with holiness (Lev. 17:10-14; Deut. 12:16, 23-25). There were restrictions on the kinds of animals which could be eaten. For example, only fish which had both fins and scales were permitted (Lev. 11:9-12; Deut. 14:9-10). Among quadrupeds only those which chewed the cud and had divided hooves were considered clean (Lev. 11:3-7; Deut. 14:4-8). Animals which crossed distinct boundaries or which did not clearly belong to certain categories were normally classified as unclean (Lev. 11:27-31).

The distinction between clean and unclean was a reminder of Israel's call to holiness (Exod. 22:31[MT 30]; Lev. 20:22-26; Deut. 14:2). Holiness implied separation from the common or the profane. Israel's vocation to holiness thus demanded separation from other nations. The restrictions on Israel's diet and its concept of the clean and the unclean defined its self-identity and kept it apart from others.

The notion of clean and unclean also served metaphorically to describe moral or ethical categories. "Unclean lips" (Isa. 6:5) stood for sinfulness, while "clean hands and pure hearts" (Ps. 24:4) were symbols of moral uprightness. Christians, who rejected Jewish purity rules because they excluded Gentiles, preferred to understand clean and unclean primarily as ethical categories (Acts 10:15; 15:19-29).

In the NT Jesus criticized Jewish purity regulations and allowed his disciples to violate them (Mark 7:1-23). He touched and healed those who were ritually unclean (lepers, Mark 1:40-45; Luke 17:11-19; the woman with a hemorrhage, Mark 5:25-34). He associated himself with known sinners. But he also drove out "unclean" spirits. Clean and unclean in the NT is often linked to the authority of Jesus and the meaning of his death and resurrection (Mark 1:27; Gal. 2:15-21).

Bibliography. M. Douglas, "The Forbidden Animals in Leviticus," *JSOT* 59 (1993): 3-23; *Purity and Danger: An Analysis of the Concepts of Pollution and Taboo* (New York, 1966); J. Milgrom, *Leviticus 1-16*. AB 3 (New York, 1991); R. D. Nelson, *Raising Up a Faithful Priest: Community and Priesthood in Biblical Theology* (Louisville, 1993); J. Neusner, *The Idea of Purity in Ancient Judaism* (Leiden, 1973).

TIMOTHY A. LENCHAK

CLEMENT (Gk. *Klḗmēs*)

A "fellow worker" who shared Paul's "struggle in the work of the gospel," among those "whose names are in the book of life"(Phil. 4:3). This indicates his value to Paul, but reveals nothing else about him. Clement was a common Latin name, appropriate for his presence in the thriving Roman colony of Philippi. Origen identifies him as Clement of Rome, the author of 1 Clement, but that identification is speculative at best. DAVID R. BECK

CLEMENT, EPISTLES OF

Two texts attributed to Clement, found in the 4th-century biblical Codex Alexandrinus and included in the Apostolic Fathers. They are in fact completely separate Christian documents written by two different authors. Both reflect a traditional piety strongly influenced by Judaism but have little else in common.

1 Clement

One of the earliest Christian documents outside the NT canon, 1 Clement is a genuine letter from the Roman church to the church in Corinth written about the turn of the 1st century. These Roman Christians were prompted to write by the report (1 Clem. 47:7) of renewed outbreak of factions and divisions in Corinth, triggered by the deposition of some of the Corinthian presbyters (44:6). In keeping with acceptable rhetorical strategy, the author(s) provides only vague allusions to the exact nature of the dispute and its cause. However, he considers its effects serious enough to warrant some response from the Roman community in the form of an appeal for the restoration of peace and concord (63:2). The letter was carried to Corinth by couriers from Rome (63:3; 65:1) who no doubt acted as mediators in the dispute.

The identity of the author(s) remains obscure, but ancient tradition from the time of Eusebius in the early 4th century (*HE* 3.16.1; 38.1) attributes the letter to a "Clement." Who this might have been remains uncertain, although many claim that he was an imperial freedman of the household of Titus Flavius Clemens and a (or *the*) leader among the Roman presbyters. He might have been the same Clement mentioned by the Shepherd of Hermas (*Visions* 2.4.3) whose duty it was to send communication from Rome "to the cities abroad," but this identification is by no means certain. However, it is certain that he did not function as a monarchical bishop, as Irenaeus later claimed (*Adv. haer.* 3.3.3), since other early sources (notably Ignatius' letter to Rome) confirm that the monarchical episcopate did not exist in Rome until at least the middle of the 2nd century. Moreover, 1 Clement uses the terms "bishops" and "presbyters" interchangeably and always in the plural.

Whoever the actual author(s) might have been, the worldview and perspective of the letter are unambiguous. The author shares a positive assessment of Roman society and government (61:1-3) and demonstrates a concern for the maintenance of hierarchical order consistent with the prevailing perspective of the well-educated "social elite" of Roman society. This stands in sharp contrast with the perspective of the contemporary book of Revelation, which sees the imperial Roman system as the "Beast" to be opposed at all costs, even at the risk of death.

Eusebius reports (*HE* 4.22.1; 23.11) that 1 Clement was successful in its attempt to end the crisis in Corinth. Moreover, the perspectives of the letter contributed significantly to the later development of a theology of ecclesiastical office in the Church.

2 Clement

2 Clement is not a letter at all but a mid-2nd-century sermon exhorting its audience to fidelity in traditional Christian virtues in the face of the coming judgment. There is nothing very distinctive about the sermon, and its main value is that it demonstrates the ordinary style of Christian preaching in the 2nd century. Written for a predominantly Gentile Christian audience of converts (2 Clem. 1:6), the preacher stresses the need for repentance and self-control, and recommends the traditional Jewish pious practices of fasting, prayer, and almsgiving. He exhorts the audience to keep pure and undefiled the "seal of baptism" (6:9; 7:6; 8:6) so that they might "gather the immortal fruit of resurrection" (19:3).

BARBARA E. BOWE

CLEOPAS (Gk. *Kleopás*)

One of two disciples to whom Jesus appeared on the road to Emmaus (Luke 24:13-32). The two were discussing Jesus' crucifixion and did not recognize Jesus until he broke bread with them in their house. Some have identified Cleopas with Clopas the husband of Mary who was at the cross of Jesus (John 19:25). The name is probably a shortened form of Cleopatros.

JOE E. LUNCEFORD

CLIMATE

Climate is associated with weather, but differs from it. Weather is often defined within short time periods, day, week, month, or year, and describes atmospheric conditions which determine levels of precipitation, wind direction and velocity, the path of the jet stream and temperature. Climate defines the status of the various factors associated with weather, but over a longer duration, years or millennia. Climate is not the summation of weather conditions, but the study of atmospheric conditions which determine weather patterns.

Two climate systems determine the weather of the Near East; (1) the westerlies, which control the weather over Greece, Turkey, Syria, Palestine, Iraq, and Iran; and (2) the monsoon, which controls the weather over east Africa and Ethiopia. The westerlies control the amount of precipitation in Turkey, where the sources of the Tigris and Euphrates rivers are located, and determine the volume of water in the river system. The African monsoon determines the amount of precipitation in Ethiopia and Lake Victoria, where the sources of the Nile River are located, and determines the volume of water in the river. Since there is little or no rainfall in southern Mesopotamia, or in Egypt, these two systems are vital for survival in the areas. The two systems work in concert. If climatic conditions cause a northerly shift of the two systems, then there would be less precipitation in Turkey and lower river levels in Mesopotamia, leading to food shortage and famine. Egypt, on the other hand, would have abundance of water and surplus of food. The reverse is also true.

A recently developed method known as archaeoclimatic modeling is site-specific and of high resolution, relating climatic conditions to specific societies in particular locations within a given period of centuries or millennium. The model starts with the variation of the heat of the earth and atmosphere based on volcanic modulation of incoming radiation and the extent of the ice cover of the surface of the earth. In addition, it includes data from atmospheric dynamics, location of the jetstream, and intertropical convergence. Past climate can be calculated for each section of the hemispheres at 200-year intervals as far back as 14 thousand years. The modeling technique has importance for the study of the ancient Near East, showing significant climatic change in the last 10 thousand years.

For Palestine the modeling has shown that climatic conditions are connected with the westerlies and in many cases, but not all, opposite to Egypt's. For example, the Predynastic Age of Egypt ended with a severe flood, while in Mesopotamia the Predynastic Age ended with a drought. In Palestine the end of Early Bronze I ended with a drought. These events occurred at about the same time, 2900/2800 B.C.E.

Bibliography. W. C. Brice, ed., *The Environmental History of the Near and Middle East Since the Last Ice Age* (New York, 1978); F. A. Hassan and S. W. Robinson, "High-precision Radiocarbon Chronology of Ancient Egypt, and Comparison with

Nubia, Palestine and Mesopotamia," *Antiquity* 61 (1987): 119-35; H. H. Lamb, *Climate: Present, Past, and Future* 1 (London, 1972); M. R. Rampino et al., eds., *Climate: History, Periodicity and Predictability* (New York, 1987), esp. 37-46.

LAWRENCE A. SINCLAIR

CLOPAS (Gk. *Klōpás*)

The husband of Mary who stood near the cross (John 19:25; the Greek construction "of Mary" also allows for husband or brother). Some identify him with Cleopas, to whom the risen Lord appeared on the road to Emmaus (Luke 24:18) and with Alphaeus, the father of James the Less.

CLOTHING

Despite the several hundred biblical references to clothing, translators face difficulties rendering accurately many of the Hebrew, Aramaic, and Greek words for specific garments. As texts took shape over some 1000 years words took on new meanings, cloth-making technology improved, and fashions changed. Biblical accounts are set in different geographic areas, with varying climates, resources, nationalities, and cultures. Dress styles can differ according to occupation (e.g., Zech. 13:4), status (e.g., 2 Sam. 13:18) and wealth (e.g., Jas. 2:2-3), and can be influenced by styles from other cultures (e.g., 2 Macc. 4:12). The complexity translators face becomes apparent when one compares translations; e.g., in Gen. 37:3, 23, 32 Joseph's *kĕṯōneṯ passîm:* "tunic of many colors" (NKJV), "long robe with sleeves" (NRSV, REB), "long tunic" (NAB), "decorated tunic" (NJB), "ornamented tunic" (NJPSV), "richly ornamented robe" (NIV).

No clothing from OT times has been recovered in Palestine. However some clothing from the end of the NT period has survived. Cloth fragments and sandals from Masada and Qumran date to 70-73 C.E. Entire tunics, mantles, and sandals from the nearby Cave of Letters date to Bar Kokhba's revolt (135).

Pictures and statues from surrounding peoples are useful. An Egyptian wall painting at Beni Hasan from Khnum-hotep III's tomb (ca. 1890 B.C.E., contemporaneous with the biblical patriarchs) shows two Egyptian officials meeting a caravan of eastern men, women, and children (*ANEP*, 3). The Black Obelisk of Assyrian King Shalmaneser III (858-824) depicts Israel's King Jehu (2 Kgs. 9–10) and 13 attendants bringing tribute (*ANEP*, 351-55). Wall carvings from Nineveh depicting the siege of Lachish (SE of Jerusalem) in 701 show Assyrian and Judean soldiers, and men, women, and children from the city (*ANEP*, 371-73).

Heb. *beged* is used as a collective term for "clothing" (Lev. 11:25) or generically for any garment (13:47). It is used of the attire of a king and his servants (2 Sam. 13:31), priestly vestments (Exod. 28:2), and women's clothing (Gen. 38:14). Gk. *himátion* functions similarly (Mark 2:21 par.). Clothing included mantles (alternately translated "coat," "cloak," "robe"), tunics ("robe"), sashes ("belt," "apron," "loincloth," "waistcloth"), headdresses ("turban," "veil," "crown"), and sandals ("shoes").

Gen. 3:7 is the first reference to clothing. The man and woman stitch fig leaves to make "waistcloths" (Heb. *ḥăgōrâ*). In 2 Sam. 18:11; 1 Kgs. 2:5 *ḥăgōrâ* describes soldiers' garb. This shirtlike garment was wrapped around the waist and covered the thighs. A "loincloth" (Heb. *'ēzôr;* Gk. *zṓnē*) was similar (Isa. 5:27; Ezek. 23:15). Either could be folded into a beltlike sash.

The fig-leaf waistcloths contrast with the "skin tunics" with which God "clothed" the man and woman (Gen. 3:21). The "tunic" (Heb. *kuttōneṯ;* Gk. *chitṓn*), a kind of shirt suspended from one or both shoulders, was worn by men (2 Sam. 15:32) and women (Cant. 5:3). A "skin loincloth" was characteristic of Elijah (2 Kgs. 1:8) and John the Baptist (Matt. 3:4 = Mark 1:6). Zech. 13:4 mentions a "garment of hair" worn by prophets; John the Baptist's clothes were of "camel's hair." Heb. 11:37 speaks of biblical saints who traveled "in sheepskins, in goatskins." Sheepskin tunics were found in the Cave of Letters.

Wool from fleece and linen from flax were Palestinian agricultural products throughout biblical times. There are frequent references to spinning (Prov. 31:19; Luke 12:27), weaving (Isa. 19:9; John 19:23), and embroidery (Exod. 28:39). Different shades of wool dyed with natural hues provided a full palette of colors. In the Beni Hasan painting the visitors' waistcloths and tunics show multiple colors and patterns, while Egyptians wear white linen waistcloths. Wool garments from the Cave of Letters have brown, tan, red, or yellow hues, with black, blue, and green stripes. Leather, wool, and linen garments might become infested (Lev. 13:47-59).

An outer garment could be worn over a tunic (Ezra 9:3, 5; Ezek. 26:16; Matt. 5:40 = Luke 6:29; John 19:23). Several words (Heb. *śimlâ, meḏew, kĕsûṯ, me'îl, 'addereṯ;* Gk. *ependýtēs, himátion, peribólaion, phainólēs*) refer to a rectangular mantle that draped over the shoulders and wrapped around the body. A mantle was essential (Job 31:19). It served as a blanket at night (Exod. 22:27; Deut. 24:12-13) and a means for carrying other items (Exod. 12:34; Ruth 3:15; Hag. 2:12). Mantles were decorated with fringes or tassels (Deut. 22:12; cf. Matt. 23:5; Luke 8:44) with blue or violet thread that reminded the wearer of the commandments (Num. 15:37-41). On the Black Obelisk Jehu and his attendants wear tunics, fringed mantles, and sashes. Yarn tassels awaiting to be attached to garments were found in the Cave of Letters.

The headdress (Heb. *pĕ'ēr, ṣānîp̱*) was a cloth draped over the head, or wrapped like a turban (Ezek. 24:17; Zech. 3:5). In the Lachish reliefs women leaving the city wear an ankle-long cloth draped over their heads and down their backs. Women sometimes used a veil (*ṣā'îp̱*) to cover their faces (Gen. 24:65; Cant. 4:1, 3). Paul uncompromisingly insisted that Corinthian women cover their hair while praying in community gatherings (1 Cor. 11:4-16).

Sandals (Heb. *na'ălāyim;* Gk. *hypodḗmata, san-*

dália) were common footwear (Deut. 29:5[MT 4]; Mark 1:7; Acts 12:8). In the Ben Hasan painting the men wear sandals or are barefoot, while the women wear shoes. On the Black Obelisk Jehu's attendants wear pointed shoes.

While biblical authors used the same words for men's and women's garments, Deut. 22:5 implies that there were differences. Decorations woven into mantles found in the Cave of Letters may reflect distinctions for men and women. Widows wore identifying clothing (Gen. 38:14; Jdt. 8:5). In Isa. 3:18-24 a detailed poem itemizes garments and ornaments of 8th-century upper-class Jerusalem women, but translations for many items remains very uncertain. Ezek. 16:13-14 metaphorically describes Jerusalem's clothing as "fine linen, rich fabric, and embroidered cloth," such as a queen might wear (cf. LXX Esth. 15:1-2; Jdt. 1-:3-4).

Distinctive clothing was associated with the sanctuary and the temple. Young Samuel (1 Sam. 2:18), the priests of Nob (1 Sam. 22:18), and David (2 Sam. 6:14) wore a linen ephod (Heb. *'ēpôḏ bāḏ),* a loincloth, while in the sanctuary. Exod. 28, 39 describe Aaron and his sons' vestments. Priests wore special linen undergarments *(miḵnĕsê pištîm)* to avoid exposing themselves while ministering. Over these were worn a linen tunic, wool mantle, and an embroidered sash. Priests also wore linen headdresses. The chief priest added a multicolored decorated ephod, jeweled breastpiece, and a gold engraved emblem on his headdress. Later levitical priests may have worn only linen vestments (Ezek. 44:15-19).

Bibliography. L. Bonfante and E. Janunzems, "Clothing and Ornament," in *Civilization of the Mediterranean,* ed. M. Grant and R. Kitzinger (New York, 1988), 3:1385-413; Y. Yadin, *Bar-Kokhba* (New York, 1971); *Masada* (New York, 1966).

JOSEPH E. JENSEN

CNIDUS (Gk. *Knídos*)

A port city on the southwestern coast of Asia Minor, located at the western tip of a long peninsula that juts out into the Mediterranean, opposite the island of Cos, in the region called Caria. A small island, artificially connected to the peninsula, was also part of Cnidus. Cnidus was famous for Praxiteles' statue of Aphrodite. Rome sent Cnidus and other cities a letter declaring support for Simon's rule over the Jewish state (1 Macc. 15:23). After a difficult voyage, the ship carrying Paul as a prisoner to Rome had to change directions off Cnidus when it was exposed to unfavorable winds (Acts 27:7). DOUGLAS LOW

COAL

While coal today is understood as a readily combustible rock primarily composed of carbonaceous material, such a mineral was not known in the biblical world. Rather, the "coal" (Heb. *gaḥeleṯ, reṣep̱, peḥām;* Gk. *ánthrax*) of the Bible was formed by placing wood, often the hard wood of the broom plant (Ps. 120:4), in a slow flame of intense heat, which turned the wood into charcoal. Coal may thus also refer to the hot coals or embers found in a charcoal fire (Lev. 16:12; Ps. 18:8[MT 9]; Prov. 6:28; Isa. 47:14; Ezek. 10:2).

Coal is used in images figuratively to represent the loss of life and one's lineage (2 Sam. 14:7) as well as guilt-inspiring acts of kindness to one's enemy (Prov. 25:22; cf. Rom. 12:20). A glowing coal is put to the lips of Isaiah by a seraphim in order to purify the prophet's unclean lips so that he might speak what is true (Isa. 6:6).

MARTHA JEAN MUGG BAILEY

COAST, COASTLAND

The shore of either the mainland (e.g., Isa. 23:2, 6) or an island (e.g., Jer. 2:10; 47:4) adjacent to or within the Mediterranean Sea (Heb. *'î, gĕḇûl*). The NRSV frequently translates *gĕḇûl* as "country" or "border" (e.g., Exod. 34:24; Josh. 13:23). "Coastlands" also indicates faraway (gentile) nations (e.g., Isa. 40-66; Jer. 31:10; Ezek. 26:15).

COAT OF MAIL

Armor consisting of 400-600 plates of metal, which were pierced and sewn to a cloth or leather undercoat. The plates overlapped to provide maximum protection; the armor was weakest at the joining of the sleeve to the tunic body and between the scales (1 Kgs. 22:34 = 2 Chr. 18:33). Such armor was probably developed to free the hands from having to hold a shield, thus enabling charioteers to drive and soldiers to wield the bow and yet still have protection.

The coat of mail was used by either foreigners (1 Sam. 17:5) or the elite (v. 38) until the time of Uzziah (2 Chr. 26:14; Neh. 4:16[MT 10]), who introduced this technology into the rank and file. The prophet Isaiah uses armor metaphorically to refer to the righteous character and actions of God (Isa. 59:17). In the NT, Paul applies Isaiah's metaphor to the righteous lifestyle of the Christian (Eph. 6:14; 1 Thess. 5:8).

Bibliography. R. Gonen, *Weapons of the Ancient World* (Minneapolis, 1976); T. R. Hobbs, *A Time for War.* OTS 3 (Wilmington, 1989).

W. E. NUNNALLY

CODEX

A wooden tablet (or tablets connected with thongs laced through holes bored near the edges). The codex, the earliest form of book — which in Roman times began to replace the more cumbersome scroll — was first used in business and legal transactions. Later Romans experimented with a codex of parchment sheets folded over and sewn together.

See BOOK; PARCHMENT.

CODEX ALEXANDRINUS

A 5th-century codex (siglum A) containing the OT, except for several mutilations, and most of the NT. Lacking are Gen. 14:14-17; 15:1-5, 16-19; 16:6-9; 1 Sam. 12:20–14:9; Pss. 49:19–79:10. Matthew up to 25:6 is lost, as are John 6:50–8:52; 2 Cor. 4:13–12:6, and, according to the table of contents, Psalms of Solomon. Included are the letters of Clement of

Rome. The manuscript now contains 773 leaves, but originally there were 822. Each leaf measures 32 by 26.3 cm. (12.6 by 10.4 in.). There are two columns to the page, and the writing is in a firm uncial hand. The work of several correctors is evident.

The nature of the text of Codex A, whose origin is unknown, is far from uniform. Hexaplaric influence is evident in Joshua, Ruth, Esther, and to a much greater extent in Samuel and Kings. Chronicles and 1-2 Esdras probably represent an early Alexandrian Text, and Lucianic elements occur in Job, Psalms, and the Prophets. The Gospels represent the Byzantine Text; the rest of the NT, with Codex Vaticanus and Codex Sinaiticus, represents the Alexandrian Text.

The codex has been in England since 1627, when it was presented to King Charles I by Cyril Lucar, patriarch of Alexandria (until 1621) and Constantinople (1621-38). Lucar obtained the manuscript from Mt. Athos in 1616. Now bound in four volumes, it is housed in the British Museum next to Codex Sinaiticus. Carroll D. Osburn

CODEX BEZAE

A 4th- or 5th-century codex (siglum D or 05) whose origin is unknown. Codex Bezae Cantabrigiensis, a principal representative of the so-called Western Text of the NT, contains parallel texts, which have been repeatedly corrected, of Greek and Old Latin on opposing pages. The manuscript includes most of the four Gospels and Acts as well as a fragment of 3 John. The Gospels are arranged in the Western order (Matthew, John, Luke, Mark). Codex Bezae's readings are unique in thousands of instances, particularly in the text of Acts, which is almost 10 percent longer than the generally accepted text. Scholars have attempted to ascertain the theological motivation behind the singularly peculiar readings in the text, but the investigation remains open. The codex was donated by the reformer Theodore Beza to Cambridge University in 1581.

Bibliography. D. C. Parker, *Codex Bezae: An Early Christian Manuscript and Its Text* (Cambridge, 1992). Paul Anthony Hartog

CODEX CLAROMONTANUS

A 6th-century codex (siglum D^p), the leading authority for the so-called Western Text of the Epistles. The codex, whose origin is unknown, contains parallel texts, which have been repeatedly corrected, of Greek and Old Latin on opposing pages. The manuscript has the epistles of Paul, including Hebrews, with the exception of Rom. 1:1-7, 27-30, and 1 Cor. 14:13-22, of which the Greek text is lost. The codex contains 533 leaves, each page measuring 24.6 by 19.5 cm. (9.7 by 7.7 in.), with one column of 21 lines per page.

Codex Claromontanus often agrees with Codex Augiensis and Codex Boernerianus. Unlike Codex Bezae, the text on the Latin side of Claromontanus is not always dependent upon the Greek. With a few exceptions, the Latin text is remarkably similar to that of Lucifer of Cagliari in the 4th century.

Both Codex Claromontanus and Codex Bezae were once owned by Theodore Beza, and they probably belonged together. As indicated by Beza on the back of the title page, Claromontanus was found in the monastery at Clermont-en-Beauvoisis; it is now housed in the National Library at Paris. Carroll D. Osburn

CODEX EPHRAEMI SYRI

A Greek codex (fully named Ephraemi Syri rescriptus Parisiensis), written in the 5th or 6th century C.E., probably in Egypt. Originally consisting of the entire Bible, the manuscript was unbound and reused in the 12th century. The codex is thus a palimpsest and owes its name to the second text, a Greek translation of treatises by the Syrian Church Father Ephraem, which was written over the original. The codex presently consists of 209 leaves: 64 leaves of the OT and 145 of the NT. Every canonical book of the NT is represented; only portions of Proverbs, Ecclesiastes, Canticles, Job, Wisdom, and Sirach from the OT are extant. Corrections were made to the biblical text in the 6th and again in the 9th century. The codex is important for textual criticism, although the manuscript remains difficult to decipher due to its palimpsest character.

Tawny L. Holm

CODEX LENINGRADENSIS

See Leningrad Codex.

CODEX SINAITICUS

A 4th-century Greek uncial manuscript (א) originally containing the entire Bible. Written on fine vellum, 390 leaves (of an original total of at least 730) were discovered by Constantin von Tischendorf in St. Catherine's Monastery at the foot of Mt. Sinai. Additional OT leaves, as yet unpublished, were discovered in 1975. While less than half of the OT is extant, the NT is complete. In addition, the Epistle of Barnabas and the first quarter of the Shepherd of Hermas are included following the book of Revelation.

The codex may have originated in either Egypt or Caesarea. The text of the OT reflects the Old Greek. In the NT Sinaiticus is frequently cited as an Alexandrian witness, but John 1–8 is more closely related to the Western tradition. The antiquity of the manuscript and the quality of its text make it one of the most important manuscripts of the Bible.

Bibliography. H. Lake and K. Lake, *Codex Sinaiticus Petropolitanus*, 2 vols. (Oxford, 1911-22).

James R. Adair

CODEX VATICANUS

One of the most important manuscripts of the Bible in Greek. Produced around the middle of the 4th century and housed in the Vatican Library at least since the 15th century, Vaticanus (siglum B) originally included the entire OT and NT and the Apocrypha or Deuterocanonicals (the books of Maccabees were omitted, apparently inadvertently, and it now lacks the first 46 chapters of Genesis, about 30 psalms, the end of Hebrews, the Pastoral Epistles, and Revelation). In Codex B the General Epistles follow the book of Acts (and therefore precede Paul's letters), and both the longer ending of Mark (16:9-19) and John 7:53–8:11 are missing. Vaticanus is one of the best representatives of the Alexandrian family of manuscripts, the most reliable ancient recension of the biblical text. It is also an important witness to the origin and growth of the LXX. JEFFREY S. ROGERS

CODEX WASHINGTONENSIS

A late 4th- or early 5th-century C.E. uncial manuscript in codex form containing the four Gospels in the so-called Western order (Matthew, John, Luke, and Mark). The manuscript (siglum W) is housed in the Freer Gallery of the Smithsonian Institution, Washington.

Behind the present text may be several fragments of different Gospel manuscripts representing different families of texts that were collected and assembled by an individual scribe. This would explain the variegated text types represented. Matthew and Luke 8:13–24:53 represent the common Byzantine Text; Mark 1:1–5:30 is Western, similar to the Old Latin; Mark 5:31–16:20 is of the Caesarean type; and Luke 1:1–8:12; John 5:12–21:25 represent the Alexandrian type.

An important variant in W is an addition to Mark 16:14, the so-called Freer Logion, in which the disciples offer an excuse for their failure to believe those who had reported Jesus' resurrection.

Bibliography. H. A. Sanders, *Facsimile of the Washington Manuscript for the Four Gospels in the Freer Collection* (Ann Arbor, 1912); *The New Testament Manuscripts in the Freer Collection,* 1: *The Washington Manuscript of the Four Gospels* (1912, repr. New York, 1972). WILLIAM R. GOODMAN

COELE-SYRIA (Gk. *Koílē Syría*)

A Hellenistic term for "all the lands of Syria." The older view is that "Coele-Syria" means "hollow Syria," but other scholars contend that the word "coele" is a Greek adaptation of Sem. *kōl,* "all." The term was used at the time of Alexander to refer to a large administrative unit, but continued through the Hellenistic and Roman periods, referring to variously defined borders that could include lands in present-day Israel, Lebanon, Jordan, and Syria, depending on the source. The term was also used to designate Transjordanian territories in the NT period (cf. Josephus *Ant.* 12.13.3; 2 Macc. 3:5, 8; 1 Esdr. 2:17, 24). DANIEL L. SMITH-CHRISTOPHER

COHORT

A Roman military unit (Gk. *speíra*) comprised generally of 600 personnel (size could vary from 500 to 1000) under the leadership of a *chilíarchos.* Cohorts were either regular, i.e., one tenth of a legion, or auxiliary, not attached to a legion. Auxiliary cohorts were often divided ca. 4:1 between infantry and cavalry; these were the units stationed in the border regions and remote areas of the empire. While stationed throughout the empire cohorts would recruit from the local population to replenish their strength (Josephus *BJ* 2.13.7), with citizenship being the reward for 20 years of service. During the reign of Claudius (41-54) the occasional practice of rewarding deserving cohorts with citizenship was made a standard procedure. No legionary troops were stationed in Judea from A.D. 6 to 66. Auxiliary units stationed in Jerusalem functioned as garrisoned troops and military police (cf. Matt. 27:27; Mark 15:16; John 18:3, 22; Acts 21:31).

Cohorts had descriptive or honorific names. The Italian Cohort, to which the centurion Cornelius was attached (Acts 10:1), was comprised of Roman citizens initially recruited in Italy and likely stationed in Caesarea from 41 to 44. Inscriptions referring to the Cohors II Italica also attest to this cohort being stationed in Syria ca. A.D. 69. The Augustan Cohort (*Cohors Augusta Sebastenorum*), to which the centurion Julius was attached (Acts 27:1), is attested by epigraphic evidence and Josephus as also being stationed in Syria. The identity and function of this cohort have been disputed. Some identify Julius and his cohort as *frumentarii,* special officers acting as liaisons between the emperor and the provinces and as imperial police, but these expanded duties are not attested to prior to the reign of Hadrian (117-138). At the time of Acts 27 the *frumentarii* had only the immediate duty of supervising the transportation of grain to Rome.

Bibliography. F. F. Bruce, *The Acts of the Apostles,* 3rd ed. (Grand Rapids, 1990), 510-12; D. B. Saddington, "The Development of the Roman Auxiliary Forces from Augustus to Trajan," *ANRW* II.3, 176-201; A. N. Sherwin-White, *Roman Society and Roman Law in the New Testament* (Oxford, 1963), 155-61. DENNIS M. SWANSON

COL-HOZEH (Heb. *kol-ḥōzeh*)

1. The father of Shallum, ruler of the district of Mizpah during the administration of Nehemiah (Neh. 3:15).

2. A Judahite, the father of Baruch and an ancestor of Ma-aseiah, who settled at Jerusalem after the Exile (Neh. 11:5). He may be the same as **1** above.

COLLECTION

Paul's collection of funds from gentile churches for the Christian community in Jerusalem in ca. 53-56 C.E. (Gal. 2:10; Rom. 15:25-32; 1 Cor. 16:1-4; 2 Cor. 8–9; cf. Acts 24:17). The Jerusalem church's understanding of the agreement at the Apostolic Council to "remember the poor" (Gal. 2:10) is best sought in their self-designation as the faithful eschatological community ("the poor"), rather than in their economic poverty. Most studies assume that Paul considered the collection a demonstration of or a method of achieving ecclesiological unity, but there are problems with this assumption. Clearly Paul initially acknowledged the Jerusalem church's eschatological priority and saw the collection as a visible connection between the two Christian missions. But after the Galatian controversy, Paul also envisioned the collection as proof of the reality of

God's grace among the Gentiles and as a symbolic gentile pilgrimage that would signal the eschaton. By the time he wrote Romans, Paul sought only to acknowledge the Gentiles' historical debt to Jerusalem through economic relief. Other interpretive issues include: the relationship of the collection to the famine relief in Acts 11 and to the temple tax; Paul's rhetoric persuading churches to contribute, and their response; and the absence of certain cities from the catalogs of participants (cf. Rom. 15:26; 1 Cor. 16:1; Acts 20:4).

Bibliography. D. Georgi, *Remembering the Poor: The History of Paul's Collection for Jerusalem* (Nashville, 1992).

JENNIFER K. BERENSON MACLEAN

COLONY

Territories administered as subordinate political units within larger governmental entities, such as empires. A colony may have some autonomy, but in many aspects it is subjugated to the empire or other ruling entity. In the ancient world, empires expanded by conquering nations and cities and turning them into colonies, with the purpose of extracting labor and wealth from them to fund the imperial bureaucracy.

When the Babylonian Empire conquered the nation of Judah (597 B.C.E.), it colonized Jerusalem and the surrounding area. This was not just a military conquest; the Babylonian Empire intentionally left behind in the Jerusalem area a sufficient number of peasants and other people to farm the ground, to pay taxes and tribute, and to provide forced labor for imperial projects. During the time of the Exile (597-539), there were Jewish communities not only in Babylon but also in the Jerusalem area.

In 539 Persia defeated the Babylonian Empire and took control of Jerusalem, which the Persian Empire called the colony of Yehud. Persia administered this colony through appointing or supporting leaders such as Sheshbazzar the governor, Joshua the high priest, Zerubbabel the governor, Ezra the priest and scribe, and Nehemiah the governor.

During the Greek and Roman periods, Judah and the Jerusalem region formed a colony or similar governmental unit within the ruling empires of the day. Rulers and administrators were known by a variety of terms, including kings, tetrarchs, and governors. Luke and Acts show an awareness of these political structures, naming several of the rulers with their titles, including King Herod of Judea (Luke 1:5), Quirinius the governor of Syria (2:2), Pontius Pilate the governor of Judea (3:1), Herod the tetrarch of Galilee (Luke 3:1, 19; 9:7-9; Acts 12:1-6, 20-23; 13:1), Gallio the proconsul of Achaia (18:12-17), Felix the governor (23:24–24:27), Festus the governor (24:27–26:32), and King Agrippa (25:13–26:32). Similar figures appear throughout the rest of the NT as well as in ancient Greek and Latin literature. Although it is not possible to determine the precise interrelationship of these various governmental officials, it is clear that early Christianity arose in an empire with a complex bureaucratic administration enforced through a number of smaller colonies.

JON L. BERQUIST

COLOR

Though the abstract term "color" is not found in the OT and not used in the NT, both parts of the Christian Bible describe various colors. Athalya Brenner identifies five basic colors mentioned in the OT: (1) red (Heb. *'āḏōm*); (2) white *(lāḇān);* (3) black *(šāḥōr);* (4) green *(yārôq);* and (5) yellow *(ṣāhōḇ)*. Though other color terms also are found in Scripture (e.g., purple), they do not fit the criteria for basic colors. These terms meet three primary characteristics: (1) monolexemic (i.e., no expressions such as reddish); (2) exclusive signification (i.e., must not be a term that can be subsumed under a broader color); and (3) unrestricted applicability (i.e., the color has a universal application; it is not restricted to a narrow class of objects). Of the five main color terms, the dominant three are red, white, and black.

White is the term used most often, and it not only describes the color of an object (hair in Lev. 13) but also has a symbolic significance. It indicates wealth (Gen. 49:12; Esth. 1:6), joy (Eccl. 9:8), or purity (Rev. 3:4; 7:9, 13-14). White was not a natural color in Israel; fullers bleached natural fabrics to achieve the color.

Black is used to describe the color of objects, such as sheep (Gen. 30:32-33, 35, 40) or hair (Cant. 5:11), but it can also symbolize trouble (Job 3:5) or judgment (2 Pet. 2:17; Rev. 6:5). Red is used to describe the color of skin (Gen. 25:25), stew (v. 30), and blood (2 Kgs. 3:22). Red also is used symbolically to describe luxury (Isa. 63:2) and war (Rev. 6:4). Tints of red include such color terms as purple, scarlet, and crimson. Purple, a symbol of luxury or kingship (Esth. 8:15; Cant. 3:10; John 19:2), was derived from the murex shellfish along the coastline of Palestine, which accounts for the name of the region — Canaan (the land of purple). Scarlet and crimson are derived from the female insect known as kermes and are used to describe the color of sin (Isa. 1:18).

Often there is a tendency to overinterpret Scripture by attaching symbolic meaning to a color in the text. Scholars might suggest that the colors of the tabernacle — predominantly blue, purple, and scarlet — have some deep, spiritual meaning attached to them. However, if the text does not allude to a deeper significance, it is best to avoid those interpretations.

Bibliography. A. Brenner, *Colour Terms in the Old Testament.* JSOTSup 21 (Sheffield, 1982).

RICK W. BYARGEON

COLOSSAE (Gk. *Kolossai*)

A city in the central highlands of Asia Minor, 201 km. (125 mi.) E of the Aegean Sea and 145 km. (90 mi.) N of the Mediterranean Sea, situated mostly on the south bank of the Lycus River. It was located along a major southern trade route that extended through Asia Minor from the Aegean coast into the Syrian Euphrates region. The fertile Lycus Valley made Colossae rich in olives and figs, and the city had a thriving wool industry, specializing in black wool and a famous woolen cloth dyed reddish-purple.

Part of the Phrygian kingdom (12th-7th centuries B.C.E.), Colossae was dominated successively by Cimmerians, Lydians, Persians, Greeks, Seleucids, Galatians, and Romans. Xenophon (ca. 401) referred to Colossae as "a large and prosperous city," but Strabo later apparently considered it only a small town (ca. 15 C.E.). In the 1st century C.E., Colossae was overshadowed by its northern neighbors, Laodicea and Hieropolis.

Roman Colossian coins indicate the worship of numerous deities, including Artemis, Helios, Demeter, Men, Isis, and Serapis. To this religious milieu could presumably be added Phrygian mysteries, the Roman imperial cult, and Judaism. The Christian community at Colossae was probably founded by Epaphras, a companion of Paul (Col. 1:7-8; 4:12-13; Phlm. 23). The letter to the Colossians may allude to aspects of Colossae's syncretistic environment.

An earthquake between 60 and 64 C.E. devastated Laodicea and Hieropolis, and presumably Colossae. Coins minted at Colossae appear from 150 to ca. 250, but not later. The population shifted to nearby Chonae, but the bishopric there retained a reference to Colossae until the 8th century.

Bibliography. M. Barth and H. Blanke, *Colossians.* AB 34B (New York, 1994); J. B. Lightfoot, *St. Paul's Epistle to the Colossians and to Philemon* (1886, repr. Wheaton, 1997). SCOTT NASH

COLOSSIANS, LETTER TO THE

A NT letter presenting itself as a communication from Paul and Timothy to Christians in Colossae, a significant city in the Lycus Valley, ca. 195 km. (120 mi.) E of Ephesus (Col. 1:1-2). It implies that the church there was never visited by Paul but founded by one of his associates, a certain Epaphras (1:7-8; 4:12). References to other Christian leaders in 4:7-17 (such as Tychichus, Onesimus, Mark, Barnabas, Luke, and Nympha) offer a lively picture of the importance of personal contacts and friendships in the Pauline churches (including congregations founded by Paul's associates and disciples). Colossians is also an official communication to a Christian community, and the writer requests (commands?) that it be read in the church there and also in the Laodicean church; he further instructs the Colossians to read "the letter from Laodicea" (presumably one written by himself). One motive for the writing of Colossians is a desire to repudiate vigorously a false religious position which may tempt the addressees (2:8-23). The letter's forceful teaching about soteriology and ethics is meant to provide a sound alternative to this false position.

The vocabulary and syntax of Colossians show similarities to the undisputed Pauline letters, notably Romans, 1-2 Corinthians, and Galatians. Many sentences, however, are comparatively long, with pleonastic expressions, and these features seem to distinguish the style of Colossians from that of Paul's undisputed letters. The general tone of the letter is less personal and more formal than that found in many of the undisputed Pauline letters. Like Romans and Ephesians, Colossians offers a clear structural division between a main section focused on doctrine and one centered on exhortation. In its attack on false "philosophy," Colossians has a special affinity to Galatians; in regard to the church leaders mentioned by name, it is very close to Philemon; in theological ideas and phraseology, it is extraordinarily similar to Ephesians (most scholars think the author of Ephesians was directly and heavily dependent on Colossians).

The authorship of Colossians has been debated since the first half of the 19th century, and a large number of critical scholars today consider it deutero-Pauline. Eduard Schweizer proposes that Timothy actually composed it, while Paul was in prison under conditions that made it impossible for the apostle to write the entire letter himself but may have allowed him to add the concluding greeting. Some scholars, however, continue to maintain that Paul directly wrote the letter. The syntax of Colossians, some of its theological ideas (Christ as head of the Church; primary emphasis on realized eschatology), and some of the ways in which Paul is described (the sufferings of Paul as "completing what is lacking in Christ's afflictions" [1:24]) make it very doubtful that Paul himself was the author. Yet the influence of Colossians on Ephesians is probably easier to explain if the letter was generally thought in the early Church to have been the work of Paul. If Paul did write Colossians, he probably did so near the end of his life, soon after composing Philemon. If Colossians was written by another in Paul's name, it must have been composed within a decade or two of his death (Ephesians, which seems to depend on Colossians, can hardly be later than about 90). The place of origin is unknown, though Ephesus and Rome are likely possibilities.

Aside from the polemic in 2:8-23, there is little argument. Most of the letter takes the form of concise assertions and injunctions, apparently expressing "previously coined and fixed views and concepts" (Gunther Bornkamm). At least in the "hymn" of 1:15-20 and the "table of household duties" in 3:18–4:1, Colossians evidently relies on authoritative traditional church materials. In contrast to a number of other Pauline letters, Colossians nowhere stresses the authority of Jewish Scriptures (there are no OT quotations, and very few allusions). Perhaps this is because the presumed Colossian readers are overwhelmingly gentile (cf. 1:27), but it also probably reflects the fact that the "false teaching" assailed in 2:8-23 has at least some Jewish features. The writer variously assumes and asserts the authority of Paul, "absent in body but present in spirit" (2:5). All his ministerial labors are on behalf of believers like the Colossians, and those labors (and teachings) are inspired by God (1:25-29).

The exact nature of the false teaching is not very clear, though Colossians suggests that its advocates called it a "philosophy" and emphasized "the elemental spirits of the universe," visions and worship of (or alongside) angels, the observance of special festivals (including sabbaths), and certain ritual and ascetic regulations (including circumcision and the avoidance of certain foods). Many modern scholars have tried to identify the teaching more precisely, linking it with pagan mystery cults (Martin Dibelius), Gnosticism (Bornkamm), or apocalyptic Judaism (Fred O. Francis). Others have urged that the "false teaching" is not Christian at all, but simply a form of diaspora Judaism (Morna Hooker, James D. G. Dunn). A sizable Jewish population is known to have existed in the area of Colossae in the 1st century.

Christology is at the heart of Colossians. The chief accusation against the "false teaching" is that it is not based on Christ and does not hold fast to him as head of the Church. The Holy Spirit is hardly mentioned (1:8), but God is emphasized often as Father of Jesus and Christians and the ultimate source of creation and salvation. Christ is the image of God, the one through whom and for whom God created all things. All the fullness (Gk. *plḗrōma*) of God dwells in Christ. His redemptive work has cosmic and universal results, though these are known at present only in the Church (his body). The ontological orientation of the christology recalls, and may be dependent on, Hellenistic Jewish concepts of Wisdom and the divine Word *(Logos)*. Special emphasis is placed on Jesus' saving death, which reconciled all things in heaven and earth to God and simultaneously constituted a victory over hostile spiritual forces allied with a legal bond threatening sinners (2:13-15). The present and future life of believers is one of participation in Christ: their present existence is "hidden" in him, and their bond with him assures future glory (1:27; 3:3-4).

The ethical teaching in 3:5–4:6 is grounded in the claim that Christians have received a new nature through dying and rising with Christ (presumably in baptism). They must "become what they already are" by giving up all sinful inclinations and practices and "putting on" a radically new selfhood marked by purity, love, and mutual forgiveness. Christ lives in them, and they are apparently all spiritual equals (3:10-11). Nonetheless, in 3:18–4:1 the duties of believers are described in relation to household positions (wives-husbands, children-parents, slaves-masters): inferiors are taught to obey, and superiors to command, everyone needing to bear in mind their common subjection to a heavenly Lord. The author deliberately affirms a hierarchical moral code that would not outwardly disturb ordinary Jewish and pagan sensibilities, but prefaces it with an egalitarian love ethic which could transform or at least make more tolerable "worldly" patterns of authority and submission.

Bibliography. C. E. Arnold, *The Colossian Syncretism.* WUNT 2/77 (Tübingen, 1995); J. E. Crouch, *The Origin and Intention of the Colossian Haustafel.* FRLANT 109 (Göttingen, 1972); J. D. G. Dunn, *The Epistles to the Colossians and to Philemon.* NIGTC (Grand Rapids, 1996); F. O. Francis and W. A. Meeks, *Conflict at Colossae.* SBLSBS 4 (Missoula, 1973); A. T. Lincoln and A. J. M. Wedderburn, *The Theology of the Later Pauline Letters* (Cambridge, 1993); E. Schweizer, *The Letter to the Colossians* (Minneapolis, 1982). DAVID M. HAY

COMFORTER

See PARACLETE.

COMMANDER

A title of authority given to military, government, civic, and religious leaders. Heb. *śar* is translated in a variety of ways in the OT. It refers to the Egyptian princes of the pharaoh (Gen. 12:15), the captains of Moses' military units (Num. 31:14), and men of honor or valor (Isa. 23:8). On the occasion of Abner's death, David said, "Do you not know that a prince and a great man has fallen today?" (2 Sam. 3:38).

In the contexts of government, civic service, and religion, several references are made concerning commanders: Judg. 9:30, the governor of a town; Gen. 40:16, the chief baker; Jer. 35:4, religious officials who served in the temple; 1 Chr. 24:5, in the organization of the priests of the sanctuary, the sons of Eleazar and the sons of Ithamar.

Daniel uses the term *śar* when referring to heavenly and divine beings. The angel Michael is called the "prince" of Judah (Dan. 10:21), and God himself is referred to as a commander, the "Prince of princes," who will face the attack of an evil king (8:25). A. PERRY HANCOCK

COMMANDMENT

A prescription or requirement, usually from God; most often a reference to God's will as revealed in the laws of the Pentateuch.

The Hebrew word for commandment (*miṣwâ;* pl. *miṣwōṯ*) is one of several synonyms for torah or "instruction." In the Pentateuch the term is used, often in conjunction with one or more of the other synonyms for torah (e.g., *ḥūqîm,* "statutes"; *mišpāṭîm,* "ordinances") to refer to a collection of laws (e.g., Gen. 26:5; Exod. 15:26; 24:12; Lev. 26:3; Num. 15:22; Deut. 5:29; 6:1; 7:11) or to the Ten Commandments in particular (Exod. 34:28; Deut. 4:13). Some commandments, such as the commandment to wear tassels (Num. 15:37-41), are intended to draw attention to the commandments as a whole. Others recall important historical events (e.g., Deut. 16:3). In the book of Psalms the divine commandments are upheld for their perfection, clarity, and truthfulness (Ps. 19:7-10[MT 8-11]; 119). Throughout Ps. 119 the psalmist delights in Yahweh's instructions by using eight different synonyms for torah in alternating fashion.

Within the context of emerging Judaism, Jesus sought to attain a unified conception of divine commandment (Matt. 5:19) by pronouncing the Great Commandment (22:34-40; Mark 12:28-34; Luke 10:25-28; cf. Rom. 13:8-10) as the sum of all commandments. For Paul, however, the commandments are an occasion for sin, and through them sin is known (Rom. 7:7-13). In the Johannine writings, the commandments refer to the commission of the Father to the Son (John 10:18; 12:49-50) or of the Son to his disciples (15:12-17), and obeying them is proof that one abides in God and walks in the truth (1 John 2:3-7; 3:22-24; 4:21; 5:2-4; 2 John 4-6).

Bibliography. F. Crüsemann, *The Torah: Theology and Social History of Old Testament Law* (Minneapolis, 1996). ARNOLD BETZ

COMMENTARY

The genre of explication of biblical texts, usually following the order of verses as they are presented. The constituent elements of the commentary generally include text-critical discussion relating to the establishment of a reliable text and philological and grammatical analysis that addresses difficult or unusual words, phrases, or syntax. Once these elements of "lower criticism" have been applied, "higher criticism" usually begins. Higher criticism is interested in the formation of the text in its historical context and includes source, form, and redaction critical analysis. Along with these more technical aspects of the commentary, a number of other characteristics of the biblical text are often analyzed, including the literary qualities of the text and its theological import. Commentaries often also include interdisciplinary approaches that bring current critical theory to bear on the analysis of texts.

The history of biblical commentary is part of the larger history of the exegesis of the Bible. Perhaps the earliest examples were Aramaic paraphrases (cf. Neh. 8:8) such as the Targums and the midrashim (cf. 2 Chr. 13:22 JB). Much of what appears in the modern genre of commentary is witnessed in commentaries from the late classical and medieval period. Modern critical commentaries often ignore the work of these early commentaries because they are considered to be "precritical." In reality, however, early commentaries share with their modern versions the awareness of ambiguities in grammar, lexicography, textual variants, and meaning in general. By and large, the difference between modern and earlier forms of commentary is not in the ability to recognize the problematics of interpreting the Bible but, rather, in the location of meaning. It has been said that prior to the "critical" approach the world was understood primarily through the Bible, but with the rise of the "critical" approach the Bible began to be understood primarily through observations about the world in general. LARRY L. LYKE

COMMISSION, GREAT

The risen Jesus' charge to his followers to "go and make disciples of all nations" (Matt. 28:18-20). This task of drawing Gentiles as well as Jews into Christian discipleship involves baptizing them and instructing them in Jesus' teachings. The command is undergirded by Jesus' assertion that he possesses divine authority, and is supported by the promise of Jesus' presence with his followers "to the end of the age." Parallels or allusions to the Great Commission are present in several strands of NT tradition (Mark 16:15; Luke 24:47-48; John 20:21; Acts 1:8; cf. Mark 13:10; Matt. 24:14). PETER K. NELSON

COMMUNITY OF GOODS

Although not found in the NT, the expression "community of goods" is a common description of the sharing of possessions in the early Jerusalem church. According to Acts 2:44-47 the Christians lived together and shared all things in common *(hápanta koiná)*, each having sold all personal possessions. Proceeds from the sale of property and buildings were given to the apostles for distribution among needy members (Acts 4:32-35).

Barnabas, who sold his property and gave the proceeds to the Church, serves as a positive example (Acts 4:36-37). However, the practice was not without problems. Ananias and Sapphira lied in their claim to be handing over all their possessions and were struck down by God (Acts 5:1-11). Complaints about unequal distribution of food necessitated the formation of a committee of seven overseers (Acts 6:1-6).

The existence of an actual communal group within the early Church is doubted by those who find contradictions within Luke's account. Others suggest that Luke is simply presenting an idealized picture based on the common Greek philosophical theme of "all things common." However, a number of commentators have suggested historical antecedents for the practice.

Some scholars look to the Rule of the Community of the Dead Sea Scrolls, which establishes how community members should share their property. Some even identify in Acts the technical terminology of property sharing as used in the Qumran text. Others look to the practice of sharing property within Essene groups (Josephus *BJ* 2.8.2-4), although many who assume the Qumran group were Essenes see Josephus' description as a variation. Other scholars connect the early Christian practice with the later rabbinic account of the *quppâ*, a weekly collection of money for the poor residents of a town, and the *tamḥûy*, a daily collection of food for poor nonresidents. However, there is some question whether this was practiced in the 1st century C.E.

The practice within the early Church soon died out. There is no mention of it elsewhere in the NT, and it quickly fades from the narrative of Acts. By Acts 11:27-30 the Judean churches are impoverished and in need of outside help (cf. Paul's collection).

Bibliography. B. J. Capper, "Community of Goods in the Early Jerusalem Church," *ANRW* II.26.2, 1730-74; K. Lake, "The Communism of Acts II. and IV.-VI. and the Appointment of the Seven," in *The Beginnings of Christianity*, 1: *The Acts of the Apostles*, ed. K. Lake and H. J. Cadbury (1933, repr. Grand Rapids, 1966), 5:140-51; D. P. Seccombe, *Possessions and the Poor in Luke-Acts*. Studien zum Neuen Testament und seiner Umwelt B/6 (Linz, 1982), esp. 197-222. RICHARD S. ASCOUGH

CONANIAH (Heb. *kônanyāhû*)

1. A Levite entrusted with the supervision of the contributions, the tithes, and the dedicated things during the reign of King Hezekiah (2 Chr. 31:12-13).

2. A chief among the Levites who contributed to the Passover offering at the time of King Josiah (2 Chr. 35:9).

CONCUBINE

A female whose status in relation to her sole legitimate sexual partner, a nonslave male, is something other than primary wife. Heb. *pîlegeš* seems clearly to be a word of non-Semitic origin. Consequently, attempts to compare the term with alleged parallel statuses in the cultures represented by those languages are of dubious value. The fact that there are clear cognates in Greek *(pallakís/pallakḗ)* and Latin (*paelex*) suggests that the word is Indo-european in origin, borrowed into all three languages from an as yet unevidenced source language (e.g., Philistine).

Some scholars maintain that the word originally was applied to non-Israelite women. The view that a *pîlegeš* was the female partner in a matrilocal, so-called *sadīqa* or *beena* marriage, has been largely abandoned. This view was based on the premises that matrilocal residence is an indicator of matriarchy, a less-evolved form of social organization than patriarchy, and everywhere preceded patriarchy, and was posited by analogy with alleged pre-Islamic connubial customs. The biblical texts typically cited in support of this view (Judg. 8:29-31; 19:1-30) have been successfully explained otherwise.

Live debate remains about whether concubines were of slave or "free" status. Scholars have noted that Bilhah is termed both a slave (e.g., Gen. 29:29; 30:3) and a concubine (35:22). Similarly, Gideon/Jerubbaal's unnamed concubine (Judg. 8:31) is also referred to as his slave (9:18). The Levite of Judg. 19–20 once refers to his concubine as a slave (19:19), but contextual considerations point toward understanding this as an instance of deferential speech. Scholars who affirm that concubines were slaves generally understand Exod. 21:7-11 as regulating men's treatment of their concubines even though *pîlegeš* is nowhere used in these verses.

Scholars who assert that concubines were not slaves generally center their argument on marriage terminology, noting that the language used to describe a concubine's marital status parallels the language used of "free" wives. Both are taken (*lāqaḥ*) by their prospective marriage partners (e.g., Judg. 19:1; Gen. 26:34), and a concubine's partner enters into a son-in-law/father-in-law relationship with her father (Judg. 19:4-5). Keturah is explicitly both wife (Gen. 25:1) and concubine (1 Chr. 1:32). Also, 2 Sam. 20:3 applies the term "widowhood" (*'almānûṯ*) to 10 of David's concubines. Some scholars speculate that concubines were of a lower status than primary wives because no brideprice (*mōhar*) was paid for them, or they brought no dowry (*šillûḥîm*), or both, but no biblical text either confirms or denies these speculations.

Sons of concubines inherited paternal land at the father's discretion (compare Gen. 25:6, where the sons of Abraham's concubines are given gifts but no property, with the tradition that the four sons of Bilhah and Zilpah — Dan, Naphtali, Gad, and Asher — were allotted land by their father Jacob/Israel). Concubines were part of the inheritance that was passed down to sons (Gen. 35:22; 2 Sam. 3:8; 16:22; 1 Kgs. 2:17-22; cf. 2 Sam. 12:8, where issues of inheritance and intercourse with concubines are juxtaposed).

To infer typical Israelite family structure from, e.g., portrayals of Jacob's household in Genesis, implicitly fails to take formal and functional considerations seriously. The fact that the word *pîlegeš* is nowhere mentioned in the legal collections of Exodus and Deuteronomy, nor in the lists of proscribed sexual relationships in Lev. 18, 20, should further caution against too quickly positing that this form of connubial arrangement was widely practiced. Various factors lead to the conclusion that kings in ancient Israel had concubines, but beyond that it is difficult to say.

Bibliography. M. Bal, *Death and Dissymmetry* (Chicago, 1988); L. M. Epstein, "The Institution of Concubinage Among the Jews," *Proceedings of the American Academy for Jewish Research* 6 (1934-35): 153-88; D. R. Mace, *Hebrew Marriage* (New York, 1953); J. Morgenstern, "*Beena* Marriage (Matriarchat) in Ancient Israel and its Historical Implications," *ZAW* 47 (1929): 91-110; "Additional Note on '*Beena* Marriage (Matriarchat) in Ancient Israel,'" *ZAW* 49 (1931): 46-58; E. Neufeld, *Ancient Hebrew Marriage Laws* (London, 1944); C. Rabin, "The Origin of the Hebrew Word Pīlegeš," *JJS* 25 (1974): 353-64.

PEGGY L. DAY

CONDUIT

In the environmental sense, generally a closed channel or passage that is filled with fluid under pressure. Geologically, it is a vertical passageway through which lava flows upward in a volcano. It can also be considered a pipe made by connecting reeds, tree trunks, tiles, bricks, or lead piping. Because water is an exceedingly important resource in arid lands, in ancient times conduits often supplied settlements with water from springs and other sources. In much of the Holy Land wells or shafts were dug to collect ground water, and conduits (or *kanats*) connected them into intricate water supply systems. Many ancient kanats are still in use today throughout the Middle East. Conduits are mentioned in the Bible as a means of getting water from springs or streams into settlements such as Jerusalem. For example, the conduit from a spring to the upper pool and then below two other pools in Jerusalem during the times of Hezekiah and Isaiah is quite well known. The conduit of the upper pool in the highway of the Fuller's Field where garments were washed was a particularly important meeting place.

RICHARD A. STEPHENSON

CONFESSION

To confess means "to say the same thing" or "to agree to a statement." Widely used in ancient legal contexts, in biblical texts the term and its cognates are used to express belief in God, acknowledge failure to keep God's laws, and praise God for salvation. These meanings are evident in the individual and communal liturgical contexts of the Psalms (Pss. 9; 22; 34; 50:14; 51; 116). To confess then served as an essential part of worship, functioning to identify, set apart, and reaffirm membership in the covenant (Deut. 6:4-9).

In the NT, likewise often within liturgical contexts, confession expresses similar meanings. However, the focus is now on the centrality of Jesus and his activity in salvation. The earliest formulations are those stating that God had raised Jesus from the dead (Rom. 1:3; 4:24; 10:9; 1 Cor. 6:14; 15:15; 2 Cor. 4:13-14; 1 Thess. 1:10). This resurrection motif is linked both to God's deliverance of Israel from Egypt and to Jesus' being raised to God's right hand and his coming role as judge (1 Cor. 16:22; Did. 10:6).

The confession of Jesus as the Christ or Lord (Mark 8:29; Rom. 10:9; 1 Cor. 8:6) is fundamental, both in the Pauline corpus (where it forms the basis of the kerygma, 1 Cor. 15:3) and in the Gospels (Mark 8:29 par.). In Rom. 10:9 the acclamation "Jesus is Lord" (like those in 1 Cor. 8:6; 12:3; Phil. 2:11) serves as a christological confession that links Jesus to the creative activity of God. Confession functions as a criterion of orthodoxy (1 John 2:22; 4:2-3, 15; 5:1, 5). It is associated with persecution, and modeled on the example of Jesus' confession itself (1 Tim. 6:13; Matt. 10:17-18).

In later Christian thought, confession is often used interchangeably with creed. However, no such systematic and comprehensive statement exists in the NT. Rather, due to the genre of the material (e.g., letters), there exist only brief statements of Jesus' lordship (Peter's confession; Mark 8:29 par.) and others of binitarian or trinitarian character (Matt. 28:19; 2 Cor. 13:13), which reflect early Christian beliefs and practices such as the confessional statements at baptism (1 Tim. 6:12; Acts 8:36-38 Western Text). From these kerygmatic, liturgical, and catechetical elements the later creeds were developed from the 2nd century onward.

Bibliography. O. Cullmann, *The Earliest Christian Confessions* (London, 1949); J. N. D. Kelly, *Early Christian Creeds,* 3rd ed. (London, 1976).

IAIN S. MACLEAN

CONFIRMATION

The practice of the early Church, well established only by the 3rd century, to anoint with oil and lay hands upon those emerging from baptismal waters for the impartation of the Holy Spirit. Scriptural justification for this dual act was found in Mark 1:10, where the Holy Spirit descended on Jesus as he came up from the Jordan; in Acts 10:38, where Jesus is said to have been "anointed" with the Holy Spirit; and in Acts 8, where the Holy Spirit was withheld awaiting the imposition of apostolic hands. This latter link between the apostolic ministry and the giving of the Holy Spirit led to the insistence that the bishop alone perform the act, and the need to postpone it until the bishop made his rounds eventually led, in the West, to its being treated as a separate sacramental action, called from the 5th century onward *confirmatio.* In the later Middle Ages it came to be regarded as renewing the sacrament of baptism and associated with a course of instruction in basic Christian beliefs or a prescribed confessional catechism.

RONALD V. HUGGINS

CONGREGATION

A gathering or assembly. Heb. *ʿēḏâ* and *qāhāl* are synonymous in many contexts, especially in reference to the political institutions of ancient Israel. While *ʿēḏâ* is used to denote the officials of Israel, *qāhāl* never appears in such contexts, suggesting that the term implies no legislative or judicial function.

The function of the *ʿēḏâ* is to bring to trial and punish violators of the covenant (Num. 35:12, 24-25; Lev. 24:14, 16); to arbitrate intertribal disputes (Judg. 21:10, 13, 16); to crown kings (1 Kgs. 12:20); and to reprimand its own leaders (Josh. 9:18-19). The *ʿēḏâ* could include the entire nation, including women and children; all adult males; or the leaders of the people. The usage of *qāhāl* is roughly equivalent to *ʿēḏâ,* though it is more general. It is used of a multitude of nations (Gen. 28:3), an army (Num. 22:4; Ezek. 17:17; 23:46), and other human gatherings of various kinds. Though *qāhāl* is relatively more frequent in the later books Chronicles, Ezra-Nehemiah, and Ezekel, both Hebrew terms are spread throughout the biblical corpus from Genesis through the Minor Prophets.

In the NT Gk. *ekklēsía* designates "the [local] assembly" or "church" (1 Cor. 11:18) and "the [universal] church" (12:28); *synagōgḗ,* "a place of assembly" (Matt. 10:17; Jas. 2:2) or a meeting for worship (Matt. 4:23); and *plḗthos,* a "crowd of people" (Luke 6:17), "community" (Acts 6:2, 4), or "the church" (15:30). The LXX always uses *synagōgḗ* to translate Heb. *ʿēḏâ,* but *qāhāl* is translated by both *ekklēsía* and *synagōgḗ.* In Classical and Hellenistic Greek literature *ekklēsía* became a technical expression for the assembly of the people, consisting of free men entitled to vote. Although the three terms are roughly synonymous in the NT, *ekklēsía* is the most common. It was adopted by the early Christians over *synagōgḗ* to designate their fellowships after the resurrection of Jesus, but not during his lifetime.

MICHAEL D. HILDENBRAND

CONIAH (Heb. *konyāhû*)

Alternate form of Jehoiachin, the last king of Judah (Jer. 22:24, 28; 37:1)..

CONQUEST: BIBLICAL NARRATIVE

In narrative parts of Exodus and Numbers, Moses leads the unified 12 tribes of Israelites delivered from Egypt through the desert to the land of Canaan. Before arriving at the Jordan River, the Israel-

CONQUEST: BIBLICAL NARRATIVE

ites conquer the lands of kings Sihon and Og east of the Jordan and carry out the ethnic cleansing of their inhabitants (Num. 21:21-35; Deut. 2:24–3:17). After distributing these lands to two and a half of the tribes (Num. 32:33-42; Josh. 13:8-32) and appointing Joshua his successor (Num. 27:18-23; Deut. 3:28; 31:7-23), Moses dies. Joshua leads the Israelites across the Jordan where, in an orgy of terror, violence, and mayhem, they conquer the land of Canaan and attempt to cleanse it of inhabitants. Joshua oversees the distribution of this land to the remaining tribes, and all the tribes settle in their new possessions (Josh. 1-19, 21–22).

This conquest is presented as the climax of the story that begins with the curse of Canaan (Gen. 9:25-26) and God's promise of the land of Canaan to Abram and his descendants (13:15). But it was not always so. The earliest narrative strands (J, E) that make up the first four books of the Bible give little or no indication how God's land grant is to be fulfilled and give no hint of an impending conquest and ethnic cleansing. These strands have many distinctive themes, and these are unrelated to conquest and conclude in Exodus (E) and Numbers (J). Neither strand leaves any trace in Deuteronomy and Joshua. Joshua's role in Exodus and Numbers is secondary to these strands, in which he is unlikely to have appeared at all.

The story of conquest purports to be about tribal warfare, but notable features point to a monarchic rather than tribal perspective, in particular of the house of David. A monarchic context is indicated by the simple unity of the tribes, the precise delineation of an immense territory to be uniformly inhabited by them, the mass slaughter based on the law of dedicating victims and booty to a central shrine (Heb. *ḥērem,* "ban"), and the requirement of strict military loyalty to a single commander, who takes counsel with no one. The bulk of the account of conquest is limited to the territory of Benjamin, immediately north of Davidic Jerusalem (Josh. 2–9). This section focuses on three Benjaminite localities which later play an important role in the rise of the house of David and its claim to monarchic sovereignty over Israel, as presented in the Deuteronomistic history: Gilgal (1 Sam. 13:8-14), Ai near Bethel (cf. Josh. 12:9; Bethel, 1 Kgs. 12:25–13:3, fulfilled in 2 Kgs. 23:15-20), and Gibeon (2 Sam. 2:12–3:1; 21:1-14). Benjamin is the tribe of the house of Saul, whom David usurped. The Conquest concludes with two stereotyped campaigns, one in Judah instigated by the king of Jerusalem, later the City of David (Josh. 10), the other against an alliance centered at Hazor in the north (11:1-15). The highland heartland of Israel plays no role in the Conquest as such: the peaceable references to Shechem in Josh. 8:30-35; 24:1-28 are secondary. In the distribution of land to the tribes, Judah receives by far the most detailed treatment (Josh. 14:6–15:63). The land distribution concludes with three episodes that likewise reflect a monarchic perspective: the cities of refuge, designed to curtail blood feuds; the towns and pasturage assigned to Levi throughout the other tribes; and a dispute over an altar built by the Transjordanian tribes in potential violation of the Deuteronomic law of centralization (Deut. 12:2-27). More than any other geographical feature the Jordan, which in the long history of Palestine was normally not regarded as a natural boundary (thus the tribe of Manasseh appeared on both sides), defines the territory conquered under Joshua; this perspective reflects Assyrian administration in Palestine in the 8th and 7th centuries B.C.E.

Thus in all likelihood the narrative of conquest reflects the interests of the house of David late in their rule over Judah, and was probably formulated at that time. After the fall of Samaria in 722, the house of David revived their claim to the territory of Israel, which became one of the chief components of the centralizing reforms of both Hezekiah and Josiah. The account of conquest in their histories of Davidic sovereignty, the basis of the so-called Deuteronomistic history, reflects their concept of how a monarchic hero once conquered — and now might reconquer — the Canaan at one time supposedly under Davidic sovereignty. An early version of the Deuteronomistic history was composed for Hezekiah to support his plan to recover the territory of Israel not long after the fall of Samaria, against Assyrian interests. In its present form the history reflects mainly the Davidic temple centralization promulgated by Josiah in 622 and extended into Israelite territory, consistent with Assyrian interests (2 Kgs. 22:1–23:25).

The relationship between Joshua and Josiah is suggested by Joshua's own royal character: he succeeds Moses as though by dynastic succession; his charge follows the form of royal installation (Josh. 1:1-9), in which the promise to the nation (Deut. 11:24-25) is concentrated on a single commander (Josh. 1:5); he studies the law day and night as prescribed for the king (Deut. 17:18-19, Josh. 1:7-8); he commands absolute obedience on pain of death; and he supervises the redistribution of conquered land to his followers. The Deuteronomistic historian uses the expression "not to deviate from the law to the right hand or the left" with respect to only Joshua and Josiah (Josh. 1:7; 23:6; 2 Kgs. 22:2), and the phrase "book of the law" with respect to only Joshua and Josiah (Josh. 1:8; 2 Kgs. 22:8, 11; cf. 14:6). Equally important, the Conquest begins with the recapitulation and keeping of Passover (Josh. 3:1–5:12), which is then not kept again, according to the history, until Josiah reinstitutes it as the climax of his reform, following the prescription of the newly discovered law (2 Kgs. 23:21-23). In sum, the biblical conquest of Canaan, though employing more ancient forms, motifs, and traditions, originated as such as a reflex of the revanchist reforms of Hezekiah and Josiah.

The episodes of Jericho, Ai, and Gibeon which form the bulk of the Conquest account involve little territory. They are complex narratives which address numerous issues, but their main purpose is to intimidate potential opponents of Davidic centralization. This they do by illustrating how the terrorizing *ḥērem,* which requires the killing of every last inhabitant of Canaan and the dedication of all booty to Yahweh — for the Deuteronomist this means the Davidic temple — is applied to redefine who belongs in and out of the Israelite camp (Deut. 20:10-18). Canaanites Rahab and her family are included (Josh. 2–6), Judahite Achan and his family are excluded (chs. 7–8), and the Gibeonite inhabitants are included (ch. 9), all based not on their original "ethnic" identity, but on loyalty or disloyalty to the project of conquest and annihilation.

Given the probable late Davidic origin of the Conquest narrative, it is not surprising that archaeological evidence comports with little of the destruction described in Joshua. Jericho, Ai, and Gibeon show no evidence of significant occupation during the Late Bronze Age. Of 16 sites said to have been destroyed, only three — Bethel, Lachish, and Hazor — show evidence of destruction, and Hazor was destroyed as much as a century before Lachish. Moreover, the archaeology of the levitical towns in Josh. 21 shows that this group of settlements could not have existed before the 8th century. Nevertheless, enthusiasm for the historical veracity of the Conquest was revived especially in the United States following World War II and in the new state of Israel in reaction to German scholarship which questioned its veracity.

By the end of the 20th century, however, it had become apparent to most authorities familiar with the archaeological, historical, and social scientific evidence regarding early Israel that Israel originated as a typical tribal formation in Late Bronze Age Palestine, and that this formation participated with others in the gradual extensive resettlement of the highlands throughout the Early Iron Age. The main impetus for this resettlement was not a concerted conquest of one people by another, but rather the complex set of factors that drive the cycle of extension and contraction of settlement and agriculture in the long-term history of Palestine.

See SETTLEMENT: ARCHAEOLOGY.

Bibliography. M. D. Coogan, "Archaeology and Biblical Studies: The Book of Joshua," in *The Hebrew Bible and Its Interpreters,* ed. W. Propp, B. Halpern, and D. N. Freedman (Winona Lake, 1990), 19-30 ; R. B. Coote, *Early Israel* (Minneapolis, 1990); I. Finkelstein and N. Na'aman, eds., *From Nomadism to Monarchy* (Washington, 1994); R. D. Nelson, "Josiah in the Book of Joshua," *JBL* 100 (1981): 531-40; L. L. Rowlett, *Joshua and the Rhetoric of Violence.* JSOTSup 226 (Sheffield, 1996); J. Van Seters, "Joshua's Campaign of Canaan and Near Eastern Historiography," *SJOT* 2 (1990): 1-12; K. L. Younger, Jr., *Ancient Conquest Accounts.* JSOTSup 98 (Sheffield, 1990). ROBERT B. COOTE

CONSCIENCE

That quality of human consciousness that allows one to be aware of moral and immoral categories of thought and behavior.

Hebrew has no specific word for conscience, although some modern translations so render Heb. *lēḇ,* "heart" (e.g., 1 Sam. 25:31). A possible reason for this lack is the Hebrew writers' perspective that one's moral awareness is not an autonomous psychological category of personhood; rather, moral awareness is a willingness to obey the commands of Yahweh God (Deut. 30:14; Eccl. 12:13b). In Hebrew thought, one's moral identity finds its meaning in relation to the moral nature of Yahweh's commands to the community of faith, not individual self-reflection or introspection (e.g., Ps. 1:1-3; 16:7-8; 24:4[MT 5]; 40:8[9]; 119:11. Respect for the Lord is the beginning of moral wisdom (Job 28:28; Ps. 111:10; Prov. 9:10; Sir. 1:11-30).

In Wis. 17:11, a text that has importance for an understanding of several NT appearances of the term, "conscience" refers to an evil moral conscience. Such a usage implies a Hellenistic understanding of the autonomous nature of the human moral decision-making process. Whereas in the OT one's moral decisions are responses to Yahweh's will and word, in Wis. 17:11 one's autonomous bad moral decisions result in a bad moral character. And, these moral decisions — whether good or bad — are not united necessarily to Yahweh's will.

Paul's use of "conscience" (Gk. *syneídēsis*) in 1 Cor. 8:7-13; 10:25-30 is significant for understanding the evolution of the term's meaning in post-Pauline literature and in Western culture. Discussing whether a Christian believer should eat meat offered to idols, Paul uses "conscience" as a practical equivalence to "self-imposed duties," "scruples," or even "perceptual awareness." The origin of conscience, therefore, would vary according to the ideology of the believer, and Paul does not limit the term to a bad conscience alone.

Elsewhere Paul elevates the term to the level of one's self-awareness of one's thoughts, knowledge, and acts in relation to the lordship of Christ (Rom. 2:15; 9:1; 2 Cor. 1:12; 4:2; 5:11). NT uses of the term in non-Pauline literature mimic Paul's application of the term to a Christian's self-aware moral perspective (e.g., Acts 23:1; 1 Tim. 1:5, 19; 2 Tim. 1:3; Tit. 1:15; Heb. 10:22; 13:18; 1 Pet. 3:16, 21). The relation of moral self-awareness (i.e., consciousness) to the resurrected Christ is an ideological identification that had far-reaching implications for a Western worldview.

Bibliography. C. A. Pierce, *Conscience in the New Testament.* SBT 15 (London, 1955); K. Stendahl, "The Apostle Paul and the Introspective Conscience of the West," *HTR* 56 (1963): 199-215.

BENNIE R. CROCKETT, JR.

CONSECRATE

To dedicate or ordain a person for sacred office (e.g., Exod. 29:33; Lev. 16:32) or an object for sacred purposes (e.g., 2 Chr. 31:6; Ezek. 43:36).

See SANCTIFY, SANCTIFICATION.

CONSOLATION

The love, concern, and comfort extended to someone in time of need. The Hebrew root *nḥm* is translated "console," "encourage," "comfort," and may appear in relation to sexual relations (Gen. 24:67; 2 Sam. 12:24; Ruth 2:13), wine (alluded to by associating the name Noah with *nḥm,* "to bring relief" out of the ground; Gen. 5:29; 9:20), visits and gifts (Job 42:11), or simply someone's presence (Lam. 1:2, 9, 16). God consoles as the good shepherd (Ps. 23:4) or by a promise (119:50, 76, 82). One can remain consoled even during affliction (Job 6:10; Ps. 94:19), or hope that God would "comfort" again (Ps. 71:21; 135:14). In anger God can withhold compassion (Hos. 13:14) and leave Jerusalem with none to comfort her (Lam. 1:17, 21), but after due punishment divine consolation will return (Isa. 12:1; Jer. 31:13). This thought is deeply embedded in Deutero-Isaiah (Isa. 49:13; 51:3, 12; 52:9) and Trito-Isaiah (66:13).

The Greek verb "to console" is *parakaléō;* nouns formed from it, *paráklēsis* and *paráklētos,* can mean "consolation," "encouragement," and "advocate." In the NT Simeon awaited the "consolation of Israel" (Luke 2:25), the messianic age (cf. Isa. 61:2). The rich receive their "consolation" here on earth (Luke 6:24); in contrast, Lazarus was "comforted" in the bosom of Abraham (16:25). The Beatitudes promise that those who mourn "will be comforted" by God (Matt. 5:4).

Paul was "encouraged" by others (1 Thess. 3:7; 2 Cor. 7:4) and asked them to "encourage one another" (1 Thess. 4:18), noting that the ability to console others comes from "the God of all consolation" (2 Cor. 1:3-4; cf. Rom. 15:5; 2 Thess. 2:16-17), in Christ (Phil. 2:1).

Jesus had promised to send another "Advocate," the Spirit of truth (John 15:26; 16:7), also sent by the Father (14:16-17), to dwell in the disciples and guide them. Jesus himself remains an "Advocate" with the Father (1 John 2:1). JOSEPH F. WIMMER

CONSTELLATIONS

The arbitrary arrangement of stars in an area of the heavens (Heb. *kĕsîlîm*). In its singular form ("stupid" or "dull") the term also refers to the constellation Orion (Job 9:9; 38:31; Amos 5:8; cf. Isa. 13:10). The identification of the Pleiades with Heb. *kîmâ* is also relatively certain (Job 9:9; 38:31; Amos 5:8). However, the identification of *ʿāš* (Job 9:9) or *ʿayiš* (38:32) is uncertain. It may refer to Arcturus, Ursa Major, or Hyades. Heb. *mazzārôṯ* is also a star or constellation whose identification is unknown (Job 38:32). According to Isaiah, the constellations and stars will not shine on the day of Yahweh (Isa. 13:10).

The priests of the *mazzālôṯ,* who were ejected from the temple by Josiah, may refer to priests of the constellations (2 Kgs. 23:5). However, *mazzālôṯ* can be taken, following Akk. *manzaltu,* as the signs of the zodiac. WILLIAM D. MATHERLY

CONVERSION

The notion of conversion as Israel's "repentance" from a failure to obey divine commands arose in the preaching of the 8th-century prophets. In Amos, who spoke against specific sins, and Hosea, who spoke of Israel's stubbornness and "harlotry," Heb. *šûḇ* was used with the sense of "returning" (to God). The term conveys motion and encompasses a range of meanings ("return, go back, turn back, come back"). Accordingly, Jeremiah played on its usage in covenantal contexts to allow *šûḇ* to bear the twofold meaning of a change of loyalty on the part of either Israel or God for the other. For Jeremiah the term could refer to both apostasy and repentance, and a people that once had departed from God could also have a change of heart and manifest the new inner reality by "repenting." Ezekiel and the Deuteronomist generally phrased the prophetic invitation negatively ("turn back from evil"), but in Jeremiah it nearly always has a positive orientation ("turn back to God"). For Jeremiah the essential ground of repentance lay not in humanity, but in the very nature of God as merciful. It is this rich view of repentance, inviting Israel to change its mind about God, that came to characterize the NT conceptions of conversion.

The Gospels open their accounts of Jesus' ministry with John the Baptist preaching "a baptism of repentance for the forgiveness of sins" (Mark 1:4). Matthew parallels the message of John and Jesus as one of repentance (Matt. 3:2; 4:17), and the Fourth Gospel depicts the Baptist and Jesus simultaneously conducting a baptismal ministry (John 3:22-23; but cf. 4:2). In graphic terms John the Baptist urged conversion because of a coming apocalyptic judgment (cf. Matt. 3:10-12 = Luke 3:9, 17). Jesus, by contrast, seems to have taken a more compassionate tack, downplaying the theme of judgment and highlighting God's love of those — especially of the house of Israel — who had become lost or (figuratively) perished (Luke 15:1-32).

Scholars ask whether Jesus himself underwent a "conversion" or suggest that the scandalous aspect of Jesus' behavior lay in his table fellowship with sinners without calling them to repent their way of life. The theme of "conversion," in this latter view, would be a retrojection into his ministry by the early Church (compare "I have come to call not the righteous but sinners to repentance" in Luke 5:32 with the shorter formulation in Mark 2:17; Matt. 9:13b). However, the preponderance of testimony from all levels (period of Jesus, the Church, the Evangelists) and forms of the Jesus tradition (beatitudes, parables, gestures of healing, prophetic actions) shows Jesus calling for a changed perspective about what God was doing through his ministry. Jesus stresses the need to heed his teaching by a change of life. Manifestations of conversion are depicted under a variety of images such as "becoming like children" (Matt. 18:3), being "born from above/again" (John 3:3), and "rebirth" (1 Pet. 1:3).

Since Paul characterized gentile conversion as a "turning to God from idols, to serve a living and true God" (1 Thess. 1:9), some prefer to describe his own reorientation on the Damascus Road (Acts 9:1-22; cf. Gal. 1:15-22) as a "call." In Pauline parenesis, great stress is laid on the radical change that has come about in believers by their association with the death and resurrection of Jesus in baptism after conversion (Rom. 6:1-11).

In the NT the once-and-for-all nature of conversion is accompanied by exhortations to allow the "fruit of the Spirit," who indwells disciples, to become manifest in their lives (Gal. 5:22-26). The salvation given by God must be "worked out with fear and trembling" (Phil. 2:12). Christian expression of the changed life includes humility, communal sharing of goods (Luke 19:8; Acts 2:42-47), and impartiality to human distinctions such as those between rich and poor (Jas. 2:1-7).

The Christian Scriptures contain a variety of views regarding the ongoing nature of conversion. Believers are urged to hold steadfast, "for it is impossible to restore again to repentance those who have once been enlightened . . . and then have fallen away" (Heb. 6:4-6). The glorified Lord Jesus addresses to the seven churches one and the same call to "repent" (Rev. 2:1–3:22).

Bibliography. R. E. Clements, *Jeremiah.* Interpretation (Atlanta, 1988); W. L. Holladay, *The Root* šûbh *in the Old Testament* (Leiden, 1958); P. W. Hollenbach, "The Conversion of Jesus: From Jesus the Baptizer to Jesus the Healer," *ANRW* II.25.1, 196-219; A. D. Nock, *Conversion: The Old and New in Religion from Alexander the Great to Augustine of Hippo* (1933, repr. Baltimore, 1998); K. Stendahl, "Call Rather than Conversion," in *Paul Among Jews and Gentiles* (Philadelphia, 1976), 7-23.

TERRENCE PRENDERGAST, S.J.

CONVOCATION

A solemn assembly, mentioned in connection with the festivals of Israel and always followed by the command to do no work. Heb. *miqrā'-qōḏeš* means lit., "a holy proclamation" or "a proclamation of a holy time" (2 Kgs. 10:20; Lev. 23:36; Num. 29:35; Deut. 16:8).

Seven days are associated with this term in Lev. 23: the first and seventh days of Unleavened Bread (vv. 4-8); Weeks (v. 21); the feast of Trumpets, the first day of the seventh month (v. 24); the Day of Atonement (v. 27); and the first and eighth days of Booths (vv. 35, 36). The sabbath is also associated with this term (Lev. 23:3).

MICHAEL D. HILDENBRAND

COPING

A structural detail mentioned in the description of Solomon's royal palace (1 Kgs. 7:9). If Heb. *ṭěpaḥ* refers to the corbels (projecting stones on the tops of which roof beams rest), then the expression "from the foundation to the coping" simply means that the entire wall — from bottom to top — was covered with precious stones.

COPPER

A common reddish metallic element. Neither Hebrew *(něḥōšeṯ)* nor Greek *(chalkós)* distinguished between copper and bronze, and modern translations are not consistent in usage (NRSV "bronze"; JB "copper" at Ezek. 22:18, but NRSV "copper"; JB "bronze" at 24:11). The metallic materials mentioned in the Bible were usually made of bronze; however, where reference is made to native metals or ore, copper is the more correct term (Deut. 8:9; Job 28:2).

Copper was one of the earliest known metals. As early as 8000 B.C. native copper was hammered to form various objects. Since most copper occurs with impurities like oxides and sulfides, they must be removed through the smelting process. Biblical tradition associated the origins of metallurgy with Tubal-cain (Gen. 4:22). The metal-working techniques of quarrying, smelting, pouring, and hammering were acquired slowly. Before 3000 metallurgy meant working with copper almost exclusively, with only some silver, gold, and lead work, but during the 3rd millennium all the metals known to ancient mankind began to be used in great variety and combination.

The great advance in copper metallurgy was the addition of a second metal to form copper alloys. Arsenic was first added to copper to improve its properties. The addition of tin, which was the dominant alloying element, produced bronze, and the addition of zinc produced brass. The alloys produced stronger, harder metals with lower melting points and greater ease in casting because of increased fluidity. As a result the alloys could form more intricate and sophisticated casts and better tools. While copper was extensively used, it was usually found in the form of an alloy.

The number of objects made from copper or copper alloys was extensive, including vessels (Exod. 27:3), tools, jewelry, musical instruments (1 Chr. 15:19), and military equipment. In NT times most of the coinage was made of silver, but smaller denominations, like the mite, were made of copper or bronze (Matt. 10:9; Mark 12:42; Luke 21:2).

Palestine was relatively poor in copper resources. However, a copper mine was located at Timnaʿ along Wadi Arabah in southern Palestine (the mine was operated by Egyptians and not King Solomon as first thought), and furnaces for smelting copper have been found at Beth-shemesh, Tell Qasile, and Ai (1 Kgs. 7:14, 45-46). One of the largest ancient sources for copper was Cyprus.

BRADFORD SCOTT HUMMEL

COPTIC

The last stage of Egyptian, linguistically an independent branch of the Afro-asiatic language family, which spreads from the eastern tip of the Arabian Peninsula to the northwestern coast of the African continent. In the early centuries of the Christian period, experiments were made in writing Egyptian, as spoken at that time, with the Greek alphabet. This writing system, along with its linguistic structure, is called Coptic. Demotic, the last stage of hieroglyphic writing, was complicated, difficult to read, and retained syntax that was no longer spoken. The advantages of the Greek alphabet, readily at hand to an educated writer, were simplicity, currency, and the addition of vowels in place of a strictly consonantal system. The Greek alphabet, however, was rearranged to fit the phonetics of spoken Coptic, and several Demotic phonograms were added to supply sounds that were not in Greek: *š, f, h, j, č, ti,* and in some dialects, *ḫ*. Coptic language, due to several hundred years of hellenization, also employs a sizable vocabulary of Greek derivation.

Use of Coptic declined in the centuries following the A.D. 640 Arab conquest of Egypt.

Coptic sentences fall into three patterns. "Nominal" sentences consist of a nominal predicate plus a subject pronoun and are characterized by the absence of the verb "to be." "Bipartite" sentences have a noun or pronoun as subject followed by a predicate consisting of a prepositional phrase, adverb, infinitive or stative verb, or the future auxiliary "going to." "Tripartite" sentences have, in strict order, a tense marker, subject, and verb, which are followed by objects, modifiers, or other sentence elements. Through a system of "second" tenses, negators, and converters, Coptic sentences are able to describe a wide and subtle range of expression. Nevertheless, Coptic does not use several features found in Greek, which should be kept in mind when studying biblical and biblically related texts, since these are, for the most part, translations from Greek. Coptic does not have a neuter gender, true adjectives, participles, a passive voice, or a verb "to have," and in other respects, such as word order, translation Coptic does not adhere to the Greek.

The codification of the writing system, translation, and copying of texts is linked, and is generally coterminous, with the development of the Christian church in Egypt and, in the earliest centuries, Christian schools outside the church such as the Valentinians. The propagation of religious teachings through written texts resulted in the use of several dialects, at least a dozen, extending up the Nile Valley from the delta to Thebes. By the 4th century, Sahidic, the dialect from around the middle of the country, began to dominate as an orthodox "standard," and most modern Coptic language reference works employ this dialect. The famous library of texts from Nag Hammadi provides useful examples of this transitional stage. From the 8th to the 11th centuries, with the gradual replacement of spoken Coptic with Arabic and the removal of the patriarchate to the desert monasteries south of Alexandria, the dialect of this region, Bohairic, was preserved and still survives, but only as a liturgical language for the Coptic Orthodox Church. "Coptic" (Copt is simply an arabicized pronunciation of the [ultimately Greek] word "Egypt") now refers broadly to Christian Egypt, and Coptic studies encompasses linguistics, archaeology, liturgy, history, and literature.

For the study of the Bible, Coptic versions of NT texts date as early as the 3rd/4th centuries. Coptic versions of many LXX passages also exist, as do important NT apocrypha found at Nag Hammadi, such as the Gospel of Thomas, as well as OT pseudepigrapha, including the Apocalypse of Elijah. Alongside these are interesting bodies of patristic, hagiographic, and magical literature in Coptic from early Christian Egypt that give us a lively picture of scriptural traditions.

RICHARD SMITH

COR (Heb. *kōr*)

Usually a dry measure a little over 220 l. (58 gal.), equal to the homer (Ezek. 45:14). Solomon's daily provision consisted of 30 cors of fine flour (ca. 6.5 kl. [185 bu.]) and 60 cors of meal (ca. 13 kl. [370 bu.]; 1 Kgs. 4:22).

CORAL

A semitranslucent to opaque piece of the hard calcareous skeleton secreted by coral polyps, a marine invertebrate, often used as a gemstone (Heb. *rā'môṯ;* Job 28:18; Ezek. 27:16). The color is most often red or orange red, but may be white, cream, brown, blue, or black. Coral was one of the goods given in payment to the merchants of Tyre (Ezek. 27:16). In Job 28:18 it is one of many stones of less value than wisdom. MARTHA JEAN MUGG BAILEY

CORBAN (Heb. *qorbān*; Gk. *Korbán*)

A term referring to religious gifts reserved for God. The gift could be an animal for sacrifice (Lev. 1:2, 3, 10), a vegetable offering (Lev. 2:1, 5), or a gift of precious metals (Num. 7:13; 31:50). In Leviticus the term distinguishes the animal separated from the rest of the herd (Lev. 22:27) or the grain sheaf taken from the harvest (23:14) as an offering to the Lord, thus removing this property from mundane uses. In the NT Jesus warns about the practice of declaring property as "corban" to evade responsibilities toward parents (Mark 7:11-13), a strategy allowing the owner to avoid spending it to support parents in their old age, thus permitting the setting aside of an obligation toward God. DENNIS GAERTNER

CORINTH (Gk. *Kórinthos*)

An important city controlling the isthmus connecting mainland Greece and the Peloponnesian Peninsula. Although its "golden age" was five centuries before Paul's visit, Corinth had enjoyed a return to prominence and a resurgence of building during the 1st century A.D.

Corinth had a leading role in the uniting of the Greek city-states into the world-wide empire of Philip of Macedon and his son Alexander. Two centuries later Corinth was a leader in the failed Achaean League's attempt to stop Roman expansion in Greece. Severely damaged and punished in 146 B.C. in the war with Rome, Corinth was restored in 44 to economic and political prominence by Julius Caesar and in 27 became the provincial capital. New colonists from many areas joined locals seeking their fortune in this commercial center.

An important city for Roman government as the capital of Achaea, Corinth was the residence of the Roman governor (before whom Paul appeared in A.D. 51 when Lucius Junius Gallio was governor). In Roman Corinth, old temples were restored and enlarged, new shops and markets built, new water supplies developed, and many public buildings added (including three governmental buildings and an amphitheater seating perhaps 14 thousand). In the 1st century Corinth's public marketplace (forum) was larger than any in Rome. All these improvements suggest that when Paul visited Corinth ca. 50 it was the most beautiful, modern, and industrious city of its size in Greece. The well-traveled Aristides commented that if beauty contests were

The *bēma,* a platform for public oration and the administration of justice, in the agora or marketplace at Corinth; constructed 44 C.E. (Phoenix Data Systems, Neal and Joel Bierling)

held among cities, as reportedly was done among goddesses, Corinth would rank with Aphrodite (i.e., first).

Commerce

The geography of Corinth determined its commercial significance. Corinth sat on a narrow (5.5 km. [3.5 mi.]) isthmus connecting upper Greece's mainland with the Peloponnese ("almost an island"). Located between the Aegean Sea on the east and the Adriatic Sea on the west and controlling two major harbors, Corinth acquired the nickname "wealthy Corinth."

There was good, but limited, farming in the Corinthia. All land trade moving between upper and lower Greece went through Corinth, and much of the marine trade between Rome and the Eastern Empire did as well. The journey around lower Greece was very dangerous, especially near the Cape of Malea ("cape of evil"). Therefore, shipping often came through Corinth's ports, Cenchreae (9.6 km. [6 mi.] east from the city) and Lechaeum (3 km. [2 mi.] to the west).

Corinth also had some light industry, manufacturing highly prized bronze works, including artful polished mirrors (cf. 1 Cor. 13:12; 2 Cor. 3:18). City artisans also made prized pottery and lamps which were exported around the Mediterranean.

Religion

About two centuries after the Roman devastation of Corinth, many of the old religions of the area were again flourishing, and they were joined by new religions brought by merchants and soldiers to this commercial center. Corinth was a place of "many gods" and "many lords" (1 Cor. 8:5).

Perhaps most familiar to Bible students is the worship of Aphrodite, whose temple atop Corinth's upper city (Acrocorinth) is infamous for its rumored "thousand sacred prostitutes." While Aphrodite was a patron of the city, this moral charge was probably never accurate. It originated in Athenian propaganda, and the lustful imagination of sailors gave it much prominence. Corinth was no worse, or better, than other port cities. Aphrodite was worshipped at several sites in the city and for many reasons, including as patroness of sailors.

Of equal fame in Corinth was Poseidon, ruler of the sea (on which Corinth's commercial life depended) and maker of earthquakes (a frequent danger in the area). Poseidon had a very large temple at a nearby village where the biennial Isthmian Games were held, second only to the Olympic Games at Delphi (cf. 1 Cor. 9:24-25).

A Corinthian temple to Asclepius, the healing god, and his daughter Hygeia included lodging facilities, baths, a swimming pool, and covered porches for the many who came to the temple seeking healing (often the prescription included baths and exercise). Excavators of the site have found a large cache of terra-cotta votive offerings left by those who came for healing. These clay copies of human body parts, which were hung around the temple by worshippers, might have given special power to Paul's image of the church as the "body" of Christ in 1 Corinthians.

The widespread Greek cult of Demeter and Kore also had a shrine on the side of Acrocorinth. Although in decline in the Roman period, a large number of dining rooms were maintained adjacent to the temple and its theater, offering insight into 1 Cor. 8, 10. These rooms were used by some who sacrificed at the temple and invited their friends to private meals in these facilities.

Some new religions from the eastern Mediterranean, including Christianity, came to Roman Corinth. Among these were cults of Isis, Serapis (an Egyptian-based mystery religion), and the Phrygian goddess Cybele, and Judaism. The famous conversion novel by Apuleius, *Metamorphoses*, which praises the mysteries of Isis, is partially set in Corinth. A door lintel from a Jewish synagogue has been found (although it is 4th-century). Both Acts and Philo mention a Jewish presence in the city.

Christianity

The earliest evidence for Christianity in Corinth is, of course, within the NT itself. Paul visited the city more often and wrote it more letters (possibly four, with two now lost) than any other of his mission points. Later 1 Clement was written to Corinth by a Roman church leader. This letter shows that the old issues of factionalism and quarreling which Paul had addressed continued among Corinthian Christians; referring to their letters from Paul, Clement rebukes some younger believers who have thrown off the leadership of the elders.

Among the archaeological finds is a dedication inscription recounting the gift of Erastus, probably the Christian Paul mentions in Rom. 16:23 as the *oikonómos* ("city commissioner").

Bibliography. D. W. Engels, *Roman Corinth* (Chicago, 1990); V. P. Furnish, "Corinth: What Can Archeology Tell Us?" *BARev* 14/3 (1988): 14-27; J. Murphy-O'Connor, *St. Paul's Corinth* (Wilmington, 1983); J. Wiseman, "Corinth and Rome, 1: 228 B.C. to A.D. 267," *ANRW* II.7.1, 438-548; B. Witherington, *Conflict and Community in Corinth* (Grand Rapids, 1995). WENDELL WILLIS

CORINTHIANS, FIRST LETTER TO THE

One of Paul's extant canonical letters to Christians in Corinth. Though called 1 Corinthians, it is not the earliest letter, for Paul wrote a letter previous to this (there was also a letter from the church to Paul), which has not survived. The character of the letter has made it one of the fundamental sources for a social description of "the first urban Christians."

Author, Provenance, Date

The authors are Paul, apostle to Gentiles, and Sosthenes (1 Cor. 1:1; cf. Acts 18:17?), about whom nothing is known. The letter was sent from Asia (16:19), probably Ephesus. The dating is less sure: the majority hold to a "late" date, based on an Acts chronology that puts Paul's first visit to Corinth at the time of Gallio (ca. 51/52 C.E.) and 1 Corinthians ca. 53-55. A minority view holds that Acts is confused about the Gallio hearing being on the first visit, that Paul's first visit to Corinth was "early" (41-42), and that 1 Corinthians was written between 46 and 49.

Corinth

The city of Corinth is well known through excavations conducted since the 19th century. Information on Corinth and its surrounding area in the Roman period is very rich and provides a general and a specific context for understanding the letter, including its economic setting. Some features of the excavations have assisted significantly in interpreting Paul's or the community's activities: dining rooms for cultic meals, benefaction inscriptions (e.g., by Erastus; Rom. 16:23), evidence for later synagogues, a meat market, houses of the wealthy, harbors, and roads.

Occasion

Following his first lengthy visit to Corinth, during which a Christian community was established, Paul went to Ephesus and Asia, from which he wrote a letter to Corinth (the "previous letter"; 5:9-13), taking a strong line on community standards, perhaps arguing for Corinthian agreement to the apostolic decree of Acts 15. This initial letter (a fragment of which may be embedded in 2 Cor. 6:14–7:1) prompted both a letter and oral messages in reply (5:1; 7:1, 25; 8:1; 12:1; 16:1, 12; cf. also 15:1; 11:2). From this information, a reconstruction can be made of the Corinthian letter to Paul and of Paul's previous letter. It is obvious that the Corinthians felt keenly about a number of issues, and raised a variety of questions.

The letter we call 1 Corinthians is Paul's response. The preceding communications made Paul feel a pressing need to instruct the Corinthians at length on matters of Christian behavior and practice: sex, grievances, marriage, betrothal, virginity, food, apostolic support, females and males at worship, Lord's Supper, charismatic gifts, resurrection, support for Jerusalem, even a visit by Apollos. Conditions in Corinth involved uncertainty and confusion at the least, dissension and opposition at the worst. The occasion was thus a difficult one for Paul: how to reply to the information he had from Corinth? The "tone" of 1 Corinthians reflects this ambivalence, at some points harsh (his handwritten autograph, 16:22; opening appeal, 1:10; admonition, 4:14, 21), at other points moderate and accommodating.

Parties and Opposition

The sense of strain is found especially in the discussion of quarrels and divisions (1:10–4:21), which begins with a suggestive identification of something akin to parties: "I belong to Paul, . . . Apollos, . . . Cephas, . . . Christ" (1:12). While Paul rejected the validity of these groupings, he continued to speak of them as if they had objective reality in the Corinthian situation (3:4-5, 21-23; 4:6). Concerns woven into chs. 1–4 that may bear on these groupings include baptism, wisdom, spirituality, maturity, precedence, leadership, power. These are different from the ethical issues of chs. 5–16; they involve qualifications to lead and direct the congregation, closely related to the party labels of 1:12 and emphasized in 4:14-21. In Corinth there were questions about Paul's role as founder and teacher (4:15-17; 3:1-3, 6-7, 10; 4:1-5; cf. also Rom. 16:17-20, written from Corinth); it was likely a matter of "patronage and power."

The evidence for a troubled community is strong, but was there deliberate opposition to Paul? Various suggestions have been made, usually deriving either from the slogans buried in the letter ("it is well for a man not to touch a woman," 7:1; "all of us possess knowledge," 8:1; "no idol in the world really exists," 8:4; "all things are lawful," 10:23; "let Jesus be cursed," 12:3), or from a mirror reading of Paul's advice (which presumes that if Paul argued for something, someone else was arguing against it). Sometimes an effort is made to link slogans and parties and leaders, but without convincing results; e.g., earlier claims about a "gnostic" opposition to Paul are rarely repeated now. Yet the tone and some of the details suggest that there was opposition; if so, it is more likely to be reflected in the body of the letter (chs. 1–4) than in the ethical advice (chs. 5–16), because this issue is more directly treated in the first main section, where rival leadership is discussed.

Closely related to this question is an analysis of who had been active leaders in Corinth. Paul and Sosthenes and Apollos had certainly been active there and were viewed as leaders, though Sosthenes did not enter the picture other than as co-author of the letter; Cephas/Peter probably had been to Corinth, since some saw him as a figurehead for a group; Timothy had represented Paul (4:17; 16:10; cf. Rom. 16:21), and Titus was soon to do so if he had not already (2 Cor. 2:13; 8:16; 12:18); Chloe (1:11) played a role, as did Stephanas and Fortunatus and Achaicus (16:15, 17; 1:16); probably Crispus and Gaius (1:14; cf. Rom. 16:23) were influential within the community; and no doubt Erastus was also (Rom. 16:23); Aquila and Prisca (16:19) and Silvanus (2 Cor. 1:19) had some role at an earlier stage. The list is long, exceeded only by the more complex list of Rom. 16:1-16. Among those persons active in Corinth were some of wealth and power and status, persons accustomed to honor and deference, who acted as patrons and reaped the prestige. While some of the persons known to be active leaders in Corinth were closely linked with Paul (Sosthenes, Timothy, Titus, Aquila and Prisca), not all were; if there were opposition to Paul, it was probably centered on the leadership of one or more of these persons, in which case Apollos and Cephas/Peter head the list.

Literary and Rhetorical Analysis

A wide variety of partition theories have been developed, arguing from repetitions, overlaps, seams, and conflicting travel plans. None has commanded wide assent; the usual view is that 1 Corinthians (possibly with one or two interpolations: 14:34-35?) is a unity. There are two main approaches to analyzing the letter's structure and unity. One using a letter-writing model argues for 1 Corinthians as a sequential response to external oral and written topics — topics raised with Paul by the Corinthians and reflected in chs. 5–16 — surrounded by typical letter elements. The other, based on rhetorical conventions of antiquity, argues for a unified letter of persuasion with its own internal logic, a rhetoric controlled by Paul, not the recipients. Both approaches come to the same conclusion on the unity of the letter, though they move in different directions with respect to Paul's purpose: in the one case he adopts a "rhetoric of reconciliation"; in the other the letter is largely a defense of Paul's attempt to bring the Corinthians into conformity with the apostolic decree, arguing that the existing tension derived from that decision.

Major Issues in Corinth

The most divisive matter is leadership (1:10–4:21), on which topic Paul is variously appealing (1:10; 4:16), threatening (4:19-21), defensive (2:1-5), condescending (3:1-4), and sarcastic (4:8-13). His main objective is to claim his precedence in the founding of the church, to minimize the roles of others, Apollos in particular, and to urge the church to avoid divisions. Much attention is given to sex (chs. 5-7), about which Paul has heard both orally (5:1) and in writing (7:1). Topics include an incestuous relationship, a civil suit, continued recourse to (sacral?) prostitutes, conjugal disputes, divorce, betrothal, and virginity. Paul also emphasizes food (chs. 8–10), dealing with eating food offered to idols and sacrificial questions, along with a defense of his own practices on support (both food and money). That focus shifts to concerns over community worship (chs. 11–14): male and female dress codes, aberrations in observing the Lord's Supper, and the use of spiritual gifts, especially the more prominent charismatic gifts such as speaking in tongues. A particular interest is Paul's attitude to women, mainly focused on 11:2-16 (women's roles in worship), but involving also the more general issues of women's sexual "equality" (ch. 7) and his laconic comment in 14:33b-36 about whether women should speak in meetings — the latter passage often viewed as an interpolation.

The one sustained doctrinal question Paul addresses is resurrection from the dead, on which there were disagreements in the congregation (esp. 15:12-19). Ch. 15 raises the more general question of Paul's knowledge and use of Jesus traditions: tradition of Jesus' death and resurrection (15:3-7); tradition of the Last Supper (11:23-26); the Lord's commands on divorce and apostolic support (7:10; 9:14; cf. 11:2). The implications of 1 Corinthians' collection of Jesus-related materials is still debated: was it more important in Corinth, compared with other communities, because some leaders had close links with Jesus? Finally, Paul describes his and Timothy's travel plans, mostly dealing with gathering and transporting a famine-support collection to Jerusalem, but also including an allusion to Apollos' refusal to return to Corinth (16:1-12; cf. 4:18-21).

Significance

Continued scholarly preoccupation with 1 Corinthians derives from several factors. (1) It is a basic resource for descriptions of Paul's ethics and some of his theological emphases. (2) Nowhere are tensions within early Christianity seen more clearly than here; these include not just matters of parties and divisions but also issues such as social status, patronage, wealth, slavery, and power. (3) Many studies focus on the pastoral dimensions of Paul's relationship with the community. (4) The letter serves as an integral part of a diachronic or longitudinal analysis of issues in one church over a period of almost 50 years (i.e., up to 1 Clement in the mid-90s) and involving a substantial number of letter exchanges, which show an ongoing concern with divisions (e.g., 1 Clem. 1:1; 3:1-4; 9:1) and a shifting dynamic. In sum, a careful reading of 1 Corinthians allows a lively sense of the spread of Christianity, of Paul's and his congregations' varied relationships, of Paul's independence of thought, and of the range of figures that emerged in the early Christian developments.

Bibliography. J. K. Chow, *Patronage and Power: A Study of Social Networks in Corinth.* JSNTSup 75 (Sheffield, 1992); A. D. Clarke, *Secular and Christian Leadership in Corinth.* AGJU 18 (Leiden, 1993); J. C. Hurd, *The Origin of 1 Corinthians,* 2nd ed. (Macon, 1983); L. A. Jervis and P. Richardson, eds., *Gospel in Paul.* JSNTSup 108 (Sheffield, 1994); W. A. Meeks, *The First Urban Christians* (New Haven, 1983); M. M. Mitchell, *Paul and the Rhetoric of Reconciliation* (Tübingen, 1991); J. Murphy-O'Connor, *St. Paul's Corinth* (Wilmington, 1983); G. Theissen, *The Social Setting of Pauline Christianity* (Philadelphia, 1982).

PETER RICHARDSON

CORINTHIANS, SECOND LETTER TO THE

Part of Paul's correspondence with Christians in the capital city of Roman Achaia.

2 Corinthians is the most personal of Paul's letters, yet also the most difficult to interpret. In terms of ancient epistolary theory, it is a mixed letter; it contains not just one literary and rhetorical style but a number of different styles and elements, including irony, self-defense, self-praise, rebukes, threats, attacks, counterattacks, prayers, appeals, and exhortations. The document also appears rather disjointed. For example, 6:14–7:1 seems to be a digression that interrupts the appeal that begins in 6:11-13 and resumes in 7:2-4. Yet 6:11–7:4 itself appears to belong to a much longer digression that begins in 2:14. The document also contains two lengthy discussions of the collection for the Jerusalem church (chs. 8–9), with the second commencing in a way that seems to ignore the preceding discussion (9:1). The tone of the document also varies considerably. In ch. 7, e.g., Paul is joyful and conciliatory, expressing confidence in the Corinthians and praising their penitence and obedience. By contrast, in chs. 10–13 Paul is ironic and argumentative, fearful about the Corinthians' devotion to Christ and castigating them for their impenitence and disobedience. Such digressions, repetitions, and differences in tone and style have led many scholars to conclude that 2 Corinthians is a composite document containing fragments of at least two and perhaps as many as five letters.

Disparate conclusions about the number of letters contained in 2 Corinthians have led to different reconstructions of the history of Paul's contact and correspondence with the Corinthian church. The church in Corinth was founded by Paul, with the assistance of Silvanus (Silas) and Timothy, on his so-called second missionary journey in ca. 50 C.E. (1:19; Acts 18:1-17). According to Acts 18:11, this initial visit to Corinth lasted about 18 months, during which time he wrote 1 Thessalonians and, if genuine, 2 Thessalonians. Following his departure from Corinth, Paul traveled eastward to Ephesus in Asia Minor (Acts 18:18-21), which was to become the focus of his evangelistic efforts on his third missionary journey (19:1). All of Paul's subsequent contact with the Corinthian church derives from this later period, which lasted some three years (Acts 20:31). This contact includes at least four letters to Corinth by Paul, at least one letter to Paul by the Corinthians (1 Cor. 7:1), two subsequent trips by Paul to the city (2 Cor. 2:1; 12:14; 13:1-2; Acts 20:2-3) as well as other trips made to Corinth by his envoys Timothy (1 Cor. 4:17; 16:10-11) and Titus (2 Cor. 7:6-7; 8:6; 12:18), and at least two trips to Paul made by people who either lived in Corinth or had visited the city (1 Cor. 1:11; 16:17).

Paul's first letter to Corinth dealt, at least in part, with the issue of associating with the sexually immoral (1 Cor. 5:9). This letter, usually referred to as Letter A or the "Previous Letter," is almost certainly lost, although some scholars believe that a fragment is preserved in 6:14–7:1. In this letter Paul enjoined the Corinthians not to associate with sexually immoral members of the Christian community (cf. Eph. 5:3-7), but the Corinthians understood him to be commanding their social separation from immoral pagans. Paul clarifies his intended meaning and addresses a number of other issues in his second letter to Corinth, the canonical 1 Corinthians (Letter B). This letter, occasioned by an oral report about the Corinthian church from Chloe's people (1 Cor. 1:11) as well as a letter from the Corinthians themselves (7:1), was written from Ephesus ca. 54 (1 Cor. 16:8). About the same time as Letter B, Paul sent Timothy to Corinth, anticipating that his co-worker would return in time to accompany him on a trip through Macedonia to Corinth (1 Cor. 4:17; 16:5-11). Precisely what happens following the dispatch of Timothy and Letter B is unclear, and all reconstructions of this later period of Paul's contact with Corinth involve inference and conjecture.

Most interpreters assume that Timothy returned to Paul in Ephesus with a disturbing report about the situation in Corinth. The troubles presumably involved the continuation of some problems addressed in Letter B (12:20-21) as well as the inception of new problems. The situation was sufficiently serious to prompt Paul to postpone or change the travel plans he had announced in 1 Cor. 16:5, when he had anticipated traveling to Corinth by way of Macedonia. He now traveled directly to Corinth in order to deal with the problems in person. Unfortunately, this second visit was a disaster; the problems were compounded rather than solved. What made this visit so painful for Paul is unknown (2:1-5). The prevailing view is that someone at Corinth, either a member of the congregation or an outsider, confronted Paul and inflicted some gross insult on him that raised serious questions about his apostolic authority. Some scholars, however, suggest that the offender was identical with the incestuous man of 1 Cor. 5; others contend that the painful episode involved money, namely, that someone either accused Paul of embezzlement or stole money from him that had been deposited with the apostle for the Jerusalem collection.

In any case, Paul left Corinth with the problems unresolved. Instead of returning to Corinth soon thereafter, as he had once intended (1:15-16), he wrote an emotionally charged letter in which he dealt decisively with the rapidly deteriorating situation. This letter (Letter C), usually called either the "Severe Letter" or the "Letter of Tears" (2:3-4; 7:8-12), was written either in Macedonia (1:16) or Ephesus (to which he eventually returned), and carried to Corinth by Titus. After sending the letter, Paul began to worry about how it would be received. He eventually left Ephesus and traveled to Troas, where he expected to meet Titus and receive his co-worker's report. Filled with so much anxiety that he could not even take advantage of the opportunity to evangelize the city, he left Troas and went to Macedonia in search of Titus (2:12-13). When they eventually met, Titus gave Paul good news about the salutary effects of the Severe Letter (7:15-16). Consoled by Titus' report, Paul now wrote a fourth letter (Letter D) in which he expressed his joy and clarified the motives that had prompted his decision to write Letter C. This letter was presumably carried back to Corinth by Titus.

The relationship of Letters C and D to 2 Corinthians is a matter of substantial scholarly dispute. According to one theory which has recently been adopted by a number of scholars, Letter C is lost and Letter D is the canonical 2 Corinthians. The great advantage of this theory is its simplicity; all others are more conjectural. The key issue is whether this hypothesis can adequately explain the textual data or whether the text itself demands a more complex explanation. The most serious problem connected with this view is the sharp break between chs. 1–9 and 10–13. Some scholars have attempted to explain the break by arguing that the final four chapters are a rhetorical peroration in which Paul makes a powerful emotional appeal to the Corinthians. Most, however, continue to doubt whether all the differences between chs. 1-9 and 10–13 can be sufficiently explained by such rhetorical analysis.

A second theory posits a change of situation for the composition of chs. 10-13. According to this theory, Letter C is lost and Paul wrote chs. 1–9 after receiving Titus' positive report. Before writing the final four chapters, however, he received another report indicating either that the situation was not as happy as Titus had indicated or that things had changed dramatically since Titus' departure. This new report led the apostle to change the tone of his letter. 2 Corinthians is, therefore, one letter (Letter D), but it was written with two different situations in view.

A third theory holds that chs. 1–9 once formed a separate letter (Letter D) that was sent after Titus gave his positive report. Chs. 10–13 are a fragment of a fifth letter (Letter E), written after Paul received a new and negative report. A variant of this theory holds that chs. 1–8 are Letter D, and ch. 9 is the fragment of a separate letter about the collection (Letter E); on this view, the envoy who carried this letter returned to Paul with the news about the dire developments in Corinth. Chs. 10–13 are thus Letter F, written in response to this troubling report.

Whereas all of the previously mentioned theories regard Paul's Severe Letter as lost, a fourth theory considers chs. 10–13 to be a fragment of that letter. Chs. 10–13 are thus Letter C, written chronologically prior to chs. 1–9 (Letter D). In this case, the Corinthian correspondence ends on a happy note.

The same is true for a fifth theory, which, however, is considerably more complex. According to this theory, Paul's third letter to Corinth was not the Severe Letter but a letter in which the apostle defended himself against charges leveled against him by opponents. This letter, preserved (except for its epistolary pre- and postscripts) in 2:14–6:13; 7:2-4, is Letter C. The failure of this first apology prompted Paul's painful visit to Corinth, after which he wrote the Severe Letter (Letter D), a second apology which is almost entirely preserved in chs. 10–13. This led to the Corinthians' repentance and Paul's fifth letter (Letter E) to them, a letter of reconciliation contained in 1:1–2:13; 7:15-16 (and 13:11-13). Following this reconciliation, Paul wrote two administrative letters, both about the collection. One of these (Letter F, to Corinth) is preserved in ch. 8, and the other (Letter G, to Achaia) in ch. 9.

According to all five theories, Paul came to Corinth not long after writing the last of his letters to the church there. This was his third visit, during which he wrote his letter to the Romans and finalized plans to journey to Jerusalem with the collection. That he was willing to leave the Aegean area indicates that he was successful in defending himself against the charges against him by his opponents, a group of Jewish Christian missionaries (11:22-23) whom he repudiates as false apostles (ch. 13). Whether these opponents were Judaizers, Gnostics, or Hellenistic-Jewish propagandists is debated, as is the time of their arrival in Corinth. Whatever their theology or time of arrival, they aggravated the problems that Paul encountered in dealing with the Corinthians. Although this was an extremely traumatic time in the apostle's life, Paul's interactions with the Corinthians and his opponents gave both form and substance to his whole theology.

One final issue is the relationship of 6:14–7:1 to Paul's theology. This section interrupts Paul's appeal in 6:11-13 and 7:2-4, contains a large number of words not found elsewhere in Paul's letters, and has affinities to the Dead Sea Scrolls. Those who defend Paul's authorship of this section offer diverse explanations, with some suggesting that it is a fragment of the "Previous Letter" mentioned in 1 Cor. 5:9, and others arguing that it is a digression in which Paul deliberately uses unusual and highly emotional language to address a problem in Corinth. Others hold that the section is non-Pauline in origin, but differ as to whether Paul himself or a later editor inserted it. Still others regard the passage as originally anti-Pauline, reflecting the theology of Paul's opponents. The continuing debates about this and other parts of 2 Corinthians suggest that this document will continue to receive attention as one of the most fascinating pieces of early Christian literature.

Bibliography. P. Barnett, *The Second Epistle to the Corinthians.* NICNT (Grand Rapids, 1997); H. D. Betz, *2 Corinthians 8 and 9.* Herm (Philadelphia, 1985); V. P. Furnish, *II Corinthians.* AB 32A (Garden City, 1984); R. P. Martin, *2 Corinthians.* WBC 40 (Waco, 1986); M. E. Thrall, *The Second Epistle to the Corinthians,* 1. ICC (Edinburgh, 1994); B. Witherington, III, *Conflict and Community in Corinth* (Grand Rapids, 1995).

John T. Fitzgerald

CORMORANT

A sea bird (*Phalacrocorax*), of which there are some 30 species. Some species spend the winter in Palestine, along the coast and the banks of the Sea of Galilee, making their nests on the rocks and in the hollows and crevices. They are exceptional swimmers and divers, able to swallow large fish whole because of the elasticity of their gullets. Their extended bodies and long, slender necks are striking.

As a predatory bird, the cormorant is included among unclean birds (Lev. 11:17; Deut. 14:17). However, scholars continue to debate the meaning of Heb. *šālāḵ* (e.g., "fisher-owl," "pelican").

CORNELIUS (Gk. *Kornḗlios*)

A centurion of the Roman army stationed in Caesarea Maritima, the seat of Roman imperial rule in Palestine. Cornelius appears as the first gentile convert to Christianity (Acts 10:1-48; 11:1-18; 15:7-9, 13-18). That his conversion is told or alluded to four times in Acts suggests something of its paradigmatic significance, particularly in the latter two instances where both Peter and James invoke the memory of Cornelius at the Jerusalem Council to justify the full inclusion of the Gentiles in the Church. Portrayed as righteous and devout, Cornelius may represent that class of Gentiles known as "God-fearers," who attached themselves to the synagogue and whom Acts presents as particularly responsive to the gospel.

After inviting Peter to his house, Cornelius, with his entire household, hears the words of salvific peace and receives the Holy Spirit in what has been described as a "Gentile Pentecost." The participation of the household in the salvation of Cornelius results in the founding of a gentile congregation and establishes the pattern for other instances of household salvation in Acts (16:14-15, 31-34; 18:8). The table fellowship that ensues between Peter and the newly converted household occasions heated criticism from certain circumcised believers back in Jerusalem (Acts 11:3), leading Peter to recount his own experience of the "cleansing" of the Gentiles (10:15, 28) and to persuade the Church to adopt his new point of view in the process (11:18). As a result, the conversion of Cornelius inaugurates the mission to the Gentiles, who eventually eclipse Jewish Christians as the dominant members in the people of God (Acts 28:28).

Bibliography. B. R. Gaventa, *From Darkness to Light: Aspects of Conversion in the New Testament.* OBT 20 (Philadelphia, 1986), 96-122; D. L. Matson, *Household Conversion Narratives in Acts.* JSNTSup 123 (Sheffield, 1996), 86-134.

David Lertis Matson

CORNERSTONE

An architectural term used in the NT as a metaphor for Christ (Matt. 21:42; Eph. 2:20; 1 Pet. 2:4-8). The NT usage of this term (Gk. *akrogōniaíos; kephalḗ gōnías*) comes from the OT (Heb. *rōʾš pinnâ;* Ps. 118:22; Isa. 8:14; 28:16-17). "Cornerstone" may refer to: (1) the stone in a new building laid first with great care and ceremony so as to ensure a straight and level foundation; (2) the interlocking cornerstones that join and strengthen two connecting walls; (3) the capstone at the top corner of a wall; or (4) the keystone of an arched door or gateway, the center and topmost stone that joins the two sides and supports the arch itself (the most important stone in which the name of the city, the ruler, and builder were often carved).

In the NT, Peter uses OT passages in a complex analogy, referring to individual believers as "stones" in a spiritual house where Christ is (1) the corner of the foundation; (2) the capstone or, more likely, keystone; and (3) the stumbling stone, upon which disobedient builders are judged for searching out a stone of their own choosing to complete the building (1 Pet. 2:4-8). Paul demonstrates that while the "apostles and prophets" are the foundation of the Church, it is Christ "in whom the whole building is fitted together" (Eph. 2:20).

Bibliography. R. J. McKelvey, "Christ the Cornerstone," *NTS* 8 (1961/62): 352-59.

Dennis M. Swanson

CORPORATE PERSONALITY

For nearly a century scholars have debated how to explain certain corporate features of Israelite religion and culture. Many biblical narratives seem untroubled by instances in which the sin of an individual or group leads to the punishment of other people not directly involved in the original offense (e.g., Josh. 7, in which the sin of Achan leads to the execution of his whole family and the destruction of all his property). H. Wheeler Robinson employed the term "corporate personality" as a conceptual key to elucidate these disturbing cases. He relied heavily on Emile Durkheim and Lucien Levy-Bruhl, who employed the notion of "primitive psychology" in attempting to explain totemism among so-called primitive peoples. According to these anthropologists, tribes with a totemic religion inhabited a very different psychic reality from that in which modern humans live. This primitive mindset was described as "synthetic thinking" or "psychical unity," implying an inability of the individual to separate himself totally from nature, and especially to differentiate himself from other members of his clan and from the totemic species that represented his clan. Often this totemic psychology was called "prelogical" and was considered a type of mystical union with reality as a whole. Robinson clearly never suggested that ancient Israelite religion was totemistic in any way. However, he did fully believe that ancient Israel, especially in the earlier period, exhibited a very similar, or perhaps even the same, psychology as these anthropologists believe they have found among "primitive" tribes.

Robinson and others applied these notions as a type of cure-all invoked to solve a host of interpretive problems in the OT. Criticisms leveled at the notion of corporate personality fall under four basic rubrics: (1) This theory creates a false dichotomy between the idea of the individual and the idea of the group, and leaves the impression that Israelite society had little awareness of the individual until the later biblical period. (2) The various cases gathered under the concept of corporate personality are sometimes better explained by ideas such as bloodguilt, ancient conceptions of property rights, and violation of holiness taboos. (3) The notion of corporate personality grew out of certain anthropological ideas now recognized to be fallacious. (4) Robinson used the term in an imprecise way and thus employed different senses of the term to solve different types of problems. In doing so he emptied the term of any clear meaning and thus of any usefulness.

Corporate Responsibility

Although the term corporate personality is now rarely used, scholars studying biblical narratives that involve the transference of the sin of an individual or group to other people or to later generations still employ the term corporate responsibility. The term corporate personality was most problematic because of the psychological connotations, which alone make the use of corporate responsibility preferable. Unfortunately that term also presents some ambiguity. It can mean a person might be liable for the action of his community or part of that community because he was not recognized as an individual with individual rights; or it might mean an individual, though not directly involved, might suffer the consequences generated by the misdeeds of his community. Although this ambiguity exists, the term is still useful as long as one makes clear exactly what meaning one has in mind. Clearly, the OT contains instances of both types of corporate responsibility and some instances in which both types seem to be exhibited at once. No modern term will ever be totally adequate in explaining all the complexities in the OT's conception of the individual's relationship to the community, but this term does seem to capture some important elements of the biblical mindset.

Individualism

One other important feature in how the OT understands the individual's relationship to the larger community is the question of whether there was a movement away from a more "primitive" type of collectivism and toward a type of individualism. Scholars have often viewed texts such as Josh. 7; 2 Sam. 21:1-14 — in which a ritual violation is followed by some type of corporate punishment — as advocating a set of primitive ideas that were eventually superseded by a superior, more individualized religious impulse. Those who argue for this position tend to label theologically troubling texts like Josh. 7 as aberrations and exceptions that do not reflect the higher aspects of Israel's religion seen in texts such as Deut. 24:16; Jer. 31:29-30; Ezek. 18. The latter are understood as signaling a radical shift toward a new individualism that rejects the older corporate ways of thinking. This viewpoint is historically inaccurate and theologically problematic. On the historical side it seems strange that a period seen to exhibit a growing individualism is the same as that in which the texts assigned to the Priestly author of the Pentateuch affirm the concept of communal solidarity (Lev. 4). This period also saw the final editing of Deuteronomy and the Deuteronomistic history, each of which utilizes notions of corporate responsibility. If in fact the individual began to emerge during the late 6th century, why did this individualism leave so little impression upon the vast literature produced during the Second Temple period? That passages within the latest strata of the OT support the idea of communal responsibility (Dan. 6:25; Esth. 9:7-10), and that this view is still alive well into NT times (Matt. 23:29-36; John 9:2; 1 Thess. 2:14-16) and beyond (*Lev. Rab.* 4:6; *b. Sanh.* 43b-44a; *Tanna Debe Eliyyahu* 12), suggests that there was no simple linear progression from older corporate to later more individualized forms of retribution. That scholars have argued for such a progression in the face of much evidence to the contrary suggests an inherent bias in some modern biblical scholarship. Certain scholars apparently have been influenced by ideas that value individualism and implicitly denigrate or reject the claims of the community as well as by ideas of linear and progressive social evolution.

Before utterly rejecting all corporate notions as primitive one should note the centrality of such corporate ideas in Israelite theology. In many respects the concept of divine mercy is predicated on being treated as a favored member of a group rather than being judged exactly according to one's own merits.

Precisely this concept stands behind notions such as God's promise after the Flood (Gen. 8:21; Isa. 54:9-10), Israel's election especially as it relates to the promise to the patriarchs (Deut. 9:4-5), and God's willingness to restore Israel after the Exile (Deut. 4:29-31; Jer. 31:31-34; Ezek. 36:22-32). Additionally, the corporate view of divine retribution recognizes that humans inevitably commit sins and thus depend on not being judged according to their ways (Job 4:12-21; 7:17-21; 1 Kgs. 8:46-53; Ps. 51:1-14[MT 3-16]; 103:8-14; 130:3; Jer. 10:24). In fact, it should be acknowledged that because the OT's theology is fundamentally corporate in its outlook, the biblical emphasis upon God's relation to a particular community cannot be treated as an early, but now irrelevant idea. The OT's message is not directed to a loose configuration of individuals but to a living community called the people of Israel.

The biblical writers were aware that our individuality can only be understood in relation to the various collectivities in which we participate and that being human means that the individual is linked to other people through the consequences that flow from each person's actions. But this does not mean that the Bible ignores the importance of the individual. The Bible has a very nuanced theology of the relationship between the individual and the community. Rather than playing off the more individualistic passages within the Bible against those that reflect a more corporate view, one can see the way in which these elements qualify and complement each other.

Bibliography. J. S. Kaminsky, *Corporate Responsibility in the Hebrew Bible.* JSOTSup 196 (Sheffield, 1995); G. Matties, *Ezekiel 18 and the Rhetoric of Moral Discourse.* SBLDS 126 (Atlanta, 1990); J. R. Porter, "The Legal Aspects of the Concept of 'Corporate Personality' in the Old Testament," *VT* 15 (1965): 361-80; H. W. Robinson, "The Hebrew Conception of Corporate Personality," in *Corporate Personality in Ancient Israel,* rev. ed. (Philadelphia, 1980), 25-44. JOEL S. KAMINSKY

CORRUPTION, MOUNT OF

The geographical mountain site (Heb. *har-hammašḥîṯ*) E of Jerusalem on which Solomon erected the high places for the worship of the deities of his foreign wives (1 Kgs. 11:7) and which was destroyed by the reforming King Josiah (2 Kgs. 23:13). The Hebrew root *šḥt* can be understood as "destroy," "corrupt," "ruin," and in one case "disfigure" (Lev. 22:25). In many contexts it carries a moral or cultic sense of violation of covenant that expects divine judgment, as with Jeremiah's prophecy against this mountain (Jer. 51:25). From the Vulgate's Lat. *Mons offensionis* has come the traditional modern name "Mount of Offense." The site is probably to be identified with the southern ridge of the Mount of Olives occupied by the Silwan village on its western side. J. RANDALL PRICE

COS (Gk. *Kṓs*)

An island in the Aegean Sea, SW of Asia Minor with a city of the same name as its major port. Flourishing as part of the trade routes, Cos was the birthplace of Hippocrates and featured a sanctuary of Asclepius and a medical school. A significant Jewish community existed on Cos. It was one of the cities to which the Roman consul wrote declaring support for Simon's rule over the Jewish state (1 Macc. 15:23). Josephus records Herod the Great's interests in Cos (*BJ* 1.21.11). While Paul was on the return leg of his third missionary journey, after leaving Miletus, he and his companions arrived on Cos (Acts 21:1). DOUGLAS LOW

COSAM (Gk. *Kōsám*)

An otherwise unknown preexilic ancestor of Jesus (Luke 3:28).

COSMETICS

In the ancient world men and women used cosmetics much the same as they are used today: to beautify and preserve the skin, to counterpoise body odors, and to adorn the hair. Perfume is the most common cosmetic found in the OT (Esth. 2:12; Prov. 27:9), worn primarily to counteract the body's natural odors. Perfumes also served hygienic purposes, providing an alternative to water in bathing. One kind of perfume, myrrh, was ground into a powder, collected in a small pouch, and worn around a woman's neck (Cant. 1:13). Henna was used for painting fingernails and dyeing hair (Cant. 4:13). Archaeological discoveries have uncovered cosmetic dishes and palettes, mirrors, and hair accessories such as combs and hairpins.

Egyptian wall paintings reveal that a black substance known as kohl was rubbed underneath the eyes, probably as a protectant against the bright rays of the sun. Kohl was used by women to outline the eyes and darken the eyebrows, thus enhancing their physical appearance. In the OT women who outlined their eyes were regarded as dishonorable (Jer. 4:30; Ezek. 23:40; cf. esp. Jezebel who, before her violent death, painted her eyes; 2 Kgs. 9:30). In addition to substances used to beautify the eyes, various ointments were applied to protect and preserve the skin from the arid climate of the Middle East. JIM OXFORD, JR.

COSMOGONY, COSMOLOGY

See WORLDVIEW.

COTTON

Cotton (*Gossypium herbaceum* L.) is native to India, and was not grown in the ancient Near East until after the conquests of Alexander the Great. Yet it is fitting that the Persian king Ahasuerus, ruler of lands "from India to Ethiopia" (Esth. 1:1), would have white cotton (Heb. *karpas*) curtains in his palace at Susa (Esth. 1:6).

Clothing in biblical times was primarily linen, which is made from the flax plant, or wool. After cotton's spread westward, it became a major crop in the Near East and remains so today.

MEGAN BISHOP MOORE

COUNCIL

The highest court of the Jews during Jesus' time, composed of 71 members from the priests, scribes, and "elders of the people," and presided over by the high priest. Traditionally the council (Gk. *synédrion*) was thought to have begun with Moses (Num. 11:16) and revived under Ezra. It tried all infractions of the law of Moses, and since there was no distinction in Jewish thought between religious and civil law, it tried cases in both areas. Its authority seems to have been limited to cases that did not involve capital punishment (John 18:31), although that is much debated. Both Jesus and Paul were tried before this august body. It condemned Jesus on a charge of blasphemy when he admitted being the Messiah (Mark 14:64), but Paul so disrupted the court by announcing he was a Pharisee that Roman soldiers had to rescue him (Acts 23:6-10). Paul eventually appealed to Caesar to avoid being brought before the council at Jerusalem again (Acts 25:11). Since the word is plural in Mark 13:9 = Matt. 10:17, there obviously were lesser councils, but except for these two passages, the references are to the high court. JOE E. LUNCEFORD

COUNSELOR

Counselors (Heb. *yô'ēṣ*) occupied a regular place in the courts of the Israelite kings (Isa. 3:3; Ezra 7:14-15, 28). Their position was perhaps next in power to the ruler himself, as suggested by the juxtaposition of "kings and counselors" (Job 3:14; 12:17-18; Mic. 4:9). David's court had two counselors, Ahithophel and Hushai. Ahithophel's counsel (Heb. *'ēṣâ*) enjoyed so extraordinary a reputation that it was likened to an oracle from heaven (2 Sam. 16:23). It was wise for the king to employ an "abundance of counselors" to advise him on national security (Prov. 11:14; 15:22) and war (20:18; 24:6). The fool ignores counsel and brings about ruin (Prov. 1:25, 30), or follows the wrong advice (1 Kgs. 12:6-14). The pharaoh of Egypt (Isa. 19:11) and Nebuchadnezzar in Babylon (Dan. 3:2) also had counselors. Artaxerxes of Persia had seven counselors (Ezra 7:14), corresponding to the "seven princes of Persia and Media" consulted by Ahasuerus (Esth. 1:14).

Outside the court, parents (Prov. 1:8), elders (Ezek. 7:26), prophets (Jer. 38:15; 2 Chr. 25:16), and wise men (Jer. 18:18; 49:7) typically acted as counselors. God is a counselor (Ps. 16:7; 32:8; 33:11; 73:24), and God's law and testimony are personified as the people's counselors (119:24). God seeks no counsel, and no one can counsel God (Isa. 40:13-14). God promised the Davidic dynasty a "wondrous counselor" (Isa. 9:6[MT 5]), upon whom shall descend "the spirit of the Lord . . . the spirit of counsel" (11:2). DANIEL GROSSBERG

COURTYARD

An unroofed enclosure surrounded by walls of a house or public building (Heb. *ḥāṣēr;* Gk. *aulḗ*). Early Israelite "courtyard-sites" (elliptically shaped sites featuring large open courtyards encircled by rooms or dwellings that opened onto it) likely developed from earlier nomadic encampment models. Courtyards might contain a well (cf. 2 Sam. 17:18). Livestock often cohabited much the same space as their owners.

Courtyards also linked intricate royal complexes. Solomon's building complex in Jerusalem, S of the temple, included multiple courtyards (1 Kgs. 7:8-12; 2 Chr. 4:9). Ahasuerus' palace in Susa included an inner and outer court, the latter serving as a reception area (Esth. 1:5). Nebuchadnezzar's southern palace boasted five courtyards flanked by offices, royal apartments, and reception rooms.

The tabernacle (Exod. 27:9-19; Num. 3:25-26), Solomon's temple (1 Kgs. 6:1-36; cf. 2 Chr. 3-4), and Ezekiel's temple (Ezek. 40-42) all had courts or courtyards. The Second Temple contained an outer courtyard for Gentiles and an inner court for Jews that was further subdivided into separate areas for women, lay males, and priests, respectively. The scene of the apostle Peter's denial of Christ began in "the courtyard" (of the temple; Mark 14:66 par.) and then moved to the "forecourt" (or gateway; 16:68).

Bibliography. I. Finkelstein, *The Archaeology of the Israelite Settlement* (Jerusalem, 1988).

MARK A. CHRISTIAN

COUSIN

The OT has no specific word for cousin other than the phrase *ben-dôḏ,* "son of an uncle" (Lev. 25:49; Jer. 32:8). Other phrases such as "son of your father's brother" or "mother's brother's daughter" also refer to a first cousin (Gen. 28:2; 29:10, 12).

In the OT a cousin had certain responsibilities. Chief among these is the expectation that a cousin would prevent land from being issued to a creditor should his cousin become impoverished (Lev. 25:49). This obligation toward one's cousin was carried out by the prophet Jeremiah (Jer. 32:7-9, 12).

In biblical times it was possible for cousins, even first cousins, to marry (Gen. 24:15; 28:2; 29:10, 19; 36:3; Num. 36:11; 1 Chr. 23:21-22). Such marriages were not considered to be incestuous (Lev. 18:6-18).

In the NT the word for cousin (Gk. *anepsiós*) occurs only once and describes the relationship of Barnabas and Mark (Col. 4:10). The nouns *syngenís* (Luke 1:36) and *syngenḗs* (v. 58), translated "cousin(s)" by the KJV, are better rendered "relative(s)." MARK F. ROOKER

COVENANT

A solemn agreement between two or more parties, made binding by some sort of oath (cf. Ger. *Bund*). What is mutually agreed upon is usually the future conduct of one or both of the parties concerned. "Covenant"-type relationships were ubiquitous in antiquity, and in the Bible they are undoubtedly alluded to more frequently than a simple study of Heb. *bĕrîṯ* and Gk. *diathḗkē* would suggest. Such relationships might include compacts or pledges between private persons (e.g., Ruth 1:16-17; 3:11-13; Exod. 21:2-6), agreements or compacts between a king and private persons (cf. Judg. 4:17; 2 Sam. 19:31-39), treaties or alliances between kings and/

or political states (1 Kgs. 5:1[MT 15]; 2 Kgs. 24:17; cf. Ps. 2:1-3; Isa. 30:1), promissory oaths proclaiming official policies (Neh. 5:11-13; 9:38–10:39[10:1-40]), and covenants between Yahweh and human beings (e.g., Gen. 25:23; 1 Kgs. 14:7-19; 2 Kgs. 9:6-10; cf. Gen. 12:1-3; 2 Sam. 7; 21:7). (The term *bĕrîṯ* does not occur in the preceding references.)

Covenant and Moral Character

The viability of covenant relationships — in stark contrast to legal ones — depends solely upon the integrity of those partners actually making promises under oath. The partners are directly accountable to one another, not to some judicial overseer. If the partners are insincere in making promises or unreliable in keeping them, then the relationship is in jeopardy; its continued viability now depends upon the repentance of the offending party and the ability of the offended party to forgive.

Because the ethical character of the covenant-makers is so crucial, almost all covenants have a spiritual dimension insofar as they depend upon a tangible commitment to such abstractions as honesty, integrity, loyalty, trust, selflessness, and love. Not surprisingly, oaths invoking the transcendent (i.e., the gods) were a common feature of covenant-making, in the hopes that this would help solidify the commitment to promise-keeping. At a time when the gods were taken seriously as monitors of human integrity and when the effective reach of state government could be quite limited, covenants filled the vacuum as functioning instruments controlling human behavior.

Old Testament

Where God Is Not a Partner

During the course of the millennium in which biblical texts were composed Heb. *bĕrîṯ* did not enjoy the same stability as the English word "covenant." When referring to certain relationships between human beings, *bĕrîṯ* indeed corresponds very closely to the English term (and Ger. *Bund*), unmistakably referring to bilateral agreements such as pacts, alliances, and treaties. Included are compacts or pledges between private persons (e.g., Gen. 31:44; 1 Sam. 18:3; 2 Kgs. 11:4; Prov. 2:17), agreements or compacts between a king and private persons (e.g., Gen. 21:27; 26:28; 2 Sam. 3:12; Dan. 9:27), treaties or alliances between kings and/or political states (e.g., 2 Sam. 5:1-3; 1 Kgs. 5:12[26]; 15:19; Hos. 12:1[2]; cf. Ps. 83:5[6]), and leagues involving different social groups (e.g., Exod. 23:32; Josh. 9).

In time, *bĕrîṯ* could be applied to the oath activating the relationship: a *bĕrîṯ* could thus be any solemn promise made binding by an oath, regardless of whether or not it constituted a bilateral agreement. Thus in later biblical texts it could be applied to "promissory oaths," where one party unilaterally pledges itself to a certain course of action or policy (e.g., Jer. 34:8-18; 2 Kgs. 23:3; 2 Chr. 15:12; at best, Yahweh was invoked [by oath?] to enhance the solemnity of the act, although in none of the latter three texts does the narrator actually depict Yahweh even being aware of the proceedings, much less being a party to them). Frequently this commitment is forcibly extracted, giving the impression that *bĕrîṯ* is not a "covenant" but an "imposed obligation" (Ger. *Verpflichtung*).

Where God Is Under Obligation

However, when referring to relationships between God and human beings, it is not immediately clear that *bĕrîṯ* conveys the same sense as the English "covenant." When God makes a solemn promise bestowing favors on certain individuals (e.g., Abraham, Phinehas, David), a special relationship is created, but it appears to resemble more of a "charter" (a grant of rights by a sovereign) than a mutually agreed-upon "covenant" (e.g., Gen. 6:18-21; 9:1-17; 15, 17; 2 Sam. 23:5; Isa. 54:9-10). Indeed, this type of *bĕrîṯ* (where God functions as the sovereign) is clearly modeled after the royal grants that were well known in the ancient Near East.

Where Israel Is Under Obligation to God: Sinai

The case is far less clear for the "Sinai covenant" associated with the Ten Commandments and the rest of the biblical laws. It is not surprising that this covenant receives the most attention in the Bible: it alone spells out what Israel must do to maintain its special relationship with God. Arguably, all biblical covenants where Israelites have sworn obligations to God (e.g., Exod. 19:5; Jer. 11:2-10; Deut. 29:1[28:69]–30:20; Josh. 24; Mal. 2:4-9 [cf. Num. 25:12-13]) are either subsumed in the Sinai *bĕrîṯ* or constitute renewals of it.

It is not even clear whether this "covenant" was initially labeled *bĕrîṯ*: Some evidence suggests that it was referred to instead as the *dĕḇārîm*, "statements (of obligation?)" or "terms (of an agreement?)," *'ālâ*, "oath," or *'ēḏûṯ*, "sworn obligation." What was this Sinai *bĕrîṯ*, and how was it originally regarded by the ancient Israelites? Was it a true "covenant" *(Bund)* between God and Israel, analogous to a treaty/pact, a mutually agreed-upon relationship? Or was it an "imposed obligation" *(Verpflichtung)*, a unilateral arrangement by God that Israel had little choice but to accept?

Later Traditions About the Sinai *bĕrîṯ*

Postexilic Period

Questions linger about how the Sinai *bĕrîṯ* was regarded by the ancient Israelites prior to the 7th-century — indeed, some scholars doubt that the idea of a Sinai *bĕrîṯ* even existed before then. The issue becomes clearer during the postexilic period with the rise of early Judaism (6th-5th centuries and later). As Mosaic law became a more dominant force in shaping Judean identity, *bĕrîṯ* became increasingly synonymous with *tôrâ*, "law": It referred to the obligations that a faithful Jew was expected to perform. Regardless of what it may have meant earlier, the Mosaic *bĕrîṯ* came to be regarded now as obligations God had imposed upon the Israelites.

Hellenistic Period: Sinai as diathḗkē

When combined with late-5th-century injunctions against intermarriage (Ezra 10:3-5), the Sinai *bĕrîṯ* came to be associated with Judean ethnicity. By the Hellenistic period it had become viewed traditionally as the special religio-cultural possession of the Jews, a sign of their "election" as God's "chosen people" (cf. Rom. 9:4). Greek-speaking Jews believed this *bĕrîṯ* to be roughly synonymous with Gk. *diathḗkē*, "an order or institution established by authority" (such as God), although in the technical sense it could refer to a deceased person's "last will and testament," yielding an interesting paradox in the claim that the *diathḗkē* was God's (cf. Gal. 3:15-18; Heb. 9:16-17)!

The Sinai *diathḗkē* — and its numerous laws (Gk. *nómoi*) — came to be viewed as God's ultimate "will" for Israel, the special cultural "heritage" or "legacy" that he had irrevocably "bequeathed" exclusively to the Jews. Readers of the Greek Bible — including apocryphal and pseudepigraphic literature — almost certainly understood God's covenants to be the unilateral and ultimate expressions of his binding will and disposition (whether toward Israel, Abraham, David, or whatever), not some mutual agreement between two parties (which would have been conveyed instead through Gk. *synthḗkē*).

New Testament

Jesus. Jesus seems not to have accepted as authoritative these later connotations, but it is difficult to plot his actual thought on the matter since he avoids using *bĕrîṯ/diathḗkē* terminology. He seems to have regarded Israel's bond with God as a dynamic process of interrelatedness (which he labeled "kingdom/rule of God"), not a theologoumenon designating Israel's traditional heritage. His reliance upon more archaic patterns of covenant thought becomes clearer when we see him as a "reformer" insisting that Israel is now *directly* accountable to God and to the higher righteousness implied in the Law (i.e., the stipulations of the Sinai *bĕrîṯ*), and no longer accountable to God *indirectly* through adherence to the *modus operandi* of accumulated religious tradition.

Perhaps in a parody of the traditional view that *bĕrîṯ* was (the "departed"?) God's final and binding "testament" (*diathḗkē*) for Israel, Jesus' parables frequently depicted God as an absentee landlord, a rich man on a journey, a king off to a distant land, whose return always spells disaster for those entrusted with the master's business (i.e., oversight of the religious community). The keepers of Jewish tradition correctly understood that such parables and similar teachings about God's "coming" kingdom were aimed at them, and they responded ruthlessly (Matt. 21:45-46). The source of conflict between them and Jesus was two competing (and authoritative) views about the essence and relevance of Israel's *bĕrîṯ* with God: for them it was a theologoumenon that sanctified the traditions over which they presided; for Jesus it was a historical enactment that had little regard for human (or Jewish) institutions or hierarchies.

At the end Jesus acquiesced to their ruthlessness, but not before speaking of a "new covenant" that would be inaugurated by his death and would draw his disciples into the ultimate relationship with Israel's God (Mark 14:24; 1 Cor. 11:25). The connection is unmistakably to the eschatological *bĕrîṯ* anticipated in Jer. 31.

Paul. When referring to Sinai, Paul uses *bĕrîṯ/diathḗkē* terminology quite sparingly and always with significant qualification. This is not surprising given his conviction that the Sinai covenant had not supplanted the Abrahamic and that it no longer has a role to play in defining the distinctive essence of Israel's religion (Gal. 3:15-18).

In Rom. 9:4 he lists *diathḗkai* (plural!) as part of the distinctive heritage or legacy that God had bequeathed Israel. While this usage is typical of 1st-century (esp. Hellenistic) Judaism, it is not clear which *diathḗkai* Paul has in mind. In 2 Cor. 3:14 he explicitly links the "old *diathḗkē*" to Mosaic legislation written in the Pentateuch, and probably understands it in the traditional sense of imposed obligations instituted by God (cf. "first *diathḗkē*" in Heb. 9:1).

Paul's animating belief that Judaism was no longer to be based on divinely-imposed obligations not only justified his use of the adjective "old" (Gk. *palaiá*) but also found expression in his allegory of Hagar and Sarah, each of whom represents a *diathḗkē* (Gal. 4:21-31). Hagar represents the Sinai (= "old"?) *diathḗkē*, which is clearly an "imposed obligation" (*douleía*, "bondage, slavery"). In fact, when referring to Sinai and its operational dynamic Paul's word of choice is usually *nómos* ("law" or "customary obligation"), not *diathḗkē*. For Paul, the equation of *diathḗkē* with "imposed obligation" or "law" adequately and accurately summarizes the current state of traditional Judaism (represented by Jerusalem, Gal. 4:25), in which religion (like Ishmael) is conceived with respect to the principle of relying on self and on the age-old way of doing things (i.e., "the flesh").

In this allegory Sarah represents a heavenly (= "new"?) *diathḗkē* for Israel that is clearly not an imposed obligation. It summarizes the Christian religious worldview, which (like Isaac) is conceived with respect to the principle of a living relationship (i.e., "the spirit") of trust in God's ability to keep his promises. In fact, when referring to this heavenly covenant and its operational dynamic Paul's word of choice is not *diathḗkē* but *epangelía*, "promise." Paul, like Jesus, thus expresses the idea that "covenant" draws one into a living relationship of direct accountability to a partner, not conformity to religious traditions, institutions, and personnel who claim to mediate that relationship.

This notion that Israel's special bond with God is not an "imposed obligation" may not be quite so "new." It could be rooted in archaic patterns of meaning that still understood God's *bĕrîṯ* with Israel — even the Sinai *bĕrîṯ* — more on the model of a mutual agreement.

Issues in Understanding the Sinai Covenant

For the past century scholars have vigorously debated the nature, antiquity, and significance of the Sinai covenant tradition. At one pole are scholars (e.g., George E. Mendenhall, Delbert R. Hillers) who claim that (1) the Sinai covenant tradition in fact goes back to Moses; (2) from the outset it was a fundamental (if not the definitive) component of Israelite religion; (3) its religious ethic actually functioned historically as the basis of Israelite life and society in the centuries before the Hebrew monarchy; and (4) when applied to the Sinai event, *bĕrîṯ* indeed meant approximately the same as the English word "covenant" *(Bund).* At the other pole are those (e.g., Lothar Perlitt, Ernest W. Nicholson) who claim that (1) the Sinai covenant tradition arose later during the Monarchy; (2) it was simply one among many elements of Israelite religion; (3) it was never more than a theological construct or idea (theologoumenon) that helped sanctify an Israelite society actually rooted in the more secular ethic of national self-interest; and (4) *bĕrîṯ* when applied to Sinai intrinsically meant "obligation" *(Verpflichtung).*

On one point they agree: Hebrew thinking about Israel's *bĕrîṯ* with Yahweh was shaped by a familiarity with the international treaty conventions prevalent in biblical times. However, here the agreement ends. Actual copies of these treaties have been uncovered, principally those of the Hittites (1400-1200 B.C. — time of Moses?) and of the Assyrians (750-650 — time of the prophets). They exhibit sufficient similarities (preambles, stipulations, witnesses, curses) to suggest a general continuity in the treaty pattern over 800 years. Yet there are important differences both in actual form and in rhetorical tone, revealing subtle but important differences in treaty conventions during biblical times. The question is *which* treaty conventions *of which period* influenced Hebrew thought about Israel's relationship to God.

The 2nd-millennium texts usually include a historical prologue depicting the history of prior good relations between the two parties, particularly the beneficent deeds of the suzerain on behalf of the vassal. The 1st-millennium texts almost always lack this.

The 2nd-millennium texts include not only curses (a litany of disasters and misfortunes to befall a disobedient vassal) but also blessings (a litany of benefits to befall a faithful vassal). The 1st-millennium texts contain only curses.

Consequently, the 2nd-millennium Hittite texts reflect a sophisticated and artful attempt to underscore the presumed good will and integrity of everyone involved: a vassal enters the relationship and willingly accepts its obligations because the relationship with his overlord is a mutually beneficial and satisfactory one. The public rhetorical appeal in these texts is to gratitude, reciprocity, fellowship, and honor. There is little doubt that these texts represent true "covenants" (i.e., mutual agreements; *Bunde*) between two parties.

The 1st-millennium Assyrian texts are comparatively unsophisticated, constituting brutally naked attempts to coerce obedience. A vassal accepts his obligations because they have been imposed upon him and because he is tangibly afraid of the consequences of disloyalty. The public rhetorical appeal is to fear and intimidation; there is not even the pretext of a real choice, much less the pretext that the vassal's interests are of any concern. Although initially labeled "(vassal) treaties," these texts are actually "loyalty oaths." They are not true "covenants," but "imposed obligations" *(Verpflichtungen).*

All scholars agree that biblical texts depicting the Sinai *bĕrîṯ* have at least been "filtered" through the 1st-millennium lens of the biblical writers, and that the parallels are striking between the Assyrian loyalty oaths and the Sinai tradition (particularly as recounted in Deuteronomy). Those who believe that the Sinai tradition arose late emphasize (1) these parallels, especially verbatim parallels between Assyrian curses and those associated with the Sinai *bĕrîṯ*; (2) the fact that *bĕrîṯ* traditionally seems to have meant "imposed obligation"; and (3) the conspicuous lack of references to a Sinai *bĕrîṯ* in the 8th-century prophets (in contrast to its emphatic use later).

Those who believe that the Sinai tradition arose early emphasize parallels with the 2nd-millennium Hittite treaties, particularly to (1) the rhetorical tone of the Sinai tradition (Yahweh attempting to "woo" rather than frighten Israel into a relationship); (2) the apparent formal analogues to the historical prologue (Exod. 20:2; cf. Josh. 24, a late text); and (3) the inclusion of blessings (even in a demonstrably late text such as Deut. 28). This suggests that the Sinai *bĕrîṯ* (or whatever it was originally called) was not originally regarded as an "imposed obligation" but as a "covenant" in the true sense of the word. If, in time, the word *bĕrîṯ* became "contaminated" (e.g., by the elevation of the Davidic charter in Judean culture), 8th-century prophets would have felt uneasy applying it to the Sinai tradition. Hosea's resort to the marriage analogy and even Amos' questioning of Israel's sense of privileged election (Amos 9:7; cf. 3:2) presuppose some type of "covenant bond" between God and Israel, as does the prophetic "lawsuit" indicting Israel for failure to keep its obligations to God.

The New Covenant

Regardless of when the Sinai tradition arose, by the late 7th–early 6th century as Deuteronomistic writers were busy promoting it as the major *bĕrîṯ* in Judean culture, other biblical writers were convinced that it had outlived its usefulness. They were anticipating a new *bĕrîṯ* between God and Israel (Isa. 55:3; 59:21; Jer. 31:31-34; 32:37-41; Ezek. 16:60; 37:26; Hos. 2:18[20]). In this *bĕrîṯ*, obligations would not be forcibly imposed but freely embraced due to a transformation of the human heart. The early Christians linked this prophetic hope with Jesus' Last Supper allusion to a "new covenant." For them, the resurrection of Jesus not only vindicated his teaching but linked God's ultimate "will" or "testament" not to the Sinai *bĕrîṯ* but to the fellowship of those who are "in Christ."

The Christian tradition of dividing the Bible into two "testaments" ("Old" and "New") indicates that Christianity has seen "covenant" as the organizing principle providing meaning and coherence to the whole of Scripture. Likewise, Judaism's emphasis on Israel's unique status as "the people of God" signals its awareness of the definitive role that "covenant" plays in shaping religious life and identity. In both these religious traditions, the covenant relationship being extolled is that between God and God's people, whether understood as the Jewish people or the faithful Church. To study the biblical notion of "covenant" is thus to study what is arguably *the* central or core concept of the entire Bible.

Bibliography. D. R. Hillers, *Covenant: The History of a Biblical Idea* (Baltimore, 1969); J. Levenson, *Sinai and Zion* (San Francisco, 1987); D. J. McCarthy, *Treaty and Covenant,* rev. ed. AB 21A (Rome, 1978); G. E. Mendenhall, "Covenant Forms in Israelite Tradition," *BA* 17 (1954): 50-76; repr. in *BAR* 3, ed. E. F. Campbell and D. N. Freedman (Garden City, 1970), 25-53; E. W. Nicholson, *God and His People: Covenant and Theology in the Old Testament* (Oxford, 1986); R. A. Oden, Jr., "The Place of Covenant in the Religion of Israel," in *Ancient Israelite Religion,* ed. P. D. Miller, P. D. Hanson, and S. D. McBride (Philadelphia, 1987), 429-47.

GARY A. HERION

COVENANT, BOOK OF THE

Exod. 20:23–23:19, a collection of words, judgments, statutes, and commandments that has been located in the Sinai theophany between the Decalogue and the covenant ceremony. This legal corpus receives its title from Exod. 24:7, which further serves to cement this collection of laws into its literary setting as a feature of the Mosaic covenant.

It is generally agreed that the Book of the Covenant is the oldest recorded Israelite compilation of laws drawn from a variety of oral traditions. It has been edited and revised as the society in which these laws were authoritative grew and developed. Evidence of this history of development is complex, and, as of yet, no compelling reconstruction of its redactional history has been put forward, due in part to the lack of an obvious structure throughout the collection. The commandments can be grouped into paragraphs by topic, but both the internal logic of paragraphs and the relationships between paragraphs seem random. This, however, is one of several similarities between the Book of the Covenant and other biblical law codes as well as those of the ancient Near East.

The Book of the Covenant has often been divided into two sections based on the type of legal material that predominates in each: Exod. 20:23–22:16 is primarily casuistic (resembling case law) in form; 22:17–23:19 is primarily apodictic (commandment-like) in form. Further divisions can be made according to general topics.

Bibliography. J. I. Durham, *Exodus.* WBC 3 (Waco, 1987), 305-38; B. M. Levinson, ed., *Theory and Method in Biblical and Cuneiform Law.* JSOTSup 181 (Sheffield, 1994); J. W. Marshall, *Israel and the Book of the Covenant.* SBLDS 140 (Atlanta, 1993); J. M. Sprinkle, *"The Book of the Covenant": A Literary Approach.* JSOTSup 174 (Sheffield, 1994).

CHERYL LYNN HUBBARD

COVET

An intense, wish-filled desire that may manifest itself in various actions, good or bad, depending upon the object of the affection and the intentions of the one in whom the desire burns. Such desires are proscribed when they take forms such as envy and jealousy, nurtured in the absence of faith in God's provision (cf. Phil. 4:5-13; *'Abot* 4:1) and neglect of his commandments (Prov. 6:20-25).

The concept of resisting covetousness anchors the Decalogue (Exod. 20:17; Deut. 5:21) and arguably precipitates all of the other sins proscribed (Philo *Leg.* 79-99). The subjects of coveting can be good (Prov. 10:24; including God: Ps. 68:16[MT 17]; Jesus: Luke 22:15) or evil (Ps. 10:3; Matt. 5:28). Likewise, the objects of coveting can be good (Ps. 132:13; Matt. 13:17; including God: Isa. 26:8-9), neutral (Deut. 12:20), or evil (Prov. 24:1; Rom. 1:24). Many biblical characters, including Eve (Gen. 3:6) and Paul (Rom. 7:7-8), are affected by this intense desire.

"Covet" and "covetousness" are translations of synonyms that derive from Heb. *ḥāmaḏ* (Exod. 20:17) and *'āwwâ* (Deut. 5:21), both rendered by Gk. *epithymeín.* Translators have also used "covet" and "covetousness" for different Hebrew words that refer to emotions or actions that are distinctly not covetousness (e.g., greed, envy, jealousy).

Bibliography. W. L. Moran, "The Conclusion of the Decalogue (Ex 20,17 = Dt 5,21)," *CBQ* 29 (1967): 543-54; J. A. Ziesler, "The Role of the Tenth Commandment in Romans 7," *JSNT* 33 (1988): 41-56.

MARK D. NANOS

COZBI (Heb. *kozbî*)

The daughter of Zur, a Midianite chief. She was the wife or concubine of Zimri, the son of Salu, a Simeonite. Cozbi, Zimri, and many Israelites were said to be involved in idolatrous activities, i.e., the worship of Baal-peor. The couple's deaths at the hands of Phinehas, grandson of Aaron, ended an Israelite plague that was understood as divine retribution for the people's illicit deeds (Num. 25:14-18).

CAROL J. DEMPSEY

COZEBA (Heb. *kōzēḇā'*)

One of the cities listed in Judah's genealogy inhabited by some of the sons of Shelah (1 Chr. 4:22). It is located in the Shephelah, considered to be the same as Chezib (Gen. 38:5) and Achzib (Josh. 15:44), which is identified as Tel el-Beiḍā/Ḥorvat Lavnin (145116).

STEVEN M. ORTIZ

CRANE

One of the 14 species of the family Gruidae, order Gruiformes. A tall (140 cm.[55 in.]) and graceful wading bird, the crane (*Grus grus*) breeds in Europe and winters in Northern Africa, thus passing the Middle East twice a year. Its ability to know when to migrate is praised in Jer. 8:7, in contrast to those who do not know the ordinances of the Lord.

The Hebrew term *(ʿāgûr)* may have been onomatopoetically motivated, as the clamor of King Hezekiah of Judah is compared to the cry of the crane (Isa. 38:14; NJPSV "swallow"; NIV "thrush"). JESPER SVARTVIK

CREATION

The concept of creation in the OT and NT exhibits at least two distinct yet interrelated meanings. Creation can refer to the primordial origination of the world, the beginning of history (e.g., *creatio ex nihilo*). In addition, biblical creation can connote the continuing order and maintenance of the world (*creatio continua* or *continuata*). To the former belong the Creation accounts of the Priestly and Yahwist compositional layers (Gen. 1:1–2:3; 2:4b-25), as well as Wisdom's description of cosmic creation in Prov. 8:22-31. Creation as work in progress or continuance is stressed in certain psalms (e.g., Pss. 8, 19, 33, 104) and Job 38:12–41:34(MT 41:26). Again, these two senses of creation are inseparably bound up. On the one hand, creation accounts that describe the originating moment of the world also say something significant about how the world is currently ordered and structured. On the other hand, passages that deal with God's continual creative activity in the world frequently have as their reference point the primal act of creation.

Related to the second meaning, a third connotation of creation is evident in the biblical literature. Creation can signify new or future creation, even the consummation of history. The theme of the new creation becomes prominent among the exilic and postexilic prophets (e.g., Ezek. 40–48; Isa. 40–55). God's new beginning of history involves a new act of creation. In this way creation as the beginning of history can anticipate the end of history; history's consummation is typically conveyed as the fulfillment or supersession of primordial creation (cf. Zech. 14:6-8; Gen. 1:3-18). As such, new creation takes on markedly redemptive or soteriological features: chaos is vanquished (Isa. 27:1); the day shall overcome the terror of night (Isa. 60:19-20; Rev. 21:23-24); and a new heaven and new earth will be an everlasting source of joy (Isa. 65:17-25; Rev. 21:1-4).

In all three senses, the biblical view of creation has little to do with modern, scientific conceptions of how the universe was brought into being or how it will end (e.g., the so-called Big Bang and Big Crunch theories). Like their ancient Near Eastern counterparts, the biblical accounts of creation do not make the modern distinction between nature and culture. Human society, its character and organization, was of utmost concern for the ancient cosmologists, whether they comprised the ruling class of Babylonian society evident in the *Enuma elish* or the priestly hierarchy of ancient Israel behind Gen. 1:1–2:3. Community and culture, by contrast, do not come into play in modern theories about the origin of life and the world. Biblical creation accounts, however, invariably indicate how human society is to be structured and organized *vis-à-vis* creation. For every text in which creation is its context, the moral life of the community is a significant subtext. Moreover, the manner of report is very different from scientific reports and theories of the origin of life and the cosmos: far from an impersonal, objective style, ancient accounts of creation are characterized by drama, poetry, and prescriptive language. They limn not only a physical but also a moral and existential order.

Most modern readers of the Bible associate biblical creation with the book of Genesis, which actually contains two creation accounts, Gen. 1:1–2:3 (P) and 2:4b-25 (J). The Priestly account (P) describes a process of creation extending over six days that begins with God's command for the creation of primordial light before the watery, dark chaos (1:3). It is doubtful that the notion of "creation out of nothing" *(creatio ex nihilo)* is meant. Nowhere are the creations of water and darkness mentioned (cf. 2 Pet. 3:5). In fact, the notion of creation out of nothing was a much later tradition in Scripture (cf. 2 Macc. 7:28; Rom. 4:17; Heb. 11:3). Moreover, Gen. 1:1-2 is syntactically an extended temporal clause that introduces the main sentence in v. 3. Light is the first creative act. Beginning with empty formlessness (*tōhû wāḇōhû*, v. 2), creation according to Priestly tradition is about the formation of interdependent structures and the separation of things into their proper categories (cf. Ezek. 44:23). Throughout the process, God is unopposed; no chaos monsters must be slain in order to bring about creation. Indeed, the "great sea monsters" come directly from God's creative power (Gen. 1:21).

The creation of primordial light, distinguished from the light of the celestial spheres (Gen. 1:14-16), functions to distinguish day from night, thereby setting in motion the progress of time. On the second day, God creates a dome or firmament that vertically separates the waters above from the waters below. Separation of the waters below results in the appearance of dry land, which is exhorted to sprout forth vegetation on the third day. With the three domains of heaven, water, and earth firmly established over the course of three days, the celestial spheres of light are created on the fourth day, with teeming life in the seas, air, and on the land appearing on the fifth and sixth days. As the culminating act of God's handiwork, humankind, male and female, is created on the sixth day. The narrative sweep of creation, however, does not end here. As the climax and completion of the narrative, the seventh day is singled out as a sanctified day of divine rest (Gen. 2:1-3). Indeed, the number seven assumes crucial significance in the account: the first two verses contain a total of 21 words (7 + 14). Certain key words such as "God," "good," and "land" appear in numbers divisible by 7. Through such numerological arrangements, the author has taken pains to demonstrate creation's goal and completeness.

In addition, the Priestly Creation account reflects a highly refined structure in which the first three days are placed in parallel with the second set of three. Indeed, the overall structure may very well reflect that of a temple, with the final day representing a temporal "holy of holies." At any rate, the process of creation is characterized by a discernible rhythm of divine command and execution, as well as approbation ("good") and differentiation of material: darkness and light, water and land, animals and humankind. Certain elements such as water, earth, and the celestial spheres assume active roles in the process and maintenance of creation (e.g., Gen. 1:11-12, 16, 20). The most critical role, however, belongs to humankind. Men and women are distinguished from the animal world by their being created in the "image of God" (Gen. 1:26-27). This language of image has little to do with humankind's essence or God's nature. Rather, as God's representatives on earth, human beings are endowed with the (royal) task of managing and exercising dominion over the whole range of life on the earth (Gen. 1:26-31). As part of humankind's stewardship of the earth, human beings are enjoined elsewhere to observe the Sabbath (Exod. 20:8-11; Lev. 23:3; Deut. 5:12-15), an act that Gen. 2:1-3 makes clear is an act of *imitatio dei.*

Though perhaps reflecting Egyptian influence, the Creation account of Gen. 1 is truly unique among the ancient Near Eastern cosmogonies. Instead of divine combat and struggle among the gods, as depicted in the Babylonian *Enuma elish* and the Ugaritic Baal epic, creation according to P is wrought peaceably and systematically through sovereign word and action. Elsewhere in the OT, however, the struggle against chaos comprises a part of the creative process (Isa. 51:9b-10; 27:1; Ps. 74:13-14; Job 26:12). In these passages, creation presupposes the defeat of watery chaos, symbolized by the sea monsters Rahab and Leviathan (cf. Ps. 104:6-7, 9, 26). By comparison, the Creation account of Gen. 1 appears more "philosophically" oriented. The "great sea monsters" created on the fifth day are reported in a matter-of-fact manner (Gen. 1:21) as part of God's good creation. Many scholars have described P's account of creation as a demythologized account of the combat motif so prevalent in the extrabiblical sources, particularly Mesopotamian. Such an intentional contrast may not be fortuitous, since the account was probably written during the time of either the late exilic period in Babylonia or the early postexilic period (late 6th century B.C.E.). In addition, modern interpreters have noted a kind of systematic, even "evolutionary," development of the created order in Gen. 1, a movement from lower to higher, more complex forms of life, culminating in humankind.

In contrast to P's account is the older Yahwist's account (J) of creation that follows (Gen. 2:4b–3:25). Here, the order of creation is reversed: man (*'āḏām*) appears first, created from the soil (*'ăḏāmâ;* Gen. 2:7), followed by the plants and animals. With the garden of Eden as the setting, J focuses on the separate creations of man and woman and their vocation in the garden. Whereas Gen. 1:26-28 depicts human beings exercising dominion over creation (cf. Ps. 8:5-9[6-10]), Gen. 2:15-17 makes man a servant of the soil, a vocation that becomes burdensome as a result of the couple's expulsion from the garden (3:17-19). The creation of woman from man (*'iššâ* from *'îš;* Gen. 2:22) in no way implies subordination of woman to man, but rather stresses their common identity, as poetically expressed in the man's jubilation in 2:23. The mutual equality of the genders breaks down only through the man's blaming the woman (Gen. 3:12) and the curse (v. 16).

In the NT there is, by comparison with the OT, a veritable dearth of cosmological models. Nevertheless, references to Creator and creation are frequent (e.g., Mark 10:6 = Matt. 19:4; Mark 13:19 = Matt. 24:21; Rom. 1:20; 8:18-30; 1 Tim. 4:4; 1 Pet. 4:19; 2 Pet. 3:4; Rev. 4:11; 10:6; 21:1; 22:1-5). Indeed, during the Hellenistic period the doctrine of creation became an essential tenet of faith for the early Church in its response to Gnosticism. Echoing both Isaiah and Genesis, the NT understands creation in light of God's action in Jesus Christ, the fulfillment of history and creation. The revelation of Christ inaugurated a new age and consequently a new creation (2 Cor. 5:17). As the revelation of God's purposes in history, Christ undergirds all of creation (John 1:1-9; Eph. 1:9-10; Col. 1:17; Heb. 1:3). Yet creation, according to Paul, remains in travail, "groaning in labor pains" (Rom. 8:22). The new age that Paul foresaw is one that involved the completion of God's purposes in Christ, in the "revealing of the children of God" (Rom. 8:19). The new age described in the apocalyptic book of Revelation recounts the primordial battle against the chaos dragon (Rev. 12:7-10; 20:2-3), whose defeat ushers in a new heaven and earth, including a New Jerusalem (21:1-2), a city without need of temple, sun, or moon, "for the glory of God is its light, and its lamp is the Lamb" (21:23; cf. Isa. 60:19-20). Moreover, the new city shall enjoy the water of life and the tree of life (Rev. 22:1-2; cf. Ezek. 47:1-12; Zech. 14:8; Gen. 2:9). Drawing from themes and images of the ancient creation accounts, the new age envisaged by John of Patmos is a new creation that shall supersede the primeval age.

Bibliography. B. W. Anderson, *From Creation to New Creation.* OBT (Minneapolis, 1994); W. P. Brown, *Structure, Role, and Ideology in the Hebrew and Greek Texts of Genesis 1:1–2:3.* SBLDS 132 (Atlanta, 1993); R. J. Clifford, *Creation Accounts in the Ancient Near East and in the Bible.* CBQMS 26 (Washington, 1994); T. Hiebert, *The Yahwist's Landscape* (Oxford, 1996); J. D. Levenson, *Creation and the Persistence of Evil* (San Francisco, 1988); R. A. Simkins, *Creator and Creation* (Peabody, 1994).

William P. Brown

CRESCENS (Gk. *Krḗskēs*)

A companion of Paul during one of his prison terms (2 Tim. 4:10). When 2 Timothy was written he had left for Galatia (some texts read Gk. *Gallía*, "Gaul"), but the text does not say why.

CRESCENTS
Moon-shaped (cf. Zakir inscription; Aram. *šhr*, equivalent of the Babylonian moon-god Sin) ornaments (Heb. *śahărōnîm*), either of gold or silver, worn by the Midianite kings or their camels (Judg. 8:26, 21). At Isa. 3:18 the crescents constitute part of the tawdry attire of the "daughters of Zion" which the Lord would remove, possibly because of their pagan association.

CRETE (Gk. *Krḗtē*)
The largest of the Greek islands, ca. 274 km. (170 mi.) S of Athens. An advanced civilization, labeled Minoan by archaeologist Arthur Evans after the legendary King Minos, began to flourish on the island in the 3rd millennium B.C.E. and reached its zenith ca. 1500, as evident in extensive palatial complexes. The Minoans exerted influence on the mainland Mycenaeans and established colonies on many Greek islands and in Asia Minor. They developed an as yet undeciphered script (Linear A). By the 15th century Crete was reflecting the influence of the Mycenaeans, who began to preserve court records in an early Greek script (Linear B). The famous Minoan palace at Knossos was destroyed ca. 1380.

The demise of Minoan civilization apparently led to immigration, perhaps influencing in part the movement of the Mediterranean Sea Peoples into various places, including Palestine and Phoenicia. In the OT Crete is called Caphtor, the original home of the Philistines (Amos 9:7). From 1100 Dorians from the Greek mainland infiltrated Crete, leading to the rise of city-states. The 8th century saw the development of the orientalizing tendencies that eventually affected other parts of Greece. While Crete lay outside the mainstream of Greek activity during the Classical and Hellenistic periods, it contributed numerous mercenaries and had a reputation for fostering piracy. When Greece became part of the Roman Empire in the 2nd century, Crete remained independent until 67 B.C.E.

In the NT Cretans were among the several Jewish groups in Jerusalem for the observance of Pentecost (Acts 2:11), and Paul describes a hazardous sea voyage along the southern coast of Crete, mentioning several Cretan sites (Acts 27). Paul's letter to Titus insinuates that he left Titus in Crete to correct problems and appoint elders in the churches (Tit. 1:5). That Paul "left" Titus there suggests a trip to Crete by Paul that is otherwise unattested. The letter to Titus quotes one of the Cretans' own prophets: "The Cretans are always liars, vicious brutes, lazy gluttons" (Tit. 1:12). While the actual source of this statement is uncertain, early Christian writers attributed it to the ancient poet Epimenides, one of the legendary seven wise men of ancient Greece.

Bibliography. P. Cameron, *Crete* (New York, 1988); M. Grant, *The Rise of the Greeks* (New York, 1987).

SCOTT NASH

CRIME, CRIMES
This English term denotes, in legal contexts, a serious, intentional violation of the order of society, subject to retaliatory sanctions. A society declares through its organs of sovereignty that certain acts are so injurious to it that the perpetrator should suffer proportionately to the damage. Minor infractions are designated "misdemeanors." Disputes between members of the legal community which are not considered violations of the order of society except to the extent that they endanger the peace among members belong to civil law ("torts").

Biblical law differs in several significant respects from modern law. According to the OT, the society does not legislate for itself, but God as creator and sovereign over Israel sets standards of justice, righteousness, and holiness for his people. Israel's neighbors shared this belief that social norms have a divine origin. Israel was distinctive in ascribing law directly to the Lord, who had formed the people as his sphere of sovereignty and made obedience to his will a component of their constitution.

Biblical Hebrew lacks terms corresponding to the English "crimes," "misdemeanors," and "torts," indicating that ancient law-givers did not operate with these categories. Hebrew has a set of terms for rules of law and another for wrong-doing, each with its own nuance, but none matches the categories of crime and tort.

It is possible for the interpreter to categorize biblical laws as criminal or civil by the kind of sanctions imposed. Offenses punished by retaliation — death, corporal punishment, banishment — clearly fall within "crime," while actions resolved by restitution are civil. When restitution involves compensation for distress and deterrence, retaliation and restitution are both involved. Israelite law had no provision for incarceration.

There is no evidence in OT legal texts of jurisdictional distinctions or differences in rules for proof for criminal and civil law.

Capital crimes are formulated differently from cases of lesser magnitude. In Exod. 21:1–23:19 formulations begin with a participle describing the offense, and the verb of the main clause is in the causative passive augmented by an intensifying infinitive. This is usually translated "whoever does X shall be put to death" (Exod. 21:12, 15, 16, 17; 22:19[MT 18]; cf. 22:18, 20[17, 19]).

While it is common to regard this as *requiring* the death penalty, it is possible that it *grants permission* to impose it. In the case of murder, all indications are that it was required to purge the land of "blood guilt" (Num. 35:31-34; Deut. 19:11-13; 21:1-9). On the other hand, it is doubtful that cursing or striking one's parents (Exod. 21:15, 17) required parents to kill their children to avert God's wrath against the community. Perhaps this formulation is the Creator's authorization of the killing of a creature made in the image of God who is otherwise under divine protection (cf. Gen. 9:1-6).

Biblical law contains many capital offenses which the modern interpreter would classify as "crimes without victims." These fall primarily under two categories, religious and sexual offenses. Worshipping gods other than the Lord (Exod. 22:20[19]; Deut. 13; 17:2-7), profaning the divine name (Lev. 24:10-16), devoting children to Molech (Lev. 20:1-5), and practicing witchcraft (Exod. 22:18[17]; cf. Lev. 20:6) are singled out as ultimate violations of the religious order. Cultic duties and rules for sacrifice, etc., are not subject to criminal or civil sanction but are under the jurisdiction of sanctuary personnel with cultic sanctions. A variety of sexual unions are condemned as "abominations" (cf. esp. Lev. 20:11-21). Since ancient Israel had neither police nor public prosecutor, charges of criminal wrong-doing would originate with witnesses (e.g., Deut. 17:2-7; 1 Kgs. 21:9-13).

Actions to remedy crimes with victims would normally originate with victims or their families. Murder, kidnapping into slavery, abuse of parents (e.g., Exod. 21:12, 15-17), and adultery (e.g., Lev. 20:10) are put under the death penalty. There is a large measure of "self-help" in the apprehension, prosecution, and punishment of a homicide, reflecting probably an earlier practice of private (kinship group) revenge; the community exercises judicial authority in granting or withholding sanctuary. Although adultery is defined in Israelite law as a crime against the husband, biblical legal texts (Deut. 22:13-27) grant legal authority to the judges to render decisions and punish; the interest of society in marital fidelity supersedes the husband's personal interests.

Criminal law extends beyond capital cases, but very little is said about lesser crimes. In Exod. 21:22-25 a case of spontaneous abortion due to physical injury is ruled upon: if the woman is not injured, it is a civil case; if the woman is injured, liability is to be assessed by the talion formula. Mutilation may not be meant literally in this formula, however, for there is only one case prescribing mutilation in all the Bible's casuistic law (Deut. 25:11-12). Whipping is mentioned in one passage (Deut. 25:1-3), but it is vague about when this penalty might be applied. The expression "be cut off from their people" (e.g., Lev. 20:6, 18) may mean banishment, though some scholars interpret it as a divine sanction.

Law governing theft, loss, and damage of property (Exod. 22:1-15[21:37–22:14]) fits the category of civil law in most respects. The victim initiates the case and has property restored with compensation for distress if he prevails. Accusations of theft or misappropriation which can only be resolved by recourse to oath (Exod. 22:7-13[6-12]) may require one of accuser as well as accused. Nevertheless, the rather steep compensation for theft doubled as a "retaliatory" sanction with a deterrent effect.

Divine sanctions are threatened for the failure of the judicial system to maintain justice in society (e.g., Exod. 22:21-27[20-26]) or render justice in the courts (e.g., 23:7). These extralegal sanctions have the same logic as in criminal law, where God authorizes capital punishment and imposes it through the agency of judges.

Bibliography. M. J. Buss, "The Distinction between Civil and Criminal Law in Ancient Israel," *Proceedings of the Sixth World Congress of Jewish Studies,* 1 (Jerusalem, 1977), 51-62; F. Crüsemann, *The Torah: Theology and Social History of Old Testament Law* (Minneapolis, 1996); M. Greenberg, "Some Postulates of Biblical Criminal Law," in *Yehezkel Kaufmann Jubilee Volume,* ed. M. Haran (Jerusalem, 1960), 5-28; D. Patrick, *Old Testament Law* (Atlanta, 1985); R. Westbrook, *Studies in Biblical and Cuneiform Law.* Cahiers de la RB 26 (Paris, 1988).

DALE PATRICK

CRIMSON

See SCARLET, CRIMSON.

CRISPUS (Gk. *Krispos*)

A former ruler of the synagogue at Corinth who was baptized with several other converts (Acts 18:8). According to 1 Cor. 1:14 he and Gaius were among the very few believers baptized by Paul himself.

CROCODILE, LAND

See Lizard.

CROCUS

Any of a vast genus (*Crocus*) of herbs of the iris family (Heb. *ḥăḇaṣeleṯ*), referred to at Isa. 35:1 to symbolize beauty and splendor. The "rose of Sharon" (so the ancient versions) may be a crocus (Cant. 2:1 NRSV mg), but it is more likely the meadow saffron (*Colchicum;* Akk. *Dabsjillatu*), which resembles the crocus.

CROSS

In the NT the Cross does not simply represent the instrument of Jesus' death but evokes a wide range of kerygmatic and theological affirmations. The Cross should not be isolated from the total Christ event, the death *and resurrection* — understood as the saving act of God (Rom. 4:24-25; 6:4-5; 2 Cor. 4:10-11). Despite the public disgrace and horror associated with Crucifixion, in a very short time the early Christians produced a sustained apologetic for the Cross along with elaborate theological reflection.

The apology for the Cross arises from the fact that, while there was precedent in Judaism for the suffering and death of martyrs (2 Macc. 6:7–7:42), as well as for the persecution of prophets and righteous people (1 Kgs. 18:4, 13; 2 Chr. 24:20-22; Jer. 26:20-23; 38:1-5), there is no pre-Christian expectation of a suffering and dying Messiah, especially one who is also not accepted by his own people. While there is no clear individual who prefigures the suffering and death of Jesus, the early Christians turned to a wide range of OT texts which were then explicitly alluded to or explicitly cited to show that Christ's death was "in accordance with the Scriptures" (1 Cor. 5:3). Chief among these was the fourth "Servant Song" of Isa. 52:13–53:12, not simply through explicit citation, but through allusion to the silent sufferer, God's Servant and a just person who was "wounded for our transgressions" (53:5) and "bore the sin of many" (53:12). This is reflected in the use of the *hypér* ("for the sake of") formula (often in pre-Pauline fragments), that Christ died "for us" or "for our sins" (1 Cor. 15:3; 11:23-25; Rom. 4:25; 8:34; 1 Tim. 2:6) and in the use of forms of *paradídōmi* ("handing over," Isa. 53:6 LXX; cf. 1 Cor. 11:23; Rom. 4:25; 8:32; Mark 9:31 par.; 10:33). Such allusions serve to root the Cross in the will of God (Mark 8:31, *deí,* "it is necessary"; 14:36, "not my will but yours be done"), which itself is then foreshadowed in Scripture. Equally influential are references to the psalms of the righteous sufferer (Pss. 22, 31, 34, 41, 69) and the similarity of Jesus to the suffering just one of Wis. 2:12-20; 5:1-12. Such texts become a storehouse for illustrating details of the Passion narrative.

By the time of Paul's letters (51-58 C.E.) significant theological reflection on the Cross has occurred. Fundamentally (and paradoxically) for Paul the death of Jesus is an expression of both the love of God (Rom. 5:8) and of Jesus (Gal. 2:20). It is also an act of obedience of the "last Adam," which reverses the disobedience of the first Adam and its disastrous effects of sin and death (Rom. 5:12-21). Paul also draws on a wide variety of images from the Hebrew Scriptures to describe the effect of the Cross. Principal among these are: justification *(dikaiosýnē, dikaioún),* an acquitting of human beings whereby they may stand before God's tribunal or judgment seat innocent, upright, or righteous (Gal. 2:16; Rom. 3:26-28; 4:25; 5:18); expiation, a wiping away of human sin by the blood of the crucified Christ who is now the new "mercy seat" superseding the *kappōreṯ* of old (Rom. 3:25); ransom/redemption (*apolýtrōsis;* cf. *lýtron* [Mark 10:45]), an emancipation or manumission of human beings bringing about their liberation through a "ransom" whereby God acquires a people in recollection of God's prototypical redemption of the people from Egypt (1 Cor. 1:30; Rom. 3:24; cf. 8:32; Eph. 1:14); and reconciliation *(katallagḗ, katallássein),* a restoring of humanity and the world *(kósmos)* to a status of friendship to God and fellow humans (2 Cor. 5:18-20; Rom. 5:10-11; 11:15; cf. Col. 1:20-22). All of these, and others such as salvation (2 Cor. 7:10; Rom. 1:16; 10:10; 13:11), freedom (Gal. 5:1, 13; Rom. 8:1-2, 21; 2 Cor. 3:17), and new creation (Gal. 6:15; 2 Cor. 5:17; Rom. 6:4; 1 Cor. 15:45), suggest a change from a state of alienation from God and neighbor to a renewal of the covenant love of God and harmony with neighbors.

Equally important is the broad application to the death of Jesus of language taken from the sacrificial cult. Christ's death is a "fragrant offering and sacrifice to God" (Eph. 5:2), a Passover sacrifice (1 Cor. 5:7-8; John 19:14), a new covenant ratified by the blood (death) of Jesus (Mark 14:24; 1 Cor. 11:25; Heb. 7:22; 8:6; 9:15), and the offering of the firstfruits (1 Cor. 15:20, 23). Christian worship is to memorialize this offering (1 Cor. 11:25-26; Luke 22:19).

The Gospels were written down retrospectively from the death and resurrection, so that they present not simply a theology of the Cross, but a narrative of the life of the Crucified One. Jesus' teaching in power (Mark 1:27) and his confrontations with sickness, death, and embodied evil (the exorcisms) prefigure God's restoration of a broken world through the death and resurrection of Jesus.

In the Gospels and elsewhere in the NT the death of Jesus becomes a paradigm for Christian life. The would-be follower must be prepared to take up the cross of Jesus (Mark 8:31 par.). Paul urges contentious Christians at Philippi to "do nothing from selfish ambition or conceit" and proposes the example of Christ who did not consider even equality with God as a thing to be grasped, but emptied himself on the Cross (Phil. 2:3-11); the Corinthians are told to limit their own freedom rather than scandalize the brother or sister for whom Christ died (1 Cor. 8:8-13; cf. Rom. 14:15). In 1 Cor. 1:17–2:5 Paul invokes the Cross as a critical principle against the pretensions of the wise and the powerful. It is a stumbling block for Jews and foolishness for Gentiles, but for those who believe it is God's power and wisdom (1:23-24). The marginal social status of a community, which nonetheless has received the gifts of God, is a paradoxical sign that the Cross is ultimately wisdom, righteousness, sanctification, and redemption (cf. 2 Cor. 4:7-15).

The wealth of images and expressions in the NT is a mandate for the Church to adapt these to different periods of history. The classical atonement theories (satisfaction, ransom), with overtones of appeasing an angry God, often have little relevance to people today, while motifs of liberation, salvation, and breaking down walls of separation (Eph. 2:14-18) are the matrix of new theological explorations. Though people turn to the image of Jesus on the Cross for solace in time of suffering, the NT does not warrant the use of the Cross by the powerful to urge people to bear suffering and injustice. It is rather the consequence of Jesus' divestment of power and self-giving for others (Phil. 2:6-11; Mark 10:42-45), and encompasses the mystery that not even God could spare his beloved son from the pain of the human condition. Yet the Cross and Resurrection are the bearers of the promise of the renewal of a broken and alienated world.

Bibliography. J. T. Carroll and J. B. Green, *The Death of Jesus in Early Christianity* (Peabody, 1995), esp. 256-79; J. A. Fitzmyer, "Reconciliation in Pauline Theology," in *To Advance the Gospel* (1981, repr. Grand Rapids, 1998), 162-85; K. Grayston, *Dying, We Live* (Oxford, 1990); H.-E. Mertens, *Not the Cross but the Crucified.* Louvain Theological and Pastoral Monographs 11 (Grand Rapids, 1992).

JOHN R. DONAHUE

CROWN

A headpiece signifying position or honor. Wearing a crown set a royal personage or an Israelite high priest apart from others. Saul (2 Sam. 1:10) and Joash (2 Kgs. 11:12 = 2 Chr. 23:11) wore crowns, as did, presumably, other Israelite and Judahite kings (cf. Ps. 89:39[MT 40]). A crown, possibly a circlet, with the words "Holy to Yahweh," formed part of the high priest's headgear (Exod. 29:6; 39:30; Lev. 8:9; cf. Exod. 28:36-38). When David captured the Ammonite capital Rabbah, he symbolized his control over Ammon by putting the crown of "their king(s)" (MT) or of the god "Milcom" (LXX) on his own head (2 Sam. 12:30 = 2 Chr. 20:2). During the Exile, Esther and her relative Mordecai wore crowns given by the Persian king (Esth. 2:17; 6:8; 8:15). The messianic leader would receive a crown (Zech. 6:9-14).

In the OT the crown (Heb. *ʿăṭārâ, keṯer, nēzer*) symbolizes personal glory (Job 19:9; Prov. 4:9). The signs of old age, such as grey hair and grandchildren, comprise such a crown (Prov. 16:31; 17:6). A crown (NRSV "garland") may symbolize godless pride (Isa. 28:1, 3, 5). God has crowned humanity with glory, honor, and steadfast love (Ps. 8:5[6]; 103:4).

In the NT the kingly crown *(diádēma)* and the wreath *(stéphanos)*, given to show honor or victory, are distinct (contrast Rev. 14:14). However, this distinction is not consistently observed by the LXX translators, the postapostolic writers, and English translators.

The kingly crown appears only three times in the NT, all in Revelation. The "great red dragon" (the devil) wears seven crowns, one for each of his seven heads (Rev. 12:3). In a similar way the "beast coming up out of the sea," who receives power and authority from the dragon, has ten crowns, one for each of his horns (13:1). "The Word of God," who sits on a white horse, the one "who is called faithful and true," is crowned with "many crowns" (19:11-13). The royal crown, then, appears only on the head of the Christ, who deserves it, or on the heads of his enemies, who hope to overthrow his rule.

CARL BRIDGES

CRUCIBLE

A vessel used for refining silver, most likely made of pottery. Heb. *maṣrēp̄* is used metaphorically to depict God's testing or judging of mankind (Prov. 17:3; 27:21).

CRUCIFIXION

A particularly horrible mode of punishment by which a person (or sometimes the corpse of an executed victim) was nailed or bound to a cross (Gk. *staurós*, †; also in the form of an X- or T-shaped structure), or to a stake or tree.

Crucifixion (from Lat. *crux*, "cross," and a form of the verb *figere*, "attach" or "fasten") was widely practiced in antiquity. Herodotus mentions it as a Median and Persian form of execution (*Hist.* 1.128.32; 3.132.2) and says that Darius crucified 3000 inhabitants of Babylon (3.159.1). Ancient sources with varying degrees of accuracy mention crucifixion among the Assyrians, peoples of India, Carthaginians, Celts, Britons, and Germans. Alexander the Great after the siege of Tyre had 2000 people crucified (Curtius Rufus *Hist. Alex.* 4.4.17); after Alexander's death rebellion against his successors was suppressed with mass crucifixions (Diodorus Siculus *Hist.* 19.67.2). Josephus reports that Antiochus IV Epiphanes after his capture of Jerusalem in 168 B.C.E. scourged and crucified Jews who resisted his forced Hellenization "while still alive and breathing" (*Ant.* 12.5.4 [256]; the corresponding account in 1 Macc. 1:54-65 does not mention crucifixion).

Under Hellenistic influence during the Hasmonean period crucifixion was practiced among the Jews. Alexander Janneus (103-76) had 800 Pharisees crucified *(anastaurṓsas)* and their wives and children killed while they watched from the crosses, which Josephus calls "the most savage of all acts" (*Ant.* 13.14.2 [380-83], *BJ* 1.4.6 [97]). This act is also alluded to in the Qumran pesher on Nahum, where Alexander is called "the Lion of Wrath" who hanged living men (4QpNah 3-4:7-8 = 4Q169). The Temple Scroll from Qumran in commenting on Deut. 21:22-23 ("for anyone hung on a tree is under God's curse") seems to refer to crucifixion as an Essene punishment for treason (11QT 64:6-13), though some authors interpret this text, as in Deuteronomy, in reference to the public hanging of an already executed person.

Under the Romans crucifixion increased in both extent and severity. Cicero (106-43) called it a "most cruel and disgusting penalty" (*In Verrem* 2.5.64[165], 66[169]; cf. Heb. 12:2). With rare exceptions, Roman citizens and the upper classes were spared crucifixion, and it came to be classed as the "the slaves' punishment" (*supplicium servile;* cf. Phil. 2:7-8). The most famous instance is the crucifixion of 6000 slaves on the Via Appia between Capua and Rome by Crassus, the victor over Spartacus in the slave revolt of 73-71 B.C.E. Crucifixion was also employed against the lower classes for treason (e.g., desertion from the army) and as a horrible public example against subject people perceived to be a threat to Roman rule. After the abortive revolt following the death of Herod (4 B.C.E.) Varrus, the Roman governor of Syria, crucified 2000 Jews (Josephus *Ant.* 17.10.10 [295]); during the reign of Caligula (37-41 C.E.) Flaccus, the Roman prefect of Egypt, tortured and crucified Jews in the amphitheater of Alexandria as a form of entertainment (Philo *In Flaccum* 83-86), and shortly before the outbreak of the Jewish War (66-72 C.E.) the procurator Gessius Florus had Jewish citizens who were also Roman knights tortured and crucified (Josephus *BJ* 2.14.9 [306-7]). Nero is the first Roman emperor to engage in mass crucifixion of Christians (Tacitus *Ann.* 15.44).

As a public mode of execution crucifixion gave free vent to the sadistic impulses of the executioners (Josephus *BJ* 5.11.1 [451]; Seneca *Dial.* 6.20.3; *Ep.* 101). It was preceded by scourging and other forms of torture. Criminals were often required to wear a placard around their necks listing the reason for execution (Suetonius *Caligula* 32.2; *Domitian* 10.1; Eusebius *HE* 5.1.44; cf. Mark 15:26 par.). Victims were nailed with long spikes or tied in various painful positions to crosses or wooden planks. There is some evidence for a saddle or *sedile* to support the body of the crucified one, which served to prolong the punishment and prevent death by asphyxiation.

Often crucified people lingered for days, and death came ultimately from loss of blood or asphyxiation. Both men and women were crucified. Normally as a horrible deterrent to future criminals, the bodies were left on the crosses to decompose.

Though virtually all the ancient sources on crucifixion are literary, the discovery in 1968 of the tomb of a crucified man NE of Jerusalem near the Nablus Road slightly north of Mt. Scopus (Givʿat ha-Mivtar) provided invaluable archaeological evidence for crucifixion. The tomb is dated to the 1st century C.E. and contained the bones of an adult male between 24 and 28 years old, most likely about 1.65 m. (5 ft. 5 in.) tall, identified by an inscription as Yehoḥanan. Though some details remain disputed, both heel bones had been transfixed by a large nail and apparently his shin bones were broken as a *coup de grace.* Though this discovery is historically unrelated to the crucifixion of Jesus, it gives good confirmatory evidence for the Gospel accounts of crucifixion.

The crucifixion of Jesus in the Gospels, though narrated with considerable reserve, reflects the ancient literary and archaeological sources. Jesus is scourged (Mark 15:15; Matt. 27:26; John 19:1) before the crucifixion. He is expected to carry the transverse beam of the cross (Mark 15:21 par.) and, though not explicitly mentioned, he is nailed to a cross (Luke 24:39; John 20:27). He is publicly crucified with *lēstaí,* "social bandits" (Mark 15:27; cf. Matt. 27:23; Luke 23:33, *kakoúrgoi,* "evil-doers") who might have been seen as a threat to the social order. Despite the general custom of denying burial to those crucified, because of Roman sensibility to Jewish laws prohibiting leaving victims exposed overnight and on a feast day, Jesus is buried. The example of Yehoḥanan shows also that friends or relatives were given permission to buy a crucified person; Josephus says that Jews are so careful about burial rights that guilty crucified people were taken down from the cross and buried before nightfall (*BJ* 4.5.2 [317]), and Philo mentions that in Alexandria the Roman governor allowed the bodies of crucified people to be removed prior to a festival (*In Flaccum* 83).

The personal loathing and public disgrace associated with crucifixion are reflected in Paul's proclamation of Christ crucified as a "stumbling block to Jews and foolishness to the Gentiles" (1 Cor. 1:23). The paradox at the heart of Christian faith follows immediately: the Crucified One is "to those who are called, both Jews and Greeks, Christ the power of God and the wisdom of God" (1 Cor. 1:24; cf. v. 18).

Bibliography. J. A. Fitzmyer, "Crucifixion in Ancient Palestine, Qumran Literature, and the New Testament," *CBQ* 40 (1978): 493-513; M. Hengel, *Crucifixion in the Ancient World and the Folly of the Message of the Cross* (Philadelphia, 1977).

JOHN R. DONAHUE

CRYSTAL

A general term for any homogeneous solid with a regularly repeating atomic arrangement. Quartz, or crystalline silica, occurs as a transparent hexagonal crystal, which may be colored by impurities. Glass, first made in ancient times, probably in the Middle East, is also composed of silica and can be formed into crystalline structures. "Crystal" may refer to either natural or manmade forms. Crystal (Heb. *gāḇîš*) is included in the list of materials that cannot purchase wisdom (Job 28:18). The dome or expanse above the four living creatures shone like *qeraḥ* (NRSV "crystal"; Ezek. 1:22); the term is more often used for frost or ice, which form crystals. Rev. 4:6 refers to a sea of glass, which was like *krýstallos,* also related to the word for frost; 22:1 describes the water of life as being clear as crystal.

MARTHA JEAN MUGG BAILEY

CUB (Heb. *kûḇ*)

An unidentified people mentioned in the prophecy against Egypt (Ezek. 30:5 NRSV mg), possibly the Libyans (LXX *Libyes;* cf. Heb. *lûḇ*) in Cyrenaica.

CUBIT

The basic unit of linear measurement in ancient Israel and other ancient Near Eastern societies.

As Heb. *'ammâ* ("forearm," "cubit") suggests, the cubit originated as the distance between the elbow and the fingertips. Subdivisions of the cubit included the span, the hand, and the finger. The actual length of the cubit varied according to date and region, with Egyptian and Mesopotamian societies each employing two cubits — a long and a shorter one. Reference in 2 Chr. 3:3 to "cubits of the old standard" suggests that also in Israel more than one cubit was in use. Ezek. 40:5; 43:13 may have a longer cubit in mind, referring as they do to a cubit that is a cubit and a hand in length.

Many attempts have been made to determine the precise value of each cubit, with varying results. Some scholars have used the 1200 cubits mentioned in the Siloam inscription and the length of the tunnel itself to calculate the length of the Israelite cubit. The probability, however, that 1200 is a round number, plus the uncertainty as to how closely the present tunnel preserves its original length, combine to make this method unreliable. A better approach is that of Gabriel Barkay, who compares measurements of Iron Age rock-cut tombs in the Jerusalem area to arrive at estimates of 52.5 cm. (20.67 in.) and 45 cm. (17.71 in.) for the long and short cubit, respectively. These results suggest that the long Israelite cubit corresponded most closely with the long Egyptian cubit of seven hands and that the shorter Israelite cubit was six hands in length.

Bibliography. G. Barkay, "Measurements in the Bible — Evidence at St. Etienne for the Length of the Cubit and the Reed," *BARev* 12/2 (1986): 37.

BRIAN P. IRWIN

CUCUMBER

The fruit of a vine cultivated in the ancient Near East (Heb. *qiššu'â*), possibly of the species *Cucumis sativus* L. or *Cucumis chate* L., garden cucumbers similar to modern varieties. They may also have been muskmelons (*Cucumis melo* L. var. chatae Nand.), green fruits similar to garden cucumbers. While in the wilderness, the Israelites pined for the cucumbers they had eaten in Egypt (Num. 11:5).

Isaiah depicts a farmer's shelter alone in a cucumber field as a symbol of Jerusalem alone in desolated Judah (Isa. 1:8). Jeremiah compares idols to scarecrows in a cucumber field (Jer. 10:5).

MEGAN BISHOP MOORE

CULT

See WORSHIP.

CULTIC PROSTITUTION

Ritual behavior, in which certain cult functionaries participated in sacred sexual acts in order to ensure fertility in the land. Biblical scholars have often suggested that although cultic prostitution was considered inappropriate by the biblical writers in the worship of Yahweh, some ancient Israelites, influenced by the religious practices of their Canaanite ancestors and also by their Babylonian contemporaries, engaged in this type activity. Recently, however, several commentators have argued that there is no clear evidence for any ancient Near Eastern or biblical ritual of cultic prostitution.

The Hebrew terms commonly translated as "cult prostitute," "sacred prostitute," or "temple prostitute" are *qāḏēš* (masc.; Deut. 23:17; 1 Kgs. 14:24; 15:12; 22:46; 2 Kgs. 23:7; Job 36:14) and *qĕḏēšâ* (fem.; Gen. 38:21, 22; Deut. 23:17; Hos. 4:14). Both stem from the root *qdš,* "to be set apart, consecrated, holy," meaning that neither has any explicit sexual connotation. But because female *qĕḏēšôṯ* (pl.) do show up in conjunction with prostitutes (*zōnôṯ*) in Hos. 4:14, biblical scholars have long argued that the "holiness" of at least the female *qĕḏēšâ* must involve ritual sexual acts. The fact that the Mesopotamian equivalent to the Israelite *qĕḏēšâ,* the *qadištu,* has commonly been understood as a functionary of Ishtar, the Mesopotamian goddess of love and fertility, further suggests a connection between the cultic office of the *qĕḏēšâ* and ritualized sexual behaviors. Indeed, whether ritualized or not, it is clear that the Mesopotamian *qadištu,* who could bear children and serve as a wet nurse, engaged in sexual activities of some sort. Herodotus, moreover, reports that in the Babylonian temples of Aphrodite (the Greek equivalent of Ishtar) ritualized sexual intercourse was a regular practice.

Yet Herodotus as a source is both late (5th century B.C.E.) and tendentious. As for the Mesopotamian *qadištu,* while it is clear she could engage in sexual behaviors, there is no evidence those behaviors were necessarily ritual in nature. Indeed, the assumption that the *qadištu* was a particular functionary of the cult of Ishtar has been questioned. Students of Mesopotamian religion have also questioned whether other Mesopotamian cultic functionaries sometimes described as "sacred prostitutes" — the *ēntu* priestess, the *nadītu,* the *ištarītu,* and the *kezertu* — in fact performed such a role. Finally, some scholars argue that the term *zōnôṯ,* "prostitutes," is used metaphorically in Hos. 4:14, as the prophet condemns those who commit apostasy in his eyes by accusing them of going "whoring" after other gods. All that is revealed in the juxtaposition of *zōnôṯ* and *qĕḏēšôṯ,* according to this interpretation, is that the cultic activities of the latter are viewed by Hosea as religiously inappropriate; that the nature of the inappropriateness is sexual misconduct remains unclear.

Bibliography. P. A. Bird, "'To Play the Harlot': An Inquiry into an Old Testament Metaphor," in *Gender and Difference in Ancient Israel,* ed. P. L. Day (Minneapolis, 1989), 75-94; E. J. Fisher, "Cultic Prostitution in the Ancient Near East? A Reassessment," *BTB* 6 (1976): 225-36; M. Gruber, "Hebrew *qĕdēšāh* and Her Canaanite and Akkadian Cognates," *UF* 18 (1986): 133-48; R. A. Oden, Jr., "Religious Identity and the Sacred Prostitution Accusation," in *The Bible Without Theology* (San Francisco, 1987), 131-53; J. G. Westenholz, "Tamar, *Qĕdēšā, Qadištu,* and Sacred Prostitution in Mesopotamia," *HTR* 82 (1989): 245-65.

SUSAN ACKERMAN

CUMIN

Cuminum cyminum L., an herb whose seeds are ground to make a pungent spice which is often added to bread. Cumin (Heb. *kammōn;* Gk. *kýminon*) is sown like grain (Isa. 28:25-27). Jesus chides the scribes and Pharisees for expending energy on the tithe of cumin (Deut. 14:22-23) and disregarding justice, mercy, and faith (Matt. 23:23).

MEGAN BISHOP MOORE

CUN (Heb. *kûn*)

A city belonging to Hadadezer of Syria from which King David pillaged a great amount of the bronze later used by Solomon for the construction of the bronze sea and other temple objects (1 Chr. 18:8; cf. 2 Sam. 8:8, Berothai). Cun, named Conna by the Romans, is sometimes identified with modern Râs Baʿalbek, a village SW of Ribleh and ca. 20 km. (12.5 mi.) N of Baalbek.

CUNEIFORM

A term for a variety of writing systems using "wedge-shaped" (Lat. *cuneatus*) graphemes. The triangular heads of the individual strokes of the symbols were created by pressing the point of a (usually) reed stylus into wet clay. The symbols were reproduced with a chisel for metal and stone inscriptions. The Sumerians developed this manner of writing in the late 3rd millennium B.C.E. to record business transactions. The symbols were originally pictographic, eventually becoming primarily syllabic. A number of language groups adopted (and adapted) the system, including Akkadian, Eblaite, Ugaritic (an alphabetic writing system), Hittite, Elamite, Hurrian, and Old Persian.

MARK ANTHONY PHELPS

CUP

A small bowl that lacked a stem or handle, typically made of pottery but sometimes of metal, such as silver (Gen. 44:2; cf. Jer. 51:7). Such cups were the most common ceramic form represented in Iron Age domestic assemblages, and were likely used for both eating and drinking. This style of shallow, stemless cup is found throughout the ancient Near East, and is evident, e.g., in King Tutankhamen's tomb and in reliefs of the Assyrian king Assurbanipal. Cups are found as well in Israelite graves, which suggests a belief in dining after death. Chalices — vessels with a shallow bowl on a high foot — were another type of drinking vessel in the biblical period.

Cups are noted in association with meals (2 Sam. 12:3; Ps. 16:5; 23:5), but they occur in the texts primarily for drinking: wine (Gen. 44:5; Prov. 23:31; Amos 6:6; Matt. 26:27) and water (10:42). The "cup of consolation" in Jer. 16:7 may indicate a custom of drinking wine while mourning the dead. Since the cup was an essential feature of everyday life, it became a symbol for holding Yahweh's impact on that life, through wrath or salvation (e.g., Isa. 51:17; Ps. 11:6). The cup of wine at Jesus' Last Supper was a feature of the meal and became a symbol holding his blood in remembrance for the disciples and the early Church (Matt. 26:27 par.; 1 Cor. 11:26).

Bibliography. R. Amiran, *Ancient Pottery of the Holy Land* (Jerusalem, 1963); J. Kelso, *The Ceramic Vocabulary of the Old Testament.* BASORSup 5-6 (New Haven, 1948): 3-48. CAREY WALSH

CUPBEARER

A prestigious position in the royal courts of the ancient Near East. The cupbearer would serve wine (Gen. 40:13), but also tasted it as protection against poison. A 9th-century B.C.E. jar from 'En-gev is inscribed "the cupbearers" and may indicate an amount of wine the cupbearers would bring from storage during any given occasion. In his prison dream, the cupbearer served Pharaoh freshly pressed grape juice in a cup (Gen. 40:11); Joseph interpreted this to mean he would be restored to his position. Nehemiah had served the Persian king Artaxerxes as cupbearer before returning to rebuild his land after the Exile (Neh. 1:11; 2:1). Jesus became the subservient and trustworthy cupbearer to his disciples when he offered them the cup at the Last Supper (Matt. 26:27). CAREY WALSH

CURSE

The concept of cursing is associated with a number of different Hebrew roots, some of which have a broad semantic range. These include verbal and/or nominal forms related to the roots *'rr* ("curse, cast a spell, ban from benefits, make anathema"), *qll* ("curse, blaspheme, disrespect, treat injuriously"), *'lh* ("curse conditionally, swear an oath, pray for punishment"), *qbb/nqb* ("revile, express contempt for"), *z'm* ("threaten"), and *ḥrm* ("ban, set aside for destruction"). Moreover, the root *brk,* meaning "bless," is used euphemistically to express cursing (e.g., Job 2:9); because God is the object of such cursing, *brk* is regarded as an early scribal substitute for either *'rr* (unlikely) or *qll* (more probable), rather than of authorial origin. The Greek equivalents also reflect this wide lexical range in verbs such as *(epi)kataráomai* ("curse, cast a spell, ban from benefits"), *(kat)anathematízō* ("make anathema"), and *kakologéō* ("revile, slander, insult") and their related nouns.

Like blessing, cursing is foremost a performative utterance, or speech act, yet it brings to its object, not goodness or favor upon its recipient as does blessing, but rather some harm, withdrawal of benefit, or negative condition. Furthermore, as a blessing is most often a relational marker, signifying the existence of some sacral, legal, or social relationship, a curse usually marks an actual or possible breach of such. Thus, a curse also has important sacral, legal, and social significance. Both God and humans may curse. God, humans, animals, and inanimate objects may be cursed.

While there is much discussion as to whether the words of a curse by humans have autonomous magical power, the bulk of recent scholarship argues that curses, both human and divine, originate in the holiness of God (Isa. 45:7). This holy power can be beneficial to that which is good or in alignment with the will of God, thereby producing blessings. Moreover, such power can be destructive to all that is evil or opposed to God, thereby bringing curses. Both divine blessing and cursing arise out of the divine-human relationship. Cursing is a means by which to discipline those who place themselves outside this relationship through disobedience and may function as either a deterrent (as in a conditional curse) or a punishment.

Divine cursing in the OT often accords with cursing in the ancient Near Eastern context. Just as the Mosaic covenant reflects a covenantal relationship similar to those of ancient Near Eastern suzerainty treaties, the biblical curses mirror those treaties' enforcement provisions, which frequently employ horrific curses, brought on by the gods, to assure compliance with their terms. Within the Holiness code and the Deuteronomistic history, God enforces the covenantal stipulations of the law through the sanctions of blessings and curses (Lev. 26; Deut. 27–28; Josh. 8:34). The prophets reenforce these sanctions through their judgment oracles (Isa. 3:17-26). Such curses may result in a variety of harm, such as some manifestation of disgrace, defilement, defeat, domination, desolation, deprivation, deportation, disease, and/or death. A divine curse *(ḥērem)* is associated with holy war. A conquered city and its items are expected to be devoted to Yahweh through burning (Deut. 7:25-26). Its people might also be completely exterminated (Deut. 7:20). One who violates the sanctity of such a curse by taking banned property may likewise become cursed, necessitating the offender's death by fire (Josh. 7:15). While nonconditional or accrued divine curses might appear to be irrevocable, the language of Jeremiah seems to indicate otherwise (Jer. 18:7-10).

Humans may also curse, this power issuing out of the divine-human relationship through either a delegation of divine power to the human or a human invocation of divine power. Thus, the act of cursing is fundamentally a sacred act over which God retains final authority for its implementation (Num. 23:8). With respect to the legal implications of human curse, a self-curse, consistent with the practice in the ancient Near East, might bind and enforce a covenant or oath made by or between individuals or nations (1 Kgs. 8:31-32). Moreover, a curse could penalize improper acts beyond those in contract or diplomacy, such as the slander of a servant to his or her master by a third party (Prov. 30:10). A curse was also part of a trial by ordeal that might be forced upon a woman suspected of marital infidelity (Num. 5:11-31). Human curses too were not irrevocable but might be overturned (Deut. 23:5; Judg. 17:2). Furthermore, the misuse of curses could give rise to the imposition of legal sentence. Cursing God (Lev. 24:10-23), the king (Exod. 22:28[MT 27]), or one's parents (Lev. 20:9) made one subject to capital punishment. Likewise, cursing the disabled, especially the deaf, could result in a penalty (Lev. 19:14). Finally, the repeated presence of cursing within Psalms indicates that cursing serves a liturgical function as well as a legal one (Ps. 37:22).

In the NT cursing remains a sign of God's power, e.g., when Jesus curses the fig tree, causing it to wither (Mark 11:12-14, 20-22). Peter utilizes the self-curse to seal his oath that he does not know Jesus (Mark 14:66-72). In Gal. 3:10-13 Paul seems to acknowledge the OT understanding of the curse as divine legal sanction, yet he argues that Christ, in becoming "a curse for us," has overturned this aspect of the law, which thus allows for God's blessings to be bestowed upon both Jew and Gentile alike. Paul is fully prepared, however, to curse those who do not love the Lord (1 Cor. 16:22) or who teach a corrupt gospel (Gal. 1:8-9). Furthermore, the author of Revelation issues conditional curses to protect the future integrity of the text (Rev. 22:18-19). NT texts also suggest, however, that curses are to be used sparingly (cf. Jas 3:8-11). Jesus counsels against swearing an oath (Matt. 5:33-37) and instructs the crowd, "bless those who curse you, pray for those who abuse you" (Luke 6:28; likewise Paul, Rom. 12:14).

Bibliography. S. H. Blank, "The Curse, Blasphemy, the Spell, and the Oath," *HUCA* 23 (1950-51): 73-95; H. C. Brichto, *The Problem of "Curse" in the Hebrew Bible.* JBLMS 13 (Philadelphia, 1963); D. R. Hiller, *Treaty-Curses and the Old Testament Prophets.* BibOr 15 (Rome, 1964).

F. RACHEL MAGDALENE

CUSH (Heb. *kûš*) **(PERSON)**

1. The eldest son of Ham and father of Nimrod (Gen. 10:6-8; 1 Chr. 1:8-10). The Table of Nations records him as the father of Seba, Havilah, Sabtah, Raamah, and Sabteca.

2. A messenger who informed David of Absalom's defeat and death (2 Sam. 18:21-23).

3. A Benjaminite and an opponent of David (Ps. 7 superscription[MT 1]). KEITH A. BURTON

CUSH (Heb. *kûš*) **(PLACE)**

The geographic area S of Egypt and immediately E of the Red Sea, encompassing areas of modern Sudan, Ethiopia, Eritrea, Saudi Arabia, and Yemen (Esth. 1:1; Isa. 11:11; 18:1; Zeph. 1:1). Modern Western scholarship differentiates between African Cush and Arabian Cush. Some feel that Cush in Gen. 2:13 is a reference to the Kassite (Cossean) territory in the Mesopotamian region. Others view the reference to the origin of Moses' wife as an indication that the Midianites also had a city or region bearing the name Cush (Num. 12:1; Hab. 3:7; cf. Exod. 2:21). While these views are widespread, the notion of multi-geographical references for Cush is challenged by contemporary scholarship.

Bibliography. C. H. Felder, *Troubling Biblical Waters* (Maryknoll, 1989); E. Ullendorff, *The Ethiopians,* 3rd ed. (Oxford, 1973). KEITH A. BURTON

CUSHAN (Heb. *kûšān*)

A people or district cited in parallel with Midian at Hab. 3:7, possibly related to or even identical with Cush.

CUSHAN-RISHATHAIM

(Heb. *kûšan riš'āṯayim*)

A king of Mesopotamia (Heb. *'aram nahărāyim*) to whom Yahweh gave his people as slaves for eight years before Othniel delivered them from his rule (Judg. 3:8-10).

CUSHI (Heb. *kûšî*)

1. The father of Shelemiah and ancestor of Jehudi who summoned Baruch and then read the law scroll to King Jehoiakim (Jer. 36:14, 21-23).

2. The father of the prophet Zephaniah (Zeph. 1:1).

CUSHITE

A gentilic term (Heb. *kûšî*) designating an Ethiopian slave who was chosen by Joab to relay the news of Absalom's death to King David (2 Sam. 18:21-23, 31-32).

Moses' wife Zipporah is identified as a Cushite woman (*kûšîṯ*), perhaps referring to a district in Midian (Num. 12:1).

CUSTODIAN

A pedagogue (Gk. *paidagōgós*), normally a slave whose job it was to take care of a young boy until he began studies with a grammarian (Gaius *Institutes* 1.19; Xenophon *Laced.* 3.1). Paul compares the relationship of a pedagogue to that of a father (1 Cor. 4:15). In a much debated text, Paul develops the metaphor of the pedagogue regarding the function of the law for Gentiles (Gal. 3:24): the law was an interim relationship for Gentiles "until Christ came" (NRSV); as sons of God, gentile believers are no longer under the tutelage of the law (v. 25).

TIMOTHY W. SEID

CUTHAH (Heb. *kûṯ, kûṯâ;* Akk. *Kutû*)

(also CUTH)

A major northern city ca. 30 km. (19 mi.) NE of ancient Babylon. The large artificial mound of Tell Ibrāhîm, almost certainly the site of ancient Cuthah, was only briefly excavated in the 1880s and subjected to surface surveys in the 20th century; hence, the political and cultic history of the site's occupation is essentially limited to written sources.

Neo-Assyrian kings anxious to legitimate their political ties to Babylonia performed sacrifices at Cuthah (Shalmaneser III, Šamši-adad V, Adad-nirari III, Tiglath-pileser III, Sargon II [?], Esarhaddon [?], Assurbanipal). Periodically Cuthah joined other Babylonian forces in resisting Neo-Assyrian imperial ambitions, and was conquered by Sennacherib and Assurbanipal, both of whom exiled Babylonians by the thousands in the 7th century B.C.E. and are thus better candidates for the unnamed Assyrian king behind the settlement of Cuthean exiles in the former northern kingdom (2 Kgs. 17:24) than the commentators' favorite, Sargon II.

Cuthah was the locus of a popular chthonic pantheon centered on the god Nergal in various manifestations, his consort Laṣ, and Ereškigal, queen of the underworld. Worship of Cuthean Nergal is attested from the reign of Naram-sîn in the 3rd millennium and continues into the Seleucid era. 2 Kgs. 17:30, part of a longer passage describing the non-Yahwistic cults practiced by peoples settled in the former northern kingdom, claims that the exiles of Cuthah (here Cuth) worshipped Nergal.

Bibliography. D. O. Edzard and M. Gallery, "Kutha," *Reallexikon der Assyriologie* 6 (Berlin, 1980-83): 384-87.

STEVEN W. HOLLOWAY

CYAMON (Gk. *Kyamōnos*)

A site associated with Holofernes' march to Bethulia (Jdt. 7:3). It may be Kammona, which Eusebius (*Onom.* 116.21) places 10 km. (6 mi.) W of Acco. The site would be Tell Qeimûn (160230), the same as Tel Yoqneʿam (Jokneam).

CYMBALS

A musical instrument (Heb. *mĕṣiltayim, ṣelṣĕlîm;* Gk. *kýmbalon*), consisting of two metal (1 Chr. 15:19, bronze) discs or bowls (cf. Gk. *kýmbē*), held in both hands and struck together. Different sounds (cf. Ps. 150:5) might be obtained from cymbals of different shapes or perhaps by holding the instruments either vertically or horizontally.

Cymbals were employed in the festive return of the ark to Jerusalem (1 Chr. 15:16, 28; cf. 13:8) and the dedication of the temple by King Solomon (2 Chr. 5:12-13). Asaph, Heman, and Jeduthun were chief cymbalists (1 Chr. 16:5, 42). Later the Levites assumed the functions of cymbalists — during the reign of Hezekiah (2 Chr. 29:25) and at the postexilic dedication of the foundation of the temple (Ezra 3:10) and of the walls of Jerusalem (Neh. 12:27).

CYPRESS

Any of a genus of trees *(Cupressus)* that are evergreen conifers, often nearly cylindrical in shape. The Italian cypress (*Cupressus sempervirens*), common in many countries bordering the Mediterranean, grows to a height of 30 m. (90 ft.).

The NRSV translates Heb. *bĕrôš* as "fir" (Ps. 104:17; Ezek. 27:5; 31:8), but more often "cypress" (e.g., 1 Kgs. 5:8[MT 22]; Hos. 14:8). As with other evergreens mentioned in the OT, the identification of this tree is uncertain.

CYPRUS (Gk. *Kýpros*)

The crossroads of the Eastern Mediterranean, an island 70 km. (44 mi.) from the south coast of Anatolia and 95 km. (64 mi.) from the Levant, making it an obvious stop for both traders and invaders. Prehistory of the island appears to date to ca. 8000-10,000 B.C.E. Its earliest prehistoric connections appear to be with Anatolia from the Neolithic period through the Middle Bronze Age. Its connections with the Levant and the greater Near East appear not to become close until the Late Bronze Age, when Aegean contacts also become apparent.

The geology of Cyprus has been particularly influential in its history. The primary formative process was the volcanic formation of the Troodos massif in the southwest — the greatest magnetic anomaly on the face of the earth. The Kyrenia mountain range by contrast is a long string of uplifted sedimentary rocks, formed during the Late Miocene period. Along the north coast, N of the Kyrenia range, is the northern coastal plain. The other major arable plain is the Mesaoria Plain, lying between the two mountain ranges. This severely divided landscape led to a particular relationship of the geographical locations of the island with one another, and with outside influences. Where people settled coastal sites, the sites seem to focus outward in the historical periods, being more heavily influenced by foreign cultures than the people of the inland sites. Sites of the Mesaoria and sites SW of the Troodos focused inward or were more purely Cypriote in culture.

The culture of the Chalcolithic period is known as the Erimi culture, after the site of Erimi Pamboula. During this period the first evidence of metal use appears in the form of copper. Some scholars claim the copper objects found in Erimi sites were not made of native Cypriote copper, implying international trade.

The Chalcolithic period produced the earliest acknowledged evidence of religious practice on the island, cruciform female figurines carved in picrolite. What appear to be cult objects, or at least a birthing ritual, have been attested at Kissonerga Mosphilia, represented by a shrine or house model and clay figurines including one of a birthing woman.

The following transitional period, the Philia culture, is variously described as Late Chalcolithic or Early Bronze. There are clear developments in metallurgy, and strong links with Anatolian material culture appear, particularly in pottery. These are the first murmurings of international connections, which characterize the following Early and Middle Cypriote periods (Early and Middle Bronze).

Legendary site of Wanassa/Aphrodite's birth "from the foam," near Paphos
(Phoenix Data Systems, Neal and Joel Bierling)

It is during the early 2nd millennium that the Mari texts first mention "Alašiya," now generally acknowledged to be the Mesopotamian name for Cyprus. This name also appears in Anatolia, Syria, Palestine, and Egypt after this time, usually in connection with copper and the copper trade. During the Middle Cypriote period the tend toward regional variation emerges on the island, which characterizes Cypriote culture to a greater or lesser extent until the present day. During this period the bulk of the population seems to have been concentrated in the eastern end of the island, perhaps centering on Kalopsidha. It has been suggested that commerce with the Levant played a role in the prosperity of the eastern region of Cyprus, which may explain the development of port cities like Enkomi and Kition at the end of this period. The northern region, represented by Lapethos, Ayia Irini, and the more northwestern Morphou, seems to have begun contacts with the Aegean at this time, in addition to continuing Anatolian contacts.

The beginning of the Late Cypriote period is the era of Enkomi. Ca. 1550 a fort was constructed beside the northern port at Enkomi, and from there the huge urban center developed, presumably based upon the copper trade. From ca. 1400 onward, the Mycenaeans became a strong presence in Cyprus, leaving great quantities of distinctive pottery at southern and eastern coastal sites. Some of those "Mycenaean" forms are known only from examples found on Cyprus. Relations with the Near East continued, with correspondence recorded between the king of Alasia and King Akhenaten of Egypt; some kind of tribute was agreed upon, although there is very little evidence of Egyptian hegemony visible in the archaeological record.

Ca. 1200 when the great urban centers of the Aegean were declining, new centers began to grow on Cyprus. New centers appeared in the southwest at Palaepaphos (Kouklia), at Maa Palaeokastro, and centrally at Sinda. All these sites have fortifications constructed of cyclopean masonry and elite architecture including palaces and temple complexes faced with well-cut ashlar blocks.

Also dating to the end of the 13th century are a number of regional "palace complexes" strongly reminiscent of Minoan culture, most notably Kalavassos Ayios Dimitrios, nearby Maroni, and Alassa Pano Mantilari in the west. Also belonging to this period is the fortified settlement of Pyla Kokkinokremmos, near Larnaca. The picture that emerges is one of regional centers of commerce, competition among which apparently was not always friendly.

Although subsequent upheavals of the eastern Mediterranean did not bypass Cyprus, ending habitation at Enkomi, Kition, and Hala Sultan Tekke, there is ample evidence of continued urban life and commerce all over the island. This continuity is exemplified by recent discoveries at Idalion. Funerary remains give evidence of continuing prosperity and international commerce.

In the 1st millennium the political geography of Cyprus coalesced into the well-known city-kingdoms, each with its own character. At Kition, the Tyrians established a new, Phoenician kingdom perhaps 50 years after the destruction of the cyclopean fortification of the Late Cypriote city. At Salamis arose the successor of abandoned Enkomi. On the south coast Amathus arose, and Idalion, Ledra, Chytroi, and Tamassos in the interior. From this time onward the name Alashiya disappears, and Cyprus is known as Kypros in the west and Yadnana in the east.

Assyrian kings Sargon II (722-705) and Esarhaddon (680-669) claimed to have had hegemony over the island. As with Egypt earlier, there is little archaeological evidence, although general Near Eastern traits appear in the artistic styles and ceramic taste of the period. Phoenician store jars are common, even at inland sites down through the 5th century, and Cypriote sculpture clings to Near Eastern "snail curls" in hair and beads long after other cultures west of the Levant have given them up. At the same time burial customs often follow the Hellenic pattern with a "dromos" leading to a burial chamber.

At the end of the 8th century the so-called Royal Tombs of Salamis with their monumental construction, wholesale sacrifices of horses, and rich grave goods demonstrate a high level of material wealth and cosmopolitan trade. There is no doubt that copper was the source of the widespread prosperity of Archaic Cyprus, with the city kingdoms minting their own coins and trading throughout the Mediterranean. Great quantities of Cypriote artifacts are found in the Levant, Naucratis, and Samos.

Religion in the 1st millennium seems to center around the cult of the Great Goddess, the "Wanassa" in native Cypriote language (except at Kition, where the traditional Phoenician pantheon held sway). The most famous shrine of the goddess was at Paphos, where the kings were priests of her cult and periodic pan-Cypriote festivals took place. The Greeks identified her with Aphrodite, and the legend of her birth in Paphos reflects the antiquity of the cult there.

In 545 Cyrus I of Persia claimed hegemony over Cyprus, but once again the foreign overlord left little mark, and city kingdoms continued to govern themselves and mint their own coins. After 500 and the Ionian Revolt, the regionalism of the island became even more pronounced. Greek influence was strong at Marion and Salamis, while Phoenician culture remained influential at Kition. "Eteocyprian" Amathus had its own Egyptian-influenced autochthonous style, and the eclectic but unmistakable native Cypriote style held sway at Paphos, Idalion, and Tamassos. The copper (Gk. *kýpros*) industry remained strong, causing many economic and military rivalries. Ca. 450 Kition conquered Idalion and took over Tamassos some time later.

Ca. 300 the Phoenician Kitians were thrown out of Idalion, presumably by the Hellenistic Greeks who then held sway until the advent of the Romans. During the second half of the 1st millennium Greek and Phoenician appear side by side in inscriptions, and presumably were the languages of commerce. At sites like Amathus and Idalion native non-Greek Cypriote inscriptions in the Cypro-syllabic script continue down through the Hellenistic period.

During the Hellenistic period Cyprus truly became a part of the greater Greek world. Only Kition attempted to hold out, whereupon in 312 Ptolemy took the city and destroyed its temples — and its Phoenician character. The Phoenician sacred quarter was never rebuilt. The Hellenistic period lasted 200 years.

In 58 B.C.E. Cyprus became part of the Roman province of Cilicia and the geographical center of gravity shifted to the southwest, with the capital city at Nea Paphos, and another important urban center at Kourion. Romans did not use the old, two-stage method of copper processing, but developed an efficient, high-temperature, one-stage smelting process, all of which was conducted at the mining sites by armies of slaves. The inland cities whose wealth had depended on the second stage of copper processing dwindled into agricultural towns. The Roman methods contributed significantly to the deforestation of the island. The Roman presence was important through the 4th century C.E., with the island regarded as a center of Greek culture in the eastern Roman Empire.

Bibliography. S. Hadjisavvas, "Excavations at the Tombs of the Kings," in *Archaeology in Cyprus, 1960-1985,* ed. V. Karageorghis (Nicosia, 1985); V. Karageorghis, *Cyprus: From the Stone Age to the Romans* (London, 1982); *Kition, Mycenaean and Phoenician Discoveries in Cyprus* (London, 1976); E. Peltenburg, ed., *Early Society in Cyprus* (Edinburgh, 1989). PAMELA GABER

CYRENE (Gk. *Kyrēnē*)

The capital of the North African Roman province of Cyrenaica (modern Libya), located ca. 8 km. (5 mi.) inland. Cyrene was, along with Berenice, Arsinoë, Ptolemais, and Apollonia, part of the region known as the Pentapolis (Pliny *Nat. hist.* 5.31). It had been settled by Greeks in the 7th century B.C. (Herodotus *Hist.* 4.145-59). During most of the Hellenistic period this region was under Ptolemaic sway, but it came under Roman hegemony in 96 B.C. During the first half of the 1st century B.C., Libya and Crete were joined together to form the Roman senatorial province of Cyrenaica.

Even though the city's design stems from the Hellenistic period, most of the extant archaeological structures come from the Roman period and include a sanctuary of Demeter, an Augusteum, a temple of Zeus, an agora, the house of Jason Magnus, Trajanic baths, an amphitheater, a hippodrome, and an altar of Apollo. Cyrene also has the most elaborate and widespread necropolis of any Greek city.

The presence of a significant Jewish community in Cyrene dates from at least the early Hellenistic period (cf. Strabo, cited in Josephus *Ant.* 16.7.2). During the early Roman period, numerous Jews from Cyrene participated in local political and civic life and were not without significant representation in the upper class (Josephus *BJ* 7.11.2 [445]). During the late 1st and early 2nd century A.D. the majority of Jews in Cyrene were susceptible, for social and economic reasons, to the rhetoric of Jewish messianic leaders. These North African Jews were participants in anti-Roman sedition during the reign of Vespasian and later, with far greater consequences, during the reign of Trajan.

Bibliography. S. Applebaum, *Jews and Greeks in Ancient Cyrene.* SJLA 28 (Leiden, 1979); P. MacKendrick, *The North African Stones Speak* (Chapel Hill, 1980); R. Stillwell, "Cyrene (Shahat)," *The Princeton Encyclopedia of Classical Sites* (Princeton, 1976), 253-55. RICHARD E. OSTER, JR.

CYRUS (Heb. *kôreš;* O. Pers. *kuruš*)

Cyrus II, king of Persia 558-530 B.C.E. Though ancient sources relate varying stories regarding Cyrus' lineage and ascent to power, it appears most likely that he was the son of a monarch who ruled nomadic tribal groups centered in the region of Pasargadae. A client-king of the Median monarchy, Cyrus was apparently solicited by Elamite nobles in 553 to revolt against their Median lord. The king of the Medes took to the field to suppress Cyrus' revolt, only to have his army turn against him, and thus he surrendered to Cyrus. By 550 Cyrus had established Ecbatana, one of the primary cities of Media, as a Persian royal residence and had solidified his rule over both Persia and Media.

From the Medes, Cyrus adopted a number of administrative and social structures, giving the Persian Empire a grounding that would serve it well. With the forging together of the "Medes and the Persians" (Dan. 5:28; Esth. 10:2), a new force emerged in the ancient Near East that was to dominate its history for the next 200 years.

As soon as he sensed the newly combined territories were stable, Cyrus began expanding his sphere of rule. Cyrus' first movement was towards the northwest, attacking the Lydian kingdom, ruled at the time by Croesus, whose legendary wealth was the result of shrewd control of overland trade between Asia and the Greek world. In 547 the Lydian capital of Sardis had fallen to the Persians, and a large portion of the interior of Asia Minor was now subject to Cyrus. Cyrus' next effort at expansion was directed westward toward Babylon, an empire that had occupied much of the territory vacated by the Assyrian Empire as it collapsed. As early as 543 Nabonidus, king of Babylon, had begun preparations for war with Cyrus. In 539 Cyrus led his armies into the Diyala Plains region E of Babylon and established himself as the legitimate monarch of the region, for several months acting to improve the irrigation systems and other public resources that the Babylonian kings had allowed to fall into disrepair. During this same time Cyrus was able to strengthen forces in the capital seeking to undercut the rule of Nabonidus, and in late 539 Cyrus and his army were able to enter Babylon without a fight. Babylon was granted special privileges in keeping with its remarkable history, and Cyrus had effectively acquired rule over the entire Near East apart from Egypt.

It is presumably during the time that Cyrus had occupied the Diyala Plain that those Jews exiled in Babylon began to sense the hand of God in shaping this unexpected change in world destiny. The second part of Isaiah speaks of Cyrus as God's "shepherd" (Isa. 44:28) and makes the audacious claim that Cyrus is God's anointed ("messiah"; 45:1). The prophet adds that God is behind Cyrus' remarkable military ability, though Cyrus is not a follower of Israel's God (Isa. 45:1-4). Cyrus' conquest of Babylon is seen as the means of Israel's redemption from exile and the beginning of a return to Zion. This same positive evaluation of Cyrus' role is reflected in the ending of Chronicles and the opening of Ezra, where God is said to have "stirred up" the spirit of Cyrus to decree the return of the exiles to Jerusalem and the reestablishment of the temple. While the authenticity of such a decree has been questioned, there are clear indications both in the wording of the decree itself and in the pattern of Persian imperial policy toward subjugated peoples to lend credibility to the decree. This same generally positive evaluation of Cyrus' role in relation to the Jewish community is reflected in subsequent narratives in Ezra where Cyrus' decree to rebuild the temple serves to protect the community from interference by surrounding peoples (Ezra 3:7; 4:3, 5; 5:13-17; 6:3, 14). Outside of these mentions, the figure of Cyrus does not play a significant role in the Bible.

Following his absorption of Babylon and its holdings, Cyrus apparently spent time attending to the infrastructure of his rule. Some of the leading capitals of the Persian Empire, such as Pasargadae, were likely founded during this time. However, there is little documentation of Cyrus' rule following the capture of Babylon. By 530 Cyrus was moving into Central Asia, apparently intending to expand the frontiers of the empire. Prior to departing on this campaign, he named his son Cambyses as his successor to the throne, and placed him as king over Babylon. In the course of the Central Asian campaign, Cyrus was killed. Even near contemporaries such as the Greek historian Herodotus admit there were several versions of the story of his demise. Cyrus' remains were interred in a simple but impressive mausoleum in Pasargadae, and ancient visitors reported an autobiographical inscription taking credit for founding the Persian Empire; no traces of the inscription survive.

Following his death, Cyrus became a figure of legend. Credited with political shrewdness and military ability, many in the Greek world saw Cyrus as an ideal leader. The Greek writer Xenophon authored a semi-fictional account of Cyrus' early education, the *Cyropaedia,* which both praised the accomplishments of the Persian king, real and exaggerated, and outlined an ideal course of study to develop such great leaders. Several centuries later, the Jewish historian Josephus had Cyrus embarking on his formation of a world empire as the result of his readings in the prophet Isaiah. This later tradition is filled with historical improbabilities, but evidences the desire of many to see Cyrus as part of their own religious and cultural tradition.

Bibliography. J. M. Cook, *The Persian Empire* (New York, 1983), 25-43; M. A. Dandamaev, *A Political History of the Achaemenid Empire* (Leiden, 1989), 10-69; A. Kuhrt, "The Cyrus Cylinder and Achaemenid Imperial Policy," *JSOT* 25 (1983): 83-97.

KENNETH G. HOGLUND

D

D

1. A symbol for the Deuteronomist, one of the literary sources of the Pentateuch, representing largely the book of Deuteronomy.

2. A symbol designating two biblical manuscripts: Codex Bezae (D) and Codex Claromontanus (D^2).

DABBESHETH (Heb. *dabbešeṯ*)
A town (or landmark; Heb. "hump") on the southern border of Zebulun (Josh. 19:11). Of the possible modern identifications Tell esh-Shammām/Tel Shem (164230), N of Tell Qeimûn/Tel Yoqneam (biblical Jokneam), is the most likely.

DABERATH (Heb. *dāḇěraṯ*)
A levitical town assigned to the Gershonites (Josh. 21:28 = 1 Chr. 6:72[MT 57]) within the tribal territory of Issachar, on the border of Zebulun (19:12). The site has been identified as Khirbet Dabūra (185233), just E of Dabûriyeh at the northwest foot of Mt. Tabor. Rabbith (Josh. 19:20) may be the same place.

DAGON (Heb. *dāḡôn*)
A major West Semitic deity who became the national god of the Philistines after their arrival in Canaan. Dagon's character remains disputed. One portrayal of Dagon as fish-god arose from a folk etymology based on Heb. *dāg*, "fish." Another suggests Dagon as god of grain *(dāgān)*, the latter word taken from the deity's name or vice versa. Yet another view sees such a fertility aspect as derived from Dagon's primary role as a storm-god and reconstructs an etymology for the name based on Arab. *dagana*, "to be gloomy, cloudy."

Dagon, whose name is commonly attested in theophoric names of the 3rd millennium B.C.E., is recognized in the inscription of Sargon of Akkad as the chief deity of upper Mesopotamia during that period (*ANET*, 268), an association that persists a millennium later at Ugarit, where he is called "Dagan of Tuttul." Dagon figures prominently at 3rd-millennium Ebla (Syria) and during the Mari period (early 2nd millennium). While Dagon is virtually absent from Ugaritic mythology, his name appears in offering lists and dedications, and a major temple of the city has been tentatively identified as his.

Early worship of Dagon by the Canaanites, from whom the Philistines inherited their god, is reflected in the place name Beth-dagon. 1 Sam. 5:1-7 portrays Dagon as the national deity of the Philistines, represented by a cult statue and served by priests in his temple at Ashdod. In Judg. 16:23-24 the Philistines celebrate a festival honoring Dagon, whom they credit with delivering up their enemy Samson. The Philistines display Saul's head in a temple of Dagon, located perhaps in Beth-shean (1 Chr. 10:10; cf. 1 Sam. 31:10). Dagon, who was still worshipped at his temple in Ashdod during the 2nd century, outlived the Philistines (1 Macc. 10:83).

Bibliography. D. E. Fleming, "Baal and Dagan in Ancient Syria," *ZA* 83 (1993): 88-98; J. F. Healey, "The Underworld Character of the God Dagan," *JNSL* 5 (1977): 43-51; F. J. Montalbano, "Canaanite Dagon: Origin, Nature," *CBQ* 13 (1951): 381-97; N. Wyatt, "The Relationship of the Deities Dagan and Hadad," *UF* 12 (1980): 375-79.

JOEL BURNETT

DAIRY PRODUCTS
Along with bread, meat, olives, grapes, and other fruits and vegetables, dairy products were important foods in the biblical world. They provided great variety and significant nutrition to the ancient diet. Included in this category were milk, butter (churned in skin or ceramic containers), curds (curdled, or coagulated, milk; Gen. 18:8; Isa. 7:15, 22), cheese (lumps made by drying or evaporating milk in the sun or by cooling; 1 Sam. 17:18; 2 Sam. 17:29), and yogurt (called *leben* in the Near East; Prov. 30:33); these products did not necessarily resemble the modern foods that bear their names. Dairy products were such an important source of food that sheep, goats, camels, and cows were often

regarded as more valuable alive (as sources of milk and wool) than dead (as sources of meat). Of course, all flocks and herds were culled systematically for their meat, hides, and horns.

The proverbial "land that flows with milk and honey" reflected the Israelite awareness that Canaan, as opposed to the desert and the wilderness, provided ample vegetation for flocks and herds. Yet, even before the Israelites reached Canaan, Moses reminded them that God had provided "curds from the herd and milk from the flock" (Deut. 32:14). At a much later time, Joel spoke of the day when "the hills shall flow with milk" (Joel 3:18[MT 4:18]). Milk was used in Canaanite religion, which meant that certain practices were forbidden to the Hebrews (cf. Exod. 23:19). Milk was stored in skin bags and served in bowls, as when Jael tricked Sisera into accepting her hospitality (Judg. 4:19; 5:25).

One of the best-known topographic features of Jerusalem in the NT era was the Tyropoeon Valley, whose name was derived from the Greek word for "cheesemakers." As an indication that the processing of dairy products was well-known in antiquity, Job's maturation is compared with the production of cheese from curdled milk (Job 10:10).

Bibliography. J. A. Thompson, *Handbook of Life in Bible Times* (Downers Grove, 1986).

Gerald L. Mattingly

DALETH (Heb. *dālet̲*)
The fourth letter of the Hebrew alphabet. The Hebrew character represents both the dental stop (transliterated *d*) and, with the daghesh, the spirantized interdental (*d̲*).

DALMANUTHA (Gk. *Dalmanouthá*)
A place on the shore of the Sea of Galilee to which Jesus withdrew following the feeding of the four thousand (Mark 8:10). Variants of the name include Dalmounai (Codex Washingtonensis), Mageda (minuscules 28, 565), Magedan (Syriac Sinaiticus), and Melegada (Codex Bezae). In the parallel passage (Matt. 15:39) Magdala/Magadan appears as the name of the district.

The location and identification of Dalmanutha is unknown, although it has been identified as a small anchorage W of Capernaum.

Zeljko Gregor

DALMATIA (Gk. *Dalmatía*)
A Roman province located on the northeastern coast of the Adriatic Sea. Dalmatia provided a model for the subsequent troublesome history of the Balkan states. This mountainous area adjacent to Macedonia came under Roman domination in 228 B.C.E. However, Rome never succeeded in completely stabilizing its control over the region. Dalmatia took its name from the Delmantae or Dalmante, tribal peoples who originally occupied the area. During NT times Dalmatia was associated with the province of Illyricum (2 Tim. 4:10). Various ancient sources testify that the church in Dalmatia was susceptible to cults, syncretism, and internal strife.

D. Larry Gregg

DALPHON (Heb. *dalp̄ôn*)
One of the 10 sons of Haman executed for trying to kill all the Jews in Persia (Esth. 9:7).

DAMARIS (Gk. *Dámaris*)
A woman of Athens singled out in Acts 17:34 (omitted in Codex D) as a believer in Paul's message concerning the Resurrection (cf. vv. 16-32). She is paired with the only other named believer, Dionysius, a member of the chief Athenian council (Areopagus). This immediate association with a civic official and the wider focus in Acts 17 on Paul's outreach to high-ranking Greek women (vv. 4, 12) suggest that Damaris herself was a person of some social standing.

Bibliography. I. Richter, *Women in the Acts of the Apostles* (Minneapolis, 1995), 246-48.

F. Scott Spencer

DAMASCUS (Heb. *dammeśeq;* Gk. *Damaskós*)
A city in southern Syria that played an important role in the political history of Israel during the 1st millennium B.C.E. Damascus also appears in the NT in connection with the conversion of Saul of Tarsus to Christianity.

The city is located in a well-watered basin along the banks of the Barada River. The fertility of the region and its location on the primary north-south trade route have made Damascus a key player in the political and economic history of Syria-Palestine.

Because the city continues to be occupied, very little excavation has been done below the Roman period levels. However, recent work in the courtyard of the Umayyad mosque has indicated that the city was occupied at least as early as the 3rd millennium. The earliest written record of Damascus comes from an inscription of the Egyptian pharaoh Thutmose III, in which he lists the names of cities who submitted to him in 1482, following an Egyptian campaign in Canaan. The city also appears in three of the Amarna Letters of the 14th century. These texts do not suggest that it was an important city during this period. Rather, it was simply one of a number of towns along the northern periphery of Egyptian political control.

The city became significant politically during the 1st millennium, when it emerged as the capital of an important Aramean kingdom, sometimes called Aram-Damascus, but usually referred to simply as Aram in the OT. The first information we have concerning Iron Age Damascus comes from 2 Sam. 8 = 1 Chr. 18, which recounts a battle between Israelite troops under King David and those of Damascus. The Israelites defeated Damascus, and David incorporated the city into his new empire. During the reign of Solomon, however, a certain Rezon proclaimed himself king in Damascus and withdrew from Israelite sovereignty (1 Kgs. 11:23-25). Solomon was unable to restore his control over the region. This represents the beginning of Aram-Damascus as a major political entity.

From the early 9th century Aram became a serious rival to the northern kingdom of Israel. Bir-hadad I (biblical Ben-hadad) attacked Israel during the reign of King Baasha, after making an anti-Israelite alliance with King Asa of Judah. During this campaign he captured and destroyed a number of cities in the northern part of Israel (1 Kgs. 15:16-22). By the mid-9th century Aram was the most powerful state in Syria-Palestine, its king Hadadezer leading a coalition of 12 states against the invasion of northern Syria by the Assyrians. The Monolith inscription of Shalmaneser III of Assyria refers to Ahab of Israel as one of the major allies of Hadadezer during the battle of Qarqar in 853.

Ca. 842/841 Hazael, an officer of the Damascene court, assassinated the king of Damascus and seized the throne (cf. 2 Kgs. 8:7-15). Following two or three further confrontations with Shalmaneser III between 841 and 837, Hazael began an expansionist policy by which he created a substantial Aramean empire that included Israel and Judah, as well as other Palestinian states, as vassals (2 Kgs. 10:32-33; 12:17-18). For ca. 40 years Aram dominated the region. But after the death of Hazael, his son Bir-hadad lost control over the empire. The Assyrians returned in 796, attacking the city of Damascus and forcing the king to pay a heavy tribute. Bir-hadad led a coalition of states against Zakkur, king of Hamath and Luash to the north of Aram, but was defeated by the latter. King Joash of Israel was able to throw off the Aramean domination of Israel during this time (2 Kgs. 13:14-19, 24-25). It is probable that the account of the two battles between Israel and Damascus described in 1 Kgs. 20 has been misattributed by later editors to the reign of Ahab, and that it is probably the account of Joash's victories over Bir-hadad, son of Hazael. During the reign of Jeroboam II (ca. 786-746), Israel actually made Damascus into a vassal (2 Kgs. 14:25, 28).

The last period of political power for Aram-Damascus came in the 730s, when King Radyan (biblical Rezin) of Aram and Pekah of Israel formed an anti-Assyrian coalition. They attempted to force Ahaz of Judah to join them, but were stopped when the Assyrian army under Tiglath-pileser III marched into the region in 734 (2 Kgs. 16:5-9; Isa. 7:1–8:15). Over the next two years the Assyrians recaptured all the rebellious states, conquering Damascus and annexing it into Assyria in 732. This was the end of Aram-Damascus as an independent state.

Damascus remained a significant city throughout the following centuries. It was a provincial capital during the Persian period (539-334), and continued to flourish in the Hellenistic and Roman periods. The city during the Roman period was laid out according to the traditional Hellenistic plan. It had a substantial wall, parts of which are still preserved, an impressive *cardo maximus,* which may be the "street called Straight" of Acts 9:11, and one of the largest temples of Roman Syria. Construction of the temple of Jupiter Damascenius (Hadad-ramman) began in the early 1st century C.E., and substantial remains of its two concentric enclosure walls still stand.

Bibliography. J. M. Miller, "The Elisha Cycle and the Accounts of the Omride Wars," *JBL* 85 (1966): 441-54; W. T. Pitard, *Ancient Damascus* (Winona Lake, 1987).

WAYNE T. PITARD

DAMASCUS DOCUMENT (CD)

A sectarian text preserved in two medieval manuscripts, discovered in the geniza of the Ben Ezra synagogue in Cairo by Solomon Schechter in 1896. Several fragmentary copies were later found at Qumran, indicating the text originated in the 1st or 2nd century B.C.E.

Because the text emphasizes the sole legitimacy of the priestly lineage of Zadok, the high priest under David and Solomon, it was first called the Zadokite Fragments. Because it alludes to a sojourn of the sect in Damascus it is also called the Damascus Document. Abbreviated CD (Cairo Damascus), the text from Cairo is included in collections of Dead Sea Scroll texts.

The text consists of two parts: Admonition and Laws. The Admonition recounts the history of the sect — how it separated from Israel to the wilderness and was eventually led by the Teacher of Righteousness. It also contains exhortations to the members of the sect, designated as the Sons of Light, to separate themselves from transgressors of the law. The Laws contain regulations governing the community, including entrance into the sect, purification, tithes, Sabbath, and punishment of transgressors.

This document shows many affinities with other Qumran texts, in particular the Rule of the Community (1QS). Following Josephus' comment that the Essenes had two types of communities (*BJ* 2.119-61), many scholars believe the Rule of the Community governed the specific group of Essenes living at Qumran while the Zadokite Fragments directed those who lived in sectarian communities spread throughout Israel. How and when the text was transmitted from the Qumran community to the Jewish community in Cairo is not certain.

Bibliography. J. M. Baumgarten and D. R. Schwartz, *Damascus Document, War Scroll, and Related Documents,* vol. 2 in *The Dead Sea Scrools,* ed. J. Charlesworth (Louisville, 1995); S. Schechter, *Documents of Jewish Sectaries,* 1: *Fragments of a Zadokite Work* (1910, repr. New York, 1970).

DAVID R. SEELY

DAMASCUS GATE

The principal gate in the northern wall of the modern Old City of Jerusalem. Constructed ca. 1538-39 C.E. by Suleiman the Magnificent, it leads to the major north-south street, the Cardo Maximus of the Roman city Aelia Capitolina. The name derives from the early Christian tradition that Paul departed from the city by this gate en route to Damascus (Acts 9). Its Arabic name is Bab el-ʿAmud ("Gate of the Column"), indicating the column erected there by Hadrian and still standing when the Arabs captured the city in 638.

DAN (Heb. *dān*) **(PERSON)**
The fifth son of Jacob and his first of two with Bilhah, Rachel's maidservant (Gen. 30:6). The close relationship between Dan and his brother Naphtali is also a matter of geographic proximity; the tribes occupied adjacent areas of the camp during the Exodus march (Num. 2:25-31) and neighboring territories in the kingdom of Israel.

Initially the Danites (Heb. *haddānî*) attempted to settle in the south, in the vicinity of Zorah and Eshtaol (Josh. 19:40-48). This attempt failed in a region crowded with indigenous Amorites (Judg. 1:34), immigrant Philistines (chs. 13–16), and Israelite groups such as the Judahites (15:9-13) and Ephraimites (1:35). As a result, the Danites migrated during the period of the judges to the extreme north (Judg. 18; Josh. 19:47). Five Danite spies set out, consulting a Levite priest in Mt. Ephraim along the way, and discovered Laish, a city both rich in resources and vulnerable to attack (Judg. 18:7-10). A war party of 600 warriors soon followed and took the city, which they renamed in honor of their tribal ancestor. The Danites forced the Levite priest to accompany them; he founded the sanctuary at Dan (Judg. 18:30-31). The Danite territory was largely confined to this single urban center. Possibly, some Danites remained in the south, the core of which Solomon's second administrative district may have preserved (1 Kgs. 4:9).

In many aspects the Danites are unusual. They apparently did not have many clans (only one is listed; Num. 26:42-43), and sometimes they are referred to as a "clan" (*mišpāḥâ;* Judg. 13:2; 18:11) rather than as a "tribe." The Danites were the only tribe who failed to hold (Judg. 1:34-35; Josh. 19:47) or receive (Judg. 18:1) a tribal allotment. They are criticized in the Song of Deborah for failing to join the Israelite coalition against the Canaanites (Judg. 5:17). The best known Danite, Samson, was the most uncharacteristic of the judges (Judg. 13–16). The tribal blessing in Gen. 49:17 ("Dan shall be a snake by the roadside, a viper along the path") may reflect a reputation for violence (nothing about the Danite conquest of Laish belies such a reputation). Jacob's deathbed words about Dan ("Dan shall judge his people *as one* of the tribes of Israel"; Gen. 49:16) have an enigmatic quality, and have left some wondering whether the Danites lacked full tribal status at some point.

Another question about the Danites is their relationship to other ethnic groups with similar names migrating in the region near the end of the 2nd millennium. Greek records name the *danaoi;* Phoenician records, the *dnym;* and Egyptian, the *denye[n]* and *danuna.* All may be linked; the evidence is inconclusive.

The Galilean tribes fell to Tiglath-pileser III's Assyrian army in 732 B.C.E. (2 Kgs. 15:29), and many Danites were among the exiles forced to resettle in Assyria. The remaining northern tribes went into exile when Samaria fell a decade later. The Danites' migrations probably ended in the districts of Assyria.

Bibliography. A. Malamat, "The Danite Migration and the Pan-Israelite Exodus-Conquest," *Bibl* 51 (1970): 1-16; Y. Yadin, "And Dan, Why Did He Remain in Ships?" *AJBA* 1 (1968-1971): 9-23.

GREGORY MOBLEY

DAN (Heb. *dān*) **(PLACE)**
A city in northern Galilee, in the Huleh Valley at the southwestern foot of Mt. Hermon. One of the springs which serves as a source of the Jordan River issues from under Tel Dan/Tell el-Qâḍi (2112.2949), the site of the ancient city. A major north-south road, connecting the Syrian city of Qatna with the Galilean city of Hazor, passed just west of Dan.

Second-millennium Mesopotamian and Egyptian records mention the city of Laish ("Lion"), the city's name before its conquest by the Danites, who renamed it after their ancestor (Judg. 18; "Leshem," Josh. 19:47).

Judg. 18 tells of the founding of the city and of its sanctuary. The Danite conquerors brought with them a levitical priest and cultic paraphernalia (Judg. 18:19-20). A priesthood which traced its roots to Moses (Judg. 18:30) served at the Danite shrine. After the split of the monarchy, the Israelite king Jeroboam made the shrine of Dan (along with Bethel) one of the two sanctuaries for the northern kingdom. Amos condemned these shrines (Amos 8:14), in which Jeroboam installed images of bull calves (1 Kgs. 12:29-30; 2 Kgs. 10:29).

Dan was conquered by Ben-hadad of Aram ca. 900 B.C.E. (1 Kgs. 15:20); this underscores the perennial threat Syria posed to Dan, which was much closer to Damascus than to Samaria, much less Jerusalem. Dan remained Israelite until 732, when Tiglath-pileser III (Pul) ended the Israelite era at Dan with his conquest of the Galilee and subsequent exile of many of its inhabitants (2 Kgs. 15:19, 29). There is archaeological evidence for settlement at the site through the Roman period.

As a frontier post, Dan was memorialized in the

Fragments A and B of the Aramaic Tel Dan inscription, which contains perhaps the only extrabiblical reference to the "house of David" (*bwt dwd*) (Tel Dan Excavations, Hebrew Union College)

common phrase "from Dan to Beersheba" (e.g., Judg. 20:1; 1 Sam. 3:20) which marked, respectively, the northern and southern limits of Israel.

Excavations at Tel Dan, led by Avraham Biran, have uncovered remains of the Israelite sacred precinct and a 9th-century Aramaic inscription which mentions the "house of David" (*byt dwd*), the sole extant extrabiblical reference to King David.

Bibliography. A. Biran, *Biblical Dan* (Jerusalem, 1994).

GREGORY MOBLEY

DANCE

Dance in the Bible is associated with various occasions. Birthdays (Matt. 14:6; Mark 6:21-22), weddings (presuming that Jer. 31:22 refers to dancing as part of a marriage ceremony and that Matt. 11:17; Luke 7:32 refer to Jesus as bridegroom), and family reunions (Luke 15:25) are all marked by dancing. Overwhelmingly, however, dance is associated with cultic events. The prophets of Baal perform some sort of limping dance around Elijah's altar on Mt. Carmel in an attempt to beseech their god to appear (1 Kgs. 18:26); Aaron and the Israelites dance before the golden calf at the base of Mt. Sinai (Exod. 32:6, 18-19); and David and the Israelites dance before the ark of the covenant as it is brought to Jerusalem (2 Sam. 6:1-23; 1 Chr. 13:1-14; 15:1-29). Dancing more generally in praise of God is described in Ps. 26:6; 87:7; 149:3; 150:4, and dancing appears as the antithesis of mourning (Ps. 30:11[MT 12]; Eccl. 3:4; Lam. 5:15). Given that mourning is a ritualized behavior in Israelite religion, the dance juxtaposed to it should be understood as ritualized as well. Also, the names of some Israelite festivals are associated lexically with dance: e.g., the Hebrew verb *pāsaḥ* (piel), "to perform a limping dance," is the root of "Pesach" or Passover.

Somewhat surprisingly in Israel's male-dominated religion, two types of cultic dancing appear to be the exclusive province of women. First, women dance in celebration of an Israelite victory in battle (Exod. 15:20-21; Judg. 11:34; 1 Sam. 18:6-7; Jdt. 15:12-13). While the religious context of such dancing may not be readily apparent, it is important to remember that war in ancient Israel was a sacred activity. A dance before two armies (Cant. 6:13[7:1]) and a dance of the virgin Israel that celebrates her restoration in Zion (Jer. 31:4) should probably also be understood as part of the women's victory dance tradition. The "hand-drum" or "tambourine" (*tōp̄*) mentioned in Jer. 31:4 was a distinctive instrument of women's victory dances.

Second, women dance as part of a cultic revel at the annual fall vineyard festival (Judg. 21:19-21; Jer. 31:12-13). Although the Mishnah (*Ta'an.* 4.8) relocates these dances to earlier in the harvest season (the 15th of Ab and Yom Kippur), this rabbinic source makes clear that the tradition of a women's harvest dance endures for the better part of a millennium.

Bibliography. J. H. Eaton, "Dancing in the Old Testament," *ExpTim* 86 (1975): 136-40; M. I. Gruber, "Ten Dance-Derived Expressions in the Hebrew Bible," *Bibl* 62 (1981): 328-46; repr. in D. Adams and D. Apostolos-Cappadona, eds., *Dance as Religious Studies* (New York, 1990), 48-66; C. L. Meyers, "Of Drums and Damsels: Women's Performance in Ancient Israel," *BA* 54 (1991): 16-27; J. Sasson, "The Worship of the Golden Calf," in *Orient and Occident*, ed. H. A. Hoffner. AOAT 22 (Neukirchen-Vluyn, 1973), 151-59.

SUSAN ACKERMAN

DANIEL (Heb. *dānī'ēl, dānîyē'l*)

1. David's second son, according to the Chronicler (1 Chr. 3:1). The author of the books of Samuel remembers his name as Chileab. Since he does not figure in the struggle for succession to David's throne (2 Sam. 9–1 Kgs. 2), he possibly died before reaching maturity or was physically or mentally incapacitated.

2. A postexilic priest who returned to the land of Israel in the time of Ezra (Ezra 8:2). He was a descendant of Ithamar and is possibly the same Daniel as the priest who supported Nehemiah's covenant (Neh. 10:6).

3. A righteous and wise individual whom Ezekiel places in the company of Noah and Job (Ezek. 14:14, 20; 28:3). Although the name is vocalized "Daniel" by the Masoretes and by most English translations, the Hebrew spelling suggests "Danel" is more correct. Thus, there may be a connection between Ezekiel's Danel and the Danel of the Aqhat text from Ugarit (2nd millennium B.C.), an esteemed judge who protected the rights of widows and orphans. The connection is more plausible when one considers that Ezekiel alludes to Danel in an oracle against Tyre (Ezek. 28), for the cultures of Ugarit and Tyre were both Canaanite.

4. The hero of the book that bears his name. The book of Daniel tells of a Jewish youth who was taken into exile in Babylon, where the Babylonians trained him to serve as one of the king's counselors.

Although some stories about Daniel might date to earlier centuries, the book of Daniel was completed in the 2nd century B.C. While there may have been a Daniel of the 6th century, the traditions have been shaped by concerns of the later era. The book was written to encourage Jews who were being persecuted by the Seleucid king Antiochus IV Epiphanes. His officers forced Jews to eat unclean food, such as pork, and thus the story of how Daniel and his friends would not defile themselves with the king's food was a reminder to the Jews to observe the dietary laws (ch. 1). Soldiers required Jews to worship the Greek gods or die, and thus the stories of the fiery furnace (ch. 3) and Daniel in the lions' den (ch. 6) encouraged faithfulness to God, which would lead to divine deliverance, or martyrdom (3:17-18) with the hope of resurrection (12:1-4).

Like the Danel of old, Daniel was noted for his righteousness and wisdom. Like Joseph, he could interpret dreams, which resulted in his promotion to a high position at court (Dan. 2:48; 5:29). Just as Moses and Aaron displayed more power to work wonders than the Egyptian magicians, Daniel exhibited more power to reveal secret things than all of the Babylonian magicians, conjurers, sorcerers, and Chaldeans (chs. 2, 4, 5). God also gave Daniel his own visions (chs. 7-12), which predict the end of the Seleucid kingdom, the coming of God's kingdom (ch. 7), the resurrection of the dead, and the final judgment (ch. 12). Daniel is mentioned in the NT at Matt. 24:15.

Bibliography. J. J. Collins, *Daniel.* Herm (Minneapolis, 1993); J. E. Goldingay, *Daniel.* WBC 30 (Dallas, 1989); L. F. Hartman and A. A. Di Lella, *The Book of Daniel.* AB 23 (Garden City, 1978).

William B. Nelson, Jr.

DANIEL, ADDITIONS TO

The "additions" to the MT of Daniel are various texts found in Greek versions of the book of Daniel. Supplementing the Hebrew/Aramaic text of Daniel, they "interpret" it by adding spoken texts to the narrative in Dan. 3 and by expanding the characterization of Daniel with two more stories about him. These additions represent different genres: two tales (Bel and the Serpent; Susanna), one prayer (the Prayer of Azariah), and one praise song (Song of the Three Young Men). Although a Semitic original is widely presumed for each of the texts, they are extant only in Greek versions: the Old Greek (closer to LXX) and Theodotion (returning towards the MT). Since the OG (LXX) translation probably occurred in Alexandria ca. 100 B.C.E., these texts should predate that era, yet each text may offer further hints about its provenance. The OG seems to have arranged the texts in this order: Daniel, Bel, and Susanna. Apparently, Theodotion had a different order: Susanna, Daniel, and Bel.

The stories are not very significant in Jewish tradition, so they are considered as "apocryphal" in Protestant circles, while Roman Catholics include them as deuterocanonical and Orthodox read them as part of the LXX. Jerome used the Hebrew text as the basis for his Latin translation, but he also translated these additions and noted their differences from the Hebrew in a preface; since the preface is usually omitted in later reprintings, many considered the additions an integral part of the Vulgate. Contemporary Bibles generally place the stories of Susanna and Bel as chs. 13 and 14 respectively. The translations in the NRSV and NAB basically follow the translation of Theodotion rather than the OG (LXX).

Prayer of Azariah

This prayer (3:24-45[Eng. 1-22]) and the following song (3:52-90[29-68]) follow the narrative about three young Jewish men thrown into a fiery furnace in Babylon because they had refused to revere a statue that Nebuchadnezzar had erected for that purpose. These two additions fall between 3:23 and 3:24 in the Masoretic tradition; they are joined by a prose addition (3:46-51[23-28]).

Azariah's prayer resembles a type common in the Second Temple period, wherein a request for deliverance and vindication is set in the framework of a prayer that also contains confessions of divine justice and mercy, of human sin, descriptions of the present humiliation, a reminder of God's covenantal promises, and a promise of contrition on the part of sinners (cf. Ezra 9:6-15; Neh. 1:5-11; 9:5-37; Dan. 9:4-19; Bar. 1:15–3:8; Ps. 106). In many ways this prayer also reminds one of Communal Lament Psalms (e.g. Pss. 44, 74, 79). An unusual feature in this prayer is the reference to "an unjust king, the most wicked in all the world" (3:32[9]); this wording may hint at Antiochus Epiphanes and the Maccabean era (similarly v. 44[21]).

This prayer fits the narrative context of Daniel awkwardly, since the predicament of the three young men occurred in spite of their apparent innocence before God; in fact, some consider their perseverance as a precursor to the martyr tradition. However, if the text comes from the Maccabean era this prayer would better fit that setting and the text of Dan. 7–12. Many scholars argue for a Semitic original, and recent commentary favors Hebrew over Aramaic as the language of composition. The prose interlude after this prayer shows no evidence of a Semitic original, so it may have been composed at the time the prayer and hymn were incorporated into Hebrew/Aramaic Daniel; then it would serve to introduce the following hymn.

Song of the Three Young Men

This song of praise to God for deliverance from the furnace resembles the genre known as hymns in recent Psalm study. It begins with six verses declaring God's glory ("blessed are you/your name, etc."; 3:52-57[29-34]); this resembles the introduction in Ps. 144:1. It also corresponds well with a line in the MT of Daniel where Nebuchadnezzar is led to praise the Lord after he witnessed the saving of these men: "Blessed be the God of Shadrach, Meshach, and Abednego, who has sent his angel and delivered his servants" (3:28). The hymn continues with typical imperatives to praise ("bless the Lord") addressed to almost all creation in the heavens and on the earth (3:58-89[35-66]); that fire and heat should praise God directly after the liberation from the fiery furnace provides an apt and ironic connection with MT Daniel. In form, this hymn resembles Pss. 136, 148. The commands to praise God in this song can be divided by content into four categories: (1) heavenly bodies (3:59-64[36-41]); (2) elements of nature (3:65-74[42-51]); (3) earth and its bodies (3:75-83[52-59]); and (4) human beings (3:83-91[60-68]). An antiphonal refrain ("sing praise to him and highly exalt him forever") is also found in each verse, and it resembles the response found throughout Ps. 136: "for his steadfast love endures forever." Such antiphons remind one of a worship setting.

Questions about the date of composition should also consider the way of describing the era: the temple serves as the place of worship, and no persecution of Jews is apparent. The Song of the Three Young Men has found a Christian liturgical usage in the Liturgy of the Hours, as a canticle paralleling some of the Psalms sung or recited in the office.

Susanna

This story about Daniel saving Susanna, a Babylonian Jewish woman, begins by describing the lust of two Jewish elders for the wife of their colleague and friend, Joakim (vv. 1-14). Soon they discover that each shares the same desires, so they concoct a plot to trap her into having sexual relations with them while she is bathing alone in her garden: they will threaten to accuse her of adultery with a young man in the garden if she refuses them (vv. 15-27). But she does refuse, preferring to fall into their wicked injustice than to sin in God's eyes. So in a public trial she is charged with adultery, the sentence for which is death (vv. 28-41). Modern readers may be amazed that the two judges also give the witness against her, and that she is never allowed to speak at the trial; but she does raise her eyes to heaven, because she trusts in God. After the assembly accepts the testimony of the elders and condemns her to death, Susanna prays a loud prayer of complaint to God, who knows all, that she has been falsely accused of actions she did not commit and is about to die despite her innocence. Finally, a young man named Daniel is led by a spirit of God to try to save this innocent woman, which he accomplishes by a wily process of interrogation of the two elders, showing how they have given conflicting versions of an important detail: under what tree did this occur? As a result, Daniel convicts them of their crime (vv. 42-64). The "whole congregation" rises up against the two elders and executes them, thus saving the innocent blood of Susanna. She receives praise from her parents and husband, and Daniel rises in stature with the people from that day.

Several theological motifs grace this story. God is all-knowing Lord of the Universe, as well as Lord of history and savior of individuals who are righteous. God responds to the outcry of the oppressed (as in the Exodus). A holy spirit inhabits the young Daniel, and God's saving activity occurs through his boldness and his investigation in the mold of a trickster. God also allows the wicked to receive as punishment what they had planned against an innocent woman, the other aspect of a saving God. This story elevates the characters of great individuals and leaves them as role models.

The story described here comes from the version of Theodotion, which differs considerably from the OG in length, amount of detail, and order of contents. The OG puts far less emphasis on Susanna as a character, focusing more on the sins of the elders. Details of her bathing are much less elaborated, nor is she the focus of the conclusion; OG, however, ends with an exhortation to search for more youths like Daniel, who will be pious and filled with knowledge and understanding (v. 62b). In the OG this story usually stands as either ch. 13 or 14. This shorter version, focusing on leadership qualities, probably served as a source for the later translation of Theodotion, which usually locates the story of Susanna before Dan. 1, effectively introducing the pious young Jewish man before the so-called court tales in Dan. 1–6.

A Hebrew original seems the best explanation of various translation anomalies, and this is most easily understood as composed in Palestine. But the OG version, which is more oriented toward social issues and categories, is often connected with Alexandria, whereas Theodotion, with its emphasis on individual character and ethics, seems more reminiscent of the Hellenistic novella, which also emerged in Diaspora settings (parallel to the Babylonian setting of the story). A hypothesis that Theodotion's translation was made in either Syria (Antioch) or in Asia Minor (Ephesus) better fits these qualities of the more popular translation. Recent feminist scholarship seems to explore both paths: with the focus on individuals, Susanna takes second place to Daniel (Theodotion), while analysis of gender and social roles (Susanna as woman and outsider) allows the story to present a subtle but challenging message: Susanna and Judaism are both viewed as "outsiders." Recent study ranges over various interpretive stances, from legal analysis of the court case to the history of Christian interpretation, especially the allegorical position developed in the patristic era. Like Judith, Susanna has provided an immensely popular biblical topic for painters. Contemporary study of these paintings tends to focus on details from the more colorful Theodotion text and may shed much interpretive light on responses to this tale throughout the centuries. In the Roman Catholic lectionary the story of Susanna has traditionally been read on a Saturday in Lent.

Bel and the Serpent

Three stories about Daniel's ridicule of Babylonian idolatry and his efforts to suppress it are joined in this addition, also known as Bel and the Dragon (or Snake). The first concerns the daily food and drink rations (sacrifices) brought to the image of Bel (Marduk) each day. The king reveres this god and questions Daniel why he does not worship Bel. Daniel responds that Bel is no god and has never eaten or drunk anything brought before the image. The king challenges 70 priests of Bel to demonstrate who actually eats the offerings. Daniel's clever wisdom allows him to demonstrate that the food and drink are actually consumed by the priests and their families, so the king turns on them and vindicates Daniel. The second story introduces a serpent which the Babylonians revered and the king's challenge to Daniel to deny that this was a living god. In this case Daniel demonstrates that the living serpent is not a god by feeding it a mixture which causes the serpent to burst after swallowing it; if the serpent had been divine it would not have eaten the deadly cakes. In the third story, Babylonians angry at their king for allowing a Jew to ridicule their gods force him to turn Daniel over to them, and they toss him into a lions' den. The prophet Habakkuk is then transported by an angel to Babylon to feed Daniel, so when the king comes later to the lions' den to mourn Daniel he finds him safe and healthy. The king then confesses the greatness of Daniel's god ("and there is no other besides you" (v. 41) and gives Daniel's enemies the treatment they had planned for him.

In each case, Daniel demonstrates the folly of Babylon's idols and those who maintain their worship: Bel is not living, and the serpent is no god. In each case the young Jewish man not only ridicules the foreign god but also shows that idol worship should not even be allowed. In each case Daniel operates with a cunning and wisdom reminiscent of some early stories of Israel (e.g., the midwives in Exod. 1). Escaping from the lions' den demonstrates again that the God of the Jews never abandons the faithful ones; in each case God effects a dramatic reversal of fortunes of the two sides in the contest. Some contend that these stories demonstrate a subtle midrash on Jer. 51:34-35, 44; if so, readers could reflect on Babylonian cruelty against Jerusalem in the 6th century B.C.E. and recognize its reversal in these stories.

The OG and Theodotion versions of this story differ much less than in Susanna, but enough to distinguish some tendencies. In OG Daniel descends from a priestly line, so this story likely predates Dan. 1–6 with its very different view of him; also the notion of a Jewish priest in the king's court may be imagined for the situation in Ptolemaic Egypt rather than others at that time. If the original language of the story is Hebrew, then a Palestinian setting before the harsh relations with Antiochus Epiphanes may be envisioned. A diaspora setting might better explain the content and theology of the story, but the evidence for either position seems less than sufficient. In the history of interpretation, this story has held far less attraction for hearers than that of Susanna.

Bibliography. J. Collins, *Daniel.* Herm (Minneapolis, 1993); M. D. Garrard, "Artemisia and Susanna," in *Feminism and Art History,* ed. N. Broude and M. D. Garrard (New York, 1982), 147-71; A.-J. Levine, "'Hemmed In on Every Side': Jews and Women in the Book of Susanna," in *A Feminist Companion to Esther, Judith and Susanna,* ed. A. Brenner (Sheffield, 1995), 303-23; C. A. Moore, *Daniel, Esther and Jeremiah: The Additions.* AB 44 (Garden City, 1977); E. Spolsky, ed., *The Judgment of Susanna.* SBLEJL 11 (Atlanta, 1996); M. J. Steussy, *Gardens in Babylon: Narrative and Faith in the Greek Legends of Daniel.* SBLDS 141 (Atlanta, 1993).

JOHN C. ENDRES, S.J.

DANIEL, BOOK OF

The account of the activity and visions of Daniel, a noble Jew exiled at Babylon.

Contents

The book of Daniel contains two collections of material: (1) stories that describe the pious wisdom of four of the exiles (Dan. 2–6) and (2) vision reports ascribed to Daniel (chs. 7–12). Both the narratives and the vision reports give expression to the conflict of cultures.

The book sets the stage for these stories by reporting on the deportation of prominent citizens by Nebuchadnezzar. Even in this first story one notices the clash between the cultures of the Jews and their captors. This remains an element in the plots in subsequent stories — accounts which have become some of the most treasured Bible stories, such as the narratives of the fiery furnace (ch. 3) and the lions' den (ch. 6). The cultural and theological conflict manifests itself in the description of the pagan rulers. Reports regarding the king who wanted a dream interpreted but refused to recount it for the interpreters (ch. 2) and Nebuchadnezzar's bizarre display of eating grass like a cow (ch. 4) depict eccentric behavior. The most pointed critique of the Babylonian captors comes in ch. 5, from which we get the phrase "handwriting on the wall" from the description of the unexpected event at Belshazzar's feast.

Themes of conflict continue in the vision reports. Now, however, the interplay between history and the celestial players becomes more explicit. Each report provides a cryptic version of the history of the empires and predicts a demise of the colonial system to be replaced by the reign of God and those faithful to God. The first vision report (ch. 7) recounts the passing of the world empires and the coming on the clouds of "one like a son of man" (7:13) who receives power from "the Ancient of Days." A parallel can be drawn between this chapter and ch. 2, which also speaks of the end of empires replaced with a new reign of God. The first two vision reports use animal depictions for the empires. Just as ch. 4 portrays the king as not acting human, the vision reports categorize the empire as the pinnacle of humanity which is anything but human. The first vision features four beasts, the second (ch. 8) a ram and a goat. The vision reports are interrupted by prayer and a prediction of the future (ch. 9). The last and longest report (chs. 10–11) recounts the conflict between the Seleucid and Ptolemaic empires. The conclusion of the book describes Daniel receiving instruction from an angel interpreter, which occurs in the other vision reports as well. In this instruction, however, the text gives one of the earliest and most explicit biblical references to resurrection, life after death. The instruction also counsels secrecy until the proper time.

Problem of Bilingualism

The book of Daniel moves from Hebrew (1:1–2:4a) into Aramaic, which was the language of diplomatic activity at this time (2:4b–7:28), and returns to Hebrew (8:1–12:13). Even the materials from Qumran indicate the bilingual nature of the book. Scholars have offered a number of suggestions to explain this phenomenon.

Such proposals typically try to explain the bilingual character of the book through reconstruction of its redaction or composition. The shift in language becomes more acutely problematic because it does not fall at the change in literary form. One theory is that there was an Aramaic text to the entire book which is no longer available. However, the retroversion of the present Hebrew text into Aramaic yields this thesis unlikely. Hence a more complex redaction history must be offered. The narratives were circulated as individual stories brought together first in a collection encompassing 3:31 through 6:28 sometime during the 3rd century B.C.E. This collection was expanded by adding ch. 2. Ch. 7 was added to the Aramaic collection probably during the early Seleucid persecution. While still in the context of persecution chs. 8–12 were affixed. It is difficult to determine whether ch. 1 was written in Hebrew to act as an *inclusio* for the Aramaic collection (chs. 2–7) or whether it was composed in Hebrew as an introduction to the entire book as we have it.

Another strategy for understanding the bilingual nature of the book focuses on sociological parallels. This approach asks the question: How does bilingualism work in communities with disproportionate power? These scholars argue that bilingualism in the book of Daniel is a reflection of the colonial system. Colonized peoples maintain an indigenous language as well as the colonial language. The book of Daniel reflects this political function of language.

Both approaches provide clues about the function of bilingualism as both rhetorical strategy and an outgrowth of a redactional history.

Date

The debated data come in three categories: linguistic, historical allusions, and knowledge of Persian and Hellenistic customs. While the narratives describe a Babylonian setting, only a minority of scholars accept this assertion at face value. The majority claim that the data suggest more realistically a 2nd-century Hellenistic context. Although the linguistic evidence is meager, the presence of Greek and Persian loanwords would seem to indicate a Hellenistic context. Historical problems plague chs. 1–6. The date of Nebuchadnezzar's campaign into Jerusalem in 606 seems unlikely according to Babylonian sources, but rather seems to be dependent on 2 Chr. 36:6. The designation of Belshazzar as king seems to be less than accurate; he was rather co-regent with his father but never king in his own right. Another problem is Darius the Mede. A number of rulers of the Persian Empire were named Darius, but none of them a Mede. No Median Empire reigned over Babylon between the Neo-Babylonian and Persian empires. While the narratives contain a number of problems with regard to historical allusions, the references in ch. 11 seem very accurate up to the description of the persecution in 167. However, the prediction about the death of Antiochus IV Epiphanes in 164 does not conform with other sources, which indicate a date a little after 167. If one understands ch. 11 as *vaticinia ex eventu* (prophecy after the fact), then a 2nd-century date seems most appropriate. However, if one accepts the possibility of detailed forecasting, then the setting depicted in the text is viable (the problems of historical accuracy alluded to above persist, nonetheless).

Placement in the Canon

The book of Daniel maintains a different placement in the Hebrew Bible than in the Christian OT. Both arrangements were informed by the location of the story line in history. The Hebrew Bible places Daniel in the collection of Writings (*Ketubim*) between Esther and Ezra-Nehemiah. This is because according to the narrative the events follow the intrigues described in the book of Esther and precede the reconstruction efforts of Ezra and Nehemiah. The Christian canon takes its order from the books of the Greek OT (LXX), in which Daniel follows Ezekiel, the last of the Major Prophets. It precedes the Book of the Twelve (the Minor Prophets).

While the Christian canon agrees on the placement of the book, there is no agreement on its scope. The Protestant Bible includes only those portions of Daniel contained in the Hebrew Bible, but Roman Catholic tradition follows the Greek text, including the Prayer of Azariah and the Song of the Three Young Men (or Children) in ch. 3 between vv. 23 and 24 and adding the stories of Susannah and Bel and the Dragon as chs. 13 and 14. In the Protestant Bible these are seen as additions and are regarded among the Apocrypha or Deuterocanonicals.

Bibliography. J. J. Collins, *Daniel.* Herm (Minneapolis, 1993); T. Craven, "Daniel and Its Additions," in *The Women's Bible Commentary,* ed. C. A. Newsom and S. H. Ringe (Louisville, 1992), 191-94; D. N. Fewell, *Circle of Sovereignty: Plotting Politics in the Book of Daniel* (Nashville, 1991); André Lacocque, *The Book of Daniel* (Atlanta, 1979); D. Smith, *The Religion of the Landless* (Bloomington, Ind., 1989).

STEPHEN BRECK REID

DAN-JAAN (Heb. *dān yaʿan*)
Part of the route that David's men traveled while taking a census of the people (2 Sam. 24:6 MT). This site was located in the extreme northern part of the land of Israel between Mt. Hermon and Sidon. The LXX reads "to Dan and from Dan." Some interpreters read *dān-yaʿar,* "Dan of the thicket," demonstrating Aramaic influence (cf. NEB "Dan-Iyyon").

PETE F. WILBANKS

DANNAH (Heb. *dannâ*)
A city in the hill country of Judah (Josh. 15:49), near Debir (Kiriath-sannah). Its location has not yet been identified.

DAPHNE (Gk. *Daphnē*)
A town in the vicinity of Antioch (Syria), ca. 8 km. (5 mi.) to the southwest. Located in a magnificent garden some 16 km. (10 mi.) in circumference, Daphne was the site of many sanctuaries, including the exquisite temple of Apollo, at the foot of the ever-flowing springs. Daphne was also a place of asylum (Strabo *Geog.* 16.2.6); Onias the high priest fled to Apollo's sanctuary after exposing Menelaus' graft (ca. 171 B.C.E.; 2 Macc. 4:32-33).

DARDA (Heb. *dardaʿ*) (also DARA)
One of four famous Israelites whose wisdom was surpassed only by King Solomon (1 Kgs. 4:31[MT 5:11]). He is called a "son of Mahol," probably des-

ignating a member of an orchestral guild. At 1 Chr. 2:6 he is included among the five descendants of Zerah of Judah (here called Dara, following MT *dāraʿ*).

DARIC

A Persian gold coin weighing ca. 8.4 g. (.3 oz.), bearing the image of Darius I Hystaspes (ca. 500 B.C.E.) and therefore assumed to have been coined by that ruler. The name may derive from Akk. *darag mana* (one sixtieth of a mina; Heb. *ʾăḏarkôn;* Ezra 8:27; cf. 1 Chr. 29:7). The coin (*darkĕmôn*) included among the exiles' offerings during the reigns of Cyrus (Ezra 2:69) and Artaxerxes (Neh. 7:70-72) may have been a drachma.

DARIUS (Heb. *dārĕyāweš;* O. Pers. *darayavahuš*)

1. Darius I, king of Persia 522-486 B.C.E. Darius, of uncertain lineage, came to the throne of Persia through suspect circumstances. His famed Behistun inscription claims a pretender attempted to take the throne from Cambyses, the son of Cyrus the Great, who had successfully conquered Egypt in 525. While returning to Persia, Cambyses died with mysterious suddenness and Darius, with the help of several Persian noble families, suppressed the pretender's revolt. Following a favorable oracle denoting him as king, Darius proceeded to consolidate his rule over an empire plagued with unrest over succession to the throne. He was successful largely due to the support of the Persian nobility. In return, Darius is credited with establishing satrapies, large administrative clusters of smaller political entities, and installing members of the Persian nobility as governors (satraps) over these larger units. Provided with a measure of independence, the satraps nonetheless seemed comfortable in remaining loyal to the Persian court throughout Darius's reign and beyond.

One of the Persian Empire's more skilled administrators, Darius is credited by the Greeks with being a lawgiver. This may well be a reflection of Darius' efforts at codifying existing legal customs in the various subject territories as he undertook the reorganization of an empire that had been created by the military prowess of his predecessors Cyrus and Cambyses, but whose legal and administrative status had been neglected. A well-known example of Darius' concern for the social order of subject territories is the mission of the Egyptian collaborator Udjahorresnet, who records he was commissioned by Darius to attend to the reorganization of scribal schools among other significant tasks. In addition, Darius undertook an extensive campaign of public works in Egypt, including completion of the precursor of the Suez Canal.

Darius' own military expansion of the empire was largely directed westward, and by 493 the Persians controlled all the Greek city-states of Asia Minor. Realizing that the free cities of the Greek mainland presented a continuing source of agitation against Persian rule in Asia Minor, Darius undertook extensive preparations prior to launching an extended campaign against the Greeks. In 490 a sizable force of perhaps 15 thousand Persian troops gathered on the plains of Marathon to do battle with a coalition of Greek forces. The battle was won by the Greeks, and the Persians withdrew with heavy losses, only to return several decades later under Xerxes I to renew the conflict with Greece. Marathon stood in the Greek consciousness as a symbol of Greek determination to remain free of foreign tyrants, though to the Persians it may have simply represented a minor reversal.

For the postexilic community of Yehud, the Persian administrative district surrounding Jerusalem, Darius served as a supportive figure in efforts to rebuild the temple. Ezra recounts how, despite returning to Jerusalem under Cyrus, work on the temple in Jerusalem did not begin in earnest until the second year of Darius' reign, ca. 520 (Ezra 4:24). During that year, the prophets Haggai and Zechariah, working with Zerubbabel the governor and Jeshua the high priest, initiated a successful community effort to rebuild the temple which had been in ruins since the Babylonian conquest of 587. Local opponents of this effort petitioned Darius to have the work stopped (Ezra 5:6-17), to which Darius responded with a clear order upholding Cyrus' earlier decree allowing for the rebuilding efforts and calling on his imperial officials to support the work (6:1-12). While the authenticity of portions of these accounts have been questioned, the general concern for proper procedure seems to be in keeping with Darius' larger role of using legislation to administer an increasingly complex and varied empire.

Among Darius' innovations was the introduction of imperial coinage, what the Greeks called the "daric." He also established several new forms of taxation, placing the empire on a firm financial base. Darius engaged in building extensive palace complexes at Susa and Persepolis, emphasizing his complete control of royal power within the heartland of the Persian Empire. Following the defeat of the Persian forces in the Battle of Marathon, he apparently undertook extensive preparations for a new military effort against the Greeks. Darius' death after 36 years of rule (and at an age beyond 60) brought these preparations to a halt until his son and successor Xerxes I could undertake a renewed attempt to defeat the Greeks.

Bibliography. J. M. Cook, *The Persian Empire* (New York, 1983), 50-182; M. A. Dandamaev, *A Political History of the Achaemenid Empire* (Leiden, 1989), 83-178. KENNETH G. HOGLUND

2. Darius II Ochus (423-404), son of Artaxerxes I; also called Nothus ("the bastard") because his mother was a Babylonian concubine. Manipulated during much of his reign by Parysatis, his half-sister and wife, Darius managed to regain Greek cities in Asia Minor by siding with Sparta during the Peloponnesian War (431-404). He is mentioned in the Jewish Aramaic papyri from Elephantine.

3. Darius III Codommanus (336-331), grandnephew of Artaxerxes III. The last Achaemenid monarch, he suffered repeated defeats at the hands of Alexander the Great and the Macedonian forces (cf. 1 Macc. 1:1-8).

4. Darius the Mede, mentioned only in the book of Daniel. He is depicted as gaining rule over the Neo-Babylonian Empire in the wake of the capture of Babylon and the death of Belshazzar (Dan. 5:30-31). Called the son of a certain Ahasuerus and a Mede by birth (Dan. 9:1), he divided the kingdom into 120 satrapies administered by three "presidents" (6:1). It was this king who ordered Daniel into the lions' den (Dan. 6:16). However, Greek and Babylonian sources indicate that it was the Persian Cyrus I who conquered Babylon, and extrabiblical accounts mention neither a Median king named Darius nor Median invasion of Babylonia. Some would identify this Darius with Nabonidus, the last king of Babylon and coregent with Belshazzar; or Cyrus I, perhaps confused with Darius I.

DARKNESS

The absence of light, a frequent image in both the OT and NT; the NT's usage is highly influenced by the OT. Darkness was present at the beginning, and God's power worked against it in creation (Gen. 1). Darkness is subsequently a master image for chaos, separation, and death, and a synonym of sin and evil. In the intertestamental period, the Dead Sea Scrolls illustrate the metaphorical use of darkness as a characteristic of the forces hostile to God and in battle with him (War of the Sons of Light and the Sons of Darkness; cf. 1 En. 108:11-15; T. Levi 19:1).

In the NT, words translated "darkness" occur often, and in virtually every case they are used in a metaphorical sense. An exception is John 6:17, where the word is literal. In the account of the death of Jesus (Mark 15:33 par.), the darkness may be both literal and figurative.

When used metaphorically, "darkness" can be equivalent to Satan (Luke 22:53) and can refer to eternal destiny without God (Matt. 8:12; 22:13; 25:30). The coming of Jesus into the world signals the beginning of the saving light's confrontation with darkness (Luke 1:79), and his ministry can be described as the bringing of light to those in darkness (Matt. 4:16, quoting Isa. 9:2[MT 1]). The response to Jesus is to choose between light and darkness, and most people prefer darkness to hide their sins (John 3:19). Accordingly, pagan life is characterized by darkness (Rom. 1:21; Eph. 5:11; 6:12), and pagans have darkness as their eternal destiny (Col. 1:13; 2 Pet. 2:17; Jude 13). The conflict between light and darkness as a description of God's work in the last days, anticipated in the OT apocalyptic hope, is heightened in the NT (Mark 13:24 par.). Acts 2:20 quotes Joel 2:31(3:4) as being fulfilled.

Because darkness and light are used to denote contrasting camps — God's and Satan's — they are also often used to designate the distinction between God's people and those who oppose him (esp. in Paul). Indeed, to turn to God is to turn away from darkness to the light (Acts 26:18; 2 Cor. 4:5). The obvious contrast between darkness and light is a strong way to state the contrast between God's people and others (2 Cor. 6:14; Eph. 5:8; 1 Thess. 5:4-5; 1 Pet. 2:9).

The fundamental opposition between God and Satan, or God's people and the unbelieving, is also manifested in the moral life. Christians must avoid the "works of darkness" and walk as "children of light" (Eph. 5:8, 11). This contrast of living, strongly presented in 1 John 1:5-6; 2:8-11, reveals the true children of God and the validity of their theological claims, thereby distinguishing them from those who are false.

Bibliography. E. Trocme, "Light and Darkness in the Fourth Gospel," *Didaskalia* 3 (1995): 3-13; D. O. Via, Jr., "Darkness, Christ, and the Church in the Fourth Gospel," *SJT* 14 (1961): 172-93.

WENDELL WILLIS

DARKON (Heb. *darqôn*)

The head of a family of "Solomon's servants" who returned from exile under Zerubbabel (Ezra 2:56 = Neh. 7:58).

DATHAN (Heb. *dāṯān*)

The son of Eliab (Num. 16:1; 26:9), who with his brother supported Korah in challenging Moses' leadership during the wilderness wanderings (16:1-40). As a result both brothers were "swallowed up" by the earth (Num. 16:27, 31-33; cf. Deut. 11:6; Ps. 106:17).

DATHEMA (Gk. *Dathema*)

A fortress in Gilead repaired by Jews and used as a refuge when persecuted by the Gentiles (1 Macc. 5:9). The siege was broken by Judas Maccabeus and his brother Jonathan. The site has not been positively identified; proposals include Tell er-Ramet (Ramatha) in Gilead and Tell Hamad, E of Carnaim/Karnaim.

ZELJKO GREGOR

DAUGHTER

In most instances, a household's female child (Heb. *baṯ*). The term may also designate a female descendant, perhaps a granddaughter (e.g., 2 Kgs. 8:26 = 2 Chr. 22:2), or the inhabitant of a city (e.g., Judg. 21:21) or region (e.g., Gen. 24:3). At times, Heb. *bēn*, "son," encompasses both sexes; like sons, daughters are regarded as blessings (Ps. 128:3) and must honor their parents (Exod. 20:10); both will prophesy in messianic times (Joel 2:28[MT 3:1]).

Daughters were highly valued because of their physical labor and because life continued through them (Gen. 29:9; Exod. 21:7). Sexual prohibitions (Lev. 18) protect daughters and forbid a man from having sexual relations with his daughter, son's daughter, daughter's daughter, daughter-in-law, a woman and her daughter, and the daughter of his father's wife.

When a daughter married, her father received a bride price; generally this was returned to her as dowry (Gen. 31:15). A father could annul his daughter's vow (Num. 30:3-5). Although genealogies primarily list firstborn sons, they also name daughters when there are no sons (Gen. 46:17; Num. 26:46 [= 1 Chr. 7:30]; 27:1-11; 36:1-12; Josh. 17:3).

The daughters of foreigners — especially the

Canaanites and Philistines — received little praise and were credited with Israel's ruin (Judg. 3:6; Mal. 2:11). The law forbade intermarriage with them (Deut. 7:3). After the Exile, the Israelites agreed not to give their daughters in marriage to the peoples around them or take foreign daughters for their sons (Neh. 10:30[31]).

In genealogical materials, towns or villages are depicted as "daughters," indicating their relationship as colonies or dependencies of a state (e.g., Ps. 48:11) or city (1 Chr. 2:3, 21, 35, 49). Elsewhere "daughter" is used metaphorically. The daughters of Jerusalem are the bride's friends (Cant. 8:4), and the "daughter of Zion" (NRSV "daughter Zion") is the personification of Jerusalem (Isa. 1:8; 62:11; Jer. 4:31; Lam. 2:8).

Jesus used "daughter" as a term of respect and endearment (e.g., Mark 5:34 par.).

Robin Gallaher Branch

DAVID (Heb. *dawîḏ*)
Israel's second king (ca. 1010-970 B.C.E.).

Sources

1 Sam. 16–1 Kgs. 2 are our main sources about David, supplemented by 1 Chronicles. Other texts name him, but in the main to emblematize either the dynasty in Jerusalem or a salvific ideal.

Some scholars maintain that, like King Arthur, David is a late invention, but this is contradicted by the depth of his embedment in the tradition. Two inscriptions indicate that by 830 (or 840) the state in Judah was identified as "the House of David" (Tel Dan inscription and probably the Mesha stone) and confirm that David was an earlier state-builder. The beginnings of his importance, attested in the 9th century, explain David's significance in the 8th century as an icon of Judah (Amos) and as the progenitor of a line of kings adopted at accession by Yahweh (Isaiah). Everything suggests that the Jerusalem court secured David's place in the literary canon long before the exilic era.

1 Sam. 16–31 represents itself as an account of David's "rise," or youthful career, in interaction with the former king Saul of the tribe of Benjamin. This text reflects two parallel sources now in combination. A representative division yields narrative sources as follows:

A. 1 Sam. 9:1–10:13; 13:1–14:52; 17:12-31, 41, 48b, 50, 55-58; 18:1-6a, 10-11, 17-19, 30; 20:1b–24:22[MT 23]; 28:3-25; 31

B. 1 Sam. 8; 10:17-27; 11-12; 15-16; 17:1-11, 32-40, 42-48a, 49, 51-54; 18:6b-9, 12-16, 20-29; 19; 25–27; 28:1-2; 29–30; 2 Sam. 1ff.

Both sources contain legendary material, including the account of David's slaying Goliath, whom 2 Sam. 21:19 identifies as the victim of Elhanan (cf. 1 Chr. 20:5; Josephus *Ant.* 7.302).

After introducing the monarchy, the A and B sources trace David's early career. In A the David narrative is interposed between materials (1 Sam. 13–14; 28; 31) focused on Saul. In B the narrative shifts from Saul to David in ch. 16 and follows David thereafter. The components of B are often misidentified, and B has been misunderstood as a late, anti-monarchic source. Its position is more complex, and its presentation concerning the origins of the monarchy, as an institution adopted by human initiative and just tolerated by Yahweh, was programmatic for Israelite theologies of the monarchy (cf. Hos. 13:10; Deut. 17:14-15; Judg. 8:22-23). It also represents a closer constitutional reconstruction of the early monarchy than scholars have until recently acknowledged. By contrast, the A source treats kingship as a given. But as it centers on Saul and ends with his death at the Philistines' hands, its date, previously thought to be early, is not clear. This source treats Saul's monarchy, much on the pattern of Abimelech's (Judg. 9), as an abortion, rather like the antedeluvian world, before the establishment of the Davidic line.

2 Samuel, the continuation of the B source, exhibits signs of near contemporary recollection. (1) 2 Samuel (like parts of B) responds to charges that David joined the Philistines in Saul's last battle and incited the assassinations of Abner, Ishbaal, Absalom, Amasa, and all but one of Saul's descendants, not to mention Uriah the Hittite; these are figures whose political relevance, and memory, had expired by the time of the Solomonic schism. (2) 2 Samuel, taken at the literal level, makes very modest claims about David's conquests, while later sources (Chronicles, Josephus, and even 2 Kgs. 14:25) make much more grandiose claims. (3) Some poetry, notably David's laments over Saul and Abner and probably his "last words," is unquestionably antique. (4) The syntax of complex sentences is not typically that of later biblical prose. (5) The geographic delineation of Israel's borders and the order in which components of her territory are enumerated differ from conceptions in biblical texts of the 8th-7th through the 5th-4th centuries. (6) The settlement patterns, especially of the Negeb and Philistia, reflected in the B source (1 Sam. 27–30) and in 2 Samuel, reflect realities of the 10th century but not of subsequent eras. (7) 1 Sam. 27:6 claims that Ziklag remained subordinate to the kings of Judah at the time of the writing of Samuel. As Ziklag lay in the immediate hinterland of Gath, it could not have belonged to kings of Judah after the 8th century, and was probably not even settled in the 9th-8th centuries. (8) 2 Samuel, a record of courtly transactions, stands at the start of a line of accounts in the books of Kings whose assertions regarding international relations are generally corroborated either by external evidence, as in the cases of Rehoboam and Shishak or of the Omrides and Mesha and Hazael, or by internal logic, as in the case of the Solomonic schism and its implications both for relations with Egypt and between Judah and Israel.

2 Samuel describes the death of Saul, David's accession in Judah and civil war with Ishbaal, David's accession to the Israelite throne, the conquest of Jerusalem and transfer of the ark there, Yahweh's promise of perpetual dynasty, David's foreign conquests, the Ammonite war and David's affair with Bathsheba, Absalom's revolt, Sheba's revolt, and Da-

vid's census and acquisition of the ground for the temple. Interspersed are details about David's offspring, officials, and army.

Much of the material in 1 Sam. 31–2 Sam. 24 is taken up in 1 Chr. 10–21, although Chronicles also omits much as irrelevant. Although non-synoptic portions of Chronicles contain some independent information, the text is usually derivative and often midrashic in supplying lists of officials. However, Chronicles is important as a textual witness for reconstructing early readings in Samuel.

Kings refers to David as the recipient of a perpetual divine dynastic grant, for whose sake Yahweh forbears from destroying Judah (but not Israel). Kings therefore holds the meritorious monarchs of Judah up against David as a standard, either directly or, through comparison with a meritorious father, indirectly (exception: Ahaz). Likewise, Amos and Hosea refer to David as the emblem of the dynasty that will regain power over Israel in the fullness of time. Isaiah, Jeremiah, and Ezekiel do much the same, as does Zech. 12–13. Ezra and Nehemiah, like Chronicles, remember David as a cult founder (Ezra 3:10; 8:20; Neh. 12:24-46). Proverbs and Ecclesiastes mention David as an ancestor of their alleged authors. Ruth presents itself as a story about David's ancestors, underscored by a genealogy. Cant. 4:4 mentions one of David's public works (cf. 2 Kgs. 11:10).

Finally, numerous psalms mention David in their superscriptions, most likely as an iconic figure, symbolizing the ruling dynasty. Several mention David as a historical figure, either in the superscription (Pss. 52, 54) or in the body of the psalm (78, 89, 122, 132, 144). Ps. 18:50(51); 72:20 mention him in colophons, while allusions to David have been found in other psalms (e.g., 83). None of this testimony is plainly early, and Pss. 89, 132, whose references are most explicit and extensive, chiefly address the dynastic promises. On the other hand, Amos 6:5 (mid-8th century) already reflects the image of David as poet-courtier.

In texts referring to later periods David embodies state relations, both domestic and international. Although references to David in Judahite contexts often contrast the dynasty to other possible lines, references concerning Israel carry the implication that "David" or "the house of David" is (the state of) Judah (1 Kgs. 12:19). The phrase is common in Isaiah (7:2, 13; 22:22; cf. 9:7[6]; 16:5; also 11:1-10) and in the postexilic era.

Name

The etymology of David's name is uncertain. Older scholars identified an Akkadian cognate meaning "leader," but this was based on a misreading of the cuneiform. The root of the term is *dwd,* usually construed as "(paternal) uncle" or "beloved." However, no text treats the term as containing a diphthong subject to contraction. It is always spelled *dwd* or even *dwyd* (the *y* representing a vowel of the *i*-class), never *dd* (as "uncle" is sometimes written).

Probably related are the names *d(w)dw* (Dodo, e.g., 2 Sam. 23:9, 24) and Dodaw(y)ahu (2 Chr. 20:37), in which the diphthong is contracted. Moreover, the Moabite king Mesha speaks of removing from Ataroth the *'r'l dwdh,* the "Ariel" of (Ataroth's) *dwd.* Here *dwd* does not refer to the house of David. The inscription attributes the fortification of Ataroth and Nebo to the Omrides, the dynasty that was to lend Israel its own name ("the house of Omri"). Nevertheless, the *dwd* of Ataroth was a significant item, whether human or not, quite as singular as Yahweh. Since "paternal uncle" is rare as an element in Israelite names, the name David should probably be construed on Mesha's unclear model. It may or may not be a throne name.

Patronym

David is called "the son of Jesse" in direct discourse in 1-2 Samuel only in derogatory contexts, mainly by Saul (e.g., Sheba's call to revolt, 2 Sam. 20:1). 1 Kgs. 12:16, regarding the Solomonic schism, is first an outcry against David, but then against his dynasty and grandson. The frozen formula, however early its origin, is evidence of David's paternity, as is Jesse's invocation as the dynasty's forebear in Isa. 11:1, 10. The single text in Samuel to denominate David as "David son of Jesse" (2 Sam. 23:1) introduces archaic poetry. This same locution in Chronicles implies only that the patronymic was fixed by the time of that work. The Chronicler supplies the patronym to punctuate his account (1 Chr. 10:14; 29:26; in poetry, 12:18), something he would not do for Moses or Aaron. This may reflect some ideological program — the Chronicler is not telling us "*which* David" was his subject, as, like other early names (patriarchs; tribes, except for Manasseh; early kings) this one does not recur in biblical times. However, the preservation of the patronymic indicates that the historical Jesse possessed means and probably influence.

Genealogy

David's genealogy is recorded at the end of Ruth and, identically, in 1 Chr. 2:3-17. The tradition's antiquity is moot, but P (late 7th or early 6th century) names David's ancestor Nahshon as Aaron's brother-in-law (Exod. 6:23) and chief of Judah (Num. 1:7). This more likely reflects the genealogy than inspires it. Nor would it be surprising were the name of David's grandfather (Obed) preserved. Some see in the story of David's entrusting his parents to the king of Moab (1 Sam. 22:4) evidence of a Moabite connection remembered in Ruth. Still, the line from David's grandfather to Nahshon, thence back to Perez and Judah, seems forced.

Location in Bethlehem

David's genealogy, Ruth, and 1 Samuel (16; 17:15, 58; 20:6, 28) all place David's family in Bethlehem, for several generations. Most convincing is the almost unconscious reference of 2 Sam. 2:32 to Asahel's ancestral tomb there. Mic. 5:2(1) indicates that this tradition was entrenched by 700. Bethlehem, despite the association of Rachel's tomb with it (Gen. 35:19; 48:7; Jer. 31:15), was a backwater suburb an hour's march S of Jerusalem. David's affiliation with the village is hardly an invention.

Early Career

1 Samuel introduces David as Yahweh's choice, by Samuel's designation, to succeed Saul. The narrative takes him to Saul's court, where he betroths one of Saul's daughters (Merab, Michal). 2 Sam. 3 continues with a story of Michal's later delivery to David from her children and former husband, and her subsequent sequestration and childlessness. Further, a ditty, occasioning Saul's anger, runs, "Saul has slain his thousands, and David his myriads" (1 Sam. 21:11). All this supports David's association with Saul's court. Conversely, when most of Samuel was written, it would have been politic to inflate David's reputation as Saul's ally and a killer of Philistines, most urgently to veil the reality that he was for a critical period a Philistine vassal and that he remained their ally throughout his reign. Likewise, David's preservation of Jonathan's son Mephibaal may have been calculated, and the implication that he had a special relationship with Jonathan derived secondarily by our author. Thus, it is unsure whether David ever served at Saul's court. None of the notices relating his men's deeds (2 Sam. 21:15-22; 23:8ff.) suggests that he did.

However, David was the vassal of Achish of Gath. This is an embarrassment to our authors: the A source denies the association altogether (1 Sam. 21:10-15[11-16]). B blunts the point of the embarrassment by alibiing David for the battle in which Saul perished. He was in the employ of the Philistine king of Gath, though driven there by Saul's rage; he was present and was Achish's bodyguard, but by virtue of this honor was detailed to the rear; he was dismissed by the other Philistine kings; he was away, even from home, chasing raiders around the south; and he killed the messenger of Saul's death, who claimed to have killed him (1 Sam. 27; 29–30; 2 Sam. 1).

Just when David, the fugitive from Saul, became king in Hebron (2 Sam. 2:2-4) is disputed. The text assigns him seven years in Hebron, while Ishbaal reigns only two and David takes Jerusalem just after his conflict with Saul's successor. Some critics posit an interregnum between Saul and Ishbaal, which is contraindicated if David had erected a competing kingdom in the south (so 2 Sam. 2:5-9, where Abner crowns Ishbaal to forestall declarations for the electioneering David). Others suggest that David became Judah's king five years before Saul's death. Most likely, however, David did not win northern loyalties or transfer his capital to Jerusalem without delay. This option explains how the tradition of conflict with Philistia arises over the taking of Jerusalem. In Hebron, David's kingship was probably unimpressive, as the poor archaeology of the site and the scant settlement of 11th-century Judah suggests, and he continued as a Philistine vassal. His takeover at Jerusalem may have been a declaration of independence.

Historical Relations with Saul's House

On Saul's death, an attack on Ziklag (1 Sam. 30:1-2) may have led David to relocate his residence in Judah's hills. This territorial expansion into Jerusalem's historical hinterland must have been a reward for service, probably in the Jezreel. From Hebron, David continued his episodic war with Israel, whose king was Ishbaal and whose chief-of-staff was Abner (2 Sam. 2-4). Finally, in consideration for a settlement, Abner and 20 retainers (re)conscripted Ishbaal's sister Michal as David's wife. At the celebratory banquet, however, David's general Joab ambushed Abner and doubtless his escort. 2 Sam. 3 presents this as Joab's treachery against a man traducing Ishbaal to hand David the kingdom. But in no case in which Joab kills for David (Uriah, Absalom, Amasa) does Joab suffer for insubordination. Likewise, Samuel alleges that Michal was betrothed to David (1 Sam. 19:11-24) before her marriage to Palti, the Israelite husband from whom and from whose sons Ishbaal and Abner strip her. This unconsummated betrothal now renders her extradition a grudging acknowledgement of a just claim, avoiding the imputation that the extradition signified peaceful alliance. David thereafter sequestered Michal: he ruptured her former union, then refused real alliance with Saul's house.

Abner's death did not propel Israel into David's arms. Instead, two non-Israelites, from the "Gibeonite" town of Beeroth, assassinated Ishbaal and rushed his head to Hebron. David, however, struck them down, proclaiming his innocence (2 Sam. 4). Contemporaries must have accused him of ordering Abner's and Ishbaal's deaths.

David retained Abner's corpse and Ishbaal's head until the consolidation of his authority over Israel. Sometime before Absalom's revolt, tracing a famine to Saul's war on the Gibeonites, he extradited to the latter Saul's surviving sons and grandsons. Only after this purge did he repatriate Saul's and Jonathan's corpses to the family sepulchre in Benjamin (2 Sam. 21:1-14).

David exempted only Saul's lame grandson. Mephibaal (Meribbaal), Jonathan's son, dwelled at the court, while a steward, Ziba, administered Saul's lands (2 Sam. 4:4; 9). After the Absalom revolt, David reassigned half the estate to the steward (16:1-4; 19:24-30[25-31]). The only other kin to survive the purge was Shimei, who accused David of murdering the entire family (2 Sam. 16:5-10). Shimei was executed in the transition to Solomon's reign.

A final "Saulide" was David's son by Saul's wife, Ahinoam of Jezreel. Amnon, David's firstborn, was assassinated by Absalom. Absalom's punishment was more severe than Joab's for other murders: three years in exile and two more under house arrest. However, Amnon's death, presented as vengeance for his rape of Absalom's sister, removed the last vestige of Saul's house from a role in the succession. In light of the overall pattern, this was not coincidental — especially since the rape was suggested to Amnon by David's nephew (2 Sam. 13:1-5).

Overall, David systematically exterminated Saul's house, maintaining Michal and Mephibaal as hostages at court, for the sake of appearance. Stories of David's youthful service at Saul's court, his relations with Jonathan, and his betrothal to Saul's daughters help alibi him for the assassinations of Abner and Ishbaal and the executions of Saul's other descendants. But all these developments served David's convenience. The contemporary accusations against which the literature responds seem far from groundless.

Rise to Kingship

David's first royal appointment was as vassal to Achish of Gath, in the town of Ziklag. From Hebron, after Saul's death, he claimed sovereignty over Judah, a territory sparsely settled in the late 11th century, especially in regions east of the Shephelah. Nonsedentary elements may also have been active in the Negeb. Nor is Judah, or its companion "tribe" Simeon, represented in any premonarchic Israelite tradition (esp. Judg. 5:13-18). Probably no such "tribe," or geographical Israelite section, existed before David, its architect, occupied Hebron. Hence Benjamin (lit., "the southerner") was originally the name for the group occupying southernmost Israel, Judah included.

David's modest establishment in Hebron remained at Achish's disposal, helping to contain the Israelite forces in the interior. David also initiated a pattern of marital diplomacy. His first wife, Ahinoam, was from Jezreel in the north (Judahite Jezreel was unoccupied in this era). The only other Ahinoam in the Bible was Jonathan's mother, suggesting that David took her from Saul. David's second wife, Abigail, also has only one alter-ego, his sister. She, in turn, had a wealthy first husband in Judah (1 Sam. 25; cf. 2 Sam. 17:25; 1 Kgs. 2:32; 1 Chr. 2:17). Through Ahinoam and Michal, David established a claim on Saul's kingdom. Through Abigail (and her husband) and by marital alliance with the king of Geshur (in the Golan), David also surrounded the north. He further added appeals to Transjordan to defect from Ishbaal (2 Sam. 2:5-7), an early alliance with the Ammonites, and, late in his reign, an alliance with Tyre. These peripheries, in combination with his Philistine allies, David activated against the northern tribes. He enfranchised the Gibeonites of the Benjaminite hills and various mercenary elements, and constructed a coalition to contain the Israelites.

After Ishbaal's death, David orchestrated subscription to his leadership by elements in Israel. Samuel portrays the collaborators as representing the whole north. But the dynamics of this development, indeed, of David's subjecting refractory elements in the north generally, are not open to our inspection. That some element of coercion was involved, however, is clear both from the defensive position adopted by 2 Samuel, probably in defense of Solomon's succession, and the rebellions against David under Absalom and against Rehoboam's succession under Jeroboam.

Administration and Achievements

2 Samuel names many of David's personnel. Often, officials are identified by gentilics (Ittay from Gath, Uriah the Hittite). While, probably on this model, 1 Samuel furnishes a brief list of Saul's officials and 1 Kgs. 4 provides a fuller list of Solomon's officials, nothing remotely similar appears for any other Israelite king. Here the reports on the United Monarchy distinguish themselves from historiography about later eras. This report of rudimentary administrative machinery attests developing state authority, whether David conquered Israel, subjecting it to imperial exploitation, or whether David was a conciliator, who inveigled support from the citizenry.

Foreign elements in David's establishment, his collusion with Gibeon in exterminating Saul's house, and the patterns of his marital (Geshur, northern Manasseh) and other (Philistia and Ammon, Tyre) diplomacy all threatened the northern tribes. Conversely, 1-2 Samuel insists that he had a popular mandate — even after David's mercenaries trounced the tribal levies in Absalom's revolt, it was politically expedient to claim popular legitimation. David's campaign for reelection after the Absalom revolt also indicates dependence on the tactic of currying popularity with his subjects.

It is Samuel's omissions that best characterize this Davidic state. David did not build a temple, but merely unified the state with the new central icon of the ark in Jerusalem (2 Sam. 6–7). David did not organize domestic provinces, as Solomon would, and he undertook no public works outside of Jerusalem — no fortification, no palace construction. Nor, in the Israelite interior, in the Jezreel Valley, does the text allege any conquests: the capture of Megiddo, Beth-shan, and other lowlands fortresses by the Israelites should therefore be assigned to Saul and Ishbaal.

It is as an engineer of empire, as warrior-hero with a grippingly tragic dimension, that David has imprinted himself on Western culture. Again, the claims of conquest lodged in Samuel are limited (contrast Kings, Chronicles). David never dominates territory west of Gezer or in Philistia proper: under Solomon Gezer remained extraterritorial. David's own encounters with Philistines are confined to the hills near Jerusalem, or cannot be located. Likewise, David subjects Aram-zobah (in the Beqaʿ), Ammon, Moab, and Edom. But nothing suggests a campaign north of Dan — the confrontation with Aram comes during the war against Ammon, in Transjordan. The northernmost activity in which David's troops are said to engage takes place at Abel-beth-maacah.

Nor is it patent how David dominated Transjordan. Samuel claims that he garrisoned (some part of the hinterland of) Damascus, versus "all of Edom," where he massacred population. His inroads into Moab are unspecified.

Ammon presents a knottier case. David initially allied with Saul's royal opponent, Nahash. On Nahash's death, David intervened in the succession, conquering the capital, and installing Hanun ben-

Nahash. This paid off during Absalom's revolt, when Hanun abetted David against the tribal militias of Israel and Judah. This in turn led to a marriage making Hanun's daughter the mother of Solomon's successor. Ammon, then, was in thrall to David's Jerusalem, but was also indispensable to the exercise of David's domestic authority.

In theory, Israel's expansion, both internal (in lowlands fortresses) and external (Transjordan), should have a prosperous foundation for "national" pride. However, resource accumulation and the innovation even of a modest monarchy, ringed about by mercenaries, left the countryside lineages in fear of losing their autonomy. David's policies (e.g., tax administration) likely led to Absalom's revolt, which was not directed against the dynasty but against David personally. It was a war concerning the succession.

The insurrection was massive: the text portrays it as recompense for David's murdering Uriah the Hittite; this exculpates the participants from charges of treason. The text insists that David actively campaigned for reelection as king after Absalom's revolt (2 Sam. 19), even supplanting his hatchet man, Joab, as national commander with the rebel general Amasa. The text then blames Amasa's assassination on Joab's, not David's, initiative (during the pretext of a failed revolt). With the army in the ascendant, the humiliating campaign for reelection and the appointment of Amasa point to claims of popular imperium, and the importance of popular support.

David's religious policies are translucent. Beyond adopting the ark from a Gibeonite city as a national symbol, he enfranchised two state priesthoods — one, probably from Judah, claiming descent from Aaron, and another linked to Eli, at the abandoned sanctuary, Shiloh. Otherwise, David prescinded from interference with clerical matters. Further, while the temple liturgy (e.g., Ps. 89) and 2 Sam. 7 would later claim that the Davidic dynasty was an unconditionalized divine gift, alternative views came to expression (e.g., Ps. 132), most obviously in Israel's secession at Solomon's death.

One major, probably Davidic, achievement was sedentarization in the Negeb. This reflects the exploitation of Arabian caravan traffic to the coast, thence abroad. The spice trade, exploited at Egypt's expense, formed a basis for state prosperity until Shishak's raid, five years after Solomon's death.

Politically, David's lasting creations were the nation (or "tribe") Judah and a dynasty whose longevity depended on his successors. Although he scrupulously observed the forms of popular sovereignty, David also created a rift between royal and countryside culture, a rift exacerbated by Solomon that later eradicated those forms.

Succession

David played the succession close to his vest. Of his sons, the third, Absalom, killed the eldest, and was in turn killed by Joab in the revolt. The second son, by Abigail, is never mentioned after his birth. The fourth, Adonijah, was widely expected to succeed.

The succession contest recapitulated the tensions of Absalom's revolt. Popular expectation focused (hopefully?) on Adonijah, and Joab's support suggests that he was David's designee. Party to the pretender was the Elide priest Abiathar. Thus traditional forces, in the court and abroad, stood behind Adonijah's candidacy.

Solomon's succession, sympathetically presented, remains a coup. Behind Solomon stand Zadok, the Judahite priest; Benaiah, the mercenary captain; and the mercenaries of the capital. Solomon's administration, with its emphasis on public works and the exactions that required, colors the contrast with the traditional candidate. Yet conciliatory maneuvers early in the reign — Rehoboam's marriage to Absalom's daughter, the writing of 2 Samuel to exculpate David from political murders and Israel's population from treason, and even the construction of the temple with its implications of tax relief for the laborers (near Jerusalem?) — all suggest that the transition was gradual. Solomon began by pursuing his father's course; only when a threat materialized from Egypt in his 24th year did the impulse to modernization assume urgency. For this reason, public works (e.g., at Megiddo) were not completed before the destruction of the Solomonic layer there.

David's Place in Tradition

David's identification as the messiah, Yahweh's "anointed" and thus son, derives from the temple royal ideology during the centuries up to the Babylonian Exile. As dynast, David personified Yahweh's reign over Judah and, by extension, Israel. Later reinterpretation of the conception of David *redivivus* — adumbrated in the comparison of Judah's kings to him in the books of Kings — and of the enthronement metaphor of his divine sonship led to their ratification as a future hope in a period without Davidic kings (the Restoration). In addition, the image of David as cult founder, full-blown in the presentation of 1 Chronicles, derives from the assignment to his reign of the dynastic charter, usually associated with temple-building, and from the superscriptions to the Psalms.

While Israel's golden age is usually associated with Solomon, the Davidic figure, far more swashbuckling and more tragically human, naturally attracted the attention and the affection of later readers.

Bibliography. D. Barthélemy, et al., *The Story of David and Goliath.* OBO 73 (Göttingen, 1986); W. Brueggemann, *David's Truth in Israel's Imagination and Memory* (Philadelphia, 1985); R. A. Carlson, *David, the Chosen King* (Stockholm, 1964); J. W. Flanagan, *David's Social Drama.* JSOTSup 73 (Sheffield, 1988); J. P. Fokkelman, *Narrative Art and Poetry in the Books of Samuel,* 1: *King David.* SSN 20 (Assen, 1981); D. M. Gunn, *The Story of King David.* JSOTSup 6 (Sheffield, 1978); P. K. McCarter, Jr., "The Historical David," *Int* 40 (1986): 117-29; L. Rost, *The Succession to the Throne of David* (Sheffield, 1982). BARUCH HALPERN

City of David, with the Millo terrace (right). To the left are the bulla house and Ahiel's house
(Phoenix Data Systems, Neal and Joel Bierling)

DAVID, CITY OF

The site David took from the Jebusites and made the capital of all the tribes, "the stronghold of Zion" (2 Sam. 5:7, 9). Located in neutral territory between the northern and southern tribes, it became both the political and religious center unifying David's rule, and here he brought the ark of the covenant (2 Sam 6:1-23). The name was also used in reference to the location of the burial of David (1 Kgs. 2:10) and Solomon (11:43) as well as other kings of Judah (14:31; 15:7, 8, 24; 22:50[MT 51]; 2 Kgs. 8:24; 9:28; 12:21[22]; 14:20; 15:38; 16:20), the southeastern hill or the oldest part of the city as distinct from the rest of Jerusalem (Neh. 3:15; 2 Chr. 32:5, 30), and, by Josephus, the city of Jerusalem as a whole. The city is mentioned in the Egyptian Execration Texts which date to the Middle Bronze period and in the Amarna Letters from the Late Bronze Age.

Historically the name is used in reference to the oldest part of Jerusalem, the eastern ridge also called Ophel. Like the Jebusites, David was attracted to the site because of its unique features. The site was comprised of a narrow north-south ridge formed by the Kidron Valley on the east and the Tyropoeon or Cheesemakers Valley on the west and south. The steep inclines to the east and west made the City of David an almost impregnable site that could be easily defended. In addition to its unique natural defense features, it also had an adequate natural water supply provided by the Gihon Spring on the east side of the ridge in the Kidron Valley. Geographically, the site was located on the north-south ridge that ran throughout the length of the land of Palestine and the major north-south highway that connected the major cities in the central hill country.

Excavations during the past century have helped provide at least a partial outline of the site's history. While evidence of habitation in the area dates back to the Neolithic Age, the first major city was established during the Middle Bronze Age when the site was fortified with a massive wall, discovered during excavations by Kathleen Kenyon from 1960 to 1968. This wall, which continued in use during the Late Bronze Age, provides valuable information about the boundaries of the Jebusite city, which covered ca. 4.5-6 ha. (11-15 a.). Other features discovered by Kenyon or more recently Yigael Shiloh include a series of terraces located on the eastern slope of the ridge, evidence of expansion of the site north toward the Temple Mount; the lower terrace house, which dates to the 8th century B.C.E.; the ashlar house with the pillared-house design typical of Iron Age Israelite houses; the house of Ahiel, so named because of an inscription on a pottery sherd discovered in the structure; the burnt room, named from the thick layer of charred remains in its floor; and the bulla house, in which were discovered 51 bulla or clay seals, four of which date to the 7th and 6th centuries.

In addition to the Gihon Spring, the City of David had several water systems. These include Warren's Shaft, which featured a stepped tunnel and vertical shaft to provide protected access to the city's water supply during times of warfare; the Shiloah water channel, which ran along the east side of the Ophel Ridge and conveyed water to the valley to the east for irrigation purposes; and Hezekiah's Tunnel, cut 558 m. (1831 ft.) through the bedrock of the ridge to convey water from Gihon Spring on the city's east side to the Siloam Pool on the southwest (2 Kgs. 18:13-18; 20:20).

During the reign of Solomon the city was expanded to the north, as the Temple Mount was added. During the 8th century, probably the reign of Hezekiah, the city expanded to the western hill.

Bibliography. D. Tarler and J. M. Cahill, "David, City of," *NEAEHL* 2:52-67. LaMoine F. DeVries

DAY

"Day" (Heb. *yôm;* Gk. *hēméra*) may designate a definite time period. When "day" is accompanied by a definite number (e.g., Gen. 1:5, 8; 7:11; Exod. 16:1; Lev. 23:34) it points only to a 24-hour period. This time extends from sunset to sunset, comprising "evening, morning, and noon" (Ps. 55:17[MT 18]). While Neh. 9:3 denotes "fourths" of a day, the OT makes no other such divisions. It speaks of the "cool of the day" (Gen. 3:8; cf. Cant. 2:17), "heat of the day" (Gen. 18:1; 1 Sam. 11:11), "high day" (Gen. 29:7), "midday" (Neh. 8:3), "broad daylight" (Amos 8:9), and "full day" (Prov. 4:18). However, the NT seems to reflect two 12-hour periods (John 11:9), with specific designations such as "first day" (Luke 24:1), divided into segments like the "sixth" and "seventh" hours (Matt. 20:1-12; cf. John 4:6, 52). Portions of a day were counted as wholes, so "three days" refer to Christ's burial, though they were not three full 24-hour periods.

The sabbath, the seventh day, is the only day specifically named (Exod. 20:8-11). The other six days are designated for work, but the sabbath is reserved for rest and worship. The divine example of six days of work, followed by a day of rest (Gen. 1–2), becomes the pattern for human activity and for explaining the sabbath.

"Day" may also represent an indefinite period of time. References to "the days of Abraham" (Gen. 26:18) or "the days of Solomon" (1 Kgs. 10:21) point to a person's lifetime (Heb. 5:7) or reign (2 Chr. 34:33; Amos 1:1).

Symbolically, salvation and righteousness are described as the day, full of light, so that a traveler may walk without stumbling (John 11:9; Rom. 13:11-13). 2 Cor. 6:2, reflecting Isa. 49:8, denotes the "acceptable time" as the "day of salvation." The Exodus is to be commemorated as such a "day of salvation," because at that time God effected the deliverance of his people from servile bondage (Exod. 12:17; Deut. 16:13). This was a constant reminder of God's willingness to save (e.g., "in the day that I brought them out of Egypt . . ."; 1 Sam. 8:8; Isa. 11:16). According to Deut. 5:12-15 God's deliverance of Israel provides a soteriological reason for observance of the sabbath.

Christians are called "children of the day" (1 Thess. 5:5, 8). The surety of the prophetic word is likened to the rising sun and a new day (2 Pet. 1:19). In John 9:4 the day for work symbolizes the period of service for salvation. Rev. 21:25 depicts eternal life with God as perpetual day.

Stock expressions like "in the latter days," "the last days" (Acts 2:17; 2 Tim. 3:1; Heb. 1:2), "the days are coming" (Amos 4:2; 8:11; Jer. 23:5, 7; 31:27, 31), "in those days" (Jer. 33:15; Zech. 8:6) seem to have an eschatological reference. These "days" point to both judgment and salvation.

Kenneth D. Mulzac

DAY OF THE LORD

The time of the decisive visitation of Yahweh, when he intervenes to punish the wicked, deliver and exalt the faithful remnant who worship him, and establish his own rule. Both judgment and salvation are especially prominent aspects. The Day of the Lord is a significant concept in biblical eschatology, especially in the OT prophetic books. Though the precise term appears only 16 times in the OT, other temporal phrases are clearly relevant (e.g., "on that day," Zeph. 1:9-10; Amos 8:9; "the day of the Lord's sacrifice," Zeph. 1:8; "the day of the wrath of the Lord," Ezek. 7:19; cf. Isa. 2:12). Some scholars consider this to be the central theme of the entire prophetic message; the books of Joel and Zephaniah are completely devoted to proclaiming the Day of the Lord and its attendant events. Indeed, preoccupation with the putative origin of the Day (e.g., the holy war traditions, an ancient enthronement festival) is not necessarily determinative of its later meaning.

The Day of the Lord brings the outpouring of Yahweh's punishment on Israel and Judah. Amos 5:18-20, probably the earliest reference, proclaims judgment on Israel and implies that the prophet overturns the people's expectations of what will happen. The covenant people, who expect God to intervene to defeat their enemies, are instead lurching towards judgment. According to the prophets, this divine judgment is not arbitrary but is prompted by idolatry (Isa. 2:8, 20; Zeph. 1:4-6), pride and arrogance (Isa. 2:11, 17), and a lack of social justice (Amos 2:6-7; Zeph. 3:1-3). It is a purging judgment, which cleanses the blot of wickedness from among God's chosen nation. Unrelenting and inescapable (Amos 5:18-19; Zeph. 1:12), it specifically targets the nation's leaders (Isa. 3:1-3; Zeph. 3:2-3). Although the punishment will come in the form of a military defeat (Amos 2:13-16; Zeph. 1:16), it is clear that Yahweh is the driving force behind it (note the 1st person verbs in Amos 8:9-11; Zeph. 1:8, 9, 11; cf. Joel 2:11).

Judgment is not limited to the covenant people, but includes certain neighboring nations (Amos 1:13-15; Zeph. 2:4-15; cf. also Joel 3:11-12[MT 4:11-12]) who are destined to reap the consequences of their heinous acts (Amos 1:13; Zeph. 2:8, 10). Several prophets depict it as of worldwide proportions (Isa. 13:9; Zeph. 3:8; Zech. 14:1-3, 9). According to Zephaniah, it is none other than the reversal of creation, a destruction more vast than even that brought about by the Flood (cf. the fish in 1:2-3). This prophetic expectation of a final, climactic event which is cosmic in scope is not inconsistent with the fact that biblical writers sometimes applied "Day of the Lord" to past events, such as the destruction of Jerusalem (Lam. 2:22) and the defeat of Egypt (Jer. 46:10). In biblical thought, these past events represent the future and tend to merge into it, foreshadowing the time when all human wickedness will be judged, human pride and arrogance will be exposed, and any power opposed to God will be deposed, preparing the way for establishment of God's own kingdom (Isa. 2:6-22).

Unfortunately, the salvific aspect has often been thought less important than or even incongruent with the judgment aspect. However, the Day is neither solely a time of judgment nor of salvation. It is a time of salvation through judgment, purification and blessing through purging. The prophets announce that a group from the covenant nation will emerge from the judgment and receive divine blessings. This group of survivors, called the remnant (Mic. 4:6-7; Zeph. 3:11-13), will be composed of people who seek Yahweh intently (Amos 5:4-6), manifest humility (Isa. 2:11-12; Zeph. 3:11-12), and live ethically (Amos 5:14-15). They will be gathered by Yahweh, restored to their own land, and enjoy Yahweh's presence in their midst (Amos 9:14-15; Zeph. 3:15, 20).

As with judgment, not only Israel but also the nations will experience future blessing. Transformed by Yahweh, foreigners will express their devotion and allegiance (Isa. 19:18; Zeph. 3:9), both making pilgrimages to Jerusalem to worship (Isa. 2:2-4; Mic. 4:1-4; Zech. 14:16-17) and venerating Yahweh while in their own countries (Isa. 19:19; Zeph. 2:11). In fact, every remaining object will be dedicated to Yahweh at that time (Zech. 14:20).

In the NT the Day of the Lord is identified with the Second Coming of Jesus Christ (2 Pet. 3:10-13; 1 Thess. 5:2; cf. 4:13-18) and is also called "the day of our Lord Jesus Christ" (1 Cor. 1:8; cf. 5:5; 2 Cor. 1:14), "the day of Jesus Christ" (Phil. 1:6), and other similar phrases. Since it is portrayed as a time of universal accountability, when final judgment is meted out and final rewards assigned, it includes the same basic range of events as the OT concept.

As for the timing of the Day, though certain events must transpire first (2 Thess. 2:1-3; cf. Mal. 4:5[3:23]), the Apostle Paul echoes the OT prophets in proclaiming that it is near (Rom. 13:11-12; cf. Isa. 13:6; Joel 1:15; Zeph. 1:7-14). This Day, the time of final vindication of the godly remnant and complete defeat of the wicked, the world still awaits.

Bibliography. G. A. King, "The Day of the Lord in Zephaniah," *BSac* 152 (1995): 16-32; W. Van Gemeren, *Interpreting the Prophetic Word* (Grand Rapids, 1990), 214-25. GREG A. KING

DAY STAR

See MORNING STAR.

DEACON

An office in early Church ministry. It is not clear when Gk. *diákonos* as used in early Christian circles passed from the generic meaning "servant" or "minister" to the specific meaning "deacon." The literal former meaning is obvious in the Gospels (Matt. 20:26; 22:13; 23:11; Mark 9:35; 10:43; for "waiters at table," cf. John 2:5, 9; Acts 6:2). Paul uses the word metaphorically in various ways to describe himself or other Christians: servant or minister (1 Cor. 3:5; Eph. 6:21; Col. 4:7); servant of the gospel (Eph. 3:7; Col. 1:23); servant of the church (Col. 1:25); servant of the new covenant (2 Cor. 3:6); servant of God (6:4); servant of Christ (11:23; Col. 1:7; cf. John 12:26; 1 Tim. 4:6); and servant of righteousness (2 Cor. 11:15). Paul also refers to Christ as a servant (Rom. 15:8; cf. Gal. 2:17) and describes the governmental authorities as servants of God (Rom. 13:4).

The meaning "deacon" seems probable in Phil. 1:1, where Paul addressed *diákonoi* along with bishops. By the time of the Pastoral Epistles, congregations received counsel on the types of person suited for the office of deacon (1 Tim. 3:8-13). The characteristics included exemplary personal, domestic, and organizational traits.

It is generally felt that the origin of the office of deacon stems from the appointment and ordination by the Twelve of seven men to administer the daily food allotment *(diakonía)* to the Hellenistic Christian widows (Acts 6:1-6, although *diákonos* does not appear). The apostles declared that they could not be diverted from proclaiming the Word to waiting *(diakonéō)* on tables. The seven, who did much more than distribute food, pioneered the proclamation of the gospel among Hellenistic Jews and Gentiles (e.g., Acts 6:8-9; 8:26-38).

See DEACONESS. WARREN C. TRENCHARD

DEACONESS

An office in early Church ministry. The only clear use of Gk. *diákonos* with reference to a woman is Rom. 16:1, where Paul introduces "our sister Phoebe" as a *diákonos* "of the church at Cenchreae" (the same form is used for masculine and feminine). The term here can be translated as the generic "servant" (e.g., KJV) or the specific "deacon" (e.g., NRSV) or "deaconess" (e.g., RSV). It is unlikely, however, that a separate order called deaconess then existed, since even by the time of the Pastoral Epistles no order separate from the office of the deacon is evident. Rather, women, probably female deacons, are mentioned in the middle (v. 11) of Paul's counsel on the types of persons suited for the office of deacon (1 Tim. 3:8-13). These women are to possess exemplary personal traits.

See DEACON. WARREN C. TRENCHARD

DEAD SEA

The large salt lake located at the southern end of the Jordan River. The Sea is bounded by the cliffs of Moab on the east and the bluffs of Judah on the west. It has the distinction of being the lowest inland body of water on the face of the earth. The surface is ca. 394 m. (1292 ft.) below sea level, and in places it reaches a depth of 396 m. (1300 ft.). It is 80 km. (50 mi.) long and at its widest 18 km. (11 mi.) across. The Dead Sea receives 6 million tons of water daily from the Jordan. There is no outlet for the sea, but until recently the level remained fairly constant because of the evaporation off the surface of the Sea due to the excessive heat from the sun. The evaporation is the cause for the high concentration of salts in the Sea, 25 percent (cf. ca. 3 percent for the ocean and ca. 5 percent for the Great Salt Lake).

The name Dead Sea does not appear in the Hebrew Bible or the Greek NT. It was first used by Pausanias (*thalassa nekra; Descr. Gr.* 5 [1.7.4-5]) and followed by other Greek and Latin authors. Several different names are used in the Bible (*yām hammelaḥ*, Salt Sea: Gen. 14:3; *yām ha'ărāḇâ*, Sea of Arabah: Deut. 3:17; Josh. 3:16; *hayyām haqqaḏmônî*, Eastern Sea: Ezek. 47:18; Joel 2:20). Josephus (*Ag. Ap.* 1.22; *Ant.* 1.9) called it Lake Asphaltitis (*asphaltitis limnas*) because of the chunks of bitumen or asphalt floating in the southern end of the Sea. In Arabic it is called Bahr Lut, "Sea of Lot."

The name Dead Sea is apropos, for there seems to be no animal or plant life in the Sea. Among the salts magnesium, sodium, calcium, and potassium are held in solution; the other salts crystallize and sink to the bottom. A large quantity of the salts comes from the Jordan River.

Along the western side are important sites: in the north, Qumran; midway, En-gedi; and in the south, Masada. Among the several streams that empty into the Sea on the eastern side are the Arnon, midway, and in the south, the Zered. Three-fourths along the eastern side is the Lisan ("Tongue"), a peninsula extending into the Sea.

Since ca. 1960 the Dead Sea has become smaller and shallower due to the increased use of water from the Jordan River system for irrigation and for household consumption in towns and cities. Also, Israel has operated a chemical plant at the southern end to extract the salts from the sea water by means of large evaporation vats. Today the Lisan is connected by dry land to the eastern shore.

Bibliography. D. Baly, *The Geography of the Bible*, rev. ed. (New York, 1974); A. E. Day, "Geology of the Dead Sea," *BSac* 81 (1924): 254-70; W. Irwin, "The Salts of the Dead Sea and the Jordan," *Geographical Journal* 61 (1923): 428-40; E. Robinson, *Biblical Researches in Palestine* 1 (1856, repr. Jerusalem, 1970).

LAWRENCE A. SINCLAIR

DEAD SEA SCROLLS

The remains of a collection of more than 800 biblical and other mostly religious manuscripts found at Khirbet Qumran ("the ruins at Qumran") and six other sites along the western side of the Dead Sea from 1947 to 1956. The majority of the texts are inscribed on leather (i.e., animal skins), but some are on papyrus, and one (3Q15) is on copper. Most are in the Hebrew language, about one fifth in Aramaic, and a few in Greek. The script for most of the Hebrew scrolls is the Jewish ("square") script; ca. 16 are in the ancient Phoenician, or Palaeo-Hebrew, script, all being the books of Moses, Joshua, or Job — i.e., believed to originate in the premonarchic period; there are also some rare examples of a cryptic script.

Near the Qumran caves where the Scrolls were found, a building complex was excavated, and it has been widely acknowledged that the Scrolls belonged to a group centered around the building. Three cemeteries were adjacent, the closest holding ca. 1100 graves aligned south-to-north with the head at the south. Of the few excavated, only males were found in the closest, but there were remains of females and children in the other parts. The date of the building and that of the manuscripts are determined by a combination of factors, including coins, pottery, palaeography, and accelerated mass spectrometry. (1) The coins unearthed in the excavations of the building date from Antiochus III (223-197 B.C.E.) to the third year of the Jewish Revolt (68 C.E.). (2) The type of pottery characterizing the jars in which a few of the manuscripts were intentionally deposited in Cave 1 is similar to that of jars and a large collection of bowls stashed in a pantry in the main building. It dates from the last centuries B.C.E. and the first centuries C.E. (3) The palaeographic date of the manuscripts in the Qumran caves, established by study of the scripts used in copying the manuscripts, extends from about the latter half of the 3rd century B.C.E. to about the middle of the 1st century C.E., though at Murabba'āt it extends to the first third of the 2nd century C.E. The early dates indicate that many scrolls were brought in from elsewhere. Some texts found at Khirbet Mird written in Arabic date as late as the 7th century C.E. (4) Accelerated mass spectrometry is a system, more advanced than Carbon-14 dating, for determining the age of ancient artifacts. Two tests were performed on a series of scrolls, including some which bore absolute dates in the hand of the original scribe, and the range of dates of the relevant manuscripts was 388 B.C.E. to 136 C.E. When these dating results are placed within the context of Jewish history, many scholars date the period of occupation at Qumran at ca. 150 B.C.E.–68 C.E. (the First Jewish Revolt), with the finds at Murabba'āt extending to ca. 135 C.E. (the Second Revolt).

Though the abandoned site of Khirbet Qumran had long been known, the first manuscript discovery was at Cave 1 by Arab Bedouin in 1947. Cave 1 is ca. 1.7 km. (1 mi.) N of the building, in the limestone cliffs towering above the littoral plane. Seven scrolls were found: one complete scroll of the book of Isaiah (1QIsa[a]), wrapped in linen and enclosed in a tall sealed pottery jar, as well as extended fragments from other scrolls, including a second copy of Isaiah (1QIsa[b]), the Rule of the Community (1QS), a *pesher* (commentary) on the book of Habakkuk (1QpHab), an imaginatively developed narrative work based on Genesis (the Genesis Apocryphon; 1QapGen ar), an apocalyptic War of the Sons of Light against the Sons of Darkness (1QM), and a collection of *hodayot* (hymns of praise) composed within the community (1QH). In subsequent scholarly excavations of Cave 1 (directed by Roland de Vaux), small fragments from an additional 72 manuscripts were unearthed. These included manuscripts of biblical books and commentaries on biblical books, as well as apocryphal, legal, and liturgical texts.

Ten more caves were found at or near Qumran. Cave 4, discovered in the immediate vicinity, was

Overview of the Qumran community and surrounding area. Four of the caves where the Dead Sea Scrolls were found can be seen left of the ravine (Werner Braun)

the richest, yielding fragments of ca. 580 scrolls. Cave 7, equally close, contained only Greek papyrus fragments, including Exodus and the Letter of Jeremiah. Cave 11 was the last discovered in the Qumran area, in 1956. Additional caves were found a few miles south at Murabbaʿāt, containing letters of Simon bar Kokhba and other documents from the Second Revolt, as well as at Naḥal Ḥever/Wadi Seiyal, and Khirbet Mird. Finally, atop the mountain fortress of Masada a mixed collection of more than 50 texts were recovered, including part of the book of Sirach in Hebrew.

The Scrolls and the OT

Indicating the importance of the Scriptures at Qumran, more than 200 scrolls, ca. 25 percent of the more than 800 found, were manuscripts of biblical books. Every book of the traditional OT, except Esther (and Nehemiah if considered a separate book from Ezra), is represented at least minimally. The most frequently attested books were Psalms (39 manuscripts), Deuteronomy (32), and Isaiah (22) — not surprisingly the three most quoted books in the NT as well.

Previously, the oldest extensive Hebrew manuscript available was from the end of the 9th century C.E. The Scrolls are older by a millennium. From the earliest days come two of the most important learnings about the biblical text. First, 1QIsa^b showed that the traditional text known from the MT had been very faithfully copied over the centuries from one ancient form of the text. Second, 1QIsa^a showed that there were variant forms of the scriptural text circulating in antiquity prior to the era of a uniform text. Whereas 1QIsa^b normally exhibited only minor variants vis-à-vis the traditional MT, 1QIsa^a displayed thousands of differences in spelling, word forms, textual variants, and cases of much longer or shorter text.

As the biblical manuscripts (now mostly published in the 38 volumes of the series *Discoveries in the Judaean Desert*) were analyzed, this pattern continued to reveal itself in ever more elaborate and instructive ways. Prior to the 2nd century C.E., when the proto-MT form of the collection of Scriptures became the only textual form transmitted in Hebrew, the text was pluriform, many books even displaying two or more literary editions. Numerous textual variants pepper all the texts, sometimes showing errors or expansions, but at other times providing superior readings where the MT has erred or expanded; thus many Qumran readings have been incorporated into recent revised translations of the Bible. The Scrolls also validate the LXX and Samaritan Pentateuch in general as faithful witnesses to an ancient Hebrew text that was simply an alternate to the textual form transmitted in the MT. They document a period in which the biblical text was still organically growing and provide evidence of how the text grew during its formative period.

The Scrolls and Judaism

The Scrolls have greatly illumined and changed scholars' understanding of Judaism at the turn of the era. Whereas it was once thought that there was a single, "mainstream" or "normative" Judaism, it is now clear that Judaism was richly pluriform. There were a variety of parties and a wide variety of views on any number of subjects, and no particular group held full authority in teaching or practice over the others, though the Jerusalem priests probably held the strongest claim to the average people's loyalty.

The Essenes, as a movement within Judaism, had previously been known only through brief descriptions written for foreigners by Josephus, Philo, and Pliny. While Josephus may have gained firsthand knowledge of the Essenes, Philo and Pliny were probably working from sources. Thus, though these descriptions help identify the Qumran group as Essene, they do not provide a standard for understanding the group's beliefs. The Scrolls themselves provide abundant correction and amplification to our knowledge of the Essenes, which though still imperfect now exceeds our knowledge of contemporary groups, the Sadducees, Pharisees, and Zealots.

The Essene movement predates the Qumran community, though its origins are not fully known. During the Maccabean period, they were led by someone called the Righteous Teacher, or Teacher of Righteousness. The Teacher, himself a priest, came into serious conflict with the leaders in Jerusalem, possibly over the legitimacy of the high priesthood, since the Maccabees installed themselves in that office in place of the traditional Zadokite priests, and the Teacher was forced into exile from Jerusalem. In time, the group settled in the wilderness at Qumran, to study Torah and so "prepare the way of the Lord" (1QS 8:12-16; Isa. 40:3).

The Scrolls reveal a dualistic worldview. There were two ways — one of light and good, the other of darkness and evil. The community believed that history was predetermined by God, and that they were part of the remnant of true Israel, living under a (re)new(ed) covenant with God, in continuity with the covenant at Sinai, but with a deeper understanding of and incentive to obedience.

In their view, like that operative in the NT as well, Scripture was written in symbolic, obscure language by prophets who may have understood one level of meaning in what they wrote but did not understand the ultimate meaning, which was revelation about the "end time." The true meaning of the text was revealed, however, to the Teacher of Righteousness. The Scriptures referred to the Essenes' own period, the "latter days," and described the events they themselves were experiencing, such as the exiling of the Teacher and Roman rule.

The Scrolls refer to other Jewish groups. They discuss conflicts with "the Seekers of Smooth Things" (probably the Pharisees) and "Manasseh" (probably the Sadducees), as well as conflicts over the high priesthood and the calendar. Some early scrolls, including the Halakhic Letter (4QMMT), contain halakhic views in common with the Sadducees, probably reflecting the group's roots in the Zadokite priesthood. Views on other subjects, however, such as predestination and resurrection, are strongly opposed to Sadducean views. The Qumran Essenes lived a life of strict observance and greater asceticism than did other groups, but it is not thought that they excluded other groups from the true Israel on that basis.

The Scrolls and the NT

The community at Qumran was destroyed before most of the NT was written, and no scrolls contain NT texts, though some unpersuasive claims of such have been made (such as claims that 7Q5 contains the Gospel of Mark). Nor is there any reference to Jesus Christ, John the Baptist, or anything specifically Christian. Nevertheless, because similarities in language, theological themes, characters, texts, and practices are pervasive, the Scrolls provide inexhaustible illumination for understanding the text and world of the NT and early Christianity.

The Scrolls reveal a common Jewish root in self-defining community practices, such as community property shared in common, a ceremonial sacred meal, and ritual bathing for purity.

The complex of messianic views characteristic of this period is further revealed in the Scrolls. More than one messiah is envisioned — a priestly and a kingly messiah, who are accompanied by a prophet: ". . . until there come the prophet and the messiahs of Aaron and Israel" (1QS 9:11). The kingly messiah was to be a victorious war hero, like David, and to rule with wisdom and justice, as prophesied in Isa. 11:1-5. The priestly messiah was still higher in authority. Christ (the Greek translation for "messiah") as king is a theme throughout the Synoptic Gospels. Hebrews speaks of Christ as a priest, though after the order of Melchizedek, not Aaron, and a minister of the heavenly sanctuary (Heb. 8:1-2; 10:12-14). A great deal was made of the so-called "Pierced Messiah" text, 4Q285, which was initially misread and thought to describe a messiah who is killed. More careful reading, however, re-

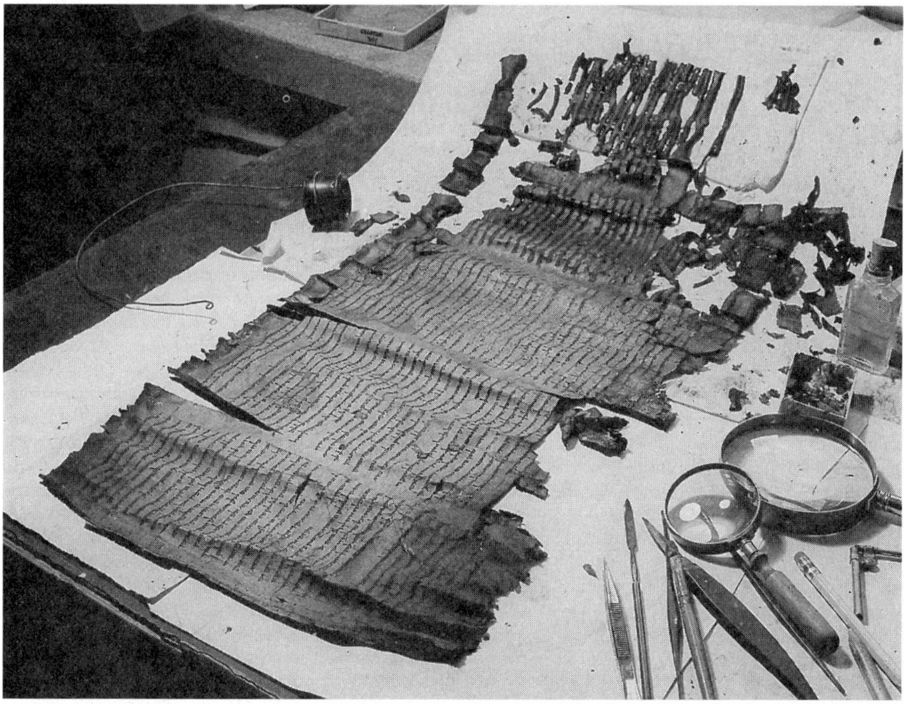

Scroll and fragments of the Genesis Apocryphon (1QapGen ar) (Photo © Israel Museum, Jerusalem)

veals that the text names Isaiah, quotes from Isa. 11, and here describes a Davidic messiah who kills someone else, as in Isa. 11:4 where the Davidic ruler kills the wicked.

In addition to "messiah," several other titles are used similarly in the Scrolls and the NT: "branch of David" (e.g., 4Q285 frag. 5:3; 4QFlor col. III:11) is similar to "Root of David" (Rev. 5:5). A striking parallel in terminology to Luke 1:32, 35 occurs in the fragmentary 4Q246, which reads, "He will be called 'the Son of God'; they will call him 'Son of the Most High.'" However, though this figure was at first hastily claimed to be a positive messianic figure, the context rather suggests a wicked leader who arrogates to himself divine status.

Like the NT, the Scrolls place messianic expectations in a dualistic (light/darkness), eschatological framework (cf. 1QS 3:13–4:26; John 1; 2 Cor. 6:14–7:1). Both read texts from the OT in an eschatological and contemporizing manner. The Scrolls and the NT also show a reverence for the same Scriptures: the Law and the Prophets plus a still undefined collection of other sacred books. They even emphasize the same texts: the Psalms interpreted prophetically, Deuteronomy, and Isaiah. But Enoch and Jubilees were both probably considered among the authoritative books, whereas the Wisdom Literature is sparsely attested.

In contrast to the earlier flat view of a distinct Christianity versus a clearly defined "normative" Judaism, the commonalities between the Scrolls and early Christianity demonstrate how thoroughly Jewish are the roots and development of Christianity. The Scrolls show a wide and diverse spectrum of beliefs and practices in Judaism, from which matrix Christianity eventually developed organically. Nascent Christianity was in most aspects an integrated part of the spectrum of general Judaism. This knowledge had simply been suppressed as Rabbinic Judaism and Christianity both developed in conscious polemical distinction from each other.

For the OT, ancient Judaism, and the NT, the Scrolls light up the ancient world, displaying for each a stage prior to the simplified picture that history had remembered: a stage of pluriformity in the biblical text, the broad spectrum of diversity within late Second Temple Judaism, and the Jewish theological world of the NT.

Bibliography. F. M. Cross, *The Ancient Library of Qumran,* 3rd ed. (Minneapolis, 1995); J. A. Fitzmyer, *Responses to 101 Questions on the Dead Sea Scrolls* (New York, 1992); F. García Martínez, *The Dead Sea Scrolls Translated,* 2nd ed. (Grand Rapids, 1996); L. H. Schiffman, *Reclaiming the Dead Sea Scrolls* (Philadelphia, 1994); E. Ulrich and J. C. VanderKam, *The Community of the Renewed Covenant* (Notre Dame, 1994); VanderKam, *The Dead Sea Scrolls Today* (Grand Rapids, 1994); G. Vermes, *The Dead Sea Scrolls in English,* 4th ed. (Baltimore, 1995); M. Wise, M. Abegg, and E. Cook, *The Dead Sea Scrolls: A New Translation* (San Francisco, 1996).

EUGENE ULRICH

DEATH

Death at the most basic level means the cessation of life in a biological sense (Gen. 25:11; Eccl. 12:6). It is also used figuratively for the forces that detract from the quality of life (Prov. 8:35-36; 1 John 3:14). Death is sometimes personified (Job 28:22; Ps. 18:4-5[MT 5-6]; 49:14[15]; Jer. 9:21[20]; Hab. 2:5; Rev. 6:8; 20:13-14). In the NT it is understood as a power that stands in opposition to the created order (Gk. *thánatos*).

In the OT physical death (Heb. *māweṯ, mûṯ*) resulted in the return of the body to the earth (Gen. 3:19), the spirit to God (Eccl. 12:7), and the departure of the soul or essence of life (Gen. 35:18; 1 Kgs. 17:21; Jonah 4:3). Death was the normal end of human life (Josh. 23:14; 1 Kgs. 2:2; Job 5:26); only God was immortal (Ps. 90:1-6). Although physical death was inevitable, the ancient Hebrews hoped that their death would come at the end of a long, distinguished life (Num. 23:10; Judg. 8:32), where children were left behind to carry on the name and bury the deceased (Gen. 35:29; 50:7-8; Job 42:16). Premature death (Gen. 21:16; Isa. 38:1-15), death as a result of violence (1 Sam. 15:32-33), the death of a childless person (2 Sam. 18:18), and death without proper burial (2 Kgs. 9:30-37) were all terrible fates. Obedience to God might result in a longer life (Deut. 30:15-20; Prov. 10:2; 11:4) and sin in premature death (1 Sam. 2:31-36; Job 36:13-14; Ps. 55:23[24]), but there were exceptions (Eccl. 7:15-18).

The ancient Hebrew law prescribed death as punishment for violations that were viewed as seriously endangering the life of the community. Among the crimes for which this ultimate penalty was stipulated were murder (Gen. 9:6; Exod. 21:12), blasphemy (Lev. 24:16), fornication (Deut. 22:20-21), sabbath violations (Exod. 35:2), kidnapping (Exod. 21:16), striking one's parents (Exod. 21:15), homosexuality (Lev. 20:13), bestiality (Lev. 20:15-16; Exod. 22:19), and a host of others. The death penalty was carried out frequently through stoning (Num. 15:32-36; Lev. 20:27; Deut. 17:2-7; 21:18-21) and sometimes by burning (Gen. 38:24; Lev. 20:14; Josh. 7:15, 25).

Even though death at the end of a full life was understood as the natural end of life, rarely was it greeted with joy (Job 3:21; Jonah 4:3); usually people were simply resigned to it. It was the contradiction of life (Jer. 21:8-9), and it meant separation from life (Ruth 1:17; Ps. 39:13[14]). The dead were believed to live in Sheol or the Pit, a shadowy place of darkness and silence (Job 10:21-22; Ps. 94:17; Prov. 2:18; Jonah 2:6[7]). God's power extended to Sheol (Ps. 139:7-8; Amos 9:2), but he was not present there (Ps. 88:5[6]; Isa. 38:18). Those who dwelt in Sheol could not praise God (Ps. 30:9[10]; 115:17) or remember him (Ps. 6:5[6]; 88:12[13]). Only Enoch (Gen. 5:24) and Elijah (2 Kgs. 1:11) escaped the usual fate. God took Enoch, and Elijah was taken to heaven in a whirlwind. Elisha raised the Shunammite woman's son from death (2 Kgs. 4:35), but presumably the young man eventually died.

In the OT death could be used in a figurative as well as literal sense. Illness (Ps. 30:2-3[3-4]), enemies (Ps. 9:13[14]; 55:1-4[2-5]), and injustice (Ps. 116:3) were all part of death in this sense. Thus, one could be biologically alive and spiritually dead (1 Sam. 25:37-38; Jonah 2:2-6[3-6]). Ultimately, one had to choose between (spiritual) life and death (Deut. 30:19).

Death was depicted as greedy (Hab. 2:5), as a force that tried to trap humans (Ps. 18:4-5[5-6]; Prov. 13:14), and as a city within which the dead were restricted (Job 38:17; Ps. 9:13[14]). Sometimes it was personified in a way that may have been influenced by pagan mythology (Job 28:22; Jer. 9:21[20]).

The finality of death was tempered somewhat by the metaphor of sleep (Job 14:10-12; Ps. 13:3[4]), though it was a sleep from which one was not expected to awaken (Jer. 51:39, 57). Nevertheless, the metaphor suggested the possibility of awakening. Isaiah stated that in the future death would be abolished (Isa. 25:8). Hannah's song affirms that God has the power to raise the dead from Sheol (1 Sam. 2:6), and Ezekiel's prophecy regarding dry bones, though it referred to the exilic community, also suggests God's power to raise the dead (Ezek. 37:1-14).

Two late passages in the OT explicitly suggest the possibility of resurrection. Isa. 26:19 affirms that the righteous dead will share in the coming deliverance. Dan. 12:2 indicates the resurrection of the righteous to everlasting life and of others to shame and everlasting contempt. By NT times many Jewish groups accepted the concept of resurrection.

In the NT, as in the OT, humans are mortals whose lives end in biological death (1 Cor. 15:21-22). Human death is a universal experience (Heb. 9:27), and the only exception mentioned in the NT is Enoch (Gen. 5:24; Heb. 11:5). Three times in the NT humans are raised from the dead (Luke 7:11-17; John 11:1-44; Acts 9:36-43), but they do not become immortal. Presumably they eventually die.

According to Paul, death is a result of human sin (Rom. 5:12; 6:23; 1 Cor. 15:21). However, through Christ's death the consequences of Adam's sin, i.e., human death, are cancelled (Rom. 5:10) and life for all is accomplished (v. 18). Christ's death destroyed the one holding the power of death (Heb. 2:14) as well as death itself (2 Tim. 1:10). Christ thus became the Lord of the living and the dead (Rom. 14:9) and has the keys of death and Hades (Rev. 1:18). This does not mean that people no longer die. However, death is viewed in a new light. Christ's resurrection from the dead is understood as the model that all believers may hope to experience (Col. 1:18; Rev. 1:5). Nothing can separate the faithful from the love of God in Christ (Rom. 8:38-39). Physical death is spoken of in positive terms, as gain (Phil. 1:21) and as departing to be with Christ (v. 23).

Just as in the OT, in the NT figurative death can be experienced while biologically alive. Rom. 7:24 speaks of a "body of death." One who has not yet met Christ is described as dead in sin (Eph. 2:1). By the same token, one who has met Christ is said already to have eternal life, even in the present mortal life (John 3:3-8). There is a tension between the "already" and the "not yet." The last enemy to be destroyed will be death (1 Cor. 15:26). Death is also personified in the NT, and it has a persona associated with Hades (Rev. 6:8; 20:13-14). In the former passage death is depicted as riding on a green horse.

Apparently the generation living during the time of the Parousia will not experience death but will be translated directly to heaven (Matt. 16:28). At this time, the translated and the resurrected will begin eternal life in its fullness (1 Thess. 4:16-18).

ALICE OGDEN BELLIS

DEBIR (Heb. *dĕḇîr*) **(PERSON)**
King of the Amorite/Canaanite city of Eglon. He was a member of the coalition of southern Canaanite kings who led by King Adonizedek of Jerusalem attacked Gibeon after it entered into a treaty relationship with Joshua and Israel (Josh. 10:3, 5). After their initial defeat at Gibeon, the kings fled westward down the Beth-horon descent, then southward through the Shephelah to the Makkedah cave area (Josh. 10:10-27).

R. DENNIS COLE

DEBIR (Heb. *dĕḇîr*) **(PLACE)** (also LIDEBIR, LO-DEBAR)

1. A city in the southern hill country of Judah, cited in the Joshua conquest narrative (Josh. 10:38-39). It has been identified tentatively with Khirbet Rabûd (1515.0933), 13 km. (ca. 8 mi.) SSW of Hebron. The site was first suggested by Kurt Galling, and excavations were led by Moshe Kochavi in 1968-69, during which they unearthed the only large Late Bronze Age (LB IIA) city in the Hebron hills dating to the 14th and 13th centuries B.C. Ample cisterns and the nearby upper and lower wells of Bir ʿAlaqa accord with the account of Achsah, daughter of Caleb (Josh. 15:15-19 = Judg. 1:11-15). Previously the site had been identified with Tell Beit Mirsim (William F. Albright) and Khirbet Tarrameh.

Earlier names for the site were Kiriath-sepher (Josh. 15:15) and Kiriath-sannah (v. 49). After conquering the city, Joshua is said to have destroyed the remnant of the Anakim of Debir (11:21).

Bibliography. M. Kochavi, "Rabud, Khirbet," *NEAEHL* 4:1252.

2. A Gadite city in the Gilead region N of Pella (Josh. 13:26; 2 Sam. 9:4-13).

The name is written Lidebir in Josh. 13:26 and Lo-debar in 2 Sam. 9:5. Jonathan's family fled there after the Israelites under Saul were defeated in the lower Jezreel Valley and the slopes of Mt. Gilboa. Mephibosheth, Jonathan's crippled son, was brought by David from Lo-debar to reside with the royal household in Jerusalem. Modern Umm el-Dabar (207219), 18 km. (11 mi.) N of Pella (Tabaqat al-Faḥl), may preserve the original name and location of the ancient city.

3. A city along Judah's northern border with Benjamin. It was located between Jerusalem and the Jordan River, above the Valley of Achor and near Gilgal (Josh. 15:7).

R. DENNIS COLE

DEBORAH (Heb. *dĕḇôrâ*)

1. One of the most notable women in the OT. Deborah ("honeybee") figures prominently in Judg. 4 and 5, which recount a decisive battle between the Canaanites, under the command of Jabin and his general Sisera, and an Israelite tribal militia force. This episode, set in the period of the judges, is one of a series of deliverer stories that constitute the central section of the book of Judges. Judg. 4 is a narrative account, usually dated to the late monarchic period. A poetic and probably much earlier version, perhaps dating to the late 12th century B.C.E., appears in Judg. 5 and is known as the Song of Deborah (although the superscription in 5:1 attributes it to both Deborah and her general Barak). Its archaic language of divine triumph over Israel's enemies represents the only extended poetic account accompanying the prose description of an episode in Judges.

Deborah is identified in Judg. 4:4 by two terms: "a prophet" (NRSV "prophetess"), lit., "a woman (Heb. *ʾiššâ*), a prophet"; and as one who was "judging Israel" at the time of a 20-year period of oppression by the heavily armed Canaanites. Between these two terms is another identifier, the phrase *ʾēšeṯ lappîḏôṯ*, typically translated "wife of Lappidoth (Torches)." However, it could equally mean "fiery (or spirited) woman" (lit., "woman of torches") because Lappidoth, elsewhere unknown in the Bible, is unlikely to be a man's name and because the noun *ʾēšeṯ* (construct of *ʾiššâ*) can mean "woman of" as well as "wife of." The need to have a woman identified in relation to a man, rather than the acknowledgement that a woman's identity could in some instances stand alone, apparently influenced virtually all modern and ancient translations. Yet the several roles Deborah plays as an autonomous woman in national life would warrant her name appearing with the epithet "fiery woman" and without reference to a man. Because of the overlap between territory and kinship groups in ancient Israel, her family identity is supplied by the information in Judg. 4:5 about her geographical locale — that she comes from a place "between Ramah and Bethel in the hill country of Ephraim" — rather than by the name of a male relative.

Deborah plays a number of vital leadership roles. As a judge, she is involved in military activity as are those other judges whom the Lord raised up "to deliver Israel." But also, uniquely among the judges, Deborah renders "judgment," or legal decisions, as she sits "under the palm of Deborah." In addition, she is the only figure in Judges who is called a prophet. That designation may be related to the song attributed to her in ch. 5, for poetic outbursts recounting Yahweh's saving (or punitive) powers are frequently related to the activity of prophets, who mediate God's word to the people. Deborah also bears the title "mother in Israel" (Judg. 5:7), perhaps because she gives wise counsel to those who seek her help (cf. 2 Sam. 20:19). More likely, "mother" is the honorific title for a female authority figure or protector in a family or the larger community, just as "father" is for a male authority (cf. 1 Sam. 24:11; Isa. 12:21).

Deborah is consulted by the Israelites, who are greatly concerned about the Canaanite threat. She summons her general Barak, who musters troops from two tribes (Judg. 4:6) or perhaps six (5:14-15). Yet, because of the superior numbers and resources of the enemy coalition, Barak is reluctant to go out to battle unless Deborah will also go. In agreeing to do so, she taunts him, saying that the victory will not be his but rather will belong to a woman. The woman is not Deborah but rather the Kenite Jael, who entices Sisera into her tent and kills him with a tent peg (Judg. 4:17-22; 5:24-27), thus assuring Israelite victory.

Both the compelling irony of the prose account, which begins and ends with the decisions and deeds of women, and the vivid passion of the poetic version, which concludes with two striking women's scenes, testify to victory against great odds in a decisive battle. Indeed, the Song of Deborah can be identified as a "victory song," a genre of stirring poetic outbursts acknowledging the miraculous intervention of Yahweh to save the people, who otherwise seem doomed. In ancient Israel, female composers and performers typically sang such songs (cf. Exod. 15:20-21, the song of the "prophet Miriam," and the account in 1 Sam. 18:6-7 of women performers heralding David's victory over the superior military power of the Philistines). Besides belonging to a genre attributed to women authors, the Song of Deborah exhibits thematic aspects, such as gender cooperation and solidarity, that characterize female texts.

The prominence of Deborah as a woman in the largely male world of military and political leadership is often viewed as unusual and remarkable. However, unless forbidden by custom or law (as for monarchs and priests), women could and did act in various public roles in Israelite society. Because they had shorter life spans than men, and because their adulthood was usually taken up with procreation, perhaps few did. And because the male biblical canon-makers typically exhibit androcentric bias, the deeds of even fewer are remembered. Yet periods such as that of the judges, with decentralized ad hoc leadership patterns, typically provide greater possibilities for the talents of women to emerge. Deborah, still visible to us millennia later, may represent many other such "mothers" in early Israel.

Bibliography. M. Bal, *Gender, Genre, and Scholarship on Sisera's Death* (Bloomington, Ind., 1988); M. D. Coogan, "A Structural and Literary Analysis of the Song of Deborah," *CBQ* 40 (1978): 143-66; F. van Dijk-Hemmes, "Mothers and a Mediator in the Song of Deborah," in *A Feminist Companion to Judges* (Sheffield, 1993), 110-14; D. N. Fewell and D. M. Gunn, "Controlling Perspectives: Women, Men, and the Authority of Violence in Judges 4 & 5," *JAAR* 58 (1990): 389-411; J. Hackett, "In the Days of Jael: Reclaiming the History of Women in Ancient Israel," in *Immaculate and Powerful: The Female in Sacred Image and Social Reality,* ed. C. W. Atkinson, C. H. Buchanan, and M. L. Miles (Boston, 1985), 15-38.

2. Rebekah's nurse, who like the judge Deborah is associated with a tree (Gen. 35:8).

3. The grandmother of Tobit (Tob. 1:8).

CAROL MEYERS

DEBT, INTEREST, LOANS

The practice of making of loans at interest was a widespread phenomenon in biblical times. The first extant legal source regulating interest rates is the Laws of Eshnunna (ca. 1800 B.C.E.) in Babylonia where interest rates were limited to 20 percent for money and 33.3 percent for grain. These (by modern standards) exorbitant figures are not untypical for OT times generally.

Two common terms for "interest" on debt in the OT are Heb. *nešeḵ* (lit., "bite") and *m/tarbîṯ* ("increase"). The exact meanings are uncertain, but *nešeḵ* may refer to interest "bitten off" beforehand (so NRSV); e.g., someone taking out a 100-unit loan might receive 80 units but owe 100. Heb. *m/tarbîṯ* may refer to regular payments of interest subsequent to the loan. Alternatively, *nešeḵ* may refer to interest on money, while *m/tarbîṯ* to interest on produce paid at the harvest.

Default could result in any collateral (a pledge or surety) being seized by the creditor (Neh. 5:3-5). If this did not cover the amount, the debtors or their children might be sold into slavery (2 Kgs. 4:1; cf. Exod. 22:3b[MT 2]; Matt. 18:25) or in later periods put into prison (Matt. 18:30; Luke 12:57-59; 1 Macc. 13:15). Debtors could temporarily avoid arrest by taking sanctuary in the temple (1 Macc. 10:43).

The Pentateuch seeks to protect the poor Israelites from economic exploitation ensuing from loans to them at interest (Exod. 22:25[24]; Lev. 25:35-38). Deut. 23:19-20(20-21) appears to narrow the earlier commands, condemning interest-taking altogether (except from foreigners), not just from the poor. On this basis, medieval Christianity, talmudic Judaism, and Islam broadly condemned all interest-taking, though legal fictions needed to be devised to avoid the practical difficulties created by this literalistic application. Against this approach, the exception made for interest from foreigners indicates that the Pentateuch does not regard all interest-taking as evil.

Calvin and the Protestant movement generally assimilated Deut. 23:19-20(20-21) to the other passages, limiting the prohibition of interest-taking to loans to the poor. Moreover, Neh. 5:1-13 suggests that all of these "laws" served as moral admonitions rather than enforced statues: hence, Nehemiah the governor cajoled rather than commanded rich Israelites to stop taking interest from poor Israelites despite Ezra's having made (assuming the priority of Ezra) the Mosaic law the law of the land (cf. Ezra 7:25-26). Interest-taking, though "legal," is discouraged by the Torah.

The Sabbatical Year (Deut. 15:1-3; 31:10) and Year of Jubilee (Lev. 25:39-55) prescribed a remission of debts (again excepting foreigners) which may mean a year's suspension of repayment rather than complete cancellation, though scholars still debate the matter. This regulation, practiced sporadically at best in OT times, was reintroduced by Nehemiah (Neh. 10:31). Creditors were admonished to respect the dignity and property rights of debtors by not barging into the house to seize a debtor's pledge (Deut. 24:10-11). Out of compassion, creditors are encouraged not to seize as pledge a person's only cloak to keep him warm or his millstone essential for preparing bread-flour (Exod. 22:26-27[25-26]; Deut. 24:6, 12-13).

Failure to address the needs of debtors could spawn civil unrest: A core element of David's first 400 followers were defaulting debtors who felt disenfranchised by Saul's administration (1 Sam. 22:2).

Proverbs condemns the exploitation of the poor via interest-taking (Prov. 28:8), but extols one who lends without interest as lending to God who will reward (19:17). Proverbs recommends avoiding debts: a borrower is the slave of the lender (22:7), and may well have his bed taken out from under him if he cannot pay (vv. 26-27). To guarantee a loan for someone, especially strangers, is asking for trouble (11:15; 17:18; 22:26), and anyone who becomes a co-signer of risky debts to foreigners or loose women can expect prudent lenders to demand collateral upfront before completing commercial dealings with them (20:16; 27:13).

Lending without interest is a virtue and blessing bestowed by the righteous (Ps. 15:5; 37:26; 112:5; Ezek. 18:7-8, 17). The wicked do the opposite and deserve death or exile (Ezek. 18:13; 22:12). Elisha, showing practical concern, performs a miracle to help a poor widow pay her debts and avoid reduction to slavery by a creditor (2 Kgs. 4:1-7).

In the NT Jesus expands on the OT moral admonitions, requiring his disciples to lend to whoever asks, not just those who can be expected to pay them back, including enemies (Matt. 5:42; Luke 6:34-35). Paul illustrates this spirit of generosity by accepting the debts of the runaway, now converted slave Onesimus (Phlm. 18).

Commercial language is used frequently in the parables: the man who hid his talent is condemned for not at least investing the money in a bank where it would receive interest (Matt. 25:27; Luke 19:23), thus illustrating that disciples must not be passive but must take risks now in view of the kingdom to come. The Unjust Steward who uses his authority to forgive debts to win friends before his impending dismissal (Luke 16:1-8) illustrates the need for the prudent use of material wealth in the present age with eternal rewards in mind. The Unmerciful Servant (Matt. 18:23-35) underscores that just as the servant was unwilling to forgive others their debts, so Jesus' Father would be unwilling to forgive anyone his sins who does not forgive his brother from the heart. The parable of the Two Debtors (Luke 7:41-43) shows that sinners forgiven many sins, just as debtors who are forgiven great debts, are more appreciative than those forgiven but a little.

The language of finance undergirds the NT's description of forgiveness. Gk. *aphíēmi*, "forgive, send away," is also the term used for forgiveness of debts. Matthew's version of the Lord's Prayer reads lit., "and forgive us our debts, as we also have forgiven our debtors" (Matt. 6:12 NRSV), the term "debt" reflecting contemporary Aramaic idiom where "debt" in the Targums is the regular translation for "sin." Luke's version substitutes "sins" for "debts"; thus, Luke interprets "debt" for his gentile audience as metaphorical for sin (Luke 11:4). In Jesus' day, where tithes, tribute, and taxes demanded as much as one half to two thirds of a peasant's produce, and where indebtedness was correspondingly common, Jesus' language represents concrete, vivid imagery and would have brought to mind both literal and figurative application.

Col. 2:13-14 probably also uses financial language to describe forgiveness. There forgiveness of sins is compared with the canceling of a "written code," i.e., probably a "certificate of debt" or "debt-bond." This bond is the IOU owed by sinners to God for violations of God's commandments (the Law), a debt that sinners are unable to pay. Like an IOU, there is a penalty clause for failure to pay, in this case death (cf. Rom. 6:23). But this debt-bond, with its penalties, has been nullified by being transferred to and paid for at Jesus' cross.

Bibliography. J. S. Kloppenborg, "Alms, Debt, and Divorce: Jesus' Ethics in the Mediterranean Context," *Toronto Journal of Theology* 6 (1990): 182-200; S. E. Loewenstamm, "נשך and מ/תרבית," *JBL* 88 (1969): 78-80; R. P. Maloney, "Usury and Restrictions on Interest-Taking in the Ancient Near East," *CBQ* 26 (1974): 1-20; P. T. O'Brien, *Colossians, Philemon.* WBC 44 (Waco, 1982), 124-25; A. Rugy, "Prohibition of Interest and Islam," *Hamdard Islamicus* 12/3 (1989): 95-98; J. R. Sutherland, "The Debate Concerning Usury in the Christian Church," *Crux* 22/2 (1986): 3-9; "Usury: God's Forgotten Doctrine," *Crux* 18/1 (1982): 9-14; C. J. H. Wright, *God's People in God's Land* (Grand Rapids, 1990), 167-73; D. Wright, "The Ethical Use of the Old Testament in Luther and Calvin," *SJT* 36 (1983): 463-85.

Joe M. Sprinkle

DECALOGUE

See Ten Commandments.

DECAPOLIS (Gk. *Dekápolis*)

A group of cities (Gk. "Ten Cities") in southern Syria and northern Jordan (except Scythopolis, located S of the Sea of Galilee just W of the Jordan River), functioning under that name in the Hellenistic and Early Roman periods. Ancient literary sources identify as many as 18 or 19 cities in the group, including Damascus, Philadelphia, Raphana, Scythopolis, Gadara, Hippos, Dion (Dium), Pella, Galasa (Gerasa) and Canatha, with Abila and several others listed as tetrarchies or kingdoms (Pliny *Nat. hist.* 5.74). Also included are Heliopolis, Abila

(Quailibah), Saana (Sanamyn), Ina, Abila of Lysanias, Capitolias (Beit Ras), Adra (Edrei, Derʿa), Gadora, and Samoulis (Ptolemy *Geog.* 5.14.22). In the NT the Decapolis is identified, but no individual cities are named (Matt. 4:25; Mark 5:20; 7:31).

A number of the cities continued into the Byzantine period and Islamic times (e.g., Damascus, Abila/Quailibah, Pella, Philadelphia, Scythopolis). Some claimed Alexander the Great as founder (Gerasa, Pella, Philadelphia, Dion), but evidence indicates that, as Decapolis cities, they were established in the 3rd century B.C., during the early Ptolemaic dynasty (Philadelphia/Amman, Nysa-Scythopolis). Still others were established as Decapolis cities during the Seleucid hegemony after the battle of Panias in 198, when Antiochus III conquered Abila (Quailibah), Gadara, Pella, Rabbatamana (Philadelphia) and Scythopolis. Identifying terms on coins, such as Antiochia (Gadara, Gerasa, Hippos) and Seleucia (Abila/Quailibah), indicate at least a remembrance of Seleucid identity and influence.

Coins of a number of the Decapolis cities often are stamped with the terms *autonomos* ("independent, living under one's own law"; Abila/Quailibah, Capitolias, Gadara), *eleutheros* ("free"; Nysa-Scythopolis), *asylos* ("sovereign, under divine protection"; Abila, Capitolias, Gadara, Hippos, Nysa-Scythopolis), and *hieros* ("hallowed, sacred, set apart"; Abila, Capitolias, Gadara, Hippos, Nysa-Scythopolis), which indicates that these cities enjoyed or at least claimed some sort of sovereign, independent, and dedicated status.

The Decapolis cities may have been bonded by strong commercial relationships fostered by well-established road systems, as well as similar Greek and Roman political affinity (the *polis*), social concepts, cultural (sculpture, painting, architecture, monuments) and religious influences (worship of the imperial cult; cf. religious figurines and other religious items found in Hellenistic and Roman tombs). This is supported by archaeological evidence from tombs, city planning, and public buildings. In Roman times (after A.D. 106) Gerasa, Philadelphia, Canatha, and Dion were organized with Nysa-Scythopolis, Hippos, Gadara, Abila, Capitolias, and Pella into Palaestina Secunda; Philadelphia, Adraʿa, Gerasa, Canatha, and Philoppopolis remained in the Provincia Arabia. Coins and inscriptions indicate that by the 2nd century a number of the cities were also identified with the name Coele-Syria: Philadelphia, under Hadrian; Gadara, Abila, Scythopolis, under Marcus Aurelius; Dion and Pella, under Caracalla.

Bibliography. M. Avi-Yonah, *The Holy Land* (Grand Rapids, 1966), 51, 69; A. N. Barghouti, "Urbanization of Palestine and Jordan in the Hellenistic and Roman Times," in *Studies in the History and Archaeology of Jordan,* I, ed. A. Hadidi (Amman, 1982), 209-29; A. H. M. Jones, *The Cities of the Eastern Roman Provinces* (Oxford, 1937), 222-94; A. Spijkerman, *The Coins of the Decapolis and Provincia Arabia,* ed. M. Piccirillo (Jerusalem, 1978).

W. HAROLD MARE

DECISION, VALLEY OF

The place (Heb. *ʿēmeq heḥārûṣ*) where God will wreak vengeance against the nations on the eschatological day of the Lord (Joel 3:14[MT 4:14]).

See JEHOSHAPHAT, VALLEY OF.

DECREE

A public declaration by a monarch or ruling body that had the force of law (cf. "edict," "interdict"). The decree would typically be spoken aloud and subsequently promulgated in written form.

Although preexilic biblical literature rarely attributes decrees to human kings (Prov. 8:15; Isa. 10:1; Jon. 3:7), later texts refer to a number of decrees issued by imperial monarchs (Esth. 1:19-22; Dan. 2:5; 1 Macc. 1:57; Acts 17:7). Cyrus' decree (Ezra 1:2-4; cf. 6:3-5) permits the Jewish exiles to return to their homeland and rebuild their temple. Several decrees calling for the annihilation of the Jewish people or the suppression of their religious practices introduce stories extolling the benefits of obedience to God's law (Esth. 3:15; 4 Macc. 4:23). A decree by Caesar Augustus provides the narrative rationale for Mary and Joseph to travel to Bethlehem for the birth of Jesus (Luke 2:1).

Several passages portray God as one who rules Israel or the world by means of decrees (Deut. 4:45; Job 28:26; Ps. 78:5, 56; Jer. 19:5; Rom. 1:32). Paul and his later interpreters assert that the salvation offered through Christ Jesus is a fulfillment of the divine wisdom decreed by God before the creation of the world (Rom. 8:29-30; 1 Cor. 2:7).

FRANK D. WULF

DECRETUM GELASIANUM

A Latin document dating in its present form to the 6th century C.E.; traditionally attributed to Pope Gelasius (492-496) but perhaps reflecting the synodical decisions of 382 under Pope Damasus. Of particular significance for the establishment of the Christian canon are its lists of canonical books of both the OT and NT, the writings of the church fathers as accepted by the early Church, "apocryphal" biblical and patristic works, and various books rejected as heretical. In addition this compilation includes pronouncements concerning the primacy of Rome and the nature of Christ and the Holy Spirit.

DEDAN (Heb. *dĕḏān*)

Name given to the al-ʿUla oasis in northwest Arabia, ca. 300 km. (186 mi.) NNW of Medina, as confirmed by its presence *(Ddn)* in the funerary inscription (JS 138) of "Kabarʾil, son of Mataʿʾil, king of Dedan" found there by the Dominican fathers Antonin J. Jaussen and Raphael Savignac in 1909/1910. Listed as a son of Keturah (Gen. 25:3; 1 Chr. 1:32) and of Raamah (Gen. 10:7), Dedan is twice associated with Edom (Jer. 49:8; Ezek. 25:13) and once with the north Arabian oasis town of Tema (Jer. 25:23). The people of Dedan are called merchants (Ezek. 27:15-20), and the "caravans of Dedanites" are said to lodge "in the forest in Arabia" (Isa. 21:13). According to records, the Babylonian king Nabonidus (555-539 B.C.) visited Dedan and defeated its unnamed king.

By the 4th century Dedan had become the site of a large trading colony of Minaean merchants from South Arabia, as attested by the Minaean inscriptions and graffiti at al-ʿUla and the occurrence of the name Dedan *(DDN)* in the hierodule inscriptions from the Rṣf temple at Qarnaw (ancient Maʿin) in Yemen. Later still it became capital of the Lihyanite kingdom, some 13 kings of which are attested epigraphically. By the late 1st century B.C. Dedan seems to have been eclipsed by the nearby Nabatean town of Hegra (Meda'in Salih).

Bibliography. W. F. Albright, "Dedan," in *Geschichte und AT. Festschrift Albrecht Alt.* Beiträge zur historischen Theologie 16 (Tübingen, 1953), 1-12. D. T. POTTS

DEDICATION, FEAST OF

A celebration in remembrance of the restoration of the Jerusalem temple and the consecration of its new altar in 165 or 164 B.C.E. under Judas Maccabeus (1 Macc. 4:36-61). The Hebrew name for the festival is Hanukkah *(ḥănukkâ),* first attested in the 1st-century-C.E. *megillat taʿanit.* The eight-day observance begins on the 25th of Kislev (Nov.-Dec.); cf. John 10:22, which refers to Jesus' being in Jerusalem in winter, during the Feast of Dedication (Gk. *enkaínia,* "renewal, restoration"). The initial celebration included the offering of sacrifices, music, and the adornment of the front of the temple and the chambers of the priests (1 Macc. 4:52-58). At this first celebration it was decided that Hanukkah should be observed annually (1 Macc. 4:59; 2 Macc. 10:8). The eight days of Hanukkah are likely based on the duration of Solomon's dedication of the first temple (1 Kgs. 8:66; 2 Chr. 7:9).

The accounts of the rededication in 1 and 2 Maccabees differ somewhat in emphases. While the focus of 1 Macc. 4:36-59 is the consecration (*enkainismós,* v. 56) of the new altar, 2 Maccabees emphasizes the purification (*katharismós,* 1:18; 2:19; 10:3, 5, 7) of the temple. 2 Macc. 10:6-7 speaks of the celebration's similarity to the Festival of Booths (including its eight-day duration, the waving of branches); the association between the two festivals is also made in 1:18.

From early on Hanukkah was associated with light and fire. Josephus (*Ant.* 12.7.7 §325) relates that Hanukkah itself was known as "Lights" (Gk. *phōtá*) and explains that the name came from "the fact that the right to worship appeared to us at a time when we hardly dared hope for it." 2 Macc. 1:18 associates Hanukkah with "the festival of the fire," recalling a legend about fire from the altar of the First Temple eventuating in the altar fire in the time of Nehemiah (2 Macc. 1:19-36). A talmudic tradition tells of a small amount of oil, found by the Maccabees upon their recovery of the temple, which miraculously burned for eight days. 1 Macc. 4:50; 2 Macc. 10:3 describe how the restoration of the temple included the candelabrum and the lighting of lamps, but the reason for the emphasis on light seems to have become obscure at an early time. JOEL BURNETT

DEEP

The chaotic and terrifying cosmic waters out of which the world originated (Heb. *tĕhôm;* Gk. *ábyssos*).

In the Babylonian creation epic, Enuma Elish, the monstrous goddess Tiamat, whose name is etymologically related to Heb. *tĕhôm,* is slain by the god Marduk in a cosmic battle. After he defeats Tiamat, Marduk cuts her body into two parts; one becomes the earth, and the other becomes the heavens. Marduk thus creates the world and establishes order out of chaos.

Even though there are echoes of this Babylonian epic in Genesis, God there creates order out of chaos by "separating the waters from the waters" and "making a firmament" and separating the waters under the firmament from those above it (Gen. 1:6-7). He does not tame a giant dragon. God divides and contains the waters with his breath (Ps. 33:6-7), and he uses "the fountains of the great deep" to wash away the violence and corruption of the world (Gen. 7:11; cf. 8:2). These waters are also the instruments of God's power and providence in leading the Israelites out of Egypt (Exod. 15:5-8).

The deep also refers to the underworld (Jon. 2:3, 5-6[MT 4, 6-7]) and the realm of the dead (Job 38:16; Rom. 10:7), and it occasionally refers to the primeval battle between God and the monsters of chaos: Rahab, Leviathan, Tannin (cf. Isa. 51:9-10).

HENRY L. CARRIGAN, JR.

DEER

Three Hebrew words are commonly identified as deer: *'ayyāl, yaḥmûr,* and *ʿōper.* All three of these animals were suitable to eat; *'ayyāl* and *yaḥmûr* were specifically designated as a clean food (Deut. 12:15; 14:5; 15:22).

Historically four species of deer have inhabited Palestine — the red deer (*Cervus elaphus*), two varieties of fallow deer (*Cervus* [*Dama*] *dama* and *D. Mesopotamica*), and the roe deer (*Capreolus capreolus*). While the rather large red deer (height 1.37 m. [54 in.]) was the predominant species in Palestine during prehistoric periods, archaeological evidence suggests their population later declined and eventually disappeared due to climatic changes and deforestation; however, bones were discovered at Hesban from levels as late as Iron II or even the Ayyubid/Mamluk periods. Roe deer are small, delicate, and shy animals (height 76 cm. [30 in.]) that congregate only in small herds and are seldom seen. Although they were undoubtedly present in Palestine throughout the biblical periods, they have seldom turned up in archaeological remains, suggesting they were seldom seen or hunted and are probably not referred to in the Bible. The slightly larger fallow deer (height 102 cm. [40 in.]) were more conspicuous since they traveled in fairly large herds. Their bones turn up more frequently than any other deer species at sites such as Hesban and Tel Dan, suggesting they were well known by ancient peoples. It is, therefore, likely that the deer the ancient Israelites were most familiar with was the fallow deer, which thus should be identified with the Heb. *'ayyāl* (Deut. 12:22; 1 Kgs. 4:23[MT 5:3]; Ps. 42:1[2]; Cant. 2:9, 17; Isa. 35:6).

Heb. *yaḥmûr* (1 Kgs. 4:23[5:3]; Deut. 14:5) carries the connotation of "red," and has been, like *'ayyāl,* associated with the fallow deer which has a pale rusty color. However, since 1 Kgs. 4:23(5:3) distinguishes between the two terms they should probably not be identified with the same species. Another possibility is the red deer, which is not only red in color, but possibly still lived in the area during the Iron Age and Arabic periods. A third suggestion is the bubal or red hartebeest (*Alcelaphus buselaphus;* cf. LXX Gk. *bubalos* for *yaḥmûr*). According to the 19th-century naturalist H. B. Tristram, Arabs claimed to have hunted this beast near springs east of the Dead Sea; although there is no other evidence that these animals ever lived as far north as Palestine, they apparently lived in Egypt during Dynastic times.

Heb. *'ōper* (Cant. 4:5; 7:3[4]) carries the connotation of "young" and should probably be identified with any young deer or deerlike animal (such as gazelle) and not equated with a particular species.

RANDALL W. YOUNKER

DELAIAH (Heb. *dĕlāyâ, dĕlāyāhû*)

1. One of the sons of Elioenai, a descendant of David through Zerubbabel (1 Chr. 3:24).

2. A descendant of Aaron; head of the twenty-third priestly division during the days of David (1 Chr. 24:18).

3. The ancestor of a group of exiles who were unable to prove their Jewish descent and thus secure their Jewish heritage (Ezra 2:60 = Neh. 7:62).

4. The son of Mehetabel and father of Shemaiah (Neh. 6:10).

5. The son of Shemaiah (Jer. 36:12); one of three princes who unsuccessfully urged King Jehoiakim not to burn Jeremiah's prophetic scroll (v. 25).

DELILAH (Heb. *dĕlîlâ*)

The woman who defeats Samson. The meaning of her name is uncertain; proposals include "devotee," "coquette," "falling curl," and "small." Given the association of the name Samson with Heb. *šemeš* ("sun"), it seems to involve a wordplay with *laylâ* ("night"). The story does not specify Delilah's ethnic identity; she is most likely Philistine, like Samson's other paramours.

The Samson stories pivot upon Samson's dangerous liaisons with three women. Samson's love for Delilah (Judg. 16:2-22) is the third and most lethal of these. Offered a large bribe by Philistine lords, Delilah agrees to discover the secret of Samson's strength. Three times she asks Samson how he may be overpowered; and is teased with a false answer. The fourth time Samson divulges his secret: his strength lies in his unshorn hair. While Samson sleeps, Delilah shaves his head, binds him, and hands him over to his enemies.

Delilah illustrates a common biblical and folkloric motif: the "strange" woman who ensnares men. Traditional interpretation portrays Delilah as the quintessential deceptive seductress. In contrast, recent feminist interpretations suggest that Delilah, like the Timnite woman who betrays Samson to save her life (Judg. 14:1-20), is a woman who does what she must in order to survive. Others note that from a Philistine perspective Delilah is like Jael, a heroine celebrated for seducing and then killing Israel's enemy, Sisera (Judg. 4:17-22; 5:24-27).

Bibliography. J. L. Crenshaw, *Samson* (Atlanta, 1978); J. C. Exum, "Aspects of Symmetry and Balance in the Samson Cycle," *JSOT* 19 (1981): 3-29; D. N. Fewell, "Judges," in *The Women's Bible Commentary,* ed. C. A. Newsom and S. H. Ringe (Louisville, 1992), 67-77.

CAROLYN J. PRESSLER

DELUGE

See FLOOD.

DEMAS (Gk. *Dēmás*)

A gentile coworker who shared Paul's first imprisonment and sent greetings to Philemon's community (Phlm. 24) and the Colossians (Col. 4:14). He apparently fell "in love with this present world," deserted Paul, and went to Thessalonica (2 Tim. 4:10), causing a rift in Paul's communities. Some scholars identify Demas (a shortened form of Demetrius, Democritus, or Demosthenes) with the Demetrius of 3 John 12. The apocryphal Acts of Paul (3:1, 4, 12-14) mentions a Demas who urges that Paul be arrested for preaching the gospel and who teaches that the resurrection has already occurred (a problem noted in canonical Thessalonians).

BONNIE THURSTON

DEMETRIUS (Gk. *Dēmḗtrios*)

1. Demetrius Poliorcetes (338-283 B.C.E.), king of Macedonia and son of Antigonus I. He twice attempted to restore Alexander's empire to a single ruler. In 307 he began to free Greece from Cassander's control by seizing Athens. The next year he took Cyprus and seaports of Asia and defeated Ptolemy I in a sea battle, after which he and his father claimed joint kingship over Alexander's empire. After failing to capture Egypt and Rhodes in 305, he returned to control Greece and by 303 planned to take Asia. This attempt failed in 301 at the battle of Ipsus, where Antigonus was killed and Demetrius defeated by an alliance of Cassander, Lysimachus, Ptolemy I, and Seleucus I.

Left with control of Cyprus and some cities in Asia Minor, Demetrius allied with Seleucus I. When this alliance fell apart in 296 over the possession of Tyre and Sidon, Demetrius set out to retake Greece once again. By 293 he ruled Macedonia and continued his domination of Greece through 289. In 289 Demetrius again planned to conquer Asia, which resulted in a new alliance of Lysimachus, Ptolemy I, and Seleucus I against him. In 285 he was forced to surrender to Seleucus I and died in captivity in 283.

2. Demetrius I Soter (162-150), king of Syria

and son of Seleucus IV. He was raised as a hostage in Rome. When the Senate refused to return him as king after the death of his uncle Antiochus IV, he escaped and returning to Phoenicia had Antiochus V killed and himself proclaimed king. He thus set out to reestablish his kingdom by settling in Antioch, freeing the Babylonian provinces from Timarchus the Milesian, and supporting Orophrenes' overthrow of Ariarathes V in Cappadocia.

Seeking to further solidify his kingdom, he took measures to stop the growing independence movement in Judah under Judas Maccabeus (1 Macc. 7–9; 2 Macc. 14–15). Demetrius appointed Alcimus as high priest from a legitimate priestly family, thus satisfying many of the concerns of the Hasidim. Nicanor was also sent to establish civil peace. But when Nicanor was ordered to arrest Judas, war again broke out resulting in Nicanor's death. Demetrius retaliated by sending Bacchides with a large force, who eventually killed Judas in battle.

Eumenes then raised up a counter-claimant to the throne, Alexander Balas. Demetrius offered Jonathan the Hasmonean military and civil leadership, but Alexander outbid him by offering Jonathan the high priesthood. By 153 Alexander formed a major coalition with Attalus II, Ariarathes V, and Ptolemy Philometor against Demetrius. Despite initial successes, Demetrius lost support of many of his troops and died in battle against Alexander.

3. Demetrius II Nicator, Seleucid king 145-140, 129-125. The son of Demetrius I, at age 14 he was sent in 148-147 with mercenaries from Crete to challenge Alexander Balas. With the support of Ptolemy VI Philometor he became king in Antioch in 145, and Alexander was defeated and killed. The Hasmonean response to Demetrius II varied according to the political situation (1 Macc. 10:67–13:30). Until his death Jonathan supported Alexander against Demetrius II. Once on the throne Demetrius confirmed Jonathan's past honors by Alexander, as well as reduced his tribute and extended his territory into Samaria. As a result Jewish troops supported Demetrius when riots broke out against him in Antioch.

When Diodotus (Trypho) placed Alexander's son Antiochus VI on the throne in Antioch, Jonathan switched his allegiance. During the ensuing battle for power Jonathan extended the political strength and independence of Judah. As a result Trypho captured Jonathan and later killed him. But when Trypho killed Antiochus VI in 143-142 and declared himself king, Simon supported Demetrius in return for Judah's independence.

In 140 Demetrius fought against the Parthians and was captured. He was freed in 129 by Antiochus VII. When the latter died in battle, Demetrius regained the throne. After a failed attempt to conquer Egypt and losing Antioch to a pretender, he was killed on board a ship at Tyre after being refused safe entry in Ptolemais.

4. Demetrius III Eucerus (95-88), son of Antiochus VIII Grypus. He proclaimed himself king in Damascus against his brothers Antiochus XI and Philip. Demetrius came to the aid of the Jews when Alexander Janneus slaughtered 6000 people during a riot at the Feast of Tabernacles, but later left when Jewish troops shifted their support to Alexander (Josephus *Ant.* 13:13-14). In 88 he attacked his brother Philip but was defeated and taken prisoner to Parthia, where he died.

5. Demetrius of Phalerum (345-283), Peripatetic governor of Athens under Cassander until 307 when Demetrius Poliorcetes (**1** above) attacked the city. Demetrius of Phalerum surrendered and was given safe passage to Egypt, where he served as president and librarian of the library in Alexandria under Ptolemy I.

The Letter of Aristeas claims that Demetrius was responsible for the translation of the Hebrew Scriptures into Greek under Ptolemy II Philadelphus, but there is no evidence that Demetrius held any position at the library under Ptolemy II.

6. Demetrius, a silversmith in Ephesus (Acts 19:23-41) who made silver shrines of Artemis. His concern about the loss of business and diminished worship of the goddess resulting from Paul's preaching provoked his fellow artisans to riot. The town clerk reminded the crowd gathered at the theater that Paul and his followers had done nothing illegal against the temple or the cult and suggested that Demetrius instead bring civil charges in the courts.

7. A person strongly commended to Gaius by the Elder in 3 John 12. Since the letter is meant as a reference letter in part, it is possible that Demetrius is also the carrier of the letter.

Bibliography. E. R. Bevan, *The House of Seleucus,* 2 vols. (1902, repr. New York, 1966).

RUSSELL NELSON

DEMON

In classical Greek a god or a small divinity (Gk. *daímōn*). In later Greek thought, demons were conceived as intermediary spiritual beings which might move either up or down (i.e., they may be either good or bad). Because of this inconsistent nature, demons became a convenient explanation for bad things that happen in this world. Jewish and early Christian writers coalesced *daimónion* with Heb. *mal'āḵ;* Gk. *ángelos* ("messenger spirit") and created a new division of good spirits (angels) and evil spirits (demons). In the NT and contemporary literature the term *daimṓnion* becomes more than pejorative, referring not only to malevolent spirits but also and more precisely to beings who in their true nature are agents of Satan and whose mission is to oppose the work of God and his people.

Jewish tradition depicts demons to be fallen angels who had joined Satan in his revolt against God (1 En. 16:1; 19:1). Gen. 6:1-4 was interpreted as narrating the fall of angels who descended on earth to mate with women, whose children became evil spirits on earth (1 En. 69:4; Jub. 4:15-22; 2 Bar. 56:12). Philo of Alexandria identified the angels of Gen. 6:1-4 with "demons" (*De gigantibus* 6). In the OT, however, good and evil spirits were thought to come from Yahweh. Thus, the "lying spirit" sent to King Zedekiah did not act on its own, but as directed by

God (1 Kgs. 22:21-23), as also the evil spirit that tormented Saul (1 Sam. 16:15-16). Satan himself operates under divine authority (Job 1:12). In the book of Tobit, which contains elaborate accounts of demonic activities, the evil demon Asmodaeus afflicts the seven successive fiancés of Sarah (daughter of Raguel) with death at her wedding night, but he is later exorcised by the angel Raphael (Tob. 8:2-3).

Demons feature prominently as adversaries in the ministry of Jesus, and as agents of Satan they must be overcome if Jesus' ministry is to be successful. Jesus himself speaks of having come to plunder Satan's goods (Luke 11:21-22); expulsion of demons from people is one means by which Jesus does so in the Gospel accounts (Matt. 12:27-28). Early Judaism taught that when the Messiah comes, he will overthrow the kingdom of Satan.

According to early Christian literature, demons do not operate in a vacuum. They "oppress," attacking people from without, or "possess," entering an individual's body and attacking it from within. They cause diseases and sicknesses of all kind, although not all sicknesses may be attributed to them (Mark 1:32; 2:10-12). For people in antiquity, certain kinds of sickness were caused by demons even if the symptoms can be explained by modern medicine. The presence of a demon in a person might sometimes not be obvious to a third party unless confronted by an exorcist (Mark 1:21-28). Most of the time, however, a demonic activity in a person's life would be obvious (Mark 5:1-19 par.; 9:14-29 par.).

Bibliography. E. Ferguson, *Demonology of the Early Christian World* (New York, 1984); E. Langston, *Essentials of Demonology* (1949, repr. New York, 1981); W. Wink, *Naming the Powers* (Philadelphia, 1986). CHARLES YEBOAH

DENARIUS (Gk. *dēnárion*)

A Roman silver coin weighing ca. 3.64 grams, approximately equal to a Greek drachma. A laborer would work all day for a denarius in Palestine during the time of Jesus (Matt. 20:2; cf. Tob. 5:15-16, where the angel Raphael agrees to work for Tobias for a drachma a day plus expenses and bonus). A hundred denarii were a significant but manageable debt (Matt. 18:28). Two hundred denarii would feed 5000 people for one meal (Mark 6:37 par. John 6:7), and a bottle of perfume could cost 300 denarii (Mark 14:5 = John 12:5). A quart of wheat, or three quarts of barley, might cost a denarius in wartime (Rev. 6:6). In Jesus' parable the good Samaritan paid the innkeeper two denarii to care for the wounded traveler, expecting the money not to cover all the costs of the man's recovery (Luke 10:35). It was a denarius that Jesus' opponents brought him when he said, "Give to Caesar what is Caesar's, and to God what is God's" (Matt. 22:19 = Mark 12:15; Luke 20:24). CARL BRIDGES

DERBE (Gk. *Dérbē*)

A city in southeastern Lyconium, a district of the Roman province of Galatia. Derbe lay on a busy main road that stretched from Iconium and Lystra east to Tarsus in Cilicia. Some archaeologists believe its ruins lie at Kerti Hüyük, 4.8 km. (3 mi.) NW of modern Zosta and 72.4 km. (45 mi.) S of Konia (Iconium). Nothing is known of the city's early history.

Paul visited Derbe on his first and second missionary journeys (Acts 14:6, 20; 16:1), possibly because it was the home of Gaius, one of his traveling companions (20:4). On Paul's first journey, after being stoned and left for dead at Lystra (14:14-19) he traveled 48.3 km. (30 mi.) southeast to Derbe, the easternmost point of that journey. He then returned to Lystra and retraced his steps through Iconium, Antioch, and Perga on his way home. Paul revisited Derbe on his second journey (16:1). We have no record of any specific events that transpired there. DALE ELLENBURG

DESCENT INTO HELL

A widely held belief in the early Church, and later an article of the Apostles' Creed, that between his crucifixion and resurrection Jesus descended into the underworld (Hades) either to proclaim victory, to release OT saints, or to proclaim the gospel. Such beliefs and their later credal development emphasized the universality of salvation offered in Jesus Christ.

No single biblical passage refers to all these elements, but the Jewish tradition had analogies to such descents (Ps. 16; 18; 42:7[MT 8]; 69:2[3]; Jonah 2:2-6; 1 Enoch). NT sources for the descent into hell are Peter's Pentecost speech (Acts 2:24-31) and passages from the Pauline corpus (Rom. 10:7; Eph. 4:9; 1 Cor. 15:54). Sayings of Jesus provided further sources for the later elaboration of the belief (Matt. 8:11; Luke 13:28-29; John 5:19-29).

Jesus' descent into hell and subsequent resurrection were commonly associated with two themes, the overthrow of evil powers or angels and the liberation of the righteous Jewish saints. The idea of Jesus' preaching to the dead was a 2nd-century development associated with 1 Pet. 3:18 by Justin, Clement of Alexandria, Origen, Irenaeus, and Hippolytus. In the late 4th century Augustine of Hippo interpreted the Petrine account allegorically as referring to Christian preaching to sinners (the "dead"). The clause "He descended into Hell" was first included in the early Roman Creed of Aquileia by Rufinus, ca. 400 C.E.

Bibliography. W. J. Dalton, *Christ's Proclamation to the Spirits,* 2nd ed. AnBib 23 (Rome, 1989); B. I. Reicke, *The Disobedient Spirits and Christian Baptism* (Copenhagen, 1946). IAIN S. MACLEAN

DESERT

Arid environment hostile to life. In the Bible, desert functions thematically as a place of revelation and a training ground for faith and obedience, in preparation for mission.

Desert is an arid region (mean annual precipitation of 25 cm. [10 in.] or less), with sparse vegetation, few animals, little or no agriculture, and

Caravansary at Nuweiba in the Sinai desert (Phoenix Data Systems, Neal and Joel Bierling)

low population density. ("Wilderness," a common misnomer, merely denotes an uninhabited region, without reference to food and water resources.) In biblical deserts temperatures are harsh, often exceeding 45° C. (113° F.) on summer days and falling below freezing on winter nights. Most precipitation occurs in winter. The chief livelihood was shepherding sheep and goats.

The various deserts mentioned in the Bible are part of the greater Saharo-Arabian desert system, but each has distinct geological, topographical, meteorological, hydrological, floral, and faunal features. Though often symbolic rather than strictly historical, biblical stories set in these deserts tend to reflect the differing conditions of each.

Physical Characteristics

Negeb

The land of Abraham and Sarah, the Negeb semidesert was limited to the Beer-sheba and Arad basins and considered part of the Promised Land. It has some fertile loose soil and a mean annual but highly fluctuating rainfall of 10-25 cm. (8-10 in.), sometimes meeting the 25 cm. (10 in.) needed for winter wheat. In normal years vegetation for grazing is found in all wadi bottoms and on most hillsides. Thus it was a land of nomadic grazing but unreliable agriculture, becoming a place of high risk in drought years (cf. stories about Abraham, Isaac, and Joseph).

Sinai

The location of the desert of Sinai, the setting for the Mt. Sinai and covenant stories, remains unknown. If correlated with the huge Sinai Peninsula, it falls into three diverse regions: (1) a northern plain of sand dunes and gravel near the Mediterranean coast, with rainfall of 7.5-10 cm. (3-4 in.); (2) the large central et-Tih plateau, drained by the el-Arish system, covered with chalk and flint toward the center and limestone toward the south, with rainfall of 2.5-5 cm. (1-2 in.); (3) the high granite mountains of the south, including Jebel Mûsā, the traditional Mt. Sinai, at 2285 m. (7296 ft.), with rainfall at 7.5-10 cm. (3-4 in.). Oases of perennial water and vegetation support a modest population, but most of the Sinai is hostile to life.

Paran

Crossed by the Israelites between Sinai and Zin, the harsh desert of Paran drains a large plateau area northeast into the Rift Valley. Its rugged limestone and chalk geology with gravel plains and alluvium, very sparse rainfall (0-5 cm. [0-2 in.]), and few perennial water sources, make most of it particularly hostile to life — a hard, hot region, deserving its description as a "great and terrible wilderness, an arid wasteland with poisonous snakes and scorpions" (Deut. 8:15). Taking the Israelites safely across this desert provided an extreme example of divine care and power, an image of God as Bedouin leader — the good shepherd of his people.

Zin

Location for much of the Israelites' "wilderness wandering," the desert of Zin is drained by the substantial Wadi Zin system, between Paran to the south and the Negeb to the north. Its mean annual rainfall of 10-20 cm. (4-8 in.) on soft chalks, marls, and clays with some alluvial loess, supports many perennial water sources and some year-round vegetation on both wadi bottoms and some north-facing slopes. It was survivable by shepherds grazing goats but supported no reliable dry farming.

Associated with Zin was the oasis region of Kadesh-barnea, portrayed as an important Israelite stopping place and central meeting point. It was apparently located in a border region between Paran and Zin, for it was linked to both (Paran: Num. 13:26; Zin: 20:1; 27:14; 33:36). and may have included all the oases of the modern 'Ain el-Qudeirat region. Stories about Moses sending the 12 scouts (Num. 13) and striking water from the rock (ch. 20) and the Israelites attempting to enter the Promised Land prematurely (14:39-45) occurred there during a lengthy stay (14:33, 35; Deut. 1:46).

Conditions and Lessons

Life in the desert teaches important lessons about faith and ethics. Surviving in this unforgiving environment requires both specialized knowledge and the discipline to apply it. Yet no amount of skill and discipline will guarantee survival, so desert life requires that people help each other, and it also generates more direct trust in God. The desert seems to facilitate revelation. People hear the voice of God more clearly, unimpeded by civilization or their own rationalizations.

Biblical Accounts

Desert played a major role in the accounts of the patriarchs (Gen. 12-50). As a whole, this cycle created a symbolic salvation geography in which the desert fringes of the Promised Land rather than the great civilizations of the day (Mesopotamia and Egypt) functioned as the chosen place for training the nascent chosen people.

The most important desert stories relate to the Exodus (Exod. 15:22; 16:1; 17:1), Sinai (18:5; 19:1-2), and 40-year sojourn (Num. 14:33; 32:13; Deut. 2:7).

The desert functioned as a place of refuge from oppression, e.g., for Hagar from Sarai (Gen. 16:7), Moses from the pharaoh (Exod. 2:15–3:1), Benjaminites from Israelites (Judg. 20:47), David from Saul (1 Sam. 23-26) and later from Absalom (2 Sam. 15-17), and Elijah from Jezebel (1 Kgs. 19:1-4).

Desert themes are similar in the NT. John the Baptist trained for his ministry and carried it out in the desert, preaching a message of repentance and justice characteristic of desert values (Matt. 3:1-12; 11:7-10; Mark 1:3-4; Luke 1:80; 3:1-20; John 1:23). There Jesus made his final preparation before embarking on his public ministry (Matt. 4:1-11; Mark 1:12-13; Luke 4:1-13) and retreated to desert places for renewal or revelation (Matt. 14:13; Mark 6:30-32; Luke 4:42; 5:16; 6:12; John 6:15; 11:54).

Bibliography. G. Brubacher, "City and Civilization Ideology in the Book of Genesis," in *Within the Perfection of Christ,* ed. T. L. Brensinger and E. M. Sider (Napanee, Ind.), 33-46; A. Danin, *Desert Vegetation of Israel and Sinai* (Jerusalem, 1983); E. Orni and E. Elisha, *Geography of Israel,* 4th ed. (Jerusalem, 1980); S. Talmon, *"midbār, 'ărābâ,"* *TDOT* 8:87-118.

GORDON BRUBACHER

DESOLATING SACRILEGE

The usurping of God's prerogative of worship by a pagan political power (Heb. *šiqqûs šōmēm;* Gk. *bdélygma tḗs erēmṓseōs*); also called the abomination of desolation. A part of the Jewish and early Christian apocalyptic traditions, the desolating sacrilege occurred in 167 B.C.E. with the desecration of the Jerusalem temple by the Seleucid ruler Antiochus IV Epiphanes (Dan. 9:27; 11:31; 12:11; 1 Macc. 1:54, 59). Antiochus forcibly ended Jewish worship and introduced the worship of Zeus Olympios (2 Macc. 6:1), placing an altar to Zeus upon the altar of burnt offerings (Josephus *Ant.* 12.253). In Daniel the phrase "desolating sacrilege" is perhaps a mocking distortion of "Lord of Heaven" *(ba'al šāmên),* the Greek Zeus Olympios.

Subsequent Jewish tradition and the NT regarded this desolating sacrilege as a prophetic paradigm for analogous idolatrous attacks on the people of God by pagans. Jesus prophesied that a desolating sacrilege would occur in Judea (Matt. 24:15; Mark 13:14), but the referent is uncertain. Proposals include Caligula's attempt to erect his statue in the temple in 39-40 C.E.; events leading to the destruction of Jerusalem in 70 C.E. (Luke 21:20), especially the activity of the Zealots in the temple (Josephus *BJ* 4.196-207); and the coming of the antichrist. Paul's man of lawlessness (2 Thess. 2:1-12) and the beast of Revelation (Rev. 13, 17) are other versions of the desolating sacrilege tradition.

Bibliography. D. Ford, *The Abomination of Desolation in Biblical Eschatology* (Washington, 1979).

DUANE F. WATSON

DESTROYER

The manifestation of Yahweh's power as the angel of death. For the final plague upon Egypt, Yahweh promises to slay the firstborn sons of the Egyptians (Exod. 11:4-8). As the agent of divine destruction passes through the land (Exod. 12:29), the Israelites avoid calamity by following Yahweh's command to smear lamb's blood on their door lintels (vv. 21-23). A destroying angel performs other acts of punishment following David's census (2 Sam. 24:16-17) and among the Assyrian camp during the siege of Jerusalem in Hezekiah's reign (Isa. 37:36). In the OT the destroyer (Heb. *mašḥîṯ, šōḏēḏ*) also refers to human agents employed as instruments of Yahweh's power (Job 15:21; Isa. 21:2; Jer. 4:7; 48:8, 15, 18).

In the NT, Paul commands the Corinthians not to complain as the Israelites did in the wilderness when Yahweh loosed the destroyer (Gk. *olothreutḗs*) upon them (1 Cor. 10:10; cf. Num. 16:13-14, 41-50). It is not clear whether Paul identifies the destroyer as Satan or as a specific angel. The latter identification represents the view in rabbinic literature.

WILLIAM D. MATHERLY

DEUEL (Heb. *dĕʿûʾēl*)
A representative of the tribe of Gad in the wilderness and the father of Eliasaph (Num. 1:14; 7:42, 47). At Num. 2:14 he is called Reuel (**4**), probably resulting from a confusion of the Hebrew consonants *daleth* and *resh.*

DEUTERO-ISAIAH
See ISAIAH, BOOK OF.

DEUTERO-ZECHARIAH
See ZECHARIAH, BOOK OF.

DEUTEROCANONICAL BOOKS
An alternate name ("second canon") which the Roman Catholic and Orthodox churches apply to those books found in the LXX and Vulgate but not in the Hebrew text of the OT. According to the decision of the Council of Trent (1548) and the First Vatican Council (1870) these books, like those of the Hebrew canon, are regarded as possessing divine and canonical authority.

See APOCRYPHA.

DEUTERONOMISTIC HISTORY
The Deuteronomistic (or Deuteronomic) history (DH) is a theoretical construct used by modern scholars to comprehend the unity exhibited by the books of Deuteronomy, Joshua, Judges, Samuel, and Kings. This scholarly consensus owes much to Martin Noth's classic study, which emphasized that the books of Deuteronomy through Kings constitute a continuous history characterized by a basic homogeneity in language, style, and content. In Noth's reconstruction, the Deuteronomist incorporated the Deuteronomic law into the beginning of his work, framing it with speeches by Moses, and then added other sources — tales of conquest and settlement, prophetic narratives and speeches, official annals and records. The Deuteronomist ordered and shaped these sources, introduced his own distinctive chronology, and inserted his own comments and speeches (often in the mouths of major characters) at critical junctures in his history. Because the Deuteronomist's compositional technique included selection, editing, and creation of new material, the resulting work was not merely a compilation of tales, annals, and sagas, but a unified work manifesting a deliberate design and a uniformity of purpose. Noth's study provided a cogent alternative both to those earlier scholars who concentrated solely upon isolated historical books without recognizing their relationship to others within the DH and to those who attempted to identify strands within the DH continuous with or analogous to pentateuchal sources.

Thematically, Noth viewed the DH as a pessimistic work that chronicled and censured the record of Israel's existence in the land. To be sure, there were high points in Israel's history, such as the dedication of the temple (1 Kgs. 8), but such positive events could neither prevent the monarchy's eventual downfall nor provide a basis for future hope. The history of Israel is thus a record of "ever-intensifying decline" that ends in disaster — the Babylonian Exile. Noth's views have been developed and refined in recent scholarship. John Van Seters defends the essential unity of the DH through a comparison with ancient Near Eastern and Greek historiography. New literary critics emphasize its unity as a carefully crafted work of art.

Many other scholars have sought to modify Noth's views. Both Gerhard von Rad and Hans Walter Wolff challenge Noth's conclusions about purpose and theme. Von Rad points to an alternation between themes of "gospel" and "law" in Samuel–Kings. The Davidic promises delay the Exile (e.g., 1 Kgs. 11:11-13, 31-35), while Jehoiachin's release from prison (2 Kgs. 25:27-30) adumbrates the ultimate revival of David's line, signalling that the DH ends with a messianic promise and not a final judgment. Wolff cites the importance of turning *(šûḇ)* to Yahweh in Deuteronomy, Judges, and Kings to argue that the DH advances an element of hope. Divine judgment does not entail Israel's doom but calls the exiles to repentance, because the people's return *(šûḇ)* to God can elicit God's compassionate return to them (1 Kgs. 8:46-53).

Frank M. Cross and Rudolf Smend challenge Noth's notion that the DH was the product of one exilic author. These scholars, and the schools of thought they have come to represent, posit a series of editions. Cross argues that the main edition of the DH was composed during the reign of Josiah as a programmatic document promoting Josiah's revival of the Davidic state. This primary edition of the DH (Dtr^1) was retouched and revised in a much less extensive edition (2 Kgs. 23:25–25:30) in the Exile (Dtr^2). Cross bases his argument on the interplay between two main themes running through most of Kings: "the sin of Jeroboam," which reverberates throughout the narration of the northern kingdom, and the promises to David, which restrain divine wrath in the history of Judah. The exilic editor (Dtr^2) retouched the earlier work, introduced the sub-theme of Manasseh's apostasy, attributing the destruction of Judah to his perfidy, and recorded Judah's exile. Adherents of Cross's theory have debated whether Dtr^2's contribution was more substantial (e.g., Brian Peckham) or less so (e.g., Steven L. McKenzie). Others have focused on the work of Dtr^1. Gary N. Knoppers, e.g., argues that the attention given to the history of the northern monarchy, the fall of Israel, and the reign of Josiah, can only be understood in the context of Dtr^1's treatment of the United Monarchy and the causes he imputes to the creation of the Divided Monarchy.

Smend construes these successive editions as present throughout much of Joshua–2 Kings, and adds a second nomistically oriented Deuteronomist (DtrN) to the historically oriented Deuteronomist posited by Noth (DtrH). To these exilic editions Walter Dietrich adds a third prophetically-oriented edition (DtrP), written after DtrH but prior to DtrN. Whereas DtrH, much like Noth's DH, functions as an etiology for the nadir of Judah, DtrP assails the political and cultic apostasy of northern royalty. The third redactor (DtrN) purportedly added assorted legal sayings, the law code itself, and the royal traditions of Jerusalem. Although Dietrich contends that all three redactions were completed by 560 B.C.E., Smend believes that DtrN stems from the early postexilic period. Other followers of Smend argue for a succession of DtrN editions. Yet others disagree with Dietrich about the nature and purpose of the major redactions — DtrH, DtrP, and DtrN.

Some recent scholars have developed new theories of multiple redactions, citing variations in the regnal formulae of northern and southern kings. Their arguments do not fall easily into any one particular pattern, but in many cases they incorporate features of the Cross or Smend hypotheses. All of these scholars (e.g., Manfred Weippert, André Lemaire, Mark A. O'Brien, Iain Provan, Baruch Halpern, and David S. Vanderhooft) speak of one or more substantial preexilic editions of the DH and of at least one exilic edition. In spite of the proliferation of different redactional hypotheses, most commentators still speak of a Deuteronomistic history, thus testifying to the profound influence of Noth's theory.

Bibliography. F. M. Cross, *Canaanite Myth and Hebrew Epic* (Cambridge, Mass., 1973); B. Halpern and D. S. Vanderhooft, "The Editions of Kings in the 7th-6th Centuries B.C.E.," *HUCA* 62 (1991): 179-244; G. N. Knoppers, *Two Nations Under God: The Deuteronomistic History of Solomon and the Dual Monarchies,* 2 vols. HSM 52-53 (Atlanta, 1993-94); S. L. McKenzie, *The Trouble with Kings: The Composition of the Book of Kings in the Deuteronomistic History.* VTSup 42 (Leiden, 1991); M. Noth, *The Deuteronomistic History.* JSOTSup 15 (1943; Eng. trans. Sheffield, 1991); M. A. O'Brien, *The Deuteronomistic History Hypothesis.* OBO 92 (Göttingen, 1989); B. Peckham, *History and Prophecy* (New York: Doubleday, 1993); I. Provan, *Hezekiah and the Book of Kings.* BZAW 172 (Berlin, 1988); G. von Rad, *Studies in Deuteronomy.* SBT 9 (Chicago, 1953); J. Van Seters, *In Search of History* (New Haven, 1983); H. W. Wolff, "The Kerygma of the Deuteronomic Historical Work," in *The Vitality of Old Testament Traditions,* ed. W. Brueggemann and Wolff (1961; Eng. trans. Atlanta, 1975), 83-100.

GARY N. KNOPPERS

DEUTERONOMY, BOOK OF

The fifth and final book of the Pentateuch. From both a literary and theological perspective, it is hard to overestimate the importance of the book of Deuteronomy. While it may not be a literary masterpiece itself, its direct literary influence is diffused through a good portion of the OT. For example, the writer responsible for telling the story of ancient Israel in its land found in Joshua, Judges, Samuel, and Kings was a Deuteronomist. Other writers using Deuteronomic language and thought edited several prophetic books, in particular, Hosea and Jeremiah. Deuteronomy, which presents itself as a written authoritative law for Israel in its land is the first book to see itself as "Scripture" (Deut. 17:19-20; 28:58; 29:19; 31:11). Deuteronomy, which sees Israel's future as determined by its observance of the Law, shaped the development of early Judaism. This book, more than any other, enabled ancient Israel to survive the loss of its religious and cultural institutions during the Babylonian crisis. It made the Law the preeminent and life-giving religious institution for Israel.

Deuteronomy presents itself as Moses' testament to Israel, which he delivers as a farewell speech to the tribes just before his death in Transjordan and their entrance into Canaan. The "testament" was a common form used in the ancient world to diffuse moral teaching. Despite this formal unity, the book of Deuteronomy as we have it is not a unified literary work. For example, it has two introductions (1:1–4:40; 4:44–11:32). There are several appendices attached to the book, e.g., the Song of Moses (32:1-43) and the Blessing of Moses (33:2-29). There is general agreement that 4:44–28:68 forms the core of the book. Still, this core is also not a homogeneous work. The law code, which is to guide Israel's life in the land, makes up chs. 11–26. Chs. 5–11 provide a homiletic introduction to the law code. Part of Deuteronomy's genius is that it consistently tries to motivate Israel to obedience so the thrust of chs. 5–11 focuses on motivation. Chs. 27 and 28 reflect a ritual by which Israel accepts the obligations of the code.

Despite the attention Deuteronomy has received from interpreters because of its importance, consensus has not been reached about several fundamental issues. For example, what circles in ancient Israel's religious leadership groups were responsible for Deuteronomy? While most interpreters recognize that ascribing the book to Moses is a theological device to legitimate its content, they have reached no consensus about the question of authorship. Priests, prophets, sages, and elders have all been suggested. Similarly, the question of the book's date is still subject to discussion. Interpreters have supported preexilic, exilic, and postexilic dates for its composition. Many favor a date in the 7th century B.C., in part because they identify the "law book" of 2 Kgs. 23:1-3 with some form of Deuteronomy.

One of the book's most significant literary issues is not obvious to those who read the book only in English translation. There are texts in the book that address their readers in the 2nd person singular and others that use the 2nd person plural. For example, 6:7-9; 11:18-20 are nearly identical in content, but the former uses the 2nd person singular while the latter uses the 2nd person plural. Does the change in person point to two sources? Is it a didactic device to address first the individual and then the group? Is it simply a matter of literary variation? This phenomenon has attracted significant attention from interpreters. Most agree that each instance of a change in person has to be examined on its own. There does not appear to be a single explanation for the changes.

While many literary issues must yet be resolved, the importance of Deuteronomy for the development of ancient Israel's religious thought is clear. First, Deuteronomy introduces a new understanding of the Divine. The expression "the place that the Lord your God chooses as the dwelling for his name" (12:11) is a constant refrain in Deuteronomy and the Deuteronomistic history. It nuances the belief of ancient peoples that their gods actually dwelt in their temples. Deuteronomy never says that God dwelt in the temple or that the temple is the "house of God." The temple is where God's *name* dwells and was built for God's *name.* God dwells in the heavens (26:15). Similarly, when speaking of the theophany on Sinai, Exod. 19:21 notes that *seeing* God posed a danger to the Israelites. For Deuteronomy, seeing God was not even an issue. It was *hearing* God that was the danger (4:32). The God that Deuteronomy describes is transcendent. This God is revealed through the Law. Obedience to that Law makes it possible for Israel to live (30:15-16).

Deuteronomy, then, is above all a law book. Still, it is not simply a repository for ancient laws. For Deuteronomy law is a living reality. The book's great achievement is how it adapts ancient legal tradition to new situations. For example, in the ancient Near East and ancient Israel sacrifices made in temples were comsumed by the gods and their priests (e.g., Exod. 22:29-30[MT 28-29]; Num. 18:15-21). In Deuteronomy it is the donor of the sacrifices who consumes them. In addition, Deuteronomy instructs the donor to invite the poor to share in the sacrificial meal (14:22-29; 15:19-23). The result of Deuteronomy's reinterpretation of ancient legal tradition is often the humanization of ancient laws. Early Judaism followed the pattern set by Deuteronomy in the production of the Mishnah and Talmud, which are new adaptations of ancient Israel's legal traditions.

Deuteronomy offers a utopian vision of Israel's life, not because it presents an unworkable plan for Israel's life in the land, but because it presents Israel with ideals rather than with laws alone. For example, the law of the king (17:14-20) is unrealistic. No ancient Near Eastern monarch would ever agree to limit his prerogatives as Deuteronomy suggests. What this law emphasizes is the equality of all Israelites under the Law. In the eyes of the Law, there are no subjects nor king but only "brothers." Similarly, Deuteronomy consistently requires people of means to remember the poor. "The widow, orphan, alien, and Levite," whom Deuteronomy never forgets (10:8; 16:11; 24:19-21; 26:12-13; 27:19), were people who had no access to land and wealth. They could not support themselves and were dependent on their fellow Israelites. Deuteronomy sides strongly with the disadvantaged.

The purpose of the Law is not simply to provide order and organization to the life of ancient Israel. For Deuteronomy, it describes a way of life that is congruent with Israel's status as the people of God (cf. 4:32-40). The idea of Israel's election stands behind the book of Deuteronomy. This election grants a status that Deuteronomy identifies when it calls Israel "a holy people" (7:6; 14:2, 21). In other ancient Israelite codes, Israel's holiness is a consequence of its observance (e.g., Exod. 22:31[30]). For Deuteronomy, holiness is a fundamental characteristic of God's people and must be the motive behind their moral choices.

Another important theological idea for Deuteronomy is the land. Deuteronomy and the Deuteronomistic literature have as a principal theme the fate of Israel in its land. God gave Israel the Law to observe in its land (12:1), and Israel's continued existence in the land is dependent on the quality of its observance (4:26; 11:17; 28:63; 30:19). For Deuteronomy, the land of Israel is not simply the setting for the story of Israel's life nor the basis for its economy. The land is the means by which Israel can have an authentic encounter with the Divine through the experience of God's providential care — especially through the gift of rain and fertility. Israel's infidelity can have only one consequence: the loss of its land and its communion with God. The importance of Deuteronomy in the development of Judaism has sealed Israel's relationship with its land.

Finally, Deuteronomy presents covenant as a basic metaphor for Israel's relationship with God. Some suggest that the book itself follows the structure of an ancient Near Eastern covenant. While that view may be hard to sustain, covenant is a fundamental Deuteronomic idea. Deuteronomy sees the covenant it envisions between God and Israel as flowing from the covenant at Horeb (Sinai; cf. esp. chs. 1–3). Still, the covenant in Deuteronomy is a new covenant that responds to a new situation (29:1[28:69]). Deuteronomy presents its readers with a notion of Israel's relationship with God that is both constant and evolving. In living out this relationship, it is important to remember the past, but it is also important to look to the changing circumstances that the people of God face. Still, the one response which must characterize Israel's reaction to these new circumstances is fidelity to its God.

Deuteronomy is the most theological book in the OT. It helped Israel survive the loss of its sacred institutions following the fall of Jerusalem to the Babylonians. It shaped the reconstitution of Judah following the restoration made possible by the Persians. Judaism, as it exists today, is a product of the book of Deuteronomy. Christianity developed its self-understanding in conversation with the theological perspectives that are at the heart of this book. From a theological perspective, it is hard to overestimate the value of the book of Deuteronomy.

Bibliography. G. Braulik, *The Theology of Deuteronomy* (North Richland Hills, Tex., 1994); D. L. Christensen, *A Song of Power and the Power of Song* (Winona Lake, 1993); F. García Martínez, ed., *Studies in Deuteronomy.* VTSup 3 (Leiden, 1994); E. W. Nicholson, *Deuteronomy and Tradition* (Philadelphia, 1967); M. Weinfeld, *Deuteronomy and the Deuteronomic School* (1972; repr. Winona Lake, 1992).

LESLIE J. HOPPE, O.F.M.

DEVIL

English translation of Gk. *diábolos,* which in both Hellenistic and Classical Greek signified an evil (human) adversary, false accuser, slanderer, calumniator.

In all but four of its 21 appearances in the LXX *diábolos* (usually with the article) translates Heb. *(haś)śāṭān*, "an adversary or plotter, one who devises means for opposing another." In a few of these instances *(ho) diábolos* denotes (1) a (divine/heavenly?) agent assigned the role of precipitating God's wrath against Israel (1 Chr. 21:1); (2) a wicked human plotter and false accuser (Ps. 109:6; Esth. 7:4; 8:1); or (3) an obstacle to Israel's faithfulness (1 Macc. 1:36). In the majority of cases, however, *diábolos* (always with the article) signifies specifically a celestial being, in particular a member of the heavenly court, responsible for indicting and prosecuting sinners before the bar of divine justice. This being is envisaged as a rigorous legalist who pursues his duties with the single-mindedness of the zealot (e.g., Job 1:6, 7, 9, 12; 2:1-7; Zech. 3:1, 2). If, as often claimed, Wis. 2:24 bears an allusion to Gen. 3 and its story of the Fall, then *diábolos* may also stand as a cipher for the beguiling serpent of Eden.

In the NT, other early Christian writings, and some contemporary Jewish pseudepigraphical literature, *diábolos* is used primarily as one among many proper names or epithets for the figure most generally known as Satan, the supernatural enemy of God and adversary of his people, who in addition to causing suffering and other ills that beset humankind, strives mightily to divert the pious from the path of obedience to God and thus break the bond between God and his servants (e.g., Mark 4:15; 8:33; 1 Cor. 7:5; cf. Eph. 4:27; 1 Tim. 3:7; 2 Tim. 2:26; 1 Pet. 5:8). His main instrument in this is *peirasmós* (usually translated "temptation," but better "a proving," "trial"), an ordeal of one sort or another which "tests" one's trust that God is faithful and thus reveals the nature and extent of one's own faithfulness to God (cf. Matt. 4:1-11 par.; 1 Thess. 3:5). The Devil is presented here as ruler of the world (Matt. 4:8-9 par.; cf. 1 John 5:19) and as chief of a host of wicked spirits (Matt. 25:41) and unseen forces (Eph. 6:12), some of whom, along with their master, are said to stand behind and direct not only the foreign nations who oppress God's people, but all apostates within Israel as well. All sources testify that in due course this *diábolos* will be subdued or vanquished, either by a divine agent such as God's Messiah or an archangel or by God himself. In the meantime, *ho diábolos* remains active, beguiling and bedeviling the elect. It is faithfulness to God and his ways that will prevent the pious from "failing in the test" and from being "delivered over" to "the evil one" (cf. Matt. 6:13; Eph. 6:11; Jas. 4:7).

In some NT occurrences *diábolos* seems to mean only "(human) calumniator," "slanderer" (1 Tim. 3:11; 2 Tim. 3:3; Tit. 2:3). Also, despite the notice of the Devil's influence upon Judas in John 13:2, in 6:70 *diábolos* (no article), referring to Judas, may mean nothing more than "wicked (human) adversary."

The choice by the LXX translators to use a term laden with connotations of malevolence as the equivalent of *(haś)śāṭān* may have been a factor in accelerating the "fall" of "the Satan" of Job and Zechariah from function to personality and from servant to opponent of God. On the other hand, it may reflect an identification that at the time of the translators' work was already (or just beginning to be) made.

Bibliography. S. H. T. Page, *Powers of Evil: A Biblical Study of Satan and Demons* (Grand Rapids, 1995); E. Pagels, "The Social History of Satan, the 'Intimate Enemy,'" *HTR* 84 (1991): 105-28; G. J. Riley, "Devil," *DDD*, 244-49; J. B. Russell, *The Devil: Perceptions of Evil from Antiquity to Primitive Christianity* (Ithaca, 1977). JEFFREY B. GIBSON

DEVOTE, DEVOTED

See BAN.

DEW

Moisture condensed upon a cool surface. This moisture carried over by west sea winds turns into the early morning fog caused by nighttime cooling (cf. Num. 11:9; Job 29:19; Cant. 5:2). During the dry summer months in Palestinian agriculture, dew (Heb. *ṭal*) is a vital supplement for rain (Deut. 32:2; 2 Sam. 1:21; 1 Kgs. 17:1; Job 38:28). Thus, it is frequently used as a metaphor of blessing from the heavens by God (Gen. 27:28, 39; Deut. 33:28; Ps. 133:3; Zech. 8:12; cf. Hos. 14:5; Hag. 1:10). By the nature of its subtle development, dew also connotes the imagery of quietude and stealth (2 Sam. 17:12; Isa. 18:4). In addition, its sudden disappearance by the rising of the sun is used to depict the transience of Israel's love for God (Hos. 6:4; 13:3).

HYUN CHUL PAUL KIM

DIAL OF AHAZ

A type of sundial formed by two sets of stairs, one ascending from the east and one from the west, which led to the roof and shared the top step. As the sun passed from east to west the steps would be illuminated and would thus delineate the passing of the day. The Lord's promise to heal Hezekiah was confirmed by the "declining sun on the 'dial' of Ahaz (Heb. *maʿălôṯ ʾāḥāz*) turn[ing] back 10 steps" (Isa. 38:8; 2 Kgs. 20:8-11).

Bibliography. Y. Yadin, "'The Dial of Ahaz,'" *ErIsr* 5 (1959): 88*-89*. CHRISTIAN M. M. BRADY

DIAMOND

A precious stone, noted for its hardness. In the oracle at Jer. 17:1 Judah's sin is etched with a diamond-tipped iron pen (Heb. *šāmîr*). At Zech. 7:12 the Hebrew term is rendered "adamant" (cf. Ezek. 3:9, "the hardest stone").

DIASPORA

See DISPERSION.

DIATESSARON

A harmony of the Gospels (Gk. *dia tessarōn*, "through [the] four") in the form of a continuous narrative, compiled ca. 170 C.E. by Tatian.

DIBLAIM (Heb. *diḇlāyim*)

The father of Gomer (Hos. 1:3). Derived from Ugar. *dblt* (lit., "cakes of dried figs"), the name may represent a continuation of Hosea's figurative use of names, a geographical location (perhaps the Moabite town Diblatayim), or a literal patronymic designation. This last sense is preferable because it stands in apposition to the personal name Gomer.

ARCHIE W. ENGLAND

DIBON (Heb. *dîḇôn*)

1. An important city located on the King's Highway in central Transjordan. Dibon is generally identified with the mound of ruins N of the modern village of Dhībān (224101), 64 km. (40 mi.) S of Amman and 3 km. (2 mi.) N of Wadi el-Mōjib (biblical Arnon). Egyptologist Kenneth A. Kitchen argues that an Egyptian equivalent for Dibon (*Tibunu*) appears in Egyptian inscriptions from the time of Rameses II. The name also appears in the Mesha inscription found at Dhībān.

According to the biblical evidence Dibon was originally a Moabite city which was subsequently taken over, first by the Amorites and then the Israelites when the latter conquered Sihon of Heshbon (Num. 21:26; 32:3-5). Although Dibon was assigned to the tribe of Reuben (Josh. 13:9, 17), it appears that the city was ultimately rebuilt by Gad and renamed Dibon-gad (Num. 32:34; 33:45-46; Mesha 10-11). During the time of the Divided Monarchy, Mesha of Moab successfully broke away from Israelite control and restored Dibon as a Moabite city (Isa. 15:2; Jer. 48:18, 22; Mesha 21, 28).

Excavations have so far revealed occupation during the Early Bronze Age II-IV, Iron Age II, Nabatean, Roman, Byzantine, and Arab periods. From EB II-IV a few segments of walls from a possible defensive system have been uncovered. At least two phases of an Iron II settlement have been reported: important finds include a gateway, large circular grain silos, a large public building (the "palace"), a "sanctuary" in which were found pieces of an Iron I incense stand and two fertility figurines, various towers, and a casemate wall. It is from the Iron II period that the Mesha stela dates. Nothing has yet been found from the Middle Bronze or Late Bronze Ages.

RANDALL W. YOUNKER

2. A town in the Negeb of Judah, toward the eastern border between Hebron and Jekabzeel, reoccupied following the Exile (Neh. 11:25). It may be the same as Dimonah (Josh. 15:22).

DIBON-GAD (Heb. *dîḇōn gāḏ*)
An alternate name ("Dibon of Gad") for Dibon **1** (Num. 33:45-46).

DIBRI (Heb. *diḇrî*)
The father of Shelomith of Dan; his grandson was stoned for cursing and blaspheming God (Lev. 24:11, 14).

DIDACHE (Gk. *Didachḗ*)
A common shorthand reference (Gk. "teaching") for the early Christian writing entitled The Teaching of (the Lord to the Gentiles by) the Twelve Apostles. Divided by modern scholars into 16 brief chapters, this is a unique collection of early Christian sayings, liturgical traditions, and community directives. Only one complete copy remains in Greek (rediscovered in 1873), though the text's ancient popularity is evident from scattered versions preserved in the Apostolic Constitutions, Apostolic Church Order, Life of Shenoute, Syntagma doctrinae, and Rule of Benedict.

An example of "evolved literature," the Didache combines ancient sayings and traditions with guidance for early Church life over as many as three stages of composition. The final form may be dated between 70 and 150 C.E., though the source materials undoubtedly are older. The author or Didachist (a term variously used to refer either to the original compiler of the sources or to the final editor) appears to have been a Jewish Christian. This is suggested by the author's focus upon OT literature and wisdom sayings (chs. 1–6), Jewish forms of baptism and thanksgiving prayers (chs. 7, 9–10), and a low Christology.

Early scholarship often assigned provenance of the text to Egypt because of its broad use there. More recent opinion favors Antioch or Syria, based upon the volatile church climate in that region. Palestinian influence certainly is possible. The purpose of the Didache is unclear. Typically referred to as an early Christian "handbook," it may have been used for the instruction of catechumens or the training of church officials. Later Christians adopted the text for both purposes.

The Didache has at least three major sections: the so-called "Two Ways" material (1.1-6.3); liturgical and ecclesiastical instructions (7:1-15:4); and a brief apocalypse (16:1-8). In a broad sense, these three divisions probably represent the socio-historical process by which the materials were assembled for use within a specific, early Christian community. Scattered throughout are subsections which no doubt reveal later alterations in the writing.

The "Two Ways" section is a call to love God and neighbor, to distinguish between the way of life (1:1-2:7) and way of death (5:1-2), and to honor ancient wisdom as an avenue toward life (3:1-4:14). The author appeals to the Decalogue as a foundation for ethical living (2:1-7) and to contemporary household codes as a basis for order (4:9-11). These teachings bear no specifically Christian imprint, except where a block of Jesus' sayings are secondarily inserted toward the beginning of the document (1:3b-2:1). Concluding verses (6:1-3), which form a warning to follow the teaching of life and to avoid food sacrificed to idols, serve as a bridge to the second major section. The "Two Ways" materials contain sayings which find a close parallel to materials in Barnabas 18-20. They would have served as appropriate instruction for new Christians and as a general community exhortation to follow an ethical life-style.

The liturgical and ecclesiastical section is a collection of intriguing topics. Preserved here are instructions about baptism (7:1-4), personal and meal prayers (8:1-10:7), wandering prophets (11:1-13:7), and community interaction (14:1-15:4). The materials reflect a church in its formative period, prior to the standardization of catholic Christianity. Three issues here serve as sources for debate: (1) The baptismal instructions reflect the common Jewish concerns of the earliest Church. (2) The eucharistic prayers (9:1-10:7) preserve either a unique approach to communion, a supplement to the scriptural words of institution used at eucharist, or an observance of an agapē feast. (3) Community regulations are addressed only to bishops and deacons, with no mention of presbyters.

The apocalypse serves to conclude the Didache much like the NT book of Revelation. It offers the hope of future reward for the righteous observance of an ethical lifestyle and appropriate church conduct. Gathered here are apocalyptic sayings which resemble materials from the NT Gospels and Pauline Epistles. Some scholars believe that this section may originally have served as a conclusion to the opening "Two Ways" section.

The Didache survives as an enigma of early Christian literature, though it appears to fit broadly into the early Church situation. The author depended heavily upon the Gospel of Matthew or some similar source, which gives the text a familiar feel. Ignatius of Antioch likely already knew of the Didache in some form by the end of the 1st century. Clement of Alexandria (early 3rd century) accepted it as Scripture, though Eusebius of Caesarea (early 4th century) rejected it as spurious. In his *Festal Epistle* 39 (367), Athanasius likewise rejected the canonical status of the text, but listed it as important reading material for instruction in the Christian faith.

Bibliography. C. N. Jefford, ed., *The Didache in Context.* NovTSup 77 (Leiden, 1995); R. A. Kraft, *Barnabas and the Didache,* vol. 3 of *The Apostolic Fathers,* ed. R. M. Grant (New York, 1965).

CLAYTON N. JEFFORD

DIDRACHMA (Gk. *dídrachmon*)
A silver coin weighing ca. 7.27 grams, equal to two Greek *drachmaí* or approximately two Roman denarii. In the LXX Gk. *dídrachmon* appears as the normal translation for Heb. *šeqel,* but in the time of Jesus the didrachma was worth a half-shekel. The half-shekel temple tax (Exod. 30:11-16; cf. Josephus *Ant.* 3.193-196) thus amounted to a didrachma. In Matt. 17:24-27 the temple tax collectors appear as "those who receive the didrachma." CARL BRIDGES

DIDYMUS (Gk. *Dídymos*)
A surname of the apostle Thomas, the Greek equivalent of Heb. *tĕ'ōm,* "twin" (so NRSV).

DIKLAH (Heb. *diqlâ*)
A descendant of Shem through Joktan (Gen. 10:27; 1 Chr. 1:21); ancestor of a South Arabian people and/or region. The name may be associated with an oasis in Saudi Arabia, perhaps in the vicinity of Ṣirwāḥ, WSW of Mārib.

DILEAN (Heb. *dilĕʻān*)
A town in the tribal allotment of Judah, one of 16 cities belonging to the Lachish district in the southwest Shephelah (Josh. 15:38). The location of the ancient settlement is unknown; one proposed site is Ras Dahinah (Dihna) (14342.10530).

STEVEN M. ORTIZ

DILL
An umbelliferous herb (*Anethum graveolens* L.) which resembles parsley (Heb. *qeṣaḥ;* Gk. *ánēthon*). The plant was cultivated for its oval-shaped brown seeds, which were used as a condiment in cooking and as a carminative medicine. According to *m. Maʻaś.* 4:5 (Aram. *šĕḇēṯa*) the dill was subject to the tithe (cf. Deut. 14:22), for which Jesus chides the Jewish leaders as paying attention to insignificant matters of the law at the expense of justice, mercy, and faith (Matt. 23:23; cf. Luke 11:42, "rue").

The plant cited in Isaiah's parable of the farmer (Isa. 28:25, 27) is probably the nutmeg flower or black cummin (*Nigella sativa* L.), a plant which can reach a height of ca. 60 cm. (2 ft.) and whose seeds can be easily severed from the husk for use as a condiment. In rabbinic use Heb. *qeṣaḥ* is translated "black cummin" (*Ber.* 40a; so LXX *melánthion*).

DIMNAH (Heb. *dimnâ*)
A levitical city of the Merarites, located in Zebulun (Josh. 21:35). The city may be the same as Rimmon **2** (Josh. 19:13) or Rimmono (1 Chr. 6:77[MT 62]).

DIMON (Heb. *dîmôn*)
A Moabite toponym mentioned in Isaiah's oracle against Moab (Isa. 15:9); also known as "Dibon" (the reading in 1QIsa^{a,b}; cf. Isa. 15:2). Jerome mentioned that in his time the village was called either Dimon or Dibon. Some amend the toponym Madmen in Jer. 48:2 to Dimon.

Both Dimon and Madmen have been identified with Dimneh (217077), 4 km. (2.5 mi.) NW of Rabbah, but this site has not yielded any Iron Age pottery. A large Iron Age site has more recently been discovered just 250 m. (820 ft.) further down the slope overlooking Wadi ibn Hammad and may be Dimon. FRIEDBERT NINOW

DIMONAH (Heb. *dîmônâ*)
A town in the Negeb near Edom, mentioned along with Kinah and Adadah (Aroer[?]; Josh. 15:22). It may be the same as Dibon **1** (Dhībān; 224101), repopulated by Jews returning from exile (Neh. 11:25). Ancient Dimonah should be distinguished from modern Dimonah SE of Beer-sheba, a city founded in 1955.

DINAH (Heb. *dînâ*)
Only daughter of the patriarch Jacob, by his wife Leah. The name is derived from Heb. *dîn,* "judgment" or "justice." In Gen. 34 Dinah is raped by Shechem, who promptly falls in love with her. Eager to marry Dinah, Shechem begs his father Hamor to negotiate marriage terms with Jacob. But Shechem's outrageous act, compounded not only by his desire to marry a Hebrew woman but also by his father's intention to negotiate a general intermarriage between Hebrews and Shechemites, incites Dinah's

brothers Simeon and Levi to plan a treacherous revenge. They insist that all male Shechemites be circumcised prior to the intermarriage, and when the Shechemites comply, the Benjaminites enter the defenseless city, put all the males to the sword, and carry Dinah away. Jacob disapproves of his sons' ruthless conduct, fearing it may encourage others to rise against him and his family. The episode closes abruptly with Simeon and Levi's retort to their father: "Should our sister be treated like a whore?"

This brief and graphic narrative contains the whole story of Dinah in Genesis. But from an early date, interpreters found an "allusion" to the Dinah narrative in a saying about Simeon and Levi in Gen. 49:5-7, part of a series of "blessings" uttered by Jacob just before his death. Modern exegetes are divided about the extent to which this text is related to Gen. 34. Whether the "blessing" was quite unrelated to the Dinah narrative or related in ways still far from clear, these two texts were understood by early interpreters to be somehow connected.

Dinah's story was reworked, retold, or alluded to in aprocryphal and pseudepigraphal works such as Judith, Theodotus *On the Jews,* Jubilees, the Testaments of Levi and Job, Joseph and Aseneth, Pseudo-Philo *Biblical Antiquities,* Josephus *Antiquities,* and the much later *Genesis Rabbah.* In some the Genesis narrative is freely expanded as a haggadic midrash to provide ethical guidance for Jews facing the tempting cultural advantages of hellenization. Most apply Dinah's story to contemporary events, to emphasize the continuity of Jewish tradition and its everlasting validity and applicability. Simeon and Levi are models of zeal and courage in dealing with Gentiles, Levi is the perfect prototype of the Jewish priest, and the Shechemites represent the forces warring against the Lord and his covenanted people. Intermarriage with foreigners is forbidden, priestly failings are severely criticized, and Dinah, the virgin daughter of Israel, is restored by her marriage to Job.

Philo's reading of Gen. 34 is allegorical: Shechem is the emblem of folly and shame; Dinah, of justice; and Simeon and Levi are the champions of truth. Philo demonstrates the power of etymology not only to disintegrate a narrative into the allegorical expression of a universal idea, but also to transform an episode of biblical history into a model for personal salvation. In this early Christian period, typological interpretation of the Dinah episode predominated (e.g., Simeon and Levi as types of the Scribes and Pharisees). But the key figure in the history of medieval interpretation of Dinah's story is Gregory the Great, for whom Dinah is a *figura* for the soul wandering into the clutches of the devil, a pawn in the cosmic struggle between God and the evil one for moral possession of the human spirit.

While the broad brushstrokes of the biblical account fail to depict Dinah's motives and feelings, the tropological readings of Gregory and his numerous followers rely consistently on the *topos* of woman as man's downfall. Though these moral readings of Gen. 34 are quite thorough and ingenious, they generally demonstrate how slight a pressure on the *sensus spiritualis* the *sensus literalis* actually exerts. Potentially positive or ambiguous or even relatively neutral features of the biblical text are made to serve the moralizing purposes of the expositors, whose interpretations fall clearly within an ascetic tradition of misogyny stretching back to Pseudo-Clement and Jerome.

One of the least explored chapters of Genesis, the Dinah narrative continues to present problems for interpretation. Unequivocally clarified neither by the Hebrew text nor by ancient and modern translations, the question remains controversial in modern exegesis: some commentators explain Dinah's plight as seduction, others as rape, and still others use the terms interchangeably or even state outright that Dinah is responsible for what happens to her. Some ideological critics have argued that blurring these distinctions constitutes a hermeneutically violent act that reflects, supports, and perpetuates the androcentric brutality of the narrative itself. LUCILLE C. THIBODEAU, P.M.

DINHABAH (Heb. *dinhāḇâ*)
The city in which the Edomite king Bela reigned (Gen. 36:32; 1 Chr. 1:43). Its location is unknown.

DIOCLETIAN
Valerius Diocletianus, the "second founder of the Roman Empire," emperor 285-305 C.E. Recognizing that a single ruler would be unable to maintain power against internal and external threats, Diocletian reorganized and transformed the empire. He created the Tetrarchy, a college of four emperors, two senior Augusti and two junior Caesars. He also reorganized the provincial structure, with smaller provinces and new larger regional structures called prefectures and dioceses. For the first time, political and military administration were completely separated. The army was thoroughly restructured and the Roman financial and judicial systems revised. These reforms reinvigorated Rome and in large part made possible the continuation of the empire for almost another 200 years.

Diocletian's program also entailed reemphasis of traditional Roman values, including religion. He and his colleague Maximian identified themselves with Jove and Hercules, respectively. Roman gods were to be honored alone or with gods of other religions by civil servants and soldiers. Large numbers of Christians, who occupied both government and military posts, refused to obey, which gave rise to their widespread persecution.

Bibliography. T. D. Barnes, *The New Empire of Diocletian and Constantine* (Cambridge, Mass., 1982); S. Williams, *Diocletian and the Roman Recovery* (New York, 1985). JOHN F. HALL

DIONYSIUS (Gk. *Dionysios*)
A convert to Christianity through Paul's ministry in Athens (Acts 17:34). Called "the Areopagite," Dionysius was a member of Athens' chief governing council, the Areopagus, and the first bishop of

Athens (Eusebius *HE* 3.4.11; 4.23.3). Tradition also names him as Athens' first Christian martyr and its patron saint. A body of pseudonymous mystic literature, melding Christian and Neo-Platonic thought, is attributed to him. His name was derived from that of Dionysus (Gk. *Diónysos*), the Greek god of wine, ecstatic experience, vegetation, and drama (cf. 2 Macc. 6:7; 14:33). ERIC F. MASON

DIONYSUS (Gk. *Diónysos*)
The Greek vegetation deity (Roman Bacchus), worshipped primarily as god of wine. His great festival was known as the Dionysia (Greece) or Bacchanalia (Rome), but Dionysiac festivals were held at different times in various locales. Worship involved ecstatic, even orgiastic behavior. Bacchanalia were banned from Rome in 186 B.C.E., but re-emerged in the 1st and 2nd centuries C.E. The ecstatic aspect of the cult and its appeal for women are commemorated in Euripides' *The Bacchae*. In Hellenistic times Dionysus was worshipped widely as a mystery deity and adopted as the patron of various voluntary associations. Aspects of the mysteries comparable to Christianity include Dionysus' association with death and rebirth and the sense of identification with the god experienced by initiates.

Antiochus IV Epiphanes compelled the Jews to wear ivy wreaths in the annual Dionysiac procession (2 Macc. 6:7). His general Nicanor sought to coerce the Jerusalem priests into handing over Judas Maccabeus by threatening to raze the temple and replace it with a temple of Dionysus (1 Macc. 14:33). Ptolemy IV Philopater registered the Egyptian Jewish community, branding them with the ivy-leaf symbol of Dionysus (3 Macc. 2:29). MARY ANN BEAVIS

DIOTREPHES (Gk. *Diotréphēs*)
Presumably the host of a house church who "liked to be first" over his congregation (3 John 9-10). He refused to receive a message or messengers from the author of 3 John and expelled from the congregation those who did show such hospitality. Nothing else is known about Diotrephes, and his motives are unclear. Some suppose that he was among the heretics mentioned in 1 and 2 John, that he suspected the elder himself of heresy, or that he simply wished to keep this controversy out of his congregation. Others suggest that issues of church structure and authority were involved: e.g., that Diotrephes was an early bishop and that the elder represented an older style of authority; or that the elder held a bishop-like office and that Diotrephes resisted this innovation. In any case, uncertainties over new developments in church authority seem to be involved, particularly troublesome for the Johannine churches with their fundamentally egalitarian tradition. Issues of personal power and honor may also have played a significant part.

Bibliography. J. M. Lieu, *The Second and Third Epistles of John* (Edinburgh, 1986); A. J. Malherbe, "Hospitality and Inhospitality in the Church," in *Social Aspects of Early Christianity*, 2nd ed. (Philadelphia, 1983), 92-112. DAVID RENSBERGER

DIPHATH (Heb. *dîpaṯ*) (also RIPHATH)
A son of Japheth's son Gomer (1 Chr. 1:6), most likely a people or region of Asia Minor; called Riphath at Gen. 10:3.

DIRGE
A song or poem that expresses mourning over death or national destruction (Heb. *qînâ, nĕhî*). Examples include David's dirge over Saul and Jonathan (2 Sam. 1:17-27) and part of the book of Lamentations (cf. the god El lamenting the death of Baal; *ANET*, 140). Dirges were often written in *qînâ* meter, with each line having five stressed syllables, the second part shorter than the first. Basic elements of the dirge include the cry, "Alas!" (*hôy*, Jer. 22:18) or "How . . .!" (*'êḵâ*, Lam. 1:1); an announcement of death or catastrophe (Lam. 1:1-4); a description of suffering (Lam. 1:5-6); contrast between the former and present situation (Ezek. 27:33-34); a call to weep or wail (Isa. 14:31); and a description of the effect upon bystanders (Lam. 1:12).

Jeremiah refers to professional women "skilled" in mourning (*mĕqônĕnôṯ*, Jer. 9:17[MT 16]; cf. 2 Chr. 35:25), and prophets often employed dirges (e.g., Isa. 5:18-22; Amos 5:16) as warnings prior to a time of calamity that would befall a sinful nation. God sings a dirge (Jer. 8:18–9:3[2]), as does Jesus (Luke 19:41-44).

The dirge is distinguished from a lament because the latter addresses God with the aim of alleviating suffering. The book of Lamentations (ca. 586 B.C.E.) contains both genres, as does the ancient Sumerian Lamentation over the Destruction of Ur (ca. 2006).

Bibliography. C. Westermann, *Lamentations: Issues and Interpretation* (Minneapolis, 1994). NANCY LEE

DISCIPLE
A follower, pupil, or adherent of a teacher or religious leader. Jewish and Greco-Roman history and literature provide examples of respected figures who gather disciples in order to teach and lead them. In the NT Gk. *mathētḗs* is used most often of followers of Jesus, although it is also used to describe followers of other figures (e.g., disciples "of John," Mark 2:18; or "of Moses," John 9:28). A general distinction between Jesus' disciples and "the crowds" may be observed, with the former as committed followers and the latter as onlookers not seriously attached to him. Yet even some of those in the larger group of "disciples" turn away from Jesus and go back to their former lives when they find his teaching difficult to accept (John 6:60, 66).

Three concentric circles of disciples may be identified in the Gospels: a large group of followers, from which the Twelve are chosen (Luke 6:13, 17; cf. Matt. 8:21) and which apparently included some women (Luke 8:1-3); "The Twelve," who were designated as "apostles" and were especially called by Jesus to travel with him and learn (Mark 3:16-19); and an inner circle of Peter, James, and John, who alone accompany Jesus on certain key occasions (e.g., the transfiguration [Mark 9:2-13] and the garden of Gethsemane [Matt. 26:36-46]).

The names of the Twelve are listed in the NT in four passages (Matt. 10:2-4; Mark 3:16-19; Luke 6:13-16; Acts 1:13 [Judas Iscariot is not named in this text]). They are: Peter, Andrew, James, John, Philip, Bartholomew, Thomas, Matthew (or Levi), James the son of Alphaeus, Thaddaeus (probably the same person referred to in some lists as Judas the son of James), Simon the zealot (also called Simon the Cananean), and Judas Iscariot (the betrayer).

Luke indicates that in the early Church the term "disciple" came to refer to the growing band of believers in Jesus, i.e., to Christians (e.g., Acts 6:7; 9:26; 14:21-22; cf. 11:26). A similar notion of an expanding circle of disciples is suggested by the "Great Commission" (Matt. 28:18-20), in which the risen Jesus commands his closest followers to "make disciples" of people from all national/ethnic groups.

The life of Christian discipleship as presented in the NT calls for supreme devotion to Jesus through the acceptance of his lofty demands. Commitment to him must come before all other attachments (Luke 9:57-62; 14:25-33). Nevertheless, a dimension of Christian discipleship that is sometimes overlooked is the promise of joy and ultimate benefits for those who take up the cross to follow Jesus (Luke 14:12-14; 18:29-30).

Bibliography. R. N. Longenecker, ed., *Patterns of Discipleship in the New Testament* (Grand Rapids, 1996); M. J. Wilkins, *The Concept of Disciple in Matthew's Gospel.* NovTSup 59 (Leiden, 1988).

PETER K. NELSON

DISEASE

See ILLNESS AND HEALTH CARE.

DISHAN (Heb. *dîšān*)

One of the sons of Seir (Gen. 36:21; 1 Chr. 1:38); the father of Uz and Aran (Gen. 36:30; 1 Chr. 1:42); a Horite chief.

DISHON (Heb. *dîšôn*)

1. One of the sons of Seir (Gen. 36:21; 1 Chr. 1:38). He was the ancestor of four Horite tribes (Gen. 36:26; MT *dîšān;* 1 Chr. 1:41).

2. The son of Anah and grandson of Seir, a chief of the Horites (Gen. 36:25; 1 Chr. 1:41); brother of Oholibamah (Gen. 36:25), the wife of Esau (vv. 1-2).

DISPERSION

The geographic and cultural spread of the Hebrew people and/or the Jewish religion and culture over time. The nations of Israel and Judah first existed as a United Monarchy (ca. 1030-922 B.C.E.) and then as a pair of separate but often interrelated kingdoms, Israel (922-722) and Judah (922-587). When Assyria conquered Israel in 722, a large number of Israelites were killed, but some may have migrated elsewhere, retaining some of their identity; their fate is uncertain. When Babylonia defeated Judah in 597 and destroyed Jerusalem in 587, they took a portion of the Judeans into exile in Mesopotamia. After that time, there were at least two communities of persons named Judeans or Jews. This began the Jewish dispersion, often called the Diaspora from a related Greek term.

In following centuries, significant Jewish populations appeared in almost every corner of the ancient world. In the 5th century there was a Jewish colony on the island of Elephantine in the Egyptian Nile. Throughout the Hellenistic period the Jewish presence in Egypt grew, to the point where the Hellenistic Egyptian city of Alexandria has often been considered the center of Judaism for several centuries during the Hellenistic period. By the time reflected in the NT there were Jewish synagogues or at least practicing Jews in most Greek and Roman cities. In particular, the book of Acts portrays Jews from all over the world and depicts Paul finding Jewish groups in a large number of cities.

JON L. BERQUIST

DIVES (Lat. *Dives*)

Traditional name of the rich man (Lat. "wealth") in Jesus' parable of the rich man and Lazarus (Luke 16:19-31).

See LAZARUS.

DIVINATION

The art of determining the future or ascertaining divine will. An important aspect of life throughout the ancient Near East, divination was not a mystical practice, but a process based upon empirical observation and cause/effect, practiced by trained specialists. The regularity of the evidence was so certain that particular omens were recorded, the precursor of the Western scientific method.

The various processes held at their core an understanding that the universe is ordered, including the mundane world. It was the gods who were responsible for maintaining this order. Given their powers, this was a routine task, but oddities did occur in nature. These anomalies were understood as allowances by the gods in order to communicate a message to humans (as more direct forms of communication were normally not possible). Thus, when one noticed an anomaly in nature, its cause was to be sought in an unusual event in the mundane human sphere, the rationale for divine contact. The certainty of this connection is celebrated in an Old Babylonian text that joyfully proclaims, "Šamaš . . . it is you who write down the oracles and indicate the divinatory decisions in the entrails of the sheep."

There was a wide variety of modes of divination, as all aspects of nature were potential mediums for this type of divine communication. The best-attested divination traditions were preserved in the extensive divination literature of 2nd- and 1st-millennia Mesopotamia, a distinct literary genre characterized by a special grammar. The texts are usually organized according to the first two words of the introductory line, the protasis, which consists of the conditional statement (e.g.,

Clay liver model, inscribed with omens and magical formulas for instructing students of divination (1st Dynasty of Babylon, ca. 1830-1550 B.C.E.). Most widely attested in Babylon, models have also been discovered at Alalakh and Hazor (Copyright British Museum)

"If a fetus has an X. . . ."). Many texts originate in observation of specific historical events. For example, a text from Mari found on a clay liver model proclaims, "When my country rebelled against Ibbi-sin [of Ur, ca. 2027-2003 B.C.E.], it is thus that the liver appeared." Other texts originate in more mundane and not readily explainable circumstances (e.g., "If a man's chest hair curls upward, then he will become a slave"). Most observations of this type are made as a person presents an animal for the priest to interpret the owner's destiny. It was assumed after a time that one could find regularity in the messages themselves. As the catalogues for types of divination expanded, a desire for completeness arose. The result was a number of theoretical events which were all but logically impossible (e.g., "If the sheep has seven livers, then the king of the universe will arise").

The notion of regularity in divine communication led to a number of practices in which one could determine the will of the gods. Rituals were regularly performed in regard to major events, such as lot casting prior to military engagements. Mesopotamians considered omens to be more reliable than more direct forms of divine communication, as evidenced in the library of Zimri-lim, king of Mari (ca. 1775). A number of ecstatic prophetic messages were delivered, generally credited to the god Dagan, which were addressed to the king during his military campaigns. These messages were accompanied by hair and garment samples from the would-be messenger of the god, to be tested by omens to confirm the validity of the message.

Among the more common mediums used in divination were animal fetuses (especially malformed ones), livers, gall bladders, kidneys, lungs, hair patterning, bird flight patterns, meteorites, weather, sleep patterns of humans, dreams, and patterns of animal behavior. The interest in interpreting internal organs of sacrificial animals is traced to two circumstances. First, examples are ubiquitous. Second, they are uncovered during the course of ritual, in which there is a heightened sense of spatial nexus between the divine and human realms.

The practice of divination was nearly universally condemned in the OT. The prime exception is the practice of cleromancy (lot casting), which is an integral activity of the high priest (Num. 27:21). Precisely what the Urim and Thummin of the high priest looked like is not clear, but the function of the objects provided a "yes" or "no" answer (cf. 2 Sam. 5:19). Lots determined the division of the land (e.g., Num. 26:55-56), divine approval of candidates for office (e.g., king, 1 Sam. 10:20-21; priest, 1 Chr. 24:5), and guilt (Num. 5:15-30; Josh. 7:14-15). A form of lot casting by manipulating arrows (belomancy) is attested in 2 Kgs. 13:14-19 involving the Judean king Joash. The same practice is attributed to Nebuchadnezzar in Ezek. 21:21, though there is no record of this practice in Neo-Babylonian literature.

Other tolerated practices (or at least not condemned in the same context) centered upon the usage of particular behaviors as signs of divine approval. In the Gideon narrative the judge asks for signs from Yahweh (Judg. 6:36-40) and then reads the sign associated with drinking water (7:4-7). Jonathan holds that the positioning of the Philistines is a sign reflecting divine approval (1 Sam. 14:8-12).

Oneiromancy, the interpretation of dreams, is tolerated in the OT (Gen. 40:5-8; Dan. 1:17). The narratives attribute interpretation completely to Yahweh, seemingly to the exclusion of the interpreter's being trained in the discipline of dream interpretation (which was of enormous interest in Egypt as well as Mesopotamia).

All other forms of divination, such as extispicy (examining the entrails of animals), astrology, necromancy (consulting the dead), hydromancy (interpretation of water patterns and interactions with foreign substances), are forbidden in the OT. A number of terms refer to fields which practice various types of divination, but unfortunately there are not enough data to decisively establish semantic boundaries for these titles. Deut. 18:10-11 lists a number of terms which denote pagan religious practitioners, including various types of diviners, that are not allowed to survive after the Israelite possession of Canaan because their continued presence could lead to syncretism. The outlawed status is illustrated in Saul's encounter with a necromancer, who is initially afraid to engage in her trade with him (1 Sam. 28:3-25). The continued presence of diviners is attested in Isa. 3:1-5, where they are listed among the elite of Jerusalem and Judah (along with judges, elders, prophets, and military leaders) who will be deported after conquest, leading to the breakdown of the social order. This underscores the degree of the revocation of the covenant, as these outlawed sorts are not only tolerated but revered in Judean society.

Otherwise, the preferred mode of divine communication in Israelite society was through ecstatic means, in sharp distinction to the subordination of all ecstatic phenomena to omen confirmation in Mesopotamian literature.

Bibliography. J. Bottero, *Mesopotamia: Writing, Reasoning, and the Gods* (Chicago, 1992).

MARK ANTHONY PHELPS

DIVINERS' OAK

A tree near Shechem (Judg. 9:37) under which divining was practiced. The tree (Heb. *'ēlôn mĕ'ônĕnîm*) was large enough to provide shade, shelter, and a recognizable location for people to meet (Judg. 9:6). Other trees are also mentioned in relation to divining and altars (Gen. 35:4; Josh. 24:26), the most famous being Abraham's oak of Mamre. That tree, a tamarisk, was a travel marker during the journey of Abram (Gen. 12:6) and the location where "the Lord appeared to Abram" (v. 7). A tree NW of Hebron has traditionally been identified as Abraham's oak of Mamre.

Bibliography. F. N. Hepper and S. Gibson, "Abraham's Oak of Mamre," *PEQ* 126 (1994): 94-105.

JOHN A. MCLEAN

DIVORCE

The legal ending of a marriage while the two parties are still living. Accordingly, it is a matter of grave seriousness and is always treated as such in the OT and NT.

The Mosaic law permitted divorce (Deut. 24:1-4), although the conditions under which it is allowed are not clear. Within a cultural context that allowed a man to divorce a woman under any circumstances or whimsy, the Israelite legal tradition would have appeared strict in that it placed limits on the right to divorce (Deut. 22:19, 29). Overall, the laws seem to protect women from some of the most flagrant endangerments of their livelihood. The divorce must be put into writing, and the woman must be sent from one house (the husband's) to another house (presumably her father's), in which she would have an opportunity for life. Other circumstances, customs, or laws regulating divorce are not known. Certainly, many marriages did not end in such an orderly fashion. The story of Samson and his first wife (an unnamed Philistine woman from Timnah; Judg. 14:1–15:8) shows a case where a marriage may not have been legally completed (depending upon the custom of seven days of feasting) or it may have been legally ended after Samson's sudden departure; in either case, Samson seems to think that he is married, when unknown to him his wife has married another. In general, the OT expresses an acceptance of divorce, although within limits and with some recognition of difficulties involved. (Mal. 2:16 is textually problematic, and even if it does refer to divorce, it deals with the cessation of a relationship between God and people).

The NT provides a much different response to divorce. In the Gospels Jesus equates divorce and adultery (Matt. 5:31-32; 19:3-9; Mark 10:2-12; Luke 16:18). Paul permits divorce when the spouse initiating the separation is not a believer, but he argues that believers should not instigate divorce (1 Cor. 7:1-16). Paul later allows remarriage of widows (1 Cor. 7:39), but remains silent about the remarriage of divorced believers.

JON L. BERQUIST

DIZAHAB (Heb. *dîzāhāḇ*)

A place associated with Moses' first address (Deut. 1:1). The word is a descriptive appellation combining an Aramaic genitive performative (*dî*, "the one of [= 'having']") and Heb. *zāhāḇ*, "gold." Some have identified the site with edh-Dheibeh, E of Heshbon in the Transjordanian plateau, while others suggest Mînâ' eḏ-Ḏhahab ("harbor of gold") in the southwestern part of the Sinai Peninsula along the Gulf of Aqaba. No location is certain.

PETE F. WILBANKS

DO NOT DESTROY

Most likely the opening words of a tune (Heb. *'al-tašḥēṯ*) according to which Pss. 57-59, 75 were to be sung, noted in the superscriptions to those psalms. An alternate suggestion is that the words represent a cultic instruction (cf. Isa. 65:8).

DOCETISM

A designation for various views regarding the humanity of Christ that began to manifest themselves in the late 1st century C.E. The term is related to Gk. *dokeín*, "to seem." Docetic thought is a by-product of the Hellenistic environment of early Christianity that, philosophically, made a radical distinction between the material and the spiritual, and thus denied that the spiritual Christ actually assumed material human form. With the denial of the Incarnation, it became logically impossible to sustain that Christ experienced genuine suffering and death on the cross, a fact that made irrelevant any discussion of authentic resurrection.

Early forms of Docetism appear to be challenged in the Johannine Epistles, and in the early 2nd century Ignatius attacks this heresy in his letters *(Trallians, Smyrnaeans)*. Clement of Alexandria opposed the doctrine, and Eusebius reports that Serapion denounced the apocryphal Gospel of Peter (ca. 190) for its docetic tendencies.

In current usage the term applies to any christological position that tends to limit or deny the full humanity of Christ.

D. LARRY GREGG

DOCUMENTARY HYPOTHESIS

See BIBLICAL CRITICISM.

DODAI (Heb. *dôḏay*)

An Ahohite, commander of the second division of David's army (1 Chr. 27:4). He is probably the same as Dodo **2** (2 Sam. 23:9 = 1 Chr. 11:12).

DODANIM (Heb. *dōḏānîm*)

An Ionian people, the descendants of Javan (Gen. 10:4). At 1 Chr. 1:7 they are called Rodanim, the people of Rhodes.

DODAVAHU (Heb. *dōḏāwāhû*)
The father of the prophet Eliezer, from Mareshah in Judah (2 Chr. 20:37).

DODO (Heb. *dôḏô*)

1. A descendant of Issachar, the father of Puah, and the grandfather of the minor judge Tola (Judg. 10:1).

2. The son of Ahohi (2 Sam. 23:9) or the Ahohite (1 Chr. 11:12); father of Eleazar, one of David's Three. He is probably the same as Dodai mentioned at 1 Chr. 27:4.

3. A Bethlehemite, the father of Elhanan who was one of David's Thirty (2 Sam. 23:24 = 1 Chr. 11:26).

DOEG (Heb. *dō'ēg*)
The Edomite chief of Saul's shepherds who observed David at Nob during David's flight from Saul. Claiming to be on a royal errand for Saul, David had deceived Ahimelech, the chief priest of Nob, who then permitted David to take both the holy bread from the sanctuary and the sword of Goliath, and consulted the Lord on his behalf (1 Sam. 21:1-9[MT 2-10]; 22:9-10). Doeg informed Saul that Ahimelech had supported David's flight, whereupon Saul summoned all the priests of Nob to Gibeah, accused them of treason, and then ordered their execution. When Saul's guards refused, Doeg obediently killed the 85 priests of Nob, except for Ahimelech's son Abiathar, who escaped and fled to David (1 Sam. 22:6-23). Doeg's betrayal of David is also mentioned in the superscription to Ps. 52.

KENNETH ATKINSON

DOG
A domesticated carnivorous mammal *(canis familiaris)*. In Palestine wild dogs roamed in packs living on the outskirts of towns. Dog skeletons excavated at Ashkelon suggest dogs were also kept as pets. Skeletons of young dogs were found carefully placed in individual graves, as one would bury a pet, rather than thrown into a pit as one would dispose of a stray animal. In the Bible the dog (Heb. *keleḇ*) carries a very negative image, representing the despised, the unclean, or the enemy waiting to devour. In the dietary laws (Exod. 22:31) the Israelites are instructed to throw food unfit for humans to dogs. Male prostitutes are called dogs (Deut. 23:18), and calling oneself a dog indicates self-debasement (1 Sam. 17:43; Job 30:1). The NT also uses the dog (Gk. *kýōn*) to refer to the unclean (Matt. 15:26-7 par.; Rev. 22:15).

Dogs were scavengers and kept towns clean by consuming garbage and unburied corpses (Ps. 59:14-15[MT 15-16]). It was considered a horrible fate to have one's corpse eaten or one's blood licked by dogs rather than having a proper burial (cf. the fate prophesied of the descendants of Jeroboam, Baasha, Jezebel, and Ahab; 1 Kgs. 14:11; 16:4; 21:23-24; fulfilled at 22:38; 2 Kgs. 9:36).

The psalmist's enemies are presented as menacing dogs (Ps. 22:16[17]), and dogs represent a fool in Prov. 26:11, where the folly or sins of the fool are compared to the filth of dog vomit. Israel's sentinels are called "silent dogs" who sleep rather than bark, while Israel's enemy is described as a voracious, devouring dog (Isa. 56:10-11).

Dogs were also cultic figures. In Egypt, as symbols of deities, dogs were often mummified and buried with their owners, and identified with the gods of the dead, Khenti-Amentiu and Anubis. In Mesopotamia dogs were used in the cult of Gula, the goddess of healing, as depicted on clay reliefs and seals. In a healing ritual a dog and a pig were waved over the patient to absorb the patient's illness, then burned. The dog and pig were also used in exorcisms of Lamaštu, the demon of sickness and fever. The use of *keleḇ* for male prostitutes (Deut. 23:18) may be a reference to such cultic activity.

Bibliography. D. W. Thomas, "*Kelebh* 'Dog': Its Origin and Some Usages of It in the Old Testament," *VT* 10 (1960): 410-27; P. Wapnish and B. Hesse, "Pampered Pooches or Plain Pariahs? The Ashkelon Dog Burials," *BA* 56 (1993): 55-80.

MICHELLE ELLIS TAYLOR

DOK (Gk. *Dṓk*)
A small fort built by Ptolemy (**17**) where in 135 B.C. Ptolemy murdered Simon Maccabeus and his two sons (1 Macc. 16:11-15). Josephus refers to the fort as Dagon, locating it N of Jericho (*Ant.* 13.8.1[230]; *BJ* 1.22.3[56]). The site is mentioned in the Copper Scroll (3Q15). The fort may have been located on Jebel Qarantal (190142), 3 km. (2 mi.) NW of Jericho. ʿAin Dûq, a spring at the base of the hill, may preserve the ancient name.

LAURA B. MAZOW

DOMINION
The translation of several Hebrew and Greek words that imply "mastery" and the power "to rule" and "to have dominion over" (e.g., Heb. *rāḏâ, māšal, šālaṭ, bāʿal;* Gk. *krátos, kuriótēs, kurieúō, exousía*).

The precise nature of the rule or dominion varies with the situation or context. Thus, the sun and moon are said to rule over the day and the night (Gen. 1:18; Job 38:33).

"Dominion" expresses political power (Judg. 14:4; 1 Kgs. 4:24) and refers to the rule of sin and death over mankind (Ps. 19:13[MT 14]; Rom. 6:9, 14) and mankind's mastery over nature (Gen. 1:26, 28). It can carry messianic overtones (Mic. 4:8) and refer to the rank or order of the angels (Eph. 1:21; Col. 1:16). The exalted Christ, however, rules over all these dominions.

The final horizon, for biblical writers in both the OT and NT, is that "dominion" ultimately belongs to God (Job 25:2; Ps. 72:8; Dan. 4:3, 34; 1 Tim. 6:16; 1 Pet. 4:11). Because God is the creator of all and his dominion will last forever, he is free to delegate authority over the works of his hand to humankind (Ps. 8:6[7]). Hence, humans are called to exercise responsibility in their dominion and care over God's creation, thereby imitating God's character and reflecting God's image in ruling over every living thing.

FRANK M. HASEL

DOMITIAN

Titus Flavius Domitianus, the younger son of Vespasian, born at Rome in 51 C.E. Unlike his brother Titus, he was not educated in the Roman court and did not join his father in military campaigns. Still, he was a key figure in the Flavian takeover in Rome in 69. At the death of Titus in 81, Domitian became emperor and ruled until his murder in 96.

Domitian was a capable administrator but autocratic in rule, largely ignoring the senate. His adoption of the titles "lord" and "god" and his construction of a luxurious palace underscored his despotism. Though he tried to raise standards of public morality, Domitian was later vilified for lustful behavior. He introduced numerous Greek elements into the games and culture of Rome, at great financial costs, which led to confiscations and heavy taxations. His generous support for the military and his involvement in several Germanic campaigns won him loyalty from the legions. In 93 Domitian began to execute numerous senators, knights, and imperial officials for suspected conspiracy. His execution of his niece's husband Flavius Clemens on the charge of atheism and his excessive taxation of Jews were associated by later writers with an alleged assault on Christians. Some understand Domitian's encouragement of the imperial cult as the background for the persecution of Christians in Asia Minor reflected in Revelation.

Bibliography. B. W. Jones, *The Emperor Domitian* (London, 1992); C. Scarre, *Chronicle of the Roman Emperors* (London, 1995). SCOTT NASH

DOOR

An opening (Heb. *peṯaḥ*) used to gain entrance into various buildings or cities, accompanied by a stone or wooden lintel, side posts, and threshold.

Blood was sprinkled on the side posts during the first Passover (Exod. 12:7, 22-23). A slave's ear was pierced against the door when he chose to remain with his master (Exod. 21:6). Doors could evidently be locked in ancient times (2 Sam. 13:17-18). The door to the temple was made of cypress wood (1 Kgs. 6:34). In the OT "door" is used figuratively to mean proximity in time and space (Gen. 4:7), as an opening to hope (Hos. 2:15[MT 17]), and as a symbol for the lips and mouth (Ps. 141:3). OT wisdom compares laziness with a door turning on its hinges (Prov. 26:14), and one who raises his door seeks destruction (17:19).

Jesus refers to himself as the "door" by which all must enter into the fold (John 10:1-9). Many sick gathered before the door of the mother-in-law of Peter because they knew that Jesus was present (Mark 1:33). Peter entered the doors of the courtyard where Jesus stood before the high priest at the time of his death (John 18:16). The doors of the prison are opened by an angel of the Lord who leads Paul out among the guards (Acts 12:6-11).

Figurative meanings are found when writers describe the imminence of Christ's coming (Matt. 24:33 = Mark 13:29; Jas. 5:9), the "door of faith" being opened to the Gentiles (Acts 14:27), the way provided for effective service (1 Cor. 16:9), the illumination of the word (Col. 4:3), and the open access to salvation that all have in Christ (Rev. 3:8). Jesus says, "Behold I stand at the door and knock" (Rev. 3:20; cf. Luke 11:10). In an apocalyptic vision John sees an open door to heaven (Rev. 4:1).

Egyptian reliefs of the 19th Dynasty depict city gates in Syria-Palestine as consisting of a lintel held in place by two side posts. These gates are shown intact before or during an attack against the city; after the battle the side posts and lintel are shown askew and the city is empty, indicating its plunder. Numerous reliefs of the Assyrian period show arched gateways and doors. Depictions of the siege of Alammu(?) and another city by the sea in Sennacherib's palace at Nineveh show arched gates with two doors. This is true also of a relief from Assurnasirpal's palace and another from the palace of Sargon II in Khorsabad portraying two soldiers torching the gate of the city Kishisim. Other Assyrian reliefs show more common building conventions.

Archaeological excavations over the last century have revealed that arched gates did exist as early as the 2nd millennium B.C. (Ashkelon and Dan). Although the doors have all disappeared due to their construction of wood overlaid with metal of various types, several limestone thresholds have been excavated at sites of all periods. These thresholds contained door sockets and fittings that indicate that the door opened toward the interior of the building/city and could be secured by closing it against the stone fittings.

Bibliography. W. Bleibtreu, "Five Ways to Conquer a City," *BARev* 16/3 (1990): 36-44; J. M. Russell, *Sennacherib's Palace Without Rival at Nineveh* (Chicago, 1991). MICHAEL G. HASEL

DOPHKAH (Heb. *dop̱qâ*)

The first wilderness campsite after the Israelites left the Wilderness of Sin (Num. 33:12-13; omitted at Exod. 17:1). Some have conjectured that the name comes from Egyp. *mfkt*, "turquoise." Consequently, the site is often identified as the Egyptian mining center, Serābîṭ el-Khâdim (999829).

PETE F. WILBANKS

DOR (Heb. *dō'r, dôr;* Gk. *Dṓra*)

A city on the Mediterranean coast below Mt. Carmel, Khirbet el-Burj/Tell Dor (142.224), 21 km. (13 mi.) S of modern Haifa. It first appears in an Egyptian document of the 13th century B.C.E. that lists towns on the coast of Palestine. Joshua defeated the king of Canaanite Dor (Josh. 12:23), and in the 12th century the Sea Peoples ("Philistines") conquered it. Incorporated into Israel, Dor was the capital of Solomon's fourth administrative district (1 Kgs. 4:11). The Assyrians conquered the city in 732, and in the 5th century the Persian king granted it to the Phoenician king of Sidon. Protected by powerful fortifications, Dor asserted its independence in the Hellenistic period until the Hasmonean Alexander Janneus added it to the Jewish kingdom ca. 100. In 63 B.C.E. the Roman general Pompey gave Dor its

Remains of the monumental Persian period building at Tel Dor. The front wall is in the foreground and to the left parts of three stone piers which supported a columned entrance porch
(E. Stern, Director, Tel Dor Project; photo by Y. Hirschberg)

freedom, and it flourished for several centuries as a seaport, only gradually succumbing in the Roman period to competition from neighboring Caesarea. In the 6th and 7th centuries, reduced to a village, it still had its own bishop.

From 1923 to 1980 various teams sporadically excavated at Tell Dor and in Lower Dor E of the mound. Since 1980 Ephraim Stern of the Hebrew University, Jerusalem, heading a consortium of foreign institutions, has explored the site continuously during summer field seasons. These excavations have recovered rich finds from the Middle Bronze Age (ca. 2000 B.C.E.) to the Late Roman period. Especially important are the sequence of fortification walls, the city's Hippodamian ("grid") street plan introduced by the Persians, and domestic and industrial quarters from several occupation periods. Other finds include a complex of large Hellenistic temples, coins featuring the Phoenician Astarte and Hellenistic Zeus, cult objects, material for studying the ancient purple dye industry, and inscribed potsherds. Another large temple, to the east of the tell, became an early Christian church, seat of the later town's bishop.

Bibliography. E. Stern, "Dor," *NEAEHL* 1:357-68; *Dor, Ruler of the Seas* (Jerusalem, 1994).

KENNETH G. HOLUM

DORCAS (Gk. *Dorkás*) (also TABITHA) (Aram. *ṭĕḇîṯā'*)

A common feminine nickname ("gazelle,""deer"), suggesting a slave; the nickname of a highly regarded Christian woman in Joppa, known for good works and presented as a model disciple (Acts 9:36-43). The feminine form of "disciple" (Gk. *mathḗtria*) is used only here in the NT (it occurs in relation to Mary Magdalene in the Gospel of Peter) and suggests a special relationship to Jesus or an office, possibly leader of the order of widows in Joppa. Her "good works and acts of charity" parallel other women's (Luke 8:1-3) and men's (Acts 6:1-7) acts. Dorcas is raised from the dead by Peter, the first such miracle by an apostle (fulfilling Matt. 10:8). In Lukan male-female pairing, Dorcas receives more attention than Aeneas (Acts 9:32-35).

BONNIE THURSTON

DOT

A minute detail of the law, cited by Jesus to emphasize the permanence and value of the OT law (Matt. 5:18; Luke 16:17). Matthew mentions it with the *iota,* the name for the smallest letter of the Greek alphabet. Gk. *keraía,* "dot" ("apex of a letter"), refers to small parts of a letter (NRSV "stroke of a letter"; KJV "tittle"), either a mark of distinction between the Hebrew letters or, more probably, a scribal ornament added to various letters.

DOTHAN (Heb. *dōṯān;* Gk. *Dōthaim*)

A major city in the territory of Ephraim located 22 km. (14 mi.) N of Shechem. Tell Dôthān (173202) covers 62 ha. (25 a.) and looms up out of the eastern end of a fertile valley; a major north-south road leading from the Samaritan hills into the Jezreel Valley ran beside the site. It was in the pastureland of Dothan that Joseph's brothers sold him to a passing Ishmaelite/Midianite caravan (Gen. 37:13-25), and there the Syrian Ben-hadad sought to capture

Elisha (2 Kgs. 6:13-14). The city is cited in connection with the attacks of Nebuchadnezzar's general Holofernes against Judea (Jdt. 3:9; 4:6; 7:3-18), but is not mentioned in any other source. Tell Dôthān was excavated by Joseph P. Free between 1953 and 1960, and again by Robert E. Cooley from 1959 to 1964.

Limited pottery evidence indicates that settlers first occupied Dothan in the late Chalcolithic period. By the Early Bronze Age it was a significant fortified city with at least seven phases of occupation. A thick defensive wall (3.3 m. [11 ft.] wide) typical of sites in this era protected the city. Ca. 2400 B.C. Dothan was abandoned, as were most Palestinian sites in the late 3rd millennium.

Dothan was resettled during the Middle Bronze Age, again with large fortifications. This city, perhaps the one indicated in the Joseph narrative, is represented by fragmentary domestic remains. Even fewer architectural remains attest Late Bronze Age Dothan, although the site appears to have been at least sporadically inhabited in the period. Cooley excavated three tombs on the western side of the tell dating from the LB II to Iron I periods; one tomb contained 3400 objects from 300-500 burials.

The Iron II remains at Dothan are the most significant, including several domestic and public buildings, a street, and many small finds. One major destruction level dated to the late 9th century may be associated with the Aramean conflicts. Later, Dothan fell to Assyrians with the destruction of the Northern Kingdom, Israel.

Bibliography. D. Ussishkin, R. E. Cooley, and G. D. Pratico, "Dothan," *NEAEHL* 1:372-74.

THOMAS V. BRISCO

DOVE

A small bird widely domesticated in biblical times and of the family *Columbidae.* The dove is Noah's messenger, signaling the Flood's end (Heb. *yônâ;* Gen. 8:8-12), and is a representation of the Holy Spirit at Jesus' baptism (Gk. *peristerá);* Matt. 3:16; Mark 1:10; Luke 3:22; John 1:32). Metaphorically, the dove is used to describe human mourning (Isa. 38:14; 59:11) and beauty (Cant. 5:12), and is a term of endearment (Cant. 2:14; 5:2; 6:9). Hiding, especially in rocks or cliffs, is an attribute of the dove (Cant. 2:14; Jer. 48:28). The Hebrew term is onomatopoeic; its root *ynh* ("the sound of rain") evokes the dove's mourning call (Ezek. 7:16; Nah. 2:7). It is the same as the proper name Jonah.

"Doves' dung" is named as food during time of famine (2 Kgs. 6:25), which sounds as unappetizing as the donkey's head mentioned there. However, doves' dung probably refers to some kind of bulbous root or cheap vegetable (NIV "seed pots"; NJB "wild onions").

English translations render the term "young pigeons" in regard to sacrifice. Young pigeons or turtledoves *(tôr)* are offered as sin and burnt offerings (Lev. 14:22, 30; 15:14, 29) and are noted as acceptable substitutes for sheep for the poor (5:7; 14:22). The parents of Jesus make such a sacrifice on the occasion of their son's birth (Luke 2:23-24), in accordance with levitical law (Lev. 12:8).

Bibliography. D. C. Allison, Jr., "The Baptism of Jesus and a New Dead Sea Scroll," *BARev* 18/2 (1992): 58-60; A. J. Hauser, "Jonah: In Pursuit of the Dove," *JBL* 104 (1985): 21-37. LISA M. WOLFE

DOVE ON FAR-OFF TEREBINTHS

Most likely the first words or line of a melody (Heb. *yônaṯ 'ēlem rĕḥōqîm*) to which Ps. 56 was to be sung (superscription[MT 1]).

DOWRY

A gift by a bride's father to the bride. Generally, a dowry is to be understood in the context of marriage, and was a common practice in ancient Near Eastern societies. One could view the dowry as the daughter's share of the parents' inheritance as she leaves the parental home for her husband's. The dowry, which may comprise different household items in addition to other valuables, could serve as an inducement to attract prospective suitors.

Laban gives his maids Zilpah and Bilhah as dowry to Leah and Rachel respectively on their marriages to Jacob (Gen. 29:24, 29). This custom is distinguished from gifts given by the groom to the bride, as in the case of Rebekah, who together with her family is lavished with gifts (Gen. 24:53). These gifts may include a payment of the bride-price to the bride's father, as in the encounter between Shechem and the brothers of Dinah (Gen. 34:11-12). If a man seduces a virgin, he is required to pay a bride-price for her and legally marry her (Exod. 22:16[MT 15]; cf. Deut. 22:29). As the woman moves from the household of her father to that of her husband, a financial transaction is entered into.

In some instances, dowry is used outside the immediate context of marriage. After Leah gives birth to Zebulun, she views the birth of her six sons as a dowry from God, which in turn she believes would bring her honor from Jacob (Gen. 30:20). In 1 Kgs. 9:16 Pharaoh gives the destroyed city of Gezer to his daughter and her husband Solomon as a dowry. In both of these instances, though used figuratively, dowry still captures the essential notion of a gift to the bride. HEMCHAND GOSSAI

DOXOLOGY

A short formula expressing praise to God (Gk. *doxología,* from *dóxa,* "glory," and *lógos,* "speaking"). Such formulaic expressions are found throughout the OT and NT.

Doxologic statements occur in the OT most frequently in the Psalms (Ps. 28:6; 31:21[MT 22]; 41:13[14]; 68:19, 35[20, 36]; 72:18; 89:52[53]; 106:48), but they are also found at the end of songs or hymns (1 Chr. 16:36) and as prayers (1 Sam. 25:32). A number of standard forms occur, most commonly describing God or God's actions as "blessed": e.g., "Blessed be the Lord" (Gen. 24:27; 1 Sam. 25:39; 2 Sam. 18:28; Ps. 28:6) or "Blessed be the Lord, the God of Israel" (1 Kgs. 1:48; 1 Chr. 16:36; Ps. 41:13[14]). These expressions are frequently completed with an enumeration of the actions performed by God. The doxology of Ps. 119:12 is the likely foundation for the rabbinic Berakot, or blessings, that developed later and attained the traditional forms that continue to be used in Jewish worship. Other common forms for doxology within the OT include "ascribe to the Lord glory" (1 Chr. 16:28) or "ascribe greatness to the Lord" (Deut. 32:3).

The object of doxology in the NT and the early Church appears to have been almost exclusively God, rather than Christ (e.g., Rom. 11:36), although such praise of God is occasionally "through" Christ (16:27). Possible doxologies directed to Christ can be found in Gal. 1:5; 2 Tim. 4:18; 1 Pet. 4:11, although the text is not entirely clear to whom praise or glory is directed. Pauline doxologies frequently take the form "to [God] be the glory forever and ever, Amen" (Gal. 1:5; Rom. 11:36; Phil. 4:20; cf. Eph. 3:20-21). These early Christian doxologies were later modified in light of Arianism and the trinitarian controversies and directed "to the Son and to the Holy Spirit." MATTHEW S. COLLINS

DRACHMA (Gk. *drachmḗ*)

A Greek "silver coin" mentioned in Jesus' parable of the lost coin (Luke 15:8). Its value was roughly the equivalent of a Roman denarius or one quarter of a silver shekel, about a laborer's daily wage. Ca. 300 B.C. a single drachma was sufficient to purchase a sheep, but it may have been worth less by the 1st century. It was not a great amount of money, and it is reported that the soldiers of Mark Antony considered his gift of 100 drachmas each proof of his stinginess. For the woman of Jesus' parable, it could represent her dowry. DAVID R. BECK

DRAGON

A mythical reptilian creature common in the mythology and iconography of the ancient Near East. It is now thought to be related to the chaos creature of Canaanite mythology (to whom also are linked such terms as "Behemoth," Job 40:15; "Leviathan," Job 41:1; "Rahab," Ps. 89:10[MT 11]; and "serpent," Isa. 27:1; Job 26:13) rather than Mesopotamian figures (cf. Heb. *tĕhôm* in Gen. 1:2, related to Ugar. *thm* rather than Akk. Tiamat). Most biblical references are polemics against the pagan gods, promoting Yahweh as the true Creator and sustainer of order in the universe.

"Dragon" is an increasingly less frequent rendering of Hebrew terminology in recent English versions of the OT. In the NT it translates Gk. *drákōn,* "serpent, dragon" (symbolic of Satan), which the LXX employs for Heb. *kĕpîr,* "lion"; *liwyāṯān,* "Leviathan"; *nāḥāš,* "serpent"; *ʿattûḏ,* "goat"; and *peṯen,* "serpent." "Jackals" is now clearly the correct reading for KJV "dragons" at Mal. 1:3 *(tannôṯ)* and in most places where *tannîm* is so rendered; Ezek. 29:3 reflects the reading of *tannîn* as "dragon(s), serpent(s), whale(s), sea monster(s), or sea creature(s)."

See SEA MONSTER. W. CREIGHTON MARLOWE

DREAMS

In the ancient Near East generally, dreams and the interpretation of dreams must be considered in the wider category of omens and omen interpretation (including reading liver deformities, the shapes and patterns of smoke, oil in water, flights of birds). However, dreams were considered among the least trustworthy forms of divining.

Although there are occasions where dreams (Heb. *ḥălôm*) are important communications from God to Hebrews (Jacob's famous dream in Gen. 28:12), this form of communication is contrasted with the directness with which God spoke to Moses (Num. 12:6-8), and dreams are certainly condemned as less than trustworthy by Jeremiah (Jer. 23:27, 32; 29:8) and of little value to the Psalmist (Ps. 73:20; 90:5). From the suspicions of prophecy by omen and dream in Deut. 13:1-5 to the late opinion of Sir. 34:7 ("For dreams have deceived many, and those who put their hope in them have perished"), one can trace this early Hebraic ambivalence with regard to dreams as trustworthy sources of information.

It seems clear, however, that not all biblical texts share this negative assessment. Although God occasionally communicates to foreigners in dreams (Abimelech in Gen. 20; Laban in Gen. 31; perhaps Amalekites and Midianites, Judg. 7:13-15), the highest incidence of dreams and dreaming in the OT surrounds the two figures of Joseph (Gen. 37–41) and Daniel. Since both cycles of Hebraic tales are likely from the same postexilic period, this is further indication that dreams became more important in the late Persian and Hellenistic periods. Both Joseph and Daniel are not only famous dreamers themselves, but become famous in foreign courts based on their successful interpretations of the dreams of the emperor, whether Pharaoh or Nebuchadnezzar. Mordecai dreams, according to the Greek Additions to Esther (Add. Esth. 11:2-12; cf. Ezra's apocalyptic dreams in 2 Esdras). Dreams are prominent, often occurring with "visions" (Gk. *hórama*) in the apocalyptic literature, and are often difficult to differentiate from visionary experiences while awake. If it is true that Hebrew interest in dreams increases in the Hellenistic period, surely this is a reflection of the widespread, and lively, Hellenistic interest in dreams. Greek sources show a serious interest in dreams, and it is from Artemidorus that we have the oldest (and surprisingly comprehensive) ancient manual of dream interpretation.

In the Gospel of Matthew, God communicates by dreams (to the "wise men," Matt. 2:12; to Joseph, 1:20; 2:13-22; and in an echo of the Hebraic literary tradition, to Pilate's wife, 27:19). Significantly, however, dreams do not occur as a major factor outside Matthew (cf. Acts 2:17, quoting Joel 2:28), which most likely reflects a certain early Christian hesitancy to be associated with pagan practices.

Bibliography. Artemidorus, *The Interpretation of Dreams,* trans. R. J. White (Park Ridge, N.J., 1975); R. Gnuse, *The Dream Theophany of Samuel* (Lanham, Md., 1984); A. L. Oppenheim, *The Inter-*

pretation of Dreams in the Ancient Near East (Philadelphia, 1956). DANIEL L. SMITH-CHRISTOPHER

DREGS

The sediment formed in the fermentation of wine (Heb. *šĕmārîm*). Wine was left in the wineskin for a time to improve its flavor and richness, then strained before drinking (Isa. 25:6; cf. Zeph. 1:12; RSV "lees"). Jer. 48:11 apparently refers to a practice of pouring wine from container to container to keep the dregs in suspension. To drink the cup of the Lord's wrath "to the dregs" means to undergo God's punishment to the end (Ps. 75:8[MT 9]; Isa. 51:17).

DRINK, DRINKING

Drink and drinking occur in various contexts: (1) consumption of fluids for bodily sustenance; (2) communal celebration and bonding; (3) cultic or sacramental usage; (4) metaphorically, denoting divine and human activity; and (5) symbolically, for the sustenance of the earth by rain.

The natural common drinks were water, milk, wine, grape juice, and vinegar. Beer was also consumed widely in the ancient Near East as early as the Early Bronze Age. Because water was such a premium commodity, abundant sources were highly treasured. Iconography is replete in the ancient Near East portraying the various liquids as gifts from the deities for the sustenance of human life. Drinking and eating were to be done to the glory of God (1 Cor. 10:31); excess and abuse were condemned (Prov. 23:21; Isa. 22:13).

People who drank and ate together formed a special communal bond, sharing joyous times (Job 1:18). Wine was a symbol of God's blessing on the land, and consumption of the best quality marked special occasions. Jesus' first recorded miracle in the Gospel of John was the turning of water into wine at a marriage feast (John 2:1-11). Offering drink to visitors was a common act of hospitality (Judg. 4:19). Giving a drink to someone in need is an act of Christian compassion (Matt. 25:35).

According to the law of the tithe, the people were to eat and drink their gifts in the presence of the Lord with rejoicing, celebrating God's beneficence (Deut. 14:22-27). A drink offering (Heb. *nesek̲*) was poured out to the Lord at the sanctuary during many of the festival offerings (e.g., Num. 28:7-8, 10).

Red wine, drunk in the Passover commemoration, was symbolic of the blood of the Passover lamb and Israel's covenant with God. In the Last Supper, the wine is reinterpreted as a symbol of a new covenant in Jesus' blood (Luke 22:7-20). The communion cup is to be drunk in remembrance, celebration, and proclamation of the death of Christ for the sins of humanity (1 Cor. 11:25-26).

Drinking is used metaphorically in contexts of human reception of divine judgment and human abuse. Since Judah had rejected the covenant and forsaken her God, the "fountain of living waters" (Jer. 2:13; 17:13), she would drink poisoned water (8:14) and drink destruction (Isa. 51:17-22; Ezek. 23:32-34; Ps. 75:8[MT 9]). In the end all nations would drink the cup of God's fury (Jer. 25:19-29; Rev. 14:9-10). Human injustice was portrayed in terms of drinking (Isa. 5:22-23) and its abuse (Jer. 35:1-9), whereas in restoration Israel drinks the wine of God's blessing (Isa. 27:2-5; 43:19-21).

Sustenance for the earth is depicted in the manner of its drinking the waters from the heavens and the earth (Gen. 2:6; Deut. 11:11; Ezek. 31:14; Heb. 6:7). R. DENNIS COLE

DRINK OFFERING

See LIBATION.

DROPSY

The symptom of a disease in the vital organs, whereby an excess of fluids collects in various parts of the body, indicating an advanced stage of the disease. Gk. *hydrōpikós* has been employed since the time of Hippocrates (4th century B.C.E.). The dropsy condition of the man healed on the sabbath was advanced (Luke 14:2).

DRUNKENNESS

Intoxication from strong drink. Drunkenness was among the more prevalent social problems of the ancient world, and its effects were long lasting on families and nations of the OT. Noah and Lot serve as examples of inebriation leading to improper sexual relationships (Gen. 9:21-27; 19:30-38). The physical effects include staggered walk (Ps. 107:27; Isa. 24:20), loss of strength (Eccl. 10:17), decreased mental alertness (1 Kgs. 16:9; 20:16), induced sleep (Joel 1:5), blindness (Isa. 29:9), or even death and destruction, as with Nabal (1 Sam. 25:36-38) and Ephraim (Isa. 28:1-3).

Inebriation can lead to derisive behavior (Ps. 69:12[MT 13]), indecent lifestyle (Rom. 13:13), quarreling and fighting, (Prov. 4:17; 20:1), or destitution (23:21). Those who lead such lives are to be avoided, for they will not inherit the kingdom (1 Cor. 5:11; 6:10). The total dissipation of life is pictured as the drunk staggering in his vomit (Isa. 19:14).

Drunkenness prevents alertness to the work of God in the world (Luke 21:34). Hence priests were prohibited from consuming wine or strong drink while in service of the sanctuary (Lev. 10:9), and the Nazirite was to abstain from all products of the vineyard during the period of dedication to God (Num. 6:2-4).

Drunkenness often is used as a metaphor for God's judgment. Many prophetic oracles against the nations surrounding Israel and Judah contained such dramatic imagery, including Moab (Jer. 48:26), Edom (49:12-13; Lam. 4:21), Babylon (Jer. 51:39), Egypt (Isa. 19:14), Assyria, and Nineveh (Nah. 1:10). Jerusalem as well, which had become God's enemy by her continued idolatry and rejection of torah, would experience horror and desolation as a result of the cup of drunkenness brought by the Lord (Ezek. 23:32-34). R. DENNIS COLE

DRUSILLA (Gk. *Droúsilla*)
The youngest daughter of Agrippa I (and sister to Agrippa II, Bernice, and Mariamme). Julia Drusilla was born ca. 38 C.E., around the time Emperor Caligula's sister of the same name died. She was engaged as a child to marry Epiphanes, son of King Antiochus IV of Commagene (Josephus *BJ* 2:220; *Ant.* 18.132; 19.354-55). After Agrippa's death (44), however, Epiphanes backed out on his commitment to convert to Judaism and so the marriage was off. In 53 Drusilla married Azizus, king of Syrian Emesa, after his circumcision.

Contrary to Jewish law she soon left Azizus to marry Antonius Felix, the gentile procurator of Judea. Drusilla's beauty (which apparently made for an abusive relationship with her likewise beautiful sister Bernice) so enamored Felix that he sent a Jewish friend named Atomus to persuade her that divorce and remarriage to Felix would make her happy (*Ant.* 20.137-43). With Felix ca. 57 she heard Paul speak about faith in Christ Jesus (Acts 24:24). Drusilla bore Felix a son named Agrippa who was killed in the eruption of Mt. Vesuvius in 79 (*Ant.* 20.144). Incidentally, of his three wives (Suetonius *Claud.* 28), Felix is reported to have married another Drusilla, the granddaughter of Cleopatra and Antony (Tacitus *Hist.* 5.9).

Bibliography. R. D. Sullivan, "The Dynasty of Judaea in the First Century," *ANRW* II.8, 329-31.

DOUGLAS S. HUFFMAN

DUALISM
Appearing first in the early 18th century, the term "dualism" took on metaphysical, ethical, and epistemological connotations in contrast to monism and pluralism. Specifically, it refers to two substances or principles that comprise reality. The term does not appear in the Bible, but the ideology associated with cosmic, metaphysical, or ethical dualism often underlies much biblical study.

In ancient Zoroastrian religion, the two opposing gods of good and evil comprise cosmic reality, with the good god ultimately gaining control of the world in the future age. By contrast, ancient Israelite religion was monotheistic; Yahweh held control over good and evil. However, in postexilic Judaism (cf. 1QM) and in subsequent Christianity (Gal. 1:4; Rom. 8:18-25; Phil. 3:20-21; Revelation), apocalyptic thought arose resembling the Zoroastrian cosmic dualism insofar as the good (God) triumphs over the present evil age (under the control of Satan and demons). Unlike Zoroastrianism's cosmic dualism with moral implications, the ethical dualism in the Bible is more pragmatic since one chooses to do good or evil. In particular, Jesus' teachings affirm that persons determine their moral identity as people in God's approaching kingdom or as people in opposition to that kingdom.

Metaphysical dualism assumes that there are two irreducible substances in the universe (i.e., matter vs. nonmatter; body vs. soul). Ancient metaphysical dualism has its widest exposure in Plato's doctrine of the sensible and the intelligible worlds, which the Hellenistic Jewish exegete Philo of Alexandria adopted. The book of Hebrews presents some interesting remarks (Heb. 9:11, 23-24; 10:1; 11:16; cf. 2 Cor. 4:18) that may be interpreted as affirming a Platonic or Philonic metaphysical dualism.

Although the anthropology in the Bible asserts the unity of persons (Gen. 2:7; 1 Cor. 15:35-50), some biblical literature may reflect the influence of an anthropological dualism (Deut. 6:5; Wis. 3:1-4; Mark 12:30 par.; Matt. 10:28; 1 Thess. 5:23; 1 Cor. 5:3; 2 Cor. 5:1-10). Paul, however, affirms that a disembodied soul is akin to nakedness (2 Cor. 5:3). Other examples of dualism's influence on biblical ideology and anthropology may be observed in some of the bipolarities of early Christian thought (light vs. dark, life vs. death, love vs. hate, and truth vs. lies).

The development of gnostic ideology intensified a dualistic understanding of personhood, causing some early Christians to separate the "bodily" aspect of personhood from the "physical or spiritual" aspect of personhood. When separated, that which is akin to God is the "spiritual" (i.e., nonphysical?), allowing one to behave in antinomian manner (cf. 1 Cor. 5:1-8; 6:12-20) or an ascetic manner (cf. Col. 2:16-23). These incipient gnostic worldviews and moralities in the NT appear more refined later in 2nd and 3rd century literatures.

Bibliography. U. Bianchi, "Dualism," in *The Encyclopedia of Religion* (New York, 1987), 4:506-12; K. Rudolph, *Gnosis* (San Francisco, 1984).

BENNIE R. CROCKETT, JR.

DUMAH (Heb. *dûmâ*) **(PERSON)**
The sixth son of Ishmael, and the presumed ancestor of an Arabian tribe (Gen. 25:14 = 1 Chr. 1:30).

RONALD A. SIMKINS

DUMAH (Heb. *dûmâ*) **(PLACE)**

1. A city in the hill country of Judah (Josh. 15:52), identified with modern Khirbet ed-Deir Dômeh (148093), ca. 10 km. (6.5 mi.) SW of Hebron.

2. A prosperous district and oasis in north central Arabia, Dumat al-Jandal (modern al-Jawf) in the Wadi Sirḥan along the major trade routes leading to Amman and Damascus. Dumah is first mentioned in the Assyrian annals of Sennacherib as Adummatu. Sennacherib launched a campaign against Dumah after his eighth campaign, between 691 and 689 B.C.E. It remained an important center in Arabia until the 8th century C.E.

3. A place mentioned in a prophetic oracle associated with the region of Edom (Isa. 21:11). The reference is probably a textual corruption for Edom itself (as read by the LXX). RONALD A. SIMKINS

DUNG
Both human and animal excrement, which the ritual and priestly material categorizes as impure. In sacrifice it is to be burned, along with other impure parts of the animal, at a place removed from the

congregation (Exod. 29:14; Lev. 4:11; 8:17; 16:27; cf. Num. 19:5 where the animal is burned altogether). Clothes stained with excrement had to be cleaned (Isa. 4:4), though fools may not notice that their clothes are dirty (Prov. 30:12).

As a means of verbal abuse, unburied dead are described as being spread over fields like manure (2 Kgs. 9:37; Ps. 83:10[MT 11]; Jer. 8:2; 9:22[21]; 16:4; Zeph. 1:17). Certainly, to be associated with dung was shameful and insulting (Job 20:7), and the dead are disrespected by having their houses made into dung heaps (Ezra 6:11). The apostatizing priests of Malachi are threatened with having dung wiped on their faces (Mal. 2:3).

Dung was used as fuel for fire, but using human dung for cooking rendered food unclean (Ezek. 4:12, 15). In ancient times as now, dung was also used as fertilizer in rural areas. Disposal of human dung in urban areas was a concern for biblical writers. One method of disposal was burning (1 Kgs. 14:10), but dung was generally removed from areas of habitation and concentrated in a dunghill (Ezra 6:11; Luke 14:35). In Jerusalem, waste was removed from the city through the Dung Gate at the southeastern corner of the city wall (Neh. 2:13; 3:13-14; 12:31). Deut. 23:13 describes proper latrine procedures for a military encampment. In times of famine and poverty, people may have consumed animal (possibly 2 Kgs. 6:25) or human dung (18:27 = Isa. 36:12).

NICOLE J. RUANE

DURA (Aram. *dûrāʾ*)

The plain upon which Nebuchadnezzar, king of Babylon, erected a great golden image (Dan. 3:1). Because they refused to bow down and worship the image, Daniel's friends Shadrach, Meshach, and Abednego were thrown into a fiery furnace. The location of the site is unknown, but the name may be related to Akk. *dūru,* "city wall" or "fortification." Jules Oppert identified the site as Tell Dēr, 27 km. (17 mi.) SW of Baghdad, where he found a massive brick structure he thought to be the platform for Nebuchadnezzar's image.

STEPHEN J. ANDREWS

DURA-EUROPOS

An ancient city located 434 km. (270 mi.) NW of Babylon where the Ḫabur River enters the Euphrates, about halfway between modern Aleppo and Baghdad. The site of the Roman frontier post Circesium, locally known in Greek as *Europos* from its founding during the Hellenistic rule of Seleucus I (311-281 B.C.E.) until at least 180 C.E., after 200 C.E. it was usually called *Doura* (Gk.), based on a Semitic name meaning "fortress." The hyphenated name is a modern construct. The city was destroyed in 256 under the rule of the Sassanid Shapur I and never rebuilt.

Following the chance discovery by British troops in 1920 of mural paintings, systematic excavations beginning in 1922 have converted the desolate town into one of the famous archaeological retrievals of the 20th century. Dura-europos is probably best known for the artwork with religious themes. This includes a standing Jewish synagogue, originally a private house, whose four walls are covered with a fascinating panorama of paintings from the OT; a Christian church, also created from a remodeled private home, containing a vaulted baptismal font; and a temple of Mithra, atypical for such temples since it was built above rather than below ground.

FLORENCE M. GILLMAN

DYE, DYEING

Linen in its natural state is white or beige, while wool is either white, brown, or black. In order to produce fabrics in colors other than these, the fibers must be dyed. There is an abundance of evidence that dyed fabrics were in use during the biblical period. A scrap of red woolen fabric, found at Naḥal Mishmar in the cliffs E of the Dead Sea, dates to the Chalcolithic period (4th millennium B.C.E.). Canaan was known for dyed fabrics. In the Song of Deborah, Sisera's mother awaits her son's triumphant return with spoils of war including "dyed stuffs embroidered" (Judg. 5:30b). The nature of textiles means that most disintegrate, so few examples from the period exist. However, depictions of Canaanites found in Egyptian art shows that richly embroidered and colored bands decorated the garments.

Dyed textiles are required in the making of the tabernacle and priestly vestments described in Exod. 25–28, 35–38. Three colors predominate: blue, purple, and crimson. The purple was produced from sea snails of the Mediterranean Sea, and crimson came from the scale insect known as Kermes, but the origin of blue is not clearly known. Blue, purple, and crimson were colors of luxury textiles and marked the owner as a person of power or wealth. Their use in the tabernacle indicates the holiness of the place. Other colors, both natural and dyed, were likely used in other garments or hangings.

To produce dyed fabrics it is necessary to have fiber for dyeing, in the form of raw wool or flax, spun yarn or thread, or woven fabric; dyes, from plant, mineral, or animal sources; tools for grinding and preparing dyes; and pots or vats to prepare the dye and color the fiber. The processes associated with the preparation of dyes produced unpleasant odors, so dyeing establishments were often located on windy promontories at the edge of settlements. Identification of installations as dyeing facilities can be difficult. William F. Albright identified stone vats at Tell Beit Mirsim as dye vats, but further research has shown them to be olive oil presses. However, excavators found piles of crushed shells of dye-producing snails and potsherds with a residue of purple dye at Tell es-Samaq/Tel Shiqmona on the northern coast of Israel, which indicates the presence of a dyeing industry. Sarepta, Tell el-Fukhkhâr/Tel Acco, and Tell Keisan/Tel Kison also produced sherds with traces of purple dye.

Bibliography. E. J. W. Barber, *Prehistoric Textiles* (Princeton, 1992), 223-43; S. Robinson, *A History of Dyed Textiles* (Cambridge, Mass., 1969).

MARY PETRINA BOYD

DYSENTERY

A disease characterized by severe diarrhea with passage of mucus and blood (Gk. *dysentérion*). This disease, due to a parasitic microbe (*Bacillus dysenteriae*) and at times fatal, has been proved to be epidemic. According to Acts 28:8 the father of Publius suffered a fever and dysentery at Malta.

DYSMAS (Gk. *Dysmás*)

The unnamed penitent thief crucified with Jesus (Luke 23:39-43), according to early Christian apocryphal stories (cf. the Acts of Pilate). Legends grew that Dysmas (also called Dismas, Demas, Titus, and Zoathan) had defended Mary, Joseph, and Jesus on their trip to Egypt, and that he was a crooked innkeeper who cheated the rich but helped the poor. Because of his kindnesses to Jesus and his repentance, he was eventually made a saint in the Greek and Latin churches. RICHARD A. SPENCER

E

E
Designation of the Elohist source, regarded as one of the principal strata of the Pentateuch.

EAGLE
A large raptor. In the OT Heb. *nešer* designates both the vulture and the eagle. The unclean carrion vulture or gier eagle (Heb. *rāḥām* or *rāḥāmâ;* Lev. 11:18; Deut. 14:17), which could not be eaten, is different than the *nešer.* Almost all uses of *nešer* refer to the eagle, and most of the time the references are metaphorical.

For the biblical writers, the eagle was a symbol of speed (Deut. 28:49; 2 Sam. 1:23; Jer. 4:13; Lam. 4:19), notable for building its nest in lofty places (Jer. 49:16), for soaring swiftly to the heights (Prov. 23:5), and for attacking its prey ferociously and swiftly (Job 9:26; Hab. 1:8). Other characteristics that were prized included its lofty grandeur (Obad. 4), its gentle and protective care for its young (Exod. 19:4-6; cf. Deut. 32:11), and its youthful vigor (Ps. 103:5; Isa. 40:31, "they shall mount up with wings like eagles"). In Ezekiel's vision of the throne chariot (Ezek. 1:10) the prophet saw four cherubim, each having four faces (of a man, a lion, an ox, and an eagle). The writer of Revelation borrowed from this image in his vision of the lamb on the throne, circled by four creatures, which are like a lion, an ox, a human, and an eagle (Rev. 4:7; Gk. *aetós*). John also employed the greatness of the eagle and its capacity for flight (or escape) in reference to the woman of Rev. 12:14 (cf. 8:13). Apart from those references, the eagle is mentioned in the NT only in Matt. 24:28 (= Luke 17:37), where the reference is clearly to carrion-eating birds and not the noble eagle of the OT. RICHARD A. SPENCER

EAR
The oral texture of Israelite religion placed great value upon the ear. Hearing, listening, understanding, and obeying were closely connected (Prov. 18:15; Job 13:1), with the ear being both instrument and symbol. Ears are the path to wisdom (Prov. 2:2) and knowledge (18:15). The ears test words and may form a defense against evil thoughts (Job 12:11). Also, the ears of the people may be blocked from heeding God's instruction, through stubbornness (Isa. 48:8) or rebellion (Ezek. 12:2).

As God's voice became the central medium for revelation, so the ear of the people of Israel became the central medium for the reception of that revelation. "Hear, O Israel" (Deut. 6:3-5) summoned them to a unique calling of obedience. Just as the servant is dedicated for life to one master (Exod. 21:6) and the sons of Aaron are consecrated with blood, on the right ear (Lev. 8:23-24), so the righteous have receptive ears (Ps. 40:6[MT 7]; cf. Jer. 6:10).

God too has ears (Isa. 59:1) and is both able and willing to save those who call on him. By contrast, Baal remained silent, in spite of Elijah's encouragement to the prophets to shout louder (1 Kgs. 18:27). Deutero-Isaiah mocks the idol who does not answer and cannot save (Isa. 46:7), while the Psalmist writes of the gold and silver deities of the nations who have ears but cannot hear (Ps. 115:6; 135:17).

Some people may close their ears, finding God's word to be offensive (Jer. 6:10), as in response to the teaching of Jesus (Matt. 13:14-15, citing Isa. 6:9-10). In a call for true hearing, which issues in obedience, Jesus commands, "Those who have ears to hear, let them hear" (Matt. 11:15 par.; cf. Rev. 2:7).

WILLIAM R. DOMERIS

EARRING
Men, women, and children of the ancient Near East adorned their ears and noses with jewelry. Ezek. 16:12 distinguishes Heb. *ʿăgîlîm,* ear ornaments, from *nezem,* a nose ring (Gen. 24:22, 30, 47; Isa. 3:21; Prov. 11:22), but *nezem* can also refer to earrings (Gen. 35:4; Exod. 32:2-3; Prov. 25:12). In other passages the distinction is not clear, and *nezem* may have simply referred to any small ring-shaped item of jewelry.

Rings are associated with the manufacture of an idol or cult object (Exod. 32:2-3; Judg. 8:27; Gen.

35:4), and they are among the pieces of jewelry offered for use in God's tent of meeting (Exod. 35:22). A ring's material, when mentioned, is always gold (Gen. 24:22, 30, 47; Exod. 32:2-3; 35:22; Judg. 8:24; Job 42:11). Gold or silver rings are infrequent among Palestinian archaeological finds, but iron, copper, and brass rings are common. Gold rings are often lunate (crescent shaped) with a point at one end for insertion into the earlobe or nose. Other rings are penannular, i.e., circular with a break and two overlapping points. Some earrings were quite heavy (Gen. 24:22; Judg. 8:24-26; cf. *ANEP,* 72). Rings sometimes had additional decorations, especially clusters of balls ("mulberry" earrings) and pendants shaped like pomegranate buds. Jewelry smiths cast these rings in engraved stone molds. See *ANEP* for pictures of various rings.

JOSEPH E. JENSEN

EARTHQUAKE

An unusual shaking or trembling of the earth or some part thereof. Both Amos (Amos 1:1) and Zechariah (Zech. 14:5) refer to a literal earthquake (Heb. *ra'aš*) during the reign of Uzziah, king of Judah. Since these two prophets refer to it as "the earthquake," without any other identification, it must have been very destructive and familiar to their readers. Beyond its literal meaning, "earthquake" became a symbol of divine activity, especially in judgment (Isa. 29:6). The earth, and Mt. Sinai in particular, are said to have quaked before the awesome presence of Yahweh (Exod. 19:18; Ps. 18:7[MT 8] = 2 Sam. 22:8; Ps. 68:8). The prophet Elijah apparently expected Yahweh to be present in an earthquake, though instead Yahweh appeared in a still small voice (1 Kgs. 19:11-12).

In the NT there is likewise a literal and a symbolic use of the term earthquake (Gk. *seismós*). An earthquake is mentioned at Jesus' crucifixion (Matt. 27:51, 54) and at his tomb (28:2). An earthquake opened the prison doors for Paul and Silas after they had been incarcerated at Philippi (Acts 16:26). The figurative use of earthquake as a symbol of God's activity is preserved in the Synoptic Gospels (Mark 13:8 par.), among several other symbols depicting the judgment of God at the end of the world. The author of the book of Revelation saw an earthquake as one of several symbols of God's judgment following the breaking of the sixth seal (Rev. 6:12), as evidence of God's activity in response to the prayers of the saints (8:5), and as the result of God's taking the "two witnesses" up into heaven (11:13). The same writer saw an earthquake as following the appearance of the ark of the covenant in the temple (Rev. 11:19) and, finally, as accompanying the judgments of the seventh bowl (16:17-21).

JOE E. LUNCEFORD

EAST

The direction of primary orientation for the Hebrews (Heb. *qeḏem*). South thus was "right" or "the right hand" *(têmān)* and north was "left" or "the left hand" *(śĕmō'l)*. This eastward orientation was shared by several other Semitic peoples including the Akkadians and the Sumerians; the Egyptians, however, used south as the primary point for orientation, probably due to the southern source of the Nile River. The Hebrew root *qdm* has several shades of meaning, including antiquity (since Abraham came from the east); front or face (facing a direction so as to gain orientation); and the "east wind" or "wind of Yahweh" (Hos. 12:1[MT 2]; cf. Gen. 41:6; Isa. 27:8). In his travels, Yahweh was viewed as coming from the east (Ezek. 10:19; 11:23; 43:1-5).

References to the "land of the east" (*'ereṣ qeḏem;* Gen. 25:6; Judg. 6:3, 33; 7:12; cf. Num. 23:7) can be translated as a proper name, "the land of Qedem." Conflicting Egyptian references to Qedem locate the region either closer to Byblos on the coast of the Mediterranean Sea in Phoenicia or E of Syria. Most scholars take the phrase descriptively as referring to the general region from northern Mesopotamia to Arabia. "People (sons, or children) of the east" (*bĕnê qeḏem*) probably refers to the people of this general region: the Edomites, Arabians, Midianites, and people of the Mesopotamian valley (Gen. 29:1; Isa. 11:14; Jer. 49:28). Job is described as the "greatest of the children of the east" (Job 1:3) and is said to have resided in the "land of Uz" in the general area of Edom.

Bibliography. M. Dahood, "The Four Cardinal Points in Psalm 75,7 and Joel 2,20," *Bibl* 52 (1971): 397; B. L. Gordon, "Sacred Directions, Orientation, and the Top of the Map," *History of Religions* 10 (1971): 211-27.

DENNIS M. SWANSON

EAST WIND

A notable climatic feature of Israel in which powerful winds blow from east to west, negating the normal sea breeze from the Mediterranean. Occurring within a 50-day period in early fall, these winds (Heb. *qāḏîm*) are known today as *khamsin* (from Arab. "50") or *sirocco.* They are notable for their strength (often 95+ kph[60+ mph]), extremely low humidity (under 7 percent), and intensely hot weather (40° temperature increases within hours have been recorded). Capable of reducing green crops to dry, brown husks in a single day, they also spawn wildfires. These winds were viewed as an instrument of God's judgment, being known as "the wind of the Lord" (Isa. 59:19; esp. Hos. 13:15). This same weather pattern is noted in Gen. 41:6; Isa. 27:8; Jer. 4:11.

DENNIS M. SWANSON

EASTER

An ancient and important Christian festival celebrating the resurrection of Jesus Christ. Originally called *Pascha* due to its association with the Jewish Passover, Easter is preceded by the 40-day season of Lent, a time of penitence and preparation. The early Church used the Lenten season as a time of preparation for baptism, administered at sunrise on Easter Sunday. The name "Easter" is derived from a spring festival honoring the Anglo-Saxon goddess Eostre.

The Quartodeciman Controversy emerged in the late 2nd century regarding the appropriate day for Easter observance. Rome observed the first

Sunday after the first full moon following the spring equinox. However, some Eastern communions, more keenly attuned to the calendar of Judaism, observed the Resurrection on the third day following the 14th of Nisan, the Passover. Since 14 Nisan, based on a lunar calendar, could come any day of the week, there was no guarantee that Easter would always be observed on Sunday. The Council of Nicaea (325 C.E.) finally determined that the Roman practice would prevail. This controversy was the first in a series of rifts that led to the eventual schism of the Eastern and Western churches.

D. LARRY GREGG

EASTERN SEA
Another name for the Dead Sea (Ezek. 47:18; Joel 2:20; Zech. 14:8; Heb. *hayyām haqqaḏmônî*).

EBAL (Heb. *ʿêḇāl*) **(PERSON)**

1. The third son of Shobal and a descendant of the Horite Seir; eponymous ancestor of an Edomite clan (Gen. 36:23; 1 Chr. 1:40).

2. A son of Joktan and descendant of Shem (1 Chr. 1:22). The parallel account in the Table of Nations gives his name as Obal (Gen. 10:28).

EBAL (Heb. *ʿêḇāl*) **(PLACE)**
A mountain just N of Shechem across the valley from Mt. Gerizim and rising 933 m. (3061 ft.) above sea level. Moses commanded the Israelites to build an altar on Mt. Ebal (the Samaritan Pentateuch reads "Mt. Gerizim") when they had crossed the Jordan, and to make a sacrifice (Deut. 27:5). The fulfillment of those commands is described in Josh. 8. In 1982 an assemblage of stones on Mt. Ebal was excavated. It has been variously interpreted as Joshua's altar, a subsequent Israelite altar, or a noncultic structure, possibly a watchtower.

Bibliography. A. Zertal et al., *Archaeology and the Bible,* 1: *Early Israel,* ed. H. Shanks and D. P. Cole (Washington, 1990), 76-107 [four articles].

ROBERT T. ANDERSON

EBED (Heb. *ʿeḇeḏ*)

1. The father of Gaal the adversary of Abimelech (Judg. 9:26-35).

2. The son of Jonathan and head of the family of Adin who, accompanied by "50 males," returned from exile with Ezra (Ezra 8:6).

EBED-MELECH (Heb. *ʿeḇeḏ meleḵ*)
An Ethiopian who reproached King Zedekiah for the decision to place Jeremiah in a cistern (Jer. 38:7-13; 39:15-18) during the Babylonian siege of Jerusalem. Ebed-melech then rescued Jeremiah from the cistern at a time when all of Jerusalem appeared to have abandoned the prophet. His name in Hebrew means "servant of a king." Traditionally, scholars have assumed that he was Zedekiah's slave, but the king's acquiescence to his request would be an unusual response to a slave's criticism. The phrase "servant of the king" occurs on numerous seals from 7th-century Judah, where it refers to high-ranking officials. Ebed-melech is called a *sāris*, a term which refers to a eunuch or an official (so used throughout the book of Jeremiah, usually in military contexts).

Ebed-melech is called "the Cushite" (Jer. 38:7). Ebed-melech was undoubtedly an African with black skin (cf. Jeremiah's reference to the skin of the Cushites, Jer. 13:23). The Cushites were soldiers and mercenaries in the army of Egypt, the primary ally of Judah in her rebellion against the Babylonians. Ebed-melech, therefore, was probably the commander of an Egyptian/Cushite military unit, exerting considerable political pressure on Zedekiah.

Bibliography. R. Deutsch and M. Heltzer, *Forty New Ancient West Semitic Inscriptions* (Tel Aviv, 1994); J. D. Hays, "The Cushites: A Black Nation in the Bible," *BSac* 153 (1996): 396-409.

J. DANIEL HAYS

EBENEZER (Heb. *ʾeḇen hāʿezer)*
The place of the battle in which the Philistines captured the ark (1 Sam. 4:1; 5:1). Ebenezer is also where the Israelites under Samuel defeated the Philistines, after which he erected a monument that he named "Ebenezer" (lit., "Stone of Help") to commemorate God's aid (1 Sam. 7:12). Scholars have debated whether this represents one place or two. Since Samuel erects and names his monument Ebenezer after the battle of 1 Sam. 4 has already occurred, two distinct locations may be inferred. Furthermore, the Ebenezer in 1 Sam. 4 is near Aphek on the road from the Philistine coast to Shiloh, while the Ebenezer in 1 Sam. 7 is near Mizpah (Tell en-Naṣbeh) just N of Jerusalem. However, there is a narrative symmetry between the two battles, and the two accounts reflect the importance of Israel's faithfulness to Yahweh in determining its fate, suggesting that the name may simply be a literary device.

Archaeologists have suggested identifying Ebenezer with ʿIzbet Ṣarṭah (14675.16795), a 4-dunam Israelite site near Aphek, if only because it is the nearest Israelite site facing Philistine Aphek. However, there is nothing other than its geographic correspondence to 1 Sam. 4 which can confirm its identity as Ebenezer.

Bibliography. I. Finkelstein, *Izbet Sartah* (Oxford, 1986).

ROBERT D. MILLER, II

EBER (Heb. *ʿēḇer)*

1. The eponymous ancestor of the Hebrews; descendant of Shelah, Arpachshad, and Shem. Two distinct lineages of Eber are given. In the Table of Nations Eber's lineage is traced through his son Joktan (Gen. 10:21-31), and Eber probably designates the "region beyond" (*ʿēber*) the River (Jordan?). That is, Eber refers to the territory of Semitic peoples, from Mesha to the hill country in the east. Eber is also listed in the genealogy from Shem to Terah, but his lineage is traced through his first son Peleg (Gen. 11:14-17). These two lineages are combined by the Chronicler (1 Chr. 1:17-27).

In the final oracle of Balaam Eber is mentioned along with Asshur (Assyria) as the place afflicted by the ships of Kittim, probably the Greeks from eastern Anatolia or Cyprus (Num. 24:24). This reference, as in the Table of Nations, probably refers to the territory beyond the river.

2. One of seven clans of the tribe of Gad, living in the land of Bashan (1 Chr. 5:13).

3. The first son of Elpaal, of the tribe of Benjamin (1 Chr. 8:12).

4. The son of Shashak, of the tribe of Benjamin (1 Chr. 8:22).

5. A postexilic priest, head of the house of Amok, during the days of Joiakim (Neh. 12:20).

RONALD A. SIMKINS

EBEZ (Heb. *'eḇeṣ*)
A city within the tribal territory of Issachar (Josh. 19:20). Its location is unknown.

EBIASAPH (Heb. *'eḇyāsāp̄*) (also ABIASAPH)
A Levite of the lineage of Kohath, said to have been the father of Assir (1 Chr. 6:23, 37) or Kore (9:19). At Exod. 6:24 he is called Abiasaph.

EBIONITES
Name for Jewish Christians first witnessed in Irenaeus (*Adv. haer.* 1.26.2; Gk. *ebionaioi*) ca. 180 C.E. The word derives from Heb. *'eḇyônîm* and means "the poor."

The precise origin and referent of the name are uncertain. Parallel usage of the Hebrew in the Qumran writings renders it virtually certain that the name was originally an honorific self-designation: the "poor" are God's favored people (e.g., 4QpPs37 2:9; 1QpHab 12:3; 1QM 11:9). The background of this usage is apparent in the OT (e.g., Amos 2:6-7; the synonym *'ānî* is also common; cf. esp. the Psalms, e.g., Ps. 35:10) and in the broader ancient Orient.

How far back the designation goes among the followers of Jesus is disputed. Some scholars see the title present already in Paul's references to a collection for the "poor" in Jerusalem (Gal. 2:10). But in Rom. 15:26 Paul distinguishes this group from the other Jerusalem believers by speaking of "the poor among the saints." In 2 Cor. 9:12 Paul further confirms the economic, or literal, aspect by speaking of the collection as making up for "the deficiencies of the saints." Nevertheless, Paul's collection for the poor doubtless had a church-political aspect that involved recognition of Jerusalem as the center of the believers. It is hard to imagine any use of the word "poor" among the early believers without some religious overtones (cf. Matt. 5:3).

Other scholars think the term was only later adopted by one group of Jewish Christians, picking up in part on the saying of Jesus in Matt. 5:3. In the 19th century Adolf Hilgenfeld accepted the historicity of a founder named Ebion, first witnessed in Tertullian (*De praescr. haer.* 33.5) and Hippolytus (*Ref.* 7.35.1). Yet most likely the supposition of the existence of an Ebion derives from the heresiological urge to attribute the "heresies" to one particular heretical figure (here perhaps originally in Hippolytus' lost *Syntagma*). No doubt the heresiologists are in part responsible for the application of the name Ebionites more broadly to all Jewish Christians. Thus Irenaeus, following his source, lumps all Jewish Christians under the title Ebionites and ascribes to them belief in the natural generation of Jesus by Joseph and Mary, use of only the Gospel of Matthew, rejection of Paul as an apostate from the law, and veneration of Jerusalem.

Stretches of modern scholarship have followed Epiphanius in distinguishing Ebionites from another branch of Jewish Christians, the Nazoreans. By linking Irenaeus' description of the Ebionites with the stricter group of Jewish Christians mentioned without specific name in Justin Martyr *Dial.* 47-48, these scholars apply the name Ebionites to the stricter Jewish Christians and leave Nazoreans for the moderate ones. This is to be discouraged because it lacks historical justification. It furthermore neglects Epiphanius' actual description of the Ebionite group or must postulate an additional "gnostic" variety of Ebionism. Epiphanius connects his Ebionites with the Pseudo-Clementines, with the anti-Pauline Ascents of James, and with a gospel conveniently called the Gospel of the Ebionites by modern scholars. While it is possible that Epiphanius received these writings from a 4th-century group who called themselves Ebionites, Epiphanius' division of the Jewish Christians into Ebionites and Nazoreans may partially be due to the pressure to come up with his announced "80 heresies"; he invented and divided when possible, here broadly picking up on the earlier heresiological view that there were two types of Jewish Christians.

Bibliography. E. Bammel, "*ptōchós*," *TDNT* 6:888-915; A. F. J. Klijn and G. J. Reinink, *Patristic Evidence for Jewish-Christian Sects.* NovTSup 36 (Leiden, 1973); G. A. Koch, *A Critical Investigation of Epiphanius' Knowledge of the Ebionites* (Philadelphia, 1976); G. Strecker, "On the Problem of Jewish Christianity," in W. Bauer, *Orthodoxy and Heresy in Earliest Christianity* (Philadelphia, 1971), 241-85.

F. STANLEY JONES

EBLA
The ancient name of Tell Mardikh in northern Syria, 65 km. (40 mi.) S of Aleppo. The mound was intermittently occupied from prehistoric times at least until the 5th century C.E. Archaeologists have discerned a long succession of occupational levels; the main areas explored belong to Middle Bronze IVA (ca. 2400-2300 B.C.E.) and Middle Bronze II (ca. 1800-1600). The site consists of a central acropolis as well as a much larger lower town, surrounded by a massive wall; at its largest expanse it covered almost 60 ha. (148 a.).

Excavations at Tell Mardikh have been conducted since 1964 under the direction of Paolo Matthiae of the University of Rome. The discovery in 1968 of an inscribed stela of King Ibbit-lim assured identification of the city as ancient Ebla, already known from other cuneiform sources. In 1975 the first inscribed clay tablets were found in Palace G on the acropolis, and eventually 15 thousand tablets and fragments were recovered. These were the remains of what was once less than 3000

Palace G with royal staircase, walls, and columned halls at Tell Mardikh/Ebla. Here were discovered some 25 thousand cuneiform tablets (Phoenix Data Systems, Neal and Joel Bierling)

texts that were left in three rooms close to the main audience hall. The date of these texts has been the subject of much debate, but it is now almost universally agreed that they were written just before the reign of Sargon of Agade in Mesopotamia (2334-2279, equivalent to Bronze Age IV A1). The destruction of Palace G has been attributed to Sargon and even to his grandson Naram-sin, as both claimed to have conquered the city, but there is no direct archaeological evidence to link either to the deed. The internal time span of the archives was likewise a matter of controversy, but it is now established that they covered the last 50 years or so before the destruction of the palace (i.e., the time of the reigns of kings Igriš-halam, Irkab-damu, and Išar-damu). The dynasty itself goes back much further, as ritual and administrative texts provide the names of 27 kings.

The texts were written in at least three languages: Sumerian, a form of early Akkadian, and a hitherto unattested Semitic language that was immediately named Eblaite. The first two were used only in literary school texts of Mesopotamian origin, while Eblaite was used in administrative, chancery, and diplomatic texts as well as in a few literary compositions, mainly incantations and lexical texts. There is much debate on the classification of the new language; the morphology suggests that it was a form of East Semitic (Akkadian), but since it uses many words that otherwise occur only in West Semitic, it has also been considered as an early form of Canaanite. It is now apparent that this was not just a local language, but one that was in use throughout Syria and Northern Mesopotamia in the 3rd millennium and is attested, with local variations, in roughly contemporary tablets from Mari and Tell Beydar. Related dialects were in use at Mari until the reign of Yaḫdun-lim (ca. 1800), when a switch to Old Babylonian was effected for administrative purposes.

The 3rd-millennium archives consist of a small number of school and ritual texts as well as a wide variety of administrative and diplomatic records. The economic documents are laconic, repetitive, and formulaic. We learn more about the written form of the Eblaite language from other types of texts. The local enthronement rituals are particularly important for our knowledge of the culture and language of the city, as are a small number of treaties, land donations, and epistolary texts. Most of the school texts were imported from Mesopotamia and are duplicated at such Sumerian sites as Abu Salabikh and Fara. The Eblaite incantations may have been local, but in addition to Syrian deities they mention such Mesopotamian gods as Enlil (Illilu). Word lists, also called lexical texts, an important part of the study of cuneiform, are well represented, some with Eblaite translations of the Sumerian words. There are also a few monolingual Eblaite word lists. The literary compositions — all of Mesopotamian origin — include a hymn to the sun-god, a text concerning the goddess of writing, and a difficult Sumerian composition mentioning the god Ama-ušumgal-ana.

The administrative texts fall into a number of categories and concern primarily the crown and its dependents; they thus reveal the workings of only a specific sector of the state. The focal point of the archives was the extended family of the ruler, crown dependents, and related elite families. The main authority for transactions in the main archives was in the hands of one person, a vizier or majordomo of the royal estate. The three persons who occupied this position were Arenum, Ibrium, and his son Ibbi-zikir. The kingdom was one of many listed in the territorial states in Syria; more than 1400 place names occur in the documents, and although many of them cannot be identified at present, a good number were undoubtedly small hamlets in the vicinity of the city. To the east lay the allied state of Emar, and further down on the Euphrates was Mari. To the north and northeast Ebla had to contend with other polities, and its influence reached as far as Carchemish. At times Ebla had to pay tribute to Mari. The population of the cities mentioned in the Ebla documents seems to have been uniformly Semitic-speaking, if one can judge by personal names. There is not a trace of Hurrian or Amorite, although a city named *mar-tu* (the Mesopotamian writing for Amorite) does occur. The archives document complex diplomatic relationships between Ebla and other Syrian states, as well as with the Mesopotamian state of Kish. Laconic receipts of deliveries and outgoing goods hide the real nature of transactions, whether they be classified, in modern terms, as tribute, gift exchange, or trade. The relationships that are registered are with other urban centers, and it is impossible to ascertain the importance of nonsedentary people in this period. Food rations for palace personnel, as well as documentation of women involved in wool production — a major part of the royal economy — provide insight into matters of the organization of dependents of the crown. In addition to the all-important cloth industry at Ebla, the texts provide detailed information on animal husbandry, primarily the care of large herds of sheep, on the cultivation of barley, wheat, oil, and grapevines, as well as on the exchange and production of large quantities of metals and metal goods, including silver, gold, tin, copper, and bronze. The sheer quantities of precious metals recorded in the texts are impressive, as exemplified by one record of deliveries made by Ebla to the city of Mari over a number of years, amounting to more than 65 kg. (140 lb.) of gold and 1000 kg. (2200 lb.) of silver.

The religious traditions of Ebla can only be glimpsed at. The chief god of the city, Kura, is otherwise unknown, as is his consort Barama. The two other prime state gods were the sun-goddess and the storm-god Hadda, also worshipped under the name Hadda-baal. Other important deities were Ashtar, Dagan, Gašru, Rašap, Kamiš, and Ishara. Offering lists and rituals provide some information on the state cult, including royal ancestor worship, but nothing is known of everyday religious practices of the population.

At the time that the Ur III dynasty was dominant in Sumer and Akkad (2100-2000) Ebla was one of the few Syrian cities mentioned in Mesopotamian texts. At Ebla this period (IIB2) is represented by a large building complex (the Archaic Palace) found in the northwestern part of the mound. Archaeological remains from the first half of the 2nd millennium (IIIA and IIIB, ca. 2000-1600) demonstrate that Ebla was a thriving city right up to the next destruction, generally ascribed to the Hittites. At this time the urban center reached its largest expansion and was surrounded by a massive brick wall. Although no archives from this period have been discovered, the rich archaeological finds, including extensive elite graves, provide much information on the culture of the times. The city would never again reach such expansion and was occupied intermittently at various times after 1600; the latest remains of human activity are from the 1st millennium C.E.

Bibliography. A. Archi, "Fifteen Years of Studies on Ebla," *OLZ* 88 (1993): 461-71; "Ebla Texts," *OEANE* 2:184-86; P. Matthiae, "Ebla," *OEANE* 2:180-83; L. Milano, "Ebla: A Third-Millennium City-State in Ancient Syria," *CANE* 2:1219-30.

PIOTR MICHALOWSKI

EBONY

The wood of two species of tree, *Diospyros ebenaster Retz.* and *Diospyros melanozylon Roxb.*, both native to the Indian sub-continent and Sri Lanka. The Phoenicians shipped the wood to Tyre from Dedan on the Persian Gulf and from there traded throughout the Mediterranean world (Ezek. 27:15). The exterior wood is white and has little value, but the interior becomes black and durable over time and it was highly valued in fine carpentry, ornaments, furniture, and some religious practices in the ancient world. Works of ebony were prized highly by Babylonians, Egyptians, Greeks, Phoenicians, and Romans. THOMAS B. SLATER

EBRON (Heb. *ʿeḇrōn*)

A town in the tribal territory of Asher (Josh. 19:28), probably the same as Abdon (21:30; 1 Chr. 6:74[MT 59]). The form is generally explained as a copyist's error, reading Heb. *resh* for *daleth.*

ECBATANA (Gk. *Ekbatana;* O. Pers. *hagmatāna;* Aram. *ʾaḥmĕṯāʾ*)

Graecized name of Hagmatana (modern Hamadan), the main city in Media. It occupies a strategic position in the main pass through the Alvand Alignment, the easternmost range of the Zagros Mountains before the Iranian plateau. Ecbatana lies along the main east-west trade route between Mesopotamia and the East. The intense urbanization in Assyria from the 9th century B.C.E. onwards and the corresponding need for foreign supplies probably gave the city its importance during the 7th century. According to Herodotus, Ecbatana was founded by King Deioces ca. 700, but the historicity of Herodotus' report of the rise of the Median state has been called into question.

Systematic archaeological investigation of Ecbatana is rendered extremely difficult, since the site is still populated. Archaeological digs at other Median sites indicate economic and cultural prosperity during the 7th century. After Cyrus the Great conquered it ca. 550, Ecbatana became the summer residence for the Achaemenid kings. In its archives, Darius I found a copy of the edict of Cyrus (Ezra 6:2).

The book of Judith, judged by scholars to be historically suspect, mentions that Ecbatana was founded by an otherwise unknown Arphaxad (Jdt. 1:1), and Nebuchadnezzar is said to have plundered the city in a campaign against Arphaxad (vv. 13-14). Ecbatana is home to Raguel and Edna and their daughter Sara, whom Tobias marries (Tob. 3:7; 5:6; 7:1); Tobias later flees Nineveh to settle in Ecbatana (14:14). GERALD M. BILKES

ECCLESIASTES, BOOK OF

In Christian Bibles, the 21st book of the OT, immediately following Proverbs. In the Hebrew Bible it is grouped with the Megilloth (the five scrolls used in the major religious celebrations of Judaism). The book is read in its entirety during Sukkoth (the Feast of Booths or Tabernacles) when Israel both remembers its sojourn in the wilderness and celebrates the end of another harvest season in the Promised Land.

Ecclesiastes is named after the principal speaker in the book, called Qoheleth ("one who assembles") in Hebrew or *ekklēsiastēs* ("member of an assembly") in Greek. In some places the term is used as a title (*the* Qoheleth in 7:27; 12:8), and in others it seems to be a person's name or a nickname (1:1, 2, 12; 12:9-10). In Hebrew *qōhelet̲* can refer to the activity of gathering together either an audience or a collection of sayings. Since tradition remembers Qoheleth as one who "taught the people knowledge, weighing and studying and arranging many proverbs" (12:9), the translation "Teacher" (NIV, NRSV) is more accurate than "Preacher" (KJV, RSV).

The Synagogue and the Church traditionally have identified Qoheleth with Solomon, but the name Solomon does not occur anywhere in the book. Solomon was known as the prototype of wisdom leadership, and 1:1 calls Qoheleth a "son of David, king in Jerusalem." But a number of statements in the book are difficult to reconcile with what we know about Solomon from other sources. In 1:12 Qoheleth says that he "*was* king over Israel in Jerusalem," implying that he speaks from a time when his reign had ended, and 1:16; 2:7 imply that many other kings had preceded the speaker on the throne in Jerusalem. Both 8:2-9 and 10:16-19 sound more like the opinions of a subject than those of a king.

The Hebrew in which the present form of the book is written represents a very late stage in the development of the language. The text contains loanwords from Persian and Aramaic and uses certain vocabulary and grammatical forms that only became common shortly before the beginning of the Christian era. Thus the present form of the book must come from the Second Temple period at the earliest (i.e., from at least four centuries later than Solomon), and Qoheleth is probably a wisdom teacher who takes on the *persona* of Solomon in order to argue that even someone as wise and as rich as Solomon would say what the Teacher says, if given a chance to do so.

Ecclesiastes has been understood in radically different ways by different readers because the central thematic metaphor (traditionally translated "all is vanity") is inherently ambiguous. Heb. *hebel* ("vanity") occurs 38 times in Ecclesiastes, compared to only 35 uses in all of the rest of the OT. In its simplest and most basic sense *hebel* means "a puff of air," "a breath," or "vapor" (e.g., Isa. 57:13; Ps. 39:5, 11[MT 6, 12]). But *hebel* acquires negative associations when used to describe the uselessness or worthlessness of idols (Jer. 2:5; 8:19; 10:8; 2 Kgs. 17:15) or the unreliability of human allies (Isa. 30:7). Thus "all is *hebel*" (1:2; 12:8) can be understood in either a positive or a negative sense.

Those who think vanity *(hebel)* is a pejorative term meaning "useless" or "meaningless" see the Teacher as a man lacking in faith and question the book's presence in the canon of Holy Scripture. Those who understand *hebel* ("vanity") to refer to that which is transitory or impermanent see the teachings of Ecclesiastes in a more positive light, especially when impermanence is understood to apply to everything "under the sun" in contrast to the permanence of God. Qoheleth thinks human life and the products of human labor are "breathlike" (impermanent, of short duration), not "meaningless."

Various parts of Ecclesiastes seem to represent conflicting points of view (compare 5:1-6[4:17–5:5] with 9:1-2 or 8:12-13 with 8:14) because the Teacher uses an ancient form of rhetoric known as "diatribe" or "disputation speech," in which a speaker quotes an opposing point of view in order to refute it. This "Yes, but . . ." style of speech is used in order to question the truth of several traditional assumptions. In effect, Ecclesiastes says to himself (or to his audience), "Yes, it may be true as the tradition tells us, that 'it will be well with those who fear God' and 'it will not be well with the wicked' (8:12-13) *but* experience tells us that '*on earth*, there are righteous people who are treated according to the conduct of the wicked, and there are wicked people who are treated according to the conduct of the righteous'" (v. 14).

Unlike the speakers in the book of Proverbs, who seem to think that the consequences of human action are relatively predictable, Qoheleth argues that human beings must choose to act without being completely sure of the ultimate results of their actions (11:1-6) and that mortals must live out their brief lives under the sun without being able to find out precisely what God has in mind to do (3:1-11; 8:17).

The book cannot be outlined as an orderly, structured, or logical argument. Topics ebb and flow, are briefly considered, abandoned for a while and then reappear for further examination. However, in general, the first six chapters consider what is good for human beings to do during their brief lives "under the sun," while the last six chapters are primarily concerned with what human beings can and cannot know.

In chs. 1–6 Ecclesiastes insists that nothing enduring or permanent can result from human efforts. Like the continually recycling elements of nature, human actions must be done over and over (1:3-9). To those who hope to make a permanent impression on the world, Qoheleth declares that fame does not endure (1:10-11). He reminds those who work to pile up the "good things in life," that they cannot take their possessions with them when they die (5:15[14]). In fact, he says, "some fool" will probably inherit what they have worked so hard to accumulate (2:18-21; 4:7-8; 5:13-17[12-16]; 6:1-3). The Teacher reminds those who work excessively hard in order to gain wisdom that, in spite of what the speakers in Proverbs say about the life-giving properties of wisdom (e.g., Prov. 13:14), "the wise die just like fools" (Eccl. 2:14-17).

Instead of working themselves to death in order to gain fame, wealth or wisdom, Ecclesiastes thinks people should "eat, drink, and find enjoyment in their toil" (2:24-26; 3:12-13; 5:18-20[17-19]; 8:15; 9:7-10) during their brief (*heḇel*-like) lives "under the sun." He does not think people should sit back and do nothing. Rather, he insists that work should be done for the sheer joy of it, for the pleasure of a job well done, or simply because it needs to be done (4:5-6; 5:18-20[17-19]; 9:9-10), not because it will bring the worker wealth, wisdom, or notoriety.

The final verse in ch. 6 introduces the questions which will dominate chs. 7–12: "Who knows what is good for mortals [to do] while they live the few days of their vain (*heḇel*-like) life? . . . For who can tell them what will be after them under the sun?" (6:12). Qoheleth doubts the claims of those who think they can predict what God will do (7:14; 8:17). Thus, he counsels his students: "Go, eat your bread with enjoyment, and drink your wine with a merry heart" (9:7). "Enjoy life with the wife whom you love, all the days of your vain (lit., breathlike) life that are given you under the sun" (9:9).

Ch. 3 brings together the major themes from both halves of the book. The Teacher uses the well-known poem in 3:2-8 to argue that because God has purposes which will always remain unknown to us and because we cannot add to or take away from God's work, therefore we ought not to work to the point of exhaustion trying to guarantee that our own actions will have permanent results (vv. 9-15).

The phrase "under the sun" plays a significant part in the development of Qoheleth's argument. In spite of what traditional wisdom teaches, Qoheleth's experience tells him that justice does not always happen "under the sun" (3:16; 7:15; 8:14; contra Prov. 10:2, 16; 11:4, 31, etc.), that sinning does not necessarily shorten the life of the sinner nor does righteousness extend the life of the righteous (Eccl. 7:15; 8:12-14; contra Prov. 10:27). However, Qoheleth leaves open the possibility that some form of judgment might take place outside the realm of human experience. Having argued that there is an appropriate time for everything "under heaven" (3:1-8), Qoheleth can continue to believe "in his heart" that God will (eventually) judge the righteous and the wicked (3:17). But he does not think anyone can really know what happens to us after we die (3:19-22).

The extended metaphor in 12:1-7, which compares old age and death to a decaying mansion on a large estate, is used to remind the reader once again that life (like everything else under the sun) is of brief duration. But lack of permanence does not mean lack of value. Life is both fleeting (*heḇel*) and sweet (11:7-10).

The book ends with a later editor's comments about Qoheleth's career (12:8-10) and some concluding advice from the editor to the reader (12:11-14).

Bibliography. J. L. Crenshaw, *Ecclesiastes.* OTL (Philadelphia, 1987); F. Crüsemann, "The Unchangeable World: The 'Crisis of Wisdom' in Koheleth," in *God of the Lowly,* ed. W. Schottroff and W. Stegemann (Maryknoll, 1984), 57-77; K. A. Farmer, *Who Knows What Is Good: A Commentary on the Books of Proverbs and Ecclesiastes.* ITC (Grand Rapids, 1991); M. V. Fox, *A Time to Tear Down and a Time to Build Up: A Rereading of Ecclesiastes* (Grand Rapids, 1999); R. B. Y. Scott, *Proverbs-Ecclesiastes.* AB 18 (Garden City, 1965); R. N. Whybray, "Qoheleth, Preacher of Joy," *JSOT* 23 (1982): 87-98.

KATHLEEN FARMER

ECCLESIASTICUS

See SIRACH, WISDOM OF JESUS THE SON OF.

ECONOMICS

Very little is known about the details of economic institutions and practices in the ancient Mediterranean world. From what is known about general conditions there, however, it is possible to infer a great deal about economic life in these times. Of primary importance is the fact that most people were very poor. As we know from our modern world, people who are very poor spend most of their incomes on food, and there is every reason to believe that such was the case in the biblical world. Consequently, the economies of the ancient Mediterranean were largely agricultural. This does not mean, however, that they were rural in the sense that farm folk lived in widely scattered locations on the plots of land they worked. Even today it is the practice in parts of that Mediterranean region for farmers to live in towns or villages and to go out to their fields to work each day.

Two other features of the ancient Mediterranean led to a high degree of self-sufficiency in agriculture rather than specialization and trade in agricultural products. The first was the high cost of land transport of bulky materials. According to the famous edict of the Roman emperor Diocletian issued ca. 300 C.E., which sought to control prices after a half century of currency debasement and inflation, the cost of delivering a wagonload of wheat would double with a journey of 480 km. (300 mi.). Water transport was much cheaper, however, and large quantities of wheat and other agricultural products were shipped by sea. High transport costs caused the prices of agricultural products to rise relatively rapidly with distance when they were shipped by land and reduced the likelihood that imported products would be cheaper than locally produced ones.

The other factor which inhibited specialization and trade in farm products is the similarity of climatic conditions in the Mediterranean basin. There are, to be sure, some dramatic special features of particular places. The annual flooding of the Nile renewed the fertility of farm land along its banks in Egypt. The Levant's location on the lee shore of the Mediterranean produced a strong seasonal pattern of rainfall which strongly influenced the time of planting of grain crops. In general, however, rainfall and temperature are similar throughout the region, so that similar crops were grown. Especially important were barley and wheat, grapes and olives. Grapes were converted to raisins and wine; although olives were eaten, they were used principally to produce olive oil, which was used for cooking, bathing, and lighting.

OT Period

The principal difference between the time of Israel and Judah and earlier times was the use of steeled iron. Steel was produced by repeated heating of iron in a charcoal fire and plunging it into cold water. The technique of steeling iron was developed ca. 1400 B.C.E., probably in the Armenian mountains. Its introduction into the Levant is usually attributed to the Philistines. Steel was cheaper than bronze, the principal metal previously used, in part because iron ores were widely available while tin, which was mixed with copper to obtain bronze, was obtainable only in a few places. When used in plowshares, steel cut deeper. It was better adapted to tools such as axes, which were used for clearing forests. Steel thus contributed both to the settlement of the highlands of Israel and to shipbuilding by the Phoenicians.

Early Israel was subject to moderately high variability both in total rainfall and in its seasonal distribution. Because of this variability, it was desirable for farmers to grow a variety of crops as insurance against the failure of some rather than to specialize in a single crop. Farmers would thus plant both barley and wheat, whose harvests were about seven weeks apart, and also grow grapes, olives, and other fruit crops which were harvested in the fall. In addition, they found it desirable to keep sheep and goats, partly as insurance and also to manure orchards and fields currently left fallow. Such a variety of products demanded attention at different times, so the farmer's labor would have been more evenly utilized throughout the year than if the whole of his effort were to be devoted to a single crop. These factors, in addition to high land transport costs and climatic similarity, tended to produce self-sufficiency in agriculture and to work against specialization and trade in farm products in ancient Israel.

Despite the production of a variety of outputs as insurance against crop failure due to weather, the variability of rainfall probably resulted in occasional losses to farmers. These losses, in turn, would have been followed by borrowing and sometimes by further losses. Some farmers probably lost their land and/or were enslaved for debts. Increasing concentration in the ownership of land and a growing population of domestic slaves might have had serious consequences for social stability. It was perhaps for this reason that institutions such as the Sabbatical Year and the Jubilee Year evolved to ameliorate the effects of losses resulting from variability of rainfall.

Two aspects of agricultural production doubtless contributed to the formation of extended family and larger social groups such as clans and of small settlements. One is the intensive effort required at certain times, especially planting and harvesting. Extended family groups would have helped supply labor beyond that of a single farmer for such periods. By staggering the planting times — and thus also the harvest times — of several farmers, each and their families could assist the others at planting and harvesting. Likewise, equipment such as plows and oxen could be more fully utilized through sharing by more than one family. Other pieces of capital equipment such as threshing floors and olive and wine presses, which no individual family would have been able to utilize fully, might have been shared by still larger groups. Thus we might expect that settlements would have developed.

Although agriculture was by far the dominant economic activity in the ancient Mediterranean, trade has probably existed almost as long. There were two major land routes in Palestine, the Way of the Sea and the King's Highway. The former ran northeastward from Egypt along the Mediterranean coast and over the Carmel ridge to Megiddo. From that point, routes went to Phoenicia, northern Syria and Damascus. The King's Highway ran northward from the Gulf of Aqaba through the hills E of the Jordan River to Rabbah and on to Damascus. Most commodities coming by sea would likely have come through the Gulf of Aqaba or through one of the Phoenician ports. Because of the high cost of transporting bulky commodities by land, one would anticipate that commodities shipped would have been relatively valuable for their weight — luxury goods, precious metals, or strategic raw materials such as tin. Our fuller knowledge of trade in NT and medieval times and the commodities noted in 1 Kgs. 10:2, 22, 25 seem to support this presumption.

There is little evidence of manufacturing beyond local handicrafts for either the OT or the NT periods. The principal evidence for the earlier of these periods is the discovery of more than 100 olive oil installations at Tel Miqne-Ekron, each of which was of relatively small scale. While olive oil was doubtless produced at many locations for local consumption, so large a number of installations suggests production at Ekron was for export, probably by water. These installations appear to have existed under the Assyrians during the 7th century but to have died out after Assyria was defeated by the Babylonians. One can only speculate as to why this may have been the case. There is no particular reason, moreover, for believing that the Ekron installations are indicative of steady and sustained industrialization and economic development during the OT period.

Like the Late Bronze Age city-states of Canaan, the economic features of governmental institutions seem to have been feudal-like or even primitive during the Iron Age. Military units appear often to have been small bands of mercenary soldiers, and these were probably supported by grants of land from the chief or king. Kings received some of their income from royal estates, and taxes were levied in kind or in the form of conscript labor. Money took the form of metals weighted to appropriate amounts instead of coins of predetermined weight and fineness.

NT Period

The Persian conquests beginning in the mid-6th century ushered in a new era of more sophisticated government that lasted well beyond the NT period. Armies were larger; e.g., Cyrus the Great's army consisted of ca. 30 thousand. They contained slingers, archers, and cavalry in addition to infantry and no longer used chariots in open country. In siege warfare blockade, siege mounds, and mines under walls were employed. The Persians and Romans established provincial governments. Taxes were received and soldiers paid in money; however, rulers continued to receive incomes from royal estates. Both the Persians and the Romans built roads, which were used for moving troops and for mail among other purposes. Perhaps the greatest difference between the OT and NT periods was the use of coinage, pieces of valuable metals of prescribed weight and fineness. Coins were first employed in Lydia ca. 600 B.C.E. and were widely used in Greek city-states from Ionia to Sicily and in Persia. While Herod the Great issued coins, the most widely used coins in NT times were the Roman silver denarius, a day's pay for a laborer or a Roman legionnaire, and the bronze sesterce, equal in value to one fourth of a denarius.

Agricultural conditions were largely the same in the NT as in the OT period. They differed largely in that there were more large land holdings or estates and hired labor was more commonly employed in agriculture. In contrast to Italy and other parts of the western Roman Empire, there was little reliance on slave labor in agriculture in Asia Minor and the Levant. Industry, too, was little different from that of OT times. Most production took the form of handicrafts for the local market. Items were produced in widely scattered locations in towns and even on the large estates. There were a few noteworthy exceptions to this pattern, however. Laodicea, Tarsus, and Alexandria, e.g., were important centers for the production of linen cloth. Production tended to be concentrated near flax-growing areas because of the weight loss inherent in the conversion of flax to linen. One of the most important examples of specialization and exchange in the Roman world was the production and export of tableware from Aretrium, modern Arezzo SE of Florence.

Like agriculture and industry, trade too was largely local during NT times. There were two interesting exceptions, however. One was waterborne commerce in agricultural commodities in the Mediterranean region. There were large-scale exports of wheat from Egypt, Sicily, and North Africa to Rome, and wheat was probably exported to some larger cities in the eastern Mediterranean. Wine was exported from Italy to Gaul in the 1st century B.C.E. and from Gaul to Italy by the late 1st century C.E. Likewise, from the late 1st century C.E. there were large-scale exports of olive oil from North Africa to Rome. In the eastern Mediterranean, Italian oil was displaced by oil from the coasts of Asia Minor and Syria.

By NT times long-distance trade in commodities of high value in relation to their weight was noteworthy. The commodities involved in this trade were principally silks, precious stones, and "spices." The last included not only seasonings such as pepper but also medicinals, dye-stuffs, and cosmetics. These commodities originated in the Far East and were exchanged especially for precious metals. They were apparently transported in stages by water to the Persian Gulf or Red Sea and by land over the famous Silk Road through central Asia. From the Persian Gulf commodities moved by land across the desert through Palmyra in Syria or Petra in what is now Jordan. Commodities also moved to the west from the southeastern Black Sea and from Alexandria, following transshipment from the Red Sea.

Bibliography. D. C. Hopkins, *The Highlands of Canaan* (Sheffield, 1985); J. D. Muhly, "How Iron Technology Changed the Ancient World — and Gave the Philistines a Military Edge," *BARev* 8/6 (1982): 40-54; R. F. Muth, "Economic Influences on Early Israel," *JSOT* 75 (1997): 77-92.

RICHARD F. MUTH

ECSTASY

A state of heightened emotion (Gk. *ékstasis,* from the verb *exístēmi,* lit., "to put out of place"). The phenomenon itself is difficult to define but is found generally throughout the whole of biblical and Greek literature (e.g., Philo *Heres* 264). The concept encompasses a variety of experiences in both the OT and NT. In Gen. 15:12 Abraham falls into a deep trance where he receives a word from the Lord. Other examples include a trance brought on by song and dance (1 Sam. 10:5, 12; 19:20; 2 Sam. 6:12-23), natural phenomena (1 Kgs. 19:11-18), and revelation of God's word (Jer. 23:9; Isa. 6; Amos 7–9).

In the NT ecstasy tends to focus more on two specific realms. The first is a state of intense astonishment or amazement to the point of being beside oneself (e.g., Mark 5:42, lit., "they were amazed with great amazement"; cf. 16:8; Luke 5:26; 24:22; Acts 3:10; 13:12). The second is a visionary state accompanied by an altered mental state. In Acts 10:10

Peter falls into a trance (cf. 11:5). Other possible occurrences of this phenomenon may be found in Jesus' temptation experience (Luke 4:1-12), the transfiguration (Mark 9:2-8), Pentecost (Acts 2), Paul's experience on the Damascus road (Acts 9, 22, 26; Gal. 1:15-16), and Paul's description of the third heaven (2 Cor. 12:1-9). VAUGHN CROWETIPTON

EDEN (Heb. *ʿēḏen*) **(PERSON)**
The son of Joah; a Gershonite Levite who ministered during the reign of King Hezekiah (2 Chr. 29:12). He may be the person mentioned at 2 Chr. 31:15 who assisted in the distribution of the freewill offering.

EDEN (Heb. *ʿēḏen;* Gk. *Edem*) **(PLACE)**
A geographic region where God planted a garden, in which the first man and woman were placed and from which they were expelled. At times the name may better connote "edenic" beauty rather than the place per se. The garden is "in" Eden only in Gen. 2:8 (with the preposition elsewhere only in Ezek. 28:13, where it is also called "the garden of God" cf. 31:9, par. "trees of Eden"). In Isa. 51:3 Eden is in parallel with "garden of Yahweh," found elsewhere only in Gen. 13:10 (where Eden is not mentioned). Eden can be equated with the garden in Ezek. 28:13; 31:9 only if its use is appositional rather than attributive.

Theories of location choose between Armenia (north) or Babylonia (south) in eastern Mesopotamia and more western regions. An important factor here is Eden as the source of four great rivers (Gen. 2:10-14). Options for the two debated "rivers" (Pishon and Gihon) have included the Indus, Ganges, canals that connect the two known rivers, lesser streams in Elam, the Nile (Blue and White), Gihon Spring in Jerusalem, and the Persian Gulf. Pivotal and persistent questions are: (1) whether to connect the etymology of Eden to a rare Akkadian (*edinu,* "plain steppe") or the closer and more common West Semitic cognate ("delight; abundance"; Ugar., Syr., and Aram. *ʿdn;* Arab. *ǵdn*), which is the traditional view (cf. LXX Gen. 2:8; 3:23-24; Isa. 51:3; Luke 23:43; 2 Cor. 12:4; Rev. 2:7); (2) whether the river of Gen. 2:10 "follows from" or "rises in" Eden, and if the four rivers are independent or interrelated; (3) whether Cush is Ethiopia or Elam (the Kassite region east of the Tigris); and (4) whether *miqqeḏem* in Gen. 2:8 means the garden was in eastern Eden, Eden was in the east, or that Eden was "of old." The Babylonian site conflicts with the eastward movement of humanity from the garden to north and south Mesopotamia in Gen. 2–11. This view also must explain how Eden as an oasis was derived from a term meaning "plain."

The significance of connecting the first couple's paradise of God's presence with the future site of the temple (cf. Gihon Spring) symbolizing God's presence and the promised Palestinian paradise (cf. Isa. 51:3; Zech. 14:8; Rev. 22:1-2) should not be missed. In ancient Near Eastern mythology a garden paradise of two rivers is where the divine council meets; and in pseudepigraphal literature Eden is associated with a "heaven" of salvation for the faithful.

In the final analysis, establishing the exact location may be impossible owing to authorial intention or to catastrophic topographical changes resulting from the Flood.

Bibliography. W. F. Albright, "The Location of the Garden of Eden," *AJSL* 39 (1922): 15-31; W. H. Gispen, "Genesis 2:10-14," in *Studia Biblica et Semitica* (Wageningen, 1966), 115-24; A. R. Millard, "The Etymology of Eden," *VT* 34 (1984): 103-6; E. A. Speiser, "The Rivers of Paradise," in *Oriental and Biblical Studies,* ed. J. J. Finkelstein and M. Greenberg (Philadelphia, 1967), 23-34; H. N. Wallace, *The Eden Narrative.* HSM 32 (Atlanta, 1985). W. CREIGHTON MARLOWE

EDER (Heb. *ʿēḏer*) **(PERSON)**

1. A postexilic Benjaminite residing at Jerusalem (1 Chr. 8:15).

2. A Levite, the second son of Mushi, and a descendant of Merari who lived during the reign of King David (1 Chr. 23:23; 24:30).

EDER (Heb. *ʿēḏer*) **(PLACE)**

1. A town in southern Judah near the border with Edom (Josh. 15:22). Identification of the site is unknown, but it has been associated with (or perhaps confused with) Arad (one LXX version of 15:22 reads Arad for Eder). However, the fact that Eder is listed together with Arad among the descendants of Judah (1 Chr. 8:15) suggests that they are separate cities.

2. Name of an ancient landmark ("tower"; Mic. 4:8, "tower of the flock") in the vicinity of Bethlehem. Jacob set up camp there soon after the death of Rachel (Gen. 35:21). Its exact location is unknown, although it has often been associated with Khirbet Siyar el-Ganam, ca. 5 km. (3 mi.) E of Bethlehem on a ridge overlooking the modern Arab village of Beit Sahur. The tower of Eder is noted as the place where the Messiah will make himself known (Tg. Ps.-J. on Gen. 35:21). WADE R. KOTTER

EDIFICATION
Literally a building or the act of building (Gk. *oikodomḗ*), especially in the Gospels (Matt. 24:1; 26:61; Mark 14:58) and Acts. Figuratively the term was used for the Church (Matt. 16:18; 1 Cor. 3:9-10), but both non-Christian and Christian writers more commonly used it to denote spiritual enrichment. Paul exhorts believers to edify each other (Rom. 14:19; 15:2; 1 Cor. 14:3; 1 Thess. 5:11) and the Church (1 Cor. 14:4-5, 12). Paul's apostolic authority is exercised for edification (2 Cor. 10:8; 13:10), and deeds are performed for edification (2 Cor. 12:19). Worship should be an edifying experience (1 Cor. 14:26). Whoever speaks in tongues edifies himself, but whoever prophesies edifies others (1 Cor. 14:4; cf. v. 17). Spiritual gifts (Eph. 4:12, 16) and all speech (v. 29) are to be used for edification (cf. 1 Cor. 8:1; 10:23). ERIC F. MASON

EDOM (Heb. *'ĕḏôm*)

The name of a nation, a geographical region, and a person in OT times. Edom is derived from a root meaning "red." The association of name with the place is usually explained by the reddish appearance of the rock and soil formations; with the person it is sometimes assumed that Edom was of ruddy complexion and, less frequently, one with red hair.

The person, Edom, is initially known as Esau, the elder of the twins born to Isaac and Rebekah; the younger was Jacob or Israel. The Gen. 25 story of Esau's birth gives two clues to his being called "Edom" or "red." Gen. 25:26 describes him as red at birth; v. 30 associates the name with the red food (pottage?) for which he traded his birthright to Jacob. He is regarded as eponymous ancestor of the Edomites.

The geographical area known as Edom is located primarily E of the Wadi Arabah, N of the Gulf of Aqabah, S of the Wadi el-Ḥesā (its boundary with Moab), and W of the Arabian Desert. There is general agreement as to the north, south, and eastern boundaries, but the western border is variously described. The biblical description of Edomite territory appears to include areas W of the Wadi Arabah. Num. 34 describes the territory of Judah as lying "against" the territory of Edom. The territory of Judah is further described in Josh. 15:1 as reaching southwest to the boundary of Edom, to the Wilderness of Zin at the farthest south. In Num. 20:16 Kadesh (probably 'Ain el-Qudeirât) is described as on the border of the king of Edom. It is important to note the existence of a major route, "the King's Highway," traversing this land. Profiting from control of travel and trade on this route must have been one of the significant economic forces at work in Edom in ancient times.

The dominant view of mid-20th-century scholarship, based primarily on Nelson Glueck's survey of the region in the 1930s and 1940s, argued that Edom lay east of the Wadi Arabah. Recent archaeological discoveries have documented a significant Edomite presence extending to the west, especially from the 7th century and later. Most likely the heartland of Edom was the area E of the Arabah, but there were from time to time Edomite presence and control to the west as well.

The early history of Edom (also called Seir) is shrouded in the uncertainties of antiquity. Early settlement dates to prehistoric times. The region was probably not known as Edom until the 13th century. The patriarchal stories, pointing to an earlier time, report that Esau/Edom along with his family settled there. These early Edomites may represent the nomadic peoples of the region mentioned in Egyptian texts (Papyrus Anastasi VI) as occasionally coming with their flocks inside the borders of Egypt.

Several references (Gen. 14:6; 36:20ff.) refer to Horites as pre-Edomite inhabitants of the land. The identity of the Horites is debated: some associate them with the Hivites, but identification with the Hurrians is more likely. Gen. 36 includes a list of kings who ruled the land of Edom before any king ruled over the Israelites. The same chapter lists wives and descendants of Esau as well as some Horite lists.

The archaeological record of Edom is based primarily on regional surface surveys with a few soundings and a small but increasing number of excavations. Survey results, but not excavated sites, indicate pre–Iron Age occupation. However, the excavated sites document the 8th-6th centuries as the time of significant occupation with fortified cities, with significantly more evidence from the 7th century. Later occupation does appear at some sites, especially for the Hellenistic period. The picture presented is only tentative, subject to continuing revision as more evidence becomes available.

The pattern of occupation seems to be one of fluctuation, likely related to climatic and ecological forces. It appears that there was considerable occupation in the latter phases of the Early Bronze Age — especially EB III and IV (mid- to late 3rd millennium) — diminishing until almost the beginning of the Iron Age. Nevertheless, there was continuing occupation in the land on through the MB and LB periods.

According to Num. 20:14-21 during the wilderness wanderings the "king of Edom" refused to permit the Israelites safe passage through his land, forcing them to circumvent Edom. No archaeological evidence of a fortified and organized settlement in this time has yet been found.

The Edomites are not mentioned as a factor at the time of the Hebrews' settlement in Canaan. Saul was the first to fight them (1 Sam. 14:47). David carried out a major campaign in Edom (2 Sam. 8:13-14), gaining and retaining control of this territory. An uprising led by Hadad, an Edomite of royal blood, forced Solomon to fight the Edomites again and again. Solomon utilized Ezion-geber in Edomite territory as a functioning port.

After Solomon's death Edom remained under the control of Judah, though unattested in the biblical narrative until the time of Jehoshaphat. According to a royal inscription in the Karnak temple, Edom was one of the territories overrun by the Egyptian Shishak on the same excursion that took him to Jerusalem in Rehoboam's time. Jehoshaphat (873-849) sought to reactivate maritime trade by way of the Red Sea, but his fleet was wrecked on rocks near Elath (1 Kgs. 22:47-50). Near the end of Jehoshaphat's reign, Edomites joined with other enemies of Judah for a raid on En-gedi (2 Chr. 20). Edom successfully revolted against Jehoram (849-842), gaining freedom from Judah (2 Kgs. 8:20-22).

There followed a time of Assyrian power and Edomite and Judean weakness. Adad-nirari III of Assyria (810-783) claims to have made expeditions to the west in 806, 805, and 797, in which tribute was received from Edom, among other places. Edom is named by this monarch as a new conquest for Assyria. But Assyria became weak for a brief period in the early 8th century, and Judah expanded her territory to include Edom once more.

Edom was subdued partially by Amaziah of Judah, who captured Sela and changed its name to Joktheel. Amaziah's son Uzziah pursued to a successful conclusion the attack upon Edom, even capturing Elath. It was in the time of Ahaz that Judah's control of Edom was permanently broken. Edom was never again to regain her former splendor but did retain some measure of independence. While Ahaz was king the Edomites were making raids on Judah to acquire slaves, prompting Ahaz to appeal to Assyria (2 Chr. 28:16-17). The Assyrian king Tiglath-pileser III (744-727) claims, in a building inscription, that he received tribute from Kaushmalaku (Qaushmalaku) of Edom. Payment of tribute to Assyria was burdensome and Edom, among other states (but not Judah), was encouraged to revolt by Egypt. Sargon II (721-705) records on his "Broken Prism" this attempted revolt which he subdued. The revolt was against paying tribute, indicating that the revolting nations, including Edom, had not been conquered as had Israel. Sennacherib claims to have received tribute from the Edomite king Aiarammu in 701, as did Esarhaddon and Assurbanipal from Qaushgabri.

The biblical accounts, as well as secular records, maintain almost complete silence concerning the role of Edom following the decline of the Assyrian Empire. Edom along with Ammon, Moab, Tyre, Sidon, and Judah plotted a revolt against Babylon ca. 592, but the revolt failed to materialize.

As to the part played by Edom and the effect of the circumstances in Palestine on Edom in the 587 destruction of Jerusalem, the historical records — biblical and nonbiblical — are silent. The only information, which is debated, is the reference in 1 Esdr. 4:45: "You also vowed to build the temple, which the Edomites burned when Judea was laid waste by the Chaldeans." This affirms Edomite support of and participation in the destruction of Jerusalem and its temple by the Babylonians.

That Edomites moved into the Negeb of Judah in the late 7th century is quite clear. Edomite ceramic remains have been found at many sites. An Edomite ostracon, which includes a reference to their chief god Qos was found at Ḥorvat ʿUza, near Arad. Edomite shrines have been found in the Arabah at ʿEn Haṣeva and at Ḥorvat Qitmit near Arad. Significant Edomite materials also have been found at Malḥata.

The Edomites are frequently mentioned in prophetic writings — almost always in words of condemnation (e.g., Obadiah, Jer. 49). The unparalleled hatred for the Edomites in the OT is usually related to either or both the Edomite encroachment into Hebrew territory and the support and/or assistance they rendered the Babylonians when Jerusalem and the temple were destroyed in 587.

The Edomites in the southern part of Cisjordanian Palestine were known as Idumaeans during the Hellenistic/Roman periods. The family of Antipater and Herod the Great were of Edomite descent. It is impossible to trace Edomites or their descendants beyond the time of the Roman campaign which resulted in the destruction of the Jerusalem temple in 70 C.E.

So thoroughgoing was the hatred of the Edomites that Edom/Edomite became a term for "the enemy," particularly applied to Rome during their oppressive actions against both Jews and Christians in the early centuries C.E.

Bibliography. Y. Aharoni, *The Land of the Bible,* 2nd ed. (Philadelphia, 1979); J. R. Bartlett, *Edom and the Edomites.* JSOTSup 77 (Sheffield, 1989); I. Beit-Arieh, "New Light on the Edomites," *BARev* 14/2 (1988): 28-41; R. Cohen and Y. Yisrael, *On the Road to Edom: Discoveries from ʾEn Hazeva* (Jerusalem, 1995); B. C. Cresson, "The Condemnation of Edom in Postexilic Judaism," in *The Use of the Old Testament in the New,* ed. J. M. Efird (Durham, 1972), 125-48; B. MacDonald, *Ammon, Moab, and Edom* (Amman, 1994). BRUCE C. CRESSON

EDREI (Heb. *ʾeḏreʿî*)

1. A major Transjordanian city and one of the residences of the Amorite king Og of Bashan. After defeating King Sihon of Heshbon, the Israelites marched north and met the army of Og just S of Edrei (Num. 21:33-35; cf. Deut. 1:4; Josh. 12:4; 13:12, 31). Together with Salecah, Edrei was a border city from where the king's army watched for an attack either from the south or the east. After the victory, Edrei was assigned to the Machirites, a clan of the tribe of Manasseh (Josh. 13:31). Edrei may be located at Derʿā, ca. 97 km. (60 mi.) S of Damascus.

2. An unidentified city in Naphtali located somewhere in upper Galilee (Josh. 19:37), probably named in the itinerary list of Thutmose III (*ANET,* 242). ZELJKO GREGOR

EDUCATION

Throughout the Bible the language of education (learning, teaching, studying), its effects (writing, knowledge, appropriate behavior), and the desire for education are very much evident. Moreover, we know the general settings where education occurred (court, cult, family, schools) and approximately what the content of much of the teaching would have been. Nevertheless, to speak of education in the Bible is to enter an area with much uncertainty precisely because of what we do not know. Who were the teachers of ancient Israel? Where, specifically, did they teach? And how did they teach? What were their methods, their pedagogy? Despite much good scholarship and study, the identity and function of the sages and teachers, their methods and particular settings in the Bible remain veiled and subject to much debate.

Development and History

Education in biblical times is best understood by looking at many interlocking and overlapping institutions and their respective traditions (e.g., cult, family, court, schools). These institutions of education were located inside and outside ancient Israel in a wide variety of settings. From the earliest times it is clear that the family was the central institution in which learning occurred and continued to be so throughout the biblical period. The "content" of family education varied widely. We assume children were taught not only the skills and way of life of their parents, but also some of the basic values of the society and an orientation to the identity of ancient Israel (who we are, where we are, how we relate to the world around us, and why). The setting presumed for this all-important education is the home.

With the advent of the monarchy (ca. 1000-587 B.C.E.) in Israel and Judah a growing need for literacy is clearly seen. Treaties, the ability to produce lists for purchases and other record-keeping activities, the need to write the histories and stories of the state — all created a special concern for an educated and literate group around the king and the court. Many of the aphorisms in the book of Proverbs can be traced to this setting. The influence of both Egyptian and Babylonian culture was seen to be important in monarchical times as the early Israelites struggled with different models of kingship and the educational needs stemming from them. In both of these cultures there were royal schools where middle-level bureaucrats were trained. While we have no direct evidence of such schools in Israel, special training was clearly necessary for some of the royal officials. The palace and its immediate environs were the probable setting for this education.

At almost all times in Israel's history the cult was an important center for education. The legal materials and the psalms offer much evidence of catechetical activity for those new to the stories and the faith of the people (cf. Deut. 6:20-25; Pss. 15, 24). Moreover, the cult is assumed to be a central place for speaking of and teaching the moral values of the society (e.g., the Decalogue, Exod. 20:1-17) and the expectations for behavior in all parts of the culture. In Judah the temple was a primary setting for both determining what needed to be taught and the actual proclamation and teaching itself.

Although many scholars believe schools must have existed in the monarchical period, the first clear references to them do not occur until postexilic times in Israel. Rabbinic Judaism, Hellenistic and then Roman culture, and the educational institutions associated with them colored and shaped what education was in Israel in the late postexilic and NT periods. Though Ben Sira and later Jewish texts refer to schools, we know very little about either the content of the curriculum or the goals of these institutions. We assume the study of Torah to be a very important part of the curriculum, but more than this is unclear. How accessible education was for all members of society at this time is subject to much debate. Surely synagogues were another place where education occurred, as witnessed to in the NT and early rabbinic materials (Luke 4:16-30).

In addition to the institutional loci of education associated with particular groups within the mainstream of society, three other sources of education deserve mention. First, the schools and other educational phenomena associated with cultures outside Israel (e.g., Babylon, Egypt, Greece, Rome) clearly influenced both the shape and the content of the education in ancient Israel. Second, a number of sectarian communities had special educational agendas (e.g., Qumran, the Essenes). Finally, there were always special people recognized for their acumen and the value of their teaching. Sometimes these people were itinerant (e.g., Jesus), sometimes not (e.g., the medium of Endor, 1 Sam. 28:7-25).

Teachers and Sages

Without explicit references to "schools" in the OT it is difficult to determine who were the teachers of ancient Israel. Though the Wisdom Literature (Job, Proverbs, Ecclesiastes) of the OT is often perceived to have been used for pedagogical purposes and authored by sages, it is still difficult to describe what a teacher might have looked like. The nature of the Wisdom Literature and the primary vocabulary used to describe learning and teaching in the Bible does not help clarify who these authors were or even in which of the settings above they were found. By the time of Ben Sira, however, the figure of the sage is associated with both teaching in schools and with special expertise in biblical interpretation. Eventually that figure would develop into the rabbi and the "sage," those whose interpretation of Torah becomes normative for the community. This development in Judaism begins in the biblical period but is completed much later.

Two interesting examples of "teachers" are the prophet Amos and Jesus. Both were itinerant. Both used forms of wisdom literature and rhetoric to express their message to the people (parables, rhetorical questions). While neither is usually seen primarily as a sage, both are given authority because of their teaching and its power. At the very least Amos and Jesus reflect the existence of wisdom teaching and its influence. Both were educated and educators.

Content and Method

Early texts from Ugarit and other Canaanite cultures (cf. e.g., the Gezer Calendar) suggest that learning was often a matter of memorization (e.g., the seasons of the year), with or without the use of writing. The cultic directives to keep the commandments in some visible place on the body or in the home reflect another attempt at learning by repetition and reminder (Deut. 6:6-9). The teaching represented in the book of Proverbs relies upon careful observation and analysis of experience, drawing some logical and theological conclusions. How such a process was "taught" to students is not known, but biblical literature contains much of this type of teaching and observation. Perhaps the most important content of biblical education and teaching, however, was not a particular skill at observation and writing, not the content of a special law code, but rather an understanding and grounding in the values upon which law, proverbs, prophetic teaching, parables, and all the rest stood. All of this was embodied in very specific oral and literary traditions witnessed to by the biblical text, with settings associated with cult and court and palace. It was probably the family above all else where the locus for passing on these values resided.

Education in ancient Israel is shrouded in mystery while at the same time the Bible reflects a significant amount of it! Education in ancient Israel was not just a copy of Babylon, Egypt, or Canaan, though we know it was influenced by their educational traditions. Education in the Bible was in transition from a family-based phenomenon to something the society saw as its primary responsibility. It was a peculiar mix of institution and individual, sage and prophet, law and aphorism, all grounded in values which could and were given humanistic rationales and, finally, attributed to God the teacher.

Bibliography. J. L. Crenshaw, "Education in Ancient Israel," *JBL* 104 (1985): 601-15; M. V. Fox, "The Pedagogy of Proverbs 2," *JBL* 113 (1994): 233-43; J. G. Gammie and L. G. Perdue, eds., *The Sage in Israel and the Ancient Near East* (Winona Lake, 1990); H. I. Marrou, *A History of Education in Antiquity* (1956, repr. Madison, 1982); R. N. Whybray, *The Intellectual Tradition in the Old Testament.* BZAW 135 (Berlin, 1974); B. Witherington, *Jesus the Sage* (Minneapolis, 1994). DONN F. MORGAN

EGLAH (Heb. *ʿeglâ*)
One of David's wives and the mother of Ithream (2 Sam. 3:5 = 1 Chr. 3:3).

EGLAIM (Heb. *ʾeglayim*)
A site mentioned in the prophecy against Moab in Isa. 15:8. Its identification is uncertain. Because of the parallelism to "border of Moab" one must look towards the periphery of the Moabite region. Together with Beer-elim (similar to Dan and Beersheba in regard to Israel) it forms a territory-defining expression. Eusebius identified a certain Agallim, 8 Roman mi. S of Areopolis (modern Rabbah). The best candidate is Rujm el-Jilîmeh (217064), SE of Kerak.

Bibliography. J. Simons, *The Geographical and Topographical Texts of the Old Testament* (Leiden, 1959), §1259; A. H. Van Zyl, *The Moabites.* Pretoria Oriental Series 3 (Leiden, 1960).

FRIEDBERT NINOW

EGLATH-SHELISHIYAH (Heb. *ʿeglaṯ šĕlišîyâ*)
A difficult term in the oracles against Moab in Isa. 15:5; Jer. 48:34, possibly an appellative or figurative expression describing some aspect of Moab and her cities ("a three-year-old heifer") or a place name ("the third Eglath"). Most modern translations follow the LXX in reading a place name, an interpretation favored by the immediate context and the differentiation of other sites of the same name by a numeral. The location of the site is unknown.

ROBERT DELSNYDER

EGLON (Heb. *ʿeglôn*) **(PERSON)**
King of Moab whom Ehud assassinated to liberate Israel from Moabite rule (Judg. 3:12-30). "Eglon" appears to be a play on words for "fat" and "calf" and may have been chosen to fit with the puns which characterize the narrative. The ease with which Moabites in general might be tricked is a continuing motif in the OT, and this king embodies that trait fully, as well as being fat.

Eglon had conquered Israel with the aid of Ammonites and Amalekites as well as the empowerment of God (Judg. 3:12-13); he is the only ruler in the book of Judges to need such help. He ruled over the Israelites for 18 years before Ehud tricked him into allowing a private conference. The story suggests that Eglon was pious enough to wish the confidential word of the gods which he understands Ehud is coming to deliver. By deceit and clever punning, the Benjaminite manipulates Eglon into a situation where he may be murdered without recourse to his guards. The Moabites in the story are all deadly dense, heightening the stupidity of their leader.

If the biblical chronology could be adapted to historical events, this king would have ruled sometime in the 12th century B.C.E. However, an expanding Moabite nation and the possibility that the story reflects local conflicts between the tribe of Benjamin and the town Eglon (Josh. 12:12; 15:39) suggest a tale no earlier than the 9th century.

Bibliography. L. K. Handy, "Uneasy Laughter: Ehud and Eglon as Ethnic Humor." *SJOT* 6 (1992): 233-246; E. A. Knauf, "Eglon and Orpah," *JSOT* 51 (1991): 25-44. LOWELL K. HANDY

EGLON (Heb. *ʿeglôn*) **(PLACE)**
A city of the Judean Shephelah or the adjacent coastal plain. Eglon's Canaanite king was part of the coalition defeated by Joshua in the Gibeon affair (Josh. 10:3, 5, 23; 12:12) and the city itself was taken on the same campaign (10:34-35). The name of the Canaanite king, Debir (Josh. 10:3), may represent a textual confusion, as everywhere else in the OT Debir refers to another city of the Shephelah region destroyed in the same campaign (Josh. 10:36-39). Eglon is listed as one of the cities in the Shephelah region of the tribe of Judah (Josh. 15:39).

The location of Eglon is disputed. Early identifications included the Philistine Plain sites of Tel Nagila/Tell Nejîleh (127101) and Khirbet ʿAjlân/Ḥorvat Egla, the latter possibly preserving an arabized form of the name Eglon. The advent of modern archaeological work placed the focus on Tell el-Ḥesī (124106), near Khirbet ʿAjlan and formerly identified with Lachish. Tell el-Ḥesī, noteworthy as the first systematic excavation in Palestine, conducted in 1890 by Flinders Petrie, has yielded finds from the Bronze and Iron Ages. It is somewhat unlikely, however, that Tell el-Ḥesī represents Eglon, as the biblical accounts seem to place the latter in the Shephelah. A more recent suggestion places Eglon at Tell ʿAitun (143099) in the Shephelah, an identification gaining more recognition due to the correspondence of the archaeological remains and topography.

Bibliography. A. F. Rainey, "The Biblical Shephelah of Judah," *BASOR* 251 (1983): 1-22.

DANIEL C. BROWNING, JR.

EGNATIAN WAY
A road that connected Macedonia's east and west coasts (Lat. *Via Egnatia*), built after Macedonia became a Roman province in 146 B.C.E. Troops and

merchants traveling from Rome would reach the eastern point of the Appian Way at Brundisium, cross the Adriatic Sea, land at Apollonia or Dyrrhachium on the west coast of Macedonia, proceed by land along the Egnatian Way as far as Neapolis (the port ca. 14 km. [9 mi.] E of Philippi), and then sail further east across the Aegean Sea.

The Apostle Paul sailed from Troas to Neapolis and then traveled to Philippi, where Lydia and her household were converted (Acts 16:11-15). He next preached in Thessalonica (Acts 17:1-9), thus traveling westward from Neapolis along the Egnatian Way (cf. 20:1-6), before going south to Beroea (17:10-14) and Athens (v. 15).

James A. Kelhoffer

EGYPT

One of the earliest and greatest civilizations of the ancient world, situated along the Nile River.

Naqada I-II

The Nile Valley has many traces of Paleolithic to Mesolithic peoples, but the earliest precursors of pharaonic culture arose from a movement of Neolithic peoples from the Sahara regions into the Nile Valley where they blended with indigenous hunter-gatherers and developed the earliest settlements. The Saharans had domesticated cattle and had acquired sheep and goats, as well as emmer wheat and barley cultivation, these probably coming from the Levant initially. In Egypt, these peoples developed two distinct cultures, the Upper Egyptian valley cultures, of which the earliest was Badarian, and in the Delta, another series of cultures, distinct from the valley.

From the Badarian later evolved the Naqada I-II cultures. Naqada I developed larger villages, and began to quarry flint from the Nile limestone cliffs. The people lived in circular houses, and formed the earliest known religious cults. They developed several types of fine pottery, including one style of decorated ware which depicts Nile-type fauna and flora and sometimes shows hunting. This culture also spread farther up and down the Nile Valley.

Naqada II (ca. 3600-3300 B.C.), which evolved directly out of Naqada I, marks the burgeoning of the valley culture and its gradually growing prosperity. The first power centers emerged in this era in areas in which the Nile Valley gave access to routes into the eastern desert, where the Naqadans found good quality stone and, more importantly, deposits of gold and copper. Two major centers developed, Nubt ("The Golden"), also called Naqada, in Middle Egypt near the Wadi Ḥammâmât, and Nekhen, farther south near the Wadi Mia. Both these centers planted cities on the eastern bank, near the wadi entrances, Koptos for Nubt and Elkab for Nekhen. Access to the desert resources greatly enriched both towns and led to the rise of an elite class. These communities also started long-distance trade, which led to the rise of other centers, Buto and Maʿadi in the north and Ta-seti and Qustul in the south. These new centers gained prosperity by controlling the long-distance trade the Naqadans desired: cedar timber and oil from Lebanon, lapis lazuli from farther afield, and in the south, ivory, ebony, panther skins, baboons, and other products. The centers involved in the trade also prospered. Maʿadi conducted the overland trade, including copper from Sinai and Canaan, while Buto maintained the sea trade with Lebanon and the ʿAmuq Valley. From the ʿAmuq region, the Egyptians came into contact with Mesopotamians via the Buto settlement.

Proto-dynastic

The Naqada II period evolved into Naqada III, or the Proto-dynastic era. In this period the elites developed into paramount chiefs. These leaders were also responsible for the beginnings of Egyptian hieroglyphic writing, which originated in the decorated buff ware of the Naqada II period. That ware frequently represented ships, reflecting an already lively Nile Valley trade. Many of the ships showed standards behind their cabins topped with signs that can be read as nome names or divine names; much of the ware was produced in the area between Abydos and Luxor, and signs linked with the nomes of this area are common on the standards. The emergent elites of Naqada III came into conflict with their neighbors, and the chiefs commemorated their victories with signs derived from the decorated ware. This gave rise to a pattern known as the pharaonic cycle, depicting a boat procession towards a palace complex. Such scenes were carved on enlarged graywacke palettes or maceheads, rock wall faces, decorated flint knife handles, or even painted on linen. As the Naqada III period progressed, such scenes proliferated and are known from Nubt, Nekhen, and Qustul in Lower Nubia. Another development during this period was the *serekh*, a decorated palace entrance such as that excavated at Nekhen. Houses since the Naqada II period were rectangular and built of mudbrick; some wattle and daub construction continued, but mainly in temporary field shelters. A type of reed fenced structure known as *zeriba* was further developed. Religious shrines became more prominent, now marked front and back with flags on poles. Some shrines boasted colossal images of the deity, such as Koptos or Min. Other shrines remained preformal, and might be a grove of trees or a niche between two boulders, as at Elephantine. Decorated palettes and maces also depict shrines, with a defined structure: a court, with standard topped by the divine emblem, then a shrine building, sometimes with a colossal depiction of the deity.

Toward the end of the Naqada III period, the power centers engaged in a series of conflicts. Nekhen apparently emerged triumphant in a conflict with Ta-seti. Its ruler, known as Scorpion, then conquered Nubt. In triumph he assumed Nubt's Red Crown. (The crown of Nekhen and Qustul was the White Crown.) Abydos, a new royal cemetery in the Nubt nome, now became the burial place of the victorious Nekhen rulers. Scorpion's successors campaigned northward and by Nar-mer's time took control of the Delta. Buto was transformed into a national shrine of Lower Egypt, as the Delta came to be known. Nekhen in Upper Egypt became a national shrine, while Elkab became Upper Egypt's tutelary center. The two deities of Buto and Elkab, a cobra and a vulture, respectively, now became national deities. On one decorated macehead, Nar-mer is depicted enthroned as king of Lower Egypt. This macehead evidently contains an enumeration of the Delta's resources, cattle, small livestock, and men (120 thousand). Extrapolating from this by adding females and children, ca. 500 to 600 thousand persons can be estimated for the Delta, and most scholars postulate a slightly larger populace for the dominant Valley culture (700 thousand). This would set the population of all Egypt at ca. 1.4 to 1.6 million around the date of the Unification (ca. 3100).

Whether Nar-mer is the real unifier, or his son and successor Aḥa, who founded the city of Memphis (then known as "White Walls"), is debated. Aḥa also created the Royal Annals, a year by year record of the deeds of the pharaohs, by stringing together the events formerly conveyed by decorated macehead or palette into a continuous sequence, linked by regularly recurring events such as the biennial cattle census. Later in the 1st Dynasty, a small box at the bottom of each year entry would record the annual height of the Nile flood. The now fragmentary list known as the Palermo Stone, which represented the annals of the Old Kingdom, preserves Aḥa's last two regnal years. The royal titulary also began to evolve. Already Nar-mer had a "Two Ladies" name. The names used for these early kings are Horus names, conveyed by the royal name atop the *serekh* topped by the falcon deity Horus of Nekhen. All the crafts developed in Naqada II-III proliferated, especially stone vases, but the early pharaohs destroyed the trade centers, Maʿadi and Qustul, as they sought to monopolize foreign trade. Metal working became better established, the pottery wheel was introduced, and woodworking flourished, with the best work done for the elites. The pharaohs also established the first bureaucracy to administer their realm. The pattern of estimating the height of the Nile flood, realigning boundary markers of fields, assessing taxes, and conducting the cattle census and taxation all developed in this era. A high official, the vizier, was appointed to administer these programs. The kings, and evidently one regnant queen, Meryt-neith, were buried in the royal ground of Abydos, complete with funerary temples of niched mudbrick and burials of hundreds of court retainers. Thus arose the pharaonic state of ancient Egypt, with a king acknowledged as a deity.

The 2nd Dynasty arose ca. 2850, and its rulers switched their burial ground to Saqqâra. Their royal names bear hints of two powers, the deities Horus of Nekhen and Seth of Nubt. Surviving records hint at troubles in the form of rebellions. Then at mid-dynasty, a major conflict burst forth. One pharaoh abandoned Horus, and instead placed Seth atop his *serekh.* This may be the rebellion of the Naqada people who had progressively lost status in the unification process. Another Horus king, Khasekhem, arose in Nekhen and progressively defeated the rebels and reunified Egypt. He now proclaimed himself pharaoh, with Horus and Seth atop his *serekh,* his Two Ladies name reading "the two powers are content in him." The rebellion was ended. The royal tomb returned to Abydos, and the later King Khasekhemwy's queen became the mother of the first two pharaohs of the 3rd Dynasty. A new royal title developed, Horus atop the gold glyph, or Horus over Nubt.

Old Kingdom

The new pharaoh Sanakht may be an enigma, but his brother Djoser shines forever as the founder of the Old Kingdom. Djoser found a master architect, Imhotep, who built for him the first complete stone structure known, the grand Step Pyramid of Saqqâra. It was surrounded by a complex enclosed in a rendition of the "White Walls" in limestone blocks the size of mudbricks, marking the evolution of Egyptian architecture from wood, reed, and mudbrick into stone. The buildings simulated a Ḥeb-sed jubilee court, and all the original detail was faithfully copied in stone. The next king, Sekhemkhet, built his complex behind Djoser's, but already the enclosure wall stones were larger blocks. The following kings were shorter lived and built unfinished step pyramids, but each complex shows a greater mastery of stone masonry. The last king, Ḥuni, built a complete step pyramid at Meidum. For the first time, the funerary temple was shifted around to the east of the pyramid and linked by a long causeway to a valley temple. (Previously, funerary temples were on the northern side of the tomb, evidently linked to a belief that the dead was resurrected to join the circumpolar stars.) Now, the dead was to join the rising sun, a powerful resurrection symbol. Also marking this transition to the solar cult, the step pyramid was altered into a true pyramid.

The true pyramid had its basis in the *benben* stone top of the sacred stone of Heliopolis, center of the solar cult. The *benben* was a short, squat obelisk, its top forming a pyramid. Sneferu, Huni's son, and founder of the 4th Dynasty, built the first true pyramids at Dahshur. He also tried transforming his father's pyramid into a true pyramid, but the monument met with disaster, collapsing at some state of its history. Now only the core of the Step Pyramid stands, with the added masonry visible at the base. Khufu (Cheops), Sneferu's son, moved his pyramid complex to Giza, perhaps viewing it as a western *benben,* where the sun set as viewed from Heliopolis. In three changes of plan, Khufu shifted his burial chamber up in the pyramid's masonry. With Sneferu and Khufu, the final two titles of the king evolved, the praenomen and nomen both in cartouches, joined by the title "son of Re," stressing the solar cult. The final solar emblem was the Great Sphinx. Known later as Hor-em-akhet, "Horus on the Horizon," it may be viewed as the deity manifest between Khufu and Khafre's (Chephren) pyramids.

Step pyramid of Djoser at Saqqâra (Third Dynasty, ca. 2700 B.C.E.). The surrounding courts and chapels featured limestone columns and carved walls and ceilings (F. J. Yurco)

The 5th Dynasty marked the triumph of the solar cult. The royal pyramid now was smaller and not as well built, but the pyramid temples grew to be exquisite. Grander still were the solar temples the kings built at Abusir in the western desert. Open to the sky, they were decorated with reliefs that celebrated the seasons and the creativity of Re in nature. The final kings of the 5th Dynasty were buried farther south at Saqqâra and built no solar temples, but the last king, Unas, was the first whose pyramid interior was carved with what became known as the Pyramid Texts. An eclectic grouping of spells, these texts include much older material with allusions to burials in the ground, in brick mastabas, and finally in stone pyramids. In one long spell the king, resurrected through Re, becomes master of heaven. Texts from later pyramids show a change. Now, the king seeks resurrection through Osiris. Yet another grand transformation of the religion had occurred. According to the Great Myth of Creation, Osiris had been ruler, but Seth was jealous of him and had him murdered. Isis, wife to Osiris, raised Osiris from death, creating the first mummy. Eventually Osiris became lord of the afterlife and the kings became Osiris, while their successor became Horus, son of Isis and Osiris. The kings of the 6th Dynasty revived the southern foreign trade, and started massive importation of Nubian archers into Egypt as mercenaries. These helped them fight foreign wars, according to several autobiographies. Pepy II of the 6th Dynasty went on to reign over 90 years, but with him the Old Kingdom tottered, only to fall in the 8th Dynasty as the Nile failed to flood in a major climate crisis. The Egyptians marked the end of the Old Kingdom as the end of an era, noting that 930 years had elapsed since the Unification in the 1st Dynasty.

Middle Kingdom

In the next hundred years, two competing dynasties arose, the 9th and 10th Dynasties at Heracleopolis and the 11th Dynasty at Thebes in the south. During this First Intermediate Period, the provincial governors aligned with one or the other, Middle Egypt with the 9th and 10th Dynasties, the south with the 11th Dynasty. By 2060 a powerful Theban king, Montuhotep II, arose, defeating the Heracleopolitans in a series of battles and emerging as the reunifier of Egypt ca. 2020. His successors tried ruling Egypt from Thebes, but it proved impractical, and the 12th Dynasty's Amenemhet I, who displaced them and initiated the Middle Kingdom period, moved the residence to Itjtawy, S of Memphis, which remained the capital into the 13th Dynasty. The 12th Dynasty also came into contact with Kish, another Nilotic powerful state that arose at Kerma near the Third Cataract of the Nile. They built powerful fortresses to hold Kush at bay, but also to help exploit the resources of Nubia, where the 12th Dynasty kings had found rich gold deposits. Senwosret III, who pushed farthest south, also developed a rich trade with Kish, funnelled through the Iken-mirgissa fortress. The Story of Sinuhe, written early in the 12th Dynasty, describes an Egyptian in self-exile in Canaan and southern Syria who took residence with a migratory chieftain (called Heka-khaswet) with a lifestyle not unlike that of Abraham and Jacob. Later in the dynasty, a governor at Beni Hasan in Middle Egypt depicted a Canaanite delegation that came to his local court to trade. The women were clad in many-colored coats, recalling the coat of Joseph.

Hyksos

In 1786, ca. 100 years after the 12th Dynasty ended, a group of foreigners with horse-drawn chariots, a new compound bow, and an improved battle-axe

Terraced mortuary temple of Hatshepsut at Deir el-Bahri, West Thebes. Nearly 200 statues and reliefs glorified her divine birth and royal exploits (F. J. Yurco)

invaded the Delta and set themselves up in a city called Avaris (Hwt-waret). These were the Hyksos, a term derived from Heka-khaswet, "rulers of foreign lands." For 108 years these people dominated Egypt. They seized Memphis and terminated the 13th Dynasty, while the 17th Dynasty barely survived in Thebes as vassals. The 14th Dynasty was a dissident group in the western Delta; the 15th Dynasty comprised the six great Hyksos kings, and the 16th Dynasty was their myriad of vassals, some Hyksos, some Egyptians. Through the oasis route the Hyksos contacted Kush and allied themselves with it. Then in 1628 a volcano erupted cataclysmically, throwing out great quantities of ash and creating tsunami, which devastated the Delta, striking the Hyksos a grave blow. This disaster evidently encouraged the Thebans to revolt under Seqenenre Ta'aa II. He died in battle, but his son Kamose continued the struggle, along with his mother, the king's widow. Finally Ahmose I, Kamose's younger brother, was able to evict the Hyksos from Egypt, pursuing them to Sharuhen in Canaan. Then the kings of the 18th Dynasty attacked Kush and destroyed its power. An officer, known as viceroy of Kush, became its ruler. However, not until Queen Hatshepsut crushed them in three campaigns were the Kushites quelled.

New Kingdom

Thutmose III in a series of 17 campaigns reduced Canaan and Syria to Egyptian hegemony and created a navy on the Mediterranean to help control it and to carry the fight to the Mitanni kingdom in northern Syria. This held until Akhenaten's time, when the Hittites destroyed Mitanni, only to have Assyria reappear as a great power. Under Amenhotep III Egypt also contacted Mycenae. Now the Mycenaeans began to trade extensively with the Levant, but some of the Anatolian and Mycenaean people also started piratical raids. Under the Ramesside dynasties Egypt first fought the Hittites for superiority over Kadesh and Amurru in Syria. The Sea Peoples raiders, however, became a greater threat, and Rameses II built a series of fortresses west of the Delta to forestall their raids. Nonetheless, they made a landing in Cyrenaica, and with the Libyans, whom they armed, attacked Egypt under Merenptah. The Hittites and Egypt earlier had signed a peace treaty, which helped Egypt now survive. Merenptah also aided the Hittites with grain and arms. However, Egypt could not resist the third onslaught of Sea Peoples that struck in Rameses III's 8th regnal year. These Sea Peoples also attacked Egypt by sea and land through Canaan. The sea raiders were annihilated, but Rameses III had to allow the land contingent to settle in coastal Canaan, where they became the Philistines and their allies, known from the Bible. Shortly thereafter, Egypt lost all her levantine empire, and at the middle of the 20th Dynasty the eruption of the volcano Hekla III in Iceland produced economic crisis in Egypt and the eastern Mediterranean. Many societies collapsed, but others like the Libyans, Arameans, and Sea Peoples set to wandering. Only Assyria and Egypt emerged intact from this disaster. The high priest of Amon, under Herihor, ended the 20th Dynasty and set up a theocratic dual state in Egypt, with kings reigning from Tanis in the eastern Delta and high priests in Thebes in Upper Egypt. Large numbers of Libyans, including Herihor's family, had settled in Egypt and came to power when Sheshonq I founded the 22nd Dynasty.

Third Intermediate Period

During the Third Intermediate period (1070-712) the high priests fought the last viceroy of Kush, and so lost Kush for Egypt. This led to a serious impoverishment, as Kush's gold mines had helped fuel the New Kingdom's expansion and its soldiers manned the Egyptian army. Now the northern realm became wealthier. Shoshenq I (biblical Shishak) also fought with Rehoboam, king of Judah, and triumphed. Later the Egyptians allied with the levantine states, as Assyria loomed as a greater threat. The 22nd Dynasty fragmented after 805 as a rival dynasty, the 23rd, arose in Leontopolis, and a little later another rival dynasty emerged in Sais in the western Delta. In Kush an indigenous dynasty had arisen, and it now intervened in Egypt. Piye campaigned against the Libyan dynasties, and Shabaka eliminated them in 712, choosing to rule Egypt from Memphis. Egyptianized, the Kushites worshipped Amon-Re, and so the Egyptians accepted them. However, in 701 they aided Hezekiah against the Assyrian king Sennacherib, and so became entangled with the Assyrians. Esarhaddon invaded Egypt in 671, and Taharqa retreated south. Taharqa, however, soon counterattacked, expelling the Assyrians. Assurbanipal, the next Assyrian king, attacked in 667, and Taharqa again retired south. When Taharqa again counterattacked, Assurbanipal retaliated once more, and made Psamtik of Sais his chief vassal. Anlamani, Taharqa's successor, attacked the Assyrians in 664, slaying Psamtik's father Necho I. This time Assurbanipal decided to attack Thebes, which had loyally supported the Kushites. In 663 he sacked Thebes, forcing the Kushites out of Egypt. Psamtik was able to make himself king, also separating from Assyria and allying with Lydia. By 656 he controlled all of Egypt and founded the 26th Saite Dynasty. He heavily fortified the eastern Delta, but his successor Necho II (biblical Neco) went to assist Assyria against the Medes and Neo-Babylonians. At Carchemish, he fought a bitter engagement, but lost and retired to Egypt. Earlier, he had killed Josiah of Judea, who had tried to block his route of advance.

Saite-Persian Period

In 601 and again in 568 the Saites defeated two Neo-Babylonian attempts to invade Egypt. The Saites built a Mediterranean navy and sought alliances with Greek states. After the fall of Jerusalem in 586, Egypt accepted some Jewish refugees and posted them to guard Aswan against the Kushites. In 539, however, the Persians and Medes defeated the Neo-Babylonians, and after Amasis died in 525, the Persian ruler Cambyses attacked and invaded Egypt, ending Saite rule. Made into a satrapy, Egypt was again a province. In 405 Egypt revolted successfully, and the 28th-29th and 30th Dynasties sought alliances with Greece in efforts to resist a Persian counterattack. In 343, however, Darius II Ochus attacked and broke into Egypt, again reducing it to a province. However, in 332 Alexander the Great attacked the Persian Empire and liberated Egypt. Now a Macedonian administration replaced the Persian.

Hellenistic-Roman Rule

Alexander's general Ptolemy I Soter claimed Egypt as his territory, and in 323 proclaimed himself king. Ruling from newly built Alexandria, he held Egypt and some overseas territories. Under the later Ptolemies, Egypt became entangled with the Seleucids of Syria, and soon had to appeal to the Roman Republic for help. The Romans answered with aid, but they too invaded the eastern Mediterranean, first crippling the Macedonian kingdom, then the Seleucid, so that only Egypt remained of the Hellenistic realms. The royal line faltered after Ptolemy X, and Ptolemy XI bankrupted Egypt in his effort to buy his legitimacy from Roman politicians.

At Ptolemy XII's death, Cleopatra VII and two younger brothers inherited Egypt, but soon fell to quarreling. Pursuing Pompey the Great, Julius Caesar followed him to Egypt in 48-47 B.C. and became enmeshed in the royal quarrel. He found Cleopatra VII the most able, and threw his support to her. Cleopatra planned marriage to Caesar in a bid to secure her realm, bearing him a son, Caesarion (Ptolemy XV). Caesar's murder in 44 forestalled her plans, and she retired to Egypt. In 42 Mark Antony summoned Cleopatra to appear in Syria, and she utterly suborned him. He had three children by Cleopatra, but Octavian tried to woo him away with his sister. Antony, though, could not resist Cleopatra, who helped his bloodied army after his attack on the Parthians failed. After revenging himself on the Armenian king, Antony decided to hold his triumph in Alexandria and to elevate Cleopatra as his consort and co-ruler, along with all her children as junior rulers. Octavian was outraged, and using a fierce propaganda campaign, attacked Antony and Cleopatra as debauched and serpentine figures. The two sides squared up for war. Cleopatra had restored Egypt to prosperity fielding 60 ships. Antony's land army bridled at Cleopatra's insistence on taking part in battle, and when the tide turned against them Cleopatra retired her ships and fled to Egypt. Antony followed her, losing most of his army. The Nabatean king burned Cleopatra's ships when she tried to transfer them to the Red Sea, and so their situation grew desperate. Antony attempted suicide, and then Cleopatra followed his example, as Octavian closed in on Egypt. So ended the last Hellenistic kingdom, and Egypt became an imperial province. Octavian so feared Egypt as a power base that he forbade any Roman senator from setting foot there.

Bibliography. M. A. Hoffman, *Egypt Before the Pharaohs,* rev. ed. (Austin, 1991); A. J. Spencer, *Early Egypt* (Norman, 1995); N.-C. Grimal, *A History of Ancient Egypt* (Oxford, 1992); K. A. Kitchen, *The Third Intermediate Period in Egypt (1100-650 B.C.),* 2nd ed. (Warminster, 1986); W. W. Tarn, *Hellenistic Civilization,* 3rd ed. (London, 1952); F. W. Walbank, *The Hellenistic World,* rev. ed. (Cambridge, Mass., 1993).

FRANK J. YURCO

EGYPT, BROOK OF

A brook or wadi (so NRSV; Heb. *naḥal miṣrayim*) that formed the southernmost border of Canaan (Num. 34:5), the tribe of Judah (Josh. 15:4, 47), and all of Israel (1 Kgs. 8:65 = 2 Chr. 7:8) and during the day of the Lord (Isa. 27:12; Ezek. 47:19; 48:28). It may have served as the border between Palestine and Egypt (2 Kgs. 24:7). Elsewhere the Shihor (Josh. 13:3; 1 Chr. 13:5) and the brook of the

Arabah (Amos 6:14) are designated as the southern border of Israel. The Brook of Egypt should be identified with Wadi el-ʿArish, which flows from the Sinai entering the Mediterranean S of Raphia and Gaza. BRADFORD SCOTT HUMMEL

EGYPTIAN (LANGUAGE)

A branch of the Afro-asiatic language group (also called Hamito-Semitic). As with other Afro-asiatic languages (Semitic, Berber, Chushitic, Chadic, Omotic), Egyptian exhibits particular linguistic features, including bi- and tri-consonantal root structures that are inflected in various ways, an original vocalic system of /i/, /a/, /u/, final feminine **at,* a qualitative or stative verb form (Old Perfective), independent and suffix pronouns, and an adjectival suffix *-I* ("nisbation").

History and Development

The history of Egyptian, extending roughly over four millennia of usage (ca. 3200 B.C.E.–1300 C.E.), is generally divided into two historical, and in some cases overlapping, phases: (1) Older Egyptian (ca. 3200-1300), encompassing Archaic Egyptian, Old Egyptian, Middle Egyptian, and Late Middle Egyptian; and (2) Later Egyptian (ca. 1300 B.C.E.–1300 C.E.), consisting of Late Egyptian, Demotic, and Coptic. The earliest examples of noncontinuous writing (late 4th millennium) consist of hieroglyphs on bone and ivory tags, clay seal impressions, pottery, and stone vases, recording the exchange of commodities. Egyptian most likely came into existence under the newly formed Egyptian state (ca. 3100), for which it served both as an administrative tool (cursive script) and a means for the public display of royal and religious ideology in the form of monumental hieroglyphic writing. The 2nd through 4th Dynasties (ca. 2840-2500) saw significant developments in writing and public display, moving from offering and title lists (in private tombs) to continuous texts in religious (Djoser at Heliopolis) and later administrative contexts. Throughout Egyptian history, writing and literacy were restricted to a very small segment of Egyptian society, probably no larger than 1 or 2 percent of the total population, and preserved texts reflect the worldview of this literary elite.

The language of the earlier dynasties (3rd to 8th), roughly contemporary with the Old Kingdom (ca. 2700-2160), is called Old Egyptian and is most widely represented in the Pyramid Texts (royal funerary spells/rituals, 5th-8th Dynasties) and private tomb biographies. The next written phase of the language, Middle or Classical Egyptian, extends roughly from the end of the Old Kingdom to the mid-18th Dynasty (ca. 2160-1400). It was during this period, especially the 12th Dynasty (1963-1786), that many of the great literary compositions of Egyptian literature were written, encompassing a variety of fully developed literary genres, including tales (e.g., Sinuhe, Shipwrecked Sailor), hymns (e.g., Hymn to the Inundation), and teachings (e.g., Merikare).

Parallel to the formal written Egyptian of the 12th-Dynasty elite, a more colloquial form of the language, Late Middle Egyptian, appears initially in practical contexts, such as letters and accounts. By the New Kingdom (1540-1069), Late Middle Egyptian is found in religious and royal monumental texts (e.g., Book of the Heavenly Cow, Pap. Leiden I 350, Nauri Decree) and continues to be used throughout the pharaonic period and beyond (e.g., Shabako Stone, Pi[ankhi] Stela, and in Greco-Roman temple inscriptions). In addition, literary classics of the Middle Kingdom, for which we possess mostly New Kingdom copies/fragments, were transmitted in Late Middle Egyptian; this literary corpus served as the classical literary core for the early New Kingdom high cultural elite.

Late Egyptian, as a written language, emerges in the second half of the New Kingdom during the Amarna period (ca. 1350-1336). In literary Late Egyptian (e.g., Wenamun, Horus and Seth), which exhibits a number of features in common with standard classical Egyptian (e.g., narrative tenses, some negative particles), one encounters literary forms not found in Middle Kingdom literature (narrative fiction, love poetry, and school texts). Nonliterary Late Egyptian refers to the language of everyday affairs contained in administrative documents, letters, and accounts of the Ramesside period (1292-1075). In the Saite period and beyond (644 B.C.E.–ca. 450 C.E.), Demotic cursive, denoting both the cursive script and the vernacular written in it, served as the language of administrative, legal, and economic concerns, with some literary texts as well (e.g., the tales of Setne Khamwas). The last phase of Egyptian is Coptic (ca. 3rd to 14th century C.E.), the language of the Christian or Coptic Church in Egypt. The Coptic script consists of letters from the Greek alphabet with an additional handful of signs taken from Demotic to represent Egyptian phonemes not found in Greek. Of its various dialects, that known as Bohairic became the official and liturgical language of the Coptic Church. In addition to early magical texts and translations of biblical books, Coptic manuscripts preserve important noncanonical writings as well, including the Gospel of Thomas and the Apocryphon of James.

Scripts

Egyptian is written in four major scripts: hieroglyphic, hieratic, Demotic, and Coptic. The latter two have already been discussed. The elaborate and decorative hieroglyphic system of writing (from Gk. "sacred carved [letters]") is the most long-lived — and widely recognized today — of the scripts, originating in the Pre-dynastic period and extending in usage down to the late 4th century C.E. As the monumental script (e.g., carved or painted in temple reliefs, tombs, stelae, statuary, etc.), hieroglyphic served the ideological needs via public display of the Egyptian state. For business and administrative needs, a cursive adaptation was devised, known as hieratic (1st dynasty down to 3rd century C.E.), written with reed pen on papyrus and ostraca. Scribes normally worked in hieratic and a more simplified hieroglyphic form; although they were literate, evidence suggests that their knowledge of decorative monumental hieroglyphic was limited.

The number of hieroglyphic signs employed in Egyptian varies through time, ranging from ca. 750 in Classical Egyptian up to ca. 6,000 in the Greco-Roman period. These signs are pictographic, depicting both objects (e.g., buildings, furniture, agricultural implements) and living things (e.g., people, animals, trees, plants). Unlike other languages of the ancient Near East, Egyptian throughout its long history retained its pictorial character as both writing and representational art. This fusion of script and representation means, for example, that the grouping, orientation, and placement of signs are determined by aesthetic or artistic considerations beyond the mere writing of a script.

Basic Principles of Writing

Egyptian pictographic signs are of two basic types: phonograms and semograms. Phonograms may represent up to three consecutive consonantal sounds; thus a given sign may be mono- (picture of a human foot = phonetic /b/), bi- (picture of a house = phonetic /p-r/), or tri-consonantal (Egyptian dung-beetle = phonetic /h-p-r/). Egyptian has 24 mono-consonantal signs, often referred to as its "alphabet," but only rarely do these function independently of semantic indicators. In addition to phonological indicators, signs could serve as semograms, either by depicting the object itself (logogram) or indicating its semantic or lexical field (generic determinative or taxogram). For example, the Egyptian word "sun" (*rʿw*) is represented by a picture of the sun itself, and the word "face" (Egyp. *ḥr*) shown as a human face. Using the rebus principle (e.g., picture of a bee + leaf = "belief"), such logograms could be used in writing various words, or portions thereof, that are unrelated in meaning, but with partially identical phonology (e.g., the "face" logogram indicates phonetic /ḥ-r/ in Egyp. *ḥrt,* "tomb, necropolis").

Generic determinatives are placed after words to indicate their semantic field (e.g., a seated man with hand to mouth often denotes actions or states such as eating, drinking, hunger, speaking, or silence). Parts of the body (e.g., ear, eye, nose, arm) may also serve as determinatives (e.g., the eye as determinative with words relating to seeing, looking, blindness, wakefulness, or weeping).

Words that are phonetically identical are distinguished in meaning by their determinatives. For example, depending on its determinative, Egyp. *ms* could be read as "child" (with a child as determinative), "calf" (with calf determinative), "bouquet" (with herb determinative), or the enclitic particle (followed by human figure with hand to mouth).

There is as well much overlap between the above types or categories, so that a given sign could function as phonogram, logogram, or semogram. For example, the rectangular house sign could be read as (1) the phonetic combination /p-r/; (2) the word "house" (with a vertical stroke to show its non-phonetic usage); or (3) a determinative with words relating to buildings or structures (e.g., "room," "sanctuary," "interior," etc.).

Loanwords in the OT

A number of Hebrew words and phrases in the OT may be explained as derivative, either directly or indirectly, from Egyptian. For example, Heb. *yĕʾōr,* "Nile River" (Gen. 41:1-3) from Egyp. *i (t) rw,* "Nile River, stream (of the Nile)"; Heb. *parʿōh,* "Pharaoh" (Gen. 12:15) from Egyp. *pr ʿ3j,* "pharaoh, king of Egypt [lit., 'great house']"; and Heb. *šûšan,* "lily, lotus" (1 Kgs. 7:19, 26) from Egyp. *ššn,* "lotus."

Bibliography. J. P. Allen, *Middle Egyptian Grammar* (Cambridge, 2000); J. Baines, "Communication and Display: The Integration of Early Egyptian Art and Writing," *Antiquity* 63 (1989): 471-82; J. Černý and S. Israelit-Groll, *A Late Egyptian Grammar,* 4th ed., Studia Pohl, ser. maior 4 (Rome, 1993); A. Gardiner, *Egyptian Grammar, Thus Wrote "Onchsheshongy": An Introductory Grammar of Demotic,* 2nd ed. SAOC 45 (Chicago, 1991); T. O. Lambdin, *Introduction to Sahidic Coptic* (Macon, 1983); A. Loprieno, *Ancient Egyptian: A Linguistic Introduction* (Cambridge, 1995).

John R. Huddlestun

EGYPTIAN, THE

One of the popular prophets in Palestine whose movements were crushed by Rome in the tense period leading up to the Jewish War (cf. Theudas). According to Josephus, "the Egyptian false prophet" led 30 thousand followers from the desert to the Mount of Olives. Claiming that the walls of Jerusalem would fall at his command, he planned to overpower the Roman garrison. The Roman procurator Felix (52-60 C.E.) struck preemptively; the Egyptian escaped while most of his followers were killed or taken prisoner (*BJ* 2.261-63; *Ant.* 20.169-72). In Acts 21:38 a Roman tribune mistakes Paul for the Egyptian, who here is credited with 4000 followers and is called a leader of the revolutionary terrorists known as the Sicarii.

The Egyptian's symbolic actions recall scriptural images of the freedom and power of Israel and its God. The desert symbolized spiritual purity and exodus from oppression, the prediction concerning the walls alluded to the conquest of Jericho (Josh. 6:20), and the Mount of Olives was understood as the place where the Lord himself would come to fight against the nations attacking Jerusalem (Zech. 14).

Bibliography. M. Hengel, *The Zealots* (Edinburgh, 1989); R. A. Horsley and J. S. Hanson, *Bandits, Prophets, and Messiahs* (Minneapolis, 1985).

Martin C. Albl

EGYPTIANS, GOSPEL ACCORDING TO THE

(III, 2; IV, 2)

An apocryphal gnostic Gospel probably created in Egypt in the mid-2nd century C.E. Although frequently referred to by the church fathers of the 2nd and 3rd centuries, all that remains of the work are a few allusions and paraphrases. Those references reveal that this treatise was a study of Jesus' teachings that support gnostic beliefs generally and several doctrines particularly: the Naasene idea that the soul is variable in form, nature, and disposition (Hippolytus *Ref.* 5.7); the Sabellian idea that the Father, Son, and Holy Spirit are one and the same (Epiphanius *Adv. haer.* 62.2.4; cf. *Excerpta ex Theodoto* 67); and, most prominently, the Encratite emphasis on celibacy, the rejection of marriage, and the eradication of the differences between male and female (by baptism) in order to restore the believer to Adam's state before the creation of Eve. A female, Salome, is prominent in this latter doctrine, but only as a setup for Jesus to enunciate Encratite doctrine. For example, she asks how long death will prevail, and Christ tells her that it will last as long as women give birth (Clement *Misc.* 3.6.45; 3.9.64; 3.13.92). This Gospel is not the same as the Coptic Gospel of the Egyptians, which is part of the Nag Hammadi literature.

Bibliography. R. Cameron, *The Other Gospels* (Philadelphia, 1982), 49-52, 186; J. K. Elliott, "The Gospel of the Egyptians," in *The Apocryphal New Testament,* rev. ed. (Oxford, 1993), 16-19.

RICHARD A. SPENCER

EHI (Heb. *'ēḥî*)
One of the sons of Benjamin (Gen. 46:21). The name is probably to be combined with the following name Rosh to read Ahiram (cf. Num. 26:38) or perhaps Aharah (1 Chr. 8:1).

EHUD (Heb. *'ēhûḏ*)

1. The second judge of Israel, the son of Gera, a Benjaminite. The story of his delivering Israel from the power of Eglon king of Moab follows the standard formula for the major judges (Judg. 3:12-30). The extent to which the narrative is history or formula is debated. According to biblical chronology, this story should have taken place during the 12th century; however, the Moabite connection makes such an early date improbable.

Ehud is depicted as "restricted in his right hand," forcing him to be left-handed; at the same time he is shown as very quick-witted. Both characteristics serve him in dealing with Eglon, who is presented as gullible. In the 18th year of Moabite rule the Israelites selected Ehud to deliver tribute to the Moabite king. The fact that Ehud could only use one hand probably caused Eglon to assume he was no threat. However, with a pun on "private word of the gods," Ehud convinces Eglon to grant him an exclusive audience. This "secret thing of God" is a dagger which Ehud uses to assassinate Eglon in his own chamber. Securing the door between himself and the unsuspecting guards, Ehud escapes out the back to raise an army in Israel under his command in order to attack, and annihilate, the Moabite troops at the Jordan River. Israel then had 80 years of peace. The text never claims that Ehud ruled over Israel as it does of other judges, although the story of Deborah begins with reference to the death of Ehud (Judg. 4:1).

Bibliography. M. Z. Brettler, "Never the Twain Shall Meet? The Ehud Story as History and Literature," *HUCA* 62 (1991): 285-304; B. Halpern, "The Assassination of Eglon," *BibRev* 4/6 (1988): 32-41, 44; L. K. Handy, "Uneasy Laughter: Ehud and Eglon as Ethnic Humor," *SJOT* 6 (1992): 233-46.

2. One of seven sons of Bilhan listed in the Benjaminite genealogy at 1 Chr. 7:10.

3. A Benjaminite, the father of Naaman, Ahijah, and Gera (1 Chr. 8:6). LOWELL K. HANDY

EKER (Heb. *'ēqer*)
The third son of Ram, a descendant of Jerahmeel (1 Chr. 2:27).

EKRON (Heb. *'eqrôn;* Gk. *Akkarōn*)
A city of the Philistine Pentapolis (Josh. 13:3). With Israel's appearance, Ekron was reckoned as a city both of Judah (Josh. 15:45-46) and Dan (19:43), perhaps situated on their border. Neither Israelite tribe, however, could successfully retain control of the city, and it frequently reverted to Philistine control (cf. Judg. 1:18).

During the early judgeship of Samuel, the Philistines controlled the city. Ekron was the staging city for returning the ark of the covenant to Judah following its capture by the Philistines in the battle of Ebenezer (1 Sam. 4, 6). The episode reflects Ekron's proximity as the northernmost of the Pentapolis cities to border Judah. Later in Samuel's judgeship, Ekron came under Israelite control (1 Sam. 7:14) only to return again to the Philistines (17:52).

Later references indicate that Ekron was outside Israelite hegemony (Jer. 25:20; Amos 1:8; Zeph. 2:4; Zech. 9:5-7). Elijah upbraided Ahaziah for inquiring concerning his health of Baalzebub, god of Ekron (2 Kgs. 1:2-16); this implies that the city was under foreign rule. Nebuchadnezzar of Babylon destroyed the entire city in 603, after which it remained essentially unoccupied. The last biblical reference to Ekron is when the city was awarded to the Hasmonean Jonathan for his loyalty to Alexander Balas (1 Macc. 10:89).

Ekron is identified with the ruins at Tel Miqne/Khirbet el-Muqanna' (1356.1315) ca. 56 km. (35 mi.) SW of Jerusalem. The site is on the eastern edge of the Shephelah which traditionally served as the frontier between the Philistines and Israel. Tel Miqne covers ca. 20 ha. (50 a.) consisting of a 16 ha. (40 a.) lower city and a 4 ha. (10 a.) acropolis.

Scattered pottery remains testify to occupation in the area for the Chalcolithic through Middle Bronze Ages. However, in the Late Bronze Age three strata, all preserving typical LB wares, provide a clearer picture of the site's occupation. These exquisite wares reflect the sudden appearance of the Philistines and are reminiscent of their Aegean heritage. In Iron Age I the Philistines fortified the site and built palatial buildings with shrines (Heb. *bāmôṯ*) which reflected Cypriot influences. At the end of the Iron Age (10th century B.C.), the city was generally abandoned, perhaps reflecting the ongoing Israelite and Egyptian campaigns in the area.

Ekron reemerged as a significant site in the 8th century during the Neo-Assyrian presence. During this period Ekron developed a trade specialty in olive oil production. More than 100 olive oil installations have been identified along the perimeter of the site, yielding an estimated 1000 tons of olive oil a year.

The site has yielded numerous stone four-horned altars which suggest some religio-political control of olive oil production. Some of the store jars indicate that oil was dedicated to the mother-goddess Asherah. A dedicatory temple inscription identifies the site as Ekron and also refers to Achish, the son of Padi, who dedicated the temple to a goddess, likely Asherat.

Bibliography. T. Dothan and S. Gitin, "Miqne, Tel (Ekron)," *NEAEHL* 3:1051-59; Gitin, "Incense Altars from Ekron, Israel and Judah," *ErIsr* 20 (1989): 52*-67*; "Philistine Silver and Jewelry Discovered at Ekron," *BA* 55 (1992): 152; "Royal Temple Inscription Found at Philistine Ekron," *BA* 59 (1996): 181-82. DALE W. MANOR

EL (Heb. *'ēl*)

In many West Semitic languages the name of El is the same as the word for "god," perhaps evidence that El was the pre-eminent god of older West Semitic pantheons (or possibly divinity incarnate). Although the etymology is uncertain, the word may derive from **'wl,* "to be in front" or "to be strong," or may be a "primitive" biradical noun, unrelated to a verbal root and meaning "chief" or "god."

Middle and Late Bronze Age Sources

Texts from Ebla, Mari, and Amarna attest to El as a theophoric element in personal names. Accordingly, it is thought that El was a major god in Syria-Palestine. In contrast, the evidence in personal names from the Mesopotamian heartland is contested. Given the lack of evidence for El's cult in Mesopotamia, these cases may involve either the generic term, "god," or the personal god, but not the proper name of El.

The most extensive source about El comes from Late Bronze Age Ugarit. In the Ugaritic mythological narratives El is the divine patriarch par excellence. He is the divine progenitor, "father" to the pantheon, which is his royal family and a royal assembly over which he exercises authority. His authority is expressed in his title, "king" *(mlk),* the same notion which seems to underlie his epithet, "bull"; like the chief and most powerful of animals, El is chief of the deities. Asherah is El's wife, with whom he has produced the pantheon (generically, but not all-inclusively, called "Asherah's 70 sons").

Both texts and iconography present El as an elderly, bearded figure, the "aged one," "father of years" (*'ab šnm,* although the meaning of the second term is debated). Anat and Asherah both affirm the eternity of El's wisdom.

As the divine patriarch, El enjoys a range of social activities. Like the well-to-do men of Ugarit, he has a social association or club *(mrzḥ),* and texts depict drunken bouts and sexual activity.

El's home is conceptualized in both terrestrial and cosmic terms. According to the Baal cycle, it is situated in the waters of the "double-deeps," located at a mountain, the terrestrial site of which is unknown. His residence is characterized further by terms which would suggest a tent. A ritual text (*KTU* 1.100.3) provides a cosmic location for El's home, placing it at a point where the upper and lower cosmic oceans meet.

El's status vis-à-vis Baal, the head of the next generation of gods, has been a matter of debate. Some scholars have argued that Baal's promotion to the head of the pantheon took place at El's expense. While this view has been severely contested, the struggle for divine kingship between Baal and El's sons is fraught with tension and intrigue. El backs the god Sea (Yamm) for divine kingship against his rival, Baal, who may have been regarded as an outsider to El's family (cf. Baal's title "son of Dagan"). Later in the Baal cycle, El supports the god Athtar, an astral deity and one of El's sons, for divine kingship. Texts depicting competition among the younger gods in the divine family, overseen by the patriarch El, may reflect two forms of divinity or cult, one astral involving El and his children and the other atmospheric involving Baal. It may be suggested (with all due caution) that the sun, moon, and stars were especially associated with El in West Semitic religion.

El attends not only to his divine family, but also to the human family. In the story of Keret, El shows solicitous care for this king, appearing to him in an incubation-dream and blessing him with progeny. Just as El engendered the divine family, so too El produced the human family. His relationship to humanity is exemplified by his titles "father of humanity" *('b 'adm)* and "creator of creatures" (*bny bnwt;* cf. Gen. 14:19, 22). The mythological texts never portray El's role as creator of the cosmos, deities, or humanity, and it would seem that this activity of his was regarded as having belonged to the distant past. Another activity posited for El is battle, based on the title "El the warrior" (*'ēl gibbôr;* Isa. 9:6[MT 5]) or "Divine Warrior."

Iron Age Sources

Outside of proper names, Heb. *'ēl* occurs ca. 230 times in the Hebrew Bible. It may designate a foreign deity (Ezek. 28:2) as well as Israel's chief deity (Num. 23:22 = 24:8). Most commonly, the word is used in conjunction with other grammatical elements (such as the definite article). It appears as a proper name of the deity in poetic books such as Psalms (Ps. 5:4[5]; 7:11[12]; 18:3, 31, 33, 48[2, 30, 32, 47] = 2 Sam. 22; Ps. 102:24[25]) and Second Isaiah (Isa. 40:18; 42:5; 45:14, 15, 20-22; 46:9). Illustrative of this usage is the shortest (and brilliantly chiastic) biblical prayer which Moses utters on Miriam's behalf: "El, please, heal her, please" (Num. 12:13; cf. Hos. 11:12[12:1]; Mic. 7:18; LXX Prov. 30:3).

According to many scholars, El's cult did not exist in Israel except as part of his identification with Yahweh. This question depends on whether Yahweh was a title of El or secondarily identified with El. Besides the grammatical questions raised against this view, the oldest biblical traditions describe

Yahweh as a storm-god from the Negeb and the Arabah, especially Edom, Teman, Paran, and Kuntillet ʿAjrud/Ḥorvat Teman (0940.9560; cf. Judg. 5; Hab. 3). These facts militate against an identification of Yahweh as originally a title of El.

Some evidence points to old Israelite traditions of El which do not involve Yahweh. Most importantly, the name of Israel does not contain the divine element of Yahweh, but rather El's name. This suggests that El was the original chief god of the group named Israel. West Semitic El lies behind the god of the patriarchs in Gen. 33:20; 46:3 (and possibly elsewhere). The Priestly theological treatment of Israel's early religious history in Exod. 6:2-3 identifies the old god El Shaddai with Yahweh, a means to gloss over the obvious difficulty that El and not Yahweh was the god of the patriarchs. Furthermore, Gen. 49:24-25 presents a series of El epithets separate from the mention of Yahweh in v. 18. At least some of these texts point to an old stage in Israelite traditions or locations where El was Israel's chief deity apart from Yahweh. It would stand to reason that El and not Yahweh was the god who accompanied the Israelites from Egypt (Num. 23:22 = 24:8; cf. El's title, "bull").

Two biblical passages suggest an accommodation of Yahweh to an Israelite pantheon headed by El. According to the LXX and one of the Dead Sea Scrolls, Deut. 32:8 regards Yahweh as one of El's sons, here called Elyon; according to v. 9, Israel was the nation which Yahweh received. The passage presupposes that El was the head of this pantheon and Yahweh was but one of its many members. Ps. 82 describes a heavenly courtroom in which Yahweh takes his stand as plaintiff. Such scenes assume another divinity as the judge, a common role for El in the Ugaritic texts (cf. the label given the heavenly council in Ps. 82:1, *ʿăḏat-ʾēl*, "the gathering of El"; Yahweh's reference to the other deities in v. 6 as "the sons of Elyon," a title of El).

The cultural process lying behind this accommodation of Yahweh can be understood better by noting the religious language and imagery associated with specific sanctuaries. 1 Sam. 1–3 describes the divine appearance to Samuel in incubation-dreams at the sanctuary at Shiloh, the divine gift of a child to Hannah, and the El name of Elkanah (suggesting an El worshipper?), all of which would cohere with the view that El was the original god at Shiloh (Judg. 18:31; cf. 17:5). The tent tradition associated with Shiloh (Ps. 78:60; Josh. 18:1; 1 Sam. 2:22) comports with Ugaritic descriptions of El's abode as a tent. It is probably no accident that Ps. 78 repeatedly uses El names and epithets in its discussion of Shiloh. Furthermore, it is arguable from the cult of Shiloh and the Egyptian names in the Shilohite lineage (Moses, Phinehas, Hopni, Merari) that the god of Moses and the levitical priesthood at Shiloh was El.

Traditions concerning the sanctuary of Shechem likewise illustrate the cultural process lying behind the inclusion of Yahweh at old cultic sites of El. At Shechem the local god was El-berith, "El of the covenant" (Judg. 9:46; cf. 8:33; 9:4). In the patriarchal narratives, the god of Shechem *(ʾēl)* is called *ʾĕlōhê yiśrāʾēl*, "the god of Israel," and is presumed to be Yahweh. In this case, a process of reinterpretation appears to be at work. In the early history of Israel, when the cult of Shechem became Yahwistic, it inherited and continued the El traditions of that site. As a result, Yahweh received the title *ʾēl bĕrîṯ*, the old title of El.

As these accounts suggest, at various points and under different circumstances Israelite religious centers based in the central highlands identified Yahweh, the god of the southern region, with their local main god, El. In identifying Yahweh secondarily with El, the priesthood at cultic sites of El, such as Shiloh, Shechem, and Jerusalem, melded the religious lore of Yahweh with the indigenous traditions about El. It is for this reason that the Hebrew Bible so rarely distinguishes between El and Yahweh or offers polemics against El. In Israel El's characteristics and epithets joined the repertoire of descriptions of Yahweh. Like El in the Ugaritic texts, Yahweh is described as an aged, patriarchal god (e.g., Ps. 102:27[28]; Job 36:26; Isa. 40:28; cf. Dan. 6:26; 2 Esdr. 8:20), seated on a throne in the assembly of divine beings (1 Kgs. 22:19; Isa. 6:1-8; cf. Ps. 82:1; 89:5-8; Isa. 14:13; Jer. 23:18, 22). Later biblical texts continued the notion of aged Yahweh enthroned before the heavenly hosts (Dan. 7:9-14, 22, the "ancient of days" and "the Most High"; cf. Rev. 7).

El and Yahweh exhibit a similar disposition towards humanity. Like El, Yahweh is a father (Deut. 32:6; Isa. 63:16; 64:8; Jer. 3:14, 19; 31:9; Mal. 1:6, 2:10; cf. Exod. 4:22; Hos. 11:1), with a compassionate disposition ("merciful and gracious god"; Exod. 34:6; Neh. 9:17; Ps. 86:15; 103:8; 145:8; Joel 2:13; Jonah 4:2). Like El, Yahweh is the progenitor of humanity (cf. Deut. 32:6-7). Both El and Yahweh appear to humans in dream-visions and function as their divine patron. Like El, Yahweh is a healing god (Gen. 20:17; Num. 12:13; 2 Kgs. 20:5, 8; Ps. 107:20). The description of Yahweh's dwelling-place as a "tent" (e.g., Ps. 15:1; 27:6), called in the Pentateuchal traditions the "tent of meeting" (Exod. 33:7-11; Num. 12:5, 10; Deut. 31:14, 15), recalls the tent of El. Furthermore, the cosmic waters of El's dwelling is a theme evoked in descriptions of Yahweh's abode in Jerusalem (Ps. 87; Isa. 33:20-22; Ezek. 47:1-12; Joel 3:18[4:18]; Zech. 14:8).

It is unknown whether some distinction between El and Yahweh in Israel extends to epigraphic evidence. It is not necessary to interpret *ʾl* in the Kuntillet ʿAjrud inscriptions as "God" and assume an identification with Yahweh. Israelite inscriptions include 557 names with Yahweh as the divine element, 77 names with **ʾl*, a handful with the divine component **bʿl*, and none referring to the goddesses ʿAnat or Asherah. The element **ʾl* in proper names may represent a title for Yahweh, but it is possible that this identification should not be assumed in all instances.

El's cult in the Levant outside of Israel is a matter of dispute. Phoenician data are quite sparse and far-flung (e.g., Karatepe, a neo-Punic inscription, a

Hellenistic inscription from Umm el-ʿAwamid, Philo of Byblos). Ezek. 28 describes the home of Tyrian El in terms similar to Ugaritic descriptions of El's abode, and the wisdom ascribed to Tyrian El also recalls El in the Ugaritic texts. Furthermore, Phoenician Bethel has been understood as a hypostasis of El, which would represent further Phoenician evidence for the cult of El in the Iron II period. This view is debated. Finally, Phoenician and Punic Baal Hamon may be a title of El. If correct, the cult of El was very widespread.

Aramaic evidence from the 8th century is more sparse but less equivocal. Panammuwa, king of Samal, mentions El in a list of deities, and the Sefire inscription is a treaty text with a list of divine witnesses including El.

Like the Phoenician evidence, the Transjordanian material for the cult of El has been debated vigorously. Ammonite personal names attest to the element *ʾl*, but it is unclear whether El is the referent. The divine element *ʾl* likewise dominates the theophoric elements in the Edomite onomastica. A 1st-millennium Transjordanian cult of El might be suggested by the Deir ʿAlla inscriptions. Some of the older poetic material in Num. 22–24 attests to El's cult in a Transjordanian setting. Like the Deir ʿAlla inscriptions, Num. 22–24 presents a Transjordanian seer whose prophecy comes from El, a role attested for this god in the Ugaritic texts. In sum, while dynastic cults of the 1st-millennium Levant had patron deities other than El, the admittedly sparse and sometimes ambiguous evidence indicates El's cult in the Levant during the 1st millennium.

Bibliography. F. M. Cross, "ēl," *TDOT* 1:242-61; *Canaanite Myth and Hebrew Epic* (Cambridge, Mass., 1973), 3-75; W. Herrmann, "El," *DDD* (Leiden, 1995), 274-80; B. A. Levine, "The Balaam Inscription from Deir ʿAlla: Historical Aspects," in *Biblical Archaeology Today* (Jerusalem, 1985), 326-39; C. E. L'Heureux, *Rank Among the Canaanite Gods.* HSM 21 (Missoula, 1979); P. D. Miller, Jr., "El the Warrior," *HTR* 60 (1967): 411-31; U. Oldenburg, *The Conflict between El and Baʿal in Canaanite Thought* (Leiden, 1969); M. H. Pope, *El in the Ugaritic Texts.* VTSup 2 (Leiden, 1955).

MARK S. SMITH

ELA (Heb. *ʾēlāʾ*)
The father of Shimei the district governor of Benjamin during the reign of Solomon (1 Kgs. 4:18).

ELAH (Heb. *ʾēlâ*)

1. One of the 11 chiefs of Esau/Edom (Gen. 36:41; 1 Chr. 1:52). The biblical texts indicate that the references probably represent a place within the territory of Edom, possibly near ʿAqaba.

2. The fourth king of Israel and son of Baasha, who ruled in Tirzah ca. 877-876 B.C.E. (1 Kgs. 16:6, 8-14). He was assassinated by Zimri, a high-ranking military officer, in an apparent military coup. Zimri executed his plot while Elah was drunk in the house of one of his palace officials. This occurred while the Israelite army was engaged in battle against the Philistine town of Gibbethon and Tirzah was relatively unprotected.

Zimri proceeded to exterminate the male family members and friends of Baasha-Elah, fulfilling the prophecy of Jehu ben Hanani that the Lord's punishment would fall upon Baasha's house (1 Kgs. 16:1-4). Elah is especially condemned for participation in idolatry.

3. The father of Hoshea, the last king of Israel (2 Kgs. 15:30; 17:1; 18:1, 9).

4. One of the three sons of Caleb ben Jephunneh (1 Chr. 4:15). He fathered one son, Kenaz. Elah here may instead refer to a place (cf. Gen. 36:41).

5. A Benjaminite who returned to Jerusalem following the Babylonian Captivity (1 Chr. 9:8). The name refers to a family living in Jerusalem during the postexilic period (but cf. Neh. 11 where the name is omitted). STEPHEN VON WYRICK

ELAH (Heb. *ʾēlâ*), **VALLEY OF**
The valley where the drama between David and Goliath was played out before Philistine forces and Saul's militia (1 Sam. 17:2-3, 19; cf. 21:9[MT 10]). The valley (Heb. *ʿēmeq hāʾēlâ,* "valley of the terebinth") is identified with the fertile Wadi es-Sanṭ ("Valley of Acacia"), 14-15 km. (8-9 mi.) WSW of Bethlehem, and provides an entrance into the Judean hill country. The fortress Azekah (Tell ez-Zakarîyeh) stood guard at the passage to the valley.

The Philistine forces positioned themselves on the western slopes near Azekah, and Saul and his forces camped in the strategic high country on the eastern side of the valley toward Socoh. The valley thus formed the battle line as the two military forces encamped on opposite sides. T. J. JENNEY

ELAM (Heb. *ʿêlām*) **(PERSON)**

1. The first of Shem's five sons (Gen. 10:22; 1 Chr. 1:17), according to the Table of Nations the progenitor of the inhabitants of Elam.

2. A Benjamite, son of Shashak (1 Chr. 8:24).

3. A son of the Korahite Meshelemiah, listed in the division of tabernacle gatekeepers (1 Chr. 26:3).

4. The head of a clan of Israelites, 1254 of whom returned to Jerusalem from the Babylonian Exile with Zerubbabel (Ezra 2:7 = Neh. 7:12). Another 70 returned with Ezra (Ezra 8:7; cf. 10:2, 26).

5. The "other Elam" (so called by Ezra 2:31 = Neh. 7:34) who returned from exile, also as leader of a group of 1254 people (cf. 1 Esdr. 5:22). The obvious similarity to **4** raises questions about distinguishing the two.

6. A leader of those who signed the covenant with Nehemiah (Neh. 10:14[MT 15]).

7. A priest among those assisting Nehemiah in his dedication of the new wall around Jerusalem (Neh. 12:42). JOHN S. VASSAR

ELAM (Heb. *ʿêlām*) **(PLACE)**
Name denoting both a region in highland Fars province (Iran) around the modern city of Shiraz, the ancient capital of which was Anshan (Tal-i

Malyan), and a state, the size of which fluctuated throughout its history and at times incorporated modern Khuzistan, parts of Luristan, and western Kerman as well as the heartland of Fars. The Table of Nations (Gen. 10:22; 1 Chr. 1:17) lists Elam, along with Assur, as a son of Shem, undoubtedly because of the historical connections between Elam and her Mesopotamian neighbors (cf. the role of Elamite archers in the Assyrian and Babylonian armies; Isa. 22:6; Jer. 49:35), rather than for any ethnolinguistic reason (Elamite is unrelated to either Akkadian or Sumerian).

More confusing for Bible commentators throughout history, however, is the statement identifying Susa (Heb. *šûšan*), a large, multi-period site in northern Khuzistan where the events played out in the book of Esther took place, as a city "in the province of Elam" (Dan. 8:2). Many of the personal names in the MT of Esther are indeed Elamite, but as the cuneiform sources clearly show, Susa (Akk. ^{kur}*Šū-šá-an/Šu-šu-un*) was the capital of Susiana (*Šu-še-en/Šu-sá-an*^{ki}), and Anshan was the capital of Elam (thus Gudea Statue B.6.64-69, "smote the city of Anshan in/of Elam"). The fact that Elam, in the sense of the political state of this name rather than the territorial homeland in Fars, periodically annexed Susiana and turned Susa into an important "Elamite" city should not obscure the fact that Elam only included Susiana in a political sense and was never synonymous with this eastern extension of the Mesopotamian alluvium in a geographical sense. This is not to deny, however, that from the distant, Israelite perspective, most people probably identified Susiana with Elam. As many commentators on Jer. 49:35-39 have noted, Elam represented, apart from anything else, one of the most remote entities on Israel's eastern geographical horizon, and as such it is scarcely surprising that an accurate understanding of the difference between Elam and Susiana escaped most of the Bible-reading public, scholars and laity alike, until quite recently. This confused perspective may be contrasted with the geographically accurate perceptions of the authors of the Babylonian Talmud who scrupulously distinguished Be Huzaë (lowland Khuzistan) from Elam (highland Fars). Similarly the Greek geographer Strabo strictly distinguished Elymais, long identified with biblical Elam, from Susis or Susiana (*Geog.* 15.3.12).

There is little of substance regarding Elam in either the OT or NT. Gen. 14:1 preserves the name of Kedor-laomer (Chedorlaomer), called "king of Elam," but he is almost certainly not Kutir-nahhunte II, the Elamite king who brought about the fall of the Kassite dynasty (ca. 1155 B.C.) and a figure with whose name he has often been assimilated. Although the story of Esther and Ahasuerus related in the book of Esther unfolded at Shushan the palace, this was in the context of Susa's role as a winter residence for the Achaemenid kings after 520 when Darius I began construction of a palace there, and postdates the last politically consolidated Elamite dynasty (of the so-called Neo-Elamite period, ca. 750-500). When Jews from Elam, along with their Median and Parthian brethren, appeared in Jerusalem at Pentecost (Acts 2:9), they served to illustrate the diverse language groups "out of every nation under heaven" present in the city and must have been viewed as foreigners from the distant east.

The biblical references to Elam give no hint of the historical importance of this, one of Mesopotamia's fiercest adversaries from the 3rd millennium until Assurbanipal's sack of Susa in 646. Contemporaries of the Old Akkadian kings, the Elamite Dynasty of Awan succumbed to the forces of Sargon of Akkad, inaugurating a period of growing Mesopotamian control over Susa and its hinterland. Nevertheless, the Elamite king Puzur-inshushinak managed to acquire control over portions of Mesopotamia before he was routed by Ur-nammu, founder of the Third Dynasty of Ur (ca. 2100). It was another Elamite king, however, Kindattu the Shimashkian, who plundered Ur and led Ibbi-sin, the last king of the Ur III dynasty, into captivity in Anshan where he died. From the late 19th to the mid-18th century, moreover, it was the *sukkal* of Elam, whom Zimri-lim of Mari, Hammurabi of Babylon, and Rim-sin of Larsa referred to as "great king of Elam," whose position in the region was paramount and marks the Elamites as one of the premier powers in Western Asia during the Old Babylonian period. Hammurabi's eventual defeat of the Elamites neutralized their power for several centuries, but a resurgence was experienced in the Middle Elamite period (ca. 1400-1100), and one of the Middle Elamite kings, Kutir-nahhunte II, is credited with bringing about the demise of the Kassite dynasty ca. 1155. Scarcely 30 years later, however, the Elamites were defeated by Nebuchadnezzar I. By the late 9th century the Elamites had again become a vexation to their western neighbors, this time the Assyrians, whose sack of Susa in 646 dealt a severe blow to the Neo-Elamite kingdom, which was, however, still extant until the coming of Cyrus the Great.

Except for the possible reference to Kedorlaomer (Gen. 14:1), none of this history is even hinted at in the Bible, but this is undoubtedly due to the fact that firsthand knowledge of Elam only came in the postexilic period, particularly after Elam had been absorbed politically into the Achaemenid Empire. By this point, however, it was scarcely a power to be reckoned with.

Bibliography. P. O. Harper, J. Aruz, and F. Tallon, eds., *The Royal City of Susa* (New York, 1992); W. G. Lambert, "The Fall of the Cassite Dynasty to the Elamites: An Historical Epic," in H. Gasche, et al., eds., *Cinquante-deux reflexions sur le Proche-Orient ancien* (Gent, 1994), 67-72; J. Simons, *The Geographical and Topographical Texts of the Old Testament* (Leiden, 1959); R. Zadok, "Notes on Esther," *ZAW* 98 (1986): 105-10.

D. T. Potts

ELASA (Gk. *Elasa*)

The site where Judas Maccabeus pitched his camp before the battle against Bacchides in 161 B.C.E.

(1 Macc. 9:5). Although most of Judas' 3000 troops deserted when confronted by the much larger Syrian forces (outnumbered more than seven to one), Judas succeeded in defeating the opponent's right wing before he was killed (1 Macc. 9:8-18). The location is probably either Khirbet Il'asa, which lies between Lower and Upper Beth-horon, or Khirbet el-'Ašši (169144), by modern Ramallah. Both sites are close to el-Bîreh. WILLARD W. WINTER

ELASAH (Heb. *'el'āśâ*)

1. A son of Pashhur the priest who promised to send away his foreign wife (Ezra 10:22).

2. The son of Shaphan; one of two emissaries sent by King Zedekiah to Nebuchadnezzar with Jeremiah's letter to the exiles at Babylon (Jer. 29:3).

ELATH (Heb. *'êlaṯ*)

A city and harbor at the head of the Gulf of Aqabah. Elath's strategic position made it an important gateway for caravan and naval commerce with Arabia and eastern Africa. In the OT Elath is frequently placed in close proximity to Ezion-geber. Some scholars consider Tell el-Kheleifeh (147884), which lies between modern Elath and Aqabah, as Elath, others as Ezion-geber, and still others as the site for both Elath and Ezion-geber. The site was also known as El-paran (Gen. 14:6). The Ptolemies changed its name to Bernice.

Elath was originally Edomite, possibly taking its name from the Edomite chief Elah (Gen. 36:41 = 1 Chr. 1:52; Eloth). Toward the end of the Exodus, the Israelites passed through Elath before turning north toward Edom and Moab (Deut. 2:8). David probably captured it during his campaign against the Edomites (2 Sam. 8:13-14). Solomon then established a navy of ships in Ezion-geber near Elath (1 Kgs. 9:26 = 2 Chr. 8:17). Apparently the Edomites had regained control, but Uzziah (Azariah, 2 Kgs. 14:22; 2 Chr. 26:2) recaptured and restored it (ca. 780 B.C.). However, under Aramean (Syrian) pressure during the Syro-Ephraimite War (ca. 735), Ahaz lost it to the Edomites permanently (2 Kgs. 16:6).

Bibliography. G. D. Pratico, *Nelson Glueck's 1938-1940 Excavations at Tell el-Kheleifeh: A Reappraisal.* ASOR Archaeological Reports 3 (Atlanta, 1993). BRADFORD SCOTT HUMMEL

EL-BERITH (Heb. *'ēl bĕrîṯ*)

A Canaanite deity ("El [or God] of the covenant") worshipped at Shechem (Judg. 9:46).

See BAAL-BERITH.

EL-BETHEL (Heb. *'ēl bêṯ-'ēl*)

The name given by Jacob to an altar he built at Bethel (Gen. 35:7). Here it occurs as an alternative name for Bethel, where God twice appeared to Jacob: after his dream of the ladder or staircase (Gen. 28:12-15) and upon his return from Paddan-aram (35:9-15), each time erecting and anointing a memorial stone. The Hebrew phrase occurs with the definite article in Gen. 31:13, where God identifies himself to Jacob as "the God of Bethel."

KEITH L. EADES

ELDAAH (Heb. *'eldā'â*)

The fifth son of Midian, one of the grandsons of Abraham and Keturah (Gen. 25:4 = 1 Chr. 1:33).

ELDAD (Heb. *'eldāḏ*)

One of 70 men chosen by Moses to receive the spirit of prophecy before the tent of meeting. When Eldad and Medad remained in the camp, Joshua became perturbed at their irregular behavior (perhaps ecstatic prophecy), to which Moses replied, "Would that all the Lord's people were prophets" (Num. 11:26-30).

ELDER

A man of authority, originally an older man in the patriarchal family and social structure. Elders of Israel (Heb. *zāqēn*) are mentioned as early as Exod. 3:16, 18, and groups called "elders" serve a variety of functions in various contexts throughout the OT. Elders sometimes represent the whole people or individual cities (e.g., Exod. 19:7-8; 24:1, 9; Deut. 21:1-9; Judg. 11:4-11); sometimes they serve as governing authorities (e.g., Josh. 20:4; 2 Kgs. 10:1, 5; Ezra 6:7-8), sometimes as judges (e.g., Deut. 21:18-21; Ruth 4:1-12; 1 Kgs. 21:8-14), and sometimes as advisors (e.g,, 2 Sam. 17:4, 15; 1 Kgs. 20:7-8). The institution continued in later times, with councils of elders (Gk. *presbýteros*) serving both administrative and judicial functions in local Jewish communities, as well as representing the community to outside authorities (e.g., Jdt. 7:23; 11:14; 1 Macc. 12:35; Mark 11:27; 15:1; Acts 4:5-8; 24:1). The highest such council was the Sanhedrin in Jerusalem. Some early Christian communities adapted this institution for their own governance. 2 John 1 and 3 John 1 are the only instances in biblical and early Christian literature where an individual is designated "the elder," with no mention of a body of elders. The exact position being claimed is therefore unclear, but evidently this "elder" was of such stature that he could be identified by the title alone.

See PRESBYTER, PRESBYTERY.

DAVID RENSBERGER

ELEAD (Heb. *'el'āḏ*)

One of the sons of Ephraim killed by the inhabitants of Gath while raiding their cattle (1 Chr. 7:21).

ELEADAH (Heb. *'el'āḏâ*)

A descendant of Ephraim (1 Chr. 7:20).

ELEALEH (Heb. *'el'ālēh*)

A Moabite town associated with nearby Heshbon in the judgment oracles in Isa. 15:4; 16:9; Jer. 48:34. Ancient Elealeh ("God is Ascending") has been identified with modern el-'Al (228136), ca. 2.5 km. (1.5 mi.) NE of Heshbon. The plateau north of the Arnon River was well-suited for grazing, so the livestock that the wealthy tribes of Reuben and Gad sought and received from Moses in return for military service made this area a valuable possession (Num. 32:3, 37). The Reubenites built (i.e., rebuilt or fortified) Heshbon and Elealeh (Num. 32:37). Though not named by the Moabite Stone among those towns taken from Israel, Elealeh and other settlements in the tableland fell under Moabite control when King Mesha revolted against Israelite rule ca. 830 B.C. It remained as such at the time of Jeremiah's oracle against Moab (ca. 600).

ROBERT DELSNYDER

ELEASAH (Heb. *'el'āśâ*)

1. A Judahite, son of Helez of the lineage of Jerahmeel (1 Chr. 2:39-40).

2. The son of Raphah, and a descendant of Saul and Jonathan (1 Chr. 8:37). At 1 Chr. 9:43 he is said to be the son of Rephaiah.

ELEAZAR (Heb. *'el'āzār*) (also AVARAN)

1. A son of Aaron, along with Nadab, Abihu, and Ithamar (Exod. 6:23), all of whom were consecrated to the priestly office (Exod. 28:1). While the Israelites were camped at the foot of Mt. Sinai, the two older brothers, Nadab and Abihu, "offered unholy fire before the Lord" and so God destroyed them with fire (Lev. 10:1-2). Eleazar and his younger brother Ithamar were then placed in charge of the tent of meeting, and through them the line of priestly descent from Aaron is traced. Eleazar seems to have held a "senior" position. In Num. 3:32; 4:16 he is described as "chief over the leaders of the Levites," in charge of all matters pertaining to transportation of the tabernacle. Moses named Joshua as his successor, but under the direction of Eleazar (Num. 27:18-23). Sixteen divisions of postexilic priests were assigned to Eleazar and eight to Ithamar (1 Chr. 24). Zadok and Ezra trace their priestly ancestry through Eleazar (1 Chr. 6:3-8, 50-53[MT 5:29-34; 6:35-38]; 24:3; Ezra 7:1-5).

2. The son of Abinadab of Kiriath-jearim (1 Sam. 7:1; 2 Sam. 6:3-4). He was a guardian of the ark of the covenant and father of Uzzah and Ahio, who transferred it to King David (2 Sam. 6:2-7).

3. The son of Dodo; one of David's three mighty men who helped in his battle against the Philistines (2 Sam. 23:9; 1 Chr. 11:12). According to 2 Sam. 23:13-17; 1 Chr. 11:15-19 the three went to Bethlehem when the Philistines occupied it and brought water from its well to David in the cave of Adullam.

4. The son of Mahli, a Merarite. He was a Levite who had no sons, so his daughters married their cousins, the sons of Kish (1 Chr. 23:21-22; 24:28).

5. The son of Phinehas, a priest who accompanied Ezra from Babylon to Jerusalem and helped inventory the returned temple treasury (Ezra 8:33).

6. A priest who took part in the dedication of the wall of Jerusalem (Neh. 12:42); perhaps the same as **5** above.

7. A son of Parosh, one of a group of men who put away their foreign wives at the insistence of Ezra (Ezra 10:25).

8. Also called Avaran; the son of Mattathias, the brother of Judas Maccabeus (1 Macc. 2:5; 6:43-44; 2 Macc. 8:23). He was crushed to death when he killed an elephant in battle at Beth-zecharaiah (1 Macc. 6:44-46).

9. The father of Jason, chosen to be part of Judas Maccabeus' emissary to Rome (1 Macc. 8:17).

10. A high-ranking scribe "in his ninetieth year" who refused to eat swine's flesh during a sacrificial meal instituted by Antiochus IV Epiphanes. Those in charge of the ritual tried to save Eleazar from martyrdom by urging him to bring his own meat to the sacrifice and only pretend to eat the pork, but Eleazar refused and was put to death (2 Macc. 6:18-31).

11. According to Matthew's genealogy, an ancestor of Joseph, the husband of Mary (Matt. 1:15).

NANCY L. DE CLAISSÉ-WALFORD

ELECT LADY

A title appearing only in 2 John 1, 5. The "elect lady" (Gk. *eklektḗ kyría*) is said to have children and an elect sister, who also has children. Some scholars identify her as a house church leader whom "the elder" is writing to encourage and warn not to receive deceivers into her house church. In that case, some of her children are grown and her physical sister lives in the city from which the elder is writing. Most scholars now believe the "elect lady" is a church, the "children" being the members of the church. The "sister" would then be the church in the city from which "the elder" is writing.

PETER H. DAVIDS

ELECTION

Although the terms "elect" and "election" do not appear with great frequency in most English translations, the range of terms associated with them indicate their importance in biblical theology. While election is associated also with such words as "call/calling," "covenant," "predestine," "foreordain," and "people of God," the primary word for expressing the concept of election is the Hebrew verb *bḥr* (Gk. *eklégomai*), commonly rendered "choose." While the term can be used in the ordinary sense of human choice (cf. Gen. 13:11; 1 Sam. 17:40), it is employed primarily to describe God's initiative in choosing a people or individuals for his purposes.

Old Testament

The classical formulation of the doctrine of election is Deut. 7:6-11. Israel is told: "You are a people holy to the Lord your God; the Lord your God has *chosen* you out of all the peoples on earth to be his people, his treasured possession" (v. 6). God *chose* Israel, not because of her superior numbers or morality, but because of his love. This election of Israel is expressed in God's redeeming power and fidelity to the oath sworn to Israel's fathers. Thus, as the author's development of this theme throughout Deuteronomy demonstrates (cf. Deut. 4:19-24; 10:14-22; 14:2; 26:18-19), God's election of Israel is the expression of his steadfast love and fidelity to the promises that he had sworn to the fathers. Indeed, Israel's history and destiny — the promises to

Abraham, the Exodus from Egypt, and the continuing promise of protection from enemies — are aspects of Israel's election (7:8-10). As a consequence of God's choice of Israel, those who are chosen are now required to keep the commandments of the One who has elected them (7:11), for the divine election demands the obedient response of God's people.

The concept of election is most thoroughly developed in the prophetic literature, especially in the work of the anonymous prophet of the Babylonian Exile known as Second Isaiah. In a period of national despair over Israel's defeat, the prophet offers a word of comfort (Isa. 40:9), indicating that Israel has not been rejected (41:9). Indeed, he refers to Israel as God's "chosen" seven times (41:8-9; 43:10, 20; 44:1-2; 45:4), of which all but one reference (43:20) connect the term with the mission of the servant who will be a "light to the nations, that my salvation may reach to the end of the earth" (49:6). Thus the language of election in 2 Isaiah serves as the assurance to a despairing people that Israel has a future that involves, not only Israel's survival, but a blessing to all nations.

Because election is associated with Israel's covenantal obligations, the prophets occasionally reflect on the consequences of Israel's failure to honor her special relationship to God. Amos appeals to the election of Israel when he announces Israel's punishment ("You only have I known of all the families of the earth; therefore I will punish you," Amos 3:2; cf. 9:7). Isa. 65 distinguishes between a "rebellious people" (v. 2) who do not keep the covenant (vv. 2-8, 11-12) and God's "chosen" (vv. 9, 15), who have remained faithful. God promises future blessings for his servants, but punishment for the rebellious people (cf. Isa. 65:15). This distinction between the promises for the "chosen" and the punishment for the disobedient reflects an initial stage in the distinction between "the chosen" and the remainder of Israel.

New Testament

The variety of NT witnesses which incorporate the vocabulary of election attests to the continuing significance of this concept in the early church. Common terms are the "elect" *(eklektós)*, "election" *(eklogḗ)*, and the verb "choose" *(eklégomai)* or terms that belong to the same semantic range (e.g., "call," *kaléō*). Although it can be used for an individual who is chosen for a specific mission (e.g., Paul in Acts 9:15), the primary significance of election lies in its designation of both Jesus Christ and the community of faith.

Jesus Christ

According to 1 Pet. 2:4, 6 Jesus Christ is the "stone" that was rejected by men but *chosen* by God. Although NT writers only rarely describe Christ as the "chosen one" (cf. the comment of scoffers in Luke 23:35; John 1:34), this christological claim plays an important role nevertheless, for the NT frequently cites passages from the OT which resonate with the election theme. 1 Peter's reference to Christ as the chosen one (2:4, 6) comes from Isa. 28:16 (cf. Matt. 21:42; Rom. 9:33; also Eph. 2:20). Similarly, numerous NT writers give a christological interpretation of the Servant Songs of Isa. 40–55 (Matt. 3:17 par.; 8:17; 20:28 par.; Acts 8:32-33; 1 Pet. 2:21-25), which describe the chosen one.

The Community of Faith

The NT most commonly employs election terminology to describe the community of faith. In the Synoptic tradition "the elect" are the faithful who appeal to God for vindication (Luke 18:7) and who withstand the eschatological tribulations (Matt. 24:22, 24) before the Christ comes to "gather his elect" (v. 31). Paul also employs election language to describe his communities. He reminds them of their election (1 Thess. 1:4; cf. Col. 3:12). Indeed, he appeals to the election tradition to explain to the Corinthians that such a community composed primarily of the lower classes is the result of God's election of the weak and foolish things of the world (1 Cor. 1:27-28). The cross itself is nothing less than an example of God's sovereign choice (1 Cor. 1:21).

The presence of the Gentiles in the Church and the rejection of the gospel by Jews provide Paul the occasion for his most thorough development of the concept of election in Rom. 9–11. The question that dominates chs. 9–11 is: Has God's election of Israel failed? In his answer, Paul affirms in 9:6-29 that the present situation, in which Gentiles predominate, is a result of God's sovereign choice. Just as Israel's entire history rests on God's election, the presence of Gentiles is a manifestation of God's choice. According to 9:30–10:21 the gospel has gone out to Israel, which bears the responsibility for its own disobedience. According to ch. 11 the present situation is not final, for the same God who elected Gentiles by grafting them onto the olive tree will also act to bring salvation to Israel. Thus God's election of Israel has not failed, for "all Israel will be saved" (11:26).

Israel's election terminology is pervasive in the NT. 1 Peter is addressed to the "elect exiles" (1 Pet. 1:1-2). This author reminds this community of Gentiles that they are "a chosen race" (2:9) insofar as they follow the stone that was chosen by God (2:4-8). The readers of 2 Peter are challenged to make their "calling and election" sure (2 Pet. 1:10). 2 John is addressed to the "elect lady" (2 John 1). Thus Israel's election language played an important role in shaping the identity of the early Church.

Bibliography. B. S. Childs, *Biblical Theology of the Old and New Testaments* (Minneapolis, 1992); W. G. Kümmel, *The Theology of the New Testament* (Nashville, 1973). JAMES W. THOMPSON

EL-ELOHE-ISRAEL (Heb. *ʾēl ʾělōhê yiśrāʾēl*)
The name of the altar that Jacob erected in Shechem after parting ways with his brother Esau (Gen. 33:20). The phrase may be rendered as "El, the God of Israel," "El is the God of Israel," or "mighty is the God of Israel." Occurring near the conclusion of the Jacob cycle (Gen. 25-35), this declaration marks a final stage in the transformation

of Jacob from trickster to father of the Israelite people. By purchasing the plot of land, erecting and naming the altar, Jacob was both confessing that the God who changed his name at Peniel was now his God (cf. Gen. 28:21) and identifying himself with the land promised to his fathers. By implication the name of the altar is also a confession of the people Israel, and in this sense the individual "Jacob" and the collective "Israel" coalesce.

Tyler F. Williams

EL ELYON (Heb. *'ēl 'elyôn*)
A name of God, translated "Most High" (cf. Ugar. *'ly*). Generally regarded as having derived from the Canaanite creator god worshipped at pre-Israelite Jerusalem (Salem; cf. Gen. 14:18-20), it was adapted as an epithet of Yahweh (cf. Gen. 14:22; Ps. 7:17; 91:9). It is found in the earliest biblical poetry (e.g., Num. 24:16; Deut. 32:8) and later archaizing poetry (e.g., Ps. 78:35; cf. Aram. *'elyônîn,* Dan. 7:18, 22, 25, 27).

ELEMENTAL SPIRITS
A term (Gk. *stoicheía*) meaning: (1) a series of letters or sounds; (2) basic constituent elements or guiding principles; (3) the stars as elemental heavenly bodies; or (4) angels, spirits, or elemental spirits. Paul appears to have either the second or fourth meanings in mind in Gal. 4:3, 9; Col. 2:8, 20. His usage of the term, however, is not clear. The close connection of these elemental spirits with the law in Galatians and philosophy in Colossians suggests that the elemental principles of human teaching may be intended. These elemental spirits might also be active spiritual powers ruling the universe and potentially worshipped by the Galatians and Colossians. This meaning appears intended in Heb. 5:12, where the author refers to the "elements of the oracles of God." In 2 Pet. 3:10, 12 the classical four elements of matter (earth, air, fire, water) are clearly intended by the suggestion that the "elements will dissolve" at the Parousia.

Matthew S. Collins

ELEPHANTINE (Gk. *Elephantinê*) **PAPYRI**
A large number of papyrus documents and fragments, written in Aramaic during the 5th century B.C.E., discovered at Elephantine, an island in the Nile River opposite Aswan (biblical Syene) which became an asylum for Judean refugees after the Babylonian conquest of Jerusalem (cf. Jer. 43–44). The papyri, which offer a comprehensive glimpse at the religious and social life of the Jewish colonists, include contracts, private letters, historical and literary texts (esp. the Aramaic Book of Ahiqar), and official correspondence with the Egyptian and Persian authorities and the Jerusalem priesthood.

In 525 the Persian king Cambyses captured Egypt, and the Jewish settlement was made a military garrison to secure the southern boundary of the empire. Even before this, the Jewish colony had established its own temple where the national God Yhw (an abbreviation of YHWH) was worshipped in association with a female counterpart (Anatyhw) and other deities of the Canaanite pantheon. In the temple, meal offering, incense, and animal sacrifices were performed by the local Jewish priesthood. Initially, the mode of worship of the Elephantine Jews (so manifestly opposed to Deuteronomistic rules) was a peculiar development of possibly North-Israelite syncretistic elements in a polytheistic Egyptian environment. A reassessment of the largely polytheistic nature of the Israelite religion before the Babylonian period has led modern scholars to reconsider the Elephantine experience as a vestige of preexilic Yahwism, which the Bible would label in retrospect as Canaanite corruption. The findings at Elephantine are strikingly similar to what was discovered in other preexilic Jewish sanctuaries, notably at 7th-century Kuntillet 'Ajrud. The religious conservatism of Elephantine was not the mere consequence of geographical isolation; it testifies to the historical process through which the Babylonian exiles struggled to impose their authority and their ideal of exclusive monotheism on Jews in and outside Jerusalem during the 5th century. The Elephantine colonists always regarded themselves as Jews and were considered as such by the Persian authorities, as testified by the sending of an official letter at the time of Darius II (419) containing regulations for the feast of Passover. When in 410 the Elephantine temple was destroyed by the Egyptians, possibly in an anti-Persian riot, the Elephantine priests appealed to the political and religious authorities in Jerusalem, the high priest Johanan and the Persian governor Bagoas (Neh. 12:22; Josephus *Ant.* 11:297-301). Apparently, the Elephantine priests received support for reconstruction of the temple, although they were no longer allowed to offer animal sacrifice. A few years later, at the beginning of the 4th century, with the end of the Persian influence in Egypt, the Jewish garrison at Elephantine was moved and the temple abandoned.

Bibliography. A. E. Cowley, *Aramaic Papyri of the Fifth Century* B.C. (1923, repr. Osnabrück, 1967); E. G. Kraeling, *The Brooklyn Museum Aramaic Papyri* (1953, repr. New York, 1969); B. Porten and A. Yardeni, *Textbook of Aramaic Documents from Ancient Egypt,* 1: *Letters* (Jerusalem, 1986).

Gabriele Boccaccini

ELEVATION OFFERING
A sacrificial offering. The precise meaning of Heb. *tĕnûpâ* has been disputed, since the LXX translators rendered it inconsistently. The traditional translation "wave offering" is unlikely and is better translated "elevation offering" because the hiphil verb *hēnîp̱* can be used for a fist outstretched to strike (Isa. 19:16) and because moving large offerings horizontally would be difficult (Lev. 8:27). Moreover, alleged Hittite parallels of waving motions occur in magical rituals, not in sacrifice; Egyptian examples of elevation offerings also exist.

Israelite priests performed this ritual within the temple precincts ("before Yahweh," Exod. 29:24-25; Lev. 7:30; Num. 8:11, 21; but "to Yahweh" in Exod. 35:22; Num. 8:13) as part of the "sin offering" (*ḥaṭṭā't*; Lev. 9:21) and at the purification of persons with skin diseases (14:12). Gold dedicated to the building of the tabernacle underwent elevation as a mark of its consecration (Exod. 35:22; 38:24-29). The elevation of a sheaf of barley marked the end of the Feast of Unleavened Bread and the deconsecration of the grain crop (Lev. 23:15). At Pentecost an elevation offering of two loaves of bread opened a series of sacrifices (Lev. 23:17, 20). A similar procedure is featured in the ordeal of the accused adulteress (Num. 5:25) and in the ritual concluding the Nazirite's vocation (6:20).

Elevating the offering apparently had several purposes. In most cases, and always when animal meat and fat constituted the sacrifice, the ritual marked a change in ownership of the sacrifice from the offerer to God, and its consecration for the presiding priest's meal (Lev. 7:24-36) Major sacrifices such as the purification, holocaust, burnt, and "sin" offerings were not elevated because they already belonged to Yahweh. Moreover, the priest lifted only those parts of the carcass that he would eat (the breast and right shank), not the parts returning to the worshipper. Exceptions to these conditions exist in the grain offerings in Lev. 23; Num. 5, all of which depart from the norm by being of barley rather than wheat and by lacking oil and incense. Also dissimilar is the offering for the person with scale disease, which cannot be paid in silver, unlike reparation offerings in other contexts.

The elevation offering could occur at various points of the ritual cycle: with grain offerings at the beginning (Lev. 23:15) and with meat and mixed offerings in the middle (Exod. 29:23-26; Num. 5:25; Lev. 14:12) or at the end (Exod. 29:27-28; Lev. 9:21) of the ceremony. Notably, the elevation offering marks the transition to the ritual exit (through blessing) in the inaugural service of the priest (Lev. 9:21), perhaps to signify his new right to preside at all sacrifices. The elevation of the offering thus marked important transitions in the ritual, especially prior to its climax.

Bibliography. B. A. Levine, *Leviticus.* JPS Torah Commentary (Philadelphia, 1989); J. Milgrom, *Leviticus 1–16.* AB 3 (New York, 1991).

MARK W. HAMILTON

ELEVEN, THE

A designation for Jesus' eleven disciples (Gk. *hoi héndeka*) in the brief period succeeding Judas' death and preceding his replacement by Matthias (Acts 1:26). The risen Savior appeared to them on two, possibly three, occasions — at Jerusalem (Luke 24:9, 33), in Galilee (Matt. 28:16), possibly elsewhere (Mark 16:14). At Acts 2:14 Peter is depicted as the representative of the Eleven, an interpretation supported by Codex Bezae (D), which reads "the ten."

ELHANAN (Heb. *'elḥānān*)

1. The son of Jair (or Jaare-oregim) of Bethlehem who slew a Philistine at Gob. There is a textual problem concerning the identity of Elhanan's father and his Philistine opponent. Likely the original name Jair (1 Chr. 20:5) was corrupted by the copyist of 2 Sam. 21:19, who also inadvertently repeated the Hebrew word *'ōreḡîm* ("weavers") and appended it to Jaare, resulting in the name Jaare-oregim. While 2 Samuel identifies Elhanan's Philistine adversary as Goliath, in 1 Chronicles he is designated as Lahmi, the brother of Goliath.

2. The son of Dodo of Bethlehem; listed among David's "Thirty" mighty men (2 Sam. 23:24; 1 Chr. 11:26). Although some consider this Elhanan to be the same individual who slew the Philistine at Gob (**1** above), the differing patronymics suggest otherwise. It is also unlikely that either Elhanan is to be identified with David. KENNETH ATKINSON

ELI (Heb. *'ēlî*)

Priest of the Shiloh sanctuary just before the emergence of monarchy (1 Sam. 1–4). In that role he wears the ephod, pronounces oracles, burns incense, and supervises sacrifice. Eli is also named judge in Israel, credited with 40 years at his death (1 Sam. 4:18).

Three related episodes cluster around Eli. First, when the childless Hannah and her husband Elkanah arrive to sacrifice at Shiloh, Hannah prays for a son, whom she promises to Yahweh's service. Eli, overhearing her prayer, misconstrues her articulation as drunkenness and chides her. Once she has corrected his misapprehension, he pronounces an oracle of fulfillment to her words, verified when Samuel is born and brought to the shrine (1 Sam. 1:9-28). A second episode occurs when Yahweh comes to the young Samuel at the shrine in a night audition and pronounces the end of Eli's priestly line, the result of the behavior of Eli's sons Hophni and Phineas: cultic violation and sexual immorality, sustained and recalcitrant (1 Sam. 2:12-36). The third event is Eli's death, occasioned by the news of devastation of Israel at the hands of the Philistines: military defeat at Aphek includes as well the death of Eli's sons and the capture of the ark of the covenant (1 Sam. 4:12-18).

Eli's priestly line both precedes and survives him. Founded before Israel leaves Egypt and descended from Aaron's son Ithamar, Elide priests are associated with Saul, who tries to extirpate them (1 Sam. 21–22); David, whose court includes the Elide Abiathar (2 Sam. 15–19); and Solomon, whose banishment of Abiathar brings the line to an end, as Yahweh had indicated to Samuel (1 Kgs. 2).

Historians discern in the fragments of Elide genealogy either genuine ancient memory or evidence of redaction and theological intent, with the Ithamar-Eli group subsidiary to the rival house of Phineas-descended Zadokites. Powerful characterization of Eli in the Deuteronomistic history shows the aged, heavy, and blind leader sitting passively on his throne to await the report of the fate of Israel, proleptically symbolizing the monarchy itself — doomed and toppled from its place as exile begins.

Bibliography. R. D. Nelson, *Raising Up a Faithful Priest* (Louisville, 1993); R. Polzin, *Samuel and the Deuteronomist* (1989, repr. Bloomington, Ind., 1993).

BARBARA GREEN, O.P.

ELI, ELI, LAMA SABACHTHANI
(Gk. *ēlí ēlí lemá sabachtháni*)
Traditionally known as the fourth word on the cross, Jesus' last response on the cross (Matt. 27:46). The sentence "My God, my God, why have you forsaken me?" is a Greek transliteration of a Hebrew version of Ps. 22:1(MT 2). The parallel question (Mark 15:34; Gk. *elōí elōí lemá sabachtháni*) is a Greek transliteration of an Aramaic version of Ps. 22:1(2). In both Matthew and Mark a Greek translation follows the transliteration.

Jesus speaks these words after a three-hour period of darkness over the whole land, one of the signs that his death anticipates the Parousia. In both Gospels bystanders think that Jesus is calling out to Elijah to help him. Those listening to or reading either Gospel know, however, that Elijah will not save Jesus since Elijah had already returned in the person of John the Baptist, whom Herod had beheaded. If Jesus' words recall to Mark's and Matthew's audiences the entirety of Ps. 22, which concludes with the psalmist's trust in God, then they may have also understood Jesus' words as an expression of his trust in God in the midst of his anguish. EMILY CHENEY

ELIAB (Heb. *'ĕlî'āḇ*)
1. The son of Helon; leader of the Zebulunites during the wilderness period (Num. 2:7; 10:16). He assisted Moses in the census of the Exodus generation (Num. 1:9) and brought an offering to the tabernacle when it was completed (7:24-29).

2. A descendant of Reuben (Num. 26:8-9); father of Dothan and Abiram, who participated in a revolt against Moses and Aaron (16:1, 12; Deut. 11:6).

3. The firstborn son of Jesse (1 Sam. 17:13; 1 Chr. 2:13). He was Samuel's first choice to be the new king of Israel (1 Sam. 16:6). While serving with Saul's forces during the Philistine wars, he chastised David for inquiring among the Israelites concerning the challenge of Goliath (1 Sam. 17:13, 28-30). Eliab's daughter Abihail married Jerimoth, the son of David, and bore Mahalath, who married Rehoboam (2 Chr. 11:18).

4. A descendant of Levi (1 Chr. 6:27) and a possible ancestor of Samuel.

5. A Gadite who joined David at Ziklag during his flight from Saul and who served as an officer in David's army (1 Chr. 12:9).

6. A Levite appointed to play harps in the worship relating to the ark of the covenant in the Jerusalem tabernacle (1 Chr. 15:18-20; 16:5).

7. An ancestor of Judith (Jdt. 8:1).

MICHAEL L. RUFFIN

ELIADA (Heb. *'elyāḏā'*) (also BEELIADA)
1. One of David's sons born in Jerusalem of an unnamed mother (2 Sam. 5:16; 1 Chr. 3:8). In a parallel list he is named Beeliada (1 Chr. 14:7).

2. The father of the Syrian king Rezon, the adversary of Solomon (1 Kgs. 11:23).

3. A Benjaminite who assumed a commanding position in the army of King Jehoshaphat (2 Chr. 17:17).

ELIAHBA (Heb. *'elyaḥbā'*)
A man from Shaalbon, one of David's Thirty (2 Sam. 23:32 = 1 Chr. 11:33).

ELIAKIM (Heb. *'elyāqîm*)
1. A court official under King Hezekiah, involved in negotiations to end Sennacherib's invasion of Judah (2 Kgs. 18:17–19:7 = Isa. 36:3–37:7). Eliakim, described as being "in charge of the palace," was sent, along with Shebnah and Joah, to meet an Assyrian delegation comprised of the Tartan, the Rabsaris, and the Rabshakeh. When the Rabshakeh pointed out the precarious position of Judah, Eliakim and his cohorts asked that he speak in Aramaic rather than Hebrew so the people of Jerusalem would not understand. When the Rabshakeh refused, the three messengers reported the news to Hezekiah. Hezekiah went into mourning and sent Eliakim, Shebna, and some priests to see Isaiah, who delivered an oracle of hope. In another oracle (which appears to predate the events described above), Isaiah proclaimed that Eliakim would usurp the role of Shebna as "master of the household," but he too seems to have lost favor (Isa. 22:15-25).

2. A son of Josiah, brother of Jehoahaz (2 Kgs. 23:29–24:7 = 2 Chr. 36:3-8). When Josiah was killed in battle with Pharaoh Neco in 609 B.C.E., Jehoahaz became king. After three months Neco deposed Jehoahaz, exiling him to Riblah, and made Eliakim king, changing his name to Jehoiakim. Eliakim ruled from 609 to 597. At first loyal to Egypt, Eliakim switched his allegiance to the Babylonian Nebuchadnezzar, only to rebel against Nebuchadnezzar in hope of siding with Egypt. According to 2 Kgs. 24:7 he died during the subsequent Babylonian siege of Jerrusalem, while according to 2 Chr. 36:6-7 he was taken captive to Babylon.

3. A priest who participated in the thanksgiving service for the completion of the walls of Jerusalem during the governorship of Nehemiah, part of a group playing trumpets (Neh. 12:41).

4. The grandson of Zerubbabel, the son of Abiud, and the father of Azor in Matthew's genealogy of Jesus (Matt. 1:13).

5. A descendant of David, son of Melea and father of Jonam in Luke's genealogy of Jesus (Luke 3:30). MICHAEL L. RUFFIN

ELIAM (Heb. *'ĕlî'ām*) (also AMMIEL)
1. The father of Bathsheba, the wife of Uriah the Hittite (2 Sam. 11:3). At 1 Chr. 3:5 he is called Ammiel.

2. The son of Ahithophel of Gilo, who became one of David's Thirty (2 Sam. 23:34).

ELIASAPH (Heb. *'elyāsāp̱*)
1. The head of the tribe of Gad, who assisted Moses in the census (Num. 1:14) and the offering (7:42, 47); son of Deuel (Num. 10:42) or Reuel (2:14).

2. The son of Lael; a chief of the Gershonites during the wilderness wanderings (Num. 3:24).

ELIASHIB (Heb. *'elyāšîḇ*)
A personal name (lit., "God restores") for seven individuals associated with the postexilic literature of the OT. Such names were once thought to be limited to the postexilic period, but the preexilic Arad Letters contain references to an Eliashib who held a position of responsibility in the Judean garrison.

1. A descendant of David who lived possibly sometime during the 4th century B.C.E. (1 Chr. 3:24).

2. A priest from the time of David and a descendant of Aaron, who was named 11th in importance (1 Chr. 24:12).

3. The father of Jehohanan, the high priest, to whose chamber Ezra retired to mourn the state of the exiles (Ezra 10:6). It is not clear whether this latter character is to be identified with the high priest in Neh. 12:23. Such an identification would affect the chronology of the missions of Ezra and Nehemiah.

4. A singer in the time of Ezra who had married and then divorced a non-Israelite wife (Ezra 10:24).

5. A descendant of Zattu, who had also married and divorced a non-Israelite wife (Ezra 10:27).

6. A descendant of Bani, who had married and divorced a non-Israelite wife (Ezra 10:36).

7. The high priest at the time of Nehemiah who supported Nehemiah in his program of rebuilding Jerusalem (Neh. 3:1, 20-21) and who was associated by marriage with Sanballat, Nehemiah's opponent (13:28).

8. A Levite, descended from Jeshua; son of Joiakim and father of Joiada (Neh. 12:10).

9. A priest of the temple staff during the period of Nehemiah who allied himself with another of Nehemiah's opponents, Tobiah (Neh. 13:4-7).

T. R. HOBBS

ELIATHAH (Heb. *'ĕlî'āṯâ*)
One of the sons of Heman who served as a temple musician during the reign of King David (1 Chr. 25:4), by lot assigned to direct the twentieth division of musicians (v. 27).

ELIDAD (Heb. *'ĕlîḏāḏ*)
The son of Chislon and representative of the tribe of Benjamin chosen to assist in the division of the land (Num. 34:21).

ELIEHOENAI (Heb. *'elyĕhô'ênay*)

1. The seventh son of Meshelemiah, a Levite and gatekeeper of the temple (1 Chr. 26:3).

2. The son of Zerahiah; head of a family of exiles returning with Ezra (Ezra 8:4).

ELIEL (Heb. *'ĕlî'ēl*)

1. Head of a Transjordanian Manassite household deported by the Assyrian king Tiglath-pileser III (1 Chr. 5:24).

2. A Levite from the family of Kohath and an ancestor of the prophet Samuel. His name appears in the levitical lists of Elihu (1 Sam. 1:1) and Eliab (1 Chr. 6:27[MT 12]). He was appointed by David to be a singer for the temple services (1 Chr. 6:34[19]).

3. A Benjaminite named in the Chronicler's genealogy as son of Shimei (**11;** 1 Chr. 8:20) and son of Shashak (v. 22).

4. A Mahavite and one of David's "mighty men" (1 Chr. 11:26, 46); another Eliel may be listed in v. 47.

5. One of the Gadites who came to David at the stronghold Ziklag (1 Chr. 12:1, 8, 11).

6. A Levite of the sons of Hebron who helped David transfer the ark to Jerusalem (1 Chr. 15:9, 11).

7. A Levite and overseer of tithes, offerings, and temple contributions under Hezekiah (2 Chr. 31:13).

CAROL J. DEMPSEY

ELIENAI (Heb. *'ĕlî'ênay*)
A Benjaminite chief, head of an ancestral house living in Jerusalem; descendant of Shimei (**11;** 1 Chr. 8:20).

ELIEZER (Heb. *'ĕlî'ezer*) (also ELEAZAR)

1. The oldest and most trusted of Abraham's servants (Gen. 15:2-3). Ancient Near Eastern texts contain references to the practice of adopting servants as heirs in the case of childlessness, and the story of Abraham here reflects such influences. Later, Eliezer chooses a wife for Isaac (Gen. 24:2).

2. The younger of the two sons of Moses and Zipporah (Exod. 18:4). In 1 Chr. 23:17 Eliezer becomes the head of a levitical family and has a son named Rehabiah. 1 Chr. 26:25 lists Jeshaiah, Joram, Zichri, and Shelomoth as Eliezer's descendants.

3. A mighty warrior, one of the sons of Becher and a member of the tribe of Benjamin (1 Chr. 7:8).

4. One of the priests who blows the trumpet before the ark of the covenant (1 Chr. 15:24).

5. The son of Zichri and chief officer of the Reubenites under the reign of David (1 Chr. 27:16).

6. The son of Dodavahu of Mareshah, who prophesies the destruction of King Jehoshaphat of Judah for his alliance with Ahaziah, Israel's wicked king (2 Chr. 20:35-37).

7. One of the priests sent by Ezra to Casiphia to find "ministers for the house of our God" in Jerusalem (Ezra 8:16-17).

8. One of the sons of priests who had pledged to divorce their foreign wives and provide a guilt offering (Ezra 10:18; called Eleazar at 1 Esdr. 9:19).

9. A Levite who divorced his foreign wife (Ezra 10:23).

10. One of the sons of Harim who divorced his foreign wife (Ezra 10:31).

11. An ancestor of Jesus (Luke 3:29).

HENRY L. CARRIGAN, JR.

ELIHOREPH (Heb. *'ĕlîḥōrep̄*)
A high official at the Solomonic court, who with his brother Ahijah served as royal secretary (1 Kgs. 4:3).

ELIHU (Heb. *'ĕlîhû*) (also ELIAB, ELIEL)

1. An Ephraimite, the son of Tohu, and great-grandfather of Samuel (1 Sam. 1:1); he is called Eliel at 1 Chr. 6:34 and Eliab at 1 Chr. 6:27.

2. A chief of a thousand from Manasseh who defected to David at Ziklag (1 Chr. 12:20).

3. A gatekeeper in the temple, of the lineage of Obed-edom (1 Chr. 26:7).

4. A brother of David, chief officer of the tribe of Issachar (1 Chr. 27:18). The LXX reads Eliab, the same as David's oldest brother mentioned at 1 Sam. 16:6-7.

5. The son of Barachel; young friend and final debater of Job (Job 32–37), the only speaker in the book with an Israelite name.

Scholars argue that these chapters are a secondary insertion into the book because: Elihu is mentioned nowhere else, including the epilogue; the style is pretentious, inferior to the remainder of the book; and the speeches disrupt the book's continuity and contribute little. Much recent scholarship refutes these arguments. Satan is also not mentioned in the epilogue, yet is integral to the book; perhaps neither is deemed worthy of mention in the epilogue. The different style may be a deliberate authorial intent to portray a self-inflated speaker.

Various opinions exist concerning the contribution of the Elihu speeches to the book. Some regard them as a critique of the prophetic tradition (J. Gerald Janzen). They act as a foil for the divine speeches: Elihu states that no one shall ever hear God speak, but then God speaks (J. G. Herder). Elihu assumes the mediator role, defender of God (Norman C. Habel). Elihu's solution of suffering as disciplinary, purging the heart of pride, is the book's climax (Karl Budde). Elihu's speeches are an early critique of the book, inserted by a later wisdom teacher (Claus Westermann). Elihu is purposefully portrayed by the author as a brash fool (Janzen, Habel). He is undercut by the divine speeches and the epilogue which ignore him and by his own speeches, where his anger and tactlessness prove him the antithesis of a wise man (cf. Prov. 12:15-16; 14:17, 29). He unwittingly characterizes himself as a windbag (Job 32:18). Elihu claims divine inspiration as his authoritative source (32:8, 18; 33:4). His main argument, that suffering is disciplinary, was already broached by Eliphaz (5:17).

Bibliography. J. G. Janzen, *Job.* Interpretation (Atlanta, 1985); M. H. Pope, *Job.* AB (Garden City, 1973).

PATRICIA A. MACNICOLL

ELIJAH (Heb. *'ēlîyāhû*)

A fiercely Yahwist prophet in the tradition of Moses. The Elijah cycle (1 Kgs. 17–19, 21; 2 Kgs. 1:1–2:18) is a collection of legends which circulated and were preserved within the prophetic community of which Elijah ("Yahweh is my God") was a part, before being incorporated into the Deuteronomistic history. Portrayed as an individual of remarkable strength and energy, Elijah was active during the 9th century B.C.E. reign of King Ahab, politically one of the great rulers of the northern kingdom.

Having come from Gilead, east of the Jordan, where Yahwism had most likely preserved its separation from other cults, Elijah was appalled by the syncretism he encountered in Israel. Ahab's wife Jezebel, a princess of Tyre, was a devotee of the Phoenician Baal. To make her feel at home, Ahab erected "a temple of Baal" in Samaria (1 Kgs. 16:32-33). The Canaanite fertility cult, ever a threat to Yahweh worship, now had a fanatical evangelist in Jezebel who imported a large number of Baal prophets from Phoenicia, supported them out of state funds (1 Kgs. 18:19), and began an enthusiastic campaign to make the Phoenician Baal the only deity of Israel. Although Ahab "served Baal a little" (2 Kgs. 10:18), he did not intend to reject Yahweh, as the names of his children — Ahaziah, Jehoram, Athaliah (all formed with the divine name, Yahweh) indicate. Rather, Ahab's tolerant position was designed to allow his wife freedom of religion, just as Solomon had done with his foreign wives. But such collaborative, permissive ideas were incompatible with Yahweh's claim for exclusive allegiance and led to the prophetic guilds' trenchant criticism of the court's "limping with two different opinions" (1 Kgs. 18:21). This was the prelude to a general persecution in which altars of Yahweh were torn down, prophets were killed, and loyal adherents were driven underground.

It was against this background of struggle between Yahwism and Baalism that Elijah appeared suddenly in Ahab's court to announce, in the name of Yahweh, that there would be a paralyzing drought. Thus Elijah threw out a potent challenge to Baal in the arena of his expertise — fertility. Indeed, the crucial question behind all of the stories in 1 Kgs. 17 is, "Who has the power of life?" Although the worshippers of Baal believed their god was the possessor of that power, the series of vignettes in 1 Kgs. 17 is designed to show that the very power attributed to Baal is controlled by Israel's God. It is Yahweh who has the power to assuage hunger (1 Kgs. 17:2-7, 8-16) and overcome death (vv. 9-24). It is noteworthy that Yahweh's power is not confined to Israel. Rather, as Elijah's replenishment of the food supply for the widow in Zarephath makes clear, Yahweh's power extends to Phoenicia as well, the special preserve of Jezebel's Baal. Further, while Baal's concern is not with widows, but with the status quo, Yahweh defends the weak and gives life to those without social power.

As drought and famine devastated the country so that even the king was forced to scour the land for water and grass to keep the animals alive, Elijah received a divine order to confront Ahab again (1 Kgs. 18:1-18). After an angry exchange, the monarch agreed to a trial of strength between Elijah and Jezebel's prophets of Baal and Asherah, i.e., between Yahweh and Baal. The description of the contest is one of the most dramatic biblical accounts. Meeting on Mt. Carmel, Elijah accused the people of syncretistic behavior, trying to keep one foot on Israel's traditional path and the other in the worship of Baal (v. 21). Thus, the clear object of the contest was to determine who was really lord and controller of rain and fertility. The author delights in stressing the unevenness of the proceedings. After all, Elijah was outnumbered 450 to 1 (v. 22), and rain was Baal's specialty. The scene on Mt. Carmel is dominated by the motifs of calling and answering, silence and responsiveness. Both parties agree to call on their deity, to perform their rites, with the understanding that "the god who answers by fire is indeed God" (v. 24). As Elijah satirically taunts their efforts, the Baal prophets rant, rave, and slash themselves (vv. 27-28). There is, however, "no voice, no answer, and no response" (v. 29). Then Elijah takes center stage, repairing an abandoned Yahweh altar and so reclaiming a cult site for Yahweh which had been under Phoenician control and used to stage Baal's ritual dances. The prophet prepares his sacrifice and then commands the people to drench the altar with water, a priceless sacrifice during a drought (vv. 33-35). Elijah calls out to Yahweh, who responds by sending fire, the traditional symbol of God's active historical presence, to consume the offering. Convinced by the spectacle, the people exclaim, "Yahweh indeed is God" (v. 39), and the Baal prophets are condemned to death (v. 40). It is important to note that the real climax of the narrative is the end of the drought (vv. 41-46). The descent of rain was proof that Yahweh, not Baal, controlled the productivity of the land and merited the people's total allegiance. Although Yahweh's resounding victory appeared definitive, royal policy was not swayed. A few years later there were enough Baal worshippers to fill a Baal temple (2 Kgs. 10:21).

When Jezebel heard of the outcome at Mt. Carmel, she swore an oath by the gods that she would do to Elijah what he had done to the Baal prophets (1 Kgs. 19:1-2). In fear, Elijah fled for his life, passing through Judah and beyond Beer-sheba into the wilderness. Broken and fatigued, Elijah fell asleep in the shade of a broom shrub, wondering how Yahweh could be sovereign when Jezebel's power was undiminished (1 Kgs. 19:3-4). Touched by a messenger of God, Elijah was divinely provided with food, a sign that he had not been deserted by Yahweh. He was thus able to continue his journey for another "40 days and 40 nights," i.e., a long time (1 Kgs. 19:5-8).

Elijah's encounter with Yahweh at Horeb (1 Kgs. 19:9-19) is set off by an inclusion ("there" and "from there"), which highlights Elijah's trip to and from the sacred space of Israel's tradition. Although allusions to Moses pervade the account and seem to present Elijah as Moses *redivivus* — the place is the same, Horeb; the visitation is accompanied by earthquake, wind, and fire, the traditional phenomena of Yahweh's revelation on the sacred mountain (Exod. 19) — it is also possible to see polemical motifs at work here. The prophet flees to Horeb, which is located in the south of Palestine, far away from Baal's domain on Mt. Casius *(Spn)* in the north. Thus, Elijah announces that *Spn* is not the center for divine inspiration. Further, although wind, earthquake, and fire accompany Yahweh's theophany, the deity is not in those violent elements. Unlike his rival, the storm-god Baal, Yahweh possesses all the attributes of a storm-god, but is not part of nature, rather above it and controlling it.

Yahweh's words to Elijah take the form of a pronouncement that has been variously translated as "a low, muttering sound," "the soft whisper of a voice," "a sound of sheer silence," "a still, small voice" (1 Kgs. 19:12). In complete contrast to the thunderous storm-god, Yahweh's was a quiet speech that could be heard only if one devoted oneself to listening for it. Yahweh commissions Elijah to anoint Hazael king of Damascus, Jehu king of Israel, and Elisha his successor (1 Kgs. 19:15-18). Although Elijah performs only one of the three commissionings (1 Kgs. 19:19-21), their mention here makes it clear that because Yahweh acts in the sphere of history, the prophets cannot hide from those places where history is being made. They may journey back to Horeb for inspiration, but they are summoned to take their stand in the current situations in which the people of God find themselves.

The well-known story of Naboth's vineyard is told as the setting for Elijah's curse on King Ahab and his house (1 Kgs. 21:1-29). Here the clash between Yahwism and the Baal cult is seen in opposing views of kingship and social relationships. Naboth, whose vineyard Ahab wants, insists that he does not have the freedom to sell the inheritance of his ancestors. Although Ahab apparently accepts Naboth's right of refusal, it is Jezebel's appearance on the scene that brings a turning point. Her Baal religion placed no limitations on the exercise of royal power. Indeed, she viewed the king in oriental fashion as an absolute despot with rights to take whatever he wanted, including land. Thus, when Ahab refuses to assert himself, Jezebel takes the matter into her own hands. In Ahab's name she orders a fast (something done only during a time of crisis) in Naboth's town. Two scoundrels bring trumped-up charges against Naboth, that he "cursed God and the king" (v. 10), a particularly heinous crime since it was believed that the spoken word was immediately effective. To wipe out the curse, Naboth is executed (v. 13) and Ahab takes over the vineyard he covets (v. 16). Directed by Yahweh, Elijah meets Ahab at the vineyard and proclaims that such behavior is condemned by God. Divine judgment is pronounced that will eventually destroy Ahab's house (vv. 21ff.).

It is interesting to note that according to 2 Kgs. 9:21-26, Ahab and not Jezebel was originally considered responsible for Naboth's death. It has been suggested that during Nehemiah and Ezra's fight against intermarriage (5th-4th centuries B.C.E.), responsibility was shifted from Ahab to Jezebel (1 Kgs. 21), the seductive, foreign woman, and through her all foreign women were stigmatized.

In the Baal cult, which supported the status quo with the aristocracy on top, there were no safeguards against a rapacious social policy of the strong against the weak. Elijah, however, proclaimed a deity who upholds a covenant community in which every person, rich or poor, king or commoner, stands equally before the law.

The Elijah cycle of stories ends with the prophet's being taken up to heaven by a whirlwind, while horses and chariots of fire interpose between Elijah and his chosen successor, Elisha (2 Kgs. 2:1-

18). Set between the obituary of King Ahaziah (2 Kgs. 1:17-18) and the accession of Jehoram (3:1-3), the narrative seems cut off from the usual flow of history. Its locale, across the Jordan which Elijah miraculously parts by striking it with his mantle, is also portrayed as removed from the ordinary world. The prophets of Jericho who were following Elijah and Elisha do not make the crossing. As during his life Elijah was depicted as an elusive wanderer, appearing and disappearing at a moment's notice, so at the end it was told that he vanished, carried heavenward by fiery horses and a chariot. The watching Elisha was left empowered. He was given the legacy of a firstborn son, a "double portion" of Elijah's spirit as well as the prophet's mantle which Elisha also uses to part the Jordan and so reenter the historical sphere where the waiting prophets recognize him as their new leader (2 Kgs. 2:19-25).

The mystery of Elijah's translation clearly made a profound impression on Israel's imagination. Indeed, that Elijah was supposed not to have experienced death like ordinary people sets the foundation for the growing role he was to play in later OT, intertestamental, and NT traditions. Thus, in Mal. 4:5-6(MT 3:23-24), Elijah was expected to return as the forerunner of the coming Day of Yahweh. He was expected to reconcile humankind (Mal. 4:6[3:24]) and to come forth from the heavenly chambers "to restore the tribes of Jacob" (Sir. 48:10). In the early Christian community, Elijah was the acknowledged precursor of the Messiah (Mark 6:14-15; 8:27-28; Matt. 16:13-14; Luke 9:7-8). Jesus was thought to be Elijah by some (Matt. 16:14), and John the Baptist was asked whether he was Elijah (John 1:21, 25). Along with Moses, Elijah appears at Jesus' transfiguration (Mark 9:4; Matt. 17:3; Luke 9:30), suggesting a tradition of two messianic forerunners (Mark 9:4-5; Rev. 11:3). In the Epistle of James, Elijah, "a human being like us," is proposed as a model of prayer (Jas. 5:17).

Bibliography. L. Bronner, *The Stories of Elijah and Elisha.* Pretoria Oriental Series 6 (Leiden, 1968); W. Brueggemann, *A Social Reading of the Old Testament* (Minneapolis, 1994); J. Jeremias, "Ēl(e)ías," *TDNT* 2:928-41; A. Rofé, "The Vineyard of Naboth: The Origin and Message of the Story," *VT* 38 (1988): 89-104. BETH GLAZIER-MCDONALD

ELIJAH, APOCALYPSE OF

References to apocalypses of Elijah and to writings by Elijah occur in postbiblical Jewish and Christian writings. Only two are extant. Their relationship is uncertain, but they may have a common source as evidenced by their traditions about the antichrist.

1. A Jewish-Christian book from 150-275 C.E., probably composed in Greek and extant in Coptic and Greek. One manuscript is titled "Apocalypse of Elijah," although Elijah is mentioned only at 4:7-19; 5:32. The source seems to have a Palestinian provenance; the later Jewish and Christian strata, an Egyptian provenance. The Jewish stratum possibly dates from before the destruction of the Jewish quarter in Alexandria (117).

The book consists of five chapters: a homily on fasting and the need for single-mindedness (ch. 1); a prophecy of events leading up to the time of the antichrist (2); a description of the antichrist (3); an account of the martyrdoms (4); and prophecies of events "on that day" when God rescues the righteous and judges the wicked (5).

2. A Jewish apocalypse written in Hebrew (mid-6th to early 7th centuries C.E.). In it appear Michael's revelations to Elijah on Mt. Carmel, details of an otherworldly journey, a discussion about the name of the last king, a description of the antichrist, events of the final year, and five visions.

Bibliography. D. Frankfurter, *Elijah in Upper Egypt: The Apocalypse of Elijah and Early Egyptian Christianity.* Studies in Antiquity and Christianity 7 (Minneapolis, 1993); O. S. Wintermute, "Apocalypse of Elijah," *OTP* 1:721-53.

R. GLENN N. WOODEN

ELIKA (Heb. *'ĕlîqā'*)

A man from Harod; one of David's Thirty (2 Sam. 23:25).

ELIM (Heb. *'êlim*)

The second named campsite of the children of Israel at least four days after the crossing of the Red Sea (Exod. 15:27–16:1; Num. 33:9-10). The name probably indicates a type of tree or an entire palm grove (cf. El-paran). Another possible meaning could be "gods" (unlikely due to the spelling). Perhaps Elim was a border oasis between the Wilderness of Shur and the Wilderness of Sin (more specifically between Marah and Sin). According to the biblical account, Elim had 12 springs of water and 70 date palms (Exod. 15:27). In the rugged terrain of the Sinai, wilderness areas do not have exact boundaries. Therefore, Elim could have served as a point of demarcation between Shur and Sin. Elim is usually located in the Wadi el-Gharandel, 90-100 km. (56-62 mi.) SE of Suez. PETE F. WILBANKS

ELIMELECH (Heb. *'ĕlîmelek̲*)

A native of Bethlehem and husband of Naomi. When a severe famine hit the land, Elimelech moved his family to neighboring Moab where he soon died (Ruth 1:1-3), leaving his widow to dispose of his land (4:3, 9). Elimelech's two sons, Mahlon and Chilion, who had married Moabite women, also died (Ruth 1:3-5). His daughter-in-law Ruth married Boaz, a kinsman, and produced a child, Obed, thus maintaining Elimelech's family line and preserving his property in Bethlehem.

ELIOENAI (Heb. *'elyô'ênay*)

1. The eldest son of Neariah, listed among the descendants of Solomon (1 Chr. 3:23-24).

2. A leader of the tribe of Simeon (1 Chr. 4:36).

3. A Benjaminite, one of the sons of Becher (1 Chr. 7:8).

4. A postexilic priest of the family of Pashhur who pledged to divorce his foreign wife (Ezra 10:22).

5. An Israelite, a member of the Zattu clan,

who was ordered to send away his foreign wife (Ezra 10:27).

6. A priest who participated in the dedication service for the restored walls of Jerusalem (Neh. 12:41).

ELIPHAL (Heb. *'ĕlîpāl*)
The son of Ur, and one of David's Thirty (1 Chr. 11:35). In a parallel list (2 Sam. 23:34) he appears as Eliphelet (**2**) the son of Ahasbai of Maacah.

ELIPHAZ (Heb. *'ĕlîpaz*)
"The Temanite," one of Job's three friends (Job 2:11). The name Eliphaz is well-attested as an Edomite name (Gen. 36:10, 11; cf. 1 Chr. 1:35, 36, where an Eliphaz is listed as the son of Esau and the father of Teman) and means, possibly, "God is fine gold." Teman was located in Edom and was renowned for its wisdom (Jer. 49:7).

Eliphaz is the first to speak after Job's self-curse and expresses the common view of ancient Near Eastern literature that no mortal can be righteous before God (Job 4:17); thus Job's best hope is to appeal to God for help (5:8). He seeks to comfort Job by reminding him that he is still alive (4:6-7), and that while God may discipline, he also heals and binds up (5:17-18).

In his later speeches Eliphaz turns to accusation and warning, first accusing Job of speaking "worthless words" and "subverting religion" (Job 15:3-4) and then recounting in great detail the ruin in store for the wicked (15:20-35). Accusation becomes even stronger with a list of Job's transgressions (22:5-9). Eliphaz's last word is a return to his original advice: that Job submit to God and be healed (22:21-30).

It is said of Eliphaz and the other two friends that "they ceased to answer Job" (Job 32:1). The last we hear of them they are reprimanded for not speaking "what is right" and are commanded to offer sacrifices, with Job, now vindicated, as intermediary (42:7). MARILYN J. LUNDBERG

ELIPHELEHU (Heb. *'ĕlîpĕlēhû*)
A Levite of the second order, and a musician appointed by David to play during celebrations (1 Chr. 15:18, 21).

ELIPHELET (Heb. *'ĕlîpeleṭ*)

1. One (two?) of 13 sons born to David's wives in Jerusalem (2 Sam. 5:16; 1 Chr. 3:6, 8; 14:5, 7). The name appears twice in the Chronicler's lists, once in the 2 Samuel list. The discrepancy may be the result of scribal dittography in the Chronicler's lists or scribal omission in 2 Samuel.

2. One of David's Thirty (2 Sam. 23:34), the son of Ahasbai of Maacah. He may be identified with Eliphal in the parallel list (1 Chr. 11:35).

3. The third son of a Benjaminite named Eshek and a distant descendant of Saul (1 Chr. 8:39).

4. A descendant of Adonikam, who returned to Judah from exile under the leadership of Ezra. He was accompanied by his two brothers(?) and a sizable company of males (Ezra 8:13; 1 Esdr. 8:39).

5. A descendant of Hashum, ordered to divorce his non-Israelite wife at the time of Ezra's religious reforms (Ezra 10:33; 1 Esdr. 9:33).

JOHN D. FORTNER

ELISHA (Heb. *'ĕlîšā'*)
The "man of God" who ministered to and succeeded Elijah, after which he performed miracles and pronounced visionary oracles. The accounts of Elisha's discipleship of Elijah (1 Kgs. 19:19-21) and succession of his Moses-like master (2 Kgs. 2:1-18) were probably added to link originally unrelated holy men and create the impression of a Mosaic prophet in each generation (cf. Deut. 18:15-19). Elisha ("my God saves") was also enlisted along with Elijah in the after-the-fact legitimation of Jehu's bloody purge of the Omride dynasty (2 Kgs. 9–10; cf. 1 Kgs. 17–19, 21). The rest of the Elisha material (2 Kgs. 2:19–8:15; 13:14-25) is a collection of originally independent miracle stories and political legends. The collection is arranged according to the principle of association: stories that have common words, themes, or locations are placed side-by-side, thereby telling the "life history" of Elisha.

Miracle Stories

The miracle stories are short, with one exception (2 Kgs. 4:8-37). Most feature the "sons of the prophets," members of a prophetic guild who looked to Elisha for guidance and help. 2 Kgs. 2:1-5 suggests that conventicles of the guild were located at Bethel and Jericho. Elisha's movements suggest that conventicles also existed at Gilgal, Mt. Carmel, and Samaria (2 Kgs. 2:25; 4:25, 38). Elisha appears as an itinerant holy man, traveling from group to group and performing miracles in response to pleas for help from his poverty-stricken disciples. He heals a spring (2 Kgs. 2:19-22), multiplies a disciple's widow's oil so that she will not lose her children to a creditor (4:1-7), nullifies the poison in a stew so that his disciples can eat during a famine (4:38-41), multiplies 20 loaves to feed 100 people (4:42-44), and floats a borrowed ax that had fallen in the river (6:1-7).

The common theme in these stories is Elisha's performance of actions that save his marginalized followers from material distress. There are no moral or religious teachings; the stories simply induce veneration of the man of God. Comparisons with shaman stories around the world suggest that Elisha's disciples told these stories in order to establish his authority as *the* man of God and their status as his disciples.

The story of Elisha cursing the boys who insulted him (2 Kgs. 2:23-25) makes it clear that establishing his authority was the aim of the miracle stories. The death of 42 of the boys seems to contradict Elisha as lifegiver, but his lifesaving acts are all directed toward those who recognize his holiness. Elisha and the boys can therefore be regarded as an inverted miracle story.

Another miracle story that does not conform to the genre, in this case in its length and complexity, is the story of the Shunammite and her son (2 Kgs. 4:8-37). Here the follower is a wealthy childless woman, who recognized Elisha as "a holy man of God" (v. 9). In return for her hospitality he gave her a son (vv. 11-17). Later, when Elisha was away, the boy died (vv. 18-20). The woman first laid the child on Elisha's bed, hoping that contact with something of Elisha's would revive him (v. 21). Then she overrode her husband's objections, went to Elisha, and shamed him into returning to save the child (vv. 22-30). Contact with Elisha's bed had done nothing, nor had Elisha's staff (v. 31). Elisha then shut the door (cf. v. 4), prayed to Yahweh, and lay on top of the boy until he grew warm (vv. 32-34). A second attempt finally revived the boy (v. 35). The story ends with Elisha summoning the Shunammite to take her child, and her silent bow before him (vv. 36-37). In contrast to the short miracle stories in which both need and saving act are tersely reported, the efforts required by the Shunammite to summon Elisha and by Elisha to revive the boy are elaborated. The resulting impression is that this was considered Elisha's most spectacular miracle, requiring a fuller telling. This impression is corroborated by the existence of a sequel (2 Kgs. 8:1-6), unique among the miracle stories.

One final miracle story is the revival of the corpse that came in contact with Elisha's bones (2 Kgs. 13:20-21). There is a touch of humor here, since the gravediggers did not ask for a resurrection and Elisha did not intend to perform one.

Political Legends

The political legends are in many ways diametrically opposed to the miracle stories. They are all elaborated; they take place in the public realm of kings and royal officers; they are set in historically known wars, mostly the late-9th-century Aramean war; and they showcase Elisha's supernatural knowledge.

A prominent theme in the political legends is Elisha's ability to save the nation when the king has failed. In the legend of the Aramean siege of Samaria (2 Kgs. 6:24–7:20), which caused a devastating famine, the king's helplessness was underscored when a woman who had eaten her own child wanted him to pass judgment on her friend who was refusing to hand over her child according to their agreement (6:26-30). In desperation the king went to Elisha, knowing that the famine was from Yahweh (6:31-33). Elisha calmly prophesied that there would be food in abundance the very next day, and that the doubting aide would suffer retribution for his disbelief (7:1-2). Events happened exactly as Elisha had foretold. Yahweh caused the Arameans to hear a huge army, prompting them to abandon their camp, and four Samarian lepers who had nothing to lose deserted to the enemy (7:3-7). Having enjoyed the abundance of the abandoned camp, they shared the good news (7:8-10). After confirming the report, the Samarians stampeded for the food, trampling the doubting aide to death (7:11-17). The legend affirms that Elisha saves when the king cannot, and that belief in him is essential to the nation's welfare.

Whether or not there was an actual Aramean siege of Samaria in the late 9th century is uncertain, but Israel was at war with Aram-Damascus throughout the reigns of Jehu, Jehoahaz, and Joash. The Aramean Hazael took advantage of Jehu's loss of military alliances after his coup and conquered Israel. The Elisha political legends, except for 2 Kgs. 3:4-27, belong in this context. They express both fear of ruin (e.g., being vastly outnumbered in battle, 2 Kgs. 6:15), and the belief that Yahweh was in control of the war (e.g., the presence of the heavenly army, vv. 16-17). If the God of Israel was directing events, then God would ultimately save the nation through his prophet.

Since Yahweh was managing the Aramean war, Yahweh was also directing political affairs in Damascus. When Elisha facilitated Hazael's murder of Ben-hadad I (in reality Hadad-ezer), it was not because he favored Hazael but because Hazael's usurpation of the Aramean throne and subsequent spoliation of Israel were part of Yahweh's plan (2 Kgs. 8:7-15). Yahweh's involvement in the Aramean war began with Hazael's succession and ended with Joash's three victories over Hazael's son Ben-hadad II, also predicted by Elisha (2 Kgs. 13:14-19, 22-25).

The legend of Naaman and Gehazi (2 Kgs. 5:1-27) includes a healing miracle, but the focus is on a reversal of the two characters. Naaman was commander of the Aramaean forces (unknown historically), but he listened to a captive Israelite maidservant and went to Elisha to be cured of his leprosy (vv. 1-9). Immersing himself in the Jordan seven times as directed, he was cured (vv. 9-14). He returned to Elisha and proclaimed his belief in Yahweh (vv. 15-19), an astonishing confession given the close relationship between nations and their gods in the ancient world. Gehazi then pursued Naaman and demanded some of the gifts that Elisha had refused, for which he received Naaman's leprosy (5:20-27). The characters' status is thus reversed: the leprous enemy commander, the ultimate outsider, is cured and confesses the God of Israel; then Elisha's aide, insider of insiders, betrays the prophet and is condemned. The legend explores the ramifications of a universal ethic based solely on fidelity to Yahweh, without regard for nationality, class, or religious status.

Deuteronomistic Edition

If Elisha was a public figure during the reigns of Jehu, Jehoahaz, and Joash, as implied by the Aramean war context of the political legends, then he was active for more than 40 years. It is unlikely that he also interacted with Jehoram (2 Kgs. 3:4-27). Elisha's hostility to Jehoram (2 Kgs. 3:13-14) is absent from the other political legends, where he works closely with the king. The similarity between 2 Kgs. 3:4-27 and 1 Kgs. 22, in which the Deuteronomistic historian identified an originally anonymous "king of Israel" as Ahab in order to assert Omride depravity, suggests that a similar process took place here. The identification of the prophet in 2 Kgs. 3:4-27 as Elisha adds his opposition against Jehoram to Elijah's opposition against Ahab (1 Kgs. 17–19, 21) and Ahaziah (2 Kgs. 1). The Deuteronomist then placed the bulk of the Elisha collection in Jehoram's reign (2 Kgs. 2:19–8:15), facilitated by the lack of historical context in the miracle stories and the nameless kings in the political legends. Because 2 Kgs. 13:14-19, 22-25 names Joash, it was separated from the rest of the collection along with the postmortem miracle story (13:20-21) fitted between the prophecy and fulfillment of the legend.

Bibliography. T. W. Overholt, *Prophecy in Cross-cultural Perspective.* SBLSBS 17 (Atlanta, 1986); W. T. Pitard, *Ancient Damascus* (Winona Lake, 1987); A. Rofē, *The Prophetical Stories* (Jerusalem, 1988); M. C. White, *The Elijah Legends and Jehu's Coup.* BJS 311 (Atlanta, 1997).

MARSHA WHITE

ELISHAH (Heb. *'ĕlîšâ*)
Reputedly the son of Javan (Greece) and grandson of Japheth listed in the Table of Nations (Gen. 10:4; 1 Chr. 1:7). The name is associated with a coastal territory renowned (even in Tyre) for high-quality purple dyes (Ezek. 27:7). Most scholars identify Elishah with Alašiya (probably derived from Sum. *alas,* "copper"), attested in 2nd-millennium B.C.E. texts from Egypt, Amarna, Ugarit, and Mari. If so, the name may designate eastern Cyprus (perhaps Enkomi) or be an alternative name for Cyprus (cf. Gk. *kýpros,* "copper"). PAUL J. KISSLING

ELISHAMA (Heb. *'ĕlîšāmā'*)

1. The son of Ammihud, and leader of the tribe of Ephraim during the time when the Israelites began their journey through the wilderness (Num. 2:18; 10:22). He assisted Moses during the journey (Num. 1:10; 7:48, 53). 1 Chr. 7:26-27 identifies him as the grandfather of Joshua.

2. One of David's sons born in Jerusalem after David was crowned king (2 Sam. 5:16; 1 Chr. 3:8; 14:7). At 1 Chr. 3:6 the name is probably a scribal error for Elishua (cf. 2 Sam. 5:15).

3. A member of the house of Judah, grandfather of Ishmael and father of Nethaniah. He was a commander of a group of Judean troops, and after the destruction of Jerusalem in 587 B.C. he murdered Gedaliah (2 Kgs. 25:25 = Jer. 41:1-3).

4. A descendant of Jerahmeel, son of Jekamiah (1 Chr. 2:41).

5. One of the two priests who formed part of Jehoshaphat's commission sent out to teach the law to the people of Judah (2 Chr. 17:8).

6. A *sōpēr,* a scribe or secretary during the reign of King Jehoiakim (Jer. 36:12, 20-21).

CAROL J. DEMPSEY

ELISHAPHAT (Heb. *'ĕlîšāpāṭ*)
One of the five army commanders who assisted Jehoiada in securing kingship for young Joash and thus aided in the overthrow of Queen Athaliah (2 Chr. 23:1).

ELISHEBA (Heb. *'ĕlîšeba'*)
The daughter of Amminadab and sister of Nahshon; mother of the priestly family. She married Moses' brother Aaron and bore four sons: Nadab, Abihu, Eleazar, and Ithamar (Exod. 6:23).

ELISHUA (Heb. *'ĕlîšûa'*)
One of David's sons born at Jerusalem by an unnamed mother (2 Sam. 5:15; 1 Chr. 14:5). Because of a scribal error he is incorrectly called Elishama (**2**) at 1 Chr. 3:6.

ELIUD (Gk. *Elioúd*)
An ancestor of Jesus, according to Matthew's genealogy (Matt. 1:14-15).

ELIZABETH (Gk. *Elisábet*)
The mother of John the Baptist, wife of Zechariah the priest, and a relative of Mary the mother of Jesus. Elizabeth was described as a righteous descendant of Aaron and obedient to the laws of God (Luke 1:5-6). She was barren and of advanced age when Zechariah received the news in the temple that she would bear a son to be named John, along with the prophetic message concerning John's mission. Her barrenness, like that of Sarah and Hannah, foreshadowed a child of great significance. Elizabeth attributed her conception to the favor of the Lord upon her (Luke 1:25).

Mary learned of Elizabeth's pregnancy from Gabriel as a sign that "nothing is impossible with God," and visited Elizabeth in the sixth month. Elizabeth was filled with the spirit at Mary's greeting and blessed Mary both for her faith and for the child that she too would bear (Luke 1:41-45). At the circumcision Elizabeth gave her child the name of John, which was confirmed by his father (Luke 1:60-63). JO ANN H. SEELY

ELIZAPHAN (Heb. *'ĕlîṣāpān*)
(also ELZAPHAN)

1. The second son of Uzziel, Aaron's kinsman, and a Levite (Num. 3:30; called Elzaphan at Exod. 6:22; Lev. 10:4). When Nadab and Abihu, the sons of Aaron, were consumed by fire before God, Moses summoned Elizaphan and his brother Mishael to carry away their corpses from the sanctuary (Lev. 10:4). He was the head of the Kohathite clans (Num. 3:30). King David appointed some of Elizaphan's descendants along with other Levites to carry the ark to Jerusalem (1 Chr. 15:8). His descendants also participated in the cleansing of the temple during Hezekiah's reign (2 Chr. 29:13).

2. The son of Parnach and the leader of the tribe of Zebulunites who participated in the distribution of the land of Canaan (Num. 34:25).

HYUN CHUL PAUL KIM

ELIZUR (Heb. *'ĕlîṣûr*)
The son of Shedeur (Num. 10:18). As a leader of the tribe of Reuben (Num. 2:10), he assisted Moses in taking the census in the wilderness (1:5) and presented an offering in behalf of his tribe (7:30, 35).

ELKANAH (Heb. *'elqānâ*)

1. A descendant of Korah of the family of Levi (Exod. 6:24). As the head of his father's house, he is called the son of Assir, Korah's son, and named father of Ebiasaph (1 Chr. 6:23[MT 8]).

2. The father of Samuel and the husband of Hannah; a resident of Ramathaim-zophim in the hill country of Ephraim (1 Sam. 1:1; 1 Chr. 6:27, 34[12, 19]).

Hannah, the favorite of Elkanah's two wives, was barren but later gave birth to the prophet Samuel; his other wife, Peninnah, was noted for her fecundity (1 Sam. 1:2). Elkanah may have been a person of some import, because he is the only commoner in the books of Samuel and Kings noted to have had more than one wife. Yearly Elkanah would take his family on a pilgrimage to Shiloh to offer sacrifices, distributing double portions of sacrificial meat to Hannah because he loved her (1 Sam. 1:5). He would also accompany Hannah on her annual visit to Samuel. The couple was blessed with three more sons and two daughters (1 Sam. 2:21).

According to Jewish tradition, Elkanah is associated with good deeds and compared to Abraham (*Ber.* 50). Hannah was his first wife and he did not marry Peninnah until 10 years later. Elkanah was so pious that he made four journeys to Shiloh each year instead of the required three. On each journey his large caravan would travel a different route, attracting attention and encouraging others along the way to worship the Lord. For his piety he is credited as responsible for all of Israel's pilgrimages to Shiloh.

3. An ancestor of Samuel and descendant of Levi (1 Chr. 6:25, 36[10, 21]).

4. Another of Samuel's ancestors (1 Chr. 6:26, 35[11, 20]), possibly the same as **3** above.

5. A Levite, ancestor of Berechiah son of Asa who lived in Jerusalem after the Exile (1 Chr. 9:16).

6. A Korahite Levite, one of David's Mighty Men who joined him at Ziklag (1 Chr. 12:6).

7. A Levite who was appointed by David as one of the two doorkeepers for the ark (1 Chr. 15:23).

8. A court official during Ahaz' reign who was next in authority to the king (2 Chr. 28:7). He forsook the Lord and was killed by the Ephraimite Zichri. Robin Gallaher Branch

ELKOSH (Heb. *'elqōšî*)

The residence of the prophet Nahum (Nah. 1:1). The location of Elkosh is unknown, but a number of sites have been proposed. The most fanciful claim has been the traditional identification of Elkosh with al-Qush, a village N of Mosul near ancient Nineveh; this tradition cannot be traced back earlier than the 16th century. Several locations in Galilee have also been proposed, including Hilkesei or Elkesi (Jerome, in the preface to his commentary on Nahum), and Capernaum, which means "village of Nahum." The political situation of Nahum's time, however, makes a Galilean location for his residence unlikely. Other traditions which locate Elkosh in southern Judah, in Simeonite territory, are more probable. The Lives of the Prophets states that Elkosh is near Beth-gabrin, probably to be identified with Eleutheropolis (modern Beit Jibrin/Beth Guvrin [140113]), ca. 51 km. (32 mi.) SW of Jerusalem. Ronald A. Simkins

ELLASAR (Heb. *'ellāsār*)

The city or kingdom ruled by Arioch, a confederate of the Elamite king Chedorlaomer who attacked Sodom, captured Lot, and thereby involved Abraham in the conflict (Gen. 14:1, 9). Ellasar has not been convincingly identified or located, but five major possibilities have been suggested: (1) Larsa, the southern Mesopotamian capital Larsa that was conquered by Hammurabi king of Babylon; (2) Telassar in northern Mesopotamia (2 Kgs. 19:12 = Isa. 37:12; (3) Assur/Assyria, on the basis of phonetics or pronunciation; (4) Ilânsura, mentioned in the Mari texts and located between Carchemish and Harran; and (5) Alişar Hüyük, a Cappadocian city located ca. 80 km. (50 mi.) SE of the Hittite capital Ḫattuša. Sheila Marie Dugger Griffith

ELMADAM (Gk. *Elmadám*)

A preexilic ancestor of Jesus (Luke 3:28).

ELNAAM (Heb. *'elnaʿam*)

The father of Jeribai and Joshaviah, two of David's warriors (1 Chr. 11:46). The LXX lists Elnaam himself as one of the warriors.

ELNATHAN (Heb. *'elnāṯān*)

1. The father of Nehushta, the wife of King Jehoiakim and mother of Jehoiachin (2 Kgs. 24:8); a resident at Jerusalem.

2.-4. Two (LXX only one) "leaders" (NRSV) and another regarded as "wise" who accompanied the returning exiles to Jerusalem (Ezra 8:16).

5. The son of Achbor who captured the fugitive prophet Uriah in Egypt and returned him to King Jehoiakim (Jer. 26:22). He also joined a number of Judahite princes in reading a scroll dictated by Jeremiah in their attempt to dissuade the king from burning the document (Jer. 36:12, 25). Some scholars identify him with the Elnathan named in Lachish Ostracon 3, father of Coniah, "commander of the host" who was dispatched to Egypt.

ELOAH (Heb. *'ĕlôah*)

A Hebrew name for God, occurring most frequently in biblical texts where non-Israelites would not be familiar with the names of God associated with the tradition history of Israel. Many scholars believe that Eloah could be a later singular form of Elohim. While the word often refers to deity in general (Job 12:6), it also functions as the name of the Israelite God (Isa. 44:8). Eloah appears mostly in poetic texts (Deut. 32:15, 17; 1 Sam. 22:32 = Ps. 18:31[MT 32]; Prov. 30:5; Hab. 3:3) ranging from the period of the Monarchy to the postexilic period. The name occurs most frequently (42 times) in the poetry of Job. Henry L. Carrigan, Jr.

ELOHIM (Heb. *'ĕlōhîm*)

The most frequent generic name for God in the OT; possibly a plural of Eloah, itself an expansion of El, "god."

Elohim most naturally refers to a plurality of gods, e.g., those of Egypt (Exod. 12:12), Syria, Sidon, Moab, the Ammonites and the Philistines (Judg. 10:6), and the Amorites (Josh. 24:15; Judg. 6:10). It is also used individually of Ashtaroth, Chemosh, and Milcom (1 Kgs. 11:33) and of Baalzebub (2 Kgs. 1:2, 3, 6, 16). This constitutes a plural of intensification, i.e., the most important of the gods of a particular group.

Elohim is used with singular verbs and/or adjectives for the focus of Israelite worship, Yahweh. Often Elohim functions as an alternative divine name, as in the Elohistic Psalter (Pss. 42-83); e.g., the only significant difference between Pss. 14 and 53 is the use of Yahweh or Elohim respectively. A similar preference is used to delineate at least two sources in the Pentateuch by proponents of the documentary hypothesis.

Num. 23:19 is representative of the ancient belief that deities were fundamentally different from humans: "God is not a human being, that he should lie, or a mortal, that he should change his mind" (cf. Isa. 31:3; 55:8-9; Hos. 11:9). An important distinction is the longevity of the gods; human mortality is a theme common to the Gilgamesh Epic (Mesopotamia), the story of Aqhat (Ugarit), and Gen. 3:22-24.

Some adjectival uses of Elohim are also best understood as intensive. For instance, since Nineveh takes three days to cross, Heb. *'îr-gĕḏôlâ lē'lōhîm* (Jonah 3:3) means "an exceedingly large city." Comparable instances include when *'ĕlōhîm* modifies the pre-creation wind (Gen. 1:2), the fear that strikes the Philistines (1 Sam. 14:15), and Solomon's wisdom (1 Kgs. 3:28). A nuance of great importance also underlies the limited use of Elohim for (living) humans: Moses will be "as God/a god" to Aaron and Pharaoh (Exod. 4:16; 7:1), and the king can be called "god" in comparison to his subjects (Ps. 45:6[MT 7]).

The characterization of Samuel's ghost (1 Sam. 28:13) as an *'ĕlōhîm* is different, reflecting the ancient belief in the deified dead (cf. the Rephaim at Ugarit). This is a possible (though not required) interpretation of *'ĕlōhîm* in parallel with "the dead" in Isa. 8:19 as well.

See GOD, NAMES OF (OLD TESTAMENT).

Bibliography. H. Ringgren, "*'elōhîm*," *TDOT* 1:267-84; K. van der Toorn, "God (I) אלהים," *DDD*, 352-65.

JOHN L. MCLAUGHLIN

ELOHIST

One of four sources or strata underlying and composing the Pentateuch. The discernment of such sources is far from assured, nor do those who see sources always agree on their features. Nevertheless, a coherent portrait of the Elohist may be attempted.

The Elohist (E) is typically understood as located in the northern kingdom of Israel in the late 10th or early 9th century B.C.E. The work, perhaps once independent or now truncated, is understood as a supplement to the Yahwist source (J), consequently sharing the J story line of events: the adventures of founding ancestors, the descent of the people to Egypt, their emergence from sojourn in the wilderness. The Elohist adds some vignettes to the Yahwist recital (e.g., the binding of Isaac in Gen. 22, Moses' meeting with Jethro in Exod. 18), contributes details (Jacob's night vision in Gen. 28:10-22), and in certain cases has distinctive vocabulary (Israel for Jacob, Jethro for Reuel, Horeb for Sinai).

The Elohist enhancement of the basic Yahwist narrative is also characterized by stylistic features. The E source is named from its propensity to call the deity Elohim (the plural word for "god"), just as the Yahwist source takes its name from its habit of naming the deity Yahweh. Elohim is more remote than the Yahwist's deity, more inclined to employ intermediaries like angels or dreams. Human beings respond appropriately, the Elohist reports, with fear of God or reverence. The Elohist multiplies episodes where sons are endangered and specifies northern sites where memorial stones are established and simple worship can occur: Shechem, Bethel, Penuel.

Scholars suggest that the Elohist's project is reformist, originating to support the act of secession from the Davidic kingdom by the 10 northern tribes, a revolution led by Jeroboam I. The Elohist is, by such reasoning, critical of the power excesses of the southern kingdom of Judah, disparaging of its priestly leadership of the Aaron-descended Zadokite line, eager to sketch forebears who resemble their own rebel king Jeroboam, and desirous of sponsoring decentralization of authority at a remove from Jerusalem. Scholars have tended to describe the Elohist texts as more ethically sensitive than some of the Yahwist's, but that claim is difficult to substantiate. Some stories credited to E rehearse more explicitly the fraught circumstances.

Dissent to the position sketched here ranges from those who deny the presence of an Elohist source at all to those who disagree on whether or not certain texts should be assigned to it; that the difference in viewpoint can be maintained by the criteria offered above is not always sufficient reason to see them operative in a long narrative like the Joseph story (Gen. 37–50), which works perfectly well, perhaps more artistically without them. As the once-strong consensus supporting the documentary hypothesis continues to crumble, so also will disintegrate confidence in the Elohist as a coherent voice in the pentateuchal symphony.

Bibliography. R. B. Coote, *In Defense of Revolution: The Elohist History* (Minneapolis, 1991).

BARBARA GREEN, O.P.

ELOI, ELOI, LAMA SABACHTHANI

See ELI, ELI, LAMA SABACHTHANI.

ELON (Heb. *'ēlôn, 'êlôn*) **(PERSON)**

1. A Hittite, the father of Basemath, one of Esau's two Hittite wives (Gen. 26:34). At Gen. 36:2 Elon's daughter is called Adah and the father of Basemath is Ishmael. A LXX tradition labels him as a Hivite.

2. One of three sons of Zebulun (Gen. 46:14), ancestor of the Elonites (Num. 26:26).

3. A Zebulunite who succeeded Ibzan of Bethlehem as judge over Israel (Judg. 12:11). Elon was judge for 10 years and was buried in Aijalon, in the land of Zebulun. The verbal similarity in Hebrew consonantal script between Elon and Aijalon suggests that this is an etiological explanation.

JESPER SVARTVIK

ELON (Heb. *'êlôn*) **(PLACE)**
A village in the tribal territory of Dan, between Aijalon and Timnah (Josh. 19:43), possibly Khirbet Wâdī ʿAlin. Some scholars think it is the same as Elon-beth-hanan (1 Kgs. 4:9).

ELON-BETH-HANAN (Heb. *'êlôn bêṯ ḥānān*)
A village in the tribal area of Dan belonging to Solomon's second administrative district (1 Kgs. 4:9). Some scholars have identified the site with Aijalon in Josh. 19:43 ("the Oak of the House of Hanan," modern Yālo; 152138), a city of refuge (1 Chr. 6:69) in the northeastern Shephelah E of Emmaus.

DAVID C. MALTSBERGER

ELOTH (Heb. *'êlôṯ*)
An alternate form of Elath.

ELPAAL (Heb. *'elpaʿal*)
The head of a Benjaminite family (1 Chr. 8:11-12, 18).

EL-PARAN (Heb. *'êl pā'rān*)
A location in Horite territory that marked the southernmost point of Chedorlaomer's military expedition (Gen. 14:6), adjacent to the Wilderness of Paran. Heb. *'êl* ("terebinth") is probably a variant of *'êlaṯ* (Elath), the modern port city on the Gulf of Aqaba (cf. LXX *terébinthos tḗs pháran,* "Terebinth of Paran").

PETE F. WILBANKS

ELPELET (Heb. *'elpāleṭ*) (also ELIPHELET)
One of David's sons born at Jerusalem, of an unnamed mother (1 Chr. 14:5). At 1 Chr. 3:6 the name occurs as Eliphelet (**1**; cf. 3:8; 14:7). Considered by some scholars to be the result of scribal error, its occurrence there may rather be a conscious effort to expand the genealogy recorded at 2 Sam. 5:14-16.

EL SHADDAI (Heb. *'ēl šadday*)
A name of God (Exod. 6:3). It was this name by which the patriarchs and matriarchs of Israel knew God (e.g., Gen. 17:1; 28:3; 35:11), in contrast to the name shared with Moses, Yahweh (Exod. 6:3). Over time, El Shaddai became identified with Yahweh.

The exact origin, history, and etymology of the name are highly debated. Traditionally, it has been connected to Heb. *šāḏaḏ,* "deal mightily with," but the verb actually has the connotation "deal violently." Other scholars associate it with Assyr. *šadu,* "mountain" or "high," thus rendering the Hebrew as "High God" or "God of the Mountains." The usual English translation, "Almighty," derives from the rendering of the Hebrew in the LXX and Vulg., which was a free translation of what was by then an obscure term.

Bibliography. W. F. Albright, "The Names *Shaddai* and *Abram,*" *JBL* 54 (1935): 173-204; D. Baile, "The God with Breasts: El Shaddai in the Bible," *HR* 21 (1982): 240-56.

LISA W. DAVISON

ELTEKEH (Heb. *'eltĕqēh*)
A levitical city (Josh. 21:23) in the southern allotment of Dan (19:44). Identified with modern Tell esh-Shallâf/Tel Shalaf (128144), the settlement grew up on the banks of the Sorek streambed (Wadi eṣ-Ṣarar/Naḥal Sorek) near the Mediterranean Sea. Surface surveys indicate that settlement continued throughout the Iron Age (ca. 1200-587 B.C.). The Taylor Prism records that during the 701 invasion of Judah, Sennacherib of Assyria captured the town along with Timnah further up the Sorek Valley.

DAVID C. MALTSBERGER

ELTEKON (Heb. *'eltĕqōn*)
A town in the hill country of Judah, named with Beth-zur and Beth-anoth (Josh. 15:59). The site is thought to be Khirbet ed-Deir (160122), ca. 9 km. (5 mi.) WSW of Bethlehem.

ELTOLAD (Heb. *'eltôlaḏ*) (also TOLAD)
A town allocated to Judah (Josh. 15:30), later reassigned to Simeon (19:4, 7). In Chr. 4:29 it is called Tolad, a name which occurs on an ostracon from Beer-sheba associated with wine distribution. A possible site identification is Khirbet Erqa Saqra, 20 km. (12.5 mi.) SE of Beer-sheba.

LAURA B. MAZOW

ELUL (Heb. *'ĕlûl*)
The sixth month of the Hebrew year (Aug.-Sept.; Akk. *elulu, ululu*).

ELUZAI (Heb. *'elʿûzay*)
A Benjaminite warrior, one of Saul's "kindred," who joined David at Ziklag (1 Chr. 12:5).

ELYMAIS (Gk. *Elymais*)
A province in the region between Persia and Babylonia, most likely the equivalent of Elam (cf. Dan. 8:2 LXX MSS) or Susiana, the capital of which was Susa (cf. Ptolemy *Geog.* 6.3; Strabo *Geog.* 15.732, 744). At 1 Macc. 6:1 it is called a city (Gk. *pólis;* cf. Josephus *Ant.* 12.9.1).

ELYMAS (Gk. *Elýmas*)
A Jewish sorcerer whom Paul encountered at Paphos on the island of Cyprus (Acts 13:6-12). Elymas opposed Paul's efforts to teach the gospel to Sergius Paulus, the Roman proconsul of the island. For his opposition, Elymas was stricken with temporary blindness. The narrative presents Christianity in contrast to religious magic.

Elymas was probably attached to the proconsul's entourage as a personal adviser who claimed to know divine will. Like many Romans, Sergius Paulus was interested in knowing any divine guidance for his affairs, and he retained Elymas for that purpose. Elymas undoubtedly perceived the efforts of Paul as a threat to his position with the proconsul.

Elymas is also known as Bar-Jesus ("son of Jesus," Acts 13:6), but Paul sarcastically calls him "son of the devil" (v. 10). The name Elymas is translated *mágos* ("magician," Acts 13:8), and it may have derived from Aram. *ḥālōmā'* ("dreamer") or *hālimā'* ("powerful").

Bibliography. A. B. Nock, "Paul and the Magus," in *The Beginnings of Christianity* 5, ed. F. J. Foakes-Jackson and K. Lake (Grand Rapids, 1979); L. Yaure, "Elymas-Nehelamite-Pethor," *JBL* 79 (1960): 297-314.

L. David McClister

ELYON (Heb. *'elyôn*)

See God, Names of (OT); Most High.

ELZABAD (Heb. *'elzāḇāḏ*)

1. The ninth of the experienced Gadite warriors who joined David at Ziklag (1 Chr. 12:8, 12[MT 9, 13]).

2. A Korahite gatekeeper in the Jerusalem temple (1 Chr. 26:7).

ELZAPHAN (Heb. *'elṣāp̄ān*) (also ELIZAPHAN) A variant form of Elizaphan (**1**), one of the sons of Uzziel ordered to remove the corpses of Nadab and Abihu (Exod. 6:22; Lev. 10:4).

EMBALMING

The process of preserving the body of the deceased (from Latin words meaning "to put into aromatic resins," referring to the use of unguents, resins, and oils to preserve the body). "Mummify" is derived from Arab. *mummiya,* "pitch" or "bitumen," a word used because some believed that the blackened corpses of Egyptian mummies had been covered with pitch. While a number of ancient peoples devised ways to preserve deceased members of their societies, the ancient Egyptians must be regarded as leading specialists in this activity. Many details of their culture are reflected in the OT, especially in Genesis and Exodus, and it is their practice of mummification — or embalming — that is directly related to biblical study. The Gospels discuss some of the preparations made for the burial of Jesus' body, but this was not embalming in the true sense, especially when compared to the elaborate processes developed by the Egyptians.

Some ancient civilizations made efforts to preserve the corpses of the dead out of respect for the individual, especially if this deceased person held a high status. The Egyptians expended great effort to preserve corpses because they believed that the survival of a physical body in recognizable form was needed for survival of the human being's immortal components, the *ka, ba,* and *akh* — the life-force, personality, and "ghost."

Through the use of various physical/surgical and chemical processes, the Egyptians devised artificial means to preserve corpses. The process of mummification was introduced very early in Egypt's dynastic history, in the first half of the 3rd millennium B.C. Even before then, the Egyptians must have noticed that the hot, dry sand of the desert often desiccated and preserved bodies without any artificial processes. A variety of techniques evolved over many centuries to conserve the bodies of Egypt's nobility; these included removing the internal organs, soaking the body in natron, and wrapping it tightly in linen. When Herodotus visited Egypt in the 5th century he documented the mummification methods that were still known, even though the art and science of embalming was not as important as it had been earlier.

According to Genesis, Joseph had become so acculturated to Egyptian life that he ordered his "physicians" to embalm the body of his father Jacob/Israel (Gen. 50:2-3). In agreement with other ancient texts, Genesis reports that the mummification process took 40 days and that the time of mourning lasted 70 days. When Joseph died, he was also mummified and placed in a coffin (Gen. 50:26); Heb. *'ărôn* corresponds to a "chest" or "box" but is an appropriate term for mummy case.

Bibliography. C. Andrews, *Egyptian Mummies* (Cambridge, Mass., 1984); C. Hobson, *The World of the Pharaohs* (New York, 1987); S. Quirke and J. Spencer, eds., *The British Museum Book of Ancient Egypt* (New York, 1992).

Gerald L. Mattingly

EMBROIDERY

The embellishment of cloth using colored or textured threads of (in biblical times) natural materials such as wool, cotton, and silk. Few examples of fabric have been found from the biblical world; our best indications are impressions created when fabric was placed against plaster or clay before these more durable materials dried. The preponderance of archaeological evidence for textiles is in the form of loom weights and copper, bronze, and bone needles. Though embroidery was a widespread activity and among the skills given by God to the tribes of Judah and Dan (Exod. 35:35), in textual records Phoenicians are most closely associated with the industry; their name may refer to the "Tyrian purple" dye they produced from murex shells. The remains of these shells in Levantine coastal sites attest to this industry, as do the textile-manufacture and dyeing facilities found at Phoenician sites abroad. Egyptian-made linen embroidery is said to have been woven into the sails of Tyrian ships (Ezek. 27:7), and embroidered cloth and garments were traded between Tyre, Edom, the Arabian Peninsula, and Mesopotamia (vv. 16, 24).

The color of embroidery was seen in the biblical world as a sign of status. Purple was associated with royalty, crimson with luxury (2 Sam. 1:24), and blue with God's covenant (Num. 15:37-40). Embroidery appears on the screens at the tabernacle's entrance (Exod. 26:36), on the gate of the court (27:16), on a bride's clothing (Ps. 45:13[MT 14]), draped over idols (Ezek. 16:18), and as booty (Judg. 5:30). The craft of embroidery is used as a metaphor for the attention God paid to Jerusalem (Ezek. 16:10, 13).

Katharine A. Mackay

EMEK-KEZIZ (Heb. *ʿēmeq qĕṣîṣ*)
A town assigned to the tribe of Benjamin (Josh. 18:21). The site is unknown. Its placement, following Jericho and Beth-hoglah and before Beth-arabah, suggests a location in the Jordan Plain SE of Jericho, although the place name ("a valley cut off") is inconsistent with this topography.

LAURA B. MAZOW

EMENDATIONS OF THE SCRIBES
An English translation of Heb. *tiqqûnê sōpĕrîm,* which was used by the Masoretes to note particular biblical texts that had been corrected or emended by earlier scribes. These textual emendations often were minor changes, such as the omission or alteration of one or more consonants. The purpose for most emendations was to remove objectionable language referring to God. Various lists include seven, 11, or 18 texts (Gen. 18:22; Num. 11:15; 12:12; 1 Sam. 3:13; 2 Sam. 16:12; 20:1; 1 Kgs. 12:16; 2 Chr. 10:16; Jer. 2:11; Ezek. 8:17; Hos. 4:7; Hab. 1:12; Zech. 2:8[MT 12]; Mal. 1:13; Ps. 106:20; Job 7:20, 32:3; Lam. 3:20).

Comparison with ancient translations suggests that some proposed emendations were genuine. Most, however, appear to be textual readings that arose to support later medieval exegesis. Scribes may have emended texts for theological reasons early in the process of textual transmission — from the 3rd century B.C.E. to the 1st century C.E. This emendation was not done systematically or comprehensively. Scholars have identified other instances — not found in these lists — that might reflect similar editorial work.

Bibliography. C. McCarthy, *The Tiqqunê Sopherim.* OBO 36 (Göttingen, 1981).

STEPHEN ALAN REED

EMERALD
The modern emerald was unknown in the ancient Near East until it began to be mined in Upper Egypt in the last two centuries B.C.E. Some translations use "emerald" when the Hebrew suggests a prized, green-colored stone. Some translations read "emerald" for *bāreqeṯ* (LXX *smáragdos*), an engraved stone on the high priest's breastpiece (Exod. 28:17; 39:10) and a stone adorning the king of Tyre (Ezek. 28:13). In those passages the NIV renders "emerald" for *yahălōm* (LXX *íaspis,* "jasper").

Gk. *smáragdos,* a course in the foundation of the city wall of the New Jerusalem (Rev. 21:19), and *smarágdinos,* an adjective describing the rainbow around God's throne (4:3), are translated "emerald" in most versions of the NT and likely refer to the gemstone as it is known today. Other translations use "beryl," "carbuncle," "crystal," "diamond," "feldspar," "garnet," "jade," "moonstone," or "turquoise" for these Hebrew and Greek terms.

JOSEPH E. JENSEN

EMIM (Heb. *ʾêmîm*)
The former inhabitants of Moab dispossessed by the Moabites (Deut. 2:10); a race of giants likened to the Anakim and also known as the Rephaim (vv. 10-11). The Emim were defeated by Chedorlaomer at Shaveh-kiriathaim, a plain E of the Dead Sea (Gen. 14:5).

EMMANUEL
See IMMANUEL.

EMMAUS (Gk. *Emmaoús*)
A village ca. 11 km. (7 mi.) from Jerusalem (30 km. [19 mi.] according to some ancient witnesses). The risen Jesus appears to two disciples on the road to Emmaus (Luke 24:13-35). Several modern sites have been proposed for the NT Emmaus, including ʿAmwâs (Khirbet Imwas, ancient Nicopolis; 149138) for the farther site, el-Quibeibeh (Crusader Castellum Emmaus, 163138), Abu Ghosh (160134), or Qalôniyeh (ancient Colonia; Motza, *j. Sukk.* 54b; 165134) for the nearer, but none has gained widespread approval.

An instance of the ancient recognition story, the Emmaus account occurs only in Luke and thus conveys a distinctive Lucan emphasis on the appearance of Jesus: Luke combines Jesus' appearance with a meal and prophecy. Jesus appears without being recognized, and the disciples' eyes are opened only when Jesus takes, blesses, breaks, and distributes bread (cf. Luke 9:16; 22:19; also 24:41-43). Yet Jesus does not share the meal; he vanishes when the pair recognizes him. Other Lucan passages also show Jesus attending meals (Luke 9:10-17; 22:14-38; Acts 10:41), and the table provides a key gathering place for the Church (Acts 2:42, 46; 20:7; 27:33-36).

The Emmaus account also emphasizes the importance of prophecy. The disciples remember Jesus as a prophet mighty in deed and word and recall their disappointment that he had been killed. But Jesus rebukes them, explaining that the Messiah's suffering had been indicated by Moses and the prophets.

Significantly, the Emmaus story begins and ends in Jerusalem. Alone among the Synoptic Gospels, the book of Luke locates Jesus' appearances and the Church's beginnings in that city.

Bibliography. R. J. Dillon, *From Eye-Witnesses to Ministers of the Word.* AnBib 82 (Rome, 1978).

GREG CAREY

EMPEROR
Originally an honorific title (Lat. *imperator*) granted to Roman commanders by their soldiers after a victory. Octavian (Augustus Caesar) began the tradition of taking the title as a part of his name, apparently to lay unique claim to military authority. Most subsequent Roman emperors adopted the title upon accession. In the later empire, an emperor might be proclaimed *imperator* several times by his army following notable victories. The term that actually communicated the status of emperor was "Augustus."

The creation of the position of emperor by Octavian had earlier precedents. Since the deposal of the last Tarquin king in 510 B.C.E., Rome had been a republic governed largely by a senate composed of aristocrats, with an assembly of common people represented by tribunes, who theoretically held veto power over senatorial legislation. However, the successes of the Roman armies resulted in the control of vast territories in the Mediterranean world and the rise to prominence and power of several generals, which threatened the traditional republican structure. The senate recognized the necessity of having powerful leaders but resisted losing its rule. The First Triumvirate — Julius Caesar, Pompey, and Crassus — represented a careful balancing of these concerns, but Caesar became prominent and was reluctantly acknowledged as "dictator" by the senate. His assassination by several senators was the death blow to the old republican government.

The Second Triumvirate, established in the crisis of Caesar's death, fell to the victories of Octavian over his rivals and led to his absolute rule. Now one person, by virtue primarily of military strength, was recognized as the supreme leader of the empire. The power of the emperor was enhanced by his role as commander of the armies, his personal praetorian guard, his presiding at public games and ceremonies, his appointive and legislative powers, his alliances with the equestrian (knights) class, his patronage of the general populace, and his bureaucracy mostly of freedmen. The status of emperors was further enhanced by the worship of Octavian and the establishment of the cult of *Divus Augustus* following his death. Though promoted through the building of temples by later emperors, only a few (e.g., Caligula, Domitian) advocated their own worship.

Bibliography. M. Cary and H. H. Scullard, *A History of Rome: Down to the Reign of Constantine,* 3rd ed. (New York, 1975); F. Millar, *The Emperor in the Roman World, 31 B.C.–A.D. 337,* 2nd ed. (Ithaca, 1992); C. Scarre, *Chronicle of the Roman Emperors* (London, 1995). SCOTT NASH

ENAIM (Heb. *ʿênayim*)
A town on the way to Timnah from Adullam. It was on the outskirts of this town that Tamar, posing as a temple prostitute, was propositioned by her father-in-law Judah (Gen. 38:14, 21). Many scholars equate Enaim with Enam in the Shephelah of Judah (Josh. 15:34). Its location is uncertain. Most place it between Zanoah and Jarmuth or near the eastern end of the valley of Elah. STEVEN M. ORTIZ

ENAM (Heb. *ʿênām*)
A village in the tribal territory of Judah, near Azekah and Socoh (Josh. 15:34), perhaps the same as Enaim.

ENAN (Heb. *ʿênān*)
The father of the Naphtalite chief Ahira (Num. 1:15; 2:29; 7:78, 83; 10:27).

EN-DOR (Heb. *ʿēn dôr, ʿên dôr, ʿên dōʾr*)
A town in northwestern Manasseh (Josh. 17:11), in the area of the Esdraelon Plain. Since the spelling varies in Hebrew, the meaning of the name is not certain. It may be connected either with a spring (Heb. *dwr*) or with the Dorians, a Greek tribal group. En-dor is the town where Barak's forces triumphed over Sisera (Ps. 83:10[MT 11]; cf. Judg. 4–5). Here lived a witch whom Saul visited on the eve of his final battle in order to gain help from the dead prophet Samuel. Perhaps, depending on exactly where one locates En-dor, Saul needed to travel behind enemy lines in order to visit the medium, hence his disguise. The name may be preserved in modern Indur, but the preferred location is Khirbet eṣ-Ṣafṣâfeh/Ḥorvat Zafzafot (187227).

Bibliography. J. P. Brown, "The Mediterranean Seer and Shamanism," *ZAW* 93 (1981): 374-400; N. Zori, "New Light on Endor," *PEQ* 84 (1952): 114-17. SAMUEL LAMERSON

EN-EGLAIM (Heb. *ʿên ʿeglayim*)
A site mentioned in Ezekiel's eschatological vision of the sacred river flowing southeast from the temple in Jerusalem to the desert (Ezek. 47:10). Ezekiel locates En-eglaim on the shore of the Dead Sea, as a place good for fishing once the life-giving water has freshened it. The actual location of En-eglaim is uncertain. Possible identifications include ʿAin Ḥajlah (197136; N of the Dead Sea), ʿAin Feshkha (192122), and/or Eglaim (217064; Isa. 15:8). MONICA L. W. BRADY

EN-GANNIM (Heb. *ʿên gannîm*) (also ANEM)
1. A settlement in the Judean Shephelah. The city was likely to the east of Zanoah and Jarmuth, coming between them in the description of the western Shephelah in Josh. 15:34. The exact location is uncertain, although some have suggested Beit Jemal, 3.2 (2 mi.) S of Beth-shemesh, or Umm Jina, 1.6 km. (1 mi.) SW of Beth-shemesh.

2. A levitical city within the tribal boundaries of Issachar (Josh. 19:21; 21:29), likely identified with Khirbet Beit Jann (196235) SW of modern Tiberius. The parallel account in 1 Chr. 6:73 calls the settlement Anem. DAVID C. MALTSBERGER

EN-GEDI (Heb. *ʿên geḏî*)
An oasis listed as one of the towns of Judah which was of sufficient size to have support villages (Josh. 15:62). A perennial spring ca. 200 m. (655 ft.) above the Dead Sea supplies the water for the site. When David fled from Saul he sought refuge in the "strongholds" (apparently caves) of the region; there David insulted Saul by cutting off the hem of his robe (1 Sam. 23:29–24:5). During the reign of Jehoshaphat, a coalition of Moabites, Ammonites, and Meunites rallied at Hazazon-tamar, which is identified with En-gedi (2 Chr. 20:1-2); however, before they had a chance to confront Judah's army the coalition forces destroyed each other (vv. 22-23).

En-gedi was known for its vineyards, date palms, and balsam (Cant. 1:14; Sir. 24:14; Josephus *Ant.* 9.1.2; Eusebius *Onom.* 86.18). Ezekiel's vision of the temple (Ezek. 47:10) lists En-gedi along with En-eglaim as geographic landmarks for a river of fresh water flowing from the temple into the Dead Sea.

En-gedi has been identified with Tel Goren/Tell ej-Jurn (187096), located about halfway down the western shore of the Dead Sea. Excavations have uncovered a well-built cult center from the Chalcolithic period on a promontory overlooking the Iron Age tell. On the tell proper, remains have been traced to the end of the Iron Age (stratum V; ca. 630-582 B.C.). The buildings are situated around courtyards. The discovery of numerous large store jars and the plentiful balsam of the region suggest that the site was a center for the production of perfume. This stratum was destroyed by Nebuchadnezzar ca. 582.

After the Exile the site was reoccupied during the Persian period (stratum IV) with a palatial dwelling of ca. 550 sq. m. (658 sq. yds.) with more than 23 rooms. This building was inexplicably destroyed ca. 400. Stratum III (Ptolemaic/Seleucid period) consisted of a fortified site which was destroyed probably in the conflict between the Hasmoneans and Herod.

The last major occupation (stratum II) occurred during the 1st century A.D. when the site was refortified with another citadel. Walls measured some 2 m. (6.5 ft.) thick. Various coins were discovered with this stratum (Agrippa I, Claudius, Nero, and coins of the second year of the First Revolt). Josephus indicates that during the rebellion against Rome the occupants of Masada raided En-gedi and massacred its inhabitants (*BJ* 4.7.2). After this destruction, stratum I consisted only of nonpermanent dwellings and agricultural terraces.

Nearby, a Roman bathhouse was built during the period between the First Revolt and the Bar Kokhba Revolt (ca. A.D. 132). After the Bar Kokhba Revolt a synagogue was built at the base of the tell and was rebuilt through several phases. It was destroyed in the 6th century.

Bibliography. D. Barg, Y. Porat, and E. Netzer, "The Synagogue at ʿEn-Gedi," in *Ancient Synagogues Revealed,* ed. L. I. Levine (Jerusalem, 1981), 116-19; B. Mazar, T. Dothan, and I. Dunayevsky, "En-Gedi: The First and Second Seasons of Excavations, 1961-1962," *ʿAtiqot* 5 (1966): 116-19; D. Ussishkin, "The Ghassulian Shrine at En-gedi," *Tel Aviv* 7 (1980): 1-44. DALE W. MANOR

ENGLISH VERSIONS

See BIBLE TRANSLATIONS.

EN-HADDAH (Heb. *ʿên ḥaddâ*)

A village in the tribal territory of Issachar (Josh. 19:21). The site is probably modern el-Hadetheh/Tel en-Hadda (196232), ca. 10 km. (6 mi.) E of Mt. Tabor.

EN-HAKKORE (Heb. *ʿên haqqôrēʾ*)

A spring at Lehi, from which Samson, wearied from battle with the Philistines, drank and regained his strength (Judg. 15:19). The name (Heb. "spring of the one who called") may derive from Samson's having first called *(qārāʾ)* upon the Lord for help (Judg. 15:18).

EN-HAZOR (Heb. *ʿên ḥāṣôr*)

A fortified city allocated to the tribe of Naphtali in the Upper Galilee (Josh. 19:37). The site is perhaps the same as *ʿn-y* in the topographical lists of Thutmose III. The location is not certain, but Yohanan Aharoni has suggested an identification with modern ʿAinitha (191281) near Bint Jbeil in southern Lebanon. STEPHEN J. ANDREWS

ENLIL (Sum. EN.LIL)

The Sumerian god of the atmosphere and the wind, worshipped at Nippur. The principal god of the Sumerian pantheon, he was later identified with Marduk.

See BEL.

EN-MISHPAT (Heb. *ʿên mišpāṭ*)

An oasis ("fountain of judgment"), and probably a cult center, in the Negeb where Chedorlaomer and his allied kings defeated the Amalekites (Gen. 14:7). It was later called Kadesh or Kadesh-barnea.

ENOCH (Heb. *ḥănôḵ*) **(PERSON)**

1. The son of Cain and father of Irad (Gen. 4:17-18). The present form of the text indicates that the first city was built by Cain and named Enoch. The context and typical form of genealogies, however, would seem to indicate that Enoch built the first city; it was thus named Irad (cf. Eridu).

2. The first son of Jared (Gen. 5:18; cf. 1 Chr. 1:3), the father of Methuselah (Gen. 5:21-22), and a 7th-generation descendant of Adam (Jude 14). Enoch's life-span of 365 years (Gen. 5:23) is comparatively short compared to other members of his family line and may suggest a connection with the solar year. In this regard Enoch has been compared with Emmeduranki, who is usually listed as the seventh of the Mesopotamian antediluvian kings, or with Utuabzu, Enmeduranki's adviser. Enoch's story ends with "then he was no more, because God took him" (Gen. 5:24). Such terminology is atypical and implies that Enoch did not die a natural, physical death (cf. Elijah; 2 Kgs. 2:1-12). This escape from death is evidently due to Enoch's piety, since he is twice described as one who "walked with God" (Gen. 5:22, 24). The first occurrence is not found in the LXX, which reads instead "and Enoch lived. . ."; furthermore, the phrase has been interpreted to mean "Enoch walked with angelic beings." Even so, the phrase is nevertheless comparable to Noah's description (Gen. 6:9) and thus probably relates to Enoch's righteousness and translation (cf. Sir. 44:16; 49:14; Heb. 11:5; cf. Wis. 4:10). This "taking" has occasioned much speculation and may be the reason why Enoch figures prominently in later literature (e.g., Jubilees, 1 Enoch [cf. Jude 14]; 2 Enoch; 3 Enoch).

Bibliography. J. C. VanderKam, *Enoch and the Growth of an Apocalyptic Tradition.* CBQMS 16 (Washington, 1984). BRENT A. STRAWN

ENOCH (Heb. *ḥănôḵ*) **(PLACE)**
A city built by Cain and named after his eldest son Enoch (Gen. 4:17).

ENOCH, BOOKS OF
Three books have come down to us under the name of Enoch: 1 (or Ethiopic) Enoch, 2 (or Slavonic) Enoch, and 3 (or Hebrew) Enoch. Much of the content of these books depends on the idea that Enoch had learned cosmological and other heavenly secrets from the angels. This is derived from the biblical account of Gen. 5:2-24 (cf. esp. vv. 21-24). Due to the Enochic tradition's distinction between *hā-'ĕlōhîm* ("the angels"; NRSV "God" in Gen. 5:22) and *'ĕlōhîm* ("God"), this pericope was understood to mean that after the birth of Methuselah Enoch spent the next 300 years with the angels and then, after a brief return to earth, was taken up to remain in heaven.

1 (Ethiopic) Enoch

1 Enoch is a collection of five books plus a few additions dating from the 3rd century B.C.E. to the 1st century C.E. (or B.C.E.). They were originally written in Aramaic, translated into Greek, and from Greek into other languages. Fragments of the Aramaic of all but Book 2 were found at Qumran. A related, fragmentary Book of the Giants, which survives in a revised form among the Manicheans, was also found at Qumran. 1 Enoch had a great deal of influence in late antiquity. It is cited explicitly in Jude 14–15, the Epistle of Barnabas, and by Tertullian and is reflected in the Synoptic Gospels, the Apocalypse of John, and other early Christian and Jewish texts. It subsequently fell out of favor and survives only in ancient Ethiopic, the version upon which all modern translations are based. A diachronic account of the separate books follows.

Book 3, the Astronomical Book (chs. 72–82), was composed in the 3rd century B.C.E. or possibly earlier. The present Ethiopic version is an abbreviated and disordered version of the Aramaic original. It consists of Enoch's tour of the heavens conducted by the angel Uriel; Enoch is shown the motions of the sun and moon, the "gates" from which they rise and into which they set, the winds, prominent geographic features, and calendrical information. A solar year of 364 days is synchronized with a lunar year of 354 days. 1 En. 80:2–82:3 (a probable later interpolation) contains a criticism of the angelic chiefs of the stars because of their failure to correspond exactly to the prescribed calendar, criticism of human sinners, and an account of Enoch's return to earth for his 365th year (suggestive of calendrical concerns) to teach wisdom to his son Methuselah and his descendants.

Book 1, the Book of the Watchers (chs. 1-36), was composed during the 3rd century. The core (chs. 6–11), based on the account of the union of the "sons of God" with the "daughters of men" in Gen. 6:1-4, is the story of the conspiracy of 200 angelic Watchers under the leadership of Shemihazah to take human wives. The giant offspring (which may function as a metaphor for the successors of Alexander the Great) of these illicit unions began to consume all of the earth's resources until God sent (an) archangel(s) to destroy the giants, imprison the Watchers, and restore the earth to a state of fruitfulness and righteousness. This core was expanded by the addition of chs. 12–16, which introduce Enoch to the narrative and describe his visionary ascent to heaven and his intercession for the Watchers. Their petition was rejected because they had defiled themselves by violating the distinction between heaven and earth (possibly a metaphor for the presumed defilement of the Jerusalem priesthood). The third stage consists of the introduction of Asael and the theme of illicit teachings of heavenly secrets throughout chs. 6–16 and one or more avenging archangels in ch. 10. Chs. 17–36 are a narrative of two of Enoch's journeys to the various places of everlasting punishment, the accursed valley of Hinnom in Jerusalem, the garden of righteousness, the mountain of God, and the four corners of the earth where the gates of the stars, winds, and various forms of precipitation are situated. Finally, chs. 1–5 were added as an introduction to the whole on the theme of final judgment and the need to do the commandments of the Lord.

Book 4, the Book of Dreams (chs. 83–90), consists of two dream visions. The first dream, of uncertain date, concerns the judgment of the wicked in the Deluge and by implication also refers to the final judgment. The second, written in 165 or 164, is an allegorical account of the history of humanity, in which animals represent human beings, humans represent angels, and stars represent the Watchers. The patriarchs from Adam to Isaac are represented by bulls, Israel by sheep, and the gentile nations by various nonkosher (usually predatory) animals. God is depicted as the sheep's owner. In response to various failures of the sheep, their owner abandons them into the hands of 70 unfaithful shepherds (angels). History culminates with God's intervention in a final battle between the sheep led by a ram (Judas Maccabeus) and the other animals. This is followed by the judgment of the stars, shepherds, and wicked sheep; the leveling and rebuilding of the sheep's house (Jerusalem, probably without a new temple); and the assembling of all the righteous animals (Jews and Gentiles) in the new house in the presence of the owner. Finally, a new white bull appears (a new Adam) and all animals are transformed into white bulls, representing the eschatological transformation of all humanity into a single Adamic race.

Book 5, the so-called Epistle of Enoch (chs. 91–105), was composed in the 2nd century B.C.E. It contains a testamentary introduction and the Apocalypse of Weeks (93:3-10 and 91:11-17). Both the apocalypse and the subsequent prophetic woes, admonitions, and predictions express a fundamental opposition of violence and deceit against righteousness and truth. The apocalypse provides the temporal framework for the subsequent prophetic judgments on the rich and powerful, who will be punished for their oppression of the righteous and deception of the many. Two brief accounts are appended at the end. The first is an account of Noah's miraculous birth and Enoch's assurance that Noah and his sons will be saved when the rest of the world is destroyed by a flood (chs. 106–107). The second is a final book of Enoch detailing the future punishment of the wicked and reward of the righteous (ch. 108).

Book 2, the Similitudes, or the Book of the Parables (chs. 37–71), consists of three "parables" and was composed in the 1st century B.C.E. or the 1st century C.E. The parables are an expansion and interpretation of earlier accounts of Enoch's visionary travels to heaven and throughout the cosmos. The first parable contains information about the fate of the righteous and sinners and astronomical secrets. The second and third parables develop the theme of eschatological judgment primarily in terms of the eschatological judge who is called "the Righteous one," "the Elect one," and "the Son of Man." Following the third parable is a final vision in which Enoch learns that he is the Son of Man.

Each of the books of 1 Enoch is an apocalypse in its present form. The Astronomical Book, the Book of the Watchers, and the Book of Parables consist largely of cosmic journeys and angelic interpretations. The oldest layers of the Book of the Watchers, however, are not apocalyptic in either form or content, and the original form of the Astronomical Book is uninterested in eschatology. The Book of Dreams and the Apocalypse of Weeks are symbolic surveys of history leading up to the eschaton. The Epistle of Enoch contains testamentary, wisdom, prophetic, and apocalyptic forms. From the point of view of their authors, the books are the heavenly wisdom revealed in Enoch's visions and travels and in the heavenly tablets.

2 (Slavonic) Enoch

2 Enoch was translated from Greek into Slavonic, the only ancient version in which it survives, having been composed probably in Hebrew (or Aramaic). The date of composition may be near the turn of the era. There are no specifically Christian ideas in it (apart from a few interpolations), nor is there very much that is specifically Jewish. Its fundamental teachings seem to be limited to monotheism and general ethics. The second half consists of Enoch's final address to his sons and subsequent ascension to heaven in his 365th year. It is reminiscent of 1 Enoch in its content and theology, with descriptions of Enoch's journey to heaven, heaven itself, cosmology, eschatology, calendar, angelology, and the secret wisdom granted to Enoch.

3 (Hebrew) Enoch

3 Enoch is a pseudepigraph written in Hebrew probably in the 5th or 6th century C.E. As a representative of Merkabah mysticism, it purports to be an account by Rabbi Ishmael (early 2nd century C.E.) of his ascension to God's throne. There he received revelations concerning angelic hierarchy and liturgy, cosmology, eschatology, and the exaltation and transformation of Enoch into God's vice-regent Meṭaṭron.

Bibliography. P. S. Alexander, "3 (Hebrew Apocalypse of) Enoch," *OTP* 1 (Garden City, 1983): 223-315; F. I. Andersen, "2 (Slavonic Apocalypse of) Enoch," *OTP* 1:91-221; M. Black, *The Book of Enoch or 1 Enoch.* SVTP 7 (Leiden, 1985); M. A. Knibb, *The Ethiopic Book of Enoch,* 2 vols. (Oxford, 1978); J. T. Milik, *The Books of Enoch: Aramaic Fragments of Qumrân Cave 4* (Oxford, 1976); D. W. Suter, *Tradition and Composition in the Parables of Enoch.* SBLDS 47 (Missoula, 1979); P. A. Tiller, *A Commentary on the Animal Apocalypse of 1 Enoch.* Early Judaism and Its Literature 4 (Atlanta, 1993); J. C. VanderKam, *Enoch, a Man for All Generations* (Columbia, S.C., 1995); *Enoch and the Growth of an Apocalyptic Tradition.* CBQMS 16 (Washington, 1984).

PATRICK A. TILLER

ENOSH (Heb. *'ĕnôš*) (also ENOS) (Gk. *Enos*)
The son of Seth and grandson of Adam (Luke 3:38). According to Gen. 5:9-11 at the age of 90 Enosh sired a son Kenan and then lived an additional 815 years. During Enosh's generation people began a new pattern of worship by invoking the name Yahweh (Gen. 4:26). This statement may imply a contrast with Gen. 4:17-24, but only if the line of Cain should indeed be interpreted as an example of wickedness.

Bibliography. A. S. Maller, "The Difficult Verse in Genesis 4:26," *JBQ* 18 (1990): 257-59, 263.

EDWIN C. HOSTETTER

EN-RIMMON (Heb. *'ên-rimmôn*)
A city in Judah assigned to the tribe of Simeon (Josh. 19:7). At 1 Chr. 4:32 (so LXX) it is assigned to Judah. Although earlier identified with Khirbet Umm er-Ramāmîm/Ḥorvat Rimmon (137086), excavations have shown that this site was not occupied during the biblical period. The city may have been located at Tel Ḥalif/Tell Khuweilifeh (1373.0879), 1 km. (.6 mi.) to the north.

LAURA B. MAZOW

EN-ROGEL (Heb. *'ên rōgēl*)
A spring near Jerusalem. An important landmark on the boundary between the tribes of Judah and Benjamin (cf. Josh. 15:7; 18:16), En-rogel served as the place where Jonathan and Ahimaaz gathered information for David during Absalom's revolt (2 Sam. 17:17). It was also where Adonijah held his sacrificial feast when he anticipated his father's death, expecting to seize the throne.

Some have interpreted the name to mean "the spring of the fuller" or "the fountain of feet," from the belief that here fullers worked their cloth with their feet. However, the meaning of *rōgēl* (also translated "spies," "explorers," "treaders") is uncertain.

En-rogel is generally identified as Bir Ayyûb ("the well of Job"), ca. 210 m. (690 ft.) beyond the junction of the Kidron and the Hinnom valleys. Some object to this association on the basis that Bir Ayyûb is a well, not a spring. However, it is possible that the original spring was covered as a result of an earthquake. Josephus (*Ant.* 9.10.4) connects En-rogel with the earthquake in the time of Uzziah (cf. Amos 1:1; Zech. 14:5). Whether or not the present well is the location of the ancient "spring," En-rogel was most certainly in this vicinity.

JOHN L. HARRIS

ENROLLMENT

A listing of people — usually by family, lineage, or tribe — who live in a particular area, belong to a particular social group, or practice a particular occupation. Ancient enrollments must be distinguished from modern censuses. A census is a regular collection of demographic data for statistical purposes; enrollments are enumerations undertaken for immediate, practical reasons, including taxation (Exod. 30:11-16), military conscription (Num. 1:1-47; 2 Sam. 24:1-9), deployment of laborers (2 Chr. 2:17-18[MT 16-17]; Neh. 3:1-32), consecration of cultic personnel (Num. 3:14-39; 26:57-62), determination of community status (Ezra 2:1-67), enforcement of legal regulations (Ezra 10:16-44), and distribution of provisions and property (Num. 26:1-51).

Beliefs concerning the potential of enrollments to incur divine wrath (Exod. 30:12; 2 Sam. 24:1, 10-25) may have arisen out of an ancient taboo based on the conviction that enrollments displayed a lack of trust in the deity.

The NT contains two apparent references to a tax enrollment conducted by P. Sulpicius Quirinius in 6 B.C.E., after he had been appointed as the Roman imperial legate to Syria. Luke seems to date Jesus' birth synchronously with this enrollment (Luke 2:1-5), and Gamaliel recalls that Judas the Galilean led a revolt against Rome in reaction to the enrollment (Acts 5:37). The difficulty of harmonizing these assertions with other ancient statements is considerable.

A few passages refer to divine enrollments of nations and people (Ps. 87:6; Heb. 12:23). Among these should no doubt be included references to the Book of Life (Ps. 69:28[29]; Phil. 4:3; Rev. 3:5).

FRANK D. WULF

EN-SHEMESH (Heb. *ʿên šemeš*)

A landmark spring ("spring of the sun") on the border between the territories of Judah (Josh. 15:7) and Benjamin (18:17; LXX "Beth-shemesh"). It is commonly identified with ʿAin el-Hôd/Ein Haud (175131), ca. 4 km. (2 mi.) E of Jerusalem. According to one tradition (ca. 15th century C.E.) the apostles drank from this spring; since then it has been called "Spring of the Apostles."

EN-TAPPUAH (Heb. *ʿên tappûaḥ*)

A spring ("spring of the apple tree") located on a ridge ca. 9 km. (7.5 mi.) S of Nablus, named after the nearby town of Tappuah (modern Sheikh Abū Zarad; 172168; Josh. 17:7-8). It was a border marker between northern Ephraim and southern Manasseh in the central plain. This area was a Canaanite stronghold at the time of Joshua's conquest, and it took the combined efforts of the tribes to dislodge the Canaanites.

JOHN A. MCLEAN

EPAENETUS (Gk. *Epaínetos*)

A Christian whom Paul greets as "my beloved" and "the first convert in Asia" (Rom. 16:5). Epaenetus probably belonged to the house church of Prisca and Aquila and was converted by them or Paul. At the time of Paul's greeting (ca. 58 C.E.), Epaenetus probably lived in Rome. Although a Roman inscription bearing the name Epaenetus, an Ephesian, exists (*CIL* 6.17171), its identification with the Epaenetus of Romans is impossible.

FLORENCE M. GILLMAN

EPAPHRAS (Gk. *Epaphrás*)

A Colossian whom Paul describes as "beloved fellow servant," "faithful minister of Christ," "servant of Christ Jesus" (Col. 1:7; 4:12-13), and "fellow prisoner" (Phlm. 23). That his name appears at the head of the list in Philemon and that Paul calls him *doúlos* and *sýndoulos,* terms used for himself but infrequently of others, indicate Paul's high regard for him. Epaphras founded the Colossian church (Col. 1:7), brought news of it to Paul (vv. 4-8), and bore responsibility for it and perhaps Laodicea and Hierapolis (4:13). His "earnest prayer" *(agonizōmenos)* for those churches is indicated by the same term used to describe Jesus' prayer in the garden of Gethsemane and Paul's own struggles for the gospel (Col. 1:29). Epaphras prays that the Colossians will be mature *(téleioi)* and fully assured *(peplērophorēménoi)* in the will of God (Col. 4:12), terms alluding to rival teachers in Colossae. Epaphras' prayer, like Paul's (Col. 1:3-12), opposes their "philosophy" (2:8). Paul's confidence in and commendation of Epaphas raise his status among the Colossians and inspire their confidence in him (as opposed to the false teachers). Epaphras is perhaps an abridgement of Epaphroditus, but no evidence connects him with the Epaphroditus of Phil. 2:25; 4:18.

Bibliography. D. E. Hiebert, "Epaphras, Man of Prayer," *BSac* 136 (1979): 54-64.

BONNIE THURSTON

EPAPHRODITUS (Gk. *Epaphróditos*)

A Christian sent by the Philippian church to deliver gifts to the imprisoned Paul and help him (Phil. 4:18). Epaphroditus then became ill and nearly died. Paul called him his brother, fellow worker (Gk. *synergós*), fellow soldier *(systratiṓtēs),* and the Philippians' messenger *(apóstolos)* and minister *(leitourgós)* to him (Phil. 2:25-30). The terms signify Paul's recognition of Epaphroditus' exemplary sacrificial service to him on behalf of the gospel. Epaphroditus was a common personal name in the 1st century C.E., related to the name of the Greek goddess of love, Aphrodite, and may shed light on his family background.

Paul refers to an Epaphras as his fellow prisoner (Phlm. 23) and identifies an Epaphras of Colossae as a beloved fellow servant *(sýndoulos)* and faithful minister *(diákonos)* and servant *(doúlos)* of Christ

(Col. 1:7; 4:12). While the name Epaphras could be a shortened form of Epaphroditus, the latter was most likely a Philippian, not a Colossian.

Bibliography. R. A. Culpepper, "Co-Workers in Suffering: Philippians 2:19-30," *RevExp* 77 (1980): 349-58.

SCOTT NASH

EPHAH (Heb. *'êpâ*) **(MEASURE)**

A dry measure, 10 times the size of an omer (Exod. 16:36). Precise volume is uncertain; an ephah equals 10-20 l. (2.6-5.3 gal.) or one-third to two-thirds of a bushel and is equal to the liquid bath (Ezek. 45:11). The term also designates a container with the capacity of an ephah (Zech. 5:6-10).

JOHN R. SPENCER

EPHAH (Heb. *'êpâ*) **(PERSON)**

1. One of the sons of Midian (Gen. 25:4; 1 Chr. 1:33). The name presumably designates a Midianite tribe, from the region SE of Palestine along the northeast shore of the Gulf of Aqaba. The tribe was famous for raising camels (Isa. 60:6).

2. Caleb's concubine, mother of Haran, Moza, and Gazez (1 Chr. 2:46).

3. A son of Jahdai (1 Chr. 2:47). Although no parentage is provided, the context suggests he is a member of the Calebite community.

Bibliography. E. A. Knauf, "Midianites and Ishmaelites," in *Midian, Moab, and Edom,* ed. J. F. A. Sawyer and D. J. A. Clines. JSOTSup 24 (Sheffield, 1983), 147-62.

JOHN R. SPENCER

EPHAI (Heb. *'êpay*)

A Netophathite whose sons were among the "leaders of the forces" who came to Gedaliah at Mizpah following the fall of Jerusalem (Jer. 40:8). There the entire assembly was murdered by Ishmael, the son of Nethaniah (Jer. 41:1-3). In the parallel account (2 Kgs. 25:23) "the sons of Ephai" are omitted.

EPHER (Heb. *'ēper*)

1. The second son of Midian and grandson of Abraham and Keturah (Gen. 25:4; 1 Chr. 1:33); eponymous ancestor of a Midianite clan.

2. The third son of Ezrah and eponymous ancestor of a Judahite clan (1 Chr. 4:17).

3. The first mentioned in a list of "mighty warriors, famous men," and heads of clans in the Transjordanian half-tribe of Manasseh (1 Chr. 5:24).

EPHES-DAMMIM (Heb. *'epes dammîm*) (also PAS-DAMMIM)

The area in which the Philistine army camped as they prepared to battle Saul preceding the battle of David and Goliath, located between Socoh and Zekah (1 Sam. 17:1). Although some scholars identify it with modern Damun, ca. 6.5 km. (4 mi.) NE of Socoh, the text suggests it should be W of Socoh. It also occurs as Pas-dammim, where Eleazar, one of David's Mighty Men, fought alongside David in the midst of a barley field (1 Chr. 11:13).

STEVEN M. ORTIZ

EPHESIANS (Gk. *Ephésioi),* **LETTER TO THE**

A letter attributed to the Apostle Paul, but actually not written to the Ephesians. The words "in Ephesus" in modern translations of Eph. 1:1 are missing in the earliest and best ancient manuscripts. Also, the statement in 3:2 that the readers "have heard" of Paul's apostolic ministry (as opposed to having a personal acquaintance with him) conflicts with Acts, which reports that Paul ministered there for almost three years. Most likely the letter was originally a circular letter to various gentile churches, probably in western Asia Minor. Some scholars have identified Ephesians with "the letter from Laodicea" (Col. 4:16), but this is doubtful. It may have been written for a general audience of Gentile Christians and at some point come to be associated with Ephesus, but how this happened is uncertain. Possibly, the letter circulated from Ephesus to churches in outlying regions; or perhaps, when Paul's letters were being collected, it was convenient to assign an unaddressed Pauline letter to the church where Paul had a lengthy ministry but which had no other letter addressed to it.

Contents

After the prescript (1:1-2) come a eulogy praising God for the spiritual benefits the Gentiles have received through God's work in Christ (1:3-14) and a prayer of thanks and petition for their spiritual enlightenment regarding those benefits (1:15-23). Then, in an anamnesis (recalling of the past to inform present attitudes or actions), the readers' past (spiritual deadness and exclusion) is contrasted with their present (spiritual life and inclusion) and they are told to "remember" in order to appreciate what God has done for them (2:1-22). More petitionary prayer follows, for power leading to even greater spiritual benefits (3:1, 14-19). Interrupting the prayer is a long digression on Paul as apostle to the Gentiles and minister of the gospel (3:2-13) showing the crucial role he has played in mediating the knowledge of the "mystery of Christ." A doxology (3:20-21) closes the first main part of the letter. Exhortation concerning the Christian life makes up the second main part. Christians should "walk worthily" of their calling, preserving the unity of the Spirit through love (4:1-16), and not "walk as the Gentiles" but as those who are renewed (4:17-24). Instructions about specific kinds of behavior are given (5:1-20), then rules governing relationships in the ancient household (5:21–6:9). A final appeal is made to prepare for spiritual battle, and in light of it, to pray (6:10-20). The letter ending contains a commendation of Tychicus and a benediction (6:21-24). The letter thus falls into two basic parts, a more theological part, followed by parenesis developing the practical implications of the theology (cf. Romans, Galatians).

Occasion, Purpose, and Literary Classification

The occasion and purpose of Ephesians are matters of debate. Errant teaching and persecution are suggested occasions (cf. 4:14; 6:10-17). Other suggestions make a more general appeal to the text, e.g., that Ephesians was written (1) as an apology to show the connection of the Church with Judaism and thus to counteract embarrassment over the Church's relatively late appearance; (2) as a polemic to deal with a crisis over the unity between Jewish and Gentile Christians in which Jewish Christianity was being marginalized by a burgeoning Gentile Christianity; and (3) as a polemic to deal with the threat of syncretistic use of magical practices by Christians. All of these are very speculative, and lack a compelling basis in the text.

According to 3:2-4 the addressees, who have only "heard" of Paul's apostolic office, will be able to perceive Paul's insight into "the mystery of Christ" by reading what he "wrote above in a few words." This suggests that the primary purpose and occasion of Ephesians is to further the readers' understanding of and rooting in Paul's gospel, given their lack of personal acquaintance with him. "The mystery of Christ" refers to the divinely revealed truth, beyond all human imagination, that the Gentiles are "fellow heirs, members of the same body, and sharers in the promise in Christ Jesus through the gospel" (3:6). Those who were excluded and without hope are now included as full participants in salvation. Paul was entrusted with preaching this mystery (3:7), and the present letter is portrayed as an attempt to carry on that task from a prison cell (3:1; 4:1). The letter is written to Gentile Christians who have already been evangelized and are thus already incorporated into the new unity of Jews and Gentiles in Christ; but they have not been evangelized or taught by Paul. Thus Ephesians takes the opportunity to inform them more fully of their equality and unity with Jewish believers and of the riches that are now theirs in Christ, and to draw out the practical implications of their position in Christ. The letter ensures that Paul's special legacy will not be lost to such gentile readers. This explanation seems to have the best foothold in the text.

A related question is the text's literary classification. Is it a letter, or something else disguised as a letter, e.g., a wisdom speech, a theological essay, a dogmatics in draft form, a homily for a baptismal occasion, a meditation, an introduction to a newly-formed collection of Paul's letters? If it is a true letter, of what kind? Some have compared it with the Greek letter of congratulations (epideictic letter) that uses praise to reinforce certain values, in this case congratulating the readers on their new state in Christ to strengthen their appreciation for the gospel. It can also be compared with the Greek letter of advice (deliberative letter) that seeks to encourage certain behavior. It seems best to view Ephesians as an actual letter, but one that blends various rhetorical, liturgical, and traditional elements to accomplish its specific purpose.

Theological Themes

In line with the purpose of reinforcing the spiritual benefits gentile believers have received through incorporation into Christ, Ephesians draws attention to their spiritual resurrection and exaltation with Christ in the heavenly places, their salvation by grace through faith apart from works, and their reconciliation to God through Christ's death "in one body." The dominant soteriological categories are union with Christ and reconciliation (e.g., as opposed to justification). The horizontal aspect of reconciliation — that Jews and Gentiles are reconciled to one another in Christ — is prominent and is developed in 2:11-22. By his death Christ destroyed the law that functioned as a "dividing wall" between Jews and Gentiles and created "one new person," the Church. Other metaphors for the Church as this new unity are building, household, holy temple, bride of Christ, and body.

Ephesians also develops the theme of unity by drawing on the exaltation and enthronement of Christ. Here the Pauline metaphor of the Church as the body of Christ is expanded to include the notion of the exalted Christ as "head" of the "body" in a figurative sense. Ephesians tailors its notion of the "Church" to this broader interest in unity, using *ekklēsía* for the church universal, not the local congregation. The interest in unity also extends to the whole cosmos: Christ is "head" over "all things," head of a cosmic unity that is the final goal of God's work in Christ, made known through the Church. It is God's purpose to "sum up all things in Christ" as their head. Christology, ecclesiology, and eschatology are thus closely wedded in Ephesians.

In keeping with its emphasis on the exaltation and enthronement of Christ, the letter stresses the present realization of salvation for those who belong to Christ, especially in the emphatic references to salvation as a past event (2:5, 8), and to co-resurrection and co-seating with Christ as having already taken place (2:6). The grandeur and graciousness of this salvation are highlighted by the fact that it is rooted in God's eternal counsel, predestination, election of believers before the foundation of the world, and preparing beforehand the good works they are to walk in. God's saving purposes, however, are not yet completely realized; Ephesians retains a future eschatological perspective alongside the stress on present fulfillment. Believers are "marked with the seal of the promised Holy Spirit" as a "pledge of our inheritance." The Church has yet to attain to "the unity of the faith," to full maturity. Christians must still "put on the whole armor of God" to wage spiritual battle against the schemes of the devil. Nevertheless, Ephesians' stress on realized eschatology leads to an omission of the mention of the return of Christ found in Col. 3:4.

Authorship, Dating, and Related Questions

In various ways Ephesians stands apart from the epistles that are accepted as authentically Pauline. It originally lacked a geographical address. It does not deal with any congregational issues, and may not even have been written for a local congregation. It is distinguished by a redundant and elaborate style, and has a significant number of words and phrases that do not occur elsewhere in Paul. Its structure is distinctive, and some of its theological perspectives are uncharacteristic.

Ephesians possesses a striking closeness to Colossians, including a large percentage of shared vocabulary, verbatim agreements, shared thematic material which appears in the same sequence in major blocks, and similarity in style. Ephesians also differs from Colossians; it develops and reconfigures some of the shared material, cites Scripture, and lacks references to controversial teaching and personal connections that would suggest a particular congregation is in view. Thus most scholars have concluded that Ephesians was written by someone using Colossians as a model. A minority view is that Ephesians was the model for Colossians, while some argue that there was a common blueprint for both.

Most scholars now see the cumulative effect of the distinctive features of Ephesians and its relationship to Colossians as casting doubt on Pauline authorship. Ephesians seems to stand too far apart from other Pauline epistles in a variety of ways, even though it clearly claims to have been written by Paul (1:1; 3:3) and its Pauline authorship was apparently never doubted in the early Church. Moreover, if someone wrote Ephesians using Colossians as a model, and Colossians itself was not authored by Paul, Ephesians could hardly have been written by Paul. Ephesians is thus most commonly judged to be pseudonymous, written by a later follower of Paul in his name. Presupposing pseudonymity, Ephesians was written sometime after Colossians, no earlier than 62 C.E., but probably between 70 and 95. Pseudonymity was a common literary practice in that time, a device to bring the intellectual or spiritual heritage of a great figure to bear on a new situation or time. The intent to deceive is not necessarily implied, and the readers of Ephesians might have known full well that the letter was written by someone assuming Paul's name. Further, canonical authority does not rest on the issue of authentic vs. pseudonymous authorship.

A minority of scholars reject the hypothesis of pseudonymity, arguing that stylistic and conceptual variations exist within the accepted Pauline corpus. Further, some of Ephesians' "uncharacteristic features" can be attributed to the different circumstances surrounding the letter, including its general rather than specific address, its conjectured occasion and purpose, developments in Paul's own situation and thinking (Roman imprisonment), his borrowing of traditional material (e.g., church liturgy in 5:14; Scripture in 4:8-10; ethical codes in 5:21–6:9), use of a secretary directly responsible for the actual formulations of the letter, or a combination of these. The closeness to Colossians can be taken to support Pauline authorship, on the condition that Colossians is Pauline: Ephesians can be viewed as Paul's reworking of Colossians for a more general audience. In that case it would have been written from Rome ca. 62.

Until better criteria are developed for assessing what Paul could have written, different assessments of the Paulineness of Ephesians will persist. Meanwhile, the majority of scholars will probably continue to be persuaded by the cumulative argument against the Pauline authorship of Ephesians and view the letter as more likely written by someone very familiar with Paul's thought. Indebtedness to Pauline thought and writings is obvious. Other influences have been suggested as well. Because of parallels with the Qumran literature, it seems likely that some thought patterns have been transmitted through sectarian Judaism. Hellenistic Greek or Jewish sources may have contributed also, as in the case of the concept of the "body." A few have proposed the influence of gnostic thought in the cosmological and soteriological ideas of Ephesians, but the parallels may be overdrawn. These probable influences would identify the author as a Jewish Christian with roots in Hellenistic Judaism, and, if not Paul himself, a keen follower of Paul.

Bibliography. M. Barth, *Ephesians 1–3.* AB 34 (Garden City, 1974); *Ephesians 4–6.* AB 34A (Garden City, 1974); A. T. Lincoln, *Ephesians.* WBC 42 (Waco, 1990); Lincoln and A. J. M. Wedderburn, *The Theology of the Later Pauline Letters* (Cambridge, 1993); R. P. Martin, "An Epistle in Search of a Life-Setting," *ExpTim* 79 (1967-68): 296-302; A. van Roon, *The Authenticity of Ephesians.* NovTSup 39 (Leiden, 1975); R. Schnackenburg, *Ephesians* (Edinburgh, 1991). JUDITH M. GUNDRY-VOLF

EPHESUS (Gk. *Éphesos*)

An early Greek colony in southwestern Ionia on the coast of Asia Minor and a member of the 12-city Ionian league (Strabo *Geog.* 8.7.1). According to legend Ephesus was founded (ca. 900 B.C.E.) by Androclus, son of Codrus, king of Athens (Strabo 14.1.3; Pausanias *Descr. Gr.* 7.2.7). The city was originally located on the south side of the Cayster River, but through centuries of silting is now located 10 km. (6 mi.) inland. Strabo described Ephesus as the largest commercial center in Asia (14.1.24). The narrowing of the entrance to the harbor by Attalos III (ca. 159-138) apparently unwittingly facilitated the silting up of the harbor (Strabo 14.1.24). Most modern estimates of the population of Ephesus during the Roman Empire are based on the supposition that the city had ca. 40 thousand male citizens, with an estimated total population of ca. 200 to 225 thousand. This is based on erroneously reading the number 40 thousand in an inscription which actually has the figure 1040, so the figures of 200 to 225 thousand, while not impossibly large, are not based on actual evidence from antiquity.

Throughout its long and complex history, Ephesus was subject to a series of kingdoms and empires. Its history can be divided into three periods. (1) Foundation to 555. Little of Ephesus is known from its foundation ca. 900 until it was captured by Croesus, king of Lydia, ca. 555 (Herodotus *Hist.* 1.26). (2) Ephesus was captured by Cyrus of Persia ca. 546, and following the Greco-Persian wars became part of the Delian League (an Athenian maritime confederacy), but revolted against Athens in 412 and sided with Sparta during the rest of the Peloponnesian War (431-404). In 386, as a result of "the King's Peace," Ephesus was again under

Colonnaded road at Ephesus, once lined with shops, leading from the harbor to the theater
(Phoenix Data Systems, Neal and Joel Bierling)

subjection to the Persians. When Ionia was liberated by Alexander in 334, Ephesus came under the control of a series of Hellenistic rulers. (3) Ephesus the Hellenistic and Roman city (ca. 290 B.C.E. to 1000 C.E.). Lysimachus controlled the region around Ephesus after the death of Alexander and pacified the region ca. 302 (Pausanias 1.9.7). He built a wall 10 km. (6 mi.) in circumference around the city ca. 287 (Strabo 14.1.21). In 197 Antiochus III of Syria conquered the southern coast of Asia Minor and made Ephesus his second capital. Ephesus was subject to Eumenes of Pergamum in 190, and was under the Pergamene rulers until 133, when Attalos III of Pergamum died and willed his empire to Rome. Thereafter it became the official residence of the governor of the Roman province of Asia. Ephesus was originally located on Mt. Pion, but was moved by the Lydian king Croesus to a level region east of Pion. The worship of Ephesian Artemis predates the Greek colonization of Ionia (Pausanias 7.2.6). Ephesian Artemis was originally an Anatolian goddess of hunting and fertility named Cybele in Phrygia and Ma in Cappadocia. The Ephesians later claimed that Apollo and Artemis had been born, not in Delos, but in Ephesus (Tacitus *Ann.* 3.60-63; cf. Strabo 14.1.20). The earliest temple to Artemis was destroyed by the Cimmerians ca. 660. This was rebuilt twice, followed by a major reconstruction begun by Croesus ca. 550 but unfinished until ca. 430. In 356 the earlier temple was destroyed by fire and rebuilt under the supervision of the Macedonian architect Deinocrates (Vitruvius 1.1.4). The resultant edifice was considered one of the seven wonders of the ancient world (Pausanias 4.31.8; 7.5.4). The Artemision (Acts 19:23-41) was located NE of the city, and was famous as a place of sanctuary in the ancient world (Pausanias 7.2.8; Strabo 14.1.23; Josephus *Ant.* 15.89). Though it was destroyed by the Ostrogoths in 263 C.E., the great altar, located west of the temple precinct, has been excavated. In 29 B.C.E. the Romans in the province of Asia received permission from Octavian, soon to become the emperor Augustus, to dedicate a temple in Ephesus to Roma and Divus Julius jointly (Dio Cassius *Hist.* 51.20.6-7). During the Roman imperial period, cities honored by being chosen as sites for the erection of temples to patron deities (i.e., Artemis) and the imperial cult assumed the title "temple-keeper" (Acts 19:35), applied to cities in Roman Asia by the mid-1st century C.E. which had been granted the right to build temples in honor of important deities. The buildings excavated by archaeologists include a library built in honor of the Roman governor of Asia, C. Julius Celsus Polemeanus (106-107), a temple in honor of Hadrian (117-138), erected toward the beginning of his reign and containing an important series of friezes, a fountain in honor of Trajan, and traces of a temple in honor of Domitian and a temple of Serapis (2nd century), with massive facade of eight stone columns 14 m. (46 ft.) high and nearly 1.5 m. (5 ft.) in diameter. The theater (cf. Acts 19:23-41), which could accommodate ca. 24 thousand people, has also been excavated.

There is very little actual evidence for the presence of Judaism in Ephesus during the Hellenistic and Roman periods. Alexander the Great had granted civil rights to the Jews of Ionia, and they actually received *isonomia* (i.e., their own laws and customs were respected equally with those of the Greeks) from Antiochus II (Josephus *Ag. Ap.* 1.22). The presence of a synagogue in

Ephesus is mentioned in Acts 18:26; 19:8, though no archaeological remains and comparatively few Jewish inscriptions have been found. Josephus indicates that there was a large Jewish community in Ephesus by the mid-3rd century B.C.E. (*Ant.* 12.125-26, 166-68, 172-73).

Ephesus was an important center for early Christianity and is frequently mentioned in the NT. The Christian community there was probably founded by Paul (Irenaeus *Adv. haer.* 3.3.4). Paul wrote 1 Corinthians from Ephesus, where he had experienced the ready acceptance of the gospel (1 Cor. 16:8-9), and he also mentions the fact that he had "fought with beasts at Ephesus" (15:32). If taken literally, this could refer to the stadium which has been excavated. However, he may have spoken metaphorically, borrowing a phrase from Hellenistic moral philosophy's description of a wise man's struggle with hedonism. Paul's first visit to Ephesus was comparatively brief (Acts 18:19-21). His second visit, however, lasted more than two years (Acts 19:1-41), though according to 20:31, he spent three years in Ephesus. While Acts 19 narrates several events in Ephesus, very little is actually revealed about the Christian community there. Acts 20:17-38 narrates a meeting at Miletus between Paul and the "elders" of the church at Ephesus, where he predicts that after he leaves (dies?) "savage wolves will come in among you, not sparing the flock. Some even from your own group will come distorting the truth in order to entice the disciples to follow them" (20:29-30). Since the deutero-Pauline letter Ephesians was probably not originally written to Ephesus, but is a circular letter of very general character, it reveals nothing about Christianity there during the late 1st century, when it was probably written. It is also striking that the message to the church at Ephesus in Rev. 2:1-7 shows no trace of Pauline influence.

Ignatius of Antioch wrote a letter to the church at Ephesus while on a forced march through the province of Asia on his way to Rome ca. 110. He mentions Onesimus as the bishop of Ephesus (*Eph.* 1:3; 6;2), whom some have tenuously linked with the runaway slave of the same name in Phlm. 10 (Col. 4:9), though the name was a relatively common slave name.

Ephesus is the traditional residence, in later life, of John the Apostle (Eusebius *HE* 3.1), who was thought to have lived into the reign of Trajan (98-117; Irenaeus *Adv. haer.* 3.3.4). According to tradition, he wrote his Gospel at Ephesus (*HE* 5.8.4), and was eventually buried there (3.39.5-6; 5.24.3). The Basilica of St. John was erected on the traditional site of his tomb during the reign of Justinian (527-565). Timothy is remembered as the first bishop of Ephesus (*HE* 3.4.5), a tradition probably based on 1 Tim. 1:3. Ephesus is also the site for Justin's dialogue with Trypho the Jew (*Dial.* 2-8; Eusebius *HE* 4.18.6).

Bibliography. F. V. Filson, "Ephesus and the New Testament," *BA* 8 (1945): 73-80, repr. in *BAR* 2, ed. D. N. Freedman and E. F. Campbell (Garden City, 1964), 343-52; S. J. Friesen, *Twice Neokoros: Ephesus, Asia and the Cult of the Flavian Imperial Family* (Leiden, 1993); G. H. R. Horsley, "The Inscriptions of Ephesos and the New Testament," *NovT* 34 (1992): 105-68; D. Magie, *Roman Rule in Asia Minor to the End of the Third Century After Christ,* 2 vols. (1950, repr. New York, 1975); R. E. Oster, *A Bibliography of Ancient Ephesus* (Metuchen, 1987); R. Strelan, *Paul, Artemis, and the Jews in Ephesus. BZNW* 80 (Berlin, 1966); P. D. Warden and R. S. Bagnall, "The Forty Thousand Citizens of Ephesus," *Classical Philology* 83 (1988): 220-23.

DAVID E. AUNE

EPHLAL (Heb. *'eplāl*)
A Judahite, the son of Zabad and father of Obed (1 Chr. 2:37).

EPHOD (Heb. *'ēpōḏ*)
An ornate, sleeveless outer garment worn by the Israelite high priest. Exod. 28:6-10 describes the ephod as a garment made of fine, twisted linen decorated with gold, blue, purple, and scarlet material. Two shoulder pieces and a woven belt made of the same materials complete the outfit. Affixed to the shoulder pieces were two onyx stones inscribed with the names of the sons of Israel. A breastplate made of the same materials and decorated with 12 precious stones, symbolizing the 12 tribes, was attached by golden rings to the front of the ephod (Exod. 28:15-28). A pocket in the breastplate stored the Urim and Thummim, the lots of divination.

The ephod also could be a common garment. David wears a linen ephod while dancing wildly in celebrating the arrival of the ark of the covenant at Jerusalem (2 Sam. 6:14). The boy Samuel wears an ephod around the temple as an everyday garment (1 Sam. 2:18).

Several passages describe an idolatrous ephod. Gideon makes an ephod with the captured gold of the Ishmaelites and places it in the city of Ophrah. It becomes a stumbling block to Gideon and his family along with all of Israel (Judg. 8:27). Gideon's ephod is not described, but it may be either a noniconic vestment employed in obtaining oracles or a garment covering an idol, such as those associated with Mesopotamian or Egyptian cultic statues (cf. Isa. 30:22). Along with teraphim, a molten image, a graven image, and a Levite priest, Micah set up an ephod in a house shrine (Judg. 17–18). Goliath's sword is wrapped in a cloth and kept behind the ephod in the sanctuary at Nob (1 Sam. 21:9). This ephod, however, may be a priestly garment hanging in front of the sword instead of an idol.

1 Samuel refers to the ephod as a tangible object of worship. Ahijah, Saul's priest, carries an ephod at the battle of Michmash (1 Sam. 14:3). By Saul's command, Doeg killed the 85 priests of the temple at Nob who carry the ephod (22:18). David is described as seeking the ephod for guidance from Yahweh (23:6, 9; 30:7). Some scholars argue that this ephod is the garment with a pocket carrying the oracular lot, the same ephod as described in Exod. 28, 39.

TERRY W. EDDINGER

EPHOD (Heb. *'ēpōḏ*) **(PERSON)**
The father of Hanniel, a leader of Manasseh chosen to assist in distributing the land among the tribes (Num. 34:23).

EPHPHATHA (Gk. *Ephphatha*)
Greek transliteration of an Aramaic term in Jesus' command that a man's ears and mouth "be opened" so that the man can hear and speak (Mark 7:34). It represents the passive imperative verb *pĕtaḥ*, "to open." Hellenistic miracles often contained unusual words which conveyed extraordinary power. If the Gospel of Mark was written primarily for people who understood Greek, then the Aramaic command may have sounded magical.

Emily Cheney

EPHRAIM (Heb. *'eprayim*) **(PERSON)**
The second son of the patriarch Joseph and eponymous ancestor of the tribe, which lent its name to the central hill country of Palestine.

Eponymous Figure

The exact etymology of the name Ephraim is unknown. The biblical text provides a popular etymology based on Heb. *prh*, "be fertile" (Gen. 41:52). Although the ending *-ayim* suggests a topographic name, there is disagreement over further elaboration of the name's meaning

The biblical figure is the second son of Joseph and Asenath, daugther of Potiphera priest of On (Gen. 41:52; 46:20). However, he received from Jacob the blessing of the firstborn instead of Manasseh, over the objections of Joseph (Gen. 48:13-20). Both Ephraim and Manasseh were adopted by Jacob as his own sons and thus reckoned among their uncles as tribal ancestors (Gen. 48:5). Ephraim was the father of nine sons who were killed by the men of Gath, and then of one additional son and a daughter (1 Chr. 7:20-24).

Tribe

The story of Ephraim replacing Manasseh as firstborn in Gen. 48 may be related to the historical situation whereby the tribe of Manasseh, at first more significant than the tribe of Ephraim (Num. 26:28-37), came to be outstripped by Ephraim, which eventually came to designate the entire northern kingdom of Israel. While some passages speak of "the land of Ephraim and Manasseh" (Deut. 34:2; 2 Chr. 30:10) as a territorial designation, in many prophetic passages "Ephraim" alone designates the sociopolitical entity of the northern kingdom (Isa. 7:2-17; 9:9, 21[MT 8, 20]; 11:13; Jer. 31:9-20; Ezek. 37:16-19; Hos. 5). The origin of this usage is uncertain, but may stem from the fact that Ephraim's territory actually constituted the geographic center of the northern kingdom, or because its first king, Jeroboam, was from the tribe of Ephraim (1 Kgs. 11:26). Hos. 5 may be a special case, in that there seems to be a distinction between Israel and Ephraim (v. 5). This may reflect a time when the northern kingdom was divided into two polities: Israel on the east bank of the Jordan (= Gilead, first annexed by Assyria), and Ephraim on the west bank remaining under Samaria's control.

Territory

The land of Ephraim comprised the central hill country of Palestine, stretching approximately from Bethel in the south to the latitude of Shechem in the north. The southern boundary ran from Jericho westward through Ai, Bethel, Gezer, and to the sea, while the northern border followed the Yarkon River in from the coast, and its tributary the Kanah River as far inland as the Ebal-Gerizim massif. East of Shechem, Ephraim's territory did not extend to the Jordan River, but turned south at Taanath-Shiloh and ran along the eastern borders of Samaria down to Jericho.

This geographic area contains several different topographic zones, as diverse as the narrow Sharon Plain along the coast and the heights of Ebal and Gerizim. Most of Ephraim was hill country of the Nablus syncline, among the most fertile areas in Palestine, boasting both good rainfall and soils. It supported an economy of both cereal farming and olive production, while the drier valleys of the Michmethath (Josh. 16:6; 17:7) and Beth-dagon were more suited to herding.

Israelite settlement in Ephraim begins with a dramatic growth in the Early Iron Age. At both the northern and southern extremes of Ephraim were regional centers at Shechem (Tell Balâtah) and Bethel (Beitin) and Ai (et-Tell), respectively. This illustrates the problem of applying the biblical tribal borders to the archaeological record, as these cities that straddle tribal boundaries seem to have governed territories that extended on "both sides" of the supposed lines. An economic polity which could be more clearly called Ephraim would be that centered on Iron I Shiloh (Khirbet Seilûn, Sailun). Here, the walled 12-dunam city appears to have been supported by a system of subordinate village centers and small hamlets extending far to the east and west. In Iron II, there was a tremendous 65 percent increase in the number of sites, more than 120 ha. (300 a.) were built up, and the entire region was under cultivation. The transition to a state economy, however, eliminated the great cities of Ephraim: Shiloh declined to a poor settlement, Shechem was replaced by northern kingdom capitals at Tirzah and Samaria, and the centers on the southern border diminished because of the political upheavals here on the border separating the kingdoms of Judah and Israel. After a sharp decrease in the Persian period, settlement in Ephraim was extensive in the Hellenistic, Roman, and Byzantine periods.

Bibliography. I. Finkelstein, *The Archaeology of the Israelite Settlement* (Jerusalem, 1988); ed., *Shiloh: The Archaeology of a Biblical Site* (Tel Aviv, 1993); D. C. Hopkins, *The Highlands of Canaan* (Sheffield, 1985); L. Watkins, "Southern Samaria, Survey of," *OEANE*, 5:66-68.

Robert D. Miller, II

EPHRAIM (Heb. *'eprayim*) **(PLACE)**
A town S of Baal-hazor and ca. 23 km. (14 mi.) N of Jersualem in the Judean hills, usually identified with modern eṭ-Ṭaiyibeh (178151). Here Absalom avenged the rape of his sister Tamar by the murder of her assailant Amnon (2 Sam. 13:23). After Lazarus' raising, Jesus went to Ephraim "near the wilderness" to be with his disciples (John 11:54). The name has been associated with biblical Ophrah (Josh. 18:23), Ephron (1 Macc. 5:46), and Aphairema (11:34). RICHARD A. SPENCER

EPHRAIM (Heb. *'eprayim*)**, FOREST OF**
The setting of the death of Absalom (2 Sam 18:6). One of perhaps several forests in Palestine during biblical times, its location has been a matter of debate. Since the forest is identified with Ephraim, some suggest it was located in the territory of Ephraim W of the Jordan River, an area to which the Bible attributes an extensive forest covering (Josh. 17:18). Others locate it E of the Jordan, based on 2 Sam. 17:24 which speaks of David traveling to Mahanaim in the territory of Gilead prior to the confrontation with Absalom. The forestry resources of Gilead are mentioned in the OT (Gen. 37:25; Jer 8:22; 46:11), and in the Prophets are ranked alongside the resources of the forest of Lebanon (Jer. 22:6; Zech. 10:10).
LAMOINE F. DEVRIES

EPHRATH (Heb. *'eprāṯ*) **(PERSON)**
(also EPHRATHAH)
The second wife of Caleb, mother of Hur and Asshur (1 Chr. 2:19); an alternate form of her name is Ephrathah (v. 24; 4:4).

EPHRATH (Heb. *'eprāṯ*) **(PLACE)**
1. A city near which Rachel died giving birth to Benjamin (Gen. 35:16), Ephrathah in southern Benjamin (1 Sam. 10:2; Jer. 31:15).
2. The place where Rachel was buried (Gen. 35:19; 48:7), generally identified with Bethlehem/Ephrathah (Ruth 4:11; Mic. 5:1).

EPHRATHAH (Heb. *'eprāṯâ*) **(PERSON)**
Another name for Ephrath, the wife of Caleb (1 Chr. 2:24; 4:4).

EPHRATHAH (Heb. *'eprāṯâ*) **(PLACE)**
A place name used in reference to Bethlehem and the surrounding region (Ruth 4:11; Mic. 5:2). Jesse, the father of David, is called an Ephrathite of Bethlehem (1 Sam. 17:12), as are Naomi, her husband, and their sons (Ruth 1:2). The LXX includes Ephrathah in the list of places near Bethlehem which it inserts after Josh. 15:59.

Ephrathah also appears as the name of a woman (1 Chr. 2:19) who is identified as an ancestor (eponymous) of Bethlehem, Tekoa, Beth-gader, and Kiriath-jearim (1 Chr. 2:24, 50-51; 4:4-5), well-known towns in northern Judah. It is unclear whether the kinship group associated with this territory took its name from such a person or whether the name is merely a personification of the territory for genealogical purposes. The inclusion of Kiriath-jearim within the boundaries of Ephrathah extends these boundaries north to the border with Benjamin (cf. Ps. 132:6, *'eproṯâ* = "fields of Jaar"). Ephrathah may also refer to Ephrath, the place to which Jacob was traveling when Rachel died (Gen. 35:16, 19; 48:7); cf. later passages that place the tomb of Rachel in southern Benjamin (1 Sam. 10:2), specifically in the vicinity of Ramah (Jer. 31:15). WADE R. KOTTER

EPHRON (Heb. *'eprôn*) **(PERSON)**
A son of Zohar; a Hittite dwelling at Hebron who sold Abraham his field and the cave of Machpelah for 400 shekels of silver (Gen. 23:8-18; cf. 25:9-10; 49:29-30; 50:13).

EPHRON (Heb. *'eprôn;* Gk. *Ephrōn*) **(PLACE)**
1. "The towns of Mt. Ephron" (Josh. 15:9), a district on the northern border of Judah near Baalah/Kiriath-jearim (modern Deir el-'Âzar). The precise location of the site is unknown, but el-Qastel near Mozah is a possibility.
2. A town taken by King Abijah of Judah from Jeroboam I of Israel (2 Chr. 13:19). It is often identified with Ophrah (Josh. 18:23) and Ephraim (2 Sam. 13:23). The site is modern eṭ-Ṭaiyibeh (178151), ca. 6.5 km. (4 mi.) NE of Bethel and 21 km. (13 mi.) NNE of Jerusalem.
3. A large and very strong town which shut and blocked the gates with stones in an attempt to prohibit the passage of Judas Maccabeus and his army, who were returning to Judah from Gilead. Judas sent a friendly message to allow them to traverse the city. After being denied, he destroyed every male and plundered the town. Afterwards, he passed through the town over the dead bodies (1 Macc. 5:46-52; 2 Macc. 12:27-29). Ephron (217216) is located E of the Jordan River, ca. 19.5 km. (12 mi.) SE of the Sea of Galilee.
JORGE L. VALDES

EPICUREANS (Gk. *Epikoúreioi*)
Epicureanism, a philosophical school deriving from Epicurus (341-271 B.C.E.), who founded a school of thought ca. 306 in Athens, based on his appreciation for nature and for practical philosophy as the medicine of the soul. Epicurus distrusted scholarly philosophy as commonly practiced and had only bad things to say about other teachers of art and science, including Plato and Aristotle. He offered a philosophy of life for simple people, intending to lead them to enjoy happiness.

Epicurus believed that the only trustworthy guide was sense perceptions. Men, women, and slaves were part of his community, which assembled in his garden. Epicurus proposed an atomic theory, that everything in the world is made of atoms, which are eternal, indestructible, and unchangeable. He accounted for difference in the nature and appearance of things by their being differing clusters of atoms. The eternity of the atoms and the randomness of their creative collisions eliminate any need for a God or Reason behind the universe. The theory also makes humans an atomic accident and their death nothing tragic or moral, but rather the alteration of atoms.

The Epicureans believed that there were gods, but that they were removed from and unconcerned with human existence, not engaged in providence or intelligent involvement with the operation of human life or the universe. Epicurus taught that one should seek pleasure and happiness — not hedonistic selfish satisfaction, but pleasure as the norm of goodness in the universe. He defined pleasure as the absence of pain and the ordinary anxieties of life. People would be happy if free from the fear of the gods and of death. In the quest for what is good, one could trust the inner sensations as a trustworthy guide. The Epicurean quest for personal pleasure led to a retreat from public activities and participation in government, which was contrary to the Greek expectation that one should be active in public life. This philosophy was a system of thought focused on the individual and mostly unconcerned with society. It was pursued by the intellectual elite and maintained that there was no universal law or moral order to the universe. The teachings of Epicurus were presented to the Roman world in the 1st century B.C.E. through Lucretius' philosophical poem, *De Rerum Natura.*

Epicureans debated with Paul at Athens (Acts 17:18). Although he used their vocabulary (e.g., Gk. *átomos,* 1 Cor. 15:52; cf. Tit. 3:3), his message of divine judgment and resurrection was contrary to their beliefs. RICHARD A. SPENCER

EPILEPSY

According to some modern medical researchers, a disorder characterized by the repeated occurrence of seizures in the absence of an acute precipitating systemic or brain insult. Some scholars see the earliest historical references to epilepsy in descriptions (from as early as the 2nd millennium B.C.E.) of the diseases known as *antašubba* and *bennu* in ancient Mesopotamia, though other interpretations are possible. In Greco-Roman literature, the "falling sickness" and the "sacred disease," a condition particularly attributed to the actions of the gods, are usually regarded as references to epilepsy.

The OT contains no clear references to epilepsy, though some scholars see the mention of the effects of the moon in Ps. 121:6 as a possible reference. The behavior of Saul (1 Sam. 16:14-16) and Ezekiel (Ezek. 3:26) has also been attributed to epilepsy by some scholars.

Many modern scholars ascribe to epilepsy the symptoms of the demon-possessed youth in Mark 9:14-29. The parallel passage in Matt. 17:15 uses Gk. *selēniázetai,* which is often translated "moonstruck," a rubric associated with epilepsy in Greco-Roman sources. More ambiguous cases of epilepsy include references to Paul's thorn in the flesh and "out-of-body" experiences (2 Cor. 12:1-7).

HECTOR AVALOS

EPISTLE (Gk. *epistolḗ*)

See LETTER.

ER (Heb. *ʿēr;* Gk. *ḗr*)

1. The firstborn son of Judah and the daughter of the Canaanite Shua (Gen. 38:1-3, 12; 46:12; Num. 26:19) or Bath-shua (1 Chr. 2:3). Er's marriage with Tamar, probably a Canaanite, ended shortly with his death, attributed to "wickedness in the sight of the Lord" (Gen. 38:7; 1 Chr. 2:3).

2. One of the sons of Shelah; the grandson of Judah and the father of Lecah (1 Chr. 4:21).

3. The father of Elmadam; listed among the ancestors of Jesus in Luke's genealogy (Luke 3:28).

ERAN (Heb. *ʿērān*)

One of Shuthelah's sons and the grandson of Ephraim; eponymous ancestor of the Eranite clan (Num. 26:36; LXX "Eden," v. 40).

ERASTUS (Gk. *Érastos*)

The city treasurer (Gk. *oikonómos*) of Corinth, from whom Paul sends greetings to the church at Rome (Rom. 16:23). Acts 19:22 mentions an Erastus sent with Timothy by Paul to Macedonia from Ephesus. 2 Tim. 4:20 refers to an Erastus who remained at Corinth. A Latin inscription excavated in a paved courtyard near the theater at Corinth reads: "Erastus laid [the pavement] at his own expense in return for his aedileship."

Rom. 16, perhaps originally directed to Ephesus rather than Rome, was probably written from Corinth. Acts is a secondary account, and 2 Timothy may be pseudo-Pauline. Still, the same Erastus was probably intended in each NT text and in the inscription. The title *oikonómos* may correspond to the questor, a lower position than aedile but also responsible for public funds; one might be questor before becoming aedile. If the same Erastus is intended by Paul and the inscription, it suggests Christianity had followers among persons of notable status in Corinth.

Bibliography. G. Theissen, *The Social Setting of Pauline Christianity* (Philadelphia, 1982).

SCOTT NASH

ERECH (Heb. *ʾereḵ*)

The biblical name of ancient Uruk (modern Warka) on the lower Euphrates River in Iraq. The early Sumerian name of the city was Unug, likely "the city"; during that time Uruk would have been the largest city in the world. According to the Sumerian King List, the First Dynasty of Uruk included Enmerkar, Lugalbanda, Gilgamesh, and Dumuzi (Tammuz), semilegendary figures who are prominent in Mesopotamian epics.

Apart from exploratory visits, excavations at Uruk began in 1912 and continued with interruptions until the 39th season in 1989. The site was first settled in the 5th millennium B.C. During the 4th millennium — the eponymous Uruk period — the site was dominated by two centers: Eanna, the location in later times of a temple to Inanna, and the so-called Anu ziggurat, a platform supporting the White temple, itself possibly dedicated to the god Anu. Protocuneiform texts found in these areas have suggested to some that writing was invented in the city at perhaps 3300. During the 3rd millennium the city grew to as much as 400 ha. (988 a.) in area and was surrounded by a large fortification wall. During the 2nd millennium the city was politically less important, although it was the site of the palace of the Old Babylonian ruler Sin-kašid. During the 1st millennium Uruk was renovated by the Assyrian king Sargon II (721-705). It experienced an economic revival in Parthian and Seleucid times, when the temples of Anu, Antum, and Gareus, and another temple the excavators called the Südbau, were built.

Erech is mentioned in the Bible as one of the cities ruled by the legendary king Nimrod in the land of Shinar, along with Babylon and Akkad (Gen. 10:10). Its citizens were among those deported to Samaria (Ezra 4:9). GEOFF EMBERLING

ERI (Heb. *'ērî*)
The fifth son of Gad (Gen. 46:16). His descendants, the Erites, are mentioned in the first census taken in the wilderness (Num. 26:16).

ERUPTION
A scab or a rash (Heb. *sappaḥaṯ*). Because the eruptions of incipient leprosy were often indistinguishable from rashes caused by something else, all such irregularities underwent ritual examination to determine whether or not they were benign (Lev. 13:2, 6; 14:56-57).

ESARHADDON (Heb. *'ēsar-ḥaddôn;* Akk. *Aššur-aḫḫa-iddina*)
King of Assyria (680-669 B.C.). Following the murder of his father Sennacherib (2 Kgs. 19:37 = Isa. 37:38), Esarhaddon was immediately confronted with a rebellion which he quelled after six weeks. After restoring Babylon, which his father had destroyed, he turned his attention to the affairs in the west in Syro-Palestine and Egypt. Continuing Sennacherib's policies, he collected heavy tribute from vassal kings in Syro-Palestine, including the rulers of Edom, Moab, Ammon, Tyre, and Sidon. He also required them to send building materials to Assyria and Babylonia. Israelite king Manasseh may have been transported to Babylon as well, which may explain the account in 2 Chr. 33:11. Late in his reign Esarhaddon required all vassals (likely including Manasseh) to sign a treaty ensuring the orderly succession of his son Assurbanipal.

Since Egypt was still a threat to seize control of the Levantine coast from the Assyrians, Esarhaddon, after a brief failure, became the first Assyrian king to enter and conquer Egypt (671). Esarhaddon's annals give a detailed description of the capture and looting of Memphis, the primary Egyptian city. Soon after the Assyrian king left, the Egyptians under Taharqa revolted, thereby precipitating another campaign by Esarhaddon, who died, however, before he was able to return.

Although not mentioned in the Assyrian annals, there is evidence that Esarhaddon sent deportees into Judah. According to Ezra 4:2, during the Achaemenid period (mid-5th century) the enemies of Judah asked to help the returned exiles in rebuilding the temple, since they had been sacrificing to God "ever since the days of King Esarhaddon of Assyria who had brought us here." It seems probable that this deportation may have come about because of Sennacherib's major campaign in the west (ca. 701) and continued during the reign of Esarhaddon.

Bibliography. S. Parpola, *Letters from Assyrian Scribes to the Kings Esarhaddon and Assurbanipal II.* AOAT 5/2 (Kevelaer, 1983); D. J. Wiseman, *The Vassal-Treaties of Esarhaddon.* Iraq 20 (1958): 1-99.

MARK W. CHAVALAS

ESAU (Heb. *'ēśāw*)
The oldest son of Isaac and Rebekah and twin brother of Jacob (Gen. 25:24-25; 1 Chr. 1:34). The etymology of Esau's name is unclear. His description as reddish in appearance (Heb. *'aḏmônî,* Gen. 25:25; cf. *hā'āḏōm,* v. 30) is etymologically related not to the name Esau but to Edom (*'ěḏôm;* 36:1, 8, 19, 43), Esau's eponymous descendants (vv. 9, 43). So too, Esau's hairiness (*śē'ār,* Gen. 25:25) is related to Seir (*śē'îr;* 36:8; Deut. 2:4-5; Josh. 24:4), the land where he finally settles.

As the eldest son Esau was entitled to the birthright and blessing of the firstborn. He sold the former to Jacob for food (Gen. 25:29-34; cf. Heb. 12:16) and lost the latter through Rebekah and Jacob's trickery (Gen. 27:1-38). Thus, Isaac could only give Esau a secondary and subordinate blessing (Gen. 27:39-40; but cf. Heb. 11:20). Such reversals where the younger brother is favored over the older are common in the Bible, and this particular instance was foretold (Gen. 25:23). Nevertheless, these reversals often come at some price — in this case Esau hates Jacob and plans to kill him (Gen. 27:41-45). The two brothers are then estranged until their reunion many years later (chs. 32–33). While this meeting caused Jacob much anxiety (note esp. Gen. 32:22-32), Esau is presented as a gracious and forgiving brother (33:4-9; cf. Rebekah's words in 27:44-45). Reconciled, Esau and Jacob then part ways, dwelling in different areas (Gen. 35:16, 21; cf. 36:6-8) but uniting again when Isaac dies (35:29).

Esau is described as a hunter and a man of the field (Gen. 25:27). He married two Hittite wives (compare Gen. 26:34 with 36:2-3; 36:10-12, 14), who made life bitter for Isaac and Rebekah (26:35; 27:46), and he also married a daughter of Ishmael (compare 28:6-9 with 36:2-3, 13), apparently to please his parents. The names of his wives are confused from one text to another, but it is clear that five sons came from these marriages: Eliphaz, Reuel, Jeush, Jalam, and Korah. A lengthy genealogy of Esau's descendants is given in Gen. 36 (cf. 1 Chr. 1:35-54).

The rest of the biblical material is somewhat ambivalent about Esau. His sibling relationship to Jacob, the ancestor of Israel, is remembered and respected at points (e.g., Deut. 2:4-5, 8, 29). Indeed, God gave Seir to Esau (Deut. 2:5, 12, 22; Josh. 24:4), not unlike the giving of Canaan to Jacob. Elsewhere, however, Esau/Edom is a rival to Israel and is judged by God (cf. Jer. 49:7-22; Obadiah). Mal. 1:2-3 states that God loved Jacob but hated Esau, a theme picked up by Paul (Rom. 9:13).

Bibliography. M. Dijkstra, "Esau," *DDD,* 306.

BRENT A. STRAWN

ESCAPE, ROCK OF

A place in the rocky wilderness of Maon, perhaps a cliff or rocky crag (Heb. *selaʿ hammaḥlĕqôṯ*), where Saul broke off his pursuit of David in order to defend Israel from Philistine aggression (1 Sam. 23:28; NRSV mg "Rock of Division"; NIV "Sela-hammohlekoth").

The narrative suggests that David was able to elude Saul and his men, whom he could see, without their being able to capture him. The place is popularly thought to be two cliffs separated by a narrow ravine, such as might exist in Wadi el-Malâqi, ca. 8 mi. (13 km.) ENE of Maon.

T. J. JENNEY

ESCHATOLOGY

Eschatology (from Gk. *éschatos,* "last") concerns expectations of an end time, whether the close of history, the world itself, or the present age. Eschatological language becomes prominent in the OT prophets and later Jewish apocalyptic texts (both canonical and extracanonical) and is a pervasive feature in early Christian literature. A rich variety of images appear in these writings: the "day of the Lord" (or "that day"), often characterized as a day of judgment (e.g., Ezek. 30:1-4; Joel 2:1-2; Amos 5:18-20; Zeph. 1:7-18; 4 Ezra 7:33-44; 1 En. 3, 45, 62-63, 100; Matt. 11:22; 25:31-46; Rom. 2:1-16; 1 Cor. 3:10-15), and preceded by a period of testing and social and political disintegration (Dan. 12:1-4; 4 Ezra 5:1-13; 2 Bar. 25, 70; T. Levi 16-18; T. Zeb. 9:5-9; T. Naph. 4:2-5; Sib. Or. 3:635-56); a decisive war in which Israel's enemies (or the forces of evil) are finally defeated and Israel (or God's people) restored (Ezek. 37–39; Joel 3[MT 4]; Zech. 12, 14; 1 En. 56; 1QM; Rev. 19:11-21; 20:7-10); restoration of the holy city and of the land (Isa. 35, 40–55; Tob. 14:5; Jub. 1:15-18); an eschatological temple (Ezek. 40–48; 11QT); the conversion or streaming of the nations to Jerusalem (Isa. 60; cf. 11:10; Zech. 8:20-23; 14:16-21; Tob. 14:6-7; cf. Rev. 21:24); a harvest in which the faithful are gathered and the wicked removed (4 Ezra 4:26-32, 39; 2 Bar. 70:2; Matt. 3:12; 13:36-43; Rev. 14:14-20); a festive eschatological banquet for God's people (Isa. 25:6; Luke 13:29; 14:15-24); resurrection (to life or judgment; Isa. 26:19; Dan. 12:2; 1 En. 51; 4 Ezra 7:32; Sib. Or. 4:179-92; John 5:25-29; 1 Cor. 15); a joyous wedding or wedding banquet (Matt. 22:1-14; Rev. 19); and simply "being with" the Lord (2 Cor. 5:8; Phil. 1:23). Characteristically, such images express the hope that deliverance or vindication for God's faithful people is imminent, and with it the final elimination of the oppressive forces of evil. Many texts, however, also reckon with a delay in eschatological fulfillment (e.g., Habakkuk; 4 Ezra 4–6; 2 Bar. 21:19-25; Matt. 25:1-13). In fact, reaffirmation of hope in the face of partial or delayed fulfillment of eschatological expectations is a regular feature of early Jewish and Christian eschatology.

Eschatological language naturally has an informational aspect, as it discloses the outcome of the historical era or specific conflict in view. Nevertheless, it is primarily expressive language; its images of judgment and vindication, of disaster and protection, of doom and rescue are designed to engage hearers' emotions and move them to a particular way of life — fidelity and persevering commitment to God even in the context of adversity. The "rhetoric of eschatology" therefore deploys its images and metaphors to sustain hope despite the ambiguities of historical existence but also, through warnings of the impending destruction of evil, to reinforce moral appeals. Extrapolating from past experience of God's goodness (whether in exodus, restoration from exile, or Jesus' death and resurrection) and from present experience of the world (banquets, harvests, courts, and battles), faith pictures the future completion: it will be like that! God is doing a new thing (Isa. 43:19), but its contours can be seen already in patterns of life and history evident to faith. Biblical eschatology is thus inescapably metaphorical in character; it does not give precise information (e.g., when the end will occur or who will participate), but enables a community to live in faith and obedience — a life that both draws its strength from and bears witness to the faithfulness of a sovereign God whose purposes for creation will yet "be done on earth as in heaven."

OT Prophets

The preexilic prophets characteristically warn the nation of approaching doom, understood as divine judgment upon a disobedient people. Amos pictures the "day of Yahweh" as a time of disaster, not deliverance, for Israel (Amos 5:18-20). For Isaiah, too, the future holds fearful retribution for the nation's injustice and infidelity (Isa. 1–5). Images of eschatological judgment receive even sharper expression in the oracles of Jeremiah, who announced the temple's demise (Jer. 7:1-15; cf. Ezek. 10:1-22). At the same time, the prophets imagined a future when God would redeem and restore the nation (Isa. 2:1-4; 4:2-6; 9:1-7[8:23–9:6]; 11:1-9; 14:1-2; Jer. 16:14-15; Hos. 14:4-7), returning justice and wisdom to the throne. Once disaster had befallen the nation, prophets of the exilic and postexilic eras awaited God's action to restore Israel's fortunes (Isa. 35, 40–55, 60; Joel 3[4]; Obad. 15-17; Zech. 10:6-12; 12–14; Ezek. 11:14-21; 20:33-44; 37:1-28; 39:21-29), yet also questioned its delayed arrival (Habakkuk). Eschatological hope of necessity wrestled with the problem of unfulfilled expectations.

Jewish Apocalyptic Literature

History brought precious little relief, however, and the dissonance between divine promise and Israel's continuing experience of weakness and subjugation (no doubt aided by ideas current in Persian and Greek cultures) became the catalyst for the emergence of apocalyptic eschatology. What if suffering and even death visited the people not because of their infidelity and disobedience but precisely because of their observance of Torah? Driven by such disturbing questions, Israel's visionaries came to view divine vindication in increasingly suprahistorical terms; faith's vision appealed to transcendent powers and outcomes not visible within history itself. God would intervene on behalf of the righteous, overturning oppressive evil and defending and restoring the nation, though that deliverance would assume many different forms (Ezek. 38–39; Zech. 12–14; Dan. 10–12; Jub. 1:15-18; T. Levi 16–18; 1 En. 38–39, 48–58, 61–63; Sib. Or. 3:657-808; 4:40-48; 1QM).

Jesus and the Gospels

Despite recurring attempts to deflect eschatological views away from Jesus to the early Church, Jesus likely expected the imminent arrival of God's mighty rule; in fact, he discerned the dawn of God's reign in his own activity (e.g., meal fellowship, the declaration of forgiveness, and exorcisms). Jesus therefore shared the intense eschatological expectancy of John the Baptizer (cf. Matt. 3:7-12), but modified it — pointing to present signs of the kingdom and also shifting the accent from impending doom to hope. In both Matthew and Mark Jesus' ministry begins (Matt. 4:17; Mark 1:15) and ends (Matt. 24–25; Mark 13) with eschatological claims. While Luke has Jesus inaugurate his ministry under the banner of fulfillment (Luke 4:16-21), this Gospel, too, gives prominence to eschatological images (12:35-48; 17:20–18:8; 21:5-36).

Yet each of the Synoptics develops this theme in its own way. Mark sharply accents the perils of faithful discipleship; Jesus, whose own way is the way of the cross, promises his followers a future marked by crisis and adversity (Mark 13:5-23). Yet they are to summon courage for their mission to the world (Mark 13:10), confident that despite the severity of their hardships, God will soon rescue the faithful (vv. 26-30), if they will remain vigilant. Pictures of eschatological deliverance, centering in the triumphant return of the Son of Humanity, reassure the community of Mark and support them in a costly mission "for the sake of the gospel." Matthew, by contrast, highlights the motif of end-time judgment, using eschatological images to underscore an appeal for a life defined by righteousness (Matt. 13:24-30, 36-43, 47-50; 25:31-46). While a wide, easy road leads many to doom, Matthew challenges readers to follow the narrow, arduous path to life (Matt. 7:13-14). Even though the "close of the age" will be deferred, thrusting the community into an era of intense conflict (Matt. 24:4-14), they must remain alert and vigorous in their service of God (24:45-51; 25:1-30). Eschatology in this Gospel serves above all to motivate a life defined by radical obedience to God and compassionate mercy toward others. Mark and to a greater degree Matthew reckon with some delay in the completion of the end-time scenario (Mark 13:5-8, 10; Matt. 24:6-8, 48; 25:1-13), yet without relinquishing expectation of the Parousia in the near future.

This pattern is even more typical of Luke, who adjusts the timetable to make room for delay (Luke 12:42-48; 17:25; 18:1-8; 19:11-27; 21:7-12; cf. Acts 1:6-8) but at the same time reaffirms hope of the Lord's imminent return (Luke 12:39-40; 17:22-37; 21:28-36). The mark of the community must therefore be persevering faith (Luke 18:1-8) and faithfulness (12:35-48; 21:12-19) in the time that remains before end-time vindication for God's people. While the narrative invests heavily in this picture of a delayed but still viable eschatological expectancy, Luke also underscores present fulfillment of hopes during the life of Jesus. The age of the Spirit (signaling the "last days," Acts 2:17-21) begins already with Jesus (Luke 4:16-21), who discerns in his own acts of healing and forgiveness the sovereign rule of God reordering human life in the present (11:20; 17:20-21). So the long deferred hopes of Israel rush to fulfillment with the advent of John and Jesus (Luke 1–2). Where Jesus works, salvation becomes reality in Israel (Luke 7:48-50; 8:43-48; 17:11-19; 19:9-10; 23:39-43; cf. 2:11, 30-32). Nevertheless, Israel's history retains its fundamental ambiguity, and even the Savior must be rejected and his kingdom thwarted for the time being (Luke 19:11-27). His community must therefore wait — and vigorously work — for the completion of the salvation inaugurated by him.

This pattern, whereby eschatological hopes find decisive, if not complete, fulfillment in the present with the person and work of Jesus, comes to its boldest expression in the Gospel of John. Jesus *is* the eschaton. Hopes ordinarily tied to the future (resurrection, eternal life, final judgment) all come to be anchored in the present, the prerogative of Jesus himself (John 3:16-21; 5:19-30; 11:23-26). Judgment for those who reject God's revealer (Jesus) is sealed even now. Eternal life for those who believe also happens now. The parousia of Jesus seems to be recast as the presence of the Spirit (the Paraclete) in the community (John 16:7-15; cf. 14:15-26). For all this accent on present realization of eschatological hopes, John does preserve eschatological elements (e.g., resurrection "on the last day," John 6:39-40, 44; cf. 5:28-29; and a personal experience of the parousia, 14:2-3). The key to this tension between present fulfillment (Jesus as eschaton) and future hope lies in the Johannine claim that the life of the disciple is utterly dependent on connection to Jesus, the source of life (John 15:1-11). True discipleship can only be validated over a lifetime of faithful witness to the Truth. Entry into life, already realized in faith now, must therefore be confirmed at the end. Eschatology undergoes radical reinterpretation in John, yet the future is not entirely absorbed into the present experience of the Johannine community. The balance swings back toward future-oriented eschatology in the letter later addressed to the same community (1 John 2:18, 28; 3:2; 4:17), without effacing, however, the conviction that eternal life is a present reality for those of faith (5:5, 11).

Paul

Paul's letters express a vibrant eschatological faith from first to last. 1 Thessalonians voices the conviction that the parousia of Jesus would occur in the near future, certainly within Paul's lifetime (1 Thess. 4:15-18). Paul deploys eschatological images (parousia, "thief in the night") to console readers distressed by the deaths of some community members before "the day" and to reinforce his appeals for moral seriousness (1 Thess. 5:1-11). While Paul's assumption that he will live to see the Parousia does give way in later letters (2 Cor. 5:1-10; Phil. 1:19-26), he reaffirms his eschatological convictions to the end (1 Cor. 7:25-31; Rom. 13:11-12; Phil. 4:5). Yet for Paul too the future is not the sole interest. His intense expectancy of imminent eschatological closure stems from his perception of the meaning of what has already occurred in the death and resurrection of Jesus. The cross is the world-shattering event that redefined the character of life in the world (1 Cor. 1:18–2:5; Gal. 6:14-15), and the resurrection of Jesus is the clear signal that history's closure events are close at hand. God's raising of Jesus is the "first fruits" that assures the full harvest is soon to follow (Rom. 8:23; 1 Cor. 15:20, 23). The presence of God's Spirit in the community is therefore a "pledge" guaranteeing full "payment" of salvation in the near future (2 Cor. 1:22; 5:5; cf. Rom. 8:11; Eph. 1:14). Paul also uses the imagery of eschatological judgment to support his moral appeals (Rom. 2:1-16; 1 Cor. 3:10-17; 2 Cor. 5:10). In Colossians and Ephesians there is a shift from temporal to spatial categories: the believer has already been raised from the dead and has taken up residence in heaven (Eph. 2:6; cf. Col. 2:12; 3:1-3). Yet the revelation of Christ in glory is still to come (Col. 3:4; cf. "day of redemption," Eph. 4:30).

General Epistles and Revelation

Eschatology remains an important feature throughout the General Epistles. 1 Peter summons the community of readers to a moral seriousness that reckons with the imminence of end-time judgment (1 Pet. 4:1-11) and reassures them that their present suffering will soon give way to eschatological salvation (1:5) and glory (v. 7). 2 Peter addresses skepticism fueled by delay in the realization of eschatological hopes: "Where is the promise of his coming?" (2 Pet. 3:4). The author attributes this delay to God's patient mercy and issues a sharp warning against surrender of eschatological faith. With the images of an imminent parousia and the eschatological judge standing at the door (Jas. 5:8, 9), James lends urgency to the appeal for congruence between faith and just, compassionate living. Hebrews, written in "these last days" (Heb. 1:2), likewise warns of the rapid approach of the day of final judgment (10:23-31).

In the book of Revelation apocalyptic visions enable readers to discern the true meaning and course of history: not Satan but God, not Rome but Christ rules the world. Of course, at present only eyes of faith can see this. Yet the forces of evil have launched a final, fierce assault upon the faithful precisely because they have suffered decisive defeat (Rev. 12:7-17), and their time has nearly run its course (v. 12). Christ the Lamb has won the victory, paradoxically through his witness unto death (Rev. 5:9-12; 12:10-11). Once again, future deliverance is assured because of what God has already accomplished. Yet readers facing the prospect of intense persecution (something John expects to occur) need encouragement, and affirmation of Jesus' speedy return becomes a prominent motif in John's Apocalypse (Rev. 1:3; 3:11; 16:15; 22:12, 20). The return of Christ, his millennial reign with martyrs, the final defeat of evil (including the "death" of death itself), and the appearance of a renewed, glorious and holy Jerusalem all loom on the horizon. Such potent images reinforce hope in a beleaguered community but also warn readers to choose their loyalties wisely. A share in "life" awaits those who persevere in their fidelity to God even at great cost.

Bibliography. D. C. Allison, Jr., *The End of the Ages Has Come: An Early Interpretation of the Passion and Resurrection of Jesus* (Philadelphia, 1985); J. J. Collins, *The Apocalyptic Imagination,* 2nd ed. (Grand Rapids, 1998); D. Gowan, *Eschatology of the Old Testament* (Philadelphia, 1986); A. A. Hoekema, *The Bible and the Future* (Grand Rapids, 1979); C. Holman, *Till Jesus Comes* (Peabody, 1996); J. Plevnik, *Paul and the Parousia* (Peabody, 1997).

John T. Carroll

ESDRAELON (Gk. *Esdrēlōn*)

The Greek form of the name "Jezreel." Although the term does not occur in the OT (it is found in the Apocrypha in Jdt.1:8; 3:9; 4:6; 7:3), it is frequently used interchangeably with Jezreel (which does occur in the OT numerous times). Technically, most archaeologists hold that Esdraelon refers to the western section of the valleys and plains that intersect Galilee just N of Mt. Carmel, separating it from Samaria, while the smaller eastern section of this area is known as the valley of Jezreel. Sometimes, however, these names are used for the whole area.

The Great Plain (1 Macc. 12:49) is triangular in shape and includes the plain of Megiddo (Zech. 12:11), stretching along the northern slopes of Mt. Carmel to the plain of En-gammin (modern Jenin) on the south, and northeast to the slopes of Mt. Tabor. Many cities were located within the Plain, the most important being Megiddo. It was a strategic site during OT times and was fortified to guard the Carmel pass. It was controlled by the Canaanites until the time of David (Judg. 1:27) when the Israelites finally gained control. The river Kishon wanders through this rich and fertile valley. As part of the Way of the Sea (Isa. 9:1[MT 8:23]), the plain of Esdraelon included the route that led from the Philistine coast through the pass at Megiddo and on to Damascus. It connected Egypt with the north and thus served as a part of a trade route from the earliest times.

Some of the famous battles here include the Philistines' defeat of Saul (1 Sam. 31) and Pharaoh Necho's defeat of Josiah (2 Kgs. 23:29). A single

NT reference to this area is found in Rev. 16:16, perhaps suggesting it as the location of an apocalyptic battle.

See JEZREEL. WATSON E. MILLS

ESDRAS, BOOKS OF

1 Esdras

The apocryphal book 1 Esdras gets its title from the standard LXX manuscripts, where it appears as Esdras A or 1 Esdras. Condemned by Jerome, it nevertheless appears in Latin Bibles as 3 Esdras. The book is canonical only for the Eastern Orthodox Churches and not for the Roman Catholic Church, although 1 Esdras appears in most collections of the Apocrypha/Deuterocanonical literature.

With the exception of 1 Esdr. 3:1–5:6, 1 Esdras is a rather free Greek version of biblical history from Josiah's Passover to Ezra's reforms. 1 Esdr. 1:1-55 duplicates 2 Chr. 35:1–36:21; 1 Esdr. 2:1-15 duplicates Ezra 1:1-11; 1 Esdr. 2:16-30 duplicates Ezra 4:7-24. 1 Esdr. 5:7-46 duplicates Ezra 2:1-70; 1 Esdr. 5:47-73 duplicates Ezra 3:1–4:5; 1 Esdr. 6:1–7:15 duplicates Ezra 4:24–6:22; and 1 Esdr. 8:1–9:55 duplicates Ezra 7:1–10:44 and Neh. 7:73–8:12.

The section without parallel in the Chronicler's work (1 Esdr. 3:1–5:6) is a story of a young man at the court of Darius, the Persian king. He solves the riddle of "what is the strongest thing in the world" with a magnificent display of wit and wisdom in a riddle contest before the king and his court. As the winner of the contest the youth wins the privilege of rebuilding the city of Jerusalem and the temple, leading the Jews home from exile, and taking back certain temple vessels which were still in captivity. By the time this narrative was joined to the rest of 1 Esdras, the winner of the riddle contest had been identified with Zerubbabel, the story becoming a "devotional legend" about Zerubbabel's wonderful opportunity in exile to influence the course of Jewish history. The success of a wise Jew at the court of a foreign king is a motif found in Daniel (1–6) and Esther, and the deuterocanonical books of Tobit, Judith, Susanna, and Bel and the Dragon.

In its present form 1 Esdras can be dated between 165 B.C.E. and 50 C.E. The linguistic and stylistic similarities to Daniel and Esther and the fact that it was used by Josephus justify this dating. There is a strong possibility that it was composed in Egypt during the latter part of the 2nd century B.C.E. This devotional legend, which had as its purpose both to entertain and educate, grew out of an original Persian court tale, discernible in 1 Esdr. 3:1–4:42. An analysis of the structure of this section shows that it is divided into a narrative framework consisting of a long prose introduction (3:1-16a) with a truncated conclusion (4:42) and four long speeches on the strength of wine, the king, women, and truth, respectively (3:16b–4:41).

There is strong evidence that the core narrative is based on the ancient Near Eastern practice of riddling as part of court entertainment. The subjects defended as the strongest by each contestant — wine, the king, and women — would suggest this. The winning answer — truth — was no doubt added at a later time when the story was moralized for religious purposes. The suggestion of the third contestant that "women" were the strongest, no doubt the winning entry in the original tale, may be a reference to a certain Apame (a wife or concubine of a Seleucid king). The cosmic and ethical nature of truth as described in the final version suggests that it could have been added at some point to celebrate the power of Asha in Zoroastrian belief, Hokmah from Hebrew wisdom literature, Greek Sophia, or Egyptian Maat.

The most famous verse in the book is the response of the assembled king and nobles at the conclusion of the hymn in praise of truth: "Great is truth, and strongest of all" (4:41). Augustine in his *City of God* (17.36) identifies the greatness of Truth in 1 Esdras with Christ the Truth.

Bibliography. J. L. Crenshaw, "The Contest of Darius' Guards," in *Images of Man and God,* ed. B. O. Long (Sheffield, 1981), 74-88; W. R. Goodman, *A Study of I Esdras 3:1–5:6* (diss., Duke, 1971); J. M. Myers, *I and II Esdras.* AB 42 (Garden City, 1974).

2 Esdras

The only apocalypse in the Apocrypha, this work bears the name Ezra or Esdras. It appears as 2 Esdras in some Latin manuscripts, the Geneva Bible, and the Authorized Version, but as 4 Ezra in most Latin manuscripts. Other manuscripts list it as 1 or 3 Esdras.

This is a composite work containing portions from the 1st and 2nd centuries C.E. and dating in its present form to the 3rd century. The major portion was originally written in a Semitic language, probably Hebrew or Aramaic, but unfortunately no Semitic versions have survived. The Greek translation of the Semitic original has also been lost.

The work consists of three distinct parts of varying length and date: 2 Esdr. 1-2; 3-14; and 15-16. The style and content of the three portions lead scholars to date each to a different period. The first section (chs. 1-2) introduces Ezra as the author receiving his commission from the Lord to deliver a message to his people. This section dates to the middle of the 2nd century and appears to have been written by a Christian author. The main body of the work (chs. 3-14) has Ezra in Babylon receiving seven revelations, some of which took the form of visions. Most scholars think that this core section was written toward the end of the 1st century in Hebrew or Aramaic by an unknown Jew. The final section (chs. 15-16) also appears to have been written, like the first two chapters, in Greek by a Christian author and appended to the core section, perhaps around the middle of the 3rd century. This final portion reflects the Parthian threat to the stability of the Roman Empire at that time.

The first section contains NT phraseology (1:30, 37; 2:42), a very strong argument in favor of Christian authorship. Ezra warns Israel that for their sins God will scatter them among the nations and choose the gentile nations instead for his people. Then innumerable saints (Christian martyrs?)

will stand on Mt. Zion and victoriously receive their rewards of crowns and palms from a young man of great stature, whom an angel identifies as "the Son of God" (2:47).

The central section contains a series of revelations mediated through the angel Uriel. The first vision (3:1–5:20) is dated to 30 years after the destruction of "our city," probably referring to Nebuchadnezzar's destruction of Jerusalem in 587/6 B.C.E. Many take this dating to mean the author was writing 30 years after the destruction of Jerusalem by the Romans in 70 C.E., thus giving an approximate date of 100 C.E. for the composition of the central portion of the book. Troubled by what he perceives to be God's unjust treatment of Israel, Ezra receives in the first dream vision the answer that God's ways are simply beyond human understanding. The seer in the second vision (5:21–6:34) again complains about the unjust way God seems to be dealing with Israel. Again, the ways of the earth and the judgments and purposes of God are beyond understanding. Such perplexing problems as the inferiority of the latter generations compared to the earlier ones in the divine plan for the world in the coming of the messianic age, and determining the time of the end of the age, are answered with a caution of not being overanxious about these things: "Believe and do not be afraid!" The third vision (6:35–9:25) deals with God's work in creation, the messianic kingdom, and the end of the world. The seer is perplexed that only a small number will be saved and there will be no intercession for the evil at the judgment day. The seer's plea to God to have mercy on his creations is answered with the word that God will rejoice in the righteous saved and forget the wicked. The seer will be among the blessed saved and should trouble his thoughts no more for the punishment of the lost sinners. The final section presents a description of the last days and the signs which will precede it. In the fourth vision (9:26–10:59) Israel's record is compared unfavorably with the Mosiac law. Israel's destruction will be devastating, but the heavenly Zion will be glorious and beautiful. In the fifth vision (11:1–12:51), known as the "eagle vision," Ezra sees the destruction of a mighty beast in eagle form, probably symbolizing the struggles in the Roman Empire after Nero's death (68 C.E.), as the interpretation of the vision (12:3b-39) would suggest. Ezra is then asked to write down his visions in a book, hide it, and then teach the visions to the "wise," who will be the only ones who can understand them. The sixth vision (13:1-58) presents to Ezra the appearance of the Messiah in the form of a man coming up from the sea and flying with the clouds of heaven, gazing at and speaking to all in judgment, finally destroying by fire the multitudes who would fight against him. In the interpretation the seer understands that he alone has been enlightened about the time of the messianic woes and the coming of the Son of God. In the seventh and final vision (14:1-48) God orders Ezra to restore the holy Scriptures, perhaps the OT, making some public but saving some for the "wise" alone. Ezra then gathers the people and pleads with them to rule over their minds and discipline their hearts so they might obtain mercy after death and live again. Ezra along with five men leaves for 40 days. Ezra receives the inspiration of the Spirit and writes 24 books, which are to be made public. Seventy books, however, are to be kept for the wise. In them "is the spring of understanding, the fountain of wisdom, and the river of knowledge." Finally Ezra is taken up into heaven.

The third division of 2 Esdras (15:1–16:78) is a Christian appendix from the 3rd century which repeats many of the themes of the apocalyptic central section, such as the vengeance of God upon the wicked and signs of the end. Nation will fight nation and cities will be places of confusion and destruction, starvation, and plunder. Babylon (Rome), Asia, Egypt, and Syria are denounced; sinners are warned not to deny their sin, and the righteous are promised that God will surely deliver them from the time of tribulation.

Bibliography. R. J. Coggins and M. A. Knibb, *The First and Second Books of Esdras* (Cambridge, 1979); W. R. Goodman, *A Study of I Esdras 3:1–5:6* (diss., Duke, 1972); J. M. Myers, *I and II Esdras.* AB 42 (Garden City, 1974); M. E. Stone, *Features of the Eschatology of IV Ezra.* HSM 35 (Atlanta, 1989).

WILLIAM R. GOODMAN, JR.

ESEK (Heb. *ʿēśeq*)
A well dug by Isaac's servants (Gen. 26:20). The name ("contention") reflects the tension between Isaac's herdsmen and those of Gerar over rights to water resources. The context of the tradition places the well between Gerar and Beer-sheba, possibly along the Naḥal Gerar (Wadi esh-Sheriah).

LAURA B. MAZOW

ESHAN (Heb. *ʾešʿān*)
A village in the hill country of Judah (Josh. 15:52). Though its exact location is unknown, Eshan may be identified with Khirbet Samaʿa (cf. LXX B Gk. *Sōma*), ca. 17 km. (10.5 mi.) SW of Hebron.

ESH-BAAL (Heb. *ʾešbāʿal*)
The original name of Ishbosheth, son and successor of King Saul (1 Chr. 8:33; 9:39).

ESHBAN (Heb. *ʾešbān*)
The second son of Dishon, ancestor of a Horite clan (Gen. 36:26; 1 Chr. 1:41).

ESHCOL (Heb. *ʾeškōl*) **(PERSON)**
An Amorite dwelling near Hebron who, like his brothers Aner and Mamre, was an ally of Abram against Chedorlaomer (Gen. 14:13, 24). The name may be a geographical designation.

ESHCOL (Heb. *ʾeškōl*) **(PLACE)**
A valley in southern Judah in the vicinity of Hebron. It was from this valley that two of the spies sent by Moses to investigate Canaan reportedly brought back a cluster of grapes so large that they had to carry it on a pole between them (Num. 14:22-23);

hence the name of the valley ("cluster"; v. 24). Num. 32:9 implies that the spies' description of this valley, together with reports of giants in the area, discouraged the Israelites from entering into the land. However, according to Deut. 1:24 the spies' report was evidence that Canaan was a good land. While the area to the north of Hebron is especially well suited to viticulture, there is not enough evidence to attempt a more precise identification. WADE R. KOTTER

ESHEK (Heb. *ʿēšeq*)
A Benjaminite, descendant of Saul and Jonathan (1 Chr. 8:39).

ESHTAOL (Heb. *ʾeštāʾōl*)
One of the lowland cities of Judah (Josh. 15:33). It is believed that Eshtaol was located just SW of Jerusalem in the Shephelah (Judg. 13:25), in the territory of Dan (Josh. 19:41). The site has been identified as Khirbet Deir Shubeib (148134) ca. 2.5 km. (1.5 mi.) E of Zorah and 21 km. (13 mi.) W of Jerusalem, near modern Ishwaʿ/Eshtaol (151132), which preserves the name. Its inhabitants are listed in a genealogy of Caleb (1 Chr. 2:53). AARON M. GALE

ESHTEMOA (Heb. *ʾeštĕmôaʿ*) **(PERSON)**
1. The son of Ishbah, and a descendant of Caleb (1 Chr. 4:17).
2. A descendant of Hodiah, Naham's sister; a Maacathite from the tribe of Judah (1 Chr. 4:19).

ESHTEMOA (Heb. *ʾeštĕmôaʿ*), **ESHTEMOH** (*ʾeštĕmōh*) **(PLACE)**
A levitical town in the central hill country of Judah (Josh. 21:14), also listed among the cities of refuge (1 Chr. 6:57[MT 42]). In the list of settlements allotted to Judah it is called Eshtemoh (Josh. 15:50). When David defeated the Amalekites he sent a portion of his booty to Eshtemoa (1 Sam. 30:28). Eusebius reports that a "very large" Jewish settlement existed here as late as the 4th century A.D. (*Onom.* 26.11; 86.20). Scholarly consensus locates ancient Eshtemoa underneath the modern Arab village of es-Samuʿ (156089), 14 km. (8.7 mi.) SW of Hebron. Although excavations have focused on the 4th-century A.D. synagogue, several Iron Age pottery vessels have also been uncovered.

Bibliography. Z. Yeivin, "Eshtemoa," *NEAEHL* 2:423-26. WADE R. KOTTER

ESHTON (Heb. *ʾeštôn*)
The son of Mehir of Judah; a descendant of Chelub (probably Caleb). He is reckoned among the people of Recah (1 Chr. 4:11-12; LXX "Rechab"), perhaps an itinerant metalworking guild.

ESLI (Gk. *Eslí*)
A postexilic descendant of Nathan and an ancestor of Jesus, known only from Luke's genealogy (Luke 3:25).

ESSENES (Gk. *Essaios, Essēnos*)
A movement within Judaism, known primarily in the late Second Temple period, especially from ca. 146 B.C.E. to ca. 70 C.E. They were a communal association, entered by initiation, and considered themselves the predestined remnant of those who truly observed God's will. They pursued their own interpretation of Torah and prophecy. Though Essenes influenced the development of Rabbinic Judaism and of Christianity, neither of those groups accepted the Essenes' self-description, and the history of the Essenes has often been considered enigmatic.

The name Essene has two forms in Greek, *Essaios* and *Essēnos;* the English pronunciation comes from the latter form, though the *Essaios* spelling is attested earlier and appears to be closer to the original Semitic form. Because the solution is crucial, more than 50 different proposals for the etymology have been offered. The Greek forms of the name Essene probably derive from a Semitic (Hebrew or Aramaic) root. The two most often repeated suggestions involve two Aramaic words, *ḥasayyāʾ* ("pious") and *ʾāsayyāʾ* ("healers"), but neither of these terms appears in any known ancient text in any reference at all to the Essenes. A Hebrew proposal is the root *ʿāśāh* in the participle form *ʿōśin* and construct form *ʿôśê hattôrâ* ("doers of torah"); this appears as a self-description in several Dead Sea Scrolls. (Most of the sectarian Scrolls are in Hebrew, not Aramaic.) It parallels some other relevant group self-understandings (e.g., Samaritans as "keepers" of torah); it corresponds with Philo's etymological guess of *hosios,* Josephus' transliteration of Heb. *ḥōšen* as *essēn,* and Epiphanius' spelling of this Jewish sect as *Ossaioi* and *Ossēnoi.* This Hebrew solution was accepted long before the Qumran discoveries (e.g., Johann Carion, *Chronica* [1532], folio 68 verso) and accords well with the evidence, but no consensus yet exists.

Several ancient descriptions of the Essenes have survived in Greek and Latin texts. Among the most important are those by the three earliest of these writers, Philo, Josephus, and Pliny. Later accounts by Hippolytus and Epiphanius, among others, also preserve important additional observations. Most of these descriptions were addressed to non-Jewish audiences, which influenced the selection of Essene characteristics and their description in terms of Greek virtues. These texts show philosophical (especially Stoic) and ethnographic interests typically found in Hellenistic histories and geographies. Several of the descriptions relied on earlier, now lost texts, including at least one Greek source earlier than Philo, whose account is the earliest extant. Posidonius, Strabo, and Marcus Vipsanius Agrippa are among the likely authors of now lost descriptions of Essenes.

Pliny located an Essene settlement near the Dead Sea. Most scholars have concluded that the ruins at Qumran and the scrolls from surrounding caves belonged to a group of Essenes. Though a few argue that Khirbet Qumran might have been a fort or a winter villa, the majority of historians and archaeologists regard Qumran as one of the Essene settlements. Other settlements or community centers were located in Jerusalem and in the "land of Damascus" (east of the Jordan River) and elsewhere. Philo also describes the Therapeutae in Egypt as a group related to Essenes.

Several of the Qumran manuscripts include parallels to the teaching, practices, and self-description of the Essenes. Surely some of the texts found at Qumran are Essene, including the *Serek hayyaḥad* (Rule of the Community), several Bible commentaries *(Pesharim),* and 4QMMT (*Miqṣat Maʿaseh ha-Torah,* "certain enactments of the Law"). Such texts as Jubilees and portions of Enoch likely are pre-Qumran texts written within the Essene movement.

Essene teachings shared much with other Jews, such as the Torah and Prophets, but claimed a special, sometimes esoteric interpretation of Scripture. Essenes regarded the Jerusalem temple high priests (sometimes associated with Sadducees) to be wrong in their practices and calendar. Though Essenes were careful in their legal deliberations, they did not call this "halakha," and used that term only as a negative pun against Pharisees as the "seekers of smooth things *(dôršê haḥălāqôṯ).*" Essenes observed Torah strictly but according to their own interpretation. Essene beliefs included predestination, important roles for angels, and resurrection, though not necessarily including bodily resurrection (Josephus and Hippolytus disagree). They expected a messiah, or, in some descriptions, priestly and royal messiahs. The Essene apocalyptic and dualistic worldview is similar to Daniel — and not to 1 and 2 Maccabees, which are not found at Qumran; God and the angels — not humans — will destroy the enemies.

The Essenes were a communal organization. They had rules for initiation and punishments, including expulsion. Some Essenes were celibate and some observed periods of celibacy limited to certain times or places. Essenes kept no slaves, and at least the full members held property in common. Agriculture was the main occupation; they made no weapons. They avoided the courts of outsiders and followed strict ritual purity rules. The extent to which they participated in the Jerusalem temple cult is still debated.

Josephus wrote that Essenes existed in 146 B.C.E. (*Ant.* 13.171), probably because his source Strabo began his *History* at that date. The exact year they originated is unknown, perhaps because the Essene movement developed more gradually and because the movement preceded the Greek form of its name. Three of the four Essene individuals mentioned in Josephus are known for prophecy and lived in Jerusalem. The fourth, John the (former) Essene who joined the zealots, is not typical; it was unusual for an Essene to rely on human weapons. Josephus also located an Essene gate in Southwest Jerusalem (*BJ* 5.145).

Qumran texts describe certain individuals, especially an Essene Teacher of Righteousness and his opponent the Wicked Priest. Though many scholars consider Jonathan (161-143/2 B.C.E.) the best candidate for the Wicked Priest, Alexander Janneus (103-76) may be preferable. Some scholars suggest there were more than one Wicked Priest and more than one Teacher of Righteousness. Though the Teacher of Righteousness has no generally agreed identity, a plausible candidate is Judah the Essene mentioned by Josephus (*BJ* 1.78-80; *Ant.* 13.311) as teaching ca. 104, soon before the rule of Alexander. In *b. Qidd.* 66a (the same?) Judah asks Alexander to give up the priesthood. The Essenes' negative view of the latter Hasmoneans was shared by Strabo, who wrote (*Geog.* 16.2.35-40) that Alexander was among the superstitious and tyrannical priests who departed from the honorable teachings of Moses (cf. Philo *Apol. Jud.* 8.11.1). The Essenes disappeared from history sometime after the war with Rome.

Many aspects of Essene history are still debated.

Bibliography. J. M. Baumgarten, "The Disqualifications of Priests in 4Q Fragments of the 'Damascus Document,'" *Madrid Qumran Congress.* STDJ 11 (Leiden, 1992), 2:503-13; F. C. Conybeare, *Philo: About the Contemplative Life* (1895, repr. New York, 1987); S. Goranson, "Posidonius, Strabo and Marcus Vipsanius Agrippa as Sources on Essenes," *JJS* 45 (1994): 295-98; G. Vermes and M. D. Goodman, *The Essenes according to the Classical Sources* (Sheffield, 1989). STEPHEN GORANSON

ESTHER, ADDITIONS TO

The book of Esther is unique in the OT for having three distinct literary editions. Most familiar is that of the MT, 10 chapters in Hebrew found in all Hebrew Bibles and most English translations. However, two Greek versions of Esther also exist, the Alpha (A) text, a Greek translation of a Hebrew version slightly different from the MT, and the LXX Esther, a translation of the MT that has been altered and expanded enough that it should be considered a separate literary work from MT Esther. The LXX version is canonical in the Orthodox churches.

The LXX Esther contains six "Additions" to the MT text, as well as internal changes. These Additions, labeled for convenience A, B, C, D, E, and F, are interspersed throughout the text. Addition A appears before ch. 1, Addition B follows 3:13, Additions C and D follow 4:17 (LXX also omits 5:1-2 of MT), Addition E follows 8:12, and Addition F ends the book. It should be noted that after the LXX had been translated into Latin, Jerome, when constructing the Vulgate edition, excised the Additions from the Latin text and placed all of them at the end of Esther, in order to bring his version into closer harmony with MT Esther. Thus in Vulgate Bibles the Additions will be found at the end of Esther and numbered 11:2–12:6; 13:1-7; 13:8–14:19; 15:1-16; 16:1-24; and 10:4-11 (F precedes the other Additions in the Vulg.).

The purpose of the Additions in LXX Esther is straightforward. MT Esther is notorious, both today and in the past, for its lack of religious language, particularly its omission of any mention of God. The Additions supply this lack, containing prayers and a prophetic dream, and giving credit for the salvation of the Jews entirely to God. Further, the Additions heighten the dramatic interest of the story by emphasizing the emotions of the characters.

Addition A contains a prophetic dream of the chief male character, Mordecai. In the dream, Mordecai sees two dragons, ancient symbols of chaos, battling while the rest of the world, in particular the Jews, looks on in fear. The conflict is resolved by God, who sends a stream of water and light. The Jews rejoice, and Mordecai wakes up. This dream, which is meant to foreshadow the story of Esther, serves to move the conflict between Mordecai and Haman, the chief antagonist, out of the realm of petty human politics and into that of cosmic struggle, where the only possible resolution comes from God. This places the book of Esther squarely in the realm of religious literature. Addition A also explains how Mordecai discovered the plot of the eunuchs against the Persian king (cf. Esth. 2:21-23), and places the blame for the plot on Haman.

Additions B and E function as a pair, Addition B giving the text of Haman's edict for the destruction of the Jews, and Addition E the text of the king's counter-edict. Both Additions, written in a rather florid Greek, are meant to give an air of historical verisimilitude to the text, although neither is actually authentic.

Additions C and D, which follow one another in the text, are the dramatic heart of LXX Esther. Addition C contains the prayers of Mordecai and Esther, which locate the plight of the Persian Jews in the context of the salvation history of Israel and place the fate of the Jews completely in the hands of God. These prayers, especially Esther's, more than compensate for the lack of religiosity in MT Esther.

Addition D, which contains Esther's unsummoned appearance before the king, is the dramatic denouement of the LXX edition. In the MT, this scene occupies a mere two verses (Esth. 5:1-2) and is rather dry. Although Esther has declared previously that to appear unsummoned before the king is to risk her life, when she actually does so she simply appears in the door, the king extends his scepter to her, and she makes her request. The scene lacks any sense of tension or danger. In Addition D, however, Esther is so agitated that she must cling to her maid for support, and when the king glares at her from the throne she is so frightened she faints, not once but twice! At this moment the real purpose of LXX Esther is revealed. Ad.Esth. 15:8 declares, "Then *God* changed the spirit of the king to gentleness," and he rushes to comfort her. Thus, for LXX Esther, the real moving force behind all the events is God, and the reader is reassured of a positive outcome.

Addition F gives the interpretation of Mordecai's dream, in which the two dragons are identified as Mordecai and Haman, and the stream as Esther. The dream and its interpretation do not quite fit the elements of the plot of Esther, indicating their secondary character.

Addition F contains a colophon, unique among biblical books, which attributes the translation to one Lysimachus, who brought it from Jerusalem to Alexandria in the 1st century B.C.E. The historical truth of this colophon cannot be verified, but it seems clear that the LXX version of Esther, with the Additions, first circulated among the Greek-speaking Jews of Alexandria in the 1st century B.C.E.

Bibliography. J. D. Levenson, *Esther.* OTL (Louisville, 1997); C. D. Moore, *Daniel, Esther and Jeremiah: The Additions.* AB 44 (Garden City, 1977); S. A. White, "Esther," in *The Women's Bible Commentary,* ed. C. A. Newsom and S. H. Ringe (Louisville, 1992), 131-37.

SIDNIE WHITE CRAWFORD

ESTHER (Heb. *'estēr*), **BOOK OF**

The fifth and last of the Megilloth, included among the Writings in the Hebrew canon.

Synopsis

The book opens with a banquet held by the Persian king Ahasuerus for all the inhabitants of his capital, Susa. After a drinking bout, the king summons his queen, Vashti, so the court might admire her great beauty. Vashti refuses, and the angry king banishes her. When he regrets losing her, his counselors suggest an empire-wide search for a new queen. All eligible virgins are gathered into his harem. Among them is Esther (Heb. "Hadassah," Esth. 2:7), the protagonist, who wins the regard of all who know her. Esther pleases Ahasuerus so greatly that he makes her his queen. Subsequently, Esther's uncle Mordecai discovers a plot to assassinate the king and reports it to Esther, thus saving Ahasuerus' life.

Some time later, the king promotes Haman the Agagite as vizier. Haman demands that all the people bow down to him, but Mordecai refuses. Angered, Haman seeks revenge by plotting to slaughter all the Jews in the Persian Empire. Mordecai learns of the plot and turns to Esther to intercede with the king. At the climax of the story, Esther, risking her life, appears unsummoned before the king in an attempt to save her people. She gains Ahasuerus' favor and then, in a series of skillful maneuvers, uncovers Haman's plot and foils his scheme. Haman is put to death, the enemies of the Jews are destroyed, and Mordecai is elevated to vizier. The book ends with Esther and Mordecai instituting the festival of Purim to commemorate these great events.

As the synopsis shows, the plot is quite simple, and there is much more emphasis upon action than character study. Indeed, the characters seem stereotypical — Mordecai and Esther are the righteous wise, struggling against the cunning Haman and his wife for the favor of the powerful but witless Ahasuerus.

Canonicity

Historically, there have been contradictory opinions on the contributions the book of Esther makes to religious doctrine(s) as well as its canonicity. Martin Luther was hostile to the book because it "judaized" too greatly and had "much pagan impropriety," but Maimonides ranked it after the Pentateuch. Esther is the only OT book not yet found among the Dead Sea Scrolls, perhaps for theological reasons. The Essenes may have rejected it because it contains no mention of God, and Esther apparently did not observe the dietary laws. Although Josephus mentions the book in his *Antiquities* and it was regarded as canonical by the Council of Jamnia in 90 C.E., the canonicity of Esther was a matter of some dispute in Judaism until after the 3rd century. The Western Church accepted the book as canonical in the 4th century, while the Eastern Church did not accept it until after the 8th.

Esther is found in different portions of the Bible. In the Hebrew MT, the book is part of the Writings (Ketubim); the LXX places it between Sirach and Judith, and English versions following the KJV put it between Nehemiah and Job.

Composition

The authorship of Esther is unknown. Most scholars agree that the story first appeared in the 4th century (during the Persian period). The final Hebrew version as transmitted in the MT dates from the Hellenistic period, at the latest the turn of the 1st century B.C.E. (cf. 2 Macc. 15:36). Supporting this dating are its Persian setting and local coloring, the absence of Greek influences, and the sympathetic attitude toward the gentile king. The writer displays a most intimate and accurate knowledge of the Persian court and customs, so much so that Esther is used to fill gaps in the accounts of classical historians. Ahasuerus has been identified as Xerxes, the fourth Achaemenid monarch (486-465). Moreover, there is a significant number of Persian nouns.

However, certain statements in the book seem to contradict extrabiblical sources. Some of these discrepancies are quite minor: e.g., Mordecai as part of Nebuchadnezzar's deportation in 597 (2:6), which would make him, and especially Esther, far too old to fit the events. Other contradictions are more significant: e.g., according to Herodotus, Persian queens had to come from one of seven noble Persian families, which would have ruled out Esther, a Jew. Taken individually, few of these problems are sufficiently notable to undermine the essential historicity of Esther. They are ultimately important only because they tend to support two more objections: (1) the striking resemblance of a number of elements to certain ancient Near Eastern legendary stories, such as *A Thousand and One Nights,* and (2) the suspicion that Purim was originally a pagan festival.

Although the core of the narrative is the clash between the two opponents Haman and Mordecai, there are also several subplots: Vashti's banishment, Esther's becoming queen, Mordecai's saving the king, the institution of Purim, and Haman as usurper of monarchical privilege. Despite the fact that the plot seems well constructed, the interweaving of these several story lines has led scholars to suggest that some of the subplots are based on individual narratives, perhaps specific Persian tales, borrowed and reformulated by the author of Esther (e.g., Henri Cazelles, Elias Bickerman, Hans Bardtke).

It is certainly true that any of the story lines could and does make for a good traditional tale, but the most compelling argument against dividing the narrative into separate sources is literary. The subplots do not separate cleanly, but instead overlap a great deal, and they cannot stand independently without key elements of the whole. Despite attempts to prove two separate strands, one focusing on the harem intrigues involving Vashti and Esther, the other on the court struggles of Mordecai and Haman, there is literary legitimacy in considering this book a single unit. Joyce G. Baldwin demonstrates the story's unity based on a role reversal, from elevation to downfall (Vashti, Haman, and the Jews' enemies) and from humiliation to victory (Esther, Mordecai, and the Jewish community).

Versions

The LXX version of Esther, produced in the late 2nd or early 1st century B.C.E., contains six passages not found in the Hebrew text. When the Christian scholar Jerome revised the Old Latin translation of the Bible, he collected them and placed these passages at the end of the canonical book. In English translations, Protestant Bibles place the Additions in the Apocrypha (either alone or integrated with the Hebrew Esther), while recent Roman Catholic Bibles (JB, NAB) translate the Hebrew Esther but insert the Greek Additions in the appropriate places. Tradition assigns the Additions the letters A-F.

These Greek Additions describe prophetic dreams, prayers of Mordecai and Esther, declarations by Esther of her loathing Persian food and bed, and other such pious trappings. Unlike the Hebrew narrative, which richly exploits comic elements of the story (Haman's and Mordecai's human vanity, Haman's fall, Ahasuerus' blindness), the Greek version presents a more somber lesson in a far more serious tone.

Genre

Various genres have been ascribed to the book, including "historicized wisdom tale"(Shemaryahu Talmon), based on characterization (Ahasuerus the foolish king, Mordecai the wise and virtuous courtier, Haman the wise but wicked courtier, and Esther the orphan adopted by a wise man who makes good), and "romance" (Edgar McKnight), depicting a successful quest entailing a perilous journey and crucial struggle in the face of death, and exaltation of the hero. Other suggestions include a traditional "comedy" (uplifting and ultimately optimistic with a cathartic release of tension and ultimate vindication for the heroes), "court tale" (the wise heroine/hero representing a "ruled ethnic group," persecution of the protagonists and their ultimate vindication), and "travesty," wherein serious subjects are treated lightly, drawing upon the incongruity of situations and sharp reversals of fate (Jack Sasson).

Most scholars view Esther as an early Jewish

novella or "diaspora novella," fictional prose that is not intended as an "accurate" historical document. It has the "traditional" narrative framework: tension develops, several complications, and ultimate resolution of the tension. Unlike longer narratives, there is only one chain of events over a limited time period, with the focus on action rather than character development.

Purpose

Most commentators agree that Esther was intended to evoke identification in an audience that was subordinated sociopolitically. Both Esther and Mordecai function in a completely heathen environment, vulnerable and relatively powerless, using skills crucial for the survival of Diaspora Jewry in a predominately gentile world which does not envision or promote the return of the Jews to Palestine. Esther in particular serves as a role model of the characteristics necessary for survival in a precarious world; by working within the system she succeeds in making the system work for her (Sidnie Ann White). Mordecai is variously admired for demonstrating reconciliation to minority status in an unpredictable environment (B. W. Jones) and reviled as inflexible, incurring the wrath of Haman and thus imperiling all Jews under Persian rule.

Others see an altogether different purpose for the book: a "call to arms." By the time of the Council of Jamnia, with Jerusalem destroyed by the Romans in 70 C.E. and their people even more scattered than before, the Jews had good cause to find consolation in the hope that another Esther or Mordecai would rise to save them from the finality of the Diaspora. Nothing in the book seems improbable, especially since the plot centers around court intrigue and ethnic prejudices. Indeed, the text takes great pains to appear as an accurate historical account of a time when the Jews were saved from almost certain extinction.

Reading the Greek text instead of the Hebrew suggests another possible purpose. The six Greek Additions began to be written shortly after the Hebrew text and radically change the nature of the narrative. The timing of the LXX version (the colophon, Addition F, attributes the translation to Lysimachus "in the fourth year of the reign of Ptolemy and Cleopatra," either 114 or 77 B.C.E.) seems to indicate that the story of Esther was soon understood or reinterpreted as conveying a religious message. Unlike the Hebrew text which mentions neither the deity nor religious observances, the LXX refers to God more than 50 times, as well as prayer, the temple, its cult, and the practice of dietary laws. Esther becomes more "Jewish" by claiming to have followed these laws and, in particular, by declaring her loathing for her heathen environment. Purim is de-emphasized, and a more strongly anti-gentile attitude espoused. The Additions, by turning what was originally a court intrigue into a cosmic conflict between Jew and Gentile, make God the champion of the chosen people, and thus the real "hero" of the book.

Recent Scholarly Issues

If the "strength" of literature can be defined by the intensity of its impact on readers, the book of Esther would doubtless qualify as one of the "strongest," most effective texts of all time. Few literary texts have provoked so many interpretations, so many exegetic passions, and so many energetic controversies. Much recent work has been among feminist scholars and tends to focus on gender issues and their implications (e.g., comparison of the Esther story and the Joseph cycle in Genesis; the "problematic" of the female figures — Esther, the beautiful, and Vashti, the headstrong). Other scholars have focused on wider matters of form, contexts, and ideology, such as the appropriate uses of regal authority, assimilation, and national identity. Now, as throughout its history, this small text continues to provoke strong emotions and stimulate academic debate.

Bibliography. J. G. Baldwin, *Esther.* TOTC 12 (Downers Grove, 1984); S. B. Berg, *The Book of Esther.* SBLDS 44 (Missoula, 1979); A. Brenner, ed., *A Feminist Companion to Esther, Judith and Susanna* (Sheffield, 1995); C. A. Moore, *Esther.* AB 7B (Garden City, 1971); J. M. Sasson, "Esther," in *The Literary Guide to the Bible,* ed. R. Alter and F. Kermode (Cambridge, Mass., 1987), 335-342; S. Talmon, "'Wisdom' in the Book of Esther," *VT* 13 (1963): 419-55; S. A. White, "Esther: A Feminine Model for Jewish Diaspora," in *Gender and Difference in Ancient Israel,* ed. P. L. Day (Minneapolis, 1989), 161-77. ILONA N. RASHKOW

ETAM (Heb. *ʿêṭām*)

1. The place where Samson lodged after his slaughter of the Philistines following the murder of his wife and stepfather (Judg. 15:8). While staying at the rock of Etam, men of Judah came to Samson with the goal of delivering him into the hands of the Philistines (Judg. 15:11). The location remains uncertain.

2. A town occupied by the descendants of Simeon (1 Chr. 4:32). The location remains uncertain.

3. A town in the hill country of Judah, listed among the towns fortified by Rehoboam (2 Chr. 11:6). The LXX includes Etam in the list of towns near Bethlehem which it inserts after Josh. 15:59. Josephus (*Ant.* 18.3.2) locates Etam 8 Roman mi. S of Jerusalem, near Pilate's aqueduct. He also claims (8.7.3) that Solomon often retreated to Etam when he wished to escape his busy capital. Due to its connections with Bethlehem and with the water supply of Jerusalem, most scholars have looked for Etam in the vicinity of ʿAin ʿAitān, a spring whose name may reflect that of the ancient town. The most suitable nearby site is Khirbet el-Khôkh (166121), situated on a ridge above the spring, ca. 3.5 km. (2 mi.) SW of Bethlehem in the vicinity of the traditional pools of Solomon. WADE R. KOTTER

ETERNAL LIFE

A blessed life freed from death. The teaching of eternal life arose gradually in the Bible, but in the NT has a central place.

The ancient Hebrews, like many surrounding cultures, believed in a shadowy underworld, a land of the dead called Sheol where departed spirits go (Deut. 32:22; Amos 9:2; Prov. 9:18). Because of its gloomy nature, this was not considered a "life after death," and the duration of any individual person in Sheol is uncertain. Contact with it was forbidden (1 Sam. 28).

The first traceable idea of eternal life comes in the postexilic period at the end of the OT. It is often attributed to Persian, Zoroastrian influence. Dan. 12:1-2 is the first certain biblical reference to eternal life. The faithful martyrs are promised a resurrection to eternal life, God's vindication of their faithfulness. That the first certain mention of eternal life is connected with the resurrection of the body is important for the NT and later Christian teaching. This distinguishes the biblical teaching from Zoroastrian and other religions' teaching, which have no place for resurrection. Almost alongside this view is the Wisdom of Solomon's more Greek-influenced teaching of the immorality of the soul, with no mention of resurrection. This was the minority view in Second Temple Judaism, but serves to refute the facile argument that early Christians had to express their faith in Jesus' eternal life only by proclaiming his resurrection.

Neither did all Second Temple period Jews believe in eternal life of any sort. The Sadducees did not believe it, as witnessed by Josephus (*Ant.* 18.11-22) and the NT (Mark 12:18-27; Acts 23:6-9). This Sadducean position reflects the older Hebrew teaching in the OT. Jesus and the early Christian Church were closer to the Pharisees on their views of eschatology, especially resurrection, judgment, and eternal life.

The center of NT belief in eternal life is the resurrection of Jesus from the dead. The NT interprets this in a variety of ways: a vindication of Jesus' faithfulness (Mark 14:62), echoing Daniel; a fulfillment of OT prophecy (Luke 24:44-46); a new creation through a new Adam (Rom. 5:12-21); a heavenly exaltation (Phil. 2:9; Eph. 4:6-8). Most of these interpretations are compatible with each other; indeed, the NT has a remarkable uniformity in its teaching on the resurrection of Jesus.

Because in Jesus the resurrection of the dead has moved from the end of time (Daniel) into the present age, eternal life in Christ has broken into the present as well. This is especially prominent in John and Paul. Jesus teaches the presence of eternal life (John 5:24). Paradoxically, death is still a reality for the believer as it was for Jesus, so a future dimension of eternal life is focused on the resurrection (John 5:28-29). In Paul, the action of the Spirit at baptism brings the death of the old self and a preliminary entrance into eternal life (Gal. 2:20).

The early Christian teaching of eternal life was often developed in response to problems and misunderstandings in various churches. In 1 Thess. 4:13-18 Paul addresses believers who think that death will separate deceased believers from living believers at the coming of the Lord. Paul responds that God will "bring with him" those who have died in Christ, which already implies life with Christ immediately at death (cf. Phil. 1:23). In 1 Corinthians Paul corrects some believers who hold that eternal life can be obtained without resurrection. He answers that, apart from resurrection, both Jesus' and the believers' (which are essentially related), there can be no eternal life and the whole Christian faith collapses (1 Cor. 4:8; 15:12-19; cf. 2 Tim. 2:17-18). In the Gospel of John the shock to some at the death of Lazarus (ch. 11) and the death of the Beloved Disciple before the return of the Lord (ch. 21) lead to further clarification of teaching on eternal life. These passages show that the NT searches for a balance on eternal life between present and future — the believer has passed in Christ from death to eternal life, but this remains to be fully realized in God's future, especially in the Resurrection and new creation at the eschaton.

The nature of eternal life is sketched only in its essential elements in the NT. The emphasis throughout is on a basic assurance of eternal life, not on a fanciful depiction of details. This accords with the notable restraint in the NT in treating the resurrection of Jesus, the center of eternal life, which is not described in any detail apart from the assertion of its actuality. (The four Gospels include resurrection *appearance* narratives, but no narrative of the Resurrection itself.) In the Synoptic Gospels Jesus teaches that eternal life is life with God in his kingdom, whether that kingdom is on earth or in heaven. Paul depicts it in terms of the fulfillment of the promise of living with Christ, especially sharing his resurrection. Even in the book of Revelation, the apocalyptic imagery of eternal life in heaven is used symbolically to encourage believers under deadly persecution to remain faithful and obtain the martyr's crown of eternal life.

Bibliography. G. B. Caird, *New Testament Theology,* ed. L. D. Hurst (Oxford, 1994), 238-78; G. W. E. Nickelsburg, *Resurrection, Immortality, and Eternal Life in Intertestamental Judaism.* HTS 26 (Cambridge, Mass., 1972); K. Stendahl, ed., *Immortality and Resurrection* (New York, 1965).

ROBERT E. VAN VOORST

ETERNITY

See TIME.

ETHAM (Heb. *'ēṯām*)

The first resting place for the Israelites after departing Succoth during the Exodus. According to Exod. 13:20; Num. 33:6-7 Etham is located "on the edge of the wilderness," suggesting a location not too distant from the eastern delta of the Nile River.

C. SHAUN LONGSTREET

ETHAN (Heb. *'ēṯān*)

1. A famous sage, one of the sons of Mahol (an orchestral guild?) and brother of Heman, Calcol, and Darda, whose wisdom was surpassed by Solomon's (1 Kgs. 4:31[MT 5:11]). He is called "the Ezrahite" (Heb. *ha'ezrāḥî;* cf. Ps. 89 superscription[1], possibly designating a member of a pre-Israelite group.

2. A descendant of Zerah, Judah's son by his daughter-in-law Tamar, and father of Azariah (1 Chr. 2:6, 8; cf. Gen. 38:30). His connection with Heman and Calcol supports his identification with Ethan **1** above.

3. The son of Zimmah and father of Adaiah, an ancestor of Asaph (1 Chr. 6:41-42[26-27]).

4. A Merarite Levite (1 Chr. 6:44[29]), the son of Kishi (or Kushaiah; cf. 15:17). He was one of the three Levites David appointed over the "service of song" in the temple (1 Chr. 6:31-48[16-33]), probably to be equated with Jeduthun in 16:41-42; 25:1-3.

TYLER F. WILLIAMS

ETHANIM (Heb. *'ēṯānîm*)
The preexilic name of the 7th month in the Hebrew year (Sept./Oct.), of Phoenician derivation. Its Babylonian counterpart was Tishri.

ETHBAAL (Heb. *'eṯba'al*)
The king of the Phoenician city of Sidon (889-856 B.C.E.). Ethbaal ("Baal is with him") was the father of Ahab's wife Jezebel. This marriage, probably one component of an alliance between Omri of Israel and Ethbaal, was regarded by the Deuteronomist as apostasy (1 Kgs. 16:31). Josephus refers to Ithobalus (Ethbaal) as a priest of Astarte who usurped the throne (*Ag. Ap.* 1.18). At an earlier period, Byblos had a king of the same name. CHRIS A. ROLLSTON

ETHER (Heb. *'eṯer*)

1. A town in the tribal allotment of Judah (Josh. 15:42). Part of the Libnah-Mareshah district in the central Shephelah, it is identified with Khirbet el-'Ater/Tel 'Eter (13855.11377), ca. 6 km. (4 mi.) NE of Lachish.

2. A town occupied by the tribe of Simeon within the tribal allotment of Judah (Josh. 19:7). It is located somewhere in the Negeb, although its exact location is unknown. It is probably the same site as Athach mentioned in 1 Sam. 30:30.

STEVEN M. ORTIZ

ETHICS
A term drawn from Greek philosophy, "ethics" denotes an effort to present norms of behavior in a systematic way that shows their internal, rational coherence. Not all biblical writings concerned with norms of behavior represent a strictly ethical stance in this sense. Many passages treat the norms simply as separate and distinct rules (e.g., much of the Torah) or bits of wise advice (e.g., Proverbs) with only minimal interconnections. Ethical thought is significant, however, in contexts such as Leviticus (with its focus on purity as the ritual expression of holiness), the prophets (with their call for justice as the primary human response to God's loving-kindness), the Gospels (e.g., in the summary of the law), and Paul (who subordinates the specifics of the law to faith and love). Such broad themes as covenant, eschatology, and discipleship may also serve as organizing principles.

Given the inherently unsystematic character of the Bible, biblical ethics often turns out to be a dimension less of the text itself than of its interpretation. Biblical commandments and proverbs and bits of wisdom may have had no need to explain themselves, but later readers often want to understand the reasons behind them in order to interpret and apply them in their own very different contexts. They need to make decisions balancing the relative importance of potentially conflicting commands or to interpret what a commandment framed in terms of a pastoral society might mean in terms of, e.g., an industrial one. Biblical ethics, then, is an inevitable, but always somewhat hybrid offspring of the biblical texts themselves.

In developing such ethical reflection, perhaps the obvious first step is to establish a hierarchy among commandments — a process that is already well under way within the Scriptures. Exod. 20 and Deut. 5, e.g., give special emphasis to the Ten Words or Commandments, perhaps suggesting that they provide a key to the commandments as a whole. Certain of the prophets insist on the duty of justice as more important than other commandments (e.g., Amos 6; Mic. 3; Jer. 7). Jesus fixes on two commandments — to love God with your whole self (Deut. 6:5) and your neighbor as yourself (Lev. 19:18) — as the two principles on which "hang all the law and the prophets" (Matt. 22:34-40; Mark 12:28-34; cf. Luke 10:25-28).

Paul, in a related but distinctive way, singles out love as the preeminent value that determines the relevance of other commandments: "The one who loves has fulfilled the rest of the law. . . . Love is the fullness of the law" (Rom. 13:8-10). Paul also gives faith a similar role: "Everything that does not proceed from faith is sin" (Rom. 14:23). In the Johannine literature, one finds something similar in the central place given to the commandment "to love one another" (e.g., John 15:12; 1 John 2:7-11).

By raising just a few principles to the highest level and making the other norms of behavior dependent on them or subordinate to them, one could link apparently independent norms of behavior to one another. Thus a famous story about Rabbi Hillel: when a Gentile insisted that Hillel teach him the whole Torah while he stood on one foot, Hillel patiently replied with the Golden Rule and then added, "Go and learn," implying that the Golden Rule was the key to something much larger and more complex (*b. Šabb.* 31a). Alternatively, one could relativize the "lesser" rules as being further from the central principles and therefore less important. Thus, Mark's Jesus, by refocusing on "purity of the heart," relativizes physical purity and makes it effectively optional (Mark 7:1-23).

The ethical thought of ancient rabbinic Judaism focused on *halakhah,* the rules of behavior found in the written Torah interpreted by the tradition of the oral Torah. Authoritative interpretations emerged from lively rabbinic debate over the meaning of particular texts — with other texts drawn in for comparison. Certain specific modes of argument, working by deduction and analogy, were recognized as legitimate. Rabbinic Judaism tended to preserve significant portions of the debate itself as well as the conclusions. It thus exhibited a dialectical quality that is still characteristic of rabbinic discourse — a quality that values the interpretive process along with the end result.

Ancient Greek-speaking Judaism followed a different procedure, as seen, e.g., in its preeminent representative, Philo of Alexandria (roughly contemporary with Paul). Philo's ethical reflections tended to resemble more the contemporary Greek philosophical discourse of Middle Platonism and Stoicism. Even when interpreting scriptural texts, Philo usually explained them in terms of basic ethical axioms giving rise to specific norms of behavior. The mainstream of early Christianity followed this pattern rather than the rabbinic one, and it has continued to be dominant in later Christianity. Christian ethics has typically been a systematic undertaking, more a subdivision of theology than of biblical interpretation; and it has tended to prize the final answer often to the neglect of the debate from which it emerged.

In contemporary biblical scholarship, ethical analysis of texts usually includes an effort to show how the norms expressed in the text fitted into the ethical systems, explicit or implicit, of the culture in which the text was written. The relevance for modern ethics may then be sought in a dynamic comparison of texts and contexts. Such comparisons may yield widely divergent results, ranging from a negative critique of the biblical text as representative of an oppressive cultural norm (so, e.g., in feminist or some liberationist hermeneutics) to the reclaiming or reuse of a text to give new direction in changed circumstances.

Bibliography. L. W. Countryman, *Dirt, Greed, and Sex* (Philadelphia, 1988); T. W. Ogletree, *The Use of the Bible in Christian Ethics* (Philadelphia, 1983); W. Schrage, *The Ethics of the New Testament* (Philadelphia, 1988); W. C. Spohn, *What Are They Saying about Scripture and Ethics?* rev. ed. (New York, 1995); P. Trible, *God and the Rhetoric of Sexuality.* OBT 2 (Philadelphia, 1978); A. Verhey, *The Great Reversal* (Grand Rapids, 1984).

L. William Countryman

ETHIOPIA (Gk. *Aithiopia*)

The ancient region S of Egypt and encompassing the entire area of modern Sudan. The northernmost point was close to the Egyptian town of Syene (Aswan), at the first cataract of the Nile River (Ezek. 29:10; Heb. *kûš*). Its southern boundaries extended to modern Ethiopia and Eritrea. On the west Ethiopia was limited by the vast desert. In its early days Ethiopia also embraced regions to the east of the Red Sea, and included some of the territory represented today by Saudi Arabia and Yemen (Homer *Od.* 1.22-23; Strabo *Geog.* 1.2.28; 2.3.8; Aeschylus *Supp.* 284-86). While the precise boundaries of ancient Ethiopia are disputed, it is generally agreed that after Herodotus and throughout the NT era Ethiopia referred to the territory directly S of Egypt and bordering the west bank of the Red Sea.

The Bible often mentions Ethiopia in conjunction with its closest neighbors, Egypt (Ps. 68:31[MT 32]; Isa. 20:3-5; Ezek. 30:4, 5; Dan. 11:43; Nah. 3:9) and Libya (2 Chr. 16:8; Ezek. 30:5; 38:5; Dan. 11:43; Nah. 3:9). Reference is also made to the rivers of Ethiopia (Isa. 18:1; Zeph. 3:10), which are commonly accepted as the White and the Blue Niles along with the Atbara. Ethiopia was rich in natural resources, and known for its wealth and trading (Job 28:19; Isa. 43:3; 45:14; Dan. 11:43; Diodorus Siculus *Hist.* 3.11.12).

The etymological root of Gk. *Aithiopia,* "burnt face," describes the pigmentation of the people who were called Ethiopians. Consequently, not only does Ethiopia refer to a geographical territory, but it also indicates ethnicity (Jer. 13:23). Historians in the Greco-Roman world believed that Ethiopians were the first humans on earth (Diodorus 3.2.1-3). There were many subgroups among the Ethiopians, each with distinct cultural and physical characteristics (cf. Herodotus *Hist.* 7.70). The ancients reported that the tallest, handsomest, and fastest of humans could be found among them (cf. Isa. 18:2; Herodotus 3.20; 4.183). There was significant interaction between Ethiopia and other ancient cultures, and Ethiopians could be found throughout Europe and Asia. Other ethnic groups could also be found living in Ethiopia, and cultural influence is evidenced by the fact that many inhabitants of Ethiopia embraced the religion of Israel (Ps. 87:4; Isa. 11:11; Acts 8:27).

The Bible identifies Cush, the son of Ham, as the father of the Ethiopians (Gen. 10:6). Much of the history of Ethiopia intertwines with that of Egypt. Ethiopian influence was evident in Egypt from the Proto-dynastic Age (ca. 2900 B.C.E.). Ethiopia was eventually conquered by the Egyptian kings of the 12th Dynasty, but regained her independence during the Second Intermediate Period (ca. 1780-1550). Following independence, Ethiopia established her capital in Napata, near the 4th Nile cataract.

Egypt managed to regain control of Ethiopia during the New Kingdom (1500-1070). The extent of Egypt's control over Ethiopia during this era is questionable, particularly in light of the biblical record of King Asa's defeat of an independent Ethiopian army (2 Chr. 14:9-15[8-14]). Under the military leadership of Piankhy and Shabako, Ethiopia overpowered Egypt and initiated the 25th (Ethiopian) Dynasty (ca. 715-663). Taharqa (Tirhakah), the best-known king of the Ethiopian dynasty, was an ally of King Hezekiah of Judah in the war against Sennacherib and the Assyrians in 701 (2 Kgs. 19:9; Isa. 37:9). Indeed, it was the Assyrians who were responsible for the eventual demise of the Ethiopian dynasty following the sack of Thebes in 664.

The diminished Ethiopian kingdom established its seat of power in Meroe, and initiated a dynasty that was to last until the early Byzantine era (ca. 350 C.E.). While certain provinces may have been briefly subjected by Persia (Esth. 1:1; 8:9; Add. Esth. 13:1; 16:1), for most of this era Ethiopia maintained her independence. During the NT era, Merotic Ethiopia was ruled by a series of queens (Candaces). By the 1st century C.E. the prominence of

Meroe was shared by Aksum, which had become the major commercial center in Ethiopia with its own prestigious dynasty. Several of the Aksumite kings were Christian.

Ethiopia is featured in a number of biblical prophecies. Isaiah speaks of judgment that is to come upon Ethiopia for her willingness to assist the rebellious Israel (Isa. 20:3-4). Ezekiel prophesies doom on Ethiopia, which together with Egypt is destined to receive punishment from Babylon (Ezek. 30:4, 5, 9); he further names Ethiopia among the allies of the defeated Gog (38:5). Zephaniah also heralds destruction on Ethiopia for her arrogance (Zeph. 2:12). But Ethiopia's judgment is no different than Israel's (Amos 9:7). In fact, the conversion of Ethiopia will allow her to share Israel's blessings (Ps. 68:31[32]; Isa. 45:14; Zeph. 3:9-10).

Several biblical personalities are identified as Ethiopian: Zipporah, the wife of Moses (Num. 12:1; since she resided in Midian [Exod. 2:21], "Ethiopian" is probably a reference to her ethnicity); Cushi, the messenger from the Israelite army who brought the news of Absalom's death to David (2 Sam. 18:21-23, 31-32); the queen of Sheba (1 Kgs. 10:1-10), also known as the queen of the South (Matt. 12:42; Luke 11:31; the Kĕbrä Nägäst ["Glory of the Kings"], which allegedly contains the royal chronicles of the Ethiopian monarchy, records an unbroken line of rulers originating with Menelek I, the legendary son of Solomon and the queen of Sheba); Zerah, the Ethiopian king who was defeated by King Asa of Judah (2 Chr. 14:9); Tirhakah, the Ethiopian king who assisted Hezekiah against Assyria (Isa. 37:9); the prophet Zephaniah (Zeph. 1:1); Ebed-melech, the court official who rescued Jeremiah (Jer. 38:7-13; 39:15-17); Amantitere, the Merotic queen who held the title *Kandake* (Acts 8:27); the eunuch, an official representative of Candace, who was also an observant Jew and the first recorded Ethiopian Christian (Acts 8:27-40).

Bibliography. E. A. W. Budge, *A History of Ethiopia, Nubia, and Abyssinia* (1928, repr. Oosterhout, 1970); C. H. Felder, *Troubling Biblical Waters* (Maryknoll, 1989); A. H. M. Jones, *A History of Ethiopia* (Oxford, 1955); H. G. Marcus, *A History of Ethiopia* (Berkeley, 1994); F. M. Snowden, *Blacks in Antiquity* (Cambridge, Mass., 1970); E. Ullendorff, *The Ethiopians*, 3rd ed. (Oxford, 1973).

KEITH A. BURTON

ETHIOPIAN EUNUCH

A Jewish-sympathizing superintendent of the Ethiopian queen's (Candace) treasury who received instruction and baptism from Philip along a desert route from Jerusalem to Gaza (Acts 8:26-39). His devotion to Judaism is evident in his pilgrimage to Jerusalem and his perusal of a personal copy of the Isaiah scroll (Acts 8:27-31). It is unlikely, however, that he was a proselyte or welcome adherent to Judaism. Although a wealthy and prominent official, as a eunuch he was defective and defiled according to traditional Jewish law, forever banned from the covenant community (cf. Lev. 21:18-21; Deut. 23:1; Josephus *Ant.* 4.290-91; Philo *Spec. leg.* 1.324-25). This marginal status is suggested in the eunuch's question concerning what might "prevent" his baptism (Acts 8:36). The focus on the "generative" potential of the shorn and shamed figure of Isa. 53:7-8 — whom Philip implicitly identifies with the crucified and risen Jesus (Acts 8:32-35) — seems particularly relevant to the eunuch's physical condition and social location.

The evangelization of the Ethiopian eunuch fulfills the inclusive vision of an Isaianic text (Isa. 56:3-8, although the foreign eunuch in Acts is accepted while moving away from, not toward, the holy city) and the expansive mission projected in Acts 1:8 "to the ends of the earth." This incident also sets the stage for outreach to Cornelius, another God-fearing Gentile (Acts 10–11).

Bibliography. F. S. Spencer, "The Ethiopian Eunuch and His Bible," *BTB* 22 (1992): 155-65; *The Portrait of Philip in Acts.* JSNTSup 67 (Sheffield, 1992), ch. 4.

F. SCOTT SPENCER

ETHIOPIC

Classical Ethiopic (Geʿez), the oldest attested member of Ethiopic Semitic, a family of about a dozen Semitic languages spoken in Eritrea and the Ethiopian highlands. Ethiopic Semitic is presumably derived from one or more forms of South Semitic brought from Yemen, probably in the first half of the 1st millennium B.C. A South Arabian colony not far from the later Ethiopian capital Aksum has been paleographically dated to ca. 500 by Old South Arabian monumental inscriptions of the Sabean type. Classical Ethiopic disappeared as a spoken language probably some time before the 10th century A.D. However, it continues today as the liturgical language of the Ethiopian Orthodox Church, and was the only official written language of Ethiopia up to practically the end of the 19th century.

The earliest attestation of Classical Ethiopic is a corpus of about a dozen royal inscriptions in Ethiopic (plus six in Greek), the most important from a king named Ezana (perhaps mid-4th century A.D.). Six of the Geʿez inscriptions are written in the Old South Arabian alphabet, two in nonvocalized Ethiopic, and four in the earliest attestation of vocalized Ethiopic script. The earliest inscriptions of Ezana are pagan, while the last few attest to the introduction of monotheism (presumably Christian) to the court at Aksum.

After Ezana the oldest core of Ethiopic literature gradually took shape in the form of translations from the Greek (in turn sometimes a rendering from Hebrew or Aramaic). This literature, preserved and recopied in churches and monasteries during a long "dark ages" when the rise of Islam in Arabia and the Red Sea area effectively cut Ethiopia off from the rest of the Near Eastern Christian world, includes an Ethiopic translation of the Bible and accompanying apocrypha (in particular a long, complete version of Enoch), many liturgical texts, some lives of saints, some patristic fragments (a few unattested elsewhere), and a version of the monastic Rules of Pachomius.

Ca. 1000 Ethiopia reestablished contact with

Egypt. A metropolitan *(abuna)* for the Ethiopian Church was regularly dispatched by the patriarch of Alexandria, and there was a new flourishing of ecclesiastical literature of all genres (much of it translated from the Arabic, in turn translated from Greek, Coptic, Syriac, or other sources). In addition, an original secular or court literature arose in the form of royal chronicles, legal texts, even a sort of national epic (the *Kĕbrä Nägäst,* "Glory of Kings," an elaboration of the legend of Solomon and Sheba). A more popular magic literature also took shape, centered around the production of amulets and "magic scrolls." The production of this, and some hymnic genres, has continued into the present century.

Bibliography. A. Dillmann, *Ethiopic Grammar,* 2nd ed. (1907, repr. Amsterdam, 1974); T. O. Lambdin, *Introduction to Classical Ethiopic (Ge'ez).* HSS 24 (Missoula, 1978); W. Leslau, *Comparative Dictionary of Ge'ez* (Wiesbaden, 1987).

GENE B. GRAGG

ETH-KAZIN (Heb. *'ittâ qāṣîn*)
A town on the eastern border of Zebulun's territory (Josh. 19:13), possibly modern Kefr Kennä, ca. 7 km. (4.5 mi.) NE of Nazareth. Tradition identifies it with Cana, where Jesus changed water to wine (John 2:1-11).

ETHNAN (Heb. *'eṯnān*)
A Judahite, the youngest son of Ashhur and Helah (1 Chr. 4:7). The name may represent a social unit from Ithnan, located in the Negeb of Judah (Josh. 15:23).

ETHNARCH (Gk. *ethnárchēs*)
A political title (lit., "ruler of the people") most commonly designating either a dependent monarch (1 Macc. 14:47; 15:1-2) or the leader of the semi-autonomous Jewish community in Alexandria (Josephus *Ant.* 14.7.2). Additional meanings have been proposed for the unnamed ethnarch under King Aretas in Damascus (2 Cor. 11:32): city governor, tribal sheik, ethnic consul, and tribal military leader. Despite no external evidence for Aretas IV's control of Damascus, most scholars accept Paul's account and suggest either that Aretas received Damascus as a benefaction from Gaius in 37 C.E. or that Aretas briefly took control of Damascus after defeating Herod Antipas in 36. A minority understands the ethnarch and Aretas' jurisdiction as outside Damascus and thus relieved of the burden of asserting Nabatean control of the city. This incident may provide a fixed point within Pauline chronology by placing Paul's Arabian mission (Gal. 1:7) between 36 and the death of Aretas in 39/40. However, the historical reliability of 2 Cor. 11:32-33 is challenged by its identification as a textual gloss and by the narrative's similarities to Josh. 2.

Bibliography. J. Taylor, "The Ethnarch of King Aretas at Damascus: A Note on 2 Cor 11,32-33," *RB* 99 (1992): 719-28.

JENNIFER K. BERENSON MACLEAN

ETHNI (Heb. *'eṯnî*) (also JEATHERAI)
A Levite of the Gershomite branch, the son of Zerah and ancestor of Asaph the singer (1 Chr. 6:41[MT 26]). At 1 Chr. 6:21[6] he is called Jeatherai.

EUBULUS (Gk. *Eúboulos*)
A Christian, presumably imprisoned with Paul at Rome, who also sent greetings to Timothy (2 Tim. 4:21).

EUCHARIST
The rite of Holy Communion or the Lord's Supper (Gk. *eucharistía,* "thanksgiving"). Among the earliest evidence for this name, which does not occur in the NT, are references in the Didache (9:1), Ignatius of Antioch (*Phld.* 4), and Justin Martyr (*Apol.* 1.66).

See LORD'S SUPPER.

EUMENES (Gk. *Eumenēs*)
Eumenes II, Attalid king who ruled in Pergamum (197-159 B.C.E.). He acquired significant portions of Seleucid Asia Minor from the Romans after their defeat of the Seleucid ruler Antiochus III at the battle of Magnesia in 190 (1 Macc. 8:8). His alliance with Rome created tension between Pergamum and its neighbors. Eumenes probably acquired the title "Soter" in 184 after victory over neighboring Bithynia. He won full control over Galatia in 180/79 after defeating Pontus. Remaining concerned about Seleucid politics, he helped Antiochus IV regain the Seleucid throne upon Antiochus' release from exile in Rome (175/4). RODNEY A. WERLINE

EUNICE (Gk. *Euníkē*)
A resident of Lystra (cf. Acts 14) and "a believer" (16:1); the mother of Timothy. Commended as having faith (2 Tim. 1:5), presumably she was the person who taught Timothy Scripture as a child (3:15). Some scholars feel Eunice was lax in her Judaism (marriage to a "Greek" [Gentile] and the fact that Timothy was not circumcised). ERIC F. MASON

EUNUCH
Typically a castrated official in the royal courts of ancient Israel and surrounding kingdoms who is appropriate to serve the queen (2 Kgs. 9:30-32; Esth. 4:4-5; Acts 8:27) or the king's harem (Esth. 2:14-15). The term (Heb. *sārîs*) can also apply to a married official (e.g., Potiphar; Gen. 39:1).

Despite the high political standing enjoyed by some eunuchs, their peculiar impairment usually rendered them among the most scorned and stigmatized members of society. In a patriarchal culture where honor was tied to male domination, the effeminate, impotent eunuch was viewed with shame and as a threatening social deviant (Lucian *Eunuch* 6-11; cf. Josephus *Ant.* 4.190-91). In the Jewish world the eunuch's alien status was compounded by his lack of wholeness (holiness) and inability to perpetuate the covenant line through circumcision and procreation. Biblical law excluded men with damaged genitals from the covenant community (Deut. 23:1) and the holy priesthood (Lev. 21:17-21; cf. Philo *Spec. leg.* 1.324-25).

Other traditions, however, offer a favored place for pious eunuchs within the Lord's house (Isa. 56:3-8; Wis. 3:14-15). In the NT a prominent, God-fearing eunuch (Gk. *eunoúchos*) from Ethiopia is baptized at the hands of Philip the Evangelist (Acts 8:26-40). Jesus' unique statement concerning self-made eunuchs "for the sake of the kingdom of heaven" (Matt. 19:12) represents a metaphor for the discipline of celibacy, reflecting either a lifelong vow or a commitment not to remarry after divorcing an unfaithful wife (cf. vv. 3-12).

F. Scott Spencer

EUODIA (Gk. *Euodía*)
A woman whose dispute with Syntyche evidently affected the entire Philippian congregation (Phil. 4:2). Paul was informed of the dispute while in prison (cf. 2:25), and he exhorts the two women "to be of the same mind in the Lord" (Phil. 4:2; cf. 2:2). These women, who had "struggled beside" the apostle "in the work of the gospel" with Clement and other "coworkers" of Paul (Phil. 4:3; cf. 1:27), evidently had prominent positions in this church, whose first converts were women (Acts 16:11-15). There is no evidence, however, that they were deaconesses. The nature of their dispute remains uncertain.

James A. Kelhoffer

EUPHRATES (Gk. *Euphrátēs*)
The longest and most important river of southwest Asia. The waters of the Euphrates nourished important cultures of Mesopotamia including the Sumerian, Akkadian, and Babylonian. Arguably no river was more important to the early development of urban civilization.

The Euphrates begins in eastern Turkey near Lake Van. Two streams, the Kara Su and Murat Su, unite near Malatya to form the Euphrates. The river descends southward for ca. 400 km. (250 mi.) and enters the Syrian Plain near Carchemish. Near ancient Emar the Euphrates bends sharply to the southeast. Two major tributaries, the Balikh and Ḫabur Rivers, join the Euphrates prior to reaching the Mesopotamian flood plain near modern Hit in Iraq. The Euphrates exhibits an anatomosing course throughout the flat, alluvial flood plain; the river follows multiple channels which separate and rejoin in an intricate pattern that, properly utilized, provided adequate irrigation possibilities in a region where rainfall was insufficient to support agriculture. The meandering courses of the lower Euphrates have shifted periodically. In antiquity the two main branches of the lower Euphrates passed Sippar, Babylon, Uruk, Nippur, Kish, and Ur. Today several of these sites lie in the desert as the two main branches of the Euphrates (the Shaṭṭ al-Hindiyah and Shaṭṭ al-Ḥillah) shifted to the east. The Euphrates and the Tigris join in the south to form the Shaṭṭ al-ʿArab, a waterway that flows into the Persian Gulf. Marshes, shallow lakes, and water channels predominate in the southern portion of the delta formed by the Tigris and Euphrates.

Life in central and southern Mesopotamia depended upon irrigation provided by the Euphrates. The Euphrates, along with the Tigris, flooded annually from late March into June. Unlike the Nile, the flooding was unpredictable, at times causing destruction of crops and cities, and at other times being insufficient for irrigation purposes. Also, the timing of the flood was less suitable to crop production. Some scholars believe this phenomenon accounts in part for a basic pessimism that underlies the Mesopotamian worldview. Salinization of the soil also was a problem for the Mesopotamian farmer. As the Euphrates slowly built up over the surrounding plain and water spilled over the levees, over a period of time salts built up in the soil. Farmers adapted by utilizing salt-tolerant crops, especially barley.

Biblical writers name or allude to the Euphrates with a frequency exceeded only by references to the Jordan and Nile Rivers. The Euphrates (Heb. *pěrāṯ*; cf. Akk. *Purattu*) first appears as one of four rivers associated with Eden (Gen. 2:14). Israel's ancestors came from "beyond the Euphrates" (Josh. 24:2), a reference to the Haran region from whence Abraham migrated. The Euphrates appears in descriptions of the land promised to Abraham and his descendants (Gen. 15:18; Deut. 1:7; 11:24; Josh. 1:4). The diviner Balaam came from Bethor on the Euphrates (Num. 22:5). David engaged Hadad-ezer, king of Hamath, as he extended his military reach to the Euphrates River (2 Sam. 8:3). Later, Josiah died at the hands of Neco II when the latter was reinforcing the Egyptian position at Carchemish on the Euphrates against the emerging Chaldean/Babylonian threat (2 Kgs. 23:29). Because the Euphrates was the natural boundary separating the Levant from Mesopotamia, the prophets referred to the Euphrates as they warned Israel and Judah of impending judgments executed by Assyria and Babylon (Isa. 7:20; 27:12; Jer. 13:4-7; 46:2-10). In the Persian period Judah was part of the Fifth Satrapy "Beyond the River," the land W of the great bend of the Euphrates (Ezra 4:10-11; 5:3; 6:6; Neh. 2:7). In the NT the Euphrates is the setting for apocalyptic events (Rev. 9:14; 16:12).

Bibliography. R. McC. Adams, *Heartland of Cities* (Chicago, 1981); S. W. Cole, "Marsh Formation in the Borsippa Region and the Course of the Lower Euphrates," *JNES* 53 (1994): 81-109; J. Zarins, "The Early Settlement of Southern Mesopotamia," *JAOS* 112 (1992): 55-77.

Thomas V. Brisco

EUSEBIUS (Gk. *Eusébios*)
Bishop of Caesarea and "Father of Church History" (ca. 260–ca. 339 C.E.). Eusebius was born in Palestine and spent the majority of his life there. As a young man he became a student of Pamphilius, a well-known Christian teacher; he adopted the name Eusebius of Pamphilius after his mentor's martyrdom in 310. Eusebius himself was imprisoned in Egypt during the final years of persecution. Shortly after the Great Persecution ended (313) he was elected bishop of Caesarea, where he served until his death.

Eusebius' most enduring contribution is his *Historia ecclesiastica (Church History),* a history of the Church to ca. 323. Here Eusebius demonstrated a concern for original sources virtually unprecedented in ancient histories; his extensive research and quotation preserve a wealth of early Church documentation otherwise lost to the Church. In addition to the *HE,* Eusebius wrote more than 40 works in such diverse areas as apologetics, theology, exegesis, gospel criticism, biblical geography, biography, chronology, and martyrology.

Eusebius' contribution to the Church was more than literary. He was also a major figure in the theological controversies and ecclesiastical politics of his day. As Constantine's primary theological advisor, Eusebius helped shape the Constantinian concept of a Christian empire. He was instrumental in achieving consensus at the Council of Nicea and was active in church councils until his death.

Bibliography. T. D. Barnes, *Constantine and Eusebius* (Cambridge, Mass., 1981); R. M Grant, *Eusebius as Church Historian* (Oxford, 1980); D. S. Wallace-Hadrill, *Eusebius of Caesarea* (London, 1960). CHARLES GUTH

EUTYCHUS (Gk. *Eútychos)*
A young man from Troas who fell two stories from his window seat when he fell asleep during one of Paul's long speeches (Acts 20:9). Luke records that Eutychus "was picked up dead," but Paul revived the youth (Acts 20:10-12).

EVANGELIST
One who proclaims the "good news" (Gk. *euangélion*) or who "preaches the gospel, brings good news" *(euangelízō).* These terms are both derived from *ángelos,* "messenger." Acts 21:8; Eph. 4:11 speak of an office; 2 Tim. 4:5 indicates an activity incumbent upon Timothy. In these passages, the evangelist *(euangelistḗs)* is distinguished from the apostolic office: the former delivers the same apostolic message, but without the same level of authority as the latter.

Although the companion word *ángelos* appears often in secular literature, *euangelistḗs* is very rare. It is used in Christian literature exclusively for one who carries on the preaching of the good news of Jesus Christ. DALE ELLENBURG

EVE (Heb. *ḥawwâ*)

OT

The first woman, according to the Creation account of Gen. 2:4b–3:24. Just as Adam was formed to remedy the earth's infertility (Gen. 2:5), so Eve is created in response to Adam's need (perhaps also his infertility; v. 18). Yahweh therefore sets about to create for the man an *ʿēzer kĕnegdô,* a "helper corresponding to him." Heb. *ʿēzer* does not carry the overtones of subordination associated with the English "helper." Rather, an *ʿēzer* is someone *capable* of helping, and in most instances the word describes God (Exod. 18:4; Deut. 33:26; Ps. 146:5; Hos. 13:9). The woman, however, is not the man's superior; she is explicitly said to *correspond* to him. Unike the animals or Adam himself, the woman is not formed of earth but built from a rib removed from Adam's side. The word "woman," is given a playful etymology in the text; she is "wo-man" because she is "from-man" (*ʾiššâ* from *ʾîš;* Gen. 2:23). The man joyfully receives this partner, and announces that a man will now leave his parents to "cling" to a woman as the two become one flesh, apparently celebrating an end to the man's sterility as well as to his loneliness.

The woman is approached in Gen. 3:1 by the snake and, as she says, is "tricked" into eating the forbidden fruit. Contrary to popular tradition, she does not then beguile her husband into eating; she "gave some to her man who was with her" (Gen. 3:6), and who was apparently party to the entire exchange between the woman and the snake. The woman is then punished with both the life-threatening pains of childbirth and with subordination to her partner (Gen. 3:16). Only now does Adam take on the authority to name the woman Eve *(ḥawwâ),* celebrating her role as "mother of all living" *(ḥay).* A connection has been proposed between the name *Ḥawwâ* and Aram. *ḥewyāʾ,* "snake," but the relation is uncertain.

In Gen. 4:1 Eve bears her first son, Cain, exclaiming, "I made a man!" Curiously, after the subsequent births of Abel and Seth Eve is not mentioned again in the OT. The figure of Eve is ambiguous. Her status as "mother of all living" suggests an affinity with the mother goddesses of the ancient Near East, but the biblical narrative pointedly consigns the universal progenitrix to mortal status.

Intertestamental Writings and NT

Eve is mentioned in various writings of the intertestamental period, during which the tradition develops that Eve (or even "woman") is responsible for introducing both sin and death to humankind: "From a woman sin had its beginning; and because of her we all die" (Sir. 25:24; cf. 2 En. 30:17; Apoc. Mos. 7.1; 21). By the NT period Paul is thus able to cite Eve (2 Cor. 11:3) as the exemplar of susceptibility to deception and even of sexual seduction. In 1 Tim. 2:12-15 Eve ("the woman") appears as the prototype whose punishment now falls on all women. The author argues (as Gen. 2 does not) that Adam's prior creation establishes his authority over Eve (Gk. *prṓtos,* "first," is taken to designate both prior creation and premier status). Moreover, because Eve was deceived by the snake (and presumably passed on the snake's words to Adam; cf. Gen. 3:17 in which Adam has "listened to the voice" of his woman) she is an unreliable authority; women are not to teach men in the church but are to maintain silence. The teaching on childbirth in 1 Tim. 2:15 is notoriously difficult. The passage, which seems to claim that modern women gain salvation through childbearing, may instead refer to Eve's sentence of life-threatening birth pains (Gen. 3:16). If the ancient translation, "she will be brought safely through childbirth," is adopted, then the author is continuing the parallel between Eve and modern women: Eve's punishment of difficult and dangerous labor may be mitigated for women who lead pious lives. The underlying premise that women's actions must be strictly regulated both as punishment for and as safeguard against the actions of Eve is striking, all the more so given the contrasting use of Adam as the redeemed type of Christ in Rom. 5; 1 Cor. 15. Eve is virtually absent from the Gospels; the single, oblique reference to Adam and Eve is Jesus' saying on divorce recorded in Matt. 19:4-6 = Mark 10:6-9. Because male and female "become one flesh" in marriage, divorce is prohibited.

Later Traditions

Eve features prominently in early Jewish and Christian texts, as the first couple increasingly take on the role (a role curiously absent from the OT) of paradigm for the human condition. In rabbinic texts Eve is generally cited as the origin of various feminine traits the rabbis found peculiar or distasteful. Thus, Eve's creation from a bone explains women's implacability, since bones are not easily softened, and so on (*Gen. Rab.* 17:8). Allegorical interpreters such as Philo cast Eve as the "sensual" side of human nature, which is corrupted by pleasure (the snake) into misleading the will (Adam) into sin. This opposition between Adam as mind or will and Eve as body or sensation anticipates the interpretation of later Christian authors who claimed that the knowledge gained by Adam and Eve was specifically carnal knowledge, resulting from Eve's seduction of Adam. In the Qur'an Adam's wife is not named, though she is known as Ḥawwāʾ in later tradition. The woman and man do not act independently of one another in this account; the two face temptation, eat the fruit, and are punished as a pair (humankind) rather than as individuals (Qur'an *Sura* 7:19-25). In addition to various traditions condemning Eve, already in the 2nd century C.E. Irenaeus posited Eve as the type of Mary, who affords a possibility of redemption for Eve parallel to that provided for Adam by Christ.

Bibliography. J. Galambush, "*ʾādām* from *ʾadāmâ* and *ʾiššâ* from *ʾîš:* Derivation and Subordination in Genesis 2.4b–3.24," in *History and Interpretation,* ed. M. P. Graham, W. P. Brown, and J. K. Kuan. JSOTSup 173 (Sheffield, 1994), 33-46; J. A. Phillips, *Eve: The History of an Idea* (San Francisco, 1984); P. Trible, *God and the Rhetoric of Sexuality.* OBT 2 (Philadelphia, 1978); H. N. Wallace, *The Eden Narrative.* HSM 32 (Atlanta, 1985).

JULIE GALAMBUSH

EVENING

The occurrence of evening (Heb. *ʿereḇ*) prior to morning indicates that the beginning of the day began with the evening. The term first occurs in Gen. 1 in reference to the evening and morning of the six creation days. That the day began in the evening is corroborated by the repeated occurrence of this time designation in Lev. 15 as the time when a ceremonially unclean person became clean again. In the NT evening (Gk. *opsía, opsé,* "late, late in the day"; *hespéra*) is also contrasted with morning (Matt. 16:2; Mark 13:35; Acts 28:23).

The Hebrew term is often associated with darkness or shadows (Prov. 7:9; Jer. 6:4; cf. Ezek. 12:4, 7; similarly *opsía* in Mark 1:32). Twilight is indicated by the phrase *bên hāʿarbāyim,* "between the two evenings" (e.g., Exod. 12:6; 30:8; Num. 9:3, 5, 11; 28:4).

MARK F. ROOKER

EVI (Heb. *ʾĕwî*)

A Midianite king and vassal of the Amorite Sihon. With four other Midianite kings he was defeated and slain by the Hebrews (Num. 31:8; Josh. 13:21) following the Israelite apostasy in the plains of Moab (Num. 25:1-3).

EVIL

A wide range of activities and conditions, both in individuals and communities, from misfortune and despair to wickedness, maliciousness, and corruption.

Although OT writers often refer to evil as a violation of Israel's covenant with God, in a number of other instances evil refers to an ontological condition. Sometimes evil is used to describe people (Prov. 11:21), their reputations or their names (Deut. 22:14, 19), and their conduct (Ps. 34:13[MT 14]). The word also relates to emotions: those who are sad or anxious are said to be "afflicted with evil" (Prov. 15:15; Gen. 44:34), and "evil is determined" by those who are angry (1 Sam. 20:7). Sometimes even land is described as evil, as when Moses directs his spies to determine whether or not the "land they [the Canaanites] dwell in is good or bad" (Num. 13:19). At the conclusion of the Holiness code God promises to "remove evil beasts from the land" (Lev. 26:6) if the Israelites walk in God's ways.

Evil also designates human immorality and corruption. According to much Wisdom Literature, evil and wickedness originate in the human heart (Prov. 6:14; Eccl. 8:11), which is evil from youth (Gen. 8:21). Acts of false witness, stealing, murder, and adultery are evil, for the Deuteronomic laws exhort the community to punish such acts by "purging the evil from your midst" (Deut. 19:18-19; 22:21-24; 24:7). The prophetic literature urges individuals and the community to turn from evil ways and to walk in the ways of the Lord (e.g., Amos 5:14-15).

Idolatry is also evil because the individual or the community is unfaithful to the covenant with God (Deut. 4:25; 1 Kgs. 11:6). Because of their idolatry and apostasy, God destroys the dynasties of both Jeroboam and Ahab (1 Kgs. 14:10; 21:29). As punishment for Judah's sins, God "brings evil from the north, and a great destruction" (Jer. 4:6) in the form of the Babylonian army. When Abimelech tries to appoint himself king in Shechem, God sends an evil spirit as punishment (Judg. 9:23). If the unfaithful repent, however, God will deliver them from evil (Jer. 18:8; 26:3, 13, 19; Jonah 3:10; 4:2).

Within this matrix of good and evil, OT writers

often question why the wicked go unpunished and the righteous suffer. Although some texts assure us that the wicked will not go unpunished (Prov. 11:21), others proclaim that the righteous may perish in their righteousness while the wicked prolong their life in their evil-doing (Eccl. 7:15). Using an ancient folktale, the writer of the book of Job presents the dilemma of the inexplicable suffering of the righteous.

In the NT, evil refers to conditions like disease ("evil sores," Rev. 16:2) and anguish and anxiety (Luke 16:25). Paul refers to the times in which he is living as "the present evil age" (Gal. 1:4). In Matthew even fruit is described as evil: "the bad tree bears evil fruit" (Matt. 7:17).

However, writers in the NT, as in the OT, describe evil primarily as moral corruption and a violation of God's laws. In his teachings, Jesus makes a clear distinction between evil and good (Matt. 5:45; 13:49), and he describes his opponents, notably the Pharisees, as an "evil and adulterous generation" (12:34, 39). Evil originates in the heart (Mark 7:21-23) and describes a person's actions (John 3:19), thoughts (Matt. 15:19), and speech (Jas. 3:8).

Contrary to OT writers, NT writers refer to the existence and power of an Evil One who can seduce individuals to do evil. Influenced by the dualism of Persian religion and Hellenistic philosophy, Christianity begins to emphasize the existence of two realms and ages, one good and the other evil. Humans are subject to the powers of the demonic forces and may even be possessed by these evil spirits. Yet the NT writers emphasize that the evil powers are limited by God's ultimate power (John 12:31; Rev. 12:9; 20:1-3). In contrast to Job, who suffers without a mediator between him and God, the NT writings offer a mediator in Jesus Christ, who, through his death, defeats the Evil One (Heb. 2:14-15).

HENRY L. CARRIGAN, JR.

EVIL-MERODACH (Heb. *'ĕwîl mĕrōḏaḵ;* Akk. *Amel-Marduk*)

Son and successor of Nebuchadnezzar II as king of Babylon in 562 B.C.E. He reigned as the third king of the Chaldean dynasty for two years. Unlike Neriglissar and Nabonidus, nothing is known of his activities prior to becoming king. Likewise, no cuneiform text detailing any military campaign the king may have conducted is yet known. In 2 Kgs. 25:27-30; Jer. 52:31 Evil-merodach is said to have released the king of Judah, Jehoiachin, from a 37-year captivity and given him an allowance. Indeed, cuneiform texts survive detailing rations given Jehoiachin while he was in Babylon. According to Berossus' *Babyloniaca* Evil-merodach was the victim of a plot organized by his brother-in-law Neriglissar (Akk. *Nergal-šarra-uṣur*). To date, no cuneiform text confirming this familial relationship has been discovered, although it is widely held that the account is true.

Evil-merodach's name is prominent in both Classical Greek and Latin sources, as well as the rabbinic commentaries. There are also indications in Babylonian apocalyptic literature and the contract tablets that Nebuchadnezzar may have established a coregency with Evil-merodach prior to his death. Berossus asserts that Evil-merodach's administration was "arbitrary and licentious," but rabbinic sources contradict this claim. Jewish folklore is replete with stories of problems involving his succession to the throne, as well as his removal of his father's body from its resting place. These stories, however, may be the result of an attempt to cast Evil-merodach in a favorable light as opposed to his father, who was forever remembered as the architect of the Babylonian Captivity and the destroyer of Solomon's temple.

Bibliography. R. H. Sack, *Amel-Marduk — 562-560 B.C.* AOAT Sond 4 (Neukirchen-Vluyn, 1972).

RONALD H. SACK

EXCOMMUNICATION

The permanent or temporary exclusion of a church member from fellowship within the community. This practice, specifically mentioned in Matthew's Gospel (Matt. 18:15-17) and the Corinthian correspondence (1 Cor. 5:5; 2 Cor. 2:6), serves two purposes. First, it protects the community from the harmful influence of the sinner (1 Cor. 5:6-7). Second, it reminds the sinner of the sin (2 Cor. 2:7) in the hope that repentance (7:9) and redemption occur. Excommunication is never an individual (2 Cor. 2:6) or judgmental activity (v. 8), and it is not a withdrawal of concern for the sinner. It always has restoration as its ultimate goal.

Although the term "excommunication" does not appear in Scripture, the concept is clearly present. Matthew instructs the Church to treat unrepentant members like "a Gentile and a tax collector" (Matt. 18:17), and Paul wants the guilty party delivered "over to Satan" (1 Cor. 5:5), i.e., delivered over to the realm of Satan, the world outside the Church.

Church discipline, ending in excommunication, should only be used for serious matters such as blatant sexual sins (1 Cor. 5:1), unrepentance (Matt. 18:15-17), factiousness (Tit. 3:10-11), and the propagation of heresy (Rom. 16:17). Sinners should be dealt with quickly and seriously for both the health of the community and the spiritual health of the offender.

Bibliography. A. Y. Collins, "The Function of 'Excommunication' in Paul," *HTR* 73 (1980): 251-63; V. Taylor, *Forgiveness and Reconciliation,* 2nd ed. (London, 1941).

SAMUEL LAMERSON

EXEGESIS

The critical explanation or interpretation of a biblical text. The term etymologically related to the Greek word meaning "to guide" or "lead out." The history of the exegesis of the Bible can be traced to the Bible itself. In particular, the case can be made that at least some of the editing of the Bible began the process of exegesis. Some scholars claim that Psalm titles are among the earliest forms of exegesis. Further evidence for this early process are texts like Deuteronomy and Chronicles, both of which appear to reinterpret and re-present material that we know from other parts of the Bible. In addition, versions of the Bible in other languages, and much in the Pseudepigrapha, can be understood as exegetical. Moreover, the history of exegesis continued in early rabbinic Judaism and early Christian sources, and onward into the medieval literature of each religious tradition.

Modern, so called "critical," exegesis began with the realization that the Bible could be understood as a product of its historical period as well as a guide to religious life. As a result, modern exegesis tends to have as its goal the pursuit of the objective realia that lie behind the text. The 20th century has seen the relativization of many of the modern critical assumptions about exegesis, with the result that exegesis now comprises an extremely wide range of approaches to reading the Bible, many of which share little other than the object of their inquiry.

LARRY L. LYKE

EXILE

The period (ca. 587/586–515 B.C.E.) when much of the population of Judah was deported to captivity in Babylonia.

Nebuchadnezzar II became crown prince of the Neo-Babylonian Empire about the time of his dramatic victory over the Egyptian forces at Carchemish in 605. After a delay of some years, he resumed his western campaign and put Jerusalem under a brief siege in March 597. After installing a king "of his liking," Nebuchadnezzar then seized much booty and removed it to Babylon. More important, after the young Judean king Jehoiachin surrendered, a number of residents were taken as exiles and resettled in the Babylonian heartland. Confirmation of these events comes not only from Babylonian royal inscriptions, but also the Weidner text, a cuneiform document listing rations issued to Jehoiachin's household in exile. Jehoiachin's father, Jehoiakim, had been placed on the throne in Jerusalem by the Egyptian pharaoh, so Nebuchadnezzar removed this line and installed Zedekiah (changing his name from Mattaniah) as a client ruler. However, Zedekiah attempted an Egyptian-supported bid for independence, and Nebuchadnezzar returned to deal with the rebellion. After a long siege, Jerusalem fell in August 587/6. The two events, the surrender in 597 and the destruction in 587/6 (and perhaps other campaigns hinted at only in Jeremiah), included the exile of significant numbers of prisoners-of-war who were deported south of the Tigris-Euphrates basin.

It is important to understand the Babylonian Exile as the conclusion of a long historical process. The destructive campaigns by Mesopotamian regimes arguably begin with the reformation of the Neo-Assyrian military and political structure of empire initiated by Tiglath-pileser III (745-727). The destruction of Jerusalem and the temple, the fall of Judah, and the deportation of a significant segment of the conquered population must be theologically and sociologically appreciated within the larger historical development of "world empire" in the Near East. The community that went into exile became perhaps the most important Jewish community by which much of the OT was either edited or written. Despite the major significance of these events, however, the Babylonian Exile is often understated in standard historical works.

Attempts to understand the impact of the Exile focus typically on three main kinds of evidence:

(1) Biblical estimates of the number of exiles taken in the surrender of 597 vary widely. 2 Kgs. 24:14 numbers the "warriors" and "officials" (the vague *śarîm*) at 10 thousand, but also implies that the number includes "artisans" and "smiths." Only the "poorest of the land" were left, perhaps to be taken as a qualitative comment on the remaining community. In 1 Kgs. 24:16 further numbers are given for "men of valor" (7000) and "artisans and smiths" (1000). Noting the round numbers and their great size, many scholars favor the far lower figures given in Jer. 52:28 as more accurate. But are only men counted? Based on various readings of these figures, estimates of the actual number of exiles vary from 3000 to over 30 thousand. Even the highest numbers, however, are dwarfed by the sheer size of the more than 3 million that the Neo-Assyrian Empire claims to have deported in various campaigns. The numbers of the community listed in the "Golah list" of Ezra 2 = Neh. 7 are not typically considered a reliable measure of the exiled community, because this late text probably represents an early census of the population within the province of "Yehud" under Persian rule (post-539).

Attempts to estimate the population of Jerusalem before the Exile, to gain some perspective, are also fraught with difficulties. Suggestions range from roughly 24 thousand (estimating 40-50 people per dunam) to 250 thousand (comparing Jerusalem to Ebla, 446 persons per dunam). These estimates vary so greatly as to make confident assessments of a quantitative impact on Judah extremely difficult. Other scholars point to the socioeconomic status of the exiles (presumably consisting mainly of the leadership, scribes, artisans, and military leaders) and thus call for a qualitative assessment of the impact of the Exile, irrespective of the actual percentages of the population. Sociologically more important is the simple fact that it was clearly a large enough number of exiles for groups to be resettled together, thus allowing them some successful continuance of familiar life (cf. the elders who meet in Ezekiel's home, Ezek. 8:1, thus reproducing the leadership role of community elders).

The text does not even attempt to number those killed and exiled in 587/6, in a horrific encounter with the full brunt of Nebuchadnezzar's militia. The state of the community left behind is a matter of some further debate. An active religious and social community may have remained in Palestine and been responsible for considerable literary activity (cf. Jer. 41:4-5). It would certainly have been in the interests of the Neo-Babylonian regime to continue economic productivity in the land, but a reading of Lamentations as more than mere stereotypical lament language suggests rather thorough devastation. All of these matters invite further consideration of archaeological evidence.

(2) Virtually all archaeological assessments of the destruction of 587/6 suggest that Jerusalem was treated severely, the walls broken down and the city plundered, with evidence of Babylonian destruction everywhere. Many nearby towns also show total cessation of occupation or destruction levels indicating Babylonian battles. It is unlikely that any viable material culture could have been maintained above a mere subsistence level.

Any archaeological survey should include royal inscriptions that relate to the events and Neo-Babylonian propaganda about the Exile. An important cuneiform inscription of Nebuchadnezzar II mentions his subjecting deported people to corvée labor, which accords with frequent references to forced labor associated with Neo-Babylonian rule over captive peoples. This accords with Robert McC. Adams' archaeological survey of the central flood plain of the Euphrates showing rapid growth in the number of settlements in the Neo-Babylonian Empire, and suggesting a campaign of transferring large masses of people in order to provide labor in the rehabilitation of that region.

(3) Finally (and, significantly, *following* an attempt to assess the social and political realities), any theories about the theological impacts of the Exile must begin with an assessment of the significance of an increasing exilic-period vocabulary referring to bonds, chains, and fetters (e.g., Isa. 45:14; 52:2; Ps. 149; Lam. 3:7) as well as various terms for places of detention (Jer. 32:2; 34:13; 38:6; Zech. 9:11) and the increasing incidence of the theme of "reversal of fortune" in exilic and postexilic literature and folklore (Daniel, Esther, Ps. 137; cf. the frequent biblical motifs "sight to blind" and "release of prisoners" as metaphors of exile, Ps. 146:7-8; Isa. 42:7; 61:1; Zech. 9:1). The Priestly writer's obvious concern with maintaining purity and separation surely reflects the strategies of a minority population preserving identity and internal structure.

Any theological assessments, however, are difficult in the face of the general underestimation of the impact of the Exile in biblical traditions. There remains a notable ambiguity by the standard works in assessing that impact. Scholars continue to seek a "balance" by taking care not to "overemphasize" the significance of the Exile, and inevitably deny that the exiles should be called "slaves" or "prisoners." Suggestions of how they would have been legally classed in ancient Neo-Babylonian society shed little light on the actual treatment of the communities in exile. The situation of the exiles is described variously as one of relative freedom and prosperity, with the opportunity to order their own affairs, yet still uncongenial. Inevitably, the presumed lack of evidence seems to have pushed 20th-century scholarship toward a benign assessment of the human and social effect of the Exile. A more severe impact, it seems to be presumed, would have left more evidence, although as argued here, more evidence exists than is often cited.

Some studies have considered a more severe influence of the Exile on the theological and textual tradition. Such attention to the sociological as well as theological impact of the Exile would lead to a re-examination of such tradition-historical themes as: (1) a reading of the Diaspora "court tales" (Daniel, Esther) which pays as much attention to the constantly threatened executions as to the high office of the Jewish characters; (2) the fact that Exile was one of the major theological motivations for the historical work of the Deuteronomic historian (cf. 1 Kgs. 8:46-53) and especially its emphasis on the sins of the monarchy; (3) the "suffering" of the servant in Isa. 40–55 as symbolic of the lifestyle of exile; (4) the theme of messianic restoration (e.g., Zechariah; Haggai; Isa. 9, 11); (5) the tradition of laments for the destruction of Jerusalem as a theological theme of repentance (Lamentations; Ps. 137); and (6) the fact that Babylon passes into the tradition as a symbol of all that is evil (already Jer. 51; cf. 1 Pet. 5:13; Rev. 14:8; 17:5; 18:10).

The Exile continued to have serious implications both internally as well as externally, long after the fall of the Neo-Babylonian Empire. Internally, the separation of the community in 597-586 began to create long-standing divisions (Ezek. 11:14-18; 33:23-27) that persisted after groups of diaspora Jews returned to Palestine under Persian patronage (thus Ezra 3–6 and the conflicts detailed there), particularly when one notes Ezra the priest using sectarian terminology ("sons of the Exile") to refer to those with diaspora lineage as the true community in Palestine (Ezra 9). Externally, the failure to regain a restored independent Israel under a Davidic ruler gave birth not only to messianic speculation (Zechariah, Haggai) but also to thoughts that the Exile was, in fact, to be a long-term condition for the Jewish people. Arguably, then, the NT should also be read with an eye toward this continued tradition of the impact and significance of the Exile.

Bibliography. P. R. Ackroyd, *Exile and Restoration.* OTL (Philadelphia, 1968); R. McC. Adams, *Heartland of Cities* (Chicago, 1981); J. L. Berquist, *Judaism in Persia's Shadow* (Minneapolis, 1996); R. W. Klein, *Israel in Exile.* OBT 6 (Philadelphia, 1979); M. A. Knibb, "The Exile in the Literature of the Intertestamental Period," *Heythrop Journal* 27 (1976): 253-72; M. Noth, *The History of Israel,* 2nd ed. (New York, 1960); D. L. Smith, *The Religion of the Landless* (Bloomington, Ind., 1989).

Daniel L. Smith-Christopher

EXODUS

The series of events experienced by the Israelites under the leadership of Moses when they left the land of Goshen, located in the northeastern Nile Delta of Lower Egypt, and made their way south to Mt. Sinai. Events preceding the Exodus include the 10 plagues and the Passover. The Exodus also had significant religious meaning for ancient Israel and is recalled by the Jewish communities today at the annual Passover celebration.

Two accounts of the Exodus appear in the Torah: (1) Exod. 12:37; 13:20; 14:2, 5; 15:22, 27; 16:1-2; 17:1; 19:1-2; (2) Num. 33:3-15. They are in essential

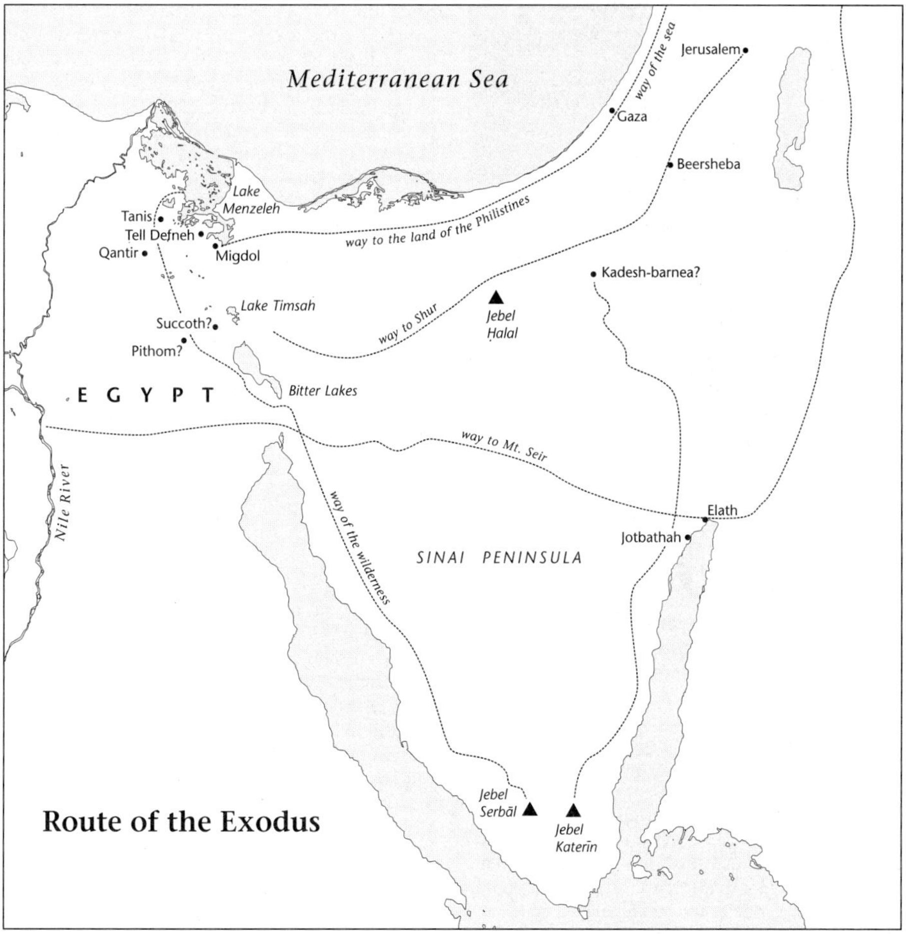

agreement, but some scholars hold that the Numbers passage is late and based on the Exodus itinerary. Numerous references to the Exodus occur in other books of the Bible (e.g., Judg. 6:8, 13; Ps. 78:12-53; 106:7-46; Isa. 63:11-13; Ezek. 20:5-26; Heb. 11:27-29), but they are based on the traditions of the Torah.

There is no mention of the Israelite Exodus in known Egyptian records. In fact, there is no contemporary reference or description in any extrabiblical source. This means we must use the biblical material carefully and correlate it with a cultural and historical context for the Nile Delta based on archaeological evidence and literary sources.

The date for the Exodus has been debated, and there are still diverse opinions. It has been dated within the reign of various Egyptian pharaohs: Queen Hatshepsut (1477 B.C.E.; Hans Goedicke), Thutmose III (1470; John J. Bimson), Thutmose III (1447; James Garstang), Rameses II (1270; Jack Finegan), or Merneptah (1220[?]; S. R. Driver). This list is not inclusive, and many scholars can be added in favor of each interpretation.

According to Exod. 1:11-15 the Israelites were forced to make mud bricks for the construction of Pithom and Rameses. These two cities have been identified with modern Tell er-Reṭâbeh and Qanṭir respectively in the northeastern Delta region. At both sites excavators have uncovered material related to Seti I and his son, Rameses II. It seems that Seti began building projects at the sites; when he died Rameses took over from his father. This situation would provide the context for the Israelites' travail as recorded in Exod. 2:23.

Another line of indirect argument for dating the Exodus uses the date of the Israelite entrance into and settlement of the hill country of Palestine under Joshua. The archaeological evidence suggests that this event took place ca. 1200. We can be somewhat more precise because Merneptah, the successor to Rameses II, mentions in a triumphal inscription that during a military campaign in Palestine he defeated the Israelites. The campaign can be dated ca. 1220. Adding 40 years for the duration of Israel's stay in the wilderness would make the date of the Exodus ca.

Monumental head of Rameses II (1290-1213 B.C.E.), **regarded as pharaoh of the Exodus, in the Rameseum at Thebes** (Phoenix Data Systems, Neal and Joel Bierling)

1260. Some scholars may argue for a date a decade or so later, but generally agree with placing the events in the 13th century.

An important geographical feature of the eastern Delta has been described which adds a new dimension to the discussion of the route of the Exodus. This new feature is the eastern canal discovered by Amihai Sneh, Tuvia Weissbrod and Itamar Perath on aerial photographs of the northeastern Delta and verified by ground exploration. One part of the canal can be traced beginning at Qanṭarah, then northeast to Tell Abu Ṣeifeh, then north to Tell el-Her and on to the Pelusiac branch of the Nile just W of Pelusium (Tell Farama). This segment is ca. 15 km. (9.3 mi.) long. The canal was 70 m. (230 ft.) wide at the banks and 20 m. (66 ft.) at the bottom. The depth could have been at least 2-3 m. (6-10 ft.). A 12 km. (7.5 mi.) section of the canal was earlier identified by the French engineer Limant de Bellafonds in 1872. This section can be traced beginning at Ismailia, then north to El Ballah. Sneh and associates suggest that these sections were connected and joined a canal through the Wadi Ṭumilât connecting the Nile to the Mediterranean Sea. The canal would have served several purposes. In addition to serving as a means of transportation, it would have provided a defense to protect the eastern Delta from attack as well as unwanted immigrants. Another purpose would have been supplying water to the numerous irrigation trenches along its course, making the land of Goshen a very good place for farming.

The Israelites left Rameses located in the area of Qanṭir at the northern limit of Goshen and traveled south to Succoth, a district at the eastern end of the Wadi Tumilât (Exod. 12:37; Num. 33:3-5). They did not use the way of the land of the Philistines, because this was a well-traveled military and commercial highway through the northern Sinai and well guarded by Egyptian forts (Exod. 13:17-18). Some scholars call this route the Way of Horus. The people were led around by the way of the wilderness toward the Sea of Reeds (LXX "Red Sea"). Next they set out from Succoth and encamped at Etham at the edge of the wilderness (Exod. 13:20; Num. 33:6). They were next told to turn back and camp near Pi-hahiroth ("mouth of the canal"), between Migdol ("fortress"; Tell el-Ḥer) and the sea, in front of Baal-zephon (Exod. 14:1-2; Num. 33:7).

Exod. 14:3 contains a piece of archaic verse:

> Pharaoh will say,
> "Trapped are they in the land (Egypt),
> The desert has barred them in."

References to the "way of the wilderness," "the edge of the wilderness," and "the desert (or wilderness) has barred them in" seem to indicate something more than just the semi-arid region of the Sinai. In fact the wilderness of the Sinai did not stop the Israelites. The way of the wilderness could refer to the water course called "the way of Horus" in the Sinuhe story. The one geographical feature that would have closed them in would have been the eastern canal. After reaching Succoth in the south the Israelites were stopped by the canal filled with crocodiles and had to turn back and go along the canal to find a safe place to cross. The exact place for the crossing is still not determined, but the biblical narrative which describes the route of the Israelites as first going south and then north makes sense in light of the eastern canal. The reference to the Sea of Reeds could refer to a marsh along the route of the canal.

The crossing of the Sea of Reeds is described in Exod. 14 and 15. In Exod. 14:21 the Lord drove the sea back by a strong east (LXX "South") wind. The dry land that appeared provided safe passage for the Israelites. Later (Exod. 14:27-28) the sea returned to its normal depth and covered the chariots of the pharaoh which had been chasing the Israelites. The poetic imagery in Exod. 15:1-18 suggests a sudden storm that capsized the boats of the Egyptians and tossed the chariots and horses into the sea. In any case, Israel praised the Lord for saving them from the Egyptians.

The group under Moses' leadership turned south and headed for Mt. Sinai. The places mentioned in the Bible, Marah (Exod. 15:23), Elim (15:27), and Rephidim (17:1), are not clearly identified with any known sites. The route would have taken them close to Serabit el-Khadem and the Egyptian turquoise mines. Mt. Sinai (Exod. 19:1-2) is located at Jebel Mûsā in the southern Sinai peninsula.

Bibliography. J. J. Bimson, *Redating the Exodus and the Conquest* (Sheffield, 1978); J. Finegan, *Let My People Go* (New York, 1963); N. M. Sarna, *Exploring Exodus* (New York, 1986); N. H. Snaith, "יַם־סוּף: The Sea of Reeds: The Red Sea," *VT* 15 (1965): 395-98; A. Sneh, T. Weissbrod, and I. Perath, "Evidence for an Ancient Egyptian Frontier Canal," *American Scientist* 63 (1975): 542-48; I. Wilson, *Exodus: The True Story* (San Francisco, 1986).

LAWRENCE A. SINCLAIR

EXODUS, BOOK OF

The second book in the OT and one of five books that make up the Torah or Pentateuch. The title "Exodus" is from the Greek or LXX translation of the Hebrew text (MT) and emphasizes the event of Israel leaving Egypt. In Hebrew the title of the book is *Šĕmôṯ*, from the opening words, "And these are the names." This emphasizes the placement of the Israelites in Egypt rather than their leaving it; the "names" are the sons of Jacob, who are now described as the children of Israel.

Canonical Context

The Hebrew title interrelates the book of Exodus with the first book of the Bible, since at the close of Genesis Jacob is described as moving to Egypt with his 11 sons in order to live with his twelfth son, Joseph, who was previously sold as a slave by his brothers. The description of the sons of Jacob as the children of Israel in the opening verse of Exodus indicates a transition from the ancestral family stories in Genesis to an account of the origins of Israel as a nation.

The opening chapters of Exodus underscore how the family of Jacob has evolved into a great nation, whose size now threatens Pharaoh, prompting oppression (Exod. 1–2). The oppression of Israel creates conflict with the divine promise to the ancestors in Genesis that their descendants would be blessed by God with many offspring and their own land (Gen. 12:1-3).

Content

Exodus is an account of God's initial faithfulness to the ancestral promise. Exod. 3–15 describes God's response to the oppression of Pharaoh in calling Moses to deliver Israel from Egyptian slavery. Exod. 16–18 describes Israel's initial journey through the wilderness to the mountain home of God. The book ends with an account of Israel's encounter with God at Mt. Sinai, where they enter into a covenant relationship with God (chs. 19, 24) and receive the divine revelation of law (chs. 20, 21-23), as well as instructions for the cultic system of the tabernacle (chs. 25–31, 35–40). In the midst of the revelation of law and sanctuary Israel breaks their newly formed covenant with God by worshipping the golden calf (ch. 32), which prompts covenant renewal (ch. 34). The revelation of the tabernacle cult continues beyond the book of Exodus through Leviticus and Num. 1–10, before Israel leaves Mt. Sinai and continues their journey through the wilderness toward the Promised Land of Canaan.

Theology and History of Composition

Biblical writers place the oppression of Israel in Egypt during the reign of Rameses II (ca. 1304-1237 B.C.E.). The lack of extrabiblical material along with the cultic and theological nature of the literature in Exodus makes the historical reconstruction of Israel's slavery in Egypt difficult. Israel is mentioned by name in one Egyptian inscription, the Merneptah Stela (ca. 1230), where they appear to be a group living in Canaan. Whatever the exact historical details may have been, the book of Exodus consistently describes salvation as divine liberation from Egyptian oppression. Essential to the event of liberation is also Israel's encounter with God in the desert. The history of composition of the book of Exodus witnesses to Israel's changing reflection on the meaning of these events.

Exodus is an anthology of liturgy and literature from nearly all periods of Israel's history. Three actions of God form the central core of Exodus: (1) Divine deliverance of Israel from Egyptian oppression; (2) Divine revelation to Israel at the mountain of God in the desert; and (3) Divine indwelling with Israel through the construction of a cult site. The book of Exodus contains some of the earliest traditions of Israel on each of these topics. (1) The Song of the Sea (15:1-18, 21) is an early poetic account of divine deliverance of Israel at the sea. In this hymn God is described as drowning Pharaoh and his army in the storm-tossed sea. (2) Exod. 19:16-19 reflects early accounts of divine revelation to Israel at God's mountain home. Other early accounts of God's mountain home in the desert include such poetry as Judg. 5:5; Ps. 68:8, 17[MT 9, 18]; Deut. 33:2. Finally, (3) Exod. 33:1-6 describes the indwelling of God with Israel as taking place in a movable desert shrine, the tent of meeting, which is located outside of the Israelite camp. These traditions most likely existed independently of each other at an early stage in Israel's worship life.

The most significant development in the compositional history of Exodus occurs when the three actions of God as savior, revealer, and indweller are interrelated into one story of national origin and salvation history. The earliest transformation of independent liturgies into an account of salvation history takes place around the character of Moses. The hymns of deliverance in 15:1-18, 21 anchor an extended narrative that includes the birth and commission of Moses, his conflict with Pharaoh through a series of plagues, which leads to the death of the Egyptian firstborn, Israel's expulsion from Egypt, and finally the confrontation at the sea. The revelation of God at the desert mountain is connected to the exodus with a wilderness journey in which Moses leads Israel. The revelation itself is fashioned into a covenant ceremony, in which the presence of God with Israel is transferred into laws that are mediated through Moses, the lawgiver.

This account of salvation history has been traditionally described as the Yahwist history, written in the 10th century during the period of the United Monarchy, when David and Solomon fashioned an empire out of the 12 tribes. More recently scholars have questioned such an early date for the writing of history in ancient Israel, favoring instead a late monarchy or even an exilic date.

Priestly writers present another interpretation of God as deliverer, revealer, and indweller. In their account of salvation history, Moses delivers Israel with the aid of his brother Aaron, the priest, who confronts Egyptian magicians with the power of Israel's God. The event of salvation incorporates imagery of a new creation. God does not simply destroy Pharaoh in the sea, but actually splits the sea in half. Such action is reminiscent of creation in the ancient Near Eastern world. As a result, for Priestly writers, salvation inaugurates a new creation. As a consequence, Israel's wilderness journey to the desert home of God becomes an exploration into a new and emerging world, in which sabbath reappears for the first time since the original creation in Gen. 1. The revelation of God at Mt. Sinai focuses on the details of the tabernacle sanctuary, with its sacrificial system and official priesthood. The revelation and construction of the tabernacle allow God to leave his mountain home and dwell in the midst of the Israelite camp as they journey on to the Promised Land.

The Priestly account of salvation history has been traditionally interpreted as a separate and independent story from the Yahwist history, and written in the exilic period. In this documentary hypothesis the two accounts were only later merged by editors. More recently scholars have questioned whether the Priestly account was ever an independent story. Some favor an interpretation of Priestly literature as an addition to the Yahwist history that is intended to reinterpret it to fit a Priestly theology. Other scholars have argued that the legal portions of the Priestly history are preexilic in origin and thus older than has traditionally been thought.

Continuing Significance

The compositional history of Exodus reflects changes in ancient Israelite society, worship, and theological reflection. As a consequence, the present form of the book contains a number of interpretations of the same event or theme. For example, salvation is both a liberation and a new creation. Revelation is focused on covenant, law (torah), and cult. God dwells with Israel both in the tent of meeting outside of the camp and in the tabernacle in the middle of the camp.

Yet throughout the many changes in the story line of Israel's salvation from Egypt and journey to God in the wilderness, the three themes of God as savior, revealer, and indweller provide points of continuity. These themes become the organizing points for worship practice in ancient Israel that continue to influence both Jewish and Christian traditions. Circumcision (4:24-26), Passover and recollection of the slaughter of the firstborn (12:21-36, 43-49), unleavened bread or *Maṣṣôṯ* (12:37-39; 13:3-10), the consecration of the firstborn and the giving of firstfruits (13:1-2, 11-16) are cultic means for participating in the power of God as savior. Sabbath (ch. 16), the formation of covenant communities (chs. 19–24), called leaders on the model of Moses, Aaron, and Miriam, the reading of sacred Scripture (20:1-17; 24:3-8), eating with God (24:9-11), and the establishment of sacred places (chs. 35–40) continue to be important ways in which God is revealed and dwells with the people of God.

Bibliography. B. S. Childs, *The Book of Exodus.* OTL (Philadelphia, 1974); F. M. Cross, *Canaanite Myth and Hebrew Epic* (Cambridge, Mass., 1973); T. B. Dozeman, *God at War: Power in the Exodus Tradition* (New York, 1996); *God on the Mountain: A Study of Redaction, Theology and Canon in Exodus 19–24.* SBLMS 37 (Atlanta, 1989); S. E. Loewenstamm, *The Evolution of the Exodus Tradition* (Jerusalem, 1992); J. Van Seters, *The Life of Moses: The Yahwist as Historian in Exodus-Numbers* (Louisville, 1994). THOMAS B. DOZEMAN

EXORCISM

An attempt to control and cast out evil spirits believed to have entered a person in order to cause harm. The Gospels (with the exception of John) contain numerous references to demon possession and exorcism. There is one major exorcism account in Acts (16:16-18), and incidental remarks about Paul and Jewish exorcists (19:13-20). Jesus performed most of the exorcisms in the Gospel accounts (e.g., Matt. 4:11, 23; Mark 1:12-13, 21-34), though the apostles also performed exorcisms. Exorcism presupposes the belief in the existence of spirit beings who can enter into an individual's body, and occupy it permanently (Mark 5:1-14) or intermittently (9:14-27). Known as demonic possession, it often involved some sort of oppression by the alien spirit.

Exorcism is traced back to the ancient Near East. An exorcist usually called on the power of a stronger, and usually good spirit, to subdue or cast out a less powerful, and usually a malevolent spirit. Methods varied from a few words of command to a full ritual ceremony and elaborate magical incantations. When necessary the exorcist will use a combination of methods to ensure success. Practices of exorcism are associated with the belief that demonic possession often brought sickness to the victim. Thus, exorcising the demon from the individual was a form of treatment of the illness believed to have been caused by the intruding spirit. There is, however, a distinction between exorcism and healing. The epilepsy that the boy in Mark 9:14-27 suffered was caused by an evil spirit, but there is no such connection made to the woman with an issue of blood (5:25-34).

Jesus exorcised demons by his commanding word with no apparent appeal to authority beyond himself. Early Christians, however, cast out demons in the name and authority of Jesus (Luke 10:17-20; Acts 16:16-17).

Bibliography. S. Eitrem, *Some Notes on Demonology* (1971); S. R. Garrett, *The Demise of the Devil* (Minneapolis, 1989); S. V. McCasland, *By the Finger of God* (New York, 1951); G. N. Twelftree, *Jesus the Exorcist* (Peabody, 1994). CHARLES YEBOAH

EXPIATION

A sacrificelike action that removes a barrier of sin which blocks fellowship between God and people. Expiatory concepts are closely linked with ideas of guilt, purity, divine judgment, and mercy. OT and NT ideas about expiation are further linked with broad patterns of sacrificial thinking in the ancient Near East and the Greco-Roman world. In modern times there has been much discussion of differences between "expiation" and "propitiation," the former suggesting divine initiative and the latter human activity (aimed at turning aside divine wrath). Such distinctions cannot be readily derived from individual Hebrew and Greek terms in the Bible. The Bible does seem to regularly assume, however, that humans cannot control or manipulate God's response to their misdeeds.

The OT generally affirms the value of expiatory sacrifices, but never presents a general interpretation or explanation of their efficacy (cf. Heb. 9:22). Naturally many statements about expiation connect it with priestly sacrifices. Leviticus in particular offers detailed prescriptions for sacrificial rituals suited to various classes of transgressions which are said to "expiate" them. A few passages speak of the deaths or executions of human beings as purifying the nation and eliciting divine forgiveness (Phinehas: Num. 25:7-13; Sir. 45:23; David: 2 Sam. 21:1-14). However, OT prophets often declare that sacrifices do not gain forgiveness when sacrificers are unrepentant. Passages like Mic. 6:6-8; Jer. 7:21-23 (cf. Ps. 51:16-17[MT 18-19]) come close to denying that any sacrificial rites expiate sin. The fourth Servant Song of Second Isaiah (Isa. 52:13–53:12) develops with unique power the idea of a voluntary human death which functions as a vicarious sacrifice for the forgiveness of the sins of others. A Hellenistic Jewish text, which may have influenced early Christian soteriology, speaks of martyrs whose deaths atone for the sins of Israel (4 Macc. 17:20-22; cf. 2 Macc. 7:30-38).

Most NT statements about expiation are connected with Jesus' death, and such statements are widespread in the NT. The influence of Isa. 53 is particularly apparent in Heb. 9:28; 1 Pet. 2:18-25; 3:18. Yet early Christian interpretations of Jesus' death as an expiation for sin often imply that that event both fulfilled and replaced sacrifices performed under the OT law.

Paul's letters, the oldest NT writings, incorporate pre-Pauline formulas interpreting Jesus' death as a sacrifice for sins (1 Cor. 11:23-26; 15:3; Rom. 3:24-26; 8:3; 2 Cor. 5:20-21). Paul appears to accept such ideas himself, though he does not explain or dwell on them. Deutero-Pauline letters also assume the validity of expiatory patterns of interpretation (Eph. 1:7; 5:2; Col. 1:20-22; 2:13-15). It is noteworthy that the Pauline and Deutero-Pauline letters explore further meanings of Jesus' death, especially freedom from the law (Gal. 2:19-21; 3:10–5:12; Rom. 7:1–8:4; cf. Eph. 2:14-16; Col. 2:13-15) and ongoing Christian experiences of suffering; Pauline interpretations of the death are not limited to expiatory ones.

In the Synoptic Gospels, sacrificial interpretations of Jesus' death are suggested especially in the Lord's Supper narrative (Mark 14:22-25 = Matt. 26:26-29) and the possibly related "ransom" saying in Mark 10:45 (= Matt. 20:28). The Gospel Passion narratives also hint that Jesus' death is specifically related to the temple and its sacrifices (Mark 15:29, 38).

A special interest in interpreting Jesus' death as an expiation for sins is shown in 1 John (esp. 1 John 2:2), and this is clearly related to an emphasis on Jesus' humanity (4:2-10; cf. Heb. 2:17). In the Gospel of John expiatory thinking surfaces in the Baptist's description of Jesus as "the Lamb of God, who takes away the sin of the world" (John 1:29; cf. 11:50), but that Gospel speaks of Jesus' death mainly in nonsacrificial ways. The book of Revelation also alludes to expiatory views of Jesus' death (Rev. 1:5; 5:9).

By far the fullest appropriation of expiation categories in the NT is found in the Letter to the Hebrews. The author presents a meticulous argument about the one-time self-offering of God's Son in the heavenly sanctuary for the sins of "many" (Heb. 9:1–10:18). Jesus' death is understood as simultaneously fulfilling and rendering obsolete the sacrificial worship of the Old Covenant.

Bibliography. C. B. Cousar, *A Theology of the Cross: The Death of Jesus in the Pauline Letters.* OBT 24 (Minneapolis, 1990); R. G. Hamerton-Kelly, *Sacred Violence: Paul's Hermeneutic of the Cross* (Minneapolis, 1992); M. Hengel, *The Atonement* (Philadelphia, 1981).
DAVID M. HAY

EYE

An essential part of the body (1 Cor. 12:16-21), enabling people and animals to see, both physically and figuratively (Deut. 3:21; 1 John 1:1). Biblical writings, however, understand the visual process very differently than does modern science. Whereas we consider the eye a receptive organ which allows light from outside to enter the brain, in most biblical thought it is an active instrument which transmits light outward from a person's interior. Thus the eye (Heb. *'ayin*; Gk. *opthalmós*) is "the lamp of the body" (Matt. 6:22-23; cf. Zech. 4:2-10), created and "enlightened" by God (Prov. 29:13; Ps. 19:8[MT 9]; 94:9), and connected with the understanding "heart" (Prov. 21:4; Eph 1:18). "Bright" eyes indicate health (1 Sam. 14:27-29), while "dim" eyes connote poor vision (Gen. 27:1; 1 Sam. 3:2; cf. Deut. 34:7). Heavenly beings (who see better than humans) can have eyes "like flaming torches" (Dan. 10:6; Rev. 1:14) or even multiple eyes (Ezek. 1:18; Rev. 4:6-8; 5:6). Eyes that are "darkened" (Ps. 69:23[24]; Rom. 11:8-10), "closed" (Isa. 6:9-10; Matt. 13:15), or "blinded" (John 12:40) often refer figuratively to a lack of understanding, while the "opening" of eyes means recognition and knowledge (Gen. 3:5-7; Luke 24:31). Eyes are also "closed" in sleep (Isa. 29:10) and death (Gen. 46:4), and "opened" when a person awakens (Job 27:19) or is restored to life (2 Kgs. 4:35; Acts 9:40; cf. Ps. 13:3[4]). People who are physically blind can also have their eyes "opened" (Isa. 35:5; John 9:1-41).

Since God can "see" everything, God's own "eyes" are mentioned frequently in the OT (e.g., Deut. 11:12; 1 Kgs. 9:3; Amos 9:8), but rarely in the NT (only Heb. 4:13; 1 Pet. 3:12). Idols also have eyes, but they cannot see (Ps. 115:5; 135:16), just like people who do not recognize God (Jer. 5:21; Mark 8:18; cf. Isa. 43:8). Human eyes rarely see God directly (Num. 24:4; Job 42:5; Isa. 6:5; cf. Exod. 33:20), but often look toward God (Ps. 25:15; Isa. 17:7).

Physically, eyes can be beautiful (1 Sam. 16:12; Cant. 1:15) or beautified with cosmetics (2 Kgs. 9:30; Jer. 4:30), yet eye color is almost never mentioned (Gen. 49:12; cf. Prov. 23:29). Priests with "blemished" eyes are restricted from certain tasks (Lev. 21:20), but few texts mention the treatment of eye diseases and ailments (Rev. 3:18; Matt. 7:3-4). Eyes can be gouged out in military action (1 Sam. 10:27b), juridical punishment (Exod. 21:23-26; Matt. 5:38), or self-mutilation (5:29), resulting in people who are "one-eyed" (18:9 = Mark 9:47) or fully "blinded" (2 Kgs. 25:7).

Because the eyes produce tears (Job 16:20; Ps. 119:136), they are often mentioned in expressions of grief (Jer. 9:1[8:23]; Lam. 1:16). Other common biblical expressions include "setting" or "fixing" the eyes on something (i.e., paying attention; Gen. 44:21; Luke 4:20) and "raising the eyes," either haughtily (2 Kgs. 19:22), or in seeking help (Ps. 121:1), or simply in observation (Gen. 13:14; Matt. 17:8). "In the eyes of the Lord" (NRSV "in the sight of") refers to God's favorable or unfavorable judgment (Exod. 33:12-13; 1 Kgs. 11:6), while "in one's own eyes" often implies self-conceit (Isa. 5:21). The eyes can be instruments of lust (Num. 15:39; 2 Pet. 2:14), while "winking the eyes" indicates wicked intentions (Ps. 35:19; Prov. 16:30).

Because events occur in the presence or "before the eyes" of people, the role of "eye-witnesses" is crucial, in both religious (Deut. 4:9; Luke 1:2) and legal contexts (Deut. 9:17; 1 Kgs. 10:7). The expression "evil eye" refers metaphorically to people who are stingy (Prov. 23:6) or envious (Mark 7:22). The phrase translated "eye of a needle" has nothing to do with the eyes, but is literally "hole of a needle" in Greek (Matt. 19:24 par.).

Bibliography. H. D. Betz, "Matt. 6:22-23 and Ancient Greek Theories of Vision," in *Essays on the Sermon on the Mount* (Philadelphia, 1985), 71-87.

FELIX JUST, S.J.

EZBAI (Heb. *'ezbāy*)
The father of Naarai, one of David's Champions (1 Chr. 11:37). The name may be a corrupted reading of "the Arbite" (Heb. *'rby*), an epithet of Paarai in the parallel list (2 Sam. 23:35).

EZBON (Heb. *'eṣbôn*) (also OZNI)

1. The fourth son of Gad (Gen. 46:16). He is called Ozni at Num. 26:16.

2. A son of Bela, of the tribe of Benjamin (1 Chr. 7:7).

EZEKIEL (Heb. *yĕḥezq'ēl*), **BOOK OF**
A book of the Major Prophets, attributed to the prophet Ezekiel.

The Prophet

Ezekiel, son of a priest named Buzi, was among the leading Judean citizens exiled, with King Jehoiachin, to Babylon in 597 B.C.E. His call to be a prophet is dated to 13 July 594, and his last recorded oracle to 10 April 574 (following the chronological equivalences of Ernst Kutsch; the reference to Ezekiel's 30th year in 1:1 has not been satisfactorily explained). We have little biographical information, and Ezekiel's marriage is only known because of the notice about his wife's death in 24:15-24. A contemporary of the Judean prophet Jeremiah, whom he does not mention, Ezekiel's primary period of activity in Babylon was ca. 25 years before the prophet known as Second Isaiah (Isa. 40–55). His knowledge of contemporary Jerusalem can be explained either by his own earlier experience there or by reports that reached the exiles in Mesopotamia. His unusual priestly behavior can almost always be interpreted as an expression of his passionate views on judgment or hope, and not as evidence for emotional imbalance or even psychosis.

The Book

The book of Ezekiel is divided into three major sections: chs. 1–24, oracles of judgment against Judah and Jerusalem; chs. 25–32, oracles against foreign nations; and chs. 33–48, words of hope. Characteristic vocabulary and expressions in the book include "mortal" as God's designation for the prophet; "house of Israel"; "you (or 'they') shall know that I am the Lord," and many words in common with the pentateuchal documents H and P. The large number of disputation words in the book indicates that the prophet experienced considerable opposition during his own lifetime. Four great vision accounts (chs. 1–3; 8–11; 37; 40–48) dominate the structure of the book.

The complex and vivid symbolism in ch. 1 connotes the reality of the God who appeared to the prophet and his mobility, shown by his presence in Babylon, away from the temple and the promised land. In the report of his call, Ezekiel is instructed to hand on obediently a message characterized as lamentation, mourning, and woe, regardless of whether the people listened or not (3:11). The watchman paragraph (3:16-21; cf. 33:1-9) limits the prophetic responsibility to the giving of a warning about God's imminent assault on Jerusalem. The account of the watchman in ch. 33 insists that Yahweh does not desire the death of the wicked, but only that they turn from their wicked ways and live.

Twelve sign actions are recorded in Ezekiel, slightly more than for his contemporary Jeremiah and far surpassing the number in earlier prophecy. Ezekiel's stoic response to his wife's death anticipates the exiles' response to the destruction of the temple and the death of their own relatives (24:15-24). His periodic speechlessness during his early years is broken only when God permits or empowers him to speak (3:22-27), but his muteness ends when a refugee from the captured city of Jerusalem arrives in Babylon (24:25-27; 33:21-22) and Ezekiel's mouth is freed to speak the longest sustained hope passage in the Bible. He acts out the siege of Jerusalem (4:1-3), bears the guilt of the people as their substitute (vv. 4-8), eats limited rations like a person in a siege (vv. 9-11), and objects to eating bread baked on coals made of human dung, only to have Yahweh mitigate this fate slightly by allowing him to use fuel made of animal dung (vv. 12-15). In 5:1-4 Ezekiel burns one third of his hair, chops up another third of it with a sword, and scatters the final third to represent what will happen to the people at the fall of Jerusalem. Verse 3 introduces the idea of a remnant through the symbol of a few hairs bound into the hem of his garment. Other sign actions are in 12:1-16, 17-20; 21:6-7, 8-13; and 37:15-28, the only sign action with a positive message.

In the great vision of judgment in chs. 8–11, Ezekiel is transported to Jerusalem to observe the abominations, or cultic sins, in the temple. He then also sees executioners pass through the city to smite old and young alike, but only after a priestly figure has placed marks on all those who sigh or groan over the abominations of the city, indicating that they will be spared punishment. The first part of this vision ends with a description of the glory of Yahweh moving from the temple to a throne chariot parked nearby and then riding off into exile. The God who pronounces judgment against Jerusalem is the same one who had called Ezekiel to be a prophet in the Exile. In the second part of this vision, Pelatiah the son of Benaiah falls dead while Ezekiel is prophesying (11:1-13). The significance of his death may lie in his name, which means something like "Yahweh delivers," the son of "Yahweh builds up." If a person with such a name cannot escape the judgment of Yahweh, who can?

In chs. 14, 18, and 33 Ezekiel develops a sophisticated theological discussion on a number of disputed issues. He holds that it is possible for the exiles to repent, and this possibility is not restricted by the behavior of previous generations or even by the conduct of the present generation in earlier stages of its life. One person's righteousness cannot reverse the retribution faced by others in the community who are wicked or even the retribution faced by that person's own wicked descendants. Unrepented evil behavior will make null and void the blessings contained in Yahweh's promises.

In ch. 20 Ezekiel symbolically retells the history of Israel, indicating that Yahweh had contemplated destroying the people before they had left Egypt (v. 8), and that exile had been determined as their fate before they entered the land (vv. 23-24). Hence inquiry of Yahweh during the Exile is ruled out of the question by Ezekiel (v. 31). Nevertheless, Yahweh would act as king to liberate his people from their several places of exile, sorting out in the process all rebels and traitors, before leading them back to Zion (vv. 32-44). Through imagery of female sexual impurity, bordering on vulgarity, Ezekiel indicts Jerusalem and Samaria (chs. 16, 23), and he compares Jerusalem unfavorably to Samaria and Sodom because of its greater wickedness (16:47-48). The patriarchal bias of both chapters is problematic to modern readers.

The oracles against the nations in chs. 25–32 address seven countries: Ammon, Moab, Edom, Philistia, Tyre, Sidon, and Egypt. Conspicuous by its absence is Babylon. This silence may be explained by political expediency or by the fact that Ezekiel lived at the beginning of the exilic period, when higher priority might be given to the fate of the nations surrounding Israel than to the great world power itself. The oracles against the nations are usually seen as a kind of middle ground between words of judgment against Israel and words of hope for Israel. Ezekiel argues that Yahweh's glory and holiness could be maintained only if the nations were judged, and if Israel, beyond its present judgment, were finally saved.

The hopeful words of chs. 33–37 climax in 37:24b-28, which promises everlasting possession of the land, an everlasting Davidic prince, an everlasting covenant, and an everlasting sanctuary in the midst of Israel. In the vision of the valley of the dry bones (37:1-14), Ezekiel asserts that a future is possible for Israel only by God's power, and he describes that power through actions that can only be performed by Yahweh, such as creation, exodus, and resurrection. The ultimate goal of deliverance is knowledge of Yahweh (37:6, 13-14).

Before spelling out the future promise in detail, the book of Ezekiel leaps ahead to a time after Israel has been restored to the land, when it is threatened by a mysterious invasion from the north (chs. 38–39). Gog of Magog (perhaps a mythological allusion to Gyges of Lydia) will be brought by Yahweh against Israel, but then will be utterly defeated in the land, with the people destroying his weapons and burying his dead. Subsequently, Yahweh will invite every kind of bird and wild animal — i.e., the entire nonhuman family — to a great victory banquet, at which the defeated soldiers and their animals are served as the main course. These chapters demonstrate that no enemy nation will ever invade the Holy Land again with success.

The theme of Yahweh's presence with his people is the central motif in the final vision of the book (chs. 40–48). Ezekiel is led around the temple and its environs and given the dimensions of the new sanctuary that will be built there (40:1–44:3). At the end of this description, Ezekiel sees the glory of the God of Israel return from the east and reenter the temple through the east gate (43:1-5). His guide informs him that the east gate will always remain shut so that no one would ever traverse the same path Yahweh took into the temple (44:2), but implying also that Yahweh would never again leave through that gate. Land is set aside for the "prince" (the term Ezekiel uses for the king or messiah of the future; cf. 34:24; 37:25), in order to give him sufficient income so that he will not be tempted to oppress those whom he rules (45:7-8). In general, Ezekiel has a low opinion of the kings during his lifetime (chs. 17, 19, 34). One of the future prince's principal roles will be as a prime figure at worship, with the result that he is assigned a favored place in the east gate during sacrificial rituals (46:2). A stream coming from the temple signifies Yahweh's renewed presence with the people, and this brings new life to the Judean desert and even to the Dead Sea (47:1-12; cf. Gen. 2:10-14; Ps. 46:4-5[MT 5-6]; Joel 3:18[4:18]; Zech. 14:8). The division of the land among the tribes gives to each the same amount of territory (implying equality), all on the west side of the Jordan (implying separation from territory deemed religiously suspect, Josh. 22:26-29), and the book conceives of the arrangement of the land in zones of holiness: the temple, its priests, and the Levites are at the center of the land, and next to this sacred area come four tribes to the north and four to the south who are descended from one of the full wives of Jacob. The three farthest tribes on the north and the farthest tribe on the south are descended from the handmaidens of the wives. The final verse of the book may well be secondary, but it expresses well the central theological idea that has been developed throughout the final vision: "The name of the city from that time on shall be, The Lord is There" (Ezek. 48:35).

Bibliography. L. C. Allen, *Ezekiel 1–19.* WBC 28 (Waco, 1994); *Ezekiel 20–48.* WBC 29 (Waco, 1990); J. Galambush, *Jerusalem in the Book of Ezekiel.* SBLDS 130 (Atlanta, 1992); M. Greenberg, *Ezekiel 1–20.* AB 22 (Garden City, 1983); R. W. Klein, *Ezekiel: The Prophet and His Message* (Columbia, S.C., 1988); W. Zimmerli, *Ezekiel 1.* Herm (Philadelphia, 1979); *Ezekiel 2.* Herm (Philadelphia, 1983).

RALPH W. KLEIN

EZEL (Heb. *hā'āzel*)
A stone where Jonathan and David agreed to meet after David fled Saul (1 Sam. 20:19) and where they bade farewell to each other (vv. 35-42). Its precise location is unknown.

EZEM (Heb. *'eṣem*)
A town allocated to Simeon (Josh. 19:3; 1 Chr. 4:29), later included in Judah when Simeon was assimilated (Josh. 15:29). The site has tentatively been identified with Umm el-'Azam (140055), ca. 36 km. (20 mi.) SE of Beer-sheba. Its possible mention on an ostracon from Tell esh-Shari'a suggests the settlement may have been located N of Beer-sheba, perhaps identified with the similarly named Umm el-'Azem.

LAURA B. MAZOW

EZER (Heb. *'ēzer, 'ēṣer*)

1. The sixth son of Seir and chief of a Horite clan in Edom (Gen. 36:21, 27, 30; 1 Chr. 1:38, 42).

2. A Judahite, the father of Hushah (1 Chr. 4:4).

3. An Ephraimite, killed by the inhabitants of Gath when he raided their cattle (1 Chr. 7:21).

4. Chief of the Gadite warriors who joined David at his stronghold at Ziklag (1 Chr. 12:9[MT 10]).

5. The son of Jeshua and ruler of Mizpah who aided in rebuilding the walls of Jerusalem at the time of Nehemiah (Neh. 3:19).

6. A priest who participated in the dedication of the rebuilt walls of Jerusalem (Neh. 12:42).

EZION-GEBER (Heb. *'eṣyôn geḇer*)
A town in Edom on the Gulf of Aqabah, listed as a resting place along the route taken in the Exodus (Num. 33:35-36). David may have captured this village when he subdued Edom (2 Sam. 8:13-14). Solomon built a fleet of ships here (1 Kgs. 9:26 = 2 Chr. 8:17; cf. 10:22). With the death of Solomon the region reverted to Edomite control. Ezion-geber was conquered by Jehoshaphat of Judah, who also built ships there, but these were destroyed (1 Kgs. 22:48; 2 Chr. 20:36) as divine retribution for his alliance with Ahaziah (v. 37). Amaziah defeated the Edomites (2 Kgs. 14:7), and his son Uzziah rebuilt the site (v. 22).

Many archaeologists, following Nelson Glueck, contend that Ezion-geber was located at modern Tell el-Kheleifeh (147884) on the northern tip of the Gulf of Aqabah, ca. 457 m. (550 yds.) from the shore. The Bible locates it "near Eloth (or 'Elath')" on the shore of the Red Sea (1 Kgs. 9:26). Although Ezion-geber and Elath are traditionally viewed as distinct settlements, many scholars regard them as different names for the same site.

The chief feature of Tell el-Kheleifeh is a series of walls with holes that Glueck took to be flues and air channels. These walls had endured such intense heat that they became kiln baked. Further they bore traces of sulphur and various other metals. Initially then, Glueck concluded that he had found the remains of a refinery specifically designed to make use of the winds from the Gulf to super-heat the fires in a copper smelter. Later, he completely revised his findings to suggest that the holes actually supported wooden crossbeams that had been destroyed by fire, and identified the structure as a storehouse and granary. Destruction of this and other buildings may be linked to the invasion of the Egyptians under Shishak ca. 925 (cf. 2 Chr. 12:4).

A more recent suggestion for location has centered on the island of Jezîrat Far'ôn/Coral Island, which appears to offer a natural harbor for ships.

WATSON E. MILLS

EZRA (Heb. *'ezrā'*)

1. A scribe and priest sent with religious and political powers by the Persian king Artaxerxes to lead a group of Jewish exiles from Babylonia to Jerusalem (Ezra 7–8). Ezra condemned mixed marriages (Ezra 9), encouraging Jews to divorce and banish their foreign wives (ch. 10). He read and interpreted the law (Neh. 8:1-12), renewed the celebration of festivals (vv. 13-18), and supported the rededication of the temple (chs. 9–10) and the rebuilding of the Jerusalem wall (12:36).

Scholarly opinion concerning the date and mission of Ezra varies widely. Most date Ezra's mission to 458 B.C.E. (13 years before Nehemiah), but others suggest 398 (after Nehemiah), and still others doubt the historicity of the mission altogether. Though Ezra and Nehemiah are presented as coworkers, many argue that passages which connect them are anachronistic redactions (Neh. 8:9; 12:26, 36). Furthermore, since Ezra's recorded actions (possibly dictated by others; cf. Ezra 9:1; 10:1-5; Neh. 8:1) differ much from his ascribed powers, many doubt the reported contents of the letter from Artaxerxes (Ezra 7:11-26) and beckon comparison with other Persian directives. Perhaps Ezra was recalled by the Persians upon the failure of his segregationalist policy since Ezra 10 ends so abruptly.

See Ezra, Book of.

2. A priest who accompanied Zerubbabel and Jeshua from Babylonia to Jerusalem (Neh. 12:1, 13; cf. Azariah, 10:2[MT 3]).

3. A priest who participated in the rededication ceremony for the Jerusalem wall (Neh. 12:33).

Bibliography. J. Blenkinsopp, *Ezra-Nehemiah.* OTL (Philadelphia, 1988); L. L. Grabbe, *Judaism from Cyrus to Hadrian,* 1: *The Persian and Greek Periods* (Minneapolis, 1992), 94-98, 136-38.

Eric F. Mason

EZRA (Heb. *'ezrā'*), **BOOK OF**

Ezra 1–10 depicts the early stages of reconstruction of Jewish life in Judah (Yehud) under Persian colonial rule in the aftermath of the destruction of Jerusalem and exile to Babylonia. In Christian Bibles the book of Ezra appears with the historical books, between Chronicles and Nehemiah. In modern Jewish Bibles, with Nehemiah it is placed among the "Writings," immediately preceding Chronicles, the last in the canon (although the oldest Hebrew manuscripts, such as the Leningrad Codex, place it last).

Date, Scope, and Structure

Written primarily between 400 and 300 B.C.E., the book of Ezra reflects Persian period politics and religiosity before the rise of Hellenism. It is the only biblical historiography that explicitly describes the transformations during the pivotal postexilic period. The author is unknown, though Ezra and Nehemiah have been suggested.

According to Ezra, the exiled Jews returned to Judah and Jerusalem *en masse* in response to a decree by Cyrus king of Persia (538; 1:1-4). Enthusiastically they restored cultic practices and rebuilt the Second Temple in Jerusalem (516/5; chs. 3–6). Later, under the leadership of Ezra the priest and scribe, they also began to implement the teachings of the Torah (458; chs. 7–8) and to rebuild the community itself by separating from foreigners (chs. 9–10). The account of the return and reconstruction continues in the book of Nehemiah, which was originally part of Ezra (as it still is in the LXX and MT). The structure of the unified Ezra-Nehemiah is as follows.

- I. Cyrus' decree (538) to restore the house of God in Jerusalem (Ezra 1:1-4)
- II. Implementation of the decree (Ezra 1:5–Neh. 7:73[MT 72])
  - A. Introduction with a list of returning exiles (Ezra 1:5–2:1-70)
  - B. Implementation of decree in three movements (Ezra 3:1–Neh. 7:73[72])
    1. First movement: Building of the temple under Zerubbabel and Joshua's leadership in 538-516/5 (Ezra 3:1–6:22)
    2. Second movement: Building community under Ezra's leadership in 458-457 (Ezra 7:1–10:44)
    3. Third movement: Building Jerusalem's walls under Nehemiah's leadership in 445-444 (Neh. 1:1–7:5)
  - C. Conclusion with a recapitulation of the list of returning exiles (Neh. 7:6-73[72])
- III. Celebration of reconstruction under Ezra and Nehemiah with Torah at the center (Neh. 8:1–13:3)
- IV. Coda: Nehemiah's report (Neh. 13:4-31)

The book contains Hebrew and Aramaic sources, the latter often as correspondence with the Persian court. Like other ancient historiography (such as Herodotus), Ezra subsumes historical data to its own point of view and purpose. Although scholars question the historical accuracy of some descriptions and the authenticity of the documents Ezra reproduces, the overall perspective of the book and the general contours of its report have gained credence in recent years because (1) archaeological studies support the influx of settlements in Judah in the 5th century; (2) the structures and practices that came to dominate Jewish life in Judah comport with those depicted in Ezra; and (3) the book's perspective on these developments *generally* agrees with extrabiblical sources.

Content and Messages

Ezra (like Ezra-Nehemiah as a whole) organizes its material to reflect the book's particular ideology, highlighting three themes: (1) the importance of the community as a whole, not only its leaders; (2) the centrality of written documents, especially the book of the Torah; (3) the expansion of the holy space to include not only the temple but the city. The book unfolds as follows:

Cyrus' decree (538) to restore the house of God in Jerusalem (1:1-4)

Cyrus' decree exhorts the people of Yahweh to build God's house in Jerusalem. Cast as Cyrus' response to Yahweh's command, the decree presents Persian rule as a benevolent instrument of Israel's God, setting the tone for the book as a whole and reflecting an important adaptation to colonial rule during the Persian period. This decree recurs in an abbreviated form in 2 Chr. 36:22-23 (Ezra 5:13-15 reproduces a different version of authorization). In form and content, Cyrus' decree in Ezra conforms to other Persian period documents such as the famous Cyrus cylinder, which similarly presents Cyrus as the emissary of the Babylonian God. Although no extrabiblical sources show specific authorization of the Jewish return and rebuilding, it is clear that Jews from Babylonia did resettle Judah and that the temple was in fact built. Such activities could not have transpired without authorization by the bureaucratic imperial court.

Implementation of the decree (Ezra 1:5–Neh. 7:73[72])

Introduction with a list of returning exiles (Ezra 1:5–2:1-70). The rest of Ezra depicts the enthusiastic compliance by the members of the families of Judah, Benjamin, and Levi, who rise up and go to Jerusalem, with the support of those they leave behind. Ezra includes two of Ezra-Nehemiah's three journeys from exile to Judah, framed by a repeated list of more than 42 thousand returnees (Ezra 2 = Neh. 7).

Implementation of decree in three movements (Ezra 3:1–Neh. 7:73[72])

First movement: Building of the temple under Zerubbabel and Joshua's leadership in 538-516/5 (Ezra 3:1–6:22). Ezra emphasizes the religious nature of the return from captivity. Accordingly, the first wave of resettlers hastens to build the altar and the temple (and establish cult personnel). Each completion is followed by celebration (of Succoth [3:4] and Passover [6:19] respectively). Ezra also highlights dual leadership by Zerubbabel (the last known Davidic descendant with authority in the OT) and Joshua the priest, setting a pattern that will continue. Finally, Ezra highlights communal dedication to the task, attributing delays in building to outside interference: Some local inhabitants, initially labeled "adversaries of Judah and Benjamin" (4:1) and then "people of the land" (v. 4), first attempt to join the builders and then, when rebuffed, incite the Persian authorities against the Jews. Consequently, the Persian government puts a stop to reconstruction.

Rebuilding resumes only at the time of Darius (520) and is completed in 516/5. To document the opposition, Ezra includes Aramaic correspondence with Artaxerxes. This correspondence raises the thorniest problem in the book, since Artaxerxes' reign *followed* Darius' and since Artaxerxes in Ezra 7; Neh. 2 supports the efforts of the Jews. Furthermore, some of the letters concern Jerusalem's walls, not the temple. Either the record was no longer clear to the writer or the period itself was confusing. The use of such correspondence in this fashion, however, may also stem from the wish to emphasize Ezra's view that the house of God extends to the city as a whole.

Second movement: Building community under Ezra's leadership in 458-457 (Ezra 7:1–10:44). Ezra 7–10 describes a shaping of the community in accordance with the book of the Torah. In 458, Ezra comes to Jerusalem, commissioned by Artaxerxes I (398 if the king is Artaxerxes II). Ezra's goal is to implement the Torah. His priestly and scribal credentials are impeccable and he remains the model leader not only in Ezra but in Ezra-Nehemiah as a whole.

The section includes an Aramaic letter from Artaxerxes delineating Ezra's extensive powers as well as substantial financial support for his mission and for the temple (7:11-27), followed by a 1st person report (conventionally labeled Ezra Memoirs) in which Ezra describes his journey to and activities in Jerusalem (7:28–9:15).

The most dramatic part here is the crisis over marriages by Jewish leaders with women from "the peoples of the lands" (9:2). Ezra interprets such marriages as a violation of the Torah and repetition of the sins that caused exile in the first place (9:6-15). The book concludes with a 3rd person report describing steps undertaken to solve the crisis and separate from foreign wives (10:1-44).

The book celebrates the return and communicates a new model for Israel in its land. The leadership is diarchic, with a governor and priest in charge, both centered in Jerusalem. Life of the people is governed by the book of the Torah, in harmony with Persian rule. Voluntary separation protects community boundaries in the midst of other nations and secures loyalty to the particular traditions of Israel (in contrast to a military solution undertaken in the preexilic period).

Historical Background

The Persian period begins with Cyrus' conquest of Babylon (539) and extends to the age of Alexander the Great (332). Initially the Persian Empire subsumed the Babylonian Empire. But by 525 it also included Egypt and was fighting with Greece for control of the region. The Persian kings Cyrus (539-530), Darius (522-486), Ahasuerus (485-464), and Artaxerxes I (465-424), all mentioned in Ezra, were deeply involved in this westward movement. The era constitutes the first major encounter between "East" (ancient Near East) and West (Greece and Europe), and its influence has been decisive for both regions. The Mediterranean became an arena of conflict, and the commercial, military, economic, and political importance of the lands around it inevitably grew.

Persian policies in Judah most likely were influenced by these conflicts even though Ezra-Nehemiah itself does not explicitly refer to them. Presumably, it served Persian interests to settle, organize, and strengthen loyal populations along the eastern Mediterranean coast and also in Judah.

Historical and Literary Issues

Several issues remain contested in Ezra studies.

1. Relation to Chronicles. The view that the Chronicler also composed Ezra-Nehemiah and shared its ideology had been held for 150 years. Sara Japhet has overturned this view, so that it now remains a minority position.
2. The identity and role of the "people(s) of the land(s)." In Haggai Judahite apathy accounts for the resistance to building the temple. In Ezra it is "people(s) of the land(s)." Ezra's emphasis on external opposition may be a retrogression (though internal and external factors could coexist). The exact identity of these opponents in Ezra 4–5 and the "foreign women" is uncertain. Although the term may designate actual Moabites, Ammonites, etc., it may also include Israelites from the north, Samarians (not to be confused with the later Samaritans), and/or Judahites who evaded exile and whose legitimacy Ezra refuses to acknowledge.
3. The Torah of Ezra. Attempts to establish the extent of the Torah that Ezra is to administer have led to diverse conclusions: that it is the Priestly law, the Deuteronomic laws, a combination of pentateuchal laws, or some form of our Pentateuch. Since Spinoza, scholars also considered the possibility that Ezra was a major, perhaps *the* major redactor of the Pentateuch.

Other questions include the historical reliability of the Aramaic correspondence, the historicity of

Ezra himself, and the authorship of the Ezra Memoirs. With few exceptions, scholars today have moved away from the radical skepticism of earlier studies on these issues.

Bibliography. J. Blenkinsopp, *Ezra-Nehemiah.* OTL (Philadelphia, 1988); T. C. Eskenazi, *In an Age of Prose: A Literary Approach to Ezra-Nehemiah.* SBLMS 36 (Atlanta, 1988); K. G. Hoglund, *Achaemenid Imperial Administration in Syria-Palestine and the Missions of Ezra and Nehemiah.* SBLDS 125 (Atlanta, 1992); S. Japhet, "The Temple in the Restoration Period: Reality and Ideology," *USQR* 44 (1991): 195-251; H. G. M. Williamson, *Ezra, Nehemiah.* WBC 16 (Waco, 1985).

TAMARA COHN ESKENAZI

EZRAH (Heb. *ʿezrâ*)
A Judahite (1 Chr. 4:17), listed among the descendants of Caleb.

EZRAHITE (Heb. *ʾezrāḥî*)
An alternate form of the gentilic Zerahite, designating the descendants of Zerah (1 Chr. 2:6). Ethan and Heman were famous members of this clan (1 Kgs. 4:31[MT 5:11]; cf. the superscriptions of Pss. 88-89).

EZRI (Heb. *ʿezrî*)
The son of Chelub; supervisor of the workers in David's crown lands (1 Chr. 27:26).

F

FABLE

A fictitious narrative or statement in which there are marvelous happenings in unusual circumstances, usually involving animals or plants which speak and act like human beings. Originating in an oral folk tradition, the fable seeks both to entertain and teach a moral lesson. The genre is known in the literature of the ancient Near East centuries before it appears in Hebrew literature. There are also pictorial representatives from the 2nd millennium B.C.E. involving animals and plants which suggest that a crucial moment in a presumed fable is being illustrated.

One of the best examples of the fable genre is found in Judg. 9:7-15, a narrative of Abimelech's efforts to establish a kingship in Israel. The negative attitude toward kingship is illustrated graphically in Jotham's fable of the thorn or bramble tree (Abimelech) which was chosen king instead of more worthy trees — the olive, fig, and vine (Jerubbaal's sons). The olive, fig, and vine each offer lengthy reasons in poetic form why they cannot agree to the request of the trees to rule over them, but the bramble accepts conditionally.

Another example of a fable featuring talking plants occurs in 2 Kgs. 14:8-10 (cf. 2 Chr. 25:18). King Jehoash sent a message to King Amaziah of Judah simply mentioning the "thornbush on Lebanon" arrogantly challenging "a cedar on Lebanon, 'Give your daughter to my son for a wife.'" This arrogance was met with a wild beast from Lebanon trampling down the thornbush.

The talking serpent in the Garden of Eden in Genesis represents a fabulistic element in this primeval tale of temptation, disobedience, and fall from grace. The folktale of Balaam's wondrous talking donkey (Num. 22:21-35) is a longer and more complete example of the genre told in a humorous and ironic way. Solomon, who spoke "of trees" and "of beasts," may have also had a reputation as a fabulist (1 Kgs. 4:33[MT 5:13]).

New translations of the NT translate Gk. *mýthos* (1 Tim. 1:4; 2 Tim. 4:4; 2 Pet. 1:16) as "myth" instead of the KJV's "fables." William R. Goodman, Jr.

FACE

In numerous contexts "face" (Heb. *panîm*) is a synonym for "surface," as in "the face of the earth" (Gen. 1:29), "the face of the ground" (2:6), and the "face of the deep" (1:2). In other contexts it assumes a close relationship with a person, so that "seeing the face of . . ." (Gen. 32:20) and "hiding the face from . . ." (Ps. 27:9) are both indicators of presence and nonpresence, acceptance and rejection. The latter is also an attempt to hide one's identity (Ps. 102:2[MT 3]; Isa. 53:3).

To "bow the face" (Luke 5:12; Gk. *prósōpon*) and "fall on the face" (Ezek. 1:28) are signs of humility and obeisance. To "turn the face" (2 Kgs. 20:2) and "set the face toward/against . . ." (Ezek. 35:2) are indicators of determination and intention. Further, to "lower the face" (Gen. 40:7) and to have a "fallen face" are signs of disrespect and dishonor, as is striking someone in the face (John 18:22). In a similar fashion, to mutilate the face (Lev. 21:18) or have a soiled face (2 Sam. 19:4-5) is an indicator of loss, mourning, and shame. By way of contrast, to "lift the face" (2 Kgs. 5:1) or converse with someone "face to face" (1 Thess. 3:10) is a sign of respect and honor in treating someone as one's equal.

In traditional Mediterranean society, which maintains a strong sense of honor among males, the face is the most obvious public expression of a person's character and standing in the social group. Thus, bowing the face or falling on the face is an appropriate gesture of obeisance to a superior. To have one's face lifted is a bestowal of honor by a superior on an inferior. The hope of believers is that they too shall see God "face to face" (1 Cor. 13:12), having received the ultimate gift of acceptance by God in Christ. T. R. Hobbs

FAIR HAVENS

A small bay on the southern coast of Crete, E of Cape Littinos and near the city of Lasea (Acts 27:8).

The name (Gk. *Kaloì Liménes*) was probably chosen by the inhabitants in order to attract commerce, but the prevailing southeasterly winds in winter would actually make the harbor unsafe (cf. Acts 27:12).

FAITH

A central theological concept representing the correct relationship to God. Heb. *'mn* and Gk. *pisteúein* demand a variety of renderings besides belief, faith, and trust, especially faithfulness. They may be used for God or human beings. A continuing question involves distinguishing personal faith with which a person believes and "the faith" with an objective content, something to be believed.

Biblical theology usually roots NT faith in the OT, and some speak of a Judeo-Christian concept, even of a "fundamentally identical" OT and NT notion. Actually, Hebrew lacks a word for "faith" (*'ĕmûnâ* is rare and equals "fidelity"). This, plus other factors, caused Martin Buber to distinguish two types of faith: OT/Judaic (*'ĕmûnâ*), which was tribal, national, communal trust and fidelity, based on the covenant; and Christian (Gk. *pístis*), which was individualistic persuasion or faith, belief in something.

In the OT, along with *'āman,* terms like *bāṭaḥ* ("trust; be confident, secure"), *qāwâ* ("hope"), *yāḥal* and *ḥāḵâ* (both "wait in hope") come into consideration. The basic idea of *'āman* is "constancy," something that is lasting (Isa. 33:16) or someone who is reliable (8:2). More important is the hiphil *he'ĕmîn,* "become steadfast, acquire stability," used of a person or of God. Applied to human beings, the term often has a negative connotation: "do not believe or rely on. . . (a person)" (Jer. 12:6; Mic. 7:5; Job 4:18) or a message (Gen. 45:26; 1 Kgs. 10:7; Isa. 53:1).

Three nouns from *'mn* appear in the OT: (1) *'ĕmeṯ,* originally meaning "stability" (Isa. 38:8; NRSV "security"), comes to denote faithfulness or truth (Gk. *alḗtheia*), on the part of a person (Exod. 18:21; NRSV "trustworthy") or God (Ps. 31:5[MT 6]; 146:6) and God's word (Ps. 119:43; 142; 160). God's works are faithful (Ps. 111:7), and the promises express faithfulness (Zech. 8:8); on this God, worshippers rely (Ps. 40:11[12], with *ḥeseḏ).* This reliability makes it possible for mortals to trust in God. (2) The noun *'ĕmûnâ* suggests conduct that grows out of a relationship, faithfulness, especially in inner attitude and conduct on the part of an individual (Prov. 14:5; 20:6; 1 Sam. 26:23) or of God (Ps. 89:2, 5, 8, 49[3, 6, 8, 50]; Deut. 32:4; Isa. 33:6). (3) Heb. *'āmēn* was used in response to God in prayer (Neh. 8:6), or with ritual curses (Deut. 27:15, 16; Neh. 5:13).

Following God's call to Abram and promise to make him and Sarah a great nation and a blessing (Gen. 12:1-3), the vision and word of the Lord present God's promise about posterity (15:1-5), followed by a covenant binding God (not Abram) to the promise (vv. 7-21). As a result, Abram acknowledged God's power to fulfill it.

In Isaiah the prophet will wait for the hidden God and hope in him during crisis times when Israel withheld faith (cf. Isa. 7:9; 30:15).

Some stress Jesus' call to faith and recognition of it in individuals; others find in Jesus only a Cynic sage, or little that is recoverable. There is some agreement that, according to the Synoptics, Jesus taught faith in God (Mark 11:12 par.) as a basis for "prayer faith" (Mark 11:24 par.) and "mountain-moving faith" (11:23 par.; 1 Cor. 13:2). Unlike the Fourth Gospel, where miracles can produce faith (John 2:11; 4:52-54; 20:30-31), for Jesus in the Synoptics "supplicating faith" leads to miracles (Mark 9:24-27; 2:5, 12 par.; 6:5-6 par.).

A new and specifically Christian use of *pístis* comes in terms of acceptance of the *kḗrygma* or apostolic proclamation about the crucified and risen Jesus (Gal. 3:2, 5). Gk. *pístis* becomes a technical term for reaction to gospel preaching, an act of faith with regard to the story about Jesus coupled with the promise of future salvation (Acts 4:4, with 3:19-26; 13:48, with vv. 38-39, 46-47; Rom. 10:9-14). This future hope was part of the kerygma (1 Thess. 1:9-10). Christians are "believers" (Acts 2:44; Rom. 1:16; 3:22), "members of the household of faith" (Gal. 6:10).

Paul inherits and exhibits much of this early Christian understanding. The personal faith that comes from hearing the word and confessing Jesus' lordship includes "the obedience of faith" or commitment (Rom. 1:5; cf. 16:26). Hence faith relates to ethics, in close relationship to its expression toward the future as "hope" and toward others as love (1 Thess. 1:3; Rom. 12:1-2, 9-10; 13:8-10).

Paul's contribution involved relating faith to righteousness and justification (cf. Gal. 3:6-14; Rom. 4). He connects faith with "gospel" for salvation (Rom. 1:16), "peace" and "access to God" (5:1-2), the Spirit (Gal. 3:2, 5,14), "in Christ" (Gal. 3:25-26). "Reconciliation" parallels justification by faith (Rom. 5:9-11), "redemption" (3:24-25). "Fellowship" *(koinōnía)* is connected with God's being faithful (1 Cor. 1:9) and our participation in Christ (Phil. 3:9-10), and "grace" is frequently linked with "faith." For Paul faith becomes the criterion, not "works of the law" such as circumcision and regulations involving clean and unclean, which marked Jews off from others and so precluded a universal mission.

Some Christians may be "weak in faith" (Rom. 14:1), while others can be regarded as "strong" or enabled (15:1). Faith is something that can grow (2 Cor. 10:15) or be lacking in some aspects (1 Thess. 3:10) but then become strong in its conviction (Rom. 4:20-22; 14:5). It is not static in the face of threats but dynamic, showing itself in action (1 Thess. 1:3), through love (Gal. 5:6).

Hebrews has 32 instances of Gk. *pístis,* mostly in ch. 11, about what people in Israel did "by faith." God is the object of faith (6:1; cf. 11:6). Those addressed have come to faith in the gospel message (4:2-3; 6:12). Faith means "full assurance" (10:22), but there is grave danger of those addressed falling away into unbelief (3:12; cf. v. 19). In 11:3–12:2 *pístis* can be trust in God's promise (11:11), accepting what God said (v. 8), or denote what motivated Abraham to sacrifice Isaac (vv. 17-18) or moved Moses (vv. 24-25) or how we understand the world's creation (v. 3; cf. 1:2).

Luke-Acts stress coming to faith as conversion, to "hear the word, believe, and be saved" (Luke 8:12-13; Acts 10:43; 13:19; 16:31; 20:21; 24:24). In miracle stories, faith saves (Luke 7:50; 17:19). "The apostles" can ask "the Lord, 'Increase our faith'" (Luke 17:5). Mary is a model of faith in the beatitude at Luke 1:45. Questions appear as to the existence of faith on the part of the disciples (Luke 8:25; 18:8). Jesus prays that Peter's faith not fail (Luke 22:32). In Acts "the faith" becomes a term for Christianity (Acts 6:7; 13:8; cf. Luke 18:8).

Faith arises out of confrontation with Jesus' word(s) (John 2:22; 4:41, 50; 5:24) as well as his deeds (miracles) and testimony to Jesus (1:7; 4:39; 17:20). Such encounter calls for decision, leading to faith or judgment (John 3:36; 5:24). The Johannine concept of believing also involves "keeping" or "remaining in" Jesus' word (John 14:23; 15:20; 8:31; 15:4), with a considerable emphasis on "knowing" (17:3, 7, 21; 16:27-30; 6:69; 1 John 4:16). The Fourth Gospel also explores the relation of "seeing" and "believing," notably in the story of Thomas (John 20:25-29; cf. 4:48).

Bibliography. A. Dulles, *The Assurance of Things Hoped For: A Theology of Christian Faith* (Oxford, 1994); J. D. G. Dunn, *The Theology of Paul the Apostle* (Grand Rapids, 1997); W. Henn, *One Faith: Biblical and Patristic Contributions Toward Understanding Unity in Faith* (New York, 1995); H.-J. Hermisson and E. Lohse, *Faith* (Nashville, 1981); J. Reumann, *Variety and Unity in New Testament Thought* (Oxford, 1991); W. H. Schmidt, *The Faith of the Old Testament* (Philadelphia, 1983); I. G. Wallis, *The Faith of Jesus Christ in Early Christian Traditions.* SNTSMS 84 (Cambridge, 1995).

JOHN REUMANN

FALCON

A bird of prey belonging to the family Falconidae (Heb. *'ayyâ*). Several species of the genus *Falco* have been attested in Palestine. The bird's keen vision would aid it in spotting and striking at its prey (Job 28:7).

FALL, THE

The fall from innocence and paradise of the primeval couple, Adam and Eve, through their temptation and disobedience (Gen. 3). Although the Genesis narrative does not refer to the couple's wrongdoing as a fall, some NT writings characterize humanity's choice to sin as a "fall into the condemnation of the devil" (1 Tim. 3:6) and a "fall under condemnation" (Jas. 5:12). Later Christian interpreters like Augustine, Dante, and John Milton develop the Genesis account of Adam and Eve's disobedience into a doctrine of the Fall in great detail.

The story of Adam and Eve is embedded in the second Creation account (Gen. 2:4b–4:1). Likely written ca. 950 B.C.E. as part of the Yahwistic history of Israel, this account is the older of the two Creation stories. In this story, God creates a male human being and a female "helper" and sets them in a lush and paradisiacal garden where all of their needs are met. God instructs the man not to eat "of the tree of the knowledge of good and evil" lest he die. The serpent, a fellow creature described as subtle and crafty, convinces the woman that the fruit of that tree is good and she will not die. When the two eat the fruit, they recognize immediately the consequences of their actions. God punishes them for their misdeeds and expels them from the garden (3:8-24). In its mythic elements the story also offers explanations for why serpents crawl on the ground (v. 14), why enmity exists between humans and serpents (v. 15), the paradox of sexual pleasure and the pain of childbearing (v. 16), and the continual conflict between humans and nature (vv. 17-19).

The Genesis account owes its rich literary symbolism to a number of other ancient Near Eastern myths. In the Babylonian Adapa myth, the wise man Adapa, having taken the advice of the jealous god Ea, rejects Anu's offer of the bread and water of life and thus loses immortality for himself and mankind. In the Sumerian Gilgamesh Epic, the hero fails to win immortality when a serpent steals from him the plant of eternal youth.

In the NT writings of Paul, the Fall takes on a universal dimension, introducing sin and mortality into the lives of all humanity. Paul acknowledges that "as sin came into the world through one man, and death came through sin, so death spread to all because all have sinned" (Rom. 5:12). In *Paradise Lost,* Milton depicts Sin and Death, Satan's children, as building a bridge to this world so that they may now move more easily between their kingdom and the new world which Satan has just conquered in the Fall.

In contrast to other Near Eastern myths where humans are the victims of jealous gods, Genesis depicts the man and woman as responsible creatures acting according to their own wills. Their disobedience is often depicted then as rebellion against God's commands. Although there is no doctrine of original sin in the Genesis story, Augustine used it to promulgate an interpretation which held that the first couple's sin was transmitted to every successive generation and thus all humans were infected with sin. While Augustine held the couple acted freely according to their will, he stated clearly that their evil act introduced corruption into God's good creation. Irenaeus used the story to demonstrate that God is a loving Father who helps his children recognize their mistakes and learn from them. Many of the Greek church fathers (e.g., Theodore of Mopsuestia) emphasize the universality of human sin.

While many commentators, from Tertullian to Milton, placed the blame for the Fall on the woman, recent feminist criticism has rejected those claims and argues that the woman acted far more rationally than the man, actually conversing with the serpent, posing questions, and making a thoughtful decision. The man, on the other hand, acted merely from appetite in taking the fruit from the woman, without question, and eating it.

Bibliography. P. Trible, *God and the Rhetoric of Sexuality.* OBT 2 (Philadelphia, 1978).

HENRY L. CARRIGAN, JR.

FALLOW GROUND

Ground that has been plowed but intentionally remains uncultivated. Every seventh year the fields in Palestine were to be left unseeded in order to give the land a rest and thus preserve its fertility (Lev. 26:34-35). Whatever grew on that land during the Sabbatical Year was to be given as sustenance for the poor and livestock (Exod. 23:11; Neh. 10:31[MT 32]; cf. Prov. 13:23). At Jer. 4:3; Hos. 10:12 the instruction "break up your fallow ground" means "cultivate a new field" or, metaphorically, "come to a renewal of your lives."

FALSE PROPHETS

Prophets who speak in the name of Baal (e.g., 1 Kgs. 18:19-40) or, more frequently, who speak lies in the name of the Lord (Mic. 3:5-8; Jer. 4:9-10).

A number of tests defined a false prophet (Gk. *pseudoprophḗtēs*). If the word of the prophet does not come true, then the prophet is false (Deut. 18:22; cf. Jer. 28:9). Yet this test is helpful only after the fact, not before disaster strikes. Furthermore, even some words of true prophets did not come true (e.g., Amos 7:11a). False prophets were condemned for dreams (Deut. 13:1-3; Jer. 23:25-38; Ezek. 13:9), but dreams were also acceptable (Gen. 28:10-22). False prophets engaged in ecstatic activity (1 Kgs. 18:19-40; 22:5-23), but ecstatic prophets were also acceptable as true prophets (1 Sam. 10:9-13). False prophets claimed to have the spirit of the Lord (1 Kgs. 22:24), but so did true prophets (Mic. 3:8; Isa. 61:1). Because of these ambiguities, people had difficulty choosing between true and false prophets.

The deciding factors seemed to be that false prophets did not attend the council of the Lord (Jer. 23:18) and were not sent by God (v. 21). They had their own visions (Jer. 23:16), using lying visions and worthless divinations (Mic. 3:7; Ezek. 13:3, 6). They gave the people false confidence, saying that the sword would not come (Jer. 4:10; 6:14; Ezek. 13:10).

The early Church was keenly aware of the perils posed by false prophets who might distract believers from the responsibilities of Christian discipleship (cf. Did. 11:3-12). Jesus warned of such individuals "who come to you in sheep's clothing but inwardly are ravenous wolves" (Matt. 7:15). They claimed supernatural powers (1 John 4:1) and practiced exorcism, using Jesus' name (Matt. 12:27; Acts 19:13-16). The Jewish magician Bar-Jesus (Elymas), who opposed Paul and Barnabas, was a false prophet (Acts 13:6). In times of social upheaval the number of false prophets seems to have increased (cf. 2 Pet. 2:1-3); consequently, they figured prominently in Christian perceptions of the end times (Mark 13:22 par.; cf. Rev. 16:13; 19:20; 20:10).

Martin Buber argues that false prophets developed their message out of the wishes and desires common to them and their people, and this message of wish fulfillment led Israel astray. False prophets may not have intended to deceive the Israelites; they were simply caught up in a world of wanting and wishing.

Bibliography. M. Buber, *The Prophetic Faith* (New York, 1960), esp. 176-80.

LAWRENCE A. SINCLAIR

FAMILY

See FATHER'S HOUSE; HOUSEHOLD; MOTHER'S HOUSE.

FAMINE

In the ancient world, the greatest of disasters (Lam. 4:9 prefers death by sword to a slow death of famine). Mentioned frequently in biblical and nonbiblical material from the ancient Near East, famine affected lives on many levels. Often seen as a major disaster along with pestilence and the sword (e.g., Jer. 14:12; Ezek. 6:11; Bar. 2:25; Matt. 24:7; Rom. 8:35), both environmental and sociopolitical changes contributed to the onset of famine. In the agrarian society of ancient Palestine, the people's lives depended on rainfall. Droughts and subsequent crop failure often led to famine (e.g., Gen. 26:1; Ruth 1:1; 2 Sam. 21:1; 1 Kgs. 18:1-2; Hag. 1:1-10; Josephus *Ant.* 15:299ff.). Pestilence such as locusts (Joel 1:4-20) only added to the threat of famine. Political changes, including siege during warfare, also fostered famine. The book of Kings recounts the siege of Samaria by King Ben-hadad of Aram (2 Kgs. 6:24–7:20) and the siege of Jerusalem by Nebuchadnezzar (2 Kgs. 25), both of which resulted in famine. Josephus tells of famine resulting from Antiochus IV's siege of Jerusalem (*Ant.* 12:375ff.; cf. 1 Macc. 6).

In the arid ancient Near East, people expected, and even prepared for, famine. The elite were able to build storehouses. Biblical accounts attest to the storehouses of the temple (e.g., 1 Chr. 26:15; Neh. 10:38-39; 13:12-13; Mal. 3:10) and of the monarchs (e.g., 2 Kgs. 20:12-15; 2 Chr. 32:27-28; Isa. 39:3-4). Such royal storehouses may have offered rulers an opportunity to enhance the extant ancient Near Eastern royal ideology of ruler as benefactor of the poor. Gen. 41:56 tells of Joseph opening the storehouses to the Egyptian people.

Ideologically, biblical texts often characterize famine as divine retribution or as a direct result of disobedience to God (Lev. 26:14-20; Isa. 3:1; 51:19; Jer. 29:17-18; Zech. 14:17) and sometimes as a threat to encourage obedience (Deut. 11:17; 28:33; Amos 4:6). 1 Kgs. 8:33-40 provides an example of biblical prayers offered in an effort to prevent famine.

The consequences of famine were vast. As demand for food increased, so would prices (e.g., 2 Kgs. 6:24-25). Sources attest to the extreme despair of famine. For Josephus (*BJ* 5.515), famine "confounded all natural passions" as people turned against each other in robbery and other violent acts (5.424ff.). Several biblical texts report cannibalism

(2 Kgs. 6:29; Lam. 2:20-21; 4:8-10). In addition to the internal strife brought on by famine, it exacerbated the vulnerability of the people and the land to external incursions. Furthermore, famine often resulted in the collapse of agrarian, subsistence-based economies which, in turn, forced people to migrate. Biblical examples of such migrations include Abraham (Gen. 12:10), Isaac (26:1), Jacob (ch. 46), and Elimelech (Ruth 1).

In the social stratification of the monarchic, agrarian society, the brief decrease in labor supply resulting from famine often increased opportunities for upward mobility. These gains, however, were short-lived and quickly counterbalanced, if not outweighed, by increased births. Thus, broadly viewed, famine did not change the propensity for peasants, who comprised the vast majority of the population, toward downward mobility. For another marginalized group, women, famine only contributed to their increasing confinement in the domestic sphere by increasing the demand for childbirth. ALICE HUNT HUDIBURG

FASTING

Deliberate and often prolonged abstinence from food and sometimes drink. Comparative anthropological literature suggests that fasting is a varied phenomenon that must be defined by context. For example, fasts in ancient Israel (Heb. *ṣôm*) are related to mourning (2 Sam. 1:12; 3:35 = 1 Chr. 10:12; Jdt. 16:24) or religious acts of piety (Lev. 16). Fasting seems to lend an air of extra dedication to religious acts such as prayer (1 Kgs. 12:27-29; Jonah 3:5). Heb. *ʿnh,* usually translated "afflict the soul," is often taken to include fasting (e.g., Lev. 16:31, which elaborates the details of the Day of Atonement), and thus an act of repentance.

In the case of mourning, the act may be intended to assuage God's anger lest the mourner be the next to die, or perhaps to avoid contamination with death itself (or spirits), as anthropological comparisons suggest. Fasting (along with sackcloth, weeping, etc.) was a part of such rituals calling for God's deliverance because they symbolized one's weakened state (cf. Ben-hadad's "reduced state" before King Ahaz, who then spared him; 1 Kgs. 20).

Fasting is associated with preparation for revelations and visions, similar to the ancient Greek practice of "incubation" (Exod. 34:28; cf. 1 Kgs. 19:8). The association of fasting with revelations and visions increases in popularity during the Hellenistic period (2 Bar. 12:5; 21:1-3; Apoc. Elijah 1:21).

Fasting is also associated with the conduct of or preparation for "Yahweh war." The Israelites practiced fasting at Mizpah in the face of the Philistine threat (1 Sam. 7:6), and Saul imposes a fast on his militia until he succeeds in seeking vengeance against the Philistines (1 Sam 14:24; cf. 2 Sam. 11:11-12; 1 Macc. 3:46; 2 Macc. 13:12).

In the postexilic period fasting was used as a means of calling on God's direct assistance when the community was in great danger (Ezra 8:21-22, 31b; Esth. 4:15-16; Dan. 9:3; 6:17-25). This notion may help to explain Jesus' otherwise enigmatic reference to demons that can be driven out "only by prayer and fasting" (Mark 9:29 = Matt. 17:21). Tertullian (*On Fasting*) notes, while commenting on 1 Sam. 7:6, that when one fasts, "Heaven fights for you" and "divine defense will be granted." Jesus' fast in the wilderness may have elements of preparing both for revelations and for "war" with Satan (Matt. 4:1-11; Gk. *nēsteúō*).

The prophets contrast outward fasting with inward corruption, stressing that social justice is the "fast" that God prefers (Isa. 58; Zech. 7:3ff.).

Bibliography. R. Arbesmann, "Fasting and Prophecy in Pagan and Christian Antiquity," *Traditio* 7 (1949): 1-71; D. L. Smith-Christopher, "Hebrew Satyagraha: The Politics of Biblical Fasting in the Post-Exilic Period (Sixth to Second Century B.C.E.)," *Food and Foodways* 5 (1993): 269-92; E. Westermark, "The Principles of Fasting," *Folklore* 18 (1907): 391-422.

DANIEL L. SMITH-CHRISTOPHER

FAT

"Fat" translates more than two dozen Hebrew and Greek words and is used literally, mainly in connection with sacrifice, and metaphorically. The Hebrews were to offer in sacrifice the best part of an animal, the fat and the blood (Lev. 7:33; 17:6; Ezek. 44:7, 15), which no human was allowed to eat (Lev. 3:17; 7:23-25). Animals kept in a stall rather than let out to pasture were being prepared for food and were known as fatted or fatling (1 Sam. 15:9; 28:24).

Fat can also refer to the size of animals (Gen. 41:2), humans (Judg. 3:17, 22), and plants such as corn (Gen. 41:5, 7). Metaphorically "fat" refers to prosperity (Deut. 31:20), fertility (Gen. 27:27-28), wealth (Jer. 5:28), strength (Ps. 78:31 MT), and insensitivity (119:70; Isa. 6:10 MT).

TIMOTHY W. SEID

FATHER

In the patriarchal worldview of biblical Israel, the father (Heb. *ʾāḇ*) was the linchpin of family life, and his house *(bêṯ ʾāḇ)* was the basic unit of biblical society. Fatherhood was the only way a man could perpetuate his name and memory after death. Thus the acquisition of male heirs is often a primary element in biblical narratives (e.g., 1 Sam. 1).

According to biblical legal codes, fathers had both privileges and obligations. Their main privilege was honor or public respect, the dominant social value in the Mediterranean world. This honor is due both parents (Exod. 20:12; Deut. 5:16; Mal. 1:6) and is demonstrated through obedience (Gen. 27:8, 13). Disrespect, physical violence, arrogant speech, or a rebellious attitude carried the death penalty (Exod. 21:15; Lev. 20:9; Deut. 22:18-21). Sons were expected to avoid any conduct that shamed their fathers (Lev. 18:7-8).

A father's central religious duty was to see that his son was circumcised into the covenant (Lev. 12:3) and instructed properly in the Lord's torah (Deut. 11:19). In the book of Proverbs, the father provides proper instruction about living well and responsibly within society for his sons. In biblical narratives sons leave their fathers' house to follow divine command (Gen. 12:1) or to escape criminal punishment (27:41-45; 2 Sam. 13:34-38). More often a father arranged endogamous marriages for his sons and welcomed his daughters-in-law into his home (Gen. 12:2-6; but cf. Cant. 4:9-10; 5:1-2). In addition, the father was responsible for supervising the behavior (Num. 12:14) and the sexuality of the women who lived within his house; in this way, he guaranteed that children born to his wife were his and that his daughters were virgins when they left his house for marriage. He exercised absolute authority over his children, but especially over his daughters, whose status within the household was inferior and precarious (2 Sam. 13). They returned to his control if they were widowed without children. If their behavior shamed him, they deserved death (Gen. 38:24; cf. Judg. 11:35-36).

Since the 2nd millennium B.C.E., ancient Near Eastern religions had addressed their national gods with the title "father" to identify them as providers and protectors. Biblical Israel followed this practice (Deut. 1:31; 8:5; Isa. 43:6; Hos. 11:1), extending the metaphor to include the Lord's creation of Israel as his people (Exod 4:22; Deut. 32:6; Isa. 63:16; 64:7). This understanding of God as father became a motive for observing the law (Deut. 14:1) and for seeking divine compassion and forgiveness (Ps. 103:13-14; Jer. 3:19; 31:9, 20; Hos. 2:1[MT 3]).

In the NT human fatherhood is partially eclipsed. Only Matthew and Luke mention Joseph as the father of Jesus. Jesus enforces the responsibility of children to care for their parents (Mark 7:10-13) and insists that his followers must leave father and mother to pursue the gospel (Matt. 10:37). The household codes maintain paternal authority and require obedience of all members of the household (Eph. 5:22–6:9; cf. Col. 3:18–4:1).

God is the father of believers whose love (Matt. 6:5-8; 10:29-31) and forgiveness (Luke 15:11-32) model the love they owe each other (Matt. 5:43-45). He is, however, the father of Jesus of Nazareth in a unique way (Matt. 11:25-27); the Synoptic Passion narratives accent this relationship (Mark 14:35-39; 15:39). The Johannine traditions further develop the father metaphor so that to see Jesus of Nazareth is to see the Father, for Jesus alone knows him (John 14:1-14). KATHLEEN S. NASH

FATHER'S HOUSE

Lit., the physical structure in which a family lived, viewed as a possession of the father due to the patriarchal orientation of biblical society (Gen. 24:23; Deut. 22:21; Judg. 19:3). In a figurative sense Heb. *bêṯ-'āḇ* means the extended family, the smallest, most intimate social structure and the basic unit of Israelite society. Many "fathers' houses" comprised a "clan," and many "clans" comprised a "tribe." The "father's house" included the patriarch and his wife, unmarried children, married sons and grandsons with their families, slaves and their families, and resident aliens. This extended family could easily approach 100 members, who resided together in a cluster of dwellings. Commanded by the patriarch, the *bêṯ-'āḇ* also served as the basic unit of the army (cf. Gen. 41:51; 46:31; Judg. 9:5; 1 Sam. 2:27-31; 2 Chr. 25:5).

In the NT Gk. *oíkos/oikíā toú patrós* has direct parallels with OT usage. It appears in reference to the literal physical structure (Acts 7:20), and also to the extended family (Luke 16:27-28). The NT includes two additional metaphorical nuances. The phrase is used by Jesus to refer to the temple (John 2:16) and to heaven (14:2; cf. Philo *Somn.* 1:43), both contexts referring to the dwelling-place of God. W. E. NUNNALLY

FATHOM

A unit of measurement (Gk. *orguiá*) representing the distance between the fingertips of both outstretched arms, equivalent to 4 cubits or 1.8 m. (6 ft.; Acts 27:28).

FEAR

Anxious dread or terror in the face of danger; also reverence to or awe of God.

Fear is a common human emotion in response to danger or the supernatural. Adam and Eve are afraid of God after they eat the forbidden fruit (Gen. 3:8-10), and Jacob is afraid of Esau after he takes Esau's blessing (32:11). When the Israelites are ready to cross the Reed Sea, they become fearful for their lives as Pharaoh and his armies draw closer (Exod. 14:10). People of the Promised Land would "melt in fear 'before'" the coming Israelites (Josh. 2:9). The prophets preach that to fear God's coming judgment is a reality none could escape (Jer. 5:22, 24; Amos 3:8; Zeph. 3:7). When Tobias begins his journey, both his father and mother have parental fear for their son's life (Tob. 5:16-21). "Fear and dread" fall upon the seacoast peoples who encounter the army of Holofernes (Jdt. 2:28). When Gabriel visits Mary she is told to "fear not" (Luke 1:30). The women who find Jesus' tomb empty are seized by "terror and amazement" and are afraid to tell others of their discovery (Mark 16:8).

While "fear of the Lord" can mean outright fear of God's presence, it also means to revere God, an idea most directly expressed in the Wisdom Literature (e.g., Prov. 2:5). Fear of God is connected to keeping the law and commandments (Eccl. 12:13) and is "the whole of wisdom" (Sir. 19:20) and "the root of wisdom" (1:20). Most succinctly stated, "Truly, the fear of the Lord, that is wisdom; and to depart from evil is understanding" (Job 28:28).

To fear God, then, is to be completely devoted to his will and its rewards while knowing the awesome consequences of not fearing him. This is the background to Paul's injunction to the Philippians to "work out your own salvation with fear and trembling" (Phil. 2:12). MARC A. JOLLEY

FEASTS, FESTIVALS

Feasts and festivals provided occasions for the Israelites to come before God and express their gratitude for successful harvests, to remember and celebrate Yahweh's saving actions on behalf of the nation, and to reflect on their status as the holy people of Yahweh. Five "festal calendars" are found in the Pentateuch: Exod. 23:14-17; 34:18-26; Lev. 23; Num. 28–29; Deut. 16:1-17 (cf. Ezek. 45:18-25). These texts and the ritual practices that they envision reflect both historical and theological development. It is important to recognize that such development does not necessarily entail the complete abandonment of earlier dynamics and concerns. Rather, it adds complexity so as to create new contexts and possibilities for reflection and enactment. Thus, e.g., the later concern to relate the festivals to specific moments in Israel's history need not mean that earlier agricultural concerns were entirely lost. The ritual remembrance and celebration of God's activity and blessing receive theological complexity precisely in the context of ritual enactment and reflection. In this way, one can understand Israel's cultic life to have been, at least in part, generative of its theological reflections.

Exod. 23:14-17; 34:18-26, the earliest festal prescriptions, call for three annual festivals: the Pilgrimage of Unleavened Bread (*ḥag hammaṣṣôṯ*), the Pilgrimage of Harvest (*ḥag haqqāṣîr*), the firstfruits of the farmer's labor (in 34:22, the Pilgrimage of Weeks [*ḥag šāḇuʿôṯ*], the firstfruits of the wheat harvest), and the Pilgrimage of Ingathering (*ḥag hāʾāsip*). The festivals of Harvest and Ingathering were clearly tied to the agricultural life of the land. Originally, the Festival of Harvest celebrated the firstfruits of the barley harvest in the spring; the Festival of Ingathering was related to the autumnal gathering of the fruits at the end of the year (Exod. 34:22). These observances were, in all probability, adapted from already existing Canaanite agricultural practices. The farmers would bring their offerings to a sacred site near their home and present their offerings to Yahweh in celebration of the fertility of the land. Such agricultural observances emphasized Israel's intimate relationship to the land and Yahweh's blessing of the people with successful crops. Harvest celebration and ritual presentation merge.

The Pilgrimage of Unleavened Bread has generally been associated with the spring harvest, although its early status as an agricultural observance is not certain. It is a seven-day observance in which no leaven is to be eaten and is, in the early texts, related to Israel's exodus from Egypt. It is not associated with Passover in either of these early texts. Thus, Unleavened Bread may reflect an early Israelite observance specifically designed to celebrate Yahweh's act of redemption. It must be noted, however, that at a later time the observance of this festival was related to the presentation of the sheaf of firstfruits (cf. Lev. 23:9-14). In this way, it came to have both agricultural and historical connotations.

It is generally recognized that a major change in the observance of the festivals took place in the 7th century. Local agricultural celebrations were transformed into national celebrations that required a pilgrimage to the central sanctuary. This requirement reflects the mandated centralization of worship in the capital city of Jerusalem which is generally associated with the reforms of King Josiah (2 Kgs. 22–23). Such a transformation is reflected in the instructions found in Deut. 16:1-17. This text emphasizes that the pilgrimages must be observed "at the place which Yahweh will choose," which in Deuteronomy refers to the temple in Jerusalem. Of particular importance, Passover (*pesaḥ*) and Unleavened Bread are now joined as two parts of one pilgrimage festival. Although it is not certain, Passover appears to have been originally a family observance that took place in the context of the individual homes (Exod. 12:21-23). Deuteronomy turns it into a national pilgrimage that requires the Passover "sacrifice" to be slaughtered at the central sanctuary. The Passover sacrifice overlaps with the first day of the seven-day Festival of Unleavened Bread. The people were not required to remain in Jerusalem for the duration of the seven days. They were required, however, to observe a solemn assembly on the seventh day.

The festal prescriptions in Deut. 16 also seek to locate the time of the Feast of Weeks more precisely (vv. 9-12). It is to be observed seven weeks from the time the sickle is first put to the standing grain. The observance of Weeks requires a freewill offering that functions as a ritual response of gratitude to the blessings of Yahweh. Further, the people are to rejoice before Yahweh and, at the same time, to remember that they were slaves in Egypt. Although it is not indicated in biblical texts, the festival would in postexilic time come to be associated with the making of the Sinai covenant (cf., e.g., the book of Jubilees).

The Pilgrimage of Ingathering is now termed the Pilgrimage of Booths (*ḥag hassukkôṯ*; Deut. 16:13-15). It is a seven-day autumn festival associated with the gathering of produce used in the making of oil and wine (generally, Sept.-Oct.). It is a time of celebration that functions both as response to and anticipation of Yahweh's blessings. Although it is not certain, it is probable that the "booths" were temporary field shelters constructed by the people during the time of harvest. When the festival was centralized, the booths were built in the capital city to provide living quarters for the pilgrims.

In Deuteronomy one detects a movement toward the historical and theological rendering of the festivals. The festivals are associated with specific moments in Israel's national story. Although the agricultural context of the festivals is not entirely lost, an effort is made to construct a ritual context that provides the occasion and opportunity for theological reflection on Yahweh's acts in history on behalf of the whole community. It is doubtful, however, that the Israelite farmer who made the pilgrimage to the central sanctuary in order to make an offering to Yahweh would fail to experience it, to some degree, in terms of agricultural blessing. Too much has been made of the supposed dichotomy between nature and history in Israelite life and thought. Both may be experienced in terms of Yahweh's blessings. Ritual offering provides the occasion for enacting one's response to the experience of divine blessings in "nature" and in "history." Thus, the festivals provided contexts not only for thinking about God and God's actions, but also for responding to the divine being in acts of thanksgiving, celebration, and offering.

The move toward a theological rendering of the sacred year is evidenced in Lev. 23 (cf. Num. 28-29). The effort to impose a ritual order on the year may reflect the loss of monarchy and the experience of exile in Babylon (6th century B.C.E.). Lev. 23 (cf. Num. 28–29) provides the details of this ritual order. Festival and ritual observance become means for establishing an orderly rhythm for the life of the community.

Lev. 23:15 locates the date of the Festival of Weeks 50 days after the presentation of the sheaf of firstfruits at the Festival of Unleavened Bread. The text requires a presentation of two loaves of bread from the Israelite settlements. A complete list of the sacrifices and offerings to be presented at this time is found in Lev. 23:15-21; Num. 28:26-31. In terms of the Festival of Booths, Lev. 23:33-36, 39-43 specifies that it is to last for seven days with a holy convocation of complete rest on the first and an additional observance on the eighth day. In addition, the booths are now associated with the booths in which the Israelites lived during their wilderness sojourn (Lev. 23:42-43). In this way, the Festival of Booths comes to be associated with the Exodus story.

Lev. 23 includes a discussion of sabbath as a significant feature of the ritual observances of the sacred year (cf. Exod. 23:12). Although the observance of sabbath appears to have been known in Israel from an early period, it began to receive more emphasis in the later years of the Monarchy and during the Babylonian Exile. The sabbath is related to a variety of issues in the biblical materials, e.g., creation (Gen. 2:1-3), the gathering of manna during the wilderness journey (Exod. 16:1-36; cf. Num. 15:32-36), the Israelites' status as slaves in Egypt and the Exodus story (Deut. 5:12-15). The sabbath was observed as a day of complete rest in which no work was done. It was also a day of joy and celebration.

Lev. 23 prescribes two additional ritual occasions. The first calls for the blowing of trumpets on the first day of the seventh month (Lev. 23:23-25). This is a day of complete rest. The sacrifices and offerings required on this day are specified in Num. 29:1-6. Although it is not the case in this text, in later Judaism the blowing of the horns was associated with the New Year.

The second additional ritual observance takes place on the tenth day of the seventh month (Lev. 23:26-32); it is the annual day of purification (the details for the enactment of this community ritual are found in Lev. 16). In this ritual, the high priest enters into the holy of holies, the only day of the year in which a person enters this most sacred of places, and sprinkles sacrificial blood on and before the ark of the covenant. He also sprinkles sacrificial blood on the outer altar of burnt offerings. After the completion of the blood rites, the priest places the sins of the community on the head of a goat which is sent out into the wilderness. The ritual functions to cleanse the camp of impurities and to remove the sins of the people from the camp.

The annual day of purification reflects the Priestly ritual system, which is primarily concerned to guard and protect the purity and holiness of the tabernacle and camp. The dynamics of ritual are no longer related primarily to harvests or history. Rather, the concern is to protect the camp and the divine presence that dwells in the midst of the camp from ritual impurities. The annual ritual of purification focuses on maintaining the holy and clean status of the holy people of Yahweh.

The "meanings" associated with the various festivals and the ways in which they were enacted continue to develop on into the 1st century. The Mishnah provides important information on the ways in which the festivals were observed and transformed. It is important to recognize that the festivals were subject to ongoing development in Judaism and its experiences of the world, God, and community. Far from being static forms of empty and mechanical activity, the festival celebrations and ritual observances provided occasions for theological reflection and adaptation to the ever-changing conditions of life.

Bibliography. R. Albertz, *A History of Israelite Religion in the Old Testament Period,* 2 vols. (Louisville, 1994); G. Fohrer, *History of Israelite Religion* (Nashville, 1972); H. L. Ginsberg, *The Israelian Heritage of Judaism* (New York, 1982); H. Ringgren, *Israelite Religion* (Philadelphia, 1966); H. H. Rowley, *Worship in Ancient Israel* (London, 1976); R. de Vaux, *Ancient Israel* (1961, repr. Grand Rapids, 1997), 269-517. FRANK H. GORMAN, JR.

FELIX (Gk. *Phḗlix;* Lat. *Felix*)

Antonius Felix, governor (procurator) of the Roman province of Judea from 52 to ca. 59 C.E., mentioned in connection with the two-year imprisonment of Paul at Caesarea, the provincial capital (Acts 23–25). Jewish leaders accused Paul of disrupting synagogues outside of Palestine and desecrating the temple in Jerusalem. Paul denied the charges, and Felix continued the case indefinitely — partly in hopes of receiving a bribe for his release. During his interrogation of Paul, the Apostle's words about justice, self-control, and future wrath alarmed Felix and his wife Drusilla. When he was recalled by Nero, Felix left Paul in prison so the Jews could not accuse him of releasing an agitator.

Other information about Felix comes from Josephus, Suetonius, and Tacitus. He was a freedman who received his office because he and his notorious brother Pallas were favorites of the emperor Claudius. His third wife was Drusilla, the daughter of Herod Agrippa I (Acts 12). Felix instigated the murder of the high priest Jonathan, routed "the Egyptian" and his followers (Acts 21:38), and allowed a pogrom against the Jews in Caesarea. He was corrupt, immoral, and oppressive. During his governorship opposition to Roman rule increased to the point that the rebellion of 66 C.E. became inevitable. JAMES A. BROOKS

FELLOWSHIP
Something that is shared, or/and those who share it (although either may be implicit rather than explicit in a particular passage). With regard particularly to Paul's use of Gk. *koinōnía* ("that which is in common") to refer to the Lord's Supper or the relationship that believers have with Christ, it is difficult to tell whether the emphasis is upon that which is shared (the Supper or belief in Christ) or the act of sharing with others (the communion).

The *koinōnía* word group was widely used in the early centuries of the Christian era (and before) and referred to a variety of situations and topics: joint undertakings in war and civic life, marriage (or sexual relationships), cultic life, business partnerships, friendships, and clubs. Before Plato, the proverb "friends have all things in common" points to sharing as establishing or manifesting a field of relationships. Thus, *koinōnía* in the NT does not imply "intimacy" or "a mystical relationship" unless those meanings are present in the context.

Paul frequently uses *koinōnía* to describe the Church. It is the mutual relationship in Christ that results from the call of God (1 Cor. 1:9), and it is sustained by the Holy Spirit (2 Cor. 13:14; Phil. 2:1). However, *koinōnía* also finds concrete expression when applied to either the relief for the Jerusalem poor (Rom. 15:26) or the money given to those who teach (Gal. 6:6). This financial sharing related to the work of the Church is manifested most clearly in Phil. 4:14-20 (cf. Heb. 13:16).

A controversial usage is in 1 Cor. 10:16-18. Nineteenth-century scholars stressed the parallels Paul makes with pagan worship to prove a "sacramental" understanding of the Lord's Supper. This view has now declined in favor, even among highly sacramental Christian groups. The fact that Paul describes Jewish, pagan, and Christian groups as examples of "fellowship" limits comparisons with alleged pagan sacramentalism and should also caution against any alleged uniqueness to the Christian meal. Rather, all three groups are examples of how partaking of a defining action (esp. eating) both creates and manifests a particular community. In biblical terms, partaking is covenantal action.

The "fellowship" of Acts 2:42 probably means the "common life" or "community," including shared meals and breaking bread. The uses in 1 John also emphasize the common life, vital in a church having just suffered division. John reminds his readers that their covenantal relationship with God is secure since it is fellowship with God, and his Son (1 John 1:6-7).

Bibliography. P. Perkins, "*Koinōnia* in 1 John 1:3-7," *CBQ* 45 (1983): 631-41; J. P. Sampley, *Pauline Partnership in Christ* (Philadelphia, 1980).

WENDELL WILLIS

FERTILE CRESCENT
Designation, coined by orientalist James H. Breasted, for that semicircular strip of land which arches between Palestine and the Persian Gulf. Contained by the Taurus, Amanus, and Lebanon mountain ranges on the west and the Zagros range to the east, this region consists of plains and foothills relatively conducive to civilization and which contrast sharply with the nearby Arabian and Syrian deserts. Cradle of the Sumerian, Babylonian, Assyrian, and Palestinian civilizations, the Fertile Crescent also served as a land bridge for commerce and military activity between Egypt and the empires of the Tigris and Euphrates valleys.

FESTUS, PORCIUS (Gk. *Pórkios Phḗstos*)
The governor (procurator) of the Roman province of Judea ca. 59 to 62 C.E. Festus is mentioned in connection with the decision to send Paul to Rome for formal trial (Acts 24–26). When Jewish leaders presented charges against Paul, at first Festus refused to send him to Jerusalem for trial. However, after a hearing in Caesarea, the provincial capital, Festus was about to change his mind when Paul took the case out of his hands by appealing as a Roman citizen to be tried before the emperor (Nero). Festus was uncertain how to charge Paul, and when Herod Agrippa II, the client king of northern and eastern Palestine, paid Festus a visit, he asked Agrippa to help. Festus interrupted Paul's defense and accused him of being insane, but Paul denied this and appealed to the king to substantiate his claim. However, neither wanted to hear anything else from Paul, and both they and their advisors agreed that Paul had done nothing worthy of death and could have been released if he had not appealed to the emperor.

Josephus describes Festus as an honest and conscientious administrator who nevertheless was unable to keep order despite taking vigorous action against the *sicarii* (the "dagger men"; *Ant.* 20.8.10; Acts 21:38, "assassins"). Festus sided with Agrippa in a dispute with Jerusalem priests, who had built a high wall to prevent Agrippa from observing temple proceedings from his nearby palace tower. Festus died in office and was succeeded by Albinus.

JAMES A. BROOKS

FIG TREE
A tree (*Ficus carica* L.; Heb. *tᵉʾēnâ*; Gk. *sýkon, sykḗ*) whose fruit has remained a staple in the diet of the ancient Mediterranean world since earliest times. The tree reaches an average height of 3-6 m. (10-20 ft.). Its large palmate leaves open in the early spring and fall at the beginning of winter. Normally the first fruit (cf. Cant. 2:13; Hos. 9:10) appears in February before the leaves appear in April/June. When the leaves appear the fruit is usually ripe. A tree produces two crops per year, one in early summer and the chief crop in the autumn. It is a dioecious tree, meaning there are both male and female varieties. The male (Lat. *caprificus*) grows wild from seeds scattered principally by birds and bats, while the female is planted from shoots of the cultivated trees and requires tending (Prov. 27:18). The fruit production of the female depends upon a process known as caprification: wasps hatched in the

caprifig's flowers bring the pollen from the male tree to fertilize the female flowers, from which the fig develops. Two- to three-year-old fig shoots will become young trees that bear the first or second year after planting. There is considerable literature on the cultivation of the fig in the Greek and Roman farming manuals (Pliny, Cato, Varro, Theophrastus, Columella).

The fig tree is the first fruit tree mentioned in the OT. The many other references to the fig indicate its significant role in the economy of Palestine. It was one of the food items that interested the Hebrews at the conquest of Canaan (Num. 13:23; Deut. 8:8), and the lack of suitability of the wilderness for the fig was a major complaint (Num. 20:5). The fruit was eaten as a delicacy fresh from the tree (Isa. 28:4), or dried individually or in strings, or pressed into cakes (1 Sam. 25:18) for the winter months. Dried figs in cakes were also used as a medicinal poltice (2 Kgs. 20:7 = Isa. 38:21).

The most common reference to the fig in the OT is metaphorical. It is generally used to depict peace, prosperity, and God's blessing ("they shall all sit under their own vines and under their own fig trees," Mic. 4:4; 1 Kgs. 4:25; Hag. 2:19; Zech. 3:10; 1 Macc. 14:12; cf. 2 Kgs. 18:31; Isa. 36:16; Joel 2:22), or God's judgment ("the vine withers, the fig tree languishes," Joel 1:7, 12; cf. Ps. 105:33; Jer. 5:17; Hos. 2:12[MT 14]; Amos 4:9; Nah. 3:12; Hab. 3:17). Other metaphorical uses occur in Judg. 9:10-11; Isa. 34:4; Jer. 8:13; 24:1-8; 29:17; Hos. 9:10; cf. Amos 8:2.

In the NT also the dominant use of the fig tree is metaphorical (Matt. 7:16 = Luke 6:44; Jas. 3:12). It depicts the imminent end of the world (Mark 13:28 = Matt. 24:32 = Luke 21:29). The most problematical passage is Jesus' cursing of the fig tree (Mark 11:12-14, 20-22 = Matt. 21:18-22). Because this account frames the cleansing of the temple, it appears that Mark regards it as an act of prophetic judgment on the temple cult for promising but not delivering true piety (Jer. 8:13; 24:1-10; cf. Matt. 7:15-20). In Luke 13:6-9 Jesus tells a parable about a barren fig tree that reflects the realistic features of farming in 1st-century Palestine. Luke does not provide an interpretation to the parable.

Bibliography. F. N. Hepper, *Baker Encyclopedia of Bible Plants* (Grand Rapids, 1992), 110-14; H. N. and A. L. Moldenke, *Plants of the Bible* (1952, repr. New York, 1986), 103-6. CHARLES W. HEDRICK

FINGER

In biblical usage, an instrument of creativity or productivity (e.g., Isa. 2:8; 17:8; Matt. 23:4; Luke 11:46), often the equivalent of the hand (cf. Isa. 59:1, 3). Used anthropomorphically, it represents divine power (e.g., Exod. 8:19; 31:18; Ps. 8:3; cf. Luke 11:20).

In various offerings, the priest was to sprinkle or smear with his finger the sacrificial blood on the horns of the altar (e.g., Exod. 29:12; Lev. 4:25), on the front of the mercy seat (16:14), or in front of the tent of meeting (Num. 19:4); in cleansing lepers, the high priest was specifically instructed to use the "right finger" (Lev. 14:16, 27). The Hebrews were to bind the pentateuchal laws in phylacteries on their fingers (Prov. 7:3).

As a unit of measure the finger is the twenty-fourth part of a cubit or 1.85 cm. (.73 in.; Jer. 52:21).

FIRE

Fire served many purposes throughout the ancient Near East. Domestically, fire was used for heat, light, and cooking. The refinement of metals necessitated fire. Light and smoke produced by fire were useful in establishing communications between neighboring towns. Fire was also used in a military context, proving effective both in sieges and open battles.

Fire is often used to execute divine judgment in the OT. God places a flaming sword to guard the road back to Eden's tree of life (Gen. 3:24), and he destroys the inhabitants of Sodom and Gomorrah with fire (19:24). Similarly, the Egyptians experience a supernatural thunderstorm, which involves hail accompanied by fire (Exod. 9:23). Aaron's sons Nadab and Abihu are consumed by fire in front of the tabernacle after they violate ritualistic protocol (Lev. 10:2), and Korah's rebellion abruptly ends when Yahweh consumes 250 men in fire (Num. 16:35). Fire likewise consumes two Israelite commanders and their soldiers when Ahaziah initially sends for Elijah (2 Kgs. 1:10-16).

Fire also played a central role in ancient Near Eastern religions, as both animal and vegetable sacrifices were most often consumed by fire. For this purpose in ancient Israel, a perpetual fire was maintained on the altar of burnt offerings (Lev. 6:12[MT 5]). Fire additionally served as the primary medium for theophanies and other divine manifestations. Yahweh is represented in Abram's dream in the form of a smoking fire pot and flaming torch (Gen. 15:17). Yahweh speaks to Moses out of a burning bush (Exod. 3:2) and descends to Mt. Sinai in fire (19:18). The wandering Israelites are nocturnally guided by a pillar of fire (Exod. 13:21). Elijah defeats the prophets of Baal on Mt. Carmel when Yahweh produces fire for a sacrifice (1 Kgs. 18:23-40), and the absence of God in the fire at Horeb is explicitly remarkable (19:12). Elsewhere, Yahweh is described as emitting fire from his mouth (Ps. 18:8[9] = 2 Sam. 22:9). Yahweh's presence in the tabernacle and temple is symbolized by the seven flames on the menorah. Also, fire often accompanies the description of angels in both the OT and NT (Judg. 6:21; 13:20; Dan. 10:6; Rev. 1:14; 2:18).

The etymology of the Hebrew word for fire (*'ēš)* is uncertain. The word may derive from a Semitic root meaning "to be sociable and friendly," or it may be onomatopoetic for the sound of fire.

MICHAEL M. HOMAN

FIRMAMENT

A thin sheet, similar to a piece of beaten metal, that stretched from horizon to horizon to form the vault of the sky. In Hebrew cosmology, the universe consisted of three parts: the waters above, the earth below, and the waters beneath the earth (cf. Exod.

20:4). Job 37:18 describes God as spreading out the heavens and making them "as hard as a mirror of cast bronze" (cf. LXX Gk. *steréōma*, suggesting an embossed or hammered-out bowl).

The firmament (Heb. *rāqîaʿ*; Lat. *firmamentum*) serves to separate the waters above from the waters below (Gen. 1:6-8), its primary function being to prevent the waters above from crashing down upon the earth below and flooding the world. However, small holes in the firmament permitted the occasional release of water in the form of rain (Gen. 7:11; Ps. 78:23-24). The moon, sun, and stars were placed along this fixed arch in the heavens (Gen. 1:14-18). In Ezekiel's chariot vision the firmament appears as an expanse over the heads of the creatures which looked like sparkling ice; above the firmament is a throne of sapphire (Ezek. 1:22-26).

W. Dennis Tucker, Jr.

FIRSTBORN

The first male offspring of both animals (also called "firstlings") and humans. They were regarded as belonging to God (Exod. 22:29-30[MT 28-29]); this was a reflection of the Passover when the firstborn males of Israel were spared during the final plague against Egypt (13:2, 14-15). In later times, the Levites were set aside for the service of the sanctuary in place of all firstborn Israelites (Num. 3:12-13). Israel was regarded as the firstborn of God among the nations (Exod. 4:22; cf. Jer. 31:9[8]).

Neither firstborn humans nor animals were to be released for secular purposes without redemption. There was to be a substitution (Exod. 13:12-13; 34:20; Lev. 27:26ff.; Num. 18:15). Firstborn impure and blemished animals were to be redeemed (by paying the assessed value of the animal plus one fifth; Lev. 27:26-27 [cf. vv. 9-13]; Exod. 34:20). Firstborn sacrificial animals were to be sanctified as either a burnt offering or a peace offering (Num. 18:17; Deut. 15:20). There is little solid evidence of the regular sacrifice of firstborn humans, in either the ancient Near East or the Bible; the incident of 2 Kgs. 3:27, where the king of Moab sacrificed his firstborn, is exceptional.

The firstborn of humans were assigned a double portion of the inheritance from the father (Deut. 21:15-17). A father could not disregard birth order in assigning the firstborn's portion of his possessions. Though the firstborn could lose his birthright either by the act of God (1 Chr. 28:4; 1 Kgs. 2:15) or by selling it (Gen. 25:31-34), the firstborn never lost the title.

The firstborn is presented first in genealogies (e.g., 1 Chr. 6:16-30[1-14]). The family line is maintained through the firstborn, even if other sons are named (1 Chr. 7:1-4). The firstborn is the base of reference for the rest of the family (cf. Gen. 36:22), indicating his status. The right of the firstborn was never extended to firstborn daughters.

In the NT Jesus is presented as the firstborn (Gk. *prōtótokos*) of Mary (Matt. 1:25; Luke 2:7) and of God (Heb. 1:6). Elsewhere he is regarded as the "firstborn of all creation" (Col. 1:15), i.e., a mediator of creation (cf. vv. 16-17), and as the "firstborn from the dead" (v. 18; Rev. 1:5), indicating his primacy in the order of resurrection. Jesus is the "firstborn of many brethren" (i.e., those who would be conformed to his image; Rom. 8:29-30). The term occurs once with regard to the "destroyer of the firstborn" in Egypt (Heb. 11:28; cf. Exod. 11:5ff.). Finally, the Church is seen as an assembly of "firstborn" people who are enrolled in heaven (Heb. 12:23).

Michael D. Hildenbrand

FIRSTFRUITS

The first of the seasonal produce from the soil (Heb. *bikkûrîm*, "first ripe"; *rēʾšîṯ*, "first processed"). It was considered to be intrinsically holy, the possession of God. In acknowledgement that Yahweh owns the land as well as the crops produced on it, and also that he brought Israel into the land, the first part of the crop was to be transferred to God before the rest could be consumed. Without that transfer, there could be no blessing on the rest of the crop (Lev. 19:23-25; 23:14; Deut. 26:1-15; Prov. 3:9-10). This transfer of the firstfruits to God was required not only from the first ripe of the crop, but also from the first processed of some products: grain, new wine, new olive oil, first syrup, leavened food, bread dough, and even wool (Lev. 2:12; Num. 15:20-21; 18:12; Deut. 18:4).

The very first sheaf of grain harvested (probably barley, since it ripened first) was to be transferred to God by the elevation ceremony ("wave" in many translations; NRSV "raise") before the Lord (Lev. 23:10ff.) preceding the consumption of any of the new harvest, along with other sacrifices. This public act proclaimed that the harvest belonged to the Lord. Seven weeks later a sacred occasion was to be proclaimed during which no laborious work could be performed.

In Greek literature up to the 1st century, Gk. *aparchḗ* is used as a term for "firstfruits" sacrificed to the gods in nonbiblical literature and to the Lord in the LXX. In the NT Paul uses this concept of firstfruits, especially relating to the OT, as a metaphor for Jesus as the first one to rise from the dead, the first in a series of those who will rise from the dead in the future (1 Cor. 15:20, 23). He also uses it to describe the first converts to Christianity in certain geographical areas (1 Cor. 16:15; Rom. 16:5). In Rom. 8:23 Paul names the gift of the Spirit as firstfruits. In Rom. 11:16 he uses a double metaphor of the dough as firstfruits to the whole lump, and secondly a tree, naming roots and branches. Both stress that Israel is holy because of her holy origin, despite unholy appearances at this time. Similarly, James (Jas. 1:18) uses the term to address Christians as the "firstfruits of (God's) creatures." In Rev. 14:4 the 144 thousand are a "firstfruit" for Christians; they are undefiled, without deceit, and spotless.

Michael D. Hildenbrand

FISH

The Bible does not identify a single species of fish. Generic terms like Heb. *dāḡ* and *dāḡâ* refer to any water-dwelling creature. Similarly, the Greek terms (*ichthýs*, the most common; *opsárion*, used only in

John's Gospel; *prosphágion,* only in John 21:5) are all general terms. This would suggest that fish played no essential part in the life of the majority of Israelites.

Unlike its Mesopotamian and Egyptian neighbors, Israel was neither a river culture nor a seagoing people. Fishing was centered around the lakes (Huleh and the Galilee) and the Jordan River. The Galilee features 19 native species. Three main kinds of fish are found in the Galilee: *Cichildae* (the famous St. Peter's fish named Tilapia); *Cyprinidae* (carplike fish of various sizes); *Siluridae* (catfish). The Dead Sea sustains no fish life, and all other Israelite water sources were insignificant for fishing. Further, the coastal Mediterranean shores were not very productive for fishing. Fish were, however, imported by Tyrian merchants (Neh. 13:16) and sold just inside the Fish Gate located on the northwestern corner of Jerusalem (Zeph. 1:10; Neh. 3:3). Obviously, imported fish must have been smoked, salted, or sun-dried for transport.

Most of the biblical terms for fishing implements are related to hunting, suggesting that fishing was not a common practice beyond the Sea of Galilee and the Jordan River. Nets and spears were the primary tools for fishing as the rod was apparently unknown. By NT times, fishing assumed a greater importance in the text. Seven of the disciples were fishermen by trade and much of the biblical record was centered in the Galilee region.

While fish were not a part of the everyday diet in Israel as they were in Egypt (Num. 11:5), they were nonetheless addressed in Israel's dietary laws. It was necessary for all fishlike creatures to possess "fins and scales" (Lev. 11:9-12; Deut. 14:9-10) in order to be "clean" or acceptable for eating; this would rule out all shellfish, sea mammals, sharks, eels, and catfish. It was also forbidden to make an image of fish (Deut. 4:18), probably in light of the goddess Atargatis, a Syrian fish deity whose temple is mentioned in 2 Macc. 12:26.

In the end days, fish would play a part in God's blessing on Israel (Ezek. 47:9). The prophet predicted that a stream would flow from the throne in Jerusalem and would purify the Dead Sea so that fish would teem there. Jesus likened the coming kingdom of heaven to fishing with a net and catching good and bad fish which symbolize the righteous and the wicked (Matt. 13:47-50).

Fish were especially important in the life and ministry of Christ. He fed bread and fish to the 5000 (Matt. 14:13-21) and later another 4000 (15:32-39). The resurrected Christ ate broiled fish with his astounded disciples (Luke 24:42). He chose to communicate his time in the grave through the experience of Jonah (Jon. 1:17[MT 2:1]), whose "great fish" was then likened to an apocalyptic sea monster (Matt. 12:40). The most famous fish story, however, is actually a postbiblical one founded on the use of the Greek word for fish as an acronym for the ancient creed "Jesus Christ, God's Son, Savior." The first letter of each of these creedal names reproduces the Greek word for fish, *ichthýs.*

DONALD FOWLER

FISHING

Fishing took place in fresh water, occasionally in the Jordan River and its tributaries, more often in Lake Huleh, but especially in the Sea of Galilee (Matt. 4:18; Mark 1:16). Fish was an inexpensive source of high quality protein and commonly served with bread (e.g., Matt. 14:17 par.; John 21:9-13; cf. Matt. 7:9-10). The Hebrews pined for the fish of the Nile (Num. 11:5). The Red Sea and the Mediterranean provided ample marine varieties of fish. Tyrians sold fish in Jerusalem which were probably salted or smoked marine fish from the Mediterranean (Neh. 13:16). Jerusalem probably had a fish market located near the Fish Gate (2 Chr. 33:14; Neh. 3:3; Zeph. 1:10), the exact location of which is unknown but thought to be one of the main entrances to the city located near the Damascus Gate. It is also possible that fish were raised in natural and constructed ponds, for which there is evidence in Egyptian and Assyrian art. The Romans widely used this method, and elaborate fish ponds were located in Rome during the time of Nero and Trajan.

Fish were normally obtained by three methods: nets, hook and line, and spears. Nets were of three varieties: a cast net, a gill net, and a drag net. The cast net (Gk. *amphíblēstron*) was a small, circular, hand-held net tossed from a boat or in shallow water (Matt. 4:18). The gill net, or trammel net *(díktyon),* was a long net with floats that would be suspended and left in the water for an extended period of time, usually overnight. Fish of the appropriate size were trapped in the net as they attempted to swim through it (Matt. 4:20-21). The seine net, or drag net *(sagḗnē),* was a long net attached to boats, pulled into a semi-circle, and hauled to the shore capturing many different sizes of fish (Matt. 13:47-48). Much labor was required to construct, clean (Luke 5:2), repair, and dry these nets (Ezek. 47:10). Fish were caught on hooks attached to lines (Job 41:1-2[MT 40:25-26]; Isa. 19:8). These lines would have been held in the hand because fishing poles or rods are never mentioned. Hooks might have been baited or used to snag fish (Matt. 17:27). Fish were also caught with spears either in shallow water or from boats (Job 41:7, 26[40:31; 41:18]).

John, James, Peter, and Andrew were all fishermen, but Jesus commissioned them to become "fishers of men" (Matt. 4:19; Mark 1:17). Fishing was a difficult work, and those who engaged in it were considered uncultured. The occupation of fisherman was one of the "most shameful occupations" according to Cicero (cf. Acts 2:7).

Bibliography. P. F. Anson, *Christ and the Sailor: A Study of the Maritime Incidents in the New Testament* (Fresno, 1954); F. S. Bodenheimer, *Animal and Man in Bible Lands* (Leiden, 1960); O. Borowski, *Every Living Thing: Daily Use of Animals in Ancient Israel* (Walnut Creek, Calif., 1998); J. D. Wineland, "Hunting and Fishing," in *By the Sweat of Thy Brow,* ed. G. L. Mattingly (Sheffield, forthcoming). JOHN D. WINELAND

FLAX, LINEN

A winter annual plant with slender long stems (*Linum usitatissimum* L.). The stem of the flax plant produces fibers for weaving into linen fabrics, while its seeds produce oil that can be used for eating and for lamp oil. However, the best fibers for spinning into linen are those that are harvested before the plant produces seed heads. The plants are harvested by pulling the plants up by their roots. After drying, a process known as retting detaches the fibers from the pectinous substances which surround them, by rotting the plant material away from the flax fibers. This can be done slowly with dew, as when Rahab laid out bundles of flax upon her roof (Josh. 2:6), or more quickly by placing the flax into ponds or streams. When the plant material has disintegrated, the flax is beaten (scrutched) and combed (hackled or heckled) to remove unwanted stem pieces and to produce the long, wavy hanks or stricks of linen fiber. Then the fibers are spun into thread. In biblical times this was done with a drop-weighted spindle.

The linen fabrics are strong and smooth. They bleach easily, but are hard to dye; hence linen is usually white or cream colored. Linen is cool to wear in hot climates, and was the primary fiber used in ancient Egypt. Along with wool, linen was the primary fabric mentioned in the Bible; however, Deut. 22:11 forbids the wearing of clothing made from the two fibers woven together (cf. Lev. 19:19). Linen was the fabric specified for the curtains, screens, and hangings of the tabernacle (Exod. 26:1, 36; 27:9) and also was used for the breastpiece, ephod, robe, tunic, turban, and sash worn by the high priest (28:4-5). The capable wife makes, wears, and sells linen garments (Prov. 31:13, 22, 24). All four Gospels describe the body of Jesus wrapped in linen cloths for burial (Matt. 27:59; Mark 15:46; Luke 23:53; John 19:40).

Bibliography. L. Barber, *Prehistoric Textiles: The Development of Cloth in the Neolithic and Bronze Ages* (Princeton, 1991), 9-15.

MARY PETRINA BOYD

FLEA

A wingless, parasitic insect of the order Siphonaptera, whose mouth is particularly adapted for piercing the skin and sucking blood. Fleas (Heb. *par'ōš*) deposit their eggs in the hair of the host animal, and the larvae thrive in dry, sandy soil such as that of Palestine. After sparing Saul's life, the rebel David deprecates himself as a minute flea on the carcass of a dead dog (1 Sam. 24:14).

FLESH

In the OT, primarily the muscular part of the body (Gen. 2:23). "Flesh" (Heb. *bāśār*) is used with reference to both humans and animals (Gen. 6:17), and to both the living and the dead (1 Sam. 17:44). The flesh of animals may be used for sacrifice and for food (1 Sam. 2:13).

In the NT flesh (Gk. *sárx*) is quite different from the body (*sṓma*), and refers to mankind's human nature. At times it does refer to the human body (Gal. 2:20), but at other times it means mankind as a whole (Matt. 24:22). Sometimes it is even used to emphasize the essential nature of humankind as soul, body, and spirit (1 John 4:2). Flesh may suggest the total experience of life, as a psychophysical being (2 Cor. 7:5). Flesh is also used to describe the commitment of a couple for each other in marriage (Matt. 19:5).

Likewise, flesh refers to the weaker aspects of the nature of humankind that are subject to temptation (Matt. 26:41; 2 Pet. 2:18). If a person does not resist temptation, then the desire to sin will increase (1 John 2:16) and the result will be spiritual bondage (Rom. 6:19). When this happens, the individual will be enslaved to the desires of the flesh (Eph. 2:3) and will have the mind-set of the flesh (Rom. 8:5-7). The consequence will be corruption (Gal. 6:8) and the inability to discern God's revelation of himself (Matt. 16:17).

Flesh, however, is not naturally sinful. Christ came in the flesh (John 1:14) and was without sin (Heb. 4:15) so that he could redeem those who are in the flesh (Gal. 2:20). Those who accept Christ as Savior remain physically in the flesh but do not live according to the sinful flesh (Rom. 8:9). They are led by the Spirit to put to death the deeds of the flesh, but not the flesh itself (Rom. 8:13).

DONALD R. POTTS

FLINT

A variety of chert; a cryptocrystalline substance consisting of chalcedony, opaline silica, or quartz. It is microscopically fine grained, very hard, and found in a variety of colors such as white, yellow, gray, and black. The mineral breaks with conchoidal fractures and can be formed into sharp cutting edges. It is usually found in association with limestone with an organic origin or as a precipitate. Flint is used for making implements of work and war (Exod. 4:25; Josh. 5:23). Domestically, it is calcined and ground down to make earthenware and porcelain in pottery as well as clay for the refractory industries. The term is used many times in a social sense in the OT. The knowledge that flint was hard gave rise to several comparisons: the impossible task of getting water or oil out of flint (Deut. 8:15; Ps. 114:8), or a facial expression like flint (Isa. 50:7), or an impenetrable obstacle.

RICHARD A. STEPHENSON

FLOCK, TOWER OF THE

See EDER (PLACE) 2.

FLOOD (Heb. *mabbûl;* Gk. *kataklysmós*)

The event narrated in Gen. 6:5–9:19, in which God destroys creation, but saves Noah and his family along with animals of every species to populate a new creation.

Terminology

Except for Ps. 29:10, Heb. *mabbûl* occurs only in Genesis, related to the Flood. In Ps. 29:10 *mabbûl* may be water above the firmament, stored in jars (cf. Gen. 1:7; 7:11). In the Hebrew of Sirach (Sir. 44:17) and the Aramaic Genesis Apocryphon (1QapGen ar 12:10) *mabbûl* refers to the Genesis Flood. The LXX always reads Gk. *kataklysmós* for *mabbûl.* In Sir. 40:10; 44:17-18; 4 Macc. 15:31 *kataklysmós* refers to the Genesis Flood. But in the LXX of Ps. 32(31):6; Nah. 1:8; Sir. 21:13; 4 Macc. 15:32 the term is generic. All four NT uses of *kataklysmós* (Matt. 24:38-39; Luke 17:27; 2 Pet. 2:5) refer to the Genesis Flood.

Biblical Narrative

When the Lord observes pervasive human wickedness, he regrets having made humanity and decides to destroy all living things. Noah, however, finds favor with the Lord. Noah is righteous, blameless, and walks with God, but the earth had become ruined, filled with lawlessness. God tells Noah of his decision to bring the Flood. God instructs Noah to build an ark and promises a covenant that, in the ark, Noah and his family will survive, along with two of every animal. Noah does as God commands (Gen. 6:5-22).

Then the Lord tells Noah to enter the ark, bringing his family and the animals, including seven pairs of clean animals. After seven days will come 40 days of rain that will destroy everything on earth. Again, Noah does as the Lord commands. They enter the ark and the Lord shuts them in. The rising water lifts the ark and covers the mountains. Every creature dies, leaving only those with Noah in the ark. The waters swell for 150 days (Gen. 7:1-24).

God remembers Noah and sends a wind. The waters begin to subside. After 150 days the ark rests among the mountains of Ararat, and mountains reappear. Noah releases a raven and a dove. The raven soars, but the dove, unable to rest, returns. After two more tries the dove does not return. At God's command, Noah, his family, and the animals leave the ark (Gen. 8:1-19).

Noah builds an altar and sacrifices some clean animals. When the Lord smells the pleasing odor, he decides never again to curse the ground or to destroy all creation, even though humanity remains inclined toward evil (Gen. 8:20-22).

God blesses Noah and his sons, and announces a new order for creation. Humans can now use animals for food, a mitigation of previous curses. God, however, demands from humans an accounting for all life. As God used Noah to preserve human and animal life for a new creation, God now uses Noah and his descendants to protect and preserve life in the new creation. Hereafter humans are responsible for limiting and punishing lawlessness and bloodshed. God then resumes the blessing formula with which he began (Gen. 9:1-7).

God then encodes his decision never again to destroy creation in a covenant with Noah and future generations, with animals, and with the earth itself. God designates the rainbow as a reminder of his eternal covenant with creation (Gen. 9:8-19).

Literary Character

Understanding the Flood story requires appreciation of the account's composite nature and its structural unity. Scholars recognize two sources within the narrative, designated Yahwist (J) and Priestly (P). Many narrative aspects are repeated with differing details. Segments attributed to J have *YHWH* ("Lord" or "Yahweh") as the divine name and anthropomorphic depictions of God. Other segments, attributed to P, have *'ĕlōhîm* ("God") for the deity and exhibit concern for precise dates. Differences include the numbers of animals (two of each in P [Gen. 6:19-20; 7:15-16], and seven pairs of clean animals and one pair of others in J [7:2-3]), the cause of the destruction (rainfall in J [7:12]; the fountains of the deep burst and the floodgates open in P [7:11]), and the length of the Flood (40 days in J [7:4, 12], over a year in P [7:11, 24; 8:3, 5, 13-14]). Scholars also recognize the unity and skillful structure of the narrative. This structure is maintained in an extended palistrophe, a literary feature in which details at the story's beginning mirror details at the end and details in the first half have corresponding details in the second half. For example, the narrative opens and closes with the names of Noah's three sons (Gen. 6:10; 9:18-19); God's covenant to preserve Noah, his family, and some animals, and God's covenant never again to destroy all life (6:18-20; 9:8-17); the mountains are covered and the mountains reappear (7:20; 8:4-5); and the waters swell for 150 days, then recede for 150 days (7:21-24; 8:3). The center, structurally and theologically, is when God remembers Noah (Gen. 8:1).

Significance

God is the story's protagonist. Noah never speaks. At the beginning, God's heart grieves because the human heart's inclination toward evil has spoiled what was a "very good" creation (Gen. 1:31). God proceeds to destroy creation, but saves righteous Noah, his family, and some animals for a renewed creation. At the end, human hearts are still inclined toward evil, but the Lord's heart decides never again to curse the ground, or destroy creation. The age prior to Noah was characterized by pervasive sin. God responded with curses upon the ground (Gen. 3:17; 4:11) and the destructive Flood. In the renewed creation, God elects a new response, characterized by blessing and covenant. God assigns to humans accountability for all life, animal and human. As images of God with God's authority, Noah and his descendants are to preserve life, keeping bloodshed and vengeance in check, so that lawlessness will never again spoil creation. This new order begins to be played out in the following story, where Noah at last speaks. Noah, not God, curses Ham and Ham's descendant Canaan for their sin. Noah blesses Shem and Japheth for their righteous behavior (Gen. 9:20-27).

Other Flood Traditions

While flood traditions exist among many civilizations, three from ancient Mesopotamia are of special interest. Components in Atraḫasis, Gilgamesh Tablet XI, and Ziusudra have parallels in the biblical accounts (*ANET,* 42-44, 93-97, 104-6). However, the similarities do not suggest direct literary dependence. The manifold differences, especially in depictions of deities and their motives and in interpretations of events, are especially significant.

Scientific Issues

Scientific evidence does not support a universal flood corresponding to the biblical account. Marine fossils commonly found in mountainous areas resulted from geological uplifts. Some claim that wood recovered on modern Mt. Ararat in Turkey is from the ark. But carbon 14 studies date the wood as only 1600 years old. Nevertheless, the absence of scientific or historical evidence, measured by modern human standards, does not detract from the biblical story's abiding theological significance as a compelling story about God and God's relationship with humanity.

Bibliography. W. Brueggemann, *Genesis*. Interpretation (Atlanta, 1982); A. Dundes, ed., *The Flood Myth* (Berkeley, 1988); G. J. Wenham, *Genesis 1–15*. WBC 1 (Waco, 1987); C. Westermann, *Genesis 1–11* (Minneapolis, 1984).

JOSEPH E. JENSEN

FLOUR

Grain was ground between stones (Num. 11:8; cf. Matt. 24:41), producing coarsely-ground meal and the more finely ground flour. The best flour required thorough cleaning and repeated grinding and sifting. Heb. *qemaḥ* designates flour or meal made from wheat or barley, and *sōleṯ* refers to very fine flour of wheat. In the NT Gk. *áleuron* designates regular flour (Matt. 13:33) and *semídalis* fine wheat flour (Rev. 18:13). Both flour and meal were stored in jars (1 Kgs. 17:12).

Flour and meal were basic staples for most meals. They could be prepared for consumption by adding water and cooked to make gruel, cake, or bread. Flour was also used as an ingredient in cakes offered to the deity as cereal offerings, made from choice wheat flour which was unleavened and mixed with oil (Lev. 2:1-7, 11).

STEPHEN ALAN REED

FLUTE

A wind instrument, actually a shawm or primitive clarinet, made of a hollow reed or wood with fingerholes to produce notes. Held vertically, the flute had a double-reed mouthpiece; a variant form was the double flute (cf. Akk. *ḫalḫallatu*), the two pipes of which could be played individually or simultaneously.

The flute was played for reveling (Job 21:12; Isa. 5:12), for ceremonial purposes such as coronations (1 Kgs. 1:40) and funerals (Matt. 9:23), and for worship (Dan. 3:5, 7, 10, 15). In several contexts, the flute is connected to the praise of God (Ps. 150:4), to the joy of the Lord (87:7; Isa. 30:29), and to the act of prophesying (1 Sam. 10:5). The sound of the flute is compared to the voice of someone weeping (Job 30:31; cf. Jer. 48:36). We may infer that flute playing was common in the Roman Empire since it is listed as one of the typical sounds that would not be heard in the apocalyptic city of Babylon (Rev. 18:22). Paul refers to the flute as an illustration of the importance of making a clear and distinct sound (1 Cor. 14:7).

TIMOTHY W. SEID/JOACHIM BRAUN

FLY

Any of various winged insects of the order Diptera. Heb. *zeḇûḇ* (Isa. 7:18; NJB "mosquito"), generally interpreted as the common housefly (*Musca domestica*), may actually refer to the larger and more annoying horsefly (*Tabunus arenivagus*).

Symbolically, the fly's filthy habits are suggested in Eccl. 10:1, which observes that even a single fly can foul a perfumer's ointment. In many parts of the world, infectious matter transported on the leg hairs of the fly still cause decay and spread disease.

Heb. *'ārôḇ*, a collective noun meaning "swarm," denotes the insects visited upon the Egyptians in the fourth plague as described in Exod. 8:20-32(16-26; JB "gadflies," NJB "horseflies," NJPSV "insects"; cf. Ps. 78:45; 105:31). This may have been the Tabanid fly *(Stomoxys calcitrans)*, whose larvae develop in cow manure and which, when mature, lives off blood by biting the arms and legs of people and animals. In rabbinical literature the word is understood to mean a mixture of wild beasts.

See BAAL-ZEBUB. JESPER SVARTVIK

FOOD

References to "food" and related themes appear in every book in the Bible, starting with Gen. 1 and ending in Rev. 22. Indeed, some of the best-known stories are those dealing with food and food getting. OT examples include Eve's temptation of Adam; Joseph saving the people of Egypt and his own family from famine; the children of Israel eating manna in the desert; Ruth gleaning wheat in Boaz' fields; David, the brave little shepherd boy; Elisha who kept the widow's oil flowing; the young Hebrew boys who would not eat the king's unclean food.

NT examples are numerous as well. They include stories about Jesus turning water into wine; helping the disciples to catch fish; feeding the 5000 with five loaves and two small fishes; his last supper. Jesus also told parables which often dealt with food-related themes, e.g., the parable of the sower; the weeds; the mustard seed and the yeast; the lost sheep; the workers in the vineyard; and the wedding banquet. To these examples many others can be added from the book of Acts and the letters of Paul, Peter, and John.

There are several reasons for the importance of food in the Bible. In antiquity most people were food producers — farmers, shepherds, and fishermen. In other words, the daily lives of almost every man, woman, and child were caught up in such activities as caring for barnyard and pasture animals, clearing and plowing, planting and tending crops, harvesting and processing crops, transporting and storing foodstuffs, preparing and consuming food, and concern about having enough left over to survive until the next harvest.

Food is also a central theme throughout the Bible because of the web of interactions it evokes — interactions between people and the land, between people as social actors, and between people and the Divine. In other words, how food was produced, distributed, prepared, and eaten had consequences which went far beyond the supply of nourishment to people's bodies. Food served in Bible times, as today, is a powerful instrument for communicating social meaning — for expressing hospitality (Abraham and his angelic visitors); commemorating evidences of Divine intervention in human affairs (the annual festivals), and sealing compacts between peoples and individuals (the Last Supper).

By far the most important ingredients in people's diets were wheat (*Triticum durum, Triticum vulgare, Triticum spelta*) and barley (*Hordeum vulgare*). In Egypt, where rainfall is practically nonexistent, wheat was grown along the banks of the Nile by means of floodwater irrigation. A similar system was used by the ancient Mesopotamians who produced their wheat in fields irrigated by an extensive network of canals linked to the Euphrates River.

In the southern Levant landscape and climatic conditions are quite different; hence different methods were used to grow grain. In this landscape of coastal plains, inland hills and valleys, mountains, and deserts — where summers are hot and dry and winters are mild and wet — a wide range of strategies was relied upon to produce cereals. Along the coastal plains and in the Jordan Valley waters from springs, rivers, and streams were diverted into aqueducts and channels to supply water to irrigated cereal fields. Along the slopes of the highland areas villagers maintained wadi diversion dams and hillside terraces to preserve moisture and retain soil for their grain crops. Others relied on transhumance — movement of people and pasture animals, especially sheep and goats — between winter grain growing areas and summer pasture lands. Still others — namely the desert Bedouin — grew little or no wheat themselves, but relied on various partnership arrangements with villagers for their wheat supply.

While wheat and barley were core to the diets of all these different groups throughout all of biblical times, other cereals (millet, rice), legumes (lentils, beans, chick peas, vetch), vegetables (onions, garlic, cucumbers), fruits (olives, grapes, pomegranates, melons, figs, dates, apples), poultry (doves, chickens), meat (sheep, goat, cattle, swine), milk, wild roots, fish, and game were also consumed, but by no means to the same degree in all times and places. What determined which and how much of these other items were included in the diet were where and when people lived, their mode of livelihood (village farming, transhumance, pastoralism), their economic situation (rich or poor), access to markets, and religious beliefs.

Given these contingencies, it follows that the meals most commonly eaten by the patriarchs, whom the Bible indicates were transhumants, differed somewhat from those of their descendants who settled permanently in villages in the highlands of Canaan. While wheat and barley were predominant in both diets, meat from male herd animals and cheese, curds, and milk produced by female animals made up the bulk of the remaining ingredients (Gen. 18:6-8). It should be noted, however, that the meat of slaughtered herd animals was not eaten every day, but rather on special occasions. Wild game, honey, dates, and spices obtained through hunting and gathering were also important to the patriarchal diet (Gen. 27:3-4).

By contrast, the diets consumed by village households in Canaan were much more varied in terms of items produced locally. For example, a typical village community would grow wheat and barley in the flatter areas, and graze sheep and goats on the stubble; it would grow olives, grapes, and other fruit trees on the lower hills, with patches of irrigated vegetables and spices around the village (Isa. 5:1-3). This traditional pattern assured that the typical village diet in Canaan included not only grains and animal by-products, but also vegetables, fruits, and nuts.

The foods consumed by the elites of larger towns and cities such as Jerusalem and Caesarea were even more varied due to the wide range of foodstuffs imported from distant places and the greater wealth with which to buy exotic foods. A rich person's diet might therefore include exotic meats and fish, vegetables, fruits, and spices imported from as far away as Southeast Asia, North Africa, or Europe. There were also many landless poor people living in and around these cities, many of whom subsisted by begging and scavenging.

Given the geographical diversity of the land of Canaan, and given the changes over time in political conditions of the region throughout biblical times, the economic conditions of various indigenous groups, including the different Israelite tribes, varied considerably over time and space. Therefore, so did their diets. Thus the foods eaten by the Benjaminites around Jerusalem at the time of David and Solomon, e.g., were not exactly the same as those eaten by the Reubenites in Transjordan. Furthermore, a millennium later, in the time of Christ, many new food items were available due to vastly increased intercontinental trade, so that diets, especially in urban areas, included items which were unheard of a thousand years earlier (e.g., garum and chicken).

Despite such regional and temporal discontinuities, cultic rules of purity served to set the Israelite diet apart wherever Jews lived. In addition to restricting animal matter to that from mammals which part the hoof and chew the cud (Lev. 11:1-8; Deut. 14:6-8) and various "clean" birds, fish, and insects (Lev. 11:9-47; Deut. 14:9-21), the regulations prohibited any food which had been contaminated by contact (through cooking or otherwise) with water defiled by an unclean carcass (Lev. 11:32-38); other legislation governed modes of preparation and combinations of foodstuffs (e.g., Exod. 23:19 par.).

ØYSTEIN S. LABIANCA

FOOL

In the Bible, foolishness is most often an ethical concept and goes beyond a lack of native intelligence. Contrasted with the wise (Prov. 1:7; 15:5), the fool first is a person who acts without counsel (12:15) and is indiscreet (v. 23; 13:16), hot-tempered (14:29; 17:12), ignorant (Eccl. 2:14), indolent (4:5), and thickheaded (2:12). He is easily led astray (Prov. 1:22), rehearsing his folly like a dog that returns to its vomit (26:11). Ruin is his end (Prov. 10:8). If he is capable of learning (Prov. 18:2; 23:9), it comes only through brutish discipline (10:13; 19:29).

The fool is the deliberate sinner who persists in evil (Eccl. 5:1[MT 4:17]), lying, slandering, and enjoying mischief like sport (Prov. 10:18, 23). Refusing to obey God (1 Sam. 13:13; cf. MT Deut. 22:21; 2 Sam. 13:11-14), a fool confides in others (2 Chr. 16:9). The fool thus "practices ungodliness" and does injustice (Isa. 32:6). Such is the example of Nabal, whose name means "fool" (1 Sam. 25:25). Elsewhere, the fool is the atheist, one who openly declares, "There is no God" (Ps 14:1; 53:1[2]).

In the NT the fool is described as witless (Luke 11:40; 1 Cor. 15:36) and dull (Matt. 23:17), one who opposes truth (2 Tim. 3:8-9) and fails to make adequate provisions (Matt. 25:1-13). Jesus contrasts the wise, who obey his teachings, with the fool who refuses (Matt. 7:24-27). When condemning intent as well as action, Jesus also denounces the use of the word "fool" as an invective (Matt. 5:22).

KENNETH D. MULZAC

FOOTWASHING

In the ancient Near East, where roads were dusty and sandals were the common footwear, making provision for guests or travelers to wash their feet was an act of common hospitality (Gen. 18:4; 19:2; 24:32; Luke 7:36-50; cf. John 12:1-8). The washing of feet also became part of the purification rituals required of priests prior to entering the sanctuary or approaching the altar (Exod. 30:19-21; 40:31).

Jesus performed the menial task of washing his disciples' feet while they were at table during the Last Supper. He commended his action as an example of the type of service the disciples should provide to each other (John 13:1-20). Some commentators view Jesus' act as a symbolic representation of the cleansing effect his death would have for humans defiled by sin. The ritual of washing "the feet of saints" is listed as one of the requisite "good deeds" of women who qualify for the order of "widows" (1 Tim. 5:9-10). The rite of footwashing is still practiced on Maundy Thursday in many churches.

Bibliography. J. D. G. Dunn, "The Washing of the Disciples' Feet in John 13," *ZNW* 61 (1970): 247-52; H. Weiss, "Foot Washing in the Johannine Community," *NovT* 21 (1979): 298-325.

JEFFREY T. TUCKER

FORCED LABOR

A type of slave labor program, commonly referred to as corvée or conscripted labor. It was by means of forced labor that rulers of the ancient Near East carried out their building enterprises, building and rebuilding cities. Also, it was through the use of forced labor that kings maintained control of minority groups in their kingdoms.

By the use of forced labor the Egyptian king, at the time of the Exodus, built the cities of Pithom and Raamses (Exod. 1:8-14) and at the same time attempted to maintain control of the Hebrews, a minority group in his kingdom. David (2 Sam. 20:23) and Solomon (1 Kgs. 9:15-21) also used forced labor programs. But while Solomon built Hazor, Megiddo, and Gezer by means of forced labor, his excessive conscription of workers from among the northern tribes (1 Kgs. 5:13-14) resulted in revolt and the division of the kingdom (12:1-19).

Egyptian records refer to rulers like Thutmose III who made campaigns annually into Palestine and Syria as a means of systematically looting those areas and collecting the resources he needed back in Egypt, including the resources of slave labor. Egyptian tomb paintings, such as that of Rameses III bringing back shackled prisoners of war or slaves, provide their own unique record.

LAMOINE F. DEVRIES

FOREIGNER

In the OT words derived from the Hebrew roots *zwr* and *nkr* are often used to describe those who are "outsiders" from the speaker's point of view. The two roots are more or less synonymous and are often used in parallel phrases (e.g., Jer. 5:19b; Prov. 27:13; also Ps. 69:8[MT 9]; 81:9[10]; Isa. 61:5; Obad. 11). But in narrative and prophetic texts, *nēḵār, ben-nēḵār,* and *noḵrî* usually connote "non-Israelite" (e.g., 1 Kgs. 8:41; Ruth 2:10) while *zār* more properly means "that which does not belong" (in whatever category is being considered). In Priestly legislation *zār* is used to designate Israelites who are not members of the levitical or Aaronic families and are thus "foreigners" as far as the performance of priestly duties is concerned (Exod. 29:33; 30:33; Lev. 22:10, 13; Num. 1:51; 3:10, 38; 16:40[17:5]; 18:4, 7; NRSV "lay person, outsider"). More frequently, *zār* takes on negative connotations when used to mean "non-Yahwistic" (and thus by implication idolatrous) forms of "otherness" (cf. Hos. 5:7).

Unlike the "sojourner" or "resident alien" (*gēr*), who was subject to and protected by Israelite laws (Exod. 12:49), the foreigner was not allowed to participate in Passover celebrations (v. 43) and could not be chosen king (Deut. 17:15). The foreigner could be charged interest on loans (Deut. 23:20[21]), and debts owed by foreigners did not have to be forgiven in the seventh year (15:2-3).

Wisdom pupils are warned against associating with the Strange Woman *('iššâ zārâ)* or with the Foreigner *(noḵrîyâ)* who represents temptation personified, not because she is sexually promiscuous (as some translators misleadingly assume) but because she represents a departure from Wisdom's (and therefore the Lord's) ways (Prov. 2:16; 5:3, 20; 6:24; 7:5; 23:27).

NT texts tend to minimize ethnic distinctions according to the principles articulated in Eph. 2:11-19, and Christians are urged to show hospitality (the giving of food, shelter, and protection) to the stranger (Gk. *xénos*) in their midst (Matt. 25:35ff.; 3 John 5). However, those who are not related to the people of Israel by birth are still sometimes called "foreigners," as in Luke 17:18 *(allogenḗs);* Acts 17:21 *(xénos);* Heb. 11:34 *(allótrios).*

Bibliography. M. Guttmann, "The Term 'Foreigner' (נכרי) Historically Considered," *HUCA* 3 (1926): 1-20; L. A. Snijders, "zûr/zār," *TDOT* 4:52-58.

KATHLEEN A. FARMER

FOREST

Biblical references to the forests and wooded areas of Palestine indicate that those areas were much more extensive during OT times than the present. Several wooded areas are referred to by name. Lebanon undoubtedly contained the largest of the forests, which consisted not only of the famous cedars, but also of pine and myrtle. Only vestiges of Lebanon's once extensive woodlands remain today. Carmel also was heavily wooded in biblical times (Cant. 7:5). David hid in the forest of Hereth after leaving Moab (1 Sam. 22:5). Josephus mentions the growths of date palms of the Jordan Valley near Jericho. The biblical references to forest fires indicate the extensive tracts of forested lands (Isa. 10:17-18; Jer. 21:14; Amos 7:4). Evidence for the once abundant woodlands is provided also by the names of localities bearing the names of trees or forests (e.g., Kiriath-jearim, "city of forests"). These areas are now devoid of such vegetation.

Heb. *ḥōreš* indicates a thicket or wooded height (Ezek. 31:3; 2 Chr. 27:4; NRSV, NIV take the word as a proper name in 1 Sam. 23:15-19). Heb. *pardēs* denotes a wooded park or orchard, though extensive enough to supply timber (Cant. 4:13; Eccl. 2:5; Neh. 2:8). The most frequently used Hebrew word for thicket or forested area is *yaʿar.*

The different soils and climates of Palestine produced a wide variety of trees and shrubs. The greater rainfall of the western and northern slopes allowed thick vegetation in the vicinities of Carmel and Galilee. The primary trees were oaks, terebinth, cedars, and Aleppo pines. The area of lower Galilee produced deciduous oaks, while the Dead Sea region grew tamarisk trees, willows, poplar, and date palms. Wild beasts, including bear and Asiatic lions, inhabited the forested areas (2 Kgs. 2:24; Amos 3:4; Jer. 5:6; 12:8).

Although the indiscriminate felling of trees was prohibited (Deut. 20:19), the once large expanses of woodlands were greatly diminished by Roman times, except for areas where access was difficult. The cutting of the forested lands caused a decrease in soil fertility and an increase in erosion. Eventually sizable areas of desert developed from these areas. Today, except for efforts at conservation and reforestation of pines, the only remnants of the ancient forests are in Carmel, Lebanon, and Transjordan. Elsewhere, shrubs predominate.

Bibliography. D. Baly, *The Geography of the Bible,* rev. ed. (New York, 1974); M. Zohary, *Plants of the Bible* (Cambridge, 1982).

HAROLD R. MOSLEY

FORK

A three-pronged utensil (Heb. *mazlēg*) used by priests to remove their portions of sacrifices (1 Sam. 2:13-14). A similar instrument *(mizlāgâ)* made of gold or polished bronze (1 Chr. 28:17; 2 Chr. 4:16) was used in sacrifices on the altar in the tabernacle and temple (e.g., Exod. 27:3; 38:3; Num. 4:14). Older translations render the term "fleshhook."

A six-pronged pitchfork (*mizreh;* Gk. *ptýon*) was used to separate chaff from grain (e.g., Jer. 15:7; Matt. 3:12 = Luke 3:17).

FORMER PROPHETS

According to Hebrew tradition, those books attributed to the "early" prophets Joshua (book of Joshua), Samuel (Judges, 1-2 Samuel), and Jeremiah (1-2 Kings). In later (particularly Christian) tradition they are regarded as the "historical books."

FORNICATION

In general, illicit sexual intercourse (Heb. *zānâ*), a sin violating the spirit of the Seventh Commandment (Exod. 20:14), which was meant to protect the integrity of the family. Fornication (Gk. *porneía*) can be linked with adultery (Matt. 5:32; 19:9) or distinguished from it (15:19 = Mark 7:21). Committing fornication is noted and rebuked (1 Cor. 6:18; 10:8; Jude 7). Paul advised monogamous marriage "because of cases of sexual immorality" (1 Cor. 7:2). Metaphorically, fornication can describe the corruption of God's people with pagan idolatry (e.g., Jer. 2:20-36; Ezek. 16:15-43; Rev. 2:14, 20-22; 17:1-18; 18:2-9). Abstaining from fornication (unchastity) was one of the four conditions demanded of the Gentiles for their admission into the Church by the Jerusalem conference (Acts 15:20, 29).

ALLISON A. TRITES

FORTRESS, FORTIFICATION

Fortresses generally consisted of walls, towers, and gates. Fortifications were built around major cities and at strategic positions near borders and trade routes. A few cities also had an inner fortress for additional protection.

Walls built around a city provided primary defense. Walls were usually built of stone, although a few were made of mud brick. Walls could be either solid (Beer-sheba stratum V) or casemate (two parallel walls connected at intervals by transverse walls; Hazor stratum X). Some walls are straight (Ashdod stratum 10) while others are offset-and-inset (Megiddo stratum VA). Several casemate walls were filled with debris for added protection (Hazor stratum VIII). Smaller villages and some cities built homes abutted together and in a circular pattern facing upward. The back wall of the homes doubled as a defense wall (Beer-sheba stratum VII).

Towers were built into walls at intervals and at strategic positions such as at gate complexes. Towers, typically taller than the walls, usually jutted out beyond the city wall, giving defenders a clear view of the city wall's foundation and anyone attempting to breach the wall.

Cities in OT times usually had only one gate complex. This complex had massive towers on each side of the entrance, multiple chambers with doors

Reconstructed Iron Age walls of Tell en-Naṣbeh (Mizpah). Built by King Asa of Judah (913-873 B.C.E.), the defenses included the city wall, a sloping revetment, retaining wall, and moat
(Badè Institute of Biblical Archaeology, Pacific School of Religion)

separating each chamber, and multiple sets of gate doors. Hazor, Megiddo, Gezer, and a few more cities had six-chamber gate complexes with four sets of doors. A few gate complexes were built sideways, creating an L-shaped turn (e.g., Lachish, Tell en-Nasbeh, Beth-shan) in order to slow down traffic or an invading army entering the gate. NT cities usually had multiple entrances and city-gate complexes.

A city needed food and water to survive a siege. Cities often built storage facilities for food and supplies along with large cisterns for water. Pillared storage rooms were discovered at Megiddo, Hazor, Tell el-Ḥesi, Beer-sheba, and Tell Qasile. Several cities (Jerusalem, Hazor, Gezer, Beer-sheba, Gibeon, and Megiddo) had the means of getting water inside the city from a hidden water supply outside the city walls via a tunnel or shaft. David's general Joab climbed up a water shaft (Warren's shaft) to enter and defeat the Jebusite city of Jerusalem (2 Sam. 5:8). Hezekiah built a tunnel from a hidden spring to a pool inside Jerusalem (2 Kgs. 20:20).

Fortresses, separate from cities, were built at strategic locations. A line of fortresses dating to the Israelite Monarchy span the Negeb. These fortresses are usually small, containing walls, towers, gates, and living spaces. They served as the first line of defense from nomads and invaders from the south.

Rehoboam, preparing for Shishak's invasion, built fortified cities and filled them with weapons and supplies (2 Chr. 14:6-7[MT 5-6]). Hezekiah repaired the walls of Jerusalem and built towers on them (2 Chr. 32:5).

In poetic literature God is frequently referred to as a fortress (2 Sam. 22:2; Jer. 16:19; Nah. 1:7; Ps. 31:2-3[3-4]; 71:3; 91:2). TERRY W. EDDINGER

FORTUNATUS (Gk. *Phortounátos;* Lat. *Fortunatus*)
A Christian from Corinth; a messenger who, with Stephanas and Achaicus, came to Paul in Ephesus bringing news of the Corinthian congregation (1 Cor. 16:17).

FORUM OF APPIUS
A station on the Appian Way (Gk. *Appíou Phóron;* Lat. *Apii Forum*), 69 km. (43 mi.) SE of Rome at modern Faiti. Probably founded during the time of Appius Claudius Caecus, who constructed the highway in 312 B.C.E., it had become by the 1st century C.E. an important town (cf. Horace *Satires* 1.5.3-6 for a traveler's critique of its accommodations and "stingy tavern keepers"). From this point a canal paralleled the road through the Pontine marshes (a haven for malarial mosquitoes) ca. 30 km. (19 mi.) to Feronia. A number of Roman Christians traveled to the Forum of Appius to greet Paul following his arrival at Puteoli (Acts 28:15).

FOX
A carnivorous member of the dog family (Canidae), genus *Vulpes.* Heb. *šûʿāl* designates both the fox and the jackal (Ps. 63:10[MT 11]; Lam. 5:18). The red fox and its desert cousin, the fennec, are small, solitary, nocturnal, and intelligent creatures. Emerging from its den to hunt at night, the fox is omnivorous, eating small game, insects, and fruit (Cant. 2:15) and scavenging if necessary. It possesses a keen sense of sight, smell, and especially hearing. The fox is regarded as a pest in rabbinical literature since it took poultry or young livestock (*Bek.* 8a; *Mak.* 24b; *Ned.* 81b; *Ketub.* 111b; *Ḥul.* 53a; *Eccl. Rab.* 98a).

Jesus points out that, unlike himself, foxes (Gk.

alṓpēx) have homes (Matt. 8:20 = Luke 9:58), and he refers to Herod metaphorically as "that fox" (Luke 13:32). DONALD FOWLER

FRANKINCENSE

A botanical product derived from a member of the Burseraceae family. Mentioned in both the OT (Heb. *lĕḇōnâ*) and NT (Gk. *líbanos*) as a highly desired and esteemed product, its enduring fame rests with the Magi account in Matt. 2:11.

Although several species of *Boswellia* produce an oleo-gum resin, *Boswellia sacra* is the only species in southwest Arabia and northern Somalia which produces the distinct resin mentioned in biblical and other historical accounts. Recent investigations clearly suggest that the plant grows in a fairly restricted habitat. Apparently never domesticated, it prefers the arid backslopes of created rain shadows beyond the reach of the summer southwest monsoon, but as a succulent it stores water derived from airborne moisture. The resin is obtained by cutting and incising the trunk, usually once a year in the winter. The exuded sap, white in color (hence Sem. *lbn,* "milk"), is left to drop to the base of the tree where it hardens and crystalizes.

Chemical analysis of frankincense suggests that the plant has certain unique characteristics of composition which may extend to discerning medicinal properties. Chemical fingerprinting of living and archaeological specimens may some day permit the detection of geographically specific groves. Frankincense may already have been traded locally as early as the Neolithic period (6th-4th millennium B.C.) and may have been known to the Sumerians by the 3rd millennium and the Egyptians sometime later. Its fame, however, derives from the greatly increased demand for the product in the late Iron Age, stimulated in part by the Israelites, the Greeks, Romans, and Persians who used it for various purposes. While harvested in Oman, Yemen, as well as Somalia, the ancient South Arabian city-states (e.g., Shabwa and Marib) were the primary beneficiaries of this trade as intermediaries. Both maritime and overland trade emanating from the southern Arabian peninsula have been documented by archaeological and literary records beginning with Herodotus. According to Levantine, Greek, Indian, and Roman texts, a very substantial price was paid for the resin. It would appear that the frankincense brought by the Magi (probably two different mixes and not gold and frankincense) came from Dhofar, which was controlled directly by the Parthians, or via northern Oman as a province of the Parthian Empire. The precipitous decline and collapse of the incense market in the 5th century A.D. coincided with the prohibition by the Christian church of lavish funerary rites involving incense.

Bibliography. N. Groom, *Frankincense and Myrrh* (London, 1981); F. N. Hepper, "Trees and Shrubs Yielding Gums and Resins in the Ancient Near East," *Bulletin on Sumerian Agriculture* 3 (1987): 107-14; A. G. Miller and M. Morris, *Plants of Dhofar* (Muscat, 1988); M. Morris, "The Harvesting of Frankincense in Dhofar, Oman," in *Profumi d'Arabia,* ed. A. Avanzini (Rome, 1997), 231-47; W. Müller, "Notes on the Use of Frankincense in South Arabia," *Seminar for Arabian Studies* 6 (1976): 124-36; K. Nielsen, *Incense in Ancient Israel.* VTSup 38 (Leiden, 1986); G. Van Beek, "Frankincense and Myrrh," *BA* 23 (1960): 70-95; "Frankincense and Myrrh in Ancient South Arabia," *JAOS* 78 (1958): 141-52; J. Zarins, "Mesopotamia and Frankincense: The Early Evidence," in *Profumi d'Arabia,* ed. A. Avanzini, 251-72; "Persia and Dhofar: Aspects of Iron Age International Politics and Trade," in *Crossing Boundaries and Linking Horizons,* ed. G. D. Young, M. W. Chavalas, and R. E. Averbeck (Bethesda, 1997), 615-89. JURIS ZARINS

FREEDMEN, SYNAGOGUE OF THE

A synagogue made up of freedmen, Cyrenians, and Alexandrians, who were Stephen's opponents (Acts 6:9). These freedmen were probably Jewish captives who had been deported from Israel but had been released and granted their citizenship (cf. Acts 22:3, 27-28; Philo *Leg.* 155; Tacitus *Ann.* 2.85; Josephus *Ant.* 12.120; 14.185-267). It seems reasonable to surmise that they had returned to Jerusalem out of devotion to God in order to observe the law and the temple sacrifices.

Evidence has been found for a synagogue of Alexandrians (*t. Meg.* 3.6 [224]) and one that was built by a certain "Theodotus," which included a guest house for diaspora Jews visiting from abroad (*CIJ* 2:1404). Scholars remain divided over the number of synagogues indicated in Acts, positing one synagogue composed of several ethnic groups, two different groups of opponents, or several groups. It would seem that one motivation for the establishment of synagogues for diaspora Jews would be to provide worship for those who spoke Greek. H. ALAN BREHM

FREER LOGION

See CODEX WASHINGTONENSIS.

FRIEND

In biblical usage, a term covering a broad spectrum of relationships, from the intimate to the remote. The OT captures the sense of these relationships in the substantives drawn basically from the roots *'hb* and *r'h.* In the LXX and NT the usual word is Gk. *phílos,* and occasionally *hetaíros.* The Vulg. almost always translates Lat. *amicus.*

In the OT the terms express quite normal human relationships that are governed by the friendship conventions of the ancient Near East. They can simply connote the relationship of neighbors and acquaintances (Lev. 19:18; Jer. 6:21; Mic. 7:5), as well as closer ones that stress equality between friends (Deut. 13:6[MT 7]) and verge on the familial (Ps. 35:14; Prov. 18:24; 27:10). Legendary in this regard is the friendship between David and Jonathan (1 Sam. 18:1-3; 20:17; 2 Sam. 1:26). Friendship with God is also possible, as Moses is called a friend of God and speaks with God face to face, as friends speak (Exod. 33:11). Judg. 5:31 reflects the conventional wisdom that one should help one's friends and harm one's enemies. The Wisdom Literature gives special attention to the importance of loyal friendship (Sir. 6:14-16), advises on its value (Prov. 18:24; Eccl. 4:9-12; Sir. 6:1; 25:1), and warns of its fragility (Prov. 19:4; Sir. 6:8-13; 9:10; 13:21; 22:20; 37:1). Sir. 22:21-22 stresses the possibility of repair for damaged friendship.

The NT does not present a unified teaching on friends and friendship, but NT authors do show some interest in the topic. Although Paul does not use the word "friend," he shows familiarity with the conventions of friendship (Rom. 5:6-8; 13:8-10; 1 Cor. 1:10; Gal. 4:12-20; Phil. 2:2-4; 4:14-16) and even employs elements of the friendly letter in his correspondence (Phil. 1:3-4, 7-8, 27; 2:12). Matthew uses Gk. *phílos* only once (Matt. 11:19), and is the only NT author to use *hetaíros,* three times in the vocative (20:13; 22:12; 26:50). Luke uses *phílos* more than other NT authors (e.g., Luke 7:6, 34; 11:5-8; 12:4; 16:9; 23:12; Acts 10:24; 19:31). Luke is the only Gospel author to include the Parable of the Persistent Friend (Luke 11:5-8). The peculiarly Lucan Parable of the Prodigal Son (Luke 15:11-32) reflects aspects of the Greco-Roman *topos* on friendship, and even challenges the reciprocity ethic (6:34-35a; 14:12-14; Acts 20:35), which governed friendship in his day. In John's Gospel the term "friend" takes on a special meaning connoting close relationship to Jesus (John 3:29; 11:11; 15:14-15). The Gospel of John reflects the common friendship motifs of sharing (John 15:15) and loyalty to the point of death (10:11, 15, 17-18; 15:13; cf. 11:16; 1 John 3:16). In these ways, NT authors appropriate and adapt to their own needs the Hellenistic-Jewish and Greco-Roman friendship traditions of their day.

Bibliography. A. C. Mitchell, "'Greet the Friends by Name': New Testament Evidence for the Greco-Roman *Topos* on Friendship," in *Greco-Roman Perspectives on Friendship,* ed. J. T. Fitzgerald. SBLRBS 34 (Atlanta, 1997), 225-62.

ALAN C. MITCHELL

FRINGE

The hem or border of a garment (Heb. *ṣîṣiṯ*). The Israelites were to make for themselves a fringe for each corner of their garments (Num. 15:37-39). Attached to each fringe was to be a blue cord. This ornamentation was not meant to be ostentatious (cf. Matt. 23:5; Gk. *kráskpedon*); rather, it was to remind the wearer of the Lord's commands and the requisite demand for holiness. It is not known exactly what the fringe looked like, although the other biblical occurrence of the Hebrew term (for a lock of hair, Ezek. 8:3) is suggestive. The practice of wearing fringes on the outer garment is well-attested in the art of the ancient Near East. Other biblical passages attach significance to the hem of the garment (1 Sam. 24:4-20; Matt. 9:20 = Luke 8:44).

KEVIN D. HALL

FROG

A class of amphibians (generally of the family Ranidae) or watery creatures. Frogs (Heb. *ṣĕpardēaʿ;* Gk. *bátrachos*) lack fins and scales and thus are unclean for food (Lev. 11:9-12); they may also qualify as "swarming creatures," also unclean (Lev. 11:41).

All OT appearances relate to the 10 plagues. Frogs are the second plague after the Nile has been turned to blood (Exod. 8:2-14[MT 7:27–8:10]). They are the third plague in Ps. 78:45 — after the bloody Nile and flies — and 105:30 — after darkness and the bloody Nile. The Wisdom of Solomon also mentions this plague (Wis. 19:10). One explanation for the phenomenon is naturalistic: frogs were driven from the Nile earlier than usual in the year because receding waters left rotting, insect-ridden fish in ponds and pools next to the river. The insects carried diseases, which killed the frogs. Another explanation is literary: frogs are a fertility symbol, associated with the frog-headed goddess Heqt (Heket), consort of the god Khnum, who fashioned human beings from clay. That Heqt assisted women in childbirth has been linked with Pharaoh's command that midwives kill the Hebrew male children (Exod. 1:16); the plague would be a response to that command. In Rev. 15–16 the seven bowls of divine wrath are modeled on the plagues; from the sixth bowl (16:13) the angel unleashes a plague of frog-shaped unclean spirits.

VICTORIA ANDREWS

FRONTLET

A headband or ornament (NRSV "emblem") which the Israelites were to wear as a reminder of the Torah (Deut. 6:6; 11:18) and God's deliverance through the Exodus (Exod. 13:9, 16).

See PHYLACTERIES.

FRUIT

Fruit (Heb. *pĕrî;* Gk. *karpós*) constituted a large and important part of the diet of the ancient Israelites. Grapes, figs, pomegranates, and olives, along with wheat and barley, were favorable attributes of the Promised Land (Deut. 8:8). Melons, dates, berries from bushes and trees, apples, peaches, apricots, and some citrus fruits were also available for consumption. Though many fruits could be gathered from the wild, domesticated fruit trees were common. Cultivated trees provide superior fruit, and the gardens in which they grew in biblical times were shady and cool.

Different fruit trees require different amounts of maintenance, including weed removal, soil aeration, and pruning. Harvesting fruit may take place as early as June (grapes) and last through October (olives). Fruit was eaten fresh and also prepared: fruit such as figs, dates, and grapes could be dried and eaten or baked into cakes; the juices of grapes and pomegranates could be made into wine; olives could provide oil for cooking and eating; and the date palm could provide honey.

The Bible attests to the importance of fruit trees. God created fruit trees on the third day (Gen. 1:11). In battle, trees that bear food may not be cut down (Deut. 20:19-20). Fruit was an acceptable offering to God (Lev. 27:30).

Fruit was also used as a symbol for offspring, e.g., "the fruit of the womb" (Deut. 28:4), and consequence, as in "the fruit of their doings" (Jer. 17:10). The fruit of the tree of knowledge (Gen. 3) traditionally has been identified as the apple; however, no textual evidence supports this claim.

MEGAN BISHOP MOORE

FUEL

A combustible material in a solid, liquid, or gaseous state, which gives off heat when ignited. It is used to produce heat energy for domestic or industrial purposes. All fuels are a combination of carbon and hydrogen compounds. Fuel can be categorized into recent plant and animal fuels such as sticks of wood, charcoal, and dung, fossil fuels such as peat, lignite, coal, and oil, as well as products of distillation of plant and fossil fuels such as today's gasoline. The burning of fuels (Heb. *peḥām*) usually results in producing a variety of harmful gases such as carbon monoxide. The Bible makes mention of coals *(gaḥeleṯ)* brought about by burning juniper (Ps. 120:4), burning dung to cook bread and fish (Ezek. 4:15), and wood being used as fuel for warmth (John 18:18). Fuel is also mentioned in connection with burnt offerings (Lev. 16:12) and the production of fire or the wrath of the Lord (Isa. 9:19).

RICHARD A. STEPHENSON

FULLER

An occupation involving the working of cloth. Heb. *kāḇas* implies treading on cloth for the purpose of cleaning it, while in the NT Gk. *gnapheús* suggests the act of carding cloth. The job included the thickening or shrinking of new cloth, as well as the cleaning and dyeing of cloth or garments. Often the washing of cloth involved treading it with the feet or beating it (Exod. 19:10; 2 Sam. 19:24). Solutions used for the cleaning of cloth consisted of lye (Mal. 3:2), white clay, ashes of special plants, or other alkaline mixtures. Archaeologists have discovered large clay pots believed to have been placed in front of the fuller's shops as public urinals in order to produce solutions which would help to separate the dirt from the cloth.

A fuller's location required both fields and ample water. After washing the cloth it was spread out on the ground to be bleached by the sun. References to the fuller's field appear in the OT (2 Kgs. 18:17; Isa. 7:3; 36:2). The fuller's work of cleansing the cloth became a metaphor for purity (Ps. 51:7[MT 9]; Jer. 2:22; 4:14; Zech. 3:3-5; Rev. 4:4).

DENNIS GAERTNER

FURNACE

An oven made of brick or other fireproof materials in which fire was placed for cooking, warmth, or refining and purifying metals. The first biblical reference to a furnace occurs in a covenant ceremony between Yahweh and Abram (Gen. 15:9-21). Abram is instructed to halve a heifer, a goat, and a ram and place the halves opposite one another. After sundown a smoking furnace ("fire pot") and a burning lamp pass between the halves of the slain animals as a seal of the covenant. In another passage, Moses takes ashes from a furnace ("kiln") and sprinkles them in the air so that they become boils on the Egyptians (Exod. 9:8, 10). As Yahweh descends upon Mt. Sinai, smoke arises like smoke from a furnace (Exod. 19:18).

When Daniel and his friends refuse to worship Nebuchadnezzar's golden image, they are thrown into a fiery furnace (Dan. 3:6-26). Nehemiah refers to a tower of furnaces in the wall of Jerusalem, possibly large ovens for baking bread (Neh. 3:11; 12:38).

The furnace is a refiner of gold (Prov. 17:3 = 27:21) and silver (Ps. 12:6[MT 7]), and that imagery is employed as a metaphor for purifying or refining Israel (Isa. 31:9; 48:10; cf. Ezek. 22:18, 20, 22; NRSV "smelter"). The furnace is also a metaphor for the Israelites' slavery in Egypt (Deut. 4:20; 1 Kgs. 8:51). The smoke from Sodom is compared to the smoke of a furnace (Gen. 19:28), again suggesting that purification took place through the destruction of evil.

In Matthew "furnace" refers to eternal punishment (Matt. 13:42, 50). "One like a son of man" has feet like shining metal heated in a furnace (Rev. 1:15). John also sees smoke from the "bottomless pit" ascending like smoke from a furnace (Rev. 9:2).

JOE E. LUNCEFORD

G

GAAL (Heb. *gaʿal*)
The son of Ebed. He led the rebellion of the Shechemites against Abimelech **2** but was repelled by Abimelech's deputy Zebul (Judg. 9:26-41).

GAASH (Heb. *gāʿaš*)
A mountain S of Timnath-serah (Timnath-heres), ca. 32 km. (20 mi.) SW of Shechem. Joshua was buried in the vicinity (Josh. 24:30; Judg. 2:9), and Hiddai (or Hurai), one of David's Thirty, was from the "torrents (or 'wadis') of Gaash" (Heb. *naḥălê gāʿaš;* 2 Sam. 23:30; 1 Chr. 11:32).

GABAEL (Gk. *Gabaḗl*)
1. A Naphtalite, an ancestor of Tobit (Tob. 1:1).
2. A friend of Tobit and brother (or son) of Gabrias who lived at Rages in Media (Tob. 1:14). Tobit deposited 14 talents of silver with him and later sent his son Tobias to retrieve the money (Tob. 4:1, 20; 5:6; 10:2). Gabael returned the sum intact at the wedding feast of Tobias and Sarah (9:2-6).

GABBAI (Heb. *gabbay*)
A Benjaminite who lived in Jerusalem following the Exile (Neh. 11:8). Some scholars regard the text as corrupt and emend to read "mighty men of valor" (Heb. *gibbōrê ḥayil;* cf. Neh. 11:14).

GABBATHA (Gk. *Gabbathá*)
The location of the judgment seat (Gk. *bḗma*), where Pilate sat for Jesus' trial (John 19:13). The name is an Aramaic word of unknown origin. Suggestions for its meaning have included "elevated," "open space," "ridge," or a transliteration of Lat. *gabata,* "platter." According to John it was also known by the Greek term *lithóstrōton,* "pavement." It was most probably a raised paved area outside Herod's palace which functioned as the Praetorium, the residence of the Roman prefects. Philo specifically references Pilate's residence there during one Jewish feast (*Leg.* 38).

Earlier attempts to identify the Gabbatha with the stone pavement excavated beneath the Sisters of Zion Convent have been discounted because of evidence that this pavement was not yet constructed at the time of the Roman destruction in A.D. 70. A more recent suggestion for its location has been provided with the discovery of the foundation of a large podium measuring 613 sq. m. (2200 sq. ft.) in the Armenian quarter of Jerusalem.

DAVID R. BECK

GABRIAS (Gk. *Gabriás*)
The brother (Tob. 1:14) or father (4:20) of Gabael **2.**

GABRIEL (Heb. *gaḇrîʾēl;* Gk. *Gabriḗl*)
A prominent angel. Gabriel reveals eschatological mysteries in Dan. 8:15-26; 9:21-27 and announces the births of John the Baptist and Jesus in Luke 1:11-20, 26-38. The etymology of the name is disputed, meaning "God is my Warrior" or perhaps "Man of God." Gabriel and Michael are the only two angels explicitly named in the OT. In the more developed angelology of Jewish apocalyptic traditions, they appear regularly together with Raphael and others as prominent archangels who stand in the presence of God (1 En. 9:1; 10:1-12; 1QM 9:14-16; Luke 1:19; cf. Rev. 8:2, 6).

In Daniel Gabriel serves primarily as interpreter of visions and mysteries; in later apocalyptic sources his functions are more varied. In 1 Enoch he is identified as one of the holy angels whose role is to oversee the garden of Eden, the serpents and the cherubim (1 En. 20:7); in 10:9-10 he is sent in judgment against the children born from the "Watchers" (fallen angels). In the War Scroll at Qumran the names of Michael, Gabriel, Sariel, and Raphael are written on the shield of the towers carried into battle (1QM 9:14-16).

In Luke's birth narrative Gabriel appears again in a revelatory role, announcing to Zechariah and Mary the fulfillment of eschatological hopes in the births of John, the Elijah-like forerunner of the Lord (Luke 1:11-20), and Jesus, the messianic king from the line of David (vv. 26-38).

MARK L. STRAUSS

GAD (Heb. *gāḏ*) **(DEITY)**
A Syrian deity worshipped along with Meni (Isa. 65:11), attested in several West Semitic languages. In English versions Gad is translated "fortune," Meni as "destiny" or "fate." It has been suggested that this deity is a late personification of the Hebrew term. NANCY L. DECLAISSÉ-WALFORD

GAD (Heb. *gāḏ*) **(PERSON)**
1. The son of Jacob and Zilpah, Leah's handmaiden. The verbal root *gdd* means "to cut off," but Leah's welcoming of Gad's birth in Gen. 30:11 indicates that name may mean "fortune"; other references suggest "troop" or "marauding band" (Gen. 49:19), "crouching lion" (Deut. 33:20), or "lion" and "gazelle" (1 Chr. 12:8). Gad took seven sons into Egypt (Gen. 46:16). During the wilderness wanderings the Gadites numbered between 45,650 (Num. 1:24-25) and 40,500 (26:18), making them tenth in size among the 12 tribes. The tribe of Gad settled in the Transjordanian highlands in eight settlements (Num. 32:24-36). Most of the sites have been identified, each showing new occupation at the beginning of the Israelite period. The Mesha inscription (mid-9th century B.C.E.) indicates that Gad expanded into the territory of Reuben.

2. David's prophet (Heb. *nāḇî'*) or seer *(ḥōzeh)*. Gad is mentioned in accounts of David fleeing from Saul (1 Sam. 22:5) and taking a census (2 Sam. 24:11-14 = 1 Chr. 21:9-12). He commanded David to build an altar on the threshing floor of Ornan the Jebusite (2 Sam. 24:18-19 = 1 Chr. 21:18-19), supervised the levitical music (2 Chr. 29:25), and was the author of a part of the history of David's reign (1 Chr. 29:29). Several passages in Chronicles connect Gad closely with Nathan.

Bibliography. H. Baruch, *The Emergence of Israel in Canaan.* SBLMS 29 (Chico, 1983); J. M. Miller and J. H. Hayes, *A History of Ancient Israel and Judah* (Philadelphia, 1986).

NANCY L. DECLAISSÉ-WALFORD

GADARA (Gk. *Gadara*)
A prominent Decapolis city from Pompey's time (63 B.C.), modern Umm Qeis, whose history goes as far back as the Hellenistic period. Gadara was near the place where Jesus cast the demons out of a man (Mark 5:1-20; two men in Matt. 8:28-34). It is located on a plateau at the northeast border of Jordan, ca. 10 km. (6 mi.) SE of the south shore of the Sea of Galilee/Tiberias; on the north it borders the steep slopes of the Yarmuk (Hieromax) River, and on the west the steep slopes extending down to the Jordan Valley.

A recent site plan established that the Gadara ruins extend for 1600 m. (1 mi.) on either side of an east-west Decumanus Maximus, and also extend 450 m. (.27 mi.) on a north-south axis.

Various remains uncovered on the terrace between the upper and lower city include a square building (ca. 23.5 m. × 23.1 m. [77 × 75.8 ft.]) in the central part of the terrace (a rectangular colonnaded building is at the north end of the terrace) with an octagonal 6th-century structure, a church, built over a Roman period floor of limestone slabs; it had an apse on the southeast, and a mosaic floor of black, blue, yellow, red, and white stone tiles/tesserae. A large public bath (30 m. × 50 m.[98.5 × 164 ft.]) was uncovered 50 m. (164 ft.) W of the church, presumably Late Roman/Early Byzantine, which with its auxiliary rooms covered ca. 2300 sq. m. (2750 sq. yds.); after its initial destruction, it was used again on a slightly smaller scale until its demise in the early 7th century, when it was reused as living/industrial quarters.

The excavation of a series of vaulted rooms along the west edge of the terrace revealed that the vaults, facing west onto a street running south at right angles to the main east-west Decumanus Maximus, were used as shops. A 34 m. (112 ft.) section excavated along the east-west Decumanus Maximus revealed that this street was 12.55 m. (41 ft.) wide, with sidewalks 3 m. (10 ft.) wide; the street was renovated in the Byzantine period. Farther west along this Decumanus some parts of a hippodrome were exposed. Also on the west a large subterranean monumental mausoleum has been excavated. In the east section of the site two theaters have been uncovered: a theater on the south side of the Decumanus, near the east wall of the city, and the other theater facing west on the east side and south of the vaulted-shops street; in the latter theater was found a life-size marble statue. A large underground aqueduct has also been found, but its full extent has not been determined.

See GERASENES.

Bibliography. B. DeVries, "The North Mausoleum at Um Qeis," *ADAJ* 18 (1973): 77; W. H. Mare, "Gadara," in *The New International Dictionary of Biblical Archaeology,* ed. E. M. Blaiklock and R. K. Harrison (Grand Rapids, 1983), 201; G. Schumacher, *Northern 'Ajlun* (London, 1890).

W. HAROLD MARE

GADDI (Heb. *gaddî;* Gk. *Gaddi*)
1. The son of Susi of the tribe of Manasseh; one of the spies that Moses sent into Canaan (Num. 13:11).

2. Nickname of John, the eldest brother of Judas Maccabeus (1 Macc. 2:2).

GADDIEL (Heb. *gaddî'ēl*)
The son of Sodi of the tribe of Zebulun; one of the spies sent by Moses into Canaan (Num. 13:10).

GADI (Heb. *gāḏî*)
The father of King Menahem of Israel (2 Kgs. 15:14, 17).

GAHAM (Heb. *gaḥam*)
A son of Nahor and his concubine Reumah (Gen. 22:24).

GAHAR (Heb. *gaḥar*)
The head of a family of temple servants who returned with Zerubbabel from the Exile (Ezra 2:47 = Neh. 7:49).

GAIUS (Gk. *Gáïos;* Lat. *Gaius*)
A common Latin name, borne by four men mentioned in the NT, of whom nothing is known beyond these mentions.

1. A Macedonian who, along with Aristarchus, had traveled with Paul to Ephesus. There the two Macedonians were caught in a riot against the Christian missionary movement (Acts 19:29).

2. A man who was among Paul's traveling companions from Corinth to Troas (Acts 20:4); probably not identical with **1** above, since he is said to have been from Derbe.

3. A Corinthian, one of the few baptized by Paul (1 Cor. 1:14) and likely identical with the man who hosted both Paul and "the entire church" in Corinth (Rom. 16:23). He must therefore have been relatively well-off.

4. The recipient of 3 John. The elder writes to encourage Gaius to continue his hospitality to traveling missionaries and to commend Demetrius to him. Gaius evidently had a close relationship with the elder, but his position in relation to the elder's opponent Diotrephes is unclear. He cannot have been a member of Diotrephes' church since the elder has to inform him of the latter's actions; yet because the elder calls Diotrephes' congregation "*the* church" (3 John 9), it is hard to think of Gaius as hosting or belonging to another house church in the same place. Whatever his position, the elder urges him not only to receive the travelers but to "send them on," i.e., to provide for their needs on the journey, implying that Gaius had the financial means to do so. DAVID RENSBERGER

GALAL (Heb. *gālāl*)

1. A postexilic Levite of the lineage of Merari (1 Chr. 9:15).

2. A Levite, son of Jeduthun and father of Shemaiah, of the lineage of Merari (1 Chr. 9:16; Neh. 11:17).

GALATIA (Gk. *Galatía*)
A region in north central Asia Minor (modern Turkey) named after Gallic/Celtic invaders. Later the name designated a Roman province.

The Gauls migrated to the region in the mid-3rd century B.C.E. and made their military presence felt. King Nicomedes I of Bithynia enlisted their support in his civil war. During the century, the Gauls fought with such powers as the Seleucid Antiochus I (281-61) and Attalus I of Pergamum (ca. 240-230). While being contained geographically, the Gauls maintained their independence. Their territory centered around the city of Ancyra (modern Ankara), in the northern half of central Asia Minor. In 64 B.C.E., the Gallic tribes became a client state of Rome, ruled however by one of their own. Upon the death of their last king, Amyntas, in 25 B.C.E., the region became a Roman province, which gradually extended south, almost to the Mediterranean Sea. Such cities as Derbe, Lystra, Iconium, and Antioch were now a part of "Galatia."

This is significant, for it has a bearing on how one understands the recipients and date of Paul's letter to the churches of Galatia. One can argue that Paul uses "Galatia" to designate the *ethnic* region in northern Asia Minor (Gal. 1:2), explaining his use of the ethnic term Galatians (3:1) in the letter. It could also correspond with Acts 16:6; 18:23, which say that Paul visited the *region* (not the *province*) of Galatia after the council meeting of Acts 15 (= Gal. 2:1-10?), requiring a date for the letter after the meeting of Acts 15. However, if Paul is using "Galatia" to denote the Roman province, the Galatian letter may be addressed to churches in the southern part of the province, churches which Paul visited early in his missionary career (cf. Acts 14:1-20), allowing one to date the letter earlier in Paul's career, *before* the meeting of Acts 15 (perhaps making Gal. 2 = Acts 11:27-30). The issue is controversial, for it affects many issues in Pauline studies: chronology, development of Paul's thought, and agreements/disagreements between Acts and Pauline letters. J. BRADLEY CHANCE

GALATIANS, LETTER TO THE
One of Paul's major letters. Galatians has played a central role in Christian theology because it provides one of the NT's most explicit teachings on justification by faith. This teaching, however, is Paul's response to a serious crisis in the churches of Galatia rather than a systematic or doctrinal presentation of justification.

Background

There is no unanimity among scholars as to the identity of the Galatians or the dating of this letter. Some argue that Paul was writing to the congregations of Antioch in Pisidia, Lystra, Iconium, and Derbe (in the Roman province of Galatia), which he established on his first missionary journey according to Acts 13–14. Others maintain that he was writing to the ethnic Galatians of Ancyra, Tavium, and Pessinus (in the old territory of Galatia), which Paul supposedly evangelized on his second and third missionary journeys (cf. Acts 16:6; 18:23). The first theory is called the South Galatian hypothesis and dates the letter ca. 49-50 C.E., making it the earliest of Paul's extant correspondence. The second is called the North Galatian hypothesis and dates the letter in the mid-50s, a period when Paul found himself in conflict with some elements of the Corinthian church.

An understanding of the situation that occasioned Galatians is more important for its interpretation than the questions discussed above, and in this regard there is some agreement, even though scholarly theories differ in detail. The background is as follows.

Paul was the first to preach the gospel to the Galatians, and they received him as if he were an "angel of God," at a moment when he was physically ill (Gal. 4:13-14). Since the Galatians were Gentiles, Paul did not require them to undergo circumcision or observe "works of the law" such as dietary prescriptions and sabbath observance. But sometime after his departure, other missionaries came to Galatia and preached a "different gospel"

(1:6) which required the Galatians to have themselves circumcised and observe these "works of the law."

The precise identity of these missionaries is disputed, but they were most likely Jewish Christian missionaries who had a strong connection to Jerusalem, and perhaps to James. Although Paul castigates their false and deceitful motives (6:12-13), there is a logic to their position. If the Galatians wish to share in the blessings of the Jewish Messiah, then they must become children of Abraham by accepting circumcision, the sign of the eternal covenant God made with Abraham and his descendants (Gen. 17). Circumcision, in turn, requires the descendants of Abraham to do the works of the law.

Paul's understanding of the gospel, especially in light of his call, led him to a deeper appreciation of Christ's work in God's salvific plan. While Jewish believers need not renounce their Jewish heritage, it was not necessary for gentile believers to adopt Jewish customs and practices in order to be justified before God. It is God's salvific work in Christ, rather than the law, which accomplishes justification and righteousness (2:21; 3:21). Therefore the Galatians are already Abraham's descendants since they belong to Christ (3:29), whereas those who seek justification through the law separate themselves from Christ (5:4).

Content

Aside from its introductory and concluding remarks (1:1-10; 6:11-18), Galatians comprises three major sections: an autobiographical section in which Paul defends the truth of the gospel that he preached to the Galatians (1:11–2:21); an intricate argument drawn from Scripture in which Paul explains that people of faith are Abraham's descendants (3:1–5:12); a moral exhortation in which Paul shows the Galatians that if they love their neighbor as themselves and walk by the Spirit, they fulfill the law of Christ (5:13–6:10). Each of these sections is an integral part of Paul's argument and is intended to persuade the Galatians not to submit to circumcision.

Truth of the Gospel (1:11–2:21)

Since his circumcision-free gospel to the Gentiles was severely criticized, Paul provides the Galatians with a brief autobiographical statement in order to demonstrate the truth of the gospel (2:5, 14) that he preaches to the Gentiles. Thus he reviews his former life as a persecutor of the Church, his apostolic call, his dealings with the church at Jerusalem, and the incident at Antioch (1:11–2:14). He then concludes with an important statement on justification by faith apart from the works of the law (2:15-21).

This biographical information supports the truth of the gospel in several ways. First, Paul did not receive the gospel from other human beings, nor did others teach it to him. The gospel that he preaches came through a "revelation of Jesus Christ" (1:11-12), i.e., Paul received the gospel when God revealed his Son to him (v. 16). Previous to his apostolic call, Paul was zealous for the traditions of his ancestors, even to the point of persecuting the church of God. But when God called him and revealed his Son to him, Paul understood that the one whom he persecuted as cursed by God (3:13) was none other than God's Son.

Paul immediately knew that he had been called to preach a circumcision-free gospel to the Gentiles, and he did so without any need to consult with those in Jerusalem (1:17). When he did go to Jerusalem, ca. three years after his call, he met only with Cephas (Peter) and James. His gospel came directly from God at the moment of his call, not from Jerusalem.

Fourteen years after his first visit Paul went to Jerusalem with Barnabas and Titus to make sure that he was not preaching in vain (2:1-10). Despite opposition from "false brethren," the pillar apostles (James, Cephas, and John) clearly approved of Paul's gospel to the Gentiles. However, when certain partisans of James came to the church of Antioch, they were not prepared for what they saw: Jewish and gentile believers sharing table fellowship, Peter among them. When Peter withdrew from this table fellowship, Paul rebuked him for betraying the truth of the gospel (2:11-14).

What Paul understood by "the truth of the gospel" is stated in the final verses of this section (2:15-21). A person is not justified on the basis of "works of the law" but through faith in (or perhaps "through the faith of") Jesus Christ. This is why Paul and other Jewish Christians now believe in Christ since they have come to realize that no one will be justified on the basis of "works of the law." If righteousness could be obtained through the law, then there was no need for Christ to die.

Children of the Promise (3:1–5:12)

Having explained the origin of the circumcision-free gospel he preaches, Paul embarks upon a rather technical argument to show that people of faith, baptized into Christ, are Abraham's descendants. The argument supposes that the promises God made to Abraham are more important in the history of salvation than the giving of the law. God had already announced the gospel to Abraham by promising that all the nations would be blessed in him. Consequently, people of faith are blessed with faithful Abraham (3:7-9). In his exegesis of Gen. 12:7, Paul argues that these promises were made to Abraham and his seed. Focusing upon the word "seed," which is in the singular, he argues that Abraham's seed is Christ (3:15-16). Consequently, all who are baptized into Christ are descendants of Abraham and children of the promise, even if not circumcised (3:26-29).

Since the law was given 430 years after the promise, it does not alter the original conditions of the promise, which depends on faith (3:17-20). The law was added later to make people aware of their transgressions, and so it functioned as a disciplinarian until the full blossoming of faith. But of itself, the law could not give life. Otherwise, righteousness would have come through the law (3:21).

Since the Galatians have not understood this

and are on the verge of circumcision, Paul reprimands them for returning to the period of their religious infancy (4:1-11). He calls them to imitate his example (4:12-20). He shows them that they are the true descendants of the free woman and her son Isaac (4:21-31), and warns them to avoid circumcision lest they separate themselves from Christ (5:1-12).

Living by the Spirit (5:13–6:10)

Although Paul has shown the Galatians that they are descendants of Abraham because they have been incorporated into Abraham's singular descendant, Christ, his argument is not complete. Paul must explain how the gentile Galatians can live a moral life if they are not "under the law," otherwise his gospel will be hollow and of no avail. The parenesis or moral exhortation of this letter, then, plays an integral role in Paul's argument that the Galatians should not submit to circumcision.

In Paul's view, the moral life is a matter of living by the Spirit (5:16), being guided by the Spirit (v. 18), and following the Spirit's lead (v. 25). People who are led by the Spirit are not "under the law" (v. 18), nor do they do the works of the flesh, which Paul catalogues in great detail (vv. 19-21). Rather, the Spirit produces its fruit in them (vv. 22-23). But if believers are no longer under the law, will they really live a moral life by following the Spirit?

Paul argues that the whole law is fulfilled in the statement, "You shall love your neighbor as yourself" (5:14, quoting Lev. 19:18). Consequently, the Galatians must serve each other through love (5:13). If they bear one another's burdens they will fulfill "the law of Christ" (6:2). This expression, which occurs only in Galatians, probably refers to the law as it was lived by Christ, i.e., in accord with the principle of self-sacrificing love (cf. 1:3-4; 2:20). To summarize, the Galatians will fulfill the law if they live in the realm of the Spirit in accord with the law of Christ.

Contemporary Discussion

Current discussion of Galatians focuses upon three areas: the social dimension of justification by faith; the faith of Jesus Christ; and the nature of Pauline ethics.

The historical context of Galatians indicates that Paul's teaching on justification was a response to a social problem: how Jewish and gentile believers should relate to each other. Do people stand in the proper covenant relationship to God on the basis of "works of the law" that identify them as Jews (circumcision, dietary prescriptions, sabbath observance), or on the basis of God's work in Christ? More than a polemic against an attempt to gain one's righteousness through good works, Paul's teaching on justification in Galatians seeks to integrate Gentiles and Jews without compelling the former to adopt a Jewish way of life.

When we ask how people are justified, the traditional answer is through faith *in* Jesus Christ. But in recent years a minority of scholars has argued that the important statement of 2:16 refers to the "faith *of* Jesus Christ." Accordingly, believers are justified on the basis of Christ's faith, i.e., Christ's faithfulness and obedience to God as demonstrated by dying on the cross. Thus Gentiles are in the proper covenant relationship to God on the basis of Christ's faithfulness, not because they have adopted a Jewish way of life. This faithful obedience of Christ, in turn, is the basis for faith *in* Christ.

Finally, new insights into the role that moral exhortation plays in Paul's argument have encouraged scholars to give greater attention to the ethical dimensions of Galatians. The integral role of the parenesis in this letter indicates that Paul's teaching on justification does not undermine the moral life of believers. Justified by what God has done in Christ and no longer under the law, believers must follow the Spirit's lead and fulfill the law of Christ through the love commandment.

Bibliography. J. M. G. Barclay, *Obeying the Truth: Paul's Ethics in Galatians* (Minneapolis, 1991); J. D. G. Dunn, *The Theology of Paul's Letter to the Galatians* (Cambridge, 1993); R. B. Hays, *The Faith of Jesus Christ: An Investigation of the Narrative Substructure of Galatians 3:1–4:11*. SBLDS 56 (Chico, 1983); R. N. Longenecker, *Galatians*. WBC 41 (Waco, 1990); F. J. Matera, *Galatians*. Sacra Pagina 9 (Collegeville, 1992). FRANK J. MATERA

GALBANUM

A resinous gum (Heb. *ḥelbĕnâ;* Gk. *chalbánē*) derived by drying the milky sap from the roots of a form of fennel or carrot (probably *Ferula galbaniflua* Boise). A herbaceous plant found in Syria, Persia, and Afghanistan, galbanum has a distinct odor which becomes unpleasant when the resin is burned; nevertheless, it was one of the ingredients used to make holy incense, probably added to improve combustion (Exod. 30:34). It was also used in antiquity as a condiment and for medicinal purposes, sometimes taken internally but usually applied as a salve.

At Sir. 24:15 galbanum is used figuratively in describing Wisdom.

GALEED (Heb. *gal'ēḏ*)

The name that Jacob gave to the stone pile he and Laban set up to commemorate their covenant and to delineate the boundary between their territories (Gen. 31:47). Laban named the pile Jegar-sahadutha, an Aramaic expression that also means "heap of witness." Etymologically the name may be related to Gilead.

GALILEE (Heb. *gālîl;* Gk. *Galilaía*)

The northern region of Palestine, shaped by geology, prehistory, and historic circumstance for an important role in the emergence of both Judaism and Christianity. Called Galilee since at least the 7th century B.C.E., the region was bounded roughly by the Esdraelon Plain to the south, the plain of Acco and the Phoenician lowlands to the west, the Litani River to the north, and the Golan Heights to the east. Josephus (*BJ* 3.3.1 [35-40]) and the Talmud (*m. Šeb.* 9:2) distinguished Upper and Lower Gali-

Sea of Galilee, from its southern end, E of Yardenit. Mt. Hermon and Golan are in the distance
(Phoenix Data Systems, Neal and Joel Bierling)

lee, marked roughly by the great escarpment on the line from Acco to Safed. Upper Galilee ranges to ca. 1200 m. (3900 ft.) above sea level, while Lower Galilee reaches only 600 m. (1970 ft.). The area around the freshwater Galilean lake (OT "Sea of Chinnereth," NT "Sea of Galilee") was considered part of Galilee; in the 1st century C.E. this included some of the eastern shore (Gamala). Fed by the Jordan River from Lake Huleh and the Lebanon range, the lake surface lies ca. 210 m. (690 ft.) below sea level. Galilean rainfall averages between 300 and 1000 mm. (12-39 in.) per year, providing ample water for perennial springs and agriculture.

The major geologic features of Galilee were established during the Cretaceous and Eocene periods when encroachments of the Mediterranean Sea laid down the sedimentary rocks so prevalent in the terrain today. Cenomanian-Turonian limestones and Senonian chalks supplied the basic building materials, with limestone making up the hills and mountains and chalks eventually eroding to become fertile valleys. The eastern part of Galilee, however, was subject to volcanic activity. Basalt rock there overlies the limestone.

Enormous tectonic forces forced the Jordan Valley to drop, creating the Galilean lake and the Jordan River, and orienting the major lines of Galilean topography east and west. Fertile valleys transect the Lower Galilean landscape, and during ancient times offered important agricultural produce — especially grain, grapes, and olives (cf. Deut. 8:8) — as well as natural avenues for human commerce. Geology also opened Galilee to the cultural and political "tectonics" of Mediterranean history.

Prehistoric Galilee was the home of important hominid activity. Neanderthals inhabited caves during the Middle Paleolithic period (Naḥal ʿAmud), and ancestral homo sapiens dwelling at Qafzeh were apparently the first humans to inter the dead. Indeed, human habitation is attested continuously in Galilee from the Paleolithic through the Bronze Ages. The agricultural revolution in the Neolithic period made possible the numerous settlements that dotted Galilee in the Bronze Age, including at times the mountain regions. Large cities like Hazor and Megiddo controlled the best land and the major routes of commerce. Nomadic ancestors of Israel may have wandered through Galilee, but little is made of this in the Bible.

Israelite Period

The biblical period of Galilee began with the Late Bronze–Early Iron Age transition. Josh. 19 perhaps contains early Israelite traditions and indicates that Asher, Zebulun, Naphtali, and Issachar received tribal allotments of land in Galilee. Dan moved at a later time to extreme Upper Galilee (Josh. 19:40-48; Judg. 18). For an accurate picture, biblical records must be supplemented by archaeological information and extrabiblical documentary material. The Egyptian Merneptah Stela provides the earliest mention (ca. 1225) of the people "Israel," suggesting a location in northern Palestine. Archaeological surveys by Yohanan Aharoni, Zvi Gal, and Rafael Frankel trace possible "Israelite" remains in the mountainous terrain of western Upper Galilee (Asher, Josh. 19:24-31) and eastern Lower Galilee (Zebulun and Naphtali, 19:10-16, 32-39), but no

Iron Age remains attest the presence of Issachar (cf. Josh. 19:17-23). The Israelites were able to settle and control mountainous regions, while the Phoenicians and Canaanites continued to dominate the rich agricultural valleys and plains, down to the time of David.

Apparently, the earliest attested usage of the Hebrew noun *gālîl* ("circle," "district"), in construct state, required a completing noun: Isa. 9:1 (MT 8:23) means lit., "The circle (region) of the nations *(gôyim)*." Late Israelite usage always includes the definite article, making *gālîl* into a proper noun, *the* Galilee (1 Kgs. 9:11; 1 Chr. 6:76[61]; cf. Josh. 20:7; 21:32). That Galilee does not appear prominently in the biblical saga is to some extent perspectival, since southern Judahite interests gave final shape to the OT. The relatively few mentions frequently concern transitory battles or military operations: Joshua at the waters of Merom in Upper Galilee (Josh. 11:1-10); Deborah's forces at the Kishon Brook (Judg. 4–5); Gideon at Harod in the Esdraelon Plain (Judg. 6–8). Solomon, moreover, fortified Megiddo and Hazor (1 Kgs. 9:15) and traded Galilean villages for Phoenician culture (vv. 10-13). During the time of the divided kingdoms, Ahab also built fortresses at Megiddo and Hazor and conducted campaigns against the king of Damascus near Galilee (1 Kgs. 20:26). Jehu's rebellion sent rivers of blood through the Jezreel Valley (Hos. 1:4-5; 2 Kgs. 9–10).

Galilee thus earns mention only when controlled or contested by powerful Canaanite, Phoenician, Syrian, Ephraimite, or Judahite interests. Isaiah's comment (Isa. 9:1[8:23]) pertains to the Assyrian removal of the northern kingdom Israel (721) and the region's transformation into Assyrian provinces. Archaeology suggests that the area was unsettled for over a century thereafter (cf. 2 Chr. 30:10-11). Seán Freyne's landmark study explores to what extent Israelites continued in the Galilee between Assyrian and Hellenistic-Roman times.

Hellenistic-Roman Period

Recent Galilean inquiries have noted Maccabean concern with northern populations loyal to Jerusalem (1 Macc. 5:1-15). Debate has centered on how to construe *Ioudaíos* as applied to regions or peoples outside of Judea proper (under Judean influence? Judean-orientation? Jew?).

A general dispatched to the Galilee during the early phases of the Judean-Roman War (66-67 C.E.), Josephus is the best historical source for Palestinian affairs in this time and gives important literary testimony to its culture and society. The historical worth of Talmudic references to 1st-century Galilee, however, is sharply debated after the form-critical work of Jacob Neusner and students has shown the difficulties of separating out early material.

Much concern understandably focuses on the historical activity of Jesus of Nazareth in Galilee. Jesus hailed from Nazareth of Galilee (Mark 6:1; John 1:46; cf. Mark 16:7). Recent excavation at Capernaum, the locale of major activity (Mark 2:1; Matt. 4:13; cf. Luke 10:13-15), corroborates the picture of Mark 1:29. Ernest Renan's picture (in his 1893 *Life of Jesus*) of the sunny rural innocence of Jesus' homeland epitomized romantic, 19th-century notions of Galilee. Albrecht Alt, William F. Albright, and others built the literary and archaeological foundations for a more sophisticated understanding. Recently, intensive literary study of the Gospel material, especially Q (apparently originating in Galilee in the 30s-40s), has provided important new baselines for historical Jesus arguments.

Concern with social history has deepened understanding of Galilean society. For example, Burton Mack sees Lower Galilee as a highly Hellenized and cosmopolitan region, and has argued that Jesus, like the ancient Cynics, identified the kingdom of God with a naturalistic life free of social convention. Eric Meyers and James Strange have investigated cultural and political connections through regional archaeology, showing that Phoenician, Syrian, and Judean influences continued in Galilee.

Early Church and Rabbis

There is little solid textual evidence, other than the scribal traditions of Q, for the perdurance of the Jesus movement in Galilee after his death. Early Christian tradition preserves surprisingly little about any sizable Christian presence in Galilee in the first several centuries C.E. However, the house of Peter at Capernaum apparently was continuously venerated until an octagonal Byzantine *martyrion* was constructed. Numerous Byzantine churches were built in the region, notably at Capernaum and Nazareth.

After the devastating revolt of Bar Kokhba (132-135), Judeans were driven north, and many rabbinic centers flourished in Galilee during late Roman and Byzantine times. The Mishnah was codified by Rabbi Judah the Prince in the early 3rd century at Sepphoris, and numerous synagogues were constructed.

Bibliography. M. Aviam, Z. Gal, and A. Ronen. "Galilee," *NEAEHL*, 2:449-58; S. Freyne, *Galilee from Alexander the Great to Hadrian, 323 B.C.E. to 135 C.E.* (Wilmington, 1980); R. A. Horsley, *Galilee: History, Politics, People* (Valley Forge, 1995); L. I. Levine, ed., *The Galilee in Late Antiquity* (New York, 1992). DOUGLAS E. OAKMAN

GALILEE, SEA OF

A freshwater lake in northern Palestine, part of the Jordan River system. The name Chinnereth or Chinneroth (Heb. *yām kinneret̲* and variants *kinnerôt̲, kinĕrôt̲*) is derived from Heb. *kinnôr*, "harp," which describes the shape of the lake (Num. 34:11; Deut. 3:17; Josh. 12:3; 13:27). It was later known as Gennesaret (Luke 5:1; 1 Macc. 11:67; Josephus *Ant.* 18.2; *BJ* 3.462, 515-16), Tiberiados (Josephus *BJ* 3.57; 4.456), and the Sea of Tiberias (John 6:1; 21:1). Gennesaret, or Gennesareth (Pliny *Nat. hist.* 5.15.71), was also the name of a town and a plain above the northwest shore. The name Tiberias comes from the town at the southwest shore named after the Roman emperor (modern Arab. *Tabariyeh*). Warm springs are located just outside Tiberias, and people would come there for the medicinal properties of the springs. Other towns around the sea were Capernaum to the northwest and Bethsaida to the north.

The lake is 14.5 km. (9 mi.) long and 8 km. (5 mi.) wide and rests in a basin formed by a geological fault. The surface of the lake is between 208.5 m. (684 ft.) and 213 m. (700 ft.) below sea level, depending on the season. The deepest point in the lake is 254 m. (833 ft.) below sea level.

Some 25 species of fish are found in the lake, and the NT includes frequent references to fishing, the size of nets and catches, and boats. Cured fish from Gennesaret were sent as far away as Rome during the 1st century. Josephus (*BJ* 3.520-21) mentions the common view of an underground connection with the Nile River because both the Sea of Galilee and the Nile were home to *coracine,* a type of black eel.

In 1986 a boat dating to the 1st century was recovered from the bottom of the lake off the northwest shore near Magdala. It provided an example of the kind of fishing craft used in the sea in biblical times.

Bibliography. N. Glueck, *The River Jordan* (1946, repr. New York, 1968); E. W. G. Masterman, "The Fisheries of Galilee," *PEQ* 40 (1908): 40-51; S. Wachsmann, "The Galilee Boat," *BARev* 14/5 (1988): 18-33. LAWRENCE A. SINCLAIR

GALL
The gall bladder (Job 20:25) and its bile (15:13). Heb. *mĕrôrâ*/*mĕrērâ* and *rō'š*/*rôš* are also employed in the OT as a metaphor for the bitterness of life, especially of a life devoid of God's blessings (e.g., Deut. 32:32). In the LXX Gk. *cholḗ* translates a number of Hebrew words meaning "gall," "poison," and "bitterness." Matt. 27:34 attests that Jesus was offered wine mixed with gall just before his crucifixion; this mocking of Jesus is at the same time a fulfillment of Ps. 69:21(MT 22). In Acts 8:23 gall is used metaphorically to describe the bondage which keeps Simon Magus from discerning the grace of God. DAVID A. DORMAN

GALLIM (Heb. *gallîm*)
A settlement in Benjamin whose name means "heaps of stones" or "ruins." After David had rejected Saul's daughter Michal, she was given to Paltiel of Gallim as his wife (1 Sam. 25:44). With Saul's capital at Bigeah, Gallim can be assumed to have been a nearby city and Paltiel the son of its prominent leader, Laish. Isaiah prophesied that although the victorious Assyrian army would pass through Gallim before conquering Jerusalem, the Lord would provide a remnant of his people to return (Isa. 10:30). Both Khirbet Ka'kûl, 1 km. (.6 mi.) NW of Anathoth, and Khirbet Erḥa, just S of Ramah, have been suggested as the modern ruins of the town. DAVID C. MALTSBERGER

GALLIO (Gk. *Galliōn*)
Eldest son of Lucius Seneca, father of the philosopher Lucius Annaeus Seneca. Annaeus Novatus (Gallio) was adopted by the senator Lucius Iunius Gallio and took his name. The banishment of his brother Seneca early in Claudius's reign (41 C.E.) may have affected Gallio's career, but soon after Seneca's return in 49 Claudius appointed Gallio proconsul of Achaia. An inscription found at Delphi, probably dating to the early summer of 52, mentions Gallio. Thus, Gallio probably began as proconsul sometime between 50 and 51 but apparently did not complete his two-year term due to his dislike for the Greek province.

Much of what can be established about Paul's chronology hinges upon the dating of Gallio's tenure. Acts 18:12 reports that while Gallio was proconsul of Achaia, the Jews in Corinth brought a case against Paul before him. Gallio refused to hear the case.

Later, Gallio was named consul under Nero in 58. Tacitus reports that when Seneca was implicated in Nero's death and forced to commit suicide, Gallio "begged for his own safety" in the senate.

Bibliography. J. Murphy-O'Connor, *St. Paul's Corinth* (Collegeville, 1983). SCOTT NASH

GAMAD (Heb. *gammāḏ*)
A place which supplied mercenaries in the defense of Tyre (Ezek. 27:11; NJB "Gammadians"). Perhaps they should be identified with Kumidi in northern Syria, mentioned in the Amarna Letters.

GAMALIEL (Heb. *gamlî'ēl;* Gk. *Gamaliḗl*)
1. The son of Pedahur; chief of the tribe of Manasseh during the wilderness period (Num. 1:10; 2:20; 7:54, 59; 10:23).

2. Gamaliel I, a well-respected and lenient Pharisee, a leader in the Sanhedrin, and master teacher of the Law who was responsible for most of Paul's rabbinic education (Acts 5:34-39; 22:3).

Josephus describes the family of Gamaliel as "very illustrious" (*Vita* 190-91; cf. Acts 5:34). Rabbinic literature pictures Gamaliel as the grandson of the great Hillel and the *nāśî'* (pharisaic leader) of the Sanhedrin (*Šabb.* 15a). The honorific title "the Elder" was bestowed upon him (*Soṭa* 9:15), as it was upon his father and grandfather. He was the first of only seven in all of rabbinic history, however, to be distinguished *Rabban* ("our teacher/master"). He may thus be understood as the greatest living authority and most revered figure in all of Judaism ca. A.D. 20-50. Gamaliel was even consulted by royalty concerning matters of Jewish law (*Pesaḥ.* 88b). Though some dispute his status, he clearly possessed significant authority (Acts 5:34), enough to persuade the Sanhedrin to spare the apostles (v. 40).

Gamaliel was the head of the school of Hillel, the most lenient and therefore most popular form of Judaism. He consistently ruled on matters of Jewish law in ways that translated his moderate pragmatism into day-to-day life. He was especially concerned to ease the burden on women and the poor. His rulings were commonly based on the guiding principles of "promotion of the common good" and "promoting the ways of peace" (*Git.* 4:2-3; *Roš Haš.* 2:5; *Yebam.* 16:7; *'Or.* 2:12; *Nid.* 9:17; *Ketub.* 10b, 28b).

Gamaliel focused on the importance of study and the teacher-student relationship (*'Abot R. Nat.* A.40; *'Abot* 1:16; *Pe'a* 2:6; *'Or.* 2:12; *Yebam.* 16:7). He reached out to Jews living in the Diaspora (*y. Ma'as.* 5:4 [56c]; *Sanh.* 11b), and was quite tolerant of Gentiles, as were his pupils and descendants after him (*t. B. Qam.* 9:30; *y. 'Abod. Zar.* 1:9; *Sifre* to Deut. 38; *Ber.* 27a). Like Hillel before him (*Sop.* 16:9), Gamaliel stood almost alone in his love for the Greek language. It was studied in his "school" and he even declared it the only language into which the Torah could be perfectly translated (*Soṭa* 49b; cf. *Gen. Rab.* 36:8; *Deut. Rab.* 1:1; *Meg.* 1:8).

W. E. Nunnally

3. Gamaliel II, grandson of Gamaliel I and successor to Johanan ben Zakkai as head of the rabbinic academy at Jabneh (Jamnia) ca. A.D. 80-120. Gamaliel strengthened Judaism in the post-temple period by reuniting the schools of Hillel and Shammai and by regulating prayer.

GAMES

Ancient games occurred as public events or pastimes for private leisure. From the time of Alexander the Great athletic festivals helped define society by being attached to religious cults and adding honor to a deity. Alexander brought the games to Tyre, and Antiochus Epiphanes introduced them to Palestine, drawing bitter opposition from the Jewish orthodox (1 Macc. 1:14-15; 2 Macc. 4:9-20; 6:7). The important Greek games — the Olympic games held at Olympia, the Pythian games at Delphi, the Nemean games at Argos, and the Isthmian games on the Corinthian isthmus — featured events like running, wrestling, discus, and javelin throwing.

Pure athletics was only one of Rome's interests. The Romans freely exploited the value of the games as entertainment, introducing chariot and horse races, boxing, bullfights, and gladiatorial shows. By the time of Augustus, games in the emperor's honor, usually connected with emperor worship, were held in every major provincial city throughout the empire. An Ephesian inscription lists the accomplishments of one Daphnus, including his presidency over a 13-day festival of games that apparently offered gladiatorial contests. Even in Palestine games were established by Herod the Great in cities like Caesarea and Jerusalem. Herod's building projects in Jerusalem included a theater, amphitheater, stadium, and hippodrome. Jericho and Tiberias also had these structures.

Roman interest in athletics was expressed in the arena of the gymnasium. More than just an area for physical training, the gymnasium also provided a public bath and a center for the social life of the city. Both cultural and athletic training were conducted in gymnasiums throughout the empire to prepare young men to fulfill their responsibilities to society. Activities associated with the gymnasium and the games are referred to frequently in the NT. Paul compares the Christian life to running a race (1 Cor. 9:24-27; Gal. 2:2; 5:7; Phil. 3:14) as do the Pastoral Epistles to fighting (1 Tim. 1:18; 2 Tim. 4:7).

Private games were also enjoyed in the ancient world. Game boards and playing pieces have been discovered in Mesopotamia and Egypt. A tomb at Ur yielded a board game that used 14 marked playing pieces and pyramidal dice, which dictated the moves of the pieces. A game called "hounds and jackals," with ivory pegs topped with carved heads of dogs and jackals, was found in the tomb of Renseneb in Thebes dating from the 12th dynasty (ca. 1990-1708 B.C.). The tomb of King Tutankhamen yielded a game board, which also served as a box to store the game pieces and pyramidal dice. Some game boards are inlaid with ivory, ebony, shell, gold, or blue paste. At Umm el-Bayyâreh a game board was carved into a flat stone on a guardpost overlooking Petra. In Palestine such games have been discovered at Kiriath-sepher, Tell al-Ajul, Beth-shemesh, and Gezer dating from as early as the 16th century. Literary references portray prisoners and soldiers playing games of chess or dice in their spare time.

Bibliography. V. C. Pfitzner, *Paul and the Agon Motif.* NovTSup 16 (Leiden, 1967); E. Schürer, *The History of the Jewish People in the Age of Jesus Christ (176 B.C.–A.D. 135)* 2, rev. ed. (Edinburgh, 1979); W. H. Stephens, *The New Testament World in Pictures* (Nashville, 1987). Dennis Gaertner

GAMUL (Heb. *gāmûl*)

A priest and leader of the 22nd division of the priesthood during the time of David (1 Chr. 24:17).

GANGRENE

In ancient Greek usage, a spreading ulcer (Gk. *gángraina*). At 2 Tim. 2:17 it describes the pernicious spread of heresy. Plutarch employs the term similarly to describe the effect of the calumnies of one Medius, a "flatterer" (i.e., a confidant with evil intent) of Alexander (*Moralia* 65D).

GARDEN

A plot of land (Heb. *gan*) where plants, fruits, vegetables, and spices were cultivated. These crops supplemented the diet of grain, dairy, and to a lesser extent meat. The garden was typically located closer to the house than were the grain fields. Smaller than a grain field, it offered shade with its trees and was a lush contrast to the arid surrounding terrain (Gen. 3:8; Isa. 36:16). Garden plots were fenced in with a stone wall or hedge to keep out unwanted intruders. They were irrigated at times, in contrast to the dry-farming characteristic of ancient Israel (Gen. 2:10; Deut. 11:10; Isa. 1:30; Jer. 31:12; Cant. 4:15). While larger farms might have had separate vineyards and olive orchards, many families probably intercultivated vines and fruit trees in their gardens (Cant. 5:1; Isa. 36:16). The garden in Eden has figs and other fruit trees (Gen.

3:7). Elsewhere, vegetable gardens are noted (Deut. 11:10; 1 Kgs. 21:2).

Palace-side gardens are attested pleasures for kings: Ahab (1 Kgs. 21:2), Manasseh (2 Kgs. 21:18), Zedekiah (25:4), and Ahasuerus (Esth. 7:7). Palace gardens gave food for the royal table, and lent prestige to the throne if stocked with plants from faraway places, as exotic plants signaled international trade. The esteem of gardens is also evident by the deity's having one (Gen. 3:24; Ezek. 28:13; Isa. 51:3). Gardens may also have been a place for social gathering (John 18:1).

Bibliography. O. Borowski, *Agriculture in Iron Age Israel* (Winona Lake, 1987); H. N. Wallace, *The Eden Narrative.* HSM 32 (Atlanta, 1985).

Carey Walsh

GAREB (Heb. *gārēḇ*) **(PERSON)**
An Ithrite and one of David's mighty men (2 Sam. 23:38 = 1 Chr. 11:40). The LXX and Syr. list his home as Jattir.

GAREB (Heb. *gārēḇ*) **(PLACE)**
An obscure site mentioned only in Jer. 31:39. Jeremiah uses the "hill Gareb" as a marker (along with Goah) for the future rebuilding and expansion of Jerusalem. This expansion will apparently include both the Kidron Valley to the east and the Hinnom Valley to the south and west. Attempts to identify this site at the so-called Mt. Zion at the southwestern extremity of the city seem clearly in error; Jeremiah's description indicates that the location of this site is across the Hinnom Valley from Jerusalem, closer to the "Shoulder of Hinnom," a well-known burial area which would fit the prophet's description in Jer. 31:40.

Bibliography. J. J. Simons, *Jerusalem in the Old Testament* (Leiden, 1952), 231-33.

Dennis M. Swanson

GARLAND
A wreath, often woven of flowers or leaves, worn around the head or neck. Linden, myrtle, bay foliage, ivy and parsley served as the wreath's framework. Flowers of various kinds, including violets and roses, were sometimes interwoven. Garlands were used for festive occasions, for funerary decorations, and for the bestowal of military, religious, and civic honors. They could symbolize victory, peace, honor, and immortality. Sacrificial animals were virtually always garlanded. The only NT use of garland (Gk. *stémma;* Acts 14:13) was probably a woolen band. The people of Lystra brought out sacrificial bulls and garlands when they mistook Paul and Barnabas for Hermes and Zeus.

Paul Anthony Hartog

GARLIC
A bulbous herb (*Allium sativum* L.) related to the onion, probably from the Kirghiz steppe, much in demand even in antiquity as a seasoning for food. The Israelites were introduced to garlic (Heb. *šûm*) and other spicy foods while laboring in Egypt (Num. 11:5). The small garlic bulbs, wrapped in their own thin skin, were woven together along strings, pressed in a mortar, and rubbed with oil. Sometimes people ate them with bread. The oil contained in the bulb cells gives garlic its sharp odor and strong flavor; in biblical times this oil was considered to stimulate activity and was used as a remedy for melancholy.

GARMITE (Heb. *garmî*)
A gentilic designating the Judahite Keilah (1 Chr. 4:19). Translated literally it means "of Gerem," but no such place is attested; it may be a descriptive term (cf. Heb. *gerem,* "bone").

GATAM (Heb. *ga'tām*)
An Edomite chieftain; a son of Eliphaz and descendant of Esau and Adah (Gen. 36:11, 16; 1 Chr. 1:36).

GATE
An entrance to a city (1 Kgs. 22:20), a camp (Exod. 32:26), the tabernacle (27:14-16), the temple (Ezek. 40–48), or a palace (Jer. 22:1-2). In ancient Israel cities defended themselves by building thick, solid or casemate (hollow) walls around the highest and most central part of the city. The gate was basically an opening in the wall through which almost everyone passed every day to get out to their fields or to take care of business inside the walls. The opening needed to be wide and easily approachable for civil needs. However, military needs required that the gate be narrow and hard to enter because it was the most vulnerable part of the city's defenses. Therefore, many entrances to city gates were built with steps or a right-angle turn to make it easier to defend. The gate was an elaborate structure with a roof (2 Sam. 18:24) and upper story (18:33[MT 19:1]). It was often flanked by two towers which, along with the top of the walls, could be used as strategic firing platforms for soldiers to protect the area in front of the gate. The gate included double doors which were attached to doorposts that turned in stone sockets (Judg. 16:3). When closed (at night, Josh. 2:5; and when attacked, 6:1) the doors were barred from the inside with a heavy beam or metal bar (1 Kgs. 4:13) inserted in slots in the doors. They could not be pushed in from the outside because they rested against an inner doorstop. Though often made of wood, they were vulnerable to fire (Neh. 1:3; Judg. 9:52). Consequently, they were sometimes plated with or made of metal (Ps. 107:16; Isa. 45:2).

The gate included a complex of two, four, or six rooms on both sides of the passage into the city (e.g., Megiddo). Each pair of rooms could have contained guards or soldiers to help prevent the enemy's passage into the city. For better protection the main gate would be built inside an outer gate with a second set of city walls.

In times of peace this gate complex was the center of city life. Elders administered justice here (Deut. 21:19; Josh. 20:4; Ruth 4:1). Kings sat at the gate to meet their subjects or administer justice (2 Sam. 19:8; 1 Kgs. 22:10). Priests and prophets delivered discourses and prophecies at the gate (Neh.

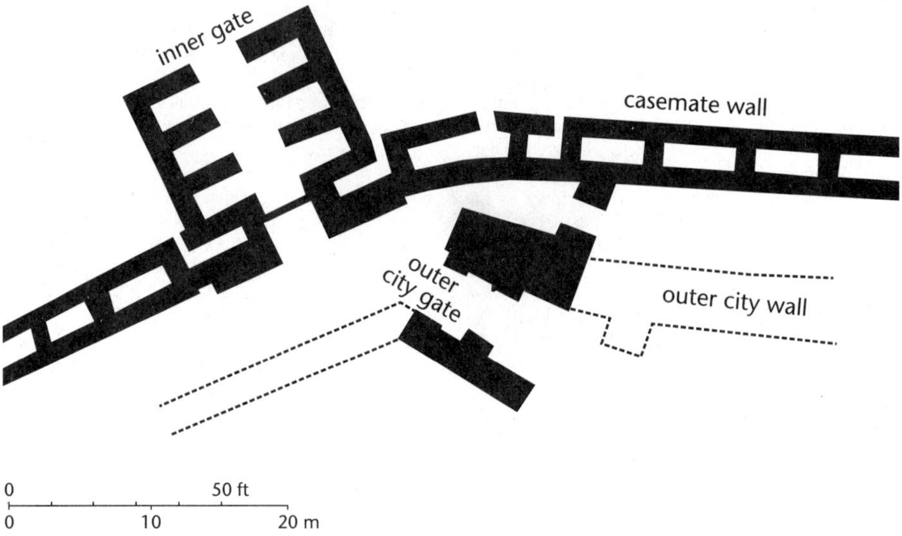

Plan of the six-chambered Iron II gate at Gezer (10th century B.C.E.)

8:1, 3; Jer. 17:19-20; 36:10). Merchants conducted business at or near the gates (Neh. 13:15-22), and some of the gates of Jerusalem took on the names of the commerce conducted there (Fish Gate, 2 Chr. 33:14; Sheep Gate, Neh. 3:1, 32).

The NT mentions gates infrequently. Jesus healed a paralytic near the Sheep Gate (John 5:2-9). Prayer was conducted outside the gate (Acts 16:13), and the dead were buried beyond the gates (Luke 7:12; Heb. 13:12).

The gate is a symbol of power (cf. Matt. 16:18), of defense and safety (Isa. 28:6), and to "possess the gate" is to capture the city (Gen. 22:17; 24:60). When a city was captured, the loss could be personified as the gates wailing (Isa. 14:31), lamenting and mourning (3:26), and languishing (Jer. 14:2). Perversion of justice for the righteous and needy can be done "in the gate" by corrupting the legal system (Amos 5:12; Prov. 22:22). Jesus used the image of the gate to illustrate the difficulty of entering the kingdom (Matt. 7:13-14).

See FORTRESS, FORTIFICATION. JAMES C. MOYER

GATEKEEPER

A guard who protected the gates of a city (2 Kgs. 7:10-11) or the Jerusalem temple (1 Chr. 9:22). King David appointed 4000 Levites to guard the temple (1 Chr. 23:3-5; 26:1-32). These guards had several duties, including caring for the ark (1 Chr. 15:23-24), overseeing the freewill offerings (2 Chr. 31:14), and guarding the storehouses at the gates (Neh. 12:25).

Esth. 2:21; 6:2 mention the eunuchs appointed by Persian King Xerxes I to guard the threshold; these men were probably the king's bodyguards. Whether this was part of the gatekeeper's tasks in ancient Israel is unknown. In the NT gatekeepers were appointed by the wealthy to guard private houses (Mark 13:34). JENNIE R. EBELING

GATH (Heb. *gaṯ*)

A city of the Philistine pentapolis, sometimes called Gath of the Philistines. Although the word Gath is usually translated "winepress," in Ugaritic texts it refers to a processing center for agricultural goods. The city is usually identified with the impressive mound known as Tell eṣ-Ṣâfi/Tel Ẓafit (1359.1237). Although other sites have been proposed (e.g., Tel Nagila [127101], Tell esh-Shariʿa/Tel Seraʿ [119088], Tell Abu Hureireh/Tel Haror [08795.11257]), none of these has garnered support.

The city's history begins in the 2nd millennium B.C.E., well before the Philistines (or Israelites) arrived in Palestine. In the 14th century the city appears in several Amarna Letters written by its ruler Šuwardata to his overlord, the Egyptian pharaoh. Gath was evidently conquered by the Philistines after their arrival on the southern coastal plain in the early 12th century. The city was still in Philistine hands in the late 11th century when David purportedly met Goliath, who came from a race of giants living in Gath, in a legendary man-to-man conflict (cf. 1 Sam. 17; 2 Sam. 21:20-22). The ark of the covenant resided there briefly after its capture by the Philistines (1 Sam. 5:8-10), and David found refuge in his flight from Saul with King Achish of Gath (1 Sam. 27). From Gath David began to curry favor with the leaders of Judah, especially round the Negeb region and the city of Hebron, and men from Gath ("Gittites") became David's most loyal supporters throughout his reign (cf. 2 Sam. 15:18). The city fell under Israelite control after the Israelites achieved independence from the Philistines.

The city was conquered by the Aramean king Hazael in the late 9th century, and its strategic location on the road leading up to Jerusalem via the Elah valley and Bethlehem was used in an attack

Iron II gate area at Tel Dan. The lower gate had two towers and four guardrooms, two on each side
(Phoenix Data Systems, Neal and Joel Bierling)

against Jerusalem (2 Kgs. 12:17). Gath was finally conquered by the Assyrian king Sargon in 712 as part of his purported conquest of Judah (cf. *ANET,* 286), and the city then passed out of the pages of history. So complete was the collapse of the legendary city of the giants that it became a proverb (Amos 6:2; cf. Mic. 1:10).

WILLIAM M. SCHNIEDEWIND

GATH-HEPHER (Heb. *gaṯ haḥēper*)
A town belonging to the tribe of Zebulun in the Lower Galilee (Josh. 19:13). The city name Gath ("winepress") was a common one, and Hepher ("pit" or "well") likely distinguished the location from other cities called Gath. The name probably referred to the primary industry of the town's residents, viticulture. Gath-hepher was the birthplace of the prophet Jonah (2 Kgs. 14:25); it was located between Nazareth and Capernaum. Jesus would have passed through the town during his ministry in Galilee. The ruins of the town are identified with modern Tel Gat Ḥefer/Khirbet ez-Zurraʿ (180238).

DAVID C. MALTSBERGER

GATH-RIMMON (Heb. *gaṯ rimmôn*)
1. A city originally allotted to the tribe of Dan (before its relocation north) (Josh. 19:45). Gath-rimmon was reallotted to the Kohathite families of the tribe of Levi according to Josh. 21:24; 1 Chr. 6:69(MT 54). Two suggestions have been offered for its location: Tell Abu Zeitun and Tell ej-Jerîshe/Tel Gerisa (1319.1665), a scant 6 km. (4 mi.) and 3.5 km. (2 mi.) respectively E of the Mediterranean, near the mouth of the Yarkon River.

2. A city reallotted from Manasseh to the Levites (Josh. 21:25). The name may be a copyist's error from Josh. 21:24.

PAUL L. REDDITT

GAULANITIS (Gk. *Gaulanitis*)
Popular name for the Golan (the plateau E of the Jordan River from Mt. Hermon to the Wadi Yarmuk) during the Hellenistic and Roman periods. The area was mostly pastoral until the Roman period, when it became a more significant region with developed road systems, better water control, and increased settlement.

Josephus and archaeological data provide most of the information regarding the history of Gaulanitis. This region was a hyparchy during the Hellenistic period, later becoming part of the eparchy of Gilead under the Seleucids. The Hasmoneans claimed it during the Maccabean revolt (83-80 B.C.), converting many inhabitants to Judaism. In 64 B.C. Rome captured Gaulanitis, but with the death of Herod's son Philip, Syria claimed it until 37 B.C. when it was given to Agrippa I. Under Agrippa II the First Jewish War was fiercely fought at Gaulanitis. Upon his death it reverted back to Syria. Jews continued to settle in the area, especially after the Bar Kokhba rebellion.

PHILLIP R. DREY

GAULS (Gk. *Galátai;* Lat. *Galli*)
A people, originally Celts, who invaded both central and western Europe (Cisalpine Gaul) and Greece and Asia Minor (Galatians). If 1 Macc. 8:2 is correct and the Romans both defeated and imposed tribute on them, then the reference would be to Cisalpine Gaul. Rome had victories over these

Gauls in 222 B.C.E. and in the 180s. The list of Roman victories in 1 Macc. 8 also seems to begin in the west and move east. If the author is merely assuming normal practice in his day, then it may refer to the victory of Gnaeus Manlius Vulso over the Galatians in 189, but no tribute was imposed at this time.

The battle in which Jewish troops defeated Celtic warriors in Babylonia (2 Macc. 8:20) must have involved Galatians, who were used as mercenaries by various kingdoms. This may have been the battle between Seleucus II and Antiochus Hierax, who used Galatian mercenaries as a major part of his army. Proposals for the time of Antiochus I or Antiochus III seem less certain.

Bibliography. J. A. Goldstein, *I Maccabees.* AB 41 (Garden City, 1976); *II Maccabees.* AB 41A (Garden City, 1983). RUSSELL NELSON

GAZA (Heb. *ʿazzâ;* Gk. *Gáza*)
An important coastal city of the southern Levant, best known in the Bible as one of the cities of Philistia. The site is Tell Ḥarube/Tell ʿAzza in the northeastern, and highest, corner of the modern city (100100). Gaza is ca. 5 km. (3 mi.) from the Mediterranean, although in Roman and Medieval times the city extended to the sea. Traditionally the southwestern boundary of Syro-Palestine (Gen. 10:19; 1 Kgs. 4:24[MT 5:4]), Gaza was the nexus of most overland commercial and military activity between Egypt and Syro-Palestine.

The Bible refers to the original inhabitants of Gaza as the Avvim, who were succeeded by the Caphtorim (Deut. 2:23), probably a variant term for the Philistines. According to Josh. 15:47 Gaza was allotted to the tribe of Judah; according to Judg. 1:18, the Judahites briefly held Gaza but v. 19 notes that they were unable to hold the cities of the coastal plain, which included Gaza. The Philistines, not the Judahites, came to control the southern coastal plain, and Gaza was one of the five major Philistine cities, the Philistine Pentapolis (Josh. 13:3; 1 Sam 6:17). Two of Samson's adventures took place in Gaza. There he visited a prostitute and, after eluding a Philistine ambush, uprooted the city gate and carried it to Hebron, 32 km. (20 mi.) away (Judg. 16:1-3). After Delilah betrayed him to the Philistines, Samson was returned to Gaza for torture and imprisonment (Judg. 16:21-25). Samson then toppled the temple of Dagon in Gaza, his final feat (Judg. 16:28-30).

The majority of biblical references to Gaza are in prophetic oracles against Philistia (e.g., Amos 1:6). Extrabiblical sources indicate that Sennacherib of Assyria captured Gaza in 734 B.C.E. Hezekiah of Judah made an incursion and attacked the city in the late 8th century (2 Kgs. 18:8). Nevertheless, Gaza maintained its independent status from ca. 1200 to nearly 600. The Egyptian pharaoh Necho II occupied the city for a time in 609, and Nebuchadnezzar captured it in 604, an event to which Jeremiah makes reference (Jer. 47:2; cf. v. 1).

The city was conquered by Cambyses in 529 and by Alexander the Great in 322. In the Hellenistic period Gaza was first an outpost of the Ptolemies and then came under Seleucid rule. The Maccabean commander Jonathan attacked the city, burning and plundering the surrounding towns before making peace on his own terms (1 Macc. 11:61-62). Alexander Janneus captured Gaza and virtually destroyed it in 96 B.C.E. after a year-long siege (Josephus *Ant.* 13.2-3; *BJ* 1.4.2). Pompey later wrested it from the Jews and the city was subsequently rebuilt.

In the NT, it is on the road to Gaza that Philip encounters and baptizes the Ethiopian eunuch (Acts 8:26-39).

Gaza endured as a major city of southern Palestine from the Late Bronze Age until the 7th century C.E. Among the remains are evidence of Philistine occupation, walls dating to the time of Necho's conquest, a dye-making industrial complex, and a 6th-century C.E. synagogue.

Bibliography. A. Ovadiah, "Gaza," *NEAEHL* 2:464-67. GREGORY MOBLEY

GAZELLE
A member of the antelope family common to the biblical world (Heb. *ṣĕḇî*). Size varies with the species; the mature gazelle measures 61 to 92 cm. (24 to 36 in.) at the shoulder and weighs ca. 18 kg. (40 lb.). Its color ranges from cinnamon to gray, with white underparts and facial highlights. Dark stripes accent its ears, flank, and short tail. The horns of both sexes are ridged, lyre-shaped, and curve gracefully to the rear. Long, delicate legs give the gazelle exceptional speed and agility. These qualities are essential for survival in the diverse regions it occupies between central Africa and Mongolia.

Many species and subspecies of gazelle are known. Common to Palestine are the mountain gazelle *(Gazella gazella),* the Arab gazelle *(G. arabica),* and the dorcas gazelle *(G. dorcas;* the name is from the Greek; cf. Acts 9:36). The distinct features of the goitered gazelle *(G. subgutturosa)* are noted specifically in Mesopotamian art, but distinguishing between these species in the archaeological record is difficult.

Gazelles were hunted for food and sport, a challenge given the fact that gazelles can reach speeds that approach 97 kph (60 mph) in short bursts. The extent to which gazelles were captured, tamed, and managed remains disputed. In the Bible these animals were considered clean, and hence edible (Deut. 12:15, 22; 14:5; 15:22). Most passages, however, refer to the gazelle figuratively, emphasizing its speed (2 Sam. 2:18; 1 Chr. 12:8[MT 9]) and beauty (Cant. 2:9, 17; 3:5; 4:5; 7:3). MARK ZIESE

GAZEZ (Heb. *gāzēz*)

1. A son of Caleb by his concubine Ephah (1 Chr. 2:46).

2. The son of Haran and grandson of Caleb (1 Chr. 2:46); nephew of **1** above.

GAZZAM (Heb. *gazzām*)
The head of a family of temple servants which returned with Zerubbabel from exile (Ezra 2:48 = Neh. 7:51).

GEBA (Heb. *geḇaʿ*)
A city identified with the modern village of Jabaʿ (175140), located 10 km. (6.2 mi.) N of Jerusalem near the northern border of the tribe of Benjamin. Its position gave rise to the expression "from Geba to Beer-sheba" as delimiting the greatest extent of the kingdom of Judah (2 Kgs. 23:8).

Geba figures prominently in the early history of the monarchy. The Philistines sent advance camps to the region of Geba and Michmash, where Saul's son Jonathan defeated them in battle (1 Sam. 10:5; 13:2–14:23). The Judean king Asa fortified Geba and Mizpeh as his northern bulwarks during the civil war with King Baasha of Israel. It was also among the towns settled by those returning from Babylonian Captivity (Ezra 2:26; Neh. 7:30).

Attempts to conflate references to Gibeah with Geba have not been convincing because both biblical and extrabiblical sources clearly distinguish two sites (e.g., Isa. 10:29). Some confusion arose among ancient scribes as a result of the similarity in spelling and meaning between Geba and two other sites in the vicinity, Gibeon (el-Jîb) and Gibeah (Tell el-Fûl) — the Hebrew root for all three words means simply "hill." For example, the reference to Geba in Judg. 20:20 should be read as Gibeah (as elsewhere in the story of Judg. 19–20), and the rout of the Philistines "from Geba to Gezer" in 2 Sam. 5:25 should be emended to "from Gibeon to Gezer," following 1 Chr. 14:16. WILLIAM M. SCHNIEDEWIND

GEBAL (Heb. *gĕḇāl*)
1. A major Canaanite and Phoenician shipping center, located ca. 30 km. (18.6 mi.) N of Beirut. Its Canaanite name was Gubla, "mountain" (Ugar. *Gbl,* transcribed in Egyptian records as *Kbn/Kpn*). The Phoenician name *Gbl* is vocalized in biblical Hebrew as Gebal. The Mycenaean Greeks called the city Byblos, either a corruption of its Canaanite name or a name derived from the classical Greek term *byblos,* also *biblos,* "papyrus, book" — whence the word Bible originated. The inhabitants of Gebal may have manufactured and/or supplied this writing material to the early Greeks, or the Greeks simply obtained papyrus from this port city.

The tell of Gebal (modern Jebeil; 210391) was explored in 1860-61 by Ernest Renan and then again by a series of archaeological excavations conducted by Pierre Montet (1921-24), Maurice Dunand (1925-52), and Jacques Cauvin (1968). The finds revealed that the settlement was occupied continuously from the Neolithic to the Roman eras. The harbor complex of Gebal consisted of three natural bays located north and south of the ancient mound.

Literary sources and archaeological finds indicate that by 2500 B.C.E. the Egyptians used this port as their primary trading outpost in the Lebanon. Excavated finds included the discovery of a new linear syllabic script, which was utilized locally during the Middle Bronze Age (2000-1550). Dunand names this writing system the "pseudo-hieroglyphic" script of Byblos. Attempts to decipher these Byblian inscriptions were made by Édouard Dhorme in 1946 and George E. Mendenhall in 1985; both efforts read the language as an early Canaanite dialect. Other epigraphic finds at Gebal included several Phoenician alphabet royal inscriptions, notably, the inscribed sarcophagus of King Ahiram (10th century or later).

From the Amarna Letters (14th century) it is known that the king of Gebal, Rib-adda, remained loyal to the Egyptian pharaohs during the upheavals in Canaan. In the 11th century Byblos was still a major trading partner of Egypt, as is known from the tale of Wenamon (ca. 1075), which provides details about Canaanite shipping partnerships. Afterward, Byblos was eclipsed by the Phoenician ports of Sidon and Tyre.

Gebal is mentioned only three times in the OT. In Josh. 13:5 the "land of the Gebalites" is described as a northern boundary of the Promised Land. Later references list the stone masons of Gebal, alongside those of Israel and Tyre, as the builders of the Solomonic temple (1 Kgs. 5:18[MT 32]). The elders and artisans of Gebal are noted in Ezek. 27:9 as members of the commercial sphere of Tyre.

Bibliography. W. F. Albright, "The Eighteenth-Century Princes of Byblos and the Chronology of Middle Bronze," *BASOR* 176 (1964): 38-46; H. Goedicke, *The Report of Wenamon* (Baltimore, 1975); G. E. Mendenhall, *The Syllabic Inscriptions from Byblos* (Beirut, 1985); R. Wallenfels, "Redating the Byblian Inscriptions," *JANES* 15 (1983): 79-118; J. M. Weinstein, "Egyptian Relations with Palestine in the Middle Kingdom," *BASOR* 217 (1975): 1-16.
ROBERT R. STIEGLITZ

2. A territory (modern Gibal) SE of the Dead Sea in the mountains of Seir near Petra, mentioned along with Moab, Ammon, Amalek, and others as continuing an alliance against Israel (Ps. 83:7[MT 8]). As Gobolitis it was part of Idumea (Josephus *Ant.* 2.1.2[6]).

GEBER (Heb. *geḇer*)
The son of Uri; the officer appointed by Solomon over the southern portion of Gilead (1 Kgs. 4:19; cf. Ben-geber, v. 13).

GEBIM (Heb. *gēḇîm*)
A village N of Jerusalem whose inhabitants fled from the approaching Assyrian army (Isa. 10:31). The site has been suggested as modern Shu'afat, ca. 3 km. (2 mi.) N of Jerusalem, but this identification is uncertain.

GEDALIAH (Heb. *gĕḏalyâ, gĕḏalyāhû*)
1. The son of Ahikam and governor of Judah after it was overrun by Babylonian forces in 586 B.C.E. (2 Kgs. 25:22-26; Jer. 40:6–44:18). Gedaliah was of royal stock (2 Kgs. 22:3, 14) and may have been the same royal steward who is mentioned on a stamp seal found at Lachish. As governor, he succeeded in effecting order in Judah with the help of the aged prophet Jeremiah and some army officers. However, his tenure lasted only two or three months. He and others were assassinated by a conspiratorial congress of Jewish nationalists led by

Ishmael, who was of the royal line. This happened because Gedaliah, who had a trusting nature, ignored prior warnings of the plot and rejected Johanan's scheme to murder Ishmael.

Gedaliah's death marked the end of a surviving Jewish community in Judah since his partisans, fearing Babylonian reprisals, fled to Egypt, forcing Jeremiah to go with them. In effect, a marked Jewish presence disappeared from Palestine until new leadership came with the return from Exile. The exiled Jews marked each anniversary of Gedaliah's death with a day of mourning and fasting (Zech. 7:5).

2. A professional musician during David's reign. His father Jeduthum was one of three leaders appointed by the king to provide music (1 Chr. 25:3, 9).

3. A priest from the family of the high priest Jeshua who divorced his pagan wife after the Exile (Ezra 10:18).

4. A Jerusalemite prince (son of Pashhur) who had pro-Egyptian leanings and agitated for Jeremiah's death because he urged submission to the Babylonians during the siege of Jerusalem (Jer. 38:1-6).

5. The grandfather of the prophet Zephaniah (Zeph. 1:1). KENNETH D. MULZAC

GEDER (Heb. *geḏer*)
One of several Canaanite cities captured by Joshua during the Israelite conquest (Josh. 12:13). A lieutenant of David's, Baal-hanan, may have hailed from Geder (1 Chr. 27:28). If the Josh. 12 conquest list is organized as either a battle itinerary or regional association, Geder might be sought near Tell Beit Mirsim in the Shephelah foothills. Yohanan Aharoni wishes to emend Geder to Gerar due to common orthographic error; so emended, the city's association with the Gerar in the Abimelech narratives of Abraham and Isaac (Gen. 20, 26) lends credence to a Shephelah location for the city.

Bibliography. Y. Aharoni, *The Land of the Bible*, 2nd ed. (Philadelphia, 1979). RYAN BYRNE

GEDERAH (Heb. *gĕḏērâ*)
1. A town in the Shephelah, part of the second district of the tribal allotment of Judah (Josh. 15:36). It should probably be identified with Khirbet Judraya (14980.12184) on the north side of the Elah River. The royal potters were from this town (1 Chr. 4:23).

2. The home town of Jozabad the Gederathite, one of David's mighty men (1 Chr. 12:4[MT 5]. It is probably located at modern Jedireh near Gibeon.
STEVEN M. ORTIZ

GEDEROTH (Heb. *gĕḏērôṯ*)
A town in the Shephelah, part of the third district of the tribal allotment of Judah (Josh. 15:41). Although its location is uncertain, it has recently been identified with Tel Milḥa (12876.09678) on the Shiqma River. Gederoth is one of the towns of the Shephelah captured by the Philistines during the weak rule of Ahaz (2 Chr. 28:18). Apparently, this town was on the often disputed border between Philistia and Judah. STEVEN M. ORTIZ

GEDEROTHAIM (Heb. *gĕḏērōṯāyim*)
A town in the lowlands of Judah (Josh. 15:36). Because this name is fifteenth in a list of 14 towns (so MT), scholars have proposed that it be read literally, "and her sheepfolds" (following LXX).

GEDOR (Heb. *gĕḏôr*) **(PERSON)**
The son of Jeiel and Maacah; eponymous ancestor of a Benjaminite family (1 Chr. 8:31; 9:37).

GEDOR (Heb. *gĕḏôr*) **(PLACE)**
(also GADARA, GEDORA)

1. A town in the Judean hill country (Josh. 15:58). Ancient Gedor is identified with Khirbet Jedur (158115), 16 km. (10 mi.) N of Hebron. Late Bronze Age remains have been found nearby, including a large number of ceramic vessels, a bronze pitchfork, and an Egyptian-style signet ring. Two Benjaminite brothers from Gedor joined David's forces at Ziklag (1 Chr. 12:7[MT 8]).

The genealogical listing of 1 Chronicles personifies the city and its history (1 Chr. 4:4). 1 Chr. 4:18 may preserve a second tradition of how the towns and villages of tribal Judah "descended" from the sons of Judah or may be a reference instead to Gederah. Mention of Gedor in the tribal list of Simeon (1 Chr. 4:39) may be a scribal error in the Hebrew text as the earliest Greek (LXX) manuscripts refer to "Gerar." Should the reading be "Gedor" in Simeon, the site is otherwise unknown.

2. A city in Gilead and capital of Perea during postexilic times, also referred to as Gedora or Gadara. The city is identified as modern Tell ʿAin-Jedûr (220160) near al-Ahalth in Jordan. The city was taken by the Roman general Vespasian prior to his siege of Jerusalem (Josephus *BJ* 4.413). Jesus' ministry "beyond the Jordan" likely included Gedor (Matt. 19:1; Mark 10:1).
DAVID C. MALTSBERGER

GE-HARASHIM (Heb. *gêʾ ḥărāšîm*)
Lit., "valley of the artisans/craftsmen," but identified as the sons of Joab, of the tribe of Judah and lineage of Kenaz, so identified "because they were artisans" (1 Chr. 4:14 NRSV). A similar term at Neh. 11:35 (Heb. *gê haḥărāšîm;* omitted in the LXX), usually translated "valley of craftsmen/artisans" in English versions, denotes a place (near Lod and Ono, perhaps Wadi esh-Shellal or Ṣarafand el-Kharab) inhabited by Benjaminites after the return from Babylonian exile. Many interpreters understand 1 Chr. 4:14 as a reference to a place, either that mentioned in Neh. 11:35 or another SE of the Dead Sea and rich with copper deposits.
ERIC F. MASON

GEHAZI (Heb. *gêḥăzî*)
The servant of the prophet Elisha (2 Kgs. 4:12-36). Elisha resides with a Shunammite woman in a roof chamber built for him. When Elisha is unsure how to repay this kindness, Gehazi reveals that the

woman has no son and that her husband is old. The servant's hint to Elisha allows him to intercede with God. When this child dies, the mother seeks Elisha, who sends Gehazi ahead with his staff to pledge his personal involvement, or to prevent the body's removal for burial on the day of death (as was the custom). Perhaps Gehazi exceeds Elisha's instructions by attempting to resuscitate the child with the help of a staff with healing properties. The boy recovers only when Elisha prays.

Naaman, commander of Syria's army, is leprous, but is healed when he washes in the Jordan at Elisha's direction. Although Elisha refuses any gift, Gehazi, seeking personal gain, follows Naaman and requests silver and clothing. Gehazi later conceals his actions from Elisha. For his greed, lying, and betrayal, Naaman's leprosy falls on Gehazi (2 Kgs. 5:20-27). No healing narrative follows, so punishment appears to be permanent, but Gehazi still enjoys social contact, without levitical restrictions (cf. Lev. 13–15).

During a famine, Elisha sends the Shunammite woman away. On returning, she seeks restoration of her property from the king. At Gehazi's intervention this request is granted (2 Kgs. 8:4-6).

Bibliography. L. Bronner, *The Stories of Elijah and Elisha.* Pretoria Oriental Series 6 (Leiden, 1968).

PATRICIA A. MACNICOLL

GEHENNA (Gk. *géenna;* Lat. *Gehenna*)

The "valley of Hinnom" (from Heb. *gê hinnōm*), a ravine (Wadi er-Rabâbi) S and SW of Jerusalem, meeting with the Kidron Valley at En-rogel. Early traditions locating the valley in the Wadi Kidron are not satisfactory. The English NT usually translates the Greek term as "hell." The OT often combines "hinnom" with "sons (or 'son') of" (NRSV "Ben-hinnom"), suggesting a possible origin in a family name.

The valley became a place of idol worship and child sacrifice during the period of the Monarchy (2 Kgs. 23:10; Jer. 32:35). The prophet Jeremiah proclaimed that the valley would become known as the "valley of Slaughter" where Yahweh would judge and punish his people (Jer. 7:30-32; 19:2, 6). Joel also envisions God's judgment as occurring in a valley just outside the city of Jerusalem (Joel 3:2, 12, 14[4:2, 12, 14]; Isa. 30:29-33; 66:24). By the time of the Maccabees, the valley was the appropriate location in which to burn the bodies of one's enemies (cf. 2 Esdr. 7:36). 1 Enoch viewed "the accursed valley" of God's judgment as outside the city of Jerusalem, the center of the world (e.g., 1 En. 27:1).

By NT times the idea of Gehenna had made a full transformation to an otherworldly place of future punishment for the wicked. The valley itself may have become a place where trash was dumped and burned, thus an "unclean" location. (This interpretation has been questioned.) In theory, one could not go directly from the Hinnom dump to the temple because of the worshipper's unclean status. This status of uncleanness ("cut-off") and the past association of the valley with a place of judgment combined to create a metaphor for "hell."

An alternative view is that the altars for pagan worship in the valley of Hinnom involved the funneling of the victim's blood directly into the earth to satisfy the gods. This may have evolved into a tradition that this was an entrance into the underworld (the opposite of Jacob's discovery of the staircase entrance to heaven).

By the time of the NT writers, the idea of a "hell" *(gehenna)* had developed into a physical place where God's enemies would suffer punishment and destruction in both body and soul (e.g., Matt. 10:28; 23:33). Slaughter, burning, and shedding of blood all became symbols for this punishment (Matt. 5:22; Mark 9:43-47).

See HINNOM. STEPHEN VON WYRICK

GELILOTH (Heb. *gĕlîlôṯ*)

A place (Heb. "circles") on the boundary separating Benjamin and Judah, situated opposite the ascent of Adummim (Josh. 18:17). The site lies along the road from Jericho to Jerusalem, ca. 10 km. (6 mi.) from Jerusalem, and has long been identified with Khan el-Aḥmar, the traditional inn of the Good Samaritan. But Geliloth may instead be ʿAraq ed-Deir (180133), 1.5 km. (1 mi.) west. It may be the same as the Gilgal (**4**) mentioned at Josh. 15:7.

GEMALLI (Heb. *gĕmallî*)

A Danite and the father of Ammiel, one of the 12 spies that Moses sent into the Promised Land (Num. 13:12).

GEMARIAH (Heb. *gĕmaryâ, gĕmaryāhû*)

1. A son of Hilkiah. Sent by King Zedekiah to Nebuchadnezzar at Babylon, he and Elasah carried a letter from the prophet Jeremiah to the exiles living there (Jer. 29:1-3).

2. A son of the king's secretary Shaphan, and brother of Ahikam. It was in his chamber within the temple that Baruch read Jeremiah's prophecies to the people (Jer. 36:10, 12). Gemariah was one of the princes who opposed King Jehoiakim's burning of the scroll (Jer. 36:25).

GEMS

A general term construed to mean any precious or semiprecious stones, especially when cut or polished for ornamental purposes. A gem can also be a cameo or an intaglio in an archaeological sense. Gems, mineralogically, are an order of minerals that are distinguished by their hardness, transparency, and nonmetallic luster. They have sufficient beauty and durability for use as a personal ornament or as symbols of authority. Gems have been used, depending on their value, in trade for many centuries. Gems mentioned in the Bible, in a liberal sense, include agate (chalcedony), alabaster, amethyst, beryl, chrysolite (topaz), diamond (Heb. *yahălōm,* which could mean onyx), emerald, jasper, and *rāʾmôṯ* (coral). RICHARD A. STEPHENSON

GENEALOGY

A record of an individual's or clan's descent from a putative ancestor(s). Genealogies (Heb. *tôlēḏôṯ*, "generations") function as an important medium of expression and interaction. Once taken at face value, biblical genealogies have come under scrutiny by critics who have recognized "apparent contradictions" and thus have considered them as artificial and tendentious creations. However, genealogies are actually accurate explanations of the milieu in which they were created, even if they do not correspond to Western notions of objective data. Lineage ties usually had little to do with ethnic identity, since no such concept existed in the ancient world, but often rather were concerned with political unity. Acknowledgment of blood ties was not the only function of a genealogy. A person received status by virtue of his kinship ties. Genealogies were altered when their function changed. Some names of ancestors disappeared (when they no longer had a relevant function), while other names were added. Thus, genealogical function varied depending upon the circumstance, and was located within domestic (to justify contemporary lineage configurations), political (to validate the incumbents or usurpers in the existing government), and religious spheres. The Bible often exhibited these functions synchronically, which accounts for the apparent contradictions.

Genealogies were a common feature of ancient West Asian historical traditions. The Sumerian King List (ca. 1900 B.C.), although dealing little with genealogies, was concerned with the succession of kingship in Sumer, maintaining the fiction that power was located in Sumer in the hands of one dynasty in any given period. A dynasty was considered legitimate if it had received a "turn of office" from the gods, not strictly because of any genealogical ties.

For the Assyrians and Babylonians, however, legitimacy was determined within the kinship structure of the Amorite tribes. These ties formed a "genealogical charter" for the legitimacy of kingship. Thus, a monarch had to claim descent from the proper lineage within a tribe. This can be seen in the Assyrian King List, a document which provides a detailed list of Assyrian rulers and their general length of reign for more than 1000 years, purporting that it was one continuous lineage. The genealogy of the Hammurabi dynasty contains the names of the kings of the First Dynasty of Babylon (to Ammiditana, 1646-1626). Both of these lists contain a consecutive roster of earlier kings and/or ancestors, most of whom have Amorite personal names. Interestingly, a number of the names are found on both lists, reflecting a common lineage tradition in Assyria and Babylonia. Moreover, Didanu, a name from both lists (as well as in the Kirta Epic from Ugarit), is likely the Dedan of Gen. 25:3.

Like the Assyrian King List and genealogy of the Hammurabi dynasty, many genealogies in the OT were composed to establish legitimacy, royal or otherwise. They are found primarily in the Pentateuch, Ruth, Chronicles, Ezra, and Nehemiah. Two types of genealogy are found in the OT. A segmented genealogy exhibited a "family tree," showing the relationship of children to other family members (e.g., Gen. 35:22-26). Linear genealogies were lists of names connecting an individual to an ancestor or ancestors and showing their relationship. An ascending linear list (e.g., Ezra 7:1-5) featured an individual as the son of another, and traced one's lineage back to an important ancestor. A descending linear list (e.g., Gen. 4:17-22) featured a father "begetting" a son, and normally provided information as to the person's age and deeds. These genealogies were not necessarily complete (i.e., listing all individuals in a direct line, one after another), since their purpose was to establish descent and thereby legitimacy from a particular ancestor or ancestors. The OT contains about 25 genealogical lists, including the descendants of Adam (Gen. 5), Noah (ch. 10), and Israel/Jacob (ch. 46). There are also registers of individuals, such as Levites (1 Chr. 6:1-53[MT 5:27–6:38) and families that had returned from the Exile (Ezra 2:2-61 = Neh. 7:7-63).

Genealogies are less frequent in the NT. Two give the ancestry of Jesus: Matt. 1:1-17, which traces his descent from Abraham; and Luke 3:23-38, which reverses the order and continues back to Adam. Matthew is interested in exhibiting symmetry, and so lists 14 individuals between Abraham, David, and the Babylonian Exile; thus a number of Judahite kings are omitted from the list to preserve the symmetry. Moreover, Luke and Matthew have a different list after David (except for two names). The lists likely serve different functions and should not be interpreted as contradictory. Departing from the tradition of tracing only male descents, Matthew's genealogy contains four women, most of whom were not Israelites. These do not appear in Luke's list.

Heb. 7:3 asserts that Melchizedek "was without genealogy" (Gk. *genealogía*). 1 Tim. 1:4; Tit. 3:9 use the term in a negative sense, describing genealogies in conjunction with myths and foolish questions; references to Jewish myths and "Teachers of the Law" may imply contemporary Jewish interpretation of biblical lineages.

Bibliography. K. R. Andriolo, "A Structural Analysis of Genealogy and Worldview in the Old Testament," *American Anthropologist* 75 (1973): 1657-69; M. W. Chavalas, "Genealogical History as 'Charter': A Study of Old Babylonian Period Historiography and the Old Testament," in *Faith, Tradition, and History,* ed. A. R. Millard, J. K. Hoffmeier, and D. W. Baker (Winona Lake, 1994), 103-28; J. W. Flanagan, "Succession and Genealogy in the Davidic Dynasty," in *The Quest for the Kingdom of God,* ed. H. Huffman, F. A. Spina, and A. R. W. Green (Winona Lake, 1983), 35-55; M. D. Johnson, *The Purpose of the Biblical Genealogies,* 2nd ed. SNTSMS 8 (Cambridge, 1988); A. Malamat, "King Lists of the Old Babylonian Period and Biblical Genealogies," *JAOS* 88 (1968): 163-73; R. R. Wilson, *Genealogy and History in the Biblical World* (New Haven, 1977).

MARK W. CHAVALAS

GENERAL EPISTLES

See CATHOLIC LETTERS.

GENERATION

A period of time (Heb. *dôr,* "circle"), generally that spanning a person's birth to the birth of his or her offspring, roughly 40 years (cf. Gk. *geneá,* Matt. 1:17); also the people of a period of time (Judg. 2:10; Jer. 2:31; Matt. 11:16; 17:17). In a crucial text relating to God's covenant with Israel, the covenant is said to be established everlastingly with Abraham and his descendants "throughout their generations" (Gen. 17:7, 9, 12); the phrase frequently describes the perpetually binding character of the law of Moses (e.g., Exod. 12:14, 17, 42).

Heb. *tôlĕḏôṯ* (always plural, from the verb "to beget [children]") introduces an account or record, often a genealogy. It occurs primarily to introduce or conclude a genealogy or historical summary (e.g., Gen. 10:32; 25:13; Exod. 6:16, 19; Num. 3:1; 1 Chr. 5:7; 7:2, 4, 9). The expression "these are the generations of ——— " gives structure to the book of Genesis, dividing it into 11 sections (e.g., Gen. 2:4; 5:1; 6:9; 37:2). Gk. *génesis,* often referring to birth (cf. Matt. 1:18), functions in a similar manner to *tôlĕḏôṯ* (v. 1). DAVID L. TURNER

GENESIS, BOOK OF

The first book of the Bible.

Name and Early Interpretation

The name "Genesis" comes from the title given to the book in the ancient Greek (LXX) translation of the book. This name in turn was taken from the Greek version of Gen. 2:4: "this is the book of generations of heaven and earth. . . ," which points to the genealogical character of Genesis. Not only does the book contain many genealogies, but it describes the "genesis" of the 12 sons of Israel. As such, Genesis forms a semi-genealogical backdrop to the emergence of the nation of Israel in Exodus and following.

The Hebrew title of the book, *bĕrē'šîṯ* ("in the beginning" or "when . . . first . . ."), derives from the first word of Genesis. This Hebrew name also points to a crucial aspect of the book. However one translates *bĕrē'šîṯ,* the expression points to the fact that Genesis stands at the outset of both the Torah narrative and the Bible as a whole. As literary critics have taught us, narrative beginnings can be quite significant. They shape the expectations of a reader as he or she moves through the following story. This has certainly been true for Genesis as it has been interpreted by both Christian and Jewish communities. Although each faith community has read the book through the lens of those beliefs it holds most dear, both have devoted disproportionate attention to Genesis.

Structure and Contents

As mentioned above, the book functions in part to give genealogical background to the "descendants of Israel" featured in Exodus and the rest of the OT. Indeed, the book is dominated by a series of labels (Gen. 2:4; 5:1; 6:9; 10:1; 11:10, 27; 25:12, 19; 36:1, 9; 37:2) which introduce many sections of Genesis as focusing on the "descendants" of a given figure. For example, Gen. 11:10 introduces the genealogy which follows as focusing on the "descendants of Shem." To be sure, there is ongoing debate about the translation of the crucial term in these labels, *tôlĕḏôṯ,* and many have argued that this term means "descendants" at some points (e.g., 5:1; 10:1; 11:10) but "history" or "story" at points where the term labels a narrative rather than a genealogy (cf. 37:2 RSV, NRSV). Nevertheless, the term *tôlĕḏōṯ* is derived from the root for "have children" (*yld*) and generally refers in Biblical Hebrew to descendants, a genealogical series, or a genealogy (cf. Num. 3:1; Ruth 4:18; 1 Chr. 1:29; 5:7; 7:2, 4, 9; 8:28; 9:9, 22; 26:31). The consistent use of this term to introduce both strict genealogies and extended narratives in Genesis gives the whole book a semi-genealogical quality.

Interpreters have generally distinguished within the whole between a "primeval history" focusing on all of humanity and an "ancestral history" (previously often termed "patriarchal history") focusing on Abraham and his descendants. The primeval history is variously defined as extending from 1:1 to 11:9, 11:26, 11:31, or even 12:3. Its primary orientation points are the Creation and Flood. First, the story of Creation leads into the rebellion and multiplication of the first family and their descendants, culminating in God's decision to destroy all human life, with the exception of Noah and his family (1:1–6:8). Then, in the Flood narrative, God destroys and then re-creates the living spaces of the cosmos, and starts over with Noah's family and the animals (6:9–9:19). Nevertheless, similar patterns of human rebellion and striving emerge in the stories that follow. The story of Noah and his sons in 9:20-27 resembles those about the first family (2:4–4:16), and the story of a human attempt to cross the divine-human boundary with the tower of Babel (11:1-9) revisits many of the same issues that dominated the brief pre-Flood story of divine beings crossing the same boundary to have children by human daughters (6:1-4). Thus both the pre-Flood (2:4–6:8) and post-Flood (6:9–11:9) narratives trace a pattern of linkage of human population growth with division between humans and threats to the divine-human boundary.

These primeval stories then set the scene for the story of promise that follows in the ancestral history. Soon after a genealogy tracing the single genealogical line leading from Noah's family to Abram (11:10-26), this ancestral history opens with God's call for Abram to go to the land God "will show" him (12:1) and God's promises (vv. 2-3), including commitments to make him into a great nation, protect, and bless him so that he becomes a paradigm of blessing for others. When Abram goes to the land of Canaan (12:4-6), God promises that land to his offspring (v. 7) and shows it to him (13:14-17). This then sets in motion an overall promise-centered narrative that extends beyond Genesis. The rest of the Abraham story (11:27–25:11) focuses in large part on Abraham and Sarah's failed attempts to secure an heir for this promise and on God's strengthening of the promise into a covenant (15:1-21; 17:1-21) and the miraculous provision of a child, Isaac, to inherit it (18:1-15; 21:1-7; 22:1-18).

After a brief digression to survey the descendants of Ishmael (25:12-18), the story of Isaac's descendants (25:19–35:29) traces another story of reception of promise and protection. In contrast to the Abraham story, Isaac's heir, Jacob, is produced early in the story (25:21-26) and soon receives the promise (28:13-15; cf. vv. 3-4; 31:3; 35:10-12). But this story is complicated by Jacob's conflicts first with his brother Esau (25:19–33:17), and then with local Canaanites and even his own sons (33:18–35:22). By the end of the Jacob narrative the 12 sons of Jacob/Israel have been born, all of whom will inherit the promise, but Esau ends up excluded from the promise and dies outside the land (36:1-43).

After diverging to survey the descendants of Esau, the Genesis narrative turns to an extensive section on Jacob's descendants, particularly Joseph (Gen. 37:2–50:26). In this subtle narrative, Joseph eventually creates the conditions for reconciling with his brothers, although they had earlier thought about killing him and did sell him into slavery. By the close of Genesis these "sons of Israel" have overcome a major challenge to their unity and stand ready *together* to inherit the promise to Abraham and become the nation of Israel. This narrative demonstrates that the issue in Genesis is not just production of those who would inherit the promise, but the move from conflictual separation of siblings into heirs and non-heirs (e.g. Isaac vs. Ishmael, Jacob vs. Esau) to the creation of a genealogically defined community of heirs where all descendants could inherit the promise and live in the land together.

Formation

Discoveries of multiple and divergent versions of texts both inside and outside Israel indicate that ancient authors diverged from us in their concept of both textual integrity and authorship. Whereas modern readers look at Genesis from the perspective of a culture where people are not allowed to add to texts authored by others, the ancient authors of Genesis worked within a culture where cherished texts were added to and where history was usually transmitted anonymously. Indeed, the Pentateuch is anonymous and nowhere claims Mosaic authorship for itself. Attribution of Genesis and the rest of the Pentateuch to Moses does not emerge explicitly until Israel had come into intense contact with the highly author-conscious Greek culture.

There are many signs that Genesis, like other important documents in Israel and elsewhere, grew over time. Already in 1753, the French physician Jean Astruc recognized signs that Genesis had been created out of at least two major sources. In subsequent centuries Astruc's insights have been expanded and refined to recognize a basic distinction in Genesis between two basic bodies of material: a Priestly set of texts (P) beginning with the seven-day Creation account in 1:1–2:3; and a largely earlier set of non-Priestly texts beginning with the garden of Eden story in 2:4–3:24. In addition to 1:1–2:3, the Priestly layer encompasses most of Genesis's genealogies, genealogical headings, a significant strand of the Flood narrative, and Priestly promise-oriented texts like 17:1-27; 26:34-35; 27:46–28:9; 35:9-15; 48:3-6. The non-Priestly layer encompasses almost everything else. In its present form the Priestly layer is integrally related to the non-Priestly material and forms an editorial framework for much of it. Scholars continue to debate, however, whether a large portion of the present Priestly layer in Genesis once may have been part of a Priestly source that originally stood separate from the non-Priestly material and even been designed to replace it.

Ever since the work of Karl Heinrich Graf and Julius Wellhausen in the late 1800s, most scholars have recognized that the earliest origins of Genesis probably are to be found in the non-Priestly material. Nevertheless, there is considerable debate about the history of the formation of that material. Over the last hundred years most scholars have maintained that the bulk of the non-Priestly material of Genesis was formed out of the combination of materials from two hypothesized pentateuchal sources: a "Yahwistic" document (J) written in the South during the reign of David or Solomon and an "Elohistic" document (E) written one or two centuries later in the northern kingdom of Israel. Recently, however, many would date crucial elements of the hypothesized Yahwistic document 400 years later to the time of the Exile. Moreover, many specialists working with Genesis no longer think there was an Elohistic source. Rather than non-Priestly material being formed out of interwoven Yahwistic and Elohistic documents, some scholars hypothesize that the earliest written origins of the non-Priestly material are to be found in hypothesized preexilic independent documents focusing on different parts of the story: e.g., primeval history, Jacob and/or Joseph. Thus, the early history of the written formation of Genesis and other pentateuchal books remains an unresolved problem in pentateuchal research.

Whatever one's theories about the written prehistory of Genesis, almost all agree that many of the book's elements were shaped by a long history of oral transmission of stories and genealogies. Overall, this traditional material falls into three categories: cosmic traditions (such as those regarding Creation and Flood), genealogies, and legendary material regarding culture heroes like Abraham, Isaac, and Jacob. The cosmic traditions of Genesis are paralleled by similar traditions in other ancient Near Eastern and Mediterranean cultures. Such materials appear to have been transmitted in temple and related contexts. The genealogical materials also have many parallels in other cultures. In particular, there is an interesting correspondence between the genealogical form of early Greek histories and that found in Genesis. Legendary material regarding culture heroes of the sort found in Genesis is also found in other cultures, and seems to have been freely transmitted in various unofficial and official oral contexts.

History

Whether cosmic tradition, genealogy, or legend — all of the materials in Genesis were shaped in the crucible of life of successive generations in Israel. As a result, the stories of Genesis tell us at least as much about the insights and beliefs of those successive generations as they do about the history of Israel before the Exodus. For example, the sabbath focus found in the 1:1–2:3 Creation account probably reflects a consciousness of the preciousness of sabbath that first arises during the Babylonian Exile. It was at that time, when Israel was far away from the land and had no temple, that the ancient practice of sabbath became a particularly central means for Israel to live out its faith. So also, although there almost certainly were figures named Abraham and Sarah, Jacob and Rachel, numerous elements of the narratives regarding them seem to have been shaped by the experience and questions of later retellers of these legends. Perhaps partly as a result of this process of reshaping of tradition over time, the book of Genesis has proven its ability to speak of people of varying cultures and times. It is not just a story about things happening in a bygone age. It is a crystallization of Israel's most fervent beliefs and hopes as expressed through traditions which have proven their theological worth over time.

Bibliography. A. Brenner, ed., *A Feminist Companion to Genesis* (Sheffield, 1993); D. M. Carr, *Reading the Fractures of Genesis* (Louisville, 1996); T. E. Fretheim, "The Book of Genesis," *NIB* 1:321-674; D. Gowan, *From Eden to Babel.* ITC (Grand Rapids, 1988); P. K. McCarter, "The Patriarchal Age: Abraham, Isaac and Jacob," in *Ancient Israel,* ed. H. Shanks (Washington, 1988), 1-29; D. Steinmetz, *From Father to Son: Kinship, Conflict and Continuity in Genesis* (Louisville, 1991). DAVID M. CARR

GENESIS APOCRYPHON (1QapGen ar)

A collection of apocryphal stories about the biblical patriarchs, among the first Dead Sea Scrolls discovered in Qumran Cave 1. This 22-column Aramaic document lacks both its beginning and end, and several of the surviving columns are either illegible or so fragmentary that reading them is impossible. While the text exhibits no uniquely Qumranic ideas, it still may have originated at Qumran in the 1st century B.C.E. As an apparent retelling and expansion of Genesis, it resembles 1 Enoch, Jubilees, and the Testaments of the Twelve Patriarchs.

The first extant story (cols. 2-5) is a version of the story of Noah's birth in 1 En. 106-7. Noah's extraordinary appearance causes his father Lamech to worry that Bitenosh had copulated with angelic beings. The text certainly also included the Flood story, but it is fragmentary at this point.

Cols. 19-22 paraphrase Gen. 12:8–15:4 and incorporate several additions to the biblical narrative. For example, Abraham has a dream that forewarns him of the Egyptians' plot to kill him and take Sarah for Pharaoh. The text also adds a description of Sarah's beauty. The account ends in the middle of the story of God's covenant with Abraham.

Bibliography. J. A. Fitzmyer, *The Genesis Apocryphon of Qumran Cave I,* 2nd ed. BibOr 18A (Rome, 1971); G. W. E. Nickelsburg, "The Bible Rewritten and Expanded," in *Jewish Writings of the Second Temple Period,* ed. M. E. Stone. CRINT 2 (Philadelphia, 1984): 89-156. RODNEY A. WERLINE

GENIZAH (Heb. *gĕnîzâ*)

The chamber of a synagogue which stores wornout copies of the Torah and other sacred writings no longer fit for use in worship as well as heretical works (from Heb. *gānaz,* "cover, hide"). Such a chamber, dating to 886 C.E., was discovered at Cairo in 1896. In addition to important biblical and apocryphal manuscripts it contained the Zadokite (or Damascus) Document (CD).

GENNESARET (Gk. *Gennēsarét*)

The coastal plain that lies to the northwest of the Sea of Galilee (also called Gennesaret; Luke 5:1), between the cities of Magadan and Capernaum. Gennesaret is probably the same as Chinnereth. The plain was boxed in by mountains and extended ca. 4.8 km. (3 mi.) along the coast and ca. 1.6 km. (1 mi.) inland. The area was quite populous and was well-known for its fertile soil, according to Josephus (*BJ* 3.10.8[516-21]) and rabbinic sources. The chief cities of the plain were the seaport towns of Magadan, Capernaum, and the small town of Gennesaret. Capernaum, Jesus' home for the latter years, was a large city with a detachment of Roman soldiers, a tax office, and the home of a Roman official. Magadan (Magdala), the home of Mary Magdalene, was reported to be a city of 40 thousand people (*BJ* 2.21.4). Extending through Gennesaret was the Via Maris, one of the major highways in the region, which ran along the northwestern coast of the Sea of Galilee and then branched inland. Most of Jesus' public ministry was in the region of Gennesaret, though the land is mentioned by name only twice in the Gospels (Matt. 14:34 = Mark 6:53). MARK R. FAIRCHILD

GENRE

A classification of literary composition characterized by particular elements of form and content.

One of the crucial insights of form criticism in biblical studies was the realization of the importance of genre recognition for textual interpretation. One cannot understand a particular text without at least some implicit knowledge of the genre to which that text belongs. There is no literary creation *ex nihilo.* Every writer who desires to communicate with an audience must draw on previously known literary conventions of one type or another. The writer starts with a specific genre or set of genres in mind. He or she may work through the conventions associated with these genres, transform them in important ways, or even totally explode them, but use them he or she must. These same genre conventions provide the reader or hearer with an initial frame of reference, some means by which to begin to extract meaning from the text.

The legacy of form criticism has been less helpful in the conception of genre which it bequeathed to the field. In particular, the belief that genres, especially oral genres, tend to be relatively short and self-contained, pure, and originate from one particular setting in life has been called into question by contemporary genre theory. Genres, both oral and written, may be realized on many different scales and involve varying degrees of complexity; generic mixture and not purity of form is the norm, and not every instance of a particular genre need necessarily reflect one putative setting in life. Genres, once known, may be imitated and exploited in all kinds of ways and for all kinds of purposes which may or may not have anything to do with the genre's ordinary setting in life. Finally, a looser concept of genre than that which has traditionally informed form criticism is to be encouraged, one which recognizes that all features, however informal, can become genre-linked and which is predicated on the notion of family resemblance instead of a more formal set theory. F. W. Dobbs-Allsopp

GENTILE

Simply put, a non-Jewish person (or non-Hebrew in the OT). This dichotomy is made clear in places where all of humanity is referred to with phrases such as "Jews and Gentiles" or "Jews and Greeks" (e.g., Acts 14:1, 5; 19:10, 17; 1 Cor. 1:22-24).

In biblical times, being a Gentile was not merely a matter of ethnicity; it was also a matter of political and territorial affiliations, and often religious faith (Deut. 12:29-30; 2 Sam. 7:23; 2 Kgs. 18:33-35 = Isa. 36:18-20; Jer. 2:11). The term "Gentile" is many times used pejoratively to speak of people who do not correctly worship God (Matt. 6:7; 18:17; Gal. 2:15; Eph. 4:17-19; 1 Thess. 4:5). Yet, in some passages the terms for "Gentile" are used for, and properly translated as, "nations" — even the Israelite nation (e.g., Gen. 12:1-2; 18:18; Exod. 19:5-6; Luke 7:5; Acts 10:22). While a person's national/political heritage often determined his or her religious identity, a person's religious commitments did not determine his/her national identity.

God's establishment of Abraham's descendants through Jacob (= Israel) brought about a sense of unique identity for the Israelite nation. This included practices to maintain a sense of separation (Lev. 18:24-30). Thus, the Israelites came to distinguish themselves from other nations, referring to all others as Gentiles. Interracial marriage was forbidden for the Israelites, not for ethnic purity concerns but for faith commitment concerns (Exod. 34:10-16; 1 Kgs. 11:1-11; Ezra 9:1-15, esp. 11-12). Other covenants with foreigners were likewise forbidden.

In conquering the Promised Land, however, the Israelites failed to chase all the foreigners out of Palestine and they disobeyed God's commands regarding interaction. These compromises eventually led to Israel's religious unfaithfulness and ultimately their exile (Judg. 1:27–2:3; 1 Kgs. 14:22-23; 2 Kgs. 16:3; 17:7-20). God exercises sovereignty over the unbelieving gentile nations, using them as tools to discipline Israel (Habakkuk) and calling them to repentance (Jonah) and declaring judgment upon them (Nahum, Obadiah).

Foreigners were allowed to convert to the Israelite faith (i.e., become proselytes; e.g., Rahab, Josh. 6:25; Jas. 2:25; Ruth, Ruth 1:16-17), but Gentiles unwilling to convert were required to be separate from Israelite faith practices if they wanted to live in Palestine (cf. Exod. 12:43-49). Those desiring to worship the God of Israel, but still unwilling to fully convert, eventually became known as "God-fearers" (cf. Acts 10:22; 13:16, 26; 17:4, 17). Gentiles were allowed in the outer courtyard of the temple of Jesus' day, but Greek and Latin inscriptions threatened death if they ventured further into the temple precincts (cf. Acts 21:28-29).

The hardened attitudes of the Jews toward non-Jews is confirmed by Tacitus: "The Jews are extremely loyal toward one another, and always ready to show compassion, but toward every other people they feel only hate and enmity" (*Hist.* 5.5). As seen in Galatians and Acts, the development of this extreme separation of Jews from Gentiles became problematic for the NT Church. The Israelite nation had too easily pictured God as a nationalistic deity uninterested in Gentiles, and this idea needed correction.

However, God is not the God of only Israel (e.g., Deut. 10:17; Acts 10:34-35; Rom. 3:29; 10:11-13). God's impartial desire to reach all nations is found embedded in the Abrahamic covenant. He promised to establish the Israelite nation as the environment from which to bring the Messiah for the whole world (Gen. 12:1-3; cf. 22:15-18; 28:10-15; Gal. 3:14). Salvation was meant to be available to all "the nations" (Isa. 2:2-4; 25:6-8; Zech. 8:20-23).

The physical sign of the Abrahamic covenant was circumcision (Gen. 17:9-14), and consequently "the uncircumcised" became another term for Gentiles, those outside of a relationship with God (Jer. 9:25[MT 24]; Acts 11:3; Rom. 3:29-30; Eph. 2:11). Yet both the OT (Lev. 26:41; Jer. 6:10; cf. Ezek. 44:7-9) and the NT (Acts 7:51; Rom. 2:25-29) testify to the symbolic nature of physical circumcision. A heart changed by faith in God through Jesus Christ becomes acknowledged as the ultimate identifier — the "circumcision" — of God's people, whether they are Jewish or Gentile (Col. 2:11-13; 3:11; Phil. 3:3). Being a Jew is not a guarantee of salvation (Acts 13:46; 18:6), nor does being a Gentile disqualify one from salvation (Acts 15:7-9; Eph. 3:6-9).

The NT clearly shows that people of both Jewish and gentile backgrounds could become Christians. Jesus taught that Gentiles could indeed be saved as God's people (Matt. 8:10-12; 28:19-20; Luke 13:28-29; Rom. 9-11; Eph. 2-3), and Paul speaks of the Church as believers no matter what their background (Gal. 3:28; Col. 3:11).

Bibliography. G. Bertram and K. L. Schmidt, "Ethnos," *TDNT* 2:364-72; H. Bietenhard, "Ethnos," *NIDNTT* 2:790-95; R. E. Clements, "Goy," *TDOT* 2:426-33; D. R. De Lacey, "Gentiles," in *Dictionary of Paul and His Letters,* ed. G. F. Hawthorne and R. P. Martin (Downers Grove, 1993), 335-39; S. McKnight, "Gentiles," in *Dictionary of Jesus and the Gospels,* ed. J. Green and S. McKnight (Downers Grove, 1992), 259-65; K. N. Schoville, "Nations, the," in *Evangelical Dictionary of Biblical Theology,* ed. W. A. Elwell (Grand Rapids, 1996), 551-52; N. Walter, "Ethnos," *EDNT* 1:381-83.

DOUGLAS S. HUFFMAN

GENUBATH (Heb. *gĕnuḇaṯ*)
The son of the exiled Edomite prince Hadad and his Egyptian wife, the sister of Queen Tahpenes (1 Kgs. 11:20). Born in Egypt, he was raised in the pharaoh's palace.

GERA (Heb. *gērāʾ*)
A common Northwest Semitic name (short form of *gēr-DN,* "client of DN") occurring in Egyptian records of the 20th Dynasty. The name also appears in Phoenician, in Samaria Ostracon 30, and in Arad Ostracon 64.

1. A son of Benjamin; most likely the eponym of a Benjaminite clan (Gen. 46:21; Jub. 44:25).

2. The father of Ehud (Judg. 3:15).

3. A Benjaminite; a member of Saul's family and the father of Shimei (2 Sam. 16:5; 19:16, 18; 1 Kgs. 2:8).

4. A name appearing three times in the Benjaminite genealogy of 1 Chr. 8:1-40, but missing in the list of Benjamin's descendants in Num. 26:38-41; 1 Chr. 7:6-12. There may be some repetition in 1 Chr. 8, and it is uncertain whether each occurrence of the name represents a separate individual or an ancient clan within the tribe of Benjamin. A Gera is listed as the second son of Bela and the grandson of Benjamin (1 Chr. 8:1-4), but he is omitted in the list of Bela's sons in 1 Chr. 7:6-12. Gera also appears as the seventh son of Bela and the grandson of Benjamin (1 Chr. 8:5). Some suggest emending 1 Chr. 8:3 to read "and Gera, father of Ehud," thus distinguishing him from the Gera of v. 5. Other scholars propose that the Gera of 1 Chr. 8:5 is the same person as Gera **5** below.

5. A son of Ehud; a Benjaminite and father of Uzza and Ahihud (1 Chr. 8:7). He is either identical with the Gera of 1 Chr. 8:5, or another Gera who is also called Heglam (v. 7; which may also be translated "Gera, he carried them into exile").

KENNETH ATKINSON

GERAH (Heb. *gērâ*)
A unit of weight equal to one twentieth of a shekel (Exod. 30:13; Lev. 27:25; Num. 3:47; 18:16; Ezek. 45:12), thus ca. .57 g. (.02 oz.).

GERAR (Heb. *gĕrār*)
A city on the southern border of Canaan, near Gaza (Gen. 10:19). Here Abraham and Sarah settled as resident aliens (Gen. 20:1-2), and Isaac and Rebekah dwelt at the command of Yahweh (26:2). Both encountered the king Abimelech, and the motif of the wife-sister switch is found in both Genesis texts.

According to LXX 1 Chr. 4:39-41 the "sons of Simeon" went to the gates of Gerar seeking pastureland (MT "Gedor"). King Asa of Judah defeated the massive army of Zerah (an Edomite name) the Cushite, and pursued it to Gerar before taking booty from all the surrounding area (2 Chr. 14:13-14). Hegmonides is called the governor of the area from Ptolemais to Gerar (2 Macc. 13:24).

Whether Gerar refers to the same place in all of these texts is uncertain, as is its exact location. Many scholars associate Gerar with Tel Haror/Tell Abû Hureireh (08795.11257) between Gaza and Beer-sheba on the bank of Naḥal Gerar. Archaeological excavations there show that the site was inhabited from the Chalcolithic period onward, with significant populations in MB II-III, LB II (although smaller than MB), Iron I, and the late Iron through the Persian periods. While the site shows evidence of being an early Philistine settlement (cf. the Genesis texts), it is not listed as part of the five Philistine cities (Josh. 13:3). Other finds at the site include a MB temple complex; grain silos; a refuse pit, which provides evidence for iron technology; public buildings; paved floors; and MB and Iron Age fortifications.

ALICE HUNT HUDIBURG

GERASA (Gk. *Gerasa*)
A Decapolis city in the late Hellenistic and Roman periods, modern Jerash located on the Transjordanian plateau just N of the Jabbok River (Nahr ez-Zarqa; Gen. 32:22).

Stone Age remains and walled Early to Middle Bronze settlements were found in the area. The main city of Gerasa, founded after the conquest of Alexander the Great, continued under the Ptolemies as a city of the Decapolis (Pliny *Nat. hist.* 5.74), and then under Seleucid rule (Antiochus III, 223-187; Antiochus IV, 175) when Gerasa became known as Antiochia ad Chrysorhoam (Antioch on the Chrysorhoas River). Later conquered by Alexander Janneus (102-67 B.C.), the city was taken over by the Romans (63) and then reached its zenith in the 2nd century A.D.

Gerasa profited from being on the lucrative spice and perfume north-south trade route between Mesopotamia, Palmyra, Damascus, Abila, and Capitalias, on to Petra and southern Arabia, and also prospered from being on a branch of the Via Triana Nova, linking with Pella, and also on routes linking the city with Judea, Galilee, and Phoenicia.

Gerasa, in Roman fashion, had a north-south Cardo Maximus, and two east-west Decumani (all colonnaded), with intersecting central tetrapylons, the one Decumanus on the south near the forum, the south theater, the temple of Zeus, a Hellenistic temple, and a soldiers' barracks, and the other Decumanus on the north, near the north theater and the western baths.

Other important archaeological remains include, to the west of the Cardo Maximus and between the two Decumani, the precinct and temple of Artemis, the nymphaeum, and a series of Byzantine church ruins.

On the south of the city are the hippodrome and Hadrian's arch, the latter commemorating the emperor's visit to the city in A.D. 129.

Bibliography. S. Applebaum and A. Segal, "Gerasa," *NEAEHL* 2:470-79; J. Finegan, *The Archaeology of the New Testament,* rev. ed. (Princeton, 1992); C. H. Kraeling, *Gerasa, City of the Decapolis* (New Haven, 1938); T. C. Mitchell, "Gerasa," in *The Illustrated Bible Dictionary,* ed. J. D. Douglas (Wheaton, 1980), 1:552-53.

See GERASENES. W. HAROLD MARE

GERASENES (Gk. *Gerasēnoí*) (also GADARENES; GERGESENES)
A Transjordanian people in whose territory Jesus encountered two "demoniacs," exorcising their demons and transferring them to a herd of swine (Mark 5:1; Luke 8:26). In the version of the incident in Matt. 8:28 they are called Gadarenes. Both forms, as well as Gergesenes, are attested in the ancient versions of each account. The name Gerasenes is associated with Jerash, N of Amman.

GERIZIM (Heb. *gĕrizîm*), **MOUNT**
A mountain 3 km. (1.9 mi.) NW of Shechem and 48 km. (30 mi.) N of Jerusalem. The summit, at 880 m. (2887 ft.), may be reached by a path from the Samaritan quarter of Nablus at the northern foot of the mount.

Mt. Gerizim is explicitly mentioned four times in the OT. God's blessings for the people of Israel are to be placed on Mt. Gerizim (Deut. 11:29), and six tribes are appointed to stand on the mount for the blessing (Deut. 27:12; Josh. 8:33). Gerizim also plays a central role in the abortive reign of Abimelech (Judg. 9). Jotham, speaking from the crest of Mt. Gerizim, delivers a tale of unqualified brambles assuming rule over qualified but unwilling trees to warn Israel of Abimelech's incompetence. Later, Abimelech successfully thwarts Gaal's revolt by sending troops down from Tabbur-erez, translated "navel" (*ómphalos*) of the world in the LXX.

In Samaritan tradition, Mt. Gerizim is considered the oldest, most central, and highest mountain in the world. It is the location of the Garden of Eden and the place where Abraham brought Isaac for sacrifice. Finally, it is the central sacred site for the Samaritan religious community (cf. John 4:20). Under Antiochus IV Epiphanes the temple was renamed in honor of Zeus-the-Friend-of-Strangers (2 Macc. 5:23; 6:2). The site was ravaged by the Hasmonean ethnarch and Jewish high priest John Hyrcanus (in 111/110 B.C.E. according to archaeological evidence). It was besieged by the Romans late in the 1st century B.C.E., and a temple to Zeus built by Hadrian in the 2nd century C.E. The site was cleared or modified by Zeno, the Roman emperor of the east, early in the 5th century for a church in honor of Mary (rebuilt by the Byzantine emperor Justinian later in that century). Between these times it was the chief center of worship for the Samaritan community, as it is today.

Remains of several structures are found on its summit. Among them are the 5th-century Theotokos church and a fortification constructed by Justinian, and a 16th-century watchtower later made into the tomb of Sheikh Ghanin. Ca. 100 m. (328 ft.) further south on the same peak are remains of three Samaritan cultic sites, and on yet another nearby mound, known as Tell er-Ras (175178), are the remains of Hadrian's temple of Zeus.

Bibliography. R. T. Anderson, "Mount Gerizim: Navel of the World," *BA* 43 (1980): 217-21.

ROBERT T. ANDERSON

GERSHOM (Heb. *gēršōm*) (also GERSHON)

1. The son of Moses and Zipporah, born in Midian (Exod. 2:22; 18:3). Gershom was the father of Jonathan, who served as priest to the Danites and whose sons maintained that position until the captivity (Judg. 18:30; MT "son of Manasseh," likely a scribal error for "Moses"). Gershom and his son Shebuel were later projected to David's time and incorporated into the levitical genealogy, with Shebuel serving as a Levite in the house of the Lord (1 Chr. 23:15-16).

2. A son of Levi, whose descendants were called Gershomites or "sons of Gershom" (1 Chr. 6:16, 62, 71[MT 1, 47. 56]; 15:7). Elsewhere the name is read "Gershon."

3. A descendant of Phinehas, who returned from Babylon with Ezra (Ezra 8:2; 1 Esdr. 8:29).

KENNETH ATKINSON

GERSHON (Heb. *gēršôn*) (also GERSHOM)
The eldest of the three sons of Levi, mentioned along with Kohath and Merari (Gen. 46:11; Exod. 6:16-17; "Gershom" in 1 Chr. 6). The name Gershon appears in various genealogies, census reports (Num. 3–4), and land allotments (Josh. 21), which describe the levitical families, their encampment and duties with regard to the desert tent of meeting, their location in tribal Israel, and their continued service in posttribal Israel.

The genealogies of Levi name Gershon as one of the priestly families who serve under Aaron. Gershon according to these genealogies had two sons, Libni and Shimei (Exod. 6:16; Num. 3:18). The census reports of Num. 3–4 assign to Gershon and his family care for the covering of the tent of meeting, the screen of the door of the tent, the hangings in the court of the tent, and the screen for the gate of the court (Num. 3:21-26; 4:21-28). The Gershonites are to encamp behind the tent on the west and, while traveling in the desert, are to transport their portion of the tent in two wagons (Num. 3:23; 7:7). The book of Joshua allots to postconquest Gershon 13 cities in the north within the boundaries of the half-tribe of Manasseh, and the tribes of Issachar, Asher, and Naphtali (Josh. 21:27-33). Chronicles attests to the continued service of the Gershonites in monarchical and in postexilic Israel, specifically pertaining to care for the temple (1 Chr. 29:8; 2 Chr. 29:12).

Bibliography. A. Cody, *A History of Old Testament Priesthood.* AnBib 35 (Rome, 1969).

JEFF H. MCCRORY, JR.

GERUTH CHIMHAM (Heb. *gērûṯ kimhām*)
The first stopping place of Johanan and company en route to Egypt (Jer. 41:17). The name may designate a caravansary or inn near Bethlehem (cf. Jer. 9:2[MT 1]; Luke 2:7). The association of this site with Chimham the son of Barzillai (2 Sam. 19:37-38[38-39]) is unclear.

GESHAN (Heb. *gêšān*)
The third son of Jahdai; a Calebite of the tribe of Judah (1 Chr. 2:47).

GESHEM (Heb. *gešem*)
The "Arab" mentioned along with Sanballat, governor of Samaria, and Tobiah, an Ammonite official, who opposed Nehemiah's plan to repair the wall around Jerusalem (Neh. 2:19). Those three sought a meeting with Nehemiah after the work commenced, but Nehemiah refused, suspecting they meant him harm (Neh. 6:2).

The Geshem of Nehemiah may be the same person called the king of Kedar in an inscription from North Arabia. If so, he ruled under Persian hegemony. The name in its more original form "Gashmu" perhaps meant "big man," and it is well attested in archaeological finds in North Arabia.

PAUL L. REDDITT

GESHUR (Heb. *gĕšûr*)

1. A small Aramean kingdom that shared a western border with the half-tribe of Manasseh in the southern part of what is now called the Golan Heights (Deut. 3:14). Geshur remained independent during the conquest of Canaan and after Joshua's death (Josh. 12:5). During the period of David and Solomon and the divided kingdoms (ca. 1020-732 B.C.) it was semi-independent. David married Maacah, who was to become the mother of Absalom, to consummate a political alliance with the Geshurite king Talmai (2 Sam. 3:3). Along with the Aramean kingdom of Maacah to the north, Geshur joined with Damascus against David (2 Sam. 10:6; 13:37; 14:23; 1 Chr. 19:7). However, it was a subject of Israel during Solomon's time. Geshur later joined with Aram Damascus to fight against the northern kingdom of Israel, and it was eventually incorporated into the Damascene state (9th century). The royal names of the kingdom reflect a Hurrian element (e.g., Talmai).

Geshur is likely listed as Ga-su-ru in one of the Amarna Letters (no. 256) from Egypt (14th century). The area of Geshur has been subject to intense archaeological surveys, which have revealed a number of sites from the Middle Bronze II to Iron I Ages (ca. 1800-1000).

Bibliography. B. Mazar, "Geshur and Maacah," *JBL* 80 (1961): 16-28.

MARK W. CHAVALAS

2. A people or region S of the Philistine pentapolis that was not taken in the Conquest (Josh. 13:2) and against whom David raided while allied with the Philistines (1 Sam. 27:8).

GESSIUS FLORUS
The last Roman procurator of the province of Judea (including Samaria), who assumed power in 64 C.E. According to Josephus he was from Clazomenae and received his procuratorship because his wife Cleopatra was a friend of Nero's wife Poppea. Josephus and Tacitus attest that Jewish patience for Roman misgovernment of Judea was exhausted under Florus. Josephus vilifies him as the worst of Roman governors and charges him with wholesale plundering of Jewish cities, going so far as to allow bands of robbers to ravage the country with immunity. When Florus sought to take funds from the Jerusalem temple treasury in 66 C.E., the citizens resisted by mocking his apparent poverty. To retaliate, he led soldiers from Caesarea to sack part of Jerusalem and to arrest numerous leading citizens, whom he had scourged and crucified, including several Jews of Roman equestrian rank. His attempt to force the Jews to show ceremonial submission to his cohorts aggravated the situation and sparked the rebellion that became the Jewish war with Rome.

Bibliography. E. Schürer, *The History of the Jewish People in the Age of Jesus Christ (175 B.C.–A.D. 135)* 1, rev. ed. (Edinburgh, 1973).

SCOTT NASH

GESTAS (Gk. *Gestas*)
The name ascribed in apocryphal writings to the unrepentant thief crucified with Jesus (cf. Luke 23:39). Other forms of the name are Gistas, Gesmas, Stegmas, and Dumachus.

GESTURES
Body movements made mainly with the head, face alone, or the limbs. Gestures are one element in a larger dimension of human behavior known as nonverbal communication. If the biblical author does not explicitly mention or describe a gesture, the reader may find it difficult to imagine the gesture appropriate to the given situation. The imaginative reader must remember that gestures in one culture often carry an entirely different — sometimes obscene — meaning in another culture. One and the same gesture does not translate readily and easily from culture to culture.

Gestures are conscious or unconscious body movements, learned or somatogenic. They serve as a primary communicative tool, dependent on or independent from verbal language, and modified by conditioning (e.g., smiles, eye movements, a gesture of beckoning, or a tic). These should be distinguished from manners (body attitudes, e.g., the way one eats) and postures (positions of the body, e.g., sitting, standing). Distinction is made between free gestures performed by a part of the body without contacting any other part or object (e.g., eye movements, head nods, hand gestures), and bound gestures where hands come into contact with each other or other body parts (e.g., scratching one's eyes, using a knife and fork, jewelry).

Four categories of gestures may be identified: (1) idiosyncratic, or unique to a person (e.g., hitting the right thigh with the palm of the right hand to express joy, surprise; cf. the earthling upon meeting his new mate in Gen. 2:23); (2) culturally induced and learned (e.g., dancing or mourning rituals; Matt. 11:17); (3) technical, therefore arbitrary and requiring prior verbal agreement (e.g., hand-signals of merchants such as fishmongers in the market place); and (4) semiotic, substitutes for speech, linked with cultural traditions (e.g., swearing an oath by placing the right hand on a body part: tip of nose, moustache or beard, phallus; Gen. 24:2, 9). Robert A. Barakat's study of Arab gestures offers an important entrée into further investigation of gestures in the Middle East; experts agree that the pre-Islamic Bedouin substratum of cultural components lives on in the folk culture of the traditional majority.

Mayer I. Gruber's mainly philological analysis of postures, gestures, and facial expressions in ancient Israel, Canaan, and Mesopotamia is helpful in understanding the literal description of gestures and the idiomatic use of phrases to convey attitudes, ideas, and feelings communicated by gestures, postures, and facial expression. The Middle Eastern world is non-, indeed anti-introspective, and a modern reader must be careful not to impose Western thought patterns upon this world.

A serious challenge is the modern reader's inability to observe the people described in the biblical record. Is it possible to imagine plausible gestures where a text does not mention them? Literary anthropology, a relatively new approach to the study of literature inspired by Fernando Poyatos, would argue in the affirmative. Clearly the investigator is dealing with signs that communicate, i.e., with the many forms of communication, mostly nonverbal, that define individuals and cultures, conveyed by the culture's narrative literature in which such information is embedded.

Illustrations

Head

"Wagging the head" is a free gesture. The movement is probably side to side horizontally, or perhaps in an arc from shoulder to shoulder rather than up and down. Dictionaries customarily explain the phrase as a "sign of scorn and derision," drawing this culturally determined meaning from Ps. 109:25. Of six occurrences in the biblical text three are free gestures (Ps. 64:8[MT 9]; 109:25; Isa. 37:22) and three are bound. Ps. 22:7, cited in Matt. 27:39, links the head with "making mouths," while Lam. 2:15 links the head with hissing and clapping of hands. These bound gestures present a fuller picture of nonverbal means of expressing scorn and derision in this culture.

Face Alone

In Middle Eastern culture, the face is a key element in the other-determined, outward-oriented character of honor. The purpose of life is to maintain or save face and never lose face. If God sets the divine face against a person or city, the consequent shame is perhaps more devastating than the withdrawal of divine protection and beneficence (cf. Lev. 20:5-6; Jer. 21:10; Ezek. 14:8; 15:7).

Further, the eyes play a significant role in the face-based gestural repertoire of biblical people. In the biblical perspective on the human person, the eyes are linked with the heart (as mouth is with ears and hands with feet) from which both good and evil can flow. Jesus expresses the cultural conviction that from the heart comes the "evil eye" (often translated "envy"; cf. Mark 7:22). Contemporary Mediterranean natives refer to the "fierce look," the "gaze," or the "stare" as reflecting the activity of an evil eye. Yet because eye behavior is predominantly involuntary and therefore more difficult to manipulate than facial expression, one can never know when an eye might slip into this look, gaze, or stare. As Sirach notes (Sir. 31:12-13), God has created nothing more evil than the evil eye. Prov. 23:6-8 warns against eating what an evil-eyed person offers; such a host feigns generosity but is actually stingy, and the guest will vomit. In his discussion of the year of release and canceling of debts, the Deuteronomist (Deut. 15:7-11) warns against ignoring the plight of a needy person (or giving such a one the "evil eye") out of (greedy) fear the debt will not be repaid. Though not explicitly mentioned in any biblical text, an interpreter can plausibly surmise that a person in a situation where the evil eye might be operative, as well as the person who reads or hears biblical texts about such situations, is very likely immediately making the appropriate protective hand gestures or stroking the appropriately colored talisman for protection against the power of this gesture. In sum, there is a wealth of cultural meaning wrapped up in the Mediterranean understanding of the eye and the gestures a person could make with it.

Limbs

When speaking of gestures, most people think of the hands. In the Middle East, the left hand is used exclusively for toilet functions. To appreciate the cultural significance of this practice, consider Jesus' statement in the Sermon on the Mount: "Do not resist one who is evil. If anyone strikes you on the right cheek, turn to him the other also" (Matt. 5:39). Here is a culturally plausible scenario for imagining that deed.

Middle Easterners routinely interact with a space of about 15-20 cm. (6-8 in.) between them (in contrast to the 30-40 cm. [12-16 in.] of personal space preferred by Westerners). The listener wants to feel the breath of the speaker against the face. The speaker routinely places the right arm on the forearm or shoulder of the listener. If the discussion should become heated or excited, the distance between both parties decreases till they are eyeball to eyeball. Should either lose control and strike at the other, there are two possibilities. One is to back away and slap at the right cheek with the back of the right hand, an insulting move. The other is to remain at close quarters which makes it impossible to bring the right arm into play but rather allows the left hand to slap the right cheek — a deeply offensive insult indeed.

This instruction, along with the entire Sermon on the Mount, is intended to guide in-group behavior. It was directed to the disciples (Matt. 5:1-2). As an example to outsiders, the insult should not be avenged. But in relationships with outsiders, the insulted party would make an appropriate response, and the one who posed the insult should hope for the intervention of a mediator to prevent escalation to further violence and bloodshed (cf. Matt. 5:9).

This exclusive function of the left hand also sheds fresh light on the gesture of "cutting off the hand." According to Deut. 25:12 a woman who interferes in a fight involving her husband by grabbing the genitals of his opponent should have her hand cut off. Force of cultural habit suggests she used her left hand, though in a moment of excitement like this it might have been her right hand. The Qur'an (5:38) prescribes amputating the right hand of a convicted thief. Matthew's Jesus recommends that a person tripped up by the right hand should personally amputate it (Matt. 5:29-30). Whether as punishment or a means to leading a better life, losing the right hand in the Middle East is the equivalent of a death sentence. It makes social life exceedingly difficult, if not impossible.

Biblical authors could safely presume that their original readers, fellow ethnics, would fill in the appropriate details such as elements of nonverbal communication or gestures that could accompany the written text. Modern students of the Bible can become similarly equipped by immersing themselves into the appropriate resources.

Bibliography. R. A. Barakat, "Arabic Gestures," *Journal of Popular Culture* 6 (1973): 749-92; J. H. Elliott, "The Evil Eye in the First Testament," in *The Bible and the Politics of Exegesis,* ed. D. Jobling, P. L. Day, and G. T. Sheppard (Cleveland, 1991), 147-59; M. I. Gruber, *Aspects of Nonverbal Communication in the Ancient Near East.* Studia Pohl 12/1-2 (Rome, 1980); R. Joseph, "Toward a Semiotics of Middle Eastern Cultures," *International Journal of Middle Eastern Studies* 12 (1980): 319-29; J. J. Pilch, "A Window into the Biblical World: Actions Speak Louder than Words," *Bible Today* 34 (1996): 172-76; F. Poyatos, ed., *Advances in Nonverbal Communication* (Amsterdam, 1988); *Literary Anthropology* (Amsterdam, 1988).

JOHN J. PILCH

GETHER (Heb. *geṯer*)
A son of Aram and grandson of Shem (Gen. 10:23; cf. 1 Chr. 1:17, son of Shem); the eponymous ancestor of an Aramean principality.

GETHSEMANE (Gk. *Gethsēmaní*)
The place where Jesus offered an anguished prayer just before his betrayal and arrest there (Matt. 26:36; Mark 14:32). Its exact location is unknown, though it was probably somewhere near the Mount of Olives since all four Gospels agree that Jesus was betrayed and arrested on or near the Mount of Olives (Matt. 26:30; Mark 14:26; Luke 22:39; John 18:1). The name Gethsemane is from Aram. *gaṯ šěmānê,* "oil press." Both olive trees and presses for extracting the oil from the olives were common in the area, and it is probable that Gethsemane contained such a press.

Matthew and Mark name the place of Jesus' prayer, betrayal, and arrest as Gethsemane and place it near the Mount of Olives. Luke does not name the place but has the events take place on the mount itself. John does not mention Jesus' prayer, nor does he name the place of Jesus' betrayal and arrest, though he locates it "across the Kidron valley" in a "garden" (John 18:1), and thus on the Mount of Olives. By combining the accounts of Jesus' anguished prayer in the Synoptic Gospels with John's account of his arrest in a garden, the traditional image of Jesus' agony in the garden of Gethsemane was constructed.

Jesus in Gethsemane was interpreted as an appropriate contrast to Adam in Eden: the sinful disobedience of the first Adam in the garden of Eden was undone because of the prayerful obedience of the last Adam in the garden of Gethsemane (cf. Rom. 5:12-21). A similar development can be seen in Heb. 5:7-9, which mentions Jesus' "prayers," "godly fear," and "obedience," which led to his "being made perfect . . . the source of eternal salvation to all who obey him."

KIM PAFFENROTH

GEUEL (Heb. *gěʼûʼēl*)
A Gadite, the son of Machi; one of the 12 spies sent into the land of Canaan (Num. 13:15).

GEZER (Heb. *gezer*)
A city attested in biblical, Egyptian, and Assyrian sources. It is to be located at Tell Jezer (Tell el-Jazari; 1425.1407), a 13.3-ha. (33 a.) mound prominently situated at the junction of the northern Shephelah and the Judean foothills, overlooking the Ayalon Valley. The site was extensively excavated in 1902-1909 by R. A. S. Macalister, briefly in 1934 by Alan Rowe; in 1964-1974 by a large multidisciplinary project directed by William G. Dever with H. Darrell Lance and Joe D. Seger; and finally by Dever in 1984 and 1990.

The principal literary references to Gezer are found first in Egyptian sources: in the annals of Thutmose III (ca. 1468 B.C.; no. 104 on the Karnak Temple inscription), in 10 of the 14th-century Amarna Letters, and in Pharaoh Merneptah's "Victory Stela" (ca. 1207). Mesopotamian references include an inscription and relief of Tiglath-pileser III, who destroyed Gezer ca. 733. Biblical references reflect the facts that Gezer remained in Canaanite hands during the period of the Judges (Josh. 10:33; 12:12), was a territorial city (21:21, an Ephraimite town allotted to the Kohathite Levites), and finally came under Israelite control through an Egyptian treaty in Solomon's day, being built up and/or fortified thereafter along with Jerusalem, Hazor, and Megiddo (1 Kgs. 9:15-17).

The following is an outline of the periods established by the most recent excavations at Gezer:

Stratum XXVI: Chalcolithic village (ca. 3600-3300)

XXV: EB I small town (ca. 3300-3100)

XXIV-XXIII: EB II unwalled town (ca. 3100-2600), followed by a gap

XXXII-XVIII: MB city (ca. 2000-1500), heavily fortified by "inner wall" and gate; many rich tombs, Macalister's "high place"; Egyptian destruction at the end (ca. 1500)

XVII: Partial gap in occupation during LB I; multiple burials in Cave 1.10A (ca. 1450-1400)

XVI-XIV: LB II urban reoccupation; several palaces and Egyptian "residences"; construction of the "outer wall"; possible destruction at end by Merneptah (ca. 1207)

XIII-XI: Ceramic continuity into early Iron Age, but Philistine bichrome wares appear; large public granary and two "patrician houses" nearby (ca. 1200-1050)

X-IX: Intermediate phases, with red-slipped unburnished pottery characteristic (ca. 1050-950)

VIII: Construction of a four-entryway monumental city gate, outer gatehouse, and casemate (double) wall system, incorporating rebuild of LB "outer wall" and towers; "Palace 10,000" adjoining city gate; heavy destruction at end, probably by Pharaoh Shishak (ca. 950-925)

VII-VI: Iron II period (ca. 925-733); city gate and "outer wall" period; domestic quarters built up; destruction at end attributable to Tiglath-pileser III.

V: Slight recovery under Judean rule, but destroyed by Babylonians (ca. 587/586)

IV: Slight Persian occupation (5th-4th centuries)

III-II: Reoccupation in Hellenistic and Hasmonean periods; city gate rebuilt a final time, during Maccabean wars

I: Mound largely deserted, but adjacent region now part of a Herodian period private estate of one "Alkios"; Macalister's "boundary stones"; only a few Byzantine tombs follow, then the founding of the Arab villages of 'Abu-shusheh in the 19th century

The principal discoveries at Gezer include the MB I-III remains, especially the massive "inner wall," "Tower 5617," the three-entryway "south gate," and the *glacis*. Also noteworthy is Macalister's "high place," now dated to the MB III period (ca. 1650-1500) and shown to have been in all likelihood an outdoor shrine utilized by a 10-city league, perhaps for covenant-renewal ceremonies.

The Late Bronze Age may be illuminated by the fortifications (the "outer wall"), the subject of much controversy but confidently dated to the 14th-13th centuries by the excavators. The various "palaces" and "residences," as well as the rich deposits in Cave 1.10A, illustrate the Amarna age and Egyptian presence particularly well.

The four-entryway city gate, outer gatehouse, stretch of casemate wall, and reused LB "outer wall" with the addition of ashlar towers, all have been taken to reflect the 10th-century Solomonic era, the destruction at the end being attributed to Shishak. Some Israeli archaeologists, however, would date these features to the 9th century.

Finally, Gezer, not far from Mod'in, has produced some of our best evidence for the period of the Maccabean wars and Hasmonean rulers.

Bibliography. W. G. Dever, "Excavations at Gezer," *BA* 30 (1967): 47-62; "Further Evidence on the Date of the Outer Wall at Gezer," *BASOR* 289 (1993): 33-54; Dever, H. D. Lance, and G. E. Wright, *Gezer I* (Jerusalem, 1970); Dever et al., "Further Excavations at Gezer, 1967-71," *BA* 34 (1971): 94-132; *Gezer II* (Jerusalem, 1974); *Gezer IV* (Jerusalem, 1986); S. Gitin, *Gezer III* (Jerusalem, 1990); J. D. Seger, *Gezer V* (Jerusalem, 1988).

William G. Dever

GIAH (Heb. *gîaḥ*)
An unidentified site along the route taken by Abner as he fled from Gibeon to the Arabah (2 Sam. 2:24). The Hebrew text may be corrupt, and recent scholarship favors a reading based on LXX Gk. *Gai* (cf. Heb. *gay'*, "valley").

GIANTS
A legendary race of imposing physical stature. These primordial inhabitants of the Promised Land went by several names. Gen. 6:4 identifies remarkably tall Nephilim (Num. 13:33) as the offspring of gods and women. According to Gen. 14:5-6 eastern kings subdued Rephaim from Bashan, Zuzim/Zamzummim from Ammon, Emim from Moab, and Horites from Edom. The Amorite king Og, who owned a bedstead 9 cubits by 4 cubits, was allegedly a remnant of the Rephaim (Deut. 3:11). Great size along with extra fingers and toes characterized descendants of the Rephaim — otherwise called the Anakim (Josh. 11:21-22) — in Philistia (2 Sam. 21:15-22; 1 Chr. 20:4-8).

Bibliography. E. C. Hostetter, *Nations Mightier and More Numerous: The Biblical View of Palestine's Pre-Israelite Peoples*. BIBALDS 3 (N. Richland Hills, Tex., 1995), 96-111. Edwin C. Hostetter

GIBBAR (Heb. *gibbār*)
The ancestral home of a family who returned with Zerubbabel from exile (Ezra 2:20). The name may be a corruption of Gibeon, which appears in the parallel list (Neh. 7:25).

GIBBETHON (Heb. *gibbeṯôn*)
A levitical city belonging to the tribe of Dan (Josh. 19:44; 21:23). During the Divided Monarchy Gibbethon was held by the Philistines. While the army of Nadab was attacking Gibbethon, Baasha assassinated Nadab and became king in his place (1 Kgs. 15:27). Some 26 years later, during the reign of Baasha's son Elah, Omri laid siege to the city as commander of Israel's army. During this attack Zimri assassinated the king and his descen-

dants at Tirzeh. Upon hearing of Zimri's coup, the troops made Omri king as they abandoned the siege and went to Tirzeh to overthrow Zimri (1 Kgs. 16:15-17).

Gibbethon appears in Thutmose III's list of conquered cities during his campaign in 1468 B.C. and in the description of the campaign of Sargon II against the kings of Ashdod (712-13).

Two sites have been proposed for biblical Gibbethon: Râs Abū Ḥamid/Ḥumeid (140145) and Tell el-Melât/Tel Malot (137140), both ca. 5 km. (3 mi.) W of Gezer. Based on initial survey and excavation results, Tell el-Malât is the more likely site.

STEVEN M. ORTIZ

GIBEA (Heb. *giḇʿāʾ*)
A Judahite, the son of Sheva and grandson of Maacah, Caleb's concubine (1 Chr. 2:48-49). The name (Heb. "highlander") may designate a site in the hill country near Hebron, perhaps founded by Sheva.

GIBEAH (Heb. *giḇʿâ*)
1. A city in the hill country of Judah SW of Jerusalem (Josh. 15:57).

2. A town in the hill country of Ephraim (Josh. 24:33), assigned to Aaron's son Eleazar, who is buried there, and subsequently the inheritance of Phinehas.

3. A Benjaminite city that was particularly prominent during the reign of Saul. The name means "hill" and often was used in place names such as Gibeah of Benjamin (1 Sam. 13:2, 15; 14:16), Gibeath-elohim ("Hill of God"; 10:5), or Gibeah of Saul (11:4; 15:34) as a synonym for Gibeah. The relationship of Gibeah to Geba is difficult to ascertain. Sometimes the two terms are used independently, but they also are used interchangeably (Judg. 19-20; 1 Sam. 13-14; Isa. 10:28-32). The use of both terms in the same passage may reflect different sources, or it may indicate that the terms are synonyms. Many scholars view Gibeah and Geba as referring to the same site.

It was at Gibeah that the Levite's concubine was raped and murdered by the Benjaminites (Judg. 19-21). The other tribes of Israel responded by killing the inhabitants of Gibeah, as well as devastating the tribe of Benjamin. According to the Deuteronomistic history, Gibeah had recovered by the time of Saul so that it became the headquarters of Saul's monarchy (1 Sam. 10:26; 11:4). Gibeah's prominence during this period is illustrated further by the presence of an important cultic site, which featured a *bāmâ* ("high place") and a tamarisk tree (1 Sam. 22:6), and a band of prophets that worshipped at it (ch. 10). The Philistines maintained a garrison in the city, which Jonathan defeated (1 Sam. 13:2-3).

After Saul's death, the city declined in importance; it rarely is mentioned in subsequent biblical texts. In Isa. 10:28-29 it appears along the path of a foreign army marching on Jerusalem, and in Hos. 5:8 it is one of the cities designated for destruction. Gibeah's cultic site probably was destroyed during the reforms of Josiah in the 7th century (2 Kgs. 23:8).

While several sites have been suggested for the location of Gibeah, two have received more support than any others. Located 5.5 km. (3.4 mi.) N of Jerusalem, Tell el-Fûl (1719.1367) was identified as Gibeah by William F. Albright. A brief excavation was conducted there in 1868 by Charles Warren, but more extensive digging was done in 1922-23 and 1933 by Albright, and in 1964 by Paul Lapp. The remains indicated occupation at various times from the Iron I Age into the Roman period. The lowest stratum was destroyed by fire in the 12th century. The next occupation contains a tower and casemate wall dating to the 11th century, perhaps Saul's fortress-palace. Although the excavators believed that the remains supported an association with Gibeah, this conclusion has been questioned.

The other major alternative for Gibeah is Jabaʿ (175140), 10 km. (6 mi.) NE of Jerusalem. Unfortunately, the site has not been excavated, but a survey yielded Iron II and Persian period sherds. Support for this identification, therefore, is based on geographical and literary descriptions.

See GEBA.

Bibliography. P. M. Arnold, *Gibeah: The Search for a Biblical City.* JSOTSup 79 (Sheffield, 1990); N. L. Lapp, ed., *The Third Campaign at Tell el-Ful.* AASOR 45 (Cambridge, Mass., 1981); J. M. Miller, "Geba/Gibeon of Benjamin," *VT* 25 (1975): 145-66; L. A. Sinclair, "An Archaeological Study of Gibeah (Tell el-Fûl)," *AASOR* 34-35 (New Haven, 1960): 1-52.

SCOTT M. LANGSTON

GIBEATH-ELOHIM (Heb. *giḇʿaṯ hāʾĕlōhîm*)
A place ("hill of God") where Samuel promised Saul he would meet a band of prophets (1 Sam. 10:5). While clearly in the hill country of Benjamin, because of the similarity of other names (Geba, Gibeah, Gibeon; all from Heb. *giḇʿâ*, "hill," the dominant topographical feature of Benjamin) the exact location of this site has seen vigorous debate. The problem is further complicated by English texts which usually translate the terms descriptively rather than as proper names. The mention of a Philistine garrison suggests that this hill was a well-known "high place" near Gibeah (cf. 1 Sam. 10:10). Gibeon has been suggested as an alternate site, but excavations there have yielded no archaeological evidence of Philistines.

Bibliography. Y. Aharoni, *The Land of the Bible,* 2nd ed. (Philadelphia, 1979); W. F. Albright, *Excavations and Results at Tell el-Fûl (Gibeah of Saul).* AASOR 4 (New Haven, 1924); A. Demsky, "Geba, Gibeah, and Gibeon: An Historico-Geographic Riddle," *BASOR* 212 (1973): 26-31; J. M. Miller, "Geba/Gibeah of Benjamin," *VT* 25 (1975): 145-66.

DENNIS M. SWANSON

GIBEATH-HAARALOTH (Heb. *giḇʿaṯ hāʿărālôṯ*)
The place, near Gilgal, where the Israelites who had been born during the journey from Egypt were circumcised after crossing the Jordan River (Josh. 5:3; "hill of foreskins"). This second circumcision

marks entrance of the Israelites into the Promised Land. The KJV associates this place with *giḇʿaṯ* in the list of Benjaminite towns in Josh. 18:28 (NRSV "Gibeah"). The site is otherwise unknown.

LAURA B. MAZOW

GIBEON (Heb. *giḇʿôn*)
A city identified with the ruin under the Arab village of el-Jib, 9 km. (5.5 mi.) NNW of Jerusalem (167139). The identification was confirmed by the discovery of 31 jar handles inscribed with the name Gibeon (*gbʿn*). The importance of the site lies in its strategic position at the crossroads of the central hill country. It guards the important roads leading eastward up from the coastal plain through the Aijalon Valley via Beth-horon and Kiriath-jearim. From Gibeon roads turn northward toward Bethel and southward toward Jerusalem. Gibeon also lies at the western edge of a relatively large and level plateau in central Benjamin which controlled north-south commerce in the hill country. As such, it was a natural hub of conflict between Israel and Judah.

Gibeon first appears in the Bible as the leader of cities (including Chephirah, Beeroth, and Kiriath-jearim) that deceived Joshua and obtained a peace treaty with Israel (Josh. 9). When the ruse is discovered, the Gibeonites are condemned to be "hewers of wood and drawers of water" in Israel forever (Josh. 9:21). The story highlights Gibeon's central position within the hill country as well as its strategic location guarding the main roads. The king of Jerusalem, Adoni-zedek, responds immediately to the threat to his territory and attacks Gibeon. Joshua is then forced into action, marching up from Gilgal and surprising the Jerusalem-led kings by attacking at sunrise and chasing them down the way of Beth-horon — miraculously aided according to the biblical account by hailstones and the sun standing still (Josh. 10:1-14). This same strategic position accounts for Cestius' pitching his camp at Gibeon on his march to Jerusalem in October 66 C.E. (Josephus *BJ* 2.515-16; cf. 2.540ff.).

Section of Iron Age water tunnel at Gibeon (el-Jib, 10th century B.C.E.). Ninety-three steps lead from inside the city wall through the hill to the spring (University Museum, University of Pennsylvania)

The sacred nature of the site is first encountered in the account of Solomon's dream (1 Kgs. 3:2-5) on the occasion of his sacrifices at a high place there. The book of Chronicles places the tent of the meeting (2 Chr. 1:3, 13) as well as the tabernacle and the altar of the burnt offering at Gibeon (1 Chr. 16:39; 21:29). The "hill of God" (Gibeath-elohim) mentioned in the Saul narratives is certainly in the general vicinity of Gibeon, and it seems likely that this "hill of God" should be equated with Gibeon. If so, the location of a Philistine garrison there (cf. 1 Sam. 10:5) would explain Saul's hostility toward the city. A famine in Israel was thought to be retribution for Saul's killing of the Gibeonites in violation of Joshua's treaty; Saul's sons were consequently executed at Gibeon in order to stay the famine (2 Sam. 21:1-14). Gibeon was also the home of Hananiah, the false prophet (Jer. 28:1). In the postexilic period, the men of Gibeon assisted in rebuilding the temple (Neh. 3:7-8).

Excavations at the site have unearthed a sophisticated water system including a huge circular pool hewn out of stone. This is undoubtedly what is referred to as the "pool of Gibeon" in biblical literature. The pool at Gibeon becomes a focal point for conflict during the civil war which followed the death of Saul. Joab and Amasa's men first meet there in a contest (2 Sam. 2:12-17); later Joab slays Amasa at the "large stone that is in Gibeon" (2 Sam. 20:8). In the early 6th century "the great pool that is in Gibeon" is mentioned as the place where Johanan came to apprehend Ishmael and the Judeans after they had slain the Babylonian governor Gedaliah (Jer. 41:11-18).

According to archaeological evidence uncovered in excavations by James Pritchard in the late 1950s, occupation of the site began in the early 2nd millennium (Middle Bronze Age). The site declined in the late 2nd millennium (Late Bronze Age), and only scant evidence from tombs attests settlement in this period. The transition to the Iron Age in the 12th century witnessed the construction of a large wall 3.2–3.4 m. (10-11 ft.) wide encircling the site. The site reached its zenith in the 7th century, when it became an industrial center for the production and distribution of wine.

WILLIAM SCHNIEDEWIND

GIDDALTI (Heb. *giddaltî*)
A son of Heman and leader of the 22nd division of musicians in the service of the sanctuary (1 Chr. 25:4, 29).

GIDDEL (Heb. *giddēl*)
1. A temple servant whose descendants returned with Zerubbabel from the Exile (Ezra 2:47 = Neh. 7:49).

2. A servant of Solomon whose descendants returned with Zerubbabel from the Exile (Ezra 2:56 = Neh. 7:58).

GIDEON (Heb. *giḏʻôn*) (also JERUBBAAL)
According to Judg. 6–8, a premonarchical leader celebrated for ridding Israel of Midianite invaders; also known as Jerubbaal. He was also remembered for divinatory activity (Judg. 6:21, 25, 36-40; 7:9-14; 8:27).

An editorial introduction (Judg. 6:1-10) sets the Gideon traditions within the redactional framework of apostasy, oppression, outcry, and deliverance. The first of the older traditions is a commissioning scene (Judg. 6:11-24). The unrecognized messenger of Yahweh commands a timorous Gideon to go and deliver Israel (cf. Judg. 13). Like Moses (Exod. 3:10-12), Gideon protests (Judg. 6:13) but is assured by God that "I will be with you" (v. 16; cf. Exod. 3:12).

The newly commissioned Gideon's first act is to tear down his father's altar to Baal and its sacred pole (asherah) and build an altar to Yahweh (Judg. 6:25-32). This story identifies Gideon with Jerubbaal (cf. 1 Sam. 12:11; 2 Sam. 11:21), and gives a Yahwistic explanation of his Baal name.

With Yahweh, not Baal, confirmed as Gideon's God, the scene is set for battle. The various traditions of Judg. 6:33–8:3 serve to establish that victory over the Midianites is wholly the work of the divine warrior. By stages 32 thousand Israelite troops are reduced to 300 men who, as at Jericho (Josh. 6), defeat the enemy without actively fighting.

The battle is followed by two mopping-up campaigns. West of the Jordan the troops earlier excused from battle, along with the Ephraimites, attack the fleeing Midianites, killing their princes, Oreb and Zeeb. This is followed by inter-Israelite tension, as Gideon diplomatically averts battle with Ephraim, a dominant tribe angered by Gideon's failure to enlist their aid and, presumably, threatened by the upstart's rise in power.

The Transjordanian campaign involves the capture and death of Midianite kings Zebah and Zamnunna. This time intertribal conflict involves Gideon's brutal vengeance against Succoth and Penuel for failing to succor his troops.

The Israelites invite the victorious Gideon to rule over them. Gideon rejects the offer for reasons of piety: Yahweh is to be their ruler. Gideon does, however, claim oracular authority, making an ephod which ensnares him and his family.

The Gideon cycle, together with the closely related story of Gideon's son Abimelech's effort to claim kingship (Judg. 9), is among the longest and most complex sets of tradition in the book of Judges. The hero's two names suggest two originally independent traditions. The view of the initial battle as a local affair involving 300 members of Gideon's clan (the Abiezrites of Manasseh) is in tension with the depiction of an intertribal alliance warring against 130 thousand Midianites. The Transjordanian campaign, depicted as a matter of blood vengeance for the previously unmentioned slaughter of Gideon's brothers, fits poorly with the military campaign narrated in Judg. 7. While there is no scholarly consensus on the details of the composition history, there is widespread agreement that a variety of originally independent local traditions have been brought together into an uneasy unity, given an "all Israel" cast, and set within the characteristic framework of Judges.

This complex composition history erodes the Gideon stories' usefulness for historical reconstruction. In particular, efforts to identify a historical basis to the Israelites' request that Gideon rule them are dubious. The passage serves as a foil for the anti-monarchical story of Abimelech (Judg. 9). Moreover, the stories have been shaped to stress a theological point: the sovereignty of Yahweh. Yahweh, not Baal, is God; Yahweh, not human armies, wins victory against Israel's enemies; Yahweh, not Gideon, shall rule.

Bibliography. A. G. Auld, "Gideon: Hacking at the Heart of the Old Testament," *VT* 39 (1989): 257-67; R. G. Boling, *Judges*. AB 6A (Garden City, 1975); J. A. Emerton, "Gideon and Jerubbaal," *JTS* n.s. 27 (1976): 289-312; J. A. Soggin, *Judges*. OTL (Philadelphia, 1981).

CAROLYN PRESSLER

GIDEONI (Heb. *giḏʻōnî*)
The father of Abidan, who led the tribe of Benjamin during the wilderness journey (Num. 1:11; 2:22; 7:60, 65; 10:24).

GIDOM (Heb. *giḏʻōm*)
A place in the vicinity of Rimmon **3**, ca. 5 km. (3 mi.) E of Bethel, to which the Israelites pursued the Benjaminites after defeating them in civil war (Judg. 20:45).

GIHON (Heb. *gîḥôn, giḥôn*)
1. One of the four rivers that branched off of that which watered the garden of Eden (Gen. 2:13). Since the Gihon flowed through the land of Cush (usually an OT reference to a region south of Egypt, i.e., Nubia or North Sudan), it has sometimes been equated with the Nile. However, because the Tigris and Euphrates are rivers in West Asia and the Cush of Gen. 2:13 may also be there, the Gihon River may have been in West Asia rather than North Africa.

2. A spring (ʻEn Sittī Maryam/ʻAin Umm ed-Daraǵ) in the Kidron Valley that was the principal water supply for Jerusalem in OT times. The water gushes from a natural cave between one and five times daily (supplying from 7000 to 40,000 cu. ft. of water), depending on the season of the year. Solomon was anointed king at this site (1 Kgs. 1:33, 38, 45). Hezekiah blocked the waters of the spring and diverted them into a reservoir (the Pool of Siloam; cf. John 9:7, 11) by means of a tunnel that he ordered dug (2 Kgs. 20:20; 2 Chr. 32:30) to protect the water supply during the Assyrian invasion of 701 B.C. In the mid-7th century Manasseh built an outer wall to bolster Jerusalem's defenses west of Gihon (2 Chr. 33:14).

Bibliography. Z. Abells and A. Arbit, "Some New Thoughts on Jerusalem's Ancient Water Systems," *PEQ* 127 (1995): 2-7; Y. Shiloh, *Excavations at the City of David* 1: *1978-1982.* Qedem 19 (Jerusalem, 1984). STEPHEN R. MILLER

GILALAI (Heb. *gilălay*)
A levitical musician who participated in the procession at the dedication of the rebuilt walls of Jerusalem (Neh. 12:36).

GILBOA, MOUNT (Heb. *har haggilbōaʿ*)
A large spur of Eocene and Cenomanian limestone that, along with the Hill of Moreh to the north, marks the separation between the Jezreel and Harod valleys. The location of Mt. Gilboa is fixed by Eusebius (*Onom.* 72.10), who writes that its name is preserved by the village Gelbus (Jelbun, 189207), 6 Roman mi. from Scythopolis (Beth-shan).

It is at the spring of Harod (Ein Jalud, 183217) at the foot of Gilboa that Gideon chooses 300 men to fight the Midianites (Judg. 7:1). Saul and his three sons meet their death on Mt. Gilboa (1 Sam. 28:4; 31:1-6). Ahab, king of Israel, appears to have established a winter capital at Jezreel (Zirin), a town at the westernmost tip of Mt. Gilboa (1 Kgs. 21:1).

Bibliography. T. Koizumi, "On the Battle of Gilboa," *Annual of the Japanese Biblical Institute* 2 (1976): 61-78. BRIAN P. IRWIN

GILEAD (Heb. *gilʿāḏ*) **(PERSON)**

1. The son of Machir and grandson of Manasseh; eponym of the tribe and territory of Gilead (Num. 26:29-30; 27:1; 36:1; 1 Chr. 2:21, 23; 7:14, 17). Gilead remained in Transjordan rather than join Deborah and Barak against Sisera (Judg. 5:17); some scholars suggest that this reflects political instability within the tribe at that time and that the tribe of Gilead was supplanted by Gad.

2. The father of the illegitimate warrior Jephthah, who judged Gilead at the time of the Ammonite invasion (Judg. 11:1-2, 8, 11). The name may be a patronymic.

3. The eponymous ancestor of a Gadite clan (1 Chr. 5:14).

GILEAD (Heb. *gilʿāḏ*) **(PLACE)**
A mountainous region in Transjordan. Its name was derived from a grandson of Manasseh (Num. 26:29). Nothing more is known about Gilead or his father Machir.

The Gilead clan may have settled in the mountainous area of Transjordan because of an earlier tribal tradition and the similarity between their name and the older name of the region (Galeed; Gen. 31:47). Judging from the many stories set in Gilead and from the fact that the Gilead clan gave its name to the entire region, one can assume that the Gileadites were the strongest family within the tribe of Manasseh. Sometimes Gilead is portrayed as a region on par with Bashan (Deut. 4:43; Josh. 17:5; 1 Chr. 5:16), while at other times Transjordan, as a whole, is referred to as Gilead (e.g., Num. 32:26, 29; Josh. 22:9, 13, 15, 32; Judg. 10:8; 20:1; 2 Sam. 2:9; Hos. 6:8). On occasion, the name Gilead was even used in place of the tribal name Manasseh (Judg. 5:17; Ps. 60:7[MT 9]; 108:8[9]) or was, at the least, an alternate name for the tribe (Judg. 12:4). During the period of the judges, Gilead was not only the strongest Israelite group in Transjordan but was probably, at times, the strongest Israelite contingent in all of Canaan (Judg. 10:3; 12:7). The Gileadites were strong enough to defeat the Ammonites and at least one interfering Israelite tribe under the leadership of Jephthah (Judg. 11:32-33; 12:4)

Due to the region's changing political fortunes, the exact geographical boundaries of Gilead are difficult to determine and are not specifically delineated. Nevertheless, Gilead proper was centered in the mountainous Transjordanian hill country WNW of modern Amman and loosely associated with the Jabbok River. Its northern neighbor was Bashan. Certainly its heartland was hill country (Gen. 31:21, 23; Cant. 4:1; Jer. 22:6). From the trees of these mountains came a soothing salve that Jeremiah compares to the healing power of God (Jer. 8:22; 46:11; cf. Gen. 37:25).

The mountainous territory was often a place of salvation or safety for the faithful. It was to Gilead that Jacob fled from Laban (Gen. 31:21), from where the Ishmaelites came and saved Joseph from the hands of his brothers (37:25), where some people hid from the Philistines in the days of Saul (1 Sam. 13:7), and where David won his victory over Absalom (2 Sam. 17:26).

The prophet Elijah is probably the most famous Gileadite (1 Kgs. 17:1). Although no story featuring Elijah occurs in Gilead, that he was recognized as a prophet of Yahweh by Cisjordan Israelites suggests that Gilead remained Israelite territory until at least the mid-9th century B.C. In the 9th-8th centuries, shortly after the time of Elijah, Gilead was no longer an independent Israelite territory (2 Kgs. 10:33; 15:29). According to the prophet Hosea, Gilead had become a place of evildoers (Hos. 6:8; 12:11[12]). It was predicted that Gilead would eventually be returned to Israelite control (Obad. 1:19; Mic. 7:14; Zech. 10:10).

Bibliography. Y. Aharoni, *The Land of the Bible,* 2nd ed. (Philadelphia, 1979), 38-39; D. Baly, *The Geography of the Bible,* rev. ed. (New York, 1974), 219-25. DAVID MERLING

GILGAL (Heb. *gilgāl*)

1. A place "opposite" Mts. Gerizim and Ebal. Deut. 11:30 describes it as both "in the land of" the Canaanites dwelling in the Arabah (which could refer to Gilgal near Jericho) and "beside" the oaks of Moreh (which would indicate another Gilgal near Shechem).

2. A place E of Jericho where the Israelites encamped after crossing the Jordan River and where they erected 12 stones from the Jordan River as a memorial of the crossing by the 12 tribes (Josh. 4:19-20). The generation of Israelites born in the wilderness was circumcised here (Josh. 5:2-9). From this action of "rolling away the disgrace of Egypt" apparently the name Gilgal was derived as a play on Heb. *gll* ("to roll [away]." In Gilgal the Israelites kept the first Passover in the land (Josh. 5:10), ate the produce of the land, and the manna ceased. They attacked Jericho from Gilgal, were deceived by the Gibeonites here (Josh. 9:6), and launched their attack on the anti-Gibeonite coalition (10:6-7, 9, 15). They also returned here from a victorious campaign into southern Canaan (Josh. 10:43) and granted Hebron to Caleb, beginning the allotment of land to the tribes (14:6).

In Judg. 2:1 the angel of the Lord goes from Gilgal to Bochim, perhaps indicating a decline in Gilgal's significance or perhaps its capture by the Moabites. From here Ehud returned to slay Eglon, their king (Judg. 3:19). In Samuel's time Gilgal seems to have regained some prominence. It was part of his circuit (1 Sam. 7:16). Samuel and the people made sacrifices here (1 Sam. 10:8), and here Saul was affirmed as king (11:15); but Saul was rebuked for presumptuously offering sacrifices (13:9-14) and for failing to destroy Amalekite flocks which he kept to sacrifice here (15:21). This mentioning of sacrifice at Gilgal perhaps indicates its importance as a sanctuary at that time. At Gilgal David was also welcomed back as king after the defeat of Absalom (2 Sam. 19:15, 40).

The 8th-century prophets condemn the use of Gilgal as a center for sacrifices (Hos. 4:15; 9:15; 12:11[MT 12]; Amos 4:4; 5:5). Micah reminds his people positively of the Israelites' journey from Shittim to Gilgal (Mic. 6:5).

Attempts by archaeologists to fix the location Gilgal near Jericho have been inconclusive. Perhaps it was just a campsite that later became a place of sacrifice which merely consisted of an altar and a few stone pillars.

Bibliography. B. M. Bennett, Jr., "The Search for Israelite Gilgal," *PEQ* 104 (1972): 111-22; J. Muilenburg, "The Site of Ancient Gilgal," *BASOR* 140 (1955): 11-27.

3. A place in Galilee, between Dor and Tirzah, whose king Joshua defeated (Josh. 12:23-24 MT). The LXX reads "Goiim in Galilee" (so NRSV).

4. A place towards which the northern border of Judah turned north, opposite the ascent of Adummim (Josh. 15:7). However, describing this same border as Benjamin's southern border, Josh. 18:17 mentions Geliloth instead of Gilgal. Excavations tentatively identify the site as ʿAraq ed-Deir (180133), 1.5 km. (mi.) W of Khan el-Aḥmar, the traditional "Inn of the Good Samaritan."

5. A site N of Bethel. From here Elijah and Elisha travelled to Jericho (2 Kgs. 2:1-4). Later, after raising the Shunammite woman's son from the dead, Elisha returned to Gilgal, where he purified a pot of foul stew (2 Kgs. 4:38). Some scholars identify the site as modern Jiljulieh, in the hill country ca. 13 km. (8 mi.) N of Bethel.

6. A site which Demetrius passed en route to his siege of Jerusalem (1 Macc. 9:2). Roger Good

GILGAMESH EPIC

Perhaps the most famous masterpiece of ancient Near Eastern literature, undoubtedly due to its flood narrative (though this is actually a late addition). Composed in Akkadian, it features the exploits of Gilgamesh, a possible king of Uruk (biblical Erech, Gen. 10:10) in southern Mesopotamia ca. 2700-2600 B.C.E. Various independent Sumerian literary works and traditions about Gilgamesh had circulated as early as the Ur III Dynasty (2100-2000). However, sometime early in the 2nd millennium these assorted works were transformed into a single composition (often referred to as the Old Babylonian Version). Its popularity is attested by the copies, fragments, and adaptations of this version that have been found at such places as Emar in north Syria, Megiddo in Canaan, and Ḫattuša, the capital of the Hittite Empire.

Neither the early Sumerian works or the Old Babylonian Version contained a flood account. This element, however, can be traced from episodic Sumerian beginnings (The Tale of Ziusudra) through successive Akkadian translations and adaptations to the final "canonical" version in 12 tablets (chapters) in what is often referred to as the Standard Version of the Gilgamesh Epic (known mainly from Neo-Assyrian copies [750-612 B.C.E.]).

The overall theme of this integrated version is the (ultimately doomed) quest for eternal life and the "consolation prize" of enduring fame which, in the case of Gilgamesh, has actually been achieved.

But it is Tablet XI of this Standard Version with its Mesopotamian story of the Deluge that is the most familiar of all biblical parallels in the epic. The tablet seems to be drawing in particular from the Akkadian myth of Atra-ḫasis. In this version, the deluge account is put into the mouth of the Flood hero himself (= Noah), known in different versions by different names but here as Utnapishtim ("I have/he has found life"). At one stage of its evolution, Tablet XI was the last tablet of the epic, and concluded with the return of Gilgamesh to Uruk. Subsequently a twelfth tablet was added by straight translation from a Sumerian prototype. It included a vision of the netherworld over which Gilgamesh presided as a deity.

Bibliography. S. Dalley, *Myths from Mesopotamia* (Oxford, 1989), 39- 153; B. R. Foster, *Before the Muses,* 2nd ed. 2 vols. (Bethesda, 1996); B. R. Foster, "Gilgamesh (1.132)," in *The Context of Scripture,* ed. W. W. Hallo (Leiden, 1997), 1:458-60; M. G. Kovacs, *The Epic of Gilgamesh* (Stanford, 1989); J. H. Tigay, *The Evolution of the Gilgamesh Epic* (Philadelphia, 1982). K. Lawson Younger, Jr.

GILOH (Heb. *gilōh*)

A town in the hill country of Judah (Josh. 15:51); the home of Ahithophel ("the Gilonite"; 2 Sam. 15:12; 23:34). Though widely accepted, the identification of Giloh with Khirbet Jala, ca. 8 km. (5 mi.) NNW of Hebron, encounters a difficulty at Josh. 15:48-51, which seems to locate Giloh SW of Hebron, perhaps near Khirbet Rabud (151093).

GIMZO (Heb. *gimzô*)

A Judahite city in the lowland region near the Philistine plain, captured by the Philistines at the time of the Syro-Ephraimite War (2 Chr. 28:18). The site is generally accepted as modern Jimzū (145148), ca. 5 km. (3 mi.) SE of Lod (biblical Lydda).

GINATH (Heb. *gînaṯ*)
The father of Tibni, who unsuccessfully rivaled Omri for the Israelite throne (1 Kgs. 16:21-22).

GINNETHOI (Heb. *ginnĕṯôy*)
A priest who returned from the Exile with Zerubbabel (Neh. 12:4). He may be the same as Ginnethon **2.**

GINNETHON (Heb. *ginnĕṯôn*)
1. A priest who set his seal to the renewed covenant at the time of Nehemiah (Neh. 10:6[MT 7]).
2. The head of a priestly family at the time of the high priest Joiakim (Neh. 12:16). If the name is an eponym for the entire family, it may encompass **1** above. Some would also identify him with Ginnethoi.

GIRGASHITES (Heb. *girgāšî*)
An indigenous ethnic group which was dispossessed by the Israelites during their acquisition of the Promised Land (Josh. 3:10; 24:11). It has been conjectured that the Girgashites inhabited an area N of the Jezreel Valley and S of the Lebanon Mountains. The NT's Gergesenes (Gk. *Gergesēnoí*) may be the same name.

Bibliography. E. C. Hostetter, *Nations Mightier and More Numerous: The Biblical View of Palestine's Pre-Israelite Peoples.* BIBALDS 3 (N. Richland Hills, Tex., 1995), 62-66. EDWIN C. HOSTETTER

GIRZITES (Heb. *girzî*)
A people, along with the Amalekites and the Geshurites, against whom David and his troops raided while at Ziklag (1 Sam. 27:8). The Girzite homeland would have been somewhere between Philistia and the Egyptian border. They are mentioned nowhere else in the OT, and many scholars suggest that "Girzite" is a corrupted dittography of Geshurite (cf. **Q** *gizrî*).
NANCY L. DECLAISSÉ-WALFORD

GISHPA (Heb. *gišpā'*)
An overseer of the temple servants at the time of Nehemiah (Neh. 11:21). Some scholars consider the name to be a corruption of Hashupa in the list at Ezra 2:43.

GITTAIM (Heb. *gittāyim*)
A town (Heb. "pair of winepresses") where Amorite inhabitants of Beeroth received permanent refuge (2 Sam. 4:3), either from Saulide hostilities against towns allied with Gibeon (21:2; Josh. 9) or from Saul in revenge for the murder of his son Ishbosheth by descendants of the Beerothite Rimmon (2 Sam. 4:2). Its location is uncertain. Some scholars prefer an identification near Beeroth in the tribal territory of Benjamin, but others prefer Gath, NW of Aijalon, where the nearby Philistine presence would have provided protection from Saul. Gittaim was inhabited after the Exile (Neh. 11:33). DAVID PAUL LATOUNDJI

GITTITE (Heb. *gittîm*)
A gentilic designating inhabitants of the Philistine city of Gath (e.g., 2 Sam. 6:10-11; 15:18).

GITTITH (Heb. *gittîṯ*)
An obscure term found in psalm superscriptions (Pss. 8, 81, 84), always as part of the phrase *'al-haggittîṯ*, typically translated "according to The Gittith" (NRSV, NIV; cf. NJPSV). Like other terms with *'al* in the psalm superscriptions, it is likely a technical term denoting a melody, perhaps one associated with Gath. Other possibilities include a type of musical instrument (e.g., the Gittite lyre), a cultic procedure, or a festal song/ceremony, perhaps associated with the New Year or Tabernacles (cf. LXX "at the wine vats," from Heb. *gaṯ*).
TYLER F. WILLIAMS

GIZONITE (Heb. *gizônî*)
A gentilic applied to Hashem, one of David's warriors (1 Chr. 11:34). No person or place named Gizo, from which the term could be derived, is known; thus scholars suggest emending the text to "Gunite" (cf. LXX) or "Gimzonite."

GLASS
Glass objects were first made at the end of the 3rd millennium B.C. Prior to the 1st century B.C. they were made by either casting or core forming. In order to cast glass, hot glass must be poured into molds or cold glass must be placed over a mold in a hot furnace. The most common cast glass objects were bowls and pendants. Core-formed vessels were produced by winding hot glass around a clay or dung core. When the glass cooled, the core was removed, leaving a hollow interior. Glassblowing was invented somewhere in Syria-Palestine in the 1st century B.C. and allowed the craftsmen to produce significantly larger quantities of glass than the casting or core-forming methods allowed, thereby reducing the cost of glass objects and making them more common.

Glass is mentioned as a precious commodity likened to gold (Job 28:17), as a possession of the daughters of Zion (Isa. 3:23; NRSV "garments of gauze"), and as a metaphor for the clearness of the gold in the New Jerusalem (Rev. 21:18, 21). References to glass as a luxury item reflect the costliness of glass objects prior to the Roman era.

A sea of glass appears in front of God's throne (Rev. 4:6; 15:2), perhaps a reference to the bronze sea in Solomon's temple (1 Kgs. 7:23-26) or to the division between the waters above and the waters below (Gen. 1:7).

Glass mirrors are referred to in Isa. 3:23; Exod. 38:8, where they are the possessions of women. They are also mentioned in relation to viewing God or seeing one's true self (1 Cor. 13:12; 2 Cor. 3:18; Jas. 1:23). It is interesting that glass is mentioned,

Green glass flask with neck coil and s-corrugations on the body, from Karanis in the Egyptian Fayoum (3rd-4th century C.E.) (Kelsey Museum of Archaeology, University of Michigan)

since prior to the Roman period mirrors were made of polished metal rather than glass.

Bibliography. M. Dayagi-Mendels, *Perfumes and Cosmetics in the Ancient World* (Jerusalem, 1989); D. F. Grose, *Early Ancient Glass* (New York, 1989).

ALYSIA FISCHER

GLEANING

The practice of gathering, mainly food. It is most often recognized in connection with the story of Ruth and Naomi (Ruth 2) where Ruth gleaned in the fields of Boaz to provide food for her mother-in-law Naomi and herself. The Torah makes provision for those in need (the poor, fatherless, aliens, widows) by commanding that the last bits of harvest be intentionally left for gleaners (Lev. 19:9-10; 23:22; Deut. 24:21).

Elsewhere, gleaning refers to a practice of collecting items that were originally put in place by someone other than the collector: the Israelites in the wilderness glean bread rained from heaven (Exod. 16); a prophet gleans herbs for stew and wild gourds (2 Kgs. 4:39); Joseph gleans money from Egypt and Canaan in preparation for dealing with the famine (Gen. 47:14); the Creator is thanked for all that is gleaned (Ps. 104:28); a lover gleans lilies (Cant. 6:2); Jonathan's servant gleans arrows (1 Sam. 20:38); and others glean stones (Gen. 31:46), food scraps (Judg. 1:7), wood (Jer. 7:18), and grapes (Judg. 8:2).

Gleaning is used metaphorically in the prophetic writings, usually to generate an image of emptiness and despair (Isa. 24:13; Jer. 49:9 = Obad. 5; Mic. 7:1). In the only metaphorical use that generates a positive image, Isaiah speaks of God's careful gleaning of each one of his people (Isa. 27:12).

Bibliography. O. Borowski, *Agriculture in Iron Age Israel* (Winona Lake, 1987).

ALICE H. HUDIBURG

GLORY

That aspect of a person or God worthy of praise, honor, or respect; often associated with brightness or splendor in theophanies. Used of people or creation, glory is that characteristic which people typically honor: wisdom (Prov. 25:2), might (2 Kgs. 14:10), wealth (Esth. 1:4; Matt. 6:29 par.). It can refer to a quality of land (Isa. 35:2) or of people: age (Prov. 16:31), strength (20:29), or outward appearance (Isa. 53:2).

Several Hebrew words are translated "glory," most commonly *kāḇôḏ,* "heavy, weighty, burdensome" (cf. Isa. 22:24). Related terms are *hāḏār* (e.g., the splendor of God's work, Ps. 90:16) and *hôḏ,* God's sovereignty over all things (Ps. 148:13), more often translated "honor." The LXX translates with Gk. *dóxa,* unifying glory with its manifestations and encompassing the greatness and majesty of God. The NT inherited this complex of meanings, also using *dóxa* in the classical Greek sense of "reputation" (cf. Luke 14:10), in the Hebrew sense of "weighty" (2 Cor. 4:17), and for the Shekinah, God's tabernacling presence (1 Pet. 4:14).

Old Testament

The Pentateuch associates God's glory (i.e., his aura, the sheer magnificence of God's presence) with theophanies, acts of salvation, and judgment. The glory is a devouring fire, shrouded with clouds on Mt. Sinai (Exod. 24:16-17). In clouds and fire God's glory accompanied Israel through the wilderness (cf. Exod. 13:21), filled the tabernacle (40:34-38) and the temple (cf. 1 Kgs. 8:10-11; 2 Chr. 7:1-3), and sanctified the beginning of the cultic service (Lev. 9:23). God shrouded his glory from Israel, but gave Moses a glimpse of its brilliance (Exod. 33:18-23). God displays his glory in salvation: in victory over Pharaoh at the Red Sea (Exod. 14:4) and by providing manna in the wilderness (16:7). When the people rebel, glory also accompanies judgment (Num. 16:42-50).

In the Prophets God's glory is again encountered in theophany (Isa. 6:3; Ezek. 43:2-5) and is declared in judgment on rebellious Israel (Isa. 2:10; Ezek. 10:18) and the nations (Isa. 10:16). In contrast to human glory, God maintains an unshakable covenant with his faithful remnant (Isa. 42:8), promising salvation (40:5; 46:13) and protection (58:5-8). Ezekiel consoles the exiles with the promise of the return of God's glory to a restored temple (Ezek. 44:4-8).

In the Psalms God's glory rests in his mighty works manifest in creation (e.g., Pss. 19, 29, 97, 104). Israel worships God for his mighty works of salvation in history (Ps. 66; 105; 145:4-12). God is the victorious king of glory (Ps. 24:7-12), whose presence now rests on Zion (26:8; 63:2[MT 3]).

The OT also proclaims the eschatological hope that the whole earth "shall be filled with the glory of the Lord" (Num. 14:21), when all nations shall bless the Lord (Ps. 66:2-4; 138:4-5). The messianic kingdom will dawn when the nations know the Messiah's glory and peace (Isa. 60:1-3; cf. 11:6-9; Hab. 2:14).

New Testament

As in the OT, glory is an essential attribute of God, "the Father of glory" (Eph. 1:17), whose radiance is displayed at Jesus' birth (Luke 2:9) and is part of eschatological hope (Rom. 5:2). In return, people are to glorify God (Acts 12:23; 1 Cor. 10:31).

The understanding of glory is here expanded to include that of Christ as well. Just as in the OT glory referred to salvation, so in the NT it is revealed in the Messiah's work of deliverance. In the Synoptic Gospels Christ shares in glory at the Parousia, when he comes with vindication and judgment (Matt. 16:27; Mark 8:38). Christ possesses his own glory through his death and resurrection (Luke 24:26). In the Transfiguration account (Luke 9:28-36 par.) Jesus' glory is experienced as theophany.

John presents Jesus as the revelation of God's glory (John 1:14), preexistent in Christ (17:24). His works are signs of the glory of God (John 2:11), inviting belief (11:4, 40). The Cross is the culminating sign, the hour of Christ's glorification (John 12:23; 13:31-32; cf. Rev. 5:12-13). God continues to glorify Christ through the work of the Spirit (John 16:14).

Participation in the glory of the resurrected Christ is a participation in the glory of God (Rom. 5:2; 2 Cor. 3:7-18). Through the Spirit the Church lets the glory of God in Christ shine through its life (2 Cor. 3:18; 4:6). Believers are the image and glory of God (1 Cor. 11:7), giving glory by leading lives worthy of the gospel (10:31; 1 Thess. 2:12), through obedience (2 Cor. 9:13), purity (1 Cor. 6:20), good deeds (1 Pet. 2:12), and willingness to suffer for Christ (Rom. 8:17-18; 1 Pet. 4:13-16). They may look forward to sharing in God's glory, living in his presence in new bodies, in a new heaven and earth (1 Cor. 15:43; Rev. 21:22-26).

Bibliography. I. Abrahams, *The Glory of God* (1925, repr. New York, 1973); H. U. von Balthasar, *The Glory of the Lord: A Theological Aesthetics*, 7 vols. (San Francisco, 1983-91); G. von Rad and G. Kittel, "dokéō, dóxa," *TDNT* 2:232-55.

Darrell D. Gwaltney, Jr./Ralph W. Vunderink

GLOSS

A scribal note, originally written in the margin or above a line, which in the process of transcription became incorporated into the text. As ascertained by textual critics, such annotations may have been intended to explain or elaborate upon a passage (e.g., Josh. 1:15, "and take possession of it"), indicate a variant reading (cf. 1 Sam. 12:13, "for whom you have asked"; lacking in LXX), or add a pious restatement or theological corrective (e.g., Ps. 51:14[MT 16], "O God of my salvation").

GNAT

A general term referring to small, winged, biting or stinging insects, perhaps the midge *(Chironomidae)*, associated with the third plague visited upon Egypt (Exod. 8:16-19[MT 12-15]; Ps. 105:31). Translations of Heb. *kinnîm* (pl.) vary (KJV, NJPSV "lice"; NJB "mosquitoes"). The image of Aaron's staff striking the dust of the earth to bring forth the plague of gnats aptly conveys their minute size, which permits them to enter the eyes, ears, and noses of their human victims. MHeb. *kinnim* means "lice," whereas the details in the Exodus account seem to indicate some sort of fast-moving flying insect.

Isa. 51:6 is problematic, since the singular form of the Hebrew term does not occur elsewhere (cf. KJV "in like manner," NJPSV "as well," following LXX).

In Matt. 23:24 Jesus criticizes those who strain out a gnat (Gk. *kṓnōps;* the lighter matter of the law — ceremonial concerns), yet swallow a camel (the weightier matter of the law — justice, mercy, and faith), forgetting that one should practice the one commandment without neglecting the other.

Jesper Svartvik

GNOSTICISM, GNOSIS

Gnosticism as a term originated in the 18th century and has functioned as the label for an ill-defined category in history of religions research. Both the term and the modern category today are under heavy criticism. The prior Greek terms *gnṓsis* ("knowledge") and *gnṓstēs* ("knower") are employed in ancient sources where they are naturally free from the modern construct "Gnosticism."

In its classic scholarly presentation, now increasingly discredited, the term Gnosticism was used as the label for what was variously described as a mostly unified protest movement against the prevailing political, religious, and philosophical structures of late antiquity. This proposed "gnostic religion," in its admittedly various forms, was said to be promoted by elitists, was parasitic of other religions, and radically dualistic in its anticosmic and antibody attitudes. Humans were understood to be in a state of blindness, sleep, and drunkenness. The inner spirit was prisoner to the fleshly body, which was prisoner of the material cosmos, both created by an inferior lower God (Gen. 1–6) sometimes said to enslave his creation with time, laws, and lust. The human story traces the attempt to transcend one's material limitations by returning to the highest and true God in the highest heaven *(plḗrōma)*. This return was achieved through the individual's receptive experience of knowledge *(gnṓsis)* which informed her of her true spiritual nature and origins in the highest heaven, her tragic fall into matter *(hýlē)*, and her eventual restoration with the true God. Attendant to this model was the idea that

Gnostics were involved in a variously described "social crisis" which exhibited itself at both the textual and mythological levels in a subversive hermeneutical revolt, a protest exegesis directed against orthodox Jewish and Christian political mythologies, often with a Jungian twist. This rebellion was characterized in texts by an exegetical value inversion of the early chapters of Genesis. On the ethical side, Gnostics were described as either ascetic or libertine. Some of these features were emphasized, deemphasized, or even absent from some heresiological reports and supposed gnostic texts, while other features were added as the complex evidences demonstrate.

This classic characterization of Gnosticism is a modern construct which has attempted to describe a social phenomenon which never existed in the ancient world, but in its failure to describe a social movement it constructed a faulty category. Scholars are divided whether the term should be retained and the category revised, or whether both the term and the category should be abandoned.

Recent studies suggest that one could instead describe the social phenomena under consideration as a varied assortment of new religious movements. These movements drew from a large pool of discrete traditions, many of which have been traced back to earlier texts and movements. Depending on its particular constellation of traditions, each movement can then be identified as to its type. The failed classic search for the origins of Gnosticism, often argued to have begun among disgruntled intellectuals (Jews, Christians, or others), has attempted to explain too many diverse phenomena in too narrow a category. This suggests that source analysis might better focus on the origins and development of individual traditions and clusters of traditions. With this emerging new model, both the term "Gnosticism" and its attendant modern category have lost all relevance to the subject at hand, and now function only to alert us to the problem of their existence.

The historical evidences which have been the focus of the modern term and category "Gnosticism" divide into two groups: ancient manuscripts and heresiological reports. Concerning manuscripts, there have been four major discoveries of Coptic papyrus codices antedating 400 C.E. including, in order of their discovery, the Askew Codex containing four texts (published in 1896), the Bruce Codex containing three texts (1891), and the Berlin Codex containing four texts (1955). In 1945 13 Coptic papyrus codices containing 52 different texts and dating to the mid-4th century were discovered in Upper Egypt near the modern village of Nag Hammadi. The books appear to have been copied and read by Christian monks. The origins mostly date from the 2nd and 3rd centuries, with some of their sources going back to the 1st century. This single discovery provides 40 new texts, 30 of which are fairly complete, but 10 highly fragmented. Many of the texts recovered from these four discoveries were placed into the category "Gnosticism" because they were seen to be similar to the texts refuted by the heresiologists. These manuscript discoveries have increased our knowledge of the breadth and diversity of the religious movements once forced into the faulty category "Gnosticism."

Heresiologists span the 2nd through 5th centuries, beginning with Justin Martyr (d. 165), the influential Irenaeus of Lyon (d. 200), Clement of Alexandria (d. 215), Tertullian (d. 225), Hippolytus of Rome (d. 235), Origen (d. 254), Epiphanius of Salamis (d. 403), Augustine (d. 430; a one-time Manichean), and Theodoret of Cyrrhus (d. 466). Heresiological evidences can be divided into reliable verbatim quotations (totaling less than 60 pages) and various descriptions. The naturally biased and sometime derivative nature of the heresiological reports is well known. Generally, these reports argued that the groups they were describing had deviated under demonic influence from the true line, and that the error had come through an earlier Jewish source (Justin and Irenaeus), a Greek philosophical source (Hippolytus and Clement), or a variety of Greek and Jewish sectarian sources (Epiphanius).

The heresiological reports evidence the existence of discrete religious movements (often called schools). Basilides of Alexandria (d. ca. 150) and his student Isidore began a successful movement which existed until the 4th century, though confined to Egypt. Valentinus of Alexandria and Rome (d. ca. 175) saw his teaching explode on the international scene during his own lifetime with the development of distinct Eastern and Western Valentinian traditions. Some of his students became influential figures in Valentinian Christian history, most notably Ptolemy, Heracleon, and Markus. Marcion of Sinope (d. ca. 160) also built a successful international movement with students like Apelles (d. ca. 200) which endured until the 4th century in the West (a target of Constantine's state persecution) but even longer in the East, where Arab authors still referred to the Marcionites in the 10th century.

Some modern researchers suggest that several NT and related texts evidence contact with "Gnosticism" in various stages of its development. Texts that especially stand out are Paul's Corinthian correspondence, Colossians, Ephesians, the Pastoral Epistles, Jude, 2 Peter, and the letters of Ignatius of Antioch (d. ca. 115) and Polycarp of Smyrna (d. ca. 165) among others. But even here the issues discussed are diverse, demonstrating a complex assortment of competing new religious movements, but no evidence of "Gnosticism."

Bibliography. H. Jonas, *The Gnostic Religion* (Boston, 1963); G. Quispel, *Gnostic Studies,* 2 vols. (Istanbul, 1974); J. M. Robinson, *The Nag Hammadi Library in English,* 3rd rev. ed. (San Francisco, 1988); K. Rudolph, *Gnosis* (San Francisco, 1984); D. M. Scholer, *Nag Hammadi Bibliography, 1948-1969* (Leiden, 1971); *Nag Hammadi Bibliography, 1970-1994* (Leiden, 1997); M. A. Williams, *Rethinking "Gnosticism"* (Princeton, 1996).

PAUL MIRECKI

GO OUT AND COME IN

An expression of military security and blessedness. In the victory stela of the Egyptian pharaoh Merneptah (19th Dynasty), the people go and come in freedom (*ANET,* 378). A successful leader must have the freedom and ability to "go out and come in" before the people (Deut. 31:2; 2 Chr. 1:10; cf. 1 Kgs. 15:17). In the blessings and curses of Deut. 28, the order of the word pair is reversed (Deut. 28:6, 19). The word combination of "come" and "go" covers a wide range of activity. It refers to the freedom to move about outside of the city gate without threat of hostility. This level of military freedom was necessary in order to grow crops successfully outside of the city walls. ARNOLD BETZ

GOAD

A pointed spike used to prod oxen when plowing. It was made from a straight branch of hard wood stripped of bark. The other end often had a flat, chisel-like piece of iron, which allowed farmers to scrape off mud and clay that clogged the plowshares. The iron-tipped variety most probably was used by Shamgar when he slew 600 Philistines (Judg. 3:31). The practice of sharpening iron goads with files is attested in 1 Sam. 13:21.

"Goad" appears metaphorically for "the sayings of the wise" in Eccl. 12:11, reminding the reader that sapiential teaching prods humankind toward wise living. Paul recalls his kicking against God's prods, i.e., stubbornly fighting against God's will for him before his conversion (Acts 26:14). J. A. VADNAIS

GOAH (Heb. *gōʿâ*)

A place mentioned in conjunction with Gareb as a point of reference for the restored, enlarged, and resanctified Jerusalem (Jer. 31:39). The precise location remains unknown, but in the context of Jeremiah's prophecy it must certainly be SE of Gareb, N of the Hinnom Valley, and W of the Kidron. The LXX, instead of rendering the term as a proper name, uses the descriptive Gk. *ex eklektṓn líthōn* ("the stone of the elect" or "stone of the chosen"); however, this yields no further indication as to an exact location.

Bibliography. J. J. Simons, *Jerusalem in the Old Testament* (Leiden, 1952). DENNIS M. SWANSON

GOAT

Indication of their importance as domesticated animals in biblical times is the occurrence of seven different Hebrew and three Greek words for "goat" in the Bible. Beyond the general term *ʿēz* (pl. *ʿizzîm*) for female goats, four Hebrew words specifically refer to the he-goat (*śāʿîr, tayiš, ʿattûḏ* [pl. only], and *ṣāp̄îr*), one to a young he-goat (*gĕḏî*), and one to the wild goat (*ʾaqqô*). The Greek words refer to a kid (*eríphion*), a young kid (*ériphos*), and a he-goat (*trágos*).

The common domestic goat in Palestine is *Capra hircus.* Goats are distinguished from their sheep cousins, with whom they are usually kept, by the latter's coats of hair (usually black [cf. 1 Sam. 19:13] or grey, but sometimes white, brown, or any combination thereof), and their flat, twisted horns. While generally not as desirable as sheep for meat, goats are a more hardy animal, less discriminating in the vegetation they will eat, and thus tend to appear in greater numbers in herds living in more marginal environments. Indeed, the ratio of goat bones to sheep bones can give archaeologists some insight into ancient local environmental conditions in antiquity. Unfortunately, the grazing habits of goats over many centuries has had a major negative impact on the vegetation of Palestine, both in the decline of several important plant communities and in inhibiting their rejuvenation.

Goat by-products have long been familiar features among Palestine's desert people from the biblical periods down to the present and include milk (Prov. 27:27), cheese, goatskin bottles for water and wine (e.g., Mark 2:22), and goat's hair clothes, pillows, and tents (Exod. 26:7; 35:26; 1 Sam. 19:13; Heb. 11:37). While adult goats have poor meat, young kids make a desirable meal (Judg. 6:19; 13:15-23). Beyond their subsistence role in ancient Israelite and Jewish society, goats, especially he-goats, played an important cultic role, serving as the key sacrifice in various religious ceremonies (e.g., Num. 7:16). RANDALL W. YOUNKER

GOB (Heb. *gôḇ*)

The site of two battles between David and the Philistines (2 Sam. 21:18-19). The parallel account gives the site as Gezer (1 Chr. 20:4).

GOD

A generic word for the deity, used to refer to the God of Israel (Heb. *ēl/ʾĕlōhîm*) and the Christian community (Gk. *theós*) as well as the gods of other peoples. The word also becomes a name for the deity of the believing community and is used in direct address (e.g., Ps. 22:1[MT 2]; Mark 15:34).

God is the central subject of the Bible and is always presented in relationship with the world, with that which is not God. God's existence is assumed from the first verse of Genesis, God's core character and most basic purposes are constant across the two testaments, and the divine speaking and acting are always in service of those purposes, whether in creation, judgment, or salvation. The person and work of Jesus Christ fill the testimony of the NT, but the Christ event is understood as a decisive act of the God witnessed to in the OT. Jesus Christ constitutes both a fuller revealing of the God of Israel and the culmination of God's salvific purposes for the world.

Issues of Genre

God is a character in every biblical tradition (except Esther). God is presented as one who speaks, is spoken to, and is spoken about (though God's direct speaking is rare in the NT), and one who acts and is affected by the actions of others (e.g., provoked to anger). Most commonly, God is presented as a character in narrative, whose presence may be depicted as both intense (Sinai, Jesus Christ) and unobtrusive (the Joseph story). Narratives provide depth to God's character without bringing closure to the depiction of God; they present God as a living reality with all the attendant ambiguity and complexity.

At the same time, the biblical texts are not content with narratives in their portrayal of God. Interwoven with narratives are more generalized ("credal") statements about God. Types of generalizing genres are those which gather claims about God in summations of divine acts (Deut. 26:5-9; cf. Acts 2:14-36; 7:1-53), in more abstract ways (Exod. 34:6-7; cf. 1 Cor. 8:4-6), and in hymns and doxologies (1 Tim. 6:15-16; Ps. 145). The integration of these types of statements within other genres suggests that they represent a centering amid the Bible's theological pluralism. The regular appeal of the book of Psalms — which presents the faith in its leaner form — to these generalizations is noteworthy. In general, the historical recitals specified those events in history that were constitutive of the community of faith and the generalizations about God provided an ongoing interpretive clue for the kind of God believed to be active in those events.

These truth claims are not presented in final formulations, and remain open to new language and content. In addition, some narrative portrayals of God do not fit the predominant confession, witnessing to a theology in process by raising up reflections and challenges regarding God that the credal statements must take into account in the ongoing discussion regarding the divine identity (e.g., creation is added in Neh. 9:6; divine repentance in Jonah 4:2). The NT continues this process in its incipient trinitarianism (Matt. 28:19) and its claims regarding Jesus and God (John 1:1; 20:28).

Another genre issue is raised by the language to God and about God in the lament and protest literature. How does one "translate" the language of these genres into theological formulation (e.g., Ps. 44:23-24[24-25])? That these expressions occur predominantly in poetry is important. The reader must sort out the rhetorical function of this language and its metaphoric character before discerning how to use it in theological formulation.

The Knowledge of God

The sources for the biblical view of God are multivocal and complex (Heb. 1:1-2). A recent emphasis upon revelation in history has given way to a more comprehensive understanding that includes Israel's history; natural events; everyday experience; personal verbal encounter; liturgical event; interaction with other ancient literature and religion, both ancient Near Eastern and Greco-Roman; the ministry, life, death, and resurrection of Jesus; the internal testimony of the Holy Spirit.

The NT presupposes the OT understanding of God and therein grounds its theological formulations, including its centering confession that Jesus is the Christ, the image of the invisible God (Col. 1:15). At the same time, the NT claims regarding Jesus Christ and the Holy Spirit result in fresh perspectives that fill out the identity of Israel's God.

Generally, language for God is drawn from at least three sources.

1. God's revealing. God is not "named" by others (Gen. 16:13 is an exception), unlike people or other gods. Though not fully revealing of character, God's names give insight into God, as does other self-identifying language (Exod. 34:6-7).
2. The ongoing experience with God, in major events, worship occasions, and everyday encounters. Language for God is almost always metaphorical, and is usually associated with the everyday, earthly, and concrete: home and family; social, commercial, and political spheres; interhuman relationships; nonhuman entities. Most fundamental to these metaphors is their relational character, revealing a God who is not aloof from the world, but has entered into genuine relationships with people, and works in and through the complexities and ambiguities of life.
3. The ancient context. The linguistic and imagistic dependence on the ancient Near Eastern and Greco-Roman cultures is not simply formal; truths about God were available to those outside the community of faith, and understandings were enriched by that contact (Acts 17:22-31). Far from diminishing the uniqueness of the biblical faith, they witness to the work of God the Creator.

Among the metaphors for God (some are also used for Jesus) are husband (Isa. 62:5), father (63:16; Heb. 12:9, most frequently by Jesus), king (Ps. 95:3; Matt. 5:35), judge (Gen. 18:25; Heb. 12:23), shepherd (Ps. 23:1; Matt. 18:10-14), redeemer-savior (Isa. 44:24; Luke 1:47), potter (Jer. 18:1-6), warrior (Exod. 15:3), rock (Ps. 18:2[3]), light (Ps. 4:6[7]; 1 John 1:5), and spirit (Isa. 63:10; John 4:24). Anthropomorphic metaphors are much more common in the OT than in the NT (Luke 11:20; Rom. 1:18); yet the NT view of God is not more spiritual, given the Incarnation. Female images are used which reflect the peculiar experiences of women, especially motherhood (Isa. 42:14; 66:13; Luke 15:8-10); the image of a child in its mother's womb or at her breast conveys a unique sense of closeness with God. All metaphors have a "Yes" and a "No" with respect; they have continuity with the reality which is God, but no one-to-one correspondence, for no image or metaphor can capture God.

Basic Claims about God

The following claims are central regarding the biblical understanding of God; texts are cited from both OT and NT and are significantly represented across various genres and traditions.

Living and eternal

God's existence is assumed in the Bible, from Gen. 1:1 on. God's life is without beginning and ending (Ps. 90:1-2; 102:26-27[27-28]; Rom. 1:23; 16:26) and is dependent upon no other for existence. God has no family tree (theogony). God alone has the power to raise from the dead and grant eternal life (2 Kgs.

5:7; Dan. 12:2), centering in the NT in the resurrection of Jesus (1 Pet. 1:21). At the same time, God, having created the world, has chosen to be dependent upon the creatures for continuing life and the ongoing care of the world (Gen. 1:22, 28).

Unity

God is one. God is not divided up into divinities or powers (cf. Baal). There is a unity to the divine identity (Deut. 6:4-5; 1 Cor. 8:4-6; Eph. 4:6). God unites in the one self everything which is God. One can discern some development in Israel's understandings in this regard, but the canonical portrayal of God is decisively monotheistic (Deut. 4:35; Isa. 45:7; 1 Tim. 1:17).

At the same time, several OT texts speak of God as acting within the *divine* realm (e.g., Ps. 103:20-21; Jer. 23:18-22). These passages testify to God as a social being, functioning within a divine community in a relationship of mutuality. The creation of human beings, e.g., is understood to be the result of an inter-divine dialogue (Gen. 1:26). These testimonies to the richness and complexity of the divine realm no doubt contribute to the NT reflections about God that move toward a trinitarian identity.

Unique, incomparable

Compared to any other powers, there is no God like Israel's God. God is incomparable (Ps. 35:10; Isa. 40:18, 25). God's holiness (Isa. 5:19, 24; John 17:11) expresses the "otherness" or transcendence of God; God is not a human being (Hos. 11:9). Yet, this Holy One dwells in Israel's midst (Isa. 12:6), Jesus is the "Holy One of God" (Mark 1:24), and the Holy Spirit is related to divine presence (John 14:26). Hence, holiness does not mean aloofness or distance. God is revealed as the transcendent one precisely in his immanence, by the way in which God is present and active among the people.

Present

God is present and active in all the world. God "fills heaven and earth" (Jer. 23:24; Ps. 139), "is above all and through all and in all" (Eph. 4:6). God is part of the map of reality and is relational to all that is not God. The earth is also "full of the steadfast love of God" (Ps. 33:5; 36:5[6]; Rom. 8:38-39). God is not simply "here and there"; God is always *lovingly* present, in every divine act. Hence, God's presence is not static or passive, but grounded in steadfast love and working for the good of all.

In developing a typology of divine presence one might speak of variations in intensification in comparing God's general (or creational) presence, accompanying presence, tabernacling presence, and theophanic presence. The Bible never speaks of God's actual absence, though that may be a perception (e.g., Ps. 22:1[2]; Mark 15:34). No *full* account of any event is possible without factoring God into the process.

According to Ps. 104:1-3 God has made the time and space of this world God's very own dwelling place. To use the language of Isa. 66:1, heaven is God's throne and earth is God's footstool. Any movement of God from heaven to earth is a movement from one part of the created order to another. God — who is other than world — works from within the world, not on the world from without (Acts 17:28).

Active

God acts in the world. The Bible witnesses to a comprehensive divine working. God's acting is focused in Israel, Jesus Christ, and the early Christian community, and God's speaking is especially articulate there, but the divine activity is not limited to them or to historical events (Rom. 3:29). Gen. 1–11, in introducing the canon, provides a universal frame of reference, portraying God as Creator of all (as does the NT: Rom. 11:36; Heb. 2:10), and also witnesses to a God whose *universal* activity includes grieving, judging, saving, electing, promising, blessing, covenant-making, and law-giving. God's actions in and for the community of faith thus occur *within* God's more comprehensive actions in the larger world and are shaped by God's overarching purposes for that world. Some texts (e.g., Amos 9:7) reinforce the understanding that even God's salvific actions are not confined to the community of faith or effected only through its mediation.

Relational

God's actions occur from within relationships established with the world. These actions are in turn grounded in the social reality of God. In other words, relationship is integral to the divine realm independent of God's relationship to the world.

This relational God freely enters into relationships with that which has been created, and in such a way that creatures have something important to say and do. This is seen in the language most common for God — that drawn from interpersonal relationships. Even where the language is not personal, it is relational (Ps. 31:2[3]). This relational focus is evident also in the emphasis on God as one who not only communicates but is desirous of the creature's voice in return (Isa. 65:1-2). Moreover, God gives God's own name(s), thereby identifying the divine self as a distinctive member of the community of those who have names. The OT view of God is no less relational and intimate than that of the NT.

Israel's God enters into committed relationships. Already in Gen. 1–11 God commits God's self to a relationship which entails a divine constraint and restraint in the exercise of power in the world (1:28; 8:21-22). Even beyond sin, God is committed to share power with human beings (Ps. 8). Moreover, the covenants into which God enters — Noah, Abraham, Israel, David, the new covenant (Heb. 8:8-12) — are relational by their very nature. God therein makes commitments which God will honor come what may (cf. Gen. 15:7-21). So, in both creation and redemption, God's actions occur from within committed relationships which God will honor come what may — because of who God is.

Intentional

God's actions are an activation of the divine will. God's actions are intentional, not idle or accidental. Every divine act is an act of will. God's acts always serve God's purposes in the world. God's word seeks to clarify and direct God's will within an already pervasive presence, and makes available a living experience (including knowledge) of the will of God. Every divine action is informed by God's ultimate salvific will for the world, by God's faithfulness to promises, and God's steadfast love for all.

Distinctions within the will of God are important for thinking about salvation and judgment. God's saving will is ultimate and absolute (Gen. 12:3; Rom. 11:32; 1 Tim. 2:4); God's will in judgment is contingent and circumstantial. Unlike love, wrath is not an attribute of God. God is "provoked" to anger (Ps. 106:29; Rom. 2:1-8) by human sin in view of divine righteousness; if there were no sin there would be no wrath or judgment. Divine wrath and judgment, common to both the OT and NT, function both temporally and eschatologically (John 3:18-19; Rom. 5:9; 13:4), with effects upon both body and spirit, individuals and communities.

Interactive

God usually takes the initiative in acting in the world (e.g., creation, Incarnation). Yet, once relationships are established, God also acts in response to creaturely initiative. For example, God hears the cries of the Israelites in Egypt and "remembers" the covenant (Exod. 2:23-25). God interacts with Moses in an extended dialogue wherein Moses' responses are taken seriously by God, and lead to new divine speech (Exod. 3–6). Moses' persistence with God increases the revelatory possibilities, and several NT texts speak of such perseverance as occasioning new directions for divine action (Luke 11:5-13; 18:1-8). Indeed, in response to prayers God may change the divine mind (Exod. 32:14; Jer. 26:19), even in response to the non-chosen (Jonah 3:10). Yet, God's core character is changeless, as is the divine purpose (Num. 23:19; 1 Sam. 15:28-29; Jas. 1:17-18; Heb. 6:13-20), and God will be steadfast in love. God's way into the future is thus not dictated solely by the divine word and will; God's word interacts with the human word and together they shape the future.

Situational

God's acting is always situationally appropriate, fitting for specific times and places (Gal. 4:4). God's seeing precedes the divine acting (Exod. 3:7-10). God is a master at discernment. In Exod. 1–15 God responds to oppression of a socio-political sort in the shape that God's salvation takes. God acts to save Israel from the effects of others' sins, not from its own. God's saving acts at the return from exile, however, have different needs in view; Israel is forgiven its sin and saved from the effects of its own sinfulness (cf. Isa. 43:25). In Jesus' life and death both senses of salvation are in view. Within those focused actions, God's more comprehensive purposes are in view (Exod. 9:16).

Effective

God's activity is effective in the world, not least in creation, Exodus, the fall of Jerusalem, Incarnation, Cross, and Pentecost. Among the effects, two more comprehensive outcomes might be noted. For one, God's acts issue in new knowledge. Promises are stated which were not known before, responsibilities delineated, and matters clarified and judged. God's acts also issue in a becoming. God's actions effect a new relationship with God and a changed status for human beings and communities, e.g., deliverance from oppression and sin (2 Cor. 5:17-21). God's actions are also effective in various forms of worship life. Israel's dramatized festivals and Christian sacraments are vehicles whereby God's salvation in historical event is made newly available to Israel. Israel's sacrificial system has a sacramental structure in and through which God acts to forgive the penitent worshipper.

God's actions may also issue in new knowledge and becoming for God, the Incarnation being the most fundamental. Human responses to God's actions may also lead to a new level of divine knowing (cf. Gen. 22:12; Deut. 8:2), which can lead to new directions in divine action. New divine commitments made and new relationships established make for a changed situation for God. In some sense one must speak of a newness in God as well.

Vulnerable

God's activity is not inevitably successful. God's word once given is in the hands of those who can misuse it. God's will may not always get done. Finitude and sin may lead to disloyalty and misunderstanding. However powerful God's word may be (Jer. 23:29), it is resisted (Ezek. 2:7), questioned (Jer. 1:6-7), rejected (Zech. 7:11), ridiculed (Gen. 18:12-13), scorned (Jer. 6:10), despised (Jer. 23:17), doubted (Judg. 6:13-17), or disbelieved (Ps. 106:24). The NT intensifies the opposition to God with its emphasis upon demonic forces (Luke 8:12; 1 Thess. 2:18). The word of God is therefore not only powerful; it is vulnerable, as is God's activity in nonverbal ways. This issues in divine suffering, evident most clearly in God's laments in the Prophets (Hos. 11:1-9; Jer. 3:19-20). The God who suffers because of, with, and for Israel and the world is brought to supreme focus in Jesus, especially in the Cross.

God will keep promises made, though it is not possible to factor out just how such promises are fulfilled. One might speak of an open future, within which human response participates in shaping life in the world, but God works purposefully within the complex of events in such a way that a new heaven and a new earth will eventually be brought into being.

Use of agents

God works through human language and various human and nonhuman agents to get things done in the world. God acts directly, but always through means. The variety of means is impressive. God works through that which is created to bring about new creations (Gen. 1:2; 11); through human language to call Abraham as well as through the dynamics of his interrupted journey to Canaan (11:31–12:3); through nonhuman agents in the plagues, at Passover, and at the Red Sea (the nonhuman is the savior of the human); through sacrificial rituals to bring about reconciliation with God; through non-Israelite kings and armies to send Israel into exile and to bring them home; through prophets and preachers (Rom. 10:14-17) to speak God's word of judgment and grace.

In such divine activity creaturely agency is not reduced to impotence; God's activity is not all-determining. There is neither a "letting go" of the creation on God's part, nor a divine retention of all such powers. God has chosen to be dependent upon creatures, and both God and creatures are effective agents. Because creatures are not perfect, God's actions through them will always have mixed results. As an example, violence is associated with God's acts for it is characteristic of those through whom the work is done.

Generally, this divine work in the world must not be viewed in either deistic or deterministic ways. God neither remains ensconced in heaven nor does God micromanage the world to control its every move so that creaturely agency counts for nothing. Between these ditches, the biblical texts do not always provide clear direction.

Mighty acts

Some divine actions are more significant than others. Israel understood this to be the case as shown by the vocabulary used ("mighty acts," Ps. 145:4, 12) and the genres employed (some divine acts are drawn into creeds; Deut. 26:5-9). The Christian community made a comparable move with respect to the Christ event, especially Jesus' death and resurrection, evident in the volume of the Passion story and Pauline emphases.

This greater level of significance is most fundamentally related to the kinds of effects produced. Regarding becoming, certain events are constitutive of the community, without which Israel or the Church would not be what it is. Regarding knowing, these events are more translucent regarding God's purposes, bringing sharper coherence and clarity to the larger range of divine purpose and activity.

Extraordinary events

These greater levels of significance may be, but are not necessarily, related to the events being "extraordinary" or miraculous. Where these elements do occur in the texts, they are not easily sorted out. The extraordinariness is not understood in terms of divine intervention or intrusion, as if God were normally not present. God's acts are not usually considered extraordinary. God is understood to act in and through the means provided by the causal continuum, but sufficient "play" exists in that continuum to allow for God to work and the unusual event to occur. For example, Job 38–41 speaks of the looseness of the causal weave with its interest in ambiguity and unexpectedness in the creation (cf. the role of chance in Eccl. 9:11; 1 Sam. 6:9; Luke 10:31).

Issues of genre and rhetoric are important. The language used for the Exodus events includes extraordinary features — plagues, passover, sea crossing. But the fall of Jerusalem and the return of the exiles are described in more mundane terms as the effects of Babylonian army movements and Persian royal policies. Isa. 40–55 uses extraordinary images to speak of a future return (including changes in nature) and links this to God's new work. But the texts descriptive of the return itself do not use such rhetoric. This difference raises questions about the genre of the Exodus material and the extent to which its extraordinariness is reflective of actual events or constitutes a rhetorical strategy more in line with that used by Deutero-Isaiah.

Bibliography. S. E. Balentine, *The Hidden God* (Oxford, 1983); W. Brueggemann, *Old Testament Theology* (Minneapolis, 1992); T. E. Fretheim, *The Suffering of God: An Old Testament Perspective.* OBT 14 (Philadelphia, 1984); A. J. Heschel, *The Prophets* (New York, 1962); P. Trible, *God and the Rhetoric of Sexuality.* OBT 2 (Philadelphia, 1978); C. Westermann and G. W. Friedemann, *What Does the Old Testament Say About God?* (Atlanta, 1979).

TERENCE E. FRETHEIM

GOD IN THE OLD TESTAMENT, NAMES OF

The most common words for God in the OT are the name Yahweh (6639 times) and Elohim ("god," 2750 times). The following discussion focuses on less frequent names and words for God.

Adon

Heb. *'āḏôn* means "lord," with the connotation of superiority, and was used of both human and divine sovereigns. In the OT it indicates Yahweh's power and control over everyone and everything. The form Adonay (*'ăḏōnāy*) is used exclusively of Yahweh. The ending *-āy* may be emphatic ("the Lord of all"). The traditional translation "my Lord" assumes a plural of majesty, with a lengthened final vowel to distinguish it from other "lords," both human and divine. When used independently of Yahweh, it takes on the character of a separate name, but the reference to Israel's God is always clear (e.g., Gen. 18:27; Exod. 5:22; 34:9; Isa. 6:1). It eventually came to be pronounced in place of the sacred name Yahweh.

Baal

Heb. *ba'al* also means "lord," but with a nuance of possession; other translations include "master" and "husband." It is frequently used in reference to non-Israelite gods in general and as the name of the Canaanite storm-god in particular. The only clear evidence for Baal as a title of Yahweh is the name Be'alyah (1 Chr. 12:5[MT 6]; "Yah(weh) is Lord"). It is not possible to determine whether other names incorporating Baal were initially understood as referring to Yahweh. For example, Saul's son Ishbaal ("man of Baal," 1 Chr. 8:33; 9:39) may also have been called Ishvi ("man of Yahweh(?)"; cf. 1 Sam. 14:49), but it is clear from the substitution of *bōšeṯ* ("shame") in almost all such names that the Deuteronomists understood the theophoric element as the Canaanite god. Ishbaal is called Ishbosheth throughout the Deuteronomistic history (e.g., 2 Sam. 2:8, 10, 12, 15), and Jonathan's crippled son Meribbaal (1 Chr. 8:34; 9:40) is called Mephibosheth (e.g., 2 Sam. 4:4). Finally, it has been suggested that Hos. 2:16[18] ("On that day, says Yahweh, you will call me 'my man' *['îšî]*, and no longer will you call me 'my *ba'al*'") rejects an established use of Baal for Yahweh as Lord. However the context is marriage, and both Hebrew terms should be translated "husband," with the prophet rejecting the latter in order to avoid any possible confusion with the pagan deity.

El

Heb. *'ēl* is the Hebrew equivalent of the common Semitic word for "god" (cf. Ugar. *'il*, Mesopotamian and Amorite *ilu*, North Arab. *'ilāh*, Phoen. *'l*). The most likely derivation is from the verbal root *'wl*, "to be strong, dominate." Although the term frequently means simply "god" in the OT, there are some instances where it preserves the name of a deity other than Yahweh. In Gen. 33:20 Jacob dedicates an altar at Shechem to *'ēl 'ĕlōhê yiśrā'ēl*, "El, the god of Israel," while in 46:3 a god identifies himself to Jacob as *'ēl 'ĕlōhê 'āḇîḵā*, "El, the god of your father." It should not be surprising, therefore, that Jacob's name was changed to "Isra-El" after his night encounter with "a man" (God?) at the Jabbok (Gen. 32:22-30[23-31]) or that the early tribal confederacy was called "Israel." This indicates that El was the deity worshipped by the group(s) who preserved the patriarchal stories and that the identification of Yahweh with "the god of Abraham, Isaac and Jacob" in Exod. 3:6 represents a later assimilation of two originally separate deities.

Often *'ēl* is followed immediately by an epithet, e.g., "El, who sees" (*'ēl ro'î*, Gen. 16:13; cf. 22:14) and "El, the eternal" (*'ēl 'ôlām*, Gen. 21:33; cf. Isa. 40:28; Jer. 10:10). The phrase *'ēl bêṯ-'ēl* in Gen. 35:7 could mean simply "the god of Bethel," but the evidence for El as the god of the patriarchs, especially Jacob, supports the rendering "El of Bethel." Similarly, *'ēl bĕrîṯ* in Judg. 9:46 is best understood as "El of the covenant"; *ba'al bĕrîṯ* ("lord of the covenant," Judg. 8:33; 9:4) is probably an epithet of El. These "El names" are associated with specific places (e.g., Beer-lahai-roi, Beersheba, Bethel, Shechem), and are generally interpreted as local manifestations of El.

El Elyon

The adjective *'elyôn* was commonly applied to kings and gods, and El Elyon (Heb. *'ēl 'elyôn*) is an appropriate title for the high god of the Canaanite pantheon as well ("El, the most high"). In Gen. 14:19 El Elyon is called "maker of heaven and earth" *(qōnēh šāmayim wā'āreṣ)*. This is an expansion of "El, creator of the earth" *('l qn 'rṣ)*, which occurs in an 8th-century B.C.E. Phoenician inscription from Karatepe and a 2nd-century Neo-Punic inscription and is reflected in the divine name ^{d}*El-ku-ni-ir-ša* from a Hittite myth discovered at Boghazköy. As for localization, apart from Ps. 78:35, the full formula occurs only during Abraham's encounter with Melchizedek, king of (Jeru)salem (Gen. 14:18-20, 22). However, it is divorced from Jerusalem in the 50 occurrences of Elyon alone (four are paralleled with El), and in Ps. 78:35 the context is the wilderness wanderings. Apart from Abraham's equation of (El) Elyon with Yahweh, the two are linked only in the Psalter (Ps. 7:17[18]; 18:13[14] [= 2 Sam. 22:14]; 21:7[8]; 47:2[3]; 83:18[19]; 91:9; 92:1[2]; cf. Ps. 97:9 and the links with the alternative name Elohim in the Elohistic Psalter: Ps. 46:4[5]; 50:14; 57:2[3]; 73:11; 78:56).

El Shaddai

Outside of the Bible this name occurs at Ugarit and in a Thamudic inscription from Teimā. The Deir 'Alla inscription mentions a group of gods called the *šdyn*. The biblical El Shaddai (Heb. *'ēl šadday*) was traditionally rendered as "God Almighty" under the influence of LXX *pantokrátōr* and Vulg. *omnipotens*. The *šadday* element is generally explained as a dual of *šaḏ* ("breast, mountain"). The translation "El of the mountains" fits well with the Ugaritic description of El's residence upon the cosmic mountain(s) and "the mountains of El" *(harĕrê-'ēl)* in Ps. 36:6(7). Since El was the god of the patriarchs, it is significant that five of the eight instances of the full formula occur in Genesis (Gen. 17:1; 28:3; 35:11; 43:14; 48:3). Shaddai's function as an El epithet is further reflected in its occurrence 13 times in parallel with El (e.g., Num. 24:4, 16; Job 8:3; 13:3) and twice with Elyon, another of El's titles (Num. 24:16; Ps. 91:1). That it was considered an ancient divine name is evidenced by the fact that 31 of the 41 occurrences of Shaddai by itself are found in the deliberately archaizing book of Job. The self-revelation of Yahweh to Moses as El Shaddai in Exod. 6:3 is part of the over-arching biblical identification of Yahweh with El (cf. Gen. 17:1; Ruth 1:21; Isa. 13:6; Joel 1:15).

Eloah

An expanded form of El and possibly the singular of Elohim, Heb. *'ĕlōah* is used as both the appellation "god" and a divine name. As with El and Elohim, some instances are ambiguous, but *'ĕlōah* is clearly a noun in 2 Chr. 32:15; Ps. 114:7; Isa. 44:8; Dan. 11:37-39. Most instances of Eloah as a name occur in the poetry of Job (including all of the 41 times in Job), where it parallels Shaddai and El. Outside of Job, Eloah is understood to be Yahweh.

Fear of Isaac

The "*paḥaḏ* of Isaac" is credited with helping Jacob during his sojourn with Laban (Gen. 31:42), and Jacob invokes "the *paḥaḏ* of his father Isaac" as a guarantor of the subsequent treaty with his father-in-law. The context and content require a nuance of divine protection, ruling out possible derivations meaning either "clan" or "thigh" (cf. Gen. 24:2, 9; 47:29). The traditional rendering as "the Fear of Isaac" denotes the dread God instills in others as a means of protecting Isaac and Jacob (cf. "the fear of Yahweh" in 1 Sam. 11:7; Isa. 2:10, 19, 21). It is more a description of God's activity than a name.

Holy One

Heb. *qāḏôš* emphasizes the essential otherness of divinity in general and of Yahweh in particular: Of the 44 instances 31 are as "the Holy One of Israel." It is a favorite term of Isaiah (30 times: 25 with the full formula; 3 others refer to Israel in the same verse). It is often used in the context of Israel's sinfulness, thereby accentuating the contrast with Yahweh (e.g., Ps. 78:41; Isa. 1:4; 30:12; 37:23; Jer. 51:5; Hos. 11:12[12:1]). The vocative in Ps. 71:22 indicates it could be used as a divine name, as does the parallel with Eloah in Hab. 3:3.

Mighty One of Jacob

The adjective *'abbîr* means "strong, mighty" and is used of humans and animals. The strong animal par excellence was the bull (cf. the parallelism in Isa. 34:7; Ps. 22:12[13]), and many translate the phrase *'ăḇîr ya'ăqōḇ* as "the Bull of Jacob," appealing to the epithet "Bull" for El at Ugarit. In Gen. 49:24 the phrase is linked with references to El Shaddai (v. 25b) and "El, your father" (v. 25a). This probably represents the preservation of another recollection of El as the god of Jacob, one which emphasizes the deity's power to look after the patriarch. Nonetheless, all other instances explicitly identify "the Mighty One" as Yahweh (Isa. 49:26; 60:16; Ps. 132:2, 5; cf. Isa. 1:24, "the Mighty One of Israel"). The Masoretic pointing without a daghesh in the middle consonant dissociates the epithet from the bull imagery of the northern Israelite cult and seeks to avoid confusion with Baal.

See further the individual entries.

Bibliography. A. Alt, "The God of the Fathers," in *Essays on Old Testament History and Religion* (1967, repr. Sheffield, 1989), 1-77; F. M. Cross, *Canaanite Myth and Hebrew Epic* (Cambridge, Mass., 1973), 31-75; O. Eissfeldt, "'āḏôn, 'ᵃḏōnāy," *TDOT* 1:59-72; T. J. Lewis, "The Identity and Function of El/Baal Berith," *JBL* 115 (1996): 401-23.

JOHN L. MCLAUGHLIN

GOD IN THE NEW TESTAMENT, NAMES OF

The three principal terms for the deity in the NT are "Lord," "God," and "Father."

The NT refers to the deity as the "Lord" (Gk. *kýrios*) ca. 180 times. More than 70 of these occurrences are in scriptural quotations and allusions, where they typically translate the Hebrew word *YHWH* ("Yahweh"). Although this usage cannot otherwise be demonstrated in the 1st century, contemporary Jews did refer to God as the Lord. While most NT references to the Lord are simple articular or anarthrous references (without any apparent difference in meaning), a few are in phrases like "Lord of heaven and earth" and "Lord God of Israel." It is unclear if some references to the Lord (e.g., Matt. 3:3) refer to the deity or Jesus.

The noun "God" *(theós)*, which is a title rather than a divine name, occurs more than 1300 times in the NT. Most of these occurrences refer to the God proclaimed by the NT; these occurrences presuppose the Jewish teaching that "the Lord our God is one" (Mark 12:29). Most of these occurrences are articular, though articular and anarthrous references are used without any difference in meaning. Many of these references to God are in scriptural quotations, where they often translate Heb. *'ĕlōhîm*. Other occurrences of *theós* refer to the devil (2 Cor. 4:4), other supernatural beings (Acts 14:1), and even a goddess (19:37).

The NT uses the epithet "Father" 261 times, usually in multi-word phrases such as "my Father," "your Father," "the Father in heaven," and "God our Father." Although this metaphor occasionally occurs in the OT, comparatively few of the NT references to the Father are in scriptural quotations. While many NT passages identify the Father as the Father of Jesus, many others identify the Father as the Father of the disciples.

The historical Jesus presupposed Jewish monotheism. Jesus was not reticent to use the term "God," especially when proclaiming the nearness of the kingdom of God. Many scholars assume that Jesus also referred to God as Father.

Mark contains 48 references to God but fewer than 10 to the Lord and only four to the Father. While the references to God occur in material in many different settings, the references to the Father are only in Jesus' prayer in Gethsemane (Mark 14:36) and his words to his disciples (8:38; 11:25; 13:32).

The Q material contains at least five references to the Lord, nine to God, and nine to the Father. In five of the references the Father is identified as the Father of Jesus (Luke 10:21bd, 22abc), in the other four as the Father of the disciples (Luke 6:36; 11:2, 13; 12:30).

Matthew contains 19 references to the Lord, 50 to God, and 44 to the Father. Matt. 1–2 stress that the Lord who spoke through the prophets is the same Lord who acted during the infancy events, and Matt. 3–4 associate God with the Scriptures and divine power. Jesus' sayings in Matt. 5:43-48 introduce the cluster of references to the Father in 6:1-8 ("your Father") which associate the Father with the divine will, prayer, forgiveness, and eschatological reward. In most of Jesus' references after the Sermon on the Mount the Father is identified as his own Father ("my Father"). While many of the Matthean references to God are in Jesus' words to his adversaries or the discourse of his adversaries, all of the references to the Father are in Jesus' prayers, his words to his disciples, or his words to audiences composed of his disciples and the crowds.

By repeatedly associating the Lord with the heritage of Israel, the Lukan Infancy narrative proclaims that the Lord who acted during the infancy events was the Lord of Israel. Luke 3–24 and Acts, however, refer much more frequently to God than to the Lord or the Father. While both Jesus and other speakers frequently refer to the deity as God, only Jesus uses the epithet "Father" in this Gospel. Though occurring only 16 or 17 times, these references to the Father stand at prominent points in the story. Many of the references to God in Acts are in speeches, where they often serve as the subjects of statements which proclaim God's acts in the story of Israel and the story of Jesus, especially the Resurrection. Since references to the Father appear only in Acts 1–2 and most of the references to the Lord are in Acts 1–15, God is virtually the only title in the last half of Acts.

The seven authentic letters of Paul contain 430 references to God but only 30 to the Lord and only 24 to the Father. Since the salutations of all of these letters introduce the deity as "God our Father" (Rom. 1:7; 1 Cor. 1:3; 2 Cor. 1:2; Gal. 1:3; Phil. 1:2; Phlm. 3) or "God the Father" (1 Thess. 1:1), they implicitly associate the Father with the subsequent references to God. Most of the other 17 references to the Father are in passages which also mention God; the only exceptions are a reference to the Father in a scriptural quotation (2 Cor. 6:18), one in traditional material (Rom. 6:4), and two references to "Abba Father" (Rom. 8:15; Gal. 4:6). Half of the references to the Lord are in scriptural quotations or allusions.

John is the only canonical Gospel which refers more frequently to the Father than to God. Most of the 120 references to the Father are in Jesus' words, and most are in passages which primarily identify the deity as Jesus' Father. Jesus also frequently refers to the deity as "the One who sent me" (e.g., John 4:34; 5:23-24). Both the narrator (John 1:1, 18) and Thomas (20:28) refer to Jesus as God. Many of the other references to God are in Jesus' words, including his assertions that God is "spirit" (John 4:24) and "the only true God" (17:3); however, the word "God" occurs much more frequently than Father in the discourse of speakers other than Jesus, including such varied speakers as Nicodemus, Peter, Martha, Caiaphas, and Pilate. This Gospel has only five references to the Lord.

The Johannine Epistles refer much more frequently to God than to the Father, with 1 John stressing that "God is light" (1 John 1:5) and "God is love" (4:8). While the other Epistles and Revelation refer much more frequently to God than to the Lord or the Father, 2 Peter and Jude contain nearly as many references to the Lord as to God.

Besides using the words "Eli" ("my God," Matt. 27:46) and "Eloi" ("my God," Mark 15:34), the NT authors occasionally use such other titles as the "Great King" (Matt. 5:35), "the One who sits on the throne" (Matt. 23:22), "Power" (Matt. 26:64; Mark 14:62), the "Blessed One" (Mark 14:61), the "Most High" (Luke 1:32), "Lord Sabaoth" (Rom. 9:29), "God our Savior" (1 Tim. 1:1), "Majesty" (Heb. 1:3; 8:1), "Father of lights" (Jas. 1:17), and "Lord God Almighty" (Rev. 4:8). Various authors also use such longer constructions as "the Father of mercies and the God of all consolation" (2 Cor. 1:3) and "the blessed and only Sovereign, the King of kings and Lord of lords" (1 Tim. 6:15). Early Christian liturgical language lies behind a number of these passages. Some NT authors indirectly refer to the deity by using divine passives and expressing divine necessity with the verb *deí* ("it is necessary").

Bibliography. D. M. Bossman, "Images of God in the Letters of Paul," *BTB* 18 (1988): 67-76; R. L. Mowery, "God, Lord and Father: The Theology of the Gospel of Matthew," *BR* 33 (1988): 24-36; "Lord, God and Father: Theological Language in Luke-Acts," *SBLSP* 34 (Atlanta, 1995): 82-101.

Robert L. Mowery

GOG (Heb. *gôg*), **MAGOG** *(māgôg)*

A ruler and his land or people, portrayed as Israel's apocalyptic foe.

Magog appears in the Table of Nations (Gen. 10:2) as a son of Japheth. He is apparently also the eponymous ancestor of a people in Anatolia (cf. Magog's "brothers," whose names are attached to the Anatolian regions of Meshech and Tubal). In Ezek. 38:2 Magog is the name of a country, again associated with Meshech and Tubal in eastern Anatolia. The threefold identification of Magog as an ancestor, a people, and a land is not unusual (cf. Israel). Unfortunately, no precise connection can be drawn to any known people or territory. Josephus (*Ant.* 1.123) identifies the people of Magog as the Scythians, but no concrete evidence supports such a specific identification.

In Ezek. 38-39 Gog is "of the land of Magog" in "the remotest parts of the north" (38:15; 39:2). He is the commander who, following Israel's return from Babylonian exile, will invade the land and so provoke a final, decisive battle with Yahweh. The battle between Gog and Yahweh is depicted in the cosmic imagery associated with the Day of Yahweh; earthquake and storm accompany the enemy's demise. Yahweh's victory will at last vindicate his holy name, proving that the Exile occurred because of Israel's sins rather than through Yahweh's weakness.

Gog's identity is a matter of continued debate. The 7th-century B.C.E. Lydian monarch Gyges (Akk. *gûgu*) has often been suggested, but it is doubtful why Ezekiel (or a later editor) would cast this distant and long-dead ruler as the great nemesis of God. Another interpretation sees Gog as chaos incarnate, the primal and ultimate enemy, whose destruction heralds God's unchallenged reign (an event foreseen in Ezek. 40–48). Certainly, Gog symbolizes all that opposes Yahweh and as such is the embodiment of chaos. Gog's symbolic role, however, does not preclude the possibility that a historical figure stands behind the symbol. In Ezekiel's historical context Nebuchadnezzar of Babylon is the monarch whose power clearly opposes Yahweh's own and whose defeat is essential for the vindication of Yahweh's name. A number of parallels between the depictions of Gog and descriptions of Nebuchadnezzar elsewhere in Ezekiel support this possibility. The prophet's Babylonian location would explain his use of a pseudonym for the Babylonian ruler.

Gog and Magog reappear in Rev. 20:7-10, identified as distant nations rather than as a ruler and his nation. The role of Gog and Magog in Revelation corresponds to that in Ezek. 38–39. Inspired by Satan, Gog and Magog will march against Jerusalem, initiating God's final victory over Satan and the triumphant reign of the Lamb from the New Jerusalem. The part played by Gog and Magog in inaugurating the eschaton has led to a number of attempts to interpret them as codes for modern nations and individuals, who in turn are seen as enemies of God and harbingers of the last days.

In 1 Chr. 5:4 an otherwise unknown Gog is listed as a "son of Joel."

Bibliography. B. F. Batto, *Slaying the Dragon: Mythmaking in the Biblical Tradition* (Louisville, 1992); S. L. Cook, *Prophecy and Apocalypticism* (Minneapolis, 1995); B. Otzen, "gôg [gôgh]," *TDOT* 2:419-25.

JULIE GALAMBUSH

GOIIM (Heb. *gôyim*)

1. A kingdom led by Tidal, an ally of Chedolaomer, king of Elam (Gen. 14:1, 9). Most scholars assume the reference is to a group of kingdoms ruled by Tidal, perhaps either in Anatolia or Mesopotamia.

2. A kingdom whose king was defeated by Joshua (Josh. 12:23). The MT adds "of Gilgal" (NIV) whereas the LXX has "of Galilee" (NRSV).

3. A general Hebrew term for the gentile "nations" (*gôyîm*). Though Israel could be called a *gôy* (sg., which had racial, governmental, and territorial implications as opposed to the familial term *ʿam*), the plural usually was used for the enemies of God's people, especially in Deuteronomistic books (e.g., Deut. 7:1-26; 18:9; 2 Kgs. 17:8-41; cf. Ezek. 20:32).

ERIC F. MASON

GOLAN (Heb. *gôlān*)

A town (Deut. 4:43), possibly Saḥm el-Jōlân (238243), allotted to Manasseh and given to the Gershonite Levites as a city of refuge (Josh. 20:8; 21:27; 1 Chr. 6:71[MT 56]). The western part of Bashan (Hauran) was known as Gaulanitis (Josephus *Ant.* 17.8.1 [189]) in the Hellenistic period and later. It was ruled by Herod the Great (23-4 B.C.) and his descendants Herod Philip (4 B.C.–A.D. 34), Agrippa I (37-44) and Agrippa II (53-85) before becoming part of the province of Syria in 106. Recent excavations and surveys indicate that the region has been occupied from Paleolithic to modern times.

Bibliography. Z. U. Maʿoz, N. Goren-Inbar, and C. Epstein, "Golan," *NEAEHL* 2:525-46.

PAUL J. RAY, JR.

GOLD

The most frequently mentioned precious metal in the Bible. In OT times gold was used for money (Gen. 44:8); jewelry (41:42); decoration, such as gilding the ark of the covenant (Exod. 25:11); thread in weaving priests' garments (28:8); and idols (20:23). Many of the tabernacle and temple artifacts and utensils were made of pure, solid gold (Exod. 25:31; 37:6; 1 Kgs. 7:49-51). Solid gold figures of mice and tumors were sent by the Philistines to the Israelites as a guilt offering (1 Sam. 6:3-5). The possession of gold indicated wealth (Gen. 24:35). Gold and silver are often mentioned together since both metals have similar physical and chemical properties and have historically been used for similar purposes, including money. Gold rings were a sign of wealth and status in the Greco-Roman world; several admonitions against wearing gold as an indication of personal wealth occur in the NT (1 Tim. 2:9; 1 Pet. 3:3).

Solomon's wealth in gold is well recorded, and a principal source for his gold was Ophir (1 Kgs. 9:28; a Hebrew ostracon from Tell Qasile reads "Gold of Ophir"). None of Solomon's gold wealth has been uncovered, but archaeological discoveries in Egypt and the Near East indicate that items similar to Solomon's do exist. Tutankhamun's throne is almost totally gold-plated. A golden goblet from Ur (ca. 2600 B.C.E.) has been found, as well as a solid gold bowl attributed to either Darius I or Darius II of Persia (ca. 522-404). Gold-plated furniture was buried with Queen Hetepheres of Egypt (ca. 2600). A clay inscription from the reign of Sargon II records "six shields of gold" as part of the booty from the conquest of the Urartian city Muṣaṣir (714; cf. Solomon, 1 Kgs. 10:16-17).

Gold coins began to circulate in Palestine in the 7th century. Croesus, king of Lydia (560-546), was likely the first to mint pure gold and silver coins. Before this time, and even afterwards, gold as a medium of exchange was measured by weight, usually in shekels (Num. 31:52) or talents (Exod. 25:39). Since the earliest coins were irregular in shape and weight due to the minting process known as "striking," coins were often reweighed and not accepted at face value.

Bibliography. M. I. Finley, *The Ancient Economy,* 2nd ed. (Berkeley, 1985); A. Mazar, *Archaeology of the Land of the Bible, 10,000-586 B.C.E.* (New York, 1990); A. R. Millard, "Does the Bible Exaggerate King Solomon's Golden Wealth?" *BARev* 15/3 (1989): 20-31, 34; L. von Mises, *The Theory of Money and Credit,* rev. ed. (Irvington-on-Hudson, 1971); C. L. Thompson, "Rings of Gold — Neither 'Modest' nor 'Sensible,'" *BibRev* 9/1 (1993): 28-33, 55.

ALAN RAY BUESCHER

GOLDEN CALF

The story of the golden or molten calf (Exod. 32) is part of the revelation of divine law and establishment of covenant at Mt. Sinai in Exod. 19-34. The account begins with Moses separated from the people on top of Mt. Sinai, where he is receiving the revelation of the tabernacle cult and a copy of the Decalogue on stone tablets. Moses' absence worries Israel, who request from Aaron gods to lead them, because they do not know what happened to Moses. Aaron collects the people's gold jewelry, only recently acquired from the Egyptians upon leaving Egypt, and he apparently fashions a golden calf in the form of a young male bovine. It is described as molten, emphasizing that it was made out of liquid metal. Construction of the calf breaks the Sinai covenant between God and Israel, as is symbolized when Moses shatters the tablets.

The golden calf becomes a central symbol of Israel's disobedience. It comes to symbolize, in particular, the danger of idolatry for ancient Israel and, through negative example, illustrates how worship of Yahweh must be image-free (aniconic). Repeated references to Exod. 32 throughout the OT reinforce this point. As a result of the construction of the golden calf, Israel loses the jewelry that symbolized their triumph over the Egyptians (Exod. 33:1-6). Moses underscores that not only did Israel make a metal or molten image but this very act of image-making was a rejection of Yahweh (Deut. 9:6-21). The sin of the golden calf is historicized in 1 Kgs. 11-12, when Jeroboam I, the first king of the northern kingdom, is condemned for building two golden calves at Dan and Bethel (1 Kgs. 12:28-29). So great is this sin that it seals the destruction of his kingship and becomes the central symbol of evil rule in the Deuteronomistic history. The prophet Hosea, too, condemns the worship of the golden calf as idolatry (Hos. 8:5; 10:5-6; cf. Ps. 106:19).

The negative symbol of the golden calf lives on in Jewish and Christian tradition. In Pseudo-Philo the blame is placed solely on the leaders of the people rather than on Aaron (*LAB* 12). Stephen refers to the incident as an illustration of Israel's stiff-necked character (Acts 7; cf. Deut. 9:6-21).

Bibliography. M. Aberbach and L. Smolar, "Aaron, Jeroboam and the Golden Calves," *JBL* 86 (1967): 129-40; J. M. Sasson, "Bovine Symbolism in the Exodus Narrative," *VT* 18 (1968): 380-87; "The Worship of the Golden Calf," in *Orient and Occident*, ed. H. A. Hoffner. AOAT 22 (Neukirchen-Vluyn, 1973), 151-59. THOMAS B. DOZEMAN

GOLDEN RULE

A popular label applied to Jesus' words recorded, in slightly different wording, in Matt. 7:12; Luke 6:31. The popularized version of those words is, "Do unto others as you would have others do unto you." Remarkably similar precepts have appeared in Judaism (Tob. 4:15; *b. Šabb.* 31a; cf. 2 En. 61:2), Confucianism (*Analects* 15:23), and Greek literature (cf. Isocrates *Nicocles* 61; Herodotus *Hist.* 3.142; 7.136). Matthew places these words immediately after Jesus' saying that even evil people know how to give good gifts to their children — and that a loving God would do so even more. Matthew also adds, ". . . for this is the law and the prophets." This phrase reflects Jesus' statement that he came to fulfill, not destroy, the law and the prophets (Matt. 5:17). Luke places Jesus' "golden rule" in the context of his command to love one's enemies. This gives the words a new dimension: we should treat not only friends and kinspeople as we want to be treated, but our enemies as well. JOE E. LUNCEFORD

GOLGOTHA (Gk. *Golgothá*)

The place of Jesus' crucifixion (Matt. 27:33; Mark 15:22; John 19:17; cf. Luke 23:33). Golgotha renders Aram. *gûlgaltā'*, "skull," and is synonymous with Lat. *calvaria*. Origen speculated that Golgotha received its name because Adam's skull was buried beneath the cross, and Jerome suggested that it was because skulls of executed prisoners littered the area. The first known reference to Golgotha as a hill is in the diary of the Bordeaux Pilgrim, who speaks of "the little hill *(monticulus)* of Golgotha," locates it a stone's throw from Jesus' tomb, and indicates that Constantine built a basilica there.

Since the mid-1800s many have identified Golgotha with the Garden Tomb area, a limestone outcropping just N of the Old City of Jerusalem. However, no one before the 19th century ever identified this site as the place of Jesus' death and resurrection. In 160 C.E. the Christian community considered Golgotha to be deep within the city (Melito *Paschal Homily* 71), not outside the walls (Heb. 13:12). Since the early 4th century Golgotha has been identified as a rock once enclosed in Constantine's 4th-century church and now covered by the Church of the Holy Sepulchre. Excavations there have revealed that Golgotha is an outcropping of bedrock that lay in the 1st century at the edge of a quarry. The rock rises to a height of 5 m. (ca. 16 ft.) above the present floor of the Church of the Holy Sepulchre.

Bibliography. J. Finegan, *The Archaeology of the New Testament*, rev. ed. (Princeton, 1992), 261-57, 282-84; C. Katsimbinus, "The Uncovering of the Eastern Side of the Hill of Calvary and Its Base," *Liber Annuus* 27 (1977): 197-208; J. Wilkinson, *Jerusalem as Jesus Knew It* (Nashville, 1983).

ROBERT HARRY SMITH

GOLIATH (Heb. *golyaṯ*)

The Philistine champion who challenged the Israelites to send out a warrior to fight with him (1 Sam. 17). This is an example of representational combat, where two heroes fight for their respective armies and the winner secures victory for his side, thus avoiding heavy casualties (1 Sam. 17:8-9).

Goliath's height was not 6 cubits and a span, ca. 2.9 m. (9.5 ft.) (MT), but 4 cubits and a span, ca. 2 m. (6.5 ft.) (NRSV mg, based on Qumran and LXX), yet he was still probably taller than the soldiers in either army. Saul, Israel's king and "giant" (1 Sam. 9:2), should have responded to the challenge. Instead, David did, and his success catapulted him to fame and eventual kingship.

Another account of this incident attributes the death of Goliath to Elhanan, a Bethlehemite (*bêṯ hallaḥmî*, 2 Sam. 21:19), and its parallel passage records that Elhanan killed Lahmi, the brother of Goliath, rather than Goliath (1 Chr. 20:5). David thus probably killed a Philistine warrior whose name was not preserved (cf. 1 Sam. 17:8, 10-11, 16). Perhaps the name Goliath found its way into 1 Sam. 17 from 2 Sam. 21:19. Some scholars regard Elhanan as David's original, preregnal name.

Bibliography. P. K. McCarter, *I Samuel*. AB 8 (Garden City, 1980); R. de Vaux, "Single Combat in the Old Testament," in *The Bible and the Ancient Near East* (Garden City, 1971), 122-35.

William B. Nelson, Jr.

GOMER (Heb. *gōmer*)

1. The oldest son of Japheth, the son of Noah, attested in the Table of Nations as eponymous ancestor of a people (Gen. 10:2-3; 1 Chr. 1:5-6). Attested also in cuneiform as *Gimirrai* and in Greek as *Kimmerioi,* their place of origin was N of the Black Sea. The Cimmerians are known in the ancient Near East from the 8th century B.C.E. when they were pressed by the Scythians. As they moved south, they became a formidable threat to Urartu and to Assyria as well. They seem to have disappeared from history by the 6th century as the Persians did not separate the Cimmerians and the Scythians. This Gomer is again named in association with the eschatological judgment scene in Ezek. 38:1-9.

2. The daughter of Diblaim, a prostitute and wife of Hosea (Hos. 1:3). She bore the three children, Jezreel ("God sows"), Lo-ruhamah ("Not pitied"), and Lo-ammi ("Not my people"). These symbolic names signify Israel's unfaithfulness, graphically expressed in Gomer's whoredom as representing religious infidelity (i.e., participation in fertility rites). Gomer's marriage with Hosea and Israel's relationship with Yahweh point out that Israel wrongfully worshipped Baal in place of Yahweh, who gave grain, wine, and oil (Hos. 2:8[MT 10]; cf. vv. 16-17[18-19]).

Aaron W. Park

GOMORRAH (Heb. *ʿămōrâ*)

A city listed in the Table of Nations as belonging to the territory of the Canaanites (Gen. 10:19). Gomorrah, along with Sodom, Admah, Zeboiim, and Bela (Zoar), comprised the five cities of the Dead Sea Valley (Gen. 14:2, 8). This pentapolis had previously served Chedorlaomer, king of Elam, for 12 years before it rebelled against him. Chedorlaomer and four eastern allies invaded and plundered Gomorrah and Sodom before taking Abraham's nephew Lot captive. Abraham gathered together a military force of 318 men and rescued Lot, along with the other captives (Gen. 14:1-16).

The Bible relates that Gomorrah, along with Sodom, was selected for destruction by the Lord because of its sin. Abraham attempted to intercede with the Lord on behalf of these cities, given that his nephew Lot had settled in the region. The Lord sent angels to take Lot, along with his family, out of Sodom. When Lot's wife ignored the angels' warning not to look back at the destruction of Gomorrah and Sodom, she was turned into a pillar of salt. Sulfur and fire from heaven destroyed Gomorrah, the inhabitants of Sodom, and adjacent cities (Gen. 19:15-29). Gomorrah is mentioned in conjunction with Sodom as an example of the Lord's judgment (e.g., Gen. 13:10; Deut. 29:23[MT 22]; Isa. 1:9-10; Amos 4:11; Matt. 10:15; Rom. 9:29; 2 Pet. 2:6). The annihilation of Gomorrah, along with Sodom, is frequently referred to in pseudepigraphal literature (Gk. Apoc. Ezra 2:19; 7:12; Jub. 16:5; 20:6). References to Gomorrah and Sodom are also found in 1QapGen 21:23–22:25 and Josephus (*Ant.* 1.170-206).

Kenneth Atkinson

GOOD

Unlike the Platonic abstract ideal of "the Good," the biblical texts portray goodness as a quality of lived experience.

In the OT trees (Gen. 2:9) and ears of grain (41:5) are described as good (Heb. *ṭôḇ*). Aspects of the human experience referred to as good include hospitality (Gen. 26:29), loyalty (1 Sam. 29:9; NRSV "blameless"), prosperity (Hos. 10:1), and old age (Gen. 15:15). Goodness describes the sensuous pleasures of sweetness (Jer. 6:20), fragrance (Cant. 1:3), and beauty (Gen. 24:16). God also brings the Israelites into a "good and broad land, flowing with milk and honey" (Exod. 3:8), "a good land" of brooks and water, of fountains and springs (Deut. 8:7-10).

The biblical writings testify everywhere to God's goodness, including creation and his faithfulness to his covenant with Israel (Exod. 18:9). However, Joshua reminds the Israelite community that the Lord "will turn and do you harm, and consume you, after having done you good," if they forsake God's ways (Josh. 24:20). The exhortation to be faithful to the covenant and walk in God's ways is common in the prophetic literature (Jer. 6:16; Hos. 3:5). The Psalmist gives thanks to God's name "for it is good" (Ps. 54:6[MT 8]), and the Spirit and its fruits are good (Ps. 143:10; Gal. 5:22). The Psalmist also emphasizes that there is no good apart from God (Ps. 16:2), for only God is good (Matt. 19:17).

In the NT Gk. *agathós* refers to the moral excellence of a person or an object. Matthew consistently contrasts *agathós* with *ponērós,* "evil," in his descriptions of individuals (Matt. 5:45; 12:34-35; 22:10; 25:21-26). Gk. *agathós* appears most often in the NT in Romans, where Paul discusses God's goodness and the good for which humans strive.

Gk. *kalós* is used frequently in the Synoptic Gospels in parables and moral exhortations. Objects such as the "good fruit" (Matt. 3:10), the "good seed" (13:38), and "fine pearls" (v. 45) all signify the goodness that resides with God. Gk. *chrēstós* appears primarily in the Pauline and Deutero-Pauline letters to refer to the goodness of God.

Henry L. Carrigan, Jr.

GOOD FRIDAY

The Friday preceding Easter, observed in commemoration of the Crucifixion (Mark 15:42; Luke 23:54; John 19:31; cf. Matt. 27:62); called Great Friday in the Eastern Church. In the church year it is traditionally a day of fasting and penance. Post-Reformation practice observed by both Roman Catholics and Protestants includes a service from noon to 3 P.M. marking Jesus' agony on the cross (Matt. 27:45; Mark 15:33; Luke 23:44).

GOPHER WOOD

The material from which Noah was instructed to build the ark. Heb. *ʿăṣê-gōp̄er* appears only at Gen.

6:14, and no cognates have been found in other ancient Near Eastern languages. Some scholars associate it with the construction of the Mesopotamian *kufa* boat, which was made of branches or reeds and palm leaves and sealed with bitumen (cf. Gilgamesh XI.20-69). Most likely this resinous wood comes from some variety of conifer, probably a cypress. ROBERT E. STONE, II

GORGIAS (Gk. *Gorgias*)
A Seleucid general whose exploits against the Jewish rebels are documented in 1 Macc. 3:38; 2 Macc. 8:9. He was one of the generals commissioned by Antiochus IV Epiphanes to quell the Jewish revolt throughout Judea. In battle against the numerically inferior Jewish rebels near Emmaus, Gorgias was strategically outmaneuvered and defeated by Judas Maccabeus (1 Macc. 4:1-24). As military governor of Idumea, he successfully repelled the unsanctioned attack of Joseph and Azariah on the garrison at Jamnia (1 Macc. 5:55-62). Subsequently Judas defeated Gorgias at Jamnia, cutting off his arm and causing him to flee to Marisa (2 Macc. 12:32-37). GENE J. LAWSON

GOSHEN (Heb. *gōšen*)
1. The territory within Egypt where the Hebrews settled to be near Joseph (Gen. 45:18) and where they sojourned until the time of the Exodus (Gen. 47:1-6; Exod. 9:26). It was called the "best of the land" (Gen. 45:18; 47:6, 11) and was considered good for grazing (46:32-34; 47:4). Goshen apparently lay toward Canaan from the Egyptian capital of the later patriarchal period, as Joseph went out to meet his father there (Gen. 46:29).

The land of Goshen is generally identified with the area around Wadi Ṭumilât, a 56 km. (35 mi.) fertile strip of land connecting the eastern part of the Nile River Delta with Lake Timsah. It provides one of only two passages for traffic between Egypt and Sinai or Palestine to the east. During the Hyksos period (1750-1550 B.C.E.) the region was inhabited by large numbers of Northwest Semites, apparently immigrants from Palestine. The Joseph account fits best in such a setting.

Following the expulsion of the Hyksos the area remained unimportant until the pharaohs of the 19th Dynasty commenced building in the Nile Delta region. The name of the area then probably changed. "Raamses" probably refers to the city of Pi-ramesse built by Rameses II (Exod. 1:11), and the area probably became known as the "Land of Rameses" (Gen. 47:11; 46:28 [LXX]).

The region constituted the 20th Egyptian nome (administrative district), called "Arabia" by classical writers. In the intertestamental period the territory of the Arabian king Geshem (ca. 450-420), a foe of Nehemiah (Neh. 2:19; 6:1-2, 6), apparently included this area; silver bowls inscribed with his name were found at Tell el-Maskhûtah there (cf. LXX *Gesem* and *Gesem Arabia* for Goshen).

2. A region in southern Canaan conquered by Joshua (Josh. 10:41; 11:16; LXX *Gosom*).

3. A town in the hill country assigned to the tribe of Judah (Josh. 15:51; LXX *Gosom*).
DANIEL C. BROWNING, JR.

GOSPEL, GOOD NEWS
The English translation of Gk. *euangélion* which, in its most general sense, in the NT refers to the word of salvation made available to the world in and through Jesus Christ.

Origin of usage

Despite impressive linguistic evidence from the wider Greco-Roman world, such as the calendar inscription from Priene (dated close to the birth of Jesus) which uses this terminology to celebrate the "salvation" of Augustus, it is doubtful that such usage can account for the central importance of *euangélion* in the NT.

Rather, the centrality of this usage stems from the perception of Jesus as the ambassador (Heb. *mĕḇaśśēr*) of a new eschatological era for Israel. Jesus' proclamation that God was about to show his saving power before the nations by bringing salvation to Zion is founded on the promise of such passages as Isa. 52:7-12; 61:1-4. The common Hebrew/Aramaic terminology for such OT proclamation is *bĕśōrâ* (= Gk. *euangélion/euangélia*, "gospel"; cf. Tg. of Isa. 51:1). According to Matt. 11:2-6 (= Luke 7:18-23) Jesus echoes Isa. 61:1 when he informs John's disciples that he is the ambassador anointed by God to bring "good news" to the poor (cf. Luke 4:14-18). If one understands that in Jesus' proclamation by word and deed the fulfillment of the Isaianic promises were taking place in his ministry, one can say that he proclaimed the gospel.

Matthew and Luke

The two foundational accounts of Jesus' life echo this perspective each in its own way. In the Matthean redactional sections (Matt. 4:23; 9:35; 24:14) Jesus' work in teaching and healing is fused together and described as an eschatological proclamation of "the gospel of the kingdom" (cf. Matt. 26:13). Luke prefers the infinitive form *euangelízesthai* (ca. 25 times in Luke-Acts); it has close affinities with the terminology of the LXX which Luke regularly imitates.

For Luke, in keeping with Isa. 40:3-5, John the Baptist is the forerunner of the gospel (Luke 3:4-6; 16:16). Consciously echoing Isa. 61:1-2; 58:6, Jesus' mission is viewed as an announcement of "good news to the poor" (Luke 4:14-18). The emphasis is that Jesus' preaching brings a reversal of status in Israel. The poor and the sick are vindicated, while the rich and proud will be put down (Luke 7:22; 8:1; 9:6; cf. 14:33; 16:13; 18:24).

This theme is continued in Acts, where the apostles and other leaders persist in a similar proclamation. However, the focus of the proclamation now moves to Jesus himself. As the one who was rejected by the leaders of Israel, he is now proclaimed (*euangelízesthai*) as the agent of salvation, since God vindicated him by raising him from the dead (Acts 5:42; 8:35; 15:35; 17:18).

Mark

Instead of the infinitive form, Mark uses the noun *euangélion*. Mark is much closer to Acts (and Paul) in portraying Jesus as both the bringer of salvation and the one in whom salvation is found.

For Mark, to tell the story of Jesus is to proclaim the gospel. It is by Jesus' teaching, deeds of healing, and conduct, especially in his Passion, that God's saving power (gospel) is shown. Thus, for Mark the gospel was first promised in Isaiah (Mark 1:1-2) but came to realization when Jesus began to preach (vv. 14-15). This preaching of the gospel demanded faith and repentance (Mark 1:15). It required a personal decision for discipleship which in Mark, in contrast to Matthew and Luke, is linked with accepting the gospel (Mark 8:35; 10:29). It is this story (gospel) that Mark's readers are called to be loyal to (Mark 14:9) and to announce to all creation (13:10; 16:15).

Paul

The preponderance of usages of "gospel" (both infinitive and noun) in the NT is found in the Pauline writings (almost 50 times in the undisputed letters). The connection between Paul and the Synoptic Gospel tradition is still somewhat unclear. However, the view that Paul picked both the terminology and general usage of "gospel" from traditions he learned from the Hellenistic church is compatible with the evidence of Acts.

Nevertheless, as in many other areas, Paul placed his unique imprint upon the concept. More clearly than any other NT writer he stresses that the gospel is the message about the salvation realized by the death, burial, and resurrection of the Messiah, Jesus of Nazareth (1 Cor. 15:1-11; Rom. 1:3; 1 Cor. 1:17). But "gospel" also included the basic doctrinal claims of the total Christian message including the hope for the return of Christ (1 Thess. 1:5, 9-10; 2 Thess. 1:8; Rom. 2:16). Indeed, for Paul, it was a synonym for the entire fabric of the Christian message (Rom. 1:16).

Paul insisted that his call as a minister of the gospel came directly as a result of a personal encounter with the risen Christ (Gal. 1:13-16; 2 Cor. 4:4-6). Through the same power made known to him by the risen Christ, in fulfillment of the OT promises that at the end time humans would announce to the world the fulfillment of God's promises, Paul became a messenger of the gospel by serving as God's special envoy to the Gentiles (Rom. 10:13-17; Gal. 1:16; Rom. 15:15-20). As God's eschatological word to the nations there is only *one* gospel (Gal. 1:6-9). The realization of what was promised beforehand to the worthies of the OT (Rom. 1:2-3; Gal. 3:8) was now to be received as a gift of God's grace and not on condition of obedience to Torah (Gal. 2:2–3:5; 2 Cor. 3:4-18). For Paul throughout, one's salvation is dependent solely upon the gospel.

Other NT Usages

Curiously, in contrast to Paul the term "gospel" occurs only once in the entire spectrum of the Johannine writings (Rev. 14:6). Here it functions as a solemn warning to a recalcitrant world. A similar warning is given in 1 Pet. 4:17.

Bibliography. C. H. Dodd, *The Apostolic Preaching and Its Developments* (Chicago, 1937); P. Stuhlmacher, ed., *The Gospel and the Gospels* (Grand Rapids, 1991). ALLAN J. MCNICOL

GOSPEL, GOSPELS

The standard term for the four books of the NT bearing that name: Matthew, Mark, Luke, and John. All four show considerable similarity, despite (at times considerable) differences in content. All four start with the figure of John the Baptist, then give long accounts of the life and teaching of Jesus, leading to an extended description of his trial and execution; moreover all four conclude with some account of his tomb being found empty and (certainly in three of the Gospels) his appearance alive to his disciples after his death. In a very real sense, therefore, it is both sensible and meaningful to treat these four books as examples of a broader single generic category.

One should note, however, that the use of the word "Gospel" to refer to these books is only established in Christian history from the second half of the 2nd century. In the 1st century and in the NT itself, especially in Paul, "gospel" refers to the whole Christian message, above all that of Jesus' death and its significance in God's saving plan. "Gospel" for Paul has very little to do with any teaching of the pre-Easter Jesus (cf. 1 Cor. 15:1ff.). So too the "gospel" for Paul is unique: there is — and can only be — one true gospel (Gal. 1:6-7), not four! Precisely when the semantic change in the meaning of the word took place cannot be certain.

However, although terminology and ideas had become fixed by the end of the 2nd century, so that there were thought to be four and only four Gospels, the situation was much more fluid in the middle of the 2nd century. Many other texts were in existence at this time, all claiming to be "gospels," but very different in scope and structure from the canonical Gospels. Some of these have become available in the texts discovered at Nag Hammadi (others were known already). Thus the Gospel of Thomas consists solely of a string of sayings of Jesus. There is no narrative, no account of Jesus' miracles or other actions, no account of his trial, passion, death, or resurrection appearances. The Gospel of Truth, also from Nag Hammadi, is an extended meditation on God and the world, with no explicit mention of Jesus at all (though scholars have detected allusions to Jesus traditions embedded in the text). The Gospel of Mary, by contrast, is concerned wholly with conversations the risen Jesus has with his disciples, and includes nothing about his suffering and death, or anything of his life prior to the Passion. All these texts claim the term "gospel," either explicitly or implicitly. It is thus clear that before the end of the 2nd century the term "gospel," even when restricted to referring to a literary document (rather than to the whole Christian message), could refer to a wide variety of texts.

For the most part, the Gospels provide our main source for any knowledge about Jesus. The value of the noncanonical Gospels in this respect is probably mostly negligible. Rather than giving any information about Jesus himself, these texts witness to the ideas of their writers and the communities that preserved them. Many are gnostic texts from a period after the time of Jesus and reflect gnostic ideas read back onto the lips of Jesus.

The one possible exception may be the Gospel of Thomas. Several have argued strenuously that Thomas preserves an independent line of the tradition and may have authentic material about Jesus. Others have argued that Thomas in fact presupposes the finished Gospels of our NT and hence witnesses only to the development of the Gospel tradition in a later period. Certainly it seems undeniable that in its present form the text of Thomas presupposes the canonical Gospels; whether other traditions are also preserved in Thomas which may be earlier is much disputed.

If we restrict attention to the four canonical Gospels, the question inevitably arises, What *kind* of documents are they? To what literary category, or "genre," do they belong?

Up to the beginning of the 20th century, it was assumed that the Gospels were in some sense "biographies," comparable to works about Socrates (by Plato or Xenophon), Epictetus (by Arrian), or Apollonius of Tyana (by Philostratus). This changed with the work of the form critics who insisted that the Gospels were really folk literature, not to be compared with literary works; the Evangelists were simply popular storytellers who did not impose their own ideas on the work as a whole. Thus Rudolf Bultmann concluded that the Gospels had no real parallels in ancient literature: they had none of the characteristic features of biography (nothing on Jesus' personality, his psychological development, his education or origin). The Gospels were thus without analogy and "*sui generis*."

Such a claim is extremely odd in literary terms. Some understanding of the genre of a text is essential if it is to be understood at all; a text without any analogy would be almost incomprehensible. Further, the rather "low" view that the Evangelists were (just) editors of their materials has been questioned in more recent Gospel studies. There has been a swing away from the older form-critical view and revival of the theory that the Gospels can be seen (in some sense at least) as "biographies." This does not mean that they are biographies in a modern sense of the word. Indeed, there is nothing on Jesus' personality, very little on his background, etc. Yet ancient writings claiming to give the "lives" (Gk. *bíoi*) of individuals also often lacked some of these features. Taking a reasonably broad spread of ancient "lives" of individuals, the Gospels can be shown to fall within the (admittedly fairly broad) parameters which such works imply. It is probably fair to say that, at least in terms of a relatively general and broad genre, the NT Gospels can be seen as sufficiently similar to some ancient "lives" or biographies to be included in that generic category.

Such a categorization does not determine precisely how the Gospels can or should be read. Certainly the category of "biography" does not necessarily imply historical veracity. Many non-Christian "biographies" were written with an author's own agenda. So too, as noted, it is now accepted that the NT Evangelists may have made a more significant contribution in their presentation of their traditions than the older form critics allowed.

Yet, as noted, the NT Gospels are virtually our only sources of information about Jesus. How reliable are they in this respect? One must remember that the Evangelists were all themselves Christians. (We have no records of Jesus by non-Christians.) As such they all believed that the Jesus who had lived and taught on earth prior to his crucifixion had somehow been raised by God from the dead and was now alive in a new way, directing and guiding his church. The "Jesus of history" was believed to be alive and still speaking to his followers; hence the teaching of Jesus preserved in the tradition was not only that of a past figure: it was also that of the Christian community's living Lord. Thus any distinctions one might wish to make between a pre-Easter and a post-Easter situation would probably have been rather unreal for 1st-century Christians.

It seems clear that the Evangelists evidently did feel free to alter their tradition at times. This can be seen most clearly in the case of the Synoptic Evangelists, where one writer has almost certainly used one of the other Gospels as a source (probably Matthew and Luke used Mark), but where in the process of using the source, a degree of freedom has been exercised to change the tradition. In relation to the fourfold Gospel canon, it is widely acknowledged that one cannot accept both John's account and the Synoptic accounts of Jesus' teaching as equally authentic. Most probably Jesus is to be seen most clearly in the Synoptic picture, and John's Gospel represents a reinterpretation and rewriting of the tradition in new categories for a different context. But John is probably not so qualitatively different from the other Evangelists in that all four have imposed their own ideas and beliefs on the tradition.

This does not mean that any quest for the historical Jesus is impossible. Far from it. Careful use of the Gospels can tell a lot about Jesus. But the Gospels also reveal much about the Evangelists and their concerns, and if we wish to use the Gospels to recover information about Jesus we shall have to be alive to the Evangelists' concerns as having shaped, perhaps significantly, the way the story is now told.

Insofar as Jesus is a unique figure in the ancient world (e.g., the Christian claims about the "resurrection" of Jesus are without real analogy), then the accounts of his life, death, and resurrection are without analogy. For example, no Jew wrote a comparable life of Johanan ben Zakkai or Hillel. But the nature of the NT Gospels as in some sense "biographies," at least as understood in the ancient world, should alert us to the riches they contain and the complexities which any reading of them involves.

Bibliography. D. E. Aune, *The New Testament in Its Literary Environment* (Philadelphia, 1988); R. A. Burridge, *What Are the Gospels?* SNTSMS 70 (Cambridge, 1992); H. Koester, *Ancient Christian Gospels* (Philadelphia, 1990); C. M. Tuckett, *Reading the New Testament* (Philadelphia, 1987).

CHRISTOPHER TUCKETT

GOTHIC VERSION

A translation of the Bible into the Gothic language by Ulfilas (ca. 310-380 C.E.), who created a special Gothic alphabet and reduced the spoken language to written form. The translation was begun ca. 341, when Ulfilas went to Byzantium and was consecrated "bishop of the Gothlands" by Eusebius of Nicomedia. It was completed sometime after 348, when Gothic Christians, including Ulfilas, were expelled and crossed the Danube into Moesia.

Other than about 50 verses from Neh. 5–7, the Gothic OT has not survived. Based on the Byzantine or Koine text, the translation of the NT is the oldest known Teutonic literary document. "Western" readings, particularly in the Pauline Epistles, were introduced from Old Latin manuscripts.

The most complete of the half-dozen fragmentary manuscripts is a 5th- or 6th-century copy in the University Library in Uppsala. Written on purple vellum with silver ink, Codex Argentus presents about one half of the text of the Gospels in the order of Matthew, John, Luke, Mark. All other manuscripts of the Gothic NT, with the exception of a vellum leaf of a bilingual Latin and Gothic manuscript now at Giessen, are palimpsests. Ca. 40 verses of the book of Romans are extant in a bilingual Latin and Gothic manuscript at Wolfenbüttel. Nothing exists of Acts, the Catholic Epistles, or Revelation.

CARROLL D. OSBURN

GOURD

The wild gourds (Heb. *paqquʿōṯ*) that Elisha's servant gathered near Gilgal were most likely the fruit of the *Citrullus colocynthis* (L.) Schrad., or colocynth (2 Kgs. 4:39). The colocynth is a ground-hugging vine which grows abundantly in dry conditions. Its fruit is round and yellow with green spots, and is approximately the size of an orange. Its pulp is poisonous, which fits the Elisha story well. Gourd-shaped carvings adorned Solomon's temple (1 Kgs. 6:18). The squirting cucumber (*Ecbalium elaterium*) and the globe cucumber (*Cucumis prophetarum*) have also been suggested for the biblical gourd.

Heb. *qîqāyôn* has also been translated gourd. As Jonah waited outside of Nineveh, this plant grew quickly to provide him shade, but it was destroyed by a worm the next day (Jonah 4:6-7). Gourds do grow rapidly; however, the Bible provides no other clues that would support any firm identification of *qîqāyôn*.

MEGAN BISHOP MOORE

GOVERNOR

Ruler of a city, territory, or province appointed by a king. Joseph became governor of all Egypt (Gen. 42:6; 45:26; cf. Acts 7:10), and Solomon named governors who exercised civic and military functions (1 Kgs. 20:14-22; 2 Chr. 9:14).

References to governors in the OT frequently designate the official administrators of Babylonia and Persia. The usual term (Heb. *peḥâ*) signifies an administrative level below a satrap, the Persian colonial governor. For example, Tattenai was governor of the province "Beyond the (Euphrates) River" (Ezra 5:6), while Zerubbabel and Nehemiah were local governors appointed by the king to rule Judah (Hag. 1:1; Neh. 5:14). Governors are also mentioned in Daniel (e.g., Dan. 2:48; 6:7[MT 8]).

In NT times "governor" (Gk. *hēgemṓn*) usually referred to the ruler of a Roman province (Mark 13:9; 1 Pet. 2:14). Matthew notes that Christians could be hauled into court "before governors and kings" for Christ's sake (Matt. 10:18; cf. Mark 13:9; Luke 21:12). In his trial Jesus was brought before Pilate, the Roman governor of Judea (Matt. 27:2, 11-26).

Three kinds of Roman officials are described as "governors" in Luke: the legate, a military ruler governing an imperial province (Quirinius of Syria, Luke 2:2); the proconsul, governing a senatorial province (Sergius Paulus of Cyprus, Acts 13:7; Gallio of Achaia, 18:12); and the perfect or procurator, governing a subdivision of a province with a settled army (Pontius Pilate, Luke 3:1; Felix, Acts 23:24; Festus, 24:27). In 2 Cor. 11:32 the "governor" *(ethnárchēs)* under King Aretas was probably his assistant.

The basic attitude inculcated in the Bible is one of respect and obedience to "the governing authorities" (Rom. 13:1-7; 1 Pet. 2:13-17; cf. Mal. 1:8). Ultimately, God is seen as the supreme governor who "rules over the nations" (Ps. 22:28[29]).

ALLISON A. TRITES

GOZAN (Heb. *gôzān;* Akk. *Guzana*)

A city (modern Tell Halaf) on the upper reaches of the Ḫabur River to which Israelites were deported following the fall of Samaria in 722/721 B.C.E. (2 Kgs. 17:6; 18:11; 1 Chr. 5:26). Traces of the deportation are found from the late 8th-7th century; persons by the names Nadbi-yahu, Neri-yahu, Palí-yahu, Halbi from Samaria, Hoshea, and Azar-yahu are attested in texts from Tell Halaf. Guzana (Bit-Baḫiani) was the capital of an Assyrian province that paid tribute to the Assyrian homeland in rye, barley, and livestock. Sennacherib's messenger claims that Gozan was recently conquered by the Assyrians (2 Kgs. 19:12 = Isa. 37:12).

Bibliography. B. Becking, *The Fall of Samaria.* SHANE 2 (Leiden, 1992), 64-69.

BOB BECKING

GRACE

A central term in the discussion of relationships between people and with the divine. Heb. *ḥēn* and *ḥeseḏ* are the primary terms indicating God's disposition to show favor toward humans, and God's continuing loyalty toward those accepted into divine favor. This favor manifested itself in acts of deliverance in time of need and provision of daily sustenance. Favor is shown in the face of the benefactor, so that "seeking God's face" (Ps. 27:8-9) and imploring God to "make God's face to shine" and to "lift up God's countenance" (Num. 6:25), are all expressions of seeking God's favor, God's disposition to help and to provide for the well-being (*šālôm*) of God's people. Favor once shown can also be withdrawn: this is commonly expressed as anger, the opposite of favor (cf. Heb. 10:26-31), represented by the hiding of the face or removal of the offender from the presence of the benefactor (Ps. 13:1[MT 2]; 51:11[13]).

The casting of the divine-human relationship in these terms reflects the manner in which human beings interacted. People in an inferior position (with regard to power or resources) would "seek the favor" of a person in a socially superior position. Joseph "finds favor" in the sight of Potiphar, the jailer, and Pharaoh's household (Gen. 39:4, 21; 50:4). This human dimension remains important in the narratives of Ruth and 1 Samuel, as well as in Proverbs. At such a level, "favor" does not necessarily create an ongoing relationship. It may be a single act of beneficence with a response of simple gratitude. Frequently, however, it does initiate an ongoing relationship in which the beneficiary returns loyal service for the favor shown by the benefactor, and the benefactor continues to provide assistance and access to resources (cf. the story of Joseph).

The relationship of "grace" between God and the people of Israel is ongoing. God's acts of "favor" in the wilderness establish a relationship which now has clearly articulated mutual obligations. An initial stance of uncoerced favor leads to the formation of a relationship in which the benefactor will continue to provide assistance, and the beneficiaries will remain singularly loyal to the Patron and offer services to the Patron. Within the Deuteronomic and prophetic traditions, this loyal service was to be fulfilled through beneficence toward one's fellow Israelites. Generosity and justice in human relationships were obligations imposed on the people as their fitting response to God's generosity toward them. God's *ḥesed*, "loyalty," remains "favor" in that where the human beneficiaries continually fail in their loyalty and service, God continues to call them back into favor, punishing for a time but always restoring those who have broken faith. Even the declaration of a "new covenant" which replaces the "old" broken by the ancestors is a declaration of God's commitment to set aside all those offenses and insults to God's favor, and approach the people anew in favor (Jer. 31:31-34).

In the NT period, "grace" (Gk. *cháris*) is embedded in the language of the Greco-Roman institution of patronage. Seneca claimed that patronage constituted the "chief bond of human society" (Seneca *de Beneficiis* 1.4.2), and so the NT proclamation of God's favor would have been heard and interpreted within this social context. Patrons gave access to goods, entertainment, and advancement. The client, who received the benefit, accepted the obligation to spread the fame of the giver and declare gratitude for the patron's gifts (cf. Seneca 2.21.1; 2.24.2). The client also accepted the obligation of loyalty and service to the patron. A third figure in this network has been called the "broker" (cf. *mesítēs*). This figure was a patron to his or her clients and a client or friend of another potential patron. The broker's chief benefaction was access to another patron and the resources at his or her disposal.

Within this social-semantic field, *cháris* has three distinct meanings. It is first the disposition of a benefactor to aid a suppliant, "not in return for something nor in the interest of him who renders it, but in that of the recipient" (Aristotle *Rhetoric* 2.7.2). In this sense it is most akin to Heb. *ḥēn.* It also refers to the client's proper return for a benefit, namely gratitude and loyal service (cf. 2 Cor. 4:15; Heb. 12:28; 13:15-16), as well as to the actual gift or benefit conferred (cf. 2 Cor. 8:6-7, 19). Paul is known as a proponent of "salvation by grace." He is concerned (e.g., in Galatians) to establish God's uncoerced initiative in reaching out to form a people from all nations through God's anointed agent, Jesus. Requiring Torah-observance from gentile converts threatens to set aside or nullify the favor of God which Jesus, the broker, has gained for his faithful clients (Gal. 2:21; 5:2-4), because it casts doubt on Jesus' ability to secure God's favor. It shows distrust toward Jesus, the immediate Patron of the new people of God formed from Jews and Gentiles, called into God's favor (Gal. 1:6). God's favor, however, seeks a response of faithfulness (*pístis*) and service from God's clients. Paul speaks, therefore, of the "obedience of faith" (Rom. 1:5; 16:26) which is the goal of his mission, calling forth the proper response of those who have benefited from God's gift. This involves the offering up of the believers' whole selves to God's service, to do what is righteous in God's sight (Rom. 12:1; 6:1-14). As in the OT, this response centers not only on honoring God, but on love, generosity, and loyal service toward one's fellow believers (Gal. 5:13-14; 6:2; Rom. 13:9-10). The giving is free and uncoerced, but the ancient hearer knew that to accept a gift meant accepting also obligation to the giver.

The author of Hebrews affords exceptional insight into the workings of "grace" within the patron-client relationship between God and human beings. Whereas humanity stood apart from God's favor on account of the sins which stained the conscience, Jesus' priestly sacrifice (brokerage) brought forgiveness and cleansing, so that Jesus' clients might have "access to the throne of favor," i.e., come into God's presence, seek God's face (favor), and receive "favor to help in time of need" (e.g., the resources to hold on in the face of opposition; Heb. 4:16). In order to attain the promised benefits of a place in God's city (Heb. 11:13-16; 13:14), the clients have need of "faith" (*pístis*) and "endurance" (10:35-39). They must remain loyal to their Patron in the face of society's hostility and not waver in their trust. To give up God's gifts (and show slight regard for God's "spirit of favor"; Heb. 10:29) for the sake of peace with society would be an outrageous insult to the Patron, a spurning of God's gifts and of Jesus' costly mediation, resulting in God's "wrath" (Heb. 10:26-31; 3:7–4:11). The author here gives insight into the reciprocal nature of *cháris:* God has accepted the believers into favor through Jesus' effective mediation; the believers, as honorable clients, are now to return "grace" for "grace," to "show gratitude" (Heb. 12:28) to God by continuing to bear witness to their Benefactor in a hostile world (13:15) and by assisting one another by love and service, encouraging and supporting one another in the face of an unsupportive society (13:1-3, 16; 6:10).

Bibliography. F. W. Danker, *Benefactor: Epigraphic Study of a Graeco-Roman and New Testament Semantic Field* (St. Louis, 1982); D. A. DeSilva, "Exchanging Favor for Wrath: Apostasy in Hebrews and Patron-Client Relationships," *JBL* 115 (1996): 91-116; R. M. Hals, *Grace and Faith in the Old Testament* (Minneapolis, 1980); K. D. Sakenfeld, *The Meaning of Ḥesed in the Hebrew Bible.* HSM 17 (Missoula, 1978); R. P. Saller, *Personal Patronage Under the Early Empire* (Cambridge, 1982).

DAVID A. DESILVA

GRAIN

Grain production relies on field crops such as cereals (Heb. *dāgān*), legumes, and other cultigens. The main cereals cultivated in the Near East are wheat *(ḥiṭṭâ)* and barley *(śeʿōrâ)*. Another group of small-grained cereal plants is known by the collective term millet, and includes broomcorn millet (*Panicum miliaceum* L.), Italian millet (*Setaria italica* [L.] Beauv.), and barnyard millet *(Echinichola crus-galli)*. The legume family includes several genera and species of which several were cultivated in the ancient Near East including lentils (*Lens culinaris* Medik.), peas (*Pisum sativum* L.), broad beans *(Vicia faba),* bitter vetch *(Vicia ervilia),* chick-peas *(Cicer arietinum),* fenugreek (*Trigonela graecum* L.), and grass peas *(Lathyrus sativus L.).*

While wheat and barley are sown in the fall (late October-December), millet is sown in the spring (March-April) and is considered a summer crop. Legumes are sown from as early as November-December (vetch), through December-January (peas, lentils), to February (chick-peas). The period for sowing legumes is referred to in the Gezer Calendar as *yrwḥw lqš* (two months of late sowing). Harvesting of grain begins with the cereals in April (barley), and continues through May (wheat, oats) and ends in late July-August (millet). Legumes start to be harvested in late April-May (vetch, peas, lentils) and end in June (chick-peas).

To be used grain must be cleared off the stalks. This is done through threshing and winnowing. The clean grain *(bār)* is ready to be used in food preparation, but the farmer must make sure that a certain amount is stored for use as seed in the next season. Transportation of the clean grain from the threshing floor *(gōren)* to the storage area was accomplished by placing it in sacks or large bags and moving it on animal backs and in wagons. Grain was stored in a variety of containers and facilities. For daily and immediate use, it was kept in large storage jars which could be placed near the food preparation area. Long-term storage required special facilities, the nature of which depended on the owner and the purpose. Individuals storing grain they themselves produced used mostly stone-lined grain pits, while the central government (the monarchy, cult centers) used a variety of facilities such as tri-partite, pillared storehouses and large underground stone-lined silos. There were other storage facilities such as above-ground granaries, but these are known mostly from Egypt and Assyria.

Grain was collected as in-kind taxes from individuals and families. Certain classes (royalty, nobility) owned large grain-producing tracts of land. Central storage facilities were constructed in towns fulfilling administrative functions in areas considered public or administrative. These were located near palaces, cult centers, city gates, and other areas designated as administrative centers. Functionaries such as the clergy, nobility, or the military were issued grain from these facilities. Written records were kept of deposit and dispatch of commodities as in the Samaria and Arad ostraca.

Bibliography. O. Borowski, *Agriculture in Iron Age Israel* (Winona Lake, 1987); "Granaries and Silos," *OEANE,* 431-33; J. M. Renfrew, *Palaeoethnobotany* (New York, 1973). ODED BOROWSKI

GRAPES

The most prominent fruit in the Bible and an important agricultural product of the ancient Near East. Grapes (Heb. *ʿēnāḇ;* Gk. *staphylḗ*) grow on grapevines (*Vitis vinifera* L.), which must be pruned to ensure abundant fruiting. Grapes ripen in the summer, and are picked quickly thereafter to avoid damage from insects and rotting. Grapes were eaten fresh and as raisins, which could be baked into cakes (Hos. 3:1). Grapes were also processed into syrup, vinegar, and wine, which was the most common use for grapes in ancient Israel. The grape juice was extracted by treading upon the grapes in a grape press. Grape-treading appears to have been a joyous occasion which involved the entire community (Judg. 9:27).

The spies that Moses sent into Canaan brought back a cluster of grapes so large that it was carried on a pole between two men (Num. 13:23). Various biblical laws apply to grapes, such as the provision which allows one to eat grapes from a neighbor's vineyard, but prohibits any from being put in a container (Deut. 23:24). Grapes also have symbolic uses. In Isaiah's Song of the Vineyard (Isa. 5:1-7) rotten grapes represent Judah's depravity. The famous proverb "the parents have eaten sour grapes, and the children's teeth are set on edge" (Jer. 31:29), pertaining to the consequence of wrongdoing for later generations, was refuted by Ezekiel (Ezek. 18:2-3). MEGAN BISHOP MOORE

GRASS

Several hundred species of plants which grow wild in Israel were represented in the Bible by Heb. *deše',* *ʿēśeḇ, ḥāṣîr,* and *yereq,* either alone or in combination. Grass is a good approximation for what these words mean, but they also refer to green vegetation in general, both grassy and herbaceous. Gk. *chórtos* also means grass or any green plant.

Grass appears in many contexts in the Bible. Ahab sends Obadiah in search of grass for his animals to eat (1 Kgs. 18:5). The Psalmist praises God for providing grass for the cattle (Ps. 104:14).

Many mentions of grass are found in similes. Eliphaz promises Job that his descendants would be as numerous as the grass of the earth (Job 5:25). "May people blossom in the cities like the grass of the field," sang the Psalmist (Ps. 72:16), who also found that the wicked "sprout like grass" (92:7[MT 8]).

Water on grass, especially dew in the morning, causes it to glisten and appear more vital. Moses sang "May . . . my speech condense like the dew; like gentle rain on grass, like showers on new growth" (Deut. 32:2). Micah's vision of a renewed Israel sees the remnant of Jacob as dew from the Lord, "like showers on the grass" (Mic. 5:7[6]). Proverbs compares the favor of a king to dew on the grass (Prov. 19:12).

In contrast, grass easily fades in the heat of the day, and is thus a symbol of fragility. Isaiah prophesies that the Assyrians would be "like grass on the housetops, blighted before it is grown" (Isa. 37:27). Likewise, Jesus speaks of the grass of the field, which one day produces beautiful flowers and the next is used as fodder (Matt. 6:30 = Luke 12:28).

MEGAN BISHOP MOORE

GRASSHOPPER

An insect of the order Orthoptera, represented by two families: the short-horned Acrididae and the long-horned Tettigonidae. Often confused with the locust, the grasshopper is a relatively solitary insect lacking the gregarious features of locusts. Nevertheless, some short-horned grasshoppers may also exhibit a gregarious phase, at which time they are properly called locusts.

The Bible contains only a few references to true grasshoppers, all within the OT. The general Hebrew term for grasshopper is *ḥāgāḇ*. The Talmud uses this term to refer to any species of short-horned grasshopper, but it can also designate gregarious locusts (2 Chr. 7:13; possibly also Eccl. 12:5). The *ḥāgāḇ* is listed as one of four exceptions to the prohibition against eating winged insects that dart about on four legs (Lev. 11:20-22). The *ḥāgāḇ* is acceptable for food because it also has a pair of jointed legs used for leaping. For the same reason, the *solʿām* and the *ḥargōl* are also listed as edible grasshoppers. The *solʿām,* usually translated "bald locust," is a short-horned grasshopper from the subfamily Tyrxalinae. According to the Talmud, the *ḥargōl* can refer to any species of the long-horned Tettigonidae. The fourth exception to the dietary prohibition is the *ʾarbeh,* the ubiquitous desert locust.

See LOCUST. RONALD A. SIMKINS

GRAVE

Burial sites, including both rock tombs and common excavated shafts or trenches (Ezek. 32:22; Jer. 26:23; Matt. 27:7). Graves were the sites of mourning and remembrance that could be preserved for centuries (1 Sam. 10:2; 2 Sam. 3:32; 2 Kgs. 23:17; Neh. 3:16). Emotional appeals concerning ancestral graves moved even monarchs (2 Sam. 19:37; Neh. 2:3, 5).

Proper or improper burial could bestow favor or disfavor from God or humans. Moses received an honorable burial by God himself (Deut. 34:6). David gave Ishbaal's decapitated head and the remains of Saul and Jonathan proper burial, while he contemptuously mutilated the bodies of Ishbaal's murderers (2 Sam. 4:12; 21:14). Jehoiakim showed his disdain for the prophet Uriah by dumping his corpse in the common people's grave (Jer. 26:23), while God in turn condemned Jehoiakim to a grave on the dung heap (22:19). The king of Babylon would be cast out of his grave because of bloodshed (Isa. 14:20; cf. 2 Chr. 16:14; 21:19-20). Failure to be buried properly or having one's bones removed from one's grave after burial was a terrible fate and judgment from God (2 Kgs. 23:16; Eccl. 6:3; Isa. 14:19; Jer. 8:1-2; cf. Deut. 21:22-23). This abhorrence may have been reinforced by the folk-religious belief that the felicity of the dead or blessings conferred on the living by the dead depended upon the descendants' practicing memorial rites honoring the deceased.

The grave, being ceremonially unclean, made tomb dwellers repugnant to God, and graves were seemingly abandoned by God (Num. 19:16, 18; Ps. 88:5, 11[MT 6, 12]; cf. Isa. 65:4). Graves were thus appropriate dumping grounds for pulverized, detestable idols (2 Kgs. 23:6; 2 Chr. 34:4).

The grave often has a figurative meaning in the Bible. English versions often translate Heb. *šĕʾôl,* "Sheol," as "grave"; e.g., "going down into Sheol" refers to being buried alive with tents and possessions (Num. 16:30). The grave is used figuratively for death itself (e.g., Job 17:1). Ideally, one would "come to the grave" at a ripe old age (Job 5:26). Death before birth makes the mother's womb the grave (Jer. 20:17). Elsewhere, passion is "fierce as the grave" (Cant. 8:6).

See BURIAL.

Bibliography. H. C. Brichto, "Kin, Cult, Land and Afterlife," *HUCA* 44 (1973): 1-54; R. L. Harris, "Why Hebrew *Sh*ᵉ*ʾōl* Was Translated 'Grave,'" in *The NIV: The Making of a Contemporary Translation,* ed. K. L. Barker (Grand Rapids, 1986), 58-71; T. J. Lewis, *Cults of the Dead in Ancient Israel and Ugarit.* HSM 39 (Atlanta, 1989); A. Mazar, *Archaeology of the Land of the Bible, 10,000–586 B.C.E.* (New York, 1990).

JOE M. SPRINKLE

GREAT SEA

The geographic designation for the Mediterranean Sea, noted as the western boundary of the Promised Land (Num. 34:6-7; Ezek. 47:20). The location of the Great Sea (W of Israel) gave rise to Heb. *yām,* "west," being used to mean "sea" (e.g., Deut. 11:24); this also holds true for Ugaritic and other Semitic languages. Because east was the main directional orientation of the Jews and other Semitic peoples, it was considered "up," the direction of the abode of the divine. West was conversely considered "down," the direction of Sheol, the place of the dead. The Jews thus viewed the Great Sea with a good deal of dread and suspicion, and in Hebrew thought there was a close connection between the sea (the deep) and Sheol (Gen. 1:2; Isa. 51:10; Jonah 2:5).

The Mediterranean or Great Sea spans more than 3400 km. (2100 mi.) west to east from Gibraltar to the coast of Lebanon and Israel. Separating the European and African continents north to south, the span varies from 160-965 km. (100-600 mi.). Until recent times sailing on the Great Sea was only safe during the late spring and summer when the wind patterns were fairly predictable. In the biblical era there would have been no sea travel from November to February because of the feared northeasterly winds. Many of the great nations around the Mediterranean basin were accomplished at sea travel; Israel, however, was not one of them. Israel lacked quality harborage, and Joppa (modern Tel Aviv), the only natural harbor on Israel's coastline, was only marginally useful. Although Solomon built a merchant fleet at the Red Sea port of Ezion-geber, he had to hire Phoenician boatwrights and sailors (1 Kgs. 9:26-27).

In the OT various terms are used for the Great Sea, including simply "the sea" (Num. 13:29; Josh. 16:8), "the western sea" (Deut. 11:24; Zech. 14:8), "sea of Joppa" (Ezra 3:7), and "sea of the Philistines" (Exod. 23:31). The only mention in the OT of a substantial voyage on the Great Sea is that of Jonah, who intended to sail west from Joppa to Tarshish.

By the time of the NT Rome had mastered the Great Sea, and, except for the unpredictable winter weather, travel was reasonably safe. Merchant ships sailed with armed protection, and piracy was held in check. With Herod the Great's construction of a harbor at Caesarea, there was increased, although still limited, sea-borne commerce through Israel. The most extensive discussion of events on the Great Sea in the NT are the travels of Paul as recorded in Acts (cf. 2 Cor. 11:25).

Bibliography. C. H. Gordon, "The Mediterranean Factor in the Old Testament," *VTSup* 9 (1963): 19-31.

DENNIS M. SWANSON

GREAVES

Protective leg coverings, part of the body armor worn during warfare. The term (Heb. *miṣḥâ*) appears in the Bible only in the description of Goliath's armor (1 Sam. 17:6). Its presence there argues for the historical accuracy of the account since the Aegean peoples, who were related to the Philistines, clearly wore this type of armor. Bronze greaves from 1400 B.C. were found at Dendra, on the Greek mainland, and greaves are mentioned prominently in the writings of Homer. They were still being worn by Greek infantrymen in their wars against the Persians. Although most ancient Near Eastern soldiers are pictured bare-legged, there is evidence that some Assyrian soldiers also wore leg coverings.

Bibliography. J. G. Warry, *Warfare in the Classical World* (1980, repr. Norman, Okla., 1995); Y. Yadin, *The Art of Warfare in Biblical Lands* (Jerusalem, 1963).

W. E. NUNNALLY

GREECE

The regions inhabited by the ancient Greeks, including the Greek peninsula, the western coast of Anatolia (Ionia), the islands in the Aegean Sea, and Magna Graecia (the 8th-century B.C.E. Greek settlement in the coastal regions of Italy). "Greeks" here refers to the inhabitants of these areas, who were conscious of sharing a common history, language, and culture. In general, there was no hard and fast division between sacred and secular for the ancient Greeks, so that religion permeated their society and provided a sense of common identity. Cultic acts performed by the ancient Greeks which conform to modern conceptions of "religion" included prayer and sacrifice (virtually inseparable), as well as votive offerings, made to various Olympian deities and heroes, visits to Panhellenic sanctuaries such as Olympia (for athletic competitions every four years), and Delphi (the most famous of the Greek oracle sanctuaries). The Greeks called themselves "Hellenes" and their country "Hellas," and labeled everyone else *bárbaroi* ("non-Greeks"). In the *Iliad* the Greeks in general are also called "Danaans" (1.42; 2.484-762), "Achaeans," and "Argives" (used as equivalent terms in 2.333-35). The Romans were the first to call the Hellenes *Graeci* (a latinized form of Gk. *Graekoi*, of uncertain etymology), and their language *Graecum* (Aristotle *Meteorologica* 1.352a; Apollodorus *Bibliotheca* 1.7.3).

Bronze Age and Archaic Period (Beginnings to 450 B.C.E.)

The Greek language belongs to the Indo-european family of languages, and more particularly to the western branch of Centum languages which includes Celtic, Italic, Germanic, Greek, and Hittite. Proto-Greek speakers arrived in the Greek peninsula toward the beginning of the 2nd millennium. In so doing, they displaced the indigenous inhabitants, now called Aegeans, whose existence is evident in such non-Greek place names as Corinth and proper nouns such as Hyacinth (the *nth* ending is the pre-Greek element). The new arrivals did not reject, but rather absorbed many features of Aegean culture including such native deities as Athena and Poseidon. These Greeks, in interaction and competition with other great civilizations (particularly the Minoans, a non–Indo-european people), ultimately grew to be a powerful warring and trading people who flourished until ca. 1200. They are now referred to as the Mycenaeans because of the striking material remains of their civilization that have been excavated at Mycenae, in the east central part of the Peloponnesus. The earliest surviving form of written Greek is called Linear B or Mycenaean Greek. Tablets inscribed with this proto-Greek syllabary of 87 signs dating from the Mycenaean and Minoan periods (1450-

Acrocorinth from ruins of Corinth; temple of Apollo (Phoenix Data Systems, Neal and Joel Bierling)

1200) have been recovered at Knossos on the island of Crete and from the mainland Greek cities of Pylos, Mycenae, and Thebes.

The collapse of Mycenaean civilization toward the end of the Bronze Age (ca. 1200) was closely followed by the migration of Dorian tribes into the western regions of mainland Greece, the last group of Greeks to arrive. The end of the 2nd millennium was a period of instability in the eastern Mediterranean theater, as indicated also by the Trojan War and the migration of the Sea Peoples to the coast of Palestine where they became known as the Philistines. This cultural collapse ushered in a Dark Age (1150-750) during which writing was forgotten and the cultural achievements of the Mycenaean and Minoan civilization remembered only in oral epic. Toward the end of the 8th century an alphabetic script from North Semitic, called Phoenician letters by the Greeks (Herodotus *Hist.* 5.58), was adapted in various forms, though the Ionic form eventually came to predominate. By the 5th century, from the perspective of modern historical linguistics, two major groups of Greek dialects are attested: West Greek, which consisted of various Doric dialects; and East Greek, which consisted of Attic-Ionic, Aeolic, and Arcado-Cypriot or Achaean. The Greeks themselves distinguished four dialects: Attic, Ionic, Doric, and Aeolic (Strabo *Geog.* 8.12.2; 14.5.26).

Toward the end of the Dark Age, in the 8th century, there are two developments of particular importance. First, a North Semitic alphabetical consonantal script (presumably acquired through trading contacts) was adapted to fit the particularities of the Greek language by giving written form to vowels as well as consonants. This new form of literacy made it possible to put the tradition of oral poetry into writing during the 7th century, as exemplified in the two monumental Homeric poems, the *Iliad* and *Odyssey.* These tales of the Trojan War *(Iliad)* and one warrior's return home from that war *(Odyssey),* attributed to the legendary Ionic poet Homer, served as sacred texts for the Greeks: retelling the glories of the Mycenaean past, exemplifying heroic behavior, identifying and characterizing the Olympic deities. These poems were, for centuries, the foundation of Greek education.

The Archaic period conventionally begins with one of the first fixed dates in Greek history: the (traditional) founding of the Olympic games in 776. By the 7th century the often hereditary *basileís* ("kings," or more accurately, "chieftains") had been overthrown in most city-states by the *kaloikagathoí* ("nobles"). During the 7th century individual members of the nobility, with popular support and often with a mercenary force, overthrew the nobility and ruled unconstitutionally as tyrants. The beginning of the Archaic period also coincided with the emergence of the most characteristic Greek form of political organization, the (normally) autonomous *pólis* or city-state. A typical polis, which originated during the mid-8th century and achieved its classic form by the close of the 5th century, consisted of an acropolis, walls, an *agorá* ("market"), temples in honor of Olympian gods, a theater, and a gymnasium. The power of aristocracies and hereditary ruling elites was strong; but movements toward democracy were made. For example, changes in warfare (from chariots and cavalry to foot soldiers) encouraged and, in fact, demanded the participation of common people. Culturally, the Archaic period is known as the Lyric

Lion gate, entrance to the citadel at Mycenae (Late Helladic IIIB, ca. 1250 B.C.E.) (B. K. Condit)

Age, when the voice of the individual poet first appears (e.g., Archilochus of Paros, Theognis of Megara, and Sappho of Lesbos). More communal-based poetry was also produced (e.g., choral lyric of Alcman and Spartan military poetry). Also, the first philosophers interested in cosmology and the problem of the one and the many appeared in Milesia in Ionia, including Thales, Anaximander, and Anaximenes. Finally, motivated by land hunger caused by an overly dense population and spurred on by merchants seeking profit, the great period of Greek colonization began in the middle of the 8th century. By the early 7th century, many Greek metropolises had established colonies in regions as widespread as Egypt, the coast of the Black Sea, the coast of Italy, and Spain.

There are several biblical references to Greece and the Greeks in this Archaic period. The Table of Nations (Gen. 10:2-5; 1 Chr. 1:5, 7) lists Javan as one of the children of Japheth. The name Javan is the linguistic equivalent of the Greek Ion, the eponymous ancestor of the Ionians. The Greeks, as "Javan" or "Javanites," are elsewhere referred to as traders (Ezek. 27:13, 19) or as one of the nations among whom Israel will be sent (Isa. 66:19; Joel 3:6[MT 4:6]).

Classical Period (450-323 B.C.E.)

The 5th century is generally considered the period when Greece (particularly Athens) reached its greatest heights of political power and cultural achievement; but this was not until it had faced its greatest national challenge up to that time: the Persian invasions during the early 5th century. However scarce direct historical links between classical Greece and Israel may be, there is a significant common history involving the nation of Persia and some of its leaders. Cyrus the Great (ruled 559-530) ordered the return of captive Jews to Jerusalem for the rebuilding of the temple (e.g., Ezra 1; Isa. 44:28); this same Cyrus extended his empire into Greek territories of Asia Minor and was later the subject of a novelistic biography, Xenophon's *Cyropaedia*, or "The Education of Cyrus." Darius I (d. 486) led the first great assault against Greece (490), which ended in the decisive defeat of the Persians at the battle of Marathon. Darius I also supported the decree of Cyrus (cf. Ezra 6) and figures prominently in the book of Daniel. Xerxes I (who does not appear in the biblical record) led a second, larger invasion in 480-79 that also failed. In 478-77 an anti-Persian alliance was formed, called the Delian League since it was headquartered on the island of Delos. Athens assumed leadership of this league and built an empire, demanding tribute from its Greek "allies" and asserting its military might to enforce Athenian interests. The great temples of the Athenian acropolis were built during this period. In various ways, these temples celebrate victory over the invading Persians (e.g., the "Greeks vs. barbarians" theme of Parthenon artwork; the temple of Athena Nike, "victory").

It was also in the 5th century that an extraordinary number of talented Athenian authors produced what is now "classical" Greek literature. Aeschylus, then Sophocles and Euripides crafted their tragic dramas; Aristophanes wrote his bawdy comedies that held a distorted mirror up to the great Athenian democracy; Herodotus and Thucydides wrote their histories that chronicled the Persian and Peloponnesian Wars respectively. This latter war, with Sparta and its allies, strained Athens but did not stop its creative output. The dramatic competitions (held in honor of the god Dionysos) continued. Sophists and the established order challenged each other; Socrates (469-399) challenged both. He was put to death on charges of impiety in 399, five years after the end of the Peloponnesian War that left Athens defeated and Sparta, for a time, as the most powerful Greek city-state.

Dynamic political and cultural forces continued to work in the 4th century. No dominant political power emerged until Philip II of Macedon (382-336) attempted to unite politically the quarrelsome and divided Greek city-states. The surviving literature of the period records the voices of the great orators who opposed Philip (e.g., Demosthenes, 384-322) and those who supported him (e.g., Isocrates, 436-338). It was also at this time that Athens secured its reputation as the seat of philosophy through the writing and teaching of Plato (429-347), the most famous student of Socrates, and Aristotle (384-322), the most famous student of Plato. A new era began, however, with the career of Philip's son Alexander III.

Hellenistic Period (323-31 B.C.E.)

The successful military campaigns of Alexander the Great (356-323), which pushed east as far as India, radically changed the political and cultural character of the Mediterranean world. Initially, Alexander intended to avenge the hardships suffered by the Greeks during the Persian invasions of the early 5th century. As a student of Aristotle, Alexander knew and embraced Greek culture and disseminated it, along with the Greek language, throughout his vast empire; this spread of "Greeklike" ways throughout the period yields the name "Hellenistic." Alexander accomplished this in part by founding many Greek city-states where large numbers of Greco-Macedonian veterans settled after serving in his army. Alexander's death in 323 ignited a complex struggle for power among the Diadochoi (the "successors") that ultimately resulted in the establishment of three dynasties, all named after their Greco-Macedonian founders: the Antigonid dynasty in Macedon and Greece, founded by Antigonus I (ca. 382-301); the Seleucid in Asia Minor and Syria, founded by Seleucus I Nicator (358-281); and the Ptolemaic in Egypt and the southern Levant, founded by Ptolemy I Soter (ca. 367-282). The Ptolemaic dynasty survived the longest, until the death of Cleopatra VII (69-30), who, following the sea battle of Actium in 31 when she and Antony were defeated by Octavian, committed suicide on 3 August 30 when Octavian captured Alexandria.

Thanks to the many thousands of papyri preserved by the dry sands of Egypt and recovered during the past century, Ptolemaic Egypt is the best-known of all the Hellenistic kingdoms. For example, papyrus documents indicate that military and administrative personnel were recruited from mainland Greece. They then contributed to the antithetic stratification of society which consisted of a Greek elite who dominated Egyptian nationals. Ptolemaic Alexandria was both the administrative capital of Egypt and seat of Greek scholarship which centered on the Museon (destroyed by fire during Julius Caesar's siege of Alexandria in 47), one of the largest libraries in the ancient world. Alexandria was home to a large Jewish diaspora community (which later included the Apollos mentioned in Acts 18:24; 19:1 and frequently in 1 Corinthians). During the 3rd century, first the Pentateuch and eventually the rest of the OT was translated into Greek and came to be known as the Septuagint (LXX, from Lat. *septuaginta,* "70"), since according to legend 70 Jewish translators took part in the project (narrated in the Epistle of Aristeas).

The rise to power of the Seleucid ruler Antiochus IV Epiphanes (ca. 215-164), as well as the career of Alexander the Great and the assumption of power by the Diadochi that preceded it, is referred to in Dan. 8; 1 Macc. 1, both written before the middle of the 2nd century. Greece itself was largely subject to the Antigonid rulers in Macedonia throughout this period until 146, when Rome, following its victory in the Fourth Macedonian War, destroyed Corinth and made both Greece and Macedonia into Roman provinces. The Roman province of Achaia was initially organized in 46 and later reestablished as a senatorial province by Augustus in 27. Achaia was the official name for the Roman province of Greece, and it is primarily by that name that Greece is referred to in the NT (e.g., Acts 18:12; 1 Thess. 1:7; 2 Cor. 1:1), though the more popular synonym Hellas also occurs once (Acts 20:2; cf. 1 Macc. 8:9).

One of the more important intellectual developments during the Hellenistic period is the development of several major schools of Greek thought, each of which regarded itself as an heir of Socratic thought. The two schools founded by Plato and Aristotle, called the Academy and the Peripatetics respectively, continued to develop throughout the Hellenistic period. The major philosophical schools or movements established somewhat later included Cynicism (founded by Diogenes, ca. 412/403–324/321), Epicureanism (founded by Epicurus, 341-270), Stoicism (founded by Zeno, 335-263, who taught in the painted Stoa "colonnade" in Athens), and Scepticism (founded by Pyrrhon of Elis, ca. 365-275, and sometimes called Pyrrhonism). All these schools regarded philosophy, not as an arcane subject, but as the "art of living" par excellence, which provided answers to the urgent human problems of human suffering, including anger and aggression, fear of death, love and sexuality, sickness and misfortune. The goal of all of these schools of thought was the attainment of *eudaimonía* (i.e., happiness or the flourishing life) through the use of reason and argumentation.

Urban life flourished in this period. Seats of power were in large cities: Alexandria (Egypt), Antioch (Syria), Pergamon (Asia Minor), Pella (Macedon); and, while not unprecedented, cities that were founded or flourished in this era shared the common elements of the Greek polis or city-state. These included the agora, essentially a large, public space that could serve as the hub of commerce, local administration, social, and religious activity (particularly in temples). A theater was obligatory, as was the Greek gymnasium, which existed not only for athletic exercise (conducted nude, Gk. *gymnós*), but also for training in the traditions of Greek culture. The gymnasium was a symbol of Greek culture, making the construction of one in Jerusalem all the more controversial (1 Macc. 1:14; 2 Macc. 4:9).

Roman Period (31 B.C.E.–476 C.E.)

In the Roman period, Greece as a nation had little to no political power; the Romans had conquered the Mediterranean world and made it their empire. Greece nevertheless exerted a strong cultural influence, providing the models for most Roman art and literature. Athens became a "university town" and was particularly distinguished, as it had been, for philosophy (cf. Acts 18:19-20; 1 Cor. 1:20-23).

The prevalence of Greek culture is reflected in the NT use of *Héllēn* ("Greek") as a cultural as well as an ethnic designation, referring to someone who is Hellenized or Greek-speaking and educated. The Pauline dichotomy of "Jew and Greek" (Rom. 1:16; 2:9-10; 3:9; 10:12; 1 Cor. 1:24; 10:32; Gal. 3:28; Col. 3:11) comes to mean Jew and "Gentile," "non-Jew" or "pagan." Also, the "Greek" woman in Mark 7:26

is actually a Syrophoenician "by birth" or "race." The ethnic designation, however, is also used (Acts 16:1; Gal. 2:3).

Bibliography. J. Boardman, G. Jasper, and M. Oswyn, eds., *The Oxford History of the Classical World* (Oxford, 1986); J. N. Colstream, *Geometric Greece* (New York, 1977); P. E. Easterling and B. M. W. Knox, eds., *The Cambridge History of Classical Literature,* 1: *Greek Literature* (Cambridge, 1985); M. I. Finley, ed., *The Legacy of Greece* (Oxford, 1981); A. H. M. Jones, *The Greek City from Alexander to Justinian* (Oxford, 1940); A. W. Lintott, *Violence, Civil Strife and Revolution in the Classical City, 750-330 B.C.* (Baltimore, 1982); C. G. Starr, *Individual and Community: The Rise of the Polis, 800-500 B.C.* (New York, 1986); F. W. Walbank, et al., *CAH,* 2nd ed., 7/1: *The Hellenistic World* (Cambridge, 1984).

DAVID E. AUNE AND HANS SVEBAKKEN

GREEK

An inflected language in which the marking of words with prefixes and suffixes encodes the syntactical structure of the sentence. Verbs are marked to express tense, mood, voice, person, and number, while adjectives, articles, pronouns, and nouns can be marked to reflect gender, number, and case. Greek has three genders: masculine, feminine, and neuter. In addition to singular and plural, classical Greek has a dual. The eight Indo-european cases were reduced to five in Greek: nominative, vocative, accusative, genitive, and dative. Greek has three voice distinctions: active, passive, and middle.

History

The Greek language consists of several related dialects (Attic, Ionic, Doric, Aeolic) which emerged from Proto-Greek, a reconstructed Indo-european language. Migrating tribes of Achaeans, speaking Proto-Greek, arrived in the Greek peninsula ca. 2000 B.C.E., where they met and fused with the indigenous Aegeans. The earliest written form of Greek is called Linear B, preserved on clay tablets found on Crete and mainland Greece and dating from the Minoan and Mycenaean period (1450-1200). The collapse of Mycenaean civilization (ca. 1250) was followed by the arrival of groups of less culturally advanced Dorian Greeks, causing a cultural upheaval which introduced the Greek Dark Ages (ca. 1100-950), during which writing was forgotten. Toward the end of the 8th century, written Greek again appeared in the form of an alphabetic script borrowed from the 22-character Phoenician alphabet, with the addition of four distinctively Greek letters.

The dominant Greek dialect of the Hellenistic and Roman periods is called Koine ("common") Greek, based primarily on 4th-century Attic Greek. Attic became the most important Greek dialect because of the political and military dominance of Athens during the 5th century. Koine was the official language of all the Hellenistic kingdoms founded by Alexander's successors, and was used as the language of government, commerce, and education, as well as of the ruling elite and the higher strata of society because Greek language and culture were thought superior to other languages. There is no evidence that written Koine had local dialects, though there was much lexical and phonological variation. The uniform character of the written language contributed to the standardization of the spoken language.

Greek in the Near East

During the Mycenaean and Minoan periods, mainland Greece and Crete had extensive commercial contacts with the Near East. The Mycenaeans brought their language to Cyprus, for the Arcado-Cypriote dialect is known from inscriptions in the Cypriote syllabary. Though contact was interrupted by the dissolution of Mycenaean-Minoan civilization, commercial contacts were renewed and extended when Greek city-states began extensive colonization in the 8th century. Throughout the Hellenistic cities of Egypt and Syria-Palestine, the middle- and upper-class Greeks lived in relative isolation from the natives, minimizing the influence of indigenous languages. Greek continued to be spoken in the Hellenistic cities in the former Persian Empire, such as Seleucia on the Tigris and Susa.

Both Latin and Greek were used in the administration of eastern Roman provinces. In the Greek East the use of the Greek language was dominant, and it was the language of local Roman administration in the provinces. In the Greek-speaking provinces, even official Roman documents were routinely written in Greek, though public works inscriptions were usually in Latin. Latin was also the medium used for communication between the central government and Roman magistrates and between Roman magistrates and Roman colonies.

In Ptolemaic Egypt Greco-Macedonian immigrants settled in the two new centers of Hellenism, Alexandria in the north and Ptolemais in the south, as well as in the ancient port of Naucratis. However, most settled in primarily rural regions along the Nile. The preservation of nonliterary Greek papyri in Egypt from the 3rd century B.C.E. through the 3rd century C.E. provides an important avenue into the written Koine of this period. During the 3rd century B.C.E. the Torah and some other parts of the Hebrew Bible were translated into a Greek version called the Septuagint (LXX). The evidence from inscriptions indicates little dialectic difference in the Koine of Egypt, Asia Minor, Italy, and Syria-Palestine. Low-status Egyptian natives continued to speak Egyptian until the 3rd century C.E. In the 2nd century the Egyptian language, at this stage known as Coptic, began to be written using Greek characters and was heavily dependent on other aspects of Greek. As much as 20 percent of the Coptic lexicon consists of Greek loanwords, and some Greek verbs were adapted to Coptic morphology. Upper-class administrators and aristocrats as well as the lower social classes (especially in Upper Egypt) were generally monolingual.

After the death of Alexander in 323 B.C.E.,

Coele-Syria, Syria, Phoenicia, and Palestine were controlled by Ptolemaic Egypt until conquered by the Seleucids in 201; Koine Greek was the administrative language of both the Ptolemies and Seleucids. From the 3rd century on, most of the inscriptions found in Syria-Palestine are in Greek. The Zenon Papyri (259-257) reflect the relationship between the Jew Tobias and Egyptian authorities. One of the oldest dated Greek inscriptions is from Jaffa in honor of Ptolemy IV, and is dated to 217. Though there were enclaves of Hellenistic culture in the Hellenistic cities in Galilee such as Sepphoris and the more northerly cities of the Decapolis, including Antiochia Hippos, Abila, Gadara, Pella, and Beth-shean, no clear picture has yet emerged regarding the exact nature of the relationship between Jewish and Hellenistic cultural worlds in Upper and Lower Galilee during the 1st century C.E.

Many Greek settlers had settled in the Phoenician coastal cities during the 3rd century B.C.E. The traditional bilingualism of these cities was replaced with a Hellenistic Koine monolingualism, though Palestine generally during the Hellenistic and Roman period was bilingual; most people spoke both Aramaic and Greek. Hellenistic Koine was spoken and written by all social classes. The use of Greek in Palestine during the Roman period has been intensely investigated because of the problem of the language or languages spoken by Jesus and the more general problem of the extent to which Palestinian Judaism was Hellenized. Jesus certainly spoke Aramaic, probably Hebrew, and possibly Greek. Hebrew was a spoken language in Palestine until the Mishnaic period, though how widely it was used remains unclear. Both Hebrew and Greek were considered prestige languages in different social contexts. During the 2nd and 1st centuries B.C.E., Hebrew was used as a literary language, by the authors of Daniel, Ben Sira, and many of the Dead Sea Scrolls. Even among the Qumran literature, however, a number of Greek manuscripts were found dating from the mid-2nd century B.C.E. to as late as the mid-1st century C.E., including fragments of four LXX scrolls; and a scroll of the Minor Prophets in Greek was discovered at Naḥal Ḥever. Two of the 15 Bar Kokhba letters (written 132-35 C.E.) from Naḥal Ḥever are written in Greek, and the Babata archive from Naḥal Ḥever consists of 36 or 37 documents written from ca. 93-132 C.E. in Nabatean, Aramaic, and Greek. The 221 Greek inscriptions from Beth-shearim in Galilee (3rd and 4th centuries C.E.) far outnumber those in Hebrew and Aramaic. The fact that there are ca. 1500 Greek loanwords in talmudic literature underlines the widespread use of Greek by Jews during the 1st centuries C.E.

Bibliography. D. E. Aune, "Greek," *OEANE* 2:434-40; J. A. Fitzmyer, "The Languages of Palestine in the First Century A.D.," in *A Wandering Aramean* (1979, repr. Grand Rapids, 1997), 29-56; W. Horbury and D. Noy, *Jewish Inscriptions of Graeco-Roman Egypt* (Cambridge, 1992); G. H. R. Horsley, "The Fiction of 'Jewish Greek,'" in *New Documents Illustrating Early Christianity* (Marrickville, New South Wales, 1989), 5:5-40; G. Mussies, "Greek in Palestine and the Diaspora," in *The Jewish People in the First Century* 2, ed. S. Safrai and M. Stern. CRINT 1 (Philadelphia, 1976), 1040-64; L. R. Palmer, *The Greek Language* (1980, repr. Norman, 1996); J. N. Sevenster, *Do You Know Greek?* NovTSup 17 (Leiden, 1968); B. Spolsky, "Triglossia and Literacy in Jewish Palestine of the First Century," *International Journal of the Sociology of Language* 42 (1983): 95-109.

DAVID E. AUNE

GREEK VERSIONS

One of the main reasons for the rise of multiple Greek versions of the Hebrew Scriptures in the early centuries C.E. was the theological discussions between Jewish and Christian scholars. However, revision of the Old Greek (so-called Septuagint or LXX) translation and/or new translations of books probably were initiated even before the beginning of the Common Era. This is known because some of the books in the LXX exhibit a close relationship with the translational characteristics in other books that are attributed to Theodotion. The fact that citations of Theodotion's material appear in the NT means that the material attributed to him must have been produced even earlier. In contrast to the Old Greek, which at times has wide departures from MT, Theodotion's version exhibits a close formal correspondence to MT. Thus, it is probable that another reason for the production of Greek versions at the beginning of the Common Era was the existence of multiple Semitic forms of some biblical books.

Beside Theodotion, there are two other famous revisions of the LXX. Aquila (128 C.E.) produced an extremely literal translation of the Hebrew. He attempted to maintain a one-to-one correspondence between the Hebrew and Greek words. In contrast to Aquila, Symmachus (late 2nd century) provided a revision that was more in the style of everyday Greek while still rendering the Hebrew text faithfully.

The primary source of knowledge of the work of Theodotion, Aquila, and Symmachus is readings preserved from the Hexapla, which was composed by Origen (ca. 230-240). In six parallel columns Origen set out: 1) the Hebrew text as he knew it; 2) a Greek transliteration of the Hebrew; 3) Aquila; 4) Symmachus; 5) the LXX; and 6) Theodotion. Origen employed Aristarchian symbols to indicate the relationship between the LXX and the Hebrew text. Greek words that had no counterpart in his Hebrew text were placed between an obelus and metobelus, while translations of Hebrew words that had no counterpart in the LXX were inserted in the text from another version (usually Theodotion) and marked by an asterisk and a metobelus. An important witness to Origen's work in the Syro-Hexaplar, a very literal translation of the 5th column into Syriac by the bishop of Tella (618).

Jerome mentions two other recensions: one by Hesychius for use in Egypt and the other by Lucian for Antioch. There is no evidence to confirm the existence of the former, while the latter can only be isolated in certain books.

Bibliography. S. Jellicoe, *The Septuagint and Modern Study* (1968, repr. Winona Lake, 1993).

TIM MCLAY

GUARD
As a verb (Heb. *šāmar*), "to watch over" or "pay careful attention to"; most frequently "to keep (safe), guard, preserve," "to watch out for (oneself)." Thus, Adam is charged with guarding the garden of Eden (Gen. 2:15; NRSV "keep") in light of the possible intrusion of evil, and God guards against Adam's return to the garden after the Fall (3:24). The verb is used both for God and humans protecting someone from danger (1 Sam. 2:9; 25:21; Neh. 4:22) and for keeping one's own nation (Isa. 26:2) or life (Prov. 10:17) from spiritual or moral danger. In this regard the appeal to the people of God is "to pay careful attention to" the words and ways of the Lord (Lev. 22:31; Deut. 4:40; Jer. 35:18; Ezek. 18:19). The term is also frequently used for guarding prisoners (Josh. 10:18) or sacred property (1 Chr. 9:23). The noun *mišmereṯ* bears the technical sense of levitical service at the sanctuary (e.g., Num. 8:26; 1 Chr. 9:27; Ezek. 40:46).

The participle and noun forms of *šmr* refer to official city watchmen (Isa. 21:11-12), gate guards (Neh. 4:22; cf. 7:3), and night watchmen (Ps. 63:6[MT 7]). The term is also used for court and cultic personnel such as gatekeepers (1 Kgs. 14:27), temple guards (2 Kgs. 12:10), field watchmen (Jer. 4:17), harem guards (Esth. 2:3, 8, 14), wardrobe managers (2 Kgs. 22:14 = 2 Chr. 34:22), and prison guards (2 Sam. 20:3; Jer. 51:12). In like manner, God takes official responsibility to protect those under his covenant as the "keeper" of Israel (Ps. 121:4), a notion so established that it became the object of the high priestly blessing for the nation (Num. 6:24).

In the NT Gk. *phylássō* and its derivatives are used for protecting the flock (Luke 2:8) and guarding prisoners (Acts 12:4; 23:35) and for the divine protection afforded the Son (John 17:12) or the saints (2 Thess. 3:3; 2 Tim. 1:12). Individuals are admonished to guard against harmful habits and practices (Luke 12:15; Acts 21:25) or to keep the commandments of God and Christ (Matt. 19:20 par.) or the apostles (Acts 16:4). Other NT terms refer to the soldier guarding the tomb of Jesus (Matt. 27:65; 28:11), the bodyguard of Herod Antipas (Mark 6:27), and the court officials (Matt. 5:25; 26:58; Mark 14:54, 65).

J. RANDALL PRICE

GUARD, COURT OF THE
A room or open area in the palace compound (Heb. *ḥăṣar hammaṭṭārâ*) where prisoners (such as Jeremiah) were detained during the Babylonian siege of Jerusalem (e.g., Jer. 32:8, 12; 38:6, 13, 28).

GUDGODAH (Heb. *guḏgōḏâ*)
(also HOR-HAGGIDGAD)
A place where the Israelites encamped during the wilderness wanderings (Deut. 10:7; LXX Gk. *Gadgad*); the first site mentioned after Moserah (Moseroth) where Aaron died. At Num. 33:32-33 it is called Hor-haggidgad.

GUNI (Heb. *gûnî*)
1. A son of Naphtali who settled with the Israelites in Egypt (Gen. 46:24; 1 Chr. 7:13); eponymous ancestor of the Gunites (Num. 26:48).
2. A Gadite, the father of Abdiel (1 Chr. 5:15).

GUR (Heb. *gûr*)
An ascent near Ibleam where Jehu fatally wounded King Ahaziah of Judah (2 Kgs. 9:27). Ahaziah was fleeing Jezreel south on the road to Beth-haggan (modern Jenin). The ascent was likely named for a nearby site. Gur may be identified with Khirbet en-Najjar (178205), which overlooks the eastern approach of Wadi Belameh, which passes between Beth-haggan and the Samaria mountains.

C. SHAUN LONGSTREET

GURBAAL (Heb. *gûr-bā'al*)
An Arab town, captured by King Uzziah in his campaign to secure Judah's western and southern boundaries (2 Chr. 26:6-8). It is probably located in the vicinity of Edom.

GYMNASIUM
A Greek institution where young men in the nude trained their bodies, minds, and souls through bodily exercise. Ancient sources note how inseparable the gymnasium was from the Greek way of life and from Greek cities (Strabo *Geog.* 5.4.7; Pausanias *Descr. Gr.* 10.4.1). The gymnasium was associated with homosexual behavior, especially pedophilia, and many Romans saw the gymnasium as a place where their youth were corrupted (Cicero *Tusc. disp.* 4.70; *De leg.* 4.4.4; Tacitus *Ann.* 14.20.4). There are no NT references to the gymnasium (but cf. *gymnázō*, "train," used metaphorically in 1 Tim. 4:7; Heb. 5:14; 12:11; 2 Pet. 2:14; *gymnasía*, "physical training," referring to ascetic disciplines in 1 Tim. 4:8).

Of particular historical significance to Judaism was the introduction of gymnasiums in Judea in the 2nd century B.C. The construction of a gymnasium in Jerusalem led to the denial of the holy covenant by many Judean Jews under the reign of Antiochus Epiphanes IV (175-164; 1 Macc. 1:10-15). Jewish participation in the gymnasium was synonymous with removal of circumcision and assimilation of pagan ways (2 Macc. 4:7-17). Introduction of this Greek institution fomented conservative Jewish reaction against assimilation, which in turn bred Jewish sects in the mid-2nd century B.C.

Bibliography. R. E. Wycherley, *How the Greeks Built Cities*, 2nd ed. (New York, 1976).

RICHARD E. OSTER, JR.

H

H
Symbol for the Holiness Code, a body of legal material (Lev. 17–26) within that portion of the Pentateuch attributed to the Priestly source.

HAAHASHTARI (Heb. *hā'ăḥaštārî*)
The offspring of Ashhur and Naarah (1 Chr. 4:6). This otherwise unknown family is listed among geographic and ethnic components of Judah.

HABAIAH (Heb. *ḥŏḇayyâ*) (also HOBAIAH)
A priest whose descendants returned from the Exile with Zerubbabel. Because they were unable to prove their priestly descent, they were excluded from the priesthood (Ezra 2:61-63). At Neh. 7:63 the name appears as Hobaiah.

HABAKKUK (Heb. *ḥăbaqqûq*), **BOOK OF**
The eighth of the Minor Prophets. In spite of its small size (three chapters) it has been the object of considerable scholarly debate, partly because of difficulties inherent in its historical-critical interpretation and also because it contains passages that have been productive in the development of later Jewish and Christian traditions.

Text

Several ancient witnesses to the text of Habakkuk exist in addition to the Masoretic textual tradition. Primary among these witnesses is the commentary found among the Dead Sea Scrolls (1QpHab). Another important witness to the Hebrew text is a 2nd-century Minor Prophets scroll discovered in 1955 in the Wadi Murabbaʿât. Early Greek versions also help in establishing the text. A 1st-century Greek manuscript of the Minor Prophets (8 Ḥev XII gr) including Habakkuk was discovered in the Naḥal Ḥever in 1952. These witnesses confirm the consonantal text of the MT as a firm basis for study, although considerable difficulties in understanding the text are evident, particularly in ch. 3.

Scholars have long questioned the status of Hab. 3 since a large part of this chapter is arguably more archaic than the rest of the book. This chapter's absence from 1QpHab leads some to conclude that it was a late addition to the book, but its inclusion in the early Murabbaʿât and Naḥal Ḥever scrolls makes this position less likely. Most scholars today consider ch. 3 to be an integral part of the book, while admitting that the author may have reused an older poem.

Form

The basic genres used within the book have been widely recognized: 1:2–2:4/5, complaints and responses; 2:6-19, woe oracles; 3:2-19, psalm. Within this broad structure, however, considerable debate has been generated about the relationship between the various parts. While some have seen these sections as integrally related in a unified composition, the majority of scholars believe that they reflect a gradual growth at the hand of the author and/or redactors. The decision made about these issues influences and is influenced by the understanding of the book's message and its historical context.

Recent studies have begun to examine the book's function within the grouping of the Minor Prophets and in the canon as a whole. How productive this approach will be in the long term remains to be seen.

Historical Context and Central Message

The superscription identifies the author as "Habakkuk the prophet." Nothing further is known of Habakkuk as a historical figure, although he is also mentioned in later literature such as Bel and the Dragon. Because of the author's apparent familiarity with the literary genres and ideology of the temple, some scholars have considered him to have been a prophet officially associated with the Jerusalem cult.

The only certain historical reference within the book is the mention of "the Chaldeans" in 1:6. This term normally refers to the Neo-Babylonian Empire which rose to power in the late 7th century B.C.E. and controlled Jerusalem until 538. While a wide range of other "meanings" has been ascribed to this reference — from the earlier Assyrians to the later Romans — there seems to be no compelling reason to discount this term as a historical reference.

Those who believe that an original oracle grew through additions by the prophet or redactors date parts of the work as late as the postexilic period. The most likely setting for the origin of the work is within the political turmoil in Judah at the end of the 7th century, probably shortly after the Babylonian defeat of an Egyptian force at Carchemish in 605. Jehoahaz, the previous king of Judah, had been deposed by Necho II of Egypt and replaced with Jehoiakim. Conflict within Judah between those who favored pro-Egyptian and pro-Babylonian positions was at a peak.

Identification of the anonymous figures of the "righteous" and the "wicked" found within the complaints is central to the issues of dating and the book's message. Habakkuk states that the righteous are being surrounded and swallowed by the wicked (1:4, 13). The complaints against the wicked and the later woe oracles appear at times to be directed against internal enemies; at other times they seem to envision an external threat. Some interpreters attribute the changing perspectives to chronological considerations, i.e., they reflect different periods within the experience of the author (or redactors). It is also possible that for the author a clear distinction between external and internal enemies was not appropriate. Both were considered enemies of "the righteous." This leaves open the possibility of a unified composition.

A central concern of the book is justice — certainly the justice of the enemies and possibly that of God. The book echoes the complaints of the Psalms when it asks, "How long shall I cry for help, and you will not listen?" (1:2). This question begins a conversation between the author and God concerning the nature of God's response to injustice. The prophet first complains of a lack of response (1:2-4). Most scholars understand the second complaint (1:13–2:1) to be a reaction to God's promise of raising the Chaldeans as an instrument of punishment. If the object of the second complaint is the Chaldeans, it appears that the prophet continues by complaining that the punishment is worse than the evil it is intended to correct. A high point is reached in 2:4, a verse with difficult grammatical problems: "the righteous because of its/his fidelity will live." The antecedent of the pronoun is disputed. It may be the fidelity of the righteous one himself. Others understand it to refer to the fidelity of the vision provided by God or even a reference directly to God. This passage becomes important in the later Christian tradition (cf. Rom. 1:17; Gal. 3:11; Heb. 10:38-39). In Jewish tradition this verse is considered a summary of the commands of the Torah (*b. Mak.* 23b-24a).

The third chapter concludes with a psalm describing a theophany which expresses the author's confidence that ultimately God and his justice will prevail. In light of this confidence the book ends with praise of God. Scholarly debate has questioned whether this chapter should be understood as a victory taking place outside history, making it one of the earliest eschatological texts. Another view, while admitting the cosmic nature of the events described in the theophany, understands the deliverance as occurring within the historical realm. The theophany of Hab. 3 is read during Shavuot (Weeks) in the Jewish tradition.

Bibliography. R. D. Haak, *Habakkuk*. VTSup 44 (Leiden, 1992); T. Hiebert, "The Book of Habakkuk," *NIB* 7 (1996): 621-55; J. J. M. Roberts, *Nahum, Habakkuk, and Zephaniah.* OTL (Louisville, 1991).

ROBERT D. HAAK

HABAZZINIAH (Heb. *ḥăḇaṣṣinyâ*)
The grandfather of Jaazaniah the Rechabite. He and his household were tested by the prophet Jeremiah in the Jerusalem temple (Jer. 35:3-10).

HABIRU
See HAPIRU, APIRU.

HABOR (Heb. *ḥāḇôr;* Akk. *Ḫabûr*)
A large tributary that drains into the middle Euphrates River in northeast Syria. The river originates in the mountains of southeast Turkey near Mardin. A number of large urban centers were in the lower Habor region in the 2nd millennium B.C., including Mari and Terqa, both inhabited by various Amorite tribes who practiced pastoralism. Habor was the "River of Gozan" (2 Kgs. 17:6; 18:11), the Assyrian provincial capital of Bīt Baḫiani, along the upper Habor to which the Israelites were exiled after the capture of Samaria in 721. Israelite personal names have been found in the texts excavated from Tell Halaf. MARK W. CHAVALAS

HACALIAH (Heb. *ḥăḵalyâ*)
The father of Nehemiah (Neh. 1:1; 10:1[MT 2]).

HACHILAH (Heb. *ḥăḵîlâ*)
A hill S of Jeshimon where the strongholds of Horesh were located (1 Sam. 23:19), also said to be "opposite Jeshimon" (26:1) and "E of Jeshimon" (v. 3). David sought asylum there while hiding from Saul, but hid in the desert when Saul himself camped at Hachilah (1 Sam. 26:3). Neither Hachilah nor Jeshimon has been identified, although Khirbet Khoreisa has been suggested for Horesh.

RYAN BYRNE

HACHMONI (Heb. *ḥaḵmônî*)
The father of Jehiel, who attended the sons of King David (1 Chr. 27:32). The Hebrew form is the same as that of the gentilic Hachmonite and may simply indicate his membership in that family.

HACHMONITE (Heb. *ben-ḥaḵmônî*)
The family of Jashobeam, a chief among David's warriors (1 Chr. 11:11; NRSV "son of Hachmoni"). The reading Tahchemonite at 2 Sam. 23:8 is a textual error.

HADAD (Heb. *hăḏaḏ*) **(DEITY)**
The West Semitic storm-god (Ugar. Haddu, Akk. Addu), better known by his epithet, Baal (lit., "lord"). Of paramount importance in a society dependent upon rain for agriculture, he was head of the Ugaritic pantheon; Mt. Saphon, N of Ugarit, was not only his home but also the assembly of the gods. The significance of Hadad is attested by its appearance as an element in names of ruling classes (e.g., OT Hadadezer, Ben-hadad; Akk. Šamši-adad).

MARK ANTHONY PHELPS

HADAD (Heb. *hăḏaḏ*) **(PERSON)**

1. A son of Ishmael and grandson of Abraham (Gen. 25:15 = 1 Chr. 1:30). Because he is listed between Tema and Massa, the eponymous ancestors of Northwest Arabian tribes, one would assume he was likewise the eponymous ancestor of a tribe.

2. A king of Edom, who ruled from Avith; the son of Bedad (Gen. 36:35-36 = 1 Chr. 1:46-47). He defeated the Midianites.

3. A king of Edom, later than **2** above, who was from the city of Pai/Pau (Gen. 36:39 = 1 Chr. 1:50-51).

4. An Edomite king who was an enemy of Solomon in the late 10th century B.C. (1 Kgs. 11:14-22). He escaped to Egypt during Israel's purge of Edomite males at the time of Solomon's predecessor, David. Similar to the rebel Jeroboam, the Egyptians treated Hadad with favor, thereby playing the Edomite noble against Israel.

Bibliography. J. R. Bartlett, "An Adversary Against Solomon, Hadad the Edomite," *ZAW* 88 (1976): 205-26.

MARK W. CHAVALAS

HADADEZER (Heb. *hăḏaḏʿezer*)

1. Aramean king of Zobah who was defeated by David; the son of Rehob (2 Sam. 8:3). The precise location of his city is not known, though scholars assume it was in the Beqaʿ Valley of Lebanon. It may be named in later Assyrian documents as a provincial center *(ṣubatu)* derived from the recently incorporated city of Damascus.

All that is known about this king are the accounts of his battle with David (2 Sam. 8:3-8 = 1 Chr. 18:3-8; 2 Sam. 10:1-19 = 1 Chr. 19:1-19). Zobah apparently exercised power throughout southern Syria, and inevitably clashed with the expanding empire of Israel. Eventually David was victorious, though the chronology and the result of the battle of 2 Sam. 10 are open to debate. Most scholars hold that it was the first battle, given the scope of the victory of 2 Sam. 8, in which Hadadezer is reduced to vassalage.

2. An early 9th-century king of Damascus, whom most scholars associate with Ben-hadad II.

MARK ANTHONY PHELPS

HADAD-RIMMON (Heb. *hăḏaḏ-rimmôn*)
A West Semitic deity. The name consists of the storm-god Hadad, followed by the epithet Rimmon (Akk. *rammānu,* "Thunderer"), which appears in Aramaic and Akkadian theophoric names and in the name of the king of Damascus, Tabrimmon (1 Kgs. 15:18). At 2 Kgs. 5:18 this deity, called Rimmon, appears as the state deity of Aram-Damascus. The Hebrew spelling *rimmôn* in the OT means "pomegranate," and is possibly an intentional parody.

Zech. 12:11 predicts a lamentation in Jerusalem that will be "as great as the mourning for Hadad-rimmon in the plain of Megiddo." An earlier interpretation of the verse understands Hadad-rimmon as a place name, identified by Jerome with Maximianopolis (modern el-Lejjun) or with the village of Rummâneh/Ḥorvat Rimona (179243) and assumed to be the place where Josiah was killed and later mourned (2 Chr. 35:23-25). More likely Zechariah refers to the god and an associated ritual. The ancient Near Eastern practice of cultic mourning was also observed in Israel (Ezek. 8:14). Ugaritic myth tells of El and Anat's lamentation for Baal-Hadad (as the storm-god was known at Ugarit) after his defeat by Mot ("Death") and of the resumption of rainfall and attendant fertility of the soil upon his return from the netherworld. In light of these traditions, a mourning rite for the storm-god, in anticipation of the returning productivity of the land, would have been right at home in the agriculturally rich area of the "plain of Megiddo."

JOEL BURNETT

HADASHAH (Heb. *hăḏāšâ*)
A town in the Shephelah, or lowland, of Judah, part of that tribe's inheritance (Josh. 15:39). Athough its location is unknown, it is part of the same district as Lachish and Eglon (Josh. 15:37-41). It may be the same place as Adasa, where Judas Maccabeus defeated Nicanor (1 Macc. 7:40-45).

A town named Hadashah ("new town") is also recorded in one of Shishak's inscriptions at Karnak. The location of this site is not positively identified, but on the basis of the Egyptian list, it may be within the Succoth Valley at the confluence of the Jabbok (Wadi Zerqā) and Jordan Rivers. It is unrelated to the biblical site.

Bibliography. S. Ahituv, *Canaanite Toponyms in Ancient Egyptian Documents* (Jerusalem, 1984).

JENNIFER L. GROVES

HADASSAH (Aram. *hăḏāssâ*)
The original Hebrew name for Esther (Esth. 2:7; Heb. "myrtle"). The earlier suggestion that it is a Babylonian title given her (from an epithet of the goddess Ishtar; Akk. *ḫadaššatu,* "bride") has been discounted.

HADES (Gk. *hádēs*)
Originally the name of the Greek god of the underworld, but later the name of the underworld itself. Found in Homer, numerous Greek papyri, the LXX, Philo, and Josephus, as well as the NT, it is translated "hell" in most English versions of the Bible. In the LXX Hades is the name used for Sheol.

In Greek religion Hades was the place where the dead went, located in the belly of the earth. It was entered through gates which were kept fast by locks which only a limited number of beings could open.

In Matt. 16 Peter is given the keys to the gates of hell; in Rev. 1 Jesus controls the keys of hell.

Hades became in Hellenistic thought a place of torment. It is this understanding of hell as the torture chamber of eternity which influenced the NT writers.
JIM WEST

HADID (Heb. *ḥāḏîḏ*) (also ADIDA)
A small city in the coastal plain, close to Lod (Ezra 2:33; Neh. 7:37). The Mishnah places it E of Diospolis/Lydda/Lod (*m. ʿArak.* 9:6). A number of Benjaminites who returned with Zerubbabel from exile in Babylon settled in Hadid (Neh. 11:34). Simon Maccabeus fortified the city, known in the Maccabean period as Adida (1 Macc. 12:38; 13:13). The site is today identified with Tel Ḥadid/el-Ḥadîtheh (145152).

Bibliography. M. Avi-Yonah, *The Holy Land,* rev. ed. (Grand Rapids, 1977).
DAVID C. MALTSBERGER

HADLAI (Heb. *ḥaḏlāy*)
The father of the Ephraimite Amasa, who would not accept Judahite captives following Ahaz' defeat by Damascus and Pekah of Israel (2 Chr. 28:12).

HADORAM (Heb. *hăḏôrām*)
(also ADONIRAM, ADORAM, JORAM)

1. A descendant of Joktan; ancestor of an Arabian tribe (Gen. 10:27; 1 Chr. 1:21).

2. The son of King Tou of Hamath, who was sent by his father to congratulate David on his victory over Hadadezer (1 Chr. 18:10). At 2 Sam. 8:10 he and his father are called Joram (**1**) and Toi.

3. An official of King Rehoboam who was taskmaster over the forced labor (2 Chr. 10:18). At 1 Kgs. 4:6; 5:14(MT 28) he is called Adoniram and at 12:18 Adoram, a shortened form of that name.

HADRACH (Heb. *ḥaḏrāḵ*)
A city in northern Syria, near modern Tell Afis, 45 km. (30 mi.) SW of Aleppo. Hadrach occurs once in the Bible, in a prophetic announcement of the destruction of various Philistine, Syrian, and Phoenician territories (Zech. 9:1-8). In an Aramaic inscription (ca. 800 B.C.E.) Zakir king of Hamath and Luʿash lauds Baalshamayn for granting him kingship in Hadrach (Aram. *Ḥazraḵ*) and also for defending him and the city of Hadrach from the coalition of Bar-hadad, son of Hazael. The Assyrian eponym chronicle mentions a campaign of Shalmaneser IV to Hadrach (ca. 772). One of Tiglath-pileser III's annals refers to his subjugation of Hadrach, and the city appears in a victory stele of Sargon II. The reference to Hadrach in Zechariah may allude to the earlier historical circumstances of the late 8th century.

Bibliography. J. C. L. Gibson, *Textbook of Syrian Semitic Inscriptions,* 2: *Aramaic Inscriptions* (Oxford, 1975); W. T. Pitard, *Ancient Damascus* (Winona Lake, 1987).
CHRIS A. ROLLSTON

HADRIAN
Ruler of the Roman Empire from 117-138 C.E. and a distant relative of his predecessor, the emperor Trajan. Hadrian succeeded Trajan with few objections since he was popular with the court and he had a letter, allegedly written by Trajan on his deathbed, designating him as heir.

Hadrian was from the province of Spain, like Trajan, and his origins may in part explain the attention he paid throughout his emperorship to provincial administration and improvement. Little expense was spared on public building in the provinces, and much was done to improve frontier fortification and defensive works. Hadrian's Wall on the boundary of England and Scotland is but one example of the massive fortifications Hadrian undertook. In fact, Hadrian supposedly spent more time in the provinces than in Rome.

Hadrian's reign witnessed the Bar Kokhba Revolt in Judea (132-135). When the revolt was finally crushed, all Jews were expelled from the province, which ceased to be named Judea and became Syria Palestina. Regarding Christianity, Hadrian maintained Trajan's policy of tolerance, as evidenced in the emperor's correspondence (122-123) with Minicius Fundanus, proconsul of Asia.

Bibliography. S. Perowne, *Hadrian* (1960, repr. London, 1986).
JOHN F. HALL

HA-ELEPH (Heb. *hāʾelep̄*)
A Benjaminite town in the vicinity of Jerusalem (Josh. 18:28). On the basis of LXX A (Gk. *Sēlaleph*), the name is probably to be read Zela-eleph.

See ZELA.

HAGAB (Heb. *ḥāḡāḇ*)
A temple servant whose descendants returned from exile with Zerubbabel (Ezra 2:46).

HAGABAH (Heb. *ḥăḡāḇâ*) (also HAGABA)
The head of a family of temple servants who returned from the Exile under Zerubbabel (Ezra 2:45; Neh. 7:48, NRSV "Hagaba").

HAGAR (Heb. *hāḡār*)
An Egyptian woman, servant to the matriarch Sarai. The story of Hagar, representing two strands of tradition in Gen. 16, 21, is one of status competition, surrogate motherhood, ethnic conflict, class struggle, abuse, exile, and triumph.

The barren Sarai gives Hagar to Abram "as a wife" (Gen. 16:3), making any would-be offspring a legal heir according to contemporary Mesopotamian law. Sarai comes to rue the day she manipulated such a union. Hagar, upon conceiving, scorns Sarai (Gen. 16:4), driving Sarai to abuse her in return. Hagar flees into the desert wilderness, pregnant and on foot, headed 240 km. (150 mi.) south to Shur. The angel of the Lord sends her back to Sarai with promises similar to those made to Abraham, Isaac, and Jacob. Her son, to be named Ishmael, would produce offspring too numerous to count (Gen. 16:10) — 12 tribes which would become a great nation (17:20).

Some years later (Gen. 21:8-21), at the weaning of Isaac, Sarah notices Ishmael laughing or playing with him. The incident, though positive, is interpreted by Sarah as bearing threat to Isaac's inheritance. She asks Abraham to rid her family of Hagar and Ishmael once and for all. Hagar, finding herself once again in the wilderness without sustenance, leaves Ishmael to die (here her son's age doesn't quite fit the context). Once again, God intervenes, providing food and water and reiterating the earlier promises to Hagar. She later finds an Egyptian wife for her near-grown son.

The Apostle Paul later allegorizes the story of Sarah and Hagar (Gal. 4:21-31) to portray Sarah's literal descendants as enslaved (like Hagar) to the old covenant, while Sarah's descendants by faith (and promise) become the essence of the new covenant of freedom. Ironically, to make his analogy work, Paul, like so many commentators before and since, overlooks the ambiguous faithfulness of both Sarah and Hagar.

Bibliography. A. O. Bellis, *Helpmates, Harlots, Heroes* (Louisville, 1994); P. E. Tarlow and E. C. Want, "Bad Guys, Textual Errors and Wordplays in Genesis 21:9-10," *Journal of Reform Judaism* 37/4 (1990): 21-29; P. Trible, "Hagar: The Desolation of Rejection," in *Texts of Terror.* OBT 13 (Philadelphia, 1984), 9-35; C. Westermann, *Genesis 12-36* (Minneapolis, 1985).

JAMES E. BRENNEMAN

HAGGADAH (Heb. *haggaḏâ*)

A noun usually understood to come from the Hebrew root *ngd,* "to tell," "correspond to," or "be in front of." Haggadah (in the Palestinian Talmud "Aggadah") is used for a number of different phenomena. As a type of midrash it is to be distinguished from Halakhah, which is primarily concerned with issues of ritual, ethical, and civil law. In contrast, midrashic Haggadah comprises almost all other types of biblical exegesis. The term Haggadah is also used to refer to almost any nonlegal text in the rabbinic corpus of literature and, as a result, it can connote biblical exegesis, stories about famous rabbis, and other rather imaginative literature that does not of necessity include biblical interpretation. With all this in mind, caution must be exercised in employing the term.

Generally, Haggadah is understood to be further contrasted with Halakhah in that the former is not binding and authoritative in the same way as is Halakhah. To whatever degree this is true, it would be a mistake to underestimate the religious nature of Haggadah. In particular, as imaginative interpretation, Haggadah is driven by the search for God in practically every word and syllable. Moreover, the playful nature of Haggadah has a religious quality missed by those with too narrow a definition of what comprises theological reflection. In many ways, Haggadah can be understood as a celebration of the religious significance of the slightest detail in Scripture and in Jewish tradition in general.

LARRY L. LYKE

HAGGAI (Heb. *ḥaggai*), **BOOK OF**

The tenth book of the so-called Book of the Twelve, the Minor Prophets of the Hebrew Bible. Haggai, which means "festival" or "of a festival," is the name of the prophet whose oracles comprise the book and may indicate that he was born on a feast day. No biographical information is provided, although he and his contemporary (First) Zechariah are mentioned in Ezra 5:1; 6:14 and are referred to in the 3rd person in the narrative frameworks in which their oracles are set.

Haggai is also linked to First Zechariah by the unique arrangement of date formulas that provide the literary structure of Haggai and Zech. 1–8. Unlike chronological information in other biblical books (Kings/Chronicles and several other prophets), in which events are keyed to the reigns of Israelite or Judean monarchs, the dates in Haggai and First Zechariah are linked to the regnal years of a foreign imperial ruler, Darius I (522-486 B.C.E.), the first of three men named Darius who headed the Achaemenid Empire. This chronological relating of prophetic oracle to Persian power is striking indication of the political situation in Yehud, the postexilic province containing the capital Jerusalem and part of the former southern kingdom of Judah. Although his words are directed to the two main leaders of Yehud — the governor Zerubbabel and the high priest Joshua — as well as to the community in general, Haggai was nonetheless acutely aware of Yehud's political status as part of a foreign empire rather than as the autonomous kingdom that its predecessor Judah had been for nearly half a millennium, since the days of King David.

The first of the five date formulas in Haggai (followed by three in Zechariah) appears in 1:1, which refers to the first day of the sixth month of Darius I's reign (29 August 520). The last formula, in 2:20, mentions (as does the fourth formula, 2:10) the date of 18 December 520, several months later. The specificity of the dates probably reflects the prophet's knowledge of and sensitivity to the oracles of earlier prophets. Jeremiah had referred to an expected 70-year period of desolation after the destruction of the First Temple in 587/586 (Jer. 25:11-12; 29:10). In 520 the imminence of the end of that period must have figured prominently in Haggai's thinking. Convinced of Yahweh's purposeful control of human affairs, he apparently saw in the emergence of the Persian Empire and its seemingly beneficent granting of semi-autonomy to many of its provinces the signals of the anticipated dawn of a new era. The fact that the dyarchic leadership structure of Yehud consisted of a priestly figure, in continuation of preexilic or even premonarchic Israelite governance, along with a political figure who was a Davidic scion, likewise encouraged Haggai's future-oriented oracles and his sense that Yehud's provincial status was only temporary and that the end of the seven decades of exile and ruin would mean the inauguration of restored independence and prosperity.

In addition to its unusual date formulas and its close thematic and lexical connections with Zech. 1–8, the book of Haggai shares with First Zechariah a literary texture that is difficult to characterize. For the most part it reads as prose, yet certain passages (e.g., 1:5-10) are rather poetic in structure, thereby lending a poetic flair to the whole, perhaps so the oracles might conform with the largely poetic prototype of earlier prophecy. The term "oracular prose," or perhaps "elevated prose," may best represent Haggai's work. The intermingling of poetic and prose sections represents the creative impulse of a prophetic figure acutely aware of the form as well as the content of his prophetic legacy.

The book of Haggai has two major parts. The first deals with the restoration of the temple and consists of two sections: 1:1-11; 1:12-15a. The second is composed of oracles of encouragement, which can be subdivided into three sections: 1:15b–2:9; 2:10-19; 2:20-23. Each of the five sub-units is associated with one of the five chronological headings, perhaps indicating separate prophetic events or proclamations. Although each of the sub-units has its own integrity, together they provide a progression of events and ideas that form a unified whole.

Prophetic Call to Work on the Temple (1:1-11)

The opening oracle links the adverse political and economic conditions of postexilic Judah with the fact that the temple, which was destroyed by the Babylonians in 587/586, still lies in ruins. Haggai attempts to convince the people that the great disparity between their expectations for a thriving restored community and the reality of economic hardship will be ameliorated if they attend to the temple, the symbol of God's presence among them. He urges that they undertake a temple reconstruction project. His oracular call to begin this project is grounded in the belief, common in the ancient Near East, that blessings will flow when the sacred center of a community — the place where its deity resides — is functioning as the locus of divine power on earth.

Response of Leaders and People (1:12-15a)

Haggai's audience responds positively to his exhortation, whereupon he assures them that God is with them in their task. The alacrity of their response is clear from the date formula with which this section closes: less than a month after Haggai's plea, the people have decided to obey God's voice as communicated by the words of the prophet.

Assurance of God's Presence (1:15b–2:9)

The second part of the book begins with further assurance that God's beneficence is with them and that they should be encouraged in the work of reconstructing the temple. Once restored, God's house will affect all humankind, for all nations will ultimately recognize Yahweh as God. The solution to the immediate problems besetting Yehud will have universal implications.

Priestly Ruling with Interpretation (2:10-19)

This proto-rabbinic pericope reveals Second Temple concepts of defilement and impurity on the one hand, and of holiness and purity on the other. The latter properties surround God and are much more difficult to transmit than are their opposites; the former categories of uncleanness are caused by immorality, sin, or disobedience to God's word, not by physical dirt, and are unfortunately all too contagious. The arcane language of the priestly ruling becomes a vehicle for the idea that the work on the temple will affect the welfare of the land and its inhabitants. Haggai's use of complex priestly concepts probably indicates the authoritative role of the priesthood at this time as well as the familiarity of his audience with priestly views.

Future Hope (2:20-23)

The concluding oracle is uniquely directed to a single individual, the governor Zerubbabel. The mention by name of this descendent of David arouses speculation that the prophet may have expected an imminent restoration of independence for Yehud, with Zerubbabel as king. Yet the language of the oracle depicts a subsidiary role for Zerubbabel as a human ruler. He is to serve as a sort of vice-regent to Yahweh ("a signet ring" on God's hand) in a theocratic scheme involving all the nations of the world. An eschatological orientation for Haggai's final utterance is thus more likely than a historical one. Haggai perceives the community's work in restoring its sacred center as an integral part of its ultimate rule as the center of God's universal redemptive plan.

Bibliography. R. Mason, *The Books of Haggai, Zechariah and Malachi.* CBC (Cambridge, 1977); C. L. Meyers and E. M. Meyers, *Haggai, Zechariah 1–8.* AB 25B (Garden City, 1987); "Haggai-Zechariah," *NAB*, rev. ed., ed. J. Jensen et al.; D. L. Petersen, *Haggai and Zechariah 1–8.* OTL (Philadelphia, 1985); "Haggai," in *Oxford Bible Commentary,* ed. J. Barton and J. Muddiman (Oxford, 1999).

CAROL MEYERS

HAGGEDOLIM (Heb. *haggĕḏôlîm*)
The father of Zabdiel the overseer, who lived in Jerusalem after the Exile (Neh. 11:14). The Hebrew term might better be translated "the great ones."

HAGGI (Heb. *ḥaggî*)
A son of Gad and grandson of Jacob and Zilpah (Gen. 46:16); ancestor of the Haggites (Num. 26:15).

HAGGIAH (Heb. *ḥaggîyâ*)
A Levite, descendant of Merari (1 Chr. 6:30[MT 15]).

HAGGITH (Heb. *ḥaggîṯ*)
One of the wives of David; the mother of Adonijah (2 Sam. 3:4 = 1 Chr. 3:2; 1 Kgs. 1:5, 11; 2:13).

HAGIOGRAPHA
The Greek word ("sacred writings") given by the church fathers to the books in the third division of the Hebrew Bible (Heb. *kĕṯûḇîm,* "Writings"). The Hagiographa include the "poetical" or wisdom books (Psalms, Proverbs, and Job), the "Five Scrolls" or Megilloth (Song of Songs, Ruth, Lamentations, Ecclesiastes, and Esther), the apocalyptic book of Daniel, and the historiographic books of

Ezra-Nehemiah and 1-2 Chronicles. The canonical order of the Hagiographa was not set until the late medieval period. A number of medieval Hebrew manuscripts differ in their placement of Chronicles, the order of Job and Proverbs, and the arrangement of the Five Scrolls, although the Five Scrolls are found together from about the 11th century C.E. The Leningrad Codex, e.g., places Chronicles at the beginning of the Writings, puts Job before Proverbs, and arranges the Five Scrolls in the order Ruth, Song of Songs, Ecclesiastes, Lamentations, and Esther. The Megilloth, read during Jewish feasts and fasts, are arranged in the modern canon to follow the liturgical order in which they are used: the Song of Songs on the eighth day of Passover; Ruth on the second day of Weeks, or Pentecost; Lamentations on the ninth day of Ab, which mourns the destruction of the temple; Ecclesiastes on the third day of Tabernacles; and Esther on Purim.

Bibliography. D. F. Morgan, *Between Text and Community: The "Writings" in Canonical Interpretation* (Minneapolis, 1990); J. A. Sanders, *Torah and Canon* (Philadelphia, 1972). MARILYN J. LUNDBERG

HAGRI (Heb. *hagrî*)
The father of Mibhar, one of David's warriors (1 Chr. 11:38). The parallel account (2 Sam. 23:36) reads "Bani the Gadite." Either Heb. *bny hgdy* in 2 Sam. 23:36 or *bn hgry* in 1 Chr. 11:38 is a textual corruption.

HAGRITES (Heb. *hagrî'îm*)
A pastoralist tribe residing in the region E of Gilead. Ps. 83:6(MT 7) enumerates Hagrites among other Transjordanian enemies of Israel from the preexilic era. In the time of King Saul the Hebrew tribes of Reuben, Gad, and half-Manasseh took control of Hagrite territory (1 Chr. 5:18-22). King David seems to have won the loyalty of at least some of them, since he gave oversight of the royal flocks to Jaziz, a Hagrite (1 Chr. 27:30). An ethnographic relationship between the Hagrites and the woman Hagar is uncertain (Bar. 3:23, "the children/descendants of Hagar").

EDWIN C. HOSTETTER

HAIR
Hair and fashion have always been important. While the Egyptians shaved their heads, the Hebrews and their neighbors favored long hair and beards, as in the case of Absalom (2 Sam. 14:26) and Jehu (note his long hair and beard on the Black Obelisk). By NT times, Greek and Roman males wore short hair and were beardless, while Roman women had highly individualistic hair styles (1 Cor. 11:6). Most well-to-do women wore their hair braided or plaited (1 Tim. 2:9; 1 Pet. 3:3), and some wore a head covering (1 Cor. 11:6). In Rome, wigs were common among wealthy women. Caracalla's wife, Plautilla, was represented in statue with removable hair so as to enable her to maintain the current fashion.

Perhaps the best-known biblical example concerning hair and religion is that of the Nazarite vow (Num. 6), whereby the participant swore an oath not to cut his hair (e.g., Samson, Judg. 16:13-31). While priests must never shave their heads (Ezek. 44:20), newly cleansed lepers must do so (Lev. 14:8). The color of the hair of infected skin determined whether the disease was leprosy (Lev. 13). Ceremonial cutting of the hair for the purpose of dedicating it to idols was repeatedly forbidden (Lev. 19:27; Jer. 9:26; Ezek. 5:1). Even the Apostle Paul had taken a Nazarite-type vow, which was consummated by a haircut (Acts 18:18). In both the OT and NT God was envisioned with hair "white like wool" (Dan. 7:9; Rev. 1:14).

The head and, therefore, its hair was the object of anointing with oil (Ps. 45:7[MT 8]) and mourning. In grief the hair could be pulled out (Ezra 9:3) or covered with dust and ashes. Mary anointed Jesus' feet with expensive perfume using her own hair (Luke 7:38; John 11:2), thereby showing both love and hospitality.

Hair also provided an effective medium for communicating idiomatic language (e.g., Matt. 10:30 par.; Luke 21:18) as well as common metaphor or simile. DONALD FOWLER

HAKKATAN (Heb. *haqqāṭān*)
A descendant of Azgad; the father of Johanan, who returned from Babylon with Ezra (Ezra 8:12; 1 Esdr. 8:38).

HAKKOZ (Heb. *haqqôṣ*)
1. The head of the seventh division of priests during the time of David (1 Chr. 24:10).

2. A postexilic family who returned with Zerubbabel from the Exile. Most were excluded from the priesthood because they could not prove their priestly descent (Ezra 2:61-62; Neh. 7:63-64); however, it appears from 3:4, 21 that priestly descent was proven for some.

HAKUPHA (Heb. *ḥăqûpā'*)
A temple servant whose family returned from the Exile with Zerubbabel (Ezra 2:51 = Neh. 7:53).

HALAH (Heb. *ḥălaḥ;* Akk. *Ḫalaḫḫu*)
An area to which Israelites were deported after 720 B.C.E. by Sargon II (2 Kgs. 17:6) and subsequently by Shalmaneser II (18:11) and Tiglath-pileser III (1 Chr. 5:26). This deportation is not reflected in Assyrian inscriptions. Fields in Halah (modern Tell al-ʿAbbāsīya), NE of the Assyrian heartland, belonged to the king. Inhabitants were obliged to perform *dullu*-duties (agricultural) for the king. Most probably Israelites were deported to Halah to assist with the Assyrian food supply.

Bibliography. B. Becking, *The Fall of Samaria*. SHANE 2 (Leiden, 1992), 62-64. BOB BECKING

HALAK, MOUNT (Heb. *hāhār heḥālāq*)
A mountain in the central Negeb demarcating the southern extent of Joshua's conquest of Canaanite territory (Josh. 11:17; 12:7). Mt. Halak is said to rise toward Seir (Edom) and may be identified with

modern Jebel Halâq, which likely preserves the place name. Ryan Byrne

HALAKHAH (Heb. *hălāḵâ*)
The teaching one is to follow, usually understood to be from the Hebrew root *hlk,* "to walk" or "go forth." Generally, Halakhah is defined in contrast to Haggadah, both of which represent the two major divisions of Midrash. While there is considerable overlap between the two, Halakhah tends to concentrate on legal matters of ritual, ethical, and civil nature and Haggadah on more discursive literary and religious concerns. Halakhah is the means by which often ambiguous legal passages are clarified and interpreted for application in new and changed circumstances. Halakhah is the name given not only to the method of midrashic interpretation applied to legal material, but also the name given to the collections of literature produced thereby. The halakhic midrashim deal with Exodus through Deuteronomy. Moreover, these midrashim are often referred to as Tannaitic, since they were produced, for the most part, during the Tannaitic period that came to a close with the fixing of the Mishnah in the early 3rd century C.E. Among the halakhic midrashim are the Mekilta de Rabbi Ishmael, the Mekilta de Rabbi Simeon ben Yohai (both mekiltas on Exodus), Sifra (on Leviticus), Sifre Numbers, and Sifre Deuteronomy. A good example of halakhic midrash can be found in the Mekilta de Rabbi Ishmael, ch. 13 of tractate Nezikin dealing with Exod. 22:1-3, a passage full of ambiguities; the midrash relies on other passages in Deuteronomy, Numbers, Genesis, and Proverbs to resolve the problematic case.

Unfortunately, the use of Halakhah for specific midrashic texts masks a much broader conception of Halakhah as a way of life. By means of Halakhah the rabbis were able to interpret the significance of the Torah for daily living. Integral to the notion of Halakhah (as a procedure) is the rabbinic concept of both a written and oral Torah. According to *m. 'Abot,* Moses received the Torah in two modes; one is represented by the written Torah found in the first five books of the OT and the other by oral traditions handed down through the ages and retaining currency among the rabbis of the Tannaitic period. As a result of this understanding of Torah, Halakhah is more than simply commentary on the Pentateuch. As a mode of interpretation, Halakhah has to do with the full engagement with the word of God, in its various manifestations, in the attempt to sanctify one's every action. With this in mind, the deeply religious and liturgical nature of Halakhah and halakhic interpretation emerges.

Larry L. Lyke

HALF-TRIBE
A reference to the two segments (Heb. *ḥăṣî šēḇeṭ*) of the tribe of Manasseh. The Machirites settled in Transjordan, in the northern part of Gilead and in Bashan N of Gad's territory (Num. 32:33-42; Deut. 3:13-15; Josh. 13:8-12). The rest of Manasseh received territory W of the Jordan River, N of Ephraim, S of Asher, Zebulun, and Issachar, extending west to the Mediterranean Sea (Josh. 17:5-11).

HALHUL (Heb. *ḥalḥûl*)
A city in the tribal territory of Judah, located in the hill country near Beth-zur (Josh. 15:58). The name has been preserved in modern Ḥalḥûl (160109), 6 km. (4 mi.) N of Hebron. According to tradition, a mosque in this city contains the grave of Jonah.

HALI (Heb. *ḥălî*)
A place on the boundary of the territory allotted to Asher (Josh. 19:25). Although the site remains uncertain, it may be Khirbet Râs Ali/Tel ʿAlil (164241), S of Tell el-Harbaj/Tel Regev (Achsaph).

HALICARNASSUS (Gk. *Halikarnassos*)
A leading city and capital on the southwestern coast of Caria in Asia Minor, modern Budrum, Turkey. It was one of six colonies founded by Dorians ca. 900 B.C.E. By the 5th century, however, the city had become Ionic (with a strong local Carian element). Because of its advantageous location, it was subject to frequent plundering and siege. Halicarnassus is famous as the home of the 5th-century Greek poet Panyassis and the historians Herodotus and Dionysius. It was the site of one of the Seven Wonders of the Ancient World, the architectural marvel called the Mausoleum with its exquisite statues which Artemisia II had built in 352 for her husband Mausolus, who had incorporated a number of villages into a single city and made it his capital.

Though it was a Greek city, Jews had favorable status there under the Romans. In 139 the senate sent a letter renewing its friendship and alliance with them (1 Macc. 15:23), and they were granted religious liberty and allowed to build a house of prayer near the sea (Josephus *Ant.* 14.10.23).

Richard A. Spencer

HALLEL
A litany of praise psalms used in Jewish festivals or morning services. Heb. *hallēl* is derived from the verb "to praise," which occurs as a command ("praise thou") in various Psalms.

The "Egyptian Hallel" (cf. Ps. 114:1) comprises Pss. 113–118. It is used in its entirety on Sukkoth, Hanukkah, the first day of Passover, and Shabuʿoth. At the Passover seder it is recited in two parts, Pss. 113–114 before the seder and 115–118 afterward. Praise is associated with Passover (2 Chr. 30:21; Wis. 18:9). It is thought that Jesus and his disciples sang from this Hallel after the Last Supper (Matt. 26:30 = Mark 14:26).

The "Great Hallel" refers to Ps. 136. It is recited at the beginning of the morning prayers on sabbaths and festivals, as well as at the seder meal at Passover. The refrain makes it amenable to responsive or antiphonal recitation. Ezra 3:11 seems to allude to such a practice.

Another Hallel is Pss. 146–150, all of which begin and end with the abbreviated Hallelujah. This

Hallel has a place in the morning prayer services in the synagogue. GERALD M. BILKES

HALLELUJAH (Heb. *halĕlû-yāh*)
A phrase translated "Praise the Lord." It is a plural imperative of the verb *hālal,* "praise," with the object *yāh* (an abbreviated form of YHWH) and is used in biblical writing from the exilic period onward. It occurs 24 times in Books Four and Five of the Psalter, in Pss. 104-6, 111-13, 115-17, 135, 146-150. The book of Chronicles attests its use in cultic worship. King David appoints Levites "to praise the Lord, the God of Israel" (e.g., 1 Chr. 16:4; 23:5). "Hallelujah" is sung by Asaph and his brothers with accompanying musical instruments in 1 Chr. 16:8-36. The congregation of Israel sings praises in 16:36 and David praises the Lord in 29:10-19.

Questions exist regarding the use of Hallelujah in the preexilic period, since the phrase does not occur in any early texts in the OT. Jewish tradition maintains that it was originally an ancient cultic shout that was not in any way connected with the name of God. Only later was the phrase appropriated for use in the cult. Although the simple verb *hālal* is used in the OT to refer to humans and objects (Gen. 12:15; 2 Sam. 14:25; Prov. 27:2; 31), in most of its occurrences, Yahweh is the object of praise.

Christian and Jewish liturgies preserve and use the phrase extensively.

NANCY L. DECLAISSÉ-WALFORD

HALLOHESH (Heb. *hallôḥēš*)
The father of Shallum (Neh. 3:12); one of the leaders who sealed the renewed covenant under Nehemiah (10:24[MT 25]).

HAM (Heb. *ḥām*) **(PERSON)**
A son of Noah. Ham is usually listed as the middle son (Gen. 5:32; 10:1; 1 Chr. 1:4), but in Gen. 9:24 he is called the "youngest." The exact etymology of the name is uncertain. Some scholars derive it from terms connoting divinity, but a (semi-)divine status for Ham is unlikely.

Ham escaped the Flood in the ark, presumably because of Noah's righteousness (Gen. 6:8-9), and received God's blessing (9:1). Later, when Noah lay drunk in his tent, Ham "the father of Canaan" (Gen. 9:18, 22) saw the "nakedness of his father," which may refer to a sexual act (cf. Lev. 18:7-19; 20:11-21). Upon waking, Noah unexpectedly cursed Ham's son Canaan (Gen. 9:25-27). The present form of the story is thus somewhat convoluted. Even so, it was not until the Middle Ages that Canaan's curse was misattributed to Ham and used for racist purposes.

Ham is also the progenitor of Cush, Egypt (cf. Ps. 78:51; 105:23, 27; 106:22), and Put (Gen. 10:6-20; 1 Chr. 1:8-16). These descendants occupy portions of Africa, Arabia, Syria-Palestine, and Mesopotamia.

Bibliography. K. van der Toorn, "Ham," *DDD,* 383-84. BRENT A. STRAWN

HAM (Heb. *hām*) **(PLACE)**
A city of the Zuzim who were defeated by Chedorlaomer and his allies (Gen. 14:5). It is listed between Ashteroth-karnaim and Shaveh-kiriathaim, ca. 16 km. (10 mi.) E of Beth-shean and mentioned as *hum* in Thutmose III's list of conquered cities in Palestine (no. 118; *ANET,* 242). A modern village on Wadi er-Rejeileh, 6.5 km. (4 mi.) S of Irbid, still bears the same name. In its close vicinity is an ancient site known as Tell Hām (226213), where three megalithic walls were discovered.

Bibliography. N. Glueck, *Exploration in Eastern Palestine* IV. AASOR 25-28 (New Haven, 1951).

ZELJKO GREGOR

HAMAN (Heb. *hāmān*)
A character in the book of Esther who is identified as the most important of the courtiers in the Persian court of King Ahasuerus (Esth. 3:1). He is identified as a descendant of Agag, thus foreshadowing his conflict with Mordecai, who as a Benjaminite is linked to the line of Saul (cf. 1 Sam. 15). In the face of Mordecai's refusal to kneel or bow to him, Haman devises a pogrom against all Persian Jews and persuades the king to agree to the plan by explaining that a "certain people" exists unassimilated in the kingdom (Esth. 3:6, 10). By means of some very subtle maneuvering, Esther and Mordecai are able to align themselves with the king and against Haman. It is not clear whether Haman falls from the king's graces because it is revealed that this "certain people" is in fact the Jews and that Queen Esther is also a Jew, or because the king suspects Haman of advances upon the queen. In either case, Haman is impaled upon the very stake on which he intended to impale Mordecai, and his planned pogrom is thwarted (Esth. 7:10).

Bibliography. T. K. Beal, *The Book of Hiding: Gender, Ethnicity, Annihilation and Esther* (London, 1997). TOD LINAFELT

HAMATH (Heb. *ḥămāṯ*)
An important city located on the Orontes River, along the primary trade route heading south from Asia Minor. The site is modern Ḥamā (312503) in Syria, ca. 210 km. (130 mi.) N of Damascus. Seven levels of Neolithic remains are attested, and Paleolithic remains are found throughout the immediate vicinity. By the 5th millennium B.C.E. trade links had been established with Mesopotamia, and with Asia Minor by the middle of the 3rd. Hamath was a major, if not the most significant, power in central Syria early in the 1st millennium. It survived as a Neo-Hittite center until the 8th century, and then was subsumed in the Aramean cultural milieu. Hamath is mentioned in Eblaite, Egyptian, Ugaritic, Luwian, and Akkadian texts.

Hamath formed the ideal northern boundary of the land of Israel (cf. Num. 13:21; Josh. 13:5; Ezek. 47:15). In the Table of Nations its inhabitants are reckoned among the descendants of Canaan (Gen. 10:18; 1 Chr. 1:16). The phrase *lĕḇō' ḥămāṯ* ("entrance to Hamath") probably denotes the boundary of the political realm associated with Hamath (though some associate this with Lebo, NW of Baalbek). David extended his boundaries to this location, establishing an alliance with Toi, king of Hamath (2 Sam. 8:9-12). Solomon extended this boundary, placing storage centers beyond the border (2 Chr. 8:4). The city was among the coalition (with Israel) which repeatedly repulsed the Assyrian armies under Shalmaneser III (853, 849, 848, and 845 B.C.E.). Jeroboam II extended the border of Israel to this point (2 Kgs. 14:25, 28). The city was ultimately incorporated into Assyria (conquered 738, incorporated as a province in 720); a number of its people were deported to Samaria (2 Kgs. 24), and some Israelites were settled in Hamath (Isa. 11:11). In its last pre-classical period mention it was incorporated into Babylon.

MARK ANTHONY PHELPS

HAMATH-ZOBAH (Heb. *ḥămāṯ ṣôḇâ*)
A city or region ("fortress of the estate/plantation") in southern Syria captured by Solomon (2 Chr. 8:3). It is uncertain whether the two names belong to a single settlement (Hamath-zobah) or a region that was alternately ruled by one or two cities (Hamath and Zobah).

Saul, David, and Solomon each battled Aramean forces settled northeast of Damascus to gain control of territory as far as the Euphrates River. Saul's forays were limited (1 Sam. 14:47), while David's army faced Hadadezer, king of Zobah, in extended battle (2 Sam. 8:3). The Chronicler refers to Hadadezer as king of Zobah Hamath (1 Chr. 18:3; NRSV "Zobah, toward Hamath"). Mercenaries from Zobah were hired by Ammon to fight David in a two-front battle, but were routed and defeated (2 Sam. 10:6). 1 Chr. 18 refers to Zobah (v. 3) and Hamath as separate city-states (v. 9).

DAVID C. MALTSBERGER

HAMITES, HAMITIC

1. The descendants of Ham, the youngest of Noah's three sons. Ham brought a curse upon his own son Canaan when he "looked upon his father's nakedness" (Gen. 9:18-27). The Bible also connects Hamites with Cushites, descended from one of Ham's sons (Gen. 10:6). Cushites have at times been called Hamitic Ethiopians. Accordingly, though difficult to confirm ethnically and geographically, many Ethiopians trace their descent through Ham.

2. Hamito-Semitic, an earlier designation of the Berber (Algeria and Morocco), Chadic (northern Nigeria, Chad, and neighboring countries; primarily Hausa), Cushitic-Omotic (Ethiopia and Somalia; primarily Oromo and Somali), and ancient Egyptian languages (later Coptic) and related cultures. Afro-asiatic has become the more common designation for this language group. The closeness of the relationship between Afro-asiatic, Egyptian, and Semitic remains unclear.

Bibliography. M. Bernal, *Black Athena: The Afroasiatic Roots of Classical Civilization* (London, 1987); E. Ullendorff, *Ethiopia and the Bible* (Oxford, 1968).

MARK A. CHRISTIAN

HAMMATH (Heb. *ḥammaṯ*) **(PERSON)**
The "father" of the house of Rechab (1 Chr. 2:55). The name may be related to the town in Naphtali mentioned in Josh. 19:35, or may indicate instead a familial relationship (Heb. "family-in-law") between the Kenites and the ancestor of the Rechabites.

HAMMATH (Heb. *ḥammaṯ*) **(PLACE)**
A fortified town within the territory of the tribe of Naphtali (Josh. 19:35). Hammath ("hot springs"; variants Hammoth-dor, Josh. 21:32; Hammon, 1 Chr. 6:76[MT 61]) has been identified with the hot springs of Ḥammam Ṭabarîyeh/Ḥame Ṭeveriya (201241), ca. 3 km. (2 mi.) S of Tiberias. Excavations have yielded three levels of occupation ranging from the 1st century B.C.E. to the 8th century C.E.

Bibliography. M. Dothan, *Hammath Tiberias* (Jerusalem, 1983).

JOHN FOTOPOULOS

HAMMEDATHA (Heb. *hammeḏāṯā'*; Pers. *mâh-dāta*)
The father of Haman (Esth. 3:1, 10; 8:5; 9:10, 24).

HAMMER
The use of hammers in the ancient Near East begins with stone hammers, stone heads with a hole bored for a wooden handle. In building Solomon's temple, iron hammers were used. Three Hebrew words represent the English "hammer": *halmûṯ* (Judg. 5:26), a "worker's hammer"; *maqqeḇeṯ* (Judg. 4:21; 1 Kgs. 6:7; Isa. 44:12; Jer. 10:4), a "hammer" with which one drives nails or pegs; and *paṭṭîš* (Isa. 41:7; Jer. 23:29; 50:23), a "forge-hammer." All are represented in the LXX by the generic Gk. *sphýra*. Heb. *halmûṯ* and *maqqeḇeṯ* appear to be interchangeable in Judg. 4:21; 5:26, where Jael drives a tent peg through Sisera's head with a hammer.

Judas' title "Maccabeus" (1 Macc. 2:4; Josephus *Ant.* 12.6.1 [265-67]) is widely believed to be based on *maqqeḇeṯ*. "Hammer" is also used metaphorically for God's word (Jer. 23:29) and for Babylon, the hammer of the earth (50:23).

THOMAS SCOTT CAULLEY

HAMMOLECHETH (Heb. *hammōleḵeṯ*)
The sister of Gilead (1 Chr. 7:18), progenitor of several Manassite clans.

HAMMON (Heb. *ḥammôn*)

1. A coastal city, S of Tyre and N of Acco, included in the territory assigned to the tribe of Asher (Josh. 19:28). It is generally identified with Umm el-ʿAwāmîd (164281) in the Wadi el-Hamûl near the spring of en-Hamûl, on the basis of the similarity of the names and two Phoenician inscriptions from the Hellenistic period.

2. A city in the territory of Naphtali assigned (with its pasture lands) as a levitical city for the descendants of Gershom (1 Chr. 6:76[MT 61]). It is usually associated with Hammoth-dor (Josh. 21:32) and Hammath (19:35) and has been identified with either Ḥammâm Ṭabarîyeh/Ḥame Ṭeveriya (201241), S of Tiberias on the western shore of the Sea of Galilee, or Tell Raqqat, N of Tiberias.

ERIC F. MASON

HAMMOTH-DOR (Heb. *ḥammōṯ dō'r*)
A levitical city in the tribal territory of Naphtali (Josh. 21:23). Hammon (1 Chr. 6:76) and Hammath (Josh. 19:35) are probably alternate names for this city.

HAMMUEL (Heb. *ḥammû'ēl*)
A Simeonite, son of Mishma and father of Zaccur (1 Chr. 4:26).

HAMMURAPI (Amor. *'ammu-rapi*)
(also HAMMURABI, AMMURAPI)
The sixth king (1792-1750 B.C.E.) of the First Dynasty of Babylon (1894-1595). This was but one of the Amorite families that came to power in Mesopotamia in the centuries following the fall of the Third Dynasty of Ur (2112-2004). Many of the kings of this dynasty had Amorite names. Hammurapi's name is probably either Amorite (*'ammu-rapi,* most probably "the paternal uncle is a healer/heals") or an Akkadianized version of such a name. When Hammurapi came to the throne, his small state was but one of the small kingdoms vying for power in Mesopotamia. To the north lay the powerful kingdom of Šamši-addu and in the south he was hemmed in by the state of Larsa. During the first years of rule, the new king expanded his territory and Babylon in the power politics of the Middle East, a regional balance of power that ranged from the Mediterranean coast to Iran. The true hegemons of the time were on the far flanks — Yamhad, centered around Aleppo, and Elam in the east. The smaller kingdoms of Larsa and Babylon in Babylonia, Eshnunna to the northeast, and Mari on the Euphrates made alliances, frequently broken, between and among themselves. These rulers pledged themselves as vassals, in theory at least, of an Elamite overlord, allowing him to arbitrate territorial disputes. After the Elamites marched into northern Syria and took over, for a short period of time, many of the local principalities, the major states created an alliance and defeated Elam and Eshnunna, creating a new political situation. The destruction of Eshnunna took place in Hammurapi's 29th year. With no major enemy on his northeastern flank, the king marched against his only Babylonian rival, Rim-sin of Larsa, who controlled all of southern Mesopotamia, took his city, and captured him alive. With the south firmly in his hands, Hammurapi now turned against his old ally, Zimri-lim of Mari, who had aided him in the wars against Elam, Eshnunna, and Larsa. His troops occupied the city for two years and then destroyed it. The Babylonians did not stay in the city and retreated back to the south after two years. Although at the beginning of his reign Hammurapi's kingdom was but one among many in Mesopotamia and Syria, at the time of his death most of the other states were gone and he stood alone between the other major powers of Aleppo and Elam. This grand kingdom did not last long; the south revolted during the reign of Hammurapi's son, Samsu-iluna. The uprising was put down, but the south of Mesopotamia was soon lost as most of the major cities

Diorite stela of Hammurapi receiving symbols of authority from the seated sun-god Šamaš (Susa, ca. 1750 B.C.E.). Below are listed 282 laws (Louvre)

along the Euphrates seem to have been abandoned at the end of his reign. The focus of the state shifted northwards, and Babylon seems to have had intermittent control of only a small area in northern Babylonia and up the Euphrates to Haradum and Terqa. The weakening kingdom apparently fell when a Hittite raid overcame Babylon.

The older levels of Babylon are, for the most part, inaccessible to archaeologists because of changes in the water table, and therefore Hammurapi's own archives have not been found. The thousands of contemporary letters from Mari provide rich documentation of the period, and include many references to Hammurapi. This city's archives gives us an outsider's view of the inner workings of the Babylonian court, and of the local and international intrigues of the time, including the draft of an anti-Elamite oath between the kings of Babylon and Mari. The information from Mari presents a distorted picture of events, however, because Hammurapi's officials took with them most of the diplomatic archives from the conquered city.

Hammurapi's administration of Babylonia is primarily documented in the correspondence between the king and his representatives in the south, as well as from economic texts from Sippar and, to a lesser extent, from other cities such as Dilbat, Larsa, and Kish. These provide extensive information on the organization of the south following the fall of Larsa, the interaction between the crown and local elite families, as well as the adjudication of legal disputes.

Hammurapi is best remembered for his so-called Law Code, a monumental inscription with a long prologue, legal provisions, and a final curse formula. The "laws" are exemplary in nature and were meant as representations of an abstract notion of royal justice. Contrary to popular understanding, they were not intended for practical legal use. Although at least three earlier texts of this genre have survived, the Hammurapi text is the longest known and the only one to survive intact in the form of a monumental stela. Although Hammurapi issued this text in a number of copies, some of which were standing in Babylonian cities for centuries, none of these have survived. The one intact version was discovered in the Elamite city of Susa, where it had been taken as war booty from Sippar in the 12th century. Like other texts of this type, portions of the Hammurapi stela were copied on tablets for scribal training, but only this one survived the Old Babylonian period. Copies of the "code" were studied in schools well into the 1st millennium. As was the custom at the time, the composition was copied, excerpted, and commented upon. Aside from this text, known in the late period as the "legal provisions of Hammurapi," the king was mentioned only a few times in chronicles and royal inscriptions. He was not remembered as one of the great ancient kings in the same league as Sargon or Naram-sin. Earlier in the 20th century scholars had identified king Amraphel of Shinar in Gen. 14 with Hammurapi, but this view is no longer held.

Although Hammurapi was a unique figure in Babylonian history, his importance should not be overestimated. His reign was actually more important for the destruction he brought on other states than for the long-term development of Mesopotamian culture.

Bibliography. J. M. Sasson, "King Hammurabi of Babylon," *CANE* 2:901-15; C. J. Gadd, "Hammurabi and the End of His Dynasty," *CAH*[3] 2/1: 176-224; M. T. Roth, *Law Collections from Mesopotamia and Asia Minor.* 2nd ed. SBLWAW 6 (Atlanta, 1997).

PIOTR MICHALOWSKI

HAMONAH (Heb. *hămônâ)*
Prophetic place name ("Multitude") given by Ezekiel as the burial site of the forces of Gog that are to be defeated by the faithful army of God (Ezek. 39:16). The site is placed in the "Valley of the Hordes of Gog" (Hamon-gog) E of the Dead Sea, in Transjordan. The burial of Israel's enemies across the Jordan will keep the Promised Land ritually pure as it is restored as holy unto God. The weapons collected from the fallen dead will be so numerous as to serve as fuel for the fires of Israel for seven years. Instead of a place name, some English translations render the term "nearby" or "great horde."

DAVID C. MALTSBERGER

HAMON-GOG (Heb. *hămôn gôg*)
The name given in Ezek. 39:11, 15 to the Valley of the Travelers where the slain armies of Gog will be interred at the latter days. The name of the valley ("Valley of the Hordes of God") seems intended to recall the "valley of the sons of Hinnom" in Jerusalem where sacrifice was offered to Moloch and where Jeremiah predicted the defeated people of Jerusalem would one day be buried (Jer. 7:31-34).

BRIAN P. IRWIN

HAMOR (Heb. *ḥămôr)*
Hivite prince of Shechem whose son, also named Shechem, raped and then sought to marry Dinah (Gen. 34). In retribution, Jacob's sons Simeon and Levi killed both Shechem and Hamor. Hamor is identified as progenitor of the Shechemites (Josh. 24:32; Judg. 9:28), who sold to Jacob the land upon which he erected an altar (Gen. 33:18-19) and where later Joseph was buried (Josh. 24:32).

HAMRAN (Heb. *ḥamrān*) (also HEMDAN)
The eldest son of Dishon (1 Chr. 1:41). At Gen. 36:26 he is called Hemdan.

HAMUL (Heb. *ḥāmûl*)
A son of Perez and grandson of Judah and Tamar (Gen. 46:12; 1 Chr. 2:5); ancestor of the Hamulite clan (Num. 26:21).

HAMUTAL (Heb. *ḥămûṭal*)
The wife of King Josiah of Judah, daughter of Jeremiah of Libnah, and the mother of kings Jehoahaz and Zedekiah (2 Kgs. 23:31; 24:18; Jer. 52:1; **K** *ḥămîṭal).* Some think that the lioness of Ezek. 19:2 is a reference to Queen Hamutal.

HANAMEL (Heb. *ḥănam'ēl*)
The son of Shallum and cousin of Jeremiah, from whom the imprisoned prophet purchased a field at Anathoth during the Chaldean siege of Jerusalem (Jer. 32:7-15).

HANAN (Heb. *ḥānān*)

1. A Benjaminite; the son of Shashak (1 Chr. 8:23).

2. A Benjaminite; the son of Azel and descendant of Saul (1 Chr. 8:38; 9:44).

3. The son of Maacah; one of David's warriors (1 Chr. 11:43).

4. The head of a family of temple servants who returned to Jerusalem following the Exile (Ezra 2:46; Neh. 7:49).

5. A Levite who helped interpret the law during Ezra's reform (Neh. 8:7). He was also among those Levites who signed a document affirming Ezra's covenant (Neh. 10:10[MT 11]).

6.-7. Two men listed among the leaders of the people (Neh. 10:22, 26 [23, 27]). It is uncertain whether these were separate individuals bearing the name Hanan, or one or more references to the Levite Hanan (**5** above).

8. The son of Zaccur. He was appointed by Nehemiah as an assistant to the storehouse treasurers who distributed the tithes (Neh. 13:13).

9. The apparent leader of a prophetic guild that occupied a chamber in the Jerusalem temple (Jer. 35:4).

KENNETH ATKINSON

HANANEL (Heb. *ḥănan'ēl*), **TOWER OF**
A tower in the northwest corner of the wall which surrounded the temple mount, rebuilt by Nehemiah (Neh. 3:1; 12:39). Some identify it with the fortress of the temple (Neh. 2:8). The tower may have been erected in the time of Manasseh (2 Chr. 33:14), and came to represent the northernmost point of the wall of Jerusalem. As such it came to be regarded as the prominent landmark in the north of Jerusalem, used in describing the circumference of the city (Zech. 14:10). As a prominent boundary point the tower of Hananel became associated with eschatological hopes for Jerusalem (Jer. 31:38).

This was the site of the Maccabean citadel (1 Macc. 13:52), rebuilt by Antiochus IV Epiphanes as the Seleucid Akra (Josephus *Ant.* 21.362-64, 369, 405-6). John Hyrcanus erected a fortress (the Baris) here which was destroyed by Pompey in 63 B.C.E. (*Ant.* 18.91). Later Herod the Great built the tower of Antonia on this location (*Ant.* 18.91; *BJ* 1.75, 118).

MARK F. ROOKER

HANANI (Heb. *ḥănānî*)

1. A seer, the father of the prophet Jehu (1 Kgs. 16:1, 7; 2 Chr. 19:2). Hanani rebuked King Asa of Judah and predicted the demise of his line because Asa had sent gold and silver to Ben-hadad in order to form a treaty which would spare Judah yet in turn freed Ben-hadad to sack the towns of Israel (2 Chr. 16:1-10).

2. One of the 14 sons of Heman who served as prophets, temple singers, and musicians for David (1 Chr. 25:4-5, 25).

3. A son of the priestly family of Immer found guilty of intermarrying with foreign women (Ezra 10:20).

4. Nehemiah's brother who brought news to him at the citadel of Susa of the poor condition of the remnant of Jews (Neh. 1:2-3). Hanani's report of their disgraceful condition prompted Nehemiah's work to rebuild the city and restore the wall. After the city's restoration, Hanani was put in charge of the administration of the city (Neh. 7:2). Although Hanani and Hananiah in the same verse may be two distinct individuals, it seems more natural to take the latter name as appositive, "Hanani, namely, Hananiah the commander of the citadel."

5. A priest and trumpeter who took part in the rededication ceremony of the wall of Jerusalem (Neh. 12:36).

Bibliography. C. G. Tuland, "Hanani-Hananiah," *JBL* 77 (1958): 157-61.

DAVID PAUL LATOUNDJI

HANANIAH (Heb. *ḥănanyāhû, ḥănanyâ*)

1. One of the four children of Zerubbabel, son of Pedaiah (1 Chr. 3:19, 21), a descendant of Solomon.

2. A postexilic individual associated with the tribe of Benjamin (1 Chr. 8:24).

3. One of the children of Heman; director of the 16th division of David's musicians (1 Chr. 25:4, 23).

4. One of King Uzziah's commanders (2 Chr. 26:11).

5. An Israelite of the family of Bebai who had to send away his foreign wife (Ezra 10:28).

6. A son of Shelemiah who helped repair the walls of Jerusalem during the time of Nehemiah (Neh. 3:30).

7. One entrusted by Nehemiah with the governance of the citadel/palace because "he was a faithful man and feared God more than many" (Neh. 7:2).

8. An Israelite leader who, on behalf of his family, set his seal to the renewed covenant under Nehemiah (Neh. 10:23).

9. A priest and head of the house of Jeremiah during the time of the high priest Joiakim who returned from Babylon with Zerubbabel and participated in the rededication of the walls (Neh. 12:12).

10. The son of Azzur who prophesied that Judah would be liberated from Babylonian oppression and that the temple vessels, which had been taken by the Babylonian army in 598, would be returned to Jerusalem within two years of his oracle (Jer. 28). This account describes a prophetic conflict in which two opposing messages claim to enjoy divine authority. During the interim between the first deportation (598) and the destruction of Jerusalem in 588/587, Jeremiah declared that Judah should not join an anti-Babylonian coalition of other Syro-Palestinian states (cf. Jer. 27) but instead accept Babylonian hegemony as a theo-political given. In contrast, Hananiah insisted that Babylonian rule would be short-lived, thus inciting rebellion against Judah's suzerain.

Although Hananiah opposes Jeremiah, the Hebrew text never refers to him as a "false prophet." He is addressed as one whose official role is assumed and whose character is not impugned. In fact, Hananiah exemplifies most, if not all, of the conventional features of Hebrew prophets: he uses the customary speech forms and symbolic actions; he speaks within legitimate religious traditions of the community and thus does not represent foreign deities or unacceptable symbol systems; and he enjoys the respect of the community, perhaps even more so than Jeremiah. One may infer from the text, therefore, that Hananiah's falsehood lies not in his person but rather in his message, which not only stands in contradistinction to prophetic oracles of the past (Jer. 28:8), but contradicts the words of Jeremiah. The ideology of Hananiah is not only untimely and out-of-touch with the historical sensibilities, but runs directly counter to the entire tradition associated with Jeremiah, that exile and suffering must be accepted and embraced as the dangerous yet necessary work of God before hopeful constructions can be articulated. Hananiah thus does not discern that many well-established preexilic social and symbolic structures (including the royal-temple ideology) are no longer part of God's program for an alternative community of the Exile. As a result, he is both "false" in content and a "dangerous" voice from the past that jeopardizes the powerful new vision of reality articulated by Jeremiah.

Bibliography. H. Mottu, "Jeremiah vs. Hananiah: Ideology and Truth in Old Testament Prophecy," in *The Bible and Liberation,* ed. N. K. Gottwald (Maryknoll, 1983), 235-51; T. W. Overholt, "Jeremiah 27–29: The Question of False Prophecy," *JAAR* 35 (1967): 241-49; *The Threat of Falsehood: A Study in the Theology of the Book of Jeremiah.* SBT, ser. 2, 16 (Naperville, 1970).

11. The father of one of the high ranking officials of King Jehoiakim who was "alarmed" (Jer. 36:16) by the contents of the scroll read by Baruch.

12. The father of Chelemiah and grandfather of Irijah, the sentinel who arrested Jeremiah and accused him of deserting to the Babylonians (Jer. 37:13).

13. One of Daniel's faithful companions whose name was changed to Shadrach (Dan. 1:6-7).

LOUIS STULMAN

HAND

In addition to the literal body part (Gen. 8:9; Matt. 8:3), a reference, by metonymy, to the whole person (Ps. 24:4). The right hand was given to seal a contract or receive a person into fellowship (Gal. 2:9), and to be at the right hand was considered a position of honor (Matt. 25:33; Heb. 12:2).

In a symbolic way the hand refers to responsibility (Gen. 4:11; Ps. 7:3[MT 4]) and authority. The expression "into (from) the hand of" may refer to the exercise of power by God or a person (Judg. 13:1, 5; 1 Sam. 9:16; Acts 12:11). The hand of God is frequently used to demonstrate God's power in creation (Ps. 95:5; Isa. 64:8), redemption (Exod. 13:9, 14, 16; Ps. 37:24; John 10:29) and judgment (Deut. 2:15; Acts 13:11). With his hand God provides blessings (Ezra 7:9; Neh. 2:18), including divine help (Ps. 119:173), protection (138:7), and prophetic ecstasy (Ezek. 1:3; 40:1).

Uplifted hands were used in prayer (1 Kgs. 8:22, 54; 1 Tim. 2:8) and signaled victory (Exod. 17:8-13); washing hands declared innocence, especially of blood-guilt (Deut. 21:6; Matt. 27:24). Hands were clapped in praise (Ps. 47:1[2]) and used to bless (Gen. 48:17; Luke 24:50), heal (Matt. 14:31), and ordain (Num. 27:18-23; Acts 6:6). People received the Holy Spirit by the laying on of hands (Acts 8:17; 1 Tim. 4:14). The hand was also used in idiomatic phrases to suggest imminence (Matt. 3:2), ownership (Rev. 13:16; 14:9), judgment (Isa. 10:32), justice (Exod. 21:24), and murder (Gen. 22:12).

KENNETH D. MULZAC

HANDBREADTH

A linear measure corresponding to the width of the hand (Heb. *ṭepaḥ, ṭōpaḥ*), ca. one sixth of a cubit or 7.4 cm. (2.92 in.; Exod. 25:25; 1 Kgs. 7:26; 2 Chr. 4:5).

HANDKERCHIEF

A cloth used for wiping the hands or face (Gk. *soudárion,* from Lat. *sudarium;* cf. *sudor,* "perspiration"). In most English translations the term is so rendered only in Acts 19:12, referring to Paul's handkerchiefs which had miraculous healing effect. These may have been the cloths tied about his head while tent making. The varied use of such cloths is seen in other NT occurrences, where the Greek word is translated "napkin" (Luke 19:20) or "(burial) cloth" (John 11:44; 20:7).

KENT L. YINGER

HANES (Heb. *ḥānēs*)

A city in Egypt, usually associated with Heracleopolis Magna (Egyp. *Ḥwt-nn-nsw,* "Palace of the Royal Child"), modern Ihnâsiyeh el-Medina, ca. 80 km. (50 mi.) S of Memphis on the west bank of the Nile. Heracleopolis was the capital of the 20th nome and an important city throughout the Late Period of Egypt. Isa. 30:4 chastises the king of Judah for sending envoys to Zoan (Tannis) and Hanes to make an alliance with Pharaoh, who would have been one of the middle kings of the 25th Dynasty, either Shabaka (716-702 B.C.E.) or Shebitku (702-690).

KEVIN A. WILSON

HANNAH (Heb. *ḥannâ*)

Mother of Samuel (1 Sam. 1:20) and wife of Elkanah the Ephraimite from Ramathaim (v. 1). Hannah, the first of Elkanah's two wives, was barren. Although Elkanah favored Hannah (he gave her a double portion each year at the Shiloh sacrifice), Peninnah (his second wife and mother of his children) made Hannah's life miserable (1 Sam. 1:6-8). One year, Hannah went before the Lord at Shiloh and vowed that if God would give her a son, she would dedicate him as a Nazarite (1:9-11). While she prayed, the Shiloh priest Eli mistakenly thought she was drunk, but she reassured him of her sobriety and pious intent (1:12-18). Upon the family's return to Ramathaim, Hannah became pregnant and bore a son whom she named Samuel ("I have asked him from the Lord," 1:19-20). Only after Samuel's weaning did Hannah finally return to Shiloh. Bringing a sacrifice of a three-year-old bull, an ephah of flour, and a skin of wine, she presented Samuel to the Lord (1:21-28) and sang a song (2:1-10). While Samuel remained with the priests at Shiloh (2:11), Hannah returned home and later bore five other children (three sons and two daughters; v. 21). Each year, Hannah returned to Shiloh and brought clothing for Samuel, who remained ministering with the priests (2:19-20).

Hannah's story contains several common literary themes: the barren wife (cf. Sarah, Gen. 11:30; Rebekah, Gen. 25:21; Rachel, Gen. 29:31; and Manoah's wife, Judg. 13:2); the rivalry between barren wives and fruitful ones (e.g., Sarah/Hagar, Gen. 16:4; Rachel/Leah, 30:1-24), and the dedication of formerly barren women's unborn sons as Nazarites (Manoah's wife, Judg. 13). What distinguishes Hannah's account from others is its ritual dimensions. Only Hannah confronts the Lord, makes a vow, and subsequently sacrifices to God at the vow's fulfillment. Moreover, Hannah's prayer is unique in the OT; rarely are we told of women's prayers, and at no other time are we given such detail as to their content. Hannah's song of praise (1 Sam. 2) is sometimes thought to be secondary to the account of Samuel's birth; its influence on Mary's Magnificat (Luke 1:46-55) is widely recognized.

Recent treatments of Hannah's story emphasize her characterization as "victim and redeemer" (Lillian Klein) and her sacrifice as an example of women's religion (Carol Meyers).

Bibliography. L. R. Klein, "Hannah: Marginalized Victim and Social Redeemer," in *A Feminist Companion to Samuel and Kings,* ed. A. Brenner (Sheffield, 1994), 77-92; C. Meyers, "The Hannah Narrative in Feminist Perspective," in *Go to the Land I Will Show You,* ed. J. E. Colesin and V. H. Matthews (Winona Lake, 1996), 117-26.

LINDA S. SCHEARING

HANNATHON (Heb. *ḥannāṯôn*)
A town on the northern tribal boundary of Zebulun (Josh. 19:14). It was located at the junction of the road leading from Acco on the coast and a branch road that split off the Via Maris at Megiddo to the south. Modern Tel Ḥannaton/Tell el-Bedeiwîyeh (174243) is identified with the ancient city.

Hannathon is mentioned twice as *Ḫinnatuna* in the 14th-century B.C. Amarna Letters. The kings of Acco and Shimron ambushed a Babylonian caravan bound for Egypt near Hannathon. Lab'ayu, king of Shechem, was set free near the city after being captured by forces loyal to the Egyptian pharaoh. The annals of Assyrian king Tiglath-pileser III describe the capture of Hannathon along with nearby Kanah and Jotbah during the 733 invasion. During the Herodian period the settlement was known as Asochis.

DAVID C. MALTSBERGER

HANNIEL (Heb. *ḥannî'ēl*)
1. The son of Ephod. A leader of the tribe of Manasseh, he represented his tribe in the division of the land of Canaan (Num. 34:23).

2. A son of Ulla; the head of an Asherite clan (1 Chr. 7:39).

HANOCH (Heb. *ḥănôḵ*)
1. A son of Midian and grandson of Abraham and Keturah (Gen. 25:4; 1 Chr. 1:33).

2. The oldest son of Reuben, Jacob's oldest son (Gen. 46:9; Exod. 6:14; 1 Chr. 5:3). His descendants became the family of the Hanochites (Num. 26:5; Heb. *haḥănōḵî*).

HANUKKAH (Heb. *ḥănukkâ*)
See DEDICATION, FEAST OF.

HANUN (Heb. *ḥānûn*)
1. The son of Nahash and his successor as Ammonite king. David sent envoys to Hanun with condolences on the death of Nahash, but the leaders of the Ammonites were suspicious and aroused Nahash against David; Nahash seized the messengers and humilated them, shaving off half their beards and cutting off one side of their garments. In the war that ensued, Hanun was defeated and his people forced into slavery (2 Sam. 10:1–11:1; 12:26-31; 1 Chr. 19:1–20:3).

2. An Israelite who aided in the restoration of the walls of Jerusalem at the time of Nehemiah (Neh. 3:13).

3. The sixth son of Zalaph who aided in the restoration of Jerusalem's walls (Neh. 3:30); possibly the same as **2** above.

HAPAX LEGOMENON
A term that is found only one time in a certain body of literature (e.g., a Hebrew term found only once in the OT; Gk. *hápax legómenon*. "once read").

HAPHARAIM (Heb. *ḥăp̄ārayim*)
A city in the territory allotted to the tribe of Issachar (Josh. 19:19). Some scholars have associated it with a site (Egyp. *ḥprm*) mentioned in Shishak (Sheshonk) I's list of conquered cities inscribed at Karnak or with two cities (*ꜣpr wr, ꜣpr šri*) in a list of Thutmose III. However, all of these suggestions have been disputed. Hapharaim is usually identified with the modern village eṭ-Ṭaiyibeh (192223), SW of the Sea of Chinnereth and NE of Jezreel. Other suggestions have included Khirbet el-Farriyeh (160226) and Afula (177223).

ERIC F. MASON

HAPIRU, APIRU
People designated *ha-pí-ru,* the syllabic cuneiform spelling of *'apīru* (less likely *'apiru*), appearing in texts from the entire 2nd millennium B.C.E. and throughout the Fertile Crescent. The term is West

Semitic in origin. Most attested names of *ʿapīru* are also West Semitic, but many are East Semitic, Hurrian, or Indo-european. The term is often written in cuneiform with the composite logogram *SA.GAZ*, which is also used for Akk. *ḫabbātu*, "robber, pillager, brigand," and probably derives from Akk. *šaggāšu*, "killer, outlaw." Not all *ʿapīru* were murderous thieves, but in the eyes of court scribes they bore these associations.

The etymology of *ʿapīru* is uncertain. Most likely it is an adjective related to Heb. *ʿāp̄ār*, "ground, earth, dirt," following the form suggested by Heb. *pālîṭ* and *śārîḏ*, both "fugitive." One reasonable suggestion is that the word labels the outlaw as "dusty" from travel, but this is improbable. The paradigm for the *ʿapīru*, from the full-fledged bandit to the merely displaced, was apparently the outlaw harboring in the highland and desert margins of society, who, in the words of Isa. 2:10, 19 ironically addressed to the ruling class, "enters the fell, hides in the *ground* . . . enters caves in the fells and holes in the *ground* " — exactly like a fox before hounds driven "to earth." The word *ʿapīru* probably represents outlaws as those who conceal themselves in holes or burrows, the ones "of the ground" (cf. Ps. 72:9).

Many references to *ʿapīru* appear to involve social bandits or outlaw gangs. An *ʿapīru* from Alalakh bore the epithet "thief." The *ʿapīru* warriors to whom the 15th-century royal refugee Idrimi fled probably represented a bandit gang. The numerous *ʿapīru* who figure in the Amarna Letters from 14th-century Syria and Palestine are best understood as social bandits in the service of various kings, even when merely the object of political name-calling. An edict of the 13th-century Hittite king Hattusilis III assured the king of Ugarit that if anyone serving in the court of that king, or anyone from another land owing debt to by that king, should flee to the territory of the *ʿapīru*, presumably the retreat of bandit gangs, within Hattusilis' jurisdiction, Hattusilis would undertake to extradite him to Ugarit (RS 17.238).

Taken as a whole, however, it is not banditry as such that most *ʿapīru* seem to have in common. The term may not have meant the same thing in all times and places, but nearly all *ʿapīru* mentioned in texts are found in the service of courts, as mercenaries, aides, servants, clients, or captive manual laborers. In personal names, *ʿapīru* apparently means a "client": e.g., Apir-baʿl, "Client-of-Baal," Apir-el, "Client of El." Furthermore, *ʿapīru* appear to be displaced persons, uprooted from home and kin, dependent on new masters — apart from the few instances in which they themselves rule. Such features are consistent with the concept of fugitive brigandage, even if not every *ʿapīru* so designated originated or acted as a bandit. Displacement could affect an individual of any social class and have many possible causes, such as war, famine, debt, simple poverty, limited opportunity, political conflict, or lengthy military service. Some displaced may have migrated and put themselves up for hire individually. Many banded together in squads or gangs (*ṣabû*, "military host," appears regularly with *ʿapīru*, in their roles both as bandits and as court forces), which pillaged and extorted or hired themselves to the highest bidder. Service to a court, which could involve elite military skills, might lead to landholding, as gang members reintegrated themselves into settled society, without always sloughing their *ʿapīru* label. In other cases, the *ʿapīru* could be rounded up and sold or otherwise dispatched as laborers.

Since first recognized in the late 19th century, the *ʿapīru* have been the subject of much debate and disagreement. In general, attempts to see them as a social class, an ethnic group, a tribal group, donkey caravaneers, pastoralists, or nomads have failed. A classic question of biblical scholarship is whether the term "Hebrew" (*ʿiḇrî*) derives from *ʿapīru*. For many the question remains unsettled, but most evidence points away from a connection. Although in syllabic cuneiform the term is always written with the *BI* sign, the Ugaritic and Egyptian writings with *p* appear to reflect the proper middle consonant, and the cuneiform sign is increasingly read without further ado as *pí*. Interchange of *p* and *b* within West Semitic is not common and within the same language even less so; it appears particularly unlikely in this case because the root *ʿbr*, "pass by, pass over, transgress," putatively behind both terms, probably also occurs in Ugaritic, where in any case a shift from *b* to *p* is attested only by regressive assimilation to an unvoiced consonant. It has further been pointed out that the consistent preservation of both internal vowels in the reflex *ha-pí-ru*, if it follows normal Akkadian rules, implies that one of the vowels must be long; if so, since neither such long vowel could have been shortened or elided, *ʿapīru* could not possibly lie behind *ʿibrî*.

It occasions some surprise, therefore, that "Hebrew," which occurs rather seldom in the OT, is almost exclusively used by non-Israelites to refer to Israelites in situations where they could be mistaken for *ʿapīru*: as refugees by Egyptians in Genesis and Exodus, and as renegades by the Philistines in 1 Samuel. This seeming agreement is apparently a coincidence, in that "Hebrew" derives in all likelihood from the patronym *ʿEber*, whose name implies a "crossing" from "beyond, over there."

The bearing of the *ʿapīru* on the history of early Israel, albeit indirect, goes well beyond an increasingly unlikely connection with the name "Hebrew." There is no reason to doubt that social dislocation and banditry played a significant role in the emergence of Israel, even if politically early Israel must be defined primarily in terms of tribalism. Social dislocation and tribalism are far from mutually exclusive, and the role of *ʿapīru* in the Amarna period has shed significant light on conditions attending the emergence of tribal Israel. A further important comparison is with particular Israelites, including Jephthah (Judg. 11:3-6) and especially David, whose career was similar to that of Idrimi and who can fairly, if anachronistically, be called an *ʿapīru* chief. As freebooters, David and his men hired themselves out as mercenaries or subsisted on plunder. In this regard, the emergence of the kingdom of Judah under David had much in common with that of the kingdom of Amurru under Abdi-ashirta and of Shechem under Labayu in the Amarna period.

Bibliography. G. Buccellati, "*ʿApirū* and *Munnabtūtu* — The Stateless of the First Cosmopolitan Age," *JNES* 36 (1977): 145-47; M. L. Chaney, "Excursus: The *ʿApiru* and Social Unrest in the Amarna Letters from Syro-Palestine," in *Palestine in Transition,* ed. D. N. Freedman and D. F. Graf (Sheffield, 1983), 72-83; M. Greenberg, *Ḫab/piru.* AOS 39 (New Haven, 1955); R. S. Hess, "Alalakh Studies and the Bible: Obstacle or Contribution?" in *Scripture and Other Artifacts,* ed. M. D. Coogan, J. C. Exum, and L. E. Stager (Philadelphia, 1994), 199-215; P. K. McCarter, "The Historical David," *Int* 40 (1986): 117-29; A. F. Rainey, "Unruly Elements in Late Bronze Canaanite Society," in *Pomegranates and Golden Bells,* ed. D. P. Wright, D. N. Freedman, and A. Hurvitz (Winona Lake, 1995), 481-96.

ROBERT B. COOTE

HAPPIZZEZ (Heb. *happiṣṣēṣ*)
The leader of the 18th division of priests during the time of David (1 Chr. 24:15).

HARA (Heb. *hārāʾ*)
One of the cities to which Israelites were exiled by Tiglath-pileser III (1 Chr. 5:26). There is some confusion about the name of the city. 1 Chr. 5:26 appears to be an incorrect or corrupt parallel of 2 Kgs. 17:6; 18:11. Instead of Hara ("mountain" or "highland"), 2 Kings reads "the cities of Media" in the MT and "the mountains of Media" in the LXX. It has been suggested that Hara in 1 Chr. 5:26 may be a corruption of either *haʿîr,* "city," or *har,* "mountain." If Hara refers to the mountains of Media, this might place the Israelite exiles in the highlands E of the Tigris River. C. SHAUN LONGSTREET

HARADAH (Heb. *ḥărādâ*)
A place where the Israelites stopped during the wilderness journey, between Mt. Shepher and Makheloth (Num. 33:24-25). The location is not known.

HARAN (Heb. *hārān*) **(PERSON)**

1. The son of Terah and brother of Abraham and Nahor. He fathered a son, Lot, and two daughters, Milcah and Iscah (Gen. 11:27-29). Haran died in the Chaldean city of Ur while his father was still alive.

2. A descendant of Judah; the son of Caleb by his concubine Ephah (1 Chr. 2:46).

3. A son of Shimei, a Gershomite Levite who was head of the family of Ladan during the time of David (1 Chr. 23:9).

HARAN (Heb. *ḥārān;* Akk. *ḫarrānu*)
(PLACE) (also HARRAN)
A cosmopolitan northern Mesopotamian city. Excavations at modern Altinbaşak, 38 km. (24 mi.) SE of Urfa, Turkey, reveal that the site was occupied no later than Early Bronze Age III. A location on the major east-west caravan route at the top of the Fertile Crescent explains both its name and its pivotal strategic, political, and economic role in the ancient Near East. Predominantly Aramean by the beginning of the Iron Age, the Haranian hinterland remained so throughout the Neo-Assyrian and Neo-Babylonian periods. Following the death of Alexander the Great, the city became a significant bridge between the intellectual traditions of ancient Mesopotamia and the Hellenistic world. Although Haran would retain its mystique for hermetic scholarship and its ancient astral cults for almost 1000 years, the economic fortunes of the city declined as the caravan routes shifted toward Palmyra and other emporia, a decline exacerbated by the fact that the region suffered the fate of a border territory actively disputed by the Parthians and succeeding Persian rulers, Romans, Byzantines, Muslims, and Mongols.

Although the cult of the moon-god Sîn of Haran is first alluded to in a treaty from the time of Zimri-lim of Mari, its origins probably lie in the Sumerian diaspora of the 3rd millennium B.C.E., as the Haranian pantheon echoes that of the southern Babylonian city of Ur. Prestige of the cult peaked under the vigorous sponsorship of the Neo-Assyrian emperors and the enigmatic Nabonidus, the last Neo-Babylonian ruler. The symbol of the Haranian moon-god cult, a tasseled lunar crescent mounted atop a pole, comprises the central visual element in eight Neo-Assyrian royal stelae and literally hundreds of cylinder and stamp seals recovered in Western Asia and Cyprus. The Roman emperors Caracalla and Julian sacrificed to the moon-god of Haran. Syriac Christian authors polemicized against the pagan practices of the Haranians. The moon-god and other members of the ancient Semitic pantheon apparently continued to be worshipped at Haran during the Islamic occupation until the city was destroyed by the Mongols in 1271.

OT Haran was the first residence of Abram after his departure with his family from Ur of the Chaldees (Gen. 11:31), the place where his father Terah died (v. 32), and the site of Abram's departure for Canaan with Lot (12:4-5). Isaac's wife Rebekah was obtained among his kinsmen in Haran (Gen. 24). Out of fear of retribution from Esau, Jacob was sent to live with his uncle Laban in Haran (Gen. 27:43; 28:10), where he acquired two wives and considerable wealth (chs. 29-31). In 2 Kgs. 19:12 = Isa. 37:12, a passage from the so-called letter of Sennacherib to Hezekiah, the Assyrian king boasts that his ancestors destroyed Haran, and its gods were unable to save it. Delivery of such a speech makes better sense during the Neo-Babylonian siege of Jerusalem, since Haran and its temple were destroyed by a Medo-Babylonian coalition in 609, whereas there is no substantive evidence for Neo-Assyrian aggression against the city.

Bibliography. T. M. Green, *The City of the Moon God: Religious Traditions of Harran.* Religions in the Graeco-Roman World 114 (Leiden, 1992); S. W.

Holloway, "Harran: Cultic Geography in the Neo-Assyrian Empire and Its Implications for Sennacherib's 'Letter to Hezekiah' in 2 Kings," in *The Pitcher Is Broken,* ed. Holloway and L. K. Handy. JSOTSup 190 (Sheffield, 1995), 276-314; J. N. Postgate, "Ḫarrān," *Reallexikon der Assyriologie* 4 (Berlin, 1972-75): 122b-25a.

STEVEN W. HOLLOWAY

HARARITE (Heb. *hahărārî, hā'rārî*)
Unidentified designation of a number of David's heroes: Shammah, the son of Agee (it may refer primarily to the father, 2 Sam. 23:11), Shamma (different spelling also in Hebrew) and Sharar (v. 33), Jonathan the son of Shagee (1 Chr. 11:34), and Ahiam the son of Sacar (v. 35). The epithet may be connected with *har,* "mountain," and thus refer to a village, a geographical area, or a dynasty in a mountainous area.

JESPER SVARTVIK

HARBONA (Heb. *ḥarĕḇônā', ḥarĕḇônâ*)
Eunuch of the Persian king Ahasuerus (Esth. 1:10). He suggested that Haman be hanged on the very gallows he had made for Mordecai (Esth. 7:9).

HARE
A herbivorous rodent of the family Leporidae, a mammal closely related to the rabbit. Various species have been attested in Palestine, including the *Lepus syriacus,* an animal slightly smaller than its European counterpart *(Lepus europaeus);* it is common in wooded and cultivated areas throughout the northern part of Palestine, particularly in the Esdraelon Valley. A smaller variety, with a light, sand-colored back, is the *Lepus aegypticus,* found in the Negeb and the Jordan Valley.

Because it "chews the cud" but "does not have divided hoofs," the hare is classified as an unclean animal (Lev. 11:6; Deut. 14:7). Actually, it is not a ruminant but may have appeared as such to ancient observers because of its constant chewing movements.

HAREPH (Heb. *ḥārēp*)
A son of Hur and grandson of Caleb, of the tribe of Judah. He was the "father" (founder) of Beth-gader (1 Chr. 2:51).

HARHAIAH (Heb. *ḥarhăyâ*)
The father of the goldsmith Uzziel, who aided in the restoration of the walls of Jerusalem under Nehemiah (Neh. 3:8).

HARHAS (Heb. *ḥarḥas*) (also HASRAH)
The grandfather of Shallum, husband of the prophetess Huldah (2 Kgs. 22:14). At 2 Chr. 34:22 he is called Hasrah (**1**).

HAR-HERES (Heb. *har-ḥeres*)
An area retained by the Amorites against the tribe of Dan (Judg. 1:35). Mentioned with the villages Aijalon and Shaalbim, Har-heres has sometimes been understood as a village, perhaps the same place as the Ir-shemesh in the territory allotted to Dan (Josh. 19:41) or the Beth-shemesh allotted to Judah (15:10; 21:16). Both *ḥeres* and *šemeš* can mean "sun." However, *har* means "mountain/hill" (and *ḥeres* can also mean "itch"; cf. LXX "the mountain of the myrtle-grove"). Thus some scholars have identified Har-heres with various sites in the mountains bordering the valley of Aijalon. It is not to be associated with the ascent of Heres (Judg. 8:13).

ERIC F. MASON

HARHUR (Heb. *ḥarḥûr*)
A temple servant whose descendants returned from the Exile with Zerubbabel (Ezra 2:51; Neh. 7:53).

HARIM (Heb. *ḥārim*)
1. The head of a priestly family in Israel, third among the 24 divisions of priests organized by David (1 Chr. 24:8). Descendants of this family were among the first returnees from Babylon (Ezra 2:39; Neh. 7:42), and five family members were among the priests who had married and subsequently pledged to divorce foreign wives (Ezra 10:21). Adna was the head of this house during the postexilic high priesthood of Joiakim (Neh. 12:15). Harim is listed as one of the priests (or priestly families) who signed the covenant during Nehemiah's administration (Neh. 10:5[MT 6]).

2. A person and/or place that identifies a lay family of exilic and postexilic Jews, who were also among the first returnees from Babylon (Ezra 2:32; Neh. 7:35). Descendants of this Harim are also listed among those who married and pledged to divorce foreign wives (Ezra 10:31). One of this family's descendants, Malchijah, worked on the rebuilding of the Jerusalem wall under Nehemiah (Neh. 3:11). The name also occurs as one of the leaders who signed the Nehemiah covenant (Neh. 10:27[28]), possibly suggesting that a representative of this lay family signed the covenant along with the priestly list of signatories.

MICHAEL L. RUFFIN

HARIPH (Heb. *ḥārîp*)
An Israelite whose descendants returned from the Exile under Zerubbabel (Neh. 7:24). He may be the same as Jorah in the parallel account (Ezra 2:18). Either he or a representative of his family set his seal to the renewed covenant under Nehemiah (Neh. 10:19[MT 20]).

HARLOT
A woman who engages in sexual intercourse for pay (Heb. *zônâ,* from a root meaning "to fornicate"; Gk. *pórnē,* from a verb meaning "to sell"). The KJV also uses "harlot" for *qĕḏēšâ* in Gen. 38:21, 22; Hos. 4:14. While *zônâ* and *qĕḏēšâ* are sometimes assumed to be completely synonymous, it is possible that the different terms imply different functions or connote different degrees of social standing.

Since the feminine *qĕḏēšâ* and its masculine equivalent *qāḏēš* come from the Hebrew root meaning "holy" or "set apart," modern scholars often assume that these words refer to men and women engaged in Canaanite fertility cult practices (as opposed to "common prostitution"). Thus, while the KJV used "whore" or "harlot" for *qĕḏēšâ* and "sodomite" for *qāḏēš*, recent versions translate both the masculine and feminine forms as "temple prostitute," "shrine prostitute," or "cult prostitute" (1 Kgs. 14:24; 15:12; 22:46; 2 Kgs. 23:7; Job 36:14).

In the OT, "harlot" *(zônâ)* is used to describe Tamar (the daughter-in-law of Judah, Gen. 38), Rahab (the woman from Jericho who sheltered the Israelite spies, Josh. 2:1-24), the unnamed mother of Jephthah (Judg. 11:1) and the two women whose quarrel over a baby was settled by Solomon (1 Kgs. 3:16). Dinah's brothers say they will not allow their sister to be treated like a *zônâ* (Gen. 34:31), Samson has intercourse with a *zônâ* (Judg. 16:1), and Israelite priests are forbidden to marry a *zônâ* (implying that some men did; Lev. 21:7). Both Tamar and Rahab are remembered by name in Matthew's genealogy of Jesus, and two of the three uses of *pórnē* in the NT refer to Rahab, whose faith in God and kindness towards the Israelite spies were thought to outweigh the negative aspect of her profession (Heb. 11:31; Jas. 2:25). Thus a harlot seems to have been a professional person whose place in society was recognized (even though she was held in low esteem).

However, the term "harlot" also appears in a variety of metaphors that are used to condemn idolatry and religious syncretism in Israel. In this figurative usage, *zônâ* takes on even more negative connotations implying adultery and promiscuity. If Israel is thought to be bound to God in an exclusive covenant relationship, then Israel can be said to commit adultery (or to "play the harlot") whenever they look to powers other than Yahweh for sustenance, comfort, or protection (e.g., Jer. 3:3; Ezek. 16:1-34; Hos. 1–4; Mic. 1:7).

While "harlot" *(zônâ)* can refer to a woman whose continued presence in the community is tolerated (though stigmatized), the terms "playing the harlot" *(znh)* and "harlotry" or "whoredom" *(zĕnûṯ/zĕnûnîm)* describe behavior that the speaker thinks can neither be tolerated nor allowed to continue. This distinction in usage may reflect a double moral standard. In Gen. 38 Judah seems perfectly willing to engage the services of a harlot and to send her an agreed-upon payment, but he plans to burn his daughter-in-law for "playing the harlot" (v. 24), until he realizes that her behavior is no worse than his own (v. 26).

Bibliography. P. A. Bird, "The Harlot as Heroine," *Semeia* 46 (1989): 119-39; S. Erlandsson, "zānâ," *TDOT* 4:99-104. KATHLEEN A. FARMER

HARMAGEDON

See ARMAGEDDON.

HARMON (Heb. *harmônâ*)

An unspecified site to which the women of Samaria were to be banished (Amos 4:3). The exact location is not known. Modern scholars repoint the Hebrew to read "Hermon" (i.e., Mt. Hermon, which lies beyond Bashan, in the general direction of Damascus; Amos 5:27). The LXX reads "the mountains of Remman" (cf. "the rock of Rimmon"; Judg. 20:45, 47). Other suggestions include "Armenia" (Targums), "the palace" (KJV), and "dunghill" (NEB).

SUJEY ADARVE-VALDES

HARNEPHER (Heb. *ḥarnep̄er*)

A son of Zophah of the tribe of Asher (1 Chr. 7:36).

HAROD (Heb. *ḥărōḏ*)

1. A spring where Gideon and his men camped (Judg. 7:1). Many scholars identify the site with the spring of ʿAin Jālûd (184217), 3.2 km. (2 mi.) E of Zerʿin below the cliffs of Mt. Gilboa. The spring flows from a rocky cave into the Jalud River and eventually reaches the Jordan. At the spring of Harod ("trembling"), Gideon tested his men before the battle against the Midianites, who were camped in the valley below. The first group dismissed by Gideon were those who "trembled" (Heb. *ḥārēḏ*). The final test came at the waters of the spring itself. Years later, before the fateful battle with the Philistines, Saul camped at a "spring" in the Jezreel Valley (1 Sam. 29:1), which some identify with Harod.

2. A town possibly identified with Khirbet el-Haredan (178126), SE of Jerusalem, although its exact location remains uncertain. Two of David's famous Thirty, Shammah and Elika, may have been from Harod (2 Sam. 23:25). However, a few manuscripts read "Harorites," and the LXX omits Elika (cf. 1 Chr. 11:27, which refers only to Shammoth [Shammah] "the Harorite"). The difference in spelling may be explained by the orthographic similarity of *daleth* and *resh*. STEPHEN VON WYRICK

HAROEH (Heb. *hārōʾeh*) (also REAIAH)

A Judahite, the son of Shobal (1 Chr. 2:52). At 1 Chr. 4:2 he is called Reaiah (**1**).

HAROSHETH-HAGOIIM (Heb. *ḥărōšeṯ haggôyim*)

The home of Sisera, Canaanite army commander of King Jabin (Judg. 4:2). Sisera assembled his army and 900 iron chariots in Harosheth-hagoiim to oppose Barak and Deborah near Mt. Tabor, and retreated there following his defeat (Judg. 4:16). The precise location is unknown, and it is not certain whether this name (Heb. "Harosheth of the Gentiles") refers to a city or a geographical region.

KENNETH ATKINSON

HARP

A stringed musical instrument primarily used in worship (Heb. *nēḇel*). Although the precise identification of this instrument is uncertain, examples and drawings of similar instruments are known from Egypt, Assyria, and Babylonia. Harps most likely consisted of 10-20 strings (cf. Ps. 144:9) stretched on an open frame perpendicular to a sound board, and were played without a plectrum. These instruments could have been a variety of sizes, judging from the known examples in the ancient Near East.

As instruments of the aristocracy, harps were made of precious woods and metals (1 Kgs. 10:12 = 2 Chr. 9:11). The instrument plays a part in the visions of Revelation (Rev. 5:8; 14:2; 15:2. Only rarely does the Bible depict the harp in secular usage (Isa. 5:12; 14:11; Amos 5:23). Along with the lyre and the shophar, the harp was part of the group of instruments used in worship by the Jerusalem priesthood (e.g., 2 Chr. 29:25; Ps. 33:2; 81:2[MT 3]).

See LYRE. JENNIE R. EBELING

HARSHA (Heb. *ḥaršā'*)
A temple servant whose descendants returned from the Exile with Zerubbabel (Ezra 2:52 = Neh. 7:54).

HARUM (Heb. *hārūm*)
A Judahite, father of Aharhel (1 Chr. 4:8).

HARUMAPH (Heb. *ḥărûmap̱*)
The father of Jedaiah, who worked on the restoration of the walls of Jerusalem (Neh. 3:10).

HARUPHITE (Heb. K *ḥărîp̱î*, Q *ḥărûp̱*)
A gentilic applied to Shephatiah, a Benjaminite who came to David's aid at Ziklag (1 Chr. 12:5[MT 6]). It appears to be based on an unknown place name, perhaps related to the clans Hareph or Hariph.

HARUZ (Heb. *ḥārûṣ*)
The father of Meshullemeth, King Manasseh's wife and the mother of Amon (2 Kgs. 21:19).

HARVEST
See AGRICULTURE.

HASADIAH (Heb. *ḥăsaḏyâ*)
1. A son of Zerubbabel (1 Chr. 3:20).
2. An ancestor of Baruch and son of Hilkiah (Bar. 1:1).

HASHABIAH (Heb. *ḥăšaḇyâ, ḥăšaḇyāhû*)
1. A Merarite Levite, the father of Malluch and son of Amaziah (1 Chr. 6:45[MT 30]). He was an ancestor of Ethan, a temple musician during David's reign.

2. A Merarite Levite, the father of Azrikam (1 Chr. 9:14) and son of Bunni (Neh. 11:15). He was an ancestor of Shemaiah, who resettled in Jerusalem.

3. One of the six sons of Jeduthun whom David set apart for prophesying, playing the harp, and thanking and praising the Lord (1 Chr. 25:3).

4. A Hebronite, leader of 1700 family members west of the Jordan. As one of David's officials, he was in charge of religious and secular matters in his area (1 Chr. 26:30).

5. The son of Kemuel; an official over the tribe of Levi (1 Chr. 27:17).

6. A chief officer of the Levites at the time of Josiah (2 Chr. 35:9).

7. A Levite and descendant of Merari from Casiphia N of Babylon whom Ezra persuaded to accompany him and the other exiles back to Jerusalem (Ezra 8:19).

8. One of the 12 leading priests whom Ezra set apart to take care of the silver, gold, and other articles that the king, officials, and people had donated to the Lord (Ezra 8:24).

9. An Israelite among the descendants of Parosh who divorced his foreign wife (Ezra 10:25).

10. A ruler of half the district of Keilah who carried out repairs on his section of the wall after the Exile (Neh. 3:17).

11. One who set his seal to the renewed covenant under Nehemiah (Neh. 10:11[MT 12]).

12. Chief officer of the Levites during the time of Nehemiah; ancestor of Uzzi and father of Bani (Neh. 11:22).

13. The head of the priestly family of Hilkiah during the days of Joiakim (Neh. 12:21).

14. A leader of the Levites who gave responsive praise and thanksgiving in the temple during the time of Nehemiah (Neh. 12:24).

ROBIN GALLAHER BRANCH

HASHABNAH (Heb. *ḥăšaḇnâ*)
An Israelite who set his seal to the renewed covenant under Nehemiah (Neh. 10:25[MT 26]). The name is an abbreviated form of Hashabneiah.

HASHABNEIAH (Heb. *ḥăšaḇnĕyâ*)
1. The father of Hattush (**2**), who worked at rebuilding the walls of Jerusalem (Neh. 3:10).

2. A Levite who participated in the ceremony preceding ratification of the covenant (Neh. 9:5). He may be the same as Hashabiah **7-8, 11-12,** or **14.**

HASHBADDANAH (Heb. *ḥašbaddānâ*)
An Israelite, possibly a Levite, who stood at Ezra's left side and interpreted the law as it was read (Neh. 8:4).

HASHEM (Heb. *hāšēm*)
A Gizonite, one of David's Champions (1 Chr. 11:34). The parallel passage at 2 Sam. 23:32 reads "the sons of Jashen."

HASHMONAH (Heb. *ḥašmōnâ*)
One of the Israelites' wilderness encampments between Mithkah and Moseroth (Num. 33:29-30). The name may derive from Heb. *šmn,* "to be fat," suggesting an area of abundance. Asemona (biblical Azmon), 'Ain el-Qeṣeimeh (099008; 16 km. [10 mi.] NW of Kadesh-barnea), and Heshmon (Josh. 15:27; in the Negeb) are possible locations.

PETE F. WILBANKS

HASHUBAH (Heb. *ḥăšuḇâ*)
A son of Zerubbabel (1 Chr. 3:20).

HASHUM (Heb. *ḥāšum*)
1. An Israelite whose descendants returned from the Exile under Zerubbabel (Ezra 2:19 = Neh. 7:22).

2. A representative of the family of Hashum **1** who stood at Ezra's left during the reading of the law (Neh. 8:4; 1 Esdr. 9:44, "Lothasubus"). It was probably he who set his seal to the renewed covenant (Neh. 10:18[MT 19]). Members of this family were required to give up their foreign wives (Ezra 10:33; 1 Esdr. 9:33).

HASIDEANS (Gk. *Asidaíoi*) (also HASIDIM)
A Jewish group in the 2nd century B.C.E. (1 Macc. 2:42; 7:13; 2 Macc. 14:6). Very little can be said with any certainty about the nature of this group and its role in the historical development of Judaism. The Greek term is a transliteration of Heb. *ḥăsîḏîm,* "Hasidim" or "pious." While the name appears to derive from Heb. *ḥasîḏ* as used in the OT, there is no evidence to suggest that Ps. 149:1 or other references in the Psalms should be used as evidence of this group.

The Hasideans are included in the account of the growth of the forces which joined Mattathias the priest and his sons in the Maccabean revolt in 167 B.C.E. (1 Macc. 2:39-48). They are described in 1 Macc. 2:2 as *ischyroí dynámei,* usually translated "mighty warriors" but which could equally well refer to "mighty men," a group of leading citizens of Judea. The members of this elite group "offered themselves willingly for the law," pledging to violate the prohibition instituted by Antiochus IV against its observance (1 Macc. 1:41-50). Included among the prohibitions were sacrifices and offerings in the temple as well as the observance of sabbaths, festivals, and the rite of circumcision.

Some scholars attribute the origins of the Pharisees and the Essenes to the Hasideans. In 1 Maccabees Mattathias and his friends are provoked to revolt when the Seleucid king's troops attack on the sabbath a group of Jews who had fled to the wilderness seeking righteousness and justice (1 Macc. 2:29-38). By relating these Jews who fled to the wilderness in 1 Macc. 2:29 to the Hasideans in v. 42, the latter are considered to be the foreparents of the two more broadly attested movements. The Essenes and the Pharisees then grow out of a split in the Hasidic movement. Other scholars have argued that apocalyptic literature such as the book of Daniel comes from this same group. All these claims can remain only hypothetical.

The leading role of the Hasideans is also described in 1 Macc. 7:12-18, where they are said to be "first among the Israelites" (v. 13), also referred to as a "company of scribes" (v. 12). Their political significance, however, is discounted by the pro-Hasmonean author of this dynastic history. The Hasideans are said to have trusted the "peaceable words" of Alcimus and Bacchides (1 Macc. 7:15), a confidence badly misplaced since it results in the murder of 60 members of their company in one day (v. 16). The use in 1 Macc. 7:17 of Ps. 79:2-3 as a proof-text explaining the fate of the Hasideans suggests that the author did regard them as legitimate but perhaps misguided martyrs on behalf of Israel. Some scholars have used this passage as evidence that they were a purely religious group uninterested in the politics of 2nd-century Judea.

In 2 Macc. 14:6 the impious high priest Alcimus names Judas Maccabeus as the leader of the Hasideans and accuses them of "keeping up war and stirring up sedition," not permitting the kingdom to find stability. It appears that this author is using the prestige of the Hasideans to exalt the reputation of Judas Maccabeus, the hero of this history.

Rabbinic literature contains references to the "first Hasidim." Their relationship to the group mentioned in Maccabees cannot be clearly established.

Bibliography. P. R. Davies, "Ḥasidim in the Maccabean Period," *JJS* 28 (1977): 127-40; M. Hengel, *Judaism and Hellenism.* 2 vols. (Philadelphia, 1974); L. Jacobs, "The Concept of Ḥasid in the Biblical and Rabbinic Literatures," *JJS* 8 (1957): 143-54; J. Kampen, *The Hasideans and the Origin of Pharisaism.* SBLSCS 24 (Atlanta, 1988). JOHN KAMPEN

HASMONEANS (Gk. *Asamōnaios*)
A prominent priestly, but non-Aaronic family from Modein. They began a revolt in 167 B.C.E. against their hegemon, Antiochus IV Epiphanes, the Seleucid king of Syria, and the Hellenized Jewish factions in Judah and Jerusalem. The latter included members of the high priestly orders and the aristocracy that supported and were supported by the Seleucids.

It is not clear whether religious persecution of non-Hellenized Jews resulted from or was the cause of the rebellion. The persecution consisted of an interdiction of sabbath keeping, feast keeping, and circumcision. It also consisted of the defilement of the temple and the priests, and the offering of sacrifices to Greek gods on a pagan altar in the Jerusalem temple as well as elsewhere in Judah and Jerusalem (Dan. 11:31-33; 12:11; 1 Macc. 1:1-64; 2 Macc. 6:1-6). Although the rebels viewed this as an attempt to suppress Judaism (1 Macc. 1-2; 2 Macc. 5:11–7:42), it was as much a sociopolitical action to sustain the pro-Syrian factions as a religious repression of those who were pro-Egyptian and/or anti-Syrian.

Mattathias killed Epiphanes' official and the first Jew to sacrifice at the pagan altar at Modein. Then Mattathias and his sons, John "Gaddi," Simon "Thassi," Judas "Maccabeus," Eleazar "Avaran," and Jonathan "Apphus," fled to the hill country, where an ever-increasing band of Jews, some of whom were Hasidim (1 Macc. 2:42-44; 7:13-14; 2 Macc. 14:6), joined them in their rebellion.

When Mattathias died, the leadership passed to Judas, surnamed Maccabeus ("the hammer"), from whence the popular name for the family derived. Although the Hasmoneans soon became sufficiently strong to fight more conventionally and to defeat the Syrian armies, they really succeeded because Epiphanes was fighting the Parthians at the same time.

Allegedly, some type of peace was declared (165) allowing Judas to enter Jerusalem, although it is more likely that after what seemed to be a miraculous victory (1 Macc. 4) he actually recaptured the city. He did not have access to the Akra, a Syrian fortress, although he tried to take it when Epiphanes died in 164/3. On returning to Jerusalem, Judas instituted an eight-day celebration as part of the rededication of the Jerusalem temple in 164 B.C.E. (1 Macc. 4:52-59), subsequently celebrated as Hanukkah (4:59; John 10:22).

Judas had not achieved independence, however. Even after Epiphanes' death, Judas continued to fight against the successor, Antiochus V Eupator. Although Judas won a great victory over the Seleucid forces, led by Nicanor, at Beth-horon in 161, his troops were defeated and he died in a later battle in 161/160. At this time, the Hellenized Jews again became ascendant in Judah and Jerusalem.

Judas' successor, Jonathan, then sided with Alexander Balas against Demetrius, each of whom having more or less overt support by different factions at Rome was vying for the Seleucid throne. Balas first appointed Jonathan high priest (153). After Demetrius' death, Balas also appointed Jonathan provincial governor of Judea (150). Jonathan's success was not long lasting. He was captured and ultimately murdered by the Syrian general Tryphon in 143 or 142.

Simon then took up the leadership, further expanding the state. In 141 he took the Akra in Jerusalem. The following year he became high priest of the Jews in Judah and Jerusalem, even though he was not of a high priestly order. He also became commander-in-chief and ethnarch of the Jews (1 Macc. 14:41-43), confirmed by the Seleucid king. Under Simon's rule the state became autonomous and free from tribute (Josephus *BJ* 1.53; *Ant.* 13.211). This does not mean that it became independent of Syrian hegemony, as many believe, because autonomy and independence were not legally the same in the Hellenistic or the Roman world.

In 134 Simon and two of his sons, Judas and Mattathias, were murdered by Simon's son-in-law Ptolemy (1 Macc. 16:11-17). When Ptolemy's bid for power failed, Simon's remaining son, John Hyrcanus, took power. After being confirmed as high priest, Hyrcanus ruled Judah and Jerusalem from 134 to 104. He extended the boundaries of his state to its greatest point since Solomon. He changed theo-political "parties," giving allegiance to the Sadducees, even though the Pharisees allegedly had the support of the masses.

After Hyrcanus died in 104, his son Aristobulus became the first Hasmonean to take the title "king." He ruled for one year, during which time he extended the kingdom. After his death in 103, Aristobulus' widow Alexandra married one of his brothers, Alexander Janneus, who ruled from 103 to 76.

Janneus fought foreign wars, extending the kingdom greatly. He also dealt with internal, religiously-based conflict by supporting the Sadducees as had his father. At his death he advised Alexandra to make peace with the Pharisees so as to ensure her rule. When Alexandra became ruler of the kingdom (76) with the support of the Pharisees, she made her son Hyrcanus II high priest. This, however, did not insure his succession.

At the death of Alexandra (66), her sons Aristobulus II and Hyrcanus II engaged in civil war. Pompey the Great was invited to intervene and did so in 64, first sending his general Scaurus. A year later Pompey came himself, captured Jerusalem, and installed Hyrcanus as high priest and ethnarch, but not king, of the state whose territory he then reduced. He took Aristobulus to Rome, parading him in his triumph.

In light of Roman foreign policy, Pompey, whose assignment under the Gabinian Law was to pacify the Mediterranean world and who was given unlimited powers under the Manilian Law, had not acted precipitously or without right. Rome's hegemony over the Hasmoneans had been established as a sort of protectorate, in accordance with Roman law, when Rome had granted Judas and his followers an *amicitia* ("friendship" or diplomatic agreement) in 161. Later, when the *amicitia* was changed into a suzerainty treaty (*societas et amicitia*, "alliance and friendship") that was renewed at the ascension of each Hasmonean except for Aristobulus and Alexander Janneus, the "client kingdom" was subject to Rome's iron-fisted rule.

Hyrcanus ruled as a Roman client from 63 to 40. After Hyrcanus' death (40), Antigonus II became, with the support of the Parthian enemies of Rome, the last ruler of the Hasmonean family. He ruled for three years (40-37), at which time Rome placed a client king, Herod, who had ties by marriage to the Hasmoneans, on the throne of Judah and Jerusalem.

Bibliography. E. Bickerman, *From Ezra to the Last of the Maccabees* (New York, 1962); S. R. Mandell, "Did the Maccabees Believe That They Had a Valid Treaty with Rome?" *CBQ* 53 (1991): 202-20; "The Beginnings of Roman Hegemony over Judah and Jerusalem," *Approaches to Ancient Judaism* N.S. 3 (Atlanta, 1991): 3-83; M. Rostovtzeff, *The Social and Economic History of the Hellenistic World*, 3 vols. (Oxford, 1941). SARA R. MANDELL

HASRAH (Heb. *ḥasrâ*) (also HARHAS)

1. The grandfather of Shallum (2 Chr. 34:22). At 2 Kgs. 22:14 the name appears as Harhas.

2. The head of a family who returned to Jerusalem with Zerubbabel following the Exile (1 Esdr. 5:31; Gk. *Asara*). The name is omitted in the parallel accounts (Ezra 2:49; Neh. 7:51).

HASSENAAH (Heb. *hassĕnā'â*)
The head of a family whose members assisted in repairing the walls of Jerusalem (Neh. 3:3). They may be associated with the family or town of Senaah.

HASSENUAH (Heb. *hassĕnu'â, hassĕnû'â*)

1. The father of Hodaviah; a Benjaminite whose descendants lived in Jerusalem after the Exile (1 Chr. 9:7).

2. The father of Judah (**5**), who was second in command of Jerusalem during the time of Nehemiah (Neh. 11:9).

HASSHUB (Heb. *ḥaššûḇ*)

1. A Levite of the line of Merari; the father of Shemaiah (1 Chr. 9:14; Neh. 11:15).

2. A son of Pahath-moab who aided in rebuilding the walls of Jerusalem (Neh. 3:11).

3. An Israelite who helped to rebuild the walls of Jerusalem (Neh. 3:23). Either he or **2** above set his seal to the renewed covenant under Nehemiah (Neh. 10:23[MT 24]).

HASSOPHERETH (Heb. *hassōpereṯ;* Gk. *Assaphiōth*)
The head of a family or guild of "Solomon's servants" who returned from the Exile with Zerubbabel (Ezra 2:55; 1 Esdr. 5:33; cf. Neh. 7:57, "Sophereth").

HASUPHA (Heb. *ḥăśûpā'*)
A temple servant whose descendants returned from the Exile with Zerubbabel (Ezra 2:43 = Neh. 7:46).

HATE
Hate is such a basic human emotion that it is not surprising to find it regularly highlighted in the Bible, even in the anthropopathisms applied to God in the OT (absent in the NT; but Rom. 9:13). While the Hebrews naturally had a whole range of such emotions ranging from outright death-seeking malice to mere preference, disregard, and rejection, they had no suitable words to express different shades of meaning. Thus words such as "love" and its opposite "hate" (Heb. *śānē'*; Gk. *miséō*) were used to express the idea of preference.

In the OT, God who is holy and jealous is described as hating the worship of false gods (Deut. 12:31); the liturgy of Israel, its sacrifices, new moons, and sabbaths because they lack deep sincerity and obedience (Isa. 1:14; Amos 5:21); injustice (Isa. 61:8); and sinners (Hos. 9:15). Two lists are collected in Prov. 6:16-19; 8:13. Yahweh hates Esau ("prefers" Jacob; Mal. 1:3). Joseph's brothers hate him because of his father's favoritism (Gen. 37:4). Isaac is hated (Gen. 26:27; cf. Jephthah, Judg. 11:7). In the OT the one clear prohibition is hatred of one's kin (Lev. 19:17-18), while one is commanded also to love the alien (Deut. 10:19). Even God is hated (1 Sam. 8:7; Jer. 14:19); this means ignoring God's commands and persecuting his people. Thus the enemies of the psalmist who range from the communal to the personal, the political to the religious, are also those who hate God (Ps. 68:1[MT 2]; 81:15[16]). They hate peace (Ps. 120:6) and discipline (50:17) and plot against God's people (83:2[3]). Naturally one hates such people (Ps. 139:21). At Qumran the community was called to separate from the wicked and to hate them (1QS 3:26–4:1), and to pursue the sons of darkness with an "everlasting hatred in a spirit of secrecy" (1:10). While God punishes the wickedness of those who hate to the third and fourth generations (Deut. 5:9), according to Ezekiel God desires not the death of the sinner (Ezek. 18:23), and Wisdom insists that God cannot hate any of the beings he has made (Wis. 11:24).

Jesus bluntly rejects hatred and insists that love is the only law, even in relation to one's enemies. This is explained as to pray for one's enemy (Matt. 5:44-45) and to "do good to those who hate you" (Luke 6:27). Paradoxically, discipleship involves a certain type of hate, or rather hierarchy of commitment, placing Jesus first in one's life before father, mother, brothers, sisters, wife, and children (Luke 14:26). Likewise a disciple must even hate oneself (John 12:25). Life in the old aeon was characterized by hate (Tit. 3:3) but in the new by love (Rom. 13:8-10; 1 John 2:10). The Johannine writings are the most prominent for the sharp contrast between the divine love and the sin of the world of darkness which is hatred for God, Christ, and God's people (John 15:23-24; 7:7; 15:18). One of the clear limitations of 1 John is its enthusiastic dedication to love (1 John 4:19) yet its bitter condemnation of former members as demonic antichrists, false prophets, and examples of lawlessness and evil (2:18-19; 4:1-6; 3:4-5). God did not send his Son to condemn the world but because he so loved the world (John 3:16).

Seán Kealy, C.S.Sp.

HATHACH (Heb. *hăṯāḵ*)
A eunuch belonging to the Persian king Ahasuerus, appointed to attend Queen Esther. It was through him that Esther learned from Mordecai about Haman's plot against the Jews (Esth. 4:5-10).

HATHATH (Heb. *ḥăṯaṯ*)
A Judahite, son of Othniel (1 Chr. 4:13).

HATIPHA (Heb. *ḥăṭîpā'*; Gk. *Atipha*)
A temple servant whose descendants returned from the Exile with Zerubbabel (Ezra 2:54 = Neh. 7:56 = 1 Esdr. 5:32).

HATITA (Heb. *ḥăṭîṭā'*; Gk. *Atēta*)
A levitical gatekeeper whose descendants returned with Zerubbabel from the Exile (Ezra 2:42 = Neh. 7:45 = 1 Esdr. 5:28).

HATTIL (Heb. *ḥaṭṭîl*)
A family of "Solomon's servants" whose descendants returned from the Exile with Zerubbabel (Ezra 2:57 = Neh. 7:59 = 1 Esdr. 5:34).

HATTIN, HORNS OF
A mountain pass in the heights above the Sea of Galilee ca. 8 km. (5 mi.) NW of Tiberias, in the saddle between two peaks connecting the Sea of Galilee with the coastal plain. Here a decisive battle of the Crusades took place. Under the leadership of Saladin (Salah ad-Din), Islam's greatest warrior, Moslems sought to recapture territory wrested from them by earlier crusading armies. On the way to Jerusalem, Saladin's forces laid siege to Tiberias. A Crusader force, led by Guy of Lusignan, king of Jerusalem, marched to relieve the besieged city. The armies met on 4 July 1187. By taking advantage of the heat, the heavy armor of the Crusaders, and a

superior strategic position, the Moslem army overwhelmed and shattered the Crusader forces. In October 1187 Jerusalem fell to Saladin as well.

D. Larry Gregg

HATTUSH (Heb. *ḥaṭṭûš*)

1. A son of Shemaiah and grandson of Shecaniah (1 Chr. 3:22); a postexilic descendant of David who returned from the Exile with Ezra (Ezra 8:2; 1 Esdr. 8:20; here called a "son" of Shecaniah; NRSV "descendant").

2. The son of Hashabneiah who repaired a portion of the walls of Jerusalem (Neh. 3:10).

3. A priest who returned from exile with Zerubbabel (Neh. 12:2). He may be the same Hattush as the priest who set his seal to the renewed covenant under Nehemiah (Neh. 10:4[MT 5]).

HAURAN (Heb. *ḥawrān*)

The area of Transjordan which extended from Mt. Hermon and the River Pharpar in the north to the Yarmuk River in the south and from the Sea of Galilee on the west to Jebel ed-Druze on the east. It encompasses basically the same territory as Bashan. The northern part is tableland with many volcanoes and rocky soil well known for its pastureland. The southern part contains an ancient layer of very fertile decomposed lava.

The name means either "hollow land" or "black-land," the latter referring evidently to the black basalt which covers much of the region. It appears for the first time in Egyptian texts of the 19th century B.C. and in Assyrian cuneiform texts as early as the 15th century. Shalmaneser III mentions the "mountains of the land of Hauran," and Assurbanipal refers to the "district of Hauran." Hauran occurs in Ezekiel's vision of restored Israel as the ideal border of the land (Ezek. 47:16, 18).

After the Exile Hauran was settled by Jews, Greeks, and Nabateans who struggled for its control. It came under Hasmonean domination in the 2nd century, only to be lost to the Nabateans in 90 B.C. By the Roman period it was known as Auranitis (Josephus *Ant* 17.11.4 [319]) and was made a part of the Decapolis by Pompey. Augustus gave it to Herod the Great ca. 23 B.C., and it was later under the control of Herod Philip, Agrippa I, Agrippa II, and the Nabateans before finally becoming part of the province of Syria (A.D. 106).

Paul J. Ray, Jr.

HAVILAH (Heb. *ḥăwîlâ*) **(PERSON)**

1. A son of Cush, according to the Table of Nations (Gen. 10:7; 1 Chr. 1:9).

2. A son of Joktan and descendant of Shem (Gen. 10:29; 1 Chr. 1:29); eponymous ancestor of an Arabian people.

HAVILAH (Heb. *ḥăwîlâ*) **(PLACE)**

A region surrounded by the Pishon River, known for its fine gold, bdellium, and onyx stone (Gen. 2:11-12). Etymologically, the name is probably derived from the West Semitic root *ḥwl* "sand," and thus refers to the "land of sand." Because of the enigmatic, or mythic, geography of Eden, it is uncertain whether Havilah refers to a specific locality known to Israel (probably in Arabia) or is used generally to refer to the desert region outside the garden.

Elsewhere, Havilah refers to a specific region of Arabia or to Arabia in general which was known for its gold, precious stones, and valuable resins. In the Table of Nations, Havilah is listed as a descendent of Cush (Gen. 10:7) and of Joktan (v. 29). In both cases it is associated with known regions of Arabia such as Sheba and Dedan. Havilah is also mentioned as the easternmost region settled by the Ishmaelites (Gen. 25:18) and later by the Amalekites (1 Sam. 15:7). Some scholars have associated Havilah with the region of Haulan in southwest Arabia, first attested in an Old Sabean inscription and preserved in the name of two modern Yemenite tribal groups.

Ronald A. Simkins

HAVVOTH-JAIR (Heb. *ḥawwōṯ yāʾîr*)

A number of villages in the region of Bashan, E of the Sea of Galilee. The Manassehite Jair captured a number of tent villages (Num. 32:41) and called them Havvoth-jair ("villages of Jair"). These villages were located in the region of Argob which was a part of Bashan (Deut. 3:4, 14). All the territory of Bashan with its 60 cities (Deut. 3:4) was then allotted to the half tribe of Manasseh (Deut. 3:14; Josh. 13:30). This seems to be confirmed by 1 Chr. 2:22-23, which reports that Geshur and Aram took Havvoth-jair (23 cities) and Kenath (37 cities), 60 towns all located in Bashan.

Later the Gileadite judge Jair gave to his 30 sons towns in Gilead known as Havvoth-jair (Judg. 10:3-5); apparently he is a different Jair from the one in Num. 32:41. In Solomon's administration the region of Argob numbered 60 walled cities (1 Kgs. 4:13). These discrepancies may represent different traditions and sources, scribal errors, or even indicate an increase in settlements due to a population explosion during the Iron I and II periods.

Bibliography. R. G. Boling, "Some Conflated Readings in Joshua-Judges," *VT* 16 (1966): 293-98.

Zeljko Gregor

HAWK

A generic term for small or medium-sized diurnal birds of prey, particularly those in the family Accipitridae. The term is sometimes extended to include certain members of the family Falconidae, which tends to create confusion in terms of classification and naming of species.

Heb. *nēṣ* is similarly generic. It occurs in the lists of nonpermitted birds (Lev. 11:16; Deut. 14:15), on both occasions followed by the clarification "of any kind." Eight to 10 different species of hawks are found in Israel today. The word is obviously related to the cognate verb *nāṣaṣ*, "to fly." The soaring flight of the *nēṣ* is noted in Job 39:26.

Heb. *taḥmās* (originally meaning "robber," "bandit") has traditionally been translated "nighthawk," but this bird of the family Caprimulgidae is seldom found in the Middle East and is not related

HAZOR-HADATTAH (Heb. *ḥāṣôr ḥădattâ*)
A city apportioned by Joshua to the tribe of Judah following the conquest of Canaan (Josh. 15:25). Its exact location is a matter of dispute. Eusebius places the city close to the Mediterranean coast (*Onom.* 20.4), while others favor a spot closer to Arad, posibly el-Hudeiria (170086). RYAN BYRNE

HAZZELELPONI (Heb. *haṣṣĕlelpônî*)
A Judahite woman from the town of Etam, designated as the sister of the "sons of Etam" (1 Chr. 4:3).

HEAD
Generally the head of the physical body, the seat of the sensory organs and the brain (Heb. *rōʾš;* Gk. *kephalḗ*). Several passages allude to particular customs pertaining to the head. The covering of one's head was an act of contrition (2 Sam. 15:30) or shame (Jer. 14:3). Casting dust upon the head was an act of grief (2 Sam. 13:19; Lam. 2:10; Ezek. 27:30; Rev. 18:19). The shaving of one's own head was also an act of grief (Job 1:20; Jer. 16:6), but the shaving of another person's head was a way of humiliating that person (1 Chr. 19:4-5; 1 Cor. 11:5-6). By anointing the head with oil a person was consecrated and received God's blessing. A ceremony of anointing accompanied the installation of new priests (Exod. 29:7; Lev. 8:12) and kings (1 Sam. 10:1; 16:13).

Often, the term "head" refers to one in a position of leadership (Josh. 11:10; Judg. 11:11). Paul blended this understanding of head with the literal concept when he spoke metaphorically of the Church as the body and Christ as the head (Eph. 1:22-23; 4:15; Col. 1:18; 2:19), thus emphasizing the unity of the Church, which is united under the leadership of Christ (the head).

"Head" also may refer to that which is most important. This is probably the sense in references to Jesus as the "main *(kephalḗ)* cornerstone" (Mark 12:10; Matt. 21:42; Luke 20:17; Acts 4:11; 1 Pet. 2:7; cf. Ps. 118:22). Similarly, Mt. Zion is referred to as the "chief of the mountains" (Isa. 2:2; Mic. 4:1), and Jerusalem is exalted above my "main joy" (Ps. 137:6). MARK R. FAIRCHILD

HEALING
See ILLNESS AND HEALTH CARE.

HEART
In general, the center or middle of things (Deut. 4:11; Matt. 12:40). The ancients did not seem as concerned about the heart (Heb. *lēḇ, lēḇāḇ;* Gk. *kardía*) as an organ as they were about such other organs as the liver and kidneys. References to the heart as a physical organ are extremely rare in the OT (cf. 1 Sam. 25:37). Even in 2 Sam. 18:14; 2 Kgs. 9:24 the meaning seems to be wider than the specific organ of the heart, indicating the internal organs generally. In Ps. 104:15 the "heart" is affected by food and drink, which could be true of the literal heart as an organ, but probably denotes a more general reference to "experience" (cf. REB, NAB).

Heart was commonly used, as today, of the center of something — whether humans or other objects, and from this usage the term was applied to the whole range of internal and central things in humans. The ancients did not use detailed psychological vocabulary to make the fine distinctions used in modern speech. The Hebrews thought of the whole human being and personality with all its physical, intellectual, and psychological attributes when they used "heart." It was considered the governing *center* for all of these. It is the heart (the core) which makes and identifies the person (Prov. 4:23). Character, personality, will, and mind are modern terms which all reflect something of the meaning of "heart" in its biblical usage.

Less often was "heart" used for emotions which are preferably expressed by such organs as the liver, or the bowels, or the kidneys, the region of the "loins." In general, Hebrew thought placed the emotional focus lower in the anatomy (liver, bowels, kidneys) than the intellectual or volitional, which was placed higher in the anatomy (heart). The same anatomical geography is generally true in English which uses the higher area of the "head" (brain or mind) to express the intellectual and volitional matters but the lower "heart" for emotional issues. Modern English translations are inclined to use "mind" to translate *lēḇ/lēḇāḇ* (cf. NRSV Eccl. 1:17; Prov. 16:23); however, "heart" is a broad term and does not make the same distinctions in reference to the rational or mental processes as did Greek philosophy.

NT usage is colored by the OT and contains very similar examples. Heart still is used in the physical sense, for it is made of "flesh" (2 Cor. 3:3), but it is also the seat of the will (Mark 3:5; 7:21-23), the intellect (2:6-8), and emotion (Luke 24:32). Thus it also means "person" in the NT.
LARRY L. WALKER

HEARTH
In its basic sense, a depression in the ground in which was built a fire for cooking or heating. In cultic usage the hearth was the upper portion of the altar of burnt offering upon which the sacrifice was burned (Lev. 6:9; Ezek. 43:15-16). The hearths in Ezekiel's ideal temple are used for boiling sacrifices (Ezek. 46:23-24).

HEAVEN
In Hebrew cosmology heaven(s) (Heb. *šāmayim*), Yahweh's dwelling place, and earth comprise God's creation. Heaven depicts skies, the upper part of the created world, and denotes the firmament (a vault or roof of the earth). It may be used literally or metaphorically, and denotes fixed or material reality. It designates God's unique home, a sanctuary, the throne of divine majesty, remoteness, and transcendence. Heaven is a space immediately surrounding the earth (e.g., atmosphere), a place of natural and supernatural signs, outer space. The firmament (Gen. 1:6-8), a solid mass (Isa. 45:12), rests on pillars (Job 26:11) and has windows (Gen. 8:2). Eschatologically, *šāmayim* concerns a new order that replaces the old or present imperfect order. Later, heaven means the destiny of and the spiritual

apex of covenantal righteousness with God, as some Jewish groups supported the resurrection of the dead and final judgment.

In the NT heaven(s) (Gk. *ouranós*) and earth comprise all of creation, though the two are distinctive (Matt. 6:9). God spoke both into existence, but humanity cannot understand either (cf. Isa. 40:12). The heavens bring on drought, house the stars, and provide atmosphere for clouds. In the eschaton, new wonders will appear. The NT relates the heavens to God's rule or kingdom on earth and to Jesus' return. Heaven, the seat of redemption and reconciliation, is beyond time; it may appear as a series (three or seven); and is foundational for this world where one experiences happiness, praise, and service. In NT postexilic Judaism, heaven symbolizes God or the divine name and ascribes divine authority. Heaven is not an idyllic place of pure light and glory, but an arena of conflict, of divine wrath. The climax of God's salvific acts occurs as an eschatological catastrophe via God's judgment. A new heaven and a new earth emerge: eternal, pure, and free from God's wrath (Rev. 21:1, 27; 22:3). Heaven, the dwelling place of God and Jesus, before and after his earthly journey, resurrection, and exaltation, produces voices, angels, the Messiah, and souls.

Theologically, heaven is God's realm. Sometimes God and heaven are used synonymously, and the opening of heaven signals God's nearness. Heaven is the dwelling place for Christ from before time with God, and also for angels, Satan, and evil spirits. For Christ, heaven is his place of origin before coming to earth, and his destination at the Ascension. It is the locus for Christ's activity on behalf of the Church, and from which he comes at the Parousia. Soteriologically, heaven is the arena of the true Jerusalem of God's mercy, blessings, and truth. The blessed reside in heaven via ascension. In the Prophets and the Psalms, heaven is the seat of divine sovereignty.

Heaven is the abode of God and of God's angels, the just, and the holy. It is the real home of Christians on earth, the treasures of the faithful, and the arena of salvation — the ultimate home of Christ's disciples. For Matthew, Jesus has authority in heaven and earth — a christological mediation from above and ecclesiological logical mediation from below. For some, the Matthean kingdom of heaven concerns a futuristic, imminent but otherworldly reality, where the present world will no longer exist. Others argue that the Matthean kingdom of heaven does not always refer to the future, as distinctive from the already begun kingdom of God. Matthew's kingdom of heaven may be already begun in Jesus' ministry, and if not recognized, shows one's spiritual hardness.

In Revelation heaven wants to send messengers so Christians may understand heavenly things. Heaven seems to be an arena of activity where basic human, societal qualities are being restated, fought for, and determined. The heavenly, spiritual world has heavenly bodies, always maintained by the divine energetic presence that was, is, and will be.

For Christians, contemporary cosmology requires a heaven of faith not contained by a hemisphere above the horizon as God's throneroom. God does not exist only in a spatial, localized sense of heaven above the world nor metaphysically, beyond the world. Our experience of heaven is not limited by infinity or finiteness of the universe in space and time. The heaven of faith is ontological, a way of being. God's heaven is God's arena of existence symbolized by the visible physical heaven, denoting an invisible, mysterious sphere of God's rule, and it completes all that is good. Heaven symbolizes resurrection hope to experience a love for life prior to and after death, being interconnected and simultaneously grounded in heaven and earth. Heaven is both now and in process, not yet. Heaven embodies the vision of eternal life with God steeped in mutuality, mercy, and justice that accords a transcendent freedom, an eschatological love, and a liberating salvation of humanity.

Bibliography. D. A. Carson, "The ὅμοιος Word-group as Introduction to Some Matthean Parables," *NTS* 31 (1985): 277-82; K. Grayston, "Heaven and Hell: A Door Opened in Heaven," *Epworth Review* 19 (1992): 19-26; H. Küng, *Eternal Life?* (Garden City, 1984); J. Michl, "Heaven," in *Sacramentum Verbi,* ed. J. B. Bauer (New York, 1970), 366-69; M. Pamment, "The Kingdom of Heaven According to the First Gospel," *NTS* 27 (1981): 211-32; G. von Rad and H. Traub, "ouranós," *TDNT* 5:497-543; K. Syreeni, "Between Heaven and Earth: On the Structure of Matthew's Symbolic Universe," *JSNT* 40 (1990): 3-13. CHERYL A. KIRK-DUGGAN

HEBER (Heb. *ḥeḇer*)

1. A son of Beriah and descendant of Asher (Gen. 46:17; 1 Chr. 7:31-32). He is the eponymous ancestor of the Hebrites (Heb. *ḥeḇri;* Num. 26:45).

2. A Kenite, descended from Hobab. He had separated from the main body of Kenites, settling near Kedesh where he coexisted peacefully with King Jabin of Hazor (Judg. 4:11, 17); it was there that Heber's wife Jael murdered Sisera by driving a tent peg through his temple as he slept (vv. 12-22).

3. A descendant of the Judahite Ezrah and his Judean wife (1 Chr. 4:18); the ancestor or founder of Soco.

4. A Benjaminite, the son of Elpaal (1 Chr. 8:17).

HEBREW, BIBLICAL

Hebrew belongs to the Semitic family of languages, a subgroup of the larger Afro-asiatic family which includes Egyptian, Berber, and the more modern Cushitic, Omotic, and Chadic (e.g., Hausa) groupings. The Semitic family, attested as early as the 3rd millennium B.C.E. (e.g., Akkadian), survives up to the present (e.g., Arabic, Hebrew), and is divided into eastern and western branches. The eastern branch is represented by Akkadian, the language of the Babylonians and Assyrians, and most likely Eblaite, known from the archive found at Tell Mardikh in Syria. In the western branch are South Semitic (Ethiopic [Geʿez] and South Arabic) and Central Semitic. The latter denotes Arabian lan-

The Hebrew alphabet with equivalent transliteration

(Five of the letters — k, m, n, p, ṣ — have final forms occurring only at the end of words)

ת	שׁ	שׂ	ר	ק	צץ	פף	ע	ס	נן	מם	ל	כך	י	ט	ח	ז	ו	ה	ד	ג	ב	א
t	š	ś	r	q	ṣ	p	ʿ	s	n	m	l	k	y	ṭ	ḥ	z	w	h	d	g	b	ʾ

	Stops/Plosives			Fricatives			Glides	Lateral	Nasal	Vibrant
	Voiced	Unvoiced	Emphatic	Voiced	Unvoiced	Emphatic	Voiced	Voiced	Voiced	Voiced
Bilabial	b	p					w		m	
Dental	d	t	ṭ	z	s	ṣ		l	n	
Palatal					š		y			r
Velar	g	k	q							
Pharyngeal				ʿ	ḥ					
Glottal		ʾ			h					

guages (e.g., Classical Arabic and several modern dialects) as well as Syro-Palestinian (Northwest Semitic) languages which are traditionally divided into Aramaic and Canaanite subgroups. Hebrew is a Northwest Semitic language which belongs to the Canaanite subgroup along with sister languages Phoenician, Ammonite, Edomite, and Moabite. Hebrew also shares an affinity to Ugaritic, though its precise position within the Northwest family is still debated.

History

Hebrew is well-known as the language of the Hebrew Bible (OT), even though it went by different names in biblical times (e.g., *śĕpat kĕnaʿan,* "the language of Canaan," Isa. 19:18; *yĕhûdît,* "Judahite," 2 Kgs. 18:26, 28; 2 Chr. 32:18; Neh. 13:24; Isa. 36:11, 13). During the Hellenistic period, the designation *Hebraios,* "Hebrew," is found in the prologue to Ben Sira and Josephus (*Ant.* 1.1:2). In rabbinic literature it came to be known as *lĕšôn haqqodeš,* "the holy language" (*m. Soṭa* 7:2).

The study of Biblical Hebrew is a very complex endeavor involving many disciplines such as linguistics, comparative Semitics, epigraphy, orthography, textual criticism (e.g., Dead Sea Scrolls, LXX, Targumic, and Masoretic studies), not to mention a basic grounding in historical-critical methodologies such as redaction criticism. Redaction criticism underscores how all of the biblical texts underwent a late editorial process making them difficult to use to reconstruct the early history of the language. Some scholars, especially those associated with the Albright school, have argued that archaic features in poems such as Exod. 15; Judg. 5; Ps. 68 give evidence of the character of Hebrew in the early Iron I period. Scholars who wish to reconstruct an even earlier stage of the language (proto-Northwest Semitic) have no biblical texts dating to the Late Bronze period and are forced to rely on cognate material such as the Ugaritic texts, Amorite personal names, and the Amarna tablets. Even though the Amarna tablets are written in Akkadian vocabulary, they reflect a distinct Northwest Semitic morphology and syntax which are attributed to their native Canaanite setting.

When it comes to the Iron Age, the character of Hebrew can be studied not only from the biblical texts, but also from extrabiblical inscriptions such as the Gezer Calendar (10th century), the Kuntillet ʿAjrud pithoi (8th century), the Khirbet el-Qom tomb inscription (8th century), Samaria ostraca (8th century), Siloam inscription (8th-7th century), Arad Letters (6th century), Lachish Letters (6th century), and numerous seals from the 8th to the 6th centuries. The Hebrew found in the Bible is broken down into archaic Hebrew (gleaned primarily from biblical poems which have preserved earlier features of the language that find corroboration in the early extrabiblical epigraphic sources), preexilic Hebrew (often called Classical Biblical Hebrew) and postexilic Hebrew (often called Late Biblical Hebrew). Some scholars have seen signs of a Transitional Biblical Hebrew between the latter two stages.

Grammar

The Hebrew alphabet, written from right to left, consists of 22 signs which are used to represent 23 consonants (the same sign was used for both /ś/ and /š/; later these were distinguished by the Tiberian Masorah with a diacritical dot to the upper left and right respectively). Two of the signs also represent the glides /w/ and /y/.

The chart above provides a very approximate schematization of the Hebrew consonants, with the vertical axis representing the place of pronunciation and the horizontal axis representing the manner in which the consonant is pronounced. It is unclear how /ś/ was pronounced originally; it becomes homophonous with /s/. It should also be noted that the Tiberian Masorah represented a distinction between stop and spirants in the six letters *b/ḇ, g/g̱, d/ḏ, k/ḵ, p/p̄, t/ṯ* (a dot was placed in the middle of the stops).

There is considerable debate over the character of the Hebrew vocalic system. The oldest form of the language did not employ vowel indicators. At a later stage several consonants (*w, y,* and *h,* known as *matres lectionis*) were used to mark final and, at a later point, medial vowels. The Tiberian system of vocalization (a mostly infralinear system of pointing used in the majority of today's Hebrew Bibles) contains signs to mark vowels (a-class: *pataḥ, qameṣ;* i-class: *segol, ṣere, ḥireq;* u-class: *ḥolem, šureq, qibbuṣ, qameṣ-ḥaṭup*) and half-vowels (known as *shewa* or *ḥaṭep-shewa;* if unstressed, the diphthongs *aw* and *ay* contracted to *ô* and *ê,* respectively). It should be underscored that this system represents a late tradition which marks quality but not quantity.

Hebrew nouns have two categories of grammatical (morphological) gender. In general, the masculine is unmarked while the feminine can be marked (*â* with *h mater lectionis, -at, -t, -et*) or unmarked. Hebrew has three categories of number: singular (unmarked), plural (most masculine nouns marked by *-îm;* most feminine by *-ôt/ōt,* although there are well-known exceptions to each and collectives also occur), and dual (*-ayim*). Some dual forms also serve as the plural form (e.g., body parts). Definiteness can be marked by the prefix *h-* on both nouns and adjectives (attributive and demonstrative). In its earliest form Hebrew nouns were marked for three cases (with *-u, -i,* and *-a* endings for the singular; *-ū* and *-ī* for plural; cf. Classical Arabic, Akkadian, Ugaritic), yet this system has all but disappeared except for some vestiges. In its place Biblical Hebrew uses what is called a "construct chain" to represent the genitive where the first of two juxtaposed nouns is in a "construct state" (or "bound") to the second; in such "bound forms" the first noun loses its definite article and can undergo vowel reduction or contraction. The accusative can be marked (although it is not obligatory) by the use of *-'eṯ* prior to the direct object (commonly when the object is a definite noun or a proper name). The nominative is unmarked.

The Hebrew verbal system is, without doubt, the most debated part of the grammar. Hebrew roots are basically triliteral, with quadriliteral roots occurring only rarely. Biliteral roots are mostly allomorphs of triliteral roots. There are seven primary stems (or "themes"; known in Hebrew as *binyanim*) including the qal (basic or simple unaugmented form), niphal (prefixed *n-;* originally medio-passive, later passive, reflexive, resultative), piel (doubled middle radical; factitive), pual (passive of piel), hiphil (some forms contain prefixed *h-;* originally causative), hophal (passive of hiphil), and hithpael (infixed *-t-* form of piel; reflexive, iterative, reciprocal). Most of the stems can also be used in forming denominative verbs, with piel and hiphil stems utilized most often. In addition to these seven stems known from the Masoretic pointing, scholars have also reconstructed the original qal passive (pointed by the Masoretes as puals and hophals). There are also rarely attested derived stems known as the polel (active), polal (passive), and hithpolel (reflexive) which reduplicate the final root letter of hollow verbs (cf. also geminate roots) as well as palal (reduplicated third root consonant) and pilpel (reduplicated biconsonantal root) stems.

Most traditional grammars describe the verbal system as including suffixal perfective ("perfect" or *qatal*) and prefixal, nonperfective ("imperfect" or *yiqtol*) conjugations as well as participles (active and passive), imperatives, jussives, and infinitives (the so-called infinitive construct can function as a verbal noun [taking pronominal suffixes], an infinitive, or a gerund; the so-called infinitive absolute is misnamed; it primarily functions as an adverb emphasizing or complementing the main verb, although it can also substitute for a finite verb). Yet, in addition to such simplified presentations, there is a vast amount of scholarly literature debating the fine points of Hebrew grammar from a linguistic perspective.

Verbal System

Diachronic vs. Synchronic Approaches

Hebrew grammarians — past and present — differ with respect to whether they see Biblical Hebrew as having a temporal or aspectual verbal system and whether it should be analyzed synchronically or diachronically. Diachronically, scholars have traditionally looked at the verbal system as having two primary conjugations: the suffixal perfective ("perfect" or *qatal*) and prefixal, nonperfective ("imperfect"; *yaqtul* > *yiqtol*). Recently, scholars using a comparative Semitic approach (especially Amarna Canaanite and Ugaritic; cf. also Akkadian) have emphasized the existence of a "short" *yaqtul* preterite/jussive form (in contrast to the "long" *yaqtulu* imperfective form) to address the vexing question of the so-called *waw*-conversive (*wayyiqtol*) forms. Synchronically, some scholars have identified five basic forms: perfect, imperfect, narrative (=*waw*-consecutive), converted perfect, and volitive (including jussive, cohortative, and imperative forms). Of these, the imperfect and the converted perfect could be paired according to function as could the perfect and the narrative forms. At the same time, discourse grammarians have paired the narrative and converted perfect forms as sequential over against the nonsequential perfect and imperfect forms.

Tense vs. Aspect

The debate over whether the Hebrew verbal system is temporal or aspectual is ongoing. The analysis of Hebrew as an absolute tense system dates back to Ibn Janah. Modern scholars who argue for Hebrew being some type of a tense system (cf. Paul Joüon–Takamitsu Muraoka, Gotthelf Bergsträsser) often theorize that Hebrew is a relative tense system in which a tense does not so much indicate the point in time of the speech-act (although it can do such) as it situates the verb in relation to the speaker (anterior or posterior). As a result of the work of H. G. A. Ewald and S. R. Driver, as well as more recent studies in the Slavic languages and Greek, the majority of modern grammars of Biblical Hebrew since the mid-19th century have emphasized that Hebrew has an aspectual verbal system (e.g., Bruce K. Waltke-Michael P. O'Connor). These works emphasize that Hebrew is a "tenseless" system; verbs are more properly analyzed according to duration or "the contour of a situation in time." Thus a perfective verb describes a complete or completed (even punctual) action, while an imperfective verb describes an incomplete or durative (even habitual) action.

Bibliography. D. J. A. Clines, ed., *The Dictionary of Classical Hebrew* (Sheffield, 1993–); P. Joüon, *A Grammar of Biblical Hebrew* (Rome, 1991); L. Koehler, W. Baumgartner, and J. J. Stamm, *The Hebrew and Aramaic Lexicon of the Old Testament* (Leiden, 1994–); T. N. D. Mettinger, "The Hebrew Verb System: A Survey of Recent Research," *ASTI* 9 (1973): 65-84; A. Sáenz-Badillos, *A History of the Hebrew Language* (Cambridge, 1993); C. L. Seow, *A Grammar for Biblical Hebrew,* rev. ed. (Nashville, 1995); B. K. Waltke and M. P. O'Connor, *An Introduction to Biblical Hebrew Syntax* (Winona Lake, 1990).

Theodore J. Lewis

HEBREW, HEBREWS

A non-ethnic term (Heb. *ʿiḇrî*) that non-Israelites used in referring to Israelites, and that Israelites used in referring to themselves when conversing with non-Israelites.

As a patronymic, the term is thought to be derived from the name of Abraham's ancestor, Eber (Gen. 10:24-25; 11:14-26; 1 Chr. 1:18-19), as suggested by the genealogical references to Abraham and his descendants (Gen. 14:13; 39:14; 40:15; 43:32; Exod. 2:6; Deut. 15:12; 1 Sam. 4:9; 29:3; Jonah 1:9; Acts 6:1; 2 Cor. 11:22; Phil.3:5). It is used for Abraham and for his posterity prior to the eschatological event in which Jacob received the name Israel.

In linguistic usage Hebrew designated the Judahite language, a member of the Canaanite branch of Northwest Semitic languages. The term "Hebrew" as a denotation of the language *per se* is first seen in the prologue to Sirach. In the NT "Hebrew" (Gk. *Hebraíos*) or "language of the Hebrews" *(Hebraïs)* denotes a language or languages used by Jews (John 5:2; 19:13, 17, 20; 20:16; Acts 21:40; 22:2; 26:14; Rev. 9:11; 16:16). There is some uncertainty as to whether references to Hebrew in the Apocrypha (4 Macc. 12:7; 16:15) and the NT denote Hebrew or Aramaic.

Various 2nd-millennium ancient Near Eastern texts refer to people classified as *habīru/ʿapīru,* a term that some think denotes "Hebrews." The *habīru* may be social outcasts, fugitives, refugees, or mercenary groups, but it is unlikely that they formed an ethnicity. Ancient Near Eastern references suggest that the *habīru* in Canaan, mentioned in the Amarna Letters, were not the Israelites. A relationship between the term *habīru* in the Nuzi servant contracts and the Hebrew slave of Exod. 21:2; Deut. 15:12 is unlikely, in part because the Nuzi archives are from a different time than the biblical narrative. In the Nuzi texts *habīru* denotes a "foreign servant" who sold himself into slavery; in Deut. 15:12 the Hebrew servant is called the "brother" of those being addressed.

The LXX translates "Abram the Hebrew" (Gen. 14:13) as "Abram, the one who crossed over" (cf. Heb. *ʿbr*). This has been tied to Abraham's having come from the other side of the Euphrates (Josh. 24:2-3) and, although not generally accepted, to the Israelites' crossing of the Jordan. Early rabbinic interpretation treats "Hebrew" as a reference to those who had crossed over the Reed/Red Sea. Since this may be eschatological, it implies that a Hebrew is one who experienced death and resurrection.

A case can be made for viewing the contrast between Egyptians and Hebrews in Gen. 43:32; Exod. 1:19; 2:11 as connoting ethnic distinctions; the parallelism between Yahweh the God of Israel (Exod. 5:1) and the God of the Hebrews (v. 3) could lead to such an understanding. However, as used in the OT or the Apocrypha, the term Hebrew does not usually denote an ethnicity. It is used by non-Israelites (OT) or non-Jews (Apocrypha) speaking of Israelites (Gen. 41:12) or Jews (Jdt. 12:11; 14:18), respectively. When used by someone who is not an Israelite, the term may have some derogatory connotation or imply that the Israelite is not free (e.g., Potiphar's wife [Gen. 39:14, 17] and the chief butler [41:12] in referring to Joseph). When used by an Israelite speaking to a non-Israelite, it frequently implies that the Israelite is not free (e.g., Joseph refers to the place from whence he comes as "the land of the Hebrews"; Gen. 40:15) or only figuratively free (e.g., when speaking to the non-Israelite sailors, Jonah defines himself as a Hebrew; Jonah 1:9). Such meanings are frequent in Gen. 30–Exod. 10, particularly when Israel is not free (e.g., in Exod. 5:1-3 Moses refers to the "God of the Hebrews" when Israel is in slavery to Egypt).

There is no ethnic connotation when "Hebrew" is used in the legislation concerning the manumission of Hebrew slaves/servants as found in Exod. 21 (social and economic rules in the Covenant Code, having a different origin from the Covenant Code that follows 22:17[MT 16]) and Deut. 15 (which forms part of the Mosaic law) and possibly Jer. 34:9, which also refers to Hebrew slaves. What is permitted regarding a Hebrew in Exod. 21 is forbidden for an Israelite in Lev. 25; and there is a distinction between voluntary nonpermanent labor and the harsh type of enforced service forbidden in Lev. 25:43-44.

There is no ethnic connotation in the reporting of the relationship between the Israelites and the Hebrews in 1 Sam. 4; 13–14; 29. The distinction may be between Israel as a whole and select groups of Israelites or of those who joined together with the Israelites, thereby becoming part of all Israel. The Hebrews of 1 Sam. 13–14 seem to be non-Israelite mercenaries at the same time that they seem identical to "all Israel." The Philistines refer to Israelites while calling them Hebrews (1 Sam. 14:11), an identification that is related to what is found in 13:19-20. But there is no ethnic reference in 1 Sam.

13:6-7, where the distinction may be between two different groups within "all Israel": v. 6 notes those excused from military service and v. 7 notes Israelite deserters from Saul's army. In 1 Sam. 14:21 those Hebrews who fought for the Philistines are to be treated as Israelite traitors. But those Hebrews who come back to Saul (1 Sam. 13:7a) together with the Israelites who had taken refuge in the hill-country of Ephraim (14:22) joined together in Saul's army.

In the NT "Hebrew" designates certain sectarian groups of Jews. It may designate someone who is superficially hellenized (Acts 6:1), or it may merely distinguish between Jews and Gentiles (2 Cor. 11:22; Phil. 3:5).

Bibliography. G. E. Mendenhall, "The Hebrew Conquest of Palestine," *BA* 25 (1962): 66-87; repr. *BA Reader* 3, ed. E. F. Campbell and D. N. Freedman (Garden City, 1970), 100-20. SARA MANDELL

HEBREWS, EPISTLE TO THE

Although Hebrews has circulated since the 2nd century among the letters of Paul and bears the apostle's name in the title of the KJV, the absence of the common characteristics of the Pauline letter indicates that it cannot easily be included within the Pauline correspondence. Indeed, the author and destination of Hebrews remain a mystery. Moreover, since the book lacks the common characteristics of epistles, its literary form also remains a matter of debate. Undebatable, however, is the fact that Hebrews is the work of a skilled rhetorician, who has provided the most sustained argument from OT Scripture within the NT. In a series of expositions, the author argues for the superiority of Jesus Christ and Christian experience to all OT institutions. Its placement after the Pauline letters and before the General Epistles reflects the distinctiveness of the book.

Literary Genre

Although Hebrews contains an epistolary conclusion (13:18-25), the remainder of the book has a totally different character from the Christian epistolary tradition that began with Paul. It lacks the epistolary opening, the common epistolary topics, and the argumentative structure of the Pauline Epistles. Indeed, the author refers to his message as a "word of exhortation" (13:22), a term which is used elsewhere (Acts 13:15) for a synagogue sermon. This was a rhetorical form that had developed in the Hellenistic Jewish synagogue consisting of 1) an indicative or exemplary section in the form of scripture quotations or theological points; 2) a conclusion based on the exemplary section; and 3) an exhortation to the community. Unlike the Pauline Epistles, Hebrews follows the common pattern of the word of exhortation. The epistolary conclusion is added to the homily because the author's sermon had to be sent.

Content

The distinctive rhetorical character of Hebrews is evident in the introduction (1:1-4), which sets the tone in both content and rhetorical power for the remainder of the homily. In these poetic lines that are filled with alliteration and assonance, the author declares that God has spoken in these last days "by a son" who, as a result of his "making purification for sins" and sitting down at the right hand of the majesty on high, is now greater than the angels. With this "overture," the author establishes the major themes of the book. He demonstrates the ultimacy of the Christian revelation in comparison with God's previous disclosures in the OT (1:1-2), and develops the high christological claim with the rhetorical device of comparison ("greater than"; cf. 6:9; 7:7, 19, 22; 8:6; 11:16, 40; 12:24). Because of the exaltation to God's right hand (Ps. 110:1), Christ is greater than all counterparts from the OT.

The remainder of the book is an amplification of the theme introduced in 1:1-4. Although the homily appears to be a series of expositions on various passages from Scripture, the unifying thread is the claim that is first established in the introduction: Christians possess a salvation through Jesus Christ that surpasses all objects of comparison. Through the interweaving of exposition and exhortation, the author indicates that the theological claims serve as a basis for exhortation. The claim that Christ is greater than the angels (1:5–2:18) is the basis for the exhortation to the community to pay attention to what it has heard (2:1-4). The comparison of Christ to Moses (3:1-6) and the assurance that he leads his people to the transcendent "rest" which Israel never attained (3:7–4:11) provide the basis for the exhortation to the community to enter that rest (4:11). After a brief reflection on the power of the word of God (4:12-13), the central section of this homily (4:14–10:31) is a comparison of the high priesthood of Christ with the high priesthood of Aaron derived from various OT passages (Ps. 110:1, 4; Lev. 16; Jer. 31:31-34). That this extended comparison of high priest, sacrifice, and sanctuary serves primarily the needs of exhortation is indicated by the exhortations which introduce (4:14-16) and conclude (10:19-31) this major section and by the extended exhortations that precede the discussion of the high priesthood of Melchizedek (5:11–6:12). A similar alternation of OT reference, comparison, and exhortation distinguishes the final section of Hebrews, which begins in 10:32. The extended depiction of examples of faithfulness among OT heroes (ch. 11) is both introduced (10:32-39) and followed (12:1-11) by the exhortation to the community to endure faithfully in the midst of hardship. Similarly, the author introduces the climactic comparison of the Sinai theophany and the Christian experience of Mt. Zion (12:18-29) with the exhortation for faithfulness (12:12-17). The final challenge for the community to go "outside the camp" (13:13) and to "offer a sacrifice of praise" (v. 15) rests on the comparison of the death of Christ "outside the city gate" (v. 12) with the levitical sacrifices (vv. 10-12).

In each comparison the author interprets the OT in order to show the superiority of Christian experience. OT institutions — angels (1:5-13), the high priesthood of Aaron (5:1-10; 7:11-28), the tabernacle (8:1-6), the sacrifices (9:1-28), and the Sinai theophany (12:18-25) — fail in comparison to Christ because they belong to the transitory world. Because Christ has sat down at the right hand of God (1:3; 8:1; 10:12), he is eternal. Hence Christians have not approached "what may be touched" (12:18) or "seen" (11:1), and the sacrifice of Christ was performed in a sanctuary "not made with hands" (9:11).

Structure

The interweaving of exposition and exhortation in Hebrews is the key element in determining the structure of this homily.

- I. The Revelation of the Word in the Son (1:1–4:13)
  - A. The Son greater than angels (1:1–2:18)
  - B. Exhortation to hear the voice of the Son (3:1–4:13)
- II. Christ the great high priest (4:14–10:31)
  - A. Exhortation to hold fast the confession (4:14-16)
  - B. Introduction of Christ the high priest (5:1-10)
  - C. Exhortation to be faithful and obtain the promises (5:11–6:20)
  - D. Christ the great high priest (7:1–10:18)
  - E. Exhortation to hold fast the confession (10:19-31)
- III. Call to faithful obedience (10:32–13:25)
  - A. Exhortation to be faithful (10:32–12:11)
  - B. Sinai and Zion (12:12-29)
  - C. Concluding exhortations to faithfulness (13:1-25)

Authorship

Although Hebrews has consistently been attributed to Paul since antiquity, the internal evidence of the book precludes authorship by the apostle. Unlike Pauline Epistles, Hebrews is anonymous. The fact that the language and style of Hebrews is far superior to that of the Pauline correspondence is further evidence that the author of Hebrews was not Paul. Although numerous candidates for authorship have been suggested — e.g., Barnabas, Apollos, Silvanus, Priscilla — the book does not supply enough information about the identity of the author to make such speculation useful. We know from internal evidence only that Hebrews is written by a skilled rhetorician of the second Christian generation (2:3).

Although the writer is anonymous, he is known to the original readers. His request that the community pray for his reunion with them (13:18-19) and his expressed desire to return to them with Timothy after the latter is released (13:23) provide further information about the author's relationship to his readers. The reference to Timothy probably indicates that the author belongs to a Pauline circle. Thus the early attribution of Hebrews to Paul may suggest that ancient readers were aware of an association between the book and Paul.

Intended Audience

The identity of the original readers is as obscure as the identity of the author. The title, "To the Hebrews," is a later conjecture based on the book's consistent appeal to the OT as the basis for the author's argument. Although this conjecture is plausible, it is by no means certain, for the book contains no direct statement that the readers are Jewish. Moreover, detailed arguments from the OT appear in books that are addressed to primarily gentile audiences in such Pauline letters as Galatians and 1 Corinthians.

The only direct indication of the location of the readers is the ambiguous statement in 13:24, "Those from Italy send you their greetings," which can be interpreted as a reference either to the location of the author or the readers. The phrase "from Italy" is used elsewhere (Acts 18:2) for Aquila and Priscilla, who have recently come "from Italy" and are now living in Corinth. This parallel suggests, therefore, that the author of Hebrews writes from a location in which he has met expatriates "from Italy" who send greetings to their home city. As in Acts 18:2, Italy is the equivalent of Rome. A Roman destination for Hebrews may also be suggested by the fact that the book is first quoted in 1 Clement, which was written from Rome at the end of the 1st century. A Roman destination for Hebrews is thus plausible but far from certain.

The author provides abundant evidence of the circumstances of his readers. Like the author, they belong to the second generation (2:3). Indeed, the distinction between the "earlier days" (10:32) of the Church's infancy and the present time (5:12) is the basic factor which lies behind the author's description of the readers' situation, for the author consistently insists that the community was exemplary in its Christian practice in the earlier days, but now faces a situation of crisis. In the earlier days the readers had demonstrated work and love in serving the saints (6:10), and had endured a "hard struggle with sufferings," including public abuse, compassion on prisoners, and the confiscation of their property (10:32-34). The author describes the present crisis as one of "drifting away" (2:1), falling away (3:12), and of committing apostasy. The nature of this apostasy may be seen in the author's description of the readers' condition. They are "dull in understanding" (5:12), and some are abandoning the assembly (10:25). They have "drooping hands and weak knees" (12:12). Hence the author's major concern throughout this work is to ensure that they maintain their endurance until the end (cf. 3:14). The author's frequent description of the condition of the readers indicates that the crisis to which Hebrews is addressed is not, despite numerous claims to the contrary, the problem of the readers' temptation to return to Judaism. Nor is the book written to counter a particular heresy. The author of Hebrews writes to encourage his community to remain faithful in the context of the lethargy and discouragement that threaten its existence.

Bibliography. H. W. Attridge, *The Epistle to the Hebrews.* Herm (Philadelphia, 1989); W. L. Lane, *Hebrews,* 2 vols. WBC 47-48 (Waco, 1991); J. W. Thompson, *The Beginnings of Christian Philosophy.* CBQMS 13 (Washington, 1982).

JAMES W. THOMPSON

HEBREWS, GOSPEL ACCORDING TO THE

A Jewish-Christian apocryphal Gospel, written in Egypt ca. 150 C.E. It was known and used by Clement of Alexandria (ca. 150-215), Origen (ca. 185-254), and Didymus the Blind (ca. 313-398), all of whom were Egyptian writers. Eusebius (ca. 260-340) also knew the Gospel and mentions it alongside the Gospel of Matthew in Hebrew and an Aramaic Gospel. Since he assigns no language to this Gospel but does to the others, it is assumed that the Gospel acording to the Hebrews was written in Greek. Jerome (ca. 342-420) claims to have translated it from Hebrew into Greek and Latin, but he is sometimes mistaken about this Gospel, on occasion believing that it, the Aramaic Gospel, and the Gospel of Matthew in Hebrew are one and the same.

The contents of the Gospel according to the Hebrews are not fully known. According to the Stichometry of Nicephorus (ca. 758-829), it contained 2200 lines, only 300 short of the Gospel of Matthew. Extant quotations of or allusions to it are found in Clement of Alexandria, Origen, Cyril of Jerusalem (ca. 315-386), Didymus the Blind, and Jerome. From them we can infer that the Gospel acording to the Hebrews covered the preexistence of Christ, his baptism, the temptations, the Last Supper, the Passion, a resurrection appearance to James the Just (cf. 1 Cor. 15:7), and three isolated sayings. None of the extant references suggests the Gospel's dependence on the canonical Gospels.

Bibliography. R. Cameron, ed., *The Other Gospels* (Philadelphia, 1982); J. K. Elliott, *The Apocryphal New Testament,* rev. ed. (Oxford, 1993), 9-10; A. F. J. Klijn, *Jewish-Christian Gospel Tradition.* Vigiliae christianae Sup 17 (Leiden, 1992).

GEORGE HOWARD

HEBRON (Heb. *ḥeḇrôn*) **(PERSON)**

1. A Levite, the third son of Kohath (Exod. 6:18; Num. 3:19; 1 Chr. 6:2, 18[MT 5:28; 6:3]; 23:12) and father of four sons (v. 19; 24:23). His descendants were called Hebronites (Heb. *ḥeḇrônî;* Num. 3:27; 26:58; 1 Chr. 26:30-31; cf. 15:9).

2. A Calebite and son of Mareshah; father of four sons (1 Chr. 2:42-43). This name and the others in the genealogy (as well as those in **1** above) may actually be place names.

HEBRON (Heb. *ḥeḇrôn*) **(PLACE)**

A city 30.6 km. (19 mi.) SSE of Jerusalem and 37 km. (23 mi.) NE of Beer-sheba, 1021 m. (3350 ft.) above sea level on the Judean mountain ridge; also known as Kiriath-arba ("city of four"; Gen. 23:2). With the possible exception of Jerusalem, probably no other site in ancient Palestine enjoys more biblical, intertestamental, and folklore attention than Hebron. Built traditionally "seven years before Zoan in Egypt" (Num. 13:22), Hebron was where Abraham pitched his tent after his separation from Lot and where he "built an altar to the Lord" (Gen. 13:18), entertained "angels" (18:1-15), pleaded for the innocents of Sodom (18:22-33), and bought the cave of Machpelah as a burial place for Sarah (23:1-20), setting the stage for subsequent burials of all the patriarchal family (25:9-10; 35:27-29). During the Exodus, Hebron's vineyards were appreciated by the spies of Moses.

After the Conquest, Hebron was "given" as an inheritance to Caleb (Josh. 14:13) and became a place of refuge (20:7) and a levitical city (21:11-13). It was in the days of David, however, that the city attained its greatest biblical renown as the capital of Judah (1 Sam. 2:11; 5:5) and, seven and a half years later, as the capital of the United Monarchy until the capture of Jerusalem. Absalom attempted to usurp his father's throne at Hebron, and Solomon, so Josephus tells us, had his vision there. With the breakup of the United Monarchy, Hebron appeared in the list of Rehoboam's refortified cities (2 Chr. 11:10) and then drops out of biblical mention.

Local folklore added much to the biblical stories, setting Hebron as the place where Adam and Eve mourned for Abel and as the location of the tombs of Jesse and Ruth, the tomb of Abner, and even the source of the red earth from which Adam was formed!

Extrabiblical evidence suggests that Hebron may have been a Canaanite royal city, and the nearby oak of Mamre, an oracular center. A possible reading in the Amarna Letters may refer to the site as early as the 14th century B.C.E., and the Medinet Habu list of Rameses III also mentions a site that may have been Hebron. Hebron may be the city noted in the conquest list of Shishak of Egypt ("a field of Abram"), against whom Rehoboam had been refortifying southern sites. During the 8th century the city appears to have functioned as a royal pottery center, as the unmistakable jar handle inscriptions found all over Palestine attest.

The first major excavation of the site (160103), with the discovery of the Middle Bronze Age walls (ca. 1728) and their characteristic "Hyksos" battering, was conducted by the American expedition to Hebron in 1965-66. Further excavations were conducted by Israeli archaeologists. Archaeological evidence carries the occupation of the area back to the Chalcolithic period, through the Early Bronze Age, to the time the city was "officially" built in the second half of the Middle Bronze Age.

No record of Hebron appears in either the Assyrian or the Neo-Babylonian conquest lists, but its prominence obviously precluded it from being overlooked by any eastern conqueror. After the fall of Jerusalem, Edomites occupied the city and were not dislodged until Judas Maccabeus took the city from their successors, the Idumeans, in 164. Later, Herod refurbished the city and built an enclosure around the traditional burial place of the patriarchs, as his characteristic masonry there still attests.

The site continued to attract attention during the later Roman period, the Islamic conquest, and the time of the Crusades. "Destroyed" by Vespasian's general Cerialis, enough remained of the city that Hadrian later built a road to its market. At the bequest of the prophet Mohammed, the city formally entered the Islamic period. During the Crusades, Hebron became a major link in the line of Frankish fortress-cities, which sustained the Latin Kingdom, under the name "Castle of St. Abraham." With the fall of the western powers, Hebron again reverted to Muslim control and became, finally, one of the major holy places in all of Palestine, even becoming a station on the *hegira* route to Mecca. The Arabic name given to the city, el-Khalil ("the Friend"), reflects its Abrahamic ties. PHILIP C. HAMMOND

HEGAI (Heb. *hēgay, hēgē'*)
A eunuch of the Persian king Ahasuerus in charge of the royal harem. He won the trust of Esther when she was preparing to meet Ahasuerus (Esth. 2:3, 8, 15).

HEGEMONIDES (Gk. *Hēgemonidēs*)
A Syrian official whom Antiochus named governor of the district from Ptolemais to Gerar at the time of Philip's attack on Antioch (2 Macc. 13:24).

HEGLAM (Heb. *heglām*)
A son of Ehud, and the father of Uzza and Ahihud; an alternate name for Gera (1 Chr. 8:7; NRSV mg "he carried them into exile").

HEIFER
A young cow (Heb. *'eglâ, 'eglaṯ bāqār*), especially one which has not produced offspring. Heifers were used for milk (Isa. 7:21) and apparently for plowing (Deut. 21:3). Heifers were occasionally used for special sacrifices (Gen. 15:9; 1 Sam. 16:2) and were designated in the ritual for the purging of bloodguilt in case of a rural murder where the culprit remained unknown (Deut. 21:1-8).

Samson likened intrigue with his wife to having "plowed with my heifer" (Judg. 14:18). Jeremiah uses heifers as symbols of carefree Egypt and Babylon (Jer. 46:20; 50:11), and Hosea pictures Ephraim as a "trained heifer" (Hos. 10:11).

Of particular significance is the ritual for purifying a person defiled by contact with a corpse (Num. 19:1-22). A "red heifer" (Heb. *pārâ*, the usual word for "cow") is slaughtered outside the camp and burned. The ashes are then mixed with spring water to produce the water of purification (Num. 19:17-19). The sacrifice is unique in that it was performed away from the altar of the sanctuary and, though the process was intended to remove impurity, individuals who contacted the cow, its ashes, or the water of purification were considered unclean (Num. 19:7-10, 21; cf. *Midr. Rabbah, Num. Rab.* 19:5-6). According to the Mishnah, the ashes were divided into three parts: one was kept on the rampart, one on the Mount of Olives, and one divided among the 24 courses of priests (*m. Para* 3:11). The water of purification was placed in a jar at the entrance to the temple court. According to *m. Para* 3:5, only seven (according to Rabbi Meir) or nine (according to the Sages) red heifers were actually burned, since after the destruction of the temple it was impossible to sacrifice more, but use of the ashes may have continued into the talmudic period. Some later traditions hold that the Messiah will prepare the last of the red heifers or otherwise emphasize an eschatological role for the sacrifice.

DANIEL C. BROWNING, JR.

HELAH (Heb. *ḥel'â*)
One of the two wives of Ashhur, the ancestor of Tekoa (1 Chr. 4:5, 7).

HELAM (Heb. *ḥêlām*)
A town E of the Sea of Galilee where David defeated and subjugated the Syrians/Arameans (2 Sam. 10:1-10). 1 Chr. 19 tells the same story without Helam. LXX Ezek. 47:16; 48:1 place Helam between Damascus and Hamath. Suggestions for its location include Haleb (Aleppo) and Alamatha on the Euphrates. It may be the same as Alema (modern Alma) in 1 Macc. 5:26, 35, possibly a district rather than a city. PHILIP R. DREY

HELBAH (Heb. *ḥelbâ*)
A town in the territorial allotment of Asher, the Canaanite inhabitants of which the Israelites were unable to expel (Judg. 1:31). The name is thought to be a duplication of Ahlab in the same verse and may be identified with Mahalab/modern Khirbet el-Maḥâlib (172303; cf. Josh. 19:29).

HELBON (Heb. *ḥelbôn*)
A city famed for its wine and honey (Ezek. 27:18), which are mentioned in inscriptions of Nebuchadnezzar and also by the Greek geographer Strabo. It is identified with modern Helbûn, a village 17 km. (11 mi.) N of Damascus in a region of the Anti-Lebanon Valley that is still a center for the cultivation of grapes.

HELDAI (Heb. *ḥelday*)

1. A Netophatite who served in David's army as one of 12 commanders responsible for the monthly course of 24 thousand men (1 Chr. 27:15). His designation "of Othniel" likely indicates his descent from the deliverer of Judg. 3:7-11. Heldai may be equated with both Heled (1 Chr. 11:30) and Heleb (2 Sam. 23:29).

2. A former Babylonian exile whom Zechariah commanded to participate in crowning Joshua (Zech. 6:10; "Helem" at v. 14 is likely a scribal error). KENNETH ATKINSON

HELEB (Heb. *ḥēleḇ*)
One of the David's Thirty; the son of Baanah of Netophah (2 Sam. 23:29). He is probably the same as Heled (1 Chr. 11:30) and Heldai (**1**; 27:15).

HELECH (Heb. *ḥêlēḵ*)
A source of the mercenary forces of Tyre (Ezek. 27:11; LXX "your army"). The name may designate Cilicia in southeastern Asia Minor (cf. Akk. *Ḫilakku*).

HELED (Heb. *ḥēleḏ*)
One of David's Thirty; the son of Baanah of Netophah (1 Chr. 11:30). He is probably the same as Heleb (2 Sam. 23:29) and Heldai **1** (1 Chr. 27:15).

HELEK (Heb. *ḥēleq*)
A son of Gilead and descendant of Manasseh (Num. 26:30; Josh. 17:2); eponymous ancestor of the Helekites.

HELEM (Heb. *hēlem*) (also HELDAI, HOTHAM)
1. A descendant of Asher (1 Chr. 7:35); called Hotham (**1**) at v. 32.
2. One responsible for the crown of the postexilic high priest (Zech. 6:14 MT). Elsewhere the name appears as Heldai (**2**).

HELEPH (Heb. *ḥēlep̄*)
A town on the border of the territory assigned to Naphtali (Josh. 19:33). A possible location is modern Khirbet ʿIrbâdeh/Ḥorvat ʿArpad (189236), slightly NE of Mt. Tabor.

HELEZ (Heb. *ḥeleṣ*)
1. A Judahite and descendant of Jerahmeel; the son of Azariah and father of Eleasah (1 Chr. 2:39).
2. A Pelonite of the tribe of Ephraim; commander of the seventh division of David's army (1 Chr. 11:27; 27:10). At 2 Sam. 23:26 he is called "the Paltite."

HELI (Gk. *'Ēlí*)
The father of Joseph, according to Luke's version of Jesus' genealogy (Luke 3:23; cf. Heb. *ʿēlî*).

HELIODORUS (Gk. *Hēliodōros*)
An official of the Seleucid court who was sent by Seleucus IV to confiscate money from the Jerusalem temple after a Jew named Simon informed Apollonius, the governor of Coele-Syria, that the temple held great wealth (2 Macc. 3). Simon's action resulted from a long rivalry between two Jewish clans. Simon, a Tobiad, thought that providing the Seleucids with information might help him prevail over the high priest Onias III. Further, Simon could deal a blow to a "renegade" family member, Hyrcanus, whom the Oniads had supported and who had considerable wealth deposited in the temple. Heliodorus' approach threw the whole city into mourning and prayer. As he neared the treasury, a heavenly horse and rider struck him and two men scourged him. Worried that Seleucus might wrongly think that the Jews had attacked Heliodorus, Onias III offered up a sacrifice to save the man's life. Heliodorus then made a sacrifice to God and returned home without the money.

RODNEY A. WERLINE

HELIOPOLIS (Gk. *hēlíou pólis*)
1. The Egyptian city On, capital of the 13th nome of Lower Egypt and center for worship of the sun-gods Atum and Re (cf. Jer. 43:13).
2. Greek name for Baalbek.

HELKAI (Heb. *ḥelqāy*)
A priest during the time of the high priest Joiakim (Neh. 12:15; perhaps a shortened form of Hilkiah).

HELKATH (Heb. *ḥelqaṯ*)
A city allotted for the tribe of Asher (Josh. 19:25), one of four levitical cities in Asher (21:31; cf. 1 Chr. 6:75[MT 60], Hukok). Its exact location in the Kishon Valley is disputed. Possible sites include Tell el-Harbaj (158240) and Tell el-Qasis (160232).

BRADFORD SCOTT HUMMEL

HELKATH-HAZZURIM (Heb. *ḥelqaṯ haṣṣūrîm*)
A place near the pool of Gibeon where 12 combatants of Joab's forces and 12 of Abner's slaughtered each other in a tournament of champions (2 Sam. 2:16; NRSV mg "Field of Sword-edges").

HELL
An English word used to translate four biblical terms. Heb. *šĕ'ôl* and Gk. *hádēs* generally refer to the world of the dead. Tartarus (cf. Gk. *tartaróō*, 2 Pet. 2:4) is the place of punishment for fallen angels awaiting final judgment. Gk. *géenna* is the place and condition of just retribution saved for the post-judgment impenitent.

Originally, all the dead had the same banal existence in Sheol. Sheol later included an eschatological dimension, a future with resurrection, final judgment, doctrines; it was the grave, and the shadowy realm of the dead, where the human spirit no longer exists. The three-tiered cosmology of heaven, earth and Sheol or Hades shifted with the realization of a planetary system. Preexilic Hebrew thought assumed the dead formed a faceless collective after death. Gk. *phylakḗ*, also the underworld or the place of punishment in hell, is where Satan is made harmless during the millennium (Rev. 20:7); though death occurs, the *pneúma* exists, and "prison" becomes the place of torture.

Gehenna first clearly occurs as a post-final judgment locus of the wicked in Enoch. In Hades, a preparatory place, the souls await their end. In rabbinic literature Gehenna refers to the final, not an intermediate, place of retribution. Apocalyptic writings announce death, resurrection, a judgment, final punishment, and a place of retribution that imply Gehenna. The term derives from "the valley of Hinnom" (or "lamentation") near Jerusalem. The pollution there signified horror, defilement, and consuming fires. Consequently, Gehenna became a metaphor for acute torment. During Jesus' time, Gehenna meant an irrevocable, eternal doom for the wholly wicked.

The Lukan Hellenistic Gehenna concerns immediate reward and punishment after death, the resurrection of the just. Following judgment, God sends the wicked to Hades or Gehenna, and the righteous go to Paradise for resurrection with Jesus at the Parousia. A Jewish-influenced Matthew omits reward and punishment at death, and ascribes a judgment day, resurrection, bodily Gehenna, and an eternal agony for the wicked. After the resurrection and judgment, Gehenna receives the evil for retribution.

Hades, the place of all the dead, is the name of the Greek underworld god. Sheol and the old concept of Hades are the dark, gloomy abodes of the dead. Increased Jewish belief in resurrection meant God would bring the dead from Hades back to life — a return of corporeal life; a life for resurrected spirits in heaven. God brings the soul from Hades and the body from the grave to be rejoined in resurrection. At the resurrection, death ceases, and Hades will be closed. Both death and Hades diminish into the lake of fire (Rev. 20:14).

In Jewish eschatology, death meant the separation of the body and soul. Yet no harm occurs after death, for the soul remains secure. Matt. 25 portrays hell as the domain of Satan and his angels, and the damned. The OT makes no reference to torture once persons are relegated to Sheol. Intertestamental literature focuses on heavenly assistance against God's enemies, a human messiah, and divine justice.

Most scholars agree that the only text (1 Pet. 3:18-20) which might imply Jesus' descent into hell does not support earlier interpretations that suggest Jesus' preaching to the dead or experiencing a passion or damnation. Recent scholars view this event as the work of the risen Christ. Some scholars contend Christ descended into hell triumphantly after his death, to show himself as the defeater and conqueror of death, Satan, and hell. The NT does not reflect any passion or activity of Jesus between death and resurrection.

Most interpreters agree that Eph. 4:8 first concerns Christ's descent (v. 9), then his triumphant ascent after his death and resurrection: from heaven to earth (incarnation) or from earth to grave (Sheol). Others contend the descent occurred after Jesus' ascension and depicts the return to the earth of the exalted Christ as the Spirit and Pentecost.

Jesus did not proclaim a doctrine of hell nor describe damnation, and spoke only marginally of hell. His proclamation of the kingdom of God invited one to choose salvation or doom, yet Jesus did not preach dualism. Many contrasting metaphors for hell indicate God's wrath and punishment. The notion of eternity indicates a final punishment, but not necessarily one that extends for all times. Ideas of complete destruction and infinite punishment over against universal love, mercy, and reconciliation exist throughout Scripture and Church history. Ultimately, damnation is not an absolute and remains contingent on God's will and grace.

Bibliography. G. Doehler, "Descent into Hell," *Springfielder* 39 (1975): 2-19; W. H. Harris, III, "The Ascent and Descent of Christ in Ephesians 4:9-10," *BSac* 151 (1994): 198-214; H. Küng, *Eternal Life?* (Garden City, 1984); C. Milikowsky, "Which Gehenna? Retribution and Eschatology in the Synoptic Gospels and in Early Jewish Texts," *NTS* 34 (1988): 238-49; H. Scharen, "Gehenna in the Synoptics," *BSac* 149 (1992): 324-37, 454-70.

Cheryl A. Kirk-Duggan

HELLENISM

A modern term for the dominative interaction of Greek culture with the cultures of people from other regions of the ancient world, particularly during the three centuries from Alexander the Great to the triumph of Rome over the last of the Greek kingdoms in the Battle of Actium (336-31 B.C.E.). This period was first designated "Hellenistic" by the 19th-century German historian J. G. Droysen, who thought that the entire epoch was primarily characterized by the mixture of Greek and Oriental culture which paved the way for Christianity. One of the most striking uses of Gk. *hellēnismós* occurs in 2 Macc. 4:13, where the terms *hellēnismós* and *allophylismós* occur in parallel. *Hellēnismós,* "the Greek way of life," is a one-word summary of Greek religious and cultural identity, while *allophylismós* is a more general term which means "the adoption of foreign customs." Both terms are pejorative and are antithetical to *Ioudaïsmós,* "the Jewish way of life," i.e., Jewish religious and cultural identity (2 Macc. 2:21; 8:1; 14:38), which was thought threatened by *hellēnismós* and *allophylismós.* The related term *Hellēnistḗs* occurs in Acts 6:1 (cf. 9:29; 11:20), where "Hellenists" and "Hebrews" are used antithetically, apparently referring to Greek-speaking Jews from the Diaspora in contrast to Aramaic-speaking Palestinian Jews, without suggesting any of the overtones of cultural assimilation found in 2 Macc. 4:13.

Though Greeks had contact with other native cultures in the eastern Mediterranean region for centuries before the formation of the Greco-Macedonian kingdom in 356, these contacts were sporadic and mutually influential. However, as part of the program of conquest initiated by Philip II (382-356) and realized by his son and successor Alexander III (356-323), Hellenism became a tool for unifying a vast and disparate empire by introducing Greek language and cultural institutions through the founding of hundreds of city-states and military garrisons throughout Asia Minor, Syria-Palestine, Egypt, and Mesopotamia. These were populated with soldiers and civilians from the Greek world who became a cultural elite who regarded their language and way of life as superior to those of the "barbarians," i.e., the indigenous population. The Greek institutions founded in each *pólis* included at least an acropolis, walls, a market, temples, a theater, and a gymnasium (Pausanias *Descr. Gr.* 10.4.1). Predictably, the natives reacted in two different ways. Those who were upwardly mobile adapted to the changed conditions by accepting the superiority of Greek language and culture and the inferiority of their own. For others Hellenism constituted a culture shock which they considered a threat to their traditional way of life and values which they resisted in a variety of ways. These antithetical reactions are dramatized in the two accounts of the conflict between Seleucid Greeks and Palestinian Jews in 2 and 4 Maccabees, which reflect a Hellenizing party in Judea alongside a group who prefer death to violating Jewish religious traditions.

Hellenism was absorbed by non-Greeks in a variety of subtle ways, including language, personal names, and architecture.

Bibliography. M. E. Boring, K. Berger, and C. Colpe, eds., *Hellenistic Commentary to the New Testament* (Nashville, 1995); S. K. Eddy, *The King Is Dead: Studies in the Near Eastern Resistance to Hellenism, 334-31 B.C.* (Lincoln, 1961); E. S. Gruen, *The Hellenistic World and the Coming of Rome,* 2 vols. (Berkeley, 1984); M. Hadas, *Hellenistic Culture* (1959, repr. New York, 1972); M. Hengel, *Judaism and Hellenism,* 2 vols. (Philadelphia, 1974); F. Millar, *The Roman Near East: 31 B.C.–A.D. 337* (Cambridge, Mass., 1993); F. W. Walbank, *The Hellenistic World,* rev. ed. (Cambridge, Mass., 1993).

David E. Aune

HELLENISTIC RELIGIONS

The conquests of Alexander the Great (336-323 B.C.E.) altered for all time the history, culture, languages, and civilizations of the peoples of the eastern Mediterranean and Asia. To fulfill his dream of uniting as much of the known world as he could under his rule, Alexander established a network of Greek cities throughout his empire which helped him transform the varied cultures into an international, cosmopolitan world. Greek was the imposed international language, but the language itself was mutated into a common (Gr. *koinē*) language which was accessible to the general public. Alexander allowed the conquered local peoples to retain their unique ways even as he imposed Greek culture on them. The result was a thorough mixing of cultures into a hybrid form called Hellenistic culture. The Hellenistic age proper lasted from the death of Alexander (323) until Rome's defeat of Egypt (30 B.C.E.), when Greek civilization was subsumed by Roman rule. The influence of Hellenism, however, continued down to the age of the emperor Constantine (d. 337 C.E.).

Significant developments occurred in religions during the Hellenistic age. Regional and national patterns of religious practice which had been mainly untouched by foreign influences and had enjoyed largely unquestioned adherence by the public were relativized or at least incorporated into an international community of religious alternatives. Travel, commerce, and the presence of military personnel throughout the world caused regional religions to become international. Sometimes the transported religions retained a form very similar to their original, while at other times they were altered by merger with other local religious traditions. The Olympic gods, which had been powerful as gods of the city-state, and the Asian and Egyptian deities which had been fixtures of their respective nations were now internationalized and venerated (or treated with skepticism) far from their native shores.

A new mentality or worldview was born, one that played down rationalism and emphasized personal spirituality and emotionalism (unlike the public, formal, and impersonal religions of the state). Hellenistic philosophies began to replace or at least to contend with religion as a means of offering people a sense of meaning and value in life. Variations of older types of philosophy shaped the views of many (e.g., Neo-Pythagoreanism, Neo-Platonism, and Neo-Aristotelianism), while the introduction of new philosophies even more directly served the needs of the Hellenistic mind (e.g., Epicureanism, which distrusted dialectic and abstract words but sought true happiness by trusting one's feelings and common sense, or Stoicism, which taught that divine reason permeated the material order of the universe and that its adherents should live a moral and tranquil life).

The new worldview was served not only by philosophies, but also by the flourishing mystery religions that developed from cults in Greece, Persia, Egypt, and Asia Minor. Their foci of worship were either personal salvation and immortality or the forces and patterns of nature or agrarian cults. The deities were often female or chthonic "earth deities" such as Isis, Demeter, Hagne, or Magna Mater, the "Great Mother." Participation in the cults was voluntary, individual, and required taking vows of secrecy regarding the practices of the group.

Not all of these mysteries were new. The worship of Demeter at Eleusis began in the 15th century B.C.E. But even the old forms of mysterious piety were re-created and rejuvenated for a new age. Priests or mediator figures effected the union of the god and the believer; sacred meals or banquets were held; speaking in unknown languages (glossalalia) was practiced; incantations and sacred recitations were performed.

Because of the dangerous and orgiastic nature of the cult of Bacchus, and because the cult spread so quickly among the lower classes and slaves, the Roman Senate suppressed the cult in 186 B.C.E. Representations of Dionysiac or Bacchic worship from Thrace depict frenzied and drunken revelry during which the devotees tore apart a live animal and ate it uncooked.

Mithraism, a Zoroastrian (Persian) cult that gained widespread following and eventually became the official cult of the Roman Empire, held that Mithras the youthful god of light who, as a solstice deity, was born on December 25, had killed a bull from whose semen and blood new life came. Initiation into this cult was by the ritual of the taurobolium, in which the initiate was drenched with the blood of a bull, which guaranteed personal salvation. The devotees of Cybele or Magna Mater practiced the gashing of their arms in worship, as well as the taurobolium.

The Egyptian cult of Isis and Osiris offered both assistance with problems during life and the promise of immortality for the afterlife. Orphism (the worship of Orpheus) offered immortality to its initiates on the example of the death and resurrection of Dionysus, and taught that the wicked would endure the tortures of hell.

Apart from participation in cults or philosophical schools, many people held as a general religious attitude the belief in chance or Fate (Gk. *Tychē*), which was personified and adopted as the protective goddess of some Hellenistic cities. Astrology and magical incantations were features of many groups that tried to influence or at least ascertain what had been fated.

Beneath all of these cults and the fear of fate lay a cosmic dualism, the sense that there were two worlds, a here and a there (heaven/hell), an ethical dualism (the contest between good and bad or truth and error, light and darkness), and sometimes a temporal dualism (the present and the future, what is already and what will come). Consequently, a dualistic worldview known as Gnosticism flourished during the period of Hellenistic influence. Gnosticism could be found in Judaism, Christianity, and pagan philosophies. It taught that salvation is based on knowledge — not a kind of knowledge available for casual acquisition, but a spiritual knowledge attained only by the elect.

All of these philosophies, mystery religions, and worldviews influenced Christianity, which emerged in their wake.

Bibliography. F. C. Grant, *Hellenistic Religions* (New York, 1953); M. C. Howatson, *The Oxford Companion to Classical Literature,* 2nd ed. (Oxford, 1990); L. H. Martin, *Hellenistic Religions* (Oxford, 1987); M. W. Meyer, *The Ancient Mysteries* (San Francisco, 1987). RICHARD A. SPENCER

HELLENISTS

One of two groups, "Hellenists" (Gk. *Hellēnistḗs*) and "Hebrews" *(Hebraíoi),* at odds with each other in the early Church (Acts 6:1). The identity of the Hellenists is usually based on the meaning of the verb *hellēnízein,* either "to speak Greek (properly)" or "to live like a Greek." The consensus view, following John Chrysostom, is that Hellenists were Jewish Christians who spoke Greek, and Hebrews were those who spoke Aramaic. Others have argued that Hellenists were either non-Jews, nonorthodox Jews who held lax views on the ritual laws and cultus, or diaspora Jews. Still other scholars claim that Hellenists represented a more progressively minded group in contrast to the particularistic Hebrews who dominated the Jerusalem congregation under James the Just. Since *Hellēnistḗs* occurs only three times in the NT (Acts 6:1; 9:29; 11:20), it is impossible to define the term conclusively as it is used in Acts.

Bibliography. H. A. Brehm, "The Meaning of Ἑλληνιστής in Acts in Light of a Diachronic Analysis of ἑλληνίζειν," in *Discourse Analysis and Other Topics in Biblical Greek,* ed. S. E. Porter and D. A. Carson, JSNTSup 113 (Sheffield, 1995), 180-99; M. Hengel, "Between Jesus and Paul: The 'Hellenists', the 'Seven' and Stephen (Acts 6.1-15; 7.54-8.3)," in *Between Jesus and Paul: Studies in the Earliest History of Christianity* (Philadelphia, 1983), 1-29; C. C. Hill, *Hellenists and Hebrews* (Minneapolis, 1992). H. ALAN BREHM

HELON (Heb. *ḥēlōn*)

The father of Eliab, leader of the tribe of Zebulun (Num. 1:9; 2:7; 7:24, 29; 10:16).

HEMAN (Heb. *hêmān*) (also HOMAM)

1. A Horite descendent of Esau, and son of Lotan (Gen. 36:22 NRSV, following LXX). The MT and most versions read more correctly Heman. In the parallel genealogy in 1 Chr. 1:39 the name is vocalized as Homam.

2. A famous wise man, son of Mahol, whose wisdom was surpassed by Solomon's (1 Kgs. 4:31[MT 5:11]). William F. Albright suggested the epithet "the Ezrahite" (Ps. 88 superscription[1]) designates a member of a pre-Israelite family, and "sons of Mahol" refers to an orchestral guild. In 1 Chr. 2:6 he is called a descendant of Zerah, Judah's son by his daughter-in-law Tamar (cf. Gen. 38:30).

3. One of the sons of Joel and the grandson of Samuel (1 Chr. 6:33[18]). He is identified as a singer (Heb. *hamšôrēr*), and was one of the three Levites David appointed over the "service of the song" (1 Chr. 6:31[16]). He is also called the "king's seer," and with his 14 sons he prophesied with lyres, harps, and cymbals during David's reign (1 Chr. 25:1, 4-6). TYLER F. WILLIAMS

HEMDAN (Heb. *ḥemdān*) (also HAMRAN)

A Horite, son of Dishon and descendant of Seir (Gen. 36:26). At 1 Chr. 1:41 he is called Hamran.

HEMORRHAGE

See BLOOD, FLOW OF.

HEN (Heb. *ḥēn*)

The son of Zephaniah, according to the MT (Zech. 6:14; so NRSV mg). The NRSV reads "Josiah" (**2**), following the Syriac and Zech. 6:10.

HENA (Heb. *hēnaʿ*)

A city named in accounts of Sennacherib's attempt to persuade the king of Judah to surrender (2 Kgs. 18:34; 19:13 = Isa. 37:13). It is cited as a city whose gods were unable to prevent conquest by the Assyrians. Although the location is unknown, it is listed with Hamath and Arpad, which are known to have been in upper Mesopotamia.

C. MACK ROARK

HENADAD (Heb. *ḥēnāḏāḏ*)

Eponymous ancestor of a levitical family or guild that helped with the postexilic restoration of the temple (Ezra 3:9). Members of this group assisted in rebuilding the walls of Jerusalem (Neh. 3:18, 24) and sealed the renewed covenant (10:9[MT 10]).

HENNA

A shrub (*Lawsonia inermis* L.) that produces extremely fragrant white flowers. Henna petals can be ground and made into a paste to dye the nails, the palms of the hands, and the soles of the feet a reddish-brown. This is considered a mark of beauty in some cultures. Egyptian mummies have been found with henna-dyed nails. Henna is also used to dye the manes and tails of horses, along with human hair and beards. Perfume is made from henna. The henna shrub may reach a height of more than 3 m. (10 ft.). It grows both cultivated and wild in Israel. Heb. *kōper* was once thought to be camphor (*Camphora officinarum* Nees), but actually is not related to that plant. Henna occurs only twice in the Bible, both times as symbols of love (Cant. 1:14; 4:13). MEGAN BISHOP MOORE

HEPHER (Heb. *ḥēp̱er*) **(PERSON)**

1. A son of Gilead and father of Zelophehad (Num. 26:32; 27:1; Josh. 17:2-3); eponymous ancestor of a Manassehite clan or other social group known as the Hepherites (Heb. *ḥep̱rî;* Num. 26:32).

2. A descendant of Judah; son of Ashhur and Naarah (1 Chr. 4:6).

3. A Mecherathite; one of David's mighty men (1 Chr. 11:36). KENNETH ATKINSON

HEPHER (Heb. *ḥēp̱er*) **(PLACE)**
A town in the tribal territory of Manasseh, whose Canaanite king was defeated by Joshua (Josh. 12:17). The city later became part of Solomon's third administrative district (1 Kgs. 4:10). Tell el-Muhaffar (170255) in the northern Dothan Valley has been suggested as the site.
KENNETH ATKINSON

HEPHZIBAH (Heb. *ḥep̱ṣî-ḇāh*)

1. The wife of King Hezekiah and mother of Manasseh (2 Kgs. 21:1).

2. A name symbolizing Jerusalem's restored status (Isa. 62:4; NRSV "My Delight Is in Her").

HERBS
A general term designating all forms of green plants suitable for human consumption. As with much biblical terminology for natural phenomena, usage is frequently imprecise by modern standards. Herbs included vegetables (Heb. *yārāq;* Prov. 15:17) and condiments such as cummin, mint, and dill (Gk. *láchanon;* Luke 11:42). Generally herbs were gathered from the fields where they grew wild (*ʿēśeḇ;* Gen. 2:5; Prov. 27:25; *ʾôrâ;* 2 Kgs. 4:39).

See BITTER HERBS.

HERDING
With agriculture, a major component of Israelite economy. Herding was prevalent during the patriarchal and settlement periods, and continued to be practiced during the Monarchy. While generally associated with nomads, it would be wrong to assume that herding took place only in open spaces such as the Judean desert and the Negeb. Much zooarchaeological evidence shows that herding was practiced also in urban and semi-urban centers.

Three production systems are found in biblical times as well as present-day Near Eastern herding societies: sedentary, transhumant, and nomadic, determined in each locale by availability of pasturage, seasonality of vegetation, and topographical and climatic conditions.

In the sedentary system, herds are kept at or close to the permanent settlement at all times. Grazing takes place during the day in the common or private grounds which include cultivated fields. At night the animals are kept inside the settlement. Shepherds accompany the herds at all times. Flocks vary in size from village flocks (200-300) to private (50-300). Smaller private flocks do exist.

Herding under the sedentary production system was practiced by the native Canaanite population before the Israelite settlement (cf. Josh. 6:21). When Gideon, who lived in the village of Ophrah, hosted the divine messenger and offered him food, a young kid was readily available for slaughter (Judg. 6:19; cf. 13:15). Maintaining herds inside the settlements continued even in the time of Hezekiah (2 Chr. 31:6).

The transhumant system demands that shepherds move their flocks to other regions depending on climatic conditions which determine temperature, humidity, and grazing conditions. When conditions improve at home, the herds return to graze or be fed there. Herds can be private or communal. In the latter case, the owners' contributions to the expenses depend on how many animals they have in the flock. Transhumant flocks are usually larger than sedentary ones (200-500). This may have been the most common system of herding in ancient Israel.

While his ancestors were nomadic herders, Jacob became acquainted with transhumance in Padan-aram in northern Mesopotamia. Laban, his uncle, lived close enough to the well for Rachel to run to her father with the news of Jacob's arrival. But when necessary, Laban kept his herds as far as three days' journey away from home (Gen. 30:36). Upon returning to Canaan, Jacob settled in Hebron, making it his home base; as apparent from the Joseph story (Gen. 37:12-14), Shechem became a point in the seasonal circuit, apparently making his sons well known to the local inhabitants who helped Joseph find his brothers (vv. 15-17).

Nomadic herds and their keepers follow the seasonal vegetation growth and migrate from region to region as dictated by grazing conditions. They do not have a home base or any form of permanent shelter. During the nomadic cycle they cover distances longer than in any other production system. For logistical reasons, the social unit of herders, the tribe or family, may have more than one flock with which they move from place to place while living in tents. Herds can be very large (150–200 thousand) and are made of one species or are mixed (sheep and goats). Wandering is a well-organized undertaking based on experience gained through years of practice. The circuit includes visits to holy sites, cemeteries, and celebrations of certain feasts.

The pastoral nature of the patriarchs is reflected in the names Rebekah (*riḇqâ,* "a row of tied animals") and Rachel (*rāḥēl,* "ewe"). Abraham is a good example of nomadic herder. Upon his arrival in Canaan, he traveled throughout the hill country (Gen. 12:6, 8), and even after pitching his tent between Bethel and Ai, continued to wander southward (v. 9). Upon returning from Egypt, where he stayed because of a drought in Canaan, he continued to wander until he came to Hebron and pitched his tent at the oaks of Mamre (Gen. 13:17-18). Abraham discovered that his flocks were too numerous to share grazing lands with those of his nephew Lot, so the latter chose the area around Sodom for his wanderings (Gen. 13:12). Abraham continued to live in a tent (Gen. 18), and to wander as far as the Negeb and Gerar (ch. 20). His son Isaac was also a nomadic herder.

The nomadic system was practiced even to the end of the Monarchy. The Rechabites are a good example of a nomadic group, being told by their ancestor Jonadab: "You shall never . . . build a house, or sow seed; nor shall you plant a vineyard, or even own one; but you shall live in tents all your days" (Jer. 35:6-7). Although herding is not specifically mentioned as their means of livelihood, it can be safely presumed.

Under all herding production systems the shepherds' responsibility for the animals includes two main activities: sheltering and feeding. Nomads house their herds near the tents in enclosures made of thorny plants piled up to form circular walls, and in natural caves. This method is used also in the transhumant system during wandering. When the herds are kept at a permanent location to which they return at the end of each day, they are housed in stone-walled pens attached to buildings or compounds and on the ground floor of houses in the city. Remains of stone-walled pens have been excavated at several sites in the hill country and Negeb.

Protecting the herds when grazing is highly important. According to 1 Sam. 17:34 David rescued his father's herd from attacks by lions and bears. The prophet Amos, who was a herder, was well familiar with such situations and used them as a metaphor for the fall of Samaria and the northern kingdom (Amos 3:12). Accordingly, dogs were used both for guarding the herd against predators and for keeping it together (Job 30:1).

Feeding the herd includes grazing on green plants during winter and on stubble and withered grass in spring/summer, and adding supplements of hay and grain to withered grass in summer and fall. To guard against overgrazing, herders must limit the size of the herd to the carrying capacity of the land (cf. Gen. 13:5-7).

Water sources are another determinant in caring for the animals. The herd is watered daily during the year and, under best conditions, twice a day in the summer heat, usually at the beginning and end of the day. If there is no water source along the daily route, the herd is watered at home before going out and upon its return. Water is drawn from a source such as a well or cistern, and poured into troughs (Gen. 30:30, 41), often made of carved stone (cf. 29:2-10). The question of water rights dominates many biblical stories depicting herding (e.g., Gen. 21:22-34; 26:15-33). ODED BOROWSKI

HERES, ASCENT OF (Heb. *maʿălēh heḥāres*)
The immediate route by which Gideon returned upon halting his pursuit of the Midianites (Judg. 8:13). It is to be distinguished from Har-heres. Some scholars read lit., "before the sun arose."

HERESH (Heb. *ḥereš*)
A Levite who lived in Jerusalem after the Exile (1 Chr. 9:15). The name is lacking in the parallel account at Neh. 11:15-16.

HERESY
Commonly, aberrant doctrine or opinion arising within the Church in opposition to biblical revelation or apostolic tradition (1 Cor. 11:19; 2 Pet. 2:1; cf. Tit. 3:10). Gk. *haíresis* originally meant "choice" and is so used in the LXX. It came to refer to a chosen way of belief, either by individuals or by groups. Pharisees (Acts 15:5; 26:5), Sadducees (5:17), and Christians (24:5, 14; 28:22) are all referred to as heresies (NRSV "sect"). The pejorative sense of the term dominates in the NT Epistles, where it refers to teaching that diverts believers from the true gospel toward doctrine that erodes the foundations of the faith, leads to ungodly living, and destroys unity in the Church. The Epistles address heresies showing Jewish, Hellenistic, and pagan tendencies, while gnostic and christological heresies greatly threatened the postapostolic Church.

Bibliography. H. O. J. Brown, *Heresies* (Garden City, 1984). JEFFREY S. LAMP

HERETH (Heb. *ḥereṯ*)
A forest in the tribal territory of Judah where David took refuge from Saul (1 Sam. 22:5). The name may be preserved in modern Kharās, 11 km. (7 mi.) NW of Hebron and E of Khirbet Qîlā (biblical Keilah). The territory may have been under Philistine control at the time (cf. 1 Sam. 23:3).

HERMAS (Gk. *Hermás*)
A Christian in Rome to whom Paul sent his greetings (Rom. 16:14).

HERMAS (Gk. *Hermás*), **SHEPHERD OF**
A long and rather complicated work belonging to the collection called since the 17th century the Apostolic Fathers. At least the first part of the work, the Visions, was written by an otherwise unknown man named Hermas who lived in Rome or its environs in the first half of the 2nd century C.E., notwithstanding Origen's attempt to identify him with the Hermas of Paul's day in Rom. 16:14 (*Comm. on Romans* 10:31). In spite of much controversy over the autobiographical details in the Visions, they do yield an outline of information about the author. At the same time, the question must be asked whether some of this information is not present for its symbolic or literary value in terms of Hermas' message to the Church.

From what we can surmise, Hermas was a Christian freedman in or near Rome at the time of writing (Rome and the Tiber on its outskirts, Vis. 1.1.1-2; the Via Campana, Vis. 4.1.2; unfortunately, the conjectured reference to Cumae in Vis. 2.1.1 is now to be rejected on the basis of the best manuscript evidence). The strong influence of Jewish theological and literary themes leads to the conjecture that Hermas may have been a Jewish Christian, of which there were certainly many in Rome at that time. A further conjecture might be that his family came to Rome as Jewish slaves after the defeat of the uprising in Palestine, 66-74 C.E. Hermas has a wife and children, probably already young adults who are not living up to their father's expectations, but still part of his extended *familia* (Vis. 2.2.2-3).

The two poles upon which dating of Hermas have hung are the reference to Clement, alive and well, as one whose function is to send letters to other cities (Vis. 2.4.3), and the reference to the Shepherd in the Muratorian Canon as having been written "recently, in our time" by a brother of bishop Pius. The Clement referred to can only be the author of 1 Clement, written in the 90s of the 1st century in the name of the church in Rome to the church in Corinth. Pius was, according to Eusebius (*HE* 4.11), bishop of Rome in the mid-2nd century, beginning in the early 140s. If both allusions are correct, this could mean a span of as much as 50 years. However, many consider the evidence of the Muratorian Canon unreliable. Even if it is correct, the time span need not be that long: Clement could be considerably older than Hermas and still functioning in the first decades of the 2nd century, and Hermas could be an older brother of Pius.

The text as we have it has three distinct sections: five Visions, 12 Mandates or Commandments, and 10 Similitudes or Parables. The fifth and last Vision is really an introduction to the Mandates, in which the revelatory figure of the Shepherd first appears. The manuscript evidence would suggest that at some very early stage the full three sections were not together as they are now. Various theories of composite authorship have been proposed. Scholarly opinion today favors rather a single author with several redactions. Considered Scripture by Irenaeus, Clement of Alexandria, and Origen, the Shepherd continued in high esteem later, though it came to be rejected from the canon. Its popularity continued longest in Egypt, and along with the Letter of Barnabas was included in Codex Sinaiticus, the earliest surviving complete NT manuscript, from the early 4th century. It was the most popular noncanonical document in the early Church.

Outside the Shepherd, Gk. *dipsychía* ("doublemindedness") with its related terms is rare in the Christian literature of this era. But Hermas is obsessed with it, using the word group at least 50 times in 24 different contexts, associated more with problems of wealth and excessive concern about business than with any other identifiable issue. The *metánoia* ("conversion") word group occurs even more often. Doublemindedness for Hermas is the inability to decide fully in one direction or another, the opposite of singlemindedness, which would enable one to be completely oriented in one direction and make all of one's decisions accordingly. It is hesitancy, vacillation, moral inconsistency, vincible doubt, and therefore lack of faith as well as of dedication. Its origins for Hermas' use are in the two-ways tradition, which is a prominent underlying theme of the moral instruction. The teaching on doublemindedness is an early and profound instruction on the discernment of spirits.

Metánoia (lit., "turning around," "conversion," "repentance") is an equally pervasive theme in the Shepherd, perhaps *the* theme of the whole book. But the theme of a proclamation of a new repentance has been misunderstood and trivialized by modern commentators who have situated the Shepherd simplistically as a key step in the development of the discipline of penance in the Church — and no more. Such an interpretation misses the point. The book is not a call to the doing of penance in some ecclesiastical structure, but to the change of heart and mind that will lead to a change of quality in Christian life. In order to convey that message to the readers, Hermas uses an extraordinary display of Jewish, Christian, and Greco-Roman images and teaching traditions. For some, ecclesiology is the central concern of Hermas. Others would say that the necessity of conversion or the proclamation of a second repentance is the major issue. Upon closer scrutiny, one sees that these proposals are not mutually contradictory. Conversion or repentance as developed in the Mandates is not individualistic, but rather very much embedded in the community context; most of the moral exhortation is intensely communal, dealing with human relationships as well as relationship to God.

There are clearly two different images of the Church presented in the book as a whole. The first is the idealized heavenly image of the woman growing ever younger, presented in the Visions. This is the transcendent, pre-existent Church already implied in Colossians and Ephesians, the perfect spouse of the pre-existent Christ (Eph. 5:23-24, 26-27). It stands in some tension with the second image, the imperfect human community that struggles with all the problems presented in the Mandates and Similitudes. The union of opposites lies in the image of the tower, which is the Church (Vis. 3.3.3; Sim. 9.13.1). It is both a transcendent eschatological image (Vis. 3.8.9; Sim. 9.32.1; 10.4.4) and a structure for which the building stones must be carefully selected and approved. What the Church is not for Hermas — and this must be emphasized over against careless characterizations — is an institution dispensing forgiveness in exchange for penance performed. Rather, it is a living community of people who struggle for forgiveness and the courage to lead an authentic Christian life.

The name Jesus appears not at all, and the title *Christós* only perhaps at Vis. 2.2.8, with great manuscript uncertainty. The glorious or great angel is identified as Michael (Sim. 8.3.3), but performs the functions of God or Christ (e.g., Vis. 5.2; Man. 5.1.7; Sim. 5.4.4; 7.2). But the glorious man, lord of the tower (Sim. 9.7.1) and Son of God (Sim. 9.12.8), may be the same as the glorious angel, though this is never stated. Meanwhile, the Holy Spirit is the

Son of God (Sim. 9.1.1; cf. 2 Cor. 3:17; 2 Clem. 14:4). The only viable conclusion is that the text cannot be pressed too hard for consistency on this question. It represents a theological world in which such clarifications have not yet been made.

The work as we now have it purports to be an apocalypse, but the long didactic and parenetic sections have raised questions throughout the history of modern scholarship as to whether the document as a whole qualifies as such. There is more certainty about Visions 1-4, where the apocalyptic structure is more clearly seen. But the format of revelatory agent and symbolic revelation is sustained from the Visions through to the end of the book. Moreover, the parenetic genre that predominates in the Mandates also appears in the Visions and Similitudes. In short, the differences of genre among the Visions, Mandates, and Similitudes are differences of degree rather than of kind. The two genres of apocalypse and parenesis have been creatively interwoven to meet a new situation. Thus one can understand why the Shepherd of Hermas was so widely popular and evoked such controversy in the early Church.

Bibliography. C. Osiek, *Rich and Poor in the Shepherd of Hermas*. CBQMS 15 (Washington, 1983); G. Snyder, *The Shepherd of Hermas,* vol. 6 of *Apostolic Fathers,* ed. R. M. Grant (New York, 1968).

CAROLYN OSIEK

HERMENEUTICS

See INTERPRETATION, BIBLICAL.

HERMES (Gk. *Hermēs*) **(DEITY)**
A Hellenic deity, the son of Zeus and Maia. Hermes' origin seems to have arisen from the *hérma,* or "stone heap," which identified boundaries, graves, and entrances. *Herms* (bearded phalluses atop stone pillars) were later placed as markers at such places, and Athenians and others continued to represent Hermes in this form. The Romans later identified him with Mercury. Credited with inventing the lyre, he was also the patron of travelers, merchants, and messengers. He was believed to conduct the souls of the dead to Hades.

According to Acts 14:2 when Paul and Barnabas visited Lystra, the inhabitants believed that they were Hermes and Zeus respectively, implying that Paul's role as the chief speaker was a cause of his association with Hermes, the god of rhetoric. The Latin poet Ovid relates a legend concerning Zeus and Hermes which takes place in the vicinity of Lystra (*Metam.* 8.611-725), and their names have been discovered in 3rd-century A.D. inscriptions in the area. Hermes was the most common theophoric personal name in the Roman Empire, and Paul addresses a Hermas and a Hermes in Rom. 16:14.

PAUL ANTHONY HARTOG

HERMES (Heb. *Hermēs*) **(PERSON)**
A Christian at Rome to whom Paul sent his greetings (Rom. 16:14).

HERMOGENES (Gk. *Hermogénēs*)
A Christian who, with Phygelus and others in the Roman province of Asia, turned away from Paul (2 Tim. 1:15). It is unclear whether the defection was over theological differences or to avoid Roman persecution.

HERMON (Heb. *ḥermôn*), **MOUNT**
The southern portion of the Anti-Lebanon mountain range, extending 29 km. (18 mi.) on the northern border of Palestine. The heights overlook much of northern Israel and southern Syria, including the valley of Lebanon, the Gilead mountains, the Jordan Valley, and the Sea of Galilee. The three peaks of the Hermon range contain the highest peak in the Levant, Mt. Hermon proper at 2814 m. (9230 ft.). The height gathers sufficient precipitation, mainly in the form of snow, to supply the sources of the Jordan and Litani Rivers. One of the mountain's Arabic names is Jebel et-Thalj, "the mountain of snow." In biblical times the mountain was thickly forested (Ezek. 27:5), the haunt of leopards and lions (Cant. 4:8).

According to Deut. 3:9 (cf. 4:48), the mountain was also called Senir or Sirion. The three names may reflect the three main peaks of the mountain cluster. The Assyrians knew it as Saniru. In a Hittite treaty the gods of Sirion are called upon as witnesses to the action. It is probable that the 18th-century B.C. Execration Texts also refer to the mountain.

The mountain has strong sacred connections. The word Hermon derives from Heb. *hrm,* "sacred" or "forbidden." The sites of Baal-hermon and Baal-gad, both probably cultic sites, lie at the foot of the mountain. Recent surveys have identified numerous shrines and possible sacred sites in the vicinity of Mt. Hermon. A classical temple near the summit has yielded coins from Antiochus III to Philip the Arab. The Hittite treaty makes it an abode of the gods. Ps. 29 celebrates the power of Yahweh in imagery reflective of the attributes of the Canaanite Baal, a storm-god; Yahweh is so powerful that he makes the seats of Baal, including Mt. Hermon, jump to his command (v. 6). 1 En. 13:9 witnesses to the sacred power of the site, recording a dream of a gathering of angels on Mt. Hermon.

Mt. Hermon has also been suggested as a location for the Transfiguration of Jesus. The "high mountain" where this took place is not identified, but it must be in the vicinity of Caesarea Philippi. The acknowledged sacredness of Mt. Hermon would have provided added veracity for the readers of the account of the encounter.

THOMAS W. DAVIS

HEROD (Gk. *Hērṓdēs*) **(FAMILY)**
A family of distinguished Idumean nobility that was converted to Judaism during the Hasmonean period and rose to prominence during the reign of Alexandra Salome. They intermarried with Nabateans, Jews, and other nearby ruling families, dominating the political fortunes of Judaism and influencing events in the eastern Mediterranean from

the mid-1st century B.C.E. to the end of the 1st century C.E. The family had particularly good relations with ruling Romans, especially with the Julio-Claudians.

1. Antipater. Idumean noble (ca. 100-43 B.C.E.), son of Antipas and father of Herod. He was a strong supporter of Hyrcanus II in the dynastic struggle between the two sons of Alexander Janneus and Alexandra Salome. His family was Idumean and had converted to Judaism during the aggressive expansion of Judea into Idumea under Alexander Janneus. Antipater married Cypros, of noble — perhaps royal — Nabatean lineage, raising four sons and one daughter: Phasael, Herod, Joseph, Pheroras, and Salome. Influential in Judea's later history in having brought Herod into prominence, there seems little doubt of his commitment to Judea, and probably also to Judaism.

Antipater became a public figure during the reign of Alexandra, assisting Hyrcanus II and opposing Aristobulus II. He was influential because of his strong base in the south of the country (*BJ* 1.123-26; *Ant.* 14.8-18), and no doubt also because of his wife's connections in Petra (Nabatea).

The dynastic quarrel in the mid-60s B.C.E. led to Rome's direct intervention in the region under Pompey and M. Aemilius Scaurus; when Rome first supported Aristobulus, Antipater and Herod fled to Petra (then under Aretas III). Before long, Pompey's view changed, perhaps as the result of Antipater's representations. In the siege of Jerusalem (63) Hyrcanus and Antipater acted with the Romans (cf. Pss. Sol. 2, 8, 17); later, Antipater acted with Gabinius on a risky expedition to Egypt. Through his links with Rome, Antipater influenced the settlement Gabinius imposed on Judea in 55 (*BJ* 1.178; *Ant.* 14.103). During this period Antipater dominated political life in Judea by managing the country's — and Hyrcanus' — relations with Rome.

Antipater probably combined military and financial responsibilities under Hyrcanus II, ethnarch in the Roman reorganization of Judea (a monogram on Hyrcanus' coins may refer to Antipater). Antipater gave his two eldest sons important appointments, Phasael as governor of Jerusalem and environs, and Herod as governor of Galilee (47). In the chaotic conditions during Rome's civil wars in the 40s, Antipater had to alter his allegiances: he first sided with Pompey, then Caesar (who rewarded him with Roman citizenship and freedom from taxation), then Cassius. In the equally volatile conditions in Judea, Antipater was poisoned by Malchus, a fellow Jew and rival supporter of Hyrcanus II (43).

2. Herod the Great. King of Judea (73-4 B.C.E.), founder of a dynasty that was influential in Judean politics and surrounding areas into the early 2nd century C.E. Herod was the son and grandson of Idumean nobles converted to Judaism during the time of Alexander Janneus. His mother Cypros was Nabatean. The family served Hyrcanus II in the struggle for the crown with Aristobulus. Both Antipater and Herod were trusted by the Romans during the period of Rome's increasing influence.

Sources on Herod include Josephus, other ancient historians, a few rabbinic references, inscriptions, coins, and archaeological remains of his buildings. The usual harshly negative evaluation of Herod, deriving from one NT reference (Matt. 2:16-18) and one side of Josephus' complex picture, does no justice to the person. While Herod was cruel and vindictive, perhaps even paranoid, in his dealings with his family, he played a crucial role in improving the lot of Jews during his long reign (40-4 B.C.E.).

Little is known of his early life and nothing of his education. He emerged publicly as a young man in command of Galilee, where he dealt severely with "brigands," as Josephus calls them — probably dispossessed peasants. In the turmoil of the Roman civil wars he was noticed by several Roman leaders (Julius Caesar, Mark Antony, Cassius, Octavian). Herod fled to Rome to seek help when Hyrcanus II was captured by Mattathiah Antigonus, who had been appointed king of Judea by Parthia, Rome's most dangerous enemy. When the Senate instead appointed Herod king of Judea (late 40), Herod and Antigonus became in effect rival kings, with both empires having a considerable stake in the outcome.

King Herod

Herod returned to Galilee in the spring of 39; a two-and-a-half year struggle for dominance in Judea ensued, won finally by Herod in the summer of 37 after a successful siege of Jerusalem with Roman help. During the 30s Herod consolidated and extended his territory, with the assistance of Mark Antony, his patron and closest ally in Rome. When Antony and Octavian fell out, Herod remained loyal to Antony; he would have fought at Actium (31) had Antony not required him to keep the Nabateans in check. Following Antony and Cleopatra's decisive defeat, Herod went to Rhodes to offer his loyalty to Octavian, becoming one of Octavian's ("Augustus" from 27 on) most trusted dependent kings. Augustus, his son-in-law Marcus Agrippa, and Herod were considered close friends.

Even in this early period Herod's personal life showed signs of strain. Herod divorced his first wife Doris and — aiming at legitimacy — became engaged to Mariamme, granddaughter of Herod's patron, Hyrcanus II (whom he later executed), and one of the last of the Hasmoneans (42). He married Mariamme in 37, when she had attained marriageable age (perhaps 16), while Jerusalem was under siege. Mariamme did not reciprocate Herod's infatuation with her during their tempestuous marriage; his suspicions resulted in charges of adultery and eventually her execution (28/27). Mariamme's mother, Alexandra (daughter of Hyrcanus II), who was implicated in Mariamme's death though she continued to live in the palace, contributed to Herod's downward slide until her execution. Herod's 10 wives and at least 15 children created very difficult family arrangements.

Herodium, mountain palace-fortress of Herod the Great (Photo by Hanan Isachar; ASAP Ltd.)

Middle Years

During the 20s, Herod triumphantly engaged in an orgy of building activity that reshaped his domains. Augustus' confidence in Herod was shown in a series of extensions to the kingdom and in the right to appoint his own successor from among his sons, most of whom were brought up in Rome. Herod's troops accompanied Aelius Gallus on a military expedition to Arabia Felix (25/24). At home, his family life became increasingly complicated by his increasing number of potential heirs, and especially by the machinations of Mariamme I's two children as they became influential youths.

Though Herod could be generous in famine relief, on the whole society probably became harsher and more exclusive. His relations with various social and religious groups are not clear; according to the NT, weakly supported by Josephus, a group developed known as Herodians. Of all the religious developments of his reign, the most significant was the rebuilding of the temple in Jerusalem, which for the first time included a court of Gentiles and a court of women. It was one of the great religious structures of the period, and continues to excite the religious imagination to this day.

Herod traveled extensively, partly, it seems, to assist in improving Diaspora Jews' security and — to a limited degree — independence; his friendship with Marcus Agrippa, Augustus' eastern lieutenant, made this readily possible. His contacts extended especially through Syria and Asia Minor, the Greek islands, and the Greek mainland (e.g., he gave benefactions to Rhodes, Chios, Cos, Pergamum, Athens, Olympia, among others); he did not build for the Jewish community itself, but offered his largesse to the city as a whole. Diaspora Jews remained attached to the homeland through the half-shekel tax; they had immunity from prosecution on the sabbath and exemption from military service.

Herod's Buildings

Herod's extensive building program included whole cities (e.g., Caesarea Maritima, Sebaste), temples (e.g., Jerusalem, three to Roma and Augustus, Baal Shamim at Si'a), palaces (e.g., Masada, Herodium, Cypros, Jericho), memorials (e.g., the patriarchs and matriarchs at Hebron, Abraham at Mamre), various pleasure buildings, infrastructure projects, unspecified donations and benefactions. It is unlikely that, as some complained after his death, he spent more on buildings outside the Holy Land than within it. His projects inside his own regions were designed partly to stimulate trade and commerce. The buildings were built with flair and technical competence, beautifully designed, often very imaginative: the northern palace at Masada, winter palace at Jericho, promontory palace at Caesarea, Herodium, and his temples — especially the awe-inspiring temple in Jerusalem. None of his palaces give evidence of pagan decorative motifs or embellishments that flout Torah. To some extent Herod was an observant Jew; some of his palaces include pools that have been interpreted as *mikvaot,* or in some cases as a cold pool that can do double duty as a *mikveh* (e.g., Masada and Cypros).

Final Years

Herod's final years were marked by public recognition (e.g., his role alongside Marcus Agrippa in the Black Sea expedition and his being named president of the Olympic games), by troubles with neighboring Nabatea, and by increased family discord. The last of these gave rise to Augustus' witticism that he would rather be Herod's pig than his son. During these last years Herod executed his two sons with Hasmonean blood (7) and his oldest son, Antipater (son of Doris; 4), all of whom had been squabbling with each other and intriguing for the succession, perhaps trying to oust him. The "massacre of the innocents" (Matt. 2:16-18) is set at this time, leading some to speculate that there has been confusion between his killing of his sons and his murder of the small children in Bethlehem. Herod died after a lingering disease in the spring of 4 B.C.E. in Jericho. He was buried in Herodium, designed as a fortified palace and mausoleum.

Evaluation

Herod was a key player in the Roman design for the eastern Mediterranean, providing a secure point in Rome's strategic extension of its kingdom. He improved Judea's economy and its place in the region's trade and commerce. Close Roman links led many of Herod's citizens to question his motives and his ties to Judaism, yet Herod appears to have been a practicing Jew. He derived great satisfaction from his rebuilding of the Jerusalem temple, his chief monument.

3. Mariamme I. Herod the Great's second wife, great-granddaughter of Alexander Janneus and Alexandra Salome on both her mother's and father's sides (ca. 54-29 B.C.E.). Her father, Alexander, continued to oppose Hyrcanus II and his chief minister Antipater (Herod's father), as well as Rome after its involvement in the East (64/63), as his father Aristobulus II had done.

Mariamme was betrothed by Hyrcanus to Herod in the late 40s, when she was still a young girl. Herod then divorced his first wife Doris, though Mariamme and he were not wed until she reached marriageable age in 37; they married in Samaria during a lull in the preparations for the siege of Jerusalem, whose conclusion meant the end of Herod's two-and-a-half year struggle to enter fully into the kingship he had been given in 40. Herod thus became a relative of Hyrcanus II, whom he had replaced as king, giving himself additional legitimacy through this close Hasmonean connection. Among Herod's 10 marriages, this was the one to which he was himself most attached, which raised his stature highest, but which troubled him most.

Mariamme was reunited with the remaining Hasmoneans in Herod's household: her grandfather Hyrcanus II (who had returned from his Parthian imprisonment), her mother Alexandra, and her brother Aristobulus III (who was briefly high priest, prior to being drowned in the pool at Jericho; Josephus *Ant.* 15.31-56). Mariamme was deeply influenced by her mother (not surprisingly, given her age), a dangerous influence given her mother's close friendship with Cleopatra VII of Egypt.

Herod was inordinately jealous of his relationship with Mariamme and suspicious of her fidelity. After Actium, he met Octavian at Rhodes (early 30), leaving Mariamme in care of Joseph and Soëmus, who apparently had orders to execute her if Herod did not return. After more misunderstanding and tension, Mariamme was found guilty of adultery and put to death (ca. 29; *Ant.* 15.185-239; *BJ* 1:441-43; *Ant.* 15.65-87); she was only about 25 years old. Alexandra continued to plot against Herod and was herself executed soon after.

According to Josephus, Mariamme was beautiful, "unexcelled in continence," but quarrelsome and fond of speaking her mind. Herod's grief and remorse over her execution led to serious neglect of the kingdom (*Ant.* 15.240-46). Mariamme was survived by several children, of whom the Hasmoneans Alexander and Aristobulus were the most important; initially they were Herod's main hope for the succession, but their hostility to him because of their resentment over Herod's murder of their mother led eventually to their own execution in 7 B.C.E.

4. Mariamme II. Herod's (seventh?) wife, married ca. 24/23 B.C.E.; daughter of Simon, son of Boethos, a priest from Alexandria whom Herod elevated to the high priesthood to improve Mariamme's status. He later divorced her; she bore him one son, Herod (Philip?), not the tetrarch of the same name, whose wife Herodias was later married to Herod Antipas (Mark 6:17-29 par.).

5. Salome. Sister of Herod, daughter of Antipater and Cypros (ca. 65 B.C.E.–10 C.E.). She first married Joseph (a friend of Herod's), then after his execution married Costobar, governor of Idumea (later divorced by Salome, then executed by Herod). She was betrothed to Syllaeus, the Nabatean second-in-command, but Herod refused them permission to marry (15 B.C.E.) when Syllaeus refused to be (re-?)circumcised. She was then married by Herod to Alexas, against her will, though at the Empress Livia's urging (Josephus *Ant.* 17.9-10).

Salome remained unfailingly loyal to Herod throughout his turbulent career, though she frequently exacerbated his problems, especially within the household. In Augustus' disposition of Herod's final will, Salome was given control of Phaselis, Yavneh (Jamnia), and Ashdod (Azotus). These toparchies she willed to Livia, wife of Augustus, at her death (*Ant.* 18.31; *BJ* 2.167). She had five children, all by Costobar: Alexander, Herod, Berenice, Antipater, and a second daughter.

6. Antipater. Eldest son of Herod and his first wife Doris (ca. 45-4 B.C.E.). When Herod divorced Doris to marry Mariamme, Antipater was banished from the royal court with his mother and was not reinstated until 14 B.C.E., at which point he arranged for his mother's remarriage to Herod. Shortly thereafter Antipater went to Rome to be presented to Augustus as one of Herod's putative heirs. The household became a battleground for the next decade as Antipater adroitly undercut the position of Alexander and Aristobulus, his two half-brothers, at court (*Ant.* 16.82-84; *BJ* 1.450). For a period Antipater may have shared rule with Herod. When Alexander and Aristobulus were executed (7 B.C.E.), Antipater was left in a strong position, with support from the military and elite. His continued machinations against his father resulted in his execution, five days before Herod's own death (4 B.C.E.), which Augustus declined to prevent.

7. Alexander and Aristobulus. Sons of Herod and Mariamme I (ca. 36 and 35, respectively-7 B.C.E.), who, because of their mother's Hasmonean credentials, represented the possibility of joining Herod's realistic politics and Hasmonean nationalist ideals. Josephus treats the brothers as a pair, though Alexander seems the more aggressive in his hatred of his father, following Herod's execution of their mother. As royal heirs of a client king, they went to Rome for their education (22-17), living for a time with Augustus himself. Herod traveled to Rome to bring them home, at the same time negotiating with Augustus their betrothals, Alexander to Glaphyra, daughter of King Archelaus of Cappadocia, and Aristobulus to his cousin Berenice, Salome's daughter. In Judea, their personal popularity and ambition made them one pole of family tensions, with Herod's sister Salome and his brother Pheroras the other pole. When Herod wished to counter the position of Alexander and Aristobulus, he recalled to court his eldest son Antipater (14), who became their chief antagonist. Herod took Alexander, Aristobulus, and Antipater to Rome to seek Augustus' help in resolving the tensions (12). The seeming reconciliation did not last, and family relationships continued to degenerate. Alexander and Aristobulus were formally charged, tried, and found guilty in Beirut, executed at Sebaste, and buried at Alexandreion. Augustus declined to intervene.

8. Mariamme. Granddaughter of Herod and Mariamme I; she married her uncle Antipater (**3**) who was executed by Herod in 4 B.C.E. Her father, Aristobulus, had been killed three years earlier.

9. Archelaus. Son of Herod the Great and Malthace (ca. 23 B.C.E.–?). Archelaus inherited Judea, Samaria, and Idumea as ethnarch on the death of Herod in 4 B.C.E.; he was deposed by Augustus in 6 C.E. According to Josephus Archelaus was a questionable appointment from the beginning because of his inept handling of disturbances following Herod's death. In the hearings in Rome concerning Herod's will, Archelaus was opposed by several family members. Both Judea and Samaria (his mother Malthace was a Samaritan) sent delegations to Rome asking for his removal from office. He was exiled to Vienne in France, after which the province was governed by prefects who were subordinate to the governor of Syria; during the rule of Cumanus, the first procurator, the census under Quirinius was taken (Luke 2:1-3; cf. Acts 5:37), an impossible action under either Herod or Archelaus. Little is known about Archelaus' reign; the parable in Luke 19:11-27 may allude to him.

10. Mariamme. Wife of Archelaus the ethnarch, then divorced by him; she may have been a Hasmonean.

11. Antipas. Son of Herod the Great and Malthace (ca. 21 B.C.E.–?). Herod regarded Antipas favorably, for he had named him sole heir in his penultimate will; on Herod's death in 4 B.C.E. Antipas had strong family support. Augustus appointed him tetrarch of Galilee and Perea, a position he held until he was deposed by Caligula in 38 C.E. after petitioning to be made king; he was sent into exile in France. Antipas' links with Rome were strong, being involved in mediating the dispute between Rome and Parthia in 36. He was especially close to Tiberius, in whose honor he founded his new capital, Tiberias, on the Sea of Galilee (ca. 18-20). Betharamphtha in Perea was renamed Julias after Augustus' widow; Antipas also restored Sepphoris as "the ornament of all Galilee." Despite these links, Josephus reports the allegation that Antipas was in league with Artabanus of Parthia and had stockpiled weapons for 70 thousand soldiers. His marriage to the daughter of the Nabatean king Aretas IV ended when he fell in love with his niece, Herodias, previously wife of his brother Herod Philip (probably not Philip, ruler of Gaulanitis, but a similarly-named brother). When Antipas' first wife fled home to Petra, Aretas inflicted a major defeat on him.

Antipas' territory comprised two parts, Galilee (home to Jesus) and Perea (home to John the Baptist). John was probably executed in Machaerus, on the border between Perea and Nabatea, a fact mentioned both by Josephus and — less explicitly — in the NT; Josephus attributes Antipas' military defeat to God's retribution on Antipas for executing John the Baptist. According to Luke 23:6-16 Antipas was involved in the trial of Jesus; while this cannot be demonstrated, it is not implausible. Antipas seems to have had some interest in Jesus; the wife of one of his trusted lieutenants was a follower and supporter (Luke 8:1-3). Some of Jesus' parables suggest some social dislocation and unrest during the reign of Antipas. To judge from the fact that Jesus alternated between Galilee and Gaulanitis, Philip's region, he may have felt threatened by the political situation in Galilee.

12. Salome. Daughter of Herod (Philip[?] not the Tetrarch) and Herodias, granddaughter of Herod and Mariamme II. Salome's mother, Herodias, had married Herod Antipas after divorcing his half brother. Salome is referred to — not by name — in Mark 6:17-29 par., where she danced at Antipas' birthday party. When Antipas offered her a gift, according to the Gospels she asked for John the Baptist's head, at the prompting of her mother.

Josephus gives a different interpretation. Antipas' first wife had been a daughter of Aretas IV of Nabatea; she had fled from the marriage when she learned of Antipas' intention to marry Herodias. Antipas' ensuing military defeat at the hands of Aretas was retribution for his execution of John the Baptist, carried out at Machaerus (*Ant.* 18.116-19). Salome, the daughter of one Herod (Philip[?]) first married her uncle Herod Philip, tetrarch of Gaulanitis and the adjacent regions. She later married Aristobulus, son of Herod of Chalcis (grandson of Herod and Mariamme I) and Mariamme (granddaughter of Herod and Malthace).

13. Philip the Tetrarch. Son of Herod and Cleopatra of Jerusalem (ca. 20 B.C.E.–34 C.E.); ruler of

Gaulanitis, Batanea, Trachonitis, Autanitis, with portions of Iturea (cf. Luke 3:1) and Hulitis, for the most part regions with a largely non-Jewish population. Philip was educated in Rome during the period of intense family troubles in Jerusalem (Josephus *BJ* 1.601-3; *Ant.* 17.20, 79-81); he was less ambitious but more able than other sibling rivals. Josephus remembered him as cooperative, reasonable, and equitable.

He embellished Panias (where Herod had built a temple of Roma and Augustus) and renamed it Caesarea Philippi in honor of the emperor and himself. His work in Bethsaida may have been significant, perhaps including another temple for imperial cult purposes. His coins, which always refer to him as "Philip, Tetrarch," were iconic (showing likenesses of Augustus, Livia and Tiberius; one showing Livia and Augustus may be associated with Philip's renaming Bethsaida Livia/Julias after Augustus' widow), with facades of a temple, probably in Caesarea Philippi.

According to John 1:43-44 (cf. v. 46; 12:20-22) several of the Twelve came from his areas, and it appears from the references to "the other side" that Jesus spent time there, perhaps as a refuge from increased tension in Galilee over his ministry.

Philip married his niece Salome, daughter of Herodias. Since she could not have been born much before 14 C.E., the marriage could not have taken place much before 30, some time after the execution of John the Baptist, in whose death they were implicated. They were childless, and there is no record of an earlier wife (cf. *BJ* 2.1-117).

14. Herod (Philip[?]). Son of Herod and Mariamme II. There may be a second Philip among Herod's children. This son figured in Herod's fourth will (ca. 7 B.C.E.) as the successor to Antipater (*Ant.* 17.53; *BJ* 1.573); it may be he who is referred to in Mark 6:17 (cf. *Ant.* 18.109) as Philip. This Herod Philip was married first to Herodias (she later married Antipas), and their daughter Salome married her uncle, Herod Philip the Tetrarch.

15. Mariamme. A granddaughter of Herod and Malthace. She married Herod IV of Chalcis, her cousin.

16. Agrippa I. Marcus Julius Herod Agrippa I (ca. 10 B.C.E.–44 C.E.); son of Aristobulus I and Berenice, and thus of the Hasmonean line through his grandmother, Mariamme I. Like other Herodians, Agrippa was brought up in the imperial court in Rome as a friend of Drusus, Claudius, and Gaius (Caligula). In his early life he was regarded as a wastrel. He first inherited Philip's and Lyania's territories (37); following Claudius's accession (41), Agrippa ruled almost all his grandfather Herod's territories, but the expectations that this engendered collapsed on Agrippa's dramatic death in Caesarea, which both Josephus and Luke (Acts 12:20-23) record. Agrippa was warmly remembered in the rabbinic literature, though it is unclear why, for he engaged in building practices similar to his grandfather, and he minted iconic coins.

Agrippa was a complex character: a romanophile (inscriptions attest to him as "friend of the emperor and friend of the Romans," yet his gathering of client kings was disbanded and he was prevented from rebuilding Jerusalem's walls), megalomaniac (he referred to himself as "great"), complaining (he was ungrateful for his uncle Antipas' kindness in making him market supervisor of Tiberias), yet he seems to have been loved by his people (they approved him when he expressed doubts about his Jewish legitimacy). He left his biggest mark in the historical literature when riots broke out in Alexandria, as he passed through the city on his way to take up his rule in Gaulanitis and Galilee (38); Philo wrote about the troubles *(De Legatione ad Gaium; Contra Flaccum)* and was a part of the delegation to Gaius.

17. Mariamme. Daughter of Agrippa I and great-granddaughter of Herod, married to Julius Archelaus, son of Helcias.

18. Agrippa II. Marcus Julius Agrippa II (27 C.E.–93 C.E.); son of Agrippa I and Cypros, great-grandson of Herod. He first inherited the kingdom of Chalcis (49/50), which was later exchanged for Philip's territory (53); when Nero added parts of Galilee and Perea he renamed Caesarea Philippi as Neronias. Agrippa was close to the Flavians (he had been a youthful friend of Titus), mostly for his support of Rome during the Jewish Revolt, when he tried to overcome dreams of Judean independence. Despite his support, he was not rewarded with the title and lands of his father and great-grandfather. Josephus was friendly with Agrippa and claims that Agrippa verified the accuracy of his historical accounts. Agrippa appears in Acts 25:13–26:32 in Paul's hearing at Caesarea Maritima.

See PHASAEL.

Bibliography. D. Braund, *Rome and the Friendly King* (London, 1984); M. Grant, *Herod the Great* (New York, 1971); H. Hoehner, *Herod Antipas* (1972, repr. Grand Rapids, 1980); A. H. M. Jones, *The Herods of Judea* (1938, repr. Oxford, 1967); P. Richardson, *Herod, King of the Jews and Friend of the Romans* (Columbia, S.C., 1996); D. R. Schwartz, *Agrippa I: The Last King of Judea* (Tübingen, 1990).

PETER RICHARDSON

HERODIANS (Gk. *Hērōdianoí*)

Partisans of the house of Herod Antipas. Although primarily a political party, they were religiously oriented and joined the Pharisees in opposing Jesus' teachings (Mark 3:6; 12:13 = Matt. 22:16).

HERODIAS (Gk. *Hērōdiás*)

The daughter of Aristobulus and Berenice. Herodias married her uncle, possibly Philip II, and bore him a daughter named Salome (Josephus *Ant.* 18.5.4 [136]). When Herod Antipas, her husband's half-brother, visited them in 29 C.E., he persuaded Herodias to divorce her husband and marry him (*Ant.* 18.5.1 [110]). John the Baptist criticized their marriage (Matt. 14:3-5; Mark 6:17-18) because Jewish law forbade a man to marry his brother's wife (Lev. 18:16, 20; 20:21) except in levirate marriage (Deut. 25:5). Angered at John's intrusion, Herodias advised her daughter to request his execution as her reward for pleasing Antipas with her dancing (Matt. 14:6-12; Mark 6:21-28). Herodias might have been just devious and cruel (*Ant.* 18.7.1 [240-44]), or she may function to excuse Antipas for John's death.

Bibliography. J. C. Anderson, "Feminist Criticism: The Dancing Daughter," in *Mark and Method,* ed. J. C. Anderson and S. D. Moore (Minneapolis, 1992), 103-34. EMILY CHENEY

HERODION (Gk. *Hērōdíōn*)
A Christian in Rome whom Paul greeted as his "relative" (Rom. 16:11; NRSV mg "compatriot").

HERODIUM (Gk. *Hērōdeíon*)
A fortress complex situated at Jebel el-Fureidis (1731.1192), 12 km. (7.5 mi.) S of Jerusalem, near Bethlehem. A hill-top fortress built by Herod the Great (ca. 23 B.C.E.), Upper Herodium is a cone- or cylinder-shaped site where Herod's five-story palace once stood. At Lower Herodium, at the base of the hill-top palace, are the remains of a pool complex, a central bathhouse, a long concourse, a monumental building, and palace. This large building complex not only functioned as Herod's summer residence but also served to preserve and commemorate Herod's name. Josephus describes the site (*Ant.* 15.9.4) and identifies it as the burial place of Herod (17.8.3; *BJ* 1.33.9).

It was at this site in 40 B.C.E. that Herod was ambushed by Antigonus, but he was able to counter and decisively defeat his Hasmonean attackers. After Herod's death the Romans selected Herodium as capital of a Palestinian toparchy. Along with Machaerus and Masada, the city was one of the last Jewish strongholds during the First Jewish Revolt, falling to the Romans in 72 C.E. It was reoccupied briefly during the Second Jewish Revolt (ca. 132).

After its identification in 1838 by Edward Robinson, there were no thorough and accurate attempts to survey and excavate the site until the mid-1960s. Recent excavations by Ehud Netzer of Hebrew University have concentrated on both the fortress of Upper Herodium and Lower Herodium, uncovering remains from the Herodian to Byzantine periods. Despite considerable discussion about the possible location of Herod's tomb at Herodium, to date it has not been unearthed.

Bibliography. G. Foerster and E. Netzer, "Herodium," *NEAEHL* 2:618-26; "Searching for Herod's Tomb," *BARev* 9/3 (1983): 31-51; J. Patrich, "Corbo's Excavations at Herodium," *IEJ* 42 (1992): 241-45.

ROBERT A. DERRENBACKER, JR.

HERODOTUS (Gk. *Hērodotos*)
A 5th-century (ca. 484-420 B.C.E.) Greek historian. The "father of history," he is known for his one great work, *The History.* Ostensibly a history of the Persian War (i.e., the wars between the Persians and the Greeks in the early 5th century), his book is actually a vast compendium of events, stories, character analyses, myths, legends, morals, ethnography, and geography. Widely traveled and insatiably curious, Herodotus wrote with remarkable openness and lack of prejudice toward other cultures and religions. Though he lacks the discriminating factual objectivity of his younger contemporary Thucydides, Herodotus writes with such superb narrative skill and brilliant classical Greek style that he becomes in many ways the model for subsequent historians in antiquity — Greek, Roman, and even Christian.

Bibliography. *Herodotus,* trans. A. D. Godly, rev. ed. Loeb Classical Library. 4 vols. (Cambridge, Mass., 1990); *The History: Herodotus,* trans. D. Grene (Chicago, 1987). J. CHRISTIAN WILSON

HESHBON (Heb. *ḥešbôn*)
A city of Moab, taken by the Israelites under Moses' leadership when its Amorite king, Sihon, refused their request for passage through his territory (Num. 21:21-31; Deut. 2:24; Josh. 12:2; Judg. 11:19-26).

According to Num. 32; Josh. 13:15-28 Heshbon ("stronghold") "and all its towns that are in the tableland" were given as an inheritance to the tribe of Reuben. Num. 32:37-38 asserts that "the Reubenites rebuilt Heshbon," and Judg. 11:26 adds that Israel occupied Heshbon, Aroer, the surrounding settlements, and all the towns along the Arnon for 300 years. Other biblical accounts indicate that the town and its surrounding territory were at various times controlled by the tribe of Gad (Josh. 21:38-39) and by the Iron Age tribal kingdoms of Ammon and Moab (Judg. 3:14-30; 11:13-28). The Heshbon region was apparently famous for its pasture lands, vineyards, wells and "pools" (Num. 21:22; Cant. 7:4; Isa. 16:8-9).

The identification of biblical Heshbon with Tell Ḥesbân (226134), a ruin located in the highland plateau of Transjordan ca. 10 km. (6 mi.) N of Madaba, has been generally supported by a series of excavations under the auspices of Andrews University, initiated in 1968 by Siegfried Horn. Perhaps most significant is what has been learned about the wide range of types of settlements at the site over the past four millennia. For example, the remains of a dry-moat from the 13th and 12th centuries B.C. suggest that some sort of stronghold, a fortified agricultural village perhaps, likely existed there then. The discovery of a variety of bowls and jars which occur contemporaneously on both sides of the Jordan during this same period adds weight to the biblical claim that there were members of the same people group (Israelites?) living in this part of Transjordan at this time.

The discovery of a 7 m. (23 ft.)-deep water reservoir dated to the 10th century suggests a process of growth involving gradual transformation of the earlier fortified village into a larger town, complete with its own large "pools" of water — possibly the "pools of Heshbon" of Cant. 7:4. For some reason, toward the end of the 10th century this larger town ceased to grow, and eventually its buildings became neglected and crumbled. Throughout the 9th and 8th centuries these ruins, along with the numerous habitation caves which are located throughout the hill of Ḥesbân, were used by people who lived very simple lives, very likely that of semi-nomadic agriculturalists who camped in the caves and ruins in order to grow wheat and barley in the fertile valleys on both sides of the tell.

In the 7th–5th centuries a large town reemerges on the hill, this time rebuilt by the Ammonites. Their presence is evidenced by a range of finds, including several ostraca with Ammonite script, pottery typical of their ceramic traditions, and a booming economy based on production and export of vine products. This town came to an end, however, and its ruins and caves again become the makeshift dwellings of semi-nomadic agriculturalists. These cycles of build-up and collapse of villages and towns on the hill of Ḥesbân repeated themselves again and again throughout the remaining centuries until the present.

However, regarding evidence for the existence of the "capital city of the Amorites" or proof of a battle over this city between the forces of Sihon and those of Moses, the archaeological data are largely silent. They neither support nor refute the biblical account, but simply are insufficient at present to illuminate this part of the biblical record.

Øystein S. LaBianca

HESHMON (Heb. *ḥešmôn*)
A town in the southern part of Judah's inheritance (Josh. 15:27). It does not appear in the LXX list, nor is it included in similar lists recording towns reassigned to Simeon (Josh. 19:2-6; 1 Chr. 4:28-30). The context suggests a location in the Negeb, near Beer-sheba.

Laura B. Mazow

HETH (Heb. *ḥet̲*)
The second son of Canaan (Gen. 10:15 = 1 Chr. 1:13). He was eponymous ancestor of the Hittites (Gen. 23:10), in biblical usage an element of the pre-Israelite population of Canaan rather than a reference to the Anatolian empire. Abraham purchased his burial cave at Machpelah from Hittites (Gen. 23; 25:10; 49:32). Rebekah and Isaac discouraged Jacob from marrying Hittite women (Gen. 27:46), whom they also referred to as "Canaanite" (28:1, 8).

Robert E. Stone, II

HETHLON (Heb. *ḥet̲lōn*)
A place on the ideal northern boundary of Israel, mentioned at Ezek. 47:15; 48:1 in connection with Damascus, Hamath, and Berothah. Its precise location is not known, but a possible identification is modern Heitela, NE of Tripolis.

HEXAPLA
An important work of biblical criticism written by Origen. The name Hexapla derives from its six columns of parallel texts (the Hebrew text, the Hebrew text transliterated into Greek characters, and the Greek versions of Aquila, Symmachus, the LXX, and Theodotion). In the LXX column, Origen marked with an obelus those passages present in Greek but not found in his Hebrew column. When the LXX lacked material found in Hebrew, Origen would insert the passage from one of the other Greek columns (which were closer textually to the Hebrew) and mark the insertion with an asterisk. Although the Hexapla in its entirety was apparently never copied, the LXX column was copied repeatedly. Unfortunately, many copies omitted Origen's textual marks, thus introducing a significant amount of contamination into the textual tradition of the LXX. Only a few fragments of copies of the Hexapla or of its fifth column are extant. One of the most important witnesses to Origen's work is the 7th-century Syriac translation of the fifth column — complete with textual marks — attributed to Paul of Tella, known as the Syro-Hexapla.

James R. Adair, jr.

HEXATEUCH
The first six (Gk. *héx*) books of the OT (Genesis–Joshua), regarded by many as a major component of the primary history of Israel. The books are related form-critically and theologically by a number of "historical credos" recalling God's mighty acts on Israel's behalf from the patriarchs through the Conquest.

See Biblical Criticism.

HEZEKIAH (Heb. *ḥizqîyâ, ḥizqîyāhû*)

1. King of Judah (probably 715-687 b.c.e.), son and successor of Ahaz. His mother was Abijah, the daughter of Zechariah. His 29-year rule began when he was 25 (2 Kgs. 18:2 = 2 Chr. 29:1) and is evaluated positively (2 Kgs. 18:3 = 2 Chr. 29:2). The Deuteronomist even claimed that "there was no one like him among all the kings of Judah after him, or among those who were before him" (2 Kgs. 18:5; but cf. 2 Chr. 32:25). Hezekiah was remembered for his piety (2 Chr. 32:20; Isa. 38:10-20), his patronage of the wise (Prov. 25:1), and his construction projects, including an underground tunnel which connected Jerusalem's Gihon spring with the pool of Siloam (2 Kgs. 20:20; 2 Chr. 32:30; Isa. 22:9-11).

When Hezekiah came to the throne, Judah was a vassal of Assyria. His father Ahaz not only paid tribute to Assyria but also modified Judean cultic practices in order to please his new masters (2 Kgs. 16:10-18). The Chronicler suggests that Ahaz even closed down the temple in Jerusalem (2 Chr. 28:24).

Hezekiah reversed the religious policies of his father. Scholars have long debated the extent of his reforms, since the Deuteronomist devotes only three verses to them (2 Kgs. 18:4, 16, 22). Chronicles, however, describes them in detail (2 Chr. 29:3–32:31). Earlier scholarship discounted the historicity of this report, but today Chronicles is generally seen as reliable. The Deuteronomist may have eliminated some of the details in order to avoid comparisons with King Josiah.

Hezekiah's reforms included the removal of the high places, the demolition of Canaanite religious symbols, and even the destruction of Nehushtan, the bronze serpent reportedly made by Moses in the desert. The king ordered the purification and restoration of Jerusalem's temple and its cult (2 Chr. 29:3-36), a renewal of the Passover celebration

(2 Chr. 30:1-27), and a reorganization of Judah's priesthood (2 Chr. 31:2-19). The centralization of the cult in Jerusalem strengthened the moral and political authority of the monarchy while tying Judah's population more closely to the capital. The remnants of the northern tribes were also invited to join Judah in a common Passover celebration (2 Chr. 30:1-11).

Eventually Hezekiah rebelled against Assyria. The biblical and extrabiblical evidence of Hezekiah's revolt, although extensive, is sometimes contradictory. It is uncertain whether Hezekiah participated in revolts which took place during the reign of Sargon II. Most likely Hezekiah planned his rebellion over a long period of time, for he carefully forged a series of alliances and fortified Jerusalem and some of the other cities of Judah. Hezekiah supported the rebellious citizens of Ekron and Ashkelon, even imprisoning Padi, Ekron's king. Most likely he had contacts with Babylon, Tyre, and Egypt (2 Kgs. 18:21; 20:12-15; Isa. 18:1-2; 30:2; 31:1). The death of Sargon II on the battlefield in 705 and Sennacherib's initial difficulties in quelling numerous revolts throughout the empire probably convinced Hezekiah to withhold tribute and to complete preparations for war. It is possible that the common Passover celebration and Judah's religious reforms took place at this time.

However, Sennacherib pacified the eastern part of his empire and then marched west. He attacked Tyre and replaced its king Luli, who fled to Cyprus. Then he moved into Philistia and conquered the rebellious cities there. Egyptian forces were routed near the city of Eltekeh. Sennacherib could now focus his attention on Judah. Assyrian annals claim that he besieged and captured 46 of its cities and deported their populations. Hezekiah was "made a prisoner in Jerusalem, his royal residence, like a bird in a cage"; *ANET,* 288). The Bible confirms that Hezekiah sued for peace and paid a heavy tribute (2 Kgs. 18:13-16).

At this point the evidence becomes ambiguous. Judah was ravaged and lost its independence, but Jerusalem was not captured or destroyed by the Assyrians. Hezekiah (a ringleader of the revolt) was again a vassal, but he did not lose his throne. In his annals Sennacherib claimed total victory over Judah, while the Bible records a slaughter of Assyrians (185 thousand according to 2 Kgs. 19:35 = Isa. 37:36; cf. 2 Chr. 32:21) by an angel of God. Rumors of political or military setbacks (2 Kgs. 19:7 = Isa. 37:7) may have induced Sennacherib to return to the Assyrian capital Nineveh, where he was later assassinated by two of his sons (2 Kgs. 19:36-37 = Isa. 37:37-38; 2 Chr. 32:21). Some scholars have claimed that the evidence points to two separate military campaigns by Sennacherib against Judah (in 701 and again 10 or 15 years later). Most scholars today prefer to see in these reports tendentious accounts of one single campaign.

There is also some ambiguity in Hezekiah's relationship with Judah's prophets. Micah and Isaiah were both his contemporaries. There is no biblical evidence that Hezekiah had contact with Micah, although a later generation credited the king with tolerance toward his message (Jer. 26:18-19). Isaiah, however, often provided guidance to Hezekiah (2 Kgs. 19:2-7, 20-34 = Isa. 37:2-7, 21-35). Although Isaiah encouraged Hezekiah to resist the Assyrians when they slandered God (2 Kgs. 19:32-34 = Isa. 37:33-35), it seems likely that he initially opposed Hezekiah's plans to rebel against Assyria (Isa. 30:1-17; 31:1-5).

Hezekiah's religious reforms were dismantled by his son Manasseh. His attempts to become politically independent brought only devastation and the burden of heavy tribute to Judah. However, Hezekiah's example of piety, faithfulness, and zeal for God gave impetus to later successful religious reforms.

Bibliography. R. E. Clements, *Isaiah and the Deliverance of Jerusalem.* JSOTSup 13 (Sheffield, 1980); R. H. Lowery, *The Reforming Kings: Cults and Society in First Temple Judah.* JSOTSup 120 (Sheffield, 1991); A. R. Millard, "Sennacherib's Attack on Hezekiah," *TynBul* 36 (1985): 61-77; F. L. Moriarty, "The Chronicler's Account of Hezekiah's Reform," *CBQ* 27 (1965): 399-406; J. Rosenbaum, "Hezekiah's Reform and the Deuteronomistic Tradition," *HTR* 72 (1979): 23-43.

TIMOTHY A. LENCHAK

2. The head of a family who returned from Babylon with Nehemiah following the Exile (Ezra 2:16 = Neh. 7:21 = 1 Esdr. 5:15). His Babylonian name was Ater, and both names are among those sealing the renewed covenant (Neh. 10:17[MT 18]).

3. An ancestor of the prophet Zephaniah (Zeph. 1:1), perhaps the same as **1** above.

HEZION (Heb. *ḥezyôn)*
The grandfather of Syrian king Ben-hadad I (1 Kgs. 15:18). He is often identified with Rezon, king of Damascus at the time of Solomon (1 Kgs. 11:23-25).

HEZIR (Heb. *ḥēzîr)*

1. The leader of the seventeenth division of priests during the time of David (1 Chr. 24:15).

2. A Levite who set his seal to the renewed covenant under Nehemiah (Neh. 10:20[MT 21]).

HEZRO (Heb. K *ḥerṣô,* Q *eḥṣray)*
A man from Judean Carmel (**2**); one of David's Thirty (2 Sam. 23:35; 1 Chr. 11:37).

HEZRON (Heb. *ḥeṣrôn, ḥeṣrōn)* **(PERSON)**

1. The third son of Reuben (Gen. 46:9; Exod. 6:14; 1 Chr. 5:3); ancestor of the Hezronite clan of Reuben (Num. 26:6).

2. A son of Perez and grandson of Judah (Gen. 46:12; 1 Chr. 2:5; 4:1). His descendants constituted the Hezronite family of the tribe of Judah (Num. 26:21; cf. 1 Chr. 2:9-33). He is listed among the direct ancestors of David and the royal house of Judah (Ruth 4:18-19) and occurs in both versions of Jesus' genealogy (Gk. *Esrōm;* Matt. 1:3; Luke 3:33).

HEZRON (Heb. *ḥeṣrôn*) **(PLACE)**
A place on the extreme southern border of the territory allotted to Judah (Josh. 15:3), apparently between Kadesh-barnea and Addar. Hazar-addar in Num. 34:4 may be a mistaken conflation of Hezron and Addar from the list at Josh. 15:3. The site may be ʿAin Qedeis (100999), one of three small wells in the vicinity of ʿAin el-Qudeirât (Kadesh-barnea), or nearby. WADE R. KOTTER

HIDDAI (Heb. *hidday*) (also HURAI)
An Israelite from "the torrents/wadis of Gaash" who was one of David's Thirty (2 Sam. 23:30). At 1 Chr. 11:32 he is called Hurai.

HIDDEKEL (Heb. *ḥiddeqel*)
The Hebrew name for the Tigris River (so NRSV; Gen. 2:14; Dan. 10:4; Akk. *Idiglat;* Sum. *Idigna*).

HIEL (Heb. *ḥîʾēl*)
A man from Bethel who rebuilt Jericho during the time of Ahab (871-852 B.C.E.). While laying the foundations of the city wall, he lost Abiran, his firstborn; while setting up the gates, he lost his youngest son, Segub (1 Kgs. 16:29-34). These deaths were understood as consequences of the curse that Joshua had placed upon anyone who would rebuild the city or its wall (Josh. 6:26). Earlier interpretations of the deaths as building sacrifices are no longer maintained. The note about Hiel may go back to court annals of the northern kingdom, but his story has become part of the negative records about Ahab.

Bibliography. C. Conroy, "Hiel between Ahab and Elijah-Elisha," *Bibl* 77 (1996): 210-18.

SIEGFRIED KREUZER

HIERAPOLIS (Gk. *Hierápolis*)
A Hellenistic commercial city and military colony located in the Lycus Valley of southwestern Asia Minor near Colossae and Laodicea. Hierapolis was known for its production of textiles and was the center of mystery cults (Strabo *Geog.* 13.4.14). The Jewish community at Hierapolis was colonized when Antiochus III transferred Jewish soldiers from Mesopotamia and Babylon to Phrygia and Lydia ca. 210-205 B.C.E. (Josephus *Ant.* 12 [147-53]; cf. *CIJ* 2.775). Paul mentions Hierapolis as a place where Epaphras ministered (Col. 4:12-13). Irenaeus regarded Papias, bishop of Hierapolis ca. 125 C.E., as a "hearer" (disciple) of John (*Adv. haer.* 5.33.3-4); although Eusebius discredits this (*HE* 3.39.2-4), Papias is considered an Apostolic Father.

Bibliography. J. M. G. Barclay, *Jews in the Mediterranean Diaspora* (Edinburgh, 1996); M. Hengel, *Between Jesus and Paul* (Philadelphia, 1983); E. M. Yamauchi, *The Archaeology of New Testament Cities in Western Asia Minor* (Grand Rapids, 1980).

LYNNE ALCOTT KOGEL

HIERONYMUS (Gk. *Hierōnymos;* Lat. *Hieronymus*)

1. A district governor at the time of Antiochus V Eupator who antagonized the Jews (2 Macc. 12:2).

2. Latin form of Jerome, translator of the Vulgate.

HIGGAION (Heb. *higgāyôn*)
A cryptic term occurring in ancient Hebrew poetry. It is likely derived from *hgh* ("moan, growl," "muse"), and may refer to reflecting/meditating (Ps. 19:14[MT 15]; Lam. 3:62; cf. Ps. 9:16[17] with *selâ*, perhaps signalling a reflective pause or an instrumental interlude) or a manner of singing or musical accompaniment, possibly a "flourish" (Ps. 92:3[4], where it occurs with *kinnôr*, "lyre"; NRSV "melody of the lyre"). TYLER F. WILLIAMS

HIGH PLACE
Most commonly a sacred site, although a precise description remains elusive. Heb. *bāmâ* (pl. *bāmôṯ*) is most commonly found in the condemnatory lists of illegitimate worship practices by Israelite and Judean kings and their subjects, but in those many instances the hated *bāmâ* is not described. The most complete description of an Israelite *bāmâ* is found in 1 Sam. 9–10, but that description is frustratingly incomplete. Because *bāmâ* was translated into Latin as *excelsus*, it is often rendered in English as "high place," a term that has itself led to confusion about what the biblical *bāmâ* actually was.

The Hebrew root *bmh* has cognates in several Semitic languages. In Ugaritic it means the back of a body. In Akkadian the singular likewise means "back," while the plural refers to terrain, possibly hilly. Despite the fact that *bmh* has no sacred association in any Canaanite dialect, most scholars have thought of the *bāmâ* as an originally Canaanite place of worship.

Four interpretations of the *bāmâ* are common to the scholarly literature. They are: an outdoor hilltop installation which included some combination of *ʾăšērâ* ("sacred pole"), *maṣṣēḇâ* ("standing stone"), and *mizbēaḥ* ("altar"); an artificially raised platform upon which religious rites were enacted; a sacrificial altar; or a mortuary installation. The first has been the most widely accepted, although neither it nor its alternatives correspond well with the rather scant biblical evidence for the *bāmâ* and the religious activities which took place there.

More recent work suggests that the *bāmâ* was a multi-roomed structure located in an urban setting. Built on an elevated site, it would have included an area in which animal sacrifice and the burning of incense could take place. Cultic furniture, including sacrificial and incense altars, would have been kept within the *bāmâ*. Among its several rooms might be a *liškâ*, in which cultic personnel and worshippers could sit to eat meals.

The most complete biblical description of the *bāmâ* comes from the tribal period, the era of the judges. 1 Sam. 9:11-25 describes religious rites at a *bāmâ* in an unnamed city within the district of Zuph, and 10:5 describes a processional of prophets leaving the *bāmâ* in Bethel. Legitimate use of the *bāmâ* by Israelites continued until the construction of the Jerusalem temple, as Solomon and the Israelites worshipped at many *bāmôṯ*, including the great *bāmâ* in Gibeon where Yahweh appeared to Solomon (1 Kgs. 3:2-5), and were not condemned for it.

During his reign, Solomon also built *bāmôṯ* for his non-Israelite wives and for the gods of Sidon, Ammon, and Moab (1 Kgs. 11:4-8). In this context, the Mesha stela is intriguing, since this late 9th-century inscription makes reference to the Moabite king Mesha's restoration of Moabite *bet bamot.* Moabite worship at *bāmôṯ* is also mentioned in Isa. 16:12; Jer. 48:35, indicating that the *bāmâ* was an Iron Age, but not exclusively an Israelite, place of worship.

Once the nation of Israel split in two late in the 10th century, Jeroboam, the first northern king, constructed royal sanctuaries at Bethel and Dan (1 Kgs. 12:25-30). To further ensure the loyalty of his people, he also built *bāmôṯ* throughout his kingdom and created a new nonlevitical priestly group, drawn from men of all social classes, to officiate at them (1 Kgs. 12:31). The fealty of these new *bāmôṯ* priests was reinforced by the fact that they also were required to serve at the royal sanctuary in Bethel (1 Kgs. 12:32).

In Judah, too, the religious needs of the population at large were not fulfilled through worship in the royal sanctuary in Jerusalem. Therefore, alongside the Jerusalem temple, Judean monarchs established a *bāmôṯ* system similar to that developed by Jeroboam in Israel (2 Kgs. 23:5). Its legitimacy is underscored by the suggestion made by officers of the late-8th-century Assyrian king Sennacherib that the Judean king Hezekiah had himself undermined loyalty to Yahweh by destroying his *bāmôṯ.* Hezekiah's ministers recognized the devastating nature of these charges and asked the Assyrians to speak in Aramaic, so that nearby Judeans could not follow the conversation (2 Kgs. 18:17-37; 2 Chr. 32:9-19).

The biblical evidence thus indicates that religion in Israel and Judah was a two-tiered affair. Royal cults in Jerusalem, Bethel, and Dan were used by the kings, their ministers, and the levitical priesthood. The many Israelite and Judean *bāmôṯ* were royally sanctioned regional sanctuaries used concurrently for worship by nonlevitical priests and by the population at large.

Initially a legitimate place for Israelite and Judean worship, the *bāmôṯ* later became the subject of Deuteronomistic diatribes accusing the kings and their subjects of lack of loyalty to Yahweh. In fact, the majority of biblical references to the *bāmâ* are found in these condemnatory pieces (e.g., 2 Kgs. 12:3; 14:4; 15:4, 35) and in their prophetical counterparts (e.g., Amos 7:9).

According to the Deuteronomistic historians, in the late 8th century Hezekiah destroyed *bāmôṯ,* along with *maṣṣēḇôṯ* and the *'ăšērâ* (2 Kgs. 18:4). Hezekiah's reforms notwithstanding, the *bāmôṯ* priesthood grew increasingly independent, so nearly a century later Josiah waged campaigns against them (2 Kgs. 23:5), hoping to eradicate their power base.

From all of this, it is apparent that the *bāmâ* was for the most part an accepted place for Israelite worship, one which met the needs of both the Israelite and Judean monarchs and of the local citizenry. At the same time, certain elements within the population, particularly the priestly and prophetic group whose ideas and traditions culminated in the work of the Deuteronomistic school, opposed this decentralizing institution and waged an ultimately successful campaign advocating the primacy of the Jerusalem temple.

Bibliography. W. B. Barrick, "What Do We Really Know About 'High-places'?" *SEÅ* 45 (1980): 50-57; A. Biran, ed., *Temples and High Places in Biblical Times* (Jerusalem, 1981); B. A. Nakhai, "What's a Bamah? How Sacred Space Functioned in Ancient Israel," *BARev* 20/3 (1994): 18-29, 77-78; P. H. Vaughan, *The Meaning of "Bama" in the Old Testament.* SOTSMS 3 (Cambridge, 1974).

BETH ALPERT NAKHAI

HIGH PRIEST

The primary official of the Israelite cultus. According to the Torah, the office of high priest goes back to the Sinaitic revelation. From Aaron, an uninterrupted hereditary chain of high priests links the portable tabernacle of the wilderness to the Second Temple in Jerusalem (Num. 25:10-13). However, from the historical perspective the actual existence of such an institution before the Babylonian Exile is very unlikely. When Ezek. 40–48 describes the temple to be rebuilt, the regulations on which the office of high priesthood is based are introduced as elements of a new order that God would establish in clear discontinuity with the past. In Ezekiel's words, the king will no longer be the owner and leader of the temple, but simply its custodian. The Levites will no longer be allowed to minister in the presence of Yahweh, and will represent a group clearly separated from the priests. Among all the priestly families the leadership will be taken by only one particular Aaronite family, the sons of Zadok. None of these conditions set by Ezekiel existed before the Exile, and without them there was no room for the institution of the high priesthood. It was among the exiles that an autonomous priestly leadership first emerged, challenging the failing power of the house of David. At the time of Darius, when the Jews were allowed to return to Jerusalem and to build a new temple, the house of Zadok was already influential enough to force the Davidic Zerubbabel to share his power with the Zadokite priest, Jeshua (Ezra 3:8). This fragile compromise lasted only a few years; construction of the Second Temple marked the end of any political role for the Davidic house. The high priest, now the supreme authority of Judaism, gained the qualities of prestige and dignity that had formerly been held by the king.

By the time the books of Chronicles were written, the process of the replacement of the authority of the king by that of the high priest was so much consolidated that the very understanding of Jewish history was changed. According to Chronicles, the kings never held any priestly duties (2 Chr. 26:16-20) and the threefold hierarchy of high priest, priests, and Levites (1 Chr. 23–24) was fully in place during the First Temple period. Any contradictory report in the previous books of Samuel and Kings was skillfully eliminated (compare 1 Chr. 18:17 and 2 Sam. 8:18).

It was during the period between Ezekiel and Chronicles that the biblical legislation concerning the high priesthood took its final shape and was made part of the Sinaitic revelation. Although some laws might have preexilic roots, they were now part of a consistent view that mapped all the world's geographical and social space in relationship to various levels of purity. As the temple with its concentric courts around the holy of holies reproduced the hierarchy of the cosmos, so the high priest was at the center of human holiness. While Gentiles, common Israelites (women and men), and the temple personnel (Levites and priests) were assigned the space reserved to each in the temple, only the high priest could enter the holy of holies, once a year for the rituals of the Day of Atonement. The high priest was bound to a degree of ritual purity, higher not only than common Jews but also than ordinary Levites and priests, with special and more restrictive laws, notably concerning marriage, contact with dead bodies, and sacrificial duties (Lev. 4:1-12; 21:10-15). The Torah also gives instructions about the investiture ceremony of the high priest (Exod. 29:1-37; Lev. 8:5-35) and a detailed description of his garments (Exod. 28:3-43).

After Jeshua, the high priesthood was hereditary and conferred for life. Despite the paucity of historical sources, it seems that in the Persian and Ptolemaic periods the leadership of the house of Zadok remained unchallenged, apart from some minor circles whose dissatisfaction toward the Second Temple found expression in the earliest Enochic literature. The end of the Zadokite priesthood at the beginning of the Seleucid period was due to political and economical factors more than to religious reasons, but had a tremendous impact on the religious authority of the office. The Zadokite Jason was able to replace his brother Onias III by bribing Antiochus IV, only to fall victim to the same trick a few years later by the non-Zadokite Menelaus (2 Macc. 4:7-27). Jason's gesture destroyed the foundations of Zadokite power. The high priesthood no longer belonged to an old hereditary line, and no longer was for life, but now depended on the ambitions of Jewish priestly families and on the interests of foreign rulers. More damaging for the office, the legitimacy of the high priesthood was no longer widely recognized but openly questioned and frequently challenged. As the experience of the Hasmoneans would prove, a reestablished hereditary line, even when based on political and military power, remained vulnerable to religious attack and dependent on political fortune.

After the death of Herod, who had relegated the high priesthood to an almost marginal role, the Roman procurators gave the office greater power in local affairs, with the intention of creating a pro-Roman aristocracy of high priests (and former high priests). On the one hand, this policy strengthened the office (and the most actively pro-Roman family of Annas and Caiaphas) but, on the other hand, made the high priests even more suspicious of those who, for political or religious reasons, opposed Roman rule. It is not surprising that one of the first goals of the radical groups that led the anti-Roman revolt in 66-70 C.E. was to disrupt the priestly elite who in recent years had already become the target of political assassination. The last high priest of Israel was a layman named Phannias, chosen by lot during the revolt (Josephus *BJ* 1:147-57).

The destruction of the temple by Titus in 70 C.E. marked the end of the high priesthood. Ironically, the long crisis of the office following the deposition of Onias III had prepared many Jews to live without a high priesthood. The memory of that powerful institution, however, continued to be an amazingly creative source of inspiration for both Christians and Jews.

Bibliography. L. L. Grabbe, *Judaism from Cyrus to Hadrian*, 2 vols. (Minneapolis, 1992); M. S. Jaffee, *Early Judaism* (Upper Saddle River, N.J., 1997).

Gabriele Boccaccini

HIGHWAY

A generally lengthy and well-maintained thoroughfare (Heb. *mĕsillâ*), in contrast to a "way" (*dereḵ, šĕḇîl*), which can range from a beaten path to a small road. References to highways in the OT include the route taken by the cows transporting the ark toward Beth-shemesh (1 Sam. 6:12) and allusions to the construction or maintenance of important roads (Isa. 40:3; 49:11; 62:10).

Highways were lifelines between the great empires of Egypt and Mesopotamia, linking Africa and Asia. Between them lay Palestine as a land bridge. Armies, merchants, and pilgrims depended on stable and well-known routes of transportation. The movement of people and goods along highways of ancient Israel was constant (Prov. 9:13-15; Lam. 2:15). The control of highways or their destruction in time of war had serious ramifications. Hence, Isa. 40:3-4 describes prosperous times in terms of smooth passage along highways.

Common routes often began as footpaths trampled by the constant passage of people and animals. An average day's travel was ca. 32 km. (20 mi.) on foot, with weather and terrain as contributing factors. Obviously, highways were constructed in relation to natural terrain such as mountain passes, valleys, lakes, and rivers, as well as the key towns and cities along the way. Major highways cited in the OT include the King's Highway (Num. 20:17; 21:22), also known in different periods as the Sultan's Highway and Trajan's Highway, and the Great Trunk Road, running from Egypt to Mesopotamia via the Fertile Crescent (Exod. 13:17; Isa. 9:1[MT 8:23]).

During the Roman period, advances in engineering marked improvements in the construction and maintenance of highways. Roman roads were layered and provided for drainage. The military, commerce, and public transport all benefited from these new methods. As in modern times, the great enemy of roads was winter weather. Annual efforts were organized to repair highways after the rainy season.

Bibliography. D. A. Dorsey, *The Roads and Highways of Ancient Israel* (Baltimore, 1991); J. J. Pilch, "Travel in the Ancient World," *TBT* 32 (1994): 100-107. J. Edward Owens

HILEN (Heb. *ḥîlēn*) (also HOLON)
A village in the hill country of Judah, allotted to the Kohathite family of Levites (1 Chr. 6:58[MT 43]). At Josh. 15:51; 21:15 it is called Holon (**1**).

HILKIAH (Heb. *ḥilqîyâ*)

1. The father of Eliakim, Hezekiah's prime minister (2 Kgs. 18:18, 26, 37; Isa. 22:20; 36:3).

2. High priest during the reign of Josiah. He was responsible for the collection and disbursement of funds that paid for the renovation of the temple, which accompanied Josiah's reform. During the renovation, he found the scroll of the law, which served as the basis for the continuing reform. He and others consulted the prophetess Huldah on Josiah's behalf in order to ascertain the word of the Lord in relation to the scroll and its implications for Judah. Hilkiah and other officials participated in the removal of implements of pagan worship from the temple (2 Kgs. 22–23; 2 Chr. 34–35; Isa. 36–37) and provided sacrifices for Josiah's Passover celebration (2 Chr. 35:8; 1 Esdr. 1:8).

3. A preexilic Levite (1 Chr. 6:13[MT 5:39]) and possibly the great-grandfather of Ezra (Ezra 7:1; 1 Esdr. 8:1). Some scholars identify this Hilkiah with the high priest of Josiah's reign (**2** above).

4. An ancestor of Merari, one of the levitical musicians appointed by David to the service of the ark of the covenant (1 Chr. 6:45[30]).

5. The father of a postexilic priest named either Azariah (1 Chr. 9:11) or Seraiah (Neh. 11:11).

6. One of the gatekeepers of the temple appointed by David. He was the second son of Hosah, a descendant of Merari (1 Chr. 26:11).

7. One of those who stood beside Ezra as he read the law before the Water Gate (Neh. 8:4).

8. One of the leaders of the priests during the time of Jeshua and Zerubbabel (Neh. 12:7); his son Hashabiah was head of the ancestral house during the high priesthood of Joiakim (v. 21).

9. A priest from Anathoth; the father of Jeremiah (Jer. 1).

10. The father of Gemariah, whom Zedekiah sent to Nebuchadnezzar (Jer. 29:3).

11. An ancestor of Judith (Jdt. 8:1).

12. An ancestor of Baruch (Bar. 1:1, 7).

13. The father of Susanna (Sus. 2, 29, 63).

Michael L. Ruffin

HILL COUNTRY
A general designation for those parts of Palestine, and the areas east of the Jordan River, that are not flat, but of less elevation than a mountain. The hill country was especially fertile (Deut. 11:11), and Moses asked that God allow him to cross over the Jordan, in order to see the "good hill country" of central Palestine (3:25). The hill country was settled by numerous peoples, including Jebusites (Josh. 11:3), Anakim (v. 21), and Amorites (Deut. 1:7; Num. 13:29). During the Conquest, Joshua instructed the tribes of Ephraim and Manasseh to clear the forest of the hill country, to provide room for settlements (Josh. 17:14-18).

Within Palestine, the hill country comprised the central mountain range, a ridge of hills that ran down the center of the country from the Galilee in the north, to the southern coastal plain and the Shephelah. Any portion of this ridge could be designated hill country, which may be divided, from north to south, into four regions: Galilee, Ephraim, Judah, and the Negeb.

The Galilee ranged in elevation from more than 915 m. (3000 ft.) in the north, to below 610 m. (2000 ft.) in the south. In antiquity the region was heavily forested, and divided by a nearly vertical slope of almost 455-610 m. (1500-2000 ft.) that hindered travel. During the time of Joshua, much of this hill country remained unconquered (Josh. 13:6). Its largest settlement was "Kedesh in Galilee in the hill country of Naphtali" (Josh. 20:7), overlooking the north Jordan Valley.

The "hill country of Ephraim" (1 Kgs. 4:8) consisted of a mountain plateau, rising to over 915 m. (3000 ft.) in its southern portion. These hills were settled by Joshua with great difficulty, because of their dense forests (Josh. 17:14-18). Northern Ephraim was lower and less fertile than the Galilean hill country and was easily traversed by accessible roads in all directions. The hill country of Ephraim was heavily developed, with major cities situated at principal road junctions, including Shechem, Tirzah, and Dothan.

The hill country of Judea (Josh. 11:21; Luke 1:39) contained the major cities of Jerusalem and Hebron. The region descended sharply in the east, more than 915 m. (3000 ft.), where it met the Judean Desert. Its southern portion contained chasms and caves that provided convenient hiding places (1 Sam. 23:14). In the NT Jesus' ministry began in the "hill country of Judea" (Luke 1:65).

The region of the Negeb declined abruptly, S of Hebron, to 455-550 m. (1500-1800 ft.), and consisted of low hills (also called the Shephelah, "Lowland").

Bibliography. Y. Aharoni, *The Land of the Bible*, 2nd ed. (Philadelphia, 1979). Kenneth Atkinson

HILLEL (Heb. *hillēl*)

1. The father of Abdon, the judge who immediately preceded Samson (Judg. 12:13-15).

2. Hillel the Elder (ca. 60 B.C.–A.D. 20), clearly the single most influential figure in postbiblical Jewish history. Born in Babylonia, he came to Israel to pursue Torah study under the greatest teachers of the time, Shemaiah and Avtalion. Hillel was eventually promoted to the presidency of the Sanhedrin and thus became the *de facto* head of the Pharisees (30 B.C.–A.D. 10). A contemporary of Herod and Jesus, he was surely among, if not the head of, the "chief priests and teachers of the Law"

(Matt. 2:4) whom Herod consulted about the birthplace of the Messiah.

In rabbinic tradition he is compared to Moses and Ezra, and it is said that he was the only one since Malachi to be worthy of the Holy Spirit resting upon him "as it did on Moses" (*t. Soṭa* 13:3; *y. Sanh.* 11a).

Hillel founded a dynasty of presidents *(nĕśî'îm)* who ruled Israel through the Sanhedrin for more than 400 years, including his grandson Gamaliel I and Yoḥanan ben Zakkai, Hillel's star pupil who almost single-handedly preserved Judaism after the destruction of A.D. 70. It is said that Hillel left a core group of 80 disciples, undoubtedly the foundation of the "School of Hillel," the pharisaic group responsible for the formation of "rabbinic Judaism." Rabbi Judah the Prince, a direct descendant of Hillel, produced the Mishnah, the basis of both Talmuds, assuring Hillel's permanent influence on Judaism.

Hillel radically transformed the pharisaic movement. He standardized methods of interpretation and application of Scripture; emphasized leniency in judgment and in halakhic responsibilities; sought out the poor, sinners, and Gentiles, and threw open to them the way to God; and sanctified all of life by teaching that even the most mundane activities are sacred when done unto God. The influence of these general emphases is readily seen in the NT.

Within Hillel's lifetime, he came to be viewed as the ideal rabbi. Not only did Hillel preach, but he practiced what he preached, and teachers were commanded to imitate his piety (*Sanh.* 11a), humility, patience, and approachability (*Šabb.* 31a), and teaching style.

Although the impact of Hillel on rabbinic Judaism was more direct, his influence on early Christianity is in another sense equally remarkable. Owing to chronological, ethnic, ideological, and geographical proximity, it should come as no surprise that Hillel's influence reached to NT teachers such as Jesus and Paul. For example, Hillel taught the principle of the "Golden Rule" (*Šabb.* 31a; cf. Matt. 7:12), that one should "Love and pursue peace" (*'Abot* 1:12; 2:8; cf. Matt. 5:9), as well as a view of divine judgment which within the Academy came to be called "measure for measure" (*'Abot* 2:7; *Sukk.* 53a; cf. Matt. 7:2). Moreover, most of the seven hermeneutical rules (*middôṯ*) which Hillel canonized for systematic interpretation and application of Scripture are used in the NT by Jesus and Paul (*t. Sanh.* 7:11; *'Abot R. Nat.* 37, 110).

Bibliography. Y. Buxbaum, *The Life and Teachings of Hillel* (Northvale, N.J., 1994); "Hillel (the Elder)," *EncJud* 8:482-85. W. E. NUNNALLY

HIN (Heb. *hîn;* Egyp. *hn*)
A liquid measure equal to one sixth of a bath, ca. 3.6. l. (1 U.S. gal.).

HIND OF THE DAWN
Perhaps the name of a tune or a similar musical instruction (Heb. *'ayyeleṯ haššaḥar*), mentioned in the superscription to Ps. 22(MT 1; NRSV "Deer of the Dawn"). The phrase suggests a common theme of the Psalms, God's help to the needy (cf. Ps. 46:5[6]).

HINNOM (Heb. *hinnōm*), **VALLEY OF**
One of three valleys which cut through the region around Jerusalem. Most scholars believe that the western valley is the one the ancients called Hinnom Valley, which joins the Kidron Valley at the southeast corner of Jerusalem. It is also called the "valley of the son of Hinnom" (Jer. 7:32) or the "valley of the children of Hinnom" (2 Kgs. 23:10; NRSV "Ben-hinnom"), and it was so familiar that it was sometimes called simply "the valley" (2 Chr. 26:9). It served as a dividing line between the tribes of Benjamin and Judah (Josh. 15:8; 18:16).

At a place called Topheth in Hinnom Valley people worshipped Baal and offered their children as burned sacrifices to the god Moloch during the reigns of Solomon, Ahaz, and Manasseh (2 Kgs. 23:10; 2 Chr. 28:3; 33:6; Jer. 32:35). This caused Jeremiah to name it the Valley of Slaughter (Jer. 7:31-32; 19:5-6). The place was made into a garbage dump to desacralize it, making it unfit even for pagan worship. For centuries constant fires burned the refuse deposited there. The fires and stench along with the recollection of the horrors practiced there and the condemnation of those evils by God's prophets generated the concept of Gehenna (lit., "valley of Hinnom"), a term designating the burning torture of condemned people, the "hell of fire" (Matt. 5:22). While the name referred to a specific geographical location, it also became for Jews and Christians a standard term for hell with its torments and punishment (Matt. 10:28; 25:30, 46).

RICHARD A. SPENCER

HIPPOS (Gk. *Híppos*)
A Greek city (Antiochia Hippos) founded by the Seleucid kings in the 3rd century B.C., located at modern Qal'at el-Ḥuṣn ("fortress of the horse"; 212242), 2 km. (1.2 mi.) E. of the Sea of Galilee. Conquered by Alexander Janneus (ca. 80 B.C.), Hippos was taken by Pompey, at which time Pliny knew it as a city of the Decapolis (*Nat. hist.* 5, 74). Augustus gave it to Herod the Great, and afterwards it became part of the province of Syria. In Byzantine times Hippos was a part of Palaestina Secunda and the seat of a bishopric. It was known in Aramaic as Sussita ("mare, horse").

Hippos, a walled city with a major gate on the east and a smaller one on the west, had on the south side of its main east-west Cardo street a nymphaeum and bath house, and on the north side a theater. Three Byzantine churches were found to the north of the Cardo and two on the south side, one of which was a cathedral triapsidal basilica, with parts of the altar screen, marble facing, and tesserae found there; it also had an adjoining triapsidal baptistery with baptismal font and mosaics with Greek inscriptions. Remains of the city's Sea of Galilee port have been found. Much of Hippos was destroyed by earthquake in A.D. 747.

Bibliography. C. Epstein, "Hippos (Sussita)," *NEAEHL* 2:634-36. W. HAROLD MARE

HIRAH (Heb. *ḥîrâ*)
An Adullamite friend (MT Heb. *rēʿēhû;* LXX, Vulg. "shepherd," from *rōʿēhû*) of Jacob's son Judah (Gen. 38:1, 12, 20-23). It was when Judah was visiting Hirah that he met the daughter of the Canaanite Shua whom he married (Gen. 38:2).

HIRAM (Heb. *ḥîrām*)
1. Hiram I, king of Tyre (969-935 B.C.E.), who lived on friendly terms with both David and Solomon. The Biblical Hebrew form of the name is a shortened version of the Phoenician Ahiram, which has been discovered on an inscribed sarcophagus at Byblos as the name of a king there. Under Hiram I Tyre enjoyed considerable expansion and prosperity — as evidenced by the establishment of colonies on Cyprus, Sardinia, and Sicily, and at Gades and Tartessus in Spain. Josephus reports that Hiram succeeded his father Abibaal and reigned for 34 years before dying at the age of 53. Hiram is credited with the construction of embankments to level the eastern part of Tyre, the enlargement of the city, the logging of timber from Lebanon for the building of temples, erection of fanes to Heracles/Melkart and Ashtarte, institution of a new feast for the former deity, demolition of a number of shrines, creation of a causeway to the temple of Zeus/Baal, and conduct of a successful campaign against Utica for its refusal to pay tribute (*Ag. Ap.* 1; *Ant.* 8).

Hiram's friendship with David and Solomon was probably based on mutual need: Israel lacked technical skills for advancing its material culture; Phoenicia lacked adequate agricultural production. The OT implies that it was shortly after David's capture of Jerusalem that Hiram sent Tyrian workers, who excelled in architecture, and also supplied raw materials for the building of David's palace (2 Sam. 5:11). Subsequently Solomon entered into a treaty with Hiram (1 Kgs. 5:12[MT 26]). 1 Kgs. 5:1(15) indicates Hiram actually made the initial contact after Solomon's accession to the throne. Palestine became Phoenicia's granary because Hiram received large quantities of barley, oil, wheat, and wine annually for both his household and his workers. In return Solomon received skilled labor besides cedar and cypress wood — shipped via sea rafts to Joppa — for his massive construction projects. Official buildings dating from this period in Israel show many signs of Phoenician influences in design and execution. By sharing experienced sailors, Hiram further aided Solomon in his maintenance of a merchant fleet which operated out of the port of Ezion-geber on the Gulf of Aqabah (1 Kgs. 9:26-28; 10:11, 22). This fleet evidently sailed along the African and Arabian coasts of the Red Sea, dealing in high-cost and low-bulk luxury items like precious stones and exotic animals. When Solomon's ambitious building program strained his treasury excessively or when his trading operations ran into serious financial trouble, he was forced to cede 20 cities in Galilee to Hiram (1 Kgs. 9:10-14).

2. A talented craftsperson and metalworker whom the king of Tyre lent to Solomon in order to decorate Yahweh's Jerusalem temple, including the erection of Jachin and Boaz (1 Kgs. 7:13-47). Hiram's father had been a Tyrian artisan in bronze. His mother was either a Naphtalite (1 Kgs. 7:14) or a Danite (2 Chr. 2:14[13]). These two labels could derive from the same memory because the city Dan lay within the territory of Naphtali. However, the Chronicler could have altered Hiram's descent to draw a parallel with the Danite Oholiab and the latter's construction of the tabernacle (cf. Exod. 31:6). Support for purposeful alteration comes from the fact that the Chronicler calls the Tyrian Huram-abi at 2 Chr. 2:13(12), a name which may have been created by joining "Hiram" to the final element "ab(i)" of Oholiab. Furthermore, the list of Hiram's abilities in 1 Kgs. 7:14; 2 Chr. 2:7, 14(6, 13) is taken from Exod. 31:1-6; 35:35.

Bibliography. J. K. Kuan, "Third Kingdoms 5:1 and Israelite-Tyrian Relations during the Reign of Solomon," *JSOT* 46 (1990): 31-46.

EDWIN C. HOSTETTER

3. Hiram II, king of Tyre (739-ca. 730), called "king of the Sidonians." He greatly expanded the territory controlled by Tyre despite the aggression of the Assyrian Empire. Texts dating to 738 and 734-32 list him among the territories paying tribute to Tiglath-pileser III (*ANET,* 283). In 733-732 he entered a coalition with Rezin of Damascus and the king of Ashkelon against Assyria; when the rebellion was quashed, Hiram alone was pardoned.

4. Hiram III, king of Tyre (551-532). Apparently a loyal vassal of Nabonidus, he was summoned from Babylon to succeed his brother Maharbal (Merbal; Josephus *Ag. Ap.* 1.158-59). With the accession of Cyrus in 539 Tyre became part of the Persian Empire.

5. Hiram IV, king of Tyre and a contemporary of the Persian king Darius I Hystaspes (521-486). Herodotus (*Hist.* 7.98) refers to him as Siromos.

Bibliography. H. J. Katzenstein, *The History of Tyre* (Jerusalem, 1973).

HIRELING
A free person who worked for a wage (Heb. *śāḵîr;* Gk. *misthōtós*). Hirelings worked as farm laborers (Lev. 25:6), shepherds (John 10:12-13), and mercenaries (Jer. 46:21). The hireling's "days" were toilsome and long (Job 7:1; 14:6). Animals were also hired for work (Exod. 22:15[MT 14]).

Hirelings served on a yearly (Lev. 25:53) or daily basis (Deut. 24:15), working the allotted time in order to receive their wages (Job 7:2). Isaiah refers to years "as a hireling would count them," indicating that a hireling would not work one day beyond the agreement with his employer (Isa. 16:14; 21:16). Some employers paid oppressive wages, though the Law forbade the oppression of a hireling (Deut. 24:14-15).

Since a hireling had no ownership in his employment, responsibility was easily lacking. Jesus referred to this lack of commitment in a hired person (John 10:12-13).

ALAN RAY BUESCHER

HISTORIOGRAPHY, BIBLICAL

The study of biblical history has focused on the Former Prophets, particularly the books of Joshua, Judges, Samuel, and Kings. Although the book of Chronicles parallels large portions of Samuel and Kings, it has been largely passed over on the assumption that its theological biases made it less reliable than its cousins. The folkloristic narratives of the patriarchs and early Israel in the Pentateuch might also be included within the broad discussion of biblical historiography. The character of the discussion will depend largely on the definition adopted for historical writing.

Definition of History

The traditional definition of the historical writing was shaped under the historical positivism of the 19th century, and emphasized the critical and scientific description and evaluation of past events (in the words of the 19th-century German historian Leopold von Ranke, "to tell it as it actually happened.") The recognition, however, that all historical writing is biased had led to a re-evaluation of the "science" of history. A definition of history emphasizing "antiquarian interests" eliminates the problem, yet still introduces the quite modern concept of antiquarianism into the definition. Although there are aspects of biblical historical narratives which are of such interest, it may be legitimately asked whether the text itself, its author, or its readers had purely antiquarian interests. A popular definition of the historical genre is that offered by the Dutch historian Johan Huizinga: "History is the intellectual form in which a civilization renders account to itself of its past" and as such it "comprises every form of historical record: that of the annalist, the writer of memoirs, the historical philosopher, and the scholarly researcher." Modern historians have tended increasingly toward this last definition, which emphasizes the use of the past for self-understanding rather than the supposedly critical and objective scientific reconstruction of the past. Notably outside the parameters of this definition is the question of historical veracity or scientific evaluation.

Survey of Research

The study of biblical history has been dominated by the question of historical reliability. With the rise of historical criticism, the origin and historicity of biblical narratives and particularly the Pentateuch became a central question. The documentary hypothesis envisioned the gradual evolution of the Pentateuch beginning with the Yahwist and Elohist historical narratives which were written in the 10th through 9th centuries B.C.E. and eventually combined. To these narratives were added the Deuteronomist's work in the 7th century and finally a Priestly writer brought the whole together in the 5th century. Once this outline was established, the hypothesis was extended to the historical books as well. The Priestly work was considered late and therefore of marginal value; the association of the historical narratives in the books of Chronicles with the Priestly writer naturally raised questions about their historical reliability.

The attempt to understand the formation of Israel's traditions has been closely associated with efforts to identify the theological threads of the various traditions. A prominent way of describing the biblical view of Israel's past has been called "Salvation History" *(Heilsgeschichte)*. Biblical theologians envisioned a special idea of history in ancient Israel which conceived of Yahweh as guiding and actively directing events towards a goal. Special claims regarding Israel's unique concept of history as linear and dynamic as opposed to the cyclical and static concepts of other Near Eastern cultures are associated with the Biblical Theology movement. This perspective overdraws the contrast between Israel and her neighbors. Its adherents painted Near Eastern cultures into an unduly narrow framework while at the same time overlooking aspects of recurrence, typology, and analogy in biblical historiography. As a result, the Biblical Theology movement along with Salvation History came under scathing criticism beginning in the early 1960s. This criticism, although largely correct, naturally tended to overreact, with the result that all distinction between ancient Israel and other Near Eastern cultures was overlooked. It remains true that ancient Israel was preoccupied with its past to a much greater degree than Mesopotamian civilizations and especially ancient Egypt. As a result, biblical historiography is shaped by a remarkable degree of introspection which is barely perceptible in Mesopotamian or Egyptian historiography. This undoubtedly reflects, first of all, the fact that biblical historiography was not state sponsored, but it also reflects the unique geographical, social, and cultural forces which shaped the history of ancient Israel.

The critique of the Biblical Theology movement spread into studies of the Patriarchal narratives. Attempts to reconstruct some historical kernel from the folkloristic patriarchal traditions were largely discredited in the 1970s, especially by John Van Seters (*Abraham in History and Tradition,* 1975) and Thomas L. Thompson (*The Historicity of the Patriarchal Narratives,* 1974). From there the critique of biblical historical narrative spread to the Conquest and Settlement period and finally to the period of the Monarchy. The new consensus is that a modern history of Israel can only begin in the 10th century with the United Monarchy (e.g., J. A. Soggin, J. Maxwell Miller, John H. Hayes). Some, however, would like to push the starting point into the Persian or even the Hellenistic period (Thompson, Philip R. Davies). This type of historical nihilism has not attracted a large following, essentially because there is too much detail in the biblical narratives corroborated by archaeological and Near Eastern sources to be dismissed as Persian or Hellenistic fiction.

Biblical Historical Writing

Biblical historical writing invariably brings the past up to the present. That is, the authors, redactors, and editors of biblical historical narratives end their accounts in their own times. So, e.g., the final composition of the book of Kings is generally attributed to the Exile, where the historical narrative ends. A broad consensus would see an early redaction of the book in the time of Josiah; it described the history of Israel up until the late 7th century. In the same way, the books of Chronicles were first composed in the early Persian period and took the history of Israel down into the writer's own day. A later editor then attached the books of Ezra-Nehemiah by repeating the last verses in Chronicles at the beginning of Ezra (compare 2 Chr. 36:22-23 with Ezra 1:1-2). This aspect of biblical historiography highlights the continuity which the writers felt with the past; they were part of a continually unfolding story. The importance of placing the present in touch with the past is also reflected in the historical psalms (e.g., Pss. 78, 105, 106, 136) and Moses' speech to Israel before they enter the land (Deut. 1:1–4:40).

Bibliography. M. Brettler, *The Creation of History in Ancient Israel* (London, 1995); P. R. Davies, *In Search of Ancient Israel.* JSOTSup 148 (Sheffield, 1992); B. Halpern, *The First Historians* (1988, repr. University Park, Pa., 1996); J. Huizinga, "A Definition of the Concept of History," in *Philosophy and History,* ed. R. Klibansky and H. J. Paton (Oxford, 1936), 1-10; I. W. Provan, "Ideologies, Literary and Critical: Reflections on Recent Writing on the History of Israel," *JBL* 114 (1995): 585-606; T. L. Thompson, *Early History of the Israelite People.* SHANE 4 (Leiden, 1992); J. Van Seters, *In Search of History* (New Haven, 1983).

William Schniedewind

HITTITES (Heb. *ḥittî*)

One of the great political powers of antiquity who during the 2nd millennium B.C. controlled much of the area comprising modern Turkey. During their heyday the Hittites built a powerful empire with its capital at Ḫattuša (ca. 200 km. [124 mi.] W of Ankara at modern Boghazköy) and stretching from the Aegean Sea as far east as the Euphrates River and into the northern Levant.

History

Though presumed to have been part of an Indo-european migration that arrived in Anatolia ca. 2300, the exact origins of the Hittites and their route into Anatolia are still disputed. While some believe they entered from the east or crossed the Black Sea, they most likely followed the traditional migration route through Thrace, across the Bosporus, and into northwestern Turkey. These immigrants, perhaps pushed by succeeding Luwian tribes, reached as far east as the Euphrates where their first influential kingdom was formed around the city of Kuššar. Pressure from the already established Hurrians in the east, however, seems to have pushed the Indo-european newcomers back into central Anatolia where they ultimately founded Ḫattuša on the site of a previously destroyed settlement.

The native culture of central Anatolia upon the arrival of the Indo-europeans was Ḫattic and the

Faience tile of a Hittite captive; mortuary temple of Rameses III (12th century B.C.E.). He wears a short kilt under a bright (perhaps Libyan) mantle (Service de Musées, Cairo)

country was known as "the Land of Ḫatti." The newcomers were rapidly integrated into the native culture and by adopting the designation "men of Ḫatti" eventually came to be known as "Hittites," a name familiar from the biblical narratives and, ultimately, through their own records. Thousands of cuneiform tablets have been found in archives at Ḫattuša as well as smaller regional centers such as Tapikka, Šapinuwa, and Šarissa. These texts are supplemented by thousands of Old Assyrian tablets found principally at Kaneš (modern Kültepe); although the Old Assyrian texts predate the Hittite state by several centuries, they illuminate the sociopolitical context from which the Hittites eventually emerged.

Hittite names found in the Old Assyrian records indicate that native Anatolians were heavily involved in the Old Assyrian trade network which flourished ca. 2000-1750. Economic and political competition between the Anatolian cities led to the demise of that commercial network by ca. 1750, and after a period of intense regional competition and slow consolidation the Old Hittite Kingdom (ca. 1650-1400) emerged with its center at Ḫattuša. While the record of this integration process remains largely unclear, evidence suggests that the Hittite state arose as the result of increasingly sophisticated interaction, first between the newly arrived Indo-europeans and the indigenous Ḫattians, and later between this mixed Anatolian population and the Assyrian traders. The lack of any evidence outside of the Hittite language indicates the full extent to which the newcomers were integrated into the native Anatolian way of life.

The first known Hittite kings, Labarna and Ḫattušili I, were tireless conquerors who integrated much of the Anatolian peninsula into a widespread political kingdom. This initial period of brilliance was capped by Muršili I's capture of Babylon (ca. 1595), but when internal factionalism led to Muršili's assassination the Old Kingdom went into decline. Other powers such as Arzawa and the Hurrians sought to capitalize on this internal discord by expanding into Hittite territory, but after a period of weakness that brought the kingdom to near extinction, the Hittites' sagging fortunes revived under Middle Hittite rulers such as Tudḫaliya II just prior to 1400.

The Hittite Empire (1400-1175) evolved from the exploits of Šuppiluliuma I and continued to develop under charismatic rulers such as Muršili II, Ḫattušili III, and Tudḫaliya IV. The empire attained its greatest influence during this period and shared the international spotlight with other major powers such as Egypt, Babylon, and Assyria. The sudden collapse of the Hittite state just after 1200 seems to have resulted from a combination of internal and external forces during the reign of Šuppiluliuma II. Neo-Hittite states that survived along the Syro-Anatolian borderland apparently maintained a degree of continuity with their Anatolian predecessor until their final incorporation into the Neo-Assyrian state.

Myths of Origin

Various myths have been associated with the Hittites, and the name itself conjures up some long-held misconceptions. One of the most common myths is that of a warrior society whose rise to power was orchestrated through a monopoly on ironworking techniques, an idea that has been rejected on numerous occasions. It has been suggested also that the rise of the Hittites was associated with mastery of the chariot, a crucial aspect of military technology thought to have been borrowed from the Hurrians. Still others visualize the invasion of Anatolia by a nomadic hoard of Indo-european invaders who "Hittitized" the native Ḫattic population soon after their arrival in Anatolia.

Such mythologies, though containing an element of truth, generally reflect beliefs based on imprecise knowledge of Hittite history and culture that date back to the early days of the discipline. Despite a rich assortment of evidence from Anatolia, both archaeological and literary sources still remain silent on many aspects of Hittite civilization, including what it actually means to be a Hittite. The general trend is to view "Hittite" in its widest sense, as a cultural term defining the material remains left by those who inhabited central Anatolia from the late 3rd millennium through the end of the Late Bronze Age.

Identity

While this may be the easiest way of treating the question of Hittite origins, it is not without its own problems. Many of the cultural traits so closely identified with the Hittites actually existed long before they came to power and survived even after their fall. Called Hittite because of their presence in the classic Hittite culture of Boghazköy/Ḫattuša, these elements result, as much as anything else, from syncretisms based on spatial proximity and the demands of the physical environment. This is particularly true of architecture, though other elements such as ceramic styles and religious iconography may well have been spread as the result of incorporation, emulation, and exchange. In all probability, a great deal of cultural borrowing must have taken place between the distinct, but closely situated, ethnic groups on the Anatolian plateau. Furthermore, the perception of cultural unity derived from this commonalty led some scholars to speculate on the presence of a strong ethnic entity in 2nd-millennium Anatolia. when in fact it was inhabited by a mixed ethnic population. Perhaps this wider cultural setting should be known more properly as "Anatolian" or "central Anatolian," reserving "Hittite" for a more specific usage.

The ethnic diversity that characterized 2nd-millennium Anatolia, however, may provide a clue as to the actual composition of the Hittite state and help clarify a number of issues. For example,

1. A Hittite is called a "man of Ḫatti" and lives in the "land of Ḫatti" but does not speak the language of Ḫatti *(Ḫattili).*
2. A Hittite is generally considered to be the

speaker of an Indo-european language now called Hittite, but which the Hittites called Nešite or a language of Kaneš *(Nešumnili).*

3. Outside of their language, little of what we now call Hittite can be said to be Indo-european in character.

The irony in all this is that, whoever the Hittites were, they seem to have passed their language on to their Anatolian neighbors while they themselves were assimilated into the cultural milieu of the central plateau, leaving no other evidence of their Indo-european background.

In contrast to the widely accepted cultural definition, the term Hittite may be understood also as a political adjective modifying the coalition of cities and lands whose political imperatives had been subsumed under the rule of Ḫattuša. Expanding from this core, the Hittites incorporated numerous lands and ethnic entities into their political system. Support was solidified through political persuasion in the form of military coercion, iconographic propaganda, marriage arrangements, the reconfiguration of religious systems, and architectural and bureaucratic expansion into the hinterland. The goal seems to have been to build a cohesive national consciousness that transcended the multiplicity of ethnic identities dotting the plateau.

One clue that the Hittite Empire was fundamentally political stems from the fact that from ca. 1400 onward Hittite culture moved away from its early Ḫattic roots and became increasingly Hurrianized. While pressures from beyond its borders left the Hittite state vulnerable at the end of the Old Hittite period, the Hittites managed to avoid disintegration. Instead they experienced a cultural metamorphosis marked by increasing Hurrian acculturation of the state. The relative ease with which this change seems to have occurred, whether through dynastic change or simply the incorporation of new values, suggests that the cultural base was modified without affecting the political superstructure to any great degree. This implies a political continuity that was not built solely along ethnic lines. Compromise and syncretism played a key role during this period as new cultural traits were incorporated into Hittite culture from conquered lands as well as influential countries such as Egypt.

While many issues remain unresolved, it appears that Hittite society was primarily a political synthesis derived from the union of migrating Indo-europeans and the indigenous Ḫattians. The system was secured by the various forms of incorporative persuasion emanating from the political center at Ḫattuša, but was not immune to change from beyond its borders. On the most basic level, Hittite leadership was always familial in nature, but their texts make clear that the realities of power led to many concessions on the local level, and this affected the formal structure of Hittite power. This was especially true with the incorporation of appendage states such as Carchemish, Aleppo, Tarḫuntašša, Ḫakpiš, Tammanna, and Išuwa in the Empire period. The Hittites can be understood, therefore, as the product of an artificial political arrangement brought together, not as the result of an orderly planned expansion, but through military necessity or political opportunism and by the most efficient integrative means possible.

Bibliography. R. H. Beal, *The Organization of the Hittite Military* (Heidelberg, 1992); K. Bittel, *Hattusha: The Capital of the Hittites* (New York, 1970); R. L. Gorny, "Environment, Archaeology, and History in Hittite Anatolia," *BA* 52 (1989): 78-96; O. R. Gurney, "Anatolia, c. 4000-2300 B.C.," *CAH*[2] 1/2:363-416; J. D. Hawkins, "The Neo-Hittite States in Syria and Anatolia," *CAH*[3] 3/1:372-441; J. G. MacQueen, *The Hittites and Their Contemporaries in Asia Minor,* rev. ed. (London, 1986); G. Steiner, "The Immigration of the First Indo-Europeans into Anatolia Reconsidered," *JIES* 18 (1990): 185-214.

RONALD L. GORNY

HIVITES (Heb. *ḥiwwî*)

According to the Table of Nations (Gen. 10:17) and its corresponding genealogy (1 Chr. 1:15), a people descended via the Canaanites from Ham, the second son of Noah. Hivites were indigenous inhabitants of the Promised Land before the Israelite settlement. Their name appears usually in the stereotypical lists of nations decreed for dispossession by the Israelites (e.g., Deut. 7:1).

The Hivites dwelled in the Lebanon and Anti-Lebanon Mountains and in the Beqaʿ Valley between them (Judg. 3:3), including the southern end of that region, the land or valley of Mizpah/Mizpeh at the foot of Mt. Hermon (Josh. 11:3, 8). Although eastern Phoenicia constituted the heartland for the Hivites, they were found farther south as well. The Gibeonites were Hivites (Josh. 9:7; 11:19; LXX "Horites"), as were Hamor, the local prince at Shechem, and his sons (Gen. 34:2).

Hivite probably originally meant "tent-dweller" from the Hebrew term for "tent-camp." It has been suggested, from the extrabiblically attested Amurru located to the north of Palestine, that the term Hivite may have designated Bedouin. If the Hivites did exist early on as nomads, they must have become sedentary by the reign of David (2 Sam. 24:7) — unless, of course, "cities" can signify "camps" there as in Num. 13:19.

Bibliography. E. C. Hostetter, *Nations Mightier and More Numerous: The Biblical View of Palestine's Pre-Israelite Peoples.* BIBALDS 3 (North Richland Hills, Tex., 1995), 72-76.

EDWIN C. HOSTETTER

HIZKI (Heb. *ḥizqî*)

A Benjaminite; son of Elpaal (1 Chr. 8:17).

HIZKIAH (Heb. *ḥizqîyâ*)

A son of Neariah and descendant of Zerubbabel, thus a member of the royal house of Judah (1 Chr. 3:23). The Hebrew name is the same as "Hezekiah."

HOBAB (Heb. *ḥōḇāḇ*)

The father-in-law of Moses (Judg. 4:11), asked to lead the Israelites through the wilderness (Num. 10:29-32). Elsewhere Moses' father-in-law is called

Jethro (Exod. 3:1; 4:18; 18:1) and Reuel (2:18). While Jethro and Reuel are consistently identified as Midianites, Hobab is called a Midianite in Numbers but a Kenite in Judges. Also, Jethro refuses to guide the Israelites, but Judg. 1:16 (LXX) suggests that Hobab did so. Accordingly, some scholars seek to allow for two separate individuals; others see the Kenite/Israelite ties being rooted in the life of Moses.

CHERYL LYNN HUBBARD

HOBAH (Heb. *ḥôḇâ*)
The site of the rout of Lot's captors by Abraham's forces N of Damascus (Gen. 14:15). Hobah is best equated with the region of Apu (Upu/Ube) known from Egyptian texts and situated around and to the north of Damascus. The Choba mentioned in LXX Judith (Jdt. 4:4; 15:4-5) may be identified with this Hobah, but it might also be the Cabul of Josh. 19:27 (LXX Choba; cf. 1 Kgs. 9:13) located in the western part of the lower Galilee (modern Kabul).

GARY P. ARBINO

HOBAIAH (Heb. *ḥăḇayyâ*) (also HABAIAH)
A family of returning exiles unable to prove their priestly descent (Neh. 7:63). Elsewhere they are called Habaiah.

HOD (Heb. *hôḏ*)
An Asherite, the son of Zophah (1 Chr. 7:37).

HODAVIAH (Heb. *hôḏawyâ, hôḏawyāhû*) (also HODEVAH)

1. A son of Elioenai and descendant of Zerubbabel (1 Chr. 3:24).

2. The head of a family in the half-tribe of Manasseh (1 Chr. 5:24).

3. A Benjaminite, the son of Hassenuah (1 Chr. 9:7). Some scholars consider the name here to be a corruption of Heb. *wîhûḏâ*, in which case he would be the same as Joed in the parallel list of Neh. 11:7.

4. A Levite whose descendants returned from the Exile with Zerubbabel (Ezra 2:40). At Neh. 7:43 he is called Hodevah. Heb. "sons of Judah" at Ezra 3:9 (so RSV) should read "sons of Hodaviah" (so NRSV) since the reference is to Levites.

HODESH (Heb. *ḥōḏeš*)
A wife of the Benjaminite Shaharaim (1 Chr. 8:9).

HODEVAH (Heb. K *hôḏĕwâ*, Q *hôḏĕyâ*)
A Levite whose family returned from exile with Zerubbabel (Neh. 7:43).

See HODAVIAH **4.**

HODIAH (Heb. *hôḏîyâ*)

1. A Judahite, brother-in-law of Naham (1 Chr. 4:19). The text lists descendants through Hodiah's wife.

2. One of the Levites who interpreted the law to the people of Jerusalem when Ezra read it publicly at the Water Gate (Neh. 8:7-8; 1 Esdr. 9:48). He also helped lead worship on the day of penitence (Neh. 9:5). He may be the same as **3** or **4** below.

3.-4. Two Levites who signed Ezra's covenant (Neh. 10:10, 13[MT 11, 14]).

5. A leader of the people, apparently not a Levite, who signed Ezra's covenant (Neh. 10:18[19]).

HOGLAH (Heb. *ḥoglâ*)
One of the five daughters of Zelophehad the Gileadite (Num. 26:33; 27:1). She and her sisters received an inheritance in Manasseh, since they had no brothers (Josh. 17:3); they married cousins, so that their inheritance would remain in the tribe of Manasseh (Num. 36:11). The name, which also occurs in Samaria Ostracon 47, may be a place name (cf. Beth-hoglah).

HOHAM (Heb. *hôhām*)
An Amorite king of Hebron who, with four other kings, sought to take vengeance upon the Gibeonites for making peace with Israel. He and his allies were defeated by Joshua at Beth-horon and hanged (Josh. 10:3-4, 23-27).

HOLINESS, HOLY
The root idea of holiness is that of "separation" or "withdrawal." It is a divine quality, part of the intrinsic nature of God, but absent from a fallen world, perhaps best described as "alienness" in a religious or divine sense. The basic theological problem is that this holy God desires to have fellowship with sinful humans living in a fallen world. Since God cannot become less holy in order to fellowship with humans, they must become more holy ("sanctified"); once gained, holiness may be lessened or contaminated by contact with various proscribed substances ("uncleanness") and by feeling, thinking, or acting in ways that God has forbidden ("sinfulness").

God used the general notion of holiness common in the ancient Near East to reveal himself and his will to Israel. This may be categorized in three levels of varying intensity. First was dedication to a deity for his/her use. This did not necessarily imply use by the god, but only that the person or object was available, just as for other "secular" uses. A higher level of holiness was attributed to a person or object the god actually used, so that something of the divine presence remained with an object after its use (e.g., Poseidon's trident, Thor's hammer, as well as the deity's human servants). The highest level was ascribed to images or idols of the gods, regarded as ideal receptacles for that specific god's presence.

Yahweh revealed holiness to be his chief attribute (Exod. 15:11; 1 Sam. 2:2; Isa. 6:3; cf. Rev. 4:8) and wanted his followers likewise to be holy. The command to "be holy as I am holy" (Lev. 11:44-45; cf. 1 Pet. 1:15-16) was for all Israelites, not just the priests. The people of Israel were to be separate from the world, a "priestly kingdom and a holy nation" (Exod. 19:6; cf. 1 Pet. 2:9). They were to limit their contact with uncleanness and adhere to the commandments of the Mosaic covenant. The Law provided for sacrifices to atone for their sins (Lev. 5:5ff.) and cleansing rituals to remove any uncleanness (e.g., Lev. 14). Holiness was to extend to the tithe, the firstborn and anything else voluntarily dedicated to God (Lev. 27:14-32).

The anointing of priests, prophets, and kings marks them as not just dedicated to God, but chosen by him for his service. Their codes of behavior, especially for priests, were stricter than for the average person (Exod. 28:1–31:11) and the consequences for their disobedience more severe (Lev. 5:5ff.; 1 Sam. 1; 1 Chr. 21).

Various objects, places, and times associated with the worship of Yahweh were considered holy. Special days of religious celebration (Lev. 23) and cultic objects (1 Kgs. 8:4; Ezra 5:14-15; 8:28), especially regarding the ark of the covenant (Lev. 16:2; 2 Sam. 6:7), were all holy. Degrees of holiness are evident in the layout of the Jerusalem temple. Most sacred was the holy of holies, the inner room in which Yahweh resided; the holy place, the court of priests, and the court of Israelites were also holy, but of decreasing intensity as one moved away from God's presence. While reverence was shown to objects associated with Yahweh in the past (e.g., the bronze serpent of the wilderness [Num. 21:9; cf. 2 Kgs. 18:4], Gideon's ephod [Judg. 8:27], and perhaps even the gold calves [Exod. 32; cf. 1 Kgs. 12:28; 2 Kgs. 17:16]), worship of them became a snare to Israel and was condemned. Contrary to the ancient Near Eastern concept of holiness, Yahweh forbade his worshippers to construct any idols, including images of him (Exod. 20:4; Deut. 4:15-19; 27:15).

The prophets condemned the actions of the people, even as the independence of Israel and Judah neared an end, but promised that God would yet cleanse the land and its inhabitants (Isa. 4; Zech. 13:1). These prophecies blurred the distinction between holiness and cleanliness (Jer. 33:8; Ezek. 36:25, 33) and set the tone for those who would follow.

The Jewish sects of NT times each worked toward holiness in their own fashion, convinced that this would keep God from exiling Israel again or even persuade him to restore Israel's independence. The Sadducees thought it critical that the temple sacrifices be maintained. The Pharisees tried to replicate the holiness required of the priests and the temple in their own homes and lives. The Zealots argued that God would aid the Jews in cleansing the land from the (gentile) Romans if only the people would have the faith to act. The Qumran Essenes founded a community on the shores of the Dead Sea so they might celebrate feasts and rituals by a calendar different from that of the Jerusalem priests, and also practiced ritual washings to remove personal uncleanness.

John the Baptist preached that Jews should repent of their sins and be baptized, a practice previously reserved for gentile converts, and prophesied that the Messiah would soon bring a much greater cleansing (Mark 1:4-8 par.). The success of John's ministry is a good measure of the widespread desire for holiness among 1st-century Jews.

The NT concept of holiness is founded on that of the OT. God is still seen as being holy and requiring that those who serve him share that quality (1 Pet. 1:15-16). Gentiles as well as Jews could become part of God's people under the new covenant (Rom. 2:28-29; Gal. 3:28; Col. 3:11). Those who accepted the invitation were called "saints" (Gk. *hágios*; Acts 9:13; 1 Cor. 1:2; Jude 3; Rev. 5:8). The Mosaic distinction between "clean" and "holy" gave way to concern for proper conduct (1 Pet. 1:15), attitude, and thought (Matt. 5-6; 1 Cor. 13; Gal. 3).

Jesus' own personal holiness was demonstrated by his conception (Luke 1:35), his public affirmation from the Father (Matt. 3:17), his deeds (Luke 5:20-24), and his resurrection (Rom. 1:3-4). The NT represents Jesus as holy and a source of holiness/cleanness. He can make his followers holy (Heb. 13:12; 1 Pet. 1:2; cf. esp. Matt. 8:1-3), something only Yahweh had done (Ps. 51:7[MT 3]; Ezek. 20:12). After Jesus' death, his followers taught that God granted forgiveness of sins ("holiness") to anyone who would have faith in him (Acts 2:22-39; Rom. 3:21-26; 1 John 1:7).

The NT also expands the role of the Holy Spirit. The Spirit convicts the world (John 16:7-11) and sanctifies those who believe in Jesus (1 Cor. 6:11; 2 Thess. 2:13; 1 Pet. 1:2). In this respect, it is like an everflowing spring of living water, always capable of cleansing others. The Spirit itself can never be made unclean (John 4:13-14; 7:38-39).

Timothy P. Jenney

HOLINESS CODE

The corpus of laws in Lev. 17–26, specifically concentrating on religious and cultic matters. The civil and criminal types of laws, found in Exodus and Deuteronomy, are conspicuously absent here. Stressing the decree to be holy because Yahweh is holy (Lev. 19:2; 20:7, 26; 21:6, 8), these laws purposely oppose Canaanite cultic practices (18:3ff.). Documentary theorists argue that, even though this corpus is a later addition to the Priestly writings, it contains material which is premonarchical and could possibly include some of the earliest laws in Israel's history. The independent nature of this corpus has been attacked on the grounds that no internal order can be found and the thematic admonishment "you shall be holy, for I am holy" appears only in Lev. 19–22 as well as outside of the corpus (11:44-45).

Bibliography. J. E. Hartley, *Leviticus.* WBC 4 (Waco, 1992); I. Knohl, *The Sanctuary of Silence: The Priestly Torah and the Holiness School* (Minneapolis, 1995); M. Noth, *The Laws in the Pentateuch and Other Studies* (1966, repr. London, 1984).

Tony S. L. Michael

HOLM TREE

In biblical usage probably the holm oak (*Quercus ilex* L.), a small evergreen resembling the holly (Heb. *tirzâ;* Isa. 44:14; cf. Sus. 58; Gk. *prínos*). The true holm tree (*Ilex aquifolium* L.) is a holly and is not found in this setting. Other possible identifications include the cypress (*Cupressus sempervirens* L.; so JB, NIV) and the plane tree (*Platanus orientalis* L.; so NJPSV). Robert E. Stone, II

HOLOFERNES (Gk. *Olophérnēs*)
The chief general of the army of Nebuchadnezzar, second in command only to the king (Jdt. 2:4). Holofernes is only known from the book of Judith, and if it was written during the Maccabean period, as many believe, then the character Holofernes may be based on Nicanor (1 Macc. 7:26-49), the Cappadocian prince Orofernes (159/8 B.C.E.) of Syria, or a combination of the two.

After gathering his officers, Holofernes installs a plan to attack Damascus (Jdt. 2:14-27) and eventually Palestine (3:9–4:15). He conquers the armies and towns of the regions and destroys the religious shrines and temples (Jdt. 3:8). When he comes to Israel, he summons the leaders of Moab and Ammon to plan his attack. Achior, the Ammonite leader, tells Holofernes of the history of Israel and her God, but Holofernes refuses to heed the warning. He leads his army to Bethulia, Judith's hometown, and cuts off the water supply. With people collapsing inside the city, Judith leaves her home, befriends Holofernes, and tells him how to defeat the people of Bethulia. After a few days Holofernes becomes drunk while in the company of Judith, and she cuts off his head. Without the leadership of Holofernes his army is routed. MARC A. JOLLEY

HOLON (Heb. *ḥōlōn, ḥōlôn*) (also HILEN)

1. A city in the hill country of Judah (Josh. 15:51) later assigned to the Levites (21:15). At 1 Chr. 6:58(MT 43) it is called Hilen. Most scholars identify the site as modern Khirbet ʿAlîn (152118), 16 km. (10 mi.) NW of Hebron in the region of Beth-zur.

2. A city in the tableland of Moab cited in an oracle of Jeremiah (Jer. 48:21). The site remains unknown.

HOLY OF HOLIES
The innermost and most sacred precinct of the Israelite sanctuary (Heb. 9:3; Gk. *hágia hagíōn*).

See MOST HOLY PLACE.

HOLY ONE OF ISRAEL
A title for Yahweh that appears primarily in Isaiah. The name emphasizes the elements of God's moral holiness and special relationship with the entire people of Israel. The title probably arose in the cultus, which emphasized God's holiness, as the theme of the Holiness Code shows: "You shall be holy, for I, Yahweh, your God, am holy."

PAUL L. REDDITT

HOLY PLACE
In both the tabernacle and the temple, the larger of the two compartments of the central sanctuary. A curtain separated the holy place from the holy of holies (Exod. 26:33). Located within the holy place were the lampstand or menorah (on the south side; Exod. 26:35; 40:4, 24-25), the table of the bread of presence (on the north side; 26:35; 40:4, 22-23), and the golden incense altar (before the curtain separating the holy place from the holy of holies; 40:5, 26-27). Though the precise dimensions of the tabernacle are uncertain, in Solomon's temple the holy place was 40 cubits long, 20 cubits wide, and 30 cubits high (1 Kgs. 6:2, 20). These dimensions are consistent with those of Ezekiel's eschatological temple (Ezek. 41:2) and of *m. Mid.* 4:7. *M. Yoma* 5:1 indicates that the holy place and the holy of holies were separated by two curtains with a one cubit space between them.

M. Tamid provides an account of the service in the holy place. Lots were cast daily to assign 12 tasks, two of which were maintenance of the incense altar and maintenance of the lampstand (*m. Tamid* 3:1; cf. *Yoma* 2:3). Procedures for these tasks are described in *m. Tamid* 3:9; 6:1-3 (cf. *Yoma* 5:1). *M. Yoma* 2:4 suggests that the burning of the incense was performed by a third priest.

The description of the tabernacle in Heb. 9:2-5 is puzzling. In this summary the incense altar is described as being in the holy of holies. Because the location of the altar is not mentioned in the prescriptions of Exod. 26, the author of Hebrews may have inserted the reference to the altar without particular concern for location, or perhaps the author associated the altar with the holy of holies (cf. 1 Kgs. 6:22). RICHARD WARREN JOHNSON

HOLY SEPULCHRE
The tomb in which Jesus' body was interred, a rock-hewn cave intended for the burial of Joseph of Arimathea (Matt. 27:57-60) located outside the walls of Jerusalem (John 19:41; Heb. 13:12).

The Church of the Holy Sepulchre, dedicated on 15 July 1149, the 50th anniversary of the Crusader conquest of Jerusalem, stands over the places identified by ancient tradition as Golgotha and the tomb of Jesus. Excavations beneath the church have shown that the site was an ancient quarry reused as a burial place in the 1st century. The area was first enclosed within city walls by Herod Agrippa (41-44), some 10 years after the crucifixion of Jesus (Josephus *BJ* 5.147-55; *Ant.* 19.326-27).

Emperor Hadrian refounded Jerusalem as Aelia Capitolina (A.D. 135) and erected over the tomb of Jesus a temple of Jupiter with a statue of Venus nearby (Eusebius *Vita Const.;* Jerome *Ep.* 58; Dio Cassius *Hist.* 69.12). After the Council of Nicea (325), Constantine ordered the pagan temple torn down and a church erected in its place. Constantine's engineers after removing the temple discovered a tomb identified as that of Jesus (Eusebius *Vita Const.* 3.25-40). A great rotunda was constructed above the tomb. Immediately to the east of the rotunda Golgotha stood in the open air in the southwest corner of a large colonnaded courtyard connecting the rotunda with a huge basilica called the Martyrium ("Witness," to the place of Jesus' death and resurrection). In 1009 Egyptian Caliph Hakim ordered the destruction of Constantine's church, and in 1048 a new church was built on the foundations of the rotunda. The Crusaders incorporated this church into their grand plan, covering the rotunda and courtyard of predecessor churches and a space once occupied by the western portion of Constantine's basilica.

Skeptics doubt that early Jewish Christians preserved the memory of the actual sites and ascribe the 4th-century identification to the desire of Constantine to propagandize his newfound faith and the desire of the Jerusalem church to exalt itself over other ecclesiastical centers. However, the location (outside the 1st-century city) has the requisite marks archaeologically, and Eusebius, no advocate of a strong Jerusalem, favors the identification, supporting the idea of continuous Christian memory.

Bibliography. M. Biddle, *The Tomb of Christ* (London, 1999); C. Couasnon, *The Church of the Holy Sepulchre in Jerusalem* (Oxford, 1974); J. Finegan, *The Archaeology of the New Testament*, rev. ed. (Princeton, 1992), 258-82; J. Wilkinson, *Jerusalem as Jesus Knew It* (Nashville, 1983).

ROBERT HARRY SMITH

HOLY SPIRIT

The tremendous repelling yet fascinating and attracting dimension of the divine. One of the most elusive themes in the Bible and theology, the actual designation Holy Spirit (Heb. *rûaḥ qāḏôš;* Gk. *pneúma hágion*) is found only in a few late pre-Christian OT texts (Isa. 63:10-11; Ps. 51:11[MT 13]; Wis. 1:5; 9:17; 1QS 3:7). According to Jerome, the fact that Heb. *rûaḥ* is mainly feminine, Gk. *pneúma* neuter, and Lat. *spiritus* masculine shows that God has no gender at all.

Old Testament

The awesome creative power of God in the universe and in preserving the lives of people and animals (Gen. 1:2; Job 33:4; Ps. 104:30) can be a destructive force which dries up the waters (Hos. 13:15) or a saving or refreshing power (Exod. 14:21; 1 Kgs. 18:45). One can have an evil spirit from, but not of, Yahweh, causing dissension (Judg. 9:23), lies, and murder (1 Sam. 19:9; 1 Kgs. 22:23).

The Spirit figures prominently in God's guidance of history, producing charismatic leaders at the necessary times. This is evident in the experience of the judges at the height of Israel's theocracy (Judg. 3:10; 6:34), in the selection of kings Saul (1 Sam. 10:1-13) and David (16:13), in Zerubbabel after the Exile (Zech. 4:6), and the enigmatic Servant of Isa. 42, and is emphasized by the prophets (Isa. 34:16; 63:10; Ezek. 18:31).

The primary manifestation of the Spirit is prophecy, as evident in Joseph's dreams (Gen. 41:38), Balaam (Num. 24:2), and Saul (1 Sam. 10:10). Note the common usage "the Spirit of Prophecy" in the Targums. For Hosea the prophet is the "man of the Spirit" (Hos. 9:7). Micah declares that he is filled "with power, with the Spirit of the Lord" (Mic. 3:8). In the exilic and postexilic periods, especially in Ezekiel, the Spirit is an inspiring agent (Ezek. 2:2; 3:24). While in the OT the Spirit is not generally a personal being, texts such as Isa. 48:16; Zech. 7:12; Neh. 9:30 describe the Spirit more personally.

Eschatological and messianic activity characterize a final age of the Spirit, when God will send his definitive salvation to Israel and the nations. The Spirit and her gifts will rest upon the king, the servant, and the prophet (Isa. 11:1-10; 42:1; 61:1), and will be poured on the whole people (Isa. 32:15; 44:3; Ezek. 39:29; Joel 2:28[3:28] [quoted by Peter at Pentecost, Acts 2:17-21]). Finally, God will pour the Spirit into the hearts of the people to turn them from stone to flesh and enable them to keep the covenant (Isa. 59:21; Ezek. 36:26-27).

Late pre-NT Judaism emphasizes the Spirit of prophecy, of revelation and guidance (Sir. 48:24), wisdom (Wis. 7:7; 9:17; 1QH 12:11-13), and occasionally praise. However, many (not all) believed that the Spirit had departed because of sin and would return at the restoration.

New Testament

In the NT the Holy Spirit, the experience of the powerful presence of God among his people, is widely treated in continuity with the OT. For 1 Peter it is the Spirit of glory (1 Pet. 4:14). The traditions of Luke, Paul, and John are particularly prominent. In the Gospels the focus is on the life and ministry of Jesus.

Gospels

In Mark the Spirit is stressed at significant moments: Jesus' future baptizing in the Spirit (Mark 1:8), Jesus' own baptism (v. 10), his constant conflict with unclean spirits (3:11; 5:12; 6:7; 7:25; 9:25), the accusation of blasphemy against the Holy Spirit (3:29).

In contrast to the extraordinary conception of John the Baptist, Matthew describes with an ascending parallelism the virginal conception of Jesus through the creative activity of the Holy Spirit. He transfers Mark's post-Easter speaking of the Spirit through the disciples (Mark 13:11) to the mission instructions (Matt. 10:17-22; 12:17-28). At the final commissioning he recalls the announcement that Jesus would baptize in the Spirit and gives an indication of the developing trinitarian understanding of the Spirit (Matt. 28:18-20).

For Luke the heart of the Church is mission, and at the heart is the movement of the Spirit for the increase of the Word, a veritable explosion of the Spirit. The Holy Spirit begins each part of his Gospel. When Jesus is conceived by the Holy Spirit, Mary, Elizabeth, Zechariah, John, and Simeon are each filled with the prophetic Holy Spirit. The Spirit descends in bodily form at Jesus' baptism and leads him in and out of the desert. Luke cites Isa. 61:2; 58:6 to describe Jesus' manifesto of "good news to the poor" at Nazareth. The Spirit again figures prominently when Jesus sets his face to go to Jerusalem (Luke 10:21; 11:13; 12:10, 12). Finally Jesus is the dispenser of the Spirit to the Church (Luke 24:49) — the Spirit is his replacement.

Not surprisingly, the Spirit plays such a prominent role in Acts that it could well be entitled "The Acts of the Holy Spirit." There is a clear parallel between the beginning of the Gospel and that of Acts. Jesus bestows his Spirit at Pentecost, the birth of the Christian community. Dramatic outpourings of the Spirit on believers are recorded at Acts 2:1-4; 4:28-

31; 8:15-17; 10:44; 19:6. All Christians now have the Holy Spirit. Peter, John, Philip, Stephen, Barnabas, and Paul are "filled with the Holy Spirit" to witness boldly and enthusiastically in proclamation, in good news and signs and wonders. Thus Luke combines God's universal saving will, Jesus' model ministry, and the worldwide mission of the early Church.

Paul

Paul, with his problem- and situation-centered theology, describes the Christian experience in terms of the Spirit ("in the Spirit," Rom. 8:9), whereas the Synoptics speak the language of the Kingdom. The Spirit is distinct from, yet clearly related to, the risen Jesus and dwells in the Christian (Rom. 15:30; 1 Cor. 6:11; 12:4).

Paul insists that the gospel comes not in word alone but in the powerful Holy Spirit bringing conviction and joy (1 Thess. 1:5-6; 2 Thess. 2:13). Paul warns, "Do not quench the Spirit" (1 Thess 5:19, his only reference using the definite article). This is a gift of God's grace but involves a struggle between the spirit (involving the full Christian person) and the flesh (the person as subject to sin).

The lively character of the Spirit is evident in the nine gifts described in 1 Cor. 12-14: wisdom, the utterance of knowledge, healing, miracles, prophecy, discernment of spirits, speaking in tongues, the interpretation of tongues. But the greatest gift is love. The Corinthians themselves are Paul's "letter" written by the Holy Spirit (2 Cor. 3:2).

In Galatians, a forerunner of Romans, Paul's reflection on the reception of the Spirit is developed quite passionately. The Spirit is received into the heart so that we can cry "Abba" as adopted children. She comes through faith rather than works of the law, from whose slavery the Christian is released and justified (Gal. 3:2-5; 5:5). The fruits of the Spirit are love, joy, peace, patience, kindness, generosity, faithfulness, gentleness, self-control (Gal. 5:22-23). A Christian is sealed with the promised Holy Spirit, "the first installment of our inheritance" (Eph. 1:11; 3:14-19).

Romans (esp. ch. 8, where the new age breaks into view) is a good summary of Paul's pneumatology. Christ has achieved what the law was unable to do. The life led by the Spirit is the life of God's free children, heirs of Christ, free from fear and sin. The Spirit helps people pray because they are too weak to pray properly. She is involved in the redemption of all creation (Rom. 8:18-27). The Spirit witnesses to Paul's great sorrow and anguish for his own people (Rom. 9:1-2).

John

While Luke stresses the external experience of the Spirit and Paul the inner experience of the person in the charismatic community, John describes the Spirit as "another Christ" (John 14:16) and stresses the individual's relationship to Christ through the Spirit. The Baptist describes his revelation of Jesus' identity "on whom you see the Spirit descend" (1:33). Rebirth comes through the Spirit "blowing where it chooses" (3:5-8). God is Spirit (4:24). Life to the fullest comes from the Spirit (6:63).

John goes further than even Paul in speaking of the Spirit as Paraclete, an advocate, counselor, or comforter. The Paraclete's functions are copied from those of Jesus: developing Jesus' teaching to meet new situations (John 16:14) — "what Jesus would have said" or what John did in writing his Gospel; stressing and teaching what has already come with Jesus, even though there are a future resurrection, judgment, and parousia (5:28-29); helping to make real the kingdom of life and love, even though the world does not see his coming (14:15-21). John's greatest contribution is this teaching of the ongoing presence of Jesus in the heart of each individual (1 John 3:24).

The Apocalypse brings together God, Jesus, and the Spirit (the sevenfold flame continually burning before God's throne; Rev. 1:4); and it is the Spirit who invites all to "come" to the gift of life-giving water (22:17). But it is Matt. 28:19, together with 1 Cor. 12:4-6; 2 Cor. 13:13; Jude 19–21, which seems to have pointed the way for the fuller development of the Christian doctrine of the Trinity.

Bibliography. R. E. Brown, *The Gospel According to John,* 2 vols. AB 29-29A (Garden City, 1966-1970); Y. Congar, *I Believe in the Holy Spirit,* 3 vols. (New York, 1983); J. D. G. Dunn, *Jesus and the Spirit* (1975, repr. Grand Rapids, 1997); Michael P. Hamilton, ed., *The Charismatic Movement* (Grand Rapids, 1975); Watson E. Mills, *The Holy Spirit: A Bibliography* (Peabody, 1988); C. F. D. Moule, *The Holy Spirit* (Grand Rapids, 1978); M. Walker, *God the Spirit* (Minneapolis, 1994).

SEÁN P. KEALY, C.S.SP.

HOMAM (Heb. *hômām*) (also HEMAN)
A son of Lotan and grandson of Seir the Horite (1 Chr. 1:39). At Gen. 36:22 his name appears as Heman (**1**).

HOMER (Heb. *ḥōmer*)
A dry measure equal to 10 ephahs or baths (Ezek. 45:11) as well as the cor (v. 14). It was the equivalent of ca. 220 l. (58 gal.).

HOMOSEXUALITY
The terms "homosexuality" and "homosexual" are coinages of the 19th century C.E. and have no equivalent in ancient Hebrew or Greek. It is debatable whether the modern idea of homosexuality (an erotic attraction focused only or primarily on persons of the same gender) existed at all in antiquity. The Bible does not appear to say anything directly about homosexuality in this modern sense of the term, but a few passages do refer to same-gender genital acts. The term "homosexual" appears in some modern English translations (usually in 1 Cor. 6:9; 1 Tim. 1:10), but the key Greek term involved *(arsenokoítēs)* is rare and of uncertain meaning.

Passages that do refer to same-gender sexual acts or life commitments may be summarized as follows:

Male-male rape

In the story of Sodom and Gomorrah (Gen. 18:16-33) the men of Sodom threaten Lot's guests by saying that they want to "know" them. Since the verb "to know" would be used in Hebrew as a euphemism for the sexual act, they may mean to commit anal rape on them, thus violating their sacred duty toward strangers. The later idea that the Sodom story condemns all male-male sexual acts does not appear in the story itself or in the references to Sodom elsewhere in the Bible, but first emerged in ancient Greek-speaking Judaism. In the NT Jude interprets the sin of Sodom as the desire to have sex with angels ("strange flesh"; Jude 7).

Same-sex intercourse as violation of purity

In Leviticus male-male sexual intercourse is condemned as an "abomination," i.e., a serious violation of purity (Lev. 18:22; 20:13). (There is no reference to female-female sexual intercourse in the OT.) In Rom. 1:18-32 Paul treats same-sex intercourse as a prime example of the impurity characteristic of Gentiles. He regards it as unclean and dishonorable and as a punishment visited on the Gentiles for their failure to worship the true God. He does not specifically say that it is sinful.

Same-sex commitments

Same-sex commitments sometimes take precedence over heterosexual household connections. Ruth left her people to go with Naomi (Ruth 1:15-18). David and Jonathan were bound by covenant and love (1 Sam. 18:1-5; 20:1-42; 2 Sam. 1:17-27). The centurion's "boy" (Gk. *país*) whom Jesus healed at a distance (Luke 7:1-10) may have been his master's *erṓmenos* ("beloved"). In none of these cases can we say with certainty whether the relationship had a genital dimension or not.

Modern discussions of homosexuality take some or all of these passages into account, but their meaning and authority are interpreted differently by different interpreters. None of them appears to address modern questions directly.

Bibliography. R. J. Brawley, ed., *Biblical Ethics and Homosexuality* (Louisville, 1996); L. W. Countryman, *Dirt, Greed, and Sex* (Philadelphia, 1988); R. Scroggs, *The New Testament and Homosexuality* (Philadelphia, 1983); M. L. Soards, *Scripture and Homosexuality* (Louisville, 1995).

L. Wm. Countryman

HONEY

A sweet viscid fluid produced by bees or derived from flowers. Honey (Heb. *dĕḇaš*) is one of the seven characteristics of the "good land," Israel (Deut. 8:7-10); according to the Talmudic sages, this is date rather than bee honey, since the other seven qualities derive from plants, not animals. The period between Passover and Pentecost is crucial for the success of the olive, grape, pomegranate, date, fig, wheat, and barley crops, but is not so for the successful production of bee honey.

The frequent references to "a land flowing with milk and honey" imply, depending on context, either blessing or destruction. In most instances the expression indicates the riches of the land; Isaiah, however, employs it with reference to the pending destruction of the land by the Assyrians (Isa. 7:22).

The references to the land of milk and honey in the Pentateuch and Joshua are to uncultivated land. These pastures, good for the grazing of sheep and goats, and therefore milk production, were rich in flowers on which wild honey bees thrived. In the OT honey was gathered from wild bees, rather than cultivated in domestic hives (Prov. 25:16; Judg. 14:8-9). 1 Sam. 14:25-26 illustrates that honey was connected to undeveloped land rather than agricultural land. Since the land was cultivated during the Monarchy, prophetic announcements of a return to a land of milk and honey indicated the deportation of the people, which would result in cultivated land returning to its natural state: a land flowing with milk and honey.

Bibliography. N. Hareuveni, *Nature in Our Biblical Heritage* (Kiryat Ono, 1980).

Alan Ray Buescher

HONOR, SHAME

Among North Americans, honor and shame often refer to a psychological state — a person's internal moral character or the actions that reflect that character. In the world of the Bible and in traditional Mediterranean societies, however, honor and shame are social values determinative of a person's identity and social status. Honor is a person's claim to self-worth and the social acknowledgment of that claim — i.e., honor is a person's public reputation which constitutes his or her identity. Shame is a person's concern for reputation. It is a positive value by which one seeks to maintain or protect his or her honor. If one is unable to maintain his honor, or if his peers do not acknowledge his claim to self-worth, then the person is shamed, i.e., dishonored and disgraced. A person with no concern for his honor or reputation is shameless.

Honor is both individual and collective. Individually, a man makes a claim to honor which is affirmed or denied by his social peers according to his own past and present behavior. A man's individual honor is dependent in large part on the man himself. But the man also shares in and commits his individual honor to the collective honor of his family, village, class, state, or other group to which he belongs. Honor can be ascribed or achieved. Ascribed honor is derived from birth — one inherits the collective honor of natural groups such as family or community — or it can be endowed from persons in power. Ascribed honor is passively received. Acquired honor is the honor that a person actively seeks and achieves. Moreover, because honor is a limited good, honor is acquired at the expense of someone else's honor, usually through the normal social interaction of challenge and response.

Honor and shame belong to both men and women and characterize their behavior as collective members of common humanity and natural groups. As individuals, however, men are associated with honor and women with shame. Their behavior is determined by their gender roles, which are rooted in the cultural understanding of their contribution in procreation.

Procreation is understood in terms of agriculture. The man sows his seed into the woman, who receives it and nurtures it like a field. Male honor is based on a man's ability to engender. It is symbolized by the penis and testicles and is an indication of his manliness and courage. Although the man has the power to create life from his seed (his honor), he does so externally to himself in the field of a woman. A man's honor is thus also dependent upon his ability to ensure that the child born is from his own seed. A woman, like soil, represents indiscriminate fecundity in which any man might sow his seed. Therefore, just as a farmer marks off soil into a field and guards it against outside intrusion, an honorable man will cover and protect his wife (and his daughters and sisters by extension), and thereby bring order to her fecundity and safeguard the legitimacy of his paternity.

Positive female shame reflects a woman's ancillary role in procreation. It is symbolized by the hymen, and it represents a woman's shyness, timidity, restraint, or sexually exclusive behavior. A woman will display honor by recognizing her position of shame and acting accordingly. She will yield to her husband's ordering of her sexuality; to do otherwise would be shameless. The sexual purity or exclusiveness of the woman is embedded in the honor of the man.

The gendered division of honor and shame is replicated in the division of labor and the arrangement of space. Just as a man's honor is rooted in his ability to engender and a woman's shame is her recognition of dependence upon a man for procreation, so a man's social orientation is outward and a woman's orientation is inward. Because a woman is indiscriminately fecund, her labor and space are ordered to ensure her exclusivity to a man. As a result, women model shame through domestic roles such as raising and educating children and managing the household economy. They carry out their tasks in the home or public spaces dominated by female activities such as the market, the well, and public ovens. In contrast, men display their honor through work and public activity in space that is common — the fields and industrial areas, city squares and gates — or exclusively male — the temple and cultic areas.

The social world described in the Bible resembles what anthropologists label an agonistic society, characterized by an intense competition among social equals which is often perceived as a battle for personal honor and family reputation. Honor is the basis of precedence among equals. The competition for honor takes the form of a confrontation through challenge and response. Every social interaction outside one's own family or close group of friends is considered to be a challenge to one's honor. It is a claim to enter into another person's social space. Yet at the same time, the challenge itself bestows honor; it proclaims that one is a person of honor and worthy of challenge. By challenging the honor of one's peer, one hopes to gain precedence over that person and thereby enhance one's own honor.

The challenge of honor is only recognized among social equals, for it implies the ability or need to respond. For a person to make a challenge against someone who is unable to defend his honor (e.g., someone of lower status, a woman, an aged or infirm person) brings dishonor upon the challenger. In such a case, a champion may take up the cause of the one challenged. If in the opposite case a man challenges his social superior, the one challenged may choose to ignore the affront of his inferior without any damage to his honor. The challenge of the inferior is unworthy and consequently brings dishonor upon him. The challenge between equals may be positive (e.g., a word of praise, a gift, a request for help, or the offer of help) or negative (e.g., an insult, a threat, or a physical affront). The challenged person in turn responds in kind to defend his honor. If the challenged person fails to respond or responds poorly, then he dishonors himself — he gets shamed. However, if the person loses the honorably fought challenge, he is not shamed; he has simply established his own lack of precedence in relation to his challenger. The *de facto* achievement of honor depends upon a person's ability to respond effectively to any challenge of his claim to honor.

Bibliography. D. D. Gilmore, ed., *Honor and Shame and the Unity of the Mediterranean* (Washington, 1987); B. J. Malina, *The New Testament World,* rev. ed. (Louisville, 1993); J. G. Peristiany and J. Pitt-Rivers, *Honor and Grace in Anthropology* (Cambridge, 1992); Pitt-Rivers, *The Fate of Shechem, or the Politics of Sex* (Cambridge, 1977).

RONALD A. SIMKINS

HOOK

Heb. *wāw* designates a hook or peg from which curtains and other hangings were suspended in the Israelite tabernacle (e.g., Exod. 26:32; 27:10-11). At Job 41:1(MT 40:25) a hook is viewed insufficient for catching the monster Leviathan (cf. Matt. 17:27; Gk. *ánkistron*). A similar device may be intended by Heb. *ḥaḥ* (e.g., 2 Chr. 33:11; Job 41:2[40:26]; Ezek. 29:4) and *ṣinnôṯ* (Amos 4:2), terms generally translated "thorn" (cf. Job 5:5; Prov. 22:5).

HOOPOE

A cinnamon- or buff-colored bird (Heb. *dûḵîpaṯ*), the sole species of the family Upupidae. Some 30 cm. (12 in.) long, the hoopoe is recognized by its high gold crest, tipped with black and white bands. For protection, it exudes an offensive smell. It eats various types of insects and worms, for which it forages in manure piles. Its zoological name (*Upupa epops*) is a combination of Lat. *upopa* and Gk. *epops,* both being onomatopoetic, imitating its hawing call.

Drawings and legends from ancient times indicate that the hoopoe was important in the Mediterranean area, probably in magical practices. The hoopoe is listed in Lev. 11:19; Deut. 14:18 as nonpermitted food. However, understanding the Hebrew word differently, the Karaites traditionally refrained from eating chicken. JESPER SVARTVIK

HOPE

While modern connotations include shades of uncertainty associated with a desired outcome (akin to "wishful thinking"), the biblical understanding of hope is a much deeper concept that contributes significantly to the worldview of biblical faith. Included are an expectation of the future, trust in attaining that future, patience while awaiting it, the desirability of the associated benefits, and confidence in the divine promises.

In the OT hope is a prominent theme especially in the poetic and prophetic books. Hope is a fundamental component of the life of the righteous (Prov. 23:18; 24:14). Without hope, life loses its meaning (Lam. 3:18; Job 7:6), and in death there is no hope (Isa. 38:18; Job 17:15). Qoheleth affirms that so long as life endures there is hope (Eccl. 9:4).

Yet for hope to be genuine hope and not foolishness or presumption, it must be grounded in God and God's promises. Often this hope is expressed in times of trouble and is closely related to trust in God. The righteous who trust or put their hope in God will be helped (Ps. 28:7), and they will not be confounded, put to shame, or disappointed (27:2-3; 30:6[MT 5]; 119:116; Isa. 49:23). The righteous who have this trustful hope in God have a general confidence in God's protection and help (Jer. 29:11) and are free from fear and anxiety (Ps. 46:2[3]; Isa. 7:4). This hope, whose fundamental position is expressed in the formulas "I trust in God" (e.g., Isa. 12:2) and "the fear of Yahweh" (e.g., Prov. 23:17-18), is manifested in quiet waiting before the Lord, who rewards trusting patience with vindication (Ps. 37:5-7; Isa. 30:15).

These positive affirmations of hope are complemented by several negative statements that speak of misplaced hope. If not grounded in God and God's promises, hope is futile, especially if it is placed in human means of attainment. Such misguided hope can turn perceptions of security into fear and anxiety (Isa. 32:9-11; Amos 6:1). Specific sources of misplaced trust that lead to ruin include riches (Ps. 52:7[9]), human righteousness (Ezek. 33:13), other people (Jer. 17:5), or objects of religious devotion such as shrines or even the temple (7:4; Hab. 2:18).

Though hope may be expressed in the desire for temporal blessing and help, it also becomes hope in an eschatological future (Isa. 25:9; 26:8; 51:5; Jer. 29:11; 31:16-17; Mic. 7:7). The restoration of the Davidic throne, the messianic expectation of the OT and apocalyptic (and later rabbinic) literature, and the resurrection of the dead were expressions of hope based on the covenant promises of God. The deliverance of the kingdom of God to the saints, the end of earthly distress through the salvation of God, and the judgment of the misplaced hope of the ungodly further characterized this eschatological hope. Its basis was a firm trust in the promises of God and confidence that they would be fulfilled.

The NT conception of hope is essentially determined by the OT view, especially in the heavily eschatological ethos of its expression. Crucial to the NT development of hope is the recognition that in Christ is found the fulfillment of the OT promises and hope (cf. Matt. 12:21; 1 Pet. 1:3). In the coming of Christ the messianic age has encroached into human history, and with it the blessings of eschatological hope. Christian hope is rooted in faith in the eschatological act of divine salvation in Christ (Gal. 5:5). So the present hope of the Christian is itself an eschatological blessing, being grounded in the salvation that is the eschatological act of God in Christ. Yet there is a paradox in the NT picture of hope, for while present hope is itself an eschatological blessing, it still retains as its focus trust and patient waiting for the future. The certainty of the eschatological consummation of God's promised future is the present confidence, trusting patience, and desire that form the hope of Christians, and this hope is engendered through the presence of the promised Holy Spirit (Rom. 8:24-25).

The stated object of Christian hope is variously identified. It is the future hope of the resurrection of the dead (Acts 23:6), the promises given to Israel (26:6-7), the redemption of the body and of the whole creation (Rom. 8:23-25), eternal glory (Col. 1:27), eternal life and the inheritance of the saints (Tit. 3:5-7), the return of Christ (2:11-14), transformation into the likeness of Christ (1 John 3:2-3), the salvation of God (1 Tim. 4:10), or simply Christ (1:1). The certainty of this blessed future is guaranteed through the indwelling of the Spirit (Rom. 8:23-25), Christ in us (Col. 1:27), and the resurrection of Christ (Acts 2:26). Again, the eschatological future is assured through the eschatological act of salvation in Christ.

The OT emphasis on trust and patient waiting is kept in the NT as well. Christians are to trust in God's continuing deliverance and protection (2 Cor. 1:10). Hope is produced by endurance through suffering (Rom. 5:2-5) and is at the same time the inspiration behind endurance and perseverance to the end (1 Thess. 1:3; Heb. 6:11; 10:22-23). Those who hope in Christ will not be put to shame, but will be given courage to see Christ exalted in life and in death (Phil. 1:20). It is on the basis of the trustworthy promises of God that believers find an anchor for hope (Heb. 6:18-19). So confident are believers in their hope of the future that they "boast" in this hope (Heb. 3:6) and exhibit great boldness in their faith (2 Cor. 3:12). By contrast, those who do not place their trust in God are said to be without hope (Eph. 2:12; 1 Thess. 4:13).

Hope is basic to the Christian view of life, and it issues forth in a changed perception of and approach to reality. Along with faith and love, hope is an enduring virtue of the Christian life (1 Cor. 13:13). In fact, faith and love spring from hope (Col. 1:4-5). Faith and hope become closely intertwined, as are faith and trust, and faith itself is the present expression of the confidence in the future hope

(Heb. 11:1). Faith and hope produce holiness in the lives of Christians (Col. 1:23), while faith, hope, and love work together to mold believers into disciples (1 Thess. 1:3).

Mentioned alone, hope produces joy and peace in believers through the power of the Spirit (Rom. 12:12; 15:13). Paul attributes his apostolic calling to the hope of eternal glory (Tit. 1:1-2), and because of this hope widows are to enter into a ministry of perpetual prayer (1 Tim. 5:5). Moreover, hope in God's promised future has ethical implications. Hope in the return of Christ is the basis for believers to purify themselves in this life (Tit. 2:11-14; 1 John 3:3), and it empowers those whose hearts have been sprinkled and whose consciences have been cleansed to spur one another to deeds of goodness and love (Heb. 10:22-24; cf. 1 Pet. 3:15-16).

While rightly identified as describing faith, Heb. 11:1 connects hope and faith, indicating that faith is the present reality and conviction of the unseen promise of God's blessed future. Hope is thereby identified as a crucial component of the Christian worldview. Attainment of this future lies beyond human abilities, for it is only through hope grounded in the promise of God that believers are able to gain the blessings of faith. In this hope believers may rest confident, for the promise of God for the future is certain because of the trustworthiness of the God who promised it.

Bibliography. J. Moltmann, *Theology of Hope* (1967, repr. Minneapolis, 1993); C. F. D. Moule, *The Meaning of Hope* (Philadelphia, 1963).

JEFFREY S. LAMP

HOPHNI (Heb. *ḥopnî*)
One of the sons of Eli (cf. Egyp. *ḥfn[r]*); a priest at Shiloh (1 Sam. 1:3). Like his brother Phinehas, he acted improperly as priest (1 Sam. 2:12-17), bringing Yahweh's judgment down upon himself (cf. vv. 27-36; 3:11-18). He was killed in the battle of Aphek in which the Philistines captured the ark of the covenant (1 Sam. 4:1-18).

HOPHRA (Heb. *ḥopraʿ*; Egyp. *wꜣḥ-ib-rʿ*; Gk. *Apriēs*)
The fourth king of the 26th (Saite) Dynasty of Egypt (589-570 B.C.E.). Hophra (Apries) continued the policy of his father, Psammeticus II, by intervening in affairs in Palestine. In 588 B.C.E. Zedekiah rebelled against Babylon, perhaps with the help of Hophra (Ezek. 17:15; Lachish Letter III). Soon afterward, the Babylonian king Nebuchadnezzar began the final siege of Jerusalem, and Zedekiah requested help from Hophra. Hophra entered Judah with an army but was forced to withdraw (Jer. 37:5). After the fall of Judah and Jerusalem, Hophra received fleeing Judahites (Jer. 43:1-7) and allowed them to settle in the city of Tahpenes in Lower Egypt. Because they had fled from Judah, Jeremiah prophesied to these Judahites that they would be destroyed and that Yahweh would punish Hophra (Jer. 44:30). Earlier, Jeremiah had prophesied that Hophra's palace in Tahpenes would be conquered by Nebuchadnezzar (Jer. 43:10; cf. 46:13-26). In 570 rebellion broke out in Egypt against Hophra, and he had to flee. Three years later, Hophra allied with Nebuchadnezzar in an attack against Egypt. The attack was repulsed, and Hophra was captured and executed.

Bibliography. G. W. Ahlström, *The History of Ancient Palestine* (Minneapolis, 1993); D. B. Redford, *Egypt, Canaan, and Israel in Ancient Times* (Princeton, 1992).

PAUL S. ASH

HOR (Heb. *hōr*)
In Hebrew always *hōr hāhār*, "Hor the mountain" or "the mountain of mountains."

1. The mountain on which Aaron died (Num. 20:22-29; 33:37-39), a site near Kadesh on the Edom border, probably Jebel Madurah. Josephus places it near Petra (*Ant.* 4.4.7), Jebel Nebī Harun ("mountain of the prophet Aaron"). The biblical account is more likely. Deut. 10:6 says Aaron died at Moserah ("chastisement"), near Kadesh, meaning Aaron was not to enter the land because of his earlier rebellion (Num. 20:24; thus "[place of] chastisement").

2. A mountain marking the "northern boundary" of Israel (Num. 34:7-8). A common designation of the extent of Israel was "from Dan to Beersheba" (Judg. 20:1), so Hor may be Mt. Hermon, near Dan. Also, Hermon is one of the most prominent mountains in that area and may well have been called the "mountain of mountains," "Mt. Hor."

EDMON L. ROWELL, JR.

HORAM (Heb. *hōrām*)
A king of Gezer who tried to aid the city of Lachish in its defense against Israel, but who was himself defeated by Joshua (Josh. 10:33).

HOREB (Heb. *ḥōrēḇ, ḥôrēḇ*)
The name for the mountain of God in a number of biblical traditions, elsewhere called Mt. Sinai. Although in the book of Exodus the name Sinai is used most frequently, Horeb appears in Moses' encounter with the burning bush (Exod. 3:1), at the waters Massah and Meribah (17:6), and after the incident of the golden calf (33:6). The book of Deuteronomy uses the name Horeb exclusively for the mountain of God (e.g., Deut. 1:2; 4:10, 15; 9:8; 18:16; 29:1[MT 28:69]), except in Moses' blessing (33:2). It is to Horeb that Elijah flees after defeating the prophets of Baal and being threatened with death by Jezebel (1 Kgs. 19:8).

Although the location of Horeb (or Sinai) is uncertain, it has traditionally been identified with Jebel Musa, "Mountain of Moses," in the southern Sinai Peninsula, near the site of the monastery of St. Catherine. Alternative sites, such as Jebel Catherine or Jebel Serbāl in the same region, have also been suggested, although there are those who suggest a location closer to Kadesh-barnea in the eastern part of the Sinai Peninsula.

Bibliography. G. I. Davies, *The Way of the Wilderness.* SOTSMS 5 (Cambridge, 1979).

MARILYN J. LUNDBERG

HOREM (Heb. *ḥŏrēm*)
A fortified city in the tribal territory of Naphtali (Josh. 19:38), presumably in northern Galilee. Its precise location is unknown.

HORESH (Heb. *ḥōreš*)
A place in the Wilderness of Ziph where David hid from Saul and made a covenant of friendship with Jonathan (1 Sam. 23:15-19). Most modern interpreters identify the site as Khirbet Khoreisa, ca. 9.6 km. (6 mi.) SE of Hebron. The name Horesh ("wood" or "wooded height") could be a description of a geographical feature, but the lack of rainfall in the Negeb raises questions about the plausibility of a wooded height. PETE F. WILBANKS

HOR-HAGGIDGAD (Heb. *ḥōr-haggiḏgāḏ*)
A place where the Israelites encamped after leaving the Wilderness of Sinai, their 17th encampment (Num. 33:32-33). Deut. 10:7 lists this site as Gudgodah (a form of Gidgad). The LXX reads *Gadgad* in both accounts; however, the Greek means "mountain of Gadgad" in contrast to the Hebrew "hole of Gidgad." While the exact location is uncertain, some identify the site in the Wadi Ghadhaghedh in eastern Sinai. PETE F. WILBANKS

HORI (Heb. *ḥōrî, ḥôrî*)
1. A son of Lotan listed in the genealogy of Esau (Gen 36:22; 1 Chr. 1:39). The name is that of the "Horites," the ancient inhabitants of Edom (Gen. 14:6).

2. The father of Shaphat, a leader of the tribe of Simeon sent by Moses to spy out Canaan (Num. 13:5). PAUL L. REDDITT

HORITES (Heb. *ḥōrî*)
1. A seminomadic people living in Seir-Edom (Gen. 14:6; 36:20; Deut. 2:12, 20; NRSV "Horim"). In Gen. 36:2 these people are called *ḥiwwî* (LXX Gk. *euaíon*), "Hivites," and thus both names probably refer to the same people.

2. Hivites are mentioned in Gen. 34:2; Josh. 9:7, where the LXX translates *chorraíos*, Horites. These people, possibly related to the Hurrians, resided in the hill country near Mt. Hermon and in Lebanon.

One suggestion for the use of both Horite and Hivite is that the letters *resh* and *waw* were easily confused in early Hebrew manuscripts. In addition, Horite is the biblical name for Hurrian, a people known in the ancient Near East as early as the middle of the 3rd millennium. Hurrians were in Palestine at the time of the Amarna Letters (14th century B.C.E.); the prince of Jerusalem had a Hurrian name; and the Egyptians called Palestine Hur or Hurru. The double *resh* preserved in the Greek, and Hurrian, was not tolerated in Hebrew, and the shift from *u* to *o* was probably normal: thus, *Hurr-* became *Hor-*. The etymology deriving Horite from the Hebrew root meaning "cave" is incorrect.

Bibliography. W. F. Albright, "The Horites in Palestine," in *From the Pyramids to Paul,* ed. L. G. Leary (New York, 1935), 9-26; E. A. Speiser, "Ethnic Movements in the Near East in the Second Millennium B.C.," *AASOR* 13 (1931-32): 13-54.

LAWRENCE A. SINCLAIR

HORMAH (Heb. *ḥormâ*)
A city described in the OT as lying on the border between the wilderness and the desert south of ancient Canaan proper. The name means "devoted" — for destruction.

Hormah was a place where the invading Hebrews sustained a crucial defeat (Num. 14:45; Deut. 1:44), the point to which the Hebrews, in a failed endeavor from the south, were driven back by the Canaanite and Amalekite inhabitants of the region. The implication is that Hormah was on the edge of the wilderness. The fact that Hormah appears in the list of 31 cities whose kings Joshua and the Israelites defeated in their campaign west of the Jordan (Josh. 12:14) also supports a Negeb provenance for the city. However, its exact location and identification are unknown. Proposed identifications with Tell Masos and Tell Sheriah have found neither unambiguous supporting evidence nor scholarly acceptance.

Hormah was first assigned to the territory of Judah (Josh. 15:30) but later reassigned to Simeon (Josh. 19:4; 1 Chr. 4:30). The city, whose original name was Zephath, was captured by men of Judah and Simeon (Judg. 1:17) and was renamed Hormah after its destruction. Another account indicates that Hormah got its name when the Israelites made good on a vow to defeat the king of Arad (Num. 21:3). It was one of the cities in the south to which David sent shares of the spoils captured after his war with the Amalekites (1 Sam. 30:30), during the time he was fleeing from King Saul.

BRUCE C. CRESSON

HORN
1. A container for liquids or the oil poured on those anointed to a specific task (1 Sam. 16:1, 13; 1 Kgs. 1:39); most likely made from an animal's horn.

2. A symbol of power, help, victory, or glory (Deut. 33:17; 1 Kgs. 22:11). The "horn of salvation" represents the king's saving power (2 Sam. 22:3 = Ps. 18:2[MT 3]). A broken horn denotes defeat (Jer. 48:25). The prophets predict the future rise of a beast with multiple horns, representing powers opposing God (Zech. 1:18-21[2:1-4]; Dan. 7:8; Rev. 13:1). At Rev. 5:6 the seven horns of the Lamb (Jesus Christ) indicate the abundance of his power.

See MUSIC, MUSICAL INSTRUMENTS.

HORNET
A large insect of the order Hymenoptera, which lives in a multicelled cellulose nest that the hornets make by chewing the bark of trees. Though they prove useful to humans by masticating large numbers of insects to feed their larvae, hornets (Heb. *ṣirʿâ*) cause great damage to ripe fruit and tree bark. Most common in the Middle East is the *Vespa orientalis,* a large yellow or reddish-brown species considered to be more malicious and aggressive

than Western varieties. Its sting is particularly painful, and the after-effects last several days, often paralyzing smaller victims. Thus the hornet occurs as a figure for divine intervention, described as being sent ahead of the Israelites to drive out the inhabitants of the land (Exod. 23:28; Deut. 7:20; NRSV "pestilence," NJPSV "plague," NEB "panic"; Josh. 24:12). JESPER SVARTVIK

HORNS OF THE ALTAR
Hornlike projections that extended upward from the four corners of the altar (Exod. 27;2; Lev. 4:7; 1 Kgs. 1:50; 2:28; Rev. 9:13). The horn was perhaps a symbolic reminder of the strength, presence, and power of God, perhaps deriving from the bull or the ox, animals known for those qualities. The generic Semitic title for God, El, was comprised of two Hebrew letters, the *aleph,* shaped like an oxhead with horns, and the *lamed,* shaped like an ox goad; combined, the two letters communicated the idea of God as active power. The horns perhaps also represented mountain peaks or a type of holy mountain, i.e., the dwelling place of the deity (reflected in the description of Ezekiel's altar; Ezek. 43:13-17; cf. also the Mesopotamian ziggurat, a type of sacred mountain associated with the home of the deity).

The horns played an important role in the sacrificial system through the cultic ritual of placing upon them some of the blood of the sin offering (Lev. 4:7). The horns also were recognized as a place of sanctuary or refuge (1 Kgs. 1:50; 2:28).

Archaeological excavations at Megiddo, Tell Beit Mirsim, and Beer-sheba have produced dismantled and intact examples. The horned altars found in the excavations of Megiddo and Tell Beit Mirsim were small limestone altars ca. .6 m. (2 ft.) tall. A larger version constructed of large blocks of stone was discovered at Beer-sheba. While offerings were apparently made on the surface of the altars, in some cases the horns may have supported a bowl or basin in which the sacrifice was made.

LAMOINE F. DEVRIES

HORONAIM (Heb. *ḥōrōnayim*)
A place in southern Moab mentioned in the oracles against Moab (Isa. 15:5; Jer. 48:3, 5, 34) and on the Moabite Stone. In Isaiah's oracle the expression "road to Horonaim" is used parallel to the "ascent of Luhith." This seems to indicate that Horonaim was located along a roadway that led from the Moabite plateau down to the Dead Sea. It may be identified with modern el-ʿIrāq (211055), ca. 15 km. (9 mi.) E of the Dead Sea, SW of Kerak, or with the northern side of Wadi el-Kerak atop ed-Der, SW of Rabbah.

Bibliography. J. A. Dearman, "Historical Reconstruction and the Meshaʿ Inscription," *Studies in the Mesha Inscription and Moab.* SBLABS 2 (Atlanta, 1989), 155-210; N. Na'aman, "The Campaign of Mesha Against Horonaim," *BN* 73 (1994): 27-30.

FRIEDBERT NINOW

HORONITE (Heb. *ḥōrōnî*)
An appellative of Sanballat, one of the rivals of Nehemiah (Neh 2:10, 19; 13:28), apparently indicating his place of birth. The name may refer to the Moabite city Horonaim, but more likely it refers to Beth-horon, located on the road from Samaria to Jerusalem. PAUL L. REDDITT

HORSE
First introduced to Palestine by the Hyksos in the early 2nd millennium B.C.E., horses are usually mentioned in contexts where they are harnessed to a chariot or ridden in the cavalry. Horses always belonged to royalty since only kings could afford their maintenance. They had little value for the ordinary Israelite, who utilized asses and mules in daily life.

The Philistines mustered 30 thousand chariots and 6000 horsemen against King Saul (1 Sam. 13:5). David kept only 100 horses for himself, choosing instead to hamstring those he had captured (2 Sam. 8:4). However, horses were a mainstay of Solomon's power — he had 4000 stalls and 12 thousand horses (1 Kgs. 4:26) — and were a prime weapon in the Israelite military. At the battle of Qarqar in 853, Ahab contributed 2000 chariots to the coalition against the Assyrians. The Horse Gate, located in the southeast corner of the city wall (Jer. 31:40; Neh. 3:28), demonstrated how horses had become essential to Jerusalem. While the text says that Solomon imported his horses from Egypt (1 Kgs. 10:28), the Egyptians must have imported them from Anatolia.

About two-thirds of the biblical references to horses are metaphorical. Horses are used to refer to the dangers of kingship and militarism (Deut. 17:14-16; Ps. 20:7[MT 8]; Isa. 2:7). They also figure in the apocalyptic imagery of Revelation (Rev. 6:2, 4-5; 19:11, 14, 19, 21). DONALD FOWLER

HOSAH (Heb. *ḥōsâ*) **(PERSON)**
A Levite from the line of Merari. He was a gatekeeper of the tent which David pitched for the ark when he brought it to Jerusalem (1 Chr. 16:38). Later Hosah, his sons, and their kin were responsible for guarding the west gate of Shallecheth (1 Chr. 26:10-11, 16).

HOSAH (Heb. *ḥōsâ*) **(PLACE)**
A city on the northern boundary of Asher, in the vicinity of Tyre (Josh. 19:29). Most likely the Usu of Egyptian and Assyrian inscriptions, Hosah may be identified with modern Tell Rashīdīyeh (170293), 4 km. (2.5 mi.) S of Tyre.

HOSANNA
An exclamation (Gk. *hōsanná*) shouted at Jesus by the crowds who greeted his triumphal entry into Jerusalem (Matt. 21:9 = Mark 11:9-10; John 12:13) and by children in the temple (Matt. 21:15). Derived from Ps. 118:25 (Heb. *hôšîʿâ-nnāʾ*, "save us, we pray"), which apparently became a liturgical cry for divine mercy through the reading of the Hallel Psalms, the expression later became associated

with Jewish eschatological hopes (cf. v. 25, quoted at Mark 11:9).

HOSEA (Heb. *hôšēaʿ*), **BOOK OF**

The first of the 12 Minor Prophets. Attributed to Hosea ben Beeri, the book condemns the inhabitants of northern Israel for their infidelity to Yahweh during the years of that nation's decline and fall (ca. 745-721 B.C.E.).

Text

With the possible exception of the book of Job, the text of Hosea is among the most difficult in the entire OT. Translations of the book vary widely depending on text-critical and philological judgments. It has been argued that much of the difficulty in the text is due to Hosea's use of a now obscure northern Israelite dialect. There is much to commend this position, especially since Hosea is the only writing prophet to have come from Israel. However, there is no other northern Israelite text tradition with which Hosea may be compared. Thus, while many proposed translations of Hosea are highly suggestive, they remain provisional attempts to understand an obscure text.

Literary Structure

The book is divided into two main sections, chs. 1–3 and 4–14. The first three chapters revolve around the relationships between Hosea and his wife and Yahweh and his people. The remaining chapters contain oracles which depict the deterioration of Israelite culture and society.

The entire book illustrates a remarkable freedom with respect to prophetic forms and genres. Chs. 1–3 exemplify this freedom, containing a 3rd person narrative (ch. 1), an oracle (ch. 2), and an autobiographical account (ch. 3). Yet this formal variety achieves metaphorical unity as the accounts of Hosea's marriage become the frame for exploring the state of Yahweh's relationship with Israel. Formal variety characterizes the remaining chapters as well. Typical prophetic judgment speeches are rare; instead there is a profusion of other prophetic forms, among them summonses to battle, calls to worship, and announcements of grievances.

Compositional History

The prevailing view is that the book went through an extended process of collecting, editing, and reshaping by Judean redactors. However, there is little agreement as to how such a process might be detected in the final form of Hosea. Nor has it been explained why the book's linguistic peculiarities would have remained intact after so much Judean editing. Nevertheless, it is assumed that certain features of the book attest to successive generations of Judean interest in the prophet's message to northern Israel.

One such feature is the superscription, which mentions the reigns of four Judean kings first and then one Israelite king, Jeroboam II. Since Hosea's ministry was to northern Israel, this focus on the regnal eras of the Judean kings has tended to support the claim that the book was redacted for a Judean audience. Other references to Judah seem to confirm the hypothesis that a later, possibly Josianic, redactor was responsible for this superscription.

However, while the superscription presupposes a date after the fall of the northern kingdom, the lack of reference to Israelite kings after Jeroboam II need not imply that the editors were addressing a strictly Judean audience. Instead, the editors may have used the superscription to continue Hosea's attack on Israelite politics which, Hosea asserted, had installed kings entirely apart from the will of God (8:4; 13:11). Since no Israelite king had the legitimation of Yahweh, there was no Israelite king after Jeroboam II.

A second feature often discussed as evidence of redactional history is the presence of eschatological elements. Each of the first three chapters ends with a vision of restoration after judgment (1:10-11[MT 2:1-2]; 2:14-23[16-25]; 3:5); similarly, 11:1-9; 14:1-9 offer a possibility of restoration and reconciliation. Where some scholars view these eschatological promises as later additions, others interpret them as an outgrowth of Hosea's understanding of Yahweh's commitment to Israel.

The lack of scholarly agreement on these features of the book illustrates the uncertainty of attempts to discern layers of tradition in the book of Hosea. It can be said with some certainty that the book sounds a call to repentance amid the chaos of a disintegrating nation, whose polity and cult can no longer shelter it from its own lies. That the book applies the lesson to Judah is also evident (11:12[12:1]).

Hosea, His Wife, and Social Location

Two aspects of Hosea's life, his marriage and social location, are often highlighted in critical discussions. Information about the former is usually derived from chs. 1 and 3, while information about the latter is scattered throughout the book in references to the prophets (4:5; 6:5; 9:7-9; 12:10-11, 13[11-12, 14]).

The biographical interpretation of chs. 1 and 3 is a recent development. Traditional Jewish and Christian interpretations viewed these chapters as visions: Hosea dreamed his marriage in much the same way that Ezekiel dreamed of a bodily translation from Babylonia to Jerusalem (Ezek. 8:1). In the past century, however, an interest in defining the Near Eastern background of Baal worship forced a more literalistic reading of these chapters. Two questions then emerged: what sort of prostitute was Gomer, and how might Hosea's experience of his marriage have led to a deeper understanding of Yahweh's disappointment with Israel?

Gomer's harlotry became understood as a form of cultic prostitution. Since the god Baal was a fertility god, it was argued, Israelites would have participated in rituals which would ensure such fertility. Such rituals, it was supposed, involved some form of sympathetic magic. It was therefore suggested that Israelite men and women took on the roles of the gods and goddesses and ritually enacted some form of sexual union. A variety of interpretations of Gomer's participation in the cult were then offered: in some reconstructions, she was a cult prostitute; in others, an ordinary Israelite girl whose participation in the sexual rites was a one-time event. In either case, Gomer's harlotry acquired religious as well as symbolic significance: not only was she straying from her husband, but she quite literally exemplified Israel's apostasy from Yahweh.

Although this interpretation gave a religious motivation to Gomer's harlotry, it was problematic on both literary and historical grounds. On the literary level, it became difficult to understand how Hosea's marriage to a known prostitute would symbolize Yahweh's commitment to Israel, who had been faithful at least at the beginning. On the historical level, there is no evidence that cultic prostitution was practiced, in Israel or elsewhere. In Hosea, the woman's seeking her lovers is a metaphorical, if pejorative, manner of describing her worship of gods other than Yahweh. Moreover, there is no evidence that such sexual rites were practiced in neighboring Canaanite religions.

Given the mixed result of these efforts to interpret chs. 1 and 3 in concrete historical and biographical terms, it seems wise to return to a symbolic reading of these chapters. Their focus is theology, not biography.

Discussions of Hosea's social location are even more tenuous, resting on ambiguous texts referring to the work of the prophets. In the 1950s Hans Walter Wolff argued that these texts established Hosea's social location as a member of the class of *nĕḇîʾîm,* whom he further identified as a group of levitical priests opposed to the established cult. This hypothesis linked Hosea to the tradition of northern Israelite prophecy and also established his lineage in the development of Deuteronomistic theology.

Despite the popularity of Wolff's thesis, it is more likely that Hosea condemned the prophets. He located them squarely in the cult (4:5); furthermore, he asserted that they were the means whereby Yahweh worked an ambiguous judgment not unlike that effected through the lying prophets of 1 Kgs. 20 (6:4-5; 9:7-9; 12:10[11]). Far from seeing himself as one of them, Hosea condemned them along with all of the other leaders of Israelite society.

Hosea's own social location is now uncertain. It is worth noting that he is not identified as a prophet in the superscription; nor, as noted earlier, does his use of prophetic forms follow normally expected conventions of prophetic speech.

Message

The superscription places the ministry of Hosea in the latter half of the 8th century. Although the allusions to historical events are vague, scholars now generally agree that certain oracles in the book reflect the prosperity of the reign of Jeroboam II (ca. 745), the tensions of the Syro-Ephraimitic War (734-32; cf. 5:8–6:10), and the diplomatic turmoil of the 720s (7:11; 11:5-7).

The oracles reflect an understanding of Yahwistic religion in which Yahweh is viewed as the guarantor of the gifts of the land. Hosea traces this understanding back to the promise to Jacob at Bethel (12:4-5[5-6]), as well as to the election and conquest traditions (11:1; 13:4-5). Israel appeals to Yahweh as its patron deity ("my God") particularly in times of national distress (8:2; 9:17).

Hosea accuses the people of a promiscuous reliance on other "saviors" as well. Frantic political maneuvers as well as the worship of other gods expose Israel's expression of faith in Yahweh as a shallow attempt to secure its safety through whatever means possible.

The primary issue in Hosea, then, is the nature of the relationship between Yahweh and people. Familial metaphors — father and son (11:1-4), husband and wife (chs. 1–3) — imply that more is involved than a contractual, covenantal relationship. What is missing is knowledge of God — a knowledge which comes from being in genuine relationship with God and which results in obedience to God's will. This knowledge is lacking because there is no loyalty *(ḥeseḏ).* Israel comes to Yahweh for the things she wants from him; but she does not come to him for his own sake. Given the prominence of familial metaphors, one might argue that the basis of Yahweh's complaint against Israel is not that Israel has broken the covenant, but that it has rebelled against more fundamental, indeed primal commitments.

Consequently, all of Israelite culture crumbles. Since Israel makes kings, but not through Yahweh, there are no kings (1:1). Altars do not remove guilt but rather increase it (8:11). Prophets lead the people into danger, and priests fail to show them the right way (9:7-9; 4:1-4). Israelite culture thus becomes a mirror of what passes for Israelite devotion, and both turn out to be hollow, false, and doomed to fail.

Nevertheless, Hosea suggests that the seed of renewal is in the relationship itself. When Israel's devotion to Yahweh corresponds to Yahweh's exclusive commitment to Israel, then the gifts of the land will once again flourish. Hosea demands of Israel exclusive worship of Yahweh, and in return promises an everlasting covenant of prosperity, fertility, and peace.

Bibliography. F. I. Andersen and D. N. Freedman, *Hosea.* AB 24 (Garden City, 1980); A. Brenner, ed., *A Feminist Companion to the Latter Prophets* (Sheffield, 1995); G. I. Davies, *Hosea.* NCBC (Grand Rapids, 1992); M. S. Odell, "Who Were the Prophets in Hosea?" *HBT* 18 (1996): 78-95; H. W. Wolff, *Hosea.* Herm (Philadelphia, 1974).

MARGARET S. ODELL

HOSHAIAH (Heb. *hôšaʿyâ*)

1. A leader of Judah who led the second contingent of Judahites in the procession at the dedication of the repaired walls of Jerusalem (Neh. 12:32).

2. The father of Jezaniah (Jer. 42:1)/Azariah (43:2), the antagonist of Jeremiah.

HOSHAMA (Heb. *hôšāmā'*)
A son of King Jeconiah (Jehoiachin), born while his father was in captivity (1 Chr. 3:18).

HOSHEA (Heb. *hôšēa'*)

1. The original name of Joshua (Num. 13:8, 16; Deut. 32:44).

2. The last king of northern Israel (732-724 B.C.E.). Hoshea, allied with Assyria, assassinated Pekah (736-732), who along with the kings of other petty nations had rebelled against Assyrian suzerainty (2 Kgs. 15:30). Tiglath-pileser III then officially named Hoshea king and received tribute from Israel. When Shalmaneser V (726-722) succeeded his father Tiglath-pileser, Hoshea aligned himself with anti-Assyrian neighbors in withholding tribute. Shalmaneser then attacked Israel and made Hoshea his vassal. When Hoshea withheld tribute again, Shalmaneser subdued Israel, imprisoned Hoshea, and continued his siege of Samaria until the city fell three years later in 722 (2 Kgs. 17:3-7). While the biblical account would seem to imply that Shalmaneser conquered Samaria, documents from the reign of Sargon II (722-705) insist that this was the real victor.

3. A chief officer whom David placed over Ephraim (1 Chr. 27:20).

4. One of the levitical priests who ratified Ezra's version of Israel's covenant with God (Neh. 10:23).

5. The 8th-century northern prophet whose name is usually transliterated Hosea. He flourished from the time of Uzziah and Jeroboam II until the reign of Hezekiah (Hos. 1:1). The dates of his career are dependent on the date of the reign of Hezekiah, which is disputed. However, there is no definitive evidence that he prophesied as late as the fall of Samaria in 722. He was probably active from 750-725.

PAUL L. REDDITT

HOSPITALITY
The practice of receiving and extending friendship to strangers. Hebrew has no specific word for the practice, but the activity is especially evident in the patriarchal traditions of Genesis and narratives in Judges. The activities and roles of both host and guest probably reflect nomadic traditions where travelers needed protection and nourishment. In the NT Gk. *philoxenía* (lit., "love of strangers") is usually translated "hospitality."

Travelers would frequently go to an open place and wait for an invitation (Gen. 19:1-3; Judg. 19:15-21) The strangers would first be tested because of their potential to pose a threat to the host or community (Gen. 19:5; Josh. 2:2). Because people's feet would get dirty from traveling in sandals, the host would provide water to wash the feet (Gen. 18:4; 19:2; 24:32; Judg. 19:21). This custom provided the point of transformation of the traveler from stranger to guest. Thus Simon the Pharisee failed in his duty as host when he did not offer to wash Jesus' feet (Luke 7:44).

Both host and guests had expected roles to play. The guests would partake of what was offered and would not insult the host. Likewise, the host was expected to honor the guests. Care and nourishment would be offered not only to the guests but to their animals as well. Abraham was viewed as an exemplary host because of the extravagance of his generosity in offering hospitality to his three heavenly visitors (Gen. 18:1-15). Not only did he prepare a meal in great haste, but a plentiful meal that included meat. As host, Abraham did not eat the meal but stood and served his guests (Gen. 18:6-8). The host was also expected to provide protection for the guests. This obligation explains why Lot offered his virgin daughters to the men of Sodom in place of the two angels (Gen. 19:4-8). A similar offer was made in the story of the rape-murder of the Levite's concubine (Judg. 19:22-26). In both stories, the abuse of hospitality by the Sodomites and Benjaminites resulted in judgment and destruction.

Israel's own experience and identity as a wandering people provided a practical and theological undergirding for its sense of obligation to provide hospitality. They too had been aliens in a strange land without legal protection and in danger of exploitation (Exod. 22:21[MT 20]; Deut. 10:17-19). Even after Israel receives the promised land, their perspective is that they remain aliens and tenants on the land with God as their host (Lev. 25:23). The prophets use the imagery of food and feasting with God as host of the banquet when envisioning the eschatological day of salvation (cf. Isa. 25:6-10).

Jesus employed the theme of a messianic banquet in his teaching about the kingdom (Matt. 8:11; 22:1-14; Luke 14:16-24). He served both as host, in the feeding miracles (Mark 6:30-44) or by washing the disciples' feet (John 13:1-11), and as guest, dependent upon the hospitality of others (Matt. 8:20). When he welcomed and ate with tax collectors and sinners, he proclaimed God's kingdom (Mark 2:15; Luke 7:34-50; 15:1-2; 19:1-10). By limiting his followers' possessions when he sent them out on mission, Jesus forced them to accept hospitality from others (Luke 10:4-12). Their actions were to follow the role of a good guest; they should stay in one house (Luke 10:7) and eat the food offered them (v. 8). The residential supporters on whom these itinerant followers were dependent had a reciprocal role of providing sustenance (Matt. 10:40-42), especially to those without the ability to pay (Luke 14:12-14).

The exhortation for the Church to practice hospitality is found in several NT writings (e.g., Heb. 13:2; 1 Pet. 4:9). The rationale for extending hospitality is multi-faceted: the recognition that Christians share the same status of resident aliens and exiles (1 Pet. 1:1; 2:4-10) or that in hosting strangers one may unwittingly be entertaining heavenly visitors (Heb. 13:2; clearly Gen. 18:1-15 is in mind). Most importantly, perhaps, is the recognition that in offering hospitality to another, one is offering it to Jesus (John 13:20; cf. the parable of the last judgment [Matt. 25:31-46], where acts of kindness performed for others are seen as acts for Jesus).

An interesting glimpse of practices of hospitality in the early Church is found in the Didache (11-12). The Church is advised not to offer hospitality to visiting itinerant preachers for more than two days. After two days, they should be sent on their way with bread. If they ask for money, they are clearly false prophets.

Bibliography. J. Koenig, *New Testament Hospitality.* OBT 17 (Philadelphia, 1985); J. J. Pilch and B. J. Malina, eds., *Handbook of Biblical Social Values* (Peabody, 1998). David B. Howell

HOST OF HEAVEN

Heavenly bodies, specifically the sun, moon, and stars (Deut. 4:19), or heavenly beings, especially angels (Neh. 9:6; Ps. 103:20-21). Israel was prohibited from worshipping heavenly bodies (Deut. 17:3, 5; 2 Kgs. 23:4-5), but it did so (Jer. 19:13; Zeph. 1:5), even during the Exodus (Acts 7:43). Such abomination (2 Kgs. 17:16; 21:3, 5) led to the nation's demise (Jer. 8:2). The "host of heaven" also refers to angels, those who attend and worship God (1 Kgs. 22:19 = 2 Chr. 18:18; cf. Luke 2:13).

The innumerable "host of heaven" is used metaphorically to denote God's rich blessings to those who maintain covenant faithfulness with him (Jer. 33:22; cf. Gen. 15:5). In prophetic symbolism, the phrase is interpreted variously as stars, angels, deities, and the persecuted people of God (Dan. 8:10-11). Kenneth D. Mulzac

HOTHAM (Heb. *ḥôṯām*) (also HELEM)

1. An Asherite; a son of Heber and grandson of Beriah (1 Chr. 7:31-32). He is called Helem at 1 Chr. 7:35.

2. A man from Aroer (1 Chr. 11:44). His sons Shama and Jeiel were among David's Champions.

HOTHIR (Heb. *hôṯîr*)

A son of the singer Heman, appointed by David to head the twenty-first division of levitical musicians (1 Chr. 25:4, 28).

HOUR

Designation of a particular time (Heb. *ʿēṯ, môʿēḏ;* Aram. *šāʿâ*), not a measure of time, with the possible exception of Dan. 4:19. The same meaning carries over into the NT (e.g., Matt. 18:1), but there an hour (Gk. *hṓra*) can also refer to the twelfth part of the time between sunrise and sunset (John 11:9; Matt. 20:1-12).

People in the OT described different times of the day in terms of nature — e.g., "about sundown" (2 Chr. 18:34; cf. Ps. 55:17[MT 18]) — while people in the NT could describe time in terms of numbered hours of the day (Matt. 20:3, 5, 6) and watches of the night (three in the Jewish system, four in the Roman; e.g., Mark 6:48; cf. Exod. 14:24; Judg. 7:19; Lam. 2:19). A "half hour" appears only in Rev. 8:1. "One hour" refers to an unspecified but relatively short time (Matt. 26:40), while longer periods can be described as lasting two (Acts 19:34) or three hours (5:7). Paul refers to temporary separation or grieving or accommodating as taking place "for an hour" (2 Cor. 7:8; Gal. 2:5; 1 Thess. 2:17; Phlm. 15; NRSV "a while"). An hour can also refer to a significant moment in salvation history, especially Jesus' suffering (Mark 14:35; John 12:27; cf. 4:23).

Carl Bridges

HOUSE

A shelter or dwelling place. Biblical and Near Eastern texts and archaeological contexts contain independent and complementary sources for the historical and cultural development of the house in Syria-Palestine.

Textual Usage

In its basic sense, Heb. *bayiṯ* designates a building. The term encompasses all social and economic levels of society and has an extended history throughout Mesopotamia, Egypt, and Syria-Palestine. It may specify a structure in which a man and his family live (Deut. 19:1; 21:12); a palace or building of a king (Gen. 12:15; Jer. 39:8); a temple (1 Sam. 5:2; 31:10), including the temple of Yahweh (Exod. 23:19; 34:26; Dan. 1:2; Arad Ostraca); and, if the complex was comprised of several buildings or rooms, a room or hall (Esth. 7:8; 2:3; Jer. 36:22; cf. Amos 3:15). The term may also designate the grave or residence of the dead (Job 17:13; 30:23; Ps. 49:11[MT 12]; Eccl. 12:5).

"House" frequently designates families, clans, or tribes. The household (or social unit) is often described in cultic contexts (e.g., Exod. 12:3-11; 20:10). The term may also refer to ruling dynasties (e.g., "house of Saul," 2 Sam. 3:1; 9:1-3; "house of David," 1 Sam. 20:16; 1 Kgs. 13:2; cf. Dan stela, Mesha stela).

The term also occurs frequently in place names, in conjunction with divine names (e.g., Bethel, Gen. 12:8; Beth-baal-meon, Josh. 13:17; Beth-horon; 16:5; 18:13), as a topographical term (Beth-arabah, Josh. 15:6, 61; 18:18; Beth-zur, 15:58), as a simple substantive (Beth-ezel, Mic. 1:11; Beth-lebaoth, Josh. 19:6), or where the second element is a proper or family name (Beth-hoglah, Josh. 15:6; 18:19, 21; Atroth-beth-joab, 1 Chr. 2:54). Parallels to many of these usages can be found in ancient Near Eastern sources.

The NT term, Gk. *oíkos,* has both literal and figurative meanings. Jesus spoke of "my Father's house" (John 2:16; 14:2) in reference to the temple. God's "house" was often applied to the Church (Eph. 2:19-22; Heb. 3:1-6), a designation partly reflecting the early Christian practice of using houses as places of meeting and fellowship (2 Tim. 4:19; Phlm. 2; 2 John 10).

Archaeological Contexts

The architectural development of houses in Syria-Palestine has been illuminated by more than a century of archaeological research. During the Early Bronze Age at least five types can be distinguished. Curvilinear houses have been associated with several ethnic groups. The elongated, oval plan of houses at Yiftaḥel was attributed to the invasive Esdraelon culture. EB II oval structures excavated in the Sinai were attributed to local populations. At Meẓer a rectilinear

Chalcolithic house is stratigraphically sandwiched between two later EB I oval houses. The rectilinear houses found in EB II Arad and Tell Chuera consist of several attached rooms which lend support to the interpretation that this was a family compound. This type, found in the southern Sinai, is closely related in function to the family compound, but is made of subcircular stone foundations with a center pillar and numerous benches.

Middle Bronze Age houses were often two-storied, with rooms surrounding a pillared hall (Tell Beit Mirsim, Megiddo, and Tell Bi'a; cf. the clay models from Emar). Late Bronze houses demonstrate continuity with the MB architectural tradition. During this period of influence from Egyptian, Hittite, Sea People, and Israelite cultural dynamics, several new house types are introduced. Egyptian-type "residencies" are introduced in Syria-Palestine (Beth-shan, Tell Farʿah [South], Tell el-Ḥesi, Tel Masos, Aphek, Pella) and have been associated with Egyptian political domination. Other houses display Hittite influences (Tell Abu Hawam, Hazor). At the end of this period and at the beginning of the Iron Age a new house type appears that is a derivative of LB architectural traditions. This "four-room house," built of stone, has a center hall with opposing sets of smaller rooms and usually is built with an upper story. It has been ethnically associated with the Israelites, but also has been identified at coastland and Transjordanian sites as well. During the Iron II period, Assyrian and Babylonian architectural elements were introduced in Syria-Palestine after the incorporation of numerous sites as vassal cities.

During the Hellenistic and Roman periods, city planning became highly advanced and houses were constructed on a rectangular plan. By Roman times, the rich were making winter homes in Jericho. Houses were typically constructed with an outer court surrounded by rooms with an inner court accompanied by more private quarters. Those in the higher levels of society added bathrooms to their homes. Herod's palace in Jerusalem, his winter palace in Jericho, and his fortress at Masada contained elaborate gardens and luxurious quarters with mosaic floors and associated bathhouses.

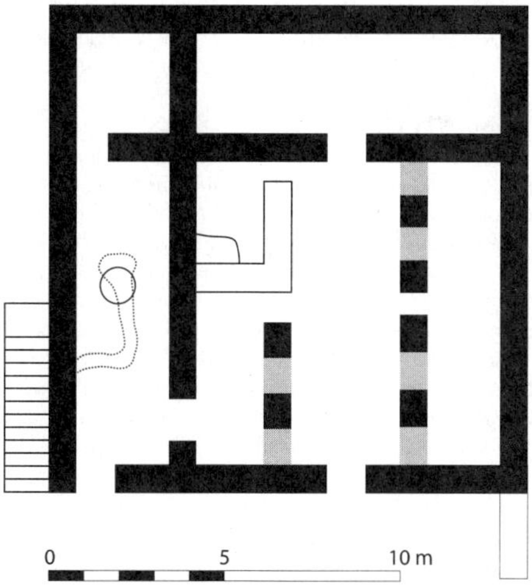

Top plan of a typical Israelite "four-room house" (Giselle S. Hasel)

Bibliography. P. M. M. Daviau, *Houses and Their Furnishings in Bronze Age Palestine.* JSOT/ASORMS 8 (Sheffield, 1993); H. A. Hoffner, "bayiṯ," *TDOT* 2:107-116; J. S. Holladay, Jr., "House: Syro-Palestinian Houses," *OEANE,* 94-114; A. Kempinski and R. Reich, eds., *The Architecture of Ancient Israel* (Jerusalem, 1992); O. Michel, "oíkos," *TDNT* 5:119-134; K. R. Veenhof, ed., *Houses and Households in Ancient Mesopotamia* (Istanbul, 1996).

Michael G. Hasel

HOUSEHOLD

The basic unit of social structure in the ancient world. The household was more extensive than in modern times and included not only immediate family but a wide spectrum of kinship groupings and retainers.

In Judaism as in gentile society, the household was the primary place for inculcation of traditional belief and morality, but in two important respects it differed. First, it was the primary means of maintaining the link between faith and ethnicity, and second, there was no distinction between the domestic and public spheres of religion. To recite the Shema was to acknowledge the sovereignty of the one Lord and to observe the commandment to teach this to one's family (Deut. 6, 11). Likewise observance of Torah governed the pattern of life both within the household and in public (the preparation of food, whom one might marry, and the rhythm of work in relation to the sabbath and festivals). The patriarchal ethos of the household is reflected along gender lines in Ps. 127; 113:9 (cf. Matt. 7:9-10; Mark 6:24; Matt. 10:35-36 par.; 1 Tim. 2:15; 3:4; 5:14).

In the early Church the household continued to play a central role as the meeting place (Acts 2:46; 5:42; 1 Cor. 1:16; Phlm. 2; cf. Acts 16:15; 18:8) and as a self-descriptive metaphor, "the household of faith" (Gal. 6:10; cf. Eph. 2:19; 1 Tim. 3:15; 1 Pet. 4:17). That description can extend in its domestic imagery to stewardship (2 Tim. 2:20; cf. 2 Cor. 4:7). The metaphorical understanding of the Church as a household may in part derive from references to Israel as a house (Num. 12:7 [Heb. 3:2, 5]; Jer. 31:31 [Heb. 8:8, 10]; Amos 5:25-27 [Acts 7:42-43]; Amos 9:11 [Acts 15:16]). The household as the primary place for the expression of faith informs the Church's recollection of Jesus' sayings about family life and domestic settings "in the house" (e.g., Mark 10:2-31). For Jesus the kingdom of God takes precedence even over family loyalty (Mark 3:31-35; Matt. 10:37; Luke 14:26), but equally it is not a means to avoid the filial duty of honoring one's parents (Mark 7:10; 10:19). The household, therefore, is both subject to and yet the context for the claims of discipleship. Indeed, the missionary pattern of the disciples (and in Luke the Seventy) in using the household as a base (Matt. 10:11 par.) would reinforce the household as a locus of evangelism (1 Cor. 7:12-16).

In the domestic code in 1 Pet. 3:1-6 the proportionate number of verses devoted to advice for wives is expressive of the delicate relationship in the patriarchal structure of the household brought about by the conversion of the wife. The Tables of Household Duty here and in Eph. 5:21–6:9; Col. 3:18–4:1 reflect the emerging Christian ethic within the household. The frequently occurring phrase "in the Lord" continues to serve as a reminder of the transcendent claims of the gospel. The sequencing of the pairs, e.g., wives-husbands, children-parents, slaves-masters, whereby the inferior is mentioned first, reflects a distinctive valuing of the example of service, no doubt aided by the particular "egalitarianism" of the Lord's Prayer ("Our Father"; cf. Matt. 23:9-12). In such ways as these one may discern the influence which Christian faith was beginning to exert upon family life and the household.

Bibliography. D. L. Balch, *Let Wives Be Submissive: The Domestic Code in 1 Peter.* SBLMS 26 (Chico, 1981); J. F. Gardner and T. Wiedemann, eds., *The Roman Household* (London, 1991).

James Francis

HOZAI (Heb. *ḥôzāy*)

The author of chronicles concerning King Manasseh of Judah, a source used by the author of 2 Chronicles (2 Chr. 33:19 MT; NRSV "the seers," following LXX (cf. v. 18).

HUKKOK (Heb. *ḥûqōq*)

A town in the tribal territory of Naphtali (Josh. 19:34), generally identified with modern Yāqûq (195254), ca. 5 km. (3 mi.) W of Chinnereth overlooking the Sea of Galilee near Jebel Habaqbuq.

HUKOK (Heb. *ḥûqōq*)

A city within the tribal territory of Asher assigned to the Gershonite Levites (1 Chr. 6:75[MT 60]). Elsewhere it may be called Helkath.

HUL (Heb. *ḥûl*)

According to the Table of Nations, a son of Aram and grandson of Shem (Gen. 10:23; cf. 1 Chr. 1:17, son of Shem and brother of Aram). The territory inhabited by his descendants cannot be identified with certainty; suggestions include the Arabian Peninsula, the region of Lake Huleh, and the Armenian border (cf. Hulia, a site mentioned in Assurnasirpal's annals).

HULDAH (Heb. *ḥuldâ*)

A prophetess from Josiah's time who predicted the destruction of Jerusalem (2 Kgs. 22:14-20 = 2 Chr. 34:22-28). She is identified as the wife of Shallum, the "keeper of the wardrobe" (2 Kgs. 22:14), which may refer to either the king's wardrobe or the priest's vestments.

When the law book was found in the temple, Josiah sent Hilkiah the priest and four others to Huldah seeking a prophecy from the Lord. She responded in typical Deuteronomistic style: a word of judgment against Judah and assurance that Josiah would be buried in peace, spared seeing the city's destruction (2 Kgs. 22:15-20). Josiah died in battle at Megiddo in 609 B.C.E. (2 Kgs. 23:29-30), but honorably before the city's siege and the people's exile.

Scholars give various reasons why Huldah, and not Jeremiah or Zephaniah, was consulted. Some speculate the male prophets were away. Rabbinic commentary, however, maintains that Josiah thought a woman would be more compassionate and more likely to intercede with God on his behalf (*Meg.* 14b).

According to Jewish tradition, Huldah had an academy or schoolhouse in Jerusalem. She and Jeremiah were kinsfolk and divided prophetic functions between them, Jeremiah preaching to the men and Huldah to the women. The rabbis call Shallum a godly and compassionate man, for which God rewarded him by letting his wife become a prophetess. The rabbis, however, call Huldah "arrogant" and thus her name ("weasel") is descriptive.

Robin Gallaher Branch

HULEH, LAKE

The northernmost and smallest of the three lakes along the course of the Jordan River. It is not mentioned in the Bible. In Arabic it is called Baheiret el-Huleh; Josephus calls it Lake Semechonitis (*Semechonitidos limnas; Ant.* 5.5.1; *BJ* 3.10.7; 4.1.1). Huleh was a body of fresh water, the basin of which was formed by the geological fault system which extended north through Syria into Turkey and south through the Jordan River Valley, the Red Sea, and to Africa. The natural dam which formed the lake was made of lava which issued from fissions in the rock. The lake was 11 km. (7 mi.) long and 4.8 (3 mi.) wide, with a large papyrus swamp in the north. Its surface was 70 m. (230 ft.) above sea level. Since the founding of the modern state of Israel the lake has been drained and the bottom used for agricultural purposes.

Bibliography. D. Baly, *The Geography of the Bible,* rev. ed. (New York, 1974); E. Robinson, *Biblical Researches in Palestine* (1856, repr. Jerusalem, 1970).

Lawrence A. Sinclair

HUMANITY

The study of humanity or of human beings in the Bible has traditionally been subsumed under such theological subjects as sin/grace, fall/redemption, creation/endtime, sexuality, ecology, suffering, and evil. With the recent emergence of theological anthropology as a distinct topic, humanity has become a focus for discussion in its own right as a study of the origin, nature, and destiny of human beings in relation to God. Theological anthropology, however, is prone to the same methodological problems as were classical descriptions of biblical humanity, namely, unacknowledged social locations and apologetic or dogmatic concerns which selectively shape the outcome of the search for the human. The Bible resists any systematic or developmental picture of human beings and opposes the imposition of overarching assumptions about human beings on texts, whether these assumptions are rooted in psychology, anthropology, philosophy, metaphysics, theology, Christology, or the historical-critical method. Contemporary feminists, womanists, and liberationists challenge the racism and sexism of current and classical anthropologies; they emphasize the necessity of understanding the totality of the human being out of lived experience and awareness of different social locations and contexts as shapers of that experience. Both the lingering Enlightenment understanding of the autonomy of the human being and today's privatized spirituality, with its psychological stress on selfishness, self-protection, and self-care, form the larger Western contemporary cultural context within which humanity in the Bible is investigated today and of which biblical anthropology can offer a critique.

Traditional OT anthropologies have focused upon the various Hebrew terms for human beings and their parts such as *nep̱eš* ("soul/person"), *bāśār* ("flesh/body"), *rûaḥ* ("spirit/breath"), *lēḇ* ("heart/ feelings"), and *kĕlāyôṯ* ("kidneys/emotions"). Of all these terms, only *nep̱eš*, which occurs 755 times, is so distinct that it is addressable in the vocative sense as the totality of the person — "my *nep̱eš*" as in Ps. 42:5, 11[MT 6, 12]; 43:5; 103:1, 2, 22; 104:1, 35. The English translation "soul" invites the body/soul dualism of Greek thought, but human beings in the OT do not have a "soul"; they are a "living soul/ *nep̱eš*" (Gen. 2:7). NT anthropologies have focused upon the various Greek terms dealing with the makeup of the human being, namely *sṓma* ("body/ person"), *sárx* ("flesh"), *pneúma* ("spirit/mind"), *psychḗ* ("soul/life"). Of these terms, *sṓma* has drawn the most attention, especially in Pauline anthropology. It is interpreted as either a term for the whole person (akin to *nep̱eš*, though it is *psychḗ* by which the LXX most often translates *nep̱eš*), or as the evil physical body in a body/soul dualism. Both OT and NT terms have been forced into systematic pictures of the human being based on now outmoded anthropological, developmental, and psychological assumptions. Such assumptions have been challenged in the OT, but NT anthropologies have resisted such critique because they have been too deeply embedded in various systematic theologies. This has resulted in a critical examination of theology or occasionally of Christology rather than of anthropology or, at the most, of Christian rather than NT understandings of the human being.

Many traditional anthropologies focus on what Henry Wheeler Robinson described as "corporate personality" in Israel, i.e., the fluidity between the individual and the group. According to Robinson, individual consciousness and morality emerged later in Israel with the classical prophets, such as Jeremiah and Ezekiel. The prophets were pioneering exceptions; only with Jesus was a direct individual relationship with God achieved. Robinson's developmentalism was undergirded by now outmoded mid-19th to early 20th-century anthropological theory which posited individualism as the transition marker from primitive (group) to modern (individualistic) thinking. It was also reinforced by the historical-critical method as formulated by Julius Wellhausen. Wellhausen declared that the prophets were the "real climax" of Israelite religion; postexilic Judaism was "a dead work." This thinking reinforced anti-Judaic tendencies in Christian theology which are still visible today. Romantic stereotypes of early Israelite nomads as brave individualists tamed by collectivity, agriculture, and cities, stereotypes which have been rejected by contemporary anthropology, also helped shape Robinson's evolutionary view. Unfortunately, many of these traditional anthropological arguments continue to be used uncritically today. Wolfhart Pannenberg, e.g., argues that the individual developed during the Exile, when act/consequence was expected to show itself in the life of each person; he ignores the much older wisdom tradition which espouses this view.

Gen. 1–3 stands at the center of classical discussions of humanity in the Bible. The NT presumes the creation faith of the OT. Most scholars agree that these creation texts proclaim that humans are creatures of God dependent upon their Creator for life (as Pss. 104, 147, 148 also attest), and that God created human beings as part of the natural world but with a special relationship to that world, to each other, and to God, the One who gives human life meaning. The nature of those relationships has been debated, with much of the discussion focusing on the Hebrew *'āḏām*, which can mean the proper name Adam, male-specific "man," or generic "humanity." The wordplay between *'āḏām* and *'ăḏāmâ* ("ground, soil") in Gen. 2:7 suggests the relatedness between humanity and the created world; indeed, human sin has consequences for the entire created order (e.g., Gen. 6:11; 7:11; Isa. 24:5-6; Jer. 4; Mark 13 par.). Yet while feminists tend to see the harmonious interrelatedness of humans and nature, womanists recognize a more conflicted relationship out of which both chaos and creativity can emerge. Classical conceptions of humanity understood Adam as historically the first human being as well as the type or paradigm of human nature, i.e., normative for humankind. Adam as type is sinner; Jesus is the new Adam who redeems corrupted humanity from the consequences of the "fall"; Jesus is the sinless anti-type of Adam, in whom sin originated (Rom. 5:12). Though Adam as first man in history is not found anywhere in the OT but only in late Jewish tradition of the 2nd century C.E. (2 Esdr. 7), this patristic view of disobedience in the garden and the consequent divine punishments for a "fallen" humanity persists today. Claus Westermann challenges the idea of an "original state" of innocence; the tightly connected events in the garden are meant to be a primeval happening. Phyllis Trible argues in her rhetorical-critical study that the divine speeches in Gen. 3 are descriptions of the consequences of disobedience rather than prescriptions for punishment and behavior.

Eve has traditionally been understood as temptress, the "devil's gateway" (Tertullian). Feminists argue that women are trapped by the unrealistic expectations created, on the one hand, by the identification of woman with Eve, self-assertion, sexuality, and sin (1 Tim. 2:9-14) and, on the other hand, by her identification with an idealized, obedient, sexless, and sinless Mary. Both models legitimate the subjugation of women in patriarchal structures. Womanists challenge the use of Christian servant language to describe humanity, noting that, for African-American women, servanthood has been unrecognized, dehumanizing servitude. Sin for them is not pride or self-assertion, but rather too much humility and self-hatred. With the emphasis upon the maleness of Jesus, and the confusion of biology with socially constructed gender roles, femaleness in many anthropologies is seen as a deviant way of being human and maleness as normative, thus legitimating social and ecclesiastical definitions of women's place. Contemporary theological anthropologies debate whether and how gender is related to humanness and how women can image Christ. Some contemporary arguments for Jesus' egalitarian approach to women contribute to an anti-Jewish dichotomy between the testaments.

Classical anthropologies have asserted the centrality of the divine image in humanity, *imago Dei,* although "image of God" is referred to only infrequently in both the OT (e.g., Gen. 1:26; 9:6; note: 1:26; 5:1 refer to the "likeness" of God) and the NT (e.g., 1 Cor. 11:7; Jas. 3:9); Christ becomes the embodiment of the divine image in 2 Cor. 4:4; Phil. 2:6; Col. 1:15. In what way humanity bears the divine image and whether or not male and female share equally in the image of God have been the center of controversy for centuries. Contemporary scholars argue that exercising dominion over creation images God, since in the ancient Near East kings ruled as the representatives of the gods. They also reject any dualistic notion of image referring to only part of the human being, such as the reason or will, rather than to the whole person. This counters Christian Platonism (Ambrose, Gregory of Nyssa), which considered the *imago Dei* to be "mind" or the "rational faculties of the soul," and the human capacity for knowledge of God over and against the ascetics (Pelagius), who believed that the divine image was autonomous self-determination rooted in the capacity to choose between good and evil and earn rewards. In his 5th century controversy with the Pelagians, Augustine fused Platonic and ascetic traditions, positing a controversial distinction between nature and grace. The natural desire for God is lost because of the "fall" of Adam; this desire is a gift of Christ's spirit, not an inalienable endowment from the Creator. Humans suffer from hereditary moral disease (original sin) and legal liability (death), from which only God's grace (for some) can save the sinner. Further, the human being is composed of two distinct elements, soul and body. The rational soul is incorporeal and thus shares in the image of God. Sex is tied exclusively to the material corporeality of the human body. The sexual body is either *vir* (man) or *femina* (woman). Woman is the image of God in her rational soul but not in her *femina;* man is God's image in both according to Augustine's interpretation of 1 Cor. 11:7. The inferiority of woman's *femina* blocks the superiority of the rational soul.

Elaine Pagels argues that with Augustine the message of human freedom in Gen. 1–3 became one of human bondage; the fall validated secular power and church authority as essential for human salvation as the Church was making the transition from sect to official religion of the Roman Empire. Augustine's views were transmitted in modified form by Thomas Aquinas in the Middle Ages, John Calvin and the Reformers, and contemporary theologians like Karl Barth. Barth's God-creature hierarchy, e.g., analogously shapes male/female relationships; humanity in its fallenness cannot respond to God except in Christ who responds for us. The legacy of Augustine is a mind/body, spirit/flesh, man/woman hierarchic dualism damaging to women. Contemporary discussions of the *imago Dei* tend to center on "God-likeness" in terms of human genderedness. Phyllis Bird argues that gender relations are not addressed in connection with the image of God in Gen. 1:26-28; "male and female [he] created them" in v. 27b is linked to the fertility blessing that follows in v. 28, a blessing which humans share with the animals, rather than to the preceding image of God in vv. 26-27a.

Paul's statements about the nature of the human being have often been taken as determinative for the anthropology of the entire NT. Scholars warn against homogenizing or spiritualizing Paul by abstracting his terms for the human being from their particular historical contexts. Krister Stendahl criticizes those who interpret Paul's justification by faith and second use of the law in Romans from a later, Western frame of reference (via Augustine and Luther) as a guide for the frustrated introspective conscience. Rather, Paul's basic concern as the Apostle to the Gentiles was with the relation between Jews and Gentiles in light of Jesus as the Messiah, which was not a real problem after the 1st century when Christianity's constituency was no longer Jewish.

In the final analysis, biblical anthropology must take seriously what Walter Brueggemann calls the dialectical, tension-filled biblical process of "core" and "counter testimonies." Core testimonies make basic claims for God that are characteristic over time; counter theologies "assault" the core testimony with fresh evidence and new questions. Thus, God is an omnipotent, transcendent ruler who guarantees order by means of reward/punishment, yet also a suffering God (Jürgen Moltmann) who shares with humans their lack of power, giving comfort and companionship. God is present as the psalm hymns attest; God is absent according to the challenge of the psalm laments. God of the saving history redeems, while the ever-present Creator God blesses. The human being in the Bible is caught between these core and counter theological testimonies and consequently relates to God in diverse ways, with stoic obedience or with protest and questioning. Humans are weak, fallen creatures prone to sin whom God the Redeemer must save, or partners in God's image who are a little less than

God (Ps. 8). A faithful biblical anthropology would take note of this dialectical tension.

Bibliography. A. Graff, ed., *In the Embrace of God: Feminist Approaches to Theological Anthropology* (Maryknoll, 1995); M. D. Guinan, *To Be Human Before God* (Collegeville, 1994); D. Hopkins, "Biblical Anthropology, Discipline of," in *Dictionary of Pastoral Care and Counseling,* ed. R. J. Hunter (Nashville, 1990), 85-88; W. Pannenberg, *Anthropology in Theological Perspective* (Philadelphia, 1985); U. Schnelle, *The Human Condition: Anthropology in the Teachings of Jesus, Paul, and John* (Minneapolis, 1996); P. Trible, *God and the Rhetoric of Sexuality.* OBT 2 (Philadelphia, 1978); H. W. Wolff, *Anthropology of the Old Testament* (Philadelphia, 1974). DENISE DOMBKOWSKI HOPKINS

HUMILITY

Concerning an individual or group, the quality of being "poor," "needy," or even "oppressed"; or more subjectively, an individual's being dependent on God and showing respect for other persons (e.g., "meekness" or "gentleness"). There is no clear distinction between humility and meekness, hence variances in translation.

Humility is often connected with low socioeconomic stature, with individuals or groups who are in affliction, poverty, and suffering (Deut. 26:6; Job 22:29). God delivers the humble and brings down the haughty (1 Sam. 2:7; 2 Sam. 22:28). Yahweh humbles individuals (Pharaoh, Exod. 10:3) and groups (Israelites, Deut. 8:2, 16), showing that their relationship before God is more important than earthly prominence or affluence; kings who humble themselves before God are exalted (1 Kgs. 21:29; 2 Kgs. 22:19; 2 Chr. 32:26; 33:12, 19), while those who do not are afflicted (2 Chr. 33:23; 36:12). Because the poor were often prey to the powerful, law codes reflect concern for them (Exod. 23:6; Deut. 15:7; 24:14). The humility of the poor is increasingly connected with righteousness (Num. 12:3; Zeph. 2:3; cf. Ps. 22:26[MT 27]; 25:9). What God desires most is not outward sacrifices but a humble spirit (Ps. 51:17; Mic. 6:8). Humility shows itself through obedience to God (Deut. 8:2), recognition of one's sinfulness (Isa. 6:5), and submission to God (2 Chr. 34:27). God accords blessings to the humble, including wisdom (Prov. 11:2), good tidings (Isa. 61:1), honor (Prov. 15:33), and even life and sometimes wealth (22:4).

Although humility is associated with righteousness in the Sermon on the Mount (Matt. 5:3-12, esp. v. 5), in the NT it is more often connected with Jesus as Messiah. Matt. 21:5 applies the messianic prophecy of Zech. 9:9 to Jesus as a king who is humble (Gk. *praús,* "gentle" or "mild," as a wild animal that has been tamed). The acts of Jesus were those of humility as well, especially washing the disciples' feet (John 13:5; cf. Matt. 11:29), an example they are to follow (John 13:15; cf. Matt. 23:12).

Humility is a consistent theme throughout the Epistles. In the Greco-Roman world many regarded humility as a sign of weakness or even a character flaw; its meanings of "lowly" or "servile" were often used disparagingly. That Christians should view humility as a virtue was therefore quite striking. Paul writes that humility is at the heart of Christ's character (Phil. 2:3-8; Gk. *tapeinós,* "lowly," "downcast"). It is an attitude of Paul himself (2 Cor. 10:1), an attitude of Christian community (Eph. 4:2; Col. 3:12), a fruit of the spirit (Gal. 5:23), which finds its source in *agápē* (1 Cor. 4:21; cf. 13:4-5). Humility is the appropriate attitude toward God (Jas. 4:10) and toward each other (1 Pet. 3:8; 5:5). T. J. JENNEY

HUMTAH (Heb. *ḥumṭâ*)

A city in the tribal territory of Judah, mentioned between Aphekah and Kiriath-arba/Hebron (Josh. 15:54). Its precise location is unknown.

HUNDRED, TOWER OF THE

A tower on the northeastern corner of the wall of Jerusalem near the tower of Hananel, between the Sheep Gate and the Fish Gate. It was restored by Nehemiah (Neh. 3:1; 12:39). The meaning of its name is unclear, perhaps indicating its height (maybe 100 cubits high or accessed by 100 steps) or its size and importance for defense (housing a garrison of a "hundred"). Some translations transliterate Heb. *hammēʼâ* and call it the Tower of Meah (or Hammēah). RICHARD A. SPENCER

HUNTING

People of biblical times hunted for food, sport, and the protection of humans, domestic animals, and crops. Hunting was an important source of food; Heb. *ṣayiḏ,* "hunting," can also mean "food" or "game." There are numerous references to wild animals such as deer, gazelles, roebuck, ibex, antelope, wild goat, mountain sheep, and various wild fowl as sources of food (e.g., Deut. 14:5; the Story of Sinuhe). Named among the descendants of Solomon's servants is Pochereth-hazzebaim ("catcher of gazelles"; Ezra 2:56 = Neh. 7:59), perhaps preserving the name of a family responsible for supplying royal provisions (cf. 1 Kgs. 4:23).

Nimrod, a heroic hunter, is identified in the Table of Nations as the founder of many cities in Mesopotamia (Gen. 10:9) and later is called a "mighty one" or warrior (cf. 1 Chr. 1:10; Mic. 5:6[MT 5]). Hunting was often connected with the activity of heroes and warriors in the ancient Near East (cf. Story of Aqhat; Gilgamesh Epic; Jer. 16:16). Many of the skills and weapons used in hunting are transferable to warfare. Some of the weapons and techniques used for hunting include the bow and arrow (Gen. 27:3), swords, knives, slings, rods, staffs (Ps. 23:4), spears, nets, pits, and traps.

Hunting is primarily a nomadic or rural activity. Esau was a skillful hunter of the open field, which endeared him to Isaac (Gen. 25:27-28). Ishmael, another inhabitant of the wilderness, is depicted as an archer (Gen. 21:20).

Hunting as a sport and symbol of royal power is common in Egyptian and Assyrian art and history. The Assyrians held lions in pits, releasing them for royal hunting purposes (cf. Benaiah, 2 Sam. 23:20 =

1 Chr. 11:22); this may explain their presence in Darius' court (Dan. 6:7-24).

Hunting as a form of protection is especially connected with a shepherd's defending the flock from predators (1 Sam. 17:34-37). Lions, bears, leopards, cheetahs, wolves, and jackals are known to have inhabited Palestine. The imagery of wild animals attacking is used to describe Israel and its enemies (Jer. 5:6). Predators and prey living in harmony are used metaphorically to describe the peace and harmony of the messianic age (Isa. 11:6-7).

Bibliography. O. Borowski, *Every Living Thing: Daily Use of Animals in Ancient Israel* (Walnut Creek, Calif., 1998); V. H. Matthews and D. C. Benjamin, *Old Testament Parallels: Laws and Stories of the Ancient Near East,* rev. ed. (New York, 1997); J. D. Wineland, "Hunting and Fishing," in *By the Sweat of Thy Brow: Labor and Laborers in the Biblical World,* ed. G. Mattingly (Sheffield, forthcoming).

JOHN D. WINELAND

HUPHAM (Heb. *ḥûpām*)
A descendant of Benjamin; eponymous ancestor of the Huphamites (Num. 26:39). He is probably the same as Huppim (Gen. 46:21), at 1 Chr. 7:12 said to be the son of Ir.

HUPPAH (Heb. *ḥuppâ*)
The head of the thirteenth division of priests at the time of King David (1 Chr. 24:13). The Hebrew name suggests the wedding baldachin in the modern synagogue (cf. Joel 2:16).

HUPPIM (Heb. *ḥuppîm*)
A descendant of Benjamin (Gen. 46:21; 1 Chr. 7:12). At 1 Chr. 7:15 he appears to be a descendant of Manasseh. The name, apparently the eponym of an Israelite subgroup, is probably a variant form of Hupham.

HUR (Heb. *ḥûr*)
Personal name probably of Egyptian background (cf. the god Hor and the personal name Pasch-ḥur). The name may have been understood in the sense of the Semitic word for "son" (Akk. *ḫuru*) of a human or an animal.

1. Companion of Moses (and Aaron), who helped keep Moses' hands raised during the battle against the Amalekites (Exod. 17:10, 12). Hur together with Aaron was entrusted with judicial responsibility while Moses ascended the mountain to receive the tablets of the law (Exod. 24:14).

2. Grandfather of Bezalel from the tribe of Judah, who designed and crafted the ark, the tabernacle, and its objects (Exod. 31:2; 35:30; 38:22; 2 Chr. 1:5). The genealogies in 1 Chr. 2 relate him to the clan of Caleb and to the town of Bethlehem (cf. 1 Chr. 4:1, 4). These postexilic texts seem to hint at a relationship to **1** above, and to underscore the claim of this Calebite/Judahite family later settled at Bethlehem (see **5** below).

3. One of the five kings slain by the Israelites in retaliation for the incident at Peor (Num. 31:8; Josh. 13:21). The names of the kings in this rather late list may also be identified with names and places in Midian.

4. The father of Solomon's governor in Ephraim (1 Kgs. 4:8).

5. The father of Rephaiah, an official of Jerusalem at the time of Nehemiah (Neh. 3:9). Ben-Hur, "son of Hur," may be understood literally or as "son of the clan Hur." The position of this "son of Hur" signifies the importance of the Hur clan in the 5th century B.C.E. (see **2** and **4** above).

SIEGFRIED KREUZER

HURAI (Heb. *ḥûray*) (also HIDDAI)
One of David's Thirty, from "the wadis of Gaash" (1 Chr. 11:32). At 2 Sam. 23:30 he is called Hiddai.

HURAM (Heb. *ḥûrām*) (also HIRAM, HURAM-ABI)

1. A Tyrian metal worker employed by Solomon for technical assistance in the ornamentation of the temple (1 Kgs. 7:13-14, 40, 45 = 2 Chr. 2:13-14; 4:11-16). His father was Tyrian and his mother an Israelite from Naphtali (1 Kgs. 7:14; 2 Chr. 2:14 identifies her as from the adjacent territory of Dan). In 1 Kings he is called Hiram (**2**), and at 2 Chr. 2:13; 4:16 his name occurs as Huram-abi.

2. Alternate form of the name Hiram, used in 2 Chronicles for Hiram I, king of Tyre.

3. A Benjaminite; the son of Bela (1 Chr. 8:5).

HURAM-ABI (Heb. *ḥûrām'āḇî*)
The Tyrian craftsman employed by Solomon for the metalwork of the temple (2 Chr. 2:13).

See HIRAM **2**; HURAM **1**.

HURI (Heb. *ḥûrî*)
A Gadite, the son of Jaroah and father of Abihail (1 Chr. 5:14).

HURRIANS (Akk. *ḫurri*)
An ancient Near Eastern people widely attested in the 3rd-2nd millennium B.C.E., founders of the powerful kingdom of Mitanni.

History

The Hurrians first appear in the archaeological record in the Sargonic levels at Tell Mozan (ancient Urkesh) in north Syria. Inscriptions with Hurrian toponyms suggest a period of settlement and occupation that preceded the documentation. The absence of Hurrian personal names in the Ebla texts indicates that their expansion from the north-northeast had not yet reached western Syria (i.e., west of the Euphrates). Similarly, the absence of Hurrian names in texts from Tel Beydar in the Ḫabûr region shows that they had not yet infiltrated northwestern Syria. Thus, their appearance, or at least their rise to prominence, must coincide with the rise of the Akkadian dynasty or shortly thereafter. Naram-sin's conquest of a coalition of Hurrians led by the kings of Simurrum and Nawar subjected the Hurrian city-states to Akkadian control at the end of the 23rd century. By the end of the Sargonic period (or the beginning of Ur III) the inscriptions of Atal-šen and Tiš-atal demonstrate a continued expanded Hurrian presence in northeastern Syria and north Mesopotamia and the adoption of writing. Šulgi, the long-reigning second king of the Ur III dynasty, fought a series of battles against Hurrian city-states along the northeastern borders of his empire. Hurrian personal names are encountered frequently in the archival texts of the Ur III bureaucracy. By the end of the 3rd millennium Hurrians are found in eastern Anatolia, northern and western Syria and Mesopotamia, with particular concentration in the hill country of northeastern Assyria and probably eastern Anatolia.

Hurrians survived the widespread disruptions that characterize the end of the 3rd millennium. In Middle Bronze Age Anatolia and Syro-Canaan they appear among the various population groups together with the Assyrians, Anatolians, Canaanites, Amorites, and Babylonians, with concentration in eastern Anatolia and most of Syria. In the 19th century they appear in the Old Assyrian merchant accounts from Kanesh (Kültepe) where they are associated with cities south of the Anti-Taurus Mountains but not yet in central Anatolia. During the Mari age Hurrian city-states are under the control of Šamši-adad, who governed from his capital at Šubat-enlil (Tell Leylan), but after his death Hurrian city-states appear as independent entities primarily in upper Mesopotamia and east of the Tigris but also as far west as Urshu and Halab (Aleppo). By the middle of the 17th century Hurrian power clashed with the emerging Hittite Old Kingdom, and Ḫattušili I campaigned to stop their expansion.

Coincident with the collapse at the end of the Middle Bronze/Old Babylonian period, the Hittites began to expand into north Syria. By the late 16th century they encountered a substantial Hurrian power east of the Euphrates called Mitanni that had previously invaded central Anatolia in the early years of Ḫattušili I and whose kings bore Indo-aryan names but whose population spoke Hurrian. Beginning with the reign of Thutmose III, Syro-Canaan was referred to as Ḫuru in Egyptian documents. Hurrian power reached its peak in the early 15th century when Kizzuwatna (Cilicia) was annexed during the reign of Zidanta II. Excavations at Nuzi in north Mesopotamia revealed the details of provincial Hurrian society over five generations with its complex social, economic, and legal customs in the 15-14th centuries. The nearly 5000 texts found at Nuzi were written in Akkadian by Hurrian-speaking scribes and were, until recently, the major source of Hurrian vocabulary. The Hurrians' capital, Wašukkani, has not yet been identified (Tell Fakhāriya?). By the late 15th century Hurrians had become a major segment of the population of Syria (e.g., at Alalakh, Halab, Qatna, Ugarit), had intermarried with the Hittite royal family, and were in communication with the kings of Egypt. Hurrian religion was widely practiced, and Hurrian gods and goddesses worshipped over a wide area. By the late 13th century Hurrian power began to wane with the conquest of Syria by Šuppiluliuma I. The Hurrian kingdom of Ḫanigalbat disappeared from contemporary records. With the devastating campaigns of the Assyrian king Tukulti-ninurta I in Syria, the deportation of large numbers of Hurrians, and the subsequent collapse of the Late Bronze Age civilizations associated with the invasions of the Sea Peoples, Hurrian power was eliminated and the Hurrians assyrianized. Subsequently they were overwhelmed by the incursions of Aramaic-speaking tribes. The Hurrian language ceased to appear in written sources in Syro-Mesopotamia, although its related language, Urartian, continued to be written and spoken in eastern Anatolia for the next few centuries.

In the Bible, the Hurrians have been associated with the Horites (Heb. *ḥōrî*), although there is no extrabiblical validation of this equation, linguistic or otherwise. Furthermore, the identification of certain royal names among the Hyksos with Hurrian personal names is no longer widely accepted. That there were Hurrians in southern Canaan and possibly in Egypt in the Middle and Late Bronze Ages is a likely but unproven possibility. Hurrians are known to have been as far north in Anatolia as Sapinuwa (Ortaköy), 50 km. (30 mi.) NE of Ḫattuša/Boghazköy, and as far west as Cyprus and possibly Crete.

Language and Literature

The Hurrians had come under Akkadian influence already in the 23rd century. Hurrian personal names and titles appear first in the seal inscriptions from Urkesh. They wrote their earliest inscriptions in Akkadian, but the underlying spoken language was Hurrian. The Hurrian language is itself an isolate possibly related to Northeast Caucasian. The earliest fully written Hurrian religious texts appear only in the 18th-century Mari archives, suggesting a tradition of written literature preceding its first occurrence at Mari. In the 3rd millennium it is known primarily from personal names. In the first half of the 2nd millennium religious texts and rituals dominate, although recently a small number of letters in Hurrian have been discovered. In the 14th-15th centuries the Hurro-Akkadian texts from Nuzi provide a substantial Hurrian vocabulary and occasional grammatical forms. Hurrian was one of the many languages spoken and written at Ugarit and is among the languages in the quadralingual dictionaries found there. The recent discovery at Boghazköy of the Hurro-Hittite bilingual "Epic of Manumission" (early 14th century, but probably originally a MB text), revealed a fully developed literary epic tradition in Hurrian previously known mostly via Hittite translations. Hitherto, the longest known Hurrian text (494 lines) had been the diplomatic letter of King Tušratta of Mitanni to Amenophis III concerning the negotiations of brideprice and dowry for Princess Tatuhepa, who was to be sent to Egypt to marry the pharaoh. There are strong indications that a rich and varied written literary tradition existed among the Hurrians as early as the 18th century. Excavations at the northern Anatolian site of Ortaköy have uncovered a large Hurrian library of more than 600 texts and fragments whose content, mostly rituals, includes many Hurrian-Hittite bilinguals.

Bibliography. G. Gragg, "Hurrian," *OEANE* 3:125-26; M. Kelly-Buccellati, "Nuzi Viewed from Irkesh, Urkesh Viewed from Nuzi: Stock Elements and Framing Devices in Northern Syro-Mesopotamia," in *Richard F. S. Starr Memorial Volume,* ed. D. I. Owen and G. Wilhelm. Studies on the Civilization and Culture of Nuzi and the Hurrians 8 (Bethesda, 1996), 247-68; N. Na'aman, "The Hurrians and the End of the Middle Bronze Age in Palestine," *Levant* 26 (1994): 175-87; D. L. Stein, "Hurrians," *OEANE* 3: 126-30; G. Wilhelm, *The Hurrians* (Warminster, 1989); "The Hurrians in the Western Parts of the Ancient Near East," in *Mutual Influences of Peoples and Cultures in the Ancient Near East,* ed. M. Malul (Haifa, 1996), 17-30; "The Kingdom of Mitanni in Second-Millennium Upper Mesopotamia," *CANE* 2:1243-54. DAVID I. OWEN

HUSHAH (Heb. *ḥûšâ*)
A "son of Ezer," founder of a place in the hill country of Judah (1 Chr. 4:4). It was the home of Sibbecai ("the Hushathite"), one of David's Mighty Men (1 Sam. 21:18; 1 Chr. 11:29; 20:4; 27:11; called Mebunnai at 2 Sam. 23:27). The site is generally identified with modern Ḥūsân (162124), SW of Bethlehem.

HUSHAI (Heb. *ḥûšay*)
A friend and confidant of King David (2 Sam. 15:37; 1 Chr. 27:33). An Archite, he was the father of Baana, an officer of Solomon (1 Kgs. 4:16). He played an important role during the rebellion of Absalom by posing as an adviser and dissuading Absalom from following Ahithophel's counsel (2 Sam. 15:32-33; 16:16–17:14); moreover, he kept David apprised through the sons of the priests Zadok and Abiathar (15:34-36).

HUSHAM (Heb. *ḥušām, ḥûšām*)
A Temanite who became king over Edom after the death of Jobab (Gen. 36:34-35; 1 Chr. 1:45-46).

HUSHATHITE (Heb. *ḥûšāṯî*)
A gentilic designating an inhabitant of Hushah (2 Sam. 21:18; 23:27; 1 Chr. 11:29; 20:4; 27:11).

HUSHIM (Heb. *ḥûšîm, ḥušîm, ḥušim*)
(also SHUHAM)

1. A son of (or a social group descended from) Dan (Gen. 46:23). The form Shuham occurs at Num. 26:42.

2. The sons of the Benjaminite Aher (1 Chr. 7:12). The Hebrew text of this verse is difficult to interpret.

3. The mother of Abitub and Elpaal; a wife of the Benjaminite Shaharaim, who later divorced her (1 Chr. 8:8, 11).

HYKSOS (Gk. *Hyksṓs*)
A Greek term, from Egyp. *ḥq3w ḫ3swt,* "rulers of foreign countries," used by the Egyptian historian Manetho (3rd century B.C.) to describe the people(s) who dominated Egypt during the 15th-16th dynasties of the Second Intermediate Period (high chronology, 1674-1550; low chronology, 1637-1529). Manetho wrongly interpreted the Egyptian phrase as "shepherd kings." In certain Egyptian writings they were also given the general designation *ʿ3mw,* "Asiatics" (lit., "speakers of a West Semitic tongue").

Ethnic Identification

Although the ethnic identification and place of origin of the Hyksos have been debated, a growing body of evidence (both textual and archaeological) indicates that the Hyksos were not Indo-european (or more specifically Hurrian), but were in the broadest sense West Semitic and perhaps, in a narrower sense, Southern Levantines.

Archaeological evidence from Tell el-Dabʿa, Tell el-Maskhuta, and elsewhere in the eastern Delta gives every indication of a West Semitic culture. The principal Hyksos site of Avaris (Tell el-Dabʿa) was an enormous city covering an area of ca. 2.5 sq. km. (1 sq. mi.). Its ceramic and artifactual content is virtually the same as the culture of the contemporary Middle Bronze IIB Levant. Its burial practices also evince Levantine origins. The tombs are of the vaulted mudbrick chamber type with donkey sacrifices appearing outside some of these tombs, normally in pairs. Similar tombs with donkey sacrifices are attested at Tell el-Maskhuta, Inshas, and Tell el-Farasha in Egypt and at Jericho, Lachish, and Tell el-ʿAjjul in the Levant. In addition, a large Canaanite temple complex has been discovered at Tell el-Dabʿa. Finally, items such as bronze daggers and axheads, jugs, and toggle pins confirm Canaanite derivation.

Textual evidence includes a slave list (Papyrus Brooklyn 35.1446) and the Execration Texts (Berlin-Mirgissa group). The slave list (dating from the 13th dynasty) consists of 77 legible names of slaves, out of which 48 are clearly Asiatic. The Execration Texts (ca. 1850-1750) reflect the magical annihilation of persons and things inimical to Pharaoh and Egypt. While these texts reflect the full range of Egyptian enemies, in the Asiatic sections they combine the *ḥq3w* of the cities of coastal Syria-Palestine with the *ʿ3mw* of the area. They are therefore an indirect witness to Hyksos origins.

Rise to Power

Scholars have long debated the arrival of the Hyksos in Egypt. For years, many scholars argued for an infiltration model in which the Hyksos assumption of power was a peaceful takeover from within by a racial element already in the majority (at least in the eastern Delta).

More recently, Egyptologists seem to understand the Hyksos takeover in more complex terms. While for a number of centuries West Semitic immigrants had infiltrated into the Delta and settled there and had, in fact, served in Egyptian paramilitary units, it may be misleading to place too much emphasis on this process of immigration as an antecedent to Hyksos rule, for the foreignness of the Hyksos was evidently something which left a deep impression on the Egyptians. Although the contemporary Egyptian sources (e.g., the Kamose stelae) are highly ideological, they nevertheless form important witnesses to a more complex process in the Hyksos ascension to power. At the beginning of the Hyksos period, a combination of various Levantine groups/tribes immigrated into the eastern Delta, as well as more mobile fighting groups, perhaps centered on or in loose federation with a main military group that fanned out and took over various Delta cities (though also leaving others still in the charge of their Egyptian rulers). Destruction levels noted at some eastern Delta sites, including Tell el-Dab'a, may record some of the more serious conflicts and indicate something more than just a peaceful infiltration.

It has sometimes been argued that the Hyksos conquered Egypt because they had superior weapons (esp. the horse and chariot). However, there is no archaeological or textual support that the Hyksos introduced the horse and chariot to Egypt or that these provided the Hyksos with the military superiority to overwhelm Syria and Egypt. This seems also to apply to the Hyksos "sloping glacis" fortifications.

End of Rule

The only potential rival to the Hyksos 15th Dynasty was in Upper Egypt, where a rump state centered at Thebes had survived the fall of the 13th Dynasty. Being hedged in by the kingdom of Kush to the south (a Hyksos ally) and the Hyksos themselves to the north, the early rulers of the 17th Dynasty that ruled this bantam state felt compelled to acknowledge Hyksos suzerainty. The political expedient of accommodation with the Hyksos promoted a political paralysis that the last rulers of the 17th Dynasty finally repudiated. Initially, Seqenenre T'aa II led a revolt against the Hyksos. But when he died in battle, his brother Kamose led a number of successful raids on Kushite territory and then on Avaris itself. Finally, Ahmose routed the Asiatics in a series of campaigns against their bases in the Delta and in Canaan itself (including the fortress at Sharuhen).

The extent of Egyptian involvement in the destructions of Middle Bronze IIC sites in Canaan after the expulsion of the Hyksos has been debated. The evidence seems to indicate a complex scenario involving a combination of factors: internal strife, conflicts between neighboring states, Egyptian campaigns, economic crisis.

Impact

The Hyksos occupation was a watershed in Egyptian history. Up to that point, the Egyptians, despite periods of internal political chaos, had been free from invasion. Generations of Egyptians would be haunted by the specter of foreign domination. The aggressive imperialism of the New Kingdom was, no doubt, a by-product of the Hyksos domination. This ideological stance may possibly serve as a backdrop to the political situation described in Exod. 1.

Bibliography. M. Bietak, *Avaris, the Capital of the Hyksos* (London, 1996): 225-90; W. G. Dever, "'Hyksos,' Egyptian Destructions, and the End of the Palestinian Middle Bronze Age," *Levant* 22 (1990): 75-81; B. J. Kemp, "Old Kingdom, Middle Kingdom and Second Intermediate Period *c.* 2686–1552 B.C.," in B. G. Trigger, et al., *Ancient Egypt: A Social History* (Cambridge, 1983), 149-82; E. D. Oren, ed., *The Hyksos: New Archaeological and Historical Perspectives* (Philadelphia, 1997); D. B. Redford, *Egypt, Canaan, and Israel in Ancient Times* (Princeton, 1992); H. S. Smith and A. Smith, "A Reconsideration of the Kamose Texts," *ZÄS* 103 (1976): 48-76; J. Van Seters, *The Hyksos* (New Haven, 1966).

K. LAWSON YOUNGER, JR.

HYMENAEUS (Gk. *Hyménaios*)

An opponent of Paul, named after the Greek god of marriage. Hymenaeus is mentioned with the false teachers Alexander (1 Tim. 1:19-20) and Philetus (2 Tim. 2:17-18). He is said to have abandoned the faith by teaching that the final resurrection had already taken place. Paul "turned [him] over to Satan" (i.e., excluded him from the Church) so that Hymenaeus might learn not to blaspheme (1 Tim. 1:20).

HYMNS, EARLY CHRISTIAN

Like the spokes of a wheel, canonical hymns display characteristics which are further developed in subsequent Christian circles to the 6th century. For example, the hymns in Revelation may reflect Roman court ceremonial, just as the symposium by Methodius of Olympus reflects dynamics of the ceremony of installation for the Roman consul Ausonius. Revelation's hymns are often structured antiphonally (chs. 4-5), a dynamic later brought to the Western Church by Ambrose. The phenomenon of martyrdom in the Revelation hymns is celebrated later by Pope Damasus, whose treatment of Agnes' martyrdom, however, lacks the explicit eroticism of the poetic treatment of Agnes by the Latin Father Prudentius. The Alleluia sung in Rev. 19 later punctuates hymns in the Odes of Solomon and is warmly welcomed by Hilary, Jerome, and Augustine as a liturgical exercise. Also, the interplay in Revelation between hymn-singing and silence in heaven (Rev. 7:10–8:1) has its analogue in hymns in the Acts of John and in the Paschal Homily of Melito of Sardis, which strike a balance between apophatic and kataphatic worship. The actual music involved in hymnic singing is scantily attested. The earliest sample is found in the musical notation of the 3rd-century Oxyrhynchus Papyrus 1786, a hymn praising the Christian God. Revelation's portrayal of instrumental accompaniment to its hymns may not of itself be sufficient to demonstrate the use of certain instruments by that community, but is at the cusp of an ensuing debate among the church fathers about the propriety of using certain instruments or any instruments at all as hymnic accompaniment.

Paul assumes that Christians who come together will spontaneously sing hymns (Gk. *psalmós,* 1 Cor. 14:26), and this practice is continued in the group reported by the Roman governor Pliny to the Emperor Trajan. However, recent studies ask if some of the materials often identified as hymnic in the Pauline corpus and in the Gospels in fact were ever sung at all but perhaps are ad hoc literary creations having closer affinities with literary encomia. This may be especially true of the hymns in Luke 1-2 and that in John 1, and in that regard they would anticipate productions such as Clement's hymn to Christ the Educator. However one decides that issue, the Lucan hymns show a strong interest in rooting the Jesus-event in the history of Israel, a trend which the Council of Laodicea (ca. 360) tried to encourage when it prohibited the production of nonbiblical hymns. The Johannine hymn marks the beginning of a trend toward celebrating Jesus using philosophical categories. Many of the hymns in the Nag Hammadi library celebrate Jesus using terms such as "form" and "matter" (Tripartite Tractate) and above all "gnosis"/knowledge (Naasene hymn), whereas the hymnic presentation of knowledge in the Acts of Andrew has a meaning determined by the cross of Jesus. The hymns of Arius in honor of Jesus as creature — albeit exceptional creature — elicit strong counter-efforts in the hymns of Athanasius, who embodies the faith of Nicea.

The almost equal number of syllables in most of the lines in 1 Tim. 3:16 displays an attention to rhythmic regularity which comes to accomplished fruition in Clement's hymn to Christ the Educator. The metric difference of the line "seen by angels/ messengers" in the Pauline verse is for some commentators a sign of editorial tampering and anticipates widespread redaction of later hymnic pieces such as those in the Apostolic Constitutions, presumably in order to make the hymns reflect current practice. Attention to the divine Name and the name of Jesus, present in Phil. 2:6-11, is continued in the hymnic portions of the Gospel of the Egyptians and the Odes of Solomon as well as in hymns of the Acts of Thomas. The hymnic presentation of Christ as image of God in whom sin is vanquished (Col. 1:15-20) is present in Ambrose's celebration of a humanity renewed morally by the Christ-event *(Aeterno Rerum Conditor).* That this Colossian Christ fulfills its role as image of God when it sings God's glory is a leitmotif also present in Ephrem's Nisibene hymn 50.

Although one cannot be certain about the pure novelty of some post-NT developments in Christian hymnody, some hymnic characteristics do seem to be developments which respond to issues different from those faced during the period of production of canonical literature. Ignatius *Eph.* 19 includes an explicit attack on the perduring attractiveness of magic in the empire. The issue of Christ's death as "sacrifice" makes explicit a motif perhaps only implicit in the canonical hymns (Melito of Sardis *Homily on the Pasch*). Dance is mentioned in the hymnic portions of the Acts of John and in the Easter hymn of Hippolytus. Prayers celebrating the Virgin's role in making Christ available are especially prominent in the Eastern Church, where numerous hymns designed for use at specific times of day were also being crafted (Gospel of Bartholomew, Cyril of Alexandria, Gregory Nazianzus). There may also be evidence that some Scriptures were being chanted in this period, which also witnesses hymnic intercessions for holders of specific church offices.

On the frontiers of research in this area one may ask about the way in which early Christian theologizing was affected by the intertwined phenomena of Hellenistic music theory and early Christian anthropology.

Bibliography. Editions of texts: F. F. Church and T. J. Mulry, *The Macmillan Book of Earliest Christian Hymns* (New York, 1988); M. Kiley, ed., *Prayer from Alexander to Constantine: A Critical Anthology* (London, 1997); E. Lodi, *Enchiridion Euchologicum fontium liturgicum.* Bibliotheca Ephemerides Liturgicae Subsidia 15 (Rome, 1979). Studies: E. Foley, *Foundations of Christian Music: The Music of Pre-Constantinian Christianity* (Collegeville, 1996); "Liturgical Music: A Bibliographic Essay," in *Liturgy and Music,* ed. R. A. Leaver and J. A. Zimmerman (Collegeville, 1998), 411-53; R. J. Karris, *A Symphony of New Testament Hymns* (Collegeville, 1996); H. M. Schueller, *The Idea of Music: An Introduction to Musical Aesthetics in Antiquity and the Middle Ages* (Kalamazoo, 1988).

MARK KILEY

HYRCANUS (Gk. *Hyrkanos)*

1. The son of Tobias (2 Macc. 3:11), but according to Josephus, the youngest son of Joseph and grandson of Tobias (*Ant.* 12.160, 186). From a family of prominent financiers, Hyrcanus donated generously to the temple treasury, and was also admired by Ptolemy for his magnanimity (*Ant.* 12.219). A pro-Egyptian stance forced Hyrcanus east of the Jordan where he built a fortress at ʿArâq el-Emîr. Hyrcanus committed suicide when the Seleucid king Antiochus IV Epiphanes rose to power (*Ant.* 12.236).

2. John (Johanan) Hyrcanus, Hasmonean high priest and ethnarch of Judea 135/4-104 B.C.E.; son of Simon Maccabeus, grandson of Mattathias. Under the leadership of John Hyrcanus, who spent most of his life in battle, an independent Judean state was greatly enlarged.

In 134, when his brother-in-law Ptolemy murdered his father, John Hyrcanus escaped to Jerusalem (1 Macc. 16:11-22; Josephus *Ant.* 13.228-29; *BJ* 1.54-55). According to Josephus Hyrcanus then besieged Ptolemy at Jericho, but Ptolemy held Hyrcanus' mother and brothers captive, threatening to throw them off the city wall if Hyrcanus did not withdraw. This delay took the siege into the Sabbatical year and the campaign was abandoned. Before

Ptolemy fled, however, he killed them (*Ant.* 13.235; *BJ* 1.60).

During Hyrcanus' first year of rule, Antiochus VII Euergetes (Sidetes) besieged him in Jerusalem. When Hyrcanus requested a truce in order to observe the Feast of Tabernacles, Antiochus sent sacrificial gifts to be offered at the temple. Encouraged by this response, Hyrcanus inquired about a settlement. The Syrian army departed after an agreement that the Jews give up their arms, pay tribute for Joppa and other towns outside Judea, and surrender hostages. In addition, Hyrcanus was compelled to pay 500 silver talents (*Ant.* 13.247). Hyrcanus then joined Antiochus in battle against the Parthians. Amply funded by 3000 talents taken from King David's tomb, Hyrcanus became the first Hasmonean to recruit mercenaries (*Ant.* 13.249).

In 129, when Antiochus died in the Parthian campaign, his successor Demetrius II immediately became involved in internal struggles. Hyrcanus took advantage of the weakened Syrian Empire by no longer paying tribute and by marching into Transjordan, conquering Medeba. Hyrcanus then turned north, capturing Shechem and Mt. Gerizim, there destroying the rival Samaritan temple. Again he turned south, attacking the Idumeans, taking Dora and Marissa, forcing the Idumeans to submit to circumcision and to Jewish law (*Ant.* 13.255-57). During his later years, Hyrcanus attacked Samaria and, after a lengthy siege, completely razed the city (*Ant.* 13.281).

Josephus attributes the gift of prophecy to Hyrcanus, relating that Hyrcanus learned about his victory over Samaria from a heavenly voice as he was presenting burnt offerings in the temple at Jerusalem (*Ant.* 13.282, 300; *BJ* 1.68).

Internal divisions involved Hyrcanus in the emerging struggle for power between the Pharisees and the Sadducees. Gradually, he shifted from Pharisee to Sadducee, finally abolishing Pharisaic rulings.

3. Hyrcanus II, elder son of Alexander Janneus and Alexandra Salome, grandson of John Hyrcanus; Hasmonean high priest (76-67, 63-40 B.C.E.) and ethnarch of Judea (47-40).

Regarded as heir to the throne, Hyrcanus II was appointed high priest during the reign of his mother (Josephus *Ant.* 13.408; *BJ* 1.109). In 67, when Alexandra died, Hyrcanus' more capable younger brother Aristobulus II challenged him for power, defeated him in battle, and forced him to surrender. While Aristobulus ruled as high priest and ethnarch, Hyrcanus accepted the advice of the Idumean governor Antipater to seek refuge and support in Petra from the Nabatean king Aretas. Antipater urged Aretas to commit his army on behalf of Hyrcanus in return for territory lost in previous wars. In 65 Aretas joined forces with Hyrcanus, besieging Aristobulus in Jerusalem, just when Pompey appeared in the east with the military forces of Rome. Both Aristobulus and Hyrcanus appealed to one of Pompey's officers, Scaurus. At first, Scaurus decided against Hyrcanus, preferring the wealthier and more politically astute Aristobulus (*Ant.* 14.30). However, Pompey, suspicious of Aristobulus, preferred the more malleable Hyrcanus, whom he appointed high priest over a smaller Judea and from whom he demanded tribute (*Ant.* 14.73).

In return for military support in Egypt, Julius Caesar appointed Hyrcanus ethnarch and high priest (*Ant.* 14.137, 143-48). Through Caesar and the Roman senate, Hyrcanus did much to enhance the lives of the Jews in the Diaspora. Yet internally, Hyrcanus could not sustain his power against the rise of Antipater and his sons, Phasael and Herod. The weakness of Hyrcanus was clearly exposed during Herod's trial (*Ant.* 14.169-70). In 40 Hyrcanus was taken prisoner by Antigonus, son of Aristobulus, and the Parthians. To disqualify Hyrcanus from a return to the high priesthood, they cut off his ears (*Ant.* 14.366). For a few years Hyrcanus lived peacefully in Babylonia. Then Herod, who married Hyrcanus' granddaughter Mariamme, invited him to live once again in Jerusalem. In 30 Herod executed Hyrcanus (*Ant.* 15.173, 181).

Bibliography. L. L. Grabbe, *Judaism from Cyrus to Hadrian,* 2 vols. (Minneapolis; 1992); E. Bickerman, *The God of the Maccabees.* SJLA 32 (Leiden, 1979); M. Hengel, *Judaism and Hellenism,* 2 vols. (Philadelphia, 1974); E. Schürer, *The History of the Jewish People in the Age of Jesus Christ (125 B.C.–A.D. 135),* rev. ed., 4 vols. (Edinburgh, 1973-1987); V. Tcherikover, *Hellenistic Civilization and the Jews* (1959, repr. New York, 1970).

LYNNE ALCOTT KOGEL

HYSSOP

In biblical usage a plant of uncertain identity. The caperbush (*Capparis spinosa* L.) is one of several candidates. It often grows in the crevices of walls, it would sprinkle liquid well, and its branches can be quite long. The Syrian hyssop (*Origanum syriacum* L.), which grows on rocks in Egypt and Israel, is also a possibility, as are some varieties of marjoram (*Origanum maru*). In any case, biblical hyssop is not European hyssop (*Hyssopus officinalis* L.), which does not grow in Egypt or Israel. Many scholars have suggested that Heb. *'ēzôḇ* refers to a number of plants and that the LXX rendering *hýssōpos* may have been an error due to the similarity of their sounds. The plant referred to as hyssop at John 19:29 may instead be Jerusalem corn (*Sorghum vulgare* var. *durra* [Forsk.] Dinsm.).

The Israelites used hyssop to daub blood on their door posts for the Passover (Exod. 12:22). Other passages associate hyssop with cleansing (e.g., Lev. 14:4, 6, 49-52; Num. 19:6; Ps. 51:7[MT 9]). Solomon knew of "the hyssop that grows in the wall" (1 Kgs. 4:33 NRSV). John notes that Jesus, while on the cross, sipped sour wine from a sponge raised on a branch of hyssop (John 19:29), but Matthew and Mark describe it as a reed (Gk. *kálamos;* Matt. 27:48; Mark 15:36).

Bibliography. H. N. Moldenke and A. L. Moldenke, *Plants of the Bible* (1952, repr. New York, 1986); M. Zohary, *Plants of the Bible* (London, 1982).

MEGAN BISHOP MOORE

I

I AM WHO I AM
Explanation of Yahweh, the covenant name of the God of Israel, given to Moses when he encountered the burning bush (Exod. 3:14; Heb. *'ehyeh 'ăšer 'ehyeh*). It is also rendered "I will be what I will be" or perhaps "I create what(ever) I create."

See Yahweh. Robert E. Stone, II

IBHAR (Heb. *yiḇḥār*)
A son of David, born in Jerusalem (2 Sam. 5:15 = 1 Chr. 14:5; 3:6).

IBLEAM (Heb. *yiḇlĕʻām*)
A city located within the tribal boundaries of Issachar and Asher but given to the tribe of Manasseh (Josh. 17:11-12; Judg. 1:27). The city was not conquered until the time of the United Monarchy. It may have been allotted to the Levites (Josh. 21:25 LXX; cf. Bileam in 1 Chr. 6:70). Pharaoh Thutmose III (15th century B.C.) lists Ibleam among his conquered cities.

Ahaziah, king of Judah, was fatally wounded near Ibleam (2 Kgs. 9:27). Jehu's soldiers had chased the king to a point near the ascent of Gur before they struck him; he died at Megiddo. Zechariah, king of Israel, may also have been assassinated at a place called Ieblaam/Ibleam (2 Kgs. 15:10 LXX^{L}; MT "in front of the people").

The site is identified with Khirbet Belʻameh (177205), ca. 1.6 km. (1 mi.) S of Jenin and 16 km. (10 mi.) SE of Megiddo. The Romans called the site Belemot. Ibleam, undoubtedly a fortress city, guarded one of the routes that provided access through the Jezreel Valley. Stephen Von Wyrick

IBNEIAH (Heb. *yiḇnĕyâ*)
A Benjaminite who lived in postexilic Jerusalem; the son of Jeroham (1 Chr. 9:8).

IBNIJAH (Heb. *yiḇnîyâ*)
A Benjaminite, ancestor of Reuel who dwelled in postexilic Jerusalem (1 Chr. 9:8).

IBRI (Heb. *ʻiḇrî*)
The son of Jaaziah, a Merarite Levite whose position was determined by lot (1 Chr. 24:27).

IBSAM (Heb. *yiḇśām*)
A descendant of Tolah, from the tribe of Issachar (1 Chr. 7:2).

IBZAN (Heb. *'iḇṣān*)
A minor judge who governed Israel for seven years after the time of Jephthah (Judg. 12:8-10). His home was Bethlehem in Zebulun, NE of Nazareth on its border with Asher (cf. Josh. 19:15). No more is known of Ibzan other than that he had 30 sons and 30 daughters, all of whom married outside the clan.

ICHABOD (Heb. *'îḵāḇôḏ*)
The son of Phinehas and grandson of Eli. His mother, who died at his birth, named him in response to the Philistine capture of the ark of the covenant (1 Sam. 4:22; "Alas! For the Glory" or "Where is the Glory?" referring to the "glory" or presence of Yahweh).

ICHTHYS
Transliteration of the Greek word for "fish." In Greek the five letters form an acrostic, "Jesus Christ, God's Son, Savior." Hence very early in Christian history the fish became a symbol for Christians. Among the earlier references indicating this fact, Tertullian refers to Christians as "little fishes after the example of our *ichthys* Jesus Christ" (*De bapt.* 1). Jesus' statement that his disciples would become fishers of men (Matt. 4:19) probably aided the development of this symbolism.

Joe E. Lunceford

ICONIUM (Gk. *Ikónion*)
A city located on a high plateau in south central Asia Minor, modern Konya, Turkey. The first literary mention of Iconium is in connection with Cyrus' visit to the city (Xenophon *Anab.* 1.2.13-14). Iconium was economically prosperous because it

was both agriculturally productive and strategically situated on several major trade routes. Its position on the border between the tableland of Lycaonia to the southeast and rugged Phrygia to the west caused its fluctuating ties between the two regions. Phrygians settled the city, but the Seleucids and later the Romans made it a chief city of Lycaonia.

Paul and Barnabas visited Iconium and won many converts among both Jews and Gentiles (Acts 13:51–14:21). However, social unrest caused the two missionaries to flee to Lystra and Derbe (cf. 2 Tim. 3:11). During the "second missionary journey," Paul and Silas visited these same cities for the purpose of strengthening the believers (Acts 15:36–16:6), and Paul may have visited Iconium again on the return leg of his "third missionary journey" (18:23). According to Acts a certain Gaius was from Iconium, and Timothy, who was from the region, had a good reputation in the city. The 2nd-century apocryphal Acts of Paul sets the legendary material about Paul and Thecla in Iconium. The church at Iconium was an important early Christian center, and a church council met there in A.D. 235.

Bibliography. C. A. Hemer, *The Book of Acts in the Setting of Hellenistic History.* WUNT 49 (Tübingen, 1989); S. E. Johnson, *Paul the Apostle and His Cities* (Wilmington, 1987).

PAUL ANTHONY HARTOG

IDALAH (Heb. *yiḏˀālâ*)

A city in the tribal territory of Zebulun (Josh. 19:15). In the Talmud it is called Ḥuryēh (*y. Meg.* 1). The site is modern Khirbet el-Ḥawârah (167236), 1 km. (.6 mi.) S of Bethlehem (**1**) in Zebulun.

IDBASH (Heb. *yiḏbāš*)

A son of Etam, from the tribe of Judah (1 Chr. 4:3).

IDDO (also ADAIAH, JADDAI)

The English translation of three distinct Hebrew names.

1. (Heb. *ˀiddô, ˀiddō*ˀ) The father of Ahinadab, one of Solomon's 12 district administrators (1 Kgs. 4:14). The ancient textual versions give this figure varying names.

2. A Levite descended from Gershom (1 Chr. 6:21[MT 6]). He is also called Adaiah (**2**; 1 Chr. 6:41[26]), and identified as an ancestor of Asaph.

3. A prophet credited with authoring a *midraš*, a "written investigation" of history (2 Chr. 9:29 [K *yeˀdî,* Q *yeˀdô*]; 12:15; 13:22). A work separate from the official Judean annals, this history must have been associated with the scribal activities of a prophetic circle with some independent power within the Jerusalemite court. The Chronicler cites the history as a source of the activities of Solomon, Rehoboam, and Abijah.

4. The grandfather of the prophet Zechariah (Zech. 1:1, 7; cf. Ezra 5:1; 6:14; 1 Esdr. 6:1; NRSV "son"). Iddo was a priest in charge of one of the priestly families that returned to Yehud from Babylonian Exile (Neh. 12:4). Zechariah eventually officiated as head of his priestly household (Neh.

12:16). Given the Zecharian traditions' kinship to those of Ezekiel, the priesthood branch of Iddo and Zechariah is best considered to be Zadokite.

5. (*yiddô, yaddô, yadday*) A tribal leader under David (1 Chr. 27:21). He was responsible for the half-tribe of Manasseh, in Gilead.

6. A Yehudite who had married a foreign woman (Ezra 10:43; 1 Esdr. 9:35). Most English translations render this figure's name "Jaddai."

7. (*ˀiddô*) A Judean leader in a diaspora settlement in Casiphia, in Babylon (Ezra 8:17; cf. 1 Esdr. 8:45-46). Ezra sent to him for Levites and Nethinim to serve in the Second Temple. STEPHEN L. COOK

IDOL, IDOLATRY

Some sort of physical representation of a deity. "Idol" is used to translate a number of words in the OT, most commonly Heb. *ˀĕlîlîm, gillûlîm, ˁăṣabbîm* (and its one-time variant *ˁōṣeḇ*), *pesel* and the related *pĕsîlîm.* It also can be used to translate Heb. *semel* (otherwise rendered as "image" or "figure"), *massēḵâ* and the less common *nesek* (otherwise rendered as "molten" or "cast image"), *tĕrāpîm* (otherwise transliterated as "teraphim" or translated as "household gods"), *šiqqûṣ* (otherwise translated as "detestable thing" or "abomination"), *ˀāwen* (otherwise a more abstract noun meaning "idolatry" or more generally "wickedness"), and *heḇel* (also a more abstract noun meaning that which is evanescent or unsubstantial). In the NT "idol" translates Gk. *eídōlon.* These terms differ somewhat in their specifics: e.g., *semel* refers generally to some sort of statue or free-standing image (2 Chr. 33:7, 15; Deut. 4:16); *pesel/pĕsîlîm* also refer to a free-standing statue carved from wood or stone (Deut. 7:5; Isa. 44:15, 17; 45:20) or cast of metal (Judg. 17:3, 4; Hab. 2:18; 2 Chr. 34:7); *gillûlîm* likewise can refer to a wood, stone, or metal statue (e.g., Deut. 29:17), but when the material used to make *ˁăṣabbîm* is identified, it is always metal (Hos. 8:4; 13:2; Ps. 115:4). Some terms for "idol" have implicit within them a value judgment: to speak of *ˀĕlîlîm,* a term which comes from a root meaning "weak" or "insignificant," is to offer a negative opinion about the worthlessness of idols; the more general meanings of "wickedness" for *ˀāwen* and "unsubstantial" for *heḇel* also indicate that a pejorative judgment is being made when these terms mean "idol." Gk. *eídōlon,* which means both "image" and "phantom," conveys a pejorative sense as well.

The reason idols are so negatively judged in the Bible is that they represent the religions of the nations, from which both the Israel of the OT and the nascent Christianity of the NT are commanded to separate themselves. In the OT, the book of Deuteronomy lists the making of idols as one of the abominations of the nations whom the Hebrews are to supplant in the land of Israel (Deut. 7:5, 25; 12:3; 29:17[MR 16]), and this sentiment is also expressed in the historical books stemming from the Deuteronomistic school. In 1 Sam. 31:9; 1 Kgs. 21:26; 2 Kgs. 17:15, e.g., idols are described as a despised component of the religions of, respectively, the Philistines, Amorites, and the nations in general.

The prophetic books further depict idol worship as a foreign abhorrence: in Isaiah idols are associated with the religion of the Egyptians (Isa. 19:1, 3) and the Babylonians (46:1), and in Jeremiah idols are likewise associated with Babylon (Jer. 50:2, 38; 51:52) and more generally with foreigners (8:19; 14:22). The same sentiment is found in the Psalms (Ps. 96:5; 106:38; 135:15) and in the NT, particularly in Acts (17:16) and the letters of Paul (1 Cor. 8).

While elsewhere in their condemnations of their neighbors the biblical writers can be guilty of polemic and hyperbole, in the case of idol worship the Bible's portrait seems fairly accurate. Both archaeological and textual evidence from throughout the West Semitic and eastern Mediterranean worlds indicate that the use of images to represent the deity was the norm in West Asian religious traditions. These images were most typically in the form of statues, although carved reliefs and wall paintings are attested. Statues, often life-sized, stood in temples and other sacred spaces, were the recipients of sacrifice and libations, and received votive offerings and prayers. They were also clothed and could be bathed. In certain ways, then, they were imagined as "alive," to the degree at least that the god was perceived to be somehow present or manifest within the image and to share its fortunes or, on occasion, misfortunes (e.g., when the cult statue of the Philistine god Dagon falls and loses both head and hands before Israel's ark of the covenant, it is as if Dagon has himself been defeated by the power of the Israelite God; 1 Sam. 5:1-5).

With respect to the biblical insistence on the lack of idols in Israel, assessing the accuracy of the biblical record, especially that of the OT, is a more complicated task. The OT's legal tradition is emphatic that the Israelites should employ no idols in the worship of their God. The most famous text rejecting Israelite idolatry is the Second Commandment: "You shall not make for yourself an idol, whether in the form of anything that is in heaven above, or that is on the earth beneath, or that is in the water under the earth" (Exod. 20:4; cf. 34:17; Lev. 19:4; 26:1; Deut. 5:8-10). Yet the narrative traditions, especially those that describe Israel's early history, are rife with accounts that involve the presence of idols, both idols of other gods and, it seems, of the God of Israel, and in these accounts, no negative judgment is rendered. Indeed, a positive judgment is often implied. Rachel's theft of her father Laban's household gods or teraphim is viewed as a good thing, as it helps her husband Jacob part from his father-in-law with the property that was rightfully his (Gen. 31:19-55[MT 32:1]). King Saul's daughter Michal is also seen as doing a good thing when she places a teraphim in her bed as a replacement for her husband David, thus helping David escape from the murderous rage of his father-in-law (the teraphim used here is presumably a full-sized figure rather than the more miniature statues Rachel stole). In Judges Micah has a shrine in which there are an ephod and a teraphim and over which a Levite, a member of Israel's priestly tribe, presides; the text invokes no note of censure (Judg. 17:5, 7-13). This man Micah has previously been expiated from stealing 1100 pieces of silver from his mother by the mother's giving of two hundred of the coins "to make an image of cast metal" (Judg. 17:1-4), and this also seems to be a laudable action from the text's point of view. Moreover, since the mother consecrated her silver "to the Lord," the implication is that the image she had cast is of the Israelite God.

Even the text that is often considered to describe the most heinous episode of idol worship in the OT, Aaron's making of the golden calf (Exod. 32), is ultimately ambivalent in its sense of what constitutes the proper and improper use of images in Israel. Note that after casting the calf Aaron declares that the next day will be a cult holiday for the Lord (Exod. 32:5), suggesting that he sees the calf as an icon appropriate to Israel's worship of its God. Since Aaron is never punished for making the calf, and, indeed, since he is elsewhere lauded as the ancestor of the priesthood of the Jerusalem temple, the impression is that many others in biblical tradition shared Aaron's judgment that the calf was an acceptable icon in the cult. Certainly Jeroboam, the first king of Israel's northern kingdom, seems to have seen the icon as appropriate, as he installed two images of bulls in the cult centers at Bethel and Dan to represent the presence of God there (1 Kgs. 12:25-33).

Archaeologists have posited that a small bronze statue of a bull found at a 12th-century site in the northern Samaritan hills represents an early Israelite icon of God as a bull or, possibly, represents an icon of a bull throne on which the Israelite God is to be imagined as sitting invisibly. This latter interpretation thus understands the bull as an object parallel to the ark of the covenant, which is often described as the footstool of a throne on which God invisibly sits (cf. 1 Chr. 28:2). But while understanding the Samaritan bull as the throne of God rather than an actual image of the divine mitigates somewhat its "idolatrous" nature, there still must be explained a small bronze of a seated figure that comes from 11th-century Hazor. Although this statue bears a striking resemblance to Canaanite representations of the god El, by the 11th century Hazor was a major city of the Israelite north, and so the figurine is most plausibly understood as a representation of Israel's God. Certainly, it is clear from other evidence that in Israelite religion God takes over many of El's attributes. If, moreover, the Israelite God takes over El's consort, the goddess Asherah, as many scholars now suggest, then the many images the Bible describes as being erected in honor of this goddess might also be seen as a legitimate part of Israelite religion, despite once more the legal traditions that condemn Israel's use of idols.

Whatever ambivalences we find regarding idols in these earlier Israelite materials, by the end of the Babylonian Exile ca. 539 those who worship idols suffer wholesale condemnation. The 6th-century part of Isaiah, e.g., contains several noteworthy texts presenting the worship of idols as futile and even absurd (Isa. 41:21-29; 44:9-20; 45:20-25; 46:1-13). This sentiment carries through into the NT period, where idolatry has so disappeared that it goes completely unmentioned in the Gospels. The issue of the worship of idols only surfaces as early Christians move into the gentile world and confront the use of images in Greek and Roman tradition. The most significant text in this regard is 1 Cor. 8, where Paul discusses whether Christians can eat meat sacrificed to the idols of Greek and Roman gods. At one level, Paul's answer is yes, as he has inherited from his Jewish past an understanding that idols are meaningless images and thus an understanding that the meat sacrificed to them is no different than any other. Yet because Paul wishes to give his followers a clear impression of the distinctiveness of their faith, he advises against eating the meat since some who witnessed Christians doing so might conclude that Christianity was, in fact, just like the gentile religions it sought to replace.

Bibliography. S. Ackerman, *Under Every Green Tree: Popular Religion in Sixth-Century Judah.* HSM 46 (Atlanta, 1992); W. G. Dever, "Archaeology Reconstructs the Lost Background of the Israelite Cult," in *Recent Archaeological Discoveries and Biblical Research* (Seattle, 1990), 119-66; "The Contribution of Archaeology to the Study of Canaanite and Early Israelite Religion," in *Ancient Israelite Religion,* ed. P. D. Miller, P. D. Hanson, and S. D. McBride (Philadelphia, 1987), 209-47; J. Faur, "The Biblical Idea of Idolatry," *JQR* 69 (1978): 1-15; J. Gutmann, "The 'Second Commandment' and the Image in Judaism," *HUCA* 32 (1961): 161-74; J. S. Holladay, "Religion in Israel and Judah Under the Monarchy," in *Ancient Israelite Religion,* 249-99; S. M. Olyan, *Asherah and the Cult of Yahweh in Israel.* SBLMS 34 (Atlanta, 1988); W. L. Willis, *Idol Meat in Corinth.* SBLDS 68 (Chico, 1985).

SUSAN ACKERMAN

IDUMEA (Gk. *Idoumaía, Idouméa*)

Designation used in the Hellenistic age for the territory stretching north to south from the southern portion of the Judean hill country to the northern part of the Negeb, and east to west from the Judean desert to the Philistine cities of Gaza and Ashdod. Its major cities included Hebron, Marisa, Adora, and Betabris. The population of the region included many Edomites, driven from their ancestral lands by the incursion of the Arabic Nabateans. It may well be from these peoples that the land derives its name (Gk. "of the Edomites," or perhaps a Hellenistic form of Semitic *'dm,* "earth"). Other inhabitants of the region included Arabs, Jews, Sidonians, and Nabateans.

Idumea was conquered by John Hyrcanus in 129 B.C.E., and its native population was forced to undergo circumcision and Judaization (1 Macc. 4:36-59; 2 Macc. 10:1-8). Soon after, the Idumeans were incorporated into the Hasmonean Empire. Alexander Janneus appointed an Idumean named Antipater as governor of the region, and he was succeeded by his son, also named Antipater. This Antipater urged the Hasmonean Hyrcanus II to contend with his brother Aristobulus II for the high priesthood (Josephus *Ant.* 14.8). He was also the father of Herod the Great, who was appointed king of Judea by the Roman senate in 39 B.C.E.

Idumea served as an important power base for Herod throughout his reign. After his death in 4 B.C.E., when his kingdom was divided Idumea fell to the ethnarch Archelaus (*Ant.* 17.319; *BJ* 2.93-98), who ruled until 6 C.E. Between 41 and 44 C.E., it was part of the kingdom of Agrippa I (*Ant.* 19.25; *BJ* 2.215). Between 6 and 41 C.E., and after 44 C.E., it was ruled by the Roman procurators as part of the province of Syria.

At the outbreak of the First Jewish Revolt against Rome (67 C.E.), Idumea was assigned its own commanders (*BJ* 2.566). John of Gischala used Idumean soldiers in his attempt to wrest control of Jerusalem from the other rebel factions (*BJ* 4.224, 228-354). Idumea suffered greatly during the war, and its population was decimated. After the defeat of the rebels, Idumea was incorporated into the Roman province of Judea. Soon after, it ceases to appear in contemporary records.

Bibliography. I. Eph'al, *The Ancient Arabs* (Leiden, 1982); A. Kasher, *Jews, Idumeans, and Ancient Arabs* (Tübingen, 1988).

ANTHONY J. TOMASINO

IEZER (Heb. *'î'ezer*)

A descendant of Manasseh; eponymous ancestor of the Iezrites (Num. 26:30). The name is an abbreviated form of Abiezer.

IGAL (Heb. *yiḡ'āl*)

1. A spy from the tribe of Issachar sent by Moses to scout the land of Canaan (Num. 13:7).

2. The son of Nathan of Zobah; one of David's Thirty (2 Sam. 23:36). 1 Chr. 11:38 lists instead Joel the brother of Nathan.

3. A son of Shemaiah, and a descendant of Zerubbabel (1 Chr. 3:22).

IGDALIAH (Heb. *yiḡdalyāhû*)

A Rechabite, the father of Hanan, whose descendants or followers had a chamber in the temple (Jer. 35:4).

IGNATIUS OF ANTIOCH

Bishop of Antioch during the reign of the Emperor Trajan (98-117 C.E.). He was taken by Roman soldiers from Antioch to Rome, where he was martyred ca. 115. During this journey he wrote six letters to churches (Ephesians, Magnesians, Trallians, Romans, Philadelphians, Smyrnaeans) and one to Polycarp, bishop of Smyrna. A longer recension of Ignatius' letters includes six spurious letters. The so-called middle recension, which contains only the seven letters named above, agrees with the list given by Eusebius (*HE* 2.36). Scholars have usually grouped Ignatius' letters together with other contemporary Christian writings in a collection called the Apostolic Fathers.

Although Ignatius' letters lack the theological depth of Paul or John, they represent in several respects a development of Christian theology from the apostolic period to the 2nd century. The Christology of Ignatius has been called "a high Christology of Johannine inspiration." Actually Ignatius moves one step further in heightening Christology than anything in the NT. Although the NT is replete with statements of the lordship and divinity of Jesus Christ, nowhere is Jesus precisely identified as being God. Ignatius makes this identification 11 times, beginning in the very salutation of his first letter, Ephesians, which refers to "Jesus Christ our God." Yet his Christology is in no way docetic. In *Smyrn.* 2.2 he refers to Jesus as "truly nailed for us in the flesh." The virgin birth and the Resurrection are important for Ignatius, but the Crucifixion is paramount. Nevertheless, he scarcely alludes to the teachings of Jesus and the events of his ministry.

The ecclesiology of Ignatius also represents a development beyond the NT. The apostles were the leaders of the earliest Church, with prophets and teachers and other spiritually gifted people forming lower ranks of leadership (1 Cor. 12:28). The deaths of the apostles usher in a new twofold church order of the offices of bishops and deacons. We see this church order in 1 Timothy and in 1 Clement and the Shepherd of Hermas in the Apostolic Fathers. Ignatius evidences movement to a threefold church order which will become the norm, of bishops, elders, and deacons. Ignatius particularly extols the office of bishop and in every letter except Romans exhorts his readers to obey the bishop. In *Eph.* 6.1 he says that "one must look upon the bishop as the Lord himself" and in *Magn.* 6.1 he says that the bishop presides in the place of God. Ignatius extols the partaking of the eucharist, though he does not speak of Christian baptism. He also notes that Christians no longer keep the sabbath (Saturday) but now celebrate the Lord's Day (Sunday).

Ignatius also goes beyond the NT in his development of a theology of martyrdom. His imagery of martyrdom, especially in *Rom.* 4–5, advances far beyond anything in the NT and points toward the theology of martyrdom that will motivate Christians through the next two centuries of Roman persecution. He himself genuinely longs for martyrdom, which he sees as true discipleship and a means to "attain to God" (*Rom.* 4.1). Ignatius received his wish in Rome toward the end of the reign of Trajan.

Bibliography. V. Corwin, *St. Ignatius and Christianity in Antioch* (New Haven, 1960); R. M. Grant, *The Apostolic Fathers,* 4: *Ignatius of Antioch* (Camden, 1966); W. R. Schoedel, *Ignatius of Antioch.* Herm (Philadelphia, 1985); M. P. Brown, *The Authentic Writings of Ignatius* (Durham, 1963).

J. Christian Wilson

IIM (Heb. *ʿîyîm*)
A town within the southern portion of Judah's inheritance (Josh. 15:29). The name is missing from similar lists recording towns reassigned to Simeon (Josh. 19:3; 1 Chr. 4:29). The context suggests a location in the Negeb, perhaps Deir el-Gawi (142068), 19 km. (12 mi.) NE of Beer-sheba.

Laura B. Mazow

IJON (Heb. *ʿiyôn*)
A small site in the southern Beqʿa Valley, on the modern Lebanon border near Merj ʿAyyûn (preserving the name; 212235), just N of Metulla on the Israel side. Most of the literary sources list Ijon together with Abel-beth-maʿacah, Dan (Laish), and Hazor in northern Israel — all border outposts between Israel and Aram-Naharaim, the Aramean states to the north.

Ijon is first mentioned in the 19th/early 18th-century B.C. Egyptian Execration Texts; later in the battle itinerary of Thutmose III on his first Asiatic campaign (ca. 1468; site no. 95 on the Karnak list); in the 14th-century Amarna Letters; and in biblical texts (1 Kgs. 15:20; 2 Chr. 16:4) as a town in Naphtali captured by Ben-hadad of Damascus. Ijon was also taken by Tiglath-pileser III ca. 733/732, during the reign of Pekah, along with Abel-beth-maʿacah (2 Kgs. 15:29), marking at that time the southern border of Aram under Assyrian rule.

Bibliography. W. G. Dever, "'Abel-Beth-Maʿacah: 'Northern Gateway of Ancient Israel,'" in *The Archaeology of Jordan and Other Studies,* ed. L. T. Geraty and L. G. Herr (Berrien Springs, 1986), 207-22; H. Tadmor, "The Southern Border of Aram," *IEJ* 12 (1962): 114-22.

William G. Dever

IKKESH (Heb. *ʿiqqēš*)
A man from Tekoa ("Tekoite"); the father of Ira, one of David's Champions (2 Sam. 23:26; 1 Chr. 11:28; 27:9).

ILAI (Heb. *ʿîlay*) (also ZALMON)
An Ahohite and one of David's warriors (1 Chr. 11:29). At 2 Sam. 23:28 he is called Zalmon.

ILLNESS AND HEALTH CARE
Healing practices have a long and complex history in biblical lands, and they should be treated as part of a health care system that includes, but is not limited to, the beliefs about the causes of illness, the options available to patients, and the role of governments in health care. Public hygiene, which refers broadly to the organized efforts of a community to promote health and prevent disease, is also part of any health care system.

Prehistoric and Early Periods

Hunter-gatherers in Syria-Palestine may have recognized the medicinal value of some plants and practiced some therapeutic rituals by the end of the Paleolithic era, the first period of human material culture ending approximately between 20,000-16,000 B.C.E. in the Near East.

During the Neolithic period (ca. 8500-4300) the domestication of animals probably introduced into human populations some new pools of diseases carried by animals (e.g., bovine tuberculosis). Human tuberculosis is reflected in skeletal material from Egypt and Bab edh-Dhra (Jordan) as early as the 4th millennium.

Throughout all prehistoric periods the family was probably the main caretaker for the ill. However, the long existence of healing specialists in Syria-Palestine is reflected in the trephinated skulls discovered at Neolithic Jericho, bone spatulas found at Tell Jemmeh (near Gaza) in the early 1st millennium, and the implantation of a bronze wire in a tooth at Horvat En Ziq, a small Nabatean fortress in the northern Negeb in the Hellenistic era. Liver models found at Hazor and Megiddo in the Late Bronze Age may have been used in medical consultations.

The Amarna Letters (14th century) mention epidemics and the traffic of physicians in Canaanite royal courts. Ugaritic texts (e.g., Keret Epic) indicate that El, the supreme god at Ugarit, was concerned with healing, especially infertility. In Tyre, Sidon, and other Phoenician city-states of the early 1st millennium, Eshmun was a healing god whose temples may have provided therapeutic services. Yahweh, Resheph, and other Near Eastern deities brought both disease and healing.

Preexilic Israel

Israel in the preexilic period probably shared many of the health problems that were common in Near Eastern settlements. The inadequate disposal of garbage and human waste was probably a constant threat to public health in Syria-Palestine. Towns (e.g., Gibeon) in areas of poor rainfall had to construct cisterns, which were vulnerable to contamination. Parts of Jericho, Tell Beit Mirsim, and other towns apparently had drains, some of which may have carried sewage, by the Middle or Late Bronze Ages. Although recent excavations in Jerusalem have recovered toilet seats (one of which was found in a separate cubicle of a house, dated to ca. 586), such amenities were probably uncommon in most of Israel.

Despite many textual references to washing and related hygienic activities (Gen. 18:4; Ps. 60:8[MT 10]), it is likely that personal hygiene was generally poor in the absence of abundant water supplies. Ruth 3:3 indicates that even bathing was sometimes seen as a special or uncommon event.

Archaeoparasitologists recently have established the probable existence of certain intestinal diseases (e.g., tapeworm [*taenia*] and whipworm [*trichuris trichiura*] infections) in ancient Israel, but the precise identification of most diseases in the Bible has been notoriously difficult, especially in cases of epidemics (Num. 25; 1 Sam. 5:6-12). Nonetheless, many plagues are viewed as the result of Israel's contact with outside groups (e.g., Midianites in Num. 25). The stories of the plagues on Egypt in Exod. 7–10 also recognize that epidemics can alter the course of history.

The condition usually translated as "leprosy" (Heb. *ṣāraʿaṭ*) receives the most attention in the Bible (Lev. 13–14), but it does not have a simple modern equivalent because it probably encompassed a large variety of diseases that produced a chronic discoloration of the skin. There are also various references to blindness (2 Sam. 5:8) and musculoskeletal disabilities (9:3). Infertility, another illness frequently mentioned in the Bible (Gen. 16:1-2; 1 Sam. 1:5-6), diminished the social status of the afflicted woman (Gen. 30:1-20).

The OT has at least two principal explanations for illness. One, represented by Deut. 28, affirms that health (Heb. *šālôm*) encompasses a physical state associated with the fulfillment of covenant stipulations that are fully disclosed to the members of the society, and illness stems from the violation of those stipulations. Therapy includes reviewing one's actions in light of the covenant.

The book of Job offers a contrasting, yet complementary, view which argues that illness may be rooted in divine plans that may not be disclosed to the patient at all, and not in the transgression of published rules. The patient must trust that God's undisclosed reasons are just.

Perhaps the most distinctive feature of the Israelite health care system depicted in the canonical texts is the division into legitimate and illegitimate consultative options for the patient. This division is partly related to monolatry, insofar as illness and healing rest ultimately upon Yahweh's control (Exod. 15:26; Job 5:18), and insofar as non-Yahwistic options are prohibited. The meaning of "magic" is in great dispute in modern scholarship, and there is no agreement on whether distinctions between "legitimate" and "illegitimate" consultants can be classified by the relative use of "magical" or "nonmagical" approaches.

Since it was accessible and inexpensive, prayer to Yahweh was probably the most common legitimate option for a patient. Petitions and thanksgiving prayers uttered from the viewpoint of the patient are attested in the Bible (e.g., Isa. 38:10-20).

Many psalms (e.g., Pss. 38, 39, 88, 102), in particular, may be intended as prayers for use by patients. These psalms also record important Hebrew concepts concerning illness and health care. In Ps. 38 the author attributes illness to Yahweh's anger and "hand" (v. 2[MT 3]). This concept is similar to the frequent Mesopotamian use of "the hand" (Akk. *qātu*) of a deity to describe the divine origin of an illness. As in many descriptions of illness in Mesopotamia, the patient in Ps. 38:4(5) attributes the deity's anger to the patient's own sin. Confession is regarded as part of the therapy (Ps. 38:18[19]), and the patient complains about the social consequences of illness (vv. 11-12[12-13]).

Tangible treatments mentioned in the Bible include "bandages" (Ezek. 30:21), "mandrakes" for infertility (Gen. 30:14), and "balsam" from Gilead, which may have been an important source of medicinal substances exported to Egypt (Jer. 46:11). Incense, oil, and combs found in various sites in various periods (e.g., Late Bronze Megiddo) may have been used to combat lice and other ectoparasites that may have been significant vectors of disease.

Illegitimate options, which were probably widely used by Israelites, included consultants designated in Hebrew as *rōpĕʾîm* (2 Chr. 16:12; NRSV "physicians"), non-Yahwistic shrines (2 Kgs. 1:2-4), and probably a large variety of "sorcerers" (Deut. 18:10-12). Female figurines found in most periods in Israel, especially in domestic contexts, may have been involved in fertility rituals. The largest known dog cemetery in the ancient world has been uncovered at Ashkelon, and may be associated with a healing cult of the Persian period.

Prophets are probably the foremost legitimate consultants in the canonical texts, and they were often in fierce competition with "illegitimate" consultants. Deut. 18:10-17 seems to advocate the monopoly by the Yahwistic prophet of all the consultation functions, including probable ones for illness, which had been previously distributed in a wide variety of consultants in Canaan. Stories of healing miracles (e.g., 2 Kgs. 4; 8) in the Deuteronomistic history may reflect an effort to promote prophets as the sole legitimate consultants. Their function was to provide prognoses (2 Kgs. 8:8) and intercede on behalf of the patient (5:11). Unlike some of the principal healing consultants in other Near Eastern societies, the Israelite prophets depended for their efficacy more on their relationship with God than on technical expertise.

Shrines of Yahweh were probably another significant legitimate option in the preexilic period. In 1 Sam. 1 Hannah visited the temple at Shiloh to help reverse her infertility. 2 Kgs. 18:4 indicates that prior to Hezekiah the bronze serpent made by Moses as a therapeutic device (Num. 21:6-9) was involved in acceptable therapeutic rituals in the temple of Jerusalem. Metal serpents have been found in temples (e.g., the Asclepieion at Pergamum) known to have been used for therapy during the 1st millennium. Metal serpents, such as those found in or near Late Bronze Age shrines at Timna, Tell Mevorakh (1441.2156), and Hazor, may have been involved in therapeutic rituals, but other functions cannot be excluded.

The centralization of the cult in Jerusalem and the reforms attributed to Hezekiah (715-687) and Josiah (640-609) may have wrought significant changes, whether in theory or in practice, to the health care system. Shrines which may have formerly functioned as therapeutic centers (e.g., Shiloh) may have been destroyed.

The prayer of Solomon (1 Kgs. 8) may be seen, in part, as an attempt to mitigate the loss of the therapeutic roles of the temple of Jerusalem and outlying shrines. The prayer in effect announces that it is not necessary to come to the temple for therapy, as extending the hands toward the temple is sufficient to receive healing (1 Kgs. 8:38-39). The story of Hezekiah's illness in 2 Kgs. 20:1-11 also shows that coming to the temple was not necessary for healing; Hezekiah, in fact, intends to go to the temple *after* he is healed (v. 5).

Postexilic Israel

By the postexilic period the Priestly code, which may be viewed as an extensive manual on public health that centralizes in the priesthood the power to define illness and health for an entire state, severely restricted access to the temple for the chronically ill (e.g., "lepers" in Lev. 13–14; cf. 2 Sam. 5:8 on the blind and the lame) because of fear of "impurity." Laws concerning pure foods (e.g., Lev. 11) were associated with the maintenance of excellent health in some biblical passages (e.g., Dan. 1:15), but the motives for the food laws may not be always restricted to health practices.

The theology of impurity, as a system of social boundaries, could serve to remove socioeconomically burdensome populations, and especially the chronically ill, from society. "Leprosy" alone probably encompassed a wide variety of patients. In effect, the Priestly code minimizes state responsibility for the chronically ill, leaving the eradication of illness for a future utopia (Ezek. 47:12; cf. Isa. 35:5-6).

Thanksgiving or "well-being" offerings (Lev. 7:11-36) after an illness were probably always acceptable and economically advantageous for the temple. Offerings after an illness also may have served as public notice of the readmission of previously ostracized patients to the society (Lev. 14:1-32).

Relative to the Priestly code, the community responsible for the *Miqsat Maʿaseh Torah* ("some precepts of the Torah," 4QMMT), the Temple Scroll (11QT), and other Qumran texts added to the list of illnesses excluded from the normal community and expanded the restrictions for "leprosy," the blind, and the lame. Socioeconomic reasons, as well as the fear of magical contamination, may be responsible for such increased restrictions.

The demise of the prophetic office in the early Second Temple period probably led to the wide legitimation of the *rōpĕʾîm* (cf. Sir. 38), but various types of folk healers and midwives (Exod. 1:15-21) may actually have been the most common health care consultants.

Early Christianity

During the 1st century a variety of health care systems were available in Palestine. These included those associated with the Egyptian goddess Isis and the Greek god Asclepius. In addition, there were secular Greco-Roman traditions associated with Hippocrates, Celsus, and other physicians.

Early Christianity may be seen, in part, as a critique of the levitical health care system. Matt. 10:8; Mark 14:3; and other passages indicate that Jesus and his disciples appear to target chronically ill populations ("lepers," blind and the lame) that may have been marginalized by the health care policies reflected in Leviticus.

In the early Christian period illness may be caused by numerous demonic entities who are not always acting at Yahweh's command (Matt. 15:22; Luke 11:14), and not necessarily by the violation of covenant stipulations (John 9:2). Illnesses mentioned include fevers (Mark 1:30), hemorrhages (Matt. 9:20), and what has been identified by some scholars as epilepsy (Mark 9:14-29). The cure for illness may be found in this world, and not simply in some utopian future.

Christianity also may have attracted patients who were too poor to afford fees charged in many Greco-Roman traditions (cf. Matt. 10:8). Some Greco-Roman traditions insisted that travel to a shrine was necessary for healing, but Christianity, with its emphasis on the value of faith alone, in effect announced that travel to a shrine was not required (Matt. 8:8). Likewise, Christianity resisted temporal restrictions on when healing could be administered (Mark 3:2-5). Nonetheless, early Christianity preserved many older Hebrew traditions regarding miraculous healings (Acts 5:16; 9:34) and collective health (Jas. 5:16), although some scholars have also seen the influence of Hellenistic healing traditions (e.g., the Asclepius traditions).

Conclusion

Most health care systems in biblical lands had a variety of options that were probably arranged hierarchically, depending in part on the needs and means of the patient. Prayer was probably one of the first, and most economical, options chosen by patients in all systems. A variety of healing specialists existed, but they were not all regarded as legitimate by biblical writers. However, it is probable that most patients availed themselves of whatever treatment they found accessible and affordable. In all biblical periods the family was probably the main caretaker of the ill (2 Sam. 13:5-6; Matt. 8:14).

The best medical technology (e.g., scalpels, forceps, dental drills, and splints) may have helped only simple problems (e.g., extraction of lodged weapons). In general, trauma (from accidents, strife), malnutrition, and disease limited life expectancy to under 40 years during the biblical periods.

The study of health care is an increasingly promising avenue of research in biblical scholarship, especially as it becomes more apparent that health care issues shape and are shaped by religion. Attention is due the role of health care consultants in ancient Israel and the role of health care in the rise of Christianity, as also the integration of medical anthropology, sociology, and biblical studies.

Bibliography. H. Avalos, *Illness and Health Care in the Ancient Near East.* HSM 54 (Atlanta, 1995); F. H. Cryer, *Divination in Ancient Israel and Its Near Eastern Environment.* JSOTSup 142 (Sheffield, 1994); G. Majno, *The Healing Hand: Man and Wound in the Ancient World* (Cambridge, Mass., 1975); J. Preuss, *Biblical and Talmudic Medicine* (1978, repr. Northvale, N.J., 1993); K. Seybold and U. B. Mueller, *Sickness and Healing* (Nashville, 1978); J. Zias, "Death and Disease in Ancient Israel," *BA* 54 (1991): 146-59.

HECTOR AVALOS

ILLYRICUM (Gk. *Illyrikón*)

A large mountainous Roman province in the northwestern Balkan Peninsula. Illyricum incorporates the territory along the eastern coast of the Adriatic Sea from Macedonia to Italy and west to the Danube River. The exact boundaries of the territory fluctuated over time. Ancient Illyrian tribes had the reputation of being wild, and they often took up piracy. The Greeks attempted unsuccessfully to colonize the coast from the 6th century B.C.E., thwarted by both geography and the native people. The name of the region comes from one of the first tribes encountered by the Greeks.

The Illyrians were defeated but not subdued by Philip II of Macedon. The Romans incorporated the full area into the empire in the 1st century C.E. under Tiberius (14-37), but it had taken them 250 years to subjugate the Illyrians, including two wars (229-28 and 219 B.C.E.). In 148-47 the southern districts were united for a time with Roman Macedonia and were thus under Macedonian jurisdiction. Augustus made Illyricum a senatorial province in 27 B.C.E. and an imperial province in 11 B.C.E. In the 1st century C.E. it was divided into the provinces of Pannonia in the north and Dalmatia in the south.

Paul claims to have "fulfilled" the gospel of Christ in the geographic circle from Jerusalem to Illyricum (Rom. 15:19), but it is unclear whether he preached in the province or whether it was the eastern boundary of his missionary activity. Illyricum is probably again referred to when Paul indicates to Timothy that Titus is working in Dalmatia (2 Tim. 4:10).

Bibliography. S. Casson, *Macedonia, Thrace and Illyria* (1926, repr. Westport, Conn., 1971), 287-327; J. Knox, "Romans 15 and Paul's Conception of His Apostolic Mission," *JBL* 83 (1964): 1-11.

RICHARD S. ASCOUGH

IMAGE

See IDOL, IDOLATRY.

IMAGE OF GOD

A phrase employed twice by the Priestly writer to describe the unique relationship between humans and God. In the opening account of creation, the Priestly writer states that humankind, male and female, is created in the image of God (Gen. 1:27). Later, in the aftermath of the Flood, the Priestly writer notes that the execution of divine justice is assigned to humans because they are created in the image of God (Gen. 9:6). However, the biblical text does not explicitly explain in what ways humans are created in that image, leading to numerous scholarly interpretations.

The basic thrust of the expression is that humans are *like* God. It is possible that the Priestly writer intends to suggest that humans are like God in appearance or form. In Gen. 5:3 the Priestly writer states that Adam begat Seth according to his image. This appears to be Paul's meaning of the expression when applied to Jesus (2 Cor. 4:4; cf. Phil. 2:6). It is also possible that the Priestly writer is deliberately ambiguous in designating humans as the image of God. In other words, the Priestly writer simply wanted to state that humans are like God without specifying in what ways. The context of Gen. 1:26-28 suggests that the image of God is closely connected to human dominion and rule over the earth. But even so, the exact connection between humans being in the image of God and having dominion over the earth is not specified. Humans might be *functionally* like God, ruling on the earth as God would rule, or humans might have dominion *because* they are like God in some unstated way. Perhaps interpreters can be no more specific. The result appears to be the same in either case: Humans are distinct from all other creatures in that they are like God and have dominion over the earth.

The Priestly writer's use of "image of God" in the context of human creation is comparable to the Yahwist's use of "knowledge of good and evil." According to the Yahwist, the human couple become like God when they eat the fruit of knowledge (Gen. 3:5, 22). With knowledge, the human couple can like God create life and produce agriculture (compare Gen. 3:16-19 with 2:7-9). Similarly, by connecting the image of God with dominion, the Priestly writer emphasizes the human ability to exercise its will over creation. Humans are not simply objects of creation, subjected to the fixed orders of creation. Like God, humans have some measure of control over the created world.

As the image of God, humans are distinct from all other creatures. Yet the Priestly writer describes only humans as male and female. The Priestly creation myth is concerned not only with the order of creation but also with the distribution and perpetuation of the created orders (Gen. 1:11, 22). The sexuality of the birds, the fish, and the animals is assumed by the Priestly writer, but such an assumption cannot be made for humans because they are in the image of God. For the Priestly writer God had no form of sexuality, no sexual differentiation. The Priestly writer thus states explicitly that humans were created male and female (Gen. 1:27). This differentiation of humans into male and female distinguishes them from God; "male and female" describes how humans are *not* in the image of God.

Human dominion has limits. The first humans' abuse of dominion resulted in God's cleansing of the earth by flood. Thus in the aftermath of the Flood, the Priestly writer sets out the limits of human dominion. Blood, which is life, belongs to God. And although humans may kill animals for food, humans themselves may not be killed. Whoever kills a human shall be killed by a human, "for in the image of God humans were made" (Gen. 9:6). The interpretation of the explanatory clause in this injunction is ambiguous. The clause could ascribe special sanctity to human life: Human life is more precious than all other life because humans are in the image of God. Such an interpretation, however, does not adequately account for the context of the Flood and the central focus of human dominion. Because humans are made in the image of God, they are given dominion over the earth. But humans abused their dominion and corrupted the earth, bringing about the catastrophic Flood (Gen. 6:11-13). So that creation will not again be destroyed by human corruption, God regulates human dominion: Humans may not kill other humans. But because humans are made in God's image, humans rather than God will impose the death penalty. Human execution of divine justice will restore the order of creation.

Bibliography. J. Barr, "The Image of God in the Book of Genesis — A Study of Terminology," *BJRL* 51 (1968/69): 11-26; P. Bird, "Genesis I-III as a Source for a Contemporary Theology of Sexuality," *Ex Auditu* 3 (1987): 31-44; J. M. Miller, "In the 'Image' and 'Likeness' of God," *JBL* 91 (1972): 289-304; J. H. Tigay, "The Image of God and the Flood," in *Studies in Jewish Education and Judaica in Honor of Louis Newman*, ed. A. M. Shapiro and B. I. Cohen (New York, 1984), 169-82; P. Trible, *God and the Rhetoric of Sexuality*. OBT 2 (Philadelphia, 1978), 12-23.

RONALD A. SIMKINS

IMAGERY

"Image" (from Lat. *imago*, "representation," "likeness," or "imitation," as in "picture," "apparition," "vision," "echo," and "figure of speech") designates the object or mental picture produced in artificial representation. "Imagery" commonly indicates both the object produced in the act of image-making (the image or mental picture itself represented), and the particular act of representation linked to the production of the image (e.g., the art of painting, sculpture, or poetic expression). Images are frequently identified according to the sense to which they appeal — though typically visual and auditory, and also organized according to the social, cultural, and discursive formations in which they are employed — artistic, literary, religious, psychological, political, and domestic, among others.

Prior to the 18th century, image and imagery were not normally applied to literature, but to things that were by definition pictorial — paintings or sculptures. Only in the 19th century, under the influence of Samuel Coleridge and his discussion of imagination — though also of course subsequently in psychoanalytic discourse and in various philosophies of language — do we see a direct association develop between the words image and imagery and metaphors and similes. The essence of imagination resides in its ability to create something apparently distinct by means of association and modification, thus lending itself to the associative powers of metaphor and simile. By the middle of the 19th century, therefore, the words image and imagery are regularly used as comprehensive synonyms for similes and metaphors. In literature and literary criticism especially, imagery comes to refer to all language that demonstrates graphic representation of a mental picture, with a general focus upon pictorial expressions and the figurative elements of metaphor and simile used to articulate abstractions.

The critical study of imagery generally seeks to demonstrate how patterns of images express a particular concept or abstraction. In psychoanalytic examination, e.g., the analyst will seek out a singular or continuous motif among various dream images in order to uncover the disturbances buried deep down in the unconscious (Freud) or collective unconscious (Jung). Similarly, the literary critic will engage a series of images in order to unveil the theme of a given literary work, as well as describe the imaginative world through which the text is produced. For example, the desperate and clashing images of a past and present River Thames in T. S. Eliot's *The Waste Land* contribute to the thematic continuity of the text whereby Eliot paints a picture of the waste and decay of human morality between the two world wars.

Images abound in the biblical literature; and certainly the study of images, including the close reading of metaphors and similes, elicits a better understanding of the various themes and perceptions of the world contained in the specific writings of the Hebrew and Christian Scriptures. Understood according to the definition of likeness or copy, imagery manifests itself in the representation of the gods of the nations — the idol or graven image — as well as in the description of humanity created in the image of the gods. But more importantly, biblical texts witness to an abundance of images metaphorically employed to elucidate a particular understanding or perception of the divine and its relation to humanity. The messenger of the Lord appears to Moses "in a flame of fire out of a bush, . . . yet the bush was not consumed" (Exod. 3:2); this image or mental picture of divine manifestation clearly portrays the power and inviolability of the Hebrew God. Ezekiel's vision of the Lord likewise employs images that communicate divine splendor and majesty: "Like the bow in a cloud on a rainy day, such was the appearance of the splendor all around" (Ezek. 1:28). In the Christian Scriptures also, such images as Mark's descending dove or the Johannine "bread from heaven" serve as metaphors to illuminate the divinely sanctioned appearance and ministry of Jesus. Studies of imagery, especially as occur in the literary-critical approaches to the Bible, have become an important part of biblical studies.

Bibliography. S. Freud, *The Interpretation of Dreams,* 8th rev. ed. (New York, 1965); N. Frye, *Anatomy of Criticism* (Princeton, 1957); P. N. Furbank, *Reflections on the Word "Image"* (London, 1970); C. G. Jung, *Dreams* (Princeton, 1974); F. Kermode, *The Romantic Image* (New York, 1964); Kermode and R. Alter, eds., *The Literary Guide to the Bible* (Cambridge, 1987); M. S. Silk, *Interaction in Poetic Imagery* (London, 1974).

MICHAEL L. HUMPHRIES

IMALKUE (Gk. *Imalkoue*)
An Arab ruler entrusted by Alexander Balas with his son Antiochus VI. Trypho persuaded Imalkue to release Antiochus and to harbor troops against Demetrius (1 Macc. 11:39).

IMITATION
The conscious or unconscious adoption of the attitudes, beliefs, or behavior of others. The biblical motif of imitation finds expression in language such as "to imitate," "to become like," "to follow after," and is often implicit in terminology like "disciples," "type," and "example."

The OT develops this theme negatively. Although exhorted not "to imitate the detestable ways of the nations" (Deut. 18:9; cf. 6:14; Exod. 23:24; Lev. 18:3), Israel aspires "to be like the nations, the tribes of the countries" (Ezek. 20:32; cf. Deut. 12:30; 1 Sam. 8:20), and thus incurs God's judgment (2 Kgs. 17:15; Ezek. 25:8). This negative aspect is also present in the NT (Rom. 12:2).

In the NT imitation is informed by the Greco-Roman context, where students were expected to imitate their teachers in philosophy, morality, and conduct (cf. Seneca *Ep.* 6.5-6; Quintilian *Inst. orat.* 2.1-15; Philostratus *Vit. Ap.* 1.19), and also by the heroic exemplars of the Maccabean literature, who urged the devout of Israel to imitate their example of faithfulness to the point of martyrdom (1 Macc. 13:1-9; 2 Macc. 6:27-28; 7:24-29; 4 Macc. 9:23). It is the person and mission of Jesus, however, which provide the definitive character of imitation for the writers of the NT.

Discipleship and imitation are inseparable. The call of Jesus to "follow me" (Matt. 4:19; Mark 10:21; Luke 5:27; John 1:43) demanded a life-long determination on the part of his disciples to pattern their values, beliefs, and behavior after their Master. For the Twelve this involved commitment to service (Mark 10:41-45; Luke 10:29-37), hardship (Mark 8:34-38), and renunciation (Matt. 19:27-29; John 12:26). For Paul too, imitation had a cruciform character (1 Cor. 11:1; cf. Phil. 2:5-8).

As a biblical motif, "the imitation of Christ" has played an important role in the life of the Church, particularly through the popular works of Thomas à Kempis *(The Imitation of Christ)* and Charles Sheldon *(In His Steps).* MOYER HUBBARD

IMLAH (Heb. *yimlâ, yimlāʾ*)
The father of the prophet Micaiah (1 Kgs. 22:8-9 = 2 Chr. 18:7-8).

IMMANUEL (Heb. *ʿimmānûʾēl;* Gk. *Emmanouḗl*) (also EMMANUEL)
The name of a child whose birth symbolizes the presence of God ("God [is] with us"). The name first appears in Isaiah (Isa. 7:14; 8:8; cf. v. 10) and is used in one of Matthew's OT fulfillment quotations (Matt. 1:23, "Emmanuel").

The context in Isaiah is the Syro-Ephraimitic crisis (735-732 B.C.). Judah was threatened by Syria and Israel because it refused to join a revolt against Assyria (cf. 2 Kgs. 16). Ahaz is warned not to depend upon Assyria for political support (Isa. 7:1-9), and Isaiah assures him of God's protection. Ahaz refuses to ask for a sign (Isa. 7:12), perhaps because he had already sought out Assyria's help (2 Kgs. 16:7-9). Nevertheless, God gives a double-edged sign of both salvation and judgment (Isa. 7:13-17): the young woman will conceive (or perhaps already has conceived), give birth to a son, and name him Immanuel. Before the child is old enough for moral discrimination, the two nations that threaten Judah will be destroyed. This word of hope is counterbalanced, however, with a word of threat that Ahaz's lack of trust in God will result in a great disaster for Judah by Assyrian domination (Isa. 7:17; 8:1-10).

Many aspects of the exact interpretation of the

sign and the identity of the child and his mother are in dispute. Some understand the child to be the king's, perhaps Hezekiah. Others suggest he is the prophet's own son, or perhaps a future reference to Jesus' birth centuries later. The latter view, however, overlooks the contemporary situation of Isaiah. The thrust of the prophecy in its OT context is not the virginity of the child's mother (Heb. *'almâ*, "young woman of marriageable age"). Normally, such a person would be a virgin given prevailing social customs, but Heb. *bĕṯûlâ* is a more common term for virgin. Moreover, the use of the article suggests a specific woman known to Isaiah and Ahaz. The child's birth and name thus give symbolic expression to the belief that God was present, caring for, and protecting his people, and its significance is in the providential timing of the sign.

Matthew's citation of Isa. 7:14 is introduced with a stereotypical fulfillment formula (Matt. 1:22) and, with some minor exceptions, follows the LXX, which renders *'almâ* by Gk. *parthénos*, a word normally used to translate *bĕṯûlâ*. Matthew uses Isa. 7:14 in his birth narrative because it supports his belief in the Davidic and divine aspects of Jesus' identity. First, Matthew's genealogy of Jesus seeks to establish Jesus' Davidic lineage (Matt. 1:1-17), and Isaiah had introduced his sign by addressing Ahaz as "the house of David" (Isa. 7:13). Second, Matthew cites Isa. 7:14 after Joseph has been told that Mary's pregnancy was by the Holy Spirit, and the reference to a "virgin" helps explain how Jesus is God's son. Matthew's interest is in the theological significance of the name, which he interprets lest his readers miss the meaning of the Hebrew (cf. Isa. 8:10). This fulfillment quotation underscores Matthew's conviction that in Jesus God is present with his people. The promise of presence in Matt. 1:23 forms a frame around the entire Gospel with 28:20, where the resurrected Jesus promises, "I am with you always, to the end of the age."

Bibliography. R. E. Brown, *The Birth of the Messiah*, rev. ed. (New York, 1993); C. Seitz, *Isaiah 1-39*. Interpretation (Louisville, 1993).

DAVID B. HOWELL

IMMER (Heb. *'immēr*) **(PERSON)**
The leader of a priestly division at the time of David (1 Chr. 24:14). Pashhur, Jeremiah's opponent, was a member of this priestly family (Jer. 20:1). Descendants of this line returned with Zerubbabel from captivity (1 Chr. 9:12; Ezra 2:37 = Neh. 7:40; 11:13) and participated in the rebuilding of the city wall (3:29). Two men of this line had taken "foreign women" as wives (Ezra 10:20).

IMMER (Heb. *'immēr*) **(PLACE)**
A city in Babylonia from which the Jewish exiles returned (Ezra 2:59; Neh. 7:61). The site is unknown.

IMMORTALITY
See AFTERLIFE, AFTERDEATH.

IMNA (Heb. *yimnā'*)
A son of Helem from the tribe of Asher (1 Chr. 7:35).

IMNAH (Heb. *yimnâ*)
1. A son of Asher (Gen. 46:17; 1 Chr. 7:30) whose descendants are called Imnites (Num. 26:44).
2. A Levite and father of Kore (2 Chr. 31:14).

IMRAH (Heb. *yimrâ*)
A son of Zophah, from the tribe of Asher (1 Chr. 7:36).

IMRI (Heb. *'imrî*)
1. An ancestor of Uthai, a Judahite who returned from exile (1 Chr. 9:4). He may be the same as Amariah (of which the name Imri is a shortened form) in the parallel account at Neh. 11:4.
2. The father of Zaccur (Neh. 3:2).

INCARNATION
The Christian belief that God has disclosed the divine self in human reality in the person and work of Jesus of Nazareth (Lat. *incarnatio*, lit., "take on flesh").

The Johannine emphasis on "the word became flesh" (John 1:14) and that of the Synoptic writers on the birth of a child to Mary both serve to protect the doctrine of incarnation from a docetic interpretation or an adoptionist Christology (cf. Rom. 8:3; Col. 1:19; 1 Tim. 3:16; 1 John 4:2; 2 John 7). In the early centuries, the believing community struggled over how to articulate belief in the Incarnation in response to outright denials and heretical revisions (Docetism, Adoptionism, Arianism, Apollinarianism, Nestorianism, Eutychianism, Monothelitism). This struggle is reflected in Nicaea's affirmation in 325 C.E. and in the reaffirmation of Chalcedon in 451.

Traditionally, the doctrine of incarnation has sought to articulate three central christological truths: (1) Jesus Christ was a divine person. (2) Jesus Christ was an authentic human being. (3) The divine nature and the human nature existed in hypostatic union in the person of Jesus Christ. It could be argued that these three truths are set forth in the affirmation of the prologue of the Gospel of John (John 1:14). The affirmation that it is the divine Logos who is incarnate emphasizes the preexistence and divine personhood of the One who is born of Mary. Gk. *sárx* here refers to the tangible, material, corporeal substance that comprises the human body. When this is seen in relation to the anti-docetic affirmation of 1 John 1:1, it is clear that the Johannine writer(s) understood Jesus as a fully human person in the same way that all others were understood to be human. Finally, Gk. *egéneto* ("became") focuses upon the dynamic union of divine and human natures in one person. The term suggests the free volitional activity of the preexistent Logos who becomes flesh without any diminution of the divine person. Further, it emphasizes that this flesh is the product of no divine subterfuge but, rather, is consistent with the corporeal nature of all human flesh.

Since the Enlightenment, the doctrine of incarnation has experienced various attempts at modification, revision, and outright rejection. Rejection is seen most clearly in the Unitarianism in some strains of post-Reformation thought and in later Deism. Revision is seen in the philosophical reformulation of the doctrine found in the thought of G. W. F. Hegel. Finally, 20th-century thought has often sought to modify the doctrine. On the one hand, some have seen the Christian doctrine of incarnation to be simply one of the various mythic manifestations of incarnational thought in generic human religious experience. On the other, the scandal of particularity within the Christian understanding of incarnation has been seen as a barrier to dialogue within a pluralistic contemporary religious environment. Such assertions remind one that the Incarnation remains at the core of Christian belief. D. LARRY GREGG

INCENSE

Odiferous plants of various origins and species growing in different parts of the ancient Middle East played important roles in the economic, political, and religious life of the region. Undoubtedly these plants were first used in the Neolithic period but came to have an increasingly greater importance with the advent of formal states in the 4th-3rd millennia B.C. However, we have virtually no etiological myths which explain how these plants came to be used in such special functions and roles. In terms of the biblical world, by the early 1st millennium these substances came to play an ever increasing role. High status and prestige for the Mediterranean world became associated with the acquisition and consumption of exotic, foreign aromata. The use of these rose to great heights during the late Iron Age.

Various odiferous substances were used by the ancient peoples of the Middle East in association with funerals, divine worship, magic ritual, for cosmetic purposes, and in medicinal applications. Cuneiform sources in Mesopotamia refer to incense as early as the 4th millennium, and in Egypt "incense" has been identified in Nagada II period burials (ca. 2500), although the term "incense" is first attested in the 5th Dynasty.

In the OT incense burners and "altars" suggest frequent use of incense (Heb. *qĕṭōreṯ*) in daily life. Specific official rituals which included incense are described in a number of OT texts (e.g., Exod. 30; Lev. 2, 10, 16; Ps. 141). Cosmetic and medicinal uses are mentioned especially in the Song of Songs. In the NT the mention of incense (Gk. *thymíama*) use is rarer, and conforms to Jewish OT tradition (e.g., Matt. 2:11; Luke 1:9-11; Rev. 5:8; 18:13; Mark 14:3-9).

The most vexing question in any discussion of incense is what plants were used and what they were called. For example, galbanum prescribed in the Exodus account may be one of 100 species of the *Ferula* genus. Recently compiled data suggest what was used and available in the 1st millennium. Some of the incense products were only available and derived from southwest Arabia or northeast Africa. These included frankincense (*Boswellia* sp.), myrrh (*commiphora* sp.), aloes (*Aloe* sp.), bdelliums (*commiphora* sp.), and balm (*Balsamodendron* sp. or *Commiphora* sp.). Other incenses were available from a larger area of the Middle East, even into the northern latitudes of Syria, Lebanon, and Asia Minor. These included sweet-smelling canes (*Acorus calamus*), sweet-smelling rushes (*Cymbopogon* sp.), tragacanth (*Astragalus* sp.), labdanum (*Cistus* sp.), storax (*Styrax* sp. or *Liquidambar* sp.), mastic (*Pistacia lentiscus*), pine (*Pinus brutia*), terebinth (*Pistacia terebinthus,* identified from a Late Bronze Age Canaanite ship in the Mediterranean; perhaps Egyp. *sntr*), and other various resins from specific trees (e.g., *Artemisia* sp. and *Acacia* sp.). Other incense materials came from southeast Asia and were transshipped to the Levant via South Arabia. The most famous of these were cinnamon and cassia (*Cinnamonium* sp.) The incense trade was conducted both by sea (cf. Hanno *Periplus;* Pliny *Nat. hist.*) and by well-known land routes up the spine of Arabia. The origins for the Iron Age trade lay well back in the Bronze Age, from which actual ship remains have been recovered and historical records attest to shipbuilding.

Bibliography. N. Groom, *Frankincense and Myrrh* (London, 1981); H. H. Hairfield, Jr., and E. M. Hairfield, "Identification of a Late Bronze Age Resin," *Analytical Chemistry* 62 (1990): 41A-45A; A. Lucas, "Cosmetics, Perfumes, and Incense in Ancient Egypt," *JEA* 16 (1930): 41-53; W. Müller, "Notes on the Use of Frankincense in South Arabia," *Proceedings of the Seminar for Arabian Studies* 6 (1976): 124-36; K. Nielsen, *Incense in Ancient Israel.* VTSup 38 (Leiden, 1986); J. Zarins, "Mesopotamia and Frankincense: The Early Evidence," in *Profumi d'Arabia,* ed. A. Avanzini (Rome, 1997), 251-72. JURIS ZARINS

INCEST

Prohibited sexual activity between kin related by blood or marriage. The Bible has no term corresponding to the English noun "incest" and instead refers to incestuous activity using verbal idioms associated either with sexual activity in general or with defilement. The Bible also does not calculate prohibited degrees of relationship but catalogues forbidden pairings (Deut. 22:30[MT 23:1]; 27:20, 22-23; Lev. 18:6-18; 20:11-12, 17, 19; cf. Ezek. 22:10-11). As a result, its treatment of incest is less comprehensive than that found in most Western law codes. Certain relationships are not specified as prohibited, notably father-daughter incest. These gaps do not mean that Israel approved such behavior since taboos against them may well have operated otherwise.

Variety in the length and focus of the biblical lists suggests development in Israel's thinking about acceptable sexual conduct. Furthermore, some incestuous behaviors prohibited in the laws seem to be permitted in certain narrative contexts (cf. Gen. 20:12; 38:1-30; 2 Sam. 13:13). The only possible NT reference to incest is in 1 Cor. 5:1-5, where Paul condemns the Corinthian church for tolerating a man living with his father's wife; Paul commands the church to expel such a man from its midst. FRANK D. WULF

INDIA

In biblical usage, the northwestern region of the subcontinent of southern Asia east of Arabia, marking the eastern boundary of Ahasuerus' territory (Esth. 1:1; 8:9; cf. Ad. Esth. 13:1; 16:1). The first important civilization in India was along the Indus River and had highly developed urban settlements; these people, akin to the Sumerians, had entered India between 4000 and 2500 B.C. Writing flourished in this culture, but only a few words of this Dravidian language have been translated by modern scholars. Communication with Mesopotamia existed, but the Indus River culture was less advanced.

Invasions by Indo-european Aryans, beginning in the middle of the 2nd millennium, introduced Vedic religion, which was assimilated into pre-Aryan elements to form Hinduism. The pre-Aryan people mainly migrated into south India, where Tamil, a Dravidian language, is now dominant.

The two chief Hindu deities are Siva, found also in the Indus River culture, and Vishnu. Siva has many functions, but especially represents creative forces. His primary symbol is a stylized phallus, which is considered to have a divine nature. Of Vishnu's many incarnations, the beautiful youth Krishna is the object of much devotion. Hinduism has a strong focus on love, both physical and romantic/emotional.

Ancient trade routes connected India and western areas as early as the Early Dynastic III period in Mesopotamia (ca. 2500). Archaeological and linguistic evidence suggests comparisons between Palestine and the land of the Tamils in the 12th century, including linguistic similarities between some Tamil/Dravidian and Hebrew names. The Seleucids employed elephants and their "Indian drivers" in warfare (1 Macc. 6:37).

Significant parallels may be seen between the Song of Solomon and the earliest surviving written literature of the Tamils, written in the Cankam Age, perhaps before the 7th century. Cankam poetry consists of both *Akam,* dealing with the interior, and *Puram,* focusing on the external world. The *Akam* love poetry involves a landscape, such as forest, mountain, cultivated lands, desert, or seashore; and the gods worshipped there and the fauna and flora. Mostly secular love poems, they exhibit deep insight into the psychology of love. Five phases of mutual love are described, all involving a kind of separation. Each landscape with its own images summons its own specific emotion and romantic situation. There is a profusion of nature imagery. The structure of the poems is drama, monologue, often with a confidante as listener.

Bibliography. S. Hikosaka and G. John Samuel, eds., *Encyclopaedia of Tamil Literature* 1 (Madras, 1990); A. Mariaselvam, *The Song of Songs and Ancient Tamil Love Poems.* AnBib 118 (Rome, 1988).

E. LYNNE HARRIS

INDIVIDUALISM

See CORPORATE PERSONALITY.

INGATHERING, FEAST OF

See TABERNACLES, FEAST OF.

INHERITANCE

Property that transfers to an heir upon the death of its owner.

The inheritance of wealth and personal property is rarely mentioned in the OT. Apart from a single law protecting the rights of a man's oldest son (Deut. 21:15-17), concerns about this aspect of inheritance are found only in a few of the ancestor narratives (Gen. 21:10; 25:5-6; cf. 31:14-16) and wisdom texts (Prov. 13:22; 19:14; cf. Job 42:15).

Most OT references to inheritance concern land. According to one strand of biblical thinking, which may have roots in the society and economy of early tribal Israel, land is not individually owned, and cannot be sold or given away in perpetuity (Lev. 25:23). Particular individuals or families obtain usufruct of the land by virtue of their membership in a larger kinship (or pseudo-kinship) community, such as a lineage, clan, or tribe.

This concept is expressed theologically through the assertion that the land is ultimately Yahweh's inheritance (Jer. 16:18; cf. Josh. 22:19), and that the Israelites are merely tenants whose tenure in the land is contingent upon loyalty and obedience to the deity (cf. Lev. 20:22-26; Deut. 30:19-20). The inheritance that is passed from generation to generation is permission to live on the land and to exploit its resources within the parameters set by the laws in the Pentateuch. Several of these laws aim at preventing the alienation of tribes and families from their ancestral inheritances (cf. Lev. 25:24-28; Num. 36:6-9; Deut. 19:14; 27:17). According to Lev. 25:8-17 agricultural and pastoral land may not be sold in perpetuity; every 50 years during the Jubilee, land which has been sold is to be returned to the family to whose ancestral inheritance it belongs. Num. 27:8-11 rules that a man's daughters are to inherit his ancestral property in the event that he dies without sons. This law does not grant women a general right to inherit or own land, but seeks to preserve a man's name by protecting his lineage from extinction and by maintaining its connection to his ancestral inheritance.

The rise of a centralized monarchy brings notions of private ownership in conflict with the ideals of tribal society. The rebellions of Sheba against David (2 Sam. 20:1-22) and of the northern tribes against Rehoboam (1 Kgs. 12:1-20) are motivated in part by a perception that the institution of kingship threatens practices of land tenure based on inheritance. The story of Naboth's vineyard (21:1-29) portrays the violent extremes to which some proponents of private ownership will go in their efforts to circumvent traditional restrictions placed upon the sale of ancestral inheritances. In a similar way, the prophet Micah condemns Jerusalem's wealthy classes for coveting and seizing the ancestral inheritances of the common people (Mic. 2:1-5).

The OT employs "inheritance" in a variety of metaphorical ways. Descriptions of Israel as God's inheritance point to the intimacy that appropriately exists between God and the chosen people (e.g., Exod. 34:9; Deut. 4:20; 2 Sam. 21:3; Jer. 10:16). The prophets draw parallels between God's rejection of sinful Israel and a landholder's abandonment of an inheritance that has become defiled (e.g., 2 Kgs. 21:14; Jer. 12:7-9; cf. Isa. 47:6). At the end of the Exile, God promises a heritage of military security to an obedient and soon to be restored Zion (Isa. 54:17). God's decrees are described as the heritage of the righteous (Ps. 119:111), whereas destruction is the inheritance of oppressors (Job 27:13-23). Eccl. 7:11 compares wisdom to a good inheritance.

The NT seldom refers to the literal inheritance of real, personal, or financial property (cf. Mark 12:1-8 par.; Luke 12:13-15; 15:11-12). More commonly, it employs ideas of inheritance in a spiritual sense. Believers are said to inherit a variety of spiritual benefits, including glorification (Rom. 8:17), redemption (Eph. 1:14), salvation (Heb. 1:14), and life (1 Pet. 3:7; cf. Luke 18:18). This inheritance is both eternal and immutable (Heb. 9:15; 1 Pet. 1:4). It is offered to all who are called through the grace of God in Jesus Christ (Acts 20:32) and is sealed by the Holy Spirit (Eph. 1:11-14). Although Col. 3:24 describes this inheritance as a reward for faithful obedience, and Eph. 5:5 declares that sinners cannot inherit the kingdom of God, other passages insist that the inheritance cannot be received through obedience to the law, but only through faith in God's promises (Gal. 3:17-18; 4:21-31; cf. Heb. 11:8-16). Those who receive this inheritance include both Gentiles (Eph. 3:6) and women (1 Pet 3:7).

FRANK D. WULF

INK

A liquid like water or oil made of the soot of burnt resin, pitch, or wood and mixed with gum for use in writing. Black was the most common color of ink in the biblical world, though other known colors were red (made with red ochre or iron oxide), yellow (most likely from iron or yellow ochre), purple (from murex shells) and even silver and gold. The ingredients were dried into cakes and then mixed with water in ink wells and applied with a reed brush. The "pens" and inkwells are described as part of a combination of writing tools kept in a case of wood, horn, ivory, or metal and worn at the scribes' girdle (Ezek. 9:2).

Because of its perishable nature, ink is rarely found in archaeological contexts, and so the textual evidence of these early periods is biased toward more permanent remains of inscribed stone or clay. The only specific biblical reference cites ink written on a scroll (Jer. 36:18), but in the few archaeological contexts available, ink is also found on the outer sides of clay vessels and on ostraca, on the walls of tombs and caves, on plaster-covered stone and on papyrus. It is used in projects of both small and monumental scales.

A characteristic of ink is its mutability — it is blotted out (Exod. 32:33; Ps. 69:28[MT 29]) and washed off (Num. 5:23). Paul compares ink-written messages to the permanence of the Holy Spirit's message on the human heart (2 Cor. 3:3).

KATHARINE A. MACKAY

INN

A place where travelers rested for the night (Heb. *mālôn,* "lodging place"). The term implies little more than a level stretch of ground on which to sleep (Gen. 42:27; Exod. 4:24; Jer. 9:2[MT 1]; NJPSV "encampment").

In the NT Gk. *katályma* (from *katá,* "down," and *lúō,* "to loose") signifies a place where travelers could loose their own burdens or that of their beasts and rest. By the 2nd century B.C.E. the term came to mean generally a lodging or dwelling place (so Luke 2:7). However, in Mark 14:14; Luke 22:11 it refers more particularly to a guest or dining room, designating the setting for the Last Supper. Another term, Gk. *pandocheíon,* means literally a place where all are received (in the NT only at Luke 10:34, in the parable of the Good Samaritan), including cattle and beasts of burden; thus, the inn of the parable was most likely a place where cattle as well as humans gathered.

DALE ELLENBURG

INNER BEING

An expression (Gk. *ho ésō ánthrōpos*) used by Paul (Eph. 3:16) apparently to describe the spiritual self, which experiences constant renewal under the guidance of God's love and mercy, as opposed to the "outer man," which is subject to sin. Such a conclusion can only be reached, however, by reading the passage through the lens of 2 Cor. 4:16 ("Though our outer nature is wasting away, our inner nature is being renewed day by day").

HENRY L. CARRIGAN, JR.

INNOCENTS, MASSACRE OF THE

A brief episode of male infanticide at Bethlehem recorded in the Infancy narrative in Matthew (Matt. 2:16-18). King Herod, duped by the astrologers from the East who are searching for the newborn king of the Jews, goes into a rage and kills all male children two years old and under in Bethlehem and the surrounding region. The 1st-century Jewish historian Josephus does not mention this specific incident, but does recount similar instances of Herod's violence and paranoia (*Ant.* 16.11.7; 17.2.4; 6.5-6). Although there are strong OT antecedents (e.g., Pharaoh's slaughter of the Hebrew male infants, Exod. 1:15-22; Rachel's traditional burial ground in Bethlehem, Gen. 35:19; her strong matriarchal role in Israelite history as reflected in Matthew's quote from Jer. 31:15; and Israel's forced gathering point and deportation from Ramah into exile in Babylon, Jer. 31:15), no other Gospel writer includes this story.

Various Christian traditions claim that from 14 thousand to 144 thousand children were killed. Historians suggest, however, that because of the probable population of Bethlehem at the time, the resulting annual birthrate, and a high infant mortality rate, the total number could not have been more than 20 boys under the age of two. That figure makes the act no less heinous. The Feast of the Holy Innocents, celebrated on 28 December, celebrates the massacred baby boys as Christian martyrs and saints. The story has been useful to scholars in setting Jesus' birth at 6 B.C.E., two years before Herod's death. For Matthew's purpose, the impending massacre prompts Joseph's decision to flee to Egypt with Mary and Jesus, thus satisfying a theme of OT prophecy, i.e., "Out of Egypt I have called my son" (Matt. 2:15; Hos. 11:1; Exod. 4:22).

Bibliography. R. E. Brown, *The Birth of the Messiah,* rev. ed. (New York, 1993); U. Luz, *Matthew 1-7* (Minneapolis, 1989). GLENNA S. JACKSON

I.N.R.I.

Abbreviation of Lat. *Iesus Nazarenus rex Iudaeorum,* "Jesus of Nazareth, King of the Jews," the inscription Pilate affixed to Jesus' cross (John 19:19-20).

INSCRIPTIONS, GREEK

Written materials preserved upon durable media such as stone and metals. While the cultures of the ancient Mediterranean basin produced inscriptions in numerous languages, Greek inscriptions are by far the most important for the study of the NT.

The systematic efforts to correlate the epigraphical discoveries of the classical world with the content of the NT began in earnest in the latter decades of the 19th century and continue, with a major hiatus in the decades following World War I, until the present. Scholars such as G. Adolph Deissman, William M. Ramsay, James H. Moulton, George Milligan, Frederick W. Danker, G. H. R. Horsley, and Ceslas Spicq have been lodestars in this academic undertaking and have made major contributions through their publications.

One of the initial and enduring results of the investigation of Greek inscriptions for NT studies was to expel older misconceptions about the uniqueness of the vocabulary of the Greek NT. Many terms which had been hitherto regarded as "Christian words" were now seen to be part of the general Greek vocabulary.

The hundreds of extant Greek Jewish inscriptions have also shed significant light on facets of Second Temple Judaism. In light of these Greek inscriptions NT scholarship clearly knows more about the date and origin of the synagogue building, the synagogue's male and female officers, the Jewish community's interaction with its pagan urban environment, and life within the larger Jewish fellowship of antiquity.

The significance of the emperor cult and general political piety in the early Roman Empire is extremely important for a proper understanding of parts of the Gospels, Acts, the General Epistles, and the Apocalypse of John. Accordingly, those Greek inscriptions which bear testimony to the local devotion to the Roman emperor, to divine epithets used of the imperial Roman family, or which highlight the divine benefits which stem from the emperor's reign provide salient insight into the ideology as well as patriotic devotion of the Roman civilization in which Christianity spread.

There are a number of political and status-based officials mentioned in the NT. Since in some instances these official positions and institutions are only adumbrated in ancient literature, Greek inscriptions are very helpful in establishing greater clarity about their significance and characteristics. This would include *asiárchēs* (Acts 19:31), *politárchēs* (17:6, 8), the city's *grammateús* ("town clerk," 19:35), the members of the Areopagus court (17:34), and the *oikonómos* ("city treasurer") of Corinth (Rom.16:23).

Since the majority of Christians who were contemporary with the writing of the books of the NT were of gentile heritage, it is crucial to understand the contours of pagan piety at that time. Greek inscriptions not only inform us about specific pagan religions mentioned in the NT such as the Ephesian Artemis, but also about many widespread facets of pagan religiosity. Pagan belief in healing miracles is widely attested in temple testimonial epigraphy and in votive inscriptions. Epigraphy attests the pagan assurance that various deities communicated to their devotees through divine dreams, visions, voices, prophecies, and written revelations. There is a collection of "confession" inscriptions found primarily in Roman Asia which bears witness to numerous individuals who became aware of their need to repent and confess violation of a deity's statute or law. One impressive inscription from the city of Philadelphia in Roman Asia focuses on the high moral standards of a cult of Zeus, violation of which standards would bring forth the wrath of the gods. In particular, the members of this cult, "men and women, slave and free," regarded abortion, pedophilia, murder, and sexual infidelity as violations of expressed divine revelation.

The social organization and characteristics of the early Church were not without parallel in the social and religious guilds and collegia of the Greco-Roman world. Many of these guilds are uniquely documented by inscriptional evidence. The activities, the specific office holders, the procedures for holding regular worship services and corporate meals, and the place of corporate discipline are all mentioned in one extensive Greek inscription of the *Iobacchi,* a group of worshippers of Bacchus at Athens.

Slavery was a ubiquitous phenomenon in the Roman world. Since this ancient phenomenon has often been anachronistically viewed through the experience of Black slavery in modern American history, Greek inscriptions have provided helpful information about the manumission of slaves in antiquity, the interaction between ancient religions and slaves, the legal obligations of slaves to their former owners, and the participation of slaves and freedmen in Greco-Roman society at large.

The last few decades have seen a burgeoning interest in "women in antiquity" studies. As a direct result of information preserved in Greek inscriptions, we are now better able to reconstruct women's life and contributions in the Roman world, particularly in religious and civic roles. Women's place in family and society as well as what their survivors, typically husbands and children, expressed about them in sepulchral epigraphy have been illumined by numerous epigraphical discoveries. At many junctures, the new evidence of Greek epigraphy has toppled older stereotypical understandings about women in the world contemporary with nascent Christianity.

There is no single corpus of Greek inscriptions. Rather, one must look to several corpora as well as technical journals to locate Greek inscriptions germane to the study of the NT. In addition to the fact that there exists no single work which contains all the relevant evidence, most of the major corpora do not contain English translations. Accordingly, the typical scholar — not to mention student — is unable to pursue his or her own studies. The best point on entry into this important, but largely inaccessible, area of study is the works by scholars such as Deissmann and Spicq as well as the more recently discovered materials assembled, translated, and interpreted by various scholars in the series *New Documents Illustrating Early Christianity* 1-5, ed. G. H. R. Horsley (Marrickville, New South Wales and Grand Rapids, 1981-1989); 6–, ed. S. R. Llewelyn (1992–).

Bibliography. G. A. Deissmann, *Light from the Ancient East* (1927, repr. Grand Rapids, 1978); F. Millar, "Epigraphy," in *Sources for History*, ed. M. Crawford (Cambridge, 1983), 80-136; C. Spicq, *Theological Lexicon of the New Testament*, 3 vols. (Peabody, 1994); *Supplementum Epigraphicum Graecum*, ed. H. W. Pleket, R. S. Stroud, J. H. M. Strubbe, 1 (Leiden, 1923), 42 (1995); A. G. Woodhead, *The Study of Greek Inscriptions*, 2nd ed. (1981, repr. Norman, 1992). RICHARD E. OSTER, JR.

INSCRIPTIONS, SEMITIC

A variety of ancient Semitic documents survives which helps to facilitate the study of the Hebrew Scriptures. It is in tracing the development of and further elucidation of the various languages that the inscriptions have the most obvious importance and value. The areas illuminated are phonology, morphology, syntax, poetics, and lexicography. The inscriptions also reveal the orthographic conventions of the various periods for the respective languages, data which help in the dating of biblical texts, for example.

In addition to their importance for philological insight, the inscriptions also shed light on history and cultures of the respective groups. Though very few shed direct light on biblical events, the inscriptions help fill in the blanks in the biblical historical record. Through the inscriptions, the succession of kings of certain states is reconstructed or the extent of relationships between different states is revealed. The researcher learns the level of literacy in a certain region and period, and legal practices are explicated.

Inscriptions are written on all kinds of materials and by all kinds of implements. Materials include stone, pottery (either whole vessels or fragments called potsherds), animal skins, papyrus, metal, and even wood. The inscriptions are chiseled, incised, written with pen and ink, and stamped — using a seal carved for that purpose — into wet clay (either a pottery vessel before it hardened or a clump of clay) to seal a document. The most common are the pen and ink texts written on potsherds (then called ostraca) and the stamp seal impressions in those clumps of clay (bullæ).

Hebrew

Pomegranate Scepter Head

The Israel Museum owns a small pomegranate-shaped scepter head which bears a late 8th-century paleo-Hebrew inscription. Unfortunately, the scepter head is broken, so the inscription is not complete. André Lemaire restored the text as follows: *lby[t yhw]h qdš khnm*, which may be translated: "Belonging to the temp[le of Yahw]eh, the priests' holy object." The dating and understanding of the text have been the subject of some debate.

Kuntillet ʿAjrud and Khirbet el-Qôm

Kuntillet ʿAjrud (Ḥorvat Teman), an ancient religious center for travelers, yielded several inscriptions which ascribe to Yahweh the goddess Asherah as a consort. For example, Kuntillet ʿAjrud no. 1 is translated by Judith M. Hadley: "X says: say to Yehal[lelʾel] and to Yoʿasah and [to Z]: I bless you by Yahweh of Samaria and by his Asherah." Interestingly, an inscription from Khirbet el-Qôm also gives Asherah to Yahweh as his consort. One is reminded of when King Manasseh put an Asherah pole in the Jerusalem temple (2 Kgs. 21:7).

Jar Impressions, Weights, Seals, and Bullæ

The most common types of inscription in Israel are seals, bullæ, weights, and jar inscriptions. Some weights were inscribed with how much they weighed. Interestingly, weights with the same title do not weigh the same (ca. 100 inscribed weights have been discovered). This brings to mind such passages as Amos 8:4-6; Prov. 20:10, which refer to differing weights and measures. Some 750 seals and bullæ have been discovered. The most famous seal (actually a bulla) reads: *lbrkyhw* | *bnnryhw* | *hspr*, "To Berechiah, the son of Neriah, the scribe." Given the patronymic (the father's name), the profession, and the paleographic date, it is virtually certain that this is the seal of Baruch, the scribe of Jeremiah.

Moabite

Mesha Stela

One of the most exciting recent finds is actually a new reading in the Mesha stela. André Lemaire's 1994 restoration in l. 31 of the first *d* in *dt dwd* has garnered wide (though not universal) support and provides the earliest reference to David outside the Bible. The mention of Yahweh in l. 18 is also the earliest mention of this deity outside the biblical text.

El-Kerak inscription, written by Moabite king Mesha or his father (9th century B.C.E.). Gray-black basalt; probably part of a longer piece, perhaps a statue (Photograph by Bruce and Kenneth Zuckerman, West Semitic Research; courtesy Department of Antiquities, Jordan)

Old Aramaic

Tell Fakhariyeh

The Tell Fakhariyeh inscription, one of the longest Old Aramaic inscriptions, is a bilingual text in both Assyrian and Aramaic carved on a statue of Hadyithi, governor of the ancient city of Gozan. It is currently dated to ca. the mid-9th century on the basis of the style of the statue and historical circumstances as related in the inscription, though paleographically it has been dated as early as the 11th century. However, the inscription also uses vowel letters *(matres lectionis),* usually considered a later development, which would support the later date.

Tel Dan

In 1993 and 1994 an Old Aramaic inscription was unearthed at Tel Dan which paleographically and archaeologically dates to somewhere in the 9th or 8th century. The text commemorates the victory of an Aramaic king (he attributes his kingship to the Aramaic deity Hadad and the language is Old Aramaic) over "the king of Israel" (l. 8) and "[the kin]g of the house of David." This latter phrase, *[ml]k. bytdwd,* has been the source of much controversy, for it was the first recognized extrabiblical reference to that famous king of Israel. William M. Schniedewind published a provocative understanding of the text whereby he attributes the stela to Hazael of Damascus, connecting it to the story of Jehu's revolt in 2 Kgs. 9-10. He translates ll. 6-9: ". . . and I slew seve[nty ki]ngs, who harnessed thou[sands of char]iots and thousands of horsemen. [And I killed Jo]ram, son of A[hab,] king of Israel, and [I] killed [Ahazi]yahu, son of [Joram, kin]g of the House of David. . ." If this interpretation is correct, it would put the date of the stela ca. 841.

Phoenician

Byblos (Aḥiram)

A recent development in Phoenician has been the new reading by Javier Teixidor of the last phrase of the Aḥiram inscription which yields the reading: "may his inscription be erased before Byblos." The sarcophagus, with its inscription, was originally dated by its archaeological context to the 13th century, but that was lowered to ca. 1000 because of some Iron Age pottery discovered in the shaft of the tomb (though some prefer the earlier date, considering the Iron Age sherds to be later contamination). The inscription itself dates, on paleographic grounds, to the first half of the 10th century, but there is a Pseudo-hieroglyphic inscription that predates the Phoenician one, the latter beginning after and, for the most part, avoiding the earlier one. (Pseudo-hieroglyphic refers to an earlier Phoenician writing system that remains undeciphered.) From the archaeological, art-historical, and paleographic arguments, one can surmise that the sarcophagus was made in the 13th century and inscribed with a Pseudo-hieroglyphic inscription, and that later (ca. 1000) Ittobaal reused the sarcophagus to bury his father Aḥiram and had a new inscription added to it.

Conclusion

Several collections of Northwest Semitic inscriptions should be consulted. In addition to the multivolume works by Herbert Donner and Wolfgang Röllig (*Kanaanäische und aramäische Inschriften,* 3rd ed. [Wiesbaden, 1971-76]) and J. C. L. Gibson (*Textbook of Syrian Semitic Inscriptions* [Oxford, 1971-1982]), one should add G. I. Davies, et al., *Ancient Hebrew Inscriptions* (Cambridge, 1991), and K. A. D. Smelik, *Writings from Ancient Israel* (Louisville, 1991). Many of these inscriptions are also translated in *ANET.* Finally, the series "Literary Sources for the History of Palestine and Syria," edited by Dennis Pardee, contains useful and convenient surveys with bibliographies of these texts plus some of the archives of the other major ancient Near Eastern cultures (*AUSS* 17 [1979]: 47-69; *BA* 47 [1984]: 6-16, 88-99; 48 [1985]: 240-53; 49 [1986]: 140-54, 228-43; 51 [1988]: 143-61, 172-89; 57 [1994]: 2-19, 110-20).

Bibliography. J. M. Hadley, "The Khirbet el-Qom Inscription," *VT* 37 (1987): 50-62; "Some Drawings and Inscriptions on Two Pithoi from Kuntillet 'Ajrud," *VT* 37 (1987): 180-213; A. Lemaire, "Probable Head of Priestly Scepter from Solomon's Temple Surfaces in Jerusalem," *BARev* 10 (1984): 24-29; G. E. Mendenhall, *The Syllabic Inscriptions from Byblos* (Beirut, 1985); W. M. Schniedewind, "Tel Dan Stele," *BASOR* 302 (1996): 75-90.

Donald R. Vance

INSECTS

Technically, creatures whose bodies are divided into three segments and which have three pairs of legs. Entomologists estimate that tens of thousands of different species inhabit Israel. Two Hebrew terms appear to refer to insects in a generic sense. Heb. *remeś* is translated "creeping things" in the RSV. Heb. *šereṣ*, from a root meaning "to swarm," "teem," probably refers to winged insects, which are included among unclean creatures (Deut. 14:19; Lev. 11:20-23); the term can also refer to creatures that swarm in the seas (e.g., Gen. 1:20; Lev. 11:10). At least 31 more Hebrew and five Greek terms also refer to insects or other invertebrates.

RANDALL W. YOUNKER

INSPIRATION

A term derived from Lat. *inspirare* (lit., "to breathe into"), referring to the claim that oral or written discourse is prompted by the Spirit. In both the biblical and nonbiblical worlds prophetic or ecstatic utterance was seen to be the result of spirit activity. For example, Balaam, the Babylonian diviner, proclaims his oracles after "the Spirit of God came upon him" (Num. 24:2-3). Philo frequently reflects the Jewish claim that all the prophets, and Moses most of all, were inspired by the Spirit of God (*Life of Moses* 1.281; 2.187-91). Postexilic Judaism believed that prophetic inspiration had ceased (Zech. 13:2-6), later to be replaced by the teaching authority of the rabbis.

Early Christian tradition saw the outpouring of the Spirit in the whole community as the fulfillment of the promise for the end time (Joel 2:28-29[MT 3:1-2]; Acts 2:16-18). Moreover, this spirit-inspired activity and speech extended to a whole host of spiritual and pastoral ministries (1 Cor. 12:8-30). Competing "spirits," however, must be "tested" to discern their truth or falsehood (1 John 4:1-3).

Beginning with both Philo and Josephus we find the belief that the Jewish Scriptures themselves had been inspired by God (Philo *Life of Moses* 2.292; Josephus *Ant.* 10.10.4). Christians accepted the belief that the Spirit spoke through the Scriptures, both in the prophetic tradition and elsewhere (2 Pet. 1:19-21; 2 Tim. 3:16-17).

From the patristic period onward Christians have sought to define precisely how, and in what manner, the inspiration of Scripture occurs. By the middle of the 2nd century, the Christian Scriptures were considered by Irenaeus, Clement of Alexandria, and Origen to be equally inspired along with the Jewish biblical texts. Various patristic analogies and metaphors were employed to explain the process of inspiration, such as playing a musical instrument or giving dictation. The human author was seen as merely the instrument of the voice of God, which had to be modulated and intoned in accord with the limits of the instrument.

Scholastic claims concerning the literal and verbal inspiration of Scripture gradually gave way to the belief in "limited inspiration," which was understood to mean divine assistance to avoid errors. Yet theories of biblical inerrancy remain firm in many fundamentalist and evangelical traditions. Contemporary hermeneutics, however, wrestles with social and historical issues of the communal character and formulation of biblical traditions and how to accommodate a theory of inspiration within such a framework. Literary critical theory, furthermore, recognizes that not just the writing of the text but also the reading and interpretation of the text are performed within the context of the spirit-inspired faith community. Such a view requires a broader and more nuanced theory of inspiration than has been formulated in the Church to date.

BARBARA E. BOWE

INTEREST

See DEBT, INTEREST, LOANS.

INTERPRETATION, BIBLICAL

OT and Judaism

Interpretation of the Bible began within the Bible itself. Later texts interpreted and appropriated earlier ones, as the book of Jeremiah illustrates. Jer. 23:1-6 includes an oracle concerning the "branch," a legitimate ruler in David's line, whose just rule will contrast with that of Judah's current leaders, whom Jeremiah indicts and threatens with severe punishment. Jer. 33:14-18 takes up and expands this oracle with reference to the permanence of David's house and the levitical priesthood, even beyond exile. Thus the early reading and interpretation of Jeremiah contributed to the growth of the book. Zechariah, in the postexilic period, then interprets Jeremiah's "branch" oracles messianically to announce the coming of a royal figure (Zech. 3:8) who will share leadership with the high priest (6:12-13). Lending urgency to Zechariah's expectations is an allusion (Zech. 1:12; cf. 7:5) to Jeremiah's prophecy that Judah's punishment would last 70 years (Jer. 25:11-12; 29:10), a formulaic number that Zechariah interprets quite literally. In thus interpreting Jeremiah's prophecy, Zechariah understood his own visions and oracles (chs. 1–6) as marking the end of Judah's punishment and the beginning of its future.

Biblical interpretation *within* the Bible implicitly acknowledged, and also established, the authority of the earlier material it used in quite varied ways. Zechariah alludes to Jeremiah and to other texts — especially from Isaiah — in elaborating, and authorizing, his vision of the future. And Jeremiah (Jer. 26:12-19) expressly cites an earlier prophet, Micah (Mic. 3:12), as precedent in a legal discussion. This process of interpretation contributed not only to the growth of the OT, but also to its eventual status as a definitive collection that tended to resist further expansion.

By the 1st century B.C.E., whether or not the Hebrew canon was in some sense closed, interpretation of the Bible was taking new forms. Pseudo-Philo's *Biblical Antiquities* retells the biblical story, adding interpretive detail. Translation offered another means of interpretation. The Jewish community in Alexandria had already produced a Greek version, the LXX, which differs in many places from the MT. From a later date, the several Targums represent another, more paraphrastic translation into Aramaic; according to rabbinic practice, they supplemented and interpreted, but did not replace, the Hebrew text in the weekly synagogue readings.

Especially after the destruction of the second temple (70 C.E.), rabbinic interpretive practices — the practice of commentary — became dominant in Judaism. The term "midrash" can serve for the mode of rabbinic commentary, which begins from a biblical text and offers legal (halakhic) or illustrative (haggadic) interpretation. Any part of the text — a sentence, a word, a letter — may be the subject of interpretation, in conversation with a living tradition of commentary: an oral Torah alongside the written Torah. Rabbinic interpretation in early Judaism was not arbitrary. In time, it articulated exegetical rules *(middôṯ)* which had been established by use; best known are the lists of 13 and seven ascribed to R. Ishmael and R. Hillel, respectively. These are rules of inference and analogy, describing legitimate means of treating the internal consistency and wholeness of the Torah, which contains all wisdom and has its origin from God.

Other forms of interpretation developed within early Judaism, in or shortly before the 1st century. Departing, physically and theologically, from the Pharisees and what would become rabbinic Judaism in Jerusalem was the group at Qumran. The Temple Scroll (11QT), a rewriting of the Torah and the longest of the Dead Sea Scrolls, reflects the group's pervasive concern for matters of cultic purity and ritual. Another group of scrolls, the *pesharim,* has similarities to rabbinic midrash. However, the pesharim quote an entire passage (sometimes only part of a verse, from a prophet or Psalms), followed by "the interpretation concerns. . . ." The pesharim assume that the Qumran community lives in the last days and can take comfort from the prophet's words, whose message for the present the pesharim decode.

Early Church and Medieval Interpretation

The Qumran community was not alone among apocalyptic Jewish groups who developed their own characteristic interpretive practices. For the followers of Jesus, these centered on Jesus himself, in the events of whose life they saw Scripture as being "fulfilled" (John 19:36). "Scripture," in the case of the NT, means primarily the Greek Bible (LXX), which in time could be called the "old covenant" or OT (cf. 2 Cor. 3:14).

The NT interprets Scripture in quite varied ways. In places it resembles Qumran's pesharim, as when Jesus in Luke 4:16-19 quotes Isa. 61:1-2 and a part of 58:6, and announces that "today this scripture has been fulfilled in your hearing" (Luke 4:21). Matthew's account of the magi (Matt. 2:1-11) can be read as a narrative realization of Isa. 60:1-6. The Letter to the Hebrews interprets in a more Platonic fashion, with Christ bearing the "imprint" or character of God (Heb. 1:3), and the old covenant as a mundane copy of a heavenly archetype (8:5; cf. Exod. 25:40). Hebrews, which is dense with quotations of Scripture, employs rabbinic exegetical techniques, but in order to show Christ's and the Church's supersession of Judaism and the "first" covenant (Heb. 8:7). Paul's letters proceed differently, employing as well as urging a spiritual and "ecclesiocentric" reading of Scripture shaped by the experience of the Spirit in the Christian community (2 Cor. 3:2-18). Paul's interpretation, and that of the NT generally, has often been called typological: establishing a figural (cor)relation between two events or entities, such as Adam and Christ (Rom. 5:14) or Israel and the Church. This provokes the question whether or to what extent Paul's use of typology may be distinguished from allegory.

Paul uses the term "allegory" in Gal. 4:21-31 (v. 24), but proceeds differently from the allegorical interpretation that Christians practiced in subsequent centuries. While Philo of Alexandria (30 B.C.E.–C.E. 40) practiced allegorical interpretation in the service of Judaism, a later Alexandrian, Origen (185-253/4), was the most able Christian allegorist. Origen's hermeneutics coheres with his tripartite anthropology — body, soul, spirit. "Body" corresponds to reading for the literal or fleshly sense of the text and "spirit" to a spiritual reading; in this way, hermeneutics corresponds to the soteriological ascent *(anagōgē)* of the soul or the mind to the divine. Interpretation of this kind not only brings but requires spiritual enlightenment; hence, the spiritual sense is hidden within the literal, and remains hidden to those incapable of discerning it. Some texts have or make no literal sense, driving the interpreter to search for their inexhaustible spiritual meaning.

Origen's contemplative and mystical hermeneutics, and the allegorical tradition in Alexandria, had their counterpart and opposition in Antioch. There people like Diodore of Tarsus and Theodore of Mopsuestia, in the 4th and 5th centuries, stressed historical and literal exegesis. Jerome (347?-420), early under the influence of Origen, was compelled as a translator (the Latin Vulgate) to study the literal sense, while recognizing other meanings as well. Augustine (354-430), especially in *On Christian Doctrine,* attended to the Bible's rhetoric, to the way God communicates through Scripture, and the distinction between words and things as signs and the spiritual realities *(res)* to which they refer. In most places, the text's literal sense is clear in its teaching of faith, love, and hope; where it is obscure, a figurative reading is required (3.9-10). The Bible's edifying purpose forms a rule for its interpretation. After Augustine, the understanding of the Bible as having a fourfold sense (literal, allegorical, tropological, anagogical) brought together the main streams of patristic hermeneutics.

Medieval hermeneutics can be thought of as a lengthy debate about the place and definition of Scripture's literal sense. Invigorating this debate was the confrontation with classical learning and its new disciplines, and with it a certain tension between monasteries and the cathedral schools. Classical texts like those of Aristotle were mediated through Arabic scholars, who affected Jewish interpretation as well. In the later Middle Ages, Jewish interpreters expressed a preference for the literal sense *(peshat)* over the applied sense *(derash)*, or sought ways to coordinate the two. In the 11th and 12th centuries, Rashi, Moses Maimonides, and Ibn Ezra exercised a profound influence on Jewish interpretation and, either directly or indirectly, on Christian interpreters as well. Hugh of St. Victor, Thomas Aquinas, and Nicholas of Lyra stressed the literal sense as the basis of all interpretation, but they defined "literal sense" in different ways. For Thomas, the literal sense was what the author intended, the ultimate author of Scripture being God. Nicholas introduced a double literal sense, so that the son promised to David in 2 Sam. 7 is literally both Solomon and, but more properly, Jesus Christ.

The Reformation and Modern Interpretation

Implicit, and often explicit, in both patristic and medieval interpretation, is that the normative sense of Scripture must be determined in accordance with the rule of faith or the analogy of faith — with what Christians believe and the Church teaches. A late medieval theologian, Jean Gerson (1363-1429), applied this to the definition of the literal meaning of Scripture, whose words *could* mean any variety of things. Its literal meaning, he argued — thus its normative meaning, its *res* — is established "by the holy doctors and expositors of sacred Scripture." He argued this against John Hus, a dissenter from the Catholic Church who demanded to be proved wrong by the plain meaning of Scripture.

Martin Luther, a century later, also dissented from the Catholic Church, while agreeing entirely with Gerson's stress on the literal sense of Scripture. Like other Reformers, such as John Calvin and Ulrich Zwingli, Luther reflected humanism's motto, *ad fontes* ("to the sources"). Their access to the biblical sources was greatly enhanced by the availability of Greek and Hebrew texts and their ability to read them. In turning to Scripture, Luther did not reject Church tradition; he appealed to it in arguments against the Anabaptists, but he held Scripture properly interpreted to be the critical norm of the Church's tradition and its teaching. Justification by faith, the hermeneutical distinction between law and gospel, and the principle that Scripture is its own interpreter lie behind the Lutheran motto, *sola scriptura* ("Scripture alone"). Calvin, like Luther, devoted much of his energy to biblical interpretation, but Calvin also wrote a handbook to guide readers of Scripture, his *Institutes of the Christian Religion*. One may read this as an effort to articulate the *res* — the reality or meaning to which Scripture bears witness.

Protestant "Orthodox" or scholastic theologians of the post-Reformation period sought to defend and advance the insights of the Reformers, after the Council of Trent (1545-1563) refined and confirmed Catholic teaching. One point of contention concerned the Protestant notion of Scripture's clarity: while only the Holy Spirit could give internal clarity, Scripture is clear in what it teaches about salvation; hence, even a layperson — even an unbeliever — could correct the bishop from Scripture. To Catholics, this amounted to private interpretation and would result in anarchy. Protestants contended that the Catholic view of multiple senses entailed that one text could signify or refer to different things, undermining Scripture's authority by placing it under the Church's. The Reformed Protestants said that interpretation must be guided by the analogy of faith — in conformity with the creeds, catechism, and confessional articles. Formally, this differed little from medieval views.

The arcane character of Protestant scholasticism and its confessionalism provoked contrasting responses in the 17th century. In the Netherlands, Benedict Spinoza and Hugo Grotius introduced historical and rigorously *critical* interpretation of the Bible. Spinoza argued that it was immaterial whether the biblical stories, or their moral lessons, or the doctrines derived from them are true, since only their meaning matters — the way they contribute to piety and behavior. Truth is for philosophy to determine. In Germany, Philip Spener and A. H. Francke urged direct engagement with Scripture, without the mediating artifice of dogmatic theology. Whereas Spinoza and Grotius required an objective stance toward the text, Spener and especially Francke said that the spiritual disposition of the interpreter must accord with the Spirit who inspired the text. While Spinoza and Grotius tended to identify the literal or primary sense of the text with its historical sense, Francke joined the literal sense with the affective sense *(sensus pius)*, and said that the text so interpreted must be applied to the interpreting subject. Pietists like Francke and J. A. Bengel were anything but unsophisticated; indeed, Bengel's work represented the most meticulous textual scholarship among Christians since Origen.

The rationalists and pietists conspired unwittingly to introduce the modern era of biblical interpretation, which pursued textual and historical study with increasing detachment from Church doctrine. In France, Richard Simon's critical study of the OT (1670) argued that the Pentateuch consisted of traditions compiled by postexilic editors. Now "tradition" could refer, not to Church tradition, but to material lying behind the biblical texts. A century later in Germany, Johann S. Semler's "Free Investigation of the Canon" proposed that the canon should be studied as a historical phenomenon, rather than as a norm, and its books regarded as witnesses to their own times. Robert Lowth's study of Hebrew poetry, in England, and Johann G. Herder's work on the same subject, in Germany, helped to combine biblical scholarship's historical interests with romanticism. These were joined early in the 19th century by the philosophy of G. W. F. Hegel (among others), which influenced the developmental theories of Ferdinand C. Baur (NT) and Wilhelm Vatke (OT), and David F. Strauss's mythic interpretation of the NT.

Hegel's colleague in Berlin, Friedrich D. E. Schleiermacher, lectured on hermeneutics, elevating that topic to renewed theological importance. He held that an interpreter must enter into the subjectivity of the author, not only through grammatical study of the text but through an act of intuition or divination — in order to understand the biblical authors better than they understood themselves. Here pietism has its echo.

Contemporary Approaches

Schleiermacher's influence on biblical interpretation was mediated by Wilhelm Dilthey, who viewed texts as expressions of life fixed in writing. This view was joined with Martin Heidegger's hermeneutic phenomenology in Rudolf Bultmann's program of "demythologizing" the NT. Bultmann wanted to understand the mythological expressions of the NT's theology in order again to hear the *kerygma* or proclamation about Jesus (and decisively the cross) as the advent of God's reign, which calls for faith — for a decision, yes or no. Faith is Bultmann's analogue to Heidegger's "authentic existence." More importantly for Bultmann, he considered his radical historical criticism and demythologizing to be consistent with Luther's (and, he believed, Paul's) doctrine of justification by faith alone.

Bultmann's work, which took shape between the two world wars, began in conversation with Karl Barth, whose Romans commentary (1918) marked a radical departure from the prevailing historical-critical interpretation of the Bible. Biblical scholarship in the 19th and early 20th centuries had been invigorated by the availability of materials from Palestine and the ancient world generally, and refinements in historical and literary analysis (form criticism, tradition history). These helped to fuel interest in the history of religion, and especially in the development of the "Israelite" and early Christian religions, each in their respective and quite different contexts. In Barth's judgment, this historicism and the liberal theology it comported with failed to engage the subject, God, and subject matter *(Sache)* of the biblical text. Bultmann accused Barth of failing critically to assess the text and its expressions in terms of its subject matter.

In North America after 1945, the Biblical Theology movement also responded to what its proponents viewed as stagnation in biblical studies and theology. Influenced by C. H. Dodd and H. H. Rowley in England, they stressed the unity of the OT and NT and the essentially historical and dynamic character of biblical theology. This attempt to join historical-critical studies with theology encountered severe criticism, but just as influential in its demise was the availability of more compelling alternatives, such as Gerhard von Rad's tradition-historical approach to the OT. In the NT field, Bultmann's students, especially Ernst Fuchs and Gerhard Ebeling, developed his views further in the "new hermeneutic."

Another of Bultmann's students, Hans-Georg Gadamer, returned to the project of a universal hermeneutics or theory of understanding that Schleiermacher initiated. However, Gadamer moved, through Heidegger, beyond Schleiermacher's subjectivism and considered understanding to be an event in which the horizon of the text and that of the interpreter are "fused." This event thus occurs within a tradition, as part of the effective history of the text. Appealing in part to theological hermeneutics, Gadamer rehabilitated such concepts as tradition, authority, and prejudice (or pre-judgment). While Gadamer did not employ these concepts naively, Jürgen Habermas criticized him for attending insufficiently to the distorting effects of tradition, which covers over varieties of injustice; Habermas proposed a counterfactual ideal-speech situation as a critical principle. Paul Ricoeur has drawn on the German tradition of philosophical and theological hermeneutics, but also on French work in structuralism and semiotics. His theory of interpretation includes a necessary step of distanciation or explanation in moving from a first to a second naiveté — the appropriation of the world projected by the text.

These developments in hermeneutics have helped biblical scholars to consider the role and character, and the aims, of their historical-critical approaches, and to pursue alternatives. In recent years, various kinds of narrative approaches have appeared, influenced both by the study of literature and theory in fields outside biblical studies and by theological concerns. Simultaneously, archaeological research and the availability of new materials — especially the Ugaritic texts, the Dead Sea Scrolls, the Nag Hammadi texts — have again invigorated historical studies. These now routinely include theories and methods drawn from the human sciences, especially anthropology and sociology.

The most significant recent development in biblical interpretation has been the inclusion of a broader range of voices and interests. Following Vatican II, Roman Catholics and Protestants have worked together. Neither has biblical interpretation remained an exclusively Christian enterprise. While Jewish scholars, especially in Israel and North America, have advanced the historical study of the Bible, they have also helped to expose the anti-Semitic biases of much biblical scholarship. Moreover, the Jewish philosophers/theologians Franz Rosenzweig and Emmanuel Levinas contribute an "other" voice to the subject-centered hermeneutics that has dominated for two centuries. Liberation and feminist interpreters have drawn attention to, or unmasked, the vested interests concealed in, and hence the political character of, the institutions and practices of biblical interpretation. These interpreters draw on experience and perspectives not represented in past practice. The significance of social location, including gender, race, class, and socio-historical context, is exhibited in biblical interpretation from around the globe. African, Asian, and Latina/Latino interpreters have expanded the theoretical and moral-political issues that hermeneutics must engage.

A critical hermeneutics of suspicion extends also to the biblical texts themselves, or to their production. The "new historicism" employs many of the methods of historical criticism but investigates the margins of texts, viewed as "sites of contestation" that reflect and participate in social "power relations." There is at the same time a call for a renewed theological interpretation of Scripture that values pre-modern interpretation and tradition, and has as its context the Church and its practices.

Biblical interpretation now embraces wide diversity, and no one mode can claim to occupy its center.

Bibliography. A. K. M. Adam, *Making Sense of New Testament Theology* (Macon, 1995); J. Bowker, *The Targums and Rabbinic Literature: An Introduction to Jewish Interpretations of Scripture* (Cambridge, 1989); M. Fishbane, *Biblical Interpretation in Ancient Israel* (Oxford, 1985); S. E. Fowl, ed., *The Theological Interpretation of Scripture* (Cambridge, Mass., 1997); R. A. Mueller, *Post-Reformation Reformed Dogmatics* 2 (Grand Rapids, 1993); J. S. Preus, *From Shadow to Promise: Old Testament Interpretation from Augustine to the Young Luther* (Cambridge, Mass., 1969); F. Segovia and M. A. Tolbert, *Reading from This Place,* 2 vols. (Minneapolis, 1995).

Ben C. Ollenburger

IOB (Heb. *yôḇ*)
A son of Issachar (Gen. 46:13). The name should probably read "Jashub" (**1**), as in the parallel accounts (Num. 26:24; 1 Chr. 7:1); LXX Gk. *Iasoub* suggests that the letter *shin* was omitted from the Hebrew through scribal error.

IOTA (Gk. *iṓta*)
The ninth letter of the Greek alphabet, corresponding to Eng. *i* and Heb. *yodh*. At Matt. 5:18 it is noted as the smallest letter in the contemporary Hebrew and Aramaic script (KJV "jot").

IPHDEIAH (Heb. *yipḏěyâ*)
The head of a Benjaminite household; a son of Shashak (1 Chr. 8:25).

IPHTAH (Heb. *yiptaḥ*)
A town in the tribal allotment of Judah, one of nine cities belonging to the Keilah district in the southern Shephelah (Josh. 15:43). Although the ancient site is uncertain, it may be identified as Atar Nehusha (14474.11456), just NE of Beit Jibrin/Bet Guvrin.

Steven M. Ortiz

IPHTAHEL (Heb. *yiptaḥ-'ēl*)
A valley along the border between the tribal territories of Zebulun and Asher (Josh. 19:14, 27). It is most likely Wadi el-Malik/Naḥal Sippori, NW of Nazareth.

IR (Heb. *'îr*)
A Benjaminite, son of Bela (1 Chr. 7:12).

IRA (Heb. *'îrā'*)
1. A Manassite of the lineage of Jair (or from Jattir), called a priest (Heb. *kōhēn*) of David (2 Sam. 20:26). The Hebrew term may designate here a special role of confidence in David's court, apparently as private priest to the king (cf. 2 Sam. 8:18; cf. 1 Chr. 18:17, "chief official").

2. The son of Ikkesh from Tekoa; one of David's Champions (2 Sam. 23:26; 1 Chr. 11:28) and captain of the division guarding the temple in the sixth month (27:9).

3. An Ithrite who was one of David's Champions (2 Sam. 23:38; 1 Chr. 11:40). On the basis of some ancient versions, which call him a Jattirite, he is sometimes identified with **1.**

IRAD (Heb. *'îrāḏ*)
The son of Enoch and grandson of Cain (Gen. 4:18). He is thought to be the same as Jared in the genealogy at Gen. 5:15-20.

IRAM (Heb. *'îrām*)
The eponymous ancestor of an Edomite clan (Gen. 36:43 = 1 Chr. 1:54).

IRI (Heb. *'îrî*)
A Benjaminite (1 Chr. 7:7); perhaps the same as Ir.

IRIJAH (Heb. *yir'îyâ*)
A sentry at the Benjamin Gate who apprehended the prophet Jeremiah as he sought to leave Jerusalem to claim his inheritance at Anathoth, charging him with deserting to the Chaldeans (Jer. 37:13-14).

IR-NAHASH (Heb. *'îr nāḥāš*)
The son of Tehinnah, listed among the descendants of Judah (1 Chr. 4:12). However, Heb. *'îr* means "city" and a cognate of *nāḥāš* is the word for copper, thus possibly "Copper City." 1 Chr. 4:12 may then indicate that Tehinnah founded Ir-nahash, just as v. 4 mentions Ephrathah as the father of Bethlehem. If Ir-nahash was a city, its location is unknown.

Paul L. Redditt

IRON
A malleable metal derived from common oxide ores such as hematite and limonite. It is the primary ingredient in wrought iron and steel. The working and use of iron is evidenced artifactually in the early 3rd millennium B.C. These early artifacts are typically high in nickel content and are apparently made of meteoric iron. The celestial origins of early iron is indicated in Old Kingdom Egyptian references to it as the "metal of heaven" and in the Sumerian cuneiform signs for "sky" and "fire" used to designate the metal in Mesopotamia. Artifacts were made of terrestrial iron in Anatolia by the middle of the 3rd millennium. Iron technology was greatly advanced by the Hittites in the 2nd millennium. Currently, the earliest physical evidence of iron mining and smelting in Canaan is from the end of the 2nd millennium at Timnah. In the 1st millennium iron became the chief utilitarian metal in the Levant, hence the designation of the period as the Iron Age.

The utilization of iron supplanted bronze as a result of technological advance, the properties of the metal, and economic factors. The development of iron was initially limited by pyrotechnology. Ancient furnaces which could melt copper from cuprous ores at 1083°C were not hot enough to melt iron from ferrous ores at 1538°C (2800°F). With a draft from blowpipes and bellows, sufficient heat could be generated to melt away impurities and to create spongelike "Iron blooms" of ca. 10 kg. (22 lb.) which had to be reheated and hammered to knock away impurities of slag and charcoal, and to make wrought iron. The iron product produced in this manner was not as tough as hardened bronze and could not be cast in molds, since it was not liquified. The use of charcoal in shaft furnaces which created a reducing atmosphere of carbon monoxide made it possible to efficiently separate iron from its oxide and carbonate ores. The subsequent steps which led to the wide expansion of iron working were carburization and tempering. The incorporation of less than 1 percent carbon in the wrought iron produced steel. This steel, when heated white hot and rapidly cooled by quenching, produced a tempered product that could attain a hardness of 6.5 on the Mohs' scale, surpassing the best bronze and having a much higher tensile strength and shock resistance. Ferrous metals thus could provide working edges on tools and weapons that could withstand intensive wear.

By the beginning of the 1st millennium, iron supplanted bronze as the standard utilitarian metal for most all metal items with the exception of those which were cast with intricate details and those in which aesthetics required a material other than iron. Economic factors contributed to this transition. Iron production utilized locally available ores and eliminated the need for expensive tin imports. A further advantage in iron production was that the process required only half the amount of fuel needed for bronze. The only disadvantage in ironworking was that it was more labor intensive, but this was no great obstacle since labor was cheap.

In the Bible the eponymous "father of metallurgists," Tubal-cain, is recognized as the forebear of those who worked in bronze and iron (Gen. 4:22). The antediluvian metalworking of Tubal-cain has been variously understood as anachronistic myth, as evidence of very early metallurgical prowess lost as a result of the Flood, or most likely as the first use of the process of heating and hammering metals and their ores, initiating a technology which developed over time. According to the biblical text iron was well known in the time of Moses. In the context of the Exodus, Canaan was recognized as a place where the Israelites could exploit local iron ores (Deut. 8:9) and where they would possibly use iron weapons (Num. 35:16) and tools (Deut. 27:5). Iron is not mentioned as being employed in the manufacture of the tabernacle, but its manufacturing process was known well enough to form a figure of speech to describe the cultural experience of the Israelites in Egypt (Deut. 4:20). In the Conquest and until the Davidic monarchy, the Israelites appear to have been at a metallurgical disadvantage to the Canaanites, whose "iron chariots" were a powerful deterrent to Israelite expansion into the plains (Josh. 17:16; Judg. 1:19; 4:3). Subsequently, the Philistines, who used iron weapons like those found in 11th-century contexts at their cities of Ekron and Tell Qasile, maintained a monopoly on metallurgy and iron in particular, which helped them to dominate the Israelites (1 Sam. 13:19-22). The metallurgical monopoly was broken by King David, who infiltrated the Philistines. He stockpiled vast quantities of iron in preparation for the Jerusalem temple construction (1 Chr. 29:2-7) and also forced subject Ammonites to work for him using iron implements such as saws, picks, and axes (2 Sam. 12:31). Iron came to be widely utilized in architecture (Jer. 1:18), particularly with iron bars and nails strengthening doors (1 Chr. 22:3; Isa. 45:2). Iron tools were widely used by the Hebrews (1 Chr. 20:3) and were of considerable value (1 Chr. 29:7). In taxonomic lists, iron is listed behind gold, silver, and bronze (Josh. 6:19; 22:8; 2 Chr. 2:14; Dan. 2:33-35) but ahead of lead (Ezek. 22:20). Iron is symbolic of strength in both the OT and NT (e.g., Job 40:18; Rev. 12:5).

Bibliography. V. C. Pigott, "Near Eastern Archaeometallurgy," in *The Study of the Ancient Near East in the Twenty-first Century,* ed. J. S. Cooper and G. M. Schwartz (Winona Lake, 1996), 139-76.

ROBERT W. SMITH

IRPEEL (Heb. *yirpĕʾēl*)
A city in the tribal territory of Benjamin (Josh. 18:27), probably located in the hill country N of Jerusalem. Some scholars place it at Khirbet Rafat (170142), N of Gibeon, ca. 10.5 km. (6.5 mi.) NW of Jerusalem.

IRRIGATION
Unlike the "hydraulic civilizations" of Egypt and Mesopotamia, which were fortunate to have major rivers for agriculture, Israel was compelled to rely upon springs and rainwater to irrigate its crops. The earliest settlements in Israel, such as Jericho, practiced fixed-plot agriculture in water-retentive soil near springs. Where available, springs continued to be exploited in the Iron Age. In Jerusalem, e.g., the Siloam Channel led the waters of the Gihon Spring south along the Kidron Valley to reservoirs at the tip of the City of David. Openings at intervals on the eastern wall of the channel, which faced the valley, allowed water to be diverted to irrigate agricultural plots in the valley below.

Population increases necessitated movement into areas without springs, where rain was the primary source of water for agriculture. Since rainfall in Israel varies drastically, settlers had to develop systems of terraces, dams, and conduits to ensure that runoff reached agricultural plots. Terraces were formed by constructing dry-stone retaining walls along the contours of steep hillsides. The result was a series of stepped, level plots that impeded the flow of water downhill, allowing it to infiltrate the soil. Terraces at Ai and Raddana date to the Iron I period.

The most impressive irrigation techniques were employed in the Negeb and the desert fringes of Transjordan. Terrace wall systems built in the Chalcolithic period retained enough water to produce wheat and barley at Shiqmim, in the Naḥal Beersheba. Farther south, irrigation systems flourished at Oboda ('Avdat), Sobata (Isbeita/Shivta), Nessana ('Auja el-Ḥafir), and other sites during the Israelite, Nabatean-Roman, and Byzantine periods. These systems included a series of walls across individual wadis, terraced fields with farmsteads known as "runoff farms," and extensive diversion systems that channeled floodwaters of main wadis into broad terraced fields where sluice gates allowed overflow from one terrace to descend to the next lower one. Iron Age runoff farms have been found in the Buqei'a region in the northeastern part of the Judean desert. Irrigation systems have been discovered at Middle Bronze Jawa, in northeastern Jordan, and Nabatean Humayma, in southern Jordan.

References to water rights and a date palm plantation in the Nessana Papyri indicate that irrigation was employed in arid regions of southern Israel into the 7th century C.E. Desert farming reached its peak in the Byzantine and Ummayid periods and ceased at about the time that the Abassids moved the caliphate to Baghdad. Runoff farming in this area required the incentive programs of strong central governments and thrived in proportion to their invested interests in the frontier.

Bibliography. O. Borowski, *Agriculture in Iron Age Israel* (Winona Lake, 1987); R. J. Forbes, "Irrigation and Drainage," in *Studies in Ancient Technology,* 3rd ed. (Leiden, 1993), 2:1-79; Ø. S. LaBianca, *Sedentarization and Nomadization: Food System Cycles at Hesban and Vicinity in Transjordan* (Berrien Springs, 1990); T. E. Levy, "How Ancient Man First Utilized the Rivers in the Desert," *BARev* 16/6 (1990): 20-31; J. P. Oleson, "The Origins and Design of Nabataean Water-Supply Systems," in *Studies in the History and Archaeology of Jordan V,* ed. K. 'Amr, F. Zayadine, and M. Zaghloul (Amman, 1995), 707-19; L. E. Stager, "The Archaeology of the Family in Ancient Israel," *BASOR* 260 (1985): 1-35; "Farming in the Judean Desert during the Iron Age," *BASOR* 221 (1976): 145-58. JAMES H. PACE

IR-SHEMESH (Heb. *'îr-šemeš*)
(also BETH-SHEMESH)
A Canaanite city ("city of the sun") allocated to the tribe of Dan (Josh. 19:41); probably the same as Har-heres, which the Danites were unable to conquer (1:35). Called elsewhere Beth-shemesh (**1**), the site has been identified as Tell er-Rumeileh (1477.1286).

IRU (Heb. *'îrû*)
A son of the Judahite Caleb, from the lineage of Jephunneh (1 Chr. 4:15).

ISAAC (Heb. *yiṣḥāq*)
The son of Abraham and Sarah. The name means "he laughs," reflecting Sarah's response when told she would have a child (Gen. 18:12); she later celebrates the birth of Isaac with laughter (21:6). Isaac is the promised offspring through whom God keeps the covenant made with Abraham in Gen. 12:1-3, although Abraham attempts to fulfill the covenant with other "heirs" (Lot, Eleazar of Damascus, Ishmael).

Isaac, as the promised offspring, is the first to be circumcised at the prescribed age of eight days (Gen. 17:12; 21:4), and Abraham marks his survival to the end of weaning with a great feast (21:8). Isaac remains the only child of Abraham and Sarah, and after the death of Sarah he marries Rebekah, the granddaughter of Abraham's brother. He becomes the father of Esau and Jacob, thereby continuing the line of descendants promised to Abraham. Isaac settles in the region of Beersheba, where God makes a promise to him (Gen. 26:3-5) similar to that given to Abraham. Isaac dies at the age of 180 and is placed by Jacob and Esau in the family tomb at Hebron (Gen. 35:27-29).

The phrase "Abraham, Isaac, and Jacob (or Israel)" occurs 23 times in the OT and 7 times in the NT, but Isaac is clearly less prominent than the other two in the remembered tradition of ancient Israel. Isaac is mentioned by name more than 70 times in Genesis, but only 33 times outside of the book.

The stories about Isaac do not form a discrete unit within the Genesis narrative. Before his marriage, Isaac's story is intertwined with that of his father and mother, and after his marriage his story is part of the story of his children. Isaac's genealogy (Gen. 25:19) follows directly after the account of Abraham's death (vv. 7-11) and directly before the birth of Jacob and Esau (vv. 21-26). The two major events in Isaac's life are tied closely to Abraham and Jacob. In Gen. 22 Isaac is more the object of than a participant in Abraham's test of faithfulness to God, as in ch. 27 he is again more the object of than a participant in Jacob's deception. Only in Gen. 24:62-67, when Isaac meets Rebekah for the first time, and in ch. 26, when Isaac encounters Abimelech, is Isaac something of a central player in the narrative.

But Isaac is linked inextricably to the promises of God to the ancestors. He is Abraham's only means of fulfilling God's promise of descendants in Gen. 12. He is the means by which God tests Abraham's (and Isaac's) fidelity to God's promises. God passes on the promise to Isaac in Gen. 25:11 after the death of Abraham, and again in 26:2-4. In Gen. 28 Isaac appears for the last time before his own death and blesses Jacob before sending him away to Paddan-aram, the home of Rebekah's brother, to find a wife. Isaac's words to his son are clearly reminiscent of God's words of promise to Abraham in Gen. 12 and to Isaac in Gen. 26.

The narratives which involve Isaac have been viewed by traditional scholarship as an amalgamation of the Yahwist, Elohist, and Priestly sources. Recent scholarship suggests that the ancestral stories were originally discrete units that originated in the various ancestral groups of which the ancient Israelites were composed. The stories of Abraham and Isaac most likely come from the southern regions of Canaan, since the narrative states that they both settled in the region of Beer-sheba; the stories of Jacob come from the northern regions, since he settled in Bethel. These units were joined together to form a single story of the successive generations of the family of Terah of Ur, the father of Abraham. The briefer stories about Isaac were woven into more extensive and detailed narratives about Abraham and Jacob. Isaac thus appears as a link between two more prominent figures in the ancestral stories of ancient Israel.

Bibliography. B. Goodnick, "Rebekah's Deceit or Isaac's Great Test," *Jewish Bible Quarterly* 23 (1995): 221-28; N. K. Gottwald, *The Hebrew Bible: A Socio-Literary Introduction* (Philadelphia, 1985), 149-78; H. Gunkel, *The Legends of Genesis* (New York, 1964); A. R. Millard and D. J. Wiseman, eds., *Essays on the Patrarchal Narratives* (1980, repr. Winona Lake, 1983).

NANCY L. DECLAISSÉ-WALFORD

ISAAC, TESTAMENT OF

A pseudonymous text in which Isaac is informed by the angel Michael of his impending death. Isaac accepts God's decree, but his son Jacob resists. Elements of the story include Isaac's short bedchamber address to Jacob on the inevitability of death; Isaac's lengthy discourse to the crowds on the subjects of the priesthood, asceticism, and the moral life; and his tour of hell and journey to heaven shortly before God takes his soul. Throughout, God's compassion on repentant sinners is emphasized.

The text is dependent on the Testament of Abraham, and while not extant in Greek, was likely composed in Greek in Egypt sometime after 100 C.E. The original Jewish text contains many Christian additions.

Bibliography. W. F. Stinespring, "Testament of Isaac," *OTP* 1:903-11. RANDAL A. ARGALL

ISAIAH, ASCENSION OF

An apocryphal work whose title is derived from the second part of the book, chs. 6–11. Chs. 1–5 are known as the Martyrdom of Isaiah. The book has a complex compositional history dating from the 2nd century B.C.E. to the 4th century C.E. The oldest part of the text (1:1–3:12 and 5:1-16) dates to the Maccabean period and tells the story of the death of the 8th-century prophet Isaiah at the hand of Manasseh. The Christian interpolation of the martyrdom (3:13–4:22) tells of Isaiah's vision of the ultimate victory of the Messiah and his army over the reign of evil and the second coming of the Lord. This interpolation served to make the text even more relevant to those who died as martyrs in the early Church.

The second half of the text, chs. 6–11, is the story of the ascension of Isaiah and is clearly a Christian work. During the 20th year of the reign of Hezekiah Isaiah receives a vision in which he journeys through the seven heavens, seeing the glory of the Lord praised in each successive heaven. Upon reaching the seventh heaven, he sees the Messiah, commissioned by God, descend from the heavens to earth. Isaiah then witnesses the miraculous birth and observes the infancy, life, crucifixion, and resurrection of the Messiah, who then ascends to the seventh heaven. The Ascension of Isaiah ends with Manasseh becoming the servant of Satan and "destroyed"; thus, ultimate victory is through the Messiah.

The book expresses themes such as faith during persecution, demonology, prophecy, the corruption of the Church, the trinity, and the Incarnation. While some have tried to connect this document to the Qumran sect, no copies have been found there. It is clear from the presence of both Jewish and Christian texts in the same composite that there was a struggle between differing groups. With an emphasis on demonology and Satan as the cause of Manasseh's evil ways, the editors of the final version make it clear that they believed that Satan was behind the other group.

Bibliography. M. A. Knibb, "Martyrdom and Ascension of Isaiah," *OTP* 2:143-76.

MARC A. JOLLEY

ISAIAH (Heb. *yĕšaʿyāhû, yĕšaʿyâ*), BOOK OF

The first and longest book of the Hebrew prophets. Essentially a hopeful book, Isaiah addresses questions of justice, righteousness, and power — its use, abuse, and limits, as well as courage, patience, and hope.

The Prophetic Scroll

Historical Questions

Questions about the unity of the Isaiah scroll have dominated scholarship for the past century. With only a few modifications, the proposals set forth by Bernard Duhm in 1892 have prevailed into our own era. Building on earlier proposals of J. G. Eichhorn (1783) and J. C. Doderlein (1789) as well as the 11th-century Jewish scholar Ibn Ezra, Duhm argued both on literary and historical grounds that chs. 40-55 must be viewed as the work of a later author, Deutero-Isaiah (Second Isaiah), who wrote after the fall of Jerusalem in 587 B.C.E. He contended that only chs. 1-39 may be viewed as source material for discerning the work of the prophet Isaiah, who lived and worked in Jerusalem in the latter half of the 8th century (750-700). Duhm did not suggest a Babylonian setting for chs. 40-55; he contended only that Second Isaiah was written from a foreign land such as Lebanon or Phoenicia. He also saw Isa. 56-66 as the work of a third author, Trito-Isaiah (Third Isaiah), who wrote in the 5th century, when exiles had returned from captivity in Babylon.

This three-part division of Isaiah has received widespread support until recent years. The only major modification has been that scholars have generally affirmed a Babylonian setting for chs. 40-55, late in the exilic era when the fall of Babylon seemed imminent and when the promises of Cyrus gave rise to new hopes for a return to Jerusalem and Judah.

In 1927 Theodore H. Robinson summarized the development of prophetic literature in terms of three stages. First, small independent oracles were collected and preserved by disciples of a prophet.

Later, disciples gathered the individual oracles into collections, adding new material and arranging the oracles into new thematic arrangements. Still later, these collections were reorganized and expanded into what today is the final form of the text. This understanding was developed from the important form-critical work of Hugo Gressmann (1914) and the concerns of Hermann Gunkel (1928) for careful attention to genre analysis. Building on the research of Gressmann and Gunkel, a generation of 20th-century scholars focused on Robinson's first stage, attempting to rediscover the actual words of the original prophetic author, Isaiah ben Amoz. Inevitably, this quest involved the distinction between what is "authentic" in the text and what is "later redaction."

More recently, the focus of Isaiah research has changed dramatically. Emphasis has moved from the quest to discover the original author to questions about the literary development and final shape of the scroll (Robinson's second and third stages). New research has focused on the work of the redactors, who are understood not just as collectors or organizers but as creative theologians who expanded earlier writing for people of faith in later eras. The redaction work is understood to be equally as "authentic" and important as earlier layers of the text.

Canonical Criticism

To a large degree, recent scholarship on Isaiah has been influenced by the work of Brevard S. Childs (*Introduction to the Old Testament as Scripture,* 1979) and his concern for canonical criticism. Childs has raised important questions about the final literary form of the biblical text as received and preserved within Jewish and Christian communities of faith. Childs contends that Isaiah is the classic example of an extended redactional process, involving repeated revisions and additions over a long period of time. But he notes that Isa. 1-39 clearly contains some material that is equally as late as material in chs. 56-66. These postexilic texts, consciously represented as the writing of the 8th-century prophet, have been purposely disconnected or "divorced" from their original historical settings precisely so that they may be held up and preserved as the living word of the Lord given to the prophet Isaiah in his vision but preserved for a new audience. Rather than simply testimony about past events, this "sacred Scripture" is a word about judgment and salvation for people in any age. Equally committed to a canonical approach, James A. Sanders focuses on the dynamic realities of those specific historical communities in which the text was preserved, examining the relationships between the text and its context, between traditions and their particular historical situations.

Some scholars have focused even more on the synchronic dimensions of Isaiah, building on their understandings of the "implied reader" of the text.

Rolf Rendtorff contends that the literary text of Isa. 40-55 is the starting point or basis for understanding the growth of the Isaiah scroll. Chs. 1-39 and 56-66 are both oriented to chs. 40-55. Various thematic and theological concepts such as the motifs of "Zion-Jerusalem," "the Holy One of Israel," and the concepts of righteousness *(ṣdq/ṣdqh)* unite the three parts and call us to consider the synchronic dimensions of the scroll. Ronald E. Clements, Christopher R. Seitz, and H. G. M. Williamson have suggested that an earlier redaction of Isaiah can be discerned within chs. 1-39, which was then enlarged and edited during the exilic and postexilic eras. Marvin A. Sweeney argues for a fourfold redactional history, working backwards from the completed scroll in the time of Ezra and Nehemiah, to a 6th-century redaction at the end of the Exile, to a collection dating from the time of Josiah, and to a collection dating from the end of Isaiah's lifetime. He contends that the final form should be understood in two parts, chs. 1-33 and chs. 34-66, each focused around a peculiar vision of Yahweh's plans for a world-wide sovereignty at Zion in a future time of restoration after the pending judgment. Chs. 1-33 anticipate such events in a future time; chs. 34-66 suggest that the process by which Yahweh's sovereignty will appear in the world has already begun.

Primary Historical Setting

There seems little doubt that the final redaction of Isaiah (chs. 1-66) should be understood against the background of the postexilic era, possibly in the era of Ezra and Nehemiah (450-400) as presupposed by chs. 56-66. At the same time, there is evidence that the present text of chs. 1-55 dates from the last years of the Exile (550-539) and that chs. 56-66 should be recognized as a postexilic addition. It seems probable that there were earlier redactions of an Isaiah scroll dating from the era of Josiah (640-609) or even from the lifetime of the prophet (cf. 8:16; 30:8-11). Certain texts within chs. 1-39 are set against the background of the era of the prophet, Isaiah ben Amoz. But because Isa. 1-39 has been so heavily redacted, the quest for an earlier edition is both problematic and difficult. What does seem certain is that those who collected and redacted these chapters believed deeply that their additions were consistent with Isaiah's prophetic vision. It is the vision that is central, not the original author.

Three factors from the late exilic era seem to have influenced the formation of chs. 1-55 in decisive ways. First, these chapters offer a response and interpretation of the painful memories of the destruction of Jerusalem in 598 and 587. There may in fact have been some within the late exilic audience who remembered the devastation of Judah, the 18-month siege of Jerusalem, the degrading feelings of humiliation at the capitulation of the city, and the forced emigration to Babylon (2 Kgs. 24-25). Undoubtedly there were others in that original audience for whom questions about faith in Yahweh seemed remote, preposterous, or irrelevant. In a very profound way, Isaiah addresses the crisis of religious faith in the aftermath of destruction (cf. Lam. 1-5). Amid the loss of family and loved ones, villages, city, temple, priesthood, and king, the vision of Isaiah still speaks of faith in a loving God and the election of Israel to a particular calling.

A second factor was the decline of Babylonian power. After the death of Nebuchadnezzar in 562, no successor emerged who could hold the empire together. Without internal stability, the throne passed to three different members of the royal family in just seven years. An old world order was crumbling. Amid the turmoil, the redactor included Isaiah's words about empires and his warnings that the arrogant abuse of power would eventually lead to judgment (10:5-19; 13:1–14:32).

The third factor was the rise of Cyrus of Persia, whose tolerant policies toward captive peoples gave hope to some within the community (44:24–45:13). The author of chs. 1-55 clearly discerned in Cyrus a sign of a new era and the basis for hope of a return to Jerusalem.

The political realities of the late exilic era inform and undergird the hopeful poetry of chs. 40-55, particularly the opening words: "Comfort, O comfort my people, says your God" (40:1). In a world dominated by futility and frustration, a world where nations and empires rise and fall, the prophetic word is set forth: "The grass withers, the flower fades, but the word of our God will stand forever" (40:8).

It is from this historical perspective that the theology of chs. 1-55 comes into focus. Judah has come through a time of judgment. She has experienced and survived a "day of Yahweh," a decisive moment of judgment that is now cited as evidence of the sovereignty of God. This is grounded in the memory that Isaiah warned beforehand of such an event (2:6-22). From the exilic perspective, Isaiah's vision about judgment for Judah and Jerusalem has been fulfilled. But Isaiah is remembered as one who also spoke words of hope.

Message

Memories of Isaiah's Vision (Chs. 1-39)

A People in Revolt (Ch. 1). Three superscriptions in chs. 1-35 shape the memories preserved in the opening chapters. In 1:1 the scroll is introduced; parallel superscriptions in 2:1; 13:1 mark the opening of the two major sections of this portion of the scroll. Ch. 1 presents a portrait of the people of Israel lost in their own pursuits, a people who have forgotten their own identity (1:3). The dominant theme of this chapter is that Yahweh, the Holy One of Israel, has been forsaken by his people (1:4-9). Religious rituals and sacrifice are carried out without sincerity while the poor, oppressed, orphan, and widow are neglected (1:10-17). In place of Yahweh, people have created little gods shaped from the earth or have made themselves into gods by their arrogance and self-centered conduct, thus inviting certain judgment upon themselves (1:18-31).

But there is hope. Humans have the capacity to change. The fundamental message of social justice which is at the heart of the Isaiah scroll is sounded in 1:16-17: "Cease to do evil, learn to do good; seek justice, rescue the oppressed, defend the orphan, plead for the widow."

Judgment for Judah and Jerusalem (Chs. 2-12). Faced with repeated human rebellion, what is Yahweh to do? The question is posed in dramatic fashion in the "parable of the vineyard" (5:1-7): people are to be "fruitful," caring for the earth and one another. But how long does one wait to see "good grapes," and what does a vinekeeper finally do with "bitter grapes"?

According to the "day of Yahweh" oracle (2:6-22), judgment is coming for Judah and Jerusalem. Nevertheless, words of promise for the faithful (2:1-5; 4:2-6) frame the opening judgment oracles (2:6-22; 3:1-12, 13-15; 3:16–4:1). A collection of memories of Isaiah (6:1–9:7) is framed by new judgment words, with 5:8-24, 25-30 structured as a preface and 9:8–10:4; 10:5-19 as a supplement. In 10:5-19 the Assyrian Empire is remembered as an "instrument" by which Yahweh will bring judgment; yet because of her own arrogance, Assyria herself will be punished. The judgment speeches in chs. 6-11 involve memories of northern Israel: ch. 7 recalls events related to the revolt of Syria and northern Israel against Assyria in 735-734. These chapters cannot be read apart from the reality that those kingdoms were destroyed and deported by the Assyrians in 721.

This section offers insight about the prophet. Isaiah ben Amoz was married to a person known as the "prophetess" (8:3), and had at least two and possibly three sons with prophetic names: Shear-jashub ("A remnant shall return," 7:3), Maher-shalal-hash-baz ("The spoil speeds, the prey hastens," 8:1-4), and perhaps Immanuel ("God with us," 7:14); all three "sign-children" lead to words of hope for Judah amid the turmoil and threats of war. Isaiah lived in Jerusalem and had personal dealings with both Ahaz (7:1-9, 10-17) and Hezekiah (cf. 37:1–39:8). His life as a social critic and as a man of conscience is confirmed not just by the words attributed to him but also by his actions, including encounters with Ahaz or walking naked in Jerusalem as a warning of impending doom (20:1-6).

Also in chs. 6-11 Isaiah speaks of an "ideal Davidic king," both in terms of his disillusionment with Ahaz and in his lofty expectations for a future "anointed One" (Messiah) (9:2-7[MT 1-6]; 11:1-9; cf. 32:1-8) who will provide wise and just leadership. In a coming era, exiles who survive the judgment will be a "remnant" community and a witness to the faith of Israel (10:20-23).

Isaiah's "call vision" (6:1-13) comes into focus when remembered from the vantage of the later exilic era. Out of a rebellious people "laden with iniquity" (1:4), Yahweh summoned one whose life he touched with a vision of heaven and with live coals (6:7). Isaiah was commissioned as a herald to speak for the living God. Later generations remembered him as a faithful servant who continued to proclaim Yahweh's word, even when the people's response had been only greater deafness and blindness. Isaiah is remembered as one whose vision remains true, even amidst the realities of the Babylonian captivity (6:9-13).

The catechetical character of Isa. 2-12 is reinforced by the doxology in ch. 12. The audience, which is to understand itself as a "remnant community of faith," is to consider the events of the past with sober reflection but also with words of thanksgiving and praise. Seen in conjunction with the opening vision of peace in 2:1-5, ch. 12 provides the concluding and hopeful framework (or inclusion) for the poetry preserved in 2:6-11:16.

Judgment for Babylon and the Nations (Chs. 13-35). Isa. 13:1 opens a second major section, declaring judgment for Babylon and the nations. Drawing on themes set forth in 10:5-19, the scroll now boldly proclaims that Yahweh is not just the "Holy One of Israel" but also the sovereign of all nations. Judah has had her "day" of judgment, but similar "days" are to come for all arrogant and boastful nations, including Babylon. "Day of Yahweh" poetry frames this section (chs. 13-14, 34-35). Many have contended that its center (chs. 24-27), the "little apocalypse," comes from a much later era, but the poetic themes here have striking similarities with other "day of Yahweh" poems and should be viewed as prophetic response to the horrors of war, not apocalyptic literature. These chapters affirm that proud rulers of the earth will be brought low (26:5) while the faithful who "wait for the Lord" (26:8) will find security and hope. In chs. 34-35 impending judgment is announced for Edom and a new word of encouragement given to the community of faith (35:10).

Isaiah and Hezekiah (Chs. 36-39). The historical prose narrative in chs. 36-39 recalls an era of military crisis from the lifetime of Isaiah ben Amoz. Dated "in the fourteenth year of King Hezekiah" (701), this was a time when the Assyrian Sennacherib captured the fortified cities of Judah and laid siege to Jerusalem (36:1). These chapters preserve a positive portrait of King Hezekiah as a man of faith (in contrast to Ahaz), and describe the sudden departure of Sennacherib as a miraculous deliverance of the city (37:36-38). The deliverance results from Hezekiah's sincerity in repentance and prayer (37:1-13, 14-20), his visit with Isaiah, and his response of faith (38:9-20).

Scholars are divided about what actually happened during this crisis. In the parallel narrative in 2 Kgs. 18:13-27, three additional verses (18:14-16) suggest that Hezekiah surrendered unconditionally to the Assyrians. This is supported by the Assyrian "Prism of Sennacherib" and also Isa. 22:1-14; 1:4-9. Regardless of what actually happened, Jerusalem is remembered as surviving a close call with destruction at the time of Sennacherib's invasion in 701.

Recently, new attention has been given to chs. 36-39, particularly in connection with the references to envoys from Babylon in 39:1-8 . Read from the perspective of the Exile, this is another memory confirming that Isaiah's words have come to pass. Hezekiah is remembered as a good king; the crisis that arose during his era was averted, but Isaiah proclaims that "days are coming" when the wealth of the palace will be carried off to Babylon (39:5-8). This chapter provides a bridge from the memories of Isaiah to the new era presupposed throughout chs. 40-55.

The Basis for Hope (Chs. 40-55)

The author of Isaiah now boldly summons people to a life of faith. In these central chapters we sense the author's confidence based both on the memories of earlier times and the political events of his own time. In 46:1-4 specific references are made to Babylonian gods, Bel and Nebo; only Yahweh, the sovereign creator and redeemer, can bring salvation (v. 4). The lengthy debates about the folly of idols (40:18-20; 41:6-7; 44:9-20), the vision of a new exodus and a highway leading back to Jerusalem (40:3-7), and the lament and taunt song over proud "daughter Babylon" (47:1-15) all complement the specific references to Cyrus (44:21-28; 45:1-8), and locate this poetry in the era between 550-539.

The exodus from Babylon has not yet come. But Yahweh is about to do something dramatically new. A new world power will bring down the might and arrogance of Babylon. Isaiah's words of judgment now apply to the realm of Nebuchadnezzar, as well as to other empires and their leaders. The new emperor, Cyrus of Persia, has declared that in a coming era captive peoples may return to their homelands. From these world events, the prophetic writer can speak anew of a "day of Yahweh"; in the same event, a proud power will be brought low and reality will be restored, vindicating Yahweh's power as sovereign over all nations. The prophet's earlier announcements of judgment now come to pass (42:9; cf. 41:22; 43:9, 18; 46:9; 48:3), evidence that the prophetic word is reliable. Even the world of nature vindicates Yahweh (42:10). The renewal of the world offers signs that Yahweh will also renew the hopes of a covenant community (41:19; 55:13).

Leadership for the community is a critical concern throughout Isaiah. The primary vision of leadership is articulated in the vision of an "ideal messianic king" (11:1-9). That portrait is shaped now by words about "servanthood" and an "ideal servant" (41:8-10; 42:1-4; 49:1-6; 50:4-11; 52:13–53:12). Even Cyrus, a foreign king, shares in this vision; in 45:1 he is referred to specifically as "Yahweh's anointed one," who performs Yahweh's will by bringing liberation to captive people.

Themes in ch. 55 suggest that this hymn of triumph was at one time a conclusion for an exilic redaction of the Isaiah scroll. Echoing the plea of 2:5, the author of 55:6 charges: "Seek the Lord while he may be found, call upon him while he is near."

Maintaining the Vision (Chs. 56-66)

A different tone marks much of the concluding 11 chapters. Chs. 56-66 evidently were written and appended to the Isaiah scroll at a time after 539 when people had returned to settled life in Judah and Jerusalem. Work on the city walls had begun and temple restoration was under way (60:10-14; 62:6-7; 66:1). These chapters suggest that the community experienced overwhelming physical hardships and economic challenges when they returned to Jerusalem, rather than the glorious journey envisioned by earlier poetry.

With considerable skill, the writer draws from earlier traditions and themes in Isaiah to renew or maintain the vision of God's sovereignty, seeking to inspire a new generation of people with a vision of how Yahweh wants the community to be: free of "weeping and distress" (65:19), a city without violence and terror. As part of the vision, the author expresses prophetic concerns for some very practical and earthy matters: sabbath observance (56:2-6; 58:13-14), apostasy (56:1-2, 4; 57:3-4, 5, 7-8; 58:1-14; 59:1-8), syncretism (57:3; 65:2), upright leadership (56:9-10, 11-12). The author now speaks of "servants of the Lord," suggesting that the postexilic community is called to be the "servant" doing the work envisioned in earlier chapters.

Like earlier sections, these chapters center around the poetic motif of the "day of Yahweh." New days of judgment are announced: in 61:1-11 the prophet announces a day of favor for Zion; in 63:1-6 Yahweh is envisioned returning from battle as a holy warrior; the wicked have been defeated, and the cause of the righteous has been vindicated for all to see (63:1).

The fundamental theme of the Isaiah scroll is sounded once again: God is sovereign over the covenant community and over all nations of the world, calling all people to responsible life. New "days" will continue to come, bringing judgment for the ruthless and the arrogant; new "days" of joy will come for those who trust and live by their faith in the vision. In 65:17-25 the summons to faith is recast as a vision of a "new heaven and a new earth" which people can anticipate by their actions in the world. Throughout this final section the words of 61:1-4 capture a fundamental aspect of the meaning of the Isaiah scroll: the people are to "provide for those who mourn in Zion," to give "a garland instead of ashes," "oil of gladness instead of mourning," to wear the "mantle of praise instead of a faint spirit," and to live as "oaks of righteousness" in the world (v. 3). This is clearly what it means to "walk in the light of the Lord."

Bibliography. R. F. Melugin, *The Formation of Isaiah 40–55.* BZAW 141 (Berlin, 1976); Melugin and M. A. Sweeney, eds., *New Visions of Isaiah.* JSOTSup 214 (Sheffield, 1996); R. Rendtorff, "The Composition of the Book of Isaiah," in *Canon and Theology.* OBT (Minneapolis, 1993), 146-69; C. R. Seitz, *Zion's Final Destiny* (Minneapolis, 1991); M. A. Sweeney, *Isaiah 1–39.* FOTL 16 (Grand Rapids, 1996); H. G. M. Williamson, *The Book Called Isaiah* (Oxford, 1994). A. Joseph Everson

ISCAH (Heb. *yiskâ*)
A daughter of Haran and sister of Milcah (**1;** Gen. 11:29).

ISH-BAAL (Heb. *'îš-ba'al*) (also ESH-BAAL)
Probable original form of the name of King Saul's son Ishbosheth (1 Chr. 8:33; 9:39). Most English versions render the name as Esh-baal.

ISHBAH (Heb. *yišbāḥ*)
A Judahite, son of Mered and the Egyptian princess Bithiah (1 Chr. 4:17). He is called the father of Eshtemoa, which may mean the founder of that city.

ISHBAK (Heb. *yišbāq*)
A son of Abraham and his concubine Keturah (Gen. 25:2; 1 Chr. 1:32); eponymous ancestor of an Arabian people.

ISHBI-BENOB (Heb. *yišbî ḇĕnōḇ*)
A Philistine, a descendant (or devotee) of the legendary giants (Rephaim). Ishbi-benob sought to kill David, but Abishai came to David's rescue and killed the Philistine instead (2 Sam. 21:16-17). The text is difficult (cf. Gob at 2 Sam. 21:18), and various alternatives have been proposed.

ISHBOSHETH (Heb. *'îš-bōšeṯ*)
The youngest son of Saul, king of Israel after Saul's death. According to 2 Sam. 2:8-10 after the "men of Judah" anoint David king over the house of Judah at Hebron, Abner, the commander of Saul's army, takes Ishbosheth to Mahanaim and makes him king over Israel. Ishbosheth's reign as rival king lasts two years, during which time Abner, following a quarrel with Ishbosheth over Saul's concubine, switches his loyalty to David (2 Sam. 3:6-11). Ishbosheth is murdered by his own men, Rechab and Baanach, while resting in his bedchamber (2 Sam. 4:5-11).

The name Ishbosheth has been the object of dispute among modern scholars. That form appears throughout the MT of Samuel. 1 Chronicles, however, uses the name Esh-baal ("man of Baal"; 1 Chr. 8:33; 9:39). The same phenomenon is reflected in the LXX, where Gk. *Iebosthe* occurs in Kingdoms, but *Asabal* in 1 Chr. 8:33 and *Isbaal* in 9:39. It is generally accepted among modern scholars that the theophoric element "bosheth" or "shame" is a euphemistic replacement for the original element "baal" or "lord," a reference to the Canaanite deity Baal. Perhaps the theophoric element "baal" was at one time an acceptable epithet for Yahweh but was later seen as offensive and therefore had to be eradicated. This shift of the theophoric element in personal names is not an isolated phenomenon in the OT.

It has, however, been suggested, on the basis of Akkadian onomastic parallels, that the theophoric element "bosheth" is genuine. Accordingly, that element reflects an honorific divine-feature epithet meaning "dignity, pride, vigor" and came to represent a type of "protective spirit." On the day of his coronation, the king may have been given the name Ishbosheth in place of his original name.

Bibliography. P. K. McCarter, Jr., *II Samuel.* AB 9 (Garden City, 1986). Arnold Betz

ISH-HAI (Heb. *'îš-ḥay*)
The father of Benaiah (**1;** 2 Sam. 23:20 **K;** NRSV mg.). Most English versions render the Hebrew "a valiant man" or a similar phrase (Heb. "son of a valiant man"; **Q** *'îš-ḥaḥ;* cf. par. 1 Chr. 11:22).

ISHHOD (Heb. *'îšhôḏ*)
A Manassite, son of Hammolecheth (1 Chr. 7:18).

ISHI (Heb. *yišʿî*)

1. The son of Appaim, a Jerahmeelite of the tribe of Judah (1 Chr. 2:31).

2. A Judahite, the father of Zoheth and Ben-zoheth (1 Chr. 4:20).

3. A Simeonite whose sons (or followers) defeated the Amalekites at Mt. Seir and then occupied the area (1 Chr. 4:42-43).

4. The head of a father's house in the Transjordanian half-tribe of Manasseh (1 Chr. 5:24).

ISHMA (Heb. *yišmā'*)
A son of Etam (so NRSV, following LXX), from the tribe of Judah (1 Chr. 4:3; MT "father of Etam").

ISHMAEL (Heb. *yišmāʿē'l*)

1. The offspring of Abraham and Hagar, the Egyptian maidservant of Sarah. In legal terms, Sarah had two first-born sons, though she herself only bore Isaac, the biological half-brother of Ishmael. Hagar was a surrogate mother whom Sarah was obliged by law to give to Abraham to provide an heir.

Though the maternal relationship of the two brothers broke down immediately upon Hagar's conception (Gen. 16:2-4), the relationship between the two brothers remained surprisingly friendly. Subsequent exegesis has strained to goad the brothers into fierce sibling rivalry along the lines of Cain and Abel or Jacob and Esau, but this was not the case. The story of Ishmael laughing with (playing with?) Isaac at his weaning ceremony (Gen. 21:9) need not be seen negatively, though some translators remain influenced by Sarah's reaction in translating the phrase as "mocking" Ishmael (NEB, KJV; cf. Gal. 4:29-30). The boys were friends.

The biblical treatment of Ishmael is remarkably congenial and parallels the positive assessment of Isaac. Though Abraham clearly had other sons through surrogacy, only Ishmael and Isaac received the unique designation "sons of Abraham." In an unusual angelic annunciation, Hagar is promised that the descendants of Ishmael would be without number (Gen. 16:10). Later, Abraham is promised that Ishmael would become the father of 12 princes (tribes) and the founder of a great nation (Gen. 17:20; 25:12-16), reiterated to Hagar in her second banishment (21:13). Ishmael is described as a "wild [i.e., undomesticated] ass," which in the context of survival skills needed for desert life was a high compliment indeed (Gen. 16:12). Abraham has a special kinship with Ishmael having been circumcised together, father and son, a sure sign of Ishmael's ongoing attachment to the clan and God of Abraham (Gen. 17:23-27). Even before Isaac's own rescue by God from the sacrificial knife (Gen. 22), Ishmael is rescued by God at his own point of starvation and dehydration in the desert (21:19). The narrator concludes the rescue story emphasizing that "God was with the boy" as he grew up in the wilderness where he became an expert archer (21:20). Finally, Ishmael's descendants would share a portion in the inheritance of the land from "the River of Egypt" to the Euphrates (Gen. 25:18).

At Abraham's death the two brothers, specifically paired as "sons of Abraham" to the exclusion of their half-brothers, reunite to bury their father (Gen. 25:9). The list of Ishmael's 12 sons leads into the account of Isaac's extended family, both closely tied to Abraham's family tree with the *tôlēḏōṯ* formula reiterating their sonship to Abraham (Gen. 25:12-15, 19-20). The traditional link between Ishmaelites and Bedouin Arabs is based on this tribal list.

Ishmael's daughter Mahalath (Basemath) married Esau (Gen. 28:9; 36:3). According to Gen. 25:17 Ishmael died at the age of 137 years.

Paul uses Ishmael allegorically as a cipher for those Jews who maintain allegiance to the Mosaic law, thus being Abraham's descendants "according to the flesh" (Gal. 4:21-28). Unfortunately, Paul's allegories have too often been historicized into aggressive rivalry between children of Isaac by flesh *and* spirit (Jews and Christians) and the children of Ishmael (Muslims).

Bibliography. I. Ephʿal, "'Ishmael' and 'Arabs': A Transformation of Ethnological Terms," *JNES* 35 (1976): 225-35; L. R. Scudder, Jr., "Ishmael and Isaac and Muslim-Christian Dialogue, *Dialog* 29 (1990): 29-32; E. C. Want and P. Tarlo, "Bad Guys, Textual Errors and Word Plays in Genesis 21:9-10," *Journal of Reform Judaism* 37/4 (1990): 21-29; C. Westermann, *Genesis 12-36* (Minneapolis, 1985).

2. The third son of Azel of Benjamin, a descendant of Saul (1 Chr. 8:38; 9:44).

3. The father of Zebediah, governor of Judah during Jehoshaphat's reign in the 9th century (2 Chr. 19:11).

4. The son of Johananan; one of the five "commanders of hundreds" involved in the revolt against Queen Athaliah of Judah (2 Chr. 23:1).

5. A son of Passhur named among sons of priests who divorced their foreign wives (Ezra 10:22).

6. The son of Nethaniah, grandson of Elishama, a member "of the royal family," who became a traitor to Judah (Jer. 40:8–41:18; cf. 2 Kgs. 25:23-25). As one of the captains of the Jewish forces, he plotted and carried out the assassination of Gedaliah, the governor of Judah, and many other faithful supporters. After capturing the inhabitants of Mizpah, including the prophet Jeremiah and the daughters of the Jewish king, he was forced to abandon his plans of deporting the captives and to flee under hot pursuit by the loyal captains of Gedaliah. He managed to escape to refuge among the Ammonites.

JAMES E. BRENNEMAN

ISHMAELITES (Heb. *yišmĕʿē'lîm*)
A people most readily identified with their eponymous ancestor Ishmael, son of Abraham and Hagar (Gen. 16, 21). They are named as the 12 "sons of Ishmael" (Gen. 25:13-16 = 1 Chr. 1:28-31), settled primarily in northern Arabia ranging from the

"River of Egypt" to the Euphrates. Tradition links them with Arab peoples.

Though they are listed in Ps. 83:6(MT 7) among the hostile neighbors of Israel (Edomites, Moabites, Hagarites, and Amalekites) competing for land and grazing rights, such striving was not unknown even among tribes within Israel. Ishmaelites held high office in David's army, including Amasa who served as commander-in-chief (2 Sam. 17:25). Another Ishmaelite, Obil, served as superintendent of David's camels (1 Chr. 27:30).

In the story of Joseph, a caravan of Ishmaelites (also called Midianites) rescued Joseph from the dry well, selling him to Egypt (Gen. 37:25-28; 39:1). Later, the defeated Ishmaelites, again associated with the kings of Midian, provided Gideon a booty of golden earrings to make an ephod for the town square of Ophrah (Judg. 8:24-26). Allusions to crescents, pendants, purple garments and collars on the necks of the defeated king's camels, suggest a stereotypical description of nomadic merchants from Arabia.

The Qur'an describes Mohammed as an Arab prophet, a descendant of the Ishmaelites through a figure known as ʿAdan. It was Mohammed's intention to return Arabs to the undefiled religion of their forefather Abraham, understanding Ishmael as the historical conjunction between Muslims and ancient Semitic monotheism. Muslims since have known their spiritual heritage to be Ishmaelite.

Bibliography. I. Ephʿal, "'Ishmael' and 'Arabs': A Transformation of Ethnological Terms," *JNES* 35 (1976): 225-35; L. R. Scudder, Jr., "Ishmael and Isaac and Muslim-Christian Dialogue, *Dialog* 29 (1990): 29-32.

JAMES E. BRENNEMAN

ISHMAIAH (Heb. *yišmaʿyâ*)

1. A Gibeonite, a leader of the Thirty; one of the warriors who came to David's aid at Ziklag (1 Chr. 12:4).

2. The son of Obadiah, chief officer of Zebulun at the time of David (1 Chr. 27:19).

ISHMERAI (Heb. *yišmĕray*)
A son of Epaal; head of a Benjaminite father's house (1 Chr. 8:18).

ISHPAH (Heb. *yišpâ*)
A Benjaminite, son of Beriah (1 Chr. 8:16).

ISHPAN (Heb. *yišpān*)
A Benjaminite, son of Shashak (1 Chr. 8:22).

ISHTAR (Akk. *Ištaru*)
The chief goddess of the Mesopotamian pantheon. In Sumerian she is identified as the goddess Inanna. Inanna/Ishtar possesses a multiplicity of characteristics, often viewed as irreconcilable — she is the goddess both of love and of war and attributed with aspects of fertility, sexuality, passion, and anger. The duality inherent in the goddess illustrates the mythological and cyclic features of an agrarian society, where survival depended upon the fertility and fecundity of the land. As an early Sumerian deity she is the consort of Dumuzi (Tammaz) and an integral participant in the *hieros gamos,* a sacred marriage ritual performed by the king and a priestess of Inanna/Ishtar to insure successful crops at the beginning of the agricultural new year. Later among the warlike Assyrians, Ishtar became the patroness of the military. Cuneiform royal inscriptions boast of her leading the Assyrian kings in battle and victorious conquests. Associated with the planet Venus, the morning and evening star, Ishtar is considered one of the astral deities: the daughter of the moon-god Nanna/Sîn, the sister of the sun-god Utu/Šamaš, and sometimes the consort of An, the god of the heavens.

Etymologically, her name was originally masculine and related to the Semitic god ʿAṯtar. In the 1st millennium B.C.E. she assimilated characteristics from other Assyrian deities as well as the complete appropriation of the Sumerian goddess Inanna. Ishtar has also been associated with the Canaanite deities Astarte and Anat. Akk. *Ištar(at)u* eventually became the generic word for goddesses.

Ishtar was worshipped universally in many temples throughout Mesopotamia, including her major cult centers at Arbela, Uruk, Akkad, Nineveh, and Babylon. Despite Ishtar's popularity, she held no political rank among the national gods Assur and Marduk, reflecting the patriarchal bias of the ancient Mesopotamian society.

The cuneiform literature contains numerous myths and hymns concerning Ishtar. In one popular myth, which has both a Sumerian and Akkadian version, Ishtar descends into the netherworld, where she passes through seven gates, is stripped of her adornments, and held prisoner by the queen of the netherworld, her older sister Ereškigal. During Ishtar's captivity procreation and fertility of the land cease. She is eventually rescued and released in exchange for her lover, Dumuzi, who must reside half of the year in the netherworld. In the Gilgamesh Epic Ishtar is presented as a seductress and an angry jilted lover. Gilgamesh, aware of her ill-treatment of her lovers, spurns her advances. His rejection fuels her wrath, and she calls upon An to send the Bull of Heaven to kill Gilgamesh.

Ishtar is not mentioned in the Bible, but some scholars have connected her with the "queen of heaven" to whom the women are making cakes and pouring libations (Jer. 7:18; 44:17-19, 25). Though Ishtar is called Akk. *malkat šamami,* "queen of heaven," this epithet is common among the Phoenician, Canaanite, and Egyptian goddesses of the ancient Near East. The biblical mention may more accurately refer to one of the Canaanite goddesses.

JULYE M. BIDMEAD

ISHVAH (Heb. *yišwâ*)
The second son of Asher (Gen. 46:17; 1 Chr. 7:30). The name is not mentioned among the Asherite clans at Num. 26:44.

ISHVI (Heb. *yišwî*)

1. The third son of Asher (Gen. 46:17; Num. 26:44; 1 Chr. 7:30), whose descendants are called the Ishvites (Num. 26:44).

2. A son of Saul and Ahinoam (1 Sam. 14:49). Attempts to identify him with Ishbosheth have been discredited.

ISIS (Egyp. *3st;* Gk. *Isis*)
One of the most popular divinities in the Greco-Roman world. She originally came from Egypt, where she was the sister and wife of the slain god-king Osiris. Possessed with great powers, Isis wandered in search of the dead Osiris, and eventually found and embalmed him, thus enabling his eventual resurrection. The son of Isis and Osiris, Horus, succeeded his father as king. In Egypt there were mysteries of Isis and Osiris, which mythologically enacted the death of one pharaoh and the succession of another.

When the worship of Isis and Osiris was imported to Greece and Rome, it took on many Hellenistic characteristics. Although the Egyptian legend remained the same, Isis in particular took on the features of other goddesses. She embodied the ideal of femininity, and was a model sister and wife and a great mother. It is not surprising that when Christianity became popular, shrines to Mary often emerged at ancient Isis worship sites.

Isis mystery cults also flourished among the Greeks and Romans. The 11th book of Apuleius' *Metamorphoses* reveals much about the initiation rites in this cult.

When Christianity triumphed, the worship of Isis, like that of many other "pagan" deities, disappeared. With the current interest in goddess worship, however, Isis enjoys some renewed popularity.

ALICIA BATTEN

ISLAND, ISLE
The islands cited in the Bible are those of the Mediterranean Sea; among those specifically mentioned are Caphtor (probably Crete), Cauda, Cyprus, Malta, and Patmos. The KJV frequently translates Heb. *'îy* as "isle" or "island" in passages where the context shows its meaning to be "coast" or "coastland" (so NRSV), i.e., the eastern Mediterranean coastland including areas from Egypt to Phoenicia (e.g., Gen. 10:5; Ps. 97:1); thus the essential meaning of the Hebrew is probably "land adjacent to the sea," whether on island or mainland.

ISMACHIAH (Heb. *yismaḵyāhû*)
An overseer of the temple tax at the time of King Hezekiah (2 Chr. 31:13).

ISRAEL (Heb. *yiśrā'ēl*)

Name

The name "Israel" occurs first in Gen. 32:28[MT 29]. The patriarch Jacob engages in a nocturnal wrestling match with a mysterious adversary whom Jacob first takes to be a man, but ultimately declares to have been God (Gen. 32:24, 30[25, 31]). The adversary finally asks to be released from Jacob's hold, but Jacob will only comply if his opponent first blesses him. The adversary renames Jacob and blesses him, explaining that he is now Israel *(yiśrā'ēl),* because he has striven *(śārîṯā)* with God and with men and has prevailed. Because the verb *śārâ* appears only here and when this event is recalled in Hos. 12:3-4(4-5), its meaning must be derived from the context. While most scholars render the verb "strive," "struggle," or "fight," some believe the root to be *śrr,* "to have dominion," and translate "prove himself ruler." One tradition divides the consonants and vocalizes *śār 'aṯā,* rendering "you are a prince *(śar)* [with God]" (*Gen. Rab.* 78:3). While Hebrew usage would dictate that "Israel" means "God fights," the story in Gen. 32 takes Jacob as the subject, and understands the meaning to be "He who fights with God." Jacob's "fighting with men" began with his intrauterine clashes with his twin Esau (Gen. 25:22), and his appropriation of Esau's birthright and blessing, actions which showed the aptness of his name Jacob ("heel-grabber," "supplanter," "deceiver"; 27:35-36; cf. 25:26). When Hosea recalls the wrestling match long after Israel has become a nation, it is to condemn Jacob/Israel's history of disobedience and fighting with God (cf. Jer. 9:4-6[3-5]). This idea of a God bestowing such a contentious name on a nation is unprecedented.

While Israel is initially a personal name, its future as the name of a people, a nation, and a monarchy is announced immediately after God reiterates the name change. In Gen. 35:11 God tells Jacob that a nation, a company of nations (tribes?), and kings will come from him, recalling his earlier promises to Abraham and Sarah when their names were changed (17:5-6, 16; cf. 12:2). In later books Israel can denote the people (sometimes as "the children of Israel" or the "house of Israel"), the nation under the United Monarchy, the northern kingdom of Israel during the Divided Monarchy, and, in the postmonarchic period, the exiles in Babylon and the purified community of Yahweh's followers. Israel can also refer to the southern kingdom of Judah before the fall of the northern kingdom (e.g., Isa. 1:3; Mic. 1:14, 15), or even to both kingdoms ("the two houses of Israel"; Isa. 8:14). Finally, Israel is a territorial name, as in the "land of Israel" (1 Sam. 13:19) and the "soil of Israel" (Ezek. 7:2).

Biblical Concept

Ironically, Israel is first called a people by the pharaoh who is oppressing them. The Egyptian king does so precisely because the 70 descendants of Jacob/Israel have miraculously grown into a people who "are too many and too mighty for us" (Exod. 1:9; cf. vv. 5-6). God tells Moses that his task is to bring "my people, the Israelites" out of Egypt (Exod. 3:10). From the time Yahweh delivers his people, he stresses that the identity and role of Israel will be unique and distinctive. Because of the oath he swore to the patriarchs and his love for the people, God has chosen Israel to be his treasured possession (Exod. 19:5; Deut. 7:6-8) and his inheritance (Exod. 34:9; Deut. 4:20; 1 Kgs. 8:53). Israel is to become a "priestly kingdom and a holy nation" (Exod. 19:6) and a people holy to the Lord (Deut. 7:6). The intimacy of God's relationship with Israel is signaled by the fact that Israel is at times referred to as God's firstborn son (Exod. 4:22), a baby whom God nurtured and raised (Deut. 32:8-14; Ezek. 16:3-7), and God's bride (Jer. 2:2; 31:32; cf. Hos. 2:14-15[16-17]).

With Israel's special status comes the obligation to obey the stipulations of the covenant Yahweh makes with Israel at Sinai (Exod. 19–23; Deut. 5–26). While no other great nation has a god so near to them, or a set of laws as righteous as those which God gave to Israel, those laws must be obeyed if Israel is not to perish from the land and be scattered among the peoples (Deut. 4:7-9, 23-40). When the Israelites of the northern kingdom disobey, the Lord tells them that they are not distinctive or special. They are like the Ethiopians to God; moreover, God has brought the Philistines and Arameans up from other lands, just as he led Israel from Egypt (Amos 9:7). When God is angry with his promiscuous "wife" Israel (Hos. 1:2; cf. Ezek. 16), he tells Hosea to marry a promiscuous woman, and then instructs him to name their third child "Not my people" (Hos. 1:2, 8-9). Nevertheless, Hosea immediately predicts a time when the people will no longer be told "You are not my people," and be told instead "You are the children of the living God" (Hos. 1:10-11[2:1-2]).

After Israel and Judah cease to exist as monarchical states, "Israel" has several different meanings. When Ezekiel addresses the "children of Israel" (Ezek. 2:3) or, more often, "the house of Israel" (3:1), he has in mind the Judean exiles in Babylon and the people in Jerusalem — all the people whose fathers were chosen by Yahweh and brought out of Egypt (20:4-10) — even though the prophet's immediate audience is the exiles in Babylon. While Deutero-Isaiah also refers to the people's past (e.g., Isa. 43:1, 21, 27), his audience is primarily the community in exile (e.g., 42:24; 43:28). Deutero-Isaiah also points to a purified concept of Israel, as when he quotes Yahweh telling the servant that he is being designated the "Israel in whom I will be glorified" (Isa. 49:3), the Israel which will be given as "a light unto the nations" (v. 6).

Late historical books also show that "Israel" can be used in a more or less inclusive sense. When Chronicles retells the history of the people, the patriarch Jacob is consistently called Israel (e.g., 1 Chr. 1:34). While the members of the northern kingdom are portrayed as having forsaken the Lord (e.g., 2 Chr. 13:11), they remain "children of Israel" and Yahweh is still the God of their fathers (v. 12). They need only to repent and accept the Jerusalem cult and the Davidic dynasty, if they want to be part of the faith community of Israel (e.g., 2 Chr. 7:14). In Ezra-Nehemiah, however, the focus is on that community which is deemed the only legitimate representative of Yahweh's Israel (Ezra 1:5; 9:1-2; 10:1-8). The distinctiveness which had been Israel's defining trait continues even into the Persian setting of the book of Esther, when Haman's hatred of his Benjaminite rival Mordecai leads him to denounce the Jews as that people "whose laws are different from those of every other people" (Esth. 3:8).

After Deutero-Isaiah and Ezra, many attempts were made to define the true Israel. Paul speaks of Christians as the true "Israel of God" (Gal. 6:16). According to 1 Pet. 2:9-10, Christians are now "God's own people," the chosen race, royal priesthood, and holy nation (cf. Exod. 19:5-6). The process of identifying Israel continues in postbiblical times, as when the Puritans saw themselves as latter-day Israelites fleeing Pharaoh George III of England for "God's American Israel."

Biblical Account of History

Wilderness to United Monarchy

After the people of Israel are delivered from slavery in Egypt and commit themselves to Yahweh's covenant and the prospect of becoming a holy nation, they balk at the prospect of confronting the gigantic Canaanites, preferring to return to Egypt (Num. 14:2-4). As punishment for putting the Lord "to the test these ten times" (14:22), they are sentenced to wander in the wilderness for 40 years, until the first generation of ex-slaves is killed off. When most of the old generation has died off, the Israelites are challenged by Canaanite and Amorite forces. In both cases, it is Israel, not Moses, who is said to respond to the crisis and to defeat the enemy (Num. 21:1-3, 21-31); in fact, when Israel is victorious over the Amorite Sihon, no action is said to be taken by either Moses or God (21:21, 24, 25).

The Israelites finally conquer Canaan under Joshua, after Moses' death. Some of the targeted indigenous peoples are allowed to remain in order to punish the Israelites for breaking the covenant with God (Judg. 2:2-3; cf. vv. 20-21) or to "test Israel" (2:22-23; 3:1-4). Repeatedly, a nation oppresses Israel, and God responds to the people's distress by sending them a "judge" as a deliverer. However, whenever a judge died, the people would go back to worshipping other gods and the cycle would begin again (Judg. 2:15-19). Only to avenge the outrage committed against the Levite's concubine do all the tribes of Israel act together "as one man" (Judg. 20:1, 8, 11). Ironically, their united action is not against a foreign nation, but their brother tribe of Benjamin, which is almost wiped out in the ensuing (and grotesque) civil war.

The period of the judges comes to an end after Saul is appointed by the prophet/judge Samuel as the first king of Israel and ruler over Yahweh's "inheritance" (1 Sam. 10:1; 13:13-15; cf. 9:16-17). In spite of his military victories over the other nations (1 Sam. 14:47-48), Saul is quickly rejected by Samuel and then by Yahweh. Nevertheless, he remains on the throne even after David has been anointed as the next king. After Saul's death, David becomes king, initially reigning over Judah, with his capital in Hebron. Then all the tribes of Israel come to David and anoint him king over Israel. From his new capital of Jerusalem, David rules over both Israel and Judah for 33 years (2 Sam. 5:1-5). Nevertheless, the northern and southern tribes are never totally united, a fact which becomes evident during and after the civil war between David and his son Absa-

Detail of Merenptah ("Israel") stela containing the name Israel (ca. 1210-1207 B.C.E.)
(Service de Musées, Cairo)

lom (2 Sam. 15:6-12; 19:8-15, 41-43; 20:1-22). After much court intrigue in David's last years, his son Solomon emerges as his successor (1 Kgs. 1–2). The narrative claims that Solomon not only rules over "all Israel" (1 Kgs. 4:1), but over "all the kingdoms from the river [the Euphrates] to the land of the Philistines and the border of Egypt" (4:21[5:1]; cf. 4:24[5:4]; 8:65), the same territory which God had promised to Abraham (Gen. 15:18). The other kingdoms enrich Solomon's empire with great gifts and tribute. Although Solomon is depicted as a typical ancient Near Eastern monarch, blessed by his God with incredible wealth, prestige, and vast territory, there are also indications that his regime has overtaxed the people, depleted the treasury, and made "all Israel" participate in forced labor (1 Kgs. 5:13-17[27–31]; cf. 9:10-14). However, Judah may enjoy a special status, for when "all Israel" (1 Kgs. 4:7) is divided into 12 administrative tax districts, Judah is not explicitly included (cf. v. 19 MT).

Kingdom of Israel

After Solomon's death and the ascension of his son Rehoboam to the throne, the northern tribes rebel against excessive taxation and oppression, with the rallying cry "To your tents, O Israel" (1 Kgs. 12:16; cf. 2 Sam. 20:1). It is at this point that Yahweh transforms united Israel into a divided monarchy composed of the northern kingdom of Israel and the southern kingdom of Judah. He does so not because of Solomon's tyrannical policies, but because Solomon introduced the worship of other gods into the kingdom through his many marriages with foreign women (presumably as part of international treaty-making; 1 Kgs. 11:1-13). God chooses Jeroboam to rule over the 10 northern tribes, leaving Judah and parts of Benjamin in the hands of the Davidic kings with whom Yahweh had made a covenant (1 Kgs. 11:13, 23-36; 12:21-23; cf. 2 Sam. 7:12-16). Jeroboam is also the choice of the northern tribes. However, because he fears that his people will switch their allegiance to Rehoboam when they go to offer sacrifices in the Jerusalem temple, and then return to assassinate him (1 Kgs. 12:26-27), Jeroboam challenges Jerusalem's claim to be the only place where Yahweh can be legitimately worshipped (Deut. 12:13-27). He fabricates two golden calf images with which he inaugurates his new cult centers in Bethel and Dan, echoing the words of the idolatrous Israelites at Sinai (1 Kgs. 12:28; Exod. 32:4). For this, and for his other alterations in the cult, Jeroboam is condemned by Yahweh and the prophet Ahijah.

After the death of Jeroboam and his sons, the government of the kingdom of Israel becomes highly unstable. Seven kings are assassinated. Nevertheless, the northern kingdom is superior to Judah in several respects: size, strategic location along international trade and communication routes, and military strength (cf. 1 Kgs. 22:4; 2 Kgs. 14:12). The two kingdoms often engaged in hostilities with one another (1 Kgs. 14:30; 15:16-22; 2 Kgs. 14:8-14; 16:5-9), sometimes forming alliances with foreign powers to gain the advantage over the other.

Of all the kings of Israel, only two built dynasties of any duration or significance. The first is the house of Omri. The Bible says relatively little about this powerful king, who built Samaria as his new capital ("Samaria" is also another name for the northern kingdom; 1 Kgs. 13:32; 2 Kgs. 17:24). Much more is said about Omri's son Ahab and his Sidonian wife Jezebel, who probably became Ahab's wife as part of a treaty. Hostilities between Israel and Judah temporarily cease when the two kingdoms are linked by the marriage of Ahab's daughter (or sister) Athaliah and the Judean king Jehoram (2 Kgs. 8:18, 26). Omride rule comes to an end after ca. 40 years (ca. 885-843) when God anoints Jehu as king and commissions him to eradicate the entire "house of Ahab" (2 Kgs. 9:6-10). The five kings of the Jehu dynasty rule for approximately a century (ca. 843-745). While God allows the Arameans to "cut off" Israelite territory during Jehu's reign (2 Kgs. 10:32), Jeroboam II, Jehu's most powerful descendant, restores the territory of Israel to the boundaries established by Solomon (14:25).

After Jeroboam's son Zechariah is assassinated after only six months on the throne, the Jehu dynasty ends. The kingship again becomes unstable and Israel goes into rapid decline. In addition, Israel has to cope with the powerful Aramean king Rezin, and the greater threat posed by the Assyrian king Tiglath-pileser III. To remain on the throne, King Menahem voluntarily pays tribute to Tiglath-pileser ("Pul"; 2 Kgs. 15:19-20). Later, during Pekah's reign, Tiglath-pileser captures a number of Israelite cities, and deports the people to Assyria (2 Kgs. 15:29). Pekah then joins Rezin of Aram against Assyria, using military power to force Judah to join their coalition. The Judean king Ahaz successfully resists the attack, with Tiglath-pileser's help (2 Kgs. 16:5-9). Tiglath-pileser kills Rezin, while Pekah is assassinated by Hoshea, the last king of the rump state of Israel (16:9; 15:30). The new Assyrian king Shalmaneser V marches against Hoshea, who at first submits and becomes an Assyrian vassal, but later rebels and refuses to pay, vainly appealing for help from Egypt (2 Kgs. 17:3-4). Samaria is then besieged for three years, and falls in 722, shortly before (or after) the death of Shalmaneser and the ascension of Sargon II (17:5; 18:9-10). "Israel" is deported to Assyria (17:6) and replaced by people brought to the new Assyrian province of Samaria from Babylon and other locations (v. 24).

Ironically, while Israel had always defined itself in terms of its distinctiveness as a people and nation, the kingdom of Israel falls to a power whose resettlement policy is designed to weaken the distinctive ethnic and political identities of conquered nations. While almost all the northern kings had been condemned for failing to turn from the sins of Jeroboam, the narrator of 2 Kgs. 17:7-23 finds the primary cause of Israel's fall to be the sinfulness and idolatry of the "children of Israel" (v. 20), although Davidic kings remain on the Judahite throne for another century and a half, when Judah falls to the Babylonians (587/586).

Extrabiblical Evidence and Theories

The earliest extant reference to Israel outside the Bible is in the stela of Pharaoh Merneptah's fifth year, ca. 1210-1207. In l. 27 we are told that "Israel is laid waste; his seed is not." A sign identifies "Israel" as a people, not a territory, and the context suggests that this people is located in Palestine. Little more can be gleaned from this tantalizing inscription, which, at present, is the only extrabiblical reference to Israel prior to the mid-9th century. Israel's demise is also announced in one of the earliest 9th-century texts, the inscription of the Moabite king Mesha (ca. 840), in which he declares that "Israel has perished forever." Mesha concedes that Moab had been humbled by "Omri, king of Israel," but insists that he triumphed during the reign of Omri's son. Ahab "the Israelite" (*[mat] Sir-'i-la-ai*) is also mentioned in the Assyrian king Shalmaneser III's monolith inscription, as a participant in the battle of Qarqar (853). Elsewhere, Shalmaneser III refers to Jehu as "son of Omri," even though it was Jehu who put an end to the Omride dynasty, according to 2 Kgs. 9-10. Later, Adad-nirari III uses "house of Omri" (*mat Ḫ-um-ri*) to refer to Israel. From this point on, extrabiblical references to the kings of Israel and Judah become more frequent and extensive.

Archaeologists have not yet located any direct extrabiblical references to the patriarchs, Moses, the Exodus and Conquest, the judges, or any king of Israel prior to Omri, with the possible exception of David. Some (but not all) scholars read the name David in the Mesha inscription (l. 12 and/or a reconstructed l. 31), and "the house of David" in a fragmentary Aramaic inscription from Tel Dan (9th or 8th century).

While the Bible stresses the distinctiveness of the Israelites, many archaeologists have concluded that nothing distinctively "Israelite" has so far been found in the material culture of the groups who settled in the highlands of Palestine during the Iron I period (1200-1000). Many argue that archaeological evidence does not support the claim that the Israelites entered and occupied Canaan by means of military conquest. Instead, some historians have suggested that the Israelite settlement occurred through a process of peaceful infiltration or an internal peasant revolt. Others contend that the existing evidence does not support these theories either. A recent tendency has been to understand the collapse of Late Bronze Age urban culture in Palestine, and increased village settlement in the hill country during Iron I, as part of a larger process of upheaval throughout the Eastern Mediterranean during the Late Bronze Age (1550-1200/1150). This process, which may have been triggered by environmental, economic, and political factors (including drought and famine), led to social and political realignments and a great increase in migration throughout the area. According to this model, the Iron I population of Canaan included pastoral groups and uprooted local groups, as well as recent arrivals to the region. Proponents of this view conclude that one cannot distinguish ethnic affiliations and national identities in Canaan until the late 11th century, when Israel became a political entity.

Bibliography. G. W. Ahlström, *Who Were the Israelites?* (Winona Lake, 1986); P. R. Davies, *In Search of "Ancient Israel."* JSOTSup 148 (Sheffield,

1992); W. G. Dever, *Recent Archaeological Discoveries and Biblical Research* (Seattle, 1990); I. Finkelstein and N. Na'aman, eds., *From Nomadism to Monarchy: Archaeological and Historical Aspects of Early Israel* (Washington, 1994); J. M. Miller and J. H. Hayes, *A History of Ancient Israel and Judah* (Philadelphia, 1986); K. W. Whitelam, "The Identity of Early Israel," *JSOT* 63 (1994): 57-87.

STUART LASINE

ISSACHAR (Heb. *yiśśāḵār*)

1. The fifth son of Leah and Jacob, and eponymous ancestor for the Israelite tribe of Issachar. The meaning of the name is difficult to discern, but the story of Issachar's conception seems to shed some light. Gen. 30 relates a story of Leah's son Reuben's finding some mandrakes (perhaps an aphrodisiac in the ancient world). Leah trades her mandrakes to her sister Rachel, in exchange for an extra night with Jacob. As a result of their time together, Leah conceives and bears Issachar. The biblical text suggests two possible etymologies for the name, both revolving around a wordplay on the Hebrew root *śkr,* "to hire, pay wages, recompense." Leah is described as having informed Jacob that he must sleep with her that night because she had "hired" him. When Issachar is born, Leah states that this child is her "compensation" for having to give her maid Zilpah to Isaac earlier when she was experiencing a time of barrenness.

Gen. 46:13 describes Issachar and his four sons immigrating with Jacob's family to Egypt. The blessing of Issachar by Jacob (Gen. 49:14-15) describes the tribe as having to bear the burden of others and become "a slave." The territory allotted to the tribe of Issachar is identified in Josh. 19:17-23 as the land between the eastern Jezreel Valley and the Jordan Valley. In the Song of Deborah (Judg. 5:15) Issachar is praised for its participation and efforts in helping to defeat the enemy.

2. The seventh son of Obed-edom, a descendant of Levi through Korah; a gatekeeper during the reign of David (1 Chr. 26:5). LISA W. DAVISON

ISSHIAH (Heb. *yiššîyâ, yiššîyāhû*)

1. A son of Izrahiah, descendant of Uzzi from the tribe of Issachar (1 Chr. 7:3).

2. One of the warriors who joined David's forces at Ziklag (1 Chr. 12:6[MT 7]).

3. A Levite, the second son of Uzziel (1 Chr. 23:20; 24:25).

4. A Levite of the family of Rehabiah (1 Chr. 24:21). ROBERT E. STONE, II

ISSHIJAH (Heb. *yiššîyâ*)

A Levite of the clan of Harim, forced by Ezra's reforms to relinquish his foreign-born wife (Ezra 10:31).

ITALA

The Old Latin (OL) translation of the Greek NT, which existed first in North Africa around Carthage, where Greek was not well known, in the 3rd century C.E. There was no one official version: Bishop Nemesianus of Tubanas, with Cyprian at the Council of Carthage in 256, used a Latin translation different from that used by Cyprian. While one translation might have been the basis, the great variety of readings in the extant manuscripts indicates that the Itala might have involved several independent translations.

Quotations in African church writers tend to be colloquial and unsophisticated, indicating that the OL was primarily for common people. The Itala usually follows the Greek rather literally, with European OL manuscripts not diverging from the Greek quite as much as African manuscripts. The textual character of the Itala is "Western."

Old Latin manuscripts passed through Italy to Gaul, Great Britain, and Ireland, each region altering the text in view of its own special interests, thus producing provincial OL texts. While the Itala was officially superseded by the Vulgate of Jerome, it appears to have been copied and used to some extent until the 9th century. CARROLL D. OSBURN

ITALY

A southern European country which forms a boot-shaped peninsula, bounded on the west by the Tyrrhenian Sea, on the east by the Adriatic Sea, on the south by the Ionian Sea, and extending north to the Alps. The Apennine mountain range extends the length of the peninsula and creates Italy's unique geography, with difficult inland terrain and fertile plains and valleys, especially in the western coastal areas.

The name may derive from Italus, the 13th-century B.C.E. chief of the Oenotri or Siculi who occupied the southwest part of the peninsula (Thucydides *Hist* 6.2; Dionysius of Halicarnassus *Rom. Ant.* 1.12.35). Another possible derivation is from Lat. *vituli,* "bull calves," in which case Italy means "the land of the bull calves." The name was applied at first only to the southwestern region and was applied to the entire peninsula much later, probably in Roman times.

Successive migrations of peoples from the north and the natural terrain which offered numerous convenient barriers between communities resulted in the coexistence of many different tribes and races in the peninsula, with their unique languages and cultures: Latins, Umbro-sabellians, Oscans, Illyrians, and Etruscans from Asia Minor. Because of Italy's good location on the Mediterranean and its seaports, a flourishing commerce fostered a rich cultural diversity. During the 8th to 6th centuries Greeks colonized southern Italy and Sicily so thoroughly that the area came to be known as Magna Graecia. While Rome was still in its primitive beginnings, Greeks were creating great and important cities in southern Italy. Through constant wars with the Italic peoples, Gallic tribes, and Celtic invaders, Rome conquered and absorbed the peoples of the peninsula, while at the same time being influenced by their languages, religions, and customs. Augustus subdivided the three locales of Italy (Upper Italy, Central Italy, and Lower Italy or Magna Graecia) into 11 regions.

Italy is mentioned several times in the NT

(sometimes "Rome" is used for all of Italy). Priscilla and Aquila, Jews from Italy, fled to Corinth in the wake of Claudius' Edict of 49 C.E., expelling Jews from Rome (Acts 18:2). Paul sailed for Italy when as a Roman citizen he appealed his capital case before Caesar (Acts 27:1, 6; cf. 28:11-16 on his reception there). He remained a prisoner in Rome for two (perhaps his last) years (Acts 28:30). The writer of Hebrews closes his treatise with the words "those from Italy send you greetings" (Heb. 13:24), indicating either that he was writing from Italy to readers outside the peninsula and was adding the greetings of the local believers, or that he was writing to Italy from elsewhere and some fellow Christians who hailed from the place to which he was sending the work sent greetings to their homeland.

Bibliography. M. C. Howatson, ed., *The Oxford Companion to Classical Literature,* 2d ed. (Oxford, 1990); R. J. A. Talbert, ed., *Atlas of Classical History* (New York, 1985), 82-123. RICHARD A. SPENCER

ITHAI (Heb. *'îṯay*) (also ITTAI)
A Benjaminite, the son of Ribai of Gibeah; a Champion of David's army (1 Chr. 11:31). In the parallel account (2 Sam. 23:29) he is called Ittai (**2**).

ITHAMAR (Heb. *'îṯāmār*)
The fourth son of Aaron (Exod. 6:23; 1 Chr. 6:3[MT 5:29]). Ithamar was commissioned for priestly service along with his brothers (Exod. 28:1). When the two oldest brothers Nadad and Abihu sinned by offering incense with a sacrifice (Lev. 10:1-3), God took their lives, leaving Eleazar and Ithamar to serve (v. 12). Ithamar had oversight of the Gershonites and the Merarites, who assisted in moving the tabernacle about (Num. 4:21-33) with the aid of oxen (7:7-8). Less numerous than the descendants of Eleazar, who functioned at the temple from the time of Solomon to its destruction, Ithamar's descendants served there also (1 Chr. 24:1-6). The Chronicler includes Zadok among the descendants of Eleazar and Abiathar of Shiloh among the descendants of Ithamar (1 Chr. 24:3, 6, 31), but this seems to be in error. In the postexilic period, Daniel, the son of Ithamar, participated in the return under Ezra (Ezra 8:2). PAUL L. REDDITT

ITHIEL (Heb. *'îṯî'ēl*)

1. A Benjaminite in postexilic Jerusalem; ancestor of Sallu (Neh. 11:7).

2. A person addressed, with Ucal, in the wisdom discourse of Agur the son of Jakeh (Prov. 30:1). The terms are not rendered as proper names in the LXX or Vulg., and various translations ("signs of God," "with me is God") and emendations (e.g., Heb. *lā'îṯî'ēl,* "I am weary, O God"; *wā'ēḵel,* "I faint" or "pine away") have been proposed.

ITHLAH (Heb. *yiṯlâ*)
A city in the early tribal territory of Dan (Josh. 19:42). The location is unknown, although some have suggested modern Siltah, 7 km. (4.3 mi.) NW of Beth-horon.

ITHMAH (Heb. *yiṯmâ*)
A Moabite, one of David's Champions (1 Chr. 11:46).

ITHNAN (Heb. *yiṯnān*)
A city apportioned by Joshua to the tribe of Judah following the conquest of Canaan (Josh. 15:23), among the southernmost towns of the Negeb. In the list of allotted cities, Ithnan follows Hazor. The LXX reading of Asorionain raises a noteworthy problem. The Greek translation may be considered corrupt, or perhaps two sites (Hazor and Ithnan) should be read as one. In either case, Ithnan's location has yet to be determined. RYAN BYRNE

ITHRA (Heb. *yiṯrā'*) (also JETHER)
The father of Amasa and husband of David's sister Abigail. At 2 Sam. 17:25 the MT calls him an Israelite (so NRSV mg), but the LXX reading "Ishmaelite" is considered correct (so 1 Chr. 2:17, "Jether the Ishmaelite").

ITHRAN (Heb. *yiṯrān*)

1. A son of Dishon and grandson of Seir the Horite (Gen. 36:26; 1 Chr. 1:41); eponymous ancestor of an Edomite clan.

2. A son of Zophah of the tribe of Asher (1 Chr. 7:37); probably the same as Jether **5.**

ITHREAM (Heb. *yiṯrĕ'ām*)
The sixth son of David, born at Hebron to his wife Eglah (2 Sam. 3:5 = 1 Chr. 3:3).

ITHRITES (Heb. *yiṯrî*)
A Judahite clan or similar unit located at Kiriath-jearim (1 Chr. 2:53). Ira and Gareb, two of David's warriors, came from this group (2 Sam. 23:38 = 1 Chr. 11:40). The Ithrites may be related to a person named Jether or a city named Jattir or Jether.

ITTAI (Heb. *'ittay, 'iṯay*) (also ITHAI)

1. A man from Gath ("the Gittite"), commander of 600 Philistines who remained loyal to David during Absalom's rebellion (2 Sam. 15:19-22). David named him, along with Joab and Abishai, to lead his forces in battle at the forest of Ephraim (2 Sam. 18:2, 5).

2. A Benjaminite, the son of Ribai from Gibea; one of David's Thirty (2 Sam. 23:29). He is called Ithai at 1 Chr. 11:31.

ITURAEA (Gk. *Itouraía*)
An area of the Beqa' Valley of southern Lebanon which came under the jurisdiction of the Tetrarch Philip, son of Herod the Great, after the latter's death in 4 B.C.E. (Luke 3:1). The name derives from that of an Arab tribe of north Transjordan that settled in the Beqa' Valley during the latter part of the 2nd century. Several Safaitic inscriptions support this migration, which has been linked to the period of the Hasmonean ruler Aristobulus (104) who forced the Ituraeans, then located in Transjordan and Galilee, to convert to Judaism (Josephus *Ant.* 13.3.318). After migrating north to escape

Aristobulus and his policies, the Ituraeans were able to maintain control over the area of Lake Huleh and Paneas (Caesarea Philippi).

After a relatively brief period of independence as a principality under the tribal leader Ptolemaios (85-40 B.C.E.), the area of Ituraea came under Roman control when, in 64/63, Pompey conquered the area and imposed a tribute on Ptolemaios. Lysanias (40-36), son of Ptolemaios, allied himself with the Parthians in 40 after they occupied Palestine, but the area soon reverted back to Rome and eventually became the possession of Herod the Great in 20 B.C.E.

The Ituraeans are listed among the offspring of Ishmael in Gen. 25:15; 1 Chr. 1:31, where Jetur is identified as their eponymous ancestor. 1 Chr. 5:18-22 recounts the events of a battle in which Reuben, Gad and half of Manasseh attack and defeat the Hagarites, Jetur, Japhish, and Nodab.

JOHN KALTNER

IVORY

A luxury good used in a variety of ways beginning in the Chalcolithic period and continuing throughout the biblical period. The use of ivory in the Levant is especially well attested in the Late Bronze II (1350-1200 B.C.) and Iron II periods (9th-8th century). The Hebrew term *(šēn)* means "tooth," a reference to the major sources for ivory — the tusk of the African and Asian elephant. The African elephant produces a larger and harder tusk preferred by ancient craftsmen. Herds of Asian (sometimes termed "Syrian") elephants were found in northwest Mesopotamia and Syria until they were hunted to extinction ca. 700. The lower teeth of hippopotami were a rare source of ivory noted for its high quality and brilliance.

Ivory was used for figurines, furniture, paneling, inlays, cosmetic boxes, spoons, gameboards and game pieces, writing tablets, combs, and pins. The ivory craftsmen utilized a variety of tools to carve, incise, saw, drill, and polish the raw material. A few workshops have been reported in excavations, but likely ivory craftsmen were mobile, moving to and from various centers known for the ivory trade. Large caches of ivory have been found in Palestine (Megiddo, Samaria), Syria and northwestern Mesopotamia (Ugarit, Arslan Tash, Tell Tainat, and Zincirli), and Assyria (Nimrud, Khorsabad, and Nineveh).

In the Levant, ivory carving can be traced back to the late 4th millennium through a remarkable group of ivory statues recovered near Beer-sheba at Tell Abu Matar/Be'er Abu Matar and Bir eṣ-Ṣafadi/Be'er Ṣafad. However, the evidence is sparse for the use of ivory in the 3rd millennium until the last third of the 2nd millennium. A hoard of ca. 300 objects found at Megiddo, including panels carved in low relief depicting scenes of banquets and military victories, suggests a blend of Egyptian, Mycenaean, and Hittite elements combined with Canaanite traditions.

By the 9th and 8th centuries two, possibly three ivory carving traditions or schools emerged, defined by the prevalence of Egyptianizing features, regional stylistic traits, and techniques. The Phoenician school adapted a variety of Egyptian motifs (e.g., a variety of Egyptian deities, sphinx figures) to Canaanite-Phoenician themes. The style is elegant, fluid, and given to Egyptian concepts of symmetry and proportion. Several non-Egyptian motifs, such as the "woman appearing in the window," also were widely utilized. The North Syrian school, by contrast, employed no Egyptian motifs and was characterized by squatter figures with unusual facial features — large eyes, receding foreheads, diminished chins — and scenes charged with action. It has yet to be proven that a South Syrian school centered on Damascus can be distinguished.

Ivory carving of a sphinx in a thicket, showing Syrian and Egyptian influence; Samaria (Iron Age) (Courtesy Israel Antiquities Authority)

The 500 ivory fragments found at Samaria dating from either the 9th or 8th centuries reflect the Phoenician school, not surprising given the contact between Israel and Phoenicia beginning at least in Solomon's reign. Solomon imported raw ivory by means of a fleet operated jointly with Hiram, king of Tyre (1 Kgs. 10:22). Phoenician craftsmen likely fashioned Solomon's ivory and gold throne (1 Kgs. 10:18). Ezek. 27:6, 15 alludes to Tyre's association with the ivory trade.

Ivory appears frequently in Assyrian booty and tribute lists throughout the 9th and 8th centuries. Menahem included ivory as tribute to Tiglath-pileser III while Sennacherib received ivory from Hezekiah in 701. Assyrian kings utilized ivory in their palaces, perhaps as paneling, but more often as decorative inlays for furniture, a fact richly confirmed by the wealth of ivory carvings recovered from Nineveh, Nimrud, and Khorsabad. Assyrian kings stockpiled ivory as a much prized measure of status and wealth. Ahab's "ivory house" (1 Kgs. 22:39) at Samaria symbolized the corrupt luxury of a pagan court condemned by Amos (Amos 3:15). Amos' condemnation of "those who recline on beds of ivory" may be a reference to a *marzēaḥ*, a pagan ritual involving sacred meals and drinking (Amos 6:4-7; cf. Jer. 16:5-9); Amos viewed them as a symptom of the callous disregard on the part of Israel's privileged class for the social abuse perpetrated upon the poor.

Bibliography. R. D. Barnett, *Ancient Ivories in the Middle East.* Qedem 14 (Jerusalem, 1982); P. R. S. Moorey, *Ancient Mesopotamian Materials and Industries* (Oxford, 1994). THOMAS V. BRISCO

IVVAH (Heb. *ʿiwwâ*)
A Syrian city-state among those captured by the Assyrians in the 8th century B.C.E. (2 Kgs. 18:34; 19:13; Isa. 37:13). It may be the same as Avva (2 Kgs. 17:24), residents of which the Assyrians uprooted and settled in Samaria after the defeat of the northern kingdom.

IYE-ABARIM (Heb. *ʿîyê hāʿăḇārîm*) (also IYIM)
A place in the desert ("ruins of Abarim"), E of Moab (Num. 21:11; 33:44), where the Israelites camped during the wilderness wanderings. At Num. 33:45 it is called Iyim. It is probably in the vicinity of Muhai, SE of the Dead Sea near the brook Zered.

IYIM (Heb. *ʿîyîm*)
A contracted form of Iye-abarim (Num. 33:45).

IYYAR (Heb. *ʾîyār*)
The second month of the Hebrew calendar (Apr./May). This name, derived from Akkadian usage, superseded the Canaanite name Ziv.

IZHAR (Heb. *yiṣhār*) (also AMMINADAB)

1. A Levite, a descendant of Kohath and father of Korah (Exod. 6:18, 21; Num. 16:1; 1 Chr. 6:18, 38[MT 3, 23]). He is the eponymous ancestor of the Izharites (Num. 3:19, 27; 1 Chr. 26:23). At 1 Chr. 6:22(7) he is called Amminadab (**2**).

2. A Judahite whose mother was Helah (1 Chr. 4:7 **K**). Some scholars view this name as a variant of Zohar (cf. **Q** *wĕṣōḥar*, "and Zohar").

IZLIAH (Heb. *yizlîʾâ*)
A Benjaminite, son of Elpaal (1 Chr. 8:18).

IZRAHIAH (Heb. *yizraḥyâ*)
The son of Uzzi and descendant of Tola, from the tribe of Issachar (1 Chr. 7:3). The Hebrew name is the same as Jezrahiah, leader of the levitical singers at the time of Nehemiah (Neh. 12:42).

IZRAHITE (Heb. *yizrāḥ*)
A gentilic applied to Shamhuth, commander of the fifth division of David's army (1 Chr. 27:8). Although some scholars interpret the name as a derivative of Izrahiah, it is probably related to the Zerahites at 1 Chr. 27:11.

IZRI (Heb. *yiṣrî*)
A leader of the fourth division of temple musicians at the time of David (1 Chr. 25:11), perhaps a "son" (guild member) of Jeduthun. He may be identified with Zeri at 1 Chr. 25:3.

IZZIAH (Heb. *yizzîyâ*)
An Israelite who had to send away his foreign wife; a son of Parosh (Ezra 10:25).

J

J
Symbol of the Yahwist (Ger. *Jahvist,* from Heb. *YHWH,* "Yahweh" or "the Lord"), the earliest of the primary sources which critics ascribe to the Pentateuch.

See Biblical Criticism; Yahwist.

JAAKAN (Heb. *yaʿăqān*) (also AKAN)
A Horite, son of Ezer and descendant of Seir (1 Chr. 1:42); called Akan at Gen. 36:27. The name occurs also in Bene-jaakan (Num. 33:31-32) and Beeroth Bene-jaakan (Deut. 10:6), where the Israelites encamped during the wilderness wanderings.

JAAKOBAH (Heb. *yaʿăqōḇâ*)
A leader of a Simeonite clan (1 Chr. 4:36).

JAALA (Heb. *yaʿălā'*), **JAALAH** (*yaʿălâ*)
One of Solomon's servants, whose descendants (or guild) returned with Zerubbabel from captivity (Neh. 7:58). At Ezra 2:56 he is called Jaalah.

JAAR (Heb. *yaʿar*)
The place where the ark of the covenant is said to have been discovered (Ps. 132:6). The name may be a form of Kiriath-jearim, where the ark had been lodged for 27 years (1 Sam. 7:1-2; 2 Chr. 1:4).

JAARE-OREGIM (Heb. *yaʿărê 'ōrĕgîm*)
A Bethlehemite, the father of Elhanan (2 Sam. 21:19). He is said to have killed Goliath at Gob. In a doublet of the passage at 1 Chr. 20:5 Elhanan kills Lahmi, Goliath's brother; here Elhanan's father is Jair. Jaare-oregim is probably an error. According to 2 Sam. 21:19 Goliath's spear is said to be as large as a weavers' beam. Oregim ("weavers"; e.g. Isa. 19:9) seems to have been repeated erroneously and joined to the name Jair. Victoria Andrews

JAARESHIAH (Heb. *yaʿărešyâ*)
The head of a Benjaminite father's house in Jerusalem (1 Chr. 8:27).

JAASIEL (Heb. *yaʿăśî'ēl*)
1. A Mezobaite, one of David's mighty men (1 Chr. 11:47).

2. The son of Abner; chief of the tribe of Benjamin at the time of David (1 Chr. 27:21). He may be the same as **1** above.

JAASU (Heb. *yaʿăśû*)
An Israelite who was required to send away his foreign wife (Ezra 10:37; **Q** *yaʿăśāy*).

JAAZANIAH (Heb. *ya'ăzanyâ, ya'ăzanyāhû*)
A popular name during the 6th century B.C.E. The name appears on a seal from Tell en-Naṣbeh (biblical Mizpah) and on Ostracon 1 from Lachish.

1. A commander of the troops of Judah under the governor Gedaliah (2 Kgs. 25:23); called Jezaniah at Jer. 40:8. He is described as the "son of the Maacathite," which suggests that he is from the Judahite clan of Maacah, the Galilean town of Abel-beth-maacah, or the Aramean kingdom of Maacah.

2. The son of Jeremiah (not the prophet) and the head of the house of the Rechabites (Jer. 35:3). During the time of King Jehoiakim the prophet Jeremiah tested Jaazaniah and his house and presented the Rechabites to the people of Judah as a model of faithfulness and obedience.

3. The son of Shaphan; one of 70 idolatrous elders of Israel seen by Ezekiel in a vision (Ezek. 8:11). Some scholars suggest that the reference to "Jaazaniah, son of Shaphan, standing among them" is a gloss.

4. The son of Azzur; one of 25 men in the temple gateway seen by Ezekiel in a vision (Ezek. 11:10). He is described as an official of the people.

Ronald A. Simkins

JAAZIAH (Heb. *yaʿăzîyāhû*)
A son (of follower) of the Levite Merari; father of Beno, Shoham, Zaccur, and Ibri (1 Chr. 24:26-27). He and his descendants are not named among the sons of Merari at Exod. 6:19; 1 Chr. 23:21.

JAAZIEL (Heb. *ya'ăzî'ēl*)
A Levite of the second order, a gatekeeper and singer at the time of David (1 Chr. 15:18). He is probably the same as Aziel at 1 Chr. 15:20 and Jeiel at 16:5.

JABAL (Heb. *yāḇāl*)
The first son of Lamech and Adah; the ancestor of nomadic and transhumant shepherds (Gen. 4:20).

JABBOK (Heb. *yabbōq*)
Along with the Yarmuk (Šerī'at el-Menādireh), Arnon (Wadi el-Môjib), and Zered (Wadi el-Ḥesa), one of the four major rivers/wadi systems that drain the Transjordanian highlands. Today called Wadi Zerqa/Nahr es-Zerqa ("blue river"), this perennial stream rises from springs and streams in the drainage basin of Amman (ancient Rabbath-ammon/Philadelphia), "the city of waters" (2 Sam. 11:16-17; 12:27). The Jabbok flows ca. 60 km. (37 mi.) before it empties into the Jordan River, 24 km. (15 mi.) N of the Dead Sea; it is one of the two major tributaries of the Jordan, along with the Yarmuk.

The Jabbok is identified as a boundary between Ammon and Israel (e.g., Num. 21:24; Deut. 2:37), between the tribal territories of Reuben and Gad and Transjordanian Manasseh (e.g., Deut. 3:16), and between the kingdoms of Sihon and Og (e.g., Josh. 12:2). This river also divides Gilead into two halves (cf. Deut. 3:12, 16; Josh. 12:2-6), but is most famous as the place where Jacob wrestled with an angel at one of the stream's fords (Gen. 32:22-32[MT 23-33]). GERALD L. MATTINGLY

JABESH (Heb. *yāḇēš*)
The father of King Shallum of Israel (2 Kgs. 15:10, 13-14). Some scholars suggest that the term is a place name indicating Shallum's provenience.

JABESH-GILEAD (Heb. *yāḇêš gil'āḏ*)
(also JABESH)
A city in northwest Gilead. It was probably located along the Wadi Yâbis, although no one site has yet been conclusively identified as Jabesh-gilead ("the dry [place] of Gilead").

The inhabitants of Jabesh-gilead were important heroic, if sometimes tragic, players in three biblical stories placed in the setting of early Israel. In Judg. 21 the male inhabitants of Jabesh-gilead were murdered so their virgin girls could be given to the Benjaminites because the other Israelite tribes had sworn, due to the Benjaminites' support for those who had committed a hideous crime, not to let the Benjaminites marry daughters from their tribes (Judg. 20:12, 13; 21:1). This event was also a judgment against the Jabesh-gileadites for their absence at the Israelite battles with the Benjaminites (Judg. 20:1ff.). In this passive way (i.e., by their death), the citizens of Jabesh-gilead were said to have saved the tribe of Benjamin from extinction (Judg. 21:17).

In a similar manner Jabesh-gilead was responsible for Saul's being accepted as king. Nahash, an Ammonite king, besieged Jabesh-gilead (1 Sam. 11:1-3). When Saul heard of the city's dilemma he rallied an Israelite army, which rescued Jabesh-gilead (1 Sam. 11:11); the victory was so inspiring that the Israelites immediately confirmed Saul as king (vv. 12-15). To grasp the fullness of the story, the tragedy of the Benjaminites, recorded in Judg. 20, must be remembered. There Jabesh-gilead saved the Benjaminites; in the victory over Nahash, Saul, a Benjaminite, saved Jabesh-gilead. As in the earlier story, the Jabesh-gileadites now have a passive part in making Saul king, when he had previously been rejected (1 Sam. 10:27; 11:7).

Finally, Jabesh-gilead played a role in rescuing the body of Saul. When the Philistines defeated Saul and his sons, they took their bodies and hung them from the wall of the city of Beth-shan (1 Sam. 31:10). The Jabesh-gileadites retrieved Saul's and his sons' bodies, burned them, and then buried their bones (1 Sam. 31:13; 1 Chr. 10:11-12). Here the tables are turned. The Jabesh-gileadites actively save Saul, while his death and their actions cause them to be blessed by the new king (2 Sam. 2:5).

Bibliography. N. Glueck, "Jabesh-Gilead," *BASOR* 89 (1943): 2-6; L. G. Herr, "The Amman Airport Structure and the Geopolitics of Ancient Transjordan," *BA* 46 (1983): 223-29.

DAVID MERLING

JABEZ (Heb. *ya'bēṣ*) **(PERSON)**
The eponymous ancestor of a Judahite family (1 Chr. 4:9). The popular etymology that his name derives from a difficult childbirth (Heb. *'ōṣeḇ*, "pain") is implicit in his prayer for protection from harm (*'oṣbî*, 1 Chr. 4:10).

JABEZ (Heb. *ya'bēṣ*) **(PLACE)**
A town in Judah, probably near Bethlehem. It was the home of several families of Kenite scribes (1 Chr. 2:55).

JABIN (Heb. *yāḇîn*)
1. The Canaanite king of Hazor (Josh. 11:1), leader of a coalition of kings who opposed Joshua in his so-called "northern campaign" at the battle of Merom. Joshua captured and destroyed the city of Hazor and put its king (not named) to death.

2. The king of Hazor to whom God delivered his people in the time of Deborah and Barak (Judg. 4:2-24). His general was Sisera. Although the narrative describes conflict only with Sisera, Judg. 4:24 mentions that Israel defeated Jabin as well.

Ostensibly, these are two different kings of Hazor with the same name. The first would have ruled Hazor during the time of Joshua; the second would have ruled a century or so later. Jabin, however, is easily extricated from Judg. 4 and does not appear in the poetic version of the battle against Sisera in ch. 5. The traditional nature of both accounts makes absolute dating out of the question. Also, the battle recorded in Judg. 4-5 may have predated that of Judg. 11, leading scholars to suggest that there was really only one Jabin, king of Hazor.

PAUL L. REDDITT

JABNEEL (Heb. *yaḇnĕ'ēl*) (also JABNEH)

1. A town on the southern border of the tribe of Judah (Josh. 15:11). Jabneel is identified with either Yibna (126141) S of Naḥal Sorek or Yavneh-yam (121147) on the Mediterranean coast. Control over Jabneel oscillated between Judah and Philistia. During Uzziah's campaign against the Philistines he recaptured Jabneel (Jabneh; 2 Chr. 26:6). During the Hellenistic period Jabneel was called Jamnia. Battles at Jamnia played an important role in securing the exclusive leadership of the Hasmoneans (1 Macc. 5:55-62; 10:69-87). It was at Jamnia that the Sanhedrin was reconstituted following the destruction of Jerusalem in 70 C.E., and there the Sanhedrin was largely responsible for the canonization of the OT.

2. A town on the southeastern border of Naphtali, S of the Sea of Galilee (Josh. 19:33). Jabneel has been identified with Khirbet Yemmā/Kfar Yamma (198233; *j. Meg.* 1.1, 70a), but archaeological evidence makes Tel Yin'am (198235) preferable.

BRADFORD SCOTT HUMMEL

JABNEH (Heb. *yaḇneh*)

An alternate name for Jabneel (**1**; 2 Chr. 26:6).

JACAN (Heb. *ya'kān*)

A man of Gad, living in Bashan during the reigns of King Jotham of Judah and King Jeroboam II of Israel (1 Chr. 5:13).

JACHIN (Heb. *yāḵîn*) (also JARIB)

1. A son of Simeon and grandson of Jacob and Leah (Gen. 46:10; Exod. 6:15), whose descendants constituted the family of the Jachinites (Num. 26:12). At 1 Chr. 4:24 he is called Jarib (**1**).

2. The leader of the twenty-first priestly division at the time of David (1 Chr. 24:17). His family was among those enlisted to repopulate postexilic Jerusalem (1 Chr. 9:10; Neh. 11:10).

JACHIN (Heb. *yāḵîn*) **AND BOAZ** (*bō'az*)

The two pillars that flanked the entrance of Solomon's temple (1 Kgs. 7:15-22, 41-42; 2 Chr. 3:15-17). Molded of bronze by Hiram of Tyre (1 Kgs. 7:13-14), the freestanding pillars were ca. 8 m. (26.5 ft.) tall (18 cubits) and had a circumference of ca. 5.3 m. (17.5 ft.; 12 cubits). The pillars were hollow, with walls ca. 7.6 cm. (3 in.) thick (four fingers). Topped with a bowl-like capital (Heb. *gullâ*) ca. 2.3 m. (7.5 ft.) high (5 cubits), the pillars had a total height of 10.3 m. (34 ft.; 23 cubits).

The biblical writer gives special attention to the elaborate design and ornamentation of the capitals. They were designed with "nets of checker work," "wreaths of chain work," "pomegranates" and "lily-work," the latter motif associated especially with the Egyptian artwork.

While the Bible provides an elaborate description of the design of Jachin and Boaz, the biblical account provides little or no information concerning the function of the two pillars. Since they seem to be described as freestanding, the pillars were apparently designed with a symbolic rather than

structural function. Freestanding pillars have been found at several ancient Near Eastern sites including Byblos, Shechem, Khorsabad, Taanach and Tell Tainat. The pillars are of special interest in light of small pillarlike offering stands or incense altars discovered in excavations at Megiddo. One such stand was designed with a bowl-like capital decorated with lotus leaves and flowers, a motif similar to the lily-work ornamentation of Jachin and Boaz. With the similarities in design and motifs, and since 1 Kings describes the capital with Heb. *gullâ* (1 Kgs. 7:41), it is possible that the two pillars that flanked the entrance of Solomon's temple were large incense altars, perhaps symbolic reminders of the divine presence in the wilderness by means of the pillar of cloud by day and the pillar of fire by night (Exod. 14:24; 33:9-10; Deut. 31:15).

But the two pillars also may have had yet another symbolic function. Since the Hebrew form of the name Jachin ("he will establish") appears also in 2 Sam. 7:12-16 ("he will establish David's throne forever"), and Boaz ("in the strength of") appears in Ps. 21:1 ("in the strength of Yahweh shall the king rejoice"), it is possible that the pillars were also symbols of the relationship between the king and Yahweh. The pillars, located in front of the royal chapel, may have functioned as symbols of the authority of the Davidic dynasty.

LaMOINE F. DeVRIES

JACINTH

A red, orange, or yellow stone. Some versions translate "jacinth" for Heb. *lešem,* an engraved stone on the high priest's breastpiece (Exod. 28:19; 39:12). The LXX renders the Hebrew term *ligýrion,* which, except in Josephus' descriptions of the breastpiece (*Ant.* 3.7.5; *BJ* 5.5.7), occurs nowhere else. At Rev. 21:20 the NAB, NIV, NKJV, and NRSV translate "jacinth" for Gk. *hyákinthos,* a course in the foundation of the city wall of the New Jerusalem. The NJB and NKJV read "hyacinth blue" for the adjective *hyakínthinos,* a color of the riders' breastplates (Rev. 9:17). Some translations render "amber," "carnelian," "feldspar," "sapphire," or "turquoise" for these Hebrew and Greek terms.   JOSEPH E. JENSEN

JACKAL

A member of the dog family common to southwest Asia and North Africa. The oriental or golden jackal *(Canus aureus)* resembles a large fox in shape and manner, with sharp face, short ears, and a bushy tail. Its fur is dirty yellow in color, mottled with reds, browns, whites, and grays. Unlike the fox, jackals are social creatures, mating for life and foraging in small packs on the fringes of human habitation. They are shy, nocturnal scavengers, feeding on carrion, refuse, vegetation, and unprotected small stock. Their eerie wail accounts for their Hebrew nickname, "the howlers" *(tannîm, tannîn).* In Egyptian mythology Anubis, the jackal-headed deity, was a guardian of the dead.

In the Bible the jackal is presented as a symbol of isolation, destruction, and abandonment (Job 30:29; Ps. 44:19[MT 20]; Jer. 9:11[10]). It is possible that the animals caught by Samson and loosed with firebrands tied to their tails were jackals (Judg. 15:4-5; NRSV "fox"), as were the "wall-breaking" creatures of Tobiah's jest (Neh. 4:3[3:25]).

Identifying jackals in the biblical tradition is difficult due to the number of Hebrew words and their Greek translations. The LXX translates Hebrew *tannîm* as Gk. *drákontes,* "dragons," or *seirḗnes,* "sirens." This produced the translations "monsters" or "sea monsters" in the KJV. Another Hebrew term, *šûʿāl,* is frequently translated "foxes" (Gk. *alṓpēx*) but may, in places, be better understood as jackals (e.g., Judg. 15:4; Ps. 63:10[11]; Ezek. 13:4; Neh. 4:3). MARK ZIESE

JACKAL'S WELL

A well or spring (Heb. *ʿên hattannîn;* perhaps also "Dragon Gate") in the Hinnom Valley, situated between the Valley Gate and the Dung Gate (Neh. 2:13). Some scholars identify the site as En-rogel.

JACOB (Heb. *yaʿăqōḇ*)

The younger son of Isaac and Rebekah, so named because he was born grasping the heel (Heb. *ʿāqēḇ*) of his older brother (Gen. 25:26). This folk etymology (the historical etymology is probably "May [God] protect") indicates Jacob's character as one who strives to overcome others, particularly his brother Esau in pursuit of the firstborn blessing. Later he gains a new name, Israel, which signals that he has "striven with God and with humans and [has] prevailed" (Gen. 32:28). Much of the thematic complexity of the Jacob narrative can be seen in the movement from Jacob to Israel, from the heel-grabber of his youth to the successful and prolific patriarch, the namesake and embodiment of Israel.

While a lad, beginning even in the womb, Jacob's adversary is his brother Esau. The eventual resolution to this conflict is predicted in Yahweh's oracle to Rebekah, specifying that the two brothers are two peoples and that "the elder shall serve the younger" (Gen. 25:23). The sibling rivalry, in which Jacob will prevail, is defined also as an ethnic conflict, in which Israel will prevail over Edom (= Esau). The dual dimension of the conflict, between siblings and between peoples, informs much of the characteristics of the two brothers and the symbolic content of their interactions. Jacob-Israel is pictured as a man of culture, who dwells in tents (Gen. 25:27), cooks (v. 29), engages in trade (v. 31), and is generally quick-witted and devious. He is a "smooth man" (Gen. 27:11), both smooth of skin and of mind. In contrast to all these traits, Esau is uncivilized, a "man of the steppe" who "knows the hunt" (Gen. 25:27), who does not understand the fine points of trade and negotiation and is ruled by his appetite (v. 32). Esau is a hairy man (Gen. 25:25), as is appropriate for a wild man of nature. The contrast between the civilized man and the wild man not only ensures that the civilized man will win (even if by deception), but also defines Israel as a civilized nation, in contrast with its culturally disadvantaged neighbors. Like the Greeks, the Israelites defined themselves as civilized and other peoples as quasi-barbarians.

Jacob's triumph over Esau, predicted in Yahweh's oracle, does not come without a price. Not only must he flee his home in fear for his life (Gen. 27:42-43), but the deceptive means by which he acquired the birthright and blessing from Esau and Isaac respectively (25:29-34; 27:1-29) are turned against him by his next adversary, Laban. Laban's deception of Jacob in Gen. 29:22-27 neatly mirrors Jacob's deception of Isaac in 27:1-29. Whereas Jacob deceived his blind father by substituting the younger son for the elder, now the father Laban deceives his son-in-law by substituting his elder daughter for the younger. Like Isaac, Jacob is deceived because he cannot see the impostor (Gen. 29:23). By this ruse Laban preserves the right of the firstborn and gains Jacob's labor for another seven years. But Jacob finally prevails over Laban by acquiring his wealth through another deception involving his ability to manipulate the flock's reproductive powers (Gen. 30:25-43).

Jacob's success in prevailing over his human adversaries and acquiring blessing, family, and wealth is intersected by two stories of encounters with God. While fleeing his home and Esau's wrath he encounters God at a place he names Bethel, "House of God" (Gen. 28:11-22). Later, while returning home and fleeing Laban's wrath, he encounters God at a place he names Penuel, "Face/Presence of God" (Gen. 32:22-32[MT 23-33]). At the first of these places God grants Jacob the patriarchal blessing and divine protection, and at the second he grants him a new name and identity as Israel, which is also defined as blessing. Jacob's return to his home as Israel is accompanied by stories of reconciliation with Laban (Gen. 31:25-54) and Esau (33:1-16). Jacob's final success is sealed by making peace with his former adversaries.

Many of the themes of the Jacob narrative are echoed in the story of Joseph and his brothers. In this story Jacob-Israel is deceived by his elder sons (Gen. 37:31-35), but the younger son, Joseph, again prevails. The older brothers finally show their worth by treating the youngest son, Benjamin, with compassion, and reconciliation among the brothers ensues. In a final turn on past deceptions, Jacob/Israel deceives his son Joseph by granting the blessing of the firstborn to Ephraim, the younger son, over Manasseh, the elder son (Gen. 48:8-21). In this story Jacob/Israel is old and blind, like old Isaac before, but the blind father now is the deceiver and grants the blessing to the younger. At this point, near death Jacob/Israel displays oracular powers, echoing the oracle given at his own birth by predicting the ascent of Ephraim and the destiny of each of his sons (Gen. 49:1-27). The transformation from heel-grabber to patriarch to seer is complete.

Outside of the Pentateuch Hosea refers to the Jacob narrative, presenting a slightly different version of Jacob's encounter at Penuel with God, who is now represented as an angel (Hos. 12:2-4[3-5]). Jeremiah also makes a disparaging allusion to Jacob's character as a heel-grabber (Jer. 9:4[3]). In later literature Jacob is uniformly depicted as a wise and pious man (e.g., Jub. 25:4-10; Heb. 11:21).

RONALD S. HENDEL

JACOB'S WELL

The location of Jesus' encounter with a Samaritan woman (John 4). The only well explicitly named in the NT, it is associated with Bir Yaʿaqûb (177179) at the base of Mt. Gerizim near Tell Balâṭah. The well is ca. 30 m. (100 ft.) deep and appears to be fed by an underground stream.

Debate continues regarding the NT association of the well with the Samaritan town of Sychar. Some hold that Sychar is to be associated with the present town of Askar N of the well. Others associate Sychar with Shechem. However, recent archaeological evidence indicates that Shechem no longer existed in the 1st century C.E. Whatever the case, the present well at Bir Yaʿaqûb accords well with the biblical evidence and is attested to by Jewish, Samaritan, Christian, and Muslim sources. Jerome reports that a church was located on the site by the end of the 4th century, and the Crusaders built a church there in the 11th century. D. LARRY GREGG

JADA (Heb. *yāḏāʿ*)

A Judahite, son of Onam and brother of Shammai; father of Jether and Jonathan (1 Chr. 2:28, 32).

JADDAI (Heb. *yadday*) (also IDDO)

An Israelite who was required to send away his foreign wife (Ezra 10:43; **K** *yaddô*). At 1 Esdr. 9:35 he is called Iddo (**6**).

JADDUA (Heb. *yaddûaʿ*)

1. One of the "leaders of the people" who set his seal to the new covenant under Nehemiah (Neh. 10:21[MT 22]).

2. The son of Jonathan (or Johanan), the last mentioned of the high priests (Neh. 12:11). According to Neh. 12:22 he was a priest about the time of the Persian king Darius III Codomannus (336-331 B.C.E.), who fell to Alexander the Great (cf. Josephus *Ant.* 11.8.4-5 [326-39]).

JADDUS (Gk. *Ioddoús*)

A priest whose descendants, because he had adopted the name of his father-in-law Barzillai the Gileadite, were unable to prove their levitical descent upon their return from exile (1 Esdr. 5:38).

See BARZILLAI **3**.

JADON (Heb. *yāḏôn*)

A Meronothite who helped repair the walls of Jerusalem (Neh. 3:7).

JAEL (Heb. *yāʿēl*)

The Kenite woman, wife of Heber, who cunningly set up Sisera, the exhausted Canaanite commander, by catering to his needs after his defeat at the hands of the Israelites and who then treacherously killed him after he had come to trust her (Judg. 4:17-22; 5:24-27). The details of this event differ in the two accounts: in Judg. 4 she slays the sleeping, exhausted Sisera by staking his head to the ground, while in the poetry of Judg. 5 she bashes in his skull while he is drinking curds from a bowl. In both accounts, however, it is quite clear that Jael is the means used by the writer to depict Sisera's total humiliation. For a warrior to die at the hands of a woman was humiliation enough, but for the warrior also to be drawn into the woman's web of deceit made the humiliation even more enjoyable to his enemies (cf. the story of Judith and Holofernes).

Jael and Deborah are the clear protagonists in this story of Israelite victory, and they stand in sharp contrast to the annihilated Sisera and the reluctant Israelite warrior Barak. Judg. 4:9 is clearly intended as a foreshadowing of Jael's ravaging of Sisera, an act which is denied Barak. It is especially noteworthy that in Judg. 5:24-26 we have the cathartic moment of the Song of Deborah, in which each blow rained down upon Sisera's head by Jael allows the Israelites to savor again the crushing of this hated Israelite enemy. In short, as Sisera falls, so fall the Canaanites, and his protracted demise embodies their defeat.

Bibliography. A. J. Hauser, "Judges 5: Parataxis in Hebrew Poetry," *JBL* 99 (1980): 23-41.

ALAN J. HAUSER

JAGUR (Heb. *yāḡûr*)

A city in the southern part of Judah near Edom (Josh. 15:21), most likely Khirbet el-Gharrah (148071), ca. 18 km. (11 mi.) E of Beer-sheba.

JAHATH (Heb. *yaḥaṯ*)

1. A Judahite, the son of Reaiah; ancestor of the Zorahite families Ahumai and Lahad (1 Chr. 4:2).

2. A Levite, son of Libni and descendant of Gershom (1 Chr. 6:20, 43[MT 5, 28]).

3. A Levite, grandson of Gershom; chief of the sons of Shimei (1 Chr. 23:10-11).

4. A Levite, son of Shelomoth and descendant of Izhar (1 Chr. 24:22).

5. A Merarite Levite, overseer of the work force repairing the temple at the time of King Josiah (1 Chr. 34:12).

JAHAZ (Heb. *yahaṣ, yahṣâ*) (also JAHZAH)

A city in Transjordan where the Amorite king Sihon of Heshbon was killed by the Israelites (Num. 21:23; Deut. 2:32-33; Judg. 11:20-21). Although the city was within the territory allocated to the tribe of Reuben, the settlement proper was assigned to the Merarite Levites (Josh. 21:36; 1 Chr. 6:78[MT 63]). Later the city fell to the Moabites during King Mesha's expansion to the north (Mesha inscription 18-20). It apparently remained in Moabite hands for some time thereafter (Isa. 15:4; Jer. 48:21 [called Jahzah], 34).

Several sites have been proposed as candidates for ancient Jahaz. These include Khirbet Libb (222112; ca. 11 km. [7 mi.] N of Dibon on the King's Highway), Khirbet Iskander (223107; ca. 6 km. [4 mi.] N of Dibon), Khirbet Remeil (228114; 5 km. [3 mi.] NE of Khirbet Iskander), Khirbet Qureiyet ʾAleiyan (233104; ca. 8 km. [5 mi.] NE of Dibon), and Tall Jalul (231125; 5 km. [3 mi.] E of Madaba).

The most recent and best proposal at this time seems to be Khirbet Medeiniyeh (236110) on the Wadi Themed (ca. 2.5 km. [1.5 mi.] NE of Khirbet Remeil). RANDALL W. YOUNKER

JAHAZIEL (Heb. *yaḥăzî'ēl*)

1. A Benjaminite who came to David in Ziklag (1 Chr. 12:4[MT 5]).

2. A priest at the time of David, appointed to sound the trumpet before the ark (1 Chr. 16:6).

3. A Kohathite Levite, third of the "sons" of Hebron (**1;** 1 Chr. 23:19; 24:23).

4. The son of Zechariah, "a Levite of the sons of Asaph" (2 Chr. 20:14) who prophesied to King Jehoshaphat that Judah would be victorious over the Moabites and Ammonites (vv. 14-17, 20-30).

5. The father of Shecaniah, who returned with Ezra from captivity in Babylon (Ezra 8:5).

JAHDAI (Heb. *yāhdāy*)
A Calebite, perhaps a concubine of Caleb, from whom are descended six offspring (1 Chr. 2:47).

JAHDIEL (Heb. *yaḥdî'ēl*)
The head of a father's house in the Transjordanian half-tribe of Manasseh (1 Chr. 5:24).

JAHDO (Heb. *yaḥdô*)
A Gadite, the son of Buz (1 Chr. 5:14).

JAHLEEL (Heb. *yaḥlĕ'ēl*)
A son of Zebulun (Gen. 46:14), and eponymous ancestor of the Jahleelites (Heb. *hayyaḥlĕ'ēlî;* Num. 26:26).

JAHMAI (Heb. *yaḥmay*)
A warrior of the tribe of Issachar, head of a father's house among the descendants of Tola (1 Chr. 7:2).

JAHZAH (Heb. *yahṣâ*)
Alternate name of Jahaz, a city in the tableland of Moab (Jer. 48:21).

JAHZEEL (Heb. *yaḥṣĕ'ēl*), **JAHZIEL** *(yaḥṣî'ēl).*
A son of Naphtali (Gen. 46:24), ancestor of the Jahzeelites (Heb. *hayyaḥṣĕ'ēlî;* Num. 26:48). At 1 Chr. 7:13 his name is given as Jahziel.

JAHZEIAH (Heb. *yaḥzĕyâ*)
The son of Tikvah; an Israelite who opposed Ezra's order to divorce foreign wives (Ezra 10:25).

JAHZERAH (Heb. *yaḥzērâ*)
A priest and the son of Meshullam (1 Chr. 9:12). He may be the same as Ahzai at Neh. 11:13.

JAIR (Heb. *yā'îr, yā'îr*)

1. A son of Manasseh who captured some of the villages of the Amorites in Bashan in Transjordan and named them Havvoth-jair, "cities of Jair" (Num. 32:41; Deut. 3:14).

2. Jair the Gileadite, a judge. He is said to have had 30 sons who rode on 30 donkeys and had 30 towns in Gilead (Judg. 10:3-5). A "minor" judge, he is otherwise unknown.

3. The father of Elhanan, who is said to have killed Lahmi the brother of Goliath (1 Chr. 20:5; Heb. *yā'îr*). However, in 2 Sam. 21:19 Jaare-oregim is named as the father of Elhanan, who is in turn credited with the slaying of Goliath. The longer form in 2 Samuel is probably a scribal error due to the inadvertent copying of the final word in the verse in MT. If in fact Jaare-oregim is to be identified with Jair, then his home was Bethlehem.

4. A Benjaminite; father of Mordecai, the cousin and guardian of Esther (Esth. 2:5).

MICHAEL L. RUFFIN

JAIRITE (Heb. *yā'irî*)
A gentilic attributed to Ira, David's priest (2 Sam. 20:26). Ira was a descendant of the Manassite Jair (**1**). Following the LXX and other versions some scholars prefer to read "Jattirite" (Heb. *yattirî*), i.e., a native of Jattir (cf. 2 Sam. 23:38 = 1 Chr. 11:40, "Ira the Ithrite").

JAIRUS (Gk. *Iáïros*)
The synagogue official ("ruler") who begged Jesus to heal his terminally ill 12-year-old daughter (Mark 5:22; Luke 8:41). In Matthew's version (Matt. 9:18) the ruler is anonymous, his daughter's age is not specified, and the girl is already dead. All three Synoptic Gospels intercalate the story of Jesus' healing of the woman with a hemorrhage between the time of the father's request and Jesus' actual resuscitation of the girl (Matt. 9:18-26; Mark 5:21-43; Luke 8:40-56). Since some reliable manuscripts of Mark also omit the name Jairus, some scholars speculate that Luke added the name because he thought it the equivalent of Heb. *yā'îr* ("he will awaken"), a view accepted by those who see this story as a resurrection legend. Several scholars have noted the similarities between the account of Jesus' healing of Jairus' daughter and Peter's resuscitation of Tabitha (Dorcas) in Acts 9:36-43.

JEFFREY T. TUCKER

JAKEH (Heb. *yāqeh*)
The father of Agur the sage (Prov. 30:1). Some scholars see Jakeh as an acronym for Heb. *YHWH, qāḏôš hû',* "Yahweh, blessed is he."

See MASSA 2.

JAKIM (Heb. *yāqîm*)

1. A son of Shimei from the tribe of Benjamin (1 Chr. 8:19).

2. The leader of the twelfth division of priests at the time of David (1 Chr. 24:12).

JALAM (Heb. *ya'lām*)
An Edomite chief, the son of Esau and Oholibamah (Gen. 36:5, 14, 18; 1 Chr. 1:35).

JALON (Heb. *yālôn*)
A son of Ezrah from the tribe of Judah (1 Chr. 4:17).

JAMBRES (Gk. *Iambrēs*)
One of two Egyptian sorcerers who opposed Moses (2 Tim. 3:8; cf. Exod. 7:11, 22). The name may be a grecized form of Heb. *mambres* (cf. *mrh*, "opponent" or "apostate").

See JANNES.

JAMBRI (Gk. *Iámbri*)
A band of robbers (Gk. "the sons of Jambri") from Medeba in Transjordan, who took captive and murdered John, a brother of the Hasmonean Jonathan (1 Macc. 9:36). Jonathan avenged his brother's death during a wedding feast (1 Macc. 9:37-42). The Jambri were probably Amorites (Josephus *Ant.* 13.1.2 [11], "sons of Amaraios"; cf. Num. 21:30-31).

JAMES (Gk. *Iákōbos*, from Heb. *yaʿăqōḇ*, "Jacob")

1. James the son of Zebedee. Among the first whom Jesus called as disciples (Mark 1:16-20 par.), James belonged with his (likely younger) brother John and Peter to the inner circle of Jesus' disciples. In the four lists of the Twelve (Matt. 10:2-4; Mark 3:16-19; Luke 6:14-16; Acts 1:13), James the son of Zebedee is always among the first three names. Zebedee was a fisherman on the Sea of Galilee, and his sons were partners with Peter and Andrew (Matt. 4:21; Luke 5:10). Matt. 27:56 may identify Salome as their mother.

Jesus named both James and John "sons of thunder" (Mark 3:17), probably for their strong, brash personalities. He rebuked them for their murderous anger toward the Samaritan village that refused him entry (Luke 9:51-56) and for their desire for precedence among the 12 disciples in the kingdom of God (Mark 10:35-45; but compare Matt. 20:20-28, where their mother made the request for them). Jesus refused this request, and predicted that they must "drink the cup that I drink," the cup of death. James did drink it when executed by Herod Agrippa I in 44 C.E. (Acts 12:2). While postbiblical Christian legend claims that all the Twelve except John were martyrs for the faith, this James is the only one of the Twelve whose martyrdom is substantiated in the biblical record.

Christian tradition has called this James "the Great/Major" to distinguish him from James the son of Alphaeus, "the Less/Minor." Legend tells how James preached in Spain and was eventually buried there; his supposed tomb in the church of Santiago [St. James] de Compostela in northwest Spain has been a major pilgrimage site since medieval times.

2. James the son of Alphaeus. In the four lists of the apostles (Matt. 10:3; Mark 3:18; Luke 6:15; Acts 1:13) a second James is listed, always called explicitly "the son of Alphaeus" to distinguish him from the more prominent James. To judge from his position in the last third of the lists, this James was of comparatively little importance; indeed, he is not mentioned in the Gospels beyond these lists. This James may possibly be the same as James the son of Mary (**3** below).

3. James the son of Mary. Not one of the Twelve, his parents likely were Clopas and the Mary who with the other women was a witness of Jesus' crucifixion (Matt. 27:56; Mark 15:40; 16:1; Luke 24:10). This James is often identified in older scholarship as James the son of Alphaeus, probably because Mark was thought to call him "the young" or "the small" in order to distinguish him from James the son of Zebedee. Nothing else is known of him.

4. James the father of Judas (not Iscariot). In the Lukan lists of the Twelve (Luke 6:16; Acts 1:13) the patronymic "son of James" is likely added to distinguish this Judas carefully from Judas Iscariot, whose name immediately follows. Nothing else is known of him.

5. James the brother of Jesus. The exact relationship of James and "the brothers of the Lord" (1 Cor. 9:5; cf. Mark 6:3 par.) to Jesus has been strongly debated in the ancient Church and in modern times. Three main positions have emerged: (1) James is the son of Joseph and Mary, the literal brother (or half-brother, given Jesus' virginal conception) of Jesus. Most Protestant and some Roman Catholic scholars hold this meaning of "brother." (2) James is a son of Joseph from a previous marriage, and hence Jesus' step-brother. This position derives from the NT apocrypha, especially the influential Protevangelium of James. Eastern Orthodox churches favor this view, but it is not a serious option in most contemporary historical scholarship. (3) James is Jesus' cousin or other near relative. Supporters of this position argue from Heb./Aram. *ʾāḥ*, which means both "brother" and "kinsman." It is the traditional Roman Catholic position in both piety and scholarship.

While not a follower of Jesus during his ministry, James seems to have been converted shortly afterwards, perhaps when the risen Jesus appeared to him (1 Cor. 15:7; cf. Acts 1:14). James gradually took over the leadership of the Jerusalem church from the leaders among the Twelve, becoming one of the most important leaders in the 1st-century Church. Paul witnesses to James' leadership in Jerusalem (Gal. 2), and in Acts 15 James presides over the Apostolic Council and issues its decision. As evidence of his position in the Church, after the death of James the son of Zebedee most references to him call him only James, although there were others by that name alive as well. This James died for the faith at the hands of the high priest Ananus, shortly before the Jewish revolt (Josephus *Ant.* 20.9.1 [197-203]; for a probably more legendary account, cf. the witness of Hegesippus cited by Eusebius *HE* 4.22.4).

James is the traditional author of the NT letter in his name. While most contemporary scholars dispute the authenticity of the letter, some stoutly defend it. The author of Jude presumably refers to this James as his own brother (Jas. 1:1). In post-NT times, James became the traditional head of the Jewish-Christian wing of the Church, figuring in Gnostic, Jewish-Christian, and Great Church writings.

Bibliography. R. Bauckham, *Jude and the Relatives of Jesus in the Early Church* (Edinburgh, 1990), 5-44; F. F. Bruce, *Peter, Stephen, James, and John*

(Grand Rapids, 1980); L. T. Johnson, *The Letter of James*. AB 37A (New York, 1995), 89-123.

ROBERT E. VAN VOORST

JAMES, APOCRYPHON OF (I,2)

The first tractate from Codex I (Jung Codex) of the Nag Hammadi discovery. The untitled text is a revelation dialogue cast in the form of a letter from James to an unknown recipient. The current title has been assigned because of an interior reference to itself as a "secret book" (Ap. Jas. 1.10).

The dialogue begins with a scene set 550 days after the Resurrection in which the Twelve are gathered together recalling the words of Jesus and recording these reminiscences in books. Jesus suddenly appears, takes James and Peter aside, and gives them his teaching.

Among the distinctive elements of this work is an exhortation to martyrdom (4.24–6.20). This section has many stylistic similarities with other discussions of this topic (cf. Origen *Ex. Mart.;* Tertullian *Ad Mart.*). What is particularly interesting is this text's positive assessment of and encouragement to voluntary martyrdom (cf. Tertullian *De fuga* 9; Clement *Misc.* 4.4).

Commentators have suggested that the Apocryphon of James should be considered a primary source of the sayings of Jesus since it contains kingdom of heaven similes (7.22-35; 12.22-30), a prophecy (9.24–10.6), and other sayings attributed to Jesus that may reflect the most ancient strata of tradition.

Bibliography. R. Cameron, *Sayings Traditions in the Apocryphon of James.* HTS 34 (Philadelphia, 1984); F. E. Williams, "The Apocryphon of James: Introduction," in *Nag Hammadi Codex I,* ed. H. W. Attridge. NHS 22 (Leiden, 1985), 13-27.

ANDREA LORENZO MOLINARI

JAMES, ASCENTS OF

A late-2nd-century Jewish-Christian book described by Epiphanius (*Adv. haer.* 30.16.6-9) and no longer extant in its original form. The book exalts James the brother of Jesus as the leader of the earliest Church and denigrates Paul as "the enemy" who prevents the conversion of the entire Jewish people. It advocates observance of Mosaic law and baptism in the name of Jesus to replace sacrifices. Originally written in Greek, it probably stems from the Transjordan and may be the main source of the 4th-century Pseudo-Clementine *Recognitions* 1.33-71, which retells from a Jewish-Christian perspective the story of Israel from Abraham through Jesus and the early Jerusalem church and features a prophet-like-Moses, preexistence Christology.

Bibliography. F. S. Jones, *An Ancient Jewish Christian Source on the History of Christianity: Pseudo-Clementine Recognitions 1.27-71.* Texts and Translations 37. Christian Apocrypha 2 (Atlanta, 1995); R. E. Van Voorst, *The Ascents of James.* SBLDS 112 (Atlanta, 1989).

ROBERT E. VAN VOORST

JAMES, LETTER OF

A NT epistle, often ascribed to James, Jesus' younger brother, leader of the church in Jerusalem (Acts 12:17; 15:13-21; 21:18; Gal. 1:19; 2:9, 12). Other men named James in the Gospels have also been proposed as the author. Following Jerome, the Roman Catholic tradition identifies the author as James, the son of Alphaeus (Mark 3:18; Acts 1:13). Also, it has been suggested that the letter is pseudonymous. It is argued that James, the son of a Galilean artisan whose native tongue was Aramaic, could not have written this letter with its elegant Greek and conscious literary style modeled on the LXX.

Evidence for James the Lord's brother being the author is strong, indicating that the letter is probably not a pseudonymous work relying on his authority. Galilee was not a literary backwater, and the possibility of Jesus' disciples being literate and influenced by Hellenistic ideas is now considered more possible. James' use of a professional secretary in the production of the letter may also explain the Greek style. James ministered to the circumcised (Gal. 2:9), and the letter seems to be addressed to a Jewish-Christian audience. This is indicated by frequent quotation and allusion to the OT and Jewish tradition, the monotheistic confession that "God is one" (Jas. 2:19), and the "assembly" in 2:2 being literally "synagogue." Also, there is little evidence of a developed or self-consciously Christian theology. These features suggest an author writing at an early date in a Jewish context such as the Jerusalem church.

According to Josephus, James was stoned to death by order of the Jewish high priest Ananus II in 62 C.E. (*Ant.* 20.197-203), while according to Eusebius he was killed just before Vespasian invaded Jerusalem in 67 (*HE* 2.23.18). On the basis of the conclusion that the author is James the brother of Jesus, the letter must be dated before these events, perhaps in the 50s. The letter's content reflects a disintegration in the social fabric of the region addressed, reminiscent of Jerusalem and Judea in the years preceding the war with Rome (66-73). Violence, anger, and killing are a key concern of the letter (1:19-21; 3:13–4:3). The only internal evidence for place of writing is the reference to earlier and latter rains (5:7), which are characteristic of the weather along the eastern coast of the Mediterranean Sea which affected Jerusalem.

The audience is poor and oppressed. Members are dragged into court by the rich (2:6) and taken advantage of by wealthy landowners (5:4-6). The audience is addressed as "the twelve tribes in the Dispersion" (1:1), a title which designates the church as the regathered and new Israel (cf. Matt. 19:28; Rev. 7:4-8). In the NT the Dispersion is a metaphor for Christians living outside their heavenly home, i.e., on earth (1 Pet. 1:1). According to Luke, after the death of Stephen in Jerusalem, the Jewish Christians (Hellenists) there were scattered (*diaspeírō*) and traveled as far as Phoenicia, Cyprus, and Antioch (Acts 11:19). James may be addressing these dispersed members of his church who once lived in Jerusalem.

Outwardly the Epistle resembles a letter, beginning with the standard salutation and greeting (1:1). However, it lacks personal reminiscences, reference to specific problems, and a closing. It is not a personal letter like those of Paul, but a more general or catholic letter meant to address more than one church. More specifically James is protreptic literature, trying to persuade an audience to live a life of virtue. It has also been classified as parenesis (moral instruction) and diatribe (dialogue and question and answer in pursuit of truth). The central portions of James are composed according to the Greco-Roman pattern of elaboration for the complete argument (2:1-13, 14-26; 3:1-12). Parenetic materials and diatribal features are incorporated into this pattern.

The letter relies heavily upon the OT, the wisdom tradition, and the Jesus tradition. James alludes to the OT (1:10; 3:9; 5:4), quotes it (2:8, 11, 23; 4:6), and uses it for examples (2:21, 25; 5:10-11, 17-18). Wisdom is a religious stance and worldview characteristic of godly people looking for understanding and insight for living, often relying on parenesis (e.g., Proverbs, Job). Although James does not quote Jesus, he does base many of his teachings on what Jesus said as transmitted in the oral tradition (2:5; cf. Matt. 5:3, 5; 5:12; cf. Matt. 5:33-37).

Theological Emphases

Wisdom

James identifies two types of wisdom: heavenly and earthly. Heavenly wisdom is nonviolent, whereas earthly wisdom is violent (3:13-18). Heavenly wisdom is a gift of God (1:5; cf. v. 17). Temptation to evil is not from God, but has its source in the human heart (1:12-16), with Satan having some role in temptation as well (4:7). Life is frail and contingent (1:9-11; 4:13-16). The righteous suffer in this world through social and economic disadvantage. They are rejected and despised by the world, and oppressed by the ungodly who have power. The righteous sufferers look to God for vindication and exaltation (5:10-11). The rich are not pious (1:9-11; 2:1-7; 5:1-6), but rather the poor (2:5), especially the widows and orphans (1:26-27) and landless laborers (5:1-6). They have God's ear (5:4), receive God's grace (4:6), and are heirs of the kingdom as part of eschatological reversal (2:5; 5:10-11). James does not espouse poverty for its own sake, but does say that the world's verdict that the poor are worthless is not God's verdict. The rich are to help the needy (1:22-27), not just spout pious platitudes (2:14-17).

Law, Faith, and Works

James teaches that profession of faith is borne out in works (1:19-26; 2:1-13). Both the "perfect law, the law of liberty" in 1:25 and the "royal law" in 2:8 refer to the law to love one's neighbor (Lev. 19:18). Love of others is the basis for action (2:12) and is especially to be demonstrated in meeting the needs of the poor (1:27; 2:15-16).

Perfection

Perfection is not being free from defects. Rather, it comes from the OT understanding of perfection as obedience to the divine commands. Perfection in the faith is not mere assent to creeds (2:19) or profession of sentiment (2:15-16). Rather, faith is perfected by works (2:22) and enduring suffering (1:3-4). Keeping the perfect law is done with deeds of kindness (1:25) and loving one's neighbor (2:8-10). Bridling the tongue is central to being a perfect person (1:26; 3:2). The opposite of being perfect is being double-minded, sinful, and disordered (1:8; 3:16; 4:8).

Eschatology

James affirms the imminent coming of Jesus as Judge (5:7-9). There will be reward to those who endure temptation (1:12), persevere in the perfect law (1:25), and use the tongue properly and show mercy to others (2:12-13). There will be judgment for those who do not use the tongue properly and do not do good works (2:12-13; 4:11-12). Judgment also falls upon teachers who misuse their position (3:1), the rich who neglect the needs of the poor (5:1-6), and those whose word cannot be trusted (5:12).

As part of the wisdom tradition with its concern for practical living, James contains much ethical material including instruction on control of speech (1:26; 3:1-12; 4:11-12; 5:9); the relationship between rich and poor (2:1-13; 5:1-6); the poor as the focus of good deeds (1:27; 2:15-16); and love, mercy, and humility as characterizing relationships with others (2:8; 3:13-18).

Bibliography. J. B. Adamson, *James, The Man and His Message* (Grand Rapids, 1989); A. Chester, "James," in *The Theology of the Letters of James, Peter, and Jude,* ed. A. Chester and R. Martin (Cambridge, 1994); L. T. Johnson, *The Letter of James.* AB 37A (New York, 1995); R. P. Martin, *James.* WBC 48 (Waco, 1988); E. Tamez, *The Scandalous Message of James* (New York, 1990); D. F. Watson, "James 2 in Light of Greco-Roman Schemes of Argumentation," *NTS* 39 (1993): 94-121; "The Rhetoric of James 3:1-12 and a Classical Pattern of Argumentation," *NovT* 35 (1993): 48-64. DUANE F. WATSON

JAMES, PROTEVANGELIUM OF

An account of the births of Mary and Jesus, arguably one of the most influential of all the apocryphal Gospels, having spawned any number of subsequent birth narratives. Mary is portrayed as the daughter of a formerly childless couple, Joachim, a rich man, and his wife Anna. Her miraculous conception and birth are based primarily on the story of Hannah (1 Sam. 1-2). The young Mary, a descendant of David, is dedicated to the service of God, and is left with priests in the Jerusalem temple at the age of three. When she reaches puberty, the priests arrange for her to marry the widower Joseph, a much older man with children from an earlier marriage. Mary then conceives while still a virgin, a fact confirmed to Joseph by an angel and demonstrated to the priests by the couple's drinking of the "water of conviction" (Num. 5); she later gives birth to Jesus in a cave near Bethlehem. The midwife Salome doubts Mary's virginal status. When she attempts to test Mary's virginity physically, her hands are severely burned, but she is healed when she touches the child. The story concludes with the visit of the Magi, the infanticide ordered by Herod, and the martyrdom of John the Baptist's father, Zacharias, in the Jerusalem temple.

The primary purposes of the book are clearly the glorification of Mary and defense of the virgin birth. The work also explains that Jesus is indeed of Davidic descent through Mary (not Joseph as in the canonical birth narratives), and that the siblings of Jesus mentioned in the NT are his half-brothers, children from Joseph's previous marriage.

The Protevangelium was written in Greek in the latter half of the 2nd century, and the provenance is most likely Syria (although Egypt is also a possibility given the attestation by Clement of Alexandria and Origen). Though banned in the West, the book was very popular in the East, as witnessed by the numerous surviving Greek manuscripts (some as early as the 3rd century) and the translations of the document into Syriac, Ethiopic, Georgian, Coptic, Armenian, and Slavonic. Though the postscript claims that it was written by Jesus' brother James, it is unlikely that the story was written by a Jew as there are numerous errors regarding Jewish customs and Palestinian geography.

Bibliography. R. F. Hock, *The Infancy Gospels of James and Thomas* (Santa Rosa, 1995); J. K. Elliott, *The Apocryphal New Testament,* rev. ed. (Oxford, 1993), 48-67. JAMES R. MUELLER

JAMES THE GREATER, ACTS OF

An apocryphal work found in Book IV of the Pseudo-Abdias' Apostolic History (and appearing with some variation in Greek, Coptic, and Ethiopic texts), thought to have evolved between the 2nd and 4th centuries. The Acts elaborate events in James' missionary career and supplement the brief mention of his martyrdom in Acts 1:13. The account describes James' conversion of the reluctant Philetus and Hermogenes by miraculous actions, his persuasion of Jews that Jesus fulfilled OT prophecies, and his conversion and baptism of a Jewish scribe. These final events correspond to a tradition known to Clement of Alexandria (Eusebius *HE* 2.9.2-3) that a guard was converted after James' arrest, only to be beheaded with James. Later tradition (6th-8th century) claims that James preached in Spain and that his body was escorted by angels to Santiago de Compostela, the site of the shrine to St. James, patron of Spain.

Bibliography. J. Charlesworth, ed., *The New Testament Apocrypha and Pseudepigrapha* (Metuchen, 1987), 217-28. MELISSA M. AUBIN

JAMIN (Heb. *yāmîn*)

1. A son of Simeon (Gen. 46:10; Exod. 6:15; 1 Chr. 4:24), eponymous ancestor of the Jaminite clan (Heb. *hayyāmînî,* Num. 26:12).

2. A Judahite, son of Ram and descendant of Jerahmeel (1 Chr. 2:27).

3. A Levite who translated into Aramaic the portions of the Law read by Ezra so the people could understand (Neh. 8:7-8).

JAMLECH (Heb. *yamlēḵ*)

A leader of the tribe of Simeon (1 Chr. 4:34).

JAMNIA (Gk. *Iamneía*)

Hebrew Yavneh, a city in the coastal plain of ancient Palestine S of Jaffa. It is mentioned in 2 Chr. 26:6 (Jabneh) and in the late Hellenistic age, in the Apocrypha (e.g., 2 Macc. 12:8-9, 40), and in classical sources. Jamnia had its own harbor during Phoenician, Hellenistic, and Roman occupation, Jamnia Paralios or Yavneh-Yam, which was 8 km. (ca. 5 mi.) away from the city on the coast. Early in the 1st century B.C.E. Alexander Janneus incorporated the city into the Hasmonean kingdom (Josephus *Ant.* 13.395), and its population became largely Jewish. When Jerusalem was destroyed in 70 C.E., Jamnia became a center for Jewish sages. In the 4th century and later it was the seat of a Christian bishop.

Yavneh-yam, 16 km. (ca. 10 mi.) S of Tel Aviv, was excavated in 1967-69 by Jacob Kaplan, and later by others doing rescue projects. The main discovery was a large square enclosure surrounded by a Middle Bronze Age rampart, which was threatened by the encroaching sea. Kaplan also excavated three superimposed gates of mud brick.

Bibliography. B. Isaac, "A Seleucid Inscription from Jamnia-on-the-Sea: Antiochus V Eupator and the Sidonians," *IEJ* 41 (1991): 132-44; J. Kaplan, "Further Aspects of Middle Bronze Age II Fortifications in Palestine," *ZDPV* 91 (1975): 1-17; E. Schürer, *The History of the Jewish People in the Age of Jesus Christ (175 B.C.–A.D. 135),* rev. ed., 2 (Edinburgh, 1979), 109-10. KENNETH G. HOLUM

JANAI (Heb. *yaʿnay*)

A descendant of Gad living in Bashan (1 Chr. 5:12).

JANIM (Heb. *yānîm*)

A place in the mountains of Judah, in the vicinity of Eshan and Beth-tappuah (Josh. 15:53). The site has not been identified, but a possibility is modern Beni Naʿim, 6 km. (4 mi.) E of Hebron.

JANNEUS (Gk. *Iannaíos*), **ALEXANDER**

See ALEXANDER 3.

JANNAI (Gk. *Iannaí*)

The father of Melchi, a postexilic ancestor of Jesus (Luke 3:24). The name does not occur in the OT.

JANNES (Gk. *Iánnēs*)

An opponent of Moses along with Jambres, and a model of those "of corrupt mind and counterfeit faith" who "oppose the truth" (2 Tim. 2:8; cf. Exod. 7:11-12, 22). Not named in Exodus, they were identified as Moses' opponents in Second Temple and rabbinic Jewish writings by the 1st century B.C.E.

(4QDamascus Document[b] [4Q266] fr. 3, 2:13-15 = CD 5:17-19) and were known by Christian and pagan writers. The pseudepigraphic work Jannes and Jambres, perhaps Christian and dated between the 1st and 3rd centuries but based on pre-Christian traditions, survives only in fragments.

Bibliography. A. Pietersma and R. T. Lutz, "Jannes and Jambres," *OTP* 2:427-42.

ERIC F. MASON

JANOAH (Heb. *yānôḥâ, yānôaḥ*)

1. A town on the eastern border of Ephraim (Josh. 16:6-7). Eusebius locates it 12 mi. E of Neas Polis (*Onom.* 108.20-21). It has been identified with Khirbet Yānûn (184173), 11 km. (7 mi.) SE of Shechem.

2. A city in the northern region of Naphtali (2 Kgs. 15:29). It was conquered by the Assyrians under Tiglath-pileser III in 733/2 B.C. Several sites have been suggested, including Tell en-Nâʿimeh (205296), 8 km. (5 mi.) NE of Kedesh, and Givʿat ha-Shoqet (203293), near Kibbutz Gilʿadi.

Bibliography. J. Kaplan, "The Identification of Abel-beth-maachah and Janoah," *IEJ* 28 (1978): 157-69.

JOHN A. MCLEAN

JAPHETH (Heb. *yep̱eṯ, yāp̱eṯ;* Gk. *Iápheth*)

1. One of the three sons of Noah, apparently the youngest since he is usually named last (although in the Table of Nations his line of descent is given first; Gen. 10; 1 Chr. 1:1-17). The derivation of the name is uncertain, but Heb. *pth,* "to be spacious," has been suggested (cf. Gen. 9:27). After the Flood, Japheth and his brother Shem walk backward into the tent of their sleeping father to cover his nakedness, which their elder brother Ham had seen; for their discretion they are blessed by Noah (Gen. 9:20-27).

In the Table of Nations seven sons and seven grandsons of Japheth are named, though they are names of peoples rather than individuals. They inhabit the region extending along the northern reaches of the entire Fertile Crescent and westward above the Mediterranean Sea. Some are readily identifiable: Madai is the Medes in ancient Iran; Ashkenaz probably refers to the Scythians in the region of the Caucasus Mountains; Gomer is the Cimmerians, who inhabited northern Anatolia; Tiras has been variously identified with Thrace or with the Etruscans; Tarshish may refer to Tartessus in Spain (cf. John 1:3); Kittim points to Cyprus or possibly Crete; and Rodanim (a correction from MT "Dodanim," based on the LXX, Samaritan Pentateuch, and Hebrew manuscripts) appears to be Rhodes.

Recent studies have associated the names of Japheth's descendants with ethnic names known from Anatolia and more widely in Mediterranean regions in the 7th and early 6th centuries B.C.E.

JEFFREY S. ROGERS

2. A region N of Arabia, perhaps in Asia Minor, where Holofernes surrounded and routed the Midianites (Jdt. 2:25).

JAPHIA (Heb. *yāp̱îaʿ*) **(PERSON)**

1. King of Lachish; one of five Canaanite kings, who at the instigation of Adonizedek, king of Jerusalem, joined the fight against the Gibeonites (Josh. 10:3). Japhia and the coalition were executed by Joshua (Josh. 10:6-27).

2. A son of David born in Jerusalem to an unnamed mother (2 Sam. 5:15; 1 Chr. 3:7; 14:6).

KENNETH ATKINSON

JAPHIA (Heb. *yāp̱îaʿ*) **(PLACE)**

A border town located on the southern edge of the territory of Zebulun (Josh. 19:12). It is identified with Yâfā (176232), located less than 3 km. (2 mi.) SW of Nazareth.

KENNETH ATKINSON

JAPHLET (Heb. *yaplēṭ*)

A son of Heber from the tribe of Asher (1 Chr. 7:32-33). He may have been the ancestor of the Japhletites (Heb. *yaplēṭî*), a group whose territory marked the southern boundary of the Joseph tribes (Josh. 16:3).

JARAH (Heb. *yaʿrâ*) (also JEHOADDAH)

A Benjaminite, the son of Ahaz and father of Alemeth, Azmaveth, and Zimri; a descendant of Saul (1 Chr. 9:42). At 1 Chr. 8:36 he is called Jehoaddah.

JAREB (Heb. *yārēḇ*)

King of Assyria to whom Israel (Ephraim) sent tribute at various times during Hosea's prophetic career (Hos. 5:13; 10:6), ca. 750-722 B.C. Because no other evidence supports the existence of a King Jareb, some interpreters read "a king who will contend," a possible Hebrew epithet for Tiglath-pileser III. The NRSV represents another common alternative, emending the Hebrew text on the basis of the Assyrian honorific title *malku rabu,* "the great king."

R. DAVID MOSEMAN

JARED (Heb. *yereḏ, yāreḏ;* Gk. *Iáret*)

A son of Mahalalel and father of Enoch, from the lineage of Seth (Gen. 5:15-20; 1 Chr. 1:2; Luke 3:37). According to Gen. 5:20, Jared lived 962 years.

JARHA (Heb. *yarḥāʿ*)

An Egyptian slave belonging to Sheshan the Jerahmeelite (1 Chr. 2:34). Because Sheshan had no sons, he gave his daughter as a wife to Jarha in order to produce an heir (1 Chr. 2:35; cf. Exod. 21:4).

JARIB (Heb. *yārîḇ*)

1. A son of Simeon (1 Chr. 4:24). Because he is called Jachin (**1**) at Gen. 46:10; Exod. 6:15; Num. 26:12, many scholars consider the reading here to be a scribal error.

2. One of the leaders whom Ezra dispatched to Casiphia to obtain ministers for the temple (Ezra 8:16; 1 Esdr. 8:44).

3. A priest whom Ezra ordered to give up his foreign wife (Ezra 10:18; 1 Esdr. 9:19).

JARMUTH (Heb. *yarmûṯ*)

1. A city in Judah (Khirbet el-Yarmûk/Tel Jarmuth; 147124), located ca. 5 km. (3 mi.) S of Beth-shemesh and 26 km. (16 mi.) SW of Jerusalem on the E edge of the Shephelah. Its king Piram joined Amorite kings in an attack on Gibeon (Josh. 10:1-27). After being pursued southward through the Shephelah, the five kings hid in the caves of Makkedah S of Beth-shemesh but were later captured by Joshua's army and executed.

Excavations at Tel Jarmuth have yielded massive Early Bronze II-III fortifications along with public, industrial, and domestic buildings of the Proto-Canaanite era and a broadroom-type pillared sanctuary measuring 11.5 × 4.75 m. (38 × 15.5 ft.). After a period of abandonment in the Middle Bronze Age, a smaller city was founded in the Late Bronze Age, occupying primarily the acropolis to the south. The mound experienced continuous settlement until the Byzantine period, including three Iron I strata. Eusebius (*Onom.* 106.24) mentioned the city Iermous in this vicinity.

2. A city in Issachar (cf. Remeth, Josh. 19:21; Ramoth, 1 Chr. 6:73[MT 58]). The city was allocated to the Levites (Josh. 21:29) and has been tentatively identified with Kôkab el-Hawā/Kokhav ha-Yarden (199222), ca. 10 km. (6 mi.) N of Beth-shan.

R. Dennis Cole

JAROAH (Heb. *yārôaḥ*)
A man of the tribe of Gad who lived in Bashan; son of Gilead and grandfather of Abihail (1 Chr. 5:14).

JASHAR (Heb. *yāšār*), **BOOK OF**
A Hebrew document, most likely a collection of songs or poetry (Josh. 10:13; 2 Sam. 1:18). Jashar means "one who is upright or honest," and thus this collection possibly served to honor the societal ideal of an upright person. The writer(s) of the book of Joshua refer to this source in telling how Joshua commanded the sun to stand still. The Samuel reference recites a song of lament entitled "Behold a Bow" and attributes it to David in his sorrow over the death of Saul and Jonathan. Some LXX manuscripts cite a "Book of Songs" for Solomon's poetic dedication of the temple (1 Kgs. 8:12-13). This may refer to the same collection attested in Joshua and Samuel, since the letters in the Hebrew word for "song" *(šyr)* transpose two of the letters in "Jashar."

Some scholars speculate that other biblical songs like the Song of Moses (Deut. 32), Song of Miriam (Exod. 15:21), Song of the Sea (15:1-18), Song of Deborah (Judg. 5), and Song of Hannah (1 Sam. 2:1-10) might have been found in this collection, which, along with several other sources in the OT (e.g., the Book of the Wars of the Lord and the Book of the Chronicles of the Kings of Israel/Judah) is no longer extant. Other scholars question whether these sources ever existed in written form.

Alice H. Hudiburg

JASHEN (Heb. *yāšēn*) (also HASHEM)
One of David's Thirty (2 Sam. 23:32). The MT reading "sons of Jashen" (Heb. *bĕnê yāšēn*) derives from a dittography with the preceding name Shaalbon (perhaps a gentilic, Shaalbonite). At 1 Chr. 11:34 he is called Hashem the Gizonite.

JASHOBEAM (Heb. *yāšoḇʿām*)

1. A Hachmonite; one of David's elite class of warriors and the chief of the Three (1 Chr. 11:11). Jashobeam apparently killed 300 men with his own sword in battle. Josheb-basshebeth the Tahchemonite (2 Sam. 23:8), who killed 800 men with his own spear, may be the same person. The LXX renders both as Ishbosheth, suggesting that Ishbaal ("man of Baal") may have been the original form of the name.

2. One of David's commanders who was responsible for 24 thousand men in the first month of rotating leadership (1 Chr. 27:2-3); the son of Zabdiel and a descendant of Perez. He could be the same person as **1** above.

3. A Korahite who defected from Saul's army to join David at Ziklag (1 Chr. 12:7). He was a great archer and sling thrower (1 Chr. 12:6).

Henry L. Carrigan, Jr.

JASHUB (Heb. *yāšûḇ*) (also IOB)

1. The third son of Issachar (Num. 26:24; 1 Chr. 7:1 **K** *yāšîḇ*); eponymous ancestor of the Jashubites. The name appears as Iob *(yōḇ)* at Gen. 46:13.

2. A returned exile who divorced his foreign wife (Ezra 10:29).

JASHUBI-LEHEM (Heb. *yāšuḇî leḥem*)
Traditionally interpreted as a place name mentioned in relation to the sons of Shelah (1 Chr. 4:22). The text is probably to be emended to read "but returned to Lehem" (cf. Vulg., LXX, Tg.).

Christian M. M. Brady

JASON (Gk. *Iásōn*)

1. Son of a certain Eleazar whom Judas Maccabeus sent with Eupolemus in 161 B.C.E. to seek a treaty with Rome (1 Macc. 8:17).

2. The father of Antipater, sent by Jonathan as an ambassador to Rome in 144 B.C.E. (1 Macc. 12:16).

3. A Cyrenian historian who composed a five-volume work on the Maccabean revolt which forms the basis for 2 Maccabees. Completed sometime after 160 B.C.E., Jason's work records battles against Antiochus IV Epiphanes and his son Antiochus V Eupator as well as the divine interventions that enabled the faithful Jews to overcome all odds (2 Macc. 2:19-23).

Benjamin C. Chapman

4. High priest from 174-171 B.C.E. who was responsible for establishing certain Hellenistic "reforms" in Jerusalem. Through bribery he got Antiochus IV Epiphanes to appoint him high priest shortly after 175. He also received permission to establish a gymnasium and an educational institution in Jerusalem and to enroll "the people of Jerusalem as citizens of Antioch" (2 Macc. 4:9). This led the author of 2 Maccabees to blame Jason for the excessive hellenization of Jerusalem (2 Macc. 4:11-17). Jason also sent envoys to the Olympic games at

Tyre with money for sacrifices to Hercules. In 171 he lost the high priesthood to Menelaus. Later, acting upon a rumor that Antiochus IV had died, Jason invaded Jerusalem and attempted to drive Menelaus out of power (2 Macc. 5:5-6). Menelaus was rescued by Antiochus upon his return from an unsuccessful Egyptian campaign. Jason became an exile and died in Egypt. JOHN KAMPEN

5. A Jewish Christian who entertained and aided Paul and Silas at Thessalonica (Acts 17:5-9). He was among those arrested because of their association with the missionaries and later released.

6. A companion and "relative" of Paul who sent greetings to the church at Rome (Rom. 16:21). He may be the same as **5** above.

BENJAMIN C. CHAPMAN

JASPER

A greenish, translucent variety of quartz of the type called chalcedony (Heb. *yāšp̄ēh;* Gk. *íaspis*). The stone is the third (and last) on the fourth row of the high priest's breastplate (the LXX places it third and last on the second row (Exod. 28:20; 39:13). Jasper is also one of the precious stones that cover the anointed cherub in Ezek. 28:13.

In the NT God appears on the throne as a light of jasper and carnelian (Rev. 4:3); the radiance of the heavenly Jerusalem is like jasper (21:11); and the walls of the city and its first foundation course are made of jasper (vv. 18-19).

TIMOTHY P. JENNEY

JATHNIEL (Heb. *yaṯnîʾēl*)

A Korahite gatekeeper of the sanctuary; the fourth son of Meshelemiah (1 Chr. 26:2).

JATTIR (Heb. *yattîr*)

A levitical city of Judah located in the hill country of Debir (Josh. 15:48; 21:14; 1 Chr. 6:57[MT 42]). After David's victory over the Amalekites (1 Sam. 30:19), he shared some of the spoils with the people of Jattir (v. 27). The town has been identified traditionally with Khirbet ʿAttîr (151084), ca. 21 km. (13 mi.) SW of Hebron.

Bibliography. W. F. Albright, "The List of Levitic Cities," in *Louis Ginzberg Jubilee Volume* (New York, 1945), 49-73. C. SHAUN LONGSTREET

JAVAN (Heb. *yāwān;* Gk. *Iōván*)

The fourth son of Noah's son Japheth and the father of Elishah, Tarshish, Kittim, and Rodanim according to the Table of Nations (Gen. 10:2-4) and its parallel genealogy (1 Chr. 1:5-7). The land of Javan is to be identified originally with Ionia, an area of Greek settlement in southwest Asia Minor. Later the name was expanded to describe the entire Greek population on both sides of the Aegean Sea.

Isa. 66:19 highlights Javan as one of the distant nations that would witness a future manifestation of Yahweh's glory. In an oracle against Tyre (Ezek. 27:13) Javan is mentioned with reference to its involvement in slave traffic and other commercial activities. The Javanites are referred to in Joel 3:6[MT 4:6) as slave traders who purchased Jewish captives from the Philistines and Phoenicians. Finally, the empire of Javan was forecast to replace that of Persia (Dan. 8:21; 10:20; 11:2). EDWIN C. HOSTETTER

JAW, JAWBONE

The lower bone structure of the human or animal mouth (Heb. *lěḥî*). Samson defeated Philistine opponents with a jawbone of an ass and commemorated the event by naming the place of slaughter Ramath-lehi, "hill of the jawbone" (Judg. 15:15-19). Metaphorically, placing a hook or bridle in the jaws indicated subjugation (Job 41:2[MT 40:26]; Isa. 30:28; Ezek. 29:4; 38:4), while breaking the jaws (or teeth) symbolized deliverance from an enemy (Job 29:17). In Ps. 22:15[16] Heb. *malqôaḥîm* (NASB "jaws") refers specifically to the gums.

J. A. VADNAIS

JAZER (Heb. *yaʿăzêr, yaʿăzēr*)

An Amorite town in central Transjordan conquered by the Israelites under Moses (Num. 21:32) and then allotted to the tribe of Gad (Josh. 13:25; Num. 32:34-35; 2 Sam. 24:5). The city was then assigned to the Merarite Levites (Josh. 21:39; 1 Chr. 6:81). The territory around Jazer was noted as suitable for grazing (Num. 32:1, 3-4) and wine production (Isa. 16:8-9; Jer. 48:32). During the 8th and 7th centuries the town apparently fell under Moabite jurisdiction (Isa. 16:8-9, 11).

The modern identity of Jazer is uncertain. Eusebius (*Onom.* 12.1-4) locates Jazer at the source of a large stream, 10 Roman mi. (15 km. [9 mi.]) W of Rabbath Ammon and 15 Roman mi. (24 km. [15 mi.]) from Esbus (Hesban). Five sites in this general vicinity have been proposed as Jazer. Khirbet eṣ-Ṣar (228150), 9 km. (5.6 mi.) W of Amman and 1.5 km. (ca. 1 mi.) SE of ʿAin eṣ-Ṣir, possesses extensive Iron Age sherds, but there is no other reason to identify it with Jazer. Yahuz (237159), 10 km. (6 mi.) N of Amman; Kom Yahuz (238160), near Yahuz; and Khirbet eṣ-Ṣireh, ca. 12.5 km. (8 mi.) W of Amman, have no evidence of Iron Age occupation. Khirbet Jazzir (219156), whose name reflects that of the ancient site, is near the location that Eusebius gives for Jazer (Azōr; *Onom.* 12.1-4) and is probably the best candidate for identification with the ancient town. RANDALL W. YOUNKER

JAZIZ (Heb. *yāzîz*)

A Hagrite overseer of the cattle belonging to David (1 Chr. 27:30[MT 31]).

JEALOUSY

Heb. *qinʾâ;* Gk. *zḗlos, phthónos* describe an intense emotional range for which English has no single word — both negative, "jealousy," and positive, "zeal," "anger," and "devotion." In the OT the term denotes a passion for justice in a particular situation and is associated more with the covenant God than with people. God is decribed as "jealous" when the prohibition of the worship of other gods is not observed (Exod. 20:5; 34:14; Deut. 4:24; 5:9; 6:15). Jealousy is like a fire (Ezek. 36:5; Zeph. 1:18) and typifies the warrior God in action (Isa. 42:13).

It is protective of the people (Isa. 26:11) and the land (Joel 2:18) and even of God (Num. 25:11). Joshua's dedication to Moses is described as jealous (Num. 11:29; cf. 1 Kgs. 19:10). The sons of Jacob were jealous of Joseph (Gen. 37:11), as were the Philistines of Isaac (26:14). Jealousy kept the Israelite kingdoms divided (Isa. 11:13). It can destroy the one who possesses it as well as its object (Job 5:2; Prov. 6:34; Cant. 8:6).

In the NT jealousy is rarely used of God. It applies to humans in the positive sense of zeal (2 Cor. 9:2; 11:2; Rom. 10:2), but also negatively, as envy (Matt. 27:18; Rom. 13:13; 1 Cor. 3:3; 13:4; 2 Cor. 12:20; Gal. 5:20; Jas. 3:14; 1 Pet. 2:1). God can be provoked to jealousy (1 Cor. 10:22). Jewish religious leaders were jealous of the success of the early Christian preaching (Acts 5:17; 17:5). But Paul mentions a pious jealousy among the Romans (Rom. 10:2; 11:11, 14). A Christian should have zeal for the Spirit (1 Cor. 12:31; 14:1), for what is right (1 Pet. 3:13), and for good deeds (Tit. 2:14). While God has made to dwell in us a spirit tending toward jealousy, he also bestows a greater grace to the humble and resists the proud (Jas. 4:5-6).

Bibliography. J. A. Fischer, "Jealousy," in *Collegeville Pastoral Dictionary of Biblical Theology,* ed. C. Stuhlmueller (Collegeville, 1996), 472-73.

SEÁN KEALY, C.S.SP.

JEARIM (Heb. *yĕʿārîm*), **MOUNT**
A mountain on the northern border of Judah (Josh. 15:10; "mountain of forests"). On this ridge is located Chesalon (Heb. *kĕsālôn,* "loins, back"), modern Keslā (154132) ca. 17 km. (10.5 mi.) W of Jerusalem. Some scholars have identified Mt. Jearim with Mt. Seir to the north across Wadi Chesalon.

JEATHERAI (Heb. *yĕʾaṯray*) (also ETHNI)
A Levite of the Gershonite line (1 Chr. 6:21; called Ethni at v. 41; one of these forms may have resulted from scribal error).

JEBERECHIAH (Heb. *yĕḇereḵyāhû*)
The father of Zechariah (**28**), who witnessed Isaiah's symbolic prophecy to King Ahaz (Isa. 8:2). Jeberechiah may have been the father-in-law of Ahaz and the grandfather of Hezekiah (cf. 2 Kgs. 18:2 = 2 Chr. 29:1).

JEBUS (Heb. *yĕḇûs*)
Pre-Israelite Jerusalem, the city David captured from the Jebusites (2 Sam. 5:6-9). The name, found only in Judg. 19:10-11; 1 Chr. 11:4-5, was perhaps derived from that of the clan that occupied the site prior to Israelite occupation. The Hebrew term means "to tread down" or "to trample," derived from a verb usually used in reference to the judgment or destruction of a city. In the Bible, the Jebusites are identified as descendants of Canaan (Gen. 10:16), one of the sons of Ham.

The name Jebus does not appear outside the biblical text. To complicate matters even more, the name Jerusalem rather than Jebus appears in the earliest extrabiblical references to the city, the Egyptian Execration Texts (19th-18th centuries B.C.E.) and the Amarna Letters (14th century). Consequently, some scholars propose that Jebus was a Canaanite village other than Jerusalem and identify it with the modern site of Shaʿfât. It is possible that the biblical writers who wrote during later periods used the term Jebus as the means to distinguish the pre-Israelite city from Israelite Jerusalem, or that they had access to an earlier tradition.

The identity of the Jebusites is also subject to debate. Some propose that they were Hurrian or Horite in background, while others suggest a Hittite background. Regardless of origin or ethnic background, the Jebusites were one of the many Canaanite groups at the time of the Conquest.

While the debate about Jebus and the origin of the Jebusites continues, according to the OT the Jebusites were a powerful people or clan that occupied Jebus, i.e., Jerusalem, prior to David's conquest of the city. Their firm grasp on the site and its territory is reflected by the fact that the Israelites did not take the site during the Conquest (Judg. 1:21). Apparently the Jebusites continued to occupy the site until the time of David.

The conquest of Jebus by David reflects the genius of the new king. While Saul is usually considered the first king of the United Kingdom of Israel, it was David who organized and established the monarchy. Having been anointed by Judah and by Israel (i.e., the tribes of the north), David then took the site of Jebus (2 Sam. 5:6-10; 1 Chr. 11:4-8), located in neutral territory between the people of the north and those of the south, and made it the capital of all the tribes. In addition to its unique location to the tribes of the north and the south, the site of Jesus was free of any tribal traditions or jealousies. But the site had other unique features. Located on a ridge, with the Kidron Valley to the east and the Tyropoeon or Cheesemakers Valley on the west, Jebus was an almost impregnable site, reflected in the Jebusite statement, "you will not come in here, even the blind and the lame will turn you back" (2 Sam. 5:6; 1 Chr. 11:5). With Gihon Spring located in the Kidron Valley to the east, the site had a plentiful water supply.

The site was perhaps first settled during the Middle Bronze Age. Archaeological evidence indicates the site was fortified with a stone wall. The discovery of a shaft, commonly referred to as Warren's shaft, provides evidence of the water system developed and used by the Jebusites. According to the Deuteronomic and the Chronistic histories, the city acquired the title "City of David" (2 Sam. 5:9; 1 Chr. 11:7) following David's conquest of the site.

LAMOINE F. DE VRIES

JECOLIAH (Heb. *yĕḵolyāhû, yĕḵolyâ*)
The wife of King Amaziah of Judah and mother of Azariah (**3;** Uzziah; 2 Kgs. 15:2 = 2 Chr. 26:3).

JECONIAH (Heb. *yĕḵonyâ, yĕḵonyāhû*),
JECHONIAH (Gk. *Iechonias*) (also CONIAH)
1. Alternate name of King Jehoiachin of Judah.

In the genealogy of Jesus at Matt. 1:11-12 he is called Jechoniah (Gk. *Iechonías*).

2. A levitical chief during King Josiah's reign (1 Esdr. 1:9). At 2 Chr. 35:9 he is called Conaniah (**2**).

3. Alternate name of King Jehoahaz of Judah (1 Esdr. 1:34).

JEDAIAH (Heb. *yĕḏaʿyâ, yĕḏāyâ*)

1. The son of Shimri; a clan leader in the tribe of Simeon (1 Chr. 4:37)

2. Eponymous ancestor of a priestly house (1 Chr. 9:10; 24:7). His descendants were mentioned among the Jews who returned with Zerubbabel to Jerusalem from the Babylonian Captivity (Ezra 2:36 = Neh. 7:39).

3. One of the people who built a part of the wall in postexilic Jerusalem (Neh. 3:10).

4. A priest who lived in Jerusalem at the time of Nehemiah (Neh. 11:10).

5-6. Two levitical chiefs who came up with Zerubbabel and Joshua to Judah in the reign of Darius I (Neh. 12:6-7). The connection between the two is not clear.

7-8. Two priests, each the head of a family, who returned following the Exile (Neh. 12:19, 21).

9. A contemporary of the prophet Zechariah, who returned from exile to Judah. Together with three other persons, he supplied silver and gold to Zechariah, who prepared a crown for Joshua the high priest as a memorial, perhaps of past apostasy (Zech. 6:10, 14).

Isaac Kalimi

JEDIAEL (Heb. *yĕḏîʿăʾēl*)

1. A Benjaminite, ancestor of mighty warriors (1 Chr. 7:6, 10-11). The genealogy in which he is named may actually be that of Zebulun, which is not listed here among the northern tribes.

2. A son of Shimri; one of David's Champions (1 Chr. 11:45).

3. A military chief from the tribe of Manasseh, who deserted to David at Ziklag (1 Chr. 12:20[MT 21]).

4. The second son of Meshelemiah; a Korahite gatekeeper for the ark at the time of David (1 Chr. 26:2).

JEDIDAH (Heb. *yĕḏîḏâ*)

The mother of King Josiah of Judah; daughter of Adaiah of Bozkath (2 Kgs. 22:1).

JEDIDIAH (Heb. *yĕḏîḏĕyâ*)

A name which Yahweh bestowed upon the infant Solomon through the prophet Nathan (2 Sam. 12:25). Some scholars suggest that this was the king's given name and Solomon his throne name.

JEDUTHUN (Heb. *yĕḏûṯûn, yĕḏîṯûn*)

1. The father of Obed-edom, who with his descendants were the Korahite levitical gatekeepers for the temple (1 Chr. 16:38, 42b; cf. 1 Chr. 26:1, 4, 8).

2. A levitical musician who served in David's tabernacle (1 Chr. 16:41-42; 25:6) and Solomon's temple (2 Chr. 5:12). Jeduthun is also described as the "king's seer" (2 Chr. 35:15), just as his descendants were appointed to prophesy with musical instruments (1 Chr. 25:1, 3; cf. 2 Chr. 29:14). Frequent descriptions of Jeduthun in association with Asaph and Heman suggest that the name Ethan can be identified as Jeduthun (1 Chr. 15:17, 19). The occurrences of the name Jeduthun in the superscriptions of Pss. 39, 62, 77 may denote his musicianship in the Davidic era or a musical form or liturgical setting associated with his name or guild (cf. Ps. 89, Ethan).

Hyun Chul Paul Kim

JEGAR-SAHADUTHA (Aram. *yĕḡar śāhăḏûṯāʾ*)

The name ("heap of witness") given by the Aramean Laban to the mount of stones erected to commemorate his covenant with Jacob (Gen. 31:47). Jacob named it, in Hebrew, Galeed.

JEHALLELEL (Heb. *yĕhallelʾēl*)

1. A descendant of Judah, probably the eponymous ancestor of a clan (1 Chr. 4:16).

2. A Merarite Levite; the father of Azariah (**18;** 2 Chr. 29:12).

JEHDEIAH (Heb. *yeḥdĕyāhû*)

1. A descendant of Shubael; a Levite at the time of David (1 Chr. 24:20).

2. A Meronothite; overseer of the donkeys of David (1 Chr. 27:30).

JEHEZKEL (Heb. *yĕḥezqēʾl*)

The leader of the twentieth division of priests at the time of David (1 Chr. 24:16).

JEHIAH (Heb. *yĕḥîyâ*)

A gatekeeper for the ark appointed by David (1 Chr. 15:24).

JEHIEL (Heb. *yĕḥîʾēl*) (also JEHIELI)

1. A Levite and musician in Jerusalem at the time of David (1 Chr. 15:18). He was a harpist appointed to the second rank of musicians who played while the ark was moved to Jerusalem (1 Chr. 15:20) and later served before the ark (16:5).

2. A Gershonite Levite, leader of the house of Laadan (1 Chr. 23:8). He was the founder of the levitical family of Jehieli (a variant spelling of his name; 1 Chr. 26:21).

3. A son of Hachmoni (or a Hachmonite), employed by David, probably as teacher or counselor (1 Chr. 27:32).

4. A Gershonite who was in charge of the temple treasury (1 Chr. 29:8); probably the same as **2.**

5. One of king Jehoshaphat's seven sons (2 Chr. 21:2).

6. A Levite, one of the overseers in the temple appointed by Hezekiah under the supervision of Conaniah (2 Chr. 31:13).

7. A prominent official at the time of King Josiah, together with Hilkiah and Zechariah called "chief officers of the house of God" (2 Chr. 35:8). He and other leaders voluntarily provided Passover offerings for the priests and Levites.

8. The father of Obadiah, of the family of Joab,

head of one of the families that together with 218 men left Babylon (Ezra 8:9).

9. The father of Shechaniah, of the family of Elam (Ezra 10:2).

10. A priest of the family of Harim, one of those who married foreign women (Ezra 10:21).

11. An Israelite of the family of Elam who had married a foreign woman (Ezra 10:26), perhaps identical with **9**. JESPER SVARTVIK

JEHIELI (Heb. *yĕḥîʾēlî*)
A levitical family descended from Jehiel **2**, responsible for the temple treasuries (1 Chr. 26:21).

JEHIZKIAH (Heb. *yĕḥizqîyāhû*)
A son of Shallum; one of the chiefs of the tribe of Ephraim at the time of King Pekah (2 Chr. 28:12).

JEHOADDAH (Heb. *yĕhôʿaddâ*) (also JARAH)
A Benjaminite; the son of Ahaz and father of Alemeth, Azmaveth, and Zimri (1 Chr. 8:36). At 1 Chr. 9:42 he is called Jarah.

JEHOADDAN (Heb. *yĕhôʿaddān*) (also JEHOADDIN)
The mother of King Amaziah of Judah (2 Chr. 25:1); called Jehoaddin at 2 Kgs. 14:2 (**K**).

JEHOAHAZ (Heb. *yĕhôʾāḥāz*) (also SHALLUM)

1. King of Judah, youngest son of Jehoram and Athaliah (2 Kgs. 8:25-29; 2 Chr. 22:1). His name is a variant of Ahaziah (2 Chr. 21:17). Jehoahaz was mortally wounded by Jehu's army and died at Megiddo (2 Kgs. 9:27-29).

2. King of Israel, the son and successor of Jehu (2 Kgs. 13:1-9). According to 2 Kgs. 13:1 he reigned 17 years, but according to v. 10 his reign lasted only 15 years.Throughout his reign he was under the subjugation of Hazael and Ben-hadad, kings of Damascus. Despite Jehoahaz' perpetuation of pagan worship, Yahweh promised him an unnamed "savior" (2 Kgs. 13:5).

3. The 17th king of Judah and one of the sons of Josiah (2 Chr. 3:15; cf. 2 Kgs. 23:31, 36). He is also called Shallum (Jer. 22:11; 2 Chr. 3:15). That may have been his personal name and Jehoahaz an assumed throne name.

Jehoahaz was 23 when proclaimed king (2 Kgs. 23:30-31), ascending the throne after Josiah's death in battle against the Egyptians. After three months on the throne, Jehoahaz was made a prisoner and removed from power by Neco II, king of Egypt, and replaced by his older brother Jehoiakim, who favored Egypt. Jehoahaz was taken first to Riblah in Syria and then in chains to Egypt, where he died. On the occasion of Jehoahaz' deportation, Jeremiah composed a lament (Jer. 22:10-12) declaring that Jehoahaz would never see his land again (cf. Ezek. 19:3-4). CLAUDE F. MARIOTTINI

JEHOASH (Heb. *yĕhôʾāš*) (also JOASH)
Alternate name of Joash (**3**), king of Judah (2 Kgs. 11-12; 2 Chr. 22:10–24:24), and Joash (**4**), king of Israel (2 Kgs. 13:10-25; 14:8-17).

JEHOHANAN (Heb. *yĕhôḥānān*)

1. A Korahite Levite gatekeeper of the temple (1 Chr. 26:3).

2. One of three Judahite "commanders of thousands" in King Jehoshaphat's army (2 Chr. 17:15).

3. The father of Ishmael, "commander of a hundred" who joined Jehoiada's coup against Queen Athaliah (2 Chr. 23:1).

4. The son (or descendant?) of Eliashib to whose chamber Ezra retreated for fasting (Ezra 10:6; 1 Esdr. 9:1). If this individual can be identified with the Johanan of Neh. 12:22-23 (apparently the grandson of Eliashib, the high priest of Nehemiah's time; cf. vv. 10-11; 3:1), his relationship with Ezra is important in the Ezra-Nehemiah chronology.

5. The son of Bebai; one of the Israelites who divorced their foreign wives (Ezra 10:28; 1 Esdr. 9:29).

6. The son of Tobiah the Ammonite, who opposed Nehemiah's rebuilding project (Neh. 6:18). He also married the daughter of Meshullam, who helped repair the walls of Jerusalem under Nehemiah (Neh. 3:4, 30).

7. A head of the priestly house of Amariah during the time of the high priest Joiakim (Neh. 12:13).

8. One of the priests officiating at the dedication ceremony of the walls that were rebuilt under Nehemiah's administration (Neh. 12:42). HAROLD R. MOSLEY

JEHOIACHIN (Heb. *yĕhôyāḵîn*) (also JECONIAH)
The throne name ("Yahweh has established") of Coniah, who succeeded his father Jehoiakim as the king of Judah. He became king at the age of 18 and reigned for three months during 598/597 B.C.E. His mother was Nehushta, daughter of Onathan, a high court official (2 Kgs. 24:8; 2 Chr. 36:9). After Babylon's decisive defeat of Egypt at Carchemish (605; 2 Kgs. 24:7; Jer. 46:2), Jehoiakim (609-598) changed his allegiance from Egypt to Babylon. Following the indecisive battle between Egypt and Babylon in 601, Jehoiakim renounced his vassalage to the Babylonian king Nebuchadnezzar (2 Kgs. 24:1). In December 598 the Babylonian army responded by marching to Judah (2 Kgs. 24:2; cf. Jer. 35:11). Jehoiakim died at this time, perhaps the result of an assassination, and it was in this context that Jehoiachin became king (2 Kgs. 24:8; cf. Jer. 22:18, 19; 36:30). Nebuchadnezzar's army arrived at Jerusalem and in March 597 the city surrendered; Jehoiachin, various relatives, and the elite and skilled population were taken into captivity in Babylon along with objects of value and prestige (2 Kgs. 24:12-17; Jer. 27:19-20; cf. 2 Kgs. 25:13-15); the king's uncle, Mattaniah (Zedekiah), succeeded him (2 Kgs. 24:17). Cuneiform sources record some of the same details. Even after his exile, some considered Jehoiachin the legitimate ruler, and certain members of the exilic community even continued to calculate their calendar according to his reign, but Jeremiah seems to have discouraged this (Ezek. 1:2; Jer. 22:24-30). In the 37th year of Jehoiachin's

exile, the Babylonian king Evil-merodach (562-560) released him from prison and gave him a regular food allowance (2 Kgs. 25:27-30; Jer. 52:31-34); cuneiform documents from the time of Nebuchadnezzar also refer to rations distributed to King Jehoiachin and his sons (*ANET*, 308; cf. 1 Chr. 3:17). Jehoiachin died in exile.

Stamped storage jar handles reading "Eliakim, steward of Yaukin" were once thought to imply that Jehoiachin continued to "administer" the crown property through Eliakim, but the paleographic and archaeological data of these epigraphs suggest that the jar handles refer to an earlier, nonroyal Jehoiachin.

Bibliography. J. J. Granowski, "Jehoiachin at the King's Table: A Reading of the Ending of the Second Book of Kings," in *Reading Between Texts: Intertextuality and the Hebrew Bible*, ed. D. N. Fewell (Louisville, 1992), 173-88; A. K. Grayson, *Assyrian and Babylonian Chronicles.* Texts from Cuneiform Sources 5 (Locust Valley, N.Y., 1975); H. G. May, "Three Hebrew Seals and the Status of Exiled Jehoiachin," *AJSL* 61 (1939): 146-48.

CHRIS A. ROLLSTON

JEHOIADA (Heb. *yĕhôyāḏā'*) (also JOIADA)

1. A priest from Kabzeel, in southern Judah. He was the father of Benaiah, chief of David's bodyguard (2 Sam. 8:18; 23:20, 22 = 1 Chr. 11:22, 24; 27:5).

2. A late-9th-century priest in Jerusalem (2 Kgs. 11–12; 2 Chr. 23:1–24:16). Jehoiada led the coup that ousted Athaliah (ca. 843-ca. 837 B.C.E.) and installed Joash (ca. 837-800?) on the Davidic throne. The 2 Kings narrative depicts his leadership, military control, and manipulation of dynastic and covenantal symbols. 2 Chronicles emphasizes his leadership in the renewal of the sanctity of the temple.

2 Kings credits Joash's correct behavior to Jehoiada's instruction. 2 Chronicles, however, limits the king's acceptable behavior to Jehoiada's lifetime in an effort to explain theologically certain negative events later in Joash's reign. In the account on the temple restoration, 2 Kings reports first Jehoiada's inaction, then his cooperation with the king's initiative to fund temple repairs. 2 Chronicles reduces Jehoiada's direct role while crediting his tenure with the proper restoration of the temple and its ritual. Rivalry between royal and religious hierarchies, typical of agrarian states, underlies both narratives.

Chronicles adds details: Jehoiada's wife was Jehosheba, he selected wives for Joash, and he was buried with the kings in the city of David. These details may have annalistic veracity but also reveal a rhetorical interest in the priest's role.

3. A son of Benaiah, successor to Ahithophel as king's counselor (1 Chr. 27:34).

4. A priest of the Second Temple period, son of the high priest Eliashib (**7;** Neh. 13:28). His son's marriage into the foreign Sanballat family was condemned by Nehemiah. Elsewhere the name appears as Joiada.

5. A priest who was replaced by Zephaniah, probably as part of factional infighting in late First Temple Judah (Jer. 29:26).

Bibliography. P. Dutcher-Walls, *Narrative Art, Political Rhetoric: The Case of Athaliah and Joash.* JSOTSup 209 (Sheffield, 1996).

PATRICIA DUTCHER-WALLS

JEHOIAKIM (Heb. *yĕhôyāqîm*)

1. King of Judah (609-598 B.C.E.), whose given name was Eliakim (2 Kgs. 23:34; 2 Chr. 36:4). His mother was Zebidah, daughter of Pedaiah of Rumah (2 Kgs. 23:36b). Jehoiakim was the second-born son of Josiah (1 Chr. 3:15) and was enthroned by Pharaoh Neco of Egypt in 609 to replace Jehoahaz (Shallum), whom the "people of the land" had chosen to succeed his father Josiah (2 Kgs. 23:30; 2 Chr. 36:1). Jehoiakim was 25 years old when he acceded the throne, and he reigned 11 years in Jerusalem (2 Kgs. 23:36). He was succeeded in 598 by his son Jehoiachin.

The death of Jehoiakim is shrouded in mystery. 2 Kings seems to indicate that Jehoiakim died peacefully in Jerusalem and "slept with his ancestors" (2 Kgs. 24:6). 2 Chronicles, however, suggests that he was taken prisoner by Nebuchadnezzar to Babylon where he eventually died (2 Chr. 36:5-8; 1 Esdr. 1:39-42). In somewhat conventional language, Jeremiah predicts the humiliating death of Jehoiakim (Jer. 22:18-19; 36:30; cf. Josephus *Ant.* 10.6.3), without reference to a specific location. The Deuteronomist presents Jehoiakim as a (compliant) vassal of Egypt who levied an oppressive tax upon the people in order to "meet Pharaoh's demand for money" (2 Kgs. 23:35). After an unspecified period (Kings makes no reference here to Egypt's defeat by the Babylonians at Carchemish in 605 [Jer. 46:2]), Jehoiakim became a servant of King Nebuchadnezzar of Babylon (2 Kgs 24:1). However, Jehoiakim was not a willing vassal; after three years of Babylonian subjugation, he revolted, only to be defeated by bands of Arameans (2 Kgs. 24:2; cf. Jer. 35:11). The writer concludes that Judah's defeat was the direct consequence of an entire history of idolatry and bloodshed. Jehoiakim is thus viewed by the Deuteronomist as simply another Judean king who "did evil in the sight of Yahweh" (2 Kgs. 23:37).

Although the account of his reign is truncated in 2 Chronicles (cf. 36:4-8), the writer adds that Jehoiakim was "bound in fetters" by Nebuchadnezzar and threatened with deportation. Whether the Babylonian king actually deported Jehoiakim or simply frightened him into submission is impossible to determine from the text. According to the Chronicler, Jehoiakim was merely an "evil king" who committed "abominations" against Yahweh (2 Chr. 36:5b, 8; cf. 1 Esdr. 1:37-39, 42).

The writer of Daniel dates to the "third year of the reign of King Jehoiakim" (Dan. 1:1-2) a siege of Jerusalem by Nebuchadnezzar (606), a reference for which there is no historical support. In Jeremiah the "fourth year of King Jehoiakim" (Jer. 25:1; 36:1; 45:1; 46:2) functions literally and as a "code word" for danger, judgment, and destruction. This date is fraught with danger because it is the accession year of Nebuchadnezzar (605), in which he overtook the Egyptian armies at Carchemish before advancing southward. Thus, the "fourth year of Jehoiakim" signals an approaching "enemy from the north" and the imminent end of Judah.

Jeremiah often contrasts the much admired Josiah and the despised Jehoiakim. The abusive reign and opulent lifestyle of Jehoiakim are compared to the just rule of his father (Jer. 22:10-30). The text commends Josiah for defending "the cause of the poor and needy" (Jer. 22:16), but condemns Jehoiakim for greed and exploitation, as well as for "shedding innocent blood and practicing oppression and violence" (v. 17). In Jer. 36 Jehoiakim is presented as one who loathes the prophetic word of God. When the king destroys the scroll of Jeremiah, one can discern in this text a deliberate contrast between Josiah's penitential response to the book of the Law (2 Kgs. 22:11) and Jehoiakim's contemptible reaction to the reading of Jeremiah's scroll. Both "hear" (Heb. *qr'*) the words of the book/scroll (2 Kgs. 22:11; Jer. 36:24), and thus are afforded an opportunity to protect the community from imminent disaster. However, whereas Josiah "rends" (Heb. *qr'*) his clothes as a sign of mourning and repentance, Jehoiakim instead "rends" the scroll. Consequently, Josiah saves the nation from destruction, at least temporarily, while Jehoiakim seals the dreadful fate of the Judean people. It is no wonder that Jehoiakim is portrayed in the Haggadah as the personification of arrogance and evil.

Bibliography. J. A. Dearman, "My Servants the Scribes: Composition and Context in Jeremiah 36," *JBL* 109 (1990): 403-21; J. M. Myers, *2 Chronicles*. AB 13 (Garden City, 1965); E. W. Nicholson, *Preaching to the Exiles: A Study of the Prose Tradition in the Book of Jeremiah* (New York, 1971); M. A. Taylor, "Jeremiah 45: The Problem of Placement," *JSOT* 37 (1987): 79-98.

LOUIS STULMAN

2. A high priest, son of Hilkiah and descendant of Shallum, to whom the exiles sent an offering (Bar. 1:7).

JEHOIARIB (Heb. *yĕhôyārîḇ*) (also JOIARIB)
A priest during the reign of David (1 Chr. 24:7); eponymous ancestor of a priestly house among the returned exiles (9:10). At Neh. 11:10 he is called Joiarib.

JEHONADAB (Heb. *yĕhônāḏāḇ*) (also JONADAB)
Alternate form of Jonadab (**2**).

JEHONATHAN (Heb. *yĕhônāṯān*)
English versions often render the Hebrew name by the shortened form Jonathan.

1. A Levite who traveled among the cities of Judah teaching the Torah during the reign of Jehoshaphat (2 Chr. 17:8).

2. A postexilic priest, head of the father's house of Shemaiah (Neh. 12:18).

See JONATHAN.

JEHORAM (Heb. *yĕhôrām*) (also JORAM)

1. The son of Ahab who succeeded his brother Ahaziah as king of the northern kingdom of Israel and reigned from 849 to 842 B.C.E. (2 Kgs. 1:17; 3:1). Jehoram is criticized for his religious practices, but is credited with removing a pillar of Baal (2 Kgs. 3:2). Portions of the Elisha cycle may have involved Jehoram (2 Kgs. 6:8–7:20).

During Jehoram's reign King Mesha of Moab withheld tribute, so Jehoram created a coalition force with Jehoshaphat of Judah and marched against Moab. The kings succeeded in routing the Moabites and driving them into the fortified city of Kir-hareseth, but the coalition forces withdrew when the Moabite king sacrificed his eldest son on the city wall (2 Kgs. 3:4-27). The Moabite Stone, commissioned by Mesha, is a record of Mesha's successful reestablishment of independence.

There is no mention of Jehoram's participation in the anti-Assyrian coalition which resisted Shalmaneser III, but it is clear that in 842 Jehoram of Israel and Ahaziah of Judah formed a coalition against the Syrian usurper Hazael. Their forces engaged Hazael's at Ramoth-gilead and Jehoram was wounded (2 Kgs. 8:28-29; 2 Chr. 22:5-6a). While he was recovering in Jezreel, Ahaziah visited him. Jehu then came to Jezreel and killed both Jehoram and Ahaziah (2 Kgs. 9:1-28; cf. 2 Chr. 22:6b-9).

Excavations at Tel Dan in 1993 and 1994 uncovered fragments of an Aramaic stela, apparently commissioned by Hazael, in which he claims to have killed [Jeho]ram king of Israel and [Ahaz]iah king of Judah. The biblical and epigraphic data seem to be in conflict, but there is biblical evidence of some sort of alliance between Hazael and Jehu (1 Kgs. 19:17). Jehu exterminated the remaining Omrides and succeeded Jehoram as king of Israel (2 Kgs. 9:30–10:11).

2. Jehoshaphat's son and successor as king of Judah. He became king at the age of 32, perhaps initially as a co-regent with his father, and reigned from 849 to 842 (1 Kgs. 22:42, 50; cf. 2 Kgs. 8:16, 17; 3:1). His wife was Athaliah, the daughter (Syr. "sister") of Ahab (2 Kgs. 8:18, 26). This marriage was probably arranged as part of an alliance between Ahab and Jehoshaphat (1 Kgs. 22:2, 44). The Deuteronomistic editor of Kings considered Jehoram an apostate and attributed his apostasy to his marriage (2 Kgs. 8:18; cf. 2 Chr. 21:6). According to the Chronicler Jehoram killed his brothers and made "high places" (2 Chr. 21:11-13).

During Jehoram's reign, the Edomites revolted. Jehoram attempted to reestablish hegemony over Edom, but was unsuccessful; Libnah also revolted during his reign (2 Kgs. 8:20-22; 2 Chr. 21:8-10). The Chronicler also indicates that because of Jehoram's sins Judah suffered a plague and was attacked by the Philistines and the Arabs, the latter resulting in the loss of Jehoram's wives and sons, with the exception of Ahaziah (2 Chr. 21:16-17 LXX). The Chronicler adds that Yahweh punished Jehoram with a bowel disease causing his premature death (2 Chr. 21:15, 18-19). He was buried in Jerusalem and succeeded by his son Ahaziah, but according to the Chronicler he was not buried in a royal tomb (2 Chr. 21:20; cf. 2 Kgs. 8:24).

3. A priest of Judah during the 9th century during the time of Jehoshaphat, commissioned to teach the law (2 Chr. 17:8-9).

Bibliography. A. Biran and J. Naveh, "The Tel Dan Inscription: A New Fragment," *IEJ* 45 (1995): 1-18; K. G. Hoglund, "Edomites," in *Peoples of the Old Testament World,* ed. A. J. Hoerth, G. L. Mattingly, and E. M. Yamauchi (Grand Rapids, 1994), 335-47; G. L. Mattingly, "Moabites," in *Peoples of the Old Testament World,* 317-33; W. Pitard, *Ancient Damascus* (Winona Lake, 1987).

Chris A. Rollston

JEHOSHABEATH (Heb. *yĕhôšab̲ʿat̲*)
(also JEHOSHEBA)
The daughter of King Jehoram of Judah. She spared Ahaziah's son Jehoiada from the queen mother Athaliah (2 Chr. 22:11). At 2 Kgs. 11:2 she is called Jehosheba.

JEHOSHAPHAT (Heb. *yĕhôšāp̄āṭ*)

1. The son of Ahilud, who served as *mazkîr* under David (2 Sam. 8:16; 20:24; 1 Chr. 18:15) and Solomon (1 Kgs. 4:3). The function of the *mazkîr* remains unknown, with suggestions ranging from recorder or archivist (cf. LXX, esp. 2 Sam. 8:16) to herald and secretary of state. Comparisons with the office of the Egyptian "speaker" *(whmw)* have led some to understand Jehoshaphat's role to be that of reporting to the king and making the king's decrees known to others.

2. The son of Paruah, who served as one of the 12 officials over Israel to furnish provisions for Solomon's household, including feed for his horses (1 Kgs. 4:27-28[MT 5:7-8]). Each officer was responsible for one month of the year, and Jehoshaphat served in this capacity over the land of Issachar (1 Kgs. 4:17).

3. King of Judah, son of Asa and Azubah daughter of Shilhi. He came to the throne at age 35, reigned for 25 years (ca. 874-850 B.C.E.), and was succeeded by his son Jehoram. 1 Kgs. 22 indicates that (1) Jehoshaphat continued the religious policies of Asa and so was faithful to Yahweh, but he did not take the "high places" away; (2) he made peace with the rulers of Israel (v. 44[MT 45]); and (3) he had "ships of Tarshish" constructed for gold trade with Ophir, but the vessels were wrecked at Ezion-geber (vv. 48-49[49-50]). 2 Chr. 20:37 construes this last matter differently, condemning Jehoshaphat for collaborating with Ahaziah in the venture and noting that the ships were built in Ezion-geber and destroyed after the prophet Eliezer rebuked Jehoshaphat for entering into an agreement with the Israelite king.

The reports about Jehoshaphat's military alliances with Ahab against the Syrians (1 Kgs. 22:1-36) and with Jehoram against Moab (2 Kgs. 3:4-27) depict the king of Judah as a godly man, who insisted on hearing the word of Yahweh's prophet before going into battle. Both accounts are problematic, however, since in each instance it seems likely that another Judean king would have been involved. In the episode involving Moab, Jehoshaphat had died before Jehoram assumed the throne of Israel, and therefore the two could not have engaged in a joint military expedition. In the case of the battle against the Syrians at Ramoth-gilead, J. Maxwell Miller has made a convincing case for placing the event in the later part of Jehu's dynasty, suggesting that originally the report did not refer to Jehoshaphat and Ahab but more vaguely to the king of Judah and the king of Israel.

Chronicles enlarges the Kings account of Jehoshephat dramatically and depicts the king more favorably, reporting that he fortified, provisioned, and garrisoned his territories against Israel and other foreign powers and that God blessed him with peace (2 Chr. 17:2, 10-19). After reproducing with few changes the Kings report about battle with Syria at Ramoth-gilead (2 Chr. 18:1-34), Chronicles notes that the seer Jehu, son of Hanani, rebuked Jehoshaphat for his alliance with Israel (19:1-3). In addition, 2 Chr. 20:1-30 describes Jehoshaphat's successful defense of his territory against an alliance of Moabites, Ammonites, and Meunites (or "inhabitants of Mt. Seir"; compare vv. 1, 23), a story with superficial parallels to 2 Kgs. 3:4-27. Jehoshaphat proclaimed a fast, appealed to God for help, and under the guidance of the Levite Jahaziel led his people out for battle, where they found that their enemies had destroyed one another. Finally, Jehoshaphat is portrayed as a diligent ruler concerned with the religious observance of his people and the administration of justice in the land. He sent princes, Levites, and priests into the cities of Judah to teach the book of the law of God (2 Chr. 17:7-9) and appointed judges throughout his kingdom, establishing in Jerusalem Levites, priests, and heads of families to judge disputes brought to them (19:4-11). The extent to which Chronicles' picture of Jehoshaphat's reign is related to actual historical events is unclear.

4. The son of Nimshi and father of Jehu, king of Israel (2 Kgs. 9:2, 14).

Bibliography. W. F. Albright, "The Judicial Reform of Jehoshaphat," in *Alexander Marx Jubilee Volume,* ed. S. Lieberman (New York, 1950), 61-82; G. N. Knoppers, "Reform and Regression: The Chronicler's Presentation of Jehoshaphat," *Bibl* 72 (1991): 500-24; J. M. Miller, "The Elisha Cycle and the Accounts of the Omride Wars," *JBL* 85 (1966): 441-54; Miller and J. H. Hayes, *A History of Ancient Israel and Judah* (Philadelphia, 1986).

M. Patrick Graham

JEHOSHAPHAT (Heb. *yĕhôšāp̄āṭ*), **VALLEY OF**
Lit., "the valley (where) Yahweh judges" (Joel 3:2, 12[MT 4:2, 12]). Identified as the Hinnom Valley, the Kidron Valley, and the King's Valley (2 Sam. 18:18), it is popularly thought to be on the eastern side of Jerusalem, between the city and the Mount of Olives. The valley is associated with God's final judgment on evil nations and his restoration of Jerusalem in the messianic age (Joel 3:14[4:14] refers

to it as the "valley of decision"), and may be a figurative rather than a geographical term.

Richard A. Spencer

JEHOSHEBA (Heb. *yĕhôšeḇaʿ*)
(also JEHOSHABEATH)
The daughter of King Joram and half-sister of King Ahaziah of Judah (2 Kgs. 11:2-3); also called Jehoshabeath, wife of Jehoiada the priest (2 Chr. 22:11-12). The story of her saving the king's infant son Joash from Athaliah's massacre and then hiding him in the temple is one of the few places in Hebrew Scriptures where women alone carry the narrative action. Jehosheba's role also reflects the close association of, and political rivalries between, the palace and temple in ancient monarchies.

Bibliography. P. Dutcher-Walls, *Narrative Art, Political Rhetoric: The Case of Athaliah and Joash.* JSOTSup 209 (Sheffield, 1996); S. Japhet, *I and II Chronicles.* OTL (Louisville, 1993).

Patricia Dutcher-Walls

JEHOVAH (Heb. *yĕhōwāh*)
A name of God, devised ca. the 16th century C.E. by artificially combining the consonants of the name Yahweh (*YHWH;* held by the Jews to be unutterable) and the vowels of the substitute name Adonai ("the Lord").

See Yahweh.

JEHOVAH-JIREH (Heb. *YHWH yirʾeh*)
The name given by Abraham to the place where God provided him a ram to be offered in place of Isaac (Gen. 22:14; NRSV "the Lord will provide"). The location remains uncertain, although tradition favors the site of the Solomonic temple; an alternate suggestion is the sanctuary of the oak of Moreh at Shechem.

JEHOVAH-NISSI (Heb. *YHWH nissî*)
Moses' name for the altar commemorating the Israelite victory over the Amalekites at Rephidim (Exod. 17:15; NRSV "The Lord is my banner").

JEHOVAH-SHALOM (Heb. *YHWH šālôm*)
The name which Gideon gave to the altar he constructed at Ophrah (Judg. 6:23; NRSV "The Lord is peace").

JEHOZABAD (Heb. *yĕhôzāḇāḏ*)

1. A servant of Joash of Judah who participated in the king's assassination. According to 2 Kgs. 12:21(MT 22) he was the son of Shomer, but 2 Chr. 24:26 calls him the son of Shimrith (a variant of Shomer), a Moabite woman. He in turn was assassinated by Joash's son and successor, Amaziah (**4;** cf. 2 Kgs. 14:5).

2. The second son of Obed-edom; a Korahite Levite and gatekeeper for the temple (1 Chr. 26:4).

3. A Benjaminite commander of thousands during the reign of Jehoshaphat (2 Chr. 17:18).

Timothy P. Jenney

JEHOZADAK (Heb. *yĕhôṣāḏāq*)
(also JOZADAK)
The son of the chief priest Seraiah who was exiled to Babylon by Nebuchadnezzar (1 Chr. 6:14-15[MT 5:40-41]); father of the postexilic high priest Joshua, who helped to rebuild the temple (Hag. 1:1, 12, 14; 2:2, 4; Zech. 6:11). In Ezra and Nehemiah the name appears as Jozadak.

Timothy P. Jenney

JEHU (Heb. *yēhûʾ*)

1. A prophetic figure in the era of King Baasha of Israel, identified as the son of Hanani (1 Kgs. 16:1-4). He received a divine oracle to deliver a judgment pronouncing the death of Baasha and the demise of the royal house. Later he confronted King Jehoshaphat of Judah and reprimanded him for his alliance with King Ahab of Israel (2 Chr. 19:2-3).

2. King of Israel for 28 years (ca. 843-816 B.C.E.). Jehu usurped the throne from Joram/Jehoram and established a dynasty that lasted almost a century.

Jehu's patronymic information is given as both "son of Nimshi" (1 Kgs. 19:16; 2 Kgs. 9:20; 2 Chr. 22:7) and "son of Jehoshaphat, son of Nimshi" (2 Kgs. 9:2, 14). Most scholars regard Jehoshaphat as the name of his father and Nimshi that of his grandfather. The designation "son of Nimshi" is, therefore, better understood as descendant of Nimshi. It has also been suggested that Nimshi is the name of the clan to which Jehu belonged. Finally, the designation "son of Jehoshaphat" may be a later addition to the text, Jehu's father then being Nimshi.

In the Assyrian inscriptions of Shalmaneser III (*ANET,* 280-81) Jehu is identified as *iaúa mār humrî* (lit., "Jehu son of Omri"). Such a designation contradicts the information provided by the OT and has confounded scholars for almost a century. Several proposals have been offered: (1) Akk. *iaúa* may merely represent the divine name Yaw, and thus be taken as a hypocoristicon for Joram or Jehu; since Joram is a descendant of Omri, *iaúa* is more likely Joram. This proposal has not won much support. (2) Akk. *mār* ——— is used to denote a citizen or native of a city or a country, and thus is a synonym for a gentilic. The Assyrians continued to refer to Israel either as *māt humrî* ("the land of Omri") or *māt bīt-humrî* ("the land of Beth-omri") until the fall of the northern kingdom. Thus, *iaúa mār humrî* is to be understood as "Jehu the (Bīt)-Humrite." (3) Jehu was a descendant of a different branch of the Omri clan than Ahab. This is one reason why the biblical texts always refer to the event of Jehu's coup as the destruction of the house of Ahab (2 Kgs. 9:7-9; 10:10-11) and not the destruction of the house of Omri.

According to 2 Kgs. 9–10 Jehu was one of the commanders of the army (*śārê haḥayil*), perhaps even the chief commander (the messenger addresses him as *haśśār,* "the commander"; 9:5). The narrator set the ascendancy of Jehu to the Israelite throne in the context of a border conflict between Israel and Aram-Damascus (now ruled by Hazael) at Ramoth-gilead. This conflict arose following the

King Jehu of Israel bowing in submission before the Assyrian Shamaneser III; Black Obelisk, Nimrud (841 B.C.E.) (Copyright British Museum)

usurpation of the Damascene throne by Hazael, which led to the collapse of the alliance of Syro-Palestinian states led by Hadadezer of Damascus and Irḫuleni of Hamath. Israel under Ahab was a major participant (*ANET*, 278-79) in this coalition, which had been successful in checking the advance of Shalmaneser III into Syria-Palestine. King Joram was wounded by the Arameans in battle and had to return to Jezreel to recuperate (2 Kgs. 8:28-29). With the king gone from the battlefield, the stage was set for Jehu's coup. The narrator of 2 Kgs. 9–10 attributes the motivation for the coup to divine initiative (cf. 1 Kgs. 19:15-17, where Elijah was commanded by Yahweh to anoint Jehu as king). The prophet Elisha summons a disciple to go anoint Jehu as king over Israel. As the disciple anoints Jehu, he delivers to him also a divine oracle, that he will "strike down the house of your master, Ahab," as vengeance on Jezebel (2 Kgs. 9:6-8). When the other officers learn what has transpired, they quickly proclaim Jehu king. While the divine initiative is meant to give legitimation to the revolt, it is nonetheless more appropriately viewed as a military coup. Taking advantage of Joram's incapacitation, Jehu leads a conspiracy and goes after the incapacitated monarch. King Ahaziah of Judah has also gone to Jezreel to visit Joram. Unsuspecting, both Joram and Ahaziah go out to meet Jehu, and Joram is killed (2 Kgs. 9:14-26). With Joram dead, Jehu continues with the killing of Ahaziah of Judah (2 Kgs. 9:27-28) and Jezebel (vv. 30-37) and masterminds the massacre of the house of Ahab (10:1-17). The final act of Jehu, according to the narrator, is the destruction of the Baal cult — its worshippers, its pillar, and its temple (2 Kgs. 10:18-27). The theological reason for the positive assessment of the coup in the 2 Kings account is quite evident, namely, that Jehu is credited for the dismantling of Baal worship in Israel in the 9th century. While the prophetic participation in the coup may not be historically accurate, it serves as a divine sanction for the revolt.

The prophet Hosea offers an entirely different assessment of Jehu's coup. According to Hosea, because of the bloodbath that took place in Jezreel, Yahweh will punish the Jehu dynasty and put an end to the northern kingdom (Hos. 1:4-5).

Shalmaneser III (858-824) mentions in his annals that he mounted a campaign against Hazael of Aram-Damascus in his 18th year (841-840). Following a devastating defeat of Hazael, the Assyrian king claims that he received tribute from the Tyrians, Sidonians, and Jehu the (Bīt)-Humrite (or "son of Omri"). Also, in a panel of the Black Obelisk relief of Shalmaneser III Jehu is depicted as bowing before the Assyrian king and presenting tribute (*ANEP*, 351; *ANET*, 281). These Assyrian texts are perhaps suggestive of a political realignment of Israel's foreign policy. In earlier campaigns of Shalmaneser in Syria-Palestine (in 853 [the famous Battle of Qarqar], 849, 848, and 845), the Assyrian king confronted a strong coalition, led by

Hadadezer of Aram-Damascus and Irhuleni of Hamath, and was forced to turn back each time at the Orontes River. Israel, under Ahab, was a major participant in the coalition. The campaign in the 18th year is markedly different from the earlier campaigns. The usurpation of Hazael of the Damascene throne probably led to the disintegration of the anti-Assyrian coalition. Without a strong coalition to thwart the advance of the Assyrians, Jehu may have found it expedient to alter Israel's foreign policy and submit to Shalmaneser. Since the Israelites were already contending with an Aramean offensive (2 Kgs. 8:28-29), Jehu's submission to Assyria was a tactical move to avoid further assault.

Bibliography. M. Elat, "The Campaigns of Shalmaneser III against Aram and Israel," *IEJ* 25 (1975): 25-35; P. K. McCarter, "'Yaw, Son of 'Omri': A Philological Note on Israelite Chronology," *BASOR* 216 (1974): 5-7; T. J. Schneider, "Rethinking Jehu," *Bibl* 77 (1996): 100-7.

3. The son of Obed and father of Azariah in the Judahite genealogy (1 Chr. 2:38).

4. The son of Joshibiah, a Simeonite (1 Chr. 4:35).

5. A Benjamite from Anathoth who served David at Ziklag as a warrior (1 Chr. 12:3).

JEFFREY K. KUAN

JEHUBBAH (Heb. *yĕḥubbâ*)
An Asherite, son of Shemer and descendant of Beriah (**K** 1 Chr. 7:34; **Q** "and Hubbah").

JEHUCAL (Heb. *yĕhûḵal*) (also JUCAL)
The son of Shelemiah, sent by King Zedekiah to solicit the prayers of the prophet Jeremiah (Jer. 37:3). At Jer. 38:1 he is called Jucal.

JEHUD (Heb. *yĕhûḏ*)
A city in the tribal territory of Dan (Josh. 19:45), probably located at modern el-Yehūdîyeh/Yehud (139159), 13 km. (8 mi.) SE of Joppa.

JEHUDI (Heb. *yĕhûḏî*)
A court officer sent by the officials to summon Baruch to bring Jeremiah's prophecies before King Jehoiakim (Jer. 36:14). Later Jehudi himself brought the scroll and read it to the king, who cut off portions and burned them (Jer. 36:21, 23). The gentilic form of the name suggests that Jehudi ("Judahite") was of foreign origin.

JEHUEL (Heb. *yĕḥû'ēl*)
A Levite of the sons of Heman who assisted with Hezekiah's reforms (**K** 2 Chr. 29:14; so NRSV); probably the same as Jehiel **6** (**Q** *yĕḥî'ēl*).

DAVID PAUL LATOUNDJI

JEIEL (Heb. *yĕ'ê'ēl*) (also JEHIEL, JEUEL)
A common levitical name from the time of David to that of Ezra and Nehemiah. The variation in the spelling of this name (Jehiel, Jeuel) is simply due to Hebrew orthography.

1. A chief of a Reubenite clan (1 Chr. 5:7).

2. The father of Gibeon and a Levite in the genealogy of Saul (1 Chr. 9:35; cf. NRSV 8:29). The Hebrew text is written Jehuel, but is to be read Jeiel (cf. NIV).

3. One of the two sons of Hotham the Aroerite; one of David's warriors (1 Chr. 11:44; **K** Jeuel).

4. A Levite harpist appointed to the second rank of musicians who played while the ark was moved from the house of Obed-edom to Jerusalem (1 Chr. 15:18; 21). This appointment became permanent after the ark was placed in the tent David built for it (1 Chr. 16:5).

5. An Asaphite Levite, ancestor of the prophet Jahaziel (2 Chr. 20:14).

6. A secretary who helped prepare a military roster for King Uzziah (2 Chr. 26:11).

7. A chief of the Levites who contributed to the Passover offering for the Levites at the time of Josiah (2 Chr. 35:9).

8. A priest and a descendant of Nebo, listed among the priests guilty of intermarriage with foreign women (Ezra 10:43).

DAVID PAUL LATOUNDJI/TIMOTHY P. JENNEY

JEKABZEEL (Heb. *yĕqaḇṣĕ'ēl*)
A city of Judah near the Edomite border (Neh. 11:25). Prior to the Exile it was called Kabzeel.

JEKAMEAM (Heb. *yĕqam'ām*)
The fourth son of Hebron (1 Chr. 23:19); head of a levitical father's house (24:23).

JEKAMIAH (Heb. *yĕqamyâ*)

1. A Judahite, son of Shallum and descendant of Jerahmeel (1 Chr. 2:41).

2. A son or descendant of King Jeconiah (Jehoiachin) of Judah (1 Chr. 3:18).

JEKUTHIEL (Heb. *yĕqûṯî'ēl*)
A Judahite, descendant of Mered and father of Zanoah (1 Chr. 4:18).

JEMIMAH (Heb. *yĕmîmâ*)
The first of Job's three daughters, born to him after his fortunes were restored (Job 42:14).

JEMUEL (Heb. *yĕmû'ēl*) (also NEMUEL)
A son of Simeon (Gen. 46:10; Exod. 6:15). At Num. 26:12; 1 Chr. 4:24 he is called Nemuel.

JEPHTHAH (Heb. *yiptaḥ*)
A military leader who successfully directed Gilead's resistance of Ammonite occupation and subsequently served as judge (Judg. 10:6–12:7). Jephthah's victory is tempered by its tragic and morally ambiguous consequences: his vow, resulting in his daughter's death, and his battle against Ephraimite kinsmen.

The main body of the Jephthah cycle, a collection of older traditions and later interpolations, begins inauspiciously with Jephthah, son of a harlot and "Gilead" (probably the personification of the territory) expelled from his home by his half-brothers. Like Abimelech (Judg. 9:4) and David (1 Sam. 22:1-2), Jephthah becomes a brigand chief.

Later, the Gileadite elders appeal to Jephthah to use his fighting skills against their Ammonite oppressors. After negotiating to become not only Gilead's temporary military commander but also permanent chief, Jephthah consents.

Jephthah attempts to press Israel's claims to the disputed Transjordanian territory diplomatically. Jephthah's diplomacy (Judg. 11:12-28) presents historical-critical problems, in that he addresses an Ammonite king with arguments pertaining to Moab. The passage may have been conflated with an account of conflict with Moab. Alternatively, by the time the passage was written Ammon, having taken over Moabite territory, may have assumed Moabite claims to the land. In any case, the attempted diplomacy fails; battle is joined.

The report of Jephthah's victory (Judg. 11:32-33) is subordinated to the story of his vow and its execution. Whether propelled by Yahweh's Spirit or despite it (Judg. 11:29), Jephthah vows that if God gives him victory, he will offer as a burnt offering whoever (or whatever) first comes to greet him when he returns home. Jephthah does triumph; the first to greet him is his daughter, an only child. Jephthah mourns but persists. The daughter submits and, after a two month delay in which to lament her maidenhood, is sacrificed. The story is editorially connected to an annual ritual of lament, possibly a rite of passage.

The final story of the cycle is also ambiguous. In a scene reminiscent of their conflict with Gideon (Judg. 8:1-3), the Ephraimites confront Jephthah over his failure to enlist their aid. While Gideon diplomatically averts intertribal warfare, here conflict leads to battle. Jephthah routs the Ephraimites. The ethnicity of Ephraimite survivors is disclosed by their inability to pronounce the "sh" sound in "Shibboleth" ("stream") and they are slaughtered. The cycle ends with the notice that Jephthah judged Israel six years, died, and was buried in Gilead.

The tradition's evaluation of Jephthah is mixed. Both OT and NT acclaim Jephthah's faithfulness (1 Sam. 12:11; Heb. 11:32). Such positive assessment is reflected in modern scholars who deem Jephthah an "exemplary judge." Other traditions condemn Jephthah's cruelty; the Haggadah recounts that Jephthah's prideful, ignorant immolation of his daughter was punished by dismemberment (*Gen. Rab.* 60:3). Modern scholars have criticized the patriarchal values of unquestioning submission and female self-sacrifice encoded in the text. Others interpret the stories of Jephthah and Samson as a portrayal of social disintegration in premonarchical Israel.

Bibliography. R. C. Boling, *Judges.* AB 6A (Garden City, 1975); P. L. Day, "From the Child Is Born the Woman: The Story of Jephthah's Daughter," in *Gender and Difference in Ancient Israel* (Minneapolis, 1989), 58-74; J. C. Exum, *Fragmented Women: Feminist (Sub)Versions of Biblical Narratives* (Valley Forge, 1993); D. Marcus, "The Bargaining between Jephthah and the Elders (Judg. 11:4-11)," *JANES* 19 (1989): 95-100; A. D. H. Mayes, *Judges.* OTG 8 (Sheffield, 1985).

Carolyn Pressler

JEPHTHAH'S DAUGHTER

A young girl sacrificed as a burnt offering in fulfillment of her father's vow (Judg. 11:34-40). While leading Gileadite resistance against Ammonite oppression, Jephthah sought to secure victory by vowing to offer up to Yahweh whatever was the first to come out of his house upon his return. (Whether Jephthah intended human sacrifice is unclear.) Jephthah does defeat the Ammonites, but his triumph turns to tragedy when he is greeted by his daughter, an only child. Jephthah mourns but persists. The daughter accepts her fate without protest, asking only for two months in which to "lament her maidenhood" with her female companions. At the end of that time, she is slaughtered.

Judg. 11:39-40 links the story to an annual ritual in which young women go into the hills for four days of lamentation. The lack of correspondence between *two* months and *four* days of the ritual suggests that the link is secondary. The ritual may have been a rite of passage in which adolescent girls mourn the passing of a life stage.

The story of Jephthah's daughter is one of several biblical passages having to do with human sacrifice. Prophetic and legal texts refer to the practice of immolating children in a desperate attempt to obtain Yahweh's favor (2 Kgs. 16:3; 17:17; Ezek. 20:25-26; Ps. 106:37-38). Gen. 22 recounts Abraham's near-sacrifice of Isaac at God's command. 1 Sam. 14:24-45 narrates Saul's vow that whoever had broken his command to fast should be put to death and his discovery that the culprit was his heir, Jonathan. But the prophetic and legal texts consistently condemn human sacrifice; God prevents Abraham from killing Isaac, and the people intervene to rescue Jonathan. Only Jephthah's daughter is sacrificed without intervention or condemnation.

Traditional appraisal of Jephthah's deed has been ambivalent. The OT and NT praise Jephthah's faithfulness (1 Sam. 12:11; Heb. 11:32). The Haggadah condemns his immolation of his daughter as ignorant and sinful. Some modern interpreters describe Jephthah as "exemplary"; others condemn the sacrifice of the girl as inhuman. Others critically assess the patriarchal values of blind obedience and female sacrifice encoded in the story, or wrest its focus away from Jephthah to mourn his daughter's fate.

Bibliography. P. L. Day, "From the Child Is Born the Woman: The Story of Jephthah's Daughter," in *Gender and Difference in Ancient Israel* (Minneapolis, 1989), 58-74; D. N. Feweli, "Judges," in *The Women's Bible Commentary,* ed. C. A. Newsom and S. H. Ringe (Louisville, 1992), 67-77; E. Fuchs, "Marginalization, Ambiguity, Silencing: The Story of Jephthah's Daughter," *JFSR* 5 (1989): 35-45; P. Trible, *Texts of Terror.* OBT 13 (Philadelphia, 1984).

Carolyn Pressler

JEPHUNNEH (Heb. *yəp̄unneh*)

1. A Judahite, the father of the spy Caleb (e.g., Num. 13:6; Josh. 14:13). He is called a Kenizzite at Num. 32:12; Josh. 14:6, 14; cf. 1 Chr. 4:15).

2. A son of Jether, from the tribe of Asher (1 Chr. 7:38).

JERAH (Heb. *yeraḥ*)
A son of Joktan and descendant of Shem (Gen. 10:26 = 1 Chr. 1:20); eponymous ancestor of a place or social unit in South Arabia.

JERAHMEEL (Heb. *yĕraḥmĕʾēl*)
1. The brother of Ram and Caleb; son of Hezron and descendant of Judah through Tamar (1 Chr. 2:4, 9). He was the eponymous ancestor of the Jerahmeelites) (1 Chr. 25-27, 33, 42), a Judahite clan living on the southern frontier of Judah ("the Negeb of the Jerahmeelites," 1 Sam. 27:10), probably in an area S of Beersheba, in the days before David became king of Israel. David first came in contact with them when he fled from Saul and established residence at Ziklag (1 Sam. 27:10; 30:29). It is possible that the Jerahmeelites were assimilated into the tribe of Judah after David became king.

2. A Levite, a son of Kish, from the clan of Merari (1 Chr. 24:29).

3. A Judean officer who served under Jehoiakim, king of Judah. He is called "son of the king" (Jer. 36:26), either an honorary title of an officer or designation of someone related to the royal family — not a son of the 30-year-old Jehoiakim. Jerahmeel was sent by Jehoiakim to seize Jeremiah and Baruch after the scroll containing Jeremiah's prophecies was burned.

Bibliography. N. Avigad, "Baruch the Scribe and Jerahmeel the King's Son," *IEJ* 28 (1978): 52-56; repr. *BA* 42 (1979): 114-18.

Claude F. Mariottini

JERED (Heb. *yereḏ*)
A son of Mered by his Jewish wife; the father of Gedor (1 Chr. 4:18).

JEREMAI (Heb. *yĕrēmay*)
A son of Hashum; an Israelite who had to divorce his foreign wife (Ezra 10:33).

JEREMIAH (Heb. *yirmĕyâ, yirmĕyāhû*)
1. A man from Libnah, the grandfather of Jehoahaz and Zedekiah, kings of Judah (2 Kgs. 23:31; 24:18). Jeremiah's daughter Hamutal was the wife of King Josiah.

2. The head of a clan of the half-tribe of Manasseh (1 Chr. 5:24). He is described as a warrior and a famous man.

3. One of the mighty Benjaminite warriors who joined David at Ziklag (1 Chr. 12:4[MT 5]). He could shoot arrows and sling stones with either hand.

4-5. Two mighty, experienced Gadite warriors who joined David at Ziklag (1 Chr. 12:10, 13[11, 14]). Both were experts with shield and sword and are described in language stereotypical of military heroes.

6. A priest who signed the covenant along with Nehemiah the governor (Neh. 10:2[3]).

7. A priest who returned from Babylon with Zerubbabel (Neh. 12:1), evidently identified with the priestly house named in v. 12.

8. One of the administrative officials of Judah who comprised the two great choirs at the dedication of the Jerusalem wall under Nehemiah (Neh. 12:34).

9. A prophet from Anathoth, whose ministry is recorded in the book of Jeremiah; son of Hilkiah (Jer. 1:1).

10. The father of Jaazaniah, a Rechabite living in Jerusalem at the time of the prophet Jeremiah (Jer. 35:3).

Gary W. Light

JEREMIAH, BOOK OF
The second book of the Latter Prophets following Isaiah and preceding Ezekiel in the Jewish canon of the Hebrew Bible, although some authorities place it as the first book (*b. B. Bat.* 14b). In the Christian OT it appears after Isaiah as the second book of the Prophets together with Lamentations. In some manuscripts the apocryphal book of Baruch and the Epistle of Jeremiah follow. The book presents the career and sayings of the prophet Jeremiah ben Hilkiah. According to the superscription in 1:1-3, Jeremiah was a priest from the village of Anathoth, who was active from the 13th year of the reign of King Josiah of Judah (ca. 626 B.C.E.) until the captivity of Jerusalem in 587. The book focuses especially on the reigns of Jehoiakim (609-598), Zedekiah (597-587), and the early years of the Babylonian Exile until the aftermath of the assassination in 582 of Gedaliah, the Babylonian-appointed governor of Judah. According to rabbinic tradition, Jeremiah was the author of his own book as well as 1-2 Kings and Lamentations (*b. B. Bat.* 15a).

The book of Jeremiah appears in two distinct but related forms: the Greek version of the LXX and the Hebrew version that is extant in the MT. The Greek version is approximately one eighth shorter than the Hebrew, and after 25:13a the two versions differ substantially in their order. The placement of the oracles against the nations constitutes a key difference between the two versions: in the MT they appear as chs. 46-51 whereas the LXX places them roughly in the center of the book where they appear as 25:14–31:44. The remaining material in MT chs. 25-45 appears for the most part as LXX chs. 32-51. Both versions conclude with the historical narrative concerning the Babylonian Exile in ch. 52. Most scholars maintain that the LXX version is a translation completed at some time between 250 and 150 of an earlier Hebrew version that was originally composed in Egypt. The Hebrew version on which the MT is based is generally believed to have originated in Babylonia. In general, the MT appears to be an expanded and rearranged version of the Hebrew underlying the LXX, but there are sufficient exceptions that point to independent transmission histories for both versions.

A particularly noteworthy aspect of the textual history of the book is the discovery of at least four Jeremiah manuscripts among the scrolls from Qumran Caves 2 and 4. The manuscript from Cave

2 (2QJer) contains fragments from Jer. 42-44 and 46-49 that date to ca. the 1st century C.E. Overall, these fragments correspond closely, although not entirely, to the MT and place the oracles against the nations at the end of the book. Among the three Cave 4 manuscripts, 4QJer[a] is the oldest, dating to ca. 200 B.C.E. The scroll contains fragments of Jer. 7-15; 17-20; 22; 26, with many corrections that apparently correspond to the MT. 4QJer[b] dates to the mid-2nd century B.C.E. and contains fragments of Jer. 9-10; 43; 50. Some see these fragments as three separate manuscripts. They are especially important in that the first two reflect the LXX text and verse order, and therefore testify to the Hebrew text underlying the LXX. 4QJer[c] dates to the Herodian period, ca. 30-1 B.C.E., and contains fragments from a proto-Masoretic version of Jer. 4; 8-10; 19-22; 25-27; 30-31; 33.

The structure of the two forms of Jeremiah is not well understood. Many maintain that the arrangement of the LXX version follows a tripartite pattern that was employed generally in the arrangement of prophetic books (e.g., Isaiah, Ezekiel, Zephaniah): oracles of judgment against Israel (chs. 1–25); oracles of judgment against the nations (LXX 26–31; cf. MT 46–51); and oracles of restoration (LXX 32–52; cf. MT 25–52). Unfortunately, this does not account for the portrayal of judgment against Jerusalem and Judah evident in the third major section of LXX Jeremiah, nor is the pattern so unambiguously apparent throughout the other prophetic books. Instead, it may point to a principle of arrangement in which the oracles of the prophet concerning Jerusalem/Judah and the nations are first presented and then followed by an account of the prophet's activities through the Babylonian Exile that relates the process by which the oracles are to be realized. The order of MT Jeremiah includes a presentation of various visions, oracles, and laments of Jeremiah concerning Jerusalem and Judah in chs. 1–24; a narrative account of various speeches and events in the life of Jeremiah from the reign of Jehoiakim through the aftermath of the Babylonian destruction of Jerusalem in chs. 25–45; the oracles against the nations in chs. 46–51; and the narrative account of the Babylonian destruction of Jerusalem and deportation of captives in ch. 52, drawn from 2 Kgs. 24:18–25:30. The identification of this arrangement is based largely on thematic and generic grounds that may well reflect the literary history of the book. A chronological principle appears to stand behind this arrangement, although repetitions, such as the dual accounts pertaining to Jeremiah's temple sermon in chs. 7 and 26, and other chronological inconsistencies disrupt the pattern. Overall, the book begins with the prophet's call or vocation account in ch. 1, which identifies him as a prophet to the nations, and continues through ch. 45 with a presentation of his life that concludes with Jeremiah's last years in Egypt. The following oracles against the nations in chs. 46-51 are to be realized at some point in the future, and the concluding historical narrative in ch. 52 summarizes the situation of Judah and Jerusalem at the conclusion of Jeremiah's life.

It is clear that the present forms of the book, both LXX and MT, are heavily edited compositions that reflect the viewpoints and concerns of the writers and editors who produced them. There is a concerted effort, e.g., to present Jeremiah as a prophet like Moses, in that he was active for a period of 40 years (1:1-3), called for adherence to the instructions or Torah of Yahweh as the basis for the relationship between the people and Yahweh, suffered abuse and rejection from both Yahweh and the people in a manner analogous to Moses' experience in the wilderness, and died outside the land of Israel. Overall, the presentation of Jeremiah in the book emerges as a sort of a theodicy, attempting to justify Yahweh's decision to destroy Jerusalem as the result of wrongdoing by the people of Israel and Judah. Scholars have long pointed to various features of the book that suggest a complex editorial history: the narrative in ch. 36 that identifies Baruch ben Neriah as the scribe responsible for writing down Jeremiah's oracles; the presence of both poetic oracular compositions, which may well constitute the words of the prophet, and prose accounts of the prophet's words and activities that clearly must stem from a writer or writers other than the prophet; and the narrative prose style that corresponds closely to that of the Deuteronomistic history, especially the books of 1-2 Kings.

An extensive debate on this question has taken place throughout much of the 20th century that highlights the difficulties in reconstructing a picture of the historical prophet from the literary presentation in the book of Jeremiah. An early influential study in German by Sigmund Mowinckel identifies four major sources within the book. Source A is the poetic material in chs. 1–25 that represents the words of the prophet. Source B is the biographical prose material in 19:1–20:6; 26; 28–29; 36–44, written by an admirer of the prophet. Mowinckel and others later identify this writer as Baruch ben Neriah. Source C is the sermonic prose material in 7:1–8:3; 11:1-17; 18:1-12; 21:1-10; 25:1-11a; 32:1-2, 6-16, 24-44; 34:1–35:19; 44:1-14, analogous to sermonic material in Deuteronomy and the Deuteronomistic history. Also included are superscriptions throughout the book and material from 3:6-13; 29:1a, 3-9, 21-23; 45. Source D constitutes postexilic oracles of consolation in chs. 30–31. Together with chs. 46–51 and 52, the whole was edited and combined together in the postexilic period.

Subsequent discussion has tended to blur these distinctions, however, as scholars have noted a great deal of affinity between Mowinckel's first three sources. John Bright maintains that there is no distinction between the B and C sources, and argues that they represent a single stream by which the words of Jeremiah are handed down. E. W. Nicholson argues that the B and C sources are both Deuteronomic, produced by Babylonian circles who employed the figure of Jeremiah in sermonic discourse as a means to convey Deuteronomic teachings in the postexilic Jewish community. A German study by Manfred Weippert argues that the Deuteronomic prose material is rooted in the poetic oracles of Mowinckel's Source A, and therefore stems from Jeremiah and his disciples. William L. Holladay likewise notes affinities between the poetic oracles and prose materials, and argues that the prose sermons constitute Jeremiah's counter-proclamations to the public readings of the book of Deuteronomy. Robert P. Carroll maintains that Deuteronomic influence is so pervasive throughout the book that it is impossible to reconstruct an accurate picture of the prophet, his words, or his ideas. According to Carroll, Baruch is the literary creation of the Deuteronomistic writers of Jeremiah, and the figure of Jeremiah as presented in the book should therefore be treated as a work of fiction. William McKane argues that chs. 1-20 contain oracles from Jeremiah, but that the book must be identified as a "rolling corpus," the product of sustained, piecemeal accretion as later writers added their exegetical and editorial comments to the original Jeremianic "kernels."

Clearly, scholarly discussion of Jeremiah points to a great deal of difficulty in reconstructing the historical figure and message of the prophet from the present literary forms of the book. Nevertheless, certain features of the prophet and his thinking, such as his priestly identity and his pro-Babylonian political stance, do emerge. Jeremiah is a priest of the Elide line that once served in the sanctuary at Shiloh during the premonarchic period (1 Sam. 1–3), but was later banished to Anathoth when Solomon replaced Abiathar with Zadok as high priest in Jerusalem (1 Kgs. 2:26-27). Jeremiah's references in the temple sermon (7:1–8:3) to the destruction of Shiloh testifies to this background as do his references to Samuel and Moses as intercessory figures (15:1). Likewise, his visions of an almond rod (1:11-12), a boiling pot (1:13), and the baskets of good and bad figs (24:1-10) all indicate his priestly role; the blossoming almond rod is the symbol of the priesthood (Num. 17:1-11), priestly duties included boiling sacrificial meat in pots (cf. 1 Sam. 2:11-17; Ezek. 24:1-14), and the reception of fruit offerings was part of the tithe due to the Levites (Num. 18:1-32; Deut. 14:22-29; 18:1-5). Although some have argued that the "laments" or "confessions" of Jeremiah (11:18–12:6; 15:10-21; 17:14-18; 18:18-23; 20:7-18) cannot be authentic to the prophet because they employ the stereotypical language of the liturgical laments of the temple, the use of such language by a priest to address his own problems can be expected. Overall, Jeremiah expresses his frustration at both Yahweh and his enemies, including men from Anathoth, for the difficulties he faced in carrying out his prophetic calling and articulating a message that was not likely to win popular support. Jeremiah's appearance in Jerusalem certainly would not win him allies among his brethren who did not come to Jerusalem after Josiah destroyed outlying sanctuaries (cf. 2 Kgs. 23:8-9). His continued call for submission to Babylon (chs. 27–28), even after the Babylonians had deported Jehoiachin in 597 (ch. 29), reflects the political stance of Josiah, who died at Megiddo in 609 in an attempt to stop the Egyptians from supporting Assyria against Babylon (2 Kgs. 23:28-30; 2 Chr. 35:20-27). Such a call would make him a natural enemy of Jehoiakim, who was placed on the throne by Pharaoh Neco as an Egyptian vassal, and Zedekiah whose revolt against Babylon led to the destruction of Jerusalem. Jeremiah's close association with the family of Ahikam ben Shaphan (cf. 26:14; 29:3; 36:10-12; 39:14; 40:5), an official in Josiah's court and the son of Josiah's secretary who reported the discovery of the book of Torah that served as the basis for Josiah's reforms, testifies to his association with the Josianic "pro-Babylonian" party in Judah. Finally, his call for observance of Yahweh's Torah as the basis for the covenant relationship between Yahweh and the people, expressed in the temple sermon as a condensed version of the Ten Commandments (7:9; cf. 11:1-17), indicates his adherence to the religious norms of Deuteronomy.

Jeremiah clearly sees the human world of social and political events as the realm of Yahweh's activity. Although Jeremiah takes a partisan stance in the Judean political world of his day, he does so out of sense of obligation, both to Yahweh and his people, to see that justice and righteousness prevail. Chs. 2–6 and 30–31 indicate that Jeremiah initially supported Josiah's bid to return the people of northern Israel to Davidic rule, but he concluded that Josiah's untimely death signaled Yahweh's intention to punish Judah for abandoning Yahweh in a manner analogous to that of northern Israel. He calls for just treatment of the underprivileged in Judean society, and severely criticizes Jehoiakim for neglecting the welfare of his people while building a sumptuous palace for himself (ch. 22). He is equally capable of chastising Yahweh for abandoning him to enemies after proclaiming Yahweh's word, and curses the day of his birth for his inability to resist his prophetic calling (20:7-18). He condemns Hananiah as a false prophet, even when Hananiah's message of salvation for Jerusalem corresponds to that of Isaiah a century before (ch. 28). He condemns Zedekiah for reneging on the release of slaves when the Babylonians temporarily lifted their siege of Jerusalem (ch. 34). When the Babylonians offered to take Jeremiah back to Babylon for his own protection in the aftermath of Jerusalem's fall in 587, Jeremiah chose to remain among his people. His redemption of family property in Anathoth during a lull in the Babylonian siege indicates his identification with his people and his confidence in the restoration of the nation following the punishment. The present form of the oracles of restoration in chs. 30-31 looks forward to the restoration and a new covenant between Yahweh and the people.

In sum, the book of Jeremiah presents Jeremiah as a priest and prophet who was heavily involved in the public affairs of his own society at a time of deep national crisis. As such, he represents a model of unswerving commitment to Yahweh, to his own people, and to the principles of righteousness and justice that stood at the foundation of Yahweh's relationship with the people of Israel and Judah.

Bibliography. J. Bright, *Jeremiah.* AB 21 (Garden City, 1965); R. P. Carroll, *Jeremiah.* OTL (Philadelphia, 1986); *Jeremiah.* Old Testament Guides (Sheffield, 1989); W. L. Holladay, Jr., *Jeremiah.* 2 vols. Herm (Philadelphia and Minneapolis, 1986-1989); W. McKane, *Jeremiah* 1. ICC (Edinburgh, 1986); E. W. Nicholson, *Preaching to the Exiles* (New York, 1971). MARVIN A. SWEENEY

JEREMIAH, LAMENTATIONS OF
Title ascribed to the book of Lamentations in several early versions. Although some ancient traditions associated the prophet Jeremiah with the book and some canonical lists reckon Jeremiah and Lamentations together (cf. LXX Prologue; Josephus *Ag. Ap.* 1.8 [38]), Jeremianic authorship is now discounted.

See LAMENTATIONS, BOOK OF.

JEREMIAH, LETTER OF
According to its superscription, a copy of a letter sent by the prophet Jeremiah to Judean prisoners who were about to be shipped to Babylon. The Letter survives in Greek and other ancient versions such as Syriac and Latin. Translation errors and linguistic usages indicate that it was translated into Greek from a lost Hebrew original. In some Greek manuscripts the Letter is separated from Baruch by Lamentations, but in others it follows Baruch. In the Vulgate, KJV, and Catholic Bibles it is included as ch. 6 of Baruch. The Letter of Jeremiah is recognized as canonical by Roman Catholics and the Orthodox communities, but classified among the Apocrypha by the Jewish and Protestant communities because it is not part of the Hebrew Bible.

The book's introduction is similar in content and purpose to the letter to the exiles already in Babylon found in Jer. 29. The contents consist of satirical parodies and polemics against idols and prophetic admonitions and warnings, all of which have literary links with the Hebrew Bible, especially Jeremiah. Whether this work is regarded as an ancient letter or a tract against idolatry depends on how flexibly the letter genre is understood.

After the introduction (vv. 1-7, following NRSV) the polemics, instructions, and exhortations may be divided into 10 sections (vv. 8-16; 17-23; 24-29; 30-40a; 40b-44; 45-52; 53-56; 57-65; 66-69; 70-73), each of which is concluded by a refrain which argues that the statues of the gods are not really gods and/or should not be feared (vv. 16, 23, 29, 65, 69; cf. vv. 40, 44, 51, 56, 72). These refrains keep before the reader the main themes of the Letter: admonitions to eschew foreign religious practices and to worship only the Lord. The Letter addresses the danger of idolatry in exile (Deut. 4:27-28) by drawing upon the prophetic and cultic polemics against idols found in Jer. 10:1-16 and elsewhere (e.g., Isa. 44:9-20; Hab. 2:18-19; Ps. 115:3-8). The extensive attacks on the foreign gods are long, detailed, and repetitious, and the virulence of the author's attack testifies to the attraction of the dominant polytheistic culture of the ancient Near East.

The Letter has been most frequently placed in the Hellenistic period (332-63 B.C.E.), a date supported by a Qumran Greek manuscript fragment of vv. 43-44 dating to ca. 100 B.C.E. A possible reference to the Letter in 2 Macc. 2:2 comes from the 2nd century. Although the polemics suggest the types of statues, processions, dressing, feeding, and care of the gods characteristic of Babylonian religion, the locus of these activities might also be the Babylonian or Judean Jewish community, and the content and purpose of the Letter are so general that they may pertain to any time in the Persian and Greek periods. ANTHONY J. SALDARINI

JEREMIEL (Lat. *Hieremihel*)
The archangel who responded to the questions of the righteous dead concerning resurrection (2 Esdr. 4:36). He is presumed to be the same as Ramiel or Ramael (so Syr; cf. 2 Bar. 55:3) or Remiel (1 En. 20:8 mg).

JEREMOTH (Heb. *yĕrēmôṯ*) (also JERIMOTH)
The slight variation in the spelling of this name (also Jerimoth) originally developed for euphonic reasons which facilitated pronunciation in Hebrew.

1. A Benjamite, one of the nine sons of Becher who served as a family head during the reign of David (1 Chr. 7:8).

2. A son of Beriah, head of a Benjamite family who lived in Jerusalem (1 Chr. 8:14, 28).

3. A Merarite Levite, one of the three sons of Mushi, who was appointed to temple service by David (1 Chr. 23:23; called Jerimoth at 24:30).

4. The son of Heman whom David and the commanders of the army appointed for the ministry of prophesying in the temple with instrumental accompaniment (1 Chr. 25:22; Jerimoth at v. 4).

5. A descendant of Elam among those who had returned from the Exile with Zerubbabel and were guilty of intermarriage with foreign women (Ezra 10:26).

6. A descendant of Zattu who divorced his foreign wife (Ezra 10:27).

7. A descendant of Bani who sent away his foreign wife and children (Ezra 10:29)

DAVID PAUL LATOUNDJI

JERIAH (Heb. *yĕrîyāhû*), **JERIJAH** *(yĕrîyâ)*
A Kohathite Levite; head of the Hebronite house at the time of King David (1 Chr. 23:19; 24:23). At 1 Chr. 26:31 he is called Jerijah.

JERIBAI (Heb. *yĕrîḇay*)
A son of Elnaam; one of David's Mighty Men (1 Chr. 11:46).

JERICHO (Heb. *yĕrîḥô*)
A town ca. 16 km. (10 mi.) N of the Dead Sea near a crossing of the Jordan River. Israelite Jericho has been associated with Tell es-Sulṭân (192142) and

Pre-pottery Neolithic fortifications at Jericho (Tell es-Sulṭân) (Jericho Excavation Fund, photo Kathleen M. Kenyon)

Roman Jericho with Tulûl Abū el-ʿAlayiq (191139). Archaeological evidence has recorded occupation near the spring (ʿAin es-Sulṭân) and at Tell es-Sulṭân and Abū el-ʿAlayiq from as early as the Mesolithic period (ca. 9000 B.C.E.), with occasional gaps, through the modern era.

Old Testament and Apocrypha

The name Jericho appears in Hebrew Scripture frequently in geographical references (e.g., Num. 22:1; 26:3, 63; Deut. 34:1, 3; also 1 Chr. 6:78[MT 63]) from beyond the Jordan. Jericho figures prominently only in the book of Joshua, which reports its miraculous conquest (Josh. 5:13–6:23); in Judges it appears as an outpost of Eglon of Moab (Judg. 3:13). David's abused emissaries recuperated at Jericho (2 Sam. 10:51 = 1 Chr. 19:5). According to 1 Kgs. 16:34 Hiel of Bethel "built Jericho," at the cost of two sons in correspondence to the curse in Josh. 6. In 2 Kgs. 2:4-18 Jericho is noted as seat of a school of prophets. Judahite captives of war were repatriated there (2 Chr. 28:15). 2 Kgs. 25:5 = Jer. 39:5 = 52:8 records the capture of the fleeing king Zedekiah near Jericho. Ezra 2:34 = Neh. 7:36 refers to a postexilic settlement (population 345) at Jericho.

Jericho regained importance in Hellenistic times. The town was fortified by Bacchides (1 Macc. 9:50) and was later the scene of the death of Simon (16:14-16). Sir. 24:14 mentions Jericho in a metaphor for wisdom.

New Testament

Jericho appears in the account of Jesus' ministry only in the Synoptic Gospels. It is the setting for the story of Zacchaeus, apparently chief tax collector for the town (Luke 19:1-10), and figures in the parable of the Good Samaritan (10:30). In Matt. 20:29; Mark 10:46; Luke 18:35 Jericho is the setting for the healing of a blind beggar(s).

Tell es-Sulṭân

Tell es-Sulṭân, first excavated by Ernst Sellin and Carl Watzinger (1907-09), later by John Garstang (1930-36) and by Kathleen M. Kenyon (1952-58), has yielded some of the most important information concerning the beginnings of urbanization. Mesolithic remains (ca. 9000), similar to Natufian artifacts, were found in a deep sounding. This narrow exposure detected a rectangular "platform" of clay purposely preserved on bedrock, interpreted by Kenyon as a shrine; however, objects tentatively understood as sockets for totems have since been identified as stone mortars.

In the succeeding four Neolithic levels (ca. 8500-4000) Tell es-Sulṭân became a large (4 ha. [10 a.]) town. The Pre-pottery Neolithic A settlement, successor to "Proto-Neolithic" villages, expanded and organized to the point that occupants constructed a large stone wall around the town. The perimeter/defense wall included in all three phases at least one tower, round in plan (8.5 m. [28 ft.] wide, surviving 7.7 m. [25 ft.] high) with an interior staircase. In the perimeter wall's second phase a ditch 9.5 m. (31 ft.) wide × 2.25 m. (7.4 ft.) deep was cut into bedrock along the outer face, a feature which provided deeper protection. Pre-pottery Neolithic B Tell es-Sulṭân, also a walled town, is most notably represented by the discovery of human skulls which had been retrieved from primary burial and onto which facial features had been molded. The skulls, examples of which have been discovered at other Neolithic sites, were kept within houses; a group of nine were found in collapsed debris of one house. Kenyon suggested that these skulls point to an ancestor cult. In the uppermost PPN B levels humanlike clay figurines, similar to those found at ʿAin Ghazal, were discovered; these Kenyon characterized as a continuation of the ancestor cult, an imitation of the decorated human skulls. Others, however, understand the figurines to represent deities.

The destruction of PPN B Tell es-Sulṭân was followed by a gap in occupation and eventually by another Neolithic settlement of the Pottery Neolithic culture. PN A consisted largely of pit-dwellings. PN B dwellings were initially built in the ruins of the PN A pits, but later tended to be constructed above ground and freestanding. PN B Tell es-Sulṭân was apparently also surrounded by a town wall. Material remains support the view that occupants were herders and hunters.

After another gap of several centuries, in the Chalcolithic/Early Bronze I era (Kenyon's "Proto-Urban"), humans again centered activities on Tell es-Sulṭân, a conclusion based on the discovery of a group of shaft tombs, all containing multiple burials. Architecture reappeared on the mound in EB IA and IB in the form of apsidal-ended houses, along with suggestions of a fortification wall and a semi-circular tower. A broad-room building, named a sanctuary by Garstang and to which he attributed several stone cultic artifacts, is included in EB I. Kenyon attributed both tombs and settlement to nomadic or semi-nomadic groups newly arrived at the site.

In Early Bronze II-III, the age of major urbanization of Palestine, Tell es-Sulṭân was again fortified, in this instance with the large brick Walls B (EB II) and C (EB III) that underwent as many as 17 phases of construction. Several hundred EB II-III tombs and houses were excavated by Garstang and Kenyon; artifact evidence depicts prosperity and trade contacts with Egypt, Anatolia, and Syria. The destruction by fire of the final EB III town, preceded by a gradual decline in the economy and the culture of EB III, once again left Tell es-Sulṭân largely abandoned for several centuries. Some 350 shaft tombs for individual burials around Tell es-Sulṭân, plus remains of a few houses on the mound, reflect the only human activity in EB IV. Most of the burials contained disarticulated skeletal remains, an indication of secondary burial practices. Kenyon interpreted the burials as reflecting a tribal organization consisting of seven affiliated groups, all of which viewed the region as a traditional locale for burial.

The Middle Bronze (Canaanite) occupation at Tell es-Sulṭân was again a well-fortified town, complete with three successive plastered ramparts. Houses and shops were set out in a town plan near the city gate. However, the fullest evidence of MB II life (and ideas of afterlife) derived from tombs on the nearby necropolis, whose preserved remains included wooden furniture, textiles, baskets, mats, scarabs, decorative ivory carvings, and even food. MB II Tell es-Sulṭân ended in destruction, probably at the hands of Egyptian forces.

The Late Bronze settlement at Tell es-Sulṭân has received much attention by biblical scholars, largely because of the account of the conquest of Jericho in Joshua. However, LB occupation appears to have been restricted to a nonfortified village in the 15-14th centuries. Kenyon's discoveries of fragmentary domestic architecture, plus limited LB remains recovered by Garstang (who had mistakenly identified an EB III fortification wall as the one in Josh. 6), fail to correspond to the story of siege and destruction of a walled Jericho. Attempts to identify archaeological remains at Tell es-Sulṭân with Jericho depicted in Josh. 6 flounder on the absence of archaeological data.

Only with the first Iron Age stratum may the name Jericho be applied successfully to Tell es-Sulṭân. From the end of the 15th to the 10th-9th centuries Tell es-Sulṭân lay unoccupied, at which time it was rebuilt, presumably by Hiel of Bethel (1 Kgs. 16:34), though artifacts from one of five known LB tombs date as late as the opening of the 14th century. By the 7th century Jericho had become an extensive settlement, which was destroyed in the 6th-century Babylonian conquest of Judah. This late Iron II settlement was the last on the mound of Tell es-Sulṭân, and occupation during the Persian through Hellenistic historical periods is little attested in the region.

Tulûl Abū el-ʿAlayiq

During the Hasmonean-Roman period occupation at the oasis moved to Tulûl Abū el-ʿAlayiq, a group of low mounds both north and south of Wadi Qelt. Excavation at these sites was done by Charles Warren (1869), Sellin and Watzinger (1913), James L. Kelso and Dimitri C. Baramki (1950), James B. Pritchard (1951), and Ehud Netzer (1973-1987). These extensive excavations exposed a two-story palace built by Hyrcanus I on the north bank of Wadi Qelt, and a large complex of buildings, complete with swimming pools, constructed by Herod the Great as a winter palace with wings connected by a bridge on both sides of Wadi Qelt. Netzer's excavations also found remains of a theater, a racing course, and a possible gymnasium built by Herod at Tell es-Samarat (1917.1413) S of Tell es-Sulṭân. Little of the town associated with NT Jericho has been discovered.

Bibliography. J. R. Bartlett, *Jericho* (Grand Rapids, 1983); P. Bienkowski, *Jericho in the Late Bronze Age* (Warminster, 1986); J. Garstang and J. B. E. Garstang, *The Story of Jericho* (London, 1940); J. L. Kelso and D. C. Baramki, "The Excavation of New Testament Jericho (Tulul Abu el-Alayiq)," in *Excavations at New Testament Jericho and Khirbet en-Nitla.* AASOR 29-30 (New Haven, 1955): 1-19; K. M. Kenyon, *Digging Up Jericho* (New York, 1957); E. Netzer, "The Hasmonean and Herodian Winter Palaces in Jericho," *IEJ* 25 (1975): 89-100; J. B. Pritchard, *Excavations at Herodian Jericho.* AASOR 32-33 (New Haven, 1958).

PAUL F. JACOBS

JERIEL (Heb. *yĕrîʾēl*)
A son (or descendant) of Tola; head of a father's house in the tribe of Issachar (1 Chr. 7:2).

JERIMOTH (Heb. *yĕrîmôṯ*) (also JEREMOTH)
Personal name, alternately spelled Jeremoth. English texts are not consistent in following the Hebrew spelling.

1. One of the five sons of Bela who served as head of an ancestral family during the reign of David (1 Chr. 7:7).

2. A Benjaminite warrior related to King Saul who joined David at Ziklag after he fled from Saul (1 Chr. 12:5[MT 6]). As with the others who attached themselves to the future king, Jerimoth was an able warrior who could shoot both the bow and sling with either hand.

3. A family head from the tribe of Levi among the descendants of Mushi assigned temple duty or administrative roles during the Davidic kingdom (1 Chr. 24:30; called Jeremoth at 23:23).

4. A temple musician and seer during David's reign (1 Chr. 25:4; called Jeremoth at v. 22).

5. The military commander of the tribal forces from Naphtali during David's reign (1 Chr. 27:19).

6. A son of King David whose daughter Mahalath married King Rehoboam of Judah (2 Chr. 11:18).

7. An overseer of the royal temple storerooms during the reign of Hezekiah (2 Chr. 31:13).

David C. Maltsberger

JERIOTH (Heb. *yĕrîʿôṯ*)
Apparently a wife of Caleb the son of Hezron (1 Chr. 2:18). The MT is not clear. Other possibilities are that Jerioth is an alternate name for Azubah or that Azubah was previously married to a man named Jerioth.

JEROBOAM (Heb. *yārobʿām*)
1. The first king of the northern state of Israel (ca. 924-903 B.C.E.); an Ephraimite from Zeredah, the son of Nebat and the widow Zeruah. Solomon set him over "all the forced labor of the house of Joseph" (1 Kgs. 11:28), but after becoming involved in rebellion (v. 27) and being designated by the prophet Ahijah the Shilonite as the one who would receive, after Solomon's death, rule over 10 tribes of Israel (vv. 29-39), Jeroboam was forced to flee to Egypt, where he remained under Pharaoh Shishak's protection until Solomon's death (v. 40). When the assembly of Israel gathered at Shechem to make Rehoboam their king, Jeroboam joined them, and after Rehoboam rejected their request for a more lenient rule, the northern tribes rejected him as king and chose Jeroboam instead (1 Kgs. 12:1-20). (The LXX gives a substantially different account of Jeroboam's rise to power and later rule, but its value for historical reconstruction is unclear.)

Jeroboam strengthened his power over Israel by building programs and cultic reforms. He built Shechem and then Penuel, presumably as his capital cities, and later apparently moved his capital to Tirzah (1 Kgs. 12:25; 14:17; 15:33). In addition, he erected golden calves at sanctuaries in Dan and Bethel, established other centers for worship at high places in the land, installed nonlevitical priests as cultic officials, and instituted changes in the cultic calendar (1 Kgs. 12:26-32; cf. 2 Chr. 11:13-16; 13:8-9). These religious innovations were probably understood in the north as an attempt to return to the more traditional Israelite cultic practices, which allowed for worship at numerous shrines, did not observe the same limits on the priesthood as were observed at Jerusalem, and regarded the gold calf (bull?) as instituted by Aaron (cf. Exod. 32:1-6) as a divine pedestal, the same function as the ark of the covenant at the Jerusalem temple. The Deuteronomistic historian, however, regarded Jeroboam's cultic policies as politically motivated attempts to dissuade Israelites from worshipping at Jerusalem, essentially idolatrous, and ultimately responsible for the destruction of the northern kingdom (1 Kgs. 12:26-32; 2 Kgs. 17:21-23). To this end, the Deuteronomistic historian reports that the Bethel cult was denounced by an unnamed prophet who traveled from Judah to Bethel to confront Jeroboam (1 Kgs. 13:1-10), and that Ahijah, who initially had named Jeroboam as king, later condemned his behavior and predicted the death of the royal son Abijah to Jeroboam's wife, who had visited the prophet to request healing (1 Kgs. 14:1-6). Subsequent references to Jeroboam in 1-2 Kings typically reflect this view of him as an idolater who led Israel to ruin (e.g., 1 Kgs. 16:2, 31; 2 Kgs. 3:3; cf. Sir. 47:23).

Jeroboam's reign was troubled by his ongoing conflict with Judah (1 Kgs. 14:30; cf. 2 Chr. 13:2b-20, which describes Abijah/Abijam's miraculous victory over Jeroboam) and by the incursion of Pharaoh Shishak's forces into Israel (1 Kgs. 14:25-26 mentions the latter only to note its effects on Judah, but the principal object of the attack was apparently Israel). Finally, the reader is told that Jeroboam's death (smitten by God, according to 2 Chr. 13:20) was followed by the succession of his son Nadab (1 Kgs. 14:20).

Bibliography. C. D. Evans, "Naram-Sin and Jeroboam: The Archetypal *Unheilsherrscher* in Mesopotamian and Biblical Historiography," in *Scripture in Context II,* ed. W. W. Hallo, J. C. Moyer, and L. G. Perdue (Winona Lake, 1983), 97-125; B. Mazar, "The Campaign of Pharaoh Shishak to Palestine," *VTSup* 4 (Leiden, 1957), 57-66; W. I. Toews, *Monarchy and Religious Institution in Israel under Jeroboam I.* SBLMS 47 (Atlanta, 1993).

2. King of Israel (ca. 785-745), son of Joash and grandson of Jehu (2 Kgs. 14:23). Jeroboam II's reign over Israel was apparently characterized by military success and economic prosperity. 2 Kgs. 14:25-27 reports that the nation's borders were extended northward to the entrance of Hamath (i.e., probably to the southern end of the Beqaʿ Valley) and southward to the Dead Sea, thus recovering the idealized extent of the land of Israel (cf. Amos 6:13-14). This expansion took place to fulfill the (otherwise unrecorded) prophecy of Jonah "son of Amittai, the prophet, who was from Gath-hepher" (i.e., the prophet for whom the book of Jonah is named) and so satisfy God's desire to rescue Israel from her affliction (2 Kgs. 14:25-26). In addition, 2 Kgs. 14:28 claims that Jeroboam II "returned Damascus and Hamath to Judah in Israel," a statement that is problematic on two counts: (1) most historians are reluctant to accept this claim that Jeroboam II conquered the two cities, and (2) it is unclear what role Judah is presumed to have played in the conquest. Various emendations of the text have been proposed to resolve these difficulties, but no consensus has been achieved. The economic prosperity of the land at this time is surmised from the prophecies of Amos and Hosea, both of whom prophesied during Jeroboam II's reign (Amos 1:1; Hos. 1:1) and condemned the extravagance of the nation's urban elite (Amos 4:1; 5:11-12; 6:4-6; Hos. 10:1; 12:8). The peculiar reference in 1 Chr. 5:17 to a census of Gadites during the reigns of Jeroboam II and Jotham of Judah, whose reigns may have barely overlapped, may point to some collaboration between Israel and Judah in the rule of the Transjordan but is itself unclear.

Little is known of Jeroboam II's religious policies, since 2 Kgs. 14:24 issues only a general condemnation of the king for continuing the practice of Jeroboam I, and Amos 7:10-17 describes a conflict between the prophet Amos and the priest Amaziah at the royal sanctuary at Bethel. The books of Amos and Hosea indicate, though, that there was a general prophetic critique of Jeroboam II's reign, addressing political affairs, social injustice, and religious infidelity. In fact, the priest Amaziah quotes Amos as predicting that Jeroboam II would "die by the sword" and that Israel would go into exile (Amos 7:11). Nevertheless, 2 Kgs. 14:29 indicates that the king died peacefully and was succeeded by his son Zechariah.

Bibliography. M. Haran, "The Rise and Decline of the Empire of Jeroboam ben Joash," *VT* 17 (1967): 266-97. M. PATRICK GRAHAM

JEROHAM (Heb. *yĕrōḥām*)

1. An Ephraimite, the father of Elkanah and grandfather of Samuel (1 Sam. 1:1; cf. 1 Chr. 6:27, 34[MT 12, 19], where he is called a Levite of the line of Korah).

2. A Benjaminite (1 Chr. 8:27), possibly the same as Jeremoth in v. 14.

3. The father or ancestor of Ibneiah, a Benjaminite who returned from exile (1 Chr. 9:8). He may be the same as **2** above.

4. The father or ancestor of Adaiah, a priest in postexilic Jerusalem (1 Chr. 9:12; Neh. 11:12).

5. A man from Gedor and the father or ancestor of Joelah and Zebadiah, two men who joined David at Ziklag (1 Chr. 12:7[8]).

6. The father or ancestor of Azarel, David's chief officer over the tribe of Dan (1 Chr. 27:22).

7. The father or ancestor of Azariah, a "commander of a hundred" who supported Jehoiada's coup against Queen Athaliah (2 Chr. 23:1).

HAROLD R. MOSLEY

JEROME

Translator of the Vulgate, a Latin translation of the Bible based on Hebrew texts of the OT and the oldest Greek texts of the NT available at the time. It was the standard Bible for Western Christendom. Commissioned by Pope Damasus I, Jerome labored upon this, his most important translation project, from 391-406 C.E.

Born Eusebius Hieronymus (ca. 347/48) into a wealthy Christian family, Jerome received a classical education at Rome and was baptized at age 19 or 20. He embraced the monastic life until his death on 30 September 419/420, but he was active in the theological debates of his day. He defended the perpetual virginity of Mary and monastic celibacy, attacked Pelagianism and Origenism, and translated the homilies of Origen and works of Eusebius. He also published commentaries on the OT prophets and Ecclesiastes and a biography of Paul the Hermit. D. LARRY GREGG

JERUBBAAL (Heb. *yĕrubba'al*) (also JERUBBESHETH)

The name ("let Baal [or 'the master'] contend" or "multiply") given to Gideon to commemorate his destruction of his father's altar to Baal at Ophrah (Judg. 6:32). At times this name is identified as an alternate appellative (Judg. 7:1; 8:35), but at others it is clearly a substitute for Gideon (e.g., ch. 9; 1 Sam. 2:11); some scholars view this as evidence of different sources. The euphemistic form Jerubbesheth occurs at 2 Sam. 11:21.

JERUBBESHETH (Heb. *yĕrubbešeṯ*)

A substitute form of the name Jerubbaal (2 Sam. 11:21; "let shame contend" or "multiply"), devised to avoid pronunciation of the Baal element.

JERUEL (Heb. *yĕrû'ēl*)

An area of the Judean wilderness between En-gedi and Tekoa, situated at the ascent of Ziz (2 Chr. 20:16). Here King Jehoshaphat defeated a coalition of Ammonites and Moabites.

JERUSALEM (Heb. *yĕrûšālayim*)

The primary city of ancient Israel, capital of Judah and the United Monarchy.

Name

The name is based on the Hebrew root *yrh* and the name of a Canaanite god Šalem. The verb *yrh* usually means "to throw" or "to shoot," but clearly has the sense of "to lay a foundation" (Job 38:6). Šalem is best known from the Ugaritic texts where he usually is associated with Šahar, both descended from El. Thus the name Jerusalem may have meant something like "founded by Šalem."

The Masoretic pointing of the name as a dual form seems to reflect a late development. Also, the notion that Jerusalem originally was called Jebus depends heavily on the Chronicler's interpolation of 2 Sam. 5:6. Where 2 Samuel reports that David and his men "went to Jerusalem against the Jebusites, the inhabitants of the land . . . ," the Chronicler reads ". . . went to Jerusalem, that is Jebus, where the Jebusites were, the inhabitants of the land" (1 Chr. 11:4). Other biblical passages refer to a place called "the Jebusite" and add "that is, Jerusalem" (Josh. 15:8; 18:28; Judg. 19:10). Close examination of the geographical details of these passages suggests that "the Jebusite" was a landmark somewhere in the immediate vicinity of Jerusalem, probably just north of the modern "Old City," rather than another name for Jerusalem per se.

Setting

Jerusalem is situated at ca. 750 m. (2460 ft.) elevation in the central Palestinian hill country. It was one of three main cities in the hill country during ancient times, connected with Shechem and Hebron by a natural land route along the north-south spine of the hill country. The earliest part of Jerusalem to be settled and fortified was the knoll immediately south of the present-day Haram esh-Sharif or temple mount. The biblical name for this knoll, or part of it, was Ophel (2 Chr. 27:3; 33:14; Neh. 3:26-27; 11:21). Ophel slopes to the south from the temple mount and is flanked on the east by the Kidron Valley (2 Sam. 15:23; John 18:1) and on the west by the Tyropoeon Valley (this name supplied by Josephus). The temple mount would have been a more naturally shaped hill in ancient times than it appears now (subsequent to Herod the Great's

Aerial view of Jerusalem from the southeast. Temple mount in foreground
(Phoenix Data Systems, Neal and Joel Bierling)

building program). Also the Tyropoeon, which joins the Kidron at the southern end of Ophel, has been largely filled with debris over time. Situated near the base of the slope on Ophel's eastern side was a spring, the biblical Gihon (2 Chr. 33:14), which served as Jerusalem's chief water supply during the city's early history. This water source was supplemented by cisterns and, during the Roman period, aqueducts from other springs S of Bethlehem.

Opposite Ophel on the east, across the Kidron, is the Mount of Olives. Opposite Ophel on the west, across the Tyropoeon, is the so-called Western Hill, which is broader and provides more gradually sloping space for buildings than Ophel. During Iron II (ca. the time of Hezekiah) and again during Hellenistic-Roman times (the Maccabean period and later) the city expanded to this western hill. Josephus referred to it as the Upper City. It seems reasonable to assume that "the stronghold of Zion" from which the Jebusites defended against David was on Ophel, and that the settlement on Ophel came to be known after David's conquest as "the city of David" (cf. 2 Sam. 5:6-10). Later, however, after the building of the temple, Zion came to refer to the temple mountain, or to the now expanded city as a whole. Eventually, apparently during the Byzantine period when the temple mount was in ruins and a major church, the basilica of Holy Zion, stood on the Western Hill, the name Zion became attached to the Western Hill.

Curving around the western and southern sides of the Western Hill, and then continuing eastward to join the Kidron just S of the southern tip of Ophel and the Tyropoeon-Kidron juncture, is another prominent valley, Wadi er-Rababa. If "the Jebusite" is to be equated not only with Jerusalem but more specifically with Ophel, on the grounds that Ophel is the oldest part of Jerusalem, then Wadi er-Rababa emerges as the best candidate for the valley of Hinnom and Bir Ayyub, in the Kidron Valley just south of where it is joined by the Tyropoeon and Rababa, as En-rogel (Josh. 15:7-11; 18:15-19, 21-28). Wadi er-Rababa has been renamed Hinnom on some modern maps.

Ancient Sources

While Jerusalem, Shechem, and Hebron were the main urban centers of the central Palestinian hill country, they were of relatively modest size as ancient cities go, even compared to some cities of the Palestinian lowlands. Jerusalem especially, while enjoying a pleasant setting, was neither overly blessed with agricultural resources nor situated particularly near a major trade route. It should not be surprising, therefore, that Jerusalem turns up only rarely in ancient written sources other than the OT. The nonbiblical epigraphical references to Jerusalem prior to Hellenistic-Roman times are as follows. (1) A place called *rwšʒmm* (usually transliterated *Roshlamem,* but possibly *Rosh-ramem*) appears in both the Berlin and Brussels groups of Execration Texts. If this is Jerusalem, as most scholars are inclined to believe, then the Egyptian pharaohs were aware of Jerusalem's existence ca. 1800 and listed it among their Asiatic enemies. (2) Two of the Amarna Letters from the mid-14th century were sent to the Egyptian court by Shuwardata, the vassal king of Gath, who accused of disloyalty ʿAbdu-ḫeba, the vassal king of Jerusalem. Five of the letters are from ʿAbdu-ḫeba himself, whose name seems to be of Hurrian origin. ʿAbdu-ḫeba insists that it is others who are disloyal to Egypt rather than he, and urges the pharaoh to send military support. (3) An Aramaic inscription fragment discovered at Tell Dan and dated by the excavator to the 9th century seems to refer to "the house of David." Presumably this is a reference to the ruling dynasty in Jerusalem which, according to the OT, would have been founded by David approximately a century and a half earlier. (4) It was during the 9th century also that the Neo-Assyrian rulers began conducting military campaigns into Syria-Palestine and, accordingly, mention local rulers of that region in their royal inscriptions. Tiglath-pileser III (744-727) provides the earliest mention of a Jerusalemite king; namely, he included Jehoahaz in a list of local Palestinian rulers who paid him tribune. Esarhaddon (680-669) and Assurbanipal (668-627) report tribute from Judah, which of course implies Jerusalem. Surely the most intriguing of the royal Assyrian inscriptions, however, are two annalistic prisms which provide almost duplicate accounts of Sennacherib's invasion of Palestine and siege of Jerusalem in 701. (5) One of the Babylonian Chronicles reports Nebuchadnezzar's conquest of Jerusalem in March 597.

Archaeological Evidence

Jerusalem's pre-Roman archaeological remains are rather meager, again not surprising because it was not a major city in ancient times. Also, the present occupation of the city, not to mention religious sensitivities and political factors, limit where archaeologists can excavate. Nevertheless, Jerusalem's archaeological profile for the Bronze and Iron Ages is fairly typical of Palestinian sites. This profile may be summarized as follows.

1. Ceramic evidence indicates some occupation of Ophel as early as the Chalcolithic period.
2. Remains of a building witness to a permanent settlement on Ophel during the early centuries (ca. 3000-2800 B.C.E.) of the Early Bronze Age.
3. Segments of a wall more than 3 m. (10 ft.) thick in places indicate that Ophel was fortified during the Middle Bronze Age.
4. Less impressive architectural remains which are more difficult to interpret and date (e.g., the "stepped structure" discussed below) suggest continued occupation through Late Bronze and Iron I.
5. Construction of a tunnel to transport water from the Gihon spring on Ophel's eastern side to a reservoir at the foot of Ophel's southwestern slope, plus fortifications on the Western Hill, verify that Jerusalem experienced a period of expansion during Iron II. An inscription discovered inside the water tunnel commemorated the completion of this project, generally attributed to Hezekiah (cf. 2 Chr. 32:30). The reservoir, which receives the water from the tunnel still today, is the pool of Siloam (John 9:1-12).
6. There are evidences that this expanded Iron II city met with destruction.
7. Settlement seems to have been limited to Ophel during the closing centuries of the Iron Age.

History

In view of the limited epigraphical and archaeological evidence, historians depend heavily on the OT for information about ancient Jerusalem. However, there has been a mood of caution during recent years. Besides the fact that the biblical writers lived long after some of the events they describe, some of what they report about Jerusalem is difficult to interpret.

Josh. 10 recounts Joshua's defeat of a coalition of five Amorite kings led by Adoni-zedek king of Jerusalem. Josh. 12:10 includes Jerusalem in a summary of Israel's conquests under Joshua. Yet Josh. 15:63 states that "the people of Judah [cf. Judg. 1:21, 'Benjaminites'] could not drive out the Jebusites, the inhabitants of Jerusalem; so the Jebusites dwell with the people of Judah in Jerusalem to this day." 2 Sam. 5:6-10 = 1 Chr. 11:4-9 report that David conquered Jerusalem from the Jebusites with no mention of either Judahite or Benjaminite presence. Finally, accusing the inhabitants of Jerusalem of abominations, Ezek. 16:45 states: "Your mother was a Hittite and your father an Amorite." It seems certain, whether (or to whatever degree) there was any Israelite conquest of Jerusalem before David, that the city had a pluralistic population.

2 Sam. 5:8 quotes David as saying, "Whoever would strike down the Jebusites, let him get up the water shaft *(ṣinnôr)* . . ." (NRSV). In 2 Sam. 5:9 he is said to have "dwelt in the stronghold . . . and built the city all around from the *millô'* inward." It is tempting to suppose that David was calling for a volunteer to climb up a particular water shaft which archaeologists have discovered in the eastern slope of Ophel above the Gihon spring (i.e., Warren's Shaft). Also it has been proposed that a stepped stone structure uncovered at the top of the slope and a short distance north of Warren's Shaft is a surviving remnant of David's rebuild. However, the meaning of *ṣinnôr* is not entirely clear, and archaeologists debate the dating of both Warren's Shaft and the stepped structure. An alternate view regarding the stepped structure is that it belongs to a pre-Davidic phase of the city.

The OT (as well as later tradition reflected in both the NT and the Qur'an) depicts Solomon's reign as one of unsurpassed splendor. Actually the epigraphical and archaeological evidence (or relative lack of same) suggests that the 10th century, when Solomon would have lived, was somewhat of a "dark age" throughout the Middle East including Palestine. Clearly this is the impression from the meager Iron I archaeological remains at Jerusalem. True, the temple mount where Solomon's temple and palace would have stood is not accessible to archaeologists, and probably was cleared by Herod the Great's builders anyhow. Nevertheless, in view of the biblical claims regarding Solomon's exceeding wealth and extensive building activities, one

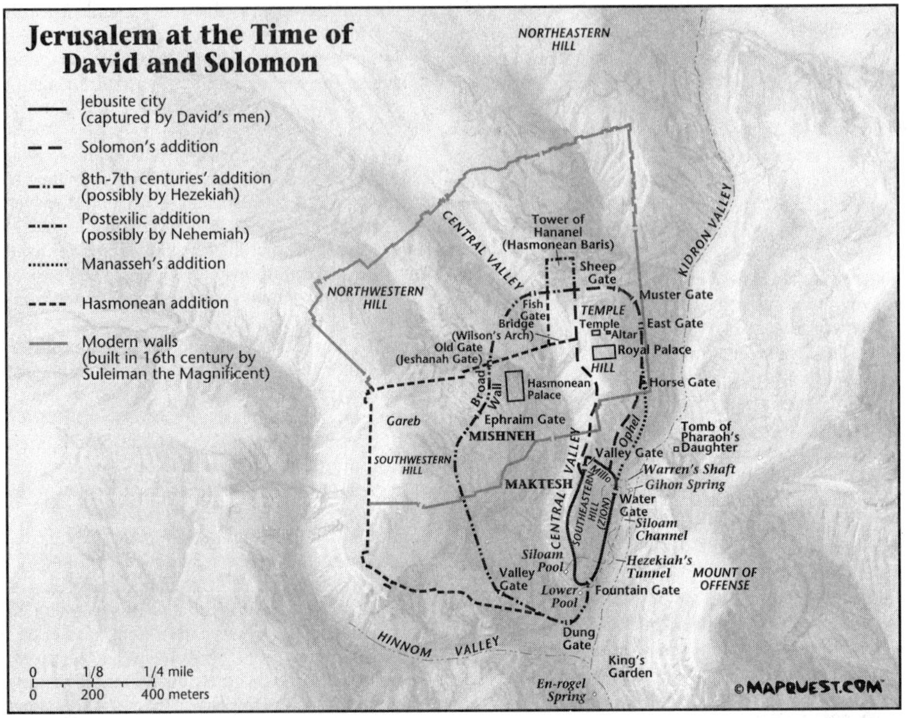

would expect more tangible and impressive archaeological remains from that brief moment of Jerusalem's history when, according to the OT, it was the center of a world-class empire.

For the later centuries of the Iron Age, it becomes much easier to coordinate the biblical materials regarding Jerusalem with archaeological and epigraphical sources. It seems reasonable to attribute the Iron II water tunnel to Hezekiah, and probably the fortification of the Western Hill as well. Jerusalemite burial practices of this period are known from several cemeteries (one immediately N of the present-day "Old City," another across the Kidron from Ophel on the western slopes of Silwan, and the so-called Ketef Hinnom cemetery SW of the Western Hill). Among the discoveries at the latter cemetery were two small, rolled silver plaques with the benediction from Num. 6:34-36. Burned building remains excavated on the eastern slopes of Ophel (built against the "stepped structure") probably witness to the Babylonian destruction of the city. One of the rooms apparently contained an archive of documents which perished at the time. Only the clay bullae which sealed the documents survive — more than 50 of them, having been fired in the conflagration.

1-2 Maccabees and Josephus are important written sources for information about Jerusalem during the Hellenistic period, and Josephus also for the early Roman period. The Maccabean rebellion was a major turning point, with Jerusalem enjoying a period of economic revival and relatively far-reaching political influence under the Hasmonean rulers, especially John Hyrcanus (135/134-104) and Alexander Janneus (103-76). Once again the city expanded to the Western Hill. The city continued to flourish after Pompey secured Roman control of the whole region and of Jerusalem in particular. Indeed, Herod the Great almost completely changed the face of Jerusalem, beginning with the temple mount on which he essentially rebuilt the modest "Second Temple," which itself had been constructed by the postexilic Jewish community during the Persian period. While the central shrine of Herod's rebuilding no doubt preserved the basic plan of the Second Temple, the overall layout was of typically Hellenistic-Roman design — i.e., the central shrine *(cella)* was surrounded by a large open court *(temenos)*, which itself was enclosed by a colonnaded portico. At the northwestern corner of the temple compound, both to protect and command it, and possibly at the site of the Hellenistic Akra (1 Macc. 1:29-36; *Ant.* 12.5.4 [252]), he built a fort named the Antonia (after Mark Antony). Other Herodian features included a palace on the Western Hill and three towers which commanded the western defenses of the city. Contemporary with Herod and active in the city were two learned and influential rabbinical teachers, Shammai and Hillel (ca. 30 B.C.E.–10 C.E.). Herod's Jerusalem also is the city that Jesus and Paul would have known, although their activities are to be associated with the generation following Herod himself. Their younger contemporary, Josephus, was involved in the First Jewish Revolt and witnessed the resulting conquest and destruction of the city by Titus in 70 C.E.

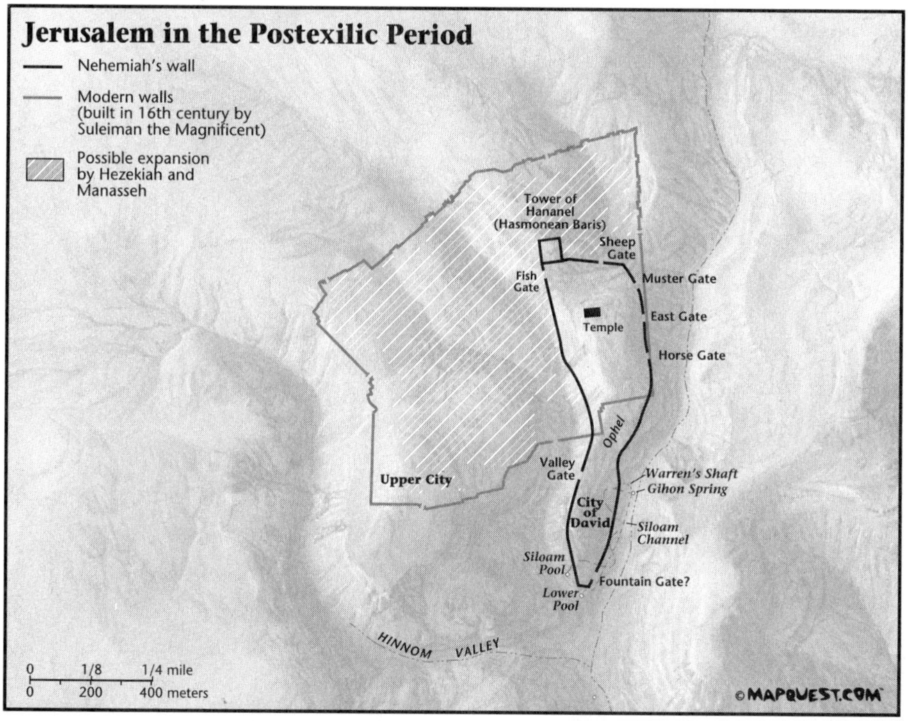

Jerusalem in the Postexilic Period

Tradition

Some landmarks in and around Jerusalem which figure in the NT can be identified confidently — e.g., the Mount of Olives, the Pool of Siloam, and the temple mount. Others are less certain, although often located by ecclesiastical traditions which date back to the Byzantine period. The following are representative examples.

John 5:2-9 reports Jesus' healing of a man at the pool of Beth-zatha (Bethesda, Bethsaida), which was said to be near the Sheep Gate and had five porticoes. Early Christian pilgrims to Jerusalem spoke of the "twin pools" of Bethsaida, and in 1888 workers clearing some ruins on the grounds of the St. Anne Church discovered an old fresco which seems to represent the healing of the man at the pool. Excavations uncovered the foundations of a Byzantine church built over what could be interpreted as the layout of twin pools with porticoes. Also, a fragment of a relief from the Roman period discovered nearby may connect the place with Asclepius, the Roman god of healing.

Matt. 26:36 = Mark 14:32 relate that Jesus' betrayal by Judas on the eve of the Crucifixion occurred at a place called Gethsemane (probably meaning "oil vat"). The other two Gospels do not actually call the place by name: Luke 22:39-40 informs us only that the incident took place on the Mount of Olives; John 18:1-11 notes that it occurred "across the Kidron Valley . . where there was a garden." Apparently Gethsemane (whether a garden, oil vat, or whatever) was located on the Mount of Olives side of the Kidron. The beautiful garden pointed out today is as likely a spot as any. However, the claim that the roots of olive trees in this garden are very old has no bearing on the question of whether it is in fact the authentic Gethsemane.

Early Christian tradition located the site of the Upper Room (Mark 14:15; Luke 22:12) on the Western Hill. It was believed that the apostles celebrated the first Pentecost in this same room (Acts 1:13) and that Caiaphas' house was located nearby (Matt. 26:57; Mark 14:53; Luke 22:54). Thus a major church, the Basilica of Mt. Zion, was erected on the Western Hill during the Byzantine period and is depicted in the Madeba mosaic map. The complex of old buildings located on the spot today date from medieval times and later.

Constantine commissioned the building of a church over what was believed at the time (326 C.E.) to be the place of Jesus' burial. According to Eusebius, bishop of Caesarea who served as consultant to Constantine, the location of the tomb had been remembered even though previous Roman authorities had covered it over with soil and erected a temple to Venus on the spot (*Vita Const.* 3.25-28). Somewhat later there arose a tradition that Helena, Constantine's mother, found the "true cross" in a cistern nearby. Originally two adjacent churches marked the traditional locations of Jesus' crucifixion (Golgotha) and burial (Joseph of Arimathea's tomb), but since the Crusader period these have been combined one roof, the Church of the Holy Sepulchre. Some scholars have objected

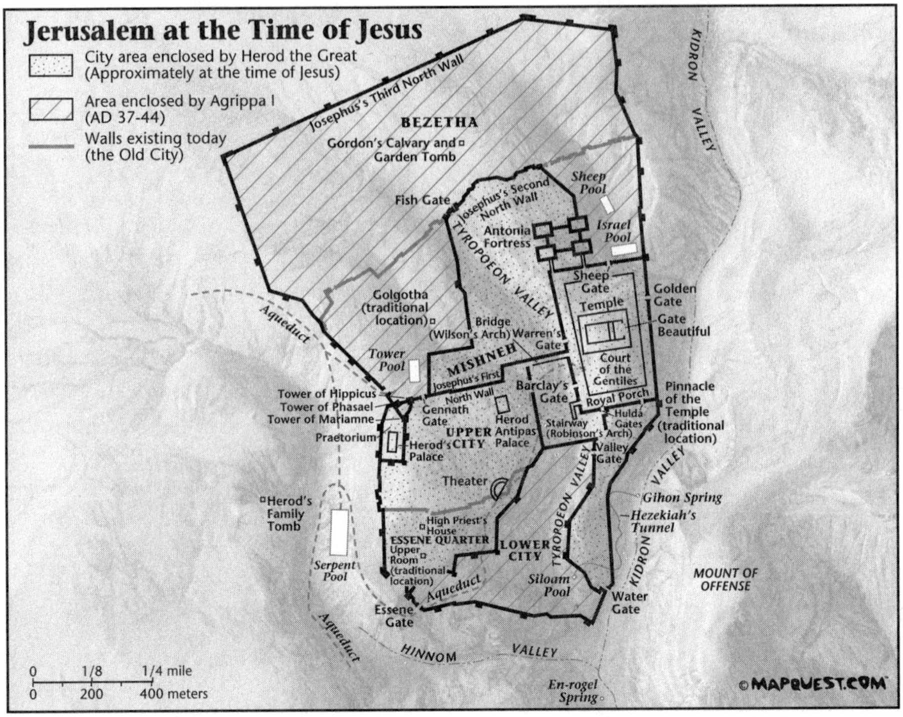

that the spot marked by the Church of the Holy Sepulchre would have been inside the city during Jesus' day, and thus an unlikely spot for crucifixions. An alternate candidate (the so-called Garden tomb) is very popular among Protestant tourists.

Jerusalem (Arab. *el-Quds,* "the holy") is a holy city for Muslims also, if for no other reason than that Islam incorporated many biblical traditions. Solomon has an important place in the Qur'an, and Mohammed himself prayed facing Jerusalem during his early career. However, Muslim reverence for Jerusalem focuses primarily on the opening verse of Qur'an *Sura* 17, which alludes to an occasion when God transported Mohammed from one holy shrine to another distant one and showed him miraculous signs. Later Muslim interpreters, connecting this verse with other passages in the Qur'an, took it to mean that God transported Mohammed from Mecca to Jerusalem in a dream and that from Jerusalem Mohammed was raised to heaven where he saw wonderful things and communicated with earlier prophets. Jerusalem, in other words, came to be identified as the "distant shrine" (*al-masjid al-Aqsa*), and Mohammed's elevation to heaven is commemorated by the Dome of the Rock monument and the nearby al-Aqsa mosque.

Bibliography. D. Bahat, *The Illustrated Atlas of Jerusalem* (New York, 1990); H. Geva, ed., *Ancient Jerusalem Revealed* (Jerusalem, 1994); W. H. Mare, *The Archaeology of the Jerusalem Area* (Grand Rapids, 1987); B. Mazar, et al., "Jerusalem," *NEAEHL* 2:698-804; F. E. Peters, *Jerusalem: The Holy City in the Eyes of Chroniclers, Visitors, Pilgrims, and Prophets* (Princeton, 1985); J. D. Purvis, *Jerusalem, the Holy City: Bibliography* (Metuchen, N.J., 1991).

J. Maxwell Miller

JERUSALEM, GATES

The construction, destruction, rebuilding and expansion of walls around Jerusalem during biblical times provided for numerous gates. Archaeological work has helped determine the placement of many of these ancient walls and gates; however, many questions still linger. Undoubtedly, some of the gates were known by more than one name, which adds to the confusion.

The construction of city walls with gates was undertaken by David (1 Chr. 11:7-8), Solomon (1 Kgs. 3:1), perhaps Uzziah (2 Chr. 26:9), Hezekiah (32:5), Manasseh (33:14), Nehemiah (Neh. 3:1–4:1), the Hasmoneans, and Herod.

Preexilic Period

Temple Gates

Evidently a gate connected the palace to the temple (2 Kgs. 11:19; 16:18). This entrance would have been to the south of the temple. References to the "gate behind the guards" and the Gate of the Foundation (2 Chr. 23:4-5; cf. the "gate of Shallecheth," 1 Chr. 26:16) may indicate additional gates connecting the palace and the temple area, as implied in "the third gate" of Jer. 38:14. Mysteriously, 1 Chr. 9:18 mentions a "king's gate on the east." Ezekiel mentions a temple gate facing the north (Ezek. 8:14; 9:2), which may be the same as Jeremiah's temple gate designated the upper Benjamin Gate (Jer. 20:2; 2 Kgs. 15:35) or the New Gate of Jer. 26:10; 36:10. The Horse Gate, which faced the east (Jer. 31:40), seems to be located in the southeast sector of the temple area near the palace (2 Kgs. 11:16). The Benjamin Gate and Horse Gate would have been city gates as well as temple gates.

City Gates

Nehemiah's inspection of the destroyed city indicates that there was a Fountain Gate on the lower eastern wall (Neh. 2:14). In the southeast corner of the city, opening to the valley of Hinnom, was the Potsherd Gate (Jer. 19:2), later referred to as the Dung Gate (Neh. 2:13; 3:13-14; 12:31). The gate's name may have been derived from a refuse heap located outside the gate in the Hinnom Valley. Also opening to the Hinnom was the Valley Gate, which is generally located in the southwest corner of the city walls. 2 Chr. 26:9 notes that Uzziah built a fortified tower at this gate. Further to the north at the northwest corner of the west wall, Uzziah built another fortified tower at the Corner Gate. According to 2 Chr. 25:23 Joash broke down the walls of Jerusalem from the Corner Gate to the Ephraim Gate for a distance of 400 cubits (200 m.[626 ft.]). Thus, the Ephraim Gate was probably in the northern wall, not far from the Corner Gate. This gate likely led to Ephraim and is probably to be identified with the "middle gate" of Jer. 39:3. The Fish Gate is difficult to place (2 Chr. 33:14); most scholars favor a location along the northern wall between the temple mount and the Ephraim Gate. This was likely a place where fish were sold or delivered.

Restoration Period

Not all of the walls of Jerusalem were broken down during the Exile. Excavations indicate that destruction was heaviest in the area of the temple and along the eastern wall. Consequently, Nehemiah's rebuilding maintained many of the gates of the old city. However, along the east, excavations reveal that Nehemiah built higher along the ridge paralleling the Kidron Valley. In the process, it seems that additional gates were added to the east.

Along the eastern wall at the north, in the temple area, lay the Muster Gate (Neh. 3:31). Further to the south, but still in the temple area, were the Horse Gate (Neh. 3:28) and the Gate of the Guard (12:39), perhaps an interior gate leading to the temple area. Further down the ravine, Nehemiah mentions the Water Gate on the east (Neh. 3:26; 12:37), which may be equated with the East Gate (3:29). The last of the east wall gates, the Fountain Gate, evidently was rebuilt higher up the ridge (Neh. 3:15).

Nehemiah mentions nothing of the Benjamin Gate, formerly located in the temple area. However, he notes that priests constructed a Sheep Gate (Neh. 3:1), which was likely facing the north in the temple area and was probably a place for selling sheep which were used for sacrifice. It cannot be determined whether or not the Sheep Gate is the former Benjamin Gate.

Elsewhere around the city, preexilic gates seem to have been restored at their original sites during this period. Thus, Nehemiah records the rebuilding of the Dung Gate and the Valley Gate, which were located 1000 cubits (500 m.[1640 ft.]) from one another (Neh. 3:13-14). Also restored was the Fish Gate (Neh. 3:3). Nehemiah, however, does not record the repair of the Ephraim Gate or the Corner Gate, though it appears that both were recognized at this time (cf. Neh. 8:16; 12:39; Zech. 14:10). Another gate repaired in the days of Nehemiah, the Old Gate, is curiously unmentioned elsewhere in Scripture. This gate should be translated the Gate of the Old (area), or perhaps the Jeshanah Gate. Prevailing opinion is that the gate was an interior gate located in the northern area of the city near the Ephraim Gate.

New Testament Period

According to Josephus there were three walls surrounding Herodian Jerusalem, though on the sides facing the valleys only one wall encompassed the city (*BJ* 5.4.1). Josephus mentions few gates, though undoubtedly many more existed. The eastern, southern, and western sections of the first wall were probably in the same area as the walls in Nehemiah's day. The northern section of this first wall extended from the tower of Hippicus (near the former Corner Gate) to the Xystus (the present-day Wilson's Arch). The only gate mentioned by Josephus in this first wall, the Gate of the Essenes (*BJ* 5.4.2), was probably close to Nehemiah's Valley Gate.

There is little agreement regarding the location of the second and third walls. Though generally known, the exact course of the second wall can only be approximated. Josephus states that it began at the Gennath Gate (E of the Hippicus Tower and perhaps identified with the Older Ephraim Gate) and circled in a northeastern direction, finally connecting with the Antonia.

The third wall was built by Herod Agrippa (*BJ* 5.4.2). In Josephus' account, the third wall began at the tower of Hippicus and went north to the tower of Psephinus. The wall then turned east past the monuments of Helena, the caverns of the kings, the Corner Tower, the Fuller's Monument, and connected to the older wall at the Kidron Valley. Some scholars believe that the northern wall was in general alignment with the north wall of the present Old City. Others, however, believe that the third wall lay further north and is to be identified with a wall discovered by E. L. Sukenik and L. A. Mayer in 1925-27.

In the area of the temple mount, Josephus mentions several gates: one on the north, four on the west, and unspecified "gates" to the south. He is silent about gates on the east. On the north was the Todi Gate. On the west, the southernmost gate, identified at the site of Robinson's Arch, led to the lower city. Robinson's Arch was one of several immense arches supporting a long staircase which descended to the valley. North of this gate, three additional western gates have been identified as Coponius Gate (popularly known as Barclay's

Gate), Wilson's Arch, and Warren's Gate. These three gates led to the western sections of the city. Wilson's Arch supported a massive causeway that bridged the Central Valley, linking the temple area to the upper city.

On the south side of the temple complex two large gates were located in the middle of the wall. The first of these, the western Huldah Gate (the Double Gate), had two portals and a broad (64 m.[210 ft.]) stairway leading down to the lower city. The second gate, the eastern Huldah Gate (the Triple Gate), had three portals. Both of these southern gates are now walled up.

Josephus recounts 10 gates which serviced the temple itself. Four were located along the north, another four along the south, and two toward the east (*BJ* 5.5.2). The two eastern gates, one inside (or west) of the other, surrounded the Women's Court on the east and west. The interior gate, leading to the Court of Israel, was probably known as the Nicanor Gate, while the easternmost gate, separating the Gentiles' Court from the Women's Court, may have been the Beautiful Gate mentioned in Acts 3:2. These identifications are not certain, and it is possible that the Beautiful Gate was the interior Nicanor Gate. Another option is that the Beautiful Gate, if Christian tradition is to be followed, may have been a gate on the eastern city wall leading to the temple area. Existing today on the eastern wall is the Golden Gate, which dates from the Byzantine period at the earliest. A recent discovery revealed another gate buried ca. 2-2.5 m.(7-8 ft.) directly beneath the Golden Gate. This newly discovered gate appears to date from pre-Herodian days and could be the Beautiful Gate.

Bibliography. W. H. Mare, *The Archaeology of the Jerusalem Area* (Grand Rapids, 1987); G. J. Wightman, *The Walls of Jerusalem: From the Canaanites to the Mamluks* (Sydney, 1993).

MARK R. FAIRCHILD

JERUSALEM COUNCIL

See APOSTOLIC COUNCIL.

JERUSHA (Heb. *yĕrûšā'*),
JERUSHAH *(yĕrûšâ)*

The daughter of Zadok and mother of King Jotham of Judah (2 Kgs. 15:33). At 2 Chr. 27:1 the form Jerushah occurs.

JESHAIAH (Heb. *yĕšaʿyâ, yĕšaʿyāhû*)

1. A grandson of Zerubbabel and son of Hananiah, listed among the descendants of Solomon (1 Chr. 3:21).

2. A son of the Levite Jeduthun chosen by David to be a temple musician (1 Chr. 25:3, 15).

3. A Levite whose family was in charge of gifts dedicated to the temple treasury; son of Rehabiah (1 Chr. 26:25).

4. The son of Athaliah and head of a family of 70 males that returned to Jerusalem with Ezra (Ezra 8:7).

5. A Merarite Levite who along with 20 kinsmen was among those recruited to accompany Ezra in returning to Jerusalem (Ezra 8:19).

6. A seventh-generation forebear of the Benjaminite Sallu, who was among those conscripted to move into Jerusalem at the time of Nehemiah (Neh. 11:7).

PAUL L. REDDITT

JESHANAH (Heb. *yĕšānâ*)

A city on the border of Israel and Judah taken by Abijah during his war with Jeroboam I (2 Chr. 13:19). It is probably also mentioned at 1 Sam. 7:12 (so NRSV, following LXX and Tg.; MT Heb. *šēn*). Later the headquarters of Antigonus' general Pappus, the city was captured by Herod the Great (Roman Isanas; Josephus *Ant.* 14.15.12 [458]). The site has been identified as modern Burj el-Isâneh (174156), 5 km. (3 mi.) N of Jefneh and 10.5 km. (17 mi.) N of Jerusalem.

JESHARELAH (Heb. *yĕśar'ēlâ*) (also ASHARELAH)

A son of Asaph; leader of the seventh division of levitical singers at the time of David (1 Chr. 25:14). He is called Asharelah at 1 Chr. 25:2.

JESHEBEAB (Heb. *yešeḇ'āḇ*)

The leader of the fourteenth division of priests at the time of David (1 Chr. 24:13).

JESHER (Heb. *yēšer, yešer*)

A Judahite, son of Caleb and Azubah and grandson of Hezron (1 Chr. 2:18).

JESHIMON (Heb. *yĕšîmôn*)

A desert region characterized by lack of rainfall and vegetation; a wasteland. Jeshimon is used to refer to desert regions in general (Deut. 32:10; Isa. 43:19; Ps. 68:7[MT 8]; 78:40; 106:14; 107:4) and to two specific desert locations.

1. A desert region E of the Judean mountains and W of the Dead Sea. It is near the region of Ziph, N of the hill of Hachilah (1 Sam. 23:19; 26:1, 3) and the desert of Maon in the Arabah (1 Sam. 23:24). It is the region to which David fled to escape the pursuit of Saul. Jeshimon refers to the region commonly known as the Judean wilderness.

2. A desert region at the northeastern end of the Dead Sea, bordering the land of Moab. It is overlooked by Mt. Pisgah (Num. 21:20) and Mt. Peor (23:28). Beth-jeshimoth (Josh. 12:3) is probably located within this region. RONALD A. SIMKINS

JESHISHAI (Heb. *yĕšîšay*)

A Gadite; son of Jahdo and father of Michael (1 Chr. 5:14).

JESHOHAIAH (Heb. *yĕšôḥāyâ*)

Leader of a Simeonite father's house (1 Chr. 4:36).

JESHUA (Heb. *yēšûaʿ*) **(PERSON)** (also JOSHUA)

Aramaic form of the name Joshua (cf. Neh. 8:17), "Yahweh is my savior," a common name of the Second Temple period.

1. The head of the ninth division of levitical priests in the Solomonic temple (1 Chr. 24:11).

2. A priest from the time of Hezekiah who aided in the distribution of the Levites' portion of the offerings (2 Chr. 31:15).

3. The son of Jehozadak, a priest who returned to Jerusalem with Zerubbabel (Ezra 2:2; Neh. 7:7; 12:1) to rebuild the temple (Ezra 3:2, 8, 9; 4:3; 5:2). He is called Joshua (**4**), the high priest, in Hag. 1:1, 12; 2:2, 4; Zech. 3:1, 8; 6:11. During the temple restoration Jeshua was overshadowed by Zerubbabel, though he is mentioned ahead of Zerubbabel in connection with the restoration of the altar. With the reestablishment of the temple and the priesthood and in the absence of a king, Jeshua rose to prominence. Zech. 3 describes the prophet's vision of the cleansing and ordination of Jeshua (cf. 6:10-15), and many interpreters (perhaps incorrectly) think 4:14 alludes to Jeshua and Zerubbabel.

4. The name of a nonpriestly clan of Pahath-moab counted among those returning from the Exile (Ezra 2:6 = Neh. 7:11).

5. A levitical house or clan among the returnees (Ezra 2:40 = Neh. 7:43; 12:8, 24).

6. Alternate form of Joshua son of Nun (Ezra 8:17).

7. Father of the Levite Jozabad, who helped weigh the treasures returned to the Jerusalem temple (Ezra 8:33).

8. A man from Mizpah, whose son Ezer rebuilt a section of the wall (Neh. 3:19).

9. A levitical singer (Neh. 12:8, 10) who signed the covenant to disassociate himself from foreigners (9:4-5; 10:9[MT 10]) and who translated the law into Aramaic for Ezra (Neh. 8:7).

10. The son of Kadmiel, a leader of the Levites at the time of the priest Joiakim (Neh. 12:24).

PAUL L. REDDITT

JESHUA (Heb. *yēšûaʿ*) **(PLACE)**
A town in southern Judah reoccupied after the return from captivity (Neh. 11:26), modern Tell es-Saʿweh/Tel Jeshuʿa (149076), 19 km. (12 mi.) ENE of Beer-sheba. It may be the same as Shema (Josh. 15:26).

JESHURUN (Heb. *yĕšurûn*)
Another name for Israel, which occurs only in poetry. Jeshurun is considered to be a hypocoristicon (diminutive, or term of endearment) that may emphasize its root meaning of "upright." The term occurs in two ancient poems: the Song of Moses (Deut. 32:15; 10th century B.C.E.) and the Blessing of Moses (33:5, 26; 11th century). It is found also in Isa. 44:2, concerning the redemption and restoration of Israel. ROBERT E. STONE, II

JESIMIEL (Heb. *yĕśîmiʾēl*)
A Simeonite chief contemporary with King Hezekiah (1 Chr. 4:36).

JESSE (Heb. *yišay, ʾîšay*)
The father of King David, son of Obed and grandson of Boaz and Ruth the Moabite. In addition to David, Jesse is traditionally credited with seven other sons (1 Sam. 16:10; 17:12) and two daughters (1 Chr. 2:16). However, 1 Chr. 2:13-15 lists only seven sons, and 2 Sam. 17:25 calls Abiga(i)l (and presumably Zeruiah) the daughter of Nahash. If this Nahash is the king of Ammon (1 Sam. 11:1), then Jesse's family would have both Moabite and Ammonite affiliations (associations certainly not emphasized in the Deuteronomistic history). Jesse plays no role in the biblical narrative apart from David: David is anointed in Jesse's family home; Jesse sends David to play the harp for Saul; Jesse sends David to the Israelite camp with food for his brothers; and Jesse sojourns in Moab during the time of David's trouble with Saul. Jesse's name appears in Isa. 11:1, 10 (the "stump of Jesse," the "root of Jesse") as a symbol of the messianic king (Rom. 15:12). JAMES R. ADAIR, JR.

JESUS (Gk. *Iēsoús*)
Greek form of the name Joshua (Heb. *yĕhôšûaʿ*, "Yahweh will save"); cf. Luke 3:29; Acts 7:45; Heb. 4:8.

1. The father of Sirach and grandfather of the author of the book of Sirach (Ecclesiasticus; Sir. Prologue).

2. Joshua ben Sira ("Jesus son of Sirach"), author of Sirach/Ecclesiasticus.

3. Surname of Justus, Paul's co-worker (Col. 4:11).

See JESUS CHRIST; BARABBAS.

BENJAMIN C. CHAPMAN

JESUS CHRIST
The founder of what became the Christian movement. For greater specificity, in his lifetime he was called "Jesus son of Joseph" (Luke 4:22; John 1:45; 6:42), "Jesus of Nazareth" (Acts 10:38), or "Jesus the Nazarene" (Mark 1:24; Luke 24:19 [some translations do not distinguish "the Nazarene" from "of Nazareth"]). "Christ" is a title, the English form of Gk. *christós*, "anointed" (which translates Heb. *māšîaḥ*, "messiah"). Acts 2:36 and other passages show knowledge that "the Christ" was properly a title, but in many NT books, including Paul's letters, the name and title are used together as Jesus' name: "Jesus Christ" or "Christ Jesus" (e.g., Rom. 1:1; 3:24). Paul sometimes simply used "Christ" as Jesus' name (e.g., Rom. 5:6).

Life

Jesus was a Galilean, whose home was Nazareth, a village near Sepphoris, one of the two major cities of Galilee. He was born shortly before the death of Herod the Great (Matt. 2; Luke 1:5), which was in 4 B.C.E. The year of Jesus' death is uncertain, probably sometime between 29 and 33.

Jesus' parents were Joseph and Mary, but according to Matthew and Luke, Joseph was only his legal father. They report that Mary was a virgin when Jesus was conceived (Matt. 1:18; cf. Luke 1:35). Joseph is said to have been a "carpenter," a craftsman who worked with his hands (Matt.

13:55); according to Mark 6:3, Jesus also was a carpenter.

Luke reports that as a child Jesus had precocious learning (Luke 2:41-52), but there is no other evidence about his childhood or early development. As a young adult, he went to be baptized by a prophet, John the Baptist, and shortly thereafter began a career as an itinerant preacher and healer (Mark 1:2-15). During this short career of less than one year he attracted considerable attention. When he went to Jerusalem to observe Passover ca. 30 C.E. (between 29 and 33), he was arrested, tried, and executed. Convinced that he still lived and had appeared to them, his disciples began to convert others to belief in him; these efforts eventually led to a new religion, Christianity.

Sources

The only substantial sources for the life and message of Jesus are the NT Gospels, Matthew, Mark, Luke, and John. Reliable (but meagre) evidence is found in the letters of Paul. There are many sayings attributed to Jesus and stories told about him in noncanonical literature, especially the apocryphal Gospels, and occasionally a reinvestigation of this material leads to the proposal that some of it is "authentic." Although possible in principle, and although a few authentic traditions probably have been preserved outside the Christian canon, it is unlikely that noncanonical sources can contribute substantially to understanding the historical Jesus. The traditions are frequently completely unlike the evidence of the canonical Gospels, and are for the most part embedded in documents that are unreliable on the whole. A few references to Jesus occur in Roman sources, but these are dependent on early Christianity and do not provide independent evidence. A reference to Jesus in Josephus (*Ant.* 18.3.3 [63-4]) has been heavily revised by Christian scribes, and the original statement cannot be recovered.

The Gospels attributed to Matthew, Mark, and Luke agree so closely that it is possible to study them together in a synopsis (arranged in parallel columns). John is remarkably different, and can be reconciled with the Synoptics only in very general ways. One may, however, distinguish John's discourse material from the narrative outline and evaluate them separately. In the Synoptic Gospels (Matthew, Mark, Luke), Jesus teaches in short aphorisms and parables, using similes and similar figures of speech, many drawn from agricultural and village life. The principal subject is the kingdom of God; he seldom refers to himself. When asked for a "sign" to prove his authority, he refuses (Mark 8:11-12). In John, however, Jesus teaches in long metaphorical discourses, in which he himself is the main subject. His miracles are described as "signs" that support the self-descriptions in the discourses and prove who he is. Faced with the choice between John and the Synoptics, scholars have almost unanimously chosen the Synoptic Gospels as giving the substance and manner of Jesus' teaching.

John's narrative outline is also different from the Synoptics, but here the choice is less clear. In the Synoptics, it appears that Jesus' ministry lasted less than one year, since they mention Passover only once during Jesus' adulthood, the occasion of his last, fatal trip to Jerusalem. John, however, cites three Passovers, and thus a ministry of more than two years. John narrates several trips to Jerusalem during Jesus' ministry. Either narrative outline is possible. A ministry of more than two years, however, leaves more questions unanswered than does a ministry of a few months. Jesus and his disciples were itinerant; they travelled around Galilee and its immediate environs, and Jesus taught and healed in various towns and villages, as well as in the countryside and by the shore of the Sea of Galilee. None of the Gospels explains how they lived (though Luke 8:1-3 mentions some female supporters), but the omission is more glaring in John.

This discussion makes clear how little we really know about the life of Jesus. The Gospels provide the information that the authors regarded as necessary in the Christian communities in which they worked. The details of Jesus' life — where he slept, how he ate, where he took refuge in bad weather — are barely mentioned. From the perspective of a modern historian, the sources are deficient in other ways as well. The characters on the whole are "flat": emotions, motives, personalities are seldom mentioned. Jesus is sometimes angry and sometimes compassionate (Mark 3:5; 6:34), but one can say little more. Because of his letters, we know more about Paul the man than about Jesus the man.

This is understandable when one considers the history of the material in the Synoptic Gospels. They consist of brief, self-contained passages called "pericopes," which the Synoptic authors arranged in different contexts as they saw fit, frequently according to similarity of subject matter. The heart of each passage has been stripped of the elements that surrounded it in real life, and the central unit applied to various situations by different users, including the authors of the Gospels.

Moreover, not all the sayings and deeds in the Gospels are reports of things that Jesus actually said and did. The early Christians believed that Jesus still lived in heaven, and they spoke to him in prayer. He sometimes answered (2 Cor. 12:7-10; cf. 1 Cor. 2:13). The early Christians did not distinguish between "the historical Jesus" and "the heavenly Lord" as firmly as most modern people do, and some sayings heard in prayer almost certainly came into the Gospels as sayings uttered by Jesus in his lifetime.

This means that we no longer have the original immediate context of Jesus' sayings and deeds, and we are somewhat uncertain as to which passages in the Gospels go back to the historical Jesus. Without context, we cannot reconstruct the original meaning of the individual passages with certainty. Jesus said, "Love your enemies" (Matt. 5:44). We do not know the original circumstances in which he said this, and so we do not know whom he had in mind. This robs us of precision in interpreting individual passages.

The Calling of the Apostles Peter and Andrew, Duccio di Buoninsegna (1308/1311)
(National Gallery of Art, Washington; Samuel H. Kress Collection)

Public Career

We can, however, find the overall context and the general history of Jesus' ministry, and this provides certainty of the thrust of his teaching as a whole. Jesus' public career began when he was baptized by John the Baptist, an eschatological prophet who proclaimed that the day of judgment was at hand. Jesus seems to have accepted this. Subsequently Jesus gathered 12 disciples, representing the 12 tribes of Israel, proclaimed the arrival of the kingdom of God, predicted the destruction of the temple and its rebuilding "without hands," and shared a final meal with his disciples in which he said that he would drink wine again with them in the kingdom of God. After Jesus' death, his disciples formed a small community which expected him to return and bring in the kingdom. This group spread, and its members continued to expect Jesus to return in the near future, inaugurating a kingdom in which the world would be transformed.

This outline of Jesus' career shows that he was an eschatological prophet, much like John the Baptist and a few other 1st-century Jewish prophets such as Theudas. Like John, Jesus believed in the coming judgment, but the thrust of his mission was more toward inclusion than condemnation.

Teaching

The Nature of the Kingdom

Jesus proclaimed the eschatological kingdom of God. "Eschatology" in this sense means "discussion or teaching of last things," rather than "of the end of the world." Ancient Jewish eschatologists actually thought of God's definitive intervention in the world, which would transform the world and its inhabitants, not destroy them. Jews believed that God had previously intervened in history (the Exodus from Egypt, the Conquest of Canaan), and hoped that he would do so again, but in an even more decisive manner. There would be peace and tranquillity in society and nature (cf. Isa. 2:2-4), and the world would be governed in accordance with the will of God.

Jesus shared this overall view. In particular, he thought that the original 12 tribes of Israel would be reassembled (Matt. 19:28; cf. the call of 12 disciples), that the order of society would be reversed, so that the meek and lowly would have plenty (Matt. 5:5), that sinners and reprobates would somehow be included (Mark 2:17; Matt. 11:19), and that he and his disciples would hold the chief positions (Mark 10:29-31, 35-40; Matt. 19:28-29).

Its Time and Place

In Jesus' view, the kingdom of God existed in heaven, and individuals would enter it on death (e.g., Mark 9:47). God's power was in some respects omnipresent, and Jesus may have seen "the kingdom" in the sense of God's presence as especially evident in his own words and deeds. But Jesus was an eschatologist: in the future, the kingdom would *come to earth* in its full power and glory, at which time God's will would be done "on earth as it is in heaven" (Matt. 6:10). Jesus died before this expectation was fulfilled, and this, coupled with the resurrection appearances, led his followers to expect his return in the near future, bringing in the kingdom and ruling in God's stead (1 Thess. 4:13-18; vv. 15-17 modify a saying of the historical Jesus about the coming Son of Man found in Matt. 24:27-28; 16:27-28; cf. 1 Cor. 15:23-28). The fact that the early Christian movement expected the kingdom to arrive in the very near future is one of the strongest indications that this had been Jesus' own expectation during his lifetime. Early in his career, Paul thought that he and most other Christians would be alive when the kingdom arrived (1 Thess. 4), but later he entertained the possibility of his own prior death (Phil. 1:20-26). One can see the diminishing expectation in the Gospels (compare Mark 9:1 and John 21:21-23), an expectation that Jesus' followers had to modify as the decades passed.

Preparation and Discipleship

Jesus called some people to follow him and to give up everything in order to do so (Mark 1:16-20). He expected others to give their possessions to the poor, even though they did not join his itinerant ministry (Mark 10:17-31). He counselled all to fix their attention on the kingdom, not on material possessions (Matt. 6:19-21, 25-34; Luke 12:13-21). Their reward would be great in the kingdom.

The Poor and Sinners

The themes of reversal and inclusion require fuller presentation. The poor, the meek, the lowly, and sinners loom large in the Synoptic Gospels. Jesus came especially to *call* them, but he seems also to have *favored* them. In the coming kingdom, the last would be first (Mark 10:31). Those who held the chief positions in the present world would be demoted (Luke 14:7-11). Those who gave up everything and followed him would receive "a hundredfold" (Mark 10:30). Sinners, typified by the tax collectors, would be included in the kingdom (Matt. 21:31). This probably rests in part on Jesus' sympathy for those who were in his own social and economic class and below it. Jesus and his disciples were not themselves from the very bottom of society; his father worked with his hands, but he was not destitute. Some of Jesus' disciples were from families who owned their own fishing boats and had houses (Mark 1:19, 29). They were not rich, but they also were not day laborers, beggars, or homeless. Jesus' sympathy, however, went out to those in the latter categories. His message had a social dimension in two respects: he thought that in the kingdom there would still be social relationships, and he thought that the disadvantaged in the present world would be in some sense advantaged in the new age (Matt. 5:3-11; Luke 6:20-23). The promise of houses and lands in Matt. 19:29-30; Mark 10:29-30 may be metaphorical, but Jesus also may have envisaged a future society in which property would still count, though it would be redistributed.

Jesus' call of sinners, according to Luke, meant that he called them to repentance (Luke 5:32; but cf. Matt. 9:13; Mark 2:17). It is probable that Jesus' message was more radical than merely that trangressors should repent. He called them, rather, to accept him and his message, and promised inclusion in the kingdom if they did so. This doubtless included moral reformation — followers of Jesus would not continue to cheat and defraud — but he probably meant that they did not have to conform precisely to the standards of righteous Jewish society, which would require repayment of money or goods, an additional fine, and presentation of a guilt-offering (Lev. 6:1-7). Accepting him and being like him and his disciples was what God required.

Self-Conception

Jesus attached enormous weight to his own mission and person. Christian preoccupation with titles (did he think that he was Messiah, Son of God, Son of Man, son of David, king, etc.?) obscures the issue. He sometimes called himself "Son of Man," and indirectly accepted "Messiah" (or "Christ") and "Son of God" (Matt. 16:16; Mark 14:61-62; but cf. the par. Mark 8:29 = Luke 9:20; Matt. 26:63-64 = Luke 22:67-70), but he did not make an issue of titles. He called people to follow him, not to give him some appellation. Jesus thought that he was God's last emissary, that he and his disciples would rule in the coming kingdom, and that people who accepted him would be included in it.

Jewish Law

Numerous passages in the Gospels concern the Jewish law. According to one set, especially prominent in the Sermon on the Mount (Matt. 5-7), Jesus admonished his followers to extremely strict observance of the law (5:17-48). According to the second set, he was deficient in strict observance and transgressed current opinions about some aspects of the law, especially the sabbath (e.g., Mark 3:1-3). It is at least conceivable that both positions were true, that he was strict about marriage and divorce (Matt. 5:31-32; Mark 10:2-12) but lax about the sabbath. The study of "Jesus and the law" is highly technical. In general, the legal disputes in the Gospels fall well within the parameters of legal disputes in 1st-century Judaism. Some people opposed minor cures on the sabbath, but others permitted them. The Sadducees regarded the Pharisees as too lax in observance of the sabbath. Some Jews washed their hands before eating (Mark 7:5), but others did not. There were many disagreements about purity, and the two main parties within Pharisaism (the Shammaites and Hillelites) disagreed over menstrual impurity, a much more serious matter than hand washing.

One statement in particular does oppose Jewish law as universally understood. All Jews agreed on a long list of prohibited foods, including pork and shellfish (cf. Lev. 11; Deut. 14), which set them apart from other people. According to Mark 7:19 Jesus "declared all foods clean," which directly opposed the law of God as given to Moses. However, this is not in the parallel passage in Matt. 15, and Peter seems to have learned it first after Jesus' death, by means of a heavenly revelation (Acts 10:9-16). Jesus did not, then, directly oppose any aspect of the sacred law.

He probably did, however, have legal disputes, in which he defended himself by quoting scriptural precedent, which would mean that he had not set himself against the law (e.g., Mark 2:23-28). However, Jesus was *autonomous;* he made his own rules with regard to how to observe the law, and he decided how to defend himself when criticized. Ordinarily legal debates were between competing camps or schools. Jesus was by no means the only person in ancient Judaism who struck out on his own, acting in accord with his own perception of God's will, and so he was not uniquely troubling in this respect, but such behavior might nevertheless be suspicious.

Ethics

Jesus demanded complete devotion to God, putting it far ahead of devotion to self and even to family (Mark 3:31-35; Matt. 10:35-37). People should be willing to give up everything in order to obtain what was most precious (Matt. 13:44-46). Observance of the law should be not only external but internal: hatred and lust, as well as murder and adultery, are wrong (Matt. 5:21-26, 27-30).

Miracles

Besides being a prophet and teacher, Jesus was also a healer and miracle worker. In the 1st century, healers and miracle workers were fairly well known, and were not considered superhuman beings. Jesus granted that others could also perform miracles, such as exorcisms, even if they did not follow him (Matt. 12:27; Mark 9:38-41; 6:7). Thus the significance of this very important aspect of his life is frequently misunderstood. In Jesus' own context, it was granted that various people could heal and perform nature miracles, such as causing rain. The question was, by what power, or spirit, they did so. Some of Jesus' opponents accused him of casting out demons by the prince of demons (Mark 3:19b-22; Matt. 12:24; Luke 11:18); he replied that he did so by the spirit of God (Matt. 12:28; Luke 11:20).

Controversy and Danger

Crowds and Autonomy

Jesus' reputation as healer had one very important historical consequence: he attracted crowds. This is the main theme of the early chapters of Mark (e.g., 1:28, 45; 2:2). Crowds meant that more people would hear his message, which was an advantage, but there were disadvantages. People who came hoping for cures often had only a selfish interest. Moreover, crowds were politically dangerous. One reason Herod Antipas executed John the Baptist was that he attracted such large crowds that Antipas feared an uprising (Josephus *Ant.* 18.5.2 [116-19]).

Jesus' message was not necessarily socially dangerous. The promise of future reversal might make some people uneasy, since it could be preliminary to social revolution, and Jesus' promise to sinners might irritate the scrupulous, but without crowds these aspects of his message would not matter much. He did not strike at the heart of the Jewish religion as such: he did not deny the election of Abraham and the requirement of circumcision; he did not denounce Moses and the law. Nevertheless, because Jesus was autonomous and therefore unpredictable, some people regarded him with hostility and suspicion.

Scribes and Pharisees

These were two largely distinct groups, though presumably some scribes were Pharisees. A scribe was someone who had legal knowledge and who drew up legal documents; every village had at least one scribe. Pharisees were members of a party who believed in resurrection and in following legal traditions that were ascribed not to the Bible but to the fathers or elders of their own party. They were also well-known legal experts, thus the partial overlap of scribes and Pharisees. It appears from subsequent rabbinic traditions, however, that most Pharisees were small landowners and tradesmen, not professional scribes.

In Mark's view, Jesus' main disputants in Galilee were scribes; according to Matthew they were Pharisees. One may accept this apparently conflicting evidence as at least generally accurate: people knowledgeable about Jewish law and tradition would have scrutinized Jesus carefully, and they doubtless sometimes challenged his behavior and teaching (e.g., Mark 2:6, 16; 3:22; Matt. 9:11; 12:2). According to Matt. 12:14; Mark 3:6 the Pharisees (Mark adds "with the Herodians") planned to destroy Jesus. If this plot was actually hatched, however, it seems that nothing came of it, since the Pharisees did not play a significant role in the events that led to Jesus' death. Only one passage in Matthew, none in Mark and Luke, gives them any role at all (Matt. 27:62).

Put another way, some people in Galilee may have distrusted Jesus, but he was never charged formally with disregard of the law, and opposition in Galilee did not lead to his death.

Jesus' Last Week

In ca. the year 30 Jesus and his disciples went to Jerusalem from Galilee to observe Passover. He presumably went a week early, as did perhaps as many as 200 or 300 thousand other Jews, in order to be purified of corpse-impurity (Num. 9:10-12; 19:1-22). The Gospels do not mention purification, but they do place Jesus in the vicinity of the temple in the days preceding Passover. Jesus entered Jerusalem on a donkey, perhaps himself intending to recall Zech. 9:9 (Matt. 21:4-5). This touched off a demonstration by his followers, who hailed him as either "Son of David" (Matt. 21:9) or "the one who comes in the name of the Lord" (Mark 11:9). Jerusalem at Passover was dangerous; it was well known to both the high priest (Caiaphas), who governed the city, and the Roman prefect (Pilate), to whom the high priest was responsible and who would intervene in case of trouble, that the festivals were likely times of uprisings. The prefect, who ordinarily lived in Caesarea, came to Jerusalem during the festivals with his troops, who patrolled the roofs of the temple porticoes. A large demonstration would probably have led to Jesus' immediate arrest. From the fact that he lived for several more days, we may infer that the crowd was relatively small.

Jesus spent some time teaching and debating (Mark 12), and told his disciples that the temple would be destroyed (13:1-2). On one of these days of purification prior to the Passover sacrifice and meal, he performed his most dramatic symbolic action. He entered the part of the temple precincts where worshippers exchanged their coins to pay the annual temple tax of two drachmas and also bought pigeons to sacrifice. Jesus turned over some of the tables (Mark 11:15-19), an action that led "the chief priests and the scribes" (Luke adds "and the principal men of the people") to plan to have him executed (Mark 11:18; Luke 19:47; cf. Mark 14:1-2 par.).

The disciples found a room for the Passover meal, and one of them bought an animal and sacrificed it in the temple (Mark 14:12-16). At the meal, Jesus blessed the bread and wine, designating the bread "my body" and the wine "the blood of the covenant" or "the new covenant in my blood" (Mark 14:22-25; the variant is in Luke 22:20; 1 Cor. 11:25).

After supper, Jesus took his disciples to the Mount of Olives to pray. While there, Judas led armed men, sent by the chief priests, who arrested him (Mark 14:43-52). Jesus was taken to the high priest, who had gathered some of his councillors (called collectively "the Sanhedrin"). He was first accused of threatening to destroy the temple, but this charge was not upheld. The high priest asked him if he were "the Christ, the Son of God." According to Mark he said "yes" and then predicted the arrival of the Son of Man. According to Matthew, he said, "You say so, *but* I tell you that you will see the Son of Man," apparently implying a negative answer to the question. According to Luke he was more ambiguous: "If I tell you, you will not believe" and "You say that I am" (Mark 14:61-62; Matt. 26:63-64; Luke 22:67-70).

Whatever the charge, the high priest had evidently already decided that Jesus had to die, and he cried "blasphemy" and rent his garments, a dramatic sign of mourning that the Bible prohibits the high priest from making (Lev. 21:10). The councillors agreed that Jesus should be sent to Pilate with the recommendation to execute him.

It is doubtful that titles were actually the issue. As Mark (followed by Matthew and generally by Luke) presents the scene, the first attempt was to have Jesus executed for threatening the temple. That did not work, and so Caiaphas employed a ruse and simply declared whatever Jesus said (about which we must remain uncertain) to be blasphemy.

Pilate did not care about the fine points of Jewish law. To him, Jesus was a potential trouble-maker, and he ordered his execution. Matthew, Luke, and John give Pilate a rather good character and show him as troubled over the decision, but yielding to Jewish insistence (Matt. 27:11-26; Luke 23:1-25; John 18:28-40). This reflects the fact that the early Church had to make its way in the Roman Empire, and did not wish its leader to be thought of as truly guilty in Roman eyes. Pilate is known from other evidence to have been callous, cruel, and given to wanton executions (Philo *Leg.* 38.302). He was finally dismissed from office for executing a group of Samaritans (Josephus *Ant.* 18.4.1-2 [85-89]). Probably he sent Jesus to his death without anguishing over the decision very much.

Jesus was crucified as would-be "king of the Jews" (Mark 15:26 par.). On the cross, he was taunted as the one who would destroy the temple (Mark 15:29). These two charges explain the decision to execute him. His own thinking was almost certainly that God would destroy the temple as part of the new kingdom, perhaps rebuilding it himself (Mark 14:58; cf. 11QT 29.8-10). Caiaphas and his advisors probably understood Jesus well enough: they knew that he was a prophet and that his small band could not damage the temple seriously. But Jesus had made a minor assault on the temple, and predicted its destruction. These were inflammatory acts in a city that, at festival time, was prone to uprisings. The high priest, under Roman rule, had the responsibility to keep the peace, and he and his advisors acted accordingly (cf. John 11:50).

Jesus' preaching of "the kingdom of God" was also potentially inflammatory. The phrase could have various meanings, but it certainly did not mean that Rome would continue to govern Judea. Many people resented Roman rule, and Rome was quick to dispatch people who became too vocal. Pilate did not think that Jesus and his followers constituted a military threat. Had he thought so, he would have had the disciples executed, either at the time or later, when they returned to Jerusalem to take up their new mission.

Thus no one thought that Jesus could actually destroy the temple, nor that he could create a serious revolt in favor of a new kingdom. Nevertheless, inflammatory speech was dangerous, Jesus had a following, the city was packed with pilgrims, who were celebrating the Exodus from Egypt and Israel's liberation from foreign bondage, and Jesus had committed a small act of violence in the sacred precincts. He was executed for being what he was: an eschatological prophet.

Jesus thought the kingdom was at hand and that he and his disciples would soon feast in it. It is possible that even to the end he expected divine intervention (cf. Mark 15:34).

The Resurrection

What happened next changed history in a way quite different from what Jesus seems to have anticipated. He appeared to some of his followers after his death. The details are uncertain, since our sources disagree on the people who saw him and the places of his appearances (cf. the final sections of Matthew, Luke, and John; the beginning of Acts; and Paul's list of appearances in 1 Cor. 15:3-9). According to Matthew, an angel showed Mary Magdalene and "the other Mary" the empty tomb, and told them to tell the disciples to go to Galilee. While still in Jerusalem, they saw Jesus, who told them the same thing. Jesus appeared just once more, to the disciples in Galilee. Matthew's account is basically implied in Mark (Mark 14:28; 16:7), though Mark lacks a Resurrection story, ending with the empty tomb. According to Luke, however, the disciples never left Jerusalem and environs. The women (Mary Magdalene, Joanna, Mary the mother of James, and "the other women") found the empty tomb. "Two men in dazzling clothes" told them that Jesus had been raised. Later, Jesus appeared to two followers on the road to Emmaus, then to Peter, then the disciples. John (including ch. 21, usually thought to be an "appendix") combines appearances in Galilee and Jerusalem. Acts, though written by the same author, has a more extended series of appearances than Luke, but like Luke places all the appearances in or near Jerusalem. Paul's long list of people to whom Jesus appeared does not agree very closely with the other accounts.

Faced with such evidence, we can hardly say "what really happened." Two points are important: (1) The sources wish to describe the resurrected Jesus as neither a resuscitated corpse, a badly wounded man staggering around, nor as a ghost. According to Luke, the first two disciples to see Jesus walked with him for several hours without recognizing him (Luke 24:13-32). He could also disappear and reappear at will (Luke 24:31, 36). According to Paul, the bodies of Christian believers will be transformed to be like the Lord's, and the resurrection body will not be "flesh and blood" (1 Cor. 15:42-53). Although substantially transformed, Jesus was not a ghost. Luke says this explicitly (Luke 24:37-39), and Paul insists on "body," choosing the term "spiritual body" rather than "spirit" or "ghost" (both Gk. *pneúma*). The authors, in other words, were trying to explain something for which they did not have a precise vocabulary.

(2) It is difficult to accuse our sources, or the first believers, of deliberate fraud. A plot to foster belief in the Resurrection would probably have resulted in a more consistent story. (We seem, instead, to have competition: "I saw him," "so did I," "the woman saw him first," "no, I did; they didn't see him at all"). Some of the witnesses of the Resurrection would give their lives for their belief, which makes fraud unlikely.

The uncertainties are substantial, but, given the accounts in our sources, certainty is unobtainable. We may say of the disciples' experiences of the Resurrection approximately what the sources allow us to say of the life and message of Jesus: we have fairly good general knowledge, though many details are uncertain or open to question.

See CHRIST.

Bibliography. M. Borg, *Jesus: A New Vision* (San Francisco, 1987); G. Bornkamm, *Jesus of Nazareth* (1960, repr. Minneapolis, 1995); J. D. Crossan, *The Historical Jesus: The Life of a Mediterranean Jewish Peasant* (San Francisco, 1991); J. P. Meier, *A Marginal Jew,* 3 vols. (New York, 1991-); E. P. Sanders, *The Historical Figure of Jesus* (London, 1993); *Jesus and Judaism* (Philadelphia, 1985); *Jewish Law from Jesus to the Mishnah* (Philadelphia, 1990); A. Schweitzer, *The Quest of the Historical Jesus* (1910, repr. New York, 1968); G. Vermes, *Jesus the Jew* (1973, repr. Philadelphia, 1981); *The Religion of Jesus the Jew* (Minneapolis, 1993); N. T. Wright, *Christian Origins and the Question of God, 2: Jesus and the Victory of God* (Minneapolis, 1996).

E. P. SANDERS

JESUS CHRIST, WISDOM OF (III, 4; BG, 3)
A Nag Hammadi tractate commonly known as the Sophia of Jesus Christ. It contains a revelation dialogue between Jesus and his disciples (the Twelve and seven women) set on a Galilean mountain after the Resurrection. Together with Eugnostos the Blessed, a non-Christian revelation dialogue cast in the form of a letter (and the major source of this tractate), it provides a dramatic example of how ancient texts were revised for new purposes. The Wisdom of Jesus Christ was probably written to non-Christian Gnostics to encourage them to accept Christ as the ultimate Revealer of Gnosis. While an Egyptian provenance has general acceptance, the text has been widely dated from the late 1st to the early 4th century C.E.

Bibliography. D. M. Parrott, ed., *Nag Hammadi Codices III,3-4 and V,1.* NHS 27 (Leiden, 1991).

ANDREA LORENZO MOLINARI

JETHER (Heb. *yeṯer*) (also ITHRA)

1. The firstborn son of Gideon (Judg. 8:20). His father ordered him to kill the Midianites Zebah and Zalmunna as vengeance, but the youthful Jether was afraid to comply.

2. The father of Absalom's commander Amasa (1 Kgs. 2:5, 32), an Ishmaelite (1 Chr. 2:17). At 2 Sam. 17:25 he is called Ithra "the Ishmaelite" (MT "Israelite"; so NRSV mg).

3. A son of Jada and descendant of Jerahmeel (1 Chr. 2:32). He died childless.

4. A son of Ezrah, from the tribe of Judah (1 Chr. 4:17).

5. An Asherite (1 Chr. 7:38), apparently identical to Ithran the son of Zophah in v. 37.

JETHETH (Heb. *yĕṯēṯ*)
A descendant of Esau; a chief and eponymous ancestor of an Edomite clan (Gen. 36:40; 1 Chr. 1:51). Jether or Ithran may be the intended form.

JETHRO (Heb. *yiṯrô*)
A priest in Midian and father-in-law of Moses (Exod. 3:1; 4:18). During his flight from Egypt Moses took refuge with Jethro in Midian. Upon hearing that Moses had defended his daughter Zipporah at the well, Jethro invited Moses into his household and gave him his daughter as a wife (Exod. 2:15-21).

Jethro is also known in the OT by the related form Jether (Exod. 4:18 MT), and as Reuel (2:18) and Hobab (Judg. 4:11). The connection with the names Reuel and Hobab is unclear (cf. Num. 10:29). Scholars are divided as to whether Hobab was the son of Moses' father-in-law, or if Reuel was the father of Moses' father-in-law. Source theory attributes Jethro to E and Reuel/Hobab to J. Other scholars attempt to distinguish three different people, try to establish different tribal names or titles for each individual, or interpret Reuel as a clan name for both Reuel and Hobab.

It is unclear which god Jethro served at Midian. Some scholars contend that Yahweh was unknown to Israel prior to Moses' encounter with the burning bush on the mountain of God in Midian (cf. Exod. 6:3) and that Jethro thus introduced the worship of Yahweh to Israel; Exod. 18 is interpreted as the initiation of Aaron and the elders into the cult. It is further postulated that, given the later antagonism between Midian and Israel, the text was revised to disassociate Yahweh from Midian. However, the majority of Jewish and Christian tradition and scholarship sees Jethro as a convert to Yahwism (cf. Exod. 18:11), although the nature of his conversion is debated.

Bibliography. W. F. Albright, "Jethro, Hobab and Reuel in Early Hebrew Tradition," *CBQ* 25 (1963): 1-11; B. Mazar, "The Sanctuary of Arad and the Family of Hobab the Kenite," *JNES* 24 (1965): 297-303.
CHERYL LYNN HUBBARD

JETUR (Heb. *yĕṭûr*)
A son of Ishmael (Gen. 25:15 = 1 Chr. 1:31). He was eponymous ancestor of the Ituraeans, one of the peoples against whom the Transjordanian tribes of Israel made war (1 Chr. 5:19; cf. LXX).

JEUEL (Heb. *yĕʿû'ēl*)

1. The head of a father's house of Zerah of the tribe of Judah; a clan listed among the returning exiles who settled in Jerusalem (1 Chr. 9:6).

2. A Levite of the sons of Elizaphan; one of 14 who cleansed the temple during Hezekiah's renewal (2 Chr. 29:13; probably to be read Jeiel, following **Q**).

3. A son of Adonikam, named among those accompanying Ezra to Jerusalem (Ezra 8:13; 1 Esdr. 8:39). The name should probably be read Jeiel, following LXX and most MSS.

JEUSH (Heb. *yĕʿûš*)

1. A son of Esau and Oholibamah; an Edomite chief (Gen. 36:5, 14 [**K** *yĕʿîš*], 18; 1 Chr. 1:35).

2. A son of Bilhan, a "mighty warrior" from the tribe of Benjamin (1 Chr. 7:10; **K** *yĕʿîš*).

3. A Benjaminite, the second son of Eshek and descendant of Saul (1 Chr. 8:39).

4. A Gershonite Levite, the son of Shimei (1 Chr. 23:10). Because he had only a few sons, his family was reckoned with that of Beriah as one father's house (1 Chr. 23:11).

5. A son of Rehoboam and Mahalath (2 Chr. 11:19).

JEUZ (Heb. *yĕʿûṣ*)
A son of Shaharaim; head of a Benjaminite father's house (1 Chr. 8:10).

JEWELRY
In the Bible, adornments are more often described as individual pieces than referred to collectively. Isa. 3:18-23 is a catalogue of jewelry including anklets, headbands, crescents, pendants, bracelets, armlets, amulets, signet rings and nose rings, as well as other items broadly classed as ornamentation. Additional pieces include necklaces (Cant. 4:9), rings (Hos. 2:13[MT 15]), earrings (Judg. 8:25), chains (Ezek. 16:11), and beads (Num. 31:50). Most of these have been found in the archaeological record, though the beads and pendants that comprised necklaces and bracelets are most common. In biblical citations, jewelry was usually made of gold, silver, and bronze. In the archaeological record, however, materials are much more diverse. Copper and bronze are more common than either gold or silver, and glass, faience, precious and semiprecious stones, shell, seeds, bone, and ivory were also fashioned into jewelry. More finely worked and rarer materials are associated with the elites, while the less wealthy apparently used the cheaper mediums as substitutes for the more expensive originals — e.g., blue glass to imitate lapis lazuli.

Evidence for the production of jewelry comes from figurative remains, tools, and the pieces of jewelry themselves. Exod. 35:30-33 states that God gave members of the tribe of Judah the skills of gold-, silver-, and bronze-working and of stone-setting, and scholars have sometimes attributed the arrival of iron-working to the Israelites. However, these technologies are also common in other regions and periods. The retrieval and working of raw materials and the finished products are displayed in the Old Kingdom mastaba of Mereruka at Saqqâra in Egypt, and an 18th-century B.C.E. sealed jar at Larsa in Mesopotamia held the tools, scrap, and metals of a jeweler. In addition, traces of flax fibers used to hang beads and pendants have been found within their stringing holes. Ancient metalworkers were familiar with manipulating pure ores and with alloying different elements to produce the desired outcome. The results are heterogeneous in form; hundreds of beads had already been classified in the 1920s. Molds for many of these shapes have been found in Palestine.

In biblical references, jewelry is considered valuable. Precious stones and pieces of jewelry are given to brides by the groom and his representatives (Gen. 24:22), brought as gifts to shrines (Num. 31:50) and kings (1 Kgs. 10:10), and are part of an inheritance (2 Chr. 21:3). Jewels are stored in the royal treasury (2 Chr. 32:27), "precious things" are taken as spoils of war (20:25), and jewelry may even have been given as tribute (cf. reliefs in Assurbanipal's palace). Archaeological evidence corroborates jewelry's worth since it is often found buried in hoards under floors. This value is connected both with the workmanship involved in producing intricate jewelry and with the cost of the materials used. Many are obtained from long distances and therefore jewelry can illuminate networks of communication and trade (cf. Ezek. 27:22): Mediterranean shells are found far inland, while the lapis lazuli of Afghanistan and the gold of sub-Saharan Africa were prized in Mesopotamia, the Levant, and Egypt. Designs that originated in one area were also widespread especially in the Late Bronze Age when internationalism caused similar styles throughout the eastern Mediterranean.

Though different types of jewelry were utilized by different social classes, biblical references to jewelry of precious metals and stones are associated with the nobility and royalty, while specific items were indicative of rank: e.g., for royalty, the armlet (2 Sam. 1:10); for priesthood, the ephod and breastplate (Exod. 28:6-30); for official power, the signet ring (Gen. 41:41-42). The connection between jewelry and social status and power is reflected in the locations of different types in the archaeological record. An analysis of LB pendants, e.g., has shown that differing classes are found according to temple, burial, and residential contexts at sites such as Megiddo and Tel Kitan (2043.2270). Of particular note in terms of religious influence are the amulets and Astarte pendants worn around the neck and waist and thought to have fertility powers, and the association of crescents, stars, and other solar images with Bronze and Iron Age cultic practices.

Jewelry is also used metaphorically to describe things of value and importance. Israel's people are described as "sacred stones . . . worth their weight in fine gold" (Lam. 4:1-2) at the time of the final siege of Jerusalem. Similarly, the 12 stones of the priest's ephod — all of which were said to have been in Eden (Ezek. 28:13) — represented the tribes of Israel (Exod. 28:17-21). Articles of jewelry are given by God to Israel, compared to an adulterous wife (Ezek. 16:11-12). Jewels are also metaphors for beauty (Cant. 5:14; 7:1). The value of jewels is not limitless, however: though knowledge is like a jewel (Prov. 20:15), real wisdom is considered to be even more precious (3:13-15; 8:11).

Bibliography. H. C. Beck, "Classification and Nomenclature of Beads and Pendants," *Archaeologia* 77 (1927); P. E. McGovern, *Late Bronze Palestinian Pendants.* JSOT/ASORMS 1 (Sheffield, 1986); K. R. Maxwell-Hyslop, *Western Asiatic Jewellery c. 3000-612 B.C.* (London, 1971); J. Ogden, *Ancient Jewellery* (Berkeley, 1992); E. E. Platt, "Jewelry of Bible Times and the Catalog of Isa 3:18-23," *AUSS* 17 (1979): 71-84, 189-201.

Katharine A. Mackay

JEWELS

See Gems.

JEWISH CHRISTIANS

The original core of a reform movement within Judaism that later emerged as a separate religion known as Christianity. Owing to the dynamics and changes within this process, scholarship has struggled to find a historically acceptable definition of Jewish Christianity. At one extreme, some have focused on all sorts of early Christian thought expressed in forms borrowed from Judaism (Jean Daniélou). At the other extreme, some have preferred to use "Jewish Christian" only for the movement's radical wing that refused to accept Gentile Christians (Hans Joachim Schoeps). The following definition allows room for diversity and development.

"Earliest Jewish Christianity" is equivalent to the body of Jews who soon confessed Jesus as a venerable person or as the messiah and thus to all of earliest Christianity. Earliest Christianity contained various underdeveloped points of view on the precise nature of Christianity.

"Early Jewish Christianity" stands for but one development out of earliest Christianity. Its characteristics are: (1) confession of Christ; (2) Jewish observance (when relevant, to a degree that separated it from the evolving Great Church, particularly including one or more of the following elements: observance of the sabbath, observance of the Jewish calendar, observance of the commands regarding sexual purity, observance of circumcision, and attendance at a synagogue); and (3) some sort of direct genetic relationship to earliest Jewish Christianity.

Part of the problem in defining early Jewish Christianity is that, as is evident from Paul's letters, the early Christians did not universally adopt a single name for themselves. One of the more widespread names was Nazoreans ("observers"). This designation was preserved among the Jewish Christians, and indeed among all Aramaic Christians, for a long period. Other self-designations for the Jewish Christians were Ebionites ("the poor") and Sampsaeans ("servants [of God]").

Sources

Paul's letters are the most important source for the earliest history of Jewish Christianity. No Jewish Christian writing has been preserved intact. While thus none of the writings of the NT are Jewish Christian in their present form, Jewish Christian sources were used in Matthew, and a stage of Q must be seen as Jewish Christian. Mark also has used traditions ultimately deriving from Jewish Christianity. Acts, however, should be used with much greater caution than has been usual in NT and early Christian studies.

Outside the NT, Jewish Christian writings have

survived in fragments. The bulk of this information is found in the patristic writers, particularly in Justin Martyr, Hegesippus, the Didascalia, and the heresiologists. There are remnants of three gospels, a Jewish Christian "acts of the apostles" found in Pseudo-Clementine *Recognitions* 1.27-71, other portions of the Pseudo-Clementines, the anti-Pauline Ascents of James, and the Book of Elchasai. Jewish Christian traditions have perhaps also been preserved in a layer of the Gospel of Thomas. While the recently recovered Greek biography of Mani adds some further information and confirms that Mani grew up as a Jewish Christian, it is doubtful whether Arabic writers have preserved any other genuine traditions.

History

The history of Jewish Christianity begins with the disciples of Jesus, who doubtless spoke Aramaic. After Jesus' death, his message was continued by his disciples in Galilee and Judea, and the memory of Jesus was venerated. Wandering charismatics traveled north, east, west (Corinth), and perhaps also south (Egypt). Jerusalem soon asserted itself as the center of the movement under the leadership of "the pillars": the apostles John, Peter, and particularly James "the Just," a brother of Jesus. An attempt was made to integrate the rising Gentile Christianity (the "collection," and a mission to correct Pauline congregations). In 62 C.E. the Sanhedrin, under the leadership of the high priest Annas, executed James for transgression of the law. Simeon, a son of Jesus' uncle Clopas, then headed up the scattered Jerusalem community, while grandsons of Jude also came to be acknowledged as authorities.

Jewish Christians continued gradually spreading among the Aramaic-speaking East. The destruction associated with the First Jewish Revolt against Rome contributed further to the disarray among the Palestinian Jewish Christians and to the dissolution of bonds with the evolving Gentile Christianity. Rabbinic Judaism institutionalized its rejection of the Jewish Christians by adding a curse of the "Nazoreans" to a synagogal prayer. In Jerusalem, Jewish Christian dominance of the church ended with the foundation of Aelia Capitolina after the Second Jewish Revolt. Elsewhere in Palestine, Syria, the Transjordan, and upper Mesopotamia, Jewish Christians survived in pockets through the end of the 4th century. The diversity among the Jewish Christians, at all periods, should not be underestimated.

Bibliography. J. Daniélou, *A History of Early Christian Doctrine before the Council of Nicaea,* 1 (Philadelphia, 1964); F. S. Jones, *An Ancient Jewish Christian Source on the History of Christianity.* Texts and Translations 37. Christian Apocrypha 2 (Atlanta, 1995); A. F. J. Klijn and G. J. Reinink, *Patristic Evidence for Jewish-Christian Sects.* NovTSup 36 (Leiden, 1973); H. J. Schoeps, *Jewish Christianity: Factional Disputes in the Early Church* (Philadelphia, 1969); M. Simon, *Verus Israel: A Study of the Relations between Christians and Jews in the Roman Empire (135-425)* (Oxford, 1986).

F. STANLEY JONES

JEWISH REVOLTS

Throughout history those people under the subjugation of others will normally revolt to throw off their oppressors when possible. The Jewish people were under the domination of one of the great Near Eastern powers through much of their history, even during the period of the Israelite monarchy. First, the Assyrians extended their empire into the Palestinian area even as early as the mid-9th century B.C.E., and the kingdom of Judah was under Assyrian control from ca. 735. In the late 6th century, Assyrian overlordship was replaced by Neo-Babylonian. It was Zedekiah's revolt against this rule which led to the destruction of Jerusalem and the Jewish state. Under Persian rule Judah became a province in the Persian Empire with some sort of Jewish local autonomy. We know of no revolts under the Persians, though it has been suggested that a hypothesized widespread revolt ca. 350 (the so-called Tennes rebellion) also included the Jews.

Greek rule replaced that of the Persians in 333. The next 500 years saw three major revolts of the Jews against their overlords. During the 3rd century Judah was under Ptolemaic rule, and to the best of our knowledge the Jews were peaceful. Things changed under Seleucid rule when the Maccabean Revolt became possibly the first Jewish revolt since the time of the Monarchy. This is described in the books of 1-2 Maccabees, from which comes most of our information on the subject. The causes of the Maccabean uprising have been much debated without a clear consensus; what does seem clear, however, is that it was a reaction to suppression of Jewish worship. In other words, according to all the information currently available, the Jews were forced into revolt to protect their religion. A struggle over the high priesthood in Jerusalem was partially to blame, however.

When Antiochus IV was driven back from his invasion of Egypt in the summer of 168, the former high priest Jason attempted to wrest back the office from the current holder Menelaus (2 Macc. 5). Antiochus thought a revolt had broken out and sent an army to put it down. A subsequent series of events, as yet unclarified and unexplained, led to the halting of the Jewish cult and the desecration of the temple in December 168 (some put it a year later). The Jewish reaction was a heroic resistance and struggle to regain the temple and reinstate the daily sacrifices. The Jews succeeded in December 165 when the temple was once again in Jewish hands and a purified cult renewed (1 Macc. 4:36-59). Antiochus accepted the de facto situation and officially withdrew the decree forbidding Judaism (2 Macc. 11:27-33).

Most of the Jews seem to have accepted the reinstatement of their religious rights as sufficient to resume their peaceable existence as a subject people under Seleucid rule, but not the Maccabees, who continued their resistance. For the next decade, especially after the death of Judas ca. 161, they seem to have had little backing and lived much as outlaws, but gradually they began to gain support. Their real opportunity came when a rival Seleucid dynasty arose to challenge the "official" one. Jonathan Maccabeus began to play one side against another to gain advantages for himself and the Jewish people. It was a dangerous game in which he eventually lost his life, but by this time he had obtained some important concessions from the Seleucids. His brother Simon continued this exercise, and Judah was officially declared independent in 140. The Seleucids did not give up their claims immediately, of course, but for almost a century Judah was, uniquely in greater Syria, a more or less independent state.

Hasmonean rule ended in 63 B.C.E. when Judah came under Roman control. Aristobulus II or his sons attempted several revolts to regain the Hasmonean throne. However, Herod became king in 40 B.C.E. and consolidated his rule by taking Jerusalem in 37. After this, Judea continued as a "client kingdom" under Herod and some of his descendants, or as a Roman province, until 66 C.E. It was a foolish conceit that they could succeed, but the Jews put up a courageous, if poorly organized, defense against the might of the Roman Empire. The causes of revolt in 66 C.E. were many: Jewish memory of their previous independence, a series of poor Roman governors, and — apparently — a strong set of apocalyptic expectations on the part of some.

No one event set off this revolt, but rather a series of events in Jerusalem, Caesarea, and elsewhere. One of the main symbolic events was the withdrawal of sacrifice for the Roman emperor on the order of the temple officer in Jerusalem. A legion sent to put down the unrest in Jerusalem was driven off, and the Roman garrison there was slaughtered. Now the Romans had to defend their authority: there could be no compromise when an eagle (the symbolic "flag" or emblem of a legion) had been taken — there could only be revenge. The Jews had some time to prepare their defense, and they set up a series of regional governors. One of those in Galilee was Josephus. His personal account of the war (his *Jewish War,* esp. books 3-6) is extremely valuable, if partisan and apologetic.

Josephus' story exemplifies one of the main problems with the revolt, that of rivalry between various Jewish leaders and groups. Much of the energy of the fighters was expended in conflicts with fellow Jews. Josephus spent a good deal of the year in Galilee struggling politically and militarily with other Jewish leaders, especially John of Gischala. Similarly, a variety of Jewish factions (the Zealots and others) in Jerusalem fought with and slaughtered one another, instead of preparing a concerted plan of resistance, until the Romans laid siege to the city. At this point, they fought like lions, but it was far too late and Jerusalem fell in the summer of 70 C.E., marking the official end of the war. However, a few fortress outposts such as Machaeus and Masada held out, and it took another three years to defeat them.

One might have thought that such a major defeat would have ended Jewish resistance to Roman rule, but it did not. It is not clear how damaged by the war the country as a whole had been, though estimates differ. Apart from Jerusalem, the rest of the country may have recovered fairly quickly. During this time there was religious reconstruction in an academy set up at Yavneh. But the continued absence of the temple cult and the ruined temple were a considerable theological problem to many, as evidenced by 4 Ezra (2 Esdras) and 2 Baruch which (like the NT book of Revelation) expected the imminent end of the Roman Empire. In the period 115-117 Jewish revolts broke out in several places: Egypt, Cyrenaica, Mesopotamia, Cyprus. We know little about these except that they seem to have been very bloody, initially pitting the Jews against the Gentiles; but then the Gentiles gained the upper hand and slaughtered the Jewish communities in Alexandria and elsewhere. The Jews in Palestine seem not to have been affected, though some speculate that even they were in some way involved.

The final Jewish effort to break the Roman yoke came in the Bar Kokhba Revolt of 132-135. The exact causes are debated, though there is evidence that Hadrian intended to restore Jerusalem, perhaps as a pagan city. Since Josephus recorded no details of the revolt, the outline of what happened has had to be pieced together from fragmented sources of varying quality. The revolt was led by Shim'on ben Kosiba, who went by the name of Bar Kokhba (Aram. "son of the star"), though a priest by the name of Eleazar (possibly his uncle) occurs on some coin legends. There is no clear evidence that Jersualem was taken by the rebels, though some think it was. Most of the land held seems to have been SE of Jerusalem in the region centering on En-gedi and W of the Dead Sea. Rabbinic and Christian sources say Bar Kokhba claimed or was declared to be the Messiah, but original letters show no evidence of this. Coin symbols are ambiguous. The country and its Jewish population suffered terribly, though so did the Roman army according to the Roman historian Dio Cassius. This ended all hope of Jewish independence for almost two millennia.

Bibliography. L. L. Grabbe, *Judaism from Cyrus to Hadrian,* 1: *Persian and Greek Periods;* 2: *Roman Period* (Minneapolis, 1992). LESTER L. GRABBE

JEWS, JUDAISM

The roughly 600-year Second Temple period is framed by the destruction of the First Temple (to be rebuilt ca. 520-515 B.C.E.) and the Babylonian Exile of 586, on the one side, and the destruction of the Second Temple in the course of a Jewish revolt against Rome in 66-73 C.E., on the other. This period witnesses the appearance of diverse Judaisms — worldviews and ways of life believed to represent God's will for the Jewish people and competing with each other for individual Jews' loyalty. Accordingly, the designation "Second Temple Judaism" is misleading, there being no single form of Judaism practiced by all Jews in this period. Still, Jewish history in this period is unified by the advent of broad social, religious, and political characteristics distinct from those of prior periods and also quite different from the modes of Jewish identity and practice that emerged after the destruction of the Second Temple. While not defining a single, unitary Judaism, the Second Temple period accordingly warrants treatment as a distinctive era, a consequential stage in the evolution of Jewish civilization.

The central feature of this period was the creation, as a result of the Babylonian Exile, of a polarity between Judaism's center, which, as in biblical times, remained Jerusalem, and the ever increasing plurality of areas of Jewish life in the Diaspora. While Jews continued to turn to Jerusalem as a spiritual center representing Jewish unity, most now chose to live and worship far from the biblical Promised Land. Thus, even as the temple and its cult continued to constitute the preeminent focus of Jewish religiosity, for most Jews the temple was no more than a distant ideal, a metaphor for Jewish peoplehood as they developed distinctive cultures in diverse areas far from the Holy Land.

Alongside the creation of the Diaspora, a second pivotal feature of the Second Temple period was that, with the exception of a brief period of Hasmonean rule, even Jews who lived in the land of Israel would now be governed by foreigners. To be sure, a gentile ruler might appoint a Jewish administrator to govern the Jews under Jewish law. Accordingly, it appears to be in this period that just such a law — the written Torah first evident in the time of Ezra — was produced. But even such home rule could not hide the reality of foreign domination or the fact that Jewish life was now to be shaped not by a distinctive Israelite culture but by the dominant culture of Hellenism, within which Jews in the land, just like those in the Diaspora, made their lives. Even as temple worship and limited governance under Jewish law continued, life for Jews even in the Holy Land was not what it had been before the Exile. Jews themselves began to recognize that biblical Judaism and the sacred history of the chosen people in the Promised Land had come to an end. This is explicit, e.g., in the book of Sirach, composed in Jerusalem ca. 190 B.C.E., which lists the Persian Jewish governor Nehemiah (538-532) as the last of the historical heroes of Judaism.

The Second Temple period's end point, the destruction of the Jerusalem temple in 70 C.E. and the Bar Kokhba Revolt of 133-135, made clear that the period's central features — diaspora, loss of sovereignty, the growing irrelevance of the temple-cult — would become permanent aspects of the Jewish condition. The beginning of this period had taught Jews to live as Jews far from their national homeland. The end of the period made firm the message to which many had begun to respond even while the temple stood: Jews would need now to worship God and practice Judaism without the priestly service and with no expectation of an immediate return of Israelite sovereignty over the land. These facts, not surprisingly, stand at the foundation of the rabbinic Judaism that arises at the end of the Second Temple period and that, in the subsequent 500 years, becomes the dominant mode of Judaism practiced by all Jews.

Little is known of the religious practices and beliefs of the Jews at the beginning of Second Temple times, in the 5th through 3rd centuries. But that this period yielded consequential developments from the Judaism of the late First Temple period is evident from the more numerous Jewish sources of the 2nd century. These depict previously unknown political institutions and leaders: the council of elders *(gerousia),* the Sanhedrin, and the sage, later called rabbi. They reveal the existence of an important new religious, social, and cultural institution, the synagogue, and depict innovative religious practices, including the use of the ritual bath *(mikveh),* new burial customs, and the institution of conversion. A variety of new sectarian religious and political groups also appear: Hasidim, Zealots, Sicarii, Pharisees, Sadducees, Essenes, among others. With these groups innovative religious ideas emerge, including, among Pharisees and Essenes, the concept of resurrection. Here we also first find the concept of canon paramount in later Judaism, which defines a three-part Written Torah (Pentateuch, Prophets, and Hagiographa) and holds that at Sinai God also transmitted to Moses an oral law that expanded and explicated the written law found in the Pentateuch.

Especially in the aftermath of the Bar Kokhba Revolt, the political and religious realities created by the Second Temple period led Jews to evaluate afresh who they were, what they believed, and how they would face an increasingly inhospitable world. At the heart of the dominant response to these questions was the recognition prompted by the ruinous Bar Kokhba Revolt, the end point of five centuries of struggles to regain control of the Holy Land, that the Jewish people were not well served by following ambitious political leaders who insisted upon military means to fulfill the biblical promise of a sovereign Jewish nation worshipping in a Jerusalem temple. The preceding centuries of nationalistic revolts had ended in the almost complete destruction of Jewish life in the Promised Land. Jews were better off now accepting Roman political domination and developing modes of piety independent of priestly and nationalistic aspirations.

The rabbinic Judaism that emerged in these centuries thus grew out of conflicting interests. On the one hand, the idea of Promised Land and the model of the temple-cult, central in Scripture, would remain primary. As a result, under rabbinic leadership, Jews prayed for the end of the Exile, the rebuilding of the temple, and the re-establishment of animal sacrifice. At the same time, these goals no longer would be concrete political and military aspirations. Instead they came to evince the advent of the messianic age, to be brought about directly by God at some undisclosed future time. The rabbis thus refocused Jewish concern from the events of political history, far beyond the people's control, to events within the power of each person and family. What came to matter were the everyday details of life, the recurring actions that, day in and day out, defined life under God's law. How did each individual relate to family and community? By what ethic did people carry out their business dealings? How did they acknowledge the debt to God for food and for the wonders of the universe evidenced in the daily rising and setting of the sun?

By making such aspects of life the central focus of Judaism and by developing explicit applications of priestly laws for every Jewish home and table, the rabbis assured that what the temple and life as a sovereign nation in the land of Israel had represented — an economy of the sacred — would be actualized in the life of every Jewish family and village. Wherever they were, the people would live as a nation of priests, eating their common food as though it were a sacrifice on the temple's altar, seeing in their personal daily prayers and in their shared deeds of loving-kindness a replacement for the sacrifices no longer offered. In place of armed military action, this observance of the detailed system of ritual and communal law was now seen as the proper way to affect God, to lead God to act on the people's behalf, to bring about the perfection of history that would cause God, finally, to bring the messiah and redeem the nation.

Rabbinic Judaism thus made the powerful point that despite the loss of temple and land, God still exists, still rules over the people of Israel. Only for this reason did the Torah still matter at all, still need to be explicated and followed. But the God who once was directly active in the sphere of world history now was understood to respond quietly to the acts of common Jews who studied divine revelation, who led their lives in accordance with divine precepts, who ate their food as though their home table were the temple altar, and who lived their lives as a kingdom of priests. In this way, rabbinic Judaism put each individual at the center of creation — where the temple and Jerusalem had always been conceived to stand — and ascribed to him or her the power to impart to the world order and meaning.

This ideology was poignant. With the temple destroyed and the land defiled, the conduct of common Jews was all that remained to deny the events of history and to affirm God's lordship. Facing the devastating events of history that had brought to an end both the First and Second Temple periods, rabbinic Judaism insisted that common Jews had the power and obligation to create a new and better world, a world of holiness and sanctification, a world as they knew it should be, wished it to be, and, if they only worked hard enough, could assure that it someday would be.

Bibliography. E. J. Bickerman, *From Ezra to the Last of the Maccabees* (New York, 1962); L. I. Levine, "The Nature and Origin of the Palestinian Synagogue Reconsidered," *JBL* 115 (1996): 425-48; J. Neusner, *From Politics to Piety,* 2nd ed. (New York, 1979); L. Schiffman, *From Text to Tradition: A History of Second Temple and Rabbinic Judaism* (Hoboken, 1991).

ALAN J. AVERY-PECK

JEZANIAH (Heb. *yĕzanyāhû*)
(also JAAZANIAH)

1. A captain of Judah's army who joined the Babylonian governor Gedaliah at Mizpah following the fall of Jerusalem (Jer. 40:8). At 2 Kgs. 25:23 his name occurs as Jaazaniah (**1**).

2. A military commander; the son of Hoshaiah (Jer. 42:2 MT; NRSV "Azariah"). He is probably the same as Azariah (**25**) at Jer. 43:2, one of the "insolent men" who disagreed with Jeremiah's advice against fleeing to Egypt.

JEZEBEL (Heb. *'îzeḇel*)

Queen of Israel, the wife of Ahab and daughter of the Sidonian (Phoenician) king Ethbaal. As vocalized in the MT the name can be read as either "islands of dung" or "no dung," generally recognized as parodies of the consonantal form meaning "no nobility" or "Where is the prince?" The latter, most likely the word's original meaning, is known from the liturgy of the Baal cult.

Conflict over the meaning of the name is replicated in a conflict over the evaluation of the character. Is Jezebel an archetypal wicked woman? (Her name is used symbolically in Rev. 2:20-23 to refer to a prophetess who is "beguiling" the congregation at Thyatira "to practice fornication and to eat food sacrificed to idols.") Or is such a characterization a way of deflecting attention away from the quite considerable power she wields? Even her first introduction into the text, as wife of Ahab and daughter of Ethbaal, signals conflict (1 Kgs. 16:31). Indeed, these two relational identifications, insofar as they also signal expectation of loyalty to two different cultures, help contextualize the several narrative episodes in which she plays a role.

Early on, it is her relationship to prophets that is highlighted — whether these be prophets of Yahweh, Baal, or Asherah. 1 Kgs. 18:3-4 (cf. vv. 13-14) comments that Jezebel has been killing off the prophets of Yahweh; refugees of this violence have resorted to hiding in caves where they subsist on bread and water. Even the highly-vaunted Elijah, fresh off his victory over the Baal prophets at Mt. Carmel, flees the country upon hearing — from a messenger sent by Jezebel — that she means to kill him. This venom on Jezebel's part toward Yahweh prophets is in contrast to her support of the prophets of Baal and Asherah. 1 Kgs. 18:19 reports that she is bestowing the hospitality of her royal table, no doubt lavishingly provendered, to no fewer than 450 prophets of Baal and 400 prophets of Asherah (no mention here of Ahab).

Another episode that provokes conflict is the Naboth incident (1 Kgs. 21:1-19). In support of her husband's desire to possess the vineyard of Naboth, Jezebel strategically arranges for the latter's death and the subsequent acquiring of his property for Ahab. In doing so, she might well be acting in accord with the royal prerogatives to which her father's upbringing had accustomed her; however, such an action is strongly counter to Israelite tradition, which demands that landed property be considered the perpetual inheritance of the family. Interestingly, though, Jezebel's means for carrying out the death sentence are actually well calibrated to the Israelite legal system: two witnesses (cf. Deut. 17:6) accuse Naboth of cursing God and the king (cf. Exod. 24:15), for which he is punished with death by stoning (cf. Lev. 24:16).

The violence evident in Jezebel's life finds a last echo in the manner of her death: cast out of a window by her own attendants, her body is trampled to death by horses (2 Kgs. 9:30-37). Israel thereby rids itself of the dangerous influences of this foreign woman. Or does it? No fewer than three of her children also come to the throne of Israelite territories: Ahaziah and Joram are, successively, kings in the north; Athaliah reigns as queen in the south.

Bibliography. C. Camp, "1 and 2 Kings," in *The Women's Bible Commentary,* ed. C. A. Newsom and S. H. Ringe (Louisville, 1992), 96-109; P. Trible, "Exegesis for Storytellers and Other Strangers," *JBL* 114 (1995): 3-19.

KARLA G. BOHMBACH

JEZER (Heb. *yēṣer*)
The third son of Naphtali (Gen. 46:24; 1 Chr. 7:13); eponymous ancestor of the Jezerites (Heb. *hayyiṣrî;* Num. 26:49).

JEZIEL (Heb. K *yĕzû'ēl;* Q *yĕzî'ēl*)
A Benjaminite, son of Azmaveth; an ambidextrous warrior who came to David at Ziklag (1 Chr. 12:3).

JEZRAHIAH (Heb. *yizraḥyâ*)
The leader of the levitical singers at the time of Nehemiah (Neh. 12:42). The name is the same as Izrahiah of Issachar at 1 Chr. 7:3.

JEZREEL (Heb. *yizrĕʿeʾl*) **(PERSON)**

1. A Judahite descent group (1 Chr. 4:3), probably a unit of the Hurites associated with the locality Jezreel in Josh. 15:56.

2. The double-edged, symbolic name of Hosea's first son. Hos. 1:4 uses the name as a threat, since the locale Jezreel connotes Jehu's bloody destruction of the Omrides (2 Kgs. 10:11). Hos. 1:5 goes further, locating the threat in the "valley of Jezreel." Hos. 2:22(MT 24), by contrast, has the name "God sows" promise future bounty (also Hos. 1:11[2:2]; cf. Ps. 81:10, 16[11, 17]). The subsequent verse repeats the name's root, "sow," in a metaphor promising Israel's post-punishment resettlement (cf. Ps. 80:8-9[9-10]).

STEPHEN L. COOK

JEZREEL (Heb. *yizrĕʿeʾl*) **(PLACE)**

1. A town in the hills of Judah, in the vicinity of Ziph and Juttah (Josh. 15:56). Its identification is unknown, but some suggest Khirbet Tarrâmā (153098), 9 km. (6 mi.) SW of Hebron. This Jezreel was the hometown of one of David's wives, Ahinoam (1 Sam. 25:43; 2 Sam. 2:2).

2. The valley of Jezreel, the eastern section of the broad valley separating Galilee from Samaria. From the pass between the hill of Moreh and Mt. Gilboa, where the town of Jezreel was located, the valley descends eastward to the Jordan, with Beth-shan commanding its eastern entrance. The broader plain to the west is known as Esdraelon — though sometimes Jezreel and Esdraelon are used interchangeably.

The valley of Jezreel comprised a rich and fertile growing area as well as one of the few routes to the Jordan Valley and the east. The famous Carmel Pass was used by traders and armies alike from Egypt, the east, and the Palestinian coast.

The Canaanites controlled the valley with chariots of iron when the Israelites entered the land (Josh. 17:16), and here Gideon met the Midianites and Amalekites in battle (Judg. 6:33–7:23). According to Hosea (Hos. 1:5) this valley was where the battle would take place that would bring an end to the kingdom of Israel.

3. A town on the southern border of Issachar (Josh. 19:18), often identified with modern Zerʿîn/Tel Yisreʿel (181218), ca. 80 km. (50 mi.) N of Jerusalem near the foot of Mt. Gilboa. Jezreel was associated with a fountain (Josh. 29:1); a fountain, ʿAin Jalud, is located near Zerʿîn.

Jezreel figured prominently in Israel's history. The Israelites encamped there before their battle with the Philistines (1 Sam. 29). Ishbosheth, son of Saul, briefly reigned over Jezreel (2 Sam. 2:9), here possibly designating more than simply the city. Jezreel was a city of Solomon's fifth administrative district (1 Kgs. 4:12). Ahab had a royal residence there (1 Kgs. 18:45-46). The city was the site of Naboth's vineyard (1 Kgs. 21; 2 Kgs. 9:24-26), and there Jezebel and the rest of Ahab's household died as prophesied (2 Kgs. 9:30–10:11).

WATSON E. MILLS

JIDLAPH (Heb. *yiḏlap*)
A son of Nahor and Milcah (Gen. 22:22).

JOAB (Heb. *yô'āḇ*)
The son of David's sister Zeruiah; commander-in-chief of David's army from the time David took Jerusalem (1 Chr. 11:4-9), and the dominant figure in David's regime, to whom more than any other David owed the success of his reign. Although an earlier line of thought ascribed to Joab command of the levies only, he always appears in command of David's professional troops (cf. 2 Sam. 10:9-14). Joab and Zeruiah's other sons, Abishai and Asahel, collectively termed "the sons of Zeruiah," provide a foil of arrogant and violent ruthlessness for David's humility and self-censure (2 Sam. 16:9-14). This is portrayed in two vignettes, when Joab slays Abner for the death of Asahel, and when he slays Amasa, with whom David has replaced Joab.

When David was pressured by his men to relinquish his field command during the Philistine wars (2 Sam. 21:15-17), a dramatic power shift in the monarchy took place. Since much of an ancient Near Eastern king's effective power rested on his military stature, David's absence from command led to a corresponding increase in Joab's power and prestige. Joab's warning to David, that he had better come up to the final assault on Rabbat-ammon lest Joab's name and not David's "be called over it" (2 Sam. 12:26-28), is a tacit admission that such a shift was taking place. Uriah the Hittite, one of David's personal retainers, actually calls Joab "my lord" in the presence of his king, David (2 Sam. 11:11). Joab's increasing stature is shown by the fact that he went from a single armor-bearer, Naharai of Beeroth, one of David's *šělōšîm,* to ten (2 Sam. 18:15).

David's attempts to replace Joab with field commanders of lesser stature, starting with Abner, indicate that David from an early date was concerned with curtailing Joab's power. Yet he was unsuccessful, since Joab appears to have been the field commander par excellence, and was willing to do whatever necessary to preserve his own position.

Indeed, Joab, though loyal to David's throne, appears to have been politically shrewder and more forceful than David, and he turned his position as commander-in-chief into an independent power base within the kingdom, from which he could defy royal policy. No account conveys this more clearly than that of Absalom's revolt, where Joab not only takes responsibility for killing David's rebellious son himself — against direct royal orders (2 Sam. 18:9-15), but where he also threatens the grieving David with the desertion of the entire army if he does not come out and acknowledge their victory (19:1-8).

Joab's slaying of Absalom seems to have created a permanent rift between David and his nephew. Thus David, only partly to reconcile the defeated Israelites after Absalom's revolt, replaced Joab with Amasa, Absalom's field commander, who was also kin to David (2 Sam. 19:13). But Amasa failed in his first assignment — calling out the levies to face the revolt of Sheba, so Joab slew him and regained his command. This apparently ended David's efforts to replace Joab, but David made further attempts to circumscribe Joab's power base. By assigning command of the bodyguard to Benaiah (2 Sam. 23:23) David put at least one military unit beyond Joab's control. Joab's position may also have been weakened by the unrecorded death of his brother Abishai, of whom we hear nothing after the revolt of Sheba.

David's personal bitterness towards Joab culminates when David instructs Solomon to use his wisdom (i.e., cunning, treachery) to bring about Joab's death (1 Kgs. 2:5-9). Solomon finds his opportunity when Joab supports the bid of his older brother Adonijah for the throne. Taking refuge at the altar, Joab forces his enemies to come in and slay him where he is, refusing to let them kill him without desecrating the sanctuary. His executioner is Benaiah, who receives Joab's command as a reward for killing him (1 Kgs. 2:35).

Despite his inglorious end, Joab represents the strength and virtue of David's old loyalists: while loyal to their king, they were not slavishly obedient as too often expected of other ancient Near Eastern courts, and as enjoined in the Wisdom tradition (cf. Prov. 16:10, 12-15). Joab also sets a model of integrity second to few in the OT. He takes responsibility for killing Absalom himself (2 Sam. 18:14) and upbraids David for not thanking his men for their victory (18:33–19:8[MT 19:1-9].

Bibliography. D. G. Schley, "Joab and David: Ties of Blood and Power," in *History and Interpretation,* ed. M. P. Graham, W. P. Brown, and J. K. Kuan (Sheffield, 1993), 90-105. DONALD G. SCHLEY

JOAH (Heb. *yôʾāḥ*)

1. The son of Asaph; a recorder in the court of King Hezekiah. He was one of the three officials sent by the king to the Assyrian representatives at the siege of Jerusalem ca. 701 B.C.E. (2 Kgs. 18:18, 26, 37 = Isa. 36:3, 11, 22).

2. A Levite and son of Zimmah from the family of Gershom (1 Chr. 6:21[MT 6]).

3. The son of Obed-edom; a Levite appointed to be a gatekeeper in the temple (1 Chr. 26:4).

4. A Gershonite Levite who, with his son Eden, participated in the temple reforms begun under King Hezekiah (2 Chr. 29:12). He is to be distinguished from **2** above.

5. The son of Joahaz; an official of King Josiah commissioned to repair the temple (2 Chr. 34:8).

JOAHAZ (Heb. *yôʾāḥāz*)
The father of Joah **5** (2 Chr. 34:8).

JOANAN (Gk. *Iōanán*)
The grandson of Zerubbabel, and an ancestor of Jesus (Luke 3:27), perhaps to be identified with Hananiah (1 Chr. 3:19).

JOANNA (Gk. *Iōánna*)
One of the women from Galilee that followed and provided assistance to Jesus. She is mentioned with Mary Magdalene, Susanna, and others as having been "cured of evil spirits and infirmities" (Luke 8:2-3). Joanna was wife of Chuza the steward of Herod Antipas.

Joanna was among the women who brought spices to anoint Jesus' body and found the empty tomb. Along with Mary Magdalene and Mary the mother of James she delivered the news of the Resurrection to the 11 apostles (Luke 24:10). Luke also notes that the women from Galilee beheld the Crucifixion (Luke 23:49) and the placement of Jesus' body in the sepulchre (v. 55). JO ANN H. SEELY

JOARIB (Gk. *Iōarib*) (also JEHOIARIB)
The head of the priestly family from which was descended Mattathias, who with his sons initiated the Maccabean Revolt (1 Macc. 2:1; 14:29). At 1 Chr. 24:7 he is called Jehoiarib.

JOASH (Heb. *yôʾāš, yěhôʾāš*) (also JEHOASH)

1. The father of Gideon (Judg. 6:11, 29-31). A member of the Abiezrite clan of the tribe of Manasseh. He was owner of "the oak at Ophrah," probably a local shrine associated with Baal and Asherah. The account emphasizes Yahwistic hegemony in Joash's refusal to contend for Baal after Gideon destroys the cult site.

2. The son of King Ahab of Israel; one of the officials ordered to take custody of the prophet Micaiah (1 Kgs. 22:26 = 2 Chr. 18:25).

3. King of Judah (ca. 837-800 B.C.E.; 2 Kgs. 11–

12; 2 Chr. 22:10–24:27). Joash (throne name Jehoash) was made king of Judah as a child by a coup d'état led by the priest Jehoiada against Athaliah, who had seized the throne and murdered all rivals seven years earlier. Narrative interest in the Kings account of the coup centers on the legitimacy of Joash as Ahaziah's son and the only survivor of Athaliah's purge, and on the necessary and authoritative restoration of the Davidic dynasty. The Chronicles account emphasizes the roles of the priest and the Levites in leading a popular uprising. While the identity of Joash as the king's son is suspect, these events are comprehensible as typical political struggles in monarchic states and as fallout from Jehu's revolt that ended the Omride dynasty in the north.

The chronology of the period is uncertain, but the attributed 40-year reign for Joash (2 Kgs. 12:1[MT 2]) seems more evocative of the reigns of David and Solomon than realistic. Joash is characterized in the Deuteronomistic-type regnal summary as a good king except for not removing the high places; Chronicles limits his right rule to Jehoiada's influence. This king is remembered for his regularizing of a financial program for the care of the temple. A power struggle with the priests for control of the finances may underlie the narrative. The Kings account demonstrates Joash's leadership in establishing an enduring arrangement (2 Kgs. 22:3-7, 9). In contrast, Chronicles highlights Joash's abandonment of the priestly ideals of Yahwistic loyalty after Jehoiada dies.

Hazael's defeat of the city of Gath and tribute from Joash reflect the dominance of Aram-Damascus in Syria-Palestine in the late 9th century. Joash's assassination by two of his officials, characteristic of royal power politics, is unexplained in Kings. In Chronicles both Hazael's victory and the assassination are retribution for Joash's transgressions. Joash was succeeded by his son Amaziah.

4. King of Israel (ca. 800-ca. 785). Joash succeeded his father Jehoahaz and ruled for 16 years early in the 8th century (2 Kgs. 13:10-25; 14:8-16; 2 Chr. 25:17-24). The regnal summary, like other Deuteronomistic judgments of northern kings, describes him as an evil king who followed in Jeroboam's sins. However, the narrative strategy of 2 Kgs. 13:14-25 portrays him according to the usually positive Deuteronomistic criterion of a king who seeks the prophetic word. The narrative focuses on Joash's responses to Elisha's commands to act out Israel's limited success in its continuing struggle against Aram. The narrative confirmation of the prophetic word comes in 2 Kgs. 13:25, where Joash defeats Ben-hadad three times.

Historically, this account reflects the changing balance of power between Aram and Assyria ca. 800. Assyria under Adadnirari III in its western campaigns between 805 and 796 controlled and then ended Aram's four decades of domination of Syria-Palestine. An Assyrian inscription, the Rimah stela, marks Adad-nirari's success and his receipt of tribute from Tyre, Sidon, and Joash of Samaria. Aram's weakness left Joash free to regain the cities (in Galilee or Transjordan?) his father had lost.

Joash figures in the report about Amaziah which describes a battle between Israel and Judah (2 Kgs. 14:8-16 = 2 Chr. 25:17-24). Narrative emphasis is on Joash's rebuff of Amaziah, Israel's defeat of Judah on its own territory, and the sacking of Jerusalem. Other than alluding to Amaziah's arrogance after defeating Edom, the report does not give reasons for the battle. While specifics cannot be known, the battle is comprehensible as typical jockeying for power or territory between smaller states after a dominating state (here, Aram) has been removed. Joash was succeeded by his son Jeroboam II.

5. A member of the Judahite genealogy in the Shelanite branch (1 Chr. 4:22).

6. A Benjaminite from the clan of Becher (1 Chr. 7:8).

7. An archer listed among the Benjaminite warriors who joined David at Ziklag (1 Chr. 12:3).

8. The overseer of David's stores of oil (1 Chr. 27:28).

Bibliography. G. W. Ahlström, *The History of Ancient Palestine* (Minneapolis, 1993); P. Dutcher-Walls, *Narrative Art, Political Rhetoric: The Case of Athaliah and Joash.* JSOTSup 209 (Sheffield, 1996); S. Japhet, *I and II Chronicles.* OTL (Louisville, 1993); J. M. Miller and J. H. Hayes, *A History of Ancient Israel and Judah* (Philadelphia, 1986).

PATRICIA DUTCHER-WALLS

JOB, BOOK OF

An extensive work of prose and poetry found in the Writings of the OT. The book recounts the moving story of a righteous individual who incurs horrendous suffering, is castigated by his friends, challenges God, and is finally vindicated and restored. Although the book is commonly associated with the wisdom books, Job holds a unique place within the biblical literature, for it broaches matters of the human condition and theology that are nowhere else conveyed with such pathos.

Composition and Structure

Dates for the composition of Job have ranged from the 10th to the 2nd century B.C.E., although most scholars contend that it was written during the exilic or early postexilic period (6h or 5th century). In Ezek. 14:14, 20 the protagonist is considered an exemplary figure of righteousness alongside Noah and Daniel. The bulk of the book is composed of poetry (3:2–42:6, with the exception of 32:1-5) and is bracketed by prose (1:1–2:13; 42:7-17). The relationship between the prose and poetry is still debated, although the traditional theory holds that the prose sections once represented an independent, early folktale about the character of Job. The poetic center, thus, is the result of later additions. It may also be the case that the poetry once stood independent of the prose, resembling the much earlier Babylonian Theodicy (ca. 1100; *ANET,* 601-4), which contains only an exchange of dialogue between a sufferer and his friend. Other Mesopotamian parallels include A Man and His God (*ANET,* 589-91) and I Will Praise the Lord of Wisdom (*ANET,* 434-37). Regardless of the compositional development of the book, the poetry stands out as central to the book on the readerly level.

The structure of the book can be illustrated as follows:

I. Prose Prologue: Job's desolation (1:1–2:13)
II. Poetic Discourse (3:1–42:6)
  A. Job's birthday curse (3:1-26)
  B. Dialogues with friends (4:1–27:23)
    1. First cycle of dialogues (4:1–14:22)
    2. Second cycle of dialogues (15:1–21:34)
    3. Third cycle of dialogues (22:1–27:23)
  C. Meditation on wisdom's elusiveness (28:1-28)
  D. Job's final defense (29:1–31:40)
    1. God's past favor (29:1-25)
    2. Job's present misery (30:1-31)
    3. Job's oaths (31:1-40)
  E. Elihu's discourse (32:1–37:24)
  F. Dialogues with God (38:1–42:6)
III. Prose Epilogue: Job's restoration (42:7-17)

Content and Movement

The prose prologue sets the stage for the poetic discourse that follows. Job, a non-Israelite, is described as one who fears God, avoids evil, and is blameless and upright (1:1). The stage is set for this folk hero to demonstrate his integrity in the face of tremendous odds. As the narrative progresses through alternating scenes of earth and heaven, Yahweh allows the *śāṭān,* a member of the divine council who specialized in the art of prosecution (1:6-8), to test Job. The issue at stake is whether Job's piety is truly disinterested (1:9), i.e., devoid of ulterior motives or self-interest. The *śāṭān* has his doubts, while Yahweh is fully confident. Consequently, the *śāṭān's* proposal, which God wholeheartedly accepts, is as much a challenge to God's credibility as it is to Job's. In two successive waves of calamity, Job is rendered without progeny and possessions. His wife urges him to curse God and die. Though often disparaged in both ancient and modern interpretations, the question posed by Job's wife is vitally important: Does persisting in integrity prompt one to keep silent or to curse God in the face of seemingly unjust suffering (2:9)? It is this question around which the rest of the book revolves. Whether rightly or wrongly, Job quickly rejects his wife's exhortation and remains a man of few words, ever deferential and stoic in accepting his fate at God's hand. In the words of the narrator, "Job did not sin or charge God with wrong-doing" (1:22).

In the poetic material that follows a different Job speaks, one who is quick to judge both his friends and God. Jas. 5:11 speaks of the enduring patience of Job, but the biblical Job is anything but patient in the discourses! Chs. 3-27 contain three cycles of conversation in which Job's three friends, Eliphaz, Bildad, and Zophar (who does not appear in the last cycle), offer a range of responses, from consolation to condemnation, over Job's plight. Indeed, they end up pinning all measure of turpitude upon him in order to make sense of his suffering (e.g., 15:7-13; 22:5-9). Relying almost exclusively upon the veracity of his experience, Job responds in kind to each of his three friends, employing an impressive arsenal of rhetorical weapons (e.g., instruction, argument, irony, sarcasm, rebuke), which turns his friends' self-righteous proverbs to "ashes" and exposes their arguments as "defenses of clay" (13:12). Job's discourse is charged with pathos and protest. Through it all, Job is adamant in maintaining his integrity (27:5-6). Moreover, in order to seek redress from God and humans alike, Job appeals to a "mediator" or "witness" in heaven, a "redeemer" who can judge between God, who has defamed and victimized him, and himself (9:33; 16:19; 19:25-27). Job, in short, comes to expect vindication from a heavenly advocate. (Christian interpreters have frequently viewed Job's "redeemer" [19:25] as Christ; however, for Job this redeemer is a heavenly being who has the power to call God to account for what he considers a flagrant travesty of justice.)

Job wraps up his defense with a wrenching resume of his present misery (30:1-31), which follows upon the heels of an effusive description of the glory days in which he enjoyed God's preeminent favor and his community's esteem (29:1-25). Job concludes with a series of powerful oaths by which he challenges God to either judge him or redress his complaint (31:1-40). In the end his friends are rendered speechless (32:1), after which a new character appears without forewarning. His name is Elihu ("He is my God"), and he represents a new generation of sapiential pedagogy, one that does not rely upon the accumulated wisdom of past sages, to which Job's friends frequently refer (e.g., 8:8; 15:17-19), but upon direct inspiration from God (33:14-15, 33; 36:2). Yet like Job's friends, Elihu finds Job guilty. As would a youth, Elihu revels in stepping on the toes of his elders (32:6-9), and his speech is to an extent theologically suspect, owing to his bombastic delivery (32:15–33:5) and accusatory tone. Yet Elihu's speech masterfully sets the stage for the Almighty's appearance before Job (37:14-24).

Yahweh's answer to Job (chs. 38–41) represents the high point of the book's development. Yet many modern readers find the speeches ultimately disappointing, since they neither address Job's insufferable condition nor solve the problem of theodicy. Some in fact accuse the author of these speeches of bad theology. In any case, the divine discourses do serve to resolve Job's case against Yahweh (cf. 42:6). These speeches from on high are filled with references to creation, embracing in order the realms of cosmology, meteorology, and zoology, the latter being most pronounced (38:39–39:30; 40:15–41:34[MT 41:26]). Indeed, it is through Yahweh's litany of the animal kingdom that Job's world is most profoundly and radically reoriented.

The animals described in this section are not domestic but wild — lion, mountain goat, deer, onager, wild ox, ostrich, hawk, and eagle. Even the war horse (39:19-25) is described as untamable and

Job begs for pity from his friends as he sits in a dunghill before his ruined house. Limbourg Brothers, *Trés riches heures du Duc de Berry,* fol. 82r (15th century); Accademia, Florence (Giraudon/Art Resource, N.Y.)

fearsome. Yahweh revels in their wildness and freedom from human control. Images of vitality and vigor abound, including some measure of violence (e.g., 38:39; 39:26-30). The majestic world which Job is shown is infinitely larger than his own accustomed world, wherein he saw himself as a patriarch of royal proportions (29:25). At one point, Job laments that he has become a "brother of jackals and a companion of ostriches" (30:29). The irony runs deep when Yahweh points out that Job is in good company with these denizens of the margin, of a "no-man's-land." Job's provincial and self-centered world is radically reoriented in Yahweh's description of the awe-inspiring creatures Behemoth and Leviathan, which together mark the apex of Yahweh's litany of creation (chs. 40-41; cf. Gen. 1:26-27). Missing is any mention of humanity in this parade of creatures, except for the slight reference to Job's creation in 40:15. Job is no longer the pinnacle of the community; Leviathan, rather, is a creature unsurpassed in strength and royal stature (41:34[26]), in somewhat the same way Job saw himself (29:25). These mythical beasts of chaos take center stage as magnificent and proud creatures. Rather than viewed as hostile beings before God, they are praised by Yahweh as integral parts of this cosmic pageant.

For Job the world is reconstructed by a fiercely loving God, the same world that Job had cursed to chaos in ch. 3. It is a world in which moral retribution has lost its force. Nevertheless, a moral sense of nature pervades these divine speeches. Creation is characterized as an arena of freedom and independence, established by Yahweh, who gratuitously balances and sustains the needs of all creatures and delights in the dignity and beauty of each thing irrespective of utility and without direct and dramatic intervention. The chaotic sea is given birth and nurtured, albeit with imposed limitations (38:8-11). Yahweh even causes the rain to shower upon the desert, "to satisfy the waste and desolate land" (38:26-27). Job's response to such a radical reorientation is enigmatic, but certainly marks both a resolution of his case against Yahweh and an embrace of a new moral vision (42:1-6). Job has emerged a different sort of patriarch operating with a different set of principles. No longer obsessed with the ideals of honor and authority, he prays to Yahweh on behalf of his friends who had unjustly condemned him. Restored with the same number of children, Job shares his inheritance equally with his daughters (cf. Num. 27:1-11). So read, the book of Job is about the transformation of human integrity, tested and refashioned, and of moral vision, reshaped and broadened.

Bibliography. D. J. A. Clines, *Job 1-20.* WBC 17 (Waco, 1989); N. C. Habel, *The Book of Job.* OTL (Philadelphia, 1985); C. A. Newsom, "The Moral Sense of Nature: Ethics in the Light of God's Speech to Job," *Princeton Seminary Bulletin* N.S. 15 (1994): 9-27; L. G. Perdue, *Wisdom in Revolt: Metaphorical Theology in the Book of Job.* BLS 29. JSOTSup 112 (Sheffield, 1991); M. Tsevat, "The Meaning of the Book of Job," *HUCA* 37 (1966): 73-106; repr. in *The Meaning of the Book of Job and Other Biblical Studies* (New York, 1980), 1-38.

WILLIAM P. BROWN

JOB, TESTAMENT OF

A pseudepigraphal book which uses the genre of testament to provide a novelistic retelling of the biblical book of Job. Job gathers his children around his deathbed and reviews events of his life in order to exhort his children to the virtue of endurance or patience (Gk. *hypomoné*).

The recasting of the biblical story is quite expansive and fanciful. For example, the first half (chs. 1-27) retells the first two chapters of the canonical book. Major roles are given to a revealing angel, to a Satan of many disguises, and to Job's impoverished wife Sitis. Unlike the biblical Job, this Job knows from the start what will happen to him and why, and he has assurance of his ultimate victory.

In the second half of the testament (chs. 28-53) Job offends his four royal friends with his talk of an eternal kingdom in heaven which is far superior to earthly kingdoms. After God restores his fortunes, Job gives his three daughters an inheritance in this earthly kingdom. He provides each of them with a magical sash which guarantees health and protection from the enemy, inspires mystical worship, and leads to the better world in heaven. When Job dies, his daughters witness his soul's ascent to heaven.

The text is extant in Greek, which was most likely the language of original composition. It was written in Egypt (Job is called "the king of all Egypt" in 28:7) by a Jewish author sometime during the 1st century C.E.

Bibliography. R. T. Spittler, "Testament of Job," *OTP* 1 (Garden City, 1983): 829-68. PAUL S. ASH

JOBAB (Heb. *yôḇāḇ*)

1. A son of Joktan; ancestor of an Arabian people (Gen. 10:29; 1 Chr. 1:23).

2. An Edomite king; the son of Zerah from Bozrah (Gen. 36:33-34 = 1 Chr. 1:44-45).

3. The king of Madon, an ally of Jabin of Hazor (Josh. 11:1); one of the kings defeated by Joshua (12:19).

4. A Benjaminite, son of Shaharaim (1 Chr. 8:9).

5. A Benjaminite, the son of Elpaal (1 Chr. 8:18).

JOCHEBED (Heb. *yôḵeḇeḏ*)

The wife of Amram and mother of Aaron, Moses, and Miriam (Num. 26:59). She was also Amran's aunt (Exod. 6:20).

JODA (Gk. *Iōdá*)

The son of Joanan and ancestor of Jesus, according to Luke's genealogy (Luke 3:26).

JOED (Heb. *yôʿēḏ*)

A Benjaminite, the grandfather of Sallu (Neh. 11:7).

JOEL (Heb. *yôʾēl*)

A common name in the OT (Heb. "Yah[weh] is God").

1. The elder son of the prophet Samuel. He and his brother Abijah were appointed by their father to be judges in Beer-sheba, but they perverted justice and accepted bribes (1 Sam. 8:1-3). According to 1 Chr. 6:33(MT 18); 15:17 he was a Kohathite Levite and the father of the singer Heman (cf. 6:28[13] MT).

2. A prince of the tribe of Simeon at the time of Hezekiah (1 Chr. 4:35).

3. A Reubenite, the father of Shemaiah (1 Chr. 5:4; cf. v. 8, "Shema").

4. A chief of the tribe of Gad who dwelled in Bashan (1 Chr. 5:12).

5. A Kohathite Levite; a son of Azariah, father of Elkanah, and ancestor of Samuel (1 Chr. 6:36[21]; cf. 1 Sam. 1:1). The name Shaul appears in the parallel genealogy at 1 Chr. 6:24(9).

6. A son of Izrahiah of the tribe of Issachar; an officer contemporary with David (1 Chr. 7:3). He may be the same as **5** above.

7. One of David's Champions and the brother of Nathan (1 Chr. 11:38). At 2 Sam. 23:36 the text has Igal the son of Nathan.

8. A chief of the Gershomite Levites who assisted David in bringing the ark to Jerusalem (1 Chr. 15:7, 11).

9. The son of Ladan (1 Chr. 23:8) who, with his brother Zetham, had charge of the temple treasuries (26:21-22; here the son of Jehieli). He may be the same as **8** above.

10. The son of Pedaiah; chief officer of the half-tribe of Manasseh at the time of David (1 Chr. 27:20).

11. A Kohathite Levite, the son of Azariah. He

assisted in cleansing the temple at the time of Hezekiah (2 Chr. 29:12).

12. One of the seven sons of Nebo; a postexilic Israelite who was required to divorce his foreign wife (Ezra 10:43; 1 Esdr. 9:35).

13. The son of Zichri; overseer of the Benjaminites in postexilic Jerusalem (Neh. 11:9).

14. The prophet Joel, the son of Pethuel (Joel 1:1; LXX "Bethuel"). His utterances comprise the book of Joel.

15. The archangel Joel; also called Jaoel, Jahoel, or Jehoel (e.g., Apoc. Mos. 29:4; 43:5; Apoc. Abr. 10:3; 17:13). MILES V. VAN PELT

JOEL (Heb. *yô'ēl*), **BOOK OF**

The second of the Minor Prophets. The book opens with a call for the elders and the people of the land to lament the unprecedented devastation caused by a locust plague. Joel links this plague to the coming day of Yahweh, compares it to an enemy assault on Jerusalem, and summons the people to return to Yahweh. In response to the people's ritual acts of mourning, Joel holds out the hope that Yahweh, at whose command the locust army advanced, will bring redemption. Indeed, Yahweh will restore the land and the agriculture ravaged by the locusts. Yahweh will also deliver the people from their oppressive neighbors. Yahweh will gather all foreign peoples to the valley of Jehoshaphat (a symbolic place meaning "Yahweh judges") to defeat them in battle and thereby restore Jerusalem as a holy city.

Previous interpretations of Joel have focused on several literary and historical problems. These include the composition and structure of the book, its date and historical setting, and its appropriation and interpretation of earlier traditions.

To even the most casual reader the book appears to consist of two distinct parts: 1:1–2:27 and 2:28–3:21(MT 3:1–4:21). The first part focuses on a natural catastrophe that is presently devastating Judah, whereas the second deals with Yahweh's future judgment on the foreign peoples who have oppressed the people of Judah. The first part is descriptive and prophetic, but the second is often characterized as apocalyptic or eschatological. However, both parts of the book display several similarities. The day of Yahweh plays a prominent role in each part, and similar phrases and literary style can be detected across both parts.

Most earlier scholars and some contemporary scholars have argued that the two parts were written by two distinct authors: the prophet Joel, who experienced the effects of an actual locust plague, and a later eschatological author who edited (by inserting references to the day of Yahweh) and supplemented the prophet's original message, giving it a more transcendent meaning. Most contemporary scholars, however, argue that Joel is the author of both parts of the book, though they often differ on the relationship of the two parts. Some scholars assert that the second part is simply a later eschatological expansion of the first, whereas others argue that both parts form an organic unity. These latter scholars have been especially effective in demonstrating that the division of the book into two distinct parts — 1:1–2:27 and 2:28–3:21(4:21) — ignores both the content and the structure of the book. The day of Yahweh is an integral theme to both parts of the book, and brings unity to the whole. Moreover, the structural midpoint of the book comes at the juncture between 2:17 and 2:18, not at the division between 2:27 and 2:28(3:1).

The structure of the book is illustrated by an outline of its contents:

- I. A natural catastrophe heralds the day of Yahweh (1:1–2:17)
  - A. Lament over a natural catastrophe (1:1-20)
    1. An unprecedented locust plague (1:1-4)
    2. A call to lament the agricultural devastation (1:5-14)
    3. Lamentation in the wake of the plague (1:15-20)
  - B. A new locust plague as Yahweh's invading army (2:1-11)
  - C. A prophetic summons for the people to return to Yahweh (2:12-17)
- II. Judgment and redemption on the day of Yahweh (2:18–3:21[4:21])
  - A. Judgment on the locust plague (2:18-32[3:5])
    1. Destruction of the locusts and restoration of the land (2:18-27)
    2. Redemption of the people on the day of Yahweh (2:28-32[3:1-5])
  - B. Judgment on foreign peoples (3:1-21[4:1-21])
    1. Crimes against the people of Judah (3:1-8[4:1-8])
    2. Yahweh summons the foreign peoples and redeems the people of Judah (3:15-21[4:15-21])

The book of Joel offers few clues to its historical setting. Consequently, scholars have dated the book from as early as the 9th century B.C.E. during the reign of King Joash of Judah to as late as the 3rd century. The growing consensus among scholars is that the book probably dates from the Persian period after the rebuilding of the temple (515), and possibly after Nehemiah rebuilt Jerusalem's walls (445; cf. 2:9), yet before the destruction of Sidon during the Tennes rebellion (345; cf. 3:4-8[4:4-8]).

The text is more explicit on the occasion for which the book was written. A locust plague had consumed Judah's agriculture (1:4), bringing even the people's participation in the temple cult to an end (v. 13). The effects of the annual summer drought further intensified the devastation (1:19-20). Moreover, a new locust infestation — described metaphorically as an invading army — was assaulting the land (2:3-9), suggesting that the locust plague extended over two agricultural seasons. The book also complains that the peoples of Tyre, Sidon, and Philistia had plundered the land of Judah and sold its people to the Greeks (3:4-8[4:4-8]). However, this complaint appears to be more indicative of Judah's weak status under the Persian Empire, intensifying the people's shame (2:17, 27), rather than the specific occasion of the book.

The book of Joel is characterized by numerous verbal parallels with earlier prophetic books. Although many of these parallels are verbatim, Joel's literary dependency on these books cannot be assumed. The highly formulaic nature of these parallels suggests that Joel was simply drawing upon common sayings and themes in the prophetic tradition. Two motifs that play a prominent role in the book of Joel are the day of Yahweh and the enemy from the north.

Employing stereotypical language, Joel identifies the locust plague with the coming day of Yahweh. Whereas the prophetic tradition identified this day with Yahweh's judgment on his enemies — his own people or foreigners — Joel transforms the day of Yahweh into a complex event that includes an assault against the land of Judah from which Yahweh will deliver his people and Yahweh's judgment on foreign peoples. Joel makes this transformation by linking the day of Yahweh with the enemy from the north tradition. Joel specifically identifies the locust army with the "northerner" (2:20; locust plagues typically enter Israel from the south). In the tradition of Ezek. 38–39, Joel compares the locusts with the enemy army that Yahweh will bring against the land of Judah for the sole purpose of destroying it and displaying Yahweh's greatness (3:1-21[4:1-21]).

The book of Joel is a response to a severe locust plague which was devastating the agriculture of Judah. In contrast to the people who found the devastation to be a source of shame, Joel recognized in the locust plague the realization of the day of Yahweh and the fulfillment of earlier prophetic expectations. Joel thus drew upon prophetic traditions to proclaim to the people Yahweh's purposes. Yahweh will restore the land and redeem the people. Just as Yahweh brought the locust army against the land of Judah only to destroy it, so also Yahweh will gather all the foreign peoples to Jerusalem to destroy them and thereby redeem his own people in Zion.

Bibliography. G. W. Ahlström, *Joel and the Temple Cult of Jerusalem.* VTSup 21 (Leiden, 1971); J. L. Crenshaw, *Joel.* AB 24C (New York, 1995); A. S. Kapelrud, *Joel Studies.* UUÅ 48/4 (Uppsala, 1948); R. A. Simkins, *Yahweh's Activity in History and Nature in the Book of Joel* (Lewiston, 1991); H. W. Wolff, *Joel and Amos.* Herm (Philadelphia, 1977).

Ronald A. Simkins

JOELAH (Heb. *yô'ē'lâ*)
A warrior who came to David's assistance at Ziklag; son of Jeroham of Gedor (1 Chr. 12:7[MT 8]).

JOEZER (Heb. *yô'ezer*)
A Benjaminite warrior who came to David at Ziklag (1 Chr. 12:6[MT 7]). He is further identified as a Korahite.

JOGBEHAH (Heb. *yogbĕhâ*)
A Transjordanian town in the kingdom of Sihon which Moses gave to Gad (Num. 32:35). It was located near a caravan route along which Gideon pursued the Midianites (Judg. 8:11). Some scholars locate Jogbehah at 'al-Gubēḥah (231159), where an Ammonite military tower has been found. Others equate it with Tell Ṣafūt, since Gubēḥah is outside Ammonite territory.

Philip R. Drey

JOGLI (Heb. *yoglî*)
The father of the Danite leader Bukki (Num. 34:22).

JOHA (Heb. *yôḥā'*)

1. A Benjaminite, son of Beriah (1 Chr. 8:16); a resident of postexilic Jerusalem.

2. A son of Shimri; one of David's Mighty Men (1 Chr. 11:45). He is given the gentilic "Tizite."

JOHANAN (Heb. *yôḥānān*)

1. The son of Kareah; one of the Judean commanders who had eluded Nebuchadnezzar's army before finally submitting to the pro-Babylonian governor Gedaliah at Mizpah (2 Kgs. 25:23-24; Jer. 40:8). Johanan reported to Gedaliah that Ishmael planned to assassinate him, but Gedaliah did not believe the report (Jer. 40:13-16). After Ishmael succeeded in killing Gedaliah (2 Kgs. 25:25), Johanan and his forces fought with Ishmael and rescued the hostages that Ishmael had taken from Mizpah (Jer. 41:11-15). Johanan and the "remnant of Judah" then fled to Egypt to elude Babylonian reprisals, taking Jeremiah and Baruch with them (Jer. 41:16–43:7; cf. 2 Kgs. 25:26).

2. The firstborn son of King Josiah (1 Chr. 3:15). Because no mention of him is made elsewhere, he probably died at an early age.

3. One of seven sons of Elioenai, and the last generation of David's descendants recorded by the Chronicler (1 Chr. 3:24).

4. The son of Azariah; a priest of the line of Aaron and Zadok who served during the reign of Solomon (1 Chr. 6:9-10[MT 5:35-36]). The Chronicler confused Johanan's father with his son, also named Azariah, to whom he attributes service in Solomon's temple.

5. A Benjaminite warrior who joined David's forces at Ziklag (1 Chr. 12:4[5]).

6. A Gadite officer who also joined David's forces at Ziklag (1 Chr. 12:12[13]).

7. An Ephraimite chief, the son of Azariah, who refused to allow Pekah and his army to bring Judean captives back to Samaria (2 Chr. 28:12; NJB, NIV "Jehohanan," following MT).

8. A descendant of Azgad who returned from Babylon with Ezra (Ezra 8:12; 1 Esdr. 8:38).

9. A high priest in postexilic Judah, the "son" (possibly grandson) of Eliashib (Neh. 12:22-23). This Johanan has been identified with the Jehohanan of the Elephantine papyri (Cowley 30:18) and, probably incorrectly, with the Johanan who killed his brother Jeshua (Josephus *Ant.* 10.297-301).

It is also tempting to identify this Johanan with Jehohanan, son of Eliashib, in whose chambers

Ezra spent the night (Ezra 10:6 KJV), but this identification is unlikely (cf. Neh. 13:4).

RONALD A. SIMKINS

JOHN (Gk. *Iōánnēs*)

1. The father of Matthias and grandfather of Judas Maccabeus; son of the priest Simeon (1 Macc. 2:1).

2. The oldest son of Matthias, surnamed Gaddi (2 Macc. 2:2). Sent to the Nabateans by his brother Jonathan to store the Maccabeans' belongings, he was ambushed and killed by "the family of Jambri" from Medeba (9:35-36; cf. vv. 37-42).

3. The father of Eupolemus and son of Accos (1 Macc. 8:17), accorded royal concessions by Antiochus III (2 Macc. 4:11).

4. John Hyrcanus I; son of Simon and nephew of Judas Maccabeus; commander of Simon's forces (1 Macc. 13:53; 16:1) and subsequently high priest.

See HYRCANUS 2.

5. John Hyrcanus II; Hasmonean high priest and ethnarch of Judea.

See HYRCANUS 3.

6. An envoy sent by the Jews to Lysias, a general of Antiochus IV (2 Macc. 11:17).

TIMOTHY P. JENNEY

7. John the Baptizer, Jesus' relative (Luke 1:36) and the forerunner of his ministry (Mark 1:1-8). The son of a priest named Zechariah (Luke 1:5), John had disciples (John 3:25) and preached repentance and the coming of one who would baptize with the Holy Spirit rather than water (Mark 1:8). He was imprisoned and beheaded by Herod the tetrarch (Mark 6:14-29). Jesus identified John with the anticipated Elijah (Mal. 4:5[MT 3:23]), the prophet who was to come before the day of the Lord (Matt. 17:10-13).

See JOHN THE BAPTIST.

8. One of the inner circle of the 12 apostles, the son of Zebedee and the brother of James the apostle, and a fishing partner with Peter (Luke 5:10). Paul notes that John was reputed to be a pillar of the Church (Gal. 2:9). One traditional view identifies this John as "the beloved disciple" (cf. John 13:23) and the author of John's Gospel (cf. 21:20-24). Another view identifies him as the author of Revelation (cf. Rev. 1:1; 22:8). The evidence for both views is inconclusive.

See JOHN THE APOSTLE.

9. The father of the Apostle Peter. He is mentioned only briefly (John 1:42; 21:15-17).

10. A friend of Annas, the high priest (Acts 4:6; the Western text has "Jonathan" instead, perhaps referring to the son of Annas). John may have been of priestly descent, but we have no further knowledge of him.

11. John Mark, the son of Mary (Acts 12:12). He occasionally accompanied Barnabas and Saul on their missionary work (12:25), but he left them to return to Jerusalem (13:13). As a result, Barnabas and Paul later were divided over whether to take John Mark with them. Barnabas took John Mark and separated from Paul (15:37-39). This may be the Mark identified as Barnabas' cousin (Col. 4:10) and the one mentioned in 2 Tim. 4:11. One tradition regards him as author of the Gospel of Mark.

See MARK, JOHN.

12. A prophet and author of the book of Revelation (Rev. 1:1, 4, 9; 22:8). We have no evidence of his background.

Bibliography. R. E. Brown, *The Community of the Beloved Disciple* (New York, 1979); C. H. Dodd, *Historical Tradition in the Fourth Gospel* (Cambridge, 1963).

PAUL K. MOSER

JOHN, ACTS OF

One of several apocryphal works purportedly written by Leucius Charinus. It was probably written in Greek in the late 2nd or early 3rd century C.E. Its provenance is unknown.

The Acts of John relates the mission, miraculous deeds, and peaceful death of the apostle in Asia Minor. John heals the sick, raises the dead, destroys the temple of Artemis in Ephesus, and converts many pagan worshippers. In one highly entertaining episode, John even commands bedbugs to gather in one spot on the bed so as not to disturb his sleep. Unlike many other apocryphal acts, John does not die a martyr's death but instead offers a final prayer commending the ascetic ideal of sexual purity and abstinence, and then lies down in a previously prepared grave and dies.

Although much in the Acts of John is not heterodox, the work was condemned as heretical by the Second Council of Nicaea (787 C.E.) because of its docetic and modalist tendencies. No complete manuscript of the work is extant, and the ca. 70 percent of the text that does survive must be reconstructed from manuscripts and secondary sources. One such source, the Acts of John by Prochorus, a 5th-century Greek collection, preserves several episodes from the earlier Acts of John but also rewords and embellishes its predecessor. The Acts were also used by Pseudo-Abdias and the Manichaean Psalm-Book, and known to Augustine, Eusebius, and Epiphanius.

Bibliography. J. K. Elliott, ed., *The Apocryphal New Testament,* rev. ed. (Oxford, 1993), 303-49; E. Junod and J.-D. Kaestli, *Acta Iohannis,* 2 vols. (Turnhout, 1983).

JAMES R. MUELLER

JOHN, APOCRYPHON OF (III, 1; IV, 1; BG, 2)

An early gnostic text, likely of the Sethian variety, concerning a vision of the Apostle John. The tractate provides an elaborate version of a gnostic mythical system. The first part emphasizes the origination of the divine and the spiritual beings, both in reference to the higher realm and the lower cosmic realm. Here attention is drawn to the fall of Wisdom (the soteriological crisis), the creation of the creator-god Yaldabaoth (vividly presented in monstrous images and equated with the OT God). The second part turns to the creation of humankind ("Adam"), with an important emphasis on salvation. Included are a discussion on the different types of souls, the creator-god's attempt to destroy those of the "immovable race" (i.e., those destined for salvation on account of their relation with the higher spiritual realm), and the descent-ascent of Pronoia ("foreknowledge") by which salvation is obtained.

The book has survived in four Coptic texts: two of a shorter version, and two of a longer version. These seem to be independent translations from a Greek original, which is no longer extant. Irenaeus (*Adv. haer.*, ca. 180 C.E.) seems to have been familiar with the Apocryphon or at least an earlier source. The closing of the longer version — the Providence Monologue — probably was an independent source later incorporated. Precise dating is difficult, although a manuscript tradition can be traced from the 2nd to 4th centuries.

This text is important for students of late antiquity. Debate continues as to whether the Apocryphon of John is primarily emergent from Jewish or Christian circles. Scholarly consensus now favors a strong Jewish connection (e.g., with Genesis, 1 Enoch, and the Wisdom of Solomon), with Christian elements being added later. Determining milieu is further complicated by the various versions of the text. The Apocryphon has also been studied in relation to Middle Platonism. Thus, this text sheds light on the cultural interrelations between various religious and philosophical groups in antiquity. The intertextual relation between the Apocryphon and biblical texts is also a significant issue (esp. Genesis and, in connection with the Providence Monologue, John 1:1-18). The descent of Wisdom, furthermore, can be seen as a gnostic example of the "descent into hell" tradition (traced back to 1 Peter and fully developed in the Acts of Pilate and the Apostles' Creed). Most important for students, however, is the elaborate gnostic system presented (yet it would be pushing too far to say that the Apocryphon of John is an exemplar of *the* gnostic system).

Bibliography. S. Giversen, *Apocryphon Johannis.* Acta Theologica Danica 5 (Copenhagen, 1963); K. Rudolph, *Gnosis* (San Francisco, 1984); J. D. Turner, "Sethian Gnosticism: A Literary History," in *Nag Hammadi, Gnosticism and Early Christianity,* ed. C. W. Hedrick and R. Hodgson, Jr. (Peabody, 1986), 55-86; M. Waldstein and F. Wisse, eds., *The Apocryphon of John.* NHMS 33 (Leiden, 1995); M. A. Williams, *The Immovable Race: A Gnostic Designation and the Theme of Stability in Late Antiquity.* NHS 29 (Leiden, 1985); F. Wisse, "The Apocryphon of John (II,*1,* III,*1,* IV,*1,* and BG 2502,*2*)," in *Nag Hammadi Library in English,* ed. J. M. Robinson, 3rd ed. (San Francisco, 1988), 104-23. PHILIP L. TITE

JOHN, GOSPEL OF

The fourth book in the NT. It tells how the Word of God became flesh in Jesus of Nazareth, who revealed God's glory and love through his words and actions. He was crucified for the sin of the world and raised that people might receive everlasting life through faith in him.

Contents

The Gospel presents the story of Jesus in two parts: Jesus' public ministry (chs. 1-12) and his Passion and Resurrection (chs. 13-21). Part 1 opens with a poetic prologue that relates how the Word entered the world and was rejected by many but welcomed by others who became God's children (1:1-18). In the narrative, John the Baptist directs people to Jesus, the Lamb of God, who gathers a circle of disciples. Jesus' teachings and healings evoke favorable responses from Samaritan villages, a royal official, a man born blind, Martha and Mary. Others misunderstand or become hostile when Jesus heals on the sabbath (ch. 5), feeds 5000 at Passover (ch. 6), announces at the Festival of Booths that he is the source of living water and the light of the world (7:1–10:20), and declares that "I and the Father are one" during the Feast of Dedication (10:22-39). Crowds wave palm branches when Jesus enters Jerusalem for the last time, but they fail to understand his allusions to his coming death, and Jesus concludes his public ministry by hiding from them (12:36).

Part 2 begins with the Last Supper when Jesus assumes the posture of a slave and washes his disciples' feet. This act displays his love for them and models the kind of service envisioned by the new commandment, to "love one another as I have loved you" (13:34). In a lengthy farewell discourse, Jesus promises to send the Spirit or "Advocate" (Gk. *parákletos*). The Spirit will be Jesus' abiding presence with people after his return to the Father, disclosing the meaning of Jesus' ministry to later generations (14:16, 26). Through dramatic irony, the account of Jesus' arrest and interrogation manifests Jesus' innocence and the culpability of his accusers. On the day of Preparation for Passover, Jesus is crucified as the Lamb of God, and his final words "it is accomplished" affirm that his death carries out God's saving work. On Easter, the risen Jesus appears to the disciples and gives them the Spirit as he promised. One week later Thomas' confession that Jesus is Lord and God brings the story to a climax. The great catch of fish in ch. 21 anticipates the spread of Christian mission.

Authorship and Composition

The Fourth Gospel does not disclose the name of its author. According to 21:24 the book preserves the testimony of "the disciple whom Jesus loved." By the late 2nd century this disciple was identified with John the son of Zebedee, since he sometimes accompanies Peter as John does in the other Gospels. Modern scholars, however, find it unlikely that the identity of a well-known figure like John would have been kept hidden. Moreover, according to the other Gospels John followed Jesus throughout his ministry, but in the Fourth Gospel the Beloved Disciple is explicitly mentioned for the first time only at the Last Supper (13:23). Some have suggested that the Beloved Disciple is the unnamed figure who encountered Jesus near the Jordan (1:35-40) and was known in the high priest's household (18:15-16), but these connections might suggest that the Beloved Disciple was actually a Judean rather than a Galilean like John. Others propose that he was Lazarus, whom Jesus loved (11:3, 5).

Many rightly acknowledge that the Beloved Disciple's identity remains unknown.

The Gospel was probably composed over a period of time in two or more editions. An early version probably ended with 20:30-31, which says that "Jesus did many other signs . . . which are not written in this book." The final chapter, which has a similar ending (21:25), was apparently added in a later, expanded edition. In an early version, Jesus' command "Rise, let us be on our way" (14:31) probably signaled the end of the Last Supper and Jesus' movement to the garden where he was arrested (18:1). The material in chs. 15-17 was probably included later. The entire Gospel is written with the same style and outlook, and the same person may have produced both the earlier and later versions. The comment that "*we* know" that the Beloved Disciple's testimony is true (21:24), however, suggests that others may have put the text in final form.

Date

The Gospel was probably completed by ca. A.D. 90. A date before the end of the 1st century is likely since the discovery of a fragment of text ($\mathfrak{P}^{52}$) shows that the Gospel was being copied in Egypt by 125-150. A date after the temple's destruction in 70 is also likely. Earlier there were various Jewish groups in Palestine — Pharisees, Sadducees, Essenes, Zealots, Herodians — but after 70 the Pharisees became dominant and other groups faded. The way the Evangelist alternately refers to "the Pharisees" and "the Jews" suggests that he wrote when other groups were no longer a factor. References to formal procedures for putting Christians out of the synagogue (9:22) and the contrasts between Jesus' followers and the Jews (e.g., v. 28) are made in ways that suggest that Christians were no longer considered a Jewish sect but were a distinct group, which was true later in the century. The author's knowledge of the deaths of Peter and the Beloved Disciple (21:19, 23) also points to composition in the final decades of the century.

Readers

John's Gospel was composed in and for an early Christian community. The many subtle allusions, wordplays, and difficult passages have led some to conclude that the earliest readers belonged to an introverted sectarian group that used language virtually unintelligible to outsiders. Others find that portraying Jesus as the light of the world, the source of living water, and the good shepherd, and explaining the meaning of words like "messiah" and "rabbi" (1:38-41) make the story accessible to a wide range of readers. Together, these perceptions indicate that the Gospel was completed with a spectrum of readers in view, perhaps because of developments within Johannine Christianity itself. The earliest members of the community were almost certainly Jewish Christians, but the Gospel suggests that the circle later included Samaritans (4:39-42) and Greeks (12:20), and the Christians mentioned in the Johannine Epistles bore Greek names and lived in various communities. The Gospel is accessible at a basic level to less-informed readers yet sophisticated enough to engage better-informed readers.

Relationship to Other NT Books

Synoptic Gospels

In all four Gospels Jesus' public ministry begins with John the Baptist and includes the gathering of disciples, performing miracles, expelling merchants from the temple, and teaching publicly. All relate that after a meal with his disciples, Jesus was arrested and tried before the Jewish authorities and Pilate, that he died by crucifixion and rose on the third day. John is different in that he recounts many actions (e.g., turning water into wine, healing at Bethesda and Siloam, raising Lazarus, washing feet) and encounters (e.g., Nicodemus, Samaritan woman, Thomas) that are not mentioned in the other Gospels. Instead of parables about the kingdom, John includes long discourses punctuated by sayings like "I am the bread of life" and "I am the light of the world." In John's Gospel Jesus makes several trips to Jerusalem during his ministry rather than just one, and the timing of key events is distinctive: the temple cleansing occurs at the beginning of Jesus' ministry rather than the end, and the Crucifixion takes place on the afternoon before rather than on the day after the Passover meal. Interpreters long thought that the Fourth Evangelist was familiar with the Synoptics and wrote his Gospel to supplement the others. Many scholars now argue that John did not know any of the other Gospels. It seems clear that the Fourth Evangelist wrote largely independently of the others, but whether he knew one or more of the Synoptics remains disputed.

Johannine Epistles

The Gospel and Letters of John are related like links in a chain. The Gospel and 1 John open with references to "the beginning," use imagery of light and darkness, and refer to the "new commandment" to love one another. 1-2 John insist that true believers confess that Jesus came in the flesh. 2-3 John were written by an "elder" who dealt with issues of whom to welcome into the communities. Many scholars think that the Letters were written later than the Gospel, since the basic conflict in the Gospel is between Christians and non-Christians while the Letters deal with conflicts that arose within the Christian community itself, seemingly at a later period. Some propose that John's Gospel was put into final form by the author of 1 John, but others suggest that these writings came from a circle of Christians who shared a common outlook.

Revelation

An early Church tradition said that the Fourth Gospel and Revelation were composed by the apostle John. This assumed that the Beloved Disciple (John 21:24) and John of Patmos (Rev. 1:9) were the same person. Both the Gospel and Revelation refer to Jesus as the Word and the Lamb, and utilize some similar symbolic language, but Revelation is written in an idiosyncratic Greek that differs markedly from the style of the Gospel. Revelation gives the author's name but does not suggest that he was an apostle or had seen the earthly Jesus, while the Gospel conceals the author's name but insists that he was an eyewitness. Revelation emphasizes the future consummation of God's saving work while the Gospel stresses the present dimension of salvation. These and other differences indicate that the two books had different authors.

Theological Emphasis

Understanding the Gospel's theological emphases requires attention to what is assumed and what is argued. Jesus' humanity is assumed throughout the Gospel; friends and foes alike recognize that he is a human being. Disputes center on whether Jesus is the Messiah and Son of God (5:18; 7:40-42; 10:33), so that the Evangelist must argue for the messianic and divine aspects of Jesus' identity. Encounters with Jesus disclose three principal dimensions of his character. First, those who meet Jesus rightly identify him in human terms as a man, a teacher, and a Jew (1:38; 4:9; 9:11). Second, they speak of him as prophet and Messiah (1:41; 4:19, 29; 9:17, 22). Third, there are indications of his divine or cosmic significance (1:51; 4:42; 9:38). Symbolic language helps to convey that Jesus is at once human, messianic, and divine, since images like light (8:12) and a good shepherd (10:11) were suitable for human leaders, the Messiah, and God. Later, some affirmed Jesus' divinity while denying his humanity (1 John 4:2-3; 2 John 7), and this view eventually became common among Gnostics. The Fourth Gospel, however, insists that Jesus' identity encompasses all three dimensions (20:30-31).

Human beings, according to John's Gospel, belong to a world that was created by God but has become hostile toward its Creator. Sin is a broken relationship with God — unbelief — and the actions that proceed from it. By giving up his Son to be crucified, God shows his love for the world that has rebelled against him (3:16). Christ's death is the sacrifice that takes away the sin of the world (1:29) because through it God overcomes sin by evoking faith. Faith brings people into life in relationship with God that begins in the present and continues beyond physical death into eternity. The Gospel affirms that there will be a future resurrection (5:28-29; 6:40; 11:25) while insisting that eternal life is also a present reality, because through faith in Christ people enter into relationship with the eternal God (5:24; 11:26; 12:44-45). Those who receive the love that God manifested in Christ are to love one another in the same way (13:34). The death of Christ establishes the source and pattern for Christian life.

Bibliography. J. Ashton, *Understanding the Fourth Gospel* (Oxford, 1991); R. E. Brown, *The Gospel According to John,* 2 vols. AB 29-29A (Garden City, 1966-1970); R. A. Culpepper, *Anatomy of the Fourth Gospel* (Philadelphia, 1983); C. R. Koester, *Symbolism in the Fourth Gospel* (Minneapolis, 1995); R. Schnackenburg, *The Gospel According to St. John,* 3 vols. (New York, 1968-1982); D. M. Smith, *The Theology of the Gospel of John* (Cambridge, 1995).

CRAIG R. KOESTER

JOHN, LETTERS OF

Three NT letters traditionally bearing the name of John. Although they are included among the "Catholic" or "General" Epistles, all three seem to be addressed to specific situations. While the first letter is anonymous, the two smaller letters give their author as "the Elder." It is doubtful that this term could be a title for the Apostle John; and though 1 John is closely related to the Fourth Gospel, it is not certain that it has the same author (whether or not the Gospel itself was written by the apostle). The situation and authorship of each of these letters thus need to be discussed.

1 John

The similarity in literary style and theology that sets the Gospel and Letters of John apart from all other NT writings is a strong argument that they were written by the same person, and this is especially true for 1 John and the Gospel. Yet there are differences between these two as well, in small details of linguistic habit; in literary quality (the Gospel uses irony and multiple meanings, while 1 John is often simply unclear); and in theology (1 John lays more stress on Jesus' atoning death and less on his mediation between God and the believer). Scholars are divided over whether these differences are natural in works written by the same author at different times, or are serious enough to suggest two different authors. The increasingly common idea of a Johannine "school" implies a group of tradition-bearers and teachers rather than single authority behind all the Johannine writings. The author of 1 John is probably also the "Elder" responsible for 2 and 3 John; at any rate, the latter are too brief to furnish enough evidence to establish a difference in authorship.

1 John lacks the typical characteristics that marked a letter in the ancient world, and it is now usually classified as an essay or sermon or the like. It has many characteristics of the rhetoric of persuasion or exhortation, e.g., repetition and the use of fixed formulations and examples to be imitated. No definite literary structure has been established for 1 John, nor is there any obvious development of thought in its repetition of important themes. Some have suggested that 1 John results from the editing of a source, but this is unlikely.

1 John is evidently a response to a crisis in the Johannine Christian community. The author speaks of certain people who "went out" from the community, whom he calls antichrists, deceivers, and false prophets, who failed to confess that Jesus is the Christ and the Son of God, or to confess "Jesus Christ having come in flesh" (2:18-27; 4:1-6). These opponents may also be in view when the author speaks about people who claim to have no sin, or to be children of God

even though they do sin (1:5–2:2; 2:28–3:10; cf. 5:16-18); who lack mutual love (2:3-11; 3:10-18; cf. 4:7-20); and who lay claim to the Spirit (4:1-6; cf. 5:6-8). The opponents are usually considered to represent an early form of Docetism, and/or to be related to the early gnostic teacher Cerinthus.

Such identifications may be too precise to be sustained by the hints of 1 John, but the opponents do seem to have devalued the physical, human reality of Jesus Christ in some way. They may have distinguished the human nature of Jesus from the divine Christ, stressing the revelation of the Christ as more meaningful for salvation than the crucifixion of the man Jesus. They may have believed that faith in the heavenly Christ and possession of the Spirit gave them not only eternal life and an intimate relationship with God, but a divine nature incapable of sin. Feeling no need for the human Jesus, either as an atoning sacrifice or as a model for sacrificial love, they correspondingly saw no spiritual value in concrete acts of human care on their own part. They may have convinced many in the Johannine Christian community to follow them into a separate fellowship.

This reinterpretation of Johannine tradition probably rose some time after the Fourth Gospel was substantially completed, when new circumstances had transplanted the Gospel's exalted claims about Jesus into the context of a more radical dualism. In this situation, the author of 1 John on the one hand reached back into the tradition. He stresses adherence to what has been essential "from the beginning": the confession of Jesus as Christ "in the flesh," i.e., in all his humanity; and the commandment to love one another within the community that makes this confession (1:1-3; 2:7-11, 22-24; 3:11-24; 4:1-16; 4:19–5:5). On the other hand, the author reached out to other forms of developing Christianity. He emphasizes more strongly than the Gospel of John themes common elsewhere in the NT: the atoning death of Jesus, the problem of sin for believers, and Jesus' future return (1:5–2:2; 2:28–3:10; 4:10, 17-18; 5:16-18).

The essential message of 1 John is that relationship with God requires both belief in incarnational christology and mutual love; and that these two are inseparably united. No new revelation can supersede the incarnation, in which the God who is love was made known in the humanity of Jesus Christ. Christian love can arise only from faith in this revelation; but faith is faith in Jesus Christ only as believers act out their love for one another.

2 John

2 John seems to derive from the same general situation as 1 John (esp. vv. 5-9). However, 2 John 10-11 proposes a more drastic solution to the problem of the opponents: refusal of hospitality to traveling teachers who do not adhere to the traditional Johannine Christology. It is possible that 2 John was addressed to a community to which the opponents' teaching had not yet come, and was meant to prevent its taking root there.

Unlike 1 John, 2 John does have the form of an ordinary letter. However, this form has been adapted to give 2 John a kind of official authority, as in the Pauline Letters. Note, e.g., the theologically expanded greeting in vv. 1-3. The "elect lady" mentioned there is probably a Christian congregation, a "sister" congregation to the author's own (vv. 1, 13). The unusual designation of the sender of the letter as "the Elder" also suggests someone in a position of respect and authority in the Johannine community, an impression confirmed by the tone of all three letters. Yet this designation, without a proper name and not as part of a *body* of elders, has no parallel in early Christian literature. No further facts are known about this "Elder."

3 John

The same "Elder" appears as the sender of 3 John, which, although closely similar to 2 John at the beginning and end, follows the conventions of ancient letter format more closely than 2 John or any other NT letter. In part, 3 John is a letter of recommendation for a Christian named Demetrius, and in part it is an exhortation to its recipient, Gaius, to follow good examples and avoid bad ones. However, it also treats a specific conflict.

3 John shows that, whoever "the Elder" may have been, his authority was not unchallenged. Someone named Diotrephes has refused to receive a letter from the Elder, and has refused hospitality to its bearers; moreover, he is expelling those who do show hospitality from the congregation. Though it seems natural to assume that this controversy is related to the one in 1 and 2 John, 3 John makes no reference to the themes of those letters. Rather, the conflict over hospitality may be related to developing structures of office and authority in the Church, or to issues of personal power and honor. The Elder's solution to the problem is to threaten a confrontation with Diotrephes in person, and to seek from Gaius the hospitality and support for traveling missionaries that Diotrephes had refused.

Dates and Location

1 and 2 John must have been written about the same time; 3 John could be a few years earlier or later. Beyond this, dates can be proposed only in relation to the Fourth Gospel, which 1 John evidently presupposes. The date of the Gospel itself is uncertain, however, and the length of time between the two is unknown. Perhaps no more than 10 to 20 years need be allowed. The tradition of the Church has always placed the Johannine writings in Ephesus. Nothing in the letters themselves positively confirms or contradicts this; one may note that Christian writers in Asia Minor are the first to show knowledge of them.

Bibliography. R. E. Brown, *The Epistles of John.* AB 30 (Garden City, 1982); J. M. Lieu, *The Second and Third Epistles of John* (Edinburgh, 1986); *The Theology of the Johannine Epistles* (Cambridge, 1991); D. Rensberger, *1 John, 2 John, 3 John.* Abingdon New Testament Commentaries (Nashville, 1997); R. Schnackenburg, *The Johannine Epistles* (New York, 1992); S. S. Smalley, *1, 2, 3 John.* WBC 51 (Waco, 1984).

David Rensberger

JOHN MARK

See MARK, JOHN.

JOHN (Gk. *Iōánnēs*) **THE APOSTLE**

The son of Zebedee and brother of James. He was a fisherman who grew up on the northern shore of the Sea of Galilee (Mark 1:19-20). Because of their fiery tempers, John and his brother were nicknamed Boanerges, "sons of thunder" (Mark 3:17).

The earliest textual evidence for John is in Paul's letter to the Galatians (ca. 52 C.E.), in which he mentions John (along with James the brother of Jesus and Cephas/Peter) as an "acknowledged pillar" in the Jerusalem church (Gal. 2:9). Mark's Gospel, used by Matthew and Luke, is the primary NT source of biographical information about John. John and Jesus' other 11 disciples play a significant role in Mark's Gospel, although primarily as negative role models. Scholars suggest that, like Paul before him, Mark portrays the disciples negatively in order to challenge their authoritative position in the Jerusalem church. If so, then John's special position as one of the inner circle of Jesus' three disciples (Mark 5:37; 9:2; 14:33; cf. Acts 3:1; 4:1) may be largely a retrojection of Mark's peculiar concern in 70 C.E. back into the ministry of Jesus. However, other biographical details about John seem less likely to have been invented by the early Church.

Five NT documents bear the name John: the Gospel of John, the three epistles of John, and Revelation. However, these titles were not originally part of the documents, and the name John occurs only in the book of Revelation. Justin Martyr (ca. 160) was the first to connect John, the visionary of the book of Revelation, with "John, an apostle of Christ." The Muratorian Canon (dated variously from 190 to 350) is probably the earliest extant evidence that attributes all five documents to the Apostle John. But with the rise of historical criticism in the late 18th century, scholars began to question whether any of the five canonical documents could legitimately be traced back to John the Apostle. Differences in literary styles and a growing appreciation for the politics of authorship in the early Church led scholars to propose two other shadowy figures as possible authors of these texts. John "the elder" (2 John 1, 3 John 1, Papias) — presumed by many to be totally different from the apostle — might be the actual author of at least two of the epistles and the Fourth Gospel. Another possibility is the "beloved disciple" who appears as a witness to Jesus' passion and validates the Fourth Gospel (John 13:23; 19:26; 20:2; 21:7, 20). Some scholars suggest that the early Church may have melded these two individuals, along with the visionary of Revelation, into a single figure named John, the disciple of Jesus.

Between the 2nd and 5th centuries, texts purporting to be written by the Apostle John and legends about him continued to appear. These traditions help solidify and legitimate the peculiarities of Johannine theology within the canon and within the Church's developing christological debates. It is during this period that Salome was identified as the mother of John (Mark 15:40-41; John 19:25), thus making John Jesus' cousin and his youngest disciple. It is also during this time that church tradition identified John as the beloved disciple of the Fourth Gospel and the author of the book of Revelation. According to some traditions, John took Mary the mother of Jesus to Ephesus (Justin Martyr *Dial.* 81.4), from which he was exiled to the island of Patmos. He was eventually released, and returned to Ephesus to teach, where the young Christian, Papias, met him and came to know him as "John, the elder." John the elder, the apostle, and beloved cousin of Jesus, then died at an advanced age ca. 100, the last of the living apostles.

Bibliography. R. E. Brown, *The Community of the Beloved Disciple* (New York, 1979); J. Charlesworth, *The Beloved Disciple* (Valley Forge, 1995); R. A. Culpepper, *John, the Son of Zebedee* (Columbia, S.C., 1994); W. H. Wuellner, *The Meaning of "Fishers of Men"* (Philadelphia, 1967).

JEFFREY L. STALEY

JOHN THE BAPTIST

Jewish religious figure at the time of Jesus, executed by Herod Antipas (4 B.C.E.–39 C.E.).

Sources

The basic sources on John the Baptist are Q, Mark, and Josephus *Ant.* 18.116-19. Information pertinent to the followers of John is found in the Gospel of John and the source of Pseudo-Clementine *Recognitions* 1.27-71. The value of the information in Acts, the special Lukan material, the Gospel of Thomas, and the Mandean writings is disputed. The presence of a non-Christian report (Josephus) to complement the Christian accounts means that the availability of sources is comparatively good.

Name

John (presumably Aram./Heb. *yôḥānān*, "God has shown favor"), a name found in the OT, is accompanied in Josephus and Mark by the sobriquet "baptist" (Aram. perhaps *tôḇeēl, ṣôḇē*ʿ, or *maṣbaʿ*), which apparently points to the distinctive aspect of John's activity.

Activity and Location

The most certain aspect of John's activity is thus that he gave instructions about proper ablution. In this regard, John fits his Jewish environment as it is becoming increasingly known through the Dead Sea Scrolls (e.g., 1QS 3:8-9) and archaeology (*miqwāʾôṯ*, ritual baths). It is uncertain whether John prescribed repeated ablutions or distinguished himself by promoting a one-time baptism (Josephus remarkably uses the singular).

The placement of John's activity in the wilderness and at the Jordan River (Mark) stands roughly in accord with the site of his execution according to Josephus (the fortress Machaerus) and with information in the Gospel of John (Bethany across the Jordan and Aenon near Salim). This location is generally accepted and would allow movement across political borders (Judea-Samaria, Perea, Decapolis) and access to natural water ("living water").

Josephus and Mark 1:5; 11:32 agree that John was enormously popular. There is no compelling reason to question the Gospels' tradition that John was active generally prior to Jesus' ministry, though the exact chronological relationship of the two cannot be specified. Josephus relates that some Jews thought that Antipas' execution of John had been avenged by God through the defeat of his army by Aretas IV, probably in 36 C.E. John's death accordingly preceded this date and probably belongs in the latter half of Antipas' reign.

Particularly in view of John's popularity, the Christian tradition that Jesus was baptized by John (and that John was soon arrested thereafter) is open to historical question. It is not clear that Q described Jesus' baptism by John. Jesus himself must nevertheless have at least heard about John and doubtless approved of him, perhaps even imitating him in some respects.

Religious Message

The exact contents and scope of John's message are difficult to determine. Josephus presents John as someone who exhorts to virtue, righteousness among fellow Jews, and reverence toward God. Given the general political and religious climate, there are likely to have been political overtones pertaining to the future of the Jewish people. Whether John used apocalyptic imagery (cf. Q) is uncertain. In any event, Christian tradition has moved John into a much more definite role as precursor of the Messiah and as Elijah.

John's teaching regarding baptism doubtless involved some discussion of repentance, purity, and forgiveness. Josephus is at pains to deny that the baptism was for forgiveness of sins, while Mark affirms this. Both positions seem to be evolved from an original connection of repentance, baptism, purity, and forgiveness, witnessed also in the writings from Qumran. The controlling idea that forgiveness comes from God will not have been displaced.

The location of John's activity outside Jerusalem, combined with baptism involving forgiveness, raises the question of to what degree John consciously challenged the Jerusalem priesthood. Increasing evidence for the prevalence of Jewish ritual ablutions renders less likely the thesis that a baptist movement must necessarily have stood in opposition to the temple cult.

Followers

Mark, Q, and John agree in speaking of a special group of "disciples of John." Remarkably, these writings witness to the continued existence of this distinct group throughout Jesus' ministry. The kernel of this group undoubtedly goes back to the lifetime of John. A group of John's adherents seems to have continued on to rival followers of Jesus even after John's death. Out of the dialogue, Johannine elements such as fasting and baptism might have been introduced into the nascent Christian faith.

John's disciples evidently believed John to be the Messiah (*Recognitions* 1.54.8; 1.60.1-2; John 1). After his execution, they seem to have thought John was hidden away by God to return soon (Mark 6:14, 16; 8:28; *Recognitions* 1.54.8). In all these aspects John's movement appears to have established a pattern for the early followers of Jesus.

Bibliography. C. H. Kraeling, *John the Baptist* (New York, 1951); E. F. Lupieri, "John the Baptist in New Testament Traditions and History," in *ANRW* II.26,1 (Berlin, 1993), 430-61; C. H. H. Scobie, *John the Baptist* (Philadelphia, 1964); R. L. Webb, *John the Baptizer and Prophet.* JSNTSup 62 (Sheffield, 1991); W. Wink, *John the Baptist in the Gospel Tradition.* SNTSMS 7 (London, 1968).

F. STANLEY JONES

JOHN THE DIVINE, DISCOURSE OF

An apocryphal Greek narrative told by John concerning the death and bodily assumption (or dormition) of the "all-holy glorious mother of God and ever-virgin Mary." It is the standard Greek version of the apocryphal Assumption of the Virgin. The many assumption accounts of Mary originated around the 4th century C.E. and have made a profound impact on both the Eastern and Western forms of Christianity. The "Assumption of the Virgin" was affirmed as an official doctrine by the Roman Catholic Church in 1950.

In this narrative Gabriel announces to Mary that her request for departure from the world will be answered. The apostles, both living and dead, are summoned to visit Mary, offer this assistance and receive her blessing. Jesus comes to take her spirit to paradise, her body is placed in a new tomb in Gethsemane, and three days later her body is taken to heaven. Mary is presented as an important link between the Trinity and humanity.

KENNETH J. ARCHER

JOIADA (Heb. *yôyāḏāʿ*) (also JEHOIADA)

1. The son of Paseah who restored the Old Gate in Jerusalem under Nehemiah (Neh. 3:6).

2. A priest during the reign of Darius and the son of the high priest Eliashib (**7;** Neh. 12:10-11, 22). At Neh. 13:28 the name appears as Jehoiada.

JOIAKIM (Heb. *yôyāqîm*)

A postexilic high priest; the son of Jeshua (**9**) and the father of Eliashib (**8;** Neh. 12:10, 12, 26).

JOIARIB (Heb. *yôyārîḇ*) (also JEHOIARIB)

1. A "man of insight" sent by Ezra to Iddo in Casiphia, requesting levitical priests for the temple (Ezra 8:16).

2. A Judahite; son of Zechariah (**25**), father of Adaiah, and ancestor of Maaseiah (Neh. 11:5).

3. A priest who returned with Zerubbabel from captivity in Babylon (Neh. 11:10; 12:6), head of a priestly house (v. 19). At 1 Chr. 9:10 he is called Jehoiarib.

JOKDEAM (Heb. *yoqdĕʿām*)

A city in the tribal territory of Judah (Josh. 15:56). The LXX reads Jorkeam (cf. 1 Chr. 2:44). The site may be modern Khirbet er-Raqaʿ (160096) between Juttah and Ziph, 7 km. (4 mi.) S of Hebron.

JOKIM (Heb. *yôqîm*)
A son of Shelah, from the tribe of Judah (1 Chr. 4:22).

JOKMEAM (Heb. *yoqmĕʿām*)
A levitical city allotted to the clan of Kohath (1 Chr. 6:68[MT 53]). In 1 Chr. 23:19; 24:23 a Hebronite levitical family bears the similar name Jekameam. Listed as one of the cities in Solomon's fifth district (1 Kgs. 4:12), Jokmeam should be identified with either the Iron I-II sites of Tell el-Mazâr (195171) or Waqf es-Samadi (195172) in the Wadi Farʿah. Many modern maps and authors have confused matters, however, by labeling both of these sites Tell es-Simadi. ROBERT D. MILLER, II

JOKNEAM (Heb. *yoqnĕʿām*)
A town allotted to the Levites of the clan of Merari on the western boundary of Zebulun (Josh. 19:11; 12:22). The king of Jokneam is said to have been killed by Joshua and the Israelites (Josh. 12:22).

As a royal Canaanite city, Jokneam appears in a topographical list of Thutmose III. Eusebius was unaware of the location of the site, although he knows of a Kammona corresponding to the locale (*Onom.* 116:21), probably the same as the Cyamon in Jdt. 7:3.

Jokneam is identified with Tel Yoqneʿam/Tell Qeimûn (1604.2289), situated at a point along the border of the Carmel range and the Jezreel Valley, 20 km. (12.5 mi.) SE of modern Haifa and 11 km. (7 mi.) NW of Megiddo. In Iron I successive Canaanite, Phoenician, and Philistine phases occupied the 4 ha. (10 a.) site, but Israelite occupation is not evident until Iron II, where a large fortified city is preserved. The site was occupied through the Persian, Hellenistic, Roman, and later periods as well.
ROBERT D. MILLER, II

JOKSHAN (Heb. *yoqšān*)
A son of Abraham and Keturah; eponymous ancestor of various Arabian peoples (Gen. 25:2-3; 1 Chr. 1:32).

JOKTAN (Heb. *yoqṭān*)
A son of Eber and descendant of Shem; eponymous ancestor of various Arabian peoples (Gen. 10:25-29 = 1 Chr. 1:19-23).

JOKTHEEL (Heb. *yoqṯĕʾēl*)
1. A town in the Shephelah, or lowland, of Judah (Josh. 15:38). It may be linked wih Jekuthiel, depicted as one of the descendants of Caleb, the "father of Zanoah" and the uncle of Socoh (1 Chr. 4:18). Both Zanoah and Socoh are sites in the Shephelah, andIoktheel may be located nearby.

2. The capital of Edomite territory. Amaziah king of Judah renamed the Edomite site of Sela (modern Petra) Joktheel after conquering it (2 Kgs. 14:7). JENNIFER L. GROVES

JONADAB (Heb. *yônāḏāḇ*) (also JEHONADAB)
1. The son of David's brother Shimeah (2 Sam. 13:3; *yĕhônāḏāḇ* in v. 5). David's son Amnon was infatuated with his half-sister Tamar, and Jonadab, who is described as a "very crafty man," counseled him to feign sickness and request of his father that Tamar prepare a meal in front of him. Amnon heeded Jonadab's advice, and when Tamar drew near Amnon seized and raped her. The scheme may have been intended to establish Amnon's claim to the throne. After Absalom had his brother Amnon slain for raping his sister, David heard a rumor that all of his sons were slain. Jonadab, however, assured him that only Amnon had been killed and that Absalom had been planning this since the rape of Tamar (2 Sam. 13:32, 35).

2. The son of Rechab (2 Kgs. 10:15), the eponymous ancestor of the Rechabite clan. According to 2 Kgs. 10:15-24, where he is referred to as Jehonadab *(yĕhônāḏāḇ)*, he accompanied Jehu in the slaughter of the survivors of the house of Ahab (vv. 15-17) as well as the priests of Baal (vv. 18-24). Jonadab's zeal for the Lord is also evidenced in Jer. 35, where the Rechabites are described as abstaining from wine, building houses, sowing seeds, and planting vineyards, as their ancestor Jonadab had enjoined them, that they might live long upon the land (vv. 6-7). Jer. 35 concludes that if Judah had followed the Lord's commands it would have prospered even as the Rechabites prospered for their faithfulness to Jonadab's command (vv. 12-19).
JOHN E. HARVEY

JONAH (Heb. *yônâ*), **BOOK OF**
The fifth book of the Minor Prophets collection, named for its chief character. This placement may function to provide a positive word about the nations after Obadiah. The reference to Jonah, son of Amittai (Jonah 1:1), relates the book to an 8th-century prophet who spoke in support of Jeroboam II, king of Israel (786-746 B.C.E.; 2 Kgs. 14:25).

The reason for this historical connection is not clear, especially in view of the nonhistorical nature of the book. It may be that Nineveh (the capital of Assyria), responsible for destroying the northern kingdom in 721, serves as a type for wicked nations opposed to God's purposes (cf. Nah. 3:1). The question posed is this: Is God's salvation available even to such people? For God to be so concerned about the positive future of nations such as Assyria was intolerable to some: How could God think of saving a nation that had so devastated God's own people? Jonah himself is a type representing certain pious Israelites who posed such a question regarding the extension of God's mercy to the wicked. This perspective constituted a challenge to the confession of faith that Yahweh is "merciful and gracious, slow to anger, and abounding in steadfast love" (Exod. 34:6-7, disputed by Jonah in 4:2). The book argues that this ancient confession — with the addition about divine repentance (cf. Joel 2:13) — is still decisive in thinking about God and God's relationship to the larger world of nations. God's way with the world, not simply with Israel, is the way of mercy in the face of deserved judgment. Such a theological dispute may have surfaced in the postexilic period, when Israel's ongoing subjugation to a prospering foreign nation (Persia), related hardships, and the seeming failure of exilic promises raised questions about the fairness of God's treatment of Israel (cf. Mal. 2:17; 3:14-15).

The book differs from other prophets in its absence of oracles (except 3:4) and its form as a story about a prophet. Unlike other prophetic oracles against the nations, Jonah is called to deliver a word of judgment against Nineveh in person. Yet, the book is prophetic in that it speaks a word of judgment and grace to a specific *Israelite* audience, seeking to elicit amendment in their thought and life.

The book is a literary unity; the four chapters constitute a carefully structured creation wherein Jonah and the heathen (sailors and Ninevites) are compared. To this end, the book makes use of earlier motifs and traditions (Gen. 18; 1 Kgs. 10; Jer. 18, 36; Joel 2). The psalm originally functioned as an independent song of thanksgiving, here adapted to accommodate Jonah's gratitude for being saved from drowning. The book is to be identified as a satire, with irony widely used in depicting Jonah and his perspective on the nations. The concluding question is designed to move readers to a new theological stance.

The plot of Jonah may be outlined as follows:

Jonah Called (1:1-3)

God's call to preach to Nineveh is rejected by Jonah. The reason becomes clear only at 4:2. This call creates the possibility that Israel's destroyers might repent and God would extend them mercy rather than judgment. Jonah's sense of justice is violated. Hence, to escape to a place where God's call is less compelling, he buys the most expensive ticket on a ship headed in the opposite direction — to Tarshish in Spain.

Jonah Pursued (1:4-16)

Because Jonah's flight subverts God's intentions for Nineveh, God pursues the prophet through a storm at sea, not to visit him with wrath but to turn him around. Jonah responds to the storm with nonchalance, and the captain — who sees that prayer does not compel God (cf. 3:9) — ironically reminds him of his religious responsibilities. When the lots pinpoint Jonah as the culprit, he confesses his faith. This confession in time moves the sailors (parallel to the Ninevites in ch. 3) to worship the god of Jonah. But the confession does not stop the storm; in fact, the weather gets worse. What is at stake for God is not Jonah's confession (Jonah is a man of faith), but his theologically informed stance regarding the nations. Jonah confesses his guilt and, given his sense of justice, offers to be thrown overboard to receive his deserved judgment. The sailors finally grant Jonah's request after making sure they are not blamed if Jonah is innocent. The storm stops; the sailors respond to God like good Israelites.

Jonah's Response to God's Deliverance (1:17–2:10[MT 2:1-11])

God sends a fish to save Jonah from drowning and return him home. Ironically, guilty Jonah is the recipient of divine mercy. God's use of the fish brackets Jonah's prayer of thanksgiving. Metaphors typically used in stating or recalling distress (cf. Pss. 30, 42) are used literally by Jonah to depict his descent to the doors of death. Jonah voices the key theme of deliverance — ironically, for he no more deserves salvation than Nineveh and would limit God's exercise of the mercy that had saved him. The prayer reveals no repentant Jonah, but God and the fish mercifully bring him home.

Nineveh and God Repent (3:1-10)

Still in need of Jonah, God repeats the call. Nineveh is described in larger-than-life terms; the entire evil city repents (even the animals!) at Jonah's minimal efforts, executed under duress. Such deliberately overdrawn details highlight the irony of his unparalleled success. Jonah's graceless word in the wake of his own experience of grace — an unprecedented countdown to doom — speaks Jonah's own mind regarding a just future for the city. Led by their king, the Ninevites engage in words and acts of repentance. Israel's God, affected by such actions, responds by reversing the announced judgment. This pattern of threat followed by human and divine repentance, common in Israel's experience, is made available to all (Jer. 18:7-11).

A Theological Debate (4:1-11)

Jonah responds with profound anger at the deliverance and presents his case for originally refusing to go — a fear that God would be merciful when judgment was called for. God has not conformed to basic standards of justice, and Jonah calls for his own death for participating in this act of injustice — Jonah will be just (cf. 1:12). God refuses the challenge and questions Jonah's response to Nineveh's salvation. But Jonah remains firm and decides to sit and wait God out (4:5). God refuses to back off and sends a plant to reinforce Jonah's shade, ironically delivering the one who is angry at God for delivering others. Jonah rejoices in his own salvation and so God pursues the issue with a worm and wind, giving him a taste of the destruction he wished upon others. In view of such give-and-take capriciousness, Jonah prefers death. God persists and questions Jonah's anger at the plant's destruction. Either answer to this clever question impales Jonah. If negative (as it should have been), then Jonah recognizes God's right to make judgments regarding God's own creatures. If positive (as it was), then he tacitly acknowledges God's right to respond to Nineveh as God pleases. Jonah has received a gift from God apart from questions of justice, and so Jonah should not begrudge God's generosity when God extends that mercy to others.

Bibliography. T. E. Fretheim, *The Message of Jonah* (Minneapolis, 1977); J. Limburg, *Jonah.* OTL (Louisville, 1993); J. D. Magonet, *Form and Mean-*

ing: Studies in Literary Techniques in the Book of Jonah (Sheffield, 1983); J. M. Sasson, *Jonah.* AB 24B (New York, 1990); P. Trible, *Rhetorical Criticism: Context, Method, and the Book of Jonah.* Guides to Biblical Scholarship (Minneapolis, 1994); H. W. Wolff, *Obadiah and Jonah* (Minneapolis, 1986).

TERENCE E. FRETHEIM

JONAM (Gk. *Iōnám*)
An ancestor of Jesus; the son of Eliakim and father of a Joseph in Luke's genealogy (Luke 3:30).

JONATHAN (Heb. *yĕhônāṯān, yônāṯān;* Gk. *Iōnathás*) (also JEHONATHAN)

1. The son of Gershom; descendant of Moses (Judg. 18:30; MT "Manasseh"). Jonathan was a Levite from Bethlehem hired by Micah to serve at Micah's personal shrine (Judg. 17–18). He later founded the priesthood at Laish (Dan) that continued until the 8th-century B.C.E. Assyrian invasions (Judg. 18:30).

2. The firstborn son of King Saul and Ahinoam (1 Sam. 14:49; 1 Chr. 8:33; 9:39); father of Meribbaal/Mephibosheth (2 Sam. 9; 1 Chr. 8:34) and friend of David.

The chief lieutenant of Saul's army, Jonathan defeated the Philistines at Geba (1 Sam. 13:3). He demonstrated particular prowess in battle at Michmash. Aided only by his armor-bearer, he entered the Philistine camp, sending it into a panic (1 Sam. 14:6-15) and setting the stage for a rout by Saul's forces.

Jonathan's devotion to David is legendary. Together they made a covenant of friendship (1 Sam. 18:1-4). When Saul plotted to kill David, Jonathan intervened (1 Sam. 19:1-7; 20:1-34, 41-42). Later at Ziph, the two renewed their covenant; Jonathan renounced his claim as Saul's heir apparent, declaring that David should be the next king and Jonathan his first minister (1 Sam. 23:16-18). Nevertheless, Jonathan remained devoted to his father, and died with Saul in the battle of Mt. Gilboah (1 Sam. 31:1-2).

3. The son of Abiathar, a priest (2 Sam. 15:27; 17:17, 20). Often mentioned with Zadok's son, Ahimaaz, Jonathan served as courier to David during Absalom's rebellion. Later, he brought the news of Solomon's appointment as king to Adonijah (1 Kgs. 1:42-43).

4. Son of Shammah the Hararite (2 Sam. 23:32; called "Shagee" in 1 Chr. 11:34). His name appears in the list of David's warriors (2 Sam. 23:8-39 = 1 Chr. 11:10-47).

5. The son of Jada; father of Peleth and Zaza; a Jerahmeelite (1 Chr. 2:32-33). Mentioned in the genealogy of "Jerahmeel, the firstborn of Hezron" (2:25-41), he is part of the line traced through Jerahmeel's "other wife," Atarah. Since Jonathan's brother Jether died childless, the line survived through Jonathan's sons.

6. The son of Shimei (called "Shimea" in 1 Chr. 20:7), David's brother (2 Sam. 21:21; 1 Chr. 20:7). He killed a 12-fingered, 12-toed Philistine giant who taunted Israel. The death was either fourth (2 Sam. 21:20-21) or third (1 Chr. 20:6-7) in a series of giant killings done by "the hands of David and his servants" (2 Sam. 21:15-22; 1 Chr. 20:4-8). In some LXX manuscripts he is called Jonadab (2 Sam. 13:3). He is sometimes identified with Jonathan, David's official (1 Chr. 27:32; **8** below).

7. The son of Uzziah (1 Chr. 27:25). One of the officials responsible for David's property, he oversaw the treasuries in the country, cities, villages and towns (but not the "king's treasuries," a duty ascribed to Azmaveth).

8. The uncle of King David (1 Chr. 27:32; NEB "nephew"; cf. 20:7). His name appears in a list of David's officials (1 Chr. 27:25-34) where he is described as "a counselor, being a man of understanding and a scribe" (NRSV). He is sometimes identified with Jethiel as tutor to David's sons (1 Chr. 27:32b) or with the "son of Shimei" (2 Sam. 21:20-21 = 1 Chr. 20:6-7; **6** above).

9. The father of Ebed; descendant of Adin (Ezra 8:6; 1 Esdr. 8:32). His son is listed among family heads who returned from the Exile with Ezra, bringing with him either 50 (Ezra 8:6) or 250 (1 Esdr. 8:32) men.

10. The son of Asahel (Ezra 10:15; 1 Esdr. 9:14). He, along with Jehzeiah, opposed either the implementation of Ezra's marital reforms, or the commission set up for the task. He was supported in this action by two Levites, Meshullam and Shabbethai. While the MT records Jonathan's opposition, the LXX reads that Jonathan agreed with Ezra.

11. The son of Joiada and father of Jaddua; a high priest during the postexilic period (Neh. 12:11), and one of the Levites who accompanied Zerubbabal to Jerusalem. He is sometimes identified with Eliashib's descendant (son, Neh. 12:23; or grandson, v. 10), in whose house Ezra stayed (Ezra 10:6; 1 Esdr. 9:1; NRSV "Jehohanan").

12. A priest and ancestral head of the house of Malluchi during Joiakim's high priesthood (Neh. 12:14).

13. The son of Shemaiah, father of Zechariah (a Levite), and a descendant of Asaph (Neh. 12:35). His son, a priestly musician, took part in the dedication of Jerusalem's walls.

14. The secretary whose house served as a temporary prison for Jeremiah (Jer. 37:15, 20; 38:26). Some translations read "Jehonathan."

15. The son of Kareah (Jer. 40:8ff.; MT reads "Johanan and Jonathan sons of Kareah" but this should be understood as a dittography of "Johanan," since it is omitted in the LXX and in the parallel passage in 2 Kgs. 25:23). Against Jeremiah's advice (Jer. 42:1-22), he and the other commanders led the people to Egypt, taking Jeremiah with them (43:1-7).

LINDA S. SCHEARING

16. The son of Mattathias who assumed the leadership of the Jewish resistance forces in the wake of the reversals they suffered after the death of Judas Maccabeus in 160 B.C.E. (1 Macc. 9:23-31). In 1 Macc. 2:5 he is the last of the five sons listed. With the assistance of his brother Simon, Jonathan launched a series of guerilla attacks on the fortresses of Seleucid troops. Rival claimants to the

Seleucid throne then attempted to enlist his support in their struggles for ascendancy. He was designated a "friend" of the king and the first Hasmonean to be appointed high priest as well as general and governor of the province by both Alexander Balas and Demetrius II Nicator (1 Macc. 10:65-66; 11:26-28). He also was the first Hasmonean authorized to recruit and equip an army.

Jonathan did besiege the citadel, the fortification which provided housing for a Seleucid garrison in Jerusalem and sometimes also sheltered Jewish opponents of the Hasmoneans. Through strategic shifts in allegiance Jonathan's power and prestige were enhanced and the territory controlled by him and Simon his brother extended, largely by force. Employing deceit, Trypho captured Jonathan in Ptolemais and then killed him, apparently in the winter of 143/142 (1 Macc. 12:24–13:24). His bones were buried in Modein, the ancestral home of the Hasmoneans. It was Jonathan who laid the groundwork to establish this dynastic family as a significant force in the waning decades of the Seleucid Empire.

Josephus includes his first reference to the Pharisees, the Sadducees, and the Essenes in the middle of the account concerning Jonathan (*Ant.* 13.171-73). This frequently has been cited as evidence of their origins by the time of or during Jonathan's reign. Some scholars have considered Jonathan to be the Wicked Priest mentioned in Pesher Habakkuk and Pesher Ps. 37. While this evidence suggests the importance of the Hasmonean period for the growth of Jewish sectarianism, it is more difficult to relate the material specifically to Jonathan. JOHN KAMPEN

17. The son of Absalom (1 Macc. 13:11), sent to Joppa by Simon Maccabeus to defend and hold the city.

18. A priest during Nehemiah's time, who led the prayer over the sacrifice (2 Macc. 1:23).

LINDA S. SCHEARING

JOPPA (Heb. *yāp̄ô*)
A city (also Jaffa, Heb. Yafo; 126162) adjoining Tel Aviv and built on a promontory jutting into the Mediterranean, with a natural harbor below protected by several rocky outcrops. Joppa is first mentioned in a 15th-century B.C.E. inscription of Thutmose III (cf. also the Harris papyrus, ca. 1300). After the Conquest it was allotted to the tribe of Dan (Josh. 19:46) and became an important seaport (2 Chr. 2:16[MT 15]; Ezra 3:7). In the 5th century the Persian king granted Joppa to the Phoenician king of Sidon. After Alexander the Great it was populated by Greeks and Greek-speaking Syrians. Under the Hasmoneans, who seized and Judaized it ca. 140 (1 Macc. 13:11), and into the Roman period it remained a port of Judea. In the early Christian period Joppa was the seat of a bishop.

The site was excavated in 1945-1950 by the Israel Department of Antiquities and Museums and in 1954-1974 by Jacob Kaplan on behalf of the Tel Aviv–Jaffa Museum of Antiquities. The site was fortified as early as the Hyksos period (18th century). Significant finds include a Late Bronze Age citadel gate that had jambs inscribed with the titles of Rameses II, an Iron Age temple with a small pillared hall where a lion's skull was found, and Persian period walls of typical Phoenician construction (ashlar pillars with fieldstone fill between them). A large ashlar building that may have been part of the Hellenistic agora and private houses of the 1st and 2nd centuries C.E. were also found.

Bibliography. J. P. Dressel, "Jaffa," *OEANE* 3:206-7; J. Kaplan, "The Archaeology and History of Tel Aviv-Jaffa," *BA* 35 (1972): 66-95; Kaplan and H. Ritter-Kaplan, "Jaffa," *NEAEHL* 2:655-59.

KENNETH G. HOLUM

JORAH (Heb. *yôrâ*) (also HARIPH)
An Israelite whose descendants returned with Zerubbabel from captivity (Ezra 2:18). At Neh. 7:24 his name is given as Hariph.

JORAI (Heb. *yôray*)
The head of a Gadite father's house in Bashan; a son of Abihail (1 Chr. 5:13).

JORAM (Heb. *yôrām*) (also HADORAM)

1. The son of King Toi of Hamath, sent by his father to congratulate David on his victory over Hadadezer (2 Sam. 8:10). In the parallel account he is called Hadoram, son of Tou (1 Chr. 18:10).

2. A contracted form of the name Jehoram (**1, 2;** Heb. *yĕhôrām*).

3. A Levite descended from Eliezer the son of Moses (1 Chr. 26:25).

JORDAN (Heb. *yardēn;* Gk. *Iordánēs*) **RIVER**
The largest and most important river in Palestine, mentioned more than any other river in the Bible. Its waters originate in four rivers that arise from the watersheds of Mt. Hermon some 65 km. (40 mi.) NE of the Sea of Galilee. Once these rivers merge, the course of the Jordan flows into and out of the now dried depression once called Lake Huleh. Some 16 km. (10 mi.) beyond, it feeds into the Sea of Galilee. On emptying from the southern end of the Sea of Galilee, the Jordan begins a 320-km. (200-mi.) circuitous journey, tripling a 105-km. (65-mi.) direct path to its final destination, the Dead Sea.

After flowing from the Sea of Galilee, the Jordan's volume is increased by a number of tributaries. Most notable is the Transjordanian Yarmuk, a river not mentioned in the Bible but one which almost doubles the volume of Jordan's water. Among the tributaries that are mentioned in the Bible are the Jabbok (Nahr ez-Zerqâ; Gen. 32:22), and the "waters of Nimrin" (possibly Wadi en-Numeirah; Isa. 15:6). Since less rain per annum falls on the western mountains than on the eastern ones, the tributaries are bigger and more numerous in Transjordan.

Due to the winter rains the tributaries are at full force during the spring. This makes the numerous shallows (the "fords"; e.g., Judg. 3:28; 12:5) that much more important for crossing, especially since

Nahr Bâniyâs, easternmost source of the Jordan River at the base of Mt. Hermon. The cave from which it originates was regarded by the Greeks as home of the god Pan
(Phoenix Data Systems, Neal and Joel Bierling)

we know of no permanent bridge before Roman times. Since a 19th-Dynasty Egyptian inquired, "The stream of Jordan, how is it crossed?" (*ANET*, 477), the crossing of the Jordan must have been a common, even international, concern.

The appearance of the Jordan is not what some hymns might suggest (e.g., "On Jordan's Stormy Banks"). South of the Sea of Galilee, River Jordan ranges from 0.6–3 m. (2-10 ft.) deep and averages ca. 30 m. (100 ft.) wide. The climate tends to be hot and dry, with an average annual rainfall at Jericho of less than 10 cm. (4 in.) and temperatures over 38°C. (100°F.) not unusual. While its appearance is mild, the waters of the Jordan are swift due to its drop in elevation averaging 1.7 m. per 1 km. (9 ft. per mi.) from the Sea of Galilee to the Dead Sea.

The Jordan Valley is the result of a tectonic fault which produced the Great Rift valley, stretching from Turkey to East Africa. The Jordan Valley S of the Sea of Galilee is made up of several levels. The river rests in the Zōr (NRSV "thickets of the Jordan"; Jer. 12:5; 49:19), while above it ca. 46 m. (150 ft.) is the Ghōr. Literally, the Zōr was the "pride" or "majesty" (Heb. *gā'ôn*) of the Jordan, a colorful description of the naturally tangled greenery along its banks.

The etymology of the name Jordan is disputed. Many have held that it is of Semitic origin with the root meaning "to go down" (from Heb. *yārad̲*). Since all rivers, by nature, "go down," why the Jordan River would have been singled out as the "one going down," is not clear. If the name is of Semitic origin, perhaps the extreme and narrow valley in which the Jordan rests, and from which settlers on both of its sides had a vigorous journey to "go down" to its waters, may have contributed to the choice of its name. However, the overwhelming number of biblical references refer to the Jordan with the definite article *(hayyardēn)*, suggesting that the word originally may have been a common, not proper, noun. Thus, "Jordan" may have been an early, widely used generic word for river, thus "The River." In support of this latter etymology, the biblical writers never refer to the "Jordan River," but always "the Jordan" or "Jordan." In only a few passages is water even associated with the Jordan (e.g., Josh. 3:8; 4:18, 23; 5:1), and the character of the Jordan is seldom described (cf. Deut. 4:49; Ps. 114:3-5).

In most cases the Jordan River plays the role of boundary marker. Before the Israelites possessed the land, "across the Jordan" was where the Canaanites lived (e.g., Deut. 11:30). Once Canaan became the homeland of the Israelites, the Jordan served as a boundary of Israel (2 Sam. 17:22; 2 Kgs. 10:33). "Beyond" or "east" or "west" or "on the other side" of the Jordan (e.g., Gen. 50:10, 11; Num. 32:19; Deut. 1:5; Josh. 12:1; 13:8; Judg. 5:17; 1 Chr. 6:78[MT 63]) is the most common use of the Jordan River in the OT (i.e., as a point of reference for the juxtaposed positions of Cisjordan and Transjordan). The Jordan serves this same purpose in the NT (e.g., Mark 10:1; John 1:28; 3:26; 10:40).

In the biblical stories several miracles occur in or near the Jordan. Like the Red Sea, as the Israelites came to claim their land, the waters of the Jordan dried up (Josh. 3:15-16). It was also near the Jordan and the holy place of Gilgal that Elijah was taken to heaven (2 Kgs. 2:6). By dipping in the river seven times, following the instructions of Elisha, the doubting Syrian general Naaman was cleansed of leprosy (2 Kgs. 5:14). Elisha also threw a wooden stick on the Jordan, which made a lost metal ax head float on its waters (2 Kgs. 6:4-6).

In the NT the Jordan River is where John, Jesus' cousin, was baptizing (Matt. 3:5-6; Mark 1:5) and where John baptized Jesus (Matt. 3:13; Mark 1:9). At what location along the Jordan these events occurred is not known, although it seems likely John would have selected a shallow pool near a large population. One of the fords near Jericho, the largest city on the lower Jordan, would have provided a large population, the nearest location to the people of Jerusalem, and would have made his preaching that much more evident to Herod, who had a palace in Jericho (Mark 6:14-29). Although John the Baptist was executed at Machaerus (Josephus *Ant.* 18.5.2), Herod may well have first heard of John's preaching about "sin" in his own Jericho palace.

Bibliography. N. Glueck, *The River Jordan,* rev. ed. (New York, 1968); J. W. Rogerson, *Atlas of the Bible* (New York, 1985). DAVID MERLING

JORIM (Gk. *Iōrím*)
An ancestor of Jesus; father of Eliezer and son of Matthat (Luke 3:29).

JORKEAM (Heb. *yorqĕʿām*)
A settlement in Judah mentioned in the list of villages settled by the house of Caleb (1 Chr. 2:44). Though the context of this chapter is a genealogy, most commentators associate the names with a list of towns in Josh. 15. The LXX reads Jokdeam and thus ties further the Chronicler's passage to Josh. 15:56. Jorkeam was most likely located S of Jerusalem, probably in the hill country around Hebron.

JOHN S. VASSAR

JOSECH (Gk. *Iōséch*)
An ancestor of Jesus listed in Luke's genealogy (Luke 3:26).

JOSEPH (Heb. *yôsēp̱, yĕhôsēp̱;* Gk. *Iōséph, Iosés*) (also JOSES)

1. The 11th son of Jacob and the older son of Rachel. Rachel, the wife whom Jacob loved, was barren for a long time before giving birth to Joseph (Gen. 29:31–30:21). Her words upon giving birth to Joseph reflect the two possible derivations of Joseph's name: "God has *taken away* (from Heb. *'sp*) my reproach" (Gen. 30:23) and "May the Lord *add* (from *ysp*) to me another son!" (v. 24).

As the firstborn of Rachel and a "son of his father's old age," Joseph was his father's favorite, a fact made clear in Gen. 37:3: "Now Israel loved Joseph more than any other of his children... and he made him a long robe with sleeves." This robe *(kĕṯōneṯ passîm)* is the traditional "coat of many colors," although the Hebrew actually refers simply to a sleeved tunic or robe reaching to the wrists and ankles (in 2 Sam. 13:18 it is the clothing of a princess). The significance of the special robe is that it set Joseph apart from his brothers and triggered hatred and jealousy in them (Gen. 37:4). To make matters worse, Joseph brought back to his father a bad report of his brothers (Gen. 37:2), then related two dreams in which his brothers, as well as his parents, bowed down to him (vv. 5-7, 9).

Joseph's brothers first conspired to kill him, then to sell him into slavery. The latter suggestion was made by Reuben who hoped to rescue Joseph and bring him back to his father (Gen. 37:22). Joseph's coat was stripped from him, and used as evidence of his death (Gen. 37:23, 31-33). Joseph himself was sold to slave traders (Gen. 37: 25-28), either Ishmaelites or Midianites (there are probably two traditions preserved here) who took him off to Egypt and sold him to Potiphar, an officer of the pharaoh.

Although Joseph was now a slave in a strange land, the narrative makes it clear throughout that "the Lord was with Joseph," and therefore everything Joseph did was successful, despite many setbacks that resulted from the actions of those in power. Joseph prospered in Potiphar's service, and soon was overseer of everything that belonged to Potiphar (Gen. 39:4). But Joseph's fortunes soon fell again. Potiphar's wife desired Joseph. Joseph refused her advances, but left behind a garment that was later used as evidence against him (Gen. 39:12-16). Once again, Joseph was cast out, this time into prison, into a state lower still than slavery. Once again, however, God was with Joseph (Gen. 39:22-23).

An opportunity for release came when Joseph was able to interpret the dreams of two of Pharaoh's officers, the chief baker and the chief cupbearer (Gen. 40), but Joseph languished for two more years (41:1).

Joseph's release finally came when his ability to interpret dreams was brought to the attention of the pharaoh, whose own magicians and wise men had failed in that regard. Joseph not only foretold seven plentiful years to be followed by seven years of famine, but also advised Pharaoh to prepare for the coming leanness by gathering the surplus of the good years (Gen. 41:14-36). As a reward, Pharaoh set Joseph "over all the land of Egypt," responsible for organizing the collection and storage of grain against the coming famine (Gen. 41:37-44). Pharaoh bestowed on Joseph the name Zephenathpaneah ("God speaks and he lives"), and gave him Asenath, the daughter of Potiphera priest of On, as a wife (Gen. 41:45). Two sons, Manasseh and Ephraim, were born to them before the famine (Gen. 41:50-52).

The famine provided the occasion for the reunion of Joseph with the brothers who had sold him into slavery. Jacob, having heard that there was grain in Egypt, sent his 10 older sons. It is Joseph they had to approach to buy the grain, bowing before him in fulfillment of Joseph's dream (Gen. 42:6-9). Although he recognized his brothers, Joseph did not reveal himself immediately, but instead accused his brothers of being spies (Gen. 42:9). He demanded that they bring their youngest brother as evidence of their innocence, and required that they leave Simeon as hostage (Gen. 42:20, 24). Jacob at first refused to let Benjamin go along, but finally agreed when the need for more grain became acute. When the brothers returned with Benjamin, Joseph questioned them concerning their welfare and that of their father (Gen. 42:16-34). At their departure Joseph ordered their sacks filled with food and the money they had paid for the grain (Gen. 44:1). In addition, he ordered his own silver cup to be placed in the sack of the youngest, Benjamin (Gen. 44:2), and used that as a pretext for bringing the brothers back to Egypt, declaring that whoever had the cup would be his slave (v. 10). Judah, out of compassion for his father Jacob, offered himself in place of Benjamin (Gen. 44:33-34), at which point Joseph finally revealed himself and reconciled himself to his brothers. Jacob and his entire household were then given a home in the land of Goshen (Gen. 46:28), and Jacob and Joseph were at last reunited (46:29-30).

Upon Jacob's (Israel's) death, Joseph made one more journey to Canaan to bury his father. Joseph again forgave his brothers and promised to provide for them. He lived the rest of his life in Egypt. Before he died at age 110, he requested that his bones be taken back to Canaan when the time came for God to take the Israelites up from the land of Egypt.

Joseph's descendants, the tribes of Ephraim and Manasseh, were among those who went out of Egypt in the Exodus as part of the people of Israel. After the Conquest Ephraim was assigned an area west of the Jordan, between Manasseh on the north and Benjamin on the south. Half of the tribe of Manasseh settled on the east side of the Jordan in the area of Gilead, while the other half was assigned land west of the Jordan north of Ephraim and south of the Sea of Chinnereth (Galilee).

Bibliography. G. von Rad, *Genesis,* rev. ed. OTL (Philadelphia, 1972); N. M. Sarna, *Genesis.* JPS Torah Commentary (Philadelphia, 1989); R. de Vaux, *Ancient Israel* (1961, repr. Grand Rapids, 1997); G. Wenham, *Genesis 16-50.* WBC 2 (Dallas, 1994); C. Westermann, *Genesis 12-36* (Minneapolis, 1985).

MARILYN J. LUNDBERG

2. The father of Igal of the tribe of Issachar, one of the 12 whom Moses selected to spy out the land of Canaan (Num. 13:7).

3. A member of the levitical guild of Asaph ("the sons of Asaph") who prophesied accompanied by music under the direction of Asaph and the king (1 Chr. 25:2, 9).

4. A descendant of Binnui who was forced to divorce his non-Israelite wife as a result of the religious reforms of Ezra (Ezra 10:42; cf. 1 Esdr. 9:34).

5. A head of the priestly house descended from Shebaniah who was a contemporary of Joiakim the high priest (Neh. 12:14).

6. The son of Oziel, an ancestor of Judith (Jdt. 8:1).

7. A son of Zechariah who with Azariah held military command in Judah under Judas Maccabeus. Through an act of insubordination and in an effort to gain renown and personal glory, both commanders attacked Jamnia (ca. 163 B.C.) but their forces were routed (1 Macc. 5:18, 55-62).

8. According to 2 Macc. 8:22 one of the brothers of Judas Maccabeus (cf. 10:19). Joseph is not named among the sons of Mattathias at 1 Macc. 2:1-5. It may be that Joseph is simply a variant for the expected John in these texts (cf. 1 Macc. 9:36).

JOHN D. FORTNER

9. The husband of Mary, the mother of Jesus. The Infancy narratives in Matt. 1-2; Luke 1-2 provide most of the information about this Joseph. In the Matthean version, Joseph is an important character who leads the story development. Being "righteous," he plans to dismiss his fiancée Mary quietly, when she has been found pregnant (Matt. 1:18-19). However, following the guidance of the angels, Joseph accepts Mary, who he has learned is pregnant through the Holy Spirit, and protects the baby from Herod's evil plot by fleeing with Mary and Jesus from Bethlehem to Egypt, later settling in Nazareth after Herod's death. Matthew provides Jesus' genealogy in the line of Joseph, in which the name of Joseph's father is mentioned as a certain Jacob, descendant of King David (Matt. 1:1-17).

In the Lucan version of the Infancy narrative, in which Mary leads the story development, the portrayal of Joseph is somewhat different. Except for a brief designation as Mary's fiancé (Luke 1:27), Joseph does not appear on the scene until the time of Jesus' birth. It is not Joseph, therefore, but Mary who receives the angel's announcement concerning the baby's conception through the Holy Spirit (Luke 1:26-38). In Luke, Joseph's home is not Bethlehem but Nazareth. Joseph and Mary only visit Bethlehem from Nazareth in order to be registered, and Mary gives birth to Jesus during the visit (Luke 2:4-7). Luke portrays Joseph mainly as a faithful observer of the torah. He circumcises the baby after eight days (Luke 2:21), dedicates the baby and offers a sacrifice for Mary's purification (vv. 21-24), and makes annual pilgrimages to Jerusalem for the Passover (v. 41). With regard to the genealogy of Jesus (Luke 3:23-38), although as in Matthew Joseph is a descendant of King David, Luke presents him as son of Heli (v. 23), not Jacob (Matt. 1:16).

Except for some minor references, this Joseph completely disappears from the rest of the NT account. Jesus is designated by Jesus' compatriots three times explicitly as the "son of Joseph" (Luke 4:22; John 1:45; 6:42) and once implicitly ("the carpenter's son" in Matt. 13:55). Mark never mentions the father of Jesus; instead, Jesus is called "the carpenter, the son of Mary" (Mark 6:3). These considerations have contributed at least partly to the later Christian tradition that Joseph had died sometime after Jesus became 12 years old (Luke 2:41-50) but before Jesus began his public ministry. In fact, the Protevangelium of James, an apocryphal gospel written probably in the 2nd century, presents Joseph as already an old man with children from a previous marriage when he took Mary as wife.

Bibliography. R. E. Brown, *The Birth of the Messiah*, rev. ed. (New York, 1993). SEUNG AI YANG

10. A brother of Jesus along with James, Simon, and Judas (Matt. 13:55; called Joses at Mark 6:3).

11. A brother of James ("the younger") and son of Mary, a woman who witnessed the crucifixion and burial of Jesus (Matt. 27:56; called Joses at Mark 15:40, 47).

12. A man from Arimathea, a small village in the Judean hill country, who asked Pilate for and received the body of Jesus for burial. He is described as a member of the council (Mark 15:43), probably the Sanhedrin. Clearly a person of high status and probably rich (Matt. 27:57), he wrapped the body of Jesus in linen cloth and buried it in his unused, rock-hewn tomb in Jerusalem.

It is possible that Joseph was motivated to bury Jesus to fulfill the Jewish law that required the burial of executed criminals on the day of their death (Deut. 21:23). As a good and righteous man who was unsympathetic to his Jewish colleagues' actions against Jesus (Luke 23:50-51), he may have intervened simply to assure that the law was obeyed (Mark 15:42).

It is also possible that Joseph was a disciple of Jesus (Matt. 27:57; cf. John 19:38) and that he wanted to bury Jesus out of love and respect for him and his followers. In this way he is like Nicodemus (John 3), whom John links with Joseph in the burial of Jesus (19:39-42).

13. The father of Jannai and son of Mattathias in Luke's genealogy of Jesus (Luke 3:24).

14. The father of Judah and son of Jonam in the genealogy of Jesus (Luke 3:30).

15. A disciple of Jesus called Barsabbas, surnamed Justus, who along with Matthias was a candidate to replace Judas Iscariot in the Twelve but was not selected when lots were cast (Acts 1:23-26).

16. A Christian Levite from Cyprus, whom the apostles named Barnabas (Acts 4:36) and who became a colleague of Paul (12:25).

WARREN C. TRENCHARD

JOSEPH, PRAYER OF

A Jewish work, apparently dating from the early Christian era. About the same length as the Wisdom of Solomon, it survives only in fragments preserved within the writings of the 3rd-century church father Origen. The few sentences which survive quote Jacob, who purports to have pre-existed as an angelic figure named Israel, one of the most powerful of the creations of God. Jacob reveals, apparently to Joseph, that his famous struggle at Penuel (Gen. 32) was actually against another angelic figure named Uriel, whom he vanquished by calling upon a very special, but unspecified, name of God. The Prayer of Joseph apparently had little impact on later Jewish literature.

IRA BIRDWHISTELL

JOSEPH AND ASENETH

An apocryphal romance now often included in the OT Pseudepigrapha. The work narrates the conversion of the gentile Aseneth to the God of Israel, her marriage to the patriarch Joseph, and the social and religious conflicts surrounding that conversion and marriage. Genesis provides the point of departure for this fictional tale with its brief references to Joseph's marriage to Asenath (LXX Aseneth), daughter of a pagan priest (Gen. 41:45, 50-52; 46:20). Joseph and Aseneth was composed in Greek and is extant in 16 Greek manuscripts and numerous versional witnesses. There is a strong, though not unanimous, consensus that it dates between ca. 100 B.C.E. and 115 C.E., that it is Jewish rather than Christian, and that it was written in Egypt. Opinion varies on the purpose of the work. Some see it as missionary propaganda designed to win Gentiles to Judaism, while others maintain that it was written for Jewish readers and designed to address such intramural issues as the status of gentile converts within the Jewish community and the propriety of marriage between a Jew by birth and a gentile convert to Judaism. Although long neglected by biblical scholars because certain influential early interpreters declared it to be a late Christian composition, Joseph and Aseneth has become the subject of considerable scholarly research. Conceptions of sin, salvation, and conversion, a positive image of women, possible ritual practices behind the language about the "bread of life," "cup of immortality," and "ointment of incorruption," and the potential of the prayers in the narrative to illuminate the history of liturgy are among the elements of this work which illustrate its importance for the study of both early Judaism and early Christianity.

RANDALL D. CHESNUTT

JOSEPH THE CARPENTER, HISTORY OF

A Coptic apocryphal work, in which Jesus tells his disciples, gathered on the Mount of Olives, the story of the life and death of his earthly father Joseph. It was composed to promote the feast day of St. Joseph, as is evident from the several blessings Jesus promises those keeping the day. The History depends on the earlier apocryphal Protevangelium of James and Gospel of Pseudo-Matthew, with which it shares, e.g., the story of Mary's rearing in the temple and subsequent placement under the care of the aged widower Joseph. On the basis of these and other considerations, scholars date the work no earlier than the 4th century. The complete text is extant in Bohairic (Lower Egypt) and Arabic, and fragments are extant in Sahidic (Upper Egypt).

Bibliography. J. K. Elliott, *The Apocryphal New Testament*, rev. ed. (Oxford, 1993), 111-17.

RONALD V. HUGGINS

JOSEPHUS

Flavius Josephus, born Yoseph bar Mattatyahu in 37 C.E., when Gaius Caligula became emperor of Rome. The year of his death is uncertain. He is significant for the Bible reader because his four surviving works, in 30 volumes, provide our main avenue for information about the environment in which Christianity was born. He is the only contemporary author outside the NT to write in any detail about the Jerusalem temple and priesthood, the Roman governors (including Pontius Pilate), the countryside of Judea and Galilee, the various groups and factions in Jewish society, and even such figures as John the Baptist and Jesus' brother James. Josephus also has a passage on Jesus, but the version that survives is inauthentic. His extensive biblical paraphrase (*Ant.* 1-11) is an extremely valuable example of Jewish biblical interpretation at the time of the NT.

Although Josephus provides considerable detail about his life, his accounts are highly rhetorical and cannot be taken at face value. In particular, the stories that readers often use to impugn his character are told in order to make him look good, according to the "wily trickster" model popular in Greek literature since Homer's *Odysseus.* Nevertheless, it seems clear that he was a priest who fought briefly against the Romans in the Judean revolt (66-74 C.E.), defending part of Galilee. He surrendered at Jotapata in the spring of 67. After a period in chains, and providing intelligence to the Romans, he was released and given a prominent role in the Flavian family's circle of clients. He accompanied the victorious Titus to Alexandria and then back to Rome for the triumph. Once settled in Rome with an imperial pension and many privileges, he began to write his four volumes on Jewish history and culture.

Open questions surrounding Josephus' life include his precise ancestry and relation to the ancient Hasmoneans, the way in which he came to prominence in the Galilean revolt, the degree of official Jerusalem support for him, his early beliefs about the advisability of the revolt, the circumstances of his surrender to the Romans, the nature of the services he provided for the conquerors, and his relation to the Jewish community in Rome after his arrival there.

His first known work, largely completed before the death of Emperor Vespasian in 79 C.E., is an account of the *Jewish War* in seven volumes. Its main point is to show that most Judeans did not support the revolt. Even though local Roman government was atrocious, Jewish tradition recognized that God chooses various powers to rule from time to time. The revolt was foisted upon the populace by some youthful and intemperate men who saw opportunities for various kinds of gain. Josephus also emphasizes that the defeat of the Jews was not the defeat of their God, who simply used the Romans to punish the impious rebels.

In 93/94 Josephus completed his 20-volume *Jewish Antiquities* and the appendix on his *Life.* The longer work is essentially a primer in Jewish history and culture. Roughly the first half is a paraphrase of the Bible from creation to the return from exile (*Ant.* 1-11). The rest covers the Persian and Greek periods, the Hasmonean revolt and dynasty, the arrival of the Romans in Judea, Herod the Great and his family, and local Roman administration to the eve of the great revolt. The precise purpose and audience of this, Josephus' magnum opus, are not clear in the scholarship. He wrote for Gentiles, but who would have had the motivation to sit through extensive readings of such material? Perhaps Josephus wrote for those Gentiles interested in Jewish culture, about whom we hear in Roman authors (e.g., Tacitus *Hist.* 5.1-13). The short appendix, *Life,* is calculated to rebut charges made by Justus of Tiberias in an account of the war that apparently portrayed Josephus as a reckless warlord.

Josephus' advocacy and defense of Jewish culture reaches its apogee in the two-volume *Against Apion.* This work defends Judaism against its numerous literary detractors from the preceding three centuries, arguing for its great antiquity and supreme nobility. The final quarter of the work is a rousing celebration of Judaism's contributions to the world. This book served as a model for Christian apologists.

Bibliography. P. Bilde, *Flavius Josephus Between Jerusalem and Rome.* JSPSup 2 (Sheffield, 1988); S. Mason, *Josephus and the New Testament* (Peabody, 1992). STEVE MASON

JOSES (Gk. *Iōsēs*) (also JOSEPH)

1. One of the brothers of Jesus (Mark 6:3). At Matt. 13:55 he is called Joseph (**10**).

2. A brother of James the younger (Mark 15:40, 47). At Matt. 27:56 he is called Joseph (**11**).

JOSHAH (Heb. *yôšâ*)
The son of Amaziah (**1**); a leader of the tribe of Simeon at the time of Hezekiah (1 Chr. 4:34).

JOSHAPHAT (Heb. *yôšāpāṭ*)

1. A Mithnite, one of David's Thirty (1 Chr. 11:43).

2. A priest responsible for blowing the trumpet before the ark of the covenant as it was brought to Jerusalem (1 Chr. 15:24).

JOSHAVIAH (Heb. *yôšawyâ*)
A son of Elnaam; one of David's Mighty Men (1 Chr. 11:46).

JOSHBEKASHAH (Heb. *yošbĕqāšâ*)
The leader of the seventeenth division of singers at the time of David; a son of Heman (1 Chr. 25:4, 24).

JOSHEB-BASSHEBETH (Heb. *yōšeḇ baššeḇeṯ*) (also JASHOBEAM)
A Tachemonite, chief of David's Three (2 Sam. 23:8). In the parallel account at 1 Chr. 11:11 the name appears as Jashobeam (**1**).

JOSHIBIAH (Heb. *yôšiḇyâ*)
The father of Jehu and son of Seraiah; leader of a Simeonite family at the time of Hezekiah (1 Chr. 4:35).

JOSHUA (Heb. *yĕhôšuaʿ*) (also JESHUA)

1. The son of Nun; "young apprentice" and successor to Moses. In the book of Joshua, he functions as military commander in the "conquest" of Canaan and as administrator of the allotment of that land to the tribes. According to Num. 13:16 Moses renamed Hoshea (Heb. *hôšēaʿ*, "salvation")

Joshua ("Yahweh saves"). He is described as a *mĕšārēṯ*, "assistant" (Exod. 24:13; Josh. 1:1), and as a *na'ar*, "youth" (Exod. 33:11); in a sense, the two terms overlap in their emphasis on Joshua's legally independent yet subordinate status in service of Moses — and ultimately God.

Apparently, Joshua had an important tribal leadership role apart from his special relationship with Moses. His selection as Ephraim's representative among the 12 spies sent into the land of Canaan (Num. 13:8) seems to support this. Among the spies, only Joshua and Caleb believed that Israel could conquer the land, and only these two would later enter Canaan.

Joshua is first introduced as a warrior leading the Israelites to victory over the Amalekites in their first military encounter after the Exodus (Exod. 17:8-13). The narration appears to stress his similarity to Moses, since both are initially presented in Exodus without reference to their fathers. This typological paralleling continues throughout the Pentateuch and is especially dominant in the book of Joshua. As Moses led the Israelites *out of* Egypt, so Joshua will lead them *into* Canaan. Canonically Joshua is deliberately depicted as parallel to Moses, yet still unequal.

God assures Joshua that he will be with him as he was with Moses (Josh. 1:5; 3:7; cf. 4:14). Joshua sends out spies as Moses did (Josh. 2). The crossing of the Jordan is clearly pictured in terms similar to the crossing of the Red Sea (Josh. 4:23). Joshua leads the people in rituals (circumcision and Passover) as did Moses (Josh. 5:1-12). The theophany of the commander of the Lord's army (Josh. 5:13–6:5) coincides with the theophany at the burning bush. Joshua defeats the Canaanite enemies of Israel through the Lord's miracles (Josh. 10–11), just as Moses defeated the Egyptian enemies of Israel through the Lord's miracle at the Red Sea. Josh. 12 juxtaposes a summary of Moses' Transjordanian military victories with Joshua's Cisjordanian victories. Joshua's assignment of the inheritances for the nine and one-half tribes west of the Jordan is paralleled to the similar work by Moses for the two and one-half Transjordanian tribes (Josh. 14:1–19:51; 13:8-33). As Moses made provisions for cities of refuge (Num. 35:6-34) and levitical towns (vv. 1-5), so did Joshua (Josh. 20-21). Joshua functions as a covenant mediator at Shechem (Josh. 8:30-35; 24:1-28) just as Moses did at Sinai (Exod. 20-24).

Joshua, however, is not equal to Moses. The characterization of Joshua in Num. 11:26-29 is quite negative, as may also be the case in Joshua's attempted intercession for Israel in the Achan incident (Josh. 7:6-15). Moses performed many more "signs and wonders" than Joshua, although Joshua's miracle concerning the sun and moon was without comparison (Josh. 10:12-14). Moses interceded for Israel far more often than Joshua, and he was the lawgiver, whereas the Law was normative for both Joshua and Israel. While there is a transferal of authority to Joshua (Num. 27:18-23), the full authority of Moses, received directly from God, was unique and could not be completely transferred (cf. Deut. 34:10). Joshua is mentioned only three times in the NT, compared to almost 80 for Moses.

The canonical presentation of Joshua includes certain monarchic elements which serve as a model for all of Israel's future kings (esp. Solomon and Josiah). The accounts of his commissioning and installation (Num. 27:15-23; Josh. 1:2-9) contain language associated with the accession of monarchs. As a leader possessing Yahweh's spirit and having prophetic sanction, he is an effective military and spiritual leader — a standard for later kings to emulate.

Later tradition describes Joshua as Moses' successor "in the prophetic office" and Israel's "great savior," a "devoted follower" of God who is an example for all (Sir. 46:1-12). He is also called a judge (1 Macc. 2:55) and is included in a list of significant intercessors (2 Esdr. 7:107) and in a list of those who passed on the Torah (*m. 'Abot* 1:1).

2. A man of Beth-shemesh, in whose field the ark stopped when the Philistines returned it to the Israelites (1 Sam. 6:14).

3. A governor of Jerusalem during Josiah's reign (2 Kgs. 23:8).

4. A high priest in postexilic Jerusalem (Hag. 1:1, 12-14; Zech. 3:1-8; also called Jeshua [**3**]).

5. An individual (Gk. *Iēsoús*) in Luke's genealogy of Jesus (Luke 3:29).

Bibliography. L. D. Hawk, *Every Promise Fulfilled: Contesting Plots in Joshua.* Literary Currents in Biblical Interpretation (Louisville, 1991); R. S. Hess, *Joshua.* TOTC 6 (Downers Grove, 1996); R. D. Nelson, "The Day the Sun Stood Frozen in Amazement," *Lutheran Theological Seminary Bulletin* 75/3[76/4] (1995): 3-10; "Josiah in the Book of Joshua," *JBL* 100 (1981): 531-40; R. M. Polzin, *Moses and the Deuteronomist* (New York, 1980); G. J. Wenham, "The Deuteronomic Theology of the Book of Joshua," *JBL* 90 (1971): 140-48.

K. LAWSON YOUNGER, JR.

JOSHUA, BOOK OF

The sixth book of the Bible, the first of the Former Prophets, the second of the Deuteronomistic history. The MT is pedantic and redundant, and the LXX, equally learned but slightly shorter and sometimes differently arranged, lacks some of its wordiness and editorial expansions.

Literary Characteristics

The book is attached to the preceding and following books in the Deuteronomistic history by repetitive links, starting (1:1-9) with a quotation from the end of Deuteronomy (Deut. 31:6-8; 34:5) and ending with a text (24:29-31) which is quoted at the beginning of Judges (Judg. 2:7-9; LXX 24:33 adds allusions to Judg. 2:6, 12; 3:12, 14). The book is organized into four parts, marked off from each other by repetition, and defined by topic and internal arrangement. The first part (chs. 1-8) portrays Joshua as the successor of Moses in the Promised Land; it begins and ends with him as guardian of the law of Moses (1:7-9; 8:30-35 [MT]). Its chapters are paired: two each on preparations for crossing the Jordan, the crossing, the rituals leading up to the capture of Jericho, and the battle of Ai. In the second part (chs. 9-11) each chapter begins with news of the preceding event, and with the reaction of all the kings (9:1) or of the kings of specific cities (10:1; 11:1). The part ends with a summary of Joshua's exploits (11:23) which alludes to the beginning of the book (1:1-6) and concludes the conquest of the land. The third part (chs. 12-21) redefines Israel's occupation of the land as an allotment to the individual tribes. It begins with an overview of the victories recounted in the first two parts and, as in the first part, all its chapters are paired. Ch. 12 limits the occupation to 31 kingdoms; ch. 13 lists the kingdoms to be conquered, and both deal with distribution of land to the Transjordanian tribes. Chs. 14-15 concern Judah, and are related to each other by recounting successive episodes in the life of Caleb (14:6-15; 15:13-19). There are two chapters each on distributions to the house of Joseph (chs. 16-17), allotments of land to the other tribes at Shiloh (chs. 18-19), and cities of refuge and the distribution of these and other cities to the Levites (chs. 20-21). This part, like the second, ends with a summary which alludes to the completion of the task and to the fulfillment of the promises mentioned at the beginning of the book (21:43-45). In the fourth part (chs. 22-24) the chapters begin with loose chronological links to the third part (22:1; 23:1; 24:1) and address the major issues left unresolved in the book. Ch. 22 deals with the Transjordanian tribes who had not received allotments in the Promised Land. Ch. 23 confronts the problem posed by a limited occupation of the land and begins like the earlier text which introduced the topic (cf. 13:1). In ch. 24 the issue is the book of the law, confided to Joshua and read to the people in the first part, which includes, according to the historical summary in Joshua's speech (24:2-13), the books from Genesis to Deuteronomy, called the law of Moses (1:7; 8:32) or the law of God (24:26).

The book does not use pentateuchal sources, but it regularly builds on texts and develops themes from the Pentateuch. Crossing the Jordan re-enacts the Exodus, ends the wilderness era which it inaugurated, and concludes, as the Exodus began, with the rite of circumcision, the celebration of Passover, and an apparition (chs. 3-5; Exod. 3:5; 4:24-26; 12:6; 16:35). The spies, unlike those of the Exodus generation, return with an encouraging report (ch. 2; Num. 13-14; Deut. 1), the Transjordanians are in the vanguard as they promised Moses (1:12-18; Num. 32:20-27), Joshua proclaims the law as the law required (8:30-35; Deut. 27:1-8), and wars follow the rules established by Moses (chs. 10-11; Deut. 20:10-18; 21:22-23). The description of tribal boundaries and the allotment of tribal territories, levitical cities, and cities of refuge complete the work that was begun by Moses and correspond to instructions he gave in Numbers and Deuteronomy (12:1-6; 13:8-33; 14:1-15; 20:2; 21:2). In the end, the Transjordanian tribes are praised for keeping their word to Moses (22:1-4; Num. 32:20-22), and Joshua, after reviewing the conditions set out on Sinai and at Horeb for the gradual dispossession of the nations (ch. 23; Exod. 23:23, 30; 34:15-16; Deut. 11:17), recalls Israel's gradual dispossession of the nations on its journey to the Promised Land (24:2-13).

The book contains narratives and lists, sometimes mixes them, and typically interrupts one or the other with some related or subordinate interest. The crossing of the Jordan is announced (1:1-6) and eventually takes place (chs. 3-4), but it is delayed by subplots that interrupt each other and gradually are resolved: the crossing takes place under the aegis of the law (1:7-9), which is carried in the ark and later becomes the focus of ceremonies at Ebal and Gerizim (8:30-35) and at Shechem (ch. 24); marshals are introduced (1:10-11) and reappear after a three-day delay (3:2); in the interval there are negotiations with the Transjordanians (1:12-18) and with Rahab (ch. 2), and while the Transjordanians are mentioned in the crossing (4:12-13), Rahab's story is left unfinished until later (ch. 6). The crossing is recounted, but it is constantly interrupted by references to priests and tribal representatives. The general reaction to the crossing is noted (5:1), but the reaction in Jericho (6:1) waits on the ceremonies at Gilgal. The kings hear the news about Jericho and Ai (9:1-2) but they do nothing until matters are settled at Gibeon. The story of the battle of Gibeon is separated from the story of the victory over Hazor by a list of cities and kings conquered at the same time (10:16-43). The distribution of land to the tribes in Canaan is announced (13:7) but delayed by allotments in Transjordan (13:8-33), reintroduced (14:1-2) but interrupted by the levitical allotments which are mentioned (14:3) in anticipation of their actual occurrence (ch. 21), delayed again by reference to Ephraim and Manasseh (14:4) before it is their turn (chs. 16-17), and again by the story of Caleb (14:6-15). Lists of boundary points are separated from lists of towns by narrative episodes (15:13-19; 17:3-6, 14-18), and the occasion of Joshua's farewell address is introduced (13:1), but he does not speak until the land has been distributed (23:1). This jagged style reflects the substance of the book, which tells interlocking versions of the same story and reflects on their significance.

Historical Features

The book manifests characteristics of the Deuteronomistic historical work. There are previews (1:1-6, 10-11, 12-18; 7:1-2; 9:1-2; 14:1-5) and summaries (5:1; 11:23; 12:1-24; 13:32-33; 19:51; 21:43-45) of the course of narrated events, and speeches explaining their significance (2:8-11; 3:9-10; 4:7, 21-24; 13:1-6; 22:1-6; chs. 23, 24). There is an incipient chronology calculated from the Exodus (5:6, 12; cf. Exod. 16:35) and, more precisely, from the first unsuccessful attempt to take the land (14:7, 10; cf. Deut. 2:14). History is based on law, events correspond to precepts (e.g., the timing of the crossing [4:19; 5:10] follows the rules of Passover [Exod. 12:3, 6]), sin frustrates Israel's relations with Yahweh, and the basic commandment is to love and worship God (22:5; 24:16-24). The book of Joshua is the work of the Deuteronomistic historian, who took material of diverse kinds and origins and arranged it in a carefully planned, skillfully written history of Israel.

The main resources available to the Deuteronomist were a narrative of the Conquest and a geography of the 12 tribes. The geography was not a literary source, but a map of the country, listing towns, delineating routes, and describing the topography, with more detail on some areas (notably Judah and Benjamin) than on others. The map was overlaid with a tribal grid (cf. 18:1-10), the kingdoms were identified by their tribal names Judah and Joseph, and the center of government was located at the tribal sanctuaries in Shiloh and Gilgal. The geography acquired a sort of historicity through the inclusion of stories and dialogue and through an implicit chronology, marked by retrospectives to the time of Moses and allusions to the present (16:10) and the future (13:6), and by dividing the allotment of tribal lands into two distinct phases (18:1-3). The narrative of the Conquest, by contrast, was a complete literary source which the Deuteronomist copied and adapted to the purposes of the history. It related how Israel, under the leadership of Joshua, invaded and conquered the land. The Conquest was exemplary, marked by the conspicuous ruins at Jericho and Ai, and illustrated the miraculous fulfillment of the Sinai covenant (3:5, 10; cf. Exod. 34:10-11), which the treaty with the Gibeonites unwittingly violated (Exod. 34:12). The battle for Jerusalem and the southern cities and the war with Hazor and the kings of Canaan gave Israel instant and complete possession of the land, as Yahweh swore to Moses and their fathers at Sinai (1:6; 11:23). This simple narrative was adapted by the history to suit its interpretation, in which the land was not conquered by Joshua but allotted by him to the tribes, by changing all the people into types, and all the narrated events into illustrations of obedience to the law of Moses.

In the narrative Joshua is the successor of Moses (1:2), but in the adaptation he is recast in the image of Moses and relives episodes from his life. In the narrative Joshua leads the people Israel, but in the history he leads the "sons of Israel" (1:2: *bĕnê yiśrā'ēl*, the 12 tribes). In the source, the people cross the Jordan at Jericho (3:16), but in the history the crossing becomes a ritual memorializing the Exodus and the wilderness wanderings. In the narrative God speaks reassuringly to Joshua, Joshua acts boldly, and astonishing things are described in realistic detail. In the history they receive a surreal touch: the amazing fall of Jericho becomes a liturgical event; God's intervention in the battle of Gibeon is matched by meteorological and cosmological wonders; everything happens predictably in the pattern of command and execution. The complete Conquest took a few days and exhausts the story of Joshua, but in the history it took many days (11:18) and was partial and occupied a small part of Joshua's career. The narrative was original, but in the history everything is modeled on past events (2:10; 9:9-10), or conforms to the law, or happens in fulfillment of prescriptions in Numbers and Deuteronomy.

These adaptations were made in the interest of historical exactitude. Even in the original the battle of Jericho was meant to illustrate the belief, expressed by Rahab, that it was Yahweh who gave the land to Israel, and the Deuteronomist emphasized this rhetorical purpose and its historical inaccuracy by turning it into a liturgy and a lesson in the law. The battle of Ai was narrated with realistic detail, but the history cast doubt on its reliability by prefacing another version which made it a lesson in obedience, by inserting a contradictory account of the ambush (8:11b-13) and by appending another lesson on observance of the law (vv. 24-29). The treaty with Gibeon is acknowledged, but there are additional negotiations (9:16-27) which relate the story to provision in Deuteronomy (Deut. 29:11 [MT 10]) and, by insisting that the Gibeonites were spared (9:18-21, 26), prepare for its sequel in the time of Saul (2 Sam. 21). The battle against Jerusalem and its allies is overwhelmed with wonders and corrected by an account of victories over a different group of cities and kings, because it was wrong (Debir was the name of a king in the source, but is the name of a place in the history [10:3, 38-39]), and because the historian had a different version of the capture of Jerusalem (Judg. 1:8, 21; 2 Sam. 5:6-9). The war with the kings of Canaan is cross-referenced, by including their horses and chariots (11:4, 6, 9) and a variant account of the battle of Hazor (11:10-15), to subsequent and quite different accounts of the wars in the north (Judg. 4-5). The summary of the wars includes battles from the time of Moses (12:14; Num. 21:1-3) and does not correspond to the original narrative. In the land that remains are included places which the narrative source supposed were under Israelite control (13:6; cf. 11:8). Joshua is the hero of the narrative source, but in the Deuteronomistic history, in agreement with the Priestly source (Num. 27:15-23), he is associated with Eleazar the priest (14:1; 17:4; 19:51; 21:1; 24:33). As the tribal borders, lists of cities, and Ephraimite affiliation of Joshua show, the purported conquest of the land by a united Israel in league with God was an amalgamation and simplification of traditions from various times and regions narrated from a Judean perspective. The narrative was designed to persuade its readers that God's promises to their fathers had been fulfilled, and made the point in charming and memorable stories appropriated from common traditions of Israel's past. The historian recognized the traditions, but thought that they had been misremembered and wrongly attributed to Joshua. Joshua's role was redefined, the Judean bias was dropped, and as the history progressed from book to book, the gradual conquest of the land was attributed to a series of heroes and kings, and came to an end only when the people were united under David.

Bibliography. S. L. McKenzie and M. P. Graham, eds., *The History of Israel's Traditions.* JSOTSup 182 (Sheffield, 1994); M. Noth, *The Deu-*

teronomistic History. JSOTSup 15 (Sheffield, 1981); E. Tov, "The Growth of the Book of Joshua in the Light of the Evidence of the LXX Translation," in *Studies in Bible, 1986,* ed. S. Japhet. ScrHier 31 (Jerusalem, 1986): 321-39; N. Winther-Nielsen, *A Functional Discourse Grammar of Joshua*. ConBOT 40 (Stockholm, 1995). BRIAN PECKHAM

JOSIAH (Heb. *yō'šîyāhû)*

1. The son of King Amon of Judah and Jedidah, daughter of Adaiah of Bozkath. Josiah (ca. 648- 609 B.C.E.) was placed on the throne of Judah at the age of eight after the assassination of his father (ca. 640). Josiah married Hamutal, daughter of Jeremiah of Libnah, and Zebudah, daughter of Pediah of Rumah. One son from each wife reigned after him: Jehoahaz succeeded to the throne upon Josiah's having being killed by Neco II of Egypt, but he was removed from the throne by Neco in favor of his older half-brother Jehoiakim after only three months.

Josiah came to the throne in a period of both internal and external turmoil for Judah. The assassination of Amon suggests wider unrest than mere unpopularity with this particular ruler, and the bloody reform measures engaged in by Josiah seem to confirm such discontent. The collapse of the Assyrian Empire, to which Judah had been a vassal, left the small nation with an uncertain place in international relations, a tenuous position perhaps reflected in archaeological remains by royal Judean stamped impressions both of scarabs (Egyptian icons) and rosettes (Babylonian icons).

The main event recorded of Josiah's reign is the cult reform of Judah in which the Yahweh temple of Jerusalem became the only accepted Judean worship site while the veneration of all other deities was treated as a capital offense; indeed, 1 Kgs. 13:2 has a prophet predict Josiah's reign for just this purpose. The polytheistic religious world of King Manasseh, as presented in Kings, had been maintained during the two-year reign of Josiah's father and the first several years of Josiah's reign, as is well documented in archaeological deposits. In addition, the prophecies of Zephaniah and Jeremiah reflect a Judean religious world of pervasive polytheism.

In the course of renovating the temple of Yahweh, during the 18th year of his reign, Josiah's workers came upon a scroll which was delivered to the king (2 Kgs. 23). Since Patristic times Christians have insisted that the scroll found was the book of Deuteronomy or some variant of it. Jewish tradition has insisted, with the Hebrew text, that it was the Torah (Pentateuch). It was unlikely to have been either in any form now known. Although no one else who saw the document was perturbed by it, Josiah instantly recognized it as condemning the religious practices of the Judeans and foretelling doom for the nation.

Josiah followed ancient Near Eastern traditions by having the veracity of the scroll verified by consulting with the divine world. The prophetess Huldah confirmed that the nation would end in destruction, but the king would die in peace (2 Kgs. 22:20). What exactly was meant by "peace" continues to be debated, since Josiah would be killed by Neco II. Josiah's actions to deflect the promise of doom for Judah included the wholesale destruction of all places of worship except the Yahweh temple in Jerusalem, the disestablishment of levitical posts away from Jerusalem, and the execution of personnel involved with cults of deities other than Yahweh, most notably at Bethel, the national temple of Israel. 2 Chr. 35 concentrates on a Passover which Josiah called for all of Judah and Israel, having given only a cursory notice (34:33) to the reform so central to 2 Kings, perhaps because the Chronicler had already assigned that reform to Hezekiah (2 Chr. 31) and Manasseh (2 Chr. 33:15-16).

Both in 2 Chronicles (2 Chr. 34:2) and Sirach (Sir. 49:4) it is stressed that Josiah was devoted to Yahweh from his youth and that he attempted to reform the religious world of Judah even before the "discovery" of the scroll in the temple. Jewish tradition has ascribed to Josiah the act of hiding the ark of the covenant from the Babylonians and attributed his death to the disregard of Jeremiah's admonitions. Matthew noted Josiah's ancestry to Jesus (Matt. 1:10-11), an item lacking in Luke.

It is generally agreed that Josiah took a contingent of soldiers to Megiddo in order to block the advance of Pharaoh Neco II and his army who were attempting to deliver the remnant of the Assyrians from annihilation at the hands of the Babylonians in 609. Josiah was slain on sight by the pharaoh according to 2 Kgs. 23:29, or in battle according to 2 Chr. 35:22-23. His body was returned to Jerusalem for burial. Jeremiah (Jer. 22:15-16) remembered Josiah as a righteous ruler who cared for the poor.

2. Son of a certain Zephaniah, whose house is to be the place for receiving gifts from the Judean exiles as decreed by the prophet Zechariah (Zech. 6:10, 14).

Bibliography. W. G. Dever, "The Silence of the Text: An Archaeological Commentary on 2 Kings 23," in *Scripture and Other Artifacts,* ed. M. D. Coogan, J. C. Exum, and L. E. Stager (Louisville, 1994), 143-68; L. K. Handy, "Historical Probability and the Narrative of Josiah's Reform in 2 Kings," in *The Pitcher Is Broken,* ed. S. W. Holloway and L. K. Handy, JSOTSup 190 (Sheffield, 1995), 252-75; A. Laato, *Josiah and David Redivivus: The Historical Josiah and the Messianic Expectations of Exilic and Postexilic Times.* ConBOT 33 (Stockholm, 1992); N. Na'man, "The Kingdom of Judah under Josiah," *Tel Aviv* 18 (1991): 3-71; Z. Talshir, "The Three Deaths of Josiah and the Strata of Biblical Historiography," *VT* 46 (1996): 213-36. LOWELL K. HANDY

JOSIPHIAH (Heb. *yôsip̱yâ)*

An Israelite whose son Shelomith returned with Ezra from captivity in Babylon (Ezra 8:10).

JOT

See IOTA.

JOTBAH (Heb. *yoṭbâ*)
The birthplace of Haruth, whose daughter Meshullemeth married Manasseh, king of Judah, and birthplace of their son Amon, who ruled two years in Jerusalem (2 Kgs. 21:19). Some scholars associate Jotbah with Jotapata, Josephus' fortress where he was besieged by Vespasian (*BJ* 3.141-334). The site is identified as Khirbet Shifāt (176248), in the valley of Zebulun, N of the Beth Netofa valley W of Lake Gennesaret. Archaeological finds and its situation correspond to Josephus' vivid description of the region. However, according to recent surveys, no Iron Age finds have been found at the site.

Bibliography. E. M. Meyers, J. F. Strange, and D. E. Groh, "The Merion Excavation Project," *BASOR* 230 (1978): 1-24. SUJEY ADARVE-VALDES

JOTBATHAH (Heb. *yoṭbāṭâ*)
A campsite during the Israelite exodus from Egypt (Num. 33:33-34), located between Hor-haggidgad and Abronah. Great difficulty accompanies the identification of all these sites, although a location in the vicinity of Wadi Ghadhaghedh is possible.

RYAN BYRNE

JOTHAM (Heb. *yôṯām*)

1. The youngest of the 70 sons of Gideon (Jerub-baal). After Gideon's death, Jotham's brother Abimelech (born of Gideon's concubine; Judg. 8:31) convinced the townsfolk of Shechem (the family home of Gideon) to support his leadership over them (9:1-4). He then murdered all his 70 brothers save Jotham, who escaped by hiding.

As the people of Shechem proceeded to declare Abimelech their king, Jotham arrived at the top of Mt. Gerizim and sought to dissuade them through his parable of the trees and thorn bush (Judg. 9:7-15). Jotham's curse (Judg. 9:19-20) was fulfilled when Abimelech was killed in his attack on Shechem (vv. 56-57).

2. King of Judah early in the second half of the 8th century B.C.E., son of Azariah (Uzziah) and father of Ahaz. The precise chronology of the kings from Jotham through Hezekiah, son of Ahaz, including the correlation with the kings of Israel at this time, is one of the most difficult in the entire monarchic period. With a probable coregency with his father, the approximate dates of Jotham's rule are 750 to the early 730s.

Jotham inherited a secure and expanded kingdom following the long and peaceful reign of Uzziah throughout the first half of the 8th century, paralleled by similar prosperity in the north under Jeroboam II. Jotham added to the defenses of Jerusalem to the north (2 Kgs. 15:35) and to the south (2 Chr. 27:4), and apparently maintained control of the seaport Elath, which Uzziah had restored from Edom (2 Kgs. 14:22). A signet ring with the inscription "belonging to Jotham" *(lytm)*, found in that region, may attest to Judean control at this time.

However, Jotham's reign also saw the rise of the Neo-Assyrian power under Tiglath-pileser III and the rapid decline of stability and security. The Syro-Ephraimite coalition (between Pekah of Israel and Rezin of Aram) was formed as an alliance against Assyria during his reign, and by the time of Ahaz Jerusalem would be invaded under pressure to join. Thus the years of Jotham's rule marked a time of transition from prosperity to crisis. According to 2 Chr. 27 Jotham was a thoroughly virtuous king, in contrast to his father. The account in 2 Kings, however, evaluates him positively only in the formulaic summary, "He did what was right in the sight of the Lord" (2 Kgs. 15:34). It also notes that he "failed to remove the high places" noted for apostate worship, as others before him had also not done (2 Kgs. 14:4; 15:4).

3. One of six sons of Jahdai listed in 1 Chr. 2:47 as one of the families descended from Caleb.

Bibliography. J. H. Hayes and P. K. Hooker, *A New Chronology for the Kings of Israel and Judah* (Atlanta, 1988); P. J. King, "The Eighth, the Greatest of Centuries?" *JBL* 108 (1989): 3-15; E. R. Thiele, *The Mysterious Numbers of the Hebrew Kings*, 3rd ed. (Grand Rapids, 1983). ANDREW H. BARTELT

JOZABAD (Heb. *yôzāḇāḏ*)

1. A Benjaminite from Gederah who joined David at Ziklag (1 Chr. 12:4[MT 5]).

2.-3. Two men of Manasseh, chiefs of thousands, who joined David at Ziklag (1 Chr. 12:20[21]).

4. One of the overseers of the temple offerings appointed by Hezekiah during his temple reform (2 Chr. 31:13). The name here may represent the Chronicler's anachronistic attempt to link Hezekiah's reform with that of Ezra and Nehemiah (cf. Ezra 8:33).

5. A Levite who contributed animals to Josiah's great Passover (2 Chr. 35:7; cf. 2 Kgs. 23:21-23).

6. A son of the priestly family of Passhur who lived in Judea and who divorced his foreign wife according to Ezra's reform (Ezra 10:22; named Gedaliah in 1 Esdr. 9:22).

The following entries may refer to the same person or to as many as four different people.

7. A son of Jeshua the Levite; an overseer of the temple treasury (Ezra 8:33 = 1 Esdr. 8:69).

8. A Levite who divorced his foreign wife according to Ezra's reform (Ezra 10:23 = 1 Esdr. 9:23).

9. One of the 13 Levites who "gave the sense" of Ezra's reading of the law (Neh. 8:7-8). If this person served as an overseer of the "work outside the house of God" (Neh. 11:16), then he served under both Ezra and Nehemiah (cf. 1 Esdr. 9:48).

C. MACK ROARK

JOZACAR (Heb. *yôzāḵār*) (also ZABAD)
A servant of King Joash of Judah who, with Jehozabad, murdered the king (2 Kgs. 12:21[MT 22]; some MSS read "Jozabad"). In the parallel account he is called Zabad (**4;** 2 Chr. 24:26).

JOZADAK (Heb. *yôṣāḏāq*) (also JEHOZADAK)
Alternate form of Jehozadak, the father of the high priest Jeshua/Joshua (Ezra 3:2, 8; 5:2; 10:18; Neh. 12:26).

JUBAL (Heb. *yûḇāl*)
A son of Lamech and Adah, and the younger brother of Jabal. He was the "father" (or "inventor") of musical instruments (Gen. 4:21).

JUBILEE, YEAR OF
The 50th year in a series of seven Sabbatical Years. The Year of Jubilee (from Heb. *yôḇēl*, "ram's horn") is the last layer in the extension of the sabbath principle that begins with the day of rest every seventh day, extended in the Sabbatical Year fallow every seventh year, to the Jubilee. It begins in the middle of the seventh sabbatical year (every 49th year) on the tenth day of the seventh month (the Day of Atonement), and extends, presumably, into the seventh month of the 50th year, thus overlapping by just over half a year with the regular Sabbatical Year. A ram's horn was to be sounded throughout the land and the Jubilee proclaimed, during which land was to be restored to its original inherited line of ownership, and Israelite debt-slaves freed to return to their own land. The Jubilee Year, like the Sabbatical Year, was also to be a year of "rest" for the land, in which sowing, reaping, and harvesting were prohibited. The redemption price of land or slave was to be pro-rated according to the number of years left until the next Jubilee. These Jubilee laws are detailed exclusively in Lev. 25, not being mentioned in the parallel legislation of Deut. 15:1-15 or the Covenant Code in Exod. 21:2-4; 23:10-12. Conversely, no mention is made in Lev. 25 of the cancellation of debts mandated in Deut. 15 (perhaps because this cancellation was predicated upon the charging of interest, whereas interest is prohibited outright in Lev. 25:35-38), though later tradition consistently connects these provisions. Nor does Lev. 25 mention the seventh-year release of debt-slaves (though the method prescribed in vv. 47-53 for the calculation of redemption price necessarily assumes it — the calculation only working when the Jubilee should happen to intervene within the normal six-year period of servitude), perhaps secondarily edited out to emphasize a political point about release from Babylonian Exile after 50 years of captivity.

The Jubilee legislation in Lev. 25 deals primarily with issues of social welfare — exhortations regarding helping the poor: providing food in the Sabbatical Years, loaning money without interest, taking them in as hired workers, redeeming them and their land. The Jubilee itself is styled as only a last resort when all other help had failed. The issues at hand were debt and debt slavery, inheritance and land tenure, kinship responsibilities and redemption, and equitable distribution of farmland (i.e., the principal means of production in agrarian societies; houses within walled cities were exempt; Lev. 25:29-30). The theological underpinning of such legislation is found in the concept that God owns all of the land and the people as well, having redeemed them from slavery in Egypt. Thus the people could not be permanently enslaved to others nor the land sold permanently. It could only be leased temporarily — the use of it sold for a limited period of time until the next Jubilee when it would be restored to the inherited line. This would prevent a few wealthy landowners from accumulating all of the land and enslaving the general population.

Aside from a few other incidental references (Lev. 27:16-25; Num. 36:4; Ezek. 46:16-18) plus Josephus *Ant.* 3.12.3, no specific mention of the Jubilee is made outside of Lev. 25, though the descriptions in Isa. 37:30 (= 2 Kgs. 19:29); 49:8-9; 61:1-2; Jer. 34:8-22; Neh. 5:1-13 may well also reflect a Jubilee tradition. There is no evidence that the Jubilee as legislated here was ever practiced, aside from fallow provisions (which were also part of the Sabbatical Year laws) during the Second Temple period (1 Macc. 6:48-54). Some scholars would see the entire Jubilee tradition as merely utopian construct or an invention of the restoration period, used to justify the usurpation of land by the returnees. Yet one wonders how effective such an appeal to "law" could be unless it already held some familiarity and respect among the people. Later tradition did, however, connect the Jubilee release of debt-slaves and restoration of property with release from the Babylonian captivity and subsequent restoration of Israel from exile (cf. Isa. 61:1-2), still later eschatologized in the Dead Sea Scrolls (11QMelch 2:1-9) and the NT (Luke 4:16-21). The book of Jubilees uses the 50-year Jubilee cycle as a normative organizing principle for history.

See SABBATICAL YEAR.

ROBIN J. DEWITT KNAUTH

JUBILEES, BOOK OF
An important postbiblical Jewish writing telling the story of Israel's origins and paralleling the narrative flow in Genesis and Exodus. Having been given a revelation at Sinai, Moses is instructed to "write it in a book," the same task assigned later to the angel of presence; in each case its revelatory value is assured. Jubilees' relation to the first two books of the Torah is so close that it has been designated as a text of "rewritten Bible," a literary work which presents and adapts a biblical narrative tradition to address issues and problems important to the writer's community. Generally, the author offers a new rendition, adding to the text, omitting aspects, or transforming its meaning by reordering the events of the tradition or refashioning the story. The author writes an adapted version of the stories of creation, the patriarchs (and matriarchs, especially Rebekah, who are more prominent here than in Genesis), and Moses' activity in Egypt, including his leadership in a covenant with God and revelation of the Torah. Jubilees expands the biblical narrative in several ways, often including rationales for Israel's festivals and laws in the early days prior to their official origin or the revelation at Sinai. This tends to collapse Israel's religious history into a single and synchronic picture, thus avoiding a notion of gradual development of religion among Judaism's forerunners. The rhetorical impact of this revelatory text strongly urges Jewish listeners to attend carefully to the living examples of their

ancestors (noting how their actions led either to blessing or disaster). It also places the laws of Judaism into a more revered position because they are so ancient, even pre-Mosaic; and it presents a challenging position, since careful adherence to the laws is absolutely crucial to life together as a community. This work offers excellent witness to one method of early biblical interpretation, especially through its "contemporizing" exegesis, similar to a preacher exhorting a congregation.

Apart from citations in a Greek translation, Jubilees first became widely known in 1861 through an incomplete Latin translation of the Greek. Later an Ethiopic translation was discovered. Many scholars had hypothesized a Hebrew original, a position strongly bolstered by the discovery of 14 or 15 Hebrew manuscripts from Qumran, representing several texts of Jubilees.

Dates from the 3rd to mid-1st centuries B.C.E. have been argued, but most likely the book was written between 170 and 140 in Palestine. This dating invites a search for evidence of a Maccabean or a Hasmonean provenance, and the results are impressive, clearly suggesting an author and community which rejected assimilation to Hellenistic cultural mores and values (particularly regarding intermarriage with Gentiles among priestly groups, which the book strongly condemns). The author's exegesis of the rape of Dinah (Gen. 34; Jub. 30) implies that the massacre of the Shechemite men was justified because of the rape of a young Jewish woman. This work offers hope for the vigilant, since it is a periodized history (jubilees of seven weeks of years [= 49 years]) which moves inexorably toward a revealed endpoint. The years are calculated according to a 364-day solar calendar, a favorite of certain priestly groups and also strongly evident in several Qumran documents. Thus we may consider Jubilees as part of the immediate literary prehistory of the Qumran group

The author apparently attempted to readjust the Enoch tradition's view of evil among humans — due to the evil actions of the disobedient divine beings who descended from the heavens for sexual relations with earthly women (Gen. 6; Jub. 5) — by including also the story of Adam and Eve, their shame in the garden, and expulsion from Eden. Human obedience to God's law is also a part of the system of covenants in Jubilees, all of which are basically the same and set out prescriptions for Jewish life from the earliest human periods. This book focuses attention on Abraham, less on Isaac, but especially on Rebekah and her central role in the era of Jacob and his family. She not only schemes for Jacob's trickery, but she also gives him a formal blessing as he prepares for action (ch. 25). Later as her death approaches she strongly urges her sons toward fraternal love in a speech resembling a testament. Levi receives high praise; for his zeal at Shechem he receives appointment as priest (ch. 30), and when Jacob takes him to visit Isaac and Rebekah he receives an important blessing from his grandfather (ch. 31). When Jacob dies he hands on all his written documents so Levi might preserve and renew them for all his descendants (45:15).

Bibliography. J. C. Endres, *Biblical Interpretation in the Book of Jubilees.* CBQMS 18 (Washington, 1987); J. C. Vanderkam, *Textual and Historical Studies in the Book of Jubilees.* HSM 14 (Missoula, 1977); O. S. Wintermute, "Jubilees," *OTP* 2 (Garden City, 1985): 35-142. JOHN C. ENDRES, S.J.

JUCAL (Heb. *yûḵāl*) (also JEHUCAL)
The son of Shelemiah; an opponent of Jeremiah who sought to kill the prophet by casting him into a cistern (Jer. 38:1-6). At Jer. 37:3 he is called Jehucal.

JUDAH (Heb. *yĕhûḏâ*)

1. The fourth son of Jacob and Leah (Gen. 29:35), who was the eponymous ancestor of the tribe and nation (i.e., he was regarded as both their origin and their representative). Hence Jacob's blessing of Judah (Gen. 49:8-12) mentions him holding the scepter and ruler's staff because David came from Judah. The prominent role of Judah among the brothers in the Joseph story (Gen. 37:26-27; 43:1-10; 44:14-34) also reflects David's elevation of Judah to a dominant position over the tribes of Israel. The story of Judah and Tamar in Gen. 38 is striking for its negative portrayal of the patriarch. It aligns the clans of Perez and Zerah genealogically with Judah and hints at their Canaanite roots.

2. The tribe of Judah, which like the patriarch in the Bible, is really a reflection of the nation's importance. The tribe's territory lay in the central hill country between, but not including, Jerusalem and Hebron. The only description of it (Josh. 14-15) actually sketches the later boundaries of the nation of Judah. Judah's independence from the Israelite tribes is suggested by its absence from the early list in the Song of Deborah (Judg. 5) and by the fact that Benjamin, immediately to the north of Judah, was regarded as the southernmost (the basic meaning of the name "Benjamin") tribe of Israel. Saul's control over Judah was sporadic and tenuous at best, to judge from the location of the stories about his reign in 1 Samuel. STEVEN L. MCKENZIE

3. A Levite, ancestor of a family that supervised work on the postexilic temple (Ezra 3:9 MT). He may be the same as Hodaviah (**4**; so NRSV).

4. A Levite who had married a foreign woman (Ezra 10:23).

5. The son of Hassenuah; second in command of postexilic Jerusalem (Neh. 11:9).

6. A Levite who returned from exile with Zerubbabel (Neh. 12:8).

7. A leader of Judah who participated in the dedication of Jerusalem's rebuilt walls (Neh. 12:34).

8. A priest and musician present at the dedication of the wall (Neh. 12:36).

9. An ancestor of Jesus, the father of Simeon and son of a Joseph (Luke 3:30).

JUDAH (Heb. *yĕhûḏâ*), **KINGDOM**
The southern kingdom, which began under David ca. 1000 B.C.E. and lasted until the Babylonian Exile of 586.

History

Sources

The main source for Judah's history is the Bible, in particular 1-2 Samuel, 1-2 Kings, 1-2 Chronicles, as well as portions of the prophetic books. All of these books are primarily religious in orientation and must be used with caution for historical reconstruction. This is especially true of 1-2 Chronicles, which is a late theological recasting of Judah's history as recorded in 1-2 Samuel and 1-2 Kings, though the Chronicler seems to have used a few other genuine sources. Much of 1-2 Kings consists of stories about northern prophets, so the information about some kings of Judah is very sparse. Archaeology provides a corrective to certain details of the biblical account and also fills in some of the gaps in our knowledge, such as the daily life of common folk and social changes over time. Occasional inscriptions and records from other countries mention persons and events from the Bible, sometimes placing them in a strikingly different light.

David and Solomon

David came from Bethlehem in the heart of the tribe of Judah. His meteoric rise in Saul's army made him a threat to Saul, who forced him to flee back south, where he became the leader of an "outlaw" band (1 Sam. 22:1-2) operating in the wilderness of Judah. David's usurpation of Nabal, a chieftain of the Calebites (1 Sam. 25), was an important step in his ascension to the throne of Judah. He was crowned in Hebron, the Calebite capital, with Abigail, Nabal's widow, at his side (2 Sam. 2:1-4). This coronation may have preceded Saul's demise. In 1 Sam. 21:11(MT 12) the Philistines already call him "the king of the land," and Ishbaal's reign accounts for only two of David's seven and one-half years as king of Judah (2 Sam. 2:11). David forged the kingdom of Judah by uniting the local clans — the Jerahmeelites and Kenites (1 Sam. 27:10, perhaps read "Kenizites"), the Calebites and Kenizites (Josh. 14:6-15; 15:13-14; Judg. 1:20; 1 Chr. 2:42-50) — and gaining control of the highlands and wilderness of Judah S of Jerusalem. He allied himself with the Philistines, who effected Saul's downfall (1 Sam. 27-31). David's subsequent defeat of Abner and Ishbaal (2 Sam. 2-4) left the elders of Israel no real option but to make him their king as well.

With his accession to the throne of Israel, David annexed Saul's kingdom in Benjamin and Ephraim and eventually added the other Israelite tribes in the north. He subjugated the Philistines (2 Sam. 5:17-25; 8:1) and conquered the enclaves of indigenous peoples, such as Jerusalem, which he transformed into his capital (2 Sam. 5:6-9). He then went on to build a small empire in Syria-Palestine by conquering Moab, Edom, and the Aramean city-states under Hadadezar (2 Sam. 8). Solomon, whose succession of David was on the order of a palace coup (1 Kgs. 1-2), established a network of administrative provinces with Jerusalem as the political and religious center (1 Kgs. 4:7-19). Both kings subordinated Israel to Judah by exempting their tribesmen from the conscription and taxation they imposed on the Israelites (cf. 2 Sam. 20:24; 24:1-9; 1 Kgs. 4-5). Resentment of this unequal treatment may have been one of the factors behind Absalom's revolt (2 Sam. 13-19). Sectional rivalry was clearly at issue in Sheba's uprising (2 Sam. 20:1-22) and in the Israelite rebellion against the Davidides after Solomon's death (1 Kgs. 12). With Rehoboam's accession ca. 922, Judah returned to the same basic status and dimensions it had when David ruled over it alone, as indicated by the list of Rehoboam's cities of defense in 2 Chr. 11:5-12.

Divided Kingdom

The reigns of the initial kings of Judah were marked by constant conflict with Israel (Rehoboam, 1 Kgs. 14:30; Abijah, 15:7; Asa, 15:16). This must have been a significant drain on the small country's resources. To make matters worse, there were foreign powers to contend with. 1 Kgs. 14:25-26 reports that Rehoboam used the royal and temple treasuries to save Judah from the Egyptian king Shishak (Shoshenq). 1 Kgs. 15:18-22 describes how Asa used what was left in those treasuries to make an alliance with Ben-hadad of Damscus against Baasha of Israel. A great deal of the royal resources were spent fortifying the frontier between Israel and Judah. When Baasha withdrew from his building activity in Ramah to deal with Ben-hadad, Asa and the people of Judah moved Baasha's own materials a few kilometers north and used them to construct the border fortresses of Mizpah and Geba. The old tribal territory of Benjamin, which had been the heart of Saul's kingdom, was now divided, part of it going to Judah.

Omride Dynasty

While Judah's monarchy consisted of a single dynasty in the line of David, Israel experienced a series of royal houses. The most important of these was the Omride dynasty, which began ca. 885. Omri's son Ahab initiated a new, peaceful relationship with Judah by making a treaty with Jehoshaphat of Judah, which was sealed with the marriage of Ahab's daughter Athaliah to Jehoshaphat's son Jehoram (2 Kgs. 8:18). Israel was clearly the superior power, and Judah may well have been a vassal, but it nevertheless prospered in the wake of the Omrides' strength. The reign of Jehoram of Judah coincided in part with the reign of J[eh]oram of Israel, and it is possible that the two kings were the same man so that Israel and Judah were briefly reunited. In any case, the Omride dynasty in Israel waned under Joram and then ended abruptly with the putsch of Jehu ca. 842, in which the new king of Judah, Ahaziah, was also assassinated.

The one remaining Omride, Athaliah, was queen mother in Judah. With the death of her son she assumed power, killing all other potential claimants except the infant Joash, who was hidden in the temple (2 Kgs. 11:1-3 = 2 Chr. 22:10-12). It seems strange that Athaliah would have overlooked one of her own grandsons, and Joash may not actually have been a member of the royal family. It was the priests, led by Jehoiada, who orchestrated Athaliah's overthrow six years later (2 Kgs. 11 = 2 Chr. 23). As a non-Davidide and a woman, they may have considered her an illegitimate ruler. That seems to be the perspective of the writer in 2 Kings, which does not include the same regnal formulas for Athaliah as for the other monarchs of Judah.

Aramean Domination

During the second half of the 9th century, all of Palestine was dominated by the Aramean king Hazael. While Judah appears to have suffered less than Israel (cf. 2 Kgs. 10:32-33; 13:3), Joash emptied the treasuries to save Jerusalem from Hazael's attack (2 Kgs. 12:17-18). The assassinations not only of Athaliah but also of Joash and his successor, Amaziah, indicate the political instability of the period. Amaziah brought some of his troubles upon himself by challenging Jehoash of Israel to war (2 Kgs. 14:8-14 = 2 Chr. 25:17-24). This took place after Hazael's death when the Aramean threat was dissipating (2 Kgs. 13:24-25) and the other kings in the region had begun vying with each other for supremacy. Jehoash's response — dismantling part of Jerusalem's city wall, plundering its treasuries, and taking hostages — made a point of demonstrating Israel's continued military superiority. Judah may once again have become Israel's vassal.

This relationship continued under the next two kings, Uzziah (also known as Azariah) and Jotham. Their reigns were overshadowed by that of Jeroboam II in Israel, but since this was a prosperous time for Israel, Judah also flourished. Although the account in 2 Chr. 26:6-8 is exaggerated, Uzziah may well have extended Judah's domain at the expense of some of the neighboring peoples. He evidently reopened Judah's commercial route to the Red Sea by reclaiming Elath (2 Kgs. 14:22 = 2 Chr. 26:2). The skin disease ("leprosy") he contracted during his reign forced a coregency with his son and successor, Jotham. It is the only documented case of coregency among the kings of Israel and Judah and one of the sources of the chronological problems for this period. The Chronicler also credits Jotham with similar victories over local foes and with extensive building projects to consolidate his new acquisitions (2 Chr. 27).

Assyrian Domination

In the reign of Ahaz, Jotham's successor, Judah came under the control of the rising Assyrian Empire. Its fate was sealed in the "Syro-Ephraimitic crisis" of 734, which is well known because of the Immanuel oracle in Isa. 7. Rezin king of Aram (Syria) and Pekah king of Israel, who were already paying tribute to Assyria, headed a coalition of Syro-Palestinian rulers intent on resisting Emperor Tiglath-pileser III (ca. 745-727). Only Ahaz refused to join the alliance. Pekah and Rezin responded by besieging Jerusalem, planning to replace Ahaz with their own puppet ruler. 2 Kgs. 16:7-9 reports that Ahaz acted against Isaiah's advice that he remain independent (Isa. 7:3-16) and sent to Tiglath-pileser III for help. By his payment of tribute, Ahaz established Judah's status for the remainder of its existence as the subject of a Mesopotamian power.

The last quarter of the 8th century was a momentous time for Judah. In 722 the Assyrians destroyed Samaria and brought an end to the kingdom of Israel. Many of its former citizens fled south, and the population of Judah, especially of its capital, Jerusalem, swelled. King Hezekiah, who is one of the heroes of both 2 Kings and 2 Chronicles, made careful preparations for rebelling against the Assyrian overlord. He fortified cities and instituted a sophisticated supply system. Jerusalem was at the heart of both initiatives (cf. 2 Chr. 32:1-8). Hezekiah's centralization of the cult in Jerusalem was part of his nationalistic reform. In a symbolic restoration of the Davidic kingdom, he enlisted the support of the remnant of Israel, which had been divided into Assyrian provinces (2 Chr. 30:1-12). He also made alliances, some forcibly, with other rulers in Palestine and Phoenicia. Then, just before the turn of the century, he withheld his annual payment of tribute to Assyria and braced for the repercussion. It was not long in coming. In 701 the emperor Sennacherib marched west. He decimated the countryside of Judah, destroying the heavily fortified city of Lachish with a massive onslaught. But he never reached Jersualem. This may have been due to the appearance of the Egyptians (2 Kgs. 19:8-9) or to a plague in his army (v. 35). Hezekiah paid a large indemnity (2 Kgs. 18:14-16) and was left on the throne, albeit over a diminshed realm. Nevertheless, his reputation as a righteous king was bolstered by what was interpreted as a miraculous deliverance.

Hezekiah's son Manasseh inherited a rump state, consisting of little more than Jerusalem and its environs, that was on the verge of economic collapse. Judah was occupied and closely watched by the Assyrians. Manasseh's submission to Assyrian policy both politically and religiously led to his harsh judgment by the biblical writers. 2 Kgs. 21:1-18 credits him with the longest (55 years) and most wicked reign of all the kings of Judah; indeed, it blames the Exile on him (21:10-15; 23:26; 24:3-4). The very different account in 2 Chr. 33:10-19, according to which Manasseh reformed after being deported to Babylon, is a foreshadowing of the Babylonian Captivity. The Chronicler invented the story to explain Manasseh's lengthy reign. Manasseh's son and successor, Amon, continued his father's submission to Assyria, to judge from the brief account of his reign in 2 Kgs. 21:19-26 = 2 Chr. 33:21-25. He was assassinated after only two years, perhaps by members of an anti-Assyrian party. The speed with which the "people of the land" executed the assassins suggests their anxiety to appease their overlords in view of the possibility of retribution.

Egyptian and Babylonian Domination

During the reign of Josiah (640-609), who followed Amon, Assyria's empire faded. Egypt seems to have replaced Assyria as Judah's foreign overlord, but its control was looser, allowing Josiah to mount a nationalistic reform after the pattern of Hezekiah. Even more than Hezekiah, Josiah laid claim to the former land of Israel, if 2 Kgs. 23:15-20 is accurate. It is impossible to know whether the details of his reforms as recounted in 2 Kings and 2 Chronicles are historical, although most of the cultic items they describe are identifiable in the archaeology of the period. The biblical writers, of course, regard Josiah, like Hezekiah, as a religious hero and credit his purge of the temple with the rediscovery of the "book of the law" presumably lost under Manasseh (2 Kgs. 22:8; 2 Chr. 34:14). Josiah's sudden death at the hands of Pharaoh Neco II, therefore, must have come as a particular shock to those who had placed their hopes for restoration of the Davidic kingdom in him. Neco was on his way to join the Assyrians in opposing the Babylonians, who had become the new imperial power. However, the exact circumstances of Josiah's death remain unknown.

The "people of the land" replaced Josiah with his son Jehoahaz. But the choice was unacceptable to Neco, who removed him three months later and made his older brother Eliakim king instead, changing his name to Jehoiakim. Jehoiakim remained loyal to Egypt until 605, when the Babylonians under Nebuchadnezzar defeated the Egyptians at Carchemish. Even as a Babylonian vassal, Jehoiakim's sympathies lay with Egypt. Ca. 600 he rebelled against Babylon, hoping for Egyptian support. His confidence was misplaced (2 Kgs. 24:7). Fortunately for Judah and Jerusalem, Jehoiakim died before Nebuchadnezzar arrived. He was succeeded by his son, Jehoiachin, also known as Jeconiah or Coniah; he also reigned only three months. In 597 Nebuchadnezzar laid siege to Jerusalem. Jehoiachin surrendered and was taken captive to Babylon, along with other leading citizens and the temple and royal treasuries. The Babylonian king placed Jehoiachin's uncle, Mattaniah, on Judah's throne, changing his name to Zedekiah. The new name, meaning "Yahweh's justice," may have been intended as a warning of divine judgment awaiting Zedekiah should he rebel against Babylon to whom he had sworn loyalty in the name of Yahweh. The warning worked for a while. But after nine years, perhaps compelled by anti-Babylonian sentiment in his court, Zedekiah rebelled. Nebuchadnezzar again besieged Jerusalem. This time the city held out for a year and a half before it finally fell in 586. The Babylonians tore down the city wall and burned the large buildings. Zedekiah, captured after an escape attempt, was forced to watch his son's executions and then blinded and led away in chains. The area north of Jerusalem in traditional Benjamin escaped heavy destruction, but most of the country was decimated. The major cities were destroyed and a significant portion of the population was deported to Babylon with Zedekiah (2 Kgs. 25).

While the destruction of 586 effectively marked the end of the kingdom of Judah, events immediately following it were closely connected and deserve mention. Nebuchadnezzar appointed Gedaliah as ruler over Judah and moved the capital to Mizpah (2 Kgs. 25:22-24; cf. Jer. 40-41). While the exact title and nature of Gedaliah's position are unknown, the fact that he was murdered by a member of the royal family (2 Kgs. 25:25) suggests that he was considered illegitimate as a ruler because he was not a Davidide. The assassination may have been the occasion for a third incursion of the Babylonians in 582 which resulted in the captivity of an additional 745 persons (Jer. 52:30).

Bibliography. G. W. Ahlström, *The History of Ancient Palestine* (Minneapolis, 1993); W. G. Dever, *Recent Archaeological Discoveries and Biblical Research* (Seattle, 1990); A. Mazar, *Archaeology of the Land of the Bible, 10,000-586* B.C.E. (New York, 1990); J. M. Miller and J. Hayes, *A History of Ancient Israel and Judah* (Philadelphia, 1986); J. A. Soggin, *An Introduction to the History of Israel and Judah,* 2nd ed. (Valley Forge, 1993).

STEVEN L. MCKENZIE

JUDAISM

See JEWS, JUDAISM.

JUDAIZING

Voluntary actions by Gentiles who adopt Jewish customs and practices, usually short of full conversion (Gk. *Ioudaízō,* "to live as a Jew"; Heb. *yāhaḏ* hithpael; used in both Jewish and Christian ancient sources). Secondarily the term refers to the actions of those who urge Judaism upon Gentiles.

Jewish and Greco-Roman usage of this verb illustrates these two meanings. When the royal edict against the Jews inspired by Haman failed and a new edict allowed Jews to destroy their enemies, many Gentiles "professed to be Jews" out of fear (Esth. 8:17); the LXX adds that they were circumcised. Josephus (*BJ* 2.17.10 [454]) says that the captured Roman general Metilius escaped death by promising to Judaize. Josephus also relates how the Syrians thought they had eliminated Judaism in their territories, "but each city had its Judaizers, who aroused suspicion" (*BJ* 2.18.2 [463]). Plutarch somewhat disdainfully relates that Caecilius, a freed slave, adopted Jewish practices (*Cic.* 7.6).

In Gal. 2:14, the only use of the term in the NT, Paul defends his law-free gospel, relating his rebuke of Peter for withdrawing, under pressure from strict Jewish Christians, from table fellowship with Gentile Christians in Antioch. Paul implies that to require Gentile Christians "to live like Jews" (NRSV) contradicts the gospel. To judge from Galatians, this Judaizing meant circumcision and keeping at least a minimum of Jewish laws, e.g., keeping kosher well enough to enable strict Jewish Christians to eat with the Galatians. Paul's argument against Judaizing is one element of his overall argument in Galatians that to force or persuade Gentile Christians to adopt Jewish customs is a betrayal of the meaning of Jesus' salvific work on the cross. He bitterly opposes those who urge adoption of Jewish laws and customs, and argues with his full rhetorical skills to keep the Galatians true to his law-free gospel.

Christian tradition and NT scholarship have

generally used the term "Judaizers," but Paul does not use this word, and thus it should not be attributed to him. Moreover, in Galatians Paul does not attack Judaism as such, but those Jewish Christians who undertake missions to the Gentiles to urge them to live as Jews. Their argument is not that Gentiles must become Jews *before* becoming Christians; rather, they want all Christians to be *Jewish* Christians, to "live as Jews" while following Christ. They do so no doubt out of a concern for the essence of Christianity and the unity of the Church, but Paul rejects this basis of faith and unity.

Second-century Christian usage of the word largely mirrors Paul's antipathy to Judaizing. Ignatius of Antioch vigorously opposes those who are Christians and yet (voluntarily) live according to Judaism (*Magn.* 8.1); "it is monstrous" to be a Christian and Judaize (10.3). Ignatius cites only the observance of Saturday rather than Sunday, but other customs are doubtless involved. A probable exception to this negative view is the apocryphal Acts of Pilate, which approvingly says that Pilate's wife revered the true God and "favored the customs of the Jews" (Acts Pil. 2:1). The Church's mainly negative attitude to Judaizing is suggested by the 4th-century Council of Laodicea, which condemned those who Judaize. To this day, Christians who adopt Jewish customs not historically practiced by the mainstream Church (e.g., Saturday observance, circumcision as a religious duty, avoidance of pork) are usually considered outside the Christian mainstream by reason of their "Judaizing."

These uses of "Judaizing" show that Jewish religious practices had a strong, continuing appeal to many ancient Christians. To judge from these passages, the initiative for this appeal came mostly from the Christian side, and not as a result of Jewish pressure or persecution. In the dynamic, sometimes difficult relationship between Jewish Christianity and Gentile Christianity, several Gentile Christian authors had to defend what they considered the essential truth and uniqueness of Christianity by warning Christians against "Judaizing."

Bibliography. L. Gaston, "Judaism of the Uncircumcised in Ignatius and Related Writers," in *Anti-Judaism in Early Christianity,* ed. P. Richardson (Waterloo, 1986), 2:33-44.

ROBERT E. VAN VOORST

JUDAS (Gk. *Ioúdas*)

1. The son of Chalphi; a commander in the army of Jonathan who with Mattathias remained with Jonathan while all others fled in the ambush at Hazor (1 Macc. 11:70).

2. A son of Simon Maccabeus and brother of John Hyrcanus. Together Judas and John defeated the Seleucid Cendebeus (1 Macc. 16:2-10).

3. One who wrote to Aristobulus and the Jews in Egypt; apparently a person of high standing in Jerusalem (2 Macc. 1:10). Some have identified him with Judas Maccabeus.

4. A brother of Jesus (Matt. 13:55; Mark 6:3). Tradition identifies him as the author of the book of Jude.

5. One of the original 12 disciples; a son (or brother) of James (Luke 6:16; Acts 1:13). This is probably the "Judas, not Iscariot" of John 14:22. He is often identified with Thaddeus (Matt. 10:3; Mark 3:18).

6. Judas of Galilee (Acts 5:37), a Zealot and leader of a revolt at the time of the census of Quirinius in 6-7 C.E. (perhaps claiming to be the Messiah).

7. One in whose house Saul of Tarsus stayed after his experience on the road to Damascus (Acts 9:11).

8. Judas Barsabbas ("son of the sabbath"), a leader of the Jerusalem church chosen to accompany Paul and Barnabas to Antioch to convey the decision of the Jerusalem church concerning placing the requirements of Jewish law on gentile converts (Acts 15:22-33).

See JUDAS ISCARIOT; JUDAS MACCABEUS.

JOE E. LUNCEFORD

JUDAS, GOSPEL OF

A lost (Cainite?) apocryphon of the mid-2nd century attested by Irenaeus and Epiphanius. Irenaeus (*Adv. haer.* 1.31.1) describes the work as transmitted by certain gnostic groups who valued its secret teaching as coming from the singular witness of "the betrayer Judas," who "alone recognized the truth and completed the mystery of the betrayal."

Bibliography. B. Layton, *The Gnostic Scriptures* (Garden City, 1987), 181; R. McL. Wilson, "The Gospel of Judas," in *New Testament Apocrypha,* ed. W. Schneemelcher and Wilson, rev. ed. 1 (Louisville, 1991), 386-87.

IRVING A. SPARKS

JUDAS ISCARIOT (Gk. *Ioúdas ho Iskariṓtēs*)

Judas Iscariot, one of the Twelve and the betrayer of Jesus. His surname was probably given to distinguish him from others named Judas in Jewish and Christian history. Various interpretations of the name have been suggested: "the assassin" (from the band of Judean Zealots who carried daggers and terrorized the Romans and their sympathizers in ancient Palestine; Lat. *sicarius*), "man from Sychar," "man of Issachar," "man from Jericho," "carrier of the leather bag," or "false one, liar, hypocrite." The most popular suggestion has been "man of Kerioth"; however, the location of Kerioth is uncertain.

The Gospels clearly characterize Judas as the betrayer of Jesus. Each Evangelist introduces Judas in a list of the Twelve with some variation on the statement that Judas would betray Jesus (Matt. 10:4; Mark 3:19; Luke 6:16; John 6:71). Little which follows convinces the reader that Judas will overcome this initial characterization. As the story of Jesus and his conflict with the Jewish authorities unfolds, Judas waits to fulfill this role. Further information in the Gospels about Judas is consistently negative. He complains about the extravagance of the anointing because he was stealing from the disciples' treasury in his care (John 12:6). Judas plots with the chief priests to betray Jesus for "30 pieces of silver" (Matt. 26:14-16). Satan enters Judas, causing him to join the plot of the priests to kill Jesus (Luke 22:3-6). None of this information suggests that Judas will do anything but betray Jesus.

This clear portrait raises other questions, however. Just as one cannot escape the idea of Judas as betrayer, one cannot escape the fact that Judas was an integral part of the Twelve. As treasurer, Judas was probably a member of Jesus' inner circle. The combination is a troubling one; Judas would be easier to accept as an outsider. His membership in the Twelve, presence at the Last Supper, and intimate greeting in the garden mark him as friend rather than enemy. If so, what motivated him to betray Jesus? John and Luke seem content to see the betrayal as a result of Judas' avarice. Matthew also mentions money, but pictures Judas in great agony after Jesus' crucifixion, committing suicide after returning the "blood money" to the authorities. Some have suggested that Judas wanted Jesus to confront the Roman authorities as a political messiah, and that his betrayal was misguided zeal. Others have suggested that Judas became disenchanted with Jesus' unwillingness to make the right "messianic" moves, and was attempting to keep Jesus from destroying the entire messianic movement with his ineffectual messiahship. More recent suggestions have interpreted Judas' actions less as betrayal and more as an attempt to force Jesus and the Jewish authorities into dialogue, to "hand over" Jesus so that he might defend and proclaim his identity as the Messiah.

Also troublesome is the manner of Judas' death. Here there is some general agreement; Judas died a gruesome death. Matthew notes that Judas, full of remorse, returned the 30 pieces of silver and hanged himself (Matt. 27:5). This "blood money" purchased a field in which to bury the poor. Luke interrupts Peter's speech in Acts 1:18-19 to report that an unrepentant Judas bought a field with "the reward of his wickedness" and, falling down, burst open in the middle and bled to death. The field became well-known in Jerusalem as the "Field of Blood."

Bibliography. W. Klassen, *Judas: Betrayer or Friend of Jesus?* (Minneapolis, 1996).

STEVEN M. SHEELEY

JUDAS MACCABEUS (Gk. *Ioúdas Makkabaíos*) The military and political leader credited with the success of the Jewish revolt against Seleucid rule during the reign of Antiochus IV Epiphanes. He is listed in 1 Macc. 2:4 as the third of five sons of Mattathias, a priest of the order of Jehoiarib; Josephus makes the less likely claim that he is the eldest son (*BJ* 1.37). While *Makkabaios* appears to be a nickname in 1 Macc. 2:4 and elsewhere, he is referred to as *Ioudas Makkabaios* ("Judas Maccabeus") in 2:66; 5:24. In 1 Macc. 5:34 and throughout much of 2 Maccabees he is simply called Maccabeus. Most scholars find the origin of the name in Aram. *maqqaḇa'* or Heb. *maqqeḇeṯ*, "hammer." There is considerable speculation as to whether this refers to a physical characteristic such as the shape of his head. By extension the term "Maccabee" is sometimes used to refer to Judas and his brothers, even though the resultant family dynasty is referred to as Hasmonean in rabbinic literature, Josephus, and elsewhere.

Modein NW of Jerusalem was most likely his ancestral home (1 Macc. 2:70; 9:19). While 1 Maccabees, the "official" Hasmonean dynastic history, and Josephus credit Mattathias with the origin of the revolt, 2 Maccabees glorifies the role of Judas Maccabeus as the hero of these events and makes no mention of his father. This has led some historians to question the significance of Mattathias' role in these developments. The two accounts do share a similar outline of the course of the battles which led to the expulsion of the Greek forces from the Jerusalem temple in 164 B.C.E.

In the account of 1 Maccabees Judas takes control of the fledgling group of revolutionaries that had been drawn together by his father, including his four brothers who accept his leadership (1 Macc. 2:65-68; 3:1-2). According to 2 Macc. 8:1 Judas secretly recruited a force of 6000 from the villages of the hill country NW of Jerusalem to resist the oppression and persecution experienced by the Jews under Antiochus IV. In 1 Macc. 3 this resistance begins with the defeat of Apollonius and Seron, commanders of the Greek forces. Vigorous Seleucid response is led by Gorgias and Nicanor. Utilizing a surprise attack at Emmaus, Judas routs these forces and the survivors flee, probably in the spring of 165. The sources agree that Judas led a growing army (1 Macc. 4:29) which by that fall had secured the temple area and other parts of Jerusalem. Sacrifices were offered on the new altar of the cleansed temple on 25 Chislev, 148 of the Seleucid Era (ca. 14 December 164). This event is commemorated annually in the Jewish festival of Hanukkah.

The texts suggest gentile resistance to this Jewish resurgence of power. Judas and his brothers defended besieged Jews in Idumea to the south, across the Jordan in Gilead, and in Galilee. In the spring of 163 Judas unsuccessfully attacked the Akra, the fortress of the Seleucid garrison and refuge of anti-Hasmonean forces in Jerusalem. After a series of battles Judas Maccabeus was killed at Elasa in 160. In the midst of the description of Judas' military campaigns, 1 Macc. 8 records a successful delegation he sent to Rome for the purpose of forming an alliance against the Seleucids.

Judas' political and military successes are largely responsible for initiating the period of Hasmonean rule which began with Jonathan his brother a few years later and continued until the Roman conquest in 63 B.C.E. But this Judean family could only come to power after it had recovered from the defeats which resulted in Judas' death. The temple, however, remained in the hands of the Jewish priesthood from the time of its rededication.

Bibliography. B. Bar-Kochva, *Judas Maccabaeus* (Cambridge, 1989); E. J. Bickerman, *The God of the Maccabees: Studies on the Meaning and Origin of the Maccabean Revolt.* SJLA 32 (Leiden, 1979); L. L. Grabbe, *Judaism from Cyrus to Hadrian,*

1: *The Persian and Greek Periods* (Minneapolis, 1992); J. Sievers, *The Hasmoneans and Their Supporters* (Atlanta, 1990); V. Tcherikover, *Hellenistic Civilization and the Jews* (1959, repr. New York, 1970).

JOHN KAMPEN

JUDE (Gk. *Ioúdas*), **LETTER OF**

One of the "Catholic" or "General" Epistles, written to encourage faithfulness in the midst of aberrance; the 26th book in the NT canon.

Literary Structure

There are three discernible types of material in Jude: the admonition (vv. 1-4, 20-25), the description of the opponents, and warning exhortations (the latter two types intermingled in vv. 5-19). Much of the confusion in the history of the interpretation of the epistle is due to failure to distinguish between forthright descriptions of the "ungodly intruders" (v. 4) and the apocalyptical warning exhortations in vv. 5-19. Only by careful attention to Jude's literary structure can one distinguish accurately these literary warnings from the actual crisis of Jude's concern.

Clearly Jude is a letter in which midrashic material supports an appeal to faithfulness. In the prologue of vv. 1-4 the salutation appears in conventional epistolary form as a greeting. The normal greeting of Hellenistic correspondence is here supplanted by the whole of v. 2. The shift from the greeting to the exhortation (vv. 3-4) is accomplished by "beloved," which here, as in vv. 17 and 20, functions as a discourse marker to highlight transition to different material. The literary thrust of the letter is expressed in vv. 3-4 as a literary petition. This vigorous petition finds precise expression in vv. 20-23, where the actual exhortation occurs in several imperatival terms. Clearly vv. 3-4 and 20-23 constitute the literary thrust of the document. Two subordinate invitations in vv. 5-16 and 17-19 to reflect upon pertinent warnings were carefully constructed to focus attention upon the exhortation in vv. 20-23.

In the first of these reminders, Jude draws from the OT and contemporary Jewish literature a few items which state in unmistakable terms the dire consequences of pursuing the course of the opponents. Vv. 5-16 is a midrashic-type commentary on the infamous incident in which the wandering Jews in the desert were destroyed for their unbelief. Woven into this midrashic material are several attempts to link the rebelliousness and fate of the traditional enemies of God with the rebelliousness and fate of these troublesome intruders and those who might opt to defect to their number. These midrashic elaborations clearly state the terrible fate destined for all who pervert the order intended by God, specifically those who reject the Christ, and warn the readers to take seriously the admonitions in vv. 20-23.

In the second reminder (vv. 17-19), Jude appeals to earlier apostolic warnings that such a situation as this was imminent. He attempts to identify these "ungodly intruders" with those whom the apostles anticipated and to dissuade anyone inclined to follow them.

Sources

Jude evidently placed value not only on Jewish texts now viewed as canonical, but also on apocryphal texts. While this may reflect Jude's own understanding, there is reason to believe that the choice of texts also reflects an attempt to use texts the readers would find convincing. In his preparations for a treatise on "salvation" (v. 3), certainly Jude would have encountered such texts. Particularly abundant are similarities to 1 Enoch, as well as passages in T. Napthali, Jubilees, and 3 Macc. The triad of references in vv. 5-7 to rebellion and fate may have been suggested by Sir. 16:6-14. Jude's references to the archangel Michael (v. 9) may be to a Jewish legend in the Assumption of Moses.

That portions of Jude and 2 Peter are similar is obvious. While it was once thought that Jude was dependent upon 2 Peter, it is now more common to view 2 Peter as dependent upon Jude. The material Jude has in common with 2 Peter occurs in a different context and lacks the verbal precision one encounters in the Synoptic Gospels. The material common to Jude and 2 Peter could well derive from a common source such as Sir. 16:6-14.

The Opponents

In deducing the characteristics of Jude's opponents, it is important to refrain from infusing into the picture elements from 2 Peter or other sources and to distinguish between literary apocalyptical warnings and historical assertions of their character in Jude. The "ungodly intruders" can then be seen as ungodly; licentious; rejecting Christ; in delusion, sexually improper, rejecting lordship, and mocking the spiritual domain; insidiously attending the love feasts where they influence the faithful; carousing together unashamedly; taking care only of themselves; disenchanted; obdurate; verbally harsh; flattering others for selfish advantage; divisive; and unspiritual. Thus these intruders have every appearance of historicity, and there is no reason why the Epistle of Jude should not be taken as a genuine attempt to counter their sinister influence.

Date

The date of the epistle has been variously estimated, from the 50s to the 2nd century. Most consider a late-1st-century date to be probable, classifying Jude as an "early Catholic" work, presupposing a certain Gnosticism, and deducing that in v. 17 the writer is looking back upon an earlier period now past. However, this reference is to earlier apostolic warnings, suggesting an earlier rather than later date. Moreover, the character of Jude's opponents is not a developed Gnosticism, so no late date is necessary.

The Epistle of Jude evidences certain primitive features and contains nothing that warrants a late date. It evidently belongs to an early Palestinian apocalyptic-type Jewish Christianity. The letter could very well be dated in the 50s, and very possibly could even be one of the earliest NT documents.

Authorship

As the epistle is attributed to "Judas, a servant of Jesus Christ and brother of James," the author has been identified traditionally as Judas, the brother of Jesus (Matt. 13:55; Mark 6:3; Eusebius *HE* 3.19.1–20.6). Since reference to one's identification is usually to one's father, this reference to a brother implies that this James must have been quite well known. In the early Church, only James the Lord's brother could have been called simply James without ambiguity.

Some suggest that the letter is pseudepigraphical and attributed to Jude by a later writer. Others counter that Jude was too obscure to have served as an authoritative pseudonym. The appeal to a blood-relationship to Jesus would have been taken by readers as an appeal to authority, but the appeal to a blood-relationship to James, while it would have carried weight, is secondary to the appeal to being "a servant of Jesus Christ."

Little is known of Judas, the brother of Jesus. Presumably he was not a follower of Jesus during his ministry (Mark 3:21, 31), but became a believer after the Resurrection (Acts 1:14). If Jude was a younger brother of Jesus, born ca. A.D. 10, he could have had grandsons about age 30 in A.D. 90, when he was about 80. That Jude could have written this letter during the mid-1st century is entirely possible.

However, linguistically the Greek of the letter is thought to be much too good to be attributable to a Galilean Jew of peasant background. The author is certainly a Semitic speaker who used the Hebrew OT and read the book of Enoch in Aramaic, but his facility with Greek is very good, especially his vocabulary. Certainly this level of Greek usage was not at all uncommon in Palestine during the 1st century. If Jude's missionary work took him among Greek-speaking Jews, even in Palestine, there is no convincing reason why he could not have acquired such competence in Greek.

Certainly the exegetical procedure used, significant use of Jewish pseudepigraphical literature, and the Jewish apocalyptical perspective are entirely consistent with authorship by a Palestinian Jewish-Christian of the first generation of Christians, as was Judas the brother of Jesus.

Destination

Nothing can be deduced for certain regarding the destination of the epistle. The formal opening (vv. 1-2) indicates that it is intended as a genuine letter, and both its *raison d'etre* (v. 4) and the particular characteristics of the opponents indicate that it is not a general letter to all Christians, but an occasional document written to a specific church or group of churches regarding an actual problem.

Both the identity of the author and the significant use of Jewish apocalyptic to illustrate his points indicate that the recipients are probably Jewish Christians. Since it is written in good Greek with no elements of translation, it is not at all improbable that the audience is a predominantly Jewish-Christian community in the Greco-Roman world.

Message

As stated in the introduction (vv. 3-4), the purpose of the epistle is to exhort the readers to remain faithful. Specifically, in view of christological aberrance and licentiousness, they are to "contend for the faith" (vv. 20-23). Having been warned that they must not become like the long-standing enemies of God in Jewish literature and tradition, the readers are told what they can do to solidify their own position (vv. 20-21) and what they can do to assist those of their number inclined to defect to the aberration in thought and life-style characteristic of the "ungodly intruders" (vv. 22-23). While the opponents are denounced decisively, Christian love and patience should be exercised with those Christians who waver between the faithful and the intruders, all the while maintaining vigilance so as not to be contaminated by ungodly influences. The masterful doxology (vv. 24-25), long lifted from this context for liturgical reasons, actually is a prayer that God will preserve the readers from disaster in this life and enable them to realize their eschatological hopes.

Bibliography. R. J. Bauckham, *Jude, 2 Peter.* WBC 50 (Waco, 1983); "The Letter of Jude: An Account of Research," in *ANRW* II.25.5 (Berlin, 1986), 3791-826; C. D. Osburn, "Discourse Analysis and Jewish Apocalyptic in the Epistle of Jude," in *Linguistics and New Testament Interpretation,* ed. D. A. Black (Nashville, 1992), 287-319; D. Watson, *Invention, Arrangement, and Style: Rhetorical Criticism of Jude and 2 Peter.* SBLDS 104 (Atlanta, 1988).

CARROLL D. OSBURN

JUDEA (Gk. *Ioudaía*)

The postexilic Greek term for Judah. Used in the LXX, Philo, Josephus, NT, and inscriptions, the term originally designated the area of southern Palestine surrounding Jerusalem previously established as a province by the Babylonian Nebuchadnezzar and retained by subsequent Persian and Hellenistic rulers. Judea extended from Bethel in the north to Beth-zur in the south (40 km.[25 mi.]), and from Emmaus in the west to the Jordan River in the east (50 km.[32 mi.]; 2000 sq. km.[800 sq. mi.]). In Persian times it was divided into six districts and was populated by Jews. Judea was a semi-independent hyparchy under the Ptolemies; and the Seleucids, who founded the Greek city Antioch in Syria, included Judea in the eparchy of Samaria along with the hyparchies of Samaria, Perea, and Galilee. The Hasmoneans brought Galilee, Samaria, Perea, Idumea, and most of the Mediterranean coast under the sway of the kingdom of Judea, and Herod the Great ruled these territories plus numerous areas east of Galilee. Archelaus was named ethnarch and inherited Judea (in the more restricted sense), Idumea, and Samaria, but he was deposed in 6 C.E. and his territory was transferred to Roman prefects of equestrian rank. Idumea officially became part of Judea, and in 41 Claudius transferred Judea and Samaria from direct Roman rule to the kingdom of Agrippa (which with the exception of three cities equaled that of Herod the Great) until the latter's death in 44. Rule of all Palestine was transferred to Roman procurators, and a series of mostly inept governors ruled until 66, the outbreak of the Jewish War.

In the NT "Judea" occurs usually in reference to Judea proper (as opposed to Samaria, Galilee, Perea, and Idumea) but also to the entire Jewish nation, specifically including Galilee (Acts 10:37) and the Transjordan territories (Matt. 19:1).

Bibliography. M. Avi-Yonah, "Historical Geography," in *The Jewish People in the First Century* 1, ed. S. Safrai and M. Stern, CRINT 1/1 (Philadelphia, 1974), 78-116.

ERIC F. MASON

JUDGE

The common Hebrew term for "judge" *(šōpēṭ)* is a participle form of the verb "decide," "rule," "govern," "vindicate," "deliver," and "judge." The conventional translation "judge" in all contexts conceals nonforensic meanings which reflect other functions of the *šōpēṭ*.

The judges' duty was to save the Israelites from their enemies and preserve domestic accord. They were to dispense absolute, impartial justice *(mišpāṭ)* and not take bribes (Deut. 16:19); they were to protect the widow, orphan, and stranger (Deut. 24:17) and not let themselves be unduly influenced by popular opinion or by the plight of the poor (Exod. 23:2-3).

In the patriarchal period family and tribal leaders acted as judges (cf. Gen. 38:24). In the wilderness period Moses alone was the judge until Jethro suggested he appoint judges for "every small matter," and reserve for himself only "a great matter" (Exod. 18:22).

The Jethro system was not operative after the settlement in Canaan when there was no tribal union. In premonarchical Israel the Lord, "Judge of all the earth" (Gen. 18:25), appointed judges by causing the spirit of God to descend upon them (Judg. 3:9) to lead armies and deliver the Israelites from their oppressors (2:16; 3:10). In this context the term *špṭ* denotes "delivering" or "saving" *(yšʿ)*. The judges were not part of regular tribal government but arose to meet a crisis and judged only during it and shortly thereafter. They judged one or several tribes, but never all. Their military heroism or personal presence enabled them to assume the juridical role also.

With the monarchy the king became supreme judge (2 Sam. 2–3), but there were also appointed local judges (Deut. 16:18). Priests, too, served as judges (Deut. 17:12; 2 Chr. 19:4-11). The elders of a city acted as judges at the gate (Judg. 8:16; Ruth 4:2; Job 29:7-8), and judges also exercised their authority going from town to town in annual circuits as did Samuel (1 Sam. 7:15-16). Judges had authority parallel to that of kings (Ps. 2:10). In Babylonia the king of Persia instructed Ezra to appoint judges and magistrates (Aram. *šāpṭîn, dayyānîn*), "all who know the laws of your God," to judge all the people "beyond the river" (Ezra 7:25). In Hellenistic times the high priest replaced the king as the principal judge (2 Chr. 19:8). In NT the Sanhedrin was the supreme court for the Jews. Jesus asserted that God alone should be judge (Luke 6:37; Jas. 4:12).

DANIEL GROSSBERG

JUDGES, BOOK OF

Part of the larger narrative from Genesis to Kings. Chronologically it is set in the period between the Conquest (Joshua) and the establishment of the monarchy (1 Samuel).

Formation

It is generally agreed that the book of Judges is composed of stories that originally circulated independent of their present context. These stories center on the exploits of local heroes (Ehud, Deborah and Barak, Gideon and Abimelech) who by their cleverness or military prowess were able to lead the people to victory over their enemies. The stories were then collected together as stories of the deliverance of Israel by Yahweh in holy war. At a later stage of development the stories were put into a framework of sin–punishment–cry for help–deliverance. The original collection of stories was supplemented by the stories of Jephthah and Samson, and the addition of brief notices about the "minor judges" (3:31; 10:1-5; 12:8-15). The framework and supplemental material are probably the work of the Deuteronomistic historian or at the very least the work of a Deuteronomic editor. At a final stage of development, the prologue (1:1–2:5) and epilogue (17:1–21:25) were added. That these sections were added at a later stage is clear from the fact that the prologue and the epilogue intrude into a story line that runs continuous from Joshua to Judges and Judges to Samuel. Moreover, in the rest of Judges the tribes are presented as united under a judge, but in the prologue and epilogue the tribes act independently. Finally, both sections focus on internal issues among the tribes, not the tribes united against a common enemy.

The Judges

The term "judge" has a broader meaning in Hebrew than in English. It can refer to someone who has a judicial function, but it can also be applied more broadly to anyone who exercises rule. For the Deuteronomistic writers the term applies to military leaders who were raised up by God to deliver the Israelites from their enemies. Six judges (Othniel, Ehud, Deborah, Gideon, Jephthah, Samson) function as military leaders and traditionally have been called the "major judges." Sometimes they are called "charismatic leaders" because it is the spirit of Yahweh that designates them as leaders; they are not appointed, nor do they inherit the office. Shamgar, Tola, Jair, Ibzan, Elon, Abdon, traditionally called the "minor judges," are said to have delivered or judged Israel, but so little is recorded of them that it is not possible to determine their rule. It has been speculated that they were judges in the sense of having a judicial function, or possibly local officials or elders of their tribes, or simply prominent individuals.

Contents

There are three major divisions in the book of Judges: 1:1–2:5, an alternate presentation of the Conquest; 2:6–16:31, the exploits of the judges; 17:1–21:25, appendices.

The Conquest (1:1–2:5)

This section is composed of ancient fragments concerning the Israelite takeover of the land of Canaan. It shows the tribes acting independently of one another, in contrast to the book of Joshua where the Conquest is presented as undertaken by all the tribes under the leadership of Joshua. In Judges the conquest of the south is attributed to the tribes of Judah and Simeon (1:2-21) and the conquest of Bethel to the tribe of Joseph (1:22-26). The other tribes fail to drive out the inhabitants of their respective territories (1:27-36). The reason for this failure is that the people disobeyed Yahweh's command (2:1-5), and consequently the inhabitants of the land were a snare to Israel.

Exploits of the Judges (2:6–16:31)

The exploits of the judges are introduced by two passages which give the theological interpretation of the period of the judges. In Judg. 2:11-23, a passage dominated by Deuteronomic language and theology, the cyclic pattern sin–punishment–cry for help–deliverance is delineated. Israel's failure to worship Yahweh and Yahweh alone sets in motion a sequence of events that is repeated again and again. The sin of apostasy leads to punishment in the form of military conquest, and only by returning to Yahweh will Israel be assured of deliverance from its enemies; Israel does not remain faithful after its deliverance and the cycle begins again. The second passage (3:1-5) explains Israel's failure to conquer the land totally as a way to test Israel's faithfulness to Yahweh. It reiterates 2:1-5.

The stories of the six "major judges" vary considerably. Othniel is little more than a name set in the Deuteronomistic framework of sin–punishment–cry for help–deliverance. The story of Ehud, in a crudely humorous manner, tells how Ehud uses "his handicap" (left-handedness) to his advantage in dispatching the king of Eglon. In the account of Deborah and Barak Israel is able to gain victory over a superior military force because Yahweh fights on Israel's behalf. The role of women (Deborah and Jael) in this story is noteworthy. The poem in ch. 5 is a victory hymn in which Yahweh is praised as the Warrior God who fights on behalf of Israel. The story of Gideon is complex, probably composed of various separate traditions that have been brought together. Victory for Israel is assured because Yahweh is with Gideon as confirmed in the account of the fleece. Issues of Israel acting as a unity (8:1-21), kingship (8:22-23; 9:1-57), and the dangers of idolatry (8:24-27) are woven into the Gideon narrative. The account of Jephthah is difficult, for it involves human sacrifice to Yahweh and as such leaves many unanswered questions. It may well have been originally an etiological story explaining the custom of ritualized yearly mourning, but in Judges it becomes another example of victory achieved by a judge. The Samson story, though set in the Deuteronomistic framework, focuses not on the relationship between Yahweh and Israel, but on the exploits of Samson. The various episodes are united by a common theme: Samson's personal vendetta against the Philistines after he is repeatedly betrayed by women. Into the exploits of the Judges are set the notices of the minor judges.

Appendices (17:1–21:25)

The last five chapters of the book of Judges are concerned with incidents in which Levites figure prominently. The first appendix (chs. 17–18) relates the sequence of events that led up to the establishment of a cultic center at Dan; the second appendix (chs. 19–21) centers on the rape of the Levite's concubine and the civil war that results from this outrage. This section is unified, not simply because both appendixes deal with Levites, but also by the recurring pro-monarchical phrase, "In those days there was no king in Israel; all the people did what was right in their own eyes" (17:6; 21:25; incomplete in 18:1a; 19:1a). The pro-monarchical stance of the appendices stands in marked contrast to the anti-monarchical sentiments expressed in the central portion of the book in Gideon's refusal to accept kingship (8:22-23) and Abimelech's attempt to establish himself as king of Shechem (9:1-57).

Themes

The Deuteronomistic theological perspective dominates thematically in the book of Judges. Its underlying theological principle is that obedience to the covenant Lord, particularly expressed in the worship of Yahweh and Yahweh alone, leads to peace and prosperity; disobedience, i.e., the worship of other gods, leads to war and dominance by one's enemies. This is clearly presented in 2:11-23 and is repeated throughout the book in the framework into which the stories of the judges are inserted. Another theme which pervades the book surrounds the issue of leadership. When under a judge Israel is able to adhere to the command to worship Yahweh and Yahweh alone; with the death of a judge Israel falls again into apostasy, suggesting that a more permanent form of leadership is needed. This becomes explicit in the epilogue with its repeated insistence that without a king the people pursue their own interests. The issue of leadership is not resolved until kingship is established in the book of Samuel, but the tension between pro- and anti-monarchical sentiment remains throughout the Deuteronomistic history.

New Directions

More recent work on the book of Judges is concerned with reading the book from a literary critical perspective focusing on the rhetorical features and unity of the book. The presence of several women characters (Deborah, Jael, Jephthah's daughter, the Levite's concubine) has drawn the attention of feminist scholars, and several studies have appeared from this interpretive stance.

Bibliography. M. Bal, *Death and Dissymmetry: The Politics of Coherence in the Book of Judges* (Chicago, 1988); J. Gray, *Joshua, Judges, Ruth.* NCBC (Grand Rapids, 1986); L. R. Klein, *The Triumph of Irony in the Book of Judges.* JSOTSup 68 (Sheffield, 1988); A. D. H. Mayes, *Judges.* Old Testament Guides 8 (Sheffield, 1985); R. H. O'Connell, *The Rhetoric of the Book of Judges.* VTSup 63 (Leiden, 1996); B. G. Webb, *The Book of Judges.* JSOTSup 46 (Sheffield, 1987); G. A. Yee, ed., *Judges and Method* (Minneapolis, 1995).

PAULINE A. VIVIANO

JUDGMENT

In the OT "judgment" (Heb. *mišpāṭ*) carries both legal and theological meanings, which reflects the embeddedness of the concept in the covenant traditions of Israel (Deut. 1:9-18, esp. v. 17). God, who is "Judge of all the earth" (Gen. 18:25), is not merely a distant magistrate but one whose judgments express the continual unfolding of the covenant relationship (Exod. 21:1; 24:3a; NRSV "ordinances"). Judgments, like commandments (*miṣwôṯ*) as expressions of the covenantal relationship, are also to be kept by the people (Exod. 24:3b; Lev. 18:4; Deut. 11:1; 26:17). In both human and divine manifestations, judgment is closely associated with another term bearing both legal and theological meanings, *ṣeḏeq* or *ṣĕḏāqâ*, usually translated "justice" or "righteousness." As God's judgment goes hand in hand with God's justice (Gen. 18:25; Jer. 9:24; cf. Deut. 10:18), so does covenant-faithful human judgment lead to justice on earth (Lev. 19:15; 2 Sam. 8:15; Jer. 23:5; Amos 5:11-15).

For the Deuteronomist, the early prophets, and the early wisdom writers, the workings of divine judgment are predictable: the wicked are punished and the righteous rewarded (Deut. 8:11; Prov. 29:25-27). Some writers, however, motivated by times of extreme national crisis, begin to lose confidence in the accustomed order of divine judgment and justice. The later prophets, Job, Ecclesiastes, and the postexilic psalmist witness the profound shift worked in biblical consciousness by the persistence of suffering among the righteous. One response, characteristic of the prophets, is to push judgment forward in time. Not only the nations but Israel herself awaits the coming "Day of the Lord" (Isa. 10:20; Hos. 1:5), to be followed by a new age of blessings and a restoration of the divine order (Isa. 65:17-25; Zech. 14:9-11).

Another response is found in Job, where the longed-for judgment and justice of God is pushed beyond earthly life to the resurrection (Job 19:25-27; cf. Isa. 26:19; Wis. 2–5). The theme of resurrection judgment becomes standard in the late Second Temple period, the time of Israel's oppression under the Syrians and the Romans (Dan. 12:1-2; 2 Macc. 12:41-45). In the apocalyptic thought of this period, the hope for a restoration of justice on earth is gone and a cosmic last judgment is in view. At the cataclysmic end of the old order, God or God's agent ("one like a Son of Man," "Messiah," "Righteous One") will come to judge the living and the (resurrected) dead. In some texts, those who die before the last judgment are resurrected and judged immediately upon death; in others, the dead rest in Sheol (in agony or peace, depending on their status as wicked or righteous) until the judgment at the last day (2 Bar. 36:11; 4 Ezra 7:95).

The NT shares in and adapts Jewish eschatological and apocalyptic notions of judgment. The English meaning of "judging" or "judgment" is carried in Greek by the verb *krínō* and the nouns *krísis* and *kríma*, but texts that imply the last judgment often do not employ these Greek terms. Other relevant vocabulary includes "the day," "those days," and terms describing the coming of the Messiah or the Son of Man at the end time. While there is considerable disagreement about Jesus' own expectations and those of his earliest followers concerning the end time, the NT authors generally look forward to a future eschatological judgment.

In the Synoptic Gospels, Jesus is the divine agent, often "Son of Man," who announces and/or effects the advent of God's rule. His second coming will bring the consummation of God's kingdom, including the final judgment of the wicked and the righteous. This judgment is variously depicted as imminent (Mark, Matthew) or delayed (Luke), but in the Synoptics it has clear future reference. The classic depiction of this future judgment is Matt. 25:31-46, where the enthroned Jesus separates the sheep from the goats (cf. 19:28, where the disciples are given authority to judge the 12 tribes of Israel). As in Jewish apocalyptic texts, the coming judgment is presaged by affliction, persecution, and cosmic catastrophe (Mark 13:3-37 par.). John's Gospel displays a heightened use of the vocabulary of judgment, but now the judgment is a decidedly present and not merely future reality. The moment of judgment may coincide with the act of belief or unbelief (John 3:19; 5:22-24, 27), and yet the eschatological reference has not disappeared: "on the last day, the word *(lógos)* . . . will serve as judge" (12:48; cf. 5:28-29).

Paul also expects an imminent judgment, the "day of the Lord" (1 Thess. 5:2; 1 Cor. 5:5; 2 Cor. 1:14; Phil. 1:6, 10). On that day, believers will be saved from the wrath of God and given eternal life (Rom. 2:7) while those who "obey wickedness" will suffer wrath and fury (v. 8). God is the ultimate judge who knows and judges the secrets of human beings (Rom. 2:16). God has appointed Christ to the judgment seat (2 Cor. 5:10; cf. Rom. 14:10) and the saints to judge the world (1 Cor. 6:2; cf. Matt. 19:28). Although God has made certain criteria of judgment known, God's judgments are finally "unsearchable" (Rom. 11:33). For Paul, divine judgment may function as a corrective (1 Cor. 11:32): even the excommunication of an immoral person from the Church may bring the salvation of his spirit in the day of the Lord (1 Cor. 5:5; cf. 3:15). There is also a sense in which for Paul the judgment of God, like the end time and the new creation, has already come upon the world. Believers and unbelievers are already being saved or destroyed insofar as they perceive or do not perceive God's saving action in the Christ event (1 Cor. 1:18; 10:11).

Judgment in the Revelation of John is highly reminiscent of Jewish apocalyptic judgment. In the present evil age of Roman domination, divine justice is inscrutable; the people cry out for God's avenging judgment on their enemies (Rev. 6:10) and are shown visions, revealed from heaven, of the coming "hour of judgment" (14:7; 18:10; cf. 11:18). In the cataclysmic end time, the "true and righteous judgments of God" (16:7; 19:2, 11) will restore justice. The Word (Logos) of God personified, mounted on a white horse, will judge and make war (Rev. 19:11). The dead will be resurrected for judgment (Rev. 20:4-5), and the saints will be rewarded in the splendor of the new heaven and new earth (21:1-4).

Bibliography. S. G. G. Brandon, *The Judgment of the Dead* (New York, 1969); P. D. Hanson, *The Dawn of Apocalyptic,* rev. ed. (Philadelphia, 1979); V. Herntrich, "krínō: The OT Term mishpat," *TDNT* 3:923-33; G. von Rad, *Old Testament Theology* 2 (New York, 1965): 119-25; D. S. Russell, *The Method and Message of Jewish Apocalyptic.* OTL (Philadelphia, 1964).

Alexandra R. Brown

JUDGMENT SEAT

A raised platform (Gk. *bḗma*) for a public speaker (Neh. 8:4 LXX; Acts 12:21) or a judge, and by extension a tribunal or court (cf. *kritḗrion*). Lysias spoke from a *bḗma* (2 Macc. 13:26), and Pilate sat on a judgment seat mounted on a raised platform when he asked the Jews what should be done with Jesus (Matt. 27:19; John 19:13). Paul appeared before the judgment seat of Gallio in Corinth (Acts 18:12-17), and before that of Festus in Caesarea (25:6, 10, 17).

Paul twice mentions the *bḗma* of divine judgment. He argues that God (Rom. 14:10) and Christ (2 Cor. 5:10) occupy a judgment seat, and all will have to appear before it and give account of their lives (cf. Rev. 20:11-15). It is doubtful that Paul has two separate judgments in mind, and all three passages probably describe the same eschatological event.

In other references, divine judgment comes when God or Christ takes his "throne" (Ps. 9:7[MT 8]; Dan. 7:9; Matt. 25:31; Rev. 20:11). Since in antiquity a judge might sit on a throne placed on a raised platform, "throne" and "judgment seat" could be identical depending on the context.

Gary S. Shogren

JUDITH (Heb. *yĕhûḏîṯ;* Gk. *Ioudíth*)

1. A wife of Esau and daughter of the Hittite Beeri (Gen. 26:34).

2. The principal character of the book of Judith; a descendant of Merari and widow of Manasseh. Characterized as beautiful, wealthy, and pious, she demonstrates great courage in delivering Jerusalem from Nebuchadnezzar's army and killing the general Holofernes.

JUDITH, BOOK OF

A book relating the heroic deeds of Judith of Bethulia. Considered canonical by Roman Catholics (among the Deuterocanonicals formally declared sacred writings in 1546 at the Council of Trent) and apocryphal by Protestants, the book was listed in 397 C.E. among the works deemed authoritative for use by the bishops gathered at the North African Council in Carthage. Jewish tradition has always enjoyed Judith, but outside of the community in classical Alexandrian Egypt, Judaism has always regarded the story as entertainment and not Scripture.

The book was written in the aftermath of the persecutions of the Jews by Antiochus IV Epiphanes and the subsequent revolt by the Hasmoneans that resulted in an independent Jewish state centered on Jerusalem during the latter half of the 2nd century B.C.E. The tendency, after Alexander the Great, for Greek rulers to take on divine attributes clearly dates this work, with its "king of the Assyrians" ordered to be the sole divinity, as a composition of the Hellenistic age in Palestine. The author of Judith appears to have been a Pharisee writing ca. 100 B.C.E. within the Hasmonean kingdom. While the earliest extant reliable versions of Judith are in Greek and Latin, it is generally agreed that the work was composed in Hebrew.

The numerous historical references in the text led the Church to treat the narrative as historical until modern times. However, the fact that the historical references tend to be retellings of biblical material with imaginative recasting of geography and nationality, by an author who knew Torah and

Judith with the Head of Holofernes, **Hendrik Goltzius (ca. 1588)** (Rijksmuseum Amsterdam)

Prophets, suggests that the intention was to compose a fictitious short story that wove elements of the traditions of Israel with historical events of more recent times into an educational narrative.

The structure of the book is fairly simple. A double chiastic structure brings the reader into the presence of Holofernes and out again twice. The first half of the book (Jdt. 1–7) describes the rise and approach of the invincible multi-national army, led by the general Holofernes, who himself worships his king (Nebuchadnezzar the Assyrian) as if he were his god. This half of the book stresses the absolute might and power of the human ruler and his unbelievably large army. The second half of the book (chs. 8–16) concerns the reception of the army by the symbolic town of Bethulia. The main figure here is Judith, a wealthy, pious, brave, and devout widow, who knows, more than do the elders of the city, that if one has faith in God one must act on it. In the face of what appears to be inescapable destruction, Judith leads her slave woman out into the camp of Holofernes, and the two women decapitate the general through some clever double entendre and the overconfidence of machismo on the part of the general. His army then flees. The two halves of the book are bridged by Achior, an Ammonite, who tells Holofernes about the God of Israel and is sent by the general to Bethulia to be part of the presumedly forthcoming slaughter; however, in Bethulia Achior becomes Jewish, apparently knowing more about the power of God than do the elders of the city. In the first half of the book Achior speaks about God clearly to Holofernes, who does not believe what Achior says though he understands it; parallel to this in the second half of the book, Judith speaks about God misleadingly to Holofernes, who in turn believes her though he misunderstands what she says by thinking she speaks about him.

The theology of the book contrasts the real, very apparent, human might of the Assyrian king with the more real, but very unseen, divine might of God. Each divine figure has its devotee: Holofernes for Nebuchadnezzar the Assyrian, and Judith for God. In many ways the two devotees are much alike, both trusting in the sole power of their divinity and acting on directives never quite stated in the narrative. Each devotee has a corresponding helper: Holofernes has at his command an invincible, powerful, male army that literally covers the land, while Judith has a powerless slave woman who carries a sack. This is the contrast: God (who does not appear) is the true might of the world and needs only a single devotee to oust all the might that the worldly human king (who does appear) can muster; this is a confrontation that clearly owes a great deal to the Gog and Magog visions of Ezek. 38–39. The speeches by Achior and Judith make it clear that the God of Israel protects Israel as long as it is righteous and keeps torah.

That the story was intended as edification can be seen even in the names of the characters. For example, Judith can mean "female Judean" or generically the Jewish people. Nebuchadnezzar, king of the Assyrians, clearly combines a Babylonian royal name with the country of Assyria; anyone familiar with the biblical histories (or ancient Near Eastern history) knows this was not a historical king; but, like Darius the Mede in Daniel, this "Great Ruler of the World" figure, by having an obviously invented name, can and does stand for all earthly rulers who trust in their own power. Achior means "my brother is light," and this Ammonite (relative of the Israelites by way of Abraham's nephew Lot) is the one who explains God's truth to both Holofernes and the elders of Bethulia (a town the name of which, though variously spelled in Greek, in Hebrew means roughly "House of God, Yahweh," itself symbolic). The name of the general appears to derive from a historical Persian military officer.

Medieval Christian interpretation of the book of Judith made it a central text in the formation of Mariology. The entire story was read both as an allegory and as a typology for the life and status of Mary, mother of Jesus. On this account many lines of the text have passed into liturgical readings used by the Catholic Church in honor of Mary.

Bibliography. M. P. Carroll, "Myth, Methodology and Transformation in the Old Testament: The Stories of Esther, Judith, and Susanna," *SR* 12 (1983): 301-12; T. Craven, *Artistry and Faith in the Book of Judith.* SBLDS 70 (Chico, 1983); C. A. Moore, *Judith.* AB 40 (Garden City, 1985); I. Nowell, "Judith: A Question of Power," *TBT* 24 (1986): 12-17; J. C. VanderKam, ed., *"No One Spoke Ill of Her": Essays on Judith* (Atlanta, 1992).

LOWELL K. HANDY

JULIA (Gk. *Ioulía*)
A Christian woman in Rome (Rom. 16:15), perhaps the wife or sister of Philologus.

JULIUS (Gk. *Ioúlios*)
The Roman centurion into whose custody Paul was placed for his journey from Caesarea to Rome as a prisoner of Caesar (Acts 27:1). Luke makes special notice of Julius' kindness to Paul (Acts 27:3, 43). Julius is identified as part of the Augustan (Imperial) division, an honorary title given to various cohorts of auxiliary troops.

The historicity of Julius' role is sometimes questioned since it is unlikely that a centurion of an auxiliary cohort would have been given charge over such an important prisoner or would have had such authority over the ship. However, Julius could have had special imperial police or envoy status.

MARK L. STRAUSS

JUNIA (Gk. *Iouvía*)
Probably the wife of Andronicus; member of a husband-wife team who, like Paul, were Jews, Christians before him, imprisoned with him, and "prominent among the apostles" (Rom. 16:7). All early sources attest Junia as female (esp. Jerome and John Chrysostom). Although the name often appears in masculine forms in English translations, they are unattested in ancient times. The only woman called "apostle" in the NT, Junia may have accompanied

Jesus' ministry, had a vision of the risen Lord, a charge of some sort, and been among the restricted leadership of the Church. Paul approved of her role, calling her "outstanding" among apostles.

Bibliography. B. Brooten, "'Junia . . . Outstanding among the Apostles' (Romans 16:7)," in *Women Priests,* ed. L. Swidler and A. Swidler (New York, 1977), 141-44. BONNIE THURSTON

JUSHAB-HESED (Heb. *yûšaḇ ḥeseḏ*)
A son of Zerubbabel (1 Chr. 3:20).

JUST, JUSTICE

In a philosophical sense, justice is understood as fairness, correct treatment, or equitable distribution of resources, but biblical justice is more than a mathematical distribution of goods. The Bible speaks of justice as a chief attribute of God, with biblical justice inextricably tied to God's mercy and grounded in the relationship between God and humankind. From the time of the wilderness wanderings when the Hebrew people were given ethical instructions about their treatment of widows, orphans, and strangers, the practice of justice has been understood as the mission of those who follow Yahweh.

The biblical tradition is alive with examples of men and women who brought justice to situations of oppression and injustice. From Deborah, the prophet and judge who administered justice, to the 8th-century prophets who called Israel and Judah to act justly toward the poor and oppressed, to Jesus who demonstrated the centrality of justice through his words and actions, biblical images of justice offer a window to God's response to injustice.

Both *ṣěḏāqâ* and *mišpāṭ,* Hebrew words for "righteousness" and "justice," can be understood in legalistic terms. Heb. *ṣěḏāqâ* can refer to ethical and moral standards or equality of all people before the law. Likewise, *mišpāṭ* can refer to law, the process of deciding a case in civil or religious government, execution of a judgment, or rights of an individual under civil or religious law.

Heb. *ṣěḏāqâ* and *mišpāṭ,* as also Gk. *díkē* and *dikaiosýnē,* often are translated as "judgment" and "righteousness," words not normally associated today with justice. However, with reference to a situation of oppression or injustice, their importance to the OT and NT concept of justice is clear.

Justice is rooted in God's character (Isa. 5:16; Deut. 32:4), and justice is what God demands of followers (16:20). A central concept is that the justice of a community is measured by their treatment of the poor and oppressed (Isa. 1:16-17; 3:15). Although the message of justice is woven throughout the Bible, the prophets especially issued a strong call for the covenant community to recognize God as the God of justice and to repent of their injustice. Their primary message can be summarized in the words of Mic. 6:8: "What does the Lord require of you but to do justice, and to love kindness, and to walk humbly with your God?"

The Jubilee tradition in Lev. 25 reflects Israel's understanding of God's demands for justice in the midst of an unjust society. Intended to be observed every 50 years, the Jubilee incorporated Sabbath Year practices of the Covenant code and the Deuteronomic code, providing for land to lie fallow and indentured servants to be set free every seven years. During the Jubilee Year, debts would be forgiven and lands sold because of indebtedness would be returned to the original owners. For agrarian societies like Israel, return of land and forgiveness of debts amounted to economic restructuring of society. Undergirding the Jubilee Year is the biblical principle of redress that corrects past wrongs to approximate equality and restores the human community to wholeness.

Bibliography. B. C. Birch, *Let Justice Roll Down* (Louisville, 1991); S. C. Mott, *Biblical Ethics and Social Change* (Oxford, 1982). MICHELLE TOOLEY

JUSTIFICATION

English Bibles render Heb. *ṣdq* and Gk. *dikaioún* as both "just, justice, justify" and "right, righteous(ness), rightwise." Righteousness/justification language occurs more than 800 times in the OT and NT.

Both the Hebrew and Greek can denote self-justification, seeking to put oneself "in the right." Job "justified himself rather than God" (Job 32:2; cf. 33:32; 9:2). The setting of such attempts may be a lawsuit, involving God and the nations (Isa. 43:9) or Israel (43:26); then it will be shown that God is righteous (45:21, 24). The lawyer in Luke 10:29 wanted "to justify himself" by asking Jesus, "Who is my neighbor?" Money-loving Pharisees are said to try to justify themselves in the sight of other people (Luke 16:15).

A further application is the justification of God. In the Lord's speech to Job from the whirlwind the issue is theodicy or defense of God's ways to mortals (Job 40:8; cf. Gen. 18:25; Ps. 37:5-6, 28-34; Jer. 12:1; Ezek. 18, esp. vv. 25-29). In the NT wisdom is justified by her deeds (Matt. 11:19) or children (Luke 7:35; Rev. 15:3-4; 16:5-7; 19:2). Paul frequently defends God's judgments (2 Thess. 1:5; cf. Rom. 2:5-11; 9:19-24) and ways of salvation (Rom. 3:4-6). Indeed, Romans contains a vindication of how, given God's plan with Israel, salvation has come to the Gentiles (3:28-30; 9:24, 30; 15:8-12) and a rebuke against Gentile Christian presumptuousness which counts Israel out (11:11-24).

Paul's justification of God is inseparably related to his major theme, especially in Romans, of the justification of the ungodly, to whom faith is reckoned as righteousness (Rom. 4:5).

Specific references to justification reflect pre-Pauline confessional slogans about Jesus' death and resurrection resulting in "our justification" (Rom. 4:25), brought home to believers as sanctification-justification via baptism, into Christ, with the Spirit (1 Cor. 6:11). Paul's was an apostolic "ministry of justification" (2 Cor. 3:9), for Jew and Gentile both, i.e., all the world (Rom. 1:16; 2:9-10; 9:24; 10:12; 1 Cor. 12:13). From his own experience and study of Scripture (esp. Gen. 15:6; Ps. 143:2; Hab. 2:4), the principle emerged that "no one is justified before God by the law" but rather by faith (Gal. 3:6-14; cf. Rom. 3:20, 28) and that God's blessing, spoken to Abraham, comes to Gentiles without their being circumcised or performing other "works of the law" (Rom. 4) that were part of Israel's identity markers for remaining in the Sinai covenant. Paul's opposition to such "covenantal nomism" or focus on the Law brought him into conflict with Cephas and "people from James" in Antioch and then into a struggle with such views in Galatia (Gal. 2:15-21; cf. 5:4-5).

In Romans Paul unfolded the gospel for a community he had not founded, precisely in terms of this biblical master theme, the righteousness *(dikaiosýnē)* of God (Rom. 1:16-17). Only after presenting Gentiles and Jews alike under God's judgment (Rom. 1:18–3:20) and a reference to "the justice of God" (3:5, God as Judge), does Paul in 3:22, 24-26 set forth our being justified by God's grace through faith in Jesus. The sacrificial death of Christ explains how God remains just while expiating sins. Justification is not merely an initial step toward salvation, in the believer's past, but also involves future vindication and living out the experience in the present (Rom. 5:1; cf. 2:13; 3:20, 24). Justification is the foundation for carrying out God's will in daily life by service to others, in church and world (Rom. 12:1-2), including "whatever is just" (Phil. 4:8).

For Paul, justification is the prime effect of the Christ event, a metaphor of salvation along with "participation 'in Christ'" and the gift of the Spirit. This theme must be considered along with the related word fields of "grace" and "faith" as well as, in English, "righteousness." Jas. 2:14-26 suggests how prominent justification was in the NT period and how Paul's view could be misunderstood, even by his followers. James follows contemporary Jewish exegesis of Gen. 15:6 by combining it with Gen. 22 (the sacrifice of Isaac), an effort by a later (Jewish) Christian to correct a view of justification that lacks the obedience of faith (Rom. 1:5) expressed in help for others (as Paul insisted in Gal. 5:6; Rom. 13:8-10).

OT and NT understandings of justification stand often in close connection with "judgment." Indeed, "righteousness" (*ṣĕḏāqâ*) and "justice" (*mišpāṭ*) can be used in synonymous parallelism (Amos 5:24; Isa. 11:4). The connection between justification and justice has been made in liberation theology.

See RIGHTEOUSNESS.

Bibliography. M. Barth, *Justification: Pauline Texts Interpreted in the Light of the Old and New Testaments* (Grand Rapids, 1971); D. A. Carson, ed., *Right with God: Justification in the Bible and the World* (Grand Rapids, 1992); N. A. Dahl, "The Doctrine of Justification," in *Studies in Paul* (Minneapolis, 1977), 95-120; J. D. G. Dunn and A. M. Suggate, *The Justice of God* (Grand Rapids, 1993); A. E. McGrath, *Iustitia Dei: A History of the Christian Doctrine of Justification,* 2nd ed. (Cambridge, 1998); H. G. Reventlow and Y. Hoffman, eds., *Justice and Righteousness.* JSOTSup 137 (Sheffield, 1992); M. A. Seifrid, *Justification by Faith.* NovTSup 68 (Leiden, 1992).

JOHN REUMANN

JUSTUS (Gk. *Ioústos*)

1. Surname of Joseph Barsabbas, unsuccessful candidate for apostleship (Acts 1:23).

2. Titius (or Titus) Justus, a "worshipper of God" in Corinth whose home was next to the synagogue and open to Christians, and with whom Paul lodged (Acts 18:7).

3. Jesus Justus, one "of the circumcision" (a fellow Jew or member of the circumcision party) and "fellow worker" with Paul who sent greetings to Colossae (Col. 4:11). His is the only name in the paragraph that does not appear in Philemon. With Mark he has been a comfort (Gk. *parēgoría*) to Paul, a strong term found in medical contexts in the sense of "assuaging" or "alleviating" and on tombstones and in condolence letters.

BONNIE THURSTON

JUTTAH (Heb. *yuṭṭâ*)
A village in tribal Judah (Josh. 15:55), designated a levitical city (21:16). Located in the hill country S of Hebron, Juttah may have been the "city of Judah" to which Mary traveled (Luke 1:39). The site is identified with modern Yaṭṭā (158095), 9 km. (5.6 mi.) S of Hebron.

DAVID C. MALTSBERGER

K

KAB (Heb. *qab*)
A unit of measurement for dry wares and liquids (2 Kgs. 6:5; from Egyp. *kb*[?]). The Mishnah recognizes the kab as one sixth of a seah, an eighteenth of an ephah, or ca. 1.2 l. (1.3 liquid qt.). According to Josephus (*Ant.* 9.4.4), a kab would equal ca. 1.91 l. (2 qt.).

KABZEEL (Heb. *qaḇṣᵉʾēl*)
A city in southern Judah, near the border of Edom (Josh. 15:21), the home of Benaiah, one of David's warriors (2 Sam. 23:20 = 1 Chr. 11:22). Following the Exile it was resettled under the name Jekabzeel (Neh. 11:25). The site may be identified with modern Khirbet Gharreh/Tell ʿIra (148071), near Wadi Mishash ca. 21 km. (13 mi.) NE of Beer-sheba.

KADESH (Heb. *qāḏēš*), **KADESH-BARNEA** (*qāḏēš barnēaʿ*)

1. Kadesh-barnea, a site in the northern Sinai (the wilderness of Zin; Num. 20:1; 33:36) where Israel encamped at least twice in their wanderings. In the narrative of Chedorlaomer's campaign into southern Canaan, Kadesh is called En-misphat, "spring of judgment" (Gen. 14:7). It was near Kadesh that Hagar received God's promise of Ishmael's birth (Gen. 16:11-14). Moses sent the spies from Kadesh to reconnoiter Canaan, but their report destroyed Israel's resolve to take the land (Num. 13–14; Deut. 1:19). For their lack of faith, God sentenced Israel to 40 years of wandering, which eventually found Israel back at Kadesh-barnea. It was also at Kadesh that Moses' sister Miriam died and was buried (Num. 20:1) and there Israel complained again about their lack of water (vv. 2-10). At Kadesh, Moses disobeyed God by striking the rock with his staff to bring forth water rather than speaking to it as God had commanded; this insubordination checked Moses' entry into Canaan (Num. 20:2-13). The site eventually served as a landmark for the southern border of Judah (Josh. 15:1-3; cf. v. 23, "Kedesh").

ʿAin el-Qudeirat (096006), the site identified as Kadesh-barnea, does not always mesh with the biblical texts. Working in part upon the identification by Nathaniel Schmidt, C. Leonard Woolley and T. E. Lawrence (1914-1915) confirmed Schmidt's conclusions. Moshe Dothan reexcavated the site in 1956, and Rudolph Cohen in 1972-1982.

Excavations reveal three superimposed fortresses dating from the 10th to the 7th-6th century B.C., followed by some Persian occupation. The 10th-century fortress was a large oval (ca. 27 m. [88 ft.] in diameter) with casemate walls. The ceramic collection and layout of the site suggest that it was constructed during Solomon's reign, probably as part of a defensive line along Judah's southern border. It was likely destroyed during Shishak's campaigns into Israel and Judah.

The fortress was rebuilt ca. two centuries later. The new fortress was rectangular (ca. 60 × 40 m.[196 × 131 ft.]) with solid walls (ca. 4 m. [13 ft.] thick) and eight projecting towers along its walls. An earth glacis and moat protected the fortification walls. Uzziah may have directed the construction of this fortress (2 Chr. 26:10). It was probably destroyed at the end of Manasseh's reign in the middle of the 7th century.

The latest fortress was built with casemate walls and followed basically the same rectangular plan as the middle fortress. The glacis and moat continued in use. In the northwestern corner of the fortress was a large circular mudbrick structure (ca. 1.9 m.[6.3 ft.] in diameter). This structure was filled with a thick layer of ashes and next to it were ceramic vessels, a small incense burner, and animal bones. This area may have been a shrine for the personnel of the site or for the region. Cohen suggests that this fortress was built during the time of Josiah and destroyed during Nebuchadnezzar's campaign when he also destroyed Jerusalem.

The excavations have produced no evidence to indicate the presence of a large number of people at the site during any period when the Exodus is thought to have occurred. Scholars have interpreted this problem differently. Conservatives may assert that the identification is an error and that Kadesh-barnea should be identified with another, yet undiscovered site. Others suggest that the biblical story is an etiological account. A growing number of scholars suggest that there was no body of people who came out of Egypt to camp at Kadesh-barnea and hence no remains should be expected.

Bibliography. R. Cohen, "Excavations at Kadesh-Barnea, 1976-1978," *BA* 44 (1981): 93-107; "The Iron Age Fortresses in the Central Negev," *BASOR* 236 (1979): 61-79; *Kadesh-barnea* (Jerusalem, 1983); M. Dothan, "The Fortress at Kadesh-Barnea," *IEJ* 15 (1965): 134-51.

2. Kadesh on the Orontes, modern Tell Nebî Mind (291444) in Syria. Although Egyptian annals mention earlier battles at the site (e.g., Thutmose III, Seti I), the more notable conflict occurred ca. 1285 when Rameses II and the Hittites under Muwatallis fought near Kadesh for control of Syria. Both sides suffered badly in the conflict and ended it with a treaty which has been preserved from both parties (*ANET,* 199-203); the Hittite version probably preserves the terms more accurately. Rameses portrayed the battle on several temple carvings in Egypt.

Bibliography. J. H. Breasted, ed., *Ancient Records of Egypt,* 5 vols. (Chicago, 1906-7).

DALE W. MANOR

KADMIEL (Heb. *qaḏmîʾēl*)
The head of a levitical family who with his descendants returned under Zerubbabel from captivity in Babylon (Ezra 2:40; Neh. 7:43; 12:8, 24). He and his sons supervised those rebuilding the temple (Ezra 3:9), took part in the public confession of sin (Neh. 9:4-5), and signed the renewed covenant (10:9[MT 10]).

KADMONITES (Heb. *qaḏmōnî*)
A people listed among the pre-Israelite inhabitants of Canaan (Gen. 15:19). The name ("Easterners") probably represents the same people as those called the "sons of Qedem" (NRSV "people of the east"; e.g., Gen. 29:1; Judg. 6:3, 33; Job 1:3).

KAIN (Heb. *qayin*) **(PEOPLE)**
A collective term singular in form, designating the Kenites (Num. 24:22; cf. Judg. 4:11).

KAIN (Heb. *qayin*) **(PLACE)**
A settlement included in the list of towns in the tribal allotment of Judah (Josh. 15:57). It has most often been identified with en-Nebi Yaqin (164100), a small site ca. 10 km. (6 mi.) SE of Hebron. Unfortunately, the site has not been systematically examined by archaeologists. However, the similarity in name and the site's location in close proximity to other well-known settlements with which Kain is grouped in the Josh. 15 list (e.g., Maon, Carmel, Ziph, and Juttah) provide strong circumstantial support for this identification.

The LXX omits Kain in Josh. 15:57, suggesting to some that Kain might be a gloss added to the MT in order to modify Zanoah ("Zanoah of Kain," or "Zanoah of the Kenites") in order to distinguish it from a different Zanoah listed in v. 34.

WADE R. KOTTER

KAIWAN (Heb. *kiyyûn;* Akk. *kayyamânu*)
The Babylonian name for the planet Saturn, which Amos calls a star-god (Amos. 5:26). Amos prophesied that since the Israelites worshipped a Babylonian deity God would send them to Babylon (presumably so they could be nearer the pagan god they wanted to worship). Stephen's quotation of this passage at Acts 7:43 follows the LXX, which reads "Rephan," apparently an error in transliteration.

KALLAI (Heb. *qallay*)
The head of the priestly family of Sallai at the time of the high priest Joiakim (Neh. 12:20).

KAMON (Heb. *qāmôn*)
The burial place of Jair the Gileadite, a minor judge of Israel (Judg. 10:5). Polybius (*Hist.* 5.70.12) refers to Kamoun which Antiochus conquered after Pella, Abila, Gadara, and other places in Gilead while battling Ptolemy Philopator. Kamon has been associated with Hanzir (207206), N of the Jabbok and 8 km. (5 mi.) E of Pella, where Iron I and Hellenistic sherds have been found. Krak-Canatha, between Derala and Souweida, and Qamm (218221), 20 km. (13 mi.) SE of the Sea of Galilee, have also been suggested.

PHILIP R. DREY

KANAH (Heb. *qānâ*)
1. A stream that defined the boundary between the territories of Ephraim and Manasseh (Josh. 16:8; 17:9). In the biblical description, Kanah flows west from the Micmethath Valley across the Sharon Plain to the Mediterranean Sea. Kanah has been identified with Wadi Qanah, which now empties into the Yarkon River before reaching the Mediterranean.

2. A town included in the territory allocated to Asher (Josh. 19:28). Many identify Kanah with modern Qânā (178290), ca. 10 km. (6 mi.) SE of Tyre. The town marks part of the northern border of Asherite territory. The town is not to be confused with the Cana in Galilee (Khirbet Qânā/Ḥorvat Qana) mentioned in the NT.

Bibliography. E. Danelius, "The Boundary of Ephraim and Manasseh in the Western Plain," *PEQ* 90 (1958): 32-43.

C. SHAUN LONGSTREET

KAREAH (Heb. *qārēaḥ*)
The father of Johanan (**1**), a military leader in Judah who escaped deportation after the Babylonian conquest of Jerusalem (2 Kgs. 25:23; Jer. 40:8; 41:11; 42:1, 8; 43:2).

KARKA (Heb. *haqqarqaʿ*)
A city on the southern border of the tribal territory of Judah, located between Addar and Azmon NW of Kadesh-barnea (Josh. 15:3). The site is perhaps to be identified with modern ʿAin el-Qeṣeimeh (089007) at the confluence of the Wadi el-ʿAin and Umm Has.

KARKOR (Heb. *qarqōr*)
The place where Gideon captured two kings of Midian (Judg. 8:10). From the Judges account the site can be assumed to be in northern Transjordan, but it is otherwise unknown. Some suggest modern Qarqar on the Wadi Sirḥân or the castle of Carcaria. PHILIP R. DREY

KARNAIM (Heb. *qarnāyím;* Gk. *Karnaim*)
A fortress-city in Gilead. Located at modern Tell Sheikh Ṣaʿd/Tel Ṣaʿd (247249), on a northern tributary of the middle Yarmuk River ca. 32 km. (20 mi.) E of the Sea of Galilee and 5 km. (3 mi.) N of Ashtaroth, it is perhaps identical with postexilic Carnaim (1 Macc. 5:26, 43-44) and near Ashteroth-karnaim (Gen. 14:5). At Amos 6:13 the prophet puns upon the names Karnaim (the "horns" of a bull, thus "strength"; cf. 1 Kgs. 22:11) and Lo-debar ("Nothing"), apparently cities captured by King Jeroboam II of Israel (2 Kgs. 14:28).

KARTAH (Heb. *qartâ*)
A levitical city in the tribal territory of Zebulun, allocated to the Gershonite family (Josh. 21:34). The site has not been identified. Because the name is missing from the similar account at 1 Chr. 6, some scholars suggest the name here may be a scribal error stemming from Kartan at Josh. 21:32.

KARTAN (Heb. *qārtān*) (also KIRIATHAIM)
A Gershonite levitical city in the territory of Naphtali (Josh. 21:32); called Kiriathaim in 1 Chr. 6:76(MT 61). No consensus exists as to the exact location of this place, but two sites are possible: Khirbet el-Quneitereh/Tell Raqqat (199245), 1 km. (.6 mi.) N of modern Tiberias on the W side of the Sea of Galilee; and Khirbet el-Qureiyeh, near the modern Lebanese village of Aytarun (194280) in the mountains of northern Galilee.

Bibliography. J. L. Peterson, *A Topographical Surface Survey of the Levitical "Cities" of Joshua 21 and 1 Chronicles 6* (diss., Seabury-Western, 1977). PETE F. WILBANKS

KATTATH (Heb. *qaṭṭāṯ*)
A city on the border of Zebulun (Josh. 19:15), probably the same as the Kitron from which the Canaanites could not be driven (Judg. 1:30). The site has not been identified, although Khirbet Quṭṭeneh (153226), 8 km. (5 mi.) SW of Tell Qeimûn (biblical Jokneam), is a possibility.

KEDAR (Heb. *qēḏār*)
The second son of Ishmael (Gen. 25:13 = 1 Chr. 1:29). Elsewhere in the OT this term refers to his descendants (the Kedarites), either specifically to the most prominent of the north Arabian "sons of Ishmael" or generally and collectively to Arabic nomads or Bedouin. In Ps. 120:5 the "tents of Kedar" are equated with peace-hating Meshech, which is probably not a region of Asia Minor (as in Gen. 10:2) but a Kedarite subgroup. Cant. 1:5 pictures them as dark skinned (cf. *qāḏar,* "to be black"), and some repoint MT "Solomon" here to "Shalmah," a tribe that lived south of the Nabateans in the 3rd century B.C. Isaiah describes them as (1) warriors and archers whose glory will end (Isa. 21:16-17; some see a reference to Nabonidus' 552 campaign; but not Jer. 49:28-29, concerned with Nebuchadnezzar's attack on Arabs ["Kedar and the kingdoms of Hazor"] S of Damascus in 599/98); (2) inhabitants of desert villages (Isa. 42:11; probably temporary, fortified enclosures); and (3) poetically paired with sheep-breeders of Nebaioth (60:7; perhaps a reference to the Nabateans of north Arabia; cf. Gen. 25:13; also Ezek. 27:21, where the "princes of Kedar" are paired with the Arabians as sheep/goat-traders with the Phoenicians). Assyrian inscriptions as well name them along with the Arabs and Nebaioth. Finally, the poetry of Jer. 2:10 uses a merism to antithetically parallel Kedar with the Kittim ("Cypriots/Greeks") as representatives, respectively, of the East and West.

Bibliography. I. Ephʿal, *The Ancient Arabs* (Leiden, 1982). W. CREIGHTON MARLOWE

KEDEMAH (Heb. *qēḏĕmâ*)
A son of Ishmael ("easterner") whose descendants constituted an Arabian tribe, possibly to be reckoned among the Kadmonites (Gen. 25:15 = 1 Chr. 1:31).

KEDEMOTH (Heb. *qĕḏēmôṯ*)
A wilderness area probably NE of the Arnon (Wadi Môjib) from which Moses contacted the king of Heshbon (Deut. 2:26). An outpost or town in this area of the same name was first assigned to the territory of Reuben (Josh. 13:18) and later given to the Levites (21:37; 1 Chr. 6:79[MT 64]). It is mentioned elsewhere only in Eusebius (*Onom.* 114.5-6). Kedemoth has been identified variously with Umm er-Rasas, Khirbet er-Remeil, Qasr ez-Zaʿferan, and ʿAleiyân. Modern es-Saliyeh is currently the best candidate in that it borders on the desert and has produced sherds from the Late Bronze and Early Iron Ages. PAUL J. RAY, JR.

KEDESH (Heb. *qeḏeš*) (also KADESH-BARNEA, KISHION)

1. A city in Upper Galilee, 10 km. (6 mi.) NW of Hazor, in the hills near Lake Huleh. Tel Kedesh/Tell Qades (199279) is the largest tell in Upper Galilee, and preliminary excavations have identified extensive occupation in the Early Bronze Age and continuing through the Muslim period. Kedesh is mentioned in the list of Canaanite kings defeated by Joshua (Josh. 12:22). It is one of the fortified cities allotted to Naphtali (Josh. 19:37), the northernmost city of refuge (20:7), and a levitical city assigned to the Gershonites (21:32 = 1 Chr. 6:76[MT 61]). Tiglath-pileser conquered the city during the time of King Pekah of Israel, and deported its citizens to Assyria (2 Kgs. 15:29).

2. A town on the southern border of Judah, usually referred to as Kadesh-barnea (Josh. 15:23).

3. A levitical city of Issachar assigned to the Gershonites (1 Chr. 6:72[57]). In the parallel passage in Joshua the city is called Kishion (Josh.

21:28), which is probably the correct name. Kedesh may be a textual corruption influenced by the Kedesh of Naphtali a few verses later.

4. A town in southern Naphtali in which Barak lived (Judg. 4:6), and near where Heber the Kenite dwelt (4:11). Kedesh is located near Zaanannim between Mt. Tabor and the Jordan River (Josh. 19:33). Barak's birthplace is usually identified with Kedesh in Upper Galilee, but this identification is impossible because Kedesh was a major Canaanite city and Judg. 4 assumes that Barak's home is the same Kedesh near Heber's dwelling in Zaanannim. This Kedesh may be identified with Ḥorvat Qedesh/ Khirbet Qedîsh (202237), a large site with Iron Age remains located on the southwestern slopes that lead down into the Sea of Galilee. Some suggest identifying Kedesh with Tel Kedesh/Tell Abu Qudeis (1706.2183), located midway between Megiddo and Taanach, because Judg. 5:19 claims that battle was "at Taanach, by the waters of Megiddo." However, Judg. 5 does not mention Kedesh, nor does Judg. 4 locate the battle near Taanach. These two texts might represent different understandings of the location of the battle.

RONALD A. SIMKINS

KEEPER

Someone granted a certain area of responsibility. The range of meaning for Heb. *šomēr, noṣēr* is one who "keeps, guards, watches, preserves, obeys."

In a general sense, one can obey God's commandments (Deut. 5:10) and the way of the Lord (Judg. 2:22), protect a stranger (Ps. 146:9) or city (2 Kgs. 9:14), and guard one's mouth. More specifically, a steward, e.g., is endowed with the oversight of a house and its affairs (Eccl. 12:3). Similar types of oversight include baggage keeper (1 Sam. 17:22) and keeper of the wardrobe (2 Kgs. 22:14). Yahweh is praised as the Keeper of Israel, the protector of his people (Ps. 121:3, 5).

In the OT various special areas of jurisdiction are the responsibility of designated officers. The temple official *(šōmrē mišmereṯ haqqōḏeš)* was a levitical position designated by Yahweh for the service, maintenance, and protection of the tabernacle or temple (Num. 3:28-38; Ezek. 44:14). The "keepers of the threshold" *(šōmrê hassap̱)* were in charge of temple income and disbursements (2 Kgs. 12:9; 22:4).

The city guard (Ps. 127:1; 130:6; Isa. 21:11; 62:6; Jer. 51:12), likely a military officer, made nightly rounds to ensure the safety and orderliness of the city (Cant. 3:3; 5:7). He provided oversight of the city walls and gates and their corresponding storehouses (Neh. 11:19; 12:25).

The palace official was responsible for the king, his palace, and his general administration. His most common task was that of doorkeeper or general palace guard (1 Kgs. 14:27; 2 Kgs. 11:5; Esth. 2:2; 2 Chr. 12:10). Other palace officials included the eunuch who kept the king's wives (Esth. 2:3), the king's bodyguard (1 Sam. 28:2), the chamberlain responsible for the king's robes (2 Kgs. 22:14 = 2 Chr. 34:22), and the keeper of the king's forest (Neh. 2:8).

Finally, the agricultural watchman was entrusted with the care and protection of fields (Jer. 4:17), flocks (1 Sam. 17:20), and orchards or vineyards (Prov. 27:18). Yahweh was metaphorically referred to as the watcher of his vineyard, Israel (Ps. 121:5; Isa. 27:2-6; cf. 5:1-30).

MILES V. VAN PELT

KEHELATHAH (Heb. *qĕhēlāṯâ*)

The seventh camp of the Israelites after they left the wilderness of Sinai, located between Rissah and Mt. Shepher (Num. 33:22-23). The place name derives from the root *qhl,* "to convoke an assembly." Kuntillet ʿAjrud (094956), 50 km. (31 mi.) S of Kadesh-barnea, is a possible location. Many hold that Kehelathah (Num. 33:22-23) and Makheloth (vv. 25-26) are the same. PETE F. WILBANKS

KEILAH (Heb. *qĕʿîlâ*) **(PERSON)**

"The Garmite," grandson of Hodiah in the list of the descendants of Judah (1 Chr. 4:19).

KEILAH (Heb. *qĕʿîlâ*) **(PLACE)**

A city in the Shephelah region of Judah (Josh. 15:44) which David defended against the Philistines before Saul forced him to flee into the wilderness of Ziph (1 Sam. 23:1-13). After the Exile the city was resettled and divided into two half-districts (Neh. 3:17-18). The city, called Qilti in the Amarna Letters, was disputed territory during the reign of the Egyptian Akhenaten just as it was in the Philistine period. It can be identified as modern Khirbet Qîlā (150113), ca. 25 km. (15.5 mi.) SW of Jerusalem and 13.6 km. (8.5 mi.) NW of Hebron.

KELAIAH (Heb. *qēlāyâ*), **KELITA** (*qĕlîṭāʾ*)

A Levite who was forced by Ezra to give up his foreign wife (Ezra 10:23). Also known as Kelita, he helped interpret as Ezra read the Law (Neh. 8:7) and signed the covenant under Nehemiah (10:10[MT 11]).

KEMUEL (Heb. *qĕmûʾēl*)

1. A son of Nahor and Milcah; the father of Aram and eponymous ancestor of the Aramean peoples (Gen. 22:21).

2. The son of Shiphtan; a chief of the Ephraimites and one of those responsible for dividing the land of Canaan (Num. 34:24).

3. The father of Hashabiah, who was chief officer of the Levites at the time of David (1 Chr. 27:17).

KENAN (Heb. *qênān*)

A son of Enosh and father of Mahalalel (Gen. 5:9-14; 1 Chr. 1:2).

KENATH (Heb. *qĕnāṯ*)

A city in eastern Gilead, captured during the Conquest by the Manassehite chieftain Nobah, who renamed it after himself (Num. 32:42). Apparently the original name persisted when the city later fell into Syrian hands (1 Chr. 2:23). Known as Kanatha in the Greco-Roman period, it was the easternmost city of the Decapolis.

The site is identified as modern Qanawât (302241), ca. 80 km. (50 mi.) SSE of Rabbath-ammon on the outskirts of ancient Auranitis.

KENAZ (Heb. *qĕnāz*), **KENIZZITE** (*qĕnizzî*)

1. A son of Eliphaz, the firstborn son of Esau and Adah (Gen. 36:11 = 1 Chr. 1:36). This Kenaz, ordinarily understood to be the eponymous ancestor of the Kenizzites, functioned as an Edomite clan chief (Gen. 36:15, 42 = 1 Chr. 1:51, 53).

The Kenizzites were one of the 10 peoples whose territory Yahweh in a theophany promised to deliver to the progeny of Abram (Gen. 15:19). At some point the Kenizzites had evidently lived in or around Edom. However, some or all of that ethnic group must have migrated into the Negeb area of Canaan — perhaps as early as the Late Bronze Age. In due course these Kenizzites became politically associated with and then thoroughly absorbed by the more dominant tribe of Judah.

2. Caleb's younger brother (Judg. 3:9), father of Othniel and Seraiah (1 Chr. 4:13).

3. The son of Elah and grandson of Caleb (1 Chr. 4:15).

Bibliography. E. C. Hostetter, *Nations Mightier and More Numerous: The Biblical View of Palestine's Pre-Israelite Peoples.* BIBALDS 3 (North Richland Hills, 1995), 95-96.

EDWIN C. HOSTETTER

KENITES (Heb. *qênî*)

A nomadic group who lived in the southern desert region of Canaan. They were owners of the land given to Abram as a result of the covenant ceremony (Gen. 15:19). The name "Kenite" may have originated from association with Cain, "smith" (Gen. 4), who built cities and established metal furnaces. The southern location of the Kenites and the presence of copper mining and smelting in that region lends credence to this assertion. The Kenites play a continuing role in the Bible as southern allies of Israel beginning in the Mosaic period and extending through the time of the judges into the Monarchy.

Moses' father-in-law (Hobab, Judg. 4:11; Jethro, Exod. 3:1; Reuel, Exod. 2:18; Num. 10:29) was a Kenite, and scholars have proposed that Moses may have learned Yahwistic worship from him (cf. Exod. 18). In addition, Jael, the wife of Heber, a descendant of Moses' father-in-law, is praised for killing Sisera (Judg. 5:24, Song of Deborah).

The Kenites settled in the south of Judah in Arad of the Negeb (Judg. 1:16) and continued their good relations with Israel. During the reign of Saul, in the Amalakite wars, the Kenites were asked to leave Amalakite cities to avoid harm (1 Sam. 15:6). Later, David carried to Arad the spoils of his raids from his camp at Ziklag (1 Sam. 27:10; 30:29). In postexilic times, in the genealogy of Judah the Chronicler lists the Rechabites, Yahwistic nomads cited as allies of Jeremiah (Jer. 35), as Kenites.

JEFF H. MCCRORY, JR.

KENIZZITE

See KENAZ, KENIZZITE.

KENOSIS

The importance of *kenosis* ("emptying") arises from its use in an ancient hymnlike text found in Phil. 2:5-11. According to Phil. 2:7 Christ Jesus "emptied himself," an action which contrasted to equality with God. During the 19th century W. F. Gess and Gottfried Thomasius taught that this emptying meant Jesus surrendered certain or all divine attributes during the Incarnation. British theologians Charles Gore and P. T. Forsyth varied this idea by asserting that some of Christ's divine attributes became only potential rather than actual during the Incarnation.

Three participles, which depend on the verb *ekénōsen,* define the verb's meaning in this context. Christ emptied himself by "taking" the form of a servant, "becoming" in the likeness of a human, and "being found" in the form of a human. The parallel phrase "he humbled himself" in Phil. 2:8 further helps to clarify the meaning of *kenosis* as Jesus' self-emptying, by becoming human, in order to die on the cross in obedience to the Father. Speculation about lost or negated attributes has no textual support.

LINDA OAKS GARRETT

KERAK (Arab. *Karak*) (also KARAK)

A major city in the western part of central Jordan; capital of a modern Jordanian administrative district (today usually Karak; 217066). The site is ca. halfway between Wadi Môjib (biblical Arnon) and Wadi el-Ḥesa (Zered), along the route traditionally known as the "King's Highway." The main part of the modern city occupies a ridge that is surrounded by deep canyons; the main valley that drains the plateau at this point is known as Wadi el-Kerak. Kerak is located 18 km. (11 mi.) E of the Dead Sea, whose glistening surface can be seen from the town's hilltop position. The city's name is derived from an Aramaic word meaning "walled town," and the place name Karakmōbā is well attested in the Hellenistic, Roman, and Byzantine periods. Apart from artifacts that have turned up in small-scale excavations or during construction, little is known about Kerak's ancient life and culture. Literary and architectural evidence from the Middle and Late Islamic periods is better represented, especially because of Kerak's role in the Crusades. Its castle is one of the best-preserved Crusader strongholds in the Levant. Much of the fortress that stands today was built by French Crusaders early in the 12th century, but major additions were made in later Islamic history, after the castle fell to Saladin's forces in 1188.

Though the identification is far from certain, Kerak is often linked with the biblical place names Kir (Isa. 15:1), Kir-heres (Jer. 48:31, 36; Isa. 16:11), and Kir-hareseth (16:7; 2 Kgs. 3:25). In Isa. 15:1 Kir is associated with Ar, another Moabite name, whose identification is also uncertain (cf. "City of Moab"). In the other OT passages Kir-heres/Kir-hareseth refers to an important Moabite town

Ruins of the Frankish period Crusader castle (early 12th century C.E.) at Kerak (modern Karak) (J. Maxwell Miller)

which was involved in Mesha's war with Israel (cf. 2 Kgs. 3), but it is possible that this site was situated N of Wadi Môjib. The discovery of a fragmentary Moabite inscription in Kerak, probably from the time of Mesha, indicates that the city was, in fact, important in the 9th century B.C. Its Aramaic name, which may have originated in the Persian period, confirms that Kerak was one of Moab's leading towns.

The famous Early Bronze III style of pottery ("Khirbet Kerak ware") is associated with another site, Khirbet Kerak (Beth-yerah; 204235), on the southwestern shore of the Sea of Galilee.

Bibliography. B. C. Jones, *Howling over Moab: Irony and Rhetoric in Isaiah 15–16.* SBLDS 157 (Atlanta, 1996); "In Search of Kir-Hareseth: A Case Study in Site Identification," *JSOT* 52 (1991): 3-24; J. M. Miller, ed., *Archaeological Survey of the Kerak Plateau.* ASOR Archaeological Reports 1 (Atlanta, 1991); W. L. Reed and F. V. Winnett, "A Fragment of an Early Moabite Inscription from Kerak," *BASOR* 172 (1963): 1-9.

GERALD L. MATTINGLY

KEREN-HAPPUCH (Heb. *qeren happûḵ*)
The youngest of three daughters born to Job after his trials had ended (Job 42:14).

KERIOTH (Heb. *qĕrîyôṯ*)
A fortified city in Moab (Jer. 48:24; Amos 2:2; cf. Jer. 48:41; NRSV "the towns," following LXX). According to the Moabite Stone, the city contained a sacred shrine for Chemosh. The site remains uncertain.

KERIOTH-HEZRON (Heb. *qĕrîyôṯ ḥeṣrôn*)
A place name designating one, possibly two, locations in southern Judah (Josh. 15:25). Some scholars separate Kerioth and Hezron, regarding them as two cities. Even if the text refers to two places, Kerioth should not be confused with Kerioth of Moab. As a separate village, Hezron may refer to the border settlement near Kadesh-barnea (Josh. 15:3). If the two names designate one locale, it is possibly the modern remains called Khirbet el-Qaryatein/ Tel Qeriyot (161083), 7 km. (4.5 mi.) S of Maon.

DAVID C. MALTSBERGER

KEROS (Heb. *qērōs, qêrōs*)
The head of a family of temple servants who returned with Zerubbabel from the Exile (Ezra 2:44 = Neh. 7:47).

KERYGMA (Gk. *kḗrygma*)
The proclamation (Gk. "preaching") of the good news in the NT and later. The word has become a quasitechnical term for the content of early Christian polemic, the "gospel" par excellence.

KETHIB (Heb. *kĕṯîḇ*) **AND QERE** (*qĕrê*)
Masoretic notations meaning "what is written" (Kethib) and "what is read" (Qere). The 1300 instances of Kethib-Qere in the MT reflect a stage in the development of the Hebrew text when the consonantal text was considered fixed and unalterable ("what is written"; **K**), but it was possible to suggest emendations in the margin ("what is read"; **Q**). The consonants of the Qere were usually written in the margin, and the vowels of the Qere, with the consonants of the Kethib, in the text. The note would lead a person reading the text to pronounce the Qere rather than the Kethib. Qere readings were intended either to correct the Kethib or to preserve variant manuscript traditions.

The Kethib-Qere fall into three categories. The *Qĕrê perpetuum,* not marked by a marginal note, is the writing of the consonants for *YHWH* with the vowels for *'ăḏōnāy.* This guarded against speaking the divine name. The *Tiqqûnê sōp̄ĕrîm* or "emendations of the scribes" are some 18 instances in which the Masoretes preserved in a note the "original" form of a text that was earlier changed by scribes to remove objectionable references to God. The *'Iṭṭûrê sōp̄ĕrîm* or "omissions of the scribes" are places where a letter was omitted, or where something either is read but not written or is written but not read.

Bibliography. E. Tov, *The Textual Criticism of the Hebrew Bible* (Minneapolis, 1992); E. Würthwein, *The Text of the Old Testament*, 2nd ed. (Grand Rapids, 1995). MICHAEL L. RUFFIN

KETURAH (Heb. *qĕṭûrâ*)
The often forgotten third wife/concubine of Abraham, first attested after the death of Sarah (Gen. 25:1-6). She is the mother of six sons by Abraham: Zimran, Jokshan, Medan, Midian, Ishbak, and Shuah (also listed in 1 Chr. 1:32-33). They settled to the east and the south of the Israelites, along what was commonly known as the "incense route" through west Arabia. Her children are usually identified with important Aramean or Arabian tribes and cities. These descendants of Abraham and Keturah helped to broaden the extent of Abraham's progeny.

There is no other known occurrence of Keturah as a personal name. Some scholars suggest that she is a personification of the incense trade (*qĕṭōreṯ*, "incense"; *qĕṭôrâ,*"incense offering"), but there is no strong evidence to prove this theory.
LISA W. DAVISON

KEZIAH (Heb. *qĕṣîʿâ*)
The second daughter born to Job after his fortunes were restored (Job 42:14).

KIBROTH-HATTAAVAH
(Heb. *qiḇrôṯ hatta'ăwâ*)
The first encampment of the Israelites, between Mt. Sinai and Hazeroth, after they left the wilderness of Sinai (Num. 33:16-17). Here the Lord sent quail for the Israelites to eat (Num. 11:31-35). The subsequent greediness of some in gathering and eating the quail prompted the Lord to plague them (cf. Deut. 9:22). Those who died were buried at this site, whose name means "graves of craving" or "graves of greediness." The location may be modern Rueis el-Ebeirij (076797), ca. 50 km. (31 mi.) NE of Mt. Sinai (Jebel Mûsā). PETE F. WILBANKS

KIBZAIM (Heb. *qiḇṣayim*)
A city in the tribal territory of Ephraim allocated to the Kohathite family of Levites (Josh. 21:22). Some scholars take it to be the same as Jokmeam in the parallel account at 1 Chr. 6:68(MT 53), but the names seem to represent two distinct sites. The location is uncertain.

KID
A young goat (Heb. *gĕḏî*). The meat of a kid was considered savory (e.g., Gen. 27:9; cf. Luke 15:29) and perhaps for this reason was associated with ritual meals (Judg. 6:19) and sacrifices (Num. 15:11; 2 Chr. 35:7). The biblical injunction against boiling a kid in its mother's milk (Exod. 23:19; 34:26; Deut. 14:21) may be a prohibition of a Canaanite religious practice (cf. *UT* 52:14); it constitutes the basis of the kosher law against eating milk and other dairy products in the same meal.

KIDNEYS
The kidneys of sacrificed animals, along with their fat, part of the liver, the broad tail, and the fat that covers the entrails, were to be burned completely by the priests (Exod. 29:13, 22; Lev. 3:4, 10, 15). At times kidneys (Heb. *kĕlāyyôṯ*; Gk. *nephroí*) represent the organs in general, e.g., as they were being formed in the womb (Ps. 139:13; NRSV "inward parts") or being pierced by archers (Job 16:13; Lam. 3:13, NRSV "vitals"). More often, however, kidneys refer to the seat of emotions and decision making. Thus, one can be called "upright in kidneys" (Ps. 7:10[MT 11]). One's kidneys may faint (Job 19:27) or rejoice (Prov. 23:16). Along with the heart they are known and searched by God (Jer. 11:20; Ps. 73:21; cf. Rev. 2:23). Those who speak well but say nothing are said to have God "in their mouths, but far from their kidneys" (Jer. 12:2).
GREGORY A. WOLFE

KIDRON (Heb. *qiḏrôn;* Gk. *Kedrṓn*)
The valley (and the brook running through it during times of heavy rain) that lies E of Jerusalem. The old walled city of Jerusalem is on its west and the Mount of Olives on its east. It is suggested that the name means "dark," "not clear," or "turbid," because the stream is thick and opaque with sediment. On the western slope of the valley is the Gihon Spring, ancient Jerusalem's primary water supply. This spring flowed into the valley, but with the building of Hezekiah's tunnel (2 Kgs. 20:20) its waters were diverted to the Pool of Siloam inside the city. On the eastern slope of the valley are many ancient tombs where certain royal officials, possibly some of Judah's kings, may have been buried. From the vicinity of Jerusalem the Kidron Valley follows a southeastern course, extending through the Wilderness of Judah, meeting the Dead Sea ca. 16 km. (10 mi.) below the mouth of the Jordan River.

This valley is first mentioned in the Bible as the place David crossed (i.e., the eastern boundary of the city) as he fled Jerusalem because of the rebellion of his son Absalom (2 Sam. 15:23). During the Monarchy it was probably to be identified as the place of the King's Garden (2 Kgs. 25:4; Neh. 3:15).

Adjacent to the temple mount, the Kidron (valley/brook/field) served as a convenient place where images and altars of idols were taken to be destroyed by reformer kings: Asa (1 Kgs. 15:13), Hezekiah (2 Chr. 29:16; 30:14), and Josiah (2 Kgs. 23:4-6; cf. v. 12).

The Kidron is mentioned only once in the NT. After the farewell discourse, Jesus along with his disciples went "across the Kidron valley to a place where there was a garden [named Gethsemane in Matt. 26:36], which he and his disciples entered" (John 18:1). Tradition identifies the Kidron Valley as the valley of Jehoshaphat ("Yahweh judges"), where God will gather all the nations and sit in judgment upon them (Joel 3:2, 12[MT 4:2, 12]).

John L. Gillman

KILN

Primarily an enclosure for firing pottery or burning lime (Heb. *kiḇšān,* in contrast with *kûr,* a smelting furnace for metals). Burnt lime was slaked and used for preparing mortar, plaster, and whitewash. Isa. 33:12 refers metaphorically to the process of burning lime. Thistles and thorns were used to fuel lime kilns.

Pottery kilns in ancient Palestine were of two types: a vertical or up-draft kiln and a horizontal or down-draft kiln (*ANEP,* 44, 344). By far the more frequently used type, the vertical kiln dates back to the Early Bronze Age and has remained essentially unchanged to the present time.

The Hebrew term is used metaphorically in reference to the billowing smoke from the burning of Sodom and Gomorrah (Gen. 19:28; NRSV "furnace") and from God's presence on Mt. Sinai (Exod. 19:18). The smoke is said to have risen like smoke from a kiln. Ashes from a kiln sprinkled into the air by Moses and Aaron inaugurate the sixth plague of boils (Exod. 9:8, 10).

Bibliography. S. Gibson, "Lime Kilns in North-East Jerusalem," *PEQ* 116 (1984): 94-102.

Stephen J. Andrews

KINAH (Heb. *qînâ*)

A city in the southern portion of the territory allotted to Judah (Josh. 15:22), probably associated with the Kenites (Heb. "smith[ville]"). The site is probably located along the Wadi el-Qeini near Arad.

KING, KINGSHIP

In the OT, king and kingship (derived from Heb. *mlk*) signify both an administrative office and a leadership role for governing peoples and territories. The concept implies at least some religious, political, social, and economic centralization, but it is not clear whether full-blown nation-statehood is necessarily envisaged. As in other Near Eastern societies, kings are suzerains (overlords) whose vassals comprise their own peoples, others whom they conquer or who willfully join allegiance, and at times lesser kings and kingdoms. Kings are responsible for maintaining socio-political order through laws, battles, rituals, and the exercise of wise judgment and effective persuasion (2 Sam. 5–8). These are meant to guarantee their vassals' general well-being and security. Unlike kingship among their neighbors, Yahwist kingship is not created by the deity, Yahwist kings do not enjoy divine filiation, and their edicts are not eternal.

The Bible depicts ambiguous attitudes toward the institution. Enthusiasm, resistance, and reluctant acceptance are all present. The ambivalence begins with the founding of kingship. Samuel, the chief proponent and prophetic impulse for monarchy, wavers (compare 1 Sam. 9:1–10:16; 11 and 1 Sam. 8; 10:17-27). Differences between Yahwist and neighboring models are desired but maintained only with difficulty, and sliding toward totalitarian practices is feared (1 Sam. 8:11-18; Amos 7:10-16). Rules of succession and inheritance seem to favor primogeniture, but the rules at times seem to be unclear, lacking, or ignored (e.g., 1 Kgs. 1:28-37; 11-12). As a result, divisiveness and intrigue lead to schism, mayhem, and even death. Divine sanction and official investiture do not guarantee competence, morality, or effectiveness. But the monarchic principle survives for several centuries (ca. 1150-587 B.C.E.), kingship can be the basis for renewal (2 Kgs. 23), and after its passing the institution is remembered favorably in the hymns and prayers of the Psalter.

The exact time and causes of biblical kingship's beginning are debated. The biblical portrayal of Saul as a divinely chosen suzerain anointed by Samuel immediately after the tribal period in the 11th century is oversimplified. Faced with Philistine domination, the Yahwists turn to Samuel to choose a centralized leader who is first Saul and then David (1 Sam. 8-16). Eventually, David is made king of Judah (2 Sam. 2:1-7) and then Israel (5:1-5) before moving his administrative center for both units to Jerusalem (5:6-10).

In this view, centralized leadership is commonly thought to date from the 10th or 9th century, when northern (Israel) and southern (Judah) Yahwists share single leadership under David and Solomon. The unity appears to have been the personal prerogative of the so-called United Monarchies, rather than a political unity of the regions. The post-Solomonic division, the Divided Monarchy, may be a shedding of a shared leader rather than a disintegration of a political and religious alliance. Whatever the exact nature and cause of the turn of events that lead to the schism separating northern and southern kingdoms, Israel survives a succession of kings until it falls to the Assyrians in 721 (2 Kgs. 17), and Judah prevails until being overrun by the Babylonians led by Nebuchadnezzar in 597 (2 Kgs. 24–25).

Archaeology and comparative sociology suggest a more gradual, prolonged, and complex process leading toward establishing kingship. Accordingly, full statehood with national kingship follows developments and pressures both within and outside the Yahwist community. Over time — suggestions range from a few decades to several centuries — Yahwist tribal units coalesce to form moieties led by paramount chiefs before further developments propel the federations to statehood. The transitions are accompanied, if not caused, by changes in economic base and residential strategy as much as by threats from foreign enemies. Developing agriculture technologies, diversification in crafts, specializations in modes of production, and introduction of iron-making all foster sedentariness and begin to supplement and shift reliance away from pastoralism and nomadism. The latter are retained in some areas and are integrated into the new economy in others. And they are valued nostalgically as socio-religious ideals imbued with mythic power from the past. But the general trend is toward sedentary agrarianism and urbanism with an accompanying need for stable permanent administrative office such as kingship.

The developments leading toward and supporting kingship parallel transformations in the Yahwist literary tradition. The palace becomes the repository and origin of tradition. There tradition is interpreted and reinterpreted in light of current needs, attitudes, and circumstances. Texts produced by court scribes bear the distinctive views of their patrons. Changes in patrons or patrons' views guide modern biblical critics in their attempts to unravel the stages of development within the biblical tradition. Identifying the stages demonstrates that as an ancient technology writing contributes directly to the propaganda and power of the centralized king. The ability to control the past by shaping its telling is an effective administrative tool. The unity and disunity, the agreements and disagreements that constitute the richness and variety of the biblical story result from the king's telling and retelling the past.

A king's personal traits are important. Good looks, physical strength, height, quick-wittedness, an even temper, and ability with weapons are valued (1 Sam. 9:1-2; 17; 1 Kgs. 4:29-34). As with other biblical figures, long years of life and ruling are signs of wisdom.

Throughout kingship's history the extent of Yahwist influence changes many times as the leaders' fate varies. Consequently, the territorial limits of kings' authority are often indistinct. Modern attempts to reconstruct them rely on census lists, battle stories, tales of journeys, and other accounts that contain place names and topographical features. However, these may be less important for marking boundaries than is the allegiance of individuals and groups that guarantee a king's power. A king's control over people and, in turn, their identification with place define the sphere of influence more than a boundary line or border such as moderns would indicate on a map.

Yahwist kingship enjoys only limited approval from Hebrew prophets, whose dire warnings eventually prove to be correct. Royal policy and behavior elicit threatening criticism and stern rebukes. Violations of covenant values bring promises of the most dire consequences, including personal punishments and loss of autonomy for the nation.

With the demise of independent political kingship among the Yahwists, priesthood emerges as the inheritor of many of the promises and expectations that Royal Theology previously invests in kings. Priesthood and priestly environments become the locus of monarchic hopes. Messianism arises from this milieu.

Bibliography. J. W. Flanagan, *David's Social Drama.* JSOTSup 74 (Sheffield, 1988); K. W. Whitelam, *The Just King: Monarchial Judicial Authority in Ancient Israel.* JSOTSup 12 (Sheffield, 1979).

JAMES W. FLANAGAN

KINGDOM OF GOD, KINGDOM OF HEAVEN

The sovereignty or realm ruled by God. The image of the kingdom of God/heaven is an important one for understanding the message and ministry of Jesus, particularly as he is portrayed in the Synoptic Gospels. This image builds on the images of kingly rule found in the OT, and it gives rise to NT discussions of the end times (or eschaton).

Old Testament

A focus on the monotheism of the Hebrew people often obscures the polytheistic reality of the ancient Near East. For Israel's neighbors, the power of their king rested in the power of the god(s) which they worshipped. The gods ruled as a result of having overthrown other evil gods in the process of creating the land; they continued to create each year, bringing fertility to the land and its inhabitants. This creative power linked them forever with the land itself, and the rule/reign of any particular god extended only as far as the political boundaries of the country which worshipped that god. In this context, armies fought not just for political gain, but for the honor and power of their god as well.

While the Hebrew concept of the kingdom or reign of Yahweh may have been influenced by this political and religious context, the land which the Hebrew people received as a result of Yahweh's "promise" came as a manifestation of God's power over other gods rather than as a result merely of God's creative abilities. After all, according to the OT, Yahweh created the entire earth and its inhabitants; the promise of a particular land was linked to Abraham's righteous response of obedience. In addition, the Hebrew idea of God's reign seems also to have been influenced by their recognition that Yahweh's power extended far beyond the boundaries of Canaan. Yahweh was able to reach down into Egypt, deliver them from Pharaoh's slavery, and provide for them in the desert of Sinai.

The OT also records some conflict concerning the kingdom of God. With the establishment of a royal line, first Saul and then David and his heirs, came a strong challenge to the idea that Yahweh was to be king over Israel. The books of the Former Prophets record the nation's fitful progress from judge to king, and suggest that God was not altogether pleased with the national outcry for a human king. The glory days of the Davidic line were short, but God's revision and renewal of the covenant with both David (2 Sam. 7) and Solomon (1 Kgs. 9) laid the foundation for a return to the idea of God's kingdom and reign.

Apocalyptic and Intertestamental Literature

The decline of Israel and her kings, which resulted in Babylonian captivity, presented a serious theological problem. Yahweh had promised David and Solomon that the royal line would continue and that the kingdom of Israel/Judah would be a sign of God's presence and rule. The fortunes of Judah, however, seemed to be moving in another direction. The Latter Prophets began to suggest that

God's rule was not dependent on the presence of an earthly king, or even a nation. The success of the nation and its king, rather, depended on their obedience to Yahweh. The history of Judah between her return from Babylonian captivity and the events of the NT is relatively devoid of kings who reigned with security and continuity. In the absence of this sense of security, apocalyptic ideas began to emerge; many of these ideas and images were linked both to the reign of God and the hope of an earthly king who would reestablish both the rule of God on earth and the line of David in Judah. That hope lay in the coming of God's "anointed one" or "messiah" who would bring about the kingdom of God in the last days. This kingdom would come with prosperity for the faithful and judgment for the enemies of God (who, coincidentally, happened also to be the enemies of Judah/Judea). God's kingdom would again be restored in Canaan, and those who occupied the land and oppressed God's people would be driven off and destroyed in the terrible judgment to come.

New Testament

The brief taste of freedom for the Hebrew people during the time of the Maccabees made the Roman occupation of Palestine even more galling. By the time Jesus began his ministry, the apocalyptic hope in the coming of God's kingdom had become a well-established idea. Only the establishment of God's rule would remove the onerous Roman rule. In fact, the Roman Empire, and the reign of Caesar, offered a serious challenge to the idea that God reigned supreme. Caesar not only held political sway over most of the Mediterranean world; he had begun to assume a divine identity as well.

Into this context John the Baptizer came, proclaiming the coming of God's kingdom and messiah and calling the nation to repent. Shortly thereafter, Jesus appeared, announcing that the kingdom of God had come/was near. In fact, the kingdom of God seems to have been the central theme of Jesus' proclamation, particularly during his Galilean ministry. (Matthew uses the circumlocution "kingdom of heaven" sometimes found in the OT, presumably out of deference to his primarily Hebrew audience who would have balked at the possible idolatry in the use of the divine name.) Scholars agree that Jesus used this image to refer to God's heavenly and eternal rule, God's rule on earth in the obedience of the faithful, and God's future rule in the eschaton. Here the scholarly agreement ceases, though, as debate rages over which of these ideas best characterizes the nature of the kingdom. An additional question has been raised concerning the present rule of God: is it merely a spiritual rule in the hearts and minds of obedient faithful, or did Jesus intend to establish the reign of God in a more political or social way?

What is clear is the importance of the kingdom of God to the message and ministry of Jesus in the Synoptic Gospels. Many of his parables are told in order to help his hearers grasp his concept of God's rule. They range in scope from stories which have their origin in peasant customs to stories of kings and landowners. They present the kingdom as a treasure beyond price, a magnificent banquet, or a wedding feast. Even the parables of Jesus which do not seem to have a surface connection to the kingdom address the need for proper behavior and relationships in the light of the coming of God's kingdom.

Outside of the Synoptic Gospels, interest in the kingdom of God seems to shift back toward the apocalyptic and/or eschatological focus of the intertestamental period. In John's Gospel Jesus denies having an earthly kingdom to Pilate, placing the emphasis more on the eternal and heavenly rule of God. Paul's focus is also apocalyptic/eschatological, perhaps in a response of urgency to Jesus' message of a kingdom now present and soon to be completed. Unlike Paul, those NT writers writing toward the end of the 1st century are dealing with the problem of Jesus' delayed return. They must find some way to emphasize the eternal power of God in a world which grows more repressive of Christians. They must find new words of hope, which the writer of Revelation offers in the form of his apocalyptic vision of the future coming of the kingdom in triumph. This final vision is the one which seems to have captured the imagination of centuries of Christians, and most of the discussion of the kingdom of God throughout the history of Christianity has centered around a conception of the kingdom of God as a time of judgment for the evil and deliverance for the faithful somewhere in the future.

Conclusion

Biblical scholars continue to debate the nature of the kingdom of God/heaven. More recently, the discussion has focused on the presence of the kingdom in the ministry of Jesus. In fact, some have suggested that the kingdom came in its full power in the earthly ministry of Jesus, and our attention must now turn to the salvation of individuals. Others have countered with attempts to see the kingdom of God in the teachings of Jesus as encompassing all of the work of Christ, from his earthly ministry, through an interim time, and culminating in a triumphal return (parousia) to rule and judge. God reigns already . . . and not yet, in the tension of Jesus' proclamation.

Bibliography. G. R. Beasley-Murray, *Jesus and the Kingdom of God* (Grand Rapids, 1986); J. Moltmann, *Theology of Hope* (1967, repr. Minneapolis, 1993); N. Perrin, *The Kingdom of God in the Teaching of Jesus* (Philadelphia, 1963); C. S. Song, *Jesus and the Reign of God* (Minneapolis, 1993).

STEVEN M. SHEELEY

KING'S GARDEN

Part of the Judean royal estate which would have also included lands, vineyards, olive groves, and vegetable plots in villages around Jerusalem. The location of this garden (Heb. *gan hammeleḵ*) is fairly certain: near the wall of the pool of Shelah (Siloam) in the Kidron Valley (Neh. 3:15), near "the gate between the two walls" (Jer. 39:4; 52:7). Excavations have revealed that this wall was part of the city wall which protected public access to the pool. Therefore the garden would have been outside this wall, probably covering the underground cistern that fed the pool and extending just south and east of the City of David across the mouth of the Tyropoeon Valley (Isa. 8:6). Terraced structures in this lower area of the city have been discovered, and even today this area holds sufficient depth of soil to be used for agriculture, being fed by surface run-off from the western side of the Kidron. Water from the well at the En-rogel spring, at the junction of the Kidron and Hinnom Valleys and dating in its lower parts to the 10th to 8th centuries B.C.E., must also have been used to water the King's Garden. The garden played a role in the last days of the kingdom of Judah, serving as part of an escape route for King Zedekiah and his army fleeing the Babylonian siege (2 Kgs. 25:4 = Jer. 39:4).

Bibliography. W. H. Mare, *The Archaeology of the Jerusalem Area* (Grand Rapids, 1987); K. M. Kenyon, *The Bible and Recent Archaeology* (Atlanta, 1978). J. RANDALL PRICE

KING'S HIGHWAY

A major route (Heb. *derek̲ hammelek̲*, "King's Highway" or "royal way"), the "main road" by which Moses sought to lead the Hebrews through Edom and Moab (Num. 20:17; 21:22; cf. Deut. 2:27). Many scholars understand the Hebrew term as a proper name for the international route that connected Damascus with Aqabah (on the Red Sea) and associate it with the itinerary mentioned in Gen. 14:5-6. A route must have traversed Transjordan from north to south, but it simply followed the passable contours and was not necessarily a well-made and officially maintained highway. In the 9th-century B.C. Moabite Stone, King Mesha claims that he repaired the highway that crossed the Arnon (Wadi Môjib). Early in the 2nd century B.C., the Romans established a road through this same region, and sections of its pavement and a few milestones survive to this day. Indeed, one of modern Jordan's north-south highways serves the same purpose, though the topography that automobiles and trucks can negotiate often varies from what pedestrians, horses, and/or beasts of burden might require. Like the ancient route, the modern "King's Highway" connects the cities of Amman, Madaba, Dhiban, Karak, Buseirah, and Aqabah.

Bibliography. D. A. Dorsey, *The Roads and Highways of Ancient Israel* (Baltimore, 1991). GERALD L. MATTINGLY

KING'S POOL

A pool (Heb. *bĕrēk̲at̲ hammelek̲*) mentioned in relation to the Fountain Gate, probably to be identified with the spring En-rogel (Bir Ayub) at the junction of the Kidron and Hinnom valleys (Neh. 2:14). Excavations by Kathleen M. Kenyon suggest that this pool is to be identified either with the still extant Pool of Siloam or the Old Pool (modern Birket el-Hamra), which was the termination point of one of two canals that flowed from the Gihon Spring down the Kidron Valley to the south. This pool must have been used to water the gardens in the valley such as the King's Garden.

Bibliography. K. M. Kenyon, *Jerusalem: Excavating 3000 Years of History* (New York, 1967); W. H. Mare, *The Archaeology of the Jerusalem Area* (Grand Rapids, 1987). J. RANDALL PRICE

KING'S VALLEY

The place where Abram met with the kings of Sodom and Salem (Gen. 14:17), originally called the "Valley of Shaveh" (Heb. *ʿēmeq šāwēh*). If the Hebrew root *šāwâ* has the cognate Ugaritic connotation of "ruler," there may be a semantic basis for this explanation (Heb. *ʿēmeq hammelek̲*), although the original designation itself may have come from a royal association, either because of imperial ownership or the presence of royal tombs. In 2 Sam. 18:18 Absalom erected a memorial stela in this place. According to some extrabiblical sources the most likely location is a plain at the confluence of the Kidron, Tyropoeon, and Hinnom valleys S of the City of David (cf. 2 Sam. 15:23).

Bibliography. J. M. Allegro, *The Treasure of the Copper Scroll*, 2nd ed. (Garden City, 1964); A. A. Wieder, "Ugaritic-Hebrew Lexicographical Notes," *JBL* 84 (1965): 160-62. J. RANDALL PRICE

KINGS, BOOKS OF

The final books of the Deuteronomistic history and the last of the Former Prophets. The title reflects the contents and core organizing principle of these books. Kings structures the history of Judah and Israel according to individual reigns and evaluates the loyalty of the whole nation on the basis of royal behavior. The kings are the focal characters, and the nations' fate hinges on their fidelity or infidelity. The Hebrew canonical tradition considers 1-2 Kings to be a single book, and the practice of partitioning the book in two did not surface until the 15th century. The division point between 1 and 2 Kings is awkward in that it splits the reign of Ahaziah and the career of Elijah. This division is associated with the formula of 2 Kgs. 1:1 ("after the death of"; cf. Josh. 1:1; Judg. 1:1; 2 Sam. 1:1). Placement within the Hebrew canonical division of *Nebi'im* or Prophets reflects the major part played by prophets in the book. The LXX preserves an alternate tradition that holds Samuel and Kings together as an overall unity divided into four books of "Kingdoms" or "Reigns." In places the Greek textual tradition in Kings is distinctive in both content and sequence.

Organization

The most obvious organizing structure is the system of opening and closing formulas for individual kings. Opening formulas synchronize each king's year of accession with the regnal year of the ruler of the other kingdom, and then give the total length of his reign. The author narrates the entire reign of a particular monarch, then backtracks to report on the king or kings of the other kingdom who came to the throne during the first king's rule. Thus after finishing a description of the 41-year reign of Asa king of Judah (1 Kgs. 15:24), the presentation turns back ca. 40 years to deal with Nadab, Baasha, Zimri, Omri, and Ahab, all of whom had succeeded to the kingship of Israel during Asa's reign. This synchronizing movement conveys the notion that the story of a single people is being told.

The opening formulas consistently evaluate the kings of Israel as having done "evil in the sight of the Lord" for sacrificing outside of Jerusalem at Bethel. Some kings of Judah are also condemned, while others receive only qualified approval. Total approval is reserved for Hezekiah and Josiah, who centralized sacrificial worship at the Jerusalem temple. The closing formulas refer to other sources and report on the king's death and his successor. Additional information is provided for the kings of Judah: age at accession, mother's name, and notice of burial. These framing notices are fragmentary until Rehoboam receives the full form (1 Kgs. 14:21-22, 29-31). Concluding statements are missing for certain kings, such as the victims of Jehu's purge, while Jehu lacks an introductory formula because of the circumstances of his accession. Jehoash of Israel is inexplicably provided with two closing formulas (2 Kgs. 13:12-13; 14:15-16). These formulas vary in wording, but become more fixed for the last rulers of each kingdom. The transfer of prophetic authority from Elijah to Elisha (2 Kgs. 2) and the story of Queen Athaliah (2 Kgs. 11) both take place outside the framework structure.

Further unity is provided by a pattern of prophetic promise and fulfillment. The prophets are Yahweh's servants, announcing divine will and judgment (2 Kgs. 17:13, 23; 21:10; 24:2). The most striking example is the unerringly precise prediction of Josiah's reform (1 Kgs. 13:1-10; 2 Kgs. 23:15-18). Other structurally important examples are the division of the united kingdom (1 Kgs. 11:29-39; 12:15), the fall of Israel (1 Kgs. 14:15-16; 2 Kgs. 17:23), the fate of Omri's dynasty (1 Kgs. 21:21-24; 2 Kgs. 9:7-10; 10:17), and the destruction of Judah (2 Kgs. 21:10-15; 22:15-17; 24:2). Unity is also promoted by analogies between paired narratives. Examples are "two mothers and their sons" (1 Kgs. 3:16-28; 2 Kgs. 6:26-31), "death of the wicked queen" (2 Kgs. 9:30-37; 11:13-16), and "wisdom and folly with visitors" (1 Kgs. 10:1-13; 2 Kgs. 20:12-19).

Contents

Kings falls into three parts. 1 Kgs. 1–11 deals with Solomon and concludes with his closing formula in 11:41-43. 1 Kgs. 12–2 Kgs. 17 tells the story of the two independent kingdoms and ends with a long evaluative discourse. 2 Kgs. 18–25 recounts the further history of Judah down to its destruction. After the segment dealing with Solomon, most kings are treated briefly, with only a few sentences supplementing the bare formulaic framework. A smaller group of kings is treated more extensively, the space between the opening and closing formulas being filled with narratives in which prophets are typically involved. These highlighted kings and prophets (Jeroboam and Ahijah, Ahab and Elijah, Jehoram of Israel and Elisha, Jehu, Hezekiah and Isaiah, Josiah and Huldah) represent turning points in history.

After an account of his accession (1 Kgs. 1–2), the career of Solomon is reported positively (chs. 3–10) under the themes of wisdom, royal power, building programs, and piety. The portrayal turns negative in ch. 11. Solomon is enticed by foreign wives into the worship of alien gods and threatened by adversaries, including a domestic rebellion by Jeroboam. Hostility between the independent kingdoms of Israel and Judah is initiated in chs. 12–14 and traced down to the accession of Ahab by chs. 15–16. 1 Kgs. 17–2 Kgs. 10 focuses on Elijah and Elisha, exploring their conflict with the apostate kings of Omri's dynasty. This culminates in the prophetically inspired revolution of Jehu. Briefer reports follow until 2 Kgs. 17, a diatribe on the reasons for the fall of Israel. The remaining history of Judah falls into a pattern of alternating righteous and wicked kings (Hezekiah, Manasseh, Josiah, Josiah's successors). The reform of Josiah (chs. 22–23) climaxes the entire book and apparently resolves the ongoing theme of apostasy and reform. Briefer reports sketch the wickedness and rebellions of Josiah's four successors. Kings ends with an enigmatic report about Jehoiachin as an honored captive in Babylon (25:27-30). This has been interpreted both positively as a sign of a potential future for the Davidic dynasty and negatively as the decisive last act in the national tragedy.

History of Composition

Kings is the last part of the Deuteronomistic history, a literary whole that begins with the introduction to Deuteronomy and chronicles Israel's life of obedience and disobedience in the land of promise. The theology of Deuteronomy pervades and inspires its presentation of history. Evaluative discourses appear at important turning points, usually in the form of speeches by main characters. These review the past and point forward to the challenges of the future. Solomon's temple dedication in 1 Kgs. 8 and the disapproving observations of 2 Kgs. 17 are two of these "end of era" summaries.

The Deuteronomistic historian used various sources to construct Kings. Three of these sources are cited by name. The "Book of the Acts of Solomon," characterized as reporting on Solomon's deeds and his "wisdom" (1 Kgs. 11:41), provided lists of an administrative nature and other historical notes, along with folkloristic narratives illustrating his glory and wisdom. Information about later kings was gleaned from two sources cited as the "Book of the Annals of the Kings of Israel" and "of Judah" (e.g., 1 Kgs. 14:19, 29). These two works provided information on wars, conspiracies, and building projects (1 Kgs. 14:19, 30; 15:23, 32; 16:20; 22:39, 45[MT 46]; 2 Kgs. 20:20). That they were accessible to readers suggests that they were not actual royal annals, but published literary works, based perhaps on inscriptions and other official sources. For 1 Kgs. 1–2, the historian employed the conclusion of the Throne Succession narrative to describe the accession of Solomon (the earlier part is found in 2 Sam. 9–20). Prophetic materials of various sorts were also utilized. Previously collected stories about Elijah and Elisha make up most of 1 Kgs. 17:1–2 Kgs. 8:15. Held together by the transfer of Elijah's mantle (2 Kgs. 2:13-14) and the completion of his mission (1 Kgs. 19:15-17), they were probably taken up as a unified whole by the historian. The appearance of narratives about other prophets (Ahijah, 1 Kgs. 11:29-39; 14:1-18; Shemaiah, 12:21-24; Micaiah, 22:1-28) suggests that other prophetic materials were used, but little can be ascertained about the character of these sources. Of these, the material about Isaiah is the most extensive and independent (2 Kgs. 18:13–20:19).

Ideology

Based on the tenets of Deuteronomy, Kings keeps up a steady critique of the nation's failure to preserve the purity and unity of the cult. For example, the charges leveled against Rehoboam and Ahaz (1 Kgs. 14:22-24; 2 Kgs. 16:3-4) closely reflect what is forbidden by Deut. 12:2-3, 29-31. One focus of this criticism is the worship of foreign gods, a practice said to have started with Solomon and continued by certain kings of both Israel and Judah. This is sometimes called the "way of the kings of Israel" (2 Kgs. 8:18; 16:3) or "of the house of Ahab" (8:27). Special contempt attaches to the worship of Baal, sponsored by Ahab and Jezebel (1 Kgs. 16:31-32), purged by Jehu (2 Kgs. 10:18-28), but then revived again by Manasseh (2 Kgs. 21:3). The second focus of criticism is noncentral sacrifice, forbidden by Deut. 12. By sacrificing at Bethel, the northern kings universally warranted condemnation for participating in the "way" or "sins of Jeroboam" (e.g., 1 Kgs. 15:34; 16:2, 19, 26, 31). In Judah noncentral sacrifice took place at local "high places." Even otherwise faithful kings of Judah received only qualified approval because "the high places were not taken away" (e.g., 1 Kgs. 15:14; 22:43). Only Hezekiah and Josiah, who shut down the high places, receive unconditional praise. These two strands of evaluation are brought together in the reform of Josiah, who removed both alien cults (2 Kgs. 23:4-5, 10-14) and local high places (vv. 8-9), even desecrating the shrine of Bethel and the high places of Israel (vv. 15-20). The infidelity of the northern kingdom resulted in its destruction by the Assyrians (2 Kgs. 17:7-18, 21-23). Judah eventually fell to Babylon as a result of similar offenses (2 Kgs. 17:19-20), especially those sponsored by Manasseh (21:10-15; 24:3-4).

Another important theme is God's special favor to David (1 Kgs. 11:12-13) and the promise of an abiding Davidic dynasty in Jerusalem (11:36; 15:4-5; 2 Kgs. 8:19). David's devotion serves as a model for measuring royal fidelity (e.g., 1 Kgs. 3:3; 11:4, 6, 38; 15:3, 11). Yahweh's special favor to David is given as the reason for the security of Jerusalem in Hezekiah's reign (2 Kgs. 19:34; 20:5-6).

Kings sometimes casts women as villains (Solomon's wives, 1 Kgs. 11:1-8; Jezebel, 18:19; Athaliah, 2 Kgs. 11). Bathsheba, however, helps plot Solomon's accession (1 Kgs. 1). Two prostitutes and the queen of Sheba enhance Solomon's reputation for wisdom (1 Kgs. 3:16-28; 10:1-10). Women also play roles in some prophetic narratives (1 Kgs. 14:1-18; 17:8-24; 2 Kgs. 4:1-37; 8:1-6), and Huldah's prophetic oracle interprets the significance of Josiah's policies (2 Kgs. 22:14-20).

Issues in Recent Study

The chronology of Kings remains in dispute. The years of reign given for the kings of Israel do not coordinate with those for the kings of Judah, and the system of sychronisms does not match the system of reign lengths. There are also discrepancies with established dates from Mesopotamia. In trying to untangle these problems, scholars postulate error in textual transmission, different calendrical conventions for the two kingdoms at various times, and coregencies in which a king and his designated successor reign concurrently (cf. 2 Kgs. 15:5).

The general reliability of Kings as a historical source is also debated. Its use of sources indicates considerable historical value in places, but the theory of historical causation in Kings is theological rather than political or economic. The short shrift given to the important northern king Omri (1 Kgs. 16:23-28) evidences a historical perspective altogether different from that of modern historians. Many of the narratives, especially the prophet legends and folk tales, cannot be used as trustworthy historical sources. It has been suggested that the narratives about the Syrian wars (1 Kgs. 20, 22; 2 Kgs. 6:8–7:20; 8:7-15) have been incorrectly assigned to the reigns of Ahab and his son Jehoram. Some scholars have concluded that the narrative of Josiah's reform (2 Kgs. 22–23) is so highly tendentious that it must be a literary creation and does not rest on any trustworthy source.

The compositional history of the Deuteronomistic history is hotly debated. Some suggest that a single exilic writer working after the death of Jehoiachin (2 Kgs. 25:27-30) authored the entire history as an explanation for the fall of the nation. Material that sounds preexilic was preserved because of this author's respect for inherited sources. Others postulate an optimistic preexilic historian writing before (contrast 2 Kgs. 22:20 with 23:29) or just after (22:1) Josiah's death, to support his reforming policies. In the Exile this was revised in a more pessimistic direction as a history of disobedience, blaming the nation's fall on the sins of Manasseh (2 Kgs. 21:10-15; 23:26; 24:3-4). Still others propose an exilic work subsequently overlaid by two redactions oriented toward prophecy and law, respectively. Other proposals suggest that the history originally ended with the reign of Hezekiah (cf. 2 Kgs. 18:5) or that a preexilic prophetic history served as the original basis for the work.

Bibliography. G. H. Jones, *1 and 2 Kings,* 2 vols. NCBC (Grand Rapids, 1984); B. O. Long, *1 Kings.* FOTL 9 (Grand Rapids, 1984); *2 Kings.* FOTL 10 (Grand Rapids, 1991); R. D. Nelson, *First and Sec-*

ond Kings. Interpretation (Atlanta, 1987); M. Noth, *The Deuteronomistic History.* JSOTSup 15 (Sheffield, 1981); I. W. Provan, *1 and 2 Kings.* New International Bible (Peabody, 1995).

RICHARD D. NELSON

KINSHIP

The heart of developing social relationships is kinship, defined in the broadest sense to include both blood and social ties. People see "who they are" based on the kinship network, in terms of descent patterns, marriage ties, and friendships. Claims and obligations, loyalties and sentiments pivot on these relationships. Basic relationships (whether kin or non-kin) may also hinge on the degree of "tolerance" (perhaps to be equated with "morality") of actions in both the long and the short term and upon recognition of the implicit rights of reciprocity. In addition, a person is judged by the reputation of his kinship group, and his own actions will have a direct influence on that group's reputation.

Kinship terms (e.g., father, mother, brother, sister, uncle, nephew) appear throughout the ancestral stories and in other sections of the OT as well. In the Bible, kinship is a portfolio describing personal identity and social standing.

Biblical genealogies, outlining kinship ties, function as historical ties to the past as well as determinants of social place or level. By using genealogies to describe their characters' kinship, storytellers tell their social status, financial worth, and how much authority they could exercise in the community as a whole. They draw their material for the genealogies from a variety of sources including oral tradition, private family archives, and administrative records.

In what may be an artful genealogical creation, each member of a tribe belongs to a lineage, and all of the lineages are believed to be related by common descent to an eponymous ancestor (i.e., Abraham). Thus, kinship is the basis for tribal unity as well as tribal identity. A tribal society may include thousands of people, each of whom belongs to several kinds of descent groups. In ancient Israel there existed a patrilineal, segmentary lineage system in which each of its households *(bêṯ 'āḇôṯ)* belonged to a lineage *(mišpāḥâ).* These lineages, in which membership and inheritance were based on the father, made up a clan. The clans formed several phratries, and the phratries comprised the tribe. Its lineages were also (once the Israelites entered Canaan) described as localized, having their own designated territories (Josh. 13-19). These social groupings are not necessarily evolutionary. They all continued to exist, even when the monarchy was established, and there was no linear progression which required each to exist in turn for the monarchy to be established.

The social and political units of ancient Israel, as portrayed in the biblical text, can thus be outlined as follows:

1. Individual nuclear families combined into an extended family *(bêṯ 'āḇ),* dependent on a *paterfamilias* (head of household)
2. Lineages *(mišpāḥâ)* comprising persons who trace their origin to a particular ancestor — including clans, like the Levites, which were nonlocalized, pan-tribal lineages
3. Sibs, which demonstrate a branching of a lineage, such as that in the Aaronic line between Zadokites and the levitical line of Abiathar
4. Phratries *(šēḇeṭ),* a major division of a tribe (i.e., Judah of the tribe of Israel), having their own designated territories
5. Tribe, a term used here in the collective sense of all of the people of "Israel," united by kinship, religion, and endogamy.

It would be inappropriate to differentiate between the social forms and stratification of Hebrew and Canaanite tribal peoples. Despite the attempts in the biblical text to draw a religious demarcation between them, their everyday existence — based as it was on the same environmental and economic concerns — would have been virtually the same. Archaeological and textual evidence, while somewhat mixed on this subject, indicate that each household consisted of an extended family of ca. 10-15 adults. It was governed by the head of the household.

The respect due to this social system may be seen in the authority of the head of household and in the commandment to "Honor your father and your mother" (Exod. 20:12). This legal pronouncement demands loyalty more than obedience to the head of the house. It represents a basic value of Israelite society, which has determined that this relationship is a key component of their covenantal community and therefore must be protected.

The transference of this position as head of the household was generational. Inheritance patterns are established which attempt to provide an orderly transition without significantly affecting the inheritance system itself. Primogeniture, for instance, is exhibited in Isaac's naming of Esau, his older son, as his heir (Gen. 27:1-4). The younger son, Jacob, if this arrangement had actually been carried out, would have received a lesser portion (see Esau's actual inheritance as the lesser heir in Gen. 27:33-40) and would have had the option of working for his brother or separating himself from the household and establishing his own.

The fragmenting of the extended family household into new units (still within the same lineage, however) is a reflection of inheritance patterns, environmental necessity, and population growth. It is the adaptability of the institution which makes this fragmentation fairly smooth while at the same time initiating changes which will in both the long and short term affect the society. For instance, in Gen. 12:1 Yahweh calls Abram to leave his "father's house" and to found his own. Burying his father is a rite of passage, which conducts Abram across the threshold of transformation. To bury his father is an exercise in severance or departure from the world of his father. It demands that Abram change the basic pattern of his life and establish a new one.

Group fission and social fluidity are basic survival components in a fragile or unstable environment. War, economic exigency, environmental catastrophe, inheritance patterns, and adventurism all contribute to the creation of new houses and the opening up of new areas to exploitation.

Households were the communities within which the Israelites crossed three important thresholds: birth, marriage, and death. It was the way in which each individual dealt with these rites of passage and the ways in which they were counseled, programmed, or restricted by the community that made them so crucial.

Although couples spontaneously conceived and gave birth to several children throughout the course of their marriage, the conception and birth of the male heir was always anticipated. This is graphically demonstrated by the "search for the heir" motif which runs throughout the ancestral narratives of Genesis. The desire for a male heir was complicated if a daughter was born first. Although not stated in the narrative, it is likely that this female child would be weaned sooner than a male in order for the mother to resume ovulating.

Another task of kinship systems within the household is the determination of which adults are eligible to marry, who actually chooses marriage partners, which children live in their parents' household, and which become heirs. Patrilineal families choose heirs only from the father's side, matrilineal families only from the mother's side, and cognate families from either side. Heirs inherit the parent's social status, financial worth, and authority in the community as a whole. In this way, the social order of the community and the principles of power and authority are perpetuated.

One example of the potential influence of preferential marriage practices is seen in Nahor's cross-cousin marriage (Gen. 11:29). It fulfills the requirements of both endogamy to marry within one's own family and exogamy to marry outside one's own family. Like Jacob who married both Leah and Rachel — his cousins who were sisters — Nahor marries a cousin who has a sister. Nahor's marriage also established a bond between him and his uncle. The avuncular relationship between a man and his uncle has been seen to be as important as the relationship between a man and his father in the ancient Near East.

Marriage was a matter of business, designed to bring together two households willing to exchange substantial goods and services over a significant period of time. When the marriage was concluded, an exchange of property took place in the form of bridewealth and dowry. This marked the transference of the rights of the bride from her father's household to that of her husband's. An elaborate legal framework was developed to administer these items to provide "a circulating pool of resources" used to arrange future family marriages, and in the event of the husband's death, to provide for the financial support of the widow.

The final obligation of a kinship group was exercised by mourners who supervised the transfer of a member from his or her place among the living to the appropriate place among the dead. In the earlier periods of Israelite history, death did not separate a member from the household. The tomb of a household reflected much the same style and many of the same amenities as its house, although in some cases a more conservative dwelling architecture was followed in the family tomb. For example, it was common enough to continue to bury villagers in cave tombs long after the village itself was constructing free-standing houses.

The rituals by which a body was transferred from the realm of the living to the realm of the dead are virtually identical to those used by midwives to transfer a newborn into the household. In both cases the body is washed, anointed, dressed and carefully placed for adoption. The newborn is placed on the lap, or "womb," of its parent, and the body of the dead in the tomb, the "womb" of Mother Earth, who is every human's adoptive parent.

After death, the memory of the deceased was preserved through rituals which suggest a cult of veneration of the dead. Ancestor worship formed a private ritual whereby the family group, without the intervention or interference of any larger political or ethnic unit, remained in contact and provided sustenance for the deceased. The private, apolitical nature of this ritual may be one reason why Saul outlawed mediums and other practitioners of communication with the dead, but then used one when personal need outweighed political concerns (1 Sam. 28:3-25).

In the 8th century B.C.E. the emergent monarchy and priestly hierarchy outlawed ancestor worship. This was to emphasize further sole adherence to Yahweh worship and to curtail magical practices which were conceived as dangerous because by definition they were "private, secret, and mysterious." Therefore these private ceremonies became a target for the government, which planned to control all aspects of worship and political expression.

Throughout the biblical period, the household and the force of kinship ties dominated relationships, provided opportunities for advancement, and determined inheritance patterns. It would be impossible to understand ancient Israel without reference to kinship ties.

Bibliography. L. Holy, *Kinship, Honour and Solidarity* (Manchester, 1989); V. H. Matthews and D. C. Benjamin, *Social World of Ancient Israel, 1250-587 B.C.E.* (Peabody, 1993); R. A. Oden, Jr., "Jacob as Father, Husband, and Nephew: Kinship Studies and the Patriarchal Narratives," *JBL* 102 (1983): 189-205; J. Pitt-Rivers, "The Kith and the Kin," in *The Character of Kinship,* ed. J. Goody (Cambridge, 1973), 89-105; D. Steinmetz, *From Father to Son: Kinship, Conflict, and Continuity in Genesis* (Louisville, 1991); R. R. Wilson, *Genealogy and History in the Biblical World* (New Haven, 1977).

VICTOR H. MATTHEWS

KIR (Heb. *qîr*)

1. The place to which the Assyrian king Tiglath-pileser III deported Syrian (Aramean) peoples after destroying Damascus in 732 B.C.E. (2 Kgs.

16:9 MT; cf. Amos 1:5). According to Amos, Kir was the original home of the Arameans (Amos 9:7). Most LXX manuscripts do not refer to Kir in 2 Kgs. 16:9, perhaps suggesting that this is a scribal gloss based on the reference in Amos.

The precise location of Kir is not certain, but an Akkadian tablet from the Late Bronze Age Syrian city of Emar refers to a certain Pilsu-Dagan, not only as the "king of the city of Emar," but also as the "king of the people of the land of Qi-ri." This may suggest that Kir was near Emar, an important city on the Euphrates River.

2. A city in Moab (Isa. 15:1). It is probably the same as Kir-hareseth (modern Kerak).

3. Apparently a city in southern Mesopotamia. In Isa. 22:6 Kir is mentioned in conjunction with the southern Mesopotamian city of Elam as a source of military support for the Assyrian army.

Bibliography. M. Cogan and H. Tadmor *II Kings*. AB 11 (Garden City, 1988); W. T. Pitard, *Ancient Damascus* (Winona Lake, 1987); R. Zadok, "Elements of Aramean Pre-History," in *Ah, Assyria*, ed. M. Cogan and I. Eph'al. ScrHier 33 (Jerusalem, 1991): 104-17.

CHRIS A. ROLLSTON

KIR-HARESETH (Heb. *qîr ḥărešeṯ*),
KIR-HERES (*qîr ḥereś*)

One of the major cities of Moab, probably the capital, and likely the same as Kir Moab (Isa. 15:1). It is mentioned in Isaiah's prophecy (Isa. 16:7, 11) and in Jeremiah's message concerning Moab (Jer. 48:31, 36). The alternate form Kir-heres appears in Isa. 16:11; Jer. 48.

Kir-hareseth has generally been identified with modern Kerak (217066), situated on a strategic plateau surrounded by steep valleys and overlooking Wadi Kerak, which flows into the Dead Sea. The city is located at an intersection of the King's Highway and a road that crosses the plateau from east to west. Kerak is mentioned on the 6th-century C.E. Madeba mosaic map ([Kar]ach Moba). Recently, Kir-hareseth has been dissociated from Kerak and identified with Qarhoh, Moab's capital near Dibon.

Archaeological remains from the biblical periods are scarce. The only considerable find is a fragmentary dedication inscription from the 9th century B.C.E. Unfortunately, the whole site is covered by modern buildings. The outstanding monument of the city is the remains of a 12th-century Crusader castle, which also houses the archaeological museum.

Bibliography. K. A. D. Smelik, *Converting the Past: Studies in Ancient Israelite and Moabite Historiography*. OTS 28 (Leiden, 1992).

FRIEDBERT NINOW

KIRIATH (Heb. *qiryaṯ*)

A city in the tribal territory of Benjamin (Josh. 18:28; cf. NRSV mg), identified with Kiriath-jearim (so NRSV).

KIRIATHAIM (Heb. *qiryāṯayim*)

1. A town E of the Jordan assigned to the Reubenites, who rebuilt it (Num. 32:27; Josh. 13:19). This region was politically unstable, and by the time of Moab's rebellion (2 Kgs. 1:1) Mesha king of Moab controlled Kiriathaim; according to the Mesha Inscription (l. 10) he rebuilt the city. Kiriathaim remained in Moab's possession until the time of Jeremiah (Jer. 48:1, 23) and Ezekiel (Ezek. 25:9). Possible locations include el-Qereiyat (215105), 8 km. (5 mi.) NW of Dibon, and Qaryat el-Mekhaiyet (220128), 5 km. (3 mi.) NW of Medeba. Shaveh-kiriathaim, "the plain of Kiriathaim" (Gen. 14:5), was probably associated with this city.

2. A city in in the territory of Naphtali assigned, with its pastures, to the Gershonite Levites (1 Chr. 6:76[MT 61]). It is probably the same as Kartan (Josh. 21:32) and to be identified with modern Khirbet el-Qureiyeh, 10 km. (6 mi.) W of Medeba.

CHRISTIAN M. M. BRADY

KIRIATH-ARBA (Heb. *qiryaṯ 'arba'*)

The ancient name ("city of four") of Hebron (Josh. 15:54). The name could mean "city of four districts" (a tetrapolis) or "city of four famous persons," as Jerome assumed by citing Adam, Abraham, Isaac, and Jacob. Josh. 14:15 traces the etymology to Arba, a great hero among the Anakim (cf. 15:13; 21:11).

KIRIATHARIM (Heb. *qiryaṯ 'ārim*)
(also KIRIATH-JEARIM)

A city named in the list of those returning from exile (Ezra 2:25). The usual form of the name, Kiriath-jearim, occurs in the parallel account at Neh. 7:29.

KIRIATH-BAAL (Heb. *qiryaṯ ba'al*)

An alternate name of Kiriath-jearim ("city of Baal"; Josh. 15:60; 18:14; cf. 15:9, "Baalah").

KIRIATH-HUZOTH (Heb. *qiryaṯ ḥuṣôṯ*)

A Moabite city to which Balaam accompanied Balak (Num. 22:39). There Balak sacrificed to Baal in an effort to coerce the deity to curse the Israelites (Num. 22:40). The site is probably N of the Arnon River.

KIRIATH-JEARIM (Heb. *qiryaṯ yĕ'ārîm*)
(also KIRIATHARIM)

A city of Judah along its northern border with Benjamin, ca. 14.5 km. (9 mi.) W of Jerusalem in the central hill country near modern Abu Ghosh. Kiriath-jearim ("city of forests") was also known as Baalah (Josh. 15:9), Baale-Judah (2 Sam. 6:2), or Kiriath-baal (Josh. 15:60; 18:14), examples of the demythologizing practice of the prophetic school, whereby names derived from natural elements were substituted for the original Canaanite deific names (Baal, Baalah). The ancient site is identified with Tell el-Achar (Deir al-'Âzar)/Tel Qiryat Ye'arim (159135).

Kiriath-jearim was among the cities of the Gibeonites, whose treaty with Joshua (Josh. 9:17) granted them protection from Israelite attack. The Israelites hence came to the aid of the Gibeonites when they were attacked by the coalition of Amorite kings led by Adoni-zedek of Jerusalem.

In the account of the journey of the ark of the covenant after its capture by the Philistines, the people of Kiriath-jearim brought the ark to the house of Abinadab. There his son Eleazar was consecrated as its custodian (1 Sam. 6:21–7:2), and it remained in the city for 20 years until David sought to bring it to Jerusalem. A new cart was prepared, but when Uzzah died from handling the ark, it was left in the house of Obed-edom the Gittite for three months, and then was transported to the City of David and housed in a special tent erected for worship of the Lord (cf. 1 Chr. 13:1-14; 15:1–16:3).

The faithful prophet Uriah ben Shemaiah, a contemporary of Jeremiah, was from Kiriath-jearim (Jer. 26:20). Two men from Kiriath-jearim, Kephirah and Beeroth, were among the exiles of Judah who returned to Jerusalem under the leadership of Zerubbabel (Neh. 7:29[MT 28]). A variant form of the name of the city, Kiriatharim, is cited in the parallel text (Ezra 2:25).

Later the Romans built an outpost on the site along the road from Jerusalem to Antipatris, where the Tenth Legion was garrisoned. An inscribed column cylinder bearing this reference was found at the site. R. Dennis Cole

KIRIATH-SANNAH (Heb. *qiryaṯ-sannâ*)
Either an alternate name or scribal error for Kiriath-sepher, identified with Debir (Josh. 15:49). This form, which occurs only in the MT, may be the result of dittography with the preceding site, Dannah.

KIRIATH-SEPHER (Heb. *qiryaṯ-sēp̄er*)
The ancient name of Debir (**1;** Josh. 15:15-16 = Judg. 1:11-12; cf. Josh. 15:49).

KISH (Heb. *qîš*) **(PERSON)**

1. A Benjaminite from Gibeah, the son of Abiel and father of Saul (1 Sam. 9:1). A wealthy man (cf. 1 Sam. 9:3), Kish is described as a *gibbôr ḥayîl,* a "man of standing" (NJPSV) or "substance" (NIV), apparently a person of privileged military or material status. Saul's claim that he comes from the "least" of the clans of Benjamin (1 Sam. 9:21) refers to status or size of the clan. Kish was buried at Zela in Benjamin, where Saul and Jonathan were also buried after their bodies were recovered from the Philistines (2 Sam. 21:14).

2. A son (or descendant) of Jeiel and Maacah (1 Chr. 8:30; 9:36). Some scholars equate this Kish with **1** above by identifying Jeiel ("Yah[weh] is God") with Abiel ("My Father is God"), but this does not resolve the difficulties raised by the disparate genealogies (1 Sam. 9:1; 1 Chr. 8:29-33; 9:35-39). Yet because the Chronicler elsewhere correctly designates the father of Saul (1 Chr. 26:28), the lineage given in 1 Chr. 8-9 could be a variant, corrupted genealogy of Kish **1** or refer to a different Kish altogether, perhaps the uncle of **1** above (cf. 1 Chr. 9:36).

3. A Levite of the Merarite clan, the son of Mahli and father of Jerahmeel, whose name became the designation for one of the levitical courses (1 Chr. 23:21-22; 24:29). His sons married their cousins, the daughters of Kish's brother Eliazar (1 Chr. 23:22).

4. A son of Abdi, also a Levite of the Merarite clan, who was involved in the cleansing of the temple during Hezekiah's reforms (2 Chr. 29:12).

5. A Benjaminite ancestor of Mordecai (Esth. 2:5). Some scholars read the Hebrew text to mean that he rather than Mordecai had been deported during the time of King Jehoiachin (Esth. 2:6). Others argue that the genealogical list of 2:5 has been condensed to link Mordecai to **1** above, making Mordecai a descendant of the first royal family of Israel. Jeffrey C. Geoghegan

KISH (Sum. *Kiš*) **(PLACE)**
The capital of an ancient city-state situated on a now dead branch of the Euphrates. The present site (in Iraq, NE of modern Hilla) consists of a series of tells ca. 14.5 km. (9 mi.) SE of ancient Babylon.

According to the Sumerian King List, Kish represented the first dynasty after the Flood; it was here that kingship descended from heaven and was given to humankind. The title "king of Kish" was of major importance in the early historic periods, and it was from Kish that Sargon set out to create the kingdom of Akkad. Kish flourished as an Early Dynastic city that was a rival of Erech; it was linked with the legendary king Etana, and Early Dynastic II king Agga opposed Gilgamesh. Kish was continuously occupied from the time of Akkad through the Old Babylonian and Kassite periods.

The site was excavated by the French (beginning in 1912), by a joint Oxford (Ashmolean Museum) and Chicago (Field Museum) expedition (1923-1933), and by a Japanese expedition led by Hideo Fuji (1989); only one season of the Japanese expedition was completed before the 1991 Persian Gulf War. The excavations have yielded a flood-deposit level (ca. 3300 B.C.), many cuneiform tablets from the earlier occupation and the 2nd millennium, graves, pottery, palaces, temples, ziggurats, and canals, and a variety of other objects. Because of the large complex of tells in the general area, much more detailed excavation and research are needed to clarify the occupations.

Larry L. Walker

KISHI (Heb. *qîšî*)
An alternate form of the name Kushaiah (1 Chr. 6:44[MT 29]).

KISHION (Heb. *qišyôn*)
A city in the territory of Issachar (Josh. 19:20) allotted to the Gershonite Levites (21:28), perhaps the *Qšn* mentioned in Thutmose III's list of conquered cities. In the parallel list of levitical cities at 1 Chr. 6:72(MT 57), its place is taken by Kedesh. Though located SW of the Sea of Chinnereth and W of the Jordan River, Kishion's precise identification is debated. Prominent suggestions include Khirbet

Qasyûn (187229) S of Mt. Tabor, Tell el-Muqarqash (194228), and Tell el-ʿAjjûl (185225).

Eric F. Mason

KISHON (Heb. *qîšôn*)
A wadi (Wadi el-Muqaṭṭaʿ) that drains the western Jezreel Valley, Esdraelon Plain, and the plain of Acco. Several wadis meet 6.5 km. (4 mi.) NE of Megiddo and feed into the Kishon: Wadi en-Nusf/ Wadi Shemmah, S of Mt. Gilboa; Wadi Muweili, from the west of Mt. Tabor; Wadi el-Mujahiyeh, with origins in Galilee; springs in the vicinity of Megiddo; and wadis from the Carmel range. The Kishon is ca. 35 km. (23 mi.) long. During the winter months it presented a formidable barrier in the midst of the Great Plain.

The Kishon was the scene of the defeat of Sisera by the armies of Deborah and Barak (Judg. 4:7, 13). The exact place of the decisive battle is unknown. The vicinity of "Taanach, by the waters of Megiddo" (Judg. 5:19) may refer to the confluence of the various wadis feeding the Kishon. Deborah and Barak engaged Sisera after a rain when the Kishon was in flood, reducing the advantage of Sisera's chariots and bogging down his army (Judg. 5:21). The Israelite victory was remembered in later times as evidence of God's protection (Ps. 83:9[MT 10]).

The Kishon was the scene of Elijah's execution of the prophets of Baal following the contest on Mt. Carmel (1 Kgs. 18:40).

Stephen Von Wyrick

KISS
Heb. *nāšaq* seems to be onomatopoetic, reflecting an inspiratory bilabial sound; Gk. *philéō, kataphiléō* ("to love") point to kissing as generally a physical expression of heartfelt affection.

In the OT kissing serves as an expression of greeting (Gen. 29:11, 13; 33:4; 45:15; 48:10; Exod. 4:27) usually involving family members, of friendship (1 Sam. 20:41; 2 Sam. 15:5; 19:39), and of erotic love (Prov. 7:13; Cant. 1:2; 8:1). It appears to refer to kissing the lips or some other area of the face, although the direct object "lips" appears only once (Prov. 24:26; cf. Cant. 1:2, "of the mouth").

In the biblical world kissing the feet is an expression of obeisance. Such a kiss is described as "licking the dust" (Ps. 72:9-11; Isa. 49:23; Mic. 7:16-17); in the latter passage the kiss of obeisance is called also "eating the dust," an expression that appears in the humiliation of the primordial serpent (Gen. 3:14). The humiliated nation of Judah is asked to "put his mouth in the dust" (Lam. 3:29-30).

The remaining OT instances of kissing involve an apostate prayer gesture (1 Kgs. 19:18; Job 31:27; Hos. 13:2), greeting the king upon enthronement (1 Sam. 10:1), and metaphors and similes based upon the kiss of greeting (Ps. 85:10[MT 11]; Prov. 27:6).

In the NT the holy kiss was a symbol of the fellowship of all Christians (Rom. 16:16; 1 Cor. 16:20; 2 Cor. 13:12; 1 Thess. 5:26; 1 Pet. 5:14), and Jesus rebukes Simon for not greeting him with a kiss (Luke 7:45; cf. vv. 36-50). Precisely because it was taken for granted that persons close to each other would kiss upon meeting, Judas was able to employ his kiss of Jesus to identify Jesus to the chief priests. Judas' deceitful kiss (Matt. 26:49; Mark 14:45; Luke 22:47) became thereby "the kiss of death."

Bibliography. M. I. Gruber, *Aspects of Nonverbal Communication in the Ancient Near East*, 2 vols. Studia Pohl 12 (Rome, 1980); W. Klassen, "Musonius Rufus, Jesus and Paul: Three First-Century Feminists," in *From Jesus to Paul*, ed. P. Richardson and J. C. Hurd (Waterloo, Ont., 1984), 185-206; C. Nyrop, *The Kiss and Its History* (1901, repr. Detroit, 1968).

Mayer I. Gruber

KITE
A predatory bird of the hawk family (Accipitridae), of the genus *Milvus*. The common kite *(Milvus milvus)* is red, almost brownish, ca. 60 cm. (2 ft.) long. It is most prevalent in the winter, when flocks are found along the Mediterranean coast, in southern Judah, W of the Dead Sea, and in the wilderness of Beer-sheba. The black kite *(Milvus migrans)* is blackish-brown with a notched tail. It arrives in March and settles for the summer near villages, where it feeds on refuse (cf. Isa. 34:15; NRSV "buzzard"). As elsewhere in biblical usage, the terms designating these species (Heb. *dāʾâ, dayyâ*) are applied imprecisely by modern standards. The KJV translates "vultures" in each of the passages cited. Lev. 11:14; Deut. 14:13 explicitly state that these birds "of every kind" shall not be eaten, implying a multitude of species.

Jesper Svartvik

KITRON (Heb. *qiṭrôn*)
A Canaanite city in the territory allotted to Zebulun which the Israelites were not able to capture initially (Judg. 1:30). It is probably the same as Kattath. The location has not yet been identified; suggestions include Khirbet Quṭṭeneh (153226), 8 km. (5 mi.) SW of Tell Qeimûn (biblical Jokneam), and Tell el-Far (160242).

KITTIM (Heb. *kittîm, kittîyîm*)
According to the Table of Nations (Gen. 10:1-32), a people descended from Japheth through Javan, thus the Ionians or Greeks (v. 4; cf. 1 Chr. 1:7). The name probably derived from the city the Phoenicians called Kitti *(kty)* and the Greeks Kition, located near modern Larnaka on the south-central coast of Cyprus. Elsewhere in the OT Kittim designated an ever-widening geographic area.

In Num. 24:24 the oracles of Balaam conclude with a reference to ships from Kittim (presumably Cyprus), which will afflict both Asshur (Assyria) and Eber (Hebrews), before coming to an end themselves. In Isa. 23:1, 12 the term refers to Cyprus as a trading partner of Tyre (cf. Ezek. 27:6), and in Jer. 2:10 its inhabitants are said to have been more faithful to their false gods than Israel has been to Yahweh. 1 Macc. 1:1; 8:5 report that Alexander the Great came from Kittim, thus identifying Greece — or at least Macedonia — with the place name Kittim. Dan. 11:30 alludes to the ships from Kittim in Num. 24:24, but applies the phrase to Roman intervention against Antiochus Epiphanes during his invasion of Egypt in 168 B.C.E. Thus Kittim came to refer to Rome too. The verse implies the further identification of the Seleucids with Asshur and Eber with the Hebrews.

In the Dead Sea Scrolls the Kittim are the eschatological foe (cf. 1QpHab). Descriptions of them often apply to either Syria or to Rome, but the commentary on Nahum (4QpNah) and the War Scroll (1QM) refer unmistakably to Rome.

PAUL L. REDDITT

KNEADING BOWL

A household utensil for the production of bread and other baked goods and thus an image of hospitality. Sarah probably uses a kneading bowl (Heb. *miš'ereṯ*) when she prepares cakes for Abraham's three visitors (Gen. 18:6). The medium at Endor kneads and bakes bread for Saul (1 Sam. 28:24), and Tamar kneads bread for Amnon (2 Sam. 13:8). Jer. 7:18 cites women kneading cakes for the queen of heaven as an example of Israel's wickedness.

The kneading bowl is also an image of life and death. During the second plague, frogs were so numerous they even got into the Egyptian's kneading bowls (Exod. 8:3[MT 7:28]). When the Israelites left Egypt, they carried their bowls, still filled with dough and bound up with their clothes, on their shoulders (Exod. 12:34). Deut. 28 mentions kneading bowls among the blessings (v. 5) and curses (v. 17).

VICTORIA ANDREWS

KNEELING

A position of humility, surrender, respect, and adoration. Bowing the knee was an expression of honor and submission to royalty and various governmental and religious authorities (Gen. 41:43). Kneeling was also a posture of giving birth (1 Sam. 4:19), and it symbolized the legal acceptance of a child (Gen. 30:3).

Most importantly, kneeling was an act, along with bowing (Ps. 95:6), that signified a reverential attitude during prayer and worship, including the worship of Baal as well as God (1 Kgs. 19:18; Rom. 11:4). Both Jesus and his followers knelt while they prayed (Luke 22:41; Acts 9:40; 20:36). When Stephen was martyred, he knelt and prayed for those who stoned him (Acts 7:60). Finally, at the second coming of Christ his lordship will be recognized when at the name of Jesus every knee will bow (Phil. 2:10).

J. GREGORY LAWSON

KNIFE

A cutting utensil, rendered by several Hebrew words. Heb. *mā'ăḵeleṯ* (from *'kl*, "to eat") is a utensil that was used to slay an animal and prepare it for food (Gen. 22:6, 10; Judg. 19:29). This cutting device was large enough to cut through human flesh and dismember the human body. It was thus probably the equivalent of a modern butcher knife (cf. Prov. 30:14, par. *ḥereḇ*, "sword").

Heb. *śakkîn* (Prov. 23:2), thought to be an Aramaic loanword, was a common word for a slaughtering knife in rabbinic literature. Biblical usage and archaeological finds do provide the precise distinction between a *mā'ăḵeleṯ* and a *śakkîn*. Heb. *ḥereḇ*, "sword," is often translated "knife" when the tool was used for circumcising and shaving (Josh. 5:2; Ezek. 5:1-2); cf. the LXX, where Gk. *máchaira* translates both *mā'ăḵeleṯ* and *ḥereḇ*. Heb. *ta'ar* refers to a shaving implement (Num. 6:5; 8:7; Isa. 7:20; Ezek. 5:1) as well as a penknife (Jer. 36:23). The word does not occur in the NT.

Knives have been discovered at almost every archaeological dig in Israel. They were made from flint, metal, copper, and iron.

MARK F. ROOKER

KNOW, KNOWLEDGE

The words for "knowledge" and "knowing" in the Bible (Heb. *yāḏa'*; Gk. *ginṓskō*) represent significant biblical concepts that are difficult to capture with a simple definition; they have a broad range of meaning. Nevertheless, some degree of generalization is useful in an attempt to characterize what is distinctive about the use of "knowledge" in the OT and NT.

In the OT knowledge is experiential and relational. The "man of sorrows" in Isa. 53:3 "is acquainted with" (Heb. "knows") grief; i.e., he has experienced grief. When the prophet Hosea announces that there is "no knowledge of God in the land" (Hos. 4:1), he is equating knowledge with loyalty and faithfulness. To know God is to be in relationship to God (Hos. 6:6). Knowledge of God involves reverent obedience to him (Prov. 1:7).

The same is true on the human plane: to know another is to have a relationship with that person. For instance, near the beginning of Exodus it is reported that "a new king arose over Egypt, who did not know Joseph" (Exod. 1:8); i.e., this new pharaoh did not acknowledge any relationship with or obligations toward the descendants of Joseph. The experiential and relational element in the OT use of knowledge is perhaps best seen in the numerous passages in which it refers to sexual intercourse (e.g., Gen. 4:1; 1 Kgs. 1:4). At the same time, knowledge can have the abstract senses of realization (Judg. 13:21), rational discourse (Job 15:2), and insight into the nature of reality (Job 12:3; Eccl. 1:16).

In the NT knowledge can also be experiential and relational, as in the OT (e.g., "the Lord knows those who are his"; 2 Tim. 2:19). In general, however, the NT uses knowledge in a more theoretical sense, consistent with its range of meaning in Greek. For instance, knowledge of Jesus is insight into a revealed truth, namely, that Jesus, against appearances, is actually the eternal Word of God (John 1:10). Because knowledge, both in Greek philosophy and in Hellenistic religion, can have an abstract, even mystical, quality, Paul could be critical of knowledge, casting it as inferior to the supreme virtue, love (1 Cor. 8:1-3). The Apostle Paul's words in 1 Cor. 13:8 ("Love never ends. But . . . as for knowledge, it will come to an end") would not make sense to an OT prophet for whom, in Hebrew terms, knowledge of God is equivalent to love for God (Ps. 91:14).

GREGORY MOBLEY

KOA (Heb. *qôaʿ*)
A people who probably lived E of the Tigris River and N of the territory occupied by Pekod (Ezek. 23:23). They are generally thought to be identical with the Guti familiar from cuneiform sources.

KOHATH (Heb. *qĕhāṯ*)
The second son of Levi (Gen. 46:11) and the father of Amram, Izhar (called Amminadab in 1 Chr. 6:22), Hebron, and Uzziel (Exod. 6:16, 18). Among his descendants were Aaron, Moses, and Miriam.

During the wilderness wanderings the Kohathites camped on the south or left side of the tent of meeting and guarded the sanctuary complex from the south. Their duties show them to be the most important of the levitical families. They were responsible for carrying the ark, table, lampstand, altars, sanctuary vessels, and screen, everything required for the service — but only after Aaron and his sons had wrapped them in cloth and placed them in leather bags. They were not permitted to touch the objects themselves (Num. 3:27-31; 4:1-20; 7:9).

Like the rest of the Levites, the Kohathites were assigned towns and pasturelands in Canaan. In the area of Ephraim these included the towns of Shechem (a city of refuge), Gezer, Kibzaim, Jokmeam, and Beth-horon. From the area of Dan they included Elteke, Gebbethon, Aijalon, and Gath-rimmon. Out of the half-tribe of Manasseh they were Taanach and Bileam (Josh. 21:20-26; 1 Chr. 6:66-70[MT 51-55]).

During the Second Temple period a branch of the Kohathites, the Korahites, were the gatekeepers, guardians of the thresholds and of the treasuries, in charge of the guarding, inventory, and upkeep of the utensils, furniture, and foodstuffs of the service (1 Chr. 9:17-33). The Kohathites were also secular officers and judges throughout the land, and probably in charge of legal decision-making, conscription, corvée labor, and taxes for the secular and cultic affairs of the temple (1 Chr. 26:22-30). During the time of the Chronicler the temple singers claimed descent from Levi, with the singer Heman claiming descent through the line of Kohath (1 Chr. 6:33-38[18-23]). At this time the Kohathites were known for their fervor in singing and praising God (2 Chr. 20:19) and for being devoted to the care, upkeep, and sanctification of the temple (29:12ff.; 34:12).

Bibliography. R. G. Boling and G. E. Wright, *Joshua.* AB 6 (Garden City, 1982); S. Japhet, *I and II Chronicles.* OTL (Louisville, 1993); B. A. Levine, *Numbers 1–20.* AB 4 (New York, 1993).

Lisbeth S. Fried

KOHELETH

See Qoheleth.

KOINE

See Greek.

KOLAIAH (Heb. *qôlāyâ*)

1. A Benjaminite; an ancestor of Sallu (Neh. 11:7).

2. The father of the false prophet Ahab, an opponent of Jeremiah (Jer. 29:21).

KORAH (Heb. *qōraḥ*)

1. A member of an Edomite clan, either a son (Gen. 36:14) or grandson (v. 16) of Esau, listed as one of the chiefs of Teman.

2. The eldest son of Izhar (Exod. 6:21-24; 1 Chr. 6:38[MT 23]), a descendant of Levi, of the Kohath division of levitical priests (1 Chr. 6:22[7] calls him the son of Amminadab). In the desert period the Korahites were gatekeepers of the tent of meeting (1 Chr. 9:19), which duties they resumed in the postexilic period. They were also a leading guild of temple singers (2 Chr. 20:19).

The book of Numbers portrays Korah and his associates as a paradigm of rebellion against Moses and the Aaronic priesthood during the desert journey (Num. 16; 26:9-11). Korah, Dathan, and Abiram, sons of Eliab, and On son of Reuben gather 250 leaders from the congregation to protest the Aaronic privilege of altar sacrifice. They appear before Moses and Aaron to affirm that the entire congregation, not just the Aaronic priests, is holy. Thus, their objection is not only against the division between levitical groups and the Aaronic priesthood, but also against any division with regard to holiness between the congregation and the priesthood. Korah's rebellion represents thus the first lay-clergy conflict in Israel. To remedy the situation, Moses suggests that Yahweh bring resolution to the conflict on the next day. Korah and his rebels are to appear with incense in their censers before the tent of meeting, where Yahweh will show whose incense will be accepted, thus settling the holiness controversy. The next day Korah and his group arrive with censers in hand. Yahweh responds, causing the ground to open up and swallow Korah, Dathan, Abiram and their families, and then sending fire to consume the remaining 250 associates. In the aftermath Yahweh commands that the burned bronze censers of the rebellion be fashioned into a covering for the altar as a warning to all future challenges to the Aaronic hegemony. When the congregation sees what Yahweh has done, they begin to murmur, which causes further problems. Angered, Yahweh sends a plague among them, killing 14,700. Finally, Moses intervenes, summoning Aaron to make atonement for the congregation, which brings to an end a grisly episode. Some have suggested that the story of the Korah rebellion is a retrojection of later priestly controversies back into the Moses period. Whether or not this is true, the episode warns against any challenge to the Aaronic priesthood.

3. A son of Hebron unrelated to either the levitical or Edomite Korah, listed among the descendants of Judah (1 Chr. 2:43).

4. Descendants of the levitical Korah. The Korahites carried on the work of gatekeepers at the tent of meeting (1 Chr. 26:19), bakers (9:31), and songwriters beginning with David and continuing in temple service during the postexilic period (6:31; 9:19). It is these Korahite singers who appear in the superscriptions of Pss. 42, 44–49, 84–85, 87-88.

Bibliography. G. W. Coats, *Rebellion in the Wilderness* (Nashville, 1968); A. Cody, *A History of Old Testament Priesthood.* AnBib 35 (Rome, 1969).

JEFF H. MCCRORY, JR.

KORE (Heb. *qōrē'*, *qôrē'*)

1. A Levite of the line of Korah; ancestor of the temple gatekeepers Shallum (1 Chr. 9:19) and Meshelemiah (26:1).

2. A Levite; the son of Imnah (2 Chr. 31:14). He was appointed by Hezekiah as keeper of the east gate of the temple (the king's gate) and was in charge of apportioning the freewill offerings.

KOZ (Heb. *qôṣ*)

A Judahite; the father of Anub and Zobebah (1 Chr. 4:8).

KUE (Heb. *qōweh, qōwē'*)

A neo-Hittite kingdom in southeastern Turkey during the first half of the 1st millennium B.C., bordered by the Taurus Mountains on the north, the Amanus Mountains in the east, and the Mediterranean on the south. The area was inhabited by Luwians and Hurrians. Solomon procured horses from Kue (1 Kgs. 10:28 = 2 Chr. 1:16). It was known as Kizzuwatna in the Hittite period (1650-1200) and Cilicia in the Greco-Roman period.

H. WAYNE HOUSE

KUSHAIAH (Heb. *qûšāyāhû*) (also KISHI)

A Levite; a descendant of Merari who ministered in song before the tabernacle at the time of King David (1 Chr. 15:17). He was the father of Ethan. At 1 Chr. 6:44(MT 29) he is called Kishi.

KYRIE ELEISON (Gk. *Kýrie eléēson*)

A prayer for divine mercy (Gk. "Lord have mercy"), often spoken or sung responsively, attested from earliest times in the liturgy of the Church (e.g., Apost. Const. 8.6). It is reminiscent of the plea uttered by the Canaanite woman in Matt. 15:22 and the blind men in 20:30-33 (cf. Dan. 9:19).

L

L

1. A designation for material found only in the Gospel of Luke that cannot be accounted for by Luke's probable dependence on Mark or on Q, the non-Markan common source of Matthew and Luke.

2. The symbol designating Codex Leningradensis B 19ă, which provides the basic text for modern editions of the Hebrew OT. The L manuscript was completed at Cairo in 1008 C.E. and was supposedly copied from exemplars of Aaron ben Moses ben Asher.

LAADAH (Heb. *la'dâ*)
A Judahite of the lineage of Shelah, progenitor of the inhabitants of Mereshah (1 Chr. 4:21; cf. Josh. 15:44).

LABAN (Heb. *lāḇān*) **(PERSON)**
An inhabitant of the city of Nahor, in the area of Haran. Haran and the surrounding region belonged to the district called Paddan-aram; thus, Laban is called "the Aramean" (Gen. 25:20; 28:5; 31:20, 24). First introduced as the brother of Rebekah (Gen. 24:29), Laban was also the grandson of Nahor (son of Bethuel and nephew of Abraham) and father of Leah and Rachel.

Laban plays a prominent role in the Gen. 24 account. It is he who offers hospitality to Abraham's servant; however, the text implies that Laban's actions were motivated by self-interest and greed. It is also Laban who decides to allow Rebekah to depart to Canaan to be Isaac's wife. Numerous ancient Near Eastern texts illustrate that in a patriarchal society the brother had important duties and powers regarding his sisters.

Laban again appears in association with Jacob. Fleeing from Esau, Jacob goes to his uncle Laban's house in Haran. After receiving Jacob into the family, Laban agrees to give his daughter Rachel to Jacob in return for seven years of service. When the time comes for Jacob to receive his bride, Laban deceitfully gives Leah in place of Rachel. Only after Jacob has agreed to an additional seven years of service is Rachel given to him to be his wife (Gen. 29:28-30).

After Jacob and his family have quietly left Haran, Laban pursues them, catching up with them in the hill country of Gilead (Gen. 31). After mutual protestations and incriminations, Laban and Jacob enter into a covenant and erect a stone structure, a kind of dividing line. Laban gives the heap an Aramaic name *(Yĕgar-śahădûṯā')*, while Jacob calls it by its Hebrew equivalent, *Gal'ēḏ* (Gen. 31:47), both meaning "heap of witness." This covenant probably represents at its earliest level an agreement between the Israelites and the Arameans concerning the borderland separating them.

Bibliography. C. Mabee, "Jacob and Laban: The Structure of Judicial Proceedings (Gen. 31:25-42)," *VT* 30 (1980): 192-207. JOHN L. HARRIS

LABAN (Heb. *lāḇān*) **(PLACE)**
A place associated with the Exodus wanderings (Deut. 1:1). Although listed with other sites which are most likely located in the Sinai, its precise location is unknown. Some scholars identify it with Libnah, which appears in Num. 33:20-21 with some of the places cited in Deut. 1:1 as well as others probably in Sinai.

Bibliography. I. Beit-Arieh, "The Route Through Sinai — Why the Israelites Fleeing Egypt Went South," *BARev* 14/3 (1988): 28-37; J. H. Tigay, "Excursus 1: The Historical Geography of Deuteronomy," in *Deuteronomy.* JPS Torah Commentary (Philadelphia, 1996), 417-22. DAVID M. VALETA

LABOR, WORK, TOIL
Human activity in the form of work, toil, and labor is expressed in a variety of ways in Scripture reflecting its economic, moral, and spiritual significance.

The term "work" covers a wide range of meaning which includes both constructive activity and that which is made. This is reflected (e.g., Ps. 145) in the nature of God, whose work is sound both in its creative power (vv. 4, 17) and in its outcome (v. 10). The Creation stories in Gen. 1–2:3; 2:4b-25 reflect two different aspects of the divine work. In Gen. 1–2:3 the sovereign grandeur of God is celebrated, whose voice commands and all is ordered by the wisdom of his measured rule. In Gen. 2:4b-25 the work of creation is more of an experiment, at times proactive (v. 7) and at times reactive (v. 18). In this story the verb "to form" (Gen. 2:7-8, 19) echoes the craftsmanship of the potter (cf. Jer. 18:1-11; Isa. 64:8). Indeed, a wide range of trades and crafts continues to shape the imagery of God's work in Scripture — e.g., refining, threshing, building, forestry, irrigation, and bleaching.

In the story of the Fall (Gen. 3:1-24) it is significant that mankind's punishment is described not as work but as toil (v. 17). Work can also lead to a temptation to pride (Gen. 11:1-9; contrast Ps. 127:1); consequently a customary prayer for blessing accompanied work (Ps. 129:8; Ruth 2:4; cf. Judg. 6:12). The creative purpose of work is commended in the Wisdom Literature (Prov. 10:4; 18:9) for both men and women (31:10-31), and bestows freedom (12:24; 22:29). However, a more pessimistic note can be sounded about the enduring nature of human endeavor (Eccl. 2:18-20; 5:13-20; cf. 2:24). This led eventually to the valuing of the study of Torah as an activity which was preferable to manual labor (Sir. 38:24-34; cf. Acts 6:2-4; the former passage presents a fine portrait of commercial activity in the ancient world; cf. Rev. 18:11-19).

Although Jesus and the disciples left their employment for the mission of the kingdom, Jesus draws upon imagery of work in his teaching (Luke 9:62). In the parables the way of God may echo patronage in working life (Mark 12:1-9; Luke 17:7-10) or it may cut across conventions (Matt. 20:1-15). Paul, however, chose to work "with his own hands" (1 Cor. 4:12; cf Acts 18:3; 20:34), even though he could claim support (1 Cor. 9:4, 14) and received it (2 Cor. 11:8). Such a practice enabled him to avoid burdening others (1 Cor. 9:18; 2 Cor. 11:9; 12:13). It also served as an exhortation to self-reliance (1 Thess. 2:9-12; 2 Thess. 3:7-13), not only for the good of the congregation but as a witness to wider society (1 Thess. 4:12).

A positive view of work is reflected especially in the Letter of James, which values faith both as practical action (Jas. 2:18-26) and as a safeguard against acquisitiveness (4:13–5:6; cf. Matt. 6:25-33). Generally speaking, mankind cannot rely on work to be justified before God (Rom. 3:20), but work is the expression of faith and a means of service (1 John 3:17-18; Matt. 25:31-46; Rev. 14:13; cf. 20:12). In the Fourth Gospel especially, work expresses the unique activity of God through Jesus (John 5:17). Jesus' miracles are his works (John 10:25; 14:11). The work of God in Jesus represents supremely the expression of the divine glory reflected in our human nature (Gen. 1:26). Thereby for John, as indeed for Scripture as a whole, the creative and redemptive understandings of work are inseparable, as are the economic and spiritual aspects of all human activity.

Bibliography. G. Agrell, *Work, Toil, and Sustenance* (Stockholm, 1976); R. J. Banks, *God the Worker* (Valley Forge, 1994). James Francis

LACEDAEMONIANS (Gk. *Lakedaimonioi*)
Inhabitants of Lacedaemon (later called Sparta), the capital of Laconia, among whom the high priest Jason sought refuge (2 Macc. 5:9).

LACHISH (Heb. *lāḵîš*)
An ancient Canaanite and biblical city located on the Naḥal Lachish/Wadi Ghafr 24 km. (15 mi.) W of Hebron. Tel Lachish/Tell ed-Duweir (1357.1083), identified as ancient Lachish, is a large mound of some 12.5 ha. (31 a.) overlooking a road from the coastal plain into the Hebron hills.

Old Testament

Lachish as Canaanite and Judahite city appears 22 times in the Bible. In antiquity Lachish was in the vicinity of Libnah, Gezer, and Eglon (Josh. 10:31, 34). Its Canaanite king Japhia entered into a military alliance with the kings of four other cities — Adoni-zedek of Jerusalem, Hoham of Hebron, Piram of Jarmuth, and Debir of Eglon (Josh. 10:3, 5) — against the Joshua-led forces of Israel. In an attempt to force the inhabitants into that military alliance, the combined forces lay siege to the town of Gibeon. Joshua routed the sieging army in response to the covenant with Gibeon. The five kings (including Japhia) escaped, but were later captured in a cave at Makkedah, and subsequently executed (Josh. 10:22-27). The two-day siege of Lachish, one of the "fortified" towns of the coalition (Josh. 10:20), by Israelite forces is specifically mentioned (v. 32). Gezer sent soldiers to relieve Lachish, but to no avail, as Joshua went on to take several sites in the south of Canaan (Josh. 10:33-39; 12:11). Lachish appears again in the list of the inheritance of the tribe of Judah (Josh. 15:39).

2 Chr. 11:9 includes Lachish in the list of cities fortified by Rehoboam of Judah, the site to which King Amaziah later fled, presumably because of its strong defenses, and was assassinated (2 Kgs. 14:19 = 2 Chr. 25:27). The Assyrian army sieged Lachish in the reign of Hezekiah (2 Kgs. 18:14, 17 = 2 Chr. 32:9; cf. 2 Kgs. 19:8), eventually taking and destroying it (Isa. 36:2; 37:8; cf. Mic. 1:13). Lachish's impending destruction in the reign of Zedekiah was reported by the prophet Jeremiah (Jer. 34:7). Finally, Lachish was listed as a village reoccupied in postexilic times (Neh. 11:30).

Other Sources

Lachish is named in extrabiblical sources as early as the 15th-century B.C.E. Papyrus Hermitage 1116A, which names it among the Canaanite cities in which Egyptian emissaries resided; Lachish likewise appears in the Amarna Letters, as well as in a letter of the same period found at Tell el-Ḥesi. Nebuchadnezzar commemorated the conquest of Lachish, naming and depicting the town on a stone relief. Eusebius refers to Lachish as located 11 km. (7 mi.) from Eleutheropolis (Beth Guvrin).

Assyrian soldiers carrying booty and escorting prisoners from the captured city of Lachish. Detail of relief from southwest palace of Sennacherib at Nineveh (704-681 B.C.E.); British Museum (Erich Lessing/Art Resource, N.Y.)

Tel Lachish/Tell ed-Duweir

Excavation of Tel Lachish/Tell ed-Duweir began in 1932-38 by John L. Starkey and was followed by Yohanan Aharoni (1966, 1968) and David Ussishkin (1972-1992). Human occupation at the site probably began as early as the Neolithic period and continued in the Chalcolithic and Early Bronze Ages; however, evidence about these settlements is sparse, though it appears likely that the entire mound had been occupied during Early Bronze II. From the EB IV period a cemetery of 120 rock-cut tombs and a small village were excavated on a low hill west of the main mound.

Lachish became an important city-state in Middle Bronze II and was fortified in depth; though no trace of the perimeter wall has been unearthed, its existence is attested by the presence of a plastered ramp or glacis and a deep ditch or fosse at the base of the mound. A well-built "palace" in the center of the site, as well as richly appointed rock-cut tombs outside the city attest to the prominence of Lachish in the region. The final level of the MB settlement was destroyed in a fire.

Not until Late Bronze II, designated Level VII, did Lachish regain the prominence as a city-state it had enjoyed in MB II. Strong ties with Egypt attest to this prominence. However, like most LB Canaanite towns, Lachish was apparently nonfortified; indeed, the fosse belonging to the MB defense was now the site of a temple which had at least three major phases of use.

Level VI, the final LB town on the tell, was built along different architectural lines, though it showed clear cultural affinities with Level VII. A large public building took the place of Level VII domestic units, and a temple was built on the summit of the mound in place of the Level VII fosse temple. Along with a group of artifacts of Egyptian origin (a cartouche of Rameses III on a bronze object and fragments of bowls with hieratic script recording taxes paid to an Egyptian religious institution), the plan of this new temple, which imitates Egyptian temples at Amarna and Deir el-Medeineh, suggests strong ties with the government of Rameses III.

Level VI LB Lachish was completely destroyed and subsequently abandoned until the 10th century. Though the destruction of this last Canaanite town would appear to fit the description of the conquest of Lachish in Josh. 10:20, the identity of the conqueror cannot be easily resolved, because of problems in correspondence of the date of the fall of Lachish with the time of Joshua. It is equally likely that Lachish Level VI met its end at the hands of the Sea Peoples. In either case, the fall of Lachish exposes Egypt's loss of control of Canaan.

The earliest Israelite settlement on Tel Lachish/Tell ed-Duweir is Level V, a nonfortified town usually assigned to the period of the United Monarchy. Besides small domestic buildings at various points on the tell, Aharoni uncovered a building dedicated to cultic activity in the vicinity of the so-called solar shrine of Level I. Recovered from this cult room were ceramic incense stands, chalices, and a stone altar. The destruction of Level V may have been by the Egyptian Sheshonq ca. 925.

Level IV Lachish, a large royal town, was heavily fortified, probably in response to changed military and political conditions. 2 Chr. 11:9 attributes the fortification of Lachish to Rehoboam, though archaeological evidence suggests a slightly later date for the founding of Level IV (Ussishkin suggests either Asa or Jehoshaphat). The massive fortification was formed with a six-chamber gateway, an outer gate which projected beyond the city wall at the crest of the tell, a second line of defense partway down the slope of the tell, and a glacis that extended between the two city walls; the new town now included a residency for the Judahite governor, a large palace-fort built atop a raised platform or podium, other government buildings, and a deep well. Few domestic structures have been uncovered within the walls of the Level IV fortress.

Parts of the Level IV town were destroyed, possibly by an earthquake, requiring major reconstruction of the city gate, part of the palace-fort (designated Palace B by the excavators, here enlarged also in Level III), a "residency" and the "enclosure wall," though not the city perimeter wall itself. This rebuilt fortress also increased in population, as shown by the additional number of domestic structures. In spite of its deep defensive system, however, an Assyrian army attacked and destroyed Lachish in 701. The siege of the town involved the construction of a massive ramp of boulders and soil which reached from the valley floor to the top of the southwest corner of the town wall, in order to permit siege weapons to breach defenses. The defenders responded with a "counter ramp" inside the perimeter wall to raise the level of defense higher than the siege. A second siege ramp atop the first sealed the fate of the defenders, who were killed or deported. Both siege ramp and "counter ramp" have been identified by the excavations of Ussishkin. The Assyrian battle for Lachish was later commemorated in relief on stone panels in the Assyrian palace in Nineveh.

Lachish was rebuilt (Level II) as a fortified town in the 7th century, probably during the reign of Josiah. This town was smaller and less well defended than the Level III city. It too suffered total destruction, in 587/586, by the forces of Nebuchadnezzar of Babylon. Correspondence by military personnel was found in the ruins of Level II; these "Lachish Letters" were probably sent to the commander of Lachish by a subordinate whose nearby location required regular reports.

Following a period of abandonment Lachish again saw occupation at the beginning of the Persian period as an administrative center. Construction on the mound included restoration of the fortifications, a small residency or palace, and a temple (called the solar shrine because of its entrance facing the rising sun). Level I lasted into the Hellenistic period, by which time the residency had been given over to "squatters." The temple, however, continued in use. The discovery of a cache of some 200 small limestone incense altars, though found outside the mound, probably relates to rituals practiced in the solar shrine. In the Hellenistic period Lachish was finally abandoned as a town or village site.

Bibliography. Y. Aharoni, *Investigations at Lachish: The Sanctuary and the Residency (Lachish V)* (Tel Aviv, 1975); H. Torczyner et al., *Lachish I: The Lachish Letters* (London, 1938); O. Tufnell et al., *Lachish II: The Fosse Temple* (London, 1940); *Lachish III: The Iron Age* (London, 1953); *Lachish IV: The Bronze Age* (London, 1958); D. Ussishkin, *The Conquest of Lachish by Sennacherib* (Tel Aviv, 1982); "Excavations at Tel Lachish — 1973-1977: Preliminary Report," *Tel Aviv* 5 (1978): 1-97; "Levels VII and VI at Tel Lachish and the End of the Bronze Age in Canaan," in *Palestine in the Bronze and Iron Ages*, ed. J. N. Tubb (London, 1985), 213-30.

PAUL F. JACOBS

LADAN (Heb. *laʿdān*)

1. An Ephraimite, and ancestor of Joshua (1 Chr. 7:26).

2. A Levite of the lineage of Gershon (1 Chr. 23:7-8; 26:21). He is apparently the same as Libni (**1**) at Exod. 6:17; Num. 3:18.

LADDER

A graded series of stages or levels. It may be a structure made of wood, metal, or rope with two side pieces and a series of rungs. The ladder symbolically represents upward movement or improvement and was considered a place where humanity and divinity interact, a means of linking heaven and earth (Gen. 28:12). Heb. *sullām*, often translated "ladder," is better rendered "stairway" because the imagery comes from the Babylonian ziggurat, a temple tower that had brick steps leading to a small temple on top. This is the place where angels ascend and descend (cf. John 1:51).

C. GILBERT ROMERO

LADDER OF TYRE

A land feature on the Palestinian coastline near Tyre (Gk. *klímax Týrou*), perhaps the ridge that extends the coastline out to a point ca. halfway between Ptolemais (Acre) and Tyre. Antiochus VI, one of the contestants for the Seleucid throne, appointed Simon Maccabeus governor "from the Ladder of Tyre to the borders of Egypt" (1 Macc. 11:59; ca. 145 B.C.E.), i.e., of the coast of Palestine.

LAEL (Heb. *lāʾēl*)

A Gershonite Levite, father of Eliasaph (Num. 3:24).

LAHAD (Heb. *lahaḏ*)

A Judahite, son of Jahath (1 Chr. 4:2). His clan was reckoned among the families of the Zorathites.

LAHMAM (Heb. *laḥmām*)

A town in the Shephelah, or lowland, of Judah and part of that tribe's inheritance (Josh. 15:40). The MT reads Heb. *laḥmās*, but most other manuscripts read *lahmām*, suggesting scribal error resulting from the very similar Hebrew letters *mem* and *samek*. While the location of the site is uncertain, it is in the same district as Lachish. Khirbet el-Laḥm (140108), 4.5 km. (3 mi.) S of Beit Jibrîn/Beth Guvrin (140113), is a possible candidate.

JENNIFER L. GROVES

LAHMI (Heb. *laḥmî*)

The brother of the giant Goliath the Gittite, killed by Elhanan (**1;** 1 Chr. 20:5). According to 2 Sam. 21:19 Elhanan's victim was Goliath himself. Some scholars regard the account in 1 Chronicles as an editorial attempt to reconcile 2 Sam. 21:19 and 1 Sam. 17:4. An alternate suggestion is that "Lahmi the brother of Goliath" may reflect a scribal error ("Lahmi" with the sign of the direct object, as at 1 Chr. 20:5, is *ʾeṯ-laḥmî;* cf. *bêṯ hallaḥmî*, "the Bethlehemite" at 2 Sam. 21:19).

LAISH (Heb. *layiš*) **(PERSON)**

The father of Palti (1 Sam. 25:44)/Paltiel (2 Sam. 3:15).

LAISH (Heb. *layiš*) **(PLACE)** (also LESHEM)

A Canaanite city in northern Palestine, captured by the Danites and renamed Dan (Judg. 18:7, 27, 29). At Josh. 19:47 it is called Leshem. The site has been identified as Tel Dan/Tell el-Qâḍi (2112.2949), 17 km. (10.5 mi.) N of the ancient Lake Huleh at the source of Nahr el-Leddan.

LAISHAH (Heb. *layšâ*)

A village likely in the territory of the tribe of Benjamin (Isa. 10:30). It is listed with other

Benjaminite cities N of Jerusalem in a vision of the prophet Isaiah (Isa. 10:28-32). This vision refers to the destruction of cities by an invasion from the north (probably the Assyrians under Sargon II or Sennacherib, at the end of the 8th century B.C.E.). Laishah is possibly to be identified with modern el-ʿIsāwiyeh (174134) or with Rās et-Tawīl (173138), located NE of Jerusalem. JOHN R. SPENCER

LAKKUM (Heb. *laqqûm*)
A border city in the tribal territory of Naphtali (Josh. 19:33). The site is generally identified as modern Khirbet el-Manṣûrah (202233), SW of the point where the Jordan River flows out of the Sea of Galilee.

LAMB
A sheep less than one year old (Lev. 17:3-4; 1 Sam. 17:34; Isa. 11:6; 65:25). In the OT lambs (Heb. *keḇeś*) are usually mentioned in relation to the sacrificial system. One lamb was to be offered in the morning and one in the evening, continually (Exod. 29:38-42; Num. 28:4). A lamb might also be offered as a freewill offering (Lev. 22:23), a burnt offering (Gen. 22:7-8), a peace offering (Lev. 3:1-7), an atonement for sin (Lev. 5:6; Num. 6:12, 14), and annually at Passover to commemorate the deliverance from Egyptian slavery (Exod. 12:3, 5, 21). At times, however, the distinction between burnt, peace, and sin offerings seems to be blurred (Ezek. 45:15). Sacrificing a lamb was also a part of the cleansing ritual for a leper who had been healed (Lev. 14:1-10, 24-25), and a firstborn donkey could be redeemed by a lamb (Exod. 13:13).

The sacrifice of a lamb was a common enough event to be used metaphorically for the suffering or death of an innocent on behalf of others (2 Sam. 12:1-6; the "suffering servant," Isa. 53:7). Jeremiah spoke of himself as a lamb brought to the slaughter (Jer. 11:10), and Hosea spoke of Yahweh as feeding backsliding Israel like a lamb (Hos. 4:16).

In the NT the word appears in only two passages outside the book of Revelation. Acts 8:32-33 quotes the "suffering servant" passage, and 1 Pet. 1:19 uses a lamb as a metaphor for Christ's sacrifice. John's usage in Revelation is similar. Here the lamb (Gk. *arníon*) is the crucified, resurrected, exalted, victorious Christ (e.g., Rev. 5:6, 8, 12-13; 6:1, 16).
JOE E. LUNCEFORD

LAMECH (Heb. *lemeḵ;* Gk. *Lámech*)
A name occurring in two genealogies in Genesis. In the Yahwist or J genealogy of the line of Cain (Gen. 4:17-24), Lamech is the son of Methushael and claims the pride of place associated with the seventh generation from Adam. The significance of this position is underscored by the fact that a linear genealogy (a single line of named descendants, Gen. 4:17-18) becomes "segmented" when it names Lamech's three sons and his daughter (vv. 20-22; cf. 5:32; 11:26). As the father of the first breeders of livestock (Jabal), the first musicians (Jubal), and the first metalworkers (Tubal-cain), Lamech is presented as a progenitor of cultural development and diversification. Thus, this list has been compared to the Mesopotamian tradition of seven preflood "sages" who originated arts and skills of culture. Of particular interest is the "song of Lamech" (Gen. 4:23-24), addressed to his two wives, Adah and Zillah. It glorifies excessive vengeance: for a wound, Lamech would kill; and he threatens 77-fold vengeance (contrast the lex talionis [Lev. 24:19-20] and the injunction of Jesus [Matt. 18:22]).

In the P genealogy of the line of Seth (Gen. 5:3-31), Lamech is the son of Methuselah and the father of Noah. As in the line of Cain, Lamech again is the only individual to speak; but this time instead of words of wrath, he speaks of hoped-for "relief" through Noah. Here Lamech is ninth in a list of 10 that concludes with Noah. A similar pattern of 10 generations ending with the hero of the Flood is attested in some editions of the Sumerian King List.

Bibliography. J. M. Sasson, "A Genealogical 'Convention' in Biblical Chronology?" *ZAW* 90 (1978): 171-85; R. R. Wilson, *Genealogy and History in the Biblical World* (New Haven, 1977).
JEFFREY S. ROGERS

LAMENESS, LIMP
In ancient Israel, which treasured notions of a complete and ordered world, and which valued wholeness, physical defects were regarded as shameful (Lev. 21:18; Deut. 15:21; Mal. 1:8; cf. 2 Sam. 5:6-8). Lame (Heb. *pissēaḥ*) or limping people were regarded as helpless and useless (Prov. 26:7). They were forbidden entry into holy spaces (Lev. 21:18), and in both the OT and NT were objects of pity and charity (2 Sam. 4:4; 19:26[MT 27]; Job 29:15; Acts 3:2; 8:7; 14:8).

In this light, Jesus' comment to his disciples that they should be prepared to enter the kingdom lame, rather than whole, was a radical statement (Luke 14:13, 21). By declaring the lame fit for the kingdom of heaven, he reverses current attitudes on wholeness and salvation.

In an unusual story, the prophets of Baal "limp *(pāsaḥ)* about [upon?] the altar that they had made" (1 Kgs. 18:26). This may be a reference to a cultic dance, but it also may be a rhetorical device to indicate the ineffectiveness of the prophets' activities.

Bibliography. J. H. Neyrey, "Wholeness," in *Biblical Social Values and Their Meaning,* ed. J. J. Pilch and B. J. Malina (Peabody, 1993), 180-84; Pilch, "Biblical Leprosy and Body Symbolism," *BTB* 11 (1981): 108-13. T. R. HOBBS

LAMENT
One of the oldest and best-attested literary genres in the ancient Near East. The OT contains at least four different kinds or subgenres of the lament: funeral dirge, city lament, individual lament, and communal lament.

The funeral dirge, common in many traditional societies like those of the ancient Near East, was sung by surviving family members or close friends as part of the ceremony for the deceased. These dirges are typically characterized by short ejaculatory phrases of the kind, "Oh, my son!"

narrative passages which contrast the gloriously depicted past of the deceased with the mournful present, and, when relevant, imprecations directed at those responsible for the death of the deceased. The OT contains only two genuine funeral dirges, 2 Sam. 3:33-34; Jer. 38:22. However, there are several literary transformations of the funeral dirge (e.g., 2 Sam. 1:19-27), and several of the dirge's more common motifs have been taken up in the city lament.

The city lament owes its original inspiration to the funeral dirge, as it mourns the destruction of a city as if the city were a deceased person. Knowledge of city laments dates back to the end of the 3rd millennium B.C.E. in ancient Mesopotamia. These laments describe the destruction of particular cities and their important shrines. The cause of the destruction is attributed to the capricious decision of the divine assembly headed by its chief god Enlil. The laments typically narrate the abandonment of the cities and shrines by their chief gods and goddesses and the onslaught of Enlil's storm — a metaphor for the military attack of the enemy. The weeping goddess, portrayed lamenting the destruction of her city, figures prominently in these poems as well. The book of Lamentations shares a large number of genre features with these Mesopotamian laments, suggesting that the poet knew of this genre and drew heavily upon it for the composition of his own Israelite city lament. The city lament as a modulating form likely occurs elsewhere in the OT as well (e.g., Ps. 137; Isa. 15:1–16:14; 47:1-15; Jer. 48:1-47; Amos 5:1-3, 16-20; Mic. 1:2-16).

The individual lament so well known from the Hebrew Psalter has precursors in similar compositions from Mesopotamia, such as the Sumerian letter prayers and the *šu-illa* prayers. The following elements are frequently found in the individual laments in the Psalms (e.g., Pss. 3, 6, 13, 22, 28, 31, 51, 88, 102): address to Yahweh, complaint describing the situation (often employing the language of sickness metaphorically), request for help, affirmation of confidence, assertion of innocence or confession of sin, and hymnic elements.

Topically, the communal laments may be divided into two groups: those which lament the destruction of the city and temple (e.g., Pss. 44, 60, 74, 79, 80, 137) and those whose focus is on other kinds of community crises (e.g., 42-43, 58, 83, 106, 125). These laments appear to have been used on fast days or in times of grave danger. The main features of the communal lament closely resemble those of the individual lament: address to Yahweh, hymnic praise, description of devastation, complaint, and plea for help.

F. W. Dobbs-Allsopp

LAMENTATIONS, BOOK OF

A sequence of five poems composed some time after the destruction of Jerusalem in 587/586 B.C.E., perhaps for ceremonies commemorating this event. In all likelihood the poems were composed in Palestine, and while the author or authors are unknown, there is no strong reason to suppose that more than one person was responsible for these poems.

Genre

The sequence as a whole exhibits a strong dependence on the city lament, a literary genre best known from ancient Mesopotamia. City laments were originally composed for cultic ceremonies during the razing of old sanctuaries just prior to their restoration. These laments describe the destruction of the city in question and its chief shrines, featuring depictions of the gods' abandonment of and eventual return to the city, the onslaught of the enemy attack, and the laments uttered by the city's chief goddess. Lamentations shares with the various Mesopotamian city laments a common subject matter, certain structural affinities, principal character roles, themes, motifs, and even occasional phrasal parallels. That Lamentations is drawing on the same literary genre as these Mesopotamian compositions seems undeniable. Yet it is equally clear that Lamentations is no mere crib of any one particular Mesopotamian city lament. The language, imagery, poetic forms and techniques, theology, and general worldview are thoroughly Israelite in nature. Moreover, city lament imagery can be found throughout the prophetic literature, dating back at least to the 8th century, suggesting that the city lament genre was in fact known in Israel for at least 200 years. The poet has taken this genre and manipulated it to serve his own purposes. The most obvious difference between Lamentations and the Mesopotamian laments lies in Lamentations' tragic trajectory. Unlike the Mesopotamian city laments, which are ultimately comic in orientation (i.e., the gods do return, the temple is rebuilt, and everyday routines are resumed), Lamentations is basically tragic in orientation. Yahweh is never heard from, and at the sequence's end the reader is not led to believe that Yahweh's return or the rebuilding of the temple will happen any time in the near future. Rather, the sequence closes with bitter statements underscoring Yahweh's continued abandonment.

Lyric and Lyric Structure

Like the Psalms and the Song of Songs, Lamentations is made up of lyrical discourse, and as such it shows no interest in reporting or narrating the events of 587/586 which form its subject matter. Rather, it seeks to explore the complex cluster of emotions — sorrow, anger, guilt, hope, despair, fear, self-loathing, revenge, compassion, forgiveness, uncertainty, disorientation — which these events have evoked in the poet and to subject them to scrutiny, deliberation, and argumentation. Lamentations as lyrical discourse does not foreground story, plot, character development, or attention to setting. Instead it depends almost solely on language and the manipulation of language as its medium of discourse. Image, perspective, and formal patterning are paramount. Parataxis is the norm. Images are piled upon and superimposed over other images in a way not dissimilar to a film montage. The poetry moves from one emotional high point to the next. Conflicting emotions can be held simultaneously and allowed to color each other. For example, in 1:18 Zion's confession ("Yahweh is in the right, for I have rebelled against his word") is immediately juxtaposed to a call for the peoples to inspect Zion's wounds, namely that her young men and women have been forced into captivity. These images evoke conflicting responses which then permeate and modulate one another. Zion's confession is softened in light of the resulting suffering and exile, and this exile is justified (at least to a point) by Zion's rebellion. This is the essence of lyric. It does not so much seek to resolve a problem or come cleanly to one final conclusion as to achieve the keenest, most genuine realization of its subject matter. Lamentations as a whole surveys, articulates, and probes the variegated tapestry of emotions provoked by the destruction of Jerusalem.

Each of the poems in Lamentations manifests its own unique lyric integrity. At the same time, they interact as a whole, modulating each other in ways analogous to the play of individual themes or images in a single lyric. Common themes, motifs, vocabulary, voices, and imagery are typically shared among varying subgroups of two or three poems. But cohesion is built into the sequence primarily through formal patterns of repetition, the most notable of which involve the alphabetic acrostic, qinah meter, and enjambed nonparallelistic lines. Each of these dominates in various ways the first four poems in Lamentations. In the concluding poem these dominant patterns are radically reduced. The alphabetic acrostic is no longer used to structure the poem (except perhaps in the number of lines, 22), and most of the individual couplets are predominantly balanced and parallelistic. This dramatic change effectively provides the sequence with a strong sense of closure. This formal closure contrasts dramatically with the thematic openness that is otherwise experienced at the sequence's end.

Contents

The first two poems are dominated by the personification of the city-temple complex, personified Zion. Lam. 1 opens with a series of 3rd person vignettes depicting Zion after the city's destruction (1:1-11). Anthropomorphisms predominate. Zion is depicted as widow, princess, and slave (1:1, 3), rejected friend or lover (v. 2), possible rape victim (v. 10), and mother (v. 5). She weeps (v. 2), remembers (v. 7), sins, and groans (v. 8). In the second half of the poem (1:12-22) the perspective shifts to that of Zion herself. Much of the same ground gone over in the first part of the poem is retraced once again, but this time from Zion's own perspective. This first poem views the destruction of Jerusalem through the person of Zion. The reader sees her own personal loss and ill treatment at the hands of the enemy and even Yahweh. The full range of emotions are explored in this initial poem, but special attention is paid to three themes in particular: Zion's own responsibility for the destruction and her resultant guilt, the absence of a comforter, and her desire for vengeance.

Lam. 2 also opens with a series of 3rd person vignettes (2:1-8). However, the perspective has shifted. Zion is still present, but the anthropomorphisms associated with her in the first poem have here receded into the background. Zion as the actual city is very much in the foreground. Moreover, Zion is no longer the topical or grammatical subject of the action. Instead, Yahweh as divine warrior takes center stage. Here the poet makes use of two traditional literary and mythopoetic motifs: the day of Yahweh and the portrayal of Yahweh as the divine warrior. Traditionally, Yahweh as the divine warrior would go into battle on his day on behalf of Israel. Victory of course was assured. Here, following in a long prophetic tradition beginning at least with Amos, the poet turns these two traditions on their heads. Yahweh is indeed portrayed as the divine warrior and he does go into battle on the day of his anger, but this time his actions are focused at Judah instead of pursued in Judah's behalf. Yahweh not only allows the enemy to attack Jerusalem, but he leads the charge and plays the central role in the destruction. Indeed, Yahweh is even depicted as the enemy. This depiction of Yahweh is exploited in at least two ways: it allows the poet to salvage Yahweh's prestige — Yahweh was not defeated by superior Mesopotamian deities, but was himself the author of the defeat. At the same time, there can be no question that Yahweh is personally responsible for the resultant suffering.

Like Lam. 1, there is a shift in perspective in the second half of the poem. A dialogue between the narrator and Zion takes up much of this part of the poem — significantly, we do not hear from Yahweh here or anywhere else in Lamentations. The poet cannot find words to describe the catastrophe and urges Zion herself to petition Yahweh on behalf of her community. But instead, Zion challenges the rightness of Yahweh's actions. She opens her speech in 2:20 with a stinging rhetorical question: "Should women have to eat their own children in order to survive?" The answer is, of course, a resounding no. The implication is that no matter Judah's guilt, nothing can justify the kind of lifestyles the survivors have been forced into as a result of Yahweh's actions.

Lam. 3 shifts perspectives once again. This time the voice is that of a male representative of the community who surveys the canvas of suffering in the vocabulary of the individual and communal laments known from the Psalms. By v. 18 the speaker has hit rock bottom. But at this point the speaker begins to reflect on the wisdom tradition which taught, among other things, that if one endured one's suffering Yahweh would eventually redress the wrongs that were encountered (vv. 25-39). It is this section of Lam. 3 where many scholars have found the only glimmer of hope in the sequence. While the possibility of hope is surely presented by the poet, it ultimately fails to speak to the speaker's experience. His reflection on hope comes to a climax in vv. 40-41 where he invites his fellow citizens to confess and repent. But then in v. 42 the tenor turns sharply to despair, as if the weight of the persistent suffering suddenly comes crashing in again on the speaker. He confesses, "We have transgressed and rebelled, and you have not forgiven." The rebuke of the second line ushers reality back in again. The remainder of the poem is plunged into despair. Whatever hope was temporarily embraced by the poet is clearly swallowed up by suffering.

Lam. 4, like the first two poems in the sequence, opens with 3rd person narrative vignettes. This time the vignettes depict the plight of specific groups representing the community as a whole: children (vv. 1-4), the rich and privileged (vv. 5, 7-8), mothers (v. 10), prophets and priests (vv. 13, 16), elders (v. 16), and even the king (v. 20). The poem closes with imprecations addressed to Edom (vv. 21-22).

Lam. 5 is the only poem which is not constrained by the alphabetic acrostic or the qinah meter. In this stark change in the formal patterns of repetition which otherwise dominate the sequence, the poet effectively announces the sequence's close. The poem draws heavily on the communal lament tradition known from the Psalms. It is significant that sin and guilt are again acknowledged in this communal voice, but nevertheless the community continues to question the rightness of Yahweh's actions: "Why have you abandoned us for so long?" "Surely you have rejected us/your anger has burned against us excessively!" F. W. DOBBS-ALLSOPP

LAMP

Fairly small vessels, much like a small bowl, holding oil into which a wick was placed.

Oil lamps are known well before the 4th millennium B.C.E. when stone bowls containing oil were burned. By the 3rd millennium a round saucer or shallow bowl evolved into a lamp, typically with four slight depressions on its rim (lamps with as many as seven "lips" have been found); these in turn developed into four open spouts, and in the 2nd millennium lamps had only one spout. This simple wheel-made bowl with one spout is what Israel borrowed from her Canaanite neighbors and used throughout the OT period.

Lamps (Heb. *nēr*) were normally made of fired clay or rarely of metal, while the wick was made of an absorbent cord, most often from flax. The wick was usually allowed to project slightly beyond the edge of the spout. The earliest fuel was animal fat, but by OT times olive oil was used widely and castor oil or sesame oil rarely. The first extraction of oil obtained by crushing the olives in a press produced a light, fat-free oil which was edible and most desirable. The best oil was also used for religious purposes (Exod. 27:20). Second and even third extractions produced oil of increasingly fatty content. This lower grade oil was widely used in lamps and was nearly smokeless and odorless. Large lamps could hold enough oil to burn throughout the night, but the wick would eventually burn down and require adjustment. Since there were no matches, some fire or pilot light had to be kept burning in the household. Smaller lamps were in danger of going out during the night (Prov. 31:18), and someone would need to get up during the night to attend to the lamp. In addition to some storage container to hold the oil, a sharp pointed instrument such as a knife or a sliver of wood was used to trim the wick as it burned. Something similar to a tweezers was probably used to extinguish the flame.

Lamps were most often placed in concave niches in the walls of houses, on a table, or in later times hung from the ceiling. If placed on a table there was probably a bowl underneath for stability and for catching any oil that slowly exuded through the clay lamp. To prevent this loss of oil through the clay, the lamp could be soaked in water and then a small layer of water placed at the bottom of the lamp on which the oil floated. Lamps also had a religious use. Up to one half of all vessels buried with the dead were oil lamps. The symbolism here is that lamp/light equals life and darkness equals death (2 Sam. 21:17). Lamps were also used in building dedications. These lamps were new with only slight traces of burning. Perhaps they were lit only at the dedication for a short time.

The lamp as a source of light is used in a number of metaphorical ways. It lights the way (Ps. 119:105), represents wise or divine precepts (Prov. 6:20, 23), and is a life spirit burning within (20:27). Yahweh is the lamp of the psalmist (Ps. 18:29[MT 30]), and David is the lamp of Israel (2 Sam. 21:17). Negatively, the lamp of the wicked will be put out (Prov. 13:9; Job 18:5-6), and haughty eyes and a proud heart — the lamp of the wicked — are sin (Prov. 21:4). The sanctuary lamp in the tabernacle is called *mā'ôr* (Exod. 25:6; 27:20; 35:28), the same term used for the sun and moon in Gen. 1:14-16.

In NT times lamps were generally smaller, often closed vessels, and featured geometric decorations. They probably burned for only four to five hours if lighted at dusk and so would go out around midnight (Matt. 25:1-12). Both John the Baptist (John 5:35) and Jesus (Rev. 21:23) were equated to lamps. Sound teaching was compared to a burning lamp (2 Pet. 1:19). To keep the lamps burning implies being ready for service (Luke 12:35).

Bibliography. R. H. Smith, "The Household Lamps of Palestine in Old Testament Times," *BA* 27 (1964): 2-31; "The Household Lamps of Palestine in Intertestamental Times," *BA* 27 (1964): 101-24; "The Household Lamps of Palestine in New Testament Times," *BA* 29 (1966): 2-27.

JAMES C. MOYER/MICHAEL D. GUINAN, O.F.M.

LAMPSTAND

A pedestal for oil-filled wick lamps, or a stand incorporating one or more such lamps into its structure.

Although lamps might be put on a shelf or niche, they were frequently set on a separate lampstand (Heb. *mĕnôrâ;* 2 Kgs. 4:10; Gk. *lychnía;* Matt. 5:15). Some lampstands were single-stemmed and held only one lamp, while others featured several branches on the pedestal.

As with the lamp, most biblical references are to lampstands intended for cultic usage: a golden, seven-branched lampstand, cylindrical in form, used in the wilderness tabernacle (Exod. 25:31-40; 37:17-24); 10 golden lampstands in Solomon's temple (1 Kgs. 7:49); the golden lampstand (perhaps two?) of the postexilic second temple, featuring a bowl with seven seven-lipped lamps (cf. Zech. 4:1-6, 11-14). The apocalyptic visions of Rev. 1:12-13, 20; 2:1 depict seven single lampstands.

The seven-branched temple lampstand from the Roman period appears in the earliest artistic depictions (cf. the arch of Titus in Rome) and forms the basis, in the Jewish tradition, for its later renderings. MICHAEL D. GUINAN, O.F.M.

LAND

The prominence of land in biblical thought has been underestimated in much 20th-century scholarship because of its strong emphasis on the historical character of biblical religion. According to this emphasis, biblical religion is about human redemption, and its God is revealed and recognized in mighty acts within the historical experiences of God's people. The natural world and the biblical landscape are consequently reduced to the stage upon which this divine-human drama takes place, or they are identified as the arena in which the pagan deities of Israel's neighbors are active. Thus land, together with the sphere of nature of which it is a part, has been considered at best a marginal domain in biblical thought and at worst a pagan realm from which Israel's historical religion dissociated itself.

Such an understanding of biblical religion has been challenged from several quarters, including those who consider the historical lens in and of itself too narrow for viewing the richness of biblical experience. Modern developments have also contributed to a new interest in the biblical landscape. Among these are the creation of the modern State of Israel and the tensions between Israelis and Palestinians concerning historical and religious claims to the lands of the Bible; new struggles worldwide over claims and rights to land between indigenous peoples and immigrants, often Christian colonists; and a new concern for the natural world and the human relationship to it arising from the environmental crisis. Partly because of such current developments, and partly because of the inadequacy of the historical reading of the Bible itself, land has been rediscovered as a crucial and indispensable player in the biblical drama. The significance of land in the Bible may be summarized under three of its key roles.

Agriculture

Arable land lay at the heart of the biblical landscape. It was the basis of Israel's physical survival as a people and of its agrarian way of life. Israel's economy throughout the biblical period was agricultural, combining the cultivation of grains and fruits with the herding of sheep and goats on small family farms. So central was this agricultural way of life to Israel's self-understanding that according to one of its creation accounts, the Eden narrative in Gen. 2:4b–3:24, the first human was made from arable soil (Heb. *ʾăḏāmâ,* 2:7) and given the task of cultivating it (2:15; 3:23). Thus working the land, the very occupation in which most Israelites were engaged, was viewed as the archetypal vocation for which humanity was created.

Agricultural land was customarily owned and farmed by multiple family households, which themselves were social adaptations to the land and labor demands of hill-country farming. Land was regarded as an ancestral inheritance (*naḥălâ,* 1 Kgs. 21:3) remaining permanently in the family. Should sale be necessary, the nearest relative had the first option to buy (Jer. 32:6-15). The strength of the connection between a family and its ancestral lands is illustrated by Naboth's refusal under great pressure to sell his ancestral vineyard to King Ahab (1 Kgs. 21:1-16). Also illustrated in this episode is the acquisition of land, not always legally, by Israel's powerful and elite, a practice criticized harshly by the prophets (1 Kgs. 21:17-19; Isa. 5:8-10; Mic. 2:1-2). According to one theological perspective, Israel's agricultural land was actually God's land, on which Israelite families were properly regarded as resident aliens and servants (Lev. 25:23).

Just as human identity was grounded in the arable land, its cultivation, and its agricultural produce, so too Israel's view of God was closely associated with this landscape. The fertility of arable soil was regarded ultimately as God's work. God, for whom the thunderstorm was a common medium of revelation (Exod. 19:9, 16; Ps. 18:7-15[MT 8-16]), brought the rain upon which Israel's dry-land farming depended (Gen. 2:5; Deut. 11:10-12). God made the soil fertile (Gen. 8:22; 27:27-28) and could render it sterile (Gen. 3:17-18; 4:11-12). In recognition of God's control over the land's production, Israel celebrated its primary religious festivals at the three harvests of its agricultural year, the harvests of barley and wheat in the spring and the harvest of fruit in the fall (Exod. 34:18-26; Lev. 23:9-22; Deut. 16:1-10). At each Israel offered to God the firstfruits of the harvest. Thus Israel's worship and liturgical calendar were shaped by its agricultural landscape.

Nationhood

Just as land was the basis of Israel's agricultural society, so it was the basis of Israel's existence as an ancient Near Eastern kingdom. Especially prominent in Israel's understanding of its land as its national territory are two beliefs. One is that Israel itself was not indigenous to its land. Its ancestral origins lay elsewhere. Abraham's family migrated to Canaan from Mesopotamia via Syria (Gen. 11:27–12:9), and Abraham's descendents later moved to Canaan from the Nile Delta of Egypt (Exod. 1–15; Josh. 1–12). The other belief is that Israel's God gave the land to Israel, as expressed in the narrative of Abraham's initial migration (Gen. 12:1-9) and in the account of the subsequent entrance of Abraham's descendants into Canaan from Egypt (Deut. 1:6-8).

The permanence of the link between biblical Israel and its land is viewed in various ways. In some texts, the relationship is described as eternal (Gen. 17:8; Deut. 4:40; 2 Sam. 7:10, 16; Amos 9:15). Other texts regard Israel's well-being in the land and its very claims to it as dependent upon its loyalty to its covenant with God and its obedience to God's commands (Deut. 4:25-27; 11:13-17; Jer. 7:1-15; Amos 6:1-8). According to this latter view, the Exile and the experience of landlessness after the fall of Samaria and Jerusalem were understood as the ultimate punishment for Israel's covenant faithlessness (2 Kgs.17:7-23; 21:1-16). Exilic prophets predicted God's new act of salvation primarily in terms of the restoration to the Israelite exiles of their preexilic lands (Isa. 40:1-11; 49:19-20; 51:1-3; Ezek. 20:40-44).

Worship

As noted, Israel's liturgical calendar, designating the times and rituals of its worship, was primarily shaped by the three harvest festivals celebrating the productivity of its agricultural lands. Just as the landscape influenced the times and rituals of Israel's worship, so it also influenced the setting of Israelite worship. Though God could be present in any place, the primary site of God's revelation in biblical Israel was the mountain top, Mt. Sinai on which the law was given and Mt. Zion on which the temple was built. Both mountains were considered sacred space (Exod. 3:5; 19:12, 23; Ps. 48:1-3[2-4]; 87:1-3). Thus a particular feature of the landscape was viewed as the special locus of divine-human communication. In its notion of sacred space, Israel shared with other cultures the notion that the landscape itself could be a medium of divine revelation.

The Jewish community in Roman Palestine, from which the first Christians came, was heir to a sense of the land that included the various roles it played in the religion of Israel. Thus the early Christian writings in the NT, especially the Gospel narratives about Jesus, reflect these same understandings. In the first place, the agricultural landscape of biblical Israel plays a prominent role in the Gospels. The small agrarian villages of Roman Palestine provide the context for the life and ministry of Jesus and his first followers, and it is with the imagery of this world — sowing and harvesting grain (Mark 4:1-20, 26-29), tending vineyards (12:1-12), herding sheep (Matt. 18:10-14) — that Jesus describes the character of the kingdom of God.

Furthermore, the political landscape of biblical Israel is reflected in a number of NT texts, where the relationship between nationhood and land is assumed. The gift of land to Abraham's descendants is recalled (Acts 7:2-7; Heb. 11:8-9), Palestine is referred to as the land of Israel (Matt. 2:20-21), and the political restoration of Israel as an independent kingdom free of Roman control is mentioned by Jesus' disciples (Acts 1:6). Finally, the sacred landscape of Israel is reflected in the Gospel narratives. The mountain figures prominently in Matthew's Gospel in which it is the location of Jesus' great sermon (Matt. 5:1–7:29) recalling the revelation to Moses on Mt. Sinai, of Jesus' transfiguration (17:1-13), and of Jesus' great commission (28:16-20). Mt. Zion and the temple, as the center of Jewish worship, provide the context of the Passion narratives in all of the Gospels, and in Luke-Acts it is here in Jerusalem that Jesus meets his followers after the Resurrection (Luke 24:33-53) and that the Church begins at Pentecost (Acts 1–2).

In spite of these lines of continuity between Judaism and early Christianity, several developments with the Christian community contributed to a distinctive view of land in the emerging Church. One of these developments was the rapid urbanization of Christianity. Within a decade of the Crucifixion of Jesus, the primary context of Christianity had shifted from the rural villages of Palestine to the cities of the Roman Empire. With this shift, the world of agriculture, which had had such a profound influence on the definition of humanity and on the understanding of divine activity in Israel, was left behind and replaced with an urban perspective. While the Gospel narratives about Jesus recall this agricultural perspective, Paul's letters that take up directly the actual urban circumstances of his audience show only faint traces of it (1 Thess. 2:1-12; Rom. 11:17-24).

A second development affecting the Christian view of land was the conversion to Christianity of large numbers of Gentiles, who did not share the close political bonds Jews felt with the territories of Judea and Samaria, once parts of the kingdom of Israel. Thus among most new Christians the link between land and nationhood was undermined, or at least altered, and the self-understanding of the early Christians as God's people no longer included a particular land as an essential element. It is noteworthy that Paul, who makes so much of Abraham's role in salvation history, does not discuss God's promise to him of land (Gal. 3:6-18; Rom. 4:1-25).

Finally, the strong apocalyptic character of early Christianity shifted its perspective on land. By stressing a future existence in a heavenly realm, unencumbered by the realities of earthy existence — whether agricultural or political survival — Christianity diminished the role of land in its religious consciousness (John 14:1-7; 1 Cor. 15:1-58; 1 Thess. 4:13-18). Still, its images of the new age never divorce it entirely from the earthly landscape: the kingdom of God does not escape earth's bounds but is established in a transformed world (Rev. 21:1, 2; 22:1-5). Thus even Christianity's apocalyptic vision consists in the natural realities — rivers, fruit trees, cities — that were a part of the biblical landscape.

Bibliography. W. Brueggemann, *The Land* (Philadelphia, 1977); W. D. Davies, *The Gospel and the Land* (Berkeley, 1974); N. C. Habel, *The Land Is Mine.* OBT (Minneapolis, 1995); T. Hiebert, *The Yahwist's Landscape* (Oxford, 1996); C. J. H. Wright, *God's People in God's Land* (Grand Rapids, 1990).

Theodore Hiebert

LAODICEA (Gk. *Laodíkeia*)

A city in Asia Minor, one of the seven churches addressed in Rev. 1–3. Laodicea ad Lycum was founded ca. 250 B.C. by the Syrian king Antiochus II, who named it after his wife Laodice. It stood on an elevated plateau in the Lychus River valley and was located ca. 10 km. (6 mi.) S of Hierapolis, 18 km. (11 mi.) W of Colossae, and 161 km. (100 mi.) E of Ephesus. Major roads made Laodicea a thoroughfare.

In the 1st century B.C. Laodicea became a banking and finance and textile center, as well as a famous site for gladiatorial games. In A.D. 60 it was devastated by an earthquake, but the wealthy inhabitants refused imperial financial assistance for rebuilding (Tacitus *Ann.* 14.27). Excavations have uncovered a stadium, gymnasium, two theaters, several churches, and a water system. Today the site is uninhabited.

The church at Laodicea, led by a woman named Nympha (Col. 4:15), probably began during Paul's lengthy Ephesian ministry (Acts 19:10) when his colleague, Epaphras, evangelized the city (Col. 4:13). Paul encourages the churches at Laodicea and Colossae to exchange the letters he had written them (Col. 4:16); the "letter to the Laodiceans" is no longer extant.

John's letter to the Laodiceans (Rev. 3:14-22) refers to the city's textile industry ("white garments," v. 18), its tepid water supply (vv. 15-16), and its eye salve (v. 18), which was known as "Phrygian powder." Apparently the Laodiceans took John's warning to heart: the church continued to prosper and became the home of famous bishops (e.g., Sagaris), debates (the proper date of Easter), and church councils (listing the NT canon, 367).

Bibliography. E. M. Blaiklock, *Cities of the New Testament* (London, 1965); C. J. Hemer, *The Letters to the Seven Churches of Asia in Their Local Setting* (1986, repr. Grand Rapids, 2000); J. McRay, *Archaeology and the New Testament* (Grand Rapids, 1991).

GARY M. BURGE

LAODICEANS, LETTER TO THE

The now lost letter that Paul exhorts the church of Colossae to obtain from Laodicea (Col. 4:16). "The Letter to the Laodiceans" also refers to a short, pseudonymous, apocryphal letter which is attributed to Paul and which purports to be the letter of Col. 4:16. The pseudonymous letter is a collection of phrases and sentences from the canonical Pauline letters, particularly Philippians (Laod. 8, cf. Phil. 1:21; Laod. 9, cf. Phil. 2:2). There is no apparent motivation for producing this letter other than to supply the missing letter of the Pauline corpus. The pseudonymous letter was written by the 4th century and was known by Theodore of Mopsuestia and Jerome. It is not found in Greek manuscripts of the NT, but by the 6th century it was found in a large number of medieval Latin manuscripts; nothing in its contents suggests that it was the Letter to the Laodiceans mentioned in the Muratorian Canon (2nd century) purported to have been written to support the Marcion heresy. The letter was considered fraudulent by the Eastern Church as early as the 4th century, but the Western Church considered it authentic until the Second Council of Nicaea (787).

Bibliography. W. Schneemelcher, "The Epistle to the Laodiceans," in *New Testament Apocrypha*, ed. W. Schneemelcher and R. McL. Wilson, rev. ed., 2 (Louisville, 1992), 42-46. DUANE F. WATSON

LAPIS LAZULI

A deep blue stone (Heb. *sappîr*) marked with traces of iron pyrite ("fool's gold"), well-known and widely used in jewelry and small decorations in the ancient Near East (cf. NRSV mg; e.g., Job 28:6, 16; Cant. 5:14; Isa. 54:11; Ezek. 28:13; NRSV "sapphire"). Because of the nature of ancient methods of classification, the precise type of stone intended cannot now be determined with certainty.

LAPPIDOTH (Heb. *lappîḏôṯ*)

The husband of the prophet and judge Deborah (Judg. 4:4). Some scholars suggest that the name is a hypocoristicon of the general Barak, since both names mean "lightning."

LASEA (Gk. *Lasaía*)

A city on the southern coast of Crete (Acts 27:8), near Fair Havens/Kaloi Limenes. It is not mentioned elsewhere in ancient literature.

LASH

A whip used in punishment. In the OT and NT the word is used both literally and metaphorically. Whipping with a lash up to 40 strokes was prescribed by Israelite law (Deut. 25:1-3); the punishment was later reduced to 39 lashes to prevent exceeding the law (2 Cor. 11:25). Lashing or scourging with a leather whip split into several thongs was practiced in the synagogues and the Sanhedrin for unacceptable behavior or for breaking religious rituals or the rules of the rabbis. Jesus warned his followers that they would be flogged in the synagogues (Matt. 10:17; 23:34).

The Romans used a stick, the rod, and the scourge or lash of leather strips with sharp pieces of bone and metal attached. Flogging with the lash was part of capital punishment and usually came before crucifixion (Matt. 20:19; Mark 10:34; Luke 18:33; John 19:1). The results were horrendous. Beating with the lash was also done to coerce a confession or as part of interrogation (Acts 22:23-29).

The word (and the related term "scourging") is used metaphorically to indicate torment, illness, trouble, or suffering (cf. Job 5:21; Isa. 10:26). Jesus healed the woman with the issue of blood from her "disease" (Gk. *mástix;* lit., "scourging"; cf. Mark 3:10; Luke 7:21). The image of scourging also represents the correction and punishment of those whom Jesus accepts (Heb. 12:6), and that image is borrowed from the OT (Prov. 3:12 LXX; 1 Kgs. 12:11, 14; 2 Chr. 10:11, 14).

RICHARD A. SPENCER

LASHA (Heb. *lešaʿ*)

A place along the ancient border of Canaan (Gen. 10:19). The name likely means "fissure" or "chasm," probably stemming from the geographical nature of the region. While the exact location of Lasha is uncertain, it is traditionally identified with Callirhoe (modern Wadi Zerqā Māʿin), E of the Dead Sea. The exact borders described in the text are uncertain, leading some to identify the site with Laash or Nuḫashe in Syria.

David C. Maltsberger

LASHARON (Heb. *laššārôn*)
A place conquered by Joshua (Josh. 12:18). Following the LXX, the text should be read "(belonging) to Sharon," the coastal plain between Carmel and Aphek.

LAST DAY(S), LATTER DAYS
A phrase (Heb. *hayyôm hāʾaḥărôn, ʾaḥărîṯ hayyāmîm*) that connotes a future time that will precede, coincide with, or follow a decisive divine reckoning. Associated terms are "day of the Lord," "day of judgment," or simply "the/that day." The earliest uses of the term in Hebrew refer to military victories and defeats. Used in this sense, the term refers to the judgment of God's enemies in battle (Num. 24:14; "days to come"). The latter days can be a time of tribulation and exile for Israel (Deut. 4:30; 31:29) or, similarly, a time when Israel will understand the wrath of the Lord (Jer. 23:20; 30:24; cf. Ezek. 38:16). The latter days may also be a time of the restoration of nations that were previously punished (Jer. 48:47; 49:39); of Israel, who will return to seek the Lord (Hos. 3:5); of Jerusalem (Isa. 2:2 = Mic. 4:1); and of justice, when the Redeemer shall stand on the earth (Job 19:25-27).

Jewish apocalyptic and Christian writers typically associate the latter days (or "last times"; Gk. *éschatos tṓn hēmerṓn*) with cosmic events: the coming tribulation, last judgment, and salvation (4 Ezra 10:59; 6:34; cf. 1 QM 1, 11; 2 Apoc. Bar. 24:1; 51:1). In Daniel the events of the latter days are mysteries to be revealed from heaven (Dan. 2:28; 10:14). In the NT the phrase is associated with the resurrection (by Jesus) at the last judgment (John 6:39-40; 11:24), the Christian era that began with the outpouring of the Holy Spirit (Acts 2:17; cf. Joel 2:28-32[MT 3:1-5]), the tribulation and disbelief before the last judgment (2 Tim. 3:1; 2 Pet. 3:3; Jas. 5:3), the time when salvation will be revealed (1 Pet. 1:5), and the present time characterized by God's revelation through Christ (Heb. 1:2).

Alexandra R. Brown

LAST SUPPER
The term "Last Supper" (rather than "Lord's Supper") broadens the focus from just the eucharistic words and actions to the entire meal, which John and Luke portray as also the context for Jesus' farewell address. The Last Supper, Jesus' final meal with his disciples before his death (1 Cor. 11:23-25; Mark 14:17-26; Matt. 26:20-30; Luke 22:14-38; John 13–17; cf. John 6:51-58), is so momentous a moment in Jesus' life, and so pivotal to beliefs and practices of most Christian denominations, that its various biblical accounts have generated frequent and sometime heated scholarly exchanges, not a few along denominational lines.

Questions regarding the Last Supper range widely. Some are narrowly textual and exegetical matters, such as how the differing versions of the Supper are related, or whether the long or the short manuscript reading of the Lukan account of the institution of the eucharist is original. Others are historical questions, e.g., whether or not the Last Supper was a Passover meal, or how much of the account goes back to the historical Jesus. Others are more theological, interpretive, and sacramental questions: the relationship between the Last Supper and the sacrifice of the Cross; its relationship to the eucharist; the meaning of the words,"This is my body," "This is my blood" (or variants).

One hotly debated question has been whether the Last Supper was a Passover meal (as implied in some of the Synoptic accounts) or held on the day of preparation before the Passover (as claimed in the Gospel of John). Proposed solutions such as the use of an alternate sectarian calendar have not prevailed. There is a consensus that the Supper was Thursday evening on the night that Jesus was betrayed, that he died on Friday before the sabbath, and that the account of the discovery of the empty tomb dated that event to Sunday morning after the sabbath as the new Christian "Lord's Day." There is also a growing agreement not to focus on the discrepancy of whether the Last Supper historically was or was not a Passover meal, since in any case all accounts treat the meal in the context of the Passover season with Passover allusions and references. These Passover resonances contribute to the NT picture of Jesus as the Lamb of God who was slain for human sins (John and Revelation), and of Jesus as the bread of life. They contribute to the Last Supper as reflecting this context of a new covenant for salvation through Jesus' sacrifice and by eating his flesh and drinking his blood (John 6:53-58; 1 Cor. 11:26-27).

Also widely discussed are the relationships of the Last Supper to the sacrifice of the Cross, the eucharist, Jesus' historical practice of eating with sinners, and early Christian *agápē* meals. Although related to Jesus' meals shared with sinners and to Christian *agápē* meals, the Last Supper has a distinctive significance beyond them as a final action and gift of Jesus to his disciples with particular reference to his death for them and to the eucharist.

Form of the Accounts

The eucharistic institution narratives have survived in two basic forms: one represented in Mark and Matthew, and the other in Paul's 1 Corinthians and Luke, with important allusions in John 6:51-58. There is no consensus on which of the two main forms is prior, or whether only the Pauline form, or also the Markan, is liturgically shaped. The most plausible solution is to argue that historical remembrances of Jesus' words and actions are needed to explain the origin of the various NT accounts of the Last Supper and treatments of eucharist, but these NT accounts have generally come down to us in language that has, to varying extents, been influenced by and corresponds to liturgical eucharistic formulations.

Frequent special questions about the Lukan version are the anomalous cup-bread-cup sequence of the longer manuscript form (Luke 22:17-20), as well as the authenticity of vv. 19b-20. With the growing awareness that Luke uses a farewell address structure, this sequence finds a natural explanation. The first cup belongs to the farewell's notice of impending death: "I will not drink of the fruit of the vine until the kingdom of God comes." The bread and (second) cup sequence is properly eucharistic: "This is my body, which is given for you; do this in memory of me"; "This cup that is poured out for you is the new covenant in my blood" (Luke 22:17-20).

Regarding John 13–17, much discussion centers on the relationship of the footwashing sign to the absence of an institution narrative in that Last Supper account. Nevertheless, while debating how much of the Bread of Life discourse in John 6 is eucharistic, most scholars agree that John 6:51-58 deals with the eucharist and has resonances with the "words of institution" present in the Synoptic and Pauline Last Supper accounts.

Meaning

From the perspective of the Christian churches, the most critical questions about NT treatments of the Last Supper concern its meaning and its relationship to the atoning sacrifice of Jesus on the Cross and to later sacramental eucharistic practices. Debates about the meaning of "This is my body," "This is my blood," have tended to follow denominational lines: Catholics, Orthodox, and some others read them in conjunction with John 6:51-58; 1 Cor. 11:23-29 as expressing the real presence of Jesus in the eucharist. Believers are to eat his flesh and drink his blood sacramentally and worthily. Others stress the lack in Jesus' original Aramaic of the linking verb "is." They emphasize parabolic or symbolic dimensions of these words, and their relationship to prophetic acted signs (such as when Ezekiel burnt one third of his hair, cut one third in pieces, and scattered one third, and then declared, "This is Jerusalem" [Ezek. 5:1-5]).

To the fundamental words about the bread and wine or cup, both the Markan and Pauline versions attach mention of at least one being "for you." Expressions like "new covenant in my blood" and "poured out for you" connote atoning significance and allude to a sacrifice (on the Cross) that saves or liberates sinners, not from an earthly "Egypt" but from Satan, "the ruler of this world" (John 14:30). Besides discussions on how the Last Supper is related to the once-for-all atoning sacrifice of Jesus on the Cross, closely related questions concern the Last Supper's relationship to the new covenant, to the institution of the eucharist, and to priestly ordination (especially in "Do this in memory of me"), and to the eschatological expectation in "You proclaim the Lord's death until he comes" (1 Cor. 11:26).

On the one hand, the several versions of the Last Supper provide multiple attestation of its basis in the life of the earthly Jesus. On the other, their variety attests for salvation (in relation to the Cross) and for on-going church life (in the eucharist). Many controversies remain over specifics of the various NT texts and their historical and theological significance. But a canonical approach to them in light of the Passover and of the Servant giving his life for "many" (Isa. 53:11-12), in relation to the many NT interpretations, and to other early Christian documents and the attested eucharistic practices, reflections, and beliefs of the churches, can unpack the richness and centrality of the NT treatments of the Last Supper for Christians of all times.

Bibliography. N. A. Beck, "The Last Supper as an Efficacious Symbolic Act," *JBL* 89 (1970): 192-98; R. J. Daly, "The Eucharist and Redemption: The Last Supper and Jesus' Understanding of His Death," *BTB* 11 (1981): 21-27; J. Jeremias, *The Eucharistic Words of Jesus* (Philadelphia, 1990); W. S. Kurz, *Farewell Addresses in the New Testament* (Collegeville, 1990); I. H. Marshall, *Last Supper and Lord's Supper* (Grand Rapids, 1981); J. Meier, "The Eucharist at the Last Supper: Did It Happen?" *TD* 42 (1995): 335-51; D. Wenham, "How Jesus Understood the Last Supper: A Parable in Action," *Themelios* 20/2 (1995): 11-16.

WILLIAM S. KURZ, S.J.

LASTHENES (Gk. *Lasthenēs*)

A Cretan who furnished Demetrius II with mercenaries in his struggle with Alexander Balas for the Seleucid throne (Josephus *Ant.* 13.4.3 [86)]. In return, Demetrius gave Lasthenes a prominent position in the kingdom, perhaps the governorship of Coele-syria or chief minister. References to a letter from Demetrius to Lasthenes (1 Macc. 11:30-37; *Ant.* 13.4.3 [126-29]) testify to his importance in the Seleucid government. In the letter, Demetrius informs him of policy changes between the Seleucids and Jonathan, the Hasmonean high priest.

RODNEY A. WERLINE

LATIN

The language of the Romans in biblical times (John 19:20). Latin is significant for biblical studies in several ways: Early Latin translations provide textual witnesses for sections of some apocryphal works; textual critics use Latin translations in their study of the Greek OT and NT and of the Hebrew OT; Latin is also the language of biblical commentary in the Latin West up to and including Reformation times.

Some of the very earliest translations of the Bible were done into Latin. These versions in Old Latin (Vetus Latina) are valued as evidence for the existence of Greek manuscript readings now lost. Likewise, the subsequent revising work of Jerome to produce the Latin Vulgate can be used to provide information on versions of the Hebrew text which no longer survive. The renewed interest in the history of exegesis gives new prominence to the commentary tradition in Latin. Some Greek commentaries have survived only in Latin translation (e.g., some of Origen's work).

At present, work continues on editing the mostly fragmentary texts of the Old Latin Bible. The convenient two-volume Stuttgart *Biblia Sacra* (ed. Robert Weber, 3rd ed., 1985) represents an abridgement (with minor revisions) of the full editions of the Vulgate OT and NT. The *Nova Vulgata* (Rome, 1979), which is used in the Nestle-Aland *Novum Testamentum Graece et Latine* (Stuttgart, 1984), is to be distinguished from Jerome's Vulgate; it is designed to provide a standard modern Latin translation for ecclesiastical use.

MICHAEL CAHILL

LATRINE

A toilet or privy, probably for public use. Using the demolished Baal temple as a latrine (or possibly a cesspool) was an obvious sign of triumph and contempt, and an illustration of the severity of Jehu's prophet-backed rebellion against the house of Omri and its worship of foreign gods (2 Kgs. 10:27).

LATTER PROPHETS

In the Hebrew canon, those books representing the major or "classical" prophets Isaiah, Jeremiah, Ezekiel, and the 12 Minor Prophets.

LAVER

A bowl or basin (so NRSV) used for ceremonial washing associated with both the wilderness tabernacle (Exod. 30:17-21) and the Jerusalem temple (1 Kgs. 7:38-39; 2 Chr. 4:6). In one instance Heb. *kiyyôr* refers to a bronze platform upon which Solomon stood in solemn assembly to offer his prayer when dedicating the temple (2 Chr. 6:13). The term can also have more profane associations, referring to a caldron or pot of fire (1 Sam. 2:14; Zech. 12:6).

The ceremonial basin associated with the wilderness tabernacle was to be made of bronze and placed between the tent of meeting and the altar so that Moses, Aaron, and his sons could wash their hands and feet whenever they approached the altar or entered the tent of meeting (Exod. 30:18-21; 40:30-32). The sacred character of the basin is indicated by the divinely-inspired skill required to construct it (Exod. 31:1-11) and the command to anoint it along with other tabernacle furnishings (30:22-29; 40:9-11).

Solomon's temple had 10 ceremonial basins used primarily for rinsing the items associated with the burnt offerings (2 Chr. 4:6). Here, the focus is on the splendor of the lavers rather than their sacred character, as in the tabernacle. The 10 bronze basins each held 40 baths (one bath was ca. 23 l. [6 gal.]), and each stood on its own bronze, wheeled stand (1 Kgs. 7:27-37). These elaborate stands were pillaged by Ahaz several centuries later in his attempt to bribe the king of Assyria (2 Kgs. 16:17).

KEVIN D. HALL

LAW

Law is a reflection of the way in which society both views and administers itself through common agreement and forms of restraint. Legal pronouncement may be recognized in relation to those acts which "mobilize" a society to react at need to protect individuals or the state. The more serious the offense, the more likely society will create a body to enforce "correct" behavior and codify a set of specific legal restraints to deal with future occurrences.

Lawgivers in Western cultures like Greece and Rome began by identifying legal principles which people took for granted. Then they drafted specific laws to apply these principles to real-life situations. But there is still little evidence that the lawgivers in Eastern cultures like ancient Israel used a system of general legal principles which they consistently applied to specific situations in the great codes from the books of Exodus, Leviticus, Numbers, and Deuteronomy. Laws in the world of the Bible seldom described typical or average or even ideal behavior in Israel. In fact, average behavior may often have been at variance with these codes.

In the world of the Bible, the basis of law was not philosophy, but crisis. Lawgivers developed specific laws to deal with households which weakened or threatened the well-being of the state. Households did this when they failed to work their own land, feed their own children, and contribute to the cooperative efforts of the state to collect taxes and raise an army. One example of such a crisis is found in the story of Zelophehad's daughters, who claim their father's inheritance when no male heir is present (Num. 27:1-11). Their appeal required legal reasoning and deliberation which expanded previous tradition regarding levirate marriage (Deut. 25:5-10) in favor of a common sense solution benefiting a household and the community at large.

Lawgivers in the Bible do not teach us as much about how Israel thought, as they do about how Israel as a community worked. For example, laws in the Bible show how Israel reacted to a particular situation or crisis (e.g., the case of the unknown homicide in Deut. 21:1-9). They also reveal Israel's basic assumptions about human nature, how Israel went about collecting evidence and using it to make legal decisions (cf. the use of the bridal sheets in Deut. 22:13-19). Finally, laws outline how Israel as a state distributed power (e.g., the admonition to judges in Exod. 23:6-8; cf. Deut. 16:18-20; 2 Sam. 15:1-4).

Law Codes

The scene in which Moses receives the law at Mt. Sinai centers on a renewal of the covenant Yahweh originally made with Abraham and then an extension of that agreement to include a more formal "treaty" with the Israelites known as the Decalogue or Ten Commandments. As part of these events, the rule of Moses as the supreme leader of the people is highlighted and enhanced. He alone speaks directly with God, and even his brother Aaron, who later serves as chief priest for the people, is portrayed as a weakling when Moses is absent (Exod. 32).

In Exod. 20:1-17 (and Deut. 5:6-21) the Decalogue is set forth in apodictic style. These are "command" laws, which do not require much explanation and do not contain the "If — Then" sequence more common in "case" law. They can be divided into two segments:

1. communal statutes, applying to the conduct of the entire nation, and
2. personal statutes, setting the code of conduct for each person.

These laws were common in other cultures and were designed to maintain order and protect the rights of property owners.

The remainder of the laws in Exodus, and those found in Numbers, Leviticus, and Deuteronomy, are primarily "case" laws. In nearly every instance, they are extensions of the legal formulas presented in the Ten Commandments and are the result of judges or individuals asking the question "But what if?" about a particular legal phrase.

Since they were designed to regulate the life of the people, it was necessary for the laws to change as the social situation of the people changed. Thus the Covenant code of Exod. 20:23–23:19 and the Deuteronomic code of Deut. 12–26 demonstrate that the people could not be governed by laws meant only for nomadic herders when they had become farmers and urban dwellers. For example, the group of laws which relate to caring for the "poor" (including widows, orphans, and resident aliens) can be traced back to the commandments to honor parents, the prohibition against theft, and the injunction against coveting. However, these case laws each speak to a particular legal situation which required an expansion of the law so that it dealt more directly with the current concerns (cf. Lev. 19:9-10; 25:35-37; Deut. 15:1-2; 16:19). At the heart of this expansion is the exhortation to remember "where they came from." The period of slavery in Egypt is continually referenced as the basis for legal restraint or legal guarantees (Deut. 5:15; 15:15; 16:12; 24:18).

Once the monarchy had ceased to exist and the priestly community became the guardians of the people's commitment to Yahweh, the Holiness code of Lev. 17–26 was formulated. It is characterized by the statement, "You shall be holy; for I, Yahweh your God, am holy" (Lev. 19:2). This group of laws, coupled with other priestly legislation (Exod. 25–31; 35–40; Lev. 1–16, 27; Num. 1–10), places additional stress on maintaining holiness or ritual purity through obedience to the law. Among their major concerns are the provision for the prescribing of sacred space (temple precincts), as well as the major festival occasions and cultic procedures.

There are many similarities between the biblical law codes and those found elsewhere in the ancient Near East. The Code of Hammurabi (18th century B.C.E.) and the Assyrian law code (8th-7th centuries) contain many laws which are similar to those in the Bible. It seems likely that legal formulas were transmitted between cultures along with other ideas, customs, technologies, and styles. For instance, both Hammurabi's code and biblical law contain the principle of *lex talionis,* "an eye for an eye." This is based on the idea of complete reciprocity for loss or injury. However, the legal codes of the Israelites demanded full equality for all of the people, with no exceptions even for the king. In ancient Babylon, there was a multitiered social system in which citizens did not receive the same punishment as slaves for similar injuries. Another difference is found in the apparent harshness of Israelite law. There are many crimes in the various legal codes for which capital punishment is prescribed (Exod. 21:12, 17; Lev. 20:9; Deut. 13:5[MT 6]). However, Israelite law does not provide for any "loophole" which would allow the convicted parties to be released or to pay a fine, as is the case in the laws from Mesopotamia. This is due to the concept of "purity" which is inherent to biblical law (cf. esp. the Holiness code in Leviticus). If the society wished to remain pure, it could not take half measure in dealing with criminal behavior which would eventually contaminate the entire nation. Thus a prodigal son is to be stoned to death (Deut. 21:18-21) in order to "purge the evil from your midst," and the leper must be excluded from society until certified by a priest as "clean" (Lev. 13).

Judicial System

In order to maintain order and administer the laws, there was more than one judicial system in ancient Israel. The judiciary included sanctuary courts, courts martial, gate courts, and the divine assembly. Each is a separate judicial system, and although they functioned contemporaneously, one did not review or appeal to the other except in extreme cases (Deut. 17:8-13).

Priests administered sanctuary courts according to a judicial system which involved divination, oracles, and the trial by ordeal (cf. Num. 5:11-31). The plaintiff came before the priest with a question to which the answer "Yes" or "No" could be given. The priest divined the answer or torah using techniques such as the Urim and Thummim (Exod. 28:30; Num. 27:21; 1 Sam. 14:41; 28:6; Ezra 2:63).

Sanctuary reform plays a prominent role in the book of Deuteronomy, which is regularly associated with the prophets. But Deuteronomy is more a royal than a prophetic reform. It is an effort on the part of Judah's kings to centralize the tax and draft system in anticipation of imminent war. Deuteronomy focuses on centralizing the economic institutions, and it also centralizes the court martial system (Deut. 12–13). Deuteronomy does not try to remedy injustice by imposing a standardized system of justice throughout Judah and preventing local distinctions. Judah's gate court institution remains decentralized, and in fact Deuteronomy argues that the legacy of Judah's cities is primarily the legal tradition of the gate court, while the legacy of Jerusalem is liturgical.

The city gate antedated the monarchy and, in a certain sense, served as a rival center of power. Gates also had strong connections with feeding and protecting. Prophets associated themselves with the gate to emphasize their function in balancing the power of the monarchs, and used the gate to direct attention to the two standard issues by which the performance of a monarch was evaluated, food and protection. This helps explain Jeremiah's execration ritual at the Potsherd Gate (Jer. 19:1-13) and the quick reprisal of the priest Pashur, placing Jeremiah in the stocks "in the upper Benjamin Gate" (20:2). Each was using a symbol of authority to heighten his own public posture.

In the Bible, prophets like any other citizen often stand at a gate to initiate their course of action (Jer. 7:1-2). But the venue of the trial is regularly transferred to the divine assembly, as in 1 Kgs. 22:1-40 where monarchs and prophets meet on the threshing floor at the city gate to discern whether or not the divine assembly has authorized Israel and Judah to go to war against Aram.

The divine assembly appears in the literatures of Egypt, Mesopotamia, and Syria-Palestine. In the Bible it is analogous to the gate court. Both are judicial bodies made up of citizens who meet at a threshold to resolve a crisis. The gate court convenes at the gate of a city, which marks the boundary between the sanctuary within its walls and the outside world (cf. Ruth 4:1-6). The divine assembly meets on the mountain, which marks the boundary between the divine and human planes. Both the gate court and the divine assembly help resolve disputes involving land and children. Residents of a single city appear before the gate court, nations before the divine assembly when they conclude treaties.

Police Power

The application of law in the state differed from the application of law in the villages, even though both functioned alongside one another. The administration of law in the village was decentralized. In villages, the fathers of the household served as its elders or lawgivers (Ruth 4:2; Prov. 31:23). They derived their authority from their own households, and served as an assembly to safeguard the rights of villagers to food and protection. Assemblies enforced their verdicts through consensus or collective agreement. Cooperation between the households in a village did not result from fear of retribution, but from a shared understanding of what each household needed to do in order for the entire village to survive. A binding consensus was possible only when every household in the village understood who initiated the complaint, what the specific indictment involved, and how the defendant responded. Consequently, elders talked with plaintiffs and defendants until they all reached an agreement on how the matter should be resolved (Deut. 16:18-20; 19:16-20; 22:13-21).

In the state, the administration of law was centralized. The monarch was the lawgiver who appointed judges to hear cases throughout the state (cf. Jehoshaphat's administration in 2 Chr. 19:4-11). The focus of village law was on the responsibility of the households to feed their members, whereas state law dealt primarily with its responsibility to protect the people. Laws dealing with incest, regulating marriage, and controlling inheritance, on the one hand, developed in villages. Laws dealing with taxes and military or public service, on the other, developed in the state. In the beginning state courts only heard complaints from households regarding their assessments and their obligation to conscript soldiers for the army (2 Sam. 15:2-4). Gradually, however, they heard cases involving all areas of public life (2 Sam. 21:2-9; 1 Kgs. 3:16-28).

State courts used police power, rather than consensus, to guarantee cooperation. A lawgiver heard the plaintiffs and then rendered a decision on the case. Since the decision was based on the judgment of a single lawgiver, there was a greater degree of judicial discretion which was not necessarily attuned to a broad consensus of opinion within the state as a whole (cf. David's judgments in 2 Sam. 12:1-6; 14:2-11). While the decision might be based on precedent, the latitude of interpretation of the precedent is more open to variation.

The centerpiece in the anthropology of state law is its characterization of the monarch as a lawgiver. Art and literature which portray monarchs as lawgivers promulgating a code of law during their coronations have been recovered by archaeologists for more than one ancient Near Eastern culture. For example, some of the most exquisite characterizations of both Lipit-ishtar and Hammurabi of Babylon portray them as lawgivers.

Although certainly each new monarch made some changes in state laws, it is unlikely that every monarch authorized a major restructuring of standing codes of law. Monarchs promulgated a code more to ratify their authority than to inaugurate a sweeping judicial reform (cf. Josiah's actions in 2 Kgs. 22:3–23:27). By doing so, monarchs imitated the actions of the divine assembly by endowing the people with a covenant or code of law by which life in the monarchy would be sustained. The ritual confirmed a monarch's responsibility to maintain order in the state. Just as the Anunnaki gods confirm Marduk as the divine lawgiver in the Enuma Elish, the divine assembly recognized monarchs as lawgivers during their coronation (Pss. 72, 101).

Law in ancient Israel functioned as a means of identifying the people with the covenant, of maintaining social order, and insuring that the authority of the palace and temple was recognized and obeyed. Although its original formulation and administration had more to do with survival in a harsh and dangerous environment, law, like Israelite society, eventually became quite complex. As a result, legal formula became more ritualistic (as in the Holiness code) and legal pronouncements took on a rigid character which may have had more to do with the maintenance of social structures than the administration of justice.

Bibliography. D. C. Benjamin, *Deuteronomy and City Life* (Lanham, 1983); H.-J. Boecker, *Law and the Administration of Justice in the Old Testament and Ancient East* (Minneapolis, 1980); V. H. Matthews, "Entrance Ways and Threshing Floors: Legally Significant Sites in the Ancient Near East,"

Fides et Historia 19/3 (1987:, 25-40; D. Patrick, *Old Testament Law* (Atlanta, 1985).

VICTOR H. MATTHEWS

LAWLESS ONE

See ANTICHRIST.

LAWSUIT

Historians of ancient law warn that the modern concept of "lawsuit" may not exactly correspond to any of the available judicial or extrajudicial means ancients had for settling their disputes. Still, one is able to find biblical examples where two disputing parties bring their claim before a third for resolution, whether that be a judge, a priest, elders, or the king (Deut. 17:8-12; Josh. 20:4; 2 Sam. 15:2-6; 1 Kgs. 3:16-27; 2 Kgs. 6:26-31). Israel's various law codes provided for the settling of such disputes throughout the centuries over which the OT was composed (Exod. 18:15-16; 23:3, 6; Deut. 19:15-19; 21:5; 2 Chr. 19:5-11).

In the past much has been written on the metaphorical understanding of a "covenant lawsuit" in certain prophetic texts, where Yahweh pressed a complaint against Israel (e.g., Isa. 1:2-3; Jer. 2:4-13; Mic. 6:1-8). More recent scholarship, however, has called into question whether one can actually identify such a form or genre in these prophetic books.

The NT has only a few references to settling disputes in a formal legal setting. Matt. 5:25-26; Luke 12:57-59 encourage people to settle their suits out of court. Matthew qualifies what may be Q material at 5:40 (cf. Luke 6:29) by rendering the confiscation of the coat as a guarantee in a lawsuit. The most extensive reference is found in 1 Cor. 6:1-11, where Paul corrects upper-status Christians in Corinth for taking lower-status Christians before provincial magistrates to settle matters of minor import. Paul reminds the Corinthians that settling their disputes this way betrays their Christian identity. As an alternative, Paul proposes private arbitration as the preferred means of settling such cases. Under arbitration, an impartial community member, acting as an arbiter, could decide the matters on a more informal and equitable basis. The proposed solution offers relief to lower-status Christians, who were at a disadvantage in the Roman legal system, and strengthens the Christian community in Corinth.

Bibliography. H.-J. Boecker, *Law and the Administration of Justice in the Old Testament and Ancient Near East* (Minneapolis, 1980); D. R. Daniels, "Is There a 'Prophetic Lawsuit' Genre?" *ZAW* 99 (1987): 339-60; D. J. Harrington, *The Gospel of Matthew.* Sacra Pagina 1 (Collegeville, 1991), 89; A. C. Mitchell, "Rich and Poor in the Courts of Corinth," *NTS* 39 (1993): 562-86.

ALAN C. MITCHELL

LAWYER

A technical term (Gk. *nomikós*) used in the NT for a learned expert in law. While the Gospels have in mind experts in Jewish law (e.g., Luke 11:45-46), it appears that Zenas the lawyer (Tit. 3:13) is proficient in Roman law. Lawyers are mentioned with the Pharisees in several places in Luke (Luke 7:30; 14:3; cf. 11:53, "scribes") and are typically in opposition to Jesus in the Gospels (cf. Matt. 22:35 = Luke 10:25).

ROBERT A. DERRENBACKER, JR.

LAYING ON OF HANDS

A ceremonial act of consecration or identification (Heb. *sāmak̲ yad̲ ʿal;* Gk. *epitíthēmi tás cheíras, epíthesis tṓn cheirṓn*). In the OT this ritual employed either one or two hands. The two-handed ritual occurred when the priest placed his hands on the scapegoat's head (Lev. 16:21), when witnesses grasped the head of a blasphemer about to be stoned (24:14; cf. Deut. 13:9[MT 10]), and when Moses ordained Joshua (Num. 27:18, 23; Deut. 34:9). In each case, the gesture identified the focus of the ritual. The one-handed ritual, meanwhile, applied to sacrifice where the offerer placed a hand on the animal just prior to slaughtering it (Lev. 1:4; 3:2, 8, 13). The purpose, as Hittite parallels confirm and the specifics of the cases demonstrate, was not to transfer guilt to the animal but to identify it as belonging to, and thus as reconsecrating, the offerer.

In the NT laying on of hands occurred in four settings: blessing, which reflected the rabbinic belief in the powers of a saint's hands (Matt. 19:13-15); healing, where the ritual was optional but often served to identify both the sickness and the healer and to dramatize the transfer of power (9:18; Mark 5:23; Acts 9:12; 28:8); the impartation of spiritual gifts, which served to distinguish charismatic Christians from other sects (Acts 8:19; 19:6); and ordination (6:6, 8; 13:3; 1 Tim. 4:14; 5:22; 2 Tim. 1:6). Finally, in all its uses (except perhaps in blessing), laying on of hands had pneumatic, miraculous overtones befitting its place in a community emphasizing the presence of the Holy Spirit.

Bibliography. D. Daube, *The New Testament and Rabbinic Judaism* (1956, repr. New York, 1973); D. P. Wright, "The Gesture of Hand Placement in the Hebrew Bible and in Hittite Literature," *JAOS* 106 (1986): 433-46.

MARK W. HAMILTON

LAZARUS (Gk. *Lázaros*)

A common Jewish name (Heb. *ʾel-ʿāzār,* "God helps"). Luke 16:19-31 reports a parable by Jesus regarding the contrasting eternal fates of a poor Lazarus (the only named character in Jesus' parables) and a rich man. A pivotal section of the Gospel of John (John 11:1–12:11) presents Jesus' raising Lazarus from the dead as the act that fixed the determination of Jesus' opponents to put him to death. Interpreters have often mused about whether these two stories are related. Some have suggested that John's account arose from Luke's parable as a demonstration that indeed Lazarus' return from death (and ultimately Jesus' own) would not change people's actions (cf. Luke 16:30-31). Others have suggested that it was John's miracle story that eventually imposed a name upon the character in Luke's parable. The consensus, to the extent that there is one, remains that the two figures are unrelated.

Much of the study of the parable of Lazarus and Dives (Lat. "rich man") in the 20th century has focused on possible literary antecedents. Hugo Gressmann argued the story is taken from the Egyptian folktale about the tour of the underworld by Si-Osiris and Setme that concluded with the moral that those who had done good in life would be rewarded in death, while those who had done evil would be punished. Others have recently argued for closer parallels in Cynic stories about trips to Hades (Lucian *Cataplus* or Menippus *Nekyia*). At a minimum, the parable of Lazarus underscores Luke's theological theme that "God helps" the poor.

The Lazarus of John's Gospel reportedly lived in Bethany with his sisters Mary and Martha. One point that is emphasized throughout the story is Jesus' special love for and relationship with Lazarus (John 11:3, 5, 11, 35-36). This emphasis has led some to propose that Lazarus may have been the "Beloved Disciple" (e.g., John 13:23; 21:7, 20) whose death seems to have been so troubling to the Johannine community (21:23). There remains, however, no scholarly consensus on the identity of the Beloved Disciple. TIMOTHY B. CARGAL

LEAD

A chemical element which is the heaviest and softest of the common metals. It is sometimes found as lead sulfide or galena, and not in its pure form. Lead has a bright metallic luster between silvery-bluish-white to bluish-gray. It is very malleable and quite ductile. It has been used for many purposes such as an official seal or as a sealant for food containers when it is mixed with linseed oil. Lead is also used in ceramics as a glaze. Lead was commonly used by the Hebrews, as it is found in Egypt, Sinai, and Palestine (cf. Sir. 47:18). Lead was used in metalwork as an inlay (cf. Job 19:24) and often smelted with other metals (Ezek. 22:18). Early glass was probably made with lead as one of the ingredients. Other uses included lead cyanide as a poison, as a base for paints, and in an alloy such as leaded bronze. It is now considered carcinogenic if ingested with water or other liquid. Quite likely many people suffered palsy or paralysis from lead poisoning, but did not know its cause.

RICHARD A. STEPHENSON

LEAH (Heb. *lēʾâ*)

The elder daughter of Laban, sister of Rachel, and first wife of Jacob. She is the mother of six sons and one daughter. Her name is thought to mean "cow" in Hebrew.

Through the trickery of her father, Leah is wed to an unknowing Jacob, who had intended to marry Rachel (Gen. 29:16-26). The text does not indicate what part Leah played in the ruse Laban pulls. As a result, however, she ends up married to a man who does not love her and sharing that husband with her sister. Due to the lack of attention shown to her by Jacob, God blesses her with great fertility, while Rachel is barren. Leah gives birth to Reuben, Simeon, Levi, Judah, Issachar, and Zebulun (Gen. 29:31-35; 30:14-20). She also arranges for her maid Zilpah to bear two sons by Jacob, Gad and Asher, who are also attributed to Leah. In addition she has a daughter, Dinah (Gen. 30:21).

Leah is often described as unattractive, in contrast to her beautiful sister. This description revolves around the interpretation of Heb. *rakkôṯ* used to describe Leah's eyes (Gen. 29:17). Most translations render the word in English as "weak," but another possible translation could be "tender" or "soft."

A key event in the stories involving Leah and her sister and their sharing of a husband occurs when one of Leah's sons, Reuben, finds some mandrakes, which may have been an ancient aphrodisiac. Leah trades her mandrakes to Rachel (who hopes to use them to conceive) for an extra night with Jacob in her bed. Leah conceives from that union (Gen. 30:14-20). Through her actions and desires, Leah becomes one of the "mothers of Israel."

Bibliography. S. P. Jeansonne, *The Women of Genesis* (Minneapolis, 1990). LISA W. DAVISON

LEATHER

The raw material for many commonly used products in ancient times, including belts, shoes, boots, and sandals (Ezek. 16:10). John the Baptist wore a leather belt (Matt. 3:4; Mark 1:6), as did Elijah (2 Kgs. 1:8). Hides of animals with the holes sewn up held milk, water, and wine (Judg. 4:19; Gen. 21:14; Mark 2:22), and other leather containers stored oil for cooking, toiletry items, medicine, and fuel for lamps. Frequently beds and chairs were made of leather, and the wall hangings of the tabernacle were leather (Exod. 25:5; Num 4:8). Military equipment included leather helmets, shields, slings, and quivers, and the care of these products included rubbing oil on the leather surface (2 Sam. 1:21; Isa. 21:5).

Leather production is implied in the Bible (Exod. 25:5; Lev. 13:48). Hair and flesh were scraped from the animal skin, which was then treated for flexibility and water-proofing. The quickly degenerating leather has left few archaeological artifacts. One exception is the Dead Sea Scrolls. The scroll of Isaiah consists of 17 sheets of leather sewn together to form a piece measuring almost 7 m. (23 ft.). Paul's parchments (2 Tim. 4:13) were probably vellum on which was written OT Scriptures.

Bibliography. R. J. Forbes, "Leather in Antiquity," in *Studies in Ancient Technology*, 3rd ed., 5 (Leiden, 1993), 1-79. DENNIS GAERTNER

LEAVEN

A fermentation agent, in the Bible always leftover dough (sourdough) mixed with new dough to facilitate rising. Yeast has replaced sourdough today, so some translations replace "leaven" with "yeast" yet retain "unleavened (bread)."

Unleavened bread is associated especially with the Feast of Passover/Unleavened Bread. The Hebrews' haste in leaving Egypt left no time for bread to rise (Exod. 12:34, 39), and thus Passover is remembered (12:1-27; Mark 14:1, 12) with unleavened bread, even today. Leavened bread could be a thank offering (Lev. 7:11-14) but never a burnt offering (cf. Exod. 23:18; Lev. 2:11).

Leaven was a common figure of speech. In Jesus' Parable of the Leaven, as leaven transforms dough, so God's rule transforms life (Matt. 13:33; Luke 13:20-21). Jesus also warned against the "leaven" of the Pharisees and Sadducees, whose teachings corrupt (Mark 8:14-21 par.; Luke 12:1). Paul admonished the Corinthians to remove the "old leaven" (cf. Exod. 12:15, 19), i.e., sin that could corrupt the whole Church, and begin anew with the "unleavened bread of sincerity and truth" (1 Cor. 5:6-8). He also warns against legalism, which, like leaven, will transform the "whole batch" (Gal. 5:9).

EDMON L. ROWELL, JR.

LEBANA, LEBANAH (Heb. *lĕḇānâ*)
The head of a family of temple servants whose descendants returned with Zerubbabel from captivity in Babylon (Ezra 2:45; 1 Esdr. 5:29, "Lebanah"; Neh. 7:48, "Lebana").

LEBANON (Heb. *lĕḇānôn*)
A mountain region north of Israel noted for its cedar forest. The name Lebanon derives from the Semitic root *lbn* meaning "white," apparently a reference to the snow-capped mountains typical of the region (cf. Jer. 18:14). Although the limits of the area are imprecise, Lebanon referred to two parallel mountain chains lying immediately E of the Phoenician coast defined on the north by the Eleutherus River (Nahr el-Kebir) and the Leontes River (Litani) to the south, an area 160 km. (100 mi.) long.

Lebanon comprises three distinct zones. The mountains of Lebanon emerge dramatically very close to the sea and reach altitudes in excess of 3048 m. (10,000 ft.); the highest elevation is 3360 m. (11,024 ft.). The western slopes of these mountains receive nearly 152 cm. (60 in.) of annual rainfall, much of it falling as snow in the higher elevations. To the east of these mountains lies the Beqaʿ, a fertile valley nestled between the two mountain chains (cf. Josh. 11:17). Although part of the same geological rift that forms the Jordan Valley further south, the Beqaʿ averages an elevation over 915 m. (3000 ft.) above sea level. The Litani River rises from the watershed near Baalbek and flows south and then west before it joins the Mediterranean Sea N of Tyre. The Orontes River emerges out of lakes and marshes lying behind basalt intrusions at the northern end of the valley. Although the Beqaʿ would seem to be a natural corridor for north-south traffic, in fact the basalt intrusions in the north and precipitously descending ridges to the south made travel difficult, especially for large armies.

The Anti-Lebanon Mountains thrust upward E of the Beqaʿ. Slightly lower and drier than their western neighbors, the Anti-Lebanons received enough rainfall to produce abundant springs along the eastern foot of the range. These springs fed the Pharphar and Abana Rivers that sustained the oasis city Damascus. Mt. Hermon (2813 m. [9230 ft.], also known as Senir or Sirion [Deut. 3:9; Cant. 4:8]) anchors the southern end of this chain. Copious springs emerge at the foot of Mt. Hermon, forming the headwaters of the Jordan River (cf. Cant. 4:15).

Lebanon was renowned for its great coniferous forests (cedar, cypress, fir, and pine) that grew in abundance upon the mountain slopes. The cedars of Lebanon often mentioned in the OT were especially prized as a building material because of their strength and size. The Egyptians imported cedar for use in pyramids and sacred barques from the early 3rd millennium. Solomon secured cedar wood from King Hiram of Tyre to build the temple and his palace, the "House of the forest of Lebanon" (1 Kgs. 5:6-14; 7:2-8; 10:17-21). Cedar from Lebanon also was used in construction of the Second Temple (Ezra 3:7). The biblical writers frequently used the cedars of Lebanon as a symbol of beauty, enduring strength, nobility, and divine bounty (Ps. 104:16; 29:5-6; 72:16; 92:12; Cant. 7:4; Hos. 14:5-7; cf. 2 Kgs. 14:9). Lebanon was known also for its wine (Hos. 14:7).

THOMAS V. BRISCO

LEBAOTH (Heb. *lĕḇāʾôṯ*)
(also BETH-LEBAOTH)
A city in the extreme south of Judah (Josh. 15:32). At Josh. 19:6 it is called Beth-lebaoth and assigned to Simeon. It is probably the same as Beth-biri (1 Chr. 4:31).

LEBBAEUS (Gk. *Lebbaíos*)
An alternative reading for Thaddaeus in some manuscripts of Matt. 10:3. Options include "Thaddaeus," "Lebbaeus," "Thaddaeus who was called Lebbaeus," and "Lebbaeus who was called Thaddaeus." Of these only the first two are viable. The name also occurs in Mark 3:18 with much less manuscript support. Possible meanings include "beloved child" or "courageous one." It is frequently identified as a descriptive designation for "Judas of James" in Luke 6:16; Acts 1:13, where neither the name Thaddaeus or Lebbaeus occurs.

DAVID R. BECK

LEBONAH (Heb. *lĕḇônâ*)
A town in the hill country of Ephraim, ca. 5 km. (3 mi.) NW of Shiloh, on the road to Shechem (Judg. 21:19). The site has been identified as the modern village el-Lubban (173164).

LEB-QAMAI (Heb. *lēḇ qāmāy*)
A cipher for Chaldea (Jer. 51:1; NRSV mg "Kasdim").

See ATHBASH.

LECAH (Heb. *lēḵâ*)
A Judahite, son of Er and descendant of Shelah (1 Chr. 4:21). The context, however, suggests that Lecah was a place in the tribal territory of Judah, founded by Er. Because Mareshah, mentioned in the same text, is located NW of Hebron, Lecah would have been in the same region, though it cannot be identified more precisely.

LEECH
A bloodsucking worm of the class Hirudinea (Prov. 30:15; Heb. *ʿălûqâ*). Various types of leech have been attested since ancient times in the stagnant or slow moving waters of Palestine. The Talmud warns against drinking water directly from a river or pond with the mouth or hands out of the fear of ingesting a leech (*ʿAbod. Zar.* 12b).

LEEK
An herb (*Allium porrum*) believed to have originated in Central Asia. Unlike the onion, its base does not form a bulb and is more aromatic. Num. 11:5 notes that leeks were craved by the Israelites of the Exodus. Heb. *ḥāṣîr,* which can mean herbs or grass, has caused some to believe that fenugreek (*Trigonella foenum-graecum*) was intended; both are found in Egypt today. Leeks were commonly considered food for the poor, which caused them to be understood as a symbol of humility. However, the Roman emperor Nero was said to have enjoyed leeks as well; after his death he was referred to by some as Porrophagus, the "leek eater."

James V. Smith

LEGEND
A genre of narrative whose content and structure typically emphasize the virtue of the protagonist. The goal of the legend is to edify its audience. "Legend" stems from *legenda,* the Latin term for "things to be read," used for the medieval Christian stories about the lives of saints. Although in popular usage today the term has come to mean an "untrue or exaggerated story" about historical events or persons, the established use of the term in scholarship does not presume either historical accuracy or inaccuracy.

The legend takes place in a real human time frame, the recent past, and is believed to be historical by those who transmit it. Legend uses static narration, i.e., the plot does not exhibit an ever increasing tension culminating in a resolution point. Rather, the plot explores the virtue of the righteous hero from all angles in order to present various examples for emulation. The hero remains one-dimensional and undeveloped, addressed only in terms of the virtue possessed. In addition, the outcome of the plot is never in doubt; God will invariably ensure a good end for the virtuous hero. For example, in Dan. 1–6 Daniel and his pious friends predictably emerge victorious in every conflict or contest in the courts of foreign kings. Their faith is the central focus of the narratives and is to be emulated.

Legends in the OT may also be about a holy place; these tend to be concerned with an explanation of the origin and history of the sacredness of a place and the customs observed there. Such legends are termed "cult legend" or "cultic aetiology" (e.g., the story of Jacob at Bethel, Gen. 28:10-22).

Legend must be distinguished from other genres with which it often overlaps. It is different from myth in that it takes place in real time and not in the long distant past at the beginning of time. It differs from tale and from the German *Märchen,* "fairy-tale," in that it is not presumed to have taken place in an unreal world beyond human experience. Finally, legend can be seen as a sub-genre of *Sage,* the German term for "folk-" or "popular-story," but it emphasizes the virtue of a great hero above any other element.

Bibliography. R. M. Hals, "Legend," *CBQ* 34 (1972): 166-76; repr. in *Saga, Legend, Tale, Novella, Fable,* ed. G. W. Coats, JSOTSup 35 (Sheffield, 1985), 45-55; J. J. Scullion, "*Märchen, Sage, Legende:* Towards a Clarification of Some Literary Terms Used by Old Testament Scholars," *VT* 34 (1984): 321-36.

Tawny L. Holm

LEGION
The principal division in the Roman army (Gk. *legiṓn,* from Lat. *legere,* "to gather"). Following the defeat of Antony at the Battle of Actium (31 B.C.), Octavian made many military reforms. He reduced the number of legions from 60 or 70 to 28 (150 thousand men, plus an equal number of auxiliaries) and changed the army from a militia to a professional military (cf. Tacitus *Ann.* 1.17). Most rulers of this period kept a small standing force of elite troops supported by civilian levies, which were no match for the professional legionnaires (cf. Josephus *BJ* 3.70-109).

The legion (ca. 6000 men), under the authority of the provincial governor or a prefect (e.g., Egypt), was often directly commanded by an imperial legate assisted by tribunes and centurions. It contained 10 cohorts: a double-strength first cohort of 960 men and nine other cohorts of 480 foot-soldiers and 120 cavalry (scouts and dispatch riders). Cohorts were further subdivided into six centuries of 80 men, each commanded by a centurion.

A legionnaire was equipped with a large rectangular shield, helmet with neck guard and cheek pieces, body armor (leather, mail, or segmented steel), a short sword, dagger, and both heavy spears and light javelins.

At Matt. 26:53; Mark 5:9, 15; Luke 8:30 the term is figurative for a large number.

Bibliography. B. Campbell, *The Roman Army, 31 B.C.–A.D. 337* (London, 1994); G. Webster, *The Roman Imperial Army of the First and Second Centuries A.D.*, 3rd ed. (Norman, Okla., 1998).

Andrea Lorenzo Molinari

LEHABIM (Heb. *lĕhāḇîm*)
A people among the sons of Ham, named as offspring of Egypt (Gen. 10:13; 1 Chr. 1:11). They are generally identified with the Libyans (perhaps an alternative spelling of Heb. *lûḇîm*).

LEHEM (Heb. *leḥem*)
An obscure Hebrew form found in 1 Chr. 4:22, possibly an unknown place (so NRSV) ruled by Joash and Saraph. Some versions regard Lehem as a shortened form of Bethlehem (e.g., NJB, REB) or read MT "Jashubi-lahem" as a personal name (cf. NRSV mg). Another possibility is to translate "and returned," rather than a name (cf. similar idiomatic forms at Deut. 5:30; 1 Sam. 26:12).

Robin Gallaher Branch

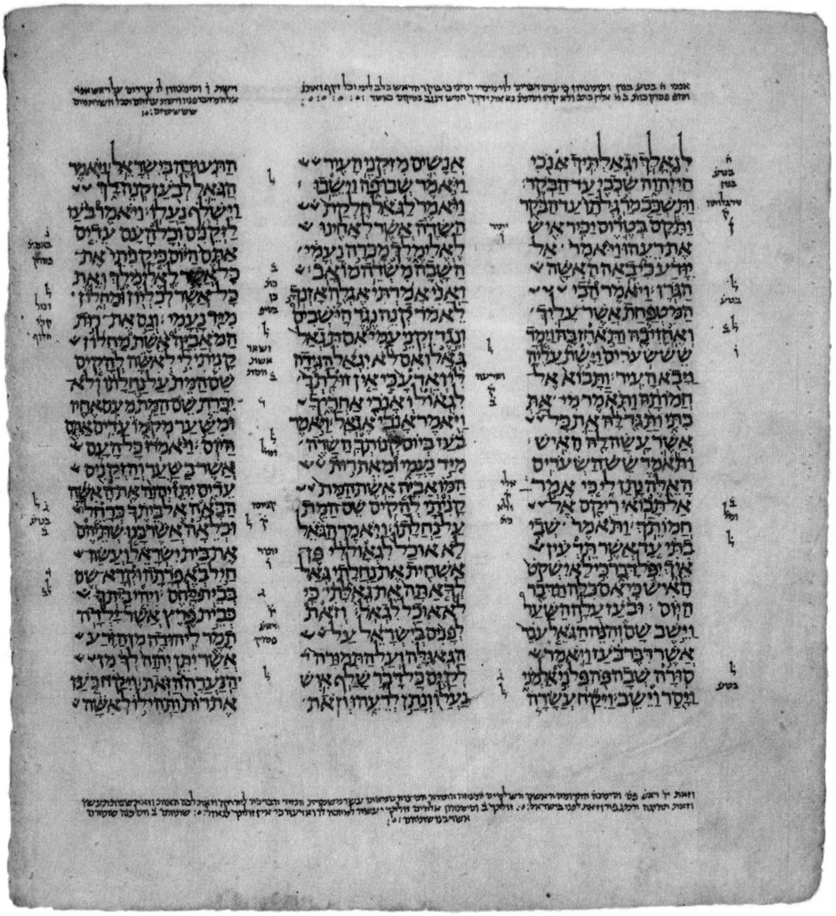

Folio 422V (Ruth 3:13b–4:13a) of the Leningrad Codex
(Photograph by Bruce and Kenneth Zuckerman, West Semitic Research)

LEHI (Heb. *leḥî*)
A Philistine camp where the imprisoned Samson broke free and killed 1000 Philistines with a "fresh jawbone (Heb. *leḥî*) of a donkey" (Judg. 15:9, 14, 19). It was subsequently called Ramath-lehi, "the high place of Lehi" (Judg. 15:17). The Philistines later deployed troops here against David (2 Sam. 23:11). Generally the Hebrew term refers to the jawbone of a human or animal, but it may also indicate a geographical feature. The site was probably located in the lowlands of Judah.

AARON M. GALE

LEMUEL (Heb. *lĕmû'ēl*)
A king ("belonging/dedicated to God") mentioned in Prov. 31:1, 4, otherwise unknown. Some conjecture that he was the king of the territory or tribe Massa, yet others assert that Lemuel refers to Solomon. The punctuation and accentuation in the Leningrad Codex (B[19]) indicate that Heb. *maśśā'* refers to what the king has been taught by his mother (NRSV "oracle"), not a place.

DAVID CLEAVER-BARTHOLOMEW

LENINGRAD CODEX
Codex Leningradensis (L), the oldest complete manuscript of the Hebrew Bible extant. It was copied ca. 1008/1009 C.E. by the scribe Shemu'el ben Ya'aqob in Cairo, following the authoritative manuscripts of Aharon ben-Moshe ben-Asher of Tiberias. The earliest complete Hebrew Bible containing vowel points and accents, the codex is particularly valued for its extensive masorah, marginal notations concerning textual matters such as occurrences and spellings. It is the base text for the third *(BHK)* and fourth *(BHS)* editions of the *Biblia Hebraica;* all Masoretic notes from the Leningrad Codex will be incorporated into the fifth edition *(BHQ).*

The codex comprises 491 folios written on thick white parchment. Each page consists of three columns, except for Psalms, Proverbs, and Job, which have two columns with poetry inserted into the text. Following the Minor Prophets, the Writings appear in "chronological" order: Chronicles, Psalms, Job, Proverbs, Ruth, Song of Songs,

Ecclesiastes, Lamentations, Esther, Daniel, Ezra-Nehemiah. An opening colophon indicates the date and place of copying; two other colophons provide the name of the scribe. The manuscript also features 16 illuminated "carpet pages" as well as Masoretic lists and poems by ben-Ya'aqob and Moshe ben-Asher.

Housed in the Russian National Library in St. Petersburg, the codex is also identified as Firkovich B 19 A, obtained from the collection of Abraham Firkovich in 1862.

Bibliography. D. N. Freedman, ed., *The Leningrad Codex: A Facsimile Edition* (Grand Rapids, 1998).

ALLEN C. MYERS

LENT

The period of preparation prior to Easter, 40 weekdays (six weeks, not counting Sundays; cf. Mark 1:13). Originally a time of fasting for baptismal candidates, it became a time of general penance and abstinence, with increased emphasis on reflection and spiritual renewal.

LENTILS

The fruit of a plant in the legume family (*Lens esculenta* Moench) cultivated since very ancient times in the Near East. Lentils grew in fields (2 Sam. 23:11), often as tall as 45 cm. (18 in.). The plant put forth a white flower followed by flat pods containing one or two seeds. Judging by the "red stuff," "pottage," or "lentil stew" Esau craved from Jacob, lentils were reddish in color (Gen. 25:30-34); Esau was, in fact, thereafter called Edom, the Hebrew word for red (Gen. 25:30).

Lentils were used to make bread (Ezek. 4:9) and even medicine, as the seeds helped ease constipation. Lentils were among the foods given to David and his troops (2 Sam. 17:28). Chiefly used as food for the poor in biblical times, lentil bread remains a part of the diet of the poor in the Middle East today.

J. RANDALL O'BRIEN

LEOPARD

A large spotted carnivore of the lion family. An adult leopard is ca. 1.5 m. (5 ft.) long, has a tail ca. 0.6-0.9 m. (2-3 ft.) long, and has a yellowish coat with dark spots (Jer. 13:23). It roamed widely in Africa, Palestine, and other parts of Asia and fed on antelope, ibex, deer, goat, sheep, and small animals. There have been few sightings of leopards in Palestine since 1960.

The leopard was an animal feared in ancient times (Cant. 4:8; Jer. 5:6; Hos. 13:7). It was also admired for its swiftness (Hab. 1:8). The leopard is used in apocalyptic imagery to represent nations that quickly conquer major regions (Dan. 7:6; Rev. 13:2). In Isaiah's prophetic vision of the messianic age, peace is exemplified by the image of a leopard lying down with a goat (Isa. 11:6).

JOHN A. MCLEAN

LEPROSY

A chronic, though not highly contagious, disease that primarily affects the skin, mucous membranes, and nerves, known also as Hansen's disease. The cause is an organism, Mycobacterium laprae, identified by the Norwegian physician G. A. H. Hansen (1841-1912).

Most scholars agree that Heb. *ṣara'aṯ*, translated "leprosy" by most English versions (Lev. 13–14), should not be equated with Hansen's disease. This term encompassed a variety of conditions characterized by chronic discoloration of surfaces, including human skin and the walls of houses (Lev. 14:34-57). Persons afflicted with *ṣara'aṯ* were regarded as impure, and Lev. 13:44-46 prescribes exile from the community for them. Some texts from Qumran apply even more comprehensive restrictions for "lepers."

The sociological implications of levitical policies, if implemented, were probably significant. Bands of persons affected with *ṣara'aṯ* roam outside of cities (2 Kgs. 7:3). The cases of Namaan (2 Kgs. 5) and Uzziah (2 Chr. 26:16-21) show that even officials and kings with *ṣara'aṯ* were not exempt from negative social consequences. Early Christianity apparently disagreed with levitical policies. Jesus touches a "leper" (Mark 1:41) and commands his disciples to minister to them (Matt. 10:8).

HECTOR AVALOS

LESHEM (Heb. *lešem*)

The alternate form of Laish, the ancient name of Dan (Josh. 19:47).

LETHECH (Heb. *leṯeḵ*)

A dry measure equivalent to one half homer (Hos. 3:2 MT; NRSV mg).

LETTER

Letters were among the most important types of written texts in antiquity, in part because they were understood to function as a substitute for the author's presence. In addition to a few handbooks on writing letters, a large number of Hellenistic letters from the period beginning in the mid-3rd century B.C.E. are extant. These materials provide an important resource for understanding the letters of the NT.

The letter is the most common literary form in the NT. Besides the nearly 20 NT books written in this form, some letters are found embedded within books of both the OT (e.g., 2 Sam. 11:15) and the NT (Acts 15:23-29).

Letters in the Hellenistic era included several conventional parts or "periods." These were: a greeting, often a thanksgiving or prayer, a body, and a closing. The greeting identified both the sender and recipient and sometimes included information about each, such as their relationship or their respective places in the social hierarchy. Thus, the greeting established a context for the rest of the correspondence. It also often included a health-wish for the recipient. When a letter included a thanksgiving or prayer to the gods, it often consisted largely of an extended health-wish, but not uncommonly it included other matters. After the letter's body, which contained the basic message and purpose of the letter, the closing was usually composed of stereotyped conventions and greetings to and from others known to both the sender and recipient.

Early in the 20th century, Adolf Deissmann divided letters into two types: epistles (which he saw as literary productions for a general/public audience) and genuine letters (which were private, strictly occasional, and nonliterary). While there were writings in epistolary form which were composed primarily as literary works, Deissmann's distinction does not satisfactorily fit either the production of letters in the Greco-Roman world generally or the NT letters. Paul's letters are clearly occasional and do not adopt the elevated style of a literary work, but they are not purely private because they are intended to be read to congregations, as are all NT letters.

Early Christian writers adapted the letter form to meet the needs of their churches. Paul often expands conventional periods so that they contribute to the purpose of the letters of which they are a part. This is most evident for thanksgivings which signal in advance the main concerns of the letter. Studies of Paul's use of each of the conventional epistolary periods reveal many patterns which contribute to our understanding of his letters. The bodies of the canonical letters draw on both epistolary and rhetorical conventions. Although early Christian writers seem to have a working knowledge of the content of handbooks on epistolary style, their letters do not indicate that these writers possessed advanced rhetorical training. Beginning in the late 2nd century, however, Christian letter writers were often trained in rhetoric and began to produce letters of a more literary nature.

The style of the canonical letters falls between everyday correspondence and literary productions. Their closest parallel seems to be letters written by philosophers to exhort and teach their readers. But even this is not an exact parallel. It is significant that NT writers chose the letter as their primary literary genre. Letters are, by their nature, occasional, i.e., designed to address specific situations. Thus, their purpose is to supply specific instructions for the particular situations in which the recipients and author(s) find themselves. Letters are also dialogical, a piece of a conversation between the sender and recipient. So modern readers need to know as much as possible about the circumstances of both the sender and the recipients to understand a letter's content.

Some NT writings which were given an epistolary framework are not actually letters. Most notably, Hebrews and James have closing or opening features of letters but are treatises of a different sort. While these writings are not genuine letters, they bear witness to the power of the epistolary genre as a means of teaching and exhortation in early Christianity.

Bibliography. S. K. Stowers, *Letter Writing in Greco-Roman Antiquity.* Library of Early Christianity 5 (Philadelphia, 1986); J. L. White, *Light from Ancient Letters.* Foundations and Facets (Philadelphia, 1986).

JERRY L. SUMNEY

LETUSHIM (Heb. *lĕṭûšim*)

An Arabian tribal group descended from Dedan, the grandson of Abraham and Keturah (Gen. 25:3).

LEUCIUS (Gk. *Leukios*)

The pseudonymous author of the 2nd-century Acts of John, supposedly a disciple of the Apostle John (Epiphanius *Adv. haer.* 51.6). Leucius was also the name ascribed to the 4th-century collector of the Acts of the Apostles, which consists of the Acts of John and four other apocryphal Acts, the Acts of Paul, Peter, Andrew, and Thomas (cf. Photius *Bibl.* 114). The Manichaeans substituted these apocryphal Acts for the canonical Acts, which led Pope Leo I to condemn these apocryphal works.

Bibliography. K. Schäferdiek, "The Acts of John," *New Testament Apocrypha,* ed. Schneemelcher and R. McL. Wilson, rev. ed., 2 (Philadelphia, 1965): 152-212.

SHEILA MARIE DUGGER GRIFFITH

LEUMMIM (Heb. *lĕ'ummîm*)

An Arabian people tracing descent from Dedan, the grandson of Abraham and Keturah (Gen. 25:3).

LEVANT

A designation for the lands of the eastern Mediterranean (from Fr. *lever,* "to rise" [i.e., the sun]), primarily Asia Minor and Syria-Palestine but often the entire coastlands from Greece to Egypt. In geological usage the Jordan Rift is sometimes called the Levant Rift Valley.

LEVI (Heb. *lēwî;* Gk. *Leuí*)

1. The eponymous ancestor of the tribe of Levi and the Levites; the third son of Jacob by his first wife Leah (Gen. 29:34). At his birth Leah says, "Now this time my husband will be joined to me," suggesting an etymology for Levi of "to be joined, attached." This is consistent with other uses of Heb. *lāwâ* (Ps. 83:8[MT 9]; Isa. 14:1). It is also consistent with the notion of the Levites being "attached to, joined to" Aaron to serve him in the cult (Num. 18:2, 4).

Levi and the Levites were characterized by zeal for Yahweh, which is exemplified in Levi by the story of the rape of his sister Dinah (Gen. 34). In that account Levi, along with his brother Simeon, avenges the rape of their sister by demanding that the rapist, who now wants to marry Dinah, circumcise himself and all the males of his town. They agree to this in order to intermarry, but while they are incapacitated from their circumcision Levi and Simeon slay them all with the sword and plunder the city. This action establishes their reputation for violence and ruthless anger on behalf of the moral imperative. It also serves to explain their scattering throughout Israel and Judah (cf. Josh. 18:7), for it was asserted that because of their temper no one would want to come into their counsel or assembly (Gen. 49:5-7).

This excessive zeal in behalf of right vs. wrong exemplified by Levi in the Dinah episode is viewed as characteristic of his descendants as well. In the story of the sin of the Golden Calf (Exod. 32), e.g., it is the Levites (as opposed to Aaron) who were willing to kill their kinsmen, neighbors, and friends on behalf of the Lord. Thus, that day they were consecrated to the Lord (Exod. 32:26-29).

LISBETH S. FRIED

2. An ancestor of Jesus, listed in Luke's genealogy as the father of Matthat and son of Melchi (Luke 3:24).

3. A tax collector (Luke 5:27, 29), the son of Alphaeus (Mark 2:14), whom Jesus called as a disciple. Levi is generally taken as the Hebrew name of Matthew in Matt. 9:9.

4. Another ancestor of Jesus, according to Luke the father of Matthat and son of Simeon (Luke 3:29).

LEVIATHAN (Heb. *liwyāṯān*)
A primeval sea serpent representing chaos.

Leviathan appears in the Ugaritic texts as Lītānū. *KTU* 1.5 I,1 describes how Baal smote Lītānū, "the twisting [cf. Arab. *lawiyā*] serpent, the tyrant with seven heads" (likewise Anat [*KTU* 1.3 III,40-42], but lacking the name Lītānū). Ancient Near Eastern iconography consistently depicts the storm-god conquering the serpent.

Yahweh's conquest of Leviathan in Ps. 74:14 (note the "heads") is part of his creative activity (vv. 12-17). This connection underlies Job 3:8 as well: while cursing his birthday (in terms reversing the creation of Gen. 1) Job invokes "those who are skilled to rouse up Leviathan." Job's reference to Yahweh piercing "the fleeing serpent" (Job 26:13) also occurs in a creation context (cf. *KTU* 1.5 I,1). In Ps. 104:26, however, the conquest motif is abandoned: Leviathan is simply one of God's creatures, and a playful one at that. Levithan is discussed at length in Job 41:1-34. Many see the crocodile here, but his ability to breath fire and smoke, the inability of humans to subdue him, and the overwhelming terror he instills all argue for a mythological creature Yahweh is able to subdue but Job cannot. In Isa. 27:1 the mythology comes full circle, with Yahweh defeating Leviathan (again) as a new creation in the eschatological age; the lexical contacts with *KTU* 1.5 I,1 are particularly striking.

The "seven-headed dragon" is equated with Satan in Rev. 12:3, 9 and echoed in the seven-headed beast of 13:1; 17:3. Postbiblical Jewish literature envisions Leviathan, along with Behemoth, as the main course at the messianic banquet (1 En. 60:7-9, 24; 2 Esdr. 6:49-52; 2 Bar. 29:4).

Bibliography. J. Day, *God's Conflict with the Dragon and the Sea* (Cambridge, 1985); C. Uehlinger, "Leviathan," *DDD*, 511-15.

JOHN L. MCLAUGHLIN

LEVIRATE MARRIAGE
A cross-cultural phenomenon whereby the nearest kinsman of a man who dies without sons marries his widow. In ancient Israel, the first son of the levirate union (from Lat. *levir*, "brother-in-law") was considered the dead man's heir.

Deut. 25:5-10 imposes the obligation of levirate marriage on a surviving brother if he and the deceased had "lived together," i.e., had not divided their patrimony. The last section of the law (Deut. 25:7-10) deals with the case where the brother refuses. The widow brings a complaint to the elders, who establish her brother-in-law's unwillingness to marry her. She then performs three acts designed to humiliate the brother-in-law for his refusal; presumably these acts release both widow and brother-in-law from further levirate obligation.

The primary purpose of the law is to provide the deceased man with a son to inherit his property and thereby establish his "name," i.e., his lineage, memory, and in some sense his continued existence. A secondary purpose of the levirate may have been to provide the deceased's wife with the economic security and social status of marriage and children. It is much less likely that law was intended to keep the deceased man's property within his family by preventing his widow from taking it into a second marriage. There is no biblical evidence that a childless widow would have inherited her husband's property (cf. Num. 27).

Two passages suggest that kinsmen other than the deceased's brother had a moral if not legal obligation to marry the widow. In Gen. 38 Tamar is deemed righteous for providing her dead husband with an heir by tricking her father-in-law into having sex with her. The book of Ruth assumes that it is an act of faithfulness for the deceased's nearest kinsman to marry his widow and provide him an heir.

Levirate marriage is discussed in the rabbinic tractate *Yebamot* and underlies the debate between Jesus and the Sadducees narrated in Matt. 22:23-33 (= Mark 12:18-27 = Luke 2:27-40).

Bibliography. S. Niditch, "The Wrong Woman Righted: An Analysis of Genesis 38," *HTR* 72 (1979): 143-49; C. Pressler, *The View of Women Found in Deuteronomic Family Laws.* BZAW 216 (Berlin, 1993); R. Westbrook, "The Law of the Biblical Levirate," *Revue internationale des droits de l'antiquité*, 3rd ser., 24 (1977): 65-87; repr. in *Property and the Family in Biblical Law.* JSOTSup 113 (Sheffield, 1981), 69-89.

CAROLYN PRESSLER

LEVITES (Heb. *lĕwî*)
Because the Levites are portrayed differently in the various biblical sources, each must be examined separately. Most secure are references in the books of Chronicles, dated to the last half of the 4th century B.C.E. Here the Levites comprise three classes of cult personnel all claiming descent from the single eponymous ancestor Levi, but carefully distinguished from each other and from the sons of Aaron by their genealogy. These are the Levites proper, who claim descent from the firstborn sons of the sons of Levi; the singers, who claim descent from the secondborn sons of the sons of Levi (1 Chr. 6); and the gatekeepers, who claim descent from Korah, son of Izhar, the second son of Kohath,

son of Levi (1 Chr. 9:19), and also from the sons of Merari (9:14; 26:19).

As described in Chronicles, the tasks of the Levites during this period indicate a well-established temple bureaucracy having both religious and secular functions. The gatekeepers are in charge of the thresholds, the chambers, and the treasuries of the temple. They collect the annual taxes and assessments and pay out from it according to the needs of the state (2 Chr. 24:6; 34:9-10). They assist the sons of Aaron in the temple service, being in charge of the furniture and utensils, the flour, wine, oil, incense, and spices — everything required for the service (1 Chr. 9:26-32; 23:24-29).

The singers accompany the sacrificial service with song and musical instruments (1 Chr. 23:30-31; 2 Chr. 29:27-28). A further role of the Levites was to instruct the populace in the law (2 Chr. 17:8-9; 19:8-10; 35:3), and it may have fallen to the temple singers to interpret, teach, and copy the law since the service of song may have included the recitation of the law.

Officers and judges were also appointed from the Levites (1 Chr. 23:4; 26:29; 2 Chr. 19:8). These were probably in charge of legal decision-making, conscription, corvée labor, and collection of taxes for the secular and cultic affairs of the temple (1 Chr. 26:22-30).

Prior to the time of the Chronicler we have a different picture. During the time of Nehemiah (446) it is still the Levites headed by an Aaronide priest who collect the tithes throughout the towns (Neh. 10:37[MT 38]), and a distinction is still made between the priests who do the work of the temple (11:12) and the Levites who do the work external to the temple. Also at this time, the temple singers had been assimilated to the levitical class (Neh. 11:17; 12:27) but not unambiguously (12:28, 45-47; 13:5, 10), but the gatekeepers were not yet considered Levites. Still earlier, in a list dating to the time of the return (between 538 and 520), neither singers nor gatekeepers were Levites (Ezra 2 = Neh. 7), and even by the time of Ezra, in the 7th year of Artaxerxes (458; Ezra 7:24; cf. Neh. 10:29, 39[30, 40]) neither of these groups had yet been assimilated into their ranks. At that time the role of the Levites was only to "read from the Law, giving the sense, and enabling the people to understand the meaning" (Neh. 8:7).

Still earlier, in Babylon in 572, Ezekiel outlines the roles and privileges of the levitical priests (Ezek. 40–48), but does not know them as either singers or gatekeepers. He knows two classes of priests: one in charge of the service of the altar, the sons of Zadok, and the other in charge of the service of the temple (Ezek. 40:45-46). As in Nehemiah both classes are counted among the levitical priests (Ezek. 43:19). According to Ezekiel, the levitical priests not of the line of Zadok administer the gates of the temple complex and have the care of the temple. They slaughter the whole burnt offering and the sacrifice of the people, and stand before the people to serve them. They have charge of the temple, the service for it, and all that is done in it (Ezek. 44:10-14), but they may not approach the altar or the sacred things (v. 13). Since Ezekiel accuses this second class of levitical priests of having led Israel astray prior to the exile (Ezek. 44:12), this class of priests must have existed prior to Ezekiel.

For his description of the role of the Levites, Ezekiel relies on references to them in the book of Numbers, which form a late addition to the Priestly corpus. Here the Levites serve the sons of Aaron (Num. 3:6; 18:2), keep the service of the tent, and do the work of the tent (Num. 3:8; 18:4, 6), but they may not approach the holy vessels or the altar (18:3). They have the duty of carrying the tabernacle and the ark, setting it up, and taking it down (Num. 1:50-51; chs. 3, 4). They slaughter the sacrifice of the people (Num. 8:19) and collect the tithes (18:26, 28). The concern of both Ezekiel and this strata of Numbers is that the Levites would "bear the iniquity" of the cult, i.e., bear responsibility for the cult and guard it against the encroachment of unauthorized personnel (Ezek. 44:11; cf. v. 7) which would incur the "wrath" of God (Num. 1:51, 53; 3:10; 18:7, 22).

The Levites may have been priests of Yahweh in the northern kingdom who fled south when the north fell in 722, and who were then incorporated into the Jerusalem priesthood as a second order of priests. According to Josh. 21 the cities given to the Aaronides were all in the areas of Judah, Simeon, and Benjamin, whereas the non-Aaronide Levites were all given cities in the north, indicating a northern province. The fall of the north may have precipitated language about the fear of the "wrath" of God in Numbers and this, or the cultic term "to bear iniquity," may have later been misinterpreted by Ezekiel or a later glossator of Ezekiel, giving rise to the polemics there.

Bibliography. S. L. Cook, "Innerbiblical Interpretation in Ezekiel 44 and the History of Israel's Priesthood," *JBL* 114 (1995): 193-208; R. K. Duke, "Punishment or Restoration? Another Look at the Levites of Ezekiel 44,6-16," *JSOT* 40 (1988): 61-81; M. Haran, *Temples and Temple-Service in Ancient Israel* (1978, repr. Winona Lake, 1985); S. Japhet, *I and II Chronicles.* OTL (Louisville, 1993); B. A. Levine, *Numbers 1–20.* AB 4 (New York, 1993); H. G. M. Williamson, *Ezra, Nehemiah.* WBC 16 (Waco, 1985).

LISBETH S. FRIED

LEVITICAL CITIES

Forty-eight cities allotted to the Levites, spread throughout the territories of the other tribes. The Bible presents Levi as unique among the Israelite tribes, receiving no allocation of land as did the other tribes (Josh. 13–19). Two texts provide the names of these cities: Josh. 21:1-42; 1 Chr. 6:54-81(MT 39-66). Num. 35:1-8 asserts that this arrangement was the divine will.

The tradition of the levitical cities reflects the early emergence of the Levites as specialists in matters of worship. They supported themselves from this service to the other tribes (Num. 18:21-24; Deut. 18:1-4; Josh. 13:14). Though at one stage in ancient Israel's life any male Israelite could offer sacrifice, texts such as Judg. 17 show that Levites were preferred. Still, the history of the priesthood in ancient Israel and the relationship of the Levites to the priests are issues that require further clarification. How to understand the levitical cities awaits the answer to these questions.

Did levitical cities as such exist in ancient Israel, or were they theological constructs? At first, scholars assumed that the levitical cities did exist to serve the purpose described in the Bible. However, archaeological evidence shows that most of the cities mentioned in the lists of Joshua and 1 Chronicles were not occupied during most of the monarchic period and that the list in Joshua was compiled in the 8th century B.C.E. Also, not all the levitical cities were part of the Israelite or Judahite kingdoms in the 8th century, nor is it clear why the list in Josh. 21 was compiled at that time. It does not seem likely that the lists fit any preexilic historical situation. They were probably the creation of postexilic writers who wanted to explain the role of the Levites in the early social and religious structure of ancient Israel. Their purpose was to help solve the problem that arose with the centralization of worship in the Jerusalem temple. Once priestly activity was limited to Jerusalem, the presence of and support for a large number of liturgical specialists without a sanctuary to serve became a serious problem.

Bibliography. A. G. Auld, "The 'Levitical Cities': Texts and History," *ZAW* 91 (1979): 194-206.

LESLIE J. HOPPE, O.F.M.

LEVITICUS, BOOK OF

The third of the Five Books of Moses that comprise the Pentateuch or Torah. Leviticus forms the core of the Priestly source (P), which comprises about half of the Torah, beginning at Exod. 24:15, extending through most of Numbers, and including scattered interpolations in Genesis and Exodus. The title Leviticus bestowed by the early Church is a misnomer, as P actually discusses Levites mainly in Numbers. Leviticus covers a wide range of topics; but its focus on sacrifice in the first 10 chapters conveys a false impression that the book will deal only with a temple cult, which slaughters animals in order to offer up choice portions like the "fat covering the entrails," "the two kidneys" and "the appendage of the liver" — all so a God called Yahweh may smell the "pleasing odor" of the burnt offering (3:1-5).

In reality, Leviticus goes far beyond the sacrificial concerns (e.g., thanks for God's bounty, atonement for sin) presented in chs. 1-10. Its topics include dietary laws defining animals fit for food and sacrifice (ch. 11); treatment of virulent but curable skin diseases (chs. 13-14); rites of atonement for individual and communal sin (ch. 16); and daily, sabbath, and festival cultic rituals observed throughout the year (chs. 23-24). The book also regulates symbolic purification of women after childbirth (ch. 12); ritual cleansing of cultic pollution caused by genital discharges (ch. 15) or contact with corpses (chs. 21-22); and most importantly, the practice of sexual intercourse and related matters (chs. 18, 20). Many scholars view the Holiness Code (chs. 17-26) as a separate source (H) adopted by P. The book concludes with laws for sabbatical and jubilee years (ch. 25), depictions of dire punishment for disobeying God's laws (ch. 26), and an appendix (ch. 27) listing the monetary value of various classes of Israelites, to be donated by one who pledges his value or that of his child to the sanctuary.

Dating and Provenance

Jewish exegetes dubbed Leviticus "the Instruction for Priests" *(tôraṯ kōhănîm),* as it is mainly a manual for conducting the Israelite cult of Yahweh. P portrays the temple in the guise of a portable sanctuary that accompanied the Israelites during their 40 years' nomadic wandering from Egypt to the Promised Land. Whether the sanctuary symbolized the First (preexilic) or Second (postexilic) Temple depends on the book's date of composition — a subject of ongoing controversy. Most scholars would date Leviticus to the 5th century B.C.E., after the 6th-century Babylonian Exile, when Israelite priests deported to Babylon by Nebuchadnezzar II (2 Kgs. 25:18; Ezra 1:5) encountered first Babylonian religion and then Persian Zoroastrianism — both of which may have influenced the writing of P. A scholarly minority would date P to preexilic times, thus viewing it as an indigenous development within Israelite culture.

Leviticus' character as a priestly manual distinguishes it from other sources of the Torah (J, E, and D) and from all other books of the OT. It is neither a myth of origins (like Genesis) nor historiography (Joshua through Kings), nor poetry (the Song of Songs), nor philosophy (Ecclesiastes), nor prophecy (Isaiah or Jeremiah). It contains little narrative and relatively few named characters, apart from the Israelite leaders Moses and Aaron. Leviticus regulates two of the Israelite castes: the high-caste hereditary priesthood called "sons of Aaron" and the common people called "sons (or 'children') of Israel." (Levites or "sons of Levi," an intermediate caste that ministered to the Aaronide priests, figure in P segments of Numbers.) Leviticus deals also with persons thought to pose a threat to holiness or cultic purity, such as sufferers from certain skin diseases (including one persistently misidentified as leprosy) and genital discharges; menstruants; and people who offended against both ethics and cult by engaging in forbidden sexual conduct, specifically adultery, incest, homosexuality, and bestiality.

Anthropological Perspectives

Its topics often introduced by the claim that "God spoke to Moses, saying . . . ," Leviticus appears to present concrete rules of divine law. But closer scrutiny reveals a concern with abstract ideas important to theology and anthropology alike. Anthropologist Mary Douglas demonstrated that laws governing food and sex embody a desire to preserve harmony in nature and society; and historian of religions Mircea Eliade showed that a concern with sacred places (like the temple in Jerusalem) and sacred times (like sabbaths and other holy days) reflects an ethnocentric belief — widely prevalent in ancient cultures — in the cosmic importance of the activities of one's own group, seen as a chosen people in a covenantal relationship with its god. In Leviticus this doctrine accounts for Priestly emphasis on "holiness" and "purity" and their connection to basic phenomena like childbirth, menstruation, sexual relations, and death.

Animal Sacrifice

Animal sacrifice, widespread in the ancient world (and still practiced in some cultures today), may strike modern readers as simply primitive. Yet it embodies sophisticated concepts characteristic of most or all religious systems. Anthropologists and scholars of religion agree that religious ideas developed from human efforts to make sense of the cosmos. An innate craving for order and harmony prompted the view that the universe was in principle orderly rather than chaotic (Gk. *kósmos* means "order"). When things went awry, whether in the form of natural disasters or societal disruptions, the disturbance of cosmic order called for symbolic action to restore the shattered equilibrium by placating the powers that rule the cosmos; and symbolic action often took the form of sacrifice to the tribal god or gods.

Conversely, if a god favored an individual or group with an abundance of crops or herds, thus tipping the scales in their favor, equilibrium could be restored by bringing a thank-offering *(quid pro quo)* from crops or herds (Lev. 1-3). Sometimes people tilted the balance toward heaven by bringing on offering in advance *(do ut des),* hoping to motivate their god(s) to restore the balance by granting an abundant harvest next time. One who had sinned by infringing some cultic regulation could appease divine wrath with a sacrifice (chs. 4-5). Leviticus prescribes offerings to fit all of these categories, the general goal being to retain or regain divine favor by symbolically righting a wrong or neutralizing some event that, for good or ill, had disturbed or threatened to disturb cosmic harmony.

Prominent among acts thought to upset cosmic balance was the commission of "sin" — a common but misleading translation of Heb. *ḥēṭ',* which in P does not carry the same moral overtones as the English word "sin." From a root meaning "to miss the mark," *ḥēṭ'* really means "error" or "mistake" (the converse of *tôrâ,* which comes from a root meaning "to hit the mark"). In the worldview of the Israelite priests, cultic infractions — even unintended ones — offended God and required a sacrifice of symbolic expiation (chs. 4, 5, 16), whereas ethical offenses against fellow human beings demanded amends by restitution or compensation (as frequently spelled out in Exodus and Deuteronomy) to restore personal and societal equilibrium.

Holiness and Purity

The primary motivators of religious practice in the priestly systems are the twin themes of holiness *(qĕḏûšâ)* and purity *(ṭohŏrâ)* — distinct but closely associated concepts that require elucidation. The demand for Israelite holiness is articulated in a thrice-repeated call for *imitatio Dei:* "You shall be holy, for I Yahweh your God am holy" (19:2; 20:7; 11:44). The meaning of holiness here may not be readily apparent to modern readers, for whom the term often evokes a pious, ascetic individual — saint, mystic, priest, or nun. The association of holiness with sexual abstinence, however, is distinctive to Christianity and rooted in particular conditions of late antiquity. To understand holiness in Leviticus, we must draw on the insights of anthropology and comparative religion.

Holiness for Israelite priests resembled similar concepts in other ancient religions like Zoroastrianism and Hinduism. It meant being "special" or "set apart." Since holiness must pervade every waking action, daily life was circumscribed by a catalogue of "thou shalts" and "thou shalt nots" encompassing both cultic acts of worship expressing love of God (chs. 1–10, 23–24) and ethical acts expressing love of neighbor (19:18, 34, and ch. 19 generally), as well as physical acts vital to the survival of individual and group — namely those involving food (ch. 11) and sex (chs. 18 and 20). Not only the priesthood but Israelites in general ("a priestly kingdom and a holy nation," Exod. 19:6) must separate themselves from others in imitation of their God Yahweh. The doctrine of election ("chosen people syndrome") is not unique to the Israelites, but is found in most ethnic or national groups (e.g., the British White Man's Burden, French *mission civilatrice,* German *Herrenvolk,* American Manifest Destiny); and in the context of religion it appears in the supersessionism of the early Church, which explicitly declared Christians to be the "Israel of God" (Gal. 6:16) and the new "chosen race" (1 Pet. 2:9).

Leviticus reinforces holiness by imposing strict standards of cultic purity in personal and communal life. Cultic purity (sometimes called ritual purity) is a concept even less accessible than holiness to the modern mind. Many ancients believed that some bodily processes triggered an intangible aura of contamination, which impeded human access to the divine. Cultic pollution could be generated by the discharge of bodily fluids associated with crucial phenomena like childbirth, menstruation, ejaculation, genital discharges, mysterious diseases, and above all by contact with death. Primitive societies lacking science and medicine viewed such events — poorly understood and largely beyond human control — as ordained by God. Not surprisingly, they became hedged around with rules of pollution and taboo and purification rituals to remove the taint that attached to people or things having physical contact with these phenomena. Such rules characterize Hinduism, Zoroastrianism, Judaism, and Islam and are still to some degree observed in the Eastern Orthodox Church. Christian baptism as a means to remove the invisible taints of sin (cf. John the Baptist in Matt. 3) evolved directly from the cleansing procedures prescribed in Leviticus.

Status of Women

In the worldview of P, a priest who contracted impurity could not "come before Yahweh" to perform his duties unless he had first purified himself by ritual immersion. The same applied to an Israelite man healed from a genital discharge, who wished to "come before Yahweh" with his offering (15:13-14). As to women, however, the omission of the crucial phrase "before Yahweh" in the case of a woman healed of a genital discharge (15:29) reflects Priestly perception of women as ineligible in principle to enter the divine presence. Cultic taboos surrounding childbirth, menstruation, and sexual relations sociologically reflect and theologically define the place of women in the patriarchal culture of ancient Israel. Even priestly-caste women could not participate actively in the temple cult; rules designed to preserve the holiness and purity of individual Israelites and of the community at large banned women's potentially polluting presence from the public cultural domain. Later, talmudic rules based on the Priestly worldview would effectively confine Jewish women to the private domain. Those laws impact the lives of women in traditional Judaism to this day, from the mandatory monthly visit to a mikveh (ritual immersion pool) to their ineligibility for public offices like rabbi, cantor, or religious court judge.

Historical Note

Ancient Israelite tradition viewed the Hebrew Bible as far more than simply "the word of God." For 2500 years, Leviticus has formed part of the political, literary, and cultural history of the Jewish people as biological and cultural heirs of those who wrote the Hebrew Bible/OT. However, it is important to distinguish the ancient Israelite priestly cult from the rabbinic Judaism practiced today, which evolved concurrently with Christianity in the 1st century, at the time of the destruction of the Second Temple. What the OT actually depicts is the religion of ancient Israel, which was destined in the time of Jesus to produce two siblings: rabbinic Judaism and Christianity.

Bibliography. M. Douglas, *Purity and Danger* (New York, 1970); B. A. Levine, *Leviticus.* JPS Torah Commentary (Philadelphia, 1989); J. Milgrom, *Leviticus 1–16.* AB 3 (New York, 1991); J. R. Wegner, *Chattel or Person? The Status of Women in the Mishnah* (Oxford, 1988); "Leviticus," in *The Women's Bible Commentary,* ed. C. A. Newsome and S. H. Ringe (Louisville, 1992), 40-48.

JUDITH ROMNEY WEGNER

LEX TALIONIS

Often taken to be a summary of biblical law, this law of retaliation demands that the guilty suffer retribution equivalent to the injury inflicted ("eye for eye, tooth for tooth"). Biblical laws of talion are found in the context of murder (Gen. 9:6; Exod. 21:12; Lev. 24:17, 21), death of an animal (Exod. 21:36; Lev. 24:18), bodily injury of a pregnant woman (Exod. 21:22-25) or of a neighbor (Lev. 24:19-20), and false testimony (Deut. 19:16-21). They also appear in Mesopotamian legal collections, most notably in the Code of Hammurabi, and are fundamental to many ancient legal systems. In contrast to ancient Near Eastern law, there is no vicarious talion in the Bible, and biblical talion is applied to all regardless of social class (except slaves). Accusations of the barbaric nature of talion have been refuted by appealing either to its intent to curb unlimited cycles of retribution or to its replacement of earlier laws that allowed monetary compensation for acts of violence, including even murder.

Whether during the biblical period talion was understood literally (either as theoretical, proverbial, or a general principle) or simply as a dictum that the punishment should fit the crime remains an open debate. Evidence against a literal interpretation is found within the OT, e.g., immediately following the application of talion to the injury of a pregnant woman (Exod. 21:26-27). Controversy over the proper interpretation of these laws continued into the Roman period (cf. Josephus *Ant.* 4.278-80; Philo *Spec. leg.* 3.181-204; *b. B. Qam.* 83b-84a). The rejection of talion in the Sermon on the Mount has been seen as problematic since Jesus claims to fulfill torah and yet condemns retaliation in favor of benevolence (Matt. 5:38; cf. Rom. 12:17; 1 Thess. 5:15; 1 Pet. 3:9). These early Christian criticisms of talion should be analyzed in the context of both contemporary Jewish discussion of talion and Greco-Roman philosophical opposition to retaliation.

Recent studies of biblical laws of talion have stressed the importance of tracing their redaction history and intertextual relationships. Calum M. Carmichael's analysis of these laws in relation to narrative (esp. Gen. 38; 1 Kgs. 21; Judg. 1) may also prove to be a fruitful approach.

Bibliography. C. M. Carmichael, "Biblical Laws of Talion," *HAR* 9 (1985): 107-26; S. M. Paul, *Studies in the Book of the Covenant in the Light of Cuneiform and Biblical Law.* VTSup 18 (Leiden, 1970).

JENNIFER K. BERENSON MACLEAN

LIBATION

A drink offering, usually of wine, poured out upon an altar or other cultic object as part of a sacrificial ceremony. Drink offerings were a common devotional practice among the peoples of the ancient Near East, and the use of libations in cultic ceremonies is well attested in the biblical literature. When Jacob erected a pillar at Bethel he poured a drink offering upon it (Gen. 35:14). The law codes of Israel contain numerous references to libations (e.g., Exod. 29:38-41; Lev. 23:13; Num. 15:5). Prophetic critiques of cultic practices contrast the intrinsic celebratory nature of libations with sharp condemnation of their idolatrous associations (Isa. 57:6; Jer. 7:18). It is possible that libations of blood were offered by some (Ps. 16:4). Libations were also known in the Greek world, and Paul made the drink offering a metaphor for his life of service to Christ (Phil. 2:17; cf. 2 Tim. 4:6). KEVIN D. HALL

LIBERATION
Liberation is expressed in Hebrew by the verbal root *nṣl,* "deliver," and *plṭ,* "rescue," along with *yšʿ,* "save," and *pdh,* "ransom." God's merciful liberation occurred especially in the Exodus (Exod. 3:8; 12:27; 18:4, 8-10; 1 Sam. 10:18), but also elsewhere. The Lord delivered the Israelites in the desert (Ps. 107:6), David (2 Sam. 22:18), Jerusalem (Isa. 31:5), Jeremiah (Jer. 1:19), Ezra (Ezra 8:31), and the psalmist (Ps. 34:4[MT 5]; 91:3; Ezek. 34:12). Awareness that God liberates because of divine mercy is often explicit: "according to your mercies" (Neh. 9:28; cf. Jer. 42:11-12), because of "steadfast love" (Ps. 33:18-19; 86:13), God's name (79:8-9), covenant (106:43-45), or promise (119:170).

Though the foundation of God's liberating action is divine power and mercy, there is a corresponding demand for faith and righteousness on the part of those who seek deliverance. When the Israelites sinned they were often abandoned to their enemies, but were rescued after they had returned to the Lord (Judg. 3:9, 15; 1 Sam. 7:3; 12:10; Ps. 106:43-45). Ezekiel, in stressing the importance of personal responsibility, taught at times that God delivers only the righteous (Ezek. 14:14, 16, 18, 20). Prov. 11:6 states that "the righteousness of the upright saves them" (cf. 10:2). The Lord rescues the righteous (Ps. 34:19[20]), those who trust in him (22:4[5]), fear him (33:18-19), love him (91:14), as well as the poor and oppressed (82:3-4; 119:134), who are being treated unjustly. Yet God delivers also from sin (Ps. 39:8[9]; 79:9).

The focus of liberation in the NT is religious and eschatological, the definitive rescue from the power of Satan and sin by God through his Son, Jesus. The Greek verbs that express liberation, *rhýomai,* "to rescue," and *exairéō,* "deliver," are used sparingly in the NT, though *sṓzō,* "save," is quite common. We have been "rescued from the hands of our enemies" (Luke 1:74) by Jesus, who was sent "to proclaim release to the captives" (4:18; cf. Isa. 61:1) through his gift of salvation from sin. In the Lord's Prayer we petition, "deliver us from evil" (Matt. 6:13; Luke 11:4), i.e., from the terrors associated with the last days of the world under the power of "the evil one" (another possible translation). Paul states that the risen Jesus "rescues us from the wrath that is coming" (1 Thess. 1:10) on judgment day, a thought echoed in 2 Pet. 2:9. It was God who had already "rescued us from the power of darkness and transferred us into the kingdom of his beloved Son" (Col. 1:13). Paul believed the Jewish people would be saved at the end, in fulfillment of the prophecy that "out of Zion will come the Deliverer. . ." (Rom. 11:26; cf. Isa. 59:20-21).

Though most NT liberation texts focus on the victory of Jesus with consequences for eternity, several passages speak of divine rescues in this life (Acts 7:10; 12:11; Rom. 15:31; 2 Tim. 3:11; 4:17). Both aspects, the material and the spiritual, safety in this world and in the next, constitute God's work of liberation. JOSEPH F. WIMMER

LIBNAH (Heb. *liḇnâ*)

1. A place of unknown location in the Sinai Peninsula that was a stopping point for the Israelites on their journey from Egypt to Canaan (Num. 33:20-21).

2. A city conquered by Joshua in his campaign through the Shephelah (Josh. 10:29-39) and the seat of one of the defeated Canaanite kings (12:15). Located in the tribal allotment of Judah (Josh. 15:42), Libnah was set aside as a levitical city (21:13; 1 Chr. 6:57[MT 42]). It rebelled during the time of Jehoram (2 Kgs. 8:22; 2 Chr. 21:10) and was the hometown of Hamutal, wife of Josiah and mother of kings Zedekiah and Jehoahaz (2 Kgs. 23:31; 24:18; Jer. 52:1). During Sennacherib's invasion of Judah, the city was besieged during or after the siege of Lachish (2 Kgs. 19:8; Isa. 37:8).

The location of Libnah remains an unresolved problem. In the 19th century, F. J. Bliss and R. A. S. Macalister placed the city at Tell eṣ-Ṣâfī/Tel Ẓafit (1359.1237; Arab. "white mound"; cf. Heb. *liḇnâ,* "white"; Eusebius *Onom.* 120-25), but the site is now generally held to be that of Philistine Gath. Another possibility, Tell el-Judeideh (141115), a naturally protected site 10 km. (6 mi.) NE of Lachish on a major east-west trade route, is more likely Moresheth-Gath. Many scholars followed William F. Albright in placing Libnah at Tell Bornât (138115), 8 km. (5 mi.) N of Lachish near the western border of Judah, but the mound is unimpressive and its vulnerable location in the low-lying area W of the Azekah ridge does not comport with a city that was the final holdout against Assyrian assault. The most likely identification for Libnah is Khirbet Tell el-Beida (145116), E of the Azekah ridge and several miles NE of Beit Jibrîn/Beth Guvrin (Eleutheropolis). Its Arabic name means "ruin of the white hill," which may well preserve the name of Libnah.

Bibliography. Z. Kallai, *Historical Geography of the Bible* (Leiden, 1986). BRIAN P. IRWIN

LIBNI (Heb. *liḇnî)*

1. A son of Gershon and descendant of Levi; a subgroup within the Gershonite clan of Levites (Exod. 6:17; Num. 3:18; 1 Chr. 6:17, 20[MT 2, 5]). He was the eponymous ancestor of the Gershonite clan known as the Libnites (Num. 3:21; 26:58); some scholars associate this clan with Libnah (**2;** cf. Josh. 21:13).

2. A Levite, descended from Merari (1 Chr. 6:29[14]).

LIBYA (Gk. *Libýē;* Egyp. *Libu*)
The land and people occupying the area west of Egypt and Ethiopia. The Greeks used the name to designate the entire continent of Africa. Under the Romans, Libya was divided into two parts: Marmarica (east) and Cyrenaica (west). In 67 B.C.E. Cyrenaica (Libya superior) combined with Crete to form a province with its capital in Cyrene.

The progenitor of the Libyans is either Put (Gen. 10:6; 1 Chr. 1:8) or Lehabim (Heb. *lĕhāḇîm;* Gen. 10:13; 1 Chr. 1:11). The earliest history of

Libya is provided by Egyptian sources from the Old Kingdom, in which we find references to the Tjehenu and Tjemehu. The dominant tribe in the New Kingdom were the *Rbw* (Libu). The Tjemehu and the Libu had several conflicts with Egypt during the reigns of Thutmose II, Sethi I, and Rameses III. Following this period, many Libyans served as mercenaries in the Egyptian army (cf. Dan. 11:43; Nah. 3:9). One of them, Shishak, rose to the rank of general and eventually seized the Egyptian throne, thus initiating the 22nd (Libyan) Dynasty. During the fifth year of Rehoboam, Shishak invaded Palestine and was successful in gaining temporary control over Judah and parts of Israel (1 Kgs. 14:25-26; 2 Chr. 12:3). Those Libyans who fought alongside Zerah and the Ethiopians were not as successful and were defeated by King Asa (2 Chr. 16:8).

Libyans in the NT include Simon of Cyrene (Matt. 27:32 par.), worshippers on the day of Pentecost (Acts 2:10), persecutors of Stephen (6:9), and members of the church in Antioch (11:20; 13:1).

Keith A. Burton

LIDEBIR (Heb. *liḏěḇir*)
A place in eastern Gilead (Josh. 13:26; NRSV mg., following MT). The name is probably the original form of that rendered elsewhere as Lo-debar.

LIFE
The basic quality of existence, in the Bible predicated primarily of God and then of humans, animals, and plants.

The Hebrew and Greek terms generally translated "life" are several and varied. In the OT *ḥayyîm*, "life" (probably an abstract pl.), often connotes the span of human existence (Gen. 23:1); sometimes it is the circumstances of life (Job 10:1). Its cognate *ḥayyâ* means "living thing." Other Hebrew terms include *nep̱eš*, "soul, life," which makes a being alive. In the NT Gk. *bíos* refers to the natural order, and *zōḗ* to God's life, and the salvation that entails eternal life. Gk. *psychḗ*, "soul, life," roughly corresponds to Heb. *nep̱eš*. Throughout the Bible, life in its various senses is often contrasted to death.

In the OT all life comes from and is sustained by God, who exists at the beginning (Gen. 1:1) and lives forever. God is the only being who is truly alive, invoked by the common oath "as God lives." God alone is "the living God" (Deut. 5:26; Jer. 10:10). While plants are indeed alive, and animals with their *nep̱eš* even more so, only humans have the life that comes from being made in God's image. This brings a qualitative meaning to "life" from the beginning of the OT. Life is not bare existence, or even longevity, but health and well-being (Prov. 3:13-17; 14:30). Life has an essential moral dimension which entails keeping God's commandments (Deut. 30:15-20). At the end of the OT period an eschatological meaning of life emerges, especially with the belief of resurrection to life (Dan. 12:2). This eschatological meaning is intensified in the intertestamentary Jewish literature (e.g., 2 Macc. 7:9; 1 En. 58:3).

The NT continues these OT meanings of life, but the emphasis shifts to eternal life. In the Synoptic Gospels almost all references to life are in the teachings of Jesus. Life *(zōḗ)* does not consist of possessions (Luke 12:15), and the *psychḗ* is more than food (v. 23). Life *(zōḗ)* comes from keeping God's commandments (Matt. 19:17), and giving up one's own life *(psychḗ)* to follow Jesus (Luke 14:26). The self-sacrificial aspect of true life is found in Jesus' saying that he came "to give his life *(psychḗ)* as a ransom for many" (Mark 10:45). The Acts of the Apostles has much the same view of life, and adds the special point that Christianity could be known as "this Life" (Acts 5:20).

While the Synoptics stress the future eschatological nature of life, the Johannine writings see the fullness of eschatological life as a present reality. Jesus says that those who hear his word and believe in the One who sent him have (present tense) eternal life because Jesus has life in himself (John 5:24-26) and has come to bring life to the world (e.g., 1:4, "the light was the life of humans"). Jesus calls himself "the bread of life," "the resurrection and the life," and "the way, the truth, and the life" (6:48; 11:25; 14:6). Despite the "realized eschatology" of the Fourth Gospel, it retains a strong future eschatology and boldly couples the two: "All who see the Son and believe in him. . . have eternal life, and I will raise them up on the last day" (6:40).

Paul views life as coming through faith in the crucified and resurrected Jesus Christ. It cannot be found by keeping the commandments, which leads instead to God's curse (Gal. 3:10-11) and death (Rom. 7:10). Jesus' resurrectional life has already become the believer's (Gal. 2:19-20). Baptism into Christ leads to living a new life in the present, which is grounded in the death of Jesus (Rom. 6:4). By the work of the Spirit, eternal life has moved into the present and will be fully realized in the Parousia with the resurrection of the body (Rom. 6:13; Gal. 5:25). Therefore, the believer lives between present down-payment and future fulfillment; Christ's resurrection is the pledge of our resurrection to full life. In the present, living by and for Christ entails living for others responsibly in every kind of social circumstance, which Paul especially emphasized in 1 Corinthians. The letters of disputed Pauline authorship emphasize this present aspect of life even more strongly, insisting that the believer has already been raised with Christ (Col. 2:12; 3:1; Eph. 2:6).

In the book of Revelation, life *(zōḗ)* is always linked to another word, often symbolic: the tree of life, which the righteous eat (Rev. 2:7; 22:2, 14, 19); the crown of life, which they wear (2:10); the book of life, the roll in which their names are written (3:5; 13:8; 17:8; 20:12, 15; 21:27); the water of life, which they drink (21:6; 22:1, 17). As fits the apocalyptic style and theology of this writing, life is eschatological and future, but it is linked to the Living One who has defeated death and is alive forever (Rev. 1:8).

Bibliography. G. Bertram, R. Bultmann, and G. von Rad, "záō," *TDNT* 2:832-75; L. Goppelt, *Theology of the New Testament* (Grand Rapids, 1982),

2:98-106; D. Hill, *Greek Words and Hebrew Meanings.* SNTSMS 5 (Cambridge, 1967), 163-201; H. W. Wolff, *Anthropology of the Old Testament* (Philadelphia, 1974).

ROBERT E. VAN VOORST

LIGHT

Light (Heb. *'ôr*) is God's creation (Gen. 1:3-5), further distinguished as the lights of the firmament, the sun, moon, and stars (vv. 14-18). "Light" can refer literally to morning light or dawn (Gen. 44:3; Judg. 16:2; 19:26; 1 Sam. 14:36) and to the light of a lamp or fire (Exod. 25:37; Num. 4:16; Neh. 9:12, 19).

Light is used figuratively as a symbol of life. To "see light" is to live (Job 3:16; Ps. 49:19), to walk in the "light of life" (Ps. 56:13[MT 14]; Job 33:30), to have that light reflected in one's eyes (Prov. 29:13). Light may be a symbol of prosperity or happiness (Esth. 8:16), which is the lot of the righteous (Ps. 97:11; Prov. 13:9), embodying God's special favor or blessing (e.g., Num. 6:25; Ps. 89:15[16]). It is a symbol of illumination, whether bringing hidden things to light (Job 28:11; Ps. 90:8) or shedding the light of instruction (Ps. 119:105, 130; Prov. 6:23). Light is also a symbol of God's majesty, of the divine glory (Ps. 104:2; Isa. 60:1-3, 19-20) which shines in deliverance (Ps. 27:1; Isa. 9:2; 60:20) or in the fire of judgment (Isa. 10:17; but cf. judgment as the withholding of light; 13:10; Jer. 4:23; Ezek. 32:7; Amos 5:18-20).

In the NT "light" (Gk. *phṓs*) is used literally to denote the radiance of the sun (Rev. 22:5), of a lamp or a torch (Luke 8:16; Acts 16:29), as well as visible light that accompanies divine presence on earth (Matt. 17:2; Acts 9:3; 12:7) or in heaven (Rev. 21:24; 22:5). By extension of the literal sense, to do something "in the light" means to do it openly (Matt. 10:27).

Figurative uses of the term include a definite ethical component (2 Cor. 6:14), so that the righteous are said to be "full of light" (Matt. 6:22; Luke 11:36) and are to radiate this light in the form of good works (Matt. 5:16), righteousness, truth (Eph. 5:8-10), and demonstrations of love (1 John 2:8-9). In this sense they are "the light of the world" (Matt. 5:14), "children of light" (Eph. 5:8; Luke 16:8), walking in the light (John 12:35; 1 John 1:7). "Light" also describes various aspects of salvation in Christ. This light shines in the witness of John the Baptist (Luke 1:79; John 5:35), Paul (Acts 13:47), and the gospel (2 Cor. 4:4) to Jesus, who is the "light for revelation to the Gentiles" (Luke 2:32), the true Light (John 1:9), the "light of the world" (8:12; 9:5; 12:46) who brings his followers the "light of life" (8:12). A chosen people stands in the marvelous light (1 Pet. 2:9) of One who is light (1 John 1:5) and "dwells in unapproachable light" (1 Tim. 6:16). Light also is associated with the various aspects of divine judgment, exposing human intentions (1 Cor. 4:5) and the "unfruitful deeds of darkness" (Eph. 5:11-13). In the Fourth Gospel light facilitates the discriminating function of judgment by provoking the rejection and hatred of those who love darkness and remain in it (John 3:19-20), a reaction which will assure their fate in the end (12:46-50).

ROBERT DELSNYDER

LIGHTNING

The electrical discharge common in thunderstorms. Lightning (Heb. *bārāq;* Gk. *astrapḗ*) is most often used in the Bible not in a literal sense but as an analogy to represent power, brilliance, and quickness. The use of lightning to represent brilliance is widespread. A sword is polished to flash like lightning (Ezek. 21:10[MT 15]), a lamp shines like lightning (Luke 11:36), and angelic visages are sometimes so brilliant that they are compared to lightning (Dan. 10:6; Matt. 28:3; cf. Luke 24:4). The metaphorical use of lightning to represent quickness is also common. Speeding chariots are said to dash about like lightning (Nah. 2:4), and a sword is said to strike like lightning (Ezek. 21:15[20]). The concept of quickness may also be present in the description that Jesus gives to the returning Seventy of Satan "falling from heaven like a flash of lightning" (Luke 10:18).

OT theophanies are generally accompanied by lightning. The appearance of God on Sinai included lightning, thunder, the sound of a trumpet, and smoke (Exod. 19:16; 20:18; cf. Deut. 33:2; Zech. 9:14). Similarly, lightning also figured in Ezekiel's vision of the four beings (Ezek. 1:13-14).

In the NT lightning is found primarily in apocalyptic contexts. The second coming of the Son of Man is described as accompanied by lightning that flashes across the sky (Matt. 24:27; Luke 17:24). In the book of Revelation lightning frequently occurs in descriptions of the throne of God (Rev. 4:5; 8:5; 11:19; 16:18), and each of the series of seven plagues (the seals, the trumpets, and the bowls of wrath) concludes with an earthly cataclysm including thunder, lightning, and an earthquake (15:1–16:21).

MARK R. FAIRCHILD

LIKHI (Heb. *liqḥî*)

A Manassite, the third son of Shemida (1 Chr. 7:19). The name may be a scribal error for Gilead's "son" Helek (cf. Num. 26:30; Josh. 17:2) and, like the accompanying names, may represent a place.

LILITH (Heb. *lîlîṯ*)

A demon attested only in Isa. 34:14, but whose Mesopotamian roots go back to the 3rd millenium B.C. The Babylonian Lilitu was a female spirit who could not bear children, but instead gave forth poison from her breasts by which she would seek to kill babies. She was also associated with stormy winds and is described as fleeing from a house through the window. Within medieval Jewish demonology Lilith is identified as the "first Eve" who was created from the earth along with Adam, but refused to accept a position subservient to him. She then fled from him and roams the earth looking for newborn infants to devour. Isa. 34:14 describes Lilith as dwelling with the wildcats and hyenas among Edom's ruins; the picture is thus one of complete desolation where only death and destruction reign.

Bibliography. M. Hutter, "Lilith," *DDD,* 520-21; G. Schakel, "Lilith," *EncJud* 11:245-49.

CHRISTIAN M. M. BRADY

LILY

A flower appearing in several different contexts in the Bible. Some occurrences of Heb. *šôšān* may refer to the white or Madonna lily (*Lilium candidum* L.), which grows wild in Israel. This flower is familiar from its association with Mary in Christian art. The lily of Cant. 5:13, which is compared to the lips of the lover, could be the Martagon lily (*Lilium chalcedonicum*), a red lily with drooping flowers. The lily appears as a flower of the field, common where animals graze (Cant. 2:16; 4:5; 6:2-3), and one that dwells in the valley (2:1). In the Song of Solomon lilies represent love in bloom. The man describes his lover's belly as "a heap of wheat, encircled with lilies" (Cant. 7:2[MT 3]).

In Solomon's temple, the brim of the "molten sea" was shaped like a lily (1 Kgs. 7:26; 2 Chr. 4:5), and the tops of the two bronze pillars set before the vestibule were adorned with lilies (1 Kgs. 7:19, 22). Analogies to these capitals may be present in two incense altars unearthed at Megiddo, both of which have bowls that suggest flowers and sculpted decorations that suggest leaves; one of these altars was painted with floral decorations. These decorations are sometimes identified with the lotus (*Nymphea lotus* L.), which often appeared in Egyptian art. Pss. 45, 60, 69, 80 contain the phrase "according to Lilies" (NRSV) in their titles, probably designating the tune. Hosea used the lily to symbolize Israel's flourishing after its reconciliation with God (Hos. 14:5[6]).

Jesus' homily on the lilies of the field demonstrated God's care (Matt. 6:28-30 = Luke 12:27-28). This lily (Gk. *krínon*) is most likely a common field flower such as the *Anemone coronora* L., which blooms in spring in many colors and is widespread in Israel. MEGAN BISHOP MOORE

LIME, LIMESTONE

Calcium oxide, a caustic, white, lumpy powder which has a number of industrial uses, and commonly is produced from limestone or shells by use of intense heat. When mixed with water, it forms whitewash, used to cover walls and other surfaces. In Deut. 27:2, 4 lime (Heb. *śîḏ*) is to be used to coat the stones in preparation for recording the words of the law following the crossing of the Jordan by the people of Israel. When bones are burned to a powder, lime is the result. Isa. 33:12 describes such burning as a total annihilation. In Amos 2:1 Moab is condemned for reducing the bones of the king of Edom to lime. MARTHA JEAN MUGG BAILEY

LIMP

See LAMENESS, LIMP.

LINEN

See FLAX, LINEN.

LINTEL

A horizontal wooden or stone beam above a door, supported by two doorposts. The lintels (Heb. *mašqôp̱*) and doorposts were sprinkled with lambs' blood in preparation for the tenth plague and in commemoration of the Passover (Exod. 12:22-23). In the description of the construction of the temple's *dᵉḇîr* (NRSV "inner sanctuary"), the lintels (*'ayil*) may have in fact been two beams set at an angle (1 Kgs. 6:31). Archaeological excavations in the Middle East have revealed the remains of doors in public and private buildings; sockets or depressions sometimes preserved in lintels and thresholds once accommodated hinges. JENNIE R. EBELING

LINUS (Gk. *Línos*)

A Christian from whom greetings are relayed at 2 Tim. 4:21. According to tradition this Linus was the son of the Claudia mentioned in the same verse and bishop of Rome for 12 years, ordained to that office by Peter and Paul and preceding Clement in it (Irenaeus *Adv. haer.* 3.3.3; Eusebius *HE* 3.2, 13).

LION

A large carnivorous member of the cat family. The Asiatic lion, *Panthera leo persica*, was once common throughout the ancient Near East and Mediterranean but has been extinct in Palestine for centuries; in Mesopotamia, it survived in the marshes of the Tigris and Euphrates until the 19th century A.D. (cf. Jer. 50:44).

Although Samson killed a lion with his bare hands (Judg. 14:6), in OT stories of encounters with lions the lions are usually victorious (1 Kgs. 13:24; 20:36; 2 Kgs. 17:25). Israel's topography naturally isolated lions from the human population, although kings bred lions in captivity to show their royal power and to punish criminals (cf. Dan. 6); the most prolific royal lion breeder was Assurnasirpal II of Assyria. Since wild prey was essential to their survival, lions were generally found in forested regions, such as the Lebanon Mountains, the area contiguous to the Jordan River, Bashan, and in suitable portions of the Negeb and Arabah. Ultimately, the lack of cover and wild game and the increasing human population resulted in the total eradication of the lion in Israel.

Due to its unmatched power and majesty, the lion leant itself to artistic and literary expression. Thus, the vast majority of biblical references refer symbolically to lions. Israel (Num. 23:24), a valiant warrior's heart (2 Sam. 17:10), the devil (1 Pet. 5:8), and the Messiah (Rev. 5:5, "the Lion of the tribe of Judah") are all compared to the lion.

The lion was very commonly used in art. Solomon's throne (1 Kgs. 10:18-20) and his temple (7:29, 36; cf. Ezek. 41:15-19) employed lion sculptures. Often a pair of lions would flank a city gate (as at the gates of Mycenae and Hattusas and Babylon's famous Ishtar Gate), offering magical protection (called *šēdû;* cf. Deut. 32:17) to the inhabitants. This protection through artwork extended to daggers, axes, decorated trappings on war horses, and afterlife items (e.g., the decorative lions flanking Tutankhamun's funeral headrest, as well as his bed). One of the most famous seals ever found in Israel (at Megiddo in 1909 belonging to "Shema the servant of Jeroboam") was dominated by its distinctive royal lion emblem. DONALD FOWLER

LITERACY

In the ancient world, writing was a specialized skill that few people possessed. The abilities to read and to write were rare, and thus they represented an expertise that would have been mostly concentrated within the control of the political, religious, and economic leadership. In the more literate cultures within the ancient world, such as Hellenistic Greece, literacy rates may have been 0.1 to 1 percent of the populace. In more rural and less centralized areas, such as ancient Israel, the literacy rates may have been significantly lower than that.

Narratives, poetry, letters, and epics — the forms used in the OT and NT — were probably very infrequent uses of writing. Instead, the most common example of writing was probably the inscriptions placed on objects, such as the frequent Hebrew inscription *lmlk* ("for the king" or "belonging to the king") found on objects presumably used within the royal palace or elsewhere within the king's service. Uses of writing such as this are difficult to describe as true literacy; people probably distinguished between a royal jar and a common jar by noticing that the royal jar had writing upon it and other jars did not. No reading ability was necessary to assign meaning to the marks.

Another frequent early use of writing was in the economic affairs of trade. Inventories required listing the goods that the owner possessed, and this list was written, possibly along with some indication of the amount. In order to facilitate trade, a copy of an inventory could be sent along with the shipment, so that a reader in another place could verify that the entire shipment was received. When trade increased, such writing would have grown in complexity and in importance as a means of communication over distances.

In Israel, governments and temples also had reasons to make written records for later reference. These might have included lists such as censuses or tax records as well as legal codes and narrative. Probably, professional scribes wrote and read these records in service to the religious and political leaders who employed them. In most of these cases, writing existed as a means for scribes to communicate with each other, rather than as a way to convey information to a variety of persons of dissimilar background. The higher literacy rate of later antiquity allowed for greater use of writing to communicate more broadly. Letters such as those from Paul to local Christian communities offer examples of communication over distance from one person to a group of others. Even in those cases, Paul probably used a scribe to write at least many of the letters attributed to him rather than wrote them himself. Paul's education implies that he could read, but even if he could write, he sometimes chose not to do so. When a local church received a letter, they probably had one person read the letter out loud to the rest of the community.

It is unknown how scribes learned to write and read in ancient Israel. Scholars have argued for the existence of formal schools or for more individualized practices of apprenticeship, but no clear evidence remains to prove either scenario. In NT times, both practices are known to exist.

Jon L. Berquist

LITERATURE, OLD TESTAMENT AS

In many ways, to speak of the OT as a work of literature seems to state the obvious. Its epic sagas, compelling dramas and lyrical poetry have long captured the imaginations of readers as well as inspired numerous writers, artists, and musicians. One need only think of John Milton's *Paradise Lost,* Cecil B. DeMille's *The Ten Commandments,* Camille Saint-Saëns's *Samson et Dalila,* or Archibald MacLeish's *J.B.* to see how the literary artistry of the Bible continues to engage creative communities and enthrall audiences.

Yet scholarly study of the OT had long been dominated by either an exploration of its religious and theological insights or an analysis of its historical settings and detail. Indeed, for many scholars, identification and examination of the Bible as a work of literature was equated with failure to take seriously into account the role of the religious, historical, social, and cultural settings of a text in the production of meaning. By the 1980s, however, analysis of the biblical text as literature — often using techniques of study developed by literary critics — received widespread recognition and acceptance as an interpretive approach to the biblical text. Examining the OT as literature does not preclude religious or historical study; rather, literary analysis brings yet another dimension to the interpretation of the biblical text and opens up the possibility of new and insightful readings.

Academic study of the OT, defined for many years by historical-critical methods, has long included some type of "literary" analysis. Form criticism, e.g., focused on the importance of classifying texts by their literary genre. The ability of a scholar to correctly determine the form of a given text, such as identifying a psalm as a hymn, lament, or thanksgiving, became a central component to understanding the *Sitz im Leben* which gave rise to that text. Ascertaining a text's "setting in life" ideally assists a scholar in understanding how that text functioned in the communities which produced and first utilized it, thereby providing clues as to social, cultural, and religious structures operative in ancient Israel.

For example, Ps. 117 often receives classification as a Thanksgiving Psalm because it expresses gratitude toward God, describes God's deliverances as the source of such thankfulness, and encourages all hearers of the word to offer similar praise to God. This psalm might be further subclassified as a community thanksgiving because of the references to a variety of persons being saved from distress as opposed to the deliverance of an individual. Given this corporate emphasis, form critics conclude that such community thanksgiving songs probably provided words for public occasions or celebrations. In this particular case, the psalm describes people traversing the dangers of desert and ocean or emerging from prison or sin in order to come to God. Many scholars thus hypothesize that this psalm was sung by groups of pilgrims traveling to Jerusalem for festal occasions. This attempt to comprehend a text's setting and purpose strives to move the interpreter closer to the world of the text and thus to meaning as intended by the author and/or received by its original audience. Such movement shows the reader not only the proper way to approach a text but also how that text functioned in its own historical milieu.

Even apart from historical-critical methods, the definition of genre still stands out as a primary task in the literary analysis of biblical texts. In the OT, a reader encounters a wide variety of literary types — from myths, to folktales, to legal texts, to prophetic oracles, to apocalyptic visions, to proverbs, to short stories, to parables. The need for such a system of classification is simple — different types of literature are read differently and generate different effects; identifying genre means associating a text with a set of defined conventions which assist the reader in making sense of a text. For example, one does not expect short stories to read like law codes; each has its own typical manner of expression and each produces different response in the reader. Thus in the biblical text, the stories of David's exploits as a warrior might invite the reader into an imaginative world of danger, challenge, and intrigue by relating how he defeated the giant Goliath as a young boy or gathered 200 Philistine foreskins to claim his bride or narrowly escaped from King Saul's murderous intent on multiple occasions. The stories have clear plots, define characters, and use action and dialogue to excite, entertain, and build up empathy for the future king. By contrast, a cataloging of divine directives such as the Ten Commandments comes across as stark and serious in its absoluteness and inflexibility. Such a text simply states its demands in a basic list format to generate ethical obligation and compliance from its readers. Recognizing the distinctive qualities of different genres provides the reader with important clues as to how to read a text and thus at least one set of guidelines for interpretation.

On occasion the form which a biblical text takes is more formally defined. One example of such formal structuring, the acrostic, comes from biblical poetry. Acrostics build words or phrases or patterns from the initial letter of each word in a line. In the biblical text a particular form of acrostic — an alphabetic acrostic — builds patterns by using each successive letter of the Hebrew alphabet as the initial letter in a line. Such structuring was perhaps initially employed as a prompt to the memory. In terms of interpretation, it assists the reader to see the poem as covering a subject "from A to Z." Texts in this format include Pss. 9-10, 25, 34, 37, 111, 112, 145; Prov. 31:10-31; and Lam. 1, 2, 3, 4. When examining a text such as Prov. 31:10-31, the reader of the Hebrew text thus sees the qualities of a good wife delineated in a virtual catalog using the alphabet as a guide.

Exploring the stylistic features of a given text also plays a vital role in literary analysis. The techniques of textual construction illustrate both the conventions operative in certain kinds of writing in ancient Israel and the artistic creativity of the biblical writers. For example, the writers of poetry in the OT often use different types of parallelisms as a

***The Creation of Eve,* from *Nine Illustrations to "Paradise Lost,"* William Blake (1757-1827)** (Gift by Subscription, 1890; Courtesy, Museum of Fine Arts, Boston)

form of expression. Parallelism simply means the repetition of an idea in slightly different terms, as in Isa. 60:2. This verse reports, in part, that darkness (Heb. *ḥōšeḵ*) will cover the earth and a thick darkness (*ʿărāpel*) the peoples. "Darkness" and "thick darkness," while different Hebrew words, convey the same idea as to earth and peoples; the ideas articulated thus receive emphasis through reinforcement of the image. On other occasions, parallelisms can denote opposites (e.g., Prov. 12:1) or build on one another to a climactic point (Judg. 5:26b).

Repetition of a key word or theme also occurs frequently in biblical texts, both poetic and narrative. The simple reiteration of a coda or line (e.g., "for his steadfast love endures forever" in Ps. 136) serves to attract the readers' attention to the central theme. Sometimes this repetition appears at both the beginning and the end of a work; this feature is called an inclusio, and it functions as a frame to illustrate the major emphasis contained within. Inclusios occur both in shorter works such as Ps. 8, which both opens and closes with "O Lord, our Lord, how majestic is your name in all the earth!" and in lengthier texts such as the book of Ecclesiastes which opens (Eccl. 1:2) and closes (12:8) with "Vanity of vanities, says the Preacher, vanity of vanities! All is vanity." Repetition also serves as a structural element in narratives. The recurrence of stock phrases such as "and there was evening and there was morning" or "and God saw that it was good" in the first Creation story (Gen. 1:1–2:4a) serves as an obvious example. The repetitions place focus on the passage of time as well as highlight the reaction of the central character. Likewise, the continual hardening of Pharaoh's heart

Naomi entreating Ruth and Orpah to return to the Land of Moab. Fresco print, William Blake (1757-1827); Tate Gallery, London
(Victoria & Albert Museum, London/Art Resource, N.Y.)

in the Exodus account prolongs the narrative while also heightening the tension in the battle between God and Pharaoh for power.

Metaphor occurs frequently in the Bible as a way to express concepts which might otherwise defy expression. Most often depictions of God and the relationship between God and the covenant people rely on metaphor. In Hosea, e.g., among the many metaphoric descriptions of God are images such as husband and lover (2:2-13[MT 3-14]), parent (11:1-4), lion (13:7), bear (13:8), or even moth and dry rot (5:12). The use of metaphor both invokes the familiar to bring the object of concern, here God, into clearer focus and engages the imagination of the reader or hearer to determine how the metaphoric figure works as a descriptive. How and why is sin like scarlet? How is forgiveness like snow? (Isa. 1:18). The use of metaphor can be within the span of a line, or it can be much more extended as in the descriptions of the people as adulterous wives of God (Ezek. 16, 23) or in the stories of the two lovers in the Song of Solomon.

Many other features of literary analysis, such as the exploration of biblical narrative in terms of stylistic features such as characterization, dialogue and plot development, rightly could be, and perhaps even should be, included in this discussion. Such a listing, however, could not cover completely all of the approaches which literary scholars take in analyzing the biblical texts. What these scholars hold in common is a concern for relating the form and construction of a text to its meaning. The shared assumption here is that words alone do not convey meaning; how words are organized and presented in a text tells as much about what they convey to a reader as do the words themselves. Moreover, seeing the texts as literature also raises questions about how these texts communicate as art. This interpretive shift often moves the question of meaning away from a strict concern with what an interpreter determines to be the intent of the texts and its author and places emphasis on the reception and understanding of a text by its readers or hearers. Such a reorientation in the understanding of where meaning resides opens up a variety of new interpretive possibilities and challenges biblical scholarship to make a place for multiple interpretive voices and a variety of readings of any given text.

Bibliography. R. Alter, *The Art of Biblical Literature* (New York, 1981); *The Art of Biblical Poetry* (New York, 1985); S. Bar-Efrat, *Narrative Art in the Bible.* JSOTSup 70 (Sheffield, 1989); A. Berlin, *Poetics and Interpretation of Biblical Narrative.* Bible and Literature 9 (Sheffield, 1983); D. M. Gunn and D. N. Fewell, *Narrative in the Hebrew Bible* (New York, 1993).

SANDRA L. GRAVETT

LITERATURE, NEW TESTAMENT AS

To read the NT as literature is to read the Bible in ways that literature in general is read. A literary reading does not diminish the understanding of Scripture, but rather enhances the meaning that is in the text. The NT is read on its own terms, which means that its figures of speech, formal organization, and other literary aspects are analyzed.

The literature of the NT may be divided into sayings, narratives, speeches, and letters. The sayings of Jesus are found in the Synoptic Gospels and the Gospel of John. Narratives are stories that have characters and plot and are found in the Gospels, the Acts of the Apostles, and Revelation. Speeches are found in Acts. The letters are conventional forms of communication in the early Church and include the letters of Paul and other NT writers.

Sayings of Jesus

The sayings of Jesus may be short, aphoristic sayings as in Matthew's Sermon on the Mount or long discourses as in the Gospel of John; but always they are artistic formulations that require a close reading on the part of the interpreter. An antithetical saying is one that is in parallelism (i.e, similar order and structure) and has a contrast or opposition in the meaning of contiguous phrases or clauses. Jesus' statement to the crowd and disciples in Mark 8:35 (cf. Matt. 16:25; Luke 9:24) is an example. Here the antithesis is a reversal of the common way of thinking about saving or losing one's life: the way to save one's life is to lose it. This example also happens to be a chiastic pattern. A chiasmus or chiasm, a cross-over pattern that resembles the Greek letter *chi* (X), reverses the elements that are parallel in syntax as follows: A : B :: B' : A'. In Mark 8:35 the terms "save" and "lose" form the chiasm save : lose :: lose : save. Another example is Jesus' saying of the first and the last (Matt. 19:30; cf. Mark 10:31). Antithetical chiasms turn upside down normal ways of thinking and common perceptions of our world. Not only does the *content* of the saying reverse natural ways of thinking, but also the *form* of the saying turns on its head the usual manner of thinking.

Jesus so consistently used metaphors and similes that any study of the Gospels as literature must pay close attention to these figures of speech. A simile compares two distinctly different things by the use of "like" or "as." In Luke 17:6 Jesus compares faith to a mustard seed. In a metaphor an implied analogy is made between one object and another that ascribes one or more qualities of the second object to the first. A metaphor has a vehicle (the metaphorical term itself) and a tenor (the subject that the metaphor is applied to). Matt. 7:6 illustrates not only the importance of identifying the vehicle and tenor, but also the difficulty at times in making the correct identification. There are several vehicles in this example: holy things, dogs, pearls, swine. But what is the tenor, the subject to which these metaphorical terms are applied? Is it the gospel? Certain esoteric teachings and practices? Fine wisdom? And whom do the dogs and swine represent? Unbelievers? The Jewish leaders? The hard-hearted and blind? Any interpretation of this difficult verse requires that an interpreter correctly identify the tenor or tenors.

Jesus' fondness of hyperbole also requires close attention. Hyperbole is a bold overstatement or extravagant exaggeration. The hyperbolic language of Matt. 7:3-5 illustrates. The hyperbole of a log protruding from one's eye is an arresting image that has a definite shock value: it forces the reader/hearer to see something that could not be seen without the use of hyperbolic language — namely, one's censorious attitude.

The sayings of Jesus in the Gospel of John contain many double entendres or statements that are deliberately ambiguous and create misunderstandings. When Jesus says to Nicodemus that "without being born from above (Gk. *ánōthen*)" he cannot see the kingdom of God (John 3:3), Nicodemus misunderstands because the Greek term can mean either "again" or "from above." Similarly, the Samaritan woman misunderstands "living water" *(hýdōr zṓn)* in John 4:10 and thinks that Jesus will provide a "flowing stream."

An understanding of irony enriches the reading of the Gospels. Verbal irony occurs when the implicit meaning by a speaker differs sharply from the ostensible meaning expressed. Words are used in a double-edged way. When Jesus tells the Jewish leaders "Destroy this temple, and in three days I will raise it up" (John 2:19), he is referring to his body, but the authorities understandably think he means the Jerusalem temple. John makes sure that the reader does not miss the irony by explaining Jesus' meaning in 2:21. Dramatic irony occurs when the reader stands in a superior position to a character in a narrative and therefore knows information that a character lacks. Caiaphas' statement concerning Jesus in John 11:50 is dramatic irony at its best. The high priest does not understand the extent to which this statement is true, although the reader does understand.

The parables of Jesus may be short similitudes that make a comparison between two distinctly different things or they may be longer, narrative parables with characters and plot. Similitudes are extended similes or metaphors that have a picture part (vehicle), a reality part (tenor), and a point of comparison between the two parts. The parable of the hidden treasure in Matt. 13:44 is an example of a similitude. The picture part is the treasure hidden in a field; the reality part is the kingdom of God; and the point of comparison is that just as the man sold all to purchase the field, one willingly sacrifices all to receive the kingdom. Other similitudes are the parables of the leaven (Matt. 13:33; Luke 13:20-21), the mustard seed (Matt. 13:31-32; Mark 4:30-32; Luke 13:18-19), the pearl (Matt. 13:45-46), the net (13:47-50), the seed growing secretly (Mark 4:26-29), the fig tree (Matt. 24:32-35; Mark 13:28-31; Luke 21:29-33), the lost sheep (15:4-7; Matt. 18:12-14), the lost coin (Luke 15:8-10), and the unprofitable servants (17:7-10).

Narrative parables are well-developed stories and should be analyzed as narrative literature with

The Prodigal Son amid the Swine, **engraving by Albrecht Dürer (ca. 1496)** (Courtesy British Museum)

attention given to the characters, rhetoric, setting, point of view, plot, and theme (see below). Examples of narrative parables are the parables of the ten virgins (Matt. 25:1-13), the talents (25:14-30; Luke 19:11-27), the sheep and the goats (Matt. 25:31-46), the rich man and Lazarus (Luke 16:19-31), the workers in the vineyard (Matt. 20:1-16), the Prodigal Son (Luke 15:11-32), the Good Samaritan (10:29-37), and the unjust steward (16:1-9).

Narratives

Narratives are stories which may be historical (e.g., passion narratives) or fictional (e.g., parables) and are related by a narrator. Narratives have characters and plot as well as point of view, rhetorical devices, and setting. Examples in the Gospels are the feeding of the five thousand (Matt. 14:13-21; Mark 6:32-44; Luke 9:10-17; John 6:1-15), the Gedarene demoniacs (Matt. 8:28-34; Mark 5:1-20; Luke 8:26-39), the stilling of the storm (Matt. 8:23-27; Mark 4:35-41; Luke 8:22-25), the Infancy narratives (Luke 1–2; Matt. 1–2), the healing of the blind man (John 9), and the Samaritan woman (John 4). The Gospels as a whole may be regarded as narratives also. Examples of narratives in Acts are the conversion of Cornelius (Acts 10:1–11:18) and the miracle of Pentecost (2:1-13). Revelation, though generally considered to be apocalyptic literature, may be interpreted as narrative literature but with special attention paid to the symbolism.

The setting of a narrative — the historical time, social circumstances, and general locale in which its action occurs — is important for interpretation of a narrative. The general setting of the Gerasene demoniac narrative in Mark 5, e.g., with its tombs, unfettered shackles and chains, and unclean spirits sets the atmosphere of the narrative. The setting indicates that this narrative is about a battle between God and Satan.

Point of view signifies the way a story is told. The actions, setting, and events are mediated through the narrator's perspective which is expressed in terms of space, time, phrases and words, insight into a character's thoughts and feelings, and the beliefs, values, and norms of the narrator. An example of spatial point of view may be seen in the way John has arranged the setting and characters in Rev. 4 and 5. At the center of the narrative are the one seated on the throne and the Lamb, and outward from the throne are expanding concentric circles of the creation: the four living creatures, followed by the 24 elders. Then the circle expands to include myriads of angels, and finally the entire creation surrounds the throne. The spatial arrangement reflects the distinct point of view of the writer, namely, that God brings order and stability (and indeed meaning) to the universe.

Rhetoric is the art of persuasion. An analysis of rhetoric looks at the devices an author uses to persuade the reader to make the "proper" interpretation of a narrative. Rhetoric includes but is not limited to such figures of speech as simile, metaphor, repetition, hyperbole, symbols, and irony. A proper understanding of rhetoric is necessary for a correct interpretation of a narrative. For example, John's Apocalypse uses symbolism so extensively that failure to recognize this rhetorical method inevitably results in misreadings of the book.

Characters in a narrative are persons with moral, dispositional, and emotional qualities that are expressed in what they say and what they do. A narrator may either show (let us see the character talking or acting) or tell (intervene authoritatively to describe or evaluate the character). God speaks only twice in Revelation: once at the beginning and then at the end of the book, and both times says, "I am the Alpha and the Omega" (Rev. 1:8; 21:6). John shows that God is the ground and goal of our existence both by God's speech and by the placement of the Alpha/Omega self-declaration. By contrast, Mark intervenes in his narrative to tell about certain characters: e.g., the disciples did not understand about the multiplication of loaves for "their hearts were hardened" (Mark 6:52); and the Sadducees "say there is no resurrection" (12:18). Whether a writer tells about a character or shows a character through dialogue or action, the point of studying characterization is to identify the main traits, the defining characteristics, of a character.

Plot is the structure of a narrative's actions that are directed toward an intended effect. A plot has a beginning, a middle, and an end. The beginning initiates the main action that causes the reader to look forward to something more. The middle presumes that something precedes and more will follow. The end follows what has gone before and requires that nothing follows. Plot is a story that begins with a stable condition, goes through some sort of disequilibrium, and concludes with a resolution, a new stable condition. The disequilibrium or instability is frequently though not always caused by conflicts. There are conflicts with the supernatural (demons, Satan, unclean spirits), nature (the sea), characters (Jesus vs. religious authorities or crowds or disciples), or within oneself (Jesus in the garden of Gethsemane). For example, the plot of Revelation is as follows. The main section of the book begins with a stable condition in heaven with God on the throne in control of the universe (chs. 4, 5). This is followed by a series of instabilities that test the resolve of Christians and the commitments of the inhabitants of the earth (plagues and persecutions by the beast in chs. 6–19). At the conclusion of the book a new stable condition is ushered in with the arrival of the millennial kingdom and the new Jerusalem (chs. 20–22). The importance of plot analysis is that it forces us to ask the fundamental question "Why?" What is the causal relationship between events in the narrative? What causes disequilibrium in a narrative, and how are the instabilities resolved? What are the consequences of the resolution?

Letters

Paul and other NT letter writers follow conventional forms of letter writing: a salutation with a greeting, followed by a thanksgiving. The body of the letter follows with often a parenetic section for ethical instruction and exhortation. Finally, the conclusion of the letter follows with a benediction.

Paul uses numerous literary forms within his letters: e.g., hymnlike material, confessional creeds, diatribes, antitheses, chiasms, poetry, typologies, anaphoras, irony, sarcasm. 1 Tim. 3:16 is representative of the artistic qualities found in NT letters. Here an interlocking chiastic structure joins together elements from two worlds: the world above and this world. The first chiasm — flesh (this world): spirit (world above) :: angels (world above) : Gentiles (this world) — is joined by a second chiasm — angels (world above) : Gentiles (this world) :: world (this world) : glory (world above). Thus, by an intricate interlocking structure the hymnlike creed proclaims that two worlds that were previously separate — the world above and this world — are now joined together and unified by Jesus Christ.

Bibliography. M. H. Abrams, *A Glossary of Literary Terms,* 5th ed. (Chicago, 1988); M. A. Powell, *What Is Narrative Criticism?* (Minneapolis, 1990); D. M. Rhoads and D. Michie, *Mark as Story* (Philadelphia, 1982). JAMES L. RESSEGUIE

LITHOSTROTON (Gk. *lithóstrōton*)
The place of judgment in the courtyard of the Fortress Antonia where Jesus was condemned to death (John 19:13; NRSV "the Stone Pavement").

See GABBATHA.

LIVER
The largest and heaviest organ in animal and human bodies. The Hebrew term *(kāḇēḏ)* apparently derives from the common Semitic root *kbd,* "to be heavy," and can refer to a physical organ or to the depths of one's being.

In all but one OT occurrence the term concerns an animal. The lobe or appendage of the sacrificed animal's liver, along with two kidneys and the fat attached to the entrails and kidneys, was consumed on the altar (e.g., Exod. 29:13, 22; Lev. 3:4, 10, 14-15).

Prov. 7:23 depicts an arrow plunging into the liver of a deer trapped in a snare, mortally wounding it, as descriptive of the man who submits to the seduction of a harlot. Lam. 2:11, the only OT reference to human liver, articulates intense grief occasioned by the tragic destruction of Jerusalem. Although the more general term "bowels" more commonly connotes passionate emotion, the expression "my liver is poured out upon the ground" serves a similar function (the Akkadian and Ugaritic cognate can denote the seat of emotions).

Assyrian and Babylonian literature have abundant references to the examination of a liver for divination purposes. Numerous textbooks on liver observation, collections of omen texts, and as many as 32 models of a liver found at Mari indicate the importance and prevalence of this practice. In his declaration that judgment would come upon Israel by means of the Babylonians, the prophet Ezekiel (Ezek. 21:21[MT 26]) depicts Nebuchadnezzar utilizing three varieties of divination to determine the proper route for his military force. According to Ezekiel, Nebuchanezzar would cast lots by shooting arrows, consult idols, and examine a liver (hepatoscopy).

Bibliography. C. Dohmen and P. Stenmans, "kāḇēḏ I," *TDOT* 7:13-22; H. W. Wolff, *Anthropology of the Old Testament* (Philadelphia, 1974).

MICHAEL A. GRISANTI

LIZARD

A reptile, usually small, of the suborder Lacertilia, a wide variety of which are found in the Middle East. Six different Hebrew words appear as designation of lizards only in Lev. 11:29-30. Because Hebrew zoological terms did not have the precision of modern scientific terminology, little is absolute about the meaning of these terms beyond the probability that they all stand for types of lizards: Heb. *ṣāḇ* (NRSV "great lizard"; KJV "tortoise"); *'ănāqâ* (NRSV "gecko"; lit., "groaning, crying," which may stand for the gecko's characteristic sound); *kōaḥ* (NRSV "land crocodile"; lit., "strength," probably used for the most powerful-appearing lizard); *lěṭā'â* (NRSV "lizard"); *ḥōmeṭ* (NRSV "sand lizard"); and *tinšemeṯ* (NRSV "chameleon"; also used for a variety of birds at Lev. 11:18; Deut. 14:16). Heb. *śěmāmîṯ* (Prov. 30:28) may be another word for some kind of lizard; in Talmudic Aramaic the word (spelled *sěmāmîṯ* or *sěmāmîṯā'*) is used for poisonous spiders as well as lizards. JESPER SVARTVIK

LO-AMMI (Heb. *lō' 'ammî*)

A symbolic name ("Not My People") that the prophet Hosea was commanded to give to his and Gomer's third child (Hos. 1:9; cf. v. 10; 2:1, 23 [MT 2:1, 3, 25]).

LOCUST

An insect of the order Orthoptera and family Acrididae, distinguished from the grasshopper by its gregarious and swarming behavior. Within Palestine three species of locusts can be found. Both the European locust (*Locusta migratoria* L.) and the Moroccan locust (*Dociostaurus moroccanus* Thnbg.) are usually harmless; rarely have gregarious swarms been observed in historic times. The desert locust (*Schistocerca gregaria* Forsk.) is most common, regularly invading Palestine from its breeding grounds along the Red Sea and in the Saharo-Sahelian region. The common Hebrew term *'arbeh* (and probably Gk. *akrís* in the NT) refers to the desert locust. Heb. *sāl'ām* designates the bald locust, which is considered clean to eat (Lev. 11:22).

Other Hebrew terms referring to locusts are not so easily identified. Heb. *gōḇay* (variant *gēḇâ?*) appears to be a synonym of *'arbeh*. Heb. *yeleq, ḥāsîl,* and *gāzām* are generally interpreted as developmental stages of the desert locust. In this case, the *yeleq* is the nymph, the *ḥāsîl* and *gāzām* are two successive stages of the juvenile hopper, and the *'arbeh* is the fully mature adult locust which is able to fly. Although this interpretation has some support from the description of locust plague in Joel 1:2–2:11, it is faced with several problems. First, four stages of the desert locust are not readily discernible (the desert locust develops through six instars). Second, these terms appear to be used interchangeably with *'arbeh* and each other (Nah. 3:15-17; Ps. 78:46; 105:34) and to represent a distinct catastrophe (1 Kgs. 8:37). The terms do not appear to be used with precision.

The Bible provides a number of realistic descriptions of locust activity. The Exodus plague narrative (Exod. 10:12-20) and the descriptions of plague in Joel (Joel 1:6-7; 2:3-9) are accurate in ecological detail. Elsewhere, the Bible notes that locust swarms reach Palestine in the spring (Amos 7:1), and that locusts are dependent upon the heat of the sun for locomotion (Nah. 3:17). Locust activity also serves as a source for metaphors. In particular, the two prominent characteristics of locusts — they swarm in vast numbers and have a voracious appetite — describe the size and destructive capability of enemy armies (Judg. 6:5; 7:12; Jer. 5:17; 46:23; 51:14).

Bibliography. B. P. Uvarov, *Grasshoppers and Locusts,* 2 vols. (Cambridge, 1966-1977).

RONALD A. SIMKINS

LOD (Heb. *lōḏ*) (also LYDDA)

A city (modern Lod/el-Ludd; 140151) 18 km. (11 mi.) SE of Joppa on the Wadi el-Kabir, near the border of the Sharon Plain; also known in the NT as Lydda. An inscription of Thutmose III at Karnak (15th century B.C.) refers to the city as an Egyptian holding. Benjaminites, the "sons of Elpaal," rebuilt the city (1 Chr. 8:12), but an early association with Dan and Ephraim is possible. Lod, Hadid, and Ono provided an ancestral homeland for 725 (Ezra 2:2) or 721 (Neh. 7:37) returning exiles.

Jonathan Maccabeus captured Lod from Demetrius Nicanor in 145 B.C. and named it Lydda (1 Macc. 11:34). Later the site was named Diospolis and became a center of Jewish studies.

STEPHEN VON WYRICK

LO-DEBAR (Heb. *lô ḏeḇār; lō' ḏeḇār*)
A city-state in northern Transjordan above the Yarmuk River. During the time of Saul Lo-debar was ruled by either Ammiel or his son Machir, who gave aid to Saul's son Mephibosheth (2 Sam. 9:3-5) and later David (17:27-29). Lo-debar came under the rule of Aram-Damascus in Iron II and later was captured by Jeroboam II (Amos 6:13).

Sites identified with Lo-debar include Tel Mghanne, Tell el-Hamme, Umm ed-Dabar (207219), Khirbet Hamid, and Ibdar, but all are south of the Yarmuk. Another possibility may be Tell Dober (209232), where evidence of Iron I and II occupation has been found.

The etymology of the name is unclear as the root letters are uncommon to Semitic languages. The quadriliteral root *ldbr* was more commonly a place name, thus the more likely rendering Lidebir (cf. Josh. 13:26). PHILIP R. DREY

LOG
A unit of liquid measure (Heb. *lōg*), probably ca. .35 l. (.63 pt.), mentioned only with reference to the olive oil accompanying the leper's purification offering (Lev. 14:10, 12, 15, 21, 24).

LOGIA
A saying, often short, generally associated with deity. In Classical Greek *lógia* was nearly equivalent to *chrēsmós*, "oracular saying." In the LXX it is usually used to translate Heb. *'ōmer* and *'imrâ* but is also used for *dāḇār* instead of the usual *lógos* ("word"). Usages of *lógion* and *lógia* in the LXX fall into four categories: (1) individual sayings of God associated with the Law (Isa. 28:13); (2) oracular pronouncements of God declared by an intermediary (Num. 24:4, 16); (3) commands, occasionally placed in parallel with covenant *(diathḗkē)*, and the Law of the Lord *(tón nómon kyríou)* (Isa. 5:24); (4) general reference to the collective sayings of a person (Ps. 19:14[18:15]), or of God (Ps. 119 [118], 17 times), often conveying promises or statements regarding a future state of affairs.

In the NT *lógia* occurs four times. In Acts 7:38 Stephen uses the phrase "living" *(zṓnta) lógia* to cite the Torah which Moses received on Mt. Sinai. He is referring to the entirety of God's revelation to Moses and stressing its living or abiding nature, and thus its contemporary efficacy. In Rom. 3:2 Paul, after speaking extensively about the OT law, proclaims the privilege of the Jews in having received the *lógia* of God. The reference is again to the entirety of God's revelation in the OT. Here, however, the Jews have forfeited their blessing because of unfaithfulness and others have benefited. In Heb. 5:12 the writer, in the context of Jesus' relation to the OT sacrificial system, chides his audience that they need instruction in the basic principles of God's *lógia.* The reference is to the entirety of the OT revelation, along with the Word which was "spoken to us by a Son" (Heb. 1:2). It is essential that this *lógia* be understood and obeyed. Finally in 1 Pet. 4:11, in reference to the proper use of a charismatic gift, the audience is cautioned to speak as one who utters the *lógia* of God. As in Num. 24:4, 16, *lógia* refers here to the oracular pronouncements of God given to an intermediary to speak on his behalf.

There are two categories of usage for *lógia* in the NT: (1) a continuation of the pre-Christian use, pronouncements from a deity relayed by a spokesperson, although the reference is to the entirety of the message and not to individual sayings (Acts 7:38; 1 Pet. 4:11); and (2) God's total revelation as it relates to salvation throughout the history of the OT and into the contemporary setting where Jesus has achieved that salvation for his people (Rom. 3:2; Heb. 5:12).

In early Church literature these same two categories continue along with a stress on individual sayings from the OT and NT, especially the sayings of Jesus. In contemporary scholarship *lógia* is a technical term for a saying, particularly with respect to a saying of Jesus, and is often associated with the oral Q source. CASEY W. DAVIS

LOGOS (Gk. *lógos*)
A prominent concept in the NT, particularly the Fourth Gospel, where it is specifically identified with Jesus of Nazareth as the preexistent Christ and the incarnate savior (John 1:1-14). The word, however, has had a variety of usages from ancient times conveyed by such English terms as "word," "speech," "narration," and "expression." For Heraclitus *lógos* meant "explanation" and by extrapolation "transcendent meaning" and an underlying cosmic principle of order and proportion in the material universe. Plato and Aristotle employed the term to mean "discourse" or "rational explanation," thus signifying the structural order in the mental and moral universe. Plato made much of the notion of a cosmic order emanating from the transcendent world or from the mind of God. The term had a central role in the worldview of the Stoic philosophers. For them God and the material world were one and *lógos* was the vital force and rational element which pervades the whole universe and controls its order, function, and life. Some identified it with fire and air, associating it with breath and spirit.

Philo Judaeus made much of the concept. For him *lógos* was the rationality in the mind of God which gave God's mind order and the potential for expression. It was the conceptual framework which arose in the mind of God for the formation of the universe(s) and the expression of that framework as the template for the creation. *Lógos* was the inner structure of natural and moral law which gives form and function to the material and moral universes, respectively. Moreover, it was the rational and epistemological structure of the human mind, as part of the created universe(s), which corresponded coherently with the structure of the creation and thus made knowledge and scientific investigation possible. It was the comprehensive system of understanding of the universe(s) that the human mind can achieve by philosophy, theology, science, and piety, thus thinking God's thoughts after him. In the LXX *lógos* usually translates Heb.

dāḇār, "word," which Philo identified rather closely with the Hebrew word for wisdom (Prov. 1–9).

The NT uses *lógos* frequently, but not in the philosophical senses of rationality or the rational or ordering principle of the universe. It simply means "word," "speech," "report," "assertion," or a "matter" under discussion. Thus it often refers to the Christian gospel preached or written. Only in the prologue of the Gospel of John does *lógos* take on cosmic dimensions when used to name Jesus Christ as the transcendent, preexistent, and incarnate Word or self-expression of God. This has some similarities to Philo's usage and that of the Stoics, except that in John *lógos* is personalized.

The term is common in the Greek Patristics and in gnostic tradition. Justin Martyr, Theophilus of Antioch, and Irenaeus of Lyon, in the late 2nd century, employ *lógos* to describe the transcendent, preexistent, and incarnational role of Jesus Christ as the facilitator of God's entire redemptive economy in creation, providence, and salvation. However, they seem more dependent upon the usages of Middle Platonism such as that of Philo, Stoicism, and the Hellenistic Jewish literature of Second Temple Judaism, than upon the prologue of the Fourth Gospel. J. Harold Ellens

LOINS

The area of the body located at the hips or lower back (Heb. *moṯnayim;* Gk. *osphýs*). The loins were the place where the belt is worn (2 Kgs. 1:8; Isa. 11:5; Jer. 13:1), the sword hung (2 Sam. 20:8), and sackcloth placed (Gen. 37:34; 1 Kgs. 20:32; Amos 8:10). When quick movement was essential, the loins were the place where the garments were tied (Exod. 12:11; 1 Kgs. 18:46; 2 Kgs. 9:1); in this capacity the expression "girding the loins" became an idiom for dressing for action or readiness (Job 38:3; 40:7; cf. Luke 12:35; Eph. 6:14; 1 Pet. 1:13). Great fear is often described as accompanied by discomforts of the loins (e.g., Ps. 69:23; Isa. 21:3).

Heb. *ḥălāṣayim* is usually associated with the genital area and thus, by extension, with progeny (Gen. 35:11; 46:26). As the area of procreation, the loins represent strength and vigor (1 Kgs. 12:10; Nah. 2:1; 2 Chr. 10:10).

Heb. *kĕsālîm* is used exclusively of the loins of sacrificial animals (Lev. 3:4, 10, 15). It is thus primarily a priestly term. Mark F. Rooker

LOIS (Gk. *Lōís*)

The mother of Eunice and grandmother of Timothy; a woman of faith at Lystra (2 Tim. 1:5).

LOOM

See Spinning, Weaving, Loom.

LORD (DIVINE TITLE)

"Lord" as a title for God is analogous to its use for human rulers; it connotes superiority and authority. In the OT its counterpoint is theophoric names containing the word "servant" (e.g., Obadiah, "servant of Yahweh"). The formulation *ʾăḏōnāy* ("my God") refers only to Yahweh and eventually was pronounced in place of the divine name itself.

In the LXX Gk. *kýrios* translates both *ʾāḏôn* and *YHWH* (the latter practice parallels the substitution of *ʾăḏōnāy*). The use of *kýrios* for God continues in the NT.

Gk. *kýrios* is a frequent title for Jesus in the NT. During his earthly ministry, it functions as a title of respect, corresponding to Aram. *mārî* ("my Lord"), which was used of rabbis in some early Jewish literature and was roughly equivalent to "Sir." Immediately after the Resurrection, however, it began to connote divinity (John 20:28). Lord as a divine title for Jesus can be found as early as the pre-Pauline hymn of Phil. 2:6-11; in light of the substitution of Lord for Yahweh in the OT and the allusion to Isa. 45:23 in Phil. 2:10, Jewish Christians certainly would have equated Jesus with Yahweh. Other OT texts and concepts referring to Yahweh are also related to Jesus in the NT. For example, he is called "King of kings and Lord of lords" (Rev. 17:14; 19:16; cf. Deut. 10:17; Ps. 136:3; Dan. 2:47), and the "day of the Lord" is used of Jesus' return (2 Pet. 3:9-10; Amos 5:18; Zeph. 1:14-18). Jesus is also the Lord of creation (Heb. 1:10-12; Ps. 102:25-27[MT 26-28]). In light of such texts, the credal formula "Jesus (Christ) is Lord" (1 Cor. 13:3; Phil. 2:11; cf. Rom. 10:9) is an assertion of his divinity.

John L. McLaughlin

LORD, MASTER

Someone who has significant authority over others. The term is sometimes found in the vocative case of address, where it indicates deference and respect toward the individual(s) addressed. The term may convey esteem to a leader from his people (Num. 32:25; cf. Acts 25:26). In Gen. 44:7-16 it indicates the respect a slave exhibits for his or her master; Jesus' parable of the wicked servant is a NT example of a similar usage (Matt. 18:23-25).

Lord also refers to secular heads of tribes or nations, as "the five lords of the Philistines" (Judg. 3:3; 1 Sam. 5:8; Isa. 16:8). It may also refer to an entire class of nobles or courtiers (Dan. 5:1). It is this kind of human lord over whom God is "King of kings and Lord of lords" (1 Tim. 6:15; Rev. 19:16). That lordship can be demonstrated even against the corrupt elite of Judah (cf. Jer. 22:8; 25:35; 34:5).

According to Mark 2:28 par. Jesus used the term to establish his authority over ancient custom: "The Son of Man is lord even of the sabbath." As a verb ("to lord it over") the term is used occasionally to describe high-handed behavior (Neh. 5:15; Eccl. 8:9), the very antithesis of the style Jesus commands of his disciples (Luke 22:24-27; cf. 2 Cor. 1:24).

See God, Names of. Watson E. Mills

LORD OF HOSTS

The most frequently used compound title for the Israelite deity in the OT (Heb. *YHWH ṣĕḇāʾôṯ*). A similar title is "Yahweh, God of hosts." These epithets describe Yahweh as both divine Warrior and divine King, with "hosts" referring to both earthly (e.g., the Israelites or their armies) and cosmic forces (celestial bodies or angels). It appears most often in the Prophets (esp. Isaiah, Jeremiah, Zechariah, and Malachi) and not at all in the Pentateuch. In 1 Sam. 1:3 it is associated with the shrine at Shiloh. During Israelite conflict with the Philistines it is paralleled with "the God of the armies" (1 Sam. 17:45), demonstrating, initially, a very militaristic understanding of the title.

Bibliography. T. N. D. Mettinger, *In Search of God: The Meaning and Message of the Everlasting Names* (Philadelphia, 1988); P. D. Miller, *The Divine Warrior in Early Israel.* HSM 5 (Cambridge, Mass., 1973). TONY S. L. MICHAEL

LORD'S DAY

The phrase "the Lord's day" is found in Scripture only in Rev. 1:10, where John is describing the circumstances in which he received his revelation. The phrase is commonly used to refer to Sunday and is often linked to the OT sabbath. There is little doubt that "the Lord" in this case refers to Jesus rather than the Father. In the early Church Christians met for worship on Sunday in honor of the day of Jesus' resurrection (Acts 20:7; 1 Cor. 16:2). In addition, Sunday was the first day of the week in the Jewish calendar, and therefore it reminded people of the first day of creation and of Jesus' re-creation through redemption. It was also called the eighth day, pointing to the coming day of judgment. Early Christians may have believed that Christ would return on his day, Sunday.

In addition to Sunday, two other possible meanings of the phrase "the Lord's day" in its context in Revelation have been proposed. Some argue that it may refer to the yearly observance of Easter. However, other early Christian uses of "the Lord's day" indicate the weekly, rather than yearly, observance. Other scholars have argued that it refers to the judgment day itself, rather than Sunday, as a type of the coming judgment day or eighth day described above. Taken in this way, it would be synonymous with "the great day" mentioned in Rev. 6:17; 16:14; however, this does not make sense in the context of Rev. 1. In order to harmonize Rev. 1 with this theory, some have suggested that John is transported in his vision to the judgment day.

Bibliography. D. A. Carson, ed., *From Sabbath to Lord's Day* (Grand Rapids, 1982). ANN COBLE

LORD'S PRAYER

The prayer attributed to Jesus in Matt. 6:9-13; Luke 11:2-4. The prayer appears in two different forms. Matthew's opening invocation ("Our Father who is in the heavens") is longer than Luke's single word address "Father." While both versions share the next two petitions ("May your name be hallowed," "May your kingdom come"), Matthew has a third not present in Luke ("May your will be done as in heaven also on earth"). The next three petitions, the "us" petitions concerning bread, forgiveness, and temptation, are essentially the same. But Matthew adds a further petition absent from Luke ("deliver us from the evil one").

The most common explanation for the differences between the two versions posits that the Lord's Prayer originated in some form with Jesus in Aramaic. It was then added to the sayings collection Q, the common source for Matthew and Luke unknown to Mark (hence the Prayer's absence from Mark). Matthew and Luke incorporated it into their Gospels, making changes to reflect their different theological outlooks and pastoral situations. Matthew, for instance, adds his extra lines. Luke changes the word "debts" to "sins," "today" to "each day," and makes the tense of "give" and "forgive" present (rather than aorist) to emphasize daily discipleship. Joachim Jeremias summarizes this view: "in *length* the shorter text of Luke is to be regarded as original, and in general *wording* the text of Matthew is to be preferred" (*New Testament Theology* 1:196).

Other ways of explaining the differences have also been proposed. One view attributes the Prayer's origin not to Jesus but to the early tradition. The Jesus Seminar thinks that Jesus taught disciples to address God as Father. He may also, at various times, have taught them to pray concerning God's name, reign, provision of bread, and forgiveness. But it was the Q tradition that assembled a prayer around these four petitions. Matthew and Luke later elaborated the Lord's Prayer.

Michael Goulder has suggested that Matthew, not Q (which Goulder thinks did not exist), created the Lord's Prayer from parts of Mark's Gospel. For example, Jesus' teaching on forgiveness in Mark 11:25-26 provides the basis for the opening address and the petition on forgiveness. The garden of Gethsemane scene (Mark 14:32-42) provides the petitions about doing God's will and being delivered from evil. On this view, Luke alters Matthew's version to accommodate it to his different situation.

Ulrich Luz proposes a further view. He has argued that while some of the changes in Matthew's version are typical Matthean redactions, others are not (e.g., the noun "earth" without an article, the singular form "heaven," the passive form "be done," the "as . . . also" construction in Matt. 6:10). He argues that the presence of Matthean and non-Matthean language indicates that while the Gospel author's language is essentially that of his tradition and community, the two are not always identical. The Gospel's author is not responsible for the Lord's Prayer in its current form. Rather, the author incorporates the Prayer in the form in which it was used in the liturgy of his community. This means, then, that in hearing the Lord's Prayer as part of the Gospel, Matthew's audience recognizes a familiar unit and recalls its liturgical experience of this prayer. The issue of origin continues, then, to be debated.

Also debated is the meaning of the Lord's Prayer. Here two questions are central: how is the Prayer answered and when? Is the Prayer completely oriented to the future when God will do these things? Or does it focus on both the future and present, with either the first three petitions more concerned with the future and the rest with the present, or with each petition involving dimensions of both present and future, of divine response and action by disciples? This last view is the most convincing.

The opening address to God as "Father" articulates a particular relation between those who pray and God. Both Gospels recognize that disciples of Jesus enter into the same relationship with God as Jesus enjoys (Matt. 2:15; 3:17; 5:16, 45, 48; Luke 2:49; 6:36). The "our" distinguishes the community of disciples. The term "in heaven" recognizes God's traditional abode and the origin of God's saving initiative (Matt. 1:18-25; 4:17).

To pray that God's name be hallowed or sanctified is to pray for the manifestation of God's power and presence. This can be done by God (Ezek. 36:22-38, return from exile) and by humans through enacting God's will now as well as in the final completion of God's purposes.

Likewise to pray for God's reign recognizes that the reign is God's dynamic, powerful presence. This reign is to be manifested in future glory, but both Gospels affirm its presence already in the ministry of Jesus (Matt. 4:17; 12:28; Luke 11:20) and in the lives of those who encounter him (Matt. 5:3, 10; 6:33; Luke 6:20; 8:10). To pray for God's will to be done similarly involves a response from both God and disciples, in the future and the present (Matt. 7:21; 12:46-50; 26:42).

Debate about the petition for bread has focused on the meaning of Gk. *epioúsios.* The word is infrequently used, and scholars have sought its meaning in possible Aramaic originals, the form (or etymology) of the word, the context of the prayer, and understandings of its meaning from Church tradition. Possible translations include "the bread necessary for existence," "bread for today," "future bread" (for the eschatological banquet), or "bread for tomorrow." The last translation is supported by the form of the word and a 2nd-century translation. The petition would be understood, then, as a request for the continuing supply of the bread needed for survival, though an additional eschatological reference cannot be ruled out.

The fifth petition continues the focus on "us" and is a petition for forgiveness. Both Gospels recognize that God's forgiveness is available through the ministry of Jesus (Matt. 1:21; 9:1-8; 26:28; Luke 5:17-26; 7:47-50). The petition recognizes that God's forgiveness mandates forgiveness of others, a theme Matthew emphasizes (Matt. 6:14-15; 18:21-35).

The next petition is problematic in several respects. The notion that God tests God's people appears for instance in Ps. 11:5; 26:2. Yet Jas. 1:13 asserts the contrary, while 1 Cor. 10:13 promises help in temptation. Some have understood "temptation" to refer to the final time of trial or testing which marks the end of the age. But it is preferable to understand the term to indicate primarily daily temptations and the petition as a request by vulnerable disciples for God's help to resist such temptations and apostasy. Matthew's addition ("deliver us from the evil one") seems to support this reading. It makes explicit the origin of the temptation in the power of the evil one, the devil, to resist God's purposes (so Matt. 4:1-11; 13:19, 38). There is, though, a future dimension in that at the end of the age God will bring about a final deliverance in the victory over all evil.

Some liturgical versions of the Lord's Prayer include a doxology ("for thine is the kingdom, the power, and the glory, for ever, Amen"). This doxology was added to some earlier manuscripts, but was probably not in the original Gospels.

Bibliography. R. E. Brown, "The Pater Noster as an Eschatological Prayer," *TS* 22 (1961): 175-208; W. Carter, *What Are They Saying About Matthew's Sermon on the Mount?* (New York, 1994), 42-45, 93-95; "Recalling the Lord's Prayer," *CBQ* 57 (1995): 514-30; M. D. Goulder, "The Composition of the Lord's Prayer," *JTS* N.S. 14 (1963): 32-45; R. Guelich, *The Sermon on the Mount* (Dallas, 1982), 272-320; J. Jeremias, *New Testament Theology* 1 (New York, 1971); *The Prayers of Jesus* (Philadelphia, 1978); U. Luz, *Matthew 1-7* (Minneapolis, 1989).

WARREN CARTER

LORD'S SUPPER

A meal celebrated in honor of Jesus Christ commemorating his last meal with his disciples. In biblical theology Lord's Supper is preferable to other synonyms: "communion" is a questionable translation of 1 Cor. 10:16, and "eucharist" does not appear as a name for this rite in the NT. In historical theology the eucharist is generally understood to refer to both the consecratory prayers and the rite of eating "the bread" and drinking "the cup," practiced separate and apart from a regular meal in the Church. This practice can be dated as early as the 2nd century.

The term (Gk. *kyriakós,* "belonging to the Lord") occurs only once in the NT (1 Cor. 11:20). The early Christian communities assembled in houses to share the main meal of the day (Gk. *deípnon,* which occurred in the Greco-Roman world later in the day) in honor of the risen Lord. The celebration of a meal in honor of Jesus Christ on the Lord's day (Rev. 1:10, the first day of the week on Jewish reckoning; cf. Acts 20:7; 1 Cor. 16:2) is hallowed in Christian tradition (cf. Luke 24:1, 13, 29, the appearance of the risen Jesus to his disciples after his crucifixion). The term "love-feast" (Gk. *agápē*) was also used in this connection (Jude 12; and some manuscripts of 2 Pet. 2:13).

Paul

1 Cor. 11:17-34

The instructions of Paul to the church at Corinth contain the earliest solid historical information about the Lord's Supper. 1 Cor. 11:17-34 addresses the problem of disunity that threatened to wreck a house church in Corinth. According to v. 21, at the time of the main meal some remained hungry while others had more than enough and even drank to excess. Apparently each one brought his or her own food, and the rich had conspicuously more than the poor. Those who did not have enough were shamed and marginalized (v. 22).

Paul interprets this as an indicator of a spiritual blight that had fallen upon the church (vv. 27-32). He urges the church to welcome and treat one another hospitably at the Lord's meal (v. 33). To substantiate his argument, Paul rehearses the apostolic tradition he received about the Lord's Supper (vv. 23b-26). That the meal had its origin on the night Jesus was betrayed (v. 23) agrees with the Synoptic accounts of what took place in the upper room. Paul apparently understands Jesus' taking bread and the words "This is my body on behalf of you" (v. 24) as occurring at the beginning of the meal. The reference can hardly be to anything other than Jesus' offering of his life (body) on the Cross. The invitation to participate ("Do this in my remembrance") was an invitation to renew sharing in the benefits of salvation accomplished through this once-and-for-all offering. Likewise, when the cup was taken (v. 25) at the end of the meal the same principle applied. Paul's point was that if all at the table were able to receive a portion of gifts of this magnitude, it was unthinkable that all of the participants would not gladly share with their fellow believers in the food and hospitality of the meal.

Indeed, since the meal was not only an offer to reclaim the benefits of salvation under the Lordship of Christ but an anticipation of participation in the future messianic banquet at the Lord's coming, it could be seen as a proclamation of the Corinthians' faith (v. 26). Clearly then, the failure to welcome and show care for fellow believers indicated some were participating unworthily, and in so doing were misconstruing and defaming the purpose of Christ's sacrifice which they supposedly intended to commemorate (vv. 27, 29).

1 Cor. 10:14-22

Paul also addresses the incompatibility of Christian participation in meals in honor of the Lord Jesus and those dedicated to other lords. Paul did not believe that the pagan gods had any real existence, but he did hold that behind them stood demonic forces with real power (1 Cor. 10:19-21). Just as spiritual food and drink did not protect the wilderness generation (vv. 1-13), neither would participation in the Lord's Supper provide a wall of protection against the demonic powers operative at meals dedicated to pagan gods. Indeed, it was incompatible with the Christian confession to eat at the two tables; the two were mutually exclusive (v. 21).

In this context, Paul gives specific teaching with reference to the claim that the Lord Jesus made upon believers (vv. 16-17). Paul uses a fragment of tradition regarding the cup of blessing that probably derived from the actual meal on the night Jesus was betrayed (v. 16; cf. Luke 22:20). This is terminology used at the Passover to denote a final cup taken at the end of the meal. Paul claims that the cup of blessing is a participation *(koinōnía)* in the blood of Christ, and the bread in the body. Some, following analogies in Greco-Roman cultic activities, understand Paul as claiming that the believer is actually united with the risen Christ, who is thought to be present at the meal. More likely the reference is only to participation in benefits of salvation won through the death (blood/body) of Christ.

Alluding to the one loaf which is taken and eaten by many (1 Cor. 10:17), Paul sees in this common action an expression on the part of all the participants of the visible oneness of the Church which, as an extension of Jesus' earthly ministry, now constitutes his presence in the world. Paul here anticipates 1 Cor. 12, where again he calls for unity within the Church under the general metaphor of a body.

Matthew and Mark

A second major tradition involves the Synoptic accounts of Matt. 26:17-30; Mark 14:12-26. Scholars have been unsuccessful in determining the priority of either account. The few variants may be explained mainly on either authorial style or differing liturgical practices in the communities that nourished these Gospels.

Both Matthew and Mark attest that the Supper was inaugurated at a Passover meal (cf. Luke 22:7-9). The reference to the cup (of blessing) after supper indicates that this was the unanimous view in the early Church (Luke 22:20; 1 Cor. 11:25). The different chronology of the Johannine Passion account (Jesus is killed while the paschal lambs were being slain; John 13:1; 18:28; 19:14, 31) suggests that John and the Synoptics reflect dependence upon different Jewish calendars or practices. John's account is also governed by a theological agenda (cf. John 1:29).

This tradition is also more developed liturgically than that in 1 Cor. 11:24-26. The account of the tradition highlights only such features of the meal that would be most useful to a later community that observed the Supper. Although such a community could not deny its historical origin in the time of the Passover festivities, it clearly differentiated it enough to be a significant new reality in the history of salvation.

A major difference from the Pauline tradition is that the bread and cup sayings (reflecting developing Christian practice) are brought close together, presumably at the end of the meal. The words of institution for the bread (Matt. 26:26; Mark 14:22) are the same as in 1 Cor. 11:24. Paul adds Gk. *hypér,* "on behalf of you," a version of which Matt. 26:28; Mark 13:24 connect to the cup (and also Isa. 53:12). Clearly, in both the Pauline and Matthean/Markan traditions Jesus' death is interpreted as something done on behalf of others (i.e., expiatory). This is underscored by Matthew's emphasis in 26:28 that it is "for the forgiveness of sins." As with the Pauline account — albeit in a more liturgical accent — the idea that the Supper is an anticipation of the banquet at the end of the age is stressed in both Matthew (26:29) and Mark (14:25).

Luke

The Lukan account seems to connect two major units (Luke 22:14-18, 19-20). The first highlights the fact that Jesus is gathering with his disciples for a final banquet together, perhaps representing the culminating act of earlier times when Jesus was at table (Luke 7:36-50; 11:37-52; 14:7-24). It also functions strongly as an anticipation of meals in the kingdom of God, fulfilled to some degree in the post-Resurrection meals with the disciples (Luke 24:30-35, 41-43).

Thus, Luke has understood the Passover meal (Luke 22:7-13) to be "a banquet meal," a glorious precursor of life in the kingdom of God. The cup, most likely the *Qiddûš* or first cup giving thanks for the wine, taken before the Passover meal itself, is incorporated into the banquet scene (Luke 22:7-18).

This enables Luke to follow the basic pattern of incorporating the bread and cup saying in the standard order of early Christian tradition (Luke 22:19-20). However, Luke not only uses elements of the other Synoptic tradition, but also incorporates elements of the Pauline tradition, or one similar to it. Thus, Luke and Paul agree that the bread is taken at the beginning of the meal and the cup at the end (Luke 22:20). Luke also uses the *hypér* saying with the body and the call to "Do this in remembrance of me" (Luke 22:19; 1 Cor. 11:24-25).

The fact that an important segment of the ancient textual tradition (Western) omits Luke 22:19b-20 has been endlessly debated. The matter is extremely technical, and for the purposes of this article these verses have been accepted as part of the genuine text.

Other Traditions

In John 6:53-58, at the end of the bread of life discourse, Jesus speaks of "eating his flesh" and "drinking his blood." Although this may echo the Johannine understanding of the meaning of the Lord's Supper, the text may also reflect the Johannine emphasis of calling one to participate in the outcome of the incarnate life of Christ in order to have eternal life. One cannot presume any additional information here on the early Christian understanding of the Lord's Supper (likewise in Heb. 6:4; 13:10).

The references to meals in Acts (e.g., 2:42, 46; 27:35, with the possible exception of 20:7, 11) reflect Luke's emphasis on the continuation of the practice of disciples sharing meals together. The term "breaking of bread" here refers to a common practice at the commencement of the meal. It is synecdochical of an ordinary meal.

Conclusion

On the last day before the Crucifixion Jesus spent an extended time in a meal with his disciples. The details of what happened there have been susceptible to various interpretations throughout history; but no one can deny that the reality of these events have left an indelible impression upon the consciousness of the Church. Every first day since then people somewhere have gathered around a table in Jesus' name. The traditions examined here indicate that central to these observances of the Lord's meal is a projection of the mind of believers both into the past and into the future. By returning to the past the believer recalls and reclaims a share in the benefits of Christ's death. Simultaneously, life with the risen Lord in the fully realized kingdom of God is anticipated in the future.

Bibliography. X. Léon-Dufour, *Sharing the Eucharistic Bread* (New York, 1984); J. Jeremias, *The Eucharistic Words of Jesus* (Philadelphia, 1990); I. H. Marshall, *Last Supper and Lord's Supper* (Grand Rapids, 1981); B. F. Meyer, ed., *One Loaf, One Cup* (Macon, 1993).

ALLAN J. MCNICOL

LO-RUHAMAH (Heb. *lōʾ rūḥāmâ*)
A symbolic name (Heb. "Not pitied") that the prophet Hosea was commanded to give to his and Gomer's daughter (Hos. 1:6; cf. 2:1, 23[MT 3, 25]).

LOT (Heb. *lôṭ*)
The son of Abraham's deceased brother Haran, who travelled with Terah and the ancestral family from Ur to Haran (Gen. 11:27-31) and then accompanied Abraham from Haran to Canaan (12:5). Once in Canaan, the two separate, Lot taking the Jordan Valley to the east and Abraham taking the land of Canaan (Gen. 13). Lot remains closely tied to Abraham, however, in the stories of the war with the kings (Gen. 14) and Sodom and Gomorrah (19:1-29). After Lot's wife dies, his two daughters enter into incestuous relationships with him, and Lot becomes the eponymous ancestor of the Ammonites and the Moabites (Gen. 19:30-38).

Other references to Lot include Deut. 2:9, 19, where the Israelites are forbidden to battle the Ammonites and Moabites since God promised them territory as Lot's children. Ps. 83:8[MT 9] reminds the reader that Moab and Ammon are the children of Lot. In 2 Pet. 2:6-8 Lot is cited as the one righteous inhabitant of Sodom and Gomorrah.

The Lot narratives have been assigned to the Yahwist (J) source, except for Gen. 14, which still eludes definite source assignment. Lot is present at the beginning of and at each stage of Abraham's initial journey in and through Canaan (Gen. 11:27, 31; 12:4-5; 13:1). His role in the Abraham-Sarah stories seems to be to introduce the central theme of their childlessness. Abraham had no children, while his brother Haran had Lot. Abraham took Lot with him to Canaan, not at the behest of God, who commanded Abraham to leave behind his land, relatives, and father's house, but perhaps as the heir he thought he might never have, a theme repeated in the stories of Eleazar of Damascus (Gen. 15:2) and Ishmael (ch. 16). When Abraham and Lot decide to separate in Gen. 13, Abraham offers Lot land to the north or to the south, indicating that he intends to share the land of Canaan with him as his heir apparent (v. 9). Lot, however, chooses the land to the east (Gen. 13:10-11), outside the boundaries of Canaan, and God appears to Abraham and promises that the land will be given to Abraham's descendants (vv. 14-17). Lot is not the promised heir. Genesis provides genealogies for Ishmael (Gen. 25:12-18) and Isaac (vv. 19-20), but none for Eleazar and Lot.

Bibliography. J. Blenkinsopp, *The Pentateuch* (New York, 1992), 98-133; L. R. Helyer, "The Separation of Abram and Lot," *JSOT* 26 (1983): 77-88; S. P. Jeansonne, "The Characterization of Lot in Genesis," *BTB* 18 (1988): 123-29.

NANCY L. DECLAISSÉ-WALFORD

LOTAN (Heb. *lôṭān*)
A son of Seir (Gen. 36:20, 22; 1 Chr. 1:38-39); a chief of Horite peoples who lived in Seir/Edom (Gen. 36:29).

LOTS
Objects cast to determine an answer beyond human comprehension or to make a decision requiring divine guidance. Heb. *gôrāl* originally meant "stone" or "pebble," but eventually came to mean "destiny" or "fate." Lots were presumably small stones or pieces of wood and are always referred to as being thrown, shaken, or cast down. The practice of lot casting is connected with the Urim and Thummin, priestly oracle devices which may have also been lots or small dice.

In the Bible lot-casting held several different purposes, both civil and cultic. Lots were cast before God in division of the land (Josh. 18:6; 19:51), distribution of goods (Nah. 3:10; Ps. 22:18[MT 19]), and selection of residents of postexilic Jerusalem (Neh. 10:34[35]). Lots were also cast to ascertain the identity of a guilty party (Josh. 7:10-26; Jonah 1:7; 1 Sam. 14:41-42), and in the selection of a king (1 Sam. 10:20) or a cultic functionary (1 Chr. 24–26). Lots were cast on the Day of Atonement for choosing the sacrificial goat (Lev. 16:8-10). In the NT the successor of Judas is selected by casting lots (Acts 1:23-26) and the Roman soldiers throw lots (Gk. *klḗros*) to divide Jesus' clothing (John 19:24; Mark. 15:24 par.).

The divinatory technique termed psephomancy or cleromancy refers to lot casting, a prevalent method of divination in the ancient world. In the Bible, however, the casting of lots was one of the few legitimate means of divine revelation (as were dreams and direct communication with the deity). Lot casting is not among the condemned mantic or divinatory practices such as soothsaying, magic, and necromancy (cf. Deut. 18:10-12). Lot casting, therefore, had divine sanction and control. Though the throwing of the lots was a human action, the revelation was a direct message from God (Prov. 16:33).

See PURIM.

Bibliography. W. W. Hallo, "The First Purim," *BA* (1983): 19-29; J. Lindblom, "Lot-Casting in the Old Testament," *VT* 12 (1962): 164-78.

JULYE BIDMEAD

LOTUS
A plant, either a thorny shrub (*Zizyphus lotus* L.) which flourishes in the hot, damp regions of North Africa and Syria, or a type of water lily (*Nymphaea lotus* L.) which grows in Egypt. The shrub seems to be indicated in Job 40:21-22, the only biblical reference to lotus. Behemoth is said to lie down under the lotus plants, which cover him with shade. This could scarcely be understood as a water lily. The translation "thorn bushes" (TEV) or "thorny lotus" (REB) makes the appropriate distinction between the two types of lotus plant. In Greek legend lotus fruit induced a state of calm forgetfulness, but this idea is nowhere found in the Bible.

JOE E. LUNCEFORD

LOVE
An inner quality expressed outwardly as a commitment to seek the well-being of the other through concrete acts of service. Love is a central biblical concept for defining the relationship between God and humans.

Several words are used in the OT to describe various aspects of love. Most common is Heb. *'āhaḇ* and its derivatives, which characterize relationships ranging from the secular to the sacred.

Secular Human Relations

Love describes the full range of relations between the sexes (e.g., Gen. 29:18, 20; Judg. 16:4; 1 Sam. 18:20). Physical attraction and sexual love are powerful inner forces (Cant. 8:6-7; Prov. 5:19-20).

Love is the bond between parent and child (Gen. 22:2; 44:20). Parental love always seeks the best for the child, which may include physical discipline (Prov. 13:24; cf. 3:12).

Love is the bond of mutual devotion and commitment expressed in a close friendship such as that between Jonathan and David (1 Sam. 18:1-4; 20:17; 2 Sam. 1:26) and the devotion of Ruth, who sought the welfare of Naomi beyond all cultural expectations or legal requirements (Ruth 4:15).

Divine-Human Relationships

Torah

The book of Deuteronomy summarizes the saving history of God's relation with Israel as the expression of Yahweh's freely bestowed love. Yahweh chose Israel and brought them out of Egypt because he entered into covenant with and loved their ancestors (Deut. 4:31-37). The entire narrative of the calling, election, covenant, and promises made to the family of Abraham, Isaac, and Jacob (Gen. 12-50) is hereby declared to be the story of God's unmerited love, bestowed on Israel as a self-motivated act of grace.

Only by embracing the unity of the divine revelation in the history of salvation as an act of Yahweh's love could the Israelites be called upon to respond with a whole-hearted love for God (Deut. 6:4-6). But because the human condition of the heart is easily drawn away from a commitment to Yahweh (Deut. 8:1-20) and stubbornly resists God's will (10:16), Yahweh in a surprising act of grace promises to enable Israel to love and obey him by circumcising the heart of Israel (Deut. 30:6). Israel's love, like

Yahweh's, is demonstrated by acts of love expressed as obedience to Yahweh's law in the daily tasks of living (Deut. 6:7-9). The law is Israel's way to imitate the love of Yahweh as experienced when Israel was redeemed from Egypt (e.g., Deut. 24:17-18).

Although Yahweh was selective in choosing Abraham and his descendants out of all the peoples of the world (Deut. 19:14-15), God's protection and providential care extends to the outsiders of society, even foreigners (v. 18; cf. Exod. 23:9). God's primary and ultimate aim in forming a people was to be a source of blessing to everyone (Gen. 12:2-3), through whom all nations will be taught about Yahweh's will for everlasting peace (Isa. 2:2-4). Israel was commanded to show concrete acts of love to their enemies and not to retaliate against those who wronged them (Prov. 24:29).

Prophets

The prophets, especially Hosea and Jeremiah, depict Yahweh's love for Israel in terms of family imagery. Israel is Yahweh's adopted son, on whom Yahweh bestowed his fatherly care by redeeming him from Egypt and providing for him along the way (Hos. 11:1-4). Israel is also the wife whom he loves (Hos. 3:1).

God demands that the Israelites have an intimate relationship with God characterized by "steadfast love" (or "loyalty"; Heb. *ḥeseḏ*) and "knowledge of God" (Hos. 4:1-2). But to Yahweh's disappointment Israel's love is as fleeting as the morning dew (Hos. 6:4-6), misdirected as sexual promiscuity with Canaanite gods in the fertility cult (3:1; 4:10-14; cf. Jer. 2:20-25; 3:6-10).

Where restoration of the relationship looks impossible, God's love transcends human love. God is the Holy One whose compassion will restore his lost son (Hos. 11:8-9; cf. Jer. 31:15-20), healing him and enabling him to return to Yahweh (Hos. 14:1-8[MT 2-9]; cf. Jer. 3:21–4:1). Likewise, Yahweh will woo back his lost bride and establish an everlasting marriage (Hos. 2:16-23[MT 18-25]). Similarly, Yahweh will bring his discouraged people out of exile because of his great love for them (Isa. 43:4-5). His momentary wrath, or judgment, will fade before this compassion and everlasting love.

Synoptic Gospels

In the NT God's love (Gk. *agápē*) for humans is enacted through Christ, and made effective through the gift of the Holy Spirit.

God's love is evident through the work of Jesus, who does acts of mercy such as healing the sick and accepting the unacceptable by eating with tax collectors and sinners, and forgiving their sins. In the parables Jesus presents God as one who bestows his love, mercy, and forgiveness as acts of undeserved grace (e.g., Matt. 18:23-35; Luke 15:11-32). Those who receive God's compassionate forgiveness are also expected to treat others with the same love.

The Great Commandment is the summary of the OT law, a double command to love God and neighbor (Matt. 22:34-40 par., quoting Deut. 6:4; Lev. 19:18). In the Parable of the Good Samaritan Jesus defines the neighbor as one who shows compassion beyond religious and ethnic boundaries (Luke 10:29-37). Love is doing good even to those who do not love you, even to your enemy (Luke 6:27-36).

Johannine Writings

In the works associated with John, God's love is clearly articulated. God's love for the world is demonstrated by sending his Son, Jesus, to die for the sins of the world that those who believe in him might have life (John 1:29; 3:16; cf. 20:31). Those who belong to the Son love him, and show their love by keeping his commandments (14:15), summarized as the commandment to love one another (15:12).

Because of God's great act of love, believers ought to love one another (1 John 4:10-11). Those born of God are enabled to love him and keep his commandments by faith (1 John 5:1-5), because love is an essential defining characteristic of God. The love that the believer shows is "perfect love," God's love which has reached its perfection, or goal, in loving others (1 John 4:17-18). Believers show God's love by concrete acts of service which meet real human need, just as Jesus showed God's love by laying down his life for them (1 John 3:16-17).

Pauline Letters

For Paul, love starts with the "God of love and peace" (2 Cor. 13:11) whose gracious act of reconciling love is revealed in Christ. Nothing in creation can separate the reconciled one from this love (Rom. 8:35-39).

According to Paul "the whole law is summed up in a single commandment, 'You shall love your neighbor as yourself'" (Gal. 5:14). Paul's famous description of Christian love in 1 Cor. 13 also could be regarded as a portrayal of Christ.

The power to love comes from God alone. The Holy Spirit pours God's love into the believer's heart, producing love as the foremost fruit of the Spirit (Rom. 5:5; Gal. 5:22), which sets believers free from the power of sin by manifesting the love of Christ in their lives (Rom. 8:1-9).

In summary, God's love is the unmerited acceptance of all people expressed in concrete acts of providence and salvation. Through faith in Christ the Christian is enabled to love with the love of God through the work of the Holy Spirit.

Bibliography. V. P. Furnish, *The Love Command in the New Testament* (Nashville, 1972); W. Klassan, *Love Your Enemies: The Way To Peace.* OBT 15 (Philadelphia, 1984); A. Nygren, *Agape and Eros* (1953, repr. Chicago, 1982). LAURIE J. BRAATEN

LOVE-FEAST

See LORD'S SUPPER.

LOVING-KINDNESS

Also rendered "kindness," "mercy," and "steadfast love," particularly when describing God. The traditional translation "loving-kindness" entered English usage through the 1535 Coverdale Bible and the KJV of 1611. The primary definition of Heb. *ḥesed* is "demonstrated loyalty," i.e., loyalty that exhibits itself in actions rather than words or sentiments (e.g., Gen. 40:14; Exod. 20:6). Furthermore, the term has a magnanimous quality. Loving-kindness is a type of loyalty that does not merely meet an obligation but goes the second mile (Jer. 2:2), just as the Israelites obeyed Moses when they followed God into a "land not sown." This linguistic compound representing one virtue piled atop another expresses a special and remarkable beneficence.

A final nuance of loving-kindness is its asymmetrical nature. Behavior worthy of the term must be generous: a virtue unilaterally bestowed and usually associated with the party that holds the social advantage. For instance, Rahab the prostitute reminds the Israelite spies that she had treated them "kindly" by hiding them and denying their presence to the king of Jericho (Josh. 2:12). This aspect of loving-kindness helps explain its popularity in descriptions of God (e.g., Ps. 107:1): God's demonstrated loyalty to creation has an uncoerced, gracious quality.

Of the many things said of God in the OT, his loving-kindness is one of the most prevalent based on its occurrence in so many formulas (e.g., Exod. 34:6; Num. 14:18; 1 Kgs. 8:23). It best describes the quality of God in the OT that attracts the obedience, praise, and love of individuals.

Bibliography. K. D. Sakenfeld, "Loyalty and Love: The Language of Human Interconnections in the Hebrew Bible," in *Backgrounds for the Bible,* ed. M. P. O'Connor and D. N. Freedman (Winona Lake, 1987), 215-29. GREGORY MOBLEY

LOWLAND

The foothills going down westward from the Judean highlands to the coastal plain of Philistia. Heb. *šĕp̄ēlâ* is usually transliterated as a proper name, Shephelah. The same word is used more broadly at Josh. 9:1; 11:2 (here probably referring to the coastal lowlands N of Carmel), 16; 12:8.

See SHEPHELAH.

LUCIFER

See MORNING STAR.

LUCIUS (Gk. *Loúkios*)

A common name in the Roman world, the Latin equivalent for the Greek name *Loukás/ós,* shortened from *Loukános.*

1. Lucius of Cyrene, one of four prophets and teachers in Antioch who are led by the Spirit to commission Barnabas and Saul (= Paul) for mission work (Acts 13:1). Cyrene, capital of the Roman province of the same name in North Africa, had a large Jewish population, and it is likely that Lucius was a Hellenistic Jew, perhaps even one of the men of Cyprus and Cyrene who traveled from Jerusalem to Antioch and evangelized there (Acts 11:20).

2. A relative of Paul. Lucius, Jason, and Sosipater are identified as Paul's relatives who send greetings to the Romans (Rom. 16:21). Since it is likely that Paul wrote to Rome from Corinth, it is probable that these men lived in Corinth. This Lucius is also a Jewish Christian, but it is very unlikely that he is the same person as Lucius of Cyrene.

The identification of either of the above persons with Luke the Evangelist is tenuous at best. When Paul refers to Luke the Evangelist, he calls him *Loukás,* not *Loúkios.* It is also likely that Luke was a Gentile, not a Jew. DAVID L. TURNER

3. A Roman consul, Lucius Caecilius Metullus, who in 142 B.C.E. addressed letters to a number of countries reaffirming a Roman protective alliance with the Jews of Judea (1 Macc. 15:15-24). The letters are in response to the Jewish embassy under Numenius that went to Rome in that year (1 Macc. 14:16-24).

LUD (Heb. *lûḏ*), **LUDIM** (*lûḏîm*)

According to the Table of Nations (Gen. 10:22) and the genealogy in 1 Chr. 1:17, Lud, a descendant of Shem. However, in Gen. 10:13; 1 Chr. 1:11 Ludim is called a son of Mizraim (Egypt), who is the second son of Ham, which could refer to an African country such as Ethiopia (Cush) and Put (Ezek. 30:5).

The area referred to by Lud is uncertain. One suggestion is that the name refers to Libya (Heb. *lûḇîm*), or to some otherwise unknown northeastern African people. In Jer. 46:9 the Ludim are presented as a bow-bearing auxiliary of Egypt (cf. Isa. 66:19), and in Ezek. 27:10 they are portrayed as mercenaries for Tyre. However, in Ezek. 30:5 both Libya and Lud are mentioned together.

The more widely held interpretation has been the identification with Akk. *Luddu,* the region of Lydia in western Asia Minor. The association in Isa. 66:19 with Tubal, Javan, and the coastlands far away agrees with the general location of Lydia near the Ionian coast. However, the historical Lydians of Asia Minor were neither Semites nor Hamites.

LARRY L. WALKER

LUHITH (Heb. *lûḥîṯ*), **ASCENT OF**

A place or road going up into the heights of southern Moab (Isa. 15:5; Jer. 48:5). The location is otherwise unknown. Eusebius (*Onom.* 122.29) identifies Luhith with Loueitha between Ar (Areopolis) and Zoar.

LUKE (Gk. *Loukás*)

The name appears three times in the NT (Col. 4:14; 2 Tim. 4:11; Phlm. 24), evidently with reference to the same person, a companion of Paul, traditionally identified as the author of the Gospel of Luke and the Acts of the Apostles.

By way of characterizing Luke, 2 Tim. 4:11 highlights Luke's faithfulness in comparison with some who are said to have deserted Paul. In Phlm. 24 Luke is identified as a "fellow worker," not simply one of Paul's "traveling companions" or "assistants," but a person of comparable stature, a "missionary colleague." Col. 4:14 refers to Luke as "beloved physician." Apparently, his knowledge and skills as a healer had won him respect, placing him in the company of those physicians, known in the

Hellenistic and Roman periods, who enjoyed high status as students of medicine and philosophy. Because Col. 4:10-11 refers to Aristarchus, Mark, and Justus as the only Jews who were present as coworkers with Paul, it emerges that Luke is a Gentile or, at least, a non-Jewish Semite. The scriptural intimacy and Jewish interests manifest in Luke-Acts do not require a hypothesis of Jewish authorship, but are equally compatible with significant exposure to Judaism by a non-Jew.

It is generally assumed that these two narrative documents were written by the same person (cf. Luke 1:1-4; Acts 1:1-2), and early traditions identify this person as Luke. The oldest Greek manuscript of the Third Gospel, Papyrus Bodmer XIV ($\mathfrak{p}^{75}$, ca. 200 C.E.), uses the title "Gospel according to Luke." The Muratorian Canon (late 2nd century) also identifies Luke, a physician and companion of Paul, as the author of the Gospel, an identification further corroborated by the 2nd-century writings of Irenaeus (*Adv. haer.* 3.1.1; 14.1) and later writers (e.g., Eusebius *HE*). Until recently, the view that Luke-Acts was penned by a companion of Paul drew additional support from the so-called "we-passages" in Acts (16:10-17; 20:5–21:18; 27–28). Some now regard these passages as literary creations.

Like the other NT Gospels, Luke and Acts are anonymous documents. Even when involved in first person narration, the writer of Acts identifies himself not as an individual with a name, but as one of a group. He may at times be present as a participant-observer, but his focus is not his individual identity. That first person narration happens in only selected portions of the account underscores that the narrator makes no claim to being a constant companion of Paul and his circle. This speaks against the tradition that Luke and Paul were "inseparable" (Irenaeus *Adv. haer.* 3.1.1, 4), but also against those who deny that Luke could have written Acts because the author of Acts could not have been a *regular* companion of Paul. It also suggests that first person narration is more than a literary device calculated to enliven the narrative.

Little reason remains not to accept the traditional identification of Luke as the author of Luke-Acts; this would make Luke responsible for the largest portion of the NT (28 percent). If Lukan authorship of these books is accepted, additional information becomes available from their language and style — e.g., that Luke is educated, probably urban, with firsthand exposure to rhetorical training and to Israel's Scriptures; a person of some economic means, writing from the social location of those who traffic in technical or professional writing; and one of the "people of the Way," a "Christian," either second- or third-generation (Luke 1:1-4).

Bibliography. J. A. Fitzmyer, "The Authorship of Luke-Acts Reconsidered," in *Luke the Theologian* (New York, 1989), 1-26.

JOEL B. GREEN

LUKE, GOSPEL OF

The third and longest book in the NT, sometimes called the Third Gospel.

Questions of introduction typically include authorship, composition, date, and provenance — all of which are problematic in the study of Luke. Concerning authorship, the most likely candidate is Luke the physician and sometime companion of Paul (Phlm. 24; Col. 4:14; cf. 2 Tim. 4:11; Acts 16:10-17; 20:5–21:18; 27-28). He is thus identified in several 2nd-century witnesses (Papyrus Bodmer XIV, the Muratorian Canon, Irenaeus *Adv. haer.*; for later testimony cf. Eusebius *HE*). However, the author himself has not included his name within or as a title to the Gospel, which suggests that his identity may not be critical to our reading. "Luke," as the voice through which the story of Jesus' mission and message is here related, functions more closely as "narrator" than "author."

The narrator refers to his use of sources and research (1:1-4), which many scholars today assume included at least the Gospel of Mark. According to the two-source theory, a second source was Q, though it remains unclear whether Q material came to Luke orally or in written form. (According to the Griesbach hypothesis, Luke used only Matthew's Gospel.) Some scholars also refer to Luke's use of the "L" tradition, including material without parallel in Matthew or Mark, but again it is unclear in what form this material might have come to Luke. Many of the distinctive features of Luke would be catalogued with "L": the parables of the Good Samaritan, the lost son, and the Pharisee and toll collector (10:29-37; 15:11-32; 18:9-14); and material concerning the positive role of women in Jesus' ministry and the problematic role of wealth and possessions for those who want to follow Jesus.

How one dates the writing of the Third Gospel rests in large part on how one understands these source-related questions. If Luke made use of Mark, then obviously he could not have written before its completion. Since Mark is typically dated in the late 60s, this would require Luke to have been written no sooner than the early 70s. Some scholars find evidence in 21:20-24 that the narrative was written in light of the actual fall of Jerusalem, but the details of this text are as likely to have been drawn from records of the siege and fall of cities in the LXX. The earliest references to Luke and Acts in other written sources come from the mid-2nd century, so the Gospel would presumably have been written in the period 70-140 C.E. Insofar as Acts seems not to evidence firsthand knowledge of the Pauline corpus, and since it is likely that Paul's letters would have been collected in the late 1st century, the writing of Luke is pushed into the earlier part of this time frame. Hence, most think in terms of a range from the mid-70s to mid-80s.

Even fewer data are available for determining the precise location from which the Gospel was written, though an urban center outside Palestine is probable. Nor can mention of Theophilus in 1:3 aid in discerning its readership. As literary patron, Theophilus would have helped to circulate Luke and Acts for copying, but this does not mean that he is Luke's primary audience or even representative of those to whom Luke is writing. What is evident is that Luke is concerned with Christian mission and identity and the forms of Christian discipleship suited to life in the Roman Empire.

The identification of the genre of the Gospel is closely tied to the question of the unity of Luke and Acts. In its current canonical position, Luke has been easily identified as a "gospel," a particular form of Greco-Roman biography. Such an identification is complicated by the book's manifest relation to the Acts of the Apostles, which claims to continue the story begun in Luke (cf. 1:1-4; Acts 1:1-2). Moreover, it is a near certainty that in Luke's day "gospel" did not exist as a literary form, so one would be amiss to think that Luke set out to write one or that his readership would have understood his work within such categories. Luke refers to his predecessors as "narratives," not "gospels."

Most now agree that Luke and Acts were written by the same person and that Acts forms some sort of sequel to the Gospel. The theological and narrative unity of Luke-Acts, largely taken for granted since the early 20th century, are now contested, On the one hand, it is easy to find in Luke-Acts the temporal sequence (beginning, middle, and end) and principal aim characteristic of narrative unity. Thus, Luke-Acts recounts the working out of God's purpose to bring salvation in all of its fullness to all people. This aim is anticipated by God's messengers and made possible by the birth and growth of John and Jesus in households oriented around the purpose of God (Luke 1:5–2:52); made probable through the preparatory mission of John and especially the life, death, and exaltation of Jesus, with its concomitant commissioning and promised empowering of Jesus' followers to extend the message to all people (Luke 3–Acts 1); realized as the Christian mission is directed by God to take the necessary steps to achieve an egalitarian, multiethnic community (Acts 2–15); and finds its denouement as Luke highlights growing Jewish antagonism to the Christian movement, and thus the increasingly gentile make-up of the Church (Acts 16–28). Accordingly, incidents in the Gospel anticipate aspects of the story narrated only (finally) in Acts. Notably, in 2:25-35 Simeon realizes that in Jesus a salvation has come that will be "a light for revelation to the Gentiles" (v. 32), but throughout the Gospel Jesus interacts only rarely with non-Jews. One must wait for Acts to see how the gentile mission is begun, legitimated, and takes firm shape at the behest of God. The last chapter of Luke closes off significant aspects of the story's plot, but there is a more overarching intent at work, the redemptive purpose of God for all people. Seen against this purpose, the Gospel is incomplete in itself, for it opens up possibilities that go unrealized in the Gospel only to materialize in Acts. On the other hand, some scholars have been more impressed by the degree to which the Third Gospel and Acts are each self-contained, each with its own aims and perspectives.

Since the seminal work by H. J. Cadbury, a broad consensus has emerged that Luke 1:1-4 belongs squarely within the literary tradition of ancient historiography. In addition to the preface, Luke's work shares many other features of Greco-Roman historiography: a genealogical record (3:23-38); the use of meal scenes as occasions for instruction; travel narratives; speeches; letters; and dramatic episodes, such as Jesus' rejection at Nazareth (4:16-30) and Paul's stormy voyage and shipwreck (Acts 27:1–28:14). This has led to the identification of Luke-Acts as historiography and to further attempts to designate the sort of history-writing it most approximates. For some Luke has always seemed too motivated by his theological agenda to be regarded as a historian, but no ancient historian was without motive, be it theological, apologetic, pedagogical, or whatever. The modern dichotomy that pits history over against interpretation has grown out of problematic philosophical (and especially epistemological) commitments and is rightly being abandoned. Others find the closest generic parallels in Greco-Roman biography. Taken on its own, the Gospel of Luke can be classified as biography; understood in relation to Acts, this designation is less easy to sustain. More importantly, the Third Gospel is primarily focused on God and the fulfillment of God's ancient purpose, so it can only in a secondary sense be classified as an account of the life of Jesus. What is nonetheless clear is that Luke, perhaps more than the other Evangelists, has been influenced by Greco-Roman literary forms, especially those related to the biographical genre, even if other formal features and the theocentric focus of his narrative preclude identification of Luke-Acts as "biography."

Identification of Luke-Acts as ancient historiography adds to the expectations we may bring to the narrative. Alongside those raised by Luke's professed intentions (1:1-4), we may anticipate a narrative in which recent history is given prominence. Issues of both causation and teleology are accorded privilege, and determined research is placed in the service of persuasive and engaging instruction.

Luke's message is fundamentally oriented toward the theme of salvation — its derivation, scope, and embodiment. Within the conflicted world of the 1st-century Mediterranean, views of the divine purpose like that sponsored in Luke-Acts — views that run roughshod over important conventions of social honor and religious status in their announcement of the nature and magnitude of salvation — would naturally have been the source of controversy and uncertainty. Against this backdrop, the purpose of Luke-Acts would have been to strengthen the Christian movement in the face of opposition by ensuring believers in their interpretation and experience of the redemptive purpose and faithfulness of God and by calling them to continued faithfulness and witness in God's salvific project. The purpose of Luke-Acts, then, would be primarily ecclesiological — concerned with the practices that define and the criteria for legitimating the community of God's people, and centered on the invitation to participate in God's redemptive project.

Not surprisingly, then, the Gospel of Luke is centered on God. Even if God does not appear often within the narrative, the design guiding the progression of the narrative is God's. He is "God my savior" (1:47), and reveals his purpose in multiple ways — the Scriptures, heavenly messengers, and the divine choreography of events. The motif of the divine purpose also surfaces via a constellation of terms expressive of God's design (e.g., "purpose," "it is necessary," "to determine"). God's will is accomplished in the Gospel through the Spirit-anointed ministry of Jesus (cf. 4:18-19), and it will be continued in Acts by means of Spirit-empowered witnesses (cf. 24:44-49). Especially in the central section of the Gospel concerned with the journey from Galilee to Jerusalem (9:51–19:46), Jesus attempts to transform the view of God held by his followers in order that they might recognize God as their Father, whose desire is to embrace them with his gracious beneficence (e.g., 11:1-13; 12:32).

Luke's emphasis on the divine purpose serves his ecclesiological and hermeneutical interests. As the Christian community struggles with its own identity, not least over against those who also read the Scriptures but refuse faith in Christ, the coherence between God's ancient agenda and the ministry of Jesus becomes crucial. In fact, Jesus' struggle with the Jewish leadership and with Jewish institutions is essentially this: Who understands God's purpose? Who interprets the Scriptures faithfully? For Luke, the advent of Jesus is deeply rooted in the ancient covenant, and his mission is fully congruent with God's intent. This is shown above all by the scriptural pattern of his life and by the divine vindication pronounced over him in his resurrection and ascension.

God may control the agenda of the story, according to Luke, but the main character in Luke's first volume is Jesus. Compared with characters within the narrative, Luke's own audience is fortunate in its ability, from the very beginning, to perceive Jesus' identity and role in God's redemptive plan. Jesus is portrayed as a prophet, but as more than a prophet; he is the long-awaited Davidic Messiah, son of God, who fulfills in his career the destiny of a regal prophet for whom death, though necessary, is not the last word. For Jesus' disciples, the struggle is not so much to discern who Jesus is, but how he can fulfill his role. Their own views of God and the world remain conventional throughout most of the Gospel; hence, almost to the very end, they lack the capacity to correlate Jesus' exalted status as God's Messiah with the prospect and experience of his heinous suffering.

Early on, Jesus is identified as savior (2:11), a role he fulfills in numerous ways. Among the most visible, his miracles of healing and the expansive nature of his table fellowship embody the truth of the in-breaking kingdom of God. Through these avenues, Jesus communicates the presence of divine salvation for those whose position in society-at-large is generally on the margins. This is "good news to the poor" (4:18-19). Such behaviors are matched by Jesus' teaching, which occupies major sections within the Gospel, especially in the accounts of his journey to Jerusalem. What is often striking about his instruction is orientation toward a reconstructed vision of God and the sort of world order that might reflect this vision. Jesus, as Son of God, is God's representative, whose life is characterized by obedience to God and who interprets for others (if they will only listen) God's nature and plan and the contours of appropriate response to God.

The call to discipleship in Luke is fundamentally an invitation for persons to align themselves with Jesus, and thus with God. This means that, for membership among the people of God, the focus is removed from issues of inherited status and a premium is placed on persons whose behaviors manifest their unmitigated embrace of the gracious God. Genuine "children of Abraham" are those who embody in their lives the beneficence of God, and who express openhanded mercy to others, especially toward those in need. Jesus thus calls on people to live as he lives, in contradistinction to the agnostic, competitive form of life marked by conventional notions of honor and status typical of the larger Roman world. Behaviors that grow out of service in the kingdom of God take a different turn: Do good to those who hate you. Extend hospitality to those who cannot reciprocate. Give without expectation of return. Such practices are possible only for those whose convictions and commitments have been reshaped by transformative encounter with the goodness of God. Within the Third Gospel, the chief competitor of this focus stems from Wealth — not so much money itself, but the rule of Money, manifest in the drive for social praise and so in forms of life designed to keep those with power and privilege segregated from those of low status, the least, the lost, and the left-out.

Throughout, the Lukan narrative focuses on a pervasive, coordinating theme: salvation. Salvation for Luke is neither ethereal nor merely future, but embraces life in the present, restoring the integrity of human life, revitalizing human communities, setting the cosmos in order, and commissioning the community of God's people to put God's grace into practice among themselves and toward ever-widening circles of others.

Bibliography. F. Bovon, *Luke the Theologian.* PTMS 12 (Allison Park, Pa., 1987); P. F. Esler, *Community and Gospel in Luke-Acts.* SNTSMS 57 (Cambridge, 1987); J. B. Green, *The Theology of the Gospel of Luke* (Cambridge, 1995); H. Moxnes, *The Economy of the Kingdom: Social Conflict and Economic Relations in Luke's Gospel.* OBT 23 (Philadelphia, 1988).

JOEL B. GREEN

LUST

The word lust today is used almost exclusively to mean strong sexual desire. In KJV usage it connotes intense pleasure or delight, or simply an inclination or wish.

In the OT "lust" as a noun translates in the KJV a variety of Hebrew words and designates, among other things, an intense desire for holy war (Exod. 15:9), a craving for food (Ps. 78), a desire so strong that "stubbornness" would be a more appropriate translation (Ps. 81:12), and sexual desire (Prov. 6:25).

In the NT Gk. *epithymía* is now more often translated "desire" for what in general the KJV instead translates "lusts" (Mark 4:19). It can be used for a strong pure desire of Christ (Luke 22:15), a longing to be with Christ (Phil. 1:23), a desire to do evil (John 8:44), and adultery (Matt. 5:28) and other impure sexual passions and practices (Rom. 1:24; 6:12; Gal. 5:16, 24). In addition to *epithymía* to indicate sexual desire, the NT also uses Gk. *órexis, thymós, hēdonḗ,* and *páthos.* The context must always be considered in choosing the appropriate translation. WILLIAM R. GOODMAN, JR.

LUTE

A musical instrument that likely had a long neck, skin head, two or three strings, and a triangular form. Heb. *šālîš* (1 Sam. 18:6) is interpreted by some as "lute"; its name (from Heb. *šālôš,* "three") refers to its three strings. In this passage, Israelite women played these instruments along with timbrels (tambourines) in celebration of David's killing of Goliath. The lute was not an instrument used in temple worship. The Hebrew term corresponds to Akk. *šalaštu,* an instrument with a long neck, similar to the modern banjo.

Representations of such instruments are known in both Egyptian tomb paintings and a relief at Carchemish; there are no known examples from Palestine. Although the NRSV translates Heb. *nēḇel* and *ʿāśôr* as lute (Ps. 150:3; 92:3[MT 4], respectively), these instruments were likely harps with more than three strings (Heb. *ʿāśôr,* "ten").

JENNIE R. EBELING

LUZ (Heb. *lûz*)

1. The site of Jacob's ladder dream. Jacob used a stone as a pillow, and when he awoke, he anointed the stone with oil and called it Bethel, "house of God" (Gen. 28:10-22; cf. 35:6; 48:3; Josh. 18:13; Judg. 1:23). Josh. 16:2 suggests that two distinct sites are intended, but most likely the two names designate a single place. Most scholars identify Luz/Bethel with modern Beitîn (172148). Others have suggested el-Bireh, ca. 3 km. (2 mi.) S of Beitîn.

2. A place established in the land of the Hittites by one who escaped Canaanite Luz/Bethel, having supplied the Israelites with information of how to capture that city (Judg. 1:26). The modern identification of this site is unknown. Once thought to be in Syria NE of the Orontes, it may simply have been a short distance W of Luz/Bethel.

Bibliography. J. J. Bimson and D. Livingstone, "Redating the Exodus," *BARev* 13/5 (1987): 40-53, 66-68; N. K. Gottwald, *The Tribes of Yahweh* (Maryknoll, 1979). DALE W. MANOR

LXX

See SEPTUAGINT.

LYCAONIA (Gk. *Lykaonía*)

In NT times, a southern region of the province of Galatia, N of the Taurus Mountains, E of Phrygia, S of ethnic Galatia, and W of Cappadocia. The area received its name from the Lukka (Lykaones), the Anatolian people who originally lived in the area. Leading Lycaonian cities included Laranda, Lystra, and Derbe, and at various times Iconium was also reckoned as part of Lycaonia.

The first literary mention of Lycaonia appears in Xenophon *Anab.* 1.2.19 (early 4th century B.C.). The region was conquered by the Persians and later by Alexander the Great (333). The Seleucids ruled the territory until they were defeated by the Romans at Magnesia (188), and Lycaonia passed into the hands of the Attalid kingdom of Pergamum. Pergamum and its territories were bequeathed to Rome in 129, and Lycaonia was subsequently ruled by dynasts. Antony gave Lycaonia to Amyntas, king of Galatia (36 B.C.). When Amyntas died in battle in 25 B.C., Augustus incorporated his kingdom into the Roman province of Galatia. Lycaonia then became a name for the southern region of this province.

Paul visited Lycaonia several times (Acts 13:51; 14:8-20; 16:1-5; 18:23). During the so-called first missionary journey he and Barnabas were received at Lystra as the gods Hermes and Zeus (14:8-18). Timothy was from Lycaonia (16:1-5), as was the lesser-known Gaius (20:4). According to the "South Galatian" theory, Paul's Epistle to the Galatians was written to the Christian communities of Lycaonia (cf. 1 Cor. 16:1). PAUL ANTHONY HARTOG

LYCIA (Gk. *Lykía;* Akk. *Lukki*)

A wooded, mountainous country on the southwest coast of Asia Minor. Lycia is bordered on the west by Caria, on the east by Pamphylia, and on the north by Phrygia and Pisidia. The coastal region is enriched by the fertile Xanthus Valley. The region was colonized early by the Greeks, whose cultural influence is evident in the presence of Greek theaters in most of the towns. The Lycians are mentioned in the *Iliad* (2.876-7; cf. 6.184) as a brave, warlike people who produced such heroes as Glaucus and Sarpedon, and who sided with the Trojans in the Trojan War. Lycia was successively dominated by the Persians, Alexander the Great, the Ptolemies, and Seleucids. When the Romans seized control in 188 B.C.E., they gave Lycia to Rhodes, which the Lycians opposed bitterly. Consequently, the Romans granted Lycia her freedom in 169. The consul Lucius Calpurnius Piso is said to have written a letter confirming an alliance with the Jews of Lycia (1 Macc. 15:23). Lycia was made a Roman province in 43 C.E. and was joined to Pamphylia as a double province in 74. The country's most important cities were the ports of Patara and Myra, where Paul changed ships on his missionary journeys (Acts 21:1; 27:5). From there a thriving commerce was carried on with Alexandria. Lycia was renowned for worship of Apollo, who spent his winters there, according to Greek mythology.

Bibliography. C. B. Avery, "Lycia," in *The New Century Handbook of Classical Geography* (New York, 1972), 187; L. Schmitz, "Lycia," in *A Dictio-*

nary of Greek and Roman Geography, ed. W. Smith (1870, repr. New York, 1966), 2:223-26.

RICHARD A. SPENCER

LYDDA (Gk. *Lýdda*)
A city (modern Lod/el-Ludd; 140151) 18 km. (11 mi.) SE of Joppa, known in the OT as Lod. During the Hellenistic period, Lod became known as Lydda, and was the capital of one of the 11 districts of Judea after having been transferred from Samaritan control (1 Macc. 11:34). Years later the city suffered under Pompey. Cassius sold the inhabitants into slavery, but Mark Antony soon granted their release by decree. Cestius Gallus burned the city in 66 C.E. while the inhabitants were celebrating the Feast of Tabernacles in Jerusalem. After the destruction of Jerusalem in 70 C.E., Lydda (now Diospolis) was known both as a center for rabbinic thinking and for its strong Christian community. The Crusaders renamed it St. George, commemorating his martyrdom there.

Lydda is the place where Peter healed the paralytic Aeneas (Acts 9:32), an event that caused many to convert in response to the Christian mission to that region.

ROBERT A. DERRENBACKER, JR./
STEPHEN VON WYRICK

LYDIA (Gk. *Lydía*) **(PERSON)**
A Gentile woman from Thyatira in the province of Asia who was a god-fearer living in Philippi (Acts 16:14-15). It is not clear whether Lydia's name is a personal name or designates her as the Lydian woman ("as a person from the country called Lydia"). Lydia worshipped the God of Judaism, perhaps originally as part of the Jewish settlement in Thyatira. She was part of a gathering of women who met for worship and prayer outside Philippi on the sabbath. Meeting in this location indicates that there were not the 10 Jewish men needed to establish a proper synagogue.

Lydia was converted by Paul, and he baptized both her and her household. She was a business woman trading in purple-dyed cloth, a trade for which Thyatira was well-known. She was apparently successful, because she had a house large enough to use as the lodging for Paul and his companions and serve as the initial meeting place of the church of Philippi (Acts 16:40). She epitomizes the role of wealthy women converts in the Pauline mission in supplying their homes as meeting places and perhaps themselves as leaders of these churches.

JOANN FORD WATSON

LYDIA (Gk. *Lydía*) **(PLACE)**
A prosperous commercial center in western Asia Minor on the Aegean Sea, a producer of textiles and purple dye (Strabo *Geog.* 13.4.14). According to Herodotus, the Lydian king Croesus, whose wealth and power were legendary (*Hist.* 1.28), allied himself with the Egyptians and Babylonians against the Persians, but was defeated and captured by Cyrus the Great in 546 B.C.E. (1.86). Under Cyrus, the Lydian capital, Sardis, became the seat of the Persian satrap (governor). Alexander the Great conquered Lydia in 334 (Diodorus Siculus *Hist.* 17.21.7). During the reign of the Seleucid king Antiochus III, Jewish soldiers (the *katoikoi*) settled in Phrygia and Lydia and became the basis of the Diaspora in Asia Minor (Josephus *Ant.* 12.147-53; *CIJ* 2.775). The Seleucids ruled until 189, when the Romans defeated Antiochus III at Magnesia (Livy *Urb. cond.* 37.44-45; 1 Macc. 8:8). Lydia was then given by the Romans to Eumenes II, king of Pergamum. In 133 the Pergamene king Attalus III bequeathed his kingdom back to the Romans in his will. Subsequently, Lydia became part of the proconsular province of Asia. According to Josephus, Hellenistic Jewish communities, including those in Lydia, obtained jurisdiction in civil matters, even before Julius Caesar (*Ant.* 14.225-64). The consigning of money for common meals and sacred festivals, and the sending of money to Jerusalem were permitted (*Ant.* 14.213-16; 16.171). A large synagogue dating from the Roman period was discovered in Sardis in 1962 and excavated.

Paul and Silas visited Lydia (Acts 16:40). A wealthy business woman known as Lydia, who came from Thyatira in Lydia, was a dealer in purple (Acts 16:14). The seven churches of Asia named in the book of Revelation were located in the area of Lydia.

Bibliography. J. M. G. Barclay, *Jews in the Mediterranean Diaspora: From Alexander to Trajan (323 B.C.E.–117 C.E.)* (Edinburgh, 1996); M. Hengel, *Judaism and Hellenism,* 2 vols. (Philadelphia, 1974); E. Schürer, *The History of the Jewish People in the Age of Jesus Christ (175 B.C.–A.D. 135),* rev. ed., 1 (Edinburgh, 1973); V. Tcherikover, *Hellenistic Civilization and the Jews* (1959, repr. New York, 1970).

LYNNE ALCOTT KOGEL

LYE, SOAP
An element for cleansing. Potassium carbonate lye was obtained from the ashes of certain plants or found naturally. A district in Egypt was known for its natural availability. Aristotle describes lye as an element that dissolves easily in water.

Soap was invented by the Phoenicians and used as a hair dye and salve during the period of the biblical writings. Not until the 2nd century C.E. is soap mentioned as a cleansing agent. Soap was formed by combining plant ashes with an oil substance. The cleansing use of soap in the Roman Empire likely resulted from contact with Germanic tribes. The paucity of reference to cleansing agents and the importance of fragrances indicate that ancient standards of cleanliness were different from modern standards.

In biblical usage lye and soap are used metaphorically for moral purification (e.g., Job 9:30; Isa. 1:25; Jer. 2:22; Mal. 3:2) or the sting of defeat (Prov. 25:20 NRSV mg).

STANLEY HARSTINE

LYING
Usually a spoken attempt to deceive, but sometimes used to refer to a deceptive action. Gk. *pseúdos* corresponds to a number of Hebrew terms with related nuances: *šqr,* "trick or treat someone falsely"; *kḥš,*

"treating someone treacherously"; *kzb,* "speaking what is untrue or being false to reality"; *pth,* "deceiving by enticing"; *šw',* "speaking vainly or without intent of accountability."

The biblical condemnation of lying stems from the testimony throughout the Scriptures that God is truthful, self-consistent, and reliable in self-revelation, and therefore cannot lie (e.g., Num. 23:19; Tit. 1:2; cf. Ps. 12:6[MT 7]; 2 Cor. 1:18). The evil in lying derives not from the falsification of facts alone, but also from the personal faithlessness to God and others that it always implies.

Humans, however, are essentially and inescapably untrustworthy, as seen in Adam and Eve's readiness to believe a lie (Gen. 3:4) and Cain's manufacture of a lie (4:9). Lying is an essential characteristic of human nature in separation from God, and of human behavior as disobedience to God (cf. Isa. 28:15; Amos 2:4; Rom. 1:25; 3:13). Lying and deception appear often in biblical narratives, sometimes even furthering God's plan (e.g., Gen. 27:35; Exod. 1:19-20). Nevertheless, even though human nature is unavoidably deceptive, lying itself can and ought always to be avoided, for the sake of both individuals and the community (e.g., Exod. 20:16; Lev. 19:11).

The NT reasserts that lying is an abomination (Rom. 3:4-9, 13; cf. Acts 5:3-5). Satan is "a liar and the father of lies" (John 8:44). In contrast, the gift of salvation is faithful and "true" (John 1:9; Tit. 1:13; 1 John 5:20; Rev. 22:6), and, in particular, Jesus Christ is the ratification of God's truthfulness (God's "yes," 2 Cor. 1:20; the "Truth," John 14:6). Christians are therefore urged to reject lying and to explore the Christian freedom of true speaking and open dealing (Eph. 4:20-25; Col. 3:9-10).

DAVID A. DORMAN

LYRE

A triangular musical instrument consisting of a sounding box with three to twelve strings, and played with either the fingers or a plectrum. Lyres (Heb. *kinnôr*) were used in festive celebrations (Gen. 31:27; Job 21:12), in public worship (Ps. 43:4; 98:5), and as a means of inducing ecstatic prophecy (1 Sam. 10:5; 1 Chr. 25:1). The *kinnôr* was the instrument played by David, and was an instrument of the aristocracy in other parts of the Near Eastern world; one well-known example was found at Ur and made of gold and other precious materials.

Aram. *qayṯĕrôs* was an instrument used only in public celebrations (Dan. 3:5, 7, 10, 15). It can be related to the classical Greek *kithára,* translated "harp" in the NT (1 Cor. 14:7; Rev. 14:2).

JENNIE R. EBELING

LYSANIAS (Gk. *Lysanías*)

The tetrarch (lit., "ruler of a fourth" of a Roman province) of Abilene (an area in Lebanon, NW of Damascus) when John the Baptist began his ministry (Luke 3:1; "the fifteenth year of Emperor Tiberius," 28-29 C.E.). Lysanias is the last and least civil ruler listed in this verse, the only mention of him in the NT. Josephus (*Ant.* 14.13.3; 15.4.1; *BJ* 1.13.1) mentions a Lysanias, the son of Ptolemy, who ruled Chalcis in Lebanon, but this Lysanias died some 60 years before the ministry of John the Baptist. Thus some have argued that Luke erred, but it is more likely that Luke refers to a later Lysanias, mentioned in inscriptions, who may also be intended by other references in Josephus (*Ant.* 19.5.1; 20.7.1) which speak of Lysanias but do not specify him as the son of Ptolemy. Luke's claim that he carefully investigated matters (Luke 1:3) is not seriously challenged in this instance.

DAVID L. TURNER

LYSIAS (Gk. *Lysías*)

A general in the Seleucid army of Antiochus IV. When Antiochus went to Persia to raise funds, he left orders for Lysias to march against Jerusalem (1 Macc. 3:32-41). In 165 B.C.E. Lysias' commanders met defeat at Emmaus in a battle with Judas Maccabeus (1 Macc. 4:1-24). Lysias marched on Israel again the next year and engaged Judas at Beth-zur (1 Macc. 4:26-35). The exact outcome of this battle is unclear. 1 Maccabees reports that Judas routed Lysias' army, while 2 Maccabees claims that the two parties signed a peace treaty (2 Macc. 11:1-15). Whatever may have happened, Lysias' departure from Israel allowed Judas to rededicate the temple (1 Macc. 4:36-59).

When Antiochus IV learned of Lysias' defeat, he appointed Philip as king. In a counter move, Lysias set up Antiochus V, the son of Antiochus IV, as king (1 Macc. 6:14-17). Philip's return from the east interrupted Lysias' second campaign against Israel, and Lysias returned to Antioch to regain control. Demetrius I killed Lysias and Antiochus V upon his return from Rome in 162 (1 Macc. 6:55–7:4).

See CLAUDIUS LYSIAS. RODNEY A. WERLINE

LYSIMACHUS (Gk. *Lysímachos*)

1. One of the generals of Alexander the Great (the Diadochi: Ptolemy Lagus, Cassander, Lysimachus, and Antigonus Monophthalmus). He gained control of Phrygia and the Hellespont after the death of Alexander (cf. Josephus *Ant.* 12.1.1). The generals are symbolized by wings, heads, horns, and winds at Dan. 7:6; 8:8, 22; 11:4.

2. A brother both of Simon the administrator of the temple and of Menelaus, the first non-Zadokite high priest appointed by the Tobiads. Menelaus appointed Lysimachus as deputy high priest during his absence from Jerusalem ca. 171 B.C.E. (2 Macc. 4:29). In collusion with Menelaus, he gradually pilfered the temple treasury. When the people of Jerusalem learned of this they became riotous, and Lysimachus sent 300 troops against them. The people routed the troops and killed Lysimachus (2 Macc. 4:39-42).

3. A son of Ptolemy of Jerusalem, known only from the colophon (unique to all other biblical manuscript traditions) found on some manuscripts of the Greek Esther (Add. Esth. F 11:1). He translated Esther into Greek sometime before 114-77 B.C.E. (depending upon the Alexander and Cleopatra to which the colophon refers), when it was taken to Alexandria by the priest Dositheus and his son Ptolemy as a "festal letter for Purim." His translation contains additions to Esther such as an interpreted dream and prayers (which also make direct reference to God), a greater distinction between Jews and Gentiles, reference to Haman as a "Macedonian," and the downplaying of the marriage of Esther to a non-Jewish king.

4. The author of an anti-Semitic history, who Josephus claimed wrote that the Jews were descendants of lepers and other such people who were expelled from Egypt, and that they were led by Moses to Judea where they called their city Hierosyla ("temple robbery") because they robbed temples, but later changed it to Hierosolyma to avoid disgrace (*Ag. Ap.* 1.34-35).

Bibliography. M. Goodman, "Jewish Literature Composed in Greek," in E. Schürer, *The History of the Jewish People in the Age of Jesus Christ (175 B.C.–A.D. 135),* rev. ed., 3/1 (Edinburgh, 1986), 505-6, 600-1; F. F. Bruce, "Tacitus on Jewish History," *JSS* 29 (1984): 33-44.

R. GLENN WOODEN

LYSTRA (Gk. *Lýstra*)

A town in the region of Lycaonia in south-central Anatolia, 40 km. (25 mi.) SSW of Iconium (modern Konya). Augustus founded a Roman colony at Lystra (on the Via Sebaste) in 26 B.C. and settled it with Roman army veterans. The hill on which Lystra stood seems to have had strategic importance as a defensive base against the surrounding mountain tribes of the south and west. Lystra remained an obscure city, and in spite of its Italian origins developed into a local Lycaonian market town.

According to Acts 14:1-23 Paul and Barnabas visited Lystra during the "first missionary journey." After Paul healed a crippled man, the amazed inhabitants identified Barnabas with Zeus and Paul with Hermes. These two gods are associated in inscriptional remains from the vicinity (3rd century A.D.), and the poet Ovid relates a story of the pair wandering in the region as unwelcomed visitors (*Metam.* 8.616-724). The Lystrans subsequently brought out sacrificial bulls and garlands, but the two missionaries refused any honors. The people's veneration turned to violence when adversaries of Paul and Barnabas arrived and incited a public riot. The mob stoned Paul, a persecution alluded to in the independent tradition of 2 Tim. 3:11. Later, during the "second missionary journey," Paul returned to Lystra and the surrounding cities (Iconium and Derbe) while accompanied by Silas (Acts 15:36–16:6). Many maintain that Paul visited these towns again on the return leg of his "third missionary journey" (Acts 18:23). Timothy was from the vicinity of Lystra, and was well-respected among the Christians of the area (16:1-2). Lystra did not play a major role in subsequent Christian history, though the foundation of a Byzantine church has been discovered at the site.

PAUL ANTHONY HARTOG

M

M
A symbol for material found only in the Gospel of Matthew; also a designation of the source of this material.

MAACAH (Heb. *ma'ăḵâ*) **(PERSON)** (also MAOCH)
A common name of both males and females in the OT.

1. A child of Nahor (brother of Abraham) and his concubine Reumah (Gen. 22:24). It is not known whether the child was male or female.

2. The mother of David's son Absalom, who temporarily overthrew his father's rule (2 Sam. 3:3 = 1 Chr. 3:2). She was the daughter of Talmai, king of Geshur, and thus represented a marriage alliance between Israel and Geshur.

3. The father of Achish, king of Gath, a contemporary of Solomon (1 Kgs. 2:39). He is called Maoch at 1 Sam. 27:2.

4. The favorite wife of King Rehoboam of Judah. She is listed as the daughter of Absalom (Abishalom, possibly the son of David) and mother of Abijah/m (1 Kgs. 15:2; 2 Chr. 11:20-22). At 2 Chr. 13:2 the mother of Abijah is identified as Micaiah, the daughter of Uriel of Gibeah. 1 Kgs. 15:10 calls Maacah the mother of Asa. Some scholars suggest she was actually the granddaughter of Abishalom (thus daughter of Uriel and Tamar; 2 Sam. 14:27) and the grandmother of Asa. One of only three mothers of kings given the title queen mother (Heb. *gĕḇîrâ*), she was discharged from her position by Asa for constructing an Asherah (1 Kgs. 15:13).

5. A concubine of Caleb; mother of Sheber, Tirhanah, Shaaph, and Sheva (1 Chr. 2:48-49).

6. The sister (1 Chr. 7:15) or wife (v. 16) of Machir, mother of Peresh (Perez) and Sheresh (Zerah).

7. The wife of Jehiel the father of Gibeon, an ancestor of King Saul (1 Chr. 8:29; 9:35).

8. The father of Hanun, one of David's Mighty Men (1 Chr. 11:43).

9. The father of Shepatiah, a tribal leader in Simeon during David's time (1 Chr. 27:16).

MARK W. CHAVALAS

MAACAH (Heb. *ma'ăḵâ*) **(PLACE)**
A tribe that shared a border with the half-tribe of Manasseh in the north of Israel during the time of Israel's entry into Palestine after the Exodus (Deut. 3:14; Josh. 13:8-13). It later became a small semi-independent Aramean kingdom S of Mt. Hermon in the Transjordan, covering the areas E of the Jordan River and possibly northern Galilee during the period of the Israelite kingdoms (ca. 1050-730 B.C.). It was often associated with the kingdom of Geshur, which along with Maacah, comprised the northern border of Israel.

A city named Abel-beth-maacah (2 Sam. 20:14) listed in the annals of Tiglath-pileser III of Assyria (745-727) has been identified as Tell Abil el-Qamḥ (204296), located W of Tel Dan. Sheba fled to this city after his unsuccessful revolt against David.

Maacah sided with the Ammonites against David's expansion in the Transjordan. The Ammonites employed 1000 soldiers from Maacah as mercenaries against Israel (2 Sam. 10:6-8; 1 Chr. 19:6-7). The kingdom appears to have become tributary to David (2 Sam. 10:19), but later was associated with the Aramean kingdom of Damascus during the reign of Solomon. Maacah was absorbed into the Damascene state soon thereafter (1 Kgs. 11:23-25).

Bibliography. B. Mazar, "Geshur and Maacah," *JBL* 80 (1961): 16-28.

MARK W. CHAVALAS

MAADAI (Heb. *ma'ăḏay*) (also MOMDIUS)
An Israelite of the line of Bani required to divorce his foreign wife (Ezra 10:34); called Momdius at 1 Esdr. 9:34).

MAADIAH (Heb. *ma'aḏyâ*)
A priest or family of priests who returned with Zerubbabel from captivity in Babylon (Neh. 12:5). He may be the same as Moadiah at Neh. 12:17 or Maaziah at 10:8(MT 9).

MAAI (Heb. *mā'ay*)
A musician in the procession during the dedication of the walls of Jerusalem (Neh. 12:36).

MAAPHA (Gk. *Máapha*)
A town or district in Gilead destroyed by Judas Maccabeus after freeing its Jewish captives (1 Macc. 5:35 NRSV). The preferred reading is "Alema."

MAARATH (Heb. *ma'ărāṯ*)
A city (Heb. "barren place") in the tribal territory of Judah linked with other cities N of Hebron. It is probably to be identified with Khirbet Qufin, a site adjacent to modern Beit Ummar (Josh. 15:59), 10.5 km. (6.5 mi.) N of Hebron. Maroth (Mic. 1:12) may be the same city.

MAASAI (Heb. *ma'ăśay*)
A priest in postexilic Jerusalem, descendant of Immer (1 Chr. 9:12). He may be the same as Amashsai (Neh. 11:13).

MAASEIAH (Heb. *ma'ăśēyâ, ma'ăśēyāhû*) (also ASAIAH)

1. A Levite of the second order who was installed as a musician when the ark was brought to Jerusalem (1 Chr. 15:18).

2. A lute player, probably the same as **1** above (1 Chr. 15:20).

3. The son of Adaiah; a captain of a hundred who supported the priest Jehoiada in overthrowing Queen Athaliah (2 Chr. 23:1).

4. An officer who under the direction of Hananiah enrolled Uzziah's army (2 Chr. 26:11).

5. The deputy or perhaps even son of Ahaz (lit., "son of"), killed by the Ephraimite Zichri during Pekah's invasion (2 Chr. 28:7).

6. A governor of Jerusalem, commissioned by King Josiah to repair the temple (2 Chr. 34:8).

7. A priest of the family of Jeshua who had married a foreign woman (Ezra 10:18; 1 Esdr. 9:19).

8. A member of the priestly family of Harim who had married a foreign woman (Ezra 10:21; 1 Esdr. 9:21).

9. A priest of the family of Pahhur who had married a foreign woman (Ezra 10:22; 1 Esdr. 9:22).

10. A member of the family of Pahath-moab who had married a foreign woman (Ezra 10:30; cf. 1 Esdr. 9:31, Moossias).

11. The father of Azariah who took part in Nehemiah's wall building in Jerusalem (Neh. 3:23). Some of the individuals named Maaseiah **11-16** may be identical.

12. A person who stood at Ezra's right hand as he read the Torah (Neh. 8:4; cf. 1 Esdr. 9:43, Baalsamus).

13. An Israelite who read the Torah in Hebrew and expounded on it, probably by translating it into Aramaic (Neh. 8:7; cf. 1 Esdr. 9:48, Maiannas).

14. One of the chiefs of the people who witnessed the sealing of the covenant under Nehemiah (Neh. 10:25[MT 26]).

15. The son of Baruch, a leader of Judah who lived in postexilic Jerusalem (Neh. 11:5). At 1 Chr. 9:5 he is called Asaiah.

16. An ancestor of the Benjamite Sallu (Neh. 11:7).

17. A priest who played the trumpet at the dedication of the wall of Jerusalem (Neh. 12:41).

18. A priest who took part in the dedication of the wall of Jerusalem (Neh. 12:42).

19. The father of the priest Zephaniah (Jer. 21:1; 29:25; 37:3).

20. The father of Zedekiah, who was accused by Jeremiah of prophesying falsely (Jer. 29:21). He may be identical with **18** above.

21. The son of Shallum, a keeper of the threshold (Jer. 35:4). JESPER SVARTVIK

MAATH (Gk. *Máath*)
A postexilic ancestor of Jesus, attested only in Luke's genealogy (Luke 3:26).

MAAZ (Heb. *ma'aṣ*)
A Judahite, firstborn son of Ram and grandson of Jerahmeel (1 Chr. 2:27).

MAAZIAH (Heb. *ma'azyâ, ma'azyāhû*)

1. The eponymous founder of the twenty-fourth division of priests during the reign of David (1 Chr. 24:18; Heb. *ma'azyāhû*).

2. A priest who participated in the sealing of the new covenant under Nehemiah (Neh. 10:8[MT 9]; *ma'azyâ*).

MACCABEES
A term designating (1) the dynasty founded by Mattathias the Hasmonean which ruled the Jews from the 160s to 63 B.C.E. when the Romans entered Jerusalem; and (2) the son of Mattathias, Judas the Maccabee, the first leader of the Jewish revolt against the Seleucids. Though the name "Maccabee" was first applied only to Judas, the use of the title "Maccabean Histories" (Gk. *Makkabaiōn*) in the Christian Church during the 2nd century for both 1–2 Maccabees resulted in the habit of referring to all the heroes of the books as "Maccabees." In this way, "Maccabean" and "Hasmonean" became synonymous in Greek and later literature. The name Maccabee is not found in rabbinic literature.

1 Macc. 2:4 introduces Judas as "Judas called Maccabeus," and each of his four brothers also are listed with nicknames. Although it is not known when or how Judas acquired the appellation, several explanations exist for its derivation and significance. The most popular explanation adduces the similarity between the name and the Hebrew term for "hammer" *(mqbt)* to explain that Judas was called "the Hammer" due to his military prowess and strength (cf. Carl Martel [Lat. the "Hammer"], 8th-century conqueror of the Saracens). Alternatively, the derivation may be from participle forms of the Hebrew roots *kb'/kbh* ("to extinguish") or *qb'* ("to overpower"), both of which may have lent themselves to association with Judas' military career. Because it is not known whether the name was given at birth, during adulthood, or as a result of

Burial site of the Maccabees near Modein/Ras Medieh (149148). The burial chambers are topped by heavy blocks (Phoenix Data Systems, Neal and Joel Bierling)

some deed or feature, however, it is not possible to determine with certainty the purpose for the appellation. Most scholars associate the name with Judas' military career rather than any other feature or event associated with him.

See HASMONEANS.

Bibliography. J. A. Goldstein, *I Maccabees.* AB 41 (Garden City, 1976); S. S. Tedesche and S. Zeitlin, *The First Book of Maccabees* (New York, 1950).

MELISSA M. AUBIN

MACCABEES, FIRST AND SECOND BOOKS OF

Books of the Apocrypha or Deuterocanonicals. Included in most modern translations, they are important for the historical information and theological interpretations they provide about persons and events in Jewish history during the 2nd century B.C.E.

Historical Background

During the 3rd century Judea was administered by the Ptolemaic dynasty based in Egypt. Ca. 200 Judea and its capital Jerusalem came under the political control of the Seleucid dynasty based in Antioch of Syria. Throughout the 2nd century the Seleucid kingship passed among the descendants of Antiochus III (223-187). These dynastic struggles provide the background for the events described and interpreted in 1–2 Maccabees.

When Antiochus IV Epiphanes gained control of the Seleucid Empire in 175, he allowed Jason to outbid his brother Onias III for the Jewish high priesthood (2 Macc. 4:7-8). Jason established Greek institutions at Jerusalem and apparently tried to make it into a Hellenistic city. In 172 Jason was outbid and replaced by Menelaus, who had no legitimate claim to the office of high priest. By 167 Antiochus IV with the help of Jason and other Jewish elites had despoiled the temple and its treasury, set up a military garrison near the temple (the Akra), abolished the traditional Jewish law, and established a new order of worship (the cult of the "lord of heaven").

Why Antiochus IV intervened in Jewish affairs remains a matter of debate. He may simply have needed money to pay his soldiers and to keep himself in power. Or he may have planned to develop the eastern equivalent of the nascent Roman Empire. Or he may have drifted or been invited into a socioeconomic and/or religious civil war among factions in Judea.

1 Maccabees

Against this background 1 Maccabees identifies the exploits of the "Maccabee" (named after Judas the "Hammer") family with the salvation of God's people, and portrays three generations of this family as the true leaders of Israel. After describing the crisis under Antiochus IV and the beginning of resistance under Mattathias the priest of Modein (1:1–2:70), it recounts the exploits of Judas (3:1–9:22) and his brothers Jonathan (9:23–12:53) and Simon (13:1–15:41), as well as Simon's son John Hyrcanus (16:1-24).

Many scholars believe that 1 Maccabees was

written in Hebrew (now lost) and translated into Greek, though it could have been deliberately composed in a biblical Greek (LXX) style. It may have been produced in the reign of John Hyrcanus (134-104) or shortly afterward in the 1st century B.C.E. Its language and style are reminiscent of the historical books in the OT.

The purpose of 1 Maccabees becomes clear with its comment on the defeat of Joseph and Azariah, who tried to engage in battle apart from the Maccabee family: "Thus the people suffered a great rout because, thinking to do a brave deed, they did not listen to Judas and his brothers. But they (Josephus and Azariah) did not belong to the family of those men through whom deliverance was given to Israel" (5:61-62). Thus the book is often described as a dynastic history or even dynastic propaganda for the Maccabee family.

Although 1 Maccabees acknowledges some Jewish initiatives in adopting the gentile way of life (1:11-15), the major villain initially is Antiochus IV. He plunders the Jerusalem temple (1:20-28), seizes Jerusalem two years later (1:29-40), and decrees that all those in his kingdom should become "one people" (1:41-64). In late 167 he had erected at the Jerusalem temple "a desolating sacrilege on the altar of burnt offering" (1:54) — what Daniel (11:31; 12:11) and the NT (Mark 13:14; Matt. 24:15) describe as the "abomination of desolation" or "desolating sacrilege."

According to 1 Macc. 2:1-70 Jewish resistance to Antiochus IV gained direction and momentum only through Mattathias and his five sons. The accounts about the Jewish martyrs (1:62-64) and the pious cave-dwellers (2:29-38) show that passive resistance was not sufficient. In carrying out his initial act of rebellion by refusing to participate in pagan worship (2:15-28), Mattathias burns with zeal for the Torah as Phinehas did (Num. 25:6-15). He joins with the Hasideans to organize an army to fight for Judaism, and agrees to wage defensive battles on the sabbath (2:41). His farewell speech (2:49-68) to his sons places his and their actions in line with those of the great heroes of the biblical tradition from Abraham to Daniel.

The military exploits of Judas Maccabeus are described in 1 Macc. 3:1–9:22. After defeating various Syrian armies (3:1–4:35), Judas purifies and rededicates the Jerusalem temple in 164 (4:36-61) — the event commemorated in the festival of Hanukkah. After a survey of the campaigns of Judas and his brothers (5:1-68), the book describes the death of Antiochus IV and the accession of Antiochus V (6:1-17). Despite Judas' triumphs, the "garrison in the citadel" or Akra (6:18) continues to cause trouble. And his efforts at fighting the Syrians at Beth-zur (6:18-63) are not successful. Judas' last great victory is against Nicanor in 161, when Demetrius I becomes the Seleucid king and Alcimus is named the Jewish high priest (7:1-50). By entering into alliance with Rome (8:1-32), Judas gains a powerful protector along with recognition of his movement as representing the Jewish people. But with the defeat of Judas by Bacchides and his death in 160 the Maccabean movement seems to be at an end.

What revived the Maccabean movement was further internal struggle for the Seleucid throne. The section about Jonathan (9:23–12:53) shows how he combined political shrewdness and military activity to win more power and territory. Jonathan succeeded by allowing one Seleucid claimant to outdo the other in promising him rewards for supporting them. The death of the Jewish high priest Alcimus in 159 and the apparent vacancy of this office between 159 and 152 made Jonathan the only serious Jewish political figure with whom one could deal. And deal Jonathan did — with the Seleucids Demetrius I (162-150), Alexander I Balas (150-145), and Antiochus VI (145-142), as well as the Egyptian Ptolemies, the Romans, and the Spartans. By supporting Alexander Balas against Demetrius I, Jonathan gained the high priesthood at the Jerusalem temple — despite not belonging to the proper Zadokite family.

After Jonathan's capture and death in 142, his brother Simon gained control of the movement. The section about Simon (13:1–15:41) narrates his military and political successes, and tells how he secured the independence of the Jewish people and renewed the alliance with Rome. According to the decree cited in 14:41-43, Simon and his descendants were to occupy the offices of high priest, military commander, and leader of the people (ethnarch). When Antiochus VII (138-129) broke his alliance with Simon, he and his generals were defeated by Simon and his son John Hyrcanus. The story of the early days of the Maccabean dynasty closes with Simon's death in 134 and the accession of John Hyrcanus (16:1-24).

1 Maccabees is the most important source for the history of Israel in the mid-2nd century. It proceeds from the perspective of a writer who viewed the Maccabee family as God's own dynasty and the leaders of the true people of Israel.

2 Maccabees

If 1 Maccabees can be described as dynastic propaganda, 2 Maccabees can be called temple propaganda. Its focus is the succession of threats against the Jerusalem temple and how it was preserved by God's agents. After two letters (1:1-9; 1:10–2:18) and a prologue (2:19-32), there are accounts of three successive attacks on the temple by Heliodorus in the time of Seleucus IV (3:1-40), by Antiochus IV (4:1–10:9), and by Nicanor in the time of Demetrius I (10:10–15:37). The book tells the story of the Maccabean movement up to Judas' defeat of Nicanor in 161.

The main part of 2 Maccabees (chs. 3–15) is, as 2:23 states, the digest of a five-volume work by Jason of Cyrene. Jason may have written his work shortly after the events that he described (160-152). The date of the first letter (cf. 1:9) suggests that the condensation may have been made ca. 124, though an early 1st-century date is also possible. The epitome was written in Greek, as was in all likelihood Jason's five-volume original. The condenser's statements in the prologue (2:19-32) and the epilogue (15:38-39) indicate that his primary goal was to make the work more attractive and entertaining.

The two letters before the prologue (1:1-9; 1:10–2:18) are from Jews in Jerusalem to Jews in Egypt. Both letters seek to encourage Jews in Egypt to celebrate the festival of Hanukkah. This suggests that Egyptian Jews needed convincing — whether because the event commemorated was so recent, or because it was so closely tied to the Maccabee family, or because it had no biblical basis.

The first attack against the Jerusalem temple (3:1-40) occurs during the reign of Seleucus IV (187-175), the brother and predecessor of Antiochus IV. In response to a request to intervene in a dispute between the pious high priest Onias and Simon over the administration of the city market, the Syrian governor Apollonius sends Heliodorus to make an inspection of the temple treasury. But in his effort to confiscate the treasury and bring the holy place "into dishonor" (v. 18), Heliodorus is miraculously struck down by a mysterious rider accompanied by two glorious young men. When revived through Onias' prayer (vv. 31-34), Heliodorus offers sacrifice to the God of Israel and comments that one should send only one's worst enemies to profane the Jerusalem temple (vv. 35-39).

The second attack against the Jerusalem temple (4:1–10:9) is occasioned by the struggles over the Jewish high priesthood. The priesthood of Jason (175-172) is portrayed as bringing "the Greek way of life" (4:10) to Jerusalem by establishing a gymnasium, enrolling the people as "citizens of Antioch," and disregarding the Torah as Israel's law. The author's own position is clear: "There was such an extreme of Hellenization and increase in the adoption of foreign ways because of the surpassing wickedness of Jason, who was ungodly and no true high priest" (4:13).

And yet Jason is outdone in wickedness by his successor Menelaus (in 172). When Jason's revolt fails, Antiochus IV captures Jerusalem (5:11), enters the temple with Menelaus as his guide, and carries off 1800 talents of money. Only in 5:27 do we first hear of Judas Maccabeus and his companions. According to 6:1-11, the Jews were forced to abandon the Torah, to deny their ancestral religion, and to transform the Jerusalem temple into the temple of Olympian Zeus.

After reflections on God's discipline toward Israel ("although he disciplines us with calamities, he does not forsake his own people," 6:16), the book describes the heroism displayed by Jewish martyrs who refuse to give up their traditional faith (6:10-11, 18-31; 7:1-42). The dialogues between the wicked king and the seven sons and their mother in 7:1-42 give particular attention to hopes for resurrection and God's judgment as motives for resisting the evil king's program.

The emergence of Judas Maccabeus and his victories over Nicanor and Timothy (8:8-36) lead to the realization that the Jews have a powerful Defender (God) and so are invulnerable because they follow God's laws (8:36). Struck down by God while robbing temples in Persia, even the arrogant Antiochus IV recognizes his errors (9:1-29). The climax of the second temple episode is the rededication of the Jerusalem temple, the restoration of Jewish worship, and the establishment of Hanukkah as a Jewish festival (10:1-9). In the second attack Judas Maccabeus and his army serve as God's instruments.

The third attack (10:10–15:37) features the Syrian general Nicanor's threat to destroy the temple and its altar, and to build in its place a temple dedicated to the Greek god Dionysus (14:33). After describing the accession of Antiochus V Eupator, 2 Maccabees discusses Judas' military victories (10:14–11:15), his correspondence (11:16-38), and further battles (12:1-45). By 161, however, there are a new Seleucid king (Demetrius I), a new Jewish high priest (Alcimus), and a new threat to the temple by Nicanor (14:1–15:37). With God's help, Judas and his army defeat Nicanor and again serve as God's instruments: "Blessed is he (God) who has kept his own place undefiled" (15:34).

2 Maccabees is perhaps most famous for its account of the Jewish martyrs and references to resurrection (12:43-45). But the author's central concern was the sanctity of God's temple in Jerusalem. He traced Israel's troubles to the internal disputes that brought the Seleucids into Jewish affairs, regarded the Greek way of life as an abomination, and considered Judas Maccabeus as God's instrument in defending the temple.

Bibliography. E. Bickerman, *The God of the Maccabees.* SJLA 32 (Leiden, 1979); R. Doran, *Temple Propaganda: The Purpose and Character of 2 Maccabees.* CBQMS 12 (Washington, 1981); J. Goldstein, *I Maccabees.* AB 41 (Garden City, 1976); *II Maccabees.* AB 41A (Garden City, 1983); D. J. Harrington, *The Maccabean Revolt* (Wilmington, 1988); V. Tcherikover, *Hellenistic Civilization and the Jews* (Philadelphia, 1959). DANIEL J. HARRINGTON, S.J.

MACCABEES, THIRD AND FOURTH BOOKS OF

3 Maccabees

A historical romance originating in the Jewish Diaspora, most probably in Alexandria, the setting of the story. Because of its literary relationship with 2 Maccabees and the Letter of Aristeas, it is usually dated between 90 B.C.E. and 40 C.E. The historicity of the tale has been questioned, due both to the lack of external corroboration of Ptolemy IV Philopator's action against the Alexandrian Jews and to Josephus' attribution of this event to the later reign of Ptolemy VIII Physcon. Similarities with the story of Esther and 2 Maccabees, moreover, suggest conscious literary creativity and patterning, rather than historiographical interest. It may well be that the anti-Jewish pogroms which arose during the reign of Gaius Caesar gave the author occasion to address the contemporary crisis through a saga of past fortitude and deliverance.

The story begins with Ptolemy's defeat of Antiochus III at Raphia, after which Ptolemy visits his client peoples to confirm their loyalty in the aftermath of the war. He visits sacred sites, lavishing gifts for the treasuries, and offering sacrifices in the temples. Everywhere he is welcome, until he attempts to enter the holy place in Jerusalem. While his intention appears to have been benevolent, the Jewish people regard this as a profanation of the temple, and flock to protest (1:1-29). The high priest Simon offers a prayer for divine intervention, and Ptolemy is driven back by God's invisible hand (2:1-24).

Outraged by such an affront from his clients based on their allegiance to indigenous customs, Ptolemy returns to Egypt hoping to prevent any problems on the home front by absorbing the Jewish population of Alexandria into the Greek citizenry, or excluding them from the political body entirely. Several hundred Jews accept the king's invitation to join in the pagan rites which accompany the gift of citizenship, while the majority refuse and are registered for the poll tax, to be treated as the native Egyptian population (2:25-33). The king then decides that reduction of status is not sufficient, so he orders all Jews in Egypt to be rounded up in the hippodrome to await execution (4:1-21). Elephants are prepared for the occasion, being intoxicated with wine and incense, but in response to the Jews' prayers, God prevents the king from carrying out his plan for several days (5:1-51). Finally, the king succeeds in giving the order to loose the elephants, but, in response to the prayer of the aged Eleazar, God turns the elephants back on Philopator's soldiers. The king praises God for delivering God's people, ordering the Jews to be sent home after a seven-day feast (6:1–7:9), The tale concludes with the punishment of apostate Jews at the hands of those Jews who remained loyal (7:10-23).

The work has striking parallels with 2 Maccabees, providing diaspora Jews with a saga about faithfulness to the ancestral Torah in the face of the threat of enforced hellenization, connecting them with the experience of Palestinian Judaism (cf. 1–2 Maccabees), and showing that they too share in the persecutions and triumphs connected with the temple and the Lord. 3 Maccabees is also very informative for understanding Jew-Gentile hostility from both sides. The Jewish author views Gentiles as "alienated from the truth" of the One God and the true religion of Torah (4:16; cf. Rom. 1:21, 25, 28); the Gentiles' failure to honor God, and their acts of outrage against the Jerusalem temple and the holy people throughout history, earn them the frequent epithet of "arrogant" (1:25-26; 2:2-9; 5:13; 6:9). Piercing through the author's bias, we also glimpse a view of the gentile viewpoint. The Jewish tendency to form tight-knit communities (necessitated by the purity and dietary regulations of Torah) becomes a cause, for the Gentiles view them with suspicion, as though Jews were unconcerned about the common good of the city and thus represented a potential source of disloyalty. Jewish commitment to one God and abhorrence of all idolatrous forms of worship prevent full participation in the life of the Greek city: attempts to enfranchise Jews as citizens meet with disaster because of the civic cult participation which is then expected. What Greeks value highly is deemed to be scorned by the Jewish population, and so mutual antagonism and misunderstanding escalate.

The insight 3 Maccabees provides into these ethnic tensions also assists our understanding of the experience of the early Church, especially the Pauline mission, which sought to break down barriers and overcome prejudices which had been firmly in place for centuries. The hostility within the Jewish community toward apostates attested here provides additional insight into Jewish (both Christian and non-Christian) reaction to Paul's relaxation of Torah in his proclamation of a new, united people (cf. Gal. 3:26-28), which could be seen as just another attempt at hellenization and the compromising of necessary boundaries.

4 Maccabees

A philosophical demonstration *(epídeixis)* of the thesis that "devout reason is sovereign over the emotions" (1:1; 7:16; 13:1,7; 16:1). The author takes as his starting point Stoic ethical philosophy with its concern for the attainment of virtue, particularly the Greek cardinal virtues of justice, courage, temperance, and wisdom. The *páthē,* which include not only emotions but also desires and physical sensations (1:20-27), might easily turn an untrained rational faculty away from pursuing that course which led to virtue. Fear of injury, or the experience of pain, might hinder the pursuit of courage on the battlefield; desire for some physical gratification might hinder the pursuit of temperance. It was the Stoic contention that reason, guided by philosophy, could master the *páthē* and choose the virtuous course even if that meant hardship, danger, or denial. 4 Maccabees is in essential agreement with this analysis, but seeks to demonstrate that only the rational faculty which has been trained and exercised by the Jewish Law will actually achieve consistent victory over the emotions, desires, and concern about pleasure or pain (1:15-17; 2:21-23; 5:22-24; 7:18-19). Only the devotee of Torah, therefore, has an accurate trainer in virtue, and therefore a sure foundation for honor and self-respect.

This thesis is demonstrated by means of examples from Israel's sacred history. Joseph, e.g., overcame sexual desire by means of his rational faculty which was strengthened by the command, "You shall not covet" (2:1-6, in striking contrast to Rom. 7:7-24). Moses, similarly, overcame wrath when provoked by Dathan and Abiram (2:16-20). The laws themselves are shown to force those who by nature are greedy to act generously (e.g., in the laws regarding canceling debts in the seventh year and regarding gleaning a field after harvest, 2:8-9). The supreme exemplars of pious reason's domination over the passions, however, are taken from more recent history, namely those who were executed for their adherence to Torah during the hellenization crisis of 167-164 B.C.E. The story from 2 Macc. 6–7 is here expanded into an encomium of Eleazar, the seven brothers, and the mother. After the suppression of the Jewish religion by the apostate Jewish leadership, supported by Antiochus IV (4:1-26), those who remained loyal to Torah were brought before Antiochus. Eleazar and each of the seven brothers are, in turn, given the opportunity to eat nonkosher foods (symbolizing their willingness to accommodate to the Greek way of life) under the threat of torture. The endurance displayed by these figures and the failure of the most severe of tortures to turn their minds away from steadfast obedience make them the ultimate proof of Torah's ability to equip the mind to choose the virtuous course no matter what the toll on the body — even above the natural love of life and the natural affection of siblings and parents (13:27–14:1; 15:24-28).

4 Maccabees is a product of the Jewish Diaspora. The precise location and the date of composition are unknown, but strong cases have been made for an Antiochene provenance during the first half of the 1st century C.E. Some scholars have read it as a speech commemorating the death of the martyrs, since it shares so much in common with Greek funeral orations. While its precise occasion must remain a mystery, 4 Maccabees shows an interest in reaffirming its audience's commitment to central Jewish cultural values in a setting where the enticements to abandon religious and ethnic particularity in favor of the Greek way of life are strong. Accommodation to Hellenism at the cost of loyalty to God offers only temporary advantage, but will bring eternal disadvantage (13:15; 15:2-3, 8, 27). The apostate Jews may for a time gain honor in the sight of Greek society, but they will ultimately lose their only abiding claim to honor (17:18; 18:3). The audience, identifying with the martyrs, are moved to remain loyal to their Divine Benefactor (16:18-22) rather than dishonor God in favor of any human patron in the Greek world, no matter what advantages are offered or disadvantages threatened (8:5-9; 12:4-5).

This work, though not regarded as canonical by any Christian communion, has nevertheless exercised a profound influence on Christianity. The author of Hebrews shares 4 Maccabees' view of faith and obligation to God as Patron, and includes the martyrs in his own encomium on faith. More generally, 4 Maccabees shares with NT authors the distinction between temporary vs. eternal safety, the depiction of society's hostility as a noble contest to be endured for the sake of a religious victory (16:16; 17:11-16), and the notion of substitutionary atonement (cf. 6:28-29; 17:21-22). This book and its heroes were frequent subjects for sermons in the first four centuries of the Church, and the anniversary of their death was celebrated as a Christian festival.

Bibliography. H. Anderson, "3 Maccabees," *OTP* 2 (Garden City, 1985), 509-29; "4 Maccabees," *OTP* 2:531-64; D. deSilva, "The Noble Contest: Honor, Shame, and the Rhetorical Strategy of *4 Maccabees*," *JSP* 13 (1995): 29-55; M. Hadas, *The Third and Fourth Books of Maccabees* (1953, repr. New York, 1976). DAVID A. DESILVA

MACEDONIA (Gk. *Makedonía*)
A region between the Balkans and the Greek Peninsula. Throughout history the borders of Macedonia have shifted, but essentially it covers the area along the northern shore of the Aegean Sea, extending west to Illyricum and east to Thrace and south along the Greek Peninsula to Thessaly. The central plain is bordered by mountains on the west and north.

During the centuries leading up to the rise of the Macedonians as a dominant power, northern Greece remained settled by Greeks from elsewhere. Macedonia came into its own as a world power in the period between 359 and 336 B.C.E., largely due to the influence of Philip II of Macedon. His son Alexander the Great expanded the Macedonian power base to include most of the eastern part of the then known world, carrying with him a policy of hellenization (cf. 1 Macc. 1:1-7).

After the death of Alexander in 332 political stability was never fully re-established in Macedonia until the arrival of the Romans in the mid-2nd century. Following the defeat of Perseus at the battle of Pydna in 168 (cf. 1 Macc. 8:5) the Romans divided Macedonia into four autonomous districts with a capital city in each (Amphipolis, Thessalonica, Pella, and Pelagonia). After the revolt led by Andriskos in 149 the Romans formed the four districts into a Macedonian *koinón* (ca. 146) with its capital at Beroea, which also became the seat of the imperial cult. At the same time a Roman governor was permanently installed at Thessalonica.

Under Augustus Macedonia was made a senatorial province. In 15 C.E. Tiberius combined Macedonia with the senatorial provinces of Achaia to the south and Moesia to the north, thus forming one large imperial province. In 44 Claudius redivided the province along the previous boundaries and Macedonia was once again a senatorial province, governed by a proconsul. However, the Macedonian "free cities" (Thessalonica, Amphipolis, and Skotoussa) and the tribute-paying cities retained their ancient forms of government (an assembly, council, and magistrates). During the *Pax Romana* new cities were founded in Macedonia and older cities were given new plans. Grand building projects were undertaken, including forums, temples, altars, and funerary buildings, all with accompanying inscriptions.

According to Acts 16:9-12 Paul received a call for help from a "man of Macedonia," whereupon he sailed from Troas to Philippi to begin his Macedonian ministry. Although Paul experienced opposition throughout this ministry (1 Thess. 2:2; cf. Acts 16:11–17:15; 2 Cor. 7:5), he succeeded in establishing churches at Philippi and Thessalonica and probably Beroea (Acts 17:10-12). Although being poor themselves, the Macedonian churches provided financial support for Paul's missionary efforts (2 Cor. 11:9; Phil. 4:15-17) and contributed generously to the collection for the Jerusalem church (2 Cor. 8:1-5; Rom. 15:26-27). Paul passed through Macedonia on a number of other occasions (1 Cor. 16:5; 2 Cor. 1:16; 2:13; cf. Acts 20:1-6).

Bibliography. N. G. L. Hammond, *The Macedonian State: Origins, Institutions, and History* (Oxford, 1989); *The Miracle That Was Macedonia* (New York, 1991); B. Laourdas and C. Makaronas, eds., *Ancient Macedonia*, 5 vols. (Thessalonica, 1970-1993). RICHARD S. ASCOUGH

MACHAERUS (Gk. *Machairous*)
A Jewish fortress strategically located E of the Dead Sea 24 km. (15 mi.) SE of the mouth of the Jordan River. A fortress built there (ca. 90 B.C.E.) by Alexander Janneus (103-76) was destroyed in 57 B.C.E. Herod the Great (37-4) rebuilt the site (ca. 30), which later passed to Herod Antipas (4 B.C.E.–39 C.E.). Josephus maintains that Herod Antipas imprisoned and beheaded John the Baptist at Machaerus (*Ant.* 18.116-19). Gospel accounts do not identify Machaerus as the location of these events (Matt. 14:3-12 = Mark 6:17-29). At the death of Herod Agrippa in 44 C.E. the fortress fell under Roman control, remaining so until the Jewish Revolt (66-70). In 72 control returned to the Romans.

Machaerus was excavated in 1978-1981, yielding detailed plans of the fortifications, confirming identification of Machaerus with Mishnaqa (209108), and providing evidence to support literary claims of occupation from 90 B.C.E. to 72 C.E. The name is preserved in the modern village of Mekawer, 1.6 km. (1 mi.) east. MONICA L. W. BRADY

MACHBANNAI (Heb. *maḵbannay*)
One of the Gadite "mighty and experienced warriors" who joined David's rebel band at Ziklag and became officers in his army (1 Chr. 12:13[MT 14]).

MACHBENAH (Heb. *maḵbēnâ*)
A name in a genealogical list of the descendants of Caleb (1 Chr. 2:49). It is more likely a place, generally believed to be in the hills of Judah S of Hebron. AARON M. GALE

MACHI (Heb. *māḵî*)
A Gadite, the father of the spy Geuel (Num. 13:15).

MACHIR (Heb. *māḵîr*)
1. The son of Manasseh (Gen. 50:23), father of Gilead, and eponymous head of the Machirite clan (Num. 26:29; 27:1). Machir's children were "born on Joseph's knees" (Gen. 50:23), an idiom for legal adoption. Thus, the Machirite group originated in Egypt and belonged to Joseph's house.

An allotment of land in the Transjordan was promised to half-Manasseh, provided they aid the other tribes in the battle for Canaan (Num. 32:39-40). The descendants of Machir captured Gilead, so Moses allotted this region to Machir (Deut. 3:15). The Song of Deborah (Judg. 5:14) describes the tribes leaving for the battle against Sisera: Machir is listed (W of the Jordan) after Ephraim-Benjamin but before Zebulun-Issachar-Naphtali. If in geographical order, this is the territory occupied by Manasseh, whose name does not appear in this list.

The relationship between the tribes of Machir/Manasseh is thus unclear. Martin Noth argues that the whole region was originally under the name Machir, a cognomen for Manasseh, meaning "rest of Manasseh." Machir may be an older appellation, Manasseh being later and secondary. Manasseh may originally have been a clan of Machir that grew powerful and replaced it or a rival tribe that drove Machir away. Machir may be a clan of Joseph's house which was later integrated into Manasseh, as Simeon was later integrated into Judah (Num. 26:29). Later OT texts do not refer to a Machirite tribe W of the Jordan.

2. The son of Ammiel from Lodebar, in whose home Saul's son Meribaal lived for a time (2 Sam. 9:4-5). The same Machir brought food to David at Mahanaim (2 Sam. 17:27). The suggested site of Lodebar is N of the Jabbok in the land of the Manasseh half-tribe, in the land allotted to Machir (see **1** above).

Bibliography. Z. Kallai, *Historical Geography of the Bible* (Leiden, 1986); R. de Vaux, *The Early History of Israel* (Philadelphia, 1978).
PATRICIA A. MACNICOLL

MACHNADEBAI (Heb. *maḵnaḏēḇay*)
A descendant of Binnui, an Israelite required to divorce his foreign wife (Ezra 10:40).

MACHPELAH (Heb. *maḵpēlâ*)
A field with a cave located in the town of Hebron (Gen. 23:19). Abraham purchased this plot from Ephron the Hittite as a burial site for his wife Sarah (Gen. 23). He desired only the cave, but Ephron insisted that Abraham buy the field as well. Ephron's actions most likely reflect Hittite law, which required an owner to be responsible for the legal obligations of the entire plot if only a portion of the land was sold. Abraham, Isaac, Rebekah, Leah, and Jacob were also buried at Machpelah (Gen. 25:9; 49:29-31; 50:13).

Herod the Great (37-4 B.C.) constructed a fortresslike stone enclosure, the only complete Herodian edifice still standing, around the site. Today a Moslem mosque (used as a church when the Crusaders conquered the city in A.D. 1188) sits within Herod's enclosure and on top of the cave. The most recent investigation of the cave took place in 1967, shortly after the Six-Day War, under the direction of Moshe Dayan.

Bibliography. M. R. Lehmann, "Abraham's Purchase of Machpelah and Hittite Law," *BASOR* 129 (1953): 15-18; N. Miller, "Patriarchal Burial Site Explored for First Time in 700 Years," *BARev* 11/3 (1985): 26-43. STEPHEN R. MILLER

MADAI (Heb. *māḏay*)
A son of Japheth (Gen. 10:2; 1 Chr. 1:5); eponymous ancestor of the Medes (cf. 2 Kgs. 17:6; Isa. 21:2).

MADMANNAH (Heb. *maḏmannâ*)
A city in the Negeb, in southern Judah, close to Beer-sheba. It may be identified with modern Khirbet Umm ed-Deimneh or Khirbet Tatrît (143084). Madmannah is one of 29 cities belonging

to the tribe of Judah that are enumerated in Josh. 15:21-32 according to some geographical principle. A parallel Simeonite list in Josh. 19:1-6 mentions 13 cities, but Madmannah is replaced by Beth-marcaboth, suggesting that Madmannah was an earlier name, later changed to Beth-marcaboth. Shaaph, the son of Caleb's concubine Maacah, is called the founder (lit., "father") of Madmannah (1 Chr. 2:49). JESPER SVARTVIK

MADMEN (Heb. *maḏmēn*)
A place mentioned only in Jeremiah's oracle against Moab (Jer. 48:2). It is generally identified with Dimon, and possibly located at Khirbet Dimneh (217077) in central Moab, 4 km. (2.5 mi.) NW of Rabbah. In Isa. 15:9 Heb. *mêḏîmôn* ("water of Dimon") may refer to a place, but this theory is unsupported. ZELJKO GREGOR

MADMENAH (Heb. *maḏmēnâ*)
A site mentioned only in Isa. 10:31 in relation to the prophet's prediction of the Assyrian campaign against Jerusalem. It is listed between Anathoth (4 km. [2.5 mi.] NE of Jerusalem) and Gebim (2.5 km. [1.5 mi.] NNE of Jerusalem). Some have identified this site as modern Shu'fat (172135), but this cannot be confirmed. The name means "dung heap" and because of similar spelling is occasionally confused with Madmannah, a town in the Negeb plains of southern Judah. DENNIS M. SWANSON

MADNESS
The ancients depicted the supernatural origin, moral nature, and behaviors that characterized madness rather than its psychological makeup. In the OT madness is viewed as a punishment God sends on disobedient Israelites or the derangement with which he will inflict people on the Day of the Lord (Heb. *šiggāʻôn;* Deut. 28:28; Zech. 12:4). The writer of Ecclesiastes contemplates the differences between what is wise, foolish, and mad (*hôlēlâ,* meaning impetuous excitement, raving and foolish actions; Eccl. 1:17; 2:12; 7:25; 9:3; 10:13). In Dan. 4 Nebuchadnezzar relates his bizarre, disturbing, and grandiose dreams to Daniel, who interprets them and then sees them come true. For a time Nebuchadnezzar grazes like an animal, detached from human community. The most extensive depiction of madness in the OT is Saul's decline. Plagued by paranoid jealousy of David, Saul becomes so violent that he has the priests and citizens of Nob murdered (1 Sam. 22:6-19), visits a medium by night at Endor, and finally commits suicide (1 Sam. 28, 31). While God is not blamed for these madnesses as acts of evil, the Hebrews saw God as the final and efficient cause of all things, so they believed that an evil spirit from God tormented Saul (1 Sam. 16:14) and a lying spirit from God brought about Ahab's death (1 Kgs. 22:19-23; cf. Luke 11:24-26 on the insanity demons cause). Madness could be imitated: David once pretended to be insane, to save his life, by drooling, marking the door, and behaving oddly (1 Sam. 21:13-15).

In the Greek world, madness (Gk. *átē*) was personified blind foolishness which came upon people and rendered them incapable of knowing right from wrong.

In the NT madness is thought to come from demon possession (Luke 8:2-3, 30; 11:14). People who have such disorders may strip themselves, live in tombs, and behave violently (Mark 5:2-13; Matt. 8:28-33). Other kinds of "madness" are the foolish ignorance of wicked teachers and religious leaders (Gk. *ánoia;* 2 Tim. 3:9; Luke 6:11), unreasonably evil and selfish foolhardiness (*paraphronía;* 2 Pet. 2:16), and delirious frenzy or eccentricity (*manía;* Festus tells Paul that too much learning has made the apostle insane, Acts 26:24).

RICHARD A. SPENCER

MADON (Heb. *māḏôn*)
A Canaanite city which joined in an ill-fated alliance against the Israelite conquest (Josh. 11:1; 12:19). Qarn Ḥaṭṭîn/Tel Qarnei Ḥittin (1933.2447), ca. 8.5 km. (5.5 mi.) NW of Tiberias, has been suggested as the site.

MAGADAN (Gk. *Magadán*)
A location in the vicinity of the Sea of Galilee. In Matt. 15:39 Jesus comes to this region after the feeding of the 4000 (KJV "Magdala"), but Mark 8:10 reads Dalmanoutha. Such great textual variants plague both the Matthean and Markan accounts that an exact location is unknown. Interpreters have offered certain phonetic connections with Magadan such as Megiddo, modern Mejdel (140105), and LXX Magdalgad (Josh. 15:37).

PETE F. WILBANKS

MAGBISH (Heb. *magbîš*)
The "ancestor" of persons returning from the Babylonian exile (Ezra 2:30). More likely, the term refers to a place. Its exact location remains a mystery; suggestions include Khirbet Qanân Mugheimis (145109), 2 km. (1.2 mi.) W of Elam, and Khirbet el-Makhbiyeh (145116), 5 km. (3 mi.) SW of Adullam. AARON M. GALE

MAGDALENE (Gk. *Magdalēnḗ*)
A gentilic from Magdala (Aram. *magdala',* "tower"), designating Mary, a principal follower of Jesus (e.g., Matt. 27:56, 61 par.; 28:1; Mark 16:9; Luke 8:2; 24:10 par.). Magdala (Tarichaeae; 198247) was an important fishing town NW of Tiberias at the western tip of the Sea of Galilee.

MAGDIEL (Heb. *magdî'ēl*)
An Edomite tribal chief (Gen. 36:43; 1 Chr. 1:54); possibly a clan or place name.

MAGI (Gk. *mágoi*)
Technical term designating the "wise men" who visit the infant Jesus (Matt. 2:1-12) and the "magician" Elymas bar Jesus who opposes Paul (Acts 13:4-12). In the LXX the term refers to those individuals who interpret King Nebuchadnezzar's dreams, in conjunction with other specialists including enchanters, sorcerers, and "the Chaldeans" (Dan. 2:2, 10, 27; 4:4[MT 1]; 5:7, 11, 15).

Herodotus mentions Magi who served as Median or Zoroastrian priests engaged in dream interpretation (*Hist.* 1.101). Philo, Tacitus, Suetonius, and Josephus also describe a range of duties for Magi, including dream interpretation, magic, astrology, and fortune-telling.

There has been much discussion as to the precise meaning of the term in Matt. 2:1, 7, 16, rendered in most English translations as "wise men," "Magi," or "astrologers." It is likely that they were astrologers, since they were interpreters and followers of the "star at its rising" (Matt. 2:2).

Bibliography. R. Brown, *The Birth of the Messiah,* rev. ed. (New York, 1993), 167-70; G. Delling, "mágos," *TDNT* 4:356-59.

ROBERT A. DERRENBACKER, JR.

MAGIC

In the literature of the ancient Mediterranean world and the ancient Near East, including the Bible, many different terms are used to designate magic and ritual power as well as the practitioners of magic and ritual power. Gk. *mageía* and related words (cf. Lat. *magia*) derive from Iranian *magus,* which designated a person from an ancient Medo-Persian tribe with priestly functions (cf. Magi, Matt. 2). During Greco-Roman times and in Judeo-Christian contexts the term magic frequently was used in a polemical fashion to distinguish between the activities of one's own group over against the opponents: "we" practice religion and perform miracles; "they" practice magic and engage in sorcery. Romans accused early Christians of practicing magic, later Christians accused pagans, and Protestant Reformers accused Roman Catholics. The word can thus be used as a club to attack outsiders, but it is not easily or precisely defined. A more neutral expression to describe the phenomena considered "magical" may be "ritual power."

Incantation bowl with spiral inscription in Jewish Aramaic for protection of the household of Babai (Photograph courtesy of the Royal Ontario Museum, ©ROM)

Ancient Mediterranean and Near East

Throughout the world of Mediterranean and Near Eastern antiquity, ritual power was employed as a means whereby power, particularly supernatural power, could be channeled through ritual activity. In many of the early traditions there was no dichotomy between magic and religion, and ritual power was accorded validity equally within organized religion and private practice. Ritual power was considered a gift of the divine, as in ancient Egypt, where Heka was the embodiment of divine power that emerged in the beginning and empowered the performance of public and private rituals. Often, but not in Egypt, malevolent ritual power (traditionally called "black magic") was condemned and declared illegal, in contrast to benevolent ritual power ("white magic"). In classical Greece the Persian roots of the word were not forgotten, and Greek discussions of philosophy, theology, and medical science led to a denigration of magic. Nonetheless, ritual power was widely practiced throughout the ancient world, and the numerous magical texts, amulets, bowls, and artifacts that have survived show practitioners using ritual power to address all sorts of medical, demonic, sexual, and social problems. For example, one parchment magical book from Coptic Egypt (Michigan 136) prescribes folk remedies and ritual spells to treat such medical concerns as gout, eye disease, pains from teething, fevers, pregnancy and childbirth, abdominal pains, malignancy, skin disease, headaches, toothaches, earaches, hemorrhoids or other sores, constipation, foot disease, and mental problems. Another magical book (Heidelberg Kopt. 686) praises the divine and invokes divine power to provide aid for such problems as demon possession, imprisonment, domestic quarrels and violence, male impotence, a wife's unfaithfulness, infant death, insomnia, and issues related to villages, workplaces, and herds of cattle.

Old Testament

Deut. 18:10-11 provides a catalog of some of the most significant terms for magic and ritual power and practitioners of magic and ritual power in the Hebrew Scriptures, and all the terms denote what is thought to be abominable to the God of Israel. Some of these terms remain difficult to translate and understand, but overall the prohibitions within this and similar passages appear to be directed against practices considered to be violations of authentic religion.

Many of the same kinds of practices that are condemned in Deut. 18, however, are condoned and even commended elsewhere in the OT. For example, prophets of God divine the future, ritual specialists interpret dreams, priests and others employ the Urim and Thummim and other oracular devices, people of God utter blessings and curses, and Elisha parts the water and curses rude boys "in the name of the Lord" (2 Kgs. 2:24), most likely with the holy name that is called the tetragrammaton (Yahweh), later used extensively in spells of ritual power. This magical use of the name of the Lord may account for the Third Commandment, not to "take the name of the Lord your God in vain" (Exod. 20:7; Deut. 5:11). In Exodus Moses and Aaron are portrayed as successful practitioners of ritual power, and the Egyptian magicians admit, "This is the finger of God" (Exod. 8:19). The image of the finger of God is also applied to Jesus as exorcist in Luke 11:20, and the divine finger is personified as Orphamiel, the great finger of God the father, in several Christian texts of ritual power.

In spite of prohibitions in the OT against magical practice, then, it appears that the practice of ritual power was as evident among the Hebrews as among other people in the ancient Near East. The Jewish use of ritual power is later reflected in the influence of Jewish themes and names for the divine in the Greek magical papyri, in the Jewish handbook of ritual power, the Sefer ha-Razim ("Book of Mysteries"), and in the Aramaic incantation bowls with spiral texts meant to eradicate evil.

New Testament and Early Christian Texts

Within the literature of early Christianity the polemical presentation of magic and magicians continues. Simon of Samaria is accused of practicing magic (Acts 8), as are Elymas or Bar-Jesus (ch. 13) and the seven sons of Sceva and other practitioners from Ephesus (ch. 19). Sorcerers are listed among the wicked to be punished in Revelation, and sorcery is included in a list of vices in Galatians.

Yet, as in the OT, materials are incorporated that portray ritual power in a more positive light. Jesus and his followers are sometimes described as exorcists and faith-healers, and Paul himself overcomes Elymas (Acts 13) with his own ritual power. Some of the NT stories of the deeds of magic or ritual power performed by Jesus are adapted from the OT (Jesus, like Moses, feeds a multitude in the wilderness and, like Elijah, heals a widow's son) or Greek mythological traditions (Jesus, like Poseidon, travels on water as on land and, like Dionysos, changes water to wine). By contrast, the story of the exorcism of the Gerasene demoniac by Jesus (Matt. 8:28-34; Mark 5:1-20; Luke 8:26-39) illustrates features typical of other stories of exorcism and spells of ritual power. Here a possessed man, violent and uncontrollable, engages in a battle of adjurations with Jesus. Jesus orders the demon, "Come out of the man, you unclean spirit," and the victim responds by adjuring Jesus to leave him alone. Jesus assumes the upper hand in the struggle when he demands the name of the demon. Thus the exorcism is accomplished, and the patient is restored to health and sanity. The demonic forces are sent into a herd of pigs in a manner somewhat reminiscent of the demon sent by Apollonios of Tyana to knock over a statue as proof of its departure from a patient. In another story Jesus uses spittle, a powerful touch, oral exhalations, and an authoritative word (preserved in Aramaic) to heal a man who is hearing-impaired and has a speech impediment (Mark 7:31-37). Such stories indicate that the historical Jesus may well have been viewed by his contemporaries as an exorcist and faith-healer, and acts of ritual power may have accompanied his proclamation of God's kingdom (Luke 11:20).

Jesus and early Christians were often accused of dabbling in magic, and the debate about whether this is so is played out in the NT and early Christian texts. The Gospels of Mark and John celebrate the miracles of Jesus but also divert the readers' attention to other ways of understanding Jesus. Another approach to this debate involves an appeal to the distinction between miracle and magic. Jesus and early Christians, it is said, do not practice magic but rather perform miracles, and the power of Christian miracles surpasses that of pagan magic. Meanwhile, Christian spells of ritual power eventually were composed in large numbers as means for the faithful to tap into power available to solve the problems in their lives. These interests in magic, miracle, and ritual power continue as a form of popular piety within Christianity and other religions to the present day.

See Divination; Miracles.

Bibliography. H. D. Betz, ed., *The Greek Magical Papyri in Translation,* 2nd ed. (Chicago, 1992); M. Meyer and P. Mirecki, eds., *Ancient Magic and Ritual Power.* Religions in the Graeco-Roman World 129 (Leiden, 1995); Meyer and R. Smith, eds., *Ancient Christian Magic: Coptic Texts of Ritual Power* (San Francisco, 1994). Marvin Meyer

MAGISTRATE

A judicial official who implemented the Torah as the official law for the Jews (Aram. *šāp̱ṭîn;* Ezra 7:25). In the NT the term refers to Roman rulers (Gk. *archḗ, árchōn;* Luke 12:11, 58; Tit. 3:1) who were annually elected and were the highest state officials of Roman colonies and towns (*stratēgós;* Acts 16:20, 22, 35-36, 38). Their official Latin titles were *duoviri* ("two men") in colonies and *quattuorviri* ("four men") in towns. Although they constituted the highest council of civil administration, their office was beneath the senatorial and equestrian orders. Magistrates built amphitheaters and maintained public works (drainage, roads, religious buildings, public baths, markets, and the food supply), often at their own expense. They also maintained civil order and dispensed justice. Every five years they revised the town census rolls for taxation. To celebrate their year in office they often sponsored games, built new public buildings, or repaved streets. Town councils often erected statues or monuments for prominent magistrates, and they were given the best seats in amphitheaters.

Bibliography. L. Keppie, *Understanding Roman Inscriptions* (Baltimore, 1991), 52-59; J. E. Sandys, *Latin Epigraphy,* 2nd ed. (1927, repr. Chicago, 1974), 228-30. Richard A. Spencer

MAGNIFICAT

The hymn or psalm of praise appearing in Luke 1:46-55, so named from the first words of the Latin translation: *Magnificat anima mea Dominum,* "My soul magnifies the Lord." It is one of several hymns in Luke's Infancy narrative (cf. Luke 1:68-79; 2:14,

29-32). This hymn is ascribed to Mary as an expression of her faith on hearing Elizabeth's blessing. It follows the pattern of traditional psalms or hymns, with expressions of praise (Luke 1:46-47) followed by the occasion for praise (vv. 48-55).

The Magnificat can be divided into two strophes or verses, the first (vv. 46-50) is Mary's expression of praise for the actions God has performed in relation to her. The paired verses or couplets each exhibit the classic parallelism of Hebrew poetry. The first couplet expresses Mary's joy (vv. 46-47). The second recounts God's salvific action in raising her from her "low estate" and her resultant status (vv. 48-49). The concluding verse in this strophe (v. 50) marks a transition to the more corporate vision of the second strophe.

In the second strophe (vv. 51-55) God's action is also described as an exaltation of the humble. However, in an echo of the prophets, this theme is expanded into an expression of God's salvific justice in exalting the humble, the poor, and the hungry, while at the same time putting down the mighty, the rich, and the rulers. This strophe can be divided into two couplets (vv. 51-52, 53-54) and a concluding verse (v. 55) that parallels the conclusion of the first strophe. Each couplet begins with a strong verb describing God's action and a parallel secondary verb providing additional emphasis. The structure and effect of the hymn as a whole make God's actions with relation to Mary a symbol or paradigm for the universal saving work of God which is now beginning in Jesus. This theme of the divine reversal inherent in God's salvific actions thus anticipates both the words and actions of Jesus' ministry.

The Magnificat appears to be modeled, to some extent, after the Song of Hannah in 1 Sam. 2:1-10. Because of these similarities and the similar situations of Elizabeth and Hannah, rather than Mary, some scholars have suggested that the hymn is mistakenly attributed to Mary. While a few minor textual variants support reading Elizabeth, the surrounding narrative and weight of manuscript evidence argue against it.

Bibliography. R. C. Tannehill, *The Narrative Unity of Luke-Acts* 1 (Philadelphia, 1986).

MATTHEW S. COLLINS

MAGOG (Heb. *māḡôḡ*)
According to the Table of Nations, a son of Japheth and the eponymous ancestor of an Anatolian people (Gen. 10:2). In Ezek. 38-39 its leader, Gog, will invade the restored Israel and provoke a final, decisive battle with Yahweh.

See GOG, MAGOG. JULIE GALAMBUSH

MAGOR-MISSABIB (Heb. *māḡôr missāḇîḇ*)
See TERROR ON EVERY SIDE.

MAGPIASH (Heb. *magpîʿāš*)
An Israelite who participated in the sealing of the new covenant under Nehemiah (Neh. 10:20 [MT 21]).

MAHALAB (Heb. *mēḥeḇel;* Akk. *Maḫallibu*)
A city in the tribal allotment of Asher. The precise form of this place name is uncertain. In Josh. 19:29 the MT has Heb. *mēḥeḇel*," while LXX B reads "from Leb and Achzob" and LXX A has "from the allotment of Achziph"; both Greek manuscripts understand the first letter of the MT form to be the Hebrew preposition "from." In LXX B the letters *b* and *l* were metathesized, but they were not in LXX A (*ḥeḇel* II, "rope, cord, allotted piece of field"; cf. Deut. 32:9). The record of Sennacherib's third campaign contains a reference to Maḫallibu (*ANET,* 287); this toponym is normally identified with Khirbet el-Maḥalîb, 6 km. (3.7 mi.) NE of Tyre. Judg. 1:31 reveals another variant form of the place name: "Ahlab" (cf. the position of the *l* and *b*) is part of the tribal allotment of Asher. Because of Sennacherib's topographic reference, a majority of scholars conclude that the precise form of the name in the MT and LXX of Josh. 19:29; Judg. 1:31 is corrupt and should be understood as Mahalab.

Bibliography. N. Na'aman, *Borders and Districts in Biblical Historiography* (Jerusalem, 1986).

CHRIS A. ROLLSTON

MAHALALEL (Heb. *mahălal'ēl*),
MAHALALEEL (Gk. *Maleleél*)

1. A son of Kenan and the father of Jared in the lineage of Seth (Gen. 5:12-17). He is called Mahalaleel in Luke's genealogy of Jesus (Luke 3:37).

2. A Judahite of the family of Perez (Neh. 11:4).

MAHALATH (Heb. *maḥălaṯ*) (also BASEMOTH)

1. The daughter of Ishmael and one of Esau's wives (Gen. 28:9). In Gen. 36:3 she is called Basemoth.

2. The wife of King Rehoboam of Judah; daughter of David's son Jerimoth and Abihail (2 Chr. 11:18)

3. A cryptic term found in the superscriptions to Ps. 53, 88 (the latter with *lĕʿannôṯ,* "to afflict"), likely a technical term denoting a melody (or musical instrument). Other suggestions include a cultic dance or flute playing associated with lamentation rites. Michael Goulder suggests that in Ps. 88 it originally refers to Mahalath-dan, a place where Danite festal rites took place; this meaning was lost, and with the addition of *lĕʿannôṯ* it was understood as referring to a completed rite of affliction. Most modern versions transliterate, e.g., "according to Mahalath."

Bibliography. M. D. Goulder, *The Psalms of the Sons of Korah.* JSOTSup 20 (Sheffield, 1982).

TYLER F. WILLIAMS

MAHANAIM (Heb. *maḥănayim*)
The place where Jacob rested on his return to Canaan (Gen. 32:2[MT 3]). Mahanaim ("two camps") later became a levitical city (Josh. 21:38; 1 Chr. 6:80) in the territory of Gad (Josh. 13:26) on the border of Manasseh (13:30). It was briefly the capital of the Saulide dynasty under Ish-bosheth (2 Sam. 2:8, 12, 29) and was later used by David as a base of operations during the coup attempt by Ab-

salom (17:24, 27; 19:32; 1 Kgs. 2:7-8). It was the seat of Solomon's 7th district (1 Kgs. 4:14) and was destroyed by Pharaoh Shishak (*ANET,* 243) in 925 B.C.

The exact location of Mahanaim is unknown. Tell edh-Dhahab el-Gharbī (214177) on the north bank of the Jabbok River (Wadi Zerqa) is currently the best candidate.

Bibliography. R. A. Coughenour, "A Search for Maḥanaim," *BASOR* 273 (1989): 57-66.

PAUL J. RAY, JR.

MAHANEH-DAN (Heb. *maḥănēh-dān*)
A place ("camp of Dan") W of Kireath-jearim and between Zorah and Eshtaol. Here the spirit of the Lord "began to stir" Samson (Judg. 13:25). An armed group of 600 Danites camped here as their tribe migrated northward (Judg. 18:12).

MAHARAI (Heb. *mahăray*)
One of David's Champions. A native of Netophah in Judah (2 Sam. 23:28; 1 Chr. 11:30) and reckoned among the clan of the Zerahites, he was commander of the tenth monthly levy of David's army (27:13).

MAHATH (Heb. *maḥaṯ*)
1. A Kohathite Levite, son of Amasai and ancestor of Samuel and the temple singer Heman (1 Chr. 6:35[MT 20]).

2. The son of Amasai; a Kohathite Levite who participated in Hezekiah's cleansing of the temple (2 Chr. 29:12). He was an overseer of the temple contributions (2 Chr. 31:13).

MAHAVITE (Heb. *hammaḥăwîm*)
A gentilic associated with Eliel, one of David's Mighty Men (1 Chr. 11:46). The term makes little sense as it stands and has been emended to *maḥănî* ("Mahanite") or *maḥănaymî* ("Mahanaimite").

MAHAZIOTH (Heb. *maḥăzî'ôṯ*)
A son of Heman the seer; leader of the twenty-third division of levitical temple musicians (1 Chr. 25:4, 30).

MAHER-SHALAL-HASH-BAZ
(Heb. *mahēr šālāl ḥāš baz*)
The portentous name ("The spoil speeds, the prey hastens"; so NRSV mg) given to Isaiah's third son to symbolize the coming Assyrian defeat of the kingdoms of Syria and Israel (Isa. 8:1-4; cf. v. 18).

MAHLAH (Heb. *maḥlâ*)
1. One of the daughters of Zelophehad for whom special provision was made to allow inheritance (Num. 26:33; 27:1; 36:11; Josh. 17:3). She may be the eponymous ancestor of a clan or town in Manasseh.

2. A son or daughter of Hammolecheth of the tribe of Manasseh (1 Chr. 7:18).

MAHLI (Heb. *maḥlî*)
1. A Levite, son of Merari and brother of Mushi (Exod. 6:19; Num. 3:20; 1 Chr. 6:29[MT 14]; 23:21). He is the ancestor of the Mahlites (Num. 3:33; 26:58).

2. A Levite, son of Mushi and grandson of Merari (1 Chr. 6:47[32]; 23:23; 24:30).

MAHLON (Heb. *maḥlôn*)
The husband of Ruth, a son of Elimelech and Naomi who died without heirs (Ruth 1:2, 5; 4:9-10).

MAHOL (Heb. *māḥôl*)
The father of Heman, Calcol, and Darda (and perhaps also of Ethan the Ezrahite; cf. the superscriptions of Pss. 88-89), wise men with whom Solomon is compared and found superior (1 Kgs. 4:31[MT 5:11]). The "sons" of Mahol here probably represent members of a musicians' guild; Heman was a temple singer (1 Chr. 6:33[16]). Ethan, Heman, Calcol, and Darda are listed among the sons of Zerah at 1 Chr. 2:6.

MAHSEIAH (Heb. *maḥsēyâ*)
The grandfather of Jeremiah's secretary, Baruch (Jer. 32:12), and of Seraiah, King Zedekiah's quartermaster (51:59).

MAKAZ (Heb. *māqaṣ*)
One of four cities in Solomon's second administrative district (1 Kgs. 4:9), administered by Ben-deker. Its location is unknown. Although some scholars have located it S of Ekron, it should actually be located in the Ajalon Valley, on the basis of the identification and location of Beth-shemesh and Shaalbim.

STEVEN M. ORTIZ

MAKHELOTH (Heb. *maqhēlōṯ*)
The tenth encampment after the Israelites left Mt. Sinai, listed between Haradah and Tahath (Num. 33:25-26). The word means "to assemble a convocation," which has led many to posit that Makheloth is the same as Kehelathah (Num. 33:22-23).

PETE F. WILBANKS

MAKKEDAH (Heb. *maqqēḏâ*)
A city to which Joshua pursued five kings heading the Amorite alliance against Gibeon, and which he subsequently captured, annihilating its population (Josh. 10:16-28). The city was among those assigned to Judah (Josh. 15:41). Biblical Makkedah has been sought at numerous sites, but seems now to be located at Khirbet el-Qôm (1465.1045). Makkedah is mentioned several times in Joshua in connection with Azekah and Lachish, in a region of natural caves. That would seem to place it somewhere in the inner Shephelah E of Lachish.

These indications might suit the location of Khirbet Beit Maqdum, but the lack of suitable archaeological data there favors the sizable mound of Khirbet el-Qôm ca. .5 km. (.3 mi.) to the southwest — ca. 10 km. (6 mi.) E of Lachish, 10 km. (6 mi.) W of Hebron. A brief survey by Moshe Kochavi in 1967 was followed by further survey and excavations by William G. Dever (1968-1971) and John S. Holladay (1971). These investigations revealed considerable Iron II occupation, a cyclopean city wall and a two-entry gate, and a cemetery of dozens or more rock-cut bench tombs. Materials salvaged from recent tomb-robbing included large amounts of 10th-7th/6th-century B.C. pottery, a group of dome-shaped shekel weights, and some important 8th-century tomb inscriptions. The general sense of Inscription 3 (T.III) seems to be:

> Uriyahu the Governor (or "singer") wrote it.
> May Uriyahu be blessed by Yahweh,
> And saved from his enemies by his Asherah.

The reference to "Yahweh and his Asherah" in a context of blessing may seem surprising, but very much the same phrase occurs in an 8th-century inscription from Kuntillet ʿAjrûd.

Later occupation of Khirbet el-Qôm is attested by several Hellenistic houses that yielded four Aramaic, one Greek, and one bilingual ostraca, one dated to "year 6," probably of Ptolemy II Philadelphus (277).

Bibliography. W. G. Dever, "Iron Age Epigraphic Material from the Area of Kh. El-Kôm," *HUCA* 40-41 (1969-1970): 139-204; D. A. Dorsey, "The Location of Biblical Makkedah," *Tel Aviv* 7 (1980): 185-93; J. S. Holladay, "Khirbet el-Qôm," *IEJ* 21 (1971): 175-77. WILLIAM G. DEVER

MALACHI (Heb. *malʾāḵî*)**, BOOK OF**

The final book of the Minor Prophets in the OT. It closes in Mal. 4:4-6(MT 3:22-24) with a look back at Moses and a look forward to the return of the prophet Elijah, which suggests that those verses were composed to conclude the first two sections of the Hebrew Bible, the Law and the Prophets. It also suggests that the book underwent a process of editing that covered a period of time.

Date

A variety of dates for the book of Malachi have been offered: 605-550 B.C.E., 515-456, or the late Persian period. Scholars offer several reasons for adopting the second option, which is the time between the completion of Zerubbabel's temple and the coming of Ezra and Nehemiah.

1. The title of the ruler is "governor" (1:8) rather than king, suggesting a time after the fall of the Davidic dynasty.
2. Bitterness toward Edom (1:2-5) also suggests a time after its complicity in the fall of Jerusalem in 586.
3. References to the functioning altar (1:7), the sanctuary in Jerusalem (2:11) and a complacent, even contemptuous priesthood (1:13), however, point to a date after the Exile, when circumstances had settled down again, at least for the priests.
4. The problem of divorce (2:14) appears to be the same as that confronted by Ezra and/or Nehemiah.
5. The language resembles Hebrew of the exilic and early postexilic periods.

Historical Background

In all likelihood, then, the book of Malachi originated in the first half of the 6th century. Local government would have been minimal, with Judah administered for the Persian Empire through its governor in Samaria. Except for the temple, a few new houses, and perhaps some government buildings, Jerusalem languished. Dissension plagued the priesthood; marriage to "foreigners" (who may have been descendants of those people sent to Palestine by the Assyrians) was not uncommon. The city wall was not repaired until the time of Nehemiah. Even at that date, the population may have numbered no more than 5000, with the population of the Judean countryside ca. 50 thousand. (The most optimistic estimates double those numbers, while the most pessimistic halve them.) The situation was not desperate, but neither did it match the promises of Deutero-Isaiah or Ezekiel.

Authorship

The superscription (1:1) attributes the book to someone called "Malachi," a term which means "my messenger." As such, it could be a proper name, but an unlikely name for a child. Consequently, some scholars have suggested that it is an abbreviated form of a name like *malʾăḵîyāhû,* which probably should be translated "Messenger of God" rather than the blasphemous "Yahweh is my Messenger." In 3:1 the same word appears again, and there it seems to refer to someone other than the prophet standing behind the book. It would seem best to conclude, then, that "Malachi" is a title, not a name, and that the book is anonymous.

The book reveals an absorbing interest in priestly matters, such as pollution, the altar, ritual, and the attitude of the priests. Consequently, many scholars consider the author a priest, and that could be correct. The difficulty is that in the postexilic period the Levites were divided into two groups: (1) Zadokites, called priests, and (2) non-Zadokites, called Levites. When the author addressed temple priests simply as Levites, he may well have been denying the distinction the priestly leaders deemed so crucial. That may have been more likely for a Levite than a Zadokite. In addition, the Levites were the officials responsible for collecting the tithes, so the insistence that farmers pay the full tithes (3:8-12) might also suggest a levitical provenance. Thus, the prophet may have been a non-Zadokite Levite interested in a purified cult and a unified priesthood. If so, it is likely his followers were mostly Levites, but perhaps included some sympathetic Zadokites.

The prophet's messages would have constituted the majority, but not the entirety of the book. Passages that betray a second hand include the superscription 1:1; 3:1b-4 plus the title "Malachi" in 3:1a; and 3:16–4:3(3:21). The people the prophet had berated in the first two chapters for despising God's covenant with Levi could scarcely be the people addressed in 3:1b-4, who are said to delight in God's covenant. Nor would the people who brought lame animals to sacrifice or the priests who accepted them with contempt for God be described as people who revered the Lord (3:16). Hence, one should posit a second audience as well as a second hand. A later redactor would have added 4:4-6(3:22-24).

Genre

The dominant view is that the book is comprised of a series of question-and-answer speeches, usually called disputation speeches. The six speeches are 1:2-5; 1:6–2:9; 2:10-16; 2:17–3:5; 3:6-12; 3:13–4:3(3:21), with 4:4-6(3:22-24) considered an addition. Another suggestion is to construe the book as a covenant lawsuit comprised of a series of "controversies" or legal proceedings. Actually, both constructions are somewhat forced, since one finds within the book a prophecy of disaster (2:1-9), a narrative (3:16), and one or more prophecies of salvation (3:17–4:6[3:24]). Thus, one should note the catechetical style of the book without trying to force the whole book or all of its components into a single genre.

Outline and Message

The book of Malachi focuses on God's covenant with the Levites and with the people. That relationship was also expressed in terms of God's parentage of the people. One primary issue is the people's abuse of that relationship. The argument of the book may be outlined under seven headings.

1:2-5 God's Love for Israel

Though the people of Judah and Jerusalem might deny it, God loved Israel. That love could be seen by contrasting the future of Israel, whom God would restore, with that of Edom, whom God would condemn.

1:6–2:9 Pollution by the Priests

The priests were not properly attentive to the worship of God. Instead of setting a table fit for a divine parent, they accepted inferior victims for sacrifice and considered the ritual for which they were responsible a bother.

2:10-16 Unfaithfulness within the Community

Consequently, the people behaved no better than their religious leaders. They committed idolatry, divorced their wives in order to marry "foreign" women, and then could not seem to understand why God rejected their offerings.

2:17–3:5 Cleansing of the Community

What was needed was a genuine cleansing from their sins. Hence, God would punish them like a refining fire.

3:6-12 Paying for Cultic Services

The people would also need to pay their tithes to support the priests and provide the offerings essential to temple worship. If they would do so, God would bless them.

3:13–4:3(3:21) Hope for the Community

If the community as a whole seemed unwilling to heed God's messenger, a loyal remnant would become God's special possession. God would spare the faithful the fury to come.

4:4-6(3:22-24) Living in the Community

The community, both parents and children alike, would heed the message of the prophet Elijah, whom God would send to them before the day of Yahweh.

Bibliography. B. Glazier-McDonald, *Malachi: The Divine Messenger.* SBLDS 98 (Atlanta, 1987); J. M. O'Brien, *Priest and Levite in Malachi.* SBLDS 121 (Atlanta, 1990); D. L. Petersen, *Zechariah 9–14 and Malachi.* OTL (Louisville, 1995); P. L. Redditt, *Haggai, Zechariah, Malachi.* NCBC (Grand Rapids, 1995).

PAUL L. REDDITT

MALCAM (Heb. *malkām*)
A Benjaminite, the son of Shaharaim and Hodesh (1 Chr. 8:9).

MALCHIAH (Heb. *malkîyâ, malkîyāhû*)

1. The father of Pashur, a chief officer of the temple in the time of Jeremiah (Jer. 21:1; 38:1). He is generally distinguished from Malchijah **2.**

2. A member of Judah's royal family and owner of the cistern into which Jeremiah was thrown (Jer. 38:6). Some scholars identify him with **1** above.

See MALCHIJAH. ROBIN GALLAHER BRANCH

MALCHIEL (Heb. *malkî'ēl*)
A son of Beriah and grandson of Asher (Gen. 46:17; 1 Chr. 7:31), ancestor to the Malchielites (Num. 26:45).

MALCHIJAH (Heb. *malkîyâ, malkîyāhû*)

1. A Gershonite Levite, one of the temple musicians. He was an ancestor of Asaph, the father of Baaseiah, and the son of Ethni (1 Chr. 6:40[MT 25]).

2. A descendant of Aaron, head of a priestly family, and leader of the fifth priestly division (1 Chr. 24:9). He was an ancestor of Adaiah, who resettled in Jerusalem after the Exile (1 Chr. 9:12; Neh. 11:12).

3. A descendant of Parosh who divorced his foreign wife (Ezra 10:25).

4. A descendant of Harim who divorced his foreign wife (Ezra 10:31).

5. The son of Harim who, along with Hasshub, repaired a section of the wall and the Tower of the Ovens (Neh. 3:11). He may be the same as **4** above.

6. The ruler of the district of Beth-hakkerem, son of Rechab. He rebuilt the Dung Gate (Neh. 3:14).

7. A goldsmith who helped repair a section of the wall (Neh. 3:31).

8. One of 13 men who stood with Ezra when he read the law of Moses to the people at the Water Gate (Neh. 8:4).

9. A priest who, along with Nehemiah the governor, signed Ezra's covenant after the Exile (Neh. 10:3[4]).

10. A priest who sang in the choir during the dedication of the wall (Neh. 12:42). He may be the same as **9** above.

See MALCHIJAH. ROBIN GALLAHER BRANCH

MALCHIRAM (Heb. *malkîrām*)
The second son of King Jeconiah/Jehoiachin (1 Chr. 3:18).

MALCHISHUA (Heb. *malkîšûa'*)
A son of King Saul (1 Sam. 14:49; 1 Chr. 8:33; 9:39), killed in battle with the Philistines on Mt. Gilboa (1 Sam. 31:2; 1 Chr. 10:2).

MALCHUS (Gk. *Málchos*)
A servant (perhaps a Nabatean) of the high priest Caiaphas whose right ear Peter inexplicably cut off at Gethsemane (John 18:10). According to Luke 22:51 Jesus restored the ear.

MALLOTHI (Heb. *mallôṯî*)
A son of Heman; chief of the nineteenth division of temple singers (1 Chr. 25:4, 26).

MALLOW
Heb. *mallûaḥ*, "mallow" (akin to *melaḥ*, "salt"), may refer to a species of the genus *Atriplex*, commonly called the saltworts. These large bushy plants abound in sandy, salty soil. *Atriplex halimus* L., called sea purslane or shrubby orache, is an excellent candidate for the biblical mallow. Job 30:1-8 indicates that mallows were the food of the poor and destitute.

Heb. *ḥallāmûṯ* (Job 6:6 NRSV), also translated "egg white," may refer to a member of the Malvaceae family, of which species of the genus *Malva* are called mallows today. These are common, mucilaginous herbs. MEGAN BISHOP MOORE

MALLUCH (Heb. *mallûḵ*)
1. A Merarite Levite and ancestor of Ethan (1 Chr. 6:44[MT 29]).
2. One of the sons of Bani required to divorce their foreign wives (Ezra 10:29; 1 Esdr. 9:30).
3. An Israelite among the sons of Harim who was compelled to "put away" his foreign wife (Ezra 10:32).
4. A priest who participated in the sealing of the new covenant under Nehemiah (Neh. 10:4[5]).
5. One of the chiefs of the people who with Nehemiah signed the covenant (Neh. 10:27[28]). He may be the same as **2** or **3.**
6. A priest who returned with Zerubbabel from Babylon (Neh. 12:2). He is perhaps the same as **4.**

MALLUCHI (Heb. *mallûḵî* K)
A priestly household headed by Jonathan at the time of the high priest Joiakim (Neh. 12:14). It is probably associated with Malluch **6.**

MALLUS (Gk. *Mallōs*)
A Cilician city whose people revolted when Antiochus IV Epiphanes gave it and nearby Tarsus to his concubine Antiochis (2 Macc. 4:30). Overlooking the Pyramus (modern Ceyhan) River Delta, the city is situated on the route taken by Alexander the Great.

MALTA (Gk. *Melítē*)
Ancient Melita, the largest of the Maltese islands, ca. 100 km. (60 mi.) S of Sicily. The Phoenicians may have established a trading colony on the island; later Carthage, another Phoenician settlement, controlled Malta, giving the island its Punic character. In the Second Punic War (218 B.C.) Malta became part of the Roman Empire.

The ship carrying Paul as a prisoner to Rome was destroyed and all those on board landed on Malta (Acts 28:1). During the three-month stay on the island, Paul survived a snake bite and worked cures (Acts 28:3-9). The inhabitants were described as *bárbaroi* (Acts 28:2), probably reflecting that they did not speak Greek (NRSV "natives"; KJV "barbarous people"). Inscriptions confirm that the local leader of the island was titled *prṓtos* ("first man" or "chief man"), which is the title of Publius in Acts 28:7. Other islands have been proposed as the site of the shipwreck, but Malta remains the most probable with the traditional St. Paul's Bay, 13 km. (8 mi.) NW of modern Valletta, as the likely spot for the landing.

Bibliography. C. J. Hemer, "Euraquilo and Melita," *JTS* N.S. 26 (1975): 100-11. DOUGLAS LOW

MAMERTINE PRISON
A prison in Rome on the east side of the Capitoline Hill and adjacent to the Forum. According to early Church tradition, Peter and Paul were held prior to their execution in this small building consisting of only two cells, one above the other. Although its name is medieval, the prison is known to have existed in the early 1st century C.E. and was possibly the oldest in the city.

MAMMON (Gk. *mamōnás, mammōnás*)
A transliteration from Aram. or Heb. *mmnw*, absent from the OT but common in rabbinic literature, denoting money or goods. Contrary to popular belief, no evidence has been found for the cult of a pagan god named Mammon.

Jesus taught that "no one can serve two masters . . . you cannot serve God and Mammon" (Matt. 6:24; Luke 16:13; quoted in 2 Clem. 6.1). Here Mammon is personified as an object of false devotion. In material unique to Luke, it appears with its conventional meaning: Make friends by means of unrighteous mammon (Luke 16:9; NRSV "wealth"), and be trustworthy in its use (v. 11).
GARY S. SHOGREN

MAMRE (Heb. *mamrē'*) **(PERSON)**
An Amorite from the vicinity of Hebron. He and his brothers, Eshcol and Aner, were allies of Abraham in the battle against the four eastern kings (Gen. 14:13, 24).

MAMRE (Heb. *mamrē'*) **(PLACE)**
A place that became the focus of Abraham's wanderings during his sojourn in southern Canaan. Abraham built an altar there (Gen 13:18), and it became the site of numerous divine visitations. While

Abraham was encamped at Mamre the Lord told him that Sarah would bear a son in her old age (Gen. 18:1-15), and there Abraham bargained with the Lord over the fate of Sodom and Gomorrah (vv. 16-33). Abraham later bought the nearby cave of Machpelah as a family burial place (Gen. 23:17-20; 25:9-10; 49:29-32; 50:13). The place shares its name with Mamre, an Amorite who is said to be one of Abraham's allies against the coalition of eastern kings led by Chedorlaomer (Gen. 14:24). Whether this character is merely a personification of the place and not a true person is a matter of continued controversy. Mamre has been traditionally identified with modern Ḥaram Râmet el-Khalîl (1088.1602), ca. 3 km. (2 mi.) N of Hebron, although definitive archaeological support of this identification is lacking. WADE R. KOTTER

MANAEN (Gk. *Manaḗn*)
A Christian prophet-teacher in Antioch (Acts 13:1), present at the commissioning of Paul and Barnabas as missionaries. Manaen was a "foster brother" (Gk. *sýntrophos;* RSV "member of the court") of Herod Antipas, tetrarch of Galilee and Perea; the title was given to boys raised as companions to royal princes and was retained in adulthood.

MANAHATH (Heb. *mānaḥaṯ*) **(PERSON)**
A son of Shobal and descendant of the Horite Seir (Gen. 36:23; 1 Chr. 1:40). He is probably the ancestor of an Edomite clan.

MANAHATH (Heb. *mānaḥaṯ*) **(PLACE)**
A town to which the inhabitants of Geba, of the Benjaminite clan of Ehud, were exiled (1 Chr. 8:6). Apparently, the Benjaminites were sent there by one of their clan leaders, Gera (1 Chr. 8:7; reading *hglm* as the verb instead of the proper noun Heglam). Manahath has been identified with el-Malḥah/Manaḥat (1289.1679), a village 5 km. (3 mi.) SW of Jerusalem. The proximity of Manahath to Geba and the agency of Gera have led several scholars to suggest that the verb *glh* be translated instead "to move, emigrate." In any case, the circumstances of this move or exile are unknown. The identification of Manahath with Manḫatu in the Amarna Letters, located in the environs of Gezer, is unlikely. RONALD A. SIMKINS

MANAHATHITES (Heb. *mānaḥtî*)
A Calebite clan whose lineage is traced in two halves, each with its own ancestor (1 Chr. 2:50-54). The first group, referred to as the Menuhoth, is part of the family of Shobal (1 Chr. 2:52; cf. Gen. 36:23). The second half of the clan is counted among the offspring of Salma (1 Chr. 2:54). JOHN KALTNER

MANASSEH (Heb. *mĕnaššeh*)
1. Firstborn son of Joseph and his Egyptian wife Asenath, daughter of Potiphera the priest of On (Gen. 46:20). In honor of Joseph, Manasseh and his younger brother Ephraim are "blessed" by their grandfather Jacob (Gen. 48:8-22) and thus elevated to the rank of tribal progenitor.

The tribe of Manasseh occupied much of the heartland of the kingdom of Israel. Its borders are discussed in Josh. 17; however, their precise delineations are not prescribed. In general, Manasseh occupies the territory immediately S of the Jezreel Valley, as well as the Transjordanian region known as Gilead. Manasseh was clearly one of the most important of the Israelite tribes, as attested by the fact that the three capitals of the northern kingdom all fell within its tribal area: Shechem (Tell Balâtah), Tirzah (Tell el-Farʿah), and Samaria (Sebasṭiyeh). Manasseh included other major cities as well: Megiddo, Taanach, Jezreel, Dor, and Beth-shan.

The exact nature of the Israelite tribes is a complex issue. The OT contains numerous lists of tribes. While these usually emphasize the tribal number as 12, they vary in detail, as well as in broad outline. Generally speaking, the tribal lists fall into two categories: (1) those that list a tribe of Joseph and a tribe of Levi; or (2) those that omit Levi and split Joseph into the two tribes of Manasseh and Ephraim. Most scholars have assumed that the Joseph lists are older, and that later Ephraim/Manasseh emerged from the old Joseph tribe. More recent research, however, has suggested that the tribe of Joseph is a later construct, meant to contrast with Judah.

Several characteristics stand out about the tribe of Manasseh. Of first importance is its preeminence. Along with the tribe of Ephraim, Manasseh dominated the heartland of Israel. Indeed Manasseh and Ephraim appear to have engaged in a long rivalry as to which tribe would ultimately take precedence. While it is clear that Manasseh is denoted as the firstborn of Joseph (Gen. 48:13-14), it is equally clear that Ephraim ultimately wins the sibling rivalry (v. 19). Note that it is an Ephraimite, Jeroboam I, that takes the throne after the monarchy splits. Indeed the term "Ephraim" eventually becomes a synonym for the kingdom of Israel (e.g., Isa. 7:2).

Manasseh is also remarkable for the persistence of its Canaanite population. Manasseh was established in an area with considerable Canaanite settlement. Shechem, Beth-shan, Taanach, Ibleam, and Megiddo — among others — are all old Canaanite cities. Even after the Israelite "conquest," Judg. 1:27 emphasizes that the Canaanites continued to dwell in their cities. The antiquity of the settlement in Manasseh clearly complicates its history. Moreover, Manasseh's relationships with the tribe of Issachar and the mysterious tribes of Machir and Jezreel (2 Sam. 2:9) further cloud the picture. The ancient Song of Deborah (Judg. 5) lists 10 tribes of northern Israel. While the tribe of Machir is mentioned, Manasseh is not. Many scholars have suggested that the term Machir is simply an archaic reference to Manasseh; others, however, have argued that Machir was originally a separate tribe that ultimately vanished or was absorbed by Manasseh.

2. King of Judah (ca. 697-642 B.C.E.). Condemned as the most evil king of Judah, Manasseh was the son of King Hezekiah and Hephzibah, father of the briefly ruling Amon, and grandfather and antithesis of good King Josiah. Manasseh's 55-year reign was the longest of any Davidic king. The excesses of his evil reign are recounted in the Deuteronomistic history (2 Kgs. 21:1-17; 23:26-27; 24:3-4), the book of Chronicles (2 Chr. 33:1-20), and Jeremiah (Jer. 15:4).

A fascinating aspect of Manasseh's reign is its divergent treatment in Kings and Chronicles. Both accounts begin with a characterization of Manasseh's tenure as one of unprecedented evil and apostasy. They decry his cultic excesses, child sacrifice, pagan altars, idolatry, and witchcraft. Both accounts also agree that Yahweh sent prophets to plead for repentance — but Manasseh refused to listen. But here the two accounts begin to diverge. The book of Kings condemns Manasseh as being so evil that his reign is the ultimate cause of the collapse of Judah. Even the righteous reign of Manasseh's successor, Josiah, is not enough to avert the wrath of God: "for the sins of Manasseh . . . the Lord was not willing to pardon" (2 Kgs. 24:3-4).

In contrast, Chronicles includes a fascinating account of exile and repentance. 2 Chr. 33 asserts that Yahweh was so angry with Manasseh that he was given over to the Assyrians and taken captive to Babylon (*sic!*). And in an account totally absent from Kings, Manasseh is said to have recognized his wickedness and contritely repented. God was so pleased with Manasseh's turn of heart that he was reinstated to the throne of Judah. After his return from Babylon, Manasseh undertook significant political, religious, and military reforms. Thus while Manasseh is depicted in Kings as the epitome of sin — the ultimate cause for Judah's demise — in Chronicles he becomes the epitome of the repentant sinner. In fact the apocryphal Prayer of Manasseh purports to be Manasseh's prayer of contrition. Traditionally most scholars have dismissed the Chronicler's account as a moralizing attempt to explain the unprecedented length of Manasseh's reign. Recently, however, several scholars have argued that more credence be given to the Chronicler's account. They argue that the Deuteronomistic writings have exaggerated Manasseh's apostasy in order to explain the ultimate failure of Josiah's reforms.

3.-5. Hebrew men who complied with Ezra's command to put away their foreign wives. The lists in Ezra 10; 1 Esdr. 9 are similar, but vary in their details. Ezra 10 refers to Manasseh son of Pahath-moab (v. 30) and a Manasseh son of Hashum (v. 33); 1 Esdr. 9 refers to "Manasseas" son of Addi (v. 31) and a Manasseh son of Hashum (v. 33).

6. Husband of Judith, the heroine of the book of Judith (Jdt. 8:2). Manasseh appears to have been a prominent, wealthy citizen (Jdt. 8:7) who died from heatstroke while supervising workers on his estate.

Bibliography. I. Finkelstein, "The Archaeology of the Days of Manasseh," in *Scripture and Other Artifacts*, ed. M. D. Coogan, J. C. Exum, and L. E. Stager (Louisville, 1994), 169-87; *The Archaeology of the Israelite Settlement* (Jerusalem, 1988); C. H. J. de Geus, *The Tribes of Israel.* SSN 18 (Amsterdam, 1976); J. W. McKay, *Religion in Judah Under the Assyrians, 732-602 B.C.* SBT 2nd ser. 26 (Naperville, 1973); L. Tatum, "King Manasseh and the Royal Fortress at Ḥorvat 'Usa," *BA* 54 (1991): 136-45.

LYNN TATUM

MANASSEH, PRAYER OF

A pseudepigraphical text purporting to be the prayer that King Manasseh offered while imprisoned in Babylon (2 Chr. 33:12-13). While included in the Apocrypha and some modern editions of the LXX, the Prayer was actually never a part of the LXX. Its primary textual witnesses are several Greek and Syriac Christian manuscripts. However, the Prayer may have a Jewish origin dating to the 2nd or 1st century B.C.E. Whether Greek is the Prayer's original language or whether it is a translation from a Semitic original remains uncertain.

Utilizing the forms of lament and penitential prayer, the Prayer borrows ideas, images, and language from the Hebrew Bible, including significant parallels to Ps. 51. It also shows awareness of and incorporates details from the story of Manasseh in 2 Kings and 2 Chronicles. Attributing a prayer to a person from Israel's past, sometimes as an addition to a text as the author has done with this prayer, is a trait of some Second Temple Jewish texts (e.g., Ezra 9; Dan. 9; Additions to Esther; Prayer of Azariah).

In the invocation (vv. 1-7) the author depicts Manasseh as praising God as the only Sovereign and almighty Creator, the God of the patriarchs and the covenant. The description of God's creative activity may include allusions to ancient pagan myths in order to leave no doubt that all gods are subject to the biblical God. Ironically, Manasseh in his idolatrous polytheism had turned his back on the God of the covenant. While the king has been unfaithful, he now calls upon God to be faithful to the promise that he forgives and delivers sinners (v. 7).

Manasseh confesses his sin in vv. 8-12. Multiple admissions typically occur in Second Temple penitential prayers and emphasize the suppliant's contrition. Manasseh's inability to lift his eyes indicates his guilt and shame (cf. Ezra 9:6; 1 En. 63:1, 5, 6, 8). Physical descriptions of his imprisonment become metaphors for his spiritual condition. His acknowledgement that God has rightfully punished him is also a traditional element of penitential prayer. He explicitly confesses his idolatry in v. 10, but assures God that he who bowed before idols now "bends the knee" of his "heart" before God (v. 11).

In vv. 13-14 Manasseh petitions God for forgiveness. Continuing a theme from the introduction, he refers to God as the "God of those who repent" (v. 13). The desperate plea for God to remove his anger, spare the petitioner's life, and remove the threat of eternal destruction are elements of lament. Manasseh's concluding promise of fidelity and praise to God (v. 15) continues the tone of lament.

This prayer shows the extravagance of God's mercy and grace which God extends to all, even the worst of sinners (v. 8). This fits the biblical tradition regarding Manasseh, as well as God's response to human repentance (cf. 2 Chr. 6; 7:14).

Bibliography. J. H. Charlesworth, "Prayer of Manasseh," *OTP* 2:625-37; G. W. E. Nickelsburg, "Prayer of Manasseh," in *Oxford Bible Commentary* (forthcoming). RODNEY A. WERLINE

MANDRAKE

A round, greenish-yellow, plumlike fruit (although some suggest that tuberous root masses are indicated) of *Mandragora vernalis,* a perennial plant most commonly known from southern Palestine and Egypt, but also appearing in Syria and, apparently, in the area of Paddan-aram.

The mandrake was thought to be an aphrodisiac (cf. Cant. 7:13 and its occurrence in traditional Egyptian love songs; cf. also the traditional translation of Heb. *dûḏay* as "love apples"). It apparently was thought to be an aid to fertility and conception (Gen. 30:14-16). However, the biblical text clearly does not endorse the idea, and in fact it may provide a polemic against it. The source of the fertility of both Leah and Rachel was not mandrakes but God's "listening to" them, apparently a response to their prayer for children. WALTER E. BROWN

MANGER

An animal-feeding trough (Heb. *'ēḇûs,* Job 39:9; Isa. 1:3; cf. Prov. 14:4) or stall (LXX Gk. *phátnē;* cf. 2 Chr. 32:28; Hab. 3:17; 2 Chr. 9:25) in a stable. Stables were situated on the ground level 46 cm. (18 in.) below a family's living quarters or in caves under a house or near it. Troughs were free-standing stone boxes placed against stable walls or boxes made by hollowing out rocks protruding into the stable area. At Megiddo archaeologists found limestone troughs, measuring 91 cm. (3 ft.) long, 46 cm. (1.5 ft.) wide, and 61 cm. (2 ft.) deep, quite ample for an infant. Tradition locates Jesus' birth in a cave stable (Justin Martyr *Dial.* 78.5; Prot. Jas. 17-18). Jesus' placement in a manger after his birth foreshadows his role as a humble Messiah for all people (Luke 2:7, 12, 16; Isa. 1:3). EMILY CHENEY

MANICHAEISM

A religion with its roots in the gnostic tradition of the Near East. Its founder, Mani, was born in Mesopotamia in 216 C.E. Manichaeism emerged out of a rich, diverse religious context. Zoroastrianism, Buddhism, Judaism, Christianity, Hellenistic philosophy, and numerous ancient indigenous religious traditions were present in western Iran in the early 3rd century C.E. Mani considered himself "the seal of the prophets" who brought the final, supreme divine revelation. Manichaeism views all previous revelations (i.e., those of Zoroaster, Moses, Buddha, and/or Jesus) to have been only partial revelations. One deficiency of these other revelations, according to Mani, was their provincialism. Manichaeism, in contrast, professes to proclaim a complete, universal revelation which will unite all people and be practiced in all lands. Its adherents were to traverse the world propagating Mani's teachings which would have been accurately copied and translated into a locally understandable language.

Manichaeism's two most basic tenets are: (1) the two eternal principles; and (2) the division of time into three epochs. In the beginning (past time) the eternal principles of good/light and evil/darkness existed separately. Present time began when representatives of the kingdom of darkness invaded the kingdom of light. This epoch may be seen as a process of regathering the elements of light that were scattered, or captured, during darkness' invasion and the reseparation of these elements from those of darkness. The final epoch will be preceded by apocalyptic events and will witness a last, great battle between the forces of light and darkness. Following this battle, a final judgment will be rendered. The good/righteous will be gathered into the kingdom of light, whereas the evil/wicked will be consigned to a bottomless pit which will be permanently sealed. The cosmos will then burn for 1468 years.

Bibliography. H.-J. Klimkeit, *Gnosis on the Silk Road* (San Francisco, 1993); S. N. C. Lieu, *Manichaeism in Mesopotamia and the Roman East* (Leiden, 1994); *Manichaeism in the Later Roman Empire and Medieval China,* 2nd ed. WUNT 63 (Tübingen, 1992); J. C. Reeves, *Jewish Lore in Manichaean Cosmogony.* HUCM 14 (Cincinnati, 1992); G. Widengren, *Mani and Manichaeism* (London, 1965). DAVID CLEAVER-BARTHOLOMEW

MANNA

A substance which fell in the night to sustain the Israelites wandering in the wilderness. God sent them manna (Heb. *mān*) for 40 years, until they celebrated the Passover at Gilgal in the Promised Land (Exod. 16:35; Josh. 5:12). Manna was a substance like coriander or frost (Exod. 16:13, 31), the color of gum resin (Num. 11:7). The Israelites collected it in the morning, gathering only enough for the day ahead, lest it spoil (Exod. 16:16-21); double provisions could be collected the day before the sabbath (v. 5). Manna was crushed and then boiled or baked (Num. 11:8; Exod. 16:23). The taste of manna was like cakes made with oil or honey (Exod. 16:31; Num. 11:8).

The appearance of manna was a miraculous occurrence that cannot be explained entirely by natural phenomena. However, some plants in the Sinai produce sweet substances that scholars have identified with manna. After sucking on the tamarisk tree (genus *Tamarix*), some insects secrete a sweet substance. Other plants also exhibit similar secretions. Lichens *(Lecanora)* have also been proposed for manna, since when dry they travel through the air and fall on the earth.

Manna is used symbolically ("bread from heaven") to represent God's care (Neh. 9:20; John 6:31; Gk. *mánna;* cf. Rev. 2:17). The Israelites were humbled and tested by manna to learn that "one does not live by bread alone, but by every word that comes from the mouth of the Lord" (Deut. 8:3). Moses commanded that a jar of manna be kept throughout the ages as a remembrance of God's safekeeping (Exod. 16:33).

MEGAN BISHOP MOORE

MAN OF GOD

A term used primarily for prophets. It serves as an appellation for Moses (the prototypical prophet for the Deuteronomistic historians), Samuel, Shemaiah, Elijah, Elisha, Igdaliah, several unnamed prophets, and even David (the latter only in the Chronicler's account). Though the term is applied far more frequently to Elisha than to any other figure, perhaps the most recognized "man of God" is the unnamed prophet of Judah of 1 Kgs. 13 who travels to Bethel to announce Yahweh's judgment on Jeroboam I and his idolatrous altar, only to be deceived by a fellow prophet and forfeit his life as punishment.

In the NT the phrase appears in the Pastoral Epistles and in some manuscript traditions of 2 Pet. 1:21. Here the prophetic connotation is absent, and the phrase is used of followers of God, especially leaders in the Church.

JAMES R. ADAIR, JR.

MANOAH (Heb. *mānôaḥ*)

The father of Samson; a Danite living in the town of Zorah. Manoah and his wife are childless when an angel of the Lord appears to them, announcing that Manoah's wife would "conceive and bear a son" (Judg. 13:3), instructs them on how he is to be brought up (vv. 4-6), and informs them that he will be a great judge and "deliver Israel from the hand of the Philistines" (v. 5). Manoah finally realizes the angel's true nature when the angel ascends "in the flame of the altar" (Judg. 13:20).

Manoah's story contains many of the common features of Palestinian and Hellenistic wisdom stories, including the foretelling by a messenger of the gods of the birth of a son of great promise and the miraculous birth of a folk-hero to barren and childless parents (cf. 1 Sam. 1:5, 9-17; Luke 1:5-17).

HENRY L. CARRIGAN, JR.

MANTIC

A term (Gk. *mantikós,* "prophetic, oracular"; *mántis,* "diviner, seer, prophet") designating wise individuals whose expertise was divination, and in particular manticism, or knowing the future through the interpretation of omens, visions, and dreams. Mantic wise men trained for the courts of Mesopotamia (cf. Dan. 1–6) have been suggested as the originators of the apocalypse genre.

"Mantological" and "mantic" are also used to specify the interpretive technique that reinterpreted oracles or that transformed nonoracular material into prediction of the future.

Bibliography. J. J. Collins, "The Court-Tales in Daniel and the Development of Apocalyptic," *JBL* 94 (1975): 218-34; M. Fishbane, *Biblical Interpretation in Ancient Israel* (Oxford, 1985); A. L. Oppenheim, *The Interpretation of Dreams in the Ancient Near East.* Transactions of the American Philosophical Society N.S. 46/3 (Philadelphia, 1956).

R. GLENN WOODEN

MANUSCRIPTS

See TEXT OF THE OLD TESTAMENT; TEXT OF THE NEW TESTAMENT.

MANY WATERS

A term (Heb. *mayim rabbîm*) commonly used in poetic contexts, often in parallel with "rivers" *(nĕhārôṯ),* "deep" *(tĕhôm),* or "sea" *(yām).* It most often denotes God's abundant provision of water, nurturing rich growth (Num. 24:7). This abundance, however, usually leads to judgment against the ungrateful, prideful recipient — whether Tyre, Egypt, or Israel (Isa. 23:2-3; Jer. 51:13; Ezek. 17:5, 8). Its roaring voice also appears as an aspect of God's glory — either the roaring of judgment (Jer. 51:55) or some other manifestation of glory — in the heavenly visions of Ezekiel (Ezek. 43:2; cf. Rev. 1:15) or perhaps as part of a storm theophany (Ps. 29:3). Alternatively it may denote the roaring of confusion or the destructive force of an enemy, from which God will surely rescue the faithful (Cant. 8:7; 2 Sam. 22:16-18 par.; Ps. 32:6; 77:17-20[MT 18-21]; Isa. 17:12-13).

In line with common ancient Near Eastern divine imagery (Canaanite Yamm/Sea, Mesopotamian Tiamat), the waters may represent a primeval force of chaos over which Israel's God is asserted to have power — either by gaining victory over it in cosmic battle (Hab. 3:13-15) or by using it as his own weapon of destruction (Ezek. 26:19; cf. Gen. 7:10-11; Exod. 15:8-10; Amos 7:4; Isa. 51:9-10, which use different but parallel phrases to express this same concept).

ROBIN J. DEWITT KNAUTH

MAOCH (Heb. *mā'ôḵ*)

The father of King Achish of Gath (1 Sam. 27:2). He may be the same as Maacah (**3;** 1 Kgs. 2:39).

MAON (Heb. *mā'ôn*) **(PERSON)**

A Calebite, the son of Shammai and father of Bethzur (1 Chr. 2:45). The name may designate here a clan or village.

MAON (Heb. *mā'ôn*) **(PLACE)**

1. A town in the hill country of Judah, identified with Ḥorvat Maon/Khirbet Ma'în (1627.0909), 14 km. (8.7 mi.) N of Arad. Perhaps named after one of Caleb's descendants (1 Chr. 2:45), the town was part of Judah's tribal inheritance (Josh. 15:55); the area east of it, near the Dead Sea, was known as the wilderness of Maon. David and his followers evaded Saul by hiding there (1 Sam. 23:24-25), and it is the setting for the story of Nabal and David (25:2). The MT reference to the wilderness of Paran (1 Sam. 25:1) should be emended to Maon, as in the LXX. The inhabitants of Maon were counted among the enemies of Israel during the period of the judges (Judg. 10:12) and the rule of Uzziah (2 Chr. 26:7). The Meunim (2 Chr. 26:7; Ezra 2:50 =

Neh. 7:52), counted among the returnees from Babylonian exile, may represent an alternative spelling of Maon.

Arad ostracon 25 (7th-6th century B.C.E.) credits Maon with the delivery of 10 hekats of barley (one hekat being just under 5 l. [4.5 qt.]).

The site was surveyed in 1968 (Moshe Kochavi), 1979 (Yizhar Hirschfeld), and 1987-1988 (Zvi Ilan and David Amit). Kochavi's survey determined that the biblical town covered 1 ha. (2.5 a.), spanning the summit, eastern, and northern slopes of the tell. The western slope was covered by later buildings. Ceramic evidence for Early Bronze, Iron, Hellenistic, Roman, Byzantine, and medieval occupation was found.

The site is best known for its 4th-7th century C.E. synagogue. While its mosaic floor was not well preserved, it features fragments of a menorah composed of marble "apples." Other finds include an underground *mikveh,* hall, and tunnel and coins from the 4th and 5th centuries C.E.

2. A town 18 km. (11 mi.) S of Gaza, modern Khirbet el-Ma'in (093.082), located near the edge of the Negeb desert by the settlement of Kibbutz Nirim, 20 km. (12.5 mi.) SW of Gaza. The site of an ancient synagogue, Maon-Nirim is renowned for its intricate 6th-century C.E. mosaic. The main motif is composed of a grapevine trellis of 55 medallions, each containing an animal, bowl, or basket. The mosaic includes such Jewish symbols as a menorah, shophar, and *lulav.* Other finds include a dedicatory inscription in Aramaic (part of the mosaic), coins from the 4th-6th centuries C.E., and a bone plaque decorated with a carved amphora.

Bibliography. Y. Aharoni, *The Land of the Bible,* 2nd ed. (Philadelphia, 1979); *Arad Inscriptions* (Jerusalem, 1981); M. Avi-Yonah, *The Holy Land,* rev. ed. (Grand Rapids, 1977); D. Barag, "Ma'on (Nirim)," *NEAEHL* 3:944-46; Department of Antiquities, "Nirim (Hurvath Ma'on)," *IEJ* 7 (1957): 265; Z. Ilan and D. Amit, "Horvat Ma'on, Synagogue," *Excavations and Surveys in Israel* 7/8 (1988-89): 123-225; "Maon (in Judea)," *NEAEHL* 3:942-44.

JENNIFER L. GROVES

MAONITES (Heb. *mā'ôn*)
A people among those who had oppressed Israel and whom God had subdued (Judg. 10:12). Although the town of Maon (modern Tell Ma'în, S of Hebron) and its surrounding area play a prominent role in David's flight from Saul, no mention is made of their earlier having invaded Israel. Many scholars emend the text to "Midianites," following LXX Gk. *Madiam.* CHRISTIAN M. M. BRADY

MARA (Heb. *mārā'*)
A name ("bitter") taken by Naomi (rather than her own, which means "my pleasant one") after God had "dealt bitterly" with her, i.e., after her husband and two sons had died (Ruth 1:20; cf. v. 13).

MARAH (Heb. *mārâ*)
An Israelite encampment in the wilderness of Shur three days after they crossed the Red Sea (Exod. 15:23; Num. 33:8, wilderness of Etham). Here the water was "bitter" (Heb. *mārâ*) or brackish, but the Lord instructed Moses to cast a tree into the water, making it sweet. *Sanh.* 56b cites Marah as the location where the earliest instructions were given for keeping the sabbath. The most accepted location for Marah is 'Ain Hawârah, 72 km. (45 mi.) SE of the Gulf of Suez ca. 11 km. (7 mi.) inland.

PETE F. WILBANKS

MARALAH (Heb. *mar'ălâ*)
See MAREAL.

MARANATHA (Gk. *maranathá*)
A transliterated Aramaic expression (1 Cor. 16:22; Did. 10:6), probably meaning "Our Lord, come!" (Aram. *māranā' ṯā'*) but possibly "our Lord has come" *(māran 'ăṯā),* depending on how one construes the original Aramaic's spelling and dialect. The contexts of both passages and its Greek translation at Rev. 22:20 suggest the former. Paul ends his correspondence with a curse and this prayer followed by a blessing (1 Cor. 16:22-24). Did. 10:6, which discusses the Eucharist ("If anyone is holy, let him come. If he is not, let him repent. *Maranatha.* Amen."), points to a liturgical use of the term. The author of Revelation records the promise of Jesus' return and prays, "Amen. Come, Lord Jesus!" (Rev. 22:20). JAMES A. KELHOFFER

MARBLE
A metamorphic rock made up of fine- to coarse-grained recrystallized calcite and/or dolomite, produced when the heat and pressure of volcanic activity works on limestone. Limestone is a sedimentary rock of organic or inorganic origin composed chiefly of calcium carbonate, but also containing dolomite, chalcedony, and other minerals. Marble, which can be very highly polished, is used primarily as an architectural and ornamental stone. It is not native to Palestine, being first imported from the Greek islands during the Persian period. However, there are some fine limestones native to Israel that are fairly common, excellent for building, and take a high polish. Heb. *šēš,* sometimes translated "marble," is more commonly translated "alabaster." In Esth. 1:6 the term is employed twice to describe building materials used in the king's palace in Susa, and it is translated "marble," probably correctly given the historical context. Marble, from Gk. *mármaros,* "glistening crystalline stone," is also listed among the goods that the merchants of earth will no longer be able to sell after the judgment and fall of the great harlot Babylon (Rev. 18:12).

MARTHA JEAN MUGG BAILEY

MARCION (Gk. *Markíōn*), **GOSPEL OF**
The first part of the 2nd-century heretic Marcion's bipartite canon. The second part consisted of an abridgement of 10 Pauline epistles. Marcion gave these two parts the names Gospel and Apostle. Behind these names was Marcion's conviction that there is only one Gospel (not four) and only one Apostle who understood it (Paul). The Gospel of

Marcion, known only through quotation by others (esp. Tertullian *Adv. Marc.* 4; Epiphanius *Adv. haer.* 42), is essentially a version of Luke, purged of what Marcion considered judaizing corruptions. His guiding principle, which he derived from his teacher Cerdo, was the gnostic rejection of the OT God of law as different from and less than the great saving NT God of grace, whom Jesus represented. Whatever the Gospel of Marcion lacked his opponents blamed on this theological bias. They saw it clearly, e.g., in its opening statement, which combined Luke 3:1; 4:31-32 to present Jesus as "coming down to Capernaum" in the 15th year of Tiberius (not however from Nazareth, as in 4:16-30, but directly from the unknown God) and astonishing the Jews by teaching against the Law and the Prophets (the absence of most of Luke 1–4 was seen as allowing Jesus to be severed from his Jewish roots). Some differences in the Gospel of Marcion, however, are better attributed to a different (esp. "Western") textual base and/or the influence of synoptic parallels. Attempts, finally, to say that canonical Luke was preceded by the Gospel of Marcion and dependent upon it are unconvincing.

Bibliography. A. von Harnack, *Marcion: The Gospel of an Alien God* (Durham, N.C., 1990); R. J. Hoffman, *Marcion: On the Restitution of Christianity.* AARAcad. 46 (Chico, 1984); J. Knox, *Marcion and the New Testament* (1942, repr. New York, 1980).

RONALD V. HUGGINS

MARDUK
(Akk. dAMAR.UTU, *dMa-ru-du-uk-ku*)
The chief deity in the Babylonian pantheon during the 1st millennium B.C.E. Originally little known, he was identified in the early 2nd millennium with the god Asalluḫi, who was the son of Enki/Ea and who was important in the cult of the southern city Eridu. Marduk's association with the increasingly prominent city of Babylon probably goes back to Hammurabi's dynasty in the Old Babylonian period. Eventually, Marduk succeeded Enlil, god of Nippur, as the supreme executive in the pantheon, and Marduk's city, Babylon, replaced Nippur as the most important religious center in Babylonia. The so-called epic of creation, Enuma Elish, celebrates Marduk's elevation to preeminent status in the pantheon; in the epic, the other gods agree to confer ultimate royal authority on him following his defeat of Tiamat, the goddess of salt water and chaos. Codified in the reign of Nebuchadnezzar I (1125-1104), Enuma Elish apparently formed part of the libretto for the New Year or Akītu Festival.

Scholars dispute the etymology of the name Marduk. Ancient scribes most often wrote the name with Sumerian logographs, dAMAR.UTU, but the most commonly suggested Sumerian etymology, "young calf of Šamaš," is probably erroneous. In Sumerian contexts it is never analyzed as a genitive, while the relation of Marduk to Šamaš is unattested elsewhere. In fact, Marduk, because of his early identification with Asalluḫi, was considered the son of Enki/Ea.

After the time of Nebuchadnezzar I, Marduk remained the chief deity of the Babylonian state and patron of its kings, including those of the Neo-Babylonian dynasty (626-539). It is in this status that the people of the Eastern Mediterranean, including Israel, encountered Marduk. In Jer. 50:2, a mid-6th century oracle, God announces the capture and shaming of Babylon and Marduk (here vocalized *mĕrōḏaḵ*). Marduk is the divine component in one biblical name, Merodach-baladan II (Isa. 39:1; the parallel in 2 Kgs. 20:12 reads *bĕrōʾḏaḵ*), a Chaldean sheik who ruled Babylonia for about a decade in the late 8th century. The common assertion that the name of Esther's cousin, Mordecai, derives from the name Marduk, remains plausible. Marduk appears elsewhere in the OT under the common title *bēl*, "Lord" (Isa. 46:1; Jer. 50:2; 51:44), his ubiquitous title. It is his temple complex in Babylon, Esagil(a), or its associated temple-tower, Etemenanki, that stands behind the narrative of the tower of Babel in Gen. 11:1-9.

Bibliography. W. G. Lambert, "The Reign of Nebuchadnezzar I: A Turning Point in the History of Ancient Mesopotamian Religion," in *The Seed of Wisdom*, ed. W. S. McCullough (Toronto, 1964), 3-13.

DAVID VANDERHOOFT

MAREAL (Heb. *marʿălâ*)
A city in the Jezreel Valley marking the southern border of Zebulun (Josh. 19:11; NRSV "Maralah"). From the context, the location must have been slightly N of Megiddo. Tell Thorah (166228) is a possible site.

MARESHAH (Heb. *mārēšâ*) **(PERSON)**

1. The firstborn son of Caleb, father of Ziph and Hebron (1 Chr. 2:42 LXX; Gk. *Marisa*). Hebrew manuscripts offer no variants, reading instead "Mesha" as father of Ziph. The LXX emendation fails to overcome the intrusion of "the sons of Mareshah, the father of Hebron" (cf. NASB "his son was Mareshah").

2. The son of Laadah and the great-grandson of Judah (1 Chr. 4:21).

R. DAVID MOSEMAN

MARESHAH (Heb. *mārēšâ*) **(PLACE)**
(also MARISA)
A prominent town in the eastern Shephelah of Judah (Josh. 15:44). It was located 2 km. (1 mi.) S of Beth Guvrin/Beit Jibrin (Eleutheropolis) and 30 km. SE of Ashkelon, identified with Tell Ṣandaḥannah (140111). One of the cities fortified by Rehoboam (2 Chr. 11:8), it was the site of the battle between Asa and Zerah the Ethiopian (14:9). Its destruction is prophesied in Mic. 1:15. During the exilic period the city was annexed by the Idumeans. Alternating between Seleucid and Ptolemaic control, the city (then called Marisa) was prominent during the Hellenistic era, featuring an "upper" and "lower" city. Judas Maccabeus captured and burned the city (Josephus *Ant.* 12.8.6), but Pompey restored it to the Idumeans in 63 B.C.E. In 47 B.C.E. Julius Caesar annexed the city to Judea. It was destroyed by the Parthians in 40 B.C.E.

Excavations in the early 20th century, along

with new efforts in 1989 and 1991 by Amos Kloner, have uncovered at least three strata: two Hellenistic and one Israelite ("Jewish"). In particular, the 1991 excavations revealed additional Hellenistic discoveries such as a residential quarter located on the northwest outside wall. Of note from the Israelite stratum was the discovery of a rich pottery repertoire believed to be from the beginning of the 3rd to the end of the 2nd centuries B.C.E. Also uncovered were numerous artifacts as well as tombs and burial caves. On the basis of such extensive finds, scholars are reassured that Mareshah played an important role economically throughout biblical times.

Bibliography. M. Avi-Yonah and A. Kloner, "Mareshah (Marisa)," *NEAEHL* 3:948-57.

AARON M. GALE

MARI (Akk. *Mari*)

An ancient city in the middle Euphrates Valley, situated on the bank of the Euphrates and on caravan routes between the East and the West, a crossroads where these cultures intersected and merged. Discovered in 1933, Tell Ḥarīrī has proved to be one of the most important Assyriological discoveries of the 20th century. Investigations led by André Parrot soon identified the city from an inscription on the statue of Lamgi-mari discovered in the palace. Excavations which have continued to the present have yielded additional monumental structures including the Ishtar temple and a ziggurat, as well as murals depicting ritual scenes and a large archive of texts.

History

Mari is first mentioned within a list of cities in a mid-3rd millennium B.C.E. document from Lagash. Mari also appears in an inscription of Sargon of Akkad (2334-2279) as one of the cities captured during his reign. During the 3rd Dynasty of Ur (2112-2004) Mari was a caravan outpost of the city-state, ruled by governors called *šakkanakku*, subordinate to the rulers of Ur. With the end of the Ur dynasty, political control of the Middle Euphrates region, including Mari, disintegrated.

Though the documentation is not entirely clear, by the late 19th century we can reconstruct an early history of an independent Mari. Yaḫdun-lim, son of Yaggid-lim, came from north of Mari from a group known as the Ḫana and united several small principalities, making Mari the center of his political realm. Within a short period, however, the Assyrian king Šamši-addu I (1812-1781) annexed Mari as part of his expanding kingdom. Šamši-addu divided his vast realm between the Tigris and Euphrates between his two sons, placing Išme-dagan I on the throne in Ekallatum in the east and Yasmaḫ-addu in Mari in the west. Letters found in the royal palace at Mari demonstrate that Šamši-addu remained the primary king in the region and regularly gave his sons political advice and counsel, if not direct assistance. Upon the death of Šamši-addu, Išme-dagan inherited his realm and continued to support his brother as a viceroy at Mari.

The Assyrian domination of Mari ended in 1775 when Zimri-lim, son of Yaḫdun-lim, regained control of the throne with the apparent assistance of Yarim-lim, king of the region of Yamḫad W of Mari, whose capital was Aleppo. Zimri-lim reigned at Mari until 1762, when the army of Hammurabi of Babylon captured and destroyed the city. In the process of destruction, the palace of Zimri-lim was burned, firing the clay tablet archives and preserving them for posterity.

Texts

The archive discovered in the palace at Mari contains texts that span almost 500 years, reaching back to the *šakkanakku* period and the 3rd dynasty of Ur and continuing to the end of the city in the 18th century. The majority of the documents come from the city's last 50 years under the final two kings, Yasmaḫ-addu and Zimri-lim. Excluding the few texts written in Hurrian and bilingual Sumerian and Akkadian inscriptions, the language of the documents is Akkadian. The Akkadian used is distinctive in that it preserves proper names and vocabulary, as well as syntactical arrangements which are clearly West Semitic in origin.

Internal administrative texts shed light on the daily workings of the palace through records of receipt and disbursement of raw materials as well as disbursement of food for royal banquets. Palace personnel are listed in records of the various types of artisans at work in royal shops within the palace and women in the royal harem. Officials appointed to various duties throughout the realm, who report directly to the king, are indicated in records of disbursement of materials for their support. Lists of disbursement of oil, clothing, and food to priests and prophetic figures indicate the segments of the ancient society which were dependent upon the palace.

Other administrative texts provide information on the external business of the palace. These record royal gifts sent to foreign kings and dignitaries. Other accounts indicate special royal gifts offered to various deities as well as regular cultic offerings. There are also records of the receipt of gifts and taxes coming into the palace at Mari or being received by the king's representatives at outlying palaces.

By far the most interesting and informative of Mari documents are the letters. These texts exist in the form of communications between individuals, but they contain information concerning the administration of the realm. Letters from royal representatives in distant capitals report their observations on the courts of foreign rulers, as well as communications from the foreign kings.

Letters to the king of Mari from palace officials, royal women of the palace, priests, and various prophetic figures indicate oracular activity in Mari. Information received through extispicy, the reading of divine messages in the entrails of sacrificed animals, ecstatic behavior, and dreams is passed on to the king in letters from a wide range of individuals. Though these documents reveal prophetic activity only as it relates to the king, it is evident that this was a key element in the ancient social structure. The number of women included in this correspondence is indicative of the prominent role of women in the palace at Mari.

Other, more personal, letters reveal private and intimate communications among family members. Beyond political advice received by Yasmaḫ-addu from his father and brother, there are letters which contain personal advice concerning his behavior. Zimri-lim received letters from Šiptum, his primary wife, as well as his daughters and older women in the palace. Whole some of these letters communicate important political and religious information to the king, many are personal familial messages which express concern for his health and well-being.

In addition to administrative and epistolary documents, there are treaty documents between the king of Mari and various allied rulers which provide considerable information on the political relationships of this period.

The importance of all the various types of documents found at Mari cannot be overestimated. It is through the decipherment and careful study of all of these documents that the history of the site has been reconstructed. Moreover, the interpersonal communications contain information about cultural practices and protocols previously unknown, such as the use of the hem of a person's garment and/or a lock of hair as verification of the message, particularly when the message emanates from a prophet.

Relationship to the Bible

Scholars have long recognized apparent similarities between the culture found at Mari and that of the patriarchs and the kingdom of Israel in the Bible. Their arguments rest on several points. First, there are cultural phenomena at Mari that seem very much like what is found in biblical material. Records of prophetic oracles sent to the king indicate a similarity in the way the people of Mari and of Israel understood the relationship between God and king.

A second point of similarity is in personal names and vocabulary. Names in Mari, such as Sumu'il and Yaqub-il, have form and meaning similar to names in the Bible. The name of a seminomadic group known as the DUMU.MEŠ *ia-mi-na* has provided interesting possibilities. If read as East Semitic, *mārī yamina,* the name seems less significant than if read as West Semitic, *benê yamina.* The homophony with the Hebrew name Benjamin is obvious.

A further point of connection is the biblical presentation of the patriarchs as having a familial connection with the people of this region. In Gen. 24, when Abraham sent his servant to obtain a wife for Isaac, he sent him to the land where his family dwelt, to Aram-naharaim and the city of Nahor. This recollection, added to the similarity of names and vocabulary, is considered by some as evidence of a genetic connection between the people of ancient Israel and Mari.

Other scholars, however, offer different explanations for these phenomena. Since the rulers and much of the population of ancient Mari were Amorites, a people of West Semitic origin, the linguistic similarities between Mari and the Bible may be attributed to their use of languages from the same language family. Furthermore, since language and culture may be considered inextricably bound together, it is only natural that we should find similarities between cultures using related languages. The common opinion is that the culture of Mari and that of the Bible are both part of the larger group of Western Semites in ancient West Asia and thus hold in common certain terms and usages, even in some cases similarities of custom and cultural practice. Without physical evidence which directly connects the two cultures, the most the linguistic argument can show is that the two are products of a common cultural milieu.

Bibliography. *Archives royales de Mari,* 1-27 (Paris, 1946-93); A. Malamat, "Prophecy at Mari," in *The Place Is Too Small for Us,* ed. R. P. Gordon (Winona Lake, 1995), 50-73; G. D. Young, ed., *Mari in Retrospect* (Winona Lake, 1992).

CLIFFORD MARK MCCORMICK

MARIAMME (Gk. *Mariámmē*)
(also MARIAMNE)
See HEROD (FAMILY).

MARISA (Gk. *Marisa*)
See MARESHAH (PLACE).

MARK

A goal or target. Paul set his aim on a lofty "mark" (Gk. *skopós*), a future goal to be attained (Phil. 3:14; cf. the cognate verb in v. 17; Rom. 16:17). Jonathan (1 Sam. 20:20) devised a plan with David that involved his shooting arrows at a prearranged target (Heb. *maṭṭārâ*). Job felt as if he were the target of God's archers (Job 16:12; cf. Lam. 3:12).

More frequently the term designates some sort of deliberate body marking, such as a scar, tattoo, or brand, that makes the bearer readily identifiable. The "mark (Heb. *'ôṯ*) of Cain" (Gen. 4:15), probably a brand or tattoo, served as a special sign to protect him from a vengeful death. Circumcision is the distinctive physical mark of Jewish males; indeed, it is a "sign *('ôṯ)* of the covenant" (Gen. 17:11). Body markings in the form of tattoos *(qa'ăqa')* are explicitly forbidden to the Israelites (Lev. 19:28), as are other forms of bodily disfiguration (21:5; Deut. 14:1). In Ezekiel's account of his vision, the ones who grieved over the idolatry in the temple were marked on the forehead with the Hebrew letter *taw* so that they would be passed over and spared by the executioners (Ezek. 9:1-6; cf. Exod. 12:13). The "mark (Gk. *cháragma*) of the beast" — the number 666, thought to be the numerological equivalent of Nero's name — authorizes its bearers to conduct business (Rev. 13:14-18); however it also marks those who submit to the beast for certain destruction (14:9-11). "The marks *(stígmata)* of Jesus" Paul bore on his body (Gal. 6:17) were probably not the scars resulting from Jesus' crucifixion, but were more likely scars that remained from the many beatings he suffered during his mission work (2 Cor. 11:23-27; cf. Acts 14:19).

JEFFREY T. TUCKER

MARK, GOSPEL OF

The shortest of the canonical Gospels. Mark gained prominence in late 19th- and 20th-century scholarship partly because of the consensus that it was the first written Gospel. Before the 19th century Mark suffered from benign neglect because almost all of its stories are contained in Matthew and/or Luke, who have a great deal of other useful material besides; the reigning view, first formulated by Augustine, was that Mark was an abbreviation of one or both of the other Synoptics. In the second half of the 19th century, however, Markan priority became the critical orthodoxy, a position it has retained to the present day, despite occasional challenges.

Convinced that Mark was the first Gospel, late 19th-century scholarship seized on it as the starting-point for reconstruction of the historical Jesus, but this approach suffered two severe blows at the beginning of the 20th century. In 1901 William Wrede argued strongly that the so-called "messianic secret motif," according to which the Markan Jesus hides his identity by silencing demons, disciples, and people whom he has healed (e.g., Mark 1:25, 34, 44; 3:12; 5:43; 8:30; 9:9), was not primarily a reflection of the practice of the historical Jesus but a creation of the early Church, which was trying to explain why Jesus' messiahship was unknown in his own day. Although this particular solution to the "messianic secret" problem has been challenged in recent scholarship, most critics would agree that the motif does to a considerable extent express the theology of the Church rather than a custom of Jesus. In 1919 Karl Ludwig Schmidt further undermined the historicity of Mark by his contention that the links between the individual Markan passages are largely the invention of the Evangelist himself, who strung together individual oral traditions; Mark is not, therefore, a reliable guide to the chronology of Jesus' ministry. This claim, too, has been widely accepted.

These challenges to Markan historicity, however, did not diminish interest in the Gospel, especially after World War II and the advent of redaction criticism, which emphasized the theological concerns of the Evangelists. These concerns were analyzed by seeing how each Evangelist edited his sources, an analysis which is more difficult in Mark's case than in those of Matthew and Luke, since the sources have to be reconstructed entirely from the Gospel itself. Recent years have seen increasing frustration with the speculativeness of this source reconstruction and the wide variance in the results, including even disagreement about the basic question of whether the Markan editing was extensive and creative or minimal and mechanical. Most, however, would agree that Mark took a crucial step by tying the traditions about Jesus together in a connected story, although he may have had a partial precedent in a narrative about Jesus' suffering and death that he incorporated into his Gospel.

But who was Mark, who took the fateful step of writing a Gospel? Papias, a bishop of Hierapolis in Asia Minor in the first part of the 2nd century who is quoted by Eusebius (*HE* 3.39.15), identifies Mark as "Peter's interpreter"; according to Papias, Mark was not himself an eyewitness of Jesus but a later Christian who made an arrangement of the Lord's oracles on the basis of Peter's preaching, presumably in Rome after Peter's death. It is logical to assume that Papias thinks this "Mark" is the only person of that name known from the NT, the "John Mark" alluded to in Acts (12:12, 25; 15:36-41) and the Pauline correspondence (Phlm. 24; Col. 4:10; 2 Tim. 4:11), a cousin of Barnabas and companion of Barnabas and Paul on their missionary journeys.

Many scholars, however, are skeptical about Papias' testimony. Its main point, the connection of Mark with Peter, has come under critical attack, since there does not seem to be anything particularly Petrine about Mark; if any Gospel concentrates especially on Peter it is Matthew rather than Mark (cf. Matt. 16:17-19; 17:24-27), and the Petrine connection could be an attempt to reconcile two wings of the Church by linking with Peter a known associate of Paul. Whether or not the author was the John Mark of Acts is also disputed. On the one hand, some 2nd-century Church leaders were interested in linking the canonical Gospels with known NT figures such as John Mark in order to refute the claims of the Gnostics for their own gospels, and Papias' testimony reveals this sort of apologetic bias, which might cast doubt on its reliability. There are in the Gospel, moreover, apparent mistakes about Palestinian geography (e.g., 7:31) and Jewish customs (e.g., v. 3) which some think disqualify the author from being John Mark, a Jewish native of Jerusalem. On the other hand, John Mark does not cut a particularly creditable figure in Acts (cf. esp. Acts 13:13; 15:36-41); if a totally fictional link were being created with an early Church figure, one might think that a more suitable candidate could have been found. Geographical ignorance, moreover, even about one's own country, was even more common in antiquity than it is today, so that Mark's apparent mistakes do not necessarily mean that he is a foreigner; and it is also possible that 7:31 is intentionally describing a geographically unrealistic but theologically significant tour of gentile regions. The exaggerated statement in 7:3 that not just the Pharisees but "all the Jews" wash their hands before eating is paralleled in Ep. Arist. 305, which is unquestionably by a Jewish author. The most reasonable verdict on the theory that the author of the Gospel is John Mark, then, is "not proven" — but not disproved either.

Papias' implication that the Gospel was written in Rome has won a more sympathetic hearing. The Markan Jesus lays great stress on the necessity of suffering for the sake of the good news, and he prophesies that his followers will undergo unparalleled persecution (e.g., 8:34; 10:30; 13:9-13, 19-20). Most scholars believe that to some extent these warnings and the Gospel's concentration on Jesus' suffering and death reflect the situation of Mark and of the community for which he writes. For some, this situation lies in the best-known 1st-century persecution of Christians, that instigated by the Emperor Nero against Roman followers of Jesus in 64 C.E. Others, however, relate the persecution envisaged to that which, it is claimed, engulfed Christians as a result of the war of Palestinian Jews against the Romans in 66-73. There is no direct evidence for such a persecution, but Mark seems to know of or to foresee the Roman destruction of the temple in 70 C.E. (13:1-2), and the references to "wars and rumors of war," "false messiahs and false prophets," and the "desolating sacrilege" (13:7, 14, 22) can all be related to occurrences during the revolt. Some of those who emphasize the background in the Jewish War place Mark close to Palestine, either in Galilee or, more frequently, in Syria; such a location, however, is not absolutely necessary, since the war was well known throughout the empire. There is no consensus on the issue of provenance, but most would locate the composition of the Gospel in temporal proximity to the Jewish War.

What is clearer is that the Gospel is addressed to a group that is predominantly non-Jewish (7:3), going through intense suffering (13:9-23), and needing to be strengthened in its faith. The frequent obtuseness of the Markan disciples, which is a striking feature of the Gospel (e.g., 4:13; 6:52; 7:18; 8:14-21), may point to misunderstandings of the faith that were widespread within Mark's community. In the 1960s and 1970s some scholars theorized that these misunderstandings were related to the view that Jesus was a "divine man," a type of Hellenistic miracle worker with whom believers were supposed to be united in glory. Mark, according to this theory, opposed the theology of glory, which he associated with Peter, the Twelve, and the Jerusalem church, by means of his own theology of the Cross. He did this by discrediting the disciples and their miracle-based faith, emphasizing crucifixion over resurrection, and relativizing the messianic title of exaltation, "Son of God," in favor of a title associated with suffering, "Son of Man" (e.g., 14:61-62). This interpretation, however, has been attacked from a number of sides. There seems to have been no fixed concept of "the divine man" in antiquity. It would, moreover, be odd that Mark presents Jesus' miracles in such numbers and detail in the first half of the Gospel, or that he places the acclamation of Jesus as "Son of God" at key points in the narrative (1:11; 9:7; 15:39), if he thought that miracles and the "Son of God" title were basically misleading.

Rather than chasing chimerical "divine men," it is probably more illuminating to compare Mark with ancient Jewish apocalyptic works such as Daniel or some of the Qumran scrolls. Such apocalyptic works often arose out of situations of persecution and suffering similar to that which Mark and his community seem to be experiencing. Apocalypticists believed that they were living in the end time, and that the very intensity of the suffering all around them was a sign that God was about to intervene decisively on the side of the righteous (cf. Dan. 12:1). These beliefs are strongly paralleled in Mark 13 and elsewhere in the Gospel (e.g., 9:1), although some exegetes have attempted to evade this conclusion by taking out of context Jesus' statement that, when the apocalyptic woes begin, the end will not yet have come (13:7). Like Mark, apocalyptic thinkers believed that God had revealed to the elect community "the mystery of the kingdom of God" which he had concealed from outsiders (e.g., CD 2:12-13; cf. Mark 4:10-12). In the short time of trial remaining before the end, however, Satan could blind even the elect (cf. 1QS 3:22-23), as seems to happen at various points to the Markan disciples; but apocalypticists also shared Mark's belief that those who endured to the end would be saved (cf. Dan. 12:12). The Markan twist is to portray a Messiah who himself seems to fall under the power of apocalyptic darkness and death, yet to insist that God has won the decisive eschatological battle against the forces of evil and inaugurated the new age of light by means of this very eclipse of messianic power (Mark 15:33-39).

Despite the general disfavor of the "divine man" approach, nearly all exegetes would agree with its partisans that the Cross is central to the Evangelist's theology and that Martin Kähler's description of the Gospels as "passion narratives with extended introductions" applies especially to Mark. This is particularly obvious if Mark deliberately ends his Gospel after the empty tomb narrative in 16:8, without describing resurrection appearances — a view that is defensible, since the conclusions that follow 16:8 in many present-day Bibles are clearly secondary, and biblical narratives often have open endings. It cannot be proven, however, since the original ending may have been lost. To be sure, even if the Gospel does end at 16:8, Mark seems to be aware of resurrection appearances, which are implied in 14:28 and 16:7; but he holds back from describing them, perhaps in order to put more emphasis on the Crucifixion as the apocalyptic turning point between the old age of evil and the new age of God's dominion (but cf. 9:9).

An ending at 16:8 would also be compatible with other enigmatic features of the Gospel, such as Jesus' seemingly arbitrary exclusion of outsiders from reflection (4:10-12), his apparently excessive anger at his disciples (8:14-21), and the strange tale about the young man who ran away naked (14:51-52) — features that Matthew and Luke regularly emend or eliminate, and that have led the literary critic Frank Kermode to compare Mark's riddling narratives to those of Kafka. These enigmas also help to explain the fascination that Mark holds for some modern theologians, who find in the Gospel's very gaps, incongruities, and paradoxes a mirror of the difficulty of speaking about a transcendent God in a broken world.

See SYNOPTIC GOSPELS; PASSION NARRATIVE.

Bibliography. S. P. Kealy, *Mark's Gospel* (New York, 1982); F. Kermode, *The Genesis of Secrecy* (Cambridge, Mass., 1979); J. D. Kingsbury, *The Christology of Mark's Gospel* (Philadelphia, 1983); J. Marcus, "The Jewish War and the *Sitz im Leben* of Mark," *JBL* 111 (1992): 441-62; W. R. Telford, ed., *The Interpretation of Mark,* 2nd ed. (Edinburgh, 1995); C. M. Tuckett, ed., *The Messianic Secret* (Philadelphia, 1983). JOEL MARCUS

MARK, JOHN (Gk. *Iōánnēs Márkos*)
An early Jewish Christian who, in canonical literature, is identified explicitly as a companion of Barnabas and Paul, implicitly as a companion of Peter, and who, in later tradition, came to be regarded as the author of the Gospel of Mark. The NT provides few facts about John Mark, called by both his Jewish (Gk. *Iōánnēs,* from Heb. *yôḥānān*) and Roman (Gk. *Márkos,* from Lat. *Marcus*) names only in Acts (12:12, 25; 15:37).

John Mark was the son of Mary, at whose house in Jerusalem Christians gathered for prayer, and to whose house Peter came after his rescue from prison (Acts 12:12). After Barnabas and Paul elected to have John Mark accompany them on their journey, for some unexplained reason he parted from their company in Cyprus and returned to Jerusalem (Acts 13:13). Paul refused to take John Mark on the next journey, even though Barnabas wanted him to come (Acts 15:37), and this resulted in a parting of the ways: Barnabas and John Mark went to Cyprus, while Paul and Silas traveled to points in Asia Minor (vv. 39-41).

Paul himself does not speak of those events, but in two letters attributed to him and supposedly written from Rome Paul refers to "Mark the cousin of Barnabas" (Col. 4:10) and a "Mark" as being one of his fellow workers (Phlm. 24). That these references are to the same person, John Mark, is not implausible — evidence enough for some scholars to conclude that John Mark and Paul reconciled their differences prior to Paul's imprisonment in Rome.

A Mark is mentioned in two other NT epistles, but because both letters are regarded as pseudepigraphs by many scholars, it is less than certain that these are trustworthy references to John Mark. 2 Tim. 4:11 builds upon the more reliable tradition that John Mark was a companion of Paul, while 1 Pet. 5:13 reflects the later tradition that a Mark was a companion of Peter, his "son" in the spiritual sense, in Rome ("Babylon"). Although it cannot be established that the latter is a specific reference to John Mark — who, it can be inferred from Acts 12, knew Peter — early church tradition clearly assumes that all the NT passages name the same figure.

According to Eusebius (*HE* 3.39.15), Papias repeated the tradition that Mark served as Peter's "interpreter" in Rome and that he recorded the Apostle's recollections of the Lord's words and deeds. However, this is not adequate proof that John Mark wrote the Gospel of Mark. Other church traditions claim that Mark was the first to evangelize Egypt and the founder of Alexandrian Christianity. Later legends depict Mark's martyrdom and reburial in Venice. That John Mark is the "young man" of Mark 14:51, and that both the Last Supper and the events of Pentecost occurred in his mother's home, are pure conjectures.

Bibliography. B. T. Holmes, "Luke's Description of John Mark," *JBL* 54 (1935): 63-72; V. Taylor, *The Gospel According to St. Mark,* 2nd ed. (Grand Rapids, 1981), 26-31. JEFFREY T. TUCKER

MARK ANTONY
Marcus Antonius (ca. 83-30 B.C.E.), Roman statesman who served as triumvir along with Octavian and Lepidus. He appointed Herod the Great as vassal king of Palestine, in reponse to which Herod named the refortified tower at Jerusalem Antonia in his honor. Antony and Cleopatra VII were defeated by Octavian at Actium in 31 and fled to Alexandria, where he committed suicide a year later as Octavian advanced on the city.

MARKETPLACE
Local markets in the ancient Near East were not always open areas in the middle of the city. Sometimes an area on the edge of the city or near the city gate was used (2 Kgs. 7:1). Marketplaces in major cities were adorned with columns and statues. Obviously the market was a place of commerce, with various shops offering needed commodities. The NT indicates that the marketplace could serve as a public forum for other activities as well, such as the hiring of laborers (Matt. 20:3), the play of children (Luke 7:32), legal complaints (Acts 16:19), and religious discussions (17:17; cf. v. 5). Pausanius *Descr. Gr.* 1.12-17 provides an ancient description of the *agorá* at Athens. DAVID L. TURNER

MAROTH (Heb. *mārôṯ*)
A town in the Shephelah, or lowland, of Judah (Mic. 1:12), possibly the same as Maarath (Khirbet Qufin; Josh. 15:59).

MARRIAGE
In ancient Israel and the Greco-Roman world, marriage signified many different social practices of household formation. Marriage is one expression of kinship and family patterns, in which typically a man and at least one woman cohabitate publicly and permanently as a basic social unit. Within most of the societies depicted in the OT and NT, the household or family created by such a marriage represents the extent of one man's ownership and control of people and property. These households interact with each other in the larger society on more or less equal terms; both custom and law respect a man's authority to operate within the household and to deal with other households on the basis of the relative social hierarchical position between the men of the households. Furthermore, the married man possesses the privilege of sexual access to the married women (and perhaps others) within the household, as limited by taboo and law. The children born of such sexual unions belong to the man and are part of the same household, under

the same terms. Thus marriage forms a unit that is social, economic, political, and sexual.

Hebrew has no particular words for "husband" or "wife." The words that are translated as such in the OT are almost always the same words more frequently translated "man" and "woman." In some versions of the OT, Heb. *ba'al,* "lord," is occasionally translated "husband." It is thus very difficult to assess the extent to which marriage functioned as a free-standing social institution within ancient Israel. Clearly, ancient Israel organized most if not all of its households around a man, and such households included both women and children under the authority of the man.

There is no clear evidence for the age at which an Israelite man or woman married or entered households, although it is likely that Israelites were involved in married, sexually active family life in their mid-teens. Likewise, the OT records no wedding ceremonies that might depict how marriages happened. It is not even known if there were wedding ceremonies in most cases, or if such occasions occurred only among wealthier families. Women may well have joined households shortly after menarche or even before; men may have waited several years before forming households of their own, because of the economic requirements for founding and maintaining households. Although there is only rare discussion in the OT of how households were formed, men may have purchased women as wives from the children of other households, and thus the entry of women into households may have been a negotiated transaction (with or without financial ramifications) between men of two households, in the roles of father and husband.

Many of the OT texts, especially in the Pentateuch and the Deuteronomistic history, depict households with one man and multiple adult women. This marriage pattern is polygyny, a type of polygamy in which there are multiple women. This pattern maximizes fertility rates, while tending to favor the political power of the sole male as leader of the household. It is not known if polygynous households were the norm in Israel or if they occurred only among the wealthier households, such as those that are more frequently represented in the extant literature. When polygyny did occur, it is likely that the women were of different ages. The household may have begun with one man and one woman, adding other women as the financial resources of the household expanded. Women's life expectancy was much shorter than that for men, and pregnancy was among the leading causes of death for Israelite women. In this situation, polygyny became a way to maintain the supply of women in the household as well as to increase its fertility. If the man of the household outlived the first wife by many years, then there may have been a great age difference between the man of the household and subsequent wives. Such a version of polygyny shares some parallels with sequential marriages.

The OT uses marriage as a metaphor to describe God's relationship with the people. In Hos. 1–3; Ezek. 16 the images contain vivid charges of betrayal and accounts of sexual violence. Separating from God is condemned (Mal. 2:10-16). Isa. 62:4-5 depicts the beauty of God's marriage to the people.

In the Hellenistic and Roman worlds polygyny was rare. The NT depicts only monogamous marriages. The Greco-Roman world practiced wedding ceremonies, and the NT records a story of Jesus at a wedding in Cana (John 2) as well as parables by Jesus about weddings. Average age at marriage had probably increased, perhaps into the early 20s, but there is little direct evidence for age at marriage of any NT figures. The NT portrays a relatively large number of single persons, although it cannot be determined if they were persons who had never married, had been previously married, or lived apart from spouses. Paul's marital status remains uncertain; as a trained Jewish religious leader, it would have been exceedingly rare for him to have not been married, and yet he advises persons considering marriage that it would be better to be single like himself (1 Cor. 7:8). Likewise, Peter's marital status remains problematic; his mother-in-law is mentioned (Mark 1:30 par.), but not a wife, making it likely that he lived apart from his wife, but it remains possible that he was a widower who had assumed some financial responsibilities for his deceased wife's mother.

The latter portions of the NT offer several household codes, which share many features in common with popular wisdom in the contemporary Greco-Roman culture (Col. 3:18–4:1; Eph. 5:21–6:9; 1 Pet. 2:11–3:12; 1 Tim. 2:8-15; 5:1-2; 6:1-2; Tit. 2:1-10; 3:1). These codes encourage wives to submit to husbands, continuing patterns of male dominance within households that were finding a number of exceptions in the diverse social patterns of the day. These codes privilege marriage and limit marriage to one man and one woman.

JON L. BERQUIST

MARRIAGE PRESENT

The gift (Heb. *mōhar*) a husband extended to the father of his bride. Shechem offers to give a "marriage present" to Jacob in exchange for his daughter Dinah (Gen. 34:12). David, unable to give either property or money, is permitted to make a gruesome "settlement" of slain Philistines for Michal, Saul's younger daughter (1 Sam. 18:25). The compensation to be paid by one who seduced a virgin may have been considered a marriage present (Exod. 22:16-17[MT 15-16]; cf. Deut. 22:29); though treated among the laws concerning property, this does not imply that the bride was to be considered such (she herself could own property; cf. Josh. 15:18-19 = Judg. 1:14-15). Rather than a purchase price intended to compensate the bride's family for the loss of their daughter and subsequent offspring, the groom's marriage present was merely reciprocation for the dowry, thus completing the exchange as expected in Israel's "gift economy."

ALLEN C. MYERS

MARS HILL
See AREOPAGUS.

MARSENA (Heb. *marsĕnāʾ*)
One of the seven nobles of King Ahasuerus who had most direct access to the king (Esth. 1:14).

MARTHA (Gk. *Mártha*)
Along with her sister Mary and her brother Lazarus, a close friend and disciple of Jesus (John 11:5). Martha (from Aram. *mārṯāʾ*, "lady") appears early in the Gospels as a worried host preoccupied with preparing a meal for Jesus. Her sister had chosen to listen to Jesus' teachings (Luke 10:38-42). Jesus gently rebukes Martha for being overly concerned about "many things," whereas only one was necessary. One plausible interpretation is that Martha was trying to prepare a multi-course meal for her honored guest and Jesus was suggesting that only one course was needed. Contrary to many interpreters, there is no comparison in this passage between Mary's listening to Jesus' teachings and Martha's serving. He says that Mary had chosen the "good" part, not the better.

Martha's next appearance involves the sickness and death of her brother Lazarus. After sending for Jesus she meets him with the gentle rebuke that if he had been there her brother would not have died. Jesus challenges her by asking if she believes that whoever believes in him will never die. She responds with one of the more lofty confessions in all the NT: "I believe that you are the Christ, the Son of God, the one coming into the world" (John 11:27).

In Martha's final appearance she is serving a meal to Jesus, Lazarus, and other, unnamed guests (John 12:2). Some interpreters locate this meal in the house of Simon the leper, assuming that this story is a variant of Mark 14:3-9. This interpretation is tenuous for at least three reasons: Mark's time frame is two days before the Passover (Mark 14:1), whereas John's is six (John 12:1); the woman who anointed Jesus is not named in Mark; and in Mark Jesus' head is anointed, whereas in John his feet are anointed. JOE E. LUNCEFORD

MARTYR
A word transliterated from Gk. *mártys, martýrion, martyría,* "witness, testimony." The word originally referred to one who was a legal witness but came to refer to one whose testimony for Jesus ends in death (i.e., martyrdom). The word is used frequently in Acts to refer to the apostles as witnesses (Acts 1:8; 2:32; 3:15; 10:39). In Acts 5:32 the reference is to one who is willing to suffer as a part of his or her testimony for Jesus. In the Apocalypse the word connotes more the idea that one dies because of his witness or testimony (Rev. 2:13; 17:6; 22:20; KJV "martyr"). Later use of the word implies only dying for one's faith in Christ (cf. Ignatius *Rom.* 2; Mart. Pol. 14:12; 17:3). EDWARD P. MYERS

MARY (Gk. *María, Mariám*)
1. Mary the mother of Jesus. Biographical information regarding Mary is limited. According to

Madonna and Child, **oil by Albrecht Dürer (1471-1528); Uffizi, Florence** (Alinari/Art Resource, N.Y.)

Luke, her home is the insignificant Galilean village of Nazareth (Luke 1:26), but Matthew places her in Nazareth only after the birth of Jesus (Matt. 2:1, 23). Both Matthew and Luke identify Joseph as Mary's husband (Matt. 1:24; Luke 1:27; 2:4-5). References to the brothers and sisters of Jesus (Mark 3:31-35; 6:3; Matt. 12:46-50; 13:55-56; Luke 8:19-21; John 2:12; Acts 1:14) indicate that she and Joseph have additional children, although the later Christian tradition of Mary's perpetual virginity leads some to speculate that these are children of Joseph by a previous marriage or cousins of Jesus. Since Luke describes the offering of Mary and Joseph following Jesus' birth as turtledoves or pigeons rather than the more costly sheep (Luke 2:24; cf. Lev. 12:8), she probably is from a poor family that managed little beyond subsistence income.

Even these slender details about Mary's life are uncertain. The insistence of Christian tradition on identifying Jesus with David may well influence Matthew when he locates Mary and Joseph in Bethlehem prior to Jesus' birth, since Bethlehem is closely identified with David. Luke's partiality for the poor may be at work when he locates Jesus' own family among the poor.

However obscure biographical information regarding Mary remains, all of the canonical Gospels make reference to her, and the portrait rendered in each is distinctive. In Mark, widely regarded as the earliest of the Gospels, Mary appears in one brief scene and is mentioned in another. Identified only as "his mother," Mary and Jesus' brothers seek Jesus, prompting his response that his family consists of those who do the will of God (Mark 3:31-35). In Mark 6:3 residents of Nazareth who find their neighbor Jesus astonishing exclaim, "Is not this the carpenter, the son of Mary . . . ?"

Matthew contains parallels to both these scenes (Matt. 12:46-50; 13:54-58), but here Mary appears as early as the genealogy of Jesus that introduces ch. 1. Her name occurs at the end of the genealogy, following those of four other women: Tamar, Rahab, Ruth, and "the wife of Uriah" or Bathsheba (Matt. 1:3, 5-6). The unusual composition of this group of women has prompted speculation for centuries, as some interpreters have identified the women as sinners, Gentiles, or participants in irregular sexual unions. At the very least, the fact that Mary is grouped with these four women suggests that some scandal will plague her story as well.

Two crises occur in the Matthean birth narrative, and both involve Mary. In response to the report of Mary's pregnancy prior to marriage, Joseph plans to dissolve his relationship with her (Matt. 1:18-25). The action Joseph contemplates would have devastating social and economic consequences for Mary and her unborn child. In the second half of the birth narrative (Matt. 2:1-23) King Herod attempts to have the infant Jesus killed; throughout this section, Matthew refers to "the child with Mary his mother" (2:11) or "the child and his mother" (vv. 13, 14, 20, 21), thereby suggesting that Herod's threat to Jesus also includes his mother, Mary. In both crises, the one initiated by Joseph and the other by Herod, angelic intervention rescues Mary and Jesus. Throughout the narrative, Mary speaks not a word and takes no independent action. She exists in the story to reveal the dangers surrounding Jesus even before his birth.

The birth narrative in Luke's Gospel consists of a series of parallel scenes which compare and contrast the birth of Jesus with that of John the Baptist. Here Mary appears both more often and in more active roles than in Matthew. When the angel Gabriel announces to this unmarried young woman that she is to bear a child, she responds with the consent of a disciple, "Here am I, the servant of the Lord" (Luke 1:38). In the presence of her relative Elizabeth, Mary interprets the anticipated birth in prophetic language that borrows from the OT figure Hannah (Luke 1:46-55; cf. 1 Sam. 2:1-10). Following the birth itself (Luke 2:1-7) and the visit of shepherds to the infant Jesus, Luke reports that Mary reflected on the events (v. 19; cf. v. 51).

Luke draws attention to the faithfulness of Mary and Joseph. They conform to the Law by having Jesus circumcised, and they take him as a newborn to the Jerusalem temple (Luke 2:21-35). They also go to Jerusalem each year for Passover (Luke 2:41-52). Luke makes no further reference to Joseph, but Mary appears in 8:19-21 (par. Mark 3:31-35). In Luke's second volume, she is among those followers of Jesus who gather in Jerusalem in anticipation of Pentecost (Acts 1:14).

John refers to "the mother of Jesus," but never uses the name Mary. She appears in two scenes, first at the wedding in Cana (John 2:1-12), where she sets events in motion by telling Jesus that there is no wine and by instructing the servants to do whatever Jesus says. Jesus' response to Mary ("Woman, what concern is that to you and to me?" John 2:4) is highly ambiguous. It can be read as a rejection of any role for Mary in Jesus' ministry, but it may be no more than another element in the enigma created by this highly complex and symbolic scene.

Mary appears again only at the Crucifixion. Along with three other women and the figure John calls the "beloved disciple," she witnesses the death of Jesus. Jesus presents the beloved disciple and Mary to one another with the words, "Woman, here is your son," and "here is your mother" (John 19:25-27). Some scholars argue that this is only an act of filial devotion, while others insist that Mary plays a highly symbolic role here in that she represents the Church and its task of nurturing Jesus' disciples.

None of the remaining NT writings demonstrates an interest in Mary. Paul identifies Jesus as "born of a woman" (Gal. 4:4) and "descended from David according to the flesh" (Rom. 1:3), expressions that serve to emphasize the normal means of Jesus' birth and his place in Israel. Rev. 12:1-6 depicts a woman "clothed with the sun," who gives birth to a messianic figure, but here the focus is on an apocalyptic confrontation rather than on the mother of Jesus.

If NT writings display little interest in Mary's life, other early Christians soon responded with stories that supplied missing information and responded to charges that Jesus' birth was illegitimate. The Protevangelium of James, written by the end of the 2nd century, draws on the language of the OT and the canonical birth narratives to construct a story about the conception, birth, and nurture of Mary. She is the child of the elderly and wealthy Anna and Joachim, and is raised in the Jerusalem temple so that her purity may be protected. At the onset of puberty, she is betrothed to the elderly Joseph. When she becomes pregnant, both Mary and Joseph undergo the test of bitter waters (prescribed in Num. 5:11-31 only for women accused of adultery) to prove their innocence. So exceptional is Mary's purity that she remains a virgin even following the birth of Jesus. Although the Protevangelium of James consists largely of late tradition that has little claim to reliability, it has exerted great influence on Christian imagination.

2. Mary Magdalene. The NT writings identify this Mary consistently by her town of origin (Magdala, on the western shore of the Sea of Galilee), not by reference to a husband or son (as in "Mary the wife of Clopas"). Probably this identification means that she has neither and that she is in control of her own property (cf. Luke 8:2-3 for the comment that Mary Magdalene and other women provided for Jesus from their own resources). Sometimes interpreters see in the association of Mary with Magdala already a hint of a bad reputation, but that exaggerates a comment in later Jewish sources about Magdala.

All four of the canonical Gospels place Mary Magdalene in the narratives of Jesus' death and resurrection. The Synoptic Gospels name Mary Magdalene first among the women present, and John draws attention to her importance through her encounter with the risen Jesus. This emphasis on Mary Magdalene suggests that she was highly revered in the memory of early Christians.

In Mark Mary Magdalene stands first in each list of the women who witness the crucifixion and burial of Jesus (Mark 15:40, 47), and who bring spices for anointing him, only to discover the empty grave (16:1). Mark explains that these women "used to follow him and provided for him," and that they had followed him to Jerusalem (Mark 15:41), all of which signals their faithfulness.

Matthew similarly identifies Mary Magdalene among the women who witnessed the Crucifixion, burial, and empty tomb (Matt. 27:56, 61; 28:1). In Matthew, by contrast with Mark, the women do not flee silently but run to tell the disciples, only to encounter the risen Lord themselves.

Luke alone introduces Mary prior to the crucifixion. In Luke 8:2 he describes Jesus' ministry to Galilee and notes that he was accompanied by the Twelve and by some women "who had been cured of evil spirits and infirmities," presumably by Jesus. Mary Magdalene, who stands first in the list that includes Joanna and Susanna, has been exorcised of seven demons. The fact that she has been demon-possessed, however, does not designate her as especially sinful, and so the tradition of identifying Mary Magdalene with the unnamed woman in Luke 7:36-50 is groundless. Luke also places women among those present at the crucifixion and burial of Jesus (Luke 23:27, 49, 55), but he does not identify them by name until the discovery of the empty tomb (24:10), and again Mary Magdalene is the first named.

Unlike the other Gospel writers, John places Mary Magdalene last among the women who witness Jesus' death (John 19:25). In this scene, however, John focuses attention on the mother of Jesus and her relationship to the beloved disciple, so that the order says nothing about the importance of Mary Magdalene. Indeed, she occupies a significant role in the Johannine Resurrection scene, for it is Mary Magdalene alone who discovers the empty tomb (John 20:1). She also becomes in John the first to encounter the risen Jesus and to proclaim the Resurrection to the other disciples (John 20:11-18).

3. Mary of Bethany. The Gospel of John identifies Mary of Bethany as the sister of Martha and Lazarus (John 11:1-44). Mary and Martha send a message to Jesus regarding their brother's illness, but he arrives only after Lazarus had already died. Following exchanges with both Martha and Mary, Jesus raises Lazarus from the dead. John also names Mary of Bethany as the woman who anoints Jesus with expensive perfume and who is criticized by Judas for so doing (John 12:1-8).

A story about Mary and Martha appears in Luke as well (Luke 10:38-42), although Luke does not associate them with either Lazarus or the village of Bethany, making an identification between the two sets of women uncertain. While Jesus is present in their home, Mary gives attention to his teaching (she "sat at the Lord's feet and listened"), while Martha tends to "many tasks." Martha asks Jesus to admonish Mary so that she might offer assistance, but Jesus responds that Mary has chosen the "better part," which will not be taken away.

4. Mary the mother of James and Joseph. The Synoptics name Mary "the mother of James and Joseph" or "James the younger and of Joses" among the women who witness the death of Jesus and who discover his tomb empty (Matt. 27:56, 61; 28:1; Mark 15:40, 47; 16:1; Luke 24:10).

5. Mary the wife of Clopas. Only John 19:25 refers to this Mary, who witnessed the crucifixion of Jesus along with Jesus' mother, her unnamed sister, and Mary Magdalene.

6. Mary the mother of John Mark. Acts 12:12 names Mary as the mother of John Mark. Because Luke refers to her house as a gathering place for believers in Jerusalem, she appears to be a woman of substantial means.

7. Mary of Rome. Among the persons greeted by Paul in Rom. 16 is Mary, whom he describes as having "worked very hard among you" (v. 6). Elsewhere that phrase applies to efforts made on behalf of the gospel, so that Mary may be among the Christian teachers or preachers in Rome (1 Cor. 15:10; Gal. 4:11).

Bibliography. R. E. Brown, K. P. Donfried, J. A. Fitzmyer, and J. Reumann, eds., *Mary in the New Testament* (Philadelphia, 1978); B. R. Gaventa, *Mary: Glimpses of the Mother of Jesus* (Columbia, S.C., 1995); C. Ricci, *Mary Magdalene and Many Others: Women Who Followed Jesus* (Minneapolis, 1994); B. Witherington, III, *Women in the Ministry of Jesus*. SNTSMS 51 (Cambridge, 1984).

Beverly Roberts Gaventa

MARY, GOSPEL OF

A 2nd- or 3rd-century gnostic Gospel, which survives in a severely damaged Coptic translation of the original Greek (P. Berolinensis 8502,1), as well as a Greek fragment (P. Rylands III 463). It presents Mary Magdalene as a revealer of secret wisdom in the post-Resurrection era. This wisdom is cosmological and soteriological in essence.

The text begins with a discourse between the Savior and the disciples on nature, sin, and ethics (1:1–9:5). Unity with the spiritual realm is central; an illness metaphor is used to explain this concept, and may reflect the Sophia myth so common in gnostic thought. The section ends with a peace wish, a warning, and an admonition to preach.

After a brief transition (9:6-24), the third section contains Mary's visions (10:1–17:7). Following the command to go preach, the disciples "wept greatly" over the suffering that they expected. Mary is then called on to speak. Her first vision discusses the nature of visions, and then, after a gap, a second vision presents a discourse on the ascent of the soul past the cosmic powers.

When Mary finishes her discourse, she is immediately challenged by Andrew and Peter (17:7-22). Her authority, as a woman, is questioned in this fourth section. In the fifth section Peter is rebuked by Levi (18:1–19:5). Peter is equated with "the adversaries" (i.e., the powers). Levi states that "the Savior made her worthy," thereby substantiating Mary's authority (thus rendering this Gospel important for feminist dialogue). After his retort, Levi instructs the group to "proclaim and preach."

Bibliography. K. L. King, G. W. MacRae, R. McL. Wilson, "The Gospel of Mary (BG 8502,*1*)," in *The Nag Hammadi Library in English*, ed. J. M. Robinson, 3rd ed. (San Francisco, 1988), 523-27; K. Rudolph, *Gnosis* (San Francisco, 1987); R. M. Wilson, "The New Testament in the Gnostic Gospel of Mary," *NTS* 3 (1957): 236-43. PHILIP L. TITE

MARY, GOSPEL OF THE BIRTH OF

A hostile anti-Jewish apocryphal book of the 2nd century C.E., attributed to the Gnostics (Lat. *Genna Marias*, "Genealogy" or "Descent of Mary"). It is known only from the reference in Epiphanius *Adv. haer.* 16.12.1-4.

MARY, REVELATION OF

A NT apocryphal apocalypse, extant in Greek, Armenian, Ethiopic, and Old Slavonic versions, and thought to be from the 9th century A.D. It shares a number of similarities with the Apocalypse of Paul. The Revelation of Mary depicts Mary, the mother of Jesus, on a visionary tour of Hades with the archangel Michael. Mary entreats Michael to show to her all the punishments given to sinners at death. Upon seeing each horrific scene, she asks for the causes of punishment. The sins include malicious talk, abortion, refusal to acknowledge the trinity, and not rising for Sunday worship. Although Mary's heart is grieved at the condition of all those whom she sees (with the exception of the Jews who had killed Jesus), it is not until she beholds the punishments of the Christians that she beseeches the Holy God on their behalf. At first Mary asks to be chastised for them in a substitutionary role. When this is denied, Michael, Moses, John, and Paul, together with the saints, join in pleading for mercy upon the Christians. Finally, God relents and Jesus is sent to earth to grant rest to the sinners (even though they had rejected him) on account of Mary.

MELISSA L. ARCHER

MARZEAH (Heb. *marzēaḥ*)

A ritual drinking feast known throughout the ancient Semitic would. Texts mentioning the *marzēaḥ* span three millennia, ranging from Ebla (24th century B.C.E.) to Madeba (6th century C.E.), with intervening attestations in Emar, Ugarit, Transjordan, Elephantine, Phoenicia, Habatea, Palmyra, and in the rabbinic literature.

The earliest substantial information comes from Ugarit, where the term denotes both the banquet and those who celebrated it. The latter comprised members *(mt mrzḥ)* with a leader *(rb)*, who levied dues, owned property, and had a patron deity. The substantial holdings included fields and vineyards, but the most important was the "*marzēaḥ* house" *(bt mrzḥ)*. The group's social importance is indicated by the size of its holdings, the number of witnesses to its transactions, and the granting of royal approval. Ugarit also provides a description of a divine *marzēaḥ*: in *KTU* 1.114 El invites the gods to his *marzēaḥ*, where they are urged to drink to the point of drunkenness; the feast ends with El collapsing in a state of intoxicated incontinence.

Although allowance must be made for divergence from place to place and over time, two common features can be discerned in subsequent instances of the *marzēaḥ*; the institution's social importance and the emphasis on drinking. In most places there is some mention of wine, often in large quantities, or at least drinking vessels, and more than once events are dated in relationship to the time of the banquet and/or the leader's presidency.

The social status of the *marzēaḥ* is evident in Amos 6. The prophet chastises the elite of Samaria (Amos 6:1) for their sumptuous banquets characterized by luxurious couches, choice meats, music, anointing with oil, and wine drunk by the bowlful (vv. 4-6). Amos announces that their *marzēaḥ* (NSRV "revelry") will end when they are taken into exile (Amos 6:7). In Jer. 16:5 the prophet is forbidden to enter the *marzēaḥ* house (not NRSV "house of mourning") to mourn those killed by the Babylonians; in v. 8 it is called "the drinking house" *(bêṯ-mišteh)*.

In light of the *marzēaḥ's* enduring significance elsewhere, it is surprising to find it mentioned only twice in the Bible. Various texts have been proposed as allusions but do not use the word (Isa. 28:1-13; Ezek. 39:17-20; Amos 4:1; cf. Isa. 56:9–57:13; Ezek. 8:7-13; Amos 2:7-8; 1 Cor. 11:20-22).

Bibliography. D. B. Bryan, *Texts Relating to the* Marzeaḥ (diss., Johns Hopkins, 1973); J. L. McLaughlin, "The *marzeaḥ* at Ugarit," *UF* 23 (1991): 265-81. JOHN L. MCLAUGHLIN

MASADA (Gk. *Masada*)

A rock fortress on an isolated high hill surrounded by precipitous cliffs and therefore nearly impregnable, located 16.5 km. (10 mi.) S of En-gedi on the western shore of the Dead Sea, across from the Lisan Peninsula. Scholars generally agree that it was the Hasmonean high priest Alexander Janneus (103-76 B.C.E.) who originally constructed the fortress, which consisted of four small palaces. In 40 B.C.E., under siege by Antigonus and the Parthians, Herod's family remained at Masada while Herod fled to Rome. His family nearly died from lack of water, but a sudden summer storm saved their lives (Josephus *Ant.* 14.390-91). Herod rebuilt the fortress, adding eight cisterns, storehouses, a palace-villa with frescoes, three terraces, and a casement wall ca. 1280 m. (1400 yds.) long with 110 rooms inside its walls and towers. In 66 C.E., during the First Jewish Revolt against the Romans, the Zealots seized Masada from a Roman garrison (Josephus *BJ* 2.408). Then, under Eleazar, they held off a prolonged Roman siege by Flavius Silva and the Tenth legion until 73/4 C.E., several years after the destruction of the temple in Jerusalem. According to Josephus, 960 Sicarii and Zealots, all the inhabitants except two women and five children, committed suicide rather than fall into the hands of the Romans (*BJ* 7.389-400). This is similar to his own experience in 68 B.C.E. when, as general of the Jewish forces in Galilee, he was defeated by Vespasian; but while other Jews in hiding with him chose to commit suicide rather than be captured by the Romans, Josephus surrendered (*BJ* 3.387-92).

Excavations by Yigael Yadin in 1963-64 yielded many remains from the Herodian period: inscriptions, ostraca, "freedom" coins from the First Jewish Revolt, and a *mikveh* (ritual bath). Also discovered were fragments of biblical and nonbiblical manuscripts similar to those found in the caves near Qumran: Leviticus, Deuteronomy, Ezekiel, a scroll of Pss. 81-85, Ps. 150, the Songs of the Sabbath Sacrifice, and Hebrew original manuscripts of Sirach and Jubilees.

Bibliography. Y. Yadin, "The Excavation of Masada — 1963-64: Preliminary Report," *IEJ* 15 (1965): 1-120; *Masada: Herod's Fortress and the Zealots' Last Stand* (New York, 1966).

LYNNE ALCOTT KOGEL

MASH (Heb. *maš*)
A son of Aram and descendant of Shem (Gen. 10:23; LXX Gk. *Mosoch*). He was the eponymous ancestor of an Aramaic tribe perhaps to be associated with Mt. Masius (Keraga Dag/Tur Abdin), a mountain range near the headwaters of the Euphrates River, or with Akk. *Māšu*, the Lebanon and Anti-Lebanon ranges. The parallel passage (1 Chr. 1:17) reads Meshech (**2**).

MASHAL (Heb. *māšāl*) **(GENRE)**
From the Hebrew root *mšl*, "represent," "be like," or "compare." A plural form, the Hebrew name of the book of Proverbs, occurs at Prov. 1:1; 10:1; 25:1. Here the term implies a pithy and ambiguous saying that requires substantial unpacking and interpretation in order to understand the multiple levels on which a comparison lay. Further, the term may signal the principle by which various sayings in Proverbs seem to have come together: what seems to guide its location in any given collection is the degree to which a saying shares some characteristic (usually verbal) with an adjacent saying.

In Ezek. 17:2 the term is found in combination with the root *ḥwd*, the nominal form of which is translated "riddle." In this instance the root *mšl* is often translated "allegory." Here the usage is probably closer to the notion of parable. In this light, several OT narratives seem to represent this notion even though they are not called *māšāl*. Judg. 9; 2 Sam. 12, 14, as well as 1 Kgs. 20 all qualify as parabolic narratives. Common to this larger sense of *māšāl* is the use of a brief story in order to force a character in the story (as well as the reader) to interpret events in view of one's own context. Characteristic of these *mĕšālîm* are the multiple interpretations suggested by narrative associations with their current settings as well as with other OT material. In rabbinic Judaism the *māšāl* emerges as a complex form of biblical interpretation in which a passage is elaborated with a story that begins "This is like. . . ." The NT parable is often understood as a form of *māšāl* but, in truth, represents only a fraction of the forms to which *māšāl* applies in the OT.

LARRY L. LYKE

MASHAL (Heb. *māšāl*) **(PLACE)**
(also MISHAL)
A levitical town in Asher (1 Chr. 6:74[MT 59]). Elsewhere it is called Mishal.

MASKIL (Heb. *maśkîl*)
A technical word used in the titles of Pss. 32, 42, 44, 45, 52-55, 74, 78, 88, 89, 142, apparently designating something about either the content or performance of each psalm. Suggested translations include "meditation," "a didactic poem," "a psalm of understanding," "a choice or delicate, skillfully composed song." The word may be derived from Heb. *śākal*, translated in the Wisdom Literature variously as "skillful," "wise," to teach," but this meaning seems appropriate only in Pss. 32, 78. More likely the word refers to some part of the musical performance of the psalm (cf. 2 Chr. 30:21-22).

MICHAEL D. HILDENBRAND

MASONS
Workers skilled in cutting stone for use in walls and buildings. Although ordinary men cut stone for use in their homes and other small-scale projects, skilled masons (Heb. *gāḏar, ḥāṣaḇ, ḥāraš*) were employed for special building projects. Well-dressed stones were used in royal constructions such as palaces, temples, and defensive city walls, projects that could afford workers specialized in the craft.

Phoenician masons were sent by Hiram of Tyre to build David's palace in Jerusalem (2 Sam. 5:11 = 1 Chr. 14:1). Structures dating to the Solomonic period show high-quality work in the cutting of stones, as do the palaces of Omri and Ahab uncovered at Samaria. Hezekiah's tunnel (2 Kgs. 20:20; 2 Chr. 32:30) shows high stone-cutting skills, as the masons carved into solid rock from both ends and worked toward the middle. Herod's buildings in Jerusalem and elsewhere show high-quality masonry skills in both the cutting and laying of stones.

Skilled masons were able to cut stones for walls so accurately that they did not need mortar. As relatively soft stone was available in Palestine for building projects, it was used extensively in the foundations of building and city walls at many sites. At Hazor the native basalt (a hard, volcanic stone) was used to make orthostats for use in wall foundations and thresholds. In Egypt, where it was costly, stone was used to build temples and royal monuments, most notably the Giza pyramids. The limestone blocks used to build the Great Pyramid at Giza show high skill in stone-cutting; in many instances, the blocks were cut and laid so accurately that a razor cannot be passed through the seams between them.

JENNIE R. EBELING

MASORAH (Heb. *māsôrâ*)
In its broadest sense, the traditions and rules, oral or written, regulating all aspects of the copying and

use of Bible manuscripts. However, the term is normally understood in its narrow sense, referring only to the Masoretic notes which are transmitted with the text. These notes are in Hebrew or Aramaic and are usually numbers or abbreviations.

There are different kinds of Masoretic notes. The Masorah Parva (Mp) consists of the notes in the side margins of manuscripts or editions (see *BHS*). These are matched with words or phrases in the text by a small circle raised over the textual item. Mp notes primarily, but not exclusively, give the number of occurrences for the textual item. For example, in *BHS, wĕlôṭ* ("and Lot") in Gen. 13:1 is matched with the Mp note *d* (daleth), the letter representing the number four. This note indicates that *wĕlôṭ* occurs four times.

The Masorah Magna (Mm) consists of notes in the upper and lower margins of the manuscripts (but in *BHS* they are in the supplementary volume, *Massorah Gedolah*). The Mm notes give a list of verses containing the occurrences enumerated by the Mp notes. Each verse is cited by a short identifying excerpt.

The Masorah Finalis (Mf) refers to the material collected at the end of a particular book, section (e.g., Writings), or manuscript. In manuscripts the Mf consists of summary lists (such as the number of verses) or other data for which there was no room in the margins of a manuscript. The term Mf also refers to the edited lists collected by Jacob Ben Chayyim which are found at the end of the *Second Rabbinic Bible* (1524-25).

The Masorah is not a unified body of material transmitted uniformly with all manuscripts. The content varies from manuscript to manuscript, although much of it is overlapping in manuscripts from the standard Tiberian tradition. The purpose of the Masorah was to safeguard the text precisely, so that nothing would be added to or deleted from the text. To this end, the notes give specific instructions regarding words and phrases where an error in writing might occur. The Masorah was an effective means of quality control by which the text was preserved without significant change.

Bibliography. A. Dotan, "Masorah," *EncJud* 16 (Jerusalem, 1971): 1401-82; C. D. Ginsburg, *Introduction to the Massoretico-Critical Edition of the Hebrew Bible* (1899, repr. New York, 1966); P. H. Kelley, D. S. Mynatt, and T. G. Crawford, *The Masorah of* Biblia Hebraica Stuttgartensia (Grand Rapids, 1998); G. E. Weil, *Massorah Gedolah* 1 (Rome, 1971); I. Yeivin, *Introduction to the Tiberian Masorah.* SBLMasS 5 (Missoula, 1980).

Daniel S. Mynatt

MASORETIC TEXT

Any text of the Hebrew Bible produced by the Masoretes (from Heb. *baʿălê hammāsôrâ*), textual scholars concerned with the precise transmission of the text who were active ca. 600- 950 C.E. There were three major groups of Masoretes: the Palestinian, Babylonian, and Tiberian. Since work of the Tiberian school gained prominence over the other two, the standard Tiberian tradition of the Hebrew text is today commonly referred to as the MT.

The Tiberian Masoretes differed with each other on minor matters, and texts produced by the ben Asher family came to be revered as the best of the Tiberian tradition. The last of this family was Aaron ben Asher, and his achievements are incorporated in two widely used Masoretic manuscripts: the Aleppo Codex (A), the basis of the Hebrew University Bible Project; and the Leningrad Codex (L), the base text for *BHS*. Tiberian manuscripts generally contain four components: the consonantal text, the vowel signs, the accent signs, and the Masoretic notes written in the margins.

There is no such thing as *the* Masoretic Text. It is more accurate to refer to representatives of the MT, such as the text of the A or L. The text of the *Second Rabbinic Bible* edited by Jacob ben Chayyim (1524-25) was for centuries considered the authoritative version of the Hebrew Bible and thus was frequently labeled the MT. Modern scholarship, however, has shown that the *Second Rabbinic Bible* was based on relatively late manuscripts, and thus is probably not the best representative of the MT. Most modern editions of the Hebrew Bible print some form of the MT, but *BHS* (based on L) is currently the standard scholarly edition of the MT in the West.

See Masorah.

Bibliography. C. D. Ginsburg, *Introduction to the Massoretico-Critical Edition of the Hebrew Bible* (1899, repr. New York, 1966); M. H. Goshen-Gottstein, "The Rise of the Tiberian Bible Text," in *Biblical and Other Studies,* ed. A. Altmann (Cambridge, Mass., 1963), 79-122; repr. in *The Canon and Masorah of the Hebrew Bible,* ed. S. Z. Leiman (New York, 1974), 666-709; H. M. Orlinsky, "Prolegomenon: The Masoretic Text: A Critical Evaluation," in *Introduction to the Massoretico-Critical Edition of the Hebrew Bible,* ed. Ginsburg, i-xlv; E. Tov, *Textual Criticism of the Hebrew Bible* (Minneapolis, 1992); E. Würthwein, *The Text of the Old Testament,* 2nd ed. (Grand Rapids, 1995); I. Yeivin, *Introduction to the Tiberian Masorah.* SBLMasS 5 (Missoula, 1980).

Daniel S. Mynatt

MASREKAH (Heb. *maśrēqâ*)

A city in Edom, the home of King Samlah (Gen. 36:36; 1 Chr. 1:47). Several attempts have been made to identify a site, ranging from Syria to southern Transjordan and northwest Arabia.

MASSA (Heb. *maśśāʾ*)

1. A son of Ishmael and eponymous ancestor of a northern Arabian tribe (Gen. 25:14; 1 Chr. 1:30). Akkadian sources (*ANET,* 283) place the Massaeans in the region of northern Arabia. Ptolemy (*Geog.* 5.18.2) mentions the "Masanoi" as situated in the area assigned to the Ishmaelites (i.e., north central Arabia).

2. A term in the heading of Prov. 30:1; 31:1, indicating perhaps a place (**1** above) or an "oracle" (cf. presence of the definite article in 30:1). Although prophetic usage of Heb. *maśśāʾ* ("burden") portends an oracle of doom (e.g., Isa. 13:1; 15:1;

Nah. 1:1; Hab. 1:1), the title of the Proverbs collections connotes no such meaning.

HAROLD R. MOSLEY

MASSAH (Heb. *massâ*), **MERIBAH** (*mĕrîḇâ*)
From the verbs "to test" and "to strive, contend," respectively, terms referring to a site where the Israelites rebelled against Yahweh in the wilderness. Three distinct traditions of these events are preserved in the Bible. In Exod. 17:1-7 the Israelites camp at Rephidim on the way to Horeb. At Rephidim they complain of thirst to Moses. Yahweh tells Moses to go ahead of the people with some elders to Horeb and strike the mountain so that water will come out of it and the people may drink. The place is called Massah and Meribah because there the Israelites "quarreled" and "tested" God (cf. Ps. 95:8; also Deut. 6:16; 9:22, where only Massah is mentioned).

A second tradition locates the rebellion near Kadesh, in the wilderness of Zin, and refers only to Meribah. The focus of this tradition is Yahweh's judgment on Moses and Aaron. Unlike the Exodus tradition, Yahweh instructs Moses to speak to the rock to produce water, but instead Moses strikes the rock twice. Because Moses and Aaron did not trust in Yahweh or display his holiness, Yahweh declares that they will not lead the Israelites into the Promised Land — they will die in the wilderness (Num. 20:1-13, 24; 27:14; Deut. 32:51; Ps. 106:32).

A third tradition, only hinted at it in the Bible, states that Yahweh tested the Levites who kept his covenant, and thus were awarded the Thummim and Urim and service before Yahweh (Deut. 33:8-11; cf. Ps. 81:7[MT 8]).

RONALD A. SIMKINS

MATRED (Heb. *maṭrēḏ*)
The daughter of Mezahab and mother of Mehetabel, the wife of King Hadad (Hadar) of Edom (Gen. 36:39; 1 Chr. 1:50; so MT; according to LXX and Syr., the father of Mehetabel).

MATRIARCHS
Symbolically considered the mothers of Israel, Sarah, Rebekah, Leah, and Rachel are the wives of the patriarchs Abraham, Isaac, and Jacob, forebears of the 12 tribes of Israel. Their stories are beautifully narrated in high literary style and form a cohesive whole in the saga of the early patriarchal age.

Sarah

Sarah/Sarai and Abram/Abraham are bonded not only in spousal obligation, but in love and devotion to each other. Sarah is intricately tied to God's repeated promises of progeny to Abraham, for she is to be the mother of nations (Gen. 17:16). At the juncture of the fulfillment of this promise, ritualized by the covenant of circumcision, their names are changed to Abraham, "father of a multitude" in Hebrew, and Sarah, "princess."

Having left Ur and then Haran, the two continue on to Canaan. Twice dire circumstances force them to sojourn south, twice the beautiful Sarah is passed off as Abraham's sister, twice she narrowly avoids violating the conjugal bond, and twice they are sent away with costly gifts and cattle.

Sarai, long barren, offers Abram her Egyptian maid Hagar so that she will obtain children through her. This seems a special variation of the recurrent theme of bitter rivalry between a barren favored wife and a fertile co-wife, or the story of a woman long barren who is given a divine promise of offspring and who then gives birth to a hero. It also mirrors the frequent malevolent sibling rivalry in the larger context of Genesis. God's promise to Abraham finally culminates in Isaac's birth when Abraham is 100 years old and Sarah is 90.

Not much is told of Sarah after this event except that she dies at the age of 127 at Hebron, that Abraham mourns her and weeps for her, and that Isaac takes his new bride, Rebekah. The cave of Machpelah, purchased intentionally for Sarah's burial (Gen. 23), is of obvious symbolic significance and represents their first permanent possession of land.

Rebekah

The story of Rebekah forms the conclusion of the Abraham saga, for Abraham's last decision revolves around his wish that Isaac, the bearer of Yahweh's promise, should not intermarry with the Canaanites. Abraham's servant is sent to find a wife from the clan of Nahor, his brother, to ensure an endogamous marriage (Gen. 24). In later years, Rebekah will again be the focal point of purposeful activity in securing the paternal blessing for her favorite son Jacob when she devises the plan to fool Isaac and thereby invokes Isaac's potential curse upon herself rather than allowing it to fall upon her son (Gen. 27).

Rebekah is the most clever and authoritative of the matriarchs, yet she epitomizes womanly beauty and virtue in her conduct, energetic speech, thoughtful courtesy, and self-assurance. The story assumes that Rebekah has been appointed by the Lord to be Isaac's wife, since events seemingly unfold according to divine providence. Her farewell from her father's house is accompanied by a shower of blessings, doubling the intentional fertility motif of the life-giving water at the well.

The theme of barrenness recurs in the story of Rebekah, for she does not conceive until after 20 years of marriage. Yahweh indicates special, yet deliberately ambiguous, intention in explaining the destiny of the two boys (nations, people) who struggle within her womb (Gen. 25:23). There is a schematic repetition in Rebekah's charge to Jacob to seek a wife from among her own clan; he later finds comfort with Rachel, just as Isaac had found comfort with Rebekah.

Leah and Rachel

The stories of Leah, Rachel, and their offspring are intertwined in competition and strife, echoing nuances of the struggle between Jacob and Esau. They are the daughters of the crafty Laban, though they will prove to be well matched with the even craftier Jacob in repetitive motifs of deception.

Jacob's journey to Haran has attributes of divine intent and promise, expressed already in the dream vision at Bethel (Gen. 28:14). Rachel then appears to Jacob at the well, and here begins Jacob's personal story of deep emotional attachment and love for her. The symbolic action of Jacob rolling away the stone at the well is thematically indicative of the numerous obstacles he must later overcome to obtain Rachel: seven years of servitude to Laban, culminating in the substitution of Leah as first wife, and seven further years of labor for Rachel.

Leah bears four sons in succession, Reuben, Simeon, Levi, and Judah, named to symbolize her yearnings for love and comfort, while Rachel remains barren. Rachel offers Jacob her maid Bilhah, who, as surrogate mother, bears Dan, then Naphtali, named to express Rachel's wrestling with her sister. Only after Leah's maid Zilpah has borne Gad and Asher and Leah has borne Issachar, Zebulun, and Dinah does God remember and bless Rachel. She bears Joseph, asking for another son in his naming.

Rachel dies on the journey back to Canaan after giving birth to her second son, Benoni ("son of my sorrow"), whom Jacob renames Benjamin. The favorite status of Rachel and envy of Jacob's special love for her are passed down to the children and become evident in their interactions with each other. Just as Jacob singles out Rachel for a special love in life, so he singles her out in death in placing a commemorative pillar on her grave to mark her tomb.

There is a thematic rhythm in the biblical narrative of the four matriarchs, emphasizing their place as divinely ordained. This in turn is reflected in the primary position they hold among Israelite ancestry. They are linked in a causal chain, a series of events firmly connected one to another, and together with the patriarchs they form the primal ancestral pattern. All four together hold the revered place as mothers of the nation.

Bibliography. R. Alter, *The Art of Biblical Narrative* (New York, 1981); A. B. Beck, "Rachel," in *ABD* 5:605-8; "Rebekah," in *ABD* 5:629-30; E. Deen, *All of the Women of the Bible* (New York, 1983); E. A. Speiser, *Genesis.* AB 1 (Garden City, 1964).

Astrid B. Beck

MATRITES (Heb. *maṭrî*)
A Benjaminite clan from which Saul was chosen king (1 Sam. 10:21).

MATTAN (Heb. *mattān*)

1. A priest of Baal slain in the coup against Queen Athaliah of Judah (2 Kgs. 11:18; 2 Chr. 23:17).

2. The father of Shephatiah, an officer of King Zedekiah (Jer. 38:1).

MATTANAH (Heb. *mattānâ*)
The first of the encampment sites in the Exodus itinerary (Num. 21:18-20) which follow Israel's song (vv. 17-18) of Yahweh's provision of well-water at Beer (cf. the meaning of the name, "gift, donation"). The context places Mattanah, understood by most scholars as a Moabite place name, E of the Jordan and beyond the Brook Zered (Num. 21:12) as far as the valley of the Arnon River (vv. 13-15). Its precise location is unknown, but a possibility is Khirbet el-Medeiyineh (236110), ca. 19 km. (12 mi.) SE of Medeba.

Bibliography. N. Glueck, *Explorations in Eastern Palestine I.* AASOR 14 (Baltimore, 1933-34); J. R. Kautz, "Tracking the Ancient Moabites," *BA* 44 (1981): 27-35; A. H. Van Zyl, *The Moabites.* Pretoria Oriental Series 3 (Leiden, 1960).

Robert Delsnyder

MATTANIAH (Heb. *mattanyâ, mattanyāhû*)
A common Hebrew name ("Gift of Yah[weh]"), attested in the Lachish Letters (1:5) and in seal bullae from the time of Jeremiah (cf. also the short form Mattan without the theophoric element).

1. The last king of Judah (ca. 597-596 B.C.E.), enthroned to replace his nephew Jehoiachin by Nebuchadnezzar of Babylon, who changed his name to Zedekiah (2 Kgs. 24:17); son of Josiah.

2. One of 14 sons of Heman whom David purportedly set apart for musical service in the planned temple (1 Chr. 25:4, 16).

3. An Asaphite Levite and great-great-grandfather of Jahaziel, court prophet for Jehoshaphat (2 Chr. 20:14).

4. A Levite at the time of Hezekiah commissioned to help reconsecrate the temple (2 Chr. 29:13).

5.-8. Four postexilic Israelites, each of whom married foreign wives and divorced them as directed by Ezra: they were from the clans of Elam (Ezra 10:26), Zattu (v. 27), Pahath-moab (v. 30), and Bani (v. 37).

9. The son of Mica(iah), an Asaphite levitical musical leader, who purportedly swelled Jerusalem's population by moving there (Neh. 11:17). The leader of the temple choir at 1 Chr. 9:15; Neh.12:8, 25 is apparently the same person, although there he is from the time of Zerubbabel. His great-grandson Uzzi was overseer of the Levites (Neh. 11:22); another great-grandson Zechariah was a precentor at the dedication of the wall (12:35).

10. Grandfather of Hanan ben Zaccur whom Nehemiah entrusted with assisting the new treasurers over the storehouses, Shelemiah and Zadok (Neh. 13:13).

Bibliography. W. E. Aufrecht, "Genealogy and History in Ancient Israel," in *Ascribe to the Lord,* ed. L. E. Eslinger and G. Taylor. JSOTSup 67 (Sheffield, 1988), 205-35; N. Avigad, *Hebrew Bullae from the Time of Jeremiah* (Jerusalem, 1986).

Paul J. Kissling

MATTATHA (Gk. *Mattathá*)
An ancestor of Jesus; grandson of King David (Luke 3:31).

MATTATHIAS (Gk. *Mattathías*)
A common name (from Heb. *mattiṯyâ,* "gift of Yahweh") in the Maccabean and Roman periods.

1. A priest of the order of Jehoiarib (1 Chr. 24:7) or Joarib (1 Macc. 2:1); son of John and grandson of Simeon. Mattathias was a descendant of Asamonaeus, whence derives the name Hasmonean, the eventual name of the ruling Jewish dynasty, which descended from Mattathias. From the village of Modein, Mattathias and his sons in 166 B.C.E. initiated a revolt against Antiochus IV, who was attempting to stamp out the Jewish religion (1 Macc. 2).

2. The son of Absalom, a general officer under Jonathan (1 Macc. 11:70).

3. The third son of Simon and grandson of Mattathias **1.** After the Maccabean revolt (134 B.C.E.), Ptolemy, an in-law of the ruling Hasmonean family, murdered this Mattathias, his brother Judas, and father Simon in their attempted coup (1 Macc. 16:14-16).

4. An envoy sent to Judas Maccabeus by Nicanor, the Syrian-appointed governor of Judea (2 Macc. 14:19).

5. An ancestor of Jesus, according to Luke's genealogy (Luke 3:25; NRSV Matthat).

6. Another ancestor of Jesus, according to Luke 3:26.

J. BRADLEY CHANCE

MATTATTAH (Heb. *mattattâ*)
An Israelite required to divorce his foreign wife (Ezra 10:33).

MATTENAI (Heb. *mattĕnay*)

1. An Israelite among the sons of Hashum required to divorce his foreign wife (Ezra 10:33).

2. One of the sons of Bani who divorced his foreign wife (Ezra 10:37).

3. Head of the priestly house of Joiarib at the time of the high priest Joiakim (Neh. 12:19).

MATTHAN (Gk. *Matthán*)
A postexilic ancestor of Jesus; grandfather of Joseph (Matt. 1:15; cf. Matthat at Luke 3:24).

MATTHAT (Gk. *Maththát*)

1. An ancestor of Jesus; according to Luke 3:24 the grandfather of Joseph (cf. Matt. 1:15, Matthan).

2. A postexilic ancestor of Jesus (Luke 3:29).

MATTHEW (Gk. *Maththaíos*)
One of Jesus' original disciples, named in all the lists of the Twelve (Matt. 10:3; Mark 3:18; Luke 6:15; Acts 1:13). In their accounts of his call to become a disciple, Mark and Luke give his name as Levi (Mark 2:14; Luke 5:27). His being a tax collector and the similarity of the details of the calling make the identification of Matthew with Levi virtually certain. Mark's account lists him as son of Alphaeus, which would seem to identify him as the brother of James (not to be confused with James, son of Zebedee).

All three Synoptic accounts of Matthew/Levi's calling are followed shortly by accounts of Jesus attending a reception with many "tax-gatherers and sinners" present. Only Luke clearly identifies the home as being that of Levi. Luke apparently wanted to show that this reception was a spontaneous and joyful response to Matthew/Levi's being called to follow Jesus.

Before he became a disciple Matthew was a tax collector in the area of Capernaum. His position would have been a very lucrative one, as he would have had opportunity to collect not only from local farmers and craftsmen as they brought their products to market, but also from caravans which often passed through the area carrying goods between Egypt and the Orient. The detail found only in Luke that he "left everything" (Luke 5:28) to follow Jesus is probably a hint as to this lucrative position.

Very little is known of Matthew/Levi beyond the Synoptic accounts of his call. Papias claims that he wrote the Gospel of Matthew in Hebrew. As with all the original disciples, legendary stories abound. According to one tradition he was martyred, but another says he died a natural death.

JOE E. LUNCEFORD

MATTHEW, GOSPEL OF
The first of the NT Gospels in canonical order. It was composed during the last decades of the 1st century, when Jews and Christians alike were faced with the task of rearticulating their self-understanding in light of the destruction of the temple and the holy city, Jerusalem. Regardless of where the Gospel was written (Syrian Antioch or one of the larger settlements in Galilee are the two settings most often proposed), the story of Jesus that Matthew tells seems well suited to clarify the identity, vocation, and practices of a community in transition and distress. Matthew uses tension and surprise, in both form and content, to address this situation, while affirming that Jesus Christ, "God with us," is the defining figure around which the community's self-understanding, imagination, and social relations are to be formed.

The ascription of this Gospel to Matthew is traditional; the earliest manuscripts are anonymous. Some scholars today argue that Matthew was the first Gospel to be written. The majority of scholars, however, hold to the priority of Mark and believe that Matthew probably used two other sources in addition to Mark, one that was shared with Luke (commonly designated "Q"), and one source that was used independently by Matthew. While earlier generations of scholars held that many of the repetitions found in Matthew were due to careless use of these sources, more recent studies affirm that Matthew employs repetition intentionally as a means to develop characters and advance the plot. Matthew also relies on citations from and allusions to the OT to guide the reader through the story and provide interpretive frameworks for the narrated events. Most prominent among these are the "fulfillment quotations" (Matt. 1:22-23; 2:15, 17-18, 23; 4:14-16; 8:17; 12:17-21; 13:35; 21:4-5; 27:9-10), which would appeal to audiences familiar with the OT, especially the prophecies concerning the Messiah. As often as one finds appeals to Jewish expectations, however, one also finds elements in this story that would have surprised readers familiar with the OT and stretched their notions about both the Messiah and

God. Jesus' description of a "scribe trained for the kingdom of heaven" as one who "brings out of his treasure what is new and what is old" (13:52) describes well this Evangelist's own work.

Matthew's manipulation of the conventions of genre also generates tension and surprise. The Gospel incorporates elements that would have led ancient audiences to associate it both with biographies of leading philosophers and kings and with Jewish historiography. Thus on the one hand, Matthew's story is about Jesus the teacher and healer, whose actions and teachings, including his death and resurrection, form a coherent, congruent, and compelling whole, worthy of emulation by faithful disciples even amidst disconcerting circumstances. In this way it functions like ancient biography. On the other hand, Matthew's story is about Jesus the messiah of Israel, whose vocation and ministry, including his death and resurrection, sum up and bring to fruition the whole history of God and the people of Israel. In this way the Gospel appears to build on and complete the historical books found in the OT. By combining biography with history, the Gospel transcends the expectations of both. The reader perceives that Jesus is a figure whose life and teachings are important in their own right, but also one whose story sums up and alters history.

Matthew also holds multiple, overlapping structural patterns in tension. The most prominent of these organizational patterns is the alternation of narrative and discourse. Five times Matthew uses the formula "and when Jesus had finished saying these things," always at the transition from one of Jesus' five major speeches to a section of narrative recording his deeds (7:28-29; 11:1; 13:53; 19:1; 26:1). Some scholars detect in the rough correspondence of themes and motifs amidst these segments of narrative and discourse an overarching chiastic arrangement (i.e., an inverted, concentric parallelism, hinging on the parables in ch. 13).

Twice Matthew uses the formula "from that time Jesus began to," each time suggesting an important shift in the narrative: at 4:17 Jesus begins his ministry and preaching in Galilee, and at 16:21 he turns toward Jerusalem, where his suffering, death, and resurrection will occur. According to this scheme, Matthew is organized into three panels, each representing a different geographical and, especially, christological aspect of the story.

More recently scholars have turned their attention to the development of the plot in Matthew, and have offered a variety of proposals regarding the Gospel's structure based on "kernels," the turning points that determine the chains of causality around which the narrative flows. This approach typically yields a six-part structure, approximately as follows: 1) the coming of the Messiah, 1:1–4:16 (kernel: 1:18-25); 2) the Messiah's ministry to Israel, 4:17–11:1 (kernel: 4:17-25); 3) conflict and crisis in the Messiah's ministry, 11:2–16:20 (kernel: 11:2-6); 4) the Messiah's journey to Jerusalem, 16:21–20:34 (kernel: 16:21-28); 5) the Messiah's final rejection and crucifixion, 21:1–27:66 (kernel: 21:1-27); and 6) resurrection of the Messiah and commissioning of the disciples, 28:1-20 (kernel: 28:1-10).

Readers should resist the temptation to pick and choose among these alternatives, since they are developed on the basis of differing but not necessarily exclusive criteria. Readings that ignore the complex intersecting and overlapping structural patterns at work in this Gospel are likely to be reductionistic. Moreover, the Evangelist sometimes establishes patterns and expectations, only to shatter them. For example, in the genealogy that opens the Gospel (and that thereby shapes the readers' generic expectations), Matthew lays out Jesus' ancestry according to a three-part structuring of Israel's history, leading from Abraham to the establishment of the Davidic kingdom, from Solomon to the Babylonian Exile, and from the return from exile to the Christ. Matthew then tells the reader explicitly that each of these three portions of Israel's history has 14 generations. A careful counting, however, yields only 13 generations in the last segment. Did Matthew make a mistake? Are we to count Jesus twice? Does the Holy Spirit count as one generation? Matthew does not resolve these questions, but leaves the readers to sort through the mystery and tension of a carefully constructed and (apparently) intentionally broken structure.

The sense of tension and surprise generated by Matthew's use of structure is matched by the thematic tensions that run throughout this Gospel. The most evident of these, and the most troubling for scholars, has been the problem posed by Matthew's relation to Judaism. Matthew is one of the most explicitly Jewish documents in the NT but also one of the most critical of Jewish leadership. Matthew seems to affirm the ongoing validity of the Law (e.g., 5:17-20), while also limiting some of its authority (e.g., 12:1-14). Does this reflect a now largely gentile community that has (perhaps long ago) left its Jewish roots behind, but not bothered to cover over the tracks of its origins? Does it reflect a predominantly Jewish community only recently emerged from a painful and definitive break with competing Jewish factions? Or is Matthew representative of a Christian (or "Christian Jewish") community that, even in its engagement in mission to the nations, understands itself as a legitimate heir and faithful embodiment of Israel's vocation and traditions, and therefore in competition with alternative expressions of Jewish identity and leadership? During recent decades most of the discussion has focused on the latter alternatives, with a growing number of voices affirming the last of these proposals.

This line of questioning, in any case, has its roots in Matthew's apparent resolve to locate Jesus' story within Israel's story or, more precisely, to establish Jesus as the fulfillment of Israel's story, while also affirming that the Messiah is the beginning of something new. In other words, Matthew affirms both continuity and discontinuity between Jesus and the vocation and traditions of Israel. Thus, Jesus both fulfills and abrogates (and radicalizes) the Law. He represents for Israel, as well as for the nations, both judgment and mercy. He is both the Davidic messiah-king (e.g., 12:23) and the humble, broken servant in whom the nations will hope (12:18-21). Matthew gives this tensive, paradoxical depiction of Jesus an almost comical expression in the story of the triumphal entry into Jerusalem (21:1-11), where Jesus apparently rides not one, but two animals — a donkey, which the kings of the OT traditionally rode to their coronation, and the colt of a pack animal, the beast of burden that symbolizes Jesus' identity as servant.

From the outset of the Gospel, Matthew uses a variety of titles and images to describe Jesus. Jesus is not only Messiah and Son of David, but Son of God, Son of Man, and the one who will save his people from their sins (1:21). In each case, Matthew twists the expectations associated with each title in order to say something new about Jesus. Matthew also explicitly names Jesus as Emmanuel, "God with us," both at the beginning and the end of the Gospel (1:23; 28:20). By "bookending" the Gospel with this identification, Matthew suggests that the whole story may be read as an explication of what this designation means. "God with us" is present in human form, in meekness (12:18-21) as well as with power (7:29; 9:8; 21:23ff.; 28:18). Jesus' actions and teachings as "God with us" blur the boundaries between the human and the divine (e.g., 9:1-8; 14:22-33), and between heaven and earth (6:10; 16:19; 18:18; 38:20). The effect of this constant redefinition of expectations and confusion of boundaries is a constant stretching of the disciples' imagination and practices, as well as the readers'.

As Matthew's story of Jesus unfolds, readers are surprised by the intrigue and violence that attend his person and ministry, from Herod's attempts to kill the baby (2:1-23) to the spasms of violence that climax in his crucifixion. According to Matthew, God's presence in the world in Jesus is met with confusion, disbelief, and rejection. Matthew depicts this response with greatest clarity with reference to the religious and political leaders, who perceive that Jesus possesses transforming power but find his ministry threatening to their own carefully cultivated power, as well as to their piety. In a key series of exchanges, Jesus traps the leaders in Jerusalem in self-condemnation (21:23-46); they articulate their own condemnation and judgment (21:31-32, 40-41). The Kingdom will be taken from them and given to others. The surprise is that the pious and powerful are not necessarily God's chosen ones.

In the course of Jesus' interactions with the Jewish leaders, Matthew makes clear that a primary issue at stake is the nature of authority. The Jewish leaders possess political, economic, and social authority, which they exercise at the expense of those whom they deem less righteous. Their power is used for self-interest and to preserve social and economic boundaries. This kind of power, according to Matthew, is human rather than coming from God. Jesus' power, by contrast, breaks down the barriers imposed by class, wealth, and piety. Jesus uses this authority to demonstrate God's mercy. The leaders' decision finally to have Jesus put to death makes it clear that their power takes life, while God's power restores it. Matthew thus uses the events leading up to Jesus' crucifixion to highlight the question of who truly represents and manifests God's authority. Here again the reader may be surprised: God's power is not manifested in the threat of death, but in the restoration of life.

Throughout Matthew only those with faith, the little ones and least ones, the children and women disciples — in other words, those whose stake in the present order is minimal — are able to discern Jesus' true identity, even if only partially. With the Crucifixion the full meaning and power of Jesus' vocation are finally manifested. His death marks the apocalyptic culmination of history. The earth is shaken, rocks broken, tombs opened, and the dead raised. The surprise is not only that God vindicates Jesus' overturning the deadly will of the leaders, but that Jesus' death and resurrection is the turning point of history.

Yet another tension in Matthew revolves around the implications of Jesus' death for the Jewish people. It is clear in Matthew that the mission to the Gentiles is dependent on the completion of Jesus' mission to the lost sheep of the house of Israel. But does the mission to the Gentiles come about because of the failure of the mission to Israel? Has God now turned away from Israel and toward the nations (i.e., to a gentile Church)? Or is the death of Jesus the means of salvation even for those who rejected and executed Jesus? Matthew does not answer these questions directly, but leaves the reader to discern the answers in the paths of discipleship (28:16-20).

Matthew's literary artistry yields a story that repays careful, attentive reading, and that stretches our imagination and deepens our insight with each new reading. Matthew points would-be disciples toward a Messiah who both fulfills hopes and surpasses expectations, and who promises to be present on the journey through difficult and confusing times, not unlike our own.

Bibliography. D. C. Allison, Jr., *The New Moses: A Matthean Typology* (Minneapolis, 1993); D. L. Balch, ed., *Social History of the Matthean Community* (Minneapolis, 1991); D. R. Bauer and M. A. Powell, eds., *Treasures New and Old: Recent Contributions to Matthean Studies.* SBL Symposium Series 1 (Atlanta, 1996); M. H. Crosby, *House of Disciples: Church, Economics, and Justice in Matthew* (Maryknoll, 1988); A. J. Saldarini, *Matthew's Christian-Jewish Community* (Chicago, 1994); G. N. Stanton, *A Gospel for New People: Studies in Matthew* (Louisville, 1993) STANLEY P. SAUNDERS

MATTHEW, HEBREW GOSPEL OF

The early Church believed that Matthew originally wrote his Gospel in the Hebrew language. The earliest to report this tradition is Papias (ca. 60-130 C.E.; Eusebius *HE* 3.39.16) A host of later writers confirm the tradition, including Irenaeus, Pantaenus, Origen, Eusebius, Epiphanius, and Jerome. These writers, however, sometimes confuse the Hebrew

Matthew with the Gospel of the Ebionites, the Gospel of the Nazoreans, and/or the Gospel according to the Hebrews, apocryphal Jewish Christian gospels written in the 2nd century. The early Christian witness to the text of the Hebrew Matthew is, consequently, unclear.

During the Middle Ages Jewish authors, writing in Hebrew, often quote the Gospel of Matthew in a text different from the canonical Greek. In 1380 the Spanish Jewish polemist Shemtob ben Isaac ibn Shaprut incorporated the entire text of Matthew in Hebrew in his treatise, *'Eben Boḥan*. His text often corresponds to the earlier Jewish quotations of Matthew in Hebrew, leading to the speculation that Shemtob's text preserves an early copy of the Hebrew Matthew.

In the 16th century Sebastian Münster and Jean du Tillet issued separate editions of Matthew in Hebrew, both reporting that they received their texts from the Jews. The versions of Münster and du Tillet, similar to each other, are distinct from the text of Shemtob. A close analysis of their differences reveals that the 16th-century editions, though based on a text like Shemtob's, have been thoroughly revised so that the Hebrew now reads closely to the Christian Greek and Latin Bibles of the Middle Ages.

Bibliography. J. K. Elliott, *The Apocryphal New Testament*, rev. ed. (Oxford, 1993); E. Hennecke and W. Schneemelcher, *New Testament Apocrypha*, rev. ed. (Louisville, 1991); G. Howard, *Hebrew Gospel of Matthew*, 2nd ed. (Macon, 1995); A. F. J. Klijn, *Jewish-Christian Gospel Tradition*. Vigiliae Christianae Sup 17 (Leiden, 1992); Klijn and G. J. Reinink, *Patristic Evidence for Jewish-Christian Sects*. NovTSup 36 (Leiden, 1973). GEORGE HOWARD

MATTHIAS (Gk. *Maththías*)
One of two persons described as an eyewitness of Jesus' ministry and a candidate for replacing Judas Iscariot (Acts 1:21-26). Matthias was chosen by prayer and casting lots to become the 12th disciple. Although the text underscores the necessity of choosing this 12th disciple, he is never mentioned again in the NT. The "necessity" was possibly the symbolism of the number 12 representing the people of God as reflected in the tribal organization of Israel. The name is a shortened form of Mattithiah, which means "gift of Yahweh." JOE E. LUNCEFORD

MATTITHIAH (Heb. *mattiṯyâ, mattiṯyāhû*)
1. A Korahite Levite who after the Exile ministered in the temple as a baker of cakes for liturgical services (1 Chr. 9:31); the first son of Shallum.

2. A levitical gatekeeper during the reign of David (1 Chr. 15:18); the son of Jeduthun (25:3). A temple musician who played the lyre as a part of prophetic activity (1 Chr. 25:1, 3, 21), he accompanied the ark to Jerusalem (16:5).

3. The son of Nebo, persuaded by Ezra to divorce his pagan wife (Ezra 10:43; 1 Esdr. 9:35). Since his name does not appear among the priests and Levites, he was probably a member of the Israelite laity.

4. An influential Israelite who accompanied Ezra when he read publicly from the book of the Law (Neh. 8:4). CAROL J. DEMPSEY

MAUNDY THURSDAY
The Thursday before Easter, a celebration of the original observance of the Lord's Supper. Also known as Holy Thursday, it is rooted in the biblical accounts of Jesus' celebration of the Passover Meal and the institution of the Eucharist with his disciples, and may be traced back to the very origins of Christian liturgical history. Later Christian practice is reflected in Justin Martyr's *First Apology* and in the liturgy of Hippolytus. Originally associated with the preparation for baptism on Easter Sunday morning, Maundy Thursday (from Lat. *mandatum*, "commandment"; Vulg. John 13:34) continues to be celebrated by many Christian communions as a time of penitence, preparation, and consecration in the midst of Holy Week. D. LARRY GREGG

MAZZAROTH (Heb. *mazzārôṯ*)
A star or constellation (Job 38:32; cf. 2 Kgs. 23:5, Heb. *mazzālôṯ*). Suggestions as to its identity include Corona Borealis (from *nēzer*, "crown") and the Zodiac (from *'āzar*, "gird, encompass"), but none is certain.

MEAL
See FLOUR.

MEALS
Meals are often mentioned in the Bible in secular as well as religious contexts. Meal customs depicted in both the OT and the NT should be interpreted in relation to their respective cultural contexts, the ancient Near East and the Greco-Roman world. In addition, there are customs specific to Jewish tradition, such as the dietary laws.

An early account of meal customs is the story of Abraham entertaining strangers at Mamre (Gen. 18:1-8; cf. 19:1-3). The story illustrates the ancient notion of hospitality, whereby one was expected to provide basic amenities for worthy strangers, including especially a meal. Here Abraham invited his guests to "stretch out" under a tree (i.e., recline) while he brought water for them to wash their feet, a custom regularly connected with meal etiquette wherever reclining was practiced. He then became both host and servant at the meal, while Sarah remained in the tent, following the widespread custom whereby a respectable woman was not to join men at the table, especially one at which guests from outside the family were present.

The Abraham story provides a snapshot of meal customs in an early period of Jewish history. Reclining can be traced as early as the 7th century B.C.E., as depicted on a relief showing the Assyrian king Assurbanipal reclining at a feast in a garden with his wife (who sits rather than reclines, indicating her station in life), eating and drinking while servants play music nearby.

The same customs are described in Amos 6:4-6. The reclining banquet is pictured here as a luxurious occasion which includes ceremonial drinking of wine, anointing with oil, and musical entertainment. Amos presents it in a negative light, as characteristic of the wealthy reprobates of Samaria, but the customs he represents were widespread in his world.

By the time of Ben Sira in the Second Temple period, the meal of luxury is something to be dealt with as part of the life of the sage. The rules of the banquet described in Sir. 31:12–32:13 present numerous parallels to the Greco-Roman banquet and illustrate the extent to which Jewish meal customs had now become intertwined with Greco-Roman meal customs, including such features as how to preside at the table (32:1-2), rules for speaking (31:31; 32:3-4, 7-9), the place of music (32:4-6), as well as injunctions to practice moderation in eating and drinking (31:12-18, 25-30).

These features are widely represented in Greco-Roman meal customs as evidenced, e.g., in Plato's *Symposium* (4th century) or in the *Table Talk* of Plutarch (1st century C.E.). They are also echoed in NT meal descriptions. For example, whenever the posture at meals of Jesus is indicated, it is always reclining (e.g., Mark 2:15; 8:6; 14:18 par.). The various Greek terms which literally mean "recline" are often translated "sit at table" in modern English versions. Diners who reclined were arranged according to standard patterns, a common one being the *triclinium* arrangement, whereby a minimum of nine diners would be arranged on three couches placed in a U-shaped configuration around a table, three diners to a couch. They reclined on their left elbows, arranged at an oblique angle on the couch and roughly parallel to each other. Diners would also be arranged by rank, proceeding around the table from left to right. Thus in John 13:23, when the Beloved Disciple is described as "reclining next to Jesus" (NRSV; Gk. "reclining on his bosom"), he is therefore represented in a position of honor, just to the right of the Lord himself. Similarly, in the parable of the rich man and Lazarus (Luke 16:19-31), the position of Lazarus in the afterlife "in the bosom" of Abraham (v. 23) is best understood as a position of honor at the messianic banquet or the banquet of the afterlife (on "eating bread in the kingdom of God," cf. 14:15).

To position guests by rank was the mark of a good host, but it could lead to tension, as in Luke 14:7-11 (cf. Plutarch *Table Talk* 1.2). Such social tension may underlie the conflict at the Lord's Supper in Corinth (1 Cor. 11:17-34), where the divisions at the table are characterized as "show(ing) contempt for the church of God and humiliat(ing) those who have nothing" (v. 22). Women and slaves were marginalized even further by not being allowed to recline, if they were present at the table at all. However, this tradition was undergoing change in the 1st century, as respectable women were beginning to appear at banquets with more frequency. In the Gospels women are often present at Jesus' meals, but these stories vary in how they depict the placement of women at the table, whether in a traditionally acceptable subservient role at the feet of Jesus (Luke 7:36-50; 10:38-42) or as possibly reclining along with men (Matt. 14:19-21; 15:35-38). By contrast, when Paul refers to women being present at the worship services in Corinth as prophets (1 Cor. 11:5), one must conclude that they were present at the table (mentioned next in Paul's argument, vv. 17-34) and presumably were reclining along with the men.

According to ancient customs, when someone hosted a meal at his home, as Levi/Matthew does for Jesus (Mark 2:15 par.), invitations were normally extended to the guests (cf. Plato *Symp.* 174E). Jesus refers to this custom in a symbolic sense when he speaks of "inviting" ("calling") not the righteous but sinners to the table, i.e., the kingdom (Mark 2:17; cf. the reference to invitations at Luke 14:10, 12, 16). Upon their arrival at the meal, guests would have their feet washed by a household servant before they took their positions upon the couches (*Symp.* 175A). This custom is referred to in Luke 7:34, where Jesus' Pharisaic host is criticized for not providing this basic act of hospitality for Jesus, and in John 13:1-16, where Jesus takes the role of servant to wash the feet of the disciples, a practice continued in some circles in the early Church (1 Tim. 5:10). Washing the hands at the table before the meal was a common practice of pagans as well as Jews (Athenaeus *Deip.* 14.641d; *m. Ḥag.* 2:5), but it had been given special religious significance in Pharisaic Judaism. Jesus, as part of his critique of the Pharisees, ignored this custom (Mark 7:1-8 par.). Guests were also routinely anointed on the head with perfumes (Josephus *Ant.* 19.238), a practice which is given symbolic significance in the Jesus tradition (Mark 14:3-9).

The ancient banquet had two primary courses, the eating course, or *deípnon* ("dinner"), followed by the drinking course, or *sympósion* (symposium). Each course began with a benediction or libation over the food and wine, a custom adapted in different ways by Greeks, Romans, and Jews (*Symp.* 176A; *m. Ber.* 6), and which is reflected in Jesus' benedictions at various meals (e.g., Mark 8:6). The Last Supper traditions refer to the two courses of the meal by indicating separate benedictions over the bread and wine (Mark 14:22-25 par.). In the Pauline and Lukan versions, these benedictions are explicitly separated by the phrase "after supper" ("after the *deípnon*"; *1 Cor. 11:23-25; Luke 22:19-20).*

The symposium course was intended to last long into the evening and was expected to include entertainment. While some Greeks and Romans tended toward prurient entertainment, philosophical Greeks and Romans often offered enlightened conversation on a philosophical topic as their symposium entertainment (e.g., *Symp.* 176E). Similarly, Jewish tradition preferred discourse on the law at the table (as in Sir. 9:15-16) and Jesus often taught at the table (e.g., Luke 14). In the early Church, it is quite likely that the worship service which began with the communal meal (or Lord's Supper) continued at the table, since "coming together as a church" (1 Cor. 11:18) included both "coming together to eat" (v. 20) and "coming together [in which] each one has a hymn, a lesson, a revelation, a tongue, or an interpretation" (14:26a).

Meals also functioned as boundary markers, helping to define who was in the community and who was not. Jewish dietary laws especially functioned to define boundaries, for those who strictly followed these laws usually could not dine at a gentile table (Dan. 1:8; Tob. 1:10). This created a problem in the early Church as its gentile membership began to grow more prominent. The issue came to a head in Antioch, in an incident described by Paul in Galatians, where Jewish Christians refused to eat at the same table with Gentile Christians (Gal. 2:11-14). Paul argued vociferously that the Church can no more have two tables than it can have two paths to salvation, for in Christ "there is no longer Jew or Greek" (Gal. 3:28). The tension over dietary laws was resolved differently according to another tradition represented in Acts 15, where Gentile Christians were enjoined to follow a modified form of Jewish dietary laws ("abstain . . . from blood and from what is strangled," v. 29), thus allowing Gentile and Jewish Christians to eat at the same table. But Mark, like Paul, envisioned no compromise on this issue, reporting that Jesus "declared all foods clean" (Mark 7:19). The table of Jesus, as related by the Gospels, was one in which inclusion of the marginalized was the rule, symbolized by his preference for eating with such impure outcasts as "tax collectors and sinners" (Mark 2:15-17 par.).

Bibliography. K. E. Corley, *Private Women, Public Meals: Social Conflict in the Synoptic Tradition* (Peabody, 1993); P. J. King, *Amos, Hosea, Micah: An Archaeological Commentary* (Philadelphia, 1988); D. E. Smith, "Table Fellowship as a Literary Motif in the Gospel of Luke," *JBL* 106 (1987): 613-38; Smith and H. Taussig, *Many Tables: The Eucharist in the New Testament and Liturgy Today* (Philadelphia, 1990).

DENNIS E. SMITH

MEARAH (Heb. *mĕʿārâ*)
A place associated with the Sidonians (Josh. 13:4). The Hebrew text is difficult, possibly to be read "from Arah" (LXX "before Gaza," reading Heb. *mēʿāzâ*). "Arah of the Sidonians" suggests a coastal site near Sidon, marking the north coastal limit of the theoretical Israelite occupation.

THOMAS W. DAVIS

MEAT
Meat (Heb. *bāśār*) was not likely a regular part of the diet in biblical times and was probably consumed only occasionally with sacrifices (1 Sam. 2:13), at seasonal gatherings, or to welcome special guests (Gen. 18:7; Judg. 13:15; Luke 15:27). It was a desired foodstuff, however, and seems to indicate bounteous dining (Exod. 16:12; Amos 6:4; Dan. 10:3). Sheep and goats were the main animals prepared for consumption, though cattle and birds were eaten too. Meat was likely roasted (Isa. 44:16) or boiled (1 Sam. 2:3; Ezek. 24:10), and various restrictions applied, such as not eating the blood of an animal (Deut. 12:23) or the sinew of the thigh (Gen. 32:32[MT 33]), or "boiling a kid in its mother's milk" (Exod. 23:19; Deut. 14:21). All animals deemed clean for sacrifice were permissible as food, and according to the levitical code they included ruminants and ungulates, birds (except for carrion), and fish with fins and scales (Lev. 11). The pig and any other unclean animals were avoided.

Bibliography. D. Brothwell and P. Brothwell, *Food in Antiquity,* rev. ed. (Baltimore, 1998); B. Rosen, "Subsistence Economy in Iron Age I," in *From Nomadism to Monarchy: Archaeological and Historical Aspects of Early Israel,* ed. I. Finkelstein and N. Na'aman (Washington, 1994), 339-51.

CAREY WALSH

MEBUNNAI (Heb. *mĕḇunnay*)
One of David's Thirty, called the Hushathite (2 Sam. 23:27). He is probably the same as Sibbecai (2 Sam. 21:18 = 1 Chr. 20:4; 11:29; 27:11).

MECHERATHITE (Heb. *mĕḵērāṯî*)
A gentilic applied to Hepher, one of David's Champions (1 Chr. 11:36). It should probably be read "Maacathite" (Heb. *maʿăḵāṯî;* cf. 2 Sam. 23:34), referring to Maacah.

MECONAH (Heb. *mĕḵōnâ*)
A city in the southern part of Judah (Neh. 11:28), resettled by returned exiles.

MEDAD (Heb. *mêḏāḏ*)
An elder who, with Eldad, prophesied in the wilderness camp outside the tent of meeting (Num. 11:26-29).

MEDAN (Heb. *mĕḏān*)
A son of Abraham and Keturah (Gen. 25:2; 1 Chr. 1:32), presumably the eponymous ancestor of an Arabian group.

MEDEBA (Heb. *mêḏĕḇāʾ*)
A city in the Transjordanian highlands, 30 km. (19 mi.) S of Rabbath-ammon (modern Amman). When the Israelites divided Canaan, the plain of Medeba (Arab. Madaba) was part of the territory assigned to the Reubenites (Josh. 13:16). It had been brought under Israelite influence when the Israelites conquered the Amorite king Sihon (Num. 21:23-30) and became an important boundary between the Reubenites and the tribe of Manasseh (Josh. 13:9, 16).

Israelite control of Medeba was short-lived, since Medeba, as a Moabite city, became a significant staging area for military activities against David (1 Chr. 19:7). David successfully defeated his foes, but Medeba again changed hands after the time of Solomon. King Mesha of Moab claims that he retook Medeba from the Israelites (Mesha Stela 7-9; *ANET,* 320). One can suppose from these accounts that Medeba was probably close to the southern border of Israelite influence and changed allegiance more often than we know. Such changing of loyalties probably generated much animosity. Medeba is listed by Isaiah among the Moabite cities that one day would be decimated (Isa. 15:2).

The consensus of archaeologists is that the modern city of Madaba (225125) rests on the ruins of ancient Medeba. This has made it difficult to uncover evidence of the early biblical periods, although Tell Jalul within sight of Medeba and 5 km. (3 mi.) east may have been one of the material cultural phases of Medeba. One outstanding find from Madaba is the 6th-century A.D. mosaic Madaba Map, a Byzantine mosaic discovered in the floor of a church and the earliest known map of Palestine.

Bibliography. M. Piccirillo, "Medeba (Madaba)," *NEAEHL* 3:992-1001; H. Donner, *The Mosaic Map of Madaba.* Palaestina Antiqua N.S. 7 (Kampen, 1992).

DAVID MERLING

MEDES, MEDIA (Heb., Aram. *māḏay;* Gk. *Mēdoi;* O. Pers. *māda*)

An Indo-iranian people who inhabited the plateau of northern Iran, around the area of modern Hamadan (ancient Ecbatana), and enjoyed a degree of military prominence during the 7th and 6th centuries B.C.E.

Our knowledge of the Medes derives mainly from archaeology, Assyrian royal inscriptions, and Herodotus. Archaeology of the northern highlands shows a clear cultural break between the Bronze and Iron Ages ca. 1500, perhaps linked with the arrival of the Iranians. During Iron I this region appears to have been rather isolated and self-contained, characterized by the so-called Early Western Grey Wares. For Iron II the patterns are more diversified and Assyrian influence is detectable.

From the 9th century on there are references to the Medes in the Assyrian royal inscriptions. Under Assurnasirpal II and Shalmaneser III the Assyrian kings extended their rule into the Zagros. In the process they came into contact with small, ethnically diverse tribes, including the Medes. From the late 9th to mid-8th century Assyrian strength was interrupted by the Urartu expanding from the north into the Zagros. With Tiglath-pileser III, the campaigns into the Zagros recommenced, also against groups designated as "the mighty Medes" and the "distant Medes." Sargon II solidified Assyrian control in the central Western Zagros from out of the center at Harhar. All the while the Medes are referred to as living in provinces or districts, and having many chieftains. The Assyrian annals do not suggest much change in Assyrian control over the region into the 7th century. However, various omen texts refer to stirrings in the East. In the late 7th century under the leadership of a certain Cyaxares, the Medes appear powerful enough to participate in the sacking of Assyrian cities such as Nineveh, Harran, and Assur. The Assyrian annals fail to explain the emergence of such Median strength at this time.

Herodotus appears to fill this gap by giving an internal account of the rise of a Median state. He narrates that a certain Deioces, who was known for justice, was declared king. Uniting various tribes, he made Ecbatana his capital. After his 53-year reign, Deioces' son Phraores succeeded him, subjugating Persia and other Asian countries as well, finally marching against the Assyrians. He was defeated and lost his own life, having reigned 22 years. His son Cyaxares, in turn, conquered Lydia and united all the land beyond the river Halys. Then he successfully campaigned against the Assyrians. Meanwhile, the Scythians, who were pursuing the Cimmerians, invaded Media and exercised tyranny over all Asia for 28 years. Then, however, Cyaxares returned to the Medes control of their former territories, including Assyria but not Babylon. Cyaxares' reign totaled 40 years including the interregnum of the Scythians. He was succeeded by his son Astyages, whose daughter Mandane was wedded to Cambyses and later bore Cyrus II. Cyrus led a revolt of Persian tribes against Astyages, deposing him, and exchanging Median rule for Persian.

Questions have been raised about the accuracy of Herodotus' account. Median sites from the 7th century indicate economic and cultural prosperity. Yet the excavated sites, which exclude Ecbatana, are without evidence of centralization and appear impoverished by the 6th century. Some scholars have argued that the developments towards state formation in the 7th century were stimulated by contact with the Assyrians. Conversely, it has been argued that with the absence of Assyrian political pressure, the Medes, who were never more than tribal groups, weakened. Other scholars have maintained that the ensuing prominence of the Medes among the Persians suggests that the Medes must have been a solidified force at some point. The debate concerning the existence of a Median state is still ongoing.

In the Bible, the Medes appear alongside of the Assyrians, Babylonians, and Persians. The Assyrians settle some of the captives from northern Israel in cities of the Medes (2 Kgs. 17:6; 18:11). Among many nations and cities and their officials, Jeremiah mentions the rulers of the Medes as objects of God's wrath (Jer. 25:25). Elsewhere Median rulers, including governors and deputies, are portrayed as a threat to Babylon (Jer. 51:11, 28; cf. Isa. 13:17; 21:2). The fact that the text uses the plural "rulers" might suggest the absence of Median centralization. The absorption of the Median Empire into the Persian is reflected in the conjunction of "the Medes and the Persians," cited frequently in Esther (Esth. 1:3, 14, 18-19; 10:2), Daniel (Dan. 5:28; 6:8, 12, 15; 8:20), and elsewhere (1 Macc. 1:1; 6:56; Jdt. 16:10; 1 Esdr. 3:1, 14). Judith contains an unhistorical reference to a certain Arphaxad, king of the Medes (Jdt. 1:1). The story of Tobit finds its setting partly in Media among exiled Jews (e.g., Tob. 1:14-15; 3:7). Diaspora Jews from Media are among those present at the Feast of Pentecost (Acts 2:9).

For Darius the Mede, *see* DARIUS **4.**

Bibliography. S. C. Brown, "Media and Secondary State Formation in the Neo-Assyrian Zagros," *JCS* 38 (1986): 107-19; H. Sancisi-Weerdenburg, "Was There Ever a Median Empire?" *Achaemenid History* 3 (1988): 197-212; T. C. Young, Jr., "The Early History of the Medes and the Persians and the Achaemenid Empire to the Death of Cambyses," *CAH* 4:1-52. GERALD M. BILKES

MEDIATOR

A person who stands between two parties to reconcile their differences or to establish a relationship between them. A mediator may be either a neutral go-between who represents the interests of each party to the other, as in the case of an arbitrator in a legal dispute, or an agent for one party who intercedes on its behalf, negotiates a settlement, or personally guarantees an agreement.

This broad array of mediatorial roles may function within the secular realm of human relationships, but religious usage elevates mediation to relationships between deity and humanity. The concept of mediation pervades Scripture, but, surprisingly, the word itself is rarely used. In fact, the OT has no precise equivalent. Occasionally it employs the participle *mēlîṣ*, which properly refers to an interpreter (Gen. 42:23), for the mediatorial role of a spokesman (Isa. 43:27), envoy (2 Chr. 32:31), or angel (Job 33:23); or it may employ the verb *pālal*, "to intervene," for praying or interceding (1 Sam. 2:25). The closest equivalent is found in Job 9:33, where the LXX translates Heb. *môḵîaḥ* ("arbitrator" or "umpire") as *mesítēs*, which is used in the NT for a mediator (Gal. 3:19-20; 1 Tim. 2:5; Heb. 8:6; 9:15; 12:24).

The biblical concept of mediation presupposes that we have been alienated from God by sin but that he desires to bridge the gulf separating us and restore harmonious relations (Isa. 59:1-2). Mediation may in principle be directed either towards God, as in intercessory prayer, or towards humans; but Scripture primarily represents it as God's initiative in reaching down to us through revelation and redemption. Finding a suitable mediator posed a problem, however, in that God cannot properly mediate himself since he is *one* (1 Sam. 2:25; Gal. 3:20), and no sinful person can enter his holy presence. God used angels to convey divine messages and assist in handing down the Law (Deut. 33:2 LXX), but the thunder and smoke on Mt. Sinai were so terrifying that the Israelites could not bear to hear God's voice and requested that Moses relay the message to them (Exod. 20:19). God also used specially chosen and anointed prophets, priests, and kings to mediate his revelation, provisional forgiveness, and theocratic rule until the true Messiah should come. Isaiah promised that the Servant of the Lord would vicariously bear God's punishment for sin and extend the light of revelation to the Gentiles (Isa. 49:6; 53).

In Jesus Christ, God's incarnate Son, the NT discovered the only one who is properly qualified to mediate between God and humanity because he is both fully human and fully divine (1 Tim. 2:5). He is the mediator and guarantor of a new covenant, which is "better" than the Mosaic covenant because it is founded upon his own blood (Luke 22:20; Heb. 7:22; 8:6). As the anointed Messiah, he fulfills all three mediatorial offices of prophet, priest, and king. In him, God has spoken his final, living, and incarnational word. By his atoning death, in which he became both high priest and sacrifice, Jesus has once and for all opened the way into God's presence. He who now rules in believers' hearts and is seated at the Father's right hand, where he intercedes for us, will one day subjugate all his enemies and mediate God's universal kingdom of righteousness and peace. During his present physical absence, the Holy Spirit mediates Christ's presence and adds his own intercession.

Bibliography. A. Oepke, "mesítēs," *TDNT* 4:598-624. DALE F. LESCHERT

MEDICINE

See ILLNESS AND HEALTH CARE.

MEDITERRANEAN SEA

See GREAT SEA.

MEDIUM, WIZARD

A person who engages in necromancy, the divinatory technique of consulting ghosts to obtain oracles about the future. In the OT these two terms most often occur together (except for 1 Sam. 28; 1 Chr. 10:13, where "medium" appears alone). Heb. *yiddĕʿōnî*, "wizard," is derived from the Semitic root *ydʿ*, "to know." Normally translated as "wizard," it refers to practitioners who possess special knowledge of the dead, and presumably other mantic arts. Heb. *ʾôḇ* may designate either the medium who consults the spirit or the ghost itself. The etymology of the word is disputed among scholars, depicting ghosts, spirits of the dead, or ancestors. In addition, *ʾôḇ* may also signify "pit" (cf. Akk. *aptu;* Ugar. *ʾēb*). Extrabiblical sources describe the digging of a ritual pit for the purpose of sacrificial offerings and to implore the spirits of the dead, a practice which Isaiah ridicules (Isa. 29:14). A related term in Deut. 18:11, *dōrēš ʾel-hammēṯîm* ("inquiring of the dead"), refers specifically to the practice of necromancy. The belief that the dead spirits possessed occult knowledge about the future was a prominent feature in ancient Near Eastern mythology and religion; the dead spirits functioned as gods, dispensing oracles, and were often venerated.

In the OT necromancy and other mantic arts were strongly polemized and listed among the abhorrent practices of the other nations. Saul, after exhausting more "legitimate" means of divine communication, seeks a female necromancer, a woman of Endor, to consult with the spirit of Samuel (1 Sam. 28). Lev. 20:27 prescribes capital punishment for anyone who practices necromancy, but in 1 Sam. 28:3-9; 2 Kgs. 23:24 the necromancers were only expelled from the land. JULYE BIDMEAD

MEGIDDO (Heb. *mĕgiddô*)

A medium-sized mound (Tell el-Mutesellim, "Mound of the Governor"/Tel Megiddo; 1675.2212) located in the southwest of the Jezreel Valley. Its significance lies in its location on a major pass leading from the coastal plain into the Jezreel Valley, part of the Via Maris which connected Egypt with the Syro-Mesopotamian world.

Aerial view of Megiddo from the east (Photo Baruch Halpern, the Megiddo Expedition)

Megiddo has been subject to three major and many minor excavations. Gottlieb Schumacher excavated from 1903 to 1905 on behalf of the German Society for Oriental Research, with some results published later by Carl Watzinger. The site was later purchased by John D. Rockefeller for the Oriental Institute of the University of Chicago, which excavated from 1924 to 1939, publishing a series of extensive reports. Yigael Yadin conducted small-scale excavations during the 1960s and 1970s in conjunction with work at Hazor. In 1994 Tel Aviv University began a long-term project directed by David Ussishkin and Israel Finkelstein. This recent project is designed to address unresolved questions left by previous excavations and to reveal entirely new aspects using modern methodologies. Since the recent excavations are on-going, and since the Chicago nomenclature has yet to be supplanted, this review follows the traditional phasing, with updates where necessary.

Stratum XX. This phase is comprised of scattered architectural elements and pottery, and should be dated to the Late Neolithic (Wadi Rabah tradition) and Chalcolithic periods.

Stratum XIX. A structure previously thought to be a "twin temple" of Early Bronze I has been shown to comprise at least two phases of a single broadroom temple dating to the late EB I (Grain Wash tradition) period. The "picture pavement" in the courtyard of this structure is dated to the same period.

Stratum XVIII. An extensive phase also dating to late EB I (Grain Wash tradition). Directly beneath the EB III "Megaron" temple, recent excavations have shown three, possibly four, large (3.5–4.5 m. [11.5–14.75 ft.]) walls of mud brick with cut stone foundations running parallel for more than 40 m. (130 ft.). The areas in between these walls were filled with pottery and animal bones. The entire area appears to have been a huge sacred precinct.

Strata XVII-XVI. Megiddo was largely unoccupied during the EB II period. At the beginning of EB III the sacred precinct was reoccupied, first by an ephemeral squatter level and then by the construction of the large "Megaron" temple circular altar. A large "palace" and massive stone fortification wall were also constructed in this phase.

Stratum XV. Also dating to late EB III, the "Megaron" temple continued in use and was supplemented by the "twin temples," but the "palace" was replaced by a smaller structure.

Stratum XIV. This poorly preserved level dates to Middle Bronze I (IIA). The EB city wall and temples went out of use, but the sacred precinct retained its function, as shown by the retention of the remains of the Megaron temple. EB IV pottery found in this stratum indicates ephemeral settlement during that period, as do tombs on the slope of the tell.

Stratum XIII-B and A. During MB I (IIA), Megiddo was fortified by a heavy mudbrick wall with stone foundations and gateway. The sacred precinct was replaced by open spaces and domestic structures, many of which had burials below the floors.

Stratum XII. In MB II (IIB) the city wall was doubled in width and the sacred precinct resumed its function, as shown by the appearance of standing stones. Domestic architec-

Temples and altar in Megiddo area J (Early Bronze I-III); strata XIX-XV, with stratum XVIII temple walls exposed. Here was discovered the largest extant EB I temple in the Levant
(Photo Baruch Halpern, the Megiddo Expedition)

ture surrounds the area. In the center of the tell a rectangular and palatial structure (the *Nordburg*) was constructed, with a series of rooms around a central court. Just to the south was the *Mittelburg,* a smaller elite residence which also had a series of large burial chambers with corbelled roofs, possibly belonging to the leaders of Megiddo.

Stratum XI. Also dating to MB II (IIB), there was little change in this period except for the addition of a stone revetment and glacis to the fortifications.

Stratum X. This phase is characterized by well-built domestic structures and dates to MB III (IIC) A large palace was also constructed in the north of the site near the fortification and gate. The structure is comprised of a central court surrounded by smaller rooms and connected to the gateway.

Stratum IX. During Late Bronze I, the northern palace was enlarged, and the domestic architecture remained impressive. The stratum was destroyed, probably by Thutmose III.

Stratum VIII. Megiddo was reconstructed in LB IB or IIA. The northern palace was enlarged and was found to contain many prestige items, especially jewelry and carved ivories in a basement treasury. In the area of the earlier sacred precinct a rectangular temple with thick walls was constructed. The fortification walls went out of use but the gate appears to be freestanding. A large administrative or elite structure was recently discovered on the lower terrace of the site and may date to this stratum.

Stratum VII-B. In LB IIB the major structures continued in use, including the palace and large temple. The stratum is heavily destroyed.

Stratum VII-A. This phase may be dated to the very end of LB or the beginning of the Iron Age. The palace and temple were poorly rebuilt, only to be destroyed again.

Stratum VI-B. An ephemeral and unfortified settlement with no public buildings.

Stratum VI-A. Rebuilt on a different plan than the preceding strata, this level contains densely arranged residential architecture and one large structure, possibly an elite residence. Sometimes attributed to the Philistines, this level was violently destroyed, producing a destruction horizon visible across the entire tell.

Stratum V-B. Another unimpressive level, typically attributed to David in the 10th century, consisting of fragmentary domestic architecture, some using pillars.

Stratum V-A–IV-B. Typically attributed to Solomon in the 10th century (cf. 1 Kgs. 9:15), this level was fortified with casement walls and gate and had several elite residences on the North Syrian *bīt ḫilāni* model. Little domestic architecture is known, indicating the site was primarily an administrative and ceremonial center. This phase may have been destroyed by Shishak, whose stela was found at the site.

Stratum IV-A. This long phase dates roughly from the 9th to late 8th centuries. A series of elaborate public buildings was constructed, including structures which may have been stables, administrative buildings, and at least two palaces, on the North Syrian *bīt ḫilāni* model. Also notable are the offset-inset fortification wall and gate, and water system with vertical shaft and tunnel. Remains of unimpressive domestic architecture have been found, suggesting again the administrative character of the site.

Stratum III. This phase dates to the Assyrian takeover of the site in 732 and its transformation into an administrative center. Three large palaces were constructed in the northwest corner, possibly using existing Israelite structures, and then joined together. The existing city wall was used as a terrace to support the new construction and the gate was rebuilt. In a later subphase an orthogonally planned settlement was constructed. The administrative buildings may also have been reused by the Babylonians.

Stratum II. Dating primarily to the Babylonian period, this unfortified phase has scant domestic architecture and one large rectangular fortress, possibly constructed by Josiah.

Stratum I. During the Persian period, the site was weak and unfortified.

Some Late Roman remains have been excavated recently on the lower terrace of the site, indicating minor utilization during that period, when the site of Leggio (el-Lejjun) assumed greater importance.

ALEXANDER H. JOFFE

MEGILLOTH (Heb. *mĕgillôṯ*)
The five books (Heb. "scrolls") of the Hebrew Bible read in synagogues on five of the annual holidays: Ecclesiastes during the Feast of Booths; Esther, Purim (cf. Esth. 9:23-28); Song of Solomon, Passover; Ruth, Pentecost; and Lamentations, the Ninth of Ab (the day of mourning for the destruction of the temple). These books appear together in the third division (the Writings) of the Hebrew canon in this order: Ruth, Song of Solomon, Ecclesiastes, Lamentations, Esther.

MEHETABEL (Heb. *mĕhêṭaḇ'ēl*)
1. The wife of King Hadar/Hadad of Edom; daughter of Matred and descendant of Mezahab (Gen. 36:39; 1 Chr. 1:50).

2. An ancestor of the false prophet Shemaiah (Neh. 6:10).

MEHIDA (Heb. *mĕḥîḏā'*)
A temple servant whose descendants returned with Zerubabbel from captivity (Ezra 2:52; Neh. 7:54).

MEHIR (Heb. *mĕḥîr*)
A Judahite, son of Chelub and father of Eshton (1 Chr. 4:11).

MEHOLATHITE (Heb. *mĕḥōlāṯî*)
A gentilic ascribed to Adriel, the husband of Saul's daughter Merab (1 Sam. 18:19; 2 Sam. 21:8). It may indicate that he was from Abel-meholah.

MEHUJAEL (Heb. *mĕḥûyā'ēl, mĕḥîyā'ēl*)
An ancestor of Lamech; the son of Irad and father of Methushael (Gen. 4:18). Some scholars identify him with Mahalalel.

MEHUMAN (Heb. *mĕhûmān*)
One of the seven eunuchs who served as chamberlains for Ahasuerus (Esth. 1:10).

ME-JARKON (Heb. *mê hayyarqôn*)
A place ("pale green water," or "waters of the Yarkon") within the original tribal allotment of Dan (Josh. 19:46). While the exact location is still uncertain, it was likely along the banks of the Yarkon River (Nahr el-ʿAujā), probably N of Joppa between the Mediterranean coast and Aphek, the large settlement at the headwaters of the Yarkon just 14 km. (9 mi.) from the sea. Since Dan was unable to capture its inheritance, Me-jarkon remained outside of early Israel's control.

DAVID C. MALTSBERGER

MELATIAH (Heb. *mĕlaṭyâ*)
A Gibeonite of Nehemiah's time who worked on the reconstruction of the walls of Jerusalem (Neh. 3:7).

MELCHIOR (Lat. *Melchior*)
The name given by Western tradition to one of three wise men bringing gifts to the child Jesus (Matt. 2:11). The earliest attestation of the name is the *Excerpta Latina Barbari,* a 7th-8th century Latin translation of a 6th-century Greek chronicle from Egypt. Melchior also appears above the representation of the Magi in the 5th-century mosaic of St. Apollinaris (Nouvo) in Ravenna, but it is a later addition. Melchior is usually associated with the gift of gold. His relics and those of his traditional companions are at Cologne.

Bibliography. B. M. Metzger, "Names for the Nameless in the New Testament," in *Kyriakon,* ed. P. Granfield and J. A. Jungmann (Münster, 1970), 1:79-99.

RONALD V. HUGGINS

MELCHIZEDEK (Heb. *malkî-ṣeḏeq;* Gk. *Melchisédek*)
A figure of disputed historicity, described as king of Salem and a priest of El Elyon who blesses Abram (Gen. 14:18-20) and mentioned in conjunction with priesthood and with respect to the Israelite king (Ps. 110:4). Several scholars have attempted to demonstrate the literary influence of one passage on the other. It is frequently suggested that Gen. 14 is a later midrash elucidating Ps. 110, but the brevity of the references and the difficulty in dating Genesis and the Psalms preclude consensus.

Genesis 14

In the present form of the narrative, Gen. 14 describes an alliance of four eastern kings subjugating five cities of the Jordan Valley and the subsequent liberation of the cities by Abram. Following Abram's victory, Melchizedek approaches him with bread and wine and pronounces a blessing upon him and upon the deity El Elyon. A number of inconsistencies in the narrative have led many scholars to conclude that this is a composite text. As such, it is generally agreed that the appearance of Melchizedek in Gen. 14:18-20 reflects a later editorial addition.

The passage has been assigned to various periods in Israelite history. Some scholars assign it to the Davidic monarchy, its purpose being to establish the legitimacy of Jerusalem (the name Salem was associated with Jerusalem from antiquity) and to support a program of religious syncretism (which fused Yahweh with the Canaanite deity El). Others suggest that Gen. 14:18-20 originated in the period of the Divided Monarchy as a polemic against the claims of Bethel, Jerusalem's rival sanctuary to the north. Still others believe the verses were inserted during the postexilic period to strengthen the authority of the postexilic priesthood at Jerusalem and to legitimate their receipt of tithes.

Psalm 110

Ps. 110 is generally classified as a royal psalm that lauds the position and attributes of the king. Textual problems, particularly in Ps. 110:3, 6-7, make it exceedingly difficult to reach positive conclusions. In Ps. 110:4 the king is called "a priest according to the order of Melchizedek," but the precise comparison is unclear. It is far from certain that Heb. *ʿal-diḇrāṯî* (commonly rendered "in the order of") refers to an official religious order per se, for elsewhere the phrase simply means "on account of." To be sure, the oracle considers the king to be "like" Melchizedek, but again, the absence of data on Melchizedek as a historical figure precludes certainty about the precise meaning of the phrase.

Uncertainty about the relationship between the two passages and Melchizedek's historicity should not obsure the fact that the name is invoked in similar literary contexts. In both Gen. 14 and Ps. 110, the primary actor (Abram and the king) is understood to be a victorious leader in warfare. Consequently, one of the primary motifs associated with Melchizedek at the time of the creation of these texts was that of deliverance. This is certainly consistent with images of Melchizedek in the NT (cf. Heb. 5:6, 10; 6:10–7:19) and other writings from the same era (e.g., 11QMelch).

Bibliography. M. C. Astour, "Political and Cosmic Symbolism in Genesis 14 and in Its Babylonian Sources," in *Biblical Motifs,* ed. A. Altmann (Cambridge, Mass., 1966), 65-112; J. A. Emerton, "The Riddle of Genesis XIV," *VT* 21 (1971): 403-39; "Some False Clues in the Study of Genesis XIV," *VT* 21 (1971): 24-47; F. L. Horton, *The Melchizedek Tradition.* SNTSMS 30 (Cambridge, 1976); J. Van Seters, *Abraham in History and Tradition* (New Haven, 1975). DEXTER E. CALLENDER, JR.

MELEA (Gk. *Meleá*)
An ancestor of Jesus, apparently from the time of the Divided Monarchy (Luke 3:31).

MELECH (Heb. *meleḵ*)
One of the sons of Micah (**3**), grandson of Meribaal and great-grandson of Saul's son Jonathan (1 Chr. 8:35; 9:41).

MELONS
The melons of Egypt for which the Israelites longed in the wilderness (Num. 11:5) may have been of more than one variety (Heb. *ʾăḇaṭṭiḥîm;* cf. Arab. *baṭīḫ*). Muskmelons (*Cucumis melo* L.) as well as watermelons (*Citrullus vulgaris*) have been cultivated in Egypt since the earliest times.

MELQART (Phoen. *mlqrt, mlk qrt*)
A god associated with Tyre. The name means "king of the city," either Tyre or (euphemistically) the underworld (cf. Melqart's association with chthonic deities such as Nergal and Resheph), but his cult was widespread throughout the Mediterranean. The first mention of Melqart dates from the 9th/8th century B.C.E. Melqart is mentioned in the theogony of Philo of Byblos, who connects him to Heracles (cf. Herodotus *Hist.* 2.44; 2 Macc 4:18-20). The evidence would suggest that Melqart was a deified king or hero who evolved into a cosmic god of prosperity.

Though the name Melqart is not found in the Bible, Ezekiel's oracle against the king of Tyre (Ezek. 28:1-19; cf. 26:11) may refer to this god. Several scholars believe that Melqart's cult was brought to Israel by Jezebel (cf. 1 Kgs. 16:31-32). The priests of Baal with whom Elijah contends (1 Kgs. 18:20-40) would thus be the priests of Melqart.

Bibliography. S. Ribichini, "Melqart," in *DDD,* 563-65. BRENT A. STRAWN

MEMORIAL PORTION
That portion of the grain offering set apart to the Lord by fire (Lev. 2:2; cf. Num. 5:26). Heb. *ʾazkārâ,* which designates this part of the offering, is based upon the verb "to remember." Its function as a token or sign of the Lord's ownership of the entire harvest, however, has led to various translations. The etymology of the term may still be pertinent though, since the verb can connote the act of remembering by naming or mentioning. Such remembrance or memorializing of Israel's God was certainly a critical component of this part of the grain offering. KEVIN D. HALL

MEMPHIS
A capital city of ancient Egypt during much of the Old Kingdom period, located ca. 20 km. (12.5 mi.) S of Cairo on the west side of the Nile near Mītrahīneh and Saqqâra; Egyp. *mn-nfr* (a name probably derived from that of the pyramid of Pharaoh Pepi I). Foundation of the city as "White Wall" (Egyp. *jnb ḥḏ*) ca. 3000 B.C.E. is traditionally attributed to Menes (cf. Herodotus *Hist.* 3.91). The modern designation of Egypt (from Gk. *Aígyptos*) derives from the name of the sacred area of Ptah's temple in Memphis, "House of the Ka of Ptah." The cult of Ptah-tatenen, the ancient creator-god, patron of artists (identified with Canaanite El and

Kothar, Greek Hephaistos), was the principal cult of Memphis, in particular in the local form of "Ptah South of his Wall." Foreign colonies and cults are attested in the trading center around the harbor (Perunefer) since the New Kingdom, including the cult of Baal Zaphon and Astarte.

The significance of Memphis as administrative center and royal residence of Egypt is reflected in the biblical prophets. Isa. 19:13 (Heb. *mōp̱*); Hos. 9:6 (*mōp̱*) may refer to the political situation in Israel and Egypt shortly before the fall of Samaria (the embassy to the king of So = Sais[?] ca. 727, 2 Kgs. 17:4; Pianchi's [Piye's] conquest of Memphis). Jer. 44:30; 46:14, 19; Ezek. 30:13, 16 may refer to Nebuchadnezzar's campaigns against the Saitic rulers Necho II, Hophra (Apries), and Ahmose II (Amasis). Some of the Jews who fled the Babylonian assault on Judah established residence at Memphis (Jer. 44:1).

Little of the glorious past of Memphis remains, because it served in medieval times as a quarry for the construction of Fostat and Cairo. Still the site shows some impressive colossal statues of Rameses II, a stela of Hophra, and embalming tables of Nekau for the Apis-bull at the south entrance of the Ptah temple. MEINDERT DIJKSTRA

MEMUCAN (Heb. *mĕmûḵān*)
One of the seven officials ("sages") who acted as legal advisers for Ahasuerus, apparently the spokesman for the group (Esth. 1:14, 16, 21).

MENAHEM (Heb. *mĕnaḥēm*)
King of Israel (ca. 746 to 737 B.C.E.). Menahem overthrew Shallum, his rival for the throne after the assassination of Zechariah, after Shallum had reigned but one month. Menahem's usurpation of power was indicative of the chaos that followed the death of Jeroboam II and that led to the decline and fall of the northern kingdom. Since Menahem came from Tirzah, the original capital of Israel under Jeroboam I until Omri founded Samaria, his coup may have been supported by a long-standing anti-Samarian faction that seized the opportunity to gain control.

Menahem's bloody coup was followed by his sack of Tiphsah (2 Kgs. 15:16) and his heavy taxation of Israel to pay off the tribute he owed Tiglath-pileser III of Assyria (vv. 19-20). Whether this was vassal tribute or a payment for military aid to secure a hold on his kingdom is not clear, but Menahem's reign was a time of pro-Assyrian compromise in the struggle against this new threat to peace. His dynasty extended to the two-year reign of his son Pekahiah, who was likely overthrown as a reaction to Menahem's policies.

Bibliography. L. D. Levine, "Menahem and Tiglath-Pileser: A New Synchronism," *BASOR* 206 (1972): 40-42. ANDREW H. BARTELT

MENE, MENE, TEKEL, UPHARSIN
(Aram. *mĕnē'*, *mĕnē'*, *tĕqel ûp̱arsîn*)
Words of judgment which the mysterious hand wrote on the wall of Belshazzar's banquet hall (Dan. 5:5, 25), reflecting God's anger against the Babylonian king for profaning the temple vessels and worshipping idols at his banquet.

Belshazzar's wise men could not make sense of the inscription (the MT of Dan. 5:8 says they could neither read nor interpret the writing), but Daniel interpreted it. The second "mene" (Dan. 5:26) may be a dittography. Belshazzar and his advisers probably would have understood the words as referring to three weights: "a mina [50 or 60 shekels], a shekel, half-shekels [or a half-mina or 'portion']." Daniel makes wordplays on the root letters of the three terms, construing them as verbal forms instead of nouns. The terms thus mean "numbered," "weighed," "divided." The divine message to Belshazzar is: God has *numbered* Belshazzar's kingdom and finished it; Belshazzar has been *weighed* and found lacking; and his kingdom has been *divided* and given to Media and Persia.

A number of scholars have argued that the terms also designate three kings, again listed in descending "value." Various identifications have been made, but Nebuchadnezzar, Belshazzar (who only ruled as regent in the absence of his father, Nabonidus), and Darius (cf. Dan. 5:31; *prsyn* is also a pun on Persia).

Bibliography. J. J. Collins, *Daniel.* Herm (Minneapolis, 1993); D. N. Freedman, "The Prayer of Nabonidus," *BASOR* 145 (1957): 31-32; J. E. Goldingay, *Daniel.* WBC 30 (Dallas, 1989); E. Kraeling, "The Handwriting on the Wall," *JBL* 63 (1944): 11-18. WILLIAM B. NELSON, JR.

MENELAUS (Gk. *Menélaos*)
High priest (ca. 172 to 162 B.C.E.) during the reign of Antiochus IV Epiphanes. A Hellenist extremist firmly against the Zadokite interpretation of Judaism, Menelaus was from a new priestly line rather than from the legitimate ancestral line of the Zadokite priesthood. Although 2 Maccabees states that Menelaus was from the tribe of Benjamin, some Old Latin and Armenian manuscripts indicate he was from the house of Bilgah, a priestly family (cf. Neh. 10:8[MT 9]). Josephus records that Menelaus was the brother of Jason and son of Onias III (*Ant.* 12.237-39), but here Josephus is unreliable.

When Jason, the high priest, sent Menelaus to Antiochus IV with large sums of money for business purposes, Menelaus, who had no qualifications for the high priesthood, nevertheless flattered and bribed Antiochus, thereby securing the high priesthood for himself, outbidding Jason by 300 silver talents (2 Macc. 4:23-24). When Menelaus removed gold vessels from the temple, he aroused the bitter opposition of Jewish traditionalists. According to 2 Macc. 2:32-34, when Onias III, a former Zadokite high priest, denounced Menelaus for the theft of the temple vessels, Menelaus bribed Andronicus, a deputy of Antiochus, urging Andronicus to murder Onias. In 167, presumably under the ill-advised counsel of Menelaus, who advocated the overthrow of the Torah as the civil constitution, Antiochus persecuted Jews who resisted enforced

Hellenism. In addition, in an endeavor to unify his empire, Antiochus imposed a syncretistic cult, perceived by traditional Jews as a desecration of the temple. While some Jews became martyrs and others acquiesced, Mattathias and his sons, with the support of the Hasidim, rose to challenge the process of Hellenization, thus beginning the Maccabean Revolt and the rise of the Hasmonean dynasty. In 164 Judas Maccabeus took control of Jerusalem. The temple was rededicated, the persecutions ended, and it became clear that the Torah would remain the civil constitution. Menelaus tried unsuccessfully to reestablish his authority in Jerusalem. Lysias, guardian of the young Antiochus, blamed Menelaus for his unwise advice to Antiochus and the resulting civil war. In 163/2 Menelaus was taken to Beroea, where he was put to death by submersion in ashes (2 Macc. 13:3-8). After the death of Menelaus, Alcimus became high priest (*Ant.* 12.385-87).

Bibliography. E. Bickerman, *The God of the Maccabees*. SJLA 32 (Leiden, 1979); L. L. Grabbe, *Judaism from Cyrus to Hadrian,* 2 vols. (Minneapolis, 1992); M. Hengel, *Judaism and Hellenism,* 2 vols. (Philadelphia, 1974); E. Schürer, *The History of the Jewish People in the Age of Jesus Christ (125 B.C.–A.D. 135),* rev. ed., 4 vols. (Edinburgh, 1973-1987); V. Tcherikover, *Hellenistic Civilization and the Jews* (1959, repr. New York, 1970).

LYNNE ALCOTT KOGEL

MENNA (Gk. *Menná*)
An ancestor of Jesus, known only from Luke's genealogy (Luke 3:31).

MENORAH
See LAMPSTAND.

MENSTRUATION
See BLOOD, FLOW OF; CLEAN AND UNCLEAN.

MENUHOTH (Heb. *mĕnuḥôṯ*)
Half of the Manahathite clan, which traced descent from Shobal (1 Chr. 2:52).

MEONOTHAI (Heb. *mĕʿônōṯay*)
A Judahite, the son of Othniel and father of Ophrah (1 Chr. 4:13-14).

MEPHAATH (Heb. *mêpaʿaṯ*)
A town in central Transjordan located within the border region between Ammon and Moab. Originally an Amorite city, it later fell within the territory allotted to the Reubenites (Josh. 13:18) and was eventually assigned to the Merarite Levites (21:37; 1 Chr. 6:79[MT 64]). By the time of Jeremiah, Mephaath had come under Moabite jurisdiction (Jer. 48:21). Eusebius mentions that in later times a Roman military camp was stationed there (*Onom.* 128.21).

Although many scholars have identified Mephaath with Tell Jâwah (239140; 10 km. [6 mi.] S of Amman) because of its proximity to a town which seems to retain a corrupted form of the name (Khirbet Nefa'ah), geographical considerations as well as recent archaeological finds suggest a location further south at Umm er-Raṣaṣ (237101). Josh. 13:18; Jer. 48:21 strongly indicate that Mephaath was located on the *Mishor* ("plain"). The line of demarcation between the hill country S of Amman and the plain (the northern portion of which is called the Madaba Plain) is quite distinctive and abrupt. Neither Tell Jâwah nor Khirbet Nefa'ah is located on the plain. Also, excavations at Tell Jâwah indicate that the material culture of this site during Iron II is distinctively Ammonite, while Jer. 48:21 would suggest that a Moabite material culture would be expected. Umm er-Raṣaṣ is not only located on the Moabite Plateau (30 km. [18.5 mi. S of Amman), but has yielded Iron II pottery, which would correspond to Moabite occupation. A mosaic in the floor of the 8th-century C.E. Church of St. Stephen preserves the name, Kastron Mefaa. It was apparently this site to which Eusebius referred (Mephaat; *Onom.* 128.21). When all of the evidence is taken together, Umm er-Raṣaṣ appears to be the best candidate for Mephaath.

RANDALL W. YOUNKER

MEPHIBOSHETH (Heb. *mĕp̄îḇōšeṯ*)
(also MERIBBAAL)

1. A son of Saul by his concubine Rizpah (2 Sam. 21:8). Along with his brother Armoni and five of Saul's grandsons, Mephibosheth was handed over to the Gibeonites for impalement in order to avenge the bloodguilt incurred by Saul's house and thus put an end to the three-year famine (2 Sam. 21:1-6).

2. Saul's grandson and the son of Jonathan. Mephibosheth had been crippled in both legs since early childhood, having fallen (or been dropped) when he and his nurse attempted to flee Gibeah upon hearing the news of the deaths of Saul and Jonathan (2 Sam. 4:4). For a long time he resided in the house of Machir at Lo-debar (2 Sam. 9:4).

In order to fulfill the covenant that he made with Jonathan (1 Sam. 20:14-17), David showed kindness to Mephibosheth, taking him into his care, and providing for him a special place in his royal household (2 Sam. 9:9-13). David again showed Mephibosheth kindness in sparing his life by refusing to hand him over to the Gibeonites along with the sons and grandsons of Saul (2 Sam. 21:7).

The name Mephibosheth ("from the mouth of shame" or "from the mouth of the god Bashtu") is disputed. Throughout the MT of Samuel the name Mephibosheth appears. 1 Chr. 8:34; 9:40, however, use the name Meribbaal. Scholars, for the most part, agree that the name Mephibosheth has replaced Meribbaal in order to conceal the theophoric element "baal," a reference to the Canaanite deity Baal. The LXX, in general, appears to confirm this interpretation. The Lucianic recension, which uses Gk. *Memphibaal,* may preserve the original name of Jonathan's son while Chronicles preserves the original name of Saul's son, the two persons having been confused in the tradition and eventually both coming to bear the same name.

Bibliography. P. K. McCarter, Jr., *2 Samuel*. AB 9 (Garden City, 1984); M. Tsevat, "Ishbosheth and Congeners: The Names and Their Study," *HUCA* 46 (1975): 71-87.

ARNOLD GOTTFRIED BETZ

MERAB (Heb. *mēraḇ*)
The elder daughter of Saul (1 Sam. 14:49), whom he promised to David but then gave to Adriel the Meholathite (18:17-19). The five sons of Adriel and Merab were handed over by David to the Gibeonites to be hung (2 Sam. 21:8-9; some MSS read "Michal").

MERAIAH (Heb. *mĕrāyâ*)
The head of the priestly family of Seraiah at the time of the postexilic high priest Joiakim (Neh. 12:12).

MERAIOTH (Heb. *mĕrāyôṯ*)
(also MEREMOTH)

1. A Levite; descendant of Aaron and ancestor of the high priest Zadok (1 Chr. 6:6-7, 52[MT 5:32-33; 6:37]) and the postexilic leader Ezra (Ezra 7:3).

2. A priest, the son of Ahitub and father of Zadok, and an ancestor of Azariah (1 Chr. 9:11) or Seraiah (Neh. 11:11).

3. A priestly family headed by Helkai at the time of the postexilic high priest Joiakim (Neh. 12:15). In the corresponding list at Neh. 12:3 he is called Meremoth (**4**).

MERARI (Heb. *mĕrārî*)

1. The third son of Levi and father of Mahli and Mushi (Gen. 46:11; Exod. 6:16, 19); eponymous ancestor of the Merarite Levites. During the wilderness wanderings the Merarites camped on the north or right side of the tabernacle, and guarded it from the north. They were in charge of transporting the boards or frames of the tabernacle, the bars, the pillars, the pedestals, and all their requirements. They were also responsible for the pillars of the courtyard, its pedestals, tent pegs and cords; these they carried in four wagons, each pulled by a pair of oxen (Num. 3:33-37; 4:29-33; 7:8).

The Merarites were assigned cities in Canaan from territories allotted to Zebulun (Jokneam, Kartah, Rimmon, and Nahalal), Reuben (Bezer, Jahaz, Kedemoth, and Mephaath), and Gad (Ramoth-in-Gilead, Mahanaim, Heshbon, and Jazer; Josh. 21:34-40; 1 Chr. 6:77-81[MT 62-66]).

During the Second Temple period the genealogy of one group of temple singers, the Ethanites, was connected to the Merarites through Ethan (1 Chr. 6:44-47[29-32]). During this period the sons of Merari were also counted among the gatekeepers. They had responsibility for the western side of the temple and for guarding the storehouses (1 Chr. 26:10, 16-19). Along with the Kohathites, the Merarites were said to have participated in the reforms of Hezekiah (2 Chr. 29:12) and Josiah (2 Chr. 34:12), and to have accompanied Ezra back from Babylon (Ezra 8:18-19).

Bibliography. R. G. Boling and G. E. Wright, *Joshua*. AB 6 (Garden City, 1982); S. Japhet, *I and II Chronicles*. OTL (Louisville, 1993); B. A. Levine, *Numbers 1–20*. AB 4 (New York, 1993).

LISBETH S. FRIED

2. The father of Judith, son of Ox (Jdt. 8:1; 16:7).

MERATHAIM (Heb. *mĕrāṯayim*)
The southern region of Babylonia where the Tigris and Euphrates rivers merge and empty into the Persian Gulf (Jer. 50:21). The Hebrew representation of the Akkadian name of the region, *māt marratîm* (taken from the name of the Persian Gulf, *nar marrâtu*, "bitter river"; cf. Heb. *mrr*), is a play on words that means "(land of) double rebellion" *(mrh)*.

MERCY
The compassionate disposition to forgive someone or to offer aid, assistance, or help to someone in need. Closely connected are such concepts as grace, goodness, love, loving-kindness, compassion, and patience.

Mercy (Heb. *rāḥam, ḥānan*) is an essential quality of God (Exod. 34:6; Deut. 4:31; Ps. 103:8). This is the quality (*ḥeseḏ*, "covenant love"), demonstrated throughout their history (cf. Deut. 30:1-6; Isa. 14:1; Ezek. 39:25-29), by which God faithfully keeps his promises and maintains his covenant relationship with his chosen people despite their unfaithfulness (Gk. *éleos;* Rom. 9:15-16, 23; Eph. 2:4). Israel was often reminded of the relationship between God's *ḥeseḏ* and their covenant with God (Deut. 7:9; 1 Kgs. 8:23; Neh. 1:5; Isa. 55:3; Dan. 9:4).

God's mercy is more than punishment withheld. It actively helps those who are miserable due to circumstances beyond their control. This is demonstrated in Jesus' healing of the blind (Matt. 9:27-31; 20:29-34) and lepers (Luke 17:11-19). The parable of the Prodigal Son (Luke 15:11-32) shows how God is "the Father of all mercies and the God of all consolation" (2 Cor. 1:3); the parable of the merciless servant (Matt. 18:23-35) puts this divine quality in a negative setting. God's merciful faithfulness is most evident in his sending Jesus and saving his people (Rom. 11:30-32; Eph. 2:4). God's mercy will be manifest at the final judgment (2 Tim. 1:18; Jas. 2:13). God is merciful and expects his children to be merciful (Matt. 5:7; Jas. 1:27).

EDWARD P. MYERS

MERCY SEAT
A rectangular slab of pure gold that covered the ark of the covenant (Exod. 25:17-22; Heb. *kappōreṯ*).

MERED (Heb. *mereḏ*)
A son of Ezrah of the tribe of Judah who apparently married both Bithiah ("daughter of Pharaoh") and a Judean woman (1 Chr. 4:17-18).

MEREMOTH (Heb. *mĕrēmôṯ*)

1. A son of Uriah; the priest who weighed the silver, gold, and temple vessels brought back from the Exile (Ezra 8:33).

2. One of the 12 sons of Bani who put away his foreign wife (Ezra 10:36).

3. A son of Uriah and grandson of Hakkoz. He assisted Nehemiah in rebuilding the city wall of Jerusalem (Neh. 3:4, 21) and, along with Nehemiah, signed a document pledging to keep the law (10:5[MT 6]).

4. A priest who returned from the Babylonian captivity with Zerubbabel and Jeshua (Neh. 12:3).

RODNEY ASHLOCK

MERENPTAH (Egyp. *Mr-n-ptḥ*)
Pharaoh of Egypt 1212-1202 B.C.; the 13th son of Rameses II and son of Queen Isis-nofret I. From early age he was trained as a soldier, and late in his father's reign served as a military general in Egypt. He married a daughter of his famous brother Kha-em-waset I, named Isis-nofret (II). They had several known sons, including Sety-merenptah, his successor, another Kha-em-waset (II), and possibly also Amenmesse, who usurped the throne, most likely at Merenptah's death.

Already aged nearly 60 at his accession, Merenptah nonetheless defended Egypt militarily against several major threats. First, he led a campaign into Canaan, probably in regnal year 2-3, against Ashkelon, Gezer, Yano'am, and, recorded for the first time in history, the people Israel. The campaign is recorded on his famed "Israel" stela (Cairo 34025) and in a series of battle reliefs at the Karnak temple. The battle reliefs depict the three cities and a battle in the open, which most probably depicts Israel. Following this campaign, Merenptah posted Egyptian troops in the highlands of Canaan, evidently to deter the Israelites' efforts to break out into the low country. A papyrus documents the Egyptians' tight control over the boundary between Egypt and the Ways of Horus, the name given the road with its fortified wells across Sinai. This explains why the fleeing Israelites took the southern route through Sinai. Merenptah's stela and battle reliefs unequivocally show that by his reign the Israelites had already departed Egypt, making his father, Rameses II, the likely pharaoh of Exodus.

Merenptah facing Re-Horakhty, the evening form of the sun-god; a conventional scene at the opening of all the Ramesside royal tombs. Wall painting from tomb of Merenptah, West Thebes (F. J. Yurco)

Merenptah next had to face an attack from the west, along the Wadi Natrun by the allied Libyans and Sea Peoples. Simultaneously, the Nubians revolted in the south. Merenptah defeated the enemy alliance near Memphis, and sent them fleeing back to Libya. As his long inscription at Karnak recounts, the Sea Peoples had interfered with his grain shipments to the Hittites, with whom Egypt had been allied since the epic peace treaty signed by Rameses II and Hattusilis III in 1258. The Sea Peoples had evidently shifted to their second phase of activity, sacking cities, as the Homeric epics record, and attacking the imperial states. The casualties stand in sober contrast to the inflated counts of other pharaohs, or the exaggerated numbers claimed in the Exodus account.

Merenptah conducted a major two-year-long inventory of the holdings of all Egypt's temples. He did not build extensively, using vacant wall space to record his victories. His funerary temple in western Thebes was largely built by quarrying away Amenhotep III's temple. So too, the "Israel" stela was usurped from Amenhotep III, who is still depicted on the front side.

Overall, Merenptah's reign reflects a successful defense of Egypt against foreign threats and revolts, coupled with continued prosperity at home. His measures in Canaan helped preserve the Egyptian Empire intact until Rameses III took over.

Bibliography. K. A. Kitchen, *Pharaoh Triumphant* (Warminster, 1983); F. J. Yurco, "Merenptah's Canaanite Campaign," *Journal of the American Research Center in Egypt* 23 (1986): 189-215; "3,200-Year-Old Pictures of Israelites Found in Egypt," *BARev* 16/5 (1990): 20-38.

FRANK J. YURCO

MERES (Heb. *meres*)
One of the seven princes who acted as advisers for Ahasuerus (Esth. 1:14).

MERIBAH
See MASSAH, MERIBAH.

MERIBATH-KADESH (Heb. *mĕrîḇaṯ qāḏēš*)
A name given to Kadesh-barnea because of the Israelites' testing of God during their wilderness journeys (Deut. 32:51; cf. Num. 20:1-3; 27:14). This new name occurs in Ezekiel's descriptions of the southern borders of the land of the new Israel (Ezek. 47:19; 48:28).

See KADESH, KADESH-BARNEA (**1**); MASSAH, MERIBAH.

MERIBBAAL (Heb. *mĕrîḇ-ba'al*)
Saul's grandson and the son of Jonathan (1 Chr. 8:34; 9:40). In 1–2 Samuel the name ("from the mouth of Baal") is changed to Mephibosheth ("from the mouth of shame").

See MEPHIBOSHETH **2.**

MERNEPTAH

See MERENPTAH.

MERODACH (Heb. *mĕrōḏāḵ*)
Hebrew form of Marduk (Jer. 50:2).

MERODACH-BALADAN (Heb. *mĕrōḏāḵ bal'ăḏān;* Akk. *marduk-apla-iddina*)
A Chaldean sheikh of the Bīt-yakin tribe and twice king of Babylon. As early as ca. 731 B.C. he was allied with Tiglath-pileser III of Assyria against another Babylonian ruler. Taking advantage of a perceived weakness in Assyria when Sargon II (721-705) usurped the throne, Merodach-baladan became king of Babylon, most likely with the help of neighboring Elam. The Assyrians were unable to remove him from Babylon until they defeated his Elamite allies in 710. Having no allies thereafter, Merodach-baladan was deposed by Sargon and once again became a local Chaldean sheikh, vassal to the Assyrian king.

Upon Sargon's death in battle in 705, Merodach-baladan helped to instigate a rebellion against Assyrian rule. It is here that the narrative in 2 Kgs. 20:12-19 (cf. Isa. 39:1-8) is likely to be placed. The Babylonian sheikh came to Jerusalem to entreat King Hezekiah of Judah to support his cause, a plan which was opposed by the prophet Isaiah. But in view of Hezekiah's actions against Assyrian rule, he apparently did act in concert with Merodach-baladan's strategy. Merodach-baladan deposed the Assyrian appointee to the Babylonian throne in 703 and ruled from nearby Borsippa until he himself was deposed that same year by Sennacherib, the new king of Assyria. Merodach-baladan fled to Elam, where he died soon thereafter.

Bibliography. J. A. Brinkman, "Merodach-Baladan II," in *Studies Presented to A. Leo Oppenheim,* ed. R. Biggs and J. A. Brinkman (Chicago, 1964), 6-53; *Prelude to Empire: Babylonian Society and Politics, 747-626 B.C.* (Philadelphia, 1984).

MARK W. CHAVALAS

MEROM (Heb. *mērôm*)
The "waters" or spring near which a coalition of Canaanite kings under the leadership of Jabin of Hazor gathered to fight Joshua and the Israelites (Josh. 11:5, 7). A major city in Upper Galilee, Merom is first mentioned in the annals of Thutmose III, Rameses II, and Tiglath-pileser III. The identification of Merom is uncertain. Traditionally, it has been identified with Meiron at the base of Jebel Jarmaq. Recent excavations, however, have indicated that Meiron was founded in the Hellenistic period, ruling out an identification with Canaanite Merom. Some suggest an identification with Tell el-Khirbeh (190275), a large Canaanite tell E of Hazor and N of the previously uninhabited wooded region which was heavily settled by early Israelites.

RONALD A. SIMKINS

MERONOTHITE (Heb. *mērōnōṯî*)
A gentilic designation of Jehdeiah, chief herder of David's donkeys (1 Chr. 27:30), and Jadon, one of the postexilic rebuilders of the walls of Jerusalem (Neh. 3:7). It is apparently related to Mizpah.

MEROZ (Heb. *mērôz*)
Town mentioned in the Song of Deborah (Judg. 5:23), whose inhabitants were condemned by an angel of the Lord for failing to participate in Deborah and Barak's battle against Sisera. Although several locations have been proposed, including Khirbet Mārûs/Ḥorvat Marish (199270) and Shimron-meron (170234), none are convincing. The town was probably situated in or near the Jezreel Valley.

KENNETH ATKINSON

MESHA (Heb. *mêšā', mêšā'*) **(PERSON)**

1. King of the Transjordanian kingdom of Moab during the early 9th century B.C.E.; son of Chemosh-yati. According to 2 Kgs. 3:4 Mesha was a sheep breeder (Heb. *nōqēḏ*) and a vassal of the "king of Israel." After the death of King Ahab of Israel in 850, Mesha withheld his tribute. Jehoram, Ahab's son, succeeded his brother Ahaziah and then requested the assistance of King Jehoshaphat of Judah and an unnamed royal Edomite vassal; their combined armies routed the Moabites. Some of the surviving Moabites entered Kir-hareseth, a fortified city. In an attempt to appease Chemosh, the national god of Moab, the Moabite king sacrificed his eldest son on the wall of the city. The appalled Israelites then lifted their siege of the city.

In 1868 the Moabite Stone was found at Dhiban (biblical Dibon), the capital of ancient Moab; the inscription was commissioned by Mesha. Here Mesha indicates that it was King Omri of Israel who subjugated Moab and initiated "40 years" (l. 8) of vassalage. But during the reign of "his son" (l. 6), Mesha regained his independence by driving the Israelites out of various cities north of the Arnon River, including Nebo. At Nebo he claims to have killed thousands of Israelites and to have taken certain vessels of Yahweh. Mesha attributes his success to Chemosh. Moab's independence was probably made possible in part because of Israel's preoccupation with resistance to Shalmaneser III.

Some consider the biblical and inscriptional materials to reflect two different episodes in the history of Israelite-Moabite relations (Cogan and Tadmor) while others consider them supplementary versions (Cross and Freedman).

Bibliography. M. Cogan and H. Tadmor, *II Kings.* AB 11 (Garden City, 1988); F. M. Cross, Jr., and D. N. Freedman, *Early Hebrew Orthography.* AOS 36 (1952, repr. New Haven, 1981); J. A. Dearman, ed., *Studies in the Mesha Inscription and Moab.* SBLABS 2 (Atlanta, 1989); G. L. Mattingly, "Moabites," in *Peoples of the Old Testament World,* ed. A. J. Hoerth, Mattingly, and E. M. Yamauchi

(Grand Rapids, 1994), 317-33; K. A. D. Smelik, *Converting the Past: Studies in Ancient Israelite and Moabite Historiography.* OuTS 28 (Leiden, 1992).

CHRIS A. ROLLSTON

2. A son of Caleb, father of Ziph (1 Chr. 2:42; LXX "Mareshah").

3. A Benjaminite, son of Shaharaim and Hodesh born in Moab (1 Chr. 8:9).

MESHA (Heb. *mēšā'*) **(PLACE)**
A boundary of the region inhabited by the descendants of Joktan (Gen. 10:30). Mesha was most likely a location in the desert of Syria or Arabia; indeed, several of the Joktanite names suggest a south Arabian origin. Some scholars identify Mesha with Massa (Gen. 25:14).

MESHACH (Heb., Aram. *mêšak*)
The Babylonian name (Akk. *Mîša-aku,* "Who is that which Aku [a Sumerian lunar deity] is") given to one of Daniel's companions (Dan. 1:7; 2:49; 3:12-30). Meshach's Hebrew name, Mishael (*mîšā'ēl*), means "Who is what God is?"

See ABEDNEGO.

MESHECH (Heb. *mešek*) (also MASH)

1. One of the seven sons of Japheth (Gen. 10:2; 1 Chr. 1:5). According to the Table of Nations the descendants of Japheth dwelled in Europe and Asia. Meshech is mentioned in Akkadian sources as early as 1100 B.C.E., as Muški, a people noted for skill in metallurgy. Meshech was located in eastern Asia, in Cappadocia according to Josephus (*Ant.* 1.6.1 [125]), but west by other ancient writers. The best known of their kings was Midas, whose touch was said to turn things to gold.

Ps. 120:5 mentions Meshech in parallelism with Kedar as a far-off, militaristic people. Gen. 10:2 associates Meshech with Tubal and Javan. In Ezekiel they are linked as trading partners with Tyre (Ezek. 27:13), and Meshech and Tubal are incorporated into the kingdom of Magog, ruled by Gog (38:2; 39:1). The kingdom and its king serve as symbols of any future enemies who would attack the Jews back in their homeland.

2. A son of Shem, eponymous ancestor of an Aramean people (1 Chr. 1:17). In Gen. 10:23 the corresponding name is Mash. PAUL L. REDDITT

MESHELEMIAH (Heb. *mĕšelemyâ, mĕšelemyāhû*)
A Korathite Levite who was a temple gatekeeper at the time of David; father of Zechariah, also a temple gatekeeper (1 Chr. 9:21; 26:1-2, 9). Meshelemiah may be the same as Shelemiah (1 Chr. 26:14) and possibly Shallum (9:17, 19, 31; Ezra 2:42 = Neh. 7:45).

MESHEZABEL (Heb. *mĕšêzab'ēl*)

1. An ancestor of Meshullam (**13**), who worked on rebuilding the walls of Jerusalem (Neh. 3:4).

2. An Israelite who participated in the sealing of the new covenant under Nehemiah (Neh. 10:21[MT 22]).

3. The father of Pethahiah of the Judahite family of Zerah (Neh. 11:24).

MESHILLEMOTH (Heb. *mĕšillēmôt*), **MESHILLEMITH** (*mĕšillēmît*)

1. An Ephraimite, the father of Berechiah (2 Chr. 28:12).

2. A priest and descendant of Immer (Neh. 11:13). At 1 Chr. 9:12 he is called Meshillemith.

MESHOBAB (Heb. *mĕšôbāb*)
One of 12 Simeonite leaders who took possession of the pastures at Gedor during the days of King Hezekiah (1 Chr. 4:34-41).

MESHULLAM (Heb. *mĕšullām*)

1. The grandfather of the scribe Shaphan and father of Azaliah (2 Kgs. 22:3).

2. A son of Zerubbabel (1 Chr. 3:19).

3. The head of a Gadite clan in Bashan (1 Chr. 5:13).

4. A son of Elpaal, a Benjaminite (1 Chr. 8:17).

5. The father of Sallu, a descendant of Benjamin; among the first Benjaminites to return from the Exile (1 Chr. 9:7; Neh. 11:7).

6. The son of Shephatiah; a Benjaminite who returned from the Exile (1 Chr. 9:8).

7. The father of Hilkiah and son of Zadok; of priestly descent (1 Chr. 9:11; Neh. 11:11).

8. The father of Jahzerah and son of Meshillemith; of priestly descent (1 Chr. 9:12).

9. A Kohathite appointed by Josiah as an overseer of the temple repairs (2 Chr. 34:12).

10. One of the "leaders" sent by Ezra to procure Levites to serve as priests in the temple (Ezra 8:16), a "man of understanding" (1 Esdr. 8:44). He may be the same as **11** and **12** below.

11. One who opposed Ezra's policy of divorcing the foreign wives (Ezra 10:15; 1 Esdr. 9:14), possibly a Levite.

12. The son of Bani who had married a foreign wife and was forced to divorce her (Ezra 10:29).

13. The son of Berechiah who helped repair the walls of Jerusalem (Neh. 3:4, 30). His daughter married Tobiah's son Jehohanan (Neh. 6:18).

14. The son of Besodeiah who helped repair the Old Gate (Neh. 3:6).

15. One who stood at Ezra's left hand during the reading of the Law (Neh. 8:4). The privilege of participating in the ceremony indicated a position of honor.

16. A priest who, along with Nehemiah, "set his seal" to the covenant between God and the people (Neh. 10:7[MT 8]).

17. A chief of the people who sealed the covenant under Nehemiah (Neh. 10:20[21]).

18. The head of the priestly house of Ezra in the time of the high priest Joiakim (Neh. 12:13).

19. The head of the priestly house of Ginnethon in the time of the high priest Joiakim (Neh. 12:16).

20. A gatekeeper who guarded the storehouses of the gates in the time of high priest Joiakim (Neh. 12:25).

21. One who participated in the procession dedicating the rebuilt walls of Jerusalem (Neh. 12:33). HAROLD R. MOSLEY

MESHULLEMETH (Heb. *mĕšullemeṯ*)
The daughter of Haruz of Jotbah, wife of King Manasseh of Judah, and mother of King Amon (2 Kgs. 21:19).

MESOPOTAMIA (Gk. *Mesopotamía*)
A Greek term meaning "(land) in the middle of the river(s)." It originally referred to a satrapy formed by Alexander the Great between the Tigris and Euphrates rivers, specifically the area east of the great bend of the Euphrates in modern Syria and northern Iraq. An earlier Hebrew term, *'ăram nahărayim,* designated only "land within the river," i.e., the area within the bend of the Euphrates itself. A still earlier Akkadian term, *bīrinārim,* referred to the same area as early as the Old Babylonian period. Aram. *beyn nahrin,* whose semantic range differed slightly from the Hebrew and Akkadian expressions, was the first to imply the area between the two rivers. English versions of the Bible render both the Hebrew and Greek terms as "Mesopotamia."

In modern archaeology, Mesopotamia is an area roughly defined by the two rivers and their tributaries. This differs from earlier usage in denoting the area between the Taurus Mountains in Anatolia and the Arabo-Persian Gulf in the south. In broad terms, this area formed a cultural unit distinct from the Levant, Anatolia, and Iran from perhaps 5000 B.C. until Alexander's conquest.

Bibliography. J. J. Finkelstein, "'Mesopotamia,'" *JNES* 21 (1962): 73-92. GEOFF EMBERLING

MESSIAH
The word "Messiah" is an adjectival form with a passive sense derived from the Hebrew verb meaning "to anoint." It can be used adjectivally ("the anointed priest"; Lev. 4:3), though its most common form is nominal (Heb. *māšîaḥ*). In the 30 occurrences of the term in the OT, there is no single occurrence of the form "the Messiah," with the definite article and no modifier. The biblical forms are "the Lord's Anointed" (used with the divine name), or "my Anointed," "his anointed," and "your anointed" (with pronominal suffixes referring to God). While used occasionally of priests and prophets, the term is used to refer principally to kings whose installation to office included a ritual anointing (cf. 1 Sam. 10:1; 16:13).

The use of "the Messiah" (or "the Christ") in the NT and subsequent Christian literature (Gk. *Messías*) and "the [King] Messiah" in later Jewish writings — referring to a single figure who needs no more qualification — presumes a history of interpretation that can be reconstructed, at least in part, from extant postbiblical literature. "The Messiah" is thus a term with roots in the OT but whose meaning arises from postbiblical usage. No simple trajectory through the OT can account for its place in later visions and dreams of the future, nor can what qualifies as "messianic" be measured simply in terms of a historical development within biblical Israel. References to "the Messiah" make little sense, however, without knowledge of the biblical tradition.

In early Christian and rabbinic tradition, "the Messiah [King]" refers to a royal figure who will play a crucial role in the last days. For a variety of reasons, traditions about the king from the Davidic line came to be projected into the future. While the king to come is not identified as "*the* Messiah" until the NT and rabbinic writings, there are precursors of such usage especially in Ps. Sol. 17 (where the coming ruler is identified as "the Anointed of Israel," "the prince," or "the branch of David").

In references to this coming king, linguistic connections with "anointing" are not always preserved. The use of "the Messiah" presumes some knowledge of the ritual of installation but also reflects the centrality of certain OT passages like Ps. 2, in which the king is identified as "anointed." The NT, the Psalms of Solomon, and the Qumran scrolls give evidence that this psalm was central to an expectation of a king to come at the end of days to rule in Israel. This royal figure, identified by the psalmist as "his [the Lord's] anointed" (Ps. 2:2) and "my king on Zion" (v. 6), whom God addresses as "son" (v. 7) is linked with the "seed" God promises David in 2 Sam. 7:10-14 — a royal figure whose throne God promises to establish for ever and whom God likewise addresses as "son."

Likewise central in the constellation of biblical "messianic" texts are Gen. 49:10; Num. 24:17; Isa. 11:1; Jer. 23:5-6; 33:14-17. Each of these passages speaks in a distinctive way about a royal figure. Later interpreters read such passages as oracles, deriving their meaning not from the historical or literary context of the verses but by relocating them in a new interpretive construct. Whatever Jeremiah or Isaiah or the authors of Genesis and Numbers thought, later readers of the Bible heard their words as predictions of "the" coming king — predictions they wove together with a variety of other biblical passages to form distinct visions of what God had in store for them.

Eschatological Variety

It is useful to distinguish between "messianic" and "eschatological." While "messianic" refers to a promised future, not all envisioned futures are "messianic." There were Jews whose future hopes were invested in a king from the line of David, "the Lord's anointed" (Ps. Sol. 17). In their visions, the king would deliver Israel from foreign bondage (Roman) and establish an ideal kingdom in which justice would rule. This "messianic eschatology" is probably the way most students of the Bible have been taught to think of "messiah" and "messianic."

Readers of the OT developed a wide variety of alternative expectations, however, in which a royal figure was either completely absent or subordinated to another deliverer. The Samaritans, e.g., who considered as "scripture" only the first five books of the Bible, invested no hopes in a king from the line of David. Their future was invested in a *Taheb* ("restorer") in the form of a new Moses, whose coming was understood in terms of such passages as Deut. 18:15-20. Others whose view of the future was cast in the form of bizarre visions (apocalyptists) often had little room for a messianic figure. While the author of 4 Ezra expected a "Messiah" from the line of David, the actual function of the royal figure is limited. At the close of the 400-year "messianic" age, the Messiah dies with the rest of the created order, and in the age to come, after the general resurrection, God alone rules and judges. Some groups expected the return of Elijah — and not simply as the precursor of the Messiah. At Qumran two "anointed ones" were expected — one a priest, the other a royal figure, with the priest clearly superior to his lay counterpart. In all these cases, biblical passages were chosen and combined to fashion diverse and distinct pictures of what was to come.

Common Themes

While there is remarkable variety among eschatological visions, and while evidence does not permit regarding "the Messiah" as the most popular deliverer, some generalizations about "the Messiah" are possible.

When the term (or its Greek equivalent) is used in the form with a definite article, whether in early Christian or rabbinic literature, it refers to a royal figure — the king to come. There is ample evidence to indicate that in the 1st century C.E. (and perhaps 1st century B.C.E.) those who heard the expression "the Messiah" would think of a king — with few exceptions, the king from the line of David who would arise at the end of days to save Israel.

While there is no uniformity even among messianic traditions, there is a constellation of biblical passages that appear with sufficient regularity so as to be viewed as constants (including Pss. 2, 89, 132; 2 Sam. 7 par.; Num. 24:17; Gen. 49:10; Isa. 11:1; Jer. 23:5-6; 33:17-22). The variety within visions of a messianic future is limited by the imagery appropriate to a king.

As a royal figure, "the Messiah" must be distinguished from prophetic and priestly deliverers who appear in eschatological traditions. While some of the traits could be exchanged, there was no general collapsing of one figure into another. Only later could Christian interpreters combine all the traits into one figure, culminating with Calvin's threefold office of prophet, priest, and king. The employment of messianic passages at Qumran offers a striking example of an eschatological vision in which at least two deliverers are expected, both of whom are "anointed."

The actual deployment of Scripture in "messianic exegesis" often resulted in the omission of texts others might have regarded as central, while passages never recognized as "messianic" could be "adopted" into interpretive traditions. An example would be the reading of Isa. 52–53 in Christian literature and in the Targum of Isaiah as a reference to the Messiah-King. Such variety makes it impossible to identify precisely a single "messianic tradition" in postbiblical Judaism, though we can note the biblical passages that seem to appear as constants among interpreters.

While there is considerable debate about how central "the Messiah" was to Jewish eschatological tradition, there can be little doubt that the importance and centrality of royal ideology has been exaggerated and the variety within Jewish tradition underestimated.

In the case of messianic tradition, as well as all other traditions, the Scriptures played a central role — but the interpretation of the biblical material was influenced by a variety of factors, including social situation and historical events. "The Messiah" exists only in particular contexts. The precise meaning of the term therefore depends upon those various contexts and can be determined only by attending to such particulars.

Bibliography. J. H. Charlesworth, ed., *The Messiah: Developments in Earliest Judaism and Christianity* (Minneapolis, 1992); N. A. Dahl, *Jesus the Christ: The Historical Origins of Christological Doctrine* (Minneapolis, 1991); D. Juel, *Messianic Exegesis: Christological Interpretation of the Old Testament in Earliest Christianity* (Minneapolis, 1988); G. Vermes, *Jesus the Jew* (Philadelphia, 1981).

DONALD JUEL

MESSIANIC WOES

A tumultuous period of eschatological distress and tribulation that, according to early Judaism, was to precede the coming of the Messiah. Characteristic features include apostasy, war, earthquakes, drought, famine, pestilence, familial strife and betrayal, cosmic signs, increasing wickedness, and the scarcity of truth and wisdom. Otherwise known in the rabbinic literature as the "birth pangs of the Messiah," these woes lead inexorably to the birth of the final state of blessedness.

The concept of messianic woes has OT roots (Isa. 13:6-8; 26:16-19; Jer. 13:21; Mic. 5:2-4[MT 1-3]; 7:1-6), more generally in OT depictions of the trauma associated with the day of the Lord (e.g., Joel 1:15–2:11; 2:30-31[3:3-4]; Zeph. 1:14-18; esp. Dan. 12:1-3).

The messianic woes pattern finds fuller development in the OT Apocrypha and Pseudepigrapha (4 Ezra 5:1-13; 2 Apoc. Bar. 25–32; Jub. 23:13-25; Apoc. Abr. 30:4-8; T. Mos. 8–9), the Dead Sea Scrolls (1QH 3:3-18), the NT, and in patristic (Did. 16:3-6; Herm. Vis. 4.1-2; Barn. 4:3-5) and rabbinic (*m. Soṭa* 9:15; *b. Sanh.* 97a-98b; *Šabb.* 118a; *Pesaḥ.* 118a; *Ketub.* 111a) literature.

The Synoptic eschatological discourse (Matt. 24; Mark 13; Luke 21) offers a striking NT parallel to the Jewish notion of messianic woes (cf. the "beginning of birth pangs," Matt. 24:8; Mark 13:8), as do the visions of the seven seals, trumpets, and bowls (Rev. 6–16). Numerous other NT texts may also share this same background (e.g., Matt. 10:17-23, 34-36; Rom. 8:17-18; 2 Cor. 4:16-17; 1 Thess. 3:3-5).

In early Judaism, the messianic woes were "messianic" not because the Messiah suffered them, but because these woes were the necessary prelude to the Messiah's arrival. In light of the Cross, however, early Christians understood that the messianic woes had indeed fallen upon the Messiah himself. As the messianic community, these Christians anticipated that just as the Messiah had suffered eschatological tribulation prior to his resurrection, they also would suffer the messianic woes until their own resurrection at the Messiah's second coming (Acts 14:22; Phil. 3:10-11; 1 Pet. 4:12-13).

Bibliography. D. C. Allison, Jr., *The End of the Ages Has Come: An Early Interpretation of the Passion and Resurrection of Jesus* (Philadelphia, 1985); E. Best, *One Body in Christ: A Study in the Relationship of the Church to Christ in the Epistles of the Apostle Paul* (London, 1955), 130-36; C. Gempf, "The Imagery of Birth Pangs in the New Testament," *TynBul* 45 (1994): 119-35; D. S. Russell, *The Method and Message of Jewish Apocalyptic, 200 B.C.–A.D. 100.* OTL (Philadelphia, 1964), 271-76.

MARK DUBIS

METALS, METALWORKING

Elements having a shiny luster that may be shaped to form tools and weapons. Stable metals such as gold and copper occur in a pure or native state. These metals were the earliest to be widely exploited. Most are chemically reactive and are found combined with nonmetals such as oxygen and sulfur in stable rock ores. The acquisition and shaping of metals was a complicated process which required determination and technical expertise. Metals were thus valuable in antiquity. OT lists identify known metals in descending order of their value as gold, silver, copper, iron, tin, and lead.

Gold is the first and most precious metal mentioned in the Bible (Gen. 2:11-12). Its distinctive luster which does not tarnish, together with its great malleability, contributed to its use in the decoration of ceremonial items (Exod. 25) and jewelry (Gen. 24:22; Exod. 28:22). Gold is easily melted, but it was rarely cast in molds because of its scarcity and subsequent value (Exod. 32:4). Typically gold was hammered out into a thin foil between layers of leather and impressed upon surfaces of base metal or wood which subsequently glittered as in the case of the interior walls and carvings of Solomon's temple (1 Kgs. 6:20-36).

Silver has long been valued for its reflective luster and used as a medium of exchange. Abraham purchased land in Machpelah for a weight of 400 shekels of silver (Gen. 23:14-16) long before silver was minted into coinage (Matt. 26:15). Silver was raised to form drinking vessels and other utilitarian objects used by the wealthy (Gen. 44:2) and was cast or hammered over base materials in the manufacture and decoration of idols (Judg. 17:1-4; Acts 19:24).

Copper is a ductile metal which was early utilized by metallurgists. Available in the Levant (Deut. 8:9), it was used mainly for decorative work and containers until tougher cuprous alloys like arsenical copper and bronze were developed. Copper alloys were used by the Israelites in sacred construction (Exod. 27:2-19; 1 Kgs. 7:15), for weaponry (2 Chr. 12:10), and a variety of tools. The Israelites used copper objects as a means of exchange (Ezek. 27:13), and eventually copper became the metal of small coinage (Mark 12:42).

Iron is a utilitarian metal commonly found in Canaan (Deut. 8:9). This metal was known prior to its extensive utilization in the period of the Israelite monarchy. Iron supplanted bronze when the refining process was improved along with the product. The Israelites employed iron tools in masonry (Deut. 27:5; 1 Kgs. 7:9), carpentry (2 Sam. 12:31; 1 Chr. 22:3), agronomy (1 Sam. 13:20), and weaponry.

Tin is rarely mentioned in the Bible. It was generally imported to the Levant, where its primary importance was as an alloy in the manufacture of bronze. While used with copper, and not readily available from local sources, it was listed after iron as a part of the Israelite plunder in the Transjordan (Num. 31:22) and a commodity for which the Israelites traded (Ezek. 27:12).

Lead is a dense but soft grey metal. Its weight was a positive attribute that led to its use in sinkers for fishing nets (Exod. 15:10) and as weights (Zech. 5:7). The softness of the metal also made it a possible writing surface for permanent documents (Job 19:24). Its low melting point made it a useful flux in the refinement of silver and a cheap component incorporated in alloys used for coins and cutlery.

Metalworking and metalworkers were not uniformly held in high regard among the Israelites, and certainly not as highly as they were held by other peoples. Those who worked in nonferrous metals and made finely finished products were held in renown (1 Kgs. 7:13; Exod. 31:2-6). The working conditions of those who processed ore and hammered hot metal were not glamorous (Isa. 44:12). The Israelites recognized that all smiths were mere mortals (Isa. 54:16). Writers of OT history and ancient generals recognized metallurgy as a strategic craft producing necessary tools and weapons (1 Sam. 13:19; 2 Kgs. 24:14; Jer. 24:1). Israelite prophets castigated metalworkers who formed hapless idols (Jer. 10:9, 14; Isa. 40:19; 41:7; 46:6-7) but also depicted God as a metalworker who shaped and refined his people through their national experience (2 Kgs. 24:14). Metalworking is depicted in the Bible as being formatively shaped by Tubal-cain (Gen. 4:22).

Archaeologists find metalworking to provide a crude chronometer as the prominent utilitarian metals proceeded from copper, to bronze, to iron with the development of metallurgical technology. The utilization of native metals for ornamentation is artifactually evidenced as early as the 8th millennium and throughout the Neolithic period when most tools were made of hard stones. Metal tools supplanted lithics as they possessed superior qualities to stone. The acquisition of metals required the location and collection of metal-rich ores. Ore was then crushed, ground to a powder, and heated to extract the metal. Pyrotechnology was important in the extraction process which is the initial task of metalworkers. Simple fires were hot enough to melt gold and for the sintering of copper. Bowl-shaped, clay-lined furnaces with air forced through blow

Jabal Hamrat Fidan (Site 120, Area C), a Pre-pottery Neolithic settlement involved in the procurement and exchange of copper ore and gateway to the Faynan district of southern Jordan, largest source of copper ore in the southern Levantine mainland (Jabal Hamrat Fidan project)

pipes facilitated the smelting of copper in the Early Bronze period. The molten copper could be separated from the lighter nonmetallic slag which floated above it. In the Late Bronze period shaft furnaces with bellows forcing a draught were developed which were hotter and produced larger quantities of copper. In these furnaces the molten slag could be drained off. In the Iron Age the use of charcoal was important, in that it created heat and carbon monoxide, making a reducing atmosphere which helped to purify iron. These furnaces were not hot enough to liquefy iron, but they were hot enough to melt away impurities and produce iron blooms. After basic extraction processes, furnaces were still important in the refinement of metals. At times, materials such as iron oxide in copper production and lead oxide in silver production would be added to act as a flux, drawing impurities from molten metals. Refined metals were at times alloyed to produce items which required metals of certain characteristics either in manufacture or in the final products. Bronze, a mixture of copper and tin, e.g., is superior in casting and produces a tougher product. Gold mixed with silver produces a tougher but cheaper product.

The physical shaping of metal is the second part of metallurgy. Initially techniques included cold hammering, grinding, and polishing. From ingots of ductile metals containers could be raised by hammering and plate metal could be formed which could be decorated in repoussé. In addition to chasing designs on surfaces, they could also be burnished with hard, smooth stones. On complex vessels decorative spouts and handles were put in place either by rivets or soldering with a softer metal alloy. Casting of liquefied metals was an option known in the 4th millennium. Simple open molds cut into stone or shaped in clay allowed for the mass production of objects like bronze axe heads. The lost wax method of casting and core casting of large objects made possible the manufacture of metal objects of complex shape with an economy of work and valuable metal. In the working of refined metals, heat continued to be important in annealing, welding, shaping, and tempering metals. In the development of both the extraction of metals and its physical manipulation the ingenuity of peoples from the past is exhibited.

Robert W. Smith

METHEG-AMMAH (Heb. *meṯeg hāʼammâ*)
A Hebrew phrase of uncertain meaning (lit., "the bridle of a cubit"; 2 Sam. 8:1). As a proper noun (so NRSV, NJPSV, REB), it refers to a town which David took from Philistine control, but no town by this name is known elsewhere. The rendering of the phrase by earlier commentators as "control of the mother city" is commonly rejected. The parallel passage in 1 Chr. 18:1 refers to "Gath and its daughter villages" (LXX "pasture-land," reading Heb. *migrāš*); this is the meaning expected from the context of 2 Samuel. Some scholars argue that the phrase should be interpreted as a metaphor for ruling; i.e., David broke the Philistine hegemony over the land.

Ronald A. Simkins

METHUSELAH (Heb. *mĕṯûšellaḥ;* Gk. *Mathousalá*)
The son of Enoch and father of Lamech in the lineage of Seth (Gen. 5:21-27; 1 Chr. 1:3). Of the extremely long-lived people before the Flood, Methuselah is credited with the longest life, 969 years. He is named among the ancestors of Jesus (Luke 3:37).

METHUSHAEL (Heb. *mĕṯûšā'ēl*)
The son of Mehujael and father of Lamech; great-grandson of Enoch in the lineage of Cain (Gen. 4:18). Similarity has been noted to Methuselah, father of Lamech and son of Enoch in the lineage of Seth (Gen. 5:21, 25).

MEUNIM, MEUNITES (Heb. *mĕʿûnîm*)
A Transjordanian people, permanently exterminated by Israelite clans seeking pasture land for their flocks (1 Chr. 4:41). In 2 Chr. 26:7 they are one of the groups in Philistia overcome by King Uzziah of Judah. Ezra 2:50 = Neh. 7:52 includes Meunim in a list of temple servants returning to Jerusalem after the Exile. Here the term, like most in the list, probably refers to a group among the temple servants, perhaps from the town of Maon.

JOHN KALTNER

MEZAHAB (Heb. *mê zāhāḇ*)
The grandmother or grandfather of Mehetabel, the wife of King Hadar (Hadad) of Edom (Gen. 36:39; 1 Chr. 1:50). The name ("waters of gold") may represent a place.

MEZOBAITE (Heb. *hammĕṣōḇāyâ*)
A gentilic ascribed to Jaasiel, one of David's Champions (1 Chr. 11:47). It should perhaps be emended to *miṣṣōḇâ*, "from Zobah" (cf. 1 Chr. 18:3).

MEZUZAH
The side posts of a city gate, door of a building, or a window (Heb. *mĕzûzâ*). The Israelites were instructed to write God's commands on their doorposts (Deut. 6:6-9). Eventually the term came to refer to the commandments that were affixed to the doorpost or, in later Jewish tradition, the glass or metal receptacle affixed to the right-hand door post of the outer entrance of a house and containing a parchment upon which certain words from Deut. 6:4-9; 11:13-21 were written. A mezuzah parchment was discovered at Qumran.

Bibliography. L. I. Rabinowitz, "Mezuzah," *EncJud* (New York, 1972), 11:1474-77.

MICHAEL A. GRISANTI

MIBHAR (Heb. *miḇḥār*)
One of David's Mighty Men; the son of Hagri (1 Chr. 11:38).

MIBSAM (Heb. *miḇśām*)

1. A son of Ishmael; eponymous ancestor of an Arabian people (Gen. 25:13; 1 Chr. 1:29).

2. A Simeonite, the son of Shallum and father of Mishma (1 Chr. 4:25). The mention of Mibsam and Mishma also at 1 Chr. 1:29-30 may suggest some relationship between Simeonite and Ishmaelite clans.

MIBZAR (Heb. *miḇṣār*)
An Edomite chief (Gen. 36:42; 1 Chr. 1:53). The name ("fortified city") probably represents a place (cf. Ps. 108:10[MT 11]), perhaps Mabsara in northern Edom (cf. Eusebius *Onom.* 124.20-21, in the region of Gebalena and subject to Petra) or Bozrah in Moab.

MICA (Heb. *mîḵā'*) (also MICAH)

1. The son of Mephibosheth (Meribbaal) and grandson of Jonathan (2 Sam. 9:12). He is called Micah (**3**) at 1 Chr. 8:34-35; 9:40-41.

2. The father of Mattaniah, a postexilic Levite of the lineage of Asaph (1 Chr. 9:15; Neh. 11:17).

3. A Levite who participated in the sealing of the new covenant under Nehemiah (Neh. 10:11 [MT 12]).

4. The father of Mattaniah and ancestor of Uzzi, a postexilic Levite of the lineage of Asaph (Neh. 11:22). He may be the same as **2** above or Micaiah (**5;** Neh. 12:35).

MICAH (Heb. *mîḵâ*) (also MICA, MICAIAH)

1. A man of the Ephraimite hill country, living during the period of the judges, whose story explains the founding of the shrine and city of Dan (Judg. 17–18). According to the story, Micah stole 1100 pieces of silver from his mother. Upon return of the silver, she dedicated 200 pieces to the Lord and gave them to Micah to make a molten and a graven image. Micah also made a shrine where he set up the images along with teraphim and an ephod (Judg. 17:1-5). He consecrated one of his sons to be a priest. Later, a young Levite from Bethlehem, who was sojourning in Micah's home, became Micah's priest. Micah paid him wages and adopted him as his own son (Judg. 17:7-12). After a while, five Danites, who were searching for a place for the clan to settle, lodged at Micah's house. They sought guidance from his priest, received a positive response, and departed to spy out the country of Laish (Judg. 18:2-6). When a 600-person army of Danites returned to take Laish, they stole Micah's idols, ephod, and teraphim and persuaded the young Levite to be their priest (Judg. 18:14-20). Micah and his neighbors pursued the Danites, but found them to be too strong and turned back without a fight (Judg. 18:22-26). The Danites conquered Laish, changed the name of the city to Dan, and set up a shrine there with Micah's cultic objects (Judg. 18:27-31).

2. The son of Shimei and the father of Reaiah; a Reubenite (1 Chr. 5:5).

3. The son of Meribbaal (Mephibosheth) and grandson of Jonathan; a Benjaminite (1 Chr. 8:33-35; 9:40-41). At 2 Sam. 9:12 he is called Mica.

4. The first son of Uzziel, a Korathite Levite (1 Chr. 23:20; 24:24-25).

5. The father of Abdon who lived before or during the reign of Josiah, king of Judah (2 Chr. 34:20). He is the same as Micaiah in 2 Kgs. 22:12.

6. Micah of Moresheth, a Judahite prophet during the reigns of Jotham, Ahaz, and Hezekiah. He is the 8th-7th century B.C.E. prophet whose words are recorded in the book of Micah (Jer. 26:18; Mic. 1:1).

TERRY W. EDDINGER

MICAH, BOOK OF
The sixth book of the Minor Prophets. The superscription attributes the book to Micah ("Who is like

Yahweh?"), a prophet from the Judean town of Moresheth. The book gives no further direct information about the prophet. According to Mic. 1:1 he was active during the reigns of Jotham, Ahaz, and Hezekiah (the latter part of the 8th century B.C.E.) and thus a contemporary of Isaiah, Amos, and Hosea. Although the book makes no unambiguous reference to major events such as the Syro-Ephraimite War, the fall of Samaria, and the Assyrian siege of Jerusalem which occurred during this period, the material attributed to Micah reflects a time of political and social upheaval when the fall of both Samaria and Jerusalem was expected.

Content

The message of the book is a complex mixture of judgment and hope. On the one hand, the prophecies announce judgment upon Israel for social evils, corrupt leadership, and idolatry. This judgment was expected to culminate in the destruction of Samaria and Jerusalem. On the other hand, the book proclaims not merely the restoration of the nation, but the transformation and exaltation of Israel and Jerusalem. The messages of hope and doom are not necessarily contradictory, however, since restoration and transformation take place only after judgment.

The book opens with the declaration that Yahweh is coming forth to judge the sins of his people (1:2-7). Judgment is announced against the capitals of Samaria and Jerusalem (1:8-9), and a series of puns describes the fate of the cities of the Shephelah (vv. 10-16). The prophetic speech in ch. 2 condemns those who are dispossessing the people of Israel (2:1-5). Claims that judgment cannot overtake Yahweh's people are rebutted with the charge that Yahweh's people have turned themselves into Yahweh's enemies (2:6-11). The chapter closes with an enigmatic declaration which seems to point to a deliverance from oppression (2:12-13).

Throughout ch. 3 the prophet condemns the rulers, priests, and prophets of Israel who exploit and mislead the people. It is because of their deeds that Jerusalem itself will be destroyed (3:9-12). The prophet's powerful declaration of judgment on Jerusalem was remembered even in the time of Jeremiah (Jer. 26:17-19).

Incorporating virtually the same oracle found in Isa. 2:2-4, Mic. 4:1-8 looks beyond the expected destruction of Jerusalem to its exaltation. The speaker proclaims the deliverance of the people who will go from Jerusalem to Babylon (vv. 9-10). The chapter concludes with an exhortation for Jerusalem to destroy the nations who have gathered against her (vv. 11-13).

Ch. 5 opens with an announcement that an ideal ruler would come from Bethlehem to defend the nation against Assyria (vv. 1-6[MT 4:14–5:5]). The prophet proclaims the triumph of the remnant of Jacob (vv. 7-9[6-8]) and foresees a day when Yahweh will purge the nation of idolatry and reliance on military might (vv. 10-15[9-14]).

In ch. 6 Israel is summoned to hear Yahweh's dispute. In response to a series of questions regarding what Yahweh requires, the prophet sets forth a powerful and concise summary of Yahweh's requirement for justice and loyalty (vv. 6-8). The remainder of ch. 6 consists of a scathing series of accusations against "the city" and announcements of judgment upon those who have followed the ways of Omri and Ahab.

In 7:1-7 the speaker laments the collapse of the social order. The book closes with a prophetic liturgy comprising elements of a lament (7:8-20). Israel confesses its sin, and is assured of deliverance through Yahweh's mighty acts (vv. 8-17). The liturgy concludes with an affirmation of Yahweh's faithfulness and willingness to forgive (vv. 18-20).

Critical Considerations

The major issue in Micah research is the question of which material can be attributed to the 8th-century prophet. Many scholars believe that only chs. 1-3 are derived from Micah. Since Micah was remembered as prophet of doom during the time of Jeremiah (cf. Jer. 26:17ff.), some have reasoned that only oracles of judgment are authentic to Micah and that his activity was confined to the time of Hezekiah. Thus, the prophecies of hope in chs. 4, 5, and 7 cannot be assigned to Micah. This assessment is re-enforced by the fact that the prophecies in chs. 4-7 seem to reflect historical settings later than the time of Micah. For example, the reference to Babylon in 4:10 would indicate a time during or after the Babylonian Exile. Other passages such as 7:12 appear to presuppose a diaspora situation. Finally, similarities in style, language, and thought to later prophetic works and the Deuteronomic school have led interpreters to conclude that material in chs. 6 and 7 has either been extensively reinterpreted or originated after the time of Micah.

A second interpretation of the book has maintained that while chs. 4-7 probably contain some material from later times, prophecies from Micah are also present in these chapters. Scholars who have taken this approach are aware of the dramatic differences in styles and themes in the material, but suggest that these differences are a reflection of the changing circumstances during the time of Micah. Especially doubtful is the assumption that Micah could not have proclaimed both doom and hope. Finally, interpreters in this second group are not convinced that the style, vocabulary, and themes of chs. 4-7 are confined exclusively to exilic and postexilic times.

Another major issue in the study of Micah is the question of the process by which the book assumed its final shape. Most interpreters believe that it underwent a long redactional process by which Micah's words were edited, reinterpreted, and expanded. Unfortunately, there is little agreement in modern scholarship on the details of this lengthy process of redaction.

Part of the problem in reconstructing the redactional process is the difficulty in discerning an underlying structure which editors might have used to unite and organize the material in the book. Some have proposed that the book was arranged according to a doom-hope scheme: two sections of doom (1:2–3:12; 6:1–7:7) are followed by oracles of hope (4:1–5:15[14]; 7:8–20). The material, unfortunately, does not fall neatly into this pattern since oracles of both kinds are found in each section. A second suggestion is that the book is arranged as three units, each beginning with the exhortation "hear!" (1:2; 3:1; 6:1). While such a division of the book is helpful, it is somewhat artificial since each unit contains material reflecting a variety of themes and genres.

Ultimately, the unity and structure of the book may be more theological than literary or historical. The widely disparate material in Micah is united by the theological conviction that both judgment and restoration are the work of Yahweh. Indeed, the constant and intricate juxtaposition of judgment and hope reflects a profound theological understanding that judgment is not mere punishment, but an integral and necessary step in the restoration of Yahweh's rule over his people. The uniting of doom and hope in one book thus reflects a complex theology which weaves judgment and restoration into the seamless work of Yahweh.

Bibliography. L. C. Allen, *The Books of Joel, Obadiah, Jonah and Micah.* NICOT (Grand Rapids, 1976); D. R. Hillers, *Micah.* Herm (Philadelphia, 1984); J. L. Mays, *Micah.* OTL (Philadelphia, 1976); J. M. P. Smith, et al., *Micah, Zephaniah, Nahum, Habakkuk, Obadiah and Joel.* ICC (Edinburgh, 1911); H. W. Wolff, *Micah* (Minneapolis, 1990).

CHARLES S. SHAW

MICAIAH (Heb. *mîḵāyâ, mîḵāyāhû*)
(also MAACAH, MICAH)

1. The son of Imlah; a 9th-century B.C.E. prophet of the northern kingdom of Israel (1 Kgs. 22:1-28; 2 Chr. 18:1-27). He and 400 other prophets were consulted by Kings Ahab of Israel and Jehoshaphat of Judah before their unsuccessful battle with the Arameans at Ramoth-gilead. The other prophets unanimously assured these two kings that God would grant them victory. Micaiah, accused of being hostile to Ahab, at first agreed with the other prophets. When Ahab challenged this prophecy, Micaiah then proclaimed defeat for the forces of Israel and Judah. This led to the first known conflict among Israel's prophets. The prophet Zedekiah even slapped Micaiah and challenged his prophetic credentials.

Micaiah is presented as a prophet who was faithful to God's word despite both prophetic and royal opposition. He insisted to the royal messenger that he would proclaim only that oracle which God revealed to him. He defended his prophecy of doom by appealing to a vision of the heavenly court, in which God permitted a lying spirit to deceive the prophets in order to mislead Ahab and bring him to disaster.

For the first time Israel had to choose from conflicting prophetic messages. Henceforth God's people would have to discern between true and false prophecy. True prophecy would often be revealed by a lone voice dissenting from the majority opinion. It might also be revealed by suffering, for Micaiah was thrown into prison to await the king's return. We never learn the prophet's fate.

2. The father of Achbor, an official of King Josiah of Judah, who was sent to Huldah the prophetess (2 Kgs. 22:12). At 2 Chr. 34:20 he is called Micah the father of Abdon.

3. The wife of King Rehoboam of Judah and mother of Abijah (2 Chr. 13:2). Elsewhere the name is spelled Maacah (1 Kgs. 15:2; 2 Chr. 11:20).

4. One of five officials sent to teach Judah during the reign of Jehoshaphat (2 Chr. 17:7).

5. An ancestor of Zechariah, a priest who played the trumpet at the dedication of Jerusalem's rebuilt wall in the days of Nehemiah (Neh. 12:35).

6. One of seven priests with trumpets at the dedication of Jerusalem's rebuilt wall in the days of Nehemiah (Neh. 12:41).

7. A son of the scribe Gemariah. He reported on the reading of Jeremiah's scroll to court officials (Jer. 36:11, 13).

Bibliography. S. J. DeVries, *Prophet Against Prophet: The Role of the Micaiah Narrative (I Kings 22) in the Development of Early Prophetic Tradition* (Grand Rapids, 1978); W. Roth, "The Story of the Prophet Micaiah (1 Kings 22) in Historical-Critical Interpretation 1876-1976," in *The Biblical Mosaic,* ed. R. Polzin and E. Rothman. SBLSS 10 (Chico, 1982), 105-37.

TIMOTHY A. LENCHAK

MICHAEL (Heb. *mîḵā'ēl*)

1. An Asherite whose son Sethur was one of the 12 spies sent to Canaan (Num. 13:13).

2. A Gadite who settled in Bashan (1 Chr. 5:13).

3. An ancestor of the Gadite Abihail (1 Chr. 5:14).

4. A Levite, the great-grandfather of Asaph (1 Chr. 6:40[MT 25]).

5. A descendant of Uzzi of the tribe of Issachar (1 Chr. 7:3).

6. One of the sons of Beraiah; head of a Benjamite ancestral house who lived in Jerusalem (1 Chr. 8:16).

7. A mighty warrior from the tribe of Manasseh who deserted Saul and joined David's ranks at Ziklag, becoming a commander (1 Chr. 12:20).

8. The father of Omri, chief officer of Issachar at the time of David (1 Chr. 27:18).

9. One of King Jehoshaphat's sons who was assassinated when his older brother Jehoram ascended the throne (2 Chr. 21:2, 4).

10. A man whose son, Zebadiah, supervised 80 returnees from Babylonian exile with Ezra, during the reign of Artaxerxes (Ezra 8:8).

11. A celestial prince or archangel, mentioned by name only in Daniel. He is "one of the chief princes" (Dan. 10:13; cf. v. 21), "the great prince who stands up" (12:1), and possibly the "prince of the host" (8:11). In the NT he is the "archangel" who disputed with the devil over the body of Moses (Jude 9) and the commander of the heavenly armies that eradicated Satan and his angels from heaven after they rebelled against God (Rev. 12:7). In each of these apocalyptic passages Michael is the leader of God's forces, in direct controversy with Satan and always victorious over him.

Jewish angelology in apocalyptic writings describes Michael as "general" and "chief captain" (2 En. 22:6; 33:10), the first of "four presences that stand before God" (1 En. 9:1; 40:9; 1QM 9:14-15). He is characterized as "merciful, charitable, and long-suffering" (1 En. 40:9; 68:2, 3), a "mediator and intercessor" (Asc. Isa. 9:23), and an intermediary between God and Moses at the time when the law was given at Sinai (cf. Jub. 1:27; 2:1; Acts 7:38). Tg. Jonathan on Deut. 34:6 claims that Michael and his angels buried Moses. As the true representative of God, identified with the "angel of Yahweh," Michael withstood Satan's accusations and vindicated Israel at the heavenly tribunal. KENNETH D. MULAC

MICHAL (Heb. *mîḵal*)

A daughter of Saul (1 Sam. 14:49; mother unknown) and wife of David (18:27), Palti/Paltiel (25:44; 2 Sam. 3:15), and, once again, David (1 Sam. 3:14-16). Michal's name appears in a list of Saul's offspring with her older sister (Merab) and three older brothers (Jonathan, Ishvi, and Malchishua; 1 Sam. 14:49-51). References to her appear in four accounts: the premarital tests Saul sets for David (1 Sam. 18:17-29); David's escape from Saul's court (19:8-17); Ishbosheth's return of Michal to David (2 Sam. 3:12-16); and Michal's criticism of David (6:15-23). While many misread "Michal" in 2 Sam. 21:8, this text is better read as a reference to Merab, Michal's older sister.

Michal's story is not a happy one. Purchased with a bride-price of 100 Philistine foreskins, she loved David, while David recognized the advantages of being the king's son-in-law. In aiding David's escape from Saul, she was separated from David and married to another from whose side she was torn, only to be "given" back to David. After she criticized David's action concerning the ark's entrance into Jerusalem, the narrator comments that "Michal the daughter of Saul had no child to the day of her death" (2 Sam. 6:23). If this is historically reliable, it may indicate that from that point on, David and Michal ceased to have marital relations.

Bibliography. A. Berlin, "Characterization in Biblical Narrative: David's Wives," *JSOT* 23 (1982): 69-85; D. J. A. Clines and T. C. Eskenazi, *Telling Queen Michal's Story.* JSOTSup 119 (Sheffield, 1991); J. C Exum, "Arrows of the Almighty: Tragic Dimensions of Biblical Narrative" (forthcoming); "Michal: The Whole Story," in *Fragmented Women: Feminist (Sub)versions of Biblical Narrative* (Valley Forge, 1993), 42-60; K. G. Shargent, "Living on the Edge: The Liminality of Daughters in Genesis to 2 Samuel," in *A Feminist Companion to Samuel and Kings,* ed. A. Brenner (Sheffield, 1994), 26-42.
LINDA S. SCHEARING

MICHMASH (Heb. *miḵmāś, miḵmās*)

An OT town located near the boundary between the tribes of Benjamin and Ephraim. The two variant spellings of the name, *miḵmāś* (1 Sam. 13–14; Neh. 11:31; Isa. 10:28) and *miḵmās* (Ezra 2:27), reflect diachronic developments in the Hebrew language.

Michmash is usually associated with the modern village of Mukhmâs (176142), ca. 11 km. (7 mi.) N of Jerusalem. The modern village stands on the northern cliff of a deep canyon, the Wadi eṣ-Ṣuweinîṭ. Recent surveying has also suggested that the ancient site can possibly be identified with Khirbet el-Hara el-Fawqa, 1 km. (ca. 0.6 mi.) N of Mukhmâs. The site guards a pass across a deep canyon, which immediately proceeds south to the biblical town of Geba (Jabaʿ) just on the other side of the canyon. This may be the pass mentioned in 1 Sam. 13:23; Isa. 10:28-29 (cf. Judg. 20:33).

Michmash figures most prominently in the early struggles between Saul's incipient monarchy and the Philistines, as described in 1 Sam. 13–14. A Philistine outpost was stationed near Michmash, while the main Philistine garrison was probably located just to the west near Gibeon.

In the postexilic period, Michmash was a village under Persian rule (Neh. 11:31). Later, the Maccabean ruler Jonathan resided at Michmash before moving to Jerusalem (1 Macc. 9:73)
WILLIAM M. SCHNIEDEWIND

MICHMETHATH (Heb. *miḵmĕṯāṯ*)

The northernmost point on the boundary between Ephraim and Manasseh (Josh. 16:6; 17:7), said to be E of Shechem. Scholars are divided as to whether Michmethath refers to a settlement or merely a prominent geographical feature. Possibilities include a mountain ridge, such as the Gebel el-Kabir; a valley, such as the Wadi Bedan; or an archaeological site, such as Khirbet 'Ibn Naser.
WADE R. KOTTER

MICHRI (Heb. *miḵrî*)

A postexilic Benjaminite, ancestor of Elah (1 Chr. 9:8).

MIDDIN (Heb. *middîn*)

A town in the Judean wilderness (Josh. 15:61) allotted to the tribe of Judah. Although controversy surrounds the exact geography of this district, which includes En-gedi, the recent archaeological discovery of three Iron Age settlements in the Buqeiʿah Valley presents the possibility of a more precise identification for Middin. It is probably to be located at Khirbet Abū Ṭabaq (188127).

Bibliography. L. E. Stager, "Farming in the Judean Desert during the Iron Age," *BASOR* 221 (1976): 145-58. RYAN BYRNE

MIDIAN (Heb. *miḏyān*)

The fourth son of Abraham and his concubine Keturah; eponymous ancestor of the Midianites (Gen. 21:1; 1 Chr. 1:32). Aside from Isaac, Sarah's only child, the fate of all of Abraham's children was to be sent into the Arabian desert where they became the eponymous ancestors of Arab tribes (Gen. 25:6).

The area associated with Midian was the northwestern corner of the Arabian Peninsula, E of the Gulf of Aqaba. This region was known to classical and medieval Arabic geographers as Madian and Madiana; its modern name is Hejaz. The region was the center of a common material culture which belies a sedentary existence (in contrast to the nomadic lifestyle ascribed to them by former generations of scholars). The indigenous pottery style of the Late Bronze period was reminiscent of Mycenean ware. Pottery kilns were found at Qurayya, one of the major population centers of the region, and at Timna, located in the Arabah (not to be confused with the Timna in the southern Arabian Peninsula). Timna also engaged in copper mining and smelting. The local pottery has been associated with dated Egyptian artifacts from the 19th dynasty (ca. 13th-12th centuries B.C.E.). The Egyptians maintained garrisons here, as part of their Palestinian empire, and an Egyptian temple was discovered at Timna. A third center, Tayma, likewise employed this pottery. Stone irrigation canals have been discovered at Qurayya and Timna, complete with walls surrounding the fields. These three major sites are located near spice trade routes. Thus, there was an urban element, connected by trade (and by military occupation to Egypt) to the rest of the urban ancient Near East.

One would expect the Midianites to be engaged in caravan trade, on the basis of their depiction in the Joseph cycle (Gen. 37:25-36). The inconsistency of the narrative in referring to them alternatively as Ishmaelite (Gen. 37:25, 27) and Midianite (vv. 28, 36) is not immediately evident. Some have suggested that Ishmaelite is a generic term for caravaneers, or for non-Hebrew descendants of Abraham, while the name Midianite is ethnically distinct.

The Midianites figure prominently in the Exodus narratives. Moses flees to Midian, where he enters the status of *gēr* ("alien"), falling under the protection of Jethro (also called Reuel and Hobab). Moses' status as *gēr* is probably attested in the confusion regarding his abandonment of his sons Gershom and Eliezer upon his return to Egypt (Exod. 18:2; however, this is attributed in the following verses to his divorcing his wife; according to 4:18-20 they were with him in Egypt). Clearly, Moses' status was inferior to his wife Zipporah, the daughter of Jethro, else his sons would have remained in his estate. Jethro helps guide the Israelites (Num. 10:29-32) and suggests to Moses a system of organizing society (Exod. 18:13-27). The Midianites among the Israelites were offered membership in the community, which they declined (Num. 10:29).

The relationship between the religion of Midian and of Israel is the matter of intense speculation. The tradition of the holy mountain in the wilderness gives birth to speculation on the relationship between the religions. A number of texts which scholars consider to be old announce that Yahweh came from the land of Seir, better known as Edom (Hab. 3:3; Deut. 33:2; Judg. 5:4-5). Southern Edom is considered to have been within the territory of the Midianites (compare Num. 22:4, 7; 31:8 with Josh. 13:21; 1 Kgs. 11:1). Moses' father-in-law was called a priest of Midian (e.g., Exod. 2:16).

Moses is pictured as passive during the events at Baal-peor (Num. 25:6), in contrast to Aaron's son Phineas, who kills the Israelite male and Midianite female in the midst of an apparent orgiastic ritual, resulting in the Aaronide covenant. Some scholars see Moses' passivity as a literary seam demarcating a later debate over the priesthood (cf. the passivity of Aaron in the incident of the golden calf in Exod. 32, perhaps the product of another priestly school). The close relationship with Midian ceases from this point, as the Midianites become just another people to exterminate upon entry into the Promised Land (Num. 31; Josh. 31:21). Gideon's heroics were set against a Midianite invasion (Judg. 6–8; Isa. 9:4[MT 3]).

MARK ANTHONY PHELPS

MIDRASH

A primary mode of rabbinic biblical interpretation. The origins of midrash (from Heb. *drš*, "to search" or "investigate") may lie within the OT itself. For example, according to 1 Chr. 5:1, because he "defiled" his father's bed, Reuben's birthright was given to the sons of Joseph; this seems to provide an elaboration on the fate of Reuben, which remains vague in Genesis, by taking up several threads there (Gen. 35:16-22; 48:5-7; 49:3-4) and tying them into a coherent whole. Interpretive strategies similar to midrash or, perhaps the antecedents thereof, can be seen in the Apocrypha and Pseudepigrapha as well as in some of the versions of the OT. Among the closest analogues to midrash is the *pesher* interpretation found in the Dead Sea Scrolls.

Whatever the origins of midrash, we know of the phenomenon best from its practice in rabbinic Judaism. Midrash, aside from being a method of interpretation, is also used to designate the literature that arose from such interpretation. Two main types of this literature correspond to the two primary ways in which the midrashic method was applied. Halakhah concentrates on ritual and civic legal matters and Haggadah on more discursive literary and religious concerns. In practice this division is simplistic due to the overlap between the two. A further way to designate and distinguish midrash is by the sources of the interpretations. Midrash produced by the rabbis prior to the coalescence of the Mishnah (ca. 200 C.E.) is called Tannaitic. Midrash produced after that date until ca. the 6th century is called Amoraic. Midrash can also be divided into the categories of expositional and homiletical. Expositional midrash, for the most part, represents a verse-by-verse interpretation of Scripture, and homiletical midrash is primarily concerned with a particular topic or issue and draws on Scripture at large. Finally, medieval Jewish interpreters distinguish midrash (or derash) from peshat or "plain sense" interpretation. This suggests something of the indeterminate nature of midrashic interpretation.

LARRY L. LYKE

MIDWIFE
A woman who assists at childbirth (Gen. 35:17; 38:28). It is unclear whether midwives (Heb. *mĕyalleḏeṯ*) constituted a professional class.
See NURSE.

MIGDAL-EL (Heb. *migdal-'ēl*)
A town in the allotment of Naphtali, most likely in Upper Galilee. Josh. 19:36 indicates that the named towns probably had associated villages included under their control. On the basis of the similar nomenclature, the town has been identified with Mejdel Islim, 26 km. (16 mi.) S of Tyre, but the site has not been systematically surveyed. The *migdal* element in the name suggests a Bronze Age fortress-temple like those at Shechem or Ebla.
THOMAS W. DAVIS

MIGDAL-GAD (Heb. *migdal-gāḏ*)
A town ("tower of Gad") in the Shephelah, or lowland, of Judah and part of that tribe's inheritance (Josh. 15:37). It is identified with Khirbet el-Mejdeleh (140105), presumably a preservation of the biblical name. Located 6 km. (3.7 mi.) SE of Lachish, the site has not been excavated.

Bibliography. A. F. Rainey, "The Administrative Division of the Shephelah," *Tel Aviv* 7 (1980): 194-202; "The Biblical Shephelah of Judah," *BASOR* 251 (1983): 1-22.
JENNIFER L. GROVES

MIGDOL (Heb. *migdōl*)
A Semitic word meaning "fortress" or "watch tower," which was taken into Egyptian and used to describe a series of military outposts guarding the eastern edge of the Delta.

1. A town in the eastern Delta that was on the route of the Exodus (Exod. 14:2; Num. 33:7).

2. A residence of Jews in Egypt (Jer. 44:1; 46:14).

3. A place in north Egypt used, with Syene, to indicate the north-south borders of Egypt.

For the identification of these places, scholars have proposed a Migdol of Seti I located in the Succoth district of Egypt, the ancient fortress of Serapeum near the north end of the Bitter Lakes, and modern Tell el-Her, which is 19 km. (12 mi.) N of Sile. None of these sites seems to fit with the biblical narrative of the Exodus. Tell el-Her is too far north, but may be identified with **2** and **3** above. Serapeum is too far west, and Succoth is where the Israelites turned back to continue their journey.
LAWRENCE A. SINCLAIR

MIGHTY MEN
See CHAMPIONS.

MIGRON (Heb. *migrôn*)
A place in Benjamin. In 1 Sam. 14:2 Saul and his 600 soldiers camp outside Gibeah (9 km. [5.5 mi.] NE of Jerusalem and S of the Wadi es-Suweiniṭ) at the "pomegranate tree" (possibly the "rock of Rimmon"; Judg. 20:45-47) "in the Migron." In Isa. 10:28 the Assyrians are viewed as passing "over Migron" through the Geba Pass. This seems to be N of Wadi es-Suweiniṭ near Michmash. Instead of a town, Migron (from Heb. *ngr,* "to gush forth") may instead refer to the region of the Wadi es-Suweiniṭ itself. The canyon of this wadi is substantial and formed a portion of the border between Judah and Israel; it runs southeast from the central hill country, joining the Wadi el-Qelt and emptying into the Jordan Valley N of Jericho. If Migron indicates a regional rather than a site name, then the problem between the two passages is resolved.
DENNIS M. SWANSON

MIJAMIN (Heb. *mîyāmîn*)

1. The leader of the sixth division of priests during the time of King David (1 Chr. 24:9).

2. An Israelite required to divorce his foreign wife (Ezra 10:25).

3. A priest who participated in the sealing of the new covenant under Nehemiah (Neh. 10:7[MT 8]). He may be the same as Miniamin **3** (cf. **2**).

4. A chief of the priests among those who returned from exile with Zerubbabel (Neh. 12:5).

MIKLOTH (Heb. *miqlôṯ*)

1. A Benjaminite who lived at Gibeon; a descendant of Jeiel and father of Shimeah/Shimeam (1 Chr. 8:32; 9:37-38).

2. The chief officer under Dodai the Ahohite of the second monthly division of David's army (1 Chr. 27:4).

MIKNEIAH (Heb. *miqnēyāhû*)
A levitical musician appointed to accompany the ark to Jerusalem (1 Chr. 15:18, 21).

MIKTAM (Heb. *miḵtām*)
An obscure technical term found in the superscripts of Pss. 16, 56-60 (perhaps also Isa. 38:9; cf. BHS). It always occurs with *lĕḏāwiḏ,* "of David," and is found in psalms of similar length and form (laments). As such it may indicate a genre classification, and mark off a small collection of psalms (Pss. 56-60). Suggestions for its meaning include "stelegraphic publication" (cf. LXX Gk. *stēlographia,* "stela inscription"; Tg.), "golden psalm" (from *ktm,* "gold"; Ibn Ezra, Luther), "atonement psalm" (from Akk. *katāmu,* "cover"); and "secret prayer." Most modern translations simply transliterate as "miktam."
TYLER F. WILLIAMS

MILALAI (Heb. *milălay*)
A levitical musician who participated in the postexilic dedication of the walls of Jerusalem (Neh. 12:36).

MILCAH (Heb. *milkâ*)

1. The daughter of Haran, sister of Lot and Iscah, wife of Nahor, mother of eight, and grandmother of Rebekah (Gen. 11:29; 22:20-23; 24:15, 24, 47).

2. One of the five daughters of Zelophehad for whom special provision was made that they might be his heirs (Num. 26:33; 27:1; 36:11; Josh. 17:3). The name may actually represent a town or tribal unit.

MILCOM (Heb. *milkōm*)
The national god of the Ammonites. Milcom was among the foreign deities whose worship in Israel was given sanction by Solomon and whose sanctuaries just outside Jerusalem were later dismantled by Josiah (1 Kgs. 11:5, 33; 2 Kgs. 23:13).

Six times in the OT the Hebrew consonants *mlkm* are most likely to be read *milkōm,* Milcom, rather than the MT rendering *malkām,* "their king." Amos 1:15 ("Milcom shall go into exile . . .") alludes to the well-known ancient Near Eastern practice of plundering the cult statues of defeated enemies. Later Jer. 49:3 takes up this same threat (as does 48:7 in reference to Chemosh, unambiguously the name of the Moabite deity), adding that "his priests" shall accompany him. The question of Jer. 49:1 ("Why has Milcom dispossessed Gad?") is phrased in accordance with the Iron Age notion of the national deity as achieving the military and territorial gains of the state. Zeph. 1:5 counts among Judah's religious offenders "those who take oaths by Milcom." In 2 Sam. 12:30 = 1 Chr. 20:2 the crown taken by David upon the capture of the Ammonite capital Rabbah most likely belonged to and rested on the head of Milcom (i.e., his cult statue); the crown would have been too heavy ("a talent of gold," ca. 34 kg. [75 lbs.]) for the head of "their king," and it would have been the "precious stone," and not the crown itself, that later rested on David's head. (In 1 Kgs. 11:7 the divine name *mōlek̠,* Molech, is probably a mistake for Milcom.)

Milcom is attested in Ammonite inscriptions from the OT period, including the Amman citadel inscription (9th century), a 7th-century seal, and theophoric personal names from a 5th-century ostracon and from 6th-century seals and bullae.

Bibliography. W. E. Aufrecht, *A Corpus of Ammonite Inscriptions* (Lewiston, 1989); P. K. McCarter, *II Samuel.* AB 9 (Garden City, 1984).

JOEL BURNETT

MILDEW
A blight that turns plants a pale green and makes them unfruitful, perhaps the result of fungus or of the hot east wind. Heb. *yērāqôn* may also indicate either paleness of the human face or a sickly paleness of plants. Mildew occurs in lists of plagues (along with scorching wind, hail, famine, fever, sword, and blight) which were understood to be punishments that God visited upon his people for their disobedience (Deut. 28:22; Amos 4:9; Hag. 2:17). Solomon petitions that, when mildew or any of the other plagues are present, God would hear the prayers of his people, forgive their sins, and deliver them (1 Kgs. 8:37 = 2 Chr. 6:28).

JOE E. LUNCEFORD

MILE
A Roman measure of distance (Gk. *mílion;* Matt. 5:41) equivalent to ca. 1480 m. (1618 yds.; the modern mile is 1760 yds.). Some English versions translate other ancient measurements into miles (particularly the *stádion,* equivalent to one eighth Roman mile).

MILETUS (Gk. *Mílētos*)
An important port with four harbors in southwestern Asia Minor, situated on a promontory where the Meander River meets the Latmian Gulf. It became a large trade center and boasted a sizable population at the time of the writing of the NT. First colonized by Cretans in the Minoan period, Miletus became a fortified outpost for the Mycenean Greeks in the 14th century B.C. It was destroyed by the Persians in 494, but soon rebuilt, and under the Romans enjoyed an abundance of wealth, trade, and architectural activity.

Paul visited Miletus on his return trip to Jerusalem at the close of his third missionary journey (Acts 20:15). While there, he summoned the elders of the church at Ephesus to come to him, warning them to be steadfast and announcing that they would not see him again (Acts 20:17-38). The mention of Paul's having "left Trophimus sick at Miletus" (2 Tim. 4:20) suggests another visit to the city.

Miletus is now more than 8 km. (5 mi.) inland, due to silting of the harbor and shifting of the Meander. The site was first excavated in 1899. Extensive Roman remains were discovered in subsequent excavations in 1938 and 1955. DALE ELLENBURG

MILK
Liquid nourishment, especially important for sustenance of newborns (cf. 2 Macc. 7:27). Milk is a basic human need (Sir. 39:26), and farmers regularly raised sheep and goats for dairy products. In the OT the goat was the primary producer of milk (Prov. 27:27). The Promised Land is called the "land flowing with milk and honey" (Exod. 3:8), referring both to the agricultural bounty of the land of Canaan and to the fact that God would nourish the Israelites there.

One cultic prohibition forbids the cooking of a kid in its mother's milk (Exod. 34:26). This puzzling regulation has provided the exegetical basis for the Jewish practice of not cooking or eating meat and milk products together.

Milk is used as a simile for whiteness (Gen. 49:12) and as a metaphor for romantic love (Cant. 4:11). Milk may refer to material wealth (Isa. 60:16) or didactic nourishment (55:1). Spiritual milk is highly desirable (1 Pet. 2:2). Referring metaphorically to communication of basic teachings and insights, "milk" is suitable food for young believers, while mature believers should eat solid food (1 Cor. 3:2).

See DAIRY PRODUCTS. STEPHEN ALAN REED

MILL
A device for grinding grain (Isa. 47:2) or other foods (Num. 11:7-8). A mill was comprised of two carved stones, a fixed lower stone and a mobile upper stone (cf. Judg. 9:53). The upper stone might range from .9–1.4 g. (2-3 lbs.) to 4.5 g. (10 lbs.). A miller would place grain on the lower stone and rub the upper stone against the lower. Later, a handle was used to move the upper stone in a circular motion. For much larger mills, the handle became a

beam to which a donkey was harnessed; the animal walked in a circle around the lower stone.

The mill was such an essential part of life that Israelites were forbidden to take a mill as collateral for a loan (Deut. 24:6), and the absence of the sound of grinding mills meant a disaster had come to the community (Jer. 25:10; Rev. 18:22). The grinding of grain was difficult work, frequently performed by women (Exod. 11:5; Isa. 47:1-2; Matt. 24:41); prisoners might also be harnessed to work mills (Judg. 16:21).

In referring to a millstone as an anchor, Jesus suggested that anyone who caused another person to sin would be better off having a great millstone tied about his neck and being cast into the sea (Matt. 18:6 par.; cf. Rev. 18:21).

Bibliography. J. G. Landels, *Engineering in the Ancient World* (Berkeley, 1978); M. Schwartz, *Machines, Buildings, Weaponry of Biblical Times* (Old Tappan, N.J., 1990).

A. Perry Hancock/Jennie R. Ebeling

MILLENNIUM

A 1000-year era in which the resurrected martyrs reign with Christ on earth. It is often understood as occurring between the destruction of this evil, temporal age ruled by Satan and the creation of a new heaven and earth in a righteous, eternal age indisputably ruled by God. While the term "millennium" is from the Latin for a "thousand years," the synonym "chiliasm" is from a Greek term, also for a "thousand years" (Rev. 20:4), which often has the pejorative connotation of sensual bliss that many associated with the millennium.

The concept of a millennium does not occur in the OT, but is derived in part from later prophecy of the coming of the Messiah to rule the nations from Jerusalem for an indeterminate length of time (Isa. 11; 40:9-11; 52:7-12; 65:17-25; Dan. 7:13-14, 27; Zech. 9:9-10). The millennium is the combination of this prophetic ideal of a messianic kingdom with an array of apocalyptic hopes. Jewish apocrypha and pseudepigrapha present various scenarios of a temporally limited reign of the faithful on earth, with or without the Messiah. It is often portrayed as an era of peace and great fertility in nature. Underlying some projections is the assumption that the earth exists for seven days of 1000 years each (cf. Ps. 90:4; 2 Pet. 3:8), to be followed by an eighth day of 1000 years of bliss followed in turn by judgment (1 En. 91:12-17; 93; 2 En. 33:1; 4 Ezra 7:26-31; 2 Apoc. Bar. 29-30; 2 Esdr. 7:26-44). Rabbinic sources describe a "day of the Messiah," a temporal messianic reign on earth of various lengths (including 1000 years) which stands in contrast to this world and the world to come (*Ber.* 34b; *Sanh.* 97a, 99a; *Šabb.* 63a, 113b). The Apocalypse of Elijah, a christianized Jewish work, mentions a 1000- year reign of Christ (5:36-39).

In the NT the millennium may be implicit in 1 Cor. 15:23-28, which indicates that Christ will rule until the cosmic powers, including death, have been conquered, and then he will hand over the kingdom to God (cf. Matt. 19:28; Col. 1:12-13). The only explicit reference to the millennium in the NT is Rev. 20:4-6, which teaches that the martyrs experience a first resurrection and rule with Christ for 1000 years (perhaps with other saints as well). Then follow the general resurrection, the judgment, and the creation of a new heaven and a new earth. The millennium vindicates and rewards those who remained faithful in spite of the antichrist's demand for allegiance.

The major question in the history of interpretation has been whether Rev. 20:4-6 is to be taken literally (millennialism) or figuratively (amillennialism). The patristic evidence is divided. Many believed in a literal millennial reign of Christ and the saints on earth from a rebuilt Jerusalem. The reign is pictured as marked by peace, harmony in the animal kingdom and between it and humanity, and great fertility in nature, to be followed by the resurrection and the judgment. The millennium is often seen as the fulfillment of the promise of Abraham that he would inherit the land (Gen. 15). Millennialists include Papias, who traced the teaching to Jesus himself (Irenaeus *Adv. haer.* 5.33.3-4; Eusebius *HE* 3.39.12), Justin Martyr (*Dial.* 80-81), Irenaeus (*Adv. haer.* 5.32-36), the Montanists, Tertullian (*Adv. Marc.* 3.25; *Apol.* 48), Lactantius (*Div. inst.* 7.14), and Victorinus of Pettau who wrote the earliest extant commentary on Revelation in Latin (cf. also Barn. 15, Mart. Isa. 4:14-18).

There was also a movement to spiritualize or allegorize the millennium (amillennialist), partly in response to chiliasm. Origen (*De prin.* 2.11.2-3; 3.6) allegorized the millennium to be the spiritual rule of Christ in the believer until Christ hands over the believer to God. Tyconius, the Donatist theologian, taught that the millennial rule was from the passion to the second coming of Christ, a position which influenced Augustine to abandon millenarianism for amillennialism. Commenting on Rev. 20:1-6, Augustine interpreted the first resurrection as death to sin and resurrection to new life in faith and baptism. The second resurrection is bodily resurrection at the end of the world. The millennium is the reign of Christ through the Church between his first and second comings (*Civ. Dei* 20.6-7). After Augustine, this was the opinion of the majority in the Western Church through the Reformation and Renaissance. The Eastern Church rejected Revelation along with millennium thinking.

In America the two traditional positions on the millennium can be readily found. Amillennialism takes a symbolic or allegorical view of Revelation, interpreting the millennium as a symbol of the saints reigning with Christ forever in victory. Millennialism assumes a literal rule of Christ on earth, with Christ's second coming preceding (premillennialism) or following (postmillennialism) the millennium. Postmillennialism assumes that God's power becomes more manifest as the second coming of Christ approaches. However, the two world wars destroyed this optimistic view of human possibilities. Also, the remainder of Revelation teaches that there is a continual increase and concentration of anti-Christian power before the second coming of Christ. Premillennialism has been a dominant position in American Christianity, often integrated into a dispensational view. Millennialism ignores the fact that in apocalyptic literature numbers, such as 1000, are often symbolic rather than literal.

Bibliography. R. G. Clouse, ed., *The Meaning of the Millennium* (Downers Grove, 1977); N. Cohn, *The Pursuit of the Millennium,* rev. ed. (New York, 1970); B. W. Snyder, "How Millennial is the Millennium? A Study in the Background of the 1000 Years in Revelation 20," *Evangelical Journal* 9 (1991): 51-74.

DUANE F. WATSON

MILLET

A grain, *Sorghum vulgare* Pers. (sorghum) or *Panicum miliaceum* L. (millet) or some other grain or variety of grains (Heb. *dōḥan*). Millet is mentioned only at Ezek. 4:9, where its apparent significance is that it is unusual as human food; siege conditions brought about the scarcity of food represented by the prophet's bread (cf. v. 6).

MILLO (Heb. *millôʾ*)

1. A fortification, or construction, at an unspecified location within Jerusalem. After David captured Jerusalem from the Jebusites, he occupied their stronghold and constructed the Millo (from *mlʾ,* "to fill"). It was somehow incorporated into David's wall of Jerusalem (2 Sam. 5:9 = 1 Chr. 11:8), and is seen to be a breach in the city wall, a filled stone tower, or a filling of the Tyropoeon Valley connecting the eastern ridge of the city with its western crest. Kathleen Kenyon identified the Millo with the 14th-13th B.C.E. Jebusite terracing she excavated on the eastern slope of the city of David, S of the present-day temple mount. This structure was further excavated by Yigal Shiloh (area G), and found to consist of stone-filled terraces, which created an additional area of approximately 200 sq. m. (240 sq. yds.) on top of the hill. Shiloh suggested that it formed the podium of the Jebusite citadel. The Millo was later repaired by Hezekiah (2 Chr. 32:5). Some scholars propose that during the divided monarchy the term Millo was replaced by "Ophel" (cf. 2 Chr. 27:3; 33:14).

2. A construction of Solomon, following his completion of a palace for his wife, Pharaoh's daughter (2 Kgs. 9:15, 24; 11:27). Whether Solomon simply repaired David's Millo, or created his own, is unknown.

3. The "House of the Millo" (spelled defectively *bêṯ millōʾ*), where Joash was assassinated (2 Kgs. 12:20[MT 21]), located on the way to Silla.

4. "Beth-millo," a city or fortress located near Shechem (Judg. 9:6, 20).

Bibliography. Y. Shiloh, *Excavations at the City of David* 1. Qedem 19 (Jerusalem, 1984).

KENNETH ATKINSON

MINA

A unit of weight (Heb. *māneh;* cf. Ugar. *mn;* 1 Kgs. 10:17; Ezra 2:69; Neh. 7:71-72) approximately equal to 571 gm. (1.26 lb.).

MIND

In the English Bible "mind" translates a number of different words with wide-ranging connotations. In the OT "mind" translates Heb. *lēḇ,* "heart," the seat of one's intellectual capacity (1 Kgs. 3:9; Isa. 65:17; cf. Num. 16:28); *nep̄eš,* "soul," one's internal intentions (1 Sam. 2:35; cf. Gen. 23:8); and *rûaḥ,* "spirit," the designation for one's life as a perceiving, thinking being (Ezek. 11:5).

The two principal Greek words translated as "mind" in the NT are *noús* and *phrónēma* and their cognates. Gk. *noús* signifies the capacity of mental perception, the mind as the source of thinking and understanding. It also refers to the results of such action, i.e., one's attitude, thought, or opinion. Since many of these references come from Paul's letters, and his Hebrew tradition held that all human faculties are bound up together in an indissoluble unit, this word connotes the higher, purposive, and hence moral aspect of humans (1 Cor. 2:16; though this capacity can be debased, Rom. 1:28). Paul also uses *noús* for the inner person (Rom. 7:23). Gk. *phrónēma* signifies one's understanding or attitude, the setting of one's mind (Rom. 8:5-7, 27).

In the NT "mind" also translates several other Greek words: *diánoia,* "understanding" or "intelligence," the seat of reason or insight (Matt. 22:37 = Mark 12:30; Heb. 8:10; 1 John 5:20); *boulḗ,* "way of thinking," "plan," or "purpose," i.e., one's considered intention (Luke 23:51; Acts 5:38; cf. 27:12); and *psychḗ,* "soul," one's committed being (Phil. 1:27; cf. Heb. 12:3).

Bibliography. R. Bultmann, *Theology of the New Testament* 1 (New York, 1951), 211-20.

RICHARD A. SPENCER

MINIAMIN (Heb. *mîyāmin, minyāmîn*)

1. A Levite who assisted in the distribution of the offerings among the levitical cities at the time of King Hezekiah (2 Chr. 31:15; LXX Benjamin).

2. A priestly father's house represented at the time of the high priest Joiakim (Neh. 12:17).

3. A priest and musician who participated in the postexilic dedication of the walls of Jerusalem (Neh. 12:41). He may be the same as Mijamin **3** (10:7 [MT 8]).

MINING AND QUARRYING

The process of obtaining minerals from the earth's lithosphere and hydrosphere, including the science, methods, and business of discovery and exploitation. Minerals can be considered a combination of two or more chemicals with distinctive physical properties or molecular structure. Mining usually means the subterranean removal of minerals, but can also include quarrying which is concerned with surface extraction, open-cast work, placer digging, alluvial dredging, and combined operations. Dimensional stone such as sandstone, marble, and granite for building purposes, and a variety of sediments like sand and clay for construction purposes are usually quarried. The mining processes are also related to obtaining useful minerals from below the earth's surface such as coal. The terms mining and quarrying are often used interchangeably outside of the scientific literature.

Mining is accomplished by using one or more methods of extraction, depending upon the characteristics of the minerals involved. The common methods of extraction are by a tunnel, shaft, and drift, each of which depends on the nature of the mineral deposit. Tunnels are subterranean passageways made horizontally or nearly so, to follow the gallery or level of a mineral seam or other mine workings. Tunnels begin from a shaft which is a vertical passage used for hoisting workers, ores, and supplies, in addition to pumping or ventilating operations. Shaft mining is accomplished by digging a shaft straight down or in a slightly inclined position cutting across mineral deposits. Drift mining tends to follow a seam of mineral ore from its outcrop on the surface and along the inclination of the bed or gallery.

Mining supplies society with its energy, mineral ores, and raw materials. There are many minerals worthy of extraction. Very seldom, however, are minerals found in a pure state. Consequently, the mineral ores which include a fairly large amount of impurities require removal before the minerals can be used. The minerals can be removed in order to improve their quality. Because of this, the process of separating the mined ores from the impurities is required, commonly at the mine site.

When minerals are believed to have economic value they are considered mineral resources. Mineral resources are either economically suitable for mining or held in reserve for extraction at a later time when they have a greater value. Some mining activities exist for hundreds of years, but other mining operations cease when the minerals peter out or become too expensive to mine.

Mines per se in the Holy Land were not located in Palestine proper but were numerous in the Sinai Peninsula, western Palestine, and along the base of the southeastern area of the Ghor. The first mines and quarries apparently began where surficial mineral deposits were discovered. As mining proceeded, tunnels and shafts were dug. Mining and quarrying is a labor-intensive activity demanding a considerable amount of manpower. Long hours of sawing and chipping stone and rock were spent by many workers under extremely enervating working conditions. Injuries and death were commonplace.

Dimension stone for buildings such as limestone was plentiful with quarries located at the site of the settlement or fortress, or very near it. Some fortresses and buildings were built from basalt, which was hard and very difficult to work into blocks as well as rafters. Stone chips for mosaics, commonly more colorful and harder than those from local mines or quarries, were carted many miles. Metallic ores such as gold and copper were mined and smelted even farther away, and precious gemstones were brought by caravans from extremely long distances. Thus, both scarcity and distance added value to the minerals and building stone used in biblical times.

RICHARD A. STEPHENSON

MINISTER, MINISTRY

The concept of serving, both secular and sacred. In the OT Heb. *šārat̠* refers especially to cultic ministry, applying to priests of the Lord who minister at the altar (Joel 1:9, 13), whether of Aaron (Exod. 28:35) or Zadok (Ezek. 40:46), or to Levites (Num. 3:6). The term also has wider application for attending or serving someone (e.g., Exod. 24:13; 1 Kgs. 1:4, 15; 10:5; Ps. 103:21). In the age to come, all Israelites would be priests and ministers (Isa. 61:6) and even foreigners would minister to the Lord (56:6). The root *ʿāḇaḏ*, "work (for someone), serve," often carries a more menial sense (e.g., Gen. 29:15). It is used for serving or worshipping God (Exod. 3:12; Ps. 22:30[MT 31]) or idols (Deut. 4:19); cf. *ʿeḇeḏ*, "servant," for God's redeemed people (e.g., Neh. 1:10) and "the servant of the Lord" (e.g., Isa. 42:1-7; 49:1-9) and *ʿăḇōḏâ*, "service" at tabernacle and temple (= "worship").

This range of meanings carries over into the NT primarily through terms related to Gk. *diakonía*, "service" or "ministry." Other words include *douleúō, doúlos*, "(be a) slave" (e.g., Rom. 1:1; NRSV "servant"); *latreúō, latreía*, "(officiate in) worship" (e.g., Heb. 13:10); and *leitourgía*, "priestly service" (e.g., Heb. 8:6; Rom. 15:16). Other words specify types of leaders in public ministry: e.g., *hypērétēs* for a synagogue attendant (Luke 4:20), Christian "ministers," or "servants of the word" (1:2); or *país* (e.g., Acts 3:13; 4:25) for Jesus as God's servant or child.

The ministry of Jesus set the pattern for development of post-Resurrection ministries in the churches. Jesus' work as teacher, prophet, and healer was taken up, under the Spirit, by itinerant teachers, prophets, and exorcists. He had sent out 12 chosen followers to preach and cure the sick (Mark 6:7 par.). These "sent-forth ones" *(apóstoloi)* became "apostles" (Acts 1:21-22), a larger group than "the Twelve" (1 Cor. 15:5, 7). Peter had a particular commission (Mark 16:7 par.; cf. Matt. 16:18-19). Paul experienced call and commission as apostle to the Gentiles (Gal. 1:15-16). There were also "congregational *apóstoloi*" such as Epaphroditus (Phil. 2:25) and likely women apostles (Rom. 16:6). "The seven" (Acts 6) seem to be a counterpart for Greek-speaking Jewish Christians to "the Twelve," preaching and evangelizing.

The fullest picture of developing mission and ministry comes in Paul's churches and letters. All Christians are there regarded as possessing "spiritual" or "grace gifts" (1 Cor. 12:4-11). Occasionally he lists functions and leaders (e.g., 1 Cor. 12:28-30; Rom. 12:4-8), somewhat ad hoc and always in connection with the Church as the body of Christ and the upbuilding of the whole community in love. Leaders emerge, but the pattern varies (cf. 1 Thess. 5:12-13; Phil. 1:1). This suggests that Paul brought and imposed no set order and allowed local creations of leadership.

In some churches — but not Paul's — "elders" *(presbýteroi)* provided leadership (cf. Acts 14:23; 15:2, 4, 6, 22-23; Jas. 5:14; 1 Pet. 5:1, 5). The model came in many instances from the Jewish synagogue or arose out of respect for those who were older in years or longer in the Christian faith. In the Pastoral Epistles elders or presbyters include some who "rule" (1 Tim. 5:17), within a council of elders (*presbytérion;* 1 Tim. 4:14). Some of these (or the "ruling elder") served as "bishop" or "overseer" (*epískopos;* 1 Tim. 3:2-7; Tit. 1:7-9). Gk. *diákonos* begins to take on a technical sense in 1 Tim. 3:8-13, but it is not yet the "liturgical" or any other type of "deacon" found later. "Ordination," from rabbinic practice, may be reflected in the "laying on of hands" (1 Tim. 4:14; 5:22; 2 Tim. 1:6). But "threefold ministry," in the particular sense of one bishop, (a college of) presbyters, and a group of *diákonoi* under him, is attested only after the NT, initially in Ignatius of Antioch, and spreads then in the late 2nd and 3rd centuries.

Eph. 4:11-12 poses the issue of whether the four groups of leaders there mentioned equip "the saints for the work of ministry" (NRSV) or equip the saints and do the work of ministry themselves (KJV). The "priesthood" (Exod. 19:6) of all baptized believers — "priest" never appears in the NT of an individual Christian leader — occurs in 1 Pet. 2:4-10 (cf. Rev. 1:5-6; 20:6). All such people, gifted by God's grace, "serve" (NRSV; 1 Pet. 4:10-11) and/or "minister" (KJV).

Bibliography. D. L. Bartlett, *Ministry in the New Testament.* OBT (Minneapolis, 1993); J. N. Collins, *Diakonia: Re-interpreting the Ancient Sources* (Oxford, 1990); J. T. Forestell, *As Ministers of Christ* (New York, 1991); N. Mitchell, *Mission and Ministry: History and Theology in the Sacrament of Order* (1982, repr. Wilmington, 1990); J. H. P. Reumann, *The Ministering People of God and Their Leaders* (Minneapolis, 1998); E. Schweizer, *Church Order in the New Testament.* SBT 32 (Naperville, 1961).

JOHN REUMANN

MINNI (Heb. *minnî*)

One of three nations summoned to war against Babylon as part of God's judgment on that nation (Jer. 51:27). Its mention with Ararat (ancient Urartu, modern Armenia) and Ashkenaz (Scythians) makes it probable that it is to be identified with the Manneans, who appear first in the inscription of Shalmaneser II (858–824 B.C.E.). The name continues to occur in Assyrian records for two more centuries, sometimes as enemy, sometimes as ally of the Assyrians. C. MACK ROARK

MINNITH (Heb. *minnîṯ*)

One of the 20 Ammonite cities captured by Jephthah (Judg. 11:33). A number of translators render Minnith in Ezek. 27:17 as the source of the wheat *(ḥiṭê minnîṯ)* Judah traded with Tyre, although others amend the text to read "wheat and olives" *(ḥiṭṭîm zayiṯ)* instead of the place name (e.g., KJV, RV, RSV).

Eusebius (*Onom.* 140.3) identifies Minnith with a village located ca. 4 Roman mi. NE of Esbus (modern Ḥesbân) on the road to Philadelphia (Amman). Eusebius' description, combined with the reference in Judg. 11:33 which describes Minnith as an opposing boundary with the southern city of Aroer, has led most scholars to place Minnith somewhere between Ḥesbân and Amman.

Currently, the most promising candidate is Umm el-Basatin (Umm el-Hanafish; 232137), a modern village situated on top of still-visible ancient ruins. Although no extensive excavation has been conducted there, surveys of the site have recovered sherds from the Ayyubid/Mamluk, Ottoman, Byzantine, Late Roman, Early Roman, Iron II/Persian, and Iron I periods.

RANDALL W. YOUNKER

MINOR PROPHETS

The 12 short prophetic books in the Hebrew canon, Hosea through Malachi.

See BOOK OF THE TWELVE.

MINT

Any of several herbs of the genus *Mentha* (family Labiatae), a number of which grow in Palestine (Gk. *hēdýosmon*). Tithing garden herbs such as mint is not explicitly required by the Pentateuch, but was considered a requirement by scribal interpretation (cf. Deut. 14:22-23). Jesus condemned not this attention to detail, but the neglect of "justice and mercy and faith" that could coexist with it (Matt. 23:23; Luke 11:42).

MINUSCULE

A modified form of Greek cursive handwriting ("rather small"), introduced in the 9th century C.E. More formal and more legible than ordinary cursive, minuscule writing enabled scribes to write more quickly and by the end of the 10th century supplanted uncial writing for literary purposes. Minuscules represent nearly 90 percent of extant NT manuscripts.

See UNCIAL.

MIRACLES

Extraordinary events that manifest divine power, that are wonders to human understanding, and therefore what human beings perceive as signs from God. The various Hebrew, Aramaic, or Greek words used in the Bible to describe "miracles" actually denote "wonders," "powers," and "signs." The manifestation of the divine power may happen with or without human agents of God.

In the OT the greatest miracle is God's creation of the world and everything in it (Gen. 1:1–2:3; 2:4–3:24). Biblical writers repetitively praise God's activity of creation (e.g., Ps. 8:3[MT 4]; 65:6-13[7-14]; Isa. 40:26; Amos 4:13). All other miracle stories are based on Israel's understanding of God's continuous sovereignty over the created world and its history. Although the stories about the manifestation of God's wonders and signs are spread throughout the OT, they are mostly concentrated in two streams of traditions, one in the Exodus and Conquest traditions, and the other in the Elijah and Elisha traditions. In the traditions of the Exodus and the Conquest, God is understood as a national God and a military warrior par excellence. Thus most miracles depict God's activity in destroying enemies and delivering God's people Israel (e.g., Exod. 19:12-25; Josh. 10:11-14). Sometimes, however, God's signs of judgment and deliverance are confined within Israel. God punishes the Israelites for their disobedience (e.g., Exod. 32:35; Num. 11:1-3) and saves them from difficulties or dangers (e.g., Exod. 16:13-31; 17:1-16). The two themes, judgment and deliverance, are sometimes combined in one story, as in the account of the serpents sent by God which killed a number of Israelites and that of the serpent of bronze which saved those bitten (Num. 21:4-9). The prominent human agents of these wonders and signs of God are the prophet Moses and other leaders of the Conquest.

In the traditions of Elijah (1 Kgs. 17-19, 21; 2 Kgs. 1) and Elisha (2 Kgs. 2-8), although the depiction of God as a national God strongly continues in the battles against the Canaanite god Baal and its worshippers, God's power as healer and sustainer is most emphasized. As the human agent of God's power, Elijah provides food (1 Kgs. 17:8-16), brings the dead back to life (vv. 17-24), and controls drought and rain (ch. 18). After Elijah is taken up to heaven, his disciple Elisha succeeds him as God's agent through the spirit of his teacher. Elisha provides water (2 Kgs. 2:19-22), food (4:38-41, 42-44) and other necessary things (4:1-7; 6:1-7), enables the barren to bear children (4:11-17), brings the dead back to life (4:18-37), and heals sick people (5:1-27). Noteworthy are the parallels between the miracle stories of Elijah and those of Elisha on the one hand (resuscitation and provision), and between miracle stories of these two prophets and those of Jesus and his disciples in the NT on the other (resuscitation, healing, and provision).

In all four canonical Gospels miracles play an important role in Jesus' ministry. About 35 miracles are ascribed to Jesus in the Gospels, and several summary statements are given (e.g., Mark 1:32-34; 3:7-12). Form criticism has conventionally categorized Jesus' miracle stories in the Gospels into four groups: healings, exorcisms, resuscitations, and nature miracles. The boundary between healings and exorcisms, however, is sometimes ambiguous due to a popular belief of the time that a demon or spirit is responsible for causing sickness or disease. For example, in the story of Peter's mother-in-law's healing, in which a demon or spirit is not explicitly mentioned as the cause of her sickness, the fever — as if it were a person — leaves her (Mark 1:31 par.) and is even rebuked by Jesus (Luke 4:39). In the story of a crippled woman's healing, she is described as being set free (Luke 13:12, 16) after having been bound by Satan by 18 years. Exorcisms and resuscitations may be regarded as belonging to healing stories in their form as well as content. Both exorcisms and resuscitations follow the same pattern of the story-telling of a typical healing story: the meeting of the healer and the sick one; detailing the nature and severity of the sickness; the healing itself; demonstration of the success; reaction of the witnesses. Regarding content, exorcisms are healings of persons possessed, and resuscitations are healings of persons who have died of illness.

Despite their overlapping ambiguity, the four categories are often quite recognizable. Although more than half of Jesus' miracles are healings, all of the four groups are present in each Gospel except John, which includes no exorcism stories at all. The absence of exorcism in John is not difficult to explain when one notes the miracles' differing significance in the Synoptic Gospels from that in the Gospel of John. In the Synoptics Jesus' miracles are the warrant for the nearness and presence of God's reign, which is the central theme of Jesus' teaching and proclamation (cf. Luke 11:20). In John, however, miracles are signs which reveal the glory of Jesus as the Son of God and Messiah who gives new life, and thus which lead people to faith in Jesus (John 2:11; cf. 20:30-31).

Jesus not only performs miracles in the Gospels, but he himself, especially in his birth and resurrection, is the ultimate miracle. In the Infancy narratives (Matt. 1–2; Luke 1–2), both Matthew and Luke describe his miraculous birth: Jesus is born from a virgin mother through the Holy Spirit. John, in his prologue, goes even further: Jesus, as the Logos who pre-existed with God even before the creation, was God who became flesh (John 1:1-3, 14). At the end of each Gospel, Jesus is raised from death as he predicted. His tomb is empty (Mark 16:1-8; Matt. 28:1-8; Luke 24:1-11; John 20:1-10), and the risen Jesus appears to his disciples (Matt. 28:9-10, 16-20; Luke 24:13-53; John 20:11-29; 21:1-23).

Although Jesus performs most of the miracles, he is not the only person mentioned as a miracle worker in the NT. In the Synoptic Gospels Jesus sends out his disciples after giving them authority to cure diseases and to cast out demons and spirits (Mark 3:15; 6:7; Matt. 10:1; Luke 9:1). Actual descriptions of miracles performed by Jesus' disciples, however, are rare in the Gospels and are concentrated in the Acts of the Apostles, where Peter and Paul are the leading figures who continue Jesus' ministry. Interestingly, the miracles ascribed to these two figures are similar both in number and kind: e.g., a man who cannot walk from birth (Acts 3:1-6; 14:8-10); Peter's shadow (5:15) and handkerchiefs or aprons which touch Paul's skin (19:11-12); punitive miracles (5:1-11; 13:6-11); resuscitation (9:36-42; 20:9-12); liberation from prison (12:6-11; 16:25-34).

The belief in miracles as well as dispute about the authenticity of miracles (e.g., Mark 3:22-30; 2 Thess. 2:9-10) is a common phenomenon in most religions, ancient or modern. Unique in the biblical understanding of miracles over against that of other religions contemporaneous with the biblical period is that it identifies the power as originating solely with the one God.

Bibliography. J. P. Meier, *A Marginal Jew: Rethinking the Historical Jesus* 2 (New York, 1994): 509-1038.

SEUNG AI YANG

MIRIAM (Heb. *miryām*)

1. A prophet(ess) remembered for leading the Israelites in singing after their deliverance from the Egyptians at the Red Sea (Exod. 15:20-21). Many scholars consider this attribution of leadership in singing more ancient than that attributed to Moses and the Israelites in the earlier verses of Exod. 15. Miriam is identified as the sister of Moses and Aaron in the genealogies of Num. 26:59; 1 Chr. 6:3(MT 5:29). The three are named together as leaders of the wilderness era in Mic. 6:4. It is possible that the sibling relationship was not biological but rather the creation of later tradition that sought to emphasize their roles in Israel's leadership. This possibility suggests to many scholars that a more extensive tradition about Miriam may once have existed.

Although Miriam is not mentioned by name in Exod. 2, tradition assumes that she is the older sister of the infant Moses who approaches the pharaoh's daughter after the baby is discovered in the floating basket. Miriam's proposal to find a Hebrew nurse serves to reunite the child with his mother.

After her leadership in singing at the Red Sea, we next hear of Miriam when she and Aaron together challenge Moses' sole authority to speak to the people on God's behalf, as well as Moses' marriage to a Cushite wife (Num. 12). The narrative makes clear God's displeasure with Aaron and Miriam and God's rejection of their claims against Moses. Yet it is reported that Miriam is punished by affliction with a skin disease that turns her white (probably to be viewed in contrast to the very dark skin of Moses' wife of Cushite descent), while Aaron is not punished at all. Upon realizing this situation, Aaron quickly petitions, "do not punish *us*," thus reaffirming his joint complicity with Miriam while begging for her healing before he too is so afflicted. God announces that Miriam's punishment will be only temporary; after seven days of purification outside the camp she rejoins the community and the wilderness journey proceeds. Various theories have been put forward to explain why Miriam alone is punished. Prominent explanations include Israel's attitudes toward priesthood (no one could serve as priest while having a skin disease; Aaron was high priest) and stages in the transmission of the tradition (perhaps the story was originally only about Miriam, with Aaron being added later). Despite such theories, the reality remains that in this story a woman and a man together commit the same sin, but the woman is punished and the man is not.

Miriam's death is recorded in a brief notice in Num. 20:1. It is symbolically significant of Miriam's full status as a leader alongside her two brothers that her death is mentioned at this point, for in the immediately following story Moses and Aaron lose their chance to enter the Promised Land (Num. 20:12). Although Aaron's death is reported only in Num. 27 and Moses' death in Deut. 34 (the two remaining stops on the wilderness journey), the three are held together here in Num. 20 as leaders who all will die outside the land.

Bibliography. R. J. Burns, *Has the Lord Indeed Spoken Only through Moses?* SBLDS 84 (Atlanta, 1987); P. Trible, "Bringing Miriam Out of the Shadows," *BibRev* 5/1 (1989): 14-25, 34.

KATHARINE DOOB SAKENFELD

2. A Judahite among the descendants of Ezrah (1 Chr. 4:17). The NRSV reconstructs this difficult text, taking Miriam as the offspring of Mered and the pharaoh's daughter Bithiah.

MIRMAH (Heb. *mirmâ*)

A Benjaminite, son of Shahariam and Hodesh (1 Chr. 8:10).

MIRROR

Ancient mirrors were made of polished metal, usually copper, gold, silver, or bronze. They were widely produced, as is attested in the Amarna Letters. Mirrors made of glass date back to the 1st century A.D. Excavations in Palestine have unearthed mirrors circular in shape, often with handles of wood, metal, or ivory.

In the OT the bronze laver of the tabernacle was constructed from the bronze mirrors of women who served at the tent of meeting (Exod. 38:8). Using the term metaphorically, Job's friend Elihu compares the firmament to a cast mirror (Job 37:18); and the author of the Wisdom of Solomon compares wisdom to "a spotless mirror of the working of God" (Wis. 7:26). In the NT the mirror is also used metaphorically. The indistinct image one sees in a mirror represents the incomplete knowledge in the present life (1 Cor. 13:12), and James uses a mirror to distinguish between hearing and doing the Word (Jas. 1:23; cf. 2 Cor. 3:18).

J. EDWARD OWENS

MISHAEL (Heb. *mîšā'ēl*)

1. A priestly figure of the wilderness period; a son of Uzziel in the line of Kohath (Exod. 6:22; Lev. 10:4).

2. An influential community member, perhaps a Levite, who stood at Ezra's left hand during his public reading of the law (Neh. 8:4; 1 Esdr. 9:44).

3. The Hebrew name ("Who is what God is?") of a companion of Daniel, also called by the Babylonian name Meshach (Dan. 1–3). 4 Macc. 16:3 highlights Mishael's special association with Dan. 3's fiery furnace. Mishael represents a brand of Israelite sage associated with bureaucratic circles. Some such circles survived, and even flourished (e.g., Dan. 2:49), in Diaspora environs through their shrewd wisdom and fresh apocalypticism. In Jewish literature subsequent to Daniel, Mishael came to serve as a classic example of heroic faith (Pr. Azar. 66; 1 Macc. 2:59; 4 Macc. 16:21; 18:12).

Bibliography. R. R. Wilson, "From Prophecy to Apocalyptic: Reflections on the Shape of Israelite Religion," *Semeia* 21 (1981): 79-95.

STEPHEN L. COOK

MISHAL (Heb. *miš'āl*) (also MASHAL)

A levitical city in the tribal territory of Asher (Josh. 19:26; 21:30); called Mashal at 1 Chr. 6:74(MT 59).

It was located somewhere near the Carmel ridge, probably in the plain of Acco. Tell Kīsân/Tel Kison (164253), 9.6 km. (6 mi.) SE of Acco, is a leading possibility.

MISHAM (Heb. *(Heb. miš'ām)*
A son of Elpaal of the tribe of Benjamin (1 Chr. 8:12).

MISHMA (Heb. *mišmā'*)
1. A son of Ishmael; eponymous ancestor of an Arabian people (Gen. 25:14; 1 Chr. 1:30).
2. A Simeonite, the son of Mibsam (1 Chr. 4:25-26). The presence of Mibsam and Mishma at both 1 Chr. 1:29-30 and 4:25 may suggest some prior relation between a Simeonite clan and what may originally have been an Ishmaelite (i.e., Arabian) tribe.

MISHMANNAH (Heb. *mišmannâ*)
One of the Gadite "mighty and experienced warriors" who joined David at Ziklag and became officers in his army (1 Chr. 12:10[MT 11]).

MISHNAH (Heb. *mišnâ*)
One of the earliest collections of rabbinic oral traditions set into writing, and probably the most influential. Redacted by R. Yehuda Ha-nasi ca. 200 C.E., it is distinguished from the other early collections, known as midrashim, by its organization. Whereas Mekilta, Torat Kohanim, and other such midrashim organize their material to follow the order of Pentateuchal texts, the Mishnah's teachings are abstracted into a topical scheme of six broad categories (*sedarim,* "orders") which divide into topics (*masektot,* "tractates"). Tractates are further subdivided into chapters, which in turn are composed of several individual *mishnayot,* "teachings," the smallest unit. Thus, the first order *Zera'im,* "seeds," the agricultural laws, contains tractates such as *Pe'a,* which deals with the requirement to leave the uncut corners of fields for the poor, and *Šebi'it,* treating the laws of the Sabbatical Year when normal farming was proscribed. Similarly, the second order, *Mo'ed,* "festive times," contains the tractates *Šabbat* and *Roš Haššana,* as well as other tractates dealing with the special laws of the individual holidays; the third order, *Našim,* "women," dealing with laws of marriage and divorce, contains the tractate *Qiddušin,* "betrothals"; and so with the latter three orders which deal, in order, with the civil criminal code *(Neẓikin),* the laws of sacrifices *(Qodašim),* and the laws of purities *(Toharot).* Within this scheme, the Mishnah encompasses the entire range of Jewish law.

The Mishnah is concise, usually citing only accepted decisions and major dissents, both in summary form. Its language is similar to yet distinct from Biblical Hebrew, and it is used with much technical precision. As its aim was to preserve and enhance the oral tradition rather than supplant it, it assumes a familiarity with the teachings it epitomizes; thus the two senses of the name Mishnah, "teaching" and "recapitulation."

Bibliography. A. Steinsaltz, *The Essential Talmud* (1976, repr. Northvale, N.J., 1992); P. Blackman, *Mishnayot,* 7 vols. (London, 1951-56).

SHMUEL KLATZKIN

MISHRAITES (Heb. *mišrā'î*)
A Judahite family of Kiriath-jearim, among the ancestors or predecessors of the Zorathites and Eshtaolites (1 Chr. 2:53).

MISPAR (Heb. *mispār*), **MISPERETH** (*misperet*)
One of the leaders who returned with Zerubbabel from Babylon (Ezra 2:2). At Neh. 7:7 he is called Mispereth.

MISREPHOTH-MAIM (Heb. *miśrěpôṯ mayim*)
A place (perhaps the "eminence over the waters"), one of the border markers for the territory of the Sidonians (Josh. 13:6). After Joshua's victory at the waters of Merom, the victorious Israelites pursued the army of the northern kings to Misrephoth-maim and the valley of Mizpah. Since Maim can be vocalized to *miyyam,* "on the west," the text might carry the secondary meaning "to Misrephoth on the west and to the valley of Mizpah on the east." This could present a literary balance and underscore the extent of Joshua's victory. The name has been taken to refer to modern Khirbet Musheirefeh/Tel Rosh ha-Niqra (161276) on the modern Israel/Lebanon border. Some scholars identify Misrephoth with the Litani River, which would accord well with its location in "Greater Sidon." The Litani River would have presented a difficult passage for a chariot army, and this obstacle may have ended the flight of the fugitives, allowing Joshua to complete his victory (Josh. 11:8). THOMAS W. DAVIS

MIST
Subterranean waters (Heb. *'ēḏ;* cf. Akk. *edû;* Sum. *a-dé-a*) used by God in the creation of plant and subsequently human life (Gen. 2:6 RSV; NRSV "stream"). According to Job 36:27 God distils the mist to produce rain. Elsewhere Heb. *něśî'îm* designates the vaporous mist, one of many forms of water and precipitation under God's control of the elements (e.g., Jer. 10:13; 51:16).

Often references to mist are figurative, depicting the transitoriness of life (Gk. *atmís;* Jas. 4:14), idols (Hos. 13:3) and false teachings (*hómichlē;* 2 Pet. 2:17), and God's forgiveness of sins (Heb. *'ānān;* Isa. 44:22). At Acts 13:11 Gk. *achlýs* describes Paul's temporary blindness.

MITANNI
A Hurrian confederacy and their vassal states, perhaps dominated by an Indo-aryan military elite, that served as an important buffer state in northern Mesopotamia during part of the patriarchal period (ca. 1500-1350 B.C.E.). While not mentioned in the biblical record, the Hurrians are probably to be identified with the Horites (Gen. 14:6; 36:20-30; Deut. 2:12, 20), who settled around Mt. Seir; however, the Horites' southerly location placed them

under Egyptian hegemony and precluded their inclusion in the Mitannian league.

The Mitannians appear in the records of the Egyptians, Hittites, and Assyrians for 250 years until they lose their independence to Assyria under Shalmaneser I (1273-1244). These records include the Amarna Letters, which indicate that Mitanni was a major regional power allied to Egypt through marriages to the pharaohs.

Mitanni's biblical significance lies in the information that the records from Nuzi, a Mitannian dependency, provide about patriarchal customs. For example, Abraham's adoption of Eliezer of Damascus (Gen. 15:2-3), the surrogate motherhood of Hagar (16:2), Bilhah, and Zilpah (30:3, 9), and the double portion to the firstborn (Deut. 21:17) all have important parallels in the Nuzi tablets. Clearly, some common northern Mesopotamian cultural habits were present during the patriarchal era.

See HURRIANS. JESSE CURTIS POPE

MITE

See COPPER.

MITHKAH (Heb. *miṯqâ*)
A place where the Israelites stopped between Terah and Hashmonah during the wilderness wanderings (Num. 33:28-29). Its location is unknown.

MITHNITE (Heb. *miṯnî*)
A term designating Joshaphat, one of David's Champions (1 Chr. 11:43). The gentilic may indicate his place of origin, possibly in Transjordan.

MITHRA
The god Mithra has a complex past extending back to ancient India, where he was a god of truth and light. He also became very popular in Persia, where again he was associated with truth and with contracts between persons. During the Hellenistic period, there is evidence of a cult of Mithra at Commagene in the south of Turkey. Here, Mithra is identified with the sun, and astrology is used in the construction of what the cult perceived to be its cosmic dimensions.

How the mystery cult of Mithra arose in Rome in the late 1st century C.E. is unclear. Some would argue that the cult gradually developed from the Persian worship of Mithra, while others attribute the cult's invention to an individual or a group of people acquainted with Persian religion. Indeed, there are similarities between the Persian worship of Mithra and the mystery cult, but there are also a great many differences. The iconography of the mystery cult, e.g., is pervaded by Greco-Roman astrological and astronomical images.

As the cult was closed and private, there is very little literary evidence describing how it functioned. There are, however, numerous Mithra monuments including the caves in which the members of the cult would worship their god. These caves (Mithraea) can be found in Rome and throughout the empire as the cult was very popular among soldiers, slaves, and freedmen. Only men could join the cult, and the iconography indicates that once initiated into the mysteries, a man could gradually ascend a symbolic ladder of grades. These initiation and ascension ceremonies were also connected with concerns about the afterlife.

With the triumph of Christianity, the worship of Mithra disappeared. Some Mithraea have been discovered, however, often underneath the churches that were built over them.

ALICIA BATTEN

MITHREDATH (Heb. *miṯrĕḏāṯ*) (also MITHRIDATES)

1. The treasurer of King Cyrus of Persia who restored to Sheshbazzar the temple treasures (Ezra 1:8; 1 Esdr. 2:11, "Mithridates").

2. One of three Persian officials who wrote to King Artaxerxes I opposing the rebuilding of Jerusalem (Ezra 4:7; 1 Esdr. 2:16, "Mithridates").

MITYLENE (Gk. *Mitylḗnē*)
A major city and port of the island of Lesbos, in the Aegean Sea, located off the northwest coast of Asia Minor. On the eastern side of the island, Mitylene (modern Mitilíni) is ca. 10 km. (6 mi.) NW of the far eastern tip of the island. The Greek poet Sappho resided there. Although liberated from the Persians by the Athenians, Mitylene was greatly diminished and brought to near ruin by the Greeks for twice refusing to honor agreements made with the Delian League. In the Roman period it was a popular resort city. On the return leg of his third missionary journey Paul sailed to Mitylene (Acts 20:14).

DOUGLAS LOW

MIXED MULTITUDE
The group of people which escaped from Egypt in the Exodus and later formed the nation of Israel (Exod. 12:38). After numbering the Israelites specifically, not including children, the text then states that in addition a "mixed multitude" (Heb. *ʿēreḇ raḇ*) joined along with them. The use of such a phrase in this context implies that the exodus group was not purely homogeneous, and certainly not comprised exclusively of the descendants of Jacob, but included various foreign elements as well. One may point specifically to the Midianites whom Moses brought along. Certainly there must have been many other Canaanites, Egyptians, and other peoples mixing in as well. Indeed, Egyptian records show that many different peoples took refuge in Egypt during times of famine, as did the Israelites, since the regular flooding of the Nile supported agriculture there even when rainfall was sparse. The Kenites and Rechabites are clearly incorporated into Israel from outside. Some would point to the Calebites as well, though they claim a Judahite descent. Some scholarly models of the Exodus would take this passage to imply a diverse coalition of slaves and other malcontents who banded together in the escape or, at least, in the subsequent settlement of the new nation. Num. 11:4 makes a similar implication in referring to "the rabble" *(hāʾsapsup)* that murmured against Moses in the wilderness

wanderings. (The LXX translates both terms with Gk. *epímiktos.*)

Even though the full phrase occurs only in Exod. 12:38, its meaning as relating to "mixing" and "foreigners" is well attested. Heb. *ʿēreḇ* alone is used in Neh. 13:3; Jer. 25:20, 24; 50:37 to describe foreigners of various types (cf. Dan. 2:41, 43). Ps. 106:35-37; Ezra 9:2 use a verbal (hithpael) form of this root for mixing with foreigners *(gôyîm)*, which leads to idolatry and human sacrifice.

ROBIN J. DEWITT KNAUTH

MIZAR (Heb. *miṣʿār*)
The "little mountain" of Ps. 42:6(MT 7). Mizar may refer to one of the foothills of Mt. Hermon, or possibly the lowest of the three peaks of Mt. Hermon itself. The term may be a veiled reference to Mt. Zion, standing in contrast to the high mountain, Mt. Hermon. Another possibility is to render "the mountains at the rim," a reference to the Canaanite underworld, attributing the Psalmist's downcast soul to the nearness of death. THOMAS W. DAVIS

MIZPAH (Heb. *miṣpâ*), **MIZPEH** (*miṣpeh*)

1. Mizpah of Gilead. The name given by Jacob as a sign of his covenant with Laban (Gen. 31:49). The so-called Mizpah benediction invokes Yahweh to monitor the parties' compliance with the covenant stipulations. Later, Israel's forces assembled here in preparation for war against Ammon (Judg. 10:17), enlisting Jephthah to head the war effort (11:11, 29, 34).

2. The "land" (Josh. 11:3) or "valley of Mizpah" (v. 8), an area N of the Sea of Galilee (Chinnereth) near Mt. Hermon. The area was inhabited by Hivites, and here King Jabin of Hazor fled from Joshua.

3. Mizpeh of Judah (Josh. 15:38), a city in the Shephelah.

4. Mizpeh of Moab. Here David met with the king of Moab during his flight from Saul and requested that his parents be granted refuge there (1 Sam. 22:3). The city's location is uncertain, although some identify it with Rujm el-Mesrefeh, a prominent height SW of Medeba.

JOHN T. STRONG

5. Mizpah of Benjamin (Josh. 18:26). There the Israelites mustered their army to avenge the rape and murder of the Levite's concubine (Judg. 20:1, 3; 21:1, 5, 8). Later they gathered there under Samuel and defeated the Philistines in battle (1 Sam. 7:5-11). Samuel performed cultic acts at Mizpah, including burnt offerings (1 Sam. 7:6, 9). There he selected and anointed Saul as king (1 Sam. 10:17-25), and along with Bethel and Gilgal it was on the yearly circuit he traveled when judging Israel (7:16). King Asa of Judah fortified Mizpah and Geba of Benjamin in the early 9th century after the Israelite king Baasha's encroachment on Judah's northern border was aborted (1 Kgs. 15:22 = 2 Chr. 16:6). After Nebuchadnezzar destroyed Jerusalem in 586, Mizpah served as the capital of the Babylonian province of Judah under Gedaliah (2 Kgs. 25:23-25; Jer. 40:6–41:16). It was still an important administrative center after the exiles returned from Babylon (Neh. 3:7, 15, 19). Mizpah is last mentioned as the gathering point for the Hasmoneans as they prepared to battle a Seleucid army (1 Macc. 3:46).

Mizpah is almost certainly to be identified with

A typical Iron Age four-room house, built of limestone blocks, just inside the city gate at Tell en-Naṣbeh. The pillars were probably roof supports (Badè Institute of Biblical Archaeology, Pacific School of Religion)

modern Tell en-Naṣbeh (1706.1436), 12 km. (8 mi.) NW of Jerusalem. The only other possible candidate, Nebī Ṣamwil, has not yielded archaeological remains matching an identification with Mizpah.

Tell en-Naṣbeh was excavated by W. F. Badè between 1926 and 1935. He cleared approximately two thirds of this 260 × 130 m. (855 × 425 ft.) site (3.25 ha. [8 a.]), making it the most broadly excavated tell in Israel. One cave contains remains from the Chalcolithic period (4500-3300). More extensive burial remains in caves and scatters of sherds on the tell from the Early Bronze I period (stratum V, 3300-3000 B.C.) point to a modest settlement at that time.

Examples of typical Iron Age I (stratum IV, 1200-1000) cooking pots, collar-rim pithoi, and Philistine bichrome wares indicate the presence of a settlement at that time. However, the only architectural elements to survive from that period are scores of rock-cut silos, cisterns, and a wine press.

Remains from the Iron Age II (stratum III, 1000-586) are extensive. The town was laid out to follow the natural slopes of the hill on which it was built; the narrow roads follow the oval outline of the hill. Houses are typically small three- or four-room structures which share walls. The initial town defenses were formed by linking together the broad back rooms of the houses along the periphery of the site into a casemate-like system. Asa's massive offset-inset wall (no less than ca. 4.5 m. [15 ft.] in thickness) and inner-outer gate complex completely enclosed the earlier town. A seal belonging to "Ja'azaniah, the servant of the King" was found in one of the tombs and likely belongs to the man of the same name mentioned as a royal officer in 2 Kgs. 25:23; Jer. 40:8. This settlement was leveled ca. 586 in order to provide construction space for the buildings of the next stratum.

Remains from the Babylonian into Persian periods (stratum II, 586-400) consist of large, well-built four-room houses and even larger administrative structures. Asa's wall continued in use, but only the outer gate still functioned. Mesopotamian-style bathtub-shaped ceramic coffins and a fragment of a bronze circlet bearing a dedicatory cuneiform inscription are examples of the Babylonian influence at the site. The reason for the destruction of the town ca. 400 is unknown.

Remains from the Hellenistic into Roman periods (stratum I) are fragmentary, but the remains of three kilns and two grape presses suggest that the mound was nothing more than an agricultural estate. The tell was not occupied in the Byzantine or later periods, though a church and tombs were found in the vicinity.

The archaeological materials from Tell en-Naṣbeh match perfectly the historical documentation relating to Mizpah and provide important data on ancient town planning. Tell en-Naṣbeh provides the only certain material remains in ancient Israel belonging to the Babylonian period.

Bibliography. T. L. McClellan, "Town Planning at Tell en-Naṣbeh," *ZDPV* 100 (1984): 53-69; C. C. McCown and J. C. Wampler, *Tell en-Nasbeh,* 2 vols. (New Haven, 1947); J. R. Zorn, *Tell en Nasbeh: A Re-evaluation of the Architecture and Stratigraphy of the Early Bronze Age, Iron Age and Later Periods,* 4 vols. (diss., Berkeley, 1993). JEFFREY R. ZORN

MIZRAIM (Heb. *miṣrayim*)
The Hebrew word for Egypt (cf. Egyp. *mṣrym*), represented in the Table of Nations as descended from Ham (Gen. 10:6, 13; 1 Chr. 1:8, 11; NRSV "Egypt").

MIZZAH (Heb. *mizzâ*)
The fourth son of Reuel (**2**) and Basemath, grandson of Esau; chief or ancestor of an Edomite clan (Gen. 36:13, 17; 1 Chr. 1:37).

MNASON (Gk. *Mnásōn*)
A Christian originally from Cyprus at whose house in Jerusalem Paul lodged during his final stay in the city (Acts 21:16). Mnason's description as an "early disciple" may mean that he was a founding member of the church in Jerusalem.

MOAB (Heb. *mô'āḇ*)
A small Iron Age kingdom in Transjordan, sharing a border with the Ammonites to the north and Edomites to the south. According to the OT, each of these ancient peoples had frequent contact with the Hebrews over a long sweep of biblical history, and all were frequently at war with each other. Specific information about the origins of these Transjordanian states is lacking, but the most important background of Ammon, Moab, and Edom was the Bronze Age occupants who lived in a small number of towns on Transjordan's tableland. The Iron Age states evolved from earlier, less organized regional groupings, as each of the Transjordanian peoples came into regular contact with and absorbed cultural features from their neighbors. The Ammonites, Moabites, and Edomites spoke related Semitic languages and shared certain aspects of material culture, but there were many differences that made each group aware of its own political, economic, and religious identity. These separate identities are reflected in the archaeological and literary evidence, and scholars are still trying to catalog the inventory of each region's material culture.

At the height of its power, Moab included an area that measured ca. 88 km. (55 mi.) from north to south and ca. 32 km. (20 mi.) from west to east. The Moabite territory was located on the high plateau immediately E of the Dead Sea, and the rim of the escarpment soars up to 1395 m. (4570 ft.) above the floor of the Jordan Valley. Moabite control sometimes extended to the north of Wadi Mujib (biblical Arnon), beyond Dibon (modern Dhībān) as far as the region of Heshbon (Hisban). Ceramic evidence, the Bible, and inscriptions (including the Mesha inscription or Moabite Stone) confirm the extent of what may be called "Greater Moab." In weaker periods, however, the Moabites controlled only their undisputed heartland between Wadi Mujib and Wadi el-Ḥesa (Zered), a territory that stretched ca. 48 km. (30 mi.) from north to south. For all practical purposes, Moab was that narrow

Khirbat al-Mudayna al-ʿAliya, Iron I site on the eastern frontier of ancient Moab. The ancient roadway in the foreground turns left at the quarry/dry moat (right center); a huge defensive wall/tower forces entry into the site along the narrow roadway
(Photo by Reuben G. Bullard, Jr.; courtesy Bruce E. Routledge, Moab Marginal Agricultural Project)

strip of cultivable land which extended less than 32 km. (20 mi.) from the edge of the plateau on the west to the "desert fringe" on the east, beyond which lived nomadic tribes.

The Moabite landscape was gently rolling, sparsely wooded tableland (Heb. *mîšôr*), sometimes called the "tableland of Medeba," and was cut into small segments by extensive wadi systems — or canyons — that drained the region's winter precipitation. The Great Rift Valley (including the Jordan River and Dead Sea), which separated Moab from Judah on the west, was an effective boundary, and the Syrian Desert established the limit of sedentary occupation on Moab's eastern border. Along the well-watered crest of the plateau was the route of the "King's Highway" (cf. Num. 20:17; 21:22). Moab's climate is Mediterranean, but its eastern frontier and the Dead Sea Valley are arid. The greatest annual precipitation generally ranges between 30.5 and 35.5 cm. (12-14 in.) in the central highlands, but this amount drops off rapidly on both east and west. In spite of Moab's topographic isolation and relatively dry environment, the Moabites managed to make a living through dry farming, pastoral activities (cf. 2 Kgs. 3:4-5), and exchanging trade goods with their neighbors.

According to the Bible, Moab, the eponymous ancestor of the Moabites, was the son of Lot (Gen. 19:37), but evidence of human occupation in this region dates back to the Paleolithic period. Deut. 2:10-11 names the Emim as giant, pre-Moabite occupants of this land. Hundreds of archaeological sites reflect a relatively continuous settlement history down to the present, though the intensity of sedentary occupation fluctuated dramatically from period to period. The 3rd millennium is well represented in the archaeological record (and in the Dead Sea Valley at sites like Bab edh-Dhraʿ and Numeira), but there was a decline in settled life during much of the Middle Bronze and Late Bronze Ages, from ca. 1900 to 1300. There is no clear explanation for this pattern, but the number of permanent sites increased steadily from the very end of LB until the end of the Iron Age. The sparse nature of Moab's LB occupation has entered into the debate concerning the date of the Hebrew Exodus and Conquest.

The Bible records regular interaction — often hostile — between Moab and the Israelites, from the time of Moses (e.g., Num. 21-24; Judg. 3:12-30; 11:26) and Ruth into the Persian period (e.g., Ezra 9:1; Neh. 13:1, 23). Most of these contacts were hostile, from the Hebrew migration through the reigns of Saul, David (1 Sam. 14:47; 2 Sam. 8:2), and the Omride dynasty (cf. 2 Kgs. 3). Solomon had Moabite women in his harem and built a shrine for their chief deity, Chemosh (1 Kgs. 11:1, 7, 33). Apart from the Bible, the most important literary evidence pertaining to the Moabites is the Mesha inscription, a basalt monument discovered at Dhībān in 1868. This 34-line Moabite text dates to ca. 930 and reports King Mesha's victory over Moab's Israelite oppressors (cf. 2 Kgs. 3). Another fragmentary memorial stela, found at Kerak in 1958, mentions Chemoshyat(ti), who also ruled at Dibon and was probably Mesha's father.

During the 8th and 7th centuries, from the time of Tiglath-pileser III through the reign of Assurbanipal, the Moabites served as a vassal state of the Assyrians. From Neo-Assyrian texts, we learn the names of four more Moabite kings (Shalamanu, Kamoshnadab, Musuri, and Kamosh'asa), but no precise chronology can be constructed. The Hebrew prophets frequently denounced the Moabites (e.g., Isa. 15–16; Jer. 9:25-26; 48:1-47; Amos 2:1-3; Zeph. 2:8-11), who — according to Josephus — fell to the Babylonians in 582. The Moabite state disappeared for good and its people were absorbed into the broad sweep of history during the Persian, Classical, and Islamic periods. During the Roman and Byzantine periods, the town and villages of Moab flourished, and the Nabatean Arabs (usually associated with Petra and the Edomite southland) were well represented in the former Moabite territory.

As noted, the archaeological evidence from Moab reflects a people whose material culture shared many features with surrounding regions. In fact, there is evidence of trade and mutual influence throughout the region. Recently excavated Moabite architecture — at sites like Khirbet al-Mudayna on Wadi eth-Themed, Khirbet al-Mudayna 'Aliya, and Mudaybi' — includes elements that are known elsewhere in the Levant (e.g., pillared buildings, multichamber gates, proto-Ionic capitals). However, some pottery forms and decorative techniques (e.g., banded painting) are distinctive to this region.

Two important basalt sculptures have been found in this territory — the Balu' stela and the Shihan Warrior stela; they date to the LB II-Iron I transition and the 8th century, respectively. These artistic monuments reflect Moab's international contacts in the portrayal of Egyptianized human figures and a warrior-figure carved in North Syrian style.

Moabite religion was polytheistic, but the god Chemosh was almost certainly viewed as a national god. According to Num. 21:29; Jer. 48:46 the Moabites were known as the "people of Chemosh"; the appearance of this deity's name in personal names is another indication of his significance. Num. 22–24 points to the Moabites' use of diviners, and a Moabite priesthood was mentioned by Jeremiah (Jer. 48:7). The existence of Moabite sanctuaries is taken for granted in the Mesha inscription, which refers to a high place for Chemosh in Qarhoh (probably part of ancient Dibon), and the OT (1 Kgs. 11:7-8; 2 Kgs. 23:13). Lines 12-13, 17 of the Mesha inscription speak of Chemosh's demand that Moab's enemies be killed in his honor; this language is virtually identical to the Hebrew notion of sacred warfare, which was often commanded by Yahweh (e.g., Deut. 7:2; 20:16-17; Josh. 6:17-19, 21; 1 Sam. 15:3, 13).

Archaeological research in this region has increased dramatically in recent decades, and much new light has been shed on Moabite history and culture. Major steps in exploration and scholarly research were made by Ulrich Seetzen (1806), Ludwig Burckhardt (1812), Henry Baker Tristram (1872), Rudolf Brünnow and Alfred von Domaszewski (1890s), and Alois Musil (1896-1902). Modern archaeological work was launched by William F. Albright (1924 and 1933), Reginald Head (1930), John W. Crowfoot (1933), and Nelson Glueck (beginning in 1933). Glueck, in particular, serves as a foundation for more recent surveys (e.g., the work of J. Maxwell Miller, Jack M. Pinkerton, and S. Thomas Parker) and archaeological excavations. Significant excavations were undertaken recently at Dhībān, 'Arā'ir, Khirbet Mudaynah al-Mu'rrajeh, Khirbet Faris, and Lejjûn. Digging continues at Tell Ḥesbān, Madaba/Medeba, Tell Jalûl, Khirbet Iskander, Khirbet al-Mudayna on Wadi eth-Themed, Lehun, Khirbet al-Bālū', Khirbet al-Mudayna 'Aliya, and Mudaybi'. The ancient site of Mephaath (Josh. 21:37; 1 Chr. 6:79[MT 64]; Jer. 48:21), which was located in Moabite territory, has been identified with modern Umm er-Reṣaṣ by means of an inscription on a 7th-century church mosaic. Many important questions remain unanswered, but ancient Moab is no longer *terra incognita.*

Bibliography. "The Archaeology of Moab," *BA* 60 (1997): 194-248 [six articles]; P. Bienkowski, ed., *Early Edom and Moab* (Sheffield, 1992); J. A. Dearman, ed., *Studies in the Mesha Inscription and Moab.* SBLABS 2 (Atlanta, 1989); G. L. Mattingly, "Moabites," in *Peoples of the Old Testament World,* ed. A. J. Hoerth, Mattingly, and E. M. Yamauchi (Grand Rapids, 1994), 317-33; J. M. Miller, ed., *Archaeological Survey of the Kerak Plateau.* ASOR Archaeological Reports 1 (Atlanta, 1991).

Gerald L. Mattingly

MOABITE STONE

A victory stela commissioned by King Mesha of Moab, who ruled during the early 9th century B.C.E.; also known as the Mesha stela. The language of the inscription is Moabite, a Northwest Semitic dialect closely related to Hebrew. The script of the stela is Paleo-Hebrew.

In the inscription Mesha states that King Omri of Israel had made Moab a vassal state, but that during the reign of Omri's "son," Mesha regained Moab's independence and even annexed certain regions traditionally associated with Israel (e.g., Nebo). Mesha attributed Israel's hegemony over Moab to the anger of the god Chemosh, clearly implying that Moab's successes were the result of the cessation of Chemosh's anger and the resumption of his favor. Disaster and success are topoi frequently associated in the Bible with the anger or favor of Israel's deity. Mesha also referred to his numerous public works in behalf of Moab, such as the (re)construction of walls, water systems, and cult structures. One of the most striking aspects of the inscription is the reference to Yahweh, the national God of Israel. Some consider the biblical and inscriptional materials to be two different episodes in the history of Israelite-Moabite relations, while others consider them supplementary versions (cf. 2 Kgs. 3:4-27).

The stone was discovered in the ruins of Dhiban, the capital of ancient Moab, by Bedouin, who brought it to the attention of F. A. Klein, an Anglican minister and medical missionary, in 1868. The stone is black basalt, ca. 1 m. × 60 cm. × 60 cm. (3.3 ft. × 23.6 in. × 23.6 in.), with an inscription of 34 lines. Klein's arrangements to purchase the stone failed; Salīm el-Qārī made a hand copy of the first few lines, and shortly thereafter Ya'qūb Karavaca made a paper squeeze. Because of complications in negotiating the purchase and delivery of the stone, the Prussian consul requested the help of the Turkish authorities. This displeased the Bedouin, who heated the stone in a fire and then poured cold water on it, causing it to break into scores of pieces. Some 57 pieces (about two-thirds of the inscription) were ultimately purchased, from which Charles Clermont-Ganneau, using the squeeze made by Karavaca, was able to reconstruct the entire inscription quite accurately.

Bibliography. J. A. Dearman, ed., *Studies in the Mesha Inscription and Moab.* SBLABS 2 (Atlanta, 1989); S. H. Horn, "The Discovery of the Moabite Stone," in *The Word of the Lord Shall Go Forth,* ed. C. L. Meyers and M. O'Connor (Winona Lake, 1983), 497-505; G. L. Mattingly, "Moabites," in *Peoples of the Old Testament World,* ed. A. J. Hoerth, Mattingly, and E. M. Yamauchi (Grand Rapids, 1994), 317-33.

CHRIS A. ROLLSTON

MOADIAH (Heb. *mô'aḏyâ*)
Ancestor of a family of priests of the time of the high priest Joiakim (Neh. 12:17). The name may be related to Maadiah.

MODEIN (Gk. *Modein*)
A small village, modern Ras Medieh (150148) ca. 29 km. (18 mi.) NW of Jerusalem, the ancestral home of the Hasmoneans and the site of the Maccabean Revolution in 167 B.C.E. The aged priest Mattathias refused to sacrifice a sow to Zeus as commanded by Antiochus IV Epiphanes and killed another priest who was going to do so, along with the king's messenger (1 Macc. 2:15-27). The Hasmonean family tombs were at Modein (1 Macc. 2:70; 9:19; 13:25-30).

JOE E. LUNCEFORD

MOLADAH (Heb. *môlāḏâ*)
A place or city in the Negeb near Beer-sheba, first assigned to Judah (Josh. 15:26), described as lying toward the boundary of Edom, then assigned to Simeon (Josh. 19:2; cf. 1 Chr. 4:28). It was reoccupied by returning exiles (Neh. 11:26). The only mention of the site outside the OT is on an ostracon found in 1984 at Ḥorvat 'Uza, but it provides no insight into its location. The most probably identification is with Tel Malḥata/Tell el-Milḥ (152069), located in the Beer-sheba Valley between Arad and Beer-sheba.

Bibliography. I. Beit-Arieh and B. C. Cresson, "Horvat 'Uza," *BA* 54 (1991): 126-35.

BRUCE C. CRESSON

MOLECH (Heb. *mōleḵ*)
A Canaanite-Israelite god (LXX *Moloch*). The longstanding response of fascination and horror stems from Molech's presumed association with the ritualistic killing of human beings. The name is typically related to a tri-radical consonantal base *m-l-k* that frequently appears in the Hebrew Bible. While its various vocalizations indicate a particular semantic value associated with rulership (e.g., *meleḵ*, "ruler"; *mĕlûḵâ*, "royalty"), the form *m-l-k* has been interpreted in about eight instances as a reference to a chthonic or a netherworld deity and patron of human sacrifice: Molech "ruler (of the netherworld"; Lev. 18:21; 20:2-5; 1 Kgs. 11:7; 2 Kgs. 23:10; Jer. 32:35; Amos 5:26? [cf. LXX]). A number of scholars, while upholding Heb. *m-l-k*'s connection with human sacrifice in these texts, would interpret these references as a technical name for child sacrifice known from Punic sources: a "*molk*-sacrifice." This is unlikely, however, as confirmed in the associated phrase "playing the harlot after Molech" (cf. Lev. 20:5; also Isa. 57:3). In its 40 or so other occurrences in the OT, the phrase "playing the harlot after. . ." refers to religious practices associated with illicit deities, their images, or numinous beings such as ghosts (e.g., the *'ōḇōṯ* and the *yiddĕ'ōnîm*). It never explicitly refers to the offering up of sacrifices. In Lev. 20:5 and elsewhere it would appear that a deity Molech is in view, rather than some technical term for sacrifice.

Recently scholars have attempted to exploit apparently relevant comparative Near Eastern data pertaining to a deity M-l-k (frequently vocalized as Malik, but nonetheless viewed as cognate to biblical Molech). Along these lines and of no little consequence is the ancient Near Eastern and biblical evidence attesting to the practice of human sacrifice more generally, irrespective of whether the sources explicitly relate said rituals to a deity M-l-k. Related references to the rite of human sacrifice underlying such biblical phrases as "the one who makes his son or daughter pass through the fire" and the "sacrifice of the firstborn to Yahweh" have been compared, contrasted, and equated with those mentioning Molech. There remains the added question of whether the ritual killing of humans was a crisis ritual or part of the sacrificial calendar. The evidence at hand suggests that human sacrifice could function in either, if not both, capacities.

The Deuteronomistic history, although critical of the practice of human sacrifice, preserves the memory of former Israelites and their neighbors who indeed ritually killed their children — Jephthah (Judg. 11:34-40); Hiel (Josh. 6:26; 1 Kgs. 16:34); Ahaz (2 Kgs. 16:3); and Manasseh (2 Kgs. 21:16). It further acknowledges the efficacious power of such a ritual as in the sacrifice of the Moabite prince offered up by his father. The performance of this ritual resulted in the wrath of the deity (Chemosh?), forcing the Israelites to retreat from Moab (2 Kgs. 3:27). It is not until much later during Josiah's reform that the Topheth in the Hinnom Valley — where human sacrifice is portrayed as having taken place — was destroyed. Even then, the practice endured well beyond the late preexilic period in Judah (cf. Jer. 2:23; 7:31; 19:5-6, 11-14; 31:40; 32:35).

Human sacrifice as more generally referred to in the phrase, "the one who makes his son or daughter pass through the fire," is frequently and exclusively attributed to Canaanite origins by some biblical writers (e.g., Deut. 12:31). Nonetheless, some form of human sacrifice was apparently part of the Yahwistic cult in preexilic (and perhaps exilic) times. Isa. 30:33 clearly connects Yahweh and human sacrifice at the Topheth (read Molech for *meleḵ* in v. 33b?); if no such connection was intended in this allusion to Assyria's anticipated destruction, one would have expected some disclaimer to that effect. The "sacrifice of the firstborn to Yahweh" and the Molech sacrifice were probably closely related, if not one and the same cult. Although the former required that the firstborn sons be sacrificed to Yahweh while the latter listed as sacrifices children generally (of both sexes), the fact that daughters could legally substitute for sons as firstborn heirs favors the equation of these two cults (cf. Num. 27:1-8 and the texts from Emar and Nuzi regarding the legal substitution of daughters for sons within the context of inheritance). The two traditions might reflect the same cult but from complementary perspectives, one from the more particular and the other from the more general (or is one a subset of the other?). Therefore, texts that refer to the sacrifice of the firstborn to Yahweh (e.g., Gen. 22:1-14; Exod. 13:2, 12-13, 15; Mic. 6:6-7) can be related to the Molech cult. Molech's associations with Baal (rather than Yahweh) in biblical traditions (cf. Jer. 2:23; 19:5; 32:35) are more likely part of the inventive Deuteronomistic rhetorical polemic to "Canaanize" what was formerly a non-Deuteronomistic, but Yahwistic, Israelite practice of human sacrifice.

As added confirmation of the endurance and pervasiveness of the practice, Ezekiel implies that Yahweh had commanded the Israelites to participate in the sacrifice of their firstborn (Ezek. 20:25-26), but qualifies this law as a form of punishment. Similarly, Exod. 22:29-30(MT 28-29) comprises an unqualified demand to make the firstborn sacrifice to Yahweh; the option to redeem the firstborn is not offered here as in later and Priestly texts. In the light of Jeremiah's condemnation of the practice and Ezekiel's recognition that Yahweh had once condoned the ritual killing of humans, it is self-evident that for many it was an acceptable form of Yahweh worship. Mic. 6:7 might imply that the most powerful sacrifice that could be offered to Yahweh was child sacrifice; he either endorses said practice or poses a rhetorically charged question eliciting an emphatic No!

Whether or not Yahweh and Molech are to be considered one and the same deity with respect to their roles in the cult of human sacrifice begs the question. Several relevant passages (e.g., Jer. 32:35; Ezek. 23:38-39; Lev. 20:3; Zeph. 1:5) indicate that the Molech cult was considered by some sectors of Israelite society as part of the Yahwistic cult. The location of the Molech cult in the nearby Hinnom Valley rather than in the Jerusalem temple precinct might be reflective of an intra-Israelite debate over its relative status within the Yahweh cult. It might well have been observed in the temple precinct in the days of Ahaz (Hezekiah?) and Manasseh, but then moved to the Hinnom Valley in the initial stages of Josiah's reign and again thereafter (cf. Jer. 7:31-32; 19:5); note too that Hezekiah never concerns himself with outlawing the existent Molech cult (cf. 2 Kgs. 18:1-4). Furthermore, 2 Kgs. 16:3; 21:6 (cf. also a form of human sacrifice as practiced by the northern kings, 17:17) do not locate that cult at the Topheth. The lack of explicit mention of the Molech cult and the failure to attribute its establishment to Ahaz or Manasseh in Josiah's defilement of the Topheth in 2 Kgs. 23:10 might be of no small consequence. The Molech cult as portrayed in Deuteronomistic and related traditions was probably not relegated to areas outside the temple precincts. Traditions like 2 Kgs. 21:3-6; 23:11-12 assume the worship of several Canaanite-Israelite deities as taking place within the Jerusalem temple precinct (e.g., Baal, Asherah, the host of heaven, and the solar deity), and the same might have applied in the case of Molech.

The lack of extrabiblical confirmation for the existence of a specifically chthonic or netherworld aspect of a deity M-l-k and for his status as patron of a cult of human sacrifice ought to elicit caution as regards a straightforward historical reading of the biblical portrayal of the Molech cult. Moreover, tensions evident in the biblical traditions regarding the nature and extent of human sacrifice suggest another instance wherein Deuteronomistic history employed a strategy of rhetorical polemic. By artificially attributing to Molech patronage over the cult of human sacrifice, the Deuteronomists sought to distance the practice from its origins in the Yahweh cult altogether. The rhetorical character of the Deuteronomistic portrayal finds its clearest confirmation in the fact that non-Deuteronomistic (and non-Priestly) biblical traditions do not distance human sacrifice from the cult of Yahweh (cf. texts preserving the sacrifice of the firstborn). If one grants that Molech was Yahweh's chthonic aspect or an independent netherworld deity of the Yahwistic cult in late preexilic Judah, one would hardly expect the Deuteronomistic and Priestly traditions to acknowledge openly that reality. Rather, in line with the Deuteronomistic tendency to reduce the divine population of heaven (as regards a Yahwistic pantheon), a deity such as Molech — real or contrived — would be portrayed as a Canaanite deity and Israel's adherence to his cult explained as the outgrowth of "syncretistic" tendencies (cf. the Deuteronomistic polemic against the goddess Asherah, known to be the consort of Yahweh in non-Deuteronomistic forms of Yahwism, but in Deuteronomistic circles identified as a Canaanite deity and wife of Baal).

Bibliography. J. Day, *Molech: A God of Human Sacrifice in the Old Testament* (Cambridge, 1989); G. C. Heider, *The Cult of Molek*. JSOTSup 43 (Sheffield, 1985); J. D. Levenson, *The Death and Resurrection of the Beloved Son* (New Haven, 1993); M. S. Smith, *The Early History of God* (San Francisco, 1990). BRIAN B. SCHMIDT

MOLID (Heb. *môlîḏ*)
A Judahite of the line of Jerahmeel; the son of Abishur and Abihail (1 Chr. 2:29).

MOLOCH
See MOLECH.

MOLTEN IMAGE
See IDOL, IDOLATRY.

MONEY
The means for exchange of goods and services. It functions as a reflex of economic intercourse, measuring relative worth, and facilitating the transaction of commodities. Coinage is the minted form of money, standardized and sanctioned by a government agency to benefit economic cooperation. A discussion of money in the Bible is the systematic treatment of the complex of biblical references to commodities of exchange.

The precursors to coinage were barter, precious metals, weights, and measures. In the biblical text metal ingots and jewelry were used as payment (Josh. 7:21; Gen. 33:19). Gold and silver were measured in various denominations. The terms for the various weights include the talent, mina, shekel, pim, bekah, and gerah. There is a great degree of continuity between practices reflected in the Bible and those of the wider ancient Near East.

References to money occur in every historical period and literary genre of the Bible. In the ancestral period, there are the transactions of Abraham (Gen. 23:15-16) and the mortgage policies of Joseph in Egypt (47:14-26). In the monarchical period, there is the royal economy of Solomon (1 Kgs. 9:10-28; 10:14-29). The legal codes contain significant data concerning money, usually in connection with tithes and offerings (e.g., Deut. 14:25; cf. Exod. 30:16; Num. 18:29), slaves (Exod. 21:21), restitution for damages (21:32), or the charging of interest (22:25[MT 24]). The prophets denounce fraudulent business practices (Hos. 12:7; Amos 8:5; Mic. 6:11) and economic oppression (Amos 2:6; 8:6).

Preexilic Hebrew inscriptions contain references to the precious metals, and ingots and jars of jewelry have been attested archaeologically. An ostracon found at Tell Qasile, dating to the time of Hezekiah (715-687 B.C.E.), demonstrates the import of gold. Two ostraca from Arad and one from Yavneh-yam refer to weighed quantities of silver, the denomination being the shekel. Hoards from this period (at Gaza, Shechem, Megiddo, Beth-shan, Beth-shemesh, and En-gedi) suggest that precious metal was becoming recognized for its transactional value and that the movement toward coinage was underway. The preexilic *lmlk* and rosette stamps, official seal impressions found on jar handles of storage pottery, constitute a precedent for the royal sanction of goods and measures. The value of money, however, was regulated by market forces and the differential was configured in weight. References to the "weights current among the merchants" (Gen. 23:16), "the royal weight" (2 Sam. 14:26), and "the shekel of the sanctuary" (Exod. 30:13) suggest that various standards were simultaneously in effect.

According to Herodotus, coinage originated in Asia Minor in the second half of the 7th century. Subsequently, many Greek cities issued coins, although the Athenian coins achieved widest circulation. The Persian imperial mints found only limited distribution, other than the gold daric issued by the Persian king Darius I ca. 515. Trade with the Phoenicians and Greeks introduced coinage into Palestine. Imported Greek silver coins predominated together with Athenian tetradrachma imitations from the Phoenician cities of Arvad, Byblos, Sidon, and Tyre. Some coins were produced and circulated by local mints, including Gaza, Samaria, Ashdod, Askelon, and Jerusalem. These coins are often designated as "Philisto-Arabian" or simply "Palestinian." They followed the Athenian standard and were exclusively silver. In addition, provincial coins with the appellation "Yehud" were in circulation from ca. 400 on into the Ptolemaic period. These were struck by the governor of the Yehud province, as is evident in another group of coins with the legend "Yehezqiyah the governor." The iconographic design of these coins imitates the Attic tradition, showing the head of the goddess Athena on the obverse and the symbol of an owl, later the lily and the falcon, together with the legend on the reverse. One Yehud coin from this era bears the representation of an enthroned deity, perhaps Yahweh, though this is debated. The impression of the enthroned deity, together with that of the goddess Athena, suggests that at this time the Jewish minting authorities had few scruples with the iconographic representation of deities. Contemporaneous with the Yehud coins of Yehezqiyah, sometime during the second half of the 4th century, are coins from Samaria bearing the legend "Jeroboam." This is likely a Samaritan governor, who assumed a name reminiscent of the northern Israelite dynasty.

Ezra and Nehemiah contain many references to money, but it is difficult to determine whether this is coinage or bullion. For the rebuilding of the temple, still during the time of Cyrus, "sixty-one thousand darics of gold, five thousand minas of silver" were donated (Ezra 2:69; cf. Neh. 7:70-71). Payments in money were made to members of guilds (Ezra 3:7). The governors of Yehud implemented a tax structure which included "shekels of silver" (Neh. 5:15; 10:32[33]). The citizens of Yehud mortgaged their property and possessions in exchange for money to pay the royal tax (Neh. 5:4, 10-11). Whether the references be to coinage or bullion, Ezra and Nehemiah suggest bustling economic activity.

The study of the relationship between the provenance of coins and their topographical distribution points to the extent and vitality of trade in Palestine during the 4th century. Economic build-up, i.e., vibrant industry and trade, has been ascertained in coastal settlements such as Achzib, Acco, Shiqmona, Dor, Jaffa, Ashdod, Askelon, and Yavneh. It is also archaeologically evident that the hinterland enjoyed benefits from coastal economic gain. Inscriptional documents from outside of Palestine, such as the Elephantine papyri, the Persepolis tablets, and the Murashu documents, indicate the democratized use of coinage for this period.

Subsequent to Alexander's conquests, the Athenian standard of coinage all but eliminated local mints. Alexander chartered the principal mints in Acco, Aradus, and Sidon, and his imperial coinage continued unchanged even during the political struggle in the aftermath of his death. This alignment of coinage seems to have continued the existing tenor of social-economic development. After 312 Palestine continued primarily under Ptolemaic control. The Ptolemies practiced an isolationalist economic policy in Egypt and throughout their territory. The silver tetradrachmas were minted at Sidon, Tyre, Acco (renamed Ptolemais), Joppa, and Gaza, and bore the legend "of Ptolemy the King (or the Savior)." Local Yehud coinage was again minted during this period, probably during the reign of Ptolemy II (ca. 285-270). Iconographically, the coins usually bear the representation of the Ptolemaic ruler on the obverse and either an eagle or a dove on the reverse. It is suggestive that some coins have eliminated symbols of deification on the representation of the ruler, and should perhaps be understood as evidence of aniconism. The Zenon archive and the Letter of Aristeas illumine the effects of the development of coinage in Ptolemaic Egypt and Palestine. The Wisdom of Solomon (Wis. 15:12), Sirach (Sir. 7:18; 18:33; 21:8; 29:5-6; 31:5; 51:28), and Tobit (Tob. 1:7; 2:11; 5:19), all from the Ptolemaic period, refer to coinage.

After 198, under the Seleucid rulers, both silver and bronze coins were in circulation in Palestine. Antiochus IV, known for his religious imperialism, propagated the Zeus cult on his coins together with a deified image of himself. The Jewish state which emerged under Hasmonean leadership issued an independent, predominately bronze mintage to supplement the larger denominations in circulation. Though 1 Macc. 15:6 intimates that Antiochus VII permitted Simon the priest to mint coins, it appears that Antiochus reversed this and other allowances (v. 27). Instead, Simon's son John Hyrcanus I (135-104) minted a series of coins, one of which bears what was to be the official Hasmonean emblem, two cornucopias with a pomegranate. The legend reads "Yehonan the high priest and the Council of the Jews." His son Alexander Janneus (103-76) used the self-designation "Jonathan the king" on his coins. Later, for unknown reasons, many of these coins were restruck with the designation "Jonathan the high priest and the Council of the Jews." After Alexander Janneus, coins are attested from the time of John Hyrcanus II (67-64) and Mattathias Antigonus (40-37).

After his triumph over Antigonus in 37 B.C.E., Herod I began a bronze mintage bearing his name and the title "king." His successors continued minting bronze coins until the end of the Herodian dynasty in Agrippa II (95 C.E.). Various Roman procurators over Palestine (6-59 C.E.), such as Pontius Pilate, issued bronze coins as well. The silver coins in circulation during this time were the shekel from Tyre and the Roman tetradrachma and denarius (the rough equivalent to the Greek drachma), minted in Rome, Tyre, Antioch, and Nabatea.

This is the setting for the NT Gospels. The coin presented to Jesus for the Roman tax (Matt. 22:19; Mark 12:15; Luke 20:24) was likely a Tyrian denarius. The imperial image on the obverse of the denarius was standard from Augustus on. The denarius was valued at about a day's labor (cf. Matt. 20:21). The temple tax of Matt. 17:24 is referred to as a didrachma, which is equal to half a shekel. The Gospels give evidence of both trade in kind and trade in money. Tenants leased the vineyard for a percentage of the harvest (Luke 16:6-7; 20:10). Tithes could be paid in kind (Luke 16:6). Sizable transactions were made in the denomination of the talent (Matt. 18:24; 25:14-28) or the mina (Luke 19:13-25). The debtor of Jesus' parable owed alternatively 10 thousand talents (Matt. 18:24) or 500 denarii (Luke 7:41). The smaller denominations, the chalkos, lepton, assarion, and quadrans, were used in more daily affairs, for which a purse would be carried (Luke 22:36). Monetary exchange was required to accommodate the variety of coinage, not in the least for cultic and sacerdotal purposes (Matt. 21:12; Mark 11:15-18; John 2:14). Luke judges the Pharisees to be "lovers of money" (Luke 16:14).

The Gospels portray Jesus' attitude toward money and riches as ranging from critical to indifferent. On the one hand, he demonized wealth (Luke 16:13) and called for the renunciation of possessions (Mark 10:21; Luke 9:3). On the other hand, he accepted support from wealthy devotees (Luke 8:2-3) and kept company with the well-to-do (Matt. 11:19). In some cases, the early Church practiced a certain communalism (Acts 4:32) and programmatically distributed to those who were economically vulnerable (6:1-6). The early Christians in the urban centers were comprised of persons of all social strata (e.g., 1 Cor. 11:22). Paul too recommends that property be regarded as relative (1 Cor. 7:30-31), and initiates collections for the rural poor in and around Jerusalem (Rom. 15:26; 1 Cor. 16:2; Acts 11:30).

During the First Jewish Revolt (66-70 C.E.), both silver and bronze coinage were minted in Jerusalem. Coinage was often minted to fund an army. The iconography of the coins was comprised of vegetation and cultic paraphernalia, and was paired with nationalistic or religious slogans. After 70, the silver tetradrachma from Tyre and Antioch became the standard coin, supplemented by bronze coins minted in Neapolis and Sebaste. Special coins commemorating the defeat of Judea were issued by the Romans. During the Second Revolt led by Simon bar Kokhba (132-135), silver tetradrachmas and denarii were overstruck with slogans referring to the leader, the city of Jerusalem, or simply "the freedom of Israel."

Bibliography. D. V. Edelman, "Tracking Observance of the Aniconic Tradition Through Numismatics," in *The Triumph of Elohim* (Grand Rapids, 1995), 185-225; A. Kindler, ed., *The Patterns of Monetary Development in Phoenicia and Palestine in Antiquity* (Tel Aviv, 1967); Y. Meshorer, *Ancient Jewish Coinage*, 2 vols. (Dix Hills, N.Y., 1982); "Ancient Jewish Coinage: Addendum I," *Israel Numismatic Journal* 11 (1990-91): 104-32; M. Rostovtzeff, *The Social and Economic History of the Hellenistic World*, 2nd ed. 2 vols. (Oxford, 1957).

GERALD M. BILKES

MONEY-CHANGER

In ancient Palestine, the banker who exchanged local currency for that of a different country or province. Coins were widely used in the Roman Empire, and many different types, weights, and sizes of coins found their way into ancient Judea. This was especially true of Jerusalem during the Passover, as Jews came to make sacrifice at the temple. In addition, each Jewish male would pay an annual temple tax of a half-shekel.

Roman coins contained images of deities and inscriptions that proclaimed Roman domination, all of which were offensive to the Jews. Therefore, Jewish authorities insisted that the temple tax be paid with coins bearing more acceptable images, usually shekels minted in Tyre. For a nominal fee, money-changers exchanged other coins for Tyrian shekels. They may also have sold sacrificial animals to the pilgrims and lent money, also for a small commission.

The money-changers' tables were set up in outlying areas approximately a month before Passover. As the pilgrims began to flow into Jerusalem for Passover, operations moved to the temple (probably the Court of the Gentiles). This is the scene of Jesus' somewhat violent confrontation with the money-changers and their comrades in commerce (Matt. 21:12-13; Mark 11:15-17; Luke 19:45-46; John 2:13-16).

STEVEN M. SHEELEY

MONOTHEISM

The conviction that there exists only one god, and no others (Gk. *mónos*, "alone, only, single" and *theós*, "god"). This is in contrast to polytheism, the belief in several deities, and henotheism or monolatry, the conviction that there exists one supreme god among lesser divinities. The principle of monotheism has become the backbone of Judaism, Christianity, and Islam. Classical inquiry into the origins of monotheism has, for the most part, followed two different trajectories. While some have advocated the notion of a primordial monotheism from which polytheistic beliefs later arose, others have seen monotheism as evolving, often in clearly defined stages, from a polytheistic climate. Most scholars today tend to follow the latter path.

Ancient Near East

Any documentation of religion in the ancient Near East presents a number of difficulties. The literary remains upon which scholarly research is based tend to favor the "official" religion of the state over the beliefs and practices of the common people.

In ancient Egypt there was a continual tension between the traditional polytheistic conception of the divine world and the tendency toward the unification of the deities and their attributes. This often led to the formation of syncretistic compounds or composite gods. The ongoing tension between local autonomy and centralized rule in Egypt may well be a counterpart to this. Most often associated with early monotheism is Pharaoh Akhenaten (ca. 1350-1334 B.C.E.). Having come to the throne as Amenophis IV, Akhenaten changed his name to reflect his strict devotion to one aspect of the sun-god (Re), the Aten, i.e., the "disk of the sun." He also began building a new capital in Middle Egypt at what is now el-Amarna. All other priesthoods and localized religious practice were condemned; even the names of the traditional gods were removed from the monuments in order to blot them out of memory. The common people could not worship the Aten itself but only the royal couple as part of the divine triad. The Hymn to the Aten (*ANET*, 369-71), often compared to Ps. 104, is the best-known literary expression of Akhenaten's monotheistic belief. After Akhenaten's death, however, there was a rapid return to traditional polytheism.

With the inception of urbanization (ca. 5th millennium), Mesopotamian religion began to exhibit a tendency toward the unification of the divine. Before the Akkadian empires Mesopotamia was comprised of a series of independent city-states, each centered around a temple complex with at least one patron god or goddess. These deities were organized in families along kinship lines. The glory of each divinity was manifest in the glory of the city and its temple; as one city gained political power and extended its sphere of influence, its patron deity was elevated to a position of prominence over deities of the subject cities and towns. The higher deity tended to take on the attributes of the lesser subject deities.

A prime example of this move toward monotheism or monolatry is the elevation of the Babylonian god Marduk. The creation epic Enuma Elish (*ANET*, 60-72), often compared with Gen. 1:1–2:4a, is an example of myth-making with the purpose of elevating Marduk to the rank of "king of the gods" by means of divine conflict. This myth, in which Marduk becomes the creator and organizer of the cosmos, was later copied by the Assyrians who substituted the name of their god Assur for the Babylonian Marduk. Tablets discovered on the Syrian coast at Ras-Shamra (Ugarit) contain a variety of myths and legends including the Baal Cycle (*ANET*, 129-42) in which the Canaanite storm-god Baal is also elevated as supreme god and ruler of the cosmos.

Ancient Israel

The text of the OT is the product of a long and complex process of literary growth, and presents an idealized portrait of Israelite religious belief and practice. Any reconstruction of Israelite religion must, therefore, draw on the material remains of ancient Palestine as a balance to the biblical account. Inscriptions discovered at Kuntillet ʿAjrud/Ḥorvat Teman and Khirbet el-Qôm permit an association between Yahweh and the goddess Asherah, suggesting that Yahweh may have at one time been worshipped along with a female consort. Monotheism in Israel, at any rate, appears to have developed over a long period of time, beginning about the 10th century up until the end of the Babylonian Exile.

Early Israelite monotheism most likely began in the highlands as localized tribal religion in which each tribe worshipped its own patron deity. The ancestral narratives in Genesis presuppose this sort of tribal religion (e.g., Gen. 24:27; 31:5, 53). With the centralization of the state under David and Solomon, there emerged certain advocates who elevated Yahweh as supreme God over all other divinities (including El, Asherah, and Baal), thus making Yahweh the "God of Israel." The combination of national religion with political might provided the monarchic state the means to exert further authority over the people, while continuing to tolerate the worship of other gods. Gradually the concept of covenant became an expression for the mutual relationship of blessedness between Yahweh and the monarchic state (1 Kgs. 8; 2 Kgs. 12 [cf. 11:17]; Pss. 2, 72, 89, 110). The continual fostering of literary activity in the royal court and temple was instrumental in promoting Yahweh as the God of the entire cosmos who possesses all the positive attributes previously associated with the traditional gods and goddesses. With the work of Second Isaiah toward the end of the Babylonian Exile, Israelite monotheism took on a more forceful form of expression. Yahweh is proclaimed as the creator of the cosmos (Isa. 40:21-23, 28). Foreign deities do not exist; there is only one true God, Yahweh (40:12-31; 43:8-13; 46:5-13). Idols are nothing more than useless objects (40:18-20; 41:21-24; 44:9-20; 46:5-7).

New Testament

The NT presupposes the monotheistic convictions expressed in the OT and early Judaism. When one of the scribes asks Jesus which is the "first of all commandments," Jesus responds by quoting the Shema (Deut. 6:4-5), the central confession of the oneness of God (cf. Matt. 22-34-40; Luke 10:25-28). Though the NT epistles do not deny the existence of other divinities, for early Christians there is one God and one Lord, Jesus Christ (1 Cor. 8:4-6). Monotheism became instrumental for early Christian mission. Since God is one, there must be only one God of both Jews and Gentiles (Rom. 3:29-30). As the early Church was faced with threats of heresy and division, the confession of one God and one Church, the body of Christ, was decisive for preserving a sense of unity (Rom. 12:3-8; 1 Cor. 12:12-31; Eph. 4:14-16; Col. 1:18, 2:19).

Bibliography. D. V. Edelman, ed., *The Triumph of Elohim: From Yahwisms to Judaisms* (Grand Rapids, 1996); T. Frymer-Kensky, *In the Wake of the Goddesses: Women, Culture, and the Biblical Transformation of Pagan Myth* (New York, 1992); E. Hornung, *Conceptions of God in Ancient Egypt* (Ithaca, 1982); P. D. Miller, Jr., P. D. Hanson, and S. D. McBride, eds., *Ancient Israelite Religion* (Philadelphia, 1987); J. C. de Moor, *The Rise of Yahwism: The Roots of Israelite Monotheism.* BETL 91 (Leuven, 1990); M. S. Smith, *The Early History of God: Yahweh and the Other Deities in Ancient Israel* (San Francisco, 1990). Arnold Gottfried Betz

MONTH

See Year.

MOON

All civilizations of the ancient Near East worshipped the waxing and waning moon; with few exceptions, the major lunar deities were portrayed as masculine. Moon gods, indigenous and international, were worshipped in ancient Palestine (Deut. 4:19; 17:3; 2 Kgs. 23:5; Job 31:26; Jer. 8:2). Abraham's links with Haran and Ur, the most prestigious centers of lunar worship in ancient Mesopotamia, probably mirror the Aramean cultic milieu familiar to the Genesis authors. Proper names in the OT reflect a recognition of moon gods from western Asia and Mesopotamia. Forms of the name of the Mesopotamian moon-god Sîn occur in Sanballat (Neh. 4:1[MT 3:33]), Sennacherib (2 Kgs. 18:13 = Isa. 36:1), and Shenazzar (1 Chr. 3:18). West Semitic Yariḫ (Heb. *yārēaḥ*) is attested in Jerah (Gen. 10:26 = 1 Chr. 1:20), and Jaroah (1 Chr. 5:14); other names based on words for the moon include Hodesh (1 Chr. 8:9) and Laban (e.g., Gen. 24:29). Place names like Beth-yeraḥ and Jericho also testify to ancient lunar worship. The iconography of Iron Age Syria-Palestine represents the moon either as a natural object — a crescent — or symbolizes it with one of the liturgical conventions of the neighboring nations, i.e., a crescent mounted atop a pole or stand (Mesopotamian Sîn of Haran, stamp and cylinder seals), a lunar barge (Egyptian mythology, amulets), or a crescent headpiece worn by a baboon or an ibis (Egyptian Thoth, amulets and scarabs).

The basis of the civil and cultic calendars in ancient Israel and Judah was the lunar month (cf. Sir. 43:7). A festive holiday was observed monthly when the new moon was first sighted (Num. 10:10; 28:11).

The figure of the moon in the Bible is usually paired with the sun and stars. As a rival to Yahweh, the moon is an object of proscribed worship (Deut. 4:19; 17:3; 2 Kgs. 23:5; Job 31:26; Jer. 8:2). Appreciation of the natural beauty and splendor of the moon inspired lyrical poetry (Job 26:9; Ps. 8:3[4]; Cant. 6:10). As a spectacular illustration of divine judgment, the apparent eternity of the moon (Ps.

72:5, 7; 89:37[38]) could be terminated: a pregnant symbol of the day of Yahweh and the eschatological conclusion of history is the extinction of the moon (Isa. 13:10; 24:23; Joel 2:31[3:4]; 3:15[4:15]; Mark 13:24 par. [Gk. *selḗnē*]; Acts 2:20; Rev. 6:12; 8:12; 2 Esdr. 7:39).

Bibliography. S. B. Freehof, "Sound the Shofar — 'ba-kesse' Psalm 81:4," *JQR* 64 (1974): 225-28; B. B. Schmidt, "Moon," in *DDD,* 585-93; M. Stol, "The Moon as Seen by the Babylonians," in *Natural Phenomena: Their Meaning, Depiction and Description in the Ancient Near East,* ed. D. J. W. Meijer. Koninklijke Nederlandse Akademie van Wetenschappen Verhandelingen, Afd. Letterkunde, N.S. 152 (Amsterdam, 1992): 245-77.

STEVEN W. HOLLOWAY

MORDECAI (Heb. *mordoḵay, mordŏḵay*)

1. A character in the book of Esther who is identified as Esther's cousin and who becomes her foster father (Esth, 2:5, 7). Mordecai's refusal to bow to Haman, the highest official of the Persian king Ahasuerus, causes Haman to plan a pogrom of all Persian Jews. By identifying Mordecai as a Benjaminite and Haman as an Agagite, the narrator subtly links their conflict with that of Saul and Agag (cf. 1 Sam. 15). When Haman decides not to wait for the pogrom to be rid of Mordecai, he erects a stake on which to impale him. Mordecai is saved by Queen Esther, however, who in the pivotal scene of Esth. 7 shifts the king's loyalties away from Haman. The narrator leaves unclear whether the shift is due to the fact that she is a Jew, and thus under threat from the planned pogrom, or that the king thinks Haman is making advances toward Esther. Queen Esther then puts Mordecai in charge of Haman's property, the king bestows upon him the royal signet ring, and together Esther and Mordecai work to thwart the pogrom.

Bibliography. T. K. Beal, *The Book of Hiding: Gender, Ethnicity, Annihilation and Esther* (London, 1997). TOD LINAFELT

2. An Israelite who returned from exile with Zerubbabel (Ezra 2:2 = Neh. 7:7).

MOREH (Heb. *môreh*)

1. A terebinth or oak tree near Shechem. Abraham built an altar there after his vision of God (Gen 12:6-7). The Hebrew term means "teacher" or "oracle giver," suggesting that the name is based on an etymology in honor of Abraham's vision. In Deut. 11:30 the tree is a landmark in the vicinity of Mt. Ebal and Mt. Gerizim, overlooking the town of Shechem. Jacob buried his idols by an oak near Shechem (Gen 35:4), which may be the same tree. Similarly, it may also be the same as the "Diviner's Oak" (Judg 9:37).

Two other trees near Shechem are mentioned in the OT (Josh 24:26; Judg 9:6), though these trees were inside the city.

2. A hill in the Jezreel Valley where the Midianites were camped on the night of Gideon's attack (Judg 7:1). Most scholars locate this hill near Nebi Daḥī, N of ʿAfula. WADE R. KOTTER

MORESHETH (Heb. *môrešeṯ*), **MORESHETH-GATH** (*môrešeṯ gaṯ*)

A satellite village of Gath in the Shephelah; hometown of the prophet Micah (Jer. 26:18; Mic. 1:1). The ancient site of Moresheth is generally identified with modern Tell ej-Judeideh (141115), ca. 2.5 km. (1.5 mi.) N of Beit Jibrin/Beth Guvrin (ancient Eleutheropolis) and ca. 10 km. (6 mi.) NE of Lachish. The form Moresheth-gath ("Possession of Gath") appears only in Mic. 1:14.

AARON W. PARK

MORIAH (Heb. *mōrîyâ*)

1. The "land of Moriah," the place where God commanded Abraham to take his son Isaac and sacrifice him (Gen. 22:2). The narrative describes this as a three-day journey from Beer-sheba (Gen. 22:4). However, "the third day" may simply be a conventional way of indicating a short distance and hence is of little help in establishing Moriah's location. In Jewish tradition the story of the sacrifice of Isaac at Moriah is referred to as the Aqedah, the "binding" of Isaac.

2. Mt. Moriah, the site in Jerusalem where Solomon built the temple (2 Chr. 3:1). The same verse identifies the site also as the place "where the Lord had appeared to his father David," who had been asked to build an altar there, on the threshing floor of Araunah/Ornan the Jebusite (cf. 2 Chr. 3:1; 2 Sam. 24:18). Today, Mt. Moriah, the temple plateau, is the site of two Muslim shrines, the al-Aqsa mosque and the Dome of the Rock. A section of the western side of the retaining wall of the temple mount is the Wailing Wall, a Jewish site of prayer.

These two places are clearly not identical. A possible explanation is that Moriah originally referred to the temple mount, and that the term replaced the original name for the site in Gen. 22, thus linking Abraham with the Jerusalem temple.

JOHN L. GILLMAN

MORNING STAR

A symbolic name of the Lord Jesus. Translated "day star" in the KJV, Gk. *phōsphóros* appears only in 2 Pet. 1:19. However, "star" (Gk. *astḗr*) as an epithet for the Messiah is not uncommon (Rev. 2:28; 22:16; cf. Num. 24:17).

At Isa. 14:12 Isaiah refers to the king of Babylon as "Day Star, son of Dawn" (Heb. *hêlēl*), which the KJV translates "Lucifer," following the Latin. The word means "light-bearer" and signified the planet Venus, which preceded or accompanied the rising of the sun. Jesus may have had reference to the Isaiah passage when he spoke of Satan falling from heaven (Luke 10:18). Lucifer thus came to be used in the Middle Ages as an appellation of Satan.

DALE ELLENBURG

MORTAR

1. A vessel, usually made of ground stone, in which substances are crushed with a pestle. The most common material crushed in a mortar was grain, although cosmetics, dye pigments, spices, and manna (Num. 11:8) were also ground using a mortar (Heb. *mĕḏōḵâ*) and pestle. Mortars were usually made of basalt (a volcanic stone native to parts of Palestine) and varied in shape from a block with a concave depression on top to more elaborate footed types. Limestone cosmetic palettes or mortars are also known.

2. A plastic building material used to bind bricks or stones. In Palestine and Egypt, mortar was usually made of the same clay used for bricks (Heb. *ḥōmer*). It was mixed with straw or other materials using the feet (Isa. 41:25; Nah. 3:14) and applied while wet. Mortar was not always used in brick or stone constructions; excavations have shown that many walls were built with stone so accurately cut that they did not need mortar. The builders of the tower of Babel used bitumen for mortar (Gen. 11:3). JENNIE R. EBELING

MORTAR, THE

A trading district in Jerusalem (Zeph. 1:11), named probably for its topography (a bowl-shaped depression, after the common mortar used with a pestle for grinding; Prov. 27:22; cf. Judg. 15:19). The northern part of the Tyropoeon Valley has been suggested as its location. JENNIE R. EBELING

MOSERAH (Heb. *môsērâ*), **MOSEROTH** (*mōsērôṯ*)

The 15th Israelite encampment after they left the wilderness of Sinai (Num. 33:30-31). Deut. 10:6 relates that Aaron died and was buried at Moserah (according to Num. 33:38-39, Mt. Hor). The itinerary of Num. 33 depicts the Israelites traveling from Moseroth to Bene-jaakan, whereas Deut. 10:6 reverses that order. If Moserah/Moseroth was near Mt. Hor, then the site is probably located NE of Kadesh-barnea, near Edom. PETE F. WILBANKS

MOSES (Heb. *mōšeh*)

Israelite liberator and lawgiver.

Biblical Accounts

Moses is born to Levite parents after Pharaoh decrees the death of all newborn Hebrew boys. Rather than drown Moses, his mother sets him in the Nile shallows, where he is discovered by Pharaoh's daughter and extracted by her maidservant. The princess raises Moses as her own son, employing his natural mother as wet nurse (Exod. 1:22–2:10). Pharaoh's daughter names him *mōšeh,* "because I rescued *(mšh)* him from the water." As a whole, the incident anticipates future events: as Pharaoh designs to drown Israel's helpless boys in the reedy Nile, from which Moses is rescued, so Yahweh and Moses will save Israel from Egypt at the Reed Sea, where Egypt's mighty men perish. Pharaoh's daughter, though a minor character, thus symbolizes God; her maidservant corresponds to Moses. Even Moses' name, if understood as Hebrew, ought to mean, not "rescued from the water," but "rescuer from the water," foreshadowing Moses' role in Israel's deliverance (cf. Isa. 63:11).

In his early manhood, Moses, hitherto an unwitting traitor to his class and kin, begins to explore life outside the palace. Coming upon a fight between an Egyptian and a Hebrew, he kills the Egyptian and hides the body. When he later interrupts a fight between two Hebrews, his previous homicide is thrown at him, and he knows he must flee (Exod. 2:11-15). These pivotal incidents, too, foreshadow Moses' destiny, to rescue Israel from Egypt, to establish justice, and yet to be rejected by his own people. These encounters demonstrate Moses' instinct for equity and capacity for swift action. They also illustrate the futility of attempting to help Israel without divine assistance.

Arriving in Midian, Moses rescues embattled shepherdesses at a well. These prove to be daughters of the local priest, called Reuel or Jethro, who welcomes Moses and gives him his daughter Zipporah in marriage. Moses and Zipporah produce two sons, Gershom and Eliezer (Exod. 2:15-22; 18:1-6). At this point one might think Moses' wanderings and story are over. But, as he is about to discover, Moses is still "a sojourner in a foreign land." The words sum up his entire career, since he will never reach the Promised Land.

Sometime later, while tending sheep, Moses encounters Israel's ancestral deity in a burning, talking bush. God reveals to him his true name, Yahweh, and reaffirms his ancient promise to bring Israel to Canaan (Exod. 3:14-17). Overruling his repeated objections, God sends Moses back to Egypt to deliver Israel, assisted by his brother Aaron and armed with the "rod of God." On the way, Moses undergoes a bizarre, hostile encounter with the deity. He nearly dies, but is saved by the blood of circumcision (Exod. 4:24-26). It seems Moses has undergone a rite of passage. He has put off his youth and the company of women for his adult role as Israel's liberator. Moses will forsake Jethro's sheep for God's "flock."

After delivering God's word to the joyous people, Moses confronts Pharaoh. But the king only makes Israel's suffering harsher, sowing dissent among people, elders, and Moses (Exod. 4:29–6:1). Moses is dismayed, but God reiterates his promise to deliver Israel (Exod. 6:2-8). At this point Moses is 80 years old (Exod. 7:7).

God sends 10 plagues against Egypt (Exod. 7:8–11:10). While he occasionally wavers, Pharaoh still refuses to release Israel; Yahweh has "hardened his heart." Finally, God kills every firstborn male, human and animal, throughout Egypt, sparing only Israel, who smear the protecting blood of a lamb or kid, the Passover, on their doorframes (Exod. 12:1-28). Now the Egyptians urge Israel to leave and even shower them with gifts (Exod. 12:29–13:16).

Yahweh leads Israel, not by the expected coastal route, but straight through the desert toward the Reed Sea. Once more the Egyptians decide to pursue, and pin Israel against the sea, but Yahweh parts the waters so that Israel may pass. When Egypt follows and Israel is safely across, Yahweh restores the waters, and Egypt drowns. Moses and Miriam lead the people in jubilation (Exod. 13:17–15:21).

Moses leads Israel through the desert, miraculously providing water, quails, and manna, defeating the Amalekites and, with Jethro's guidance, establishing the Israelite judiciary. Throughout, the people complain against Moses, but he is continually vindicated by God (Exod. 15:22–18:27). Finally they reach Sinai, where Israel will camp for 11 months (cf. Num. 10:11). Israel formally enters into a covenant with God (Exod. 19; 24). Yahweh's covenant obligation is to give Israel prosperity in its own land. Israel's obligation is to worship Yahweh alone and to obey all God's moral and ritual laws received by Moses atop Mt. Sinai. These are detailed in Exod. 20–Num. 10.

In Moses' absence, Aaron builds a golden calf for the people to worship. God proposes to wipe out Israel and create a new nation out of Moses, but Moses declines the honor and placates the deity. Returning from the mountain, Moses smashes the tablets of the covenant and orders all idolaters killed. A new covenant is enacted, and Moses bears new tablets down from the mountain. During this second revelation he has an almost direct experience of God and is somehow transformed: his face is either radiant or burnt (Exod. 32–34).

Finally, after a census is taken, Israel sets forth from Sinai, bearing the ritual tabernacle they have built to house Yahweh's presence (Num. 1–10). But their rebellions continue. Frustrated, Moses demands more assistance from God, who invests 70 prophets to help him. This leads his own brother and sister, Aaron and Miriam, to question Moses' unique leadership (they are also bothered by his second marriage to an Ethiopian). Moses declines to defend himself, but Yahweh afflicts Miriam with temporary leprosy (Num. 11–12).

Moses dispatches 12 spies to reconnoiter Canaan. When all but Caleb and Joshua report that the land is impregnable, the people again wish they were back in Egypt. Moses once more dissuades Yahweh from destroying Israel. But now God decrees that all the people, except Caleb and Joshua, must die in the wilderness; Israel will wander for 40 years. Chastened, the people attempt to enter the land without divine sanction, but it is too late (Num. 13–14). During this period God reveals more religious laws (Num. 15; 18–19; 28–30; 35).

At some point during the 40 years, the Levite Korah and the Reubenites Dathan and Abiram rebel against Moses and Aaron, contesting their unique claim to religious office and blaming their apparent inability to bring Israel to Canaan. Yahweh kills Korah, Dathan, and Abiram. At God's behest, Aaron and the other tribal leaders deposit their rods in the tabernacle. Aaron's sprouts blossoms and almonds, showing that he is Yahweh's elect. His rod is to be kept as a sign against future challenges to authority (Num. 16–17).

When Israel again rebels, demanding water, Yahweh commands Moses to take Aaron's rod and to address a rock face, which will yield water. Instead, Moses strikes the rock. Water gushes forth, but the miracle is less impressive. For his imperfect obedience both Moses and Aaron are condemned to die in the desert (Num. 20:2-13).

At the end of 40 years, Israel is back (or still) at Kadesh, preparing to enter the land. Various peoples contest Israel's passage south and east of Canaan. Some are circumvented and others defeated. During this time Moses averts a plague of fiery serpents by affixing a bronze snake to a pole (Num. 21:6-9; cf. 2 Kgs. 18:4).

Final preparations for the conquest of Canaan include a new census and delineation of the Promised Land (Num. 26:1–27:11; 32; 34–36). Moses appoints Joshua as his successor (27:12-23; Deut. 31:14-23). Moses then ascends Mt. Nebo to deliver his farewell address, basically the book of Deuteronomy. He recapitulates Israel's recent history and the laws of the covenant (Deut. 1:5–31:23), predicting that God will send other prophets like himself (18:15-18). Moses sings a prophetic song, blesses the tribes, beholds Canaan from afar, and dies at the age of 120 (Deut. 32–34). He is buried by Yahweh himself (Deut. 32:6).

Moses is among the Bible's most complex and vivid characters. This is partly because varying accounts of his life and teachings have been fused. To some extent Moses is idealized: he is the epitome of pious humility (Num. 12:3) and functions as prophet, priest, judge, and king. Later figures may be depicted as Moses-like — Joshua, Elijah, Elisha, Josiah, Jesus — yet Moses remains a unique phenomenon, not so much by his internal greatness as by his unparalleled intimacy with God (Exod. 33–34; Num. 12:6-8; Deut. 34:10). He is father of his people — and arguably mother, too (cf. Num. 11:12), assuaging the wrath of Israel's Father in heaven. Moses twice forgoes the supreme honor of begetting a new nation (Exod. 32:10; Num. 14:12) and instead is condemned to die in the wilderness for his people's sins (Deut. 1:37; 3:27; 4:21), buried in an unknown, unvisited grave (34:6). Moses is even described as a god to Aaron and Pharaoh (Exod. 4:16; 7:1), and, by one interpretation, his face shines with divine splendor (34:29-35). Still, in all sources Moses is a flawed character. Throughout his career his faith wavers; he is given to mood swings, is inconsistently obedient to Yahweh, and is a somewhat reluctant leader.

Moses rarely appears in biblical poetry, which in general is more mythic and less historical than the prose sources and accordingly emphasizes Yahweh's role in saving Israel over Moses'. But in later Judaism Moses' importance grew. The entire Torah was attributed to his authorship, along with innumerable other principles supposedly passed down orally (*m. 'Abot.* 1:1). Tales of his exploits developed along folkloric lines (Exodus Rabbah). For Hellenistic Jews and sympathetic pagans, Moses was a kind of philosopher king (e.g., Philo of Alexandria). For the Jews' opponents, he was a pestilential crank (cf. Josephus *Contra Apion*).

The NT depicts Jesus as essentially affirming Moses' law (e.g., Matt. 5:17-20; Luke 16:16-17), citing an apparition of Moses and Elijah as a validation of Jesus (Matt. 17:1-8; Mark 9:2-8; Luke 9:28-36). Moses in many ways serves as a literary prototype for Jesus (cf. Acts 7:37). Each is endangered from birth but protected by his parents (Matt. 2).

Each returns with his family from exile after the oppressor's death (Matt. 2:19-20). Each comes out of Egypt (Matt. 2:13-21). Each preaches from a mountain (Matt. 5) or after descending from a mountain (Luke 6:12-49). Each fasts for 40 days and nights (Matt. 4:2; Luke 4:2). Each feeds humanity with divine drink (John 7:37-38) and food (Matt. 14:13-21; 15:32-39; Mark 6:31-44; 8:1-10; Luke 9:10-17; John 6). Even Moses' saving standard, a snake on a pole, supposedly anticipates Jesus' resurrection (John 3:14). Each is rejected by the very people to whom he has brought salvation (Acts 7:27-53). Luke 9:31 calls Jesus' death his *éxodos* (lit., "departure"). Yet Moses is not just Jesus' prototype, but also his antitype. Moses' Law is superseded by Christianity, whose New Covenant offers a more immediate and universal relationship with God (John 9:28-29; 2 Cor. 3; Galatians; Heb. 3:2-6). In the NT's ambivalent attitude toward Moses we recognize the early Church's ambivalence toward its Jewish roots.

History

We can say little for certain about the historical Moses — not even when he lived. Biblical chronology places his birth ca. 1520 B.C.E. (Exod. 7:7; 1 Kgs. 6:1), but few critical scholars would endorse so early a date. Moreover, Moses' life story consists largely of stereotypical narratives widely paralleled in world literature: the abandoned and rescued baby; the prince who discovers suffering; the exile who returns from the desert with a family and a mission; the reluctant prophet. Tales of his interactions with Aaron and the Levites are retrojections of later priestly squabbles. As for Moses' literary activity, scholars believe that virtually all "Mosaic" legislation is centuries younger, codified ca. 400. The entire Torah, in fact, is composed of several strands, written perhaps between the 10th and 5th centuries. By its spelling, language, and content, the Pentateuch in its present form cannot be Moses' work.

What remains? First, *mōšeh* is a genuine Egyptian name meaning "is born," short for such names as Thutmose ("Thoth is born"). In fact, several Levites bear Egyptian names: Merari, Hophni, Phinehas, Pashhur, and perhaps others. This corroborates the tradition that some Israelites came out from Egypt.

That some Israelite ancestors were slaves who escaped or were expelled from Egypt is quite plausible. The Egyptians possessed many Semitic slaves, especially in the late 2nd millennium. Since Moses' clan, Levi, would become Israel's priestly caste and the only tribe without a territory, most scholars assume that the historical Exodus was experienced principally by the Levites, who infiltrated and in effect converted the already landed tribes. Other Israelite ancestors, perhaps the majority, may have been true Canaanites, dominated by the Egyptian Empire for centuries. Some of these were probably descended from the Hyksos, erstwhile Semitic rulers of Egypt since ca. 1800, expelled ca. 1500. If the traditional date of Moses' birth is perchance correct, he must in fact have been an ousted Hyksos.

Most scholars, however, would place Moses and the "real" Exodus in the 13th century in the reign of Rameses II. Rameses' self-portrayal as a vigorous warmonger fits the biblical portrait well. Moreover, his name appears twice in tradition, albeit not as a personal name (Gen. 47:11; Exod. 1:11). In fact, Israel first appears, as a tribal people settled in Canaan, in an inscription of Rameses' successor Merneptah, ca. 1220. At just this time, archaeology informs us, the Canaanite highlands saw rapid population growth. In short, while the tradition of expulsion/liberation may combine different historical processes transpiring over three centuries, the events with which tradition associates Moses belong chiefly to the 13th century.

More than one scholar has observed that, were there no tradition of a Moses, we would have to posit his existence anyway. Israelite religion vis-à-vis the ancient Near East seems a deliberate innovation, not a natural outgrowth. As there was a Mohammed, a Paul, a Jesus, a Zoroaster, and a Buddha, so must there have been a Moses. But because our written traditions are so much later, it is impossible to distinguish his teachings from those of his followers.

Is nothing then Mosaic? The Song of the Sea features linguistic and stylistic archaisms and might conceivably be by Moses (Exod. 15:1b-18). Many suspect that the Ten Commandments derive from a Mosaic prototype (Exod. 20:2-17; Deut 5:6-21). Perhaps, too, we should credit Moses with the two most characteristic teachings of Israelite religion: the covenant with God and aniconic (idolless) monotheism. The Israelite covenant, we now know, is modeled on ancient Near Eastern treaties between vassals and suzerains. One of the key provisions of such contracts is exclusive allegiance to a single ruler — for Israel, Yahweh.

If Moses invented Israelite monotheism, he surely relied also upon the doctrine of Pharaoh Akhenaten (reigned 1377-1361?), who broke with Egyptian tradition by worshipping the Sun alone, without images. Just as the Sun exclusively loves his son Akhenaten, so Yahweh loves his covenanted "son" Israel. The idea of a connection between Akhenaten and Moses is often dismissed as implausible, but that two aniconic monotheisms should have arisen independently out of Egypt is even less plausible. The acknowledged dependence of Ps. 104 upon Akhenaten's "Hymn to the Sun" is sufficient to prove the endurance of the pharaoh's peculiar theology.

As for how Moses would have encountered Akhenaten's teaching, the biblical tradition that he was raised as an Egyptian is not as romantic as it sounds. Although closely following folkloric prototypes, Moses' nativity story reverses a key motif: he is a commoner raised at court, not a prince raised in obscurity. This may indicate a historical kernel. We know that Semitic leaders' sons were raised in the palaces of New Kingdom pharaohs, the better to ensure their fathers' loyalty, as well as the eventual loyalty of the sons (cf. 1 Kgs. 11:18-20).

Apart from the influence of Akhenaten, there is

also evidence that Yahweh was worshipped as a god — not necessarily the only God — near Midian in the 14th century. Also, Israelite concepts of deity owe a profound debt to Canaan. In sum, Moses was doubtless a religious revolutionary. But his achievement was, at most, a synthesis of pre-existing ideas.

Bibliography. F. M. Cross, *Canaanite Myth and Hebrew Epic* (Cambridge, Mass., 1973); R. E. Friedman, *Who Wrote the Bible?* (New York, 1987); B. Halpern, "The Exodus and the Israelite Historians," *ErIsr* 24 (1993): 89*-96*; W. A. Meeks, "Moses in the NT," *IDBSup* 605-7 (Nashville, 1976); W. H. C. Propp, *Exodus 1-18.* AB 2 (New York, 1999); D. B. Redford, *Egypt, Canaan, and Israel in Ancient Times* (Princeton, 1992). WILLIAM H. C. PROPP

MOSES, TESTAMENT OF

A prophecy of Moses preserved in a single, incomplete, 6th-century C.E. Latin manuscript translated from a Greek text, itself likely translated from a Hebrew original. Ancient lists of apocryphal books record both a Testament of Moses and an Assumption of Moses. Whether these were two distinct works or a single composition is unclear. Because the Testament of Moses lacks its original ending, it is possible that it once contained the Assumption of Moses or some other account of Moses' death.

The 12 extant chapters of the Testament of Moses contain the final exhortation of Moses to his successor Joshua. The book loosely rewrites Deut. 31–34, and follows the basic Deuteronomic pattern of sin and punishment. In ch. 1 Moses tells of his impending death and appoints Joshua as his successor. In ch. 2 Moses predicts the Conquest, the period of the judges, and the Divided Monarchy. Ch. 3 foretells the fall of Jerusalem to the Babylonians and views the Exile as a punishment for sin. In ch. 4 Moses predicts the return from captivity and the rebuilding of Jerusalem. In chs. 5 through 7 Moses foresees Jewish idolatry during the Hellenistic period, the degeneration of the Hasmoneans, the rise of Herod the Great, and the campaign of Varus in 4 B.C.E. Ch. 8 then recounts the prior persecution under Antiochus IV Epiphanes. In ch. 9 the Levite Taxo and his seven sons resolve to die, rather than break the laws. Ch. 10 is an apocalyptic hymn prophesying the coming kingdom of God. The work concludes with a dialogue between Joshua and Moses, in which Moses promises Joshua that God will keep the covenant. The text then breaks off in the middle of a sentence.

The date and author of the Testament of Moses are subject to debate. Some scholars argue for an early 1st century C.E. composition, while others propose a date in the early stages of the Maccabean Revolt (168-165 B.C.E.), with later post-Herodian interpolations (4 B.C.E.–30 C.E.). The unknown author of the Testament of Moses has been variously identified as a Hasidim of the Maccabean period, a Pharisee, an Essene, or a pious member of an unknown Jewish sect.

Bibliography. J. Licht, "Taxo, or the Apocalyptic Doctrine of Vengeance," *JJS* 12 (1961): 95-103; G. W. E. Nickelsburg, ed., *Studies on the Testament of Moses* (Cambridge, Mass., 1973); J. Tromp, *The Assumption of Moses.* SVTP 10 (Leiden, 1993).

KENNETH ATKINSON

MOST HIGH

An epithet of God (Heb. *'elyôn*). Similar to forms attested in Ugaritic literature (Ugar. *'ly;* cf. *UT,* no. 1855), it occurs in the most archaic Hebrew poetry within the patriarchal accounts (e.g., Num. 24:16; Deut. 32:8; cf. 2 Sam. 22:14 = Ps. 18:13 [MT 14]; cf. Acts 7:48). It appears also in the compound form God Most High (*'ēl 'elyôn;* e.g., Gen. 14:18-20; cf. Mark 5:7).

MOST HOLY PLACE

The innermost compartment of the tabernacle and subsequent temple, perhaps reflecting the conception of holiness as fundamentally a matter of separation from that which is common or profane. The designation (Heb. *qōdeš haqqŏdāšîm*) utilizes a common Hebrew idiom for forming the superlative degree and was also used to describe the meat offered in sacrifices that was eaten by the priests (Num. 18:9-10), the supreme holiness of the temple as a whole (Ezek. 45:3), the idealized apportionment of land to the priests (48:12), and possibly a person (Dan. 9:24; cf. NRSV mg).

The limits of "the most holy place" were demarcated in the tabernacle by a hanging veil (Heb. *pārōket*). Although understood by the rabbis to be a vertical partition between "the most holy" and "the holy" places (the latter containing the incense altar, lampstands, and table for the bread of the presence), the veil may have stretched horizontally over the ark of the covenant as a covering (Heb. *sukkâ;* cf. Num. 4:5). Perhaps the olivewood doors separating the "holy" and "most holy" places of the Solomonic temple (1 Kgs. 6:31-32), which were apparently replaced by curtains in the second temple (cf. 2 Chr. 3:14; Heb. 9:2-3), led to the confusion on this point. The dimensions between the cherubim's wings in "the most holy place" of Solomon's temple would have allowed the tabernacle proper to have been erected there (cf. 1 Chr. 6:48[MT 33]; 23:32; 2 Chr. 24:6; Lam. 2:6-7).

The cultic significance of "the most holy place" arises from the regulations concerning access to this most sacred space. Only when the high priest placed blood upon the covering of the ark of the covenant during the ritual of the Day of Atonement (Lev. 16) was anyone allowed to enter it. This rite was allegorized under the influence of Neo-Platonic philosophy by the author of Hebrews to explain the atoning value of Jesus' death (Heb. 9:6-28).

Bibliography. R. E. Friedman, "The Tabernacle in the Temple," *BA* 43 (1980): 241-48.

TIMOTHY B. CARGAL

MOTH

The Palestinian clothes moth, *Tineola biselliella* of the order Lepidoptera, whose larvae feed on wool and fur. The moth (Heb. *'āš;* Gk. *sḗs*) is pictured as frail, but the human being, considered hyperbolically, is even more frail (Job 4:19). Similarly, a moth-eaten garment also illustrates the frailty of human existence (Job 13:28; Isa. 50:9; 51:8). God is pictured as a consuming moth, e.g., the moth's larva (Ps. 39:11[MT 12]; Hos. 5:12). The destruction of garments by moths is an indication of the temporariness of earthly possessions (Matt. 6:19-20; Luke 12:33; Jas. 5:2). At Job 27:18 LXX and Syr. read "spider" (so RSV, JB; cf. 8:14), probably correctly, in place of MT "moth."

MOTHER

According to a number of biblical texts, most women desire motherhood. Male narrators define motherhood as the social role that brings women honor and happiness, a view that disregards the frequency of miscarriage and infant mortality in antiquity and the possibility that a woman might object to risking her life repeatedly in pregnancy and childbirth. The ideas that many children are a blessing and that woman's self-importance derives from giving birth are cultural constructs designed to encourage large families that promote agricultural prosperity, to insure social prestige for the fathers, and to divert feminine energy into maintaining a patriarchal structure whose margins house women and their children. The linkage of multiple pregnancies to curse and punishment in Gen. 3:16 probably catches more accurately the biblical woman's ambivalence toward motherhood. When women do suffer and die in childbirth, their experiences are reinterpreted by male characters; e.g., acknowledging her suffering the dying Rachel names her new son *ben-'ônî* ("son of my sorrow"), but Jacob renames him *ben-yāmîn* ("son of my right hand"), an expression of delight in his own virility.

Often a woman's inability to conceive allows the storyteller to showcase divine power and potency. The heroes of Israel are born to women with shriveled wombs, who cannot conceive without divine assistance. Their stories glorify the might of Israel's God at the expense of women like Sarah, Rebekah, Rachel, Hannah, and Samson's nameless mother. Their wombs are closed and opened in order to emphasize that, from the beginning, Israel's existence has depended upon a divine graciousness at work in its circumcised members. Few female characters echo Eve's joyful cry (Gen. 4:1) honoring woman's active role in birth. Once mothers deliver their sons, they generally disappear from the story.

The prophets' use of maternal imagery to describe God's attitude toward Israel is also problematic. If the male Yahweh can provide a mother's love for Israel, there is no need for a divine mother. In the same way, women themselves are seldom described acting as mothers, other than giving birth. Absent from the divine world, mothers are quickly dispatched to the fringes of their narratives. Rebekah and Bathsheba are notable exceptions; they guide and direct their favored sons long after Jacob and Solomon have attained adulthood. Sarah likewise intervenes to secure Isaac's birthright by having Hagar and Ishmael banished from Abraham's household. While the actions of these women benefit their sons, they also reinforce the misogyny within the biblical text, portraying women as divisive and manipulative, often at odds with their husbands, a potential threat to household order as they champion their favorites. Wisdom Literature offers a more positive view. The male narrator of Proverbs urges the young male reader to pay attention to his mother's teachings. These teachings are the teachings of Woman Wisdom, who is lover, builder, teacher, prophet, wife, mother, divine companion, pattern for creation, Torah. Like the instruction of Wisdom, maternal instruction preserves the androcentric and patriarchal status quo.

In the NT, the pregnancies of Elizabeth and Mary celebrate divine power and favor, not female fertility and sexuality. Mary praises God for being so pleased with her lowliness that he has done great things for her (Luke 1:48-49). She later surfaces as an anxious mother searching for her adolescent son, whose words intrigue and puzzle her (Luke 2:41-51). Jesus' response to praise of his mother in Matt. 12:46-50 subverts biological motherhood as a suitable definition for woman in the Christian community; even more blessed than his own mother are those who do the will of his father in heaven. In John's Gospel Mary is doubly a sorrowful mother; she witnesses her son's execution and is passed, without consultation, into the hand of the disciple he loved (John 19:25-27).

KATHLEEN S. NASH

MOTHER-OF-PEARL

The iridescent inner layer of mollusk shells (Heb. *dar;* cf. Arab. *durr,* "pearl"), one of the materials used in the mosaic pavement at Ahasuerus' extravagant banquet (Esth. 1:6).

MOTHER'S HOUSE

More accurately "mother's household" (Heb. *bêṯ 'ēm*), indicating not simply a dwelling place but rather a social unit. It is the female-oriented counterpart to "father's house(hold)" *(bêṯ 'āḇ),* the normal term for the primary living group, used widely in reference to an extended or compound family group that may also have included nonfamily members such as servants or resident aliens. In addition to its human members, the household, as the basic economic unit of society, consisted of property (land), animals, pottery vessels, farm implements, and even objects of household religion. The attachment of the term "father" to "house" in the scores of instances in which the family household is mentioned leads to the conclusion that the household unit was male-dominated and patriarchal in nature, with the senior male figure controlling the dynamics and decisions of family life. The appearance of the term "mother's house" in a small but significant set of passages calls that traditional interpretation into question.

In Gen. 24:28, in the endearing story of how Rebekah became Isaac's wife, "mother's household" apparently refers to the same entity ("father's house") mentioned several verses previously (v. 23; cf. 24:27). When Rebekah herself is depicted as going home, it is to her mother's household that she runs. Ruth's memorable statement of loyalty to her mother-in-law (Ruth 1:16) follows Naomi's exhortation for both Ruth and Orpah to return, each to her "mother's house" (v. 8). In the female-dominated Song of Solomon, the female expresses how dear her beloved is by speaking of bringing him to her "mother's house" (Cant. 3:4; 8:2).

Several indirect references to a woman's household appear in Proverbs. In Prov. 9:1 Woman Wisdom is depicted as having "built her house," and in the succeeding verses she is shown managing her household. A reference to wise women building their houses appears in the Hebrew of Prov. 14:1 (the difficult Hebrew here means that English translations often delete the word "women"; cf. 24:3). The "worthy woman" poem of Prov. 31:10-31 describes a woman, clearly a mother (vv. 15, 28), skillfully managing her household's functions, notably its economic ones.

Several characteristics found in most or all of these contexts are noteworthy: a woman's story is being told; a wisdom association is present; women are agents in their own destiny; the agency of women affects others; the setting is domestic; marriage is involved. The term "mother's house" apparently reflects the family household viewed from the female perspective. The household was the major arena of daily life for most Israelite women (and most men too); within that setting women's voices were heard and their activities were essential. Women and their deeds shaped the dynamics of ancient Israel's fundamental social unit. In the androcentric Hebrew Bible, these few instances in which the household is designated in relation to its senior female members provide a rare female angle of vision on the internal workings of family life. As anthropologists have noted, the formal documents of a society do not always map accurately the informal reality, which in this case may have been the way in which females were powerful actors in the daily affairs of Israelite households.

Bibliography. C. Meyers, *Discovering Eve: Ancient Israelite Women in Context* (Oxford, 1988); "'To Her Mother's House': Considering a Counterpart to the Israelite *Bêt'āb*," in *The Bible and the Politics of Exegesis*, ed. D. Jobling, P. L. Day, and G. T. Sheppard (Cleveland, 1991), 39-51, 304-7; L. Stager, "The Archaeology of the Family in Ancient Israel," *BASOR* 260 (1985): 1-35. CAROL MEYERS

MOUNT(AIN) OF GOD

Because two large mountain ranges dominate the geography of Israel, it is not surprising that mountains figure prominently in the Bible and in Israel's symbolism. Reflecting the religious mythology of Israel's neighbors, the sacred mountain was the meeting place of the divine council (cf. Isa. 14:13), and divine decisions/decrees were made there (cf. Exod. 19–20). The sacred mountain symbolized fertility and was a source of water (cf. Hab. 3:10; Zech. 14:8). Moreover, it was the site of primeval conflict/combat or creation. These elements are widespread and found, e.g., in Ugaritic descriptions of Mt. Zaphon, the mythological abode of Baal (cf. Ps. 48:2[MT 3]; 89:12[13]), and in ancient Near Eastern art in the "scale-pattern" of Mesopotamian glyptic.

In the biblical accounts mountains are holy (Obad. 16), ancient (Job 15:7), eternal (Gen. 49:26; Hab. 3:6), and a place where theophanies occur (e.g., Exod. 3–4; 32–34; 1 Kgs. 19; cf. Rev. 21:10). Diverse mountains are associated with the Lord, "a god of the mountains" (1 Kgs. 20:28) — e.g., Ebal, Gerizim, and Seir — but the mountains of God in the OT are usually Sinai/Horeb (Exod. 18:5; 24:13; Num. 10:33) and Zion (Ps. 68:16[17]; Isa. 2:2; 1 Macc. 11:37). Despite John 4:21, mountains also figure prominently and (probably) symbolically in the Gospels. Jesus is often found praying, teaching, and healing on mountains (Matt. 5:1–7:27; 14:23; 15:29; Mark 3:13; 6:46). Part of Jesus' temptation takes place on a mountain (Matt. 4:8), as do the Transfiguration (Mark 9:2) and Ascension (Luke 24:50).

Bibliography. R. J. Clifford, *The Cosmic Mountain in Canaan and the Old Testament*. HSM 4 (Cambridge, Mass., 1972); D. Pardee and P. Xella, "Mountains-and-Valleys," in *DDD*, 604-5.

BRENT A. STRAWN

MOURNING

The expression of grief over death or national calamity. The most frequent mourning practices were tearing one's garments (Gen. 37:34) and wearing sackcloth (2 Sam. 3:31; cf. Ezek. 27:31). Other observances included fasting (2 Sam. 1:12) and receiving "mourners' bread" (Hos. 9:4) and the "cup of consolation" (Jer. 16:7). Mourners would sing or chant dirges (*qînâ, nĕhî;* David's dirge, 2 Sam. 1:17-27). The mourner might be grief-stricken *(ʿāṣab̲),* weep *(bāk̲â),* and cry out (*zāʿaq;* 2 Sam. 18:33[MT 19:1]). Also attested are wailing (*sāpad̲,* "beat the breast"; Amos 5:16-17), crying "Alas, my brother!" or "sister!" (*hôy,* Jer. 22:18), putting dust on the head (2 Sam. 1:2), and sitting in ashes/dust (Jonah 3:16).

Mosaic law prohibited shaving the beard and making the head bald (Lev. 21:5; cf. Moabites, Isa. 15:2), although other texts suggest acceptance of these activities (Ezra 9:3). Also prohibited were gashing the body (Deut. 14:1; Jer. 47:5; but cf. 16:6), food/drink offerings to the dead (Deut. 26:14), and seeking oracles from the dead (2 Kgs. 21:6). Because a corpse defiled, priests could mourn only for their next-of-kin (Lev. 21:2-3). High priests and Nazirites were prohibited from mourning (Lev. 21:10-11; Num. 6:6-7).

Initially the period of mourning lasted seven days (Gen. 50:10; cf. 30 days for Moses [Deut. 34:8] and Aaron [Num. 20:29]; cf. the ignominious lack of mourning for Jehoiakim compared to his father, Josiah [Jer. 22:18-19]). Jeremiah refers to professional women "skilled" in mourning (*mĕqônĕnôt̲,* Jer. 9:17[16]; 2 Chr. 35:25) who sang dirges. Mourning was conducted in the home (Matt. 9:23), at other places of everyday activity, and at the burial site, but not in the sanctuary. Mourners were to refrain from dancing and jubilant music (Isa. 24:8; Job 30:31; cf. Ps. 30:11[12]).

Prophets adapted mourning motifs and dirges (Amos 5:16) for judgment speeches as dire warnings (Isa. 5:18-22) *prior to* the deadly calamity that were to befall a sinful nation. The author of Lamentations employs the dirge and "lament" prayer genres to render Judah's suffering.

Bibliography. A. Rothkoff, "Mourning," in *EncJud* 12:485-93. NANCY C. LEE

MOUSE

In biblical usage, any of a number of rodents of family Muridae, including mice, rats, and field mice (Heb. *ʿaḵbār*). Such creatures were not acceptable according to the Pentateuchal food laws (Lev. 11:29; cf. Isa. 66:17, which depicts pagan observances). In answer to a divinely sent invasion of mice the Philistines included five golden mice as part of a guilt offering when they returned the ark of the covenant to Israel (1 Sam. 6:4-18).

MOZA (Heb. *môṣāʾ*)

1. A son of Caleb and his concubine Ephath (1 Chr. 2:46).

2. A Benjaminite, son of Zimri and father of Binea; descendant of King Saul through his son Jonathan (1 Chr. 8:36-37; 9:42-43).

MOZAH (Heb. *mōṣâ*)

A city assigned to the tribe of Benjamin (Josh. 18:26). Later, as Colonia Emmaus, it was colonized in 75 C.E. by Roman veterans of Vespasian's war against Jerusalem. The site is modern Qâlūnya/Moza (166134), ca. 6.5 km. (4 mi.) NW of Jerusalem.

MUGHARA, WADI EL-

1. Wadi el-Mughara (near modern Haifa), located on the western side of Mt. Carmel, ca. 3 km. (2 mi.) from the Mediterranean Sea. Four caves in this wadi produced important archaeological remains, predominantly from the Paleolithic period, but also including some significant Natufian remains: (1) Mugharet el-Ward ("Cave of the Valley"); (2) Mugharet ej-Jamal ("Cave of the Carmel"); (3) Mugharet es-Sukhul ("Cave of the Kid"); (4) Mugharet et-Tabun ("Cave of the Oven"). The site was excavated from 1929-1934 by Dorothy Garrod of the British School of Archaeology in Jerusalem. In addition to yielding an important prehistoric flint sequence, the caves also contained human skeletal remains (several articulated ones); most significantly, some of the human bones in Mugharet es-Sukhul have features characteristic of both Neanderthal humans and Homo sapiens (i.e., modern humanoid). In the caves, animal bones (important evidence for the faunal record and for human food consumption patterns) were also found, as were a few "art" objects.

2. Wadi el-Mughara (in the southwestern Sinai), an ancient mining region, a particularly important source of turquoise for the ancient Egyptians as clearly demonstrated by numerous Egyptian inscriptions discovered in this general vicinity. This epigraphic evidence suggests that the native inhabitants of the region as well as various southern Canaanites were hired or conscripted to participate in the mining. Significantly, alphabetic inscriptions dating to ca. 1500 B.C.E. have been found in the region, particularly at the nearby site of Serabiṭ el-Ḥadem. Referred to as the Proto-Sinaitic inscriptions, they are among the earliest known alphabetic inscriptions; they were apparently produced by the Canaanites working in the region.

Bibliography. D. A. E. Garrod and D. M. A. Bate, *The Stone Age of Mount Carmel: Excavations at the Wady el-Mughara* 1 (Oxford, 1937); P. K. McCarter, Jr., *Ancient Inscriptions* (Washington, 1996); J. S. Jorgensen, "Inscription Sites," in *OEANE* 3:171-72; J. Naveh, *Early History of the Alphabet*, 2nd ed. (Leiden, 1987); D. B. Redford, *Egypt, Canaan, and Israel in Ancient Times* (Princeton, 1992). CHRIS A. ROLLSTON

MULBERRY

Gk. *sykáminos* (Luke 17:6), sometimes translated "sycamine tree," is generally thought to refer to the black mulberry tree or bush (*Morus nigra* L.). The juice of the mulberry was used to arouse the elephants of Antiochus V's army for battle against Judas Maccabeus (1 Macc. 6:34; Gk. *móron*). Some suggest that Heb. *bāḵāʾ* (2 Sam. 5:23-24; 1 Chr. 14:14-15) refers to this same plant, but others argue this term refers to the poplar or aspen tree.

RANDALL W. YOUNKER

MULE

A member of the equid family, the offspring of a donkey and horse, or a donkey and onager (wild ass). Male (Heb. *pereḏ*) is distinguished from female *(pirdâ)* in the biblical text. As a hybrid, the mule is almost always sterile, yet exhibits qualities of size, strength, and endurance. For these reasons, mules were valued in the ancient world as royal mounts (2 Sam. 13:29; 1 Kgs. 1:44), objects of tribute (10:25), and animals of traction (2 Kgs. 5:17; 1 Chr. 12:40[MT 41]). As crossbreeding was seemingly prohibited in biblical Israel (Lev. 19:19), it is possible that these sure-footed animals were obtained through import or trade (Ezek. 27:14).

MARK ZIESE

MUPPIM (Heb. *muppîm*) (also SHEPHUPHAM

A son of Benjamin (Gen. 46:21). At Num. 26:39 he is called Shephupham (cf. 1 Chr. 8:5, "Shephuphan") and his descendants Shuphamites. The plural form of Muppim and Huppim suggests that they may actually have been populations that joined themselves to the tribe of Benjamin (cf. 1 Chr. 7:12, 15).

MURATORIAN FRAGMENT

A portion of an early Christian document that discusses the books of the NT that were accepted by the churches known to the anonymous author of the fragment. The fragment, probably of the 8th century, is written in vulgar Latin but is almost certainly a translation of a much earlier Greek document. The fragment begins with a probably mutilated reference to Mark; Luke and John are then mentioned as the third and fourth Gospels, respectively. It is probable that Matthew was discussed in a missing portion of the original. Thirteen letters are attributed to Paul; Jude and two letters of John are mentioned approvingly, as are the Wisdom of Solomon and the apocalypses of John and Peter (although the latter is said to be rejected by some).

Scholarly tradition has placed composition of the original Greek version in the 2nd century because of the statement that the Shepherd of Hermas was written "very recently in our times." However, some scholars have argued for a 4th-century date for the original.

Bibliography. G. M. Hahneman, *The Muratorian Fragment and the Development of the Canon* (Oxford, 1992); A. C. Sundberg, Jr., "Canon Muratori: A Fourth-Century List," *HTR* 66 (1973): 1-41. JAMES R. ADAIR, JR.

MURDER

Strictly speaking, the willful or premeditated deprivation of human life. Because of the complications of determining motive, the discussion of murder in the Bible is placed in a broader context of the deprivation of life. A basic distinction is made between premeditation and an act of God (Exod. 21:12-13). Furthermore, distinction is made between premeditation and inadvertence, or accident. Premeditation is determined by previous enmity (Num. 35:20-21; Deut. 4:42), the act of ambush (Num. 35:20; Deut. 19:11) or possession of a weapon of lethal potentiality (Num. 35:17-19). Inadvertence is designated as "without intent" (Num. 35:11, 15; Deut. 19:4).

The punishment stipulated for murder is capital (Exod. 21:12; Lev. 24:17). Asylums were designated to ensure proper trials (Num. 35:9-34; Deut. 4:41-43; 19:1-13; Josh. 20:1-9). The practice of asylum appears designed to regulate the custom of blood vengeance and vendetta (Num. 35:19; Deut. 19:12). Other provisions were the multiplicity of witness (Num. 35:30), and the rejection of bail (v. 32; cf. one exception in Exod. 21:28-30). Unlike other ancient near Eastern law codes, the biblical codes do not discriminate according to class, though it is impossible to gauge to what extent this was the actual practice.

Distinctions are applied within the intentional deprivation of life. The killing of a murderer was not considered murder. Killing someone out of self-defense could also be excluded from being considered murder (Exod. 22:2[MT 1]). Killing in war is also excluded (Deut. 20:13). In the case of unsolved murders, the community enacts a ritual of expiation (Deut. 21:1-9).

The Decalogue compactly prohibits the unlawful deprivation of life (Exod. 20:13; Deut. 5:17). The command is often translated "You shall not murder," yet the Hebrew word *(rāṣaḥ)* can also refer to unintentional homicide (Num. 35:25-28; Deut. 4:41-42; Josh. 20:3). Thus the impulse of the commandment seems to extend further than mere murder, to the deprivation of life in general. Connected to this is the recognition that external acts reach back to internal inclinations. Sirach designates economic oppression as murder (Sir. 34:24-27). The NT closely aligns murder with inclinations of enmity (Matt. 5:21-26, 38-48; 1 John 3:15), but this is present in principle in the OT (Lev. 19:17-18).

As foreign empires began to exercise increasing control over Judea, jurisdiction over murder moved into the hands of the foreign states (Ezra 7:25-26). Paul affirms this authority as derivative from God (Rom. 13:4).

Bibliography. M. Greenberg, "Some Postulates of Biblical Criminal Law," in *Yehezkel Kaufmann Jubilee Volume,* ed. M. Haran (Jerusalem, 1960), 5-28; B. S. Jackson, "Reflections on Biblical Criminal Law," *JJS* 24 (1973): 8-38; repr. in *Essays on Jewish and Comparative Legal History.* SJLA 10 (Leiden, 1975), 25-63. GERALD M. BILKES

MURMURING

An overtly vocal or subdued expression of deep pain, grief, distress, discontent, dissatisfaction, or anger. Murmurings, at times, functioned as prayers to God that called for action. Examples include complaints (Heb. *lûn*) by the Israelites in the wilderness (Exod. 15:24; 16:2, 7-8; 17:3; Num. 14:2, 27, 29, 36). These murmurings had concrete ground, namely, hunger or thirst. God responded to such cries by "hearing favorably" and providing food and water and thus alleviating the people's anguish.

However, murmurings are also presented as clandestine, malicious whisperings of slander against God or his appointed leaders. Korah complained against Moses and Aaron (Num. 16), and the people of Israel are said to have been murmuring against the leadership of Moses (ch. 17). The Israelites are also portrayed as grumbling *(rāgan)* in their tents (Deut. 1:27; Ps. 106:25) in response to the report of the spies. This is a graphic picture of the people sulking in their tents instead of preparing for the march upon Canaan. Such murmuring is a scorning of God and his appointed leaders and calls for severe punishment. Those who refused to enter the Promised Land would die in the wilderness. In addition, the people of Israel justifiably murmured in the Promised Land when they believed that the leaders of the nation were disobedient to the rules established by God (Josh. 9:18).

In the NT "murmuring" (Gk. *gongýzō*) generally refers to the complaining of the Pharisees and scribes (Luke 5:30; 15:2; cf. 19:7; Matt. 20:11). The NT church experienced the murmuring of the Hellenists against the Hebrews because their widows were being neglected in the daily distribution (Acts 6:1).Paul exhorted the Corinthians not to murmur as the Hebrews had done in the wilderness, for their murmurings had brought destruction (1 Cor. 10:10; cf. Phil. 2:14).

Bibliography. G. W. Coats, *Rebellion in the Wilderness: The Murmuring Motif in the Wilderness Traditions of the Old Testament* (Nashville, 1968).

JOHN L. HARRIS

MUSHI (Heb. *mûšî*)
A Levite, the second son of Merari (Exod. 6:19; Num. 3:20; 1 Chr. 6:19, 47[MT 4, 32]; 23:21, 23; 24:26, 30). He was the eponymous ancestor of a levitical family, the Mushites (Num. 3:33; 26:58).

MUSIC, MUSICAL INSTRUMENTS
Music and its tools of production, musical instruments, as mentioned in the Bible are among the most perplexing phenomena of the past. This stems from both the ephemeral nature of music itself and the indirect sources of study — written, archaeological-iconographical, comparative — and the fact that only a few musical instruments discovered in excavations (e.g., cymbals, rattles) are still able to produce sound.

The oldest documentation of the oral tradition of biblical recitation is preserved in the Codex Cairo (9th cent.), where the biblical text is provided with *ṭaʿamê hammiqrāʾ* (biblical accents), a type of ekphonetic writing, which can serve as a comparative source, albeit not reliable for recreating the cantillation of ancient Israel (likewise Ugarit cuneiform notation or the transcription of contemporary Jewish traditional music as frequently used for this purpose). The Bible, considered the main source for the study of music in ancient Israel, may be helpful only for the study of its social context: e.g., the sacred service (1 Chr. 23; 2 Chr. 29:25) and praise of God (Isa. 12:5-6; Ps. 150); the apotropaic-prophylactic (Exod. 28:33; 1 Sam. 16:16), ecstatic-prophetic (10:5), or supernatural (Exod. 19:19) media; communication (Num. 10:1-9); war (2 Chr. 20:28); events of joy (Exod. 15:20) and sorrow (2 Sam. 1:17-27); or symbol of sin and prostitution (Isa. 5:12; 14:11). The accounts are sometimes ambiguous: e.g., the advance of David with the ark as a kind of orgy, with dominant percussion instruments of a Dionysiac character (2 Sam. 6:5), or a somewhat ceremonial occasion with singing and trumpet fanfare (2 Chr. 13:8).

Various accounts suggest that different styles of singing were employed: solo (2 Sam. 23:1), choral (2 Chr. 20:21; Exod. 32:18-19), a capella (15:1) or with instrumental accompaniment (15:20-21; Ps. 149:1-3), responsorial (1 Sam. 29:5; Ezra 3:10-11), or antiphonal (1 Sam. 18:6-7).

The greatest potential for information concerning music as described in the Bible is the study of the instruments recorded, but this information is similarly limited. The precise character of the music is never described, except for some general terms regarding the shophar and trumpet signals (Num. 10:2-10). Only three verses mention the material of which a musical instrument is made (Num. 10:2; 1 Kgs. 10:12; 1 Chr. 15:19), and seldom is the performance technique mentioned (1 Sam. 16:23).

The names of musical instruments are not entirely clear. The LXX, Peshitta, and Vulgate translate them with no precise understanding of their meaning. One version may render the same word in several different ways: e.g., the LXX translates Heb. *kinnôr* as *kithára, kinýra, psaltḗrion, órganon,* and *nábla; ʿûgāḇ* as *kithára, psalmós,* and *órganon.* Ambiguous information is available from postbiblical sources: the writings of Josephus Flavius and Philo from Alexandria, the Talmud, and the Qumran scrolls.

Mosaic of flute player; Caesarea Vaults, trench CV11 (5th-6th century C.E.) (Photo by Aaron Levin; courtesy Combined Caesarea Expeditions)

For these reasons, and particularly the historical and chronological uncertainty of the biblical record, archaeology must be regarded the primary source for the study of the musical cultures of the biblical world. At present some 700 artifacts — actual remains of musical instruments and artistic depictions — have been excavated. Statistical analysis of these artifacts provides an important indication of musical instruments present in ancient Israel/Palestine. For instance, harps are not attested, so consequently there is no reason to interpret Heb. *nēḇel* as "harp," the instrument King David is commonly depicted as playing. From the Babylonian-Persian period, which the books of Ezra, Nehemiah, and Chronicles report as having developed an exceptionally rich musical liturgy and musical life, no significant musical evidence has survived.

The most common instruments in Iron Age Israel were derived from Canaanite culture. They seem to have been of modest construction, yet of great variety and capable of relatively sophisticated performance technique. Among those instruments available to the masses were clay rattles (probably *mĕnaʿanʿîm*), round frame drums *(tōp̄)*, and double pipes similar to the oboe and clarinet (probably *ḥālîl*). The elaborate Egyptian lyres with eight or more strings gave way to the smaller *kinnôr* and *nēḇel* with fewer strings, mainly used in cultic and court music. During the Babylonian-Persian period a decline in musical life was apparent, perhaps reflective of local religious and social constraints (cf. Isa. 5:12; 24:8-9; Hos. 9:1). The Hellenistic-Roman period brought a blossoming of all kinds of musical activities and the introduction of many new types of instruments (e.g., new varieties of harps and lutes, bone pipes with bronze overlay). This was met with resistance in orthodox circles, who cited biblical admonishments regarding licentious activities associated with music (*m. Soṭa* 9:11; *b. Soṭa* 48a-b; *Giṭ.* 7a-b).

Old Testament

bĕḵōl ʿăṣê ḇĕrôšîm

Instruments made of various kinds of wood (2 Sam. 6:5; 1 Chr. 13:8 reads *bĕḵol-ʿōz ûḇšîrîm*, "with all might and singing"). These may be the cypresswood double-clappers used by the masses (in contrast to the Egyptian-type ivory or bone Hathor-clappers of the wealthy).

ḥālîl

Single or double-pipe reed instrument similar to the clarinet or oboe (from *ḥll*, "hollow, empty," also "profane"). It accompanied ecstatic prophecy (1 Sam. 10:5), and was used in both joyful revelry (1 Kgs. 1:40) and mourning (Jer. 48:36) as well as secular debaucheries (Isa. 5:12). Simple bone instruments as well as elaborate ones dressed in bronze have been found from the Hellenistic-Roman period, and numerous artistic representations from all strata as early as the 14th century B.C.E. portray goddesses and erotic dancers, priests and satyrs, mourners and the joyful playing double-pipes.

ḥăṣōṣĕrâ

The trumpet, made of hammered silver (Num. 10:2) or bronze. It was originally to be blown only by the priests for communication (to assemble the congregation and leaders) or alarm, in times of war, celebration, or on solemn days, at the beginning of the month and for the burnt offering (Num. 10:2-10). In the Babylonian-Persian period the trumpet was blown at the temple service (2 Kgs. 12:13[MT 14]), at coronations (11:14; 2 Chr. 23:13), construction of the temple (Ezra 3:10), and in connection with vows to God (2 Chr. 15:14). Some passages describing trumpet blowing should be considered later additions reflecting liturgical practices (cf. 2 Sam. 6:5; 1 Chr. 13:8). Depictions believed to represent the temple trumpets on the Bar Kokhba coins and the arch of Titus are now questioned. Num. 10:4-5 and especially the Qumran scrolls (1QM 2:15; 3:1; 7:9; 9:9) contain general descriptions of techniques for playing the trumpet (sustained sound, short blast, quavering blast, sharp sound, battle alarm).

kinnôr

The lyre, a popular instrument attested in various ancient Near Eastern texts, as well as in the names of gods and place names, and in Syro-Palestinian iconography. It was a symbol of early professional musical activities (Gen. 4:21) and associated with nearly every type of musical occasion, from praise of God (Ps. 150:3) and prophecy (1 Sam. 10:5) to grief (Job 30:31), secular celebrations (Gen. 31:27) and debauchery (Isa. 23:16). Lyres were made of almug wood (1 Kgs. 10:11-12), with 10 (Josephus *Ant.* 8.3.8) or seven (*m. Qinnim* 3:6) thin gut strings, and usually played with a plectrum (1 Sam. 16:16 specifies plucking). The *kinnôr* changed form over time, although regional differences were less apparent in the multicultural biblical society.

mĕnaʿanʿîm

An idiophone, probably a clay rattle (from *nûaʿ*, "shake") of various shapes (geometric, zoo- and anthropomorphic; 5-12 cm. [2-5 in.] long), as suggested by more than 70 archaeological finds from the Bronze to Babylonian periods. It was a popular instrument used in orgiastic cultic activities (2 Sam. 6:5), and so not favored by the theocratic establishment (cf. 1 Chr. 13:8).

mĕṣiltayim, ṣelṣĕlîm

Cymbals (occurs only in the dual form), mentioned as early as the 14th century. Examples have been recovered ranging from Canaanite occupations to Hellenistic-Roman sites nearly a thousand years later. Two types have been found: saucerlike plates (7-12 cm. [3-5 in.]) held by hand loops, beaten mainly in a vertical position, and smaller cymbals (3-7 cm. [1-3 in.]), fastened to two fingers of one hand. Cymbals "of brass" are mentioned only in postexilic texts (1 Chr. 15:19; cf. Ezra 3:10; Neh. 12:27); they are to be played by the Levites (1 Chr. 15:16) and at cultic events (2 Chr. 5:13). The *ṣelṣĕlîm* mentioned at 2 Sam. 6:5 may have been simply small noise-making instruments, a kind of metal rattle, while the *mĕṣiltayim* in 1 Chr. 13:8 are larger and so better suited to temple worship. Ps.150:5 mentions *ṣilṣĕlê-šāmaʿ* ("clanging *ṣelṣĕlim*") and *ṣilṣĕlê-tĕrûʿâ* ("loud, crashing *ṣelṣelîm*"), perhaps the two types attested by archaeology.

nēḇel, nēḇel ʿāśôr

A type of lyre. Like the *kinnôr*, with which it is generally mentioned, the *nēḇel* was made of almug wood (1 Kgs. 10:12), but it had 12 thick strings (*m. Qinnim* 3:6) and was always plucked (Josephus *Ant.* 7.12.3). Archaeological evidence discounts its identification as a harp (NRSV), suggesting instead that the *nēḇel* was a large, lower-pitched bass lyre. The *nēḇel ʿāśôr* was a ten-stringed lyre (Ps. 33:2; 144:9). The *nēḇel* was played by Levites (1 Chr. 15:16; 25:1) at cultic events (1 Chr 13:8; Ps. 150:3), victory celebrations (2 Chr. 20:28), and accompanying ecstatic prophecies (1 Sam. 10:5), as well as orgiastic revels (Isa. 5:12).

paʿămôn

Bell (from Heb. *pʿm*, "beat"). "Bells of gold," placed between pomegranates, were attached to the lower hem of the high priest's robe (Exod. 28:33, 34; 39:25, 26) and had apotropaic-prophylactic significance (28:35). Attested in the Near East as early as the 15th century, bells appear in ancient Israel from the 9th-8th centuries on. Finds from the Hellenistic-Roman period include bells accompanied by remnants of fabric which indicate their placement on a garment. The recently discovered mosaic from the Sepphoris synagogue (early 5th century) depicts Aaron with bells fastened to his robe.

šôp̱ār

Ram's horn (cf. Akk. *šappāru,* "wild goat"). The most frequently mentioned musical instrument in the Bible, used from at least the Iron Age until today. It is capable of producing two or three sounds of different pitch and alarming nature, characterized as *tēqaʿ* ("blast"), *tĕrûʿâ* ("shout of jubilation"), and *yabbāḇâ* ("sobbing, moaning; trembling"). The earliest known musical notation for the *šôp̱ār* is recorded in Sa'adia Gaon's *Siddur* (10th century C.E.). The *šôp̱ār* was a solo instrument at significant cultic and national events: theophanies (Exod. 19:13, 16), the Day of Atonement (Lev. 25:9), the New Moon feast (Ps. 81:3[MT 4]), the day of judgment (Joel 2:1), transporting the ark (2 Sam. 6:5), during battle (Judg. 3:27), and in victory celebrations (1 Sam. 13:3). From the 3rd century C.E. the *šôp̱ār* appears as a symbol in synagogue mosaics (Hammath-Tiberias, Beth-shan), on fragments of columns, oil lamps, etc.

qeren hayyôḇēl

Ram's horn, mentioned only once in connection with the destruction of the walls of Jericho (Josh. 6:5). It may have been a variety of the *šôp̱ār.*

tōp̱

Drum, tambourine, timbrel. An instrument widely attested throughout the ancient Near East, its most common form in Syria-Palestine was a 25-40 cm. (8-16 in.) frame over which was stretched a skin or membrane. It had both cultic and secular use, accompanying singing and dancing (Ps. 149:3) and prophetic ecstasy (1 Sam. 10:5). Drums were played for feasts (Ps. 81:2[3]), processions (2 Sam. 6:5; Ps. 68:25[26]), and other celebrations (Gen. 31:27), but apparently not for temple worship. The *tōp̱* seems to have been played most often by women, frequently as a solo instrument and in connection with dancing, also a female activity. Numerous terracotta figurines of female drummers have been found from the Iron Age on; two types are common, seemingly reflecting the synthesis of sacral and secular in the musical culture of ancient Israel: women in long, bell-form dresses, without jewelry, or partly unclad and wearing rich jewelry.

ʿûgāḇ

Often identfied as a vertical flute (cf. Egyp. *maʿt*), although the LXX and Josephus consider it a stringed instrument (cf. Gen. 4:21; NRSV "pipe"). It occurs as an instrument of praise (Ps. 150:4), joy (Job 21:12), and mourning (30:31).

Daniel

The names of the six musical instruments listed in Dan. 3:5, 7, 10, 15 are of Aramaic or Greek origin: *qarnāʾ* (cf. Heb. *qeren,* "animal horn"), here a brass trumpet known from Neo-Babylonian sources; *mašrôqîṯāʾ* (from *šrq,* "to whistle"), probably a kind of reed instrument; *qayṯrōs* (Gk. *kithára*), a Greco-Roman lyre; *sabbĕḵāʾ,* Greek or Phoenician angular harp, attested in the Seleucid period; *pĕsantērîn* (cf. Gk. *psaltḗrion*), a large, angular horizontally-held harp, beaten with two sticks; *sûmpōnyâ,* variously understood as the bagpipe or kettledrum or perhaps a designation for "the entire ensemble" *(kōl zĕnê zĕmārāʾ).*

Collective Terms

A number of other terms occur designating classes or varieties of instruments, mostly string instruments: *kēlîm,* lit., "vessels, implements," a generic term for instruments (1 Chr. 23:5); *kĕlê-ḏāwîḏ,* "instruments of David" (2 Chr. 29:26); *kĕlî-neḇel* (Ps. 71:22; 1 Chr. 16:5; NRSV "harp"); *kĕlê-ʿōz,* "loud instruments" (2 Chr. 30:21); *kĕlê-šîr,* "instruments of song" (e.g., Amos 6:5); *minnîm,* "strings" (Ps. 150:4).

Superscriptions to the Psalms

Musical terms in the headings of the Psalms are among the most difficult problems in translating the Bible. Modern musicologists consider many to be notations regarding performance techniques or perhaps catchwords for popular melodies. Heb. *lamĕnaṣṣēaḥ,* "For the choirmaster" (or "Master of Victory"), which occurs 55 times in the Psalms and also with Hab. 3, may indicate instructions for the leader. Heb. *mizmôr,* which occurs in 57 Psalms, may specify singing with instrumental accompaniment. Many of the notations remain highly uncertain. For example, *ʿal-ʿălāmôṯ* (Ps. 46:1) may mean "with a string instrument" (cf. 1 Chr. 15:20) or "drum" (cf. Ps. 68:25[26]) or perhaps "on the eighth (tone or mode)" (cf. 1 Chr. 15:20-21). Heb. *ʿal-haggittîṯ* (Pss. 8, 81, 84) may specify "in the style of Gath" or "on the instrument of Gath."

New Testament

Four or perhaps five musical instruments are mentioned in the NT.

Single or double-pipe (Gk. *aulós;* Lat. *tibia*). This popular Greco-Roman reed instrument was played both at weddings and funerals (1 Cor. 14:7; cf. Matt. 9:23; 11:17).

Lyre (Gk. *kithára*). Comparison of the sound of lyres with the voice of many waters and great thunder (Rev. 14:2) may indicate the larger Roman instrument (NRSV "harp").

Trumpet (Gk. *sálpinx;* Lat. *tuba*). The most frequently mentioned instrument in the NT (11 times), its sound symbolized supernatural power ("God's trumpet," 1 Thess. 4:16) and the apocalyptic "last trump" heralding the Parousia (1 Cor. 15:52).

Cymbals (Gk. *kýmbalon*). The "noisy gong"

(*chalkós ēchṓn,* 1 Cor. 13:1) was probably a resonating device, a bronze vase at the back of the Greek theater (KJV "sounding brass").

Gk. *symphōnía* (Luke 15:25) may designate another instrument, but is more likely a collective term for a consort of musical instruments or perhaps a general term for "music."

1 Cor. 14:7-8 is particularly significant for music history. Here for the first time in the Bible is reference to "distinct notes." This and the parallel concern regarding "indistinct sound" suggest emergent aesthetic regard for musical precision.

Bibliography. B. Bayer, "The Finds That Could Not Be," *BAR* 8/1 (1982): 20-33; J. Braun, *Music in Ancient Palestine* (Grand Rapids, 2000); C. Sachs, *The History of Musical Instruments* (New York, 1940); A. Sendrey, *Music in Ancient Israel* (New York, 1969); W. W. Smith, *Musical Aspects of the New Testament* (Amsterdam, 1962).

JOACHIM BRAUN

MUSTARD

A plant cultivated in both gardens and fields for its seeds, ground for spice, and for the oil in the seeds (Gk. *sínapi;* Matt. 13:31-32 par.; 17:20 par.). The variety grown in Palestine was black mustard (*Brassica nigra* Koch or *Sinapis nigra* L.), which can grow to 3 m. (10 ft.) in height but which had the smallest seed of plants then cultivated.

MUTH-LABBEN (Heb. *mûṯ labbēn*)

A term in the superscription of Ps. 9(MT v. 1) meaning "death of a son." It may be the name of a well-known melody to which the psalm was to be sung.

MYRA (Gk. *Mýra*)

A major city of Lycia (near modern Dembre), ca. 4-5 km. (2.5-3 mi.) from the Mediterranean. Under the Romans it was capital of the province of Lycia. With its port Andriaca, Myra was an important trading center. Here the escort taking Paul to Rome changed ships (Acts 27:5-6). Some manuscripts add "and Myra" after "Patara" in the account of Paul's journey toward Jerusalem in Acts 21:1. The apocryphal Acts of Paul contains stories of Paul's preaching and cures at Myra. St. Nicholas was a 4th-century bishop of Myra, later revered as Santa Claus.

DOUGLAS LOW

MYRRH

Like frankincense, a plant product derived from members of the Burseraceae family. As an incense, it is often mentioned in biblical and other ancient sources together with frankincense. Like frankincense, its reddish gum oleoresin had numerous uses in ritual, medicine, and fumigation. Mentioned in tandem with frankincense in the Matthew magi account (Matt. 2:11), myrrh (Heb. *mōr;* Gk. *múrra, smýrna,* perhaps originally meaning "bitter") is more difficult to identify with Linnean classification botanical terms. This is because hundreds of species of *Commiphora* are known from Arabia and Africa, only several of which apparently produce the odiferous substance labeled "myrrh." According to botanists, true myrrh (formerly called *balsamodendron myrrh*) comes from *Commiphora myrrha,* which is found only in southwest Arabia and northern Somalia. True myrrh at present may not overlap with frankincense in its territorial distribution. The three species found in Dhofar do not include true myrrh; only *C. Habessinica* and *C. Fileadensis* (called balm or balsam of Gilead) are reported with myrrh-like properties. In Yemen, six other species of *Commiphora* are known, including bdelliums and the balm of Mecca.

As with frankincense, myrrh was originally traded locally as early as the Neolithic period (6th millennium B.C.), and it is perhaps documented in Egyptian Red Sea trade as early as the Old Kingdom (if Egyp. *'ntyw* is to be equated with the product). The well-known New Kingdom Hatshepsut expedition to Punt may well depict the removal of myrrh trees. Its mention in Mesopotamia only occurs with the beginning of the Old Assyrian period. The burgeoning Iron Age trade and biblical involvement are well documented. Actual pollen grains of myrrh have been found at Qana from a Classical period level of the famous seaport. As with frankincense, the international trade of myrrh collapsed in the 5th century A.D., although the resin is still harvested and used in the more restricted Near Eastern markets.

Bibliography. P. Dolara et al., "Analgesic Effects of Myrrh," *Nature* 379 (1996): 29; N. St.J Groom, *Frankincense and Myrrh* (London, 1981); A. Lucas, "Cosmetics, Perfumes, and Incense in Ancient Egypt," *JEA* 16 (1930): 41-53; A. G. Miller and M. Morris, *Plants of Dhofar* (Muscat, 1988); K. Nielsen, *Incense in Ancient Israel.* VTSup 38 (Leiden, 1986); G. Van Beek, "Frankincense and Myrrh," *BA* 23 (1960): 70-95; "Frankincense and Myrrh in Ancient South Arabia," *JAOS* 78 (1958): 141-52.

JURIS ZARINS

MYRTLE

Myrtus communis L., a fragrant evergreen shrub with dark oval leaves, white or pink flowers, and black berries common in Syria and Palestine and elsewhere in the Mediterranean region (Zech. 1:8, 10-11). Myrtle (Heb. *hăḏas*) is associated with the eschatological transformation of the desert into a well-watered place (Isa. 41:19; 55:13). After the postexilic restoration of the Feast of Tabernacles, myrtle branches were used in constructing the booths (Neh. 8:15).

MYSIA (Gk. *Mysía*)

A mountainous region in northwestern Asia Minor, with Bithynia to the northeast and Lydia to the south. Originally settled by Thracians, the region was successively ruled by the Lydians, Seleucids, and Attalids before being incorporated into the Roman province of Asia (ca. 129-126 B.C.E.). The Mysians were known as mercenaries and played a role in an expedition against Jerusalem in the Maccabean era (2 Macc. 5:23-26; cf. 1 Macc. 1:29-

35). By the 1st century B.C.E. Jewish communities were located in at least two of its prominent cities, Adramyttium and Pergamum (Cicero *Pro Flacco* 28.68; Josephus *Ant.* 14.247-55; cf. Rev. 1:11; 2:12-17). Paul and his companions have a brief stay in the city of Troas (Acts 16:7-8; cf. 20:5-12; 2 Cor. 2:12-13); later, Paul stopped over at the coastal city of Assos (Acts 20:13-14).

Bibliography. D. Magie, *Roman Rule in Asia Minor* (1950, repr. New York, 1975).

PHILIP A. HARLAND

MYSTERY

Something revealed by God, at least to a few. The meaning is different from the usual English sense of an unsolved problem. An exact equivalent for Gk. *mystḗrion* does not occur in the OT, though the idea of secret knowledge revealed by God is found in Isa. 48:3, 6; Amos 3:7. In Daniel this knowledge is the coming of a new age in which God will reign.

The Greek term occurs only once in the Gospels (Mark 4:11 = Matt. 13:11 = Luke 8:10), where Jesus relates it to the kingdom of God. Its principal occurrences are in Pauline literature, where it is found 21 times.

In the Hellenistic world, mystery religions flourished in which participants were taught secrets they were obliged to conceal. An important issue is the relationship between these mystery religions and the Pauline use of the term "mystery." Although the NT writers may have used the term in part as an evangelistic strategy to gain gentile converts, the background for their understanding of it was probably more Semitic than Hellenistic.

Paul's use of the term contrasts with that of the mystery religions, connecting it with Jesus' crucifixion rather than with esoteric forms of knowledge (1 Cor. 1:23; 2:1-7). For Paul the mystery that has been revealed is God's plan of salvation. In Eph. 6:19 he speaks of the mystery of the gospel. Similarly, in Col. 2:2 he calls God's mystery Christ himself. The mystery is ancient. According to Rom. 16:25 it was kept secret for long ages, but in the following verse and in Eph. 3:9-10 Paul indicates that it was revealed in the fullness of time. The mystery relates to the inclusion of the Gentiles as well as the Jews in God's plan of salvation (Rom. 16:25-26; Col. 1:26-27; Eph. 3:3-6).

The term is used elsewhere in Paul and the NT in secondary meanings. In 1 Cor. 13:2 understanding of mysteries is attributed to prophets. In 1 Cor. 14:2 the content of tongues speaking is said to be mysteries in the Spirit. The word "mystery" is also used in a derivative sense in several passages where the terms to which it applies are significant in the divine plan of salvation which has been revealed. Israel's destiny is called a mystery (Rom. 11:25). In 1 Cor. 15:51 the resurrection of the dead at the end of time is called a mystery. In Eph. 5:31-32 the application of Gen. 2:24 (marriage) to the relationship between Christ and the Church is described as a mystery. In 1 Tim. 3:9, 16 mystery refers to faith and religion respectively, meaning the good news about Jesus. In 2 Thess. 2:7 it applies to the man of lawlessness; in Rev. 17:5-7 to the scarlet woman Babylon. In Rev. 1:20 the seven stars seen in Christ's right hand and the seven lampstands are called a mystery and then explained as the angels of the seven churches and the churches themselves.

ALICE OGDEN BELLIS

MYSTERY CULTS

"Mystery cults" or "mystery religions" refer to a pattern of religious expression in the Greco-Roman world. The "mysteries" were initiation rituals in which the initiate *(mýstēs)* had an extraordinary experience about which participants were forbidden to speak afterwards. Elements of these rituals (*teletaí*, "completions") could include: *legómena* ("things spoken"), recitations or enactments of ritual words or the myth of the cult deities; *deiknýmena* ("things shown"), cult objects often hidden in a basket; and *drṓmena* ("things performed"), ritual actions or dramatic enactments. The word "mystery," from Gk. *mýein* ("to close"), indicates the initiate's closed eyes, later opened to see what was revealed in the ritual, as well as the initiate's closed mouth keeping secrecy.

Beyond the common factor of the initiation ritual, the mystery cults varied in origin and organization. Various themes figured in the initiations: life and death, suffering, sexuality, fertility, and well-being. Cult worship was not confined to initiation rituals but also included public ceremonies and personal devotional acts. Initiation was an individual choice, but most cults did not require exclusive loyalty.

Similarities which characterize these cults as mysteries can be attributed to their development within the framework of common social institutions and conditions in the Greco-Roman world. In a context of social dislocation, individuals sought personal ritual experiences to connect them to their deities. The mysteries provided one opportunity.

The mysteries are best understood as particular cults. The Eleusinian mysteries, commemorating the myth of Demeter and Persephone, were based at Eleusis, 21 km. (13 mi.) from Athens. Most Athenians were initiated, and members from all levels of society were admitted. Primary positions in the cult were filled by two prominent Athenian families. The Greater Mysteries, the second of three stages of initiation, were celebrated annually in autumn. Initiates were purified at the seashore, where each brought a piglet which was ritually washed and killed and the blood sprinkled on the initiate. A few days later, the initiates formed a procession from Athens to Eleusis along the Sacred Way, carrying the sacred objects and statues, crying *"Iache! Iacce!"* (lit., "Shout!"). They arrived at night, carrying torches, and entered the Telesterion, the temple of initiation, where a distinctive sacred meal was part of the ritual. Initiation promised a better afterlife in the underworld.

On the Aegean island of Samothrace, the Samothracian mysteries honored deities known simply as the Great Gods *(Theoi Megaloi).* In

Greco-Roman times, visitors came from throughout the Mediterranean world to experience initiation there. Samothracian initiation was said to protect seafarers. The initiation took place in two stages, the *mýēsis* in a large central torchlit chamber, and then the *epopteía* for a more limited group in a smaller room. The nocturnal rituals included sacrifices and dancing, and probably a water purification ceremony. The Rule of the Andanian mysteries, an inscription from the Peloponnesus dated 92/91 B.C.E., provides information about the rules and organization of another such cult of several deities, but does not reveal the secrets of the cult.

The mysteries of Dionysus (Bacchus) had no central sanctuary and took diverse forms throughout the Hellenistic world. The cult was noted for frenzied wine-drinking rituals in which participants wandered the forested mountainsides wearing fawn skins and carrying staffs *(thýrsoi)* adorned with ivy leaves and a pine cone. They also reputedly tore live animals to pieces with their bare hands and ate the flesh raw. Many of the participants were women, known as *maenads.* Euripides' play, *The Bacchae,* provides an image of their orgiastic cult. Other evidence suggests more sedate rituals and regulated cult associations. The cult was especially associated with actors. A fresco from the Villa Item near Pompeii probably provides images of a Dionysiac mystery initiation. Orphism was also related to Dionysian mysteries.

The mysteries of Isis and Osiris, the ancient Egyptian goddess and her brother and lover (also known as Sarapis), spread from Egypt to become one of the most prominent mysteries across the Greco-Roman world. In ancient Egypt, Isis and her divine family had played a role in the orderly succession of the pharaohs. Ceremonies using actual or symbolic water from the Nile played a central role in the cult, and sacred meals were held in honor of Sarapis. The closest to an eyewitness account from any mystery cult is found in Apuleius' *Metamorphoses* (Book 11), which describes a *mýstēs'* experience of initiation into the Isis cult with an approach to death and a revelation of the light as essential elements. Extant Isis aretalogies from the cult list the mighty deeds of the goddess in the form of "I am" statements.

Evidence of the cult of Cybele and Attis spans the Roman Empire. The cult center was the Anatolian city of Pessinus. In 204 B.C.E. a meteorite identified with the goddess was brought to Rome, where her temple occupied a prominent location on the Palatine. Her annual festivals there took place on successive days in late March. The most notable personal experience of initiation was that of the *galli* of the goddess, who castrated themselves during her annual frenzied rituals and afterwards became her permanent servants, dressed in feminine cultic garb. In the late Roman era, another form of initiation became prevalent. In the *taurobolium* or *criobolium,* the initiate descended into a pit covered by grillwork and was showered in the blood of a bull or ram sacrificed above. The cult of the Syrian goddess Atargatis with her *galli* bears many similarities to that of Cybele, but was a distinct cult throughout the Roman era.

The cult of Mithra rose to popularity as a Greco-Roman mystery cult during the 2nd century C.E. Scholars debate the relationship of Mithra's Persian origins to the mystery cult of Greco-Roman times. The cult was restricted to men and especially popular among Roman soldiers. Most sanctuaries of Mithra from the Roman era were partially underground to replicate the cave which figures in the Mithra myth. Such a Mithraeum was often decorated with artwork representing the figure of Mithra as the bull-slayer *(tauroktonos)* and with astronomical images. Mithraic initiation took place in seven stages. Each level was named by a different symbol and protected by a different celestial body. A common meal was also an important cultic activity.

The rituals and initiation ceremonies of early Christianity developed in a context in which these mystery cults were also developing. Similarities between early Christianity and the mysteries are not surprising, and the nature of the relationship has been the subject of scholarly debate.

Bibliography. U. Bianchi, *The Greek Mysteries.* Iconography of Religions 17/3 (Leiden, 1976); W. Burkert, *Ancient Mystery Cults* (Cambridge, Mass., 1987); B. M. Metzger, "A Classified Bibliography of the Graeco-Roman Mystery Religions, 1924-1973, with a Supplement 1974-77," in *ANRW* II.17,3 (Berlin, 1984), 1259-1423; M. M. Meyer, *The Ancient Mysteries: A Sourcebook* (San Francisco, 1987); J. Z. Smith, *Drudgery Divine: On the Comparison of Early Christianities and the Religions of Late Antiquity.* Jordan Lectures in Comparative Religions 14 (Chicago, 1990).

SUSAN (ELLI) ELLIOTT

MYSTICISM, EARLY CHRISTIAN

Evidence of mysticism within early Christian literature is determined by the way in which the term is defined. The actual noun "mysticism" (Gk. *mystēriōdía*) occurs nowhere within these materials, but came into use only toward the end of the 5th century through the work of Pseudo-Dionysius (or Denys) the Areopagite. Prior to this time, widespread use was made of Lat. *contemplatio* ("contemplation"), a term which continued to be popular within the Western Church well into the Medieval period.

In its most general sense, ancient mysticism may be characterized both as the spiritual union of the human with the divine and as an introduction to some specific secret or mystery. It is in both of these senses that Hellenistic mystery religions employed such concepts as "mystery," "mystical," and "the mysteries." Similar terminology quickly entered Christian vocabulary, but unlike pantheistic religions, the idea of a personal God in biblical religion has restricted any true sense of unification between human and divine. Evidence suggests that ancient movements such as Gnosticism, Jewish mysticism, Greek speculation, and Neoplatonic doctrine ultimately had great influence upon

Christian views. And yet, Christianity's unique view of mysticism maintained a special quality because of its focus upon the believer's union with the person of Jesus Christ.

Mystical thought occasionally has been identified within the NT. The central message of Jesus that all humanity must "turn/repent" *(metanoéō)* and enter the Kingdom of God (cf. Mark 1:14-15) certainly led many early Christians to seek some special mystical association with God. The miracles of Jesus and his disciples have sometimes been cited as proof of such spiritual union. The author of Acts observes that God's Spirit descended as "tongues of fire" upon the church in Jerusalem (Acts 2:1-4) and was bestowed upon those whom Paul baptized in Ephesus (19:1-7). Mark even identifies specific charisms which were to accompany the disciples as they spread the gospel message (Mark 16:17-18).

A further witness to the spirit of mysticism may be considered within the Pauline literature. In 2 Cor. 12:2-4 the Apostle speaks grudgingly about visions and revelations as a rhetorical foil to the claims of his Corinthian audience. Paul's self-reference in the 3rd person undoubtedly signals his reluctance to focus upon mystical experiences in general. Nowhere does he mention his own conversion, an event dramatically portrayed in Acts 9:1-9. Elsewhere, Paul refers to the living Christ within his life (Gal. 2:20) and explains the Church as the body of Christ (Rom. 12:4-5; 1 Cor. 12:27). But these are not descriptions of separate mystical experiences, only clear statements of the continual communion which he feels with the spirit of Christ. While it is true that the Pauline spiritual center revolves around what is called "the mystery" (Col. 1:27), this idea has little in common with contemporary mystery religions. Instead, Paul's mystery is the revelation of God's plan for human salvation as proclaimed by Christ Jesus and witnessed in the power of the Cross and Resurrection.

Johannine literature also hints at some mystical speculation. In the Gospel of John the metaphors of the Good Shepherd (John 10:1-18) and of the vine and branches (15:1-8) serve as possible examples of mystical thought. To these may be added the short oration of Jesus concerning his role as the bread of life (John 6:35-40), a text which has often come to be viewed as a direct comment upon the mystical aspect of the eucharistic celebration. Such limited texts, however, even when coupled with the ever-present Johannine motif of the close relationship among the Father, Son, and believer, nowhere portray mysticism as an extended activity of the broader Christian community. Even the bold testimony of the prophet at Rev. 1:10 attests only to individual participation in mystical activities.

Whether any of these scriptural examples may actually serve as possible evidence of mysticism in the early Church is much debated. And yet it is clear that primitive Christian faith was driven by two specific experiences which bore some directly spiritual association with Christ — baptism and eucharist. These were community events which guided individual believers in their spiritual lives and became the foundation of later mystical experiences within Christian history.

Thus, while the evidence is limited and uncertain, the specter of mysticism is clearly evident within early Church consciousness. A broad witness to visions, miracles, and prayers speaks to some broad sense of mystical awareness in the personal life of ancient Christians. On the liturgical level, certain authors specifically refer to doctrines and sacraments as "mysteries" of the common Christian experience (e.g., Ignatius *Eph.* 19.1; *Trall.* 2.3, "deacons of the mysteries of Jesus Christ"; Didache 11:11, "worldly mystery of the Church"). During the 2nd century, the "peak experience" of mysticism became identified with martyrdom, depicted as a sweet reunion with Christ (cf. Mart. Pol. 15.1-2).

During these early years, certain segments of the Church were greatly influenced by the rise of mysticism in Judaism. Jewish speculation became a dynamic force as it sought to find the heavenly God within the common elements of daily life. Prominent in this quest during the 1st century was Philo of Alexandria, whose philosophy came to argue that the "spirit" (Gk. *pneúma*) of God resides at the center of the human will in the form of the "mind" (Gk. *noús*). His ideas influenced Christian speculation in Alexandria and Egyptian asceticism in general. Philo stands prominently behind the principles of Clement of Alexandria, who insisted upon gnosis (i.e., divine knowledge) as the ultimate goal of the Christian experience, and of Origen, who sought to wed the human soul with the divine Logos as the ultimate union between the believer and God.

The rise of mysticism within patristic literature is most fully evident during the 4th through 6th centuries under the influence of Cappadocian thought. Key among 4th-century authors was Pseudo-Macarius, an Egyptian anchorite who spoke of the mystical experience as that point when the soul embraces God and becomes "a spiritual eye and entirely light." His contemporary, Evagrius of Pontus, sought mystical union with God through a progression of stages whose culmination in the full knowledge of the trinity brought freedom from all passion.

True systematic treatises on Christian mysticism appeared only at the end of the 5th century. Noteworthy here is the *Mystical Theology* of Pseudo-Dionysius the Areopagite of Syria, as well as *The Ladder of Divine Ascent* of John Climacus, written as a practical guide for the monastic life. Eastern spirituality ultimately had a great influence upon later Western views of mysticism, as evident from the mystical speculations of Ambrose of Milan and his pupil Augustine of Hippo (cf. his *Confessions*). To this tradition should be added the names of Jerome, Gregory the Great, and Maximus Confessor, to name but a few late patristic voices.

Bibliography. L. Bouyer, *History of Christian Spirituality,* 1: *The Spirituality of the New Testament and the Fathers* (London, 1963); E. C. Butler, *West-*

ern Mysticism, 3rd ed. (New York, 1968); A. Louth, *The Origins of the Christian Mystical Tradition from Plato to Denys* (Oxford, 1981); "Mysticism," in *Early Christianity*, ed. I. Hazlett (Nashville, 1991), 208-17; M. Smith, *Studies in Early Mysticism in the Near and Middle East* (London, 1931), repr. *The Way of the Mystics* (London, 1976).

CLAYTON N. JEFFORD

MYTH

A story or narrative that conveys the fundamental structure of knowledge upon which the ideologies and customs of a particular culture rest. Though myth is frequently invested with elements of the fantastic, and generally associated with religious and ritual practice, scholarship has clearly extended its understanding of myth (from Gk. *mýthos*) beyond earlier associations with noble savages and primitive mentalities. Notwithstanding its customary fictional character, consensus proposes that the power of myth lies in its capacity to construct worldviews wherein origins, identities, and behaviors are established and legitimated. Thus, analogous to its many and diverse religious expressions, myth simultaneously embraces the numerous post-Enlightenment formations of the sciences, social sciences, and humanities clearly affiliated with our endeavor to define a person, family, or culture.

"Mythology" designates a body of myths associated with particular cultures. The term concurrently refers to a designated academic field concerned with the study of myth and mythologies: history of religions and comparative religions, biblical studies, linguistics, cultural anthropology, sociology, psychoanalysis, classics, literature and literary theory.

In addition to cultural identification, ethnological and literary sensibilities suggest comparative analyses and the classification of myths according to principal themes. Customary categories include cosmology (myths about the origins of the universe, the gods, and humanity; e.g., creation stories, flood stories, and stories about the fall of mankind); myths about the afterlife and apocalypse (e.g., Homer's description of the land of the dead in the *Odyssey*, or the end of the *Age of Kali* in Hindu scripture); myths about dying and rising gods (e.g., Osiris, Dionysus, and Christ); myths about the Goddess or Great Mother (e.g., Mesopotamian Inanna-Ishtar and Greek Demeter); myths about heroes and heroic quests (e.g., Gilgamesh, Moses, Odysseus, Aeneas, Buddha, Parcival, and Hiawatha); and myths about important places and objects (e.g., Mt. Sinai, Delphi, Golgotha, and Mohammed's Cave).

Reflection on the meaning of myth occurs as early as the 6th century B.C.E. in the philosophical work of Thales of Miletus, followed 200 years later in the work of the 4th-century Greek mythographer Euhemerus, and subsequently addressed in the early 2nd century C.E. by the Neoplatonic and Christian allegorists. However, the systematic collection and analysis of myth does not emerge until the period of the Enlightenment in the second half of the 18th century when hundreds of travel narratives began flowing into Europe detailing bizarre rituals and mythologies from around the world. These materials furnished data for comparative analyses between the new-found mythologies and the well-known and textually-based stories of the Hebrews, Greeks, and Romans, thereby facilitating the systematic study of mythology. Early studies focused upon the language of myth in association with supposed primitive mentalities, proposing that its linguistic attributes reflect graphic instances of primal irrationality. Scholars were reluctant to identify such privileged myths as the Hebraic and Greco-Roman mythologies with the language of irrationality. In the context of literary studies, the Romantic movement sought to displace this disquieting association, suggesting that myth signals a primeval and poetic language fundamental to humanity and its organic development. Cultural anthropology likewise addressed such difficulties. Anthropologists such as Sir James Frazer, E. B. Tylor, Franz Boas, Emile Durkheim, and Bronislaw Malinowski generally proposed that primitive mythology mirrors the fundamental elements of modern civilization, and that its proper comparative study should assist in the development of our own contemporary understanding of humanity's cultural and social formations. These observations were also welcomed and studied by such classicists as Gilbert Murray, Jane Harrison, A. B. Cook, and F. M. Cornford, and similarly engaged by such historians of religion as Franz Cumont and Rudolf Otto. Moreover, the trajectory finds its way into the studies of modern psychology where analysis turns more directly to the constitution of the human psyche. Both Sigmund Freud and Carl Jung recognized motifs and patterns essential to the mythic and subconscious worlds: Freud's "Oedipus complex" and "Elektra complex," Jung's "archetypes" and "collective unconscious." In the field of cultural anthropology, Claude Lévi-Strauss continues the anthropological study of mythology, introducing the important structuralist component to the analysis of myth, while Joseph Campbell's highly popular theories on the relationship between mythology and universal archetypes carry forward the psychoanalytic perspectives of Jung. In the field of the history of religions, the analysis of mythology is advanced in Mircea Eliade's work on mythic and existential time, while studies in literature and literary theory maintain a focus upon the poetic nature of mythic language exemplified in such diverse critical perspectives as Northrop Frye's formalism and Roland Barthes' structuralism/poststructuralism.

Congruent to the influx of foreign mythologies into late-18th-century Europe, exploration also recovered ancient Egyptian and Babylonian artifacts that shortly thereafter generated the decipherment of hieroglyphics and cuneiform writings. A new library of Near Eastern antiquity emerged, and scholars discovered discomforting similarities between the stories of these pagan religions and the sacred texts of Judeo-Christianity. Until this time, scholarship resisted any comparison that might compromise the privileged position of these sanctioned texts, but German scholarship, in particular, moved forward in the application of its higher criticism. In the wake of Johann Salomo Semler's (1725-1791) contested distinction between dogma (theology or the teachings of the Church) and religion (historical experience), J. G. Eichhorn (1752-1827) drew attention to similarities between the creation and flood stories in classical and biblical narrative, using the word "myth" for the first time to describe them. These stories were not records of actual happenings, but the expressions of a religious and pre-scientific consciousness. Although "myth" became one of the most contentious of higher critical terms, biblical scholarship continued to use the comparative study of mythology as a means to elucidate its understanding of biblical history. Nowhere was this more in evidence than in the work of David Friedrich Strauss (1808-1874), whose demonstration of early Christian myth in *Das Leben Jesu* generated a new era of scholarship focused upon the issue of mythology and Christian history. Despite many attempts to delimit if not erase the proximity of the mythological to the Christian gospel, success was not forthcoming; it became evident that the perception which Christianity shared with the rest of the 1st-century Mediterranean world was a perception fastened to the mythological. Efforts then focused upon the act of interpretation as a means to address the truth of Christianity's mythic quality, culminating early in the 20th century with the introduction of demythology by the German NT scholar Rudolf Bultmann. These analyses sought not to eliminate the mythological but to recast its message in the language of Heideggerian existentialism, a hermeneutical procedure whereby the essential substance *(Sache)* of the early Christian proclamation *(kḗrygma)* was divested of its mythological element and invested with the language of postenlightenment sensibilities, thereby preserving the essence of the Christian gospel.

Although subsequent studies have not appreciably advanced our understanding of the relationship between Judeo-Christian literature and the language of myth, there is renewed effort to reassess demythology's narrow understanding of myth, and to address the issue of Christian origins in view of contemporary cultural anthropological observations and postmodernist theories of language and literature.

Bibliography. R. Bultmann, *Jesus Christ and Mythology* (New York, 1958); M. Detienne, *The Creation of Mythology* (Chicago, 1986); M. Eliade, *Myth and Reality* (New York, 1963); T. Gaster, *Myth, Legend and Custom in the Old Testament* (1969, repr. Gloucester, 1981); G. S. Kirk, *Myth: Its Meaning and Function in Ancient and Other Cultures* (Berkeley, 1970); I. Strenski, *Four Theories of Myth in Twentieth-Century History: Cassirer, Eliade, Lévi-Strauss and Malinowski* (Iowa City, 1987); J.-P. Vernant, *Myth and Society in Ancient Greece* (New York, 1990).

Michael L. Humphries

N

NAAM (Heb. *na'am*)
A Judahite, son of Caleb and grandson of Jephunneh (1 Chr. 4:15).

NAAMAH (Heb. *na'ămâ*) **(PERSON)**

1. The daughter of Lamech and Zillah, and the sister of Tubal-cain in the lineage of Cain (Gen. 4:22).

2. An Ammonite woman who married Solomon; the mother of Rehoboam (1 Kgs. 14:21, 31; 2 Chr. 12:13).

NAAMAH (Heb. *na'ămâ*) **(PLACE)**
A town in the Shephelah of Judah, part of that tribe's inheritance (Josh. 15:41). It is included in the Lachish district, but the exact location remains uncertain. Some scholars have suggested sites in the Sorek Valley near Timnah on the basis of toponymic evidence, while others believe it should be located nearer Lachish.

Bibliography. W. F. Albright, "Topographical Researches in Judæa," *BASOR* 18 (1925): 6-11.

JENNIFER L. GROVES

NAAMAN (Heb. *na'ămān*)

1. A son of Benjamin (Gen. 46:21).

2. A son of Bela, the son of Benjamin, eponymous ancestor of the Naamanites (Num. 26:40; 1 Chr. 8:4).

3. A son of Ehud, the great-grandson of Benjamin (1 Chr. 8:7).

4. The commander of the Aramean army who was cured of his leprosy by bathing in the Jordan (2 Kgs. 5). An Israelite maidservant told Naaman's wife that a prophet from Samaria, Elisha, could heal Naaman of his leprosy. Informed of this in a letter from the king of Aram, the king of Israel interpreted it as a pretext for conflict between Aram and Israel. Through the intervention of Elisha Naaman nevertheless came to Israel, but he was cured only after his servants compelled him to follow Elisha's instructions to bathe in the Jordan. Naaman then confessed his allegiance to the Lord and departed. Telling Naaman the prophet had changed his mind, Elisha's servant Gehazi deceptively obtained gifts of silver and clothing from Naaman. Upon being confronted by Elisha, Gehazi was thereupon struck by the leprosy of which Naaman was cured.

The narrative demonstrates that although Israel was the locus of the Lord's activity, the Gentiles also participated in the Lord's beneficence: in spite of his objections to the contrary, Naaman could be cleansed only in the Jordan (2 Kgs. 5:11-14); he confessed that there was no God in the whole world except in Israel (v. 15); and he wished to return to Aram with Israelite earth, for he would sacrifice only to the Lord in the future (v. 17). Jesus' recalls the story in Luke 4:27 to emphasize that God's beneficence extends beyond Israel to the Gentiles.

JOHN E. HARVEY

NAAMATHITE (Heb. *na'ămāṯî*)
A gentilic attributed to Job's friend Zophar (Job 2:11; 11:1; 20:1; 42:9; cf. LXX "the Minean"). It apparently derives from Naamah or Naameh, a city (or district) in northwest Arabia (possibly Jebel el-Na'ameh) or Edom.

NAAMITES (Heb. *na'ămî*)
A clan of the Benjaminites, the descendants of Naaman (Num. 26:40).

NAARAH (Heb. *na'ărâ*) **(PERSON)**
One of the two wives of Ashhur, the father of Tekoa. She was the mother of Ahuzzam, Hepher, Temeni, and Haahashtari (1 Chr. 4:5-6).

NAARAH (Heb. *na'ărâ*) **(PLACE)**
A town on the eastern border of Ephraim (Josh. 16:7). 1 Chr. 7:28 lists Naaran, which is probably the same site. Josephus refers to a town named Naara (*Ant.* 17.13.1[340]), and Eusebius describes a Jewish settlement, Noarath, located 8 km. (4.5 mi.) from Jericho (*Onom.* 136.24). The exact location is uncertain, but Naarah has been identified with Iron Age sites near Jericho, including Khirbet el-'Ayâsh,

el-Aujeh, and most commonly with Tell el-Jisr (190144), ca. 6 km. (3.5 mi.) NW of Jericho.

LAURA B. MAZOW

NAARAI (Heb. *na'ăray*) (also PAARAI)
The son of Ezbai; one of David's Mighty Men (1 Chr. 11:37). At 2 Sam. 23:35 he is called Paarai the Arbite.

NAARAN (Heb. *na'ărān*)
Alternate form of Naarah (1 Chr. 7:28).

NABAL (Heb. *nāḇāl*)
A wealthy Calebite shepherd from Maon (1 Sam. 25). Although it is unlikely that his given name was Nabal ("fool"), his actions in the story portray him to be such, while his contrastingly cunning and sharp-witted wife Abigail cleverly works her way into the future king's harem. This story also depicts David's early relationship with the power structure near Hebron, where he would subsequently be crowned king first of Judah and then of all Israel. David, an outlaw from Saul's court who had been residing with his men near Nabal's herds, seeks gifts from Nabal during the festive shearing season, reminding Nabal that David's men have been with Nabal's herds and shepherds, but have done them no harm. There certainly is a bit of a threat interwoven with David's request, as becomes obvious when Nabal, in his foolishness, refuses David's request and insults him (1 Sam. 25:10-11), calling him merely one of many servants who were breaking away from their masters. Upon hearing this response, David prepares his warriors to attack Nabal. The quick-witted Abigail meets David on the road with gifts, diverting the disaster which would have fallen upon Nabal (as emphasized by David's words in 1 Sam. 25:34, where he asserts that without Abigail's intervention not a male would have been left to Nabal by morning). When Nabal sobers up from his wine in the morning and learns how close he came to disaster, "his heart dies within him" and he becomes "like a stone" (1 Sam. 25:37). When Nabal dies 10 days later, David takes Abigail as his wife. She eventually bears him Chileab, a son who does not figure in the succession.

Abigail is the heroine of this story, successfully mediating between her foolish husband and David, the future king who has been offended by Nabal's rebuff. Furthermore, it is on her lips that we encounter the words about David becoming the prince of Israel and not having bloodguilt on his hands (1 Sam. 25:28-31). Nabal is the fool who cannot see what lies in David's (or his own) future, while Abigail sees all and shrewdly orchestrates events to the advantage of the future king of Israel. Thus, the foolish Nabal is a foil to Abigail, and the writer uses Nabal's story to show the folly of those who see David only as an outlaw cast out from Saul's court, and therefore not worthy of support (1 Sam. 25:10-11).

Bibliography. J. D. Levinson, "1 Samuel 25 as Literature and as History," *CBQ* 40 (1978): 11-28.

ALAN J. HAUSER

NABATEANS (Gk. *Nabataíoi*)
A people who first emerge as an independent group in the report by Diodorus Siculus of a raid by the Seleucid general Antigonus in 312 B.C.E. However, other classical authors refer to a people situated along the western edge of the Arabian Peninsula, the Nabaṭû, who, after failing as pirates in the Red Sea, make their way northward along the coast. The Nabaṭû apparently represented a confederacy of seminomads seeking a more permanent lifestyle. It is at Petra, the southernmost stronghold of the biblical Edomites, that they finally found their refuge, amalgamated with the sedentary Edomites, and became the Nabateans of history. Edomites resisting symbiosis with the Bedouin group moved westward, to become known as Idumeans, but ties between the two groups long remained, as is illustrated by the ancestry of Herod the Great, whose father was an Idumean and his mother a Nabatean.

The joining of a vigorous wandering people with a sedentary population led to the formation of one of the most important commercial bodies in the Middle East during the last few centuries B.C.E. through the 4th century C.E. Utilizing their earlier knowledge of the trade routes of the Arabian Peninsula, the Nabateans were able to secure the sources and the markets of the lucrative frankincense and myrrh trade, add to it spices, gems, balsams, bitumen, and even the China silk trade in the course of time.

Monarchy had soon followed tribal sheikdom and with it came the urge to emulate neighboring, more sophisticated, cultures. Under the hand of King Aretas IV (9 B.C.E.–40 C.E.), Petra became an urban capital city, complete with an oversized theater, nymphaeum, public bath, temples, and more than 800 rock-carved funerary monuments, some of which reached monumental proportions.

Commerce required expansion, and by the 1st century C.E. the Nabateans controlled more than 1000 sites throughout Coele-Syria and Saudi Arabia, with the contacts reaching from Damascus to the north to Medain Selah to the south, through the Sinai Peninsula, into Egypt, and into the Roman West.

Such a rich and expanding provincial kingdom attracted the attention of Rome as early as the conquest of Syro-Palestine by Pompey in 64 B.C.E. Early attempts to subdue the Nabateans failed for one reason or another, and they were permitted to exist in a quasi-autonomous state. Emperor Augustus had raised an investiture objection to the accession of Aretas IV, but had done nothing formally to claim the kingdom. Trajan, however, found it necessary to consolidate Roman holdings in the Middle East, and when his legions marched into Petra in 106 C.E. the Nabatean kingdom, as a political entity, ceased to exist. However, contrary to views held earlier in Nabatean studies, current evidence suggests that the takeover actually disrupted neither the economy nor the lifestyle of the people.

Along with commercial brilliance, the widespread connections of the traders opened the way for an equally impressive borrowing of all of the lifestyle advantages of the greater world around them. This habit of extensive borrowing clouds the issue of the degree to which any given attributes of Nabatean culture are really Nabatean in origin, or whether individual aspects represent adoption, adaptation, or actual innovation. Regardless of the confusion, however, the native abilities of the people resulted in the creation of a most unique mosaic of technology, art, architecture, religion, and all other facets of daily life.

Perhaps the most striking feature of Nabatean technology appears in their hydrological achievements, both for water collection and distribution in the capital city and for agricultural use in the arid and semi-arid portions of the kingdom. Ceramic pipelines, reservoirs, gravity feeds, runnels, and capacious cisterns all served the urban environments. Outside, dams closed off wadis to collect water during the rainy season, circles of stone retarded runoff from slopes, and irrigation lines fed crops. It is possibly in regard to the conservation of water supplies that the seminomadic background of the Nabateans may be seen to emerge most obviously.

The same degree of technological sophistication may be seen in other aspects of Nabatean life: architecture, ceramics, metallurgy, chemistry, mathematics, construction, and even toxicology. Greco-Roman architectural forms were borrowed, adapted, and put to use, especially for the facades of funerary monuments; common ware pottery of the period was simply copied, whereas fine thin ("eggshell") wares, plain and painted, emerged as perhaps the best ceramics produced in the Middle East up to that time; mining, processing, and manufacturing of iron, copper, bronze, lead, gold, and silver objects was on a par with the rest of the Roman world; and so it was with virtually every facet of life.

Cultural sophistication and eclecticism followed technological, to be seen in art and architectural forms, religion, dress, diplomatic relations, and even in communication. The Aramaic-speaking Nabateans even created another script to add to those in use in the Middle East of their day. A running cursive writing form developed, used both for lapidary and more common graffiti. It was this script that would somewhat later be transformed into the "Arabic" writing still in use today.

Prior to the excavations of George Horsfield at Petra beginning in 1929, the only indicator of Nabatean presence on a site was epigraphic evidence. Horsfield linked the fine thin pottery of Petra to the Nabateans, permitting identification of sites throughout all of the ancient kingdom and along its trade routes, regardless of whether graffiti or other inscribed materials were present. Survey activity began to pinpoint Nabatean sites and to reveal the extent of their influence. Excavations followed slowly, beginning at Petra and, more recently, at other major sites on both sides of the Jordan River.

As a result of a disastrous earthquake which occurred on 19 May 363 C.E., Petra was virtually destroyed and its people sought other home sites. With the loss of the dominance of the capital city, the Nabateans as a nation were themselves virtually lost as well, except for the sparse classical references, those in the intertestamental biblical sources, and the myriad of graffiti spread throughout the regions of their ancient realm. More extensive excavations, especially at Petra, and research in the classical and biblical records, have continued, gradually piecing together more and more of Nabatean life. Lack of official records, annals, and similar materials is still a major problem, and many elements of Nabatean customs, history, and other details are still missing. Likewise missing are details of presence of the people, as they both lingered on earlier sites and sought new areas to exercise their expertise in commerce and their myriad of skills borrowed and developed during the life of the kingdom.

PHILIP C. HAMMOND

NABLUS (Arab. *Nablus*)
A city just W of Tell Balâṭah (biblical Shechem), founded by Vespasian in 72 C.E. as Flavius Neapolis (Gk. "new city"), a settlement for Roman army veterans. Justin Martyr was born nearby ca. 100. The city is home to the modern Samaritan community.

NABONIDUS (Akk. *Nabû-na'id*)
The last king of Babylon (556-539 B.C.). The son of a priest of the moon-god Sîn from Harran in Upper Mesopotamia, he was apparently not from the royal line and thus usurped the throne. In a pseudo-autobiographical account of her life, his mother Adad-guppi (who lived for more than 100 years) claimed to have been instrumental in Nabonidus' rise to power. He favored the Sîn cult over that of Marduk, the chief god of Babylon, and thus caused friction between himself and the religious establishment in Babylon.

For some unstated reason, Nabonidus left Babylon for the oasis of Tema in the Arabian desert and stayed there ca. 10 years (ca. 553-543). His son Belshazzar ruled Babylon in his place, taking care of administrative and military duties. Thus Nabonidus was not present to fulfill his role as king in the New Year festivals of Marduk, thereby incurring the wrath of the Marduk priests. Nabonidus had returned to Babylon for only a short time before his kingdom was attacked by Cyrus of Persia, who captured the city in 539. According to the Babylonian writer Berossus (ca. 250), Cyrus later made Nabonidus a governor in Carmania.

Nabonidus was considered an "evil king" by later historical traditions. The Verse Account of Nabû-na'id was a propagandistic text composed by the Marduk priests to justify the takeover of Babylon by the Persians. Nabonidus' crime was his ignoring of the Marduk cult. The priests even claim to have helped the Persian cause. The Persian Cyrus Cylinder extolled the greatness of Cyrus, while listing the sins of Nabonidus.

Although Nabonidus is not mentioned in the Bible, he is found in the folkloristic Prayer of Nabonidus, a 1st-century B.C. text written in Aramaic. The depiction of the Babylonian king is similar to that in the Verse Account. Furthermore, Nabonidus was said to have been afflicted with a bad inflammation which caused him to be "put away from men" for seven years, not unlike the description of Nebuchadnezzar II in the book of Daniel. The marked similarities between the two Babylonian kings in later traditions has been the subject of much scholarly discussion, but there has been no consensus to explain this.

Bibliography. C. J. Gadd, "The Harran Inscriptions of Nabonidus," *Anatolian Studies* 8 (1958): 35-92; R. H. Sack, "Nebuchadnezzar and Nabonidus in Folklore and History," *Mesopotamia* 17 (1982): 67-131; "Nabonidus of Babylon," in *Crossing Boundaries and Linking Horizons,* ed. R. E. Averbeck, M. W. Chavalas, and G. D. Young (Bethesda, 1997), 455-73.

MARK W. CHAVALAS

NABOTH (Heb. *nāḇôṯ*)
A Jezreelite judicially murdered by Jezebel and Ahab in order to confiscate his vineyard, presumably located next to Ahab's palace in Jezreel. The story of Naboth's vineyard (1 Kgs. 21:1-16) raises issues of royal power and prerogative, especially concerning the ownership of land in ancient Israel. Naboth upholds the old tribal ethos that land remain in the tribe (Lev. 25:23; Num. 26:5-9), the inheritance (Heb. *naḥălâ*) of his fathers and an inalienable trust from Yahweh.

1 Kgs. 21 places the blame for Naboth's death on Jezebel. She declares a fast in Ahab's name, then hires two scoundrels to falsely accuse Naboth of committing treason against God and the king, ensuring Naboth's death by stoning (Deut. 13:10; 17:5; Exod. 22:28[MT 27]). She devises this plan only after Naboth refuses to sell his vineyard to Ahab for a vegetable garden. Upon Naboth's death, Ahab takes possession of the land. As a result, both Jezebel and Ahab are punished by God as prophesied by Elijah (1 Kgs. 21:17-24).

In 2 Kgs. 9:21-37 these events are cited as the reason for the demise of Ahab's dynasty. Here only Ahab is responsible for Naboth's death (2 Kgs. 9:26); the vineyard is in riding distance from Ahab's palace (v. 21) instead of next to it; and both Naboth and his sons are killed by Ahab. According to the rabbis, Ahab is Naboth's cousin and the rightful heir of his property (*Sanh.* 48b). They also suggest that it is Naboth's revengeful spirit that entices Ahab to engage in the battle that ultimately leads to Ahab's death (*Yalquṭ Šimʿoni* Kgs. 221).

DEBORAH A. APPLER

NACON (Heb. *nāḵôn*)
The threshing floor on the way to Jerusalem, where the oxen stumbled during a cultic procession and Uzzah, an officiating priest, reached out to the ark of God, took hold of it, and died (2 Sam. 6:6). An editorial note (2 Sam. 6:8) adds that David called the place Perez-uzzah ("Uzzah's breach"). In the parallel in 1 Chr. 13:9 the threshing floor is called Kidon (cf. Gk. *Cheidṓn,* Josephus *Ant.* 7.81). One LXX tradition reads Nodab, another Nachor, and in a Qumran manuscript it is called Nodan. The Hebrew has been variously translated as a proper name or a passive participle of the verb *kûn* ("certain," "secure," "permanent," or "prepared" [i.e., threshing floor]).

JESPER SVARTVIK

NADAB (Heb. *nāḏāḇ*)
1. Firstborn son of Aaron and Elisheba (Exod. 6:23; Num. 3:2; 26:60; 1 Chr. 6:3[MT 5:29]; 24:1). Nadab accompanied Moses, Aaron, the 70 elders, and his brother Abihu up Mt. Sinai, where they saw the God of Israel (Exod. 24:1-2, 9-11). He and his father and brothers were appointed priests (Exod. 28:1). Nadab transgressed the law (Exod. 30:9) with Abihu in offering "unauthorized" (NRSV 'illicit') fire" in burning incense before the Lord (Num. 26:61). Drunkenness may have been an element in the sin (Lev. 10:8-9).

2. A king of Israel, successor to his father Jeroboam I. He is said to have reigned for two years (1 Kgs. 14:20; 15:25-31). Nadab's murder after such a short reign indicated how unstable the political situation was in the northern kingdom. His evil reign was ended when he was assassinated by Baasha of Issachar, ending the dynasty of Jereboam and fulfilling Ahijah's prophecy (1 Kgs. 14:1-20). The only noteworthy event during his reign was the Israelites' siege of Gibbethon (1 Kgs. 15:27).

3. A son of Shammai, of the house of Jerahmeel, and a descendant of Tamar, daughter-in-law of Judah (1 Chr. 2:28, 30).

4. A Benjaminite, son of Jeiel and Maacah; brother of Kish, who was the father of King Saul (1 Chr. 8:30; 9:36).

5. Relative of Ahikar (Tob. 11:18), and one of the guests at the wedding of Tobias. When Tobias returned with Sarah, his bride, Nadab and his uncle came to the marriage ceremony, which was celebrated for seven days with great festivity.

LARRY L. WALKER

NADABATH (Gk. *Nadabath*)
A village in Transjordan. A wedding party traveling from Nadabath to Madaba was ambushed by Jonathan and Simon Maccabeus to avenge the death of their brother John, who was captured and executed by the Jambrites of Madaba (1 Macc. 9:37). This village might be the same as one mentioned by Josephus (*Ant.* 3.1.4). Suggestions for its location include Main (219120), 7 km. (4 mi.) SW of Madeba; en-Nebâ (ancient Nebo) NW of Madeba; and Khirbet et-Teim (223123), 2 km. (1.25 miles) S of Madeba.

Bibliography. N. Glueck, *Explorations in Eastern Palestine I.* AASOR 14 (Baltimore, 1933-34).

ZELJKO GREGOR

NAG HAMMADI
A modern city in Upper Egypt, 556 km. (345 mi.) S of Cairo and 118 km. (74 mi.) N of Luxor on the west bank of the Nile River. The name of the city has been applied to a collection of papyrus manuscripts that shed light on religious and philosophical issues during the early Christian period.

Discovery of the Codices

According to James M. Robinson, the Nag Hammadi codices (NHC) were discovered by Egyptian fellahin, including Muhammad Ali of the al-Samman clan, ca. December 1945 in a large storage jar buried at the base of the Jebel el-Tarif, the cliff that flanks the Nile River near the village of Hamra Dum and across from the city of Nag Hammadi. Although portions may have been burned, the rest of the collection is now conserved and stored in the library of the Coptic Museum in Old Cairo.

Contents

The Nag Hammadi codices constitute a collection of 12 papyrus books (called codices, from Latin) and eight leaves from a 13th. They represent some of the earliest examples of bound books, as opposed to scrolls. These codices and extra leaves contain more than 50 separate texts and 48 separate titles (less the duplicate texts, according to one means of enumeration). The texts are preserved in Coptic, though most scholars conclude that they were originally composed in Greek. Dated material from the cartonnage, or scrap papyrus lining the leather covers of the codices, indicates that at least some of the codices may have been assembled ca. the mid-4th century. The evidence from the cartonnage and other circumstantial evidence, including archaeological data, may link the manufacture of the covers and codices to a nearby site such as Pabau (modern Faw Qibli) and the Pachomian monastic movement, but the evidence is not conclusive. Some scholars guess that the occasion for the burial of the codices may be the promulgation of the Easter letter of Athanasius of Alexandria in 367 with its condemnation of heretics and their books, but that also remains uncertain.

The texts exhibit a wide range of religious and philosophical perspectives. Christian, esoteric, and ascetic tendencies predominate, but the codices also contain non-Christian and marginally or secondarily christianized texts, Jewish gnostic texts, and even a fragment from Plato's *Republic.* Among the numerous gnostic texts are Sethian and Valentinian texts, as well as Hermetic texts. Still, the variety of supposedly gnostic and nongnostic perspectives among Nag Hammadi texts has raised fundamental questions about the nature of Gnosticism and the ways in which scholars define and classify Gnosticism and gnostic schools of thought.

The texts also exhibit a range of genres of literature. Like the NT canon, the Nag Hammadi codices contain texts that may be termed gospels, acts, letters, and apocalypses. Among the gospels are the Gospel of Truth (NHC I,3; XII,2), the Gospel of Thomas (II,2), the Gospel of Philip (II,3), and the Gospel of the Egyptians (III,2; IV,2). (The fragmentary Gospel of Mary is in a related codex, Berolinensis Gnosticus [BG]8502,1.) These gospels, however, are quite different from the NT narrative gospels, which focus upon the salvific death and resurrection of Jesus as the occasion for interpreting the life of Jesus. The gospels from the Nag Hammadi codices are more concerned with interpreting sayings and offering revelatory discourses of Jesus, and meditating upon the deeper meaning of Jesus. The Acts of Peter and the Twelve Apostles (VI,I) and the Letter of Peter to Philip (VIII,2) include materials similar to that found in the NT and apocryphal acts. (The Act of Peter, from the apocryphal Acts of Peter, is preserved within the same codex from Berlin, BG 8502,4.) The Letter of Peter to Philip (also identified, according to reports, in another unpublished papyrus codex) opens with a letter, and other Nag Hammadi texts also are cast in the form of letters. Several Nag Hammadi texts are described as revelations or apocalypses (one of Paul, two of James, one of Adam). These are located in Codex V.

Other genres are also attested. Several contain revelatory discourses of Jesus or dialogues between the resurrected Christ and his disciples, such as those in the Apocryphon (Secret Book) of James (I,2) and the Apocryphon of John (II,1; III,1; IV,1; BG 8502,2). The Apocryphon of John, a Jewish gnostic text that has been secondarily christianized, includes a revolutionary interpretation of the opening chapters of Genesis that gives a mythological vision of the devolution and restoration of the divine and all who manifest the spirit of the divine. Four copies of this text exist (in two recensions), and heresiologists likewise wrote about materials similar to this text. The Apocryphon of John thus seems to offer a classic gnostic presentation of the origin, fall, and salvation of humankind.

Significance for Ancient Religion and Philosophy

The publication of the Nag Hammadi codices has disclosed remarkable new possibilities for exploring religion and philosophy during the first centuries C.E., particularly as these issues come to expression in early Christianity. The discovery of the codices has highlighted the importance of the Nag Hammadi region as a center of early Christian life and thought, particularly when this discovery is considered along with the renewed study of the Dishna papers (sometimes called the Bodmer Papyri), which derive from the same general area in Upper Egypt, and the archaeological work undertaken at monastic sites and other Christian locales in the region.

The Nag Hammadi texts illumine varieties of Judaism, Christianity, and Gnosticism previously understood in a much more limited way. For example, esoteric Jewish traditions, reminiscent of what is to be read in other Jewish apocryphal and pseudepigraphical documents, are reflected in such texts as the Apocryphon of John, the Apocalypse of Adam (V,5), the Three Stelas of Seth (VII,5), Zostrianos (VIII,1), the Thought of Norea (IX,2), Marsanes (X,1), and Allogenes (XI,3). The Teachings of Silvanus (VII,4) is essentially a work of Jewish wisdom that has been Christianized to a degree. Several of these sorts of Nag Hammadi texts also show clear familiarity with Neoplatonic thought and demonstrate the development of Gnosticism in a Neoplatonic thought-world.

The study of Gnosticism itself has been fundamentally transformed by the discovery and publication of the Nag Hammadi codices. These texts carry the study of Gnosticism far beyond the heresiologists and the church fathers, whose polemical portrayals of gnostic life and thought often provide only a caricature of Gnosticism. The gnostic texts within the codices disclose a rich diversity of mystical, mythological, syncretistic expressions in Gnosticism. They suggest that some gnostic traditions were deeply rooted in Judaism: in Jewish wisdom, in apocalyptic Jewish groups, in alienated types of Jewish piety that raised troubling questions about the divine, in concerns for Seth as the enlightened son of Adam and eventually a gnostic redeemer. The appearance of Seth, Derdekeas, and other gnostic redeemers in Nag Hammadi texts gives evidence of a developed redeemer myth apart from early Christianity. This evidence contributes to the ongoing discussion of whether Gnosticism should be viewed merely as a Christian heresy or rather as a religion in its own right, with non-Christian and perhaps pre-Christian manifestations. After the publication of the Nag Hammadi texts, the latter position seems tenable to many scholars, and gnostic religion is emerging as a highly reflective and self-consciously provocative form of spirituality.

Significance for the NT and Early Christian Literature

The Gospel of Thomas (II,2) has attracted more attention than any other Nag Hammadi text on account of its significance for NT and early Christian studies. Thomas is a gospel of wisdom that presents "the living Jesus" uttering a series of sayings (conventionally considered to be 114 in number); and although the sayings cannot be classified as gnostic without qualification, they all are said to be capable of being interpreted in such a way as to bring readers to a state in which they will not "taste death." As a collection of sayings of Jesus, the Gospel of Thomas resembles other Jewish, Greco-Roman, and Christian collections of sayings, especially the synoptic sayings source Q. Debate continues about whether the Gospel of Thomas is essentially dependent upon or independent of the original NT Gospels, but a good case can be made for it as an independent source for the Jesus tradition. Some sayings in the Gospel of Thomas are presented in a form that is earlier than that of the sayings in the NT, e.g., parables of Jesus that are given without allegorical embellishment in Thomas. Other sayings that are without parallel in the NT and early Christian literature may be helpful in the quest of the historical Jesus and the sayings of the historical Jesus, e.g., the parable of the jar of meal (saying 97) and the parable of the assassin (saying 98). A form of saying 17 ("I shall give you what no eye has seen . . .") may be alluded to in 1 Cor. 2:9. The Gospel of Thomas could have been originally composed in the 1st century, and it should take its place alongside Q as a primary source for sayings of Jesus and an early example of Christianity with an orientation toward wisdom.

In addition, the Nag Hammadi codices contribute substantially to the study of the Gospel of John and Johannine literature. It has been claimed by some scholars that the author of John uses terms, motifs, and styles familiar from gnostic literature, and writes within the context of a gnostic world of ideas. Nag Hammadi texts support this claim by providing examples of revelatory discourses, "I am" aretalogical statements, and reflections upon the divine Logos (Word). The Trimorphic Protennoia (XIII,1) features the divine Word revealing itself in an aretalogical manner and describing its descent to the world, its appearance in human likeness, and its work of restoring to the light those who belong to the Word, all in a way much like the Gospel of John. Further, the Johannine tradition about "doubting Thomas" may now be interpreted, in the light of the Gospel of Thomas and the Book of Thomas (the Contender) (II,7), as a part of the controversy about the place and role of Thomas in early Christianity.

The Nag Hammadi codices also contribute to the study of traditions about the Resurrection and resurrection appearances within early Christianity. The Letter of Peter to Philip (VIII,2), like other Christian gnostic texts from the Nag Hammadi codices, portrays the risen Christ appearing as "a great light" on the Mount of Olives and revealing himself through a voice calling out from the light, in the form of an "I am" statement, "I am Jesus Christ who is with you forever." While such a presentation of an appearance of the risen Christ may be contrasted with NT passages that stress the physical reality of the body of the risen Christ, this gnostic description recalls the appearance of Christ to Paul as a light and voice on the Damascus road according to Acts 9, 22, 26; the discussion of Paul on the glorious, spiritual nature of the Resurrection in 1 Cor. 15; and the brilliant apocalyptic vision of the risen Christ in Rev. 1. There is a Nag Hammadi text, the Treatise on Resurrection (I,4), that is devoted entirely to an evaluation of the Resurrection, and this text concludes that the spiritual resurrection is something that has already happened. Although this is precisely what is condemned in 2 Tim. 2:17-18 as the ungodly teaching of Hymenaeus and Philetus, the author of the Treatise substantiates the argument on the Resurrection given in this text with a citation of the Apostle Paul himself.

Bibliography. M. Meyer, *The Gospel of Thomas* (San Francisco, 1992); J. M. Robinson, ed., *The Nag Hammadi Library in English*, 3rd ed. (San Francisco, 1988); D. M. Scholer, *Nag Hammadi Bibliography, 1948-1969.* Nag Hammadi Studies 1 (Leiden, 1971); *Nag Hammadi Bibliography, 1970-1994.* Nag Hammadi and Manichaean Studies 32 (Leiden, 1997).

Marvin Meyer

NAGGAI (Gk. *Naggaí*)
An otherwise unknown ancestor of Jesus (Luke 3:25).

NAHALAL (Heb. *nahălāl*) (also NAHALOL)
A levitical city allotted to the Merarites (Josh. 21:35) from the territory of the tribe of Zebulun (19:15). It is not mentioned in the list of levitical cities at 1 Chr. 6:77[MT 62]). According to Judg. 1:30 (Nahalol) the Zebulunites were unable to drive out its Canaanite inhabitants but did subject them to forced labor. Two sites have been proposed. Tell el-Beiḍā (168231) lies in the Esdraelon Plain NW of Jokneam (cf. Josh. 19:11) but lacks traditional support. Tell en-Naḥl (156245), whose name is similar to Nahalal, lies on the Mediterranean coastal plain S of Acco and NE of the Kishon River, an area associated with the tribe of Asher, not Zebulun.

Eric F. Mason

NAHALIEL (Heb. *naḥălî'ēl*)
An Israelite encampment near the end of the wilderness journey, E of the Dead Sea between Mattanah and Bamoth, and near the land of Moab. Nahaliel is not listed in the itinerary of Num. 33. Possible locations for the site are Wadi Wâlā, which flows into the Arnon River from the north; and Wadi Zerqā Ma'în, which flows into the Dead Sea 17-18 km. (10.5-11 mi.) N of the Arnon.

Pete F. Wilbanks

NAHAM (Heb. *naḥam*)
A Judahite, the sister of Hodiah's wife (1 Chr. 4:19).

NAHAMANI (Heb. *naḥămānî*)
One of the leaders of the Israelites who returned with Nehemiah from exile in Babylon (Neh. 7:7).

NAHARAI (Heb. *naḥăray*)
One of David's Mighty Men and Joab's armor-bearer whose hometown was Beeroth (2 Sam. 23:37 = 1 Chr. 11:39).

NAHASH (Heb. *nāḥāš*)

1. A king of Ammon during the late 11th century B.C.E. In a narrative intended to demonstrate the validity of Saul's kingship (1 Sam. 12:12), the MT indicates that Nahash surrounded the Transjordanian Israelite city of Jabesh-gilead and demanded its capitulation. Saul heard about the Ammonite threat, summoned an army, and routed the Ammonites (1 Sam. 11:1-11). A Qumran scroll (4QSam*a*) preserves not only the same material regarding Nahash as the MT, but also a prologue to the Nahash pericope which is also contained in Josephus (*Ant.* 6.5.1[68-71]). According to this supplemental text, Nahash had been oppressing the Transjordanian tribes of Reuben and Gad, and 7000 men had escaped from Nahash and fled to Jabesh-gilead. The longer form of the narrative is considered original by some scholars but secondary by others.

Nahash and his son Shobi apparently had a congenial relationship with David (2 Sam 10:2; 17:27-29). After Nahash's death, David sent envoys to his son Hanun, ostensibly to console him, but Hanun considered them to be spies and humiliated them. This led to a military confrontation (2 Sam. 10:1-19; 1 Chr. 19:1-19).

2. The sister of Zeruiah (Joab's mother) and the father of Abigal. Nahash's daughter Abigal (the mother of Amasa) was married to Ithra, who is identified both as an Israelite (2 Sam. 17:25) and an Ishmaelite (1 Chr. 2:17). The materials regarding this Nahash are problematic textually.

Bibliography. A. Rofé, "The Acts of Nahash according to 4QSam[a]," *IEJ* 32 (1982): 129-33; E. C. Ulrich, Jr., *The Qumran Text of Samuel and Josephus.* HSM 19 (Missoula, 1978); R. W. Younker, "Ammonites," in *Peoples of the Old Testament World,* ed. A. J. Hoerth, G. L. Mattingly, and E. M. Yamauchi (Grand Rapids, 1994), 293-316.

Chris A. Rollston

NAHATH (Heb. *naḥaṯ*)

1. The firstborn son of Reuel and grandson of Esau (Gen. 36:13; 1 Chr. 1:37); an Edomite tribal chief (Gen. 36:17).

2. A descendant of Levi (1 Chr. 6:26[MT 11]). It has been suggested that the name here be read as Toah in conjunction with 1 Chr. 6:34(19) or Tohu in accordance with 1 Sam. 1:1.

3. One of the assistants appointed by Hezekiah to work under the supervision of Conaniah the Levite and his brother Shimei and take charge of the storage chamber where contributions to the clergy were kept (2 Chr. 31:13).

Arnold Gottfried Betz

NAHBI (Heb. *naḥbî*)
A Naphtalite, the son of Vophsi. He was one of the 12 spies Moses sent into Canaan (Num. 13:14).

NAHOR (Heb. *nāḥôr*) **(PERSON)**

1. A son of Serug, the sixth recorded generation from Shem. At age 29 Nahor fathered Terah, who later became the father of Abram. Dying when 148 years old, Nahor lived well into the life of Abram (Gen. 11:22-26).

2. A son of Terah and brother of Abram (Gen. 11:27-29). Nahor married his brother Haran's daughter Milcah, who gave birth to eight children (Gen. 22:20-23). One of these, Bethuel, was the father of Rebekah, who married Isaac. Nahor's concubine Reumah bore him four additional offspring (Gen. 22:24). If the names here have the function of eponyms, this account would present Nahor — similar to Ishmael (Gen. 25:16) and Jacob (49:28) — as the progenitor of 12 kindred tribes.

Edwin C. Hostetter

NAHOR (Heb. *nāḥôr*) **(PLACE)**
A city in northwest Mesopotamia to which Abraham sent his servant to obtain a wife for Isaac (Gen. 24:10). The Mari Letters mention a Naḫur situated E of the upper Baliḫ River near Haran (cf. Gen. 29:4-5).

NAHSHON (Heb. *naḥšôn;* Gk. *Naassṓn*)
A son of Amminadab and brother of Elisheba the wife of Aaron (Exod. 6:23). He represented Judah in

assisting Moses with the first census (Num. 1:7) and led that tribe during the wilderness wanderings (2:3; 10:14; cf. 7:12, 17). Nahshon is reckoned among the ancestors of David (Ruth 4:20; 1 Chr. 2:10-11) and Jesus (Matt. 1:4; Luke 3:32).

NAHUM (Heb. *naḥûm;* Gk. *Naoúm)*

1. One of the 12 Minor Prophets, whose words are recorded in the book of Nahum. He was a native of Elkosh (Nah. 1:1), a village in southern Judah.

2. The father of Amos and son of Esli, listed among the ancestors of Jesus (Luke 3:25).

NAHUM (Heb. *naḥûm*), **BOOK OF**

The seventh book of the Minor Prophets. The heading indicates that Nahum is from Elkosh, a location not otherwise mentioned in the Bible. The time and location of Nahum's activity are not identified, but the date can be inferred as between the destruction of Thebes in 663 C.E. (3:8) and Nineveh in 612. Interpreters who understand the text as a prediction suggest various dates prior to the actual collapse of Nineveh, ranging from the reported reforms of Manasseh ca. 650 (2 Chr. 33:14-16), to the period after Assurbanipal's death ca. 630, to the months of the siege of Nineveh in 612. Interpreters who view the text as an explication of the significance of Nineveh's demise propose dates close to or shortly after the actual destruction. If Nineveh is viewed as paradigmatic of evil, the exact date is of less importance, thus permitting exilic and even postexilic dates.

The book of Nahum has been regarded as an example of self-serving, nationalistic prophecy. Interpreters have been uncomfortable with the lack of moral challenge directed toward Judah. Although the heading of the book labels Nineveh as the subject matter (1:1), Judah is addressed with words of assurance (v. 15[MT 2:1]). Judah's yoke and bond will be broken (1:13); the power of Assyria will come to an end (chs. 2-3). Hope can even be derived from the name of the prophet; Nahum means "comfort" or "consolation." The harsh words directed toward Assyria are, in fact, designed for Judean ears. Nahum offers refuge for Judah (1:7) and announces destruction for Assyria (2:10[11]). Nahum has been compared to false prophets like Hananiah (Jer. 28). More positive assessments of the book have tended to stress the cruel, violent character of Assyrian tactics and control; the demise of Assyria, so graphically depicted, is termed acceptable when viewed from the perspective of the victim, namely, Judah. The destruction of Assyria is necessary for the moral coherence of history.

Several recent interpretations have challenged the notion that Nahum is uncritically comforting. Marvin A. Sweeney has argued that Nahum opposes those who doubted God's capacity to deliver. The fall of Nineveh requires both Judeans and Assyrians to rethink their view of God's sovereignty. The central form of the book follows that of the "refutation pattern of the disputation speech." Judah and Assyria are addressed in the opening unit (1:2-10), Judah in the second (1:11-15[2:1]), and Assyria in the third (2:1[2]-3:19). Michael H. Floyd has suggested that Nahum was interrogating his Judean audience, accusing them of plotting against God. The question in 1:6 ("Who can stand before his indignation?") requires the answer that no one has the capacity to oppose God. The question in 1:9 ("Why do you plot against the Lord?") in effect argues that one should not oppose God because the consequences are disastrous. Floyd argues that 1:2-10 should not be understood as either acrostic in technique (e.g., too many letters are missing) or hymnic in character (e.g., hymns do not contain confrontative questions); rather these opening verses are best characterized as "prophetic interrogation."

These studies also indicate a shift toward a more unified reading of the book. The shifting gender of the 2nd person pronouns in 1:9-14 has often stood in the way of a unified reading. Many have concluded that the variation is the result of a complex redactional history, with independent units being conflated at various stages extending into the postexilic period. Sweeney directly argues for a literary coherence, and Bob Becking has argued for a conceptual coherence centered on the metaphor of the wrath of God, a protective refuge for the faithful and a definitive no to oppressive forces.

Nahum is not a facile word of comfort. The words are filled with a biblical memory that recollects Israel/Judah's own rebellious past (and likely future?). Judeans and subsequent readers are not invited simply to be cheerleaders at the scene of Nineveh's demise. This point is made directly by the latter part of 1:12: "Though I have afflicted you, I will afflict you no more." Nahum depicts the addressee as afflicted specifically by God. The hard words directed against Nineveh/Assyria are introduced by words that deeply position the Judeans as people who are also in a turbulent relationship with God. The Judean addressees have already experienced the indignation of God; they know better than anyone the heat of God's anger. The refuge provided by God is a refuge from the day of trouble, a day which God is initiating.

In addition, when read in the context of the larger canon, the hard words directed at Nineveh/Assyria have been or will be directed to Israel/Judah. This includes the most abrasive words in Nahum. Nah. 2:13[14] asserts: "I am against you [= Nineveh], says the Lord of hosts, and I will burn your chariots in smoke, and the sword shall devour your young lions" (cf. Ezek. 5:8; Amos 1-2; Jer. 21:5). The double-edged character of the threats extends to even the most gruesome images. Assyria/Nineveh will suffer what happen to Thebes: "She became an exile, she went into captivity; even her infants were dashed in pieces at the head of every street"(3:10; cf. Hos. 10:14-15). Compare the image of sexual violence directed against Nineveh (3:5) with that against Jerusalem (Jer. 13:26). The language of violence must be used cautiously, if at all, today, but it should be noted that what is directed against Nineveh/Assyria is remembered canonically as also directed against Israel and Judah.

Bibliography. B. Becking, "Divine Wrath and the Conceptual Coherence of the Book of Nahum," *SJOT* 9 (1995): 277-96; M. H. Floyd, "The Chimerical Acrostic of Nahum 1:2-10," *JBL* 113 (1994): 421-37; J. J. M. Roberts, *Nahum, Habakkuk, and Zephaniah.* OTL (Louisville, 1991); M. A. Sweeney, "Concerning the Structure and Generic Character of the Book of Nahum," *ZAW* 104 (1992): 364-77.

RICHARD NYSSE

NAIN (Gk. *Naín*)
A city in Galilee where Jesus raised from the dead a widow's only son (Luke 7:11-17). The site is modern Nein (183226), a small village on the slopes of Mt. Moreh (Nebi Dahi), 9 km. (5.5 mi.) SE of Nazareth. It overlooks the plain of Esdraelon, perhaps the reason it was named "lovely" (*Gen. Rab.* 98:12).

NAIOTH (Heb. *nāyôṯ*)
A place "in Ramah" to which David fled after escaping from Saul with the help of Michal (1 Sam. 19:18-24). David dwelt in Naioth with Samuel and a band of prophets. As Saul pursued David to Naioth, he was seized by an ecstatic frenzy and prophesied. David fled Naioth to meet Jonathan (1 Sam. 20:1). The repeated references to Naioth "in Ramah" indicates that Naioth is not a separate place name. Although its linguistic form is uncertain, Naioth should be related to Heb. *nāweh,* which is a shepherd's camp pitched outside a city. Such a camp was apparently also the dwelling of Samuel and his disciples.

RONALD A. SIMKINS

NAKEDNESS
Unlike contemporary English usage, nakedness in the Bible can refer to a range of undress from total nudity to being inadequately clothed (Job 22:6; Ezek. 18:7; Matt. 25:36; 2 Cor. 11:27). As in contemporary English usage, however, even the more literal uses of the Hebrew and Greek terms are loaded with figurative and symbolic meanings and allusions.

Although total nudity could be associated with the innocence of a newborn child (Job 1:21; cf. Gen. 2:25; Ezek. 16:7), it was most often a euphemism for sexual organs or sexual activity (Lev. 18:1-23; 20:10-21; Ezek. 16:8). This range of euphemistic meaning has complicated attempts to understand the precise nature of Ham's offense against Noah when he "saw his father's nakedness" (Gen. 9:22). Commentators have suggested that Ham may have taken the occasion of Noah's drunkenness to engage in either some form of sexual conduct with his father or an incestuous relationship with Noah's wife. More likely the phrase is to be understood quite literally in this instance (cf. Gen. 9:21, 23), and the severity of Noah's response relates to the affront to his dignity and Ham's disrespect.

Adam and Eve's own shame at the recognition of their nakedness in the wake of their disobedience (Gen. 3:7) is but one example of the fact that nakedness was associated with a variety of human conditions often considered shameful or humiliating (cf. Isa. 47:3). Nakedness symbolized adulterers (1 Sam. 20:30) and was often the defining characteristic in metaphors depicting those who rejected God as either adulterers or prostitutes (Lam. 1:8; Ezek. 16:36-37; Rev. 17:16). Nakedness in the sense of being inadequately clothed is one of several deprivations used to represent both poverty (Job 24:10; Isa. 58:7; Jas. 2:15) and oppression by one's enemies (Deut. 28:48; Rom. 8:35). Consequently it was often used as a figure of judgment against either Israel (Ezek. 23:29), the nations (Isa. 20:2-4), or even individuals (Hos. 2:3[MT 5]).

Nakedness was also associated with ecstatic spiritual states, both positively (1 Sam. 19:24; 2 Sam. 6:20-21) and negatively (Luke 8:27). The laws regarding the attire of priests and the construction of altars showed a particular concern that they avoid accidentally exposing themselves during the performance of their duties (Exod. 20:26; 28:42). Whether these laws were a direct reaction against aspects of Canaanite religious practice, as some have suggested, or reflected a more general taboo regarding nakedness is subject to debate.

TIMOTHY B. CARGAL

NAMES AND NAMING
When Shakespeare asserted that "a rose by any other name would smell as sweet" (*Romeo and Juliet* II.ii.43) he was emphatically not expressing an idea that had any warrant in the biblical world — or anywhere else in the ancient Near East. In the ancient world generally, a name was not merely a convenient collocation of sounds by which a person, place, or thing could be identified; rather, a name expressed something of the very essence of that which was being named. Hence, to know the name was to know something of the fundamental traits, nature, or destiny of that to which the name belonged.

In the Bible, this connection between the name and what is named is particularized in a number of different ways. For instance, a name may denote some feature considered fundamental to that which is being so designated — whether that feature is physical or something more abstract. Giving a town the name of Gibeah indicated that its physical positioning on a hill was probably deemed its most significant feature, since "hill" is precisely the Hebrew meaning of Gibeah (so too the name Gibeon). Similarly, the name Esau, meaning "hairy," is quite fitting for the firstborn son of Rebekah and Isaac, since what was most noticed about him, physically, was his hairy body (Gen. 25:25; cf. 27:11). In terms of more abstract features, a preeminent example is found in the person of Nabal; the name means "fool," and sure enough, as his wife points out, "folly is with him" (1 Sam. 25:25). Consider, too, the name Bethlehem, "house of bread"; the town so named likely has the reputation for the bountiful production of grain.

The practice of highlighting a significant feature by means of the name given to it is also found in those instances in which a person's name is that of a plant or animal. Presumably such a name is bestowed when the outstanding qualities of a particular plant or animal are also identifiable — or at least hoped for — in the person so named. Deborah means "bee," and the idea that bees are a busy and industrious insect certainly intersects with the many and varied positions this woman took on in her life (judge, prophetess, wife, mother, warrior, singer; cf. Judg. 4-5). Jonah means "dove," and, regarding the prophet who holds that name, the intention seems to be an ironic comment on that person's character; Jonah's life was actually far from being peaceful, a characteristic normally associated with the dove (esp. Jonah 1, 4).

A second particularity of the name-named connection, though relevant only for personal names, centers on the circumstances of a child's birth. Jacob comes out of the womb gripping his older twin brother's heel: Jacob means "heel-grabber" (Gen. 25:26). Here the birth circumstances (and the name) foreshadow the adult character of the person, as evident later both when Jacob steals the birthright that rightfully belongs to his older brother Esau (Gen. 27:1-45), and when he tricks his father-in-law Laban and so becomes extremely wealthy (30:25-43).

Sometimes the connection between the name and the circumstances of the child's birth has little actually to do with the child itself; instead, the name concerns itself more generally with the broader situation of the community into which the child has been born. Ichabod, which means "Where is the glory?" is the name given to a child born at the time of a great Israelite catastrophe: Israel's defeat at the hands of the Philistines, which resulted further in the loss of the ark of the covenant (Israel's "glory"; 1 Sam. 4:5-11, 19-22). When the prophet Hosea names his daughter Lo-rahama ("Not pitied"), it is done in order to signify the lack of pity that Yahweh now has towards the entire northern kingdom of Israel (Hos. 1:6).

A third way in which the connection between the name and the named is particularized focuses on the destiny of a person; here the name somehow presages that person's future. Jesus is the Greek form of the Hebrew name Joshua; its meaning is "savior," which Matt. 1:21 understands as an adumbration of the child's future task of saving his people from their sins (cf. Luke 1:31). Jesus' foremost disciple is named Peter, meaning "Rock," which alludes to this person's foundational role in the future establishment of the Christian Church (Matt. 16:18-19). Moses, which in Hebrew means "draw out," is a reference to this child's eventual task of drawing out his people from Egypt and leading them toward the Promised Land. Of course, the name may also relate to the circumstances of the child's birth, since by being drawn out of the Nile River Moses was saved from the annihilation that Pharaoh was visiting upon the Hebrew male babies at the time (Exod. 2:1-10). Thus a name can do double duty (cf. Jacob), referring both to the circumstances of the person's birth and that person's adult role.

Because a name is so inextricably bound to that which is named, if a change occurs in the conditions of a person or place, the name must also be altered so as to reflect the new and different situation. When Saul becomes a missionary to the Gentiles, his name becomes Paul, a Roman version of the Hebraic Saul; the name change befits his new vocation as evangelizer to the peoples of the wider Roman world (Acts 13:9). When Naomi returns to Bethlehem, having lost her husband and both her sons while in the foreign land of Moab, she asks that her name no longer be Naomi, which means "Pleasant"; instead, she wants to be known as Mara, "Bitter" (Ruth 1:20). Although a person rarely experiences more than one name change, place names in the Bible can be altered again and again, a consequence of their oftentimes longer, and hence more complex histories. The city known as Jerusalem, for instance, is also referred to by such names as Moriah, Jebus, Zion, Ariel, and City of David. Some of these name changes were provoked by political events, as when David, after conquering and claiming it as his own city, renamed it City of David (2 Sam. 5:6-9). Other times the reason for the name change is unrecorded, and so remains unknown (a feature more characteristic of place names than the names of persons).

Types of Names

Most of the names so far considered are of the simple type, i.e., they consist of one element (e.g., Nabal, "Fool"; Deborah, "Bee"). The other main type is the compound; in it two or more elements are combined, sometimes as a descriptive phrase (Obadiah, "servant of Yahweh"), but more often as a full sentence (Ichabod, "Where is the glory?"). Compound names quite often have some religious significance. Indeed, the vast majority of compound names are of the sort where one element is some form of the divine name (usually either El or Yah/Yahu [short for Yahweh]); the other part then offers some commentary on that divine name. Names of this sort are termed theophoric (Gk. "God-possessed"); they are relatively frequent in the OT, with ca. 135 compounded with the name El (e.g., Elimelech, "God [or 'My god'] is king"; Elisha, "God is salvation"; Elhanan, "God has been gracious"; Nathaniel, "God has given") and more than 150 compounded with the name Yah (e.g., Jehoshaphat, "Yahu has judged"; Jehonathan/Jonathan, "Yahu has given"; Yehoshua/Joshua, "Yahu is salvation"; Zechariah, "Yahu has remembered"). Note too the name Elijah, which combines both divine names into the statement "God (or 'My god') is Yah." Theophoric names can also appear in a shortened form, wherein the divine name is omitted (though implicitly understood); this shortened form is known as a hypocoristicon (e.g., Nathan, "[God/Yahu has] given"; Baruch [Baruchiah], "[Yahu has] blessed").

Name-givers

After being created, the first explicit task carried out by Adam is the naming of the animals (Gen. 2:19); Adam thereby becomes a participant in their very creation, since names call forth the true nature or essence of that which is named. From the very beginning of the Bible, then, humans are involved in naming, an endeavor that not only requires discernment, but also has the potential, if not actual, function of signaling the name-giver's authority over that which is named.

In the OT the name-givers of children are almost always their parents. However, the biblical couple rarely, if ever, works together on this task; naming is, instead, done by either one or the other parent so that naming is, in effect, a rather individualistic enterprise. Out of the ca. 46 accounts where the name-giver is specified, at least 25 involve mothers (e.g., Gen. 4:1, 25; 19:37-38; 30:6-24; 1 Sam. 1:20; 2 Sam. 12:24; 1 Chr. 4:9). Eighteen involve the father (e.g., Gen. 5:3, 29; 16:15; 35:18; 41:51-52; Exod. 18:3-4; 1 Chr. 7:23; Hos. 1:4-9). A very few involve a relationship other than that of the parent, as when Man names Woman (Gen. 2:23), Adam names Eve (3:20), and the women friends of Naomi name Ruth's child Obed (Ruth 4:17). That the majority of name-givers are women is attributable at least partly to the intimacy of the relationship between mothers and children in the latter's early years. This focus on females does not extend, however, to the recipients of the names: in the 46 naming accounts referred to above, only seven females are named; two of these accounts involve the "First Woman" (Gen. 2:23; 3:20). The naming of female children by their parents is recorded in only five instances in the OT, and only once does a mother name a daughter (Gen. 30:21).

In the OT children are named shortly after their birth. The NT records the practice of waiting eight days (at least for sons), so that naming occurs concurrently with circumcision (Luke 1:59; 2:21). Also evident in the NT is the practice of naming a boy after some male relative (also attested in other texts of the Second Temple period, e.g., Josephus, but generally not found in the OT). Finally, the NT, along with both the Apocrypha and the post-5th century B.C.E. OT texts, often demonstrates the assigning of both a Hebrew and a non-Hebrew name, a reflection of the diaspora situation in which the majority of Jews were then finding themselves (e.g., Hadassah/Esther, Esth. 2:7; Simon Peter, Matt. 4:18; Acts 10:5).

If names are so essential to personhood, what then of those persons who are without names? Anonymity can have an appreciable literary function, either by shifting attention towards the other characters of the narrative, or by throwing into sharper relief the role(s) assumed by the anonymous individual. Still, given the high value accorded to names in the biblical tradition, it is not surprising that many of the nameless persons of both the OT and NT have names bestowed upon them in the pseudepigraphal literature. Jubilees, in its commentary on Genesis and the first part of Exodus, assigns names to such nameless individuals as Noah's wife (Emzara), Pharaoh's daughter (Tharmuth), and the wife of Cain (Awan) — with the latter being explained as a daughter of Eve, though in the OT her origins are not identified. NT examples include the three magi who bring gifts to the child Jesus: nameless in the Gospel of Matthew, a text known as the Excerpta Latina Barbari (a Latin translation of a 6th-century Greek chronicle) identifies them as Balthasar, Melchior, and Gaspar.

Bibliography. G. B. Gray, *Studies in Hebrew Proper Names* (London, 1896); I. Ljung, "Women and Personal Names," in *Silence or Suppression: Attitudes Towards Women in the Old Testament.* Women in Religion 2 (Uppsala, 1989), 15-33; A. Reinhartz, "Anonymity and Character in the Books of Samuel," *Semeia* 63 (1993): 117-41; R. de Vaux, *Ancient Israel* (1961, repr. Grand Rapids, 1997), 43-46.

KARLA G. BOHMBACH

NANEA (Gk. *Nanaía*)

A Mesopotamian goddess whose temple Antiochus IV Epiphanes attempted to plunder, resulting in his death (2 Macc. 1:13-17). The temple of Nanea, located in Elymais (Elam), probably in the city of Susa, was famous for its wealth, including the golden shields, breastplates, and weapons deposited by Alexander (1 Macc. 6:1-2). In order to plunder the temple, Antiochus deceptively entered into a sacred marriage ritual with Nanea, hoping to claim the temple treasures as her dowry. However, the priests of Nanea trapped him and his men in the temple precinct, then stoned them through a secret opening in the ceiling.

Nanea, known as Nanâ and Nanay(a) in Mesopotamian sources, was primarily a goddess of erotic love. Originally at home in Uruk, in the 1st millennium B.C.E. she was associated with Borsippa and Babylon, where sacred marriage rituals were performed between her and Nabû. The Persians identified her with Anahita, and her cult was widely promoted by Artaxerxes II. She was a prominent member of the Aramean pantheon until the 5th century C.E. In addition to Susa, she had prominent temples at Assur, Palmyra, and Dura-Europos. The Greeks later identified her with Artemis, Aphrodite, and Isis.

The tradition of the death of Antiochus IV Epiphanes recorded in 2 Maccabees certainly reflects Antiochus' reputation for plundering temples (cf. 2 Macc. 9:1-2). However, the depiction of his death is probably confused with that of his predecessor Antiochus III, who according to other sources was similarly killed in an attempt to plunder a temple of Belus in Elymais.

RONALD A. SIMKINS

NAOMI (Heb. *noʿŏmî*)

A primary character in the symbol-laden book of Ruth; the mother-in-law of Ruth and Orpah, mother of Mahlon and Chilion, and wife of Elimelech.

Sojourning in the land of Moab, Naomi ("pleasant one") is left bereaving the deaths of her husband and her two sons. Accompanied by Ruth, she returns to her homeland, Bethlehem in Judah, where she renames herself Mara ("bitter"). Naomi frequently portrays the reversal of cultural norms: she lives in a foreign land; she insists that her daughters-in-law return to the house of their mothers; she returns to her homeland with her foreign daughter-in-law; she owns a parcel of land; and she sends Ruth to the threshing floor to solidify her relationship with Boaz. In a narrative full of contrasts and irony, Naomi is pivotal for the development of the plot. Naomi leaves Judah "full," with her entire family, and returns "empty," poor and without social status (Ruth 1:21). Naomi is an old Israelite; Ruth is a young Moabite. Naomi is poor; Boaz is wealthy. Naomi, after losing her sons, is too old to bear children; Ruth bears Obed ("restorer of life"), the grandfather of David, who, according to the women of Bethlehem, is the son of Naomi (4:17).

Bibliography. E. F. Campbell, Jr., *Ruth.* AB 7 (Garden City, 1975); D. N. Fewell and D. M. Gunn, *Compromising Redemption: Relating Characters in the Book of Ruth* (Louisville, 1990); J. M. Sasson, *Ruth,* 2nd ed. (Sheffield, 1979).

ALICE H. HUDIBURG

NAPHATH (Heb. *nāpeṯ*)
A village assigned to Manasseh, which they were unable to capture (Josh. 17:11). It is apparently to be distinguished from Dor and En-dor. The Hebrew text is obscure.

NAPHATH-DOR (Heb. *nāpaṯ dôr*),
NAPHOTH-DOR (Heb. *nāpôṯ dôr*)
A city in the territory of Manasseh that participated in the league of northern kings led by Jabin, king of Hazor (Josh. 11:2; Naphoth-dor). It is considered to be the same as Dor. Although the ruler of Dor was defeated by Joshua (Josh. 12:23), Manasseh apparently did not take possession of the city (17:11-12; Judg. 1:27) and no Israelite cities were established. David conquered Dor during his reign, and Solomon later appointed Ben-abinadab as its district governor (1 Kgs. 4:11). Dor is identified with modern Khirbet el-Burj (142224), 14.5 km. (9 mi.) N of Caesarea and 19 km. (12 mi.) S of Mt. Carmel.

STEPHEN VON WYRICK

NAPHISH (Heb. *nāpîš*)
A son of Ishmael (Gen. 25:15; 1 Chr. 1:31); ancestor of an Arabian tribe attacked by a coalition of Reubenites, Gadites, and the Transjordanian half-tribe of Manasseh (5:19).

NAPHTALI (Heb. *naptālî*)
The sixth son of Jacob, the second born by Bilhah, Rachel's handmaiden. His birth narrative is recorded in Gen. 30:1-8. Jacob's first four sons were born to him by Leah, and the barren Rachel was jealous. Rachel offered her servant Bilhah to Jacob as a wife; any children conceived would be "born upon Rachel's knees," an idiom for legal adoption. The name Naphtali in Hebrew means "my wrestling," a wordplay on Rachel's statement "with mighty wrestlings I have wrestled with my sister" (Gen. 30:8). The birth mother's status seems to contribute no inequalities within the tribal system. While some tribes of full descent (Simeon, Reuben) early lost significance, some "concubine" tribes such as Naphtali contributed leaders to Israel. When Jacob escaped famine in Egypt, Naphtali and his four sons accompanied him (Gen. 46:24-26; Exod. 1:4).

In the census taken in the second year after leaving Egypt, Naphtali's descendants totaled 53,400 men 20 years and older, able-bodied for war (Num. 1:42-43; 2:29-30). According to a second census for the apportionment of the land among the tribes, Naphtali totaled 45,400 (Num. 26:50).

The book of Judges records several narratives emphasizing military and leadership capabilities of Naphtali's tribe. During the settlement process, Naphtali did not drive out all Canaanite inhabitants, but pressed some into forced labor (Judg. 1:33). When Deborah led the Israelites against King Jabin of Canaan, the tribes of Naphtali and Zebulun were summoned for military duty with Barak, a Naphtalite from Kedesh, as military commander (Judg. 4:6-10). Gideon called Naphtali's forces against the Midianites and Amalekites (Judg. 6:35; 7:23).

The territory of Naphtali lay along the western shore of the Sea of Galilee and extended north; it touched the territory of Zebulun in the south, Asher on the west, with the Jordan River as its eastern boundary. No northern border is given (Josh. 19:34). Naphtali's region was mountainous and heavily forested; thus it was both aesthetically and politically attractive. Major trade routes connecting the port of Acco and the coastal plains with points north passed through this area, and it included many fortified towns (Josh. 19:35-38).

Naphtali was conquered by Ben-hadad of Syria ca. 900 B.C.E. (1 Kgs. 15:20 = 2 Chr. 16:4) and later annexed by Assyria (2 Kgs. 15:29).

Bibliography. Y. Aharoni, *The Land of the Bible,* 2nd ed. (Philadelphia, 1979); R. G. Boling, *Joshua.* AB 6 (Garden City, 1982); N. K. Gottwald, *The Tribes of Yahweh* (Maryknoll, 1979).

PATRICIA A. MACNICOLL

NAPHTHA (Gk. *náphtha*)
A flammable substance used to stoke the furnace into which Azariah/Abednego, Shadrach, and Meshach were thrown (Song of the Three 23); an ancient name for petroleum. It is described as a "thick liquid" (so NRSV) that caught fire after the sun shown on it, igniting Nehemiah's sacrifice (2 Macc. 1:20-22); accordingly, the term is linked with "purification" (v. 36, "nephthar"; cf. Num. 31:23).

NAPHTUHIM (Heb. *naptuḥîm*)
A descendant of Egypt (Mizraim) listed in the Table of Nations (Gen. 10:13 = 1 Chr. 1:11), perhaps indicating inhabitants of the Nile Delta (cf. Egyp. *na-patoḥ,* "dwellers of the Delta").

NARCISSUS (Gk. *Nárkissos*)
The head of a household in Rome of which some members were Christians. They are greeted by Paul in his Epistle to the Romans (Rom. 16:11).

NARD

An ointment (Heb. *nērd;* Gk. *nárdos*) extracted from the *Nardostachys jatamansi* plant found in the Himalayas of India. The distance required to import the ointment to Palestine added to its value. The roots and stems of the plant are used to produce an aromatic oil that serves as a cosmetic, a perfume (Cant. 1:12; 4:13-14), and a stimulant. This expensive ointment was often stored in alabaster boxes and opened only on special occasions, e.g., to anoint people of honor, as seen in the anointing of Jesus (Mark 14:3; John 12:3). Nard is often referred to as "spikenard" due to the shape of the plant. In the NT the Greek adj. *pistikós* means "genuine" or "pure," though often translated "spike" based upon a Sanskrit derivative. L. THOMAS STRONG, III

NASH PAPYRUS

A 2nd-century B.C.E Egyptian papyrus containing one of the oldest fragments of the biblical text. Described by Stanley A. Cook in 1903, the papyrus contains versions of the Decalogue and Shema which have textual affinities to the LXX. Probably copied from a liturgical work, the papyrus' affinities with the LXX and Philo, as well as the provenance of its discovery, suggest a form of the Hebrew text current in Egypt that differed significantly from the text later preserved by the Masoretes.

JAMES R. ADAIR, JR.

NATHAN (Heb. *nāṯān*)

1. A son of David by Bathshua (Bathsheba) daughter of Ammiel; full brother of Solomon (2 Sam. 5:14; 1 Chr. 3:5; 14:4). He is mentioned in an eschatological prophecy (Zech. 12:12), which may account for Luke's genealogy of Jesus through Nathan (Luke 3:31) rather than through Solomon (Matt. 1:6).

2. Prophet at the time of David. He arrives, with no pedigree of birthplace or genealogy, to mediate Yahweh's dynastic grant to David (2 Sam. 7:1-17 = 1 Chr. 17:1-15), confront David with his sin against Uriah (2 Sam. 12:1-25; cf. Ps. 51 superscription[MT 2]), and conspire with Bathsheba to convince David that he had sworn that Solomon would succeed him (1 Kgs. 1:1-40).

The dynastic grant (2 Sam. 7:1-17) is comprised of two literary sources, the History of David's Rise (7:1-7) and a Deuteronomistic addition (vv. 8-17). In ancient Near Eastern ideology, kingship was tied to temple-building; gods were represented as guaranteeing dynasties in return for the (re)building of temples. The aim of the History of David's Rise (1 Sam. 15–2 Sam. 8) was to establish David's kingship in place of Saul's dynasty by proving that Yahweh chose him. However, Yahweh's chosen one never built the expected temple. The explanation is that although David wished to build it, Yahweh forbade it, based on the precedent of the judges (2 Sam. 7:1-7).

More than three centuries later the Deuteronomist incorporated the History of David's Rise in a comprehensive history written in support of a reform that included an attempted restoration of the Davidic kingdom and centralization of all worship in the temple. An eternal Davidic dynasty established by Yahweh and closely tied to the temple was key to the reform; hence this addition (2 Sam. 7:8-17). The addition is integrated with the preexisting text by a wordplay between *bayiṯ*, "house," as "temple" (2 Sam. 7:1-7) and *bayiṯ*, "house," as "dynasty" (vv. 11b-16); the prophecy that David's son will build the temple and his throne will be established forever (v. 13) provides the missing symmetry between dynast and temple.

Nathan also mediates an oracle to David after his adultery with Bathsheba and murder of her husband Uriah (2 Sam. 12:1-25). Rather than confront the king directly, he leads David to convict himself by telling a juridical parable, a fictitious case that asks the king to pronounce judgment in his capacity as judge (2 Sam. 12:1-4; cf. 14:1-20; 1 Kgs. 20:35-43). The story of the rich man with many flocks and herds who takes the poor man's beloved lamb to prepare a meal for a traveler provokes David's rage and prompts him to declare the offender a dead man (2 Sam. 12:5-6). When Nathan delivers the punch line, "That man is you!" (2 Sam. 12:7a), David repents and is spared the death penalty, which is transferred to the child who is the product of the adultery (vv. 13-23). Without the intervening judgment (2 Sam. 12:7b-12), there is a clear connection between the death sentence that David unwittingly passes on himself and its transference to his child. The intervening judgment is redundant, since the redirection of David's murder and adultery against himself creates a duplicate sentence. The interpolation was added by the author of Solomon's Succession Narrative (2 Sam. 10–12; 1 Kgs. 1–2) to magnify David's crimes and to connect them to the story of Absalom's revolt (2 Sam. 9, 13-20; cf. esp. 16:20-22). By inserting the David and Bathsheba story near the beginning of the revolt account, David's enhanced adultery and murder are made to appear the cause of Amnon's rape of Tamar, Absalom's murder of Amnon, and Absalom's revolt. In contrast, Solomon's ruthless consolidation measures appear necessary to restore order (1 Kgs. 2).

In 1 Kgs. 1:1-40 Nathan is not a mediator of Yahweh's word, but a court prophet embroiled in a conspiracy. An aged David's lack of intimacy with the exceedingly beautiful Abishag indicates that the succession is imminent (1 Kgs. 1:1-4). As the eldest, Adonijah presumes that he will be the successor, and holds a sacrificial feast that Nathan intentionally or unintentionally misinterprets as a coronation feast (1 Kgs. 1:5-10). Since the court has split into Adonijah and Solomon factions, Nathan enlists Bathsheba's help in a plot. He persuades her to "remind" David that he had sworn that Solomon would succeed him, and Nathan then corroborates her words (1 Kgs. 1:11-27). The scheme works because of David's faulty memory, and David directs Nathan and Zadok to anoint Solomon (1 Kgs. 1:28-40). This account by Solomon's historian acknowledges a palace coup while asserting the legality of Solomon's succession (cf. Gen. 27).

3. The father of Igal, one of David's elite 30 warriors (2 Sam. 23:36; 1 Chr. 11:38).

4. The father of Azariah and Zabud, two of Solomon's officers (1 Kgs. 4:5).

5. A Judahite in the line of Jerahmeel; son of Attai and father of Zabad (1 Chr. 2:36).

6. One of those sent by Ezra to Iddo to bring back Levites (Ezra 8:16). He may be the same as Nathan, a descendant of Binnui, who divorced his foreign wife (Ezra 10:39).

Bibliography. P. K. McCarter, *II Samuel*. AB 9 (Garden City, 1984); J. W. Flanagan, "Court History or Succession Document? A Study of 2 Samuel 9-20 and 1 Kings 1–2," *JBL* 91 (1972): 172-81.

MARSHA WHITE

NATHANAEL (Gk. *Nathanaḗl*)

1. An ancestor of Judith (Jdt. 8:1).

2. A priest ordered to divorce his non-Israelite wife (1 Esdr. 9:22).

3. An Israelite mentioned only in the first and last chapters of the Gospel of John. Introduced to Jesus by Philip, he acknowledges Jesus as the Son of God and King of Israel (John 1:45-49); Jesus calls him "truly an Israelite in whom is no deceit" (v. 47). His presence with other disciples at the Sea of Galilee after Jesus' resurrection suggests that he was one of the Twelve (John 21:2). Some have identified him with Bartholomew, in part because Bartholomew means "son of Ptolemy," which would imply that he had another name. Also, Nathanael does not appear in the Synoptic accounts nor is Bartholomew mentioned in John.

JOE E. LUNCEFORD

NATHAN-MELECH (Heb. *nĕṯan-meleḵ*)

A chamberlain or eunuch (Heb. *sārîs,* from Akk. *ša rēši,* "at the head [of the king]") at the time of Josiah's reforms. Josiah removed the horses which earlier kings had dedicated to the sun-god Šamaš, which were quartered near Nathan-melech's room at the temple entrance (2 Kgs. 23:11).

ROBIN GALLAHER BRANCH

NATIONS

In the OT the concept of "nation" (usually Heb. *gôy;* LXX Gk. *éthnos*) included at least four components: (1) a related group of people (2) living in its own territory (3) with its own government and (4) worshipping its own god or gods. Consequently, Israel and other groups could be nations. "People" (Heb. *ʿam;* LXX *laós*) was a more general term with no particular political significance, though the two terms could be used as synonyms (Exod. 33:13; Deut. 4:6). The NT seems to maintain the distinction of the terms *éthnos* and *laós.* The words *gôy* and *éthnos* also meant "Gentiles," and only context establishes the correct meaning.

The political meaning of "nations" is clear in several well-known passages. The Table of Nations (Gen. 10:1-32) depicts humanity already divided into nations, not as a unity. The people of Israel appealed to Samuel to find them a king "like other nations" (1 Sam. 8:5). On the day of Pentecost "Jews from every nation under heaven" were present in Jerusalem (Acts 2:5).

The Hebrew prophets in particular spoke of specific nations as deserving future punishment: e.g., Edom, Ammon, and Moab (Amos 1:11–2:3); Babylonia, Assyria, and Egypt (Isa. 13–14, 19). However, in places eschatological speculation about the elevation of Israel also took note of the "nations" almost as a foil for the special attention Israel would receive (e.g., Zech. 14).

PAUL L. REDDITT

NATURE

For the larger part of the 20th century biblical scholars gave little attention to the role of the natural world in the Bible. They emphasized instead that the Bible presented a God who acted in and for human history. Yahweh was unlike the gods of Mesopotamia, Egypt, and Canaan, who were bound by the endless and unchanging cycles of nature. Nature was regarded as the stage for Yahweh's historical drama of salvation or as Yahweh's instrument in that drama, but the natural world was not deemed significant in its own right.

Interest in the Bible's view of nature has intensified in recent decades due largely to the public's growing environmental awareness. The claim by many that the Bible's objectification of nature was the foundation for our exploitation of the natural environment led many scholars to reassess the biblical view of nature. By first giving attention to the biblical understanding of creation, scholars have begun to recognize that the Bible contains multiple views of nature and that the natural world played a significant role in the formation and expression of the religion of Israel. The various biblical views of nature can be grouped into three distinct value orientations, shared by the people of the Bible, but expressed under different circumstances: harmony with nature, mastery over nature, and subjugation to nature.

Harmony with nature is the most frequently expressed value in the biblical texts. This value orientation assumes that humans and nature are united in a precarious balance so that human actions cause consequences in nature which inevitably affect humans themselves. In texts reflecting the covenant tradition, the condition of the natural world is linked to the people's faithfulness to the stipulations of the covenant. If the Israelites follow God's commandments, then Yahweh will send the rains so that the land abundantly yields its produce. Otherwise, God will withhold the rains and the land will become desolate, resulting in the people's death (Deut. 11:13-17). The prophets similarly link human actions to the environment. Both Hosea and Jeremiah attribute drought to the people's crimes against one another and against God (Hos. 4:1-3; Jer. 3:1-3). Haggai blames drought on the people's dereliction to rebuild Yahweh's temple (Hag. 1:9-10). Second Isaiah offers the eschatological hope that Yahweh will redeem the natural world even as the people are redeemed (Isa. 51:3).

In the Yahwist Creation myth (Gen. 2:4b–3:24)

the first human is described as being born from the earth, made of the dirt of the ground, and returning to the earth when he dies. Although the account expresses the harmony-with-nature value, it qualifies it with the mastery-over-nature value. The acquisition of knowledge has freed the human couple from the determinism of nature. They are distinct from the animals, which are also made from the dirt, and can transform the natural world to create civilization (Gen. 4). Yet in the end humans are bound to the natural world of which they are a part.

The Priestly Creation myth (Gen. 1:1–2:3) is the foremost biblical example of the mastery-over-nature value orientation — that nature can and should be manipulated for human purposes. According to the account, humans are commanded to subdue the earth and are given dominion over all other creatures (Gen. 1:28). However, within the larger context of the Priestly narrative this mastery-over-nature value is qualified by the harmony-with-nature value, which emphasizes the order of creation. Human dominion must be exercised within the constraints of the created order lest human actions corrupt the creation (Gen. 6:11-13). As a result, only certain animals are acceptable for food (Lev. 11), men are limited with whom and when they may have sexual relations (18:6-23), and the land may not be farmed in Sabbatical Years (25:1-12).

The mastery-over-nature value is also expressed by the cosmic metaphors of Jerusalem's royal ideology. According to this ideology, human kingship replicates divine kingship. The king's reign in Jerusalem was based on a manifestation of Yahweh's reign over creation. Therefore, just as Yahweh defeated all threats to the created order — typically personified as the sea (Ps. 89:9-11[MT 10-12]; 93) — the king secures the order of creation by defeating his enemies (89:22-25[23-26]). The king's actions are world-ordering, bringing righteousness — fertility and abundance — to the land (Ps. 72). Yet the king's mastery over nature is not absolute. It is only by virtue of God's covenant, bestowed upon him as a gift, and should be characterized by God's righteousness.

Subjugation to nature — that humans have no control over nature and are subject to its inevitable effects — was probably the dominant value orientation of the ancient Israelite peasants. However, the biblical texts, which come from elite groups, only sporadically reflect this value. The book of Job is a notable exception. Contrary to covenant theology, Job emphasizes that there is no necessary correlation between human actions and the condition of the creation. Moreover, the speeches of Yahweh (Job 38–41) underscore the inability of humans to either control or replicate the creation.

Joel also expresses the subjugation-to-nature value. The prophet calls the people to lament the devastation caused by a locust plague, but unlike other prophets does not attribute the natural catastrophe to the people's sins. The people's actions are not responsible for the plague, nor can they prevent it. Their only hope of deliverance is God, and thus Joel summons them to return to Yahweh with fasting, weeping, and mourning (Joel 2:12-14).

As a result of the recent scholarly attention to the Bible's view of nature, God's presence and activity in the world can no longer be understood in historical categories and metaphors exclusively. The Bible attests that God's activity is visible also in the cycles of nature, in blessing. As the Creator, God brings the advent of seasonal rains, makes the land agriculturally productive, and increases the reproduction of flocks and herds. The Bible usually links God's presence to natural locations — predominantly mountain tops, but also springs, rivers, and trees. Moreover, God's appearance in theophany is often presented in natural form: God is associated with the thunderstorm and the related phenomena of downpours, clouds, and lightning; the voice of God shakes the earth like an earthquake (or the rumbling of thunder); and God appears in a burning bush and a pillar of cloud and fire.

Bibliography. B. W. Anderson, *From Creation to New Creation.* OBT (Minneapolis, 1994); T. Hiebert, *The Yahwist's Landscape* (Oxford, 1996); R. A. Simkins, *Creator and Creation: Nature in the Worldview of Ancient Israel* (Peabody, 1994); O. H. Steck, *World and Environment* (Nashville, 1980).

RONALD A. SIMKINS

NAVE

The main room of the temple (Heb. *hêḵal*), between the vestibule and the holy of holies (1 Kgs. 6; 7:50; 2 Chr. 3:4-5, 13; 4:22; Ezek. 41). The Hebrew term can refer to either this room or the entire temple (cf. Sum. *e-gal,* "great house").

NAZARENE

A gentilic (Gk. *Nazarēnós, Nazōraíos*) normally used to distinguish someone from the city of Nazareth. In the NT "Nazarene" is used most frequently to clarify the identity of Jesus by associating him with his hometown of Nazareth (Mark 10:47; John 18:7). In the early history of the Church, the term took on a further connotation and referred by extension to Jesus' followers, who were called "the sect of the Nazarenes" (Acts 24:5).

A difficult use of *Nazōraíos* appears in Matt. 2:23, which states that the family of Jesus settled in Nazareth as a fulfillment of the prophetic teaching that he would be called a Nazarene. The problem is that no OT passage explicitly connects the Messiah with Nazareth. Apparently, Matthew was referring rather to the general expectation of the prophets that the Messiah would be despised and rejected (Ps. 22:6-8[MT 7-9]; 118:22; Isa. 49:7; 53:2-3). Jesus' association with Nazareth, a despised city (John 1:46), caused him to be scorned by some (cf. John 7:41-42, 52). Elsewhere in his Gospel, Matthew quotes the OT to emphasize this theme of Jesus as a humble Messiah, rejected by his people (Matt. 12:16-21; 13:13-15; 21:42; 27:39-44).

Bibliography. W. F. Albright, "The Names 'Nazareth' and 'Nazoraean,'" *JBL* 65 (1946): 397-401; R. T. France, "The Formula-Quotations of Matthew

2 and the Problem of Communication," *NTS* 27 (1981): 233-51. JOEL F. WILLIAMS

NAZARETH (Gk. *Nazarét, Nazaréth*)
A city in central Galilee located on a ridge overlooking the Jezreel Valley to the south and the Beth-neṭofa Valley (Sahl el-Baṭṭof) to the north (170234). There are no literary references to Nazareth prior to the NT, and Josephus never mentions the site. Variant spellings in the Greek NT (Matt. 4:13; Luke 4:16 read *Nazará;* all others read *Nazaréth* or *Nazarét*) and the Greek manuscript traditions accentuate its relative anonymity prior to Christendom. At the time of Jesus, Nazareth was an obscure village S of Sepphoris. Excavations under several churches and convents have found dwellings dug into bedrock and around caves. Silos, olive and wine presses, as well as storage jar receptacles are indicative of the village's agricultural base. Evidence for a necropolis helps determine the extent of the 1st-century ruins, which correlate to a population of well under 500. Nathanael's exclamation in John 1:46, "Can anything good come out of Nazareth?" aptly symbolizes the town's obscurity in the 1st century. In the NT Nazareth is at times referred to as a city (Gk. *pólis;* e.g., Matt. 2:23), but this can hardly be taken in the proper technical sense. According to Luke 2:4-5 Nazareth was the hometown of both Mary and Joseph (Matt. 2 seems to imply it was Bethlehem). It was considered Jesus' hometown (Matt. 13:54; Mark 6:1; Luke 4:16), from which he departed to Capernaum at the beginning of his ministry (Matt. 4:13). The Gospels concur that Jesus' ministry was less than successful in Nazareth, precisely because it was his hometown (Matt. 13:54-58; Mark 6:1-6; Luke 4:16-30). Jesus is often referred to as "the Nazarene" (Mark 1:24; 10:46; John 18:5, 7; Acts 2:22; 3:6), and in Acts 24:5 his followers are even called "Nazarenes," with no apparent connection to the Nazirites.

A 3rd-century C.E. synagogue mosaic inscription from Caesarea locates one of the Jewish priestly courses at Nazareth after the destruction of the temple. It is doubtful that a priestly connection can be retrojected into the 1st century, but it does indicate that Nazareth was acceptable for Jewish priests to settle. Nazareth did not rise to prominence among Christian pilgrims until the late Byzantine period, when Christian building projects began, many of which still leave their mark on the modern city, such as the Church of St. Joseph and the Church of the Annunciation.

Bibliography. B. Bagatti, *Excavations at Nazareth I* (Jerusalem, 1969); E. M. Meyers and J. F. Strange, *Archaeology, the Rabbis, and Early Christianity* (Nashville, 1981); J. E. Taylor, *Christians and the Holy Places* (Oxford, 1993).

JONATHAN L. REED

NAZIRITE (Heb. *nāzîr*)
Men or women who consecrated themselves to God for a specific time by a special vow (Num. 6:1-21). During the period of consecration, Nazirites had to abstain from alcoholic drink and leave their hair uncut. Their special status as "holy to the Lord" also required that they be especially careful to avoid contact with a corpse even if a member of their family died during the time their vow was in force (Num. 6:6-7). Both deliberate and accidental contact with a corpse nullified the time served in compliance with the vow. Special sacrifices had to be offered and the period of consecration begun anew (Num. 6:9-12). After the completion of the vow, special offerings had to be made including the cutting of the hair and burning it with an offering for well-being (Num. 6:13-20). The exacting regulations that circumscribed the period of Nazirite service underscore the seriousness of this state.

The law in Numbers implies that living as a Nazirite was a matter of personal choice. In other OT texts this is not as clear. Samson was consecrated as a Nazirite while still in his mother's womb (Judg. 13:4-14), and Samuel's mother made the consecration for him (1 Sam. 1:11). Amos 2:11 implies that living as a Nazirite was a divine charism rather than a personal choice. Apparently, at one time Nazirites were a charismatic group like early prophetic circles. Later individuals might choose to live like these Nazirites for a time, and Num. 6 served to regulate this practice. This practice continued into the 1st century A.D. Acts 18:18; 21:20-26 imply that Paul participated in the rituals connected with the conclusion of Nazirite observance. Matt. 2:23 may allude to the Nazirite status and may imply that Jesus, like Samson and Samuel, was a consecrated person.

The Bible does not explicitly state the reasons for becoming a Nazirite. Abstaining from alcoholic drink recalls the Rechabites of Jer. 35:1-11. Their abstinence is explicitly related to the rejection of a settled existence that made viticulture possible. Though the Heb. *nāzîr* usually means "consecrated person," Lev. 25:5 uses it to mean "untrimmed vine." Perhaps the Nazirite lifestyle is a protest against the cultivation of grapes for use in the production of wine. The reason for allowing the hair to grow without cutting is unclear. Other religious traditions entail specific renunciations and the following of certain disciplines for those who seek a specially close relationship with God. The Nazirite vow may be an ancient Israelite example of this pattern.

LESLIE J. HOPPE

NAZOREANS, GOSPEL OF THE
A Jewish-Christian apocryphal Gospel, written in Hebrew or Aramaic in Palestine ca. 100-150 C.E. It was apparently known and used by Hegesippus (ca. 110-180), Eusebius (ca. 260-340), Jerome (ca. 342-420), and the Nazoreans, an early Jewish Christian sect who lived in Beroea. Quotations from this Gospel are also found in the Latin translation of Origen's commentary on Matthew and in the marginal notations of five medieval manuscripts of the NT that refer to *To Ioudaïkon,* "The Jewish (Gospel)."

According to Jerome, the Gospel of the Nazoreans was present in the library of Caesarea which Pamphilus had collected. Jerome himself received permission from the Nazoreans of Beroea to make a copy of their version of it. Eusebius, who speaks of the Gospel in "Hebrew letters," apparently also had access to the Gospel in the library of Caesarea.

The contents of the Gospel are not fully known, but they may be inferred from its extant fragments as including the baptism of John, the temptation of Jesus, the Sermon on the Mount, the ministry of Jesus (miracles, parables, various narratives and sayings), the sending out of the Twelve, Peter's confession at Caesarea Philippi, predictions of the Passion, Peter's denial at the trial, the Crucifixion, and burial.

Although the Gospel of the Nazoreans is closely associated with Matthew, its accounts of the rich young man (Matt. 19:16-24) and the parable of the talents (25:14-30) are sufficiently different from Matthew to suggest a separate origin from the canonical Gospel. Both Gospels appear to come from a common environment in which traditions used by one were also used by the other.

Bibliography. R. Cameron, ed., *The Other Gospels* (Philadelphia, 1982), 97-106; J. K. Elliott, "The Gospel of the Nazaraeans," in *The Apocryphal New Testament,* rev. ed. (Oxford, 1993), 10-14; A. F. J. Klijn, *Jewish-Christian Gospel Tradition.* VCSup 17 (Leiden, 1992); Klijn and G. J. Reinink, *Patristic Evidence for Jewish-Christian Sects.* NovTSup 36 (Leiden, 1973); P. Vielhauer, "The Gospel of the Nazaraeans," in *New Testament Apocrypha,* ed. E. Hennecke-W. Schneemelcher, 1 (Philadelphia, 1963), 139-53. GEORGE HOWARD

NEAH (Heb. *nēʿâ*)
A city on the northeastern boundary of Zebulun, located somewhere between Rimmon and Hannathon (Josh. 19:13). The city may be the Noa mentioned on Samarian pottery fragments dating from the time of King Ahab.

NEAPOLIS (Gk. *Neápolis*)
The seaport of Philippi located 16 km. (10 mi.) SE of Philippi on an inclined strip of land that extended to the Aegean Sea with a harbor on both sides. Neapolis ("new city") was controlled by various empires throughout its history. During the Byzantine era it was called Christoupolis (modern Kavalla). Archaeological discoveries include an aqueduct, remnants of a Hellenistic village, and a sanctuary of the goddess Parthenos, the chief deity of Neapolis. Some Latin inscriptions have confirmed Neapolis' military and economic dependence on Philippi during the Roman era and that Neapolis was the residence of some prominent people of Philippi.

Following his Macedonian dream, Paul left Troas for Europe. Neapolis was the first city he visited there (Acts 16:11). Paul again traveled through Neapolis on his third missionary journey (cf. Acts 20:6). STEVEN L. COX

NEARIAH (Heb. *nĕʿaryâ*)
1. A descendant of Solomon; the son of Shemaiah and father of Elioenai, Hizkiah, and Azrikam (1 Chr. 3:22-23).

2. One of the four sons of Ishi who led 500 Simeonites in driving out the remnant of Amalekites from Mt. Seir (1 Chr. 4:42-43).

NEBAI (Heb. **Q** *nêḇāy*)
One of the "leaders of the people" who set his seal to the new covenant under Nehemiah (Neh. 10:19[MT 20]; **K** *nôḇāy*).

NEBAIOTH (Heb. *nĕḇāyôṯ, nĕḇāyōṯ*)
The first son of Ishmael (Gen. 25:13; 28:9; 36:3; 1 Chr. 1:29). Isaiah (Isa. 60:7) names him as eponymous ancestor of a people paired with the north Arabian descendants of Kedar. Assyrian documents name them, along with Kedar, among northern Arabs that were defeated by Tiglath-pileser III. Recent scholarship discounts any connection with the later Nabateans (Arab. *Nabaṭ*) for linguistic and historical reasons. W. CREIGHTON MARLOWE

NEBALLAT (Heb. *nĕḇallaṭ*)
A city in which the Benjaminites settled following the Exile (Neh. 11:34). It has been identified with modern Beit Nabala (146154), 32 km. (20 mi.) W of Hazor and 7 km. (4.3 mi.) NE of Lod.

NEBAT (Heb. *nĕḇāṭ*)
The father of Jeroboam I; an Ephraimite from Zereda (1 Kgs. 11:26). The appellative "son of Nebat" occurs frequently in the OT to distinguish between Jeroboam I and Jeroboam II, the son of Joash.

NEBO (Heb. *nĕḇô;* Akk. *nabû*) **(DEITY)**
One of two principal gods of the Babylonian pantheon. The name is found as early as the early 2nd millennium B.C., but Nebo worship began its ascendancy ca. 925 and was at its peak in Babylon by the 7th century, roughly the time of Isaiah. As son of Marduk, Nebo was considered to be the keeper of the tablets of the gods, and thus a scribe. As such he had access to secrets that others who could not read did not, granting him wisdom, and so he could control religious rites. He wrote down the decisions of the gods and kept accounts of human dealings, especially on his "tablet of life" and "tablet of destiny" (cf. Exod. 32:32-33; Ps. 69:28[MT 29]; Rev. 20:12, 15). Isa. 46:1 depicts Nebo, with Bel, being carried in the New Year procession, unable to help his people (in contrast to the God of Israel).
MICHAEL D. HILDENBRAND

NEBO (Heb. *nĕḇô*) **(PLACE)**
1. A town which was taken from the Amorite king Sihon and allotted to the tribe of Reuben (Num. 32:3; 37–38). The Reubenites rebuilt it at some point (1 Chr. 5:8), but later lost it to the Moabites under Mesha (Mesha stela 14-18). Its destruction is recorded in Isa. 15:2; Jer. 48:1, 22. This town is usually connected with the Iron Age site of Khirbet el-Mekhayyat (221131) on the southern peak of Mukhayyat, 8 km. (5 mi.) SW of Heshbon.

2. A town in western Palestine, settled in the postexilic period (Ezra 2:29 = Neh. 7:33). It is usually identified with Nûbā (153112), 5 km. (3 mi.) NW of Beth-zur. PAUL J. RAY, JR.

NEBO (Heb. *nĕḇô*), **MOUNT**

The mountain on which Moses died and was buried, following his preview of the Promised Land (Deut. 32:49-52; 34:1-8). The area is also claimed by the two and one half Transjordanian tribes (Num. 32:3). The name Nebo appears to refer to the Mesopotamian deity Nabû, or may rather be cognate to a Semitic root implying height.

Mt. Nebo is located in west Jordan, ancient Moab, near the Dead Sea, ca. 19 km. (12 mi.) E of the Jordan River's mouth. About 3 km. (2 mi.) SE of the summit lies the ancient town of Nebo (**1**), modern Khirbet el-Mekhayyat (221131), a city which prospered in the Iron I-II periods, exemplified by its inclusion in the Moabite Stone. Mt. Nebo (Jebel en-Nebā) is part of the Abarim range mentioned in Num. 33:47, with its peak resting 835 m. (2740 ft.) above sea level and 1247 m. (4030 ft.) above the Dead Sea. Consequently, the mountain's summit offers a spectacular view of Israel.

MICHAEL M. HOMAN

NEBUCHADNEZZAR (Heb. *nĕḇûḵaḏne'ṣṣar*), **NEBUCHADREZZAR** (*nĕḇûḵaḏre'ṣṣar*)

King of Babylon for 43 years (605-562 B.C.E.), more than any other monarch of the Chaldean dynasty. He succeeded his father Nabopolassar (Akk. *Nabû-apla-uṣur*), who founded the dynasty. Nebuchadnezzar II (Akk. *Nabû-kudurri-uṣur*) had considerable prior military experience, having campaigned against the Egyptian armies just south of Carchemish and won an important victory. Shortly thereafter, he received word of his father's death and hastened to Babylon to claim the throne. For ca. the next three years, he waged war in Syria and exacted tribute from a number of cities, including Damascus. He then campaigned against the forces of Neco II (610-595) of Egypt and in Arabia, where he appears to have had successes. By March 597 he was in Palestine, where he besieged Jerusalem and placed a certain Zedekiah, the uncle of the former ruler of Judah, Jehoiachim, on the throne. According to Josephus' *Antiquities,* Nebuchadnezzar returned to besiege Jerusalem a second time in 586. The book of Jeremiah states that this campaign resulted in the taking of the city, the destruction of Solomon's temple, and the deportation of the Hebrews into captivity (which was to last until 538). Unfortunately, no contemporary cuneiform account of this event is known to exist, since the Babylonian Chronicle is incomplete after 594. Such is also the case with the accounts of campaigns against Tyre and Egypt referred to in Josephus; however, it is likely that they did occur. The king died in 562 and was succeeded by his son, Amel-marduk (OT Evil-merodach), who is said to have released Jehoiachin, former king of Judah (Jer. 52:31) and to have provided him with an allowance.

When Nebuchadnezzar gained the throne in Babylon, he faced several challenges. Although Babylon had been rebuilt by the Assyrian king Esarhaddon (681-669), it was not suited to be the headquarters of an imperial administrative bureaucracy. In order to restore Marduk to supremacy as "king of the gods," his temple, the Esagila, and the ziggurat Etemenanki (the biblical tower of Babel) had to be restored and fortified. Furthermore, as recorded in inscriptions, Nebuchadnezzar had to build a royal residence of his own. Excavations by Robert Koldewey and his successors have revealed remains of no fewer than five walls, with three comprising an outer ring and two an inner rampart, built of both sun-dried and baked bricks and of varying degrees of thickness. Projecting towers were at spaced intervals, and the entire city was surrounded by a moat. Although Nebuchadnezzar at first lived in his father's palace, he later built a residence of his own to the west of it. As the political situation became more stable, he also built the so-called Summer Palace in the part of the city still carrying the name Babil. The Southern Palace was the most important, not only because of its size but because it was located near the Ishtar gate and the "Processional Way." Lavish materials were used in construction of the palace, including cedar, ivory, gold, silver, and lapis lazuli.

Attending to the traditional responsibility of Babylonian kings, Nebuchadnezzar repaired temple sanctuaries and restored divine images. He oversaw construction work in no fewer than 12 cities throughout the realm. He also refurbished the Esagila and Ezida (the temple of Nabû), and supposedly created the Hanging Gardens, which later Greek writers regarded as one of the seven wonders of the ancient world. Unfortunately, Koldewey turned up little or no evidence of work on these temples, nor is there any trace of the Etemenanki or the ziggurat north of the Esagila. However, excavations by Iraqi archaeologists have yielded traces of an elevation on the north side of the city that may support Nebuchadnezzar's reputation.

Even though contemporary cuneiform sources are incomplete or, in some instances, silent on the extent of his achievements and activities, Nebuchadnezzar's name occurs in more secondary sources for the Chaldean period than that of any other member of his dynasty. Apart from Jeremiah, 2 Kings, 2 Chronicles, and Daniel of the OT, he appears in no fewer than 10 rabbinic commentaries, six books of the Apocrypha, several Arabic commentaries, and in the extant writings of classical and medieval Greek and Latin authors. Some of these, most notably Berossus' *Babyloniaca,* stress his building activities throughout Babylonia. Since the Greek mind clearly idolized the monumental, it should be no surprise to see Nebuchadnezzar's name associated with some structure of enduring quality, such as the fortification walls around Babylon or the ziggurat of Marduk itself. Writers such as Megasthenes characterize his achievements as the result of Marduk giving the king the ability to create something of eternal greatness, while authors such as Strabo and Diodorus Siculus speak to his achievements as if they were the creation of some superhuman figure who was god or godlike.

Conversely, Hebrew writers had to preserve an image of a conqueror-king who captured the city of Jerusalem, dismantled the temple of Solomon, and deported captives back to Babylonia. All of these acts could not be construed positively. Destruction and wickedness had to be emphasized, as seen in the didactic message of the book of Daniel. To better strengthen his point, the OT author liberally drew from the sources for the reign of Nabonidus (556-539), who had not only introduced the worship of the god Sin of Harran into Babylonia but also forsook his kingdom for a campaign to the Arabian oasis of Tema. What resulted from this distortion of historical accuracy was a picture of a Babylonian monarch whose deeds could be applied to any later king who accomplished the same things. The concrete became subordinate to the abstract, and Nebuchadnezzar's "character" could be applied to virtually any period of history.

Bibliography. R. H. Sack, *Images of Nebuchadnezzar* (Cranbury, N.J., 1991); D. J. Wiseman, *Chronicles of Chaldean Kings* (1961, repr. London, 1974); *Nebuchadrezzar and Babylon* (Oxford, 1985).

RONALD H. SACK

NEBUSHAZBAN (Heb. *nĕḇûšazbān*)
The Rabsaris, or chief eunuch, of Nebuchadnezzar, dispatched by the Babylonian king to protect Jeremiah after the fall of Jerusalem (Jer. 39:13; Akk. *Nabû-šûzibanni,* "Nabû save me").

NEBUZARADAN (Heb. *nĕḇûzar'ăḏān;* Akk. *Nabû-zer-iddinam*)
The "chief cook" mentioned in a list of high officials of Nebuchadnezzar II of Babylon (605-562 B.C.; *ANET,* 307-8). He is also noted in the biblical account of the fall of Jerusalem as commanding the forces of the Babylonian king. The title chief cook, like that of chief cupbearer, was an archaic term for those in high positions in Assyrian and Babylonian courts. They were often sent on military and diplomatic missions (cf. the Rabshekah, 2 Kgs. 18:17). Nebuzaradan ("Nabu has given me offspring") was responsible for the destruction of the city of Jerusalem, for sending Judahite officials to be executed (2 Kgs. 25:8-12, 18-21), and for the deportation of a number of the Judahites a few years later (ca. 582; Jer. 52.24-30). He was also given orders to release the prophet Jeremiah (Jer. 39:11-14; 40:1-6; 43:6). Because of invoking the name of the Lord when speaking to Jeremiah, Nebuzaradan was considered a convert in later Jewish tradition (cf. Jer. 40:2-6).

MARK W. CHAVALAS

NECO (Heb. *nĕḵōh, nĕḵô;* Egyp. *nk'w*) (also NECHO)
Neco II (610-594 B.C.E.), king of the 26th (Saite) dynasty of Egypt. In 609 Neco (also Necho) led his army north through Palestine and Syria to aid the Assyrian army in their desperate stand at Harran against the Babylonians under Nabopolassar. Josiah, king of Judah, engaged the Egyptian force at the Megiddo pass (Wadi ʿAra) to stop, or at least slow, the march of the Egyptian troops. In the battle Josiah was mortally wounded and his army routed (2 Kgs. 23:28-30; LXX 4 Kgs. 23:29-30; 2 Chr. 35:20-25; compare MT 2 Chr. 35:20-27; 1 Esdr. 1:25-31, which confuse this battle with a later one at Carchemish). Neco was not able to prevent the fall of the Assyrians but did claim suzerainty over Palestine and Syria. He deposed Jehoahaz and took him to Egypt, placing on the throne of Jerusalem Eliakim, son of Josiah, who changed his name to Jehoiakim (2 Kgs. 23:31-35).

In 605 Neco and his army engaged in battle against Nebuchadnezzar, the Babylonian crown prince, at Carchemish (Jer. 46:2; Josephus *Ant.* 10.6). The Egyptians were soundly defeated and driven back to their borders. In 601 Neco had to defend his country against the incursions of Nebuchadnezzar. Both armies suffered heavy losses, and Nebuchadnezzar was forced to withdraw. There is no other mention of Neco in the historical records.

Bibliography. A. Gardiner, *Egypt of the Pharaohs* (Oxford, 1961); D. J. Wiseman, *Chronicles of Chaldaean Kings (626-552 B.C.)* (1956, repr. London, 1974); *Nebuchadrezzar and Babylon* (Oxford, 1985).

LAWRENCE A. SINCLAIR

NECROMANCY
See MEDIUM, WIZARD.

NEDEBIAH (Heb. *nĕḏaḇyâ*)
The seventh son of King Jeconiah/Jehoiachin (1 Chr. 3:18).

NEEDLE
A slender implement, sharp at one end, with an eye for thread or a leather thong. Archaeologists have found needles of bone, ivory, bronze, and iron throughout the ancient world, some dating back to the 6th millennium B.C.E. Skill in embroidery was considered a gift from God and was used in the making of the tabernacle (Exod. 31:6-10). Indeed, the difficulty involved in sewing in biblical times was one of the factors in the popularity of tunics as the common style of clothing for men and women — they involved few seams and little sewing. When necessary, Paul supported himself as a tentmaker, which involved sewing strips of cloth together (Acts 18:3).

The use of needles is implied when Adam and Eve "sewed fig leaves together" (Gen. 3:7). The word "needle" appears only in Matt. 19:24 (= Mark 10:25; Luke 18:25). Matthew and Mark use Gk. *rhaphís,* a sewing needle, while Luke uses *belónē.* Some have speculated that Luke's choice reflects his medical background, and that a *belónē* was a surgical needle, but there is no clear evidence for this idea. In all three Gospel accounts, the eye of a needle, one of the smallest openings common to the household, is contrasted with a camel, one of the largest animals commonly seen in Palestine. Early interpreters contended that the "eye of a needle" was the name of a narrow gate in Jerusalem, but this view is no longer accepted. Such an interpretation would not explain the disciples' conclusion that salvation is impossible; the expression is simply a typical oriental hyperbole used to communicate the great difficulty faced by those who are rich in leaving all to follow Christ. JOHN S. HAMMETT

NEGEB (Heb. *negeḇ*)
The southern area of ancient Palestine. Unlike the biblical term (apparently from the Semitic root "dry") the modern designation "Negev" refers to the southern half of the modern state of Israel — from Beer-sheba southward to the Gulf of Aqaba. Only the northern portion of this region was extensively settled in biblical times; therefore the biblical term essentially refers to the Beer-sheba drainage basin.

The environment of the Beer-sheba region consists of a semi-desert environment with an average annual rainfall of 200 mm. (7.9 in.), which allows for only subsistence agriculture. This region included urban centers, fortresses, and village settlements throughout most of the biblical era. Archaeologists have uncovered numerous Chalcolithic and Early Bronze Age sites, leading many to argue that the Negeb must have had a significantly wetter climate prior to ca. 2500. South of the Beer-sheba basin lies the Negeb "highlands." Here, annual rainfall ranges from 150–50 mm. (5.9–2 in.). This is below the minimum necessary for agriculture. The settlements in this area were associated primarily with forts or caravansaries to protect the trade routes. Two commodities in particular played a role in the highlands trade: copper and incense/spices.

The Patriarchs, whom many would place in the Middle Bronze Age, are reported to have sojourned in the Beer-sheba area. While MB remains have been uncovered at other Negeb sites, Beer-sheba has yet to reveal any significant MB remains. The wilderness wanderings center around the oasis of Kadesh-barnea, which lies on the western edge of the Negeb highlands. The Hebrews are also reported to have fought the Canaanites at Arad and Hormah (Num. 21:1-3; 33:40; Josh. 12:14). However, there has been little evidence found of any LB settlement in either the Beer-sheba basin or in the highlands; in the south, 13th-century copper mines have been excavated at Timna.

With the monarchy, Negeb activity increased. Saul and David fought the Amalekites (1 Sam. 14–15; 30), and Solomon established a naval outpost at Ezion-geber (1 Kgs. 9:26). In the 8th century, Uzziah reinvigorated the Negeb, reestablishing the Ezion-geber trade. Transshipment of copper and other goods from Ezion-geber required the establishment of royal forts to safeguard the routes (2 Chr. 26:10). A latter 7th-century building boom can be attributed to either Manasseh or Josiah. In its final years, Judah increasingly lost control over the Negeb to the Edomites. Edomite names, ostraca, and cult sites appear throughout the Negeb (e.g., Qitmit).

Archaeological evidence from the Persian and Hellenistic period is almost totally absent. Written sources discuss the presence of the Nabateans, but few remains of these tent-dwelling people have been found. By the turn of the eras, the Nabateans had come into their own as spice traders and merchants. The Petra-ʿAvdat-Gaza road was built, along with caravansaries to guard the frankincense and myrrh route. Nabatean cities and forts were constructed, trade flourished, and agricultural projects were even introduced. Ultimately, the Romans annexed the Negeb and its highlands to Palestina Tertia. In the Byzantine era, the area experienced its greatest flowering. Cities expanded, churches were built, monasteries founded, and settlement increased.

Bibliography. Y. Aharoni, "The Negeb and the Southern Borders," in *The World History of the Jewish People,* 4/1: *The Age of the Monarchies: Political History,* ed. A. Malamat (Jerusalem, 1979), 290-307; J. R. Bartlett, *Edom and the Edomites.* JSOTSup 77 (Sheffield, 1989); I. Beit-Arieh, ed., *Horvat Qitmit: An Edomite Shrine in the Biblical Negev* (Tel Aviv, 1995); R. Cohen, "Negev: Hellenistic, Roman, and Byzantine Sites in the Negev Hills," in *NEAEHL* 3:1135-45; "Negev: Middle Bronze Age I and Iron Age II Sites in the Negev Hills," in *NEAEHL* 3:1123-33; "Negev: The Persian to Byzantine Periods," in *NEAEHL* 3:1133-35; N. Glueck, *Rivers in the Desert,* rev. ed. (Philadelphia, 1968). LYNN TATUM

NEHELAM (Heb. *hanneḥĕlāmî*)
"The Nehelamite," an appellative of the false prophet Shemaiah who opposed Jeremiah (Jer. 29:24, 31-32). The term, otherwise unattested, may indicate either a family name or a location (NRSV "of Nehelam"). Another suggestion is that it represents a wordplay on Heb. *ḥālam,* "dream," and so means "Shemaiah the dreamer."

NEHEMIAH (Heb. *nĕḥemyâ*)

1. A leader of the Israelites, who returned with Zerubbabel from captivity in 538 B.C.E. (Ezra 2:2; Neh. 7:7).

2. The son of Hacaliah (Neh. 1:1); postexilic governor of Jerusalem, whose public ministry is recorded in the book of Nehemiah.

3. The son of Azbuk, ruler of half the district of Beth-zur, who helped repair the walls of Jerusalem (Neh. 3:16).

NEHEMIAH (Heb. *nĕḥemyâ*), **BOOK OF**
The second part of Ezra-Nehemiah recording the events of Nehemiah's governorship. In English versions it is a separate book.

Name and Canonical Setting

That Ezra-Nehemiah was originally a single work called Ezra is indicated by the earliest manuscripts of the LXX (Vaticanus, Sinaiticus, Alexandrinus) that treat the two books as one, calling them Esdras B, and the Masoretic annotations that deal with both books but occur only at the end of Nehemiah. The division into two books first appears with Origen (3rd century C.E.) and Jerome's Vulgate (4th century), which refers to Nehemiah as *liber secundus Esdrae.* In Hebrew Bibles there is no separation before 1448 C.E. While the Hebrew canon assigns Nehemiah to its third division, the Writings, and places it after Ezra but before Chronicles, the Alexandrian Greek canon, which forms the basis for our modern English sequence, places Nehemiah among the historical books following Chronicles. Frequently, the apocryphal book 1 Esdras appears between Chronicles and Ezra-Nehemiah.

Authorship

Vigorous debate concerning the authorship of Chronicles, Ezra, and Nehemiah continues to rage. The older consensus position that all three were the work of "the Chronicler" was based upon four arguments: 1) the repetition of the first verses of Ezra at the end of 2 Chronicles; 2) the evidence of 1 Esdras, which begins with 2 Chr. 35–36 and continues through Ezra including Neh. 7:73(MT 72)–8:13a; 3) linguistic similarity; and 4) similarity of theological conception. Recently, a growing number of scholars have been convinced that while the first three arguments are inconclusive on the matter of authorship, research on the fourth has yielded at least four areas of differing theological conception: 1) the emphasis upon David and the Davidic covenant, so prominent in Chronicles, is lacking in Ezra-Nehemiah; 2) the exodus traditions, so prominent in Ezra-Nehemiah, are virtually ignored in Chronicles; 3) Ezra-Nehemiah's negative stance against marriages with foreigners is difficult to explain in light of the tolerant attitude expressed towards Solomon's mixed marriages in 2 Chronicles; and 4) Chronicles' pervasive use of immediate retribution as a theological lodestone is absent in Ezra-Nehemiah.

Date and Place of Composition

Widely varying dates have been proposed for the final form of Ezra-Nehemiah, due in large measure to the variety of positions held regarding the extent, authorship, and compositional theory of this material, as well as conflicting chronologies reconstructed from Josephus. Recent scholarly opinion seems to favor a date of ca. 400 B.C.E. The first quarter of the 4th century has also been suggested to account for the occurrence of "Johanan," the last-mentioned high priest, who held office until 410, and "Darius the Persian" (Darius II, 425-405) in Neh. 12:22. While the dating of these books remains an open question, there is a strong consensus that Jerusalem, or at least Palestine, is the place of composition.

Sources

The frequent switch between 1st person and 3rd person speech is but one indication that a variety of sources have been utilized in the composition of Nehemiah. Chief among these is the so-called Nehemiah Memoir, a 1st person, autobiographical narrative that presents Nehemiah's own interpretation of the early events of his career. There is widespread scholarly agreement that the Memoir consists of Neh. 1–7; parts of 12:27-43; and 13:4-31, with the understanding that the lists contained in ch. 3 (a list of those involved in building the wall) and 7:5b-73a(72a) (a list of those returning from exile virtually identical with Ezra 2), while originally compiled by others, were included by Nehemiah in the Memoir. More controversial is the material contained in Neh. 5 (esp. vv. 14-19) which interrupts the flow of the wall-building narrative that is the Memoir's primary concern and seems to come from a later period; 11:1-2, which reports the completion of Nehemiah's plan to repopulate Jerusalem initiated in ch. 7; and 12:31-43, which describes the joyous dedication of the wall.

Extensive debate concerning the genre of the Nehemiah Memoir continues in the scholarly literature. Royal inscriptions, votive inscriptions (cf. the repeated requests that Nehemiah be "remembered": 5:19; 6:14; 13:14, 22, 29, 31), Egyptian tomb inscriptions, Solomon's poems, prayers of the unjustly accused, and justifications of one's activities before the king have all been suggested as possible parallels, though none of these suggestions has gained widespread support. Even the title "Memoir" has been challenged on the grounds that it assumes Nehemiah is the author of the work and that it is essentially an autobiographical piece. The lack of agreement regarding the form of the passage, however, should not deceive us into thinking it is without structure. On the contrary, the first section of the Memoir (1:1–7:3) is carefully arranged, falling into an extensive concentric agreement punctuated by seven similarly introduced episodes of opposition:

The History of Nehemiah (1:1–7:3)

A Hanani's report, Nehemiah to rebuild Jerusalem (1:1–2:8)
B Letters to governors vouch for Nehemiah (2:9)
C Opposition (2:10)
D Inspection by night, reproach of Jerusalem (2:11-18)
E Opposition, Geshem charges sedition (2:19-20)
F Wall building (3:1-32)
G Opposition (4:1[3:33])
H Ridicule (4:2-3[3:34-35])
I Prayer (4:4-5[3:36-37])
J Wall "joined" to half its height (4:6[3:38])
J′ Opposition "joined together" (4:7-8[1-2])
I′ Prayer (4:9[3])
H′ Ridicule's effect (4:10-14[4-8])
G′ Opposition (4:15[9])
F′ Wall building with defense (4:16-23[10-17])
[Problems of Nehemiah's second period (5:1-19)]
E′ Opposition, Geshem charges sedition (6:1-9)
D′ Nehemiah: threats by night, reproach (6:10-14)
C′ Opposition (6:15-16)
B′ Letters to Tobiah defame Nehemiah (6:17-19)
A′ Hanani placed in charge of rebuilt Jerusalem (7:1-3)

Other sources, probably documents from the temple archives and related to Neh. 3:1-32; 7:6-73(72); 11:1-2; 12:31-43, have also been detected in various passages: 1) Neh. 9:38; 10:28-39(10:1, 29-40), the people's resolution to abide by the stipulations of God's law; 2) 10:1-27(2-28), the list of those who signed the previous resolution; 3) 11:4b-20, the residents of Jerusalem; and 4) 13:1-3, a description of the people's banishment of all those of mixed descent from Israel. Two lists, 11:21-36 (listing the residents of Benjamin and Judah), and 12:1-26 (listing priests and Levites from several different periods) are best seen as much later additions to the book. It is unclear whether the 3rd person portions of the so-called Ezra Memoir (cf. Ezra 7:1–9:15) that appear in Neh. 8; 9:1-5 derive from the final redactor or some other source.

The Order of the Reformers

The traditional view holds that Ezra arrived in Jerusalem in 458, in the "seventh year of King Artaxerxes" (Ezra 7:7) and that Nehemiah followed him in 445, in the "20th year" of Artaxerxes (Neh. 1:1; 2:1; 5:14). Several anomalies arise from this reading of the material, however. Chief among them are the troubling gap of 13 years between Ezra's arrival and his reading of the Law in Neh. 8:1-8 and Nehemiah's apparent ignorance of Ezra's work. Confusion increases with the realization that there were three Persian kings named Artaxerxes: I, Longimanus (465-424); II, Mnemon (404-359); and III, Ochus (359-338).

As early as 1890 Albin van Hoonacker suggested that Ezra's Artaxerxes was Artaxerxes II. By assigning the "seventh year of Artaxerxes" to Artaxerxes II he arrived at a date of 398 for Ezra's arrival in Jerusalem. This resulted in the reversal of the order of the reformers, a denial that they were contemporaries, and the deletion of those verses that speak of both reformers together (Neh. 8:9; 12:26, 36).

An intermediate position associated with John Bright and Wilhelm Rudolph seeks to preserve the contemporaneity of the reformers by placing Ezra after Nehemiah in the reign of Artaxerxes I. This is accomplished by emending the text of Ezra 7:7 from the "seventh year of Artaxerxes" to the "27th/37th year of Artaxerxes (I)." On this reading, Ezra would have arrived in Jerusalem after Nehemiah in either 438 or 428. Richard J. Saley's tentative suggestion that we place Nehemiah in the reign of Artaxerxes II has not enjoyed much support.

Virtually all agree that Nehemiah came to Jerusalem under the auspices of Artaxerxes I. Among the late 5th-century Aramaic papyri discovered at Elephantine is a letter to the governor of Judah complaining that Johanan the high priest in Jerusalem has ignored the request for help in temple rebuilding. This must be the Johanan mentioned in Neh. 12:22. Sanballat, the governor of Samaria and Nehemiah's primary nemesis (cf. 2:9-10), is also mentioned in conjunction with his sons, who appear to be governing in his stead. If Sanballat is governor in name only in 407, this serves as a confirmation of Nehemiah's description of his old enemy in his prime (445), during the reign of Artaxerxes I. It is unlikely that agreement will be reached about Ezra's dates without further discoveries.

Nehemiah, the Person

Nehemiah (Heb. "Yahweh comforts") was a governor of Judah during the Persian period (mid-5th century), best known for overseeing the rebuilding of the walls of Jerusalem. What we know of Nehemiah's activities comes from the 1st person Nehemiah Memoir, which forms the basic source for the book of Nehemiah. Prior to his governorship, Nehemiah was a high ranking official in the court of Artaxerxes I (465-424). When Nehemiah heard of the ruinous state of Jerusalem's defenses and the deplorable conditions suffered by his fellow Jews in Palestine at the hands of their neighbors, he was moved to petition his God and then his king for help (Neh. 1–2). This resulted in credentials, monetary support, and a 12-year political appointment as governor (445-433).

Nehemiah's major achievement is the refortification of Jerusalem despite the threats, intrigues, and plots of the surrounding governors: Sanballat of Samaria, Tobiah the Ammonite, and Geshem the Arab, who unjustly accused him of sedition (chs. 2, 4, 6). Josephus reports that the reconstruction took almost two years and four months (*Ant.* 11.5.8), though the text of Nehemiah claims the project was completed in a remarkable 52 days (6:15).

Nehemiah was also responsible for a series of social and religious reforms. Poor harvests and the usurious practices of the upper classes at the expense of the less fortunate led to serious economic difficulties among the community during his tenure as governor, including the enslavement of children (5:1-5). Nehemiah's capable leadership and unselfish example led to the restoration of decency (5:6-16). The resettlement of a representative tithe of the outlying population solved the defensive problem of an underpopulated Jerusalem and illustrates the administrative ingenuity of the reformer (7:4-5; 11:1-2), while the joyous dedication of the walls indicates that the governor was keenly aware of the importance of morale (12:27-43). Following a brief absence, Nehemiah carried out a series of reforms having to do with the misuse of the temple (13:4-9), financial support of the Levites (vv. 10-14), observance of the sabbath regulations (vv. 15-22), and the dissolution of mixed marriages (vv. 23-27).

Bibliography. J. Blenkinsopp, *Ezra-Nehemiah.* OTL (Philadelphia, 1988); T. C. Eskenazi, *In an Age of Prose: A Literary Approach to Ezra-Nehemiah.* SBLMS 36 (Atlanta, 1988); K. G. Hoglund, *Achaemenid Imperial Administration in Syria-Palestine and the Missions of Ezra and Nehemiah.* SBLDS 125 (Atlanta, 1992); M. A. Throntveit, *Ezra-Nehemiah.* Interpretation (Louisville, 1992); H. G. M. Williamson, *Ezra, Nehemiah.* WBC (Waco, 1985).

Mark A. Throntveit

NEHUM (Heb. *nĕḥûm*)
One of the leaders who returned with Zerubbabel from captivity in Babylon (Neh. 7:7). The name should probably read Rehum (**1**), as at Ezra 2:2.

NEHUSHTA (Heb. *nĕḥuštā'*)
The daughter of Elnathan of Jerusalem; wife of Jehoiakim and mother of Jehoiachin, kings of Judah (2 Kgs. 24:8). She was taken captive to Babylon by Nebuchadnezzar in 598/597 B.C.E. (2 Kgs. 24:12, 15; Jer. 13:18; 29:2).

NEHUSHTAN (Heb. *nĕḥuštān*)
A proper name or a pun based on Heb. *nĕḥōšeṯ*, "bronze/copper," and *nāḥāš*, "serpent" (i.e., "only a bit of brass"; cf. Heb. "serpent of bronze," Num. 21:9). Such crafted creatures were common in the ancient Near East. During Hezekiah's reforms aimed at the removal of idolatry from Judah (2 Kgs. 18:4), this appellation was applied to the bronze serpent made by Moses during Israel's wilderness wanderings, which ministered divine healing when gazed upon by anyone with a deadly snake bite (Num. 21:4-9; cf. 1 Cor. 10:9-11). Righteous King Hezekiah smashed this serpentine statue because it was being worshipped as a god with offerings from the people of Israel (2 Kgs. 18:1-4; cf. 17:35-40). A question is whether the final phrase in 2 Kgs. 18:4 (*wayyiqrā'-lô nĕḥuštān*) means this title was the popular, pre-existing name for the idol ("Now it was called Nehushtan") or was provided contemptuously at that point by Hezekiah ("Now he [Hezekiah] called/named it Nehushtan"). Some suggest the term sounds like the Hebrew for "unclean thing."

Bibliography. K. R. Joines, "The Bronze Serpent in the Israelite Cult," *JBL* 87 (1968): 245-56; *Serpent Symbolism in the Old Testament* (Haddonfield, N.J., 1974); J. A. Montgomery, "Hebraica," *JAOS* 58 (1938): 131. W. CREIGHTON MARLOWE

NEIEL (Heb. *nĕ'î'ēl*)
A border city in the tribal territory of Asher (Josh. 19:27), called Inhi in the Egyptian text of Seth. The city has been identified as Khirbet Ya'nîn (171255), 3 km. (2 mi.) N of Cabul on the edge of the plain of Acco. The site has yielded remains from the Bronze and Iron Ages.

NEIGHBOR
The word usually translated "neighbor" in the OT (Heb. *rē'â*) is from the verb *r'h*, "to associate with." The word therefore describes a relationship, although the nature of this relationship varies with the context. A "neighbor" may simply be another person (Gen. 11:3), friend (or co-conspirator, 2 Sam. 13:3), an apparent rival (1 Sam. 28:17), lover (Jer. 3:1), or spouse (v. 20). Usually, the word does not describe one's immediate family (however, cf. Jer. 9:4) but someone who lives or works nearby (Prov. 3:29).

In many instances the word acquires the specific meaning "fellow Israelite" or "member of the covenant" (Jer. 31:34). This is especially the case in texts where mutual responsibilities, both positive and negative, are described. Israelites are not to bear false witness (Exod. 20:16; Deut. 5:20; cf. Ps. 101:5) or covet their neighbor's house, wife, slave, ox, donkey, or any other possession (Exod. 20:17; Deut. 5:21). They are not to defraud their neighbor, steal from their neighbor, or keep a laborer's wages until morning (Lev. 19:13). In general, one is to do no evil to a neighbor (Ps. 15:3).

In fact, Israelites are to do certain things for their neighbors. They are to judge their neighbors justly (Lev. 19:15) and love their neighbors as themselves (v. 18). It should be noted that the responsibilities listed in Lev. 19 are extended to include the resident alien in Israel as well (vv. 33-34).

In the NT the love for one's neighbor is an important concept; the majority of appearances of the word "neighbor" in the NT (Gk. *plēsíon*) are quotations of Lev. 19:18. Jesus quotes this verse as the commandment second only to "Love the Lord your God" (Mark 10:17-31; Matt. 19:16-30). In Luke this is amplified by the question, "And who is my neighbor?" (Luke 10:29). The story of the good Samaritan follows, in which Jesus shows that being a neighbor by showing mercy is more important than determining just who is a neighbor. Jesus also shows that we are to love more than only our neighbors (Matt. 5:43-44).

Other uses of "neighbor" in the NT reveal that the earlier denotation of close association is still at work. Although Jesus seems to apply the word "neighbor" to any and all, other NT passages suggest that "neighbor" is restricted, or perhaps applies primarily, to fellow Christians (Rom. 15:2; Eph. 4:25; Jas. 2:8). MICHAEL B. COMPTON

NEKODA (Heb. *neqôḏā'*)

1. The head or founder of a family of temple servants who returned with Zerubbabel from captivity in Babylon (Ezra 2:48 = Neh. 7:50).

2. The head of a family who returned from Exile but were unable to prove their Israelite ancestry (Ezra 2:60 = Neh. 7:62).

NEMUEL (Heb. *nĕmû'ēl*) (also JEMUEL)

1. A Reubenite; the elder brother of Dathan and Abiram, who sided with Korah against Moses and Aaron (Num. 26:9).

2. A Simeonite, eponymous ancestor of the Nemuelites (Num. 26:12; 1 Chr. 4:24). At Gen. 46:10; Exod. 6:15 he is called Jemuel.

NEPHEG (Heb. *nepeg*)

1. A Levite, son of Izhar and brother of Korah and Zichri (Exod. 6:21).

2. One of the 13 sons of David born in Jerusalem (2 Sam. 5:15; 1 Chr. 3:7; 14:6).

NEPHILIM (Heb. *nĕp̱îlîm*)
The offspring of heavenly beings ("sons of God"; cf. Job 1:6; 2:1; Ps. 29:1; 82:6) who had sexual relations with human women ("daughters of men"; Gen. 6:1-4). Since the boundary between the divine realm and the earthly was not supposed to be crossed in this way, this was the final abomination that led to God's decision to destroy the Nephilim and all people in the Flood (Gen. 6:3, 5-7).

Prior to the conquest of Canaan Israelite spies reported that there was a gigantic race of people,

Nephilim, living in the land of Canaan (Num. 13:33). These people seem to be survivors of the Flood (cf. Gen. 6:4), but there is no explanation of how they survived the disaster. Perhaps there were two conflicting traditions, one in which the Nephilim perished in the Flood and another in which they survived and settled in Canaan. Alternatively, it may be that the giants in the Promised Land came to be called Nephilim by analogy with the earlier race of mighty heroes.

Bibliography. R. S. Hendel, "Of Demigods and the Deluge: Toward an Interpretation of Genesis 6:1-4," *JBL* 106 (1987): 13-26; "When the Sons of God Cavorted with the Daughters of Men," *BibRev* 3/2 (1987): 8-13, 37. WILLIAM B. NELSON, JR.

NEPHISIM (Heb. K *nĕp̄îsîm*) (also NEPHUSHESIM)
The head of a family of temple servants who returned with Zerubbabel from captivity (Ezra 2:50; **Q** *nĕp̄ûsîm*). In the parallel list at Neh. 7:52 he is called Nephushesim.

NEPHTHAR (Gk. *néphthar*)
See NAPHTHA.

NEPHTOAH (Heb. *nep̄tôaḥ*)**, WATERS OF**
A named spring on the border between Judah and Benjamin (Josh. 15:9; 18:15). The site is identified as modern Liftā/Me Neftoah (168133), ca. 5 km. (3 mi.) NW of Jersualem. Some have connected the naming of this spring with Pharaoh Merenptah (whose name is nearly identical with the Hebrew phrase). If that is the case, the site is mentioned in the Egyptian Papyrus Anastasi (13th century B.C.; *ANET*, 258). DENNIS M. SWANSON

NEPHUSHESHIM (Heb. K *nĕp̄ûšĕsîm*)
The ancestor of a group of temple servants; alternate form of Nephisim (Neh. 7:52; **Q** *nĕp̄îšĕsîm*).

NER (Heb. *nēr*)
A Benjaminite, the son of Abiel and father of Abner (1 Sam. 14:50-51). Nothing is known of his life, and his relationship to Saul is unclear. It is uncertain whether "Saul's uncle" in 1 Sam. 14:50 refers to Ner or Abner. Ner is called the brother of Kish and son of Jeiel at 1 Chr. 9:36. Elsewhere he appears as the father of Kish (2 Chr. 8:33; 9:39). Josephus (*Ant.* 6.130) considers Ner to be the uncle of Saul and the brother of Kish. KENNETH ATKINSON

NEREUS (Gk. *Nēreús*)
A Christian in Rome to whom Paul sent his greetings (Rom. 16:15). Scholars variously identify him as the son of Philologus or the brother of Philologus and Julia.

NERGAL (Heb. *nērgal*)
The Babylonian god of the netherworld, worshipped by peoples resettled in Samaria after its fall in 722 B.C.E. (2 Kgs. 17:30). The name is a transliteration of Sum. [E]N.ER[I].GAL, lit., "lord of the big city" (i.e., the underworld). His cult was centered in Kutha (biblical Cuth), 32 km. (20 mi.) NE of Babylon. The Akkadians identified Nergal with their underworld deity Erra, and by the 1st millennium the two were synonymous. The West Semitic peoples later identified him with Resheph. Nergal was associated with pestilence, drought, famine, fire, and sudden death. Thus, he was called upon by Assyrian and Babylonian kings to aid in their foreign campaigns. MARK ANTHONY PHELPS

NERGAL-SHAREZER (Heb. *nērgal šar-'eṣer*)
Successor to Amel-marduk (OT Evil-merodach) as king of Babylon in 560 B.C.E., ruling until April 556. The earliest known mention of Nergal-sharezer (Akk. *Nergal-šarra-uṣur,* Classical *Neriglissar*) occurs in a contract dated in the ninth year of Nebuchadnezzar. Our present evidence suggests that he was a member of a prominent family known for its business activities in northern Babylonia and was well advanced in age when he became king. According to Berossus *Babyloniaca,* he seized the throne through a coup d'etat which resulted in the assassination of his predecessor. Berossus also claims that Nergal-sharezer was Amel-marduk's brother-in-law, although no cuneiform text definitely confirming this relationship has yet been produced. Nergal-sharezer seemingly formed an alliance with the *šatammu* of the Ezida temple in Borsippa, Nabû-šuma-ukin, and requested the hand of the king's daughter, Gigitum, in marriage before the end of his accession year. He was also long involved with the Ebabbar temple in Sippar and its important personnel, and seemingly interfered in the affairs of the Eanna temple in Uruk by replacing officials with individuals of his own choosing.

Formulaic royal inscriptions indicate that Nergal-sharezer restored the Esagila and Ezida temples in Babylon and Borsippa, repaired a palace on the bank of the Euphrates for his own use, and worked on some of Babylon's canals. He also conducted a campaign into southeast Anatolia during the third year of his reign, which resulted in the defeat of the state of Pirindu and its ruler, a certain Appuašu. Nergal-sharezer died in 556, probably only two months after returning home from his campaign into Cilicia. He was succeeded by his son Labaši-marduk, who reigned about two months before being dethroned by Nabonidus.

In Jer. 39:3 Nergal-sharezer is connected with the fall of Jerusalem (also Josephus *Antiquities*) and the release of Jeremiah. There seems to be little, if any, doubt about the connection between the Nergal-šarra-uṣur of the cuneiform sources and the Nergal-sharezer of Jer. 39. The mention of Nergal-sharezer as the prince of Sin-magir in Jer. 39:3, 13 represents, most likely, a misinterpretation or misunderstanding of a title designating a Babylonian administrative official long known from cuneiform temple records in Babylonia.

Bibliography. R. H. Sack, "Nergal-šarra-uṣur, King of Babylon, as Seen in the Cuneiform, Greek, Latin and Hebrew Sources," *ZA* 68 (1978): 129-49;

Neriglissar, King of Babylon. AOAT 236 (Neukirchen-Vluyn, 1994). RONALD H. SACK

NERI (Gk. *Nērí*)
The father of Shealtiel in Luke's genealogy of Jesus (Luke 3:27).

NERIAH (Heb. *nērîyâ;* Gk. *Nḗrias*)
The son of Mahseiah (Jer. 32:12); father of Jeremiah's scribe Baruch (v. 16; 36:4, 8; 43:3; 45:1; Bar. 1:1) and the prophet's quartermaster Seraiah (Jer. 51:59).

NERO (Lat. *Nero*)
The fifth Roman emperor and the last from the family of the Caesars. Born L. Domitius Ahenobarbus during the reign of his uncle the emperor Gaius (Caligula), as the son of Agrippina, great-granddaughter of Augustus, he was adopted by his mother's uncle and husband, the emperor Claudius, and received the name Nero Claudius Caesar Germanicus. Nero was married to Claudius' daughter Octavia and preferred in the succession to Claudius' natural son, the young Britannicus. Nero ruled from 54 C.E. until his suicide in the year 68. He died trying to escape Rome after he had been declared public enemy by the Senate. Upon his death the line of the Julio-Claudian emperors came to an end, largely because Nero had himself seen to the execution of other members of the family whom he imagined potential rivals.

Nero's reign began quite well. Its first five years are considered a time of excellent government. Sources, ancient and modern, disagree as to whether the success was attributable to Nero himself, to his mother Agrippina, or to his advisors, the philosopher Seneca and the praetorian prefect Burrus. Probably under the guidance of Seneca, Nero was careful to recognize senatorial prerogatives in certain areas of civil administration and particularly in respect to juridical administration. Good relations with the Senate prevailed for much of Nero's reign.

Nero followed the Julio-Claudian foreign policy as established by Augustus. Persistent harassment on the eastern frontier by Parthia was checked by the appointment of the experienced general Domitius Corbulo to an extraordinary post over governors of the eastern provinces. Corbulo's generals were successful in asserting Roman arms and Corbulo was able to negotiate a solution to Roman-Parthian rivalry over Armenia. Under Nero's reign Roman troops were detailed to Judea to suppress the Zealots, whose guerrilla activities resulted in death and property loss for both Jew and Gentile in Judea, and whose seizure of Jerusalem brought appeals from Jewish leaders for a restoration of order. After the defeat of troops under Cestius Gallus, governor of Syria, Corbulo's lieutenant, the future emperor Vespasian, was dispatched at the head of Roman legions to prosecute the Jewish War.

Nero's popularity at Rome declined after the deaths of Seneca and Burrus, for which he himself may have been ultimately responsible. The new praetorian prefect Tigellinus encouraged Nero in his behavioral excesses and cruelty. The emperor's extreme philhellenism and image of himself as a great artist in the Greek sense further contributed to continued extreme behaviors and lack of esteem with the upper classes at Rome. Paranoia about plots to overthrow his rule resulted in the execution of various generals and senators, further destroying Nero's credibility as a ruler. Only the common people whose favor was bought by "bread and circuses" seemed to continue to proclaim Nero as emperor.

Nero's popularity was further damaged by the great fire of 64, which reduced to ruin three of the city's 14 regions and heavily damaged eight others. It was rumored that Nero was somehow involved, in an attempt to provide land for the great palace complex he wanted to build at the south end of the Forum. Despite Nero's efforts to lay blame for the fire on Christians, the rumors and the emperor's unpopularity grew. Cruel punishments were exacted from the Christians for their alleged crime, including Nero's use of Christians as living torches to illumine races at the Vatican Circus, an act which according to Tacitus met with disgust from the senatorial class.

Whether Nero's actions toward the Christians at Rome can be properly defined as a "persecution" has engendered debate among religious scholars, Roman historians, and students of Roman law. Were the Christians prosecuted as criminals guilty of arson? Were their punishments a result of the power of a Roman magistrate, in this case the highest Roman magistrate — the emperor — to exercise *coercitio* ("force") against a criminal? Was the charge of *maiestas* ("treason") applied in this as in so many other prosecutions in the early Empire? Was this the first instance of persecution *suo nomine* ("for the sake of the name itself") — in other words, simply because they were Christians? The evidence is unavailable for any definite conclusion, but that this action was confined to the Christians at Rome and did not extend to Christians elsewhere in the Empire makes unlikely the latter option. The time of the Christian persecutions *per se* simply had not yet arrived, and even Nero's excessive cruelty does not make it so.

Bibliography. M. T. Griffin, *Nero: The End of a Dynasty* (London, 1984); H. Mattingly, *Christianity in the Roman Empire* (1954, repr. New York, 1967); B. H. Warmington, *Nero: Reality and Legend* (London, 1969). JOHN F. HALL

NET
Nets of various types of cord provided tools of trade for hunters, trappers, fowlers, and fishers. Hunters hung nets between trees or along game paths (Ps. 140:5[MT 6]) to entrap antelope or similar game (Job 18:8; Isa. 51:20) or, in conjunction with pits, used nets to trap lions (Ezek. 19:1-9). Metaphorically, nets represented God's judgment (Lam. 1:13; Ezek. 12:13) or symbolized the schemes of the wicked to trap the righteous (Ps. 10:9). The imagery imparts a sense of hidden danger (Hos. 9:8) or the inability of the prey to escape the meshes of the net (Ezek. 32:3; Mic. 7:2).

The fowler suspended a net, secretly (Prov.

1:17), and lay in wait. At the right moment the net was released over feeding birds (Jer. 5:26; Amos 3:5). Flocks of birds, like quail, who had taken refuge in the undergrowth were trapped by having a net thrown over them (Hos. 7:12). So too, bad times fall like nets upon people (Eccl. 9:12). Death is the entangling cords of a net (Ps. 18:4-5[5-6] = 2 Sam. 22:5-6), but God delivers the righteous, like birds out of the broken nets of the fowler (Ps. 124:7).

Fishers also used nets (Matt. 4:20-21), either smaller cast nets (Isa. 19:8; Matt. 4:18) or dragnets (seine) requiring a group of people, in boats or on the shore (Hab. 1:15; Ezek. 47:10). Matt. 13:47-48 suggests fishers, as in Galilee, sorting edible fish (*Cichlidae,* musht or St. Peter's fish; *Cyprinidae,* carp, both barbel and sardine) from inedible by Jewish law (*Siluridae,* catfish).

Bibliography. M. Nun, "Cast Your Net upon the Waters," *BARev* 19/6 (1993): 46-56, 70; S. Wachsmann, "The Galilee Boat," *BARev* 14/5 (1988): 18-23.

William R. Domeris

NETAIM (Heb. *nĕṭāʿîm*)
A place in Judah where royal potters resided (1 Chr. 4:23). Although its exact location is unknown, Netaim is believed to be located in the Shephelah, near the city of Gederah. Some have suggested Khirbet en-Nuweitiʿ, S of the Wadi Elah.

Aaron M. Gale

NETHANEL (Heb. *nĕṯan'ēl*)

1. The son of Zuar, head of the tribe of Issachar (Num. 1:8).

2. The fourth son of Jesse, and one of David's six older brothers (1 Chr. 2:14).

3. One of seven priests who sounded the trumpets before the ark of God when it was brought to Jerusalem (1 Chr. 15:24).

4. The father of Shemaiah, a clerk and Levite (1 Chr. 24:6).

5. A son of the door-keeper Obed-edom (1 Chr. 26:4).

6. One of the officers Jehoshaphat sent in the third year of his reign to teach the Torah in Judah (2 Chr. 17:7).

7. A chief of the Levites, the brother of Shemaiah; one of those who gave an additional Passover sacrifice (2 Chr. 35:9; cf. 1 Esdr. 1:9).

8. A member of the family of Pashhur, who had married a foreign woman (Ezra 10:22; cf. 1 Esdr. 9:22).

9. A priest, head of the family of Jedaiah in the days of Jehoiakim (Neh. 12:21).

10. One of the Levites who contributed with thanksgiving and song at the dedication of the walls of Jerusalem (Neh. 12:36).

Jesper Svartvik

NETHANIAH (Heb. *nĕṯanyâ, nĕṯanyāhû*)

1. The father of Ishmael, one of the men who murdered Gedaliah (2 Kgs. 25:23, 25; Jer. 40:8, 14-15; 41:1-9).

2. A Levite of the line of Asaph who prophesied with lyres, harps, and cymbal (1 Chr. 25:2); leader of the fifth division of levitical singers (v. 12).

3. A Levite sent to teach in the cities of Judah during the reign of King Jehoshaphat (2 Chr. 17:8).

4. The father of Jehudi, who conveyed Jeremiah's scroll to Jehoiakim (Jer. 36:14).

NETHINIM (Heb. *nĕṯînîm*)
A class of temple servants (lit., "given ones"; cf. Ezra 8:20). Apart from 1 Chr. 9:2 (= Neh. 11:3), they are mentioned only in Ezra and Nehemiah. Modern translations translate "temple servants" or "temple slaves."

The Nethinim are listed with four other groups in what is possibly a descending order of status: priests, Levites, singers, gatekeepers, and temple servants (Ezra 2:70; 7:7; Neh. 10:28) — all exempt from taxes (Ezra 7:24).

The foreign names in the lists (cf. Ezra 2:43-58) plus the possibility that some of them may be descendants of prisoners of war have led to the conclusion that the Nethinim were probably of foreign origin. Some scholars have compared them to the Gibeonites of Josh. 9:27. In 1 Esdr. 5:29 and Josephus *Ant.* 11:128 they are called "temple slaves" (Gk. *hierodoúloi*).

The Nethinim are listed among the 392 exiles who accompanied Zerubbabel to Jerusalem after the Exile. In Ezra 2:43-58 they are grouped with the "sons of Solomon's servants," perhaps a technical term for a class of temple workers. They had special quarters in the Ophel district of Jerusalem near the temple (Neh. 3:26, 31; 11:21). This may have been where they lived when they were on duty, since Ezra 2:70; Neh. 7:73 refer to cities in which they lived; it is possible, however, that the reference here is to the period before the rebuilding of the temple.

Larry L. Walker

NETOPHAH (Heb. *nĕṭōpâ*)
A town in the hill country of Judah near Bethlehem (1 Chr. 2:54). Ancient Netophah is most often identified with modern Khirbet Bedd Fālûḥ (171119), situated on a ridge top ca. 5.5 km. (3.5 mi.) SE of Bethlehem. Unfortunately there is no direct archaeological evidence to support this identification. The ancient name is possibly preserved at ʿAin en-Natûf, a nearby spring.

Maharai and Heleb, two of David's Mighty Men, came from Netophah (2 Sam. 23:28-29; 1 Chr. 11:30; 27:13,15). Seraiah, another Netophathite, supported Gedaliah after his appointment as governor by Nebuchadnezzar (2 Kgs. 25:23), as did Ephai and his sons (Jer. 40:8). Several inhabitants of Netophah joined Zerubbabel on his return from exile in Babylon (Ezra 2:22; Neh. 7:26). A few returning Levites also settled in Netophah; some apparently sang at the dedication of the rebuilt wall of Jerusalem (Neh. 12:28).

Wade R. Kotter

NETTLES
Any of the coarse herbs of the genus *Urtica,* having leaves covered with hairs that secrete a fluid that stings the skin on contact (Heb. *qimmôś, ḥārûl*).

Stinging nettles grow throughout Palestine, particularly *Urtica ureus* L. and *Urtica pilulifera* L. They are common in fallow fields, unkempt gardens, and on ruins. In ancient times nettles were viewed as a sign of desolation (Isa. 34:13; Hos. 9:6; Zeph. 2:9).

Heb. *ḥārûl* (Zeph. 2:9; Job 30:7) may actually be a general term for weeds, or perhaps a specific term for wild mustard (*Brassica nigra* [L.] Koch or *Sinapis arvensis* L.), which tends to grow on abandoned sites (cf. parallel occurrences of the two terms, Prov. 24:31).

NETWORK

Any pattern with a "netlike" reticulation, primarily associated with the embellishments of the tabernacle and temple. Heb. *rešeṯ* designates the bronze latticework that covered the ark of the covenant, extending from just below the ledge to halfway down the side. Four rings were fastened to this grating at the corners, and poles were inserted through these rings when the ark had to be carried (Exod. 27:4-5; 38:4). A "network" *(śeḇāḵâ)* of interwoven chains (1 Kgs. 7:17; NRSV "nets of checker work") adorned the capitals of the two pillars that stood in front of the temple; the capitals were further decorated with pomegranates and lilies (vv. 17-42; 2 Kgs. 25:17; 2 Chr. 4:12-13; Jer. 52:22-23).

NEW MOON

The monthly festival marking the first sighting of the new moon (Heb. *ḥōḏeš*), celebrated 11 times every year (the new moon that began the month of Tishri commenced the autumnal New Year's celebration). The cultural importance of this festival is difficult for modern Westerners to grasp; the handful of references to it in the OT probably belies its significance to the peoples of ancient Palestine. Most if not all of the civilizations of the ancient Near East experienced the monthly darkening of the moon as an ominous event; restoration of the lunar disk was greeted with rejoicing that became ritualized. Festivals of the new moon are attested in 3rd-millennium texts from Egypt and Mesopotamia, playing a prominent role in the cultic life of both civilizations. The principal cultic and civil calendar described in the OT has its origins in the ancient calendar of Nippur, in which lunar months, empirically established by observation, were adjusted to correspond to the (solar) seasons by periodic proclamation of a leap month.

The OT suggests that the monthly new moon festival was more popular and cultically eventful than weekly sabbath observance in Palestine during the pre-Hasmonean period. Several texts emphasize the festive nature of the holiday (Num. 10:10; 1 Sam. 20:5, 18-19, 24-29; Ps. 81:3[MT 4]; Hos. 2:11[13]). Celebration of the new moon in Jerusalem is reminiscent of the sabbath observance: normal business is suspended (Amos 8:5), special sacrifices are initiated (Num. 28:11-15; 2 Chr. 31:3), and festive meals may have been common (1 Sam. 20:18). If a normative practice can be extrapolated from Jdt. 8:6, fasting was forbidden on the day of the new moon.

M. Roš Haš. 1.3–3.1 relates that the Sanhedrin was responsible for proclaiming the advent of a new moon, based on sightings by reliable witnesses; the Jewish lunar calendar was not calculated mathematically until the 4th century C.E. The Jewish new moon festival maintained its popularity during the first centuries C.E., when some early Christian authors used it for drawing invidious contrasts between Jewish and Christian ritual observance (Col. 2:16; Justin Martyr).

Bibliography. M. E. Cohen, *The Cultic Calendars of the Ancient Near East* (Bethesda, 1993); W. W. Hallo, "New Moons and Sabbaths," *HUCA* 48 (1977): 1-18; H. A. McKay, "New Moon or Sabbath?" in *The Sabbath in Jewish and Christian Traditions,* ed. T. C. Ezkenazi, D. J. Harrington, and W. H. Shea (New York, 1991), 12-27; T. C. G. Thornton, "Jewish New Moon Festivals, Galatians 4:3-11 and Colossians 2:16," *JTS* N.S. 40 (1989): 97-100.

STEVEN W. HOLLOWAY

NEW YEAR

Traditionally a time of celebration, renewal, and ritual. In the agrarian societies of the ancient Near East, the New Year festivities corresponded to the cyclical agricultural season; elaborate ceremonies marked the phenomenon of transition from one season into the next. The peoples of the ancient Near East celebrated New Year's festivals during both sowing and harvest seasons, at the beginning or end of the agricultural year. In early Mesopotamian societies the *akītu* festival, often referred to as the New Year's festival, first occurred in Tishri around the time of the fall equinox; in the later periods, especially at Babylon, it was observed at the vernal equinox during the first 12 days of Nisan. Similarly, ancient Israel observed agricultural festivals which may have been New Year celebrations.

The timing of the New Year in ancient Israel is uncertain and debated among scholars. Some suggest that there were two New Year's days, the spring New Year commemorating the cultic new year and the fall festival celebrating the civic new year. The OT contains scarce evidence of a New Year's celebration and its accompanying rituals. In the early period of Israelite history the autumnal festival (*heḥāg;* 1 Kgs. 8:2, 65) and the festival of the Lord (*ḥag-YHWH*; Judg. 21:19) celebrated in the seventh month (Tishri) marked the turn of the new year. Jeroboam (1 Kgs. 12:32) celebrated this same festival in the eighth month. Ezek. 40:1 reports *rō'š haššānâ* (the "head of the year") as 10 Tishri. These autumnal celebrations reflect the influence of the solar calendar; after the Exile, when the lunar calendar was adopted, the New Year was celebrated on the first day of the new moon in the month of Nisan. In Lev. 25:9 the blowing of the shofar on the tenth day of the seventh month may designate the beginning of the new year, as it does in later Jewish Rosh Hashanah celebrations. Drawing upon comparative evidence of cult ritual drama in the ancient Near East, Sigmund Mowinckel theorized that Pss. 47, 93, 96-100 were Enthronement Psalms, each containing liturgy that celebrated the enthronement of Yahweh. The *Sitz im Leben* of these Psalms was the annual reenactment of the ritual cult drama when Yahweh was celebrated as king, creator, and savior of the world.

New Year's festivals in the ancient Near East included a number of similar elements — processions of the king and the deities, intricate sacrifices, prayers, rites of purification and cleansing of the temple, and celebrations to commemorate the overcoming of chaos and restoration of order. In the Ugaritic literature, the myth of the death and resurrection of Baal, as a fertility god, celebrating his triumph over Mot and the building of his palace, has been connected to the autumn New Year festivities in Canaan. In Egyptian New Year rituals at the temple of Edfu, the statue of the god Horus was removed from his temple and exposed to the rays of the sun to reunite his body with his soul. The Babylonian *akītu* festival, which became the most important religious and political celebration in Mesopotamian history, also involved complex and elaborate rituals. The temples of Marduk and Nabu were ritually purified, decorated with splendid adornments, and filled with lavish offerings and banquets. The creation epic, the Enuma Elish, commemorating Marduk's victory over chaos, was recited before his statue. The *akītu* festival celebrated the supremacy of Marduk as the national deity, as well as the sovereignty of the king as the chosen representative of Marduk. The king underwent a ritual humiliation, stripped of his crown, scepter, and sword, forced to his knees and required to swear an oath stating that he had not neglected his duties as king and to promise to respect Marduk and the people of Babylon. The king "took the hand" of Marduk and led a procession of the statues of Marduk and neighboring deities through the city, in magnificent view of the Babylon citizens, to the *akītu* house, which lay on the outskirts of the city walls. The destinies of the land, presumably for the upcoming year, were fixed and the festival ended with the gods returning to their temples.

JULYE BIDMEAD

NEZIAH (Heb. *nĕṣîaḥ*)
A temple servant whose descendants returned with Zerubbabel from captivity in Babylon (Ezra 2:54 = Neh. 7:56).

NEZIB (Heb. *nĕṣîḇ*)
A town in the Shephelah of Judah and part of that tribe's inheritance (Josh. 15:43). Eusebius places it 14 km. (9 mi.) E of Beit Guvrin/Beth Jibrin (Eleutheropolis) in the direction of Hebron (according to Jerome, 11 km. [7 mi.]). The location is identified as Khirbet Beit Neṣîb esh-Sharqiyeh (150110), in the north-south valley that separates the Shephelah from the Judean hills. The biblical name has apparently been preserved.

Bibliography. A. F. Rainey, "The Administrative Division of the Shephelah," *Tel Aviv* 7 (1980): 194-202; "The Biblical Shephelah of Judah," *BASOR* 251 (1983): 1-22.

JENNIFER L. GROVES

NIBHAZ (Heb. *niḇḥaz*)
One of two gods worshipped by the Avvites, a Syrian people whom the Assyrians resettled at Samaria (2 Kgs. 17:31). He has been identified variously as "Nebo the Seer" or "Nebo of the face," a Babylonian deity revered in Syria, or an Elamite deity Ibnaḫaza.

NIBSHAN (Heb. *hanniḇšān*)
A city in the wilderness of Judah (Josh. 15:62). The site has been identified as Khirbet el-Maqârī (186123) in the valley of Achor, 17 km. (10.5 mi.) SE of Jerusalem.

NICANOR (Gk. *Nikánōr*)
1. One of four commanders whom Lysias sent against Judas Maccabeus (1 Macc. 3:38; 2 Macc. 8). Although 1 Maccabees suggests that Gorgias led this campaign (1 Macc 4:1), 2 Maccabees depicts Nicanor as the prominent figure. According to 2 Macc. 8 he sold captured Jews from the campaign as slaves in order to pay tribute to Rome (190 B.C.E.). Judas attacked Nicanor's forces at Emmaus and defeated them. During Demetrius I's rule (162-150), Nicanor led another attack on the Jews. On this occasion, he planned to lure Judas into a meeting with him where he could kill Judas. Learning of the plot, Judas spoiled Nicanor's plan. The two engaged in battle at Caphar-salama, where Judas won. He and Judas had one last battle at Adasa in which Syria lost and Nicanor died (1 Macc. 7:26-50; 2 Macc 14:12–15:36).

2. One of the seven men chosen to oversee the food distribution to the Hellenists' widows in the Jerusalem church after the Hellenists complained that they were being neglected (Acts 6:5).

RODNEY A. WERLINE

NICODEMUS (Gk. *Nikódēmos*)
A Pharisee, a member of the Sanhedrin ("leader of the Jews"), and a scribe ("teacher of Israel"; John 3:1-14). Nicodemus came to Jesus at night (possibly so as not to compromise his position) as a person perplexed by Jesus' discourse about the new birth. He later defends Jesus before the Sanhedrin (John 7:50-52). After Jesus' death, Nicodemus provides an enormous amount of spices for Jesus' burial, thus implying that he was wealthy (John 19:39-40).

The Babylonian Talmud mentions a certain Nakdimon (the Hebrew equivalent of Gk. *Nikódēmos*) who flourished ca. A.D. 66-70, but the biblical Nicodemus was probably dead by then. Nakdimon, however, could have been a member of his family. In several NT apocryphal works Nicodemus defends Jesus at his trial, is converted to Christianity, expelled from the Sanhedrin, and dies a martyr's death. However, such legends probably bear little truth.

JAMES A. BROOKS

NICODEMUS, GOSPEL OF
The name ascribed by Latin traditions of the 13th-14th centuries C.E. to the Acts of Pilate.

NICOLAITANS (Gk. *Nikolaḯtēs*)
A sect of the early Church associated with the cities of Ephesus and Pergamum (Rev. 2:6, 15). The group was apparently accused of the sins of eating meat offered to idols and (probably ritual) sexual immo-

rality (Rev. 2:14). The association of these same antinomian practices (proscribed by the Apostolic Council at Jerusalem; Acts 15:20, 28-29; cf. 21:25) with the prophetess Jezebel at Thyatira (Rev. 2:20) may indicate activity by the sect in that city as well.

Two explanations have been offered for the name of this group. Irenaeus (*Adv. haer.* 7.24) reported that this sect traced its origins to Nicolaus of Antioch, one of the seven Hellenists chosen to assist the apostles (Acts 6:1-5). Clement of Alexandria (*Misc.* 2.20) concurred with Irenaeus but argued that the group's 2nd-century adherents had corrupted Nicolaus's teachings. Most modern scholars are dubious of any connection between the sect and Nicolaus of Antioch, and many even doubt that the libertine gnostic sects known to the apologists by this name are the same as those mentioned in Revelation.

Most scholars now tend to interpret the name symbolically as a wordplay on the name Balaam (Rev. 2:14-15). That name can be construed as a contracted form of Heb. *bālaʿ ʿam,* "he destroyed the people," and so parallels the name Nicolaus from Gk. *níkē laoú,* "conqueror of the people." Balaam was traditionally associated with antinomian practices during this period (2 Pet. 2:15; cf. Jude 11). TIMOTHY B. CARGAL

NICOLAUS (Gk. *Nikólaos*)
One of the seven men appointed and ordained by the 12 apostles to administer the daily food distribution among the Hellenistic Christian widows in the early Jerusalem church (Acts 6:5). He was "a proselyte of Antioch," i.e., a Gentile.

The early church fathers are divided on whether or not Nicolaus later apostatized and founded the heretical sect known as the Nicolaitans (Rev. 2:6).
WARREN C. TRENCHARD

NICOPOLIS (Gk. *Nikópolis*)
A common name ("city of victory") in antiquity. Paul asks Titus to visit him at Nicopolis as he had decided to spend the winter there (Tit. 3:12). This was probably the city located on the isthmus of the Bay of Actium in northwestern Greece, founded by Augustus after his victory over Antony and Cleopatra in 31 B.C.E. It was a Roman colony and the capital of the province of Epirus. Herod the Great built most of the public buildings, and Epictetus resided there after his expulsion from Rome. The note in Codex Alexandrinus ascribing the writing of Titus to Nicopolis is incorrect. RICHARD S. ASCOUGH

NIGER (Gk. *Níger*)
The surname of Simeon, a prophet and teacher who lived in Antioch (Acts 13:1). The name is derived from Lat. *niger,* "black," suggesting his African origin. Some scholars identify him with Simon of Cyrene (Mark 15:21).

NIGHT
"Night" occurs in the Bible in both a literal (the period between sunset and sunrise) and metaphorical sense. In both cases it is related to the idea, and often the word, "darkness," even at creation when God's word separates light from darkness ("night"). However, night is not demonized in the OT since the central religious festival, Passover, is a nocturnal meal recalling the "night of deliverance" (Exod. 11–12).

OT references to "night" often occur in combination or contrast with "day" and thus become a mode of describing time. Night is the time for restful sleep, and thus a sleepless night is agony (Job 7:3-4). When employed literally, the night is often divided into three or four watches (1 Sam. 11:11; Ps. 63:6[MT 7]; 119:148; Matt. 14:25; Luke 12:38). Although it is often associated with danger or calamity (Job 24:13-15; Ps. 91:5; Mic. 3:6), night is also the time for "dreams," frequently valued as a medium of divine communication (Gen. 40:5; 41:11; Dan. 7:2).

Within OT apocalyptic writings, night becomes a symbol for evil in a fuller, almost cosmic, sense ended by God's coming (Zech. 14:7). This metaphorical use is expanded in the intertestamental period, especially in the Qumran community. Night is the power of darkness (1QS 6:6; 1QH 8:29; 10:15). Thus, in the War Scroll (1QM) the final conflict is a battle between the "sons of light" and the "sons of darkness."

The Gospel of John uses "night" as a symbol of death (John 9:4; 11:10), part of what opposes God. Thus, when Judas leaves to betray Jesus, it is "night" (John 13:30), which can be understood both literally and figuratively. Jesus can then say it is the "hour of darkness."

For Paul, for whom Jesus represents the shift of the eons, night is a metaphor for the fading rule of evil as salvation (i.e., "light") increasingly brings the rule of God (Rom. 13:2). Because of this contrast, Paul uses night to describe life apart from faith (1 Thess. 5:3-7). Believers are now removed from the night, and it no longer shapes their lives. Here night is used metaphorically to describe a moral life apart from God (cf. Paul's plea to live as "children of light"; Eph. 5:8-11).

Night is absent in the new Jerusalem. Because God has defeated that which opposes him, there is "no night there" (Rev. 21:25; 22:5).
WENDELL WILLIS

NIGHT HAG
A term (Heb. *lîlîṯ*) variously translated (Isa. 34:14) "night hag/creature/monster," "screech owl," and "Lilith" (NRSV). The LXX reads Gk. *onokéntauros* ("a tailess monkey" or "a demon of desolate areas") and the Vulg. Lat. *lamia* ("witch"). Lilith was a female demon of Babylonian/Assyrian mythology. Nighttime is associated because of similarity with Heb. *laylâ* ("night"). The context is God's judgment of desolation on Edom. A hyperbolic picture of creatures of desolate places, including imaginary ones, is possible; however, a mythological interpretation is less likely since most, if not all, of the other creatures in Isa. 34:11-15 are actual animals.

Bibliography. H. Torczyner, "A Hebrew Incantation against Night-Demons from Biblical Times," *JNES* 6 (1947): 18-29. W. CREIGHTON MARLOWE

NIGHTHAWK
A small nocturnal bird related to the owl and the hawk (Heb. *taḥmās*); also known as the nightjar *(Caprimulgus europaeus)* or "goatsucker." Some 95 known species exist, including those which flourish in parts of Europe, Asia, and Palestine. At least one species, *Caprimulgus nubicus,* is found in North Africa, though only when migrating.

It is unlikely, however, that *taḥmās* designates the nighthawk since it is seldom found in the Middle East. Rather, a small predator owl is probably meant (cf. NJB, NIV "screech owl"; LXX Gk. *glaúx*). These small nocturnal birds feed on prey at night and roost in trees in daylight throughout the forests of Galilee. This bird was considered unclean and thus could not be eaten (Lev. 11:16; Deut. 14:15).

T. J. Jenney

NILE (Gk. *Neílos;* Lat. *Nilos)*
One of the principal forces shaping Egyptian history (Heb. *yĕʾōr;* Egyp. *i[t]rw*). The political division of the land into two areas, Upper and Lower Egypt, had its origin in the Predynastic Age. The terms Upper and Lower are determined by the direction of the flow of the Nile. Since the river flows north, Lower Egypt or downstream was located in the north and Upper Egypt or upstream in the south. Lower Egypt lies between the Mediterranean and Cairo. This flat, fertile area is in the shape of a triangle with the apex at Cairo and formed by the fanning out of the branches of the Nile, of which only two of the original seven remain open. Herodotus first called the area the Delta because of its triangular shape, like the capital "D" in the Greek alphabet. Upper Egypt lies between Cairo and Aswan.

Egypt receives scarcely any rain, and the desert encroaches on either side of the fertile area watered by the Nile and irrigation. The Nile is formed by two rivers with their sources in Africa. These are the White Nile (Baḥr al-Abyad) and the Blue Nile (Baḥr al-Azrâq), with the Atbara tributary. The White Nile begins in Lake Victoria and joins the Blue Nile at Khartoum. The other sources are in the western plateau of Ethiopia, which has the headwaters of the Sobat which flows into the White Nile. The headwaters for the Blue Nile are found in the Goiam highlands at Lake Tana, and the river runs north to Khartoum. The Atbara River rises in the Begemir and Simen region of Ethiopia and is joined by the Tekeze River in the Sudan and enters the Blue Nile ca. 320 km. (200 mi.) N of Khartoum. The Blue and White Nile receive their waters from two separate, but related monsoon storm systems. The Blue Nile and its tributaries receive water from the monsoons that reach Ethiopia from the Indian Ocean. The White Nile receives its water from the branch of the Atlantic monsoon which comes across Africa to the Lake Plateau region. The Blue Nile and its tributaries account for 75 percent of the total annual discharge, but during the annual flooding of the summer and fall contribute 90-95 percent of the total discharge. During the spring and early summer when the Blue Nile is low, the White Nile contributes 75 percent of the total discharge.

The length of the Nile from Lake Victoria to the Mediterranean is 6450 km. (4000 mi.). Before it reaches Aswan, the river passes over six cataracts or waterfalls and rapids, which makes navigating the length of the river almost impossible. Before the modern hydroelectric dam was built, Egypt relied on the annual flooding of the Nile for silt and moisture to grow crops. The flooding was regular and not destructive as is the case with many other rivers, but it was not consistent year to year. In the years that the Nile was high, more land was available for growing crops and there would be a surplus of food. If it were extremely high, the flood could destroy towns and villages. It is possible that some of the flood waters flowed into the Fayum and would increase the amount of farm land in that area, but the high water could also be destructive. When the Nile was low, there would be less land and less food. If there were a succession of low Niles over a period of years, famine could occur.

Bibliography. M. S. Abu al-Izz, *Landforms of Egypt* (Cairo, 1971); J. Baines and J. Malik, *Atlas of Ancient Egypt* (New York, 1980); K. W. Butzer, *Early Hydraulic Civilization in Egypt* (Chicago, 1976); W. B. Fisher, *The Middle East,* 7th ed. (London, 1978); F. A. Hassan and B. R. Stucki, "Nile Floods and Climactic Change," in *Climate, History, Periodicity and Predictability,* ed. M. R. Rampino et al. (New York, 1987), 37-46. Lawrence A. Sinclair

NIMRAH (Heb. *nimrâ*)
Alternate form of Beth-nimrah (Num. 32:3).

NIMRIM (Heb. *nimrîm*), **WATERS OF**
A place in Moab known for its abundant water resources and lush vegetation. In the oracles of judgment against Moab (Isa. 15:6; Jer. 48:34) the prophets announce that the waters would dry up and the once fertile ground would turn into a desert.

Eusebius located Nimrim at Bennamarein, N of Zoar at the southeastern corner of the Dead Sea. Some scholars equate Nimrim with Tell Nimrîn (Beth-nimrah, Num. 32:36; Josh. 13:27), but most identify the waters of Nimrim with Seil en-Numeirah, a perennial stream ca. 16 km. (10 mi.) N of Wadi el-Ḥesa, and Nimrim with Numeirah, an Early Bronze Age site located on a cliff overlooking the entrance of the wadi and the Dead Sea plain. The site was surrounded by a wide city wall. Among various industrial installations are unusual storage bins or drainage pits. Evidence of a fiery destruction in the Early Bronze period is abundant.

Bibliography. W. E. Rast, "Settlement at Numeira," in *The Southeastern Dead Sea Plain Expedition,* ed. Rast and R. T. Schaub. AASOR 46 (Cambridge, Mass., 1981), 35-44; Rast and Schaub, "Preliminary Report of the 1979 Expedition to the Dead Sea Plain, Jordan," *BASOR* 240 (1980): 21-61.

Friedbert Ninow

NIMROD (Heb. *nimrôḏ*)
A famed war hero and hunter (Gen. 10:8-12; 1 Chr. 1:10; Mic. 5:6[MT 5]), subject also of pre- and postbiblical literature and legends. At face value the

biblical texts relate to the Hamitic Cush of Gen. 10:6-7, but the Cush of v. 8 may be a Kassite (Akk. *kaššû/kuššû*). Theories of identification include (1) a Mesopotamian god; (2) a legendary Mesopotamian hero or eponym; or (3) a historical Mesopotamian or Egyptian king. Gen. 10:10-11 regionalizes his kingdom or range of influence by naming five to eight cities in southern (Babel, Erech, and Akkad; possibly "Calneh," alternatively repointed and interpreted as "all of them") and northern Mesopotamia (Nineveh and Calah; possibly Rehoboth-ir and Resen, thought otherwise to mean "public square" and "canal," respectively). The data argue most for Nimrod as a human, historical figure, but his identity remains unclear.

Bibliography. K. van der Toorn and P. W. van der Horst, "Nimrod before and after the Bible," *HTR* 83 (1990): 1-29; E. A. Speiser, "In Search of Nimrod," in *Oriental and Biblical Studies,* ed. J. J. Finkelstein and M. Greenberg (Philadelphia, 1967), 41-52.

W. Creighton Marlowe

NIMSHI (Heb. *nimšî*)
The father of Jehoshaphat and grandfather (or "ancestor") of King Jehu of Israel (2 Kgs. 9:2, 14).

NINEVEH (Heb. *nînĕwēh;* Akk. *Ninu[w]a*)
A site on the outskirts of modern Mosul, at the confluence of the Tigris and Khosr rivers. Nineveh is best known as one of the capitals of the Assyrian Empire, but it was also the longest-lived settlement in the region, having been founded by the 7th millennium B.C. Its prominence was due to the abundance of agricultural land round it, as well as its location at the intersection of two routes: one following the Tigris to the north and south, and one crossing the Tigris and the Assyrian plains to the east and west.

Nineveh was one of the first Mesopotamian sites to be visited and excavated, having to date been excavated by 13 different French, British, Iraqi, and American projects. The site consists of two large mounds — Kuyunjik and Nebi Yunus — separated from one another by the course of the Khosr River, and surrounded by a lower settlement of as much as 750 ha. (1850 a.). Early settlement was concentrated on the Kuyunjik mound, which in time grew to a height of 30 m. (98 ft.) and an area of 40 ha. (100 a.). A Muslim shrine to the prophet Yunus (Jonah) has prevented much excavation on Nebi Yunus.

Nineveh is said to have been founded by King Nimrod, grandson of Noah (Gen. 10:11). Actually, we have very little evidence about early occupation at Nineveh. Occupation up to the 3rd millennium was excavated in a deep sounding; apart from a mudbrick building with vaulted rooms dating to the late Uruk period, few architectural remains were recovered. The long-lived temple of Ishtar, the city goddess, may have been founded in the early 3rd millennium, the eponymous Ninevite V period. During the Akkadian period a fortification wall was built around Kuyunjik, and the Ishtar temple was renovated by rulers of the Akkadian dynasty; the famous copper head of an Akkadian ruler was found in Neo-Assyrian layers of the Ishtar temple. In the Ur III period a ruler of Nineveh named Tish-atal was in contact with, but independent of, the kings of Ur. No excavated material and virtually no textual references to Nineveh survive for the first half of the 2nd millennium. During the second half of the 2nd millennium, Nineveh was ruled by the Mitanni state and then by the rising state at Assur. Nineveh expanded greatly during the earlier part of the 1st millennium. Rulers built royal residences on Kuyunjik, and settlement expanded to the north of Kuyunjik in the recently identified "Old Town Mound." Nineveh became the capital of the Assyrian Empire in the reign of Sennacherib (704-681). Sennacherib built his palace on Kuyunjik and called it the "Palace Without a Rival." It contained more than 3 km. (1.9 mi.) of carved stone reliefs, including the famous scenes of Sennacherib's siege of Lachish. Sennacherib also constructed gardens and orchards, in addition to waterworks 80 km. (50 mi.) long to bring water from the mountains. It has recently been suggested that these waterworks and gardens together constituted the famed Hanging Gardens of antiquity. Among Sennacherib's other constructions were a royal road from the palace to the Nergal Gate at the northern end of the city; an arsenal on the Nebi Yunus mound; and a double fortification wall around the city, which had grown to its largest size of 750 ha. (1850 a.). Sennacherib's murder by his sons in the temple at Nineveh is reported in 2 Kgs. 19:36-37 = Isa. 37:37-38.

Sennacherib's grandson Assurbanipal (668-627) also built a palace on Kuyunjik. It is known for, among other things, a series of reliefs depicting the royal lion hunt. The palace also contained a large library of cuneiform texts that included literary accounts of the Flood.

The end of the Assyrian Empire was marked by the sack of Nineveh in 612 by Babylonians and Medes; remains of the slaughter have been excavated in the Hatzi Gate on the southeast of the city wall. The site was not completely abandoned after that event as has previously been assumed, but continued to be occupied through the Hellenistic and Parthian periods. In recent times, the inhabitants of Mosul have begun to live within the perimeter of Sennacherib's wall, particularly in the area between Kuyunjik and Nebi Yunus.

Most biblical references to Nineveh relate to its role as capital of the Assyrian Empire and to predictions of its fall (Jonah; Nahum; Zeph. 2:13). The lack of detail in these accounts suggests, however, that the authors did not have first-hand knowledge of the city.

Bibliography. S. Dalley, "Nineveh, Babylon and the Hanging Gardens: Cuneiform and Classical Sources Reconciled," *Iraq* 56 (1994): 45-58; D. Stronach, "Village to Metropolis: Nineveh and the Beginnings of Urbanism in Northern Mesopotamia," in *Nuove fondazioni nel vicino oriente antioco,* ed. S. Mazzoni (Pisa, 1994), 85-114.

Geoff Emberling

Fragment of a clay tablet with a plan of Nippur showing the locations of temples, walls, gates, and canals. Early Period (Kassite period, ca. 1300 B.C.E.) (Friedrich-Schiller-Universität, Jena)

NIPPUR (Sum. *Nibru*)
A city with a unique role in Mesopotamian history and society as its millennia-long religious center yet never a political base. Nippur (Tell Nuffar) was established on the bank of the Euphrates River during the 6th millennium B.C.E. and, except for relatively brief periods, was continuously occupied until its abandonment in the 9th century C.E. At some stage it became the primary dwelling of the chief god of the Sumerian pantheon, Enlil, and control of the city provided legitimacy to a ruler's control over Mesopotamia. At its maximum, the city covered ca. 150 ha. (370 a.) surrounded by a roughly rectangular wall breached by nine main gates. At times a branch of the Euphrates ran through the city itself while others flowed west of the city.

The triple mounds of Nippur — Tablet Hill, Temple Hill, and West Mound — were the focus of the first American excavations in Ottoman Iraq from 1889-1890, undertaken by the University of Pennsylvania Museum. Subsequent excavations from 1948-1952 were by the joint University Museum–Oriental Institute expedition, augmented in 1953-1962 by the American Schools of Oriental Research and culminating in 10 seasons of work between 1964 and 1989 by the Oriental Institute.

The city was dominated by the great ziggurat complex, built by Ur-Nammu (ca. 2100), situated in the Ekur, the sacred temple precinct dedicated to Enlil from at least the early 4th until the mid-1st millennium. Other sacred temple precincts also existed in the city, including the temple of Inanna on Temple Hill and the North Temple. Tablet Hill appears to have contained both administrative structures and private dwellings; here were found the major finds of perhaps 50 thousand tablets and fragments constituting the majority of known Sumerian literary and lexical texts and numerous private administrative archives from many periods. The West Mound revealed additional private dwellings, a temple founded in the 3rd millennium, a Kassite palace (ca. 1300), a Parthian villa, and the major settlement of the Islamic period.

The earliest levels of Nippur are not very well explored because of their depth beneath later accumulations of occupation debris. Sumerian sources attribute the building of the Tammal, a temple complex dedicated to Enlil, to the reign of Enmebaragesi of Kish who lived in the Early Dynastic II period. But it was not until the rise of the Akkadian dynasty under Sargon the Great in the 23rd century that major construction in the Enlil temple complex took place. The North Temple was built during the same period; a contemporary archive of a governor of Nippur was excavated on the West Mound.

In the subsequent Ur III period (21st century)

Ur-Nammu initiated the construction of the three-tiered ziggurat for Enlil and an accompanying sacred complex that was to dominate the city for the following 1500 years. After the collapse of the Ur III dynasty and the subsequent Amorite settlement, Nippur quickly regained its prominence under the Hammurabi dynasty with its capital in Babylon. It was during this period that the worship of Enlil was partially combined with that of Marduk, the patron god of Hammurabi. Towards the latter part of the Old Babylonian period (late 18th-17th centuries), Nippur appears to have been abandoned or greatly reduced in size, perhaps due to a shift in the course of the Euphrates.

By the late 15th century the ruling Kassite dynasty had established a palace on West Hill and instituted a major building and reconstruction of temples at Nippur as well as the restoration of the city walls depicted on the remarkable map preserved on a clay tablet of the period. During the mid-13th century the city was attacked, possibly by Elamites, and mostly abandoned except perhaps for the sacred Ekur area. However, the city recovered after a hiatus and by the mid-8th century was once again a flourishing town, well documented by the Governor's Archive.

During the 7th century Nippur came under Assyrian control and once again underwent major restoration of the Ekur. With Assyrian troops stationed there, it remained under Assyrian rule until it was captured by the Babylonians after a prolonged siege in 612. It remained under their control until they too were defeated in 539 by Cyrus. Under Achaemenid rule the city flourished and is well documented in the archives of the great merchant family of Murashu. The city continued as an important center through the Seleucid era and into the Parthian period, when it was subjected to massive alterations due to the construction of a huge fortress which incorporated the ziggurat and Ekur. The subsequent Sassanian occupation from the 3rd to 7th centuries C.E. is best known from Talmudic sources, which attest to a prosperous Jewish community at the site. Hundreds of incantation bowls written in Judeo-Aramaic, Mandaic, and Syriac are vivid reminders of their presence. After the Arab conquest in the 7th century the city remained under Islamic rule until the shifting course of the Euphrates River deprived it of its major source of water. The city was abandoned in the 9th century and the region slowly reverted to a desert.

Bibliography. S. W. Cole, *Nippur, 4: The Early Neo-Babylonian Governor's Archive from Nippur.* OIP 114 (Chicago, 1996); M. Gibson, "Patterns of Occupation at Nippur," in M. deJ. Ellis, ed., *Nippur at the Centennial* (Philadelphia, 1992), 33-54; D. E. McCown, R. C. Haines, and D. P. Hansen, *Nippur, 1: Temple of Enlil, Scribal Quarter, and Soundings.* OIP 78 (Chicago, 1978); M. W. Stolper, *Entrepreneurs and Empire: The Murašu Archive, the Murašu Firm, and Persian Rule in Babylonia* (Istanbul, 1985); E. C. Stone, *Nippur Neighborhoods.* SAOC 44 (Chicago, 1987); Stone and D. I. Owen, *Adaption in Old Babylonian Nippur and the Archive of Mannum-mešu-lissur.* Mesopotamian Civilizations 3 (Winona Lake, 1991); R. L. Zettler, "Nippur," *OEANE* 4:148-52.

DAVID I. OWEN

NISAN (Heb. *nîsān;* Gk. *Nisan;* Akk. *nisānu*)
The first month of the Hebrew calendar (Mar./Apr.; Neh. 2:1; Esth. 3:7), called Abib in preexilic times.

NISROCH (Heb. *nisrōḵ*)
The Assyrian deity in whose temple in Nineveh Sennacherib was worshipping when he was murdered by his sons (2 Kgs. 19:37 = Isa. 27:38). As there is no reference to Nisroch among the Mesopotamian pantheon or in any of the cuneiform texts, scholars are unsure of the identity of this deity. Nisroch may be an epithet for the national deity, Assur, though this interpretation is speculative and no similar parallels have been found. Most likely the name is the result of a scribal error and refers to Ninurta, the Assyrian god of war.

JULYE BIDMEAD

NOADIAH (Heb. *nôʿaḏyâ*)

1. The son of Binnui; a Levite to whom the temple vessels were returned after the Exile (Ezra 8:33).

2. A prophetess among those who tried to discourage Nehemiah from rebuilding Jerusalem's walls (Neh. 6:14).

NOAH (Heb. *nōaḥ;* Gk. *Nṓe*)
Son of Lamech and father of Shem, Ham, and Japheth; the central human character of the Flood story (Gen. 6–9).

Name

Lamech's folk etymology ties Noah's name to Heb. *nḥm,* "to provide comfort" (Gen. 5:29), alluding to the curse of 3:17-19: by "toil" and "labor" the ground yields food. Lamech's prediction is fulfilled when God allows animals as food, bringing respite from the curse (Gen. 9:3). Then Noah, "a man of the soil," plants and harvests a vineyard (9:20). Noah's name also reflects *nwḥ,* "to give rest." "Rest" and "comfort" are two of many recurring concepts in the Flood story: e.g., "the ark came to rest *(wattānaḥ),*" 8:4; "the dove found no resting place *(mānôaḥ),*" 8:9; "then the Lord smelled the restful *(hannîḥōaḥ)* aroma," 8:21. Less obvious are Hebrew puns: e.g., "the Lord was grieved *(wayyinnāḥem)* that he had made humankind," 6:6; "Noah found favor *(ḥēn)* in the sight of the Lord," 6:8; "the earth was filled with violence *(ḥāmās),*" 6:11, 13.

Genealogy

Noah is the ninth descendant in Adam's genealogy through Seth (Gen. 5:1–6:8). Each descendant's account is fairly consistent, giving the age when the individual fathered the next descendant, the additional years the individual lived, and the individual's total years. With Noah, the genealogy breaks off with Noah's age when he fathered his three sons (Gen. 5:32). The formula closes at the end of Noah's story (Gen. 9:28-29), giving the additional years

Noah lived and his age at death. Noah's story is framed by the genealogical formula's opening and closing.

The Story of Noah

Noah's story has three components. An account of humanity's depraved condition before the Flood (Gen. 6:1-8) concludes the list of Adam's descendants, emphasizing the increasing pervasiveness of sin. This depravity contrasts with Noah, who "found favor in the sight of the Lord" (6:8). This component is paralleled in an account of Noah and his sons after the Flood (Gen. 9:18-27). The depraved behavior of Ham, Noah's son, and by implication, Canaan, Ham's son (perhaps incest with Noah's wife, cf. Lev. 18:7-8), contrasts with the behavior of Shem and Japheth. These accounts frame the central component, the Flood account (Gen. 6:9–9:17) where Noah, "blameless in his generation," alone is "righteous" among his contemporaries and "walked with God" (6:9; 7:1).

God reveals to Noah his intention to destroy humanity and the earth, and gives instructions to build an ark, in which Noah and his family will survive, along with a male and female of every creature. God directs Noah to gather enough food. Noah does as God commanded (Gen. 6:13-22).

The Lord then tells Noah to bring his household and the animals, including seven pairs of clean animals, into the ark. After seven days, 40 days of rain will destroy all life on earth. Again, Noah does as the Lord commanded. Noah is 600 years old when the Lord shuts him in the ark. When the Flood comes, everything on earth dies, leaving only those with Noah in the ark (Gen. 7:1-24).

Then God remembers Noah. He sends a wind and the waters recede. After the ark rests among the mountains of Ararat, Noah releases a raven and a dove. Unable to find a resting place, the dove returns. Seven days later, Noah releases the dove again, and it returns with an olive leaf. When Noah releases the dove after seven more days, it does not return. The ground is dry (Gen. 8:1-14).

At God's command Noah, with his family and animals, leaves the ark. Noah builds an altar, and sacrifices some clean animals. Smelling the aroma, the Lord decides never again to curse the ground or destroy all life, despite humanity's continuing inclination to evil (Gen. 8:15-22).

God blesses Noah and his sons as he had the first humans in Gen. 1:28. God also announces a new world order. Noah and his descendants have dominion over animals and plants, and animals can be used for food. However, Noah and his descendants must control lawlessness and revenge, using animals responsibly and punishing murder. God closes this announcement of a new order, continuing the blessing with which he began (Gen. 9:1-7).

In a covenant with Noah, his descendants, the animals, and the earth itself, God codifies his decision never again to destroy his creation. The rainbow will remind God of this eternal covenant with his creation (Gen. 9:8-17).

Significance

Gen. 5:1–6:8 begins, "This is the list of the descendants of Adam," and ends, "But Noah found favor in the sight of the Lord." Noah is the last patriarch of the former age, an age characterized by curses (Gen. 3:17-19; 4:11-12), inclination toward evil (6:5), and lawlessness (6:11, 13). That age ends with God's decision to destroy creation (Gen. 6:7). Gen. 6:9 begins a new story, "These are the descendants of Noah." Noah, the first patriarch of a new age, is "righteous," "walked with God" (Gen. 6:9; cf. 7:1), and "did all that God had commanded him" (6:22; 7:5). Humans in the new age remain unchanged, still inclined toward evil (Gen. 8:21). But characteristic of the new age are God's mitigation of previous curses and God's covenant never again to destroy creation. God had used Noah to preserve humanity and animals for a new creation. Now, in that new creation, God uses Noah and his descendants to keep lawlessness in check, protecting and preserving all life, animal and human.

Later References

In Isa. 54:9 God's promise no longer to be angry with Israel parallels God's promise that "the waters of Noah would never again go over the earth." In Ezek. 14:14-20 Noah, along with Daniel and Job, is considered righteous. Ben Sira notes that it was Noah's righteousness and perfection that led to a remnant left upon earth (Sir. 44:17-18). In the NT Noah is among Jesus' ancestors (Luke 3:36). Jesus compares his contemporaries' lifestyles to those of "the days of Noah" prior to the Flood (Matt. 24:37-38). Noah is "a herald of righteousness" (2 Pet. 2:5), "an heir to the righteousness that is in accordance with faith" because he heeded God (Heb. 11:7). The author of 1 Peter notes God's patience in "the days of Noah" while the ark was being built (1 Pet. 3:20).

Bibliography. W. Brueggemann, *Genesis.* Interpretation (Atlanta, 1982); G. J. Wenham, *Genesis 1–15.* WBC 1 (Waco, 1987); C. Westermann, *Genesis 1–11* (Minneapolis, 1984).

Joseph E. Jensen

NOAH, BOOK OF

A pseudepigraphal writing composed by the beginning of the 2nd century B.C.E. Alluded to in Jub. 10:13; 21:10; T. Levi 2:3; 17:2 (one manuscript), the book survives only in summaries and remnants in Jubilees, 1 Enoch, 1QapGen ar, 4QMess ar, 1QNoah, and 4QAramaic N, C. It seems to have included accounts of the fall of the Watchers, the unnatural features of Noah at his birth, the assurances about his real father given by Enoch in Paradise, the Flood, his post-Flood sacrifice and covenant with God, and the division of the earth among his sons. The older designation for the book is the "Apocalypse of Noah."

Bibliography. F. Garcia Martinez, *Qumran and Apocalyptic.* STDJ 9 (Leiden, 1992), 1-44.

R. Glenn Wooden

NO-AMON (Heb. *nō' 'āmôn*)

An alternate form of the Hebrew name for Thebes (Heb. *nō';* Nah. 3:8; NRSV mg), intermittently the capital of Egypt ca. 2000-661 B.C.E.

NOB (Heb. *nōḇ*)
A site in the territory of Benjamin, N of Jerusalem. When fleeing Saul, David comes to Nob (1 Sam. 21:1-11[MT 2-12]). There he meets the priest Ahimelech, who gives David loaves of sacred bread ("bread of the presence"; cf. Matt. 12:3-4; Mark 2:25-26; Luke 6:3-4) and the sword of Goliath. When the Edomite Doeg reports that David has been seen with Ahimelech (1 Sam. 22:9), Saul summons Ahimelech and the other priests from Nob (v. 11) and accuses them of conspiring against him. Saul then orders Doeg to kill the 85 priests from Nob, but instead Doeg puts "to the sword" all the inhabitants of Nob (1 Sam. 22:11-19).

Isa. 10:32 mentions the city as the last stop of the Assyrian army before reaching Jerusalem (Isa. 10:27d-32). The leader of this Assyrian invasion is either Tiglath-pileser III or Sennacherib. Finally, Nob is named, in the postexilic period (Neh. 11:32), as one of the Benjaminite cities, located between Jerusalem and Bethel.

The location of Nob is not entirely clear, but the site is perhaps to be identified with el-ʿIsāwîyeh (173134) or Râs el-Mešârif, on Mt. Scopus just N of Jerusalem. Some scholars have suggested that the city of Nebo (Ezra 2:29; Neh. 7:33), located in the Benjaminite region N of Jerusalem, should instead be read as Nob.

Bibliography. Y. Aharoni, *The Land of the Bible,* 2nd ed. (Philadelphia, 1979); W. F. Albright, "The Assyrian March on Jersualem," in *Excavations and Results at Tell el-Fûl (Gibeah of Saul).* AASOR 4 (1924): 134-40; J. Blenkinsopp, *Ezra-Nehemiah.* OTL (Philadelphia, 1988); P. K. McCarter, Jr., *I Samuel.* AB 8 (Garden City, 1980). John R. Spencer

NOBAH (Heb. *nōḇaḥ*) **(PERSON)**
A Manassite who captured Kenath and its villages in Transjordan and renamed the city after himself (Num. 32:42).

NOBAH (Heb. *nōḇaḥ*) **(PLACE)**

1. A region in Gilead conquered by Nobah the Manassite (Num. 32:40-42). After the Amorite kings Sihon and Og were defeated by the Israelites, the land was divided among the tribes of Reuben, Gad, and Manasseh. This particular area belonged to Kenath and was renamed after Nobah. Its location is not certain, but modern Qanawât (302241) is possible.

2. A city in eastern Gilead near Jogbehah (Judg. 8:10-11). Gideon used the caravan route E of Nobah and Jogbehah to surprise Midianites at Karkor. Its location is not known, although it may be the same as Nobah **1** above. Zeljko Gregor

NOBILITY
Ancient Israel as a society held strong equalitarian ideals, rooted early in their history. The origin of the Israelite tribes in the Arabian steppes gave them a system of authority based on tribal and clan chieftains, family heads, and tribal elders. Under this complex system of tradition, authority, and family, where social rank was based on age, experience (wisdom), and merit, a rough equality was administered between members by those in authority, and real justice was expected from those in power. After the settlement of these tribes in Canaan, this system remained in place, with vestiges surviving into the period of the Monarchy. Indeed, its equalitarian aspects were strengthened as Israel developed from a semi-nomadic tribal society to a society based on a landed peasantry, with the contempt for rank based on status that such societies engender.

By the period of the Divided Monarchy, although the tribal system could still play a decisive political role — as in the revolt of the northern tribes against Rehoboam — a real class society had emerged, with a real nobility. Rehoboam's rash decision not to conciliate the demands of the Israelites reflects the emergence of an influential nobility at court. At the outset of Rehoboam's reign, this nobility was young, upstart, and lacking in sympathy for the peasantry (1 Kgs. 12:6-11). Throughout the subsequent years of the Israelite monarchies, the division widened between the landed (or unlanded) peasantry and the nobles in their "great houses" (cf. Amos 3:15). Various terms attest to this noble class, e.g., Heb. *gāḏôl,* "the great"; *nāgîḏ,* "designated one"; and *partĕmîm,* "nobles, grandees" (Persian loanword). Sem. *śār* is used widely in contexts where it can be applied to military officers, commanders, rulers, or nobles (cf. Hos. 7:16).

In any society based on peasant agriculture, where the possibility of buying and selling land exists, a gradual and natural impoverishment of small landowners, caught in the vicissitudes of weather and other natural setbacks or disasters, or between the variable qualities of land, leads to increasing divisions between the large, wealthy landowners and the peasantry. As large landowners acquire increasing amounts of land they are, by honest means, able to apply economies of scale to agricultural production, thus increasing not only their income but their hedge against economic disaster. As the small landowners are forced to turn to their more prosperous neighbors for loans and other kinds of assistance, their relative economic position is further eroded. Those who borrow could well find themselves having to sell their land to their more prosperous neighbors, signing themselves on as tenants, being reduced to field laborers, or selling oneself or one's family members into "debt slavery." The bitter — and nearly universal — prophetic invective against the rich and noble reflects this progressive degradation of the native Israelite peasantry. Thus, we may consider that the formation of a landed nobility in Israel came about at least partly through and in conjunction with the decline of small landholders. The process was exacerbated by the exertion of power, either by the great landowners or the royal administrations, or both, to suspend the ancient laws designed to prevent just such a development (cf. Exod. 21:2-11; Deut. 15:7-18; Lev. 25).

Militarization provided another means by which aristocracies or nobilities could be formed. To meet the threats posed by the Philistines to the west and the rising Semitic states to the east, Israelite leaders such as Jephthah and Saul began to build private armies of professional soldiers, using booty as the primary means of remuneration. As Saul and later David moved to regularize the military, more satisfactory means of payment — relieving the ruler of the need to pay his troops out of his own resources — may have included distribution of the lands of conquered peoples among the soldiery. Because of the intractability of Israel's native land tenure system (cf. 1 Kgs. 21), such practice may have been feasible only in the conquered or annexed lands of the Canaanite city-states of the Jezreel and Sharon. Land and position were the most likely means to secure the long-term loyalty of the professional soldiery to the king, rather than to the people of Israel.

Another factor was the creation of actual feudal sinecures for members of the warrior class. Solomon instituted a chariot corps, perhaps necessitating creation of a class of warriors similar to the Canaanite *maryannu* to support this mode of fighting. By annexing the Canaanite city-states, David or, more likely, Solomon may have integrated the *maryannu* into the military. The later Israelite nobility may well have grown out of this Canaanite nobility, drawn wholesale into Israelite society as a part of Solomon's military expansion and reform. Support for this class would have been made more palatable to the largely peasant Israelite population because it required relatively little new taxation (unlike his building projects, which required corvée service). The *maryannu* would quickly have become integrated into Israel's life and culture; indeed, the later prophets make no such distinction between Israelite and old Canaanite nobility (but cf. Isa. 2:6-7). However, the injection of a strong element of foreign nobility into Israelite society would have placed the native peasantry at an even greater disadvantage in confronting the challenge to their ancestral rights.

The prophets chastised the Israelite and Judean nobility for failing to provide the just political and social leadership required of persons in positions of power and authority: justice, integrity, and knowledge of the law (cf. Jer. 5:4-5). The abuse of position and power, or the neglect of the responsibilities inherent therein, elicits terrible divine judgment (Amos 5:10-13; 6:1-7; 8:4-8).

DONALD G. SCHLEY

NOD (Heb. *nôḏ*)
The land E of Eden where Cain settled after having killed Abel (Gen. 4:16). The name (from Heb. *nwd*, "to wander") is probably symbolic, playing on Cain's punishment.

NODAB (Heb. *nôḏāḇ*)
A clan attacked by the Transjordanian tribes of Israel (1 Chr. 5:19). Associated with Jetur and Naphish, Ishmaelite groups descended from Hagar, they may be the same as Kedemah named at Gen. 25:15; 1 Chr. 1:31.

NOGAH (Heb. *nōḡah*)
A son of David, born in Jerusalem (1 Chr. 3:7; 14:6). The name is missing in the parallel list at 2 Sam. 5:15, suggesting that the name may be a dittographical error for Nepheg.

NOHAH (Heb. *nôḥâ*) **(PERSON)**
The fourth son of Benjamin (1 Chr. 8:2). The name is missing from other lists of the sons of Benjamin (e.g., Gen. 46:21).

NOHAH (Heb. *nôḥâ*) **(PLACE)**
A place inhabited by the descendants of Nohah, from which the other tribes pursued the Benjaminites (Judg. 20:43 LXX; NRSV mg "from their resting place," following MT).

NOMADISM, PASTORALISM
Grazing, water, and proper herd management are basic essentials in any pastoral economy. The difficulty that arises in the Near East is that grazing land is often unavailable year-round in any one region, and water, in this mainly arid zone, is a precious commodity which is jealously protected and often fought over. Herd management thus becomes the skill of juggling these two realities. In addition, several other factors are of concern: the hiring of sufficient help; proper harvesting of wool, milk, and meat; the judicious use of markets; and the protection of herds from predatory animals, raiders, and the designs of local rulers.

The most common form of migratory pastoralism is termed semi-nomadic pastoralism. This is distinguished by nearly constant pastoral activity and the periodic change of pastures during the greater part of each year. Since pastoralism is not a self-sufficient mode of subsistence, nomadic groups also must supplement their diet by engaging in seasonal agriculture and by trade with settled communities. This brings the tribes into more intimate contact with these communities and also directs their migratory routes.

Categories, of course, do not tell the whole story of a people, especially one so large as "semi-nomad." Variants may reflect the physical and/or political environment which they inhabit or may be a reflection of the transition from a single to a multi-faceted tribal economy.

Another category of pastoralism is herdsman husbandry, in which the majority of the population leads a sedentary life and is occupied primarily with agriculture. Their livestock, or some of it, is maintained year round on pastures, sometimes quite far from the settlement, and tended by herdsmen especially assigned to this task. These herdsmen function as a complementary group to the village agriculturalists. They may be a permanent part of the area's population, or they may act as migratory workers, moving from one herding situation to another. In either case, their function is to supplement the economy of the village, not compete with it.

A somewhat similar form of pastoralism is yaylag pastoralism. This corresponds fairly closely to what is often called transhumance. While the agricultural base is maintained by the majority of the people, the livestock is periodically moved from mountain pastures to lower zones. This is sometimes confused with seasonal pastoralism or vertical pastoralism. However, this type of economic activity is designed to deal with particular environmental conditions. It cannot be indiscriminately applied to every seemingly similar situation.

Most other categories involve village pastoralism. Sedentary animal husbandry is generally a supplementary activity to the agricultural pursuits of the settlement and generally does not involve the management of herds as large as non-village-based pastoralists. Stock-breeding, the establishment of feed lots and free grazing within fairly close proximity, and the use of enclosures are other variants in this category.

Pastoral nomadic activity, such as that described in the ancestral narratives, appears to include aspects of both semi-nomadic pastoralism and herdsman husbandry (cf. esp. Gen. 13:5-12; 21:25-34; 26:17-33; 29:1-10; 37:12-17). A basic sketch of the differences between these two categories includes: the size and mix of herds, timing of migratory activity, areas of pasturage, and percentage of the group involved in pastoral activity. The fact that the herds of semi-nomadic tribes may be larger and consist of a different mix of breeding stock (generally sheep and goats in ancient times) is based on the route of travel, markets, and available pasturage. Since semi-nomads are not always tied to the grazing and water restrictions of their immediate area, a greater flexibility is therefore to be found in their herd-management decisions.

At the same time, the semi-nomadic pastoral groups also must operate within the political and economic spheres of various regions and states. This makes them cautious in their dealings with sedentary peoples. They also develop predatory or at least trickster-like attitudes toward all groups other than their own. As a result, relations between the villages and pastoral nomads, and governments and pastoral nomads were often strained at best.

Another difference between sedentary and semi-nomadic pastoralists involves basic group dynamics. The members of semi-nomadic kinship groups rely on their own judgment in determining route of march, division of herds to take maximum advantage of grazing zones, and parceling out of water rights. Those pastoralists associated with a village culture are often told what to do by higher authorities. These same authorities may try to manage the activities and movements of the semi-nomadic groups, but this can lead to conflict and is certainly not always a successful policy (as can be seen in numerous 18th-century B.C.E. texts from ancient Mari; *ARM* 3.38; 6.30; 14.121).

For this reason, governments that rule areas in which pastoral nomadic peoples operate try to restrict the freedom of movement of these peoples for their own national security purposes. If a group or groups are allowed to pass with impunity from one area to another, important military information may be transmitted to an enemy, or scarce natural resources may be exhausted — thereby depriving village pastoralists of their livelihood — with no significant return in taxes or labor service for these losses. In addition, these transient pastoralists may engage in raiding or other unsanctioned activities which will drain the local economy and force the government to expend time and effort in order to bring them under control or drive them from the area.

It is a continual struggle by the government to either settle the nomadic pastoralists into villages (a process still under way in modern Israel) or to control the resources of their area and channel the activity of the semi-nomadic group's young men, who may be underemployed in some seasons of the year, into harvesting or some other constructive activity. This can be seen in the struggle by Israel's kings to control their southern border by building a series of fortresses and forcing the desert tribes (Amalekites, etc.) into submission and a sedentary existence. However, they eventually were too weakened by foreign invaders (Assyrians, Egyptians, Babylonians) to maintain this policy, and the tribes simply reverted back to pastoral nomadic activity.

Bibliography. F. Barth, "A General Perspective on Nomad-Sedentary Relations in the Middle East," in *The Desert and the Sown,* ed. D. Nelson (Berkeley, 1973), 11-21; D. G. Bates, "The Role of the State in Peasant-Nomad Mutualism," *Anthropological Quarterly* 44 (1971): 109-31; A. M. Khazanov, *Nomads and the Outside World,* 2nd ed. (Madison, 1994); Ø. S. LaBianca, *Sedentarization and Nomadization: Food System Cycles at Hesban and Vicinity in Transjordan* (Berrien Springs, 1990); V. H. Matthews, "Pastoralists and Patriarchs," *BA* 44 (1981): 215-18; M. A. Morrison, "The Jacob and Laban Narrative in Light of Near Eastern Sources," *BA* 46 (1983): 155-64.

VICTOR H. MATTHEWS

NOPHAH (Heb. *nōpaḥ*)

A city in Moab N of Dibon (Num. 21:30 MT; NRSV "fire spread," following LXX, Samaritan Pentateuch).

NORTH

Since the development of the compass, geographic orientation has been toward magnetic north. In the ancient world, however, the rising sun served as one's orientation ("orient" means "east"). The most common word used for east (Heb. *qeḏem*) means lit., "in front" or "before." Thus "north" is often designated as "the left" (*śĕmō'l;* Gen. 14:15).

Directional north came to take on various connotations for the Hebrews. With the Mediterranean Sea on the west and the desert on the east, Israel watched for invading armies only from the south (the Egyptians) or the north (e.g., the Hittites, Damascus, Persia). From the time of the later monarchy danger threatened especially from the nations who would attack from the north. Thus the prophetic literature is stamped with an expectation of disaster from the north (e.g., Jer. 1:14; Ezek. 1:4). Babylon (Jer. 25:9-11; Ezek. 26:7) and Gog (38:14-

16) are specifically mentioned, but more generally God's judgment itself is expected from the north (e.g., Jer. 4:6). Likewise, prophecies of the return of the exiles speak of them arriving from "out of the north" (Jer. 23:8).

The idea of God's judgment coming from the north dovetails with an assumption in common with other ancient Near Eastern civilizations that the gods dwell in a mountain toward the north. Thus the theophany of Ezek. 1:4-5 arises in the north, and the evil one of Isa. 14:13 is tempted to supplant God in the north. This idea clashes somewhat with the idea of the lordship of God over the whole earth (Job 26:7) and with God's dwelling in the temple, but it comes to interesting expression in Ps. 48:1-3(MT 2-4), which identifies Mt. Zion as a northern mountain. DAVID A. DORMAN

NORTHEASTER

Euraquilo (Gk. *eurakýlōn,* a compound word meaning "north and east wind"), the violent storm that threw the ship carrying Paul and other prisoners off course near Crete (Acts 27:14). Named for the major storm systems which can develop throughout the winter, northeasters are a major concern for mariners on the Mediterranean Sea. Typically these storms blow from the north-northeast (60° N of east) and were the reason that shipping virtually ceased in the Roman world from November through February. The great danger was that the wind would either capsize the large-sailed barges or drive ships out of control into shallows of the Syrtes, the quicksand off the Libyan coast. These winds are known today as the *grigale.*

DENNIS M. SWANSON

NOT MY PEOPLE

Lo-ammi (Heb. *lōʾ ʿammî*), the name of Hosea's third child, a son. God tells the prophet to name his son accordingly, thus symbolizing the broken covenant (Hos. 1:9). When Yahweh later promises to restore Israel he will say paronomastically, "You are my people" (Hos. 2:23[MT 25]).

NOT PITIED

Lo-ruhamah (Heb. *lōʾ ruḥāmâ*), the symbolic name given to Hosea's second child, a daughter, indicating that Yahweh would no longer forgive the house of Israel (Hos. 1:6). When the covenant is later restored God will again "have pity" on Israel (Hos. 2:23[MT 25]).

NUMBERS

Although archaeological discoveries of a monetary system evidence a concept of numbering in the "preliterate" Middle East, one does not encounter written examples of numerics until the Proto-Sumerian era with the inscriptions on clay tablets from Uruk in southern Mesopotamia (3000 B.C.E.). These display decimal (10), duodecimal (12), and sexagesimal (60) units of numbering. The oldest mathematical text indicating an advanced use of numbers has been located at the Sumerian city of Shuruppak (ca. 2650). The Egyptians had a comprehensive decimal system which included symbols for whole numbers as high as 1 million and also some fractions. Ebla texts also provide evidence for a decimal system of numbering from as early as the 3rd millennium in Syro-Palestine. Probably influenced by the Egyptians, Israel showed a preference for the decimal system of numbering.

It is apparent that the majority of literate ancient cultures used symbols as the preferred method to express numbers. However, other forms were also used. Some cultures employed the acrophonic system, using the first letter of a word naming or suggesting the number to represent the number. Others used the alphabetic system, representing the numeric units by the successive characters of the alphabet. Still others wrote the number out in full alphabetic script.

The sacred literature of Israel was biased toward writing numbers out in full. However, archaeological finds indicate that symbols were commonly used in the public literary practices of ancient Israel. During the Maccabean period (168-40), Greek influence led to Jewish adaptation of an alphabetic system of numbering. Although the Greeks utilized acrophonic, alphabetic, and symbolic methods, numbers in the Greek NT are always written in full.

Five Hebrew terms are used in the OT: *sāpar,* "to count" (Lev. 25:8; 2 Sam. 24:10); *mispār,* "numeric amount" (Judg. 7:6; Ps. 147:4); *mānâ,* "to enumerate" (Gen. 13:16; Num. 23:10; 2 Kgs. 12:11); *minyān,* "a specific number" (Ezra 6:17); *pāqaḏ,* "to take inventory/a census" (1 Sam. 11:8; 13:5). Three Greek terms are used in the NT: *arithméō,* "to count" (Matt. 10:30 par.; Rev. 7:9); *arithmós,* "a number" (Luke 22:3; John 6:10; Acts 6:7; Rev. 13:18); *psēphízō,* "to calculate" (Luke 14:28; Rev. 13:18).

While critical scholarship questions the validity of the apparently inflated numbers that often occur in the biblical record, the original authors intended them to be taken at face value. The high ages of the prediluvian patriarchs are obviously meant to be taken literally, since the ages of the postdiluvian patriarchs come from the same source (e.g., Gen. 5; 9:28-29; 11; 25:7; 47:28). Also, the census numbers of the Israelite population and various armies are meant to show Israel's strength (e.g., Num. 1-3; Judg. 20).

Symbolic Numbers

Numbers in the Bible often have symbolic or idiomatic application. Three (Heb. *šālōš;* Gk. *treís*) indicates completeness. There are three major pilgrimage feasts for Israelite males (Exod. 23:14-19); three standard times for Jewish prayers (Dan. 6:10; Ps. 55:17[MT 18]); three sections to the universe (Phil. 2:10); three sections in the sanctuary (1 Kgs. 6:2-22); and special efficacy of three-year-old sacrifices (Gen. 15:9; 1 Sam. 1:24). Jonah was in the sea creature's belly three days and three nights (Jonah 1:17), and Jesus was in the tomb three days (Matt. 12:40).

Four (Heb. *ʾarbaʿ;* Gk. *téssares*) indicates boundaries. There are four corners of the earth (Isa. 11:12); four winds (Jer. 49:36; Dan. 7:2); four chariots patrolling the earth (Zech. 6:1-5); four rivers proceeding from Eden (Gen. 2:10-14); four living creatures surrounding the divine throne (Ezek. 1:10; Rev. 4:6-7); and four horsemen (6:2-8).

Seven (Heb. *šeḇa'*; Gk. *heptá*) indicates rest, fulfillment, and restoration: God rested on the seventh day (Gen. 2:2-3; Exod. 20:11); seven animals seal a business transaction (Gen. 21:28); Pharaoh dreams of seven lean years and seven plentiful ones (41:1-36); the land is to lie fallow every seven years (Lev. 25:2-7); seven men are appointed as administrators in the early Church (Acts 6:1-6); the most potent anti-Christ beast has seven heads (Rev. 17:7); the restoration of the earth takes place during the seventh seal and the seventh trumpet (8:1–9:21; 11:15), and after the seventh plague (16:17-21).

Multiples of seven also have significance: e.g., 70 elders (Exod. 24:1, 9); Judah's captivity in Babylon is 70 years (Jer. 25:12; 29:10; Dan. 9:2); 70 prophetic weeks (490 years) are decreed for the Jews (Dan. 9:24). Jesus commissions 70 disciples (Luke 10:1-17); Jubilee occurs after 49 years when debts are canceled and slaves released (Lev. 25:8-55); the number of times to forgive is 70 times seven (Matt. 18:21-22); the extent of vengeance is 77-fold (Gen. 4:24).

Ten (Heb. *'eśer;* Gk. *déka*) indicates completion. God gave Moses 10 commandments (Exod. 34:28); there were 10 plagues against Egypt (Exod. 7:8–11:10); the tithe was 10 percent of a person's increase (Deut. 26:12); 10 virgins await the coming of the bridegroom (Matt. 25:1-13); the final apocalyptic anti-Christ power is represented by 10 horns, 10 kings, and 10 toes (Dan. 2:42; 7:7, 24; Rev. 17:7, 12).

Twelve (Heb. *šĕnêm 'āśār;* Gk. *dṓdeka*) indicates order. There are 12 tribes of Israel (Gen. 49:28; Exod. 28:21; Josh. 3:12); 12 sons of Ishmael; 12 apostles (Matt. 10:1; Luke 9:1); 12 baskets spare after the feeding of the 5 thousand (Matt. 14:20); 12 gates, 12 foundations, and 12 fruits in the New Jerusalem (Rev. 21:12, 14, 21). Multiples of 12 include the total number of the eschatological saved, 144 thousand (Rev. 7:4-17; 14:3-5); the New Jerusalem is 12 thousand furlongs (21:16).

Forty (Heb. *'arbā'îm;* Gk. *tessarákonta*) indicates a complete cycle. The flood rains fell on the earth for 40 days and 40 nights (Gen. 7:12); it took 40 days and nights for Moses to receive instructions about the sanctuary (Exod. 24:18); the wilderness generation wandered for 40 years (Exod. 16:35; Num. 14:20-23); the periods of the judges are sometimes enumerated by 40-year intervals (Judg. 3:11; 5:31; 8:28); Nineveh is given 40 days notice of impeding destruction (Jonah 3:4); Jesus is tempted for 40 days (Mark 1:12 par.).

One thousand (Heb. *'elep̱;* Gk. *chiliás, chílioi*) indicates a very large number. God's love is extended to the thousandth generation of commandment keepers (Deut. 5:10); a thousand days is used to define an indefinite period of time (Ps. 84:10[11]; 2 Pet. 3:8); the 144 thousand comprise a group that none can number (Rev. 7:9); Satan is bound for a thousand years (20:3, 7), the span of the interval between the first resurrection and the second death (20:6, 11-15).

Bibliography. J. J. Davis, *Biblical Numerology* (Grand Rapids, 1968). KEITH A. BURTON

NUMBERS, BOOK OF

The fourth book of the Pentateuch. It recounts the story of the Israelites' preparations for departure from Mt. Sinai and their journey through the wilderness to the Plains of Moab, across the Jordan River from the city of Jericho.

Name

The English name of the book, based on its traditional name in Greek *(Arithmoi)* and Latin *(Numeri)* manuscripts, alludes to the several occasions in which Moses is instructed to "number the people" (i.e., take a census; chs. 1, 3–4, 26). The Hebrew name *Bamidbar* means "In the Wilderness" and better describes the overall content of the book.

Structure

The book is a mixture of dramatic narratives, instructions for camp organization, liturgical calendars, itinerary lists, and laws on subjects as diverse as vows, contact with dead bodies, and the penalty for gathering sticks on the sabbath. It is difficult to discern an outline that accounts for all the details of the book, and proposals are as numerous as the books on the subject. Broadly speaking, there are two main sections introduced by the censuses in chs. 1 and 26. Num. 1–25 covers the period of the generation of those who originally departed from Egypt until their death; it highlights their many acts of disobedience against the God who had delivered them from slavery. Ch. 26 enumerates the second generation, those who had not been in Egypt, and the following chapters picture them by contrast as a people of complete obedience. Thus the name "Numbers" points to a theologically significant theme in the book.

Composition

Tradition holds that the Pentateuch, including Numbers, was written by Moses. The connection of the material in the Pentateuch with Moses as the founding figure of the Israelite community is theologically important because it gives the status of "constitution" to the record of the pre-land, pre-state period of the people's history. This foundational status of early traditions became crucial for identity and survival in later eras, especially during the Second Temple period (after 520 B.C.E.). Despite the traditional attribution to Moses, it is widely believed by modern scholars that material in the book of Numbers comes from many different periods. Some may be as old as the era of Moses himself, and some stems from the era of the Monarchy, but much comes from the exilic and restoration periods of the people's life as a community. From this perspective, the book offers insights not primarily into the history of the wilderness era itself, but more into the ways in which memories of the founding era were shaped to give guidance to later generations.

The materials from the era of the Monarchy are commonly attributed to an "Old Epic" source, while those from exilic and restoration times are labeled "Priestly." Recent scholarship on Numbers tends to deemphasize this "source-critical" analysis in favor of more attention to literary design and theological perspectives discernable in individual passages regardless of their exact date of composition.

It should be noted that as with the OT generally, Numbers is an androcentric composition. It is apparently written by men who consciously or unconsciously presume the interests and concerns of a male audience. Even the story concerning the daughters of Zelophehad (chs. 27, 36) and the legislation concerning vows made by women (ch. 30) function to lay out the rights and responsibilities of men in Israelite culture. Passages such as 14:1-4 in which "all the Israelites" are pictured as worrying about their wives and children also reveal the androcentric orientation of the ancient text.

Historical Value

As noted, most of the material in Numbers is believed to have been written down centuries after the events it purports to describe. Many (although not all) scholars presume that a band of slaves did depart from Egypt and eventually make their way to the territory that became the ancient land of biblical Israel. Rock formations have been identified that can make sense out of the traditions of water gushing from a split rock (ch. 20; Exod. 17). The manna stories fit well with the existence of a sticky substance (excretion from scale lice on tamarisk trees) known in the Sinai Peninsula even today. Yet many of the specific features attributed to the wilderness Israelites may well be later retrojection. The organization of the priesthood as described in Numbers is likely to be the product either of the monarchical period or of the Second Temple era. Many scholars associate the emergence of the 12-tribe organizational pattern with the period of the judges or even later. The itinerary described cannot be reconstructed, as most of the place names given are not identifiable today. Just as with compositional questions, so also the answers to questions about historical details are not essential to an appreciation of the theological themes of the book.

Theological Themes

Among many themes present in the book, three are prominently featured: the holiness of God, the forgiveness of God, and the providence of God.

Holiness

Israel's God is by definition the Holy One (although this phrase does not appear in Numbers), and that which is profane or impure must not come into contact with the holy. Regulations concerning who may come in contact with the tabernacle and its furnishings (ch. 4), the instructions for consecration of the Levites (ch. 8), the ritual for purification after contact with a dead body (ch. 19), and the procedures for atonement in cases of unintentional ritual infractions (ch. 15) are among the many reminders that Israel must be constituted as a holy people in the presence of the holy God.

Forgiveness

The story of the 12 spies and the people's refusal to go up into the land promised to them (chs. 13-14) is paradigmatic for understanding divine forgiveness. The unfaithful and disobedient people express their intention to choose new leadership and return to Egypt, thus "despising" God (14:11). Through Moses' intercessory prayer, God is persuaded not to destroy the people, but to maintain the covenant relationship with the community. There is judgment, to be sure, as the original generation to leave Egypt does not itself enter the Promised Land. Nonetheless, God's faithfulness to the unfaithful people, as manifest in forgiveness that refuses to break God's side of the covenant relationship, is foundational for understanding the nature of this Holy God whom Israel worships.

Providence

Divine providence refers to the undergirding care by which God sustains the life of the community. The theme is first highlighted in the giving of the so-called Aaronic benediction or blessing (6:24-26). The significance of God's will to bless Israel is seen concretely in the dramatic story of Balaam, a foreigner hired by the king of Moab to curse the Israelites. Although Balaam is popularly most famous for his talking donkey, he should better be remembered as the one who repeatedly blesses Israel even though he has been hired to utter curses. The narrator is deliberately ambiguous about whether Balaam speaks the words of blessing of his own will or because God enters his mouth and "compels" him to do so. In a world which took the power of spoken blessings or curses very literally, God's providential care for Israel was made manifest through Balaam's words and proclaimed whenever the Aaronic blessing was spoken.

Bibliography. P. D. Miller, "The Blessing of God: An Interpretation of Numbers 6:22-27," *Int* 29 (1975): 240-51; D. T. Olson, *The Death of the Old and the Birth of the New.* BJS 71 (Chico, 1985); *Numbers.* Interpretation (Louisville, 1996); K. D. Sakenfeld, *Journeying with God: A Commentary on the Book of Numbers.* ITC (Grand Rapids, 1995).

KATHARINE DOOB SAKENFELD

NUMENIUS (Gk. *Nouménios*)

The son of Antiochus, chosen by the Maccabean high priest Jonathan as a Jewish ambassador to Rome and the Spartans (1 Macc. 12:16). The high priest Simon later dispatched him to Rome with a large shield to confirm the alliance (1 Macc. 14:24). He returned with letters from the consul Lucius detailing the Romans' support (1 Macc. 15:15; cf. Josephus *Ant.* 14.8.5 [143-48]).

BENJAMIN C. CHAPMAN

NUN (Heb. *nûn*)
An Ephraimite, the father of Joshua (Exod. 33:11; Josh. 1:1; 1 Chr. 7:27; cf. Num. 13:8, 16).

NUNC DIMITTIS
Latin name derived from the opening words ("now You are dismissing") of Simeon's canticle (Luke 2:29-32), sung — since the 5th century — every evening at Compline, the last of the daily monastic offices.

The "prophet" Simeon ("the Holy Spirit rested on him"; Luke 2:25) declared that his life had found completion with the realization of the Holy Spirit's promise that he would not die before he had seen the Lord's messiah (v. 26). Simeon's declaration that the Messiah's advent was "for glory to your people Israel" and its context (the Jerusalem temple, Jesus' parents following the Jewish ritual of offering a firstborn child, along with Simeon and Anna both personifying expectant Israel) cohere with mention of the Gentiles to suggest the universality of salvation, a common Lukan theme (cf. Luke 3:4-6; 4:16-30; Acts 13:47; 26:23). The hymn is replete with OT allusions, particularly from Second Isaiah (cf. Isa. 40:5; 42:6; 46:13; 49:6; 52:9-10). To a promise-fulfillment motif, the hymn adds direct praise of God.

Scholars differ on the origins of the Nunc Dimittis. Some see it as a free composition by Luke; others warrant Luke is citing a primitive hymn, either from Jewish or Jewish-Christian sources. With the Nunc Dimittis, the Magnificat (Luke 1:46-55), and Benedictus (1:68-79), the early Jewish Christian community and subsequent Christian generations have expressed gratitude that Jesus, the long-awaited one, has come into their midst.

Bibliography. R. E. Brown, *The Birth of the Messiah*, rev. ed. (New York, 1993); S. Farris, *The Hymns of Luke's Infancy Narratives*. JSNTSup 9 (Sheffield, 1985). TERRENCE PRENDERGAST, S.J.

NURSE
Nurses (Heb. *mêneqeṯ, 'ōmeneṯ*) and midwives *(mĕyalleḏeṯ)* helped households determine which women would bear children, when couples would have intercourse, who would adopt children, and who would nurse them. In many households only one wife conceived, bore, adopted, and nursed its sons and daughters (Gen. 21:7; Exod. 2:7; 1 Sam. 1:23; 1 Kgs. 3:21; Cant. 8:1; 2 Macc. 7:27), but in some households a child could be carried by one woman, adopted by another, and nursed by yet another (Gen. 24:59; 35:8; Ruth 4:13-17; 2 Kgs. 11:2 = 2 Chr. 22:11). Jochebed (Exod. 6:20) conceives and breast-feeds Moses, but the daughter of Pharaoh adopts him (1:22–2:10); Ruth conceives Obed, but Naomi adopts and nurses him (Ruth 4:13-17). Breast-feeding immunized children against disease and reduced the chance of a mother conceiving again before she had weaned the child she was nursing; females were weaned in 18 months, males in 30.

The Bible celebrates God as mother, midwife, and nurse. God cradles humanity in his arms (Isa. 46:3-4; Hos. 11:3-4), breast-feeds humanity (Deut. 32:13-14; Isa. 49:15; Hos. 11:4; 2 Esdr. 1:28-29; John 7:37-38; 1 Pet. 2:2-3), and weans humanity to solid food (Wis. 16:20-21; Ps. 131:1-2). Midwives and nurses are metaphors for God creating the cosmos, birthing the first humans, beginning each day, and delivering the eschaton (Lam. 4:4; Joel 2:16). The governing of a state (Num. 11:12; Esth. 2:7; Isa. 49:23) and the care of Christian communities (1 Thess. 2:7) are also modeled on the service of midwives and nurses in the biblical world.

Bibliography. D. C. Benjamin, "Israel's God: Mother and Midwife," *BTB* 19 (1989): 115-20; B. Jordan, *Birth in Four Cultures*, 4th ed. (Prospect Heights, Ill., 1993). DON C. BENJAMIN

NUTS
The edible seeds of several species of fruit trees. "Nut" is used both as a generic term and also to refer specifically to the walnut *(Juglans regia)*. Although the walnut is native to Persia, it was introduced into Palestine, where it flourished in the hills of Palestine and around Lake Gennesaret and the upper course of the Jabbok River. The trees apparently grew wild, though they were sometimes cultivated (Cant. 6:11; Heb. *'ĕgôz*).

Pistachio nuts were among the "choice fruits of the land" sent by Jacob down to Egypt (Gen. 43:11; *boṭnîm*). They were considered a delicacy in the Near East and a particularly appropriate gift. The city Betonim (Josh. 13:26), E of the Jordan River, may have received its name from plentiful orchards of the same.

The almond *(Amygdalus communis)* is also native to Palestine; the hazel nut, however, is not (cf. Gen. 30:37, *lûz*). Heb. *šāqēḏ* probably refers to almonds in Gen. 43:11.

Bibliography. H. N. Moldenke and A. L. Moldenke, *Plants of the Bible* (1952, repr. New York, 1986), 118-20, 179-80. T. J. JENNEY

NUZI (Akk. *Nuzi*)
Since the early 20th century the Nuzi texts have played a major role in the comparative study of the OT. More than 4000 cuneiform texts were uncovered from the Hurrian site of Nuzi (modern Yorghan Tepe) in northern Iraq. Most documents date from ca. 1500-1350 B.C. and deal with legal matters, social and family customs, and myths. Nuzi was apparently part of the small principality of Arrapḫa, which was subject to the large kingdom of Mitanni. A significant percentage of the personal names at Nuzi are Hurrian, although the texts are written in Akkadian. These texts reveal a thriving palace, textile production, and metalworking industry.

As land could not be legally sold but only inherited, Nuzi had an institution of pseudo-adoption, whereby one was adopted by presenting his or her "father" a gift which was in fact the purchase price. The practice of indenture is also attested. An individual pledged to serve a family for a period of time after which he was free; in return, the family of the indentured person gained access to various resources. A number of institutions existed at Nuzi which are generally analogous to those in early Israelite society, including levirate marriage, a system of bridewealth and dowry, and the formal adoption of daughters in the absence of male offspring. These women were allowed to act legally like male heads of families, and thus could arrange their own marriages, care for the family domestic gods, and have their husbands move into their homes.

The Nuzi marriage contracts, adoptions, and herding agreements provide important comparative material for interpreting many of the patriarchal narratives, especially those concerning Jacob and Laban. Moreover, the Nuzi texts allowed a father to provide security for his daughters by selling them into adoption for purposes of marriage. The law in Exod. 21:7-11 somewhat resembles the Nuzi texts in that it allows a father to sell his daughter to a buyer who was then required to see that she was married. The adoption of the daughter, however, is never mentioned in the biblical text.

The Nuzi texts in general appear to reflect common Mesopotamian legal practice (as now known from Emar on the Syrian Euphrates), and thus cannot be used to fix the date of certain biblical traditions in the 2nd millennium.

Bibliography. B. L. Eichler, "Nuzi and the Bible: A Retrospective," in *Dumu-E2-dub-ba-a,* ed. H. Behrens, D. Loding, and M. T. Roth (Philadelphia, 1989), 107-19; M. J. Selman, "Comparative Customs and the Patriarchial Age," in *Essays on the Patriarchal Narratives,* ed. A. Millard and D. Wiseman (Winona Lake, 1983), 91-139; *Studies on the Civilization and Culture of Nuzi and the Hurrians* 1-5 (Winona Lake, 1981-1995), 7– (Baltimore, 1995–).

MARK W. CHAVALAS

NYMPHA (Gk. *Nýmpha*)

A Laodicean Christian whom Paul greeted (Col. 4:15). The Greek name (possibly a rare contraction of Nymphodoras) occurs unaccented in the accusative. It is uncertain whether the noun is "Nymphas" (masc.) or "Nympha" (fem.). Textual variants read "his" *(autoú),* "her" *(autḗs),* and "their" *(autṓn)* house. Nympha appears as a woman's name in Latin inscriptions and Greek literature; textually uncertain, that seems the case here. Introduced without male associate, Nympha would have been a widow or single woman head of a household where a church met (cf. Acts 16:15, 40; Rom. 16:5). She provides evidence of Paul's female associates and friendships in areas he had not visited.

BONNIE THURSTON

O

OAK

Many species of oak (genus *Quercus*) inhabit Israel. Several of these have been identified with the biblical oak (Heb. *'allôn, 'ēlôn*), but no scholarly consensus exists. For instance, the Tabor oak (*Quercus ithaburensis* Decne.) is a grand deciduous tree that may reach 23 m. (75 ft.) in height and 18 m. (60 ft.) in crown circumference, a stature that coincides with the biblical reverence for the oak's strength. The Valonia oak *(Q. Aegilops)* still inhabits Bashan, and may be one of the species of the "oaks of Bashan" (Isa. 2:13; Ezek. 27:6; Zech. 11:2). Oaks are known for their longevity, up to 500 years.

Oaks symbolize strength and power (Amos 2:9), which may explain their association with gods and ritual customs in the Bible. Large trees were also a burial site; Deborah, Rebecca's nurse, was buried under an oak tree (Gen. 35:8). The prophets condemn idol worship that took place under oaks and other large trees (Ezek. 6:13; Hos. 4:13). In Gen. 18:1 God appears to Abraham at the oaks of Mamre.

In some translations, *'allôn* and *'ēlôn* have also been rendered "terebinth," and *'ēlâ* and *'allâ* have been translated "oak." Debate over these terms still exists. It is possible that they refer to large, stately trees in general, since many types of oak and the terebinth fit this description.

MEGAN BISHOP MOORE

OATH

A sacred promise to keep one's word (Num. 30:2) and to honor one's covenants and agreements (Gen. 26:28; 2 Kgs. 11:4). As such, oaths are solemn declarations, which invoke God (Gen. 24:3; 31:53; Deut. 10:20) or some sacred object (Gen. 24:2; 47:29; cf. Matt. 5:33-37; 23:16-22) in order to guarantee the truth of what is declared. The power of the promise itself is binding in biblical oaths and is premised on the understanding that an oath confirms the obligation of the spoken word (Judg. 11:35; 1 Sam. 14:24-27; Jdt. 8:30; cf. Matt. 14:9). The sacral nature of oaths is emphasized by the invocation of God as the guarantor or witness to the sworn word (Gen. 21:23; Josh. 9:19; 1 Kgs. 2:8, 23, 42), and not uncommonly God swears an oath in the OT. Often these concern the promises made to Israel, e.g., those made to Abraham and other ancestral figures (Gen. 22:16-18; 24:7; Deut. 19:8; Josh. 21:43-44; Jer. 11:5; Sir. 44:21), but sometimes they involve threats and sanctions against those who would violate the covenant (Josh. 5:6; 1 Sam. 3:14; Ezek. 17:16-19).

The need for fundamental trust and unequivocal veracity in oaths is so serious as to require the provision of punishments for those who fail to keep them, and any violation of an oath may bring dire consequences (Ezek. 16:59; Dan. 9:11). Therefore, the Bible warns against swearing false oaths and provides sanctions for those who are disingenuous in making them (Exod. 20:7 = Deut. 5:11; Lev. 5:4; 19:12; Zech. 8:17; Wis. 14:29-30). To do so is to devalue the spoken word, which, when given under oath, is the most solemn promise a person makes. Conversely, the one who swears truthfully and with purity of heart receives a blessing (Ps. 24:4-5; Jer. 4:2). Although most oaths seem to be absolutely binding (Num. 30:2, 4, 6-7, 9-11, 14), sometimes conditions placed on them or circumstances under which they are made may mitigate the obligations they carry (vv. 5, 8, 12-13; Gen. 24:41; Josh. 2:17, 20).

The NT understanding of the nature and function of oaths and their value is varied. Some NT authors seem to share the attitude of Philo Judaeus that oaths should be seldom or never sworn. When a person is too quick to make an oath it may not indicate good faith and may actually devalue on the oath itself (Philo *De spec. leg.* 2.8). Therefore, oaths should be sworn only when they are absolutely necessary (*De spec. leg.* 2.9). Matthew's Jesus advises against swearing oaths at all (Matt. 5:33-37) and criticizes the casuistry that can sometimes accompany oath-making (23:16-20). Jas. 5:12 follows the tradition of Matt. 5:33-37 in prohibiting the swearing of oaths. It is interesting, however, that, in the Passion narrative Matthew adds that Peter swore on oath in his second denial of Jesus (Matt. 26:72). In Peter's third denial, Matthew follows Mark 14:71, where Peter invokes a curse on himself in order to strengthen his claim that he does not know Jesus (Matt. 26:74).

Other NT authors look more positively upon oaths. Paul employs oath formulas in Rom. 1:9; 2 Cor. 1:23; Gal. 1:20; Phil. 1:8. In Hebrews God's oath to Abraham is recalled as a reminder of the guarantee of God's promises and the surety of God's word (Heb. 6:13-19). Elsewhere in the NT an oath sworn by God is remembered in Luke 1:73 (cf. v. 55); Acts 2:30; Rom. 14:11; Heb. 3:11, 18; 4:3. Thus the attitude of NT authors on swearing oaths depends on whom one consults. ALAN C. MITCHELL

OBADIAH (Heb. *ʿōḇaḏyâ, ʿōḇaḏyāhû*)

1. The steward or manager in charge of King Ahab's household (1 Kgs. 18:3-16) who supervised Ahab's estate and probably was responsible for royal trade and mining. As a devout worshipper of Yahweh, he hid 100 prophets of Yahweh during Jezebel's pogram and, at Elijah's request, arranged an audience for Elijah with Ahab, a meeting that led to the contest between Elijah and the prophets of Baal.

Bibliography. T. N. D. Mettinger, *Solomonic State Officials.* ConBOT 5 (Lund, 1971).

2. A postexilic descendant of David, one of the sons of Hananiah (1 Chr. 3:21).

3. A chief of the tribe of Issachar; son of Izrahiah (1 Chr. 7:3).

4. A Benjamite, the son of Azel and a descendant of Saul (1 Chr. 8:38; 9:44).

5. A Levite who was among the first to return to Jerusalem (1 Chr. 9:16). He may also be called Abda (Neh. 11:17).

6. A Gadite leader who joined David's army at Ziklag and served as a warrior and officer (1 Chr. 12:9).

7. The father of Ishmaiah, who was a ruler over the tribe of Zebulon during the last days of David (1 Chr. 27:19).

8. A prince commissioned by King Jehoshaphat to teach the "law of the Lord" to the people throughout Judah (2 Chr. 17:7-9).

9. A Merarite Levite who helped oversee the repair of the temple during Josiah's reign (2 Chr. 34:12).

10. A family head who returned to Jerusalem with Ezra; descendant of Joab (Ezra 8:9).

11. A leader who added his seal to the renewal of the covenant under Ezra and Nehemiah's leadership (Neh. 10:5[6]). He may be the same individual as **10** above.

12. A gatekeeper during the high priesthood of Joiakim whose task was to guard the storehouses of the gates (Neh. 12:25).

13. Obadiah the prophet, who most likely lived and ministered ca. the mid-5th century B.C.

MICHAEL A. GRISANTI

OBADIAH (Heb. *ʿōḇaḏyâ*), **BOOK OF**

One of the 12 Minor Prophets; with only 21 verses, the shortest book in the Hebrew Bible. In the MT it follows Amos, perhaps because the canonical compilers wanted to connect it with Amos 9:12; the LXX groups the three undated books (Joel, Obadiah, Jonah) together following the three 8th-century books (Hosea, Amos, Micah).

Text

The Hebrew text of Obadiah has been well preserved. The oldest extant text is in the Minor Prophets scroll from Wadi Murabbaʿat (ca. A.D. 135), a proto-Masoretic text that differs from the Leningrad Codex (A.D. 1008) in only a few places. The ancient versions also attest to texts that generally agree with the Leningrad Codex.

Style

The book consists of a poetic composition (vv. 1-18) with a prose conclusion (vv. 19-21). The poetry exhibits the systematic and dominant use of parallelism that operates "horizontally" between two contiguous lines or cola and "vertically" among larger groupings of lines or cola. The poetic lines are terse, usually 4-10 syllables and 2-4 accents in length. The poetry also draws from a common stock of imagery, although no one image is developed beyond a single verse: e.g., v. 4 compares Edom's lofty abode with that of an eagle's nest; v. 10 equates shame with a garment that will cover Edom; v. 16 employs the cup-of-wrath metaphor; and v. 18 likens Israel to fire and Edom to stubble.

Composition

Much scholarly debate has concentrated on the book's compositional history and unity. Assessments vary from a unity originally composed by one person named Obadiah to a collection of eight originally independent fragments. Some scholars presuppose an original disunity but consider the book in its final form to reflect a redactional cohesion. What causes the debate is the amount of diversity evident in the book in terms of style, emphasis, and perspective. If the reader assumes that prophetic discourse can employ divergent and even dissonant perspectives, emphases, and styles within the same composition, then there is no reason to doubt the original unity of this small book.

Biblical Parallels

Obadiah offers a study in intertextuality since so many of its expressions, images, and motifs appear elsewhere in the OT. Nearly every verse reflects parallels with other biblical texts. Particularly significant is the overlap between Obadiah and Jeremiah's Edom prophecy (vv. 1-4 = Jer. 49:14-16; vv. 5-6 = Jer. 49:9-10; vv. 7-8 = Jer. 49:7) and between Obadiah and parts of Joel (v. 10 = Joel 3:19[MT 4:19]; v. 11 = Joel 3:3[4:3]; v. 15a = Joel 1:15; 2:1; 3:14[4:14]; v. 15b = Joel 3:4, 7[4:4, 7]; v. 17 = Joel 2:32[3:5]; 3:17[4:17]). The degree of overlap raises the question of dependence. Most scholars contend that Obadiah depended on Jeremiah or they both used a third source, and Joel depended on Obadiah.

Date and Historical Setting

Unlike other prophetic books, the title provides no chronological information. We only know the prophet's name ("one who serves Yahweh"), a very common name in ancient Israel. Any other information must be inferred from the contents of the prophecy. Early Jewish traditions, followed by Jerome, identified the prophet with the Obadiah in 1 Kgs. 18, the official in charge of Ahab's palace who hid 100 prophets. Some scholars locate him at the time of Edom's revolt against Jehoram ca. 845 B.C. (2 Kgs. 8:20-22; 2 Chr. 21:8-17). Both suggested dates would make our prophet the earliest of the writing prophets, almost a century before Amos. Other scholars date Obadiah in the mid-to-late 5th century during the Persian period. Luther and Calvin located him after the fall of Jerusalem in 587/586, and most recent scholars agree in placing at least the core of the book within Babylonian exile.

The book seems to fit best in the first half of the exilic period, after the fall of Judah and Jerusalem to Babylon in 587/586 and before the demise of Edom in 553. According to vv. 10-14 the Edomites took the side of the "strangers" and "foreigners" who attacked Judah and Jerusalem. The prophet condemns the Edomites for gloating over Judah's downfall, looting Judah's towns, and capturing Judah's refugees (cf. Ezek. 25:12-14; 35–36; Ps. 137; Lam. 4:21-22). Recent archaeological work has revealed a significant Edomite presence in the Negeb during the 7th–early 6th centuries, so some Edomites had the opportunity to take advantage of Judah's troubles. Perhaps this presence provides the background for the statement in v. 20: "the exiles of Jerusalem who are in Sepharad will possess the cities of the Negeb" (the returning exiles will retrieve the Negeb's towns from Edomite control). The process of Edomite settlement in southern Judah continued so that later this area was called Idumea. According to the Nabonidus Chronicle, Nabonidus of Babylon campaigned against Edom in 553 (cf. vv. 7, 11); archaeology seems to attest to this campaign, since several Edomite sites reveal evidence of destruction in the 6th century. During the Persian period the Nabateans began to migrate into the land of Edom.

Structure and Genre

The book can be divided into five parts: vv. 1-4; 5-7; 8-15; 16-18; 19-21, connected by the use of grammatical links and catchwords.

The authorial voice of the book is the prophet Obadiah, who functions as Yahweh's mouthpiece and addresses Yahweh's speech to Edom in vv. 1-15 and to Judah in vv. 16-18. The use of the plural form of "you" in v. 16a signals the shift in addressee to the Judahites. The final three verses are presented as the prophet's own expansion. The opening two thirds of the book (vv. 1-15) consist of announcements of doom, accusation, and warning for Edom, whereas the final one third (vv. 16-21) contains promises of restoration and victory for Israel. Much of the book concerns the Edomites who, according to biblical tradition, are the descendants of Esau. Prophetic judgment speeches against Edom occur also in Isaiah, Jeremiah, Ezekiel, Joel, Amos, and Malachi. This is part of a larger category, prophecies against foreign nations.

Contents

Obadiah announces Edom's coming doom. God has recruited the nations to attack Edom and thereby will bring Edom down, despite Edom's sense of security based on its location high in the Edomite mountains (vv. 1-4). Edom's hiding places and hidden treasures will not go undetected (vv. 5-7); the attacking nations will turn out to be Edom's own covenant partners (i.e., the Babylonians?). God will destroy Edom's wise men and terrify its warriors so that everyone will be cut off from Edom (vv. 8-9). The prophet attempts to persuade Edom that none of its strengths and defenses can fend off the coming destruction: its status among the nations, inaccessible location, hiding places and wealth, allies, wisdom, and military power.

Obadiah then explains the basis for Edom's future judgment as grounded on Edom's past violence against its own brother, Jacob (v. 10). Instead of coming to the defense of their brother, the Edomites sided with the invading "strangers" and "foreigners" and even acted like one of these outsiders (v. 11). Verses 12-14 serve a twofold function. First, they specify the charges: Edom gloated over Judah's demise and took advantage of the situation by looting and capturing Judah's survivors. Second, they serve as warnings for Edom to stop its anti-Judahite hostilities before it is too late (v. 15a). On that day Yahweh will judge Edom (and presumably the other nations; v. 15b).

Beginning in v. 16 the prophet addresses the question of Israel's future status. While Edom's judgment is based on Edom's past actions, Israel's future restoration is based solely on God's unconditional commitment to Jacob and Zion. This is depicted as a reversal of the judgment recently experienced by Israel. Just as the Judahites and the Jerusalemites drank the cup of Yahweh's wrath, so also the other nations including Edom will have to drink it (v. 16; Jer. 25:15-29). But Mt. Zion will be the place of escape from the impending divine judgment (v. 17a). Whereas it was profaned by "strangers" and "foreigners" in the past (v. 11), in the future Zion will regain its sacred status (v. 17a; cf. Joel 3:17[4:17]). The Israelites will repossess their land (v. 17b), and they will completely defeat and eradicate Edom (v. 18).

The conclusion expands on the divine promises made in vv. 17-18. All of Israel, including the exiles, will regain the full extent of their land (vv. 19-20), and Mt. Zion will rule over Mt. Esau (v. 21a). Yahweh will definitively manifest his rule over all nations (v. 21b). Both these themes of the eschatological kingdom of Yahweh and the eschatological day of Yahweh (v. 15) became important in the NT and thus contribute to Obadiah's continuing significance.

Bibliography. J. R. Bartlett, *Edom and the Edomites.* JSOTSup 77 (Sheffield, 1989); E. Ben Zvi, *A Historical-Critical Study of the Book of Obadiah.* BZAW 242 (Berlin, 1996); P. R. Raabe, *Obadiah.* AB

24 (New York, 1996); "Why Prophetic Oracles against the Nations?" in *Fortunate the Eyes That See,* ed. A. B. Beck et al. (Grand Rapids, 1995), 236-57; H. W. Wolff, *Obadiah and Jonah* (Minneapolis, 1986). PAUL R. RAABE

OBAL (Heb. *ʿôḇāl*) (also EBAL)
One of the sons of Joktan, and the eponymous ancestor of a south Arabian tribe (Gen. 10:28). He is called Ebal at 1 Chr. 1:22.

OBED (Heb. *ʿôḇēḏ;* Gk. *Iōbēd*) (also EBED)
1. The son of Ruth, the widowed Moabitess (Ruth 4:21), and Boaz, the "close relative" (2:21) of her deceased husband Mahlon. Obed became the grandfather of King David (Ruth 4:16; 1 Chr. 2:12) and ancestor of Jesus Christ (Matt. 1:5; Luke 3:32). Curiously, he was named Obed ("worshipper") by the women of Bethlehem rather than by his parents (Ruth 4:17). The birth of Obed was possible because of levirate law (Deut. 25:5-10), which required the eldest brother or closest relative of the deceased husband to marry the widow.

2. A son of Ephlal (1 Chr. 2:37) and descendant of Jerahmeel (1 Chr. 2:37-38).

3. One of David's Mighty Men (1 Chr. 11:47). His name is missing in the parallel account (2 Sam. 23).

4. A son of Shemaiah, a Korahite gatekeeper whose four sons were said to be "men of great ability" (1 Chr. 26:6-7).

5. The father of the military commander Azariah, who followed the priest Jehoiada in executing Queen Athaliah and installing the child Joash as king (2 Chr. 23:1).

6. A son of Jonathan; one of the men who returned from Babylon to Palestine with Ezra (1 Esdr. 8:32); called Ebed at Ezra 8:6. DONALD FOWLER

OBED-EDOM (Heb. *ʿōḇēḏ-ʾěḏôm*)
1. A Gittite in whose house David stored the ark of the Lord for three months, following the death of Uzzah for having touched the ark (2 Sam. 6:10-11; 1 Chr. 13:13-14). When David heard that Obed-edom was blessed because of the ark's presence, he ordered its removal to the tent in Jerusalem (2 Sam. 6:12; 1 Chr. 15:25). His name and origin, in the city of Gath, may indicate that he was also among those Philistines loyal to David (cf. 2 Sam. 15:18-22; 18:2).

2. The son of Jeduthun; a levitical musician and gatekeeper at the tent of meeting (1 Chr. 15:18, 21, 24). He was appointed by David, along with his 68 brothers, to minister with harp and lyre before the ark (1 Chr. 16:5, 38).

3. A son of Korah; a gatekeeper who, with his 62 descendants, served at the temple precinct's southern gate and storehouses (1 Chr. 26:4-8, 15).

4. The custodian of the temple treasures when King Joash of Israel captured Amaziah of Judah (2 Chr. 25:24). It is uncertain from the MT whether Obed-edom was taken captive (so LXX) or is simply named as the official in charge at the time. His name is absent from the parallel account in 2 Kgs. 14:14. KENNETH ATKINSON

OBEDIENCE
The English translation of Heb. *šamaʿ,* referring to the physical act of hearing and, in certain contexts, the combination of hearing with the intent to obey (Exod. 19:5, 8; Deut. 28:1; 30:11-14). If one truly hears the word of God, then obedience is inevitable. Thus, if people fail to obey, the prophets often accuse the Israelites of being deaf (Isa. 6:9-10). Obedience is what is expected of one's relationship to God (Jer. 3:13, 25) and a son's relationship to his father (Prov. 4:1-2). Clearly, there is an implied expectation of obedience in "hearing" a message (Gen. 3:17; 23:15; Exod. 24:7).

In the NT there is also the expectation of obedience when hearing a message. In the Sermon on the Mount, Jesus summarizes his entire message with the parable of the two builders (Matt. 7:21-27). The one who hears the words of the sermon and then translates that hearing into action is like the one who builds his house upon a rock — he is on solid foundation. Not only is obedience the expected response to the ethical injunctions of Christ, but it also should be one's response to the gospel (Gal. 3:2). Paul reminds the readers of the Philippian letter that Jesus Christ's death on the cross is the ultimate example of obedience (Phil. 2:8; Gk. *hypḗkoos*). RICK W. BYARGEON

OBEISANCE
The act of honoring someone by bowing or prostrating oneself. Gk. *proskynéō* and Heb. *šḥh (hištaḥăwâ)* express both the idea of physical prostration and of honor. One may bow down to honor a powerful person (1 Kgs. 1:16, 23, 31, 53; Matt. 18:26) or to worship a god (Ps. 95:6; Isa. 44:17; Rev. 19:10; 22:8-9). Occasionally the words express the idea of worship or honor where physical prostration is impossible or unlikely (2 Sam. 16:4; Heb. 11:21). CARL BRIDGES

OBELISK
A sacred monument native to ancient Egypt in the shape of a tall, four-sided pillar that rises to a pyramidal point. Built of stone, its four sides were usually covered in royal or religious inscriptions. Numerous examples of obelisks survive to this day in Egypt.

In the only biblical reference to an Egyptian obelisk (Jer. 43:13), Jeremiah prophesies that Nebuchadnezzar would destroy the obelisks of Heliopolis. The obelisk likely originated in this Egyptian cultic center, and was apparently associated with the sun-god Amon-Re. In earlier periods, it was believed that the god both lived in and rested on the obelisk; in New Kingdom times, however, obelisks were raised to commemorate the celebration of the pharaoh's Thirty Year festival.
JENNIE R. EBELING

OBIL (Heb. *ʾôḇîl*)
An Ishmaelite who was the overseer of King David's camels (1 Chr. 27:30).

OBLATION
The evening temple sacrifice (1 Kgs. 18:29, 36; Heb. *minḥâ*).

OBOTH (Heb. *ʾōḇōṯ*)
An Israelite encampment near the end of the wilderness journey, located between Punon and Iye-abarim (Num. 21:10-11; 33:43-44). Oboth was probably E of the Dead Sea on the King's Highway (Num. 20:17; 21:22) between the lands of Edom and Moab. Possible locations include ʿAin el-Weiba, ʿAin Ḥoṣob, and various places N of Feinân and N of Bozrah. PETE F. WILBANKS

OCHRAN (Heb. *ʿoḵrān*)
The father of Pagiel, chief of the tribe of Asher (Num. 1:13; 2:27; 7:72, 77; 10:26).

OCINA (Gk. *Okina*)
A coastal town S of Tyre (Jdt. 2:28). Some scholars identify it with Acco, largely on the basis of name similarity and general location.

ODED (Heb. *ʿôḏēḏ*)

1. The father of the prophet Azariah (**11;** 2 Chr. 15:1, 8).

2. A prophet at Samaria who ordered the victorious Israelite army of King Pekah to free their Judahite prisoners. Oded rebuked the soldiers for their slaughter and reminded them of their own sins against Yahweh, whereupon they fed, clothed, and released their captives (2 Chr. 28:8-15).

ODOR
The scent of a sacrifice, in ancient Near Eastern mythology held to be pleasing to the gods and thus attracting their attention (e.g., Atrahasis III.5.30-35). This is reflected in the account of Noah's post-Flood offering (Gen. 8:20-21).

Heb. *rēaḥ* is well attested as the common word for odor or scent (e.g., Cant. 4:10), but the phrase *rēaḥ nîḥ nîḥōaḥ*, "pleasing odor," occurs only in cultic contexts, particularly as a technical term designating an offering by fire. Sacrifices which did not include frankincense or incense were also described with this term, so it must have been the nature of the sacrifice, not the often unpleasant smell of burning meat, which was envisioned as pleasing. The only burnt offering to which this term is never applied is the reparations (guilt) offering (Lev. 5:14–6:7[MT 5:26]). It appears only once in connection with the purification (sin) offering (Lev. 4:31), and many scholars regard this attestation as a later addition to the text. All of the attestations of "pleasing odor" in Exodus, Leviticus, and Numbers may be the work of the Holiness school.

Ezek. 6:13; 16:41; 20:28 refer to pagan cults. Ezek. 20:41 is a metaphorical reference to the people of Israel as a whole.

Bibliography. W. R. Scott, *The Booths of Ancient Israel's Autumn Festival* (diss., Johns Hopkins, 1993). WILLIAM R. SCOTT

OFFERING

See SACRIFICES AND OFFERINGS.

OFFICE
An official position or responsibility. A clearly defined office means that authority and legitimation of leadership are secure and can be transferred from generation to generation. Three basic types of authority give legitimation to an office: legal authority (based on rules or precedent), traditional authority (based on sacral traditions and beliefs), and charismatic authority (based upon the extraordinary leadership skills of an individual).

In tribal Israel, offices were derived from a combination of traditional and charismatic authority. The "judges" came into temporary positions of leadership by uniting the tribes against a common enemy. Leadership on the local level was derived more from traditional authority. Samuel administered his authority as prophet and judge through a regular "circuit" of three cities: Bethel, Gilgal, and Mizpah (1 Sam. 7:16). In the same period, kings such as Abimelech of Shechem ruled their small city-states through the power of legal authority (Judg. 9).

A clear administration with offices based more upon legal authority began to appear at the time of the Israelite United Monarchy. The difficulty of the transition from the traditional administration of a prophet-priest to that of a king is demonstrated by the people's having to plead with Samuel for a king. The king would have the authority for taxation, conscription for military and labor purposes, and organization of the economy into a "royal" economy (1 Sam. 8:10-17).

The Israelite United Monarchy and the monarchies of Judah and Samaria served in the institutionalization of various offices throughout ancient Israel. The uniqueness of Israelite religion within its ancient Near Eastern context is attested by the prophetic tradition that was able to bring a critique against the office of the king.

Bibliography. R. R. Hutton, *Charisma and Authority in Israelite Society* (Minneapolis, 1994).

BRUCE W. GENTRY

OFFICER, OFFICIAL
A person imbued with civil, political, military, or religious responsibility. No one word in Hebrew is used for "office" or "official" in the OT because the office of an individual was implied through the description of the position. The roles of officials vary greatly because of the different types of administrative structures found throughout biblical history: tribal government, the monarchy, and the government of the ruling empire. The palace, temple, and military contained a complete contingent of officers for administration. Heb. *śar* is most widely used for a variety of official titles, often translated "prince," "chief," "noble," or "official." Leadership roles are also evidenced by more general terms such as "head" (*rōʾš;* Josh. 22:14; 1 Sam. 15:17); "great" (*raḇ;* Dan. 4:22[MT 19]); "servant" (*ʿeḇeḏ;* Gen. 40:20; 1 Sam. 18:5); "boy" (*naʿar;* 2 Sam. 16:1;

often translated "steward" or "household servant"); and the preposition "over" (*'al;* 2 Kgs. 10:5; Isa. 36:3).

The scribe *(sōpēr)* served as the personal secretary to the king or other official, such as a priest or prophet (2 Sam. 8:17; Neh. 8:1; Jer. 36:32). The *nĕṣîḇ* was a regional administrative official of the Philistines (often translated "garrison," 1 Sam. 10:5; 13:3) and of the Solomonic districts (1 Kgs. 4:7). Other words designate a certain type of official, although in some cases, precise meanings have been lost through time. The *sagan* (MT only pl.) was described as an official of Babylon, Assyria (Ezek. 23:6), and Judah (Neh. 2:16). The *sarîs* was a eunuch who held a distinguished office in the governments of such countries as Egypt (Gen. 37:36), Babylon (2 Kgs. 20:18; Dan. 1:7), and Persia (Esth. 2:3). It has been suggested that *sārîs* in the OT may not refer to a specific officer who was a eunuch but may be a general term for an officer; however, eunuchs were apparently present in the administration of ancient Israel (1 Sam. 8:15; 1 Kgs. 22:9; 2 Kgs. 24:15; 1 Chr. 28:1). The *šōṭēr* (MT usually pl.) was a secondary officer in Israel (Num. 11:16; Josh. 8:33).

In the NT a variety of terms denote officials and officers. Gk. *hypērétēs* denotes officials, guards, or servants (John 18:3; Mark 14:54; 1 Cor. 4:1). Gk. *hekatontárchēs* denotes the Roman centurion (Matt. 8:5) and *chilíarchos,* a commander or general (Acts 21:31; Rev. 6:15). BRUCE W. GENTRY

OG (Heb. *'ôg*)
The king of the Transjordanian territory of Bashan, whom the Israelites under Moses claim to have conquered at Edrei. They then captured the 60 towns contained within his kingdom, which were fenced with high walls, gates, and bars (Num. 21:33-35; Deut. 3:1-10). He and another Amorite king, Sihon, were massacred and depossessed of land that Reuben, Gad, and half of the tribe of Manasseh would inherit (Deut. 3:13). This event became legendary among the Israelites, and was celebrated in many subsequent writings (e.g., Josh. 12:4; 13:12, 30-31; 1 Kgs. 4:19; Neh. 9:22; Ps. 135:11; 136:20). Og is also remembered as the last remnant of the Rephaim, or giants, and his famous giant "bed of iron" (9 cubits × 4 cubits) may be a reference to his sarcophagus (Deut. 3:11).

Bibliography. A. R. Millard, "King Og's Bed and Other Ancient Ironmongery," in *Ascribe to the Lord.* JSOTSup 67 (Sheffield, 1988), 481-92; W. S. Sumner, "Israel's Encounters with Edom, Moab, Ammon, Sihon, and Og according to the Deuteronomist," *VT* 18 (1968): 216-28. TONY S. L. MICHAEL

OHAD (Heb. *'ōhaḏ*)
The third son of Simeon (Gen. 46:10; Exod. 6:15). He is not mentioned in the genealogies at Num. 26:12-14; 1 Chr. 4:24-25.

OHEL (Heb. *'ōhel*)
A descendant (perhaps a son) of Zerubbabel (1 Chr. 3:20).

OHOLAH (Heb. *'ohŏlâ*), **OHOLIBAH** (*'ohŏlîḇâ*)
The names given in Ezek. 23 to two sisters, the personified cities of Samaria and Jerusalem, respectively. In a metaphor that draws heavily on Jer. 3:6-11; Ezek. 16, the capital cities are represented as Yahweh's wives, and their various international liaisons as a series of sexual encounters — all acts of adultery against Yahweh. The cities' destruction is thus justified as an enraged husband's legally sanctioned execution of his spouse. The angry desperation of this oracle against Jerusalem is conveyed through its crude sexual imagery and depictions of savage violence against the two women.

The sisters' names symbolize their religious identities: "Oholah" (Samaria) may be translated "a tent belongs to her" and "Oholibah" (Jerusalem), "my tent is in her." The cities' "tents" are their worship centers: Samaria has her own tent while Jerusalem houses Yahweh's sanctuary. In a transparent recapitulation of the northern kingdom's international relations, Oholah is censured for her liaison with Assyria and for her continued flirtations with Egypt, infidelities culminating in her death, i.e., the destruction of Samaria in 722 B.C.E. Oholibah follows her sister's example, entertaining both Assyrian and Babylonian lovers, but continuing to lust after the Egyptians. The metaphor reflects Judah's situation in the early 580s, when Jerusalem had transferred loyalty from Assyria to Babylonia but continued to maintain relations with Egypt. In response, Yahweh announces that he is about to punish Oholibah and, surprisingly, the previously executed Oholah as well: i.e., all of Israel will be destroyed. JULIE GALAMBUSH

OHOLIAB (Heb. *'ohŏlî'āḇ*)
The son of Ahisamach of the tribe of Dan, a craftsman and designer. He and Bezalel were responsible for construction of the tabernacle (Exod. 31:6; 35:34; 36:1-2; 38:23).

OHOLIBAMAH (Heb. *'ohŏlîḇāmâ*)

1. A wife of Esau, and the daughter of Anah the son of Zibeon the Hivite (Gen. 36:2, 25). She bore three sons (Gen. 36:5, 14, 18). Oholibamah is not named among Esau's wives at Gen. 26:34; 28:9.

2. The chief of an Edomite clan (Gen. 36:41; 1 Chr. 1:52).

OIL, OINTMENT
Most of the oil noted in the Bible is olive oil. Extracting the oil from the berry varied from place to place and time to time. Yet the basics are clear. Olives were harvested between September and December. Earlier in the season olives were green; later the olive turned black and the oil content increased. Oil extraction required the berries to be bruised or crushed. This was done by tramping on them with the feet (Mic. 6:15), pounding them in a mortar, or pressing them with a large stone. The olive pulp was then placed in open-weave baskets with plenty of spaces for the oil to seep through. This first extraction was the most valuable and was

used with food, for religious use (Exod. 29:40), and for trade (1 Kgs. 5:11[MT 25]). The remaining pulp was heated and then placed in a vat. By using a lever, beam, and heavy stones the oil was pressed from the pulp. This second extraction, and even a third extraction, produced a type of oil that was commonly used for oil lamps and other household use. Mills were used for very large quantities of olives. These mills included a rather large circular stone basin (up to 2.5 m. [8 ft.] in diameter) in which the olives were placed. Then a heavy vertical stone wheel was rotated around the basin to crush the olives. One or two people or an animal turned the stone by pushing a bar around a pivot.

The use of olive oil was extensive. Olive oil, wine, and grain were the three most important agricultural products of the Promised Land (Deut. 7:13). Olives and olive oil were staples in the diet and were served at almost every meal. Bread was commonly eaten with olive oil. It, and rarely other oils such as castor oil and sesame oil, took the place of butter and animal fat. It was mixed with meal to make cakes or bread (1 Kgs. 17:12-16), and it was often mentioned with other food such as fine flour (Lev. 2:1-4), wine (Rev. 6:6), and honey (Ezek. 16:13).

Because olive oil burned brightly without much of an odor or smell, it was used in oil lamps for illumination. First-grade olive oil was used for the continual light in the tabernacle (Exod. 27:20) and provided the light in the temple candelabrum (25:6). It was used to anoint kings (1 Sam. 16:1-13; 2 Kgs. 9:1-3), priests (Exod. 29:7-35; Lev. 8:12), a prophet (Isa. 61:1), stelae (Gen. 28:18), as well as the tabernacle and its contents (Exod. 30:23-29). Oil was used in purification rituals (Lev. 14:10-29), food offerings (Exod. 29:40), meal offerings (Lev. 2), and with animal sacrifices (Num. 15:1-16).

Oil was used widely in the ancient Near East to anoint the body. It was a protection from sunburn and flies, and it kept the skin soft. The oil was applied to the body after bathing (Ruth 3:3), but in times of mourning no oil was used (2 Sam. 14:2; cf. 12:20). Guests had their feet washed and their heads anointed with oil (Luke 7:46). Oil was used on bruises, sores, and wounds (Isa. 1:6), and the sick were anointed with oil (Mark 6:13). Elders of the Church prayed for the sick and anointed them (Jas. 5:14). The Good Samaritan poured oil and wine on the wounds of the beaten traveler (Luke 10:34).

Because of its unique importance olive oil was frequently exported. The largest trading partner was Phoenicia. Solomon gave Hiram of Tyre ca. 435 thousand l. (115 thousand gal.) of oil in exchange for assistance in building the temple (1 Kgs. 5:11[25]). In both Egypt and Mesopotamia little or no olive oil was produced, and it had to be imported as a luxury item. Israel supplied at least some of it (Hos. 12:1[2]). It was also a good cash crop within the country (2 Kgs. 4:7; Luke 16:6).

Oil was a symbol of prosperity (Deut. 32:13), hospitality (Ps. 23:5), and joy (45:7[8]). The words of deceit were softer than oil (Ps. 55:21[22]), as was the speech of a loose woman (Prov. 5:3).

The OT does not distinguish between oil and ointment, which is not surprising since olive oil was a part of most ointments. Various spices were used with olive oil to make perfumes and ointments. These included myrrh (Esth. 2:12; Matt. 2:11), nard (Mark 14:3), balsam or balm (Gen. 37:25; Jer. 8:22), and aloes (Ps. 45:8[9]; John 19:39). Alabaster or glass flasks or jars were used to hold the ointment.

Ointments were used in religious ceremonies (Exod. 30:22-25), in preparation for burial (Luke 23:56), for protection of the skin and beautification (Esth. 2:3, 9, 12), and in the hospitality for a guest (Luke 7:46).

Bibliography. R. Frankel, S. Avitsur, and E. Ayalon, *History and Technology of Olive Oil in the Holy Land* (Arlington, 1994). James C. Moyer

OLD LATIN VERSIONS

A Latin textual tradition of the Bible that preceded Jerome's Vulgate. It is unclear whether the Old Latin proceeded from one original or from several independent translations, but as various Roman provinces altered texts in their own ways, they differed more and more from the earliest text and from one another. Two forms, African and European, are prominent, with slight provincial variations, such as in Spain and Ireland.

The African texts of the 5th and 6th centuries are practically identical with quotations in Cyprian (Codex Bobbiensis, copied in North Africa ca. 400; Fleury Palimpsest, 5th century) or Augustine.

The unity of European texts is shown by their agreement in readings unlike that of the African text; the texts show agreement with Novatian in the mid-3rd century (Codex Vercellensis, copied in northern Italy before 370) and Lucifer of Cagliari (d. 371, Sardinia). All other European manuscripts of the Gospels agree with Codex Veronensis (5th or 6th century) more than with each other; Veronensis may represent the type of text Jerome used as the basis of the Vulgate. In the Epistles, Codex Claromontanus agrees closely with Lucifer of Cagliari; Codex Boernerianus agrees frequently with Ambrosiaster (ca. 375, Rome). Speculum exhibits in the Catholic Epistles a Spanish form of the African text, agreeing with quotations in Priscillian (d. 385). Whether the text on the northern side of the Mediterranean arose independently or as a development of the African text is uncertain.

Even after the appearance of Jerome's Vulgate, many kept to the Old Latin text. Codex Colbertinus (12th century, France) reflects traces of African readings in a European text contaminated at places by the Vulgate. Codex Gigas (13th century, Bohemia) agrees with Lucifer of Cagliari, particularly in Acts and Revelation. Carroll D. Osburn

OLIVE

A slow-growing evergreen tree *(Olea europeae)* reaching 4.5-6 m. (15-20 ft.) at maturity if pruned or 12 m. (40 ft.) if unpruned. Indigenous to western Asia, it is attested as early as the 4th millennium B.C. The wet cool winters and hot dry summers of the Mediterranean region are ideal for the olive tree

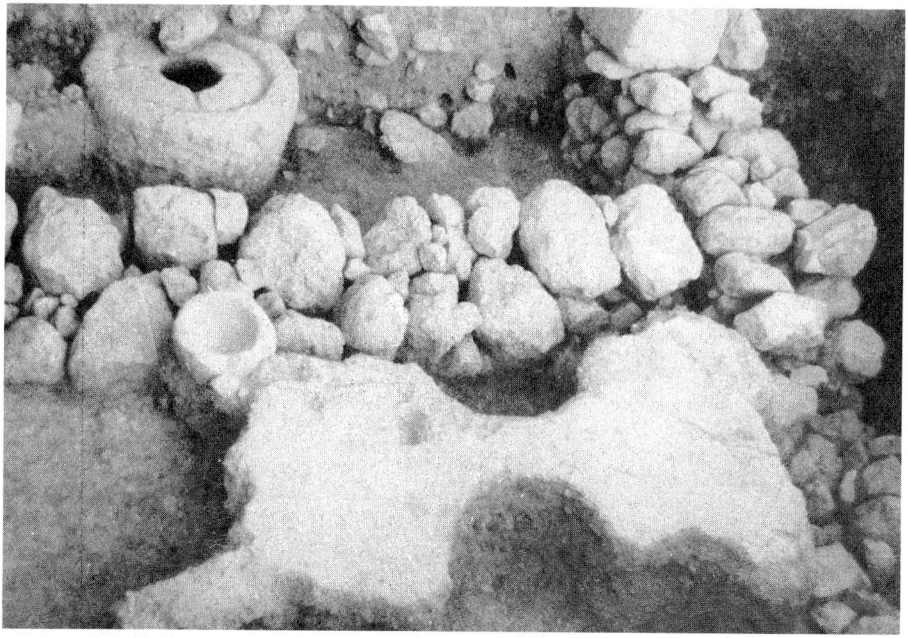

Olive press at Gezer, Field VII (Iron II) (Phoenix Data Systems, Neal and Joel Bierling)

(Heb. *zayiṯ*; Gk. *elaía*). An extensive though shallow root system enables it to survive the hot dry summers. Young trees have a smooth silvery-gray bark, but older trees have hollow gnarled trunks and holes where the side branches have rotted away. Flowering and fruit begins when trees are five to six years old, and peak production is reached between 40 and 50 years. Production can continue for hundreds or even 1000 years. The olive tree grows well in the rocky hillsides of Samaria, Judea, and the Shephelah, though the elevation around Hebron is too high for successful cultivation. The tree is hardy, but a hard frost will kill it. The "wild olive" (Gk. *agriélaios;* Rom. 11:17, 24) has been identified with either the wild or Russian olive (*Elaeagnus angustifolia,* unrelated to the true olive) or the oleaster *(Olea europaea* var. *sylvestris).*

Olive trees can be grown from seeds if they are subsequently grafted onto older trees. However, cutting a slip from an older tree and rooting it or grafting it is more common. Cutting off very old trees at the base of the trunk also produces new shoots. Resembling a willow leaf, the leaf is narrow (1.3 cm. [.5 in.]) and long (5-7.6 cm. [2-3 in.]), green on the upper side and white on the lower side, with minute scales to prevent water loss from the tree. Despite the small leaf size numerous branches form excellent shade for animals.

The olive tree produces clusters of small white flowers in May, and the fruit forms after the flowers fall. Green table olives can be harvested in September-October, but most olives are harvested in December when they turn black and the oil content is greatest (as much as 50 percent). The ripe fruit is ca. 2 cm. (.75 in.) long, 1.3 cm. (.5 in.) wide, and has skin, flesh, and a stone. The fruit can be carefully handpicked or beaten or shaken off the trees (Isa. 17:6). Gleanings must be left on the tree for the resident alien, orphan, and widow (Deut. 24:20). Each tree produces ca. 9-20 kg. (20-45 lbs.) of fruit every other year; with irrigation and fertilization the best trees can produce good crops every year. The wood of the olive tree is very beautiful and was used throughout the temple (1 Kgs. 6:23, 33).

The olive was a staple in the diet. The fruit or its oil was served at almost every meal. In addition, the oil was used for lighting, cosmetics, medicine, and a variety of rituals, including purification rituals (Lev. 12:32) and the anointing of kings (1 Sam. 16:1-13), priests (Exod. 29:7), stelae (Gen. 28:18), and the tabernacle and its contents (Exod. 30:23-29). It was one of the three most important agricultural products of the Promised Land (Deut. 7:13).

The olive or olive tree was a symbol of fertility (Ps. 128:3), beauty (Jer. 11:16), perpetual usefulness (Ps. 52:8[MT 10]), and dignity (Judg. 9:9). In Rom. 11 Paul compares the inclusion of Gentiles in the covenant of God with the grafting of the olive tree.

Bibliography. F. N. Hepper, *Baker Encyclopedia of Bible Plants* (Grand Rapids, 1992).

James C. Moyer

OLIVES, MOUNT OF

A north-south ridge just E of Jerusalem. The ridge has three main summits, the northernmost of which is the highest, ca. 820 m. (2700 ft.) above sea level. This northern section has been identified as Mt. Scopus, meaning the mountain of the "lookout" (Josephus *BJ* 5.67-70). The central peak directly across the Kidron Valley from the temple is the

Mount of Olives proper. The southernmost and lowest peak is usually identified as the Mount of Offense (or Corruption) where Solomon built shrines to foreign gods in "the high places that were east of Jerusalem" (2 Kgs. 23:13). The Mount of Olives has also been identified with Nob (1 Sam. 21:1[MT 20:42]; Isa. 10:32), but this is less certain.

The Mount of Olives is so named because it is composed of a limestone soil that is relatively fertile for the area, and therefore olive groves have long been cultivated on it. Gethsemane (from Heb. "oil press") was probably on or near the Mount of Olives (Matt. 26:36; Mark 14:32). The villages of Bethany and Bethphage were located on the eastern slopes of the mount (Mark 11:1).

In the OT the Mount of Olives is mentioned explicitly only twice. The first is an image of humiliation and defeat, when David is fleeing after the successful revolt led by his son Absalom (2 Sam. 15:30). Zech. 14 also associates the mount with defeat and destruction, describing an eschatological devastation of Jerusalem by her enemies. But this defeat will be reversed when Yahweh appears on the Mount of Olives, standing on the Mount of Olives, which "shall be split in two from east to west" (Zech. 14:4). A very similar description of Yahweh forsaking Jerusalem and then returning to her is also found in Ezek. 11:23, a passage that probably refers to the Mount of Olives; later the glory of Yahweh returns to the temple from the east (43:2-5). The Mount of Olives thus held implications of both defeat and ultimate redemption.

These implications of humiliating defeat and triumphant victory can also be seen in the NT references to the mount. Jesus' triumphal entry into Jerusalem is placed at the Mount of Olives (Matt. 21:1-9; Mark 11:1-10; Luke 19:29-38). Luke, however, follows this with Jesus' weeping over the city and prophesying her terrible defeat (Luke 19:41-44). Similarly, Jesus' discourse of eschatological woes is given on the Mount of Olives (Matt. 24:3; Mark 13:3). The theme of defeat and sorrow can also be seen in the events of Jesus' passion that are located on the mount. All four Gospels locate Jesus' betrayal and arrest on or near the Mount of Olives (Matt. 26:30; Mark 14:26; Luke 22:39; John 18:1). The Synoptics also place Jesus' agonized prayer there (Matt. 26:36-41; Mark 14:32-38; Luke 22:39-46). But Jesus' ultimate triumph is also associated with the Mount of Olives, as it is there that he ascends into heaven (Luke 24:50; Acts 1:12).

Bibliography. J. Finegan, *The Archeology of the New Testament,* rev. ed. (Princeton, 1992), 154-83.

Kim Paffenroth

OLIVET

Alternate name for the Mount of Olives (Acts 1:12; Gk. *elaiōn,* "of olive trees"; from Lat. *olivetum,* "olive grove").

OLYMPAS (Gk. *Olympás*)

A Christian at Rome to whom Paul sent his greetings (Rom. 16:15).

OMAR (Heb. *'ômār*)

An Edomite chief, the second son of Eliphaz and grandson (or descendant) of Esau (Gen. 36:11, 15; 1 Chr. 1:36).

OMEGA

The twenty-fourth and last letter of the Greek alphabet. Phonetically it represents a long "o" sound; its numerical value is 800. It is used figuratively with Alpha, the first letter of the Greek alphabet, to signify God (Rev. 1:8; 21:6) and Christ (22:13) as "the beginning and the end" (cf. 1:17; 2:8).

See Alpha and Omega.

OMER (Heb. *'ōmer*)

1. A dry measure equal to one tenth of an ephah (Exod. 16:16-36). The measure was probably not exact, indicating basically the capacity of a common-sized bowl.

2. A sheaf of grain (so NRSV, Lev. 23:11-12, 15; Deut. 24:19). The probable measure was 2.2 l. (2.3 qts.), although suggestions range as high as 4 l. (4 qts., ca. one half of a peck basket).

OMRI (Heb. *'omrî*)

1. A king of the northern kingdom of Israel. Omri was the founder of a dynasty of Israelite kings ("Omride") who ruled the northern kingdom during the first half of the 9th century B.C. The account of his rise and reign is found in 1 Kgs. 16:15-28.

Establishing a precise chronology for the reign of Omri is difficult. Various proposals for his accession and death dates have been made, ranging from 886-875 to 879-869. Any proposal for dating his reign must account for the fact that Omri's son Ahab was on the Israelite throne at least as late as 853, since Ahab is mentioned as king of Israel by Shalmaneser III in his inscription describing the Assyrian western campaign of that year. If one assumes that 853 is also Ahab's final year and that he is to be credited with reigning the full 22 years accorded him by 1 Kgs. 16:29, then the death of Omri and accession of Ahab could be dated as early as 875. Giving Omri credit for the 12 years ascribed to him in 1 Kgs. 16:23 would place his accession in 887/886. However, these dates fall afoul of the synchronisms with the reign of Asa of Judah given in 1 Kgs. 16:23, 29. In 1 Kgs. 16:23 Omri's accession takes place in the 31st year of Asa, and the accession of Ahab occurs in the 38th, leaving only a span of seven years for the reign of Omri. One is thus forced to choose between shortening the 12-year figure for the length of Omri's reign, disregarding the synchronisms in either 1 Kgs. 16:23 or 29, or explaining the discrepancy by some other means (e.g., that the seven-year span between the 31st and 38th years of Asa reflects the length of Omri's reign after the founding of Samaria). In any event, an accession date for Omri in the period between the mid-880s and 879 seems appropriate on the basis of available information.

Omri acceded to the Israelite throne amid political tumult. His predecessor, Elah, was apparently incompetent or unpopular or both; the text indicates that while the Israelite army was engaged with the Philistines at Gibbethon, Elah was at home in Tirzah "drinking himself drunk" (1 Kgs. 16:9). Zimri, a commander in the chariot force, seized upon the occasion to assassinate Elah, massacre the royal family, and claim the throne for himself. However, when word reached the troops at Gibbethon, they rallied behind their own commander, Omri, and marched on Tirzah. Zimri barricaded himself in the palace, but the situation soon became hopeless. In a final gesture of defiance, Zimri set fire to the palace and perished in the flames.

Zimri's death did not leave Omri on the Israelite throne uncontested. At some point early in his reign, Omri faced opposition by a certain Tibni son of Ginath. 1 Kgs. 16:21 makes clear that the kingdom was sorely divided between the two. After a civil war, Omri was able to overcome and put to death Tibni; only thereafter did Omri manage to rule without serious rival.

Despite the negative evaluation of Omri offered by 1 Kgs. 16:25-26, a number of important achievements are clear during his reign. First among those accomplishments is the construction of a new Israelite capital at Samaria (modern Sebastiyeh). The fire in which Zimri died probably caused such extensive damage to the royal palace in Tirzah that it was not worth rebuilding. But the need to build a new capital also provided the opportunity to move the entire governmental complex to a site located closer to the major roads leading from the Jezreel Valley to the Philistine coast. Omri's selection of Samaria meant that the Israelite capital would be a stop on the great trade routes that carried commerce along the Fertile Crescent, and would thus be a cosmopolitan city as well as a political center. Excavations at Sebastiyeh I and II have revealed a number of ivory pieces of Phoenician manufacture, testifying to the cultural cross-pollination occurring in Omride Samaria.

Omride construction was not limited to Samaria, however. Storage buildings, formerly identified as stables, at Megiddo are certainly of Omride origin. In addition, an extensive tunnel and shaft system for delivering water inside the city walls at Megiddo is also an Omride engineering achievement. City walls and other large public buildings at Megiddo and Hazor (stratum VIII) also date from this period. All this testifies to the relative wealth and technological sophistication of Omri and his successors.

Omri was the first of the Israelite kings to become a player in international politics. The mid-9th century Mesha inscription (Moabite Stone) states that Omri ". . . occupied the whole land of Medeba and . . . dwelt in it during his days. . . ." Reaching to the west, Omri also became involved with the Phoenician city-state of Sidon. He concluded an alliance with Ethbaal of Sidon, sealed by the marriage of his son Ahab to Ethbaal's daughter Jezebel (1 Kgs. 16:31). In the years following Omri's death, Ahab was involved in a large 12-nation coalition to oppose the advance of Assyrian forces under Shalmaneser III into Syria-Palestine. Ahab's contribution to the force was substantial enough to merit comment from Shalmaneser in his own account of the confrontation (Monolith inscription; *ANET,* 278-79). In this and in subsequent Assyrian inscriptions, even those recorded long after Omri's death and the end of the dynasty he founded, Assyrian monarchs referred to Israel as *Bīt Ḫumrî,* "the land of Omri," testifying to Omri's enduring historical legacy. Omri's reign was in all probability a period of significant economic growth, as can be deduced from both the large-scale building activity at Samaria and other cities, and from the likely opportunities in international trade opened to Israel by virtue of its alliance with the Phoenicians. But the economic prosperity would undoubtedly have brought with it a significant increase in religious syncretism, especially with the Baal cult of Phoenicia and Canaan, in both court and kingdom. Jezebel, the Baalist wife of Ahab, serves as a symbol of this influence, but surely the growth in Baalistic worship and practice was more widespread than she could account for on her own. Undoubtedly, this waxing influence of the Baal cult during his reign contributes to Omri's extreme negative assessment at the hands of the Deuteronomistic editors of 1 Kings.

With his death (sometime between 874 and 869, depending on the chosen chronology) and the succession of his son, Omri founded the first of the two great dynasties to rule Israel. In all, one son and two grandsons (Ahaziah and Jehoram) acceded to the Israelite throne, and one daughter (Athaliah) ruled Judah.

Bibliography. J. M. Miller, "The Elisha Cycle and the Accounts of the Omride Wars," *JBL* 85 (1966): 441-55; "So Tibni Died (1 Kings xvi 22)," *VT* 18 (1968): 392-94; Miller and J. H. Hayes, *A History of Ancient Israel and Judah* (Philadelphia, 1986), 251-87.

2. A member of the Benjamite clan, son of Becher and grandson of Benjamin (1 Chr. 7:8).

3. An inhabitant of postexilic Jerusalem, probably of Judahite, Benjaminite, or Manassite origin (1 Chr. 9:4).

4. An Issacharite tribal leader from the time of David (1 Chr. 27:18). PAUL K. HOOKER

ON (Heb. *'ôn*) **(PERSON)**
A Reubenite, the son of Peleth who joined with Korah in rebelling against Moses (Num. 16:1).

ON (Heb. *'ôn;* Egyp. *iwnw, inw*) **(PLACE)**
The Egyptian city Heliopolis ("city of the sun"). Located at the southern tip of the Nile Delta, On (modern Tell Hisn, in Matariyeh, a suburb NE of Cairo) was the capital of an Egyptian district and from Early Dynastic times to the Saitic dynasty the main cult center of the sun-god Re (Egyp. "pillar[-town]," from the stone fetishes, later obelisks, of the god; cf. Jer. 43:13). One pillar of Sesotris I is still standing, but the site has yielded few remains. It may be the "City of the Sun" mentioned in Isa. 19:18.

Joseph's father-in-law Potiphera is called the priest of On (Gen. 41:50; 46:20). At Ezek. 30:17 the MT renders the name *'āwen,* "evil."

Bibliography. M. Abd el-Gelil, M. Shaker, and D. Raue, "Recent Excavations at Helopolis," *Or* 65 (1996): 136-46. MEINDERT DIJKSTRA

ONAM (Heb. *'ônām*)

1. The fifth son of Shobal; eponymous ancestor of a Horite clan (Gen. 36:23; 1 Chr. 1:40).

2. The son of Jerahmeel and Atarah (1 Chr. 2:26, 28); eponymous ancestor of a Judahite clan.

ONAN (Heb. *'ônān*)

The second son of Judah and the Canaanite Shua. After his older brother Er died an early death because of his wickedness, Er's wife Tamar was left without a son. According to the custom Onan's father Judah asked him to enter a levirate marriage with his sister-in-law in order to raise an offspring who would preserve the name of his brother (Gen. 38:8; cf. Deut. 25:6). Onan, however, repeatedly frustrated his union with Tamar by spilling his semen on the ground, thereby avoiding his responsibility toward his deceased brother. For this reason the Lord brought about Onan's death.

The name Onan ("vigor, wealth") connotes generative or reproductive power. Some have surmised that the name perhaps also encompasses the connotation of "wicked," "sinful"; but this remains without solid evidence. FRANK HASEL

ONESIMUS (Gk. *Onḗsimos*)

A slave who is the subject of Paul's Letter to Philemon. Paul plays on the meaning of his name ("useful" or "profitable," a common slave name) in his appeal on behalf of Onesimus because of his usefulness during Paul's imprisonment (Phlm. 11). Onesimus had apparently run away from Philemon and encountered Paul during his captivity in Rome. Why he traveled to Rome from Colossae (a considerable distance) and how he avoided capture as a fugitive slave remains a mystery. Paul converted Onesimus and returned him to Philemon bearing the intercessory letter on his behalf, and perhaps the letter to the Colossians (cf. Col. 4:9) as well. It is unclear if Onesimus had wronged his master (Phlm. 18-19) or had simply run away. In either case, as a slave he was liable to the whims of his master regarding the severity of his punishment. Paul's appeal suggests the return of Onesimus to him in Rome and leniency from Philemon because of Onesimus' conversion. He implores Philemon to receive the slave as a "beloved brother" and does not specifically request emancipation, although it may be implied.

Ignatius' letter to the Ephesians (ca. 115 C.E.) mentions a bishop named Onesimus. While it is not impossible that this is the same figure, it is highly unlikely given the dating of Ignatius' letter and the fact that the name Onesimus became more common within Christian circles in imitation of Philemon. MATTHEW S. COLLINS

ONESIPHORUS (Gk. *Onēsiphóros*)

A Christian from Ephesus who found Paul in Rome and aided him during his imprisonment (2 Tim. 1:16-18). The name means "profit-bearing" and may indicate a slave or freedman. The phrasing of 1 Tim. 1:18 and the greetings to his household in v. 16; 4:19 suggest that he may have already died. Onesiphorus plays a significant role in the apocryphal Acts of Paul. MATTHEW S. COLLINS

ONIAS (Gk. *Onias*)

A recurrent name in a priestly family prominent in Palestine during the Hellenistic period from the rule of the Ptolemies into the Maccabean period. Of Zadokite lineage, this family of hereditary high priests is frequently referred to as the Oniads.

1. Onias I, the son of Jaddua who served in the priesthood with his brother Manasses during the early reign of Alexander the Great (Josephus *Ant.* 11.8.7). Onias I ascended to the high priesthood sometime after the death of both his father and Alexander the Great. Some suggest that Onias I was the Onias mentioned as a correspondent with Arius, a Spartan king (1 Macc. 12:7, 19-20), while others see Onias II or Onias III (*Ant.* 12.4.10) as the more likely candidate. Onias I was the father of Simon I.

2. Onias II. Son of Simon I and grandson of Onias I, he did not become high priest immediately following his father's early death. According to Josephus (*Ant.* 12.4), both his uncle Eleazar and his great uncle Manasses preceded his priestly tenure. Onias II served as high priest during the Ptolemaic rule over ancient Palestine and found himself, at least periodically, in opposition to the secular rulers. Josephus notes his conflict with Ptolemy III Euergetes over taxes and characterizes Onias II as avaricious. Others see Onias as politically supporting the Seleucids over against the Ptolemies. Whether Onias' motivation was personal or political, this conflict was a critical element in the long-term struggle between the Oniads and the Tobiads, a wealthy family related to the Oniads by the marriage of Onias' sister to the head of the Tobiads. Eventually Onias' nephew Joseph Tobiad gained control of the tax collection system as well as considerable political power.

Onias was succeeded by his son, Simon II (the Just), around the time that the Seleucids finally took Palestine from the Ptolemies.

3. Onias III. Son of Simon II and grandson of Onias II, he served as high priest during the reign of Seleucus IV Philopator. Onias III is noted in 2 Maccabees for his piety and his "hatred of wickedness" (2 Macc. 3:1). He continued what his predecessors had begun in his political opposition to the Tobiad family. Simon, the Tobiad overseer of the temple, was a particular adversary. Eventually, Simon denounced Onias to the Seleucid overlords as pro-Ptolemaic and as one who mishandled finances. In an attempt to quiet mounting tension, Seleucus sent one of his chief ministers, Heliodorus, to the temple. Heliodorus mysteriously fell deathly ill and was restored to life upon Onias' prayers and sacrifices to God. Heliodorus returned to Seleucus and Onias survived a round of scrutiny; however, he continued to face Simon's accusations so that he eventually made a personal trip to Antioch to defend himself directly before the Seleucid king. Upon his arrival (175 B.C.E.), Onias found that Heliodorus had murdered Seleucus and Seleucus' brother, Antiochus IV Epiphanes, was king. Meanwhile, in Onias' absence, his brother Jason purchased the position of high priest from the financially strapped Antiochus. Onias did not return to Palestine. Some think he remained exiled, voluntarily or involuntarily, in Antioch. Others think he fled to Egypt and established a Jewish temple in Leontopolis. Some associate Onias III with the Teacher of Righteousness mentioned in the Dead Sea Scrolls.

4. Onias Menelaus, usually referred to as Menelaus. The brother of Simon, the overseer of the temple, Onias Menelaus was allied with Jason, the brother of Onias III, before usurping him as high priest in 172. Under Menelaus' tenure, a series of events occurred that precipitated the Maccabean Revolt.

5. Onias IV, son of Onias III. Some report Onias IV as the priest who fled to Egypt and received funds from the rulers of Egypt to build a Jewish temple at Leontopolis, to run a military colony, and to serve as a Ptolemaic general. Josephus offers conflicting accounts in *Antiquities* and *Jewish War.*

ALICE HUNT HUDIBURG

ONION

One of the vegetables for which Israel longed in the wilderness (Num. 11:5; Heb. *bāṣal*). Of the several varieties of onions grown throughout the ancient Near East, the Egyptian onion (*Alium cepa* L.) was reputedly among the most flavorful, eaten raw, boiled, and as a condiment in lentil dishes. In Palestine the Israelites ate the mature onions, but not the leaves, which they considered to be harmful. Onions were employed medicinally as an antiseptic and laxative, and the onion skin was used as a dye.

ONO (Heb. *'ônô*)

A city in the Shephelah, identified with Kafr ʿAnā (137159), 10 km. (6 mi.) NW of Lod. Ono and Lod are closely associated throughout; Neh. 11:35 refers to the cities as "the valley of artisans." Thutmose III (15th century) includes Ono in his Karnak list of conquered sites.

According to 1 Chr. 8:12 Shemed, son of Elpaal the Benjamite, built the city of Ono, but an early association with Dan and Ephraim is possible. Lod, Hadid, and Ono provided an ancestral homeland for 725 (Ezra 2:33) or 721 (Neh. 7:37) returning exiles (or more, if the figures indicate only men). During the rebuilding of the walls of Jerusalem, Sanballat and Geshem requested a parley with Nehemiah "in one of the villages in the plain of Ono" (Neh. 6:2), identified with Wadi Muṣrarah.

STEPHEN VON WYRICK

ONOMASTICON

A list of proper names, usually personal but sometimes geographical sites. In the first instance the list of names may be derived from a given document (e.g., David's Mighty Men, 2 Sam. 23:8-39; cf. 1 Chr. 11:26-47) or compiled from various sources with a common point of reference (e.g., onomasticon of names in Jerusalem ossuary inscriptions). Onomastic study of personal names not only contributes understanding of their meaning, but also provides insight into the ethnic and linguistic background of those named. This can be valuable in evaluating population movement, social intercourse, and acculturation (e.g., the presence of Greek names in 1st-century synagogue inscriptions provides significant insight into the hellenization of Jewish society).

When the term is used in a geographical sense it usually indicates a gazetteer of place names. Eusebius' *Onomasticon* of biblical sites includes almost 1000 entries ranging in length from a few words to as much as a page. The entries are categorized by the first letter of the alphabet, then by their order of occurrence in the biblical text. They include such information as location, distance from other places, events that occurred at the site, contemporary (4th-century) name, and state of the site (inhabited or ruined, and if inhabited the religious orientation of inhabitants).

Bibliography. T. D. Barnes, "Composition of Eusebius' *Onomasticon*," *JTS* N.S. 26 (1975): 412-15; N. G. Cohen, "The Names of the Translators in the Letter of Aristeas," *JSJ* 15 (1984): 32-64; D. E. Groh, "The *Onomasticon* of Eusebius and the Rise of Christian Palestine," in *Studia Patristica* 18/1, ed. E. A. Livingstone (Kalamazoo, 1985), 23-31; J. P. Kane, "The Ossuary Inscriptions of Jerusalem," *JSS* 23 (1978): 268-82; M. P. O'Connor, "The Ammonite Onomasticon: Semantic Problems," *AUSS* 25 (1987): 51-64; A. B. Tataki, *Macedonian Edessa: Prosopography and Onomasticon* (Athens, 1994); C. U. Wolf, "Eusebius of Caesarea and the Onomasticon," *BA* 27 (1964): 66-96.

CHARLES GUTH

ONYCHA

A spice which when burned emits a musky odor. It may be derived from the rockrose or ladanum, the stem and leaves of which produce a dark brown resin. More likely, onchya was obtained from the operculum or closing muscles of a mollusk called the stromb or wing shell, found in the waters of the Red Sea.

Onchya, along with equal parts of stacte, galbanum, and frankincense, was a pungent component of the holy incense used in the temple (Exod. 30:34-36). Such formulas for both holy incense and oil were not to be duplicated for nonsacred use (Exod. 30:33, 37-38).

JAMES V. SMITH

ONYX

A banded quartzite stone prized as material for carving or engraving. The onyx (Heb. *šōham*) was a stone equal in value to gold (Gen. 2:12; Job 28:16). Each shoulder of the high priest's ephod bore an onyx engraved with the names of Israel's sons (Exod. 28:9; 39:6), and an engraved onyx was present on the high priest's breastpiece (28:20; 39:13). A *šōham* adorned the king of Tyre (Ezek. 28:13). The LXX uses a number of words to translate *šōham*, reflecting confusion as to the type and color of stone represented: green or blue (Gen. 2:12; Exod. 28:9) and red or brown (25:7). The NRSV reads "onyx" for Gk. *sardónyx*, a course in the foundation of the city wall of the New Jerusalem (Rev. 21:20). English translations also use "beryl," "carnelian," "emerald," "lapis lazuli," and "sardonus" for the Hebrew and Greek terms. JOSEPH E. JENSEN

OPHEL (Heb. *'ōpel*)
The southeast ridge between the Kidron and Tyropoeon Valleys, fortified by David as his capital (cf. 2 Sam. 5:9). The Ophel was the site of construction activity by Jotham (2 Chr. 27:3) and Manasseh (33:14), and following the Exile temple servants who lived on the Ophel repaired its walls (Neh. 3:26-27; 11:21). In the mid-8th century B.C.E. (2 Chr. 27:3) the word "ophel" may have replaced the earlier term "millo" to specifically designate the citadel of Jerusalem. The area was called Ophlas by Josephus (*BJ* 5.145; 5.254), a Greek transliteration of Aram. *'apla*, and was considered by Josephus to be situated below the southeast corner of the present-day temple mount. Josephus distinguished the Ophel from the Akra fortress, farther down the same ridge (*BJ* 5.253; 6.354). The area has been excavated by Kathleen Kenyon and Yigal Shiloh.

The Hebrew term means "hill," "mound," or "bulge" (Isa. 32:14; Mic. 4:8), and with the definite article can designate a specific hill, e.g., Samaria, where Elisha's house stood (2 Kgs. 5:24; NRSV "citadel"). The term is also used in the Mesha stela from Dibon, which mentions a "wall of the Ophel" in Kerak.

Bibliography. Y. Shiloh, *Excavations at the City of David* 1. Qedem 19 (Jerusalem, 1984).

KENNETH ATKINSON

OPHIR (Heb. *'ôpîr*) **(PERSON)**
According to the Table of Nations, a descendant of Shem, the son of Joktan and brother of Havilah (Gen. 10:29; 1 Chr. 1:23). He is presumably the eponymous ancestor of a South Arabian region.

OPHIR (Heb. *'ôpîr*) **(PLACE)**
A nation with whom Israel conducted maritime relations from as early as the time of Solomon (1 Kgs. 9:28; 10:11; 22:48; 2 Chr. 8:18; 9:10). Ophir supplied gold, precious stones, and wood to both Solomon and Hiram of Tyre through Ezion-geber on the Red Sea. Ophir's gold was so well known that it came to symbolize wealth and decadence in contrast with wisdom and faith (Job 22:24; 28:16; Isa. 13:12).

The identification of Ophir has yielded a number of possibilities. If an association is believed between Ophir and the descendant of Joktan (Gen. 10:29-30), then the eastern hill country of v. 30 makes a case of an Arabian identification. The mention of Ophir (1 Kgs. 10:11) within the queen of Sheba narrative may bolster Ophir's identification with Seba in southwest Arabia. India remains a possibility with its ivory and exotic primates (1 Kgs. 10:22), although ch. 10 may imply a different trading partner. Africa also possesses the commodities imported from Ophir. An inscription from Tell Qasile provides the only surviving extrabiblical reference to Ophir, but it lacks useful geographical information.

Bibliography. B. Maisler, "Two Hebrew Ostraca from Tell Qasîle," *JNES* 10 (1951): 265-67.

RYAN BYRNE

OPHNI (Heb. *'opnî*)
A town in the territory of Benjamin, listed between Chepar-ammoni and Geba (Josh. 18:24). The exact location is unknown, but the other cities listed in this grouping suggest a site NE of Jerusalem. Ophni is often identified with modern Jifna (170152), ca. 5 km. (3 mi.) NW of Bethel. Josephus calls the town Gophna, which he indicates was the capital of its toparchy (*BJ* 3.3.5.55). WILLARD W. WINTER

OPHRAH (Heb. *'oprâ*) **(PERSON)**
The son of Meonothai of Judah (1 Chr. 4:14).

OPHRAH (Heb. *'oprâ*) **(PLACE)**
1. A city in the territory of the tribe of Benjamin (Josh. 18:23), probably identical to the city of Ephraim (2 Sam. 13:23) near Baal-hazor, as well as the city of Ephron mentioned in 2 Chr. 13:19. Ophrah is situated at modern eṭ-Ṭaiyibeh (178151), 6.5 km. (4 mi.) NE of Bethel. Ophrah was the destination of one of the Philistine raiding parties during the reign of Saul. Departing from Michmash, one Philistine party moved toward Beth-horon in the west, one toward the valley of Zeboim in the east, and the third toward Ophrah, which was in a northerly direction (1 Sam. 13:17). Ephron is listed among the cities recaptured by King Abijah of Judah from Jeroboam I (2 Chr. 13:19). Ophrah was the capital of one of the three Samaritan districts given to Jonathan Maccabeus by Demetrius II (1 Macc. 11:34, Aphairema). On the basis of the early church father Jerome, the city is equated with Ephraim in John 11:54, as a site to which Jesus went to hide at the beginning of his persecution. Ophrah was the site of yet another confrontation when Vespasian conquered the city, along with Bethel, en route to Jerusalem (Josephus *BJ* 4.9.9).

2. Ophrah of Abiezer, associated with the judge Gideon (Judg. 6–8). The clan name Abiezer indicates the city was part of the territory of the tribe of Manasseh. Located in the valley of Jezreel, near Mt. Tabor, it was the home of Gideon and the place where he received a divine commission to deliver Israel from the oppressing Midianites. It is also the site where Gideon built an altar inscribed "the Lord is Peace" (Judg. 6:24) to commemorate the appearance of the angel of the Lord. Later Gideon made an ephod here, which became a source of apostasy for

Gideon, his family, and his fellow Israelites (Judg. 8:22-28). Gideon died at Ophrah as an old man (Judg. 8:29-32), and his son Abimelech, ambitious for power and the kingship, murdered all but one of his 70 brothers there; Jotham was the only one to escape (9:1-6). The site may be modern el-ʿAffuleh/ʿAfula (177223). WILLARD W. WINTER

ORACLE

A message from God to an individual or group of people, usually delivered by a prophet. Heb. *maśśāʾ*, in its basic meaning "burden," frequently refers to the prophetic communication from God to humankind (cf. the double usage in Jer. 23:33-40). When associated with prophetic speech, *maśśāʾ* usually, but not always, has a negative connotation. It is frequently associated with oracles of judgment against the nations (e.g., Isa. 13:1; Nah. 1:1), but also of oracles against Judah (Isa. 22:1) and Israel (Ezek. 12:10). Later texts associate *maśśāʾ* with the "word of Yahweh," effectively removing any negative connotation (Zech. 9:1; 12:1; Mal. 1:1).

Richard D. Weis has suggested that *maśśāʾ* should be understood as a distinct prophetic genre in which the words of the prophet rather than the words of Yahweh predominate. Thus the term would be more accurately translated "a prophetic exposition of divine revelation" and the initiative for a *maśśāʾ* would lie neither with God nor the prophet, but with the community that was requesting clarification concerning the divine will.

While texts labeled *maśśāʾ* are properly distinguished from other types of prophetic speech such as messenger speeches or prophetic judgment speeches, it is unclear whether they are sufficiently distinct from others not so designated but which contain similar material (cf. esp. the various units in Isa. 13–23).

Bibliography. R. D. Weis, *A Definition of the Genre* Maśśāʾ *in the Hebrew Bible* (diss., Claremont, 1986). JAMES R. ADAIR, JR.

ORAL COMPOSITION

Composers of the materials which now make up the OT and NT (and nearly all other materials of the time) expected the majority of people who came in contact with their compositions to hear, rather than read, them. The literacy rate was less than 10 percent, so compositions were structured for the ear rather than the eye. Audiences heard clues to meaning and structure because they had learned to communicate in a world where those clues were essential to understanding, much as periods and paragraph indentations in modern English literature.

In a "primary oral culture," one which has no contact with writing, attitudes and actions toward issues are more dependent on interpersonal interaction than on an abstract set of values. Many scholars relate the development of the vowelized phonetic alphabet to the development of abstract thinking. Philosophical thinking, then, is minimal in such cultures. For example, the principle of righteousness is not defined but is demonstrated in epic illustrations. One acts a certain way not because it is "right" but in order to follow the example of a hero. Indeed, the epic tales of the oral culture are the primary means of education. Moral norms, trade skills, history, and every aspect of communal life are passed on in oral poetry.

As a natural consequence of the necessity of preserving the traditional material, the stress is on the community rather than on individualism and individual thought. Traditional materials also deal with matters of high practicality and interest. If an idea or procedure loses its validity or usefulness, it is forgotten. Thus, these societies tend to be very conservative, maintaining an equilibrium for generations.

The primary characteristic of oral composition is the use of formulaic and thematic style. Formulas are preset groups of expressions or figures of speech used to communicate given ideas within the poetic meter. They do not indicate theme, structure, or style. Themes are groups of topics which are normally associated with one another in the composition of traditional songs. Various themes such as birth, the council, and marriage follow one another in recognizable patterns and are found in oral compositions of nearly all primary oral societies. Oral poets do not seek the originality of a literary author. They simply follow a theme and, for the most part, use formulas associated with that theme to fill in the meter of their song.

In a primary oral society poets learn the formulaic technique through apprenticeship, and it is assimilated by the rest of the society. This formulaic (and thematic) style leads both to consistency and inconsistency. While using formulas and themes which characteristically fall into place within conventional songs makes the stories easy to remember, it also leads to substitution of similar but different formulas and themes when retelling the story. Verbatim memorization is extremely rare. Thus, oral poets may tell a song hundreds of times with very little change in the general content but they are unlikely to tell it exactly the same way twice.

Oral compositions in the form of poetry and song are present in all societies, and the reciprocal influence which flows between literature and oral artistry must not be underestimated. This is especially true in cultures with a high degree of residual orality, such as those which produced the Bible and early Church literature. The biblical documents were written by authors who were influenced by their own literacy. However, these authors never forgot that they were addressing hearing audiences (cf. Rev. 1:3). Aural structural and mnemonic clues were just as important in the literary compositions of the OT and NT as in oral compositions in primary oral societies.

There is a high degree of interplay between a storyteller or teacher and the audience in an oral culture. Authors in a culture with a high degree of residual orality tend to be more aware of the speaker/audience relationship. They dialogue with their audience and create adversaries to argue against in order to make their point. They are more concerned with how relationships are affected by a topic than a philosophical position of "right" versus "wrong." They are more likely to give examples to follow and instances of praise and blame rather than setting forth a logical argument designed to promote a certain action.

Since unused information tends to be forgotten, outside of traditional stock phrases (e.g., in parenesis), authors in cultures with a high degree of residual orality tend to deal with topics which are immediately applicable to the present situation, either of the author or audience, rather than theoretical. Authors will bring themselves and their audience into the discussion rather than looking at a topic from a distance.

Figures of speech, which are widely used in all forms of communication, are especially important in oral composition. From the time of Cicero onward, the primary rhetorical criterion for judging the merit of a speech was the proper use of the metaphor and other figures. Major figures of speech include antithesis, synonymy, vagueness, metaphor, and wordplay.

Repetition, as evidenced in structural patterns such as inclusio and chiasm, has to this point been the major emphasis of most oral biblical criticism. Forms of repetition include sounds, grammatical constructions, words, and topics. Repetition can be used to group elements into high frequency blocks to indicate units or be fashioned into inclusio and chiasm to show structure. Especially in the case of word and topic repetition, it can be spread over large blocks of material to designate major structures.

Oral composers use rare words because of aural and rhetorical considerations. With respect to aural considerations, rare words may be chosen in order to avoid hiatus, form a rhyming couplet, or give added emphasis to a unit in which a certain sound is grouped. Rhetorically, a rare word may be used to gain the audience's attention or to influence their emotions.

An author's use of oral formulas may indicate material which the author discusses frequently. In a culture with no literacy, formulas are words and phrases dealing with a specified topic and fitting a certain rhythm. In an oral/literary environment, where meter is not nearly so much of a concern, a formula is more of a cliche or standard phrase used to express a certain thought. It is the use of an expression in a grammatical or contextual setting simply because of its habitual association with that setting. There is little or no conscious deliberation with respect to its use.

An awareness of the influence of the principles of orality is particularly helpful with regard to determining the structure of a book and individual units within that book. It also provides insight into the usages of many words and forms which may seem unusual to readers in a fully literate society.

Bibliography. C. W. Davis, *Oral Biblical Criticism: The Influence of the Principles of Orality on the Literary Structure of Paul's Epistle to the Philippians.* JSNTSup 172 (Sheffield, 1999); J. Goody and I. Watt, "The Consequences of Literacy," in *Literacy in Traditional Societies,* ed. J. Goody (Cambridge, 1968), 27-68; W. V. Harris, *Ancient Literacy* (Cambridge, Mass., 1989) E. A. Havelock, *The Literate Revolution in Greece and Its Cultural Consequences* (Princeton, 1982); A. B. Lord, *The Singer of Tales.* Harvard Studies in Comparative Literature 24 (Cambridge, Mass., 1960); W. J. Ong, *Orality and Literacy* (1982, repr. London, 1991).

CASEY W. DAVIS

ORDAIN, ORDINATION

The appointment or installation of religious officials. Clothing with the garments of the priesthood and anointing with olive oil were the basic elements of the installation of priests in Israel (Exod. 29; Lev. 8). In Herodian-Roman times investiture appears to have been constitutive in making the high priest (Josephus *Ant.* 20.6; *m. Hor.* 3.4; *b. Yoma* 12a-b). Christianity's break with the priestly traditions of the OT is well symbolized by the absence of anointing and giving of distinctive dress in ordination until well into the Middle Ages. Heb. *ml'*, "ordain" (lit., "to fill"; e.g., Exod. 29:9), was used in the sense "to appoint." The full phrase "to fill the hand" (Judg. 17:5, 12) may refer to an earlier practice of placing portions of the sacrificial animal (cf. Lev. 8:27) or of sacred lots (Deut. 33:8) in the hands of the priest. Anointing indicated the divine choice in the appointment of kings (1 Sam. 10:1; 16:13). No ceremony of installation for judges and elders is recorded in the OT. Later practice in the greater and lesser Sanhedrins was to appoint persons by a solemn seating in the council (*m. Sanh.* 4.3-4; *Sipre Num.* 27; cf. As. Mos. 12.2). Information fails on any special method of installation of synagogue functionaries and leaders at Qumran.

Two episodes from the OT became important for rabbinic and Christian ordination. In Num. 8:10 the Israelites lay hands on the Levites in setting them apart for service at the tabernacle, an event assimilated to the form of a sacrifice, the principal occasion for this gesture in the OT. In Num. 27:15-23 Moses lays hands on Joshua when he commissions him to lead the people. Deut. 34:9 seems to attribute Joshua's possession of the spirit to this act, but Num. 27:18 says Joshua's possession of the spirit was the reason Moses laid hands on him. Perhaps the "spirit of wisdom" in Deuteronomy was an added gift, or perhaps Deuteronomy implies that the laying on of hands is an evidence for possession of the spirit rather than the means of imparting it. These accounts employ Heb. *sāmak̠*, "to lean upon," from which rabbinic literature developed its technical terminology for ordination *(semikuth).* Rabbinic ordination by leaning on with the hands is not certainly attested before 70 C.E.

The Gospels describe no method by which Jesus appointed the apostles other than his naming them (Mark 3:14), an omission supplied by the apocryphal Acts Pet. 10, which reflects later Church practice by adding an imposition of hands.

Acts and the Pastoral Epistles provide the principal NT passages pertaining to ordination. Where details are given, there is mention of prayer accompanied by the laying on of hands and sometimes fasting, both of which served to support and reinforce prayer. The fullest account of an appointment to church office concerns the Seven in Acts 6:1-6, which records the following elements: recognition of a need, statement of qualifications, examination and selection by the congregation, presentation of the chosen persons to the apostles, prayer and the laying on of hands. Fasting, prayer, and the laying on of hands are mentioned in the sending out of Paul and Barnabas in Acts 13:1-3, and prayer and fasting in the appointment of elders in 14:23. The latter passage uses the verb *cheirotonéō*, from which the later Christian technical terminology for ordination derived. Here it is not clear whether the word refers to selection (closer to its original sense of "elect by show of hands") or to appointment (a Hellenistic usage that prepared for the Christian meaning of "ordain"). It is commonly thought that the Christian "laying on of hands" has its background in Heb. *sāmaḵ*, but Christian usage favors another Hebrew practice, the gentle touching with the hand in blessing (Gen. 48:14, 17-18). This would account for the constant association of the gesture with prayer, which is always given the priority in the Christian accounts. The meaning of the incident in Acts 13:3 is explained by 14:26, "commended to the grace of God for the work."

Timothy was designated for ministry by prophecy (cf. Acts 20:28), and Paul and the elders laid hands on him (1 Tim. 1:18; 4:14; 2 Tim. 1:6). A special gift was imparted by Paul; the laying on of hands by the elders was an accompanying circumstance. These NT passages provided the basis on which later ordination practices in the Church were developed.

See also Laying on of Hands.

Bibliography. E. Ferguson, *The Church of Christ* (Grand Rapids, 1996), 310-16; "Laying on of Hands: Its Significance in Ordination," *JTS* n.s. 26 (1975): 1-12; J. Newman, *Semikhah* (Manchester, 1950); M. Warkentin, *Ordination: A Biblical-Historical View* (Grand Rapids, 1982).

Everett Ferguson

ORDER

A society or class of people united by certain common characteristics. According to 1 Chr. 6–7, 24 David arranged the priests and Levites into labor divisions based on family units (cf. 2 Kgs. 23:4; 1 Chr. 15:18). The "order of Melchizedek" (Heb. *diḇrâ;* Ps. 110:4; Gk. *táxis;* Heb. 5:6, 10; 6:20; 7:11, 17) is an appeal to a tradition of legitimate priests outside of the levitical ranks; it refers not only to the position of Melchizedek but also to the distinctive nature of his (and thus Christ's) priesthood.

OREB (Heb. *ʿōrēḇ, ʿôrēḇ*)

One of two Midianite princes beheaded by the Ephraimites at the time of Gideon (Judg. 7:25; 8:3; cf. Ps. 83:11[MT 12]). Subsequently his name was given to the rock where he was killed (Judg. 7:25; Isa. 10:26).

OREN (Heb. *ʾōren*)

A Judahite, son of Jerahmeel (1 Chr. 2:25).

ORIGINAL SIN

The term "original sin" was coined by Augustine (Lat. *peccatum originale*), though its roots are patristic and biblical. Infants are "reborn" in baptism (Irenaeus), cleansed from the "true stains of sin" in them (Origen), the "contagion of the ancient death" (Cyprian). The most important OT contribution is its teaching about the universality of sin (1 Kgs. 8:46; Job 4:17; 14:4; 15:14; 25:4; Ps. 130:3; 143:2; Eccl. 7:20). Gen. 3 should be added to this list, though it had very little direct impact on the rest of the OT (only on Ezek. 28; Wis. 2:24; Sir. 25:24). Judaism does not have a concept of original sin; instead it speaks of an "evil inclination" (Heb. *yēṣer hāraʿ*) in the heart of everyone, on the basis of Gen. 6:5; 8:21 (cf. Deut. 31:21), but teaches that people can overcome it by vigilantly keeping the law. Gen. 2:4b–3:24 is the beginning of an ancient Yahwistic etiological narrative of origins (chs. 2–11) and stresses that human sinfulness does not derive from God. Its relationship to original sin was first seen by Paul.

Though other NT texts point to original sin (e.g., Heb. 9:26; John 1:29; 8:44), its clearest expression is found in the Pauline literature, always in a context of salvation by Christ. "All have sinned" (Rom. 3:23) and "all, both Jews and Greeks, are under the power of sin" (v. 9). They can be justified only by God's "grace as a gift, through the redemption that is in Christ Jesus, whom God put forward as a sacrifice of atonement, by his blood, effective through faith" (Rom. 3:24-25). The universal dimension of Adam's sin and Christ's redemption is stated succinctly in 1 Cor. 15:22 ("as all die in Adam, so all will be made alive in Christ") and in greater detail in Rom. 5:12-21: "Sin came into the world" through Adam and "death came through sin, and so death spread to all because all have sinned" (v. 12). The full meaning of the final clause, "because all have sinned," is unclear. It implies personal guilt for committing sin, but in light of statements that Adam's sin "led to condemnation for all" (Rom. 5:18) and that by his disobedience "the many were made sinners" (v. 19), the connection between Adam's sin and that of all others must be very intimate. Paul is aware of the dominion of Adam's sin over all humanity, but does not yet speak of heredity; that was the later contribution of Augustine.

Joseph F. Wimmer, O.S.A.

ORION

A constellation named for the mythological Greek hunter represented as a man of great strength, a worker in iron, who at his death was transferred to the heavens, bound to the sky, and became this constellation. Located E of Taurus, the constellation features Betelgeuse and Rigel, two stars of the first magnitude. Generally mentioned with Pleiades, Orion occurs as testimony to God's creative power (Amos 5:8; Job 9:9; 38:81; Targ., Peshitta "giant"). The plural of Heb. *kĕsîl* is used for constellations in general (Isa. 13:10); elsewhere the Hebrew term means "fool" (Prov. 9:13).

Bibliography. G. R. Driver, "Two Astronomical Passages in the Old Testament," *JTS* N.S. 4 (1953): 208-12. AARON W. PARK

ORNAMENTS
Adornments (Heb. *ʿăḏî*) worn by both men and women for decoration. Jewelry of all types is included in this designation, as are scarves, headdresses, sashes, robes, mantles, cloaks, turbans, veils (Isa. 3:18-23), and tiaras (Jdt. 10:3; Gk. *mítra*). The ornaments described in biblical references are most often of gold (e.g., 2 Sam. 1:24), but archaeology reveals other metals, most significantly bronze. Perhaps the most commonly found items of adornment in the Bronze and Iron Ages are the copper or bronze toggle pins that would have performed both a decorative and a functional purpose in holding together pieces of clothing. Most adornments were made of expensive materials or were labor intensive to make, and they were therefore a symbol of wealth, power, and God's favor. They were worn on special occasions, particularly by a bride on her wedding day (Ezek. 16:10-13; Isa. 49:18; Jer. 2:32), but not at times of sadness and mourning (Exod. 33:4-6). Ornaments also appear in religious contexts in the shape of golden bells that hung between the multi-colored yarn pomegranates on the fringe of the high priest's robe (Exod. 28:33-34). Idols were draped with embroidered cloth (Ezek. 16:16-18), considered elsewhere among ornamentation. Cosmetics and perfumes are included in this category: the perfumed boxes in Isaiah's list of ornaments (Isa. 3:20) have their counterpart in the archaeological record in the ceramic, glass, stone, and shell palettes, bottles, and juglets that date to the biblical periods. KATHARINE A. MACKAY

ORNAN (Heb. *ʾornān*)
An alternate form of Araunah.

ORONTES
The main river of western Syria (modern Nahr el-ʿAṣī), known for the important trade routes that followed it, strategic military campaigns in its area, and the major cities built along its course, especially Antioch-on-the-Orontes (modern Antakya, Turkey). Originating on the eastern side of the Lebanon Mountains, the Orontes flows north some 400 km. (250 mi.) through Syria into southern Turkey before it bends to the southwest; it flows into the Mediterranean 26 km. (16 mi.) below Antioch.

Founded ca. 300 B.C.E. by Seleucus I, Antioch lies on the southeastern side of the Orontes. Cargo was moved on the river to and from Antioch to its Mediterranean port, Seleucia (also known as Seleucia Pieria; Acts 13:4; cf. 14:26; 15:39-41). Seleucia's ancient harbor (near modern Samandag, Turkey) has now become a flat, marshy area due to silt flowing down the Orontes through the centuries. Other important cities in the Orontes Valley include Riblah, Kadesh-on-the-Orontes, Emessa, Hamath, and Alalakh. In 853 an alliance of Ben-hadad of Damascus, Irḫuleni of Hamath, and Ahab of Israel battled to a standstill the Assyrian king Shalmaneser III at Qarqar on the lower Orontes, and there in 720 Sargon II routed the rebels of Hamath and Damascus. JOHN L. GILLMAN

ORPAH (Heb. *ʿorpâ*)
A Moabite woman, daughter-in-law of Naomi. After her husband Chilion died, Orpah sought to accompany Naomi to Bethlehem, but at her mother-in-law's insistence returned to her kin in Moab (Ruth 1:4-14).

ORPHAN
A fatherless child (Heb. *yāṯôm*, from the root "to be alone, deprived"; cf. Lam. 5:3). In cultures throughout the ancient Near East, orphans (along with widows and resident aliens) were among the *personae miserabilis*, with a special claim on a community's justice and care because they were often under divine protection. In a social system where the male head of the family safeguarded the welfare of its members, orphans were particularly vulnerable. Without a voice to advocate on their behalf within the clan, these fatherless children were outsiders and their property an easy mark for the greedy.

Within the community constituted by the Sinai covenant, the treatment of orphans determines Israel's fate before the Lord. This Lord is their father (Ps. 68:6), watching over them (Ps. 146:9) and executing justice for them (Deut. 10:18; Ps. 10:14, 18). This protection extends even to Edomite orphans whom the Lord promises to keep alive (Jer. 49:11). Consequently, if the Israelites deprive orphans of justice (Deut. 24:17) or oppress them (Zech. 7:10), the Lord will kill them and make their own children orphans (Exod. 22:23-24). If the people of Judah care for orphans as the Lord cared for the Hebrew slaves in Egypt, the Lord will remain with them (Jer. 7:6) and Davidic kingship will continue (22:3). Job invokes his regard for orphans as evidence that he suffers unjustly (Job 29:12; 31:17, 21). Isaiah, however, observes that Israel's evil is so great that it smothers the Lord's concern for orphans (Isa. 9:17[16]). Similarly, angered at God's refusal to answer him directly, Job declares that God casts lots for the life of orphans (Job 6:27).

The wicked snatch orphans from their mother's breast and make them slaves (Job 24:9); driving away their donkeys (v. 3), they victimize (Isa. 10:2) and kill them (Ps. 94:6). Israel is evil because it does not allow orphans to prosper (Jer. 5:28). Thus, Eliphaz thinks Job's suffering stems from his having "crushed the arms of the orphans" (Job 22:9).

Jesus of Nazareth promises the Johannine community that he will not leave them orphans (John 14:15-24), i.e., unprotected amid the evils of this world; he will send them an advocate to aid them in their struggles. The Letter of James argues that loving attention to the needs of widows and orphans, often the silent and the invisible within the community, is necessary for a faith-filled relationship with the Lord (Jas. 1:26-27). KATHLEEN S. NASH

OSIRIS
See Serapis.

OSNAPPAR (Aram. *'osnappar*)
An Assyrian king who deported conquered peoples and resettled them at Samaria (Ezra 4:10). Although Shalmaneser V and Sargon best fit the circumstances of siege and resettlement, the name may be a corrupt form of Assurbanipal.

OSPREY
A bird or prey mentioned only in the lists of unclean animals (Lev. 11:13; Deut. 14:12; Heb. *'ozniyâ*). The exact species is impossible to determine based on the scant biblical references, but talmudic tradition supports the bird's identification as the osprey *(Pandion haliaëtus)*, a large fish-eating hawk. Other possible candidates are the harrier (or short-toed) eagle (*Circaëtus gallicus;* cf. Aram. *'ûzyā'*, "sea-eagle"; so LXX), the bearded vulture *(Gypaëtus barbatus aureus),* or the black vulture *(Aegypius* [or *Vultur*] *monachus).*

OSTRACA (Gk. *óstraka*)
Sherds of pottery which preserve inscriptions. The Greek word refers sometimes to an earthen vessel, but more frequently only to broken fragments (cf. Ps. 22:15[LXX 21:16]).

In archaeological contexts, ostraca are usually potsherds that preserve inscriptions of various genres. The term can include, however, inscriptions preserved on other materials, such as shell or small stones. Ostraca usually were written in ink, but sometimes were incised. Ostraca occur most frequently in Syria, Palestine, and Egypt and are rather rare in Mesopotamia, where cuneiform was more prevalent in the earlier periods.

Ostraca were used more in the context of routine daily writing activities rather than for more permanent literary preservation. They often preserve only names, numbers, or lists, but were also used for administrative missives (Arad and Samaria), occasional legal appeals (Meẓad Ḥashavyahu), and even as military communiqués (Arad, Ḥorvat 'Uza). Such inscriptions often provide valuable glimpses into the daily affairs and concerns of the people. Additionally, they are important sources of evidence for studying the development of languages and writing.

Bibliography. G. I. Davies et al., *Ancient Hebrew Inscriptions* (Cambridge, 1991); J. Naveh, "Writing and Scripts in Seventh-Century B.C.E. Philistia," *IEJ* 35 (1985): 8-21. Dale W. Manor

OSTRICH
A large, richly plumed, swift moving, flightless bird of the genus *Struthio.* Now found in the wild only in Africa, in ancient times ostriches were also plentiful in the barren plains of Western Asia. The biblical writers frequently mention the ostrich (Heb. *baṯ hayya'ănâ; rĕnāîm*) as an image of desolation (Isa. 13:21; 34:13; 43:20; Jer. 50:39; cf. Job 30:29; Mic. 1:8).

Though many Western Asian peoples hunted it for food, the Israelites considered the omnivorous ostrich unclean (Lev. 11:16; Deut. 14:15). The ostrich is described as neglectful of its eggs (Job 39:14-16; Lam. 4:3), leaving them to be warmed by the sun during the day and incubated at night. The description of the ostrich as stupid (Job 39:17) arises from this supposed neglect and its inability to take evasive action when pursued.

Nicole J. Ruane

OTHNI (Heb. *'oṯnî*)
The eldest son of Shemaiah; a levitical gatekeeper during the reign of King David (1 Chr. 26:7).

OTHNIEL (Heb. *'oṯnî'ēl*)
An Israelite judge, the son of Kenaz and the nephew (less likely the younger brother) of Caleb, who became Caleb's son-in-law by capturing Debir (Kiriath-sepher) and thus winning Achsah, the daughter of Caleb, as wife (Josh. 15:15-19 = Judg. 1:11-15). Othniel later delivered the people from the oppressive hand of Cushan-rishathaim of Aramnaharaim (Judg. 3:7-11). The name Othniel functions as a clan name in a genealogical list of commissioned officers (1 Chr. 27:15). Caleb and Othniel may represent, respectively, eponymous ancestors of elder and younger clans of the tribe of Kenaz (the Kenizzites) that were absorbed into Judah.

Rick R. Marrs

OVEN
A small cooking device (Exod. 8:3[MT 7:28]; Lev. 11:35) employed to bake various kinds of bread (2:4; 7:9; 26:26). Cylindrical in shape, the most common ovens (Heb. *tannûr*) were made of clay and could be embedded in the ground or raised above it. The oven floor was lined with pebbles, on which the fire was built. Bread dough was placed on the hot stones or against the wall of the oven to cook. Fuels included dry grass (Matt. 6:30; Luke 12:28) and cakes of animal dung (cf. Ezek. 4:12, 15). Commercial bakers may have lived in a specific area of a city (cf. Neh. 3:11; 12:38).

For Abraham, a portable, smoking oven was a sign of the Lord's presence (Gen. 15:17; NRSV "fire pot"). An oven blazing with fire was seen as a symbol of the wrath of the Lord (Ps. 21:9[10]; Isa. 31:9; NRSV "furnace"; Mal. 4:1[3:19]; cf. Lam. 5:10). The wicked are also likened to an oven burning with desire, evil deeds, and treason (Hos. 7:4, 6-7).

Stephen J. Andrews

OVENS, TOWER OF THE
A tower defending the northwestern angle of Jerusalem's city wall, possibly constructed first by King Uzziah (cf. 2 Chr. 26:9) and later rebuilt by Nehemiah (Neh. 3:11; 12:38). The precise location of the tower (Heb. *migdal hattannûrîm*), as well as its position relative to the Corner Gate, is a matter of dispute. According to Nehemiah it was situated somewhere S of the Broad Wall and N of the Valley Gate. The name may point to a location near the "bakers' street" of Jer. 37:21, although this reference dates before the time of Nehemiah.

John R. Huddlestun

OWL
A nocturnal bird of prey of the order *Strigiformes*, listed among birds forbidden to eat (Lev. 11:17; Deut. 14:16). The owl is characterized by exceptionally large eyes that are directed forward rather than to the sides. The feathers around the eyes radiate from a common center and enhance the apparent size of the eyes. Yet, in spite of this, owls trust their ears far more often than their eyes in their search for prey. They fly extremely quietly, though slowly, and surprise their prey by descending from above. Their sharp talons and short, hooked beak are extremely powerful and make escape difficult.

A number of Hebrew terms *(kôs, qā'aṯ, yanšûp̱, qip̱ôḏ)* are variously translated by the NRSV as "owl," "screech owl," and "desert owl" (Zeph. 2:14) and "little owl" and "great owl" (Lev. 11:17; Deut. 14:16). Attempts to associate Hebrew terms with particular species are extremely problematic and may never be accomplished. From this list it is quite obvious that translations vary due to the necessity to distinguish between different Hebrew words for owls, not between different species.

JESPER SVARTVIK

OX (ANIMAL)
A castrated male bovine *(Bos taurus)* managed for traction, meat, hide, and other by-products. Breeds that have been identified in artistic and archaeological contexts include varieties of the *Bos primigenius, Bos longifrons,* and *Bos indicus,* the zebu or "humpback." The fact that several Hebrew and Greek words are used for the ox suggests that a wide variety of breeds, sexes, grades, or uses existed (Heb. *bāqār, 'eleṗ, pār, šôr;* Gk. *bous, taúros*). Cattle domestication and management began no later than 6000 B.C. There is probably a link between the intensification of cattle raising and periods of sedentism or village life.

The ox was important in the agricultural societies of the biblical world. Castration tempered the aggressive nature of the ox and rendered its immense strength and endurance manageable. Care and control of the ox rested with its owner (e.g., Exod. 21:28-29), and there were rules of use and misuse. Tools and implements that channeled the power of the ox included goads, yoke-harnesses and ropes, plows, harrows, threshing sledges, and possibly large rotary querns or mills.

The investment of resources required to raise these animals made the ox very valuable. It is frequently mentioned as an indicator of wealth or an object of booty. Correspondingly, the ox is almost always listed first in sacrifice lists (e.g., Deut. 17:1; 2 Sam. 24:22). Apart from such expensive offerings, only the young or very old were probably harvested for meat and hides.

MARK ZIESE

OX (Gk. *Ṓx*) **(PERSON)**
The paternal grandfather of Judith; father of Merari and descendant of Israel (Jdt. 8:1).

OXYRHYNCHUS FRAGMENTS
Oxyrhynchus, an ancient Egyptian site (modern Behnesa), lies at the edge of the desert ca. 193 km. (120 mi.) S of Cairo and 16 km. (10 mi.) W of the Nile. Excavations at the end of the 19th century uncovered, in its rubbish heaps, a treasure chest of ancient texts of all sorts, dating from the 1st to the 9th century B.C. By 1995 more than 60 volumes of the Oxyrhynchus Papyri series were published, presenting the Greek text of several thousand separate documents. Among the official documents, correspondence, personal letters, informal notes, and other texts were fragments of Matt. 1 (now at the University of Pennsylvania), parts of Rom. 1 and 1 John 4 (at the Semitic Museum, Harvard University), parts of 1 Corinthians and Philippians (now in Cairo), and a leaf from Revelation (at Princeton Theological Seminary). Also found at Oxyrhynchus were fragments of a papyrus codex preserving several sayings of Jesus from the Gospel of Thomas.

CARROLL D. OSBURN

OZEM (Heb. *'ōṣem*)
1. The sixth son of Jesse, and the brother of King David (1 Chr. 2:15).

2. A Judahite, the fourth son of Jerahmeel (1 Chr. 2:25).

OZNI (Heb. *'oznî*) (also EZBON)
A son of Gad and ancestor of the Oznite clan (Num. 26:16). He is called Ezbon at Gen. 46:16.

P

P
A designation of the Priestly source of the Pentateuch.
See PRIESTLY DOCUMENT.

PAARAI (Heb. *paʿăray*) (also NAARAI)
An Arbite; one of David's Thirty (2 Sam. 23:35). At 1 Chr. 11:37 he is called Naarai the son of Ezbai.

PADDAN-ARAM (Heb. *paddan-ʾărām*) (also PADDAN)
An area around Haran in upper Mesopotamia. Usually translated "Field of Aram" (cf. Hos. 12:12[MT 13]), Paddan-aram is generally regarded as an alternate designation for Aram-naharaim, the territory encompassed by the great bend of the Euphrates River. A few scholars have argued that the term was an Aramaic rendering of the city name Haran. The exact location of Paddan-aram is not known.

All biblical occurrences refer to the homeland of Abraham's family. Rebekah was from Paddan-aram (Gen. 25:20); Isaac sent Jacob there to procure a wife (28:2-7); Jacob sojourned with Laban at Paddan-aram, and most of his sons were born there (35:26; 46:15; cf. 48:7, Paddan).

STEPHEN J. ANDREWS

PADON (Heb. *pāḏôn*)
A temple servant whose descendants returned with Zerubbabel from captivity in Babylon (Ezra 2:44 = Neh. 7:47).

PAGANS
A designation for non-Christian Gentiles in contrast to the Christian Gentiles addressed by Paul (Gk. *éthnē*; 1 Cor. 5:1; 10:20).

PAGIEL (Heb. *pagʿîʾēl*)
The son of Ochran; the chief of Asher during the wilderness wanderings (Num. 2:27; 10:26) who assisted Moses in the census (1:13) and who brought an offering for the tabernacle (7:72, 77).

PAHATH-MOAB (Heb. *paḥaṯ-môʾāḇ*)
A name (lit., "governor of Moab") probably given to the founding ancestor of a clan which returned from the Babylonian Exile (Ezra 2:6; 8:4; Neh. 7:11). Pahath-moab is listed as one of the "leaders of the people" who signed a covenant with Nehemiah to uphold the Law (Neh. 10:14[MT 15]). This clan consisted of two families, descended from Jeshua and Joab. One of their number, "Hasshub son of Pahath-moab," repaired a section of Jerusalem's walls and the Tower of the Ovens (Neh. 3:11). Eight members of the clan are mentioned in Ezra 10:30 as having taken foreign wives.

CHRISTIAN M. M. BRADY

PAI (Heb. *pāʿî*)
Alternate form of Pau, the residence of the Edomite king Hadar (1 Chr. 1:50).

PALACE
Even without the ancient literary references to palaces, the existence of a sociopolitical hierarchy could be discerned archaeologically. Remains of many palaces, which served as residences and administrative centers for royalty, have been discovered in the biblical world. Their identity is evident in their size, layout, elaborate decorations, and contents, including expensive furniture, costly domestic utensils, and state archives (e.g., collections of cuneiform tablets or ostraca). The earliest identifiable palaces date to the early 3rd millennium B.C.; these examples come from Mesopotamia, where competition for land and resources fostered the evolution of government and placed power in the hands of an aristocracy.

The ancient terminology was no more precise than the English translations, and the same words can often refer to a "temple," "palace," or "citadel" (e.g., Heb. *bayiṯ, hêḵāl, ʾarmôn*). Some of the earliest Sumerian palaces and Persian royal residences from a much later period are known from their size, lavish interiors, and facilities. Mari's palace, which dates to the 1st Dynasty of Babylon, includes some 300 rooms. A palace at Ai dates to ca. 2500 and reflects the presence of a ruling class in Palestine. Other Early Bronze Age palaces have been found at Tell Mardikh (ancient Ebla) in Syria and at Tell Jarmuth/Yarmut and Arad in Israel. Impressive Middle Bronze palaces include those at Ur, Eshnunna, Larsa, and Uruk in Mesopotamia and those at Shechem, Hazor, Megiddo, and Lachish. Other royal residences and administrative centers have been found in Luxor, Tell el-Amarna, Knossos, Mycenae, and Boghazköy. Smaller but readily identifiable palaces have been unearthed in Palestine at Gezer, Tell Jemmeh, Tell el-Ḥesi, and Aphek. In the Iron Age the Assyrians built elaborate palaces in their capitals of Nineveh, Nimrud, and Khorsabad. The Assyrian-style palace, the *bīt ḫilāni* or "open court building," has parallels at palaces in Megiddo and Gezer.

No remains have been linked with the palaces of David (2 Sam. 5:9; 7:1-2) or Solomon (1 Kgs. 7:1-12) in Jerusalem, but some scholars detect Syrian influences in the account of Solomon's temple. Palatial residences from Hazor and Megiddo have been dated to Solomonic times. Equally famous is the palace of Omri and Ahab at Samaria. Excavations at this site recovered ivory furniture inlay and decoration (1 Kgs. 22:39). The OT also mentions Ahab's palace at Jezreel (1 Kgs. 21:1), the Assyrian palace at Nineveh (Nah. 2:6), and the palace of Babylon (2 Kgs. 20:18; Dan. 4:4, 29[MT 1, 26]). The Persian palace at Susa is featured prominently throughout the book of Esther.

Royal residences from NT times include Herod's palaces at Jericho and Jerusalem (near the Jaffa Gate) and a series of fortress-palace complexes, the most famous of which was located at Masada. Palaces were common enough that they appear in figurative language of the OT prophets — especially as symbols of national-political life (e.g., Isa. 34:13; Jer. 17:27; Amos 2:5).

Bibliography. A. Kempinski and R. Reich, eds., *The Architecture of Ancient Israel* (Jerusalem, 1992); G. R. H. Wright, *Ancient Building in South Syria and Palestine,* 2 vols. HO 7, 1/2 B/3 (Leiden, 1985). GERALD L. MATTINGLY

PALAL (Heb. *pālāl*)
The son of Uzai who repaired a portion of the walls of Jerusalem (Neh. 3:25).

PALESTINE, LAND OF
In describing Palestine from a geographical point of view, the physical facts as defined by modern research must be combined with the ancient nomenclature of the Bible and other ancient sources. Caution must be exercised in using ancient terms which have acquired modern connotations different from their original meaning.

Names and Definition

The Bible never uses the term "Promised Land," but that concept is behind passages such as Gen. 15:18-21. The territory encompassed there is the modern "Levant," used here to mean the eastern Mediterranean littoral. It extends from the Euphrates, "The Great River," to "the River of Egypt," the eastern branch of the Nile which passed in antiquity along the Sinai-Egyptian border (not to be confused with the Brook of Egypt). To the east and south the Levant is bordered by deserts.

In OT times the area from the modern Lebanese border with north Syria down to the Wadi el-ʿArîsh was known as Canaan. Its boundary descriptions (Num. 34:1-2; Josh. 13:4; Ezek. 47:15-20) are quite explicit; they encompass the modern state of Lebanon, the area around Damascus, and western Palestine. Transjordan was excluded. Canaan extended from the Eleutheros (modern Nahr el-Kebîr) to Wadi el-ʿArîsh. It differed, therefore, from the land of promise in Gen. 15 and also from the "land of Israel" as settled by the Israelite tribes.

The territory originally occupied by the Israelite tribes was "all Israel from Dan to Beer-sheba" (1 Sam. 3:20; 2 Sam. 17:11; cf. 1 Kgs. 4:25[MT 5:5], "Judah and Israel"). When Transjordan is expressly included it is "from Dan to Beer-sheba, including the land of Gilead" (Judg. 20:1).

In Roman times Judea came to be applied not only to ancient Judah but to the whole country (Strabo *Geog.* 16.2.34; Ptolemy *Geog.* 5.16.1); Herod was king of Judea. After the Bar Kokhba Revolt (A.D. 135), Hadrian changed the name to Syria Palaestina, a term which had originally applied only to Philistia (Herodotus *Hist.* 7.89). By the 4th century it was called simply Palaestina.

Physical Description

The terrain is clearly depicted as a land of brooks of water, of fountains and springs and valleys, which "drinks water by the rain from heaven" (Deut. 11:11). Unlike the great nations of Mesopotamia with its Tigris and Euphrates and Egypt with its Nile, Palestine had no such natural water source that could be used for irrigation. The two main types of topographical formations, hills and valleys, are stressed time and again. Due to the great Jordan depression, general north-south orientation is given to the entire landscape with coastal and mountain zones running parallel. But regional faulting has led to further divisions of these north-south bands into east-west units that influenced the distribution of human settlement throughout the ages and often find echo in the administrative divisions of the country. From earliest times the communal settlements tended to group themselves around the water sources at the edge of the plains. They thus insured for themselves a source of water near cultivable land. The country's lines of communication also tended to follow the valleys and less difficult mountain passes often formed by the exposure of soft Senonian chalk between the strata of Cenomanian and Eocene limestones.

The terrain will be briefly described from north to south and west to east. Stress is upon the biblical terminology as applied in OT times, though later terms (esp. Greco-Roman) and even some modern names are unavoidable.

Coastal Plain

Phoenicia. The northern coast, that of modern Lebanon, is characterized by the closeness of the mountains to the shore. The major harbors of the east Mediterranean were the Phoenician cities Byblos, Beirut, Sidon, and especially the islands, Tyre and Arvad. Cultivable land is scarce on the plain, but the mountains of the hinterland provided the timber and other products so famous in antiquity. The northern coastal zone is called Phoenicia in Greco-Roman times but has no name in the OT except Canaan or simply Sidon. The population was mainly engaged in maritime activities. The promontory of Ras en-Naqûra/Rosh ha-Niqra, called Ladder of Tyre in Crusader times, sets off the plain to the south of it from the rest of Phoenicia. On the south it is bounded by the Carmel.

Mt. Carmel is the mass of Cenomanian limestone running northwest-southeast from its headland to Wadi el-Milḥ/Naḥal Yoqneʿam. It forms a wedge-shaped barrier that divides the coastal plain; within its ridges were plentiful orchards and vineyards, making it a symbol of fertility (Isa. 33:9; Amos 1:2; Nah. 1:4). The Carmel formed its watershed along the northeast ridge; the main streams flow westward through steep ravines, the caves of which gave shelter to prehistoric humans.

The coastal zone from the Carmel headland south to the Crocodile River (Naḥal Tanninim) was evidently called Naphoth-(dor). It is bounded by ridges of sandstone along the shore which shelter a fertile plain at the foot of the Carmel.

Sharon Plain. From Naphoth-dor to Joppa the Sharon (Eusebius *Onom.* 162.5-6) consists of alluvial soil from the Samaria hills on the east, a band of red Mouseterian sand in the middle, and then ridges of sandstone (Kurkar) which blocked the passage of the several streams crossing the plain from east to west. This caused swamps and scrub forests to develop behind the sandstone ridges. The Wadi ʿAuja (modern Yarkon) cuts across the southern third of the plain, forming an additional barrier. Thus, the ancient towns grew up along the eastern side of the Sharon where the ground was higher, more fertile, and rich in water sources. In OT times the plain was mostly used for pasturage. From Aphek north to Gath-padalla ran a key segment of the great coastal trunk route connecting Egypt with Syria and Mesopotamia.

At Aphek the waters of the Yarkon rise and flow in a tortuous course to the sea N of Joppa. The ancient route led eastward around Aphek because of this barrier.

According to the Phoenician inscription of Ešmunʿazer (l. 19) the hinterland of Joppa was also included in "the mighty grain lands in the territory of Sharon" (cf. Eusebius *Onom.* 162.5-6). The southern border of the Sharon must be placed at the valley of Sorek (Wadi eṣ-Ṣarar/Naḥal Sorek), which was also the southern border of the Danite inheritance. Another wadi (Wadi Muṣrarah; modern Naḥal Ayalon) runs from the valley of Aijalon diagonally across the plain toward Joppa.

Philistia. From the border of Joppa southward was the coast occupied by the Canaanites. While Joppa and Ashkelon stood right on the shore, along with Yavneh-yam, two other major towns, Ashdod and Gaza, were located inland behind the sand dunes. They had access to the sea by means of small harbor settlements on the coast, usually at the mouth of a wadi.

The plain of Philistia is much wider in the south, 25 km. (15 mi.), and narrows progressively toward the north to ca. 17 km. (10 mi.). Just behind the sands there is a sort of topographic corridor, somewhat troughlike, which gradually rises toward the Shephelah foothills to the east.

Along the sand dunes, especially around Gaza, were extensive vineyards. The inland soils are excellent for grain crops and olive orchards. The area supported a dense human population from earliest antiquity.

The great trunk route from Egypt across northern Sinai and northwards to Damascus and the Phoenician coast followed the "trough" east of the line of dunes. After Jabneel it turned northeast toward Aphek.

Several wadis cut across the Philistine plain, some of them forced to turn northwards in order to find passage through the dunes.

The commercial route from Egypt to Mesopotamia was not the only source of caravan trade. The seaports of Philistia were the destination of the caravans coming from Arabia across the Negeb to the Mediterranean. This heavy commercial traffic led to the frequent alliances between the Philistine cities and the Edomites and Arabs.

Central Range

Lebanon. The mountains of Lebanon, a range ca. 160 km. (100 mi.) long, are the most prominent orographic features of the Levant. They were the source of timber for both Egypt and Mesopotamia. The southern extension of this range, beyond the Liṭani River, forms the western highlands of Palestine, which consist of several distinct units. The foothills behind the coastal plain of Tyre and of Acco were called Shephelah ("lowlands").

Galilee. The northernmost district, Galilee, is divided into Upper and Lower (Josephus *BJ* 3.3.1; cf. the order of towns in Josh. 19:35-38). The plateau in the north is lower to the northwest and slopes upwards toward the south. It was an area of Canaanite cities. The southern part of Upper Galilee is a massif (Jebel Jarmuq, now wrongly called Mt. Meiron), largely uninhabited until the Israelite period. It looks down on the valley of Beth-kerem which separates it from Lower Galilee.

Lower Galilee consists of a series of ridges running east-west, the most important being Mt. Atzmon and the Nazareth hills. In between these ridges were some latitudinal valleys, especially that of Beth-netopha/Sahl el-Baṭṭôf, the plain of Asochis in Greco-Roman sources. The watershed between east and west is east of the center line of Galilee; to the east the ridges slope steeply down to the Huleh Valley and the Sea of Galilee; to the west

Foothills of "the hill country of Ephraim" in Samaria (Werner Braun)

they point long slender fingers down to the coastal plain. There is considerable basalt on the east, while the west is limestone.

Jezreel. This triangular depression between the hills of Lower Galilee and Samaria was the main thoroughfare between the coast and the Jordan Valley. Its name in Greek and Latin sources is Esdraelon. On its eastern edge stood Mt. Tabor and the Hill of Moreh, and to the east of these two hills is a basalt plateau comprising the inheritance of Issachar. The ʿEn-harod Valley led from Jezreel down to Beth-shean. The Jezreel Valley (also called Esdraelon) was famous for its grain production. Megiddo stood near the mouth of the main thoroughfare from Egypt as it enters the valley.

The low-lying plateau behind Megiddo and Jokneam (Bilâd er-Rûhah/Ramat Menashe) separates the valley of Jezreel from the Sharon Plain and connects the Carmel range with the mountains of Samaria. The southeastern point of the Jezreel, partly encircled by the arm of Mt. Gilboa, is bounded by a low ridge leading up the valley of Dothan, which provided another easy passage to the Sharon.

Samaria. The mountains of Samaria are called Mt. Shechem in an Egyptian source from the Canaanite period (Papyrus Anastasi I). Opinions are divided as to whether it could all be called Mt. Ephraim. A central feature is the Shechem Valley between Mt. Gerizim on the south and Mt. Ebal on the north. Samaria had several valleys leading out to the west, providing easy access to the mountain area. The Dothan Valley and the Shechem Valley in the north and east respectively are matched by the Wadi Farʿah, a dramatic gash in the mountains running down to the Jordan Valley at Adam(ah). Southwest from the Shechem Valley, via the valley of Michmethath, ran the valley of Kanah, the principal boundary between Manasseh and Ephraim.

The foothills slope naturally down to the west in a gentle continuity. The eastern side is largely steppe, while the west is good for vineyards, orchards, and grain, the latter especially in the valleys.

The hill country of Ephraim and Benjamin is a

Nahal Zin, boundary between the north and central Negeb (Phoenix Data Systems, Neal and Joel Bierling)

continuity. One major subdivision, the district occupied by the people of Gibeon (Josh. 9:3), forms a topographic saddle between Mt. Ephraim and Mt. Judah and includes the ridge of Nebī Samwîl and the plain through which passes the road to Beth-horon. This latter joins the "highway" (Judg. 21:19) that follows the watershed from Shechem past Lebonah to Ramah in Benjamin, going west of Jerusalem to Bethlehem, Halhul, Hebron, and finally to Beer-sheba.

Jerusalem. In the vicinity of Jerusalem are two ravines, the Wadi Beit Ḥanînah and the valley of Rephaim, which bisect the mountain chain from the watershed west. They are steep and dangerous, and anyone approaching from the west was easily threatened by ambushes. Accordingly, the route through Gibeon to Beth-horon was the favorite link between Jerusalem and the coast. Jerusalem is situated, therefore, at a point where three major approaches connect the shore with the central range. To the east was the Jericho road, facilitating passage to the Jordan Valley and beyond. The ridge W of Jerusalem above the valley of Hinnom was a link between Mt. Ephraim to the north and Mt. Judah to the south.

Mt. Judah. The heart of Cisjordan is the high watershed zone known as Mt. Judah or the hill country of Judah. Comprised of limestone and dolomite strata with layers of chalk and marl, the hill country forms a massive block incised from the west by some deep ravines and bordered on that side by a trough of Senonian chalk. To the east lies the wilderness of Judah.

The highest point in the Judean hills is at Ḥalḥûl (ca. 1000 m. [3300 ft.]). The central plateau is dominated by Hebron, situated in a depression, the meeting place of deep valleys running westward. The southern district was the Negeb of Caleb, the principal town being Debir.

Shephelah. The "Lowland" or Shephelah is a separate unit of later limestone on the western flank of the Judean hills, separated from it by a trough valley of soft chalk running north-south. The rounded hills of the Shephelah are fairly uniform in height, ca. 200 m. (1200 ft.) above sea level. The zone reaches to the area around Gezer in the north and the southern end trails off toward Beer-sheba. Several wadis bisect the Shephelah from east to west, the most prominent being the valley of Ajalon, the Sorek, the vale of Elah, and the valley of Zephatha. The Shephelah was divided into three districts from north to south, following the pattern of the wadis.

Wilderness of Judah. This zone had few towns because it was the chalky waste in the rain shadow to the east of the Judean watershed. The infertile soil and lack of water left the area unsuitable for cultivation except with special care for water collection; even then the territory remained a steppe land, a pastoral zone for the flocks of the hill country settlements. Actually, there are several "wildernesses," e.g., the wilderness of Tekoa, Ziph, and Ma'on. The areas above the cliffs bordering on the Dead Sea were even more wild and could be accurately called "wasteland."

Negeb. To the south of the hill country was a zone often translated "South" or "extreme south." The biblical Negeb was mainly the valley E of Beer-sheba and the rolling plain encircled by the brook Besor to the west. This Negeb of Judah was in fact inhabited by various satellite tribes or ethnic groups (e.g., Simeon, the Kenites, the Jerahmeelites, and the Cherethites).

The local administrative center was at Beer-sheba during the United Monarchy. It is beside the junction of the Hebron wadi from the hill country and the Beer-sheba wadi from the east; after they join they form the Besor, which winds its way west and northwest to empty into the sea S of Gaza.

The Negeb should not be thought of as wilderness, though it is a zone of very marginal rainfall. Its main significance was as a link in the caravan route from the Arabah to the Philistine seacoast. It was to the kingdom of Judah what the Jezreel Valley was to the northern kingdom of Israel; control of the Negeb was a sign of Judean strength and prosperity; loss of the Negeb with incursions from the Philistines and the Edomites or the Arabs meant a time of weakness and lack of political power.

Just S of the Negeb was a steppe land called the wilderness of Beer-sheba, which passed the way of Shur (leading to Egypt). Kadesh was in another zone, the wilderness of Zin, which bordered on the wilderness of Paran (the Sinai expanse). The highlands S of the Negeb were considered by the author of Chronicles to be Mt. Seir (1 Chr. 4:42; probably also 2 Chr. 20:10).

The modern term "Negev" encompasses all the area from Beer-sheba to Elath, but this derives from a misconception of the biblical term.

"Rift" Valley

Determining the north-south orientation of the main physical feature of the entire land is the Great Rift running the length of the Levant and extending down into Africa.

Beqaʿ. In the north the Rift is known as the Beqaʿ "Valley" (biblical "valley of Lebanon"), the rich plain between the mountains of Lebanon and the Hermon-Sirion (Anti-Lebanons). At its watershed was Lebo-hamath; northwards it is drained by the Orontes, southwards by the Liṭani. The valley at the foot of Hermon was called valley or land of Mizpeh.

Mt. Hermon. This is the highest mountain in the land of Israel (2814 m. [9166 ft.]). Its snows furnish most of the water for the Jordan, of which there are four sources, two from the ʿAyûn Valley and two from Hermon.

Hûleh Valley. The principal sources for the Jordan are the waters by Tell el-Qadi (Tel Dan) and the spring at Banias (Paneas). They join in the Hûleh Valley (Josephus "Ulatha") and formed the shallow Lake Hûleh. This latter has generally been taken to be the waters of Merom, but the site of Merom must be located in the plateau above, near Marûn er-Ras. The lake was surrounded by swamps and served as a filter cleansing the waters of the Jordan before they flowed down to the Sea of Galilee.

From the north, one entered the Hûleh via the pass beside Abel-beth-maacah or that coming down past Dan. The major town in the valley was Hazor, the largest urban center of the Canaanite period.

Between the swampy basin in the northern part of the valley and the Sea of Galilee is a massive dyke of ancient basalt. The Jordan cuts its way through this lava deposit in a narrow gorge on the eastern side of the valley.

Sea of Galilee. The river comes out of the gorge, crosses a small alluvial plain, and enters the lake of Chinnereth, or the Sea of Galilee. This is a heart-shaped body of water, ca. 200 m. (600 ft.) below sea level. It is 18 km. long × 12 km. across (ca. 12 × 7 mi.) and is shut in by basalt hills on nearly all sides. The waters are generally fresh, though highly mineral springs once fed the northwestern shore. Hot springs break forth along the western side, leaving a small arm of land isolated to the east.

Jordan River. The Jordan flows in a tortuous course through the deep Rift Valley down to the Dead Sea. In a straight line it covers ca. 105 km. (65 mi.) and descends from 200 m. (600 ft.) below sea level to nearly 400 m. (1200 ft.) below. The first part of its course is through steep clay banks until it reaches the confluence of the Jabbok from the east and the Wadi Farʿah on the west. At this point, denoted by the town of Adam (modern ed-Damiyah), the riverbed cut through a more open plain.

The valley was part of the biblical Arabah and served as the boundary of Canaan. Along the eastern edge of the valley were rich water sources that encouraged the rise of towns in the Canaanite period (e.g., Pella, Succoth), while the western side was more arid except for the Beth-shean Valley and the Jericho region, which was a tropical paradise (Josephus *BJ* 4.8.3).

Dead Sea. The biblical Sea of Salt or Sea of the Arabah (Asphalitis, Josephus *Ant.* 1.9.1) was called the Dead Sea by Greco-Roman writers in the latter half of the 2nd century A.D. It formerly received ca. 6 million tons of water every 24 hours from the Jordan. On the east it is bordered by steep cliffs of Moab with only the "Tongue" (Arab. *Lisan*), a boot-shaped peninsula projecting across its width. South of the Lisan it is a shallow basin, but on the northeastern side it is over 400 m. (1200 ft.) deep. At times one could cross dryshod from the Lisan to the western shore. The water of the Dead Sea is of such a high mineral content as to be poisonous to normal life forms. The arid valley S of the Dead Sea was called the valley of Salt.

Southern Arabah. The name Arabah was preserved in Arabic only with relation to the valley S of the Dead Sea. The valley floor rises gradually southward to ca. 200 m. (600 ft.) above sea level before sloping down again on the gulf of Elath. It is a desert area with heavy alluvial sands in the middle and salty soils just S of the Dead Sea. The red cliffs of Mt. Seir rise to the east, and the yellow limestone of the Cisjordan desert highlands stand on the west. The two main oases are ʿAin Ḥuṣb in the north and ʿAin Ghaḍyân in the south. The Arabah was a natural border between Israel and Edom but was also a line of communication with south Arabia, by land and also by sea. As such it was a contested zone between the neighboring states.

Reed Sea. The Gulf of Elath, the eastern arm of the Red Sea, is called the "Reed Sea," often rendered "Red Sea" (1 Kgs. 9:26), following Greek usage (Herodotus *Hist.* 11.8).

Transjordan

In Transjordan the history of biblical times touches mainly on those districts bordering on the deep valley of the rift; they were bounded on the east by the wastes of the Arabian desert. The geopolitical importance of Transjordan was due to the King's Highway, the route from Damascus to Elath which also led to Midian and then to south Arabia.

Bashan. The northern districts, often disputed with Aram-Damascus, were part of the land of Apum/Upe in the Canaanite period. The biblical name for the whole district was Bashan, which included various territories including the "whole region of Argob," with its 60 walled cities. In Greco-Roman times it was divided into Gaulanitis (named after the town Golan) along the western edge of the plateau and east to the Nahr Allân; Batanea (from the Aramaic form of Bashan), the zone E of the same Allan Valley; and Auranitis (from OT Hauran), mainly the mountain called Jebel ed-Druze, the highest peak of which is Jebel Ḥaurân. The lava region NW of the Hauran mountains was called Trachonitis (Gk. "rough country"), modern el-Leja.

The entire area was included in Canaan and contained the Aramean district of Geshur (just E of Chinnereth). Its southern border was the Yarmuk Valley. The Yarmuk is the largest river in Transjordan, and flows through a steep gorge to join the Jordan below the Sea of Galilee. Its waters originate in stream beds far to the east, especially from the Hauran region. The Yarmuk Valley thus separated Bashan/Golan from Gilead.

Gilead. Central Transjordan (biblical Gilead) is a mountainous area of Cenomanian limestone like the hills of Ephraim and Judah. It is not reckoned as part of Canaan, but was occupied by the tribe of Gad as well as Bashan. Thus, the division of the area into two halves by the Jabbok was recognized in the Israelite settlement.

The mountains reach over 900 m. (3000 ft.), the highest point being at ʿAjlûn. The western slopes and the hills take up most of the area; to the east is a narrow tableland bordering on the desert. There is a double watershed, one near the west from whence steep ravines flow into the Jordan Valley; the easterly flowing streams are largely collected by the course of the Jabbok, which runs north along the eastern plateau before turning west to bisect the entire uplifted dome reaching the valley by Mahanaim and Succoth.

Ammon. Rabbath-ammon, the center of Ammonite territory, is located on the east at the head of another series of valleys separating Gilead from the tableland of Moab. Ammon is structurally a basin 32 × 16 km. (20 × 10 mi.) from northeast to southwest.

Moab. The tableland, the northern half of the territory claimed by the Moabites (disputed by Israel), consists of a plain behind the ridges sloping down to the Dead Sea (from Mt. Nebo-Pisgah). The entire plateau E of the Dead Sea is divided into two halves by the Arnon Valley (Wadi el-Môjib), which formed the border between Israel and Moab proper. The term *mîšôr,* "tableland," applies only to this northern plain, while the area between the Arnon and the Zered (Wadi el-Ḥesā) was considered as Moab's original home since the tableland had belonged to the Amorites.

Edom. Southern Transjordan was known as Mt. Seir or Edom. The name may have designated also the high country S of the Negeb, but during the Monarchy the red sandstone mountains S of the Zered are meant. Some of the peaks reach as high as 1736 m. (5704 ft.). The territory of Edom proper, though 120 km. (75 mi.) long, is only about 20 km. (12-13 mi.) wide. The embayment behind Feinân (biblical Punon) divides the area into two halves. The OT capital was Sela (Arab. Silaʿ), while the Nabatean and Roman capital moved to Rekem (Petra in Greek sources). The people of Edom were in constant rivalry with Judah for control of the Arabah S of the Dead Sea, and Elath/Ezion-geber changed hands several times. To the south of Edom was the territory of Midian and to the east was Kedar, whose king gained control of the entire area across to Gaza and Egypt during the Persian period.

Climate

Although rabbinic tradition knows four seasons, the OT recognizes only two: "seedtime and harvest," winter and summer. The year is divided into two halves, one beginning with Nisan, the first month, and another with Tishri, the seventh. The OT sacred festivals fall in the seven-month period embracing Passover (in Nisan) and Tabernacles (in Tishri). During the winter, the main agricultural activities are devoted to grain crops expected in the spring and summer; in the summer the work is on vines and orchards, for the summer fruits.

The weather pattern in winter consists of low pressure systems that arrive from the west and northwest. Those from northern Italy pass along the Adriatic to Greece and the Aegean, reaching Syria. The others come from southern Italy to the central Mediterranean and across to Palestine. The rains of a given year usually come in three phases: the "rain," "early rain," and "latter rain." The "early rain," a light sprinkling to soften the hard earth and facilitate plowing, may come in September but usually arrives sometime in October. The principal phase of the rain, ca. 75 percent, falls between December and February. The main sowing takes place in November through December, and late sowing usually is done during a break in the rains in January. By March the grass is high enough to cut for fodder, and in April the "latter rain" is needed as a final dose to swell the grain. But if the rain in April/May is too heavy, it can bring disaster.

The rains are deposited more intensively on the mountain ranges of Judah, Ephraim, and Galilee. There is a difference of several degrees in temperature during the winter between Jerusalem and the seacoast, the latter being the milder. Beyond the watershed in Ephraim and Judah there is a rain shadow, since most of the precipitation has fallen on the hills; thus the dry chalk wastes of the Judean wilderness have little chance of getting moisture.

However, the same winds that brought the rains from the west descend again to the humid depression of the Jordan Valley and the Dead Sea, where they pick up more moisture to be deposited in the ranges of Gilead and Moab. In a drought year for western Palestine, the dry winds and high temperatures cause higher evaporation in the Rift Valley so that Transjordan actually may have a slightly higher precipitation for a change.

The snows of Mt. Hermon provide the principal water source for the Jordan. Most of the winter rainwater is absorbed by the limestone mountains of Cisjordan and descends to a deep underground water table. This was not utilized in antiquity, but some of the water did break through to the surface in the form of springs and wells generally located along the edge of the plains at the foot of the hill ranges.

Bibliography. Y. Aharoni, *The Land of the Bible,* 2nd ed. (Philadelphia, 1979), 21-42; D. Baly, *The Geography of the Bible,* rev. ed. (New York, 1974); A. Horowitz, *The Quaternary of Israel* (New York, 1979), 11-43; Y. Karmon, *Israel, a Regional Geography* (London, 1971); A. F. Rainey, review of D. Baly, *The Geography of the Bible,* 2nd ed. *JBL* 94 (1976): 634-35. ANSON F. RAINEY

PALLU (Heb. *pallû'*)
A son of Reuben (Gen. 46:9; Exod. 6:14; 1 Chr. 5:3). He was the father of Eliab (Num. 26:8) and ancestor of the Palluites (v. 5).

PALM SUNDAY
The day commemorating Jesus' final entry into Jerusalem, during which the multitude spread palm branches in front of Jesus as he came into the city. The event is attested in all four Gospels (Matt. 21:1-11; Mark 11:1-10; Luke 19:28-38; John 12:12-18), although only John 12:13 mentions palm branches specifically. Palm Sunday is celebrated the Sunday before Easter and thereby marks the beginning of Holy Week in both the Eastern and Western Church traditions. ANN COBLE

PALM TREE
The date palm (Heb. *tāmār, timōrâ;* Gk. *phoínix*), a magnificent, tall tree that grows abundantly in the Near East. Its large leaves radiate from the top of a single trunk that can grow to more than 15 m. (50 ft.) tall. Date palms (*Phoenix dactylifera* L.) grow well in hot conditions in saline soil. They may grow alone, but a clump of palm trees in the desert likely signals an oasis (cf. Elim, Exod. 15:27; Num. 33:9). Jericho, which to this day is a verdant oasis, was known as the city of palm trees (Deut. 34:3; 2 Chr. 28:15).

In the Bible, the palm tree appears as a symbol of grandeur and steadfastness. Deborah judged underneath a palm tree, probably due to both its shade and its prominence (Judg. 4:5). The youth of Cant. 7:7(MT 8) calls his bride "stately as a palm tree." The likeness of the palm tree appeared in several places in Solomon's temple (1 Kgs. 6:29-35). Palm branches figured in many celebrations and are used in the construction of booths for Succoth (Lev. 23:40; Neh. 8:15). Following the Maccabean Revolt, the Jews rededicated the temple carrying palm branches (1 Macc. 13:51). Jesus was greeted in Jerusalem by people holding palm branches (John 12:13).

The palm tree was a frequent symbol of Israel, both in the Bible (Isa. 9:14; Joel 1:12) and in ancient society. The Hasmonean rulers put palm branches on several of their coins, and the Romans celebrated the capture of Judea in A.D. 70 by minting various coins reading *Ioudaias Ealokuias* ("Judea has been captured") and depicting palm branches.

Almost every part of the palm tree can be utilized. Baskets, sandals, mats, and ropes are made from palm branches and fibers. The palm tree provides oil, a sweet liquor, and honey (cf. Deut. 8:8). Dates, the fruit of the palm tree, grow in large clusters and were a staple of ancient Near Eastern diets. Therefore, palm trees were a valuable crop and were actively cultivated. Palm trees are either male or female. Though the extent of the ancients' understanding of tree fertilization is unknown, the practice of putting the pollen from male trees near female trees was apparently carried on for centuries. MEGAN BISHOP MOORE

PALMYRA
A major oasis in the Syrian Desert (modern Tadmor). The city's perennial spring, which still provides water for Palmyra's agriculture and population, explains why this site rose to prominence in antiquity. Presumably the name of the ancient city is derived from its concentration of palm trees and production of various types of dates. The sedentary population of the oasis grew wealthy because Palmyra was located halfway between the Euphrates River and Damascus, and tariffs were charged for goods carried by passing caravans. These camel caravans transported local products and luxury cargoes obtained through long-distance trade; products from the Arabian Peninsula and from India and the Far East passed through Palmyra en route to the cities of the Roman Empire. In this regard, Palmyra was an important trading partner with Rome, like those described in Rev. 18. In A.D. 269, however, Palmyra's Queen Zenobia rebelled against Roman hegemony, and the city was destroyed in 272. Though the site was not totally abandoned, Palmyra never recovered its former glory. It was brought to the attention of the West through visits to the ruins by Robert Wood and James Dawkins in 1751.

2 Chr. 8:4 refers to Solomon's construction of "Tadmor in the wilderness" (Palmyra's ancient Semitic name, to which it has reverted today). Almost all of the remains uncovered at Palmyra date to the Roman period, and the city's art and architecture reflect international connections in this late period. A difficulty arises with regard to the Solomonic link with Palmyra/Tadmor, since 1 Kgs. 9:18 refers to Solomon's construction of "Tamar in the wilderness" (in the territory of Judah). Some scholars assume that it was unlikely that Hebrew building pro-

jects were carried out as far as Tadmor in the Syrian Desert and think that 2 Chronicles has inserted "Tadmor" for the correct reading "Tamar." On the basis of 2 Sam. 8:3-6, it is possible that Solomon was involved in building activities at Palmyra/Tadmor, and the antiquity of this site is demonstrated by its appearance (as Tadmor) in cuneiform texts from Kültepe (in Anatolia), Mari, and Assyria. European and Syrian archaeologists have cleared and reconstructed a fair proportion of the ruins, but considerable work remains.

Bibliography. S. Abou Zayd, ed., "Palmyra and the Aramaeans," *ARAM Periodical* 7 (1995) [22 articles]; I. Browning, *Palmyra* (London, 1979); R. Stoneman, *Palmyra and Its Empire* (Ann Arbor, 1992).

GERALD L. MATTINGLY

PALTI (Heb. *palṭî*) (also PALTIEL)

1. The son of Raphu of the tribe of Benjamin; one of the 12 Israelite spies sent into Canaan (Num. 13:9).

2. A Benjaminite from Gallim, the son of Laish, to whom Saul punitively gave David's wife Michal as his own wife (1 Sam. 25:44). According to 2 Sam. 2:15-16 (where he is called Paltiel) when Abner and Ish-bosheth took Michal from him to return her to David, Palti(el) followed, weeping, as far as Bahurim.

PALTIEL (Heb. *palṭî'ēl*)

1. The son of Azzan; a leader of Issachar who assisted Moses in the division of Canaan (Num. 34:26).

2. Alternate form of Palti **2.**

PALTITE (Heb. *happalṭî*)

A gentilic ascribed to Helez, one of David's Thirty (2 Sam. 23:26). The name may indicate that Helez was from Beth-pelet (Josh. 15:27; Neh. 11:26) or that he was a descendant of the Calebite Pelet (1 Chr. 2:47) or perhaps Palti. At 1 Chr. 11:27; 27:10 Helez is called "the Pelonite."

PAMPHYLIA (Gk. *Pamphylía*)

A region (lit., the land of "all tribes") located E of Lycia on the southern coast of Asia Minor and inhabited by people of both native and Greek origin (cf. Herodotus *Hist.* 7.91; Strabo *Geog.* 14.4.3). Its large fertile plain on the Gulf of Antalya provided olive oil, fruits, and grains; its mountainous areas were rich in forest of pine and oak. Trade and communication was facilitated through access to the sea and two main roads, which both led north from Perga to the main southern highway. The major Hellenic cities in the plain included Attalia, Perga, Sillyum, Aspendus, and Side, and further inland were Selge and Termessus. Pamphylia was incorporated into the Roman province of Cilicia from 102-44 B.C.E. Subsequently it was included as part of the provinces of Asia and Galatia, respectively; it was finally joined with its neighbor to the west by Vespasian (ca. 69-79 C.E.) to form the province of Lycia-Pamphylia.

Jewish communities lived in Pamphylia from Hellenistic times (cf. 1 Macc. 15:23; Philo *Ad Gaium* 281), and Jews from Pamphylia were present on the day of Pentecost (Acts 2:10). During the first missionary journey, Paul, Barnabas, and John Mark landed at Pamphylia, specifically the city of Perga, on the way to Pisidian Antioch (Acts 13:13-14), and they preached in that city on their return before sailing from Attalia (14:24-26). John Mark had left their company after entering Perga, which later led to divisions in travel plans from Syrian Antioch between Barnabas and John Mark, on the one hand, and Paul and Silas, on the other (15:36-41).

Bibliography. D. Magie, *Roman Rule in Asia Minor*, 2 vols. (1950, repr. New York, 1975); R. Syme, "Galatia and Pamphylia under Augustus," *Klio* 27 (1934): 122-48.

PHILIP A. HARLAND

PAPHOS (Gk. *Páphos*)

A city on the southwest coast of Cyprus, visited by Paul and Barnabas on their first missionary journey (Acts 13:6-13). Their visit was actually to New Paphos, established in the 4th century B.C. as a port town at the site of modern Baffo, some 15 km. (9 mi.) distant from the older inland city (modern Kouklia). When Cyprus became part of the Roman Empire in 58 B.C., New Paphos became the capital of the island. At the time of Paul it was the most important city on Cyprus.

Old Paphos was renowned in antiquity for its temple of Aphrodite. According to legend, it was off the coast near Paphos that this goddess was born of sea foam and first appeared to humankind. Traveling on the Roman road from Salalmis to Paphos, Paul and Barnabas would have descended from the hills of central Cyprus to a view of the temple and the two towns with the sea beyond. It was here that they met the proconsul Sergius Paulus and the magician Elymas. Paphos retained its importance until the Byzantine era when Salamis, rebuilt as Constantia, became the island's capital.

DAVID A. DORMAN

PAPIAS

Bishop of Hierapolis in Asia Minor in the early 2nd century. Papias (ca. 60-130) wrote a work in five books (chapters) titled An Exposition of the Dominical Oracles, which is now lost. At least 13 fragments have been preserved in writings of various church fathers, primarily Irenaeus and Eusebius, and as late as the 9th-century *Chronicon* of George the Sinner.

The most important of the Papias traditions is his writing on the Gospel of Mark. Papias says that he heard from John the Elder that Mark was a translator for Peter, writing "all that [Peter] remembered accurately but not in order as to what was either said or done by the Lord" (Eusebius *HE* 3.39.15). Papias' work is an apology for the disorderliness of Mark and a defense of Mark's accuracy, and is the sole source of the idea that Mark got his information from Peter. Many scholars have disputed this tradition, contending that it is an effort of the early Church to link Mark, who was not an eyewitness to the life of Jesus, to a source who was the preeminent eyewitness. Yet this critique presupposes that Papias seeks to establish the canonicity of Mark on the criterion of apostolicity. Such presupposition is anachronistic; Papias has no idea of a NT canon, and he prefers the oral traditions of the elders over books (*HE* 3.39.4).

Papias also wrote that Matthew "made an ordered arrangement of the oracles in the Hebrew language," which others then translated (*HE* 3.39.16). Although most scholars doubt Papias on this, some do support the idea of a Semitic origin of Matthew. A number of the church fathers express disdain for Papias because of his chiliasm, belief in the coming thousand-year reign of Christ. This belief indicates likelihood that Papias knew the book of Revelation.

Bibliography. J. A. Kleist, *Rereading the Papias Fragment on St. Mark* (St. Louis, 1945); W. R. Schoedel, *Polycarp, Martyrdom of Polycarp, Fragments of Papias. The Apostolic Fathers* 5, ed. R. M. Grant (New York, 1967). J. CHRISTIAN WILSON

PAPYRUS

A tall, aquatic, reed plant abundant in marshy areas of lower Egypt in ancient times (cf. Job 8:11), although no longer found there. Papyrus *(Cyperus papyrus)* was used in a number of products in ancient Egypt, including baskets, ropes, boats, sandals, and mats. Its most extensive use, however, was as a tough and inexpensive paper. (The English word "paper" comes from "papyrus," although paper was invented in China and is made from wood or cotton fibers.) Papyrus is made by cutting strips of pith from inside the stalks of the plant, laying the strips out in two layers at right angles, fusing the layers together by pounding, and drying and smoothing the resulting sheet with shell or stone tools (cf. Pliny the Elder *Nat. hist.* 13.11-13). The sheets could then be joined together to form scrolls of any prescribed length. The longest existing roll is 39.6 m. (130 ft.).

Papyrus was used as a writing material in Egypt from ca. 3000 B.C.E. until well into the 1st millennium C.E. and was preferred over clay tablets, stone, and wood. Leather, however, was also used extensively as a writing medium. Papyrus was a significant trade item for ancient Egypt (*ANET,* 28), and was exported to Syria-Palestine, Greece, and Italy. Ancient papyrus documents exist in many languages, including Egyptian, Greek, Aramaic, Hebrew, Coptic, and Latin. Direct and indirect archaeological evidence suggests that papyrus was a common writing material in Palestine during the 1st millennium B.C.E. A few fragments of papyrus documents have been found at a number of locations, including a cave in Wadi Murabba'at (7th century), a cave in Wadi ed-Daliyeh (4th century), caves around Qumran (3rd century B.C.E.–1st century C.E.), and in Naḥal Ḥever (2nd century C.E.). In addition, at Samaria, Lachish, Tell el-Hesi, Beth-zur, and Jerusalem, hundreds of clay bullae used to seal contracts and letters have been found with traces of papyrus fibers attached, indicating that the documents to which they were attached were papyrus. The evidence confirms the suggestion that papyrus was used extensively in Palestine, but the climate was too damp to permit the preservation of papyrus documents except in sheltered, dry areas. Texts of the OT were written mainly on leather (although some may have been written on papyrus), while texts of the NT, especially the letters, were probably written first on papyrus.

The only clear biblical reference to papyrus as a writing material is found in 2 John 12. Gk. *chártēs* refers to the papyrus roll or sheet on which a letter is written. Isa. 18:2 mentions the use of papyrus stalks to make sailing vessels. Baby Moses is hidden in a papyrus basket (Exod. 2:3), and the "reeds and rushes" in Isa. 35:7 undoubtedly refer to papyrus.

Bibliography. J. Černy, *Papers and Books in Ancient Egypt* (London, 1952); R. S. Hanson, "Ancient Scribes and Scripts and the Clues They Leave," *BA* 48 (1985): 83-88; Y. Shiloh, "A Group of Hebrew Bullae from the City of David," *IEJ* 36 (1986): 16-38; B. Watterson, *Introducing Egyptian Hieroglyphs* (Edinburgh, 1981).

NANCY L. DECLAISSÉ-WALFORD

PARABLES

Transliteration of Gk *parabolḗ,* used in the NT to identify a variety of literary forms. Literally the word signifies something cast alongside another thing to clarify it. However, literary units identified as parables in the NT themselves generally require clarification and are frequently, but not always, accompanied by explanations provided by the Evangelist.

The Gospels are not consistent in what they describe as a parable. The term is used to identify: stories having a beginning, middle, and end (Mark 4:2-9); brief images (13:28); aphorisms (7:15-17); and traditional proverbs (Luke 4:23). Luke (14:8-10) even regards Jesus' advice about seating etiquette at a marriage banquet as a parable (v. 7). The Evangelists do not always agree among themselves that particular literary units are parables. For example, Luke 5:36-38 designates twin aphorisms as a single *parabolḗ,* while Matt. 9:16-17; Mark 2:21-22 do not. Generally NT scholars reserve the designation *parabolḗ* for the stories and use other terms more consistent with their character for the other literary forms.

The Evangelists do agree that parables are obscure and need explanation. They usually provide the parable with a literary introduction (e.g., Luke 18:1, 9) and/or an interpretation (vv. 6-8). The literary setting clarifies how they understand the parable. Some parables, however, have neither introduction nor interpretation to clarify how the Evangelists understood them (e.g., Luke 3:7-9). Parables are not always introduced by a literary frame calling for comparison (Luke 12:16-20; 15:8-9). Also, some parables are used as examples (Luke 10:25-37) rather than comparatively. Twelve parables out of about 38 preserved in early Christian literature are compared to the kingdom (i.e., reign) of God.

The usual way of explaining parables in the Gospels is the attachment of a contiguous "moral" at the end, relating the parable to some aspect of Christian life in the church community (e.g., Luke 18:6-8: the return of the Lord). Some interpretations treat the parabolic stories as allegories. In an allegory multiple elements in the story have a one-to-one relationship with things outside the story. There are only three fully developed allegorical interpretations of the parables in the canonical Gospels: the Sower (Mark 4:14-20 par.), the Weeds in the Field (Matt. 13:36-43), and the Fishnet (13:47-50).

Stories attributed to Jesus of Nazareth can be found in the canonical Gospels of Matthew, Mark, and Luke and in two Nag Hammadi texts, the Gospel of Thomas and the Apocryphon of James. The Gospel of John preserves no parabolic stories, and does not even use the word *parabolḗ*. Instead, John uses *paroimía*, which seems best translated as "figure" or "cryptic saying," since such language in John is contrasted to open or clear language (John 10:1-6; 16:16-30).

The canonical Gospels provide reasons to explain why Jesus spoke in parables. According to Mark 4:10-12 Jesus used the parables in order to keep outsiders from understanding his teaching about God's reign, for if they understood they would "repent and be forgiven." Hence the teaching about God's reign in Mark was meant for the disciples only. Luke's explanation (Luke 8:9-10) is like Mark's, except that Luke does not include the offensive phrase about repenting and being forgiven. Matt. 13:10-17, on the other hand, cites Isa. 6:9-10 as a prophetic anticipation that people would not understand the parables. Matthew explains that people could have understood the parables had they wanted to. The reason they did not is that they deliberately hardened their hearts and in so doing fulfilled Isaiah's prophecy. These explanations for Jesus' use of the parables are generally regarded as early ecclesiastical traditions. They demonstrate that the Church in the latter half of the 1st century had difficulty understanding the parables. The stories could not easily be related to the cultural and theological changes that had taken place in the Church since the time of Jesus, such as the shift from a Semitic to a Hellenistic environment.

The stories are realistic portrayals of village life in 1st-century Palestine. They treat such topics as the hazards of farming (a Sower, Mark 4:3-8 par.), the ownership of real estate and property (the Hidden Treasure, Matt. 13:44 par.), household activities (the Lost Coin, Luke 15:8-9), Jewish worship (the Pharisee and Toll Collector, 18:10-13), family relationships (the Prodigal Son/Elder Brother, 15:11-32), and cooking (the Leaven, Matt. 13:33 par.). Since the latter part of the 1st century their realistic character, portraying aspects of ancient Palestinian village life, has regularly been bypassed in favor of insights into early Christian theology and morality. For example, Matthew appends a circulating saying (Matt. 20:16; cf. Mark 10:31; Luke 13:30) to the Laborers in the Vineyard (Matt. 20:1-15), a story dealing with employer-employee relations in Palestinian antiquity, to indicate that the story illustrates reversal of rank at the last judgment. The story of the Lost Sheep (Matt. 18:12-13) serves Matthew as an allegory on the preservation of the Christian disciple (v. 14), while in Luke (Luke 15:4-6) it is an allegory on the conversion of sinners who are outside the Church (vv. 1-2, 7). These distinctly Christian interpretations strike many interpreters as out of place with the thoroughly Jewish stories.

The Hebrew Scriptures contain only a few narratives that resemble the characteristic story parable typical of Jesus. Ezek. 17:2-10 (the Eagles and the Vine) is an allegory *(māšāl)*, followed by an allegorical interpretation (vv. 11-21) similar to the parable of the Sower. Ezek. 19:1-9 (the Lions) and 19:10-14 (the Vine) are called lamentations *(qînâ)*. Judg. 9:8-15 (the Trees and the Bramble) is a fable that serves an allegorical function. 2 Sam. 12:1-4 (the Ewe Lamb) is a story that functions as an allegory. 2 Sam. 14:5-7 (the Wise Woman of Tekoa) is a brief fictional narrative (vv. 1-3 show it to be a fabricated story) used neither comparatively or figuratively. Eccl. 9:14-15 is a brief story (the Besieged City) followed by a summarizing moral on the superiority of wisdom (v. 16). These last two are most like the typical parable of the early Christian Gospels.

In the LXX Heb. *māšāl* is regularly translated as *parabolḗ*, and is used to characterize a variety of literary forms. *Māšāl* describes: allegories that are both narratives (Ezek. 17:2-10) and brief figures (24:3-5); traditional proverbs (Jer. 23:28; 1 Sam. 24:13; Ezek. 18:2); and lamentations that are brief narratives (Ezek. 19:1-9, 10-14) and sayings (Hab. 2:5-6; Mic. 2:4). In general, a *māšāl* appears to describe any literary unit whose meaning is not immediately clear or easily understood (Ps. 49:4[MT 3]; 78:2, Prov. 1:6).

The ecclesiastical and allegorical interpretations of the parables were not challenged until the end of the 19th century. The rise of the modern critical study of the parables began with rejection of the idea that parables were allegories requiring interpretations like Mark's explanation of the Sower (Mark 4:14-20). In 1886 Adolf Jülicher rejected the allegorical method, and reduced the many points of allegorical interpretation to a general one point moral against a hypothetical background in the life of Jesus. The literary settings of the parables in the Gospels were not regarded as the original settings of the parables in the social life of Palestinian antiquity. Thus a story about the hazards of farming in 1st-century Palestine becomes "a warning to the converted against a failure to stand fast in time of persecution and against worldiness" (Jeremias, 150).

The next shift in understanding the character of the parables occurred in 1935 when C. H. Dodd argued that a parable was "a metaphor or simile drawn from nature or common life, arresting the hearer by its vividness or strangeness, and leaving the mind in sufficient doubt about its precise application to tease it into active thought" (Dodd, 5). Metaphors and similes are figures of speech that are used to describe one thing as another thing. For

Dodd, the parables presented the reign of God under the guise of realistic stories about common life in small Palestinian villages. Thus the Sower becomes a parable of growth. It "illustrates . . . the coming of the Kingdom of God in the ministry of Jesus, under the figure of harvest" (Dodd, 149).

In 1967 Dan O. Via argued that parables were brief narrative fictions that refracted a particular understanding of human existence. When one reads the parables one engages Jesus' understanding of human existence. Thus the parable of the Talents (Matt. 25:14-30) describes a man whose quest for security produces his own death, for in his quest for security he becomes "the slave of the very realities which he hopes will give him security . . . Risking is life, for in it one is free from the anxious effort to provide one's own security through the world" (Via, 120-21).

A modification of Via's approach is that Jesus' parables are not existential, theological, or moral stories but rather political and economic ones. They are about political power and the exploitation of the peasant classes. Thus the parable of the Wicked Tenants (Mark 12:1-12 par.) describes the spiral of violence attending a local peasant "revolt" against a landed elite class.

A recent approach argues that the parables are freely invented narrative fictions that are to be read in the context of the ways that 1st-century Palestinian Jews understood themselves. They are not referential, but are designed to bring the reader into the story where discoveries about self and the world may be made. The parables are open-ended stories that do not teach, direct, or answer; rather they confront and tease, and are capable of a rather wide range of reasonable readings, as the history of parables interpretation attests. Thus the parable of the Pharisee and the Tax Collector (Luke 18:10-13) confronts the reader with the conundrum: which of the two flawed characters in the story will in the final analysis be able to "stand before the Lord," i.e., will be pleasing to God.

Today there is no common agreement among scholars on what a parable is or how it functions. Parables are read in many different ways: as allegories, as stories with a religious moral, as examples of Christian morality, as metaphors, as stories that refract a particular understanding of human existence, as political and economic stories, and as poetic fictions.

Bibliography. C. H. Dodd, *The Parables of the Kingdom* (New York, 1961); C. W. Hedrick, *Parables as Poetic Fictions: The Creative Voice of Jesus* (Peabody, 1994); W. R. Herzog, II, *Parables as Subversive Speech* (Louisville, 1994); J. Jeremias, *The Parables of Jesus,* rev. ed. (New York, 1963); B. B. Scott, *Hear Then the Parable* (Minneapolis, 1989); D. O. Via, *The Parables: Their Literary and Existential Dimension* (Philadelphia, 1967). CHARLES W. HEDRICK

PARACLETE

Transliteration of Gk. *parákl̄etos,* derived from the verb meaning "to call alongside," often for the sake of exhorting or encouraging. Therefore, some have interpreted the term as "Comforter." Others have pointed to the use of *paráklētos* in Greek and Hellenistic legal contexts, entailing a judicial meaning similar to "Advocate." This sense is certainly present in 1 John 2:1, which states that Jesus Christ acts as the sinning believer's *paráklētos* before the Father. The remaining NT occurrences all appear in the "Farewell Discourses" of the Gospel of John (John 14:16, 26; 15:26; 16:7). An editorial comment inserted at John 7:39 identifies this Paraclete with the Holy Spirit, who was to come after Jesus' glorification. The Evangelist portrays the Paraclete as a teacher of truth, a reminder of Jesus' teachings, a witness to Jesus, and a source of conviction in the world. Such activities may suggest a general meaning such as "Helper" or "Supporter." Various parallels to the Paraclete have been suggested, including Michael and the Spirit of Truth from Qumran documents, the *angelus interpres* of apocalyptic literature, and the successor motif in the OT (Joshua/Moses, Elisha/Elijah). Such parallels may illuminate the character of the Paraclete, but primary emphasis should fall upon the Johannine contexts.

Bibliography. R. E. Brown, "The Paraclete in the Fourth Gospel," *NTS* 13 (1966-67): 113-32; K. Grayston, "The Meaning of *PARAKLĒTOS,*" *JSNT* 13 (1981): 67-82; G. Johnston, *The Spirit-Paraclete in the Gospel of John.* SOTSMS 12 (Cambridge, 1970). PAUL ANTHONY HARTOG

PARADISE

Originally a "walled enclosure" or a "wooded parklike garden" (O. Pers. *pairi-daēza*). In ancient Iran it referred primarily to a royal enclosed "park" with streams, trees, and hunting grounds. Many ancient sources indicate that royal paradises were located throughout the Persian Empire, perhaps one for each satrapy. During travel the royal caravan would use such oases as a base for royal activity. Persian and Greek sources mention Cyrus' tomb and burial in the "paradise" at Pasargadae, the first capital of the empire.

In the OT, Asaph was "keeper of the royal paradise" (Heb. *pardēs*), responsible for obtaining timber for Nehemiah's rebuilding project (Neh. 2:8). The bride in the Song of Solomon is described as a paradise or orchard of "pomegranates with all choicest fruits," spices, and life-giving water (Cant. 4:13-15). Eccl. 2:5 mentions gardens and "parks" with a variety of fruit trees.

In Hellenistic times the word refers increasingly to the garden of Eden and the place of reward for the faithful. In the LXX the Greek loanword *parádeisos* is used for the garden of Eden which God planted for Adam and Eve. In writings of the intertestamental period (e.g., 1–2 Enoch), Paradise is a future lush garden of Eden (2 En. 8). By the 2nd century B.C.E. resurrection became a hope for certain Jewish groups, longing for a future home free from earthly troubles, and belief in a paradise which would become their abode — whether temporary or permanent — gained popularity. A future "Eden" for the righteous after death took on the characteristics of the ideal "paradise." By the end of the 1st century C.E. the term is used for both the garden of Eden of Genesis and the final dwelling place of the righteous dead (2 Esdras).

In the NT paradise could refer to a temporary dwelling place for the righteous dead prior to their resurrection, a possible meaning of Jesus' response to the repentant thief from the cross that that day he would be with him in Paradise (Luke 23:43). Paul's reference to a "third heaven" (2 Cor. 12:2-4) may also indicate that he was taken up into Paradise. In Revelation those who "conquer" will be granted "permission to eat from the tree of life that is in the paradise of God" (Rev. 2:7).

Paradise in the Qur'an appears as a future garden for the righteous who drink, usually in the company of beautiful women, a beverage (probably wine) which produces neither intoxication nor madness (*Sura* 18:32). WILLIAM R. GOODWIN, JR.

PARAH (Heb. *pārâ*)
A city in the tribal territory of Benjamin (Josh. 18:23), identifiable with Tell Fâr'ah (177137), 10 km. (6 mi.) NE of Jerusalem.

PARAN (Heb. *pā'rān*)
A desert region S of Judah, W of Edom, and N of the wilderness of Sinai, and probably encompassing Kadesh-barnea. According to the stories of Israel's journey through the wilderness, the Israelites went from the wilderness of Sinai to the wilderness of Paran (Num. 10:11-12) via Hazeroth (12:16). Moses then sent out spies from Paran to explore the land of Canaan, and they returned to Kadesh, identifying the two locations (Num. 13:3, 26; in Deut. 1:19-25 the spies are sent out from Kadesh-barnea). In the wilderness itinerary of Num. 33, Paran is not mentioned and Kadesh is associated with the wilderness of Zin (Num. 33:36); however, the LXX identifies Kadesh with Paran, suggesting a textual corruption in the MT.

Other references to Paran are consistent with the region around Kadesh-barnea (e.g., Gen. 14:6). Ishmael lived in Paran after being banished by Abraham (Gen. 21:21). After Samuel's death, David obtained his wife Abigail while visiting the region of Paran (2 Sam. 25:1). The Edomite Hadad passed through Paran while fleeing from Midian to Egypt (1 Kgs. 11:18). Two poetic references associate Paran with Yahweh's southern dwelling, from which he marches to fight Israel's enemies (Deut. 33:2; Hab. 3:3). RONALD A. SIMKINS

PARAPET
A low wall built around the outer edge of a roof to prevent people from falling (Heb. *ma'ăqeh;* Deut. 22:8). The flat roof of a house was commonly used as part of the living and working quarters (cf. Josh. 2:6; 1 Sam. 9:25-26; 2 Sam. 11:2; 16:22).

PARBAR (Heb. *parbār*)
A structure connected with the temple (1 Chr. 26:18; cf. Heb. *parwārîm,* "precincts"; 2 Sam. 23:11). The etymology and meaning of the term are uncertain, possibly a loanword from Sumerian ("shining house," or "sun temple"), Egyptian (a room in a temple), or Persian (a court or colonnade). Interpretations range from a toilet or water closet for the high priest or king to a suburb of Jerusalem.
RICHARD A. SPENCER

PARCHMENT
A writing material produced from the skins of domestic animals such as sheep and cattle. The origin of the word is attributed to the city of Pergamum. According to Pliny the Elder (*Nat. hist.* 12.21), parchment came into existence through the rivalry between the libraries of Ptolemy V Theos Epiphanes of Egypt (205-182 B.C.) and Eumenes II of Pergamum (197-159); an embargo on the export of papyrus caused the invention and manufacturing of parchment in Pergamum.

Vellum, which is generally of superior quality, was produced from goats, calves, lambs, and sometimes antelopes. Pigs produced inferior parchment and were usually avoided. The skins were washed and the hair scraped off, rubbed with pumice to make them smooth, and finally chalked.

The older papyrus scroll was inconvenient to use, as two hands had to be employed to roll and unroll the scroll simultaneously. In addition, parchment could be written on both sides, whereas papyrus could not. From the 4th century A.D. onward, demand for the Christian Scriptures in their entirety made the parchment codex (a book with leaves) preferable over the papyrus roll.
JAMES V. SMITH

PARMASHTA (Heb. *parmaštā'*)
One of the 10 sons of Haman killed by the Jews after their father was hanged (Esth. 9:9).

PARMENAS (Gk. *Parmenás*)
One of the seven chosen to assist the apostles in the distribution to the widows of the Church (Acts 6:5).

PARNACH (Heb. *parnāḵ*)
The father of Elizaphan; leader of Zebulun who helped distribute the land (Num. 34:25).

PAROSH (Heb. *par'ōš*)
1. An Israelite whose descendants returned with Zerubbabel (Ezra 2:3; Neh. 7:8) and Ezra from exile in Babylon (Ezra 8:3). Among the descendants of Parosh were some of the men who divorced their foreign wives (Ezra 10:25) and one of those who repaired the walls of Jerusalem (Neh. 3:25).

2. A chief of the people who participated in the sealing of the covenant under Nehemiah (Neh. 10:14[MT 15]).

PAROUSIA (Gk. *parousía*)
A Greek noun, used of persons or things, meaning "arrival" or active "presence" (from the verb *páreimi,* "to be present"). Before the Christian era, broad Hellenistic use of *parousía* for the divine presence at meals gave the word a sacral ring. Gradually the noun gained technical force, denoting the local visit of a ruler or other high personage, heal-

ing manifestations by the gods, or the divine presence implicit in philosophical insight. In a world otherwise dominated by a view of events as recurring in eternal cycles, however, it was interaction with Jewish belief that lent this term a new sense of finality.

Pre-Christian Jewish tradition uses the image of God's "coming" to mark specific moments God has chosen to judge humanity, or events which reveal God's powerful presence and purpose. Such tradition sees God's presence in concrete terms like "the day," "the time," or "the year" of the Lord, or through graphic images such as the ark of the covenant, the meeting tent, the holy place, the cloud, the Spirit, the Hand, or the Word of God. The LXX, reflecting the Hellenistic origin of *parousía,* uses it only in works first written in Greek, only in its profane sense, and clearly prefers the verb.

Israel's growing sense of God's regal stature, however, demanded worldwide submission to God's rule, and the notion of direct, definitive divine appearances gave way to those agents deemed divinely chosen to wield such authority in the world. The later decline of Jewish kingship provoked deep disputes over the authority of the priestly cultus to express God's will. In this vacuum, prophetic, otherworldly, elliptical, apocalyptic visions of God's final self-manifestation flourished. By the 1st century C.E., beyond Christian circles Jewish use of *parousía* remained limited. The first-century B.C.E. Alexandrian Jewish philosopher Philo never uses it. Even after Rome destroyed the Jerusalem temple, priesthood, and cultus with impunity in 70 C.E., the 1st-century Jewish historian Josephus still employs *parousía* for God's potent, saving presence on behalf of Israel. But the overt, apocalyptic, political overtones of such terminology have faded. In subsequent rabbinic usage the vivid, complex vision associated with God's promised parousia loses most of its earlier apocalyptic force.

Parousia enters early Christian usage from several directions. But the main vector is Paul, who joins older, traditional Jewish terminology with Hellenistic notions about the visit of a ruling personage (e.g., 1 Cor. 15:23; 1 Thess. 2:19). The resulting blend envisions an imminent, future "coming" of Jesus with cataclysmic, global finality. Paul's fusion of judicial with covenantal imagery, combined with a temporal ambiguity in his views about the end of the world, produces conflicts that continue to challenge his modern interpreters. Although the Synoptic tradition clearly presumes Jesus' coming global assertion of God's authority over this world, the noun *parousía* is entirely missing from Mark, from Q, and from Luke and Acts. The verb *páreimi* does appear, but mainly in its common, secular sense. Mark and Q prefer standard Jewish expressions such as "the day of the Lord" for Jesus' imminent return in power as God's final messianic judge. By comparison, Matthew inserts *parousía* into his source material, giving his own special connotation to this term by portraying the Risen Jesus as already present, but hidden, within his Church until the end of time (Matt. 24:27, 37, 39). In the post-Pauline Pastoral Letters *parousía* yields to the still more abstract *epipháneia,* usage already presaged in 2 Thess. 2:8 (cf. Acts 2:20). This complements 2nd-century Christian trends away from historical, messianic thinking about Jesus in favor of more logocentric, timeless, universalized Christology. Modern biblical scholarship has seen much lively debate over the historical impact of Jesus' delayed parousia in changing Christianity from a fluid, charismatic movement to a more stable, institutionalized, worldly entity.

Bibliography. A. Oepke, "parousia, pareimi," *TDNT* 5:858-71. F. CONNOLLY-WEINERT

PARSHANDATHA (Heb. *paršandāṯā'*)
One of the 10 sons of Haman killed by the Jews after their father was hanged (Esth. 9:7).

PARTHIANS
An Iranian tribe from the region SE of the Caspian Sea. They threw off Seleucid domination in the mid-3rd century B.C.E. and developed an empire that would endure for nearly 500 years. During most of that time, Parthia would successfully vie with Rome for power in the Near East.

Thought by the Persians to be of Scythian origin, the Parthians used the same mounted archery tactics as their barbarian kin to build an empire extending from the Euphrates River in Syria to the Indus in modern Pakistan. One of a few nations to be seen by the Romans as a persistent threat to their military dominance, the Parthians inflicted upon the Romans one of their most crushing and humiliating defeats at Carrhae (OT Haran) in 53 B.C.E. One reason for this defeat was the effective use of the Parthian or "parting shot," which combined an archery volley while charging with another over their horses' tails as they retreated. It is perhaps the Parthian threat in general, and this tactic in particular, that is alluded to in Rev. 9:13-19; 16:12.

The only specific biblical mention of the Parthians is in Acts 2:9 where Parthian Jews, or proselytes, are among the nationalities that hear their own language on Pentecost. Some take this, along with other evidence, as indicating that while maintaining a reputation for barbarism, the Parthians exercised religious toleration toward a diverse population. Their empire finally collapsed ca. 226 at the hands of the Sassanian Persians, still unconquered by Rome. JESSE CURTIS POPE

PARTRIDGE
Two main species of partridge (Heb. *qōrē'*) are found in Palestine. The rock partridge *(Alectoris graeca)* has white cheeks on black with barred sides and is ca. 35 cm. (14 in.) in length. It inhabits the coastal plain to the lower hills of central Palestine. The desert partridge *(Ammoperdix heyi)* is smaller and sandy in color and inhabits the rocky desert regions of the central to southern wilderness of the Dead Sea and Negeb. The female lays between six and twelve eggs, and the partridge can be an intrusive bird that steals other birds' eggs (Jer. 17:11). It

feeds on insects and seeds. Both species are kosher and are hunted because of their delicious breast meat (cf. 1 Sam. 26:20). Sir. 11:30 notes the use of caged partridges as decoys.

Bibliography. J. F. A. Sawyer, "A Note on the Brooding Partridge in Jeremiah XVII 11," *VT* 28 (1978): 324-29. JOHN A. MCLEAN

PARUAH (Heb. *pārûaḥ*)
The father of Jehoshaphat (**2**), Solomon's officer in Issachar (1 Kgs. 4:17).

PARVAIM (Heb. *parwāyim*)
A region from which Solomon imported gold for the temple (2 Chr. 3:6). Although locations in Yemen or northeastern Arabia have been suggested, the exact site is unknown.

PASACH (Heb. *pāsaḵ*)
An Asherite, the son of Japhlet (1 Chr. 7:33).

PASCHAL (Gk. *páscha*)
Pertaining to the Passover, specifically the lamb slain for the Passover (cf. Exod. 12:3-8, 21), a metaphor for the death of Christ (1 Cor. 5:7).

PAS-DAMMIM (Heb. *pas dammîm*)
A variant form of Ephes-dammim; a place where David's forces defeated the Philistines (1 Chr. 11:13). STEVEN M. ORTIZ

PASEAH (Heb. *pāsēaḥ*)

1. A son of Eshton of the tribe of Judah (1 Chr. 4:12).

2. A temple servant whose descendants returned from exile with Zerubbabel (Ezra 2:49 = Neh. 7:51).

3. The father of Joiada, who repaired the Old Gate of Jerusalem (Neh. 3:6).

PASHHUR (Heb. *pašḥûr*)

1. The son of Malchiah and a descendant of Immer, identified in 1 Chr. 9:12; Neh. 11:12 as the grandfather of Adaiah, a priest in Jerusalem after the Exile. He may be the same as the Pashhur (**5**) in Jer. 21, 38, although that individual is not identified as a priest.

2. The head of a priestly family that returned from exile with Zerubbabel (Ezra 2:38 = Neh. 7:41; 1 Esdr. 5:25). Several members of the family gave up their foreign wives in response to Nehemiah's urging (Ezra 10:22; 1 Esdr. 9:22).

3. A postexilic priest who attached his name to the covenant which the returned Israelites made under the direction of Nehemiah (Neh. 10:3[MT 4]).

4. A son of Immer; priest and chief officer in the Jerusalem temple during the time of Jeremiah (Jer. 20:1-6). One of his duties was to maintain order in the temple precincts, and after Jeremiah preached his prophecy of doom in the court of the temple, Pashhur ordered Jeremiah beaten and put in stocks. When Pashhur released him the next day, Jeremiah pronounced upon him the judgment of seeing his family and nation carried into exile. Jeremiah also renamed Pashhur *māgôr missābîḇ*, "Terror-all-around." Pashhur was most likely among the temple officials deported to Babylon in 598 B.C.E., since soon afterward his position was taken by Zephaniah (Jer. 29:25).

5. The son of Malchiah; a prince of Judah (Jer. 21:1). King Zedekiah sent Pashhur to request an oracle from Jeremiah when Jerusalem was under siege, and the prophet pronounced an oracle of doom (Jer. 21:3). Later he was part of a group that heard Jeremiah advise Judah to surrender to Babylon, and he requested of the king permission to have Jeremiah put to death. Zedekiah turned Jeremiah over to the group, and they lowered him into a cistern (Jer. 38:1-6).

NANCY L. DECLAISSÉ-WALFORD

PASSION NARRATIVES
Accounts of the suffering and death of Jesus. Both the Passion narratives and references to the passion of Christ that are preserved in canonical and extrabiblical early Christian writings are testimony to the importance of the Passion narratives in the early life of the Church. The first preserved written reference to the oral tradition of the Passion in early Christianity is Paul's rhetorical question in Gal. 3:1, "O foolish Galatians, who bewitched you — before whose eyes Jesus Christ was publicly set forth as having been crucified?" Paul's impassioned remark points to the central theme of his preaching, but it indicates that Paul proclaimed more than *that* Jesus Christ was crucified (a possible understanding of texts such as 1 Cor. 2:2) or, taking one small interpretive step, *that* Christ died for the sins of humanity (e.g., 15:3). The striking reminiscence of Jesus Christ's having been publicly set forth crucified before the eyes of the Galatians employs verbs and the metaphor of seeing which denote vivid, even graphic portrayal beyond the mere statement of fact or the terse character of creedal formulation. Unfortunately, Paul neither amplifies nor illustrates this preaching of Jesus Christ's being crucified, so that one is unable to reconstruct the apostle's preaching of the Passion. At other points in his writings, however, we do learn of certain events of the Passion of which Paul had knowledge, and which he *could* (and likely did?) narrate in his preaching. These include that Jesus instituted the Lord's Supper (1 Cor. 11:23-26), was betrayed — at night (v. 23), was crucified (Gal. 3:1), died (1 Cor. 11:26), and was buried (Rom. 6:4). Thus, in what are likely the earliest preserved pieces of Christian writing one finds evidence of the oral tradition of the passion of Christ.

Thus, from the advent of form criticism interpreters contended that prior to the composition of the first written Gospel there existed a fairly wellformed, perhaps even definitely set, version of the Passion narrative. The expanse of time between the death of Jesus in A.D. 30/33 and the writing of the first Gospel in the mid-60s to 70 required a process of oral transmission of tradition. Comparison of the Passion narrative to the other stories and sections of the Gospels found the Passion narrative to be an extended, logically progressive sequence of scenes which were interconnected and even dependent upon one another in forming a larger coherent account. By contrast the portions of the Gospels prior to the Passion narrative were short, seemingly independent units which could be, and perhaps were, arranged in whatever order the Evangelists desired. Moreover, whereas the pericope composing the account of Jesus' ministry prior to the Passion could stand alone and communicate a purposeful message, certain elements of the Passion narrative had no discernible function outside of the larger account and seemed unlikely ever to have existed independently. Although there has never been consensus about where the pre-Gospel Passion narrative began, items seemingly incapable of an independent existence included the brief memory of Judas' agreement to betray Jesus, the mention of the young man who fled naked from Jesus' arrest, Simon Peter's denials of Jesus, the Barabbas incident, and the reference to Simon of Cyrene. In isolation from the other Passion narrative material interpreters did not believe that such items would have been preserved.

The contentions of the early form critics have undergone serious criticism by scholars attempting to disprove the existence of a pre-Gospels Passion narrative. Yet, there are many scholars who, although dubious about the numerous and different, but precise, reconstructions of the pre-Gospels Passion narratives, still find the basic logic of the argument for a pre-Gospels Passion narrative persuasive. While this important interpretive issue may never be settled finally, one should not miss the central agreement by all parties in this controversy, that all agree there were Passion narrative traditions in early Christianity prior to the composition of the Gospels; otherwise we would seek to identify the author of the Passion narrative fiction.

Without attempting to settle the issues of the existence and shape of a pre-Gospels Passion narrative or narratives, one may ask whether there is evidence in the Gospels Passion narratives of the oral tradition(s) from the period prior to the writing of the Gospels. Analysis of five prominent early Christian Gospels reveals a plethora of special materials in each of the works that comprehensively suggests an active interest in the passion of Jesus and implies steady elaboration of the most basic story. When one encounters a story element in a single Gospel, it is possible that the item is a mere invention of the Evangelist; however, from observing several such features in each of the Gospels, one suspects that the Evangelists are drawing upon more than their imaginations. Volume of particularity is no guarantee of dependence on oral tradition(s), but the more unique features an Evangelist incorporates into the Passion narratives, the more likely he is to be relying upon some external stimulus rather than sheer inventiveness. That many story items are preserved in a single Gospel is not by itself a forceful argument for the influence of oral tradition on the Evangelists, but when coupled with additional evidence this phenomenon may enhance the strength of a case for the existence and influence of oral tradition on the formation and transmission of the Passion narratives.

In Matthew's account (Matt. 26:1–27:66) one finds Jesus' questioning of Judas after he is kissed, the story of the death of Judas, the story of Pilate's wife, Pilate's washing of his hands and the accompanying cry of the people, the offer of wine mixed with gall, the signs after Jesus' death, and the posting of a guard at the tomb.

In Mark's Passion narrative (Mark 14:1–15:47) alone one reads of the young man who fled nude from Jesus' arrest, the offer of wine mixed with myrrh (similar to Matthew, but not exactly the same), and Pilate's confirmation of Jesus' death.

Luke (Luke 22:1–23:56) offers still other items, including Jesus confronting Judas and apparently preventing the kiss, the presence of the Jewish leaders at Jesus' arrest, Jesus' healing of the man whose ear was cut off, Jesus being mocked as he waits at the home of the high priest, the morning assembly of the Jewish leaders to consider Jesus' fate, Jesus before Herod Antipas, Jesus and the daughters of Jerusalem, two or three words of Jesus from the cross, the report of the exchange between Jesus and those with whom he was crucified, the reaction of the assembled crowds who watch and see Jesus' death, and the mention of the acquaintances being present with the women and seeing the Crucifixion.

John's narrative (John 18:1–19:42) is even more distinguished by its special materials: the exchange between Jesus and the crowd that came to arrest him, including his saying "I am" (Gk. *egṓ eími*) and their falling to the ground; the details that Simon Peter wielded the sword and that Malchus lost his ear; the soldiers' seizing Jesus; another disciple's accompanying Peter to the house of the high priest; Jesus' being interrogated by the high priest, Annas; the officer striking Jesus for his answer to the high priest and Jesus' words to the officer; Annas' sending Jesus bound to Caiaphas; conversations between Jesus and Pilate; Pilate and the Jews in dialogue; the declaration by the Jews, "We have no King but Caesar"; Jesus' bearing of his own cross; three words of Jesus from the cross; the Jews' request that Jesus' legs be broken, but since he is already dead his side is pierced; and Nicodemus' bringing 100 pounds of spices to use in burying Jesus.

The Gospel of Peter, though a fragment, offers a Passion narrative plot with elements similar to those of the canonical accounts. However, this Gospel contains many striking ideas and additional story elements: Herod is cast as a law-observant Jew; he is also a king, who seems to have authority over Pilate; the people execute Jesus; Jesus, both as subject and object throughout this narrative, is referred to as "the Lord"; as he is mocked, Jesus is challenged, "Judge righteously!"; the placard over Jesus reads, "This is the King of Israel," and seems to be posted by the people; the crucified Jesus "holds his peace, as if he feels no pain"; one malefactor rails at those crucifying the Lord, because he does not deserve it; the darkness causes the executioners anxiety, since Jesus is still alive, and if the sun sets they are in violation of the law; giving Jesus gall with vinegar completes the Jewish sin, but it is not related to the fulfillment of a messianic prophecy in the narrative; Jesus cries, "My power, O power, thou has forsaken me"; the earth quakes when Jesus' body is placed upon it; the Jews hand the body over to Joseph; the Jews and the leaders lament their evil and relate it explicitly to "the [forthcoming] end of Jerusalem"; the reader is informed, as if by Peter, that the disciples hide, fast, mourn, and weep; the leaders ask Pilate for a guard for the tomb because they know "he" was righteous and now they fear the wrathful remorse of the people; "Petronius the centurion with soldiers" watches the tomb; they all roll a great stone over the tomb's entrance; seven seals are set on the tomb; and the guards pitch tents at the site.

No firm conclusion comes from observing these items in the Gospel Passion narratives. But whatever theory of Synoptic interrelatedness one holds, clearly there is additional material incorporated into the Passion narrative by the subsequent Evangelists; in turn, whatever, if any, the relationship of the Fourth Gospel and the Gospel of Peter to the Synoptics, their authors offer a wealth of additional Passion narrative material. While each of these unique items in the earliest Passion narratives would require individual analysis to determine whether the material is more likely to result from the influence of oral tradition or from the author's own meditation and composition, it seems highly unlikely that all of these added traditions were the results of the authors' meditations.

Furthermore, examination of materials beyond these documents of earliest Christianity — ranging from the 2nd through the 5th century (including Eusebius citing Papias [*HE* 3.39.2-4], Barnabas, Ignatius [*Trall.* 9.1], Odes Sol. 28, Justin Martyr [*Apol.* 35; *Dial.* 98-106], Melito of Sardis [*Homily on the Passion*], the Ascents of James [Ps.-Clem. 1.41.3], Asc. Isa. 11, Tertullian [*Apol.* 21.15-26; *Adv. Marc.* 4.42.5], Didascalia 21.5.17-19, Julius Africanus [*Epistle to Aristides* 18.1], and the Gospel of Nicodemus [containing the Acts of Pilate]) — shows that a marked tendency to add details and even scenes to the Passion narrative became the normal manner of recounting the story of Jesus' death. The Passion narrative was told often.

Given the tendencies observed in these writings and given the natural restrictions related to ancient written materials, throughout the early centuries of the Church, one can safely conclude that the Passion narrative was more often told than written, more often heard than read, more often known than physically held. The process of elaboration was normal. The difficulty of the interpreter confronting the evidences of this process is twofold and sets the agenda for future studies: scholars must determine whether the additions are creations of the authors or reflections of oral traditions; and they must assess the antiquity of the traditions when these are present in Passion narrative accounts.

Bibliography. R. E. Brown, *The Death of the Messiah,* 2 vols. ABRL (New York, 1994); J. T. Carroll and J. B. Green, *The Death of Jesus in Early Christianity* (Peabody, 1995); J. D. Crossan, *The Cross That Spoke: The Origins of the Passion Narrative* (San Francisco, 1988); J. R. Donahue, *Are You the Christ? The Trial Narrative in the Gospel of Mark.* SBLDS 10 (Missoula, 1973); D. Senior, *The Passion of Jesus in the Gospel of John* (Collegeville, 1991); *The Passion of Jesus in the Gospel of Luke* (Collegeville, 1989); *The Passion of Jesus in the Gospel of Mark* (Collegeville, 1984); *The Passion of Jesus in the Gospel of Matthew* (Collegeville, 1985); H. Wansbrough, ed., *Jesus and the Oral Tradition.* JSNTSup 64 (Sheffield, 1991). MARION L. SOARDS

PASSOVER, FEAST OF

A ritual observance of Israel that celebrates Yahweh's deliverance of the community from Egypt. The observance took place on the 14th day of Nisan (Apr.-May; Abib in older calendars) and included the slaughter of a lamb and its consumption in a meal shared by the whole family. Passover (Heb. *pesaḥ*) eventually became associated with the seven-day Festival of Unleavened Bread that began on the 15th of Nisan.

It has long been argued that Passover reflects an ancient nomadic observance. In this older context, the blood of the slaughtered animal was thought to provide protection for the nomadic community as it made its annual migration. The concern for a "safe journey" provided the thematic linkage that allowed Israel to adapt the festival to its commemoration of the Exodus journey from Egypt.

The most extensive discussion of Passover is found in Exod. 12–13. These chapters reflect a complex literary development with several distinct layers of traditions. In these chapters the primary prescriptions for the observance are delivered to Israel in the context of and in relation to the final plague of Yahweh against Egypt, the death of the firstborn. It is important to recognize that the ritual of Passover is situated within a larger narrative context that provides details not only for the narrative enactment of the ritual "in the past" but also for the enactment of the ritual "in the future." The genres of "story" and "instruction" are complementary and interactive.

In these chapters, the observance takes place within the context of the family. A pre-selected lamb is slaughtered at twilight on the 14th day of Nisan (Exod. 12:1-6). Its blood is placed on the frame of the door (Exod. 12:7). In the context of the Exodus story, the blood serves to protect the Israelite families from the divine plague that will kill the firstborn. The lamb is roasted and then shared by the family in a meal which includes unleavened bread and bitter herbs (Exod. 12:8-11). The seven-day Festival of Unleavened Bread that follows Passover requires a pilgrimage to a sacred site on the seventh day of the festival (Exod. 13:6).

The family meal provides the context for the head of the family to explain the nature of the observance to the children (Exod. 12:25-27; cf. the similar feature of Unleavened Bread in 13:6-10). "Remembering" is combined with "retelling" in such a way that the events of the past are actualized for every Israelite in the context of the observance. Passover celebrates not only what God has done in the past, but also what God is doing in the present. Ritualized activity provides the occasion for celebration, reflection, and the formation of community identity.

It is important to note that Passover was celebrated at Gilgal when the Israelites first entered the land of Canaan (Josh. 5:10-12). The Israelites began to eat the produce of the land on the following day. Thus, Passover not only marks the exit from Egypt, but also marks the entry into the land of promise. As such, it provides a ritual frame for the larger story of redemption which includes both exit out of slavery and entry into the freedom of the land.

Changes in the observance of Passover appear with the move toward centralization of worship associated with Deuteronomy. In Deut. 16:1-8 Passover is viewed as a pilgrimage festival which requires that an animal be sacrificed (v. 2, "the Passover sacrifice") at the central sanctuary. The day of the slaughter is also viewed as the first day of the Feast of Unleavened Bread. Deuteronomy is very specific in relating both Passover and Unleavened Bread to aspects of the Exodus story. The animal is to be sacrificed in the evening at sunset (Deut. 16:6) and all of its meat is to be eaten on that night (v. 4). The people are then allowed to return to their tents, where they are to refrain from eating unleavened bread. They are to observe a solemn assembly on the seventh day (Deut. 16:8).

What was once a family observance in the home is transformed into a national pilgrimage festival. This shift brought several changes in the observance of Passover and Unleavened Bread. First, the time of the slaughter of the animal was shifted to an earlier time of the day (Deut. 16:6; cf. Exod. 12:6). This made it easier for the pilgrims to arrive and the sacrifices to be offered in a timely fashion. In addition, this allowed the Passover sacrifice to mark the beginning of the seven days of Unleavened Bread. Second, the Israelites could now choose either sheep or cattle for sacrifice (Deut. 16:2; cf. Exod. 12:3). Third, the method of cooking was changed from roasting to boiling (Deut. 16:7; cf. Exod. 12:9). Fourth, the observance is now constructed in terms of a national experience. This does not, however, preclude a family from eating together at the pilgrimage site. Finally, it is probable that Passover and Unleavened Bread were first linked at the time of the Deuteronomic reforms.

The descriptions of the Passovers observed by Hezekiah (2 Chr. 30) and Josiah (35:1-19) emphasize the pilgrimage aspects of the Passover/Unleavened Bread ritual complex. One can detect the ideological concerns of the Chronicler in these texts as more detailed information is provided on the role of the priests and Levites in the presentation of the blood of the Passover sacrifices. Both texts emphasize the large number of people present in the capital city and the extravagance of the celebrations.

Passover and Unleavened Bread receive extensive discussion in nonbiblical texts. For example, Jub. 49 (ca. 150 B.C.E.) provides instructions for the observance and emphasizes the time of the sacrificial slaughter at the central sanctuary. It adds to the observance the drinking of wine at the meal (Jub. 49:6). Philo and Josephus also include discussions of the celebration in their works. Both emphasize the extravagant nature of the joyous celebrations and the large number of pilgrims that participate in the activities. Finally, *Mishnah Pesaḥim* (ca. 200 C.E.) provides extensive details on various aspects of the observance. In particular, it seeks to restructure the observance in light of the destruction of the Jerusalem temple.

Passover plays a prominent role in the NT accounts of the death of Jesus. All four Gospels locate his death in relation to the celebration of Passover and Unleavened Bread (Mark 14:1-52; Matt. 26:1-46; Luke 22:1-53; John 13:1-38). The Synoptic Gospels locate Jesus' last meal with the disciples and his arrest on the night in which the Passover sacrifice was slaughtered and the Passover meal eaten (Mark 14:12-16; Matt. 26:17-19; Luke 22:7-13). For the Synoptic writers, the Last Supper was itself a Passover meal that was reinterpreted in light of the theological reflections of the early Church. John, however, seeks to link Jesus' death with the actual slaughter of the Passover sacrifices (cf. John 13:1; 19:14, 31, 42). In this way, John interprets the death of Jesus in terms of the sacrificial slaughter of the Passover sheep (cf. John 1:29; 19:36). The association of the death of Jesus and the Passover sacrifice had already been made by Paul (1 Cor. 5:7-8). Thus, the Israelite ritual observance of Passover was appropriated and adapted by the Christian community as it sought to understand and interpret the life and death of Jesus in relationship to its own ritual practices.

Bibliography. B. M. Bokser, *The Origins of the Seder* (Berkeley, 1984); H. L. Ginsberg, *The Israelian Heritage of Judaism* (New York, 1982); A. J. Saldarini, *Jesus and Passover* (New York, 1984); J. B. Segal, *The Hebrew Passover, from the Earliest Times to A.D. 70* (London, 1963).

FRANK H. GORMAN, JR.

PASTORAL EPISTLES

1-2 Timothy and Titus, three letters which constitute a distinct group within the Pauline corpus. These once highly esteemed texts fell under a shadow with the rise of higher criticism. Thereafter conservatives labored to rehabilitate them, while more liberal scholars found their views of church, society, and theology increasingly objectionable. The strategy of those defending Pauline composition required assigning the Pastoral Epistles to the latest possible date while seeking to conform their contents to the undisputed epistles. This strategy has not been especially successful. If written by Paul, the Pastoral Epistles represent a dim conclusion to a brilliant career. If post-Pauline, they are interesting witnesses to later conflicts over Paul's heritage. Recognition that alleged authorship has more to do with authority than with composition and that secondary writings are not necessarily inferior (cf. Isa. 40–66) has eased tensions. The world of the Pastoral Epistles is more readily explicable in the light of 1 Clement, the Acts of Paul, and the Letter of Polycarp than from Paul's career. A probable date is ca. 100-125.

The addressees of the Pastoral Epistles are not communities but co-workers of Paul. Timothy and Titus appear here as relatively youthful (Titus 2:7, 15; 1 Tim. 4:12) successors of Paul. These letters, which are parenetic (advisory) in form, have a twofold aim: to show Paul's work and thought and to provide models for the organization of Christian communities in a hostile world. The former polytheist Titus (Titus 3:4-5) is developing a new mission area, Crete, while Timothy, the scion of devout forebears (2 Tim. 1:3-14; 3:15), supervises the established church of Ephesus.

These leaders face challenges from false teachers both within (1 Timothy) and without (Titus) the community. Because some of the charges, such as the motivation of greed, are polemical stereotypes while others are terse, it is difficult to establish whether one or more "heresies" are in view. Reference to myths, genealogies, speculative thought, and asceticism (e.g., 1 Tim. 1:3-7; Titus 3:9-11) evokes incipient Gnosticism. "Jewish" (Titus 1:14) *may* be no more than a hostile epithet. The Pastoral Epistles advocate that false teachers be shunned rather than refuted (2 Tim. 3:5). Particularly objectionable is the disruption of conventional social life through nonconformist behavior, especially by women (1 Tim. 2:8-15; 4:7; 5:13). The gradient is clear: Paul favors celibacy, but states that it is better to marry than to burn (1 Cor. 7). In the Acts of Paul his dutiful convert Thecla quite literally prefers burning to marriage. 1 Tim. 2 requires women to be married. The Pastoral Epistles seek to preserve Paul's thought by smoothing out its potentially speculative edges and underlining the normality of its morality.

The Church is not the enemy of ancient "family values"; it is the "household of God" (1 Tim. 3:15). Officials (bishops/overseers, presbyters, elders and deacons/servant ministers) possess the qualities of both household heads and organizational leaders (e.g., 1 Tim. 3:1-13). Their task is formation. What we call "ethics" was for ancients largely the performance of tasks and duties appropriate to one's role and station in life. Grace is not simply liberating; it is educative (Titus 2:12). The Pastoral Epistles accept the possibility of persecution (1 Tim. 6:13), but wish to condemn conduct that would injure the Church's reputation. Today it is easy to see how much of this advice is culture-specific and to lament apparent concessions to worldly standards. What is more important than its cultural coloration is the witness of the Pastoral Epistles to the beginnings of a structure that would, over centuries, gradually make the Church a moral force in the Greco-Roman and, later, the "barbarian" world.

Bibliography. J. C. Beker, *Heirs of Paul* (1991, repr. Grand Rapids, 1996); M. Dibelius and H. Conzelmann, *The Pastoral Epistles.* Herm. (Philadelphia, 1972); G. W. Knight III, *The Pastoral Epistles.* NIGTC (Grand Rapids, 1992); D. R. MacDonald, *The Legend and the Apostle* (Philadelphia, 1983); F. M. Young, *The Theology of the Pastoral Letters* (Cambridge, 1994). RICHARD I. PERVO

PATARA (Gk. *Pátara*)

The major port of Lycia situated on the southwest coast opposite Rhodes, 9.6 km. (6 mi.) E of the mouth of the Xanthus River. A prosperous city, Patara was one of the six largest cities of the Lycian league (Strabo *Geog.* 14.3.2-3). Here Paul changed ships to sail to Phoenicia during his final journey to Jerusalem (Acts 21:1; some texts read "Patara and Myra").

PATHROS (Heb. *paṯrôs*), **PATHRUSIM** *(paṯrusîm)*

Upper Egypt, i.e., the southern part of Egypt (Egyp. *p3-t3-rsy,* "southern land") from just S of Memphis to the first cataract at Syene, to which some of the exiled Israelites fled (Isa. 11:11; Jer. 44:1, 15; Ezek. 30:14). According to Ezek. 29:14 "the land of Pathros" was the original home of the Egyptians (cf. Gen. 10:14; 1 Chr. 1:12, "Pathrusim").

PATRIARCHS

The leaders of families and clans within ancient Israel. The term derives from Heb. *rā'šê 'ăḇôṯ* ("heads of the fathers"), translated in the LXX as "rulers of the fathers" (Gk. *archaí patriós*) and simplified as *patriárchēs* in the NT and Apocrypha. Within the discipline of biblical studies the term has come to refer more specifically to the four generations of Israel's founders described in Gen. 12–50: Abraham, Isaac, Jacob, and his 12 sons (esp. Joseph). This leads into the realm of ethnicity, an organizing social principle based on the perception that members of the group share a common ancestral heritage. Ethnicity is a very powerful mode of identity because it extends the natural sentiments of kinship affiliation from the immediate family to the society as a whole. Sentiments of ethnicity are commonly associated with original forefathers through whom all members of the group trace their lineage — in the case of ancient Israel, Abraham, Isaac, and Jacob. Research in ethnicity has demonstrated that, although a forefather might be a historical figure, it is also quite common to find that the tradition was invented to foster group cohesiveness. This raises an important question about the patriarchal stories themselves. To what extent do the narratives provide historical information?

History and Genre

Early in the 20th century it was increasingly common for scholars to view the patriarchal narratives as family legends and sagas rather than as historical compositions. But in later decades it was proposed that they derive from ancient epics which preserve historical accounts of the forefathers' movements in

Mesopotamia and Palestine. In addition, some have argued that the geopolitical and cultural details of the stories find their closest affinities with ancient texts from Ebla, Mari, and Nuzi (from 2300-1500 B.C.E.), and this is taken as evidence for a supposed 2nd-millennium "patriarchal age" (ca. 2000-1800). Recent work has called this archaeological and textual evidence into question, so that most now concede there is little solid evidence to connect the patriarchal stories exclusively with such an early historical period. A survey of the ideological landscape shows that four views of the patriarchal narratives predominate. First, in both Christian and Jewish quarters there remain religiously conservative scholars who view the texts as accurate historical narratives. Second, some scholars continue to adhere to the "epic" interpretation of the stories and see them as a useful — albeit cloudy — historical window into early Israel's patriarchal origins under Abraham and/or forefathers like him. Third, some view the narratives not as history but rather as ancient family and tribal sagas acted out by literary characters — Abraham, Isaac, Jacob, and his sons. These first three approaches have in common the view that the patriarchal narratives preserve within them a good deal of ancient material. The fourth perspective differs in that, while acknowledging some older materials, it views the patriarchal story as a later, invented tradition that tells more about the period in which the narrative was constructed (exilic or postexilic periods) than it does about ancient Israelite history. Although many scholars would not go this far in denying the historical value of the patriarchal narratives, at present nearly all scholars recognize that Genesis does not provide us with history like that provided by the historical books of Samuel and Kings. Accordingly, it has become common for those writing the history of ancient Israel to begin with the period of David and Solomon rather than of Abraham and Jacob.

Literary Considerations

Although the patriarchal stories of Genesis are preserved as a single literary work, scholars generally believe that a very complex process has created them. Various literary sources from different historical periods lie behind the narratives, and these have been written or edited by several authors and redactors. In addition, these literary sources were composed of smaller units of tradition, e.g., Jacob traditions from the northern kingdom, the Abraham/Isaac traditions from the southern kingdom, and a self-contained short story about the forefather Joseph. Whether these materials originated orally or as smaller literary works is often difficult to determine. The process by which the various traditions were combined is also debated, with some viewing it as the work of a few authors or editors and others as a gradual and accidental process which resulted in the accumulation of many traditions into one narrative.

Theological Significance

The complex literary origin of the narratives does not negate their theological importance for Jewish and Christian traditions. Especially important is the concept of "promise." God promised the patriarchs that they would receive blessings — a posterity — and a homeland. The fulfillment of these promises became a preoccupation in other portions of the OT, including the remaining parts of the Pentateuch, the historical books, and much of the prophetic material. While in the OT this promise was inherited primarily by the ethnic community of ancient Israel — Abraham's posterity — in the NT the promise was spiritualized (cf. Heb. 4:1-11) and extended to non-Jews by "grafting" them into the people of God (Rom. 11:17-24). However, this theological innovation did not necessarily render inconsequential the ethnic boundaries that separated Jews from Gentiles, as Rom. 11:25-32 shows.

"Faith justification" is another important theological concept in the patriarchal narratives. This perspective maintains that one is in right standing with the deity by virtue of trust in God (Gen. 15:1-6), a view subsequently taken up in both Jewish and Christian traditions (Isa. 51:1-2; Rom. 4).

Bibliography. W. F. Albright, *Yahweh and the Gods of Canaan* (1968, repr. Winona Lake, 1990); P. G. Kirkpatrick, "Folklore Studies and the Genre of the Patriarchal Narratives," in *The Old Testament and Folklore Study.* JSOTSup 62 (Sheffield, 1988), 73-114; W. McKane, *Studies in the Patriarchal Narratives* (Winona Lake, 1983); A. R. Millard and D. J. Wiseman, *Essays on the Patriarchal Narratives* (Winona Lake, 1983); J. Van Seters, *Prologue to History: The Yahwist as Historian in Genesis* (Louisville, 1992); C. Westermann, *Genesis,* 3 vols. (Minneapolis, 1984-86), esp. 2:23-131.

KENTON LANE SPARKS

PATROBAS (Gk. *Patrobás*)
A Christian in Rome to whom Paul sent his greetings (Rom. 16:14). The name is a shortened form of Patrobias.

PAU (Heb. *pāʿû*) (also PAI)
An Edomite city, the capital of King Hadad (Gen. 36:39); called Pai at 1 Chr. 1:50. Its location is unknown. The LXX reads Gk. *Phogōr,* its usual designation for Peor.

PAUL (Gk. *Paúlos*)
Except for Jesus, no one influenced the development of early Christianity more than Paul. He was the foremost apologist for the gentile mission, and the most eloquent defender of the centrality of Jewish traditions, Scriptures, deity, and morality for his predominantly gentile churches. That 13 of the 27 books of the NT are attributed to Paul gives eloquent testimony to the importance he had for the early Jesus movement. That legacy remained to inspire such theological titans as Augustine, Luther, Calvin, and Wesley, and to profoundly influence the intellectual history of the West.

Athena temple on the acropolis at Lindos, Rhodes, overlooking St. Paul's Bay
(Phoenix Data Systems, Neal and Joel Bierling)

Sources

The seven letters which came from Paul's hand (1 Thessalonians, 1 Corinthians, Philippians, Philemon, 2 Corinthians, Galatians, and Romans) serve as the primary sources for our knowledge about the apostle; Acts, though secondary, is nevertheless useful when judiciously used. The disputed letters (2 Thessalonians, Colossians, and Ephesians) merit consideration, and the pseudepigraphic letters (1 and 2 Timothy, Titus, and Hebrews) and later apocryphal literature assist with the history of Pauline interpretation.

"Pre-Christian" Period

Paul was born, lived, and died a Jew. He writes that he was of the tribe of Benjamin, circumcised on the eighth day, was blameless before the law, followed the Pharisaic interpretation (Phil. 3:5-6), and was zealously observant of the ancestral traditions (Gal. 1:14). He was probably born in Tarsus (Acts 22:3), a thriving, cosmopolitan, urban gateway to the eastern Mediterranean, a vibrant intellectual center, and a transportation hub of strategic importance. There Paul learned his first language, Greek, was taught a trade, and received his schooling. This background and Gal. 1:22 contradict the view of Acts 22:3 that Paul was brought to Jerusalem at an early age to sit at the feet of the great teacher Gamaliel (26:4). Whatever its source, no one disputes that Paul was a learned man and creative thinker. The length and complexity of his letters, the sophistication of his arguments, his knowledge of the LXX, his familiarity with Jewish law and traditions, and his persuasive skills used to found churches and hold them together all suggest that Paul was an educated man. Unfortunately, we know very little about the exact nature of his formal schooling.

In addition, Paul benefitted from a rich informal education. The urban setting in which he grew up acquainted him with important literary and rhetorical skills. He owed his use of the diatribe (Rom. 6:1, 15; 7:7; 11:1) and his knowledge of the law of nature (2:14-15) to Stoicism, and his anthropology and views of celibacy, conscience, and self-control were influenced by Hellenistic popular religion. His style of argumentation reflects a selective appropriation of Hellenistic rhetoric. By contrast, his apocalypticism, his spiritualization of the sacrificial cult (Rom. 12:1), his monotheism, and moral convictions came from Jewish sources, and his knowledge of Jesus' passion, death, resurrection, teaching, and the sacramental cult came from the messianists. His letters reveal how this fertile mind absorbed, synthesized, and interpreted these traditions for his churches.

His learning, however, hardly presupposes high status or Roman citizenship. Given the rarity of Roman citizenship in the East, Paul's silence about it even though threatened with execution (2 Cor. 1:8-9), and the theological importance of Paul's citizenship to Luke (Acts 22:22-29), it is unlikely that Paul was a Roman citizen. Instead, he was probably a member of a *políteuma* or Jewish community accorded relative political autonomy and given the freedom to govern itself by Jewish law and institutions. Instead of high class origins, his training as a leatherworker or tentmaker probably came from his artisan father; he would later use that skill to support himself in his mission to the Gentiles (Acts 18:3; 1 Thess. 2:9; 1 Cor. 9:6-18).

Though haunted by the painful memory of his persecution of Christians, Paul nowhere tells us where he waged the persecution, what the nature of the persecution was, who its victims were, or what inspired it. Did the proclamation of the kingdom of God make Jews already nervous about Roman reprisals eager to squelch this messianism? Did a law-free gospel invite reprisals from those who saw their identity threatened? Was it a hostile response to deviant convictions, or to criticism of the temple cult? We cannot answer these questions with certainty. In any case, Paul's dramatic about-face, he tells us, came in response to an epiphany of the risen Christ (Gal. 1:16-17) which turned the adversary into an apostle of Christ.

Apostleship

From the beginning critics questioned the authenticity of Paul's apostleship. Unlike Peter, James, and John, he had never seen Jesus in the flesh; he had never been instructed by the "pillar" apostles, and he had been a vicious enemy of the early Church (Gal. 1:23). Recognizing this, Jewish-Christian apostles attacked both the legitimacy of Paul's apostleship and the integrity of his gospel. Paul responded to these attacks with autobiographical information (Gal. 1–2), creative exegesis of the key texts of his adversaries (Gal. 3), and appeals to the cross of Christ (3:10-14). In an autobiographical remark reminiscent of the prophetic call of Jeremiah and Isaiah, he claimed to have been set aside by God from his mother's womb (Gal. 1:15; Jer. 1:5; Isa. 49:1-6). He shifted the locus of his authority from the teaching of the earthly Jesus to the revelation of the risen Christ (Gal. 1:12, 16). He recited a chronology of sparse contacts with the Jerusalem "pillars" — "after three years" and "after fourteen years" (1:18; 2:1) — to support his claim of independence from the Jerusalem "pillars" (2:9-10). Three times in the letter (Gal. 1:7-9; 4:16-18; 6:12-13) Paul turned on his opponents, confronting them directly, pronouncing a divine curse on them, belittling them, and denouncing them. The apostle, however, went beyond denunciation by seeking to persuade his converts of the legitimacy of his gospel and apostleship by reminding them of tender moments between them (Gal. 4:12-20), and of their baptismal experience (3:26-29).

2 Corinthians reports that Jewish-Christian charismatic apostles armed with testimonials from other congregations enjoyed some success in undermining confidence in Paul's apostleship. These rivals used his fragile physique and unskilled speech (2 Cor. 10:10; 11:6), his physical affliction and uncharismatic appearance (12:7), and his financial independence (vv. 15-16) and unwillingness to boast of charismatic prowess to question his apostleship. Paul appeals to his suffering and weaknesses as authenticating signs of his apostleship (2 Cor. 11:21-29; 12:7-10; 6:4-10), and with appeals to autobiography (12:1-10), to a catalogue of sufferings (6:3-10; 11:22-29), and God's raising of Christ from the dead, Paul defended himself by showing how God's strength is manifested in weakness.

For 25 years after his death an awkward silence about Paul hovered over the early Christian landscape. Then in Luke's Acts Paul emerges as an important figure, and nothing seems able to stop the march of his gospel westward. Soon afterward, pseudepigraphical letters began to appear that offered interpretations and defenses of Paul's theology.

Letter Writer

Given the cost of writing materials, the low literacy rate, and the absence of a delivery network for private correspondence, the survival of thousands of papyrus letters from the Hellenistic period is astonishing. Diplomacy, trade, and travel fostered letter writing both official and unofficial, and the increasing use of letters by the imperial court and by the wealthy who could afford couriers or slaves to deliver them contributed to their growing popularity. A thriving business sprang up to support letter writing. Handbooks on letter writing appeared. Scribes served government agencies, wealthy households, and the illiterate poor. Under the influence of Hellenistic rhetoric the letter became an artistic form with a high level of aesthetic expression. Paul drew on this rich, venerable, and pervasive epistolary tradition to pen his letters. These letters were not private but public events written to exhort, instruct, remind, and console churches. They were not theological treatises, but real letters dealing with real situations. Even Romans, Paul's most theological letter, reveals the apostle's defense against false charges and malicious rumors (Rom. 3:8) and deals with factionalism in the church (ch. 14). In time these letters were collected, copied, circulated, and even imitated to strengthen other churches as well.

These letters had multiple functions. They served as a substitute for the presence of the apostle until his coming. They provided a means for exhortation and advice (1 Thess. 5:23; 1 Cor. 1:8; Phil. 2:15). They offered consolation (2 Cor. 1:3-7), provided a vehicle for responding to critics (esp. in Galatians and 2 Corinthians), and presented a means for relating the gospel to everyday concerns.

While the form of Paul's letters resembles that of the traditional Hellenistic letter, Paul bent the form to his ends. In Romans he expanded the salutation to include an affirmation to counter the charge that his gospel was an outrageous novelty. In Galatians he substituted an expression of astonishment for the typical thanksgiving to rebuke his addressees (Gal. 1:6). In 1 Thessalonians he expanded the closing to exhort the disheartened to readiness for the coming of Christ (1 Thess. 5:23-24). These modifications for stereotypical epistolary forms offer valuable clues to his purposes.

Chronology

Difficulty besets any attempt to synchronize the chronology of Acts with Paul's letters. Acts records three missionary journeys which only partially conform to the accounts in Paul's letters, and Acts reports five Pauline visits to Jerusalem where the letters record only three. Acts 18:12, 14, 17, however, refer to Paul's arraignment before the Roman proconsul Gallio in Achaea, which most judge to be historical since the reference serves no theological agenda. If so judged, the reference would require Paul's presence there in 51-52 C.E. during Gallio's proconsulship. Furthermore, if Acts is correct that Paul was in Corinth for 18 months (Acts 18:11), then his ministry there probably began in 50. From that date one can work backward and forward to approximate a Pauline chronology. Before that date he had founded the churches in Galatia, Thessalonica, and Philippi (ca. 49), and before that mission he had been in Antioch for a time (Gal. 2:11-14). A bit more than 17 years intervened between Paul's apostolic call (ca. 31) and his Antioch visit (Gal. 1:17-18; 2:1). During those years (31-48) Paul spent three years in Arabia before his first visit to Jerusalem, and 14 years in Syria and Cilicia before his second visit.

After his arraignment before Gallio Paul wrote all of the letters we possess (except for 1 Thessalonians) between 52–58, but their exact order is disputed. A possible arrangement would place the composition of several of these letters during his 27-month stay in Ephesus after his mission to Corinth (53–56; Acts 19:8-10). Although neither Paul's letters nor Acts refers explicitly to an imprisonment in Ephesus, it is likely that he was in custody there. Paul speaks metaphorically of fighting with beasts at Ephesus (1 Cor. 15:32) and of a great affliction in Asia that left him so "utterly, unbearably crushed" that he despaired of life itself, and felt he was under the sentence of death (2 Cor. 1:8-9). Paul also refers to being in prison many times (2 Cor. 11:23), and an Ephesian imprisonment may be confirmed by the apocryphal Acts of Paul. During such an imprisonment, Paul could have written Philippians and Philemon (ca. 55). During his mission in Ephesus he wrote multiple letters to Corinth and our letter to Galatia. He wrote the fourth Corinthian letter (possibly 2 Cor. 1:1–9:15 minus 6:14–7:1) en route to visit the church there (late in 56), and Romans came as he embarked or was about to embark from Corinth on his trip to Jerusalem with the offering for the "poor among the saints" (57; Rom. 15:25-27). Fearful of the "unbelievers" in Judea (Rom. 15:31), Paul requested the prayers of the Roman church. Thereafter his voice abruptly fell silent. Acts attempts to complete the story by suggesting that Paul's premonition was tragically realized. He was arrested, brought before the Roman procurator Festus (59), made an appeal based on his "Roman citizenship," and was taken to Rome for trial. Luke, however, does not tell us how Paul died; if he were beheaded in Rome, as the 3rd-century Acts of Paul suggests (10:5), his execution would have come before the end of 62.

Theologizer

Paul hardly launched his mission with a developed systematic theology which he could lay like a template over every situation. Since he was a pastoral rather than a systematic theologian his theologizing had an ad hoc character, developed for each new situation. Disturbances created by rival missionary apostles, charismatic factions, judaizers, disillusioned believers, and popular religionists provoked Paul's thinking in varying ways. These points of friction mark the issues Paul deemed worth fighting for, and they offer a window onto Paul's theologizing in process.

This theologizing though situational was, nevertheless, rooted in deep, underlying convictions embedded in the sacred story of Israel. Of primary significance was the supremacy of the one God of Israel, the creator, redeemer, and guarantor of the future. Crucial to the narrative of God's people were the election and the giving of the law recorded in the Scriptures. In those sacred texts Paul found prescripts of the dawning eschaton, anticipations of the Christ, and authority for his gospel. In addition to these texts and Israel's sacred story, Paul's experience of the revelation of the risen Christ offered him added evidence that the new age was breaking in (Gal. 1:12; 1 Cor. 9:1; 15:8) which led to an apocalyptic conclusion. The revelation of Christ meant that, as Paul repeatedly says, God had raised him up (Rom. 4:24; 8:11; 10:9; 1 Cor. 6:14; 15:15; 2 Cor. 4:14; Gal. 1:1; 1 Thess. 1:10) as the firstfruits of the general resurrection (1 Cor. 15:20), and he would soon return to gather his own and judge the world (1 Thess. 4:14). Thus those in Christ were already given a glimpse of their vindication in the world to come. This apocalyptic vision caused Paul to view Scripture, his native Judaism, the temple, the world, natural disasters, and his celibacy and suffering in a radically new way. His sense of the imminent denouement gave his apostleship its urgency, and suffused his letters (e.g., 1 Cor. 7:26; Rom. 14:10-12; 1 Cor. 11:32; Rom. 13:11-14) from the first letter (1 Thess. 4:15) to the last (Rom. 13:12). The feverish intensity of Paul's expectation dimmed only slightly if at all throughout his apostolic period.

Paul believed Jesus the Christ had brought the world to its final, climactic moment. While Paul recognized the importance of the earthly Jesus (Rom. 1:3; 9:5), he appealed to his teaching less than 10 times in all of the letters. He focuses instead on the suffering, dying, and resurrected Jesus who, he believed, would soon return, but his treatment of the death was highly nuanced. It served as an example for the persecuted (1 Thess. 1:6), as an instance of Christ's obedience (Phil. 2:8), as a device for the redemption of Gentiles (Gal. 3:13-14), as a sacrifice (Rom. 3:25), as a medium through which the righteousness of God is revealed (Rom. 3:22), and as a vehicle for subverting the Corinthian charismatic hierarchy (1 Cor. 2:1-5). While he clearly recognized Jesus as Messiah (Rom. 9:5), more often he used the name Christ as a proper name referring to him as Jesus Christ, Christ Jesus, Christ, and Jesus Christ our Lord.

Paul fervently believed that the God who had raised the crucified Jesus from the dead had established him as Lord and would send him soon to gather the elect and judge the world. The title "lord," so highly idiomatic in Hellenistic circles, was richly polysemous. It was a title for respect for the gods and goddesses like Isis, Asclepius, and Chronos, and also ruling authorities like Augustus, Herod, or Agrippa. It expressed deference to anyone of importance in the social or political hierarchy. In the LXX it frequently translated "Yahweh," but nowhere in the letters did Paul call Jesus "God." 1 Cor. 11:3 makes clear the line of origin that subordinates Jesus to God. Following early Church tradition (Phil. 2:6-11) Paul often used the title Lord as an ascription of the one whom God raised from the dead, thereby establishing him as Lord over death and the demonic powers.

An important feature of Paul's messianism was a mystical participation in Christ. Paul regularly addressed his letters to those "in Christ Jesus" or its variants (1 Cor. 1:2; Phil. 1:1; 1 Thess. 1:1). He spoke to his converts in Galatia as those who had been "baptized into Christ," who had "put on Christ," and who were all "one in Christ Jesus" (Gal. 3:26-28), and he noted that those who partake of the eucharist participate in the body of Christ (1 Cor. 10:15-17). He spoke synonymously of being "in the Lord" and "in Christ." This mystical identification was a corporate not an isolated, private experience, and it was always shaped to fit each situation. For example, those grieving over the unexpected death of believers in Thessalonica were reassured that both the living and the dead are "in Christ," joined in a common bond across the gulf of separation (1 Thess. 4:16-17).

The theologizing we see in the letters developed over the decade of the 50s, and the profundity and practical issues they contained helps explain why these letters became Scripture by the end of the 2nd century.

Bibliography. J. C. Beker, *Paul the Apostle* (Philadelphia, 1980); N. A. Dahl, *Studies in Paul: Theology for the Early Christian Mission* (Minneapolis, 1977); D. Georgi, *The Opponents of Paul in Second Corinthians* (Philadelphia, 1986); *Theocracy in Paul's Praxis and Theology* (Minneapolis, 1991); J. C. Lentz, Jr., *Luke's Portrait of Paul.* SNTSMS 77 (Cambridge, 1993); H. Räisänen, *Paul and the Law,* 2nd ed. WUNT 29 (Tübingen, 1987); C. J. Roetzel, *The Letters of Paul: Conversations in Context,* 3rd ed. (Louisville, 1991); E. P. Sanders, *Paul, the Law, and the Jewish People* (Philadelphia, 1983); K. Stendahl, *Paul among Jews and Gentiles and Other Essays* (Philadelphia, 1976).

CALVIN J. ROETZEL

PAUL, ACTS OF

An apocryphal acts of various traditions about the Apostle Paul. According to the 9th-century Stichometry of Nicephoros, it contained 3600 lines (compare the 2800 lines of the canonical Acts). About one third of the work is missing. Originally written in Greek, substantial parts of the text are extant only in Coptic translation. Since Tertullian refers to it in *De Baptismo,* it must have been composed before 200, probably in the last quarter of the 2nd century. Several distinct units (the Acts of Paul and Thecla, 3 Corinthians, and the Martydrom of Paul) appear to predate the composition of the entire book. Authorship is unknown, though some recent scholarship contend for a female author, at least of the source for the Acts of Paul and Thecla.

The work tells of missionary journeys of Paul and his miracles and preaching on these journeys. Many of the places are the same as in canonical Acts but none of the stories. The constantly recurring theme is the need for asceticism in general and celibacy in particular. Among many other acts, Paul baptizes a talking lion, who becomes a Christian. After Paul is beheaded in Rome, he rises from the dead, appears to the emperor Nero, and condemns him.

Bibliography. D. R. MacDonald, ed., *The Apocryphal Acts of the Apostles.* Semeia 38 (Atlanta, 1986); *The Legend and the Apostle* (Philadelphia, 1983); W. Schneemelcher, "Acts of Paul," in *New Testament Apocrypha,* ed. E. Henncke-Schneemelcher, 2 (Philadelphia, 1965): 322-90.

J. CHRISTIAN WILSON

PAUL, APOCALYPSE OF (V, 2)

A pseudonymous apocalypse, especially popular among early Christians. The Apocalypse of Paul elaborates upon 2 Cor. 12:2-4, Paul's account of a man (probably himself) who had journeyed to the third heaven. The narrative, originally composed in Greek but existing in several versions, describes its own discovery ca. 388 C.E. Paul sees the contrasting deaths of righteous persons and sinners, visits paradise and the city of Christ, meets important persons of faith like Abraham, Moses, and Mary, and tours hell.

Bibliography. H. Duensing and A. de Santos Otero, "Apocalypse of Paul," in *New Testament Apocrypha,* ed. E. Hennecke and W. Schneemelcher, rev. ed., 2 (Louisville, 1992): 712-48; J. K. Elliott, "The Apocalypse of Paul (Visio Pauli)," *The Apocryphal New Testament,* rev. ed. (Oxford, 1993), 616-44.

GREG CAREY

PAUL, PRAYER OF THE APOSTLE

An early Christian writing, most likely produced in Greek in the late 2nd or early 3rd century, surviving in Coptic in the 4th-century Nag Hammadi codices. It most likely emerges from Valentinian Gnostic Christianity, as indicated by both its language and theology.

The work is a magical invocational prayer that is primarily concerned with attaining perfection ("redemption"), specifically revelatory knowledge and unity with the spiritual realm. It contains a string of invoked names or titles (attributed to Jesus). The five requests (which have an ascendancy from least to greatest) may reflect the five Valentinian sacraments listed in the Gospel of Philip (baptism, chrism, eucharist, redemption, bridal chamber), although the exact terms vary between these two Valentinian texts.

The Prayer illustrates the importance of Paul among early Christians and provides insights into early Christian rituals, views on holiness, use of magic, and mystical (visionary) experiences.

Bibliography. M. R. Desjardins, *Sin in Valentinianism.* SBLDS 108 (Atlanta, 1990); D. Mueller, "Prayer of the Apostle Paul I, 1: A.1–B.10," in *Nag Hammadi Codex I,* ed. H. W. Attridge. NHS 22 (Leiden, 1985), 5-11; K. Rudolph, *Gnosis* (San Francisco, 1987). PHILIP L. TITE

PAUL AND SENECA, LETTERS OF

A collection of 14 Latin letters purportedly exchanged between the apostle and the 1st-century Roman philosopher. Known to both Jerome and Augustine, the correspondence, which includes eight brief letters by Seneca and six by Paul, probably dates to the 4th century (although two or more may be later). Jerome notes that the letters were "read by many" in his age, and the letters remained popular through the Middle Ages as evidenced by the numerous manuscripts from that period. Seneca's letters to Paul contain praise for Paul's "admirable exhortation to an upright life" (letter 1); agreement with Paul's sentiments as expressed in his letters to the Galatians, Corinthians, and Achaeans (letter 7); and an expression of sadness regarding the wrongful persecution of the Christians (letter 11). Paul's responses are full of flattery, caution in terms of the emperor, and concern for proper epistolary etiquette, with an occasional encouragement to respectful treatment of others. None of the letters expresses any of the well-known thought of either correspondent, instead highlighting the friendship and mutual respect between two equals.

There seem to be two purposes behind the pseudepigraphical correspondence. On the one hand, the letters clearly commend Christianity as worthy of respect by pagans after the example of Seneca. In fact, some traditions even posit that Seneca converted to Christianity, although there is no evidence of such a conversion in his authentic writings. On the other hand, the letters also exhibit an early Christian understanding of the compatibility of Pauline and Stoic ideas, perhaps acknowledging what some modern scholars see as influences of pagan moral philosophy in Paul's letters.

Bibliography. J. K. Elliot, ed., "The Correspondence of Paul and Seneca," *The Apocryphal New Testament,* rev. ed. (Oxford, 1993), 547-53; J. N. Sevenster, *Paul and Seneca.* NovTSup 4 (Leiden, 1996), 11-14. JAMES R. MUELLER

PAUL AND THECLA, ACTS OF

A component in the larger apocryphal Acts of Paul. Edited on the basis of 11 Greek manuscripts in addition to Latin, Greek, Slavic, and Arabic versions, the narrative may have circulated independently; the earliest attestation (2nd century; Tertullian *De bapt.* 17) is inconclusive about its relationship to the Acts of Paul. It has been suggested that early 2nd-century, ascetic Christian groups, including women, generated the text, propagating a pro-ascetic understanding of Pauline Christianity.

The narrative begins with Thecla's acceptance of Paul's appeals to chastity which lead her to reject her betrothed, Thamyris. Consequently, Thecla's mother condemns her to the funeral pyre, and Paul is imprisoned due to his anti-establishment, ascetic teachings. Miraculously, rain spares Thecla from the flames and she escapes to meet Paul. Thecla asks Paul to baptize her, but Paul refuses, despite Thecla's status as a confessor. They both travel to Antioch, where a leading citizen publicly attacks Thecla. Paul fails to defend her, and Thecla is again arrested and sentenced to death. Thecla requests a custodian to guard her virginity the night before she is to die, and she receives the protection of a recently bereft aristocratic woman, Theocleia. Sentenced to be mauled by beasts, Thecla baptizes herself in the theater lest she die unconsecrated, though female beasts keep Thecla from harm. Thecla is spared once her accuser calls off the games for fear that Theocleia would use political means to avenge Thecla's death. Thecla then returns to Paul, who commissions her to preach in her own mission throughout Seleucia.

Bibliography. D. R. MacDonald, *The Legend and the Apostle* (Philadelphia, 1983); W. Schneemelcher, "Acts of Paul and Thecla," in *New Testament Apocrypha,* ed. E. Henncke-Schneemelcher, 2 (Philadelphia, 1965): 353-64. MELISSA M. AUBIN

PAVEMENT, THE

The place of judgment outside the Praetorium where Pilate tried Jesus (John 19:13; Gk. *lithóstrōtos*).

See GABBATHA.

PEACE

The Hebrew term for peace *(šālôm)* is derived from the verb "to complete, make sound." This verb is often used to express the finish of major buildings (e.g., the temple, 1 Kgs. 7:51 = 2 Chr. 5:1; or walls of Jerusalem, Neh. 6:15). The term is used in the sense of restoration in Lev. 6:5ff.(MT 5:24ff.) or repaying debts in Jer. 16:18; Lev. 24:18-21. The noun has an even broader use. As a greeting, the root *šlm* is used to inquire of the welfare of individuals or groups (Gen. 29:6; 43:27; Exod. 18:7; 1 Sam. 17:18; cf. Ezek. 13:16, "visions of peace"; similarly Isa. 38:17). There is further the sense of *šālôm* as state of being, as in contentment or tranquility. Isa. 32:17 draws a parallel between "peace" and "quietness and trust forever" as the results of righteousness. The idea of peacefulness at death is a common theme (Gen. 15:15; 1 Kgs. 2:6). The sense of friendship, or even a contractually arranged "friendship" (implied in "covenants of peace," Num. 25:12), can also be noted (Isa. 54:10; Ps. 28:3; Prov. 12:20). Justice is frequently combined with "peace" (Isa. 32:16-17, cf. Jas. 3:18).

In the Bible "peace" is quintessentially the absence of war. Judg. 4:17; 1 Sam. 7:14; 1 Kgs. 5:12(26)

imply treaty relations as times of peace as opposed to warfare. Times of *šālôm* are contrasted with war in 1 Kgs. 2:5-6; Josh. 9:15. The term is also used of a desired state of permanent *šālôm* (cf. Lev. 26:6, where peace is a part of tranquility, absence of war and enemies). In the prophets (esp. later prophets, Deutero-Isaiah, Zechariah) peace becomes an ethical standard and characteristic of the messianic age (cf. Mic. 5:4-5[3-4]). In Isa. 2:2-4; 9:2-7, and profoundly in 19:24-25 these postexilic insertions contain themes of peace that are interwoven with the theme of destruction of weapons and reconciliation of former enemies (cf. Zech. 9:9-10; Jonah). Although there is often debate as to whether some forms of "peace" result from God's annihilation of enemies (an Israelite version of Pax Romana), this is not universally the case in all texts that deal with release from enemies. Indeed, not only are Israel's own weapons included in an envisioned destruction (Isa. 2), enemies are as often converted rather than annihilated (Jonah; Isa. 19:24-25).

NT use of forms of Gk. *eirḗnē,* as well as in the intertestamental literature (cf. Tob. 7:11-12; 10:12), is only somewhat more limited in its range of meaning than *šālôm.* The typical use of "peace" is a reference to a personal state of being (1 Tim. 2:2), thus equivalent to the use of "well-being" or "welfare." An individual can be told to "Go in peace" (e.g., Mark 5:34; Luke 7:50; 8:48; Acts 16:36) or to "be at peace" (Luke 24:36; John 20:19, 21, 26). Paul frequently enjoins "peace" in opening greetings (Rom. 1:7; 1 Cor. 1:3; 2 Cor. 1:2; Gal. 1:3; cf. 1 Pet. 1:2). "Peace" can also refer to an attribute of a relationship with God (Acts 10:36; Rom. 5:1; 8:6; 15:13; Phil. 4:7; cf. Eph. 6:15). The Greek terms also include the absence of, or contrast with, war and interpersonal violence (Matt. 5:9; Luke 14:32; Rom. 12:18; Jas. 3:18). If the proclamation of "peace" in early Christian preaching is taken, on occasion, to refer to the messianic age of peacefulness as opposed to present realities of warfare and suffering, then the connection to Hebraic notions of peace as "absence of war" is even clearer (Acts 10:36; Rom. 10:15; Col. 3:15). Thus, the somewhat limited meaning of the Greek terms should not suggest that the late Hebrew notion of nonviolence is absent from NT ethical discourse. NT conceptions must also take into consideration the entire ethical context of peacefulness and peacemaking in the teachings of Jesus and the practice of the early Church. For this reason, any discussion of peace that is exclusively based on a lexical analysis, particularly in the NT, is inadequate to a full appreciation of either the biblical concept or the ethic of peace.

Whether resulting from the impossibility of a Hebrew military presence in the sociopolitical circumstance of subordination under the Assyrian, Babylonian, Persian, and Hellenistic rulers, or whether to be attributed to the increasingly ironic visions of the messianic age, late biblical teaching tends toward the praise of a wise restraint (Sir. 41:14; 44:6) and nonviolent piety (Daniel, esp. 11:33-34, against the Maccabean uprising; Joseph in Testament of the Twelve Patriarchs; Taxo in T. Moses 9, cf. antiwar ethos in classical Greek sources) in studied contrast to the period of the Monarchy. Early Christianity thus combines the Davidic royal themes with the equally messianic expectations of an age of peace where swords are made into plowshares. The resulting image in Matthew and Luke, particularly, is a "militant nonviolent" Messiah — both Davidic and unarmed, and thus consistent with Jesus' teaching to "love enemies" (Matt. 5:44) and "put away swords" (26:52). This ironic combination results further in Pauline imagery of "weapons" of the spirit, where the "war" is "not against blood and flesh" (Eph. 6:10-17; drawing on Isa. 59:17; cf. spiritual battle in Rev. 19, etc.). The apocalyptic context of early Christian nonviolence is unmistakable, and clearly relates to themes such as the angelic battles in Dan. 7–12 and at Qumran. Prohibitions against even killing in the military are widely documented in the first three centuries of Christianity, and these prohibitions also draw from this Hebraic and early Christian interpretive tradition. Such Hebraic traditions of peacefulness and nonviolence are also discernible in early rabbinic teaching as well, most notably in the teachings of the 1st-century C.E. rabbinic teacher Yohanan ben Zakkai.

Bibliography. S. S. Schwarzschild, "Shalom," in *The Challenge of Shalom,* ed. M. Polner and N. Goodman (Philadelphia, 1994), 16-25; J. H. Yoder, *The Politics of Jesus,* 2nd ed. (Grand Rapids, 1994).

DANIEL L. SMITH-CHRISTOPHER

PEACE OFFERING

A covenant meal which served to affirm the relationship between the worshipper, God, and the community of believers. The name derives from Heb. *šālôm,* though "sacrifice of well-being" is also appropriate (so NRSV).

Like all other animal offerings, the animal to be sacrificed, male or female, must be unblemished, and could be a cow, bull, sheep, or goat (Lev. 3). The blood and fat of the sacrificial animal are reserved for God (Lev. 3:16-17). The right thigh of the animal is reserved for the particular priest who officiates at the sacrifice, while the other priests will be given the breast (Lev. 7:30-36). The worshipper bringing the offering receives the rest of the animal.

Three categories of peace offering are attested: thanksgiving, votive, or freewill. A thanksgiving offering differs from the freewill and votive offerings in that it is to include cakes of unleavened bread, in addition to the sacrificial animal (Lev. 7:12-14). The votive offering is given for repayment of a vow (Lev. 27), while a freewill offering is not limited to any special occasion. The meat and cakes of a thanksgiving offering must be eaten within the day of the offering, while the meat of the votive or freewill offering could be eaten the following day (Lev. 7:15-16).

HEMCHAND GOSSAI

PEARL

A dense spherical concretion of aragonite or calcite, deposited about a foreign particle by various marine and freshwater mollusks. Pearls are usually white or light-colored, and have a nacreous luster. Heb. *pĕnînîm* is translated either as pearls or corals. Pearl refers to the third of three precious stones (the first is coral) which are not valuable enough to purchase wisdom (Job 28:18).

Pearls (Gk. *margarítēs*) were very valuable, and so not to be thrown before swine (Matt. 7:6), but it may be worth selling all to acquire one of great value (13:45-46). Wealthy women wear pearls, but proper Christian women are to be discreet and not wear such valuables (1 Tim. 2:9), as does the woman on the scarlet beast in John's vision (Rev. 17:4). The merchants of earth weep when there is no longer anyone to buy their goods, which include pearls, and mourn the loss of the city clothed in such (Rev. 18:12, 16). When the heavenly Jerusalem emerges, each of its 12 gates is a single pearl (Rev. 21:21). MARTHA JEAN MUGG BAILEY

PEASANTRY

In the anthropological sense, a class of rural cultivators whose surpluses were exploited by the dominant class(es). Characterized as autonomous/independent and conservative/traditional, they embody the transition and contradiction between two opposing types of social formation: "feudalism" and the nation-state. Because written sources, including the Bible, are the product of the scribal class as a subsidiary of the royal court, the peasantry is largely undocumented.

The agrarian basis of Israelite life was characterized by a combination of grain-farming, stock-breeding, and cultivation of vine and tree crops. The Israelite farmer produced and lived off his varied yield: grain (wheat and to a lesser extent, barley); milk, meat, and skins of sheep and goats; and olive oil, figs, and wine from his orchard and vineyard. Some products were used in trade and barter for needed materials such as tools. In semiarid Israel, with variable rainfall and few perennial rivers, famine and want remained a constant threat (Gen. 12:10; 26:1; 41:56; 47:4, 13; Ruth 1:1; 2 Sam. 21:1; 1 Kgs. 18:2; 2 Kgs. 6:25; 25:3). Farming was a family enterprise, with all members performing the various daily chores.

The Israelite house, typified by the pillared multi-roomed house with a courtyard, was as much an agricultural facility as it was living space for the family. Large storage jars filled with grain, wine, and oil would likely have been stored in several of the rooms, along with other ceramics and tools. Animals may have been stabled within the house during the night. The courtyard often served as a work area where agricultural installations were found, and also as an outdoor pen for animals.

Archaeology and biblical accounts suggest that much of the population lived in small villages or cities. Heb. *pĕrāzôn* (Judg. 5:7, 11) probably represents the inhabitants of unfortified villages in the open country surrounding walled cities (cf. Esth. 9:19; Ezek. 38:11); in time of warfare they were permitted refuge within the walls in exchange for service as warriors (cf. Hab. 3:14; Heb. *przw*). Some scholars propose a peasant revolt model for the Israelite conquest.

Bibliography. O. Borowski, *Agriculture in Iron Age Israel* (Winona Lake, 1987); M. Broshi and I. Finkelstein, "The Population of Palestine in Iron Age II," *BASOR* 287 (1992): 47-60; B. Rosen, "Subsistence Economy in Iron Age I," in *From Nomadism to Monarchy*, ed. I. Finkelstein and N. Na'aman (Washington, 1994), 339-51; Y. Shiloh, "The Four-Room House: Its Situation and Function in the Israelite City," *IEJ* 20 (1970): 180-90; L. Stager, "The Archaeology of the Family in Ancient Israel," *BASOR* 260 (1985): 1-35; E. R. Wolf, *Peasants* (Englewood Cliffs, 1966).

CAREY WALSH/ALLEN C. MYERS

PEDAHEL (Heb. *pĕḏah'ēl*)

A leader of the tribe of Naphtali who helped Moses divide the land of Canaan (Num. 34:28).

PEDAHZUR (Heb. *pĕḏâṣûr*)

The father of Gamaliel (**1**), who led Manasseh in the wilderness journeys (Num. 1:10; 2:20; 7:54, 59; 10:23).

PEDAIAH (Heb. *pĕḏāyâ, pĕḏāyāhû*)

1. The maternal grandfather of Jehoiakim, king of Judah (2 Kgs. 23:36).

2. A son of King Jeconiah/Jehoiachin of Judah; father of Zerubbabel (1 Chr. 3:18-19). Elsewhere his brother Shealtiel is given as the father of Zerubbabel (e.g., Ezra 3:2, 8; Neh. 12:1; Hag. 1:1, 12, 14; Matt. 1:12; Luke 3:27).

3. The father of Joel, who was the chief officer of the half-tribe of Manasseh (1 Chr. 27:20).

4. The son of Parosh; one of the workers who repaired the wall of the city opposite the Water Gate (Neh. 3:25-26).

5. One of the men who stood at Ezra's left hand as he read the book of the law in the square before the Water Gate (Neh. 8:4; cf. 1 Esdr. 9:44).

6. A Benjaminite living in postexilic Jerusalem (Neh. 11:7).

7. One of three Levites appointed to administer the temple tithes (Neh. 13:13). C. MACK ROARK

PEKAH (Heb. *peqaḥ*)

King of Israel ca. 735-732 B.C.E. Identified as the "son of Remaliah," Pekah overthrew Pekahiah, whom he served as officer (2 Kgs. 15:25) and from whom he may have usurped also his throne-name. It is likely that Pekah represented an anti-Assyrian movement that sought independence from the heavy tribute exacted as payment to Tiglath-pileser III by Pekahiah's father, Menahem (2 Kgs. 15:19).

Pekah formed an alliance with Rezin of Syria against Assyria. 2 Kgs. 16:5-20 (cf. Isa. 7:1-9) reports that this coalition attacked Jerusalem in order to depose Ahaz of Judah and place the "son of Tabeel" (whose name suggests an Aramean) on the Judean throne. 2 Chr. 28:5-7 describes a massive slaughter and plunder. As a response, Ahaz appealed to Assyria for help (2 Kgs. 16:7; 2 Chr. 28:16). This led to the fall of Damascus to Assyria in 732, the loss of much of Gilead and Galilee

(2 Kgs. 15:29), and the overthrow of Pekah by Hoshea (v. 30), which, according to Assyrian annals, was instigated by Tiglath-pileser himself.

Pekah's exact regnal years are part of the very difficult chronology of this period. According to 2 Kgs. 15:27 he reigned 20 years, which cannot fit between a *terminus a quo* in the early 730s and a *terminus ad quem* of 732/731 when Hoshea took the throne. It is quite possible that Pekah actually controlled a large part of Gilead as a rival to Menahem and was taken into Pekahiah's court as an effort to consolidate territory. This strategy backfired when Pekah took control with "fifty of the Gileadites" and quickly (re?)-established contact with Rezin of Syria, which may indicate his previous leadership east of Samaria. The numeration of his 20 years would then include at least 10-15 years before he became king in Samaria.

Bibliography. J. H. Hayes and P. K. Hooker, *A New Chronology for the Kings of Israel and Judah* (Atlanta, 1988); E. R. Thiele, *The Mysterious Numbers of the Hebrew Kings,* rev. ed. (Grand Rapids, 1994). ANDREW H. BARTELT

PEKAHIAH (Heb. *pĕqaḥyâ*)
King of Israel for two years (ca. 737-735 B.C.E.) following his father Menahem (2 Kgs. 15:23). Pekahiah apparently continued the pro-Assyrian policies of his father, and he was soon overthrown by Pekah (2 Kgs. 15:25), likely as a response to the heavy tribute exacted from Israel as payment to Assyria.

No details are known of Pekahiah's reign other than the formulaic negative description of 2 Kgs. 15:24. His short reign would suggest that he was a weaker ruler than his father, and the usurper Pekah is identified as one of his own officers. The inability of any king of Israel to hold a dynasty after that of Jehu (2 Kgs. 15:12) reflects the chaos that followed the rise of the Neo-Assyrian Empire and led to the fall of Samaria in 722. ANDREW H. BARTELT

PEKOD (Heb. *pĕqôḏ;* Akk. *puqûdu*)
An Aramean tribe inhabiting the plain E of the lower (southern) Tigris River. Recorded among the conquests of various Assyrian kings, Pekod is associated with Babylonia in the oracles of Jeremiah (Jer. 50:21; cf. NRSV mg "Punishment") and Ezekiel (Ezek. 23:23).

PELAIAH (Heb. *pĕlāyâ*)
1. A son of Elioenai and descendant of David (1 Chr. 3:24).

2. A Levite who helped interpret the Book of the Law for the people as Ezra read it (Neh. 8:7). He was among the participants in the sealing of the covenant under Nehemiah (Neh. 10:10[MT 11]).

PELALIAH (Heb. *pĕlalyâ*)
An ancestor of Adaiah, a priest during Nehemiah's time (Neh. 11:12).

PELATIAH (Heb. *pĕlāṭyâ, pĕlāṭyāhû*)
1. A descendant of David and the first son of Hananiah; possibly the grandson of Zerubbabel (1 Chr. 3:21).

2. One of the sons of Simeonite Ishi. A captain during the reign of Hezekiah, king of Judah (727-698 B.C.), he drove out a group of Amalekites on Mt. Seir and settled there (1 Chr. 4:42).

3. A postexilic leader in Jerusalem who signed the covenant under Nehemiah (Neh. 10:22[MT 23]).

4. The son of Benaiah (Ezek. 11:1, 13). He was a corrupt Judean leader who died after Ezekiel cast judgment upon him. CAROL J. DEMPSEY

PELEG (Heb. *peleḡ;* Gk. *Phalek*)
A son of Eber; an ancestor of Abraham (Gen. 10:25; 11:16-19; 1 Chr. 1:19-25) and, by Luke's reckoning, Jesus (Luke 3:35). The etymological remark that "in his days the earth was divided (Heb. *plg*)" (Gen. 10:25; 1 Chr. 1:19) may refer to the dispersion of mankind following the building of the tower of Babel (Gen. 11:8-9), or perhaps to irrigation practices (cf. Akk. *palgu,* "canal") or a form of geographical or political organization associated with his descendants.

PELET (Heb. *peleṭ*)
1. A Calebite, son of Jahdai (1 Chr. 2:47).

2. A Benjaminite warrior, one of the two sons of Azmaveth who joined David at Ziklag (1 Chr. 12:3).

PELETH (Heb. *peleṯ*)
1. A Reubenite, the father of On, who participated in Korah's rebellion (Num. 16:1). The name should probably be Pallu (Num. 26:5, 8).

2. One of the two sons of Jonathan, a descendant of Jerahmeel of the tribe of Judah (1 Chr. 2:33).

PELETHITES (Heb. *pĕlēṯî*)
Part of King David's personal bodyguard and mercenary force (2 Sam. 8:18; 20:23; 1 Chr. 18:17), like the Cherethites recruited when David was stationed at Ziklag (1 Sam. 27). The Pelethites and Cherethites formed an effective, cohesive fighting force in David's military during all of his campaigns and suppressing of rebellions (2 Sam. 15:18; 20:7; 1 Kgs. 1:38, 44). Since they were so closely identified with the Cherethites, it is generally thought that they too were of Aegean origin, but there is little supportive evidence.

BRUCE W. GENTRY

PELLA (Gk. *Péll*a)
A city in Transjordan (207206), modern Tabaqat Faḥil (from Sem. *Piḥil[um],* occurring in Egyptian texts as early as 1800 B.C.), 11 km. (7 mi.) SE of Scythopolis/Beth-shean and 8 km. (5 mi.) E of the Jordan River. It was prominent in the Roman period as a city of the Decapolis (Pliny *Nat. hist.* 5, 74). The city received the name Pella in the Hellenistic period, from the Macedonian home of Alexander the Great. Following a brief period of occupation in the Late Chalcolithic period (Pre-Pottery

Neolithic and Pottery Neolithic sherds [8th-5th millennia] have also been found on the main tell), Pella's history extends from the Bronze Age Egyptian era (e.g., tombs on the north, east, and south) into Late Hellenistic (destroyed by Alexander Jannaeus) and Roman times (Pompey's conquest, 63 B.C.), through its zenith in the Byzantine era, and on into the Islamic periods.

Archaeological excavations at Pella have uncovered the West Church complex and considerable burial remains from the 17th century B.C. to the 6th century A.D., excavated from the slope E of the 400 m. (1312 ft.)-long main tell. Also uncovered are a civic complex, extending from the low southern slope of the main tell and on down into the wadi; a complex composed of an *odeon* and bath of the Early Roman period; a Byzantine church; an East Church; and a Mamluk mosque. The city, which was already in decline in Late Byzantine times, finally collapsed in the earthquake of A.D. 747.

Bibliography. A. W. McNicoll, R. H. Smith, and J. B. Hennessy, *Pella in Jordan,* 1: *1979-1981* (Canberra, 1982); McNicoll et al., *Pella in Jordan,* 2: *1982-1985* (Sydney, 1992); R. H. Smith, *Pella of the Decapolis,* 1: *1967* (Wooster, 1973); Smith and L. P. Day, *Pella of the Decapolis,* 2: *1979-1981* (Wooster, 1989).

W. HAROLD MARE

PELONITE (Heb. *pĕlōnî*)
A gentilic designating Helez and Ahijah, two of David's Mighty Men (1 Chr. 11:27, 36; 27:10). The term probably arises from separate errors; Helez is called "the Paltite" at 2 Sam. 23:26, and Ahijah is called "Eliam son of Ahithophel the Gilonite" at v. 34.

PELUSIUM (Gk. *Pēlusion*)
An Egyptian border fortress located at Tell el-Faramâ in the northeastern corner of the Delta on the defunct Pelusiac branch of the Nile, ca. 29 km. (18 mi.) W of the Suez Canal and ca. 3 km. (2 mi.) inland. Ezek. 30:15 describes the city as a stonghold of Egypt (cf. v. 16). Strabo (*Geog.* 27.1.24) suggests that Pelusium was a seaport with access to the Mediterranean through the Pelusiac branch of the Nile. Herodotus (*Hist.* 2.14) was the first to name the site *(Pēlousios).* Strabo indicates the name was derived from Gk. *pēlós,* "mud," because of the marsh area to the west and south of the city. The earliest mentions of Pelusium (Egyp. *Snw;* cf. Heb. *sin*) are in the records of the Old Kingdom as a wine-producing area and later in those of the New Kingdom as an important military outpost (cf. Josephus *Ag. Ap.* 1. 274, 291, 302). Herodotus (*Hist.* 2.141) describes the defeat of Sennacherib's army by the Egyptians at Pelusium as helped by fieldmice who ate the quivers, bows, and handles of the Assyrians' shields (cf. 2 Kgs. 18). Rameses in the route of the Exodus was once thought to be located at Pelusium, but that identification has been abandoned.

Bibliography. J. Baines and J. Malik, *Atlas of Ancient Egypt* (New York, 1980); A. Sneh and T. Weissbrod, "Nile Delta: The Defunct Pelusiac Branch Identified," *Science* 180 (1973): 59-61.

LAWRENCE A. SINCLAIR

PENIEL (Heb. *pĕnî'ēl*) (also PENUEL)
The name ("face of God") given the place where Jacob wrestled with a divine being and "saw God face to face" and yet survived (Gen. 32:30[MT 31]). Elsewhere the name occurs as Penuel.

PENINNAH (Heb. *pĕninnâ*)
One of Elkanah's two wives. Because she had borne children, she taunted Elkanah's other wife Hannah, who was barren (1 Sam. 1:2-6).

PENNY
One of two Roman bronze coins: the *quadrans* (Gk. *kodrn̄tēs;* Matt. 5:26; Mark 12:42), representing one sixty-fourth of a denarius, and the *as* (Gk. *assárion;* Matt. 10:29; Luke 12:6), one sixteenth of a denarius.

PENTAPOLIS
The Five Cities of the plain/valley (Wis. 10:6), who rebelled against Chedorlaomer (Gen. 14) and four of which were destroyed because of their corruption (19:24-29). According to Philo, the cities represent the five senses (*De Abrahamo* 147). Another pentapolis was the league of five Philistine cities (Josh. 13:3; cf. 1 Sam. 7:7).

PENTATEUCH
The first five books (Gk. *pénta teúchos*) of the Bible, the Torah (Heb. "law, instruction"). In antiquity these books were ascribed to Mosaic authorship (e.g., 4QMMT C.10; Josephus *Ag. Ap.* 1.39; Luke 24:44), hence the traditional designation, Five Books of Moses. The content of these books comprises the history of the world from creation to the dispersal of nations (Gen. 1–11), and the history of Israel from Abraham to the death of Moses (Gen. 12–Deut. 34). The extended crescendo of the work is the covenant between Yahweh and Israel at Mt. Sinai/Horeb, which comprises Exod. 19–Num. 10 and which is recapitulated in Deut. 4–26. The largest part of the Pentateuch consists of the stipulations of the covenant.

The modern study of the Pentateuch has concentrated on the history of its literary composition, with increasing attention in recent years to methods of comprehending its final form. The textual transmission of the Pentateuch has also seen increasing attention due to the discovery of the Dead Sea Scrolls. This article will explore the dominant scholarly models in the study of the Pentateuch, while cautioning the reader that other models have been proposed, but which have not been shown to accommodate the data as comprehensively.

Textual Transmission

The study of the Dead Sea Scrolls fragments of pentateuchal books indicates that the traditional Hebrew text (MT) is a faithful reproduction of one of the text-types in circulation in the Hasmonean and Herodian period. The Samaritan Pentateuch and the Greek LXX appear to belong to two other text-types, though all three text-types are closely related and descend from a single textual ancestor. It is unclear whether other text-types existed and the extent to which mixing among text-types has affected the surviving texts.

Although all pentateuchal texts descend from a common ancestor, there is evidence that some sections were inserted, revised, or expanded after the three major text-types separated. The most extensive revision, amounting to a new edition, occurs in the account of the construction of the tabernacle in Exod. 35–40. The LXX contains a shorter text of this account, in which numerous items occur in a different sequence than the account in the Masoretic (and Samaritan) Text. It has been cogently argued that the LXX preserves an earlier stage of this text, which was subsequently revised and expanded in the edition preserved in the Masoretic and Samaritan texts. One important implication of this case of textual expansion is that the type of literary activity attributed to the sources and editors of the Pentateuch is detectable in some instances in the textual history of the Pentateuch. This result substantiates to some extent the methods by which scholars have explored the literary history of the Pentateuch.

Literary Sources

The Pentateuch is composed of a number of different literary sources that have been combined in a series of redactions. The primary literary sources are identified as J (Yahwist), E (Elohist), P (Priestly source), and D (Deuteronomist). The series of redactions by which these sources were combined are referred to as R^{JE}, R^{JEP}, and R^{JEPD}. While it is difficult to set absolute dates on the compositions and redactions, it is possible within reasonable bounds to determine relative dates, as several of the sources appear to be directly influenced by their predecessors. The clearest case of literary dependency is the reliance of D on R^{JE}, as D quotes from and expands upon this work in many instances, both in legal and narrative sections. Hence D, composed in the main by the late 7th century B.C.E. (the era of Josiah), provides a *terminus ad quem* for the date of J, E, and R^{JE}. It is possible that the "book of the Torah" that Ezra reads to the public in Neh. 8 is the Pentateuch in final or near-final form (ca. 458).

The use of literary sources in the composition of the Pentateuch is explicit in Num. 21:14-15, where a verse is quoted from the "Scroll of Yahweh's Wars," and in Gen. 5:1, which refers to the "Scroll of Adam's Genealogy." Other than these instances the presence of diverse sources must be inferred by internal criteria, including the following:

1. *Doublets.* There are roughly 25 occasions in the pentateuchal narrative when a story is told in two or more versions (e.g., Gen. 12:10-20; 20:1-18; cf. 26:6-11). Often these versions contradict each other in details. There are more than 50 occasions where a law is given in two or more versions, where one often expands or revises the other (e.g., Lev. 11:1-47; Num. 14:3-20).
2. *Terminology.* Different sections of the Pentateuch have consistently different terminology for certain names, places, and ordinary items of vocabulary. The different sets of terminology consistently correspond to the different sets of doublets.
3. *Narrative continuity.* Sections isolated by the correspondences of doublets and terminology often connect with each other to create a more coherent narrative continuity than that possessed by the composite text. For example, the details of the Flood narrative in Gen. 6–9 are more intelligible when read as two parallel versions of the Flood (J and P). The rebellion of Dathan, Abiram, and Korah in Num. 16 is more intelligible when separated into its constituent stories (Dathan and Abiram is J; Korah is P; note that Deut. 11:6 knows only the J version). God's revelations of the name Yahweh to Moses in Exod. 3 (E) and 6:2-8 (P) are intelligible when separated from each other and from the J source, where Enosh is the first to call on the name of Yahweh (Gen. 4:26). There are numerous such instances.
4. *Theology.* Different sources of the Pentateuch, each marked by distinctive doublets, terminology, and narrative continuity, have different theologies. Concepts of God, the relationship between God and humans, and issues of free will and ethical ideals differ considerably among the pentateuchal sources. Whereas J's God is fallible and sometimes changes his mind, as in the Flood story (compare Gen. 6:5-8 with 8:21), and his human characters have free will (e.g., Gen. 3:6), E's and P's God is the author of human events in which humans are often the unwitting actors (for E, Gen. 20:6; 45:5-8; for P, Exod. 7:3). In P God's numinous presence in the tabernacle is the culmination of creation and the mediator between humans and God (Exod. 29:42-46; 40:33-34; cf. Gen. 2:1-3), whereas in D it is God's word and the tablets of his law that mediate between human and divine (Deut. 5:22-33; 10:1-5). In many respects the various sources are arguing among themselves on crucial issues of religious theory and practice.

Unity and Diversity

The series of redactions of the pentateuchal sources created a composite text that possesses a unique character. Each of the versions of sacred history, when combined together, takes on a new character as commentary, development, and counterpoint to the other versions. Thus God's compassionate nature in J, emphasized in his title "Yahweh, a compassionate and merciful God" (Exod. 34:6), provides a counterbalance to the juristic quality of God in P. The corporeality of J's God walking about in the garden (Gen. 3:8) or eating with Abraham (18:8) is balanced by the invisibility of God in D (Deut. 4:12-15). The virtue of absolute obedience to God in E (Gen. 22) is balanced by the virtue of personal ethical commitment, even where it may conflict with God, in J (18:23-32). Human free will, with its inherent responsibilities and consequences, dominant in J and D, is counterbalanced by God's providential predestination in E (Gen. 45:5-8; 50:20) and by the divinely ordained periodicity of time, measured by covenants, in P. A wide range of possibilities for living are encompassed by this complex work, enabling in no small measure the ability of the Pentateuch to respond to the religious needs of the faithful over the last two millennia and more. In a very tangible sense the Pentateuch, as a unified diversity, creates a nearly unlimited potential for meaningful interpretation.

Bibliography. J. Blenkinsopp, *The Pentateuch* (New York, 1992); S. R. Driver, *An Introduction to the Literature of the Old Testament*, 6th ed. (Edinburgh, 1897); T. E. Fretheim, *The Pentateuch* (Nashville, 1996); R. E. Friedman, *Who Wrote the Bible?* (New York, 1987).

RONALD S. HENDEL

PENTATEUCH, SAMARITAN

See SAMARITAN PENTATEUCH.

PENTECOST

The Greek name (meaning "50th") for the Israelite Feast of Weeks which celebrated the spring harvest. This feast took place 50 days after the offering of the sheaf of firstfruits at the time of Passover and Unleavened Bread (cf. Lev. 23:9-14). In later Judaism, the festival became associated with the giving of the law and the making of the covenant at Sinai. In Christian history, the day of Pentecost is associated specifically with the descent of the Spirit on the believing community in Jerusalem (Acts 2). At this time, the community began to proclaim the good news of God's activity in the languages of all the nations of the world (Acts 2:1-13). Although the text of Acts fails to make any specific reference to Sinai or the Sinai covenant, it is probable that the writer of Acts understood the descent of the Spirit to mark the sacred beginning of the Christian community in a way that paralleled the sacred origin of the Israelite community at Sinai. As such, Pentecost functions as a celebration of the founding of the Christian community and the beginning of its evangelistic mission.

See WEEKS, FEAST OF.

Bibliography. I. H. Marshall, "The Significance of Pentecost," *SJT* 30 (1977): 347-69.

FRANK H. GORMAN, JR.

PENUEL (Heb. *pĕnûʾēl*) **(PERSON)**

1. A son of Hur, and grandson of the patriarch Judah (1 Chr. 4:4).

2. A son of Shashak of the tribe of Benjamin (1 Chr. 8:25; **K** Peniel).

PENUEL (Heb. *pĕnûʾēl*) **(PLACE)**

The place in Transjordan where Jacob wrestled with a "man" (Gen. 32:22-32[MT 23-33]; cf. Hos. 12:4). Jacob named the spot Peniel (Gen. 32:30[31]), "the face of God." Gideon destroyed a tower built at Penuel because the inhabitants refused to help him pursue the Midianites (Judg. 8:8-9, 17). Jeroboam I later rebuilt the town (1 Kgs. 12:25). The exact location, somewhere between Mahanaim and Succoth, is debated, although many identify it as Tell edh-Dhahab esh-Sherqîyeh (215176) on the Jabbok River (Nahr ez-Zerqā) E of Succoth.

BRENT A. STRAWN

PEOPLE OF THE LAND

Although in some instances a designation for all humanity (i.e., "all the peoples of the earth"), Heb. *ʿam hāʾāreṣ* differs in meaning in texts from the premonarchic through rabbinic eras. In texts referring to the premonarchic era, the term simply signifies the free citizens of the particular locale under discussion (e.g., the Egyptians in Gen. 42:6); here the term appears to exclude slaves and foreigners.

Regarding the monarchic era, the people of the land are involved in the overthrow of wicked Queen Athaliah (2 Kgs. 11:13-20), the transition from the assassinated Amon to King Josiah (21:24), the succession of King Josiah's son Jehoahaz (23:30), and the transition from the leprous King Uzziah to his son Jotham (15:5). The people of the land have been identified variously as the lower social classes, the powerful landed elite, and the free citizenry of the state. There has been particular debate over whether *ʿam hāʾāreṣ* is a *terminus technicus* that refers to a specific body of Judeans.

Ernst Würthwein argued that the term refers to the representatives of the fully enfranchised Judean citizenry. He and other scholars have noted a recurrent struggle in Judean history between the centralizing policies of the Davidic monarchy and the traditional decentralized polity of the old tribal league. This interpretation has led to a loose consensus that the people of the land should be seen in contrast to, and often in opposition to, the royal administration in Jerusalem. They champion a sort of traditional Yahwism which stood as a check against the syncretistic excesses of the royal establishment. Rather than viewing the people of the land as a subset of the traditional Judean citizenry, the best evidence indicates that they should be seen as the free citizenry — *in toto.*

A semantic shift occurs in the postexilic period, when the term takes on a negative aura. It is used — usually in the plural form — to refer to those who opposed the righteous reforms of Ezra and Nehemiah. The *ʿam hāʾāreṣ* are viewed — along with the priests and royalty — as responsible for the catastrophe of the Exile. It is now the returnees, those purified by the Exile, which represent the true congregation in contradistinction to all the "peoples of the land(s)." Note that the plural forms now dominate.

A final shift in meaning occurs in postbiblical rabbinic texts. There the term means the ignorant, nonobservant transgressors of the Torah. They are to be seen in contrast to the revered scholars of Torah, who detested the people of the land.

Bibliography. A. H. J. Gunneweg, "עם הארץ — A Semantic Revolution," *ZAW* 95 (1983): 437-40; B. Halpern, *The Constitution of the Monarchy in Israel.* HSM 25 (Chico, 1981), 190-216; E. W. Nicholson, "The Meaning of the Expression **עם הארץ** in the Old Testament," *JSS* 10 (1965): 59-66; A. Oppenheimer, *The ʿAM HA-ARETZ.* ALGHJ 8 (Leiden, 1977); E. Würthwein, *Der ʿamm haʾarez im Alten Testament.* BWANT 4/17[69] (Stuttgart, 1936); S. Zeitlin, "The Am Haarez," *JQR* 23 (1933): 45-61.

LYNN TATUM

PEOR (Heb. *pĕʿôr*)
A mountain of the Abarim range in northwestern Moab, also called Baal-peor because it was the focal point for the worship of a local manifestation of Baal (also known as Baal-peor or simply Peor). Many Israelites fell into apostasy by worshipping the god of this mountain (Num. 25:3, 5, 18; 31:16; Deut. 4:3; Josh. 22:17; Ps. 106:28). It was from this mountain that Balaam attempted to curse Israel.

It had generally been understood that Mt. Peor is located somewhere near Mt. Nebo (Jebel en-Nebu), since the biblical text indicates that Balaam could observe the camp of Israel at Shittim (on the Plain of Moab) from its summit (Num. 23:28; 24:2; 25:1), a vantage point that Nebo also provides. The proximity of these two mountains to each other is further supported by Deut. 34:1-6, which indicates that Moses died on or near Mt. Nebo, but was buried in an unknown location in the valley "opposite Beth-peor." Egeria claimed she could see the prominence of Peor (Fogor) at a site called Agri Specula, located to the "left" of the mountain where the Byzantine church known as the Memorial of Moses stands, "toward the Dead Sea" (i.e., SW of Râs es-Siyagha, the western prominence of Mt. Nebo). Another possibility would be the Mushaqqar ridge immediately N of Siyagha. Indeed, at least two sites on this ridge (220131), Khirbet el-Meḥaṭṭa/Khirbet esh-Sheikj Jayil and Khirbet ʿAyûn Mûsā, have been proposed as candidates for Beth-peor, the cult center for Baal-peor. RANDALL W. YOUNKER

PERAZIM (Heb. *pĕrāṣîm*)**, MOUNT**
A mountain named in Isaiah's oracle against the leaders of Jerusalem (Isa. 28:21).

See BAAL-PERAZIM.

PEREA (Gk. *Peraía*)
A Transjordanian territory extending south-north from Machaerus to Pella, or roughly from the river Arnon (Wadi Mojib) to the Wadi el-Yābis (since Pella was part of the Decapolis and therefore not included), and east-west from Philadelphia (Amman) to the Jordan River (Josephus *BJ* 3.3.3 [46]). In the NT the term occurs only in variant readings of Luke 6:17. It is evidently derived from the phrase "beyond the Jordan" (Gk. *péran toú Iorodanou*), from Heb. *ʿēḇer hayyardēn.*

Following the exile of Jews from this area in 732 B.C. (2 Kgs. 15:29), it was resettled by Gentiles after the conquest of Alexander. The latter threatened a minority of postexilic Jews in Maccabean times (1 Macc. 5:9, 45-54), which led to conquest of the area by Jonathan, expanded upon by John Hyrcanus and Alexander Jannaeus. Perea became an administrative district under Rome ca. 57 B.C. In 20 B.C. it became part of Herod's kingdom and subsequently passed back and forth between his descendants (Antipas, 4 B.C.–A.D. 39; Agrippa I, 39-44; Agrippa II, 54-ca. 100), finally becoming part of the Roman province of Syria. PAUL J. RAY, JR.

PERESH (Heb. *pereš*)
A Manassite, son of Machir and Maacah (1 Chr. 7:16).

PEREZ (Heb. *pereṣ;* Gk. *Pháres*)
A son of Judah and Tamar, the twin brother of Zerah, and an ancestor of David (Gen. 38:29; 46:12) and Jesus (Matt. 1:3; Luke 3:33). He was the eponymous ancestor of the Perezites (Num. 26:20).

PEREZ-UZZA (Heb. *pereṣ ʿuzzāʾ, pereṣ ʿuzzâ*)
The name ("breach of Uzza") given to the place where Uzza was killed by Yahweh after having taken hold of the ark of the covenant to keep it from falling as it was transported to Jerusalem (2 Sam. 6:8; 1 Chr. 13:11). Located somewhere W of Jerusalem, it is perhaps to be identified with the threshing floor of Nacon/Chidon.

PERFECTION
Heb. *tāmîm, šālēm;* Gk. *téleios* and cognates typically mean "complete," "whole," "mature," "unblemished," or "undivided." It is in contexts where the focus is on human or divine disposition that the theological conception of perfection becomes sharpened.

Apart from Matt. 5:48, there is no direct biblical statement that God is by nature perfect. Absent also is any abstract notion of perfection as found in Greek philosophy, though Jewish and Christian philosophical speculation certainly addressed this matter. Christian apologists utilized philosophical categories to describe God's nature, and Philo called God "the perfect" in Greek fashion.

The biblical focus is largely upon that which makes human beings "perfect" in relation to God. In the OT *šālēm* is frequently used with "heart" to describe persons undivided in their exclusive worship of Yahweh (1 Kgs. 8:61; 11:4; 15:3, 14; 1 Chr. 28:9), while *tāmîm* is used of those commanded to be blameless in obedience to God's commands (Deut. 18:13; cf. Gen. 6:9). Frequently in Psalms (e.g., Ps. 119:1; 101:6) and Proverbs (e.g., Prov. 11:20; 28:18) *tāmîm* is used with "walk" to describe blamelessness in obedience to God's law.

In the NT perfection is understood positionally. Christians stand perfect in relation to God as partakers of the divine nature (2 Pet. 1:4). They are given the Spirit and embrace God's wisdom in Christ crucified (1 Cor. 2:6-16) and are enabled to appear before God by virtue of Christ's perfect priestly work (Heb. 7:19; 10:1). Perfection is also understood in terms of maturity, defined as living and growing in the power of the cross and resurrection of Christ (Rom. 12:2; 1 Cor. 2:6; 14:20; Eph. 4:13; Phil. 3:15). Perseverance is thus crucial for progressing in maturity and perfection (Jas. 1:4), and producing this maturity is the goal of Paul's apostolic ministry (Col. 1:28). Perfection also entails an ethical component. This is clear in Matt. 5:48, where believers are commanded to be perfect as God is perfect. The immediate context suggests that the focus of this perfection is love. Believers must love all persons as God loves them. The love of God for humanity, demonstrated in the sacrifice of Christ, is the foundation of the Christian's ability to love God and one another and thereby be perfected in divine love (1 John 2:5; 4:12, 18). The path to perfection is obedience to the commandment to love God and neighbor completely (Mark 12:30-31). Love is the bond through which all other Christian virtues are perfected (Col. 3:14).

Perfection is related to sanctification, suggesting that relative perfection is presently attainable. While absolute sinless perfection is available only in eternity, perfection in the present is a goal worthy of aspiration (Phil. 3:12-15). Paul's dictum in Phil. 3:16 is programmatic: "Only let us live up to what we have already attained" (NIV).

Bibliography. H. K. La Rondelle, *Perfection and Perfectionism* (Berrien Springs, 1971).

JEFFREY S. LAMP

PERFUME

Perfumes, liquid, gelatinous, or dry substances known for their aromatic qualities, play an important part in the economic, social, and religious culture of the ancient, biblical world. Words translated by "perfume" come from the Hebrew root *rāqaḥ*, "to prepare perfume," and are associated with incense and ointment as well. Most perfumes were derivatives of plants, while a few were extracts from animals. Most sources of perfume came to Canaan through trade routes along the Fertile Crescent and include such substances as frankincense and myrrh from Arabia, nard from Nepal, aloes and saffron from India, cinnamon from Sri Lanka, and onycha, derived from a Red Sea mollusk. Trade in perfumes and spices became a significant part of the economy of the ancient Near East and the Greco-Roman world.

Those who manufactured perfumes, called perfumers, were often connected to religious or priestly communities. Exod. 30:37-32; 37:29 describe the scented oils used for anointing the ark of the covenant, and the sacred objects in the tent of meeting. Perfumers extracted essential oils from plants, flowers, and fruits, and used gums, resins, spices, and animal secretions in various recipes. Packaging of perfumes ranged from a simple cloth satchel to elaborate alabaster jars and perfume boxes. Oils were used to anoint people as well as objects, while dry mixtures were burned as incense at sacrifices and in sanctuaries.

In addition to community religious ceremonies, perfumed oils and balms were used for a variety of medical purposes. In desert climates, ointments protected the skin against the harsh, arid conditions, while oils were poured into wounds to facilitate closure and stem infections. Myrrh mixed with wine was given to Jesus as an anesthetic during his crucifixion (John 19:39). Further, many ancient Near Easterners used perfumes as part of their death and funeral rituals, in embalming or cremation.

Perfumes were also used in social, secular situations. In the Greco-Roman world, individuals used scented oils after bathing or participation in athletic contests, often to counteract body odors. Perfumed sachets were worn or carried with clothes for personal use or were chewed to sweeten one's breath. Perfumes were used by both men and women for cosmetic purposes, to increase attractiveness and demonstrate social or economic status. Pliny notes that guests, arriving for dinner parties, had their hands and feet bathed and perfumed before coming into a banquet hall. The anointing of Jesus at Bethany (Mark 14:3) may indicate this practice among 1st-century C.E. Jews, and was seen as an act of hospitality and kindness. Perfumes were associated with the pleasure of life and were used to give fragrance to furniture such as sofas and wedding beds.

JOSEPH A. CORAY

PERGA (Gk. *Pérgē*)

A prominent Greco-Roman city located near the Cestrus River in the region of Pamphylia (cf. Strabo *Geog.* 14.4.2), ca. 12 km. (8 mi.) N of the Mediterranean coast in southern Asia Minor. Important roads led north from the city into the interior of Asia Minor. The prosperity of the city (whose patron deity was Artemis) can still be witnessed in the impressive architectural remains, which include a stadium, theater, Roman baths, and a gymnasium dedicated to the emperor Claudius.

After preaching on Cyprus during his first missionary journey, Paul sailed from Paphos to Perga, through which he passed on his way to Pisidian Antioch in Galatia. At this point John Mark left his company (Acts 13:13-14). At the end of this journey, Paul and Barnabas returned to Perga to preach before sailing from the nearby coastal city of Attalia back to Syrian Antioch (Acts 14:24-26).

Bibliography. D. Magie, *Roman Rule in Asia Minor.* 2 vols. (1950, repr. New York, 1975); A. M. Mansel and A. Akarca, *Excavations and Researches at Perge* (Ankara, 1949).

PHILIP A. HARLAND

PERGAMUM (Gk. *Pérgamos, Pérgamon*)

A city in western Asia Minor listed among the seven churches of Rev. 1:11 (also 2:12-17). Located 24 km. (15 mi.) from the Aegean Sea and 113 km. (70 mi.) N of Smyrna, Pergamum was a famous and important city that enjoyed a rich history from the 3rd century B.C. to the 4th century A.D. Its acropolis was located strategically atop a steep cliff nearly 396 m. (1300 ft.) above the Caicus River, giving it an excellent view of the Bay of Lesbos. Ancient Greek kingdoms based their power here as a means of controlling vast regions and as a refuge during assault. With the conquest of Alexander the Great (334 B.C.) Pergamum rose in prominence as a major military and political center.

Rome conquered the area in 133 B.C. Pergamum became the chief city of Asia, locus of the beginnings of the imperial cult in the east and a continued center of intellectual and economic influence. In 88 B.C. Pergamum joined a revolt against Rome, prompting Antony to give its beloved library to rival Alexandria. Since 350 Pergamum was also known for its worship of Asklepios, god of healing, and many came to visit its *asclepium*, or healing sanctuary.

When John wrote the book of Revelation, Pergamum had been a major seat of government for 400 years. Evidence of a Jewish community can be found in literary sources. The Christian church probably developed here during Paul's two-year stay in Ephesus. John's letter commends the church for its perseverance — particularly in light of its life "where Satan's throne is" (Rev. 2:13), perhaps a reference to the temple of Zeus or Asklepios. John also warns against "the Nicolaitans" (Rev. 2:15), apparently a sect that had urged a compromise with paganism (cf. 2 Pet. 2:15; Jude 11).

Examples of the city's magnificence are its 12 m. (40 ft.) high altar to Zeus, its numerous temples, theater, enlarged agora, and library (200 thousand scrolls), making it an important intellectual center in antiquity.

Bibliography. E. M. Blaiklock, *Cities of the New Testament* (London, 1965), 103-6; C. Foss, "Archaeology and the 'Twenty Cities' of Byzantine Asia," *AJA* 81 (1977): 469-86; C. Hemer, *The Letters to the Seven Churches of Asia in Their Local Setting.* JSNTSup 11 (1986, repr. Grand Rapids, 2000); J. McRay, *Archaeology and the New Testament* (Grand Rapids, 1991). GARY M. BURGE

PERIDA (Heb. *pĕrîḏāʾ*) (also PERUDA)
The head of a family or guild of Solomon's servants who returned from exile with Zerubbabel (Neh. 7:57). In the parallel account (Ezra 2:55) the name occurs as Peruda.

PERIZZITES (Heb. *pĕrizzî*)
A population group occupying Palestine from patriarchal times, encountered by the emerging nation of Israel. A plausible etymology links Perizzite to Heb. *pĕrāzôn,* "rural person." In such case, the Perizzites would originally have been country folks as opposed to city dwellers (Judg. 1:4-5). The tremendous increase in the number of small villages in the Cisjordanian highlands by the Iron Age I period may relate to the existence of the Perizzites and their name. Apparently the term Perizzite eventually shifted from primarily designating a social category to more often indicating an ethnic group — specifically in the lists of pre-Israelite peoples (e.g., Neh. 9:8). Josh. 11:3 locates the Perizzites among the highlands of Canaan, while 17:15 places with greater precision this people's central home in the forested hill country of Samaria, where Ephraim and Manasseh later settled.

Bibliography. E. C. Hostetter, *Nations Mightier and More Numerous: The Biblical View of Palestine's Pre-Israelite Peoples.* BIBAL DS 3 (Fort Worth, 1995), 80-83. EDWIN C. HOSTETTER

PERSECUTION
Suffering imposed on persons or groups, a common theme throughout the Bible (e.g., Esth. 3:6). God's servants frequently faced opposition and hostility (1 Kgs. 18:13; Matt. 23:34-37; 1 Thess. 2:14-15). The psalmists struggled with hostile pursuers and sought divine deliverance (Ps. 7:1, 5[MT 2, 6]; 31:15[16]; 69:26-29[27-30]). The prophets also wrestled with opposition (cf. Acts 7:52) and prayed for vindication (Jer. 15:15; 17:18).

The intertestamental period saw intense suffering inflicted by Antiochus IV Epiphanes. The horrible Maccabean martyrdoms, vividly described in 2 Macc. 6–7, challenged Jews and Christians to be faithful.

The NT contains frequent references to persecution (Mark 10:30; Luke 11:49-51; Gal. 6:12). Jesus was persecuted (Luke 4:29; John 5:16) and suffered mocking, beating, and crucifixion. He told his followers to expect similar treatment (Matt. 10:23; 24:9; Mark 13:9; Luke 21:12; John 15:20; 16:2). These occasions were not to be feared, for the Holy Spirit would give them courage (Luke 12:11-12; 21:15; Acts 1:8).

Persecution continued in the early Church (Acts 5:17-42; 8:1; 11:19; 13:50; 14:19; 16:19-24); note the militant pre-Christian activities of Saul of Tarsus (8:3; 9:1-13; 22:4-8; 26:9-15). Herod Agrippa I put James to death (Acts 12:2), Stephen was martyred (7:54–8:1a), and Christians were persecuted by the emperors Nero and Domitian. Nevertheless the Spirit would empower disciples to bear witness in such unpromising circumstances (Acts 2:4; 4:8-13; 6:10; 7:55).

Paul wrote of his shame for having persecuted disciples (1 Cor. 15:9; Gal. 1:13, 23; Phil. 3:6; cf. 1 Tim. 1:13) and counseled Christians to bless those who persecute them (Rom. 12:14; 1 Cor. 4:12-13). Paul declared that the resources he had discovered in Christ enabled believers to cope with any form of persecution (Rom. 8:31-39). He mentioned his own persecutions to encourage them in facing theirs (2 Cor. 1:5-7; 4:8-12; 12:10; cf. 2 Thess. 1:4; 2 Tim. 3:11-12).

1 Peter recalled the example of Christ's suffering to strengthen believers who faced persecution and social ostracism (1 Pet. 2:18-25; 3:13-18; 4:1-2, 12-19). Similarly, Hebrews reminded readers to take encouragement in facing persecution from the example of Jesus and other heroes of faith (Heb. 12:1-4; 11:4-40). John likewise called Christians to follow Jesus, "the faithful and true witness" (Rev. 1:5; 3:14). Antipas had already suffered martyrdom (Rev. 2:13), and others might face similar persecution. However, they would overcome the demonic forces by using the same spiritual weapons which Christ had used (Rev. 12:11; 17:14; 21:7).

Persecution is taken seriously in the Bible, and the righteous are told to expect it (2 Tim. 3:12). Despite its painfulness, persecution can become a means of blessing to those who handle it in the right manner (Matt. 5:10-12; 1 Pet. 4:12-14).

Bibliography. G. Ebel and R. Schippers, "Persecution, Tribulation, Affliction" *NIDNTT* 2 (Grand Rapids, 1976): 805-9; C. G. Kruse, "Afflictions, Trials, Hardships," in *Dictionary of Paul and His Letters,* ed. G. Hawthorne, R. P. Martin, and D. G. Reid (Downers Grove, 1993), 18-20.

ALLISON A. TRITES

PERSEPOLIS (Gk. *Persépolis*)
An Achaemenid royal capital (along with Babylon, Susa, and Ecbatana) until the end of the Achaemenid Empire in 330 B.C. Its Old Persian name was Parsa, meaning "Persian," hence "city of

Portico of the Hall of a Hundred Columns, audience hall of Xerxes I at Persepolis
(Courtesy of the Oriental Institute of the University of Chicago)

the Persians." The modern site is Takht-i Jamshid, located NE of Shiraz in the Marvdasht Plain of the Zagros Mountains. Most of the excavated portion of Persepolis was built from 500 to 460. In particular, Persepolis was the center of ceremonial display for the empire. It must be emphasized, however, that much of the site — including other palatial structures and the nonroyal settlement — has not yet been excavated and would presumably show both earlier and later occupation. The royal tombs at Naqsh-i Rustam, where four Achaemenid rulers were buried, is within 6 km. (3.7 mi.) of Persepolis and must be considered part of the settlement area.

The site of Persepolis as presently known consists of several well-preserved buildings, including a striking number of standing stone columns with capitals in the form of bulls or lions. The site was noted by many early explorers and first excavated by Ernst Herzfeld and Erich Schmidt during the 1930s. Excavation later continued under Iranian directorship. The palace complex is located on a stone platform 14 m. (643 ft.) high and provided with a drainage system. Darius I built a residential palace, an audience hall (Apadana), and a treasury building. Xerxes I built a larger palace and harem, fortification walls including the Gate of All Nations with a double stairway decorated with relief carving, and another audience hall, the Hall of a Hundred Columns. Subsequent construction included a palace of Artaxerxes I and an expansion of the Hall of a Hundred Columns. Many of the buildings were decorated in carved reliefs, notably the stairway to the Apadana. The reliefs depict a variety of scenes, including delivery of tribute from all the provinces ruled by the Achaemenids, as well as rows of soldiers. The ensemble demonstrated the successful unification of the empire and the power of its rulers. Excavations recovered two large groups of tablets: the Fortification tablets and the slightly later Treasury tablets. Written mostly in Elamite, with a minority in Aramaic, they record food disbursements to people of a wide range of statuses.

The Bible mentions Persepolis only once (2 Macc. 9:2), as one of several cities that rebelled successfully against the Seleucid king Antiochus IV (175-164 B.C.). GEOFF EMBERLING

PERSEUS (Gk. *Perséus*)
The last king of Macedonia, successor of Philip V (ca. 212-162 B.C.E.). His perceived aggression precipitated in 171 the Third Macedonian War with Rome. After the battle of Pydna in Thessaly (168), Perseus was removed from power and his kingdom became a Roman province (1 Macc. 8:5; NRSV mg "king of Kittim").

PERSIA (Heb. *pāras;* Gk. *Persís;* O. Pers. *Pārsa*)
An ancient Near Eastern empire which at the height of its power spanned from the borders of India in the east to Ionia in the west. The people themselves called the empire Aryana, from a term in the Zoroastrian scriptures derived from Sanskrit *arya,* "noble" (cf. "Iran," "Aryan").

Geography

The area in which Persia was established is a plateau ca. 777,000 sq. km. (300,000 sq. mi.), consisting of a series of high valleys and dry basins, ca. 900-2500 m. (3000-8000 ft.) above sea level. The plateau is ringed by a variety of mountain ranges (the

Tomb of Cyrus II at Pasargadae (Courtesy of the Oriental Institute of the University of Chicago)

Kurdistan and Zagros on the west, Elburz on the north, and Hindu Kush to the east). To the south, along the Persian Gulf and Gulf of Oman, lie inhospitable plains. Two vast, salt-caked deserts, the Dasht-i-Kavir and Dasht-i-Lut, occupy most of central eastern Persia.

History

Early Period

Archaeological evidence indicates that plants and animals were domesticated at several sites in the Zagros Mountain region as early as 9000 B.C.E. (the "Neolithic Revolution") and that here were formed the earliest village civilizations relying on irrigation agriculture.

The kingdom of Elam, which predated the formation of the Persian Empire, was located in southwestern Iran along the northern coast of the Persian Gulf. It supplied Sumer with such minerals as copper, tin, silver, lead, and alabaster. Precious gems, timber, and horses were also exported from Elam.

Toward the end of the 2nd millennium ethnic groups from south and east of the Caspian Sea entered Elam. This wave of Aryan peoples included Cimmerians, Scythians, Medes, and Persians. By the 9th century the latter two groups had settled in northwest Iran, but they were hemmed in by the power of Urartu, Assyria, Elam, and Babylonia. An inscription of the Assyrian king Shalmaneser III (859-825) includes the first reference to the Medes (Akk. *Madai*) and Persians *(Parsu)*, whom he deported in large numbers in 837. These peoples also paid tribute to Tiglath-pileser III (745-727) and Sargon II (721-705).

Attacks by the Assyrians and Urartians in the 7th century forced the Medes to unite, founding a capital at Ecbatana (modern Hamadân). Their leader was Deioces (or Dayakku), who was taken to Assyria in 715 and thence exiled to Hamath in Syria. His successor, Phraortes (Khshathrita), who ruled from 675 to 653, died while his forces conquered the Persians in the southwest. The Medians lived under Scythian rule for 28 years, until Cyaxares (Uvakshatra, 653-585) liberated them. Allied with the Babylonians and Scythians, Cyaxares participated in the siege and destruction of Nineveh. He then concluded a treaty with Babylon and married his granddaughter Amytis to Nabopolassar's son Nebuchadnezzar II (605-562); it was for Amytis that the famed "Hanging Gardens" of Babylon were built.

The Persians gradually settled east of Elam, led by a dynasty founded by Achaemenes (Hakhamanish) ca. 700. His successor Teispes added Anshan to Persian territory; his sons Ariaramnes (Ariyaramna, 640-590) and Cyrus I (Kurash, 640-600) annexed lands in the west. Cambyses I (Kanbujiya, 600-559) married Mandane, daughter of the Median Astyages, who bore him Cyrus II. The Achaemenid dynasty was founded when Cyrus II successfully revolted against Astyages in 549.

Persian Empire

Babylonian preoccupation with westward expansion gave Cyrus II opportunity to add Assyria, Cilicia, Sardis, and the Ionian Greek cities to his realm. Newly acquired lands were organized into satrapies, initially ca. 20 administrative units headed by royal appointees from noble families. King Nabonidus' unpopular decision to remove the images of most of

Xerxes I's Gate of All Nations at Persepolis, featuring massive winged bulls
(Courtesy of the Oriental Institute of the University of Chicago)

the deities of Babylon to the capital paved the way for Cyrus' conquest of Babylonia, and the Persians (aided by disgruntled Babylonians) entered the city on 13 October 539.

In a stroke of diplomatic genius, Cyrus returned the images to their temples and decreed that all subject peoples of the Babylonians return to their homelands (cf. 2 Chr. 36:23; Ezra 1:1-4). Persian rulers were careful to be crowned king of conquered lands in accordance with local custom; the Babylonian "Cyrus cylinder" depicts Cyrus as chosen by Marduk to topple Nabonidus and praises him for not looting the temples in Babylon (*ANET*, 15-16). Cyrus died in battle against the Massagetae on the northeastern frontier in 530.

Cambyses II, Cyrus' eldest son, was quick to continue the expansion of the empire. Egypt, Cyprus, and the Greek islands fell in quick succession, but the Persians were stopped at Nubia. At this juncture the throne was seized by Gaumata ("Pseudo-Smerdis"), a member of the *magi* who masqueraded as Cambyses' younger brother Bardiya ("Smerdis," killed by Cambyses in 526). Revolts broke out in Media, Armenia, and Babylonia. Gaumata hastened to consolidate his position by offering exemptions from military service and taxes, but his rule lasted only six months. Cambyses died under mysterious circumstances, perhaps by suicide, as he returned to Babylon.

Darius I (Daryavaush, 522-486), son of Hystaspes (Vishtāspa) and satrap of Parthia and Hyrcania, took Gaumata prisoner and executed him at Ecbatana in 522. It took Darius two years to quell the revolts around the empire, but by 518 satrapies as distant as Ionia and Egypt acknowledged his rule. Persian troops campaigned as far west as the Danube River, but they were defeated by Greek forces at Marathon in 490. A huge bas relief on a high cliff at Behistun (modern Bisitun) on the Ecbatana-Babylon trade route depicts Darius, under the protection of Ahura Mazda, trampling Gaumata, with nine rebel leaders in attendance; the inscription in Old Persian, Akkadian, and Elamite proved invaluable in deciphering these ancient languages. Subsequently peace prevailed throughout the empire until the first Ionian revolt (500-494), which ended with the destruction of Miletus.

Darius was an able administrator who reorganized the empire into 22 satrapies. A good road network, royal postal service, and the use of Aramaic as the language of government (replacing Elamite) served to promote efficiency. Darius introduced unified systems of taxation, weights and measures, and currency. Trade flourished, banking houses were established, and Darius had a canal constructed linking the Nile River and Red Sea. An opulent new palace was built at Susa in 521 and work was started on the new capital at Persepolis (Parsa) in 518. It was during Darius' reign that reconstruction of the Jerusalem temple finally was undertaken by the returned exiles; when local officials challenged the work, Darius commanded that construction continue (Ezra 5:1–6:15). When Darius died Persia was at the height of its territorial expansion and material wealth. Its borders ranged from the Indus and Jaxartes (Syr Darya) rivers in the east to Egypt and the Aegean in the west, and from the Persian Gulf in the south to the Caspian and Black seas in the north. All Persian kings after Darius were involved in maintaining the size and prestige the empire had attained in his reign.

Formerly viceroy of Babylon, Xerxes I (485-465) ruled Egypt and Babylonia with a heavy hand. In 480 a Persian army, accompanied by ships served by Phoenicians, Egyptians, Ionians, and Cypriotes, moved against Greece. After a temporary delay at Thermopylae, the Persians took Thebes and Athens. However, the reverses they suffered at Salamis, Miletus, Plataea, and Mycale forced Xerxes to relinquish control of all lands beyond Asia Minor. He was assassinated in 465 and succeeded by Artaxerxes I.

During much of his early reign, Artaxerxes was plagued by revolts in Egypt (460-454), encouraged by the Greeks. Other rebellions resulted in the loss of some eastern territories. Peace was restored by the treaty of Callias in 449. Darius II ascended the throne as Greece was rent by the Peloponnesian War. Despite interference by his consort Parysatis, by siding with the Spartans he was able to recapture various Greek cities in Asia Minor. A weak ruler, Artaxerxes II Mnemon (404-359) faced revolt in Egypt that lasted 60 years and involved the Egyptians in anti-Persian activities along with Sparta, Athens, and Cyprus. Artaxerxes made peace with the Greeks in 386, but his subsequent invasion of Egypt was blunted by the skillful defense of Pharaoh Nectanebo I. A brutal but ambitious ruler, Artaxerxes III Ochus (359-338) mounted another expedition against Egypt. Nectanebo II repelled his forces in 351, and the Egyptians continued their tradition of stirring unrest against Persia by supporting a revolt in Phoenicia. Artaxerxes finally defeated the Egyptians in 343, but was murdered in 338 by Bagoas, his vizier and eunuch. His troops defeated by Alexander the Great at Issus, Darius III Codommannus (336-330) fled to Bactria, where he died, the last of the Achaemenid dynasty. Alexander captured Persepolis in February 330 and sent its treasures to Ecbatana.

Post-Achaemenid Persia

Alexander's death in 323 loosened Persia from Greek domination. The Seleucids retained control of the region but briefly. Parthians from eastern Iran established their capital at Ctesiphon (Casiphia) and under the Arsacid dynasty gradually took over the country. The Parthians revived trade in Iran, and served as intermediaries in commerce between the Mediterranean and Far East which was centered in the mid-Euphrates city of Dura-Europus.

Roman absorption of Syria led to several unsuccessful attempts to extend Roman influence into Persia. In 40 B.C.E. the Parthians, who invaded the Roman province of Syria, were considered liberators by the Jews. They placed Antigonus, son of Aristobulus, on Jerusalem's throne (40-37) and gave military support to that city during Titus' siege. Jews and Parthians worked together against Rome during the reigns of Trajan and Hadrian.

The Parthians were succeeded by the Sassanians (223-651 C.E.), who annexed part of northwest India, northern Mesopotamia, and Armenia. In their battles with Rome they once captured the emperor Valerian (260).

Religion

Initially, India and Persia shared a number of deities, as was common throughout the ancient Near East. At some point the god Ahura Mazda was elevated to a supreme position. Other deities included Mithra (Indian Mitra), god of contract and war; Haoma (Soma), personification of an intoxicating drink; Anahita, goddess of rivers and fertility; and Tishtrya, bringer of rain.

In the 6th century B.C.E. the prophet Zarathustra (perhaps "he who drives camels") appeared on the scene. According to Zoroastrian tradition, he enjoyed the patronage of his convert, the local chief Vishtāspa. Zarathustra's teachings, preserved in the Gāthās (the earliest portion of the Avesta), admonish persons to side with good against evil by exercising free choice. Other topics, such as the merits of animal husbandry and cattle breeding, are found in Zarathustra's discourses.

While Zoroastrianism leans toward monotheism in the figure of Ahura Mazda, it contains strong elements of dualism, as *aša*, "truth," stands in opposition to *druj*, "falsehood." How pervasive Zoroastrianism was in the Achaemenid dynasty is unclear, but Ahura Mazda appears in many reliefs and inscriptions.

Bibliography. G. G. Cameron, *History of Early Iran* (1936, repr. Chicago, 1976); J. M. Cook, *The Persian Empire* (New York, 1983); R. N. Frye, *The History of Ancient Iran.* Handbuch der Altertumswissenschaft 3/7 (Munich, 1984); A. T. Olmstead, *History of the Persian Empire* (1948, repr. Chicago, 1959). ROBERT E. STONE, II

PERSIS (Gk. *Persís*)
A Christian in Rome to whom Paul sends his greetings (Rom. 16:12; "the beloved Persis"). The name was common among Roman female slaves.

PERUDA (Heb. *pĕrûḏā'*)
Alternate form of Perida (Ezra 2:55).

PESHIṬTA
The Syriac translation of the Bible. This late Eastern Aramaic rendering is the second oldest of the primary versions and one of the earliest documents of Syrian literature. The word *peshiṭta* (Eastern, Nestorian pronunciation; cf. Jacobite "Peshiṭto") functions as an adjective meaning "simple." The translation was apparently the "simple" or "common version." (Most believe the designation was to distinguish this standard Syriac version from the more sophisticated, annotated Syro-Hexapla.)

It is a matter of debate where and when the translation originated, and why the translation was made and by whom. The consensus is that the Peshiṭta was the work of more than one translator and was produced over an extended period of time, possibly as early as the 1st or 2nd century C.E. Evidence shows that the biblical books were translated individually, and that the translation points to a Hebrew original very close to the MT. Some books exhibit a link with Jewish targumic traditions; others give evidence of

LXX influence. Debate continues as to whether the Peshiṭta is a Jewish or Christian translation.

The value of the Peshiṭta to textual criticism and to the study of textual history has been recognized by scholars since the 16th century. Not only is the Peshiṭta a textual witness in its own right, but Syriac readings of this primary version provide insight into the history of the Hebrew text and Hebrew textual traditions that deviate from the MT.

See Syriac Versions.

Bibliography. P. B. Dirksen, "The Old Testament Peshitta," in *Mikra,* ed. M. J. Mulder. CRINT 2/1 (Philadelphia, 1988), 255-97; Dirksen et al., eds., *The Peshitta: Its Early Text and History.* Monographs of the Peshitta Institute 4 (Leiden, 1988).

Dennis R. Magary

PESTILENCE

In the Bible, pestilence (Heb. *deḇer, māweṯ;* Gk. *loimós; thánatos*) usually refers to divine intervention into human history in the form of human sickness in order to punish human misbehavior. Pestilence is often associated with other calamities (e.g., Exod. 9:3-15; Lev. 26:25; Amos 4:10; Hab. 3:5; Luke 21:11). It also served as a threat to bring about correct human behavior (e.g., Num. 14:12; cf. 16:46).

Although pestilence and plague are often associated in ancient writings, some modern writers argue that this does not mean that the two are interchangeable. Scourges such as bubonic plague, cholera, dysentery, smallpox, and typhoid fever are generally described as "plagues," while "pestilence" is most often associated with sicknesses which result from contaminated water supplies that often accompany the sieging of a city. However, some passages refer to smallpox and bubonic plague as forms of pestilence. It could very well be that antiquity did not make such a distinction between "pestilence" and "plague" (cf. Lat. *pestilentia,* which is related to *pestis,* "plague"). Thomas B. Slater

PETER (Gk. *Pétros*)

Simon bar Jonah, nicknamed Cephas or Peter (Aramaic and Greek for "rock") by Jesus. Since Simon was a common Jewish name and a number of others are mentioned in the Gospels and Acts, the nickname became the common designation for the man, although the Gospels report Jesus often calling him Simon.

Peter was the son of a Galilean fisherman, Jonah (Matt. 16:17) or John (John 21:15), who never appears in the Gospel narratives. Peter and his brother Andrew were themselves fishermen and partners of another pair of brothers, James and John bar Zebedee (Luke 5:10). The Gospels introduce the reader to Peter three different ways: as called by Jesus while fishing (Mark 1:16-17 par.), as called by Jesus through a miraculous catch of fish (Luke 5:1-11), and as a disciple of John the Baptist introduced to Jesus by his brother (John 1:35-42). All three stories agree that Peter became a committed disciple of Jesus. The Synoptics also mention that Jesus later visited Peter's house in Capernaum (Mark 1:29), where he healed Peter's mother-in-law. The picture painted of Peter, then, is that of a somewhat better-off Galilean peasant who was a semi-observant Jew in the eyes of the Pharisees (i.e., he was one of the *'am hā'āreṣ*) and yet religious (or nationalistic) enough to follow Jesus, having perhaps first followed John the Baptist.

Despite, or maybe because of, his humble origins, Peter is pictured as a disciple who was chosen to be one of the Twelve (Mark 3:16 par.; he is on every list of the Twelve), and then one of the inner core of three, a group which excluded his brother Andrew (Mark 5:37; 9:2 par.). All four Gospels record Peter as expressing the Twelve's conviction that Jesus was the Messiah, although they place it in different contexts (Mark 8:29 par.; John 6:68-69). All agree that Peter was present during some of the core events of Jesus' ministry. Futhermore, there is agreement that Jesus predicted that Peter would betray him and that in the courtyard of the high priest's home Peter did in fact three times deny that he knew Jesus. Three of the Gospels place Peter among the disciples during the resurrection appearances, Luke 24:34 agreeing with Paul (1 Cor. 15:5) that Jesus also appeared separately to Peter.

It is obvious that the early Church did not disqualify Peter because of his denial of Jesus, for in both Acts (esp. chs. 1–5) and Paul (Gal. 1:18; 2:1-10) one discovers Peter as an acknowledged central leader of the early Church, along with Jesus' brother James and the bar Zebedee brothers. Yet since Peter had a traveling ministry (again confirmed by both Acts and Paul), Jesus' brother James soon became the main leader of the Jerusalem church. Indeed, Acts 15 (ca. A.D. 49) pictures James as the chief leader even when Peter was present.

Peter's life was not without controversy. The Gospels report that Jesus had to correct him on occasion (e.g., Mark 8:32-33 par.). Acts pictures him as the center of controversy over his acceptance of table fellowship from the gentile Cornelius (Acts 11:2-3, although the story also indicates his vindication). Paul reports that when Peter visited Antioch Paul censored his behavior in public (Gal. 2:11-14). In this case Peter appears to have had no personal scruples about table fellowship (probably meaning celebrating the Lord's Supper, which for the first two centuries was a full meal) with Gentile Christians. This fits the picture of Peter as a semi-observant Jew (including his willingness to live with a tanner in Acts 9:43). However, when "some from James" appeared he withdrew from that table fellowship to a strictly Jewish mealtime practice. According to Paul, this was due to his "fear of the circumcision," meaning either Jewish Christians or Jews in general. We are not informed whether these people from James were sent by James with a message which caused Peter's behavior or whether they arrived on other business and on their own caused Peter's behavior, but it is clear that Peter was sensitive to what Jews or Jewish Christians thought about him. This fits with Paul's description of him as a missionary to the Jews (Gal. 2:7-8). In the light of this it is somewhat surprising to discover that 1 Peter is addressed to gentile converts, although the letter comes from a different period of Peter's life and is probably co-authored by one of Paul's companions.

Other than the attribution of two letters to Peter, he disappears from the pages of the NT ca. A.D. 50. It should be noted, however, that when it came to writing the Gospels, the author of Matthew showed a special interest in him, including in his Gospel five blocks of unique material about Peter (Matt. 14:28-31; 15:15-20; 16:18-19; 17:24-27; 18:21-22).

According to tradition Peter eventually traveled to Rome, although the church there arose well before his arrival. In Rome, tradition adds, his evangelistic preaching became the basis of Mark's Gospel, although there is disagreement as to whether or not this pre-dated or followed Peter's death (Papias in Eusebius *HE* 3.39; Irenaeus *Adv. haer.* 3.1.1). Finally, as John 21:18-19 implies, Peter is said to have been martyred by crucifixion, probably after the great fire in Rome in 64 and certainly before Nero's death in 68 (Acts Peter 30–41; Eusebius *HE* 2.25.5-8; 3.1.2–3; Tertullian *Scorpiace* 15; cf. Apoc. Peter; 1 Clem. 5:4). He would most likely have been in his mid-60s at the time. While this tradition is the strongest, some scholars argue that Peter survived Nero and lived into his 80s, even ordaining Clement as his successor (Tertullian *De praescr. haer.* 32; Epistle of Clement to James 2). However, this latter tradition may be simply an attempt to support Roman primacy.

Bibliography. R. Bauckham, "The Martyrdom of Peter in Early Christian Literature," *ANRW* 26,1 (Berlin, 1992): 539-95; R. E. Brown, K. P. Donfried, and J. Reumann, eds., *Peter in the New Testament* (Minneapolis, 1973); O. Cullmann, *Peter: Disciple, Apostle, Martyr,* 2nd ed. (Philadelphia, 1962); W. R. Farmer and R. Kerestzy, *Peter and Paul in the Church of Rome* (New York, 1990); J. R. Michaels, *1 Peter.* WBC 49 (Waco, 1988); "Peter," in *Dictionary of Paul and His Letters,* ed. G. H. Hawthorne and R. P. Martin (Downers Grove, 1993), 701-3.

PETER H. DAVIDS

PETER, ACTS OF (BG, 4)

One of the miracle-filled apocryphal acts, centering on a contest between Peter and Simon Magus in Rome (an elaboration on the encounter in the canonical Acts) and on the martyrdom of the apostle. In the competition with Simon, Peter enlists the aid of a dog and a baby, both of which are given the power of speech, and restores three men to life. In a last, desperate attempt to reassert his power over those in attendance, Simon flies over the city of Rome. By means of prayer Peter is able to bring Simon to earth. In the martyrdom, Peter is crucified upside-down as a result of having angered two prominent Roman citizens by preaching chastity to their wives and concubines. Each of the two episodes portrays a major theme of the Acts: the restoration of the faith of those who have been lured away by pagan cults and the insistence on sexual abstinence even within marriage.

The document was almost certainly composed in Greek in the latter half of the 2nd century C.E. Approximately the first third of the document is missing, although it is likely that the stories of Peter temporarily healing his paralyzed daughter (preserved only in a Coptic translation and known as the Act of Peter) and of his healing a gardener's daughter (summarized in the Epistle of Pseudo-Titus) are from the missing chapters. The remainder of the work is preserved in Latin in the Vercelli manuscript, and the martyrdom, which also circulated independently, is preserved in Greek, Syriac, Ethiopic, Arabic, Armenian, Georgian, Slavonic, and Coptic. The author is unknown, and the most likely candidates for the place of writing are Rome or Asia Minor.

Bibliography. J. K. Elliott, ed., *The Apocryphal New Testament,* rev. ed. (New York, 1993), 390-430; W. Schneemelcher, "The Acts of Peter," in *New Testament Apocrypha,* ed. Schneemelcher-R. McL. Wilson, rev. ed., 2 (Louisville, 1992): 271-321.

JAMES R. MUELLER

PETER, APOCALYPSE OF

The name of two early Christian texts, one from the first half of the 2nd century, and a gnostic discourse (VII,3), probably from the 3rd century. These are distinct from the later Arabic Apocalypse of Peter.

The earlier Apocalypse of Peter is treated as Scripture in the Muratorian Fragment and by Clement of Alexandria, both late 2nd-century witnesses. Originally composed in Greek, its fullest text is in Ethiopic. The apocalypse begins with Jesus and his disciples seated on the Mount of Olives (cf. Mark 13:3 par.). In a version of the fig tree parable (cf. Mark 13:28-29 par.), Jesus warns of persecution in the last days by a false messiah. Jesus extends his right hand, and in it Peter perceives hell and heaven. Preoccupation with martyrdom and apostasy motivate this revelation. Punishments for the wicked match their sins, and the righteous watch their counterparts suffer. The narrative closes with Jesus' ascension.

The gnostic apocalypse is a revelatory dialogue between the Savior and Peter. It also shows a preoccupation with persecution, in this case of Gnostics by other Christians. The Savior explains that Peter's opponents, who include bishops and deacons, are "without perception." Especially striking is its vision of the "living Jesus" laughing from the cross.

Bibliography. J. Brashler and R. A. Bullard, "Apocalypse of Peter (VII, 3)," in *The Nag Hammadi Library in English,* ed. J. M. Robinson, 3rd ed. (San Francisco, 1988), 372-78; D. D. Buchholz, *Your Eyes Will Be Opened: A Study of the Greek (Ethiopic) Apocalypse of Peter.* SBLDS 97 (Atlanta, 1988).

GREG CAREY

PETER, FIRST LETTER OF

A letter of encouragement addressed to the "exiles of the Dispersion" in the northwest corner of Asia Minor. Beyond the fact of genre and addressees, 1 Peter remains a disputed letter which shows how early Christians encouraged one another in a situation of persecution.

Recipients

The "exiles" live in a series of Roman provinces which could be reached by a journey from the Black Sea shore of Pontus and circling through Galatia, Cappadocia, and Asia, ending with the messenger taking ship from Bithynia. 1 Peter presents itself, then, as a circular letter which does not address any particular congregation.

The term "of the Dispersion" would normally make the addressees Jews (or Jewish Christians) living outside (and thus exiled from) Palestine. However, several references in the letter imply that the readers are Gentile Christians (e.g., 1:14, 18; 2:9-10; 4:3-4). Thus it appears that the author is taking a Jewish term and applying it to Gentile Christians who are exiled from their heavenly home. This sense of presently being a "foreigner" or "exile" in the very country one was born in permeates the letter.

Author

The author identifies himself as (Simon) Peter, the most prominent of Jesus' 12 apostles. However, the fact that Peter's mission was to the Jews, not Gentiles; the excellent quality of the Greek, especially in ch. 1; the use of traditional teaching rather than original ideas; the appearance of terms and phrases typical of Paul; and the lack of any tradition connecting Peter with the area of the recipients have all raised questions about authorship. Many scholars therefore believe that the letter is pseudonymous, coming from a "Petrine circle" in Rome in the last quarter of the 1st century. Others argue that the use of Silvanus (5:12), probably indicating Paul's colleague Silas, as the secretary as well as the messenger would account for the quality of Greek (including the use of the Greek OT rather than Hebrew or Aramaic) and the Pauline phrases. The other issues could be explained by the letter's being addressed to those Peter does not know personally, but whose plight he had heard about. In that case the letter was most likely written around the traditional date of Peter's martyrdom, A.D. 64 (unless Peter was not martyred, as some argue). This would make the letter's self-designation of its authorship accurate.

What is clear is that the letter presents itself as written by that Simon whom Jesus nicknamed Cephas ("rock" in Aramaic) or Peter (the Greek form of Cephas). This author locates himself in "Babylon" (5:13) along with Mark (probably John Mark, the companion of Paul on his first missionary journey). Because of the identification in Rev. 17:5, 9 of Babylon with a city built on seven hills, a common description of Rome, this location has traditionally been thought to be Rome. However, recent commentators on Revelation have pointed out that Jerusalem was also built on seven hills. Moreover, Babylon was the location of the Jewish exile and so could stand for any place of exile rather than the capital of an empire. Thus while the Roman identification has much to commend it, including the weight of tradition, the author's emphasis is not so much on his physical location, but more on his also being an exile like the Christians he addresses.

Purpose

The recipients of the letter are, in the view of the author, experiencing persecution. There are no references to official legal processes against them, much less to anyone's having been executed, nor is the persecution viewed as inevitable for every believer (3:13-14, 17). Its form appears to be social ostracism, personal rejection, and, in the case of slaves, unfair punishment (1:6-7; 2:12, 20; 3:14-17; 4:4, 12-16; 5:9), all of which were extremely significant in a society which was based on social standing (honor and shame). In the face of this 1 Peter appears to have two purposes. First, the author wants to give his readers a sense of belonging to the true people of God, and thus a reason to stand firm in the persecution. Their future is secure; they have an inheritance no one can confiscate. They are God's people and have a true home. Furthermore, their experience in life is no worse than that of Jesus Christ himself, and he has now been exalted to God's right hand.

Second, the author wants to remind his readers to give no cause for persecution other than their being Christians. He thus calls them to holy behavior and the upholding of their social roles in ways that were thought just and honorable in pagan society. This would reduce persecution to a minimum and make sure that the persecution they did experience was based on their specifically Christian behavior, including their holy life-style (4:3-5).

Form and Structure

The book is a letter of exhortation or encouragement. The traditional opening structures of the salutation and thanksgiving (expanded into a longer prayer, as in the case of the Pauline letters) flow into the opening exhortation. Three themes are addressed: their eschatological security in God; their duty to live as God's children in the light of coming judgment; and their identity as the people of God joined to Jesus Christ. We notice that it is their collective identity as a people which is described, not their individual identity, which was not the critical issue.

The central exhortation of the letter body regards living in pagan society. It is assumed that the leaders of the state, the slave's master, and the wife's husband are not Christians (although Christian husbands are addressed in a one-verse aside, 3:7). It is accepted that the Christian will persist in his or her Christian belief, even though society rejected such independent judgment on the part of citizens and especially on the part of slaves and wives. Yet because of their commitment to Christ these people can choose to live a virtuous life according to their Christian commitment and social standards, in that order. All of this is put into an eschatological setting of final judgment, which relativizes any human judgments of honor or shame.

Finally, in the last part of the letter body the situation of persecution is addressed directly, starting with the arena of conflict (society), then moving to the arena in which there should be solidarity (the Christian community), and finally moving back to the arena of conflict, this time viewed as a conflict with the devil rather than with people in society. The letter ends with the greetings (often in the hand of the author if a secretary was used), starting with the commendation of the messenger and continuing on to general greetings, which are in line with a circular letter to groups whom the author does not know personally. Thus the outline is as follows:

I. Address (1:1-12)
 A. Salutation (1:1-2)
 B. Thanksgiving (1:3-12)
II. Opening Exhortation (1:13–2:10)
 A. Exhortation on Holiness (1:13-25)
 B. Exhortation on Commitment (2:1-10)
III. Living as a Christian in Pagan Society (2:11–4:11)
 A. Introductory Exhortation (2:11-12)
 B. Living with the State (2:13-17)
 C. Living as a Slave (2:18-25)
 D. Living as the Wife of a Pagan (3:1-7)
 E. Summary on Virtuous Living (3:8-22)
 F. Exhortation in the Light of Eschatology (4:1-11)
IV. Living with Persecution (4:12–5:11)
 A. Persecution and Society (4:12-19)
 B. Persecution and Christian Solidarity (5:1-5)
 C. Persecution and Spiritual Warfare (5:6-11)
V. Conclusion and Greetings (5:12-14)

Theology

While 1 Peter has been considered by some a catechetical document or a baptismal homily because of the basic nature of its teaching, it is not that systematic or all-inclusive. What it does do is apply central themes of Christian theology to the perceived situation of the readers. God is presented as the one in control of history (5:6). He is the creator (4:19) and judge (1:17) of the world, and yet also the father of his people (1:17). Because of this, while persecution may make life appear chaotic, order and control remain. Jesus is presented in two ways. First, he is the savior who gave his life for his people (1:19; 2:24; 3:18). Second, he is an example to the believers of one who was rejected and suffered yet was resurrected and ascended triumphantly. It is this picture, drawing on Jewish interpretations of Gen. 6:1-4, which appears in 3:18-22, showing Jesus proclaiming his triumph to the fallen "sons of God" imprisoned in the second heaven. The persecuted Gentile Christians are presented as the people of God, receiving the titles and peoplehood of God's people Israel. History is viewed in terms of conflict with the devil and those he controls, but a conflict in which God's apocalyptic intervention and final judgment is sure. Suffering, then, is the experience of persecution now as one participates in this conflict. The hope presented is that in the present one already belongs to the people of God and in the future one will receive the full inheritance to which that belonging entitles him or her.

Bibliography. P. H. Davids, *The First Epistle of Peter.* NICNT (Grand Rapids, 1990); N. Hillyer, *1 and 2 Peter, Jude.* NIBC (Peabody, 1992); J. N. D. Kelly, *A Commentary on the Epistles of Peter and Jude* (1969, repr. Grand Rapids, 1981); T. W. Martin, *Metaphor and Composition in 1 Peter.* SBLDS 131 (Atlanta, 1992); J. R. Michaels, *1 Peter.* WBC 49 (Waco, 1988); P. Perkins, *First and Second Peter, James, and Jude.* Interpretation (Louisville, 1995).

PETER H. DAVIDS

PETER, GOSPEL OF

A 2nd-century C.E. pseudonymous work literarily related to the Synoptic Gospels. A Greek Gospel manuscript from the 7th century purporting to have been written by Peter was found by French archaeologists in 1886-87 in Egypt. Scholars identified it as the Gospel of Peter, witnessed only twice in antiquity, by Eusebius (*HE* 6.12.2-6) and Origen (*Comm. on Matt.* 10.17). The manuscript, only partially preserved, abruptly begins in the trial of Jesus before Pilate, continues with his death, burial, and resurrection, and breaks off at the beginning of an appearance of the risen Lord to several disciples in Galilee. Two fragments from the Oxyrhynchus Papyri were identified in 1972 as the Gospel of Peter and demonstrate this book to be circulating by 200.

Past scholarship viewed the Gospel of Peter as gnostic or docetic, following Eusebius. More recently it is viewed as mainly a Great Church document (probably used by Justin and almost certainly by Mileto of Sardis), but one also usable by Gnostics. Most current research focuses on its relation to the canonical Gospels. John Dominic Crossan, following Helmut Koester, has argued that a source which he isolates in the Gospel of Peter, "The Cross Gospel," goes back to the mid-1st century and was a source of all four canonical Passion narratives. Others have sharply contested this, maintaining that the Gospel of Peter is literarily dependent for most of its composition on the Synoptics, especially Matthew, and supplemented with 2nd-century oral tradition from popular mainstream Christianity.

Bibliography. R. E. Brown, "*The Gospel of Peter — A Noncanonical Passion Narrative*," in *The Death of the Messiah* (New York, 1994) 2:1317-49; J. D. Crossan, *The Cross That Spoke* (San Francisco, 1988); C. Maurer and W. Schneemelcher, "The Gospel of Peter," in *New Testament Apocrypha,* ed. Schneemelcher and R. McL. Wilson, rev. ed., 1 (Philadelphia, 1991): 216-27.

ROBERT E. VAN VOORST

PETER, PREACHING OF

An early Christian work extant only in fragmentary quotations, primarily in Clement of Alexandria (*Misc.* 1.29.182; 2.15.68; 6.5.39-41; 6.5.43; 6.6.48; 6.7.58; 6.15.128; *Ecl. proph.* 58). While Clement attributes it to the Apostle Peter, Origen doubts its authenticity (*Comm. in Jn.* 13.17), and Eusebius considers it noncanonical (*HE* 3.3.2). The gnostic writer Heracleon quoted it, and the apologists Theophilus and Aristides seem to have known it. These witnesses point toward an early 2nd-century composition, possibly in Egypt.

The fragments feature missionary speeches by Peter, but also include the resurrected Christ's instructions as he sends the apostles to preach to all the world. The work emphasizes monotheism, rejecting both Greek and Jewish worship in favor of that of Christians, the "third race." Proof from Scripture is valued: the apostles "say nothing apart from Scripture"; Peter claims that Christ's coming, his suffering, death, resurrection, and ascension are all found in Scripture.

The Preaching is related both to early Christian apologetic works (emphasis on monotheism, attacks on pagan and Jewish worship) and to early missionary literature (e.g., Acts of the Apostles).

Bibliography. W. Schneemelcher, "The Kerygma Petri," in *New Testament Apocrypha,* ed. W. Schneemelcher and R. McL. Wilson, rev. ed., 2 (Louisville, 1992): 34-41. MARTIN C. ALBL

PETER, SECOND LETTER OF

One of the seven "catholic" or "general" epistles. On the basis of 3:1 ("this is . . . the second letter I am writing to you") it is assumed that the same audience is intended as in 1 Peter, although no such specific reference occurs. The situation, style, and content indicate that both the writer and the intended readers lived in pluralistic Hellenistic environments.

Literary Structure

2 Peter may be outlined as follows:

1:1-15	*Introduction*
1:1-2	Greeting
1:3-9	Core of Peter's definitive teaching
1:10-11	Admonition to make "calling and election sure"
1:12-15	Reminder: Peter's testament
1:16–3:13	*Body*
1:16-21	Authentication of traditional Christian teaching
2:1-22	Denunciation of the "false teachers"
3:1-13	Eschatological certainty and Christian ethics
3:14-18	*Conclusion*

2 Peter evidences two literary genres: the letter and the testament. In 3:1 the writer refers to the document as a letter. Its opening (1:1-2) conforms to customary Jewish and early Christian letter openings. The introduction, stating the theme (1:3-11), followed by the statement of the occasion for the letter (vv. 12-15), is typical. The letter was sent to specific addressees, i.e., the recipients of the letter of 1 Peter (3:1). So in spite of the general address (1:1), it is not a "catholic" letter addressed to all Christians, but an occasional letter aimed at a specific problem.

2 Peter is also a testament, or farewell speech. This genre, common in the intertestamental period, is characterized by two features: ethical admonitions and revelations of the future (cf. Acts 20:17-34; 2 Timothy; also Acts of Peter, Acts of John, Acts of Thomas). 2 Pet. 1:3-11 is a homily which follows a pattern found, e.g., in the farewell speeches of Ezra (2 Esdr. 14:28-36). 2 Pet. 1:12-15 is replete with language typical of farewell addresses, and specifically mentions Peter's knowledge of his approaching death. 2 Pet. 2:1-3a; 3:1-4 predict the arrival of false teachers.

Literary Relationships

It is commonly supposed that 2 Peter is a revision of Jude. Unlike Jude, 2 Peter contains only a few OT allusions, usually to the LXX, and no OT citations or references to Assumption of Moses and 1 Enoch, the latter a very popular book in 2nd-century Christianity but used in the 1st century in Palestinian Jewish circles. Since Jude's midrash is based on traditional material with which the readers were already familiar (Jude 5), 2 Peter may also use a similar tradition. Jude's careful midrashic structure is absent from 2 Peter. Contrary to common assumptions, the two letters derive from different situations, oppose different opponents, and therefore make appropriate use of and adjustments to whatever material they may have in common.

The author of 2 Peter knew a collection of Pauline letters and regarded them as "scriptures," authoritative alongside the OT (3:15-16). However, there is little, if any, sign of Pauline influence in 2 Peter, even though the author states that Paul dealt with his subject matter. Although 2 Peter contains four allusions to gospel traditions (1:14; 1:16-18; 2:20; 3:10), it is impossible to tell whether it is dependent upon any of the four canonical Gospels. The account of the Transfiguration (1:16-18) is rather primitive and not at all like the strongly hellenized 2nd-century accounts.

The difference in vocabulary and style between 1 and 2 Peter is significant. Both letters are relatively brief and are directed to quite different situations. Unlike the Pauline letters, common terminology in 1 and 2 Peter is negligible and common themes are mostly those ideas common throughout early Christianity. While the author of 2 Peter knew 1 Peter, he did not follow the common 2nd-century pseudepigraphic practice of echoing writings attributed to their pseudonyms.

2 Peter is quite unlike other NT documents, and seems to represent a Christian situation and style of discourse not otherwise found in the NT. However, there are many parallels in ideas and terminology with 1–2 Clement and the Shepherd of Hermas, all claiming dates in the last decade of the 1st century. It is possible that 2 Peter shares with these works a common indebtedness to some tradition of Roman Christianity.

The Opponents

2 Peter is a polemical document intended to counter the influence of certain teachers who were denouncing early Christian eschatological expectations as a mere apostolic invention (1:16a; 2:3b; 3:4,

9a). As this skepticism lent itself to ignoring moral restraint, they laughed at warnings of a coming judgment, as well as at the supposed power of Satan and his angels (2:10). Freedom for them meant lack of restraint regarding sexuality, drunkenness, and sensual excess (2:2, 10, 13-14, 18).

Nowhere does 2 Peter mention any claims to spirituality, prophetic revelations, or perversion of grace as addressed in Jude's epistle. Unlike the "ungodly intruders" in Jude, who are characterized by christological neglect and an antinomian understanding of grace, the "false teachers" in 2 Peter teach ethical libertinism rooted in eschatological skepticism. The only real resemblance between the opponents in the two epistles is their ethical libertinism.

The opponents here are not Gnostics. No evidence links them with cosmic dualism, nor does the delay of the Parousia figure in gnostic argument against traditional Christian eschatology. "Myths" in 1:16 does not refer to gnostic myths, but the opponents' charge against the apostles. "Knowledge" here has no polemical overtones. Only with regard to eschatological disillusionment could the opponents in 2 Peter be considered primitive precursors of Gnosticism or even "incipient Gnostics."

The most plausible background for the "false teachers" is the pagan environment with which they have compromised. Jerome H. Neyrey has shown the commonality between the eschatological debate in 2 Peter and pagan Hellenistic controversy over the views of the Epicureans on eschatology. The sexual immorality of the opponents is rooted in accommodation to pagan society. If the "false teachers" could rid Christianity of its eschatology and ethical standards, they could be done with elements embarrassing in their culture. To what extent they held other traditional Christian views is not known. A basically negative theological construct could have appeared impressive (2:18).

Theological Character

2 Peter has been called the classic example of "early Catholicism," demonstrating decreasing emphasis on the eschatological hope, increasing institutionalization in the Church, and crystallization of the faith into set forms. Certainly the author does not abandon the expectation of the Parousia common to early Christianity (1:19; 3:14), but 2 Peter makes no reference to ecclesiastical officeholders. While the author refers to Christian knowledge, there is nothing approaching formalized creedal orthodoxy. 2 Peter's response to the opponents is not the "early Catholic" response of insistence upon institutional authority and creedal orthodoxy, but an appeal to return to the eschatological perspective common to early Christianity. Seeking to promote the ancient apostolic message in a postapostolic situation, the writer combines his own background in Hellenistic Judaism with a mixture of apocalypticism characteristic of the earlier Church (cf. 1–2 Clement, Hermas).

Date

2 Peter has been variously dated from A.D. 60-160. Peter's death occurred ca. 66-67. 2 Peter knows the Pauline letters, which date from the mid-1st century but were collected somewhat later. The Apocalypse of Peter, dating from the first half of the 2nd century, knows 2 Peter. The lack of reference to 1 Enoch indicates a 1st-century date. Also, the absence of "early Catholic" stress on institutional officeholders may suggest an earlier date. The opponents are certainly not 2nd-century Gnostics. 2 Pet. 3:4 may reflect that the first generation of Christians, that of the apostles, are dead. The scoffers' objection in 3:4 is plausible in the period 75-90, marked by great disillusionment regarding the Parousia. There is certainly no basis for viewing 2 Peter as the latest composition in the NT.

Authorship and Pseudonymity

Peter is portrayed as an eyewitness and authenticator of the historical Jesus (1:16-19) who had the authority to interpret Scripture and prophecy (vv. 20-21) and to correct false interpretations (3:15-16). While Peter could have been martyred in Rome as early as 65, it is more likely that he was imprisoned there shortly after the outbreak of the Jewish War in 66 and killed in 67. If 2 Peter was written by Peter, the changes brought about by the war and his own impending death could account for the differences in content and tone between 1 and 2 Peter. The letter, written to specific churches (3:15), could have originated in Rome. 2 Pet. 3:1 suggests that the churches addressed are those which 1 Peter addressed from Rome (1 Pet. 5:13).

However, certain factors militate against Petrine authorship. The author of 2 Peter was likely Jewish, but a strongly hellenized Jew. 2 Peter evidences the highest proportion of *hapax legomena* in the NT: 57 words do not occur elsewhere in the NT, and 32 of these do not occur in the LXX either. The vocabulary reflects that of other Hellenistic Jewish writers of the period (e.g., Philo and Josephus) and the Apostolic Fathers. This suggests that the writer is widely read, fond of literary and poetic terms, and aims at creating a decidedly literary effect not unlike contemporary Greek rhetoric.

It is generally held that the document is pseudonymous, employing the testament genre to address current issues as a prediction of a venerable figure of the past. This does not imply a fraudulent means of claiming apostolic authority, but faithfulness to the apostolic message.

Along with 1 Peter and a large body of noncanonical Petrine literature (including the Gospel of Peter, Preaching of Peter, Acts of Peter, Apocalypse of Peter), 2 Peter illustrates the importance attributed to the Apostle Peter in both orthodox and heterodox circles. Even so, no NT document is so weakly attested among the church fathers or was so slowly accepted into the NT canon as 2 Peter.

Bibliography. R. J. Bauckham, *Jude, 2 Peter*. WBC 50 (Waco, 1983); T. Fornberg, *An Early Church in a Pluralistic Society: A Study of 2 Peter.*

ConBNT 9 (Lund, 1977); B. M. Metzger, "Literary Forgeries and Canonical Pseudepigrapha," *JBL* 91 (1972): 3-24; J. H. Neyrey, "The Form and Background of the Polemic in 2 Peter," *JBL* 99 (1980): 407-31.

CARROLL D. OSBURN

PETER AND PAUL, THE PASSION OF

Two different narratives, each attributed to Marcellus, a follower of Peter, recounting the passion of Peter and Paul. The longer version of the two, dating perhaps to the 6th century, is attested in Slavonic, Latin, and Greek and appears to be later than the apocryphal Acts of Peter and Paul. The Passion narrates the apostles' adversarial encounters with Simon Magus and Nero in Rome and features the apocryphal Letter of Pilate to the emperor Claudius. The narrative culminates with descriptions of the executions of Peter and Paul and the disposition of their relics at sites associated with the apostles' death. The shorter Latin version (6th-7th century) inserts different narrative details drawn from the Acts of Peter, omits the Letter of Pilate, and terminates at the apostles' sentencing. Paul is eclipsed by the more prominent Peter in both accounts, perhaps due to the authors' dependence on the pro-Petrine Acts of Peter.

Bibliography. J. Charlesworth, *New Testament Apocrypha and Pseudepigrapha* (Metuchen, N.J., 1987), 329-30.

MELISSA M. AUBIN

PETER AND THE TWELVE APOSTLES, ACTS OF

A gnostic tractate, the first 12 pages of the sixth codex discovered at Nag Hammadi. Like the majority of texts in that corpus, it exists only in a Coptic translation, although it was originally written in Greek.

On the basis of internal evidence, this work apparently received its final redaction in the years immediately following the Decian persecution (ca. A.D. 249-251). This is well within the previous estimates of a 2nd- or 3rd-century dating. While the provenance has not received extended analysis, an Alexandrian locale is likely. The text itself is a combination of two previous sources (a *narratio fabulosa* or heavenly journey and a resurrection appearance) sewn together by a later redactor who added a commissioning scene, creating the effect of a revelation dialogue.

This allegorical text describes the arrival of Peter and the other disciples at the island city of Habitation (earth) where Peter encounters the mysterious figure of Lithargoel, a traveling pearl merchant. After offering his pearls (salvation/knowledge) to the city's inhabitants (the rich, the poor, and the disciples represent the three classes of people — the fleshly, the psychic, and spiritual), Lithargoel talks with Peter and invites him to come to receive a pearl, a treasure which is only attained by making the hazardous journey (through the hostile realms of the archons) to the merchant's city of Nine Gates (heaven). Upon their arrival at Nine Gates, the disciples re-encounter Lithargoel (disguised as a physician), who finally reveals himself as Jesus. The commission, both practical and extremely community-oriented, includes commands to teach, care for the poor, heal as "physicians of bodies and souls," and an absolute rejection of the rich as potential Church members.

Bibliography. A. L. Molinari, *The Acts of Peter and the Twelve Apostles (NHC 6.1)*(diss., Marquette, 1997); S. J. Patterson, "Sources, Redaction and *Tendenz* in the Acts of Peter and the Twelve Apostles (NH VI,1)," *VC* 45 (1991): 1-17.

ANDREA LORENZO MOLINARI

PETER TO JAMES, LETTER OF

An epistle written in the name of the Apostle Peter in order to claim his authority for the continuing validity of the law in opposition to Paul's law-free understanding of Christian faith. The James to whom this pseudonymous letter is addressed is the brother of Jesus and major leader of the Jerusalem church (Gal. 2:9). The letter serves as the introduction to the *Kerygmata Petrou* (Preachings of Peter), most likely a 2nd-century work from Syria which presents Peter's teachings and debates advocating a form of Jewish Christianity. In this letter Peter warns that his teachings have been distorted, specifically those about the law. He requests that James "pass on the books of my preachings" (Ep.P. 3:1) only to those who have been properly trained in order to prevent a distortion of Peter's true teaching on the law. The letter reflects debates about the role of the law in the Church of the 2nd century and claims the authority of Peter for an understanding of Christian faith requiring obedience to the law.

JAMES J. H. PRICE

PETER TO PHILIP, LETTER OF

A brief tractate from the Nag Hammadi library, attributed to the Apostle Peter. By the end of the 1st century Peter was regarded as the preeminent authority for the apostolic tradition in an emerging orthodox Church. This pseudonymous writing represents Peter as the central recipient of a gnostic revelation that should be the content of the apostolic preaching. The actual letter, consisting of only a few lines (Ep.Pet.Phil. 132:10–133:7a), invites Philip and his group, who are said to be "separate from us" (133:2), to come together to receive instructions from the risen Christ.

The epistle consists chiefly of a gnostic revelation discourse given by Jesus in response to a series of questions from the apostles. A distinctive feature of the work is a sermon delivered by Peter in which he affirms the gnostic conviction that "Jesus is stranger to this suffering" (139:21). The epistle is a Coptic translation of an original Greek version from the late 2nd or early 3rd century C.E.

JAMES J. H. PRICE

PETHAHIAH (Heb. *pĕṯaḥyâ*)

1. The leader of the nineteenth priestly division during the days of David (1 Chr. 24:16).

2. A Levite among those who divorced their foreign wives at Ezra's direction (Ezra 10:23).

3. A Levite who participated in the corporate

confession of sins under Ezra (Neh. 9:5). He is probably the same as **2** above.

4. A Judahite, the son of Meshezabel. He was a postexilic administrator for the king of Persia in Judea, perhaps an advisor to the Persian court (Neh. 11:24).

PETHOR (Heb. *pěṯôr;* Akk. *Pitru*)
A place on the western shore of the Euphrates River in northern Mesopotamia, the home of Balaam (Num. 22:5; Deut. 23:4). It is mentioned in a list of Pharaoh Thutmose III conquered in 856 B.C.E. The site may be Tell Aḥmar, 19 km. (12 mi.) S of Carchemish.

PETHUEL (Heb. *pěṯû'ēl*)
The father of the prophet Joel (Joel 1:1).

PETRA (Gk. *Pétra*)
An ancient capital city in the southeastern desert of modern Jordan. The Petra Basin was most certainly occupied from Neolithic times but gained its first prominence as a stronghold, if not the capital city, of the biblical Edomites. The towering mountain today called el-Habis is regarded by some as the biblical Sela, from whose peak King Amaziah is said to have cast down some 10 thousand Edomites (2 Kgs. 14:7).

Guarded on the east and west by mountain ranges, with a defensible cleft as an entry and ample springs, and adjacent to the major trade routes of the day, Petra provided both security and potential for commercial enterprise. In the later times the site served as the seat of an alliance between a seminomadic Bedouin group that had drifted upward along the coast of the Arabian Peninsula and the sedentary Edomites. The amalgamation of the two peoples became known as the Nabateans, with dissident Edomites withdrawing into southern Palestine and becoming known as Idumeans. Through successful Nabatean commercial ventures, especially because of the lucrative frankincense and myrrh trade, Petra became urbanized, most probably during the reign of King Aretas IV (9 B.C.E.–40 C.E.).

Relative isolation in the eastern desert permitted the Nabateans to escape immediate occupation by Rome after the invasion of Pompey in 64 B.C.E., but Greco-Roman influence in art, architecture, and virtually all aspects of daily life was brought back to Petra by traders. Ultimately Emperor Trajan was forced to consolidate the eastern regions of the empire, and Petra was officially occupied in 110 C.E. Neither this occupation or later Byzantine influence, however, had much effect on Nabatean daily life.

On 19 May 363, a major earthquake destroyed the city. Modern excavations indicate that no major rebuilding was done, and occupation thereafter was relatively slight.

In the late 6th century, Christian influence resulted in a resurgence of Petra, and at least two churches were constructed, but with the Islamic conquest the site ceased to be of strategic importance. The Crusader period brought new interest in the area because of its proximity to taxable routes

The Great Temple at Petra, probably constructed in the early 1st century C.E. and used into the Byzantine period. The 7000 sq. m. precinct is comprised of a propylaea, a lower temenos, and a monumental grand stairway which leads to the upper temenos, the sacred enclosure for the temple proper
(photograph, A. A. W. Joukowsky; courtesy of the Brown University Excavations)

of Muslim caravans. A major fortress was constructed just outside the western rim of the basin, with a smaller one placed atop el-Habis inside the ancient city center. By this period Petra had accrued considerable biblical folklore, especially connected to Moses and the Exodus, which it maintains to this day.

With the fall of the Latin kingdom, Petra disappeared from Western view, and it was not until the epic journey of Johann Burckhardt in 1812 that the site was "rediscovered" and interest in its people revived. Because of the political situation in the region, no excavations were possible at Petra until those begun in 1929 by George Horsfield, during which the distinctive fine, thin pottery found there became the marker for identifying Nabatean sites throughout Syro-Palestine. Petra today ranks as one of the major tourist sites in the Middle East, both for its natural beauty and for the magnificence of its rock-carved monuments.

PHILIP C. HAMMOND

PEULLETHAI (Heb. *pĕʿullĕṯay*)
The eighth son of Obed-edom, a gatekeeper, whose family was assigned to the South Gate of the temple and the temple storerooms (1 Chr. 26:5, 15).

PHANUEL (Gk. *Phanouḗl*)
The father of the prophetess Anna of the tribe of Asher (Luke 2:36).

PHARAOH
Egyp. *pr-ʿꜣ* (lit., "Great House"), originally designating the royal palace of the king of Egypt. By the 18th Dynasty (ca. 1560-1320 B.C.) "pharaoh" designated not only the royal residence, but royal authority, personified in the king himself, much like "White House" might refer to the U.S. President's residence or the President (e.g., "The White House said . . .").

The title occurs in the OT as a generic locution for the "king of Egypt." Episodes involving (unnamed) pharaohs include Abraham's sojourn to Egypt (Gen. 12:10-20); Joseph's rise to power and Israel's sojourn to Egypt (Gen. 39–50); Israel's deliverance from Egypt (Exod. 1–15); and Solomon's marriage to Pharaoh's daughter (1 Kgs. 3:1). Specifically named are pharaohs Shishak (1 Kgs. 11:40; 14:25-26), So (2 Kgs. 17:4), Neco (23:29-30), Tirhakah (19:9 = Isa. 37:9), and Hophra (Jer. 44:30).

In the NT the term "pharaoh" occurs in references to Israel's sojourn and deliverance (Acts 7:10, 13, 21; Rom. 9:17; Heb. 11:24).

Bibliography. A. F. Rainey, ed., *Egypt, Israel, Sinai: Archaeological and Historical Relationships in the Biblical Period* (Tel Aviv, 1987).

JEFFREY C. GEOGHEGAN

PHARATHON (Gk. *Pharathōn*)
A city in Judea, one of those fortified by Bacchides, Seleucid governor of the province Beyond the River (1 Macc. 9:50). The city should not be identified with Ephraimite Pirathon (Judg. 12:13-15).

PHARISEES (Gk. *Pharisaíoi*)
An important group within Judaism of the late Second Temple period (2nd century B.C.E.–1st century C.E.). Because we have no surviving text written by a committed Pharisee and no archaeological finds that mention them, the reconstruction of the Pharisees' aims and views must depend on the writings of third parties: the NT writers, the 1st-century Jewish historian Flavius Josephus, and the authors of rabbinic literature. None of these outsiders, however, was primarily interested in explaining who the Pharisees were.

All three source collections, although they understand the Pharisees very differently, support the conclusions that: they were a lay (not priestly) association who were thought to be expert in the laws; they were, in a sociological sense, "retainers" who brokered power between the aristocracy and the masses; they promoted a special living tradition in addition to the laws; they were very interested in issues of ritual purity and tithing; and they believed in afterlife, judgment, and a densely populated, organized spirit world. Few critics today would make the confident statements that characterized scholarship of a generation ago concerning the meaning of the Pharisees' name ("separatists," "the consecrated," "Persians," "specifiers"), the date and circumstances of their origin (in Ezra's time, after the Maccabean Revolt, from the Hasidim), the degree of their involvement with apocalypticism, and their political platform. It is plausible that the Pharisees emerged from the turmoil following the Maccabean Revolt, but no more can be said at this point.

The most vigorously contested issue today concerns the degree and manner of the Pharisees' influence over the Judean-Galilean populace in the time of Jesus and Paul. The NT authors use the Pharisees mainly as a negative foil for Jesus. Paul is the only writer known to us who actually lived as a Pharisee (Phil. 3:5), but because his writings are thoroughly conditioned by his encounter with the risen Christ (he dismisses his Pharisaic past as "dung"; v. 8), it is hazardous to make inferences about Pharisaism from them. Paul's expert biblical knowledge doubtless comes from his former life as a Pharisee, and certain aspects of his worldview (belief in resurrection and spiritual powers) probably also continue from that past.

Mark and John portray the Pharisees as key elements of the cosmic battle between Jesus and the evil spirits. Lumped together in a scarcely differentiated Jewish leadership, they are presented as hostile to Jesus from the outset and in league with the devil (Mark 3:6, 19-30; John 8:13, 22, 44). In both texts the Pharisees appear as the most prominent Jewish group in Jesus' environment. Mark shows them as preoccupied with issues of purity, tithing, and legal interpretation (Mark 2:1–3:6). Mark also attributes to them a special extrabiblical tradition, which Jesus denounces as merely human contrivance (Mark 7:5-8).

Matthew often couples the Pharisees with the Sadducees, even with the chief priests, to portray them all as the leadership of old Israel (Matt. 3:7; 16:1, 6), from whom the kingdom will be taken away (8:12; 21:43-45). However, tensions remain, perhaps partly as a result of Matthew's conflicting sources. The Pharisees are both "blind guides," whose teachings are harmful (Matt. 15:14; 16:11-12), and those who "sit on Moses' seat," whose teachings should be observed even while their practices are eschewed (23:2-3). Matthew introduces specific remarks about the Pharisees' wearing of phylacteries and fringes and about their concern for tithing (Matt. 23:5, 23). This Gospel assumes their prominence in Galilean-Judean life.

Luke's portrayal of the Pharisees recalls portraits of the Sophists in Hellenistic texts: the respected teachers of the common people, who come out to scrutinize Jesus' activities (Luke 5:17). Though sometimes critical of him, they nevertheless address him respectfully as a fellow teacher, regularly invite him to dinner, and even try to help him in trouble (Luke 7:36; 11:37; 13:31; 14:1). Jesus is much more strident in his critique of them for typical Sophist's faults — for being money-hungry, complacent, and ineffective in bringing about real change (Luke 11:39-44; 12:1; 16:14-15; 18:9-14). The Pharisees of Luke remain outside Jerusalem, and so are sharply distinguished from the temple authorities.

In Acts this openness continues at first, especially in the person of Gamaliel, an influential member of the Sanhedrin (Acts 5:33-39). But with the execution of Stephen, Acts presents a galvanizing Jewish opposition to the Christian "Path" (Acts 8:1-3). Some Pharisees convert, and they remain most zealous for the precise observance of torah (Acts 15:5). Indeed, Acts claims that the Pharisees are the most scrupulously precise of the schools (Acts 22:3; 26:5). When he is brought before the Sanhedrin, Acts' Paul is able to make clever use of the Pharisees' famous opposition to the Sadducees on the issue of resurrection (and angels) to deflect the charges against him.

Flavius Josephus, a representative of the priestly aristocracy, wrote the *Jewish War* in the late 70s C.E. to persuade Greek readers that the recent Jewish loss to Rome (66-74) was not a defeat of the Jewish God and that most Jews had nothing to do with the revolt. In recounting earlier history as evidence of the Jews' good citizenship, he mentions the Pharisees incidentally as a destructive force, because of the inordinate power they wielded under the Hasmonean Queen Alexandra (*BJ* 1.110-14) and later under Herod (1.571). When the revolt against Rome finally broke out, however, the most eminent Pharisees joined with the temple authorities in trying to dissuade the revolutionaries, but they were equally unsuccessful (*BJ* 2.411). Describing the Jews' philosophical traditions, Josephus briefly mentions that the Pharisees, in contrast to the Sadducees, believe in after life after death, judgment, and fate or providence (*BJ* 2.162-66).

In the *Jewish Antiquities/Life*, Josephus presents the Pharisees as the most influential of the Jewish parties, even though they do not officially control the organs of power, which are centered in the temple. He consistently and caustically repudiates their activities, whether under the Hasmonean prince John Hyrcanus, Alexandra, Herod the Great, or himself as commander of Galilean forces in the revolt: they allegedly use their vast popular support to cause problems for the proper leaders — i.e., for Josephus and the aristocrats (*Ant.* 13.288, 400-432; 17.41-45; *Vita* 189-98). He again cites their doctrine of the afterlife and their special extrabiblical tradition, which Josephus claims endear them to the masses (*Ant.* 13.297-98; 18.12-15). Throughout all his works, Josephus reiterates the Pharisees' reputation as the most precise of the schools in interpreting the laws (*BJ* 1.110; 2.162; *Ant.* 17.41; *Vita* 191).

Rabbinic literature is extremely complex and multi-layered, written in Hebrew and Aramaic from the 3rd-6th centuries C.E., in Galilee and Babylonia. Because this literature mentions among its founding figures some who are elsewhere connected with the Pharisees (esp. Hillel and Shammai and the family of Gamaliel), scholars have traditionally identified the Pharisees with the rabbis. Those who liked what they found in rabbinic literature saw the Pharisees as a progressive party committed to making the Torah practicable for everyone. Those who were baffled and alienated by rabbinic style found support for their view of the Pharisees as petty legalists. Curiously, when these texts refer to a group called the *pĕrûšîm*, more often than not the tone is unfavorable (e.g., *m. Soṭa* 3.4); the rabbis do not call their own forebears *pĕrûšîm*. Scholars disagree, also for linguistic reasons, on the extent to which these *pĕrûšîm* should even be identified with the Pharisees (Gk. *Pharisaíoi*) of Josephus and the NT.

The general trend today is to see early rabbinic literature as the product of a small elite, which only gradually came to exert influence over larger circles of Jews toward the end of the 2nd century C.E. That elite claimed notable Pharisees among its founders, but it also took over the role of temple-related teaching. It probably originated not simply among the Pharisees but in a surviving coalition of priests, scribes, Pharisees, Sadducees, and others. Rabbinic literature should no longer be used, therefore, as direct evidence for the Pharisees.

Bibliography. L. L. Grabbe, *Judaism from Cyrus to Hadrian*, 2 vols. (Minneapolis, 1992); S. N. Mason, "Chief Priests, Sadducees, Pharisees, and Sanhedrin in Acts," in *The Book of Acts in Its First Century Setting*, 4: *Palestinian Setting*, ed. R. Bauckham (Grand Rapids, 1995), 115-77; *Flavius Josephus on the Pharisees*. SPB 39 (Leiden, 1991); J. Neusner, *The Rabbinic Traditions About the Pharisees before 70*, 3 vols. (Leiden, 1971); A. J. Saldarini, *Pharisees, Scribes, and Sadducees in Palestinian Society* (1988, repr. Grand Rapids, forthcoming); E. P. Sanders, *Judaism: Practice and Belief, 63 B.C.E.–66 C.E.* (Philadelphia, 1992); G. Stemberger, *Jewish Contemporaries of Jesus: Pharisees, Sadducees, Essenes* (Minneapolis, 1995).

STEVE MASON

PHARPAR (Heb. *parpar*)
A river in Syria mentioned with the Abana at 2 Kgs. 5:12. It is generally thought to be the modern Nahr el-Aʿwaj, 16 km. (10 mi.) S of Damascus.

PHASAEL (Gk. *Phasaḗlos*)
Older brother of Herod I the Great. Their father Antipater, procurator over the Jewish territories (Josephus *Ant.* 14.143), appointed Phasael as governor of Judea and made Herod governor over Galilee.

According to Josephus Phasael's governorship was peaceful and marked with restraint (*Ant.* 14.158-62). Phasael and his father prevented Herod from attacking Jerusalem after the latter had been incensed by the Sanhedrin's attempt to pronounce sentence on Herod for military actions in Galilee (*Ant.* 14.168-85). However, the Antipatrids were viewed by Jews as usurpers of the Hasmonean dynasty, whose heirs (Aristobulus II and his sons Antigonus and Alexander) were the focus of several rebellions throughout the 50s and 40s B.C. Various Jewish delegations called for the removal of Antipater and his sons. The murder of Antipater in 43 renewed these calls, but Antony supported Phasael and Herod, appointing them tetrarchs in 42 (*Ant.* 14.326).

Parthian invasions in 40 gave opportunity to Antigonus, the sole surviving son of Aristobulus, to reclaim the Hasmonean kingdom. The invasion forced Phasael, Herod, and Hyrcanus II on the defensive. Trapped in Jerusalem, Phasael and Hyrcanus sought a negotiated settlement and traveled to Ptolemais to meet with the Parthians. Both were placed under arrest; realizing that escape was impossible, Phasael committed suicide (*Ant.* 14.366-69). Herod fled to Rome, where the Senate ratified his nomination by Antony as king of the Jews.

Herod later commemorated the memory of his brother by naming the largest of the three towers north of his palace in Jerusalem Phasael (*BJ* 5.166). Known in Byzantine times as David's tower, it was one of the few structures to survive Titus' destruction of Jerusalem in A.D. 70. THOMAS V. BRISCO

PHASAELIS (Gk. *Phasaḗlis*)
A town in the Jordan Valley (Khirbet el-Fasayil), 16 km. (10 mi.) N of Jericho. Built by Herod the Great in memory of his brother Phasael, it was given to his sister Salome in 4 B.C. with the division of Herod's kingdom. It appears on the 6th-century mosaic map from Madeba. LAURA B. MAZOW

PHASELIS (Gk. *Phasḗlis*)
A city in the region of Lycia, on the southern coast of Asia Minor, and an important trading point between east and west. In 139 B.C. the Roman consul Lucius mentioned it in a letter to various government leaders (1 Macc. 15:23) instructing them to treat the Jews in their region with favor. Phaselis was seized in 77 B.C. by the Romans because it had become a base for Cilician pirates.
H. WAYNE HOUSE

PHICOL (Heb. *pîḵōl*)
The Philistine commander in chief who witnessed Abimelech's covenants with Abraham at Beer-sheba (Gen. 21:22, 32) and Isaac at Gerar (26:26). The name may be a title rather than a personal name.

PHILADELPHIA (Gk. *Philadélphia*)
1. A city in the Roman province of Asia, in western Asia Minor (Rev. 1:11; 3:7-13). Since Philadelphia lies beneath the modern Turkish city of Alaşehir, it has never been systematically excavated. The city was founded in the 2nd century B.C. by Attalos II of Pergamum. It experienced severe earthquake damage in the period of the early Roman Empire; the earthquake of unparalleled magnitude which occurred during the reign of the emperor Tiberius (A.D. 17; Pliny *Nat. hist.* 2.86, 200; Tacitus *Ann.* 2.47) and destroyed several Asiatic cities also devastated Philadelphia (cf. Strabo *Geog.* 12.8.18; 13.4.10).

The earliest sources for Christianity in Philadelphia come from the book of Revelation and the Letter to the Philadelphians written by Ignatius of Antioch in the early 2nd century. It is clear from these that there was continuing animosity between Christianity and the local Jewish community (Rev. 3:9; Ignatius *Phld.* 6:1). Efforts to interpret the Johannine message to the church at Philadelphia in light of Philadelphia's social and political history have often been very subjective.

The numerous epigraphical remains from the city and its vicinity have not been seriously investigated by NT scholars. One rather noteworthy inscription from the 1st century B.C. records the moral imperatives required of members in a cult of the pagan god Zeus. In addition to demonstrating a close connection between pagan piety and ethical standards, this lengthy inscription gives insight about pagan resistance to participation in promiscuous sexual relations, use of abortifacients, use of magical spells, and participation in pedophilia. Moreover this inscription explicitly informs us that the members of the religious guild represented "men and women, free and slave."

Bibliography. S. C. Barton and G. H. R. Horsley, "A Hellenistic Cult Group and the New Testament Churches," *JAC* 24 (1981): 7-41; C. J. Hemer, *The Letters to the Seven Churches of Asia in Their Local Setting* (1986, repr. Grand Rapids, 2000); D. Magie, *Roman Rule in Asia Minor,* 2 vols. (1950, repr. New York, 1975). RICHARD E. OSTER, JR.

2. A city in the Decapolis, modern Amman.
See RABBAH.

PHILEMON (Gk. *Philḗmōn*)
The recipient of Paul's Epistle to Philemon, written on behalf of Philemon's slave Onesimus who was with Paul in Rome. This epistle is our only source of information about Philemon, with inferences possible from the accompanying Epistle to the Colossians (cf. Phlm. 12; Col. 4:9). Although uncertain, Apphia and Archippus whom Paul greets in Phlm. 2 may be Philemon's wife and son, respectively (cf.

Col. 4:17). Since Onesimus and Archippus reside with Philemon (Phlm. 2, 10-21) and belong to the church of Colossae (Col. 4:9, 17), we can surmise that Philemon also resided in Colossae in the Lycus Valley of the Roman province of Asia.

Philemon was one of Paul's converts (Phlm. 19), perhaps when Paul was ministering in Ephesus on his third journey and the province of Asia was evangelized (Acts 19:10). Paul considers Philemon a fellow worker (Gk. *synergós*), possibly because he was instrumental in founding the church of Colossae. Philemon was a wealthy patron of a house church in his home in Colossae (Phlm. 2) and was known for his hospitality (vv. 5-7). Paul tried to convince Philemon that the conversion of Onesimus to Christianity transcended the relationship of master and slave, seeming to imply that one option open to Philemon was to set Onesimus free.

Bibliography. J. M. G. Barclay, "Paul, Philemon and the Dilemma of Christian Slave-Ownership," *NTS* 37 (1991): 161-86; N. R. Petersen, *Rediscovering Paul: Philemon and the Sociology of Paul's Narrative World.* Guides to Biblical Scholarship (Philadelphia, 1985). DUANE F. WATSON

PHILEMON (Gk. *Philḗmōn*)**, LETTER TO**

Paul's briefest preserved correspondence, in its comparative brevity more like the majority of preserved ancient Greek letters than Paul's other writings. Unlike Paul's other letters, Philemon does not deal with theological controversies or ethical difficulties in the lives of his audience.

Philemon is universally accepted as an authentic letter of Paul, and its authenticity has only rarely been questioned in the past. However, questions have persisted from earliest times regarding the value of the letter. Interpreters ancient and modern have responded to criticisms of Philemon by drawing out from it a variety of moral lessons, pointing to its value for showing the depths of Paul's humility and caring as an example to all Christians, and emphasizing the letter's value in showing how Christian persons from different social levels are to relate to one another.

Structure

The entire letter to Philemon divides into four or five parts. Most common is the following five-part delineation:

1. Verses 1-3 form a salutation, which names the senders, the recipients, and issues a greeting.
2. Verses 4-7 offer a thanksgiving to God for a specific memory of Philemon's life. Verse 7 is a bridge to the main portion of the letter.
3. Verses 8-21 are the body of the letter, discussing the return of Onesimus the slave. In the first section of the body (vv. 8-14) Paul appeals to Philemon in Onesimus' behalf by declaring his affection for the slave and by telling Philemon of his desire to have Onesimus with him in his imprisonment for the gospel. In the second section of the body (vv. 15-20) Paul both reflects upon the change in Onesimus that came through his conversion and promises to stand good for anything that Onesimus might owe Philemon.
4. Verses 21-22 are parenesis, coupling a declaration of Paul's confidence in Philemon with a request that quarters be prepared that Paul may pay an anticipated visit to the church.
5. Verses 23-25 form the closing of the letter, passing greetings from Paul's companions to Philemon and the others and speaking a final, somewhat formal, word.

Content

Paul, who was in prison, writes a letter with some assistance from Timothy; he opens the letter with a greeting to Philemon, Apphia, Archippus, and the church that met in Philemon's house. It is impossible to say with certainty where Paul was located at the time of the writing. The traditional site of Rome has lost some favor because of the improbability that Paul would backtrack from Rome to visit a congregation in the East after arriving in Italy and planning to work in Spain. A case has been made for Caesarea, but the most commonly advanced theory today is that Paul was in prison in Ephesus (cf. 1 Cor. 15:32; 2 Cor. 1:8-11). The location of the church in Philemon's house is also a puzzle, although the similarities between portions of Philemon and Colossians (whether or not authentically Pauline) lead many scholars to conclude that Philemon lived in Colossae.

Paul then turns toward Philemon in particular. Based upon his knowledge of Philemon's character and secure in his own commission from Christ, Paul addresses the situation. Apparently Onesimus was a slave who belonged to Philemon, one whom Philemon would have regarded as useless, not least because he had fled from his master. Nevertheless, in a rich combination both of metaphors and wordplays Paul fashions his testimony concerning the conversion of Onesimus to Christ — a conversion that had the practical effect of changing Onesimus from being of no account to being highly valuable. Indeed Paul found Onesimus, after his conversion, of such usefulness in his apostolic ministry that he desired to retain Onesimus to assist him rather than return him to Philemon. Paul assumed that Philemon himself would have gladly provided such assistance had he been present, and he was desirous of having Onesimus to assist him in Philemon's behalf; but rather than presume upon Philemon's known generosity, Paul decided to return Onesimus to Philemon and leave the matter to Philemon's volition.

Paul continues his appeal by pleading for Philemon to recognize the transformation and to receive the slave as if he were the apostle himself. Moreover, Paul interjects that should Onesimus owe Philemon in terms of a wrong or a debt, that he (Paul) would himself stand good for the sum; Paul goes so far in this matter as to write the promissory note in his own hand. Yet, Paul moves beyond the appeal and the promise of reimbursement, declaring his confidence in Philemon to do even more than Paul said.

Purpose

There are at least two recognized purposes for Paul's writing to Philemon concerning Onesimus. First, he sought to convince the master to take back the servant without anger or the kinds of harsh punishments permitted by Roman law. Second, and equally important, the apostle sought to secure Onesimus from Philemon for service to him in the gospel ministry. Whether or not this development would include Onesimus' being freed by Philemon is a debatable and irresolvable issue.

Bibliography. E. Lohse, *Colossians and Philemon.* Herm (Philadelphia, 1971); P. T. O'Brien, *Colossians, Philemon.* WBC 44 (Waco, 1982); N. R. Petersen, *Rediscovering Paul: Philemon and the Sociology of Paul's Narrative World* (Philadelphia, 1985); M. L. Soards, "Some Neglected Theological Dimensions of Paul's Letter to Philemon," *Perspectives in Religious Studies* 17 (1990): 209-19; S. K. Stowers, *Letter Writing in Greco-Roman Antiquity.* Library of Early Christianity 5 (Philadelphia, 1986).

MARION L. SOARDS

PHILETUS (Gk. *Phílētos)*
One who, with Hymenaeus, taught that the resurrection had already taken place (2 Tim. 2:17-18).

PHILIP (Gk. *Phílippos)*

1. Philip II, king of Macedon (359-336 B.C.E.). The father of Alexander the Great (1 Macc. 1:1), he was assassinated before embarking on a military expedition against Persia (Josephus *Ant.* 11.304-5). He unified Macedonia, adopted Greek culture, and dominated Greece through the League of Corinth.

2. Philip V, king of Macedon (221-179 B.C.E.). He took up arms against Rome and was decisively defeated in the battle of Cynoscephale (198; 1 Macc. 8:5). Rome left him on a weakened throne, acting as a buffer with Syria under the powerful Antiochus III (for a Judean view, cf. *Ant.* 12.414).

3. Philip the Phrygian, governor of Jerusalem under Antiochus IV Epiphanes, on whose death he was appointed regent over Antiochus V (1 Macc. 6:14-17, 55; 2 Macc. 9:29). According to 1 Macc. 6:63 when Philip tried to assume control himself, Lysias (the young Antiochus' guardian according to *Ant.* 13.296, 360) defeated him in a battle for Antioch (ca. 164/63 B.C.E.).

4. Philip the Tetrarch (ca. 20 B.C.E.–34 C.E.). *See* HEROD (FAMILY) **13.**

5. Herod (Philip?), son of Herod and Mariamme II.
See HEROD (FAMILY) **14.** PETER RICHARDSON

6. Philip the Apostle and Evangelist. In the Synoptic Gospels the name Philip for a follower of Jesus occurs only in the lists of the names of the twelve disciples/apostles (Mark 3:16-19; Matt. 10:2-4; Luke 6:14-16; cf. Acts 1:13). In each instance Philip is presented in fifth position. In John, however, Philip plays a narrative role in 1:43-46; 6:5-7; 12:20-22; 14:8-9. He is said to be from Bethsaida (John 1:44; 12:21), is connected with Greeks seeking Jesus (12:20-21), and serves as a foil for the Johannine Jesus (6:5-7; 14:8-11). It is tempting to conclude that the figure of Philip was "known" by both the author and the readers of the Fourth Gospel.

Ostensibly another early Christian named Philip is introduced in Acts 6:1-7 as a member of the "Seven" appointed by the apostles to care for the Hellenist widows. Luke, the author of Acts, possessed additional traditional material concerning this figure's activity and significance and used it in Acts 8, which attributes to Philip the expansion of the gospel outside Jerusalem: first to Samaria (vv. 5-13), and then to the "ends of the earth" (vv. 26-40), represented in the person of an Ethiopian convert. This groundbreaking "evangelizing" (cf. 8:4, [5], 12, 35, 40) beyond the bounds of Judaism represents a significant fulfillment of Jesus' commission to the apostles in 1:8. After Acts 8 Philip's sole appearance is at 21:8-9, along with his four prophetic daughters, as one of Paul's hosts on the latter's final journey to Jerusalem. Philip's designation as the "evangelist" in 21:8 represents a commonsense conclusion based on his earlier activity in Acts.

Second-century sources are unanimous in their assumption that the Philip Luke is concerned with (i.e., the Philip with four prophetically gifted daughters, Acts 21:9) was, in fact, Philip the apostle. Polycrates understood this Philip to be "one of the Twelve apostles" (cf. Eusebius *HE* 3.31.3; 5.24.2). Even more significant is the identification presupposed by Papias (*HE* 3.39.9), who personally knew the daughters of Philip. Since Philip, along with his daughters, is often invoked in 2nd-century polemical contexts to legitimate this or that group's theological position (in polemical exchanges between Rome and the Montanist/New Prophecy movement in Asia Minor [cf. Proclus in *HE* 3.31.4], by Heracleon for his antimartyr position [cf. Clement of Alexandria *Misc.* 4.71.2-3], by Tatian in support of his contention that true disciples must be unmarried), it can hardly be imagined that the appeal is to anyone other than a clearly recognized authority, i.e., an apostle. Although scholars persistently explain all of these witnesses as "confused," the documentary evidence of the 2nd century should not be so casually discounted.

It is at least possible that Luke does not identify Philip as an apostle in Acts because of his theme that in the earliest period the Twelve remain in Jerusalem (e.g., Acts 8:1). Such a narrative strategy on Luke's part would be directly comparable to his denial of the title "apostle" to Paul (except Acts 14:4, 14) in deference to his conception that only the Twelve were apostles.

Bibliography. C. R. Matthews, *Trajectories through the Philip Tradition* (diss., Harvard, 1993); F. S. Spencer, *The Portrait of Philip in Acts.* JSNTSup 67 (Sheffield, 1992). CHRISTOPHER R. MATTHEWS

PHILIP, ACTS OF
A fragmentary apocryphal work from the 4th or 5th century A.D., surviving in Greek, Syriac, and Latin. It reports 15 acts and the martyrdom of Philip: the apostle raises the dead, heals blind men

with magical words, converses with animals, makes the earth swallow 7000 men, and smiles while hanged upside down by his pierced ankles and thighs. He preaches a severe encratite philosophy of chastity, and his nature metamorphoses from beastly to mild.

Bibliography. J. K. Elliott, *The Apocryphal New Testament*, rev. ed. (Oxford, 1993), 512-18, 531.

RICHARD A. SPENCER

PHILIP, GOSPEL OF (II,3)

A Gospel discovered at Nag Hammadi in 1945. This Coptic translation from a Greek original exists in only one recension and probably dates from the 2nd century. It is not to be confused with the other Gospel of Philip quoted by Epiphanius (*Haer.* 26.13.2-3). The name of the text is attested in the incipit, but its positioning suggests that it may have been a later insertion, possibly suggested because Philip is the only apostle named (Gos. Phil. 73:8).

Variously described as a florilegium, a Valentinian anthology, and sermon notes, the Gospel is probably best understood as a loosely organized "notebook for speculation" (cf. Clement of Alexandria *Excerpta ex Theodoto*). This compilation of several divergent sources is best divided into two major sections: (1) the first three fourths of the text (51:29–77:15) and (2) the final one fourth (77:16–86:19). The first of these two major sections contains a variety of materials including segments related to Thomas traditions (e.g., Gospel of Thomas, Acts of Thomas, Thomas the Contender), traditions reflecting a more classical Gnosticism (e.g., references to a fallen Sophia), and some Valentinian material. The second major section, which speaks with a more coherent voice, includes longer rhetorical units and reflects a primitive Valentinianism, displaying conceptual similarities with the Gospel of Truth (e.g., Gos. Phil. 83:30–84:13; Gos. Truth 18:7-11; 24:28-32).

Despite its textual complexities, the Gospel of Philip remains alluring predominantly because of its discussion of Christian sacramentalism from a gnostic viewpoint. It lists five sacraments including baptism, chrism, eucharist, redemption, and the bridal chamber (67:27-30) and discusses the last of these in some detail (e.g., 70:5-9, 17-22). Among other things it is also unique in its use of the term "Christian" (62:31-32; 74:12-16), which only appears one other time in the Nag Hammadi corpus (Testim. Truth 31:25).

Bibliography. M. L. Turner, *The Gospel According to Philip.* NHMS 38 (Leiden, 1996); R. McL. Wilson, *The Gospel of Philip* (New York, 1962).

ANDREA LORENZO MOLINARI

PHILIPPI (Gk. *Phílippoi*)

A city in Macedonia, northeastern Greece, ca. 17 km. (10 mi.) inland from the Aegean Sea and NW of the port city of Kavala (ancient Neapolis). It was first occupied in the 6th century B.C.E. by settlers from Thasos who named it Krenides ("the springs") because water sources in the region were abundant. The particular feature which drew settlers to the area was the enormous deposits of gold discovered in nearby Mt. Pangeo. The site was renamed Philippoi by Philip II of Macedon (Philip the Great, father of Alexander the Great) ca. 358 when he established a settlement of Macedonians to protect the gold mines from looters. Philippi was brought under Roman rule in 168.

The archaeological site of ancient Philippi lies on the Via Egnatia, which runs through it. Excavations have revealed ruins of Roman baths at the end of a colonnaded street, basilicas on either side of the street, temples, a Roman forum, a 4th-century theater which the Romans renovated for gladiatorial contests, remnants of several Christian churches, and an acropolis which gives evidence of occupation for the Macedonian to the Byzantine ages. The rocky slope on the north side of the road is dotted with numerous inscriptions, shrines, reliefs, and votive carvings which represent numerous religions, myths, cults, and deities that were part of this vibrant and pluralistic society. These include religious movements that spread widely throughout the Mediterranean (e.g., the veneration of Isis and Osiris) as well as purely local deities (e.g., Bendix and the Thracian rider-god).

Philippi was the site of one of the most significant military engagements in Roman history. In a series of battles there in 42 B.C.E., Mark Antony and Octavian (later endowed with the title "Augustus") conquered the republican forces of the assassins of Julius Caesar, Cassius and Brutus. In some ways this battle marked the turning point between the Roman Republic and the Roman Empire. The poet Horace fought in this battle, on the side of Cassius and Brutus, though he reports that he threw away his shield and ran for his life when his defeated leader Brutus killed himself. Little more than a decade later, when Augustus defeated Antony, his sole remaining competitor for Roman rule, at the battle of Actium (31 B.C.E.), Augustus turned Philippi into a Roman colony which he named Colonia Julia Augusta Victrix Philippensis. Here he planted veterans of the civil wars and the supporters of Mark Antony whose lands he took over and whom he dismissed from Italy. Special privileges were allowed to these Roman colonists, such as exemption from taxes and the right to own and market property.

According to Acts 16:9 Paul had a vision that he was to leave Asia Minor and come to Macedonia. He landed at Neapolis, where the major Roman highway, the Via Egnatia, came to its end. Ca. 50 C.E. he, Luke, and Silas came to Philippi and established a Christian fellowship there, founding the first church on European soil. He returned to the city on his second and third journeys. Paul found Philippi to be a cosmopolitan area, with Romans, Greeks, Jews, and people of quite diverse national and ethnic derivation. Because a considerable portion of the citizenry were Romans who enjoyed special privileges as colonists, Paul encountered there a community with a pronounced devotion to and pride in the Roman Empire. The political and religious loyalties of the people appear to have been an issue for Paul. Only in Philippians does he use language that speaks of civil or political identity, when he tells his readers to live in a way that is worthy of the gospel of Christ (Gk. *politeúesthe;* Phil. 1:27) and when he reminds them that they are citizens of heaven (*políteuma;* 3:20). Paul appears to have been trying to get the Philippian Christians to see themselves as Christians first and Romans second, not Romans first and Christians second.

Bibliography. C. Bakirtzis and H. Koester, eds., *Philippi at the Time of Paul and after His Death* (Harrisburg, 1998); S. E. Johnson, *Paul the Apostle and His Cities* (Wilmington, 1987), 70-76.

RICHARD A. SPENCER

PHILIPPIANS, LETTER TO THE

One of the "captivity" epistles (along with Ephesians, Colossians, and Philemon), so called because of internal references to imprisonment (1:7, 12-14, 17, 19; 2:17). Philippians is one of Paul's epistles that best reveals his own struggles and his ongoing relationships with communities he founded. While some doubts were raised about authorship in European scholarship of the last century, today the letter is universally accepted as genuine. After a typical address (1:1-2) and a prolonged thanksgiving (1:3-11), Paul launches an exposition of his present status (1:12-26) followed by an impassioned appeal for community unity (1:27–2:18), news about colleagues (2:19–3:1), a warning about opponents and appeal to follow his example (3:2–4:9), thanks for a gift received (4:10-20), and concluding greetings (4:21-23). Because the letter seems to move suddenly and jarringly from one topic to another and even to conclude several times (3:1a; 4:9, 20), many scholars consider it to be not a literary unity but a compilation of several letters. Phil. 3:1b implies a previous letter, and Polycarp, writing to the same church a century later, knows of more than one letter of Paul to them (*Phil.* 3.2). Phil. 4:10-20 could be an independent acknowledgement of a gift from the Philippians, perhaps written first. Phil. 1:1–3:1; 4:2-9 would be another letter written with the express purpose of exhorting the Philippians to unity. Phil. 3:2–4:1 would be a third letter to warn about judaizing opponents, who do not appear elsewhere in the letter. One of the difficulties with this theory, however, is the way parts of the letter seem to relate to other parts, e.g., the self-emptying of Christ (2:6-11) is paralleled by Paul's account of his own self-emptying (3:4-14), but this could also be the result of later editing.

Philippi was founded under the name Krenides ("springs") by colonists from Thasos ca. 360 B.C.E. It is situated on a plateau about 21 km. (13 mi.) N of its seaport, Neapolis (modern Kavalla) in Macedonia. It was located on the Via Egnatia, a principal Roman road linking the route from Brundisium in Italy across the Adriatic, across Macedonia, to Byzantium. Already part of the Roman province of Macedonia in the 2nd century, the city became a Roman military colony after the nearby victory of Octavian and Antony over Cassius and Brutus in 42 B.C.E., receiving the name Colonia Julia Augusta Philippensis from Augustus a few years later.

Paul writes to the Philippians during an imprisonment (1:7, 12-14, 17) whose outcome is uncertain (1:19-26). The traditional place and time of composition are Rome just before Paul died, sometime toward the end of the reign of Nero, between 64 and 68 C.E. Another possible location is Caesarea during Paul's two-year confinement there, just before he was sent to Rome (Acts 23–27). The problem with both of these locations is the great distance to Philippi and therefore long travel time of a month or more, whereas the letter presupposes numerous visits back and forth (2:19-30; 4:16-18). A third location suggested more recently is Ephesus, from which Philippi could be reached in about one week of travel. According to Acts, Paul spent several years there (Acts 19), but there is no mention of imprisonment. Yet chance comments elsewhere by Paul (2 Cor. 1:8-10; 6:5; 11:23; and 1 Cor. 15:32, which is to be taken figuratively) indicate that he was in prison more than once before his final arrest and that something terrible happened in the province of Asia, of which Ephesus was the most prominent city. Paul's references to the praetorium and the household of Caesar (1:13; 4:22) are often thought to compel a Roman place of origin, but they can apply to any city where there was a contingent of the Praetorian guard and the imperial civil service. Rome, Caesarea, and Ephesus all qualify. If Ephesus is the place of writing, the date would be as much as 10 years earlier, in the mid-50s.

Acts 16 narrates Paul's dream at Troas of a Macedonian asking him to come over and help them. In two days Paul and Silas traveled by sea to Neapolis and took the Roman road up into the hills to Philippi. There on the sabbath at the river outside the western gate they encountered Lydia, a purple-dye merchant from Thyatira, the first convert, whose house became the center of the first Christian community of the city. Acts goes on to tell of Paul's exorcism of a slave girl with a prophetic spirit, his subsequent imprisonment with Silas, their miraculous deliverance by means of an earthquake, the conversion and baptism of the jailkeeper and his household, and the departure of Paul and Silas west down the Via Egnatia to Thessalonica.

Unfortunately, none of the characters or situations narrated in Acts can be seen reflected in Paul's letter. There his traveling companions are Timothy (Acts 16:1 suggests that Timothy also accompanied Paul, but vv. 19, 25, 29 exclude him) and his other assistant, Epaphroditus (1:1; 2:19-30). The names of Philippian Christians mentioned are Euodia and Syntyche, Syzygus (which may be not a proper name but an appellation, "partner"), and Clement (4:2-3). The presence of the Roman name Clement (Clemens) is not surprising given the heavy Roman presence in the city as witnessed by the preponderance of Latin funerary inscriptions from the Roman period.

The Philippian church shows an early tendency to organize. They were apparently the first Pauline church to adopt the secular titles *epískopoi* and *diákonoi* (here "supervisors" and "assistants") for their collegial group of leaders (1:1). The reference to the *diákonos* Phoebe in Rom. 16:1 cautions us not to assume that all these figures in Philippi were male; Euodia and Syntyche, two women whose disagreement with each other is affecting the whole community, are probably among them. Syzygus is likely a male member of the same leadership group who has a gift for reconciliation. Paul asks him to intervene (4:2-3).

Paul seems to have a special affection for the first of his churches on European soil. The thanksgiving section (1:3-11) is the longest of any authentic Pauline letter. There he assures them of a special place in his heart and his longing for them because of their sharing in his apostolic work and suffering (1:7-8). Undoubtedly part of Paul's special affection for them is owing to their extraordinary generosity in the past: they were the only Macedonian church to fund his further travel from there, and they twice sent other monetary gifts besides the present one for which he thanks them (4:15-18; probably 2 Cor. 11:9).

The central message of the letter is the appeal for union of hearts and minds in the face of several community problems, among them disagreements about the significance of circumcision and law observance for believers (3:2-3) and dissensions, such as that between Euodia and Syntyche (4:2), which may be personal or more likely between two house churches of which they are the leaders. It is out of these concerns that Paul incorporates into the letter the "Philippian hymn" (2:6-11) and the autobiographical reflection that provides valuable information about Paul's social and religious background as well as his spiritual account of his relationship with Christ (3:4-15).

The christological hymn in 2:6-11 is one of the earliest poetic statements of the significance of Christ. There is general consensus among scholars that its composition is pre-Pauline, perhaps for liturgical use, and that Paul has incorporated it here for specific effect. There are two general directions of interpretation, depending on the meaning of "equal to God" (Gk. *ísa theṓ*) and self-emptying to take on the form of a slave (vv. 6-7). The traditional interpretation is that the equal status with God refers to Christ's pre-existence, and the self-emptying to the form of a slave refers to incarnation with its result of death. A more recent interpretation that has found significant following is that the equal status with God refers rather to the immortality originally intended for humanity, but spoiled by sin which brings death (Wisd. 2:23-24; Rom. 5:12). This immortality belonged by right to the sinless Christ, who nevertheless emptied himself and took the form of a slave by taking on death as well, even the death of the Cross. The first interpretation emphasizes pre-existence; the second, immortality. There is no general agreement among scholars about the intended meaning or the precise origins of the hymn.

The self-emptying of Christ in 2:6-11 has something of a parallel in Paul's own account of his blameless Jewish background that enables him to boast of his own qualifications in the face of rival claims (3:4-6). The security of his religious status in Pharisaism was forever altered by his encounter with the risen Christ, for whom he suffered the loss of everything (3:7-14). These verses are written, not for the purpose of self-revelation, but of inspiring his readers to imitate him by putting Christ first in their lives without reliance on Jewish ritual practices (3:15-17). While "they" (those who oppose Paul's way of being Christian) glory in physical qualifications and satisfactions (3:19), Paul has adopted the Stoic attitude of *autárkeia,* the freedom by which he enjoys what he has but does not suffer when he does not have it (4:11-13). Nevertheless, his reflections in 3:7-14 are a poignant reminder of the personal cost of Paul's apostleship and his own centering in the mystery of Christ.

CAROLYN OSIEK

PHILISTINES (Heb. *pĕlištîm*)
An Aegean people who migrated to the southern coast of Palestine in the late 13th and early 12th century B.C.E. and became one of the Israelites' fiercest rivals. One of five peoples defeated by Rameses III in his 8th year, they settled on the plain from Raphia north to Joppa. According to the Bible, the Philistines had a league of five major cities (Pentapolis): Ashdod, Ashkelon, Ekron (Tel Miqne; Khirbet el-Muqanna'), Gaza, and Gath. Other sites in the Philistine Plain include Tell Qasile, Tel Gerisa, Tel Ẓafit/Tell eṣ-Ṣafi, Tell Jemmeh, and Tell el-Far'ah. Elsewhere in Palestine evidence of the Philistines has been found at Megiddo, Beth-shean, and Deir 'Alla. The modern name Palestine is derived from the Hebrew term for the people and their territory.

The history of the Philistines can be traced from the period of the judges to the fall of Jerusalem. The Song of Deborah (Judg. 5:6) mentions Shamgar ben Anath, who killed 600 Philistines (3:31). The Samson stories (Judg. 13–16) further relate the tension heightened by Philistine expansion eastward. When Egypt withdrew their control over Palestine ca. 1070, the Philistines filled the power vacuum and within several decades engaged in full-scale war with the Israelites. During the time of Samuel, Israel was defeated at the battle of Ebenezer (1 Sam. 4:1–7:1), Shiloh was destroyed (Jer. 7:12-14), and the ark of the covenant captured. It was the Philistine threat that fired the Israelites' demand for a king. Saul fought the Philistines throughout his reign (1 Sam. 14:47, 48, 52). Israel was victorious at the Battle of Michmash (1 Sam. 13:2-7, 13-23; 14:16-30). David defeated Goliath at Socoh (1 Sam. 17:1-54); the description of Goliath with his weapons and armor matches that of Aegean warriors. Saul was killed when the Israelite army was defeated at the battle of Mt. Gilboa (1 Sam. 31:1-13). His successor, David, pursued the Philistines "from Geba all the way to Gezer" (2 Sam. 5:17-25). Through a series of victories he broke the Philistines' strength (2 Sam. 8:1; 21:15-18) and drove them back to the coastal plain and broke the Pentapolis alliance. Solomon received Gezer as dowry from the Egyptian pharaoh (1 Kgs. 9:16). Nevertheless, war with the Philistines continued during the Divided Monarchy (e.g., 1 Kgs. 15:27; 16:15; 2 Chr. 26:6-7; 28:18; cf. Isa. 9:12[MT 11]). In 712 the Assyrian king Sargon II ordered an attack on

Ashdod (Isa. 20; *ANET,* 84-87) and captured Gath. The Philistines rebelled upon Sargon's death, but Sennacherib recaptured Ashdod in 701 and went on to take Ashkelon, Ekron, and Gaza (*ANET,* 287-88). Under Esarhaddon the Philistine cities were reduced to vassals of Assyria (cf. *ANET,* 291). Although Egypt under Pharaoh Neco II reasserted control over Philistine territory in 612, the end for the Philistines came in 604 with the attack of Nebuchadnezzar II and subsequent deportation (Jer. 25:20).

The main literary source for information about the Philistines is the Bible, which can be supplemented by Egyptian, Assyrian, and Babylonian records. Most important have been the numerous archaeological discoveries in the eastern Mediterranean basin, particularly in Palestine.

Philistine occupation can easily be identified by the distinctive pottery which differs from Egyptian, Israelite, and Canaanite styles. Philistine pottery has been identified as Mycenaean and classified as Myc (Late Helladic) IIIC 1b, dating to the 12th century. The repertoire of forms follows that of Mycenaean pottery, with bell-shaped bowls that have two horizontal handles, large kraters with profile rims and handles, stirrup jars (small globular jars with two handles and a false spout), large globular jars with strainer spouts, pyxides, and two types of bottles. Decoration on the pottery initially copied the monochrome style of Myc IIIC ware, but later the Philistines developed their own style of bichrome ware using black and red on a white slip. The decorations were painted in bands around the body of the pottery and divided into panels. Some of the artistic motifs included looped spirals, concentric circles, half circles in a fishscale pattern, checkers, net design, and stylized birds.

A large monumental building discovered at Tel Miqne features a large hall with two pillars and a freestanding hearth; three square rooms on the east open to the hall. The freestanding hearth was an architectural feature otherwise unknown in Palestine, but characteristic of the Aegean, Anatolia, and Cyprus. Excavations at Tell Qasile (1309.1678) uncovered three stages of a Philistine temple, again reminiscent of Mycenaean form.

1 Sam. 13:19-21 has been interpreted to mean that the Philistines had a monopoly on smelting iron. However, iron was not widely used in Palestine until the 10th century. Excavations at Tel Miqne (Ekron) indicate that under Assyrian rule the city was a major center for the production of olive oil.

Excavations at Deir ʿAlla found in the Philistine level a clay tablet inscribed with a linear script containing 50 characters, grouped into 15 words in a writing tyle related to Minoan A. Two seals (from Ashdod and Tel Batash) also contain letters of a linear script. These short inscriptions have defied translation. A few Philistine loanwords can be identified in the Bible. The lords of the Philistines are called *seren,* which is probably cognate with Gk. *týrannos,* "tyrant." The *-yat* ending of the name Goliath (Heb. *golyāṯ*) is cognate with Hittite *-wattas.* Scholars do not agree on the derivation of the name Achish, king of Gath.

A Pelester (Philistine) prisoner, with feathered headdress. Relief from main temple of Rameses III (20th Dynasty; 1183-1152 B.C.E.), Medinet Habu, West Thebes (Erich Lessing/Art Resource, N.Y.)

The Bible records three gods in connection with the Philistines. Dagon (1 Sam. 5) was more than a grain-god, having broader powers of weather and fertility. Ashtaroth (Judg. 10:6; 1 Sam. 31:8-13) was a mother goddess. Baal-zebub (2 Kgs. 1), "Lord of the Flies," may be a corruption of Baal-zebul, "Baal-Prince" (cf. Ugar. *zbl bʿl*). Excavations have produced several cultic vessels, including a clay figurine called Ashdoda, which depicts a seated goddess in the Mycenaean tradition. Other cult objects include kernoi (tubular rings with attached spouts in the shape of animals), kernos bowls (with tubular rims), and a female-shaped libation vessel.

Bibliography. W. F. Albright, "Syria, the Philistines and Phoenicia," *CAH*³ (Cambridge, 1975) 2/2:507-136; M. Dothan and T. Dothan, *People of the Sea: The Search for the Philistines* (New York, 1992); T. Dothan, *The Philistines and Their Material Culture* (New Haven, 1982); A. Mazar, "The Emergence of Philistine Material Culture," *IEJ* 35 (1985): 95-107; B. Mazar, "The Philistines and the Rise of Israel and Tyre," *Proceedings of the Israel Academy of Sciences and Humanities* 1/7 (Jerusalem, 1964): 1-22; T. C. Mitchell, "Philistia," in *Archaeology and Old Testament Study,* ed. D. W. Thomas (Oxford, 1967), 405-27; G. E. Wright, "Fresh Evidence for the Philistine Story," *BA* 29 (1966): 70-86.

Lawrence A. Sinclair

.ILO OF ALEXANDRIA

Jewish statesman and philosopher (ca. 20 B.C.E.–ca. 50 C.E.). One of the more prolific writers of antiquity, his writings are the most important witnesses to the religious culture of Hellenistic Judaism. We know of only one event in his life: ca. 40 C.E. he led a Jewish delegation to Rome to complain to the emperor Caligula about gentile riots against the Jewish community of Alexandria. The embassy seems to have been modestly successful, and in any case it implies that Philo was an experienced political leader who was widely trusted by Alexandrian Jews.

Whatever his other involvements in public affairs, Philo found time to write a large number of commentaries on books of the Pentateuch (esp. Genesis and Exodus). Indeed, he composed three distinct series of exegetical treatises: the Allegorical Commentary (18 treatises survive), the Exposition of the Law (seven treatises extant), and the Questions and Answers on Genesis and Exodus (partially extant). All three series offer both literal and allegorical interpretations, though the latter are most fully developed in the first series. Philo refers quite often to exegetical predecessors and contemporaries, though never by name; clearly he worked within a tradition of Jewish biblical study, perhaps within some kind of "school" environment. His writings show rhetorical sophistication and a profound knowledge of the Jewish Scriptures and pagan learning. His allegorical explanations often blend Judaism with Middle Platonism. They give particular attention to the spiritual pilgrimage of the human individual from materialism to spiritual monotheism and from bodily passions to virtue through human reason yielding obedience to the divine Logos. Philo regards Moses as the supreme revealer of divine truth, but he does not seem to limit the highest spiritual and intellectual fulfillment to Jews.

Besides scriptural commentaries, Philo wrote a series of thematic treatises on philosophical and apologetic themes (one of the most famous, *On the Contemplative Life,* describes the Therapeutae, a group of Jewish ascetics living near Alexandria; another provides an invaluable account of Palestinian Essenes).

Philo's works must have been appreciated and first preserved by Jews of his own time, but there is virtually no record of Jewish readers of his treatises until the 16th century. By contrast, Christian thinkers such as Clement of Alexandria, Origen, Ambrose, and Augustine read Philo and were heavily influenced by his philosophical theology and allegorical methods. It is not possible to prove that any NT writer knew Philo's works, but some (esp. the authors of Colossians, Hebrews, and the Gospel of John) may have been influenced by Hellenistic Jewish traditions which are also attested by Philo.

Bibliography. Philo of Alexandria, *The Contemplative Life, The Giants, and Selections,* trans. D. Winston (New York, 1981).

DAVID M. HAY

PHILOLOGUS (Gk. *Philólogos*)

A Gentile Christian in Rome greeted by Paul (Rom. 16:15).

PHILOSOPHY

A word used negatively in the Bible to refer to human understanding in contrast with divinely revealed knowledge. In Classical Greek, philosophy (Gk. *philosophía*) could refer to the systematic investigation of a subject or to a distinct body of knowledge. By the 1st century, the term became more generalized to include moral philosophy and religious speculation. Many religious groups tried to convey the impression that they were imparting philosophy, as did many persons employing magic and spells. In Hellenistic Judaism, the term was used in both of its classical senses to designate the search for knowledge by reason and to designate a body of knowledge espoused by a particular group. In 4 Maccabees, e.g., philosophy designates the use of reason over emotions (1:1) to counter the charge that Judaism is a "foolish philosophy" (5:11). The Jewish historian Josephus, on the other hand, uses the term more narrowly and refers to Pharisees, Sadducees, and Essenes as Jewish philosophical schools.

The admonition of Col. 2:8 regarding "philosophy and empty deceit" must be understood in light of these possible meanings. It is highly unlikely that the classical understanding of the term as the pursuit of knowledge through reason is envisioned here. Paul is referring instead to the self-designation of a particular group claiming to hold a special knowledge of or power with relation to the "elements of the universe." This Colossian philosophy apparently involved dietary restrictions (Col. 2:16, 21) and may have involved a syncretistic mix of Jewish traditions involving the sabbath and new moon festivals (2:16). Based upon the supremacy of Christ demonstrated in Col. 1:15-20, however, the letter's polemic points out that such teachings are founded upon human tradition and as a result are empty deceit.

The related term "philosopher" (Gk. *philósophos*) occurs in Acts 17:18, designating adherents to classical philosophical schools of Epicureanism and Stoicism who confront Paul.

Bibliography. E. Lohse, *Colossians and Philemon.* Herm (Philadelphia, 1971).

MATTHEW S. COLLINS

PHINEHAS (Heb. *pînĕḥās;* Egyp. *p'nḥsy*)

1. The son of Eleazar and grandson of Aaron (Exod. 6:25), who settled at Gibeah (Josh. 24:33). Ps. 106:30-31 memorializes Phinehas for his righteous act of slaying Zimri for consorting with a Midianite woman in the Israelite camp (Num. 25:1-18). Moses sent Phinehas to accompany the Israelites in battle against the Midianites (Num. 31:6) and later established him as leader of the Korahite gatekeepers (1 Chr. 9:20). Josh. 22:9-34 recounts Phinehas' role in settling the dispute between the 10 tribes and the Reubenites, Gadites, and the half tribe of Manasseh because of the great altar constructed on the eastern side of the Jordan River. Phinehas' last recorded act as high priest (Judg. 20:28) occurred during the Benjaminite civil war. Phinehas delivered the oracle of God to the Israelites, instructing them to fight the next day (cf. 1 Esdr. 5:5; Sir. 45:23-24; 1 Macc. 2:26, 54).

2. The younger son of Eli (1 Sam. 1:3; 2 Esdr. 1:2), who defiled himself through sexual intercourse with women serving the shrine at Shiloh and dishonored the Lord by improper sacrifices (1 Sam. 2:15-17, 22-25). The Philistines slew Phinehas and his brother Hophni as they escorted the ark of the covenant at the second battle of Aphek-Ebenezer (4:1b-11). Learning of this disaster, Phinehas' wife died in premature childbirth, having her son Ichabod, "The glory has departed from Israel." Later genealogies (Ezra 7:1-2; 1 Chr. 6:4ff.[MT 5:30ff.]; 1 Esdr. 8:1-2) omit this second Phinehas (though they do mention his son Atihub), thereby fulfilling God's judgment against any of Eli's future descendants who dishonored the Lord while serving as a priest (1 Sam. 2:30).

3. Father of a postexilic priest (Ezra 8:33), perhaps the Levite named as the father of Eleazar (1 Esdr. 8:2, 63). ARCHIE W. ENGLAND

PHLEGON (Gk. *Phlégōn*)
A Christian in Rome to whom Paul sent his greetings (Rom. 16:14).

PHOEBE (Gk. *Phoíbē*)
A leading woman and deacon of the church at Cenchreae, the eastern port of Corinth. She carried Paul's letter to the Roman church (Rom. 16:1-2). Phoebe appears first in a long list, indicating her importance to Paul. The formulaic opening of Rom. 16 suggests it may be a letter of commendation for her as she travels. Mentioned without male associate, her freedom to travel suggests Phoebe was single or a widow, would have been in danger traveling alone, and provides evidence that women served the Church in itinerant capacities. Three important terms describe Phoebe. She is "our sister" (Gk. *adephḗ*), a fellow Christian. She is a "deacon" (*diákonon,* not "deaconess"; no distinction is made between female and male activity), a technical term of office whose duties are not self-evidently clear (cf. 1 Tim. 3:8-13). She was a "benefactor" *(prostátis)* or patron, used only here in the NT but a common legal term for technical patronage, indicating her responsibility for a church which probably met in her home (the masculine form appears three times in 1 Clement for Jesus as "patron" of Christians). In this role she helped the church in Cenchreae and Paul himself. A Gentile Christian, highly recommended and approved of by Paul, Phoebe was a prominent deacon who served, worked in, supported, and traveled for an apostolic church.

Bibliography. W. D. Thomas, "Phoebe: A Helper of Many," *ExpT* 95 (1984): 336-37.

BONNIE THURSTON

PHOENICIA (Gk. *Phoinikē*)
The name by which the Greeks and Romans called ancient Canaan, the coastal region of southern Syria-Lebanon-Israel. Extending roughly from the city of Arwad (Aradus) in the north to Ascalon in the south, the region was inhabited in antiquity by a Northwest Semitic people calling themselves Canaanites or Pon(n)im, the origin of the name Phoenicia(n). In the strictest and narrowest sense, as used by the Phoenicians themselves, Canaan denoted this coastal region alone, dominated politically and culturally in the 1st millennium B.C. by the city-states of Tyre and Sidon.

Phoenician overseas expansion and colonization in the western Mediterranean, undertaken as early as ca. 1200 by the Tyrians and Sidonians, resulted in the emergence of a Greater Phoenicia, comprising two subregions, Phoenicia proper, the historical homeland; and Western Phoenicia. Western Phoenicia comprised the coastal regions of North Africa (from Cyrenaica to Western Morocco), southern and southwestern Spain, northwestern and western Sicily, as well as the islands of Malta, Gozo, Sardinia, Majorca, and Minorca. Most important of the Western Phoenician states was Carthage in Tunisia, founded in 825 or 814 by Tyre. By ca. 500 Carthage had become the dominant political and cultural center of the Western Phoenicians, and in a real sense it supplanted Tyre in importance in the Classical period. At its height, Carthage rivaled Greece and Rome, and Western Phoenician (called Punic, so to differentiate it from Phoenician) was a world-class language as significant as Greek and Latin. Although Carthage was defeated and destroyed by Rome in 146, Western Phoenician language, religion, and culture continued to flourish in Africa and elsewhere well into the 5th century C.E. In this period the Punic language counted among its native speakers the Roman emperor Septimius Severus, the poet Appuleius, and the church father Augustine.

People and Language

Inasmuch as the cities of Tyre and Sidon held hegemony over Eastern and Western Phoenicia throughout the 1st millennium, "Tyrian" and "Sidonian," used as cultural terms, came also to be functionally equivalent to "Phoenician." Indeed, already in the 9th century the dialect of Tyre and Sidon had been accepted by all Phoenicians as a standard literary language; the language of Western Phoenicia (Punic) is merely a subdialect of this language.

In broader historical perspective, the Phoenicians were one of the several peoples of the ethnolinguistic "Canaanite" subgroup of the Semitic peoples, to which belonged Israelites, Moabites, Ammonites, and Edomites. Although politically distinct at an early period, these peoples traced historical descent from a common culture, speaking closely related languages and possessing related cultural and religious traditions and institutions. Thus, in the late Classical period, the Phoenicians themselves traced their origins to an ancestor

The Tophet or "Precinct of Tanit" at Carthage, burial ground for the victims of the rite of child sacrifice. Excavation of square CT 6 shows urns and stelae in situ
(Photograph by Gradon Wood, ASOR Punic Project; copyright President and Fellows of Harvard College for the Semitic Museum)

named *Khna* ("Canaan"), said by them to have been the brother of *Isirilos* ("Israel"). This lineage indicates awareness of an historical and cultural bond to the Israelites.

Religion

Gods

The religion of the Phoenicians was a conservative expression of the ancient religion of Canaan, preserving forms, traditions, and practices that Israelite religion had long rejected and abolished. Phoenician religion remained polytheistic and iconic and, to the end, tolerant and accommodating of diversity. Possessing no central or coherent doctrine or "truth," it was always ready to absorb the gods and practices of other religions, including those of the Israelites.

The Phoenicians possessed numerous words for "god(s)" or "goddess(es)," the most common being *ilim,* used for "god," "goddess," and "gods." A god was normally addressed and referred to by the title "Lord" *(adum)* and a goddess by "Lady" *(ribbot* or *adot)* or "Our Lady" *(ribbaton).* Two common epithets of a god or goddess were "holy" *(qiddis)* and "powerful, great" *(iddir).*

The gods of the Phoenicians were organized in the Pantheon in three orders, in the manner of earlier Canaanite religion: the High Gods, largely otiose; the active gods, those of common worship; and the Infernal Gods. Nothing of the rich mythology of the High Gods other than their names and titles survives: Il, Creator of Earth (chief of the gods), Semes (sun-goddess), Yerah (moon-god), Khusor (artisan-god, in his female form Khusart identified in late Classical antiquity with the Israelite "goddess" Turo, the Torah), and Balsamem (lord of the heavens, Uranos). Curiously, Il's consort, the goddess Ashirat, is never mentioned in Phoenician religion of the 1st millennium.

For the active gods, the most prominent were Baal, Baalhammun, Esmun (Baal Sidon, "proprietary god of Sidon," identified with Greek Asklepios), Milqart (Baal Sor, "proprietary god of Tyre"), Milkastart (god of the city of Hammun, near Tyre), Meskar, Osiris (the Egyptian god), Rasap, and Sikkun. Most important of the female gods was Astarte, patron deity of the kings and queens of Sidon, who were her priests. Other prominent goddesses were Anat, Isis (the Egyptian goddess), and Tinnit. Ruling the netherworld were the god Nergal and the goddess Hawwit, called Amma, "Mother."

Major gods, like Baal or Astarte, had their cults in many cities and were specified, e.g., as "Baal/Astarte (who is) in Tyre" or "Baal/Astarte of Tyre." As held in the theology of the pre-Persian period, the gods resided in their cities, in the temple built for them, and were the divine proprietors of the cities and peoples they ruled. Thus, Milqart was "proprietor of Tyre" (Baal Sor) and Esmun "proprietor of Sidon" (Baal Sidon). The inhabitants of a city understood themselves to be in the custodial care of their proprietary gods and under their protection. An altogether similar relationship existed between a god and a family, especially a ruling family or royal dynasty.

In the Persian period, a new theology emerged which held that the gods permanently resided not in their cities but "in the Great Heavens." Thus, in the Roman period, we find the fellowship of the god Meskar praying to the god "facing Heaven."

Another theological innovation, related to the new theology of heaven, appeared in the late period: the duality of god. This belief held that a god *(ilim)* was actually two gods *(allonim),* the first (called by his simple name) being his heavenly manifestation, the other (called by his name prefixed by the word *mal'ak*) being his earthly manifestation. For instance, Milkastart and Mal'ak-Milkastart designate the same god, yet at the same time, discrete gods: one as two or two in one, a celestial form and a terrestrial form. In historical perspective we have here the evolution of the concept of the divine messenger *(mal'ak):* in the 2nd millennium, in early Canaanite mythology, every major god had a messenger or two to do his bidding; in the 1st millennium, in Phoenician religion, a god was his own messenger, assuming that role and appropriate form, when among humans.

Temple

A Phoenician temple was the "house of a god/goddess" *(bet ilim),* also called simply a "house" *(bet);* thus, Baal's temple was "Baal's house" *(bet Baal).* The temple, a complex consisting of the "house of the god" and a courtyard *(haser),* was situated upon a hill, called "the mountain of the gods," inside a large protected area or precinct, surrounded by a wall or fence. The inauguration of a new temple was known as the day when "the god entered the sacntuary," i.e., when the statue of the god/goddess was brought into the temple; it was at this time that the sacred implements for the cult were "given over to the priests" by the municipal officials "in charge of temples."

Many kinds of temple edifices existed, but the most common form was that built by Phoenician (Tyrian) architects for the god of Israel in the time of Solomon. It was a three-room structure, consisting of an anteroom or vestibule; a main sanctuary; and, in the rear, a small private room or holy of holies, containing the statue of the god/goddess and the divan upon which the god/goddess slept.

Associated with the temple, either an annex or separate structure, was the "depository," in which were stored images, statues, altars, and other such furniture and equipment required by the priests; the depository had its own administrator. Included was the temple treasury, from which expenses were paid, such as the salaries of the priests and other hired personnel, as well as ransoms to secure the release of citizens from imprisonment and arrest in neighboring cities.

Temple Personnel

The Phoenician temple had a large staff, consisting of religious and lay personnel. Four classes of priests are known: (1) the *kuhen,* the principal class of priest, headed by the "Chief of Priests"; a "priestess" served primarily female deities, like Astarte; (2) the *kumir,* whose function is not known; (3) the "watch-priest" *(sufe);* and (4) the "sacrifical priest" *(zabah),* charged with administering the rite of the "Surrender of the Firstborn," i.e., the cult of infant sacrifice. Assisting the consecrated priests was an order of lay priests called "helpers" *('ozrim),* headed by the "Prefect of Helpers." Also attached to the cult was the "man of the god/goddess" *(is ilim),* a cultic prophet, known also in Israelite religion *('îš hā'ĕlōhîm);* nothing substantive is known of the role of this cultic functionary.

The professional staff of the temple were assisted by a large staff of "service personnel," headed by a lay person called the "Head of the Service Personnel." Many of this staff were salaried employees, among them young boys *(na'arim)* and young women *('alamut),* as well as technical service people (professional scribes, barbers, bakers, singers), artisans (architects and builders), and workers. The latter appear to have been members of a special "labor force" who were in the charge of "taskmasters."

Daily Sacred Liturgy

The divine service (lit., "sacred work") resembled to some degree that performed in the Egyptian temple. At dawn, a specialized priest called the "Awakener of the Gods" entered the holy of holies and bade the sleeping god/goddess (i.e., the statue lying on its divan) to awaken (cf. 1 Kgs. 18:27). (This same act was performed in the Jerusalem temple by levitical priests called the "Awakeners" *(mĕ'ôrĕrîm),* who stood on a platform in front of the holy of holies; the practice and priesthood were abolished by John Hyrcanus.) Once roused, the statue of the god/goddess underwent an elaborate divine toilette. After being shaved, washed, and dressed, the statue was served freshly baked "loaves of bread"; these are the so-called "shewbread" or "loaves of the presence [properly, 'placed before God']" of the Israelite temple.

Sacrifice

Sacrifice to the gods at the temple was strictly controlled by public and religious law administered by a municipal bureau called the "Thirty men in charge of (Sacrificial) Prices." The charge for every animal available to purchase for sacrifice at the temple, specification of what parts of the animal belonged to the person sacrificing and to the priest, proper practice required of the priests and the public, including fines to be exacted for violations all were published in a book kept by the Thirty and in condensed form in a tariff (lit., "sales document") posted at the temple. As in Israelite practice, sacrifices were of two basic kinds: the "whole burnt offering" and the cereal offering. Animals offered on the altar included bovines, sheep and goats, fowl, wild game; also offered were oil, fat, and milk.

Three major seasonal public or communal sacrifices were observed: the periodic sacrifice of an ox; a lamb at plowing time; and a lamb at harvest time. In addition, there were the daily sacrifice and the monthly sacrifice on the new moon and the full moon. The latter were offered to ensure the welfare of the royal family and one's own family.

Child Sacrifice

Child sacrifice was an essential element of Phoenician religion. Although this ancient rite seems to have been obsolete in the Phoenician motherland, it continued to be practiced vigorously by the Western Phoenicians well into the Late Roman period. Two related rites were connected with the sacrifice: the "Vow in Distress," entailing the immolation of a child in fulfillment of a vow made to obtain divine intervention to overcome a personal or national difficulty; and the "Surrender of the Firstborn/Firstling," the tendering of the firstborn son of one's own flesh to the god(s), presumably as an expression of obedience.

The sacrifice itself was called "a *molk*-offering of a human being." The human victim was called an *izrim,* "one snatched away before one's time at the age of a few days"; another term for the victim was "one brought to the god(s)." The qualification that the child be of the sacrificer's own flesh was an assurance of compliance with strict orthopraxis, which disallowed the substitution of the child of a slave for one's own to circumvent the law.

The immolation was performed by a specialized class of priest called the "Sacrificer" *(zabbah).* The cremated remains were placed in urns, which were deposited in a large open-air precinct (perhaps called the "sacred field"); the sites were marked by small stelae inscribed with religious symbols and the formula of presentation containing the name of the person(s) who made the sacrifice.

The Phoenicians shrouded child sacrifice in euphemisms in order to deny its horrific character. Until the Roman period, the word "sacrifice" *(zaboh)* was never used in connection with the rite; rather, the parent is said only to have "brought" or "carried" his child to the god. Yet more telling is the deceptive name "Good and Happy Day" to describe the day of the sacrifice. Justification of the rite was the belief that the children were elevated to special godhood in the netherworld, they constituting a distinct class of the dead called "the gods who were sacrificed."

Death and the Netherworld

The Phoenicians shared the common Canaanite belief in a netherworld where the dead lived on as gods, called the "Rafa'im gods." When one died, one went to have "rest among the Rafa'im." According to Western Phoenician belief, the netherworld, called the "Dark Chamber(s)," was ruled by "Hawwit, the goddess who rules the Dead," also known as "Mother." Her male companion was probably the god Nergal. Entry into the netherworld may perhaps not have been automatic but earned through righteous conduct during one's lifetime; this may be inferred from the term *miske* ("those who died innocent") for the dead over whom Hawwit ruled. Other epitaphs note that the deceased "died an innocent person," "was honest during his lifetime," or "was righteous." This aspect of Phoenician funerary belief may have been deeply influenced by the cult of Isis and Osiris, which was popular in both Western and Eastern Phoenicia.

Society and Its Values

Phoenician society, East and West, was powerfully motivated by a profound sense of civic and religious responsibility on the part of the individual and the collective. Primary and most highly esteemed of virtues was the "performance of service on behalf of the community," or "(public) service" *(misrat).* Service entailed sustained effort to benefit the welfare of one's community and one's god(s); it was incumbent upon every individual and group, with the promise of public reward and acclaim for action but social ostracism and divine condemnation for inaction.

Dedication to public service was also a primary focus of the most important of all Phoenician social institutions, the men's fellowships or clubs: the *marzih ilim* and the *mizrah ilim.* These were essentially eating and drinking clubs (cf. Amos 6:4-6). Known by the general term "fellowship" the clubs were organized of a general membership of "fellows," headed by an elected president called the "convenor." The club's financial affairs, including renting quarters for its meetings, were attended to by an elected "treasurer." Not merely humans belonged to such clubs but the gods as well, as depicted in the ancient Canaanite mythology, which provides an account of the god Il's eating and drinking to intoxication at the banquet of his *marzih.* Indeed, in Canaanite society it was the duty of a good son to carry his drunken father home. While organized primarily for social pursuits, the clubs were each affiliated with a particular god/goddess. It was to the service of their patron god that the membership devoted itself assiduously, together to pray and to sacrifice jointly to their patron deity.

Bibliography. D. C. Baramki, *Phoenicia and the Phoenicians* (Beirut, 1961); D. B. Harden, *The Phoenicians,* 3rd ed. (New York, 1980); S. Lancel, *Carthage: A History* (Oxford, 1995); P. MacKendrick, *The North African Stones Speak* (Chapel Hill, 1980); S. Moscati, *The World of the Phoenicians* (London, 1968); B. H. Warmington, *Carthage,* 2nd ed. (New York, 1969).

CHARLES R. KRAHMALKOV

PHOENIX (Gk. *Phoínix*)

A town and anchorage on the southwestern coast of Crete which Paul's ship unsuccessfully attempted to reach (Acts 27:12). It may be located at the northeast corner of Cape Mouros (the modern village of Loutro), or more likely a bay at the northwest corner of the cape, the site of a chapel called Phoinika. Cape Mouros has a fair harbor but offers little protection against the northeast winter wind. The bay to the northwest would have provided protection and fits the description in Acts. Today it has no satisfactory anchorage, but earthquakes in the 6th century may have altered the ocean depth.

JAMES A. BROOKS

PHRYGIA (Gk. *Phrygía*)
A territory in west central Asia Minor (Acts 2:10; 18:23), a plateau which includes rock mesas and mountains as well as broad river basins. Phrygia's pine forests and sheep herds yielded timber and wool, and Phrygian artisans produced fine metal work, embroidery, and carpets.

The Phrygians probably migrated from Thrace at the end of the 2nd millennium B.C.E. Following Hittite domination of central Asia Minor, they ruled a more loosely organized confederation, flourishing during the middle of the 1st millennium. The short-lived Phrygian Empire (ca. 725-675), founded by King Midas, ruled western Asia Minor until the Cimmerian invasion allowed the Lydians to gain ascendancy. The Phrygian capital was at Gordion. Pessinus, the temple-state of the Mother of the Gods (Cybele), was also a major Phrygian city.

Many settlements in the Phrygian highlands centered around "kales," fortified rock mesas. At these sites, the Phrygians left behind huge rock-cut monuments, flat facades carved with geometric designs surrounding niches for huge images of the Mother of the Gods. Some are inscribed in Old Phrygian. The most prominent is the Midas monument at the remains of Midas City, a village near modern Eskisehir.

In the Roman era, Phrygia was recognized as an ethnic territory comprising the eastern portion of the Roman province of Asia. The eastern part of what had been the Phrygian kingdom was absorbed into the province Galatia. The ethnic name Phrygian was frequently synonymous with "slave" during the Greco-Roman era. Inscriptions from as late as the 3rd century C.E. are found in the Neo-Phrygian language.

Bibliography. E. Akurgal, *Ancient Civilizations and Ruins of Turkey,* 8th ed. (Istanbul, 1993); C. H. Haspels, *The Highlands of Phrygia,* 2 vols. (Princeton, 1971). SUSAN (ELLI) ELLIOTT

PHYGELUS (Gk. *Phýgelos*)
A Christian from the province of Asia, who, together with Hermogenes and other Asian Christians, abandoned the imprisoned Paul (2 Tim. 1:15).

PHYLACTERIES
A pair of small black leather boxes (Heb. *tĕpillîn*) containing parchment slips inscribed with biblical commandments (Exod. 13:1-10, 11-16; Deut. 6:4-9; 11:13-21). Although the command to "bind them [the words of the Torah] as a sign on your hand and they shall be as a frontlet on your forehead" (Deut. 6:8) was probably not originally intended to be taken literally, the Jews developed the practice of binding *tĕpillîn* to their left arm and head. Made of the skins of "clean" animals, they were attached to the body by leather straps of any color except blood red. Sometimes in the 1st century and before, other passages from the Torah (e.g., the Decalogue and Deut. 5:22-23) were also included, as attested by the *tĕpillîn* found among the Dead Sea Scrolls.

Gk. *phylaktḗrion* (only in Matt. 23:5) is derived from the verb *phylássō,* "to guard/protect." Accordingly, some scholars have suggested that the phylactery served as a magical amulet (cf. *b. Ber.* 6a, 23b, 30b; *Menaḥ.* 43b). The vast amount of evidence, however, suggests another primary purpose. The verb *phylássō* sometimes has the nuance "to observe (the commandments)" (so Ep. Arist. 159). The rabbis, Targums, and Peshitta all refer to the same objects by Aram. *tĕpillîn,* which derives from either *pll* ("to pray") or *plh* ("to separate/distinguish [Jews from non-Jews]").

Rabbinic sources suggest that in the 1st century C.E. and before it was customary for the observant to wear phylacteries all day; today, "laying *tĕpillîn*" occurs only during morning prayers in weekday services. W. E. NUNNALLY

PI-BESETH (Heb. *pî-ḇeseṯ*)
A city in Lower Egypt on the easternmost branch of the Nile Delta, at modern Tell Basṭa 1.5 km. (1 mi.) SE of modern Zagazig and 63 km. (39 mi.) NNE of Cairo. Pi-beseth (Egyp. *Pr-Bȝst,* "home of Bastet (the cat-goddess]") is mentioned with On, another city in Lower Egypt, in Ezekiel's oracle against Egypt (Ezek. 30:17).

PIGEON
Any of several birds of the family Columbidae. The NRSV translates Heb. *yônâ* as "pigeon" when referring to sacrificial animals (elsewhere "dove"). Birds were usually offered for sacrifice as an alternative to larger animals; their use for sacrifice is, therefore, an indication of relative poverty (e.g., Lev. 5:7; Luke 2:24), although a cereal offering might be an even greater indication of poverty (Lev. 5:11).

In the NT Gk. *peristerá* is translated "dove" with reference to birds sacrificed at the temple (Matt. 21:12; Mark 11:15; John 2:14, 16). "Pigeons" are mentioned only at Luke 2:24 to distinguish between two species of birds in a quotation from Lev. 12:8.

Heb. *gôzāl* is translated "young pigeon" in recounting animals cut in half for a covenant ritual (Gen. 15:9; cf. Deut. 32:11). JESPER SVARTVIK

PI-HAHIROTH (Heb. *pî-haḥîrôṯ*)
A place of encampment on the route of the Exodus, in the eastern Delta near Migdol and Baal-Zephon (Exod. 14:2, 9; Num. 33:7-8). The name cannot be identified with any known site. The LXX and Syriac have variant readings, including "the mouth of Heritha, the canal" (Num. 33:7 Syr.), which may refer to irrigation trenches connected to the eastern canal (cf. William F. Albright, who suggests that the name is a Semitized form meaning "mouth of the canals"; Roland de Vaux, "mouth of the channels").

LAWRENCE A. SINCLAIR

PILATE, ACTS OF
Originally written in Greek, an apocryphal work surviving in many medieval manuscripts, the oldest from the 12th century, and in Latin, Coptic, Syriac, Armenian, and Arabic translations. In a number of medieval manuscripts it is found together with another work, Christ's Descent into

Hell, and entitled the Gospel of Nicodemus. The date is uncertain. Justin Martyr (mid-2nd century) refers to an Acts of Pontius Pilate (*Apol.* 5, 21), but scholars are unsure that this is the same document. Eusebius refers to the Acts of Pilate in the early 4th century (*HE* 1.9.3; 9.5.1). A 5th-century revision (Recension B) makes numerous changes and additions.

The work follows the outline of the Passion and Resurrection narratives of the canonical Gospels. The author depends most heavily on Matthew and John, but knows the longer ending of Mark. He greatly expands this basic outline with much additional material, and is particularly interested in Pilate, Joseph of Arimathea, and Nicodemus.

When Jesus is brought before Pilate, the standards, which bear images of the emperor, bow before Jesus. The Jewish authorities claim that the standard-bearers lowered them. Pilate tells them to choose 12 men of their own to bear the standards. When they do so, the standards again bow on their own accord before Jesus.

After the Crucifixion and burial the Jewish authorities lock up Joseph of Arimathea in a building without a window. He escapes and later tells them that the building was lifted up from the ground and the risen Jesus let him out, took him to the now empty tomb, then to his house, and put him in his bed.

Other Jews tell the Jewish authorities and the people how they saw Jesus speak to his disciples on Mt. Mamlich in Galilee and how he was then taken up bodily into heaven. The authorities reserve judgment about this, and the people praise God for his fulfilling the Scriptures.

Bibliography. F. Scheidweiler, "The Gospel of Nicodemus; Acts of Pilate, and Christ's Descent into Hell," in *New Testament Apocrypha,* ed. W. Schneemelcher and R. McL. Wilson, rev. ed., 1 (Louisville, 1991): 501-36. J. Christian Wilson

PILATE, PONTIUS (Gk. *Póntios Pilátos*)
Roman governor or procurator of Judea, 26-36 C.E. (Matt. 27:2; Josephus *Ant.* 18.2.2 [35]; 18.3.1 [55]; *BJ* 2.9.2 [169]; Philo *Leg.* 299). According to an inscription found at Caesarea, he was a *praefectus Iudaeae,* a commander of auxiliary troops (500-1000 soldiers).

The Gospel accounts depict Pilate as an equitable but weak governor, probably to promote positive relations between the Roman government and Christianity (Mark 15:1-15 par.). The Jewish leaders ask Pilate for Jesus' death sentence on the grounds of treason (esp. Luke 23:1-2). After interrogation, Pilate pronounces Jesus innocent; yet he yields to the crowds' demands for Jesus' execution. Pilate acquiesces to satisfy the crowd (Mark 15:15), to stop a riot (Matt. 27:24), to silence the people's pleas for Jesus' death (Luke 23:18-25), and to affirm his loyalty to the emperor (John 19:12-13). Additional incidents function to shift the responsibility for Jesus' death away from Pilate. In Matt. 27:19-25 Pilate, heeding his wife's advice, disassociates himself from Jesus and "washes" his hands; then the crowds claim responsibility for his death. In Luke 23:6-12 Pilate sends Jesus to Herod to be tried, who then returns him to Pilate without condemnation, thereby confirming Pilate's judgment of innocence.

Josephus and Philo, however, describe Pilate as extremely offensive, cruel, and corrupt. Josephus reports that Pilate violated the Jewish law against graven images when he brought into Jerusalem the emperor's images attached to the Roman standards (*Ant.* 18.3.1 [55-59], *BJ* 2.9.2-3 [169-74]). According to Philo, Pilate also offended the Jews when he put shields bearing the emperor's name in the former palace of Herod in Jerusalem (*Leg.* 299-305). His misappropriation of temple funds to finance the building of an aqueduct in Jerusalem provoked a riot that left many Jews dead (*Ant.* 18.3.2 [60-62]; *BJ* 2.9.4 [175-77]). After a cruel massacre of the Samaritans, Pilate was summoned to Rome (*Ant.* 18.4.1-2 [85-89]). He was not reappointed as governor. Emily Cheney

PILDASH (Heb. *pildāš*)
A son of Abraham's brother Nahor and Milcah (Gen. 22:22).

PILGRIMAGE
Travel to a holy site to participate in special rites was common in the ancient Mediterranean (Olympus, Epidauros) and Near Eastern (Harran, Teman) worlds. In Israel too pilgrims visited key sites, including Mt. Sinai, Jerusalem, and others (Bethel, Hos. 4:15 [cf. the temple etiology in Gen. 28]; Gilgal, 1 Sam. 10:8; Hos. 4:15; and Shiloh, 1 Sam. 1). From very early times, the primary pilgrimage festivals were Passover, Pentecost, and Tabernacles (Exod. 23:14), even if their precise dates varied by region (cf. 1 Kgs. 12:32-33). Pilgrimage was an occasion for dancing and singing (Ps. 42:4[MT 5]).

The Bible indirectly attests a practice of pilgrimage to Sinai. Elijah makes a 40-day trek to Horeb (1 Kgs. 19) in order to receive a revelation. The duration of the journey corresponds to the 40-year sojourn of Israel in the wilderness. The itinerary of Num. 33 probably reflects stops along the pilgrimage route to Sinai. One of these stops may have been the khan at Kuntillet ʿAjrud/Ḥorvat Teman (0940.9560), where the excavator Zeev Meshel has found pots inscribed "to Yahweh and his Asherah" and fabric-blended cloth with possible cultic significance.

Jerusalem's stature as a pilgrimage site owes much to the royal ideology associated with the Davidide dynasty. The city became the mythical center of the universe and the cosmic mountain (Isa. 2; cf. Ps. 2). Pilgrims sang a series of hymns while approaching the city (Pss. 120–134). These picturesque "songs of ascents" capture the religious feelings of the community coming to the Solomonic temple from the surrounding hills (Pss. 121–122). They also celebrate Yahweh's commitment to Jerusalem (Pss. 126–127, 133) and its rulers (132).

In the Second Temple period the sacred precinct became an important regional banking center while maintaining its ideological significance for the formative Jewish and Christian communities. Pilgrims gathered outside Jerusalem from throughout the Diaspora and traveled via Ashkelon, Gaza, or Jaffa into the city (*b. Sanh.* 11a; cf. Luke 2:41-52). Numerous burial inscriptions and other memoria of pilgrims survive. Despite Jesus' ambivalence toward the temple (Mark 13), his disciples continued to visit, and even Paul is reported to have made a pilgrimage in fulfillment of a vow (Acts 21:23-26). While the destruction of the temple in 70 C.E. and expulsion of Jews from the city in 138 altered the rhythms of pilgrimage, the city retained its attractions. Constantine's legalization of Christianity ushered in a period of imperially sponsored construction of churches (notably the Church of the Holy Sepulchre under St. Helena and later emperors; cf. the Bourdeaux pilgrim). Jerusalem became the magnet for three faiths, which it remains today.

Bibliography. J. D. Levenson, *Sinai and Zion: An Entry into the Jewish Bible* (Minneapolis, 1985); Z. Meshel, *Kuntillet Ajrud* (Jerusalem, 1978).

MARK W. HAMILTON

PILHA (Heb. *pilḥā'*)
One of the chiefs of the people who set his seal to the new covenant under Nehemiah (Neh. 10:24[MT 25]).

PILLAR
A standing stone (Heb. *maṣṣēḇâ*) erected as a memorial or an object of worship. During the period of the patriarchs, stones were set up as memorials (Gen. 28:18; 31:45-52; 35:14, 20; Exod. 24:4; 2 Sam. 18:18), sometimes representing God's dwelling (Gen. 28:22). Sometimes translated as "image" (KJV), the Hebrew term also refers to stones set up to represent Canaanite deities, a practice abhorred by the biblical writers. This practice of erecting stones to represent deities was adopted by the Israelites (Exod. 23:24; Lev. 26:1; 1 Kgs. 14:23; 2 Chr. 31:1). As these stones were associated with the Canaanite god Baal and were possibly erected alongside a wooden pillar symbolizing the female deity Asherah, they may have in some cases been phallic symbols. The term is also used to refer to an Egyptian obelisk (Jer. 43:13); Isaiah refers to a *maṣṣēḇâ* which shall be erected on the border of Egypt to signify God's lordship over foreign nations (Isa. 19:19). Both of these references affirm that the *maṣṣēḇâ* is a monument of the god's presence (the Egyptian sun-god Amon-Re and the Hebrew god, respectively) and thus an object of worship.

Many examples of pillars are known from Bronze and Iron Age Palestine. Architectural pillars used as supports are found made of either roughly shaped stones or well-cut stones with capitals (as at Megiddo and Samaria). Stones found standing alone or in rows can be interpreted quite differently, however, as they have no structural purpose, often have smooth rounded tops, and are found in association with materials of a cultic nature. The Middle Bronze Age "high place" at Gezer consists of 10 large standing stones with smooth tops and a basinlike structure, and has been interpreted by some as standing for living persons or clans united in the worship of a deity embodied by the sacred pillar. A Late Bronze Age temple at Hazor includes a row of basalt standing stones with smooth rounded tops, found in association with a basalt figure of a male deity. One of the stones has an engraved representation of two arms upraised in a gesture of adoration beneath the emblem of the sun-god.

Heb. *'ammûḏ* usually refers to architectural pillars and columns (Exod. 26:32, 37; 1 Kgs. 7:15-22) and the pillar of fire and pillar of cloud in the Exodus story.

JENNIE R. EBELING

PILLAR OF CLOUD, PILLAR OF FIRE
Complementary manifestations of the divine presence, cloud by day and fire by night, to guide the Israelites through the wilderness (Exod. 13:21). The combined term only occurs in Exod. 14:24. This pattern is interrupted once by the Sea of Reeds; here the pillar of cloud moves into a defensive position behind the Israelites at night, apparently to supplement the darkness of night for the Egyptians and thus prevent any nighttime attack. In addition, the pillar of cloud is associated with the presence of God in the tent of meeting (Exod. 33:9-10).

Fire and cloud are both common symbols of God throughout the Bible. The cloud both reveals God's presence and conceals God's person (e.g., Exod. 16:10; Lev. 16:2), while fire signifies God's power, passion, and purity (e.g., Exod. 19:18; Mal. 3:2). These images both reach back to the theophanies of the patriarchs and point forward to the theophany on Mt. Sinai and beyond to those of the prophets.

Scholars have tried to connect the pillar of fire and cloud with either the pillar torches used in religious and military ceremonies or the pillars of the Solomonic temple, as well as storms and volcanic eruptions, but such efforts remain conjecture.

Bibliography. J. I. Durham, *Exodus.* WBC 3 (Waco, 1987); T. W. Mann, "The Pillar of Cloud in the Reed Sea Narrative," *JBL* 90 (1971): 15-30.

CHERYL LYNN HUBBARD

PILTAI (Heb. *pilṭāy*)
The chief of a priestly family during the time of the postexilic high priest Joiakim (Neh. 12:17).

PIM (Heb. *pîm*)
A unit of weight equal to two thirds of a shekel, or ca. 7.8 gm. (0.27 oz.) (1 Sam. 13:21).

PINE
Any of the various coniferous evergreens with long, slender needles, of the genus *Pinus.* Pines were common in biblical lands, although they are seldom mentioned in the Bible. The stone pine *(Pinus pinea)* thrives in the sandy soil and warm climate of the Palestinian coastal plain. This tree matures into an umbrella-shaped tree (also called the umbrella pine) growing up to 24 m. (80 ft.) tall. Its bark is gray-brown with light brown patches (due to peel-

ing). Its needles grow in pairs along the tip of the branch, which ends with a round glossy brown cone. In three years the cones produce mature seeds, which are edible and marketed as pignolia nuts. Ezekiel describes a Tyrian ship with a deck made of *tĕʼaššûr* wood, likely the stone pine, from the coasts of Cyprus. The spiring cypress, the majestic strength of the plane, and the towering canopy of the stone pine suggest a fitting image for the luxuriant richness of Yahweh's saving work (Isa. 41:19; 60:13).

The Aleppo pine *(Pinus halepensis)* prefers a moister soil and can withstand harsher climates than the stone pine. It reaches a height of 20 m. (65 ft.). The ash-gray bark becomes reddish brown as it matures. The sparse needles grow in twos, and the cones produce winged seeds which mature in two years. The Romans used its strong and durable wood for shipbuilding, piles, and pitprops. The bark is rich in tannin and was widely used in the tanning of leather. The resin of the tree may have suggested the name *ʿēṣ šemen* (lit., "oil tree"), which some scholars now believe to be the Aleppo pine (Neh. 8:15; NRSV "olive"). It was mentioned as a sign of Yahweh's new creation in the wilderness (Isa. 41:19).

Bibliography. F. N. Hepper, *Baker Encyclopedia of Bible Plants* (Grand Rapids, 1992); M. Zohary, *Plants of the Bible* (Cambridge, 1982).

LAURIE J. BRAATEN

PINNACLE

An architectural feature of the Jerusalem temple, the place where the devil took Jesus for one of the three temptations (the second in Matt. 4:5, the third in Luke 4:9). Gk. *pterýgion*, "pinnacle" or "parapet," means lit., "small wing" and figuratively refers to the extreme point or tip of something. Although its precise location in unknown, from Byzantine times the pinnacle has usually been taken to be the Royal Portico of the temple on the southeast side of the outer court. Josephus describes this colonnade as a high place overlooking a deep ravine, probably the Kidron Valley. Another suggestion is that the pinnacle was part of the superstructure or lintel of one of the gates of the temple. JOHN L. GILLMAN

PINON (Heb. *pînōn*)

The ancestor of an Edomite clan (Gen. 36:41; 1 Chr. 1:52); subsequently the name of the people or region. Pinon should probably be associated with Punon (Khirbet Fênān; 197004), where the Israelites encamped shortly before entering the plains of Moab (Num. 33:42-43).

PIPE

See MUSIC, MUSICAL INSTRUMENTS.

PIRAM (Heb. *pirʼām*)

The Amorite king of Jarmuth at the time of the conquest of Canaan (Josh. 10:3). Along with the other allies of King Adonizedek of Jerusalem who attacked Gibeon, he was defeated and killed by Joshua (Josh. 10:22-26).

PIRATHON (Heb. *pirʿāṯôn*)

The home of the judge Abdon (Judg. 12:13-15) and of Benaiah, one of David's Thirty (2 Sam. 23:30; 1 Chr. 11:31). Situated "in the land of Ephraim" (Judg. 12:15; cf. 1 Chr. 27:14), Pirathon has been identified with modern Farʿâtā (165177), ca. 10 km. (6 mi.) WSW of Nablus.

PISGAH (Heb. *pisgâ*)

A mountain or mountain range (Heb. "peak" or "slope") in northwestern Moab in close proximity to Mt. Nebo (Num. 21:20; Deut. 3:17; 4:49; Josh. 12:3; 13:20). It is part of the Abarim promontory of the Moabite Plateau that slopes toward the Dead Sea and the Jordan Rift Valley. Balak built seven altars atop Pisgah, and from there Balaam spoke his oracle over Israel (Num. 23:14). From Pisgah Moses was shown the Promised Land and there he died (Deut. 3:27; 34:1).

Most scholars identify Pisgah with Râs es-Siyaghah just N of Jebel en-Nebā (Mt. Nebo). Although Pisgah's location is lower than Mt. Nebo, it commands a breathtaking view of the Rift Valley and beyond, as far as Jerusalem and Mt. Hermon on clear days. Excavations on top of Pisgah have revealed a Byzantine church erected to the memory of Moses.

Bibliography. M. Piccirillo, *The Mosaics of Jordan* (Amman, 1993), 133-51. FRIEDBERT NINOW

PISHON (Heb. *pîšôn*)

One of the four rivers of Eden, said to have flowed around the land of Havilah (Gen. 2:11). Attempts to identify the Pishon have included the Ganges, the Indus, and tributaries of the Euphrates.

PISIDIA (Gk. *Pisidía*)

A region in southwest Galatia, N of the Taurus Mountains, and bordered by Asia, Pamphylia, Phrytia, and Lycaonia. This region consisted of mountains, fertile valleys, and lakes, which produced quality pastures, forests, olive trees, and vineyards.

The Pisidians were a people of violence and brigandage (2 Cor. 11:26-27). Politically, the region was dominated by the Persians and later the Romans, with brief periods of independence. The Romans made Antioch the capital of Galatia before NT times.

Paul and Barnabas passed through Pisidia (Acts 13:14; 14:24), but their ministry was limited because of a small number of Jews as a point of contact. At Pisidia Paul decided to focus on Gentiles in his missionary strategy (Acts 13:46).

STEVEN L. COX

PISPA (Heb. *pispâ*)

An Asherite, the son of Jether (1 Chr. 7:38).

PISTIS SOPHIA

A gnostic document whose title means "faith-wisdom," perhaps originally titled the Book of the Savior. It was discovered in 1772 by A. Askew and bought by the British Museum in 1785 but not made public until 1905. Perhaps written in Egypt during the 3rd or 4th century and belonging to the genre of discussions between the resurrected Christ and his followers, it contains four sections treating two distinct subjects. Sections 1-3 contain 46 questions asked mostly by Mary Magdalene about the origin of sin and evil, heaven, the fall, and redemption of Pistis Sophia (representing humanity) to Jesus in his 12th year of teaching after the Resurrection. Personified Faith-Wisdom gives thanks to the "First Mystery" in a series of hymns of praise, after each of which a disciple interprets the hymn. A promise of equality with God for those who discover the unknowable truth of the mysteries concludes this part. Section 4 does not mention Pistis Sophia, but contains Jesus' answers given on the day of Resurrection about heavenly powers, visions, a description of punishments for sins, magical words and rites (such as offering wine, bread, and water along with sacred words), and a prayer for compassion. RICHARD A. SPENCER

PIT (Heb. *bôr, bĕʾēr, šaḥaṯ, paḥaṯ*)
In biblical sources, physical pits may be of natural formation (Ps. 40:2[MT 3]) and bitumen pits (Gen. 14:10)], of unexplained origin (37:22), or manmade (Ps. 57:6[7]). The latter were dug into the ground and sometimes modified with lining materials such as stone slabs or clay. They were used to collect and store water and other substances, as graves (2 Sam. 18:17), to trap animals and people both accidentally (Exod. 21:33) and deliberately (Gen. 37:22; Ezek. 19:4), and to hold prisoners (Isa. 24:22). Pits are described as a structural feature of a wine press (Mark 12:1). Many examples of these have been recognized archaeologically, as have pits created for the subterranean part of houses of the Chalcolithic period.

Since pits were recognized in the ancient world as a source of danger (Exod. 21:33), they are consequently used symbolically to describe the destruction awaiting those who turn to evil: those who concoct evil plots will fall into the very "pit" they have dug (Ps. 7:15[16]; Prov. 26:27); a man who associates with a loose woman will fall into the "pit" of her mouth (22:14); and others who have sinned will fall into the pit created by divine judgment (Isa. 24:17-18). The Pit is also a synonym for Sheol, the place of the dead (Ps. 16:10; Prov. 1:12), and for the source of the destruction of the earth and the location of demons and the devil (Rev. 9:1-11; 11:7).
KATHARINE A. MACKAY

PITCH
A naturally occurring combustible substance used in antiquity as an adhesive and a sealant. The related English words "asphalt" and "tar" reflect something of the nature of the material, although they indicate manufactured materials. Pitch apparently was common in the Dead Sea area but was also available to other regions and was used by different peoples. Words for pitch appear in both Akkadian and Arabic, and references to its use exist in the Babylonian flood story. In the biblical narrative, Noah was to cover the ark with pitch (Heb. *kōp̱er*) to seal it (Gen. 6:14), and Moses' mother used pitch to seal the little "ark" that would hold him during his journey down the Nile (Exod. 2:3). Isaiah uses streams of pitch to describe the burning judgment that Edom would endure, a judgment reminiscent of the destruction of Sodom and Gomorrah (Isa. 34:9). WALTER E. BROWN

PITHOM (Heb. *piṯōm*)
One of the Egyptian store-cities built by Israelite forced labor (Exod. 1:11). The name (Egyp. *Pr-ỉtm*) means "House of Atum," the Egyptian solar-deity Re (cf. Jer. 43:13, Beth-shemesh; LXX Heliopolis; the LXX of Exod. 1:11 mentions Pithom along with "On, which is Heliopolis").

Early excavators identified Pithom with Tell el-Maskhûṭah at the eastern end of the Wadi Tumilât in the district of Succoth. Several Egyptian inscriptions bearing the cartouche of Rameses II were discovered at the site, but later excavations found no architectural remains dated before the 7th century B.C.E. Current consensus identifies Pithom with Tell er-Reṭâbeh farther W in the Wadi Tumilât. Clear evidence indicates occupation during the 19th Dynasty (Seti I, Rameses II, and Merneptah).

Bibliography. B. MacDonald, "Excavations at Tell el-Maskhuṭa," *BA* 43 (1980): 49-58; E. P. Uphill, "Pithom and Raamses: Their Location and Significance," *JNES* 27 (1968): 291-316; 28 (1969): 15-39.
LAWRENCE A. SINCLAIR

PITHON (Heb. *pîṯôn*)
A Benjaminite, son of Micah and descendant of Saul (1 Chr. 8:35; 9:41).

PLAGUE
A general term for a judgment, usually inflicted by God. Sometimes used to refer to what is now understood as epidemic disease (e.g., 1 Sam. 6:4), it usually designates a more comprehensive range of calamities including endemic disease, battle casualties, and natural disasters (e.g., 1 Kgs. 8:37). The 10 plagues of Egypt, rarely called plagues in Exodus itself (Exod. 9:3, 14-15; 11:1), are more frequently known as signs and wonders (e.g., 7:3; Deut. 6:22; 7:19; 26:8; 34:11; Neh. 9:10; Ps. 135:9; Jer. 32:20-21) and judgments (Exod. 6:6; Num. 33:4).

The English word is used to translate a number of Hebrew and Greek terms. The Hebrew verb *nāḡap̱* and nouns *maggēp̱â, negep̱,* and *makkâ,* lit., "hit," "strike," or "touch," indicating injury, a fatal blow, slaughter in battle, or military defeat, are often translated synonymously as "plague." Gk. *plēgḗ* is translated "plague" in Revelation, and *mástix* as "plague" (KJV Mark 5:29, 34) or "disease" in the Gospels, but elsewhere mean "beating" or "flogging." The emphasis here may be on the calamity's sudden and unusual onset. An epidemic or outbreak of acute infectious disease may be described only in some instances (Exod. 32; Num. 16, 25; 1 Sam. 5–6; cf. Zech. 14:12, 15, 18).

Heb. *deḇer* (usually translated "pestilence") always refers to an outbreak of disease. The triad "sword, famine, and pestilence," found frequently in Jeremiah and Ezekiel, describes the devastating effect of depleted food supplies and polluted water associated with siege warfare. Likewise, Gk. *loimós* indicates a severe disease with a high mortality affecting large numbers of people at the same time (Luke 21:1).

Heb. *nega*ʿ (KJV "plague"; RSV "disease") refers in Lev. 13–14 to various skin disorders (not Hansen's disease, as the traditional translation "leprosy" seems to indicate), and to rot in clothing and houses. Heb. *rešep̄*, apparently cognate to the name of the Canaanite god of plague, is personified in Hab. 3:5 (RSV); Deut. 32:24 (NJPSV), as is *deḇer* in Ps. 91:6.

Where epidemic disease seems to be indicated, it is still extremely difficult to read modern medical diagnoses into the biblical text in order to pinpoint specific diseases. A possible exception is the plague on the Philistines (1 Sam. 5–6): here an infestation of rats or mice coupled with a disease involving swellings may describe bubonic plague. However, even here other diseases such as dysentery have been postulated, and the LXX seems to suggest that the plague is exclusively one of mice.

Plague, in its more restricted meaning of disease, was a prevalent fact of life in the ancient Near East. Endemic disease, in the absence of effective treatment and exacerbated by urbanization and inadequate diet and sanitation, accounted for at least half of all deaths; warfare and epidemics, events that were often related, caused a further increase in mortality rates. Ancient Near Eastern texts show an awareness of epidemic diseases (e.g., the plague prayers of the Hittite king Mursilis; *ANET*, 394-96), attributing them to various deities or demons. Likewise, in the Bible it is God who brings or threatens plague.

Plague first appears in the Bible in Gen. 12:17 as a divine punishment of Pharaoh for taking Sarai, Abram's wife, into his harem. The Israelites experience plague in the wilderness because of their apostasy with the golden calf (Exod. 32:35), their craving for meat (Num. 11:33), their complaints and rebellion (14:37; 16:41-50), and their worship of the Baal of Peor (25:9). They are threatened with plague if they break the covenant with their God (Lev. 26:21, 25; Num. 14:12; Deut. 28:21, 58-61). David chooses a three-day pestilence as punishment for his census (2 Sam. 24; 1 Chr. 21), and Solomon's prayer at the dedication of the temple lists plague as a possible consequence of covenant disloyalty (1 Kgs. 8:37 = 2 Chr. 6:28). The arrival of God is associated with plague in Hab. 3:5.

The Philistines, upon capturing the ark of the covenant, suffer a plague (1 Sam. 5:6, 11; cf. Ps. 32:4) underlining the sovereignty of Israel's god Yahweh over the Philistine Dagon (1 Sam. 5:4). The same kind of contest appears in the 10 plagues of Egypt, where Yahweh's sovereignty must be established over against Pharaoh (Exod. 9:3).

Plagues of Egypt

Egypt is associated preeminently with the plagues of Exod. 7–12. The traditional enumeration of 10 plagues does not appear in Exodus and is first explicitly attested in the book of Jubilees (Jub. 48:7). The accounts in Pss. 78, 105 seem to list only seven or eight plagues, and in different order. The meditation on the plagues in the Wisdom of Solomon (Wis. 11–19) presents seven contrasts between the treatment of Egypt and Israel at the hands of God (cf. Rev. 8–11, 15–16).

The 10 plagues are (1) blood; (2) frogs; (3) gnats; (4) flies; (5) livestock pestilence; (6) boils; (7) hail; (8) locusts; (9) darkness; (10) death of the firstborn. The nature of the third and fourth plagues is especially uncertain; the *kinnim* or gnats (RSV) of Exod. 8:16-18(MT 12-14) have also been understood as lice (NJPSV) or maggots (NEB), and the *ʿārōḇ* (lit., "mixture") or swarms of flies (RSV) of 8:20-32(16-28) could be a swarm of a number of insects (NJPSV) or, as in rabbinic literature, wild animals.

Complex variations between the presentation of the individual plagues, such as the fluctuation between Moses, Aaron, and God as the agent who induces each plague or the erratic reactions of Pharaoh to the individual plagues, as well as discrepancies such as the reappearance of Egyptian livestock in the seventh plague after they have all died in the fifth (Exod. 9:6), have led to the theory that the Exodus narrative is a composite of several traditions. In its classic formulation, an early account of seven plagues (usually identified with J) was gradually combined with, or supplemented by, other sources or traditions, finally giving shape to the present 10-plague account.

Against this source-critical approach, others have stressed the unitive structure and balance of the plague narrative in its completed form. Already recognized by the medieval rabbinic commentators was a formulaic pattern of three triplets of plagues (1, 2, 3 + 4, 5, 6 + 7, 8, 9) capped by a further 10th plague. (This is similar to the 3 + 3 + 1 pattern of the Creation account in Gen. 1.) Another commonly recognized pattern is that of five contiguous pairs, based on content: 1, 2 (Nile); 3, 4 (insects); 5, 6 (diseases); 7, 8 (crop damage); 9, 10 (darkness).

The 10 plagues have also been interpreted as a sequence of catastrophic natural phenomena exhibiting a scientific cause-and-effect relationship. Thus, reddish-colored mud and algae turned the Nile blood-red (1), killing the fish and causing the frogs to migrate onto land (2). The dead frogs provided a breeding ground for gnats and flies (3 and 4), which in turn transmitted diseases to livestock and humans (5 and 6). Hail and locusts (7 and 8) were common natural disasters, while the darkness of the ninth plague was caused by a sandstorm or solar eclipse. Such naturalizing explanations, however, not only stumble over details such as the selective or instantaneous nature of some of the plagues, but they also discredit the ideological depiction of the plagues in the biblical narrative as clearly supernatural or miraculous events happening by divine instigation.

Two major themes stand out in the narrative of the 10 plagues: "that you may know that there is no one like the Lord our God" (Exod. 8:10[6]; cf. 9:14), and "that you may know that the Lord makes a distinction between Egypt and Israel" (11:7). The plagues demonstrate the superiority of Israel's God over an Egypt which, under its semidivine Pharaoh, increasingly reverts to a pre-creational state of chaos. At the same time, the plagues are the birthing of Israel as a separate or distinct entity from its Egyptian matrix.

Bibliography. T. E. Fretheim, "The Plagues as Ecological Signs of Historical Disaster," *JBL* 110 (1991): 385-96; R. M. Martinez, "Epidemic Disease, Ecology, and Culture in the Ancient Near East," in *The Bible in the Light of Cuneiform Literature,* ed. W. H. Hallo, B. W. Jones, and G. L. Mattingly. Scripture in Context 3 (Lewiston, 1990), 413-57.

F. V. GREIFENHAGEN

PLANTS

At least 128 plant names appear in the OT and NT, a small number when compared with the more than 2780 species which modern botanists have identified in Israel. For convenience, the herbaceous plants described in the Bible are grouped here according to use and/or natural habitats.

Field Crops and Garden Plants

Three important grains mentioned in the Bible are wheat, barley, and millet. Wheat *(Triticum aestivum* and *T. Compositum),* one of the oldest cultivated grains in the world, is represented by Heb. *ḥiṭṭâ* and Gk. *sítos áleuron* and *semídālis.* This is the "corn" of Pharaoh's dream (Gen. 41:5). Heb. *kussemeṯ* (Exod. 9:32; Isa. 28:25; Ezek. 4:9) probably refers to emmer *(Triticum dicoccum).* Barley (*Hordeum vulgare* L.) is Heb. *śĕʿōrâ* (Exod. 9:31; Lev. 27:16; Deut. 8:8; Ruth 1:22; 2 Kgs. 4:42) and Gk. *krīthḗ* (John 6:9; Rev. 6:6). Millet *(Panicum miliaceum)* or sorghum *(Sorghum bicolor),* used for porridge and bread, is Heb. *dōhan* (Ezek. 4:9).

Important biblical pulses include the lentil, chickpea (garbanzo bean), and broad bean. Heb. *ʿăḏāšâ* (2 Sam. 17:28; 23:11) is associated with the lentil *(Lens culinaris),* also used for Jacob's pottage (Gen. 25:34). The chickpea *(Cicer arietinum)* is Heb. *ḥāmîṣ* (Arab. *humus;* Isa. 30:24). The broad bean *(Vicia faba)* is Gk. *kerátion* (Luke 15:16).

Leeks, onions, and garlics were among the Egyptian vegetables the Israelites craved while wandering through the wilderness (Num. 11:5-6). The leek (Heb. *ḥāṣîr)* is generally identified with *Allium kurrat,* although some have suggested the fenugreek *(Trigonella foenum-graecum).* The onion *(Allium cepa)* is Heb. *bāṣāl,* while the garlic *(Allium sativum)* is *šûm.* The cucumbers and melons the Israelites also pined for are Heb. *qiššûʾâ* (Num. 11:54; Isa. 1:8), probably the muskmelon *(Cucumis melo)* and the *ʾăḇaṭṭîaḥ* (Num. 11:5) or watermelon *(Citrullus lanatus).*

Condiments used by biblical people to spice up their foods included cummin, dill, and mint. Cummin *(Cuminum cyminum)* is confidently identified with Heb. *kammōn* (Isa. 28:25, 27) and Gk. *kýmīnon* (Matt. 23:23). Heb. *qeṣaḥ* (Isa. 28:25, 27) probably refers to the black cummin *(Negella sativa).* Manna reminded the Israelites of *gaḏ* (Exod. 16:31; Num. 11:7), i.e., the coriander seed *(Coriander satovum).* Dill *(Anethum graveolens)* is referred to in Matt. 23:23 (Gk. *ánēthon*), as is mint *(Mentha longifolia;* Gk. *kedyosmon).* Rue *(Ruta chalepensis)* is probably Gk. *pḗganon* (Luke 11:42). Jesus refers to the seed of a *sinapi* (Matt. 17:20 par.; Mark 4:31 par.) as an illustration of the power of faith; this plant is the mustard (probably *Brassica nigra*). The slimy vegetable mentioned in Job 6:6 *(ḥallomûṯ)* is probably purlane *(Portulaca oleracea)* or mallow *(Malva sylvestris, M. nicaeensis, Alcea setosa).* Heb. *qinnāmôn* (Exod. 30:23; Prov. 7:17; Cant. 4:14) and Gk. *kinnámōmon* (Rev. 18:13) are confidently identified with cinnamon *(Cinnamonoum verum),* a spice that was imported into Palestine. Heb. *qiddâ* (Exod. 30:24; Ezek. 27:19; cf. 45:8[MT 9]) is probably cassia *(Cinnamonum cassia),* another imported plant that was inferior to true cinnamon.

Two important plants that were used for textiles rather than subsidence were flax and cotton. Heb. *pištâ* (Exod. 9:21) and Gk. *línon* (Matt. 12:20; Rev. 15:6), *bý* (Luke 16:19), *sindōn* (Mark 15:46 par.), and *othónion* (John 19:40; 20:5, 7) are identified with the flax plant *(Linum usitatissimum),* whose stem fibers are extracted to make fine linen. The seeds are the source for linseed oil. Cotton *(Gossypium herbaceum)* is Heb. *karpas* (Esth. 1:6); it was used for the curtains in King Ahasuerus' banquet hall.

Many plants were used for medicinal purposes. Heb. *ṣōrî* (Gen. 37:25; Jer. 8:22) is usually translated as balm, although balm itself is a general term for any healing ointment. Undoubtedly several plants were used in antiquity to create balms. Balms were made from the resin from the lentisk bush *(Pistacia lentiscus),* the seeds of the Atlantic terebinth *(P. Atlantica),* ladanum resin from the Turkish rockrose *(Cistus laurifolius),* and oil from the fruit of the Jericho balsam *(Balanites aegyptiaca).* Opobalsamum is derived from the resin of the Balm of Judea *(Commiphoroa gileadensis).* Heb. *nĕḵʾōṯ* (Gen. 37:25) is the gum tragacanth extracted from the roots of leguminous plants from the genus *Astragalus (A. Gummifer, A. Bethlehemicus).* It has been suggested that castor oil, derived from *Ricinus communis,* may be associated with Heb. *qîqāyôn* (Jonah 4:6-10).

A number of plants were also used as fragrant incense. Heb. *ḥelbĕnâ* (Exod. 30:34) is galbanum *(Ferula galbaniflua).* Heb. *nērd* (Cant. 1:12; 4:13-14) and Gk. *nárdos* (Mark 14:3; John 12:3), the spice Mary used to anoint Jesus, are often translated as nard or spikenard *(Nardostachys jatamansi),* although some botanists believe the Hebrew term is probably to be identified with camel grass *(Cymbopogon schoenanthus).* Heb. *karkōm* (Cant. 4:14), saffron, comes from the saffron crocus *(Crocus sativus)* and was used both as incense and a dye. Some have suggested since Heb. *qāneh* appears in Cant. 1:14, it must have been an aromatic grass which could have been used as incense; if so, sweet flag *(Acorus calamus)* is probably the best candidate.

Wild Herbs

It is estimated that there are at least 200 palatable grasses and herbs in Palestine. Hebrew words that refer to this broad category of plants include *ḥāṣîr* and *'ēśeḇ*. Heb. *mĕrôrîm* (Exod. 12:8; Num. 9:11) specifically refer to the "bitter herbs." Plants included in this category, according to the Mishnah, include lettuce *(Lactuca),* chicory *(Cichorium intybus* and *C. Pumilum),* eryngo *(Eryngium creticum),* horseradish *(Armoracia rusticana),* and sow thistle *(Sonchus oleraceus).* Other plants that have been grouped in this category include dandelion *(Taraxacum officinale),* endive *(Cichorium endivia),* reichardia *(Reichardia tingitana),* sorrel *(Rumex acetosella),* and watercress *(Nasturtium officinale).*

Waterway Plants

Heb. *qāneh* and Gk. *kálamos* (1 Kgs. 14:15; Matt. 27:29) have sometimes been identified with the common reed *(Phragmites communis = P. australis),* although sweet flag *(Acorus calamus)* has also been proposed. Heb. *'agmôn* (Isa. 9:14[13]; 58:5) probably covers sedges and rushes and includes the six local species of *Scirpus* as well as several species of *Juncus.* Two species of cattail (*Typha* sp.) are probably included under the class of water plants known in Hebrew as *sûp̱* (Exod. 2:3; Isa. 19:6; Jonah 2:5). Papyrus *(Cyperus papyrys)* is probably to be identified with *gōmeh* (Exod. 2:3; Isa. 18:2).

Wilderness Plants

Wilderness plants include senna bush, white broom, and shrubby orache. The senna bush *(Cassia senna)* is probably Heb. *sĕneh* (Exod. 3:2-4; cf. Arab. *sene*). The white broom *(Retama raetam)* has been identified with Heb. *rōṯem* (1 Kgs. 19:4; Job 30:4). Heb. *malûaḥ* (Job 30:4) is similar to Arab. *mulaḥ,* which is identified with several species of *Atriplex* or orache.

Thorns and Thistles

Because of the relatively dry Mediterranean environment, thorny plants are plentiful in Palestine. More than 70 varieties have been identified by modern botanists while at least 20 Hebrew and Greek terms refer to this category of plants. Those probably indicated include Christ thorn; thorny burnet; bramble; Syrian, holy, and globe thistles; Spanish thistle; golden thistle; nettle, gray nightshade; Syrian acanthus; and spiny zilla.

Matt. 13:24-25 refers to the tares or weeds (Gk. *zizánion*) that grow among the good plants. The tare is mostly likely the darnel *(Lolium temulentum),* a noxious weed that routinely invades crops in Palestine. Heb. *rō'š* (Hos. 10:4) also refers to a noxious weed, probably the Syrian scabious *(Cephalaria syriaca)* or the henbane *(Hyoscyamus reticulatus).* These same species may be what Job had in mind (Job 31:40; Heb. *bo'šâ*).

Flowers of the Field

It is extremely difficult to identify specific species of flowering plants with Hebrew terms. Three Hebrew terms refer to flowers in a generic sense: *peraḥ, ṣîṣ, niṣṣâ.* Heb. *niṣṣānîm* (Cant. 2:12) probably refers collectively to those flowers that are the first to bloom in the spring. This would include anemones (*Anemone coronaria* L.), tulips (*Tulipa montana* Lindl.), poppies (*Papaver rhoeas* L.), and crowfoots *(Ranunculus asiaticus).* Another group is the "flowers of the field" (Isa. 40:6, 8; 1 Pet. 1:24-25), which probably includes daisies and daisy-like flowers such as the dog chamomile (*Anthemis* sp.), scarlet crowfoot (*Ranunculus asiaticus* L.), and crown daisy (*Chrysanthemum coronarium* L.). Some suggest that the "lily of the field" (Gk. *krínon;* Matt. 6:28 par.) is the anemone *(Anemone coronaria).* Several flowers have been identified with Heb. *šûšan* (1 Kgs. 7:19, 26; Cant. 2:2), including the white lily (*Lilium candidum* L.), chamomile *(Anthrmis noblis, A. tinctoria),* narcissus *(Narcissus tazetta),* sea daffodil *(Pancratium maritimum),* sternbergia *(Sternbergia lutea, S. clusiana),* and crowfoot (*Ranunculus asiaticus* L.). The "rose of Sharon" (Heb. *ḥăḇaṣṣeleṯ;* Cant. 2:1; Isa. 35:1) likely also refers to this lily, although some have suggested the Phoenician rose *(Rosa phoenicia).*

Bibliography. M. Zohary, *Plants of the Bible* (London, 1982). RANDALL W. YOUNKER

PLEIADES (Gk. *Pleíados*)
According to Greek mythology, the seven daughters of Atlas and Pleione, later transformed into a group of stars (cf. Amos 5:8 KJV) when Orion the hunter was about to molest them. In the OT (Heb. *kîmâ,* from the root "to heap up, accumulate") they are created by Yahweh (Job 9:9; Amos 5:8) and under Yahweh's control (Job 38:31).

Bibliography. G. R. Driver, "Two Astronomical Passages in the Old Testament," *JTS* N.S. 4 (1953): 208-12. AARON W. PARK

PLOW, PLOWSHARE
The single-furrow plow was a straight pole (a thin trunk or long branch) that ran parallel to the ground. A yoke enabled the plowman to attach one end to a draft animal; a branch or arm projected down from the pole's other end at an angle, with a plow point or plowshare secured at the arm's end. The farmer pushed the plow down so that the plowshare came into contact with the ground and pierced its surface. Before the invention of iron, plow points were made of stone, hardwood, or bronze; even after iron came into use (after ca. 1200 B.C.), many plowshares were still fashioned from bronze. These points have survived at many archaeological sites.

In biblical times the plow was quite primitive and farmers were able to do little more than scratch the surface and cut a shallow furrow into the soil. The point of the plow broke up hard-packed, sun-baked ground to give seeds a place to germinate and allow the winter precipitation to soak in. Therefore it required sharpening to be effective (1 Sam. 13:19-22). Once a farmer broke the soil, it was necessary to smash the clods and level the surface with a hoe or harrow (Isa. 28:24-25). Plows were usually yoked to oxen, but cows, mules, and asses were also used. Mosaic law prohibited yoking an ox with an ass (Deut. 22:10). When the early rains of late autumn began, plowing for winter crops could take place (cf. Prov. 20:4).

Plowing was used metaphorically throughout the OT (e.g., Job 4:8; Ps. 129:3; Jer. 26:18 = Mic. 3:12; Hos. 10:11). For example, an era of peace will arrive when people turn swords into plowshares (Isa. 2:4; Mic. 4:3; but Joel 3:10[MT 4:10]). Jesus used the plowing process to emphasize the importance of commitment to the kingdom of God (Luke 9:62).

Bibliography. O. Borowski, *Agriculture in Iron Age Israel* (Winona Lake, 1987); J. A. Thompson, *Handbook of Life in Bible Times* (Downers Grove, 1986). GERALD L. MATTINGLY

PLUMB LINE, PLUMMET

A builders' device consisting of a string with a weight, or plummet, on one end. The weight forces the cord to hang vertically so that builders and renovators are able to check the alignment of walls they are constructing and make sure that they are perpendicular to the center of gravity of the earth. The plumb line is also used to recognize walls that are tilted and need to be torn down. Used metaphorically in the Bible, the plumb line is a tool to enable the people of Israel to delineate righteousness and truth from apostasy (Amos 7:7-9). It also occurs as a testing tool: justice is the line and righteousness the plummet that test rebuilt Jerusalem (Isa. 28:17). The measuring line and plummet used to condemn Ahab's Samaria also condemn Jerusalem (2 Kgs. 21:13), while chaos and confusion are brought to Edom by God's line and plummet (Isa. 34:11). Zerubbabel's holding a plummet in his hands at the time of the temple's reconstruction (Zech. 4:10) may be a literal reference to its normal usage, but this passage may also be interpreted metaphorically. KATHARINE A. MACKAY

POCHERETH-HAZZEBAIM (Heb. *pōḵereṯ haṣṣēḇāyîm*)

The progenitor of a family of Solomon's servants whose descendants returned from exile (Ezra 2:57 = Neh. 7:59). The Hebrew term appears to be a feminine proper name or the name of an office, meaning "gazelle hunter."

POETRY

Most of the religious literature of the ancient Near East was poetic in form, as is much of the literature in the Bible. The Psalms, of course, have been widely recognized as poetic compositions, but to this poetry may be added as well the two major reflections on human wisdom: the book of Proverbs, a collection of short poetic aphorisms, and the book of Job, a succession of extended poetic dialogues. Themes as different as distress, in the book of Lamentations, and love, in the Song of Solomon, are treated in poetic form. But the major type of poetic speech in the Bible is prophecy. The prophets delivered divine oracles in poetry. Nearly all of the speeches of the major prophets — Isaiah, Jeremiah, Ezekiel — and of the 12 Minor Prophets are poetry. Some have even suggested that Israel's great historical prose narrative, in which are embedded some poetic compositions (e.g., Gen. 49; Exod. 15; Deut. 32, 33), was a poetic narrative in its original (perhaps oral) form. Much less of the NT, composed primarily of Gospel narratives and letters, is poetry, though these prose genres contain an occasional poem, such as the Magnificat of Mary (Luke 1:46-55) and an occasional hymn in the letters (e.g., Eph. 1:3-14; Phil. 2:6-11).

Literary critics have always been at a loss to say exactly what defines poetry or makes it different from prose, regardless of the particular language within which they are working. Yet there is almost universal agreement that poetry is a distinct and unique kind of language. Definitions often describe it as intensified language, an especially concentrated and condensed form of literature. Poetry relies more heavily than does prose on recurrent patterns of words and of sounds, and it makes more concentrated use of imagery, symbol, and metaphor. Furthermore, it appeals to a broad range of human experience, engaging not just the intellect but the senses, the emotions, and the intuition of the hearer or reader as well.

The basic building block of biblical Hebrew poetry is a repetitive pattern called parallelism. This is a device by which the poet expresses an idea in one line of verse, and then in a second line repeats — better, reshapes — that idea through nuance, extension, contrast, or another kind of development. The result is an image or thought richer than possible through a single statement. An example is three verse units from the prophecy of peace in Isa. 2:4:

> He shall judge between the nations,
>   and shall arbitrate for many peoples;
> they shall beat their swords into plowshares,
>   and their spears into pruninghooks;
> nation shall not lift up sword against nation,
>   neither shall they learn war any more.

In each of these three two-line verses, the idea expressed in the first line is parallel and enriched in some way in the second line. In the first, the verb "judge" in l. 1 is paralleled by "arbitrate" in l. 2, and "nations" is paralleled by "many peoples." But more than mechanical repetition by the use of synonyms is involved here. For example, the term "arbitrate" amplifies the term "judge," since it has the sharper connotation in Hebrew of calling to account, and thus it emphasizes, within the idea of the adjudication of a dispute, the idea of "reprimand" or "admonishment." Likewise in the second verse unit, "spears" parallels "swords" and "pruning hooks" parallels "plowshares." As is common in parallelism, the verb ("beat") is expressed only in the first line but also assumed in the second. Again, more than mechanical repetition is involved in this parallelism. The unifying idea in both lines is the shift from a wartime economy to a peacetime or agricultural economy, but in parallel lines the poet is able to call to mind the two major branches of Israelite agriculture: the cultivation of grain in l. 1 ("plowshares") and the production of fruit crops ("pruninghooks") in l. 2. In the third verse, both lines describe the end of war, but the idea is deepened when the laying down of arms in l. 1 is followed by the absence of the study of warfare in l. 2.

While by far the most common verse unit in Hebrew poetry is composed of two parallel lines like those above, three-line units also occur, as illustrated by this verse from Isaiah's indictment against corrupt leaders (Isa. 2:12):

> For the Lord of hosts has a day
> against all that is proud and lofty,
> against all that is lifted up and high. . . .

In this case the opening line sets the topic as the "day of the Lord," a phrase that could mean either salvation or judgment. The following lines describe the kind of day it will be: a day of judgment, in particular against the proud and elite of the nation.

The nature of the relationship between the two, or three, parallel lines in a verse of Hebrew poetry can vary widely; poets exercised a great deal of creativity in their use of this conventional device. For example, the two lines of a verse can be almost entirely synonymous:

> The voice of the Lord is powerful;
> the voice of the Lord is full of majesty.
> (Ps. 29:4)

Here only the descriptive elements, "powerful" and "full of majesty," break the exact repetition at the beginning of each line. However, repetition can be avoided almost completely, when the second line simply continues the thought of the first line, a practice literary critics refer to as enjambment.

> From where [God] sits enthroned he watches
> all the inhabitants of the earth. . . . (Ps. 33:14)

All sorts of variations on parallelistic structure that fall between these two extremes are present in Hebrew verse. One such variation employs two contrasting images to present a single idea from opposite sides:

> For the Lord watches over the way of the righteous,
> but the way of the wicked will perish.
> (Ps. 1:6)

This contrastive type of parallelism is especially common in the short wisdom sayings in the book of Proverbs, in which wisdom and folly are frequently contrasted in a single verse of poetry.

All Biblical Hebrew poetry, whether in a psalm or a prophetic speech or a wisdom saying, is built upon these two- (or three-) line verse units composed according to the conventions of parallelism. Older translations, such as the original King James Version, did not present the poetic sections of the Bible in lines and verses so that their poetic form and parallelistic pattern was readily recognizable; the entire Bible was simply printed as prose. Recent translations, such as the NRSV, lay out the poetic sections in lines and verses to represent the parallelistic pattern according to which this poetry was originally written. Verse numbers were added long after the poetry was composed, and while they frequently coincide with actual verse units, this is not always the case (cf. Isa. 2:4 above).

The power of poetic parallelism lies in its ability to represent the multifaceted character of religious experience. It does not approach experience primarily through the logic of a linear argument built on closely related propositions or through an expository description of ideas and illustrative details, though these are not absent in poetic parallelism. Rather, parallelism approaches experience through the presentation of multiple images, images that are at once related and different. It is as if the object of the poet's attention were a gem, which the poet turns and describes the changing appearance of its different facets. It is as if the poet assumes different positions in a landscape, and tries to show how the same landscape appears differently from different perspectives. Such an approach represents a great appreciation for the complexity of religious experience, and achieves insight through the probing of its multifaceted character.

A great deal of attention has been devoted to the question of whether this repetitive pattern in content is accompanied by a repetitive pattern of sound. Does biblical poetry have meter, a repeating pattern of stressed and unstressed syllables according to which individual lines of verse were composed? One major theory proposes a metrical system in which a line of verse is built on three primary stresses accompanied by a varying number of unstressed syllables. Thus a unit of verse would be scanned, or analyzed, as follows, with each section divided by a dash containing a primary stress and one or more unstressed syllables:

> He shall judge — between — the nations,
> and arbitrate — for many — peoples.
> (Isa. 2:4)

According to this theory, lines could also be composed of a two-stress pattern, and verse units could be constructed of 3:3 meter, like the one above, or 2:2 or 3:2 meter, the latter being supposedly selected most often for the poetry of lamentation. An alternative theory proposes that poetic lines can be better analyzed according to their length in terms of total number of syllables, with long lines composed of seven or more syllables, short lines of six or less. According to this theory, poets were not mechanically counting syllables, but were working within the general constraints of long lines or short lines of verse.

Both of these theories are able to bring to light a kind of symmetry within verse units, but neither works with the kind of regularity that might be expected if biblical poetry in fact employed a distinct meter and if the particular theory actually understands it properly. The central, and possibly insurmountable, problem for detecting and describing the meter of biblical poetry is that Biblical Hebrew is no longer a living language that can be heard as originally spoken, and, moreover, its pronunciation has changed over the years since the biblical period. Thus contemporary theories about meter appear to be approximations of the actual metrical conventions used in the composition of biblical poetry rather than precise descriptions.

The repetition of sound for effect is present in biblical poetry in other ways besides its use in larger metrical patterns. Assonance, the repetition of vowel sounds, and alliteration, the repetition of consonants, are frequently present in lines of verse, though rhyme is seldom employed. A common device is the practice of playing on words that sound alike. Isaiah concludes the Song of the Vineyard (Isa. 5:1-7) by contrasting God's expectations for Israel with their actual behavior:

> [God] expected justice *(mišpāṭ)*, but saw
> bloodshed *(miśpāḥ)*;
> righteousness *(ṣĕḏāqâ)*, but heard a cry
> *(ṣĕʿāqâ)*. (5:7)

In each line of this verse, Isaiah uses terms for God's will and Israel's failure to follow it that sound almost exactly alike but are vastly different in meaning. The similarity of sound clashes with the difference in meaning and makes the disparity between divine expectation and human reality sharper and more unsettling. This effect is highlighted by the fact that such plays on similar sounding words in Hebrew are usually employed to reinforce their similar meanings. The opposite case here makes the point even more jarring and incredible.

Unfortunately, the sounds of Hebrew poetry, whether in metrical rhythms or wordplays, can almost never be rendered properly with English words or pronunciations, as the above example from Isaiah illustrates. Thus the English reader will unavoidably miss many patterns and connections imbedded in the Hebrew original. Because poetry relies so heavily on the precise placement of sounds, and because these sound patterns cannot be duplicated in another language, some have argued that poetry is the one kind of language that is essentially untranslatable. Occasionally, however, modern translators will alert readers to such uses of sound in Hebrew in notes to the translation.

One further aspect of biblical poetry that deserves attention is its heavy reliance on images and symbols to explore and communicate the central elements of religious life. A fine example is Isaiah's Song of the Vineyard (Isa. 5:1-7), in which the prophet uses the vineyard as a metaphor for God's people. In this poem, Isaiah describes a vineyard for which the ground has been thoroughly cleared, and in which the best vines have been planted and have been tended with great care; but the vineyard, against all agricultural logic, produces only rancid fruit. Through this representation of Israel as a well-tended but worthless vineyard, Isaiah is able to place the blame squarely on Israel for its failures and to depict such behavior as contradicting the very orders of nature itself. The poetry of the Psalms is also full of imagery aimed at describing the character of God and the experience of the psalmist. For example, God is pictured as shield (Ps. 3:3[MT 4]), rock (18:2[3]), shepherd (23:1), light (27:1), king (47:2[3]), and judge (50:6). To communicate the experience of the psalmist, such images as trees (Ps. 1:3), deer (42:1[2]), sheep (100:3), and the prey of the lion (17:12) are common.

Through the use of symbolism such as this, insight is achieved through a comparison of things that are at once different and alike. At the beginning of the narrative of the vineyard the listener has no reason to connect it with the people of Israel at all. But when the connection is finally made at the end, the listener is forced to recognize certain things about Israel's faithlessness that are uniquely clear by this comparison. Symbols used for such comparison are taken from common experience, and are thus familiar and readily understandable. This quality of the poet's symbols means that biblical poetry is concrete and vivid, not theoretical and abstract. It communicates religious truth with reference to the ordinary realities of experience rather than through ideas and concepts that appeal to the intellect alone.

While building poems from the two- and three-line verse units described above, biblical poets also followed well-defined conventions in their creation of larger compositions. These conventions prescribed certain structures for particular types of compositions. Psalms, e.g., are by and large composed according to a number of major forms or genres that provided the basic framework for the poet's creative expression. The two most common psalm forms are the hymn and the lament, each with its own distinctive pattern. The hymn contains three major parts: a call to praise God; a description of the reasons to praise God, focusing on God's beneficent deeds; and a renewed call to praise. Some noteworthy examples of the hymn form include Pss. 8, 19, 33, 100, 104. The lament is a more complex form, containing in its most complete examples six parts: an address to God; a description of the problem faced by the psalmist; a confession of trust in God; a plea for help; words of assurance delivered to the psalmist promising God's help; and the psalmist's vow to praise God after help arrives. Noteworthy examples include Pss. 3, 22, 42–43 (originally a single psalm, as its reflection of the lament form proves), 51, 90, 130. Psalmists did not follow these forms woodenly, but adapted them creatively so that each psalm is a unique variation on the typical pattern. Yet there is enough consistency in the use of these patterns to indicate that the psalmists employed them consciously in their compositions.

Just as there are formal patterns according to which the psalms were composed, so there are larger patterns according to which prophetic poetry was composed. One of the most common of all prophetic speech forms is the judgment speech, within which the prophet delivered an indictment of Israel's behavior followed by an announcement of the judgment imposed by God to punish it. An example is Amos 6:1-8 in which Amos indicts Israel's leadership for its self-indulgence and luxury (vv. 1-6) and announces their coming judgment as exile (vv. 7-8). The following two-line verse unit illustrates well the larger indictment of which it is a part:

> Alas for those who lie on beds of ivory,
> and lounge on their couches . . . (v. 4)

The salvation speech, in which a description of distress is followed by an announcement of salvation, is a kind of positive counterpart to the judgment speech (cf. Amos 9:11-15). An almost bewildering array of larger speech forms are employed by prophets, two of which are the woe oracle (Amos 5:18-20) and the prayer (7:2, 5).

Within Wisdom Literature, the most characteristic literary form is the proverb, a two-line aphorism that coincides with the ordinary two-line verse unit employing parallelism. An example is this proverb lauding the value of hard work:

> A slack hand causes poverty,
> but the hand of the diligent makes rich.
> (Prov. 10:4)

Most of the book of Proverbs (chs. 10–31) is made up of such two-line sayings that have been collected and simply listed one after the other, sometimes apparently organized by subject but often arranged quite randomly in the eye of the modern reader. Prov. 1–9 is composed of more extended poems on wisdom, still making use of the two- and three-line verse units characteristic of biblical Hebrew poetry. Such is also the case in the book of Job, in which the truth of divine justice and the value of wisdom are debated by Job and his friends in the form of long poetic discourses organized as a lengthy dialogue.

These observations on biblical poetry have been directed primarily to the OT, which contains major kinds of literature — psalms, wisdom, prophecy — in which poetry was the primary medium of expression. Since the NT is composed primarily of Gospels and letters, both of which employ prose for narrative and exposition, little poetry is found here. The few instances include occasional quotations in the Gospels of OT poetic texts, primarily from the prophets (e.g., Matt. 4:15-16; 12:18-21; Luke 3:4-6; 4:18-19). These quotations are already the product of a translation, since they are taken not directly from the Hebrew but from the LXX. Even in Greek translation, however, the parallelism of the Hebrew is still obvious. In other cases, the Gospels employ hymnic material, such as the poetic compositions in Luke 1:46-55, 68-79, which resemble, and appear to be drawn from, various psalms. Outside of the Gospels, early Christian hymns or hymnic fragments, reflecting the poetic parallelism of Hebrew poetry, appear to be preserved in some of the NT letters: Rom. 11:33-36; Eph. 1:3-14; Phil. 2:6-11; Col. 1:12-14, 15-20; 1 Pet. 1:3-5. Though the major genres of the NT are not poetic, it is clear that the early Church was familiar with the use of poetry for religious expression, as can be seen in its contact with poetic texts from the Hebrew Scriptures and in the hymns preserved from its liturgical life.

Bibliography. R. Alter, *The Art of Biblical Poetry* (New York, 1985); A. Berlin, *The Dynamics of Biblical Parallelism* (Bloomington, Ind., 1985); J. L. Kugel, *The Idea of Biblical Poetry* (1981, repr. Baltimore, 1998); D. L. Petersen and K. H. Richards, *Interpreting Hebrew Poetry* (Minneapolis, 1992); W. G. E. Watson, *Classical Hebrew Poetry.* JSOTSup 26 (Sheffield, 1984). THEODORE HIEBERT

POLYCARP, EPISTLE OF

The so-called Epistle of Polycarp to the Philippians is the only surviving text from the hand of the Christian martyr Polycarp, 2nd-century bishop of Smyrna. His prominence among the ancient churches of Asia Minor is renowned, as evidenced elsewhere by the portrayal of his death (ca. 156) in the Martyrdom of Polycarp and the fictional 5th-century account of his career, A Life of Polycarp. According to Irenaeus and Eusebius, Polycarp stood as a direct link between the testimony of the Apostle John and the faith witness of the later Church. A close friend of Ignatius of Antioch, Polycarp was a reputed enemy of the gnostic Marcion.

Certain circumstances behind the Epistle are clear. The opening address establishes the city of Smyrna as the place of composition and the church at Philippi as the intended recipient. The focal concern for the epistle (now divided into 14 chapters) is the theme of righteousness, a motif which the Philippians had previously requested Polycarp to address (Pol. Phil. 3:1).

Other aspects of the epistle are debated. Polycarp's references to the situation of Ignatius, housed temporarily in Philippi on his way to martyrdom in Rome (cf. 1:1; 9:1; 13:2), have led to speculation concerning questions of integrity and date behind the epistle. Traditionally, these references have been accepted as an indication that the text was written soon after the death of Ignatius, sometime ca. 110-120. The witness of Ignatius' faith and the circumstances of his tragic demise would have been of immediate concern to those Christians who had known him. Some more recent scholars, however, have asked whether the epistle is not actually a combination of two short letters (both from Polycarp), the earlier preserved in chs. 13–14 and the latter in chs. 1–12. One observes, e.g., that the theme of righteousness is abandoned in ch. 13 in favor of a discussion of the letters of Ignatius. The Philippians had requested copies of those letters, and Polycarp apparently intended for chs. 13–14 to serve as a brief cover letter for that collection. At the same time, Polycarp himself requested specific information from the Philippians about the fate of Ignatius, which suggests that he wrote soon after Ignatius' martyrdom. Elsewhere in the epistle, Polycarp's references to Ignatius (1:1; 9:1) reveal no particular urgency about the situation, perhaps because some years had now passed. If his phrase "first-born of Satan" (7:1) can be taken as a reference to Marcion, whom Polycarp met shortly before 140, then chs. 1–12 may preserve a second, later letter sent to Philippi during the years 120-135. Our current epistle thus may actually preserve two separate letters, the more recent work now placed in advance of the older text.

Polycarp's epistle reveals his role as an acknowledged authority among early Christian communities. He reveals a breadth of acquaintance with the writings of ancient Israel, as well as with later Christian authors, especially the letters of Paul. Much like Ignatius himself, Polycarp stands as a beacon of warning against the divisive threat of docetism (ch. 7) and as an advocate of church unity. He addresses specific issues of leadership at Philippi, specifically in the case of the "fallen presbyter" Valens and his wife (ch. 11). Most notably, Polycarp forwards the vision of a youthful, growing Church whose members are "citizens" who are worthy of God's community (5:2), whose offices and functions are firmly organized according to the standards of ecclesiastical faith and order (chs. 4-6), and whose "eternal high priest" in Jesus Christ himself (12:2).

Bibliography. L. W. Barnard, "The Problem of St. Polycarp's Epistle to the Philippians," in *Studies in the Apostolic Fathers and Their Background* (New York, 1966), 31-39; P. N. Harrison, *Polycarp's Two Epistles to the Philippians* (Cambridge, 1936); W. R. Schoedel, *Polycarp, Martyrdom of Polycarp, Fragments of Papias. The Apostolic Fathers* 5, ed. R. M. Grant (New York, 1967). CLAYTON N. JEFFORD

POLYCARP, MARTYRDOM

Apart from the NT account of the death of Stephen (Acts 7:54-60), the Martyrdom of Polycarp preserves Christianity's earliest example of a martyrdom. The Martyrdom is a stylized portrayal of the death of Polycarp, bishop of Smyrna, who served the Church through the advanced age of 86 (Mart. Pol. 9:3). The portrayal of his death ultimately came to serve as a prototypical example for subsequent martyrological accounts, with focus upon the themes of faithfulness, courage, and piety in the face of danger and death.

The actual account of the martyrdom is preserved within the framework of a letter which was sent from the Christians at Smyrna (the site of Polycarp's death) to the church at Philomelium in central Asia Minor. Its purpose was to honor the memory of the slain bishop, as well as to encourage other Christians who faced the threat of persecution. The account was undoubtedly recorded soon after Polycarp's death, though the date of that event (and hence of the text) is much debated. The closing portion of the text (ch. 21) places the death on 22 (or 23?) February, but no year is indicated. Internal evidence argues for 154-155, though Eusebius preferred 166 (or 167). Recent scholars observe that the general context of persecution under Marcus Aurelius could permit a date at any point prior to 181.

Apart from the general Christian community at Smyrna, no single author is clearly identified for the writing. The name Evarestus is offered as the author of the letter itself (20:2), and certain later Christians are recorded in the closing chapter as those who forwarded the text in antiquity. Use of the plural pronoun "we" (15:1) suggests that more than one individual may have served as author (or at least as witness) for the actual martyrdom account.

Scholars assume that the Martyrdom does indeed offer some large element of authenticity as a witness to Polycarp's death. Because of the polemical nature of the document, however, it is certain that the event has been recounted through the eyes of faith. This is best exemplified through the numerous similarities which the final days of Polycarp's life, trial, and death find in the story of Jesus of Nazareth in the NT Gospels. Like Jesus, Polycarp enters the city (here Smyrna) on a donkey. He prays for the Church at large (5:1), is betrayed to the authorities by someone close to him (6:1-2), serves as head of the table at a final meal (7:2), and offers an extended prayer before his arrest (7:2-3). He then is interrogated by an official named Herod (8:2-3), made the object of derision by the Jews (12:2–13:1), crucified on a Friday (7:1), and his body removed by loyal followers after his death (18:2-3). The emphasis upon these elements is clear to even the most casual reader, and reflects traditions which were borrowed from all of the NT Gospels.

The Martyrdom has become famous within the Christian tradition for the various elements of a heroic sacrifice which are modeled here as a pattern for later martyrological accounts. Most noteworthy is the focus upon a "noble death" tradition, i.e., the ancient view that in certain circumstances it becomes necessary for one person to be sacrificed for the benefit of the larger community. This sacrifice comes in the midst of a struggle between the forces of good and evil, the latter represented here by the "evil one," the Jews, and the civil authorities of the Roman Empire. The death of a faithful martyr is depicted as a sweet conclusion to a prayerful life — Polycarp's body is baked as bread which produces the smell of incense and perfume. Finally, the anniversary of the event (the "birthday of the martyrdom," 18:3) becomes an occasion of reverence and discernment, and contributes to the developing stream of growing "martyr cult" mentality which characterized so much of subsequent Christian spirituality.

Bibliography. W. H. C. Frend, *Martyrdom and Persecution in the Early Church* (Oxford, 1965), 268-302; C. N. Jefford, K. J. Harder, and L. D. Amezaga, Jr., *Reading the Apostolic Fathers* (Peabody, 1996), 84-97. CLAYTON N. JEFFORD

POMEGRANATE

Punica granatum, a small tree (Heb. *rimmôn*) which usually resembles a rounded bush but can sometimes grow fairly large (cf. 1 Sam. 14:2). One of the seven species associated with the Promised Land (Deut. 8:8), its fruit is red with a crownlike calix, about the size of an orange. Dye from the fruit's rind is used in tanning leather. Inside the pomegranate fruit are several compartments which surround a jellylike pulp and several seeds which are eaten both raw and dried. The juice is refreshing and is sometimes made into syrup or spiced wine (Cant. 8:2). While in the wilderness, the Israelites longed for the pomegranates they ate in Egypt (Num. 20:5). Spies brought pomegranates and grapes back from Canaan to show the fertility of the land (Num. 13:23).

The pomegranate symbolizes beauty in the Bible. The maiden of the Song of Solomon has cheeks "like halves of a pomegranate" (Cant. 4:3; 6:7). The spring blossoming of pomegranates symbolizes the awakening of love (Cant. 6:11; 7:12). Pomegranates were commonly associated with places of worship and deities in the ancient Near East. The fruit and blossoms adorned the bottom of the priest's ephod (Exod. 28:33-34) and appeared in Solomon's temple as decorations above the pillars (1 Kgs. 7:18, 20, 42; 2 Kgs. 25:17 par.). Dying pomegranates symbolized the destruction of the prosperity of Judah (Joel 1:12), and their restoration was included in the Lord's promise to reestablish the nation (Hag. 2:19).

Heb. *rimmôn* also appears as a man's name (2 Sam. 4:2, 5, 9) and a place name (Judg. 20:45; Josh. 15:32). MEGAN BISHOP MOORE

PONTUS (Gk. *Póntos*)
A region in northeastern Asia Minor on the south shore of the Black Sea (Pontus Euxinus), with Galatia, Cappadocia, and Armenia bordering to the south. The region consists of narrow fertile coastal plains and rugged mountains to the interior that extend to portions of the coast. In ancient times these mountainous protrusions prevented a continuous coastal road, thus forcing people to travel by sea or inland roads. The coast was colonized by the Greeks ca. 700 B.C.E., with Sinope and Amisus the chief ports. The natives of the rugged interior were free from Greek influence, and had close ties with Armenia and Cappadocia. Important products of the region included corn, fruit, olives, and timber.

Pontus had been under the Assyrian, Hittite, Greek, and Persian empires before attaining independence under Mithradates I in 302. Mithradates VI Eupator led Pontus in three defensive wars against Rome, culminating in defeat by Pompey in 63 B.C.E. The Mithridatic dynasty ended with Caesar's defeat of Pharnace II's revolt in 47.

Judaism was widespread in Pontus by the NT era. Acts 2:9 confirms that some Jews from Pontus were in Jerusalem at Pentecost, thus taking the gospel back to the region. 1 Peter confirms the presence of Christians in Pontus and neighboring areas (1 Pet. 1:1-2).

Notable people from this region include Paul's associate Aquila; Strabo the geographer, from the ancient capital Amasia; Aquila, a proselyte and contemporary of Hadrian, who translated the OT into Greek; Alexander of Abonuteichos, the founder of a pagan cult; and Carcion, from Sinope.

Bibliography. C. J. Hemer, "The Address of 1 Peter," *ExpT* 89 (1977/78): 239-43.

STEVEN L. COX

POOL
Natural pools were simply depressions holding rain water (e.g., Exod. 7:19; 2 Kgs. 3:16; Ps. 84:6[MT 7]; 114:8; Isa. 14:23; 41:18). Artificial pools were large, unroofed reservoirs used to store runoff water or water diverted from nearby springs. Longer in length and width than depth, they were often partially hewn in rock with sides heightened by additional stone blocks. As public water sources, they are mentioned in connection with the names of the towns which they supplied (e.g., Gibeon, 2 Sam. 2:13; cf. Jer. 41:12; Hebron, 2 Sam. 4:12; Samaria, 1 Kgs. 22:38; Heshbon, Cant. 7:4). The size of Jerusalem required numerous pools (e.g., 2 Kgs. 20:20), some of which bear specific designations such as the lower pool (Isa. 22:9), upper pool (2 Kgs. 18:17 = Isa. 36:2; 7:3), old pool (22:11), King's Pool (Neh. 2:14), pool of Shelah (3:15), artificial pool (v. 16), Bethzatha (John 5:2), and pool of Siloam (9:7). They provided water for households, livestock, industry, healing (John 5:2; 9:7), and irrigation (Eccl. 2:6; Neh. 3:15).

Archaeologists have uncovered a cylindrical shaft at el-Jib, which some speculate is the "pool of Gibeon." In Jerusalem, the pool of Siloam continues to hold the waters of the Gihon Spring at the southern end of Hezekiah's tunnel. Below that was a reservoir known today as Birket el-Ḥamra. Two pools on the grounds of the Church of St. Anne are identified with Bethzatha. Known from Josephus are the Amygdalon (Tower Pool), near the Jaffa Gate (*BJ* 5.468); the Serpent's Pool, SW of the Jaffa Gate (5.108); and the Struthion, at the northwest corner of the temple mount (5.467). The pool of Israel lay at the eastern end of the northern wall of the temple mount.

Bibliography. D. Adan (Bayewitz), "The 'Fountain of Siloam' and 'Solomon's Pool' in First-Century C.E. Jerusalem," *IEJ* 29 (1979): 92-100; H. Geva, "Jerusalem: The Second Temple Period: Water Supply," *NEAEHL* 2:746-47; J. B. Pritchard, *The Water System of Gibeon* (Philadelphia, 1961); Y. Shiloh, "Jerusalem: The Early Periods and the First Temple Period: The Water-Supply Systems," *NEAEHL* 2:709-12; T. Tsuk, "Pools," *OEANE* 4:350-51; "Reservoirs," *OEANE* 4:422. JAMES M. PACE

POOR
One lacking material goods, honor, and power. Recent anthropological and sociological studies have shown that the "poor" is not just an economic concept, but is more especially a question of honor, social status, a lack of power that led to oppression.

In the OT different blocks of traditions emphasize different aspects. The legal texts regulate the treatment of the poor, seeking to protect the poor, widows, orphans, or strangers (Lev. 19:9-10; 25:25, 35). The prophets show a concern for those economically exploited. They protest the oppression of the poor at the hands of the greedy. Isaiah attacks those landowners who amass vast properties (Isa. 5:8), and condemns the denial of rights to the poor (10:2). Amos draws attention to the oppression of the poor (Amos 2:7; 4:1; 5:11). The wisdom traditions view poverty from different perspectives. Proverbs sees poverty as one's own fault (Prov. 6:10-11; 10:4, 15; 13:18; 21:17), while for Job poverty results from political and economic exploitation. Job argues his innocence through his defense of the poor (Job 29:12, 16; 30:25; 31:16). The Psalms present God as the defender of the poor (Ps. 22:26[MT 27]; 35:10). The narrative literature of the Pentateuch and Deuteronomistic history show little interest in the poor, concerned more with critiquing the kingship.

Three groups within Israelite society — widows, orphans, and strangers — experienced poverty as particularly harsh. In a society structured upon the male as the worker, the widow and orphan struggled to survive: powerless, they depended upon the good will of others (Deut. 24:17). The strangers, as ones who did not belong, had no bonds to their new society. These groups shared a common poverty: a lack of status whereby the powerful and unscrupulous took advantage. Concern is expressed for their precarious social status (Prov. 31:9; Ps. 82:3) — what others had done to them to cause their poverty (Ps. 10:2; Isa. 32:7).

In addition to economic considerations the NT also focuses on the lack of honor, social status, and powerlessness which led to the oppression of the poor. The Epistle of James stands out as a writing concerned for the poor, who lack power — they are at the mercy of the rich. The rich "have dishonored the poor" who have no rights — the poor are brought to court by the rich (Jas. 2:6). The rich are boastful and arrogant, relying solely upon their own power (Jas. 4:13-17). Wealth has brought honor to the rich and shame to the poor (Jas. 2:1-7). True religion is defined as "caring for orphans and widows in their distress" (Jas. 1:27) — two groups identified with the poor in the OT because they have no rights or power to defend themselves.

In the Synoptic Gospels the life-styles of John the Baptist (Mark 1:6), Jesus (vv. 38-39; 11:12), and the disciples (1:18, 20; 2:23-25) embrace poverty. Matthew opens Jesus' teaching with a blessing on "the poor in spirit" (Matt. 5:3), while Luke 6:20 has simply "the poor" whose status is lowly, whose spirit is crushed by their powerlessness. This saying implies that the poor also enter the kingdom. It challenges the arrogance of those who deny status to the poor by refusing them their rights. They will be part of God's kingdom that reinstates their honor and power. The Gospel of Luke shows an empathy for the poor and hostility toward the rich that is more pronounced than in the other Gospels. Again the status of the poor is championed, e.g., in the parables of admission to the messianic banquet (Luke 14:15-24) and the rich man and Lazarus (16:19-31).

The other NT writings pay scant attention to the poor. Paul is chiefly concerned with the collection for the poor in Jerusalem (Gal. 2:10; Rom. 15:26). In 2 Cor. 8–9 Paul calls upon the wealthy to give as much as possible so that economic inequality could be bridged. 1 Peter is written to the "homeless" in the Diaspora. In a sense it reflects the "strangers" of the OT. The good news proclaimed to them (1 Pet. 1:12, 25) imparts a sense of dignity and status (1:5, 9; 2:9-10).

Bibliography. T. R. Hobbs, "Reflections on 'The Poor' and the Old Testament," *ExpT* 100 (1989): 291-94; P. U. Maynard-Reid, *Poverty and Wealth in James* (Maryknoll, 1987).

PATRICK J. HARTIN

POPLAR

Two types of poplar were widespread in biblical lands. The white poplar *(Populus alba;* Heb. *liḇneh)* is so named for its bark and the white underside of its leaves. This fast-growing tree thrives in damp soil such as riverbanks where it can reach a height of 30 m. (100 ft.). The soft wood could be used for tools or roof beams. The grayish-white bark contains salicin, which reduces fevers or inflammation of the joints. Jacob placed stripped branches of white poplar, almond, and plane in the drinking troughs of Laban's goats to obtain the desired offspring (Gen. 30:37). The white poplar is one of the shade trees on the mountains where Israel practiced their idolatry (Hos. 4:13). Cuttings from this tree root easily (cf. Hos. 14:5[MT 6]).

Another tall poplar, the Euphrates poplar *(Populus euphratica;* Heb. *ʿărāḇâ),* grows well in the salty soil near the Jordan and brackish desert springs. It was probably among the trees Elisha's prophets cut near the Jordan (2 Kgs. 6:4). Its immature leaves look like willow leaves, so the tree is sometimes confused with the willow. The "poplars by the stream" were large enough to conceal the behemoth (Job 40:22 NIV; cf. Isa. 44:4). It was among the four branches used in the lulab ceremony in the Festival of Booths (Lev. 23:40), and is probably the tree upon which the exiles hung their harps in Babylon (Ps. 137:2).

Bibliography. F. N. Hepper, *Baker Encyclopedia of Bible Plants* (Grand Rapids, 1992); M. Zohary, *Plants of the Bible* (Cambridge, 1982).

LAURIE J. BRAATEN

PORATHA (Heb. *pôrāṯā'*)

One of Haman's 10 sons who were slain by the Jews (Esth. 9:8).

PORCIUS FESTUS

See FESTUS, PORCIUS.

PORPHYRY

A red or purple stone consisting of white or pink feldspar crystals in a dark red groundmass (Heb. *bahaṭ*). In biblical times porphyry usually was brought from the Red Sea coast of Egypt and cut and polished for ornamental purposes (Esth. 1:6).

PORTION, SHARE

That which is distributed and received, e.g., spoils of war (Gen. 14:24; 1 Sam. 30:24) and food eaten in ceremonial meals (Exod. 29:26; Lev. 7:33; 1 Sam. 1:4-5). The terms (Heb. *ḥēleq, ḥeḇel, mānâ;* Gk. *méros, merís*) are used in a technical sense with regard to inheritances (Gen. 31:14; Luke 15:12) and land (Deut. 10:9) as that entrusted or allotted to Israel by Yahweh, the true owner of the land. Expressions such as "to have a portion in (someone)" mean to be affiliated with that person or to belong to that person's company or community (2 Sam. 20:1; 1 Kgs. 12:16; cf. John 13:8). Words translated "portion" can also be used with reference to that which is dear and close to a person; thus Israel is called the portion of the Lord (Deut. 32:9), as Yahweh is likewise Israel's portion (Ps. 16:5; 73:26; 119:57; 142:5; Jer. 10:16; Lam. 3:24). "Portion" can also refer to the lot or fate that befalls a person at the hand of the Lord (Job 31:2; Jer. 13:25).

POSIDONIUS (Gk. *Posidṓnios*)
An envoy sent by Nicanor in the face of certain defeat to negotiate a truce with Judas Maccabeus (2 Macc. 14:19).

POTIPHAR (Heb. *pôṭîp̱ar*)
The individual who purchased Joseph from the Ishmaelites (or Midianites) in Egypt after he was sold by his brothers (Gen. 37:36; 39:1-6). His name was apparently a short form of Potiphera, the name of Joseph's father-in-law (Gen. 41:45; 46:20), which means "he whom Re (the sun-god) has given" (LXX Gk. *Petephrēs* for both). He was described as an "official" or "officer" of Pharaoh and the "captain" or "chief" of "the (body)guard." The last description is problematic. The key word in the phrase seems to have the sense of "slaughter," and perhaps by extension "cook," resulting in "chief steward," functionally like a modern "lord chamberlain," or lit., "captain of the slaughterers," the commanding officer of the royal guard which carried out the king's capital sentences. The latter rendering may be supported by identifying Potiphar with the "captain of the guard" over the royal prison (Gen. 39:20; 40:3-4; 41:10, 12).

See Wife of Potiphar. WALTER E. BROWN

POTIPHERA (Heb. *pôṭî p̱eraʿ*; Egyp. *p3-dî-p3-Rʿ*)
A priest ("the one given [sent] by [the sun-deity] Re") in the Egyptian city of On (Heliopolis, "city of the sun"), whose daughter Asenath became Joseph's wife (Gen. 41:45, 50; 46:20).

POTTER'S FIELD
See Akeldama.

POTTERY
Pottery is one of the most common and abundant finds at ancient Near Eastern sites. This is because everyone possessed ceramic vessels, and because once the clay was fired in a kiln, it could break but not disintegrate like organic materials. Pottery can provide a great deal of information about various aspects of ancient life, including trading patterns, ethnicity, diet and culinary habits, and cult and ritual. However, pottery is still used primarily as a means of dating. Though petrographic and neutron activation analysis can help determine the source of the clay, absolute dates are arrived at by creating systems of classification, or typologies, which group ceramic vessels on the basis of stylistic characteristics

Stylistic Characteristics

The stylistic characteristics used to classify pottery include ware, technique, firing, morphology, and decoration/surface treatment. The ware is the material from which the vessel is made. It includes the clay and trace elements in the soil, inclusions, and temper. Inclusions are impurities that remain after the clay has been cleaned by the potter.

Temper is material such as ground rock or straw that is added by the potter to the clay as a binding agent. The technique refers to the process of manufacture: by hand (pinching, coiling), on a wheel, or in a mold, or any combination of these. The earliest vessels were made by hand, and handmade pottery continued to be manufactured in various parts of the Near East up to modern times. Wheelmade pottery became dominant once it was introduced ca. 2000 B.C.E. Molds, which were introduced in the Hellenistic period, were usually used for the production of oil lamps and certain types of bowls.

The process of firing dehydrates the vessel and thus determines its relative hardness. The temperature of the kiln and the amount of oxygen it contains also affect the color of the vessel. For example, vessels fired in a kiln with little or no oxygen will absorb the smoke and turn grey or black, while a kiln with lots of oxygen will produce red-colored vessels.

Morphology refers to the overall shape, size, and proportions of the vessel. Open vessels, such as bowls, cups, and plates, are those whose largest diameter is at the rim. Closed vessels, such as jars, jugs, and juglets, are those whose rim is narrower than the width of the body. Partially open or closed vessels, such as cooking pots, fall between these two categories.

There are many kinds of decoration or surface treatment, most of which are applied before the vessel is fired in the kiln. Among the most common is a slip, a thin solution of clay mixed with water that is applied to the surface of the vessel before firing (if applied after firing it is called a wash). Paint can be similar in composition to a slip, but is applied with a brush to form patterns. Different incised designs such as combing, grooving, puncturing, and engraving can be made using various instruments. Plastic decoration refers to pieces or strips of clay applied to the surface of the vessel. Ribbing, which first appeared in the Persian and Hellenistic periods, consists of undulating horizontal bands created by the potter while turning the vessel on the wheel. Burnishing is the polishing of the vessel's surface by rubbing it with a pebble, a shell, or even a handful of grass. Burnishing can be applied directly to the surface of the vessel or over a slip. It can also be used to create a pattern of darker lines contrasting with the unburnished areas. True glaze consisting of a glassy coating over the vessel's surface did not become common outside of Iran and Iraq before the early 9th century C.E.

Though the precise use of every vessel type cannot always be determined with certainty, it is possible to establish broad functional categories based on the stylistic characteristics outlined above. Table wares include vessels used for eating or drinking, such as plates, bowls, and cups, and dishes used for serving, such as jugs and decanters. Like contemporary fine china, table wares tend to be more highly decorated than other categories of vessels. Cooking vessels include cooking pots, which have a relatively narrow rim diameter, and casseroles, which are more open in form. Proceeding from the largest to the smallest in size, storage vessels include pithoi, jars (usually two-handled), jugs (one-handled), and juglets (smaller versions of jugs). The small size and narrow neck of juglets reflects their use as containers for precious liquids such as perfumes and scented oils. Oil lamps lit interior spaces. They developed in form from ordinary open bowls to bowls with a pinched spout to closed, moldmade vessels.

Ceramic Types

Following are the main ceramic types characteristic of Palestine from the Neolithic to Byzantine periods.

Pottery Neolithic Period (ca. 6000-4000 B.C.E.)

Pottery appeared throughout the Near East ca. 6000 B.C.E. The Neolithic period witnessed the transition from an economy of food-gatherers (hunting and collecting) to an economy of production (livestock and agriculture). Whether pottery was introduced from outside Palestine or developed locally from such pre-pottery Neolithic features as polished plaster floors and plastered human skulls is still debated. Neolithic vessels are handmade and have simple shapes, with flat bases and globular bodies. The clay contains a great deal of straw temper and grits, and tends to be friable due to low firing temperatures. Some vessels are decorated with cream slip that is partially covered by a burnished red slip, with the reserved portions of the cream slip forming chevrons, triangles, or similar designs. Others have bands containing herringbone incision with a red slip covering the rest of the vessel.

Chalcolithic Period (ca. 4000-3300)

The pottery of this period is still handmade. Impressions on the flat bases of some of the vessels suggest that they were manufactured while being turned slowly on a mat. Common types of decoration include red paint on the rims of bowls and cornets, and heavy rope-molding on large jars. Common vessel shapes include V-shaped bowls, which have straight walls and slightly flaring rims; cornets, a distinctive Chalcolithic shape resembling an ice cream cone; goblets, which are cups on a high ring base; footed bowls and chalices; holemouth jars with loop or lug handles; pithoi decorated with bands of rope-molding; and churns, which have a horizontal barrel-shaped body with loop handles at either end and a short, narrow neck. The last, which represent a distinctive Chalcolithic type, are thought to have been used for churning milk into yogurt, butter, or cheese.

Early Bronze Age (ca. 3300-2000)

The Early Bronze Age is subdivided into four major phases: Early Bronze I, II, III, and IV, based primarily on changes in ceramic types. Most of the pottery is still handmade. Three main groups of pottery distinguished in form and decoration are found in the EB I period. The first is characterized by a hand-burnished red slip, which decorates hemispherical bowls with an omphalos (concave) base, large bowls with an incurved rim, jugs and juglets with a high loop handle, and teapots (jugs with spouts). The second group is characterized by red or brown lines painted in groups or smeared in streaks over a buff background, with shapes corresponding to those of the first group. The third group is a grey-burnished ware with sharply carinated shapes imitating metal vessels. It is called Jezreel Valley or Esdraelon ware, after the area where it is most commonly found. The pottery of the EB II-III periods forms a single corpus. The vessels have thick, heavy walls and large, flat bases. The decoration consists mostly of an evenly burnished or pattern-burnished red slip. The pattern-combing found on some vessels gives them a metallic ring. Characteristic shapes include platters; piriform (pear-shaped) juglets; tall, slender jars with a flat base and flaring rim; and so-called Abydos jugs, which have a tall, elegant body, small flat base, and flaring rim with single handle. During the EB III period a distinctive type of pottery called Khirbet Kerak ware makes a brief appearance, named after the only site where it is found in abundance. The profiles of these vessels are characterized by an S-shape and by the highly burnished black exterior with a red rim and red interior, produced by firing.

The pottery of the EB IV period (William F. Albright's MB I and K. M. Kenyon's Intermediate EB-MB) demonstrates elements of continuity and change from the previous period. Some vessels are partly handmade and partly wheelmade. Most tend to have relatively thin walls, with a light yellow or tan fabric common in the south and a dark grey fabric common in the north. New shapes include teapots with a very broad, flat base; small cups; goblets; and open, four-spouted oil lamps. Though some red-burnishing continues, new types of decoration include incised straight or wavy lines and white-painted lines on dark clay. The new vessel shapes and dark ware with light painted decoration reflect Syrian influence.

Middle Bronze Age (ca. 2000-1500)

The pottery of the Middle Bronze Age represents an almost complete break with the EB traditions, both in terms of forms and decoration. Though burnished red slip is still common at the beginning of the period, later vessels tend to be plain. Painted decoration is rare. The technique changes too, with a fast wheel facilitating the production of thin-walled, carinated vessels with high ring bases. The characteristic shapes include bowls with carinated walls and high ring bases, at first with a burnished

Pottery Types Characteristic of the Various Archaeological Periods

From the Chacolithic till the Byzantine Periods

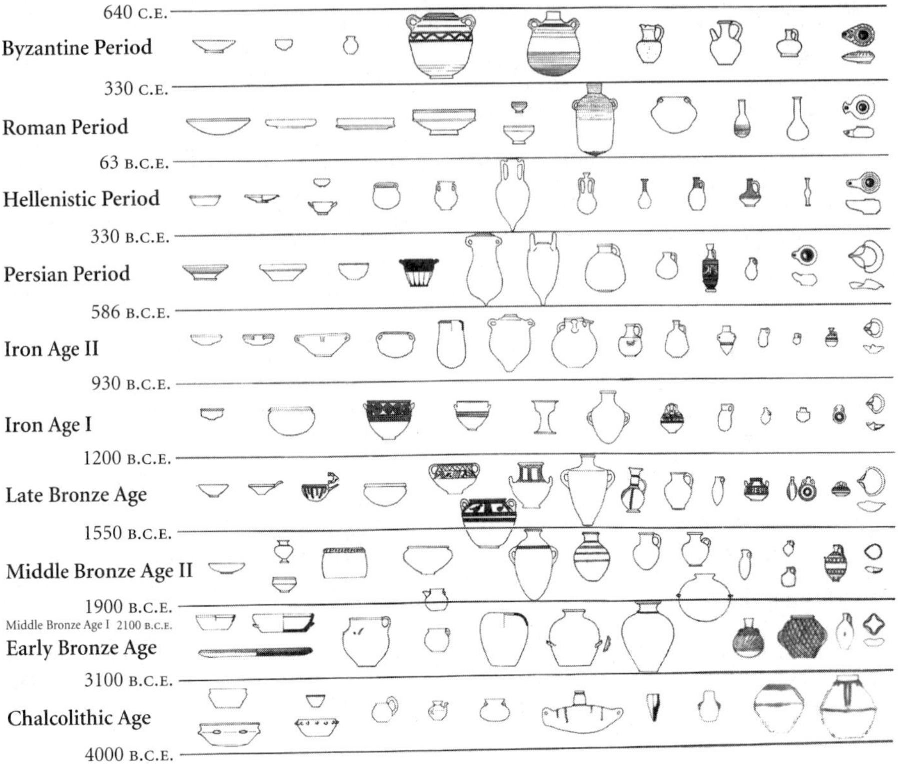

(Israel Department of Antiquities and Museums)

red slip, but later made of a thin, white ("eggshell") ware. A special shape now appears for cooking pots, instead of holemouth jars which were previously used for this purpose. At the beginning of the period the cooking pots have a flat base and straight walls with rope molding. These are replaced by deep bowls with carinated walls and flaring rim, which continue to develop into the Late Bronze Age. Jars have a rounded or small flat base, an egg-shaped body, and loop handles or no handles. Juglets have an egg-shaped body, a small flattened base, and multiple (double or triple) loop handles. Oil lamps consist of a deep bowl with a single, slightly pinched nozzle. One distinctive type of the latter part of the period is Tell el-Yehudiyeh ware, named after the Egyptian site where it was first found. It is usually represented by piriform juglets with a loop handle and button base made of a dark ware with burnished grey slip, punctured by incised lines and dots filled with white chalk.

Late Bronze Age (ca. 1500-1200)

Although some new wares and elements appeared in Palestine during the Late Bronze Age, most of the pottery represents a development of MB types. In general, there is a marked deterioration of the local wares during LB. At the same time, the number of imports increases, especially from Cyprus and Mycenaean Greece. Two fine painted wares are characteristic of the transition from MB to LB. The first, Cypriot bichrome ware, has black and red painted designs on a light background. The painted decoration is divided into zones containing animals. The second, local "chocolate on white" ware, is covered with a burnished creamy white slip over which geometric designs in a thick dark brown or reddish brown paint are drawn. The influence of these two wares is reflected in the popularity of painted decoration on local LB pottery. At the beginning of the period, much of the painting is bichrome (red and black or brown), and the motifs are elaborate and well executed. A later deterioration is reflected by the use of monochrome brown paint and simpler motifs. In addition, the carination of the bowls gradually becomes less pronounced, and their walls and bases become thicker. The shoulders of the cooking pots become more carinated, and they develop a thicker, undercut rim. The egg-shaped jars of MB develop angular shoulders and an elongated, pointed base. Oil lamps become larger and heavier, the nozzle is more deeply pinched, and the bowl develops a flange (rim) all the way around.

Iron Age (ca. 1200-586)

The pottery found at the small hill country sites usually associated with the Israelite settlement during the early Iron Age is crudely made. The walls are thick and poorly fired, and the vessels seem to have been turned on a slow wheel. There is little decoration aside from a light buff slip. Many of the shapes, such as the cooking pots, represent developments of LB forms. Collared rim jars, a type of large storage jar common at these sites, have an elliptical body, a thick rim with a raised ridge at the base of the neck, and two loop handles on the body. At the same time, a distinctive type of fine decorated table ware is found at sites associated with the Philistine settlement in the coastal region. The painted decoration (at first brown, and later black and red), geometric and bird motifs framed by "metopes," and shapes (including kraters with horizontal handles, stirrup jars, and "beer jugs") reflect the apparent Aegean origin of the Philistines. During the latter part of the Iron Age (after the establishment of the United Kingdom), this ware disappears, and Phoenician influence becomes evident in terms of form and decoration. There is also an overall improvement in the quality of the local pottery. Painted decoration is rare, and many vessels are now covered with a burnished red slip. At first, the slip is dark red and the burnish covers the entire vessel in irregular patterns. On later vessels the slip is orange-red, and the burnishing was done on the wheel. This produces a spiral pattern, with the burnished lines becoming spaced more widely apart as time progresses. Characteristic Iron II shapes include large carinated bowls with thick walls and everted rim; cooking pots with a short triangular rim; decanters (jugs with a tall ridged neck); asymmetrical flasks; and small open oil lamps with deeply pinched nozzles and wide flanges.

Persian, Hellenistic, Roman, and Byzantine Periods (ca. 586 B.C.E.–640 C.E.)

The period of Persian rule over Palestine corresponds with the flourishing of classical Athens. However, it was not until Alexander the Great's conquest (332 B.C.E.) that Greek culture began to make a significant impact on the material culture of Palestine. In terms of pottery, this is reflected mainly by the oil lamps, which become closed, moldmade, and decorated, and by changes in fine table wares. From the 5th to 3rd centuries, table wares covered with a shiny black slip (misnamed black glaze) were popular in Greece. Imported fragments of this ware are occasionally found at Near Eastern sites. During the 2nd and 1st centuries, it was gradually replaced by pottery covered with a shiny red slip (misnamed red glaze). By the 1st century B.C.E., red-slipped pottery, called terra sigillata, was produced at sites around the eastern Mediterranean and is common at Roman sites throughout Palestine. Red-slipped table

Iron II pottery in situ, Gezer Field VII (Phoenix Data Systems, photo by Robert A. Lyons)

wares remained popular until the Muslim conquest; those produced from the 4th to 7th centuries C.E. are called Late Roman red wares. The more utilitarian types of pottery continue the local traditions, with storage jars having the bag-shaped body, and cooking pots the globular body that appeared during the Iron Age.

Bibliography. R. Amiran, *Ancient Pottery of the Holy Land* (Jerusalem, 1969); J. W. Hayes, *Late Roman Pottery* (London, 1972); P. W. Lapp, *Palestinian Ceramic Chronology, 200 B.C.–A.D. 70* (New Haven, 1961); J. Magness, *Jerusalem Ceramic Chronology circa 200-800 C.E.* JSOTSup 103. ASORMS 9 (Sheffield, 1993); A. O. Shephard, *Ceramics for the Archaeologist* (Washington, 1971); E. Stern, *The Material Culture of the Land of the Bible in the Persian Period, 538-332 B.C.* (Warminster, 1982).

JODI MAGNESS

POVERTY

See POOR.

POWER

A common translation for several Hebrew and Greek words (Heb. *ḥayil, kōaḥ, ʿōz, gĕḇûrâ;* Gk. *dýnamis, exousía*) that refer to the ability to accomplish a task. As applied to people, the words generally refer to physical strength or ability. Thus, Caleb boasts of his strength (Josh. 14:11), and Samson's great strength is similarly described (Judg. 16:5-6). Heb. *gĕḇûrâ* frequently is used politically to refer to the power of the king, e.g, the "mighty deeds" recorded in the chronicles of the kings of Israel and Judah (e.g., 1 Kgs. 16:5, 27). As applied to God, the words commonly mention God's unlimited ability to act. God's deliverance through the Exodus is frequently cited as an example of God's unbounded power (Deut. 4:37). Heb. *ʿōz* refers primarily to the power of God and is found frequently in the Psalms (e.g., Ps. 59:11[MT 12]).

In the NT Gk. *dýnamis* refers primarily to the powers of God or to powers and abilities that God gives to people. Jesus tells the disciples to wait for the Holy Spirit, who will give them power for ministry (Acts 1:8). The Holy Spirit is frequently mentioned in connection with God giving power. In many cases the supernatural power of God is meant, and translations frequently render the word "miracle" or "miraculous powers." Rarely, Paul uses *dýnamis* to refer to evil demonic forces (Eph. 6:12).

When referring to the power of rulers, the NT prefers Gk. *exousía,* most commonly translated "authority," though sometimes rendered "power." Paul explains that all authority comes from God and that political "powers" administer God's power (Rom. 13:1-7). In the case of Jesus, the miracles demonstrate his divine authority. Jesus assumes the divine office of forgiving the sins of a paralytic (Mark 2:1-12, esp. v. 10; cf. Matt. 28:18).

MARK R. FAIRCHILD

PRAETORIAN GUARD

Established by Octavian in 27 B.C., an elite bodyguard *(cohors praetoria)* with superior pay, shorter terms of service, and more elaborate uniforms. Although its numbers fluctuated until it was disbanded in A.D. 312, during the 1st century it had nine cohorts of 500 men.

Six cohorts were stationed in other Italian towns (cf. Phil. 1:13), and three cohorts were reserved for constant attendance on the emperor. These guards typically appeared in civilian dress due to the traditional senatorial aversion to having troops stationed within the city limits. In A.D. 23, Tiberius concentrated the Praetorians in one camp inside the city.

The Guard was commanded by the emperor himself with one or two Praetorian prefects of equestrian rank as subordinate officers. Its members were primarily recruited from Italian towns.

Although established to protect the emperor, the Guard would eventually become an actual threat to his safety. As early as A.D. 31, the Praetorian prefect Sejanus was charged before the senate with treason and executed. In 41 Caligula was murdered by a Praetorian tribune; in the confusion that followed, Claudius, found hiding in the palace, was brought to the camp and hailed as emperor. A similar occurrence led to Nero's accession, and during the Civil War of 67-69 the Praetorians raised their own candidate, Otho, as emperor. This trend reached its pinnacle in 193, when two rivals stood near the Praetorian camp and traded bids for the emperorship (cf. Dio Cassius *Hist.* 74.2.3-6).

Bibliography. M. Grant, *The Army of the Caesars* (1974, repr. New York, 1992).

ANDREA LORENZO MOLINARI

PRAETORIUM

Originally a general's tent, the word "praetorium" in NT times was commonly used of the residence of a provincial governor (Acts 23:35; cf. Phil. 1:13).

The Gospels report that Jesus was interrogated by Pontius Pilate at "the praetorium" (Gk. *aulḗ,* "palace"; Mark 15:16; cf. Matt. 27:27; John 18:28, 33; 19:9). This was once widely held to be the Fortress Antonia at the northwest corner of the temple mount. In 35-37 B.C. Herod the Great rebuilt an existing Hasmonean fortress, renaming it Antonia in honor of his patron Mark Antony (Josephus *BJ* 1.75, 117, 401-2). The Antonia surfaces in the NT in reference to "the barracks" (*parembolḗ;* Acts 21:34, 37; 22:24; 23:10, 16, 32). The Via Dolorosa begins at this site. Across the street at the modern Ecce Homo convent is a pavement once thought to be part of a 1st-century courtyard (*Lithóstrōton,* John 19:13) of the Antonia, but the pavement is now identified as part of the eastern forum of the city as rebuilt by Hadrian (A.D. 132-135).

Herod's Hasmonean predecessors had a palace at the edge of the upper city across the Tyropoeon Valley from the temple (Josephus *Ant.* 20.189-96; *BJ* 2.344). Early Christian tradition leads Bargil Pixner to favor this identification. Excavations in the area (in the modern Jewish Quarter) have uncovered mansions of ancient Jerusalem's aristocracy but no Hasmonean palace.

The leading candidate for the praetorium is the new palace of Herod the Great, located on the western edge of the city at the Citadel next to the present Jaffa Gate. Constructed in 24-23 B.C., Herod's palace was most impressive, rivaling the temple itself in size and splendor. Josephus writes of its huge towers and high walls, banquet halls and guest rooms, ornamented ceilings and furniture, porticoes and gardens with statues and canals (*BJ* 5.176-183; *Ant.* 15.318). Philo (*Leg.* 299, 306) writes that Herod's palace served as "residence of the governors." Archaeology has shown that it extended into the present Armenian Quarter nearly to the south wall of the Old City and so covered an area larger than that of the Citadel, which today sits at the northern end of the site.

Bibliography. J. Finegan, *The Archaeology of the New Testament,* rev. ed. (Princeton, 1992), 246-53; R. M. Mackowski, *Jerusalem, City of Jesus* (Grand Rapids, 1980), 89-111. ROBERT HARRY SMITH

PRAISE

An expression of worship which recognizes and acknowledges God as the ultimate source and giver of all good gifts. In the Bible it encompasses a number of elements. (1) The call to praise can be expressed in a variety of ways, including "praise" (Heb. *hll;* e.g., Ps. 113:1, 3; 117:1); "thank" (*ydh;* 136:1-3); "bless" (*brk;* 34:1[MT 2]; 113:2; 134:1); "magnify" (*gdl;* 34:3[4]; 69:30[31]); "glorify" (*šbḥ;* 117:1); "sing" (*šîr;* Ps. 33:3; Exod. 15:21). Scholars discuss nuances of difference among the various terms, but they clearly belong to the same semantic field. (2) This call is addressed to a diverse audience: the inner self (Ps. 103:1-2), the community of Israel

(113:1; 135:1-2), all peoples and nations (117:1), even creation itself (148:3-10). Humans, in fact, are to be the voice for the praise rendered by all creatures. (3) The ground or motive of praise (often introduced by *ki,* "for, because") is some action of God on my/our behalf. It can be an act of redemption or deliverance when we were in need (Ps. 22:23-31[24-32]; 30:1-12[2-13]) or, more generally, God's acts of creation (103), steadfastness, and constancy (117:1-2). In form critical terms, the former have been designated "thanksgivings" and the latter "hymns." Claus Westermann proposes seeing the former as psalms of "narrative praise" and the latter as "descriptive praise." As lament is prayer prayed in distress, from experiences of curse and brokenness, so praise is prayer prayed from experiences of blessing, life, and wholeness; as such it focuses on the Giver and the gift.

In the NT the work of God in Jesus is similarly marked by praise. Praise attends his birth (Luke 1:46-55, 68-79; 2:13-14) as well as his triumphal entry into Jerusalem (19:37-38 par.). The Christian community is called to praise God constantly (Col. 3:16-17); Gk. *eucharístein* means basically "to render thanks and praise." The book of Revelation abounds in cosmic hymns of praise (e.g., Rev. 19:1-2, 5, 6-8).

Bibliography. P. D. Miller, *They Cried to the Lord: The Form and Theology of Biblical Prayer* (Minneapolis, 1994); C. Westermann, *Praise and Lament in the Psalms* (Atlanta, 1981).

MICHAEL D. GUINAN, O.F.M.

PRAYER

A primary means of communication that binds together God and humankind in intimate and reciprocal relationship. Its foundational assumption is the belief that the Creator of the world is both available for human address and committed to a divine-human partnership that sustains, and when necessary restores, the world in accordance with God's creational design.

In its broadest sense prayer is communication with God that comprises both word and deed, both verbal discourse and nonverbal, performative acts. As word, prayer consists of the special speech directed from people to God that is preserved in the recorded prayers of the Bible. As act, prayer establishes connection with God through a variety of nonverbal means such as sacrifice, dance, and bodily gestures and postures. Thus, one may verbalize praise and thanksgiving and also enact it, through ritual acts of eating, anointing with oil, robing in festal attire (Ps. 66:13-17; 116:12-14; cf. 30:11-12[MT 12-13]). One may speak lamentation and mourning and also dramatize it, through symbolic acts of fasting, putting dust on the head, and rending the garments (Josh. 7:6; Ezra 9:3, 5; Neh. 1:4; Dan. 9:3-4; Joel 2:12-13). In short, prayer is both a linguistic and a gestural construal of the fundamental realities that define relationship with God.

The development of prayer is difficult to trace precisely, although historical and sociological data support a general understanding. In the pre-state period the family and the village community provide the social context for a personal piety in which prayer is expressed primarily through brief addresses to God that arise directly and naturally from situations in daily life. Such prayers typically require no formal cultic setting and no cultic specialist. With the emergence of the monarchy and the establishment of the cult in Jerusalem, an official context for religion is institutionalized and ritualized. Prayer assumes more formulaic and prescribed forms as patterned rituals orient individuals toward corporate concerns that reinforce national solidarity. With the dissolution of the monarchy in the exilic and postexilic periods, the cult loses its institutional base and prayer assumes a variety of different forms and expressions that embody the legacies of both personal piety and official religion. This trend continues in early Judaism and through the first centuries of the early Church (ca. 250 B.C.E.–200 C.E.) as both statutory and spontaneous prayers are offered in the temple, synagogue, and home. Although these shifting historical and social contexts suggest something of a linear development in the stages of prayer, from the spontaneous to the prescribed and formal, there is a genetic connection between conventional and extemporized modes of praying that indicates both existed coevally during the biblical period.

The vocabulary of prayer in the Hebrew Bible is varied in keeping with different forms, settings, and degrees of formality or informality. A number of key technical expressions may be prefaced to or included within a verbal address that clearly distinguish it as prayer: Heb. *pll,* "pray"; *'tr,* "entreat"; *ḥnn* hithpael, "plea," "make supplication"; *qr' bšm YHWH,* "call on the name of the Lord." In other cases, however, prayer is conveyed not with special terminology but with the language of ordinary everyday discourse. A large number of recorded prayers, particularly in prose narratives, begin with the simple statement "and X said *('mr)* to God," an introduction that depicts prayer in theologically significant ways as analogous to the conversational dialogue routinely exchanged between persons of equal stature. What distinguishes such divine-human conversations from ordinary intra-human dialogue is the weighty nature of what is discussed. These "conversational prayers" typically emerge out of some crisis, which if left unaddressed threatens to destabilize or subvert trust in God.

A distinction may be made between prose prayers and those that are poetic in style. Prose prayers function as integral parts of narrative contexts and derive their meaning directly from what precedes and follows in a specifically defined situation. Approximately 100 recorded prose prayers occur throughout the OT, especially in Genesis-Kings where narrative is the primary literary style. Some are quite brief, containing little more than a simple petition for something concrete and practical (e.g., information, a child, healing), the granting of which may be verified (cf. Gen. 15:2, 3, 8; Judg. 13:8; 2 Sam. 15:31; 2 Kgs. 6:17, 18, 20). Other prose prayers contain petitions of a more abstract nature, e.g., for blessing, remembrance, hearing. Such prayers are often accompanied by lengthy elaborations that offer added incentive for God to hear and respond favorably (cf. 2 Sam. 7:18-29; 1 Kgs. 8:22-61; 2 Kgs. 19:15-19).

Prose prayers serve a variety of literary and theological functions within narrative contexts. They function as a literary means for portraying the character of actors, both human and divine, in a narrative drama. The prayers of Elijah (1 Kgs. 17:17-24), Solomon (3:4-15), and Hezekiah (2 Kgs. 20:2-3 [= Isa. 38:2-3) serve to confirm these persons as exemplary models of piety. The prayers of Jacob (Gen. 32:9-12[10-13]) and Jonah (Jonah 4:2-3; cf. 2:2-9[3-10] [poetic]), by contrast, function subtly to caricature or parody the piety professed by these persons. A number of postexilic prayers of penitence (Ezra 9:6-15; Neh. 1:5-11; 9:6-37; Dan. 9:4-19) are governed rhetorically by the repeating affirmation that God's character, especially as manifest in divine forgiveness, is defined primarily by the qualities of sovereignty, mercy, and justice. Further, a number of prose prayers contain a petition for divine justice that is located at the critical narrative juncture between some crisis in the relationship with God and its subsequent resolution (Gen. 18:22-33; Exod. 32:11-14; Num. 11:11-15; 14:13-19; Josh. 7:7-9; 1 Kgs. 17:17-19). The aggregate narrative sequence — crisis, prayer, resolution — portrays prayer theologically as an important resource for addressing theodicean issues.

The Psalms represent the largest collection of poetic prayers in the OT, although poetic addresses also occur within narrative contexts (1 Sam. 2:1-10; 2 Sam. 22:2-51; Jonah 2:1-9[2-10]). The distinguishing feature of these prayers is the formulaic language that renders them appropriate for repetition by a variety of persons in different contexts. The Psalter's mixture of individual and collective prayers, along with the regular and spontaneous ritual ceremonies that accompany them, reflect the convergence of personal piety and official religion that appears to characterize Israel's worship in the postexilic period.

Prayers occur in a variety of forms in the Psalter — hymns, dirges, blessings, imprecations — but two basic types dominate: lament and praise. Lament prayers (individual and collective) are more numerous than any other single type, comprising approximately one third of the collection (Pss. 3, 12, 22, 42–43, 44, 69, 79, 88, 130). Along with the "confessions" of Jeremiah (Jer. 11:18-23; 12:1-6; 15:10-21; 17:14-18; 18:18-23; 20:7-13, 14-18), the laments of Habakkuk (Hab. 1:2-17) and Job (Job 3:3-26; 6:1-30; 10:18-22; 13:20–14:22; 19:7-22; 30:16-31), and prophetic liturgies of lamentation (Jer. 14:7-9, 19-22; Isa. 63:7–64:12[11]; Joel 1–2), these prayers offer a profound witness to a lament tradition that authorized and promoted the practice of bringing before God a wide range of difficult and threatening circumstances. The typical pattern of these prayers — invocation, lament, petition, affirmation/hope of divine response — provides a rhetorical and substantive vehicle for articulating and coping with pain and suffering.

Prayers of praise and thanksgiving (individual and collective) are also well attested in the Psalter (Pss. 8, 30, 33, 66, 100, 113, 138, 146–150). They too follow a general pattern: invocation and summons to praise; reasons and motivations for praise (God's saving deeds and God's abiding nature and character); and concluding exhortation to praise. Both in form and in content praise prayers are connected to lament and thus to a central affirmation of biblical faith: when people who are in distress call to God, God hears and responds, thereby evoking in return heartfelt gratitude and adoration.

The NT uses a variety of terms with reference to prayer (*proseúchomai*, "pray"; *déomai*, "ask/seek"; *eucharistéō*, "give thanks"; *krázō*, "cry"). But in contrast with the OT, which preserves more than 250 prose and psalmic prayers, the NT contains relatively few recorded prayers: the prayers of Jesus (Matt. 11:25-27 = Luke 10:21-22; Matt. 26:39 = Mark 14:36 = Luke 22:42; Matt. 27:46 = Mark 15:34; Luke 23:34, 46; John 11:41-42; 12:27-28; 17:1-26); the prayers of Peter and the assembly (Acts 1:24-25) and of Peter and John (4:24-30); the prayer of Stephen (7:59-60). Prayer is prominent in Paul, particularly in the introductory thanksgivings (Rom. 1:8; 1 Cor. 1:4) and the benedictory blessings (Rom. 16:25-27; 2 Cor. 13:13) that conclude the letters, but otherwise the actual words of Paul's prayers are not recorded. Also in contrast with the OT, which offers very little instruction in prayer (cf. Job 8:5-6; 11:13-15; 22:23-27), is the significant attention in the NT to teaching about prayer.

The NT offers both a continuation of the forms and traditions of Israelite and Jewish prayer and a distinctive Christian perspective on them. Jesus continues the practice of lament (Matt. 27:46 = Mark 15:34 [Ps. 22:1(2)]; Luke 23:46 [Ps. 31:5(6)] and praise/thanksgiving (Matt. 11:25-27 = Luke 10:21-22; John 11:41-42) and is thus revered by his followers as one who modeled the essence of Hebraic prayer (cf. Heb. 5:7). The Gospel of Luke portrays Jesus as having prayed at critical junctures in his life — at baptism (Luke 3:21), the choosing of the disciples (6:12), transfiguration (9:28-29), in Gethsemane (22:32, 41-42), and at his crucifixion (23:46) — thus modeling the legacy preserved especially in Hebrew narratives of the importance of prayer in life's decisive situations.

The NT's distinctive perspective is especially evident in its instructions concerning how to pray. In the Sermon on the Mount Jesus cautions against impious and pretentious prayer (Matt. 6:5-8) and offers the Lord's Prayer as a pattern for his disciples (Matt. 6:9-13 = Luke 11:2-4). This model prayer, which combines praise and petition in a simple, personal, and spontaneous form, is itself rooted in Jewish antecedents (cf. the Amidah or Prayer of Eighteen Benedictions). A further emphasis in Jesus' teaching in the Sermon on the Mount is the exhortation to be persistent in prayer (Matt. 7:7-11 = Luke 11:9-13), a theme also prominent in Paul, who calls believers to "pray without ceasing" (1 Thess. 5:17; cf. Rom. 12:12; Eph. 6:18; Col. 4:2). Luke's Gospel elaborates further on this theme in two parables, Luke 11:5-8; 18:1-8, the latter of which connects persistent prayer with the promise of justice for the disadvantaged and the oppressed.

A further distinctive of prayer in the NT is the importance of intercession. In the high priestly prayer of John 17, Jesus embodies the role of intercessor as he entrusts the faith community and the efficaciousness of its witness in the world to God. Paul frequently exhorts congregations to become communities of intercession for him and for the success of his mission (Rom. 15:30-32; Col. 4:3; 2 Thess. 3:1). Peter and Paul pray for the healing of the sick (Acts 9:40; 28:8), a practice that the Letter of James commends to the elders of the church (Jas. 5:13-16). Elsewhere intercessions are offered for spiritual growth (Eph. 1:16-17; Phil. 1:9), sustenance in times of peril (Acts 12:5; Phil 1:19; Heb. 13:18), and for the civil authorities (1 Tim. 2:1-2). Especially noteworthy is Jesus' admonition to his followers to pray for the forgiveness of their persecutors (Matt. 5:44 = Luke 6:28). Jesus himself models such intercession in his last words from the cross (Luke 23:34). Stephen reflects Jesus' example in his own last words (Acts 7:60). The theology of the Cross in turn shapes Christian prayer definitively, and the principle of blessing, not cursing, one's enemies becomes a foundational imperative for Christian piety and practice (Matt. 5:39-48; Luke 6:27-36; Rom. 12:14).

In sum, both the OT and the NT portray prayer as a principal means by which Creator and creature are bound together in an ongoing, vital, and mutually important partnership. The ultimate goal of this partnership, as articulated in Jesus' model prayer, is that God's will be done "on earth as in heaven."

Bibliography. S. E. Balentine, *Prayer in the Hebrew Bible* (Minneapolis, 1993); O. Cullmann, *Prayer in the New Testament* (Minneapolis, 1995); M. Greenberg, *Biblical Prose Prayer as a Window to the Popular Religion of Ancient Israel* (Berkeley, 1983); J. Koenig, *Rediscovering New Testament Prayer* (San Francisco, 1992); P. D. Miller, *They Cried to the Lord: The Form and Theology of Biblical Prayer* (Minneapolis, 1994); G. P. Wiles, *Paul's Intercessory Prayers* (Cambridge, 1974).

SAMUEL E. BALENTINE

PREACHING, PROCLAMATION

In both the OT and NT, the oral address plays a decisive role in shaping the identity of the people of God. God's spokesmen "preach" and "proclaim" God's deed to the people, challenging them to acknowledge the divine will for their lives. In the NT the English verbs commonly render Gk. *kēryssō* and *euangelízō*, which may be used synonymously. The content of the preaching may be described with the corresponding nouns *kḗrygma* and *euangélion.* Other terms belonging to the same semantic domain include "to speak the word of God," "exhort," and "witness."

The LXX rarely employs *kērýssō* and *euangelízō* for the proclamation of the prophets (cf. Jonah 1:2; Jer. 20:8). NT usage is based primarily on the language of Isa. 40–66. Isa. 52:7 employs *euangelízō* twice to describe the one who "brings good news" and "proclaims peace." In Isa. 61:1 the prophet declares God's call for him to "preach good news *(euangelízō)* to the poor" and "proclaim *(kerýssō)* liberty to the captives."

C. H. Dodd's definition of preaching as "the public proclamation to the non-Christian world" is only partially valid, inasmuch as the verbs "preach" and "proclaim" (as well as synonyms) are also used for the oral address to the believing community (Rom. 1:15; 1 Thess. 2:9; cf. 2 Tim. 4:2). However, the verbs are most commonly employed for the prophetic announcement of God's eschatological acts and the call to believe, often in terms that echo Isa. 52:7; 61:1. John the Baptist (Matt. 3:1) and Jesus "proclaim" (4:17) the gospel of the kingdom (4:23). Similarly, the Synoptic Gospels portray Jesus' mission in terms of his "proclaiming" the kingdom (Mark 1:14; cf. vv. 38-39, 45). According to Luke 4:18, Jesus identifies himself as the prophet of Isa. 61:1, whose mission is to "proclaim good news to the poor." When he calls disciples, he sends them out to "preach" to the lost sheep of the house of Israel (Matt. 10:7, 27). The disciples continue this ministry by preaching the kingdom (Acts 20:25; 28:31).

A common topic in Paul's letters is his own recollection of his preaching ministry, which began in the missionary proclamation and continued in his work with the churches. He understands his mission as that of the herald of Isa. 52:7 (Rom. 10:15). He describes the content of his message variously as "Christ crucified" (1 Cor. 1:23), "Christ Jesus" (2 Cor. 1:19), "Jesus Christ as Lord" (4:5), and the gospel (11:7; Gal 1:11; 2:2; 1 Thess. 2:2, 9). He recalls the creedal formula of 1 Cor. 15:3 as the content of the preaching which the community had originally believed (v. 11). Paul indicates the relationship between the original proclamation and the subsequent pastoral ministry in 1 Thess. 2:9-13, where he equates his preaching of the gospel (v. 9) with the task of community formation in which he took on the paternal role of "encouraging, comforting, and urging" his community to "live lives worthy of God" (v. 12).

Bibliography. C. Brown, "Proclamation," *NIDNTT* 3:44-68; C. H. Dodd, *The Apostolic Preaching and Its Developments* (Chicago, 1937).

JAMES W. THOMPSON

PRECINCTS

See PARBAR.

PRECIOUS STONES

See GEMS.

PREDESTINATION

In its broad definition, the theological affirmation that God has sovereignly and graciously planned for the unfolding history of all things. It is more commonly known according to a narrower definition, that God has decreed either the final salvation or the final reprobation of each person. Election and reprobation, then, are subcategories of the doctrine of predestination. This doctrine is associated primarily with John Calvin and Calvinism, although it finds its biblical roots in a variety of OT and NT texts, was given classic form by Augustine, and was treated by many Patristic and medieval theologians as well as the Reformers. The doctrine of predestination has a number of vexing logical difficulties, having to do mainly with the issues of divine sovereignty and human freedom. It also raises acute pastoral difficulties. Because of these difficulties, the doctrine has frequently come under attack.

In the OT the doctrine of predestination is related to call or election. God corporately calls the people of Israel to be the covenant people (cf. Deut. 7:6-10) and individually calls persons (cf. Exod. 3, Moses; Judg. 2:16, judges; Jer. 1:4-8, Jeremiah). This election was for the purpose of fulfilling the will of God, for blessing the nations, and for executing the judgment of God. Several Psalms also express the confidence, comfort, and wonder of God's election and foreknowledge (e.g., Ps.139:16; 115:1, 3, 12, 13). In the NT the several Greek words which are translated variously as "predestine," "decree," "foreordain," or "foresee" indicate a wide range of God's activity which centers on Jesus Christ as the means of salvation and includes human persons in this saving plan. The classic predestination texts include Rom. 8:28-30; Gal. 1:15; Eph. 1:4, 5; 2 Thess. 2:13. In these texts the background of predestination is humanity's disobedience and rebellion against God; humanity thus earns God's rightful condemnation. However, God does not leave humanity bereft. God graciously elects those whom God wills to elect. The implications of election, for humanity, are gratitude and service to God and all God's people.

Several options exist in the Christian tradition on stating and understanding the doctrine of predestination. One version, which might be called the "softer" version, states that God elects on the basis of God's foreknowledge. That is, either election or reprobation is contingent on God foreseeing how each person would freely respond to the gospel. On this reading of the doctrine, the justice and fairness issues are somewhat mitigated. Each person, so to speak, gets what he or she deserves. An example of a theologian who has taken, or has tended to take, the approach of identifying God's foreknowledge with predestination is John Wesley, as well as the broad Arminian tradition.

Another option in the history of this doctrine can be identified with Martin Luther. Although Luther had a very strong understanding of election, with related affirmations of the sovereignty of God, he did not wish to state a corresponding doctrine of reprobation. His can perhaps be called a "middle" position, a position with the necessary ingredients for a stronger stand, but one which avoids the most excruciating questions and dilemmas by simply moving them off to one side.

The "harder" version of predestination asserts that God does not merely foresee but actually foreordains. That is, God's election or reprobation is a primal divine decree and does not depend on God's foreknowledge of free human action or decision. Calvin is the name most identified with this position. Although Calvin constantly emphasized the primary purpose of the doctrine of predestination as a call to gratitude and praise, he did not hold back from a full statement of both election and reprobation. The pastoral difficulties of this version of predestination are immediate and extremely difficult. Why does God choose only some and reject others? Calvin said that to ask such questions was to stretch well beyond the limited capabilities of the human mind. The best course of action, according to Calvin, is for believers to thank God for their election and not to probe further the mysteries of God. Calvin's approach to predestination affirms a full and undiluted divine sovereignty; it nonetheless holds human beings responsible and then warns against the folly of a morbid curiosity about these matters.

A bold new approach to the doctrine of election was offered by Karl Barth. As a theologian of the Reformed tradition, Barth shared with Calvin the convictions concerning God's sovereignty and the reality of sin. However, he interpreted election as accomplished through Jesus Christ, who is the elect of God. Humanity, as united with Jesus Christ, shares in that election.

At its best, the doctrine of predestination emphasizes the free gracious saving activity of God and the grateful response of the believer. At its worst, it suggests that God arbitrarily saves some and condemns others, thus implying a God with lower standards of neighborly love than Christians are enjoined to display. The most helpful way of approaching the doctrine of predestination is to cast its conceptual net widely: it affirms a divine plan and determination for all humanity that conforms to God's eternal will. In these terms, predestination doctrine is not so much interested in the final fate of individual persons, but is a broad affirmation that the love of God, the wisdom of God, and the righteousness of God are the underlying realities of all created life, including each human person. It is God who has made us, and we belong to God.

LEANNE VANDYKE

PREPARATION, DAY OF

The evening before a holy day (Matt. 27:62; Luke 23:54; John 19:14, 31, 42). Mark further specifies "the day before the sabbath" (Mark 15:42; cf. Jdt. 8:6; 2 Macc. 8:26; Josephus *Ant.* 3.255; 16.163).

According to Exod. 16:23 the day before the sabbath was to function as a time of preparation for the celebration of the sabbath. Everyday responsibilities were to be performed in advance, so that the holy day could be enjoyed in as much comfort as possible. Such responsibilities came to include bathing, donning festive dress, lighting lamps, and preparing food. By the time of Christ, all such activities had to be completed by 3 P.M. (*Ant.* 16.163; cf. *BJ* 6.423).

Citing rabbinic literature, most commentators assume that "day of Preparation" could also refer to the day before the first day of each festival, since these days were also considered "sabbaths" (cf. Exod. 34:22; Lev. 16:31; 23). D. A. Carson, however, notes that such usage is attested nowhere outside John 19:14; thus the phrase "the day of Preparation for the Passover" may be better rendered "the day of the Preparation of the sabbath occurring during Passover week."

Bibliography. D. A. Carson, *The Gospel According to John* (Grand Rapids, 1992).

W. E. NUNNALLY

PRESBYTER, PRESBYTERY

A group of elders (Gk. *presbytérion,* from *presbýteros,* "elder"). Some early Christian communities adopted and adapted this institution of governance from Jewish precedents and from the bodies of elders known in Greek and Egyptian society. Elders were appointed in new Christian congregations (Acts 14:23) and appear in Jerusalem both alone (11:30; 21:18) and alongside (15:2-6, 22-23; 16:4) the apostles. The presbytery as a body of elders was active in ordination (1 Tim. 4:14), and in the Pastoral and Catholic Epistles elders had both leadership (5:17, 19) and liturgical (Jas. 5:14) functions. The terms "elder" and "bishop" may be interchangeable (Acts 20:17, 28; Titus 1:5, 7). A council of elders surrounds God on his heavenly throne (Rev. 4:4, 9-11; 5:6-14).

Bibliography. J. M. Lieu, *The Second and Third Epistles of John* (Edinburgh, 1986).

DAVID RENSBERGER

PRESENCE

The Hebrews believed that they had a unique relationship with their God (Exod. 19:5; Jer. 30:22; 31:3). But even God's revelations were shrouded with mystery to protect the glory of the deity (Heb. *kāḇôḏ, šĕḵînâ;* Exod. 3; 33:17-23, esp. 20; cf. John 1:18). Abram and Jacob commemorated their experiences of God's presence by erecting sanctuaries (at Shechem, Beer-sheba, Bethel, and Peniel). Yahweh prescribed the tent of meeting (Exod. 40:34-38) and the ark of the covenant (25:10-30) as aids to celebrate his presence. Later, the temple served this purpose (1 Kgs. 8; cf. Ps. 24:7-10). The people eventually took for granted the temple as a symbol of God's presence and wrongly saw it as a guarantee of divine, protective favor (Jer. 7:1-4). The principal biblical word for "presence" is "face" (Heb. *pānîm;* Gk. *prósōpon*). Adam and Eve hid from the face (presence) of God (Gen. 3:8); Yahweh promised that his face (presence) would accompany Moses (Exod. 33:14); and the face (presence) of God is the fullness of joy (Ps. 16:11). Whenever displeased with his people, God would withdraw his face or presence (Ezek. 10:18; Ps. 22:1-21[MT 2-22]).

In the NT the presence of God is shaped by the doctrine of the incarnation, that God was made flesh in Jesus Christ. Though he was human (Gal. 4:4-5; Phil. 2:5-11), he was the means of reconciling the world to God (2 Cor. 5:19; cf. John 1:1-18; 20:28; Col. 1:15-20; Heb. 1:1-4) whose glory shone in the face (presence) of Jesus Christ (2 Cor. 4:6). God is present also as the Holy Spirit or Paraclete (e.g., John 14:25; Acts 2:1-47) and through angelic messengers (Matt. 1:18-25; Luke 1:26-38; 2:8-20). The ultimate hope for the unmediated presence of God is expressed as the coming (Gk. *parousía,* lit., "presence") of Christ (1 Thess. 1:10; 2:19; 3:13; 4:13–5:11). Finally, John envisions the end time when God will be present with his people immediately and forever (Rev. 21:1-4).

Bibliography. S. E. Balentine, *The Hidden God: The Hiding of the Face of God in the Old Testament* (Oxford, 1983); L. H. Brockington, "Presence," in *A Theological Word Book of the Bible,* ed. A. Richardson (New York, 1950), 172-76; S. L. Terrien, *The Elusive Presence* (San Francisco, 1978).

RICHARD A. SPENCER

PRIESTHOOD, ISRAELITE

This article focuses on the Israelite priesthood in the wider context of the ancient Near East, because that is where it was active. Exercising caution against parallelomania, either pan-babylonianism or pan-ugaritism, we will see that the Israelite priesthood shows many affinities with the obviously more complex picture of that in Mesopotamia with its more than 3000 years of history. Egypt had its own unique theology which surprisingly influences Israel very little, though its close proximity would suggest otherwise.

Practices in Israel reflected those of the peoples immediately surrounding them, so the Hebrews could be considered a kind of "Canaanite." For the Canaanite cult, we rely upon archaeology and look far north to the Ugaritic tablets, and east to the Amorites as reflected in the Mari Letters. Furthermore, Mesopotamian sources represent vast land areas, thousands of years of history, and many tens of thousands of texts, many of which had sacerdotal elements, in the areas of historiography, royal annals, geography, economics, marriage, mathematics, astronomy, law, medicine, school, wisdom, divination, magic, liturgy, lexicography, grammar, all interpreted by art of many varieties.

By contrast, the ancient Hebrew writings provide quite limited data. To obtain sufficient information about the Israelite priesthood then, we must consider the whole gamut of writings in the Bible, but even then we are asking questions of the Bible which it was not designed to answer.

Another limitation is that we know almost nothing of the priesthood in the northern kingdom, and what is described in our texts is from the standpoint of their rivals. The OT professes to represent practices extending over perhaps a 1000-year period, but much of this material may have been edited rather late in Israelite history.

Every civilization had its own way of handling sacred space and sacred time. In all of them one figure is chosen to represent the movement both human to divine and divine to human, and so does the liturgy in the name of humanity. In Israel, the Deuteronomic stratum assumes one worship place, the temple in Jerusalem. Archaeologists have discovered, however, that there were other places where some kind of worship was carried on. Worship at the enigmatic *bāmôṯ* ("high places"), whose configuration is unclear, appears often. Excavations at the sites of Arad, Hazor, Beth-shan, Shechem, Bethel, and many others show worship activities. All of these used cultic officials, in Hebrew called by the general term *kōhēn*.

Another term for a priestly office, *kōmer*, appears rarely. Zeph. 1:4 prophesies in the vein of the other preexilic prophets that the names of both the *kōhănîm* and the *kĕmārîm* will be cut off, i.e., their priesthood will be nullified. In a typical Deuteronomic criticism, 2 Kgs. 23:5 tells of Josiah deposing the *kĕmārîm* for making offerings in the "high places," as well as to Baal, the sun, moon, and stars. However, it says that the kings of Israel had assigned them these offices (cf. 1 Kgs. 13:33)! Hos. 10:5 sardonically describes them as exulting with ritual joy over the calves of Beth-aven.

The root *kmr* is an old one in Semitic languages, appearing as Akk. *kumruy* in Old Assyrian (19th century) and at Mari (18th century), where there was an Amorite society. The term continues into Aramaic, and in Syriac appears alongside *knh* designating a priest. In Mesopotamia dozens of titles were given to cultic officiants, in Israel only a few.

The root of *kōhēn*, by contrast, appears in almost all Semitic languages, although not all have the same meaning. An exception is Ugaritic, where it appears with much the same definition as in Hebrew. The Western word "priest" comes ultimately from Gk. *presbýteros*, "elder"; this later meaning should not be read back onto the original word. The norm for the OT, then, is the Jerusalem temple, with the *kōhēn* as the cultic official. The status of the *kōhēn* is shown by the theology that the Israelites are to be a "kingdom of priests" (Exod. 19:6). The subject of the priesthood overarches much of the narrative of Exodus-Deuteronomy as well as Psalms.

The *kōhēn* was "ordained" (Heb. *millē'*, lit., "fill up his hand"; Exod. 28:41; Judg. 17:5). In this ceremony he was anointed (Exod. 29:7) and consecrated (28:41; *qiddēš*, lit., "treat as holy"). He wore an ornate garb (Ezek. 44:17), of linen rather than wool, which he changed upon leaving the sanctuary (v. 19). His principal vestment, the ephod, is described in great detail in Exod. 28, 39. David acting in a priestly role wore an ephod (2 Sam. 6:14). The *kōhēn* also had a special tonsure (Ezek. 44:20).

Duties

The *kōhēn*'s tasks were quite varied, and the literary evidence is sporadic. Thus, it must suffice to say that *at some time in Hebrew history* the tradition records the priest as doing this-or-that. The priest was essentially the guardian of the holy place (Num. 18:5). To do this he took on the holiness of the sanctuary. This invested him with a kind of authority, but responsibility also. He had to bear the guilt for any lapse of propriety in the sanctuary (v. 1). Though all the people were to follow the *tôrâ* and are commanded to be holy (Lev. 19:2), the priests were the paradigm holy people (Ezra 8:28). They were to be as the people they prayed for should be, because the stones woven into the ephod had written on them the names of the sons of Israel (Exod. 28:9-12).

The *kōhēn*'s liturgical functions were first and foremost to preside over the many types of sacrifice at the main altar; Num. 28–29 list the main ones. The food items then became part of their sustenance (1 Sam. 2:29; Ezek. 44:29-30). No details of what must have been a highly physical and dirty operation are described in our sources except obliquely.

A major part of the *kōhēn*'s duties was to pray (1 Sam. 7:5), although praying was not exclusively his duty (cf. 2 Kgs. 6:18; Jer. 37:3; also Job 42:8; 1 Sam. 2:1-10). As an aspect of this, the priest asked Yahweh questions on behalf of others (Judg. 18:5), reminiscent of the *ša'ilu* (masculine) and *ša'iltu* (feminine) "questioner" in Mesopotamia. A more literary function was to pronounce the blessing (Deut. 10:8). The poetical form of Num. 6:24-26 suggests that it may have been chanted; it is unclear whether the blessing was said once only or repeated, or if it was part of a longer prayer.

The physical actions of the priest may be inferred from words in the psalms and elsewhere: processing into the sacred area (Ps. 68:24-27[MT 25-28]), lifting the hands (134:2), kneeling (95:6), dancing (149:3), singing (149:1), blowing the horn (Num. 10:10). These ritual acts were not so much embellishments to the liturgy, but represented symbolically the very heart of the belief which lay behind it. Other cultic activities included burning the incense (Exod. 30:7-9), tending the oil lamps (27:21), setting out the bread of the presence (25:30; 1 Sam. 21:4-6[5-7]), sprinkling salt (Ezek. 43:24), sprinkling blood (Lev. 3:2), and pouring drink offerings (Exod. 37:16), the latter a prevalent act in Mesopotamia.

Analogy with Mesopotamian practices suggests a cultic character to some of the narratives in Genesis and Exodus, perhaps indications of a cultic drama. There are ties between religion and drama in most of the world's religions. Joshua orchestrates a procession of priests to circumambulate the walls of Jericho, blowing horns and carrying the ark (Josh. 6). References to the movements, garments, responses, limits, and trumpets may indicate a ritual performed at the base of Mt. Sinai (Exod. 19:10-13), acted out by Moses, as a priest.

Outside the altar area, the priest's duties included consultation of the sacred lots Urim and Thummim (Num. 27:21), used in cases of difficult decisions. Some think they could give only yes or no answers, but there may have been various configurations of their falling (we do not know their shape nor their number) or there could have been multiple castings, and so they might have given a more complex answer. The fact that both words are in the plural would indicate that. In some literary strata they were described as kept in the breastplate, bound to the ephod (Exod. 28:30). Casting lots was common in ancient Israel, used in the scapegoat ceremony by Aaron in his holy vestments (Lev. 16) and in the division of the land by lot by a priest and Joshua (Josh. 14:1-2). The use of lots apparently continued into postexilic times (cf. Neh. 10:34[35]). In late Assyrian times *puru,* "lots," were used to determine the *limmu*-official, for whom the year was named.

The OT offers no indication of a physician, and the priest sometimes took on the role of healer. He made decisions in some cases of leprosy (Lev. 13:30-46; Deut. 24:8), but this could also be done by the prophet (2 Kgs. 5:1-14).

The priest shared judicial office with those entitled judge (Deut. 17:8-9). In difficult cases he used the ordeal, a cultic act performed "before Yahweh," i.e., the altar. Num. 5:11-31 vividly describes the case of a woman suspected of adultery.

The priestly office at times had a teaching function (Lev. 10:11), a role shared with the prophet (Isa. 28:9; Mic. 3:11), responsible for transmitting *tôrâ* (Deut. 33:10).

Responsibility for distinguishing between clean and unclean (Lev. 10:10) was wholly under the aegis of the priest. Among the numerous acts rendering a person unclean was contact with certain animals, birds, seafood, and insects.

The priest also had administrative duties. The money that came into the temple was probably overseen by the priests. In 2 Kgs. 22:4 the "keepers of the threshold" collected the money and the high priest handled it. In postexilic times the priest had the title "treasurer" (Neh. 13:13).

The priest also operated, although astutely, in the political realm. Zadok's anointing of Solomon as king (1 Kgs. 1:39) hearkened back to a practice described in 1 Sam. 10:1, described perhaps from a later perspective. In a reform context, the king would obtain and read "this *tôrâ,*" monitored by the "levitical priests" (Deut. 17:18-19), the latter a term especially used by the Deuteronomist.

The priesthood shared some of the sacerdotal tasks with the king, as was true of Mesopotamia, where one of the king's titles actually was "priest" *(šangu).* David made the offering (2 Sam. 6:17; cf. Ezek. 46:4). Solomon prayed at the altar (1 Kgs. 8:22) and blessed the people (v. 14). Jeroboam burned incense (1 Kgs. 13:1). In later Maccabean times, the ruler took over some of the priestly prerogatives, e.g., pronouncing the blessing (Sir. 50:20), and he finally assumed the title "high priest" (1 Macc. 16:24).

To give a balanced account, mention must also be made of the many times the prophets accused the priest of wrongdoing. He was a sinner (Hos. 4:8-9) and was like a robber (6:9). He taught for money and was complacent of being taken care of by his God (Mic. 3:11). He became intoxicated (Isa. 28:7), worshipped false gods (Jer. 2:27; 8:1-2), did not distinguish between clean and unclean (Ezek. 22:26), and gave wrong instructions (Mal. 2:8). All of this must be exegeted, and some statements are probably metaphorical.

History and Development

The above has treated the texts synchronically, as if they all were written at the same time and by the same group. Nevertheless, there was a history to and development of the Israelite priesthood, although it is difficult to determine what that was, being limited by the probable later editing of the texts. The few notes that can be gleaned show that the office was held from the earliest times by the tribe of Levi (Deut. 10:9; 33:8, probably from an old stratum), with Aaron the eponymous priest (Exod. 28:1). A priest became such through training (1 Sam. 3:1) or inheritance (Jer. 1:1; cf. 1 Kgs. 2:26). At the time of Solomon there is an indication of a new order or family heading the priesthood. Zadok (1 Kgs. 2:35) is found in a leadership position, and this continued to the end of the state (Ezek. 48:11). Ezra also was a Zadokite (Ezra 7:1-2). Zadok's origin goes unmentioned.

Little is known about another order (*dib̠râ,* lit., "manner") in the priesthood, that of Melchizedek. Ps. 110:4 is the only mention of it in the OT in an Israelite stratum, though Gen. 14:18 narrates the old tradition. The Qumran scroll 11QMelch and the gnostic Nag Hammadi Melchizedek present him as an end-time figure, not a priest. The reference to Melchizedek in 2 En. 71–72, telling of his originating a line of priests, is a later commentary on the Genesis passage, as is Heb. 7:15-17.

Even though all priests were supposed to be from the family of Levi, non-Levites also served (1 Kgs. 12:31). Some of the lesser roles were assigned to Levites. Num. 4:17-45 tells of three families, the Kohathites, Gershonites, and Merarites, who had other than priestly duties in the sanctuary, keeping the implements and trappings. Postexilic data shows singers and doorkeepers among the Levites (Neh. 10–12), but listed separately from the priests. If 1 Chr. 24:7-19 represents a postexilic arrangement, the priesthood then appeared in 24 divisions, each one taking its turn (cf. Luke 1:8).

After the Exile the office of high priest plays a significant role, recorded especially in the postexilic and intertestamental literature (Hag. 1:1; Sir. 50:1) and the Synoptic Gospels, though the term had appeared earlier (Josh. 20:6). Earlier the head was usually called simply priest (1 Kgs. 4:2-4) or chief priest (2 Kgs. 25:18; Jer. 52:24).

With the capture of the temple in 70 C.E., the cultic functions of the priesthood ceased, although priestly families continued to bless the people in synagogue service.

See WOMEN IN THE ISRAELITE CULT.

Bibliography. M. Haran, "Priests and Priesthood: Function of the Priests," *EncJud* (New York, 1971) 13:1076-80; R. A. Henshaw, *Female and Male: The Cultic Personnel: The Bible and the Rest of the Ancient Near East.* PTMS 31 (Allison Park, 1994), §1.4; B. A. Levine, "Priesthood: Jewish Priesthood," *Encyclopedia of Religion* (New York, 1987) 11:534-36; J. Pedersen, *Israel, Its Life and Culture* III (London, 1940).

RICHARD A. HENSHAW

PRIESTLY DOCUMENT

One of the hypothetical sources of the Pentateuch, commonly referred to as "P." To the Priestly Document are ascribed the first Creation account (Gen. 1:1–2:4a), the genealogies in the Pentateuch, and the largest part of the laws pertaining to the priestly and sacrificial system in Exodus, Leviticus, and Numbers. It is thought to have originated in priestly circles no later than the 8th century B.C.E.

PRINCIPALITY

A class of spiritual being (Gk. *archḗ*), most often evil (cf. Rom. 8:38; 1 Cor. 15:24; Eph. 1:21; 3:10; 6:12; Col. 1:16; 2:10, 15). The term always occurs with other similar terms also denoting evil spiritual beings: power *(exousía),* authority *(dýnamis),* throne *(thrónos),* dominion *(kyriótēs),* world-rulers of this age *(kosmokrátōr toú skótous toútou),* evil spiritual force in the heavens *(pneumatikón tḗs ponērías en toís epouraníois).* The use of different terms probably indicates different ranks or types of evil spiritual beings. In Eph. 2:2; 6:11-12 Paul identifies one evil spiritual being to which these others seem to be subject: "the ruler of the power of the air" or "the devil." In Dan. 7 "dominion" (LXX Gk. *archḗ*) denotes the earthly power of the fourth beast (vv. 12, 26) hostile to Israel and standing in contrast to the power of God and the one like a son of man (v. 14); that lurking in the background of earthly kingdoms — esp. the fourth kingdom — are evil spiritual beings, is clear from Dan. 10.

The notion of different classes of spiritual beings is not unique to the NT (cf. 1 En. 41:9; 61:10; T. Levi 3:8; T. Sol. 20:15). Similar lists are found in the Greek magical papyri (*PGM* 1.215; 3.35; 4.1193, 1275, 1599, 2199-99; 22b.2, 4, 7).

In Pauline theology, Christ shall destroy every "principality, power, and authority" at the end, when he hands over to God the kingdom (1 Cor. 15:24). Nevertheless, in the present these evil spiritual beings are subject to Christ, for Christ has been seated at the right hand of God in the heavenlies (Eph. 1:20-21). Because of this, believers can resist the evil influences of these spiritual beings (Eph. 6:10-17; cf. 2:1-5). Colossians stresses the superiority of Christ over all spiritual beings (Col. 1:15-20; 2:10), and attributes the heresy rampant among the recipients of the letter to the influence of the "elemental principles of the world," a collective name for these evil spiritual beings (2:8). The cross of Christ was the means by which all evil spiritual beings were defeated and rendered ineffectual (Col. 2:15).

Bibliography. C. E. Arnold, *Ephesians: Power and Magic.* SNTSMS 63 (Cambridge, 1989); G. B. Caird, *Principalities and Powers* (Oxford, 1956).

BARRY D. SMITH

PRISCA (Gk. *Príska*), **PRISCILLA** (*Prískilla*)

A woman Christian missionary, teacher and leader of the Pauline missionary circle. She was probably freeborn, and married Aquila, a Jewish tentmaker from Pontus in Bithynia. Prisca and Aquila were Christians in Rome when Christians still worshipped alongside Jews in the synagogues. Controversy between Jews and Christians in Rome about the gospel led the emperor Claudius to expel Jews from Rome (49 C.E.), and Prisca and Aquila moved to Corinth (Acts 18:2). There they met Paul, and he stayed with them over a year and a half, working alongside them as a tentmaker (Acts 18:1-3, 11).

At the end of Paul's stay at Corinth Prisca and Aquila moved to Ephesus (Acts 18:18-19). There they hosted a house church (1 Cor. 16:19). One notable event was their further instruction of the Alexandrian Jewish Christian, Apollos (Acts 18:26).

Prisca and Aquila returned to Rome in the mid-50s and founded another house church. Paul sends them and their congregation greetings in his epistle to the Romans and calls them missionary co-workers (Gk. *synergoí;* Rom. 16:3-5). They may have returned to Ephesus in the early 60s (2 Tim. 4:19).

Prisca's name in most instances precedes that of her husband, indicating that she was the more prominent of the two in missionary activity. Together they were partners with Paul and partners with one another in the missionary work of the early Church, heading churches and gathering worshippers in their homes in the urban centers of Rome, Corinth, and Ephesus.

JOANN FORD WATSON

PRISON

People were imprisoned for a variety of reasons in biblical times. Joseph was charged with sexual impropriety by Potiphar's wife and held in the house of the captain of the guard (Gen. 40:3). The Mosaic code permitted imprisonment to allow time for clarifying the facts of a case (Lev. 24:12; Num. 15:34). Other accounts refer to confinement in non-Israelite prisons (Gen. 39:20; 2 Kgs. 17:4; 25:27, 29; Jer. 52:11; Judg. 16:21).

Later, Jewish prisons kept in custody people who were awaiting trial (Matt. 5:25; Acts 4:3; 5:18-23). Roman imprisonment could be used to coerce a prisoner into testifying (Matt. 18:30) and as punishment for disorderly conduct (11:2; Acts 16:26). Early Christians experienced imprisonment (2 Cor. 6:5; 11:23), often at the hands of religious opponents. Paul called this a service for Christ (Phlm. 1, 9; Eph. 3:1; 4:1; 2 Tim. 1:8). Other passages describe miraculous releases from prison (Acts 12:6-10; 16:25-26).

Conditions in ancient prisons were harsh. Prisoners were often chained (Heb. 11:36) either to posts or to guards (Acts 12:6). Wooden stocks were sometimes used to confine prisoners (Acts 16:24) in inner chambers with no windows. The sexes were not separated, and the lack of ventilation and facilities for good hygiene encouraged rats and disease. Such conditions explain the frequent encouragement to visit believers in prison (Matt. 25:36; 2 Tim. 1:8; Heb. 13:3).

Bibliography. B. Rapske, *Paul in Roman Custody,* vol. 3 of *The Book of Acts in Its First Century Setting,* ed. B. K. Winter (Grand Rapids, 1994).

DENNIS GAERTNER

PRISON LETTERS
The four letters (Ephesians, Colossians, Philippians, and Philemon) in the Pauline corpus that claim to have been penned while Paul was in prison (Eph. 3:1; 4:1; Col. 4:3, 10, 18; Phil. 1:7, 13-14, 16-17; Phlm. 1, 9-10, 13, 23). Traditionally, Paul's Roman imprisonment has been considered the most likely place of their origin (Acts 28), and this still remains the view of the majority of scholars, at least for those letters that scholars regard as genuinely written by Paul. However, a strong case can also be made for Caesarea (Acts 23:33–26:32) or Ephesus (cf. 1 Cor. 15:32; 2 Cor. 1:8-10). The evidence is not conclusive. Some would assign Philippians to a different imprisonment than the other three prison letters. Of course, if Ephesians or Colossians are pseudonymous, their prison setting is then of little historical value. Although 2 Timothy also asserts a prison origin (2 Tim. 1:8), it is normally grouped with the Pastoral Epistles (1-2 Timothy, Titus).

KENT L. YINGER

PROCHORUS (Gk. *Próchoros*)
One of the seven charged with the care of the Hellenistic widows in the early Church (Acts 6:5). Tradition regards him as the scribe to whom John dictated the Fourth Gospel.

See JOHN, ACTS OF.

PROCONSUL
Roman civil and military officials who were former consuls, serving one-year terms of office. Provinces where legions were stationed to deal with potential insurrections were under the direct control of the emperor and administered by either a legate, procurator, or prefect. Provinces that did not require a standing army to pacify resistance to Rome were under the control of the senate and administered by proconsuls (Gk. *anthýpatos*).

Two proconsuls are mentioned in the NT. Sergius Paulus administered Cyprus and apparently was converted to Christianity by Paul (Acts 13:7-10). Gallio administered Achaia and refused to adjudicate what he considered an intrareligious dispute between Paul and his Jewish opponents (Acts 18:12-17).

TIMOTHY B. CARGAL

PROCURATOR
The official title of governors of equestrian rank of the lesser Roman imperial provinces, such as Judea, from the time of Claudius (A.D. 41-54) onward. Earlier, the proper title of these officials was prefect.

Judea was an imperial province (ruled by the emperor rather than the senate) between A.D. 6-41 (the first procuratorship) and between 44-66 (the second procuratorship). At other times it and other portions of Palestine were client kingdoms. The legates/procurators were both personal representatives of the emperor and state officials. They had jurisdiction in fiscal, judicial, and military matters. Most of those appointed to govern Judea were men of below average ability, insensitive to Jewish culture and religion, corrupt, and oppressive. Much of the blame for the Jewish Revolt of 66-70 must be placed upon them.

Neither "procurator" nor "prefect" appear in English translations of the NT, but are instead usually rendered "governor" (e.g., Matt. 27:2; Acts 23:24). One prefect (Pilate, whose official title is on an inscription found at Caesarea, the provincial capital) and two procurators (Felix and Festus) are mentioned in the NT. The names and approximate dates of all 14 governors of Judea between A.D. 6-66 are known.

JAMES A. BROOKS

PROMISE
According to the ancient Yahwistic narrative, the Lord promised Abraham offspring, land, divine guidance, and to become a blessing for the whole world (Gen. 12:1-4a, 6-9). The birth of Isaac was promised (Gen. 18:9-15) and fulfilled (21:1-2a), and the land that had been promised (12:7) was granted, beginning with the purchase of the field in Machpelah (23:2-20). A pattern thus emerges whereby God is recognized as the faithful one whose promises are fulfilled. Significant events are seen not so much as the accomplishment of human endeavor but rather the work of God.

Moses was called as God's instrument to bring about the Exodus (Exod. 3:7-8, 16-17) and was promised divine presence and success (vv. 10-12). During the Monarchy God assured David that his dynasty would rule forever in justice and peace (2 Sam. 7:4-17), a promise that led to messianic hope (Isa. 9:2-7; 11:1-9).

The prophets threatened punishment for sin but promised deliverance for the repentant (Hos. 2:14-16[MT 16-18]; 14:1-7; Isa. 1:18). Jeremiah promised a new covenant (Jer. 31:31-34), and Ezekiel, a new heart (Ezek. 36:26-27).

In the Psalms God is praised for fidelity to promises made (Ps. 18:30[31]; 105:9, 42), trusted because of them (12:6[7]; 119:50), but reminded in petitions to remember them (77:8[9]; 119:38, 41, 58).

In the NT Jesus promises satiety, laughter, the kingdom of God, a great reward in heaven (Luke 6:20-23; cf. Matt. 5:1-12), and eternal life (John 4:14; 6:35, 51; 11:26). Those who pray, fast, or give alms will be rewarded by the Father who sees in secret (Matt. 6:4, 6, 18). Those who ask will receive; those who seek, find; and to those who knock, it will be opened (Matt. 7:7).

The Pauline Letters teach that the promise made to Abraham is being fulfilled by Christians through faith and grace (Gal. 3:16-18; Rom. 4:13-21; 9:8-9). Paul was called to be an apostle "for the sake of the promise of life that is in Christ Jesus" (2 Tim. 1:1), in whom "every one of God's promises is a 'Yes'" (2 Cor. 1:20), which the Gentiles share through the gospel (Eph. 3:6). The Letter to the Hebrews speaks of "better promises" (Heb. 8:6), the "promise" of eternal life (4:1; 9:15) inherited through "faith and patience" (6:12). Those who accept God's "precious and very great promises" become "participants of the divine nature" (2 Pet. 1:4).

JOSEPH F. WIMMER, O.S.A.

PROPHET, PROPHECY

A religious intermediary (Heb. *nāḇîʾ*; Gk. *prophḗtēs*) whose function is to carry messages back and forth between human beings and a deity. Persons performing this social function have been found in a wide range of times, places, and societies, though they may not locally be known by the title prophet.

The OT refers to a number of figures as prophets. Fifteen of these are associated with written collections that bear their names — the books from Isaiah through Malachi, excluding Daniel. References to others appear in the prophetic and Deuteronomistic history books. These include Nathan (2 Sam. 7, 12; 1 Kgs. 1), Gad (1 Sam. 22:5; 2 Sam. 24:11), Ahijah (1 Kgs. 11:29; 14:2, 18), Elijah (1 Kgs. 17–2 Kgs. 2), Elisha (2 Kgs. 2–9), Micaiah (1 Kgs. 22), Jonah (2 Kgs. 14:25), Huldah (22:14), and Hananiah (Jer. 28). These books also refer generically to prophets whom they do not name (1 Sam. 28:6; 1 Kgs. 13; 2 Kgs. 17:13, 23; 21:10; 23:2; 24:2; Amos 2:11-12; Mic. 3:5-6, 11; Jer. 14:13-16; 23:9-22), and sometimes these operate in groups (1 Sam. 10:5, 10-12; in 1 Kgs. 22 there are 400). The story of Elijah's contest with 450 prophets of Baal and 400 of ʿAnat indicates that prophets of other deities than Yahweh could be found in Israel (1 Kgs. 18).

OT prophecy is not a homogeneous phenomenon. The bands of anonymous ecstatic prophets referred to in Samuel and Kings contrast with the likes of Amos and Jeremiah, who carried out their function as individuals. Elijah and Elisha, who are referred to as "man of God" more often than "prophet," have affinities with both the ecstatics (cf. 1 Kgs. 18:46; 2 Kgs. 3:13-20) and the others and add some peculiarities of their own.

The historical and cultural context of OT prophecy is the period of the Israelite and Judean monarchies, continuing through the Exile into the early postexilic period. This context affects the functioning and message of the biblical prophets.

Social Role

There have been various attempts to argue that the OT prophets had their base of operations in the cult, but there is insufficient evidence to support such a generalization. Samuel and the anonymous prophets were associated with places of worship (1 Sam. 3:20; 10:5). Jeremiah (Jer. 1:1) and Ezekiel (Ezek. 1:3) came from priestly families, but this does not seem to have determined the location of their activity as prophets. Amos appears to have had no prior connection with the cult (Amos 7:14-15). Rather, where the texts allow us to identify the location of a prophet's activity it is most often in interaction with kings or other leaders of the nation. Sometimes they were summoned to provide counsel in times of crisis, as when the kings of Israel and Judah consulted the 400 prophets and Micaiah about the advisability of going to war (1 Kgs. 22), Hezekiah summoned Isaiah at the time of an impending Assyrian invasion (Isa. 37 = 2 Kgs. 19), or Zedekiah asked Jeremiah to inquire of Yahweh about Judah's military fortunes (Jer. 37).

Prophets often appear unsummoned to offer words of encouragement or criticism (e.g., 2 Sam. 7:1-17; 12:1-14; Amos 7:10-17; Jer. 26). They were sometimes involved in partisan political struggles. Elijah opposed Ahab and Ahaziah (1 Kgs. 17–19, 21; 2 Kgs. 1), and his successor, Elisha, was instrumental in the coup that brought the Omri dynasty to an end and established Jehu as king of Israel (2 Kgs. 9). Amaziah, the priest at Bethel's royal sanctuary, accused Amos of conspiracy against Jeroboam (Amos 7:10-11), and Jeremiah was a vocal member of one the parties struggling to control Judah's foreign policy in the years prior to the Exile (Jer. 27–29).

In general, then, prophets were religious intermediaries who functioned at the national level. Elijah and Elisha interacted with lesser individuals as well as with kings, but they are significantly different from other prophets in important respects.

It was understood that the prophets' activity and message were grounded in some type of communication from Yahweh. There are several accounts of initial contacts that inaugurated a prophet's career (Amos 7:15; Isa. 6; Jer. 1:4-10; Ezek. 1–3) and other references to visions or dreams that were the source of a prophet's claim to speak for God (e.g., 1 Kgs. 19:9-18; 22:17-23; Amos 7:1-9; 8:1-3; 9:1; Jer. 1:11-19; 13:1-11; 14:14; 23:16).

It is further assumed that when prophets spoke they were transmitting the deity's message to their audience. However, they were not simply one-way channels of information from Yahweh to the people. Like all communication, prophetic speech involved a dynamic interaction between speaker and audience. Feedback was integral to the process, and in their position between deity and audience prophets received and carried messages in both directions. People were free to accept or reject a prophet's words (Amos 2:10-12; 7:10-17; Jer. 5:12-13; 11:18-20; 20:7-8), and prophets could belabor God with their own concerns (Amos 7:1-6; Jer. 11:18–12:6; 17:14-18).

Sometimes prophets with conflicting messages from Yahweh appeared on the scene (e.g., 1 Kgs. 22; Jer. 14:11-16; 28:1-17), and believing members of the populace would have had to decide among them. The story of Jeremiah's confrontation with Hananiah illustrates the difficulties inherent in making such judgments. In this story Jeremiah appears to invoke the criterion of fulfillment as the appropriate way to resolve the conflicting claims to speak for Yahweh (Jer. 28:5-9; cf. Deut. 18:21-22), but in the end he does not wait the amount of time required to prove Hananiah's claim false. Other passages suggest additional criteria for judging true from false prophecy (personal immorality, Jer. 23:14; 29:23; lack of a valid commission, 14:13-14), but none were really useful for people faced with the immediate necessity of adjudicating between competing prophetic claims.

The narrative of Saul's consulting the medium at Endor mentions prophets in the same breath with standard methods of divination, dreams, and Urim (1 Sam. 28:6). The function of prophets, to facilitate communication between Yahweh and his people, is broadly speaking the same as that of diviners, who occupied another (though often condemned; cf. Deut. 18:9-14) established religious role within Israelite society. A distinction is often drawn between these two roles on the grounds that diviners wait to be consulted and rely on mechanical means such as lots to arrive at their message, while prophets come forward at Yahweh's direction and have their message directly from the deity. This is not quite accurate, since there are examples of prophets being consulted (1 Sam. 28:6; 1 Kgs. 22:5-8, 13-14; Jer. 42:1-6) and of diviners coming forward unasked (1 Sam. 10:17-24; 14:36-37). Prophetic utterances can be referred to as divination (Mic. 3:11; Jer. 14:14) and the words of diviners as prophecy (Jer. 29:8-9). Within the Israelite conceptual world, the results of divination, like the words of prophets, were considered to be "wholly from Yahweh" (Prov. 16:33).

Conceptual World

The perceived existence of prophets in any society is predicated upon belief in the reality of a deity or deities who are able to influence events in this world and are at least potentially susceptible to influence from humans. In this respect biblical Israel was not unique. What gives much of biblical prophecy its distinctive flavor is the prevalence of the Deuteronomistic idea of a prophet like Moses who would speak Yahweh's word and to whom obedience was required (Deut. 18:15-22). As a result, the OT presents prophets as the privileged intermediaries between Yahweh and his people. The message of the prophets tends to mirror Deuteronomistic theology in assuming that a special relationship existed between Israel and Yahweh, one defined by a covenant which required obedience to certain commandments. The result of such obedience would be prosperity and peace, but disobedience would result in punishment at the hands of foreign invaders, over whose activities it was assumed Yahweh had power. 2 Kgs. 17 is a classic statement of this theology within the Deuteronomistic history itself, and these ideas appear in Jer. 11:1-13 in much the same language. This basic interpretation of national history may be found in many standard poetic oracles throughout the prophetic books (e.g., Amos 2:4-5, 6-16; Jer. 2:4-37).

In the case of Elijah and Elisha we find evidence of other ideas that reflect a cultural background not evident in the Deuteronomistic history as a whole. Insofar as they are champions of Yahweh and critics of kings, Elijah and Elisha fit within the conceptual world of the Deuteronomists. In addition, however, the stories about these two "men of God" include accounts of the miraculous multiplication of food, calling down fire from heaven, floating ax-heads, curing lepers, raising the dead, and murderous attacks on other humans. Such accounts, unique in the prophetic literature, seem to assume the conceptual world of shamanism, a set of beliefs fairly common among tribal peoples. Like OT prophets, shamans are thought to be intermediaries between humans and deities. They have ecstatic experiences, and besides conveying messages from the deities have a variety of functions, including curing and divination. Such beliefs are at odds with the Deuteronomistic theology, so these narratives provide a hint of complexity of the cultural and religious situation in monarchic Israel.

Historicity

Though Abraham (Gen. 20:7), Miriam (Exod. 15:20), Eldad and Medad (Num. 11:26-30), and Deborah (Judg. 4:4) are referred to as prophets, the primary historical context of OT prophecy is the periods of the Monarchy, Exile, and Restoration (11th-6th centuries B.C.E.). The narratives speak of both Samuel (1 Sam. 3:20) and bands of anonymous prophets in the time of Saul, of Nathan and Gad in the court of David, of Elijah opposing Ahab (1 Kgs. 17), and of Elisha's role in the coup that brought Jehu to the throne of Israel (2 Kgs. 9). All but six of the prophetic books (Joel, Obadiah, Jonah, Nahum, Habakkuk, and Malachi) begin with superscriptions that locate the prophet's activity during the reign of specific kings, from Amos and Hosea in the mid-8th century to Haggai and Zechariah in the late 6th century. Prophetic texts refer to events and situations in the life of the nation, including foreign invasions (e.g., Amos 6:14; Isa. 36–39; Jer. 39), internal political struggles (e.g., 2 Kgs. 9; Amos 7:10-17; Jer. 37–38), social injustice (e.g., Amos 2:6-7; 5:6-7, 10-15), and religious malpractice (e.g., 5:21-24; Jer. 2; Mal. 1:6–2:9) or indifference (e.g., Jer. 5:12; Haggai).

Despite these specific references, it is not safe to assume that the accounts of the prophets' activities are always historically accurate. This is because both the collected oracles (prophetic speeches) and the stories about them are dominated by ideas like those outlined above. Elijah provides one obvious example. The stories depict him in part as an ardent champion of Yahweh, and model his character on the figure of Moses. In 1 Kgs. 19, e.g., he flees for his life to the desert, encounters Yahweh in a theophany on Horeb (Sinai), and complains about his mission, which Yahweh in turn reaffirms (cf. Exod. 2–6). This suggests that the Deuteronomistic compilers of these narratives have presented us with a picture of the prophet that is not merely biographical. The stories also represent Elijah as a healer and wonder-worker, suggesting another element in his cultural background, but given the fantastic nature of some of the occurrences it is unlikely that these accounts are historically accurate. The same model of the "prophet like Moses" is evident in the account of Jeremiah's call (Jer. 1:4-10) and elsewhere in the book of Jeremiah.

One can, therefore, ask whether prophetic books and narratives about prophets provide any access to Israelite and Judean history and society in the days of the prophets themselves or only to the period during and after the Exile. At the very least we can be confident that "prophet" was a well-established social role in preexilic monarchic society, and evidence points to the level of national government as the primary sphere of prophetic activity. In addition, the existence of collections of materials bearing the names of individual prophets (or in the case of Elijah and Elisha, a sizable collection of stories about them) makes it reasonable to assume that these persons really existed, though it may not be possible to be confident about identifying their exact words and will certainly be impossible to write their biographies.

Literary Considerations

It is evident that not all of the words in prophetic books can be attributed to the prophets themselves. For example, Amos 7 begins with three reports of visions narrated in the 1st person; Amos would appear to be the speaker (v. 8). However, with v. 10 there begins a 3rd person account in which an anonymous narrator tells about a confrontation between Amos and Amaziah. Though the narrative quotes both these men, neither appears to be its author.

Any quest for the authentic words of a given prophet is complicated by the recognition that the process by which the books that bear the names of individual prophets came into being was often lengthy and complicated. From this point of view, one may think of prophetic books as the products of literary activity that begins with the composition and collection of material by and about the prophetic figures, its eventual collection into a "book" (scroll), and subsequent editing and revising of the collection. There is not enough evidence to trace this process exactly, but it is often possible to form plausible hypotheses about it. The branch of biblical scholarship actively concerned with such matters is called redaction criticism.

The book of Jeremiah illustrates the complexity of the redactional process. It contains several kinds of material (poetic oracles addressed to Judah, individual laments, prose sermons reflecting an interpretation of the nation's history similar to that of the Deuteronomists, 3rd person narratives about the prophet, oracles against foreign nations, a historical narrative largely duplicating 2 Kgs. 24–25). The book has no obvious overall organization. It is sometimes internally contradictory, e.g., counseling submission to Babylon (chs. 27–29) in one place while in another inveighing against that nation in the harshest terms (chs. 50–51). The Greek translation of the book (LXX) is one eighth shorter than the Hebrew text, and incorporates the collection of oracles against foreign nations in the middle of the book rather than near the end. Nevertheless, the book has a broad thematic unity, interpreting developments in Judah's history as the result of the people's past and present infractions of their covenant agreement with Yahweh ("falsehood" is one of the operative terms in this analysis). It is no longer possible to discern exactly how the book came to have its present shape, but passages that mention the restoration of the people to their land (e.g., 3:14-18; 23:1-4, 7-8; 24:4-7; 27:22; 29:10-14) signal exilic or postexilic editorial activity. Because this editorial activity reflects a reinterpretation of the Jeremiah tradition in light of the interests of a later time, we must be cautious about assuming that we can construct a biography of the prophet from such material.

In light of these problems, some scholars have taken a more strictly literary approach to the complexity of prophetic books which views them as literary monuments from the distant past and attempts to discover and describe their aesthetic coherence without reference to any specific historical background.

The "End" of Prophecy

After the early postexilic period the OT reports no figures comparable to the prophets of the monarchic period, and the dominant opinion is that Israelite prophecy had come to an end. At the very least, it had been transformed into something else, like the kind of visionary activity leading to apocalyptic. This interpretation is the result of a too narrow understanding that defines prophecy in terms of the classical OT figures. As long as there are people who believe in a deity able and willing to be involved in the affairs of this world and who have a tradition of intermediaries bridging the gap between the divine and the human spheres, it is unlikely that prophecy has come to a complete end. Jewish texts from the last centuries B.C.E. indicate a continued belief in the possibility of prophecy, and the NT attests to prophecy both in Judaism (John 11:49-52) and in the early Christian Church (Acts 11:27; 15:32), where prophets occupied a recognized religious role alongside apostles, teachers, and other functionaries (Acts 13:1; 1 Cor. 12:27-31). When Mark reports that some who encountered Jesus thought he was a prophet (Mark 8:28; cf. 6:4, 15), we can infer that within the culture of 1st-century C.E. Palestinian Judaism there were people both familiar with that religious role and open to its continuation. In the 2nd century Christian prophetic activity continued in the Montanist movement. Prophecy thrived in monarchic Israel, but we can expect to find it at other times and places where persons identify and acknowledge others among their contemporaries performing the prophetic function of intermediation.

Bibliography. J. Blenkinsopp, *A History of Prophecy in Israel* (Philadelphia, 1983); T. Collins, *The Mantle of Elijah: The Redaction Criticism of the Prophetical Books* (Sheffield, 1993); E. W. Conrad, *Reading Isaiah.* OBT 27 (Minneapolis, 1991); T. W. Overholt, *Channels of Prophecy: The Social Dynamics of Prophetic Activity* (Minneapolis, 1989); D. L. Petersen, *The Role of Israel's Prophets.* JSOTSup 17 (Sheffield, 1981); R. R. Wilson, *Prophecy and Society in Ancient Israel* (Philadelphia, 1980).

THOMAS W. OVERHOLT

PROPHETS, THE

The second of the three divisions of the Hebrew canon (Heb. *nĕḇîʾîm*), subdivided into the "Former Prophets," which include Joshua, Judges, 1-2 Samuel, and 1-2 Kings (placed among the "historical books" in the LXX and Christian versions of the

OT), and the "Latter Prophets," comprised of Isaiah, Jeremiah, Ezekiel, and the Book of the Twelve (Hosea, Joel, Amos, Obadiah, Jonah, Micah, Nahum, Habakkuk, Zephaniah, Haggai, Zechariah, and Malachi, often called the "Minor Prophets"; cf. Sir. 49:10).

PROPITIATION

See Expiation.

PROSELYTE

A convert from one faith or community to another. In the LXX Gk. *prosēlytos* translates Heb. *gēr,* "resident alien" or "stranger" (e.g., Exod. 20:10); this status was higher than the *nok̲rî,* "temporary resident," and thus equal to the native-born Israelite (cf. Exod. 12:49; Num. 15:16, 29).

In OT times there seems to have been no official conversion "process." The resident alien simply affiliated with the covenant community (e.g., 2 Sam. 11:3–12:10), renounced foreign gods in favor of Yahweh (e.g., Josh. 2:11; Ruth 1:16), and submitted to circumcision (Exod. 12:48).

Throughout the OT the ideal Israel was not only open but also actively sought to include outsiders (cf. Gen. 12:3; Exod. 12:38; Isa. 44:5). Although certain persons (e.g., Jonah) and periods (cf. Ezra 9:1-2) do not accord with this general rule, they are clearly the exception.

The number of gentile converts to Judaism appears to have increased greatly during the Second Temple period, due partly to greater interaction of Jews with Gentiles during the Diaspora and partly to the missionary activities of the Pharisees (cf. Tob. 1:8; CD 14:4; Philo *Spec. leg.* 1.51-52; Josephus *Ag. Ap.* 2.282-84; *Šabb.* 31a; *Pesaḥ.* 87b). Jesus refers to the effort of proselytism (Matt. 23:15), but suggests that its results are negative (cf. v. 4 and the dictum of some rabbis requiring that the proselyte accept responsiblity for every rule of both the written and oral law; *t. Dem.* 2:5; *Sopra Qod.* 8:5).

Toward the end of the Second Temple period a conversion process can be discerned, which for most rabbinic authorities included circumcision, baptism, and sacrifice (*Ker.* 2:1; *Yebam.* 46a,b). Of these Christianity adopted only baptism (e.g., Acts 2:38, 41; 10:47-48). The proselyte was "like a new creation, newborn child" (*Gen. Rab.* 39:14; *y. Yebam.* 4a; cf. John 3:3, 7; 2 Cor. 5:17; 2 Pet. 1:23).

Women seem more likely to become proselytes (Josephus *BJ* 2.20.2; *Ant.* 18.3.5; *Sukk.* 23a,b), possibly for the lack of need for circumcision (despite the absence of this requirement in Christianity; cf. Acts 13:50; 16:30; 17:4, 12).

Although the rabbis often differed on the number of legal requirements for proselytes, the consensus seems to have settled upon the "laws of Noah" (*ʿAbod. Zar.* 64b; *Yebam.* 8d). Early Christianity, in deference to Jewish Christians from the Pharisaic party, applied these same rules to gentile converts (Acts 15:20, 29). It appears the rabbis had to fight for equality of these gentile converts to Judaism (*ʿAbod. Zar.* 65a; *Pesaḥ.* 21a) as did Paul for gentile converts to Christianity (Gal. 3:28-29; cf. Eph. 2:14-20).

W. E. Nunnally

PROSTITUTION

See Cultic Prostitution; Harlot.

PROVERB

Heb. *māšāl* (commonly translated "proverb" or "saying") is difficult to define precisely. Its etymology can be associated with the Hebrew verb "to rule" and with the concept of "comparison." The former suggests that a *māšāl* is an authoritative word that enables one to master living; the latter implies that it offers trustworthy counsel based upon a perceived order in the world. In the OT, *māšāl* refers broadly to many literary types and is used in diverse contexts (cf. 1 Sam. 10:12; Deut. 28:37; 1 Kgs. 9:7; Isa. 14:4-11; Ezek. 17:2). As a genre in instructional texts, the term is used generally for any sapiential form (e.g., poems, parables, dialogues). The most common is the "proverb," a pithy saying characteristically comprised of two parallel lines written in the indicative mood. Such a form is widely attested in didactic texts throughout the ancient Near East, including the Egyptian Instruction of Ani, the Instruction of Amenemope, the Instruction of Onchscheshonqy, the Sumerian Instruction of Shuruppak, and the Aramaic Words of Ahikar. It is best represented biblically in the book of Proverbs.

The two lines of a proverb may be related to one another synonymously, antithetically, or synthetically. In a synonymous construction, the second line restates the point of the first, occasionally adding a nuance or twist: "An evildoer listens to wicked lips; and a liar gives heed to a mischievous tongue" (Prov. 17:4; cf. 16:11; 19:5; 21:12). Antithetical parallelism occurs when the two lines contrast with one another: "The wise are cautious and turn away from evil, but the fool throws off restraint and is careless" (Prov. 14:16; cf. 11:12-15; 14:5-6, 8-9). In synthetic proverbs, the second line continues and develops the thought of the first: "The eyes of the Lord are in every place, keeping watch on the evil and the good" (Prov. 15:3; cf. 16:31; 17:2; 21:6-7). Proverbs may also be comparative, identifying shared aspects of different objects in order to offer insight into one or the other; two particular types are the "like" sayings ("Like cold water to a thirsty soul, so is good news from a far country"; Prov. 25:25; cf. 10:26; 26:6-11) and those employing the formula "if x, then how much more or less y" ("Sheol and Abaddon lie open before the Lord, how much more human hearts"; Prov. 15:11; cf. 11:31; 19:10). "Better than" proverbs compare two things with the judgment that one is preferable to the other ("Better is a dry morsel with quiet than a house full of feasting with strife"; Prov. 17:1; cf. 15:16-17; 16:8) while "happy" (or "blessed") proverbs declare that those who choose to live wisely will experience joy ("Those who despise their neighbors are sinners, but happy are those who are kind to the poor"; Prov. 14:21; cf. 8:32, 34; 16:20; 29:18). Finally, numerical proverbs contain a title line followed by a list of two, three, four, or seven items that share the feature(s) of the title line: "Three things are too wonderful for me; four I do not understand: the way of an eagle in the sky, the way of a serpent on a rock, the way of a ship on the high seas, and the way of a man with a maiden" (Prov. 30:18-19; cf. vv. 15-31).

Concise and creative, the proverb is an artistic literary form in which content and aesthetics are intertwined. As is evident in Hebrew, proverbs frequently contain alliteration, assonance, rhyme, and wordplay. There is also extended use of metaphor, simile, paradox, and other imagery. Such crafting results in poetic and terse sayings which, in their gathering of observations and conclusions drawn from human reason and experience, are striking and easily memorized. Proverbs thereby function effectively as didactic tools for the education of youth, as ethical and/or legal instructions, and as entertainment. They may offer observations about reality or, more forcefully, instruct or influence the reader to uphold certain values or behaviors. In all, proverbial wisdom demonstrates a self-conscious attempt to provoke human thinking and imagination in a manner that is aware of the ambiguities of life and of wisdom's own limitations; it is instruction that reflects the human effort to find order and "steer" through the complexities of reality.

Bibliography. L. G. Perdue, *Wisdom and Creation* (Nashville, 1994); G. von Rad, *Wisdom in Israel* (Nashville, 1972). CHRISTINE ROY YODER

PROVERBS, BOOK OF

A collection of various wisdom sayings that seem to come from a wide span of centuries and from several separate sources and life settings. The name of the book derives from the heading found at 1:1 and again at the start of a second major collection at 10:1, "The *měšālîm* (proverbs) of Solomon." Heb. *měšālîm* generally signifies didactic sayings which use a comparison or illustrative lesson, together with a poetic form or style of presentation. Its singular form, *māšāl,* describes a number of diverse literary genres: the simple proverb or folk saying (1 Sam. 10:12; Jer. 31:29), an oracular vision of Balaam (Num. 23:7-10), an extended allegory (Ezek. 17:1-10), or a psalm on the meaning of life (Ps. 49). Some of the simple sayings stem from the everyday life of the village and home (Jer. 23:28; Ezek. 16:44), but a great number that occur in Proverbs are directed at students from a master, and so seem to have been cultivated by a professional class of teachers. From Sumerian and Egyptian sources, we know that rote learning of lessons was favored in schools, and that often these consisted of lists of proverbial maxims about successful behavior. We can reasonably conclude that Proverbs developed from such school texts.

Outline

Proverbs contains six major groupings which can be identified as separate collections:

1:1–9:18	made up of 10 rather large instruction discourses from a teacher to his pupil and three speeches by personified wisdom;
10:1–22:16	a collection of the proverbs of "Solomon," the largest body of sayings in the book;
22:17–24:22	The "Thirty Sayings" (cf. the NAB translation of 22:17-20), another collection of proverbs, which have a decided relationship to an Egyptian work, the Thirty Precepts of Amenemope;
24:23-34	listed as an appendix of proverbs to the previous collection;
25:1-29:27	a second collection of proverbs attributed to Solomon;
30:1-31:31	two collections from foreign kings, Agur and Lemuel.

As is evident from chs. 30–31, which combine two sources, and from the note at 25:1 that Hezekiah's men copied older proverbs, these six groupings themselves may have been gathered from smaller and earlier collections. The book can also be divided differently, into two major parts: chs. 1–9, which contain a number of larger "instruction genres" with only a few individual proverbs; and chs. 10–31, which contain just short proverbial sentences.

The entire book, however, has been unified by two devices: a general introduction in 1:2-7 that states the purpose is to help all to gain wisdom by both learning and piety; and several reflections on "woman wisdom" which are carefully positioned to organize the whole. She speaks on her own behalf in 1:20-33; 9:1-18 to open and close the first part, and is described in 31:10-31 as the ideal woman for a "wise husband" to marry, matching the general summons of 1:1-7. This editorial use of personified wisdom serves as a structural unifier, but it also makes the book more than a general textbook of maxims by announcing a religious claim on the reader who must first embrace the call of wisdom and then live by it, seeing it both as a gift from God and as a daily way of response to God.

Date

Since proverbs occur in the earliest known literary works in Sumer, and examples of the "instruction genre" (chs. 1–9) are known from Egypt in the early 2nd millennium, the book of Proverbs stems from very ancient roots. Many of the individual instructions and sayings may be among the oldest written parts of the Bible, but the question remains open whether the cultivation of learned proverbs and the editorial gathering of these collections did not occur at a later time. Solomon in 1 Kgs. 4:32(MT 5:12) is credited with composing many proverbs, and royalty are especially associated with the gift of divine wisdom in the ancient Near East (cf. 1 Kgs 3:9-28). Thus there is nothing improbable in a tradition that many proverbs came from the court of the kings of Judah or of northern Israel. Indeed, it is common scholarly opinion today that although some individual wisdom sayings and maxims might well have originated in the home or village life where elders were the respository of folk wisdom, the present books of wisdom stemmed from either the royal court and its training of government and priestly officials (e.g., Job and Proverbs) or from later schools for upper-class educated youths in postexilic Judah (e.g., Ecclesiastes and Sirach).

In particular, Proverbs' lack of interest in sacred history and its failure to group sayings by subject matter (qualities found in 2nd-century Sirach) probably reflects preexilic wisdom composition during the Monarchy, even if the book later received some editorial refinement in the early Second Temple period. Scholars half a century ago judged that its theology of righteousness and evil reflected either Deuteronomic influence or a postexilic piety of the "Fear of the Lord." As a result they tended to date all wisdom books in the Hellenistic era. Now that most themes in Proverbs are well known in ancient Near Eastern wisdom sources prior to David, general consensus agrees that the basic book in Hebrew reflects the period of the Monarchy, confirming what the individual headings claim. Not one of the six collections needs to be dated after the Exile. The fact that the LXX contains 130 additional proverbs, mostly very Hellenistic in nature, supports this conclusion since it indicates that the text in Greek had a lively period of growth after the MT was fixed and closed.

The Individual Sections

1:1-7

Challenging the reader to cultivate wisdom, this general preface piles up a number of synonyms that seem to be technical terms for aspects of being wise. The different terms reflect professional interest in distinctions that can be used as teaching tools. It ends with the clear identification of proper religious observance ("fear of the Lord") with obtaining wisdom.

1:8–9:18

The body of the first part of the book is made up of distinct instructions from teacher to pupil, built around the search for wisdom during the educational period of youth and around a sharp metaphorical contrast between "woman wisdom" and "dame folly" who seduces the young both sexually and intellectually away from prudence and wisdom. The units are 1:8-19; 1:20-33; 2:1-22; 3:1-12; 3:13-35; 4:1-9; 4:10-27; 5:1-23; 6:1-19; 6:20-35; 7:1-27; 8:1-36; 9:1-18. No single "plot" runs through all the instructions, and they frequently return to the same themes. But as a whole, they create a model for conduct and decision making based on trust in and faithfulness to the God of Israel. Unlike the proverb collections in chs. 10–31, God is frequently mentioned as the source of wisdom in these chapters, and the instructions shape a vision by which the student will find guidance in life's decisions.

10:1–22:16

This collection contains 375 individual sayings, and they include practical advice on how to succeed in life (e.g., 12:9, "better a lowly man who supports himself than one of apparent dignity who lacks bread"), as well as specifically Israelite piety (e.g., 16:6, "By kindness and piety guilt is atoned for, and by fear of the Lord one avoids evil"). Major topics include the contrast between the ways of the wicked and of the righteous, parental advice on the education of children, proper treatment of the poor, developing good work habits, and the right use of speech. A single plan for grouping sayings has eluded commentators until now, and the principle seems to be that repetition and variation is the mother of learning.

22:17–24:22

There are decided parallels between this collection and the Egyptian Teaching of Amenemope. Since the latter was composed between 1000 and 600 B.C.E., it is likely that Israelite sages knew of it and composed their own table of 30 sayings using pieces of the Egyptian work. In general, its themes are similar to those of chs. 10–22.

24:23-34

The heading in v. 23, "These also are sayings of the wise," marks this as an appendix to the previous section. Its few proverbs focus on work habits and justice in the courts and may be from a much older text now lost.

25:1–29:27

This second collection attributed to Solomon repeats many of the topics in the first collection. It echoes the practical wisdom of success, and God's name occurs rarely. The heading says it was gathered by Hezekiah's scribes in the late 8th century, and there is no reason to doubt this. Sharp contrasts are drawn between the wise and the fool, and the lazy versus the hardworking. The problems of wealth, poverty, speech, trust between coworkers, and friendship all receive attention.

30:1–31:31

From the headings at 30:1; 31:1, it seems there are two collections, the words of Agur and those of Lemuel. But by form and content, there appear to be four units (30:1-6; 7-33; 31:1-9, 10-33). The latter is more likely, especially since 31:10-33 is an alphabetic acrostic poem seemingly composed as a final conclusion to the whole book. The stress in both chapters is on foreign (eastern) kings or sages who also search for the wisdom found in this book.

Theological Themes

Wisdom's spirituality is practical and prudent. It counsels caution in matters between sexes, commitment to work as a source of success; careful and coolheaded speech, respect for authority, personal humility, and control of the passions in general. These were the qualities of leadership and were highly prized personal virtues for all social interaction. They are usually assumed to be indications of the upper-class audience for whom the book was written.

The most frequent message of individual proverbs and sayings is to avoid the way of the "wicked," which involves scoffers, slanderers, troublemakers, heedless behavior, arrogance, rash actions, hotheaded reactions, and even practical atheism about the divine consequences from human actions. The "wicked" can range from the senseless and naive to the cruel and brutish.

The way of the "righteous" involves understanding, discipline, skill in setting a life course, and taking or giving good advice about God and the world. These contrasts betwen the "wicked" and the "righteous" are scattered in every chapter of the book and form a thread of unity among the diverse counsels. Interestingly enough, they are expressed altogether only in one place, Ps. 1, which appears to interpret the Psalter in light of the wisdom of Proverbs.

Utterances and instructions are often contradictory: e.g., "the mouth of the righteous is a source of life" (10:11); "A man of understanding remains silent" (11:12). This does not matter, for proper conduct means choosing the right option for each situation. Discretion in new circumstances and wonder at the mystery of life with its limits and boundaries are tolerated as respectfully as the traditional knowledge passed down by the masters.

The questions of why God permits suffering or injustice or death are rarely posed in Proverbs. They are addressed only where specific behavior reveals how acts bear evil consequences, where cause leads to effect. In these cases the wise pupil must master the lessons on how to avoid evil. Where experience offers no clear explanations or guidelines, Proverbs counsels staying close to the way of the Lord known by traditional faith or seen in the good order of creation.

A remarkable exaltation of wisdom as the expression of the divine will is provided by 8:22-31 (and less clearly in personified wisdom at 1:20-33; 9:1-12). After describing the role of wisdom in everything that God made, 8:30-31 suggests wisdom was the *'āmôn,* the "architect" or "divine delight" (i.e., God's beloved child), who was both inspirer and designer of the universe by being at play with God. Behind this imagery, wisdom is clearly seen as a gift of God to help us understand the divine personal creator.

Finally, the portrait of the ideal wife in the closing passages of 31:10-33 sums up the model of the wise, and extends the message of the book clearly beyond a targeted audience of promising young males in higher education to all men and women alike with the same lesson for all: wisdom comes to fruition in fear of the Lord, the same point at which the book started in 1:7.

See WISDOM, WISDOM LITERATURE.

Bibliography. L. Boadt, *Introduction to Wisdom Literature and the Book of Proverbs.* Collegeville Bible Commentary 18 (Collegeville, 1986); W. McKane, *Proverbs.* OTL (Philadelphia, 1970); R. N. Whybray, *Proverbs.* NCBC (Grand Rapids, 1994).

LAWRENCE BOADT

PROVIDENCE

The term "providence" derives from the Latin noun *providentia,* "foresight, forethought," and the related verb *providere,* "to provide for, take precautions for or against" something. Its secular usage included the common belief that a benevolent ordering principle governed the universe and human history, that nothing happens solely by chance or is merely haphazard, but rather that there is a guiding purpose ordering all things toward an end. Stoicism saw this principle as the "world soul" or "world reason." At other times the notion of providence also led to a more pessimistic worldview marked by determinism or fatalism. This idea contributed to a passive sense of human resignation before the whimsy of uncontrollable fates.

The biblical concept of God's providence, however, signals a universally confident belief in God's loving care and protection of the world, It is grounded in the belief in God as Creator, one who continues at all times to preserve and order the world, holding chaos at bay, and leading the world and all human history toward life and full happiness. Sometimes through unpredictable turns of fate God's providence can be written "straight with crooked lines," as in the case of Joseph who was sold into slavery by his brothers and who later became God's instrument of protection for the family of Jacob in Egypt. Joseph attests to God's loving hand at work with the words: "Even though you intended to do harm to me, God intended it for good . . ." (Gen. 50:20). Time and again God promises that the divine presence will remain in the world and with those who need divine protection (Exod. 3:12). God's very name revealed to Moses at the burning bush in the enigmatic tetragrammaton YHWH (Exod. 3:14) has sometimes been translated "I will be with you," signaling the irrevocable covenantal and protective presence of God among the people in the midst of the world.

God's provident presence can be manifest in both merciful care and righteous chastisement, but the biblical emphasis surely rests with the affirmation of God's ultimate care. An old cultic confession acclaiming God's steadfast love and mercy reverberates through the OT tradition (Exod. 34:6-7; Num. 14:18; Neh. 9:17, 31; Ps. 103:8; Jer. 32:18; Jonah 4:2). This confession does not negate the need for God's judgment upon sin, but promises that mercy and forgiveness will be God's ultimate providence. The affirmation of God's providence neither nullifies human freedom nor cancels the mysterious problem of the presence of evil in the world. It promises, however, simply that God will be a loving God in the midst of the world, leading it and all creation toward a future full of hope (Jer. 29:11-14).

The Christian tradition reiterates the same confidence in God's provident care. "Consider the lilies of the field . . . ," Jesus says (Matt. 6:26-30), and be certain of a loving God who cares for the smallest living thing. Paul expands this notion even further to see God's providence and loving presence drawing all creation, the entire cosmos itself, toward the divine intention (Rom. 8:28-39). Given this conviction, Christian prayer is marked by trust and certainty that God hears the cries of humanity and responds with love and care (Matt 6:8; 7:7-8).

BARBARA E. BOWE

PSALMS, BOOK OF

Often called the hymnal of the Second Temple, the book of Psalms provides a window through which ancient Israel's response to God's presence, or absence, may be viewed. The 150 psalms in the MT give voice to a panoply of human emotions, sometimes sublime but at other times embarrassingly vengeful. The psalms arose in the experience of worship; in them both individual prayer and communal praise find expression, as do private reflection and learned instruction. Hardly a "little Bible," as Martin Luther claimed, the book of Psalms differs from the overwhelming majority of the other biblical writings which purport to declare divine revelation to Israel.

The human voice within the psalms resonates with that of later worshippers, Christian and Jewish, who have found ways to recite the laments and hymns during worship. According to the Mishnah, Levites recited a specific psalm on each day of the week: Ps. 24 on Sunday, 48 on Monday, 82 on Tuesday, 94 on Wednesday, 81 on Thursday, 93 on Friday, and 92 on Saturday. *M. Ta'an.* 2:3 assigns Ps. 102 to days of fasting; 104 was used by Christians at the Feast of Pentecost. Ps. 136 is the Great Hallel for sabbath services, 113–118 the Egyptian Hallel. Several psalms are known as penitential psalms (6, 32, 38, 51, 102, 130, 143), and 79 is recited at the western wall in the Old City of Jerusalem on Friday evening, the 9th of Ab. The LXX and Talmud assign Ps. 93 to the eve of the sabbath when God completed the creation of the world, and rabbinic tradition associates 95 with a New Year's festival.

Inspired by these biblical psalms, later worshippers wrote their own. One of these actually became canonical, Ps. 151 in the LXX (included in Codex Sinaiticus, Vaticanus, and Alexandrinus, which notes that this psalm is "outside the number"). An unknown Jewish author wrote 18 psalms in the 1st century B.C.E., now called the Psalms of Solomon. The sectarians at Qumran were particularly fond of psalms. Besides writing their own Hodayot comprising some 25 psalms, they left behind an extensive cache of biblical psalms. Fragments of 115 psalms have survived, along with a scroll (11QPs[a]) containing 39 biblical psalms; 2 Sam. 23:1-7 ("a Prose Statement on David's Compositions"); Sir. 51:13-30 ("an Apostrophe to Zion"); Pss. 151, 154 ("a Plea for Deliverance"), 155; 149–150 is "a Hymn to the Creator." Cave 11 yielded another scroll with fragments of Pss. 141, 133, 144. Yet another has noncanonical psalms but concludes with biblical 91. Nearby sites (S of En-gedi, Masada) have also yielded Hebrew texts of Psalms. Four commentary texts have portions of psalms.

One of the oldest Hebrew manuscripts, the Aleppo Codex, lacks 15:1–25:2; among Greek codices, Vaticanus does not have 105:27–137:6 (added in the 15th century), and Alexandrinus lacks 49:20–79:11. The order in the MT differs from that in the LXX:

MT	LXX
1–8	1–8
9–10	9
11–113	10–112
114–115	113
116	114–115
117–146	116–145
147	146–147
	148–150
148–150	151

The sequence in the LXX is supported by the fact that Pss. 9–10 were originally a single psalm, but the separation of 114 from 115 favors the order of the MT. Both LXX and MT divide a single psalm into 42–43. Confusion also results from the MT's reckoning of titles as the first verse. Some English versions follow this practice (NAB, NJPSV); others do not (e.g., RSV, KJV, NIV, TEV).

The early Christians sang hymns, although it is not clear whether these were taken from the OT or composed by Christians (cf. Mark 14:26; Acts 4:24; 1 Cor. 14:26; Eph. 5:19; Col. 3:16). It has been estimated that the NT cites psalms (55 citations of 365 psalms) from memory, but establishing actual quotations is difficult. Christian writers (e.g., Clement of Rome) frequently cite Psalms (49 citations from 32 psalms), as does the Didache. Justin's *Dialogue with Trypho* contains 47 references to 24 psalms.

The name "Psalms" derives from Gk. *psalmoí,* "songs of praise" (Vaticanus has *psalmoí* as the title for Psalms; Sinaiticus has no title, but concludes with "*psalmoí* of David.") "Psalter" comes from the title in Alexandrinus *(psaltḗrion)* and indicates a musical instrument, presumably to accompany the singing of Psalms. The MT lacks a title, but that is typical for all the books of the OT; at the end of Ps. 72 is the notation "the prayers *(tĕpillôt)* of David have come to an end." Rabbinic literature prefers the terms *tĕhillîm* or *tillîm* ("praises") to the Masoretic "prayers." Together these two, praise and prayer, describe the contents of the Psalter.

Like the Torah (Pentateuch), Psalms is divided into five books (1–41; 42–72; 73–89; 90–106; 107–150). Each of these books concludes with a doxology (41:13[MT 14]; 72:19; 89:52[53]; 106:48; 150). In Book I, closely associated with David by means of superscriptions, laments dominate, but by Books IV and V praise comes to the forefront. The final five psalms are framed by the expression, "Praise the Lord," which suggests that the book of Psalms leads worshippers through grief to thanksgiving, from lament to praise.

Of the 150 psalms in the MT, 116 have superscriptions. Virtually all of the psalms in Book I have superscriptions linking them to David. The exceptions are 1–2, 10, 33, but the first two introduce the whole book of Psalms, whereas 10, 33 are linked with the immediately preceding psalms. Book II duplicates two psalms in Book I (53 and 14; 70 and 40:13-17[14-18]). An unusual feature of Books II-III is their preference for the divine name Elohim over Yahweh, but inconsistency abounds. Although Elohim occurs 244 times, Yahweh appears 44 times in 42–83. In Book I Elohim is used only 49 times, and it occurs only 70 times in 84–150. With 44 psalms, including the unique 119, Book V is the longest of the five. An alphabetic acrostic, 119 has eight lines beginning with the 22 letters of the Hebrew alphabet in sequence. Furthermore, each line has one of eight synonyms for the law (except 90, which has a ninth synonym, and 122). Less complex acrostics include 25, 34, 111, 112, 145 (cf. the irregular pattern in 9–10, where every second verse begins with a letter of the alphabet in sequence).

The titles of individual psalms range from a single word in 98 (*mizmôr,* "a psalm") to extensive comment (e.g., 18). Only 34 psalms lack titles (I: 1–2, 10, 33; II: 43, 71; IV: 91, 93, 94–97, 99, 104–106; V: 107, 111–119, 135–137, 146-150). Perhaps the invitation to praise the Lord functioned as a substitute for a title in 111–113, 117, 135, 146–150. Thirteen titles recall particular events in David's life (3, 7, 18, 51, 52, 54, 56–57, 59–60, 63, 142). Another 55 have a specific liturgical instruction, "to the leader," while others refer to musical instruments and to as yet unknown things. Still others record genre designations such as prayer, praise, song, *maskîl, miktām,* and *šiggāyôn.* Considerably more variation in titles from the MT exists in Books IV and V in the Qumran manuscripts. The term *mizmôr* is found 57 times, and *selâ* ("pause"?) occurs in the body of some psalms (it also appears in psalms outside the book of Psalms, e.g., in Hab. 3:3, 9, 13; in 3:19 one also finds "To the choirmaster: with stringed instruments").

The tendency during the postexilic period to attribute sacred writings to revered leaders — the Pentateuch to Moses, the Wisdom Literature to Solomon, prophetic texts like Isa. 40–66 to Isaiah — led to an identification of David as the author of numerous psalms. The attribution of psalms to him in 2 Sam. 1:10-27; 22:2-51 (which also appears as Ps. 18), together with the tradition that he was a musician (1 Sam. 18:10; Amos 6:5), encouraged this trend. The LXX carries it even beyond the point reached by the MT, increasing the number of psalms attributed to David from 73 to 85. Although Heb. *lĕḏāwiḏ* does not necessarily mean Davidic authorship, its intent seems to have been that in many instances. It could also suggest that the particular psalm was written for a collection honoring David. The Qumran sectarians left no doubt about their view; a note states that David composed 3600 psalms and 446 songs, plus four for the stricken, totaling 4050 (cf. 1 Kgs. 4:32[5:12] for a similar comment about Solomon's literary productivity — 3000 proverbs, 1005 songs).

Not every psalm is credited to David, or even associated with him in some manner. Other persons honored in this way include Jeduthun (39, 62, 77), Heman (88), Solomon (72, 127), Moses (90), Ethan (89), and two musical guilds, the Korahites (42, 44–49, 84–85, 87–88) and the Asaphites (50, 70–83). The family of Asaph is said to have been active as late as the Josianic reforms (621 B.C.E.) and during the time of Ezra and Nehemiah nearly two centuries later.

When were the psalms written? Certain similarities with Canaanite texts from Ugarit have suggested an early date for 29; 82; 19:2-7, but late texts (cf. Daniel) also show affinities with this literature. Plausible connections with David make 2, 10, 18 viable candidates for the 10th century, or at the very least they imply a date during the Monarchy. Several psalms reflect interests in the north, leading some critics to think they derive from the northern kingdom prior to its defeat by Assyrian soldiers in 722. Other psalms seem to assume the existence of a monarchy (e.g., 2, 18, 20–21, 45, 72, 89, 101, 110, 132, 144). Linguistic features point to a postexilic date for 103, 117, 119, 124–125, 145. Content alone places 137 in postexilic times. Every attempt to date psalms encounters enormous difficulty, for their content is altogether indifferent to historical events except those serving paradigmatically (e.g., the Exodus from Egypt).

The early Church understood the psalms as personal expressions of worship in definite historical contexts. That view prevailed until the 19th century, when critical scholars began to emphasize the genres of individual psalms and to stress their congregational origin. The groundbreaking work of Hermann Gunkel elevated form criticism to pride of place, and this approach has continued to the present. Essentially, it distinguishes the following literary types: lament (both individual and communal), thanksgiving hymn (individual and communal), royal enthronement psalms, wisdom and torah psalms, entrance liturgies, prophetic exhortation, and mixed forms. Laments routinely include an opening address, description of trouble, petition, expression of confidence, and a vow. Thanksgiving songs include praise, description of past trouble, testimony, and exhortation. Naturally, individual psalms vary the elements, and it is often impossible to distinguish between a lament and a song of thanksgiving which presupposes the situation described in laments, whereas the expression of confidence resembles thanksgiving. Moreover, some designations of genre are based on content; that is true of royal psalms, songs of Zion, wisdom and torah psalms.

Form critics sought to illuminate the social setting of individual psalms. Accordingly, they posited special festivals (e.g., enthronement festival, royal Zion festival, covenant renewal ceremony, liturgical sermons). The Akitu, or New Year, festival in ancient Babylonia was often assumed to have a corollary in Judah, with annual coronation of the Davidic king. For this occasion Royal Psalms (e.g., 2, 18, 20, 21, 72, 89, 101, 110, 132, 144) are thought to have been used. Entrance liturgies would have served to prepare worshippers before they entered the holy temple (15, 24). A royal wedding gave rise to 45; didactic or learned instruction produced many psalms (e.g., 19, 119, 78, 89); and prophetic exhortation yielded 50, 81, 95. Songs of Zion give voice to the people's fondness for Jerusalem as the divine dwelling place (46, 48, 76, 84, 87, 122). Another group of psalms is presumed to have been sung as pilgrims made their way to Jerusalem (120–134) or as priests ascended the steps within the temple.

Some psalms seem to relate to individuals during times of extraordinary suffering brought on by illness, attack by foreign armies, slander, magical practices, and the like. Others give voice to private joy and public expressions of honor. Individuals express their deepest emotions in prayer, sometimes in near despair and at other times barely able to contain their jubilation. Locating precise settings for all of these has resulted in little more than vague generalities.

For this and other reasons, interpreters have begun to emphasize the rhetoric of psalms, their persuasive use of language. Advances in the understanding of poetry have isolated numerous features of the psalms. The balancing of one colon with another is achieved through various means, but prominence is usually given to chiasm (the forming of an X by structuring a poem as follows: ABB′ A′). Repetition takes place in a number of ways, e.g., question and answer; statement and quotation; a "better than" expression; A varies and B repeats: abstract and concrete; whole and synecdoche; two terms as a merismus; simile and reality.

In some scholarly circles, rhetorical criticism has virtually superseded form criticism, resulting in special emphasis on repetition, chiasm, inclusions, structure, and figurative language. Whether many of the features isolated in this manner result from authorial intention or not has yet to be established. That judgment applies particularly to analysis of structure, often the result of highly subjective reading, and to inclusions, which may be accidental, given the repetitive demands of Hebrew poetry and the limited vocabulary available to composers.

Not every interpreter focuses on the structure of a single psalm. Some critics examine the macrostructure, hoping to explain the overall shaping of the book of Psalms. Gerald H. Wilson has argued that the complete collection of five books is arranged to show how the covenant between God and David as king became bankrupt and the kingship of Yahweh took its place. Wilson thinks the presence of royal psalms at the beginning of Book I (2) and at the conclusion of Books II and III (72, 89) documents a move from an intimate relationship between the king and God and its reinforcement through ritualistic ceremony to a rehearsal of a wrenching rejection of the covenant with David. The purpose of these psalms (specifically 2, 72, 89) was to document the failure of the Davidic covenant. The initial psalm (1) emphasizes the individual relationship with God, whereas 2 stresses the corporate dimension. Books IV and V move in another direction entirely, demonstrating that Israel's true home is God, the only dependable ruler. The heart of the Psalter, in this reading, resides in Book IV. This theological center clarifies the real nature of monarchy, a theocracy. Book V transfers to the people the former royal claims associated with David. The result is a resounding triumph of eschatological praise. The Psalter defines happiness (cf. 1:1, "Happy is the one who . . .") in quite concrete ways, but at the heart of the definition is the concept of trust and refuge.

Other interpreters understand the overall structure of Psalms differently. Two of these views merit attention here: a movement from lament to praise, and an increasingly liturgical movement. The first attributes significance to the early positioning of laments, for praise cannot achieve its goal until religious people have wrestled with their own doubts and emerged from them in the way described so effectively in 73. The second approach acknowledges that the early laments emphasize David's humanity and consequently the demise of his dynasty, but it recognizes the growing importance of liturgical guilds (Book III) and cultic events (pilgrimages and festivals; Book V: 120–134 for pilgrims, 113–118 for three major festivals). Notably, the opening word in 1:1 *('ašrê)* is more secular than *bārûḵ* ("blessed"). The closing exhortation, "Praise the Lord," belongs to sacred discourse. This final psalm (150) has 10 *hallĕlûyāhs* (or *hallĕlûhûs*), or 13 if one counts the conclusion in v. 6 and the opening and closing ones. Carroll Stuhlmueller suggests that these numbers correspond to the Decalogue and the 13 attributes of Yahweh revealed to Moses in Exod. 34:6-7, or the 13 times God spoke in Gen. 1.

The rich theological dimension of the Psalter continues to press itself on Jews and Christians. The metaphors for God serve in prayer and worship to convey deep feelings of trust and abandonment. The psalmists praise God as king, judge, shepherd, rock, portion, light, warrior, father, and farmer. They describe the people in a role of dependency as vine, tree, sheep, quiver, and the like. They distinguish between the righteous and wicked, promising life in its fullness to the former and destruction to the latter. Such evil practitioners are likened to grass, chaff, and dust; in the language of Ps. 1, their roots lack adequate water. Sinners did prosper, much to the chagrin of psalmists, but their prosperity was believed to be short-lived. A few psalmists probe deeply into traditional belief, in one instance breaking new ground and approaching, if not actually attaining, belief in life beyond the grave (73).

The book of Psalms has provided a reservoir from which poets draw in composing hymns, a practice already engaged in by composers of some psalms who produced mosaics of biblical passages (cf. 96–97, 119, 135). Individual psalms have contributed both language and sentiment for meditating about God and the law, and one psalm (23) has become a virtual icon in the United States. Another psalm (46) is the basis of Martin Luther's hymn, "Ein Feste Burg." The psalms may be Israel's response to God's self-manifestation, but to many modern worshippers they represent authentic worship. They plumb the depths of despair through which many pass at one time or another, and they soar to lofty heights of adoration, to which good people aspire. In short, from these majestic psalms one learns how to pray.

Bibliography. W. Brueggemann, *The Message of the Psalms* (Minneapolis, 1984); H. Gunkel, *The Psalms: A Form-Critical Introduction* (Philadelphia, 1967); W. L. Holladay, *The Psalms Through Three*

Thousand Years (Minneapolis, 1993); H.-J. Kraus, *Psalms 1–59* (Minneapolis, 1988); *Psalms 60–150* (Minneapolis, 1989); J. L. Mays, *Psalms.* Interpretation (Louisville, 1994); P. D. Miller, *Interpreting the Psalms* (Philadelphia, 1986); S. Mowinckel, *The Psalms in Israel's Worship* (Nashville, 1962); C. Westermann, *Praise and Lament in the Psalms* (Atlanta, 1981); G. H. Wilson, *The Editing of the Hebrew Psalter.* SBLDS 76 (Chico, 1985).

JAMES L. CRENSHAW

PSALMS OF SOLOMON

See SOLOMON, PSALMS OF.

PSALTER

A name for the book of Psalms.

PSEUDEPIGRAPHA

Lit., "falsely ascribed writings." This anachronistic term describes a variety of ancient noncanonical Jewish documents from the Hellenistic and Roman periods (ca. 250 B.C.E.–200 C.E.). The texts are not a part of the Hebrew Bible (Protestant OT) or the OT Apocrypha (roughly equivalent to the Roman Catholic Deuterocanonicals), but such a delineation does not do justice to the fluidity of this "modern" category. There is no widespread agreement as to what texts should be included in this corpus for there is no consensus on the criteria for inclusion. A maximalist view includes nearly any text associated with a character, or passage, from the OT, whether the text is considered Jewish or not, and whether the text derives from the Hellenistic and Roman periods or not (e.g., Vision of Ezra). Minimalists would tend to restrict the category to those works that are clearly Jewish, and almost certainly date from ca. 250 B.C.E.–200 C.E. Confusion arises in that a sizable majority of the texts often included in the Pseudepigrapha were clearly transmitted and altered by Christians, thus making strict categorization impossible.

Though not included in any of the major Western canons of Scripture, these texts, along with the Dead Sea Scrolls, are important for any attempt to understand the religious, political, and social world at the turn of the eras. They represent the multifaceted Jewish responses to the encroachment of Hellenism, the establishment of Maccabean power, Roman conquest and hegemony, the destruction of the Jerusalem temple, and the rise of Christianity. Christian preservation and adaptation of nearly all of these texts also enhance our knowledge of Jewish-Christian relations in the first several centuries C.E. In addition, many theological notions present in embryonic form in the OT are explored and expressed with increased sophistication within the Pseudepigrapha, making this literature an invaluable resource for the study of both early rabbinic Judaism and Christianity. For example, the NT book of Jude includes an extracanonical prophecy attributed to the antediluvian figure Enoch found only in the noncanonical 1 (Ethiopic Apocalypse of) Enoch. Judging from the context, the author of Jude clearly approved of this writing. He may even have considered this pseudepigraph "canonical." Jude's use of 1 Enoch helps us to understand the processes of canonization of both the OT and the NT.

Many, but not all, of these texts are associated with a figure or character from the Hebrew Scriptures such as Enoch. He was a prime candidate for "authorship" because of the OT's description of his fate (Gen. 5:24). The ancient authors expanded on this passage and built a significant interpretative framework in which Enoch becomes a scribe in heaven, recording both the secrets of creation and of the eschaton, and then revealing these secrets to a select group. The characters Ezra and Baruch are also employed because of their historical connection with the destruction of the first Jewish temple by the Babylonians. Later authors, attempting to come to grips with the destruction of the Jerusalem temple by the Romans in 70 C.E., used Ezra and Baruch to draw parallels between the two disastrous events. However, instead of an historical restoration as in the Persian period when the Jews were allowed to return from exile and rebuild the temple, the authors of the later pseudepigrapha look forward to a final, eschatological restoration. As one might surmise there are documents associated with many other great heroes of Israel, including Adam, Abraham, Isaac, Jacob, Joseph, Moses, Elijah, and Jeremiah.

Other texts attempt to fill in gaps in specific OT stories, or to smooth over theological problems perceived to be present in such stories. One of the best examples of this type of pseudepigrapha involves the marriage of Joseph and Asenath. In the OT, Asenath is described as the daughter of an Egyptian priest (Gen. 41:45). The text does not address the theologically thorny issue of a marriage between a foreign woman and a Jewish man, a union heavily discouraged in other parts of the OT (cf. 1 Kgs. 11:1-4; Neh. 13:26-27), but a later author composed a full narrative that details Asenath's conversion to Judaism, followed by her marriage to Joseph. The expansion of the biblical story eliminates the problem of Joseph having entered into a potentially corrupting marriage to a foreigner. Other such narrative expansions, or rewritings, include the story of Adam's ritual atonement for eating the forbidden fruit in the garden of Eden (he stands up to his neck in the Jordan River for 40 days; Life of Adam and Eve), a narrative that relates Abraham's discovery of the worthlessness of his father's idols (Apocalypse of Abraham), deathbed testamentary speeches by Jacob/Israel to each of his 12 sons (Testaments of the Twelve Patriarchs), tales about the Egyptian magicians who opposed Moses (Jannes and Jambres; cf. 2 Tim. 3:8-9), and a full and graphic description of the martyrdom of seven sons and their mother that is presented in abbreviated form in 2 Macc. 6–7 (4 Maccabees). Each "new" story tends to address issues of concern for the actual author's contemporaries, concerns directly related to the text being expounded and/or to the unstable religious and social situation of the period.

In addition to expansions or retellings of limited portions of the OT, some texts offer nearly complete reworkings of whole sections of the biblical text. Jubilees recounts the history of Israel from creation to the giving of the Law to Moses on Mt. Sinai. This pseudepigraphical text recasts, supplements, and sometimes eliminates the familiar stories of the OT so that its narrative supports the reckoning of dates according to the solar calendar (as opposed to the lunar/solar calendar which predominated within Judaism). Pseudo-Philo's *Liber Antiquitatum Biblicarum (Biblical Antiquities)* describes the period from Adam to David, interweaving adaptations of the biblical text with legendary elements in order to emphasize the Law and its eternal validity. It is by the Law that God will judge the whole world at the eschaton. The righteous will be granted peace and happiness in the age to come while the wicked will be destroyed. Beyond any attempt to understand the particular theological and religious emphases of the individual pseudepigraphical works described here, it is also important to note the freedom with which the Hellenistic and Roman period authors treated the texts of the OT. The biblical texts were not considered untouchable or final, but instead served as starting points for these new narratives.

Still other biblical texts served as models or templates for several of the Pseudepigrapha. This is most evident in the hymns, prayers, and wisdom texts generally included in the corpus. The 18 Psalms of Solomon, which clearly imitate the biblical psalms, describe the lawlessness of those who have established a non-Davidic monarchy and who have profaned the temple, but also relate the anticipation of the righteous as they await the appearance of the Messiah. The Prayer of Manasseh (sometimes classified among the OT Apocrypha), based on 2 Chr. 33, provides the content of the wicked king's penitential prayer in which he details his own abominable actions and prays for divine forgiveness. Several apocryphal psalms, some of which are found in a Qumran scroll interspersed with biblical psalms (11QPs), highlight the fluidity and malleability of the biblical canon in this period. Several wisdom texts included among the Pseudepigrapha (e.g., Pseudo-Phokylides, Syriac Menander, Aristobulus) clearly incorporate Hellenistic traditions, often concealing by means of style and substance any distinctive Jewish elements. In such cases the authors may very well have been trying to demonstrate the compatibility of Jewish and Greco-Roman wisdom traditions.

At least a few other pseudepigrapha consciously imitate Greek epic poetry. The Sibylline Oracles, e.g., are claimed to be the ecstatic prophecies of a legendary character from the distant past. The Jewish and Christian oracles focus on both ritual and ethical violations that have led, or will lead, to punishment by God, although they also contain some hope for future restoration. Several other fragmentary poetic texts, preserved only in later Christian works, include a history of Jerusalem (Philo the Epic Poet), an extended reworking of the story of the rape of Dinah in Gen. 34 (Theodotus), a dramatic rendering of the Exodus story (Ezekiel the Tragedian), a reconstruction of the life of Job based on the Greek version of the canonical story (Aristeas the Exegete), to name just a few.

As is evident from this survey, the Pseudepigrapha covers a wide range of theologies within Hellenistic and Roman period Judaism. This diversity incorporates attempts to contemporize traditional biblical stories as well as efforts to reconcile Hellenistic and Jewish philosophical notions. However, the most persistent theme within the corpus is the eschatological hope centering on the renewal of all creation by God or God's Messiah. In nearly every genre represented in the Pseudepigrapha, the hopelessness of the present is balanced by the expectation that God will judge the world, punishing the wicked and those who oppress Israel, and will reward the righteous for their steadfast faithfulness to the commandments.

Bibliography. J. H. Charlesworth, ed., *The Old Testament Pseudepigrapha,* 2 vols. (Garden City, 1983-85); M. de Jonge, *Outside the Old Testament* (Cambridge, 1995); G. W. E. Nickelsburg, *Jewish Literature between the Bible and the Mishnah* (Philadelphia, 1981); H. F. D. Sparks, ed., *The Apocryphal Old Testament* (Oxford, 1984); M. E. Stone, ed., *Jewish Writings of the Second Temple Period.* CRINT 2/2 (Philadelphia, 1984).

JAMES R. MUELLER

PSEUDO-MATTHEW, GOSPEL OF

A Latin apocryphal gospel of the 6th or 7th century, which borrows extensively from the earlier Protoevangelium of James and the Infancy Gospel of Thomas. Its major "original" material concerns the travels of the Holy Family to Egypt, only briefly noted in Matt. 2:14-15. On the journey, the infant Jesus rebukes attacking dragons (who then worship him, fulfilling Ps. 148:7), commands a palm tree to bend down to provide fruit and water to the travelers, and miraculously shortens the journey by days. Upon their arrival in Egypt, the very presence of the infant topples and shatters the idols of the Egyptians (fulfilling Isa. 19:1). Pseudo-Matthew, which seems to have been popular during the medieval period, also is the first to mention the "ox and ass" (cf. Isa. 1:3) which overlooked the manger in Bethlehem, a detail almost universally noted in medieval art.

IRA BIRDWHISTELL

PTOLEMAIS (Gk. *Ptolemaïs*)

An important city on the Mediterranean coast (modern Tel Acco/Tell el-Fukhkhar; 1585.2585). Known first as Acco, the city is mentioned in a number of extrabiblical sources including the Egyptian Middle Kingdom Execration Texts, the Amarna Letters, the temple at Karnak, and Ugaritic, Assyrian, and Persian texts.

The city was renamed during the Hellenistic period in honor of Ptolemy II Philadelphus. Later during the Hellenistic period, Antiochus VI again renamed it Antiochia-at-Ptolemais. The Seleucid ruler Antiochus V named Hegemonides as governor appointed over the region from Ptolemais to Gerar (2 Macc. 13:24-25). The city's name changed again during the Middle Ages to Acre to commemorate St. Jean d'Acre.

According to Judg. 1:31, the only OT reference to Acco, the tribe of Asher was unable to conquer Acco. Acts 21:7 notes Paul's visit to Ptolemais as he traveled on from Tyre to Caesarea.

ALICE H. HUDIBURG

PTOLEMY (Gk. *Ptolemaíos*)

1. Ptolemy I Soter ([323]305-282 B.C.E.) was a worthy founder of the Ptolemaic dynasty (his father was Lagus, which is why the dynasty is sometimes called the Lagids). He was a true polymath, not only being a general and strategist of considerable ability but also a statesman and a man of learning and culture, and apparently even a good drinking companion. He wrote a history of Alexander's conquests which still serves as the basis of the most reliable account extant, and he perhaps began the famous library of Alexandria (the Museon), though possibly this was done by his son. Shortly after Alexander's death he established himself in Egypt, and during the 40-year period of military and political maneuvering (the period of the Diadochi or "Successors" to Alexander), he played his cards well, with one clear aim: to preserve Egypt as his fiefdom, and in this he succeeded well. He aided Seleucus I in returning to Babylon after the latter was driven out by Antigonus. This is why when Ptolemy seized southern Syria and Palestine after the battle of Ipsus in 301 Seleucus did not press his legitimate claim to the territory. Ptolemy took the title king in 305 or 304.

2. Ptolemy II Philadelphus ([285]282-246) had a long reign in which he pursued cultural as well as political matters, such as building the famous lighthouse Pharos and bringing the library of Alexandria to completion, if he did not begin it. Known most widely as the Ptolemy of the Letter of Aristeas, he established diplomatic relations with Rome, who was engaged in the First Punic War with Carthage (264-241). His attempts to influence events in the Aegean area were thwarted by the Macedonian king Antigonus Gonatas (283-239) in the Chremonidean War (267-261). We know little of the First Syrian War (274-271) with Antiochus I (281-261), but some Egyptian holdings in Asia were lost in the Second Syrian War (ca. 260-253) with Antiochus II (261-246). Ptolemy II made peace with Antiochus by giving him his daughter Berenice Syra in marriage (which led to disastrous consequences for Antiochus' son Seleucus II). Ptolemy divorced his first wife to marry his sister Arsinoë, a strong and independent woman, though her influence on her brother has often been exaggerated. Ptolemy's reign has regularly been interpreted in idyllic terms as one of economic prosperity as well as cultural achievement, but recent studies have suggested that his fiscal policies were in fact disastrous, spending more than the economy could sustain, and led to the financial crisis in his son's reign.

Ptolemy II with his sister and wife Arsinoë II. Ptolemaic cameo (278 B.C.E.) cut out of the nine layers of an Indian sardonyx; Kunsthistorisches Museum, Vienna (Erich Lessing/Art Resource, N.Y.)

3. Ptolemy III Euergetes I (246-221) began his career by putting down a revolt in Cyrenaica while still crown prince. Shortly after taking the throne, he received an urgent message for help from his sister Berenice. She had married Antiochus II but after his death she was under siege from Antiochus' first wife. Ptolemy took an army to her aid but found she had already been killed. He used the occasion to take Antioch, then to move on eastward to take Babylon and Seleucia-on-the-Tigris and perhaps even other areas (the Third Syrian War, 246-241). However, he was forced to make peace with Seleucus II and return home when a number of low Nile floods produced a famine in Egypt.

4. Ptolemy IV Philopator (221-204) is generally regarded as a weak ruler under domination of palace functionaries, though some recent scholars have evaluated his reign more positively. Regardless of this, his main achievement was to defeat Antiochus III at the battle of Raphia in the Fourth Syrian War (219-217), though in order to do so he used native Egyptian troops. This was thought to lay the ground for future civil disorders since the Egyptians naturally expected some civic rights in return, though some recent scholars think this is exaggerated. The battle of Raphia and a possibly authentic visit to Jerusalem are mentioned in 3 Macc. 1.

5. Ptolemy V Theos Epiphanes (204-180) was a minor for the first 15 years of his reign, and Egypt suffered considerably during this time including loss of most territories in the Aegean and Asia Minor. The main event was the loss of Palestine and southern Syria to Antiochus III in 200. An agreement was finally sealed with a marriage to Cleopatra I, a daughter of Antiochus. His coronation is the event described on the Rosetta Stone. Ptolemy V had not given up his claim to the Syria possessions, however, but was assassinated before he could do anything about it.

6.-15. Ptolemy VI Philometor (180-145) was only a young boy when he came to the throne, but his regents planned an invasion of Anitochus IV's realm which they launched ca. 170. Antiochus was victorious and made Ptolemy his ward; the regents then put his brother Ptolemy VIII Euergetes II (Physcon) (145-116) on the throne where he ruled jointly with Ptolemy VI and the latter's sister-wife Cleopatra II for several years. This cooperation led to another invasion by Antiochus in 168, but this time the Romans warned the Seleucid king off. Ptolemy VI then ruled alone, though his younger brother was given Cyrenaica. After Philometor's death, Euergetes took the throne, becoming guardian to Philometor's son Ptolemy VII Neos Philopator but soon had him executed. His two wives, Cleopatra II and Cleopatra III (mother and daughter), become rivals. Cleopatra II drove him out of Egypt for a number of years, during which time she reigned in his stead, but he soon returned and established an uneasy truce with his wives.

After Ptolemy VIII's death the two Cleopatras again became rivals, each apparently championing one of the two sons, though Cleopatra III became the main player and reigned jointly with each son in turn. The elder son Ptolemy IX Soter II (Lathyrus) (116-107, 88-80) ruled first but was displaced by his younger brother Ptolemy X Alexander I (107-88) and set up his own rule in Cyprus. In the meantime, an illegitimate son of Ptolemy VIII named Ptolemy Apion took up rule in Cyrenaica. At his death in 96, his will left the region to Rome. Ptolemy X also decided to leave Egypt to Rome in his will; however, he was driven from Egypt by a revolt (dying soon afterward), and Ptolemy IX returned to take up his second period of rulership. An embassy from Rome came in 86 and was well received, but the Romans were impressed only by Egypt's apparent wealth.

When Ptolemy IX died, the Romans now began the first of a series of increasing interventions in Egypt. Ptolemy IX's half sister Berenice took the throne, but the Romans sent as king a son of Ptolemy X (and stepson of Berenice), Ptolemy XI Alexander II, who murdered Berenice. However, the Alexandrians in turn quickly assassinated him. A son of Ptolemy IX, Ptolemy XII Neo Dionysys (Auletes) (80-58, 55-51) took over rule, apparently without Roman intervention, but Rome was an ever present power to be reckoned with. Pompey did not interfere in his activities in the east in 65-63; nevertheless, he took control of territory right up to Egypt's border. When Rome took over Cyprus, Ptolemy XII was driven out by his own people and his daughter Berenice ruled in his place. He sought Roman help and retook his throne, after which he had his daughter killed. (The one who brought him back to Egypt was Gabinius, who was accompanied by Antipater the father of Herod the Great.)

When Ptolemy XII died, he left instructions that his daughter Cleopatra VII (51-30) should marry her younger brother Ptolemy XIII (51-47). Cleopatra worked hard to strengthen her relations within her own country and became the only Ptolemy to speak the Egyptian language; however, she was only 17 and was opposed by powerful functionaries. She fled to Syria, and the Romans became involved in her attempt to regain her throne. Ptolemy XIII was killed in the fighting, and Cleopatra ruled jointly with her younger brother Ptolemy XIV (47-44) until she had him assassinated. Her involvement with Caesar and later Mark Antony demonstrated her skill in manipulating circumstances to gain the best deal for Egypt in a difficult period. This included regaining Cyprus for Egypt. She was also a major thorn in the side of Herod and would probably have had him disposed if he had not been so useful to Mark Antony. Nevertheless, the Romans as a whole opposed her, so when Mark Antony was defeated in Actium in 31 B.C.E. she had nowhere else to turn and committed suicide. She had associated her son Ptolemy XV Caesar (Caesarion) (36-30) with her on the throne, claiming that Julius Caesar was his father. He was executed on Octavian's orders.

Bibliography. *CAH*[2], esp. 7/1: *The Hellenistic World,* ed. F. W. Walbank et al. (Cambridge, 1984); 8: *Rome and the Mediterranean to 133 B.C.,* ed. A. E. Astin et al. (Cambridge, 1989); 9: *The Last Age of the Roman Republic, 146-43 B.C.,* ed. J. A. Crook, A. Lintott, and E. Rawson (Cambridge, 1994); N. Davis and C. M. Kraay, *The Hellenistic Kingdoms: Portrait Coins and History* (London, 1973).

LESTER L. GRABBE

16. The son of Dositheus and father of Lysimachus who, during the reign of Ptolemy IX and Cleopatra III, brought to Alexandria the Letter about Purim (Add. Esth. 11:1).

17. The son of Abubas and son-in-law of the high priest; governor of the region N of the Dead Sea ("the plain of Jericho"). Led by ambition, he ambushed and murdered his father-in-law Simon Maccabeus and two of Simon's sons, Mattathias and Judas, during a feast at Dok (1 Macc. 16:11-17). Enraged by this vile act and the perpetrator's boastfulness, John Hyrcanus retaliated, slaying Ptolemy and his cohorts (1 Macc. 16:18-22).

18. Ptolemy Macron, son of Dorymenes. Appointed governor of Cyprus by Ptolemy Vi, he transferred his loyalties to the Seleucid Antiochus IV Epiphanes. Bribed by Menelaus, he convinced Antiochus to clear the priest of complicity in Lysimachus' plundering of the temple (1 Macc. 4:45-47). Regarded as a traitor for his pro-Jewish stance, he committed suicide (1 Macc. 10:12-13; but cf. 8:8-9).

PUAH (Heb. *pûʿâ, pûʾâ*) (also PUVAH)

1. One of the two midwives to the Hebrew women in Egypt (Exod. 1:15). It is unclear if the two women, Shiphrah and Puah, were Hebrew or Egyptian. Summoned to assist in Pharaoh's plan of genocide for Hebrew male babies, they disobeyed and let them live. The two women feared Yahweh and were rewarded for their obedience to God.

2. A man from the tribe of Issachar, father of the judge Tola (Judg. 10:1).

3. A descendant of Issachar (1 Chr. 7:1). Ancestor of the clan of the Punites, he is called Puvah at Gen. 46:13; Num. 26:23. MICHELLE TOOLEY

PUBLICAN
See TAX.

PUBLIUS (Gk. *Poplios;* Lat. *Publius*)
The leading Roman official (Gk. *prṓtos*) on the island of Malta, where Paul landed after surviving a shipwreck. Publius provided lodging for Paul and his companions and acted kindly to them during their three-day stay (Acts 28:7), and Paul cured Publius' father of a fever and dysentery (v. 8).

PUDENS (Gk. *Poúdēs;* Lat. *Pudens*)
A Christian in Rome who, with Paul, sent greetings to Timothy (2 Tim. 4:21).

PUL (Heb. *pûl*)
A nickname for Tiglath-pileser III, king of Assyria (2 Kgs. 15:19; 1 Chr. 5:26). Although the name occurs in the Babylonian King List A (Akk. *Pulu; ANET,* 219), it is not attested in cuneiform sources contemporary with Tiglath-pileser's reign. It does not appear to have been a throne name.

PUNITES (Heb. *pûnî*)
The descendants of Puvah (Num. 26:23; some versions read Heb. *pû'î,* perhaps Puah or Puites).

PUNON (Heb. *pûnōn*)
A campsite during the Israelite exodus from Egypt, located between Zalmonah and Oboth (Num. 33:42-43). Punon is commonly associated with modern Fênân (197004), a copper smelting site active in the Chalcolithic, Early Bronze, and Iron Ages. Excavations at the site have yielded Edomite, Roman, and Byzantine occupation strata. Punon is associated with *pwnw,* a region inhabited by the nomadic Shasu as mentioned by Rameses II (13th century B.C.E.). RYAN BYRNE

PUR (Heb. *pûr*)
See PURIM.

PURAH (Heb. *purâ*)
Gideon's servant who accompanied him in spying on the Midianite camp (Judg. 7:10-11).

PURIM (Heb. *pûrîm*)
A springtime holiday in the Jewish liturgical calendar, falling on the 14th of Adar, that celebrates the defeat of Haman and the survival of the Jews in the book of Esther. The word *Purim* is a Hebraized Akkadian word meaning "lots," and is thus linked to the lots (Heb. *pûr*) cast by Haman in order to decide on the date for his planned pogrom against all Persian Jews (Esth. 3:7; 9:24-28). It is not clear which came first, the book of Esther or the festival of Purim. In either case, the two have become inextricably linked, with the scroll of Esther being read in full in the evening synagogue service. Purim encourages a carnival atmosphere, with children bringing noisemakers to the synagogue and the congregation stamping their feet every time Haman's name is read from the scroll. The Talmud (*Meg.* 7b) commands adult Jews to drink so much wine on Purim that they cannot tell the difference between "blessed by Mordecai" and "cursed be Haman." But it is also clear that, given the threat of annihilation described by the book of Esther and the many persecutions endured by Jews throughout the centuries, the festivities of Purim harbor more serious themes.

Bibliography. T. K. Beal, *The Book of Hiding: Gender, Ethnicity, Annihilation, and Esther* (London, 1997); A. Waskow, *Seasons of Our Joy* (1982, repr. Boston, 1990); E. Wiesel, *The Trial of God* (1979, repr. New York, 1995). TOD LINAFELT

PURPLE
Purple fabrics were highly prized in the ancient world. The Phoenicians developed the purple dye industry, centered in Tyre and Sidon (Ezek. 27:7, 16). The source of the dye was one of several carnivorous snails that lived in the Mediterranean Sea: *Murex brandaris, Murex trunculus,* and *Purpura haemostoma.* The hypobranchial glands of these shellfish produce a colorless liquid, which upon exposure to air dyed fabrics a colorfast purple. Archaeologists find evidence of the industry in the piles of crushed mollusk shells.

The process of extracting the dye was complex. First, wicker baskets, baited with fish or meat scraps, were lowered into the water to catch the shellfish. When the shellfish were drawn up, the dye was extracted from the hypobranchial gland by crushing the shell. The resulting liquid was mixed with salt and allowed to set for three days. Then the mixture was simmered for 10 days, reducing it to one sixth of its original volume. Wool was placed in the resulting dye bath for five hours. Sometimes the wool was dyed twice to produce a richer color. Twelve thousand shells would produce less than 2 g. (.07 oz.) of dye. The process was costly, and thus purple fabrics were associated with royalty and wealth.

Skilled artisans used purple fibers, along with blue and crimson, for the curtains of the tabernacle and for Aaron's priestly vestments (Exod. 26:1; 28:15-33); Gideon received purple garments worn by the kings of Midian (Judg. 8:26); and King Belshazzar clothed Daniel in purple (Dan. 5:29). The soldiers clothed Jesus in purple as they mocked him (Mark 15:17-20; John 19:2-5); Lydia dealt in purple cloth (Acts 16:14); and purple was associated with the decadence of "Babylon" (Rev. 17:4; 18:12, 16).

Bibliography. I. I. Ziderman, "Seashells and Ancient Purple Dyeing," *BA* 53 (1990): 98-101.
MARY PETRINA BOYD

PUT (Heb. *pûṭ*)
Either a person (son of Ham, Gen. 10:6; 1 Chr. 1:8) or the people or place related to his descendants in

Africa; military allies of Egypt (Jer. 46:9; Ezek. 30:5), Tyre (27:10), Gog (38:5), and No-amon (Thebes) in its fall to Assyria (Nah. 3:9). In all but one passage Put is listed along with Ethiopia (Cush, or Nubia); Josephus equates it with Libya. Some suggest Punt (Somalia) in light of "Put" and "Libya" (Heb. *lûḇîm*) in Nah. 3:9, but these probably refer to separate Libyan tribes, as with Libya (lit., Lubiim) and Sukkim in 2 Chr. 12:3.

W. Creighton Marlowe

PUTEOLI (Gk. *Potioloi;* Lat. *Puteoli*)
A major port on the Gulf of Naples (modern Pozzuoli), W of Naples. Founded in the 6th century as the Greek colony Dicaearchia, it later flourished as a Roman colony of ca. 65 thousand residents and was the main port of entry for large ships bringing grain to Rome from the East. Josephus mentions a sizable Jewish population (*Ant.* 17.328; 18.160), and Paul spent seven days there with local Christians en route to Rome (Acts 28:13-14). This cosmopolitan and entrepreneurial city boasted several of the oriental cults (e.g., Serapis) as well as the normal imperial worship during the 1st century

Kent L. Yinger

PUTHITES (Heb. *pûṯî*)
A family who lived in the region of Kiriath-jearim, mentioned in a Judahite list (1 Chr. 2:53).

PUTIEL (Heb. *pûṭî'ēl*)
The father-in-law of Aaron's son Eleazar (Exod. 6:25; Egyp. *pꜣ-d'i-* + Heb. *'ēl,* "the one given by God" [?]).

PUVAH (Heb. *puwwâ*) (also PUAH)
The second son of Issachar, among those who accompanied Jacob to Egypt (Gen. 46:13). He is called Puah (**3**) at 1 Chr. 7:1. He was the ancestor of the Punites (Num. 26:23).

PYRRHUS (Gk. *Pýrros*)
The father of Sopater, one of Paul's companions on his final journey to Jerusalem (Acts 20:4).

Q

Q

A hypothetical collection of Jesus' sayings that is thought to have circulated in the 1st century and used independently by the authors of Matthew and Luke. The Q hypothesis was first developed among German scholars as a component of the two-source theory in the 19th century, the solution to the Synoptic problem in which Mark is the first Gospel (and the most reliable for describing the ministry of Jesus) and Q an early source of Jesus' sayings. The designation Q derives from German *Quelle,* "source." The Q hypothesis explains (1) the remarkable verbal agreement between large blocks of Jesus' teachings found both in Matthew and Luke but not Mark (hence Q is sometimes called the "double tradition"), (2) why the sequence of sayings in Matthew for the most part follows the relative Lukan sequence, and (3) why Matthew especially has doublet sayings (i.e., similar sayings, one adopted from Mark and one from Q). Perhaps one of the sources explicitly mentioned in Luke 1:1-4, Q contains some of the most characteristic parables and ethical teachings of Jesus, such as the Beatitudes, love of enemies, and the Lord's Prayer. There are only two narrative stories in Q, the temptation and the healing of the centurion's servant, but even in these passages the primary focus is Jesus' dialogue.

Interest in Q was revived in the late 1960s in the wake of redaction criticism and the discovery of the Gospel of Thomas in 1947. Redaction criticism's interest in the Gospel writers' style and theology analyzed the use of their sources, including the sayings in Q. The 114 sayings of Jesus collected under the title Gospel of Thomas, part of the Nag Hammadi library, provided an early Christian document analogous in genre to Q and bolstered claims of its existence. Several scholars have attempted to reconstruct Q's original text by carefully analyzing the differences between Matthew's and Luke's readings, and then determining which of the two preserves Q's reading and which edited Q's reading. Recent studies have focused on Q's own and distinct theology, particularly its concerted condemnation of "this generation" and its views on Judaism and Gentiles. Sociologically oriented studies have speculated on the community behind the document: the sayings may have been recorded by early wandering missionaries or prophets, or among the communities in or near Galilee which supported them. Q's theology and its community are found not only in what it contained, but also in what it did not: strikingly absent are references to a eucharistic meal or Jesus' resurrection, explicit references to the Crucifixion, church leadership, or primacy of any disciples. Whether these aspects were simply assumed, rejected, or not yet developed by the tradents of Q has been disputed. While some scholars still dispute that Q was a written document, others have speculated that Q itself contained two written layers, an early sapientially oriented collection of sayings blocks that was later supplemented with apocalyptically oriented sayings.

Proposed Q Material (Following Luke)

3:7-9	11:2-4	12:(49,)51-53	16:13
3:16-17	11:9-20	12:57-59	16:16-18
4:1-13	11:21-22	13:18-21	(17:1-2)
6:20b-23	11:23-26	13:23-30	17:3-4
6:27-49	11:29-35(36)	13:34-35	17:(5-)6
7:1-10	11:39-52	14:11 (18:14)	17:23-24
7:18-35	12:2-12	14:16-24	17:26-30
9:57-60	12:22-31(32)	14:26-27	17:33-37
10:2-16	12:33-34	14:34-35	19:12-27
10:21-24	12:39-46	15:4-7	22:28-30

Since Luke follows the Markan sequence of pericope closely, many posit that Luke also follows the order of Q more closely, and hence Q passages are often cited with the Lukan versification (e.g., Q 11:2-4 for the Lord's Prayer). Alternatively, Q passages are referred to by citing both parallel passages (e.g., Matt. 6:9-11 = Luke 11:2-4 for the Lord's Prayer).

Bibliography. I. Havener, *Q: The Sayings of Jesus.* Good News Studies 19 (Wilmington, 1987); J. S. Kloppenborg, ed., *The Shape of Q* (Minneapolis, 1994).

JONATHAN L. REED

QERE
See KETHIB AND QERE.

QESITAH (Heb. *qĕśîṭâ*)
A unit of weight of unknown quantity used as a monetary measure (Gen. 33:19; Josh. 24:32; Job 42:11; so NRSV mg; NRSV "piece [of money]").

QOHELETH (Heb. *qōheleṯ*) (also KOHELETH)
The Hebrew title of the book of Ecclesiastes and the name of the primary speaker in the book. The term is a verbal noun from Heb. *qhl* ("to assemble") and thus can be translated as "the one who assembles" or "the one who calls (people) together" (RSV "the Preacher"; NRSV "the Teacher"). Based on Eccl. 1:1, which states that Qoheleth is the son of David, some have contended that Qoheleth should be identified with Solomon. The date of the book, however, seems to warrant against such a conclusion. Elsewhere in the book the term appears in a variety of functions (Eccl. 1:2, 12; 7:27; 12:8-10). Overall, the primary function of Qoheleth more closely resembles that of a sage than a king.

W. DENNIS TUCKER, JR.

QUAIL
Coturnix coturnix, a small pheasant-type bird 19 cm. (7.5 in.) in length and weighing 100 g. (3.5 oz.). In the wilderness, God is twice reported as supplying the Israelites with quail (Heb. *śĕlāw*) to eat (Exod. 16:13; Num. 11:31-32). Quail pass over the Mediterranean during their annual migrations and were captured by the millions until the 1930s, when their numbers dropped (cf. Num. 11:31).

Bibliography. *Fauna and Flora of the Bible.* 2nd ed. Helps for Translators 11 (New York, 1980); A. Parmelee, *All the Birds of the Bible* (1959, repr. New Canaan, Conn., 1988).

MATTHEW A. THOMAS

QUARTERMASTER
The title of Seraiah, one of Zedekiah's officers (Jer. 51:59; Heb. *śar mĕnûḥâ,* lit., "officer of rest" or "officer of the resting place"). NRSV "quartermaster" is probably based on emendation to *śar maḥăneh,* "officer of the camp," suggested by the Syriac text. The LXX and Targum reflect *śar mĕnāḥôṯ,* "officer of tribute."

QUARTUS (Gk. *Koúartos;* Lat. *Quartus*)
A Christian (Lat. "fourth") in Corinth whose greetings to the Roman Christians are passed on in Paul's letter (Rom. 16:23). The epithet "our brother" identifies him as a fellow Christian rather than as a sibling of Erastus or Paul.

QUEEN
A king's wife, mother, or a ruler in her own right. Five foreign queens are mentioned in the Bible: the queen of Sheba (1 Kgs. 10), Taphenes of Egypt (11:19-20), Vashti of Persia (Esth. 1), Esther of Persia (Esth. 2–10), and Candace of Ethiopia (Acts 8:27). Of these, only those of Sheba and Ethiopia are presented as sovereign rulers, while those of Persia are dependent on their husband's status.

Royal marriages helped establish alliances and strengthen treaties. Four (perhaps five) specific instances of intermarriage between Israel and Judah's royal houses and those of other nations are: David and Maacah of Geshur (2 Sam. 3:3); Solomon and Pharaoh's daughter (1 Kgs. 3:1); Ahab and Jezebel (16:31); Jehoram and Athaliah (2 Kgs. 8:18); and possibly Solomon and Naamah (LXX 1 Kgs. 12:24). Other unions — both royal and common — are implied (cf. 1 Kgs. 11:1-2).

In spite of the warning in Deut. 17:17, some Judean and Israelite kings had numerous wives: Saul (2 Sam. 3:7; 12:8); David (3:2-5; 5:13; 11:27; 15:16; 16:21-22; 20:3); Solomon (700 wives, 300 concubines; 1 Kgs. 11:3); Rehoboam (18 wives, 60 concubines; 2 Chr. 11:21); Abijah (14 wives; 13:21); Ahab (1 Kgs. 20:3-7); Jehoiachin (2 Kgs. 24:15); Jehoram (2 Chr. 21:14, 17); and Zedekiah (Jer. 38:23).

Perhaps the most influential position occupied by a royal wife was that of the king's mother. These women, often mentioned as part of their son's introductory regnal formulas, rarely have narratives detailing their activities. Only Bathsheba, Maacah, Hamutal, Jezebel, Athaliah, and Nehushta have more than cursory mention in their son's accounts. Of these, only Athaliah of Judah (2 Kgs. 11) attained the power base necessary for independent rule.

Scholars debate whether or not queen mother was an institutional position in Judah or Israel, whether such a position arose from outside influence (i.e., the Hittites) or from within Israel (i.e., a prior matriarchal social structure), and whether its duties and powers were primarily cultic, political, or personal. Zafrira Ben-Barak argues that individuals like Bathsheba, Maacah, Hamutal, and Nehushta gained power by enlisting support for a younger son with no claim to succession, thereby grasping power normally outside the reach of kings' mothers. The queen mother's influence then would be personally rather than institutionally or religiously derived. In contrast, Susan Ackerman argues that the queen mother's duties were both political (king's advisor) and cultic (Asherah's representative in the Judean royal court, perhaps even the surrogate of Asherah). The queen mother would then be second in power only to her son, the king.

Bibliography. S. Ackerman, "The Queen Mother and the Cult in Ancient Israel," *JBL* 112 (1993): 385-401; Z. Ben-Barak, "The Status and Right of the *Gĕbîrâ,*" *JBL* 110 (1991): 23-24; L. S. Schearing, "Queen," *ABD* 5:583-86; K. Spanier, "The Queen Mother in the Judaean Royal Court: Maacha — A Case Study," in *A Feminist Companion to Samuel and Kings,* ed. A. Brenner (Sheffield, 1994), 186-95.

LINDA S. SCHEARING

QUEEN OF HEAVEN
A goddess worshipped first in Judah in the late 7th century and then by Judahites who fled to Egypt after the Babylonian destruction of 586 B.C.E. (Jer. 7:16-20; 44:15-28). Jeremiah's remarks associate the goddess with fertility and somewhat with war; she also, as her

title indicates, has astral characteristics. Her cult is described as one particularly attractive to women, who bake offering cakes in the goddess' image.

The Canaanite goddess who best fits this description is Astarte, who is associated with both fertility and war and who has astral features. Phoenician inscriptions also ascribe to Astarte the title "Queen." Astarte's cult, however, is not known to be one in which women play a special role. Yet women do have an important place in the cult of Astarte's Mesopotamian counterpart, Ishtar, whose female devotees ritually weep in imitation of the goddess' lamentations over her dead lover, Tammuz (cf. Ezek. 8:14). Ishtar's cult also involves the offering of cakes called *kamānu,* an Akkadian word cognate to Heb. *kawwānîm* used for cakes in Jeremiah. The Queen of Heaven is thus best identified as a syncretism of Canaanite Astarte and Mesopotamian Ishtar.

SUSAN ACKERMAN

QUIRINIUS (Gk. *Kyrēnios;* Lat. *Quirinius*)
Publius Sulpicius Quirinius, governor (legate) and consul of Syria. Possibly as a result of distinguished military service during Augustus' campaigns in Actium (31 B.C.E.) and Spain (20s), Quirinius rose from the plebeian class to be elected consul in 12 B.C.E. When Augustus removed Archelaus, the son of Herod the Great, as ruler of Judea in 6 B.C.E., Quirinius was appointed governor (legate) and charged with the task of completing the formal annexation of Judea. He enjoyed considerable political favor and power during the reigns of both Augustus and Tiberius Caesar until his death in 21 C.E.

Both Josephus (*Ant.* 27.13.5; 28.1.1) and an inscription discovered in Aleppo report that Quirinius conducted a census of Judea for tax purposes as part of this process (cf. Acts 5:37). Luke associates Jesus' birth with both this census (Luke 2:1-7) and the "days of Herod the King" (1:5), who died in 4 B.C.E.. Thus, there is a discrepancy of at least a decade regarding the nativity.

TIMOTHY B. CARGAL

QUMRAN
Khirbet Qumrân (193127), 14 km. (8.5 mi.) S of Jericho overlooking the northwest shore of the Dead Sea, ruins of the site inhabited by the community that produced the Dead Sea Scrolls.

QUOTATIONS
The OT contains a number of direct quotations, all poetic, from books no longer extant, including the Book of Jashar (Josh. 10:12-13; 2 Sam. 1:18-27) and the Book of the Wars of the Lord (Num. 21:14-15). Indirect quotations from such works also appear. The books of the Chronicles of the Kings of Israel and Judah are major sources for 1-2 Kings (e.g., 1 Kgs. 14:19; 2 Kgs. 24:5). 1 Kgs. 11:41 refers to a Book of the Acts of Solomon. A genealogical Book of the Kings of Israel was used by the Chronicler (1 Chr. 9:1), as were a Commentary on the Book of the Kings (2 Kgs. 24:27) and other works (1 Chr. 27:24; 29:29; 2 Chr. 12:15; 33:18-19). The Chronicler also drew on the Pentateuch and the books of Samuel and Kings (perhaps referring to the latter by name at, e.g., 2 Chr. 16:11; 32:32). A shorter quotation of a canonical book is the quotation of Mic. 3:12 at Jer. 26:18.

The NT contains more than 1000 quotations from and allusions to each of the three divisions of the OT. These function in a variety of ways, largely to underscore the authority of a NT statement or to show an event as divinely ordained. The fundamental assumption underlying such quotations is that the divine origin of the salvation in Jesus and of the proclamation and possession of that salvation by the Church is recognizable only because in the events so noted has the OT reached its fulfillment; the quotation formulas (e.g., "to fulfill what the Lord has spoken by the prophet," Matt. 2:15) make this clear. Elsewhere the teaching of the OT is held up as exemplary moral teaching (e.g., Mark 10:19), or it may be cited only for the sake of criticism and revision (e.g., vv. 2-9).

The NT quotes the OT most often according to the LXX. Matthew is the most significant exception to this rule; 32 of his quotations differ from the LXX, which may indicate that he used the MT or that he had access to a now lost Greek version of the OT. Some quotations are targumic in style (e.g., Rom. 12:19, quoting Deut. 32:35), while others join interpretation closely to quotation in a manner somewhat like that of the Qumran commentaries (e.g., Mark 1:2-4, quoting Mal. 3:1; Isa. 40:3). Effort generally is made in the choice of text and in its presentation to show clearly the correspondence between the OT text and that aspect of the coming redemption in Christ that constitutes fulfillment of the particular text. Sometimes the meaning of an OT passage in its original historical context is set aside in its application to a new situation in the NT; e.g., what is said of Solomon at 2 Sam. 7:14 is applied to believers in Christ at 2 Cor. 6:18. In such cases, a typological correlation between the original form of the statement and the new focus is assumed, as is the underlying continuity of salvation history.

The pseudepigraphal book of 1 Enoch is quoted in Jude 14-15 (1 En. 1:9). Greek poets are quoted in the Epistles: the Cretan Epimenides at Titus 1:12; Epimenides and Aratus of Cilicia at Acts 17:28; and the Athenian Menander at 1 Cor. 15:33.

Each of the Gospel writers was dependent upon earlier sources, both oral and written, as the basis for his work. These sources were quoted liberally, as can be seen in the way in which Mark serves as a source for Matthew and Luke, at times quoted verbatim and at others changed significantly by the later Gospels. Authors apart from the Evangelists quote liberally from hymnic and poetic sources (e.g., Phil. 2:6-11; 1 Tim. 3:16; and hymns found in the book of Revelation). Some later NT books were written with knowledge of others written earlier, and contain a development of the thinking found in the earlier works. 2 Peter, e.g., is partly based on the Epistle of Jude, and Ephesians is apparently a development of the thought in Colossians and its application to a new situation.

Bibliography. J. M. Efird, ed., *The Use of the Old Testament in the New* (Durha, 1972); R. H. Gundry, *The Use of the Old Testament in St. Matthew's Gospel.* NovTSup 18 (Leiden, 1967).

LEE E. KLOSINSKI

R

RAAMA (Heb. *ra'mā'*), **RAAMAH** (*ra'mâ*)
A son of Cush (Gen. 10:7; 1 Chr. 1:9); eponymous ancestor of Sheba and Dedan, Arabian peoples and territories. Located in southwestern Arabia (possibly modern Naǵrān), Raamah was a place rich in spices, gems, and gold, and thus a trading partner with Tyre (Ezek. 27:22). It is mentioned in various Old South Arabian inscriptions (cf. Strabo *Geog.* 16.4.24).

RAAMIAH (Heb. *ra'amyâ*) (also REELAIAH; RESAIAH)
An Israelite who returned with Zerubbabel from exile (Neh. 7:7). He is called Reelaiah at Ezra 2:2 and Resaiah at 1 Esdr. 5:8.

RAAMSES (Heb. *ra'amsēs*)
Alternate form of Rameses, an Egyptian store-city built by the Israelites and later the Ramesside capital (Exod. 1:11).

RABBAH (Heb. *rabbâ*)
(also RABBATH-AMMON)

1. A city in the tribal territory of Judah near Kiriath-jearim (Josh. 15:60), generally identified with Rubutu in the Amarna Letters and Rubute in Egyptian texts. The site was likely Khirbet Bîr el-Ḥilu/Khirbet Ḥamîdeh (149137), a short distance S of Emmaus.

2. A city (modern Amman; 238151) on the Transjordan plateau, ca. 88-105 km. (55-65 mi.) by road from Jerusalem and ca. 39 km. (24 mi.) E of the Jordan River at the headwaters of the Jabbok. Rabbah ("great" or "large") was the center of surrounding cities and villages (cf. Ezek. 25:1-11). It is found most often in direct reference to the Ammonites (Rabbath bene Ammon, Rabbath-ammon, or Bīt-ammanu in the Assyrian texts).

Rabbah physically consisted of two parts. The upper city or acropolis, known as the "royal city" (2 Sam. 12:26), a citadel with attached terraces, was situated on Jebel Qal'a. The lower city, the "city of waters" (2 Sam. 12:27), ran along two wadis at the base of the hill in the valley. The two were connected by a long underground passageway leading from the "city of waters" up to a cistern on Jebel Qal'a. This 16 × 6 × 7 m. (52 × 19 × 23 ft.) high reservoir was apparently in use as early as the Middle Bronze Age and as late as the Hellenistic period.

The site has been occupied at least since the Neolithic and Chalcolithic periods. MB II structures are substantial, and by LB II the city had grown considerably. The best LB architecture is represented by the temple at the old Amman airport. Continuous rebuilding, especially in modern times, has destroyed so much that it is seldom possible to discern city plans. Fortunately, some significant structures remain. Tombs carved into hillsides and defense systems on the acropolis attest to almost every period.

Rabbath-ammon showplaced the "iron bed" taken from King Og of Bashan (Deut. 3:11). David captured Rabbah and crowned himself with the gold crown of Milcom, the tutelary deity (2 Sam. 12:30). He looted and reportedly destroyed Rabbah and "all the Ammonite cities," but they rebuilt and later supplied David with food, clothing, and other goods in his time of need (2 Sam. 17:27-29).

The city fared relatively well under the Persians. It became a Hellenistic city under Ptolemy II Philadelphus (285-246 B.C.), who officially changed its name to Philadelphia. The city came under Seleucid rule for a short time, then under Nabatean, and finally Roman rule in 63 B.C., when it flourished greatly as evidenced in a propylaeum, colonnaded street, large theater, nymphaeum, temenos, and temple of Hercules. In Byzantine times it sent bishops to the Councils of Nicea (A.D. 325), Antioch (341), and Calcedon (451). Under Arab rule, an Umayyad palace crowned the acropolis.

Bibliography. M. Burdajewicz, "Rabbath-Ammon," *NEAEHL* 4:1243-49; R. H. Dornemann, "Amman," *OEANE* 1:98-102. DONALD H. WIMMER

RABBI (Gk. *rhabbí*), **RABBONI** (*rhabbouní*)
A title of respect (from Heb. *raḇ*, "great" or "big"). By the 1st century C.E. "rabbi" was a loose designa-

tion for a teacher, meaning "my master" or "my great one." This term appears in three of the four Gospels, typically in reference to Jesus.

In Mark only the disciples call Jesus "rabbi," and this address typically follows a miraculous event (Mark 9:5; 11:21; 14:45; "rabboni" at 10:51). In Matthew the only person to address Jesus as "rabbi" is Judas (Matt. 25:26, 49). The remainder of the disciples choose other titles, thus suggesting the polemical natures of Judas and the remaining eleven. In a speech by Jesus, the term seems to refer to one who is a teacher of the law (Matt. 23:7-8). Luke's gentile audience would have found little meaning in a term like "rabbi" that developed in the Jewish culture. Luke prefers Gk. *epistátēs,* "school-master" or a supervising official (Luke 5:5; 8:24, 45; 9:33, 49; 17:13). In the Gospel of John "rabbi" is used by both the disciples and outsiders to designate Jesus (John 1:38, 49; 3:26; 4:31; 6:25; 9:2; 11:8). When Mary Magdalene encounters the risen Christ, she exclaims "rabbouni" (John 20:16). Twice the term is glossed with *didáskalos,* "teacher" (John 1:38; 20:16).

In 1st-century Judaism the word maintained a loose designation, meaning "teacher." The use of rabbi as an official term for an ordained scholar actually belongs to the period following the destruction of the temple in 70 C.E. In the rabbinic literature individuals from the predestruction era (e.g., Hillel and Shammai) are not referred to as "rabbi," while those who are associated with the period following the destruction (e.g., Akiba) are consistently given the title "rabbi."

W. DENNIS TUCKER, JR.

RABBITH (Heb. *rabbîṯ*)
A city in the tribal territory of Issachar (Josh. 19:20; LXX B Gk. *Dabirōn*). It is probably to be identified with Daberath, a levitical town (Josh. 21:28) on the border of Zebulun (19:12).

RABMAG (Heb. *raḇ-māg̱*)
The title of Nergal-sharezer, one of Nebuchadnezzar's officials (Jer. 39:3, 13). The term is derived from the Assyrian title *rab-mūgi,* the exact meaning of which is unknown.

RABSARIS (Heb. *rab-sārîs*)
An Assyrian official. Most scholars hold that the title is a conflation of Akk. *rab-ša-rēšu,* lit., "chief eunuch." The bearer of this title often took the role of military leadership in the absence of the king. The Rabsaris appears among the Assyrian officials who encouraged the capitulation of the Judean king Hezekiah during the siege of Jerusalem (2 Kgs. 18:17; Jer. 39:13). MARK ANTHONY PHELPS

RABSHAKEH (Heb. *rab-šāqēh*)
Title of an Assyrian official, well attested in Akkadian literature (*rab shāqē,* lit., "chief cupbearer"). Though the office of cupbearer is attested in its literal sense in Akkadian, the title denotes a high ranking governmental official. In eponym lists, this title usually follows the king, the *turtānu* (the highest ranking military official), and the *nagir ekalli.* One text may suggest a military function for the *rab shāqē,* while a number of other texts speak of the administrative districts and private holding of these officials. His precise function remains unknown, though his access to power is indubitable (2 Kgs. 18:17–19:8 = Isa. 36:2–37:8).

MARK ANTHONY PHELPS

RACA (Gk. *rhaká*)
An expression of contempt, perhaps a transliteration or derivative of Aram. *rêqāʾ,* "stupid fool" (Matt. 5:22; NRSV "insult" [paraphrase]).

RACAL (Heb. *rāḵāl*)
A place in Judah to which David sent a portion of the spoil taken in battle against the Amalekite soldiers who had destroyed Ziklag (1 Sam. 20:29). The LXX reading "Carmel" (**2**) is probably correct.

RACHEL (Heb. *rāḥēl*)
The younger daughter of Laban, sister of Leah, and one of the wives of Jacob. Her name probably means "ewe" and she was said to be "fair of form and of fair appearance."

Rachel was watching her father's sheep when she was first greeted by Jacob, who had gone to Haran either to escape his brother Esau's anger (Gen. 27:41-45) or to seek a wife from his mother's kin (27:46–28:5). Jacob went to work for Laban, who was also his mother's brother. When asked what his wages should be, Jacob asked for the hand of Rachel, whom he loved. In return for seven years of service, Rachel would become his wife (Gen. 29:15-20).

Although Laban seemed to agree to the terms (Gen. 29:19), when the time came to give Rachel to Jacob Laban substituted Leah. Laban's reason for doing so is heavily ironic: it was not the custom to marry off the younger daughter first. Jacob, who had stolen the blessing from his other brother, himself had to accept as a wife the older daughter rather than the younger he had chosen. Jacob was forced to give another seven years of service for Rachel, although he was allowed to marry her within a week (Gen. 29:28).

Ironically Rachel, the wife Jacob chose and "loved," remained for a long time barren, while her sister Leah, the "hated" one, bore children for Jacob. This led to tension and conflict between the two sisters as Leah bore four sons in succession and Rachel remained childless (Gen. 29:31-35). To overcome this state Rachel offered as wife to Jacob her maid Bilhah, who bore two sons (Gen. 30:1-8). Leah in her turn offered her maid Zilpah, who also bore two sons (Gen. 30:9-13). This practice seems to reflect a legal procedure by which childless women could acquire their handmaids' children by adoption; by resorting to this practice Rachel probably hoped to remove the shame brought by barrenness.

As Rachel's desperation increased, she even traded a night with Jacob for a mandrake, or "love-apple," found by Leah's son Reuben (Gen. 30:14-16). The fruit of the mandrake (or yellow flowering mandragora) was regarded as an aphrodisiac, promoting fertility.

After Leah gave birth to two more sons and a

daughter, Rachel finally bore a son, Joseph, and the conflict, or contest, between the two women ended, although not without Rachel's hope for another son (Gen. 30:24). Although the birth of Joseph occurred soon after Rachel gained possession of the mandrake, the narrator is careful to attribute the conception of Joseph to the fact that "God remembered Rachel, and God heeded her and opened her womb" (Gen. 30:22).

After Joseph's birth Jacob made plans to leave the house of Laban secretly, with the consent of his wives. Rachel took with her the teraphim (small cultic objects, images of gods or possibly of the ancestors), hiding them in the camel's saddle. Rachel's reasons for doing so are unclear, but it is possible that the teraphim represent the blessing, or well-being, of the family, which she takes in compensation for the injustice perpetrated by her father (Gen. 31:14-16). In doing so she very nearly brought death upon herself. Jacob, innocent of either theft or knowledge of theft, promised Laban that whoever had taken the teraphim would die. Rachel used trickery to avoid discovery, claiming that it was the time of her menstrual period.

Rachel's desire for another son was not fulfilled until after Jacob had returned to Bethel (Gen. 35). On the journey from Bethel to Ephrath (Bethlehem), Rachel gave birth to a second son, called Benjamin by his father, but died in childbirth (Gen. 35:16-18). Jacob buried her there on the way, with a pillar to mark the place (Gen. 35:19-20), which later became part of the "territory of Benjamin at Zelzah" (1 Sam. 10:2).

Rachel is remembered in Israel as the one who, together with Leah, built up the house of Israel (Ruth 4:11). The prophet Jeremiah speaks of Rachel weeping in Ramah for her lost children, the northern tribes descended from Joseph and Benjamin (Jer. 31:15). MARILYN J. LUNDBERG

RADDAI (Heb. *radday*)
The fifth son of Jesse, and a brother of David (1 Chr. 2:14).

RAGES (Gk. *Rhagoí;* O.Pers. *Râgâ*)
(also RAGAE)
A city in Media where Tobit hid 10 talents of silver at the home of his kinsman Gabael (Tob. 4:1, 20; cf. 1:14). The angel Raphael guided Tobit's son Tobiah to and from this city to retrieve the money (Tob. 5:5; 6:12[LXX v. 10]; 9:2). Nebuchadnezzar waged war against Arphaxad in the mountainous region of "Ragae" (Jdt. 1:5, 15). The ruins of Rages are immediately S of modern Tehran.

RAGUEL (Gk. *Rhagouḗl*)

1. The father of Sarah (**2**) and father-in-law of Tobias (**1;** Tob. 3:7-8).

2. An archangel (1 En. 20:4; 23:4).

RAHAB (Heb. *rāḥāḇ;* Gk. *Racháb*)

1. A prostitute (Heb. *zōnâ*) whose house adjoined Jericho's outer wall (Josh. 2:15). According to Josh. 2:1-24 the king of Jericho discovered that Joshua's spies (sent to spy out Jericho) were at Rahab's house. When ordered to turn them over, Rahab insisted the two men were gone (though secretly they were hiding on her roof with the stalks of flax). In return for her help, the spies agreed to spare Rahab's family in the coming battle. They told her to tie a crimson cord on the window through which the spies would soon leave; all of her family was to remain in the house during the battle (Josh. 2:18), and she was to tell no one of their visit (v. 14). Rahab lowered the spies through the window, and they returned to Joshua's camp (Josh. 2:22-24). Later, at the battle of Jericho (Josh. 6) Joshua spared Rahab and her family and she "lived in Israel ever since" (v. 25). Rahab is not mentioned in the OT outside Josh. 2 and 6.

In Heb. 11:31 she appears in a list of heroes of the faith. According to Jas. 2:25 Rahab was "justified by works" because she "welcomed the messengers and sent them out by another road." In both references she is identified as "Rahab the prostitute."

Bibliography. P. A. Bird, "The Harlot as Heroine," *Semeia* 46 (1989): 119-39; M. L. Newmann, "Rahab and the Conquest," in *Understanding the Word,* ed. J. T. Butler, E. W. Conrad, and B. C. Ollenburger. JSOTSup 37 (Shefffield, 1985), 167-81.

2. The mother of Salmon and wife of Boaz (Matt. 1:5). She is the second of four women mentioned in Jesus' lineage according to Matthew's genealogy.

3. The primeval dragon of chaos (Heb. *rāhaḇ*) defeated by Yahweh during creation (Job 9:13; 26:12; Ps. 89:10[MT 11]; Isa. 51:9). Yahweh's battle with and victory over this mythological chaos beast represents one of four distinct creation traditions in the OT.

Bibliography. J. Day, *God's Conflict with the Dragon and the Sea.* University of Cambridge Oriental Publications 35 (Cambridge, 1985).

4. A poetic name for Egypt (Ps. 87:4; Isa. 30:7).
LINDA S. SCHEARING

RAHAM (Heb. *raḥam*)
The son of Shema; a Calebite and descendant of Judah (1 Chr. 2:44).

RAINBOW
An arc of colored bands in the sky produced by the double refraction and single reflection of the sun's rays by mist or rain (Heb. *qešeṯ;* Gk. *íris*). This familiar meteorological phenomenon is used symbolically in the Bible to represent God's glorious majesty (Ezek. 1:28; Sir. 43:11; 50:7; Rev. 4:3; 10:1), in visions of his throne room, or as one of his creative splendors. It is most familiar as the sign after the Flood of God's covenant with Noah never again to destroy all life in such a manner (Gen. 9:8-17). In this context Heb. *qešeṯ,* which also indicates a warrior's bow (Ps. 7:12[MT 13]; Lam. 2:4; Hab. 3:9-11), recalls the ancient Near Eastern image of the warrior storm-god (cf. Ps. 18:7-15[8-16]). God is setting his war bow aside in the clouds to indicate a covenant of peace — a divine disarmament by which God has promised to withhold ultimate de-

structive judgment. Instead, part of the responsibility for judgment is given to mankind in the form of self-enforced laws (Gen. 9:4-6).

ROBIN J. DEWITT KNAUTH

RAISIN CAKES

Apparently a delicacy (Cant. 2:5; Isa. 16:7), raisin cakes were said to be distributed to all people of Israel by David after his great celebration that brought the ark of the covenant into Jerusalem (2 Sam. 6:19 = 1 Chr. 16:3). Raisin cakes may also be connected with cultic observance in Hos. 3:1, although there the cakes seem to be dedicated to the worship of a deity or deities other than Yahweh. Yet this should come as no surprise, for the making of grain or bread offerings is a cult act associated with most, if not all, ancient Near Eastern gods and goddesses. The Bible, e.g., describes how cakes were made as offerings to a goddess called by the epithet "Queen of Heaven" (Jer. 7:16-20; 44:15-28). It should be noted, however, that these particular cakes do not seem to contain raisins.

SUSAN ACKERMAN

RAKEM (Heb. *rāqem*)

A son of Sheresh and descendant of Manasseh (1 Chr. 7:16).

RAKKATH (Heb. *raqqaṯ*)

A fortified city in the tribal territory of Naphtali (Josh. 19:35). Talmudic tradition associated it with the site of later Tiberias (201242), but some scholars now place it 2.4 km. (1.5 mi.) N of Tiberias but still on the shore of the Sea of Galilee at Khirbet el-Quneiṭireh/Tel Raqqat (199245).

RAKKON (Heb. *raqqôn*)

A city in the original southern tribal territory of Dan (Josh. 19:46), located perhaps at Tell er-Reqqeit, a short distance N of the Nahr el-ʿAujā on the Mediterranean N of Joppa.

RAM (ANIMAL)

A male sheep (Heb. *'ayîl*), frequently used in sacrifices (e.g., Lev. 5:15; 6:6; cf. 1:10). Rams' skins were used as a covering for the tabernacle (Exod. 36:19), and their horns (Heb. *šôpār*) were used to signal in worship and battle (e.g., Josh. 6; 2 Sam. 6:15). When the obedient Abraham attempted to sacrifice Isaac, the Lord provided a ram as a substitute burnt offering (Gen. 22:13).

RAM (Heb. *rām*) **(PERSON)**

1. A son of Hezron, and ancestor of David (Ruth 4:19; 1 Chr. 2:9-10) and Jesus (Matt. 1:3-4; Gk. *Aram;* cf. Luke 3:33).

2. A son of Jerahmeel of the tribe of Judah (1 Chr. 2:25, 27).

3. An ancestor of Elihu (Job 32:2).

RAMAH (Heb. *rāmâ*)

Common designation for elevated towns and villages in ancient Israel (Heb. "the height").

1. A town allotted to Benjamin (Josh. 18:25), located on the border of Ephraim. It is usually identified with modern er-Râm (172140), 8 km. (5 mi.) N of Jerusalem. Deborah the prophetess would sit under a palm tree between Ramah and Bethel and decide Israelite disputes (Judg. 4:5). Ca. 900 B.C. King Baasha of Israel captured Ramah and fortified the city in an attempt to cut off northern access to Jerusalem. Baasha's occupation of Ramah ended when King Asa of Judah bribed Ben-hadad of Aram to attack Israel (1 Kgs. 15:16-22; 2 Chr. 16:1-6). In the late 8th century both Hosea (Hos. 5:8) and Isaiah (Isa. 10:29) allude to an attack on the city (probably by the Assyrians, though some have suggested the Syro-Ephraimite coalition). Captives seem to have been collected at Ramah for deportation to Babylon (Jer. 40:1). Jeremiah portrays Rachel (the mother of Benjamin whose tomb was nearby) as "weeping for her children," i.e., for the Jews being taken into exile (Jer. 31:15). Matthew applies Jeremiah's lamentation to the sorrow experienced when Herod massacred the babies at Bethlehem (Matt. 2:18). Ramah is mentioned in several postexilic contexts (Ezra 2:26; Neh. 7:30; 11:33).

2. Ramah of the Negeb; a town in the territory of Simeon (also called Baalath-beer; Josh. 19:8). David sent some of the plunder taken from the Amalekites to a town near Ziklag called Ramoth of the Negeb (1 Sam. 30:27), undoubtedly the same place. The site has not been certainly identified.

3. A village near the northern border of Asher, in the vicinity of Tyre (Josh. 19:29). Modern Ramieh (180280) has sometimes been identified as the biblical site, though this is uncertain.

4. A fortified city in Naphtali (Josh. 19:36), usually identified with modern Khirbet Zeitûn er-Râmeh/Khirbet Jûl (187259), 13 km. (8 mi.) SW of Safed.

5. The hometown of Samuel. Many scholars equate Samuel's birthplace with Ramah of Benjamin, arguing that Samuel's father Elkanah was a descendant of Zuph (1 Sam. 1:1), a Levite of the Kohathites who settled in northern Benjamin (9:5; cf. Josh. 21:5; 1 Chr. 6:22-26, 35, 66-70), or that Ramah (near the border of Ephraim) was inhabited by Zuphites. Others understand 1 Sam. 1:1 to mean that Ramathaim ("two heights"), usually called Ramah (cf. v. 19; 2:11), was located in the territory of Ephraim. The latter has sometimes been associated with NT Arimathea, modern Rentîs (151159; cf. Eusebius *Onom.* 32.21-23). Samuel was born in Ramah (1 Sam. 1:19-20), grew up in Shiloh (v. 24), but after the tabernacle was moved from Shiloh returned to Ramah where he spent most of his adult life (7:17; 25:1).

6. A shortened form of the name for Transjordanian Ramoth-gilead (2 Kgs. 8:29 = 2 Chr. 22:6).

STEPHEN R. MILLER

RAMATH-LEHI (Heb. *rāmaṯ lĕḥî*)

Name given to the place ("hill of the jawbone") where Samson killed 1000 Philistines using a jawbone as a weapon (Judg. 15:17).

RAMATH-MIZPEH (Heb. *rāmaṯ hammiṣpeh*)
A border town of Gad, named along with Heshbon and Betonim (Josh. 13:26), and possibly the home of Jephthah. This town has been identified with a number of sites including Khirbet Jelʿad, Khirbet eṣ-ṣSire, Khirbet el-Qarʾa, and ʿAraq el-Emir. Tell Rāmîth is a possibility if Mizpah in Gilead and Ramoth-gilead are to be equated. PAUL J. RAY, JR.

RAMATHAIM-ZOPHIM
(Heb. *rāmāṯayim ṣôp̱îm*)
The home of Elkanah, Samuel's father (1 Sam. 1:1 MT; NRSV "Ramathaim").
See RAMAH **5.**

RAMATHITE (Heb. *rāmāṯî*)
The gentilic designation of Shimei (**13**), overseer of David's vineyards, indicating that he was from one of the places named Ramah (1 Chr. 27:27).

RAMESES (Egyp. *Rʿ-ms-sw*) **(PERSON)**
A royal name used by a number of Egyptian kings of the 19th and 20th (or Ramesside) Dynasties of the New Kingdom.

1. Rameses I. General and vizier of Horemheb, the last king of the 18th Dynasty, who became the successor of Horemheb and the founder of the 19th Dynasty. He is credited with a reign of two years (1306-1305 B.C.E.) and was succeeded by his son Seti I (1305-1290).

2. Rameses II. The son of Seti I, who reigned for some 67 years (1290-1224). In the fifth year of his reign he fought a major campaign against the Hittites, and in his 21st year he concluded a treaty with the Hittite king Ḫattušili which established Egypt's control over Canaan. The treaty has survived in Egyptian in inscriptions in the temple at Karnak and in the Ramesseum and in a Babylonian cuneiform copy recovered from the Hittite capital. Rameses was also responsible for monumental construction projects, including colossal statues; the temples at Abu Simbel; and his mortuary temple, the Ramesseum. Some interpreters identify the cities of Pithom and Rameses (Exod. 1:11) with Per-Atum and Per-Rameses in the eastern Delta and suggest that Rameses II may have been the king of Egypt at the time of the Israelite Exodus. A monument erected by his son and successor Merneptah (1224-1204) includes the first known extrabiblical reference to Israel as a people in the territory of Canaan.

3. Rameses III (1183-1152). The son of Setnakht, who had founded the 20th Dynasty and ruled ca. two years. During his reign he dealt with incursions by Libyans and others into Egyptian territory. Reliefs at the mortuary temple of Rameses III at Medinet Habu depict his battles against the Sea Peoples in the eighth year of his reign. One of these groups, called the Peleset by the Egyptians, settled on the southern coastal plain of Canaan and are known in the OT as the Philistines and perhaps also the Pelethites of David's bodyguard (2 Sam. 8:18).

4. Rameses IV-XI. Rameses III was followed on the throne by a series of kings who also took the name Rameses and who ruled until 1085. During the reigns of these kings the power of the Egyptian Empire declined, and there were growing internal problems. A number of factors were probably involved in the decreasing effectiveness of the Egyptian monarchy evidenced during the latter years of the 20th Dynasty, including an unusual pattern of succession — a number of elderly kings with relatively short reigns who followed Rameses III, administrative inefficiency, and changing relationships between the king and the civil government and the army.

Colossi of Rameses II. Exterior of Great Temple, Abu Simbel (Courtesy of the Oriental Institute of the University of Chicago)

Bibliography. K. A. Kitchen, *Pharaoh Triumphant: The Life and Times of Ramesses II* (Warminster, 1983); A. B. Knapp, *The History and Culture of Ancient Western Asia and Egypt* (Chicago, 1988); B. G. Trigger et al., *Ancient Egypt: A Social History* (Cambridge, 1983). KEITH L. EADES

RAMESES (Heb. *Ramʿamsēs*) **(PLACE)**
(also RAAMSES)
The region in which the Hebrews settled during their Egyptian sojourn (Gen. 47:11) and the name of a store-city they were forced to build (Exod. 1:11, Raamses). Rameses was the starting point for the Exodus (Exod. 12:37; Num. 33:3, 5). The city was named after Rameses II of the 19th Dynasty (Egyp. *pr-rʿ-ms-sw*, "House of Rameses"). It was during this time that the capital of Egypt was moved from Thebes in the south to Rameses in the Delta.

Rameses was long identified with Tanis (Zoan; modern San el-Hagar) based on the presence of numerous monuments of Rameses II, but the site was unoccupied before the 21st Dynasty and the monuments were found to have been moved there from other locations. Earlier scholars had suggested Tell er-Raṭabeh and Pelusium. Current consensus places Rameses at Qantir (Khatana), 24 km. (15 mi.) S of San el-Hagar and 14 km. (9 mi.) N of Fagus. Evidence of occupation includes palaces and administrative buildings of the Ramesside period. Important finds in the surrounding area indicate that the city of Rameses extended out from Qantir which was the center and included such sites at Tell el-Dabʿa (location of Avaris, the Hyksos capital) and Tell Abu el-Shafiʿa.

Bibliography. M. Bietak, "Avaris and Piramesse," *Proceedings of the British Academy* 65 (1979): 225-89; *Avaris, the Capital of the Hyksos* (London, 1996); E. P. Uphill, "Pithom and Raamses: Their Location and Significance," *JNES* 27 (1968): 291-316; 28 (1969): 15-39. LAWRENCE A. SINCLAIR

RAMIAH (Heb. *ramyâ*)
An Israelite of the family of Parosh; a returnee from exile compelled to divorce his foreign wife (Ezra 10:25).

RAMOTH (Heb. *rā'môṯ, rāmōṯ, rā'mōṯ*)

1. Ramoth in Gilead (Deut. 4:43; Josh. 20:8; 21:38; 1 Chr. 6:80[MT 65]).

See RAMOTH-GILEAD.

2. Ramoth of the Negeb, a Simeonite town to which David sent spoils from the Amalekite raiders of Ziklag (1 Sam. 30:27).

See RAMAH **2.**

3. A levitical city in the tribal territory of Issachar, assigned to the Gershomites (1 Chr. 6:73[58]). It was probably the same as Jarmuth (**2;** Josh. 21:29) and Remeth (19:21).

RAMOTH-GILEAD (Heb. *rāmôṯ [hag]gilʿāḏ*)
A Transjordanian city of refuge located in the eastern portion of Gad's territory (Deut. 4:43; Josh. 20:8; 21:38).

Ben-hadad of Syria apparently captured the city from Israel in the middle of the 9th century B.C.E. (1 Kgs. 20, 22). The king of Israel (probably Ahab) subsequently asked Jehoshaphat of Judah to assist him in recovering the city from Aram (1 Kgs. 22:3), over the objections of the prophet Micaiah, who predicted failure (vv. 15-17). A second allied attempt to recover Ramoth-gilead was undertaken by Jehoram of Israel and Ahaziah of Judah against Ben-hadad's successor Hazael, some 12 years later (ca. 840; 2 Kgs. 8:28-29), although Jehoram was wounded in the attempt. The resulting confusion in Israel (which led to the rise of Jehu) enabled Hazael to recapture not only Ramoth-gilead, but also the rest of Israel's holdings in Transjordan (2 Kgs. 10:32-33).

There is no consensus on the modern identity of Ramoth-gilead, although Tell el-Ḥusn (232210; 16 km. [10 mi.] SW of Ramtha) and Tell Rāmîth (244210; 7 km. [4 mi.] S of Ramtha, near the modern border of Syria) have been proposed. Tell Rāmîth has the advantage of etymological ties with Ramoth, a strategic location as a "height," and Iron Age pottery that dates from the time of Solomon to that of Tiglath-pileser III. RANDALL W. YOUNKER

RANSOM
A price paid to release a captive or seized property, or the act of procuring release in this manner. Heb. *kōper* (from *kpr,* "to cover"; cf. Akk. *kapāru,* "wipe off") is most often used in the positive sense of ransom money (e.g., Exod. 21:30; Num. 35:31-32; Isa. 43:3; cf. Ps. 49:7-8[MT 8-9]). Negatively, the term can refer to a "bribe" (so NRSV, 1 Sam. 12:3; Amos 5:12). Though among the Greeks Gk. *lýtron* could refer to the redemption of a slave, in NT usage it specifies also "atonement money." Matt. 20:28 = Mark 10:45 clarify the substitutionary nature of Christ's atonement as "a ransom for many" (cf. Isa. 53:4-12; cf. 1 Tim. 2:6).

See REDEMPTION. MICHAEL SPENCE

RAPHA (Heb. *rāpā'*)
The fifth son of Benjamin (1 Chr. 8:2). Rapha is omitted from the genealogy at Gen. 46:21.

RAPHAEL (Gk. *Raphaḗl*)
An angel, first mentioned in two postexilic Jewish books, Tobit and 1 Enoch. In 1 Enoch Raphael ("God heals") is prominent in the angelic hierarchy (1 En. 20:3; 40:2, 8–9), and is one of the angels responsible for binding the armies of Azazel and casting them into the valley of fire (54:6). Tobit depicts Raphael along comparable lines, as "one of the seven angels who stand ready and enter before the glory of the Lord" (Tob. 12:15). He follows the demon Asmodeus to the remote parts of Egypt and binds him there (Tob. 8:3).

Tobit, however, goes further in its depiction of angelic activity entering the human sphere. Raphael is dispatched by God in answer to the prayers of Tobit and Sarah "to heal them" (Tob. 3:17). He appears in human form as Azariah ("Yah helps"), and aids Tobias as guide, servant, mentor, and matchmaker. Toward the end of the book, when Tobit and Tobias are about to pay him for his services, Raphael reveals his true identity to them (Tob. 12:6-21). He exhorts them to piety, explains that he only appeared to eat and drink, commissions them to write an account of what has happened, and ascends to heaven while Tobit and Tobias praise God. WILL SOLL

RAPHAH (Heb. *rāpâ*) (also REPHAIAH)
A Benjaminite, son of Binea and descendant of King Saul (1 Chr. 8:37). At 1 Chr. 9:43 he is called Rephaiah (**4**).

RAPHON (Gk. *Raphṓn*)
A city near one of the major sources of the Yarmuk River, ca. 55.5 km. (34.5 mi.) directly E of the upper Jordan as it enters the Sea of Galilee; modern er-Râfeh. The Ammonite general Timothy encamped with his forces opposite the city, but Judas Maccabeus crossed the wadi and defeated him (1 Macc. 5:37).

RAPHU (Heb. *rāp̄ûʾ*)
A Benjaminite, father of the spy Palti (Num. 13:9).

RAPTURE
The "catching up" (from Lat. *raptio*) of the saints to meet the Lord in the air, mentioned by Paul in 1 Thess. 4:17. Paul's comments in 1 Thess. 4:14-18 are prompted by the expressions of excessive grief by some in the young congregation at the loss of loved ones. He comforts them by deepening their hope of resurrection, which he assures them will not disadvantage the deceased at all, but will mark the reunion of all believers and their permanent abiding with the Lord in resurrected glory.

Clement of Alexandria curiously referred Paul's statements to the experience of the believer at the time of death, but the association with the Parousia is evident in the text and is recognized by the great majority of interpreters. In the 18th century J. N. Darby popularized, though evidently did not originate, the notion of a "secret rapture" to come without warning or accompaniment, leaving the world bereft of Christians to face the antichrist, seven years of tribulation, and the wrath of God. All this would precede Christ's return to earth and the ensuing millennial reign. Darby's understanding has become a hallmark of dispensational premillennialism.

Paul, however, apparently refers to the rapture again in 2 Thess. 2:1-2 as "our being gathered together with him" (cf. Matt. 13:30; 24:31), which he links to "the coming of Christ" and "the day of the Lord." This means the rapture too awaits, as 2 Thess. 2:3 indicates, the coming "apostasy" or rebellion and the advent of the "man of lawlessness." The rapture of the saints then is that aspect of the return of Christ which effects the fathering of all believers, those alive at that time and those who have gone before in death, to be with the Lord forever.

Bibliography. E. Best, *The First and Second Epistles to the Thessalonians.* BNTC 13 (Peabody, 1993); E. R. Sandeen, *The Roots of Fundamentalism: British and American Millenarianism, 1800-1930* (Grand Rapids, 1978); G. Vos, *The Pauline Eschatology* (Grand Rapids, 1961).
CHARLES E. HILL

RAS SHAMRA
See UGARIT.

RASSIS (Gk. *Rhássis*)
A city that was plundered by Holofernes' army (Jdt. 2:23; NRSV "the Rassisites"). The author appears to place it somewhere in the region of Cilicia. Some consider Rassis a corruption of the name Tarsus (Vulg. *Tharsis*), while others believe it is the Rossos (modern Arsos) mentioned by Strabo (*Geog.* 14.5.19; 16.2.8) and Ptolemy (*Geog.* 5.14).
H. WAYNE HOUSE

RATHAMIN (Gk. *Rháthamin*)
One of the districts taken from Samaria and given by Demetrius to Jonathan Maccabeus ca. 150 B.C.E. (1 Macc. 11:34). The place is otherwise unknown, but some scholars identify it (through a transposition of consonants) with Ramathaim(-zophim), the birthplace of Samuel.
See RAMAH **5**. BENJAMIN C. CHAPMAN

RAVEN
A large, strong, black bird ca. 61 cm. (2 ft.) in length with a large 7.6 cm. (3 in.) beak. The raven (Heb. *ʿōrēḇ;* Gk. *kórax*) is widely distributed throughout Europe, Asia, and Africa. It feeds on birds and small animals, as well as seeds, berries, and fruits. It is also partially a carrion eater and was designated as an unclean bird probably because of this fact and the wide variety of its diet (Lev. 11:15; Deut. 14:14). Palestine has eight different species of ravens (order Passeres). These birds are particularly loud with their caws. Noah sent out a raven to find dry land because of its strength of long flight and ability to feed on many different sources (Gen. 8:7). Ravens fed Elijah when he was hiding from Ahab (1 Kgs. 17:4-6). This would have been contrary to the pattern of the raven, which usually took care of itself even to the neglect of its young (Job 38:41; Ps. 147:9). Jesus taught that God's care of the raven was an indication of God's greater value of human beings (Luke 12:24). JOHN A. MCLEAN

REAIAH (Heb. *rĕʾāyâ*) (also HAROEH)

1. A Judahite, the son of Shobal (1 Chr. 4:2). He is called Haroeh at 1 Chr. 2:52.

2. A Reubenite, the son of Micah of the family of Joel (1 Chr. 5:5).

3. A temple servant whose descendants returned with Zerubbabel from exile in Babylon (Ezra 2:47 = Neh. 7:50).

REBA (Heb. *reḇaʿ*)
One of the five kings of the Midianites, all vassals of King Sihon of the Amorites, who were killed by the Israelites in war (Num. 31:8; Josh. 13:21). His territory was later assigned to the Reubenites.

REBEKAH (Heb. *riḇqâ*)
The wife of Isaac and the mother of Jacob and Esau; daughter of Bethuel and sister of Laban (Gen. 22:23; 24:29). When Abraham sends his servant to find a wife for Isaac from his Mesopotamian homeland, Rebekah is encountered at a well outside the city of Nahor (Gen. 24:11-49). She is described as beautiful, and her actions reveal her not to be a passive woman. Initially, her brother and father arrange with the servant to send Rebekah as a wife for Isaac. Ultimately, though, the text suggests that Rebekah chooses for herself to return with Abraham's servant and marry Isaac (Gen. 24:58). The first encounter between the betrothed, Isaac and Rebekah, reads like a scene from a romance novel. Isaac readily accepts his new bride, and the text says that "he loved her" (Gen. 24:67). After a prayer by her husband, Rebekah's barrenness is overcome and she conceives. During a difficult pregnancy, she prays to God and is told that she will give birth to two sons, two nations, and that the elder will serve the younger. After her children are born, Rebekah recognizes

the differences between the two boys. She is fond of the younger one, Jacob, but Isaac loves Esau more (Gen. 25:21-28). When she overhears Jacob telling Esau that he is going to give his oldest son a blessing, Rebekah devises a plan to trick her husband into giving the blessing to Jacob instead. She instructs her son of everything he is to do in order to pull the ruse on his father, and her plan succeeds (Gen. 27:5-40). When Rebekah sees the intense anger of Esau toward Jacob, she decides that she must do something to protect her son. She convinces Isaac that Jacob should marry a woman from her own land. So, Jacob is sent away to find a wife, and his life is temporarily spared (Gen. 27:41-46). After this final act of insurance for her favorite son, Rebekah disappears from the narrative. Her death is not mentioned. In Gen. 49:31, however, her burial place is identified as being in the family cave in Machpelah, along with Abraham, Sarah, Isaac, Jacob, and Leah. Through her trickery and extraordinary insight, Rebekah insures that the word of the Lord concerning her two sons, given to her during her pregnancy, is ultimately fulfilled. She is recognized as one of the four matriarchs of the Israelites.

Bibliography. S. P. Jeansonne, *The Women of Genesis* (Minneapolis, 1990); S. Niditch, "Genesis," in *The Women's Bible Commentary*, ed. C. A. Newsom and S. Ringe (Louisville, 1992), 13-29.

LISA W. DAVISON

RECAH (Heb. *rēḵâ*)
The home of a branch of the Judahites (1 Chr. 4:12). The location of this place is unknown, and the text may well be corrupt. A major recension of the LXX suggests that the name referred to is Rechab, in which case it might be not a place name but a gentilic form designating those listed here as Rechabites (cf. 1 Chr. 2:55).

RECHAB (Heb. *rēḵāḇ*)

1. A son of Rimmon of Beeroth who with his brother Baanah murdered Ishbosheth the son of Saul (2 Sam. 4:2, 5-8). For this act Rechab and Baanah were executed by David (2 Sam. 4:9-12).

2. The father of Jehonadab/Jonadab, whose descendants were the Rechabites (2 Kgs. 10:15, 23; 1 Chr. 2:55; Jer. 35).

3. The father of Malchijah, the postexilic ruler of the district of Beth-haccherem (Neh. 3:14). He may be the same as **2** above.

RECHABITES (Heb. *rēḵāḇîm*)
Followers of Jehonadab, who joined Jehu in his revolt against the house of Ahab (2 Kgs. 10:15-17); named after Rechab, the father or ancestor of Jehonadab. During the reign of Jehoiakim the Rechabites are described as a religiously conservative group (Jer. 35), characterized by a vow not to drink wine and strong opposition against Baalism and some practices of a settled agricultural society. Jeremiah uses the Rechabites as an example of religious obedience, in stark contrast to the people of Israel and Judah. The Rechabites also appear in genealogical lists where they seem to be associated with the Kenites (1 Chr. 2:55; 4:11-12). Also, a pseudepigraphon variously titled The History of the Rechabites or The Story of Zosimus contains an expanded exegesis of Jer. 35.

Developmentalist anthropological theory used the "doctrine of cultural survivals" to interpret the Rechabites' abstention from wine, their dwelling in tents, and their disdain of agriculture as remnants of a much older nomadic way of life. Diffusionist theories led to the rejection of the Rechabites as survivors of earlier nomadism and reinterpreted them as the result of the contact and interaction between different groups within a given culture. Their way of life is compared to that of the prophets, abstaining because alcohol would impair their prophetic capacity and itinerating in protest of the evils of urban society. The occurrence of Rechabites in genealogies gave rise to the view that they were a guild of ancient metalworkers, organized on the model of families and known for their endogamous lines and lengthy genealogies.

Comparative research on the role of ritual self-demarcation as a substitute for actual power and the need for symbolical self-assertion by marginalized communities may provide more satisfactory hypotheses in the future to understand the enigmatic Rechabites.

Bibliography. F. S. Frick, "The Rechabites Reconsidered," *JBL* 90 (1971): 279-87; C. Knights, "Who Were the Rechabites?" *ExpTim* 107 (1995-96): 137-40; K. van der Toorn, "Ritual Resistance and Self-Assertion: The Rechabites in Early Israelite Religion," in *Pluralism and Identity*, ed. J. Platvoet and van der Toorn (Leiden, 1995), 229-59.

HENDRIK L. BOSMAN

RECONCILIATION
To "reconcile" or bring about "reconciliation" is to restore harmony or friendship between two entities formerly divided. In the biblical tradition, reconciliation denotes the fundamental fact of a restored relationship, either between human persons, among various elements in the cosmos, or between humans and God.

This biblical idea assumes that relationships have indeed been broken, as the narrative of Gen. 3 so poignantly relates. In that story, moreover, all relationships of human existence stand in need of reconciliation: relations between creatures and their Creator, gender relationships made hostile by the effects of sin, and the relationships between human creatures and the earth itself which have been marred as well by the sin of the garden.

The covenant people of Israel understood reconciliation primarily in a cultic sense whereby "sin offerings and guilt offerings" would restore the harmony between themselves and God, a harmony which had been broken by sin and covenant violation. Heb. *kāpar*, "to cover, make atonement," conveys the intent of these cultic offerings (Lev. 8:15; 16:1-34; Ezek. 45:15, 17, 20) to purify and restore the people's relationship with God. In the OT acts of reconciliation or atonement are performed by the people through the mediation of the priests.

In the NT reconciliation also denotes a changed relationship in which formerly estranged persons or elements experience a restored harmony. Christians should seek reconciliation between themselves and any estranged community member, especially before offering a gift at the altar (Matt. 5:24) or going to settle disputes before a magistrate (Luke 12:58).

The Pauline tradition, however, develops the theme of reconciliation more fully than any other biblical texts. Paul can use the term "reconciliation" in a very human way, as in 1 Cor. 7:11 when urging spouses to be reconciled with one another. But, for Paul, the dominant emphasis falls not on efforts at human reconciliation but on what God has done in the world, through Christ. This Pauline conviction appears especially in 2 Cor. 5:14-21; Rom. 5:8-11; 11:15 (cf. Col. 1:20-22; Eph. 2:12-17).

Christ's death and resurrection have redefined and restored all relationships in the "new creation" (2 Cor. 5:17); God, now, has become the perfect Reconciler. Through Christ, God has restored all people to a right relationship with the divine Creator and has summoned every believer to cooperate in this "ministry of reconciliation" (2 Cor. 5:18). The whole cosmos now stands reconciled before God, invited into this reconciliation: "in Christ God was reconciling the world" (2 Cor. 5:19). In Romans Paul draws on the sacrificial language of his Jewish heritage to understand Christ's atoning death as the perfect act of reconciliation (Rom. 5:10-11) effected by God, in and through Christ.

Finally, Colossians and Ephesians draw the implications of God's act of reconciliation to their cosmic heights. In Christ, God was reconciling "all things, whether on earth or in heaven" (Col. 1:20) so as to enable a "holy and blameless and irreproachable" offering (v. 22). For the author of Ephesians, the fundamental religious division between Jew and Gentile has finally been reconciled; Christ has himself become the "peace between us" (Eph. 2:14). The effect of this reconciliation is nothing less than the creation of a "new humanity" (Eph. 2:15) built on Christ, the one who "fills all in all" (1:23).

Bibliography. R. J. Schreiter, *Reconciliation: Mission and Ministry in a Changing Social Order* (Maryknoll, 1996).

BARBARA E. BOWE

RECORDER

A prominent administrative position in the Hebrew government similar to that of the Egyptian grand vizier. Though specific duties are not described in the biblical record, the recorder (Heb. *mazkîr*) served as a secretary of state, advising the king on important governmental affairs. The office was held by Jehoshaphat during the reign of David and Solomon (2 Sam. 8:16; 20:24; 1 Kgs. 4:3; 1 Chr. 18:15). Joah, the son of Asaph, served under Hezekiah and represented the king in his negotiations with the Rabshakeh (2 Kgs. 18:18, 37 = Isa. 36:3, 22). Another Joah, the son of Joahaz, served under Josiah and was placed in charge of temple repairs (2 Chr. 34:8).

Bibliography. D. J. Elazar, *Covenant and Polity in Biblical Israel* (New Brunswick, 1995); D. R. Gordan, *Old Testament in Its Cultural, Historical, and Religious Context* (1985, repr. Lanham, 1994).

A. PERRY HANCOCK

RED

Red (Heb. *'āḏōm;* Gk. *pyrrós*) may encompass shades as divergent as brown, as well as the bright colors yellow and pink. Hence, the brownish color of animal hide is described as red (Num. 19:2; Zech. 1:8; 6:2), as well as the yellowish-brown color of lintel soup (Gen. 25:30) and a person's healthy countenance (Cant. 5:10; Lam. 4:7). Some OT passages refer to objects dyed red, such as ram skins (Exod. 25:5) and shields (Nah. 2:3[MT 4]). Gen. 25:25-30 makes a wordplay with the adj. *'aḏmônî,* "reddish," and Esau, a figure associated with Edom *('ěḏōm),* the land of red clay. Isa. 63:1-2 has a similar wordplay with Edom *('ěḏôm)* and red *('adōm).* Over time new terms were introduced to create finer nuances of color.

In the NT red describes the color of the evening sky, a popular folk image indicating fair weather to come (Matt. 16:2-3). The book of Revelation includes red as one of four primary colors in apocalyptic imagery, representing war, bloodshed, and the forces of evil (Rev. 6:4; 12:3).

Bibliography. A. Brenner, *Colour Terms in the Old Testament.* JSOTSup 21 (Sheffield, 1982).

J. EDWARD OWENS

RED SEA

The large body of water which extends south from the Sinai Peninsula to the Strait of Bab el-Mandeb, separating northeastern Africa from the Arabian Peninsula. The term does not appear in the OT or the NT (cf. Isa. 11:15, "sea of Egypt"). In the LXX Gk. *thálassa erythrá* ("Red Sea") translates Heb. *yam sûp,* "Reed Sea," which refers to a body of water E of the Nile Delta. Herotodus (*Hist.* 2.158) and Strabo (*Geog.* 17.1.25-26) both use the term "Red Sea" to include the Gulf of Suez.

The basin of the sea was formed by the geological fault system extending north through the Jordan River Valley, Syria, and into Turkey. From the head of the Gulf of Suez to the strait is ca. 2175 km. (1350 mi.), and the widest point is 370 km. (230 mi.). In places the sea is more than 1830 m. (6000 ft.) deep. No rivers empty into the sea, but the depth is stabilized, despite severe evaporation, by water from the Gulf of Adan through the strait. Coral reefs parallel both shores, but with breaks to allow access to the harbors. The name Red Sea comes from the red algae bloom in the summer giving the sea a reddish-brown color.

Solomon conducted trade on the Red Sea with both south Arabia and Africa. The queen of Sheba visited Solomon and brought gifts of spices, gold, and precious stones (1 Kgs. 10:1-10, 13). From later discoveries it appears that south Arabia also exported incense and frankincense. Solomon's ships also traded with Ophir in Africa, for gold, silver, ivory, apes, and baboons (1 Kgs. 10:11, 22).

Identification of the "Sea of Reeds" crossed by the Israelites as they left Egypt (e.g., Exod. 15:4, 22; Deut. 11:4; Josh. 4:23; 24:6; Ps. 136:13, 15) remains uncertain. Scholars have variously proposed the Bitter Lakes region, Lake Menzaleh, Lake Sorbonis, and the Gulf of Suez as possible sites.

Bibliography. M. S. Abu al-'Izz, *Landforms of Egypt* (Cairo, 1971); C. L. Drake and R. W. Girdler, "A Geophysical Study of the Red Sea," *Geophysical Journal* 8 (1964): 473-95; Girdler, "The Relationship of the Red Sea to the East Africa Rift System," *Quarterly Journal of the Geological Society* 114 (1958): 79-105; A. F. Mohamed, "The Egyptian Exploration of the Red Sea," *Proceedings of the Royal Society of London* B/128 (1940): 306-16; W. Phillips, *Qataban and Sheba* (New York, 1955).

LAWRENCE A. SINCLAIR

REDEMPTION

Release from legal obligation or deliverance from desperate circumstances, closely connected with a payment necessary to effect that release. In the OT the primary words used to express this concept are Heb. *pāḏâ* and *gā'al.* The NT uses primarily cognates of Gk. *lytróō* and *agorázō.*

In the Mosaic law, the basic idea is that of monetary payments required to free persons or property from an obligation. It is applied to the redemption of the firstborn (Exod. 13:11-15; 34:19-20; Num. 3:44-51; 18:15-17), to the redemption of property (Lev. 25:23-34; Ruth 4:1-12), and to the redemption of individuals (Lev. 25:35-55). It is also applied to the process of securing release from a difficult vow or a tithe (Lev. 27:1-33).

The idea of release from obligation continues in the Prophets and Writings (Ps. 49:7-8[MT 8-9]; Jer. 32:7-8). More frequently, however, the word is synonymous with the concept of rescuing or delivering (Ps. 25:22; 26:11; 44:26[27]; Mic. 4:10), occasionally in parallel with the notion of "ransom" (Ps. 49:7[8]; Hos. 13:14). This deliverance may be from any number of circumstances, including famine and war (Job 5:20), oppression and violence (Ps. 72:14), adversaries (Job 6:23; Ps. 69:18[19]; Jer. 15:21), Sheol and death (Ps. 49:15[16]; Hos. 13:14), and iniquities (Ps. 130:7-8). Above all, God is the redeemer (Ps. 19:14[15]; 78:35; Isa. 41:14; 44:6; 49:26; 50:2) who will come to Zion (Isa. 59:20) to bring rest to Israel and judgment to her foes (Jer. 50:34).

These OT emphases are present in the NT, but they are applied foremost to what Christ has done for the believer (1 Cor. 1:30) and only secondarily to what God will do for Israel (Luke 1:68; 2:38; 24:21). The concept of legal obligation is clear in that the believer is "bought with a price" (1 Cor. 6:20; 1 Pet. 1:18-19; Rev. 5:9; 14:3-4) and so is "redeemed from the curse of the law" (Gal. 3:13; 4:5). The idea of ransom is present in Jesus' statement that he came to "give his life a ransom for many" (Matt. 20:28; Mark 10:45) and in Paul's affirmation that Jesus "gave himself a ransom for all" (1 Tim. 2:6). The idea of deliverance has both past and present aspects. Jesus' death has accomplished redemption in securing the forgiveness of sins (Rom. 3:24; Eph. 1:7; Col. 1:14; Titus 2:14; Heb. 9:11-15). Yet believers still await the redemption of the body at his return (Luke 21:28; Rom. 8:23; Eph. 1:14; 4:30).

JOHN D. HARVEY

REED, RUSH

Water-abiding plants that the Bible refers to by various names. Heb. *qāneh* is usually translated reed but also has the specific meaning of a measuring rod equal to 6 cubits (Ezek. 40:3, 5); thus from it we have the word "canon" to denote the standard holy texts of the Bible. Gk. *kálamos* follows the Hebrew in duality of meaning: it is the name of the plant Jesus was given to resemble a scepter when he was mocked (Matt. 27:29), and it is a unit of measure (Rev. 11, 21).

Reeds grow in swamps, marshes, and next to bodies of water. They are hollow and can be over 3 m. (10 ft.) tall. Reeds are easily bruised, bent, and broken (Luke 7:24). The Rabshakeh of Assyria compared Egypt to a broken reed, "which will pierce the hand of anyone who leans on it" (2 Kgs. 18:21 = Isa. 36:6). Reeds that grow in the Near East include *Arundo donax* and several species of *Phragmites.* Heb. *'āḥû, 'agmôn, 'ăḡam, 'ēḇeh,* and *sûp̱* also refer to marsh-dwelling plants and have been inconsistently translated both reed and rush. Rushes are similar to reeds. The cattail (*Typha australis* sp.) is one rushlike plant that thrives in Israel and Egypt.

Rushes and reeds were utilized in a number of industries. Mats, baskets, shoes, pens, brushes, and even houses were constructed of these water plants. One reed, the papyrus (*Cyperus papyrus* L.) was processed into paper. Papyrus is also buoyant and therefore was used in boat construction (Isa. 18:2). The baby Moses was placed in a basket of papyrus *(gōme'),* which floated on the Nile (Exod. 2:3-5). The biblical name for the Red Sea is *yam sûp̱,* or Sea of Reeds.

MEGAN BISHOP MOORE

REEDS, SEA OF

See RED SEA.

REELAIAH (Heb. *rěʿēlāyâ*)
(also RAAMIAH; RESAIAH)

A prominent Israelite who returned from captivity with Zerubbabel (Ezra 2:2). He is called Raamiah at Neh. 7:7 and Resaiah at 1 Esdr. 5:8.

REFUGE

Shelter or relief from danger or anxiety. The OT concept owes its richness to several Hebrew words: *miśgāḇ,* a high rock (e.g., Isa. 33:16); *mā'ōnâ,* a secure dwelling place (e.g., Deut. 33:27); *mānôs,* a place to flee to (Ps. 142:4[MT 5]); and *maḥseh,* a shelter (Isa. 4:6).

Zion is a refuge against invaders (Isa. 14:32); likewise righteous kings and princes can be a refuge for the people as a whole (32:2). On a personal level, the "fear of the Lord" is a source of confidence and refuge (Prov. 14:26); it is foolish to seek a "refuge of lies" (Isa. 28:15-17).

The Psalms proclaim that God himself is ultimately our only refuge (e.g., Ps. 14:6; 46:1[2]; 62:7-8[8-9]; 71:7). To affirm that "God is my refuge" is often a turning point in the prayers of the Psalms, moving the supplicant into confidence and praise (e.g., Ps. 18:2, 30[3, 31]; 34:8, 22[9, 23]) and a life of positive testimony to the power of God (71:7; 73:28).

Surprisingly perhaps, refuge is not as prominent in the NT. Peace and restoration are certainly a part of the gospel message (Luke 12:32), but the emphasis tends to be placed on the active witness and ministry that arises from it. Jesus offers rest (Matt. 11:28-30) not as a hiding place but as a yoke. The "refuge" of Christians is in the hope of the eschatological triumph of God in Christ (Heb. 6:18).

DAVID A. DORMAN

REGEM (Heb. *regem*)
A son of Jahdai of the Calebite clan of Judah (1 Chr. 2:47).

REGEM-MELECH (Heb. *regem melek̠*)
An inhabitant of Bethel who was sent with Sharezer to Jerusalem to ask the priests and prophets whether certain days of fasting and repentance were still in effect (Zech. 7:2). The Peshiṭta suggests an original Hebrew form *rab̠-mag hammelek̠*, a title adapted from Akkadian (cf. Jer. 39:3, 13).

REGENERATION
The regeneration of life, conceived literally or figuratively, is a recurrent theme in Jewish and Christian literature, especially in contexts of recovery after personal or national catastrophe and/or in cosmic, eschatological contexts. Technically, "regeneration" translates Gk. *palingenesía* ("to create again"). This term, which occurs only twice in the NT (Matt. 19:28; Titus 3:5), is strongly attested in Stoic teachings about cyclical conflagration and regeneration of the cosmos. Philo uses the same term to refer to the restoration of life to the earth after the Flood (*Life of Moses* 2.65), and Josephus writes of the regeneration of the people Israel after exile (*Ant.* 2.66). It is likely that Matthew, following Jewish apocalyptic sensibilities, envisions cosmic destruction and renewal once and for all at the last judgment. In Titus the focus is personal, not cosmic: salvation comes to the individual through the "washing of regeneration and renewal *(anakaínōsis)* by the Holy Spirit." And yet for Titus, as for other NT writers concerned with spiritual regeneration of the person (cf. Rom. 12:2; 2 Cor. 4:16; Col. 3:10), individual renewal is but a part of the awaited eschatological "blessed hope, the appearing of the glory of our great God and Savior Jesus Christ" (Titus 2:13).

The idea of regeneration is also conveyed by various other terms in both Hebrew and Greek. In Hebrew, the terms *ḥāḏaš* ("renew") and *ḥalap̠* ("change, renew") convey related meanings, i.e., respectively, the renewal of "right spirit" in Ps. 51:10(MT 12) and of "strength" in Isa. 40:31; 41:1. Several other verb stems, when combined with the idea of newness *(ḥāḏāš)*, behave similarly: hence, *bārā'* ("create") and *kārat̠* ("cut, make") render, respectively, "a new heart" in Ps. 51:10(12) and "a new covenant" in Jer. 31:31-34. Notably, the notion of cosmic regeneration, first attested in Isaiah's prophecy of the creation of the new heaven and earth (Isa. 65:17; 66:22), is reused and extended in both Jewish and Christian apocalyptic literature (e.g., 1 En. 45:4; 72:1; 2 Bar. 32:6; 57:2; 2 En. 65:7; 2 Pet. 3:13; Rev. 21:1).

Elsewhere in the NT the notion of regeneration may also be conveyed by the Greek terms *anagennáōmai* ("be born anew"; 1 Pet. 2:2), *anakainóō* ("renew"; 2 Cor. 4:16; Col. 3:10), *anakaínōsis* ("renewal"; Rom. 12:2; Titus 3:5), and *anakainízō* ("renew, restore"; Heb. 6:6). In John's Gospel regeneration is in view in the pointedly ambiguous imperative, "You must be born *ánōthen* ('from above'; 'anew')." In the NT generally, regeneration motifs denote both the salvific, spiritual transformation already begun in human beings by the work of Christ and the expectation of a future new creation. The NT language of personal regeneration has given rise to different and often conflicting theological views on the nature of baptism.

ALEXANDRA R. BROWN

REHABIAH (Heb. *rĕḥab̠yâ, rĕḥab̠yāhû*)
The son of Eliezer and grandson of Moses (1 Chr. 23:17; 24:21; 26:25).

REHOB (Heb. *rĕḥôb̠, rĕḥōb̠*) **(PERSON)**

1. The father of King Hadadezer of Zobah, who was defeated by David (2 Sam. 8:3, 12). "Son of Rehob" may mean "of the house (i.e., dynasty) of Rehob," indicating a relationship between the two Aramean states of Beth-rehob and Zobah.

2. A Levite who sealed the covenant under Nehemiah (Neh. 10:11[MT 12]).

REHOB (Heb. *rĕḥôb̠, rĕḥōb̠*) **(PLACE)**

1. A place in extreme northern Canaan near the entrance to Hamath in modern Lebanon (Num. 13:21). Rehob is here used to represent the northern limit of the territory explored by the spies sent by Moses to investigate the land of Canaan. It is probably the same place as Beth-rehob. The location of the ancient settlement remains unidentified.

2. A town allotted to Asher (Josh. 19:28). Its association with Cabul, Ebron, Hammon, Kanah, and especially Sidon clearly places it in the northern part of Asher's territory. It might also be the Rehob within Asher that was assigned to the Levites (Josh. 21:31; 1 Chr. 6:75[MT 60]) and the Rehob from which the people of Asher were unable to evict the Canaanites (Judg. 1:9). Two identifications have been suggested: Tell el-Balaṭ (177280), ca. 16.5 km. (10 mi.) E of Rosh ha-Niqra (inside modern Lebanon), and Tell er-Raḥb (180275), ca. 6.5 km. (4 mi.) SE of Tell el-Balaṭ (on the Israeli side of the border). Unfortunately, neither site has been extensively investigated by archaeologists.

3. Another town within the territory allotted to the tribe of Asher (Josh. 19:30). Its association with Achzib and Aphek appears to place it in the Plain of Acco. The name Ummah *(ʿmh),* also associated with Rehob in the list, may well be a corruption of Acco *(ʿkh).* It may also be the Rehob within Asher that was assigned to the Levites (Josh. 21:32; 1 Chr. 6:75[60]) and the Rehob from which the people of Asher were unable to evict the Canaanites (Judg. 1:9). Most scholars identify Rehob in the plain of Acco with Tell Bir el-Gharbī/Tel Bira (166256) on the edge of the plain near the Galilee foothills. Archaeological evidence documents occupation during the Middle Bronze, Iron I-II, Persian, and Hellenistic periods. WADE R. KOTTER

4. The principal city of the Beth-shean Valley during Egyptian rule of Canaan, ca. 7 km. (4 mi.) S of Beth-shean. Although not mentioned in the Bible, references to Rehob occur in a number of Egyptian documents. Excavations at Tel Rehob/Tell eṣ-Ṣârem (197207) attest occupation from the early 3rd-1st millennia B.C.E.

REHOBOAM (Heb. *rĕḥaḇʿām*)

King of Judah (ca. 924-907 B.C.E.), son of Solomon and the Ammonitess Naamah (1 Kgs. 14:31), and the father of Abijah/Abijam. He came to the throne at 41 and reigned for 17 years (1 Kgs. 14:21). 2 Chr. 11:18-23 identifies two of his 18 wives as Mahalath and Maacah (mother of Abijah) and notes that he had 60 concubines, 28 sons, and 60 daughters. Rehoboam's reign is described in 1 Kgs. 12:1-24; 14:21-31, which apparently derives from the royal annals of Judah (1 Kgs. 14:29), and 2 Chr. 10:1–12:16, which is based on 1 Kings and perhaps a prophetic source (cf. 2 Chr. 12:15).

At his accession to the throne, Rehoboam met at Shechem with representatives of the northern tribes of Israel, who demanded relief from the oppressive policies of Solomon. After three days and consultation with his advisors, the king rejected the counsel of his older and more experienced officials that he acquiesce temporarily to the demands of Israel, and foolishly accepted the advice of his younger associates, who urged him to assert his authority. Consequently, the northern tribes revolted and elected as their king Jeroboam, who had fled to Egypt when Solomon suspected him of treason (1 Kgs. 12:1-16). This disaster is explained as God's punishment for Solomon's religious unfaithfulness (1 Kgs. 11:9-13, 29-39; 12:15; cf. 2 Chr. 10:15). When Rehoboam sent Adoram/Hadoram, his officer over forced labor, to quell the revolt, the official was stoned to death, and the king fled to Jerusalem (1 Kgs. 12:17-18). Conflict between the two kingdoms continued throughout the reigns of Rehoboam and Jeroboam (1 Kgs. 14:30; cf. 2 Chr. 12:15b).

In the fifth year of Rehoboam's reign an Egyptian army under Pharaoh Shishak (Shoshenq I) attacked Palestine (1 Kgs. 14:25-28; cf. 2 Chr. 12:1-12), not to install Egyptian officials over the land but to plunder its wealth and perhaps to assert Egyptian influence. Although the biblical accounts leave the impression that the attack was aimed at Judah and constituted divine punishment for Rehoboam's religious unfaithfulness (explicitly stated in 2 Chr. 12:1-2; implied by juxtaposition in 1 Kgs. 14:21-24, 25-26), Shishak's inscription at the temple of Amon at Karnak lists the places that the Egyptians had conquered and suggests that Israel, rather than Judah, was the primary object of the attack. Jerusalem is not mentioned in the list, but a few sites in the Negeb are, perhaps an indication of the pharaoh's efforts to protect his troops from raids by nomadic peoples in the region. Apparently, Rehoboam paid tribute to the Egyptians to avoid further trouble (cf. 1 Kgs. 14:25-26). The report of these events is greatly expanded in Chronicles, where the prophet Shemaiah announces that Shishak's conquest of the fortified cities of Judah (cf. 2 Chr. 11:5-12) is God's punishment for their sin, the leaders repent, and Shemaiah proclaims a partial deliverance: the leaders will remain in power, but the Egyptians will take away much of their wealth (2 Chr. 12:3-8).

In addition, 2 Chr. 11:5-12 reports, as evidence of divine blessing, that Rehoboam built and provisioned 15 "cities for defense." Although the king may have undertaken this to protect his land from Egyptian attack before Shishak's invasion, as is indicated by the position of the report in Chronicles, others have suggested that Rehoboam's strategy was to secure his kingdom against further internal rebellion, and still others have dated the list of fortified cities to the reigns of Josiah or Hezekiah.

1 Kgs. 14:22-24 characterizes Rehoboam's religious policies as idolatrous, while Chronicles portrays them more ambiguously, reporting that northern priests and Levites moved to Judah because of Jeroboam's religious innovations. These were followed by others who were faithful to God, and together they strengthened Rehoboam for three years (2 Chr. 11:13-17; cf. 12:14).

Bibliography. G. N. Knoppers, "Rehoboam in Chronicles: Villain or Victim?" *JBL* 109 (1990): 423-40; B. Mazar, "The Campaign of Pharaoh Shishak to Palestine," *VTSup* 4 (Leiden, 1957): 57-66; J. M. Miller, "Rehoboam's Cities of Defense and the Levitical City List," in *Archaeology and Biblical Interpretation,* ed. L. G. Perdue, L. E. Toombs, and G. L. Lance (Atlanta, 1987), 273-86.

M. PATRICK GRAHAM

REHOBOTH (Heb. *rĕḥōḇôṯ*)

1. The third of three wells dug by Isaac's servants in the valley of Gerar (Gen. 26:22). The tradition reflects tension between the herders over water rights. The well's location has been associated with Wadi Ruḥeibeh/Naḥal Shunra, SW of Beer-sheba, which may preserve the ancient name.

2. Rehoboth ha-Nahar (*rĕḥōḇôṯ hannāhār,* "Rehoboth on the river"), the home of Shaul, one of the early kings of Edom (Gen. 36:37; 1 Chr. 1:48). The location is uncertain. "The river" has been assumed to describe the Euphrates (NRSV), as elsewhere (e.g., Gen. 31:21), but in this context it may refer to a location in Edom. It may perhaps be identified with Brook Zered (modern Wadi el-Ḥesa), which marked the border between Moab and Edom (Deut. 2:8-14). The site may be modern Râs er-Rihâb (208038). LAURA B. MAZOW

REHOBOTH-IR (Heb. *rĕḥōḇōṯ ʿîr*)
One of the four cities that Nimrod built in Assyria (Gen. 10:11). Although Nineveh and Calah are well known, Resin and Rehoboth-ir have not been easily explained. Rehoboth-ir seems best explained by Akk. *rêbīt āli,* a generic term meaning "the public square of a city." In the context of Gen. 11, the term is thus connected to Nineveh, meaning "the public square of the city of Nineveh." Nineveh had a large square complex that was enlarged by Sennacherib in the late 8th century B.C.E.

Bibliography. J. M. Sasson, "Reḥōvōt-'Īr," *RB* 90 (1983): 94-96. MARK W. CHAVALAS

REHUM (Heb. *rĕḥûm, rĕḥum*)
1. One of 10 leaders who accompanied Zerubbabel from Babylon back to Judea (Ezra 2:2; cf. Neh. 7:7, Nehum).
2. The Persian commanding officer in Samaria who, along with Shimshai, wrote a letter to King Xerxes protesting the Jews' work of restoring the walls and repairing the foundations of Jerusalem (Ezra 4:8). Xerxes replied, ordering the work to cease, and Rehum stopped the work by force (Ezra 4:17-23).
3. A Levite, son of Bani, and supervisor of other Levites during the rebuilding of a section of the wall in Jerusalem near the tomb of David (Neh. 3:17).
4. A leader of the people who signed a long prayer of praise, confession, and petition asking the Lord for help in a time of distress after return from the Exile (Neh. 10:25[MT 26]). The governor Nehemiah, priests, and Levites also signed.
5. A priest and Levite who returned with Zerubbabel (Neh. 12:3; cf. Harim in v. 15; 1 Chr. 24:8). ROBIN GALLAHER BRANCH

REI (Heb. *rēʿî*)
A warrior (and perhaps court official) who continued to support David during Adonijah's revolt (1 Kgs. 1:8).

REKEM (Heb. *reqem*) **(PERSON)**
The name of three individuals, perhaps the eponymous ancestors of clans. The names may also represent places.
1. One of the five kings of Midian who were vassals of the Amorite king Sihon and who were killed by the Israelites en route to Canaan (Num. 31:18; Josh. 13:21).
2. A son of Hebron of the tribe of Judah (1 Chr. 2:43-44).
3. A grandson of Machir and Maacah (1 Chr. 7:16).

REKEM (Heb. *reqem*) **(PLACE)**
A city in the western portion of the territory of Benjamin (Josh. 18:27). Its location and modern identification are unknown. It may be associated with the Midianite ruler of the same name (Num. 31:8; Josh. 13:21). Josephus (*Ant.* 4.161) identifies Rekem with Petra. JOHN R. SPENCER

REMALIAH (Heb. *rĕmalyāhû*)
The father of King Pekah of Israel (2 Kgs. 15:25; Isa. 7:1). In Isa. 7:4-5, 9; 8:6 Pekah is not named but called simply "the son of Remaliah."

REMETH (Heb. *remeṯ*)
A city on the border of Issachar (Josh. 19:21). It is probably to be identified with Jarmuth (**2;** Josh. 21:29) and Ramoth (**3;** 1 Chr. 6:73[MT 58]).

REMISSION, YEAR OF (also RELEASE, YEAR OF)
See SABBATICAL YEAR.

REMNANT
That part of a nation, tribe, clan, or family which survives a divine catastrophe, whether natural (flood, famine, pestilence) or not (war, exile). This group forms the nucleus for the possible future rebuilding of the community. The remnant, therefore, functions within the theological framework of judgment and salvation.

In the OT remnant terminology (the stems *šʾr, plṭ, mlṭ, ytr,* and the nouns *śārîḏ* and *ʾăḥarîṯ*) appears more than 500 times in contexts indicating that this concept is rooted in existential concerns in the face of mortal threats: will there be total annihilation or will a company survive to preserve existence? In most instances, both the destructive and constructive elements are underlined, highlighting the fact that God's gracious salvation preserves a faithful group.

The first explicit reference appears with the Flood (Gen. 6:5–7:23). Other examples include Lot and the destruction of Sodom (Gen. 18:22-33; 19:15-29); the famine in Egypt (45:7); and the escape at the Red Sea (Exod. 14:28). However, only covenant fidelity could ensure God's continual protection over Israel (Lev. 26:27-39; Deut. 4:27).

Remnants of the Canaanites (the Anakim and Amalekites; Josh. 11:21-22; Judg. 6:1-6; 1 Chr. 4:43) were used to test Israel's faithfulness (Judg. 2:21-23; 3:1-6). In a theophany God revealed to Elijah that he had preserved 7000 faithful followers (1 Kgs. 19:17-18). Ezra (Ezra 9:8-15) and Nehemiah (Neh. 1:2-3) designate both the returnees and those who remained in the land as the remnant.

The Prophets have the most to say concerning the remnant. Amos declares that only an insignificant group would survive the Assyrian crisis (Amos 3:12; 5:3), but God's grace will rejuvenate the faithful "remnant of Joseph" (5:15; 9:11-15). Isaiah denotes the remnant as a "holy seed" (Isa. 6:13) which will survive divine judgment (4:2-4), embrace the election promises, and become the center of a new faithful community, rebuilt by God (10:20-23; 28:5ff.). This is clearly evident in the name of Isaiah's firstborn son, Shear-jashub, "A remnant shall return" (Isa. 7:3). Micah and Zephaniah speak of a regathered remnant which is forgiven (Mic. 2:12; 7:18), characterized by new life, strength (5:7-8), humility, and purity (Zeph. 3:12-13). For Jeremiah and Ezekiel, the exiles constitute the true remnant since they carry the election promises. God will regather them, blessing them with the new covenant (Jer. 23:1-8; 31:31-34) and a new heart (Ezek. 11:16-21; 36:26), so that they could again be his people (cf. Zech. 13:7-9). Those left in Judah comprised an insignificant, poor assemblage (Jer. 8:3; 21:8-10).

The remnant concept is implicit in the Gospels, although the actual noun "remnant" is absent. Jesus, like John the Baptist, made a universal appeal for the faithful and penitent to enter God's kingdom (Mark 1:3-8, 15). But only a few accepted the invitation. This emphasis on the "few" (Matt. 7:14; Luke 13:23), the "chosen" (Matt. 20:14-16), and the "little ones" (Luke 17:2) points to the remnant of faith in Jesus' teachings. Further, metaphors such as "sheep" (Matt. 10:6; Luke 12:32), "shepherds" (John 10:16), and the separation of sheep and goats (Matt. 25:32-34) demonstrate association with OT remnant concepts.

Rom. 9–11 (citing the OT) insists that "only a remnant will be saved" (9:27). These are the faithful, not necessarily of Jewish lineage, who comprise a new spiritual community, the Church (Rom. 10:4, 9-13). In the metaphor of the olive tree, Paul asserts that believing Gentiles will be grafted in while unbelieving Jews will be cut off. Yet, if they repent, God will reattach them (Rom. 11:17-24) so that one tree, comprised of "all Israel[,] will be saved" (v. 26). God's final goal is salvation.

The book of Revelation uses Gk. *loipós* several times; the faithful in Thyatira (Rev. 2:24); the unsullied "few" in Sardis (3:2, 4); a surviving group which praises God for his salvation (11:13); those faithful to God's commandments and having the testimony of Jesus (12:17; cf. 14:12; 19:10), while the "rest" (the unfaithful) are destroyed by God (19:21).

Bibliography. G. F. Hasel, *The Remnant,* 3rd ed. AUM 5 (Berrien Springs, 1980); V. Herntrich and G. Schrenk, "leímma," *TDNT* 4:194-214; K. D. Mulzac, "The Remnant and the New Covenant in the Book of Jeremiah," *AUSS* 34 (1996): 239-48; *The Remnant Motif in the Context of Judgment and Salvation in the Book of Jeremiah* (diss., Berrien Springs, 1995); J. W. Watts, *A Critique of Interpretations of the Remnant Theme in the New Testament* (diss., Louisville, 1986).

KENNETH D. MULZAC

REPENTANCE

A biblical concept ranging from regret or remorse (Heb. *nāḥam,* "to pant, sigh, or grieve") to a complete change of mind or behavior (*šûḇ,* "to turn").

Heb. *nāḥam* usually refers to God's repenting, rather than that of people, although occasionally it refers to human grief over sin (Exod. 13:17; Job 42:6; Jer. 8:6; 31:19). The term typically describes God's gracious response to human repentance, in which God relents from punishment.

In the OT the basic idea of human repentance is represented by *šûḇ*. It implies turning from sin to righteousness, often with accompanying sorrow. A clear example of this religious sense of the term appears in 1 Kgs. 8:47, where Solomon entreats God to hear the prayers of a repentant people who return to God. Repentance often involves reverting from idolatry to true worship of Yahweh and its corresponding moral behavior (Isa. 1:10-17; Ezek. 14:6; 18:30; Amos 4:6-11). In response to this repentance, God forgives and restores.

In the NT repentance primarily relates to the Greek words *metanoéō* and *metńoia,* meaning to understand something differently after thinking it over. This change of mind necessarily leads to changed actions, in keeping with the Greek view that the mind *(noús)* controlled the body. Repentance comprises a central theme in the preaching of Jesus, Peter, and Paul.

Jesus began his ministry with a call to repentance as the prerequisite for entering the kingdom of God (Mark 1:15; Matt. 4:17). Mark 6:12-13 summarizes Jesus ministry by saying that Jesus preached repentance, cast our demons, and healed sick people. At the conclusion of his earthly ministry Jesus commissioned his disciples to preach repentance and forgiveness to all nations in his name (Luke 24:47). A call to repentance characterizes the content of his preaching.

Peter, Paul, and the rest of the apostles proclaimed a gospel of repentance (Mark 6:12). Peter's sermon at Pentecost instructed people to repent and believe in Jesus (Acts 2:38); later, he echoed this message before the Sanhedrin (Acts 3:19). Paul also condensed his gospel as a call to repentance and righteous living (Acts 17:30; 26:20). Because the Gospels emphasize the centrality of repentance in Jesus' preaching, and both Peter and Paul taught that repentance was the correct response to the gospel, the importance of repentance to the theology of the NT cannot be overemphasized.

The early church fathers gave little attention to the doctrine of repentance, but by the 2nd century church tradition equated repentance with the act of baptism, leading to the difficulty of Christians gaining forgiveness for postbaptismal sins (Herm. Man. 4:1-3). Tertullian attempted to revolve this problem by positing a public confession of sins *(exomologḗsis)* to cleanse postbaptismal sins, but denied it to those who were guilty of adultery, fornication, murder, or idolatry.

By the Middle Ages the Church had developed the idea of public confession into the doctrine of penance. Repentant Catholics were to make confession to a priest at least once a year. Thomas Aquinas itemized penance into the elements of contrition, confession, satisfaction, and absolution. Abuse of indulgences provoked a rejection of the sacrament of penance among Reformation writers, although they discussed repentance in connection with the Calvinist/Arminian debate over free will. Calvinists regarded repentance as an absolute gift of God, while Arminians thought repentance involved human response to God's initiative.

Repentance, faith, and election form a closely

interwoven set of ideas which express the gospel. God's elective call for people to enter God's kingdom arises as a summons to repentance. Faith in the word of God initiates repentance (Rom. 10:11-17; Hos. 6:1-6; Joel 2:32[MT 3:5]). The person who repents repudiates the wickedness of sin, understanding it as serious and repulsive. The Holy Spirit generates life within human believers through repentance and faith. The elect accept the call to turn from their rejected status of not being God's people, to those whom God claims as children (Rom. 9:25-26; Joel 2:25). LINDA OAKS GARRETT

REPHAEL (Heb. *rĕp̄āʾēl*)
A levitical temple gatekeeper, the son of Shemaiah of the family of Obed-edom (1 Chr. 26:7).

REPHAH (Heb. *rep̄aḥ*)
An Ephraimite, and an ancestor of Joshua (1 Chr. 7:25).

REPHAIAH (Heb. *rĕp̄āyâ*) (also RAPHAH)

1. A descendant of Zerubbabel (1 Chr. 3:21 MT).

2. One of the sons of Ishi who led 500 Simeonites in supplanting the Amalekite remnant on Mt. Seir (1 Chr. 4:42-43).

3. A son of Tola of the tribe of Issachar (1 Chr. 7:2).

4. A descendant of Saul through Jonathan (1 Chr. 9:43). He is also called Raphah (1 Chr. 8:37).

5. The son of Hur; chief of half of the district of Jerusalem in the days of Nehemiah (Neh. 3:9).

REPHAIM (Heb. *rĕp̄āʾîm*)
The Rephaim have been repeatedly identified as the deified, dead, royal ancestors and thereby exemplary of the early Israelite belief in the supernatural beneficent power of the dead. This in turn has generated a virtual consensus that the biblical Rephaim reflect an underlying Canaanite-Israelite royal ancestor or death cult designed to manipulate the powers of those dead. Modern interpreters suppose that it is against such a background that the biblical writers aim to convince their audiences that the dead possess no power nor are they worthy objects of religious performance. More likely, however, the Rephaim simply represent the weakened, common dead — the lot of all mankind, a perpetual weakened existence in a shadowy netherworld. Only later, with the development of beatific notions of the afterlife in the Hellenistic period, did such a state of insignificance come to be abhorred and eventually replaced by the belief in the eternal reward of the righteous and punishment of the wicked.

Etymology of the term is commonly explained as derived from *rp'*, "to heal," thus "healers" (cf. LXX Ps. 88:11; Isa. 26:14), but this healing aspect is marginal at best. Biblical and extrabiblical texts might better support another Semitic root *rp'* (< *rb'*), "to be great, large," thus "the Mighty Ones," referring to their memorable feats while living or as portrayed in legend. Some scholars have pointed out the possible connection with Heb. *rph*, "to become weak" (cf. references in the historical narratives to them as "descendants of the Weak One"); this probably reflects a popular etymology designed to diminish rhetorically the power of the living or legendary Mighty Ones.

Old Testament

The OT testifies to two distinct traditions with regard to the Rephaim: (1) the ancient, autochthonous populations of Palestine as depicted in the narratives of the Pentateuch and Deuteronomistic history (e.g., Gen. 14:5; 15:20; Josh. 12:4; 13:12); (2) in the prophetic, psalmic, and sapiential traditions, those Rephaim who, as weakened shades of the dead, inhabit the netherworld (e.g., Isa. 14:9; Ps. 88:10[MT 11]; Job 26:5). The biblical traditions themselves never explicitly associate the "prehistoric ethnic" Rephaim and the Rephaim who are shades. Nevertheless, in the history of interpretation some organic connection between the two has been assumed: what were once living entities from the distant past died and then came to inhabit the netherworld. 1 En. 6–14 elaborates upon Gen. 6:1-4 by describing how the giants or Nephilim — which came to include the Rephaim of the OT historical narratives — were cast into the netherworld.

The status of the biblical Rephaim as shades finds analogy in the funerary contexts of two 6th-century B.C.E. Phoenician inscriptions (cf. the phrase ". . . a place of rest with the *rp'm*"). Neither the biblical nor Phoenician texts indicate that they possessed the social status of royalty or the powers of lesser gods. Isa. 14 has been cited as an exception, but the Rephaim in v. 9 are parallel to "Sheol," here representative of the common dead; only beginning with v. 14 are the deceased from among the social elites introduced with mention of "the leaders of the earth" and "kings of the nations."

Ugaritic Texts

The once common view that the Phoenician and biblical references to the Rephaim as shades preserved an older Canaanite tradition now, according to many, finds direct confirmation in the alphabetic cuneiform texts discovered at Late Bronze Age Ugarit. The consensus is that these texts refer to the Rephaim or Rapi'uma *(rp'um)* as epitomizing the powerful, Canaanite, royal dead on behalf of whom an ancestor or death cult emerged at Ugarit. Accordingly, the texts indicate that the Rapi'uma were once a living collective reality, then a mythologized, heroic group, long before they became inhabitants of the netherworld as the powerful dead. This reconstruction of the Ugaritic traditions is routinely cited in support of the notion that a similar set of circumstances underlies what must have been the original connection between the Rephaim as gigantic autochthons and the Rephaim as the powerful dead in Hebrew tradition.

The major datum for the Rapi'uma as the deified dead is the Shapsh hymn that concludes the Baal-Mot cycle (*KTU* 1.6 VI, 5-49). The central evidence for their deceased, royal, ancestral status is

KTU 1.161, a royal litany on the occasion of a new king's coronation to which all living warriors and social elites are summoned, including the mighty ones or *rp'um*. The litany does include some minor elements that are mortuary in nature and associated with the death of the new king's predecessor, but the dead mentioned in the text, the ancient Mighty Ones *(rp'im qdmym),* are portrayed as weak and are required only to receive the newly deceased king's throne as it ritually descends to them below in the netherworld.

The Shapsh hymn mentions four entities: the *rp'im* ("mighty ones"), *'ilnym* ("divinities"), *'ilm* ("gods"), and *mtm* ("men, mortals"). The cycle nowhere presents humanity as dead or deified. Humanity is threatened with the prospects of its annihilation, but it is never actualized. Likewise, the goddess Shapsh is nowhere located in the netherworld. Instead she assists Anat in retrieving Baal's corpse at the edge of earth and netherworld, in the outback or steppe. Elsewhere in the cycle she is portrayed as possessing wisdom and authority to fix the fates of both gods and mortals alike by restricting the powers of Mot, god of death. The aim of these lines is to underscore the goddess' all-encompassing authority to decide the fates, above and below on the earth, of humanity, mortal heroes, lesser divinities, and the gods.

The Rephaim of the OT are ghosts of inconsequential power and in need of care. They are not the supernatural beneficent ghosts of the dead, nor is such a status polemicized against anywhere in the biblical traditions. There is no ancestor or death cult underlying the Rephaim traditions. At most, a commemorative cult might underlie the references in the historical narratives as these traditions presuppose these Rephaim to be legendary living heroes of immense size and stature. They are described as "the descendants of the Weak One" in an attempt to negate their former powers. If an anti-Rephaim polemic exists anywhere, it appears here in the narrative contexts where the *rph* base is associated with the prehistoric ethnic Rephaim.

Bibliography. C. E. L'Heureux, *Rank among the Canaanite Gods.* HSM 21 (Missoula, 1979); T. J. Lewis, *Cults of the Dead in Ancient Israel and Ugarit.* HSM 39 (Atlanta, 1989); B. B. Schmidt, *Israel's Beneficent Dead* (Winona Lake, 1996).

Brian B. Schmidt

REPHAN (Gk. *Rhaiphán*)
A transliteration of Heb. *kiyyûn* ("Kaiwan"), the planet Saturn worshipped by the Israelites during their wilderness wanderings (Acts 7:43; from LXX Amos 5:26).

REPHIDIM (Heb. *rĕpîḏîm*)
A stopping point on the Exodus between the wilderness of Sin and the wilderness of Sinai (Exod. 17:1; 19:2; Num. 33:14-15). Here Moses, in response to the incessant demands of the Israelites, struck a rock to provide water (Exod. 17:2-7). Because of this, Rephidim also became known as Massah ("testing") or Meribah ("contention"), and the Israelites were repeatedly reminded of what had happened there (Deut. 6:16; 9:22; 33:8). Shortly thereafter, the Israelites fought the Amalekites at Rephidim (Exod. 17:8-16). The present context of Exod. 18 suggests that Jethro's advice regarding the appointment of judges was also given while the Israelites camped at Rephidim. Tradition has long identified Wadi Feirân near Jebul Mûsâ as the location of Rephidim, although more recent scholarship prefers the nearby Wadi Refayid because of the similarity in name. Neither site has been the subject of intensive archaeological investigation.

Wade R. Kotter

RESEN (Heb. *resen*)
An Assyrian city between Nineveh and Calah (Gen. 10:12). The exact location of the city is uncertain, and the city is unattested in cuneiform sources.

RESHEPH (Heb. *rešep̄*) **(DEITY)**
A Canaanite deity of plague (Ugar. *ršp;* cf. Heb. *rešep̄,* "flame," perhaps related to fever; cf. Akk. Nergal), attested as early as the mid-2nd millennium B.C.E. at Ebla. Such mythological sense may underlie biblical usage of the Hebrew term, often translated "plague" (Deut. 32:24, "burning consumption"; cf. Cant. 8:6). The usage at Job 5:7 (NRSV mg "sons of Resheph"); Ps. 76:3(MT 4); 78:48 connoting the flash of flying (perhaps flaming) arrows may derive from the Ugaritic epithet of Resheph, *b'l ḥs,* "lord of the arrow" (cf. his identification in inscriptions from Cyprus with Apollo, whose arrows bring sickness). At Hab. 3:5 "pestilence" and "plague" (Heb. *deḇer*) escort Yahweh as he marches in theophany, reminiscent of Ugaritic paired deities.

Bibliography. W. J. Fulco, *The Canaanite God Rešep.* AOS 8 (New Haven, 1976).

Allen C. Myers

RESHEPH (Heb. *rešep̄*) **(PERSON)**
An Ephraimite, son of Rephah and father of Telah (1 Chr. 7:25). The name may represent a clan or town.

RESURRECTION
Concept of a person being brought back from a mortal death to a state of immortality, usually involving the reunification of the spirit or the soul with an immortal body. In the OT there is no single word for resurrection; in the NT the most common Greek term is *anástasis,* "rise up."

Old Testament

Evidence for belief in resurrection in the OT is scarce and often ambiguous. As God formed man's body from the dust of the earth and gave him life by breathing the breath of life into him (Gen. 2:7), so upon death the breath leaves the body and the body returns to the dust (Ps. 104:29). The realm of the dead in the OT is Sheol. On the one hand, Sheol is described as a dark and gloomy place, a place where the dead are separated from the living and God (Ps. 6:5[MT 6]; 30:9[10]; 88:1-12[2-13];

115:17), where they are forgotten (Ps. 88:14[15]; Eccl. 3:19-21; 9:5-10), and as a final destination and a place "of no return" (Job 7:9-10; 16:22; Isa. 38:10). On the other hand, several texts describe the power of God over Sheol (Job 12:22; 26:6; Ps. 139:8; Prov. 15:11; Amos 9:2), and that the Lord will deliver from Sheol (Ps. 49:15[16]). Several passages specifically allude to Yahweh's power over death (Deut. 32:39; 1 Sam. 2:6; Isa. 25:7). Likewise, three passages directly allude to resurrection in the context of national restoration (Isa. 26:19; Ezek. 37:13-14; Hos. 6:1-2).

The first clear and uneqivocal statement of belief in the resurrection of the dead in the OT is found in Daniel (Dan. 12:2). The fact that the first explicit statement of resurrection occurs in such a late book has led many scholars to suppose that the concept of resurrection gradually developed through the OT period and reached its complete form only in the apocalyptic circles of the intertestamental period. These scholars dismiss as figurative the earlier passages in the OT referring to God's power over Sheol and death, and the passages referring to resurrection in the context of national restoration. Other scholars believe these allusions presuppose an early belief in resurrection.

Intertestamental Literature

The ambiguity of the OT evidence is reflected in the beliefs of the sects of Judaism in the intertestamental period. According to Josephus the Pharisees believed in a bodily resurrection, the Sadducees and the Samaritans did not, and the Essenes believed in the immortality of the soul but not the body (*BJ* 2.8.11, 14, 154, 163, 165; *Ant.* 19.1.3-5, 14, 16, 18). Ancient evidence bears out Josephus in regard to the Pharisees and Sadducees, but the evidence concerning the Samaritans and the Essenes is not decisive. Recently published texts from Qumran suggest that there was a belief in resurrection at Qumran. 4Q521 1:12 reads: "he will heal the wounded, give life to the dead, and proclaim good tidings to the poor" — a passage considered by many scholars to be a clear statement of belief in resurrection at Qumran.

In texts from this period the concept of resurrection is fully expressed. Sirach echoes OT passages about the finality of death, that those in Sheol are cut off from God (Sir. 17:27-28), and all that remains of an individual after death is honor and a good name (37:26), but he says about the judges and prophets, "may their bones send forth new life from where they lie" (46:12; 49:10). Wis. 1–6 includes a long discussion of immortality. Resurrection is usually mentioned in the context of rewards and punishments, as in Dan. 12, and is reserved for the righteous and not the wicked. 1 Enoch describes the division of the righteous from the wicked in the afterlife as they await judgment (1 En. 22) and alludes to a resurrection of the righteous only (91:10). In 2 Maccabees the martyrs express their belief in the resurrection of the righteous (2 Macc. 7:9, 11, 14); allusion is made for the offering of prayers and sin offerings to the dead in hope of resurrection (12:43-45); and physical restoration of a mutilated body is described (14:46). However, a passage in 2 Esdras suggests a resurrection for all (2 Esdr. 7:32, 37).

New Testament

Resurrection is a pivotal doctrine in the NT. The resurrection of Jesus Christ is presented as the central event of history. It is the fulfillment of OT prophecy and teaching and the most important sign that Jesus was the Messiah (Acts 2:32-36; 13:33; Rom. 1:3-4; 1 Cor. 15:12). It represents a reversal of the consequences of the fall brought about by Adam and Eve (1 Cor. 15:22).

In the Gospel accounts the Resurrection is prominent in the discussions between Jesus and the Pharisees and the Sadducees. Jesus clearly sides with the Pharisees citing OT passages as evidence of resurrection (Matt. 22:23-33; Mark 12:18-27; Luke 20:27-40). Throughout his ministry Jesus prophesied his rising on the third day (Matt. 16:21; Mark 8:31; Luke 9:22) as a fulfillment of OT prophecy (Hos. 6:1-2). Jesus raised three people from the dead, Jairus' daughter, the widow's son, and Lazarus — on which occasion he said, "I am the resurrection and the life. Those who believe in me, even though they die, will live" (John 11:25). These episodes demonstrate Jesus' power over death and foreshadow his ability to raise himself from the dead. The resurrection of Jesus Christ signaled his power over death which he gave to all mankind: the righteous to a resurrection of life and the wicked to a resurrection of condemnation (John 5:25, 29). Matthew says others rose from the dead after the resurrection of Jesus "and appeared to many" (Matt. 27:53).

The symbol of the resurrection of Jesus in the NT is the empty tomb, but the evidence of his resurrection is his several appearances before and after his ascension. On one occasion he clarified the nature of his resurrected body: "Touch me and see; for a ghost does not have flesh and bones as you see that I have" (Luke 24:39).

Paul gives the most extensive theological exposition of resurrection in the NT in 1 Cor. 15. Paul cited as evidence of the Resurrection the Scriptures and Jesus' appearances to Cephas, to the Twelve, to 500, to James, and to himself (1 Cor. 15:1-11), and taught that the resurrection of Jesus had universal significance: "for as all die in Adam, so all will be made alive in Christ" (vv. 20-22). Paul explains that resurrection necessitates transformation, since "flesh and blood cannot inherit the kingdom of God" (1 Cor. 15:50). Thus resurrection involves transformation from the perishable to the imperishable, from dishonor to glory, from weakness to power, from physical to spiritual (1 Cor. 15:42-46).

The Resurrection symbolizes the power of Jesus Christ to give new life to his followers, both in a spiritual as well as in a literal sense. Belief in resurrection offers Christians a distinctive perspective on the significance of mortal life as a temporary state of probation to be followed by death, judgment, and resurrection.

Bibliography. J. J. Collins, "Excursus: On Resurrection," *Daniel.* Herm (Minneapolis, 1993), 394-98; R. Martin-Achard, *From Death to Life: A Study of the Development of the Doctrine of the Resurrection in the Old Testament* (1960); G. W. E. Nickelsburg, Jr., *Resurrection, Immortality, and Eternal Life in Intertestamental Judaism.* HTS 26 (Cambridge, Mass., 1972); P. Perkins, *Resurrection: New Testament Witness and Contemporary Reflection* (Garden City, 1984); N. J. Tromp, *Primitive Conceptions of Death and the Nether World in the Old Testament.* BibOr 21 (Rome, 1969).

DAVID ROLPH SEELY

RETRIBUTION

The dispensing of or receiving recompense or payment. Whether between God and humans or between human beings, retribution is the act of getting what one deserves, either by human standards or by divine decree. In the earliest traditions the legal material dictated that individuals should be punished accordingly for their wrongdoings. Both the Covenant code (Exod. 20–23) and the Holiness code (Lev. 17–26) are the classic texts for seeing the clarity with which the laws were written regarding retribution. Both sets of laws speak to both the divine-human relationship and the human-human relationship. To break any law, however, was to damage the relationship with God. All the commandments were given by God to give direction and instruction to the community of faith (Deut. 4:5-8; 5:28-33). Retribution must be made to correct any wrong or to reward any right.

With the law as its foundation, the history of Israel was a continuous cycle of making retribution. Even in the narrative of Cain and Abel, Cain is punished by being forced to leave his home (Gen. 4). All the earth is punished by a devastating flood for widespread sin (Gen. 6–9). For obeying God's voice and going to Canaan, Abraham and Sarah are rewarded with a son, Isaac, to fulfill the promise (Gen. 12–25; 12:1-3; 21:1-7). The Jacob-Esau-Laban narratives are full of interesting twists on the theme of retribution (Gen. 26–36). Later, after Moses has led the children of Israel from bondage in Egypt, the people rebel against God and Moses and are punished by being denied entry into the Promised Land; it would be their children instead who would enter. The whole Deuteronomistic history is filled with one act of retribution after another (e.g., Judg. 10–20).

The problem of retribution, however, is serious. Throughout the Deuteronomistic history and the book of Proverbs, and even in the legal material and elsewhere, the idea is that everyone gets what they deserve. Deut. 5:28-33 (and many other places as well) states that if the people will just keep the commandments then all will go well and they will live in the land a long time. The Proverbs are similar, but on an individual level (cf. Prov. 3:1-2). The theology on which such texts are based is that the universe is right, and if one will but do the right things then good things will happen to such people.

While the point of such texts can be understood as to their intent, the book of Job, the questions of Jeremiah, the laments of the Psalms, and the story of the incarnation of Jesus Christ suggest that such a theology of retribution must include a lifelong search for an answer to Jeremiah's question: "Why does the way of the guilty prosper?/Why do all who are treacherous thrive?" (Jer. 12:1). Retribution, then, is closely connected to any discussion of theodicy.

In Job a righteous man loses all he has except for his life and his wife. His friends, proponents of the "national" theology of retribution, are convinced that he has sinned. Even Job's wife is so convinced. But Job knows that he has done nothing wrong. He is a threat to the accepted theology. Like Jeremiah, Job has serious questions for God (Jer. 12:1-4; Job 33; cf. Hab. 1:1–2:5). And, like Jeremiah, Job is answered by God, but the expected answer is not to be found (Jer. 12:5-6; Job 38–41). Both are told that the world will not change. The order of creation is not yet perfect. Indeed, the answer is not to be found in this lifetime. Retribution proper belongs solely to God and will be administered in the life to come (Matt. 25:31-46; Rev. 21:1-8; 22:1-5). Then and only then does the theology of the Deuteronomistic history and Proverbs come to fruition. Until then, bad will happen to the good and good will happen to the bad, and vice versa.

Bibliography. W. Brueggemann, *Old Testament Theology* (Minneapolis, 1992); K. Koch, "Is There a Doctrine of Retribution in the Old Testament?" in *Theodicy in the Old Testament,* ed. J. L. Crenshaw. IRT 4 (Philadelphia, 1983), 57-87.

MARC A. JOLLEY

RETURN

The immediate postexilic period, during which the exiled Israelites left Mesopotamia and resettled in their Palestinian homeland.

For biblical use of the verb "to return" (Heb. *šûḇ;* Gk. *metanoéō*), *see* REPENTANCE.

RETURN OF CHRIST

See SECOND COMING.

REU (Heb. *rĕʿû;* Gk. *Rhagau*)

A son of Peleg, descendant of Shem, and ancestor of Abraham (Gen. 11:18-21; 1 Chr. 1:25) and Jesus (Luke 3:35).

REUBEN (Heb. *rĕʾûḇēn*)

The first son born of Leah and Jacob and the eponymous ancestor of the tribe of Reuben. In Gen. 29:31-32 his name is given a symbolic explanation connected to the events surrounding his birth. Leah was blessed by God and conceived because she was not loved by her husband, Jacob. When the son is born, Leah declares, "Because Yahweh has looked on my affliction; surely now my husband will love me." Most scholars accept the meaning of "behold a son" from the Hebrew. However, various other meanings have been suggested for the name: "substitute" or "chief" from the Arabic.

In Gen. 30:14ff. Reuben is portrayed as a devoted son to his mother. He is the child who found the mandrakes (perhaps an ancient aphrodisiac) and brought them to Leah. This provided her with sufficient leverage to get an extra night with Jacob and to conceive and bear another son. In keeping with his maternal devotion, after Rachel's death, Reuben sleeps with her maid, Bilhah, thus making it improper for Jacob to have sexual relations with her again. His motivation may have been to force his father to return to Leah's tent. Some scholars, though, relate this incident to the account in 1 Sam. 16:20-22, where Absalom takes David's 10 concubines, and they attribute Reuben's actions to an attempt at wresting away his father's authority. The outcome of this event was that Reuben lost his father's favor and eventually his birthright to the descendants of Joseph and Judah (Gen. 49:4; 1 Chr. 5:1). In the Joseph story (Gen. 37) Reuben is presented in a more positive light. His attempt to save Joseph's life from the hands of his brothers is seen as an underscoring of his position as Jacob's firstborn son. He also is the one who offers his own two sons to Jacob as insurance for Benjamin's safe return (Gen. 42:37).

Reuben had four sons: Hanoch, Pallu, Hezron, and Carmi. The land allotted to his descendants was in the Transjordan, S of Gilead and N of the Arnon River. There are, however, conflicting biblical descriptions of the exact settlement of the tribe of Reuben (Josh. 15:6; 18:17). In Josh. 22 Reuben is accused, along with Gad and Manasseh, by the Cisjordanian tribes of having set up a rival altar for worship in their own territory. A war among the tribes is prevented when the Transjordanian tribes affirm that the altar is only a model of the real altar and not used for cultic purposes. The rest of the history of the tribe of Reuben is a challenge to reconstruct. Reuben is mentioned in the Song of Deborah (Judg. 5) and admonished for not supporting the battle against Sisera. In 1 Chr. 5:10, 19 the tribe of Reuben is named as fighting with Manasseh and Gad against the Hagrites during the reign of Saul. The last historical mention of this tribe is among those whom Tiglath-pileser of Assyria exiled (1 Chr. 5:6). Lisa W. Davison

REUEL (Heb. *rĕʿûʾēl*)

1. A son of Keturah (Gen. 25:3 LXX).

2. The son of Esau and Basemath who founded the Edomite clan consisting of the tribes of his sons Nahath, Zerah, Shammah, and Mizzah (Gen. 36:4, 10-17; 1 Chr. 1:35-37).

3. The father-in-law of Moses and the father of Hobab (Exod. 2:18; Num. 10:29). Moses' father-in-law is known also as Jethro (Exod. 3:1; 4:18; 18:1) and Hobab (Judg. 4:11; 1:16 LXX). Since there are no discrepancies besides their names, most scholars tend to see Jethro and Reuel as a single character. Interestingly, the names Hobab "beloved (of God)" and Reuel "friend of God" are essentially synonymous.

4. The father of Eliasaph, captain of the tribe of Gad (Num. 2:14 LXX; MT Deuel).

5. The son of Ibnijah and grandfather of Meshullam, a Benjaminite living in Jerusalem (1 Chr. 9:8). Cheryl Lynn Hubbard

REUMAH (Heb. *rĕûmâ*)

The concubine of Abraham's brother Nahor; mother of Tebah, Gaham, Tahash, and Maacah, apparently the eponymous ancestors of Aramean peoples (Gen. 22:24).

REVELATION

The "opening" or "uncovering" of a previously hidden reality. God is hidden from humankind because of human sinfulness and can only be known through a special revelation. While the creation itself reveals something of the invisible or hidden Creator (Ps. 19:1-6[MT 2-7]; Wis. 13:5; Rom. 1:20), the biblical concept most often relates to an act of God in history which reveals God as Savior. Although the terminology of revelation may apply to personal secrets (Prov. 11:13) or private messages (Luke 2:26; Gal. 2:2) or esoteric matters (1 Cor. 14:26; 2 Cor. 12:1-7), the biblical references are usually intended for public dissemination and communal benefit. That is, God's actions reveal his desire to save Israel (Jer. 33:6) and the nations (Isa. 40:5).

Old Testament

The broad scope of the Hebrew verb "to reveal" is illustrated by the fact that it often appears in conjunction with related terms such as those meaning "to see," "to hear," and "to speak." The emphasis falls on visions or auditions, and these combine in the theophany in which manifestations of God's presence are seen and his voice heard. This is the case in the key revelatory event of the OT when the Lord descends on Sinai to give the Law to the people redeemed from Egypt (Exod. 19–20). In addition, Moses is portrayed as the mediator of this revelation, a role that was also extended to include the angels (Acts 7:53). The commitments of the nation of Israel to God its Savior are reflected in the maxim, "The secret things belong to the Lord our God, but the revealed things belong to us and to our children forever, to observe all the words of this law" (Deut. 29:29).

The emergence of technical expressions in the OT further illustrates the concept of revelation: God "opens the eyes" (Num. 22:31), or "opens the ear" and "says . . ." (2 Sam. 7:27). Similarly, the prophets see a vision (Isa. 1:1) or the Word of the Lord comes to them (Jer. 1:4). God's secret is revealed to prophets (Amos 3:7) and later to seers (Dan. 2:19). Perhaps the most telling technical expression is: "God reveals himself to someone" (Gen. 35:7; 1 Sam. 2:27). Fundamentally, revelation in the OT is the self-disclosure of God to his chosen servants so that God's people may know his saving deeds and live in harmony with his will.

Postbiblical Jewish Literature

In the Second Temple period, revelation is often regarded as the disclosure of something hidden in a sacred book or in heaven. For instance, Ben Sira teaches that Scripture contains hidden wisdom.

Personified Wisdom hides in the Torah (Sir. 24:23) and reveals her secrets to those who diligently seek her (4:18; 38:34–39:3; 39:6-8). As a scribe who finds wisdom in the Torah, Ben Sira is a bearer of revelation to his students.

The texts unique to the Qumran community portray its founder, the Teacher of Righteousness, as a mediator of revelation. God has revealed himself and his marvelous mysteries to the Teacher (1QH 4:23, 27). The mysteries involve things hidden in the law of Moses and the prophets which are now revealed to the remnant community through the interpretations of the Teacher (CD 1:11; 3:13-14; 1QpHab 7:4). Community members freely pledge to practice all that has been revealed (1QS 1:3; 8-9; 5:8-12).

There is a large body of pseudepigraphal literature in which the revealer figures are great biblical characters of the past. These texts may state that Moses was given the (additional) revelation on Sinai (Jubilees, Apoc. Moses) or texts may relate how a great figure such as Enoch or Abraham journeyed to heaven and returned with revelation (1 Enoch, T. Abraham). The obscure nature of what is seen in heaven necessitates the role of an angel as the "interpreter of revelations" (3 Apoc. Bar. 11:7).

In short, revelatory claims abound in the period between the testaments. The content of the revelation may reinforce peculiar observances of the law, lay bare the structure and operation of the cosmos, shed light on the hardships being faced by the readers, or describe the coming judgment.

New Testament

The kingdom of God is a mystery or secret that is disclosed to the chosen (Mark 4:11). Jesus proclaimed the kingdom of God and demonstrated its arrival with his deeds of power, but this activity did not always move the recipients or witnesses to repentance. The Father has "hidden these things" from the wise and intelligent and has "revealed them to infants" (Matt. 11:25; Luke 10:21). The Father reveals that Jesus is the Messiah, the Son of God (Mark 8:29; Matt. 16:16-17; Luke 9:20). Although the term "to reveal" does not occur in John's Gospel, it is there that Jesus is preeminently the revealer figure (John 14:9; cf. Matt. 11:27; Luke 10:22). Moreover, in each of the Gospels, when Jesus opens the eyes of the blind or unstops the ears of the deaf, there are definite allusions to the OT phenomenon of revelation. The self-disclosure of God is experienced by the person who sees Jesus and hears his message. Finally, the Gospel tradition looks to the future when it describes the day of judgment as a time when everything covered will be revealed (Matt. 10:26; Luke 12:2) and the Son of Man will be revealed (Luke 17:30).

The death and resurrection of Jesus have resulted in his hiddenness until the Parousia. The mystery of the kingdom is now more properly the mystery of the Servant King who was crucified and raised in glory. God granted the Apostle Paul a vision of the risen Son and commissioned Paul to proclaim him among the Gentiles (Gal. 1:12, 16). Along with Christ, faith is now revealed as the way of salvation (Gal. 3:23). The gospel or kerygma reveals the crucified Lord of glory and, when attended by the Spirit (1 Cor. 2:10; Eph. 1:17), imparts God's saving power to the person of faith (Rom. 1:16-17; 16:25-26). The revelation of the mystery includes the union of Jews and Gentiles in one body (Eph. 3:3-6). In the future, there will be a revelation of judgment (Rom. 2:5) and glory (8:18) when Jesus Christ returns to bring salvation to his own and eternal destruction to the wicked (2 Thess. 1:7-10; 2:3-8; 1 Pet. 1:5, 13; 4:13; 5:1). This theme is carried forward within the developing literary genre apocalypse by the last book of the NT, which describes itself as the "revelation *(apokálypsis)* of Jesus Christ" (Rev. 1:1).

Bibliography. M. N. A. Bockmuehl, *Revelation and Mystery in Ancient Judaism and Pauline Christianity* (1990, repr. Grand Rapids, 1997); A. Oepke, "apokalýptō," *TDNT* 3:563-92; H.-J. Zobel, "gālâ (gālāh)," *TDOT* 2:476-88. RANDAL A. ARGALL

REVELATION, BOOK OF

The last book of the NT, also called the Apocalypse (or Revelation) of John.

Genre

The book of Revelation is widely regarded as an apocalypse, a genre of revelatory literature widely represented in early Judaism from ca. 200 B.C.E. to 200 C.E. The term "apocalypse" itself, used as a modern generic designation for revelatory literature similar to the Revelation of John (e.g., 1-2 Enoch, 2-3 Baruch, 4 Ezra), was derived from the title of the book as found in its opening words: "the revelation (Gk. *apokálypsis*) of Jesus Christ" (Rev. 1:1). The book is formally framed as a letter, with an epistolary prescript which concludes with a doxology (1:4-6) and an epistolary postscription consisting in a grace benediction (22:21), though typical epistolary features are not found in the body of the work. It contains a number of characteristics which are often said to characterize apocalypses including pseudonymity, reports of visions, reviews of history presented as prophecies, number speculation, the presence of an "interpreting angel," expectation of an imminent end, pessimism, dualism, determinism, and bizarre imagery. Such lists are problematic since many of these features are found in eschatological literary contexts which are clearly not apocalypses. A more adequate description of the apocalyptic genre takes into account the three related generic dimensions of form, content, and function: (1) Form: an apocalypse is a 1st person prose narrative, with an episodic structure consisting of revelatory visions often mediated to the author by a supernatural revealer, so structured that the central revelatory message constitutes a literary climax, and framed by a narrative of the circumstances surrounding the primary revelatory experience. (2) Content: the communication of a transcendent, usually eschatological, perspective on human experience through a variety of literary devices, structures, and imagery, which (3) function so that the recipients of the message will be encouraged to continue to pursue, or if necessary to modify, their thinking and behavior in conformity with transcendent perspectives.

Authorship

The author of Revelation tells us that his name is John four times in the framework of the book (1:1, 4, 9; 22:8). Since John (the anglicized form of Ioannes, in turn a graecized form of the Hebrew name Yohanan, meaning "Yahweh is gracious") was a relatively common Jewish name in antiquity, it is not immediately evident who this particular John actually was. The author further identifies himself as "his (God's) servant" (1:1), as well as "your brother and companion in the tribulation, kingdom, and endurance in Jesus" (v. 9), but this does not help very much except that it indicates that the author regards his audience as equals. The book is traditionally part of the Johannine corpus, which consists of five compositions: the Gospel of John, the three Letters of John, and the Revelation of John. However, the name John occurs only in the *titles* of the Gospel and Letters of John, which appear to have been added to these works sometime in the 2nd century C.E. While there was some doubt in the ancient Church that Revelation was written by John the Apostle (the dissenting opinions of the elder Gaius and Dionysius, bishop of Alexandria, were preserved by Eusebius *HE* 7.25), the common view among the church fathers of the 2nd and 3rd centuries was that all of these works were written by the Apostle John, the son of Zebedee and the brother of James. Modern critical scholars, aware of the striking differences in the grammar, vocabulary, style, and theological perspective between the Gospel and Letters of John and the Revelation of John, generally assign these works to at least two different authors, neither of which is thought to be the Apostle John. Various scholars have proposed that Revelation was written by the shadowy figure of John the Elder (Eusebius *HE* 3.29.2-4), or by John Mark or by John the Baptist or the heretic Cerinthus (3.28.2; Epiphanius *Adv. haer.* 51.3-6).

Even though it is no longer possible to know who this John was who wrote Revelation, it is possible to construct a basic profile of his social identity. Since the name John was exclusively a Jewish name until it came to be used by Christians beginning in the 2nd century, the Jewish origin of the author is certain. The grammar of Revelation indicates that the author was a native speaker of Hebrew or Aramaic, who reveals an interest in Jerusalem and the Jewish temple and exhibits an intimate familiarity with the OT, usually in Hebrew, though occasionally in Greek. Further, the author was a Christian who considered himself a prophet in the Judaeo-Christian tradition. Though the author does not explicitly identify himself as a prophet, he does describe the book he is writing as a "prophecy" (1:3) and a "prophetic book" (22:7, 10, 18-19). His prophetic

***The Four Horsemen* (Rev. 6:2-8), woodcut from *The Apocalypse* by Albrecht Dürer (probably 1496/1498). Death, Famine, Pestilence, and War trample their victims** (Rosenwald Collection, © 2000 Board of Trustees, National Gallery of Art, Washington)

self-consciousness is also revealed by the presence of two commissions in the book (1:9-20; 10:1-11) which are similar to prophetic call narratives in the OT (Isa. 6:1-13; Jer. 1:4-10; Ezek. 2:8–3:3; cf. 1 En. 14:8-25). The author comes closest to identifying himself as a prophet in the words attributed to the revelatory angel in Rev. 22:9: "I am your fellow servant with you and your brothers the prophets." John appears to have been a member of a prophetic circle or guild, perhaps as a master prophet, who exercised a prophetic ministry among the Christian churches of Roman Asia. It is likely that the author was a Palestinian Jew who became a Christian and emigrated to Roman Asia in the wake of the First Jewish Revolt (66-73).

Date

During the 19th century the prevailing opinion among scholars was that Revelation was written between 64 and 70 C.E. Since the early 20th century, however, there has been a gradual shift toward the new consensus that Revelation was written ca. 95, toward the end of the reign of Domitian (81-96). The main reason for this shift in opinion is that the proponents of the earlier date read Revelation against the background of the Neronian persecution which took place in Rome following the great fire in 64, while advocates of the later date read Revelation against the background of the supposed Domitianic persecution of the late 90s. Among the weaknesses of the earlier date is the fact that "Babylon" was not used as a symbol for Rome before the First Jewish Revolt in 66-73, and the fact that the Nero *redux* ("returned") or *redivivus* ("returned to life") myth, reflected in Rev. 13 and 17, did not begin to become current until some time after Nero's suicide on 9 June 68. The chief weakness of the Domitianic date lies in the fact that scholars now recognize that no widespread, officially sanctioned persecution of Christians took place under that emperor. Both the earlier and later dates proposed for Revelation contain aspects of the correct solution, for it appears that the book was written over a 30-year period beginning with the mid-60s and not completed until the end of the 1st or very beginning of the 2nd century.

Purpose and Setting

Throughout Revelation there is an emphasis on the repression and persecution experienced by the followers of Jesus. Rev. 6:9-11 describes the cry for vengeance of those slain for the word of God and the witness they had borne. Rev. 2:13 indicates that Antipas of Pergamon had been executed for his faith. The whore on the Beast, representing Rome, is said to be "drunk with the blood of the saints and martyrs of Jesus" (17:6). Until recently, it was thought that a persecution under the emperor Domitian provided the historical and temporal setting for the composition of the book: the end of the reign of Domitian (81-96). It is now known that the so-called Domitianic persecution was largely the invention of church fathers from the 3rd century on, who were probably extrapolating the historical situation within which Revelation was written from the book itself. While it is clear that some persecution has actually occurred (e.g., the execution of Antipas of Pergamon), it is less clear whether other references to persecution refer to the past or to the author's expectations for the future. The author does regard the present time as a critical period in the history of the world and imminently expected the final conflict between God and Satan to be enacted through the people of God against those people held in thrall by the Roman Empire. While no official persecution of Christians was put in motion by Domitian, it is likely that sporadic opposition to Christians took various forms in Roman Asia, and that these incidents were regarded by John of Patmos as presaging the eschatological conflict to come. In this situation of tension and conflict, the author provided his audience with the divine assurance that their God was fully in control of historical events and that they would eventually be vindicated by him.

Sources and Integrity

The author of Revelation exhibits a close familiarity with many of the works which came to comprise the OT, particularly with such prophetic books as Isaiah, Jeremiah, Ezekiel, and the apocalypse of Daniel. Though he alludes to the OT from 300 to 400 times (scholarly assessments vary considerably), he never formally quotes a biblical text. Nevertheless, the OT is used in a variety of ways in Revelation. Frequently the author uses phrases and motifs from the OT (often a pastiche of allusions to two or more books) as a vehicle for expressing his own theological perspectives. While other early Christian authors characteristically use the OT to demonstrate that the biblical promises have been fulfilled in Christ, the author of Revelation rarely uses the OT in this way. Occasionally he uses larger segments of books such as Ezekiel and Daniel to structure sections of his visionary narratives.

In addition to allusions to the OT the author also makes frequent use of apocalyptic traditions which are also reflected in such nearly contemporary works as the Similitudes of Enoch (1 En. 37–41), 4 Ezra, and 2 Baruch, though it does not appear likely that he alludes to these works directly.

Structure

Revelation exhibits the most complex structure of any Jewish or Christian apocalypse. One of the most obvious features is the significance to the author of the number seven, which occurs 54 times throughout the book. The author makes extensive use of groupings of seven, such as the seven proclamations to the seven churches (chs. 2–3), and the visionary narratives of the seven seals (6:1–8:1), the seven trumpets (8:2–11:18), and the seven bowls (15:1–16:21). Various attempts to arrange other unnumbered vision sequences in groups of seven have not proven convincing (e.g., A. Y. Collins, *The Combat Myth*). These series of seven are juxtaposed with other units of text which have little to do either with the heptads within which they are embedded or the larger context of Revelation. These quasi-independent textual units, often called "interludes," include 7:1-17 (the sealing of the 144 thousand); 10:1-11 (the angel with the little scroll); 11:1-13 (the two witnesses); the woman, the child, and the dragon (12:1-18); the beasts from the sea and the land (13:1-18); the whore of Babylon (17:1-18); the fall of Babylon (18:1-24); the rider on the white horse (19:11-16). These units are very different from each other. Some are symbolic visions whose meaning is not explicated (12:1-18), while the meaning of other symbolic visions is explained by an interpreting angel (17:1-18). Others are not visions at all but prophetic narratives (11:1-13; 13:1-18). All of these texts are extremely important to the author, who has embedded them in unifying literary structures. The diversity of form, style, and structure suggests that these textual units were not originally written for inclusion in their present literary contexts, but were rather adapted to the context when the author produced a finished composition toward the end of the 1st century.

While the four series of seven dominate Rev. 1–16, chs. 17–22 are dominated by a very different literary structure. Rev. 17:1–19:10 and 21:9–22:9 are a pair of angelic revelations with a very similar beginning and concluding structure:

Rev. 17:1–19:10	Rev. 21:9–22:9
17:1 Then came one of the seven angels with the seven bowls	21:9 Then came one of the seven angels with the seven bowls full of the seven last plagues
and he spoke with me saying, "Come, I will show you the judgment of the great Whore. . . ."	And he spoke to me saying, "Come, I will show you the bride, the wife of the Lamb. . . ."
17:3 He then transported me to the desert in prophetic ecstasy	21:10 He then transported me in prophetic ecstasy to a great and high mountain.
Then I saw . . . [Vision reports 17:3b–19:9]	Then he showed me . . . [Vision reports 21:10b–22:5]
19:9b Then he said to me, "These are the true words of God . . ."	22:6 Then he said to me, "These words are trustworthy and true . . ."
19:10 Then I fell before his feet to worship him	22:8b And when I heard and saw this I fell down to worship before the feet of the angel who showed me these things.
But he said to me, "Don't do that! I am a fellow servant with you and your brothers who maintain the witness to Jesus.	But he said to me, "Don't do that! I am a fellow servant with you and your brothers the prophets and with those who keep the commands of this book.
Worship God!"	Worship God."

These formal parallel structures each frame a sequence of visions. Rev. 17:1-3; 19:9-10 frame three vision sequences: the whore on the scarlet beast (17:4-18), the fall of Babylon (18:1-24), and the victory celebration in the heavenly throne room (19:1-8). Rev. 21:9-10; 22:6-9 frame the vision of the new Jerusalem (21:11–22:5). These paired angelic revelations in 17:1–19:10 and 21:9–22:9 also frame, and thereby emphasize, the intervening text in 19:11–21:8, which contains visions narrating the final defeat of God's foes.

Bibliography. D. E. Aune, *Revelation,* 3 vols. WBC 52 (Nashville, 1997-98); R. Bauckham, *The Climax of Prophecy: Studies on the Book of Revelation* (Edinburgh, 1993); G. K. Beale, *The Book of Revelation.* NIGTC (Grand Rapids, 1999); A. Y. Collins, *The Combat Myth in the Book of Revelation.* HDR 9 (Missoula, 1976); *Crisis and Catharsis: The Power of the Apocalypse* (Philadelphia, 1984); J. J. Collins, ed., *The Origins of Apocalypticism in Judaism and Christianity,* vol. 1 of *Encyclopedia of Apocalypticism* (New York, 1998); L. L. Thompson, *The Book of Revelation: Apocalypse and Empire* (Oxford, 1990). DAVID E. AUNE

REZEPH (Heb. *reṣep*)
A town included in a list read by a messenger of the Assyrian king Sennacherib to King Hezekiah of Judah (2 Kgs. 19:12 = Isa. 37:12). The list consisted of cities destroyed by the Assyrians in earlier campaigns and suggests that Rezeph (Akk. *Raṣappa*) may be located in the vicinity of a northern tributary system of the Euphrates River. The message was intended to undermine the will to resist the invading Assyrian army. Most likely Rezeph was incorporated into the Assyrian Empire by Shalmaneser III (858-824 B.C.). The town then became an important trading center and was a provincial capital within the empire. C. SHAUN LONGSTREET

REZIN (Heb. *rĕṣîn*)
1. The last king of Syria (Aram) before Damascus fell to the Assyrians in 732 B.C.E. Rezin formed a coalition with Pekah of Israel (and possibly others) against the rising power of the Assyrians under Tiglath-pileser III, probably after 738, when an Assyrian text lists him among others who paid tribute. This "Syro-Ephraimite league" put pressure on Ahaz of Judah to join, and Ahaz' apparent refusal (or simple failure to act) prompted the invasion referenced in 2 Kgs. 16:5; 2 Chr. 28:5; Isa. 7:1-9.

2 Kgs. 16:6 suggests that Rezin even restored Elath for Aram at this time, but the spelling of Aram is possibly a scribal error for Edom. In either case, the moment was a time of crisis for Judah. The force of Rezin and Pekah caused Ahaz to appeal to Assyria for help (2 Kgs. 16:7), quite against the counsel of Isaiah (Isa. 7:3-9). Assyria responded by moving against the coastal cities and then turned east toward Damascus in 732. Rezin was killed at this time and Aramean power and influence came to an end.

2. One of the families listed in Ezra 2:48 = Neh. 7:50 among the temple personnel returning from exile.

Bibliography. W. T. Pitard, *Ancient Damascus* (Winona Lake, 1987). ANDREW H. BARTELT

REZON (Heb. *rĕzôn*)
The son of Eliada who escaped from his master, King Hadadezer of Zobah, and headed a "marauding band." Subsequently he founded the Syrian kingdom of Damascus and became, as the ruler of much of Syria, an enemy of Solomon (1 Kgs. 11:23-25). Some scholars identify him with Hezion, but evidence is lacking (1 Kgs. 15:18).

RHEGIUM (Gk. *Rhḗgion*)
A city founded by Greek colonists ca. 720 B.C.E. in the extreme southwestern tip of the Italian peninsula. In Greek mythology the site is associated with the navigational hazards of Scylla (a rock outcrop) and Charybdis (a whirlpool). The city became allied with Rome during the Punic Wars. It was destroyed by an earthquake in 91 B.C.E. and rebuilt by Caesar Augustus as Rhegium Julium in the early 1st century C.E. Separated from the island of Sicily by the Straits of Messina, Rhegium became a stopping place for shipping traveling from the west coast of Italy to the eastern Mediterranean. Acts 28:13 indicates that Paul and his companions waited for one day there on their journey to Rome.
D. LARRY GREGG

RHESA (Gk. *Rhēsá*)
A descendant of Zerubbabel and ancestor of Jesus named only in Luke's genealogy (Luke 3:27).

RHODA (Gk. *Rhódē*)
A servant in the house of Mary the mother of John Mark (Acts 12:13). Answering Peter's knock after his miraculous escape from prison, she was so excited at seeing him there that she forgot to open the gate and was unable to convince members of the household gathered for prayer that the apostle was actually standing outside (Acts 12:14-15).

RHODES (Gk. *Rhódos*)
A large island in the Aegean Sea, SW of Asia Minor, with a port city of the same name. Strategically located at the entrance to the Aegean, Rhodes flourished in trade and politics, founding colonies in Sicily and Italy. The city of Rhodes was founded on the northeast part of the island in the late 5th century B.C. The Colossus of Rhodes, one of the seven wonders of the ancient world, was a statue of the sun-god Helios, more than 30 m. (100 ft.) high located at the entrance to the city (but not straddling the harbor). Cato and Julius Caesar were students at the school of rhetoric on Rhodes.

The earliest biblical reference to the island's inhabitants may be in the Table of Nations (Gen. 10:4), where some Hebrew manuscripts and the Samaritan Pentateuch read Rodanim (so NRSV, NIV; MT "Dodanim"), as does the par. 1 Chr. 1:7 (cf. Ezek. 27:15, MT "the men of Dedan"; NRSV "Rhodians").

Rome sent Rhodes and other cities a letter declaring support for Simon's rule over the Jewish state (1 Macc. 15:23). Herod the Great's submission to and acceptance by Octavian occurred on Rhodes (Josephus *BJ* 1.20.1), and Herod had various interests there (1.21.11). On the return leg of his third missionary journey Paul stopped at Rhodes (Acts 21:1). DOUGLAS LOW

RIB
A curved bone, often cartilaginous, attached to the spine and protecting the viscera (Heb. *ṣēlāʿ*; Aram. *ʿalaʿ*). It was from one of Adam's ribs that God formed Eve (Gen. 2:21-23). The second beast in Daniel's vision has three ribs in its mouth (Dan. 7:5; NRSV "tusks"). Elsewhere biblical usage is less precise, rendering the Hebrew term as "side," with reference to cultic furnishings (e.g., Exod. 25:12, 14; 26:20), side chambers of the temple (1 Kgs. 6:5-6; Ezek. 41:5), the leaves of a door (1 Kgs. 6:34), and the slope of a hill (2 Sam. 16:13).

RIBAI (Heb. *rîḇay*)
The father of Ittai (Ithai), one of David's Thirty (2 Sam. 23:29 = 1 Chr. 11:31).

RIBLAH (Heb. *riḇlâ*)
A city (modern Ribleh) located on the east bank of the Orantes River, occupying a strategic position in the northern Beqaʿ Valley. In 609 B.C.E. the Egyptians under Neco II asserted control over Syria-Palestine and deposed Jehoahaz of Judah, imprisoning him at Riblah and placing his brother Eliakim (Jehoiakim) on the throne in Jerusalem (2 Kgs. 23:31-35). Twenty years later, it was at Riblah that Nebuchadnezzar punished Zedekiah of Judah before exiling him to Babylon (Jer. 39:5-7 = 52:9-11 = 2 Kgs. 25:6-7). The Riblah mentioned as part of the territory of the Israelites in Num. 34:11 is a different site, as yet unidentified. GARY P. ARBINO

RIDDLE
A wisdom genre common in the literature of the ancient Near East. Examples abound in Sumerian, Babylonian, Assyrian, Egyptian, Iranian, and Greek sources. One Sumerian riddle proposes a classic riddle question: "What is the most useful thing for mankind?" The widespread riddle, "What is the strongest thing in the world?" is represented in the Samson stories (Judges) and in 1 Esdr. 3:1–5:6.

Riddles appear throughout the OT and are related to fables, parables, and metaphors, all of which require that the hearer or reader look behind the words and images to discern the meaning or hidden wisdom therein. Some scholars speak of the "clue" and "trap" form which riddles take. Riddles probably had their origin in some specific situation in the life of a people. They were probably originally independent of the tales and stories in which they appeared, and as riddles were passed on from generation to generation.

One function of the riddle form is to test the participants and hearers in order to discern some truth. But this quest for truth can take a playful turn during the riddling. The riddle contest in the Samson narrative, in which the Israelite is matched with the Philistines in both intellectual and physical contests, is an example of this playfulness, occurring in a setting with quite high stakes (Judg. 14:14, 18).

The OT Wisdom Literature contains many riddles. 1 Kgs. 10:1-3 tells of Solomon, Israel's patron and purveyor of wisdom par excellence, engaging in a riddle contest with the queen of Sheba. Josephus reports a tradition of an exchange of "tricky problems and enigmatic sayings" between Solomon and Hiram, king of Tyre (*Ant.* 18.143).

1 Esdras preserves a tale of a riddle contest at the court of Darius in which one of the oldest riddles in the world is proposed to three youths, presumed guards of the king. Whoever can solve the riddle "What is the strongest thing in the world?" will be rewarded handsomely. The three youths offer separate answers: wine, the king, and women, respectively. In the original, secular version of the contest the third page wins, with the answer "women," but in a later version "truth" is added as the winning entry, thus moralizing the tale.

Riddles also appear in prophetic oracles (e.g., Amos 6:12). Many of the riddles in the Bible, especially those associated with Samson and Solomon (Song of Songs, Proverbs), may reflect an underlying erotic context. WILLIAM R. GOODMAN

RIGHT HAND

The term "right hand" (Heb. *yāmîn*) often refers to one's literal right hand (Ezek. 39:3; Jon. 4:11). However, it is also symbolic of authority and power: the signet ring was worn on the royal right hand (Jer. 22:24), the elder son received the greater blessing via the right hand (Gen. 48:14, 17), and the position of honor was at one's right hand (Ps. 110:1, 5; cf. Mark 14:62; Col. 3:1). If one was dishonest, the right hand was said to be false (Ps. 144:8, 11).

The right hand of God performs acts of deliverance (Exod. 15:6), victory (Ps. 20:6[MT 7]), and might (Isa. 62:8). Defeat is seen as the inactivity or withdrawal of God's right hand (Ps. 74:11; Lam. 2:3). The right hand of God gives support (Ps. 18:35[36]) and blessings (16:11).

As an adjective *yāmîn* can refer to the right eye (Zech. 11:17) or thigh (Judg. 3:16) or simply to the right side (Deut. 17:11; Josh. 1:7; Ezek. 1:10). Additionally, it refers to the direction "south," since the right hand of one facing east would be to the south (2 Kgs. 23:13). GREGORY A. WOLFE

RIGHTEOUSNESS

English treatments often separate Heb. *ṣdq* and Gk. *dikaioún* into "justification" and "righteousness," reflecting historical differences over whether the sense was "declare (a person) righteous," as in a law court, or actually "make righteous," implying moral transformation. In a basic sense, the terms imply "relation to a norm" or "covenant" or "power" or "order."

There is a certain general parallelism of development between *ṣdq* and *dikaioún* language. Legal uses develop for both (Ps. 9:4[MT 5]; Isa. 5:7), a sense of "proper order, proper comportment" (*ṣeḏeq-ṣěḏēqâ* and *mišpāṭ*, "righteousness and justice"; doing the "right" thing); and hence an ethical sense (Ps. 15). The NT inherits the forensic, law-court aspects and the moral connotations (cf. the plural of *ṣěḏāqâ* for the "triumphs [of Yahweh]," e.g., Judg. 5:11; cf. also 1 Sam. 12:7; Mic. 6:5, "saving acts"; Ps. 103:6, "vindication"). Paul emphasizes such saving righteousness/justification in Rom. 3:21-26.

But whose righteousness is involved, God's or Israel's, and how do they relate? Some scholars attempt to arrange the evidence in terms of *ṣdq* as an activity of God and as human activity or behavior. A "two-way relationship" between God and Israel (as in the covenant) may be the starting point, preexilic in terms of national righteousness (Jer. 31:28, cf. 30; 22:3) but after the Exile more concerned with righteousness of the devout individual before God (Ezek. 18:2, 5-9, 25-29). The covenant relationship especially assumed the king was responsible for maintaining righteousness in Israel (Ps. 72:1-7). God's *ṣěḏāqâ* as saving action is projected into the future (Isa. 62:1; 63:1).

While there is considerable emphasis on righteousness as involving certain traits of pious behavior, the forensic and salvific aspects in what God does or will do continue, especially in the Dead Sea Scrolls. The Qumran community's radical, apocalyptic outlook stressed election, sin, grace, and God's righteousness as saving activity as well as judgment. The priestly Teacher of Righteousness at Qumran taught righteousness (CD 6:10-11; 1QpHab 8:1-3) in terms of a rigorist understanding of the Law, but was hardly a parallel to Jesus of Nazareth.

Though doubtless aware of this rich background in the Hebrew Scriptures, Jesus did not often use righteousness/justification terminology. Likely he did see his mission as directed to "sinners," not the pious "righteous" in terms of his day (Mark 2:17 par.), and saw himself and John the Baptist as messengers who "justified" God's wisdom (Luke 7:35 = Matt. 11:19). In the parable of the Pharisee and the tax collector, it is the latter who goes home vindicated or accounted righteous (Luke 18:14). Luke 10:29; 16:15 suggest a Jesus who was hard on those seeking self-justification.

The Matthean development of the Jesus tradition in a Jewish-Christian world exhibits a particular interest in righteousness. Matt. 5:6; 6:33 suggest God's righteousness as a gift eschatologically, like the kingdom. Matt. 5:10, 20; 6:1 call for righteous living; 3:15; 21:32 may reflect a view of salvation history incorporating both divine gift and human response.

Among the considerable uses of terms from *dikaioún* in Acts, the most significant is Paul's sermon (Acts 13:39) about "everyone who believes" being "set free" from all those sins "from which you could not be freed by the law of Moses." Paul himself did not speak of being justified "from sins" but liberated from sin (Rom. 6:18).

It is in Paul that righteousness/justification comes into greatest prominence in the NT. Several factors in the pre-Pauline period help explain the prominence of this OT theme in Paul's mature thought and that of other early Christian writers, including use of the OT phrase "the righteous one" (cf. Isa. 53; Wis. 2:12-20) to describe Jesus (e.g., Matt. 27:19; Luke 23:47; Acts 3:14; 7:52; 22:14; 1 Pet. 3:18; 1 John 2:1). The phrase "the righteousness of God" has been claimed as a technical term, possibly going back to Deut. 33:21 and developing in apocalyptic literature, including Qumran (cf. 2 Cor. 5:21; cf. Rom. 1:17; 3:21, 22, 25, 26; 10:3; Phil. 3:9; Matt. 6:33; Jas. 1:20; 2 Pet. 1:1).

Paul's contribution was to bring together his entire gospel message under "righteousness/justification" to a degree accomplished with no other metaphor of salvation. His call and conversion are often given a key place, but coming to distinguish fully "righteousness from the law" and "righteousness through faith in Christ" (Phil. 3:9; Rom. 9:30-31; 10:5-11) represents a longer process of reflection, shaped by Jewish-Christian formulations about Jesus' death and by Scripture.

The justice *(dikaiosýnē)* of God which can reveal wrath (Rom. 3:5; 1:18ff.) and the salvific righteousness of God (3:21-26) both come into play, the latter through the death of Christ and his being raised by God. To be united with this Christ by hearing and believing this message (Rom. 10:10-17) and by conversion-baptism (6:4-7) carries with it the imperative to present the whole self henceforth as "weapons" in the war against sin and unrighteousness (6:13-14). Paul developed righteousness/justification out of the apocalyptical and missionary situation, especially so as to include Gentiles by faith along with Jews by faith, as the heart of his overall vision of God's plan (Rom. 3:28-30; 4:11-12, 23-24; 10:5-13). Paul's understanding of God's kind of righteousness now available in Christ removes all boasting and illusions of self-achievement, for it rests upon God (1 Cor. 1:29-31) and justifies God in calling the Gentiles (Rom. 9:23-26; 15:8a, 9-12) and for the hopes Paul holds for Israel (Rom. 11:11-12, 25-32; 15:8).

Paul's experience and presentation of righteousness/justification, as participation in Christ's righteousness and the benefits of justification (Rom. 5:1-5; 8:3-4, 10-11; 12:3-8) in the overlap of the old and new ages, inevitably changed as time went on without the end coming, as the Church grew more Greco-Roman and OT/Jewish roots were obscured. In Eph. 2:4-10 Paul's emphasis on grace and faith continues, but the verb is not "be justified" but "be saved"; the forensic, judgment note is muted, and the absence of future eschatology opens the way to new ethical application (4:24; 5:9; cf. Titus 3:3-7).

James not only uses the phrase "righteousness of God" (Jas. 1:20) but in 2:14-26 stresses justification, not involving an impotent, merely intellectual "faith" but faith and one's life and deeds.

In the Johannine literature the Gospel of John speaks of righteousness in connection with Jesus' vindication, in a forensic setting (John 16:8, 10; cf. 5:30; 7:24). 1 John 2:1 presents Jesus as the Righteous One, a sacrifice for sins. From the life arising out of this follows the ethical admonition to "do righteousness" (1 John 2:29; 3:7, 10).

See JUSTIFICATION.

Bibliography. D. A. Carson, ed., *Right with God: Justification in the Bible and the World* (Grand Rapids, 1992); J. D. G. Dunn, *The Theology of Paul the Apostle* (Grand Rapids, 1998); B. Przybylski, *Righteousness in Matthew and His World of Thought*. SNTSMS 41 (Cambridge, 1980); J. Reumann, *Righteousness in the New Testament* (Philadelphia, 1982); H. H. Schmid, "Creation, Righteousness, and Salvation," in *Creation in the Old Testament*, ed. B. W. Anderson. IRT 6 (Philadelphia, 1984), 102-17; M. A. Seifrid, *Justification by Faith*. NovTSup 68 (Leiden, 1992); J. A. Ziesler, *The Meaning of Righteousness in Paul*. SNTSMS 20 (Cambridge, 1972).

JOHN REUMANN

RIMMON (Heb. *rimmôn;* Aram. *rammān;* Akk. *ramānu*) **(DEITY)**

An epithet of the Syrian deity Hadad, whom the Syrian commander Naaman worshipped at Damascus (2 Kgs. 5:18; cf. Zech. 12:11, "Hadad-rimmon").

RIMMON (Heb. *rimmôn*) **(PERSON)**

An inhabitant of Beeroth in Benjamin whose sons Baanah and Rechab, in an attempt to gain David's favor, murdered Saul's son Ishbosheth as he slept (2 Sam. 4:2, 5-12).

RIMMON (Heb. *rimmôn*) **(PLACE)**

1. En-rimmon ("pomegranate spring"); a city allotted originally to Simeon (Josh. 19:7) that eventually became part of a southern district of Judah (15:32). In the postexilic period, En-rimmon was one of the cities in which Judeans settled (Neh. 11:29). A late text appended to Zechariah refers to the whole land of Judah "from Geba to Rimmon," suggesting that this Rimmon was the southernmost town of Judean occupation during that period (Zech. 14:10). It has traditionally been identified with Ḥorvat Rimmon/Khirbet Umm er-Ramāmîm (137086), Eusebius located a town called Eremmon ca. 28 km. (16 mi.) from Eleutheropolis (Bethguvrin) in the vicinity of Ḥorvat Rimmon. Recent excavations, however, have demonstrated that Ḥorvat Rimmon was not occupied in the Iron Age. A more likely identification is Tel Ḥalif/Tell Khuweilifeh (1373.0879), less than 1.6 km. (1 mi.) NW of Ḥorvat Rimmon.

2. A levitical city assigned to the Merarites and belonging to the tribe of Zebulun. In Zebulun's list of levitical cities (Josh. 21:35), Dimnah is an unknown location and probably a scribal mistake for Rimmon (cf. 1 Chr. 6:77[MT 62], "Rimmono"). The town is usually identified with modern Rummâneh/Ḥorvat Rimona (179243), ca. 10 km. (6 mi.) N of Nazareth.

3. An outcropping of rocks to which 600 Benjaminites fled from Gibeah after being defeated by the other Israelite tribes (Judg. 20:45-47). They remained there four months until the Israelites offered them peace (Judg. 21:13). The rock of Rimmon has traditionally been identified with on outcropping of rock ca. 6.5 km. (4 mi.) E of Bethel, the site of the modern village of Rammûn.

RONALD A. SIMKINS

RIMMONO (Heb. *rimmônô*)

Alternate form of Rimmon **2** (1 Chr. 6:77[MT 62]); probably the same as Dimnah (Josh. 21:35).

RIMMON-PEREZ (Heb. *rimmōn pereṣ*)

The fourth camp during the wilderness journey after the Israelites left the wilderness of Sinai. Num. 33:19-20 places the site between Rithmah and Libnah. No exact location is known, but it is probably located on the southeastern side of the Sinai Peninsula.

PETE F. WILBANKS

RING

Rings described in the Bible are most often of gold or bronze, while those found in the archaeological record are also of silver, iron, copper, and bone. On a woman, rings were worn on the fingers, nose (Gen. 24:22), and ears for decoration. For a man, they were connected with identity or authority and generally took the form of signet rings (Gen. 41:41-42); cf. the irrevocability of a decree sealed with a signet ring (Esth. 8:8). Rings were considered luxury items (Isa. 3:21) and represented status (Jas.

2:2). They were among the goods collected by Aaron to make the golden calves in Sinai (Exod. 32:2-4).

Rings were associated with the sacred. In addition to being part of the worship of other gods (Gen. 35:4) and the improper worship of Yahweh (Exod. 32:4), rings were part of the frame (26:24), table, and altar (25:26-27) of the tabernacle. Gold rings were used to attach the priest's ephod to his breastplate (Exod. 28:26-28).

Rings were also functional devices. Silver rings held back the curtains in the palace of the Persian king (Esth. 1:6), and poles would have been inserted into rings attached to the sides of the ark to enable its transport (Exod. 25:12). Rings were used figuratively as a metaphor for beauty (Prov. 11:22), value (25:12), and powerful people (Jer. 22:24; Hag. 2:23). KATHARINE A. MACKAY

RINNAH (Heb. *rinnâ*)
A Judahite, the son of Shimon (1 Chr. 4:20).

RIPHATH (Heb. *rîpat̲*) (also DIPHATH)
A people descended from Gomer (Gen. 10:3; called Diphath at 1 Chr. 1:6). Josephus identified them with the Paphlagonians. Their association with Ashkenaz and Togarmah underscores their identification with Asia Minor.

RISSAH (Heb. *rissâ*)
A place where the Israelites camped after their escape from Egypt (Num. 33:21-22). The exact location is unknown.

RITHMAH (Heb. *rit̲mâ*)
One of the places where the Israelites camped after their escape from Egypt (Num. 33:18-19). Its exact location, W of the Gulf of Aqabah, is unknown.

RITUAL
Ritual plays a significant role in the religious practice of early Israel, later Judaism, and early Christianity. Efforts to construct a definition of ritual that does justice to the variety of specific ritual acts envisioned in biblical materials have been unsuccessful. The religious rituals of the Bible provide a means for the faith community to discover, enact, and reflect upon its faith. Ritual enactments provide occasions for engaging the divine being and for responding to the full range of life experiences in the context of the sacred. Ritual practices provide a means for maintaining traditional types of beliefs. They also function, however, as a creative force in the construction of new forms of faith.

The religious practices of Israel as evidenced in the biblical materials exhibit at least three distinct dynamics. First, the festal prescriptions of early Israel took shape within an agricultural context that reflects the rhythms of the annual harvests. Ritual presentations of firstfruits and offerings from one's harvests provided a means to enact a response of thanksgiving to the blessings of Yahweh. At the same time, these ritual presentations provided a means by which one could gain the ongoing blessings of Yahweh.

Second, Israelite ritual practices also demonstrate an engagement with the dynamics of history. Passover is an excellent example. The Passover meal provided the occasion for a "remembering" of Yahweh's saving acts on behalf of the Israelite community. "Remembering," however, gave rise to a "retelling" of the Exodus story. In this ritualized narration, the Exodus from Egypt was actualized in such a way that the story of God's actions in the past became a present reality. Israel recognized the power of ritualized memory and narration.

Finally, the Priestly traditions of the Pentateuch reflect a ritual dynamic focused on the holiness of the tabernacle and the divine presence that resides within the holy of holies. The Priestly concern for holiness shows a concern for the very good order of creation (cf. Gen. 1:1–2:4a). Thus, priestly rituals may function to bring into being some aspect of the very good order of creation (Lev. 8, 9), to maintain the already existing order (Num. 28–29), or to restore order when it has been disrupted through sin or impurity (Lev. 13–14, 16). This ritual system seeks to maintain the purity and holiness of the sacred community so that the divine presence may continue to reside in its midst.

The writings of the early Church reflect two movements in relation to ritual activity. On the one hand, some texts reject certain aspects of the Jewish purity system (Mark 7:1-23) and the Jewish sacrificial system (Hebrews). Paul's discussion of Christian freedom from the law (Gal. 2:15–3:29; Rom. 1–8) has often been understood as a rejection of Jewish ritual. In this view, ritual activity is understood as a primary example of "righteousness based on works" from which the Christian is free.

On the other hand, some texts clearly recognize that ritual activity is central to the Christian faith. In the biblical texts two rituals in particular are emphasized: baptism and communion. Baptism functions, in part, as a ritualized means of entering into and becoming a part of the Christian community. Paul views baptism as a means of dying to the old self and rising to newness of life in Christ (Rom. 6:1-11). It provides one means by which a person may become a member of the community understood as the body of Christ (1 Cor. 12:12-26).

Paul's understanding of the ritual meal of communion includes "remembering" and "retelling," re-enactment of the original supper and proclamation of the story (1 Cor. 11:23-26). The ritualized meal allows one to identify with the death of Jesus in such a way that his story becomes the believer's story. At the same time, the meal allows the story of Jesus to become the story of the community. Thus communion functions, in part, to actualize the past in the present for the believing community. In this way, ritualized activity contributes to the construction and formulation of Christian identity.

Bibliography. F. H. Gorman, Jr., *The Ideology of Ritual.* JSOTSup 91 (Sheffield, 1990); "Ritual Studies and Biblical Studies," *Semeia* 67 (1994): 13-36; R. L. Grimes, *Ritual Criticism* (Columbia, S.C., 1990). FRANK H. GORMAN, JR.

RIZIA (Heb. *riṣyā'*)
A son of Ulla of the tribe of Asher (1 Chr. 7:39).

RIZPAH (Heb. *riṣpâ*)
The concubine of Saul and daughter of Aiah, known for her devotion to her sons and her insistence that they have a proper burial. She became a minor player in the great sport of kingship, and an important factor between the ruling houses of Saul and of David.

After Saul's suicide, his son Ishbosheth became king, in name only. He accused Abner, his father's general, of having sexual relations with Rizpah (2 Sam. 3:6-11), a sign that Abner was usurping the kingship and claiming the throne as his own (cf. 2 Sam. 16:20-22; 1 Kgs. 2:22). Ishbosheth's objection gave Abner an excuse to negotiate with David for the kingship, vowing to transfer the kingdom from the house of Saul and establish David's throne (2 Sam. 3:6-10).

Some 27 years later (ca. 970 B.C.E.) blame for a three-year famine was placed on Saul's having violated Israel's covenant with Gibeon (Josh. 9:3, 15-20). As recompense, David gave the Gibeonites seven of Saul's descendants: Rizpah's two sons, Armoni and Mephibosheth, and five sons of Saul's daughter Merab (2 Sam. 21:5-6, 8). The seven were put to death and their bodies left exposed on a hill (2 Sam. 21:9). Rizpah spread sackcloth over a rock — a public sign the nation had repented — and began her vigil for a proper burial, from the barley harvest (Apr.) until the season of early rains (Oct.; 2 Sam. 21:10). Learning of her devotion, David ordered a public burial for the members of Saul's household (2 Sam. 21:11-14).

Robin Gallaher Branch

ROADS
Roads and streets during the OT period were generally two or more lanes in width (at least 3-4 m. [10-13 ft.]), wide enough to accommodate the traffic of chariots, carts, and wagons. During the Roman period roads ranged from two to five lanes in width. Until Roman times roads were generally unpaved, although city streets were occasionally paved. Although the technology of paving did exist, no paved road from the pre-Roman period has been found in Palestine, and unpaved thoroughfares are assumed in the biblical literature (cf. Hos. 2:6[MT 8]; Prov. 15:19; 22:5). Streets in ancient Mesopotamia were sometimes paved with techniques almost matching that of the Romans, comprising a foundation layer of bricks set in asphalt, over which was laid a surface of heavy limestone slabs, with the joints between them sealed with asphalt. In Israel the paving of city streets is attested as early as the Early Bronze Age. The Iron Age streets at Tell Deir ʿAlla were paved, and the paving was regularly refurbished. The main street of Israelite Dan was paved with stone. Cobbled streets from the Iron Age include the 3.5 m. (11.5 ft.)-wide street discovered at Ashdod and the 10th-century street at Gezer. The process of road building during the OT period is alluded to in Isa. 40:3; 57:14; 62:10; Mal. 3:1. The procedure simply involved "clearing" (Heb. *pnh*) the roadway and "smoothing" *(yšr)* and "leveling" *(sll)* the surface. The Romans introduced the practice of paving open highways. Their technology featured superb foundations, adequate drainage, and one or more layers of cement or stone paving designed to last for centuries. The remains of many of these paved Roman highways still exist today.

Roads were generally named according to their destinations. For example, the "Beth-shemesh road" mentioned in 1 Sam. 6:12 was the road which led to the town of Beth-shemesh, the "Bashan road" (Num. 14:25; Deut. 3:1) led to Bashan, and the Beth-haggan road (2 Kgs. 9:27) led to Beth-haggan.

Since few physical traces of pre-Roman roads have been discovered, determining the locations of these earlier thoroughfares is inferential. First, there may be evidence of a particular road in the historical sources. Judg. 21:19 mentions a highway from Bethel to Shechem, passing W of Shiloh. Second, lines of ancient settlements, as revealed by archaeological excavations or surveys, often testify to the existence of ancient thoroughfares, since roads determined settlement patterns. Cities, towns, villages, way stations, and forts generally sprung up along roads; even after a road fell into disuse and disappeared, the ruins of settlements which once flourished along the road continued to attest the former road's existence. Third, the courses of later routes, including Roman, medieval, and 19th-century roads, frequently preserve the courses of OT period roads, since these later roads usually simply followed the courses of earlier roads. Finally, the geographical and topographical conditions of an area determined to a large degree the courses taken by roads. Mountain passes, river fords, harbors, easily traversed valleys, ascents, and springs attracted roads, while deep canyons, high mountains, swamps, deserts, and unfordable rivers were natural barriers avoided by roads.

The courses of many roads of Israel from both OT and NT periods have been traced. Some 245 OT period roads have been identified, including 62 roads running north-south through Israel's coastal plain, 42 roads connecting the northern Sharon Plain with Transjordan and the Beqaʿ Valley, 34 north-south roads through the highlands of Judea and Samaria, five north-south roads through the western Jordan Valley, 14 local roads in Galilee, 29 in Samaria, and 59 in Judea. Of these, six were particularly important in biblical times, including two north-south highways and four east-west roads. The most important was undoubtedly the main international coastal highway and its northern branches. This highway connected Egypt in the south with Phoenicia, Syria, and Mesopotamia in the north. Coming from Egypt, the road entered Canaan near Gaza and proceeded northward through the coastal plain, passing Ashkelon, Ashdod, Aphek, and then skirting along the eastern edge of the Sharon Plain (which was swampy in biblical times). From the northern end of the Sharon Plain several passes

Roadway (possibly the King's Highway) running north-south through Moabite territory (J. R. Kautz)

led through the lower Mt. Carmel range and into the Jezreel Valley, the most important of which came out at Megiddo. From the Jezreel Valley one branch turned westward, passing north of Mt. Carmel and thence to Phoenicia. A second branch turned east and passed through Beth-shean to Transjordan. A third branch continued northward, passing Mt. Tabor, the Sea of Galilee, Hazor, and eventually reaching Mesopotamia.

The second important north-south highway was the Beer-sheba–Jerusalem–Jezreel road which ran along the crest of the Israelite highlands. This road led from Beer-sheba to Hebron, Bethlehem, Jerusalem, Gibeah, Ramah, Mizpeh, Bethel, Shiloh, Shechem, Samaria, Dothan, Ibleam, and Jezreel. The highway has been called the "Way of the Patriarchs," since Abraham, Isaac, and Jacob and his sons frequently traveled it; it is the road most often mentioned in biblical narratives.

The four important east-west roads provided passage across the Israelite highlands, linking the coastal plain and the Jordan Valley. The northernmost was the Jezreel Valley pass, which led through the Jezreel and Beth-shean valleys, passing the towns of Jokneam, Megiddo, Taanach, Jezreel, and Beth-shean. The second east-west route led past Samaria, the pass between Mts. Gerizim and Ebal, Shechem, and the Fari'a Valley. The third pass linked the coast with the Jordan Valley by way of Gezer, the Beth-horon ascent, Gibeon, Jerusalem (or, alternately, by Bethel and Ai), and Jericho. The fourth pass connected Gaza with southern Transjordan by way of Gaza and Beer-sheba.

Bibliography. M. Avi-Yonah, "Map of Roman Palestine," *Quarterly of the Department of Antiquities of Palestine* 5 (1936): 139-93; L. Casson, *Travel in the Ancient World* (1974, repr. Baltimore, 1994), 163-75; D. A. Dorsey, *The Roads and Highways of Ancient Israel* (Baltimore, 1991); R. J. Forbes, "Land Transport and Road-Building," in *Studies in Ancient Technology,* 3rd ed. (Leiden, 1993) 2:131-92; *Notes on the History of Ancient Roads and Their Construction* (Amsterdam, 1934).

DAVID A. DORSEY

ROCK

The rocky terrain of Canaan provided the background for a rich imagery found in the Bible. From its obvious use for literal hardness (Jer. 5:3; 23:29; cf. Isa. 50:7), "rock" (Heb. *sela'*, *ṣûr;* Gk. *pétra*) also included the idea of stable and secure support, such as the stability that God gives to life (Ps. 40:2[MT 3]; Matt. 7:24-27; Luke 6:48). Similarly, it is used of an immovable foundation; to remove "the rock" is equivalent to shaking the world (cf. Job 18:4).

Its literal use of providing shade from an overhanging "rock/cliff" in the desert sun (Isa. 32:2) was extended to the figurative use of God providing refuge for his people. God is described as a rock (2 Sam. 22:2 = Ps. 18:2[3]; 71:3) that gives security and safety to his people (cf. 2 Sam. 22:32, 47 par.; cf. Ps. 62:2, 7[3, 8]; 89:26[27]). Since rock is hard, the power of God is revealed when he breaks it (Jer. 23:29; cf. 1 Kgs. 19:11).

The Israelites are urged to recall the solidity of their heritage with rock imagery: "the Rock that bore you" (Deut. 32:18) and "the rock from which you were hewn" (Isa. 51:1). The Church is said to be founded upon a rock and therefore able to withstand enemy assaults (Matt. 16:18).

In Isa. 8:14 *ṣûr* is used of the messianic stone rejected by the Jewish "temple builders" (cf. Ps. 118:22; Isa. 28:16). Following these passages, "rock" becomes important for NT typology: Jesus Christ, the rejected "rock of offence," becomes the cornerstone of God's true temple, the Christian Church (1 Pet. 2:6-8). As a rock, Christ is portrayed as smitten in order that the spirit of life may flow from him to all who will drink (John 4:13-14; 7:37-39; 1 Cor. 10:4). LARRY L. WALKER

ROD

A long piece of wood used for support and as a weapon. A long staff (Heb. *maṭṭeh*) was used by travelers for support and shepherds for guiding their flocks (Exod. 4:2; Isa. 10:26). It was also the miraculous rod of Aaron and the Egyptian magicians (Exod. 7:9-12) and was used figuratively for oppression and punishment (Isa. 30:32). Both *maṭṭeh* and *šēḇeṭ* figuratively meant "tribe," presumably from the notion that a group of people were led by a chief with a rod. Heb. *šēḇeṭ* also carries the stronger connotation of smiting and may have been a shorter, clublike instrument (Ps. 23:4; Mic. 7:14). It also was a scepter, a symbol of authority (Judg. 5:14). In the NT Gk. *rhábdos* designates both a rod for support (Matt. 10:10) and for chastisement (1 Cor. 4:21). CHRISTIAN M. M. BRADY

RODANIM (Heb. *rôḏānîm*)

A people descended from Javan (i.e., Greece; 1 Chr. 1:7).

See DODANIM; RHODES.

ROE, ROEBUCK

See DEER.

ROGELIM (Heb. *rōḡĕlîm*)

A town in Transjordan, the home of Barzillai the Gileadite, who escorted David to the Jordan River (2 Sam. 17:27; 19:31[MT 32]). The name comes from Heb. *regel*, "foot," and means "treaders" or "fullers" (artisans who worked with wool and cloth). Possible sites for Rogelim are Tell Barsînyā (223215), 9 km. (5.5 mi.) SW of Irbid, and Ẓaharet Soq'ah. PETE F. WILBANKS

ROHGAH (Heb. Q *rohgâ*, K *rôhăgâ*)

A son of Shemer of the tribe of Asher (1 Chr. 7:34).

ROMAMTI-EZER (Heb. *rōmamtî ʿezer*)

A Levite and son of Heman; leader of the 24th division of singers at the time of David (1 Chr. 25:4, 31). Though the names in 1 Chr. 25:4 are regarded as personal names later in the same chapter (vv. 13-31), many scholars suggest that beginning with Hananiah (v. 23) or Hanani (v. 25) the passage is actually a confused bit of poetic prayer. Rather than a name, the text would read, "I will exalt (my) helper."

ROMAN RELIGION

At every stage that we know it, Roman religious practice was an amalgam of native Latin elements with foreign influence and overlay. Because religion in all societies is conservative and because Rome was an unusually conservative society, survivals of archaic practices in the later Roman state religion provide precious clues about the practices and beliefs of the earliest Roman community.

The native Roman religion consisted of rituals designed to protect or enhance the agricultural and family life of the household on the one hand and the integrity of the community on the other. The Romans perceived all functions, social as well as natural, as manifestations of a divine power. Indeed, the divine power was as much present in the function as it was in control of it. Such powers could be negative as well as positive. That is, the Romans understood a destructive process as resulting from the presence of a negative force, rather than the absence of its opposite. Rituals were intended either to encourage a positive power in its activity or to ward off a dangerous or destructive power.

Some of the best-known powers include the Lares and Penates, which protected the household and its contents. The *genius* presided over the reproductive continuity of the family and was associated specifically with the male. Juno originated as a spirit of female fertility. Vesta protected the hearth and its fire. St. Augustine preserves a long list of agricultural functionaries, remarking that the Romans were not satisfied with a single god of agriculture, but recognized separate powers for each process, from seed to fruit. The most frequently cited example of a negative functionary is *robigus,* the power that attacked crops in the form of a rusty mildew. On the level of the community, *terminus* guaranteed the integrity of boundaries between one household and the next. The cult of Vesta, presided over by the young women of the household, had its urban counterpart in the college of Vestal Virgins.

Religious ceremonies marked the changing of the seasons, both natural and civil. The *fontinalia* celebrated the power of springs and wells. The *tubilustrium* protected the trumpets used to summon the people to assembly, while the *armilustrium* purified weapons after their return from hostile territory.

It follows from the narrowly functionary nature of these divine powers that the native Roman religion was not anthropomorphic and that there was no mythology. From the earliest known times, however, this native religion was overlaid with elements assimilated from Rome's neighbors. According to Roman tradition, an Etruscan dynasty seized power during the 6th century B.C., bringing with them religious traditions of Greek as well as Etruscan origin. Whether the Etruscans were a pre-Italiote native people or immigrants from Asia Minor remains a subject for debate. In either case, it was under Etruscan domination that the Romans first built a temple and installed on the capital their tutelary deities — Jupiter, Juno, and Minerva. The names are Latin, and Jupiter at least derives from the primordial Indo-european sky-father; but the anthropomorphic conception, with the attendant notion that these powers required a temple, is something new. So great was the Etruscan influence on religious matters that the Roman word from which we derive our word "sacred," which is not linguistically Latin, may be of Etruscan origin.

After the expulsion of the Etruscans, during the early Republican period, the Romans continued to welcome deities of foreign origin. The Greek cities of southern Italy were the single most significant influence, but the Romans also received deities of Semitic (Phoenician) origin during the wars with Carthage. Some of these deities came to Rome through the procedure known as *evocaton,* whereby the tutelary power of an enemy city was "called out" and invited to take up residence in Rome. An example is the Phoenician goddess Astarte, brought from Sicilian Eryx under the Greek name of Aphrodite and assimilated with the native Venus. By another process, during the Second Carthaginian War, in response to an oracle allegedly found in the Sibylline books, the Romans brought with great ceremony from Asia Minor a black stone in which resided the power of the Great Earth Mother.

While most of these importations were carefully controlled by Roman religious officials, the city was also of course exposed to influences brought by immigrants and travelers. The most famous example is the cult of Bacchus, or Bacchanalia, outlawed by the Roman senate in 186, but permitted to non-Romans under controlled conditions. This was the first of many so-called mystery religions that developed during the Hellenistic period from more traditional cults such as that of Demeter at Eleusis and Isis in Egypt. Resistance to such religions by the Roman elite was futile, and we know of no further attempts to legislate against them after 186, until the short-lived and sporadic attempts to extirpate Christianity (and Manicheanism) during the late 3rd and early 4th century.

With the rise of these more individualistic religions, traditional Roman religion seems to have declined, at least within the city itself. The emperor Augustus, whose program included restoration of traditional values and traditional religion, boasts of having restored some 82 cults in one year alone. At the same time, he fostered a new cult of Roma, especially in the eastern provinces, with which his own person was closely associated. Nevertheless, while it became customary to honor the emperor's *genius,* the emperor was not himself (a few megalomaniacal exceptions aside) directly worshipped while still alive. The Roman senate would honor the memory of a deceased emperor of whom they approved by declaring him to be of semi-divine status and establishing a cult in his honor.

Despite the ruse of the mystery religions and the evidence for decline of traditional cults during the turmoil of the late Republic, the resilience and vitality of the traditional Roman religion must not be underestimated. The traditional religion was closely associated with the idea of Rome itself, and the Roman elite clung to it long after the emperors themselves had embraced Christianity. In rural areas, traditional dedications to the traditional gods persisted against all efforts of the later empire to suppress them. Evidence of the ancient Roman religion can still be found in Europe today. Shrines at the crossroads dedicated to a Christian saint are the direct descendant of the ancient Roman *compitalia.* The Church of the Virgin Mary on Mt. Eryx in Sicily is the modern counterpart of the Phoenician cult of Astarte, adopted by the Romans as Venus. The practice of associating each Christian saint with cognizance over some specific activity, such as health or travel, may be regarded as the descendant of the ancient Roman "functionary" conception.

Bibliography. C. Bailey, *Phases in the Religion of Ancient Rome* (1932, repr. Westport, Conn., 1972); J. H. W. G. Liebeschutz, *Continuity and Change in Roman Religion* (Oxford, 1979); R. MacMullen, *Paganism in the Roman Empire* (New Haven, 1981); L. H. Martin, *Hellenistic Religions* (Oxford, 1987); R. M. Ogilvie, *The Romans and Their Gods in the Age of Augustus* (New York, 1970); H. J. Rose, *Religion in Greece and Rome* (New York, 1959).

ALDEN A. MOSSHAMMER

ROMANS (Gk. *Rhōmaíoi*)
A designation of persons in one or more of four categories: representatives of the foreign government to which the Jews were subject (John 11:48; Acts 25:16; 28:17); Jews who had been born in Rome or who lived there (2:10); those who claimed an allegiance to the Roman Empire that (it is implied) others did not possess (16:21); and those who possessed Roman citizenship (vv. 37-38; 22:25-29; 23:27). By law Roman citizens could not be flogged or crucified, and when on trial could appeal to the emperor.

ROMANS, LETTER TO THE
The longest of Paul's epistles, placed in most Bibles at the head of the Pauline corpus. It has had enormous influence, attracting such commentators as Origen, Thomas Aquinas, Philip Melanchthon, John Calvin, and Karl Barth. Romans was decisive in the life and thought of Augustine of Hippo, in his conversion and battles with Pelagius over "original sin"; Luther, regarding law and gospel; Calvin, for (double) predestination; and Wesley, on justification and sanctification. In the last century of scholarship, there has been wide agreement on many major points, but new interpretative possibilities have also arisen.

Author, Date, Place

Paul (1:1), apostle to the Gentiles (11:13; cf. 1:5; 15:16, 18), writes from Corinth, during a three-month Greek sojourn, before going to Jerusalem with the collection for the poor among the Christian saints there from his Aegean congregations (Acts 20:3; Rom. 15:25-26). The time of writing is between A.D. 54/55 and 58/59, depending on the chronology followed (51/52, if the less likely "early" chronology). Reconstruction of the circumstances relates to decisions about the text.

Text

The address at 1:7 is "To all God's saints in Rome," but there is no reference to a church there until ch. 16, and then only to the house church of Prisca and

Aquila (16:5). That "in Rome" is lacking in a few manuscripts at 1:7, 15 is likely due to scribes who wished to give the document a less specific and more universal reference. More important, the doxology found in some of the best Greek manuscripts at 16:25-27, with its pattern of "long kept secret, now disclosed," appears in many manuscripts at 14:23, in 𝔓[46] at 15:33, in some manuscripts after both 14:23 and 16:23, and is omitted in some sources (cf. NRSV mg). Some Latin versions lack ch. 15. All this had led to conjectures about a 14-chapter version, known to Origen and used by Marcion; a 15-chapter version; and a 16-chapter one found in most English Bibles. In the 1950s the view came to dominate that Paul sent a 15-chapter version to Rome, and what is now ch. 16 (at least 16:1-20, perhaps with a copy of 1-15 also) to Ephesus. That meant that the 28 people greeted in 16:3-16, including Prisca and Aquila, were in Ephesus, not Rome. But since 1970 the tide has turned, especially in light of the argument that ch. 16 provides a necessary conclusion to the typical Pauline letter. That means that the five to seven house churches mentioned are in Rome, and further that they are to be connected with disputes between "the strong" (in faith) and "the weak" in 14:1–15:3, likely Gentile and Jewish Christians. While the pertinence of ch. 16 remains disputed, the trend is toward acknowledging, in light of the decision that chs. 1-16 went to Rome, that Paul knew a great deal about the situation among fragmented believers in the capital city.

Circumstances and Purposes

The origins of Christianity at Rome are unknown. Belief in Jesus probably arose in the large Jewish community there through (merchants') contacts with Palestine. According to the Roman historian Seutonius (*Claud.* 25.4), the emperor Claudius expelled many Jews because of disturbances "instigated by Chrestus" (Christ), between Jewish followers and other Jews, or between Jewish Christians who had begun to share their good news with Gentiles and Jewish Christians who opposed a gentile mission. This occurred in the year 49 (less likely, earlier, in 42). Some of these Jewish Christians moved eastward; Paul came into contact with them in Corinth (e.g., Aquila and Prisca/Priscilla, Acts 18:1-3; 1 Cor. 16:19), Ephesus, and elsewhere. Later, when tensions cooled (Claudius died in 54), some of these Jewish Christians returned to Rome. But in the interim gentile followers of Jesus had become the dominant form of Christianity in Rome. Through these returning exiles Paul had some knowledge of house churches in Rome for the letter which would be carried there by Phoebe, a minister from the Corinthian seaport of Cenchreae, whom Paul commends (16:1-2). Another historical detail may lie behind Rom. 13, in the fact that Nero, then in his five years of good rule, considered in 58 abolishing indirect taxes, about the unjust collection of which by *publicani* there had been wise protest (Tacitus *Ann.* 13.50-51). In 13:6-7 Paul specifically advises Christians in Rome to pay their taxes as good citizens and not get caught up in movements of unrest.

Several purposes emerge for writing Romans to a now basically gentile group of house churches, with some Jewish Christian returnees.

1. The apostle clearly wants to introduce himself and his gospel to all the Christian communities in Rome. He did not found the churches, and we know of no significant "founder," but the notion that Paul wanted to provide an "apostolic" foundation is not convincing. Paul writes diplomatically, with a certain mutuality (1:11-15), aware of rumors about himself in some quarters (3:7-8; 6:1-2; 9:1-2). But it is by no means clear that he confronts Jewish Christian counter-missionaries who disputed his positions, as in Galatia. Paul presents his gospel therefore apologetically and winsomely, but without its being a "systematic theology."
2. Paul seeks rapport in order to have support in Rome for his proposed mission work in Spain (15:23-29; cf. vv. 14-22). Romans is missionary in interest.
3. Paul asks prayers from Roman Christians for his journey to Jerusalem with the collection for the saints there (15:25-27, 30). That he is angling for contributions from Rome is not clearly implied. That he had fears as to how this gift would be received in Jerusalem is likely (15:30-32). But to see the Jerusalem Jewish Christian community as the "secret addressee" for Romans (perhaps through a "carbon copy" sent there) is a view not as strongly supported as a few decades ago in scholarship.
4. That Paul is concerned to have the "strong" and "weak" in Rome mutually accept each other can be seen in chs. 14–15, esp. 15:7. To this extent the letter has an ecclesiological purpose of church unity, while allowing considerable liberty to each position (Paul himself sides with the gentile "strong" against laws concerning food, drink, and special days; 14:2, 5, 17, 21). This has been called a "pastoral" aim, but it is not without its theological aspects (15:7b-13), and Paul's other aims have pastoral aspects to them.

Romans has been called Paul's "last will and testament." It turns out, on certain assumptions, to be the final letter we possess from him. But Paul wrote vibrantly, as he was completing goals in the East, with new ventures in mind in the western Mediterranean (15:28).

Genre and Other Proposals

Romans reflects the letter form in its opening (1:1-17) and closing (15:14–16:23). The pattern of "doctrinal" section (1:18–8:39 or 11:36), followed by parenesis or the ethics section (12:1–15:13), is typically Pauline. But the body of the letter (1:18–15:13) is thus so lengthy that some term such as "letter essay" is warranted. More recently, categories from ancient rhetoric have been applied, designating Romans as predominantly "epideictic" (Lat. *demonstrativus,* "praising" or "blaming," strengthening an audience's ethos), or "deliberative" (persuasive, as in an assembly), or at times "judicial" (as in a law court), even as an "ambassadorial letter" or a "speech of exhortation" (Gk. *lógos protréptikos*). Much more widely acknowledged is the presence of the "diatribe" form (e.g., 2:1-5, 17-29; 3:27–4:2), where the attempt is made, in interchanges with an (imaginary) interlocator, Jewish or Christian, to criticize arrogant views and persuade to the speaker's position. Literarily, Paul's extensive use of OT material (e.g., 1:17; 3:10-20; chs. 9–11; 15:3-12), at times with rabbinic principles of interpretation (which also reflect Greek logic), as at 4:3-12 (the Abraham story), is apparent. There are citations of what many agree are earlier formulations, often Jewish Christian, used to establish common ground with the believers in Rome who had not been taught by Paul (e.g., 1:3-4; 3:24-26a; 4:25; 10:9; 11:33-36). There may be later additions like 16:25-27 (post-Paul, to round out and universalize Romans), but attempts to designate 2:16 or 6:17b, e.g., as glosses have often met with the response that they are the very key to Paul's argument.

Outline

There is general agreement on major divisions.

I. Introduction: salutation (1:1-7), thanksgiving (1:8-15), theme *(propositio)*, 1:16-17: the gospel as God's power for salvation — the righteousness of God, by faith, for Jew and Greek alike

II. The need for God's righteousness in a world (or "the old age") where divine wrath is being revealed (1:18–3:20)
   - A. Upon all of gentile humanity (1:18-32) — failure to honor and thank God results in idolatry and all sorts of sinning
   - B. Upon Jews too, judgment and wrath (2:1–3:9) — relying on the law of Moses leads to boasting, not keeping the law
   - C. All humanity is accountable, unrighteous, under sin, not justified before God (3:10-20, with scriptural support)

III. The gospel as God's righteouness revealed in justification of ungodly sinners, through Christ by faith (3:21–4:25)
   - A. Without distinction, all share in God's righteousness, through Christ Jesus' sacrificial death (3:21-26)
   - B. Justification by faith excludes boasting about works by Jew or Gentile (3:27-31)
   - C. Exemplified in Abraham, who was justified by faith, not works, prior to circumcision or the Mosaic law (4:1-25)

IV. Meaning of justification and new life in Christ: the new age now, but its freedoms not yet enirely here (chs. 5–8)
   - A. Free from wrath and death (ch. 5) — Adam/Christ contrast
   - B. Free from sin and self (ch. 6) to walk in newness of life
   - C. Free from the law (ch. 7) — the dilemma of the "I"
   - D. Free for life in the Holy Spirit and for hope (ch. 8), living not yet by sight, awaiting redemption (8:23b-25)

V. The gospel of God's righteousness and the unbelief of (much of) Israel (chs. 9–11)
   - A. God's sovereignty and promises: a failure? (ch. 9)
   - B. Israel's failure to respond to righteousness by faith in Christ (ch. 10)
   - C. Paul's hopes for the future (ch. 11): Gentile Christians, no presumptions; Israel, to receive mercy

VI. The meaning of God's justifying righteousness for everyday life (12:1–15:13)
   - A. Exhortations for Christians in community (ch. 12), with regard to the state (13:1-7), and looking toward "the end" (13:8-14, the love-command and eschatology)
   - B. Love and mutual welcome among believers (14:1–15:13, the "strong" and the "weak")

VII. Letter closing: travel section, Paul's plans for visiting Rome and a mission to Spain (15:14-33); a recommendation for Phoebe (16:1-2), greetings (16:3-16, 21-23), a warning about those who cause dissensions (16:17-19). Benediction, 16:20; v. 24 omitted on textual grounds; vv. 25-27 (added), doxology

Reading Romans

Romans has long been treated with emphasis on chs. 1–8 and such themes as sin and grace; righteousness/justification; faith as belief, trust, obedience, and God's faithfulness to the divine promises; peace with God and other blessings of the new life in Christ, including the Spirit. Chs. 9–11, about Israel or theodicy (justifying that God's word has not failed), have sometimes been seen as intrusive or a subsidiary theme. Often statements about predestination (beginning at 8:29; ch. 9) have been the chief concern of interpreters. More recently the focus has been on "salvation history" (Adam, Abraham, Moses, Christ) and the application to Jews (in interreligious conversation), so as to make chs. 9–11 the center of the entire letter. The ethical teachings in chs. 12–15 have at times been the focus of attention — Paul wants to show how his gospel works out in sacrificial service by Christians, not to God but to others in the workaday world (12:1-2). Even if the exhortations in 12:3-21 seem general, not arising directly out of the justification theme, they do rest on all that has been said in 3:21–8:39 (12:1: "therefore," "by the mercies of God" enumerated in prior chapters). Ch. 13, on the state, reflects the context in which Paul writes, and chs. 14–15 address real problems in Rome of integrating divided ethnic house churches. To "welcome one another" (15:7) can then be termed the climax toward which Paul builds his presentation. Or is the goal to be united for the mission to Spain?

Different eras and interpreters have seen different aspects of Romans as especially pertinent. A balanced reading regards the whole as coherent, in light — and as a development — of Paul's theme (1:16-17) about righteousness, God's Christ, and faith.

Bibliography. B. Byrne, *Romans.* Sacra Pagina 6 (Collegeville, 1996); K. P. Donfried, ed., *The Romans Debate,* rev. ed. (Peabody, 1991); J. D. G. Dunn, *Romans 1–8.* WBC 38A; *Romans 9–16.* WBC 38B (Waco, 1988); J. A. Fitzmyer, *Romans.* AB 33 (New York, 1993); E. Käsemann, *Commentary on Romans* (Grand Rapids, 1980); S. K. Stowers, *A Rereading of Romans: Justice, Jews, and Gentiles* (New Haven, 1994); P. Stuhlmacher, *Paul's Letter to the Romans* (Louisville, 1994).

John Reumann

ROME (Lat. *Roma;* Gk. *Rhṓmē*)
A designation both for the ancient city on the Tiber River, located 16 km. (10 mi.) inland from the port of Ostia, as well as for the expansive empire which began to grow during the Republic and continued to increase in size until it reached its greatest extent in the early 2nd century C.E. At its widest extent toward the end of Trajan's reign (98-117), the Roman Empire circled the Mediterranean basin, encompassing all southern Europe, Britain (to the Scottish border), North Africa (to the Sahara), Egypt (to well beyond the first cataract), Asia Minor, the north coast of the Black Sea, Armenia and regions south of the Caucasus, Mesopotamia (to the Euphrates), Syria, and Palestine: 9650 km. (6000 mi.) of frontier.

A knowledge of Roman history and culture sheds light on a number of passages in the OT, Apocrypha, and NT. Heb. *kittîm* is an ambiguous term found in the OT (Isa. 23:1; Jer. 2:10; Ezek. 27:6), where it very likely refers to the Greeks. In the Apocrypha Kittim also seems to refer to the Greeks (1 Macc. 1:1; 8:5), though in the nearly contemporaneous literature of Qumran, the term probably refers to the Romans (1QpHab 2.12-13; 3.9; 4.5-6; 6.1-4; 4QpNah frags. 3-4.I.3). Jews were very much aware of the presence of Roman power in the western Mediterranean, as suggested by the list of Roman conquests to the mid-160s B.C.E. found in 1 Macc. 8:1-16. The significant political links between the Maccabees and Rome are narrated in 1 Macc. 8:17-32; 12:1-4. In the NT the author of Luke-Acts was particularly aware of the ubiquitous political presence of Rome, and carefully weaves allusions to Roman history and culture throughout his work, beginning with explicit mention of the reign of Tiberius in Luke 3:1 and continued through numerous references to Roman political and social institutions in the Acts of the Apostles.

Environment

The soil of Italy is more fertile than that of Greece, though the climate is similar. The topographical system is also very different from that of Greece, for the Apennine Mountains form the backbone of the peninsula with arable land both east and west of the mountain range. Italy is divided into two parts. Continental Italy centers on the Po Valley with the Po River running through the center. Peninsular Italy is divided into three parts: the east coast, west coast, and southern boot. Italy had few good harbors, such as the Bay of Naples, which together with the fact that the Po and the Tiber are the only navigable rivers impeded the development of trade and commerce. Throughout their long history the Romans remained landlubbers. The east coast was sparsely inhabited in antiquity, with little sailing on the Adriatic and no shipping until the time of the Crusades. The west coast consisted of excellent farmland, while the northwest part of the peninsula had mineral resources. The southern tip also had an abundance of arable land, but was particularly vulnerable to invasion. Unlike Greece, Italy was a land suitable for raising cattle.

Origins to the End of the Monarchy (753-509 B.C.E.)

According to Varro, Rome was ritually founded on 21 April 753, one of several legendary 8th-century dates proposed in antiquity (the birthday of Rome was celebrated during the Republic as the *Parilia,* and in the Empire as the *natalis Urbis*). There were in fact two competing legends of the founding of Rome which were ultimately linked in various ways, both going back to the 4th century B.C.E. One centered on the eponymous founder Romulus and his twin brother Remus, the other on Aeneas (whom Augustus claimed as an ancestor), a prince of Troy who fled to the west following the sack of Troy by the Greeks and eventually founded Rome (Dionysius of Halicarnassus *Rom. arch.* 1.72.2), narrated in epic length in Vergil's *Aeneid.* The fact that the Romans regarded themselves as descended from the Trojans meant that they differentiated themselves from both Greeks and Etruscans. After the mid-1st century B.C.E., Rome became known as the *Septimontium* (*septem montes,* "seven hills"), a conception popularized by Varro (*De ling. lat.* 5.41-54; 7.41), though his list (which quickly became canonical) differs considerably from earlier lists of seven hills. The earliest settlement of Rome was on the Palatine and the Forum Romanum (used as a cemetery) by the 10th century, and then after 650 spread to the Quirinal, the Esquiline, and other hills not identical with Varro's list. Throughout the history of Rome, the territory of the city itself (though occasionally enlarged) was called *urbs* and defined by a sacred boundary, the *pomerium,* which was surrounded by the *ager Romanus,* the "Roman territory" (which also increased in size). Roman kingship was nonhereditary and Roman political organization followed the Indo-european pattern of king-council-assembly. While new kings were nominated by the senate, they were approved when the popular assembly *(comitia curiata)* passed a *lex de imperio* conferring the rights of *imperium* on the king. The mythical Romulus (temporarily sharing kingship with the Sabine Titus Tatius) was the first of a canonical succession of seven kings including Numa Pompilius (a Sabine), Tullus Hostilius, Ancus Marcus, Lucius Tarquinius Priscus (the

Roman Forum from Capitoline Hill. The oldest of the city's public squares, it comprised a complex of open spaces and government buildings, temples, and shops (Allen C. Myers)

Etruscan founder of the Tarquin dynasty), Servius Tullius, and Tarquinius Superbus (expelled in 508 according to tradition), a patently artificial list since the names of other kings survive in various sources. The seven kings mentioned in Rev. 17:9 may allude to the tradition that the seven Roman kings represented a complete and predestined number of rulers.

The Romans are descended from a group of related tribes called Latini who originated in central Europe, settling in the region of Latium by the 10th century. Latin, the language spoken by the people of Latium, belongs to the Italic group of Indo-european, which has two major divisions, Oscan-Ubrian and Latin-Faliscan. Oscan was the standardized common language of central Italy until the area was subjugated by the Romans during the Republic. Originally the language of Latium and the city of Rome, Latin eventually displaced the other Italic languages as a result of the increasing political and military power which Rome exerted in central Italy and then throughout the Italian peninsula.

Republic (509-27 B.C.E.)

The monarchy was replaced by a republic whose chief magistrates were two consuls elected annually (thus avoiding concentrating power in the hands of one person), lists of whom, together with significant events, were preserved in the *annales maximi,* a chronicle compiled by the *pontifex maximus* and which served as a major source for such Roman historians as Q. Fabius Pictor and L. Cincius Alimentus (3rd century), Gnaeus Gellius (late 2nd century), and Licinius Macer (1st century). These historians were in turn major sources for Livy and Dionysius of Halicarnassus (*Rom. arch.* 1.6.2), the two historians of the early period of Roman history, major portions of whose works have survived.

The political history of republican Rome falls naturally into two periods, 509-265 and 264-27. During the first period Rome expanded locally (509-336), came to dominate central Italy (336-290), and eventually gained control of the entire peninsula (290-265). This control was partially facilitated by the founding of colonies in areas newly under Roman control as well as by Roman support for local aristocracies. Roman expansionism, which continued through the early 2nd century C.E., was not motivated by the desire to build an empire but rather to protect Rome's existing holdings. During this period, Rome experienced the Gallic invasion which climaxed in the catastrophic sack of Rome ca. 386 B.C.E., resulting in the rebuilding of the city, reorganization of the army, and elimination of the Etruscans as a dominant power. Greek colonists in Magna Graecia, harassed by the Samnites, appealed to Rome for aid, which was forthcoming. The consequent Samnite wars lasted from 325-306, leading to Roman control of the west coast of the peninsula. The conflict was facilitated by the construction of the Via Appia, the first Roman road, in 312 under the censor Appius Claudius. A second series of wars was fought from 298-290 against the Samnites who had allied themselves with Gauls and Etruscans. However, allied with Tarentum, the Romans defeated the Samnite coalition and found themselves in control of most of central Italy. Conflict with Tarentum in the Bay of Naples led to open warfare from 281-272, ending with the fall of Tarentum.

The second period (264-27) saw Roman expansion outside of peninsular Italy, beginning with a series of wars with Carthage (264-201), its primary economic and political rival in the western Mediterranean region, followed by Roman interventions in the Greek east (201-146), and concluded by the gradual dissolution of the Republican constitution and the institution of the principate (146-27). In 264, because of a dispute with Sicily, Rome went to war with Carthage, a Punic city in North Africa colonized in the 8th century by Phoenicians from the

Palestinian coast. The war concluded in 241 when the Carthaginians ceded Sicily to Rome. The Second Punic War (220-201) erupted when Carthaginian expansion in Spain came into conflict with Roman interests there. In the subsequent conflict, Hannibal led an army with elephants through Spain and over the mountains to Italy. Though he won many battles in peninsular Italy, he never quite managed to conquer Rome itself. Hannibal's defeat at Zama in 201 led to the surrender of Carthage, destruction of her fleet, and payment of an enormous indemnity. The period of the first two Carthaginian wars coincided with a complex series of power struggles between the Hellenistic monarchies in the Greek east established by the *diadochoi* or "successors" of Alexander the Great (who died in 323). The three major players (all founders of dynasties in their respective spheres of rule) were Ptolemy in Egypt, Seleucus in Mesopotamia, and Antigonus in Greece and Macedonia. Rome opposed Philip of Macedonia, an Antigonid, because of his aid to Carthage. The Second Macedonian War (200-196), prosecuted by the Roman general Flamininus, led to Philip's defeat and Flamininus' proclamation of the freedom of Greece at the Isthmian games in Corinth in 196. Following two more Macedonian wars, Rome destroyed Corinth in 146 and incorporated Greece and Macedonia as Roman provinces. The Fourth Macedonian War (148-146) largely coincided with the Third Punic War (149-146), an uneven conflict which resulted in the destruction of Carthage in 146 (both Corinth and Carthage were rebuilt by Julius Caesar in 46 on the hundredth anniversary of their destruction). Finally, the year 133 became a landmark in Roman history when Attalus III of Pergamon died and bequeathed his kingdom to Rome, which became the Roman province of Asia in 129. Rome had by this time acquired much of the desirable real estate around the Mediterranean (Spain, Carthage, Pergamon, Macedonia), with the exception of Egypt.

The social history of Rome during the Republic is dominated by the so-called Conflict of the Orders, a major emphasis of late republican historians whose work was preserved by the Roman historian Livy (59 B.C.E.–17 C.E.) and the contemporary Greek historian of Rome, Dionysius of Halicarnassus (ca. 60 B.C.E.–ca. 30 C.E.). This Conflict of the Orders centered on the twin problems of debt and availability of farmland. Political and social power was concentrated in the hands of the aristocratic patricians (*patres,* "fathers") who belonged to privileged clans *(gentes).* The plebs constituted the commons and may have originated as the clients of patricians. The plebs was itself divided into two groups: those who belonged to prominent families and those who were poor. The former considered themselves equal in status to the *gentes,* but were constitutionally prevented from enjoying an egalitarian status with the patricians. By the end of the monarchy, there were four basic rights *(ius),* all four possessed by the patricians, though only two by the plebeians. Of the two public rights, *ius suffragii* (right to participate in the assembly) and *ius honoris* (right to hold office), only the first was held by plebeians. Likewise, of the two private rights, the *ius commercium* (right to buy and sell) and the *ius conubii* (right of intermarriage), only the first was held by plebeians. The prohibition of intermarriage, found in the Twelve Tables (cf. Livy *Urb. cond.* 4.4.5; Dionysius *Rom. arch.* 10.60.5; Cicero *Republic* 2.37.63), the earliest surviving codification of Roman law, was critical in keeping the two orders separate. Patricians monopolized the priesthoods, principal magistracies, the *interregnum* procedure, senate membership, and effectively controlled the popular assembly through patron-client relationships. The two distinctively plebeian magistracies were the tribunate and aedileship. The senate originated during the monarchy as a council of kings, appointed first by kings and then during the Republic by the chief magistrates. By the end of the monarchy there were 300 senators (perhaps based on three Roman tribes, each consisting of 10 *curiae*). The *comitia,* or assemblies, were three in number: the *comitia curiata,* in which each of 30 original *curiae* (a clan-type form of social organization) had a single vote; the *comitia centuriata,* a military assembly based on landed wealth; and the *comitia tributa,* the plebeian assembly. Following the *secessio plebis,* the temporary emigration of the plebs from Rome to the Aventine in 494, they formed their own state within a state with an assembly *(concilium plebis)* and annually elected their own magistrates (10 tribunes, two aediles) for nearly two centuries. The codification of the Twelve Tables of Roman law by two successive committees of 10 men (Decemvirs) in 451 and 450, replacing the consulship and the tribunate, represents a major plebeian success (Livy 3.33-57; Diodorus 12.24-26). The Sexto-Licinian laws of 367 allowed plebeians to hold the consulship. Equality of the plebs became more or less complete by 287 with the enactment of the *lex Hortensia,* which turned the decrees of the plebs *(plebiscita)* into laws binding on all the people including patricians. From the time of the Gracchi (last third of the 2nd century), Roman political life was polarized by the *optimates* (who sided with the senate) and the *populares* (who worked with the popular assembly and the tribunate).

The Greeks, who had colonized Magna Graecia in southern Italy by the mid-8th century, came to dominate Roman cultural life by the mid-1st century. Greek literature, mythology, and history were central in Roman education, and Greek was the first language of Roman education. By the end of the 1st century B.C.E. many young Roman aristocrats were routinely educated in Greece and were thus bilingual. By the 1st century, only a small percentage of the population of the residents of Rome were of Roman or Italian ancestry, perhaps 10 percent. Within Rome itself various national groups often maintained linguistic and cultural traditions; the extensive Jewish community, e.g., which numbered from 30 to 50 thousand, was a Greek-speaking community, doubtless because of the hellenization of Palestine.

Empire (27 B.C.E.–476 C.E.)

The Roman Empire, from its foundation by Augustus in 27 B.C.E. through the fall of the western empire in 476 C.E., falls roughly into two periods, the Principate (27 B.C.E.-283 C.E.), when the emperors took the title *princeps* ("first man"); and the Dominate (284-476), when emperors assumed the title *dominus* ("lord") and the principate was transformed into a bureaucratic and totalitarian monarchy.

In the eight years following the civil unrest sparked by Julius Caesar's assassination on 15 March 44 B.C.E., Octavian gained control of Italy and the west (43-35) and after that the east at the decisive sea battle at Actium where he defeated Antony and Cleopatra VII (31), ending the chaotic civil wars. Octavian, given the name Augustus by the senate in 27 (he was almost given the name Romulus, the legendary founder of Rome), ruled as the *princeps* from 27 B.C.E. to 14 C.E. At the beginning, the age of Augustus was regarded by some as the restoration of the Republic (Velleius *Hist. rom.* 2.89; Ovid *Fasti* 1.589), but by others as the beginning of autocracy (Dio *Hist.* 52.11.1; 53.11.4). The latter view proved to be the more correct one. While Augustus began by laying down extraordinary dictatorial powers, he gradually assumed a series of political and civil powers and offices including the title *imperator* ("emperor"), the *tribunicia potestas* ("tribunician powers") in 23 (Dio 53.32.5), and *pontifex maximus* ("high priest") in 12 B.C.E. According to Tacitus, Augustus "gradually increased his power, and drew into his own hands the functions of the senate, the magistracies, and the laws" (*Ann.* 1.2). Augustus, the adopted son of Julius Caesar under the title *divi filius* ("son of the god [Julius]"), continued the Julio-Claudian dynasty which included Tiberius (14-37 C.E.), Gaius (37-41, nicknamed Caligula "baby boots"), Claudius (41-54), and concluded with Nero (54-68). Following the unstable period of 68-69, when three emperors reigned, Vespasian (69-79) and his sons Titus (79-81) and Domitian (81-96) established the short-lived Flavian dynasty. Nerva, who reigned only briefly (96-98), established a new imperial dynasty consisting of a series of adoptions, by adopting Trajan (98-117), of Spanish descent the first emperor to originate in the provinces. When Trajan died the empire was at its greatest extent before or after. Trajan's adopted successor Hadrian (117-138) was a relative on his father's side. Hadrian in turn adopted Antoninus Pius (138-161) who, following Hadrian's recommendation, adopted Marcus Aurelius (161-180), a relative of Hadrian and a devotee of Stoicism who has been widely admired as a model philosopher-ruler. Finally, the son of Marcus Aurelius, Commodus (181-190) was the last of the five imperial successors of Trajan.

During the early empire, there were two new social developments: (1) the social pyramid (consisting of an upper class numbering not more than 5 percent of the population, no middle class, and a vast lower class) received a new summit which consisted of the imperial household, and (2) the

Augustus of Prima Porta **(shortly after 20 B.C.E.). Marble with traces of polychrome; Chiaramonti Museum, Vatican** (Photo Philip Gendreau, N.Y.)

provincials and provinces were integrated into the Roman system. The traditional Roman orders which constituted the upper-class minority, the senate (whose members numbered ca. 600 during the 1st and early 2nd centuries), and the equites or knights (numbering ca. 20 thousand during the same period), came to include the urban decurions, aristocratic members of the councils of provincial cities. Under Augustus and his successors, the senate retained a formal role (such as the investiture of emperors) but lost all real political power. While the equites only held public office as judges and officers during the late Republic, under Augustus they were employed as *procuratores Augusti,* placed in charge of the administration of imperial property as well as the economic and financial administration of the whole empire. There were two very different kinds of relationships in the Roman social structure between members of the upper and lower classes. The emperor treated senators and equites as *amici* ("friends") or equals, while his relationship to the masses was that of a powerful patron to dependent clients. Augustus took the title *pater patriae* ("father of the fatherland") in 2 B.C.E. as a formal expression of this dependency relationship.

Augustus extended the Roman Empire to include Egypt, parts of Asia Minor, the areas S of the Danube from the Alps to the Black Sea, and northern Spain. Increasing urbanization was a characteristic of the early empire, which included some 1000 cities of varying populations. While most cities had a population of 10-15 thousand, Pergamum was a mid-range city with a population of ca. 50 thousand, Antioch and Alexandria had populations in the hundreds of thousands, and Rome, the largest city of the empire, an estimated 1 million inhabitants. The entire population of the Mediterranean world during the reign of Augustus is estimated at 50 to 80 million; at least 20 percent were slaves, 10 percent Jews, and 90 percent lived on the land (giving an agricultural base to the imperial economy). During the reign of Augustus, a dual provincial system was developed consisting of imperial provinces (originally Gaul, Spain, and Syria) and senatorial provinces governed by proconsuls (such as Asia and Africa) who nevertheless had first to be approved by the emperor. Roman provinces were integrated into the structure of the empire by several means: (1) construction of a network of roads begun during the late Republic; (2) introduction of coherent provincial administration; (3) admission of provincials into Roman military service; (4) extension of Roman citizenship to provincials; and (5) the process of urbanization. The extension of Roman citizenship was particularly significant. Under Augustus, according to his "testament" called the *Res Gestae Divi Augusti* ("The Achievements of the Divine Augustus"), there were 4,937,000 Roman citizens in 14 C.E., a number which increased to 5,984,071 by 48 (Tacitus *Ann.* 11.25). Under Caracalla (211-217), citizenship was given to all free inhabitants of the empire. Paul of Tarsus is an example of a provincial who possessed Roman citizenship. The distinction between provincials and Roman citizens which existed early in the 1st century C.E. was gradually transformed during the 2nd century into the distinction between the *honestiores* (the high born) and *humiliores* (the low born). These received unequal treatment under Roman law. Capital offenses for Roman citizens during the 1st century and *honestiores* during the 2nd century and beyond frequently consisted of exile, while capital offenses committed by noncitizens or *humiliores* was punished by crucifixion.

The *pax Romana* ("Roman peace"), which began initially as the achievement of Augustus, was a period extending from his reign to that of Antoninus Pius (138-161) which enjoyed relative tranquility both domestically and on the frontiers. Exceptions to this peaceful era included the First and Second Jewish Revolts (66-73 and 132-135) and the intervening Jewish revolts under Trajan in Cyrenaica, Egypt, and Mesopotamia (115-117). The attempt of the emperor Gaius to introduce a golden statue of himself into the Jewish temple in Jerusalem (an act virtually guaranteed to trigger a Jewish revolt) came to nothing when Gaius was assassinated in 41 C.E. by members of the Praetorian Guard (Philo *Leg.* 197-337; Josephus *BJ* 2.184-203; *Ant.* 18.256-309).

The various aspects of Roman religion, such as Roman civic religion, Roman army religion, and Mithraism, had little significant impact on non-Romans with the exception of the Roman imperial cult, i.e., the worship of deceased and even living Roman emperors, primarily by provincials in the east and west. From Augustus to Constantine, no less than 36 of 60 emperors were apotheosized and given the title *divus*, "divine." In Rome, certain deceased emperors were posthumously designated divine by the Roman senate and worshipped alongside Dea Roma (the goddess Roma, a personification of the city of Rome), and the more traditional romanized divinities of Greek cult and myth. In the Greek east, living emperors were sometimes accorded divine worship, which was as political as it was religious. In the earliest Christian martyrdom, the Martyrdom of Polycarp (written during the third quarter of the 2nd century), Polycarp is required to sacrifice to the imperial cult or suffer martyrdom. Rev. 13 suggests that Christians found themselves in the same predicament late in the 1st century.

Bibliography. G. Alföldy, *The Social History of Rome* (Baltimore, 1988); *The Book of Acts in Its First Century Setting*, 2: *Greco-Roman Setting*, ed. D. W. J. Gill and C. Gempf (Grand Rapids, 1994); *CAH*, 2nd ed., 3: *Rome and the Mediterranean to 133 B.C.*, ed. A. E. Astin et al. (Cambridge, 1989); 7/2: *The Rise of Rome to 220 B.C.*, ed. F. W. Walbank et al. (Cambridge, 1989); F. Millar, *The Roman Near East: 31 B.C.–A.D. 337* (Cambridge, Mass., 1993); H. H. Scullard, *From the Gracchi to Nero: A History of Rome from 133 B.C. to A.D. 68*, 5th ed. (London, 1982); *A History of the Roman World, 753 to 146 B.C.*, 4th ed. (London, 1980); J. E. Stambaugh, *The Ancient Roman City* (Baltimore, 1988).

DAVID E. AUNE

ROOF

In biblical times, roofs were usually flat and used for many domestic activities. Roofs were built upon lintels and beams made of wood or stone; wooden poles were placed across these supports and then covered with mud and other organic materials. Roof-rollers are known in the Middle East today, and stone examples have been found in archaeological contexts; they are used to flatten the mud and further protect the building from rain.

In ancient Israel guest quarters were built on roofs (2 Kgs. 4:10), and families often slept on their roof (1 Sam. 9:25). People engaged in mourning on their roofs (Isa. 15:3; 22:1), and worshipped and offered sacrifices there as well (Jer. 19:13; 32:29; Zeph. 1:5). Excavations at the site of Ashkelon uncovered a small incense altar found above preserved roof remains. Josh. 2:6 suggests that foodstuffs and other agricultural products were dried and processed on roofs, a practice still common in the Middle East. Deut. 22:8 demands the construction of parapets around house roofs, recognizing the potential danger of these well-used areas. JENNIE R. EBELING

ROSE

A flower (Heb. *ḥăḇaṣṣeleṯ*) that has been called the rose in many translations (Isa. 35:1), but actually refers to a bulb plant (NRSV "crocus"). Likely candidates are the narcissus *(Narcissus tazetta)* and the lily *(Lilium candidum)*. The rose of Sharon in Cant. 2:1 may be one of these plants or another plant such as the *Tulipa montana*. Later writings (Wis. 2:8; Sir.

24:14; 39:13; 50:8; 3 Macc. 7:17; 2 Esdr. 2:19) mention the rose (Gk. *rhódon*), probably either the Phoenician rose (*Rosa phoenicia* L.) or the oleander (*Nerium oleander* L.). In Rabbinic and Modern Hebrew, the rose is Heb. *wered.*

MEGAN BISHOP MOORE

ROSH (Heb. *rō'š*)
A son (or grandson) of Benjamin, among those who accompanied Jacob to Egypt (Gen. 46:21; "head" or "chief"). His name does not occur in other lists of Benjamin's descendants (Num. 26:38-41; 1 Chr. 7:6-12; 8:1-5).

RUBY
Rubies were unknown in the ancient Near East. Some translations use "ruby" when Hebrew suggests a prized red-colored stone. Heb. *kaḏkōḏ* (NAB, NIV, NJB, NKJV, NRSV "ruby") is a product from Syria (or Edom), traded for Tyre's merchandise (Ezek. 27:16). The battlements of an idealized Zion are of *kaḏkōḏ* (Isa. 54:12). Heb. *pĕnînîm* (NJPSV, NIV, NKJV "rubies") designates gems of great value (Job 28:18; Prov. 3:15; 8:11; 31:10). The NIV renders "ruby" for *'ōḏem,* an engraved stone on the high priest's breastpiece (Exod. 28:17; 39:10) and a stone adorning the king of Tyre (Ezek. 28:13). Some translations read "agate," "amber," "carnelian," "coral," "garnet," "jasper," "pearl," or "sardius" for these terms.

JOSEPH E. JENSEN

RUE
A strong-scented perennial herb (*Ruta graveolens* L.), the green-gray leaves of which produce a bitter etheric oil prized as a purgative and as a condiment (Gk. *pḗganon*). In NT times this plant was imported from Greece. According to Luke 11:42 Jesus referred to a Pharisaic practice of tithing rue, but the text may have originally mentioned not rue but dill (Gk. *melánthion;* cf. the variant reading in Matt. 23:23); dill was, in fact, tithed, but rue was not (*m. Ma'as.* 4:5; *Šeb.* 9:1).

RUFUS (Gk. *Rhoúphos;* Lat. *Rufus*)
1. The son of Simon the Cyrene and brother of Alexander (Mark 15:21). The reference suggests that he was well known to the readers of Mark.

2. One whom Paul greets, along with his mother, in Rom. 16:13. He is called "chosen in the Lord." If Mark's Gospel was written in Rome, he may be the same as **1** above.

JOE E. LUNCEFORD

RUHAMAH (Heb. *ruḥāmâ*)
"Pitied," a name given to Hosea's daughter (Hos. 2:1[MT 3]).

RULER OF THE SYNAGOGUE
One of several offices of the Jewish synagogue. The ruler or "elder" or "head" (Gk. *archisynágōgos*) was responsible for maintaining order in the assembly (Luke 13:14), deciding who was to conduct public worship (Acts 13:15), and keeping the congregation faithful to the Torah (18:1-17).

The ruler was not a scribe, but stood in rank immediately after the office of scribe. A group of elders directed the activities of the local synagogues, and the ruler was probably chosen from among those elders. Jairus (Mark 5:22), Crispus (Acts 18:8), and Sosthenes (v. 17) are mentioned by name in the NT as ruler or head of the synagogue.

Bibliography. L. L. Grabbe, "Synagogues in Pre-70 Palestine: A Re-assessment," *JTS* N.S. 39 (1988): 401-10; J. Gutmann, ed., *The Synagogue* (New York, 1975).

DALE ELLENBURG

RUMAH (Heb. *rûmâ*)
The home of Zebidah the mother of King Jehoiakim (2 Kgs. 23:36). Rumah has been variously identified with Arumah (Khirbet el-'Ormah; 180172) near Shechem (Judg. 9:41) and with Khirbet er-Rûmeh/Ḫorvat Ruma (177243), ca. 10 km. (6 mi.) N of Nazareth.

RUSH
See REED, RUSH.

RUTH (Heb. *rûṯ;* Gk. *Rhouth*)
A Moabite, the widow of the Judahite Mahlon (Ruth 1:2-5); the central figure of the book of Ruth, and an ancestor of David and Jesus (Matt. 1:5; cf. Ruth 4:17-22).

RUTH (Heb. *rûṯ*), **BOOK OF**
The book of Ruth has no named author, no named date of origin, and there is modern debate as whether or not the purpose of the story was to settle the issues of universalism versus exclusivism, matriarchy versus patriarchy, the status of the levirate marriage, the status of the poor, land rights, or the Davidic genealogy. The book, therefore, appears in various orders in the predecessors to the Hebrew Bible and the LXX. Ruth is assigned to be read in the synagogue for the Festival of Shavuot (Feast of Weeks or Pentecost), which celebrates the spring grain harvest as well as the giving of the Torah. The story of Ruth is a perfectly crafted Hebrew folktale, in that it incorporates complex social and religious issues into an entertaining and romantic narrative.

Ruth is a story of relationships between family members, between nations, between God and Israel. The story begins with Elimelech and Naomi, along with their two sons, Mahlon and Chilion, journeying to the foreign country of Moab because their own city of Bethlehem in Judah is famine stricken. During the 10 years that the family lives in Moab, the sons marry women named Ruth and Orpah. Eventually, all three men in the family die, leaving Naomi alone with her two daughters-in-law. Naomi decides to return to her native Judah when she hears that the Lord has visited the people there and provided them with food. As the three women set out, Naomi tells Ruth and Orpah to return to their own mothers' homes. Both of the young widows at first refuse to leave Naomi, but eventually Orpah kisses her mother-in-law goodbye; Ruth continues with Naomi to Bethlehem.

Ruth and Orpah are not ordinary daughters-in-law to the Israelite Naomi: they are Moabites, i.e., traditional enemies, temptresses and corrupters of Israel. Moabites serve other gods, and the Israelites are often in trouble for mingling with the foreigners (Judg. 10:6; cf. Num. 22–25; Deut. 23:2-6; Ezra 9:1-2; Neh. 13:1-2; Ps. 83; Zeph. 2:9).

Orpah returns to her own people and gods, but Ruth clings to Naomi and Naomi's God. Naomi makes one more plea to which Ruth replies with what has become a familiar phrase, "entreat me not to leave thee." Naomi finally accepts Ruth's resolve to stay with her, and the two journey in search for a more prosperous land.

The rabbis of the 1st century were so impressed with this story of friendship and commitment that they used it to explain how the enemies of Israel would become part of the house of Israel even though certain laws prohibited it. The story became a paradigm for conversion in the faith. Naomi's requests and Ruth's rejections constitute a rabbinic form for a prospective proselyte to follow in order to become a Jew:

1. *Request:* But Naomi said to her two daughters-in-law, "Go, return each of you to the house of her mother." (1:8a)

   Rejection: And they said to her, "No, we will return with you to your people." (1:10)

2. *Request:* But Naomi said, "Turn back, my daughters; why will you go with me?" (1:11a)

   Rejection (anticipated): "Do I still have sons in my womb that they may become your husbands?" (1:11b)

3. *Request:* "Turn back, my daughters, go your way." (1:12)

   Rejection: Then they lifted up their voices and wept again. Orpah kissed her mother-in-law, but Ruth clung to her. (1:14)

4. *Request:* And she said, "See, your sister-in-law has gone back to her people and to her gods; return after your sister-in-law." (1:15)

   Response: But Ruth said, "Do not press me to leave you or to return from following you; for where you go I will go, and where you lodge I will lodge; your people shall be my people, and your God my God." (1:16)

   Accceptance: When Naomi saw that she was determined to go with her, she said no more. (1:18)

Noting that Naomi told Ruth three different times to "turn" or "return," early rabbis correspondingly stated that a would-be proselyte was to be repulsed three times; if the proselyte persists after that, he or she would be accepted. Prospective converts were to be discouraged in order to determine their sincerity, as well as to let them know that it is not easy to be a Jew. But the discouragement was not to be for too long, because when Naomi saw that Ruth was steadfastly minded to go with her, "she said no more." The Moabite Ruth is, therefore, the model convert because of her declaration of fidelity to Naomi.

Boaz, a wealthy kinsman of Naomi's husband Elimelech whom Ruth eventually marries, recounts the ways in which Ruth has been faithful (2:11). According to Boaz, Ruth demonstrates her faithfulness by staying with Naomi and by leaving her own parents and homeland and going into a foreign country. In that same speech to Ruth, Boaz concludes: "The Lord recompense you for what you have done, and a full reward be given you by the Lord, the God of Israel, under whose wings you have come to take refuge" (2:12).

The phrase "under whose wings you have come to take refuge" is also a formal metaphor for proselytism meaning "in your protective care." The image is suggested by the watchful care of a mother bird (cf. Deut. 32:11; Ps. 57:1[MT 2]). It is in the interpretation of the book of Ruth that the phrase first appears with the meaning of "to be converted to Judaism." As in the case of other foreign-born women (e.g., Tamar the Canaanite, Gen. 28; Rahab the Canaanite, Josh. 2–6; Bathsheba the Hittite, 2 Sam. 11), God chooses Ruth the Moabite to properly fulfill the obligations of the Jewish community.

The community in Bethlehem prays a benediction for Boaz as he tells the people and elders of his plans to marry Ruth (4:11-12). In spite of the fact that Ruth is of a people who are considered to be noted enemies of Israel, her commitment and friendship with Naomi win God's favor, and God uses her to "build up the house of Israel."

Ruth and Boaz do build up the house of Israel and are the great-grandparents of King David, but the house is also built by Naomi. Even though she is old and cannot bear more children and her sons are dead, the Lord has blessed her with a child through her daughter-in-law Ruth (4:14-15). The compliment cannot be overlooked or overrated. Ruth demonstrates her friendship and devotion to Naomi by sharing her child with her mother-in-law (4:16-17a). The son's name was Obed and he became the father of Jesse and the grandfather of the future King David.

The beautifully artistic book of Ruth serves many purposes in the Jewish tradition, including the importance of women in Israel's history: Naomi and Ruth; Leah, Rachel, and Tamar before them. That purpose moves forward in history as the writer of the Gospel of Matthew capitalizes on the tradition and includes in the genealogy as forebears of Jesus both Tamar and Ruth, as well as two other enemy women, Rahab and Bathsheba (Matt. 1:3, 5, 6b).

Bibliography. D. R. G. Beattie, *Jewish Exegesis of the Book of Ruth.* JSOTSup 2 (Sheffield, 1977); A. Brenner, ed., *A Feminist Companion to Ruth* (Sheffield, 1993); D. N. Fewell and D. M. Gunn, *Compromising Redemption: Relating Characters in the Book of Ruth* (Louisville, 1990); J. A. Kates and G. T. Reimer, eds., *Reading Ruth: Contemporary Women Reclaim a Sacred Story* (New York, 1994); J. Neusner, *The Mother of the Messiah in Judaism: The Book of Ruth* (Valley Forge, 1993); I. Pardes, "The Book of Ruth: Idyllic Revisionism," in *Countertraditions in the Bible* (Cambridge, Mass., 1992), 98-117; J. M. Sasson, *Ruth: A New Translation with a Philological Commentary and a Formalist-Folklorist Interpretation,* 2nd ed. (Sheffield, 1989).

GLENNA S. JACKSON

S

SABA (Heb. *šĕḇāʾ*), **SABEANS** (*šĕḇāʾyîm*)
A tribe and a kingdom in Arabia variously designated in three OT genealogies as a son of Cush (Gen. 10:7; 1 Chr. 1:9; NRSV "Seba"), a son of Joktan (Gen. 10:28; 1 Chr. 1:22; NRSV "Sheba"), and a son of Keturah (Gen. 25:3; 1 Chr. 1:32). The association of Saba and Dedan among the sons of Keturah and the account of a raid on the oxen and asses of Job by a group of Sabeans (Job 1:15) have led some scholars to posit the presence of Sabeans in north Arabia. Conversely, the association of Saba (cf. Epigraphic South Arabian *S^{l}bʾ*) with Hazarmaveth (Wadi Ḥadramaut in Yemen) among the sons of Joktan points certainly to south Arabia. The LXX of Ps. 72:10, 15 reads *Arábōn, Arabía* for Heb. *šĕḇāʾ*, perhaps following a Greek convention attested from the time of Herodotus (*Hist.* 3.107) whereby "Arabia" designated the frankincense-producing region of south Arabia.

The earliest biblical attestation of Saba is, however, the account of the visit of the queen of Saba to Solomon (1 Kgs. 10:1-13; NRSV "Sheba") in the 10th century B.C.E. Although the wealth attributed to the queen scarcely suggests that she came out of a north Arabian milieu in the early 1st millennium, and is much more consistent with the early Sabean kingdom of south Arabia, it is nevertheless true that frankincense, the quintessential south Arabian product, was not among her gifts to the Israelite king. The earliest biblical references to explicitly Sabean incense occur at Jer. 6:20; Isa. 60:6 (cf. Herodotus 3.97, 107). Whereas argument once raged over the unacceptably early date of a Sabean kingdom in south Arabia at 1000 to which the queen mentioned in 1 Kings could be assigned, recent archaeological discoveries have pushed back the date of sedentary settlement in the highlands of northern Yemen well into the 2nd millennium. By the 8th century Sabeans (*^{lú}sabaʿayya*) are mentioned in the annals of Tiglath-pileser III (744-727), and slightly earlier they appear in a text from Sur Jurʿeh on the Middle Euphrates (near Ana, Iraq) which describes the attack on one of their caravans by Ninurta-kudurri-uṣur, governor of Suḫu. Itaʿmara "the Sabean" sent tribute to Sargon II (722-705) just as Karibʾil, designated "king of Saba," did to Sennacherib (705-681). On analogy with the later south Arabian (Minean) trading colony at Dedan, it has sometimes been suggested that the growth of the Sabean state in south Arabia led to Sabean expansion into north Arabia, accounting for the appearance of both a northern and a southern Saba.

Bibliography. I. Ephʿal, *The Ancient Arabs* (Leiden, 1982).

D. T. Potts

SABBATH (Heb. *šabbāṯ*)
The seventh day in a seven-day week, established in the OT as a day of rest. The OT records the institution of the sabbath in the laws given to Moses. The first command concerning the observance of the sabbath is found in Exod. 16:22-30. The Israelites were given manna daily and were told to gather twice as much on the sixth day so they would not have to gather on the seventh day. The inclusion of the sabbath law in the Decalogue both in Exodus and Deuteronomy established this command as a permanent law of the nation of Israel. In Exod. 20:8-11 the requirements of the law explicitly state no work shall be done by any person or livestock on the sabbath day. The theological defense for resting on the seventh day is derived from Gen. 2:1-3, in which God rests on the seventh day of creation. Israel is to rest because God rested.

Once the sabbath had been instituted, specific commands and prohibitions were given. The sabbath was not only a day of rest, but also a feast day. Because of this, the requirements of feast days were enforced, including holy convocations, public worship, and worship in the home. Special sacrifices were to be offered and the bread of the presence was to be renewed.

While the sabbath was to be considered a joy and privilege, it was also of such supreme importance that a violation of sabbath law carried the death penalty (Num. 15:35). This reflects the sabbath's two-sided nature: it was both a blessing and a requirement for the nation of Israel.

In the intertestamental period, two rabbinic traditions developed concerning the sabbath. One maintained a strict sabbath observance, with an emphasis on the rules of the sabbath, while the other emphasized the concept of internal, spiritual rest.

There are six recorded confrontations between Jesus and Jewish religious leaders over sabbath observance. Five involve healing on the sabbath, and the remaining incident involves picking corn on the sabbath (Mark 2:23-26 par.). This was a violation of the law according to the Pharisees. Using the legal format of finding a similar case, Jesus argued that this was like the situation in 1 Sam. 21:1-6, in which David and his men eat the consecrated bread. The similarity was that human need overrides ritual law.

In Mark 3:1-6 par. Jesus heals a man with a withered hand. In Luke 13:10-17 he heals a woman who was bent over in sickness caused by evil spirits. In Luke 14:1-6 Jesus takes the offensive and asks the Pharisees if it is right to heal on the sabbath. Receiving no response, he heals a sick man. Jesus defends his actions by pointing out that any one of the Pharisees would rescue an animal who had fallen in a well on the sabbath day. In John 5:1-17 Jesus makes the Jewish leaders angry by healing a sick man and telling the healed man to carry his pallet. This was a twofold problem, because Jesus was both healing on the sabbath and encouraging the healed man to violate the sabbath by carrying a pallet. In John 7:21-24 Jesus is still being sought because of healing this man. He points out that the Jewish leaders circumcise on the eighth day, even if it falls on the sabbath. How much more important is it to heal an entire man. In John 9:1-34 Jesus heals a blind man by making clay and putting it on the man's eyes. Not only does Jesus heal on the sabbath, but he also makes clay, which is against the law of the Pharisees. In all six sabbath confrontations, Jesus did not question the principle of a day of rest. Rather, the right use of the day is at the heart of these controversies. In some cases, such as in the picking of grain on the sabbath, human need overrides the ritual law. In other cases, Jesus is challenging the kind of regulations which go against the purpose of the law, which is to bring healing and wholeness. Although Jesus broke with rabbinic traditions about the sabbath, he did not seek to annul the observance of the sabbath day.

Considering the role of sabbath laws in the OT and in the Gospels, one might expect to find much more about the sabbath. If the sabbath is to be kept, one would assume that the gentile converts would need to be instructed in this. If the sabbath is to be annulled, one would assume that the Jewish believers would need to have this explained to them.

Six NT texts outside the Gospels and Acts impact discussions of sabbath theology and practice. There is evidence in Acts 20:7 that the first day of the week, Sunday, became a regular day of worship, but it does not replace or override the Jewish sabbath observance at this time. Rom. 14:5-6 contains no direct mention of the sabbath, but these verses renounce the idea of sacred days. All days are to be considered God's days, and no day has any special sacredness. Galatians contains an argument against Gentiles adopting Jewish practices and upholding Jewish ritual laws. In Gal. 4:10 there is an injunction against observing Jewish ritual time; although the sabbath is not specifically mentioned, it seems to fall under the idea of observing special days. In Col. 2:16 the argument is that the sabbath (along with food and festival regulations) was a type, a shadow, of what was to come in Christ. Therefore, now that Christ has come, there is no need for the shadow. Heb. 4:9 states that the sabbath rest in some way remains. This describes a sabbath rest which is probably not the once-a-week day of rest, but a rest of heart, provided by Christ. This rest appears to be spiritual rather than temporal, but this text has caused some confusion about a post-Gospels understanding of the sabbath.

Rev. 1:10 describes "the Lord's Day," which refers to Sunday, the day on which Jesus was resurrected. However, this early practice of meeting for worship on Sunday was not linked to the sabbath rest until much later. Therefore, this reference to the Lord's day does not appear to be linked to the sabbath laws at this time.

The Scriptures have left some questions concerning the sabbath unanswered. Not only are some particulars of sabbath regulations unclear, but the fundamental question of whether or not the sabbath was completely fulfilled by Christ's first coming has plagued Christianity and is still a debated topic. The choice of the day also presents a point of disagreement, with some groups continuing to adhere to the Jewish practice of a Saturday sabbath. Lastly, the relationship of the sabbath to the Lord's Day becomes an issue in later centuries.

Bibliography. N.-E. A. Andreasen, *The Old Testament Sabbath* (Missoula, 1972); D. A. Carson, ed., *From Sabbath to Lord's Day* (Grand Rapids, 1982); W. Stott, "Sabbath, Lord's Day," *NIDNTT* 3:405-15; K. A. Strand, ed., *The Sabbath in Scripture and History* (Washington, 1982). ANN COBLE

SABBATH DAY'S JOURNEY

The distance of travel permissible on the sabbath. Work was prohibited on the sabbath, and travel was considered work (Exod. 16:29). Therefore, scholars of the law had to determine what distance of travel was permissible. In the wilderness a sabbath day's journey was the distance between the ark and the camp, which was 2000 cubits or ca. 914 m. (1000 yds.; Josh. 3:4). The same distance existed between the levitical cities and the boundaries of their pasture lands (Num. 35:4-5). In NT times a sabbath day's journey was about the distance from the Mount of Olives to the temple (Acts 1:12).

Debates grew around the question of how much travel was permitted. Some Jews redefined their "home" by depositing food 2000 cubits from their home. This spot became a new home, and travel could extend another 2000 cubits from there. In some cases entire towns were declared one's domicile, and thus travel could extend from the border (hence the importance of boundary markers).

Bibliography. D. A. Carson, ed., *From Sabbath to Lord's Day* (Grand Rapids, 1982); E. P. Sanders, *Jewish Law from Jesus to the Mishnah* (Philadelphia, 1990), 6-23.

GARY M. BURGE

SABBATICAL YEAR

The "seventh year" in a seven-year cycle, designated as a "year of resting" and a "year of release." The Sabbatical Year extends the weekly sabbath principle of resting the seventh day, foundational to the covenant community (Exod. 31:12-17). The Ten Commandments motivate sabbath as imitating God's act of rest after creating the world (Exod. 20:8-11) or in remembrance of Israel's release from slavery in Egypt (Deut. 5:12-15) and thus as a relief measure for the poor (Exod. 23:12). This principle is then extended into the whole seventh year, to be set apart for rest from labor, providing food to the poor, cancellation of debt, and reading the law. The cancellation of debt is later connected with forgiveness of sins in the Dead Sea Scrolls (11QMelch 2; 1QDM 3). Freeing slaves is also mandated on a seven-year cycle, but in the seventh year after the indenture of a given individual, rather than in a universal release (Exod. 21:2-4; Deut. 15:12-15). An ancient Near Eastern parallel is the Mesopotamian tradition of *mīšarum* edicts (e.g., the Edict of Ammisaduqa), issued upon accession of a new king, also providing for cancellation of debt and freeing of debt slaves. Finally, the Sabbath Year is further extended in the Jubilee Year, every seventh Sabbatical Year, when land ownership reverts to the inherited line (Lev. 25:8-17, 23-28).

The main text on the Sabbatical Year is Lev. 25:1-7, 20-22, emphasizing "rest for the land." Sowing fields, pruning vineyards, and harvesting crops are prohibited. The produce of the untended land will be food for slaves, hired workers, aliens, livestock, and wild animals. The legislation in Exod. 23:9-12 is almost identical (here called the "seventh year").

What this means and how to apply it is debated. A system of rotating fallow, allowing revitalization of the soil as in modern farming, is attractive but without basis. A universally observed fallow year threatens severe hardship to a subsistence-level, agriculturally based economy. Such hardship would seem to be inconsistent with the stated purpose of this legislation as providing food and relief for the poor. Another possibility, given that the Jewish calendar year begins with harvest and ends with planting, is that the law envisions a full crop planted in the sixth year which is then exempt from harvest in the seventh, but is left for the poor and for animals as food, some of which will naturally reseed itself when sowing is prohibited later that year. This would allow minimal hardship to the community and maximum benefit to the poor, but little of the environmental benefit expected in our modern understanding of "fallow."

Parallel laws in Deut. 14:28–15:18 do not mention a fallow, but provide for feeding the poor by allocating a tithe of produce every three years for Levites, aliens, widows, and orphans. The "seventh year" is designated a "year of release" (NRSV "year of remission") for canceling debts. Deut. 31:10-13 further mandates a public assembly in the "year of release" every seventh year in which the Law will be read, possibly as part of a regular covenant renewal ceremony.

As with the release of slaves in the seventh year, reckoned on an individual basis from whenever the enslavement began, it is possible that the cancellation of debt "at the end of seven years" (Deut. 15) originally meant seven years from whenever the debt was incurred, after which time full repayment would have been completed with interest, just as six years of slave labor calculated according to the standard yearly wage of a hired worker would pay off the price of a slave (cf. Lev. 25:47-53). Hammurabi §88 and Eshnunna §§18a, 20, 21 specify a yearly interest rate of 20 percent. Such excessive interest was forbidden outright in Lev. 25:35-38, which may explain its failure to mention any cancellation of loans after seven years. This rate of payment, if observed in Israel, would have paid back the full original debt within five years, plus an extra 40 percent the sixth and seventh years before cancellation.

Deut. 15:9 would seem to imply, however, that (at least in later years) the "year of release" was universally observed. If so, it is possible that the cancellation of debt was temporary, as necessitated by the lack of agriculturally related income to be expected in a fallow year. Only the interest or payment due for that year was cancelled, or full repayment postponed for that one year. The same verbal root used here for the "dropping" of debt *(šmṭ)* is also used for the temporary cessation of agricultural work during the fallow year. Otherwise the pressure to refrain from lending shortly before the "release" (as warned in Deut. 15:7-11), or to circumvent the law, becomes overpowering.

Biblical references to these laws (as with many other laws) often record noncompliance (Lev. 26:43; 2 Chr. 36:20-21; Jer. 34:8-22; Neh. 5:1-13), but later practice is attested in 1 Macc. 6:48-54; Josephus *Ant.* 11.8.6(343-44); 13.8.1(234-35); 14.10.6(202); 16.2(475); 15.1.2(7); *BJ* 1.2.4(60); 1QM 2:6-9. These mention a policy of not waging war in Sabbatical Years, remission of Jewish taxes/annual tribute in consideration of the Sabbatical Year fallow, and food shortages caused by the fallow.

See JUBILEE, YEAR OF.

ROBIN J. DEWITT KNAUTH

SABTA (Heb. *sabtā'*), **SABTAH** *(sabtâ)*

A son of Cush (Gen. 10:7; 1 Chr. 1:9); eponymous ancestor of a south Arabian people. The name may be preserved in modern Sabota, a city in Ḥaḍramaut, or Ḏū s-Saphtha, a city near the Persian Gulf mentioned by Ptolemy (*Geog.* 6.7.38).

SABTECA (Heb. *saḇtĕkāʾ*)

A son of Cush; eponymous ancestor of a place or people in southern Arabia (Gen. 10:7; 1 Chr. 1:9).

SACHAR (Heb. *śāḵār*) (also SHARAR)

1. A Hararite; the father of Ahiam, one of David's Thirty (1 Chr. 11:35). At 2 Sam. 23:33 Ahiam's father is called Sharar.

2. The leader of one of the divisions of temple gatekeepers (1 Chr. 26:4); a son of Obed-edom and thus assigned watch over the storehouse (v. 15).

SACHIA (Heb. *śāḵĕyâ*)

A Benjaminite, son of Shaharaim and Hodesh (1 Chr. 8:10).

SACKCLOTH

A type of coarse fabric made from goat's (or camel's) hair. Sackcloth (Heb. *śaq*; Gk. *sákkos*) appears most often in the Bible (as elsewhere in the ancient Near East) as a material worn as clothing during times of distress and mourning. Because goats in the Mediterranean world were mostly dark brown or black, sackcloth itself was dark in color (cf. Isa. 50:3; Rev. 6:12). A sackcloth garment could cover the whole body, in which case it was worn loosely and fastened around the waist with a girdle or rope, or it could be a simple loincloth. The wearing of sackcloth could symbolize grief or penitence on either a personal (Gen. 37:34; Joel 1:8) or a national level (Jdt. 4:10; Jonah 3:8; in both of these examples, even animals are clothed in sackcloth!); it is also portrayed as prophetic clothing in Rev. 11:3. The material was also used for making tents, sails, and carpets.   James R. Adair, Jr.

SACRIFICE, HUMAN.

See Molech.

SACRIFICES AND OFFERINGS

The phenomenon of sacrifice cannot be appreciated apart from the mythic notion that the temple serves as the very house of God. In order to concretize the fact of this physical or sacramental encounter, biblical law took special care to outline the responsibilities that accompanied it. Chief among these were the requirements to attend to the daily needs of this resident deity and to dispose of material which the deity found offensive. The former concern resulted in the sacrificial system, whereas the latter led to the concern for purity.

The laws of sacrifice presume a sacramental mentality that believes that God makes his presence manifest within the confines of the material world (Exod. 20:24). Rituals such as sacrifice evolved to help concretize the manner in which the deity was truly present in the human community. Though God is beyond nature and history, through the medium of his temple he makes his presence manifest. But this presence cannot be merely stated; it must be lived and experienced. Thus — following through with this logic — if the deity assumes residence in this temple, then he must be revered and honored with the proper trappings of such a setting. These would include an elaborate throne room, finely crafted paneling, handsome vestments for his servants, and most importantly sumptuous food for his consumption. What holds together all of these images is the notion of God's assuming and maintaining residence within a particular place. Sacrifice, considered here as the provisioning of the deity's banquet table, is simply one among a number of ritual acts that symbolize the miraculous availability of the deity within the temple and allow this reality to be lived and experienced by the human community.

Within the biblical narratives, the act of sacrifice is the single most important feature of the liturgical life of the temple. The tremendous importance of the sacrificial system is certainly related to the fact that it — unlike most other dimensions of temple life — requires daily maintenance and upkeep by the community of worshippers. In other words, this mode of affording honor and reverence toward the deity is unique in so far as it requires constant human attention. It should cause no surprise that the same word for service (Heb. *ʿăḇōḏâ*) is also the term for [divine] worship. For in the act of providing a sacrifice the Israelite was not only providing a service to the deity, but also setting himself in a position of subservience to that very deity.

The performative role of sacrifice has long been a topic of reflection among anthropologists. This role has sometimes been caricatured as nothing more than the secondary application of the fundamental principle of secular mercantile exchange: *do ut des*, "I have given [a gift to the god], so grant me [a blessing in return]." Though no one would doubt that an aspect of exchange is present in the sacrificial act — people do present sacrifices in hope of gaining a blessing in return — recent thinking on the topic of sacrifice has suggested a more subtle aspect to the type of exchange that is envisioned. For gift exchange among unequal partners is never a purely mercantile affair; that is one party giving merely with intention of securing a future benefit. Rather, the very act of exchange itself serves to embody and communicate the relative status of the partners in question. Thus, when a person offers a mere animal in the hope that God will in turn grant him a child, the unequal nature of the items exchanged cannot help but create within the person a feeling of dependency and gratitude. Understood in this manner, *do ut des* could well be translated as "I have given [so precious little], and yet may you grant [so very much]." In this view, the exchange that has taken place is hardly a crude bargain oriented at "twisting the arm" of the deity, but rather a cultic "realization" of the absolute dependence of the human giver upon the graces of his God. Sacrifice is an essential vehicle for establishing and expressing this relationship of God to mankind; it could hardly be considered optional.

Priestly Source

Sinai Narrative

When one first looks at the P source in its entirety, the laws of sacrifice seem to be ordered in a rather haphazard way. Beginning at Exod. 25 and continuing to the end of Numbers, the sacrificial laws of P are interwoven among the various narrative materials of J and E. It is difficult, especially in Numbers, to understand the editorial function of this structure. Yet there are clear signs of editorial design within this larger framework. One might note the structure of Exod. 25–Lev. 9. Exod. 25–40 describes the delivery of the architectural plans for the tabernacle to Moses (chs. 25–31) and the subsequent execution of those plans (chs. 35–40). This particular section comes to a climax with the appearance of the divine presence ("glory of the Lord") in the tabernacle (Exod. 30:34-38). After the tabernacle has been revealed, the laws of sacrifice are laid out in a very general way (Lev. 1–7). Then follows the narrative of the ordination of Aaron and the ceremony of the eighth day (Lev. 8–9). This section concludes with the first appearance of the Lord to the entire gathered throng of Israelites (Lev. 9:23-24).

Laws for Sacrifice

The Torah has both general rules for the performance of individual sacrifices and particular applications for the individual sacrifices or sets of sacrifices. General rules for all of the sacrificial types are found primarily in one location, Lev. 1–7. These general rules provide full details about how to administer the burnt offering: where to bring the animal, how to lay on hands, where to kill it, how to handle its blood, how to prepare the altar, and what to burn on the altar. The section closes with the statement: "This is the law of the holocaust, the cereal offering, of the purification offering, of the reparation offering, of the consecration offering, and of the peace-offering which the Lord commanded Moses on Mt. Sinai" (Lev. 7:37-38).

Yet it is only on the rarest of occasions that an Israelite would offer only a holocaust or cereal offering. Israelite rituals usually required a specific combination of these individual types in order to be efficacious. Thus the rest of the laws of sacrifice in the Pentateuch can be viewed as the specific ritual application of the rather abstract and general rules of Lev. 1–7 (excluding the doublets to Lev. 1–7; e.g., Num. 5:5-8; 15:22-31). The specific applications of the general rules of Lev. 1–7 can be grouped into three categories:

1. foundational sequences: ordination of priests and Levites (Lev. 8–9; Num. 8), dedication of the tabernacle (Num. 7);
2. festival laws and the *tāmîḏ*, "daily burnt offering" (Lev. 16, 23; Num. 28–29); and
3. specific rituals pertaining to the life cycle of the individual: e.g., childbirth (Lev. 12), "leprosy" (Lev. 13–14), vows of the Nazirite (Num. 6), impurity from discharge (Lev. 15:13-15), corpse defilement (Num. 19).

Basic Types of Animal Sacrifice

Burnt offering. At its most basic level, the *ʿôlâ* was considered a gift to the deity, which the deity consumes as a "soothing odor." The burnt offering constituted the daily food for the deity (cf. Exod. 29:38-42; Num. 28:3-8). These sacrifices took place in the morning and the evening and were offered along with a cereal and drink offering.

Peace offering (Lev. 3). In the P source the *šĕlāmîm* sacrifice is broken down into three subtypes: the "thanksgiving" sacrifice, the "vowed sacrifice," and the "freewill offering" (Lev. 7:11-18). The *šĕlāmîm* sacrifice is primarily a sacrifice intended for human festivity and consumption. This role helps to explain why the *ʿôlâ* and the *šĕlāmîm* are routinely paired in biblical ritual. The *ʿôlâ* was the sacrifice that constituted the basic nourishment for the deity, while the *šĕlāmîm* in turn nourished the people.

Purification offering (Lev. 4). The traditional translation of Heb. *ḥaṭṭāʾṯ* has been "sin offering" (e.g., Lev. 4:1–5:13; Num. 15:22-31). This translation, followed by the LXX, is based on etymological considerations. The term would better be understood as referring to the process of purification.

Atonement and Sacrifice. The purification function of the *ḥaṭṭāʾṯ* challenges us to reconsider its role in rituals that seem to have an atoning function. Can these rituals also be understood in a purificatory sense? In order to understand this role one must pay particular attention to the role of blood manipulation in each of the rituals described here, for it is the blood itself which acts as the purging agent. In light of this, it is significant to note that the blood is never placed upon the individual. If the individual himself was being cleansed then one would expect the blood to be placed on him or her. Instead the blood is placed on various cultic appurtenances. Even more telling is the variability of this blood ritual with respect to the status of the sinner. Lev. 4 makes very careful distinctions between the status of various classes of people. The inadvertent sins of the priest and community as a whole are more serious than the sins of the individual, whether a commoner or a ruler. Most serious of all are the advertent offenses of any kind. In each of these cases, as the seriousness of the sin becomes more pronounced, the blood is brought closer to the very inner sanctum of the holy of holies. Thus the blood used for the commoner is placed on the altar of the holocaust outside the sanctuary per se (Lev. 4:30). The blood used for the sin of the priest or of the community as a whole is placed within the sanctuary itself. It is sprinkled on the veil separating the holy of holies from the outer chamber and placed on the incense altar. Finally, the blood of the purification offering on the Day of Atonement, which atones for advertent sins (so would seem the sense of Heb. *pešaʿ* in Lev. 16:16), is sprinkled "in front of the mercy seat" within the holy of holies itself (v. 14).

Jacob Milgrom has argued that his sequence of the graded usage of blood in respect to the grid of the sacred shrine shows that what is being purged is not the sin from the sinner, but the effects of sin, i.e., cultic impurity, from the sanctums within the sanctuary. Since the blood is understood to be a purging agent, one would expect the sinner to receive this material (if the primary intention of the ritual were to eliminate his sinful condition). Such an understanding would accord well with what is said about the purificatory role of the *ḥaṭṭāʾṯ* blood in the case of those suffering from discharge: "Thus you shall keep the people of Israel separate from their uncleanness so that they do not die in their uncleanness by defiling my tabernacle that is in their midst" (Lev. 15:31; cf. Num. 19:13). Impurity, conceived in this fashion, becomes akin to a physical substance which is attracted almost magnetically to the Holy. The purification offering is designed to remove this material from the sanctuary itself. If the impurity is allowed to accumulate, the deity will be forced to leave the sanctuary.

Prophetic Critique

It has been common for scholars to denigrate the enterprise of biblical sacrifice. One scholar went so far as to describe the system as a means of "self-help." This criticism is certainly supported by such prophetic invective as found in Jeremiah: ". . . I did not speak to [your ancestors in Egypt] or command them concerning burnt offerings and sacrifices. But this command I gave them, 'Obey my voice, and I will be your God . . .'" (Jer. 7:21-23). One scholar characterized this prophetic text as a "slap in the face of the Priestly code." It seems to overturn the Priestly notion that all cultic laws had been part of Mosaic law.

Yet one should be careful about what types of conclusions should be drawn from such a piece of fiery rhetoric. In other prophetic texts one can find both fasting and intercessory prayer condemned. In sum, one should not mistake the prophetic critique of the cult for systematic theology. Prophetic discourse occurs in a highly charged atmosphere. It is a mixture of hyperbole, exalted rhetoric, and even polemic. It would be fairer to say that the Bible contains two models for dealing with human sin. The most prominent would be that of the P code. In P the harmful effect of sins is ameliorated by a system of sacrificial atonement. The sins envisioned to fall within this framework are those acts of disobedience which are committed within the context of a larger covenantal bond. The prophets, by contrast, are concerned with sins of a vastly different nature: sins that represent advertent, gross rebellion against the very fabric of the covenant charter. So heinous are these deeds that the whole covenant framework is called into question. It is not a question of rejecting P, but rather finding oneself in such a radically new context that P's norms are no longer believed to apply.

Viewed this way, one could argue that the "prophetic" understanding of sacrifice was also a Priestly one. For in a text such as Lev. 26, one finds a long list of the curses that will fall upon Israel should she neglect her covenantal responsibilities. This chapter moves beyond the concerns of purification and atonement found in Lev. 1–25. Israel's wanton disobedience, which is foreshadowed here, calls for measures of divine punishment that cannot be altered by the sphere of the cult. The language of judgment found in Lev. 26, especially the threat to terminate the cultic order itself, is very close to prophetic thought. What is important to note is that within the P code itself are allusions to the type of criticism of the cult that one finds within the prophetic materials. This evidence, in and of itself, should call into question any overly rigid typological distinctions which would isolate Priestly concepts of the cult from those of the prophets. The difference has to do with emphasis and rhetorical purpose rather than with outright contradictory evaluations of Israel's spiritual heritage.

Bibliography. G. A. Anderson, "Sacrifice and Sacrificial Offerings: Old Testament," *ABD* 5:870-86; B. A. Levine, *In the Presence of the Lord.* SJLA 5 (Leiden, 1974); J. Milgrom, *Leviticus 1-16.* AB 3 (New York, 1991).

GARY A. ANDERSON

SADDUCEES (Gk. *Saddoukaíoi*)

An important group within Palestinian Judaism from the 2nd century B.C.E. to the 1st century C.E. As also for the Pharisees, reconstructing the historical Sadducees means weaving a plausible historical portrait from educated ingenuity and sparse clues in the three main source collections: the NT, Josephus, and the rabbinic literature. The Sadducees receive far less attention than even the Pharisees. A possible fourth source is the Dead Sea Scrolls.

The Sadducees hardly appear in the NT. They are absent from Paul's letters. Mark presents them as flat, two-dimensional characters "who say there is no resurrection" (Mark 12:18). John collapses them altogether into an undifferentiated Jewish leadership; they do not appear by name. In addition to preserving Mark's question about the resurrection, Matthew simply couples them with the Pharisees to represent the joint leadership of the old Israel who reject Jesus (Matt. 3:7; 16:1-12). Only Luke-Acts offers a nuanced portrait. In Acts 4:1; 5:17 the author indicates that the high priest and temple authorities were Sadducees. This clarifies the closing section of Luke, where the more or less friendly Pharisees leave the story at Jesus' entry into Jerusalem (Luke 19:39). In dealing with the disciples, these figures continue the policy of aggressive hostility that they (not the Pharisees) had begun with Jesus. Near the end of Acts, the author reintroduces the Sadducees' denial of resurrection as an issue that Paul uses to divide the Sanhedrin; only now Luke adds the unparalleled statement that they also deny the existence of angels or spirits (Acts 23:8).

Although Josephus was himself a proud member of the temple-based priestly aristocracy, neither of the two incidents he reports of the Sadducees expresses any admiration. First, he relates a story about the Hasmonean John Hyrcanus' rejection of the Pharisees in favor of the Sadducees, which occurred because a Sadducee named Jonathan inflamed the prince's anger toward the Pharisees. In this story we learn that the Sadducees were more severe than the Pharisees in punishing offenders (*Ant.* 13.294). Josephus also indicates that the Sadducees' rejection of the Pharisees' tradition "of the fathers" and insistence upon observing only the laws of Moses was a cause of major conflict between the two groups (*Ant.* 13.297), but that the Sadducees had only the support of "the well fixed." He repeats these points in *Ant.* 18.16-17, where he admits that although the Sadducees include men of the highest standing, they must defer to the program of the Pharisees because of the latter's popular support (18.17).

Although much of this might seem congenial to the aristocrat Josephus, sharp conflicts with his views come in the Sadducees' outright and Epicurean-like denial of an afterlife and rejection of fate in favor of unfettered free will (*BJ* 2.164-65; *Ant.* 13.173; 18.16-17; cf. 10.277-81). And when he relates the second incident that involves Sadducees he is markedly hostile. That story concerns the execution by stoning of Jesus' brother James and others, after the death in office of the Roman governor Festus but before the arrival of the new governor Albinus. The high priest Ananus, who instigated the proceedings, appears as a member of the Sadducees, who "when it comes to judgments, are savage in contrast to all other Jews" (*Ant.* 20.199). Although Josephus elsewhere praises the severity of the Jewish laws against wrongdoers (*Ag. Ap.* 2.276-78), he considers the Sadducees altogether too cruel.

Rabbinic literature from the 3rd to 6th centuries C.E. contains a number of references to the *ṣĕḏûqîm* (Hebrew), the etymology of which is uncertain. Scholars have usually taken it to approximate Gk. *Saddoukaíoi* and link it with the biblically authorized high-priestly family of Zadok (1 Kgs. 2:35; Ezek. 40:46), who lost power under Antiochus IV; however, this presents a linguistic difficulty in the double *d* of the Greek, and it is unclear why the non-Zadokite priesthood would perpetuate that name. The rabbinic *ṣĕḏûqîm* generally appear allied with the mysterious Boethusians (a Greek name) and in dispute with the sages and/or the *pĕrûšîm.* The *ṣĕḏûqîm* have their own date for Pentecost (*m. Ḥag.* 2.4; *Menaḥ.* 10.3) and purity laws that differ from those of the majority (*m. Yad.* 4.6-7). Although they apparently seek to find fault with the others' ritual prescriptions (*m. Para* 3.3), they do not appear as wealthy aristocrats in the early rabbinic literature. They can be isolated from "Israel" as much as the Samaritans (*m. Nidd.* 4.2).

Early rabbinic literature does preserve some hint that the priestly aristocracy (though not identified as Sadducean) was compelled to follow the prescriptions of "the elders" (though not named as Pharisees; cf. *m. Yoma* 1.1-7). By the time of the 6th-century Babylonian Talmud, we have the explicit claim that the Sadducean chief priests had to follow Pharisaic dictates (*b. Yoma* 19b). But this is vary late and hardly useful for reconstructing 1st-century conditions.

Lawrence Schiffman has argued that small correspondences between positions attributed to the rabbinic *ṣĕḏûqîm* and those advocated by the authors of a halakhic letter from Qumran (4QMMT) suggest that the original group behind the Dead Sea Scrolls were proto-Sadducees. Both groups claimed loyalty to the priestly line of Zadok. This view has not yet won wide acceptance because of the major disagreements between the views of the Scrolls' authors (with strong emphasis on spiritual powers, heavenly intervention, and coming judgment) and those attributed to the Sadducees in the NT and Josephus.

What can be said with confidence about the Sadducees? It seems that they found their base in the priestly aristocracy, though not all of that group were Sadducees (witness Josephus). Rejection of the Pharisees' living tradition, of the afterlife, and of (at least) an elaborate angelology or demonology would all fit together, since the Pentateuch does not elaborate such views. Nevertheless, they must have had an interpretive tradition besides the Law of Moses. Whatever form that tradition took, whether oral or written, explicitly recognized or unconsciously supplied, they must have had one, for the Torah itself requires clarification if one is to live by it. Speculations about the Sadducees' precise religious program, motives, attitudes, and political platform, or even their role in the Jewish Revolt, must so far remain speculations because of the lack of confirming evidence.

Bibliography. S. Mason, "Chief Priests, Sadducees, Pharisees, and Sanhedrin in Acts," in *The Book of Acts in Its First Century Setting,* 4: *Palestinian Setting,* ed. R. Bauckham (Grand Rapids, 1995), 115-77; A. J. Saldarini, *Pharisees, Scribes, and Sadducees in Palestinian Society* (Wilmington, 1988); E. P. Sanders, *Judaism: Practice and Belief, 63 B.C.E.–66 C.E.* (Philadelphia, 1992); L. H. Schiffman, *Reclaiming the Dead Sea Scrolls: The History of Judaism, the Background of Christianity, the Lost Library of Qumran* (Philadelphia, 1994); G. Stemberger, *Jewish Contemporaries of Jesus: Pharisees, Sadducees, Essenes* (Minneapolis, 1995). STEVE MASON

SAFFRON

A pungent bright orange spice (Heb. *karkōm*) made from dried stigmas of *Crocus sativus* L. The saffron of Cant. 4:14, which is among spices and plants in a description of a young woman as an ideal garden, may have been from *Curcuma longa* or *Carthamus tinctorius.*

SAINTS

In biblical usage not restricted to specially holy individuals, but a term for the people of God in both the OT and NT (e.g., Ps. 31:23[MT 24]; Eph. 1:1, 15; 2 Thess. 1:10; Rev. 5:9; 18:20). They are called God's "holy ones" (Heb. *qĕḏôšîm,* Ps. 16:3; 34:9[10]) or "faithful ones" (*ḥăsîḏîm,* 30:4[5]; 85:8[9]; 145:10). They rejoice in God's goodness and trust in his care (2 Chr. 6:41; Prov. 2:8). Their death is precious "in the sight of the Lord" (Ps. 116:15).

The NT frequently speaks of "saints" (Gk. *hágioi*). Matthew notes that after Christ's resurrection "many bodies of the saints" who had died were raised (Matt. 27:52). Ananias protests against helping Saul of Tarsus, for he has heard of his persecution of the "saints" in Jerusalem (i.e., Christians, Acts 9:13; cf. 26:10); 9:32, 41 mention "saints" living in Lydda and Joppa who are "believers." Similarly, Paul refers to Christians (1 Cor. 6:1-2; Phil. 4:21-22; Phlm. 5, 7), who are "called to be saints" (Rom. 1:7), addressing Christian communities as "all the saints" (2 Cor. 1:1; 1 Thess. 3:13; Phil. 1:1; cf. Col. 1:4; Eph. 3:8, 18). Sometimes they need help (Rom. 8:27; 16:2; 2 Cor. 8:4; 9:1, 12); sometimes they give it (Rom. 12:13; 15:25-31; 1 Cor. 16:1, 15; cf. Heb. 6:10). Saints prepare for Christ's coming (1 Thess. 3:13; 2 Thess. 1:10).

Colossians views Christians sharing "the inheritance of the saints in light," and notes the christocentric mystery as something revealed to the "saints" (Col. 1:12, 26-27; cf. Eph. 1:18). Ephesians highlights equipping the saints "for the work of ministry" and calls for vigilance in Christian living and intercessory prayer (Eph. 4:12; 5:3; 6:18). In the Pastorals church-supported widows are expected to wash the "feet of the saints" (1 Tim. 5:10). Christianity was "once for all entrusted to the saints" (Jude 3). In Revelation the "saints" are persecuted Christians (Rev. 13:7, 10; 14:12; 16:6; 17:6; 18:24) who pray to remain faithful (note "the prayers of the saints," Rev. 5:8; 8:3, 4). The Apocalypse closes with a benediction for "all the saints" (Rev. 22:21).

Allison A. Trites

SAKKUTH

A name *(skwt)* occurring as Heb. *sikkûṯ* in Amos 5:26 followed by Kaiwan *(kiyyûn)*. The Masoretic pronunciation suggests that both are idols (abominations). Early Jewish tradition (LXX, Qumran) interpreted the word as a holy object. Modern translations therefore differ between "Sakkuth your king" (NRSV, NJB) and "the shrine of your king" (REB, NIV). If Kaiwan is the deified planet Saturn, Sakkuth might have been another planet, or a star, associated with the Babylonian god Ninurta. A god Sakkut (< ^{d}SAG.KUD), cup-bearer of the gods, sometimes identified with Ninurta, is known. His name may be of Elamite origin. The same god may also be mentioned in the composite divine name Sukkoth-benoth *(skwt,* now pronounced as *sukkôṯ)*, perhaps originally Sakkut of (the goddess) Bānītu. Both gods are suggested to have been worshipped by the Babylonians resettled in Samaria (2 Kgs. 17:30). It is unclear whether this astral cult of Sakkuth spread west before or after the Neo-Assyrian expansion in the 8th century B.C.E. If it arrived with the settlers, it implies that the text is a later insertion in Amos. However, the forms of the names suggest a West Semitic intermediary.

Bibliography. M. Cogan, "Sukkoth-benoth," *DDD,* 821-22; M. Stol, "Sakkuth," *DDD,* 722-23.

Meindert Dijkstra

SALA (Gk. *Salá*)

In Luke's geneaology of Jesus, the father of Boaz (Luke 3:32; NRSV mg "Salmon" [**1**]).

SALAMIS (Gk. *Salamís*)

A major port city on the eastern coast of Cyprus, 5 km. (3 mi.) N of Famagusta near modern Seryios. According to tradition, Salamis was founded by Teucer after the Trojan War. The town possessed a good harbor and was the chief city of Cyprus through the Roman period, even though Paphos, on the west coast, was the capital of Cyprus. On the first missionary journey Barnabas, a native Cypriote (Acts 4:36), led Paul and John Mark to Salamis, where they began to preach the gospel in the city's synagogues (13:5). On the second missionary journey Barnabas and Mark parted company with Paul and returned to Cyprus, likely putting in at Salamis (Acts 15:39). Tradition claims that Barnabas was martyred at Salamis in A.D. 61.

Mark R. Fairchild

SALATHIEL (Gk. *Salathiḗl*)

See Shealtiel.

SALECAH (Heb. *salkâ*)

A city on the eastern boundary of Og's kingdom (Deut. 3:10; Josh. 12:5). It was captured by the invading Israelites and given to Gadites (1 Chr. 5:11). Salecah was probably an outer limit of the Bashan territory.

The city is almost unanimously identified as modern Ṣalkhad (311212), a place built on a lava plug of an extinct volcano. According to a Nabatean inscription found at the site, it was captured by the Nabatean king Malik in A.D. 17, and at that time was named Ẓalhad.

Zeljko Gregor

SALEM (Heb. *šālēm*)

The city where Melchizedek was king (Gen. 14:18; cf. Heb. 7:2). It is identified with Zion in Ps. 76:2(MT 3), hence, Jerusalem — a tradition that was widespread in antiquity. It is likely that the early vocalization of Jerusalem was *yerûšālēm.* Targ. Onkelos, Neofiti, and Pseudo-Jonathan all assent to the equation of Salem with Jerusalem by rendering "Salem" in Gen. 14:18 as "Jerusalem." Similarly, the Genesis Apocryphon from Qumran glosses Gen. 14:18 "Salem, that is Jerusalem" (1QapGen 22:13).

Still, this view was not held in unanimity. One possible early divergent tradition is found in the ambiguously worded phrase of Gen. 33:18, translated by the KJV "and Jacob came to Salem, a city of Shechem." Targ. Onkelos and Pseudo-Jonathan interpret *šlm* here as another name for Shechem ("Salem, the city of Shechem"). The phrase might also, however, be understood with the RSV, "and Jacob came safely to Shechem." Another tradition is seen in Eusebius (*Onom.* 152), who equates Salem with Salumias (Salim, John 3:23), 12 km. (7.5 mi.) S of Scythopolis (ancient Beth-shean). Despite the scant evidence, most commentators accept the view identifying Salem with Jerusalem.

Dexter E. Callender, Jr.

SALIM (Gk. *Salím*)

A place near Aenon, where during the early part of Jesus' ministry John the Baptist was baptizing (John 3:23). Although various sites have been proposed W of the Jordan River, the location is not certain.

SALLAI (Heb. *sallay*) (also SALLU)

1. A postexilic Benjaminite who settled in Jerusalem (Neh. 11:8).

2. A priestly family of the time of Joiakim the high priest (Neh. 12:20), called Sallu (**2**) at v. 7.

SALLU (Heb. *sallûʾ, salluʾ, sallû*)

1. A postexilic Benjaminite living in Jerusalem (1 Chr. 9:7; Heb. *sallûʾ;* Neh. 11:7; *salluʾ*).

2. A postexilic priestly family (Neh. 12:7; Heb. *sallû*), probably the same as Sallai (**2**) at v. 20.

SALMA (Heb. *śalmāʾ*) (also SALA; SALMON)

1. According to 1 Chr. 2:11, the father of Boaz. Elsewhere the name appears as Salmon and Sala.

2. A Calebite, the son of Hur, founder ("father") of Bethlehem (1 Chr. 2:51) and Atroth-beth-joab; ancestor of the Netophanthites, the Zorite half of the Manahathites (v. 54), and possibly also the "families of the scribes" named at v. 55.

SALMON (Heb. *śalmôn;* Gk. *Salmṓn*) (also SALA, SALMA)

A Judahite, the father of Boaz and an ancestor of David and Jesus (Ruth 4:20-21; Matt. 1:4-5). At Ruth 4:20 the name occurs as Heb. *śalmâ,* at 1 Chr. 2:11 as Salma (**1;** *śalmāʾ),* and at Luke 3:32 as Sala.

SALMONE (Gk. *Salmṓnē*)

A promontory pointing toward the north from the eastern end of the island of Crete, modern Cape Sidero. Apparently a wind out of the northwest prevented the ship bearing Paul, en route to Rome, from staying close to the Asian mainland and reaching Cnidus, leading to the decision to sail toward Crete. The ship sailed "under the lee of Crete" (i.e., along the island's southern coast), having come in past Salmone (Acts 27:7).

SALOME (Gk. *Salṓmē*)

1. Sister of Herod, daughter of Antipater and Cypros.

See Herod (Family) **5.**

2. Daughter of Herod (Philip? not the Tetrarch) and Herodias, granddaughter of Herod and Mariamme II.

See Herod (Family) **12.**

3. A follower of Jesus, who ministered to him in Galilee and traveled with him to Jerusalem (Mark 15:40; if Matt. 27:56 is a parallel, she may be mother of James and John, the sons of Zebedee). Salome, with the two Marys, brought spices for Jesus' burial (Mark 16:1). Peter Richardson

SALT

A crystallized compound chemically known as sodium chloride. It was used generously in the arid climate of the Near East where excess perspiration resulted in the loss of natural body salts. For the inhabitants of the Bible lands, salt (Heb. *mělaḥ;* Gk. *hálas, háls*) was necessary for life (Sir. 39:26). The Dead Sea provided a major source for salt, and it was mined both from the shores and the surrounding hills. Zephaniah refers to salt pits that were probably located in the region of Jebel Usdum, S of the Dead Sea (Zeph. 2:9). Dead Sea salt was not the best, and the people of Palestine often purchased the superior specimens of the northern traders.

Salt had a variety of uses in antiquity, most frequently as a common condiment to flavor a variety of foods (Job 6:6). Possibly even animal food was flavored with salt (cf. Isa. 30:24). As with all cultures before the technology of refrigeration, salt was also used as a preservative. In addition to culinary usage, salt was valued medicinally and was rubbed on newborn babies (Ezek. 16:4).

Salt was an element of Israelite worship. The people were to ensure that salt was applied to every grain offering as an indication of the covenant (Lev. 2:13). Salt was also used to "season" certain burnt offerings (Ezek. 43:24; Josephus *Ant.* 3.9.1). A covenant sealed by salt was believed to be everlasting (Num. 18:19; 2 Chr. 13:5).

Ancient armies used salt as an agent of destruction, pouring it over the ground of conquered territories (Judg. 9:45). Land that has been contaminated by salt becomes barren (Job 39:6). However, in an ironic reversal it is Elisha's application of salt that provides the antidote for the harmful water that hampered plant growth at Jericho (2 Kgs. 2:19-22).

The NT often speaks of salt in figurative terms. Jesus refers to his disciples as "the salt of the earth" (Matt. 5:13); while some have seen this as a reference to the "preservative" nature of salt, in light of the emphasis on taste it is more likely a reference to its seasoning ability. Col. 4:6 applies the seasoning metaphor to human speech. If salt loses its distinctiveness it has no value (Mark 9:50; Luke 14:34).

Keith A. Burton

SALT, VALLEY OF

The site of two Israelite military victories over the Edomites, the first during the reign of David (2 Sam. 8:13; 1 Chr. 18:12; Ps. 60 Superscription[MT 1]) and the second by Amaziah (2 Kgs. 14:7; 2 Chr. 25:11). Its identification with Wadi el-Milḥ (cf. Heb. *gêʾ hammelaḥ*) E of Beer-sheba is commonly suggested, although a site within territories traditionally attributed to Edom warrants consideration.

Ryan Byrne

SALT SEA

A name for the Dead Sea (Heb. *yām hammelaḥ*) in the Pentateuch and Joshua.

SALU (Heb. *sālûʾ*)

A family chief of the tribe of Simeon whose son Zimri, together with a Midianite woman, was killed by Phinehas (Num. 25:14).

SALVATION, SAVE, SAVIOR

God's deliverance of a people or an individual from a threatening situation from which that group or person is unable to rescue itself. The threatening situation may range from political oppression, unjust accusations, military disaster, difficult labor or physical illness to a spiritual consequence of sinful behavior or the experience of God's wrath. The agent of salvation may be a human liberator, king, or judge; nevertheless, clearly it is God who provides the agent, and it is God alone who ultimately saves.

Salvation is the theme of much of the Bible. In the life of the Hebrew people, God is the one who delivers from oppression, trouble, or destruction. This conviction is expressed through a variety of terms other than the word "salvation" (Heb. *hôšîaʿ* or related terms from the verb *yāšaʿ*): *hiṣṣîl* ("remove someone from trouble"), *ʿāzar* ("help"), *gāʾal* ("buy back," "vindicate," or "redeem"), *pādâ* ("ransom"), *pālaṭ* ("bring to safety, cause to escape, rescue"). Such deliverance is the gracious working out of God's own salvific purpose for Israel and does not depend upon the merits of the people.

Heb. *yāšaʿ* can also describe the help that human beings offer one another (2 Sam. 10:11). Even in the areas of human activity, however, the working of God is evident (1 Sam. 23:2-5; Josh. 10:6-11). Thus Israel's faith expressed its experiences in warfare as God's salvation (e.g., Judg. 6–7) and through human agency in the juridical process (Deut. 22:25-27). Even the king is to be the "savior" *(môšîaʿ)* of the helpless (e.g., 2 Sam. 14). God provides human agents whose responsibilities include the working out of justice or righteousness to bring about the salvation of someone in need.

The faith claim of the OT is that Israel has both already experienced and still anticipates the promised salvation of God within the arena of history. The paradigmatic experience of Israel's salvation is the Exodus event, God's deliverance of his people from slavery in Egypt. Each new generation recites these events in a confession of faith that not merely recalls the historical facts, but enables each generation to participate anew in the event (Deut. 6:21b-23).

In its worship Israel characteristically recited in detail its experiences of God's salvation within historical events (e.g., Ps. 105). Other Psalms make it clear that Israel envisioned other historical events as revealing God's saving purpose for Israel. Ps. 72:12 recites creation as a historic, salvific act of God. Ps. 136 extends the range of these events from creation through the wilderness wandering to Israel's possession of the Promised Land. Ps. 107 speaks of God's redeeming work in general terms so that God's saving acts for the desert wanderer, the prisoner, the sick, and the shipwrecked are also available in the present to those who dwell in Israel.

God's salvation is the reception of his steadfast love *(ḥesed)* and peace *(šālōm)* in the life of the nation and of the individual (Ps. 29:11; 55:18[MT 19]), even in the midst of trouble. Salvation is expressed not only in the release from captivity, but also the forgiveness of sin (Ps. 85), characterized not only by the manifestation of God's loving-kindness and peace but also God's righteousness *(ṣedeq)* and truth *(ʾemet)*.

The experience of salvation has a communal as well as an individual nature. This bipolar understanding of salvation and the resulting tension is maintained throughout the Bible. Nevertheless, the OT gives evidence of a shift in emphasis from the collective nature of salvation to the salvation of the individual which is then maintained in the NT. This shift seems to have been accelerated by the experience of exile. Both Jeremiah and Ezekiel emphasize the individual nature of sin and judgment and the individual nature of repentance and forgiveness (Jer. 31:29; Ezek. 18:2b). This is not to deny the communal nature of faith but to insure that individuals recognize their personal responsibility rather than blaming others. Nevertheless, such an emphasis opened the way to a focusing upon the personal experience of salvation as often expressed in the Psalter (e.g., Ps. 88:1-3[2-4]).

In both the prophetic literature and the emerging apocalyptic literature, God's salvation was increasingly projected into the future. Even from the giving of the promises to the patriarchs in Genesis there had always been a future element in the nature of salvation, but the promises were never completely fulfilled. The restoration had raised the hopes of an age of salvation to begin with a new temple and all nations bringing tribute to Israel (Isa. 49; Zech. 2). Yet Haggai and Malachi indicate that the restoration of the people to Israel and the rebuilding of the temple led to disappointment and disillusionment. Therefore, the final saving acts of God were placed in the future with even more radical metaphors of salvation: a new heaven and a new earth (Isa. 65). While previous prophets had seen God's salvation as a future event within history (Hos. 2), the biblical writings after the Restoration move toward apocalyptic imagery until finally salvation will be fully expressed in the arena of eternity after the resurrection of the dead (Dan. 12; Isa. 26:19). These concepts continued to be developed in the intertestamental literature (e.g., Enoch, 2 Esdras, the Apocalypse of Baruch, and the Assumption of Moses), and their influence is felt in the NT.

The NT's contribution to the understanding of salvation lies in its witness to Jesus, the Christ (Messiah), the Savior (Gk. *sōtḗr*) of the world (John 4:42; Luke 2:11). Jesus (from Heb. *yāšaʿ*, "to save") was born to save his people from their sin (Matt. 1:21). It is Jesus, and Jesus alone, who is the agent of God's salvation (Acts 4:12).

The NT speaks of salvation as deliverance from physical danger such as sickness, deformity, demon possession, death, or the "evil one," as well as deliverance from sin. Salvation does include a concern for the earthly needs of people, as evidenced by the miracles of Jesus as well as the teachings of James and 1 John, but its major focus is more spiritual in nature. Salvation means entry into the kingdom of God, or the kingdom of heaven. Jesus was interested in giving abundant life to the whole person (John 10:10). This life in the kingdom is life within the reign of God, which is actually present and yet remains future in its complete realization (cf. Rom. 8:1, 9). This present reality of salvation is the proleptic experience of the believer of eternal life in the presence of God by means of faith in Jesus Christ, the crucified and resurrected Lord.

The NT also knows of the communal nature of salvation. The Church, not just individuals, was the object of Christ's saving love as demonstrated on the cross (cf. Eph. 5:25-27).

The NT, like the OT, bears witness to the ultimately eschatological nature of salvation. Salvation has yet to be realized completely in the life of believers. Jesus speaks of an end to history and the coming of the Son of Man, the final saving act of God (Mark 13:27). But even Jesus does not claim to know when this "day of the Lord" will come. It is the book of Revelation that gives greatest expression to the concept that the final salvation of God will be revealed on a stage beyond history, beyond time, and beyond this earth (Rev. 21–22). That day will be one in which God's salvation will be available to all the world (Matt. 28:19-20; Eph. 1:9-10; Phil. 2:9-11; Col. 1:20). This universal scope of God's love was not unknown in the OT (cf. Gen. 12:3; Isa. 19:24-25; Ezek. 29:9). Nevertheless, it is the NT which gives salvation its widest scope, its greatest motivation, and its unique means (John 3:16). GARY W. LIGHT

SAMARIA (Heb. *šōmrôn;* Aram. *šāmĕrāyin;* Gk. *Samáreia*)

Region

Though never explicitly delineated in the OT, the region of Samaria included mainly the mountainous territories S of Lower Galilee and the Jezreel Valley (below the Mt. Carmel–Mt. Gilboa line), W of the Beth-shan and Jordan River valleys, and E of the Sharon and Acco plains. The southern border fluctuated with the political vicissitudes between north and south (1 Kgs. 14:30; 15:15ff.; 2 Chr. 13:19) until King Asa of Jerusalem established it in the area between Bethel and Mizpah (Tell en-Naṣbeh), which served henceforth as border stations. The sons of Joseph, Manasseh and Ephraim (Josh. 16:1-4), became the eponymous ancestors for Israelite tribes occupying this north central hill country region, but Ephraim emerged as the dominant tribe early on, and consequently the entire area took on his name (cf. Gen. 48:14). Later, under the political influence of Omri, the territory assumed the same name as the capital city Samaria (1 Kgs. 13:32 notwithstanding). Still, some 8th-century Judahite prophets preserved a distinction between region and city by referring both to Ephraim, with its ties to the house of Joseph, and to Samaria, in relationship to the broader kingdom of Israel (Isa. 7:9; 9:8-9; Mic. 1:5; compare Amos 3:12; 6:1 with 6:6).

Shechem quickly became the religious and political hub of Samaria because it controlled a crucial pass between the centrally located mountains of Ebal and Gerizim. We may therefore speak of "North Samaria," the area N of Shechem which correlated roughly with the tribe of Manasseh (Josh. 17:7-10), and "South Samaria," the territory south of Shechem which basically represented tribal Ephraim (16:5-10). These areas reveal different geological formations which helped determine patterns of settlement. The mountains of South Samaria were formed primarily of hard, uplifted, Cenomanian limestone and rose to greater heights (915 m. [3000 ft.]) than the ranges N of Shechem. Deeply cut drainage systems on both sides of the southern Ephraimite watershed made access to it more difficult and restricted travel to primary ridge routes stretching longitudinally between eastern and central Samaria. That the book of Joshua failed to provide a list of cities for Ephraim, unlike other tribal territories, may reflect the difficulties encountered in settling this area. Once the area was populated, however, terrace farmers made good use of the shallow but fertile terra rosa soil produced by the deteriorating rock formations.

By contrast, North Samaria presented a more variegated geological portrait as the Ephraim arch declined toward the northern valleys. Uplifted strata of Cenomanian limestone dominated the eastern sector of this area, while an even harder Eocene limestone base (which decomposed into a less-than-fertile brown forest soil) characterized the central portion from Gilboa to Ebal and Gerizim. West of these areas, a mixture of limestones and chalks which had experienced more moderate degrees of faulting facilitated the establishment of a local and regional network of roadways that prompted denser settlements and made for greater communication and trade. Here the principal roads either followed the Naḥal Shechem to the coastal route or proceeded northward through the Dothan Valley to Jezreel and points farther north and east. Though forested throughout initially, the entire area of Samaria underwent significant ecological change resulting from intense deforestation as the area absorbed large numbers of inhabitants starting in the early Iron Age (Josh. 17:14-18).

Settlement patterns of the Iron Age resemble those of Early Bronze I (3500-3100) and Middle Bronze IIA (2000-1800). In all three phases, survey data seem to suggest that peoples spread generally from east to west and north to south. Those who see the highland population emerging from processes of de-urbanization among the Canaanite city-states of the western lowlands must reckon with this pattern of occupation. In Iron I a mixture of sedentary settlements and interspersed, seasonal campsites lay mainly in the dry forest ecozone just E of the watershed, where rainfall averaged ca. 200-400 mm. (8-16 in.) annually. Both the nature of sites surveyed and their concentration in this particular zone point to a localized, dimorphic, socioeconomic base in which pastoralists and agriculturists existed in a symbiotic relationship.

The main approach to the central country of Samaria from the east lay in the deeply faulted Wadi Fâriʿa, which ascended toward Tell el-Fârʿa (biblical Tirzah) from el-Mahruq in the Rift Valley S of the fords of the Jordan River at Adam. During Iron I this main road turned south from Tirzah and continued to Shechem. A secondary road diverged just prior to reaching Tirzah and led directly to Shechem from the northwest end of the wadi. A

Ruins of the Omride royal residence at Samaria (Phoenix Data Systems, Neal and Joel Bierling)

string of more than a dozen Iron I-II sites along those routes attests to their maintenance and use in both periods. This eastern access to Shechem served mainly North Samaria, while another Iron I route linking Shiloh and the Jordan River Valley served South Samaria. The latter passageway has yielded few Iron II remains, reflecting developments associated with the nascent monarchy in Jerusalem and the demise of Shiloh as a cultic and political center. Instead, a new road followed a more northerly course from the valley area E of Shiloh and proceeded along the Ephraim-Manasseh border through Khirbet Yānûn (biblical Janoah?) to Shechem.

By the time the population spread west in Iron II, highland society had become more complex in its political and economic structure. Numerous settlements of a more uniform character (with virtually no ephemeral campsites) appeared on the seaward slopes of Samaria and survived or thrived as part of a much larger network of trade, while locally a new type of dimorphism resided in the symbiosis between capital and countryside. Early Iron II chronologies for the late 10th and early 9th centuries are not yet archaeologically secure enough to determine precisely how many of these sites arose as a result of Solomon's administrative districts versus Omri's economic programs and demands. But clearly these sites both served the capital at Samaria and participated in interregional trade, if only by offering auxiliary services such as overnight lodging and animal care to passing caravans. In this way, they facilitated trade between the highland centers and the main coastal route leading north to Phoenicia or northeast through the Jezreel Valley past Hazor to Damascus. The close spatial distribution of these new western settlements indicates that not all represented mere caravan stops; rather, many of these villages bolstered their own local economies by producing and trading commodities such as wine and oil.

Omri's shift of the region's political center from Tirzah W of the watershed to the city of Samaria in the early 9th century prompted significant demographic and economic change throughout the region. Few Iron I sites had existed in this area (e.g., Khirbet Kabuba, Khirbet el-Babariya, Khirbet Husein es-Sahel, Khirbet Qaraqaf, Khirbet ed-Duweir/Tel Lachish), and they had all remained quite small and very near Shemer's family estate, the site of the future capital city (1 Kgs. 16:24). But Iron II western expansion of rural villages left a footprint of settlements which has allowed identification of at least 11 lateral and local roadways connecting the highlands in the Samaria-Shechem area with the lucrative trade along the coastal route. Most notable among these routes were those which: (1) connected the villages of South Samaria to the major center at Aphek via the lateral valley systems north of Shiloh (Naḥal Qanah), and (2) utilized the more northerly Naḥal Shechem to link the highland towns of North Samaria to Socoh by intersecting the coastal route just S of the southwest entrances to the strategic Jezreel Valley. Undoubtedly, both Socoh and Aphek became trading stations or clearing houses for goods and commodities produced by or transported through the matrix of highland villages leading down from the Israelite capital and other large centers at high elevations (Samaria, Tirzah, Tubas, Tappuah, Dothan, Shechem).

City

Ca. 884 Omri transferred his political capital to Samaria, located near the center of the northern kingdom. Situated 56 km. (35 mi.) N of Jerusalem and W of the Ephraimite watershed, its summit rose to a height of 430 m. (1410 ft.) above sea level and overlooked the main coastal road (Via Maris) connecting Egypt and Judah with the Jezreel Valley and northern routes to Phoenicia and Damascus. The site's biblical names, *Šāmîr* (Judg. 10:1-2) and, somewhat later, *Šōmrôn* (1 Kgs. 16:24), mean "watch" or "watchman."

Gottlieb Schumacher initiated the archaeological exploration of Samaria (1908), followed by George Andrew Reisner and architect Clarence Fisher (1909-10). Focusing on the western half of the summit, these excavations revealed much of the Israelite royal palace and, immediately to its west, a sizable storeroom complex. The latter became known as the Ostraca house due to the discovery of dozens of laconic shipping dockets recording the transfer of various commodities from outlying villages to the capital during the reigns of Jehoash and Jeroboam II in the first half of the 8th century.

A consortium directed by John W. Crowfoot renewed excavations at Samaria from 1932 to 1935. Kathleen M. Kenyon, who supervised all work in the royal quarter, introduced new techniques of debris-layer analysis. After exposing a north-south section across the entire summit, Kenyon concluded that pottery found there provided crucial evidence which justified a redating of the stratigraphic history and ceramic traditions at other Iron II sites in Palestine, such as Megiddo and Hazor.

Though the rock surface yielded clear signs of EB I occupation, most of the material remains pointed to Iron Age cultures. The date of the earliest Iron Age settlement, however, proved problematic. Kenyon interpreted 1 Kgs. 16:24 as precluding any occupation of the site prior to Omri's reign. From there, she outlined eight major building phases, with periods I-VI spanning from Omri to the fall of Samaria to Assyria in 722/721. Additionally, the Kenyon construct argued that new ceramic traditions accompanied each new building phase. But other scholars proposed maintaining a distinction between the ceramic and architectural developments at Samaria, with the earliest Iron Age pottery providing evidence of pre-Omride occupation.

The resulting controversy stemmed mainly from differences in archaeological method and interpretation. Whereas Kenyon dated floor levels based on material found beneath them (sometimes by as much as several depositional layers), George Ernest Wright and others dated surfaces according to material lying directly on them. While Kenyon's system offers the earliest possible date of the surface's construction, Wright's approach identifies the span of time the floor was actually used. Recent reevaluations of the Samaria evidence, from both ceramic and stratigraphical starting points, have confirmed an Iron I occupation but have shown (with Kenyon) that this phase lacked any monumental architectural features. Instead, installations either resting on or cut into the rock surface seem to indicate the presence of a modest family estate which produced oil and wine already during the late pre-monarchic era.

Unfortunately, much of the pottery and other materials came from disturbed or secondary contexts. As a result, many fewer stratigraphically secure archaeological data are available from the city for the 9th century than Kenyon's official report implied. Without further field work, we cannot rely on this evidence alone when establishing or adjusting chronologies at other sites in Israel or the Aegean world.

History

The region of Samaria experienced three successive models of social, economic, and political organization: (1) locally controlled tribal allotments under Joshua in the days of the judges (Josh. 16–17; 19:49-50); (2) centrally controlled administrative districts under Solomon (1 Kgs. 4:7-19); and (3) a foreign controlled imperial province, beginning with Assyrian hegemony in the second half of the 8th century (2 Kgs. 17:24ff.).

Though in the judges phase the region embodied the "cradle of Israelite civilization," it attained its greatest prominence following Omri's rise to power in the early 9th century. Quickly transferring the country's political center from Tirzah to Samaria (1 Kgs. 16:21-24), Omri and his successors — particularly his son Ahab — transferred this onetime family estate into a relatively small but cosmopolitan royal city. So impressive appeared the fortification walls, palace, large courtyards with rectangular pools, public buildings, and storerooms, that writers spoke of Samaria as the undisputed "head of Ephraim" (Isa. 7:9), or as Jerusalem's "elder sister" who ruled and influenced numerous "daughters" (outlying villages) of her own (Ezek. 16:46, 53, 55, 61; 23:4-5). Bountiful archaeological discoveries of ivory fragments and furnishings spanning the period from Ahab to Jeroboam II correlate well with later biblical memories of opulent, ivory-appointed houses and royal banquets in the capital (1 Kgs. 22:39; Ps. 45:8[MT 9]; Amos 3:15; 6:4). That the city now gave its name to the larger region bespeaks the power which emanated from this new, stately center. Even the villagers themselves came to be known as Samaritans rather than Israelites (2 Kgs. 17:29).

Omri's new economic orientation toward the open markets of the Mediterranean brought the entire region into greater contact with foreign cultures. With Ahab's politically motivated marriage to Jezebel, Samaria gained access to Phoenician wealth but also exposure to its religious beliefs and customs. As it became increasingly syncretistic under this influence, the political leadership incurred the scorn of Elijah and the orthodox religious establishment generally (1 Kgs. 17–19). Ultra-conservative factions with both religious and political aspirations arose. With backing from the prophetic leadership, conservative social groups such as the Rechabites, and zealous segments of the military, the populist Jehu seized the throne of Samaria in 842 (2 Kgs. 9–10). Yet even in the late 8th century the Assyrians continued referring to Samaria as the "House of Omri" and, like contemporary Hebrew prophets, often distinguished between the capital city/kingdom of Israel *(bît Ḫu-um-ri-ia)* and the countryside of Manasseh/Ephraim (*Sa-me-ri-na-a-a,* though they also employed this term interchangeably for the city).

From ca. 884-722/721, 14 Israelite kings ruled from Samaria. But the regional and even international prominence which they brought to the area also presented its capital and religious centers (e.g., Bethel) as the clearest and most dangerous symbols of opposition to the southern kingdom and its cult at Jerusalem. This deeply rooted north-south schism and the Judahite perspective taken in the final Deuteronomistic history produced a critical treatment of the rulers and activities at Samaria in the OT, while extrabiblical sources (Mesha stela; Assyrian annals) often pointed to the capital's political, military, and economic successes, despite periods of severe drought and famine (1 Kgs. 17:1, 7; 18:2).

By the late 8th century the Assyrian provinces of Dor, Megiddo, and Gilead encompassed the Ephraimite hill country on the west, north, and east, respectively. In 722/721 armies led by Shalmaneser V and Sargon II penetrated the highlands, besieged and occupied the city of Samaria, deported large numbers of Israelites, and resettled the city primarily with captives from distant Syro-Mesopotamian locations as well as from southern Arabia (2 Kgs. 17:24). In this manner, Assyria effectually transformed the highland region into the province of Samerina. Though its southern border remained fixed between Bethel and Mizpah (2 Kgs. 17:28), it appears that Samerina now subsumed the coastal district of Dor.

Archaeologists have recovered only a few remains from the Assyrian occupation, including a stela fragment (apparently from the time of Sargon II) and appreciable quantities of palace ware. But fragments from various cuneiform tablets, some apparently representing a letter to Abi-aḫi, the local governor, strongly suggest that Samaria served as the administrative center of Samerina.

Following the decline of Assyrian influence at home and abroad after 633, Josiah reannexed to Judah at least the southern extent of Samerina, as far as Bethel, and perhaps the province in full measure. His political and religious reforms led him to desecrate local shrines in the north and to execute their priests (1 Kgs. 13:1-2; 2 Kgs. 23:15-20), while merely closing the high places of the south and recalling local priests to Jerusalem. After the fall of Jerusalem to Nebuchadnezzar in 587/586, Gedaliah, the Babylonian-appointed governor of Judah, established his administrative center at Mizpah rather than in Jerusalem (Jer. 41:1); this may belie the south's orientation toward Samaria more than Jerusalem at this time, possibly because those who survived the scourge of Judah needed the stores of grain, honey, and oil which remained available in the region (vv. 4-8). Some have suggested that the Babylonians now officially considered the ravaged south as part of Samaria.

When Persia conquered Babylon in 539, Cyrus and his successors retained Samaria as the administrative center in the "Province Beyond the River (Euphrates)" and placed it under the governorship of Sanballat. Athenian and Sidonian coins, Aramaic ostraca, plus significant quantities of pottery imported from Aegean centers all attest to the solvency of the Ephraimite economy, which Persia apparently underwrote. It seems likely that the economic dependence of Judah upon Samaria increased during this period (cf. Neh. 5:1-5). As a result, northern leaders viewed efforts to revitalize Jerusalem as a fortified center of activity late in this period to be an act of sedition against Samaria and the Persian Empire alike (Ezra 4; Neh. 2, 4, 6; 1 Esdr. 2).

The local and international economies of the north continued to flourish throughout most of the turbulent Hellenistic period. In the late 4th century, when locals assassinated Andromachus, a Greek general installed by Alexander the Great as prefect of Syria, Samaria incurred Alexander's full wrath. Citizens who could fled eastward with numerous legal and administrative documents written in Aramaic (Samaria papyri), only to have Alexander's army overtake and execute them in a cave in the precipitous Wadi ed-Daliyeh. As the city they abandoned became more fully Greek in character, the center of Samaritan activity shifted to Shechem. A series of beautifully built round towers at Samaria and a subsequent massive defense wall with square towers bear witness to the current political vicissitudes, as the successors of Alexander, the Ptolemies and Seleucids, competed for control over the region. The greatest setback to Samaria, however, emerged more locally. Late in this period (ca. 108/107), the Hasmonean priest John Hyrcanus gained *de facto* independence in Judea following the death of the Seleucid ruler Antiochus VII in 128 and planned a frontal assault on the region and city of Samaria. Following the capture of Shechem and the burning of the Samaritan temple on Mt. Gerizim, a year-long siege against Samaria destroyed much of the fortress wall and brought the entire region temporarily under Judean control (Josephus *Ant.* 13.275-81; *BJ* 1.64-65).

The Roman conquest of Palestine by Pompey in 63 B.C.E. set the stage for the climactic resurgence of Samaria, beginning with the tenure of Gabinius (57-55) as provincial governor. He rebuilt the city walls, created new residential areas, and constructed a forum with an adjoining basilica northeast of the summit. Soon after the earthquake in 31 B.C.E., Herod the Great expanded the city's fortifications, apportioned both city and territorial properties among his former allies (Josephus records 6000 colonists), offered them special constitutional rights, and consequently considered Samaria "a third rampart against the entire nation," behind only his own palace in Jerusalem and the fortress Antonia (*Ant.* 15.292-98; *BJ* 1.403). Even the street which led into the city became a thriving bazaar, and additional temples and altars as well as a stadium and theater adorned the summit and slopes of the city. To honor Emperor Augustus, Herod named this magnificent place Sebaste (the Greek equivalent of Lat. *Augusta*). It became a center of celebration, ceremony, and magic (cf. Acts 8:9). Perhaps for these reasons, and because of the Samaritan-Jewish schism, natives of Judea generally circumnavigated the entire region when traveling to and from Jerusalem (Matt. 19:1; Luke 17:11; cf. John 4:4-9), and the followers of Jesus treated it as a virtual foreign territory in their early missionary and church-planting efforts (Acts 1:8; 8:1-25; 9:31; 15:3).

The grandeur of Samaria-Sebaste gradually faded during the late Roman/Byzantine period. Archaeologists have recovered few remains from this time.

Bibliography. B. Becking, *The Fall of Samaria* (Leiden, 1992); D. A. Dorsey, "Shechem and the Road Network of Central Samaria," *BASOR* 268 (1987): 57-70; I. T. Kaufman, "The Samaria Ostraca: An Early Witness to Hebrew Writing," *BA* 45 (1982): 229-39; R. E. Tappy, *The Archaeology of Israelite Samaria,* 1: *Early Iron Age through the Ninth Century* B.C.E. HSS 44 (Atlanta, 1992).

RON E. TAPPY

SAMARITAN PENTATEUCH

The distinctive form of the Torah handed down in the Samaritan community. These five books constitute the only Scripture in the Samaritan tradition.

Among the Samaritan Pentateuch's most notable features is its adaption to Samaritan theology, preeminently exhibited in the expansion of the Ten Commandments by incorporating the commands of Moses in Deut. 11:29-30; 27:2-7 after Exod. 20:17 in order to make worship on Mt. Gerizim the Tenth Commandment. Following this insertion, the Samaritan Pentateuch's version of Exod. 20:24 reads, "in *the* place where I *have caused* my name to be remembered," instead of "in *every* place where I *will cause* my name to be remembered." This adjustment (also made throughout Deuteronomy) effectively rules out Jerusalem as an acceptable place of worship. Other elements of Samaritan theology featured in this Torah include defending the honor of God (by removing anthropomorphisms and by incorporating an angel of God in place of a direct encounter between the deity and humans) and occasional legal differences rooted in Samaritan interpretation of the law.

Textual critics generally agree that the Samaritan Pentateuch probably arose ca. 100 B.C.E. However, the type of text that the Samaritans adopted at that time was already in use more widely among Jews in Palestine in the Hasmonean period. For example, an important scroll of the book of Exodus from Qumran, 4QpaleoExod^m, exhibits all of the textual characteristics of the Samaritan Pentateuch, lacking only the so-called "sectarian commandment" concerning Mt. Gerizim. This "proto-Samaritan" textual tradition, as it is called, is characterized by expansions of the text to achieve harmony within and between biblical books, by "modernization" of archaic or difficult elements in the Hebrew text, and by extensive use of *matres lectiones* (Hebrew consonants employed as vowels to assist in reading).

Bibliography. J. D. Purvis, *The Samaritan Pentateuch and the Origin of the Samaritan Sect.* HSM 2 (Cambridge, Mass., 1968); J. E. Sanderson, *An Exodus Scroll from Qumran: 4QpaleoExod^m and the Samaritan Tradition.* HSS 30 (Atlanta, 1986).

JEFFREY S. ROGERS

SAMARITANS (Heb. *hachššōmĕrōnîm;* Gk. *Samareítēs*)

A Hebrew religious sect geographically focused on Mt. Gerizim and claiming to be descendants of Ephraim and Manasseh among the tribes of the northern kingdom. They believe they preserve the original Mosaic religion. Several hundred survive today, about equally divided between Nablus at the foot of Mt. Gerizim and Holon, a suburb of Tel Aviv.

Josephus traces their origins to the foreigners (he calls them Cutheans) forcibly brought into the territory of Israel after its defeat by the Assyrians in 722 B.C.E. (2 Kgs. 17). The earliest evidence of the schism between Jew and Samaritan comes from the Persian period. This includes the more ambiguous mention of Samaritans in Ezra 4, which could be a geographical designation of peoples rather than a reference to a religious group. But the 5th-century B.C.E. Elephantine papyri contain explicit religious reference to Samaritans. Included are letters from both Samaritan and Jewish priests, each pleading for support to build temples for their respective communities. The only source of information on the Samaritans during the Greek period, Josephus claims a temple was built on Mt. Gerizim at that time. Both Jewish and Samaritan tradition affirm that it was the most sacred place for the Samaritans during this period, and most agree that it was devastated by the Hasmonean ethnarch and Jewish high priest John Hyrcanus in 111/110.

The NT includes several references to Samaritans. Jesus had trouble in the Samaritan villages (Luke 9:52-53) and instructed his disciples not to go there (Matt. 10:5-6). Nevertheless, he talked to the Samaritan woman (John 4) and used Samaritans as favorable characters in some of his stories, particularly the account of the 10 lepers (Luke 17:11-19) and the parable of the Good Samaritan (Luke 10:29-37). Samaria was an early mission field for the growing Church (Acts 8).

Most of our knowledge of the Samaritans comes from their own literature produced during two major periods of renaissance, in the 3rd and the 14th centuries C.E. It is during the first period that Baba Raba organized a council of priests and laity and facilitated the building of several synagogues. Marqah wrote his theological work, Memar Marqah, which became the base of Samaritan theology, and Amram Darrah wrote poetry that became the core of the Samaritan liturgy.

In the 14th century a reformation was intentionally instituted by the high priest Phineas, in part to reconcile a variety of Samaritan sects. Abu'l Fath, commissioned by Phineas to write a history of the sect, drew from the Bible, traditional stories, and previous chronicles to create a single, integrated narrative. The revered Abisha Scroll, a pentateuchal manuscript attributed to the great grandson of Aaron but generally considered to date from ca. 1000 C.E., was discovered in 1355 and survives today as the most important artifact of the Samaritan community. A historical commentary with parallels to the book of Joshua was also completed at this time. Dating shortly before this period is a book of stories (Asatir), parallel to the Pseudepigrapha, attributed to Moses which preserves stories of significant figures from Noah to Moses.

The Samaritans became a focus of modern European scholarship in the 17th century when a copy of their Pentateuch arrived in Paris. The text represented by this Pentateuch became the focus of continuing hostilities between Roman Catholics and Protestants. Roman Catholics under the leadership of Jean Morin, a scholar at the Oratory in Paris, argued that the Samaritan Pentateuch supported the LXX, the favored text of Roman Catholics, over against the Hebrew MT endorsed by Protestants. More recent scholarship demonstrates that the Samaritan Pentateuch derives readings from both the LXX and the Masoretic traditions and is not exclusively aligned with either. The text type of the Samaritan Pentateuch is represented at Qumran and becomes part of the discussion of the earliest textual development.

Only the Torah is canonical in Samaritan tradition, and the earliest manuscripts date from ca. the 10th century C.E. The period of greatest production of surviving manuscripts was during the 14th and 15th centuries. The Samaritan Pentateuch differs most dramatically from the MT in its exaltation of Mt. Gerizim as the site of Joshua's altar (added as one of the commandments in Exod. 20:17) and the reading of "Gerizim" for "Ebal" at Deut. 27:4. It also protects the oneness of God by changing the word "God" (Elohim) from plural to singular and makes textual changes to protect the honor of Moses and to be more consistent with Samaritan beliefs and practices.

Samaritan religion focuses on five affirmations. Central to their faith is the one God, Yahweh (anglicized as Jehovah). His chief mediator is Moses. The vehicle of the mediation is the Torah. According to their version of the law (Deut. 27:4), Moses, at God's command, instructed Joshua to build an altar on Mt. Gerizim, which thus became the central site of worship for the community. Finally, the Samaritans anticipate a coming Day of Vengeance and Recompense initiated by the Messiah (who was called Taheb).

Samaritans celebrate Passover, the feasts of Unleavened Bread, Weeks, the Seventh Month, Yom Kippur, Booths, and the "80 days of solemn assembly" in addition to regular sabbath services. Passover, chief among the annual festivals, is celebrated on Mt. Gerizim with animal sacrifice in accordance with the book of Deuteronomy.

During the 19th century the Samaritans were denied access to Mt. Gerizim, their literary efforts had dwindled, and approaching the 20th century their total population was less than 200. That number has more than doubled during the 20th century.

Bibliography. A. D. Crown, ed., *The Samaritans* (Tübingen, 1989); Crown, R. Pummer, and A. Tals, eds., *A Companion to Samaritan Studies* (Tübingen, 1993). ROBERT T. ANDERSON

SAMGAR-NEBO (Heb. *samgar-nĕḇô)*
An official in Nebuchadnezzar's government who had a role in the 587 B.C.E. Babylonian siege of Jerusalem (Jer. 39:3). The term is usually taken as the combination of "Simmagar" (a title) or "Samgar" (a territory) with the beginning of "Nebo-sarsechim" (a personal name), probably a confused form of the "Nebushazban" of Jer. 39:13.

SAMLAH (Heb. *śamlâ)*
An early king of Edom, resident of Masrekah (Gen. 36:36-37; 1 Chr. 1:47-48).

SAMOS (Gk. *Sámos)*
A mountainous island in the Aegean Sea, ca. 1.6 km. (1 mi.) from the coast of Asia Minor, SW of Ephesus, with a city of the same name as its capital. A cultural and naval center, Samos was the birthplace of Pythagoras. Rome sent Samos and other cities a letter declaring support for Simon's rule over the Jewish state (1 Macc. 15:23). For a time part of the Roman province of Asia, Samos was made a free state by Augustus in 17 B.C. Herod the Great later visited Samos (Josephus *BJ* 1.21.11).

On the return leg of his third missionary journey Paul sailed near or stopped at Samos (Acts 20:15). The Greek text is ambiguous, and a few manuscripts thus add "and after remaining at Trogyllium" (a promontory jutting out from the mainland close to Samos). DOUGLAS LOW

SAMOTHRACE (Gk. *Samothrákē)*
A mountainous island in the northeastern Aegean Sea, ca. 32 km. (20 mi.) from the Thracian coast. Although the island has no natural harbor, the ship carrying Paul's party stopped there en route from Troas in northwestern Asia Minor to Neapolis in Macedonia (Acts 16:11).

SAMSON (Heb. *šimšôn)*
The last of the great judges (Judg. 13–16) who led premonarchic Israel. The Danite Samson is said to have begun delivering Israel from the Philistines, their most persistent and threatening enemy.

As with all of the judges, the depiction of Samson (diminutive of *šemeš,* "sun") as a national leader is an editor's work. In the case of Samson, the notion is held very lightly. Samson engages in a personal vendetta, not a national liberation movement. He acts alone, not as a military leader. The Samson stories have their origins in folktales about a local hero celebrated for the audacity and strength with which he harassed Philistine men and for the prowess and naiveté with which he loved Philistine women. The stories would have circulated independently and were crafted by compilers into a balanced artistic whole.

The Samson cycle begins as a messenger of Yahweh announces to a barren woman that she will bear a son (Judg. 13). In true folkloric fashion, the miraculous quality of his birth sets Samson up as a hero. The messenger specifies the nature of Samson's heroics ("he shall begin to deliver Israel from the hand of the Philistines," Judg. 13:5) and enjoins Nazirite restrictions on both mother and child. Finally, the story assures the reader that Samson, a bawdy, amoral hero, is nonetheless Yahweh's man; Samson is the only judge whom Yahweh is said to bless (Judg. 13:24).

The main body of the cycle is organized around Samson's liaisons with and betrayal by two women. In both cases, Samson's seeming defeat leads to destruction of his enemies, the Philistines. Samson's determination to marry a woman from the Philistine village of Timnah sets in motion a series of events narrated in Judg. 14–15. A journey to Timnah is the setting for Samson's first superhuman feat, ripping apart a lion. The wedding celebration occasions his first conflict with the Philistines. Samson bets his Philistine attendants they cannot solve a riddle. His bride, threatened with death unless she helps, cajoles Samson into telling her the answer and passes it on to her compatriots. Enraged, Samson kills 30 Philistines for booty to pay off his wager. Vengeance leads to countervengeance, culminating in Samson's slaying 1000 Philistines with the jawbone of an ass.

Samson's entanglement with another woman leads to both death and triumph. Delilah, like the Timnite woman, is persuaded by the Philistines to coax secret information from Samson. Like the Timnite, Delilah persists, insisting Samson prove his love, until he reveals the secret of his strength, his hair, which in obedience to Nazirite regulations is unshorn. This time disclosure is fatal. Delilah uses the information to turn Samson over to the Philistines.

The tone of the story shifts from ribald humor and erotic teasing to pathos. The Philistines blind, shackle, and imprison Samson, finally forcing him to dance for them in the temple of Dagon, their god. Once again, betrayal and seeming defeat become the occasion for Samson to destroy his enemies. Samson, praying for vengeance, pulls the temple down. "Those he killed in his death were more than those he had killed during his life" (Judg. 16:30).

The stories are marked as folklore by their hyperbole and their humor. Samson tears a lion apart with bare hands and slays 1000 men with a bone. He later evades capture in walled Gaza, where he has been visiting a whore, by pulling up the city gates and carrying them some 40 miles to Hebron. Samson quite literally "possesses the gates of his enemies" (cf. Gen. 22:17). The stories are full of etiologies, riddles, and outrageous events such as Samson tying torches to the tails of 300 foxes to set fire to Philistine fields. They are marked by folkloric motifs such as Samson's miraculous birth. These narratives are first of all adventure tales intended to entertain. The stories of a nose-thumbing underdog, they also served to vent frustration.

Interpreters debate the stories' theological message. Given Samson's violent and amorous character, many argue that he serves as a negative example. Some see Samson as a foil for Samuel's greatness. Others view the stories as demonstrating the consequences of breaking a Nazirite vow or of interethnic marriage. In contrast, several scholars view the Samson stories as illustrations of God at work to fulfill the divine purpose of liberating Israel from its oppressors. The latter is more plausible. The storytellers and compilers do not censure Samson. Nor is the motif of the Nazirite vow, found only in Judg. 13 and 16, sufficiently integrated with the rest of the Samson cycle to serve as its overall theme. Moreover, Yahweh is thoroughly implicated in Samson's actions. Yahweh stirs up Samson (Judg. 13:25) and is behind his passion for the Timnite woman (14:4). The spirit of Yahweh empowers Samson to kill not only a lion (Judg. 14:6) but also 30 (14:19) and then 1000 (15:14-15) Philistines. Yahweh is also involved in Samson's self-destruction. Samson, captive, blind, humiliated, asks Yahweh for vengeance and death (Judg. 16:28-30); his prayer is granted. As J. Cheryl Exum has shown, the stories portray Yahweh working secretly, through human actions, with all their ambiguity, and openly, in direct answer to prayer, to defeat Israel's enemies and the enemies' god.

Bibliography. J. L. Crenshaw, *Samson* (Atlanta, 1978); J. C. Exum, "Aspects of Symmetry and Balance in the Samson Cycle," *JSOT* 19 (1981): 3-29; "The Theological Dimension of the Samson Saga," *VT* 33 (1983): 30-45; S. Niditch, "Samson as Culture Hero, Trickster, and Bandit," *CBQ* 52 (1990): 608-24; J. A. Soggin, *Judges*. OTL (Philadelphia, 1981); J. L. Wharton, "The Secret of Yahweh: Story and Affirmation in Judges 13–16," *Int* 27 (1973): 48-66.

Carolyn Pressler

SAMUEL (Heb. *šĕmû'ēl*)

Samuel gave leadership to Israel in the critical period of transition from tribal existence under the judges to the establishment of monarchy. He is the central character of the first half of 1 Samuel, which bears his name. In these stories he appears in multiple roles of authority: priest, prophet, judge, military leader. Samuel occupies a unique role in Israel's story. He is the representative and defender of an older tribal covenant order in Israel, yet he is God's prophetic agent for ushering in the new day of kingship.

It is difficult to determine which traditions reflect the historical Samuel. Older independent traditions have been reworked by historians incorporating the stories of Samuel into larger works with particular interests. It seems likely that Samuel's prophetic role has been emphasized and enhanced by circles interested in the prophets as the legitimizers and confronters of kings (1 Sam.

9:1–10:16; 13:8-15; 15:1-35; 28:3-25). The Deuteronomistic historian, working at the time of Babylonian Exile, used Samuel to voice negative views toward kingship (1 Sam. 8:1-22; 12:1-25). However, what seems beyond doubt is that Samuel played a catalytic role in the establishment of kingship in Israel. He is a central figure in all of the stories on Saul's elevation to the kingship. Samuel was also the key figure in keeping Israel's identity and religious tradition alive during a period of defeat and occupation by the Philistines (1 Sam. 4). In this time of confusion and dissolution it may well have been possible and necessary for Samuel to exercise authority in roles that would normally not converge in a single individual (priest, prophet, judge).

Samuel's birth story (1 Sam. 1) reports that his father Elkanah was an Ephraimite from Ramathaim-zophim. His mother Hannah was barren and was given the child Samuel as God's response to her fervent prayer. In return she devoted the boy to the service of the Lord, and he came to Shiloh to serve under the priest Eli, presumably to take up priestly duties himself. In a direct revelatory experience from the Lord (1 Sam. 3) Samuel is given an oracle to deliver to Eli denouncing the corruption that Eli's sons have brought on the priesthood and announcing judgment against Israel and the house of Eli (3:11-14). From this beginning Samuel becomes widely recognized in Israel as a prophet (1 Sam. 3:19–4:1a). When the Philistines defeat Israel and capture the ark, Eli's sons are killed and Eli himself collapses in death (1 Sam. 4:10-18). Later texts indicate that Shiloh was also destroyed at this time (cf. Jer. 7:14; 26:9).

In the time of Philistine occupation, Samuel is portrayed as single-handedly maintaining Israelite tradition and identity. Assembling the people at Mizpah, he challenges them to maintain covenant obedience (1 Sam. 7:3-6). He is said to "judge" the people (1 Sam. 7:6, 15, 16), which includes traveling a circuit of towns in the central hill country and "administering justice" from his home in Ramah (vv. 16-17). When the Philistines threaten to attack, Samuel presides over sacrifices (1 Sam. 7:7-9) and calls to the Lord on the people's behalf. The Lord sends a panic upon the Philistines and the Israelites win a military victory over them (1 Sam. 7:10-11). Samuel is credited with subduing the Philistines all his days (1 Sam. 7:13). 1 Sam. 7 is often said to picture Samuel as the last of the judges. His role is broader than that, and the portrait here is probably idealized to make the elders' request for a king (1 Sam. 8) seem unnecessary.

Samuel appears as a key figure in all of the differing traditions on the beginning of kingship in Israel. The elders of Israel come to Samuel and request him to "appoint for us a king to govern us, like other nations" (1 Sam. 8:5; cf. vv. 19-20). Samuel interprets this as a personal rejection and is reluctant to comply. God tells him that the people's request is a rejection of divine kingship but that he should make them a king after issuing a severe warning on the dangers of kingship (1 Sam. 8:11-18).

Three stories follow that show Samuel in the key role of designating or installing Saul as Israel's first king. In the first (1 Sam. 9:1–10:16), Samuel appears as a seer encountered by Saul while seeking his father's lost asses. God reveals to Samuel that Saul is the one God has designated to deliver Israel from the Philistines. Samuel privately anoints Saul, after which he is possessed by God's spirit. This account stresses Samuel's role as a prophet, anointing and authorizing Saul for kingship. In the second account (1 Sam. 10:17-27), Samuel assembles the people at Mizpah where Saul is selected king by the casting of lots. Samuel installs him as king in a public ceremony that includes instructions in the "rights and duties of kingship" (v. 25). Finally, following Saul's heroic deliverance of the people of Jabesh-gilead (1 Sam. 11:1-13), Samuel "made Saul king before the Lord in Gilgal" (v. 15).

In a final public assembly Samuel declares the integrity of his own leadership in Israel (1 Sam. 12:1-5) and admonishes the people and their king to give obedience to the commandments of the Lord (vv. 6-25). He promises to continue to pray for them and to instruct them in "the good and the right" (1 Sam. 12:23). Public addresses such as this often mark transitions between major periods in the Deuteronomistic history, and 1 Sam. 12 is usually regarded as the dividing point between the period of judges and that of kings.

Samuel appears as the prophet announcing judgment against Saul in two stories describing Saul's rejection by God for failure to carry out God's word as made known by Samuel. In 1 Sam. 13:8-15 Samuel condemns Saul for proceeding with sacrifices that Samuel was to have made. The rejection takes the form of denying future dynasty to Saul. In 1 Sam. 15:1-35 Samuel pronounces judgment on Saul for failing to carry out the full extermination of the Amalekites in a campaign declared by Samuel as God's holy war. This time Saul himself is rejected as God's king. Samuel, as God's prophet, can withdraw divine authority from kings as well as bestow it.

Samuel grieves over the failure of Saul, and God must call him from his grief to undertake the mission to annoint a new king (1 Sam. 15:35–16:1). In Bethlehem Samuel wants to anoint the first of Jesse's sons brought to him, but God chides him to look on the heart and not on appearances. At last Samuel anoints David, Jesse's eighth son who was off tending sheep. Again, the emphasis is on the need for kings to be anointed and authorized by God's prophet.

Samuel encounters Saul twice more. While Samuel is leading the group of prophets in his home of Ramah, Saul comes searching for David and is seized up in the frenzy of their prophesying, strips of his clothes, and lies naked before Samuel all day and night (1 Sam. 19:18-24). Although Samuel dies (1 Sam. 25:1), Saul is humiliated before the prophet one last time. Fearful over a coming battle with the Philistines, Saul has a medium call up the ghost of Samuel (1 Sam. 28). Samuel reiterates God's rejection of Saul as king and predicts a Philistine victory in which Saul and his sons will die.

BRUCE C. BIRCH

SAMUEL, BOOKS OF

First and Second Samuel, included in the Former Prophets of the Hebrew canon, which is regarded as part of the Deuteronomistic history. In the Hebrew Bible Samuel was one book, but in the LXX it was divided into two books and appears as part of a four-volume collection in the historical books entitled 1-4 Kings, corresponding to 1-2 Samuel and 1-2 Kings. The name of the book probably derives from the first key character, Samuel, who appears as priest (1 Sam. 3), judge/charismatic leader (ch. 7), and prophet (chs. 8-28). Samuel does not appear in 2 Samuel.

Contents and Plot

1-2 Samuel concerns the close of the period of the judges (1 Sam. 1–7) and the rise of the Monarchy in Israel (chs. 8–12). It details the reigns of Saul (1 Sam. 13–31) and David (2 Sam. 1–24). 1 Samuel can be divided into the following subsections: Hannah's miraculous delivery, her Song, Eli's priesthood, and Samuel's life at Shiloh (chs. 1–3); the Ark narrative, where the Philistines defeat Israel, capture the ark of the covenant, place it in the temple of Dagan, and then return it (chs. 4–6); Samuel as judge (ch. 7); three different versions of the establishment of the monarchy, with Saul as Israel's first king (chs. 8–11); Samuel's "Farewell Speech," bringing to a close the period of the judges (ch. 12); Jonathan's victory over the Philistines and Saul's rejection as king (chs. 13-15); the secret anointing of David, his induction into Saul's court as harpist, and slaying of Goliath (chs. 16–17); David and Saul as adversaries and David's life as renegade, marauder, and Philistine vassal (chs. 18–30); the death of Saul and his sons in battle (ch. 31). 2 Samuel records alternative reports on the death of Saul and David's elegy over Saul and Jonathan (ch. 1); the aborted reign of Ishbosheth, David's anointing as king of Judah and Israel, and his establishment of Jerusalem as his capital (chs. 2–5); the end of the Ark narrative, placement of the ark in Jerusalem, and David's conflict with Michal (ch. 6); promise of dynastic succession for the Davidic line (ch. 7); David's foreign wars and his administrative structure (ch. 8); David's bringing Mephibosheth to Jerusalem (ch. 9); the Ammonite wars and accounts of David and Bathsheba, Nathan's parable, and the birth of Solomon (chs. 10–12); the rape of Tamar, banishment and redemption of Absalom (chs. 13–14); Absalom's revolt (chs. 15–18); restoration of David after a second revolt (chs. 19–20); David's appeasement of the Gibeonites (ch. 21); the Prayer of David (ch. 22); the Song of David and list of his warriors (ch. 23); and David's census and the subsequent divine punishment (ch. 24).

Text

The books are fraught with text critical problems, in that the MT appears to have many scribal errors and the LXX version is longer and was considered more reliable (contrary to the usual text critical rule that the shorter and more difficult text is the more original). Since many difficulties in the Hebrew text stem from words and phrases appearing to have dropped out in transmission, the Greek is not viewed as expansionistic. With the discoveries at Qumran, the possibilities of different Hebrew texts of Samuel have called into question some of the earlier assessments while confirming others.

Authorship

Because of the many text critical problems, source critical work on authorship was not fully developed until the early 20th century. One marked feature of the book is the several duplicate narratives, such as the rise of Saul to kingship (1 Sam. 8; 9:1–10:16; 10:17-27; 11); the rejection of Saul as king (chs. 13, 15); David's arrival at the court of Saul (16:14-23; 18); David and Goliath (ch. 17); David and Jonathan's discussion of Saul's attempts to kill David (chs. 19, 20); David's sparing Saul's life (chs. 24, 26); the death of Saul (1 Sam. 31; 2 Sam. 1); and lists of David's officials (2 Sam. 8:15-18; 20:23-26). The position of these duplicate narratives in the book underscores their disagreements. For instance, in 1 Sam. 19 Jonathan tells David about Saul's plot to kill him, while in ch. 20, when David reports the plot Jonathan is ignorant of it. Had the chapters been reversed, the plot line would be smoother and the duplication less problematic.

The earliest source critical studies therefore attempted to trace the pentateuchal sources J and E into Samuel, along with some recognition of Deuteronomic materials as a way of explaining the duplication. Others attempted to identify pro- and antimonarchic sources. However, unlike in the Pentateuch the differences in the duplicate accounts lack sufficient continuity to argue for continuous sources. Still others suggest a prophetic source to account for the duplicates.

Succession Narrative

In 1976 Leonhard Rost suggested a Succession narrative, arguing for an old source encompassing 1 Sam. 9–20 and 1 Kgs. 1–2 that was intended to answer the question raised in 1 Kgs. 1, "Who will sit on the throne of David?" Rost contended this material was written by an eyewitness familiar with the inner workings of the court in an attempt to glorify Solomon, who although not first in line did succeed David. Rost also posited two other independent collections, the Ark narrative (1 Sam. 4:1–7:1; 2 Sam. 6:1-16) and the Ammonite war narratives (2 Sam. 10:1–11:1; 12:26-31), as historical documents written close to the events.

Since the 1960s scholars have chipped away at Rost's theory of a Succession narrative. R. A. Carlson argues that 2 Samuel was heavily influenced by Deuteronomic retributive theology and divides thematically into David under the blessing (chs. 1–10) and David under the curse (chs. 13–24), with the David-Bathsheba-Nathan complex as the turning point. R. N. Whybray, followed by Carole Fontaine, identifies wisdom influence on the work. James Flanagan suggests a court history in 2 Sam. 15–20, separate and apart from the Succession document which was later added to it. Charles Conroy argues for a strong difference in language between 2 Sam. 9–12 and 13–20. Ernst Würthwein contends that the work is political propaganda. John Van Seters proposes that the Succession narratives were late, postexilic additions. Randall C. Bailey argues that the complex in 2 Sam. 10–12 is a Deuteronomic construction, revealing the hands of the First and Second Deuteronomists, and that the David-Bathsheba marriage was a political marriage on the order of those with Michal and Abigail. He further maintains that the events took place after Absalom's revolt, but were placed in their present location to create the Deuteronomic retributive justice theology.

Historical Reliability and Genre

The historicity of the materials in Samuel is buttressed by the work of Albrecht Alt, who sees behind the battle narratives and lists of officials and conquest accounts historically reliable materials. According to Martin Noth and his followers, one cannot speak of a "History of Israel" until the Monarchy, so the Samuel materials are the major source for historical reconstruction. Other arguments for large blocks of material in Samuel come from Artur Weiser, who identifies 1 Sam. 16–2 Sam. 5 as the "History of the Rise of David," intentionally pro-Davidic.

Evidence of Rost's strong influence is seen in Noth's 1943 *Überlieferungsgeschichtlichte Studien*, in which he argues for the existence of a Deuteronomistic historian writing in Judah during the exilic period and using older sources. Noth accepts Rost's designations of blocks of materials and sees little Deuteronomic editing in Samuel, except for the Farewell Address of Samuel in 1 Sam. 12 and a reworking of the dynastic promise in 2 Sam. 7. In essence, Noth contends the Deuteronomic work was one of setting the pre-existent blocks of materials in their current arrangement, with minor editing. Noth's work all but puts an end to the argument for pentateuchal sources in Samuel. Interestingly, those who follow Noth's theory of a Deuteronomic historian, and those who follow Frank M. Cross on a double redaction theory, base their position on books other than Samuel. However, some German scholars who maintain prophetic or nomistic (legal) Deuteronomic strands (Rudolf Smend, Timo Veijola) base their positions on Samuel.

Gerhard von Rad goes even further, claiming that the Succession narrative was the earliest example of history writing in the ancient world, noting that the books contain only three notices of divine intention or intervention and pointing to heavy emphasis on behind the scenes work, an almost "secular" notion that when one reads the book of Samuel one has struck "pay dirt" in terms of historically reliable materials in the Bible. These studies are reinforced by Walter Brueggemann's work on the books' theology in the presentation of David as monarch.

New Literary Criticism

Moving beyond historical questions, new literary critics began reclaiming the whole book of Samuel and moved back to studies in 1 Samuel as well as 2 Samuel. More interested in questions of plot and characterization, David M. Gunn maintains that Saul was a tragic hero in the Greek sense, who is fated not to succeed. He also argues for viewing the whole of 2 Samuel as a novel about David, rather than breaking up the units into smaller genres. Gunn identifies subplots with the cycles of good and evil directing the narrative. Naomi Sternberg argues for the role of ambiguity in the narrative as key to the portrayal of character and plot in 2 Samuel; in this regard she is followed by Gail Yee. I. P. Fokkelman suggests multiple dualistic categories repeated throughout the David materials. Peter D. Miscall focuses on complication of characters and plot, with attention to characters and especially to deconstruction of older readings which essentialize. David Jobling maintains that the subject of heredity is key to the book of Samuel, which revolves around the question of kingship. Robert Polzin proposes reading Samuel as a message to the exiles in which kingship is called into question. Most particularly he concentrates on characterization, taking issue with Gunn's sympathetic reading of Saul, viewing him instead as an overly superstitious character who brings the house down on himself. Polzin sees Saul as a negative character, calling into question the older "pro-prophetic readings." David is a shadowy figure whose true self is not revealed until 2 Samuel. Bailey furthers Polzin's message to the exiles, arguing that not only the monarchy but also the priesthood and prophetic institutions were called into question. Along with these literary critical approaches, Flanagan addresses social world issues associated with David.

Canonical Shaping

Brevard S. Childs addresses the book's canonical shaping, arguing that the Songs of Hannah and David (1 Sam. 2; 2 Sam. 23) framed the book, such that the account ends where it begins. Brueggemann maintains that this framing was intended to depict the history of Israel, not as blood and guts but rather as the story of Yahweh's salvation. According to Bailey, this framing characterizes Yahweh as God of reversal and savior, in contrast to the portrayal of the deity in the remainder of the book.

Post-Colonial Interpretation: Feminist, Racialist, Sexual Orientation Criticism

Feminist interpretation of the book of Samuel has called into question the basic presupposition of all the above research, namely that Samuel (1 Sam. 1–12), Saul (1 Sam. 13–31), and David (2 Samuel) are the key characters in all the narratives and that the other characters are only present as foils. Adele Berlin concentrates on the wives of David and their characterizations in the narrative. J. Cheryl Exum confronts patriarchal ideology in the narrative, especially in the depiction of Michal. Alice Bach moves away from patriarchal readings, arguing that Abigail is the central character who directs the action in 1 Sam. 25 and not a foil to David. JoAnn Hackett notes that Samuel revolves around the three main males, but then questions this long-held strategy of reading and details the roles of women in the work.

Race and sexual orientation issues have come to the fore in Samuel studies. C. B. Copher notes the long history of racialist interpretations, most markedly in the treatment of the Cushite in 2 Sam. 18. G. D. Comstock identifies a homosexual relationship between David and Jonathan in the elegy of 2 Sam. 1.

Message

As reader response criticism has shown, the message of the book depends in large part on the reading strategy of the reader. God's faithfulness to Hannah meets us at the very beginning, as does Hannah's faith and faithfulness to God. The warnings to clergy like Eli loom large.

The different readings of Samuel, from paragon of virtue, to sacred prophet, to self-absorbed individual; the different readings of Saul, from victim to disobedient one; the different readings of David, from "one after God's own heart" to scoundrel; the different readings of God, from Almighty to elusive presence, are all possible readings of this book. The richness for nurture and questioning abounds on each page. The intrigue of the political dealings and the theological manipulations shout out for clarification.

Is Samuel only a priest because his mother dedicated him (1 Sam. 1)? What would this say for a theology of call? Is Saul's visitation by the "evil spirit from God" a paradigm of psychological distress (1 Sam. 16)? If so, how do we come to understand the nature of mental illness? Is David the original "Teflon king" (1 Sam. 21–22)? If so, is the ethic today of "just don't get caught" germane? Does God really repay adultery with rape (2 Sam. 11–13)? If so, how do we trust divine justice?

The messages are as varied as the interpreters.

Bibliography. R. C. Bailey, *David in Love and War: The Pursuit of Power in 2 Samuel 10–12.* JSOTSup 75 (Sheffield, 1990); B. Birch, *The Rise of the Israelite Monarchy: The Growth and Development of 1 Samuel 7–15.* SBLDS 27 (Missoula, 1976); W. Brueggemann, *David's Truth in Israel's Imagination and Memory* (Philadelphia, 1985); D. M. Gunn, *The Fate of King Saul.* JSOTSup 14 (Sheffield, 1980); *The Story of King David.* JSOTSup 6 (Sheffield, 1978); P. K. McCarter, Jr., *I Samuel.* AB 8 (Garden City, 1980); *II Samuel.* AB 9 (Garden City, 1984); L. Rost, *The Succession to the Throne of David* (Sheffield, 1982).

RANDALL C. BAILEY

SANBALLAT (Heb. *sanballaṭ*)

A leader of the opposition to Nehemiah's rebuilding the walls of Jerusalem. Derived from Akk. *Sin-ubal-lit,* the name means "may [the god] Sin give him life." In view of this foreign name, scholars speculate that Sanballat may have descended from a family settled in Israel by the Assyrians in the 8th century (2 Kgs. 17:24; cf. Ezra 4:1-3). However, one of the Elephantine papyri gives the names of his two sons as Delaiah and Shelemiah, both compounded with the shortened name of God, Yah. In addition, one of the grandsons of the high priest Eliashib was his son-in-law. It seems likely, then, that Sanballat thought of himself as a loyal Yahwist.

Sanballat is also called "the Horonite." Given his Akkadian name, scholars have suggested variously that he came from Haran in northern Mesopotamia, which was the center of worship of the moon-god Sin; from Hauran, a former Assyrian province in northern Transjordan; or from Horonamim in Moab. A more likely possibility is that the name derived from one of the cities named Beth-horon settled by the Ephraimites.

The aforementioned Elephantine papyrus calls Sanballat governor of Samaria, and as such he was also responsible for Judah and Jerusalem. He may well have thought he had jurisdiction over Nehemiah, who instead claimed to be the agent of King Artaxerxes and thus beyond Sanballat's control.

Sanballat joined with Tobiah the Ammonite and Geshem the Arab to oppose Nehemiah's plans on behalf of Jerusalem (Neh. 2:10-19). They charged Nehemiah with plotting to commit treason, specifically with wanting to reestablish the monarchy and revolt against Persian control — hence, the need for a wall around Jerusalem (Neh. 6:6-7). Nehemiah repudiated such thinking as a product of their own imaginations, but he probably did hope the city and its environs would be separated from Samaria and granted a modicum of self-rule. A wall would also allow further economic growth. Sanballat and his companions were prepared to use force to stop Nehemiah (Neh. 4:8[MT 2]). When the three proposed a meeting with Nehemiah (Neh. 6:1-9), he was suspicious of their motives and refused to meet with them. Despite Nehemiah's success, Sanballat did not easily relinquish control over Jerusalem, as the marriage of his daughter to the grandson of the high priest Eliashib proves (Neh. 13:28).

Bibliography. J. Blenkinsopp, *Ezra-Nehemiah.* OTL (Philadelphia, 1988); P. L. Redditt, "Nehemiah's First Mission and the Date of Zechariah 14," *CBQ* 56 (1994): 664-78.

PAUL L. REDDITT

SANCTIFY, SANCTIFICATION

The act of making something or someone clean or holy. In Christian theology, sanctification is usually understood as an act or process subsequent to salvation which renders the believer holy in fact (as opposed to justification, which is a legal declaration of innocence).

In the OT, especially in the prophets, sanctification was understood as the whole process by which God is cleansing our world and its people. His ultimate goal is that everything — animate and inanimate — be cleansed from any taint of sin or uncleanness (Ezek. 36:25-29; 37:21-23). Heb. *qdš* occurs as a verb, "to be set apart, consecrated," and an adjective ("sacred, holy" [thing, place, person, etc.]), whether that quality was applied to God, or places, things, persons, or times sanctified by (or to) God. The people were to be a "holy nation" (Exod. 19:6). In order to facilitate their sanctification, God established a holy priesthood (Exod. 29:1; 1 Sam. 7:1).

A less frequent term, Heb. *ṭhr* ("to be clean, pure"), describes cleansing in a physical, ceremonial, and moral sense. There are "clean" animals (Gen. 7:2, 8; 8:20) and "pure" metals (Exod. 25:11-39), "clean" people and things (Num. 18–19). The Lord's words are "pure" (Ps. 12:6[MT 7]), his eyes "too pure to look on evil" (Hab. 1:13).

Something may be separated from God by sin and uncleanness. One can obtain forgiveness from sin by offering the appropriate sacrifice for sin; cleansing from uncleanness requires the appropriate purification ritual. Such rituals can be divided into water rituals, for people and things that can be cleaned, and fire rituals (usually destructive), for severely contaminated things, especially those which cannot be cleansed.

A person who has contracted uncleanness must bathe, wash his clothes, and wait until evening (Lev. 11:38; 15:1-32; Num. 19:11-13). Greater amounts of uncleanness required more complicated ceremonies and additional ingredients (Lev. 14:1-9; Num. 19:1-22). Under the right conditions, even water could be made unclean (Lev. 11:33-35). However, water from a spring ("living water") or underground cistern was always considered clean. This is why "living water" became so important (Lev. 14:5, 6, 50-52; 14:52; 15:2, 13; cf. John 4:10, 11; 7:38).

Ultimately, the NT teaches that the sanctification of the world takes place at a personal and individual level. Those who choose to be sanctified by the Spirit must cooperate in the process (1 John 3:3; Rev. 22:11) — just as in the water purification rites of the OT. This process removes the sin but "saves" the individual. The Spirit's role in sanctification begins before conversion with conviction (John 16:8-11), includes cleansing the believer at conversion (1 Cor. 6:11; 2 Thess. 2:13; 1 Pet. 1:1-2), continually washing him or her from sin after conversion (John 4:10-14; 7:38-39; cf. 1 John 1:7-9), through guiding him or her in righteous living (John 14:26; Rom. 8:5-13; 1 Cor. 2:9-16).

Purification by fire included a variety of materials: clothing or leather with any kind of destructive mildew (Lev. 13:47-59) or a house from which mildew could not be cleansed (Lev. 14:33ff.; cf. Sodom and Gomorrah, Gen. 19:24; cf. Luke 17:29-30; and idolatrous Jerusalem, Jer. 4:4).

People who refuse to cooperate with the Spirit's work of sanctification are punished with fire. God will use this method to "cleanse" the earth of the presence of sinful people (Isa. 66:24; cf. Matt. 25:30, 41, 46; Rev. 20:11–21:1; cf. 2 Pet. 3:10-13).

TIMOTHY P. JENNEY

SANDALS, SHOES

Ancient footwear is well known from paintings, sculpture, and reliefs. While most persons wore a simple sandal, slippers of soft leather were not uncommon. Assyrian soldiers at times are depicted wearing a high boot; in later periods, Roman soldiers often wore a larger, more substantial leather boot. The ancient world considered shoes the humblest article of clothing; although they were often repaired, sandals and shoes could be purchased inexpensively.

Heb. *naʿălāyîm* serves interchangeably for shoes and sandals. During the NT era Gk. *hypódēma* (Matt. 3:11; 10:10) was a simple leather sole attached with a strap at the front. The less frequent term *sandálion* signifies a sole bound to the foot (Mark 6:9).

A wall painting from the Egyptian tomb of Beni Hasan depicts tribute-bearing Semites shod in a variety of sandals. Some of the shoes bind the sole to the foot with straps around the ankle, across the instep, up the leg, or across the toes; females wear a low boot. Peasants in ancient Egypt wore sandals of leather, papyrus, or woven palm bast commonly held by two woven straps across the arch of the foot and joining between the toes. The Golden Throne of Tutankhamen (ca. 1340 B.C.E.) shows the youthful pharaoh wearing a simple sandal held by a single strap. Later Roman sculptures portray some sandals with an intricate open-woven pattern of straps covering the toes.

Shoes were removed at the doorway of a tent or home before entering (Luke 7:38, 44) or during extended periods of mourning (2 Sam. 15:30). Removal of a houseguest's shoes was the duty of the lowliest slave or servant in the home. A student also would stoop to loosen and remove the shoes of his teacher. However, rabbinic literature warned students not to do so before strangers lest they be mistaken for servants rather than scholars.

In the presence of a superior the shoes often were removed, as on the occasion of a theophany (Exod. 3:5; cf. Josh. 5:15). The Lachish reliefs from Sennacherib's palace at Nineveh (ca. 700) picture the defeated residents of the city coming barefooted before their vanquisher as a sign of humility.

A sandal might also be used to seal a legal contract (Ruth 4:6-10) or to designate ownership or lordship of property (Ps. 60:8[MT 10]). To go barefoot indicated poverty, reproach, or impending judgment (Isa. 20:2). In contrast, being shod gave evidence of readiness for a journey or task (Exod. 12:11; Mark 6:9).

Bibliography. E. A. Speiser, "Of Shoes and Shekels," *BASOR* 77 (1940): 15-20.

DAVID C. MALTSBERGER

SANHEDRIN

The hebraized form of Gk. *synédrion,* meaning "a counsel or assembly." Sanhedrin is first used in the Mishnah (ca. A.D. 200) as the name of a tractate and occasionally as a term for courts (the ordinary Mishnaic Hebrew word for court is *bêt dîn,* lit., "house of judgment"). The use of "Sanhedrin" in some NT versions to translate the Greek term is anachronistic.

The terms for courts and councils are very imprecise in the NT, Mishnah, and Greek culture in general, and the historical reconstruction of these institutions is similarly uncertain. In the NT *synédrion* is used for judicial courts in general (Matt. 5:22; 10:17; Mark 13:9) and the supreme judicial and legislative court in Jerusalem presided over by the high priest (e.g., Matt. 26:59; Mark 14:55; Acts 5:21). But the terminology is imprecise and mutable. In Acts 5:21 the *synédrion* is linked to "the whole council of the elders *(gerousía)* of Israel." In Luke 22:66 the "*presbytérion* (another word for 'council of elders') of people," consisting of the chief priests and scribes, is said to have gathered and then to have brought Jesus into their *synédrion.* Here *synédrion* simply means "gathering" or "assembly" and the official name of the group is *presbytérion.* Similarly, in Acts 22:5 Paul claims that the high priest and the whole *presbytérion* had given him the authority to arrest Jewish followers of Jesus in Damascus. The Gospel of Mark (Mark 15:1) refers to this supreme council as a *symboúlion* (yet another word for "council"). In general, the Greek NT terms for the Jerusalem legislative and judicial body vary greatly and the English translations of these terms are similarly imprecise.

Josephus speaks of many local and national councils *(synédria)* whose powers and memberships changed with political circumstances. Gabinius, the Roman governor, set up five regional councils in Judea and Samaria in 457 B.C. Herod the Great assembled frequent councils of his family and friends. The Roman senate is referred to as a *synédrion* or a *boulḗ* (city council in a Hellenistic city), and Josephus uses both terms for councils in Jerusalem. Josephus does not describe a single, continuous body functioning as supreme council in Jerusalem nor does he refer to such a body by one name or specify its membership or powers, probably because the council's nature varied over time.

The mishnaic use of the term "Sanhedrin" reflects the later rabbinic sages' reconstruction of temple institutions. The "Great Court" *(bêt dîn)* or "Great Sanhedrin" had 71 members and met in the Chamber of Hewn Stone in the temple complex (*m. Sanh.* 11:2; *Mid.* 5:4). It made final decisions in legal disputes (*m. Sanh.* 11:2), judged the fitness of priests to serve in the temple (*m. Mid.* 5:4; *Qidd.* 4:5), and decided on additions to the temple (*m. Šeb.* 2:2). The sages' exalted and nostalgic view of the Jerusalem council can be seen in two statements: the "Great Court" on the temple mount was the place from which "Torah goes forth to all Israel" (*m. Sanh.* 11:2) and its loss in A.D. 70 caused an end to singing at wedding feasts (*m. Soṭa* 9:11). The word "Sanhedrin" is also used in the Mishnah for courts of 23 judges that decide capital cases inside or outside of Israel (*m. Mak.* 1:10). These courts, which have sages for judges seated in a semi-circle (*m. Sanh.* 4:3-4), seem to reflect 3rd-century realities contemporary with the Mishnah, rather than the Second Temple period.

The NT, Mishnah, and Josephus do not present a consistent picture of Jewish governance and the role of various councils, but they testify to the frequency of councils with legislative and judicial functions within the political contest of the Roman Empire. Such councils would have been composed of the elders and respected members of the literate governing classes (ca. 10 percent of the population). In Jerusalem high officials and the senior members of the most powerful priestly and wealthy aristocratic families would have constituted the supreme council. Since religious laws and practices were thoroughly embedded in political and social life, no distinction should be made between a secular and religious council or Sanhedrin, nor should the religious scholars of the rabbinic period and their legal concerns be projected back into the 1st century. The Jerusalem council probably legislated and ruled in limited ways, depending on the political strength of the ruling high priest and on the freedom given by Roman governors and their Herodian clients. As members of the governing class, the Jerusalem councilors probably busied themselves with maintaining public order, preserving their own power and position in Judean society, and mediating between the empire and the people.

ANTHONY J. SALDARINI

SANSANNAH (Heb. *sansannâ*)
A town in the southern district of Judah (Josh. 15:31). It does not occur in similar lists of Simeonite towns, where Hazar-susah (Josh. 19:5) and Hazar-susim (1 Chr. 4:31) appear as possible variants of the name. The site is identified with Khirbet esh-Shamsanīyât (140083), ca. 15.5 km. (9.6 mi.) NW of Beer-sheba. LAURA B. MAZOW

SAPH (Heb. *sap̱*) (also SIPPAI)
A giant who fought for the Philistines. He was defeated by Sibbecai the Hushathite at Gob (2 Sam. 21:18). At 1 Chr. 20:4 he is called Sippai.

SAPPHIRA (Gk. *Sápphira*)
The wife of Ananias (**1**; from Aram. *šappîrā'*, "beautiful"). Together they agreed to withhold from the church part of the money gained from sale of property, while apparently claiming to bring it all. Since this amounted to a lie against the Holy Spirit, both were struck dead (Acts 5:1-10).

SAPPHIRE
In biblical usage probably lapis lazuli, a semiprecious azure stone that contained golden flecks of iron pyrite (cf. Job 28:6, 16). References to the sapphire (Heb. *sappîr;* Gk. *sáppîrâ*) are found in descriptions of the glory of divine epiphanies (Exod. 24:10; Ezek. 1:26), in prophetic-apocalyptic descriptions of the glory of the New Jerusalem (Isa. 54:11; Rev. 21:19), and in poetic descriptions of the majesty of a personage (Cant. 5:14; Lam. 4:7; Ezek. 28:13). It is one of the stones representing a tribe of Israel on the priest's breastplate (Exod. 28:18).

JEFFREY S. LAMP

SARAH (Heb. *śārâ*) (also SARAI)
1. The primary ancestress of the Jewish people, and of Christians and Muslims as well. Introduced late in Gen. 11 as Sarai, wife of Abram, she functions between Gen. 11 and 23 as companion to Abraham. Called by God from their dwelling in the East (Ur of Babylon via Haran), they start their bib-

lical lives in old age struggling to discern implications of the promises God has made with them: land, progeny, blessing. Stories involving Sarah may be seen as the struggle of herself and Abraham to understand their role in receiving land, in begetting offspring, and in being blessing for and blessed by the peoples around them. In no instance is their path particularly clear.

They no sooner arrive in the promised Canaan when famine drives them to Egypt, where Abram's survival strategy lands Sarai in Pharaoh's palace (Gen. 12, and with minor changes, Gen. 20). Once God intervenes with disapproval, the couple and their household depart and re-enter the land of Canaan, enriched by their encounter with the foreigner. Other episodes involving peoples of the land specify groups to whom their descendants eventually stand in relationship: Moabites, Ammonites, Canaanite kings, peoples of the Dead Sea neighborhood (Gen. 13, 14, 18–19).

But the primary promise, for Sarah, is the begetting of an heir through which the Jewish people will be descended. All of the episodes in which she figures may be seen as complications of her role as ancestress. No sooner is Sarai introduced than it is noted that she and Abram go childless; the promise of numerous descendants does not include directions for accomplishment of it. Abraham evidently has other alternatives to Sarah's being the mother of the son: his sponsorship of his nephew Lot, perhaps even his temporary disclaiming of his wife when in foreign territory, and his adopting a slave of his household are plausible solutions to the prolonged childlessness of Sarah. Sarah herself eventually suggests that her husband beget a son by her Egyptian maidservant Hagar; that child, Ishmael, though blessed by God, is not the child of promise. But finally with orchestration by God about conception, naming, and circumcising, Sarah bears to Abraham the appropriate heir, Isaac, when she is 90 and Abraham 100 (Gen. 16–21). Having accomplished that deed, she vanishes, absent when Isaac's life is threatened on Mt. Moriah (Gen. 22), dead at the age of 127.

Modern biblical scholarship poses several questions to the stories of Sarah and Abraham. Historians question whether and how to retrieve relevant social, political, and economic information. But the originating circumstances, time of composition, and reference of the materials remain opaque. Those who attempt to date the events of the narratives tend to place them midway through the 2nd millennium B.C.E. Those dating the composition of the sources differ; competent suggestions range from the 10th to the 5th centuries.

Social scientific criticism clarifies the efforts at childbearing in particular. Once rather confident at having found a 14th-century extrabiblical parallel to Abraham's claiming his wife as his sister, recent scholars have been concerned to understand issues of marriage, kinship, and economics more systemically. Sarah's urgency to bear is not an abstraction or ideal but a need to provide for Abraham a clear determination of who will inherit vertically the name, the land, the property rights; she needs a son to clarify her own status and ensure a potential caretaker for herself. Hence the episodes involving Sarah's failure to produce an heir involve a mix of details historical, legal, sociological, and psychological as well as religious or theological.

Literary analysis of the stories, while still positing several voices or sources for the stories (most agree that texts emerge from the Yahwist [e.g., Gen. 12], Elohist [ch. 20], and Priestly [chs. 17, 23] strata), also undertakes a more wholistic analysis of the ancestral texts. The genealogies, once dismissed as secondary and tedious, now set agendas embellished by supplementing episodes. For Sarah, the question posed is how, despite her age and apparent barrenness and that of her husband, she will produce the "direct" vertical heir for Abraham. A detail such as Sarah's silence when consigned by Abraham to the foreigner is assessed in terms of characterization or ideology. Caught between difficult circumstances, she may choose not to contribute to her own oppression, or she may wordlessly dread its approach — or her words may seem moot. Similarly, her competitive relationship with Hagar is shown to arise less from malevolence than from the threat Sarah must feel to her status as she continues childless or from narrative presuppositions.

References to Sarah outside Genesis are derivative of her roles as wife and progenitrix. In the OT she is mentioned only in Isa. 51, where her name (with Abraham's) is lent to postexilic factions. Paul makes similar reference (Rom. 9; Gal. 4), where Sarah and Isaac represent being chosen, promised, freeborn, over against Hagar and her son who represent opposite values. Her aged barrenness is also briefly referenced in Rom. 4; Heb. 11 as part of Abraham's challenge to faith. Finally, having traveled some distance from the episodes of Genesis, she is named obedient to Abraham (1 Pet. 3).

Bibliography. A. Brenner, ed., *A Feminist Companion to Genesis* (Sheffield, 1993); N. Steinberg, *Kinship and Marriage in Genesis: A Household Economics Approach* (Minneapolis, 1993).

BARBARA GREEN, O.P.

2. The daughter of Raguel and wife of Tobias (Tob. 3:7-8). She had been married to seven husbands, each of whom had been killed by the demon Asmodeus before the marriage was consummated.

SARDIS (Gk. *Sárdeis*)

A city in Asia Minor listed among the seven churches of Rev. 1:11 (cf. 3:1-6). Founded as early as 1200 B.C., Sardis was an ancient capital of the kingdom of Lydia which was conquered by the Persians in the 6th century. Alexander's defeat of the Persians in 334 brought independence, but it was once again conquered and made a provincial capital by the Seleucids. Roman occupation began in 189, and for two centuries Sardis lived under the government of Pergamum.

Excavations at Sardis have uncovered the acropolis, impressive monumental buildings, a gymnasium, and a temple dedicated to Artemis (which imitated that of Diana in Ephesus). The most important find is a basilica that was transformed into a synagogue in the 3rd century A.D.; its monumental size and decor suggest that the Jewish community enjoyed considerable wealth and prestige — and may have lived in some competition with the young church growing in the city (cf. Rev. 3:9). This discovery puts in question the assumption that the Jewish (and Jewish-Christian) communities lived in some seclusion or in their own religious enclave.

Sardis and Laodicea receive the harshest criticism in the letters of Revelation. Even though the church was in severe spiritual jeopardy, some of its members were faithful and had not "soiled their clothes" (Rev. 3:4).

The church of Sardis continued to grow in the Patristic period. Melito was bishop of Sardis in the 2nd century and wrote prolifically — especially criticizing the rival Jewish community. By the 4th century Christianity was growing rapidly in the empire, and at Sardis a large basilica complex was built. Bishops are recorded for Sardis till the 14th century, but the subsequent Turkish conquests put an end to the city's ecclesiastical leadership.

Bibliography. C. Foss, *Byzantine and Turkish Sardis* (Cambridge, Mass., 1976); G. M. A. Hanfmann, *Sardis from Prehistoric to Roman Times* (Cambridge, Mass., 1975); J. G. Pedley, *Ancient Literary Sources on Sardis* (Cambridge, Mass., 1972); A. R. Seager, "The Building History of the Sardis Synagogue," *AJA* 76 (1972): 425-35.

GARY M. BURGE

SARGON (Heb. *sargôn;* Akk. *Šarru-kēn*)
Sargon II, king of Assyria (721-705). Although the name Sargon means "the king is legitimate" in Akkadian, Sargon II's legitimacy to the throne is uncertain. He refers to Tiglath-pileser III (744-727) as his father only once in his inscriptions, and gained the throne upon the murder of Shalmaneser V, his possible brother, during the siege of Samaria. After his first regnal year of fighting in Assyria he silenced the rebellion at home by freeing the citizens of Assur from "the call to arms of the land and the summons of the tax-collector" apparently imposed on them by his predecessor. His next battle with Babylon, now ruled by the Aramaean Marduk-apal-iddina II (biblical Merodach-baladan) with support of Elam, ended in a temporary stalemate.

During the period between rulers in Assyria rebellions broke out in Syro-Palestine. Sargon claims responsibility for the capture and exile of the citizens of Samaria (2 Kgs. 17). He defeated allied forces including Hamath, Arpad, and Carchemish (Isa. 10) and continued south to Judah where he defeated an Egyptian army at Gaza, Egypt's border. Sargon launched a campaign against the rebels, punishing and deporting large numbers. He was then concerned with defeating his enemies to the north, Mushki and Urartu. His famous "Letters to the Gods" employs vivid terminology to describe his campaign and defeat of Urartu.

Later in his career Sargon again turned to the problem of Babylon. Marduk-apal-iddina II escaped to Elam and Sargon made himself king of Babylon. Another rebellion in the west, led by the king of Ashdod, was crushed (Isa. 20:1); a small fragment of a stela of Sargon was found in the excavations at Ashdod. Sargon was killed in a rather minor campaign in Anatolia.

Sargon built his new capital city named Dur-Sharruken ("Fortress of Sargon," Khorsabad) near Nineveh. While it was one of the more ambitious projects in Assyria, it was abandoned almost as soon as it was inhabited. TAMMI J. SCHNEIDER

SARID (Heb. *śārîḏ*)
A place that defined the southern limit of the tribal territory of Zebulun (Josh. 19:10, 12). Sarid is probably to be identified with Tell Shadûd (172229), in the Jezreel Valley ca. 8 km. (5 mi.) SW of Nazareth.

SARSECHIM (Heb. *sarsĕḵîm*)
"Sarsechim the Rab-saris," a Babylonian official (Jer. 39:3). It is unclear whether this is the name of an official or an official title. Many contemporary scholars correct this verse based on Jer. 39:13, thus reading: "Nergal-sharezer, prince of Simmagar, the Rab-mag; Nebuchazban, the Rab-saris. . . ." The assumption is that the confusion occurs with Babylonian titles of officials at the time of the fall of Jerusalem. DANIEL L. SMITH-CHRISTOPHER

SATAN (Heb. *śāṭān*)
Lit., an adversary or plotter, one who devises means for opposing another. In the OT the term (usually accompanied by the article) is applied to both human and heavenly figures who have been assigned the role of blocking the way of the wrongdoer and to act as an agent of divine judgment (e.g., Num. 22:22, 32; 1 Kgs. 11:14, 23; Ps. 109:6; 1 Chr. 21:1; Job 1–2; Zech. 3:1, 2; cf. 1 Sam. 29:4, where it denotes a potential saboteur in the ranks). The sense here is clearly not a being or personality but a function or status which a being takes up temporarily.

In the prologue of Job and Zech. 3 "the" *śāṭān* is identified specifically as one of "the sons of Elohim," a full-fledged member of the heavenly court, upon whom lies the task of indicting and prosecuting sinners before the bar of divine justice. Toward that end he takes up the mantle not only of the oriental spy, the intelligence gathering "eyes and ears of the king," who wanders to and fro on the earth observing humans and reports back to court on the state of their loyalty to their suzerain; but also the *agent provocateur* who coaxes people into committing crimes for which they can then be punished. In 1 Chr. 21:1 he who acts as "a" *śāṭān* is also a heavenly being who may very well be God himself.

In intertestamental, NT, and contemporary Jewish (esp. apocalyptic) literature, the term is used as a proper name to denote a supramundane being who stands in complete opposition to God and is dedicated to frustrating his work. He is known also by such epithets as Azazel (1 En. 13:1), Mastema (1QM 13:4, 11; Jub. 10:8), Beelzebul (Mark 3:22; Matt. 10:25; 12:24), Sammael (Mart. Isa. 1:8, 11; 2:1), Belial/Beliar

(2 Cor. 6:15; 1QS 1:18; 1QM 13:12; Mart. Isa. 2:4), "the devil" (Matt. 4:1; 25:41; Luke 4:2; 8:12; John 13:2; Acts 10:38; T. Job 3:3; cf. Wis. 2:24), "the evil one" (Matt. 13:19; John 17:15; 1 John 5:18, 19; cf. Matt. 6:13; 2 Thess. 3:3), "the ruler of the demons" (Mark 3:22 par.), "the enemy" (Matt. 13:25, 28, 39; Luke 10:19), and "the ruler of this world" (John 12:31; 14:30). Often regarded — along with "minioned" demons (called "satans" in 1 En. 64:4) and other evil spirits — as the cause of suffering, disease, frenzy, pestilence, and even national calamity, this figure was regarded primarily as one who "tests" the pious or the elect (never the "wicked" who are already in his grasp) by placing them in a forced position where the nature and extent of their dedication to God will be revealed — thus his designation in Matt. 4:3; 1 Thess. 3:5 as "the tempter." His ultimate aim is to disrupt or destroy their faithfulness to, and trust in, God, and thereby induce in them the seeds, if not the flowering, of disobedience to convenantal obligations. According to classic descriptions of Satan "at work" (e.g., Matt. 4:1-11 par., Jesus' wilderness temptation), Satan most frequently employs a tactic consonant with his character as both "a liar and the father of lies" (John 8:44) and one who nevertheless often disguises himself as "an angel of light" (2 Cor. 11:14), namely, to use cunning arguments, often grounded in Scripture itself, to persuade those whom he "tests" to "see" and accept that what God has commanded them to do (or put their trust in) cannot possibly be "of God." But afflictions, persecutions, and various other "trials" are also part of the arsenal used in the attempt to turn the pious from whatever task God has laid upon them (cf. 1 Pet. 5:8).

This same Satan seems also to have always been known as one who acts only within and under God's permissive will (note the coordination of divine and satanic purposes in Matt. 4:1) and even in his wickedness functions still as a divine servant, wittingly fostering in the world various aspects of God's righteousness. In Luke 22:31-34, e.g., Satan is described by Jesus as sifting out for God the impurities in the disciples' commitment. In 1 Cor. 5:1-5; 1 Tim. 1:20 Satan is one who can aid the sinner and the blasphemer respectively in returning to the fold. According to CD 8:2 at the final judgment, when the wicked are punished and the righteous rewarded, it is Satan who shall "visit" all apostates with destruction (cf. Matt. 25:41). As Rev. 12:7-12 notes, until he was relieved of office by the atoning work of Christ which nullifies all charges against God's elect, Satan was still God's Satan who executed his appointed role as Great Accuser from heaven.

Nevertheless, except within Pharisaic Judaism (where Satan is strictly a servant of God), the emphasis upon Satan as primarily "the evil one" hostile to God and his people tends to predominate. Accounting for this are (1) identification of Satan in the intertestamental period with the serpent of Eden (2 En. 31:3; Life of Adam and Eve 15-16; cf. Wis. 2:24; cf. also Rev. 20:2) and with the chaos dragon of the creation myth; (2) the subjection of Jews, during Persian rule, to the machinations of overzealous surveillants and prosecutors who used entrapment to gain convictions and were satisfied only with a capital sentence (cf. Eccl. 10:20); and (3) the flowering within Jewish thought (due to contact with Persian Zoroastrianism?) of moral and ontological dualism, coupled with a growing dissatisfaction with traditional or orthodox explanations of the origin and persistence of evil which seemed no longer adequate to account for the sheer, massive amount of apparently undeserved, noneducative, and nonredemptive sufferings with which the faithful among postexilic Israel were continually confronted.

All sources agree, however, that at some point Satan's activities will be halted, and Satan himself permanently restrained from pursuing any of his ends. Still, the depiction of the manner and means by which this will be brought about, as well as the degree to which Satan will resist his own curtailment and demise, varies considerably, even within a corpus emanating from an otherwise like-minded group, and seems to depend on how independent or hostile to the purposes of God Satan was thought to be. One such depiction deserves note, namely, that of Revelation. Here, within a work in which Satan's opposition to God and his people is as implacable as it is furious, where Satan is said to strive mightily against his "casting out," and where he is ultimately consigned for his wickedness to an eternal punishment, Satan is envisioned nonetheless as having to endure his torture not in the underworld (cf. Matt. 25:41; 1 En. 54:6), but in the throne room of the Ancient of Days. Satan is subdued by being lifted up to God.

Bibliography. P. L. Day, *An Adversary in Heaven: śāṭān in the Hebrew Bible.* HSM 43 (Atlanta, 1988); J. B. Gibson, *The Temptations of Jesus in Early Christianity.* JSNTSup 112 (Sheffield, 1995); L. Jung, *Fallen Angels in Jewish, Christian, and Mohammedan Literature* (1926, repr. New York, 1974); S. H. T. Page, *Powers of Evil: A Biblical Study of Satan and Demons* (Grand Rapids, 1995); E. Pagels, *The Origin of Satan* (New York, 1995); J. B. Russell, *The Devil: Perceptions of Evil from Antiquity to Primitive Christianity* (Ithaca, 1977); W. Wink, *Unmasking the Powers* (Philadelphia, 1986).

Jeffrey B. Gibson

SATRAP

Title of provincial governors in the Persian Empire (Heb., Aram. *ʼăḥašdarpān;* O.Pers. *xšaśapāvana;* Ezra 8:36; Esth. 3:12; 9:3; Dan. 3:2-3; 6:1-7). Esth. 1:1; 8:9 reports some 127 provinces in the empire, and Dan. 6:1-2 notes 120 satraps under three presidents. Herodotus lists 20 satrapies in the empire as organized under Darius Hystapes (*Hist.* 3.89-94).

SAUL (Heb. *šāʼûl*)

A Benjaminite, the son of Kish from the town of Gibeah, who became the first king of Israel. His story begins with his anointing by the prophet Samuel in 1 Sam. 9 and ends with his death by his own hand in 2 Sam. 1.

The story of Saul as it now stands incorporates

traditions with varying viewpoints on Saul and on kingship itself. The Deuteronomistic historian, working at the time of the Babylonian Exile, sets Saul's accession to kingship in a framework that sees kingship as a sinful rejection of God (1 Sam. 8:1-22; 12:1-25). Saul himself is introduced in a folktale manner, as a young man who is searching for his father's lost asses, but instead encounters the prophet Samuel who anoints him as Israel's future king (1 Sam. 9:1–10:16). In general this tale is quite positive toward Saul. He receives God's spirit after the anointing, and his task is to be the deliverance of Israel from the oppressive power of the Philistines. This account and the two stories of Saul's rejection by Samuel are from circles concerned to emphasize the role of prophets in anointing kings and holding them accountable to God.

A second story detailing how Saul became king (1 Sam. 10:17-27) opens with Samuel's reminder to the people at Mizpah that kingship itself is a sinful request by the people, but the account goes on to speak of Saul as God's choice for king, designated through a ceremony of casting lots. Saul is found hiding in the baggage and is brought out to be acclaimed king by the people and to hear Samuel read a document on the duties of kingship.

In a final narrative describing Saul's accession (1 Sam. 11:1-15), Saul is described as a military deliverer in a style reminiscent of the judges in the book of Judges. Word arrives that the people of Jabesh-gilead are under siege by Nahash, the king of Ammon. Saul is seized by God's spirit and leads a force of Israelites to victory over the Ammonites. Following this triumph, the people make Saul king at Gilgal. An editorial hand has tried to harmonize by calling this ceremony a "renewal" of kingship (1 Sam. 11:14). Many believe Saul's role as an effective military commander, as reflected in this account, is the probable historical basis of Saul's kingship. In the beginning Saul was probably little more than a local chieftain, but his military successes in the crisis with the Philistines led toward the development of a monarchy in Israel. A significant victory over Philistine forces in the territory of Benjamin is attributed to Saul and his son Jonathan in 1 Sam. 14:1-46. A notice in 1 Sam. 14:47-48 attributes victories to Saul over Moab, Ammonites, Edom, kings of Zobah, Philistines, and Amalekites. Saul's life ends in the context of a lost battle with the Philistines.

The customary accession formula for kings in the Deuteronomistic history signals the beginning of Saul's reign in 1 Sam. 13:1, but Saul almost immediately runs into conflict with the prophet Samuel over issues of obedience to God's word. There are two stories of Samuel's rejection of Saul. Both emphasize the role of prophet as mediator of the divine will to kings, and both reflect the conflicts which arise between older and emerging offices of authority in Israel. In 1 Sam. 13:7-14 Saul proceeds with a sacrifice before battle that was to be conducted by Samuel. When Samuel discovers this, he pronounces a judgment that denies the possibility of dynasty to Saul's descendants. In 1 Sam. 15:1-35 Saul disobeys the command of the Lord through Samuel to exterminate an Amalekite enemy according to the practices of holy war. Saul brings back livestock for his own provisions and the Amalekite king as prisoner. This time Samuel's judgment against Saul for disobedience to the word of the Lord is a rejection of Saul himself as God's legitimate king on the throne of Israel. In both of these rejection stories there is an allusion to David as the future of Israel rather than Saul.

The accounts of Saul's reign after this rejection are part of a narrative detailing David's rise to power and kingship (1 Sam. 16–31). In these stories Saul appears primarily as a rejected king, increasingly driven by his own jealousy and anger toward David, who is portrayed as God's chosen king. Saul takes David into his own court, as a musician (1 Sam. 16:14-23) and as a warrior (17:1-58), but he is plagued by an "evil spirit from God" (16:14; 18:10) and consumed by jealousy of David's success (18:1-9). He gives his daughter Michal to David in marriage, but even this is a plot to kill David by asking the bride-price of a hundred Philistine foreskins (1 Sam. 18:20-29). Saul's son, Jonathan, and daughter, Michal, both love David (1 Sam. 18:1-3, 20) and aid him against their father when Saul determines to kill David (19:1-17; 20:1-42). Much of the energy of Saul's final days as king is spent in pursuit of David in the wilderness areas of Judah (1 Sam. 22–24, 26). Saul seems obsessed and driven in this period of his life. He turns on those who have supported him (1 Sam. 22:6-10) and even slaughters 85 priests at Nob for their supposed aid to David (vv. 11-23). After David twice spares Saul's life, Saul seems resigned to the eventual transfer of power to David and breaks off his pursuit of him (1 Sam. 24, 26).

In a pathos-filled scene, Saul calls up the ghost of Samuel on the eve of battle with a large Philistine army (1 Sam. 28). He seeks solace and a hopeful word, but even from the grave, the prophet Samuel condemns him and foretells Saul's death, along with his sons, on the following day. Saul watches from Mt. Gilboa on the next day and sees his army defeated and his sons go down in battle. In despair he falls upon his own sword (1 Sam. 31:1-13; 2 Sam. 1:1-10). Although David eloquently laments the death of Saul and Jonathan (2 Sam. 1:17-27), the way is now open for his assumption of the kingship in Israel.

Saul's kingdom probably never extended effective control beyond the territory of Benjamin and adjacent territory in the central highlands of Israel. He did establish a court in Gibeah and the beginnings of a royal bureaucracy and a standing army for Israel (1 Sam. 14:49-52). In this sense he did lay the foundations for a more fully developed monarchy under David. Without Saul's military successes and the existence of his fledgling kingdom, Israel's distinct identity might well have been swallowed up in the Philistine occupation of the land. Although portrayed as a failed king in later tradition, his kingship made David's successes possible.

BRUCE C. BIRCH

SAVE, SAVIOR
See Salvation, Save, Savior.

SCALE ARMOR
See Coat of Mail.

SCAPEGOAT
See Azazel.

SCARLET, CRIMSON
Dyes obtained from the shield louse *(Kermococcus vermilio),* which is found on the kermes oak. Harvesters collect the female insect and spray it with an acid solution to kill it. The insects are dried, then dissolved in water to produce a colorfast red dye. Lat. *kermes,* from which English carmine and crimson are derived, means "worm," as does Heb. *tôlā'*, "scarlet."

Scarlet was expensive to produce, since 70 thousand insects were needed to produce one pound of dye. It was less costly than purple, but still marked the wearer as a person of wealth or privilege (2 Sam. 1:24; Jer. 4:30; Rev. 18:16). Scarlet usually refers to the dyed thread or cloth, used to mark Tamar's firstborn child (Gen. 38:28-30) and Rahab's house (Josh. 2:18) or used in ritual cleansings (Lev. 14:4, 6; Num. 19:6). Artisans used scarlet threads, along with blue and purple, to make the hangings of the tabernacle (Exod 25:4; 26:1) and Aaron's vestments (28:5) and in the veil of Solomon's temple (2 Chr. 3:14).

Isa. 1:18 speaks of sin as being like scarlet and crimson; this metaphor refers to the colorfast nature of dyed fabric, which God alone can transform to white.

Bibliography. A. Brenner, *Colour Terms in the Old Testament.* JSOTSup 21 (Sheffield, 1982), 143-45; F. Brunello, *The Art of Dyeing in the History of Mankind* (Vincenza, 1973). Mary Petrina Boyd

SCEPTER
The baton or staff employed as a symbol of authority by kings and chiefs (from Homeric Gk. *skḗpteron;* cf. Isa. 14:5; Ezek. 19:11; Ps. 60:7[MT 9]; 110:2). Originally the term designated a stick or club used as a weapon (cf. Num. 21:18). The OT terminology includes Heb. *maṭṭeh, šēḇeṭ, mĕḥōqēq,* and *šarbîṭ).*

King Ahasuerus' holding out the golden scepter to welcome *persona grata* (Esth. 4:11; 5:2; 8:4) is a form of the gesture of extending the hand in welcome frequently depicted in Mesopotamian art. The scepter as a symbol for royal authority in the OT, ancient Near East, and Hellenic world derives from the use of a stick or club much as the modern police officer's nightstick to punish enemies (Ps. 110:2; Ezek. 19:14). In Amos 1:5, 8 and in Mesopotamian royal inscriptions the king is referred to as "the one who holds the scepter"; by metonymy the OT refers to kings and kingship as "the scepter" (Gen. 49:10; Num. 24:17; Jer. 48:17; Zech. 10:11).

In some Greek manuscripts of Heb. 1:8 Gk. *skḗpteron* translates Heb. *šēḇeṭ* in the quotation from Ps. 45:6(LXX 44:7), but many Greek versions read *rhábdos,* the term used throughout the LXX. Heb. 1:8 transforms the twin emblems of temporal kingship — throne and scepter — into symbols of divine sovereignty. Mayer I. Gruber

SCEVA (Gk. *Skeuás*)
A Jewish chief priest (Gk. *archiereús*) whose seven sons attempt to exorcise demons in Ephesus through the name of "Jesus whom Paul proclaims" (Acts 19:14). They meet with disastrous results, as an evil spirit ridicules their misappropriation of Paul's authority and violently assaults them (Acts 19:11-16).

Nothing is known outside of Acts concerning a Jewish high priest with the Latin name of Sceva *(Scaeva).* Historically, this suggests that Sceva either had some broader priestly connection (the Western text calls him "a certain priest") or, more likely, that he masqueraded as the high priest to boost his reputation as a powerful broker of holy names.

Within the Acts narrative, the superiority of Paul's miraculous ministry over the pretentious schemes of Jewish exorcists and other practitioners of magic (Acts 19:17-20) recalls Paul's earlier defeat of the diabolical Jewish *mágos* and false prophet Bar-Jesus (13:6-12). Also, humiliating a putative high priest and his sons in Ephesus fits a pattern of exposing the futile opposition of the high priest family in Jerusalem to the expanding Christian mission (Acts 4:1-22; 5:17-42; 22:30–23:11).

Bibliography. S. R. Garrett, *The Demise of the Devil: Magic and the Demonic in Luke's Writings* (Minneapolis, 1989), ch. 5. F. Scott Spencer

SCORPION (Heb. *'aqrāḇ;* Gk. *skorpíos*).
An *Arachnid* (a class which includes spiders) of the order Scorpiones. Scorpions are nocturnal, inhabiting warm, dry climates, and are prone to enter houses and seek asylum in clothing, beds, cracks, and crevices.

Approximately 12 varieties of scorpions inhabit Israel. The largest and most dangerous is the rock scorpion which is 127-177 mm. (5-7 in.) long. The most common scorpions in Israel are the yellow scorpion *(Buthus questriatus)* and the black scorpion *(Buthus judaicus).*

The scorpion has a poison sting at the tip of its tail used to paralyze its prey. Scorpions do not intentionally attack humans, but they will sting a human out of self-defense.

In the OT scorpions (Heb. *'aqrāḇ*) are associated with the dangers of the wilderness (Deut. 8:15). Rehoboam refers to scorpions analogously in reference to his proposed harsh, stinging rule over the people (1 Kgs. 12:11, 14 = 2 Chr. 10:11, 14). Ezekiel's call by God includes an analogy of the sting of the scorpion to the rebellious nature of the people (Ezek. 2:6).

Jesus speaks of scorpions (Gk. *skorpíos*) as dangerous (Luke 10:19) and undesirable (11:12). In Revelation an analogy is made to the sting of scorpions as an indication of torture and harm (Rev. 9:3, 5, 10). Alan Ray Buescher

SCOURGING

Beating with a rod or staff (Heb. *šēḇeṭ*) was a punishment for children (Prov. 13:24), fools, or slaves (Exod. 21:20). More severe was the scourging with a leather whip *(šôṭ)*, a punishment comparable to a scorpion's sting (1 Kgs. 12:11). The prophets described the punishment that God administers to a disobedient people as a national scourging (Isa. 10:26).

Judicial punishment in the Mosaic code limited the number of strokes applied to the victim to 40 (Deut. 25:1-3). Jewish practice subtracted one stroke to keep from exceeding 40, and "40 minus one" became a standard reference to a Jewish beating (2 Cor. 11:24). The Mishnah describes a scourging, which included a determination of how many stripes the victim could endure, binding the hands to either side of a pillar, baring the chest and back, and lashing the victim so that one third of the stripes fell on the front and two thirds on the back (*m. Mak.* 3:10-14).

Roman scourging ignored the limits of the Mosaic law and varied the severity according to the status of the victim. A freeman, like Paul, could be beaten with rods (Gk. *hrábdos*) of elm or birch by Roman lictors (Acts 16:22; 2 Cor. 11:25). Slaves or non-Romans could be scourged with straps *(mástix)* or whips of leather cords knotted at the ends and weighted with pieces of metal or bone (*phragéllion;* Matt. 27:26; John 2:15).

Bibliography. B. Rapske, *Paul in Roman Custody,* vol. 3 of *The Book of Acts in Its First Century Setting,* ed. B. K. Winter (Grand Rapids, 1994).

DENNIS GAERTNER

SCRIBES

Persons who can read and write. Their education made them indispensable in many civilizations, as they were needed to keep all military, government, legal, and financial records. Such secular roles for scribes are found in the earliest biblical references to them (e.g., Judg. 5:14; 2 Sam. 8:17; 1 Kgs. 4:3; 2 Kgs. 12:10; 18:18; 22:3, 12; Jer. 36:10). Jeremiah's secretary Baruch is a scribe, assisting with business transactions (Jer. 32:12) as well as taking dictation (36:18, 32).

Although scribes continue to perform such roles in the postexilic period (cf. Neh. 13:13, where a scribe named Zadok is appointed as a treasurer over the storehouses where tithes are kept), the term begins to be more specifically associated with the transmission and interpretation of Torah. The scribes were Torah scholars who preserved and interpreted the Law in order to maintain its centrality in Judaism after the Exile and in the Diaspora. Ezra is an epitome of this kind of scribe (Ezra 7:6, 10).

Ben Sira (ca. 180 B.C.E.) describes the scribe as one whose study of God's revelation translates into great power in the government and courts (Sir. 38:24–39:11). The scribe's learning extends to all Israelite (and even non-Israelite) traditions: he "devotes himself to the study of the law of the Most High. He seeks out the wisdom of all the ancients, and is concerned with prophecies; he preserves the sayings of the famous and penetrates the subtleties of parables" (Sir. 38:34–39:2). Only the scribe has "eminence in the public assembly"; he is the one who can "sit in the judge's seat" and can "expound discipline or judgment" (Sir. 38:33). The scribe "serves among the great and appears before rulers; he travels in foreign lands and learns what is good and evil in the human lot. . . . The Lord will direct his counsel and knowledge, as he meditates on his mysteries" (Sir. 39:4, 7).

Such a description of scribes as both pious and influential is found in 1 and 2 Maccabees (late 2nd century B.C.E.). In 1 Macc. 7:12 a group of scribes negotiates with the Syrians, indicating they were in a position of some authority and power. Later a scribe, Eleazar, is held up as a model of piety for the rest of the community (2 Macc. 6:18-20).

Scribes are again presented as influential interpreters of Torah in the NT, though with a decidedly negative portrayal of them. They are usually presented together with other Jewish groups, especially Pharisees (e.g., Matt. 5:20; 23:2). As interpreters of the Torah, the scribes probably would have been most often associated with the Pharisees, who sought to broaden the applicability of the Torah. On a very few occasions scribes are shown as responding positively to Jesus (Matt. 8:19; 13:52; Mark 12:32), but they are most frequently portrayed as his enemies (Mark 8:31; 10:33; 11:18; 14:1, 43, 53; 15:1). Not surprisingly, their conflicts with Jesus often have to do with how the law of Moses should be observed (Mark 2:15-17; 7:1-8; Luke 6:6-11).

Matthew's depiction of the scribes is at once the most negative and the most positive in the NT. On the one hand, probably due to the opposition his own community was experiencing from Jewish officials, Matthew views the Jewish scribes as corrupt and false, having Jesus attack them with the refrain, "Woe to you, scribes and Pharisees, hypocrites!" (Matt. 23). But while he may view the current interpreters of the law as misguided (Matt. 23:16), Matthew still accepts their legitimacy and authority (vv. 2-3). Also, Matthew does not believe that Jesus has come to abolish the old laws and institutions, but rather to fulfill and complete them, giving them their proper authority and place (Matt. 5:17). Matthew therefore believes that there will still be scribes in the new Christian community, and they will continue their function of making the past traditions relevant and alive to believers, preserving them as precious treasures (Matt. 13:52; cf. 23:34).

KIM PAFFENROTH

SCROLL

A roll used by ancient scribes for writing significant literary works or important and detailed letters. Scrolls (Heb. *mĕgillâ;* Gk. *biblíon*) were made by gluing together, side by side, separate strips of papyrus, leather, parchment, or vellum and then winding the long strip around a pole, which would often have handles at both ends to facilitate transporting and reading the scroll. Papyrus, or specifically the pith of the papyrus reed, had been used as a writing surface since the early 3rd millennium B.C.E. It was probably a papyrus scroll, written by Baruch while Jeremiah dictated, that King Jehoiakim ordered burned (Jer. 36). The leather of tanned animal skins was also employed, but rarely used because papyrus existed in abundance. The OT makes no specific reference to leather scrolls, though some were found at Qumran. Parchment, which gradually replaced papyrus, was made by removing the hair and rubbing very smooth the skins of sheep, calves, or goats. The major advantage of parchment was that it could be used more than once by simply erasing the text (cf. Num. 5:23). A reused scroll is called a palimpsest (lit., "rescraped"). Vellum was simply a finer grade of parchment made from kids and calves that became popular for more important texts.

Scrolls was seldom longer than 9 m. (30 ft.); the Isaiah scroll from Qumran included 17 sheets of sheepskin joined by linen thread and measured 7.3 m. (24 ft.). The English word "volume" is derived from Lat. *volumen,* "a roll or scroll of writing." The restrictions on length saw the scroll eventually replaced by the codex since it could include several books in a single volume.

Scrolls figure in the visionary experiences of Ezekiel (Ezek. 2:8–3:3), Zechariah (Zech. 5:1-4), and Revelation (Rev. 5:1-14; 10:1-11).

TONY S. L. MICHAEL

SCYTHIANS

A collection of nomadic tribes associated with the area of the Ukraine and renowned in antiquity for their cruelty and barbarism. First identified in Assyrian annals of the 7th century B.C.E., Scythians (Akk. *Ašguzai*) descended from the north and, according to Herodotus (*Hist.* 1), dominated the Near East for 28 years until eventually driven back across the Caucasus by the Medes. They participated in the Persian defeat of Babylon in 538 (Jer. 51:27). Associated with Ashkenaz, the grandson of Japheth (Gen. 10:3; 1 Chr. 1:6), their chief biblical significance lies in their reputation for savagery.

Some biblical scholars reject the traditional association of the Babylonians with Jeremiah's enemies "from the north" (Jer. 1:14; 4:29; 5:15-17; 6:22-26; 50:41-42) and see in the Scythians a more consistent picture of the mounted archers described. It may be that this or subsequent raids on Palestine and possible Scythian settlement account for Beth-shan being renamed Scythopolis. Modern interest in the Scythians has been fueled by Herodotus' mention of their ceremonial and recreational use of hemp. While historical reference to the Scythians dies out in the early centuries C.E., some scholars see surviving elements of their culture in the Ossetian people of Caucasian Russia and the Georgian Republic.

In Col. 3:11 the Scythians are mentioned as an extreme example of barbarian peoples and an indication of the potential for renewal and the unifying power of the gospel of Christ. JESSE CURTIS POPE

SCYTHOPOLIS (Gk. *Skythópolis*)

A Decapolis city (Pliny *Nat. hist.* 5.74). Nysa Scythopolis, containing Hellenistic, Roman, Byzantine, and early Arab archaeological materials, is located at the foot of the tell of Beth-shean (Tell el-Ḥuṣn, 1977.2124). A wall surrounded the city in the Byzantine period, and a necropolis surrounded parts of the city.

Excavations have revealed that the general plan of the city was established in the 2nd century A.D., with main streets extending at northeast-southwest and southeast-northwest angles due to the limitations of the terrain. Along the streets numbers of public buildings had been erected. A Roman theater, elaborately decorated with marble and granite (late 2nd-3rd centuries; there is evidence also of a 1st-century theater there), was built to the south of the NE-SW street; its *scaenae frons,* decorated with marble and granite, had a facade of two or three stories, and was adorned with columns, capitals, and entablature. Flanked by a colonnaded, covered sidewalk and a row of about 20 shops, the colonnaded NE-SW street (Palladius Street, from a dedicatory inscription), which was paved with rectangular basalt blocks, ran from the theater some 180 m. (590 ft.) to the foot of the Beth-shean tell. Along the west side of this NE-SW street have been excavated remains of a propylaeum which led to the large T-shaped bathhouse complex; and next to it an *odeon* (or *bouleuterion*), with orchestra paved with flagstones.

In the civic center near the crossroads was a temple (possibly for Dionysus or Tyche) facing northwest, with monumental stairs extending up to a four-columned prostyle which led to the temple itself; in the plaza in front of the temple was a circular pedestal for a statue (the pedestal's Greek inscription states that the citizens of this Coele-Syria city dedicated it to Marcus Aurelius). Just to the east on this SE-NW street (the Valley Street) are ruins of a nymphaeum/fountain, including a 4th-century Greek inscription on the architrave; other architectural ornamentation there points to an earlier late 2nd-century Roman phase. Just east of the nymphaeum is a 4 m. (13 ft.)-high stone platform for a columnar monument, and south of it is a 2nd-century basilica building with an apse and four rows of columns and corner pillars to sustain the ceiling. Farther to the southeast and just to the south of the SE-NW street, a colonnaded stoa (2nd century) was built, ca. 56 m. (185 ft.) long, with 18 monolithic, limestone columns and Ionic capitals, over which a series of shops was later built in the Late Byzantine period. Another broad colonnaded street (the eastern street) with covered sidewalks (total, 23 m. [75 ft.] wide), and with shops bordering the street, extended from the Roman bridge crossing the Harod River and ran southwest toward an open square in front of the columnar monument on the SE-NW street; and an additional street, from as far as the amphitheater on the south, came to join the SE-NW street, east of the open square. To the west of the city center a villa and a synagogue ("House of Leontius") were excavated, the latter featuring a mosaic floor depicting a vine-trellis and a menorah.

Just south of the theater are remains of a large,

rectangular amphitheater (possible 2nd century) which was used for gladiatorial games.

See Beth-shan, Beth-shean.

Bibliography. G. Foerster, "Beth-Shean at the Foot of the Mound," *NEAEHL* 1:223-35; "Glorious Beth-Shean," *BARev* 16/4 (1990): 16-31.

W. Harold Mare

SEA, MOLTEN

An enormous bronze basin constructed by Hiram of Tyre that was placed in the courtyard of Solomon's temple in Jerusalem (1 Kgs. 7:23-26; 2 Chr. 4:2-5; cf. 2 Kgs. 25:13; 1 Chr. 18:8, "bronze sea"). "Molten" refers to the bronze casting technique employed in the sea's construction. The basin was ca. 2.3 m. (7.5 ft.; 5 cubits) deep and ca. 4.6 m. (15 ft.; 10 cubits) from rim to rim. It had a tremendous capacity, holding at least 41,640 l. (11,000 gal.; cf. 1 Kgs. 7:26; 2 Chr. 4:5).

The only specific reference to the sea's purpose is that it was for the priests to wash in (2 Chr. 4:6). Two factors, however, suggest that this was a specialized and limited purpose of the sea which the Chronicler chose to highlight: the courtyard also contained 10 basins designed for ritual washings that would have been, because of the height of the sea, more feasible for regular use; and the elaborate nature of the sea's construction suggests its symbolic value. Resting as it did upon 12 oxen in four groups of three facing toward the four points of the compass, its elaborately paneled bowl (1 Kgs. 7:24-26) would have made a powerful impression upon the public by displaying in a formidable fashion the sovereignty and might of Israel's God who ruled even the sea (cf. Ps. 93:1-4).

Kevin D. Hall

SEA GULL

An unclean bird (Lev. 11:16; Deut. 14:15) of uncertain identity (Heb. *šaḥap̱*). Gulls (family Laridae) are aquatic birds with webbed feet and wings long in proportion to their bodies. They feed on fish, insects, and other small animals. Several varieties of gulls are found on the Palestinian coast and the Sea of Galilee.

SEAH (Heb. *sᵉʾâ;* Gk. *sáton*)

A unit of dry capacity, the equivalent of 2 hins or 7.3 l. (2 gal.) (Gen. 16:6; Matt. 13:33; NRSV "measure").

SEAL, SIGNET

A device engraved with a reverse design for making an impression. Seal use in the ancient Near East preceded the development of writing, probably appearing during the second half of the 4th millennium. Early seal impressions likely denoted the ownership of goods and materials or acted as a magical safeguard over the item. Stamp seals, often a conical stone with a carved base, are the earliest known forms of seals and were popular in Egypt and Palestine. While most seals were cut upon stone, other media included wood, bone, and ivory. Greek and Roman period seals were often delicately carved on semi-precious stones.

Seals authenticated copies of laws, treaties, public contractual agreements, the sale and purchase of government holdings, and certified the quality or quantity of a container's contents. Seals commemorated important political events such as marriage, treaties, and public celebrations. Private seal impressions witnessed sales, purchases, contractual agreements, letters, wills, and adoptions. Believed by their owners to possess magical properties, seals also were utilized in religious ceremonies. Personal seals often were worn as amulets or left as votive gifts in the temples of various deities. Seals accompanying burials may have been given by relatives as gifts for use by the deceased in the afterlife, or as prayers to help speed the deceased on his passage through the underworld.

The Bible describes the use of seals in both bu-

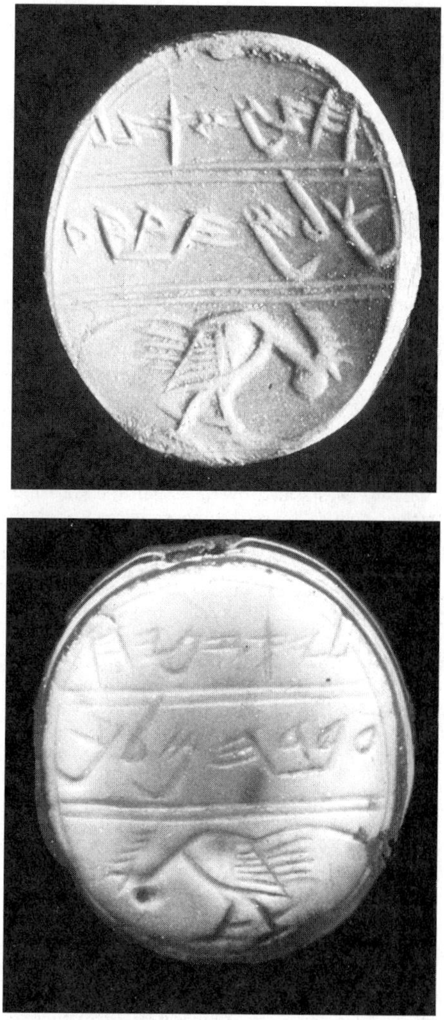

Jaazaniah seal from Tell en-Naṣbeh and impression (Badè Institute of Biblical Archaeology, Pacific School of Religion)

reaucratic and nonbureaucratic terms. A seal might be given as a pledge (Gen. 38:18) or worn as a ring to symbolize political authority (41:42). Letters bearing the seal of a king were considered as binding as his verbal command (1 Kgs. 21:8). Love is metaphorically compared to the inviolable nature of a seal (Cant. 8:6). Isaiah prayed to Yahweh, calling upon God to "seal the law" among the faithful disciples, closing it from the sight of the unworthy (Isa. 8:16; 29:11). Jeremiah placed his seal upon a deed as evidence of his purchase of a field in Anathoth (Jer. 32:10-14, 44). A seal impressed upon a container verified that the vessel contained an appropriately full measure (Ezek. 28:12). After Daniel was cast into the lions' den, the entrance was sealed with the signet of the king and his advisors to evidence the royal decree of death (Dan. 6:17). A seal impressed to prevent the reading of a document also is attested to during the Exile (Dan. 12:4, 9). A public proclamation of fealty to Yahweh and the cultic law was sealed by Nehemiah the governor, various political representatives, and the leaders of the levitical priesthood on behalf of the people (Neh. 9:38–10:27[MT 10:1-28]). The Revelation of John mentions several scrolls that were sealed both to attest to their authority and to hide their contents from outsiders.

Bibliography. *The Iron Age Stamp Seals* (c. 1200-350 B.C.) (Oxford, 1988), xii; D. Collon, *First Impressions: Cylinder Seals in the Ancient Near East* (Chicago, 1988), 6-13; L. Gorelick, "Ancient Seals and the Bible: An Overview," in *Ancient Seals and the Bible*, ed. Gorelick and E. Williams-Forte. Occasional Papers on the Ancient Near East 2/1 (Malibu, 1983).

DAVID C. MALTSBERGER

SEA MONSTER

A large sea creature, real or mythological (also "dragon"/"serpent"). Significant are passages where Heb. *tannîn* is parallel or paired with terms like "Leviathan" (*lwytn;* cf. the Canaanite god Lotan; Ps. 74:13; Isa. 27:1) and/or where the context is "the sea/deep." Such texts are comparative correctives to Canaanite beliefs about the terrifying, divine power and danger of the Sea (cf. Gen. 1:21; Ps. 148:7) and creation concepts about creatures of chaos within OT polemics for the uniqueness of Yahweh, who created, controls, and has and will conquer them (Job 7:12; Isa. 51:9; Ezek. 29:3; 32:2).

Bibliography. W. F. Albright, *Yahweh and the Gods of Canaan* (1968, repr. Winona Lake, 1978); J. Day, *God's Conflict with the Dragon and the Sea.* University of Cambridge Oriental Publications 35 (Cambridge, 1985).

W. CREIGHTON MARLOWE

SEA PEOPLES

A designation used by the Egyptians to describe attackers ("Foreigners from the sea") who invaded Egypt during the reigns of Merneptah (19th Dynasty) and Rameses III (20th Dynasty). The term encompasses more than 20 groups of people, named by their place of origin. Of the names which can be identified, two can be traced to North Africa, but most are related to the Aegean Sea area, particularly western Asia Minor (Turkey), or to Lycia (southwestern Asia Minor) or Cilicia (southeastern Asia Minor), and the islands of Cyprus and Crete. Several of these groups are known from earlier Egyptian records.

Four invasions of Egypt are recorded, but two, one in the 5th year of Merneptah and the other in the 8th year of Rameses III (ca. 1174 B.C.E.), were the most significant and related to severe crises that occurred in the eastern Mediterranean basin. Merneptah comments that the people came with their families, women and children, and that he killed 6000 and captured 9000. Some of the captives were used as mercenary troops. Rameses III's encounter with the Sea People, depicted in a relief on the wall of the funerary temple of Medinet Habu, shows the Sea People wearing kilts and adorned with either feathered headdress or horned helmets. The bows of their boats featured a bird's head. Carts bearing women and children follow the ships by land. In both cases, the Sea People were not just engaging in a foray into Egypt, but were looking for a place to settle.

It is during the attack on Egypt in the 8th year of Rameses III that we hear of the Peleset, or Philistines, whom Rameses allowed to settle in Palestine on the Philistine Plain from Raphia in the south to Joppa. A second group, Tjikkar, settled around the city of Dor.

Bibliography. W. F. Albright, "Syria, the Philistines, and Phoenicia," *CAH*[3] (1975) 2/2: 507-16; R. D. Barnett, "The Sea People," *CAH*[3] (1975) 2/2: 359-78; M. Dothan, "Archaeological Evidence for Movements of Early 'Sea People' in Canaan," *AASOR* 49 (1989): 59-70; N. K. Sandars, *The Sea Peoples: Warriors of the Ancient Mediterranean, 1250-1150 B.C.*, rev. ed. (London, 1985).

LAWRENCE A. SINCLAIR

SEAT, SEATING

Chairs date from ancient times throughout the Near Eastern world, consisting of seat, legs, and sometimes backrest and arms. For centuries they were used only by the affluent or powerful. Biblical terminology (Heb. *môšāḇ, šeḇeṯ, kissēʾ;* Gk. *kathédra, prōtokathedría, prōtoklisía*) often makes it difficult to distinguish seat, chair, stool, and sometimes throne.

Most biblical references to seating pertain to honor and authority, with the seat synonymous with the office of the person (but cf. Ps. 1:1; Prov. 9:14). To be seated on a throne, such as Solomon's ornate gold and ivory throne (1 Kgs. 10:18-20; Heb. *kissēʾ*), was synonymous with possessing royal authority (16:11; 2 Kgs. 11:19; Acts 12:21-22). Gk. *thrónos,* "throne," is used metonymically for royal power (Luke 1:52). The imagery of a king seated in regnal authority looking down on his subjects depicts God's majesty and sovereignty over nature and all of creation (Ps. 113:5-6; cf. Ezek. 1:26). Sennacherib's list of tribute received from Hezekiah of Judah (ca. 701 B.C.) mentions both couches and chairs (*ANET,* 288). The seat of Solomon's carriage, like the carriage itself, was one of ornate splendor (Cant. 3:9-10).

Those seated in the royal courts were carefully placed with attention to relative power and honor as well as dishonor (1 Sam. 2:8; 1 Kgs. 10:5; Ps. 113:8; cf. 1 Kgs. 2:19; Esth. 3:1; also Jer. 13:18).

Rulers and judges heard cases and pronounced sentences seated in a public place (2 Chr. 19:8; Ps. 122:5; Matt. 27:19; John 19:13; Acts 25:6), often near a gate (2 Sam. 19:8; cf. Jer. 26:10). Imagery of a seated judge often depicts eschatological judgment (Dan. 7:9; Rom. 14:10; Rev. 20:4, 11).

Seating was important in the synagogues as well. The "best seats" (Mark 12:39 par.) were reserved for the elders, who sat at the front with backs to the ark, facing the congregation. Jesus mentions "Moses' Seat" (Matt. 23:2), both a figurative office of interpreting the law and a literal stone chair in the front of many synagogues, allotted to an elder, presumably a scholar of distinction. The 3rd-century A.D. synagogue excavated at Capernaum has two stone benches along each of two sides.

The cathedra (Gk. *kathédra*), originally a portable chair used by Roman and Greek women, gave its name to a type of chair from which philosophers lectured. In the early Church the term was applied to a chair in which the bishop sat, hence the name "cathedral."

Ordinary seats play significant roles in Scripture, including Eli's seat at the door of the Shiloh sanctuary (1 Sam. 1:9) and by the roadside or the gate (4:13, 18), Elisha's seat in his roof chamber (2 Kgs. 4:10), Job's seat in the town market or square, and the places the sellers took in the temple (Mark 11:15 par.). T. J. JENNEY

SEBA (Heb. *sĕḇā'*)
A son of Cush (i.e., Ethiopia); eponymous ancestor of a land in Africa or south Arabia (Gen. 10:7; 1 Chr. 1:9; Ps. 72:10; Isa. 43:3). Seba may have been the home of the Sabeans (Isa. 45:14) or perhaps a colony of Arabian Sheba (**2**).

SEBAM (Heb. *śĕḇām*)
Alternate form of Sibmah, a city in Moab claimed by Reuben after the defeat of Sihon (Num. 32:3).

SECACAH (Heb. *sĕḵāḵâ*)
A town in the Judean wilderness (Josh. 15:61) allotted to the tribe of Judah. Although controversy surrounds the exact geography of this district, which includes En-gedi, the archaeological discovery of three Iron Age settlements in the Buqei'ah Valley presents the possibility of a more precise identification for Secacah.

Bibliography. L. E. Stager, "Farming in the Judean Desert during the Iron Age," *BASOR* 221 (1976): 145-58. RYAN BYRNE

SECOND COMING
Pre-Christian Jewish tradition uses the metaphor of God's "coming" for special moments God has chosen to judge humanity, or events which reveal God's powerful presence and plan for Israel as God's covenant people. A vivid sense of God's active presence emerges in graphic images such as "the day," "the time," or "the year" of the Lord, the ark of the covenant, the meeting tent, the holy place, the cloud, the Spirit, the Hand, or the Word of God. The memory of Israel enduring covenant relations with God from the time of Abraham stirred abiding trust in God's protective intervention. The major refinements of this covenant conviction under Moses and David themselves arose in the face of grave impending moral and political crisis for Israel. The same is true for many crucial moments in Israel's history, as its prophetic tradition shows. Visions about future reassertion of covenant rights recur in the classic oracles of Isaiah, Jeremiah, Ezekiel, exilic and postexilic Isaiah, and Zechariah.

Despite dramatic rescue from past threats, their stubborn recurrence challenged Israel's confidence, spurring hope for a full and final intervention by God. Emerging Jewish hope for God's "second" coming represents a potent metaphor for long-awaited, definitive divine confirmation of the covenant. God's accumulated acts in Israel's history dictated there could be only one "second" coming, whose dimensions grew in proportion to the success and failure of past "comings." Eventually God's latter coming merges with the end of all present time and history, marking the boundary between this world and all that lies beyond. Such tension drives the apocalyptic imagery that colors the oracles of Daniel, the Qumran community, John the Baptizer, and Jesus of Nazareth. Although various scenarios of how this would occur abounded in late Jewish and early Christian writing, some shared features shine through, i.e., a chain of woes climaxed by assertion of messianic authority, the raising of the dead, and divine judgment on humanity, marking the start of a new age.

This tension between past and future deliverance recurs in the oldest levels of the Jesus tradition, which both presume and proclaim an imminent, final change in Israel's fate. The awaited shift fuels a deep ambivalence in the teaching of Jesus, reflected in views of John the Baptizer as unsurpassed, and yet a prelude of much more to come (Matt. 11:9-15; Luke 7:26-28; 16:16; cf. Gos. Thom. 46). The main streams of earliest Christian apostolic written tradition variously portray Jesus' own mission as prefacing still greater events at hand. Jesus' teaching clearly evoked differing messianic expectations, positive and negative, from his audiences. From early on, his disciples suffer public scrutiny for the unusual behavior evoked by their trust in him as God's final messianic agent. Early Christians thus invested the tension between God's former and latter coming in Jesus himself, whose life becomes a basic Christian key for interpreting Israel's past and future history. In adapting older Jewish notions and scenarios for God's second coming, early Christianity generated a distinctive eschatology which concretizes Jewish apocalyptic symbols while apotheosizing the specifics of Jesus' own person and story.

The trend toward logocentric, timeless, vertical Christology that flourished as 2nd-century Christianity diverged from rabbinic Judaism gradually eclipsed older Christian views about Jesus' second coming. Such belief gradually shifted to a more in-

…ical, spiritual key. But the vigor … tanism shows that vivid hope to… tangible, majestic return remain… …any Christian circles. Intermittent, pow…ful resurgence of such hope betrays enduring Christian ambivalence on this matter. Amid changing Christian fortunes from Constantine to Charlemagne to the Crusades, from Joachim of Fiore through the late Middle Ages to the Reformation and beyond, the awesome prospect of Jesus' impending return has remained a flame easily fanned by threat of famine, plague, war, moral scandal, or foreign invasion.

Modern idealism, secularism, and rationalism have pushed such hope in a second coming to the margin of acceptable public discourse and visibility. Academically, the scientific view of time as a linear, uniform train of discrete moments has burdened our rediscovery of Christian eschatology in this century with undue stress on the temporal side of Jesus' return. Recent biblical study, however, has begun recasting such discussion in more spatial, interpersonal, and rhetorical terms. Popularly speaking, apparitions, oracular disclosures, and urgent calls for moral reform, driven by deeply rooted Christian belief in Jesus' eventual return, still persist. The vitality of dipensationalist, revivalist, and adventist Christian movements in our own time reflects an enduring Christian need for closure concerning God's moral claim on humanity as invested in Jesus' second coming.

Bibliography. J. D. G. Dunn, "He Will Come Again," *Int* 51 (1997): 42-56; L. J. Kreitzer, "Eschatology," in *Dictionary of Paul and His Letters,* ed. G. F. Hawthorne, R. P. Martin, and D. G. Reid (Downers Grove, 1993), 253-69; D. C. Allison, Jr., "Apocalyptic," in *Dictionary of Jesus and the Gospels* (Downers Grove, 1992), 17-20; "Eschatology," in *Dictionary of Jesus and the Gospels,* 206-9.

F. CONNOLLY-WEINERT

SECOND MAN

A term Paul applies to Christ in view of his being the first to be resurrected and, therefore, a second beginning (after Adam, "the first man") of the human race (1 Cor. 15:47; Gk. *ho deúteros ánthrōpos*).

SECOND QUARTER

A section of Jerusalem (Heb. *hammišneh,* "the second") that developed in the 8th-7th centuries B.C.E., W of the City of David across the Tyropoeon Valley in the southern part of what is now called the Upper City (2 Kgs. 22:14 = 2 Chr. 34:22; Zeph. 1:10).

SECOND TEMPLE

See JEWS; JUDAISM.

SECRET

See MYSTERY.

SECRETARY

A person skilled in the art of writing (Heb. *sōp̄ēr;* Gk. *grammateús*). Such a person could serve in various capacities in the ancient world, including a royal court record keeper who drafted official correspondence and decrees (2 Kgs. 12:10), military secretary (25:19), or the personal scribe of a prophet (Jer. 36:4). As one who was literate and familiar with royal communications, a secretary naturally might provide wise counsel (1 Chr. 27:32).

In the NT the term appears only in the related sense of an important civic official (Acts 19:35). However, Paul regularly employed a secretary (amanuensis) in writing letters, a practice common in antiquity (cf. Cicero *Ep. ad Fam.* 5.20.1; Plutarch *Vit. Caes.* 17.3; Pliny *Ep.* 9.36). The only secretary known by name is Tertius, secretary of Paul's letter to Rome (Rom. 16:22). Elsewhere Paul tells the reader specifically at what point he is adding his conclusion in his own hand (Gal. 6:11; Phlm. 19; cf. Col. 4:18; 2 Thess. 3:17; 1 Pet. 5:12).

GERALD L. STEVENS

SECT

A subset of the whole (Gk. *haíresis;* LXX Lev. 22:18, 21; Neh. 12:40; 1 Macc. 8:30; also rabbinic literature, Josephus, Philo, and NT). The Sadducees are understood as a party, group, or society which functioned within the rubric of greater Judaism (Acts 5:17; 23:6-8; Josephus *BJ* 2.119, 164-66; *Ant.* 13.171-73, 297-98; 18.16-17; 20.199). The Boethusians are a group related to the Sadducees, although the connection is not entirely clear (cf. *'Abot R. Nat.* 5; *b. Pesaḥ.* 57a). Likewise, the Pharisees, the largest and most popular group within 1st-century Judaism, are also called a "sect" (Acts 15:5; 26:5; *BJ* 1.110-12; 2.119, 162-63, 166, 411; *Ant.* 13.171-79, 288-98, 401-2, 408-9; 18.12-15). The party of the Zealots (*BJ* 4.161; 5.3-8; 7.268-74; *Ant.* 18.1-9, 23) held beliefs similar to the Pharisees, but had also concluded that submission to any foreign power was tantamount to idolatry. Their goal was to implement the kingdom of God on earth by force of arms (cf. Matt. 11:12). The Sicarii were apparently a radical subset of the Zealots (*BJ* 2.254-57, 425-26; 4.400-405, 516; 7.253-63, 410-19, 437; *Ant.* 20.164-66, 185-88; Acts 21:38); their preferred method of accomplishing the Zealot ideal was assassination. The Essenes (*BJ* 2.119-61; *Ant.* 13.172; 15.373-79; 18.18-22; Philo *Quod omn.* 75-91; *Hypothetica* 11.1-18) were ascetics who had withdrawn from society to create a new eschatological society which would be pure and prepared for the messianic age. The Herodians (Matt. 22:16; Mark 3:6; 12:13) may have been Jews who favored a reunited Israel under a ruler from the Herodian dynasty.

A negative nuance of sects seems to have developed during NT times, becoming even more pronounced in the writings of post-NT Christian apologists. Christianity itself is described by others within Judaism as a "sect" with somewhat negative connotations (Acts 24:5, 14; 28:22; cf. *b. Ber.* 28b). Christians soon came to apply the term to groups within the Church who were following after personalities (1 Cor. 11:19; Gal. 5:20) or departing from the teachings of the apostles (2 Pet. 2:1, often "heresies").

W. E. NUNNALLY

SECU (Heb. *śek̲û*)
A site in the territory of Benjamin visited by Saul in his pursuit of David (1 Sam. 19:22). It has a well and is located near, or perhaps in, the city of Ramah. Some manuscripts (e.g., LXX B) read "on the bare hilltop," and thus some scholars have altered the MT to Heb. *špy,* "bare height." This suggests that Secu is a location and not a city or village.

JOHN R. SPENCER

SECUNDUS (Gk. *Sekoúndos*)
A Christian who, along with Aristarchus, represented the city of Thessalonica on Paul's last trip to Jerusalem (Acts 20:4). The two probably were responsible for administering in Thessalonica the collection for the church in Jerusalem (cf. 2 Cor. 8:3), and may have accompanied Paul on the trip both for accountability and protection. The name (from Lat. *Secundus,* "following" or "second") is common in the Greek papyri and is found among the list of politarchs on the triumphal arch in Thessalonica.

CHARLES A. RAY, JR.

SEDRACH, APOCALYPSE OF
Echoing the questions about divine mercy and justice found in other "Ezra" apocalypses (4 Ezra, Greek Apocalypse of Ezra, Questions of Ezra), this pseudepigraph begins with a sermon on God's love for humankind (including the sacrifice of his Son). Immediately following the sermon, Sedrach hears the voice of an angel and is transported into the presence of God in the third heaven, where he engages God in a discussion of divine punishment and the presence of evil in the world. God responds that humans are created with free will, and thus are responsible for evil. God then commands his "only begotten Son" to take Sedrach's soul to paradise, but Sedrach pleads for mercy on behalf of sinful humanity and presses God to forgive any person who repents for 20 days. As soon as God agrees to Sedrach's terms, Sedrach allows his soul to be taken.

This apocalypse is extant in a single 15th-century Greek manuscript, but its contents derive from a much earlier time. It is likely that the opening sermon dates to the Byzantine period, and equally likely that the ascent text dates to the first few centuries C.E. The coupled text is clearly Christian, but many elements of the ascent text bear strong resemblances to early Jewish apocalypses. There are no internal or external clues as to the provenance of the work. In addition to its preoccupation with divine justice, the work also presents readers with the legend of Satan's refusal to worship humans (cf. Life of Adam and Eve), and an idealized, positive view of the human body.

Bibliography. S. Agourides, "Apocalypse of Sedrach," *OTP* 1:605-13; R. J. H. Shutt, "The Apocalypse of Sedrach," in *The Apocryphal Old Testament,* ed. H. F. D. Sparks (Oxford, 1984), 953-66.

JAMES R. MUELLER

SEER
One who experiences and reports or interprets a dream or vision (e.g., 1 Sam. 9:9; Amos 7:12; 2 Chr. 9:29). Such figures (Heb. *rōʾeh, ḥōzeh*) are frequently associated with ecstatic states (cf. 2 Chr. 29:25, 30). Visionaries may have been associated with the royal court (e.g., 2 Sam. 24:11; 1 Chr. 25:5).

See PROPHET, PROPHECY.

SEGUB (Heb. *śeg̲ûb̲*)
1. A Judahite, son of Hezron and the daughter of Machir (1 Chr. 2:21-22).

2. The youngest son of Hiel of Bethel who (with his older brother Abiram) died, possibly as a human sacrifice, when Hiel refounded Jericho at the time of King Ahab (1 Kgs. 16:34). Segub's death fulfilled Joshua's curse upon the city (Josh. 6:26).

SEIR (Heb. *śēʿîr*) **(PERSON)**
The progenitor of the Horites, the original inhabitants of Mt. Seir (Gen. 36:20-21; 1 Chr. 1:38; cf. Gen. 14:6; Deut. 2:12, 22).

SEIR (Heb. *śēʿîr*) **(PLACE)**
1. A high hilly plateau within the region of Edom. Seir is identified with modern Jebel esh-Sharah, a mountain range between Wadi el-Ḥesā in the north and Râs en-Naqb in the south, and running between the Arabah on the west and the desert on the east. The edges of the mountain range are quite arid, rugged, and inhospitable, but until the early 20th century the high plateau was thickly forested. Seir, which means "hairy," undoubtedly referred to this forest. According to the biblical tradition, Seir was originally inhabited by Horites (Gen. 14:6; 36:20-30). The descendants of Esau, the Edomites, drove out the Horites and settled in Seir (Gen. 36:8). Although Edom refers to a much larger region than Seir, the two names are often used interchangeably in the Bible (cf. Judg. 5:4, where Seir and the land of Edom are in poetic parallelism). 1 Chr. 4:42-43 claims that 500 Simeonites invaded the hill country of Seir during the days of King Hezekiah, destroyed the remnant of the Amalekites there, and continued to dwell through the period of the Chronicler.

2. A mountain on the northern border of Judah (Josh. 15:10). Some identify the mountain with Sārîs, ca. 14.5 km. (9 mi.) W of Jerusalem. This is a forested region, as the name Seir suggests. The Seir of Judah could also be the northernmost point which the Israelites reached when they invaded the Canaanite hill country from the south against the command of God. According to the biblical text, the Amorites drove the Israelites back "from Seir as far as Hormah" (Deut. 1:44; cf. Num. 14:45). The identification of this Seir with the Seir of Edom is unlikely due to the number of geographical problems which it would pose for the story.

RONALD A. SIMKINS

SEIRAH (Heb. *śĕʿîrâ*)
The place to which Ehud escaped after killing King Eglon of Moab (Judg. 3:26). Perhaps a city or topographical feature, Seirah was probably in Ephraim (cf. Judg. 3:27).

SELA (Heb. *sela'*)
A place name ("rock") referring to several cities E of the Jordan River. It is most commonly associated with the Nabatean city Petra in the Wadi Mûsā, the name of which also means "rock."

1. A site designating a portion of the Amorite border (Judg. 1:36). Although mentioned near the ascent of 'Aqrabim ("scorpions"), Sela may not necessarily be sought in Judah, but perhaps along the same latitude. The LXX reading "Edomites" may acknowledge the common border of Edom and Ammon. If so, it is possible to interpret this occurrence of Sela as a reference to an Edomite city, rather than Judahite or Amorite.

2. A fortified Edomite settlement conquered by King Amaziah of Judah and renamed Joktheel (2 Kgs. 14:7). It is traditionally identified with Umm el-Bayyârah, overlooking the Nabatean city of Petra, ca. 75 km. (46.5 mi.) S of the Dead Sea in Jordan. Failure to locate Edomite occupation earlier than the 7th century B.C.E. at Umm el-Bayyârah (192971) has prompted some to seek the site at modern es-Sela' (205020), which is slightly N of Buṣeira. The material culture unearthed at this location reflects 9th-7th century occupation and better satisfies the Bible's chronological account.

3. A place mentioned in a woe-oracle against Moab (Isa. 16:1). The exact location of the site has yet to be determined. The description is minimal, so this Sela might be sought in either Moab or Edom.

4. A place named as one of a series of representative distant places (Isa. 42:11), perhaps the same as **2** above.

Bibliography. S. Hart, "Sela: The Rock of Edom?" *PEQ* 118 (1986): 91-95. RYAN BYRNE

SELAH (Heb. *selâ*)
Likely a musical or liturgical notation, occurring 71 times in 39 Psalms and 3 times in the psalm of Hab. 3. In the LXX Selah is rendered as Greek *diápsalma* ("pause in singing"), suggesting some type of caesura. According to the Targ., followed by Jerome, the term means "forever" or "everlasting." Perhaps this was a directive to insert a benediction, refrain, or prayer collect at that point. Proposals based on etymology include "voice modulation," "increase in volume," "prostration," and "prayer ritual." Others have suggested that the consonants of Selah form an acronym for "voice modulation" or "repetition."
GERALD M. BILKES

SELED (Heb. *seleḏ*)
The elder son of Nadab of the tribe of Judah (1 Chr. 2:30). Seled died childless.

SELEUCIA (Gk. *Seleúkia, Seleúkeia*)
The name of at least 10 cities, four of them in northern Syria, founded by Seleucus I Nicator in the 4th century B.C. and named after himself.

Seleucia Pieria on the northern coast of Syria was built on the southern slope of Mt. Pierius, ca. 8 km. (5 mi.) N of the mouth of the Orontes River. It functioned as a seaport for Antioch on the Orontes (modern Samandağ, Turkey), 26 km. (16 mi.) to the east. It gradually increased in importance as a commercial city and frontier fortress until the Roman period. However, all the land routes connecting Asia Minor to Syria and Mesopotamia ran through Antioch, and Seleucia eventually became largely an outlet for Antioch to the western part of the empire via the Mediterranean. The city changed hands several times, falling to Ptolemy III of Egypt during the Third Syrian War (246-241) and to the Seleucid Antiochus III in 219. After 146 Seleucia briefly marked the northern terminus of Ptolemy VII's dominion along the Mediterranean coast (1 Macc. 11:8), but in 138 it reverted to the Seleucids. It became a free city under Pompey (60 B.C.). When Paul and Barnabas set out to the west on their first missionary journey, they sailed along with John Mark from Seleucia to Cyprus (Acts 13:4).

Today the port has silted up, as have many ports on the Turkish coast, and has been replaced in importance by the port of İskenderun (or Alexandretta) several miles to the north.
JOHN MCRAY

SELEUCID EMPIRE
One of the largest empires formed from the division of territory conquered by Alexander the Great. The history of the Seleucid Empire is characterized by two main considerations: (1) it was enormously diverse and decentralized, which made it much harder to govern than the Ptolemaic Empire; (2) it began to decline from the very first, its greatest period being under its founder Seleucus I. Antiochus II's half brother Antiochus Hierax rebelled ca. 240 B.C.E. and set up an independent kingdom in Asia Minor. The eastern provinces began to fall away quite quickly. In the middle of the 2nd century a rival dynasty arose, and the ruling house essentially split into two warring factions. This allowed the Maccabees to set up an independent Jewish state, further weakening the Seleucid Empire. By the time the Romans ended the dynasty, the Seleucid Empire had been reduced to a small amount of territory in northern Syria.

In the wake of Alexander the Great's conquests from Greece to northern India, and then his death, his empire was fought over for about 40 years by his generals (the Diadochi, "successors"). The Asian part of Alexander's empire was essentially divided between the Seleucid Empire from Syria to Afghanistan and the Ptolemaic Empire which was mainly in Egypt.

Alexander originally made Babylon the capital of his empire, but with the founding of the Seleucid Empire the capital moved to Antioch. This was unfortunate in some ways because it was far to the west of the center of gravity, since Babylonia was an important part of the empire. The eastern section was harder to govern, and ca. 250 the Parthians founded their own empire which endured for another 500 years. This began the loss of the eastern provinces, eventually leaving the Selecuids in control mainly of Asia Minor and Syria, though periodically a Seleucid ruler would march east to try to take back some of the old territory.

During the struggle between the Diadochi, 301 B.C.E. was a crucial point when a treaty and division of territory were agreed on. At that time, the area of Palestine and southern Syria was assigned to Seleucus. However, Ptolemy seized it and refused to give it up. This became the occasion of a series of four "Syrian Wars" fought over the next century in which the Seleucids attempted to regain what they regarded as rightfully theirs. Finally, in 200 in the Fifth Syrian War Antiochus III retook this territory for the Seleucid Empire. Antiochus III's expansion of his empire was brought to a halt by the Romans, who similarly restrained Anitochus IV's ambitions with regard to Egypt. After this, the Seleucid Empire gradually declined as Roman power increased. Ca. 150 we find the beginning of rival dynasties, each claiming to be the rightful line of rulers. By 96 B.C.E. a multiplicity of individuals were claiming to sit on the Seleucid throne. The last ruler (Antiochus XIII) was a puppet king put on the throne by the Romans, but they removed him in 65 B.C.E., bringing the Seleucid Empire formally to an end.

Bibliography. *CAH*², esp. 7/1: *The Hellenistic World,* ed. F. Walbank et al. (Cambridge, 1984); 8: *Rome and the Mediterranean to 133 B.C.*, ed. A. E. Astin et al. (Cambridge, 1989); 9: *The Last Age of the Roman Republic, 146-43 B.C.*, ed. J. A. Crook, A. Lintott, and E. Rawson (Cambridge, 1994); P. Grimal, ed., *Hellenism and the Rise of Rome* (New York, 1968); Walbank, *The Hellenistic World,* rev. ed. (Cambridge, Mass., 1993). LESTER L. GRABBE

SELEUCUS (Gk. *Seleúkos*)

1. Seleucus I Nicator ([321]312-281 B.C.E.); one of the Diadochi ("Successors") who divided up Alexander's empire after his death. A childhood companion of Alexander, he had served Alexander well as chief of his elite body guard. Seleucus I was satrap of Babylon at the time or Alexander's death, and after Perdiccus' assassination received Babylonia as his portion. However, he was driven from Babylon by Antigonus Monophthalmus (another of the Diadochi) in 316 and fled to Egypt for the protection of Ptolemy I. With Ptolemy's help he returned to retake Babylon in 312 and began the system of the "Seleucid era," a widely used system of dating in antiquity. The peace treaty of 301 assigned Palestine and southern Syria to Seleucus; however, Ptolemy seized the territory and refused to turn it over. Seleucus refrained from pressing his entitlement because of the earlier assistance of Ptolemy; nevertheless, he did not give up the claim, and his successors pursued it in a series of "Syrian Wars." The Seleucid Empire reached its greatest extent under his rule.

2. Seleucus II Callinicus (246-226); son of Antiochus II (261-246). Shortly after he was proclaimed king, the Seleucid realm was invaded by Ptolemy III in the Third Syrian or Laodicean War (246-241). The Syrians were not in a position to resist, but a famine in Egypt forced the Ptolemaic army home. Seleucus' younger brother Antiochus Hierax was given authority in Asia Minor; there he established an independent rule which Seleucus could not tolerate, initiating the "War of the Brothers" (ca. 240-237). Seleucus was defeated and came to an agreement, but then Hierax was himself defeated in a succession of fights with Attalus I of Pergamum, which had become an independent power. The rise of the Arsacid dynasty in Persia began the erosion of that part of the empire, though Seleucus may have taken back some of the eastern provinces before his death.

3. Seleucus III (226-223). The elder son of Seleucus II, he proved to be immature and impetuous. He tried to bring Attalus I of Pergamum to heel. Whether there was one attempt or two is disputed, but in any case the invasion failed. Losing confidence in Seleucus, some of his officers brought his short reign to an end. An uncle of Seleucus restored discipline, and the much more capable younger brother was crowned to become Antiochus III.

4. Seleucus IV Philopator (187-175). He was a weak ruler according to the ancient sources; however, this may be slander since he maintained a state of peace for his entire reign by astute dealings with Rome. According to 2 Macc. 3 Seleucus sent his officer Heliodorus to confiscate the treasure of the Jerusalem temple, but an angel fought him off. The precise event behind this story is unclear, though Seleucus may have regarded the current high priest as disloyal since he was holding funds for the Ptolemaic supporter Hyrcanus Tobiad (2 Macc. 3:11). Seleucus was assassinated by Heliodorus not long after the Jerusalem incident and possibly as a direct result of it.

Bibliography. E. R. Bevan, *The House of Seleucus,* 2 vols. (1902, repr. New York, 1966); *CAH*², esp. 7/1: *The Hellenistic World,* ed. F. W. Walbank et al. (Cambridge, 1984); 8: *Rome and the Mediterranean to 133 B.C.*, ed. A. E. Astin et al. (Cambridge, 1989); N. Davis and C. M. Kraay, *The Hellenistic Kingdoms: Portrait Coins and History* (London, 1973). LESTER L. GRABBE

SEMACHIAH (Heb. *sĕmaḵyāhû*)
A levitical gatekeeper, son of Shemaiah and descendant of Obed-edom (1 Chr. 26:7).

SEMEIN (Gk. *Semeïn*)
A postexilic ancestor of Jesus in Luke's genealogy linking Joseph to Adam (Luke 3:26).

SEMITES, SEMITIC LANGUAGES
Although the word "Semite" does not occur in the biblical materials, we can nonetheless properly speak of the biblical Semites. These people first appear in the Table of Nations (Gen. 10), an early Israelite ethnographic list. The Table conceptualizes Israel's ancient neighbors as the descendants of Noah's three sons, with the Semites being the progeny of the eldest, Shem. Although identifying these progeny with particular nations is sometimes difficult, it is nonetheless clear that Shem is to be associated especially with peoples to the east of Israel (e.g., Persia, Assyria, Babylon) and also with the Arameans to the northeast and with some regions

of Africa. Most important perhaps is that Shem is the ethnic forefather of the Israelites, being an ancestor three generations removed from Eber (the Hebrew eponymous ancestor) and 10 generations removed from the patriarch Abraham. The author of the Table thus viewed Israel as having ancient genealogical links to the great civilizations of the east.

The rationale behind the construction of the Table is not entirely clear, but it seems certain that linguistic similarities played an important role in the threefold division it offers, as is evident from its own testimony: "These are the sons of Shem, by their families, their languages, their lands, and their nations." On the other hand, ideological factors also influenced its composition, as indicated by the fact that the Canaanites — a group closely related to the Hebrews both linguistically and culturally — are listed as Hamites rather than as Semites. Other explanations for the Table's organization, particularly socioeconomic and sociocultural criteria, have also been suggested. However, our efforts to understand the scheme of the Table are hindered somewhat by the fact that some editorial changes have probably been made to the text.

The Table of Nations has exerted a considerable influence on the history of Western anthropology, primarily because for much of its history Europe viewed the biblical material as an authoritative historical source. As a result, early efforts to catalogue the peoples and languages of the world followed the contours laid out in the Table. The peoples encountered during Western imperial expansion — Indians, Japanese, Chinese, and Native Americans — were frequently inserted into the threefold taxonomy provided by the biblical lists. Critical study of the biblical text and its genre during the 19th and 20th centuries has changed this, since for many scholars the Table's literary character is no longer viewed as historiographic but rather as early Israelite speculation about the origins of nations and peoples. So although some conservative Jewish and Christian scholars still view the Table as a helpful taxonomic source, this is generally not the case.

Semitic Languages

Despite this change in perspective, linguists nonetheless continue to speak of Semites and Semitic peoples, not in an ethnic sense but rather in a linguistic sense (although the ethnic/linguistic distinction has been frequently blurred). The Semitic language family is represented by both ancient and modern tongues and is chiefly characterized by the fact that nouns, verbs, and adjectives generally derive from roots of three consonants. So, e.g., in Hebrew the verb "to speak" *(dāḇar)* and the nouns "word" *(dāḇār)* and "oracle" *(dĕḇîr)* derive from the same consonantal combination, *d-b-r.* Although one often finds that the same three-consonant combination is used in various Semitic languages, this is not always the case. And even when it is, the root meanings can be quite different. Using the above example of *d-b-r,* Akk. *dabāru,* "to push back," is not very close to the Hebrew meaning "to speak." However, Akk. *dabābu,* which uses the somewhat different combination *d-b-b,* does mean "to speak." So although we cannot always explain the similarities and differences between these languages, our efforts to compare the various Semitic tongues presuppose their essential similarity.

The Semitic languages, which stem from an original "Proto-Semitic" used in the Fertile Crescent region, made their first literary appearance in the East Semitic languages of the Akkadians and Eblaites (3rd millennium B.C.E.). At roughly the same time another branch of the language family developed in the western part of the region (hence called West Semitic) which is considered the linguistic ancestor of the biblical languages, Hebrew and Aramaic. Closely related to the development of Hebrew, both historically and linguistically, are Phoenician, Moabite, Ammonite, and Edomite. However, although the early forms of Hebrew appeared sometime after 1200, the language of the Hebrew Bible is somewhat different because much of the Bible was written in a later period (and so with later forms of the language) and because the text has undergone a continuing process of "modernization," i.e., the replacement of older forms and constructions with newer ones. Three major Semitic tongues continue to be used in modern times: Arabic, Amharic (= Ethiopic), and Israeli Hebrew.

New Testament

Beginning with the Babylonian Exile and then accelerating with the advent of the 6th-century Persian conquests, the language of Palestinian Judaism was increasingly influenced by Aramaic, so that by the NT period it was the common language of the region. As a result, the ministry of Jesus and his disciples was carried out in this language, and this in turn influenced the composition of the NT Gospels — despite the fact that the Gospels were written in Greek, not Aramaic. These Semitic influences are sometimes explicit (cf. the Aramaic quote of Jesus in Mark 5:41) but are more often subtle changes in the language of the Greek text called aramaisms or semiticisms. These Semitic linguistic features are carefully identified by scholars and their import for the interpretive task is weighed accordingly.

Bibliography. G. Bergsträsser, *Introduction to the Semitic Languages* (Winona Lake, 1983); S. Moscati, *The Semites in Ancient History* (Cardiff, 1959); Moscati, ed., *An Introduction to the Comparative Grammar of the Semitic Languages* (Wiesbaden, 1964), 3-21; B. Oded, "The Table of Nations (Genesis 10): A Socio-cultural Approach," *ZAW* 98 (1986): 14-31; G. M. Schramm, "The Semitic Languages: An Overview," in *Current Trends in Linguistics,* ed. T. A. Sebeok, 6: *Linguistics in South West Asia and North Africa* (Hague, 1976), 257-60.

Kenton Lane Sparks

SENAAH (Heb. *sĕnāʾâ*)

A group of Babylonian exiles listed as returning with Zerubbabel (Ezra 2:35 = Neh. 7:38). It is unclear whether the name refers to a place (possibly identified with Magdalsenna, ca. 13 km. [8 mi.] NE of Jericho) or a family name. It may be related to "the sons of Hassennah" who helped rebuild the walls of Jerusalem (Neh. 3:3) or the Benjaminite family of Hassenuah (1 Chr. 9:7; Neh. 11:9).

LAURA B. MAZOW

SENEH (Heb. *senneh*)
One of two rocky crags flanking a pass along the Wadi eṣ-Ṣuweinîṭ between Michmash and Geba (1 Sam. 14:4). Seneh (cf. Heb. *sĕneh,* "thorn bush") is on the south side of the wadi, ca. 11 km. (7 mi.) NNE of Jerusalem.

SENIR (Heb. *śĕnîr*)
The Amorites' name for Mt. Hermon (Deut. 3:9). At 1 Chr. 5:23 Senir and Mt. Hermon are distinguished (unless "and" should be taken as epexegetic "even"); furthermore, Senir is known to have been a name for the entire Anti-Lebanon range (as opposed to the single peak of Hermon; cf. Cant. 4:8; Ezek. 27:5).

SENNACHERIB (Heb. *sanĕḥērîḇ;* Akk. *Sin-aḫḫē-rība*)
The king of Assyria (704-681 B.C.E.) who invaded Judah during the reign of Hezekiah. Sennacherib inherited a vast empire from his father Sargon II. While he had to mount some major campaigns, primarily to curb rebellions, nonetheless he was able to turn his attention to other matters, especially great building projects. He rebuilt Nineveh, converted it into a metropolis, and made it Assyria's capital. Sennacherib is also remembered as having destroyed Babylon in 689. Sources for the reign of this king are abundant, including annals, letters, astrological reports, and legal and administrative texts. Biblical texts relating to this king are found in 2 Kgs. 18:13–19:37; 2 Chr. 32:1-23; Isa. 36–37.

Arguably, the most important event for Judah involving Sennacherib was the Assyrian invasion in 701. Following the death of Sargon II, widespread rebellion broke out throughout the empire — in Anatolia, Babylonia, and Syria-Palestine. As a part of this revolt, Merodach-baladan of Babylon sent envoys to Hezekiah (2 Kgs. 20:12-15). In fact, Hezekiah had been making preparations for the revolt, rebuilding the walls of Jerusalem, strengthening and reorganizing his military (2 Chr. 32:5-6), building storehouses for food and stalls for animals (vv. 28-29), and constructing the Siloam tunnel to transport water from the Gihon spring inside the walls (2 Kgs. 20:20; 2 Chr. 32:30; *ANET,* 321; cf. the *lmlk* jar handles, dated to the reign of Hezekiah, discovered throughout Judah). Sennacherib's inscriptions suggest that Hezekiah's revolt was coordinated with those of other Syro-Palestinian rulers. 2 Kgs. 18:8 notes that Hezekiah attacked Philistine states, probably because of their noncooperation in the rebellion.

Sennacherib spent his early years dealing with the rebellion in Babylon, before he was able to turn his attention to Syria-Palestine in 701. Two inscriptions, the Oriental Institute Prism (*ANET,* 287-88) and the Rassam Cylinder (*ARAB* II, §284), describe this campaign in detail. The Assyrian king began by marching down the Phoenician coast without encountering major opposition until he reached Philistine territory. At Ashkelon, he captured its king and his family and deported them to Assyria. The campaign in Philistia continued with the conquest of a number of cities under Ashkelon's influence. From there, Sennacherib turned his attention toward Hezekiah, first taking Eltekeh, Timnah, and Ekron, cities under Hezekiah's control. Sennacherib claims to have captured 46 strong walled cities of Hezekiah. One of these would have been Lachish, prominently depicted in reliefs at his palace in Nineveh (*ANEP,* 371-74). The Assyrian then laid siege to Jerusalem — making Hezekiah prisoner in his royal residence — and plundered surrounding cities, returning them to Philistine control. Inscriptions note that Sennacherib then imposed a huge tribute on Hezekiah. There is general agreement that the content of 2 Kgs. 18:13-16 converges with that described in the Assyrian texts for this campaign (dating the campaign to the 14th year of Hezekiah, generally accepted as 701). The text further describes Sennacherib as having captured "all the fortified cities of Judah," while making no mention of the capture of Jerusalem, and receiving a huge tribute from Hezekiah.

Discrepancies within the Kings account (between 2 Kgs. 18:13-16 and 18:17–19:37) and between the Assyrian sources and the biblical texts have led scholars to question whether Sennacherib conducted only one campaign against Judah. Given the two divergent courses of action taken by Hezekiah in response to the Assyrian attack — capitulation (2 Kgs. 18:14-15) and resistance (19:19) — and the prominence of the conquest of Lachish in Sennacherib's relief from Nineveh but with no mention of it in any annalistic narrative of the 701 campaign, it has long been suggested that Sennacherib conducted a second campaign against Judah, perhaps in 688-687. This is the campaign reflected in 2 Kgs. 18:17–19:36, in a new text of Sennacherib, and the Lachish relief. It was during this campaign that the Judean cities of Azekah, Lachish (2 Kgs. 18:17–19:7), and Libnah (19:8) were conquered.

Bibliography. N. Na'aman, "Sennacherib's 'Letter to God' on His Campaign to Judah," *BASOR* 214 (1974): 25-39; W. H. Shea, "Sennacherib's Second Palestinian Campaign," *JBL* 104 (1985): 401-18.

JEFFREY K. KUAN

SENTINEL
A lookout responsible to keep vigil (Heb. *ṣōp̄eh, šōmēr*), often on a tower or wall, whether for the king (1 Sam. 14:16; 2 Sam. 18:24-27; 2 Kgs. 9:17-20), over a city (Ps. 127:1 [figurative for the Lord]; Cant. 3:3; 5:7), or over a field (Isa. 56:10; cf. Jer. 4:17), and often at night (Ps. 127:1; 130:6; Isa. 21:11-12).

The prophet Ezekiel is appointed a watchman for the house of Israel, and it becomes his particular responsibility to warn his people to turn from their wicked ways (Ezek. 3:17; 33:2-7; cf. Hos. 9:8).

SEORIM (Heb. *śĕʿōrîm*)
The leader of the fourth division of priests appointed at the time of David (1 Chr. 24:8).

SEPHAR (Heb. *sĕpār*)
A place named in the description of the limit of the Joktanite settlements (Gen. 10:30). Located in south Arabia, Sephar may be identified with Ẓafār in Hadramaut.

SEPHARAD (Heb. *sĕpārad̠*)
One of the places of exile for some of the Jews of Jerusalem (Obad. 20). The biblical text, however, does not indicate exactly where this is. Possibilities include Sefarad, a location in modern Spain; a city in Media; and the city of Sardis, capital of the Lydian Empire (Asia Minor) just before Cyrus conquered it in 546. Sepharad was made the center of a Persian satrapy and renamed Sparda (O.Pers.). This lends further support to the idea that Jews may have resided there from the time of the Persian conquests, since the Persians, after Darius, made Sardis/Sparda a major stop on the trade routes from Susa.
DANIEL L. SMITH-CHRISTOPHER

SEPHARVAIM (Heb. *sĕp̄arwayim*)
A Mesopotamian city of unknown location whose citizens were brought by Sargon II to Samaria after its fall in 722 B.C.E. (2 Kgs. 17:24). Apparently they were devotees of Adrammelech and Anammelech, whose worship included the sacrifice of children by fire (2 Kgs. 17:31).

Sepharvaim is one of the towns mentioned in Sennacherib's attempt, through his envoy the Rabshakeh, to show Judah the folly of her resistance to Assyria (2 Kgs. 18:34 = Isa. 36:19; 2 Kgs. 19:13 = Isa. 37:13). If the kings and gods of these cities could not effect their rescue, neither should Judah expect it of her kings and gods. C. MACK ROARK

SEPPHORIS (Heb. *Zippori*)
A city strategically located in the center of the Galilee, on a hill overlooking the Beth-netofa Valley, which connects the Sea of Galilee with the Mediterranean.

According to Josephus the Romans made Sepphoris the seat of the Galilean council in 57-55 B.C.E. and then burned it to the ground after a revolt in the wake of Herod the Great's death in 4 B.C.E. (*Ant.* 14.91; 17.289). Herod Antipas refounded it as his capital of the Galilee shortly thereafter, and it remained a leading regional city for centuries, even after Herod Antipas relocated his capital to Tiberias between 18 and 20 C.E. Josephus presents a picture of Sepphoris as the largest and most cosmopolitan city in the Galilee, describing it as "the ornament of all Galilee" (*Ant.* 18.27). During the First Jewish War, Sepphoris remained pro-Roman, and coins minted there even contain the epigraph *Eirenopolis,* "City of Peace." Sepphoris is also known as an important center of Jewish learning in rabbinic literature, and it was there that Rabbi Judah the Prince codified the Mishnah.

Archaeological excavations have added significantly to our knowledge of the city during the Roman-Byzantine periods. The domestic quarters contain many stone vessels (related to a concern for ritual purity) and Jewish ritual baths; these, coupled with a general absence of swine bones in the early centuries, confirm the literary record's identi-

Colonnaded street at Roman Sepphoris, paved with rectangular limestone blocks. The parallel sidewalk was roofed and paved with mosaics (Phoenix Data Systems, Neal and Joel Bierling)

fication of the city as primarily Jewish. The building materials, however, such as plaster, mosaic, fresco, and the basic grid pattern of the city show an acceptance of Roman architectural materials as early as the 1st century. Coins from the late 1st century even depict a pagan temple, and a theater seating ca. 4500 also dates to some time in that century. Nevertheless, most of the architectural structures which are Roman in orientation date to after the First Jewish War, including the aqueduct, the porticoed agora or market, and the many mosaics with pagan themes that begin to appear in the 3rd century. Ironically, the surge in pagan imagery, Greco-Roman architecture, and the city's designation as Diocaesarea ("City of Zeus and the Emperor") beginning in the 2nd century coincides precisely with the time when Sepphoris became known as one of the most important centers of rabbinic learning.

Archaeological excavations have also uncovered remains of an Iron Age village at Ein Zippori, the springs of Sepphoris, just S of the Roman-Byzantine city.

Since Jesus' hometown Nazareth is only 6.5 km. (4 mi.) to the south, it is curious that Sepphoris is never mentioned in the NT. Perhaps the city's cosmopolitan character, gentile presence, or wealth in comparison to the Galilean villages led to Jesus' aversion. Jesus' awareness that Herod Antipas had executed John the Baptist most likely led him to avoid Sepphoris as a seat of political power. However, given the relative infrequence with which any place names occur in the Gospels, perhaps Jesus' contacts with Sepphoris went unrecorded.

Bibliography. E. M. Meyers, E. Netzer, and C. L. Meyers, *Sepphoris* (Winona Lake, 1992); S. S. Miller, *Studies in the History and Traditions of Sepphoris*. SJLA 37 (Leiden, 1984); R. M. Nagy et al., *Sepphoris in Galilee* (Winona Lake, 1996).

JONATHAN L. REED

SEPTUAGINT

General designation for the Jewish-Greek Scriptures, which consist primarily of various translations of the books of the Hebrew Bible. Also included are additions to some books of the Hebrew Bible as well as independent works, some of which are translations while others were composed in Greek. The texts are believed to have been produced from the 3rd to the 2nd or 1st centuries B.C.E., and at least partly in Alexandria, Egypt. The name Septuagint derives from the tradition in the Letter of Aristeas that 72 (or 70; hence the symbol LXX) elders translated the Pentateuch into Greek.

The term "Septuagint" is actually a cause of difficulty for the field. Many nonspecialists employ a reading from one of the standard printed editions (Rahlfs or Brooke-McLean) or a manuscript and designate it as the definitive reading of the LXX, as though this represents the oldest recoverable form of the Greek text. For this reason, specialists now reserve the term "Old Greek" (OG) or other, more specific terminology to designate a text that in the judgment of scholars most likely represents what was originally written. Critical editions for many books of the LXX are now available and continue to be published in the Göttingen *Septuaginta*.

There are three main areas of interest in LXX studies. First, the study of the LXX and the later recensions offers insights into the beliefs and thoughts of the Jewish community in antiquity. Second, next to the Dead Sea Scrolls the LXX is the most important witness for textual criticism of the Hebrew Bible. For the most part the LXX text is very close to the Hebrew; however, there are significant differences between the two, in certain sections (e.g., Exod. 35–40; Dan. 4–6) or even entire books (e.g., the LXX version of Job is 17 percent shorter and Jeremiah, 12 percent shorter). Any comparison of the Greek to the Hebrew must treat each book individually. Third, Greek versions were employed with equal authority to the Hebrew Bible in the early Church. Consequently, the LXX had an enormous impact on the language and theology of the early Church.

Bibliography. A. Aejmelaeus, "What Can We Know about the Hebrew *Vorlage* of the Septuagint?" *ZAW* 99 (1981): 58-89; C. E. Cox, ed., *VII Congress of the IOSCS* (Atlanta, 1991); L. Greenspoon, "The Use and Abuse of the Term 'LXX' and Related Terminology in Recent Scholarship," *BIOSCS* 20 (1987): 21-29; S. Jellicoe, *The Septuagint and Modern Study* (1968, repr. Winona Lake, 1993).

TIM MCLAY

SERAH (Heb. *śeraḥ*)

The daughter of the patriarch Asher (Gen. 46:17; Num. 26:46; 1 Chr. 7:30). The name may represent a clan or place.

SERAIAH (Heb. *śĕrāyâ, śĕrāyāhû*)

(also AZARIAH, SHAVSHA, SHEVA, SHISHA)

1. The royal secretary during the reign of King David (2 Sam. 8:17). In the other lists of David's state officials he is called Sheva (**1;** 2 Sam. 20:25) and Shavsha (1 Chr. 18:16). In the list of Solomon's administration, under whom his two sons served, he is called Shisha (1 Kgs. 4:3).

2. The chief priest, a descendant of Zadok, who served in the temple of Jerusalem when Nebuchadnezzar conquered the city in 587/586 B.C.E. Along with other officials of the city, he was executed before Nebuchadnezzar at Riblah (2 Kgs. 25:18-21 = Jer. 52:24-27). Ezra is called the son of Seraiah (Ezra 7:1), but this must refer to his lineage rather than his actual parentage.

3. The son of Tanhumeth the Netophathite; one of the Judean commanders who had eluded Nebuchadnezzar's army. He and his troops submitted to Gedaliah at Mizpah with assurances of being treated well. He fled to Egypt when Gedaliah was murdered (2 Kgs. 25:23-24; Jer. 40:7-9).

4. The son of Kenaz, brother of Othniel, and father of Joab of the tribe of Judah (1 Chr. 4:13-14).

5. A prince of a Simeonite clan; the son of Asiel, father of Joshibiah, and grandfather of Jehu (1 Chr. 4:35).

6. One of the exiles who returned from Babylon to Judah with Zerubbabel (Ezra 2:2). He is called Azariah (**23**) in Neh. 7:7.

7. A priest who sealed the covenant to support the temple during the administration of Nehemiah (Neh. 10:2[MT 3]).

8. A postexilic priest (Neh. 11:11). A similar list of priests reads Azariah instead of Seraiah (1 Chr. 9:11).

9. One of the "chiefs of the priests" who came up with Zerubbabel from Babylon (Neh. 12:1). During the days of Joiakim, the son and successor of Jeshua, Meraiah was the head of the priestly house of Seraiah (Neh. 12:12).

10. An official of King Jehoiakim; the son of Azriel. Jehoiakim sent Seraiah, along with Jerahmeel and Shelemiah, to arrest Baruch and Jeremiah, but both escaped (Jer. 36:26).

11. The son of Neriah, brother of Baruch; quartermaster under King Zedekiah. He went with Zedekiah to Babylon during the fourth year of his reign (594/593 B.C.E.; Jer. 51:59-64). A seal impression reading "Belonging to Seraiah, (son of) Neriah" has been found in Jerusalem.

RONALD A. SIMKINS

SERAPHIM

Heavenly beings seen by Isaiah in his inaugural vision (Isa. 6:1-7), probably so called because they shone brightly like fire (from Heb. *śrp*, "to burn"). Seraphim have six wings: two for covering their faces, lest they look directly at God; two for covering their "feet" (a euphemism for the genitals, which speaks of modesty and warns against the Canaanite fertility cult); and two for flying. When Isaiah complains of his unclean lips, the seraphs purify him with a coal taken from the altar.

The seraphim were most likely serpentine in shape, as suggested by the "fiery (NRSV 'poisonous') serpents" sent to bite the Israelites when they complained in the wilderness (Num. 21:6; Deut. 8:15); here the name may refer to their shiny skins or to the burning pain associated with their bites. Moses is instructed to fashion a bronze serpent *(śārāp)* and mount it on a pole (Num. 21:8-9); it was still in the temple at the time of Isaiah's call (2 Kgs. 18:4). Isaiah twice refers to "flying fiery seraphs" or "serpents" (Isa. 14:29; 30:6), mythological creatures rather than the heavenly seraphim. Excavations have unearthed a number of scarab seals with winged serpents, some from the approximate time of Isaiah. In addition, winged serpents surround the throne of Pharaoh in Egyptian art (cf. Isa. 6, a vision of the heavenly king on his throne).

Bibliography. K. R. Joines, *Serpent Symbolism in the Old Testament* (Haddonfield, N.J., 1974); A. Reifenberg, *Ancient Hebrew Seals* (London, 1950); W. A. Ward, "The Four-winged Serpent on Hebrew Seals," *RSO* 43 (1968): 135-43.

WILLIAM B. NELSON, JR.

SERAPIS (Gk. *Sarapis*)

A god created by a fusion of Osiris and the spirit of the Apis bull which was entombed at Memphis, thus also called Osorapis. Ptolemy I is attributed with creating Serapis in order to accentuate his own power, and imported a huge statue from Sinope to represent the god.

The cult of Serapis became quite popular within the Greek world. Serapis is a good example of the syncretism of the Hellenistic age, for not only did he have characteristics of Osiris, a god of the dead, he acquired healing powers, like Asclepius, and was even represented as Zeus Serapis. The only Egyptian god whom he could not rival was Isis, whose popularity in the Greco-Roman world was immense.

The cult of Serapis spread throughout the Roman Empire, evidenced in Africa, France, northwest Europe, and Britain. By the 2nd or 3rd century C.E., the Romans were reported to have entirely adopted the cult. The emperor Julian expressed admiration for Serapis and condoned the identification of Zeus with the god.

By the end of the 4th century, however, this formerly thriving cult was finished when the Christian patriarch of Alexandria destroyed a statue of the god and ordered the burning of the Serapis temple.

ALICIA BATTEN

SERED (Heb. *sereḏ*)

A son of the patriarch Zebulun (Gen. 46:14); ancestor of the Seredites (Num. 26:26).

SERGIUS PAULUS (Gk. *Sérgios Paúlos*)

The proconsul of Cyprus who was converted when Paul visited the island on his first missionary journey (Acts 13:4-12; A.D. 47/48). He is described as an intelligent man who believed through Paul's teaching and through the power displayed when Paul struck blind the Jewish sorcerer Bar-Jesus (or Elymas), an advisor to the proconsul who opposed Paul's preaching. Though the Roman family name Sergius is well attested, attempts to identify this Sergius Paulus through inscriptional evidence have proven inconclusive.

Since the apostle is first called "Paulus" in Acts 13:9, some have suggested that the apostle took his Roman name from this first gentile convert. It is more likely that the similarity of names is a coincidence.

Bibliography. C. A. Hemer, *The Book of Acts in the Setting of Hellenistic History.* WUNT 49 (Tübingen, 1989).

MARK L. STRAUSS

SERMON ON THE MOUNT/PLAIN

The first of Jesus' discourses (Matt. 5:1–7:28), which summarizes his moral demand upon Israel. The account opens with a short narrative introduction (4:23–5:2) and closes with a short narrative conclusion (7:28–8:1). These two units share several words and phrases — "great crowds followed him," "the mountain," "going up/down," and "teaching" — which mark the intervening material as a distinct literary unit.

The discourse proper is symmetrical. Eschatological blessings (Matt. 5:3-12) are at the beginning, eschatological warnings (7:13-27) at the end. In between are three major sections, each primarily a compilation of imperatives: Jesus and the Torah

(5:17-48), Jesus on the cult (6:1-18), Jesus on social issues (6:19–7:12). Preceding these sections are the prefatory sayings on salt and light in 5:13-16. These move from the life of the blessed future (depicted in 5:3-12) to demands in the present and so signal the point at which the theme switches from gift to task.

Exegetical history offers various approaches to the Sermon. Some medieval exegetes, living in a world with two sorts of Christians, the so-called religious (priests, monks, nuns, ascetics) and the nonreligious, urged that some of the imperatives (e.g., the call not to store up treasure on earth) can only be kept by those with a special religious calling. Leo Tolstoy propounded a literal interpretation applicable to all: Christians should not take oaths, even though this would result in the abolition of courts, and they should love enemies and so not serve in any army or police force. Many Protestants have distinguished between the spiritual order and the civil order and contended that the Sermon applies only to the former. The Sermon, then, does not prescribe public policy but individual morality. The victim of a crime may, for instance, forgo personal revenge and yet support the state in exacting justice. Other Protestants have, in Pauline fashion, maintained that the Sermon cannot be lived: like the law of Moses its demands are too high. It rather teaches the need for grace. For when one seeks to obey Jesus one fails, but this only leads one to acknowledge personal inadequacy, which throws one back upon God's grace. The Sermon is preparation for the gospel.

While judging the merit of these and other interpretations one should always keep in mind that the Sermon is not an adequate summation of anybody's religion. It was never intended to stand by itself. It is rather part of a larger whole. Its demands are perverted when isolated from the grace and Christology which appear from Matthew in its entirety.

Indeed, the Sermon is itself a christological document. Isa. 61:1, 2, 7 speak of good news for the poor (cf. Matt. 5:3), of comforting those who mourn (cf. 5:4), and of inheriting the land (cf. 5:5). So Matthew's beatitudes make an implicit claim: Jesus is the anointed one of Isa. 61. Beyond this, the qualities mentioned in the Beatitudes — such as meekness and mercy — are manifested throughout the ministry (cf. 9:27-31; 11:29; 20:29-34; 21:5). So the Sermon is partly a summary of its speaker's deeds. Matt. 5–7 proclaims likeness to the God of Israel (5:48) through the virtues of Jesus Christ.

One must also always remember that Matthew's Sermon must be associated with the kingdom of God. The Sermon does not speak to ordinary circumstances. It instead addresses itself to people overtaken by an overwhelming reality which can remake the individual and beget a new life. Furthermore, the Sermon sees all through the eyes of eternity. It does not so much look forward, from the present to the consummation, as from the consummation to the present. Matt. 5–7 presents the unadulterated will of God because it proclaims the will of God as it will be lived when the kingdom comes in its fullness. This is why the Sermon is so heedless of all earthly contingencies, why it always blasts shallow moralism.

The most difficult section of the Sermon is Matt. 5:21-48, the six so-called antitheses. But four proposals regarding it seem more probable than not. First, the antitheses do not set Jesus' words over against Jewish interpretations of the Mosaic law; rather, there is contrast with the Bible itself: "You have heard that it was said to those of ancient times" refers to Sinai. Second, although Jesus' words are contrasted with the Torah, the two are not, according to the Sermon itself, contradictory (cf. 5:17-20). Those who obey 5:21-48 will not break any Jewish law. Third, the section is not Jesus' interpretation of the law. The declaration that remarriage is adultery, e.g., is a new teaching grounded not in exegesis but Jesus' authority. Fourth, Jesus here illustrates through concrete examples what sort of attitude and behavior he requires and how his demands surpass those of the Torah without contradicting it.

Many have complained that the teaching of Matt. 5:21-48 is impractical. But the Sermon, which is so dramatic and pictorial, offers not a set of rules — the ruling on divorce is the exception — but rather seeks to instill a moral vision. The text, which implies that God demands a radical obedience which cannot be casuistically formulated, functions more like a story than a legal code. Its primary purpose is to instill principles and qualities through a vivid inspiration of the moral imagination. One comes away not with an incomplete set of statutes but an unjaded impression of a challenging moral ideal. That ideal may remain beyond grasp, but that is what enables it ever to beckon one forward.

Apart from the woes (Luke 6:24-26) and two short proverbs (vv. 39-40), all of the units in Luke's Sermon on the Plain (Luke 6:20–7:1) have parallels in Matthew's Sermon; and even the two proverbs appear elsewhere in Matthew (Matt. 10:24-25; 15:14). Indeed, all of the materials common to the two sermons, with the sole exception of the Golden Rule, are in the same order:

Luke 6:20a	cf. Matt. 5:1-2
Luke 6:20b-23	cf. Matt. 5:3-12
Luke 6:24-26	
Luke 6:27-36	cf. Matt. 5:38-48; 7:12
Luke 6:37-38	cf. Matt. 7:1
Luke 6:39	(cf. Matt. 15:14)
Luke 6:40	(cf. Matt. 10:24-25)
Luke 6:41-42	cf. Matt. 7:3-5
Luke 6:43-45	cf. Matt. 7:16-18
Luke 6:46	cf. Matt. 7:21
Luke 6:47-49	cf. Matt. 7:24-27
Luke 7:1	cf. Matt. 7:28–8:1

Matthew's Sermon was composed by the author of the rest of the Gospel. Drawing upon Q, Mark, and his distinctive tradition (M), he forged the discourse in accordance with his own interests. But Luke 6:20-49 is usually regarded as a speech which Luke only lightly retouched: it brings us very close to Q.

Luke's Sermon opens with four beatitudes (Luke 6:20-23). These are followed by a subsection on loving enemies and doing good (vv. 27-36). This subsection as a whole has the Golden Rule at its center (v. 31). On one side of it is a series of eight parallel imperatives (vv. 27-30) and on the other a series of three questions (vv. 32-34) and a conclusion (vv. 35-36). The opening imperatives are neatly arranged into two quatrains, with the first set using the 2nd person plural, the second set the 2nd person singular.

Luke 6:37-38 continues the theme of doing good to outsiders. It contains four related, parallel imperatives — do not judge, do not condemn, forgive, give. The first two are structural twins, as are the last two. But the long final member, like the long fourth beatitude, breaks the parallelism in order to add emphasis.

The subject of the discourse appears to shift with Luke 6:39-42, which contains the sayings about the blind leading the blind (v. 39), the disciple not being above the master (v. 40), and the splinter in the eye (vv. 41-42). The harshness of the address ("hypocrites," v. 42) is new. New too is the ecclesiastical orientation, signaled by the use of "brother" (vv. 41, 42). Unlike vv. 27-38, in which the issue is how disciples should act toward their enemies, in vv. 39-42 the issue is how they should relate to one another. In other words, the first half of the Sermon on the Plain seems concerned with how disciples should behave toward outsiders whereas the second half has to do with communal relations.

Luke 6:43-45, which speaks about good trees and bad fruit and bad fruit and good trees, continues the call for community members to examine themselves. The focus on fraternal relations, in contrast to vv. 27-38, explains the tension between v. 35, where the "wicked" are clearly outside the community, and vv. 43-45, where the "wicked" are plainly inside. That is, Luke 6:43-45, like the sayings in vv. 39-42 and the parable of the two builders in vv. 46-49, draws the line not between insiders and outsiders but between disciples good and bad. In theological terms, Luke 6:39-49, which demands that one judge not others but oneself, addresses the reality of sin within the Christian community.

Bibliography. H. D. Betz, *The Sermon on the Mount.* Herm (Minneapolis, 1995); W. Carter, *What Are They Saying about Matthew's Sermon on the Mount?* (New York, 1994); R. A. Guelich, *The Sermon on the Mount* (Waco, 1982).

DALE C. ALLISON, JR.

SERPENT

A general term for the various snakelike creatures found in the ancient Near East (Heb. *nāḥāš, śārāp̄;* Gk. *óphis*).

Representations of serpents in literature and other media (chiefly clay and bronze) occur throughout the ancient Near East. Serpents functioned largely as objects of worship or charms against evil, often that of snakebite. Enuma Elish depicts Tiamat, herself perhaps a serpentlike creature, as allied with a horde of creatures — many serpentine — in her battle with Marduk. While Gilgamesh is swimming, a serpent steals the plant that is to give immortality.

In the Gen. 3 story of the fall of humanity, a crafty serpent (cf. Matt. 10:16) talks Eve into eating the fruit of the tree of the knowledge of good and evil, which she then hands to Adam. God pronounces the consequences on the serpent, Eve, Adam, and the ground (only the serpent and the ground are cursed). This explains why the serpent has no legs; for humanity, it means — among other things — the loss of immortality (cf. Gilgamesh). In Gen. 3 the serpent is simply one of God's creatures. The explicit equation of the serpent with the satan, the accuser, comes in later Jewish and Christian apocalyptic works (e.g., 2 Enoch, Revelation).

In Num. 21 God commands Moses to craft a bronze serpent (Heb. *śārāp̄*) to relieve the effects of a plague of poisonous serpents *(nĕḥāšîm)* which God had sent to punish the people. This serpent image was later erected in the Jerusalem temple, but the association of this serpent (Nĕhuštān) with Canaanite religious practice eventually led Hezekiah to destroy it (2 Kgs. 18:4). The healing aspects of the bronze serpent reflect other ancient cultures (perhaps underlying the reference to Jesus in John 3:14).

The vision of Isa. 6 includes fiery, winged serpents *(śĕrāp̄îm)* which hover around the divine throne, symbols of God's regal glory. Similar depictions of winged serpents have been found in Egypt, where the erect image of the cobra (uraeus) was a symbol of the royalty of the pharaoh and the gods.

Bibliography. R. S. Boraas, "Of Serpents and Gods," *Dialog* 17 (1978): 273-79; J. Milgrom, "Excursus 52: The Copper Snake," in *Numbers.* JPS Torah Commentary (Philadelphia, 1990), 459-60; J. Tabick, "The Snake in the Grass: The Problems of Interpreting a Symbol in the Hebrew Bible and Rabbinic Writings," *Religion* 16 (1986): 155-67.

MATTHEW A. THOMAS

SERPENT'S STONE

A landmark also rendered "stone of Zoheleth" (Heb. *'eb̄en hazzōḥeleṯ;* 1 Kgs. 1:9), apparently a place of Jebusite worship prior to the area's capture by David. Here Adonijah, Solomon's rival for David's throne, was making a sacrifice as he prepared his attempt to usurp the throne. From 1 Kgs. 1:41 it is clear that the location is out of sight of Jerusalem, but still close enough for Adonijah and his companions to hear the celebration of Solomon's anointing as king. Locating the site at the confluence of the Kidron and Hinnom Valleys near En-rogel provides the only adequate solution.

Bibliography. J. J. Simons, *Jerusalem in the Old Testament* (Leiden, 1952). DENNIS M. SWANSON

SERUG (Heb. *śĕrûg;* Gk. *Seroúch*)

A son of Reu; the father of Nahor, hence an ancestor of Abraham (Gen. 11:20-23; 1 Chr. 1:26) and Jesus (Luke 3:35).

SERVANT

A person employed or otherwise bound to serve and discharge duties for another. Many servants mentioned in the Bible are clearly not slaves, but in a form of dependent labor different from actual chattel slavery. Heb. *ʿeḇeḏ* and Gk. *doúlos* each cover wide semantic domains that name a variety of inferiors and are often nontechnical in ancient vernacular.

"Servants of the king" include soldiers and sailors in a professional army (1 Sam. 18:5; 2 Sam. 2:13-17; 1 Kgs. 9:26-28; 2 Chr. 8:18). Because they receive pay and are made "commanders of thousands and commanders of hundreds," these clearly are not chattel slaves but free subjects commissioned as military officers (1 Sam. 22:6-10; cf. 1 Kgs. 9:22). Others are civil servants of the king: royal counselors (1 Sam. 16:15; 2 Sam. 15:34), secretarial or financial administrators (2 Kgs. 22:3-13; 2 Chr. 34:8-18), labor overseers (1 Sam. 21:7[MT 8]; 1 Kgs. 9:23; 11:26; 2 Chr. 13:6), political ambassadors (2 Sam. 10:2-4; 2 Kgs. 19:23; Isa. 37:24), and royal courtiers (2 Sam. 8:14; 11:9, 13). These servants hold respect and command as functionaries of the monarch.

Other OT references designate people not with honor but in military surrender and political submission (e.g., the Gibeonites before Joshua, Josh. 9:11; the guardians of Ahab's descendants in Samaria writing to Jehu, 2 Kgs. 10:5). In this connection, even monarchs can be described as servants (e.g., Ahaz' message to Tiglath-pileser III of Assyria, 2 Kgs. 16:7; cf. 2 Sam. 10:19; 2 Kgs. 18:24). Further examples of such negative designations — a few linked with being called "dog" — carry humiliation, dishonor, and lament (2 Kgs. 8:13; 2 Sam. 9:8).

The religious term "servant of God" appears as a humble self-deprecation before a deity. Its highest concentration occurs in a section of Deutero-Isaiah (Isa. 40–55). Although 13 of the occurrences refer clearly to the nation of Israel as the servant, the remaining verses are unclear and scholars debate whether the songs refer to Israel or a distinct individual. Whatever its referent, the servant resembles the preexilic kings and especially prophets. Privy to Yahweh's divine plan, the Isaian servant-prophet has a call to lead the people toward obedience to Yahweh (Isa. 49:1-6; modeled after the call of Moses in Exod. 3–4). The NT authors later apply these "Servant Songs" to Jesus Christ.

OT individuals called a servant of Yahweh (or God) include Abraham (Gen. 26:24; Ps. 105:6, 42), Jacob (Ezek. 28:25), Caleb (Num. 14:24), Joshua (Josh. 24:29), David (Ps. 144:10; Isa. 37:35; Ezek. 37:24-25), Ahiah of Shiloh (1 Kgs. 14:18; 15:29), Elijah (2 Kgs. 9:36; 10:10), Jonah "son of Amittai, the prophet" (14:25), Isaiah (Isa. 20:3), Eliakim (22:20), Job (Job 1:8; 2:3), Zerubbabel (Hag. 2:23), and especially the great prophet Moses (Exod. 4:10; Num. 11:11; 12:7; Deut. 3:24; Neh. 10:29[30]; Dan. 9:11; Mal. 4:4[3:22]). These references illustrate the term's designation for the pious and faithful in Israel and Judah, especially prophets and rulers. NT authors build on this metaphorical usage, especially Paul (Rom. 1:1; Gal. 1:10; Phil. 1:1; the Christian apostle as a "servant of Christ"), Luke (Luke 12:41-46; the managerial slaves clearly represent church leaders), and the author of Revelation (Rev. 1:1; 2:20; 19:5; 22:6; recipients of prophecy are called God's slaves, as is John himself).

The most important NT term for servant is Gk. *diákonos,* which in ancient Greek sources denotes an emissary and spokesperson of another. Paul provides the earliest and most ample evidence of this meaning in early Christianity. He describes himself and Apollos as *diákonos* ("emissary"), conveying that they both belong to a deity, are entrusted with the deity's message, have the commission to announce it, and so have a right to be heard and believed (1 Cor. 3:5; cf. 2 Cor. 3:6; 6:4). With *diákonos,* Paul expresses his specific entitlement as an authoritative spokesman and ambassador of God. Paul, in turn, has his own emissaries among the churches, such as Phoebe (Rom. 16:1-2), Timothy (1 Thess. 3:2), and perhaps Onesimus (Phlm. 13). According to the Synoptic Gospels, this understanding of early Christian ministry as ambassadorship comes from Jesus: "whoever wishes to become great among you must be your servant . . . for the Son of Man came not to be served but to serve" (Mark 10:43-45 par.; cf. Luke 22:26-27). The meaning is in areas of message, agency, and attendance, as an emissary of heaven (the other possibility, "serving tables," is unparalleled in other Christian sources and unprecedented in non-Christian sources and so is unlikely here). Related concepts of the servant as an assistant of a higher authority include *hypērétēs* (most often in John) and *therápōn* (Heb. 3:5, of Moses).

Bibliography. J. N. Collins, *Diakonia: Re-interpreting the Ancient Sources* (Oxford, 1990); W. Zimmerli and J. Jeremias, *The Servant of God,* rev. ed. SBT 20 (London, 1965).

J. Albert Harrill

SERVANT OF THE LORD

One who belongs to Yahweh and seeks to do his will. The OT designates many individuals as servants of Yahweh *(ʿeḇeḏ YHWH):* Abraham (Gen. 26:24), Moses (e.g., Exod. 14:31; Deut. 34:5; Josh. 1:2, 13), Joshua (Judg. 2:8), David (e.g., 2 Sam. 3:18; Ezek. 34:23-24), Hezekiah (2 Chr. 32:16), Isaiah (Isa. 20:3), and Zerubbabel (Hag. 2:23). The prophets as a group are also called Yahweh's servants (2 Kgs. 17:13; Amos 3:7; Jer. 7:25; 26:5).

Second Isaiah

Four poems in Second Isaiah (Isa. 40–45) center around the theme of the Servant of Yahweh: Isa. 42:1-4 [5-9]; 49:1-6 [7]; 50:4-9 [10-11]; 52:13–53:12 (bracketed verses are included by some scholars and excluded by others). Scattered references to the same theme occur in Isa. 41:8-9; 42:19; 43:10; 44:1-2, 21, 26; 45:4; 48:20; 50:10.

In the first poem (Isa. 42:1-4 [5-9]) Yahweh describes his servant as chosen, endowed with the Spirit, humble, and compassionate. He will persevere until he brings justice to the nations. In the second poem the servant testifies that he is called before birth, prepared as Yahweh's special, hidden weapon;

the servant feels that his labor is in vain, yet he will trust in God to vindicate him (49:1-4). Here Israel is identified as the servant (49:3), whose mission, paradoxically, is to restore fallen Israel and to be a light to the nations (vv. 5-6). Although the term "servant" is missing from 50:4-9 [10-11], most scholars consider this passage to be part of the series. Here the servant is Yahweh's faithful, obedient disciple, enduring scorn, abuse, and painful beatings, yet continuing to trust in God to vindicate him. In the fourth poem (52:13–53:12) a group, probably the nations, speaks of the servant's vicarious sufferings on their behalf and his ultimate exaltation.

Scholars have identified various individuals as Yahweh's servant. Cyrus is highlighted as someone God has ordained to subdue kingdoms so that Jerusalem and the temple can be rebuilt (Isa. 44:28–45:1). Remarkably, he is even designated Yahweh's messiah, or anointed one (Isa. 45:1). However, Cyrus hardly fulfills the suffering imagery of the third and fourth poems. Another candidate, Jeremiah, suffered, but unlike the servant of Isa. 53:7 who was silent, he complained bitterly (Jer. 15:18; 20:7-8). Since Second Isaiah predicts a new exodus (Isa. 40:3-5; 43:16-19; 48:20-21; 51:9-11), he may have been thinking of a new Moses who would lead the people out of Babylon and back to the Promised Land. However, Second Isaiah very clearly states that the servant is Israel (Isa. 41:8; 44:1-2, 21; 45:4; 49:3), thus a collective servant rather than an individual. In the second Song (Isa. 49:1-6 [7]), "servant" is used equivocally. How can Israel be both the fallen people in need of restoration and the obedient ones who restore the others? There are two Israels: one sinful and the other righteous. Yahweh's servant, then, at least in the 6th century B.C.E., is the group of faithful ones who suffer on behalf of the rest of Israel, purchase their redemption from exile (Isa. 40:1-2), restore fallen Israel, and witness to the Gentiles.

Second Temple Judaism

Second Isaiah's message for the 6th century became a paradigm for all time. Judaism came to believe that vicarious suffering of righteous ones could atone for sin. Death was especially efficacious. The deaths of high priests, innocent children, and martyrs had redemptive power. Furthermore, Yahweh's servant was identified with the Messiah, beginning when David is called "my servant" (2 Sam. 3:18; 7:5, 8), in later passages invoking Zion and David traditions (2 Kgs. 19:34 = Isa. 37:35), and in passages anticipating a future messiah (Ezek. 34:23-24; 37:24-25). In the postexilic period the governor Zerubbabel, a Davidide, was called "my servant the branch" (Zech 3:8; cf. Isa. 11:1; 53:2). In some circles Palestinian Judaism regarded the suffering servant of Isa. 53 as the Messiah (cf. Targum of Isa. 52:13).

New Testament

It is no wonder that NT writers identified Jesus as the Servant of the Lord. According to Matt. 8:17 Jesus' healing the sick fulfills Isa. 53:4. Similarly, Matt. 12:18-21 quotes the second Servant Song, Isa. 42:1-4 (cf. also Mark 1:11 and Isa. 42:1). When Jesus predicts his suffering and death (Mark 9:12, 31; 10:33; Luke 24:7) he is probably reflecting on the Servant Songs. In more specific parallels, Jesus came to serve and to give his life a ransom for many (Matt. 20:28 = Mark 10:45; Isa. 53:11-12); he was silent before his accusers (Matt. 26:63; 27:12, 14 par.; Luke 23:9; John 19:9; Isa. 53:7) and interceded for sinners on the cross (Luke 23:34; Isa. 53:12). When the people would not believe Jesus' signs, John saw it as a fulfillment of Isa. 53:1 (John 12:38; cf. Rom. 10:16). Peter calls Jesus the servant (Acts 3:26; 4:27, 30), and Philip teaches the Ethiopian eunuch to believe that Jesus fulfilled Isa. 53 (Acts 8:32-35). Paul includes a hymn exalting Jesus as the suffering servant of Isaiah (Phil. 2:6-11). Peter teaches that the sinless Lord suffered silently, bearing the sins of others so they might be forgiven (1 Pet. 2:22-25; 3:18).

Bibliography. J. Jeremias, *The Eucharistic Words of Jesus* (Philadelphia, 1990); H. H. Rowley, *The Servant of the Lord,* 2nd ed. (Oxford, 1965); W. Zimmerli and J. Jeremias. "país theoú," *TDNT* 5:654-717.

William B. Nelson, Jr.

SETH (Heb. *šēṯ;* Gk. *Sḗth*)
The third son of Adam and Eve, born to replace his older brother Abel who was murdered by Cain (Gen. 4:25; 5:3). Seth was the father of Enosh and the ancestor of Noah (Gen. 5:6-7; 1 Chr. 1:1; Luke 3:38). Sir. 49:16 refers to Seth and Shem as "honored among men."

SETHUR (Heb. *sēṯûr*)
An Asherite, the son of Michael. He was one of the 12 spies sent into Canaan (Num. 13:13).

SETTLEMENT: ARCHAEOLOGY
As the discipline of Palestinian archaeology developed in the 1920s-1930s, at least in the guise of "biblical archaeology," it inevitably became embroiled in a historiographical and theological controversy that had long been crucial in biblical studies: Is there any *historical* evidence for the biblical "Exodus" or "conquest of Canaan"?

Conventional Models

In the formative period two classic "models" advanced by biblical scholars to explain Israelite origins began to be subjected to archaeological testing: (1) The first envisioned the "peaceful infiltration" of pastoral nomads, first forwarded by Albrecht Alt, Martin Noth, and other Continental scholars. (2) The "invasion hypothesis" was based largely on the book of Joshua and was advocated by the "Baltimore school" of William F. Albright, John Bright, G. Ernest Wright, and others. The first model accorded reasonably well with the "nomadic ideal" of some strands of the patriarchal narratives, but it turned out to be naïve ethnographically and never found any archaeological confirmation, since pastoral nomads characteristically leave few traces in the archaeological record. The second model relied on a rather literalistic and exclusive reading of

Joshua, as well as positivist notions of archaeological "proofs" of historiographical (not to mention theological) issues that were current at the time.

By the 1960s-1970s, as Palestinian archaeology began to mature as a professional and largely secular discipline, it became apparent that neither traditional model of Israelite origins could be sustained in the light of the growing body of archaeological evidence. By the 1980s, e.g., the "invasion" model had been almost completely discredited by the fact that Jericho, 'Ai, and Gibeon — all central to the Conquest accounts in Joshua — had been shown not to have had any occupation in the mid-late 13th century B.C.E., which the narratives would have required as a historical setting. To sum matters up, of the 16 Canaanite sites claimed to have been destroyed by Joshua's forces, a number have been identified and/or excavated, but only two — Bethel and Hazor — have produced any possible evidence for an "Israelite destruction," and even that is debatable.

In the 1960s-1970s, two American biblical scholars, George E. Mendenhall and Norman K. Gottwald, put forward versions of a "peasants' revolt" model, in which "Israel" was seen as emerging out of the collapse of Late Bronze Age Canaanite society in the 13th-12th centuries. The picture was of various groups of peoples "displaced" both geographically and ideologically, and in process of developing a new ethnic and religio-cultural identity in the Early Iron Age. The emphasis on indigenous rather than foreign derivation turned out to be prescient. But little real archaeological evidence of "peasants' wars" in the Late Bronze/Iron I period was forthcoming then or subsequently, and in any case the model was too Marxist to attract wide support.

New Models

By the 1980s, a wealth of new archaeological data had begun to accumulate, which required more sophisticated attempts at explanatory models. Much of the new data came from surface surveys carried out by Israeli archaeologists in the occupied West Bank — "Judea" and "Samaria," the heartland of early Israel. These data were first synthesized and presented in English by Israel Finkelstein in 1988 in *The Archaeology of the Israelite Settlement.* This volume described some 300 late 13th-11th century (or Iron I) small unwalled villages, most of which were in the hill country extending from the lower Galilee to the northern Negeb, located not on the ruins of destroyed Canaanite cities but founded *de novo.* The ceramic repertoire was still recognizably in the Late Bronze Age tradition, but absent were either imported wares or Philistine bichrome pottery. On the other hand, elements of cultural discontinuity were seen in new technologies, including extensive hillside terracing; the widespread use of plastered cisterns and stone-lined silos; the gradual introduction of iron implements; and the development of an innovative "four-room" courtyard house well suited to the needs of a family-based agricultural society and economy.

The most significant implication of the new data was that there had been a large-scale shift in settlement type and pattern with the transition from the Late Bronze Age to the early Iron Age — a move, as it were, from declining urban sites and life-styles to the "hill country frontier," and *perhaps* to a new cultural and ethnic identity (as Mendenhall and Gottwald thought). It has been estimated that in the Samarian and Judean hill country the population grew from ca. 12 thousand in the 13th century to ca. 40 thousand in the 12th century, then to ca. 75 thousand by the late 11th century — a demographic change that cannot be attributed to natural birthrates, but must reflect a major influx of new population elements. The only questions then concerned the origins and hopefully the ethnic identity of these newcomers.

The marked ceramic continuity with the Late Bronze Age repertoire suggested to nearly all archaeologists indigenous (i.e., "Canaanite") origins for the hill country settlers. Finkelstein, however, saw them as mostly local pastoral nomads in the process of sedentarization; his fellow surveyor Adam Zertal agreed on nomadic origins, but argued strongly for a movement of peoples from Transjordan (along the lines of the old Alt-Noth hypothesis).

In a series of studies, William G. Dever proposed that the hill country settlers had comprised a motley collection of urban dropouts, displaced peasant farmers, refugees from various strata of decaying Canaanite society, a few local pastoral nomads (such as the "Shasu" of Egyptian texts), and perhaps even some newcomers from Egypt. "Early Israel" would then have made up one element within an exceedingly complex multiethnic society in 13th-12th century Canaan, including Canaanites, Egyptians, "Sea Peoples"/Philistines, and others (all not only textually documented, but ethnically identifiable in the archaeological remains). Dever suggested connecting the distinctive *hill country* Iron I material culture assemblage with the "Israel" of Pharaoh Merneptah's well-known Victory stela (ca. 1207), but to separate the group involved from *biblical* Israel by designating them "Proto-Israelites." Finkelstein initially agreed, but by the early 1990s he had come to question any ethnic identification whatsoever. Despite such disagreements, today all archaeologists and most biblical scholars are agreed upon some variation of an "indigenous origin" or "symbiosis" model for the Iron I peoples of central Canaan. Yet it must be asked: If these are not Merneptah's "Israelites," where *are* they? And who *were* the authentic progenitors of the "Israel" that all would agree had emerged by the early Monarchy in the 10th-9th centuries?

The "minimalist" position would be that of Finkelstein currently, along with the minority "revisionist" biblical schools of Philip R. Davies, Niels P. Lemche, Thomas L. Thompson, and Keith W. Whitelam. The "maximalist" position, if there is one, would have to espouse some sort of large-scale military conquest by incoming Israelites from Transjordan, or even ultimately from Egypt, for which there is simply no archaeological evidence. The present treatment has tried to outline a middle-ground position, representing a growing consensus of scholars of several different schools, including virtually all archaeologists.

Toward a Theological Rationalization?

There remains only the problem created for biblical history and theology by the newer archaeological formulations, namely how to account for the fundamental and persistent stories of "exodus from Egypt" and "conquest of Canaan," if the earliest Israelites had originally been elements of Late Bronze Age Canaanite society. Most archaeologists have simply ignored the biblical traditions as unhistorical, or else have offered halfhearted and theologically naïve rationalizations. A more sophisticated attempt to reconcile the two sources of data for history writing (i.e., texts and artifacts) might see the biblical stories as originating from within the clan traditions of the "house of Joseph." Elements of these small groups, later identified with the tribes of Benjamin and Judah, may actually have come out of Egypt. When they told their "story," it was one of miraculous liberation from bondage and victory over the enemies of Yahweh. And in time, because these southern groups had a disproportionate influence on the shaping of the literary traditions in the OT in their final form, this version of distant origins became the story of "all Israel." Thus the Exodus and Conquest narratives must be taken seriously, at least as a sort of "Passover Haggadah," true theologically if not historically, and therefore preserved and even celebrated today.

See Conquest: Biblical Narrrative.

Bibliography. R. B. Coote and K. W. Whitelam, *The Emergence of Early Israel in Historical Perspective* (Sheffield, 1987); W. G. Dever, "Archaeology and the Emergence of Early Israel," in *Archaeology and Biblical Interpretation,* ed. J. R. Bartlett (London, 1997), 20-50; "Ceramics, Ethnicity, and the Question of Israel's Origins," *BA* 58 (1995): 200-213; "The Identity of Early Israel," *JSOT* 72 (1996): 3-24; I. Finkelstein, *The Archaeology of the Israelite Settlement* (Jerusalem, 1988); "Pots and People Revisited: Ethnic Boundaries in the Iron Age I," in *The Archaeology of Israel,* ed. N. A. Silberman and D. Small (Sheffield, 1997), 216-37; Finkelstein and N. Na'aman, eds., *From Nomadism to Monarchy: Archaeological and Historical Aspects of Early Israel* (Washington, 1994); V. Fritz, "Conquest of Settlement? The Early Iron Age in Palestine," *BA* 50 (1987): 84-100; N. K. Gottwald, *The Tribes of Yahweh* (Maryknoll, 1979); G. E. Mendenhall, "The Hebrew Conquest of Palestine," *BA* 25 (1962): 66-87 (repr. *BA Reader* 3, ed. E. F. Campbell and D. N. Freedman [Garden City, 1970], 100-120); L. E. Stager, "The Archaeology of the Family in Ancient Israel," *BASOR* 260 (1985): 1-35.

William G. Dever

SEVEN, THE

A designation for the seven men (Gk. *hoi heptá*) appointed by the Church and ordained by the apostles to "wait on tables" (NRSV mg "keep accounts") and minister to the widows (Acts 6:1-6; cf. 21:8).

See Deacon.

SEVEN WORDS, THE

The sayings of Jesus uttered while he was on the Cross. The traditional order of the seven recorded "words" is (1) "Father, forgive them; for they do not know what they are doing" (Luke 23:34); (2) to one of those being crucified with him, "Truly, I tell you, today you will be with me in Paradise" (v. 43); (3) to Mary his mother and "the disciple whom he loved," "Woman, here is your son" and "Here is your mother" (John 19:26-27); (4) "Eli, Eli, lema sabachthani?" (Matt. 27:46 = Mark 15:34); (5) "I am thirsty" (John 19:28); (6) "It is finished" (v. 30); and (7) "Father, into your hands I commend my spirit" (Luke 23:46).

SEX

When investigating the attitude toward sexual intercourse in ancient Israel, it is important not to impose modern assumptions about sexuality on an ancient culture.

In ancient Israelite thought humans have been given a sexual desire to create life through the production of children (Gen. 3:16), so sexual intercourse establishes people's tie to God who is the perpetuator of life (implied by the name Yahweh) and to nature. Although the full meaning of the word "Yahweh" is not known, some scholars feel that the name is related to the causative (hiphil) future (imperfect) of the verb "to be or exist." Since this Hebrew tense implies a flow from the present into the future, the causative imperfect would suggest that God sustains and perpetuates being/existence from the present onward. Consequently, because sexual intercourse ties people to the divine, its power is highly valued and considered the greatest power that humans possess. The idea of sex being inherently dirty is out of the question. Male and female sexual roles follow the patterns of nature where the male is the "fertilizer" and the female is the "producer," so through sexual intercourse humans participate in the flow of God's creation.

In small agricultural communities which require abundant and intense labor (such as ancient Israel), sexual intercourse is central for the physical survival of the household and the overall society. Because individuals have a sense of the continuation of their lives through children, sexual intercourse is central for their psychological sense of salvation. Women, as the "co-producers" of children with Yahweh (cf. Gen. 4:1), are the co-producers of salvation; there is no greater power, no greater functioning in this kind of society. Therefore, women have significant power and value within the society. Because women receive social status from the number of children they produce, they are sexually aggressive (e.g., Tamar or Ruth). But sexual intercourse is also a threatening power, in that it can produce either life (birth) or death of the infant and/or mother in childbirth. So sexual intercourse embodies both the risk and the pleasure of life; it entails living fully and authentically.

In Hebrew Scripture sex has two primary functions: the production of progeny which lead to salvation, and the creation of the strong ties or oneness which are essential for holding the household and the community together. Sex is the physical bonding together of what appears physically different in order to produce life, suggesting that the uniting of opposites is both creative and essential to the divine life process. In Gen. 1 God creates by separating what is different in the original chaos, but in Gen. 2:24 sexual intercourse reunites what is separate and different into a physical (a child) and psychological unity. Likewise, the oneness between Israel and God is often envisioned in terms of the sexual bonding of marriage. Sexual intercourse is associated with love, which in the OT is perceived in physical and psychological terms as the bonding together of different things in oneness.

Sexual intercourse is a boundary crossing that requires the relaxing of the boundaries that the ego uses to define its identity and as a defense mechanism. In sex, identity and defense mechanisms are penetrated or enveloped. This is symbolized in the OT by the association of sex with nakedness, which entails the removal of the protective barrier of culturally prescribed clothing. Nakedness exposes people's vulnerability, both the vulnerable parts of the body, the genitals (the site of fundamental human power critical to continued life), and the vulnerable self deprived of its artificial ego defenses. But when humans do not relax ego boundaries and defenses in intimate relationships with one another, they can become barriers to intimate, genuine love and oneness. If people cannot loosen these barriers with one another, most probably they will not be able to loosen them in relationship with God. Because of the association of sexual intercourse with intimacy, it is also connected to "knowing," which encompasses broad intellectual, experiential, and sexual knowing. Since sexual intercourse involves boundary crossing, vulnerability, intimacy, and oneness, it should entail "knowing" a person in the fullest sense.

Since sexual intercourse is a critical yet threatening power that impacts the life/salvation of the household, it must be used with great care and control. For example, the male is to "control" the female's sexual desire (Gen. 3:17) because it can produce either life or death and because if it is used outside the household or society, it squanders the salvific power of the group and "builds the house" of outsiders. But the word "control" (Heb. *māšal*) connotes a noncoercive power that encourages and enhances potential within limitation. So the male's control of the female's sexual desire is set within the context of potential not being unlimited and limitation not destroying potential.

There is also casual sex or sex that does not create marital or family bonding and obligation (e.g., Deut. 22:28-29) or that violates existing marital or family bonding and obligation (e.g., vv. 23-24). This kind of sex is considered foolish and shameful, an "inadequacy" or "failure" to live up to internalized, societal goals and ideals because it violates the purpose of sex and therefore does not participate in the divine life process. Thus the prostitute is tolerated, but her sexual activity is marginal because it does not create bonding and does not build the household or community. Rape, which entails a man overpowering a woman, who cries out for help but with no one to rescue her, is a hostile, exploitative crime against a woman and society (e.g., Deut. 22:25-27; 2 Sam. 13:11-14). This kind of sexual activity is usually employed for purposes of building the individual ego with power and control, not for building the community. Sexual intercourse in ancient Israel is intended to be an activity that builds the community first and therein fills the needs of the individual.

LYN M. BECHTEL

SHAALBIM (Heb. *šaʿalbîm*)
(also SHAALABBIN)

A city allotted to the tribe of Dan (Josh. 19:42; "Shaalabbin"). Though the Danites were unable to capture the city, its Amorite inhabitants subsequently were subjected to forced labor by "the house of Joseph" (Ephraim; Judg. 1:35). Later it was included in Solomon's second administrative district (1 Kgs. 4:9). Shaalbim is likely to be equated with Shaalbon, hometown of Eliahba, one of David's Thirty (2 Sam. 23:32; 1 Chr. 11:33). As has Shual, it has also been associated by some with the "land of Shaalim" through which Saul passed in search of his donkeys (1 Sam. 9:4). Archaeologists identify Shaalbim with modern Selbît/Tel Shaʿalevim (148141), 5 km. (3 mi.) NW of Aijalon.

ERIC F. MASON

SHAALBON (Heb. *šaʿaləḇōn*)

The home of Eliahba, one of David's Mighty Men (2 Sam. 23:32 = 1 Chr. 11:33). The name occurs as the Hebrew gentilic *hašaaʿalbōnî,* perhaps derived from Shaalbim, Shaalabbin.

SHAALIM (Heb. *šaʿălîm*)

A region of unknown location, probably near a border of Benjaminite territory and perhaps named after a city or a prominent natural landmark. Saul and a servant passed through this region while looking for Kish's asses (1 Sam. 9:4). It is generally associated with Shaalbim, Shaalabbin, but a connection with Shual N of Bethel is also possible.

SHAAPH (Heb. *šaʿaḇ*)

1. A son of Jahdai; a Judahite and descendant of Caleb (1 Chr. 2:47).

2. A son of Maacah and Caleb; father (founder) of Madmannah (1 Chr. 2:49).

SHAARAIM (Heb. *šaʿărayim*)

1. A town in the Shephelah, or lowland, of Judah and part of that tribe's inheritance (Josh. 15:36). It is located in the northern part of the valley of Elah, NW of Socoh and Azekah. After David conquered Goliath, the Israelites chased the Philistines from the valley of Elah northwestward toward Gath and Ekron via the road to Shaaraim (1 Sam. 17:52; LXX ". . . the wounded of the Philistines fell on the road of the gates to Gath and to Ekron" is not widely accepted). Khirbet es-Saʿîreh, ESE of Beth-shemesh, has been proposed as the site, but a location further west seems more likely.

2. A Negeb town in the tribal inheritance of Simeon (1 Chr. 4:31). The parallel list in Josh. 19:6 does not mention Shaaraim, but includes Sharuhen; 15:32, which lists towns in the Judean Negeb, includes Shilhim but not Shaaraim or Sharuhen. These may represent three separate sites, two sites, or three different names for the same location, but most likely the variations reflect different political or historical situations. Most likely Shaaraim is to be linked with Sharuhen because the lists in 1 Chr. 4; Josh. 19 are so similar in other respects. Alternatively, the use of Sharuhen may be based on an Egyptian transcription of Shilhim which was later corrupted to Shaaraim, which suggests there was only one Negeb site. Sharuhen is commonly identified with Tell el-Far'ah (South; 100076) or Tell el-Ajjul (0934.0976), both located along the southern bank of Naḥal Besor.

Bibliography. Y. Aharoni, *The Land of the Bible*, 2nd ed. (Philadelphia, 1979); S. Ahituv, *Canaanite Toponyms in Ancient Egyptian Documents* (Jerusalem, 1984); N. Na'aman, "The Kingdom of Judah under Josiah," *Tel Aviv* 18 (1991): 3-71; A. F. Rainey, "The Administrative Division of the Shephelah," *Tel Aviv* 7 (1980): 194-202; "The Biblical Shephelah of Judah," *BASOR* 251 (1983): 1-22.

JENNIFER L. GROVES

SHAASHGAZ (Heb. *ša'ašgaz*)
A eunuch in the court of King Ahasuerus who was in charge of the king's second harem (Esth. 2:14).

SHABBETHAI (Heb. *šabbĕṯay;* Gk. *Sabbataíos*)
The name of three postexilic Levites, possibly all the same person.

1. One who opposed Ezra's solution to the problem of mixed marriages (Ezra 10:15) or, perhaps, assisted in carrying it out (so 1 Esdr. 9:14).

2. A Levite who interpreted the law for the people while Ezra read it (Neh. 8:7).

3. A chief of the Levites who supervised the outside work of the temple (Neh. 11:16).

SHADES

See REPHAIM.

SHADRACH (Heb. *šaḏraḵ*)
The name (cf. Akk. *Šudur-Aku*, "command of Aku [a Mesopotamian lunar deity]") given by King Nebuchadnezzar's chief eunuch to Hananiah, one of Daniel's companions (Dan. 1:7; 2:49; ch. 3).

See ABEDNEGO.

SHAGEE (Heb. *šāgēh, šāgē'*)
A Hararite; father of Jonathan, one of David's Thirty (1 Chr. 11:34). The parallel account at 2 Sam. 23:32-33 reads "Jonathan son of Shammah the Hararite" (LXX; cf. v. 11, "Shammah son of Agee, the Hararite").

SHAHARAIM (Heb. *šaḥărayim*)
A Benjaminite living in Moab who had numerous offspring and who sent away two of his wives (1 Chr. 8:8-11).

SHAHAZUMAH (Heb. K *šaḥăṣûmâ*, Q *šaḥăṣîmâ)*
A city on the border of Issachar's tribal territory (Josh. 19:22). Various sites have been suggested between Tabor and Beth-shemesh.

SHALISHAH (Heb. *šālišâ*)
A region through which Saul and a servant passed while looking for his father's lost asses (1 Sam. 9:4). Little is certain about the location of this region. Baal-shalishah (2 Kgs. 4:42), midway between modern Tel Aviv and Nablus, may have been located there.

SHALLUM (Heb. *šallûm, šallūm*)
(also MESHULLAM, SHILLEM)

1. King of Israel who overthrew Zechariah and ended the dynasty of Jehu (2 Kgs. 15:10, 13). His one-month reign ca. 750 B.C.E. signaled the beginning of a period of chaos leading to the fall of the northern kingdom to Assyria in 722. Hosea speaks both of the fall of the house of Jehu (Hos. 1:4) and of such assassinations (7:7), and Shallum himself was soon struck down by Menahem, who may have been a rival already at the murder of Zechariah.

Nothing is known of Shallum's background. The identification "son of Jabesh" may be a geographic rather than patronymic designation, indicating that the coup against Zechariah (and Samaria in general) began in Transjordan (cf. Pekah, who came from this area).

2. The husband of Huldah the prophetess (2 Kgs. 22:14) and son of Tikvah. 2 Chr. 34:22 identifies him as the son of Tokhath.

3. A descendant of Judah, son of Sismai and father of Jekamiah (1 Chr. 2:40-41).

4. The fourth son of Josiah (1 Chr. 3:15), who succeeded his father to the throne of Judah in 609 (Jer. 22:11) and took the throne name Jehoahaz (2 Kgs. 23:30; 2 Chr. 36:1). He reigned for three months, when he was deposed and removed from Jerusalem by Pharaoh Neco (2 Kgs. 23:33-34), who replaced him with his brother Eliakim (Jehoiakim).

5. A descendant of Simeon, son of Shaul and father of Mibsam (1 Chr. 4:24-25).

6. The son of Zadok and father of Hilkiah, listed among the descendants of Levi through Kohath, Amram, Aaron, and Eleazar (1 Chr. 6:12-13[5:38-39]). Ezra 7:2 includes him in the genealogy of Ezra. He is called Meshullam at 1 Chr. 9:11.

7. A son of Naphtali (1 Chr. 7:13), called Shillem in Gen. 46:24; Num. 26:49.

8. Chief of the gatekeepers and descendant of the Korahites, listed in 1 Chr. 9:17-19 among those who returned first from Babylon. Ezra 2:42 = Neh. 7:45 lists the gatekeepers as "sons of Shallum" (and others). According to 1 Chr. 9:19 Shallum held the important post at the eastern Kings' Gate, through which the king would enter the temple (Ezek. 46:1-2).

9. The father of Jehizkiah, an Ephraimite leader opposed to the subjugation of Judean captives taken in the Syro-Ephraimite attack on Jerusalem (2 Chr. 28:12).

10. A levitical gatekeeper among those in the postexilic community required to divorce their foreign wives (Ezra 10:24).

11. One of the sons of Bannui listed in Ezra 10:42 among those who had married a foreign wife at the time of Ezra.

12. The son of Hallohesh, a high-ranking Jerusalem district official who with his daughters helped repair the walls of Jerusalem at the time of Nehemiah (Neh. 3:12).

13. The son of Col-hozeh, the ruler of Mizpeh, who helped repair the walls and gates of Jerusalem at the time of Nehemiah (Neh. 3:15).

14. The father of Maaseiah, doorkeeper of the temple when Jeremiah brought the Rechabites there as an object lesson on obedience (Jer. 5:4).

15. Jeremiah's uncle (Jer. 32:7), whose son Hanamel sold the field at their family's hometown Anathoth to Jeremiah. ANDREW H. BARTELT

SHALMAI (Heb. *šalmay*) (also SHAMLAI)
The ancestor of a family of temple servants who returned from exile in Babylonia (Neh. 7:48). Ezra 2:46 records a variant reading, "Shamlai" (Heb. *šamlay*).

SHALMAN (Heb. *šalman*)
A name appearing in an allusion to an apparently well-known battle in which Beth-arbel was destroyed (Hos. 10:14). Possible identifications include Shalmaneser V of Assyria who attacked Samaria in 722 B.C.E., Shalmaneser III who invaded Israel in 841, and the 8th-century Moabite king Shalmanu, whose assault on Gilead was roughly contemporaneous with Hosea.

SHALMANESER (Heb. *šalman'eser;* Akk. *šulmānu-ašarid*)

1. Shalmaneser I, king of Assyria 1274-1245 B.C.E.; son of Adad-nirari I. He conquered Hanigalbat (the remnant of Mitanni), deporting its populace, and subdued the formative confederation of Urartu. Kalhu (biblical Calah) was founded during his reign.

2. Shalmaneser II (1031-1020), son of Asshurnasirpal I.

3. Shalmaneser III (858-824), son and successor of Assurnasirpal II, the first great king and founder of the Neo-Assyrian Empire. When Shalmaneser succeeded his father, he continued his father's expansionistic policy, but concentrated his attention on the north and west. Written sources from his reign are numerous, including the eponym chronicle, annalistic texts, and reliefs with accompanying inscriptions.

Shalmaneser's northern campaigns were focused on the kingdom of Urartu, penetrating the heartland of Urartu as early as 856. In the latter part of his reign he conducted a number of other Assyrian campaigns in the region, but these campaigns were led by by his *turtanu,* Dayyan-ashur, rather than the king himself.

Shalmaneser's advance into the west began in his first regnal year. In a number of successive campaigns he was able to crush Bit-adini and annex it to the Assyrian Empire. His campaigns west of the Euphrates were presumably conducted to establish dominance over the trade routes and to set up trade colonies in the region. In several of these campaigns Shalmaneser was confronted by western coalitions, including the formidable Syro-Palestinian coalition of 12 states headed by Hadadezer of Aram-Damascus and Irḫuleni of Hamath. Ahab of Israel was also an important participant in the coalition. According to his annals, Shalmaneser fought this coalition in 853, 849, 848, and 845. The first of these confrontations was the battle of Qarqar in 853, recorded in detail in the Kurkh Monolith inscription (*ANET,* 278-79). With northern Syria firmly under his control, Shalmaneser turned his attention to central Syria, where he plundered and burned three of Irḫuleni's cities. He then advanced against the royal city of Qarqar on the Orontes. Following that city's destruction, the Assyrian army was confronted with the Syro-Palestinian coalition. According to the Assyrian inscription, Ahab of Israel is noted to have supplied 2000 chariots (more than any of the partners) and 10 thousand soldiers (figures intended to exaggerate the military size of Assyria's enemy while also claiming their devastating defeat). Lack of any further movement of the Assyrian army beyond Qarqar calls into question this grandiose claim; more likely the coalition was able to thwart the Assyrian advance into the region. Accounts of the other campaigns (*ANET,* 279-80) report Shalmaneser's confronting Hadadezer of Aram-Damascus, Irḫuleni of Hamath, and the 12 kings of the seacoast and accomplishing their defeat. This, however, is doubtful, since he never seems to have pushed farther westward than just beyond the Orontes.

Not until 841 was Shalmaneser able to establish a strong Assyrian presence in Syria-Palestine. On this campaign in his 18th year, he marched beyond the Orontes and encountered only the forces of Aram-Damascus. The account of this campaign mentions Hazael rather than Hadadezer as king of Aram-Damascus; Irḫuleni, in earlier texts a coleader of the coalition, does not appear, nor do the "12 kings of the seacoast"; and now tribute is paid by Tyre, Sidon, and Jehu of Israel. From this one can infer the dissolution of the coalition, perhaps precipitated by the dynastic change in Aram-Damascus. In another text of Shalmaneser III, Hazael is referred to as "the son of a nobody," not as a descendant of Hadadezer. Like other states, Tyre, Sidon, and Israel evidently altered their foreign policies and submitted to the Assyrians. Hamath may have done the same, thereby allowing the Assyrian army passage through its territory without any resistance. A final western campaign was conducted in 838, primarily to deal with Hazael of Aram-Damascus.

4. Shalmaneser IV (782-773), son of Adad-nirari III. Most of his reign was devoted to defense against the encroaching Urartians.

5. Shalmaneser V (726-722), son and successor

of Tiglath-pileser III. 2 Kgs. 17:1-6; 18:9-12 remember him as the king who laid siege to Samaria, which according to the Babylonian Chronicle was his only achievement of any consequence. He is perhaps the Shalman mentioned in Hos. 10:14. According to 2 Kgs. 17:3 Shalmaneser led a campaign against Israel (probably in the beginning of his reign), and Hoshea submitted and paid tribute. However, Hoshea soon rebelled and sent representatives to Egypt to request assistance (2 Kgs. 17:4a). In response to the revolt, Shalmaneser launched another campaign against Samaria and arrested Hoshea. Eventually, the Assyrian invaded Israel and put Samaria under siege for three years (2 Kgs. 17:5; 18:9). The city finally fell to the Assyrians in 722-721 and segments of the population were taken into exile in Assyria (2 Kgs. 17:6; 18:10-11). Questions have arisen whether Shalmaneser V was responsible for the capture of Samaria and the deportation of Israelites, since 2 Kgs. 17:5-6 does not mention the Assyrian king by name. One view suggests that it was Shalmaneser who captured Samaria but that his successor Sargon II deported the Israelites. A second view suggests that Shalmaneser was only responsible for attacking Hoshea, arresting him, and deporting him; it was Sargon II (the Assyrian king mentioned in 2 Kgs. 17:5-6) who besieged Samaria and conquered it, and deported the Israelites. A third view, on the basis of a straightforward reading of 2 Kgs. 17:3-6, argues that only one Assyrian king, Shalmaneser V, is intended throughout.

Bibliography. M. Elat, "The Campaigns of Shalmaneser III against Aram and Israel," *IEJ* 25 (1975): 25-35; G. Galil, "The Last Years of the Kingdom of Israel and the Fall of Samaria," *CBQ* 57 (1995): 52-65; J. H. Hayes and J. K. Kuan, "The Final Years of Samaria (730-720 B.C.)," *Bibl* 72 (1991): 153-81.

JEFFREY K. KUAN

SHAMA (Heb. *šāmāʿ*)
A son of Hotham the Aroerite; one of David's Mighty Men (1 Chr. 11:44).

SHAMGAR (Heb. *šamgar*)
The "son of Anath" (perhaps from Beth-anath in Galilee or a follower of the goddess Anath), probably a mercenary who delivered Israel by killing 600 Philistines with an ox goad (Judg. 3:31). In "the days of Shamgar" (perhaps Hurrian *Shimig-ari*, "Shimike [a deity] gave"), travelers had to keep to secondary routes and caravans were impossible because of raiders (Judg. 5:6).

SHAMHUTH (Heb. *šamhûṯ*)
An Izrahite, commander of the fifth division of David's army (1 Chr. 27:8). He is sometimes identified with Shammah (**4;** 2 Sam. 23:25)/Shammoth (1 Chr. 11:27) of Harod.

SHAMIR (Heb. *šāmîr*) **(PERSON)**
A Kohathite Levite, the son of Micah (**4;** 1 Chr. 24:24; cf. 23:12, 20).

SHAMIR (Heb. *šāmîr*) **(PLACE)**

1. A town in the hill country of southwest Judah, one of 38 towns inherited by the tribe of Judah (Josh. 15:48). Located in the same district as Debir, the site may be modern el-Bîreh. Other possible locations include Khirbet es-Sumara (143092), 20 km. (12 mi.) WSW of Hebron, or Khirbet Raddana on the northern side of modern Ramallah (1695.1468).

2. A town in the hill country of Ephraim, where the minor judge Tola lived and was buried (Judg. 10:1-2).

AARON M. GALE

SHAMLAI (Heb. *šamlay*) (also SHALMAI)
The head or ancestor of a family of temple servants who returned from the Exile (Ezra 2:46). Neh. 7:48 reads "Shalmai."

SHAMMA (Heb. *šammāʾ*)
An Asherite, son of Zopha (1 Chr. 7:37).

SHAMMAH (Heb. *šammâ*) (also SHIMEA, SHIMEAH, SHIMEI, SHAMMOTH)

1. A descendant of Esau, and a chief in Edom (Gen. 36:13, 17; 1 Chr. 1:37).

2. The third son of Jesse, an elder brother of David, and the father of Jonadab (1 Sam. 16:9; 17:13). He is also known as Shimeah (**1;** 2 Sam. 13:3, 32), Shimea (**1;** 1 Chr. 2:13; 20:7), and Shimei (**3;** 2 Sam. 21:21).

3. One of the leading members of David's Mighty Men, the son of Agee the Hararite (2 Sam. 23:11-12, 33; cf. 1 Chr. 11:34).

4. Shammah of Harod, one of David's Mighty Men (2 Sam. 23:25); also known as Shammoth (1 Chr. 11:27).

JOHN R. HUDDLESTUN

SHAMMAI (Heb. *šammay*)

1. A Judahite, a son of Onam and father of Nadab and Abishur (1 Chr. 2:28).

2. A Judahite, son of Rekem and father of Maon (1 Chr. 2:44-45).

3. A son of the Judahite Mered and Bithiah the daughter of Pharaoh (1 Chr. 4:17).

SHAMMOTH (Heb. *šammôṯ*)
Alternate name of Shammah (**4;** 1 Chr. 11:27).

SHAMMUA (Heb. *šammûaʿ*) (also SHEMAIAH, SHIMEA)

1. The son of Zaccur; the Reubenite chosen to spy out Canaan (Num. 13:4).

2. One of the sons born to David at Jerusalem (2 Sam. 5:14). At 1 Chr. 3:5 he is called Shimea (**1**).

3. The father of Abda, a postexilic Levite (Neh. 11:17). In the account at 1 Chr. 9:16 he appears as Shemaiah (**6**).

4. The head of the priestly family of Bilgah at the time of the postexilic high priest Joiakim (Neh. 12:18).

GREGORY D. JORDAN

SHAMSHERAI (Heb. *šamšĕray*)
A son of Jehoram; head of a Benjaminite family dwelling in postexilic Jerusalem (1 Chr. 8:26).

SHAPHAM (Heb. *šāpām*)
A leader of the tribe of Gad living in Bashan, son of Abihail (1 Chr. 5:12).

SHAPHAN (Heb. *šāpān*)

1. The son of Aziliah; a scribe to King Josiah (2 Kgs. 22:9; 2 Chr. 34:15). His grandfather Meshullam and three of his sons — Ahikam, Elasah, and Gemariah — were also scribes (2 Kgs. 22:3, 12; Jer. 29:3; 36:10). Shaphan's grandson Gedaliah was appointed by Nebuchadnezzar as governor of Judah after the fall of Jerusalem (2 Kgs. 25:22).

Josiah commissioned Shaphan to distribute wages to workers who were renovating the Jerusalem temple in 622 B.C.E. While Shaphan was at the temple, the workers discovered "the book of the law." Hilkiah the high priest gave the book to Shaphan, who read it to Josiah. Josiah tore his clothes when he heard the words of the law and commanded Shappan and a number of others to take the book to Huldah the prophetess to verify its authenticity as the word of the Lord (2 Kgs. 22:13-20; 2 Chr. 34:20-30). Josiah then instituted cultic reforms to purify the worship of Yahweh at the Jerusalem temple (2 Kgs. 23).

2. The father of Jaazaniah (Ezek. 8:11), one of the 70 elders whom in a vision Ezekiel saw committing idolatrous acts in the temple in Jerusalem (vv. 10-12). This Shaphan may be the same as **1** above, but, if so, Jaazaniah has departed from the beliefs of his father.

NANCY L. DE CLAISSÉ-WALFORD

SHAPHAT (Heb. *šāpāṭ*)

1. One of the 12 Israelite spies sent into Canaan, the son of Hori of the tribe of Simeon (Num. 13:5).

2. The father of the prophet Elisha (1 Kgs. 19:16, 19-20; 2 Kgs. 3:11; 6:31).

3. A son of Shemaiah and descendant of Zerubbabel (1 Chr. 3:22).

4. A Gadite leader who lived in Bashan, son of Abihail (1 Chr. 5:12).

5. The son of Adlai; overseer of David's cattle "in the valleys" (1 Chr. 27:29).

SHAPHIR (Heb. *šāpîr*)
A city probably located in the Philistine Plain, mentioned in Mic. 1:11 along with a number of other cities destroyed by Sennacherib in his march from the southwest toward Jerusalem. Micah appears to play on the names of the cities, to emphasize the destruction brought by the enemy. That Sennacherib destroyed Shaphir ("glittering" or "beautiful") heightens his crime. Perhaps, too, the word is a play on Heb. *šôpār,* and the prophet calls on the inhabitants of Shaphir to sound the alarm.

RICHARD A. SPENCER

SHARAI (Heb. *šāray*)
One of the sons of Binnui among those required by Ezra to divorce their foreign wives (Ezra 10:40).

SHARAR (Heb. *šārār*) (also SACHAR)
A Hararite and the father of Ahiam, one of David's Thirty (2 Sam. 23:33). He is called Sachar at 1 Chr. 11:35).

SHAREZER (Heb. *śar'eṣer*)

1. One of the two sons of Sennacherib who murdered the Assyrian king (2 Kgs. 19:37 = Isa. 37:38), plunging the empire into a short dynastic crisis until the youngest son, Esarhaddon, returned from exile and assumed the throne in 680 B.C.E. Other than the Bible, however, there is no Mesopotamian source for the names of these sons, although the murder of Sennacherib at the hand of his own sons is apparently historical (Nabonidus inscription; *ANET,* 309). Based on the construction of Akkadian names, Sharezer here is only a partial name ("[The God X] protect the king" = *šar-uṣur*), and a divine name should be included (e.g., Nebu, thus Nebusharezer).

2. One of the emissaries sent by the people of Bethel in 518 to ask about continuing to fast (more frequent fasting was instituted after the Exile; Zech. 7:2). Many scholars suggest that the text should actually read Bethelsharezer, "May Bethel (the deity) protect the King."

DANIEL L. SMITH-CHRISTOPHER

SHARON (Heb. *šārôn*)
A fertile coastal region in Palestine ("plain" or "level country"). Ca. 80 km. (50 mi.) long by 16 km. (10 mi.) wide, it extends north along the Mediterranean from Joppa to south of Mt. Carmel. A caravan route ran along this maritime plain in ancient times connecting Mesopotamia and Asia Minor with Egypt. 1 Chr. 5:16 locates the "pastureland of Sharon" E of the Jordan River; one interpretation equates this reference to pastures near Mt. Hermon, while an alternative rendering views Sharon as a reference to the tableland of Gilead.

The first undisputed biblical reference to the plain of Sharon is found in 1 Chr. 27:29, where Shitrai the Sharonite is cited for overseeing David's herds that grazed in Sharon. Figurative references to the area include the rose of Sharon, a metaphor for unsurpassed beauty (Cant. 2:1). Also, the status of the plain of Sharon, either parched or flourishing, symbolizes in Isa. 33:9; 35:2; 65:10 the spiritual state of Israel.

The "Lasharon" associated with a defeated king in Josh. 12:18 is most likely a reference to the plain of Sharon. Sharon (Gk. *Sarōn*) at Acts 9:35 is the same, as evidenced by its association with the town of Lydda.

ERIC HOLLEYMAN

SHARUHEN (Heb. *šārûḥen*)
A city in the tribal teritory of Simeon (Josh. 19:6, lacking in LXX), usually identified with Shilhim (15:32, assigned to Judah) and Shaaraim (1 Chr. 4:31). Sharuhen is mentioned in an Egyptian document from before the Israelite occupation (*ANET,* 233), where it is the first stronghold of the Asiatic Hyksos after their expulsion from Egypt in the 16th century B.C.E. The site is generally believed to have

been located in the southwest. Possible identifications include Tell el-Fâr'ah (South; 100076), Tell el-'Ajjûl (0934.0976), and more recently Tell Abu Hureirah/Tel Haror (08795.11257).

LAURA B. MAZOW

SHASHAI (Heb. *šāšay*)
A returned exile required by Ezra to divorce his foreign wife (Ezra 10:40).

SHASHAK (Heb. *šāšāq*)
The head of a Benjaminite father's house who had several sons (1 Chr. 8:14, 22-25). He lived in postexilic Jerusalem.

SHAUL (Heb. *šā'ûl*)
1. One of the early Edomite kings, a native of Rehoboth on the Euphrates (Gen. 36:37-38; KJV "Saul"; 1 Chr. 4:24).
2. A son of the patriarch Simeon and an unnamed Canaanite woman (Gen. 46:10; Exod. 6:15; 1 Chr. 4:24). His descendants are called the Shaulites (Num. 26:13).
3. A Levite of the Kohathite line; son of Uzziah (1 Chr. 6:24[MT 9]). He may be the same as the Joel at 1 Chr. 6:36(21).

GREGORY D. JORDAN

SHAVEH (Heb. *šāweh*), **VALLEY OF**
The valley where Abram met the king of Sodom and Melchizedek after his victory over the kings of the east (Gen. 14:17). It was later known as the King's Valley.

SHAVEH-KIRIATHAIM
(Heb. *šāwēh qiryāṯayim*)
The place in Moab where Chedorlaomer and the kings allied with him defeated the Emim (Gen. 14:5). A number of sites have been proposed for Shaveh-kiriathaim with the thought that it was a city. It is likely, however, that the name designates the plain (Heb. *šāwēh*) around the city of Kiriathaim.

SHAVSHA (Heb. *šawšā'*) (also SERAIAH, SHEVA, SHISHA)
The secretary at the court of David (1 Chr. 18:16). Elsewhere he is called Seraiah (**1;** 2 Sam. 8:17), Sheva (**1;** 20:25), and Shisha (1 Kgs. 4:3).

SHEAL (Heb. *šě'āl*)
A returned exile required to send away his foreign wife and their children; descendant of Bani (Ezra 10:29).

SHEALTIEL (Heb. *šě'altî'ēl, šaltî'ēl*)
(also SALATHIEL)
The son of King Jeconiah (Jehoiachin) of Judah, who was taken captive into exile by Nebuchadnezzar in 597 B.C.E. (1 Chr. 3:17; Matt. 1:12). He is not the son of Neri as claimed by Luke's genealogy of Jesus (Luke 3:27; Gk. *Salathiel*). Shealtiel is more widely known in the biblical tradition as the father of Zerubbabel, the Persian governor of postexilic Judah under Darius I of Persia (Ezra 3:2, 8; 5:2; Neh. 12:1; Hag. 1:1, 12, 14; 2:2, 23). In the Chronicler's list of David's descendants, however, Zerubbabel is called the son of Pedaiah (1 Chr. 3:19). The Chronicler might be in error, or he might have conflated his sources by identifying the governor Zerubbabel with a cousin of the same name.

In the apocalypse of 4 Ezra Shealtiel is equated with the scribe Ezra, who lived ca. 100 years later (2 Esdr. 3:1; NRSV "Salathiel"). This equation serves the literary purpose of placing Ezra 30 years after the Babylonian destruction of Jerusalem, thereby associating Ezra's time with that of the author — 30 years after the destruction of Jerusalem by the Romans.

RONALD A. SIMKINS

SHEARIAH (Heb. *šě'aryâ*)
A Benjaminite, son of Azel and descendant of King Saul (1 Chr. 8:38; 9:44).

SHEAR-JASHUB (Heb. *šě'ār yāšûḇ*)
A son of the prophet Isaiah (Isa. 7:3), so named (Heb. "A remnant will return") to symbolize the promise that only a remnant of the Israelite army would return home from their siege of Jerusalem (vv. 4-9; cf. 8:18). Later the name became a promise applied to Israel in the face of eschatological destruction (Isa. 10:21-23; cf. 11:11, 16).

SHEBA (Heb. *šěḇā', šěḇā'*) **(PERSON)**
1. The son of Raamah and great-grandson of Noah's son Ham (Gen. 10:7; 1 Chr. 1:9).
2. The son of Joktan and a descendant of Noah through the line of Shem (Gen. 10:28; 1 Chr. 1:22).
3. The son of Jokshan and grandson of Abraham and Keturah (Gen. 25:3; 1 Chr. 1:32).
4. The son of Bichri, a Benjaminite who led a rebellion against David which was potentially more dangerous than that of Absalom (2 Sam. 20:6), perhaps because of long-standing regional tensions between the northern and southern tribes. David's appeal to Judah after the failure of Absalom's rebellion — which had involved disaffected members of all the tribes, Judah's support for David, and Judah's leading role in bringing David back to Jerusalem (2 Sam. 19:8-15[MT 9-16]) — caused resentment among the northern tribes, who probably assumed that Judah would be especially favored by the king (vv. 41-43[42-44]). Sheba used the dispute between the tribes to initiate his own rebellion against David among the northern tribes (2 Sam. 20:1-2). David's clemency to Shimei the Benjaminite (2 Sam. 19:16-23[17-24]) and his appointment of Amasa, who had been Absalom's general, to replace Joab (v. 13[14]; 20:4-5) may have helped David regain the support of the northern tribes. When Amasa did not return at the appointed time with Judah's troops, he was killed by Joab, who led the army in the pursuit of Sheba. Sheba took refuge in Abel of Beth-maacah, a fortified city on Israel's northern border. When Joab and the army began to besiege the city, a wise woman negotiated with Joab (2 Sam. 20:16; cf. 14:2). Sheba was beheaded and his head thrown over the city wall, and Joab left the city in peace.
5. A descendant of Gad (1 Chr. 5:13).

KEITH L. EADES

SHEBA (Heb. *šĕḇā', šĕḇā'*) **(PLACE)**
  1. One of the towns listed in Josh. 19:2-6 defining a portion of land transferred from the tribe of Judah to the tribe of Simeon. Sheba, often equated with the Shema of Josh. 15:26, is omitted from a parallel list in 1 Chr. 4:28. Since the towns are numbered at 13 in v. 6, many scholars regard the Sheba of Josh. 19:2 as a dittography for Beer-sheba, which precedes it in the list. Two accounts in Genesis support this association. When Abraham sealed a treaty and settled a dispute over a well with Abimelech, the location of this transaction was identified as Beer-sheba (Gen. 21:31). Isaac also sealed a treaty with Abimelech at Beer-sheba, followed by the completion of a well which he named Shibah (Gen. 26:33). These wells of Abraham and Isaac may be the deep wells of present-day Bir es-Seba.
  2. A country in southwest Arabia noted for its international trade during the reign of Solomon. The queen of Sheba visited Solomon in order to investigate the report of his wisdom and achievements.
  See SABA, SABEANS.   ERIC HOLLEYMAN

SHEBA (Heb. *šĕḇā'*), **QUEEN OF**
The queen, identified only by her country, who visited King Solomon (1 Kgs. 10:1-13 = 2 Chr. 9:1-12). In 1 Kgs. 10 her visit follows reports of Solomon's building (9:15-25) and commercial (9:26-28) projects, and is set within the context of Solomon's great wealth and achievements (10:11-12, 14-29). In response to rumors of Solomon's fame, the queen (accompanied by a large and costly retinue; cf. 1 Kgs. 10:2) came to Jerusalem to "test him [Solomon] with hard questions" (v. 1). Not only did Solomon answer her questions satisfactorily (1 Kgs. 10:3), he so impressed her with the quality of his household that there "was no more spirit in her" (vv. 4-5). After praising Solomon at great length (1 Kgs. 10:6-9) the queen gave Solomon numerous and costly gifts (v. 10). In return, Solomon gave the queen of Sheba "every desire that she expressed" (the content of this gift is not specified) and she returned home with her servants (1 Kgs. 10:13).
  While the content of the Chronicler's account parallels that in Kings, its context is different. Since 2 Chronicles has no tensions surrounding Solomon's accession (compare 1 Chr. 29 to 1 Kgs. 1–2); no mention prior to 2 Chr. 9 of Solomon's accession (compare to 1 Kgs. 3:16-28; 4:29-34); and no subsequent political catastrophe due to Solomon's apostasy (compare 2 Chr. 9:13-29 to 1 Kgs. 11), the queen's visit in 2 Chr. 9 becomes the showcase example of Solomon's wisdom and the climax of his peaceful and prosperous reign.
  Although the NT does not mention the queen of Sheba, Matt. 12:42 (= Luke 11:31) does refer to a "queen of the South" who "came from the ends of the earth to listen to the wisdom of Solomon." Another identification, linking Candace queen of the Ethiopians (Acts 8:27) with the queen of Sheba, is more problematic.

Bibliography. L. S. Schearing, "A Wealth of Women: Looking Behind, Within, and Beyond Solomon's Story," in *The Age of Solomon,* ed. L. K. Handy. SHANE 11 (Leiden, 1997).
                                           LINDA S. SCHEARING

SHEBANIAH (Heb. *šĕḇanyâ, šĕḇanyāhû*)
  1. One of the priests appointed by the Levites whose function was to blow the trumpet before the ark of God (1 Chr. 15:24).
  2. One of the leaders who led the people in praise and confession during the postexilic covenant renewal ceremony led by Ezra (Neh. 9). The name Shebaniah appears twice in this context: in the list of those who "stood on the stairs of the Levites" and cried out (Neh. 9:4) and in the list of Levites who summoned the people to praise God (v. 5). He, along with four other Levites named in both lists, may have led in both parts of the worship process. This Shebaniah may be the same as one of the Shebaniahs who signed Nehemiah's covenant of support for the temple (see **3-5** below).
  3. A postexilic priestly house of which a Joseph is said to have been the head during the time of the high priest Joiakim (Neh. 12:14). This family name may designate a signatory to the covenant of Nehemiah (Neh. 10:4[MT 5]). Some manuscripts and versions read "Shecaniah."
  4.-5. The name given to two Levites who signed the Nehemiah covenant (Neh. 10:10, 12[11, 13]). Some scholars prefer the explanation of dittography for this repetition rather than admit a problem in textual transmission or assume that the names represent two different people.
                                           MICHAEL L. RUFFIN

SHEBARIM (Heb. *haššĕḇārîm*)
A place to which the men of Ai chased the Israelites after rebuffing their attempt to capture Ai (Josh. 7:5). The name may refer to a topographical feature (e.g., "the quarries").

SHEBAT (Heb. *šĕḇāṭ*)
The eleventh month of the Jewish calendar (Jan./Feb.; Zech. 1:7; cf. Akk. *šabaṭu;* 1 Macc. 16:14; Gk. *Sabat*).

SHEBER (Heb. *šeḇer*)
A Judahite, son of Caleb and his concubine Maacah (1 Chr. 2:48).

SHEBNA, SHEBNAH (Heb. *šeḇnā', šeḇnâ*)
A court official under King Hezekiah of Judah, apparently once master of the household. According to a prophecy of Isaiah, however, he had attempted to appropriate too much authority and/or prestige to himself and thus would be replaced in his position by Eliakim (Isa. 22:15-25). The oracle emphasizes the arrogance of Shebna in carving out a fine tomb for himself, although some scholars believe that Shebna may have incurred Isaiah's wrath by being involved in anti-Assyrian plans. Shebna's demotion had occurred by the time of the Sennacherib invasion(s) described in 2 Kgs. 18:18-37;

19:2-7 = Isa. 36:3-22; 37:2-7. In those passages Shebna is described as "the secretary." He accompanied Eliakim, now "in charge of the palace," and Joah "the recorder" in negotiations with the Tartan, the Rabsaris, and the Rabshakeh, representatives of Sennacherib. MICHAEL L. RUFFIN

SHEBUEL (Heb. *šĕḇû'ēl*), **SHUBAEL** *(šûḇā'ēl)*

1. A Levite of the "sons of Gershom," descendant of Moses; chief treasury officer in David's organization of the Levites for temple service (1 Chr. 23:16; 26:24; called Shubael at 24:20).

2. A son of Heman and leader (or ancestor) of the 13th division of temple musicians (1 Chr. 25:4; Shubael at v. 20).

SHECANIAH (Heb. *šĕḵanyāhû*)

1. A descendant of David and Jehoiachin (Jeconiah), grandson of Zerubbabel, and father of Shemaiah (1 Chr. 3:21-22). He is probably the same Shecaniah as in Ezra 8:3; 1 Esdr. 8:29, head of a clan that returned from exile. Deleting "and the sons of Shemaiah" (1 Chr. 3:22) makes the "six" at the end of the verse appropriate.

2. A priest chosen by lot to perform temple duties at time of David's organization of the temple personnel, head of the 10th division (1 Chr. 24:11).

3. A Levite who assisted in the distribution of temple offerings during Hezekiah's reign (1 Chr. 31:15).

4. A son of Jahaziel who returned with Ezra to Judah after the Exile (Ezra 8:5; 1 Esdr. 8:32).

5. A son of Jehiel who proposed to Ezra the policy of putting away the foreign wives and their children (Ezra 10:2; cf. 1 Esdr. 8:92).

6. The father of Shemaiah, a gatekeeper who helped with the rebuilding of the walls of Jerusalem under Nehemiah (Neh. 3:29).

7. A son of Arah and father-in-law of Tobiah the Ammonite, who opposed Nehemiah in the rebuilding effort. Tobiah's influence was due in part to Shecaniah's status (Neh. 6:18).

8. A priest who returned to Judah with Zerubbabel after the Exile (Neh. 12:3).

Several manuscripts read "Shecaniah" rather than "Shebaniah" in Neh. 10:4(MT 5); 12:14.

HAROLD R. MOSLEY

SHECHEM (Heb. *šĕḵem*) **(PERSON)**

1. A son of Hamor, Hivite prince of the Shechemites (Gen. 34:2). After raping Dinah, the daughter of Jacob and Leah, he becomes enamored with her and asks his father to arrange a marriage (Gen. 34:4). Outraged by Shechem's violent act, as well as his desire to marry a Hebrew woman and Hamor's proposal of a general intermarriage alliance between Hebrews and Shechemites, Dinah's brothers insist that all males of the city be circumcised as a partial concession to Israelite ways (Gen. 34:13-17). While the Shechemites are incapacitated by the operation, two of Jacob's sons, Simeon and Levi, enter and plunder the defenseless city, kill all the men including Shechem and Hamor, and carry off Dinah (Gen. 34:25-29).

LUCILLE C. THIBODEAU, P. M.

2. A descendant of Manasseh and progenitor of the Shechemite branch of Manasseh (Num. 26:31; Josh. 17:2).

3. A son of Shemida of the tribe of Manasseh (1 Chr. 7:19), perhaps the same as **2** above.

SHECHEM (Heb. *šĕḵem*) **(PLACE)**

A city in the heartland of the Ephraimite hill country (Josh. 20:7). The 6 ha. (15 a.) site is 67 km. (40 mi.) N of Jerusalem, 2 km. (1.2 mi.) E of Roman Neapolis (modern Nablus), and 10 km. (6 mi.) SE of Samaria. Though certain classical sources affiliated biblical Shechem with Neapolis, founded by Vespasian in 72 C.E. (Josephus *BJ* 4.8.1; Jerome), other early sources located pre-Roman Shechem at modern Tell Balâṭah (177179), 2.5 km. (1.5 mi.) SE of Neapolis, nearer to Mt. Ebal (Eusebius *Onom.*, Bordeaux Pilgrim, Medeba Map). First investigated in 1903 by Hermann Thiersch, scholars generally accept this identification. The NT reference to a site in this region called Sychar (John 4:5; cf. Sychem, Acts 7:16) apparently indicates the Hellenistic and Roman ruins situated beneath modern ʿAskar, just NE of Balâṭah.

Influenced by Gen. 33:18-19, classical writers (Eusebius) and early modern explorers (Edward Robinson) derived the name Shechem from traditions surrounding the son of Hamor who violated Dinah (Josh. 24:32; Judg. 9:28; cf. genealogies of Manasseh, Num. 26:31; Josh. 17:2; 1 Chr. 7:19). The name more likely reflects the physical setting of the city on the "shoulder" (slope) of Mt. Ebal or its opposing proximity to Gerizim, a prominent topographical feature once called the "navel of the land" (Judg. 9:37).

Situated in a strategic pass between Mt. Ebal to its north and Mt. Gerizim to its south, Shechem quickly became an urbane hub of political, economic, and, eventually, religious activity within the region of Samaria. The system of latitudinal and longitudinal roads which converged in this valley of very fertile soil undoubtedly accounted for the founding and flourishing of the city here rather than at higher, more defensible elevations on Ebal or Gerizim. The primary ascent to the central hill country of Samaria from the Jordan River proceeded up the deeply faulted Wadi Fariʿa from just south of the river fords at Adam and continued on to Shechem by way of biblical Tirzah. By Iron Age I (1200-1000 B.C.E.), many small settlements lay along this route, which gained even greater prominence during Iron II (1000-587/586) as the former cultic and political center at Shiloh (S of Shechem) declined. At that time, an alternate road diverged from the former route to Shiloh, assumed a more northerly course from the valley area east of that site, and followed the Ephraim-Manasseh border to Shechem (cf. Josh. 17:7-9). From there, innermontane highways provided passage either to the lucrative coastal route through the Naḥal Shechem or to points farther north and east by way of the

Great standing stone in forecourt of Late Bronze I fortress temple at Shechem (ca. 1450 B.C.E.) (Allen C. Myers)

Dothan Valley and Jezreel. These crossroads distinguished Shechem as a strategic juncture between northern and southern Samaria (roughly the tribal allotments of Manasseh and Ephraim).

Excavation

Field exploration of Tell Balâṭah and its vicinity has involved two extended series of excavations, first under Austro-German leadership and later by an American joint expedition. After small-scale work at the site by Carl Watzinger (1907-9), Ernst Sellin in 1913-14 exposed some 75 m. (245 ft.) of a wall (wall A) previously observed by Thiersch on the northwest side of the site. Incorporated into this wall was a massive three-entryway gate complex. Sellin also cut a 52 m. (170 ft.) trench from the north side of the mound toward its center, revealing four main occupational phases, subsequently identified as Hellenistic, Israelite, Middle Bronze, and Chalcolithic–Early Bronze I. Sellin undertook five additional campaigns from 1926 to 1928, together with architect Gabriel Welter. In addition to a palace area immediately inside the northwest gate complex, they discovered a huge fortress-temple with foundation walls 5 m. (16 ft.) wide, dating to Late Bronze I (ca. 1550-1400). In the eastern sector of the city they uncovered an offsets-insets wall (wall B) with a two-entryway gate (the east gate), which they dated to LB II (ca. 1400-1200). Sellin's official report, completed in 1943, all the field records, and numerous artifacts were destroyed during World War II.

From 1956-1973 Drew University, McCormick Theological Seminary, the ASOR, and Harvard University collaborated to renew fieldwork under the direction of George Ernest Wright. Over seven full seasons and three shorter ones, the team opened 14 "fields" of excavation and employed improved techniques of debris-layer analysis and ceramic study to distinguish 24 strata ranging from the Chalcolithic to the late Hellenistic periods, during which time four lengthy occupational gaps disrupted settlement at the site. Excavators also discovered a domestic quarter on the northern side of the city and related it stratigraphically to the public architecture situated on the acropolis to the west. Supplementing this on-site work, Edward F. Campbell conducted a regional survey from 1964-1972.

Settlement History

Separate fields in strata XXIV-XXIII, which lay immediately on bedrock, yielded scant remains of circular mud-brick structures from the Chalcolithic period (ca. 4000-3500). Sherd collections indicate that this occupation may have extended into EB I (ca. 3500-3300). Following this limited occupation, the site was abandoned until ca. 1900. From here to the city's final destruction, three further occupational gaps would divide the history of Shechem into four major phases: MB II (1900-1550), LB IB–Iron IA (1450-1150/1125), Iron II–Persian (975-475), and Hellenistic (331-107).

Shechem developed from an unfortified, domestic settlement in MB IIA (ca. 1900; strata XXII-XXI) to a city with a heavily defended acropolis flanked by substantial domestic quarters in MB IIB (ca. 1750-1650; strata XX-XVII) to a powerful city state center in MB IIC (ca. 1650-1550; strata XVI-XV). Early in this period, Shechem appeared in the Egyptian Execration Texts as the principal center in the Ephraimite hill country (complementing Jerusalem in the southern highlands), and its regional prominence may even have attracted Egyptian military activity by the late 19th century. On the acropolis in the western precinct of the city, an MB IIB courtyard revealed a complex of structures which underwent at least four phases of construction. Wright's interpretation of these as temples has encountered serious opposition more recently. During MB IIC were built the "cyclopean wall A," northwest gate complex, fortress temple, and, on the eastern side of the site, the east gate and fortification wall B. Also, what Sellin believed represented a palace seems instead to have served as a central sanctuary surrounded by guard rooms. North of the acropolis and its enclosure wall, a quarter of fine domestic houses may have included the private residences of some city officials. The heavy destruction debris that overlay stratum XV likely stemmed from Egyptian retaliation against the Hyksos ca. 1550. A century-long occupational gap followed.

During LB and Early Iron (strata XIV-XI), occupants rebuilt the northwest and east gates. A new temple, somewhat smaller than its *migdal* predecessor but complete with altar and large *maṣṣeba* ("standing stones"), stood on the acropolis. This structure likely correlates to the "house of Baal-berith/El-berith" (also called the "tower of Shechem") in Judg. 9:4, 46 (excavators found a bronze figurine of a standing male deity — an apparent representation of Baal — in the succeeding stratum). Stratum XIII, corresponding to the Amarna age (14th century) during which the aggressive Lab'ayu ruled a sizable kingdom from Shechem, again revealed a well-planned domestic quarter in field XIII on the north side of the site, while the area to the east accommodated a large public building in field III. The correspondence from Tell el-Amarna (EA 289; cf. nos. 244-45, 249, 252-55, 263, 280) indicates that Shechem not only dominated the entire north-central hill country, as the earlier Execration Texts reveal, but that Lab'ayu at times extended its influence as far as the Sharon Plain (EA 250). A violent destruction, traced across the site, marked the end of stratum XIII and of Lab'ayu's principality sometime ca. 1300. The ensuing strata XII and XI reflect a less affluent society whose diminished political power might provide the historical backdrop to the city's amenable treaty and social relations with the Israelites (Josh. 24). Not until Abimelech attempted to impose kingship upon the city did these relations end in disaster, as reflected in the massive destruction of stratum XI ca. 1125-1100 and in the textual traditions of Judg. 9.

Following another century without appreciable occupation (1100-1000), Shechem and the entire area around it managed only a modest recovery during the United Monarchy (stratum X; note the political vicissitudes hinted at in Ps. 60:6-7[MT 7-8] = 108:8-9[9-10]). The site reverted to town status as part of Solomon's administrative network (1 Kgs. 4:8ff.). Though Shechem also appears in both rosters of levitical cities (Josh. 21:21; 1 Chr. 6:67), many interpret this as a secondary addition due to its position now as a city of refuge (Josh. 20:7). Ceramic dating confirms the destruction of stratum X during the invasion by Pharaoh Shishak ca. 925 (cf. 1 Kgs. 14:25). Jeroboam I subsequently rebuilt the site (stratum IX) and temporarily made it his capital (1 Kgs. 12:25). The mention of Shechem in an early 8th-century Samaria ostracon (no. 44) indicates that the city now served the economic needs of the monarchic regime ensconced in the north; a large building, possibly a granary, in stratum VIII, supports this function. Rather than representing the primary partner, as it had in the earlier patron-client relationships between Lab'ayu and various pastoralist and mercenary classes (*'apiru*), Shechem apparently now had to subordinate itself in a new political and social order between capital and countryside.

Strata VI-V, spanning the Assyrian and Persian periods, yielded only meager material remains. Though overall the prosperity and political influence of the city seem to have diminished during this time, excavation of fields I, VII, and IX yielded a substantial quantity of Attic black-glazed ware and an assemblage of small finds which included an electrum coin and various seal impressions. Jer. 41:4-8 records that early in the 6th century a party of Shechemites arrived in Jerusalem with cereal and incense offerings and the claim that they had stores of wheat, barley, oil, and honey hidden in the north.

The site once again lay abandoned from ca. 475 until the appearance in Canaan of Alexander the Great. As Samaritans fled eastward under the punitive raids of Alexander, Shechem regained its status as a fortified center of activity (Josephus *Ant.* 11.8.6). In strata IV-III (ca. 323-190), dated by the recovery of a series of Ptolemaic coins, massive quantities of fill covered the partially exposed remains from previous periods and provided a level building area for well-planned homes over the earlier terraces in field VII. The arrangement of the new fortifications approximated that of the MB II plan; the east gate area itself was cleared to MB levels. A conspicuous shift to Seleucid coinage in stratum II reflects the influence gained throughout the region by Antiochus III and Antiochus IV Epiphanes following the former's military victory in 198 at Panias in northern Israel. Although Josephus records that the final destruction of Shechem occurred in 128 (*Ant.* 13.254-56, 275-81), both ceramic and numismatic evidence suggest lowering the date to 108/107 and correlating the disaster to the mayhem associated with the northern raids of the Hasmonean priest John Hyrcanus, who not only destroyed the Samaritan temple on nearby Tell er-Ras (on Mt. Gerizim) but devastated and then buried the city occupying Tell Balâṭah.

Bibliography. E. F. Campbell, *Shechem II: Portrait of a Hill Country Vale.* ASOR Archaeological Report 2 (Atlanta, 1991); Campbell and J. F. Ross, "The Excavation of Shechem and the Biblical Tradition," *BA* 26 (1963): 1-27, repr. in *BAR* 2, ed. D. N. Freedman and E. F. Campbell (Garden City, 1964), 275-300; W. G. Dever, "The MB IIC Stratification in the Northwest Gate Area at Shechem," *BASOR* 216

(1974): 31-52; J. D. Seger, "The Middle Bronze IIC Date of the East Gate at Shechem," *Levant* 6 (1974): 117-30; L. E. Toombs, "The Stratification of Tell Balâṭah (Shechem)," *BASOR* 223 (1976): 57-59; G. E. Wright, *Shechem: The Biography of a Biblical City* (New York, 1965); G. R. H. Wright, "Temples at Shechem," *ZAW* 80 (1968): 1-35. RON E. TAPPY

SHEDEUR (Heb. *šĕḏêʾûr*)
The father of Elizur, who represented the tribe of Reuben and assisted Moses during Israel's travels through the wilderness (Num. 1:5; 2:10).

SHEEP
Along with goats, the most common domesticated animals during biblical times, evidenced linguistically in biblical and extrabiblical sources and supported by zooarchaeological finds at many sites. Biblical references to herding and to small cattle (Heb. *ṣōʾn, miqneh*) are numerous, including the two main components of the group, sheep *(kebeś)* and goats *(ʿēz)*. Furthermore, in the ancient Near East riches were measured, in part, by the size of the herd a person owned.

Sheep were raised for wool or hair, milk and its products (yogurt, butter, cheeses), meat, skins, bones and horns, and dung. The significance of milk *(ḥālāḇ)* in the biblical diet is apparent since it connotes plenty and nutritional richness, especially when mentioned with another whole and complete food, honey *(dĕḇaš)*, a combination used in many ancient societies for sacrifice (cf. the expression describing the land of Israel as "flowing with milk and honey"; e.g., Exod. 3:8).

Milking in pre-industrial societies was done by setting the ewes one opposite the other and tying them in pairs by a long rope, creating two long rows *(riḇqâ)*. While sheep were raised also for their meat, it was not consumed on a daily basis. In antiquity, meat and milk production were very important endeavors in which private individuals, as well as temples and the royal palace, participated (1 Chr. 27:29, 31; 2 Chr. 26:10). The Levites were given large tracts of land where they were supposed to "keep their cattle, their livestock, and all their animals" (Num. 35:3; cf. Josh. 14:4). A small number of animals was kept for fattening. Apparently raising and selling fattened animals were lucrative because even kings (2 Kgs. 3:4) and other leaders (Ezek. 27:21) were involved. Fat *(ḥēleḇ)* was considered a nutritious food element, therefore from very early times (Gen. 4:4) it was a major component of sacrifices (Exod. 29:13).

Artistic representations from Ur (Uruk III), Assyria, Arabia, and Israel suggest that the sheep raised in antiquity were closely related to the fat-tail Awassi sheep, the most numerous and widespread breed in the Near East today (cf. also Herodotus). The Awassi sheep is usually white with brown head and feet; entire whiteness, or black heads and feet, are frequent. However, entirely black or gray as well as dappled are uncommon, which may explain Laban's willing acceptance of Jacob's offer to take "every speckled and spotted sheep and every black lamb" as his wages (Gen. 30:31-32).

The process of domestication led to animals becoming less resistant and, even worse, more susceptible to diseases. Biblical references to flock diseases are infrequent and in general terms. The curses accompanying the Covenant include the broad statement: "Cursed shall be . . . the increase of your cattle and the issue of your flock" (Deut. 28:18), but there is no enumeration as in the curses concerning humans or crops.

Wool is an important by-product of sheep. Shearing of wool (*gēz*, Deut. 18:4) is done once a year in April-May, just before the summer heat commences. If water is available, the sheep are washed beforehand (Cant. 4:2; 6:6), but otherwise the wool is sold by the fleece and not by weight, since it is dirty and heavy. Shearing was an event that brought together many people engaged in caring for the animals, and like during the ingathering of other crops was an occasion for great celebration (1 Sam. 25; 2 Sam. 13:23-28).

Bibliography. D. Brothwell and P. Brothwell, *Food in Antiquity*, rev. ed. (Baltimore, 1998); H. Epstein, *The Awassi Sheep* (Rome, 1985); S. Hirsch, *Sheep and Goats in Palestine* (Tel Aviv, 1933).

ODED BOROWSKI

SHEERAH (Heb. *šeʾĕrâ*)
The daughter of Ephraim (or perhaps Beriah **2**) who built Upper and Lower Beth-horon and Uzzen-sheerah (1 Chr. 7:24).

SHEHARIAH (Heb. *šĕḥaryâ*)
A son of Jehoram; head of a Benjaminite family living in postexilic Jerusalem (1 Chr. 8:26).

SHEKEL (Heb. *šeqel*)
The standard unit of weight in the OT. Its name is derived from a Semitic root meaning "to weigh." Although it varied significantly, the average weight of an Israelite shekel seems to have been just over 11.4 gm. (.4 oz.). With the large-scale introduction of standard coinage into Israel during the intertestimental and NT periods, the word shekel commonly refers to a silver coin weighing ca. 14.5 gm. (.5 oz.). MICHAEL HOMAN

SHEKINAH
A Hebrew term *(šĕḵînâ)* in the Targums and rabbinic literature which reverently expresses the divine Presence. It is derived from Heb. *škn*, "to dwell, abide, settle down." The term does not appear in the OT or NT. The historical background for the correlation of Shekinah ("that which dwells") with God's Presence may be found in Exod. 25:8; 40:34. When the ark of the Lord is placed in the temple in Jerusalem, a cloud representing the Shekinah subsequently fills the temple, thereby symbolizing its new habitation (1 Kgs. 8:10). The Judeo-Christian biblical tradition portrays the Shekinah as leaving the temple and going into exile with the Israelites following the first temple's destruction (cf. Ezek. 10; 11:16, 22-25). A different tradition claims that the Shekinah returned

to heaven, whereas another tradition claims that it remains in the Western (Wailing) Wall on the temple mount. In the intertestamental period, the Shekinah was also thought to dwell in synagogues and among assemblies of the faithful (cf. *m. 'Abot* 3.2; 1QS 8:4-10). Several passages in the NT imply the belief that the Shekinah was first incarnate in Jesus of Nazareth (e.g., John 1:14) and later in the Church (e.g., Eph. 2:19-22).

Bibliography. M. E. Lodahl, *Shekhinah/Spirit: Divine Presence in Jewish and Christian Religion* (New York, 1992); E. M. Umansky, "Shekinah," *The Encyclopedia of Religion* (New York, 1987) 13:236-39.

DAVID CLEAVER-BARTHOLOMEW

SHELAH (Heb. *šelaḥ, šēlâ;* Gk. *Salá*)

1. A son of Arpachshad (Arphaxad), descendant of Shem, and father of Eber (Gen. 10:24; 11:12-15; 1 Chr. 1:18, 24). Luke 3:35-36 follows the LXX in listing Shelah as the son of Cainan and grandson of Arpachshad.

2. The third son of the patriarch Judah and the daughter of Shua, a Canaanite (Gen. 38:5, 11, 14, 26; 46:12; 1 Chr. 2:3; 4:21). He was the eponymous ancestor of the Shelanites (Heb. *šēlānî;* Num. 26:20).

SHELAH, POOL OF (Heb. *bĕrēḵaṯ haššelaḥ*)
A reservoir in the King's Garden (Neh. 3:15; cf. John 9:7, "pool of Siloam"), perhaps the same as the King's Pool (2:14) or the "lower pool" (Isa. 22:9).

SHELEMIAH (Heb. *šelemyâ, šelemiyāhû*) (also MESHELEMIAH)

1. A Korahite, grandson of Asaph, and gatekeeper during the time of David (1 Chr. 26:14). He is called Meshelemiah at 1 Chr. 26:1 and may be the same as Shallum (**8**) at 9:17, 19, 31.

2.-3. Two descendants of Bani or Binnui who had married foreign women (Ezra 10:39, 41).

4. The father of Hananiah, the man who repaired a section of the wall in Jerusalem next to the East Gate (Neh. 3:30).

5. A priest whom Nehemiah put in charge of the temple storerooms along with Zadok the scribe and a Levite named Pedaiah because the three were found to be trustworthy (Neh. 13:13).

6. A son of Cushi and grandfather of Jehudi, whom Jerusalem officials sent to tell Baruch to read from the scroll of Jeremiah (Jer. 36:14).

7. One of three men King Jehoiakim sent to arrest Baruch and Jeremiah (Jer. 36:26); the son of Abdeel.

8. The father of Jehucal (Jucal), whom King Zedekiah sent to ask Jeremiah to pray for the nation (Jer. 37:3) and who subsequently recommended that Jeremiah be put to death (38:1).

9. The son of Hanniah and father of Irijah, captain of the guard sent to arrest Jeremiah (Jer. 37:13).

ROBIN GALLAHER BRANCH

SHELEPH (Heb. *šelep*)
A son of Joktan and descendant of Shem (Gen. 10:26; 1 Chr. 1:20); ancestor of a south Arabian people.

SHELESH (Heb. *šēleš*)
A son of Helem; head of an Asherite father's house (1 Chr. 7:35).

SHELOMI (Heb. *šĕlōmî*)
The father of Ahihud, who was the representative of the tribe of Asher in the division of Canaan (Num. 34:27).

SHELOMITH (Heb. *šĕlōmîṯ*)
The name applies to both men and women. Originally, Shelomith may have been the feminine form and Shelomoth masculine.

1. The daughter of Dibri of the tribe of Dan. Her son blasphemed the name of God and was stoned to death (Lev. 24:10-23).

2. A daughter of Zerubbabel, sister of Meshullam and Hananiah (1 Chr. 3:19).

3. A son of Shimei (**Q** 1 Chr. 23:9; **K** "Shelomoth").

4. The son of Izhar, a chief Levite (1 Chr. 23:18). At 1 Chr. 24:22 he is called Shelomoth.

5. A child of King Rehabeam and Maacah (2 Chr. 11:20).

6. The son of Josiphiah, a descendant of Bani; head of one of the families that returned with Ezra (Ezra 8:10).

See SHELOMOTH. JESPER SVARTVIK

SHELOMOTH (Heb. *šĕlōmôṯ*)

1. A Levite, the son of Shimei and a descendant of Gershom (**K** 1 Chr. 23:9).

2. A Levite of the Kohathite line, the son of Izhar (1 Chr. 24:22). The MT calls him Shelomith at 1 Chr. 23:18.

3. A Levite, the son of Zichri and descendant of Moses' son Eliezer. He and his brothers guarded the treasuries of the dedicated gifts acquired as spoil during the reign of David (1 Chr. 26:25-28).

JESPER SVARTVIK

SHELUMIEL (Heb. *šĕlumî'ēl*) (also SALAMIEL)
The son of Zurishaddai; a representative to Moses and leader of the Simeonites during Israel's wilderness wanderings (Num. 1:6; 2:12; 7:36-41; 10:19). Judith's ancestry is traced through Shelumiel (Jdt. 8:1; Gk. *Salamiēl*).

SHEM (Heb. *šēm;* Gk. *Sēm*)
A son of Noah, brother of Ham and Japheth (Gen. 5:32). Shem is listed as the first and eldest (cf. Gen. 9:24; 10:21) son of Noah, though in genealogical accounts he appears last (Gen. 10:21-31; 1 Chr. 1:4, 17-27), perhaps to emphasize his paternity of the individuals who follow. Shem accompanied his wife on the ark (Gen. 7:13) and escaped the Flood, apparently because of Noah's righteousness (6:8-9). Later he received God's blessing (Gen. 9:1). After Ham saw Noah's nakedness, it was Shem and Japheth who covered Noah and were blessed at Canaan's expense (Gen. 9:23-27).

Shem is the ancestor of diverse peoples, both Semitic — to whom he lends his name — and non-Semitic (Elam), who inhabited various areas (Gen.

10:21-31; 11:10-26). Shem is also the ancestor of the Hebrews (through Eber) and hence the forefather of Abraham. Perhaps for this reason Sirach calls him "honored" (Sir. 49:16); Luke explicitly mentions him in the genealogy of Jesus (Luke 3:36).

Shem means "name" or "fame." Despite some evidence that *šm* was used as an epithet or name for a god(s), a (semi-)divine status for Shem is unlikely.

Bibliography. B. Becking, "Shem," *DDD*, 763-64; M. Lubetski, "*ŠM* as a Deity," *Religion* 17 (1987): 1-14. BRENT A. STRAWN

SHEMA (Heb. *šĕma'*) **(PERSON)**
(also SHIMEI)

1. A son of Hebron of the tribe of Judah, possibly a place name (1 Chr. 2:43-44).

2. The son of Joel of the tribe of Reuben (1 Chr. 5:8). He may be the same as Shemaiah or Shimei (1 Chr. 5:4).

3. A son of Elpaal of the tribe of Benjamin. He was an inhabitant of Aijalon, whose citizens fought with Gath and won (1 Chr. 8:13). At 1 Chr. 8:21 he is called Shimei.

4. One of the lay leaders who stood at Ezra's right hand in support of Ezra during his public reading of the law (Neh. 8:4). KEVIN D. HALL

SHEMA (Heb. *šĕma'*) **(PLACE)**
A town in the southern district of Judah (Josh. 15:26). "Sheba" may be a variant of the name in the Simeonite town list (Josh. 19:2). Neither name occurs in the parallel list at 1 Chr. 4:28. The location is unknown, but it was probably in the vicinity of Beer-sheba. LAURA B. MAZOW

SHEMA (Heb. *šĕma'*), **THE**
The foundational statement of Jewish belief: "Hear, O Israel, Yahweh our God, Yahweh is one" (Deut. 6:4). The name derives from the first Hebrew word in the verse, the command to "hear." The declaration that "Yahweh is one" rules out local manifestations of Yahweh, but also connotes Yahweh's exclusiveness. Thus, although "alone" is an inaccurate translation of Heb. *'eḥāḏ* ("one"), the assertion of unity contains within it the idea of uniqueness. In Hebrew manuscripts, the last letters of the first and last words are written larger than the others to form the word *'ēḏ* ("witness"), reflecting the verse's testimony to the uncompromising monotheism of Judaism. It has been the final utterance of Jewish martyrs throughout history.

The prayer came to include Deut. 6:4-9; 11:13-21; Num. 15:37-41, and is recited in the morning and evening (cf. Deut. 6:7). The text of Deut. 6:4-9 is placed inside phylacteries, bound to the forehead and arm during prayer, and in a mezuzah attached to the entrance of houses (cf. vv. 8-9). Jesus identified Deut. 6:5 as the greatest commandment (Mark 12:29). JOHN L. MCLAUGHLIN

SHEMAAH (Heb. *šĕmā'â*)
The father of Ahiezer and Joash, two Benjaminite warriors who joined David at Ziklag (1 Chr. 12:3).

SHEMAIAH (Heb. *šĕma'yâ, šĕma'yāhû*)
(also SHAMMUA)

1. A Judean prophet at the time of the division of the monarchy following the death of Solomon. Shemaiah was sent by Yahweh to admonish Rehoboam, king of Judah, to return to Jerusalem and not wage war against Jeroboam (1 Kgs. 12:21-22; 2 Chr. 11:2-4). Later, when Yahweh punished Rehoboam and Judah because of their idolatrous practices, it was Shemaiah who declared to the leaders of Judah that the invasion by an Egyptian army led by Shishak was the consequence of their unfaithfulness. He also declared that final judgment over their idolatry would not come by the hands of Shishak (2 Chr. 12:5-8). Shemaiah also was a historian of the court and wrote a book containing the events of Rehoboam's reign (2 Chr. 12:15).

2. The son of Shecaniah; a descendant of David (1 Chr. 3:22).

3. A leader of the tribe of Simeon, the father of Shimri (1 Chr. 4:37).

4. One of the leaders of the tribe of Reuben, the son of Joel (1 Chr. 5:4).

5. A Levite, the son of Hasshub, from the clan of Merari (1 Chr. 9:14), who lived in Jerusalem at the time the exiles returned from Babylon. He was one of the Levites responsible for the work outside the house of God (Neh. 11:15-16).

6. A Levite, the father of Obadiah and the son of Galal, from the clan of Jeduthun (1 Chr. 9:16). His name and the name of his son appear abbreviated in Neh. 11:17 as Shammua (**3**) and Abda.

7. The leader of a levitical family, descendant of Elizaphan. Shemaiah and 200 Levites carried the ark of the covenant when it was removed from the house of Obed-edom to the tent that David had prepared in Jerusalem (1 Chr. 15:8-11).

8. A Levite, the son of Nethanel, and the scribe who, in the days of David, recorded the names of the men who constituted the 24 divisions of priests (1 Chr. 24:6).

9. A Levite from the clan of Korah; firstborn son of Obed-edom (1 Chr. 26:4). Shemaiah and his sons were gatekeepers of the temple (1 Chr. 26:6-8).

10. One of the Levites sent by Jehoshaphat, king of Judah, to teach the law to the people of Judah (2 Chr. 17:8).

11. The son of Jeduthun; one of the Levites who went through a process of ritual cleansing in order to help purify the temple during the time of Hezekiah (2 Chr. 29:14-15).

12. A Levite at the time of Hezekiah who helped distribute the freewill offering and gifts given to the Levites who lived in the towns of the priests (2 Chr. 31:15).

13. One of the leaders of the Levites who contributed 5000 sheep and goats and 500 bulls to help the Levites celebrate Passover in Josiah's time (2 Chr. 35:9).

14. One of the sons of Adonikam who came to Judah with Ezra from Babylon during the reign of King Artaxerxes (Ezra 8:13).

15. One of the leaders of the people who returned from exile in Babylon. Ezra sent him and others to Iddo, the leader in Casiphia, to bring Levites to attend to the service of God (Ezra 8:16-17). He may be the same person as **14** above.

16. A priest from the family of Harim who divorced his foreign wife (Ezra 10:21).

17. An Israelite from the family of Harim who divorced his foreign wife (Ezra 10:31).

18. A Levite, the son of Shecaniah. Shemaiah was the keeper of the East Gate of the temple and helped to repair a section of the walls of Jerusalem in the days of Nehemiah (Neh. 3:29).

19. The son of Delaiah, a prophet hired by Tobiah and Sanballat to intimidate Nehemiah and to discredit him (Neh. 6:10-13). Shemaiah tried to coerce Nehemiah to enter the temple and thus violate religious law because he was not a priest.

20. One of the priests who signed the binding agreement with Nehemiah and the leaders of the nation (Neh. 10:8[MT 9]) that required the leaders of Judah, the priests, and the Levites to follow all the commandments and regulations of the law of God (v. 29[30]). He had returned from Babylon with Zerubbabel (Neh. 12:6) and was probably the father of Jehonathan (v. 18).

21. One of the leaders of Judah who participated in the dedication of the new walls of Jerusalem (Neh. 12:34).

22. A priest, the son of Mattaniah, from the clan of Asaph. His grandson Zechariah played the trumpet during the dedication of the new walls of Jerusalem in the days of Jeremiah (Neh. 12:35).

23. A Levite who was among the musicians celebrating the dedication of the new walls of Jerusalem (Neh. 12:36).

24. One of the Levites who accompanied Nehemiah in the procession during the dedication of the new wall (Neh. 12:42).

25. The father of Uriah, a prophet from Kiriath-jearim killed by order of Jehoiakim (Jer. 26:20).

26. A Nehelamite and false prophet who lived among the exiles in Babylon. He prophesied the imminent return of the people to Judah and wanted priests in Jerusalem to reprimand and imprison Jeremiah for preaching that the Exile would last many years. When Jeremiah heard Shemaiah's word, he prophesied that Shemaiah would not have descendants among the people of Judah and would not live long enough to see the return of the people from exile (Jer. 29:24-32).

27. The father of Delaiah, one of the officials who served in the court of Jehoiakim, king of Judah (Jer. 36:12). He was present when Baruch reread the scroll of Jeremiah's prophecies before a group of royal officials gathered in the king's palace.

CLAUDE F. MARIOTTINI

SHEMARIAH (Heb. *šĕmaryâ, šĕmaryāhû*)

1. A Benjaminite who joined David's rebel force at Ziklag (1 Chr. 12:5[MT 6]).

2. A son of King Rehoboam of Judah and his wife Mahalath (2 Chr. 11:19).

3. An Israelite among the sons of Harim required by Ezra to divorce his foreign wife (Ezra 10:32).

4. One of the sons of Binnui who divorced his non-Israelite wife (Ezra 10:41).

SHEMEBER (Heb. *šem'ēḇer*)

The king of Zeboiim, one of the five kings who rebelled against Chedorlaomer and fought unsuccessfully against his alliance in the valley of Siddim (Gen. 14:2).

SHEMED (Heb. *šemeḏ*)

A Benjaminite; one of the sons of Elpaal who rebuilt the cities of Ono and Lod after the Exile (1 Chr. 8:12; some manuscripts have Heb. *šemer*).

SHEMER (Heb. *šemer*) (also SHOMER)

1. Owner of the hill that Omri purchased for the site of Samaria (1 Kgs. 16:24).

2. A Merarite Levite, son of Mahli (1 Chr. 6:46[MT 31]).

3. An Asherite (1 Chr. 7:34), called Shomer at v. 32.

SHEMIDA (Heb. *šĕmîḏāʿ*)

A son of Gilead of the tribe of Manasseh (Num. 26:32; Josh. 17:2; 1 Chr. 7:19), ancestor of the Shemidaite clan (Heb. *šĕmîḏāʿî*).

SHEMINITH

A term (Heb. *ʿal haššĕmînîṯ*, "on the eighth") occurring in the superscriptions of Pss. 6, 12 and at 1 Chr. 15:21. Among suggestions as to its meaning are "octave" (perhaps indicating voices an octave lower), "on an eight-stringed instrument," and "for the eighth stage of the liturgy."

SHEMIRAMOTH (Heb. *šĕmîrāmôṯ*)

1. A levitical musician of the second order appointed to play the harp, accompanying the ark as it was brought to Jerusalem (1 Chr. 15:18, 20; 16:5).

2. One of the Levites sent by King Jehoshaphat to instruct the people of Judah in the law (2 Chr. 17:8).

SHEMUEL (Heb. *šĕmû'ēl*)

1. The representative of Simeon in the division of Canaan; son of Ammihud (Num. 34:20).

2. A son of Tola; head of a household in the tribe of Issachar (1 Chr. 7:2).

SHENAZZAR (Heb. *šen'aṣṣar*)

A son of Jehoiachin (Jeconiah), the captive king of Judah (1 Chr. 3:18). Some would identify Shenazzar (cf. Akk. *Sin-ab-uṣur*) with Sheshbazzar (Ezra 1:8, 11; 5:14, 16).

SHEOL (Heb. *šĕ'ôl*)

The netherworld, the abode of the dead. Derived from the verb *š'h,* "to be extinguished," "to have misfortune," the noun is translated by Gk. *hádēs* and Lat. *infernum* or *inferi.* The English translation "hell" is misleading. Often synonymous with death itself (e.g., 1 Kgs. 2:6, 9), Sheol is depicted as in the depths of the earth (Job 11:8; Prov. 15:24; Ezek.

31:15-18), a place of gloom (10:21-22) and decay (Isa. 14:11).

The concept of an afterlife was relatively undeveloped in Israel's early period. The story of the "witch" of Endor is an excellent example of the concept of Sheol in Israel's Monarchic period. Samuel appears after death as a shadowy figure, appearing much as he had in old age (1 Sam. 28:14). Thus Sheol is a place where the conditions of life are unchanged. From 1 Sam. 28:15 it seems that those in Sheol are in some state of rest and can be disturbed from that calm.

Later passages of the OT portray Sheol as a place of punishment for the unrighteous (Ps. 31:17[MT 18]). The righteous are there as well (cf. Ezek. 32:21, 27), but God is capable of delivering the righteous from Sheol's icy grip (Ps. 49:15[16]). Still, the OT does not describe the alternative to Sheol for those delivered from it.

JIM WEST

SHEPHAM (Heb. *šĕp̄ām*)

A town named as part of the northeast border of the land, N of the Sea of Galilee (Num. 34:10-11). The exact location is still unknown. If the Riblah mentioned later in the passage is correctly identified with Riblah on the Orontes, Shepham would be a place on the Upper Orontes. The expansive boundaries delineated in this passage are not just geographic information, but also serve to illustrate the bounty of the God of Israel.

THOMAS W. DAVIS

SHEPHATIAH (Heb. *šĕp̄aṭyâ, šĕp̄aṭyāhû*)

1. A son of David and his wife Abital born in Hebron (2 Sam. 3:4; 1 Chr. 3:3).

2. An ancestor of a group of Benjaminites who dwelled in Jerusalem after the Exile (1 Chr. 9:8).

3. A Haruphite of the tribe of Benjamin who joined David's rebel force in Ziklag (1 Chr. 12:5 [MT 6]).

4. The son of Maacah; chief of the tribe of Simeon during the reign of David (1 Chr. 27:16).

5. A son of King Jehoshaphat of Judah (2 Chr. 21:2). He and five of his brothers were killed by their brother Jehoram, Jehoshaphat's oldest son, after Jehoram's accession to the throne (2 Chr. 21:4).

6. The ancestor of two groups of people who returned to Judah after the Exile (Ezra 2:4 = Neh. 7:9; Ezra 8:8).

7. One of Solomon's servants whose descendants returned with Zerubbabel from exile in Babylon (Ezra 2:57; Neh. 7:59).

8. A Judahite whose descendants lived in Jerusalem after the Exile (Neh. 11:4).

9. One of four princes of Judah who demanded that King Zedekiah put Jeremiah to death because of his prophecies (Jer. 38:1-4). This occurred during a lull in the Babylonian siege of Jerusalem (Jer. 37:11; 588 B.C.E.). Zedekiah granted their request and gave Jeremiah over to them, and they cast him into a dry cistern to die (Jer. 38:5-6).

STEVEN C. BOUMA-PREDIGER

SHEPHELAH (Heb. *šĕp̄ēlâ*)

The lowland region between the coastal plain in the west and the Judean hills to the east. The Sharon Plain and Negeb Desert comprise the northern and southern boundaries, respectively — an area between the latitudes of modern Tel Aviv and Gaza. The Shephelah encompasses an area 20 km. (12.5 mi.) east-west by 65 km. (40 mi.) north-south. Elevations range from 90-400 m. (300-1300 ft.).

Situated as it is between elevations at sea level to the west and up to 1000 m. (3300 ft.) on the Judean plateau, one can easily understand why the Hebrew term is variously translated as "lowland, low country," "foothills," "vale, valley," and "plain." At Josh. 11:2, 16 it refers to the Shephelah of Israel, an area N of the Carmel range and W of the mountains of Ephraim, or just E of the southern coast of Lebanon.

Geologically, the Shephelah is classified as a synclinal depression, composed of limestone and chalk hills of the Eocene epoch, in contrast to the alluvium and marine sediments of the coastal plain and the harder Cenomanian limestone and dolomite of the Judean plateau. The western side of the plateau is comprised of softer Senonian chalk which has extensively eroded, creating a longitudinal valley between the Shephelah and the plateau.

The Shephelah is intersected by several east-west alluvial valleys which have traditionally served as pathways between cities on the coast and those on the plateau. From north to south, the primary valleys include: Aijalon, Sorek, Elah, Zephatha, Lachish, and el-Hesi. Strategically located cities (Aijalon, Zorah, Gath, Azekah, Mareshah, and Lachish) guarded these valley routes, creating a line of defense for Judah's western boundary and cities in the hill country, including Jerusalem.

The Shephelah is agriculturally fertile, receiving 46 cm. (18 in.) of rain annually. The original vegetation, prior to the onset of deforestation which may have begun before the Early Bronze Age (ca. 3200 B.C.E.), included lentisk bushes and carob trees in the west and oak, terebinth, and Aleppo pine in the east, as well as sycamore-fig trees (1 Chr. 27:28; 1 Kgs. 10:27). The primary crops in ancient times were cereals, olives, and grapes.

According to the tribal allotments in Josh. 15, the Shephelah was part of Judahite territory. Judg. 1 may presuppose an inheritance of Dan in the Shephelah as well (cf. Josh. 19:40-48; 21:23-24; Judg. 1:34-35; 18). The Shephelah may have functioned as one of the administrative divisions of the kingdom, further subdivided unto four districts (Josh. 15:33-44). A fifth Shephelah district (Josh. 15:45-47) included the heart of Philistine territory and was not always under Judahite control.

The Shephelah served as a staging ground for numerous battles, including Joshua's fight against the Amorite coalition (Josh. 10) and Samson's exploits with the Philistines (Judg. 13–16). Rehoboam fortified many cities in the region following Jeroboam's rebellion (2 Chr. 11:5-12). These same fortifications have also been attributed to Hezekiah and Josiah. Archaeological surveys show that the region prospered from the 9th to the 8th centuries, abruptly ending with Sennacherib's invasion and defeat of Lachish and other lowland cities in 701. Cities such as Ekron and Timnah were rebuilt in the 7th century and flourished only to be destroyed a century later at the hands of the Babylonians (604-600). Under Persian rule, the southern part of the Shephelah may have been included as part of Idumea. This arrangement continued into the Hellenistic period. The Maccabean Revolt began in the northern end of the Shephelah and the area was once again a staging ground for battles.

A survey of the Shephelah was conducted in 1979 by Yehuda Dagan as part of the Lachish Expedition of the Institute of Archaeology at Tel Aviv University under the auspices of the Israel Exploration Society. A survey conducted in 1986-87 by Zvi Ilan identified 20 sites as synagogues, most dating to the Roman and Byzantine periods. Remains of other buildings, including churches, were also identified.

Bibliography. H. Brodsky, "The Shephelah — Guardian of Judea," *BibRev* 3/4 (1987): 48-52; I. Finkelstein, "The Shephelah of Israel," *Tel Aviv* 8 (1981): 84-94; N. Na'aman, *Borders and Districts in Biblical Historiography* (Jerusalem, 1986); A. F. Rainey, "The Administrative Division of the Shephelah," *Tel Aviv* 7 (1980): 194-202; "The Biblical Shephelah of Judah," *BASOR* 251 (1983): 1-22.

JENNIFER L. GROVES

SHEPHER, MOUNT (Heb. *har šeper*)
A place where the Israelites stopped during their journey through the wilderness after Sinai (Num. 33:23-24). Its location is unknown.

SHEPHERD
Sheep and goats were the most important domestic animals in the biblical world, and the Bible contains numerous literal and figurative references to these animals — and to those who cared for them. The earliest biblical shepherd was Abel, "a keeper of sheep" (Gen. 4:2). Many people in Hebrew history spent part of their lives as pastoralists (e.g., Abraham, Isaac, Jacob and Rachel and their sons, Moses, and David). In the OT the shepherd's status ranged from that of a lowly herdsman (cf. Amos 7:14-15) to a master breeder of sheep (cf. 2 Kgs. 3:4). In fact, the Bible contrasts David's pastoral and royal careers (2 Sam. 7:8; cf. Ps. 78:70-71). Naturally, nomadic peoples like the Amalekites and Midianites engaged in pastoral activities, but many sedentary farmers also tended flocks or hired shepherds to work for them.

Shepherds spent most of their time in the monotonous work of guarding their flocks. Sheep and goats require constant care, since they are practically defenseless (Ezek. 34:5-6; Matt. 7:15; 18:12). Sheep are submissive (Isa. 53:7; Jer. 11:19) and trust the shepherd (John 10:3-5). Because shepherds had to locate food and water for their flocks, they often ranged far from home and endured numerous hardships (Gen. 31:40; Isa. 38:12; Cant. 1:8). The shepherd guarded against thieves (Gen. 31:39; John 10:1, 8, 10), but the greatest threat came from wild animals, e.g., lions, bears, and wolves (1 Sam. 17:34-35; Isa. 31:4; Amos 3:12; Mic. 5:8; John 10:12).

Sheep are highly gregarious, and the shepherd had to watch for strays and count the animals as they returned to the fold at night (Lev. 27:32; Jer. 33:13; Ezek. 20:37). The shepherd was responsible to find any lost sheep (Ezek. 34:11-12; Matt. 18:11-14). Expectant ewes, newborn lambs, and sick animals received special attention (Isa. 40:11; Ezek. 34:16). The shepherd's work was accomplished with simple equipment — a heavy cloak (cf. Jer. 43:12), a rod and staff (Ps. 23:4), a bag for food, and a sling (1 Sam. 17:40). Even in antiquity, shepherds used dogs to help manage sheep (Job 30:1).

Ancient authors, including the Bible's writers, made extensive use of shepherd imagery. Biblical passages frequently use the customs of shepherds to illustrate spiritual principles (e.g., Num. 27:16-17; Eccl. 12:11; Matt. 9:36; Mark 6:34; John 21:15-17). Ancient peoples also illustrated the sovereignty of their deities by referring to them as shepherds (cf. Gen. 48:15; 49:24); the Hebrew writer thought of Yahweh in this way, as seen most clearly in Ps. 23; Ezek. 34 and in many other psalms and prophetic utterances.

Other ancient Near Eastern literature refers to kings and princes as shepherds (cf. Nah. 3:18), but the OT normally applies this title to political leaders in a negative way. Since God was the true shepherd of Israel, human rulers often fell short of God's standards and were condemned for their stupidity and mismanagement (e.g., Jer. 10:21; 22:22; 23:1-4; 25:34-38; Ezek. 34:1-10; Zech. 10:3; 11:4-17). David, however, was a shepherd who ruled with an "upright heart" and a "skillful hand" (Ps. 78:70-72), and Isaiah refers to Cyrus as God's shepherd (Isa. 44:28). Jeremiah (Jer. 3:15; 23:4) promised that God would raise up new shepherds; this pledge eventually took on messianic significance (Ezek. 34:23; 37:22, 24). It was held that God's shepherd would come from Davidic lineage and would suffer on behalf of the sheep (Zech. 13:7; cf. 12:10).

Surprisingly, the only literal reference to shepherds in the NT is found in Luke 2:8-20; elsewhere they appear in parables and figures of speech, most often in the Gospels. Jesus claims that his mission is "to the lost sheep of the house of Israel" (Matt. 10:6; 15:24). He also tells a famous parable about lost sheep (Matt. 18:12-14; Luke 15:3-7) and compares the shepherd's separation of sheep and goats to judgment (Matt. 25:32-33). In a well-known allegory, Jesus refers to himself as the "good shepherd" who "lays down his life for the sheep" (John 10:1-29).

Outside of the Gospels, Jesus is called "the great shepherd of the sheep" (Heb. 13:20), "the shepherd and guardian of your souls" (1 Pet. 2:25), and "the chief shepherd" (5:4). In his warning about "fierce wolves" (i.e., false teachers), Paul tells the Ephesian elders to oversee and care for the flock — i.e., "the church of God" (Acts 20:28-30). This role is included in the English word "pastor," the normal translation in Eph. 4:11, but Gk. *poimḗn* in this verse is usually rendered "shepherd" (cf. 1 Pet. 5:1-4). GERALD L. MATTINGLY

SHEPHERD OF HERMAS
See HERMAS, SHEPHERD OF.

SHEPHI (Heb. *šĕp̄î*), **SHEPHO** *(šĕp̄ô)*
The fourth son of the Horite clan chief Shobal (**1;** Gen. 36:23; 1 Chr. 1:40).

SHEPHUPHAM (Heb. *šĕp̄ûp̄ām)*
A son of the patriarch Benjamin, and ancestor of the Shuphamites (Num. 26:39). The similarity of the name to names of other descendants of Benjamin — Muppim (Gen. 46:21), Shuppim (1 Chr. 7:21, 15), and Shephuphan (8:5) — suggests that one person, the ancestor of an important Benjaminite line, may be in view.

SHEPHUPHAN (Heb. *šĕp̄ûp̄ān)*
A son of Bela and grandson of the patriarch Benjamin (1 Chr. 8:5).

SHEREBIAH (Heb. *šērēḇyâ)*
1. A "man of discretion" sent from Casiphia with his sons and kinsmen to "minister for the house of God" (Ezra 8:18, 24).
2. A Levite (so 1 Esdr. 9:48; the MT distinguishes him from the Levites) among those who interpreted the Book of the Law for the people as Ezra read it (Neh. 8:7) and who gave the call to praise during the subsequent assembly of fasting and repentance (9:4-5).
3. A Levite who participated in the sealing of the covenant under Nehemiah (Neh. 10:12[MT 13]).
4. A chief of the Levites who returned with Zerubbabel from exile (Neh. 12:8, 24).

SHERESH (Heb. *šereš)*
A Manassite, son of Machir and Maacah (1 Chr. 7:16).

SHESHACH (Heb. *šēšaḵ)*
A cryptogram for Babylon, substituting the consonants *ššk* for *bbl* (Jer. 25:26; 51:41).

SHESHAI (Heb. *šēšay)*
One of three descendants (or clans) of Anak who lived at Hebron when the Israelite spies explored the land of Canaan (Num. 13:22). When Caleb took possession of Hebron, he drove the three out (Josh. 15:14; Judg. 1:10, 20).

SHESHAN (Heb. *šēšān)*
The son of Ishi of the tribe of Judah (1 Chr. 2:31). Sheshan had no sons and, to perpetuate his family, gave one of his daughters to Jarha, his Egyptian slave (1 Chr. 2:34-35).

SHESHBAZZAR (Heb. *šešbaṣṣar;* Akk. *Sin-ab-uṣur)*
The "prince of Judah" (Ezra 1:8), the first Babylonian governor of Judah charged with rebuilding the temple (5:15); the titles may have been more honorific than precise. Apparently he did begin the project during the reign of Cyrus (i.e., before 530 B.C.E.), but was unable to complete it (Ezra 5:16). That he is not mentioned in Haggai or Zechariah is not surprising, given at least Zechariah's insistence that Zerubbabel had founded and would complete the temple. Some scholars equate Sheshbazzar and Zerubbabel, but that is unlikely. If he is the same as the Shenazzar mentioned in 1 Chr. 3:18, he was Zerubbabel's uncle. PAUL L. REDDITT

SHETH (Heb. *šēṯ)*
1. Hebrew spelling of Seth, the son of Adam and Eve (Gen. 4:25; 1 Chr. 1:1).
2. "The sons of Sheth," apparently a designation of Moab in Balaam's prediction of Moab's defeat by Israel (Num. 24:17; NRSV "Shethites"). The Hebrew term should perhaps be emended to *śĕ'ēṯ,* "exaltation, defiance" (cf. NIV mg "noisy boasters"), or *šē'ṯ,* "desolation" (cf. *šā'ôn,* "tumult" at Jer. 48:45, which deliberately echoes Num. 24:17).

SHETHAR (Heb. *šēṯār)*
One of the seven chief advisors to King Ahasuerus (Esth. 1:14).

SHETHAR-BOZENAI (Heb. *šĕṯar bôzĕnay)*
A Persian official who tried to interfere with the rebuilding of the temple in Jerusalem (Ezra 5:3, 6; 6:6, 13; cf. 1 Esdr. 6:3, 7, 27; 7:1, "Sathrabuzanes"), apparently a subordinate of the governor Tattenai.

SHEVA (Heb. *šĕwā'*) (also SERAIAH, SHAVSHA, SHISHA)
1. David's secretary (**Q** 2 Sam. 20:25; **K** *šy'*). He is also known as Seraiah (**2;** 2 Sam. 8:17), Shisha (1 Kgs. 4:3), and Shavsha (1 Chr. 18:16).
2. A son of Caleb and his concubine Maacah (1 Chr. 2:49).

SHIBAH (Heb. *šiḇ'â)*
A well (Heb. "oath") dug by Isaac's servants (Gen. 26:33). Its completion coincided with the making of an oath between Isaac and Abimelech, the Philistine king of Gerar. This account provides a second aetiology for the site (cf. Gen. 21:25-31). Shibah is identified with Tell Beer-sheba/Bir es-Saba (130472), 3 km. (2 mi.) E of the modern town of Beer-sheba. LAURA B. MAZOW

SHIBBOLETH (Heb. *šibbōleṯ)*
A word ("ear of grain" or "torrent") used as a test by Gileadite guards to detect Ephraimites attempting to cross the Jordan (Judg. 12:5-6). Because they spoke a distinct dialect of Hebrew, the Ephraimites would pronounce the word's initial *šin* (a sibilant) as the consonant *sin* (a spirant, originally *that* [*ṯ*], which merged with *šin* at an earlier time in Palestinian usage than in Transjordanian), producing *sibbōleṯ* (written, as in the originally unpointed Hebrew, with a *samech* to distinguish the sounds).

SHIELD
The use of shields in battle is attested as early as the 3rd millennium B.C. in scenes from Egypt and Mesopotamia. The long shield of the Sumerians covered a soldier from the neck to the ankles. With the

advances in construction of body armor in the Late Bronze Age, shields became smaller and lighter, varying in size and shape depending on the country of origin.

Shields commonly consisted of a wooden frame covered with hide or leather, which was oiled to prevent cracking and to ward off more effectively glancing blows (2 Sam. 1:21; Isa. 21:5). Although metal provided greater protection, military shields made entirely of metal were rare since the increased weight impeded a soldier's mobility. Metal was used primarily to strengthen wooden shields.

Gold or bronze shields were hung on the walls of the temple and palace as decoration and as trophies taken in battle (2 Sam. 8:7; 1 Kgs. 10:17; 14:27). Battlements of walls and towers of a besieged city were sometimes covered with the shields of the defenders (Ezek. 27:11). This enabled the owner to be free of the weight yet still enjoy a measure of protection, and it protected the battlements from missiles. At the same time the shield could be taken up for hand-to-hand combat when needed.

"Shield" is often used figuratively to denote God's relation to his people. God is a shield about his servants (Gen. 15:1; Ps. 3:3[MT 4]). The shield is a symbol of divine deliverance (2 Sam. 22:36 = Ps. 18:35[36]) and of God's anointed (84:9[10]). In the NT it is a symbol for the content of the faith, one of the Christian's vital defenses (Eph. 6:16).

Bibliography. R. Gonen, *Weapons of the Ancient World* (Minneapolis, 1976); Y. Yadin, *The Art of Warfare in Biblical Lands* (Jerusalem, 1963).

W. E. Nunnally

SHIGGAION (Heb. *šiggāyôn*), **SHIGIONOTH** (*šigyōnôṯ*)
A term appearing in the superscription of Ps. 7 and in a plural form at Hab. 3:1, which is the superscription of a psalm (vv. 2-19). The term may indicate that these are songs to be performed in a lament or dirge style (cf. Akk. *šegu,* "lament") or that their structure and performance are varied from part to part (cf. Heb. *šāgâ,* "wander").

SHIHOR (Heb. *šîḥôr, šīḥôr, šīḥōr*)
A river marking the boundary between Egypt and Palestine. The name may derive from Egyp. *P3-š-Ḥr* ("Pool of Horus"), the ancient name for a body of water of uncertain location, or may be related to Heb. *šāḥōr,* "black"; it was no longer understood by the time of the translators of the LXX (cf. Josh. 13:3, Gk. *aoíkētos,* "uninhabited"; 1 Chr. 13:5, *hória,* "boundaries"; Jer. 2:18, *Gēōn,* "Gihon"). The term probably designates the Bubastite or Pelusiac branches of the Nile (e.g., Josh. 13:3; 1 Chr. 13:5; Isa. 23:3). Otherwise, the term may refer to the Nile itself (Jer. 2:18).

SHIHOR-LIBNATH (Heb. *šîḥôr liḇnāṯ*)
A place on the western boundary of the territory allotted to the tribe of Asher, in the vicinity of Carmel (Josh. 19:26). Since Heb. *šîḥôr* was used by biblical writers to refer to the Nile (Isa. 23:3; Jer. 2:18) or a river which served as the southern boundary of Canaan (Josh. 13:3) and Israel (1 Chr. 13:5), and the word seems to be derived from an Egyptian word meaning "lake/river of Horus," Shihor-libnath most likely refers to a river near Carmel. It is often identified with the lower branch of the Kishon River (Naḥal Qishon/Nahr el-Muqattaʿ), which runs roughly northwest from Mt. Gilboa to the Mediterranean Sea near Libnath (Tell Abu Huwam) NE of Mt. Carmel. However, other identifications (including the Naḥal Dāyah and Naḥal Tanninim) have been suggested. Eric F. Mason

SHIKKERON (Heb. *šikkĕrôn*)
A city on the northern border of the tribal allotment of Judah (Josh. 15:11), located between Ekron and Mt. Baalah on the northern Philistine Plain. It has been identified with Tell el-Fûl (132136), a small mound ca. 8 km. (5 mi.) SE of Yavne.

Steven M. Ortiz

SHILHI (Heb. *šilḥî*)
The father of Azuba, wife of King Asa and mother of Jehoshaphat (1 Kgs. 22:42; 2 Chr. 20:31).

SHILHIM (Heb. *šilḥîm*)
A city apportioned by Joshua to the tribe of Judah (Josh. 15:32). The parallel list in Simeon's allotment (Josh. 19:6) may reflect Simeon's territorial assimilation with Judah, as well as Shilhim's geographical association with Sharuhen and Shaaraim (1 Chr. 4:31). Ryan Byrne

SHILLEM (Heb. *šillēm*) (also SHALLUM)
A son of Naphtali (Gen. 46:24); ancestor of the Shillemites (Num. 26:49). He is called Shallum (7) at 1 Chr. 7:13.

SHILOAH, WATERS OF (Heb. *mê haššilōaḥ*)
A pool and aqueduct in Jerusalem, part of the Siloam Channel water system (Isa. 8:6).

SHILOH (Heb. *šilōh*)
An ancient holy site in the north-central territory of Ephraim, some 27 km. (17 mi.) N of Bethel, 3 km. (2 mi.) E of the main road, at Tell Seilûn (178162). It was the chief northern shrine through much of the premonarchic period, the site of the ark (1 Sam. 1–3), the tent of meeting (Josh. 18:1; 19:51b; 1 Sam. 2:22b), and the altar (Josh. 22:9-34). According to Josh. 18:9 Shiloh was the early site of the war camp as well. Early traditions also associate Shiloh with the Aaronite priesthood of Phinehas (Josh. 22:13, 30-32; 24:33). Moreover, Shiloh is one of only two shrines, both northern, hallowed in the Priestly traditions of the Hexateuch, the other being Bethel (Gen. 35:9-15). Thus, it is not inappropriate to regard Shiloh as the locus of the Priestly traditions, and to regard these as therefore northern, since both shrines were considered by Jerusalem to have been heretical (cf. Ps. 78:56-72; 1 Kgs. 12:25-33). Shiloh may also have been the chief sanctuary which supported Saul, as the disaster re-

ferred to in Ps.78:56-72 is better associated with Saul's demise on Mt. Gilboa than with an earlier Philistine victory. The histories of both Shiloh and Saul have been edited to convey the Davidic view that the kingship of Saul was illegitimate, since it stood without either ark or sanctuary. Yet the ark does appear, cryptically, during the reign of Saul, in 1 Sam.14:18, where it is borne by a Shilonite priest named Ahijah, a name later associated with the shrine (1 Kgs. 11:29-40).

After the reign of Saul, Shiloh was superseded in importance by the Jebusite city of Jerusalem, where David brought the ark, thus appropriating the heritage of Shiloh to his own regime (probably presaged in the cryptic passage Gen. 49:10). By this means David sought to bind the sacral traditions of the north to his own southern house. Still, the prophet Ahijah the Shilonite may have represented the sacral traditions of Shiloh, and it appears toward the end of the monarchy as a place from which pilgrims travel to the destroyed site of the Jerusalem temple (Jer. 41:5). For the prophet Jeremiah, the demise of the Shiloh sanctuary served as a warning to Jerusalem of the fate that was about to befall it (Jer. 7:12-15; 26:6-9).

Historical debate over Shiloh has centered on the date and circumstances of its destruction. On the basis of Ps. 78:52-72, E. W. Hengstenberg in 1839 first postulated an actual destruction of the site, explaining why the central shrine could legitimately be moved from Shiloh to Jerusalem without any violation of the centralization law in Deuteronomy. Archaeological investigations by the Danes under Aage Schmidt in 1922-1932 seemed to support a destruction of Shiloh during the early Iron I period. William F. Albright dated this destruction to 1050, at the end of the premonarchic period and immediately before the reign of Saul. Subsequent excavations by Marie-Louise Buhl and Svend Holm-Nielsen in 1963 reversed this position, attributing the destruction to sometime in Iron II. Further excavations by Israel Finkelstein in the 1980s seem to confirm the earlier position of Albright and Schmidt. However, the only biblical references to any destruction of Shiloh come from the late date of Jeremiah's ministry. A destruction of the site in Iron I is nowhere recorded.

Dating of the Iron I destruction layer should be undertaken with extreme caution. The suggestion that such a destruction occurred at the end of Saul's reign — in conflict with a more traditional view that the disaster suffered by the Elide priesthood in 1 Sam. 4, and reflected in Ps. 78, came before the reign of Saul — would be difficult to justify or refute given the broad expanse of time which the destruction layer at Tell-Seilûn can fit, even within Iron I.

Bibliography. I. Finkelstein, *The Archaeology of the Israelite Settlement* (Jerusalem, 1988); Finkelstein, ed., *Shiloh: The Archaeology of a Biblical Site* (Tel Aviv, 1993); D. G. Schley, *Shiloh: A Biblical City in Tradition and History.* JSOTSup 63 (Sheffield, 1989).

DONALD G. SCHLEY

SHILONITE (Heb. *šîlōnî, šilônî*)

1. A designation of the prophet Ahijah, perhaps identifying him with the shrine at Shiloh (1 Kgs. 11:29; 12:15; 15:29; 2 Chr. 9:29; 10:15).

2. A gentilic designating a family of returnees from exile (1 Chr. 9:5; Neh. 11:5). The reference may be to descendants of Shelah (**2**); the term should then be rendered "Shelanites" (cf. Num. 26:20).

SHILSHAH (Heb. *šilšâ*)

An Asherite, son of Zophah (1 Chr. 7:37). The name probably represents a clan or region.

SHIMEA (Heb. *šimʿāʾ*) (also SHAMMAH, SHAMMUA, SHIMEAH, SHIMEI)

1. The third son of Jesse; a brother of David (1 Chr. 2:13) and father of Jonathan (**4**)/Jonadab (**1**), who killed a Philistine giant (20:7). Shimea is also known as Shammah (**2;** 1 Sam. 16:9; 17:13), Shimeah (**1;** 2 Sam. 13:3, 32), and Shimei (**3;** 21:21).

2. A son of David born after he had become king of all Israel in Jerusalem (1 Chr. 3:5). He is also called Shammua (**2;** 2 Sam. 5:14; 1 Chr. 14:4).

3. A Levite of the house of Merari (1 Chr. 6:30[MT 15]).

4. A Gershomite Levite, the father of Berechiah (1 Chr. 6:39[24]).

SHIMEAH (Heb. *šimʿâ, šimʾâ*) (also SHIMEA, SHIMEAM)

1. The third son of Jesse, David's father (2 Sam. 13:3, 32). At 1 Chr. 2:13 the name appears as Shimea (**1**).

2. A Benjaminite, the son of Mikloth (1 Chr. 8:32); called Shimeam at 9:38.

SHIMEAM (Heb. *šimʾām*) (also SHIMEAH)

A Benjaminite, the son of Mikloth (1 Chr. 9:38). He also occurs as Shimeah (**2;** 1 Chr. 8:32).

SHIMEATH (Heb. *šimʿāṯ*)

An Ammonite woman whose son Jozacar/Zabad was among those who killed King Joash (Jehoash) of Judah (2 Kgs. 12:21[MT 22]; 2 Chr. 24:6).

SHIMEATHITES (Heb. *šimʿāṯîm*)

One of "the families of the scribes that lived at Jabez," listed among the descendants of Caleb and regarded as a Kenite or Rechabite group (1 Chr. 2:55).

SHIMEI (Heb. *šimʿî*)

1. The second son of Gershon (Gershom), son of Levi (Exod. 6:17; Num. 3:18; 1 Chr. 6:17; 23:7). The Shimeites comprised one of the major levitical families both before and after the Exile (cf. Num. 3:21; Zech. 12:13).

2. The son of Gera, a Benjaminite relative of Saul in Haburim who publicly cursed David and accused him of bloodguilt in an illicit supplanting of the royal house of Saul (2 Sam. 16:5-13). Later, with the rebellion of Absalom quelled, Shimei petitioned David for his life, whereupon David extended to him his oath of clemency (2 Sam. 19:16-

23[MT 17-24]). Nevertheless, on his deathbed, David revealed his continuing suspicion of Shimei and his desire to vindicate the royal house from the power of Shimei's curse. David charged Solomon to find pretext and opportunity to put Shimei to death (1 Kgs. 2:8-9). In return for his oath, Solomon put Shimei on parole and on pain of death confined him to the city of Jerusalem. However, after three years Shimei violated his oath, whereupon Solomon ordered his death (1 Kgs. 2:36-46).

3. The third son of Jesse (2 Sam. 21:21 **K** "Shimei") is an error for Shimea (Heb. *šimʿāʾ* ***Q;*** cf. 2 Sam. 13:3, 32; 1 Chr. 2:13; 20:7).

4. A leader during the last days of David's rule who did not support the usurpation of Adonijah (1 Kgs. 1:8).

5. The son of Ela, one of Solomon's 12 administrators whose responsibility was to provide food for the king and the royal household, responsible for Benjamin (1 Kgs. 4:18). He may be the same as **4** above.

6. The brother of Zerubbabel, son of Pedaiah, and grandson of Jehoiachin (1 Chr. 3:19).

7. A descendant of Mishma and head of a large Simeonite clan (1 Chr. 4:27).

8. The son of Gog and head of a Reubenite family or clan (1 Chr. 5:4).

9. A Levite, one of the descendants of Merari (1 Chr. 6:29[14]).

10. A Levite, son of Jahath, one of the descendants of Gershom (1 Chr. 6:42-43[27-28]).

11. A Benjaminite (1 Chr. 8:21), probably an error for Shema (cf. v. 13).

12. One of the six sons of Jeduthun who was head of the 10th order of temple musicians appointed by David (1 Chr. 25:3, 17).

13. A Ramathite appointed by David over the royal vineyards (1 Chr. 27:27).

14. A Levite descended from Heman who participated in the temple cleansing and cultic reforms at the beginning of Hezekiah's reign (2 Chr. 29:14).

15. A Levite and brother of Conaniah who was second in charge of a team of overseers who received contributions, tithes, and dedicated materials for the temple and the Levites during the cultic reforms of Hezekiah (2 Chr. 31:12-13). He may be the same as **14** above.

16. A Levite who sent away his non-Israelite wife and children (Ezra 10:23; cf. 1 Esdr. 9:23).

17. A descendant of Hashum, a lay person who divorced his non-Israelite wife (Ezra 10:33; cf. 1 Esdr. 9:33).

18. A descendant of Binnui, a lay person who divorced his non-Israelite wife (Ezra 10:38; cf. 1 Esdr. 9:34).

19. A Benjaminite descendant of Kish who was an ancestor of Mordecai (Esth. 2:5; cf. Add. Esth. 11:2). He may be the same as **2** above.

JOHN D. FORTNER

SHIMEON (Heb. *šimʿôn*)
A descendant of Harim, required by Ezra to divorce his foreign wife (Ezra 10:31).

SHIMON (Heb. *šîmôn*)
The head of a Judahite family (1 Chr. 4:20).

SHIMRATH (Heb. *šimrāṯ*)
A son of Shimei (**11**) of the tribe of Benjamin (1 Chr. 8:21), resident of postexilic Jerusalem.

SHIMRI (Heb. *šimrî*)

1. The son of Shemaiah (**3**) of the tribe of Simeon (1 Chr. 4:37).

2. The father of Jediael and Joha, two of David's Mighty Men (1 Chr. 11:45).

3. A levitical gatekeeper, the son of Hosah of the house of Merari (1 Chr. 26:10).

4. A descendant of Elizaphan who was among the Levites who cleansed the temple during the reign of King Hezekiah (2 Chr. 29:13).

SHIMRITH (Heb. *šimrîṯ*) (also SHOMER)
A Moabite woman whose son, Jehozabad, was one of the murderers of King Joash (Jehoash) of Judah (2 Chr. 24:26). At 2 Kgs. 12:21(MT 22) she is called Shomer (**1**).

SHIMRON (Heb. *šimrôn*) **(PERSON)**
A son of the patriarch Issachar (Gen. 46:13; 1 Chr. 7:1), ancestor (or head) of the Shimronites (Heb. *šimrōnî;* Num. 26:24).

SHIMRON (Heb. *šimrôn*),
SHIMRON-MERON (*šimrôn mĕrʾôn)*
A royal Canaanite town that allied with King Jabin of Hazor's confederation against the Israelites (Josh. 11:1). The alliance was defeated by the Israelites under Joshua's leadership (Josh. 12:19-20). The defeated town appears in the MT as Shimron-meron, but the LXX is probably more accurate in listing two separate towns. Shimron was later allotted to the territory of Zebulun (Josh. 19:15). The town is traditionally identified with Khirbet Sammûniyeh/Tel Shimron (170234), ca. 8 km. (5 mi.) W of Nazareth.

Bibliography. W. F. Albright, "Bronze Age Mounds of Northern Palestine and the Hauran," *BASOR* 19 (1925): 9-10.

C. SHAUN LONGSTREET

SHIMSHAI (Aram. *šimšai*)
A high official ("scribe") in the western province of "Beyond the River" (which included Palestine) during the reign of King Artaxerxes I of Persia (465-424 B.C.E.). Shimshai and other officials of the province protested the rebuilding of Jerusalem by Jews who had returned from exile, thinking that the Jews intended rebellion (Ezra 4:8-16). The king's initial response was to agree that the rebuilding should cease (Ezra 4:17-23).

SHINAB (Heb. *šinʾāḇ;* Akk. *Sin-a-bi*)
The king of Admah, one of the five cities that rebelled against Chedorlaomer during the time of Abraham (Gen. 14:2).

SHINAR (Heb. *šin'ār*)
A place name (Akk. *Šanhara;* Egyp. *Sngr*) referring to Babylonia ("the land of Sumer and Akkad"), particularly by peoples dwelling west of the Euphrates, when Babylonia was under Kassite rule during the second half of the 2nd millennium B.C.E.

Shinar is first mentioned in Egyptian documents (Thutmose III, 1457) and also in the Amarna Letters (the Hurrian letter sent from Ittanni [EA 24:95] and that sent from Alašia [Cyprus] to Egypt [EA 35:39]).

In the Table of Nations (Gen. 10:10) Babel, Akkad, Erech, and Calneh were located in "the land of Shinar." However, according to Gen. 11:2, 9 Shinar is parallel to Babel (cf. Isa. 11:11; Zech 5:11). Nebuchadnezzar placed some of the vessels from the Jerusalem temple in his own temple in "the land of Shinar" (Dan. 1:1-2; cf. 2 Chr. 36:6-7). A Neo-Hittite document reports the campaign of Muršili I against "Babylon," while the Babylonian account uses the name Shinar (^{uru}Ša-an-ha-ra).

Amraphel king of Shinar was one of the four kings who defeated Abraham (Gen. 14:1, 9). According to Josh. 7:21 Achan had stolen from the booty of Ai "a beautiful mantle from Shinar."

Bibliography. I. Kalimi, "History of Interpretation: The Book of Chronicles in Jewish Tradition — from Daniel to Spinoza," *RB* 105 (1998): 5-41, esp. 8-10; R. Zadok, "The Origin of the Name Shinar," *ZA* 74 (1984): 240-44. ISAAC KALIMI

SHION (Heb. *šî'ōn*)
A city in the tribal territory of Issachar (Josh. 19:19). Possible locations include Sirin, 22.5 km. (14 mi.) SE of Mt. Tabor, and 'Ayun esh-Sha'in, ca. 5 km. (3 mi.) E of Nazareth.

SHIPHI (Heb. *šip'î*)
The son of Allon; leader of a Simeonite family (1 Chr. 4:37).

SHIPHMITE (Heb. *šipmî*)
A gentilic ascribed to Zabdi, overseer of David's royal vineyards (1 Chr. 27:27). The term may indicate his origin at Shepham (cf. Num. 34:10-11) or Siphmoth (cf. 1 Sam. 30:28).

SHIPHRAH (Heb. *šiprâ;* Egyp. *Šp-ra*)
One of two Hebrew midwives commanded by Pharaoh to kill all male children born to the Israelites (Exod. 1:15-16).

SHIPHTAN (Heb. *šipṭān*)
The father of Kemuel, the representative of Ephraim among those who assisted Moses in the division of the land (Num. 34:24).

SHIPS AND SAILING
As the historic era dawned in the Bible lands, ca. 3000 B.C.E., blue-water sailing on the Mediterranean (and perhaps the Red Sea) already had a venerable tradition. Although the advent of maritime travel and the identity of the first mariners who bravely sailed beyond sight of the shore remain unknown, archaeological evidence from Greece, Cyprus, and Crete indicates that such voyages commenced at least 10 thousand years ago. Very likely the beginning of humankind's adventure with the sea is far older than our evidence currently suggests. For now, the scanty archaeological data for this prehistoric era allow little more than broad generalizations.

Phoenician *hippos* ships with horsehead-shaped prows, transporting lumber from Lebanon for construction of Sargon II's palace at Dur-šarrukin. Alabaster relief from Khorsabad; Louvre (Caisse Nationale des Monuments Historiques et des Sites/ S.P.A.D.E.M.)

Water transport on the great river systems of Egypt and Mesopotamia most likely predated seafaring, but the geographical origins of riverine travel in the Middle East remain uncertain. Does the nod for this great transportation breakthrough belong to the early inhabitants of the Nile corridor or to their counterparts who inhabited the banks of the Euphrates or the Tigris? Wherever primacy of invention belongs, the earliest river boats were probably made from reeds lashed together or were skins stretched taut over wicker. Wooden boats, originally canoelike in appearance, appeared later. Construction techniques for vessels built of planks evolved later to accommodate more goods and passengers. Sumerian craft may have been built with edge-to-edge planking, with fastening achieved through the use of mortise-tenon joinery. In predynastic Egypt, plank boats may have been lashed together with ropes.

The first seagoing vessels were structural cousins or clones of early riverine craft, but the greater rigors of sea travel and the distances to be sailed encouraged the development of more durable wooden boats. The early use of reed rafts, skin craft, and dugout canoes gave way to sturdy plank-built hulls sometime in the Neolithic Age, although when or where this technological advance occurred or if it preceded or followed the appearance of similarly constructed riverine craft cannot be determined.

In the Mediterranean, the ships of antiquity eventually evolved into extraordinarily sophisticated machines, each featuring mortise and tenons to secure the edge-to-edge planking. At present, all ancient wrecks recovered from the Mediterranean that have been dated from the Roman period or earlier were constructed in this fashion. Today, this type of joint is not common in wooden boats, but rather in the most expensive wooden furniture.

Pharaonic Egypt, however, seems to have followed and then modified its nautical tradition of rope lashings to strengthen its wooden ships for the challenges of blue-water sailing. While Egyptian vessels performed superbly on the Nile, their capabilities in deep water were another matter, particularly for trade with Punt down the Red Sea. The failure of Egyptian shipwrights to develop or copy the use of mortise-tenon joints assured a continuing structural weakness in their hulls.

Propulsion of antiquity's ships was limited to wind power, oars, or a combination of the two. Paddles may have been used for riverine craft, but would not have been practical for larger blue-water vessels. By modern standards, ancient vessels did not carry much sail and were not very efficient. One large linen square sail was common, meant to sail before the wind. Sailing windward was far more difficult, but not impossible, particularly after an innovation dating from the late Bronze Age. Sometime late in the 2nd millennium the lower boom of the mainsail, commonly used in earlier vessels, fell from favor and was removed. Brailing lines took place. By adjusting these ropes, which ran through lead rings up the sail and over the yard, the sail's shape or size could be altered to better accommodate prevailing winds.

With such ships, the ancients transformed the Mediterranean and the Red Sea from barriers to highways. The evolution of blue-water sailing was a great step forward. Seafaring played a major, if not completely understood, role in advancing the development of civilization. The ancient seas became communication and transportation conduits for the transfer of culture, commodities, and ideas. Certainly land travel between the Bible lands occurred routinely, but the sea offered a better transportation alternative. Travel by ship was faster, easier, and probably safer.

Although mention of ships dispatched to the Levant to obtain cedar trees appears in some of the earliest Egyptian records, the national origin of the ships that carried this trade is unknown. These early merchants may have been Egyptian or Syro-Canaanite in origin. Later Cypriots, Phoenicians (e.g., Solomon's Red Sea activities with sailors from Hiram of Tyre; 1 Kgs. 10:22; 2 Chr. 9:21), Greeks, and finally Romans dominated waterborne trade to and from the Middle East. Not every civilization that arose around or controlled a part of the littoral of the eastern Mediterranean, however, became a maritime power. The Hittites, e.g., never developed a thalassocracy.

While it is certain that maritime trade began deep in humankind's collective past, its organization, motivation (profit as we understand that term today or "gift" exchanges between rulers and/or societal elites), evolution, and extent at different periods of ancient history remain some of many questions for which there is no scholarly consensus.

Warfare at sea appears in the earliest records as well. Ships were first used as troop transports and fighting platforms. The earliest extant depiction of a naval battle appears as a relief on the wall of Rameses III's mortuary temple at Medinet Habu. There the pharaoh's artists portray his triumph over the invading "Sea Peoples," raiders and/or pirates who had ravaged lands throughout the eastern Mediterranean before meeting their defeat in the Nile Delta (ca. 1190). But was this proclamation of victory truth or hyperbole? Scholars continue to debate the significance of this important monument.

In the Iron Age, specialized warships appeared equipped with a unique weapon. The bronze battle ram, fitted at the waterline of the prow, distinguished a new class of vessels designed specifically to utilize its potential fully. These new instruments of war, the battering ram and the warship equipped with it, became the dominant naval weapon system of the day. Battles at sea became far more common and often decisive for the fate of states and specific rulers. International aspirations and dreams frequently disappeared beneath the sea along with the warships that failed in naval combat, as Mark Antony learned at Actium in 31 B.C.E.

Although artistic depictions of ships and maritime themes like Medinet Habu and literary sources are limited in number, a new and promising window to the ancient maritime past has opened in recent decades. Marine archaeology has begun to realize the potential of the Mediterranean and, to some extent, the Red Sea as archives of unique information about ancient seafaring and ships.

This avenue of research has already confirmed its promise with some remarkable discoveries. George Bass and his team of diving archaeologists have uncovered two early shipwrecks off the Turkish coast. The oldest, found off the headland known today as Uluburun, dated from the later 14th century B.C.E. The other, discovered at Cape Gelidonya, foundered ca. 1200. Together these two excavations have provided invaluable and often unique data about the nature of ship construction and size, cargoes carried, and the geographical scope of maritime trade in the Bronze Age.

Much underwater work is being done in Israel. Shelley Wachsmann headed a team that recovered the hull of a fishing boat from the Sea of Galilee dating from the early Roman Empire. He also has explored a veritable graveyard of ancient ships in Tantura Lagoon near the site of Dor. Kurt Raveh and Sean Kingsley have also excavated at the same site with extraordinary results. Ehud Galili, Avner Raban, and Elisha Linder have also added to our understanding of ships and seafaring along this section of the Levantine coast.

Bibliography. L. Casson, *The Ancient Mariners*, 2nd ed. (Princeton, 1991); *Ships and Seamanship in the Ancient World* (1971, repr. Baltimore, 1995).

ROBERT L. HOHLFELDER

SHISHA (Heb. *šîšā'*) (also SERAIAH, SHAVSHA, SHEVA)
The father of Elihoreph and Ahijah, secretaries for King Solomon (1 Kgs. 4:3). Shisha was probably David's secretary, known as Shavsha (1 Chr. 18:16), Seraiah (**1;** 2 Sam. 8:17), and Sheva (**1;** 20:25).

SHISHAK (Heb. *šîšaq;* Egyp. *ššnq)*
Sheshonq I, first king of the 22nd Dynasty of Egypt. Due to uncertainty regarding the length of several kings of this dynasty, the exact dates and length of his reign are unclear. His accession occurred ca. 950 B.C.E., and he probably reigned 21 years. Shishak reunited Upper and Lower Egypt through a variety of astute political means, such as intermarriage and appointment of his relatives to high offices.

According to 1 Kgs. 14:25-28, during the fifth year of Rehoboam, Shishak invaded Palestine and exacted tribute from Rehoboam — the golden shields Solomon had made for the palace. 2 Chr. 12:1-12 provides further details about the size and ethnic makeup of Shishak's army, but the historical value of these details is uncertain. Most likely, they are exaggerated and reflect the postexilic milieu of the Chronicler.

Shishak's invasion of Palestine is attested on the Bubastite portal of the Karnak temple of Amon in Thebes. One scene contains an inscription describing the battle in stereotypical terms. Below this inscription is a list of cities conquered or visited by Shishak. About two dozen towns in Palestine have been identified in this list, but unfortunately the text is badly damaged in places, hampering efforts to determine Shishak's itinerary. Shishak seems to have bypassed Judah and concentrated on northern Israel and the Negeb.

Bibliography. K. A. Kitchen, *The Third Intermediate Period in Egypt (1100-650 B.C.),* 2nd ed. (Warminster, 1986); D. B. Redford, *Egypt, Canaan, and Israel in Ancient Times* (Princeton, 1992).

PAUL S. ASH

SHITRAI (Heb. *šiṭray)*
A Sharonite, overseer of David's cattle in Sharon (1 Chr. 27:29).

SHITTIM (Hheb. *šiṭṭîm)*
1. The last campsite of the Israelites on the plains of Moab before crossing the Jordan River (Num. 33:49). The name is the abbreviated form of the full toponym Abel-shittim, "Meadow of Acacias" (Num. 33:49). Here, the Moabite king Balak tried to curse Israel through Balaam (Num. 22–24), Israel's men participated in idolatrous relations and immoral practices with Moabite and Midian women (ch. 25), the census was taken (ch. 26), and Joshua was publicly proclaimed the successor of Moses (27:12-23), who delivered his final address to the people here (Deut. 31–33). From here Joshua dispatched two spies (Josh. 2:1) before the Israelites prepared to cross the Jordan (3:1). The prophet Micah urged Israel to remember what God had done for them during the people's journey from Shittim to Gilgal while they entered the Promised Land (Mic. 6:5).

Josephus mentions a place "Abila" in this area. F.-M. Abel first equated Shittim with Tell el-Kefrein (210139), but Nelson Glueck argued for the larger Tell el-Ḥammâm (214138), which during the Iron Age consisted of a fortress with massive towers and a strong glacis.

Bibliography. N. Glueck, "Some Ancient Towns in the Plains of Moab," *BASOR* 91 (1943): 7-26.

2. The "Valley of Shittim" (Joel 3:18[MT 4:18]), an area W of the Jordan. It is probably Wadi en-Nâr, a continuation of the Kidron Valley which extends through the wilderness of Judah up to the Dead Sea.

FRIEDBERT NINOW

SHIZA (Heb. *šîzā'*)
A Reubenite; the father of Adina, one of David's warriors (1 Chr. 11:42).

SHOA (Heb. *šôa'*)
A people whose soldiers, probably mercenaries, accompany Babylonian invaders in a vision of an attack against Jerusalem (Ezek. 23:23). They are commonly identified with the Sutu, a nomadic Aramean tribe known from inscriptions and other sources, but this is far from certain.

SHOBAB (Heb. *šôḇāḇ)*
1. A Judahite, son of Caleb and Azubah (1 Chr. 2:18).

2. A son of David and Bathsheba born in Jerusalem (2 Sam. 5:14; 1 Chr. 3:5; 14:4).

SHOBACH (Heb. *šôḇaḵ*), **SHOPHACH** *(šôpaḵ)*
The commander of the army of the Aramean king Hadadezer of Zobah. David's army defeated Shobach's forces at Helam, and David himself killed Shobach in the battle (2 Sam. 10:16-18 = 1 Chr. 19:16-18, Shophach).

SHOBAI (Heb. *šōḇāy)*
The head of a family of levitical gatekeepers who returned with Zerubbabel from captivity in Babylon (Ezra 2:42 = Neh. 7:45).

SHOBAL (Heb. *šôḇāl)*
1. A Horite chief, son of Seir (Gen. 36:20, 23, 29; 1 Chr. 1:38, 40).

2. A Judahite, son of Hur and ancestor of the inhabitants of Kiriath-jearim (1 Chr. 2:50, 52; 4:1-2).

SHOBEK (Heb. *šôḇēq)*
A participant in the sealing of the covenant under Nehemiah (Neh. 10:24[MT 25]).

SHOBI (Heb. *šōḇî*)
A son of the Ammonite king Nahash who provided food for David and his supporters at Mahanaim as they fled from Absalom (2 Sam. 17:27).

SHOES
See SANDALS, SHOES.

SHOHAM (Heb. *šōham*)
A Levite of the house of Merari, son of Jaaziah (1 Chr. 24:27).

SHOMER (Heb. *šōmēr*)
(also SHEMER, SHIMRITH)
1. The mother of Jehozabad, one of those who killed King Joash (Jehoash) of Judah (2 Kgs. 12:21). She is also known as Shimrith the Moabitess (2 Chr. 24:26).
2. One of the sons of Heber of the tribe of Asher (1 Chr. 7:32). He is also called Shemer (**3;** 1 Chr. 7:34).

SHOPHACH (Heb. *šôpaḵ*)
An alternate name of Shobach (1 Chr. 19:16, 18).

SHOPHAR
A curved musical instrument made of a ram's horn (Heb. *šôpār,* "trumpet" or "horn"). The shophar produces two tones, and is important for its signaling quality rather than its musicality. Its sound carried a long way, and thus it was used to signal attack (Josh. 6:4; Judg. 3:27), sound the alarm of war (Jer. 4:19), prepare for war (51:27), suspend battle and recall troops (2 Sam. 2:28; 18:16), and declare victory (1 Sam. 13:3). It was also used to praise God in worship (Ps. 98:6; 150:3), announce the accession of a king (2 Sam. 15:10; 1 Kgs. 1:34, 39; 2 Kgs. 9:13), summon the Israelites to Sinai (Exod. 19:13, 16, 19; 20:18; cf. Heb. 12:19), proclaim the New Year Festival (Lev. 23:24; Num. 29:1), and herald the arrival of the ark of the covenant into Jerusalem (1 Chr. 15:28). It warns of God's judgment (Hos. 5:8; Amos 2:2), the day of the Lord (Joel 2:1; Zeph. 1:16), and eschatological revelation (Isa. 27:13; Zech. 9:14; Rev. 8:2, 6, 12; 9:1, 13). RICHARD A. SPENCER

SHOWBREAD
In older English translations the name for the bread of the presence.

SHRINE
A structure holding sacred objects, a sanctuary, or a place of worship. A shrine can be a tent (Exod. 33:7), a high place (2 Kgs. 23:19), or a temple (Acts 17:24).
The early Hebrew clans and tribes established shrines both before and after the conquest of Canaan, often occupying abandoned Canaanite shrines or consecrating places where sacred events had occurred. For example, Abraham built an altar at Mamre to commemorate his covenant with God (Gen. 13:18). The tribal confederation also possessed its own traveling shrine, the ark of the covenant, which was later located at various permanent shrines, including Shechem (Josh. 24), Gibeah (Judg. 20:27), Gilgal (Josh. 3–4), and Shiloh (1 Sam. 3:3). Eventually the temple in Jerusalem became the central shrine. Many kings of Israel erected shrines to pagan gods; these were destroyed in the Josianic reform of 622 B.C.E. HENRY L. CARRIGAN, JR.

SHUA (Heb. *šûaʿ*, *šûʿā'*)
1. The father of Judah's Canaanite wife (Gen. 38:2, 12). At 1 Chr. 2:3 recent English versions transliterate *baṯ-šûaʿ* as the proper name ("Bathshua") of Judah's wife rather than translating "daughter of Shua."
2. An Asherite, the daughter of Heber (1 Chr. 7:32).

SHUAH (Heb. *šûaḥ*)
One of the sons of Abraham and his concubine Keturah (Gen. 25:2; 1 Chr. 1:32). Shuah is thought to be associated with Šûḫu, a land on the Euphrates River in Syria known from Assyrian inscriptions, and with the Shuhites, to whom Bildad, one of Job's friends, belonged (Job 2:11).

SHUAL (Heb. *šûʿāl*) **(PERSON)**
A son of Zophah of the tribe of Asher (1 Chr. 7:36). The name may represent a clan or place.

SHUAL (Heb. *šûʿāl*) **(PLACE)**
A region to which one of three groups of Philistine raiders turned as they came out of their camp at Michmash (1 Sam. 13:17). The direction of this group of raiders is also said to be "toward Ophrah"; from this it is known that they were heading northward from Michmash. A connection with Shaalim is possible.

SHUBAEL (Heb. *šûḇā'ēl*)
Alternate form of Shebuel (**2;** 1 Chr. 25:20).

SHUHAH (Heb. *šûḥâ*)
The brother of Chelub of the tribe of Judah (1 Chr. 4:11).

SHUHAM (Heb. *šûḥām*) (also HUSHIM)
A Danite, ancestor of the Shuhamite clans (Num. 26:42-43). At Gen. 46:23 he is called Hushim.

SHUHITE (Heb. *šûḥî*)
A designation of Job's friend Bildad, probably identifying him as a descendant of Shuah (Job 2:11; 8:1; 18:1; 25:1; 42:9).

SHULAMMITE (Heb. *šûlammîṯ*)
A gentilic designating the woman in the Song of Solomon being sought by her lover (Cant. 6:13[MT 7:1]). Four possibilities for the word's origin are suggested: (1) Since the Song of Solomon is ascribed to Solomon, and the name Solomon occurs a number of times in the text (Cant. 1:5; 3:7, 11; 8:11, 12), Shulammite may be a feminine form of Heb. *šĕlōmōh* (Solomon). The Shulammite ("the one belonging to Solomon") is the female counterpart to the Solomon of the Song. (2) The name may

indicate an inhabitant of the town of Shunem, identified with modern Sôlem. Abishag, the young woman who cared for David in his old age and was sought later as a wife by David's son Adonijah, comes from Shunem (1 Kgs. 1–2). (3) Shulammite may be a nickname for Ishtar, the Mesopotamian goddess of war and love, or for Anat, the consort of Baal. (4) The name may be a noun derived from the Hebrew root *šlm* ("well, whole, at peace").

NANCY L. DECLAISSÉ-WALFORD

SHUMATHITES (Heb. *šumāṯî*)
A family residing in Kiriath-jearim descended from Shobal the son of Hur (1 Chr. 2:53).

SHUNEM (Heb. *šûnēm*), **SHUNAMMITE** (*šûnammîṯ*)
A town in the territory of Issachar (Josh. 19:18), located near Mt. Gilboa at the foot of the hill of Moreh, on the eastern edge of the Jezreel Plain. The site is ca. 8 km. (5 mi.) S of Mt. Tabor on the lower southwest slope of the Nebī Daḥī. The valley between Shunem and the city of Jezreel to its south forms a natural pass to the Jordan River. Scholars identify the site as the modern village of Sôlem (181223), 14.5 km. (9 mi.) N of Jenîn.

Surveys of the site indicate that the earliest occupation began in the Middle Bronze Age and continued through the Islamic period. During the Canaanite period, the city held power as a small city-state. Thutmose III (15th century) conquered the city (Shunama), and the Amarna Letters (14th century) mention its defeat by Labʿayu of Shechem and its inhabitants being pressed into forced labor. Biridiya, prince of Megiddo, soon rebuilt the city.

Shunem falls within the tribal territory of Issacher (Josh. 19:18). In the late 11th century, the Philistine army assembled at Shunem prior to the final battle in which Saul was killed (1 Sam. 28:4). Abishag, the young woman brought to David in his old age, was from Shunem (1 Kgs. 1:3); it was Adonijah's request for Abishag as wife that led to Solomon's orders to execute his brother. Following the division of the kingdom, Pharaoh Sheshonk (Shishak) listed the city among his conquered cities in the Karnak list, although the biblical record is silent concerning the Egyptian conquest of northern cities. A Shunammite woman fed and housed the prophet Elisha, and he later revived her son (2 Kgs. 4:8-37). Some interpreters connect Shunem with the Shulammite of the Song of Solomon (Cant. 6:13[MT 7:1]).

NANCY L. DECLAISSÉ-WALFORD/STEPHEN VON WYRICK

SHUNI (Heb. *šûnî*)
A son of Gad and grandson of Jacob and Zilpah (Gen. 46:16); eponymous ancestor of the Shunites (Heb. *haššûnî;* Num. 26:15).

SHUPHAMITES (Heb. *šûp̄āmîm*)
A Benjaminite clan claiming Shephupham as eponymous ancestor (Num. 26:39).

SHUPPIM (Heb. *šuppîm*)

1. One of the two sons of Ir of the tribe of Benjamin (1 Chr. 7:12). "Shuppim" and "Huppim" are probably alternate forms of "Shephupham" and "Hupham," which also appear in a Benjaminite genealogy list (Num. 26:39; cf. Gen. 46:21; 1 Chr. 8:5). Their appearance in a quite confused Manassite list (1 Chr. 7:15) is probably the result of textual corruption.

2. A levitical gatekeeper at the west gate of the temple at the time of David (1 Chr. 26:16).

SHUR (Heb. *šûr*)
A desert region in the northeast Sinai, S of the Mediterranean coast and between Egypt and the Brook of Egypt (Wadi el-ʾArish). The wilderness of Sur, also called the wilderness of Etham (Num. 33:8), was the southwestern border of Canaan. For a time Abraham settled between Kadesh and Shur (Gen. 20:1), and Abraham's handmaid Hagar fled toward Shur to a well, where an angel found her (16:7). The descendants of Ishmael settled from Havilah to Shur (Gen. 25:18). Later, Moses led the Israelites through the wilderness of Shur for three days until they came to the bitter waters of Marah (Exod. 15:22). Shur was used to indicate the direction from Palestine toward Egypt (1 Sam. 15:7; 27:8).

Shur (Heb. "wall") may also have referred to a series of border forts established by the Egyptians to control the influx of foreigners from the east. The Way to Shur was a major caravan route that ran east-west from the King's Highway through the wildernesses of Zin and Shur to Egypt (Gen. 16:7).

BRADFORD SCOTT HUMMEL

SHUTHELAH (Heb. *šûṯelaḥ*)

1. A son of Ephraim, ancestor of the Shuthelahite clan (Num. 26:35-36; 1 Chr. 7:20).

2. An Ephraimite, the son of Zabad (1 Chr. 7:21). The text is unclear whether he is the same as **1** above or a descendant.

SIA (Heb. *sîʿāʾ*), **SIAHA** (*sîʿăhāʾ*)
The head of a family of temple servants who returned with Zerubbabel from captivity in Babylon (Ezra 2:44, "Siaha"; Neh. 7:47, "Sia").

SIBBECAI (Heb. *sibbĕḵay*) (also MEBUNNAI)
A Hushathite, and one of David's Mighty Men who served as commander of the eighth division of David's army (1 Chr. 11:29; 27:11) and defeated the giant Saph/Sippai (2 Sam. 21:18 = 1 Chr. 20:4). At 2 Sam. 23:27 he is called Mebunnai.

SIBBOLETH (Heb. *sîbbōleṯ*)
See SHIBBOLETH.

SIBMAH (Heb. *śiḇmâ*) (also SEBAM)
A Moabite town on the east side of the Jordan River, near Heshbon, given to the tribe of Reuben following the defeat of the Amorite king Sihon (Josh. 13:19). The name of this town is misspelled as Sebam in the MT of Num. 32:3, and appears correctly in v. 38. Sibmah, known for its vineyards, was

later retaken by the Moabites, and is condemned in the oracles against Moab (Isa. 16:8-13; Jer. 48:32-33). The site is traditionally identified with Khirbet Qarn el-Qibsh, situated between Heshbon and Nebo. KENNETH ATKINSON

SIBRAIM (Heb. *sib̲rayim*)
A place in Syria mentioned in Ezekiel's description of Israel's ideal northern boundary (Ezek. 47:16). A location at the northern end of the Lebanon and Anti-Lebanon ranges and the source of the Orontes River is indicated by Sibraim's description as "between the border of Damascus and the border of Hamath."

SIBYLLINE ORACLES
A collection of oracles included among the Pseudepigrapha. Ancient Greek tradition, later accepted by the Romans and Jews, viewed the Sibyl as an old woman to whom ecstatic predictions were attributed. She was thought to have been a wanderer, and by the 1st century B.C. 10 Sibyls were mentioned by Varro in association with 10 geographic locales. Few people claimed to have actually seen a Sibyl, and the Oracles were known primarily through various collections that circulated. From the earliest days, the Sibylline Oracles were written down in hexameter form while the use of the acrostic was viewed as a mark of authenticity. The most famous collection was to be found in Rome. These books were only consulted in times of crisis and by the order of the senate. When the temple of Jupiter burned down in 83 B.C. this collection was lost to fire. A commission was formed to collect "new" oracles. This second Roman collection remained important until they were destroyed in the reign of the Christian emperor Theodosios in A.D. 408. Only fragments survived.

Jews and Christians wrote their own oracles attributed to the Sibyls. Jews explained that the Sibyl was one of the daughters-in-law of Noah (Sib. Or. 3:827), while Christians explicitly stated that the Sibyl was pagan yet prophesied the coming of Jesus Christ. Some of the pagan fragments which remained may be found in the present 14-book collection of the Jews and Christians, the books ranging in date from ca. 250 B.C. until ca. A.D. 550. Christians accepted the Jewish oracles and occasionally added their own interpolations. These Oracles enjoyed great popularity among Patristic, medieval, and Renaissance writers and artists.

Bibliography. J. J. Collins, "Sibylline Oracles," *OTP* 1:317-472. JAMES V. SMITH

SICKLE
A handheld, curved cutting tool for harvesting standing grain (Deut. 16:9; 23:25[MT 26]). In the Early Bronze Age a sickle's blade was constructed by inserting serrated flints into a curved wooden frame. Along with other agricultural blade tools, the "Canaanean" blade was made from a high-quality imported flint. This hard flint allowed the blades to be resharpened. Later, metal sickles with wooden handles appeared.

The sickle is symbolic of God's wrath and fulfilled judgment in both Joel 3:13(4:13) and the NT (Mark 4:19; Rev. 14:14-19).

Bibliography. S. A. Rosen, "The Canaanean Blade and the Early Bronze Age," *IEJ* 33 (1983): 15-29. J. A. VADNAIS

SIDDIM (Heb. *śiddîm*), **VALLEY OF**
The valley where King Chedorlaomer of Elam and his allies conquered the armies of Sodom, Gomorrah, Admah, Bela (Zoar), and Zeboiim (Gen. 14). Identified in Gen. 14:3 as the Salt Sea (Dead Sea), Siddim is often associated with the sea's southern end, where modern bitumen deposits are reminiscent of the tar pits mentioned in v. 10, into which soldiers from the armies of Sodom and Gomorrah fell during their retreat. In equating the Salt Sea with the valley of Siddim, Gen. 14 seems to imply a later submersion of the valley as a result of the destruction of Sodom and Gomorrah (Gen. 19). RYAN BYRNE

SIDON (Heb. *ṣîd̲ôn*; Gk. *Sidṓn*)
Phoenician metropolis and famous harbor in southern Lebanon, some 40 km. (25 mi.) S of Beirut. The modern town of Ṣaidā lies over the ancient site, and only its perimeter has been explored by archaeology. Sidon had a complex double port consisting of an off-shore island anchorage, with multiple landing places on the shore north of the city. On the south was a large natural haven called the Round Bay. The latest ancient description of the ports of Sidon is in the writings of the 3rd-century C.E. Alexandrian Greek mathematician Achilleus Tatius.

The city is mentioned in Egyptian *(Ḏdn)*, Hittite, Ugaritic *(Ṣdyn)*, and Assyrian records of the 2nd millennium B.C.E. During the Amarna Age (14th century), its king Zimr-adda supported the local rebellions against Egyptian authority in the Lebanon. Its Canaanite name was *Ṣidunu*, probably derived from the root *ṣwd*, "hunting, fishing" (cf. Heb. *ṣayid̲*). In later Phoenician and Hebrew the name was Ṣîd̲ôn, the form also attested in Greek (the Roman author Justin regarded this as a Phoenician word for "fish").

The statement of Gen. 10:15 that Sidon was the firstborn of Canaan appears to be an allusion to the prominent role played by this city in Canaanite culture. According to Josh. 11:8; 19:29 the Hebrew conquest of the Promised Land extended as far as the territory of Great Sidon *(ṣîd̲ôn rabbâ)*, and the region was then allotted to the tribe of Asher. Other biblical accounts, however, indicate that Hebrews were not settled in that area of the Lebanon (cf. Judg. 18:28). Greco-Roman writers (Strabo *Geog.* 16.2.13; Justin 18.3.5) record a tradition that Sidonian refugees rebuilt Tyre after its destruction in the era of the Trojan War.

These later traditions concerning the leading role of Sidon in Phoenicia were also well known to the early Greeks. In the epics of Homer, the title Sidonian is synonymous to the word "Phoenician," just as in the Bible Sidonian can also refer to the coastal Canaanites in general (1 Kgs. 5:6[MT 20]). Deut. 3:9 preserves a tradition that the Sidonians spoke a distinct dialect, presumably what we now call Phoenician. Among the numerous foreign women Solomon married were "Sidonian" ladies (1 Kgs. 11:1), and Ethbaal, the father of Queen Jezebel, was known to the Hebrews as the "King of Sidonians" (1 Kgs. 16:31) although he was a king of Tyre.

Sidon lost much of her power and prestige under the Assyrian and Babylonian domination of the Levant beginning in the 9th century. Allusions to the decline of Sidon, along with other kingdoms in the region, under the crushing blows of invading imperial armies are found in several prophetic passages in the Bible (Isa. 23:4; Jer. 25:22; 47:4; Ezek. 28:20-27; Joel 3:4[4:4]).

Under the Persian kings, Sidon regained much of her lost glory, territory, and political influence. The Persian emperor Darius I (522-486) ceded the fertile coastal strip from Dor to Jaffa to the Sidonian king Eshmunazor II (ca. 501-487), an act which led to the founding of several Sidonian settlements in this region. During that generation, when the Judeans rebuilt the temple in Jerusalem, the cedars of the Lebanon for its construction were transported by both Sidonians and Tyrians to "the Sea of Jaffa" (Ezra 3:7), perhaps to the settlement at Tell Qasile.

In the Hellenistic era, when Sidon was still competing with Tyre for primacy in Phoenicia, the city minted coins inscribed with the legend "belonging to the Sidonians, metropolis of Cambe, Hipp, Citium, Tyre." Cambe refers to Carthage — a city founded by Tyrians — while Tyre, located only 35 km. (22 mi.) from Sidon, is listed last. The region of Tyre and Sidon is mentioned in the NT narrative about Jesus and the Canaanite woman (Matt. 15:21-28; cf. Mark 7:24-31).

Bibliography. W. F. Albright, "The Role of the Canaanites in the History of Civilization," in *The Bible and the Ancient Near East,* ed. G. E. Wright (1961, repr. Garden City, 1965), 438-87; H. Frost, "The Offshore Island Harbour at Sidon and Other Phoenician Sites in the Light of New Dating Evidence," *International Journal of Nautical Archaeology* 2 (1973): 75-94; N. Jidejian, *Sidon through the Ages* (Beirut, 1971); T. Kelly, "Herodotus and the Chronology of the Kings of Sidon," *BASOR* 268 (1987): 39-56.

ROBERT R. STIEGLITZ

SIEGE

A warfare strategy involving the surrounding of a city until its population either surrendered or was weakened enough to be overcome. An effective siege cut off all lines of communication of a city as well as all nearby water supplies. Although siege warfare was practiced as early as Middle Kingdom Egypt and known throughout the ancient Near East, the Assyrians and later Babylonians became true masters of this type of warfare.

The siege of Rabbah (2 Sam. 12:27) is the earliest recorded siege of the Israelites; prior to this direct assault was the preferred means of capturing a city. When the Israelites besieged a city, they built a siege wall or earthen mound to protect the attackers down below (2 Sam. 20:15; 2 Kgs. 19:32 = Isa. 37:33; Jer. 6:6; 32:24; 33:4; Ezek. 4:2; 17:17; 21:22). Examples of such works have been found at sites throughout Palestine, as have water tunnels that allowed for the collection of water without leaving the safety of a walled city (as at Hazor, Megiddo, and Jerusalem).

Assyrian siege methods are well attested in both reliefs and cuneiform sources. The Assyrians used battering rams and other war machines to knock down a city's gates and walls; walls were further weakened by digging trenches along the outside of the city wall. When the city's defenses were sufficiently weakened, the heavily armed attackers ascended tall scaling ladders, fending off arrows and boiling oil hurled by the besieged. It is believed that the extremely thick, well-built city walls and gates of Middle Bronze Age Palestine were constructed with the battering ram in mind.

The Seleucids also employed Assyrian and Babylonian methods of siege warfare, notably in their 2nd-century B.C.E. siege of Jerusalem (1 Macc. 6:48). The Seleucids had various methods for hurling fire and stones into besieged Jerusalem; it is unclear if catapults or similar machines were known to the Assyrians.

JENNIE R. EBELING

SIGN

An act or manifestation that points to something beyond the sign itself, in most biblical instances God's purpose or the relationship between God and his people.

In the OT signs (Heb. *'ôṯ, môpeṯ*) refer primarily to divine or prophetic acts. To understand the symbolism of any sign, a word from the Lord is necessary. Signs in the OT cluster around two major works of God: the Exodus, with frequent reference to "signs and wonders" miraculously performed by God through Moses (Exod. 7:3); and less spectacular symbolic signs employed by the prophet, attesting the prophet as God's messenger (Isa. 7:14; 8:18; cf. Ezek. 12:6, 11; 24:24, 27). Nothing miraculous is present in Isaiah's walking "stripped and barefoot" for three years as a sign of judgment on Egypt and Cush (Isa. 20:3; cf. Jer. 19:1-6; Ezek. 4:1-8). Prophetic signs have two revelatory elements: the prophetic word and the act's intrinsic symbolism. Both converge, so when the sign is accomplished, the prophet's word is authenticated as divine.

In the NT signs (Gk. *sēmeíon*) reflect OT roots, referring to actions or things that carry symbolic meaning (e.g., Judas's kiss, Matt. 26:48; cf. Luke 2:12; Rom. 4:11). Tongues-speaking is a sign of God's judgment on unbelief (1 Cor. 14:22; cf. Isa. 28:11-12). Cosmic signs are indications of the last days (Matt. 24:30; Luke 21:11, 25; Acts 2:19; Rev. 12:1, 3; 15:1). "Signs and wonders" accompany the apostles to attest them and their divine message (Rom. 15:19; Acts 2:22, 43; 5:12; 6:8; 14:3; 15:12; Heb. 2:4).

Jesus' signs are public acts. Though most are miraculous (John 2:1-11; 4:41-54; 5:1-15; 6:1-14; 9:1-41; 11:1-57), the symbolic function of the sign takes precedence, for every sign points away from itself and from the earthly realm to that which it symbolizes in the heavenly realm. Hence, the cleansing of the temple (John 2:13-25; cf. v. 23; 3:2) also functions as a prophetic-symbolic sign, pointing to the true temple where humans meet God, namely Jesus' body.

Bibliography. F. J. Helfmeyer, "'ôṯ ['ôth]," *TDOT* 1:167-88; C. R. Koester, *Symbolism in the Fourth Gospel* (Minneapolis, 1996); A. J. Köstenberger, "The Seventh Johannine Sign," *BBR* 5 (1995): 87-103; K. H. Rengstorf, "sēmeíon," *TDNT* 7:200-261.

A. B. CANEDAY

SIGNET

See SEAL, SIGNET.

SIHON (Heb. *sîḥōn, sîḥôn*)

One of the Amorite kings of Transjordan whom the Israelites defeated before entering Canaan. Sihon's capital was Heshbon (Deut. 2:26, 30), and the borders of his kingdom extended south to the Arnon River and north to the Jabbok (Num. 21:24). Since Sihon's territory lay between the Israelites and Canaan, Moses requested peaceful passage (Num. 21:22). Not only did Sihon refuse Moses' request, he engaged the Israelites in battle at Jahaz (Num. 21:23). The Israelites slew Sihon and defeated his forces, thus gaining control of southern Transjordan. This newly acquired territory was assigned to the tribes of Reuben, Gad, and the half-tribe of Manasseh on the condition that they cross over into Canaan to help the other tribes dispossess the inhabitants of the land (Num. 32:33). In his final speech, Moses refers back to this victory as "down payment" of what God would do for Israel in Canaan (Deut. 29:7[MT 6]; 31:4). Moreover, the Canaanites themselves understood this victory as evidence that God was fighting for Israel (Josh. 2:10; 9:10). Often paired with the subsequent Israelite conquest of Og of Bashan (Num. 21:33-35; Deut. 3:8), this battle symbolized God's power and faithfulness (Neh. 9:22; Ps. 135:10-12; 136:19-20).

Bibliography. A. Haldar, *Who Were the Amorites?* (Leiden, 1970). JEFFREY C. GEOGHEGAN

SILAS (Gk. *Sílas*) (also SILVANUS)

A leader of the Jerusalem church and companion of Paul on his second missionary journey (Acts 15:22–18:5). He is the same as Silvanus in the Epistles (2 Cor. 1:19; 1 Thess. 1:1; 2 Thess. 1:1; cf. Acts 16:19-24; 18:1-5; 1 Thess. 2:2). Silvanus is the Latin form and Silas either a Semitic name or Greek abbreviation.

Silas is one of the "leading men" from the Jerusalem church who was chosen to deliver and explain to the believers in Syria and Cilicia the decision of the Jerusalem council (Acts 15:22). He and Judas (Barsabbas) accompanied Paul and Barnabas on this important mission, and as prophets (Acts 15:32) they encouraged and strengthened those in Antioch. Apparently after Silas reported back to Jerusalem (Acts 15:33) he returned to Antioch.

Following his disagreement with Barnabas, Paul chose Silas to accompany him on his second missionary journey (Acts 15:40) beginning in Syria and Cilicia. Silas' presence gave to their ministry the sanction of Jerusalem (cf. Acts 16:4), and like Paul he was a Roman citizen (16:37-38), another benefit in their travels. Joined at Lystra by Timothy and at Troas by Luke, they ventured into Macedonia (Acts 16:8-11), where they ministered in Philippi and were briefly imprisoned (vv. 19-40), and then to Thessalonica and Beroea before Paul was forced to flee to Athens. Although Silas and Timothy may have come to Paul at Athens for a time (Acts 17:15), they apparently ministered in Macedonia before rejoining Paul at Corinth (Acts 18:5; 2 Cor. 1:19). There Silas is listed along with Paul and Timothy as a co-sender of the Thessalonian epistles (1 Thess. 1:1; 2 Thess. 1:1).

Silas (Silvanus) was apparently later at Rome, where he assisted Peter with his first letter (1 Pet. 5:12), either as Peter's amanuensis or courier. Peter's personal commendation of Silas and the absence of a salutation from Silas to the recipients (cf. Mark in 1 Pet. 5:13) favor the latter.

Bibliography. F. F. Bruce, *The Pauline Circle* (Grand Rapids, 1985), 23-28; D. E. Hiebert, *Personalities Around Paul* (Chicago, 1973), 88-97; B. N. Kaye, "Acts' Portrait of Silas," *NovT* 21 (1979): 13-26.

W. EDWARD GLENNY

SILK

A rare and valuable textile produced by the larvae of the Chinese moth *(Bombyx mori)* and obtained by unwinding its cocoon. This tedious labor yields a lustrous, fine, yet strong filament, which can be dyed, spun, and woven. Known in the West by the 4th century B.C., true silk (Gk. *sērikós*) has an unmistakable Eastern origin (*Sḗrēs,* "Chinese"). The extravagance of this commodity is suggested by Josephus, who mentions silk robes as a part of the victory spectacle of Rome (*BJ* 7.126), and by Rev. 18:12, which includes silk in a list of precious items from "Babylon."

In the OT Heb. *mešî* (Ezek. 16:10, 13) and *šēš* (Exod. 25:4; Prov. 31:22) have been translated as "silk" (KJV). These may refer to an inferior silk associated with the island of Cos in the Aegean, or to a type of fine linen (so NRSV).

MARK ZIESE

SILLA (Heb. *sillā'*)

Perhaps a landmark or section of the City of David, mentioned in connection with the house of Millo (**3**; 2 Kgs. 12:20[MT 21]).

SILOAM (Gk. *Silōam;* Heb. *šilōaḥ*) **CHANNEL**

Channel II, the water supply system in ancient Jerusalem that opened ca. 3 m. (10 ft.) above the floor of the Gihon Spring and followed a course that ran outside the fortification wall on the City of David's east slope. It is a composite system, con-

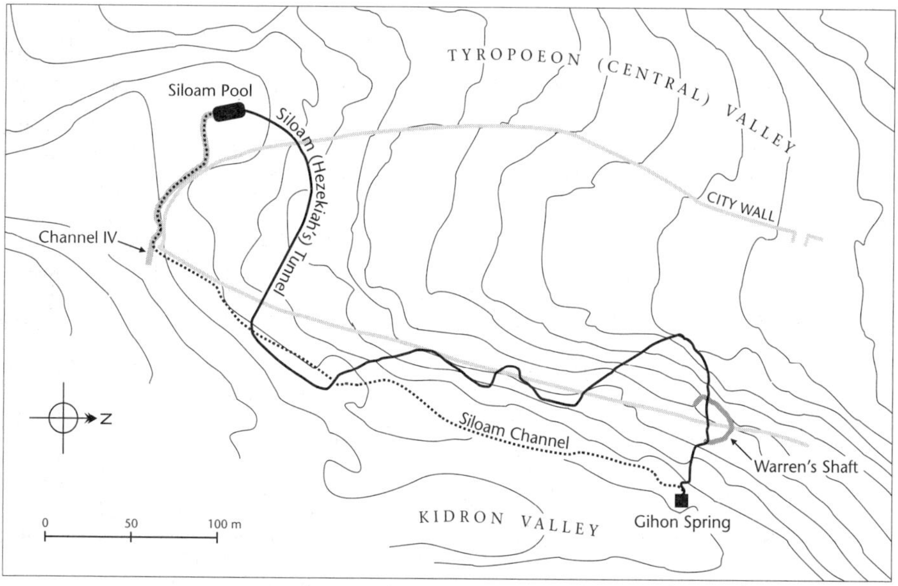

Iron Age II water systems in the City of David (strata 14-10), featuring the Siloam channel
(City of David Archaeological Project)

sisting partly of a rock-hewn tunnel and partly of a rock-hewn and stone-capped channel, that varies in width from 0.4-0.6 m. (1.3-2 ft.) and in height from 1.4-2.75 m. (4.6-9 ft.). Roughly half of its estimated 400 m. (1312 ft.) length has been investigated.

Because the Gihon is a siphon-type, karstic spring whose outflow gushed forth intermittently, its excess waters could not be used efficiently unless they could be captured, stored, and distributed. The Siloam Channel was designed to control the excess waters of the Gihon in three ways: by conveying them to a reservoir located in the southern reaches of the Tyropoeon Valley; by releasing them onto agricultural plots in the Kidron Valley through windowlike openings in its east wall; and by supplementing them with runoff collected through openings in its roof.

The Siloam Channel was superseded and partly canceled by the Siloam Tunnel, which diverted its waters and changed the direction in which water flowed through its south end. Thus, although the Siloam Channel's precise date of construction is not known, it must predate the Siloam Tunnel and may be identified with "the waters of Shiloah (Siloam) that flow gently" (Isa. 8:6) and the "upper watercourse of Gihon" (2 Chr. 32:30) that Hezekiah stopped and brought down to the west side of the City of David.

Bibliography. Y. Shiloh, *Excavations in the City of David,* 1: *1978-1982: Interim Report of the First Five Seasons.* Qedem 19 (Jerusalem, 1984); L. H. Vincent, *Underground Jerusalem: Discoveries on the Hill of Ophel (1909-11)* (London, 1911).

JANE M. CAHILL

SILOAM (Gk. *Silōam;* Heb. *šilōaḥ*) **TUNNEL**
The subterranean water supply system in ancient Jerusalem attributed to King Hezekiah that carried water from the Gihon Spring, the city's only perennial source of water, to the Siloam Pool, a reservoir located in the southern reaches of the Tyropoeon Valley. It consists of four component parts: a spring, a rock-cut tunnel, a reservoir, and an overflow channel.

Located in the Kidron Valley outside the city's fortification wall, the Gihon Spring is a siphon-type, karstic spring whose outflow varied with the seasons and whose waters could not be used efficiently unless they could be captured, stored, and distributed. Because the first water supply system designed to exploit the excess waters of the Gihon — the Siloam Channel — lay outside the city's fortification wall, it served no strategic function. Therefore, when the Assyrians threatened Jerusalem during the reign of Hezekiah, the Siloam Tunnel was designed to exploit and protect the excess waters of the Gihon by bringing them into the fortified area of the city.

From the Gihon, a sinuous tunnel cut through the bedrock carried water for a distance of 533 m. (1750 ft.) to the Siloam Pool located only 320 m. (1050 ft.) away. While the tunnel exhibits only slight variations in width, ranging from .58-.65 m. (1.9-2.1 ft.), it exhibits extreme variations in height, ranging from 1.5-5.0 m. (4.9–16.4 ft.). The difference in level between its starting point and its present ending poiht is a minute 33 cm. (13 in.). Toolmarks visible on its walls indicate that it was quarried by two teams of tunnelers working toward each other from opposite directions. The meeting of the two teams is described in a monumental inscription — the Siloam inscription — carved into the rock wall near the tunnel's south end.

The tunnel's sinuous shape, its length, the variability of its height, and the way in which two teams of tunnelers working toward each other managed to meet have been subjects of considerable debate. Scholarly explanations for these anomalies include: the need to follow a soft, easily quarried stratum in the bedrock; the desire to avoid the tombs of the Davidic kings; and the ability to follow a natural fissure. In his hydro-geological survey of the City of David, Dan Gil demonstrates that the tunnel's anomalous features resulted from the enlargement of a preexisting natural solution conduit that originally carried water toward the spring. Gil's survey shows that the entire tunnel is cut through hard *(mizzi ahmar)* limestone and that its variation in height evidences the down-cutting required to reverse the water flow from the direction of the spring to the direction of the reservoir.

The rock-cut tunnel empties into a small reservoir called the Siloam Pool, known also as the pool of Shiloah and Birket es-Silwan. Excavations conducted in its vicinity have yielded evidence of reservoirs dating to the Roman and Byzantine periods. Although physical remains of earlier reservoirs have yet to be found, they were probably located in the same vicinity.

Beyond the Siloam Pool, a rock-cut channel — known as Channel IV — carried water in an easterly direction around the southern tip of the City of David toward the Kidron Valley either for purposes of irrigation or for storage in additional reservoirs. At its southeastern extremity, Channel IV incorporated the south end of the Siloam Channel and reversed the flow of water through it. Channel IV's excavator, Raymond Weill, believed that it represented an addition to the Siloam Tunnel. However, David Ussishkin identifies it as the final segment of the Siloam Tunnel which, he believes, emptied in the vicinity of the Kidron rather than the Tyropoeon Valley.

The ascription of the Siloam Tunnel to Hezekiah (ca. late 8th century B.C.E.) is based on evidence in the Bible (2 Kgs. 20:20; 2 Chr. 32:30) and the Apocrypha (Sir. 48:17), as well as on the paleography of the Siloam inscription. Although aqueducts replaced the Gihon Spring as Jerusalem's primary source of water during the Hellenistic and Roman periods, the Siloam Tunnel and Pool remained in use (John 9:7; Luke 13:4). During the Byzantine period, a church depicted on the Madeba Map was built above the Siloam Pool. Today a mosque stands above remains of the church. Channel IV remained in use until the Middle Ages when it was blocked by a stone wall.

Bibliography. D. Gil, "The Geology of the City of David and Its Ancient Subterranean Waterworks," in *Excavations at the City of David,* 4: *1978-1985: Various Reports,* ed. D. T. Ariel and A. DeGroot. Qedem 35 (Jerusalem, 1996); "How They Met: Geology Solves Long-standing Mystery of Hezekiah's Tunnelers," *BARev* 20/4 (1994): 20-33, 64; Y. Shiloh, *Excavations at the City of David,* 1: *1978-1982: Interim Report of the First Five Seasons.* Qedem 19 (Jerusalem, 1984); D. Ussishkin, "The Original Length of the Siloam Tunnel in Jerusalem," *Levant* 8 (1976): 82-95.

JANE M. CAHILL

SILVANUS (Gk. *Silouanós*)
An alternate name of Silas in the Epistles.

SILVER
A precious metal having multiple uses. In biblical times silver (Heb. *kesep;* Gk. *árgyros*) was used for money (Gen. 23:15-16; Matt. 26:15; Acts 3:6), jewelry (Exod. 3:22), a variety of utensils such as cups, dishes, and bowls (Gen. 44:2; Num. 7:13; 2 Tim. 2:20), idols (Exod. 20:23; Acts 17:29; Rev. 9:20), and trumpets (Num. 10:2). Silver was used in the construction of the tabernacle (Exod. 26–27) and in some of the temple utensils (1 Chr. 28:15-17; 2 Chr. 24:14). The possession of silver indicated wealth as did gold, cattle, and servants (Gen. 13:2; 24:35).

Gold is often mentioned in conjunction with silver in the Bible since both metals have similar physical and chemical properties, and have historically been used for similar purposes, including money. Because of their similar abilities to satisfy human wants and needs, mankind has wavered for thousands of years between choosing gold or silver exclusively for use as money. In biblical times, silver was the primary medium of exchange. The use of money in any form requires a division of labor in the economy as well as a market of free exchange; therefore, the use of gold, silver, and bronze as money in biblical times indicates such a market economy based upon a division of labor.

Croesus, the king of Lydia (560-546 B.C.E.), was likely the first to mint pure gold and silver coins. Before this time, and even later, silver used as a medium of exchange was measured by weight, usually in shekels (Gen. 23:16) or talents (1 Kgs. 16:24). Other units of weight were used, but most of these were based upon shekels or talents. Since the earliest coins were irregular in shape and weight due to the minting process known as "striking," coins were sometimes weighed to ascertain their weight, and not accepted at face value.

Silver used in the ancient Near East was obtained primarily from Asia Minor until the 1st millennium B.C.E., during which it became more plentiful and less valuable relative to gold (cf. 1 Kgs. 10:21, 27). Five clay jars containing 28 kg. (62 lb.) of silver, probably representing taxes belonging to the state, were unearthed in the Judean hills at Eshtemoa, 19 km. (12 mi.) S of Hebron. Some of the hoard was melted and had no particular shape; other pieces consisted of jewelry cut to fit into the mouths of the jars. The pieces vary from 78 to 97 percent pure, suggesting that the silver came from several sources. The hoard dates to the 10th century at the earliest, and no later than the 8th century.

In NT times, silver money was still sometimes weighed, but coins were in greater use than earlier. The principal denomination of silver coinage in the

Roman Empire was the denarius (Matt. 18:28). Other silver coins occurring in the NT are the argurion (Matt. 26:15), usually translated "pieces of silver," and the drachma (Luke 15:8), a Greek coin.

Bibliography. A. R. Burns, *Money and Monetary Policy in Early Times* (1927, repr. New York, 1965); M. I. Finley, *The Ancient Economy,* 2nd ed. (Berkley, 1985); A. Mazar, *Archaeology of the Land of the Bible 10,000-586 B.C.E.* (New York, 1990); L. von Mises, *The Theory of Money and Credit,* 4th ed. (Indianapolis, 1980); D. R. Sear, *Roman Coins and Their Values,* 4th ed. (London, 1988); Z. Yeiven, "The Mysterious Silver Hoard from Eshtemoa," *BARev* 13 (1987): 38-44. ALAN RAY BUESCHER

SIMEON (Heb. *šimʿôn*)

1. The second son of Jacob (Gen. 35:23); the eponymous ancestor of the tribe whose territory was within the southern limits of Judah (Josh. 19:1-9). Simeon and his brother Levi exacted treacherous and violent revenge for the rape of their sister Dinah by a local prince called Shechem (Gen. 34); consequently Jacob's testament singles out Simeon and Levi for chastisement (49:5-7). Ultimately Simeon lost its distinctiveness as a tribe. During David's reign the concept of a territory for Simeon was absent altogether, perhaps because of administrative changes (cf. 1 Chr. 4:31). During the reign of Hezekiah Simeonites took pasturelands by force from non-Israelites both to the west and southeast or south of their original territory (1 Chr. 4:34-43).

2. Grandfather of the Hasmonean priest Mattathias and great-grandfather of Judas Maccabeus (1 Macc. 1:1-5).

3. Simon Maccabeus, a son of Matthias and elder brother of Judas Maccabeus (1 Macc. 2:65).

4. A righteous and devout man who encountered Joseph and Mary when they brought the infant Jesus to the temple for presentation. Under the inspiration of the Holy Spirit, Simeon recognized the baby to be Israel's messiah. He offered a prayer to God ("Nunc Dimittis") and then a prophecy to Mary (Luke 2:25-35).

5. An ancestor of Jesus in the Lukan genealogy (Luke 3:30).

6. One of the prophets and teachers in the church at Antioch (Acts 13:1-3). His Latin nickname Niger suggests that he was of African origin. He was among those who commissioned Barnabas and Saul.

7. The Hebrew equivalent of Gk. Simon, another name for the Apostle Peter (Acts 15:14; 2 Pet. 1:1).

Bibliography. B. Goodnick, "Simeon the Scapegoat," *Jewish Bible Quarterly* 20 (1992): 168-73, 181; S. F. Plymale, "The Prayer of Simeon (Luke 2:29-33)," in *The Lord's Prayer and Other Prayer Texts from the Greco-Roman Era,* ed. J. H. Charlesworth (Valley Forge, 1994), 28-38. EDWIN C. HOSTETTER

SIMON (Gk. *Símon;* Heb. *šimʿôn*)

1. Simon, surnamed the Just (Gk. *dikaios,* also meaning "righteous"), who according to Josephus (*Ant.* 12.43) succeeded his father Onias in the high priesthood. This places him within the period of Ptolemy I's rule over Judea (301-282 B.C.E.). A scholion to Megillat Taʿanit (par. *b. Yoma* 69a) tells of an encounter between Simon and Alexander the Great. Since it is doubtful that Alexander would have prostrated himself before any Jewish priest, the story is usually considered to be largely legendary. While the existence of a priest by the name of Simon at the time of Ptolemy I seems quite likely, other evidence suggests that the surname should be applied to Simon II.

2. Simon II, the son of Onias II, high priest in Jerusalem ca. 219-196 B.C.E. He is praised for his leadership in the repair of the temple and the fortification of Jersualem in Sir. 50:1-21, an account which describes at length his presence at and participation in the daily sacrifice. This appears to be the high priest also called the Just (**1** above) by Josephus in *Ant.* 12.157 (cf. 12.224). *M. ʾAbot* 1:2 states that Simon the Just was among the survivors of the Great Assembly and ascribes a major rabbinic maxim to him. It is probably because of the pious reputation of Simon II that the rabbis made such an attribution.

3. Simon the Benjaminite. In 2 Macc. 3:4-6 he is described as the captain of the temple who informed Seleucus IV Philopator that there were treasures in the temple beyond those required to sustain the daily sacrifice. The king sends Heliodorus to seize these funds, thereby violating the sanctity of the temple. In this case "Benjaminite" is probably a textual corruption of Bilgah, one of the priestly clans listed in 1 Chr. 24:14. This evidence suggests that the story reflects a dispute between priestly clans, with Simon a member of the pro-Seleucid camp (cf. 2 Macc. 4:1-6). JOHN KAMPEN

4. Simon (surnamed Thassi, 1 Macc. 2:3), the second son of Mattathias and brother of Judas Maccabeus and Jonathan, whom he succeeded as high priest (143-135 B.C.E.). Though older than his predecessors, Judas and Jonathan, he was the last son of Mattathias to lead the Jews against the Seleucids (1 Macc. 13:8; 14:41ff.). He won independence for Judea (142), thus establishing the Hasmonean dynasty, which endured until 63 B.C.E. Simon enlarged the territory of the Jews and advanced their fortunes (1 Macc. 13–16), until his treacherous murder by his son-in-law Ptolemy (16:14-19). 1 Macc. 14:4-15 is a poem extolling Simon's glory.

See HASMONEANS.

5. Simon Chosamaeus (Gk. *Chosamaias*), the son of Annas, listed in 1 Esdr. 9:32 among those who had married foreign wives (cf. Shimeon in Ezra 10:31).

6. Simon Peter, son of Jonah (Matt. 16:17) or John (John 1:42; 21:15-17) and brother of Andrew, who led him to Christ (1:40-42). All three were fishermen and natives of Bethsaida (John 1:44). Surnamed Peter ("stone") or Cephas (Aram. "rock") by Jesus (Matt. 4:18; 16:17-18; 1 Cor. 1:12; esp. John 1:42), he belonged to the inner group of three disciples (Matt. 17:1; 26:37) and became the most prominent of the Twelve (Matt. 10:2-4; Mark 3:16-19; Luke 6:13-16; Acts 1:13). He was a leader in the early Church (cf. esp. Acts 1–15; Gal. 1–2) and two NT letters bear his name. Tradition places his martyrdom at Rome.

7. Simon the Zealot, one of the Twelve (Matt. 10:4; Mark 3:18; Luke 6:15; Acts 1:13). Before becoming a disciple of Jesus, he was a member of the Zealots, a party of patriotic Jews, who believed that to submit to Rome's authority was to deny God's lordship. In Matthew and Mark he is called "the Cananaean," a transliteration of Aram. *qan'ān,* "zealot." It does not mean he is from Cana or a "Canaanite," as the KJV reads in Matt. 10:4; Mark 3:18.

8. Simon, the half brother of Jesus (Matt. 13:55; Mark 6:3). He apparently came to believe in Jesus after the Resurrection (John 7:5; Acts 1:14; 1 Cor. 9:5).

9. Simon the Leper, who owned the house at Bethany in which Mary anointed Jesus (Matt. 26:6; Mark 14:3; John 12:1-8). He may have been the father of Mary, Martha, and Lazarus, or perhaps Martha's husband. If he had once been afflicted with leprosy, he had obviously been cured, possibly by Jesus.

10. The father of Judas Iscariot (John 6:71; 13:2, 26).

11. A man from Cyrene in North Africa who was compelled to carry Jesus' cross to Golgotha (Mark 15:21; Matt. 27:32; Luke 23:26). Mark notes that he was the father of Alexander and Rufus, men obviously known to the reader of his Gospel, which was probably written to the church at Rome (cf. Rom. 16:13).

12. A Pharisee who invited Jesus to dinner in his home, where a penitent woman anointed Jesus' feet with her tears, and Jesus in a parable taught the relationship between appreciation and forgiveness (Luke 7:36-50).

13. Simon, called Magus because he practiced magic (Acts 8:9, 11). He believed and was baptized when Philip preached the gospel in Samaria (Acts 8:5-13). When Peter and John followed up on Philip's ministry, Simon attempted to buy from them the authority to bestow the Holy Spirit, and they severely rebuked him (Acts 8:14-24). The English word "simony," which means "the buying or selling of sacred things," derives from Simon Magus.

14. A tanner who lived in Joppa, in whose house Peter stayed "many days" (Acts 9:43; 10:6, 32). His house was outside the city "by the sea" (Acts 10:6), apparently separated from the Jewish community, because contact with dead bodies made tanning an unclean trade.

15. Simon bar Kosiba, leader of the Second Jewish Revolt (132-135 C.E.).

See BAR KOKHBA. W. EDWARD GLENNY

SIN

A reality signifying the broken relationship between God and humanity. The occasions by which this relationship breaks, the need to recognize this rupture, and the avenues for salvation are detailed in endless situations throughout the Scriptures.

Old Testament

Ancient Israel's concern for sin reflected the basic ethical nature of the early Jewish faith and the diversity of theological approaches to the problems of evil. Several Hebrew terms are used to signify sin. Most frequent is *ḥṭ',* "to miss a goal or way." Though ethical implications often are intended, the term may indicate some simple error, deficiency, or fault. The person who "fails to find" wisdom is at risk (Prov. 8:36). Similarly, a hasty person often will "miss" the better way (Prov. 19:2). Abimelech questions how he has "wronged" Abraham (Gen. 20:9), while Jonathan counsels Saul not to "act against" the innocent David (1 Sam. 19:4). Such "sins" ultimately become an offense toward God, because one misses the path of duty (1 Kgs. 18:9; 2 Kgs. 18:14) or incurs guilt through some action, either by conscious error (Lev. 5:5) or unwittingly (Num. 15:28).

The second most common term for sin is *'wn,* which signifies guilt or iniquity. This is primarily a religious term, one which was used originally to specify sins associated with guilt and punishment. Included here are actions undertaken against God or in defiance of God's stated commandments. Hence, a person who purposefully acts against God's commandments "bears sin" (Num. 15:30), a single witness cannot convict someone of a "crime" (Deut. 19:15), and children may be punished by God for the "iniquities" of their parents (Exod. 20:5). In certain instances the term offers no real distinction between the crime and its punishment, perhaps as a reflection of the belief that sin carries within itself the seeds of consequence. Cain thus despairs that he cannot bear his "punishment" (crime before God?; Gen. 4:13). In similar manner, Second Isaiah claims that the coming suffering servant shall assume the "iniquities" (penalties?; Isa. 53:11) of those whom he will make righteous.

The final term of significance is *pš'.* Most often translated "transgression," it indicates a willful crime of an individual against another, a nation against other nations, or a sinner against God (Gen. 31:36; Amos 1:3; Ezek. 21:24[MT 29], respectively). The implication of "rebellion" is associated with the word, especially rebellion against the terms of a covenant. As with *'wn,* the term encompasses the notion of crime and consequence. Daniel laments that the people of Israel have brought "calamity" (sin's penalty; Dan. 9:12-13) upon themselves. Likewise, Micah asks whether the sacrifice of a firstborn child will atone "for transgression" (as penance?; Mic. 6:7). As might be expected, the focus upon sin as broken covenant lends itself aptly to the teachings of Israel's prophets.

The concept of rebellion, or revolt, against God's commandments appears early in the biblical narrative. After the creation of the world and the formation of Adam and Eve, Gen. 3:1-7 offers a scenario in which humanity is presented with its first common dilemma — the choice between obedience to divine will or pursuit of human desire. The occasion seems to cover both conscious decision (Eve) and unwitting participation (Adam). No specific word for sin appears here, but the seeds of separation between God and humanity are clearly sown. Curiously, this revolt against God finds no further mention in the OT, yet its implications continue to dominate both the actions of history's earliest participants (Gen. 1–11) and the progression of Israel's own response to God. Later Christian interpreters of the text, from Paul to Augustine, make specific, extended usage of this episode of the "fall" of Adam.

Gen. 3 reflects a common ancient notion that sin is both basic to the human experience and universal in its scope (cf. Prov. 20:9). A recognition of the reality of sin in the life of Israel brought into existence the need for repentance and atonement. As with competing Near Eastern civilizations, Israel soon adopted a sacrificial system designed to restore broken relationships between God and the chosen people. A priestly system emerged in the name of Moses and under the aegis of Aaron's sons for this very purpose. Despite the several covenants which Israel made with God throughout this journey (Exod. 24; Josh. 24; Deut. 27), the temptation to sin remained. Thus, the priestly order and cultus provided opportunity for restoration through votive offerings, expiation sacrifices, blood rites, incense offerings, and other rituals of appeasement to a God who had been wronged. The priestly system of atonement recognized the sin of both the individual and the corporate community, and sought to satisfy the requirements which God demanded in order to restore the severed covenant.

While sin most often relates to humanity's own actions in response to the will of God, it likewise seems to have a life of its own. God tells Cain that if he should not do well, then sin "lurks at the door, having desire for him" (Gen. 4:7). The temptation to link the essence of sin with the reality of an independent source of evil (e.g., the serpent in Paradise or the Satan of intertestamental literature) was always available for ancient Israel's theologians. Curiously, however, the biblical authors rarely speculated upon this connection within the literature. Instead, as with Israel's own prophets, sin usually was associated with the pursuit of individual greed or the dependence of Israel upon foreign alliances. Reflecting on Ps. 1, the prophets called both the people and the rulers of Israel and Judah to a recognition of their sin (Isa. 1:2-20; Jer. 3:1-5; 5:1-31; Hos. 4:1-19; Amos 5:10-13), to a return to justice and repentance, trust and righteousness. According to the Deuteronomist, only after the sinner has repented of apostasy (individual or corporate) does God choose to restore covenant agreements and provide salvation.

By the Second Temple period Judaism had become utterly dependent upon the Torah as the standard by which sin was to be measured. To transgress against the Law of Moses was to rebel against God (1 Sam. 2:17). It was a violation of the sacred covenant between God and Israel. Less emphasis was placed upon corporate responsibility during this period. More focus was given to the individual, especially since Judaism had come to recognize that all peoples must ultimately fall prey to sin. The avenues of atonement as defined by the cultic system of the temple (sacrifice and penance) became essential to the restoration of the individual to a right relationship with God.

New Testament

The basic NT term for sin is Gk. *hamartía,* which bears a wide variety of meanings, including reflections of parallel Hebrew terminology: fall short, error, deficiency, fault, transgression, rebellion, and revolt (cf. LXX).

While Judaism traditionally defined sin as the separation of humanity from God, classical Greek thought recognized guilt under three basic conditions: rebellion against destiny *(moíra);* violation of the rules of hospitality and honor *(timḗ);* and breach of cultic obligation. Such conditions brought the retaliation of the gods and, hence, effected acts of divine punishment which continue to plague the human condition. This eventually led to Hellenistic beliefs that human existence is ultimately sinful, since human activities consistently violate the norms of the natural world. The result of ignorance, such violations are inevitable and lead humanity to suffer the consequences of despair and guilt.

Early Christianity's view of sin reflected the merger of Jewish and Greek traditions. All people ultimately sin, either through their violation of God's Torah and cultic obligations, or through their rebellion against codes of honor and the divine purpose for their lives. It was the very recognition of this sinful state and the means by which atonement may be achieved that helped early Christians to define the nature of their faith.

The NT suggests that Paul offered Christianity its first systematic understanding of sin within the context of salvation through the resurrection of Christ Jesus. Paul argues, from the perspective of Greek tradition, that all persons have sinned (Rom. 3:23). Based upon the Judaic tradition, he traces the roots of this dilemma to the actions of Adam (Rom. 5:12; cf. Gen. 3:1-7). This interpretation was consistent with the convictions of intertestamental Judaism (Wis. 2:24; 2 Esdr. 3:21, 26). Paul's own special contribution to this view was that the coming of Christ Jesus, a free gift of God's grace, stands as the means by which the inevitability of human sinfulness is resolved. While Adam's first sin led to death, the Christ event has conquered both sin and death.

Paul encouraged his followers to live "blameless and innocent" lives (Phil. 2:15), but many who heard him came to believe that they already fully shared in the glory of Christ. As suggested by the context of 1 Corinthians, forgiveness of sin was interpreted by these persons as support for an antinomian position. Similar conclusions could be drawn from the Gospel of John, which seems to suggest that those who hear the words of Christ may live in a sinless state (John 15:22, 24) and perhaps from 1 John, which indicates that sin cannot reside where love is present (1 John 4:12-17). Certain later interpreters, especially those who followed gnostic interpretations of Scripture, become convinced by such conclusions (Origen *Com. John* 2.15).

Ultimately, it is the interpretation of sin in the Synoptic Gospels and Acts which came to dominate the mainstream Church. In the Gospel accounts Jesus rarely teaches about the nature of sin and its consequences directly (but cf. Mark 3:28-30 par.). Instead, the reader is quickly made aware that the gospel message was (and is) addressed to sinners on behalf of sinners, always as Jesus undertook his ministry among those whose lives were afflicted by sin. He is portrayed as a friend of sinners (Matt. 11:19), a messenger whose task was to call sinners specifically (Mark 2:17). Luke 5:8 even recalls that Jesus' most prominent disciple, Simon Peter, identified himself as a sinner.

Luke's account bears the majority of references and allusions to sin among the Synoptic texts. Luke emphasizes that the followers of Jesus were those whom 1st-century Judaism considered to be sinners: the poor, sick and lame, lepers, tax collectors and prostitutes, and impure. The constant theme in the Lukan vision is that such persons were deemed to be sinners because they had broken cultic obligations or had brought some calamity upon themselves, presumably because of their sin. The concept was widespread (cf. John 9:2). The parable of the Prodigal Son perhaps offers the apex of Jesus' message about sin: all humanity is prone to sin; yet anyone who seeks forgiveness may freely receive it from God, who is merciful and gracious. The community which Jesus gathered was exactly that, a collection of sinners in quest of forgiveness.

The Matthean vision of sin is much more closely tied with late Jewish concerns for Torah and righteousness. As is illustrated by the Sermon on the Mount (Matt. 5-7), the demands of Jesus' message surpassed the old understanding of Torah requirements. It is not sufficient simply to "keep the laws" of God's commandments; the truly righteous person must comply with God's will through an acknowledgement of the divine intention behind such laws. While murder, adultery, and judgment are evils to be avoided, so too are hate, lust, and judging itself! In the vision of Matthew the world follows a distinctly dualistic track, the choice between good and evil (Matt. 7:13-14) and the separation of the good from the bad (25:31-46). As with intertestamental Judaism in general (cf. T. Asher 2) and the Qumran community in specific (1QS 3:12–4:26), Matthew's Jesus depicts sin as a warring element within the human experience. While the potential for failure is great, there is always a choice to be made between sin and salvation.

The early Christian conception of sin as understood through the crucifixion and resurrection of Jesus is perhaps best viewed through the words of institution at the Last Supper (Matt. 26:26-29 par.). The imagery of ancient Israel is specifically preserved in the Matthean version, where the cup is offered as the "blood of the covenant, which is poured out for many for the forgiveness of sins." Here is a classic reflection of the Jewish understanding of sin as the broken relationship between God and humanity, defined specifically by the words of covenant. In the NT vision, the Cross signified in some sense the establishment of yet a new covenant between God and those who would be forgiven and saved. This view is already evident in Paul's theology (cf. 1 Cor. 11:23-26), where the Christ event serves to conquer sin in the same way that God is victorious over evil.

The core NT views of sin assume, then, three basic perceptions: (1) The world is by nature inherently sinful. While "original sin" as such is never explicitly stated or defined by the Scriptures, its reality is strongly implied. (2) Sin is humanity's rebellious attitude toward God's will. The forms of this rebellion manifest themselves in numerous ways. (3) Salvation derives from the remission of sin as understood through the Christ event. Through the gospel message of Jesus, the reign of God has been declared and sinners are forgiven through the restoration of humanity to God in righteousness. The early Christian message stands as a direct answer to the perception of sin in the world, a message of hope for the hopeless and forgiveness for the condemned.

Bibliography. H. Conzelmann, *An Outline of the Theology of the New Testament* (New York, 1969); B. A. Levine, *In the Presence of the Lord.* SJLA 5 (Leiden, 1974); S. Lyonnet and L. Sabourin, *Sin, Redemption, and Sacrifice.* AnBib 48 (Rome, 1970); P. D. Miller, Jr., *Sin and Judgment in the Prophets.* SBLMS 27 (Chico, 1982); G. Quell, G. Bertram, G. Stählin, and W. Grundmann, "Hamartáno, hamártēma, hamartía," *TDNT* 1:267-316; E. P. Sanders, *Paul and Palestinian Judaism* (Philadelphia, 1977).

CLAYTON N. JEFFORD

SIN (Heb. *sîn*) **(PLACE)**

1. A wilderness area between Elim and Mt. Sinai through which Moses and the Israelites crossed. Sin is either on the southwestern side of the Sinai Peninsula (southern Exodus route) or in the vicinity of central Sinai (northern route). The wilderness of Sin (Exod. 16-17; Num. 33:11-12) is to be distinguished from the wilderness of Zin (v. 36); the Israelites crossed the wilderness of Sin at the beginning of the Exodus and entered the wilderness of Zin more than a year later. In the wilderness of Sin God first gave manna to the grumbling Israelites (Exod. 16:2-21), and there God provided quail (Num. 11:31-32). The similarity between Sin *(sîn)* and Sinai *(sînay)* suggests a morphological connection.

2. An Egyptian border fortress in the northeastern corner of the Nile Delta (Ezek. 30:15-16).

See PELUSIUM.

PETE F. WILBANKS

SIN OFFERING

A special type of offering (Heb. *ḥaṭṭā't,* "error or wrongdoing"), since ancient times universally called the sin offering (Lev. 4:1–5:13; Num. 15:22-31). However, it was in fact a purification offering which had the purpose, not of expiating a person of sin, but of purifying the sanctuary from contamination brought about by any sort of pollution. Throughout the ancient Near East, including Israel, it was considered of utmost importance to keep sanctuaries free of contamination caused by error or uncleanness, as such could render a sanctuary repugnant to its god.

The offering was required in several cases in which no sin or wrongdoing was involved: e.g., recovery from childbirth (Lev. 12), completion of a Nazirite vow (Num. 6), dedication of a new altar (Lev. 8), and the induction of Levite priests (Num. 8). In the case of impurity brought about by inadvertent wrongdoing (Lev. 6), an animal sacrifice commensurate with the status of the offender (which could be the entire community) was touched by the one causing the contamination (or the high priest on behalf of the community); the priest would then smear some of the blood on the horn of the sanctuary altar.

Bibliography. J. Milgrom, *Leviticus 1–16*. AB 3 (New York, 1991), 226-92. WILLIAM R. SCOTT

SINAI (Heb. *sînay*)

The name for both a wilderness area and the mountain at which the people of Israel made a covenant with God. It has also been used to refer to the peninsula lying between Egypt and Palestine. Mt. Sinai is called Horeb in many of the biblical traditions, particularly in Deuteronomy and Kings, and according to some is identical to Mt. Paran (Deut. 33:2).

Sinai Peninsula

The Sinai Peninsula is bounded on the west by the Gulf of Suez and the Suez Canal, on the east by the Gulf of Aqabah and the Negeb Desert, on the north by the Mediterranean Sea, and on the south by the Red Sea. In area it occupies ca. 60,865 sq. km. (23,500 sq. mi.), most of which is arid land or desert. The southern part of the peninsula is made up of huge granite mountains and deep wadis that drain off most of the rainfall into the gulfs of Suez or Aqabah. The northern two thirds of the peninsula consists of a large plateau that slopes down toward the Mediterranean. This plateau is drained by the Wadi el-ʿArish (the biblical Brook of Egypt). This wadi in ancient times often formed the natural border between Palestine and Egypt.

In prehistoric times there seems to have been much more rainfall on Sinai than today, since hunters seem to have been plentiful both there and in the Negeb Desert. Settlements have been found dating back as far as the 9th millennium in the southern Sinai. Southern and eastern Sinai seem to have been home to pastoralists and copper miners during the 4th millennium. Connections between Egypt and Palestine are attested by Egyptian inscriptions with Arabic names at copper mines in Sinai from the 3rd and 2nd millennia.

The northern part of the Sinai Peninsula formed the only land bridge between Asia and Africa in ancient times. A road leading from Egypt across the top of Sinai joined the Via Maris, the "Way of the Sea." Along this road has been found evidence of many small settlements dating from the 4th millennium onward, and later a number of forts guarding the way. It was because of these forts that the Israelites are said to have avoided the northern route, the "way of the land of the Philistines" into Canaan (Exod. 13:17).

Wilderness and Mt. Sinai

In the Exodus account the Israelites came to the wilderness of Sinai after passing through the wilderness of Shur, the oasis of Elim, the wilderness of Sin and Rephidim. The location of the wilderness, like that of Mt. Sinai, is uncertain, but tradition locates it in the southern part of the peninsula, in the area of huge granite mountains.

The problem of identifying both the wilderness and the mountain arises because of uncertainty about the route the Israelites took after leaving Egypt. Num. 33 gives a summary of the route taken from the city of Rameses to the plains of Moab, but none of the stations between "the Sea" and Ezion-geber (Elath) at the head of the Gulf of Aqabah can be identified with certainty.

Since the 4th century C.E. tradition has identified Mt. Sinai with Jebel Mûsā (Arab. "Mountain of Moses," 2300 m. [7486 ft.]) in the southern part of the peninsula, near the monastery of St. Catherine, established in the 6th century and still inhabited by Orthodox monks. Other nearby mountains such as Jebel Katerīn (2600 m. [8652 ft.]) or Jebel Serbāl (2075 m. [6791 ft.]) have also been suggested.

Some scholars argue that all of the sites mentioned in Num. 33 should be located in the southern Negeb, in proximity to Kadesh-barnea, which seems to have been a central place during the wilderness period. Deut. 33:2; Judg. 5:4-5; Hab. 3:3 seem to associate God's revelation in the wilderness in association with Seir, or Edom. In that case Mt. Sinai is to be identified with Jebel Ḥalal (Har Karkom), 35 km. (22 mi.) W of Kadesh-barnea.

Other suggestions locate Mt. Sinai in northwest Arabia, near Midian (cf. Exod. 3:1), or in the north or west of the Sinai Peninsula.

For many scholars the most likely location of Sinai is still in the southern part of the peninsula. The reference in Deut. 1:2 to "eleven days' journey" from Horeb to Kadesh-barnea by way of Mt. Seir fits that location, as does the ancient tradition linking Mt. Sinai to Jebel Mûsā. The account in 1 Kgs. 19:8 of Elijah's journey of "forty days and forty nights" from Beer-sheba to Horeb supports the idea that Sinai/Horeb was a long way from Kadesh-barnea. However, identification remains uncertain, since the temporary nature of any Israelite settlements make the recovery of archaeological evidence unlikely.

Biblical Traditions

The most extensive account of the events at Sinai is found from Exod. 19 through Num. 10. In addition, several passages in Deuteronomy retell parts of the Sinai narrative, although there the mountain is called Horeb.

The narrative begins in Exod. 19:1 with the Isra-

Aerial view of Jebel Mûsā, traditionally identified with Mt. Sinai (Werner Braun)

elites' arrival at the wilderness of Sinai. There they camp in front of the mountain, after which the people are constituted as the people of God. The narrative in Exod. 19–40 is characterized by the movement of Moses, the leader of the people and their mediator with God, between the mountain and the camp. Within this pattern of movement occurs the promise of covenant (Exod. 19:3-8a), theophany (19:8b-20b), the giving of the Ten Commandments (19:20b–20:21a) and the law found in the Book of the Covenant, and the making of the covenant (20:21b–24:8). The climactic threefold movement up the mountain begins with Exod. 24:9. In Exod. 24:9 Moses goes up the mountain with Aaron, Nadab, Abihu, and 70 of the elders. He next goes up with only his servant Joshua (Exod. 24:13). Finally, in Exod. 24:15 Moses goes up the mountain alone, remaining for 40 days and 40 nights. Here he receives the instructions for the tabernacle, in which God will dwell in the midst of his people (Exod. 25–31).

The pattern is disrupted in Exod. 32 by the activity in the camp below: the building of the golden calf, an "antitabernacle," and Moses' breaking of the "tables of testimony." The movement is resumed in Exod. 34, as Moses returns up the mountain to receive again the tablets of the covenant. He descends for the building of the tabernacle in Exod. 35–40. The final movement is not by Moses but God, who moves down from the mountain to dwell among his people (Exod. 40:34).

The placement of Leviticus right after the glory *(kāḇôḏ)* of the Lord fills the tabernacle is intended to signal that it is from the tabernacle that the instructions found in the book of Leviticus are given, even though later in that book Mt. Sinai is again mentioned as the place of revelation (Exod. 25:1; 27:34).

Num. 1–10 deals with the formation of God's holy army, laid out as a camp in concentric circles. In the center of the camp is the Lord himself, surrounded by the Levites, with the other tribes encamped on every side (Num. 2). In Num. 10:11-12 the people leave Sinai for the wilderness of Paran.

The parallel account of revelation and covenant in Deuteronomy speaks of Horeb rather than Sinai (Deut. 1:2, 6, 19; 4:10, 15; 5:2; 9:8; 18:16; 29:1[28:69]), except in Moses' blessing in 33:2. It is also to Horeb that Elijah flees after being threatened with death by Queen Jezebel (1 Kgs. 19:8).

Bibliography. Y. Aharoni, *The Land of the Bible,* 2nd ed. (Philadelphia, 1979); G. I. Davies, *The Way of the Wilderness.* SOTSMS 5 (Cambridge, 1979); A. Mazar, *Archaeology of the Land of the Bible, 10,000-586 B.C.E.* (New York, 1990); R. W. L. Moberly, *At the Mountain of God.* JSOTSup 22 (Sheffield, 1983); E. W. Nicholson, *Exodus and Sinai in History and Tradition* (Richmond, 1973).

MARILYN J. LUNDBERG

SINEW OF THE HIP

A phrase (Heb. *gîḏ hannāšeh*) referring to that part of Jacob's body which was dislocated in his wrestling with the "man" at Penuel (Gen. 32:32[MT 33]). Heb. *gîḏ* is used elsewhere in the OT to refer to sinew. The noun *nāšeh* is usually translated "hip," but since it is not used elsewhere in the OT, this rendering is dubious. It is usually identified with the sciatic nerve, but the connection between the sinew (tendon) of the thigh and this nerve is not clear. The account provides an etiology of the Jewish taboo against eating part of the thigh of animals.

GREGORY A. WOLFE

SINITES (Heb. *sînî*)
A Canaanite people named in the Table of Nations (Gen. 10:17; 1 Chr. 1:15). Early historians associated the Sinites with Sinnu or other sites in Lebanon or with Siyyān (Akk. *Sianu*) in northern Phoenicia.

SIPHMOTH (Heb. *śipmôṯ*)
A town in southern Judah to whose inhabitants David sent part of the booty taken from the Amalekites (1 Sam. 30:28). The location of Siphmoth is unknown. Zabdi "the Shiphmite," David's vineyard overseer (1 Chr. 27:27), may have been from Siphmoth.

SIPPAI (Heb. *sippay*) (also SAPH)
A giant who fought for the Philistines and was defeated by Sibbecai the Hushathite (1 Chr. 20:4). At 2 Sam. 21:18 he is called Saph.

SIRACH (Gk. *Sirach*), **WISDOM OF JESUS THE SON OF**
Also called the Wisdom of Ben Sira, after the name of the author (Heb. *ben sîrā'*), or the Latin title, Ecclesiasticus ("the church [book]"). It is classified among the deuterocanonical or apocryphal works, absent from the Jewish and Protestant canon, but regarded as Scripture by Roman Catholics and the Orthodox. It was written in Hebrew ca. 180 B.C.E. and translated into Greek by the author's grandson (who introduced it with an important prologue) ca. 130. Sirach has had an unusual history. From the time of Jerome to about 1900 the Hebrew text was practically unknown to the Western world, and the book was transmitted in Greek, Latin, and other ancient versions. The discoveries of portions of the Hebrew text in a Cairo geniza and recently at Masada and Qumran have yielded about two thirds of the Hebrew. This has resulted in better modern translations (e.g., NRSV, whose chapter/verse numbering is to be followed).

Ben Sira died before the critical Maccabean period convulsed Palestine. He was aware of the threat of Hellenism (cf. his prayer in 36:1-22), and his strategy was to meet it by a strong exhortation to be faithful to traditional Israelite belief. He does this in the form of wisdom teaching that resembles the book of Proverbs: short sayings (usually included in relatively smooth longer units), instructions (favoring 22 and 23 lines in length; e.g., 1:11-30), hymns of praise (e.g., 39:12-35; 42:15–43:33), and didactic historical narrative ("the praise of the ancestors," 44:1–49:16). He was a scribe, most probably a Jerusalemite, who appreciated his craft, as his celebrated description of the various trades demonstrates (38:24–39:11).

Contents

The book does not lend itself to a simple outline. Here we can only select some of the more outstanding topics that he dealt with. Wisdom is, of course, the most important. The work opens with a poem on the origin of wisdom (1:1-10): She is from God, who has poured her out on all his works and lavished her upon friends. This succinct summary is developed at length in the famous ch. 24, where Wisdom is clearly personified as a woman. Before the members of the heavenly court she describes her origins "from the mouth of the Most High" before creation (cf. Prov. 8:22-31), and her dominion over all nature and peoples (24:5-6). But she wants to dwell somewhere, and the "Creator of all" gives her Jacob/Israel as her inheritance. In the holy city of Zion she ministers before God. She describes her excellence in terms of images of trees and plants, and issues an invitation to all to partake of her fruit, a fruit that will make them hunger for her all the more. When she finishes her speech Ben Sira identifies her outright with the "book of the covenant," "the law that Moses commanded" (24:23). For the first time, the elusive figure of OT Wisdom is explicitly identified. This equation of Wisdom and Torah is hinted at in Deut. 4:6-8, but it is affirmed several times in Sirach (e.g., 15:1; 19:20).

Equally important is "fear of the Lord," long a favorite concern in Wisdom Literature (Prov. 1:7). The very first chapter has a lengthy poem on fear of the Lord: it is "the beginning of wisdom"; indeed it *is* wisdom, and also the "root," "crown," and "fullness" of wisdom. "Those who fear the Lord will have a happy end; on the day of their death they will be blessed" (1:13). Because in modern times "fear" of God is usually considered a negative term, it is important to recognize that in the Wisdom Literature it has the sense of reverence, obedience, and even of love. In 2:15-16 fear and love appear together and indicate loving service, just as fear and love are frequently paired in the exhortations of Deuteronomy (Deut. 6:13, 24; 10:12-13; cf. Job 28:28).

Ben Sira shares the typical OT view on sin and suffering, and the doctrine of retribution. He does allow for periods of testing and adversity, but urges perseverance and steadfastness (2:1-6); things will right themselves in the end (11:26-27). He was not unaware of the difficulties in this doctrine, but he remained firm in his views: virtue is to be rewarded with health and prosperity, children and a long life, and an enduring "name" (41:12-13) or reputation. The wicked will lack these blessings. Despite appearances to the contrary, sooner or later they will receive their just punishment from God. Of course, the divine retribution had to take place in this life, since there was no real life after death; there was only Sheol, where everyone, good and bad alike, would find themselves on equal terms. There was no loving contact with the Lord (17:27-28), just as the psalmists also complained (Ps. 6:5[MT 6]; 30:9[10]).

The OT displays a certain ambivalence in the description of human acts. On the one hand, the agency of the Lord is always at work. As Jeremiah put it (Jer. 10:23), "the way of human beings is not in their control" (cf. Sir. 33:12; Prov. 16:9). But on the other hand, human responsibility is presumed and even affirmed. Sirach leaves no doubt: "Do not say, 'It was the Lord's doing that I fell away'. . . . It was he who created humankind in the beginning, and he left them in the power of their own free choice" (15:11-14). Sirach differs from the usual wisdom stance in that he explicitly envisions conversion for sinners (17:25-26). He shares in the OT warning that sacrifice is futile unless it is accompanied by moral integrity: "The Most High is not pleased with the offerings of the ungodly, nor for a multitude of sacrifices does he forgive sins" (34:23). He shows admirable balance in judging ritual and morality: sacrifice is in order, but almsgiving is also a "sacrifice of praise" (35:1-11).

Less convincing is Sirach's view of the polarities he finds in this world. He composes several beautiful hymns in praise of the works of the Lord (39:12-35; 42:15–43:33). Their strength lies in their lively imagery. But his boundless optimism is difficult to accept: "All the works of the Lord are very good. . . . The works of all (humankind) are before him. . . . No one can say, 'What is this?' or 'Why is that?'" (39:16-21). However, there is the inevitable distinction between the virtuous and the sinner: good things for the good, but for the sinner, good things and bad (39:25). The second hymn (42:15–43:33) is in praise of creation, somewhat reminiscent of Pss. 144–145; Job 38–41. He plays with the idea that all things come in pairs (e.g., night and day) and this match catches his imagination. But when such a doctrine of opposites is applied to Providence, the weakness of his views appears, as in 33:7-15: "Why is one day more important than another?" After exemplifying several polarities he concludes that just as good is the opposite of evil, and life contrasts with death, so the sinner is the opposite of the godly person (33:14): "Look at all the works of the Most High; they come in pairs, one the opposite of the other" (33:15). His enthusiasm for the polarities is off the mark; they do nothing to solve the mystery which confronted both the author of Job and Qohelet in a traumatic way.

Sirach's "Hymn in Honor of Our Ancestors" (an early title appended to 44:1–49:16) succeeds in covering a significant portion of Israelite traditions. He is the first sage to have incorporated historical material into wisdom teaching, and he is followed in this by the author of the Wisdom of Solomon (Wis. 10–19). The abrupt beginning with Enoch in 44:16 is followed by descriptions of people Sirach obviously favors, such as Moses and Aaron, Joshua, Samuel, David, Elijah and Elisha, Hezekiah (but the kings generally receive blame, 49:4-5), and Ezekiel. The mention of the prophet contains a reference to Job (cf. Ezek. 14:14, 20) so casual as to give the impression that Sirach never struggled with the problem of Job. Ch. 50, which is really apart from the hymn, gives full attention to the role of Simon, son of Onias, high priest ca. 200, whose priestly activities are described and admired by Ben Sira.

Finally, we may examine Sirach's own view of his life and activity. As already noted, he exalted the work of the scribe (39:1-11), a class to which he doubtless belonged. He also betrayed an understandable pride in his own role as a wisdom teacher. After he identifies Woman Wisdom with the Torah in ch. 24, Sirach likens his role to a small stream that becomes a sea, and compares his teaching to prophecy (vv. 30-34). In the final chapter he offers a hymn of thanksgiving in the traditional style of a psalm, but we are unable to determine the situation that called it forth (51:1-12). There follows an acrostic poem, the text and meaning of which has been considerably enhanced by the discovery of its Hebrew form in Cave 11 at Qumran. Sirach describes his ardent pursuit of Woman Wisdom, and invites the reader to share in his teaching.

Bibliography. R. E. Murphy, *The Tree of Life,* 2nd ed. (Grand Rapids, 1996); P. W. Skehan and A. A. DiLella, *The Wisdom of Ben Sira.* AB 39 (New York, 1987).

ROLAND E. MURPHY, O. CARM.

SIRAH, CISTERN OF (Heb. *bôr hassirâ*)
A place from which Joab summoned Abner before killing him (2 Sam. 3:26), according to Josephus (*Ant.* 7.1.5 [34]) 4 km. (2.5 mi.) N of Hebron. More than one location has been suggested, including Ṣîret el-Bellāʿ (159108).

SIRION (Heb. *śiryōn*)
The Sidonian name for Mt. Hermon (Deut. 3:9; cf. 4:48, Heb. *śîʾōn*). At Ps. 29:6b Sirion is the parallel for Lebanon in v. 6a, here perhaps designating the entire Anti-Lebanon range, of which Mt. Hermon is the southern part, or possibly both the Lebanon and Anti-Lebanon ranges. Jer. 18:14 (*śāḏay,* "field"; so NRSV mg) is associated with Lebanon and is often corrected to Sirion (so NRSV).

SISERA (Heb. *sîsĕrāʾ*)

1. Commander of the Canaanite forces which Israel, led by Deborah and Barak, decisively defeated near Tanaak in the valley of Jezreel. Judg. 4:2 describes Sisera as the commander of the army of Jabin, king of Hazor, while 5:19-20 simply presumes he is the leader of a coalition of Canaanite kings (cf. 1 Sam. 12:9; Ps. 83:9[MT 10]). In both chapters the defeat of the Canaanites is expressed most pointedly through the moment of Sisera's death. The Canaanites, with their powerful horse-drawn chariots, had repeatedly defeated Israel in the plains areas of Palestine (cf. Judg. 1:19, 27-36), making the defeat of the coalition especially sweet to Israel. Since Sisera embodies in himself the hated Canaanite forces, his death provides Israel the moment of cathartic release.

In the prose account of Judg. 4 Sisera flees the battlefield in desperate need of sanctuary from his enemy. The Bedouin woman Jael provides this, speaking soothing words and seeming to provide him protection. However, when the exhausted warrior falls asleep on the ground, she drives a tent peg through his temple, staking him to the ground (Judg. 4:17-21). In Judg. 5 she again gains Sisera's confidence by seeming to cater to his needs, but here bashes in his head while he is still standing, drinking the curds she has provided. The highly repetitive description of Jael's killing of Sisera and his fall to the ground (Judg. 5:26-27) allows the Israelite audience to savor in detail not only the demise of Sisera, but also of the Canaanite forces he led.

Sisera's death at the hands of a woman adds to the joy of Israel's victory, as does the fact that the chief force behind Israel's gathering for battle, Deborah, is also a woman. Adding to Sisera's humiliation is his thirst, the result of his panicked flight (Judg. 4:15, 17; cf. the irony of the torrent in 5:20-21).

Sisera's final humiliation comes in Judg. 5:28-30. Sisera's aristocratic mother and her ladies in waiting are troubled by his long delay in returning from battle, yet can bring themselves to consider no outcome other than victory. The utterance of this folly just after the gruesome picture of Sisera lying dead underscores the joy of Israel's victory.

2. "Sons of Sisera," listed among the temple servants who returned from exile (Ezra 2:53; Neh. 7:55; 1 Esdr. 5:32). Their precise status is unknown, but use of the name Sisera could imply that they were considered outsiders in Israel, perhaps even descendants of the defeated Canaanite leader.

Bibliography. N. K. Gottwald, *The Tribes of Yahweh* (Maryknoll, 1979); A. J. Hauser, "Judges 5: Parataxis in Hebrew Poetry," *JBL* 99 (1980): 23-41.

ALAN J. HAUSER

SISMAI (Heb. *sismāy*)
A Judahite descendant of Jerahmeel, son of Eleasah and father of Shallum (1 Chr. 2:40).

SISTER
Heb. *'aḥâ* generally relates a woman to a man or another woman as a blood sibling with one or both parents in common. Abram asks Sarai to misrepresent the nature of their relationship to the pharaoh; as her husband he would be killed so Pharaoh could take her into the royal harem, but as her brother he is safe and could even benefit from Pharaoh's delight in her (Gen. 12:10-20; cf. 20:1-17). Jacob takes as his wives the two sisters Leah and Rachel (Gen. 29:15-30), a domestic situation Lev. 18:11 sought to avoid. Occasionally, the term identifies women of the same nationality (Num. 25:8; Hos. 2:1[MT 3]) and sometimes is a title showing familial affection (Gen. 24:59-60).

The lover in the Song of Songs frequently addresses his beloved as "sister" (paired four times with Heb. *kallâ*, "bride"). This vocabulary expresses the intimacy the two lovers share; they are as familiar as children who share the same womb. If Job calls the worm "my mother" or "my sister," he is too friendly with death (Job 17:14). To avoid the lure of a smooth-talking woman, the teacher encourages his young student to court Lady Wisdom, saying to her, "You are my sister" (Prov. 7:4-5).

Jeremiah links Israel and Judah as sisters who share a propensity for infidelity (Jer. 3:7-10). In two misogynist allegories, Ezekiel describes Jerusalem, Samaria, and Sodom (Ezek. 16) and Jerusalem and Samaria (ch. 23) as a trio of sisters whose maternal bloodline shows itself in their sexual perversions, a figure for religious betrayal.

The sister relationship plays a part in a few OT narratives. Rachel and Leah are the only pair of sisters mentioned; following the tendency to represent women at odds with other women (cf. Gen. 16:4-6, 9; 21:8-14) lest female solidarity threaten the patriarchal system, they compete for Jacob's sexual favors. Dinah is the only sister to Jacob's 12 sons. When Hamor's son Shechem rapes her and then proposes marriage, her brothers reject marriage to the uncircumcised Shechem because it would dishonor them. In order to avenge their sister, whose desires are unspoken and unsolicited, they destroy the city and claim all its wealth. Miriam is the sister of Moses and Aaron, a genealogical ploy that doubly subverts Miriam's role as a leader of the Israelite community (Exod. 15:20-21; cf. Num. 12). The sisterly solidarity of Zelophehad's five daughters and their insistence that Moses allow them to preserve their father's name compel him to broaden Israelite inheritance law (Num. 27:1-11). In 2 Sam. 13 Tamar is the sister of Amnon and Absalom, sons of David. At the request of his well-loved Amnon, David sends Tamar to take food to Amnon who covets her. Despite her protests (she knows Israelite law better than he; cf. Lev. 18:9), he rapes her and then drives her away. Absalom plots to avenge his sister and murders Amnon, at the same time conveniently clearing his way to the throne. The episode commences the unraveling of David's immediate family while his dynasty continues in Solomon; it also conveys what many women already know: sisters and daughters are not safe in patriarchal homes.

KATHLEEN S. NASH

SITHRI (Heb. *siṯrî*)
A Kohathite Levite, the son of Uzziel (Exod. 6:22).

SITNAH (Heb. *śiṭnâ*)
One of two wells in the valley of Gerar over which Isaac's servants and the herdsmen of Gerar fought (Gen. 46:21). It was apparently S of Gerar and N of Rehoboth (**1**), somewhere W of Beer-sheba.

SIVAN (Heb. *sîwān;* Akk. *simānu*)
The third month of the Hebrew year (May/June; Esth. 8:9).

SIX HUNDRED SIXTY-SIX
The "human number" of the beast of the Apocalypse according to Rev. 13:18. This riddle has perplexed popular and scholarly readers alike. Because 666 is "a human number," and because Greek and Hebrew characters had numerical values, many have tried to identify a person's name with the number.

One popular solution has tied the name to the emperor Nero (54-68 C.E.), noting that a transliteration of Caesar Nero into Hebrew *(neron qesar)* yields a numerical value of 666. This approach is especially intriguing because Revelation apparently alludes to a popular myth that Nero would return after his death (Rev. 13:3; 17:8, 11; cf. Sib. Or. 4.137-39; 5.33-34, 93-110). It also explains those ancient witnesses in which the number is 616: Latin pronunciation would omit the final *n* of Neron, which has a numerical value of 50, leading to the value 616.

The allusion may characterize the emperor

Domitian (81-96), within whose reign most scholars date Revelation, as a second Nero, associating Domitian with Nero's brutal persecution of Roman Christians and Jews in 64. Similar identifications in Revelation label Rome as Babylon (Rev. 16:17–19:3) and apply the biblical names Balaam and Jezebel to two Christian prophets (2:14, 20).

Theologically oriented readings follow a symbolic rather than mathematical logic. In the late 2nd century Irenaeus suggested that since six precedes the perfect number seven, 666 embodies the original, present, and final revolts against God (*Adv. haer.* 5.28.2). Others have contrasted 666 with 888, the numerical value of Jesus in Greek.

GREG CAREY

SKULL, THE

See GOLGOTHA.

SLAVE

A person held in servitude by violence, natal alienation, and personal dishonor as the chattel of another. Unlike modern slavery, ancient slavery was not based on race. The authors of the Bible assume slave ownership to be an unquestioned part of daily life, as normal as possessing oxen, donkeys, and farm equipment. This assumption reflects the perspective of the biblical writers themselves, many of whom most likely came from slaveholding orders of their respective societies.

Most OT material on slaves (Heb. *ʿeḇeḏ*) is legal, proverbial, anecdotal, and mentioned only in passing (e.g., Prov. 12:9; 22:7; 29:19, 21; Sir. 7:20). While a few slaves are key figures of ancient Israelite history (e.g., Joseph, Gen. 39–41; Moses, Exod. 2–15), the vast majority are indistinct background figures often lacking a name. "Male and female slaves," acquired as gifts or purchases (e.g., Gen. 12:16; 17:23), included miscellaneous workers (26:25) and domestics (Exod. 11:5; Judg. 3:24; Job 31:13). Solomon forced foreigners into slave labor to rebuild Israelite cities and to erect the Jerusalem temple (1 Kgs. 9:20-22 = 2 Chr. 8:7-10). Such foreign slaves apparently were numerous, serving in a variety of royal and priestly functions for the Israelite monarchy (1 Sam. 8:10-18; 1 Kgs. 10:2-5 = 2 Chr. 9:3-4).

Slaves appear most prominently in the OT laws concerning debt-bondage and manumission (Exod. 21; Lev. 25; Deut. 15), important evidence for Israelite enslavement of both foreigners and fellow Hebrews. Although designed to curtail and perhaps even to end debt-slavery, these Deuteronomistic laws apparently went unheeded, as debt-slavery of fellow Hebrews continued to be common throughout the biblical period (2 Kgs. 4:1; Amos 2:6; 8:6; Mic. 2:9). King Zedekiah of Judah tried to end the practice with his own large-scale manumission legislation (Jer. 34:8-22).

A recurring theme in the OT is the people's history as slaves in Egypt, forced into manual labor, refused basic supplies such as straw for brickmaking, and beaten by rod-wielding taskmasters (Exod. 5:1-23). Admonishments to serve Yahweh by remembering Moses and the Exodus recur throughout (Exod. 13:3; 20:2; Lev. 25:42; Deut. 6:21; Josh. 24:17). This Exodus theme echoes in accounts of the Babylonian Captivity (Ezra 9:8-9; cf. 2 Chr. 36:20).

Slaves (Gk. *doúlos*) mentioned in the NT include Onesimus (Phlm. 10-21), the Ethiopian eunuch (Acts 8:27-39), the maid Rhoda (12:13-15), the clairvoyant slave girl of Philippi (16:16-24), the Roman centurion's slave (Luke 7:1-10 = Matt. 8:5-13), and slaves of the high priest Caiaphas (Mark 14:47, 66-69 par.). Slaves also appear as stock characters in the parables of Jesus (e.g., Luke 16:1-13). Dealing ostensibly with the problem of debt among domestic slave stewards, the parable of the unforgiving slave (Matt. 18:23-25) is not about slaves as a social order, but early Christians in Matthew's church (who may or may not be actual slaves). Synoptic admonitions to watchfulness aim to inform not about the ancient treatment of slaves but about the eschatological judgment of God (Luke 12:35-48; Matt. 24:45-51). This allegorical use of slavery reveals that slavery was taken for granted in that period; no extant saying of Jesus condemns the institution as intrinsically evil.

Paul, self-identified as "slave of Jesus Christ" (Rom. 1:1) and even "slave to all" (1 Cor. 9:19), employs metaphorical use of slavery. Among baptized Christians "there is no longer slave or free" (Gal. 3:28; Col. 3:11). In 1 Cor. 7:21-24 Paul advises believers who were baptized while slaves to "not be concerned" about being a slave unless they have manumission opportunities. Early Christian adaptations of Greco-Roman domestic codes of household management command slaves to "obey your earthly masters with fear and trembling, in singleness of heart, as you obey Christ" (Eph. 6:5; Col. 3:22; cf. 1 Tim. 6:2; 1 Pet. 2:18-21). This evidence shows that early Christians such as Paul and his followers held attitudes about chattel slavery that resembled those in the wider Greco-Roman world.

Bibliography. G. C. Chirichigno, *Debt-Slavery in Israel and the Ancient Near East.* JSOTSup 141 (Sheffield, 1993); J. A. Harrill, *The Manumission of Slaves in Early Christianity.* Hermeneutische Untersuchungen zur Theologie 32 (Tübingen, 1995).

J. ALBERT HARRILL

SLEEP

The regular suspension of consciousness wherein the body is refreshed (Gen. 28:16; Ps. 3:5[MT 6]; Matt. 25:5). Creatures must sleep, but not the Lord (Ps. 121:4), who indeed cares for us while we sleep (vv. 5-6) and communicates through dreams (Gen. 20:6-7; Matt. 1:20; 2:12-13, 22). God created Eve while Adam slept (Gen. 2:21) and made a covenant with Abram while he slept (15:12). Though God does not sleep, poetic imagery calls upon him to arise as if he were asleep (Ps. 44:23, 26[24, 27]; cf. 78:65).

Sleep appears metaphorically for physical death, whether of the righteous or of the wicked (Ps. 13:3[4]; 76:5[6]; Jer. 51:57; Dan. 12:2; cf. 1 Cor. 11:30). In the NT, however, Christ will awaken believers (1 Thess. 5:10), for those who die "fall asleep" in Jesus (4:14). In the OT the use of sleep for death as a reversible condition anticipated the resurrection (cf. esp. Dan 12:2). Jesus confirmed this when he raised Lazarus, who had "fallen asleep," from the dead; Jesus came to "wake him up" (John 11:11) as a sign of his authority to resurrect the dead on the last day.

Sleep is also used metaphorically for spiritual dullness and spiritual death. Throughout Proverbs sleep is the occupation of the lazy, yielding poverty and hunger (Prov. 6:9-11; 19:15; 20:13; 24:33-34). In the NT sleep represents spiritual indolence (Mark 14:32-40), a drowsiness from which one must rise, be awakened spiritually, and prepare for the day of salvation about to dawn (13:36; Rom. 13:11; Eph. 5:14; 1 Thess. 5:6-9). A. B. CANEDAY

SLING

A weapon consisting of two thongs made of rushes, animal sinews, leather, cloth, or hair attached to a wider pocket that held the projectile. The projectile was placed in the pocket and swung above the head one to three times. When the desired centrifugal force had been generated, one thong was released, discharging the missile. The sling was inexpensively manufactured and required little technical know-how to produce. Optimum accuracy (Judg. 20:16) was achieved only by years of practice. Stones were carried into battle in a bag (1 Sam. 17:40). During a siege they were piled at the slinger's feet. The average slingstone was slightly smaller than a tennis ball.

As evidenced in wall paintings, reliefs, and statues, the sling has been used as a weapon since at least 8000 B.C. It appeared first as a weapon of herdsmen, who used it to protect animals from predators. By the Middle Bronze Age slingers were found among the light infantry in Egypt.

The bow and sling were the two primary long-range weapons. The intent of the slinger was to incapacitate the enemy so that the fatal blow could be delivered by the infantry (2 Kgs. 3:25). Biconical missiles could pierce armor, and even if penetration did not result, the impact could cause fatal internal injury. Slingers can be seen to have had a decided tactical advantage when pitted against soldiers outfitted with short-range weapons (1 Sam. 17:40-51).

Bibliography. R. Gonen, *Weapons of the Ancient World* (Minneapolis, 1976); Y. Yadin, *The Art of Warfare in Biblical Lands in the Light of Archaeological Study,* 2 vols. (Jerusalem, 1963).

W. E. NUNNALLY

SMITH

The number of specialists who worked with metals must have increased dramatically with the introduction of bronze and iron in the late 4th and late 2nd millennium B.C., respectively. Long before copper and tin were alloyed to produce bronze, copper was used to forge various implements, and work in silver and gold developed along with the more utilitarian metals. The ancient metallurgists and artisans contributed much to the rise of alchemy and early chemistry, and their skills were vital to the rise of ancient Near Eastern civilizations. The smith produced a full array of tools and weapons, along with tack for horses and draft animals, parts for vehicles (including chariots), and fittings on furniture. Where soil chemistry and other conditions allow, archaeological excavations recover large numbers of metal artifacts, objects that were used in many aspects of ancient life.

In a narrative that explains the origin of many components of human culture, Tubal-cain is identified as an early smith "who forged all kinds of tools out of bronze and iron" (Gen. 4:22). Later, the Philistines attempted to maintain a monopoly on producing tools and weapons, and thereby prohibit the flow of weapons into the hands of the Israelites, by denying the Israelites skilled blacksmiths (1 Sam. 13:19-21). The Hebrews did have a number of objects made by blacksmiths, however, such as the standard inventory of agricultural implements in the early Iron Age (i.e., plowshares, mattocks, axes, sickles, and forks; cf. 1 Sam. 13:20-21).

The prophet Isaiah wrote a remarkable satire on idolatry that included a description of the blacksmith's and carpenter's role in fashioning idols by means of human strength and technology (Isa. 44:9-20). Reference is made to the smith's work in casting metal and shaping or forging his product by means of his furnace, hammer, and muscles (Isa. 44:10, 12; cf. v. 19; 54:16). The tools of the smith are mentioned in Sir. 38:28, where work at the forge is contrasted with that of the scribe or scholar. Jer. 6:29 mentions the bellows by which high temperatures were achieved in smelting furnaces; the common Akkadian term for "smith" actually meant "blower" of the bellows. GERALD L. MATTINGLY

SMYRNA (Gk. *Smýrna*)

A city (modern Izmir) located at the terminus of inland trade routes that followed the Hermus (Gediz) and Maeander valleys out of the east. From its sheltered harbor in the southern Aegean, trade made its way west to the Greek mainland. A Greek colony dominated the area as early as the 10th century B.C., claiming to be the birthplace of Homer. In the Roman era, the city was invited to be one of the custodians for the temple of Augustus. It is listed among the seven churches of Asia Minor in Rev. 1:11 (cf. 2:8-11).

In NT times Smyrna was an important commercial city. It competed with and was comparable to Ephesus to the south. John's letter in Revelation is our first hint at a Christian community in Smyrna. He commends the Christians for their strength against formidable persecution by a local synagogue. That courage in the faith is also cited later by Ignatius (d. A.D. 120), who stopped in Smyrna en route to Rome and martyrdom and wrote four letters there. Polycarp was martyred in the city's stadium in 156, evidence of continued Jewish-Christian animosity. Irenaeus (d. 202), bishop of Gaul, came from Smyrna. In 1932 and 1941 the agora was excavated, but the remains are under the modern city (pop. 500,000).

Bibliography. E. M. Blaiklock, *Cities of the New Testament* (London, 1965), 98-103; C. J. Cadoux, *Ancient Smyrna* (Oxford, 1938); C. Foss, "Archaeology and the 'Twenty Cities' of Byzantine Asia," *AJA* 81 (1977): 469-86; C. J. Hemer, *The Letters to the Seven Churches of Asia in Their Local Setting* (1986, repr. Grand Rapids, 2000). GARY M. BURGE

SNAIL
A gastropod mollusk usually enclosed in a spiral shell (Heb. *šabbělûl*). The Talmud suggests some kind of gastropod at Ps. 58:8(MT 9), whether a slug (so NJB, NIV) or a snail. The term parallels "untimely birth" in the second half of the verse, suggesting the ephemeral nature of life or the psalmist's wish that his enemies had never been born (cf. Job 3:16; 10:18-19).

SNARES AND TRAPS
Trapping relied on snares (nooses placed on game paths to catch anything from rabbits to pheasants; Amos 3:5), fine meshed nets (for birds; Jer. 5:26-27), large nets (for antelope; Isa. 28:13), and pits, used with nets or wooden spikes (for lions; Ezek. 19:4, 8). Trapping provided supplies for the royal court (1 Kgs. 4:23[MT 5:3]) and, especially in times of famine, for peasants.

Traps and snares are also used metaphorically in the Bible. Female prophets who make charms are like bird traps (Ezek. 13:17-23). Jerusalem is a hunted animal caught in a net (Isa. 28:13). An innocent person, snared in court, is deprived of justice (Isa. 29:21). Hidden dangers (Prov. 22:14) lie in the path of the innocent (Ps. 35:8). The righteous are at risk (Ps. 119:85) from those who seek to entrap them in immoral actions (Prov. 23:27) or in false worship (Deut. 7:16, 25).

In the NT a trap describes the unexpected arrival of the kingdom of God (Luke 21:34-35), the snare of the devil (1 Tim. 3:7; 2 Tim. 2:26), or the lure of riches (1 Tim. 6:9). Other metaphorical uses include the description of Jesus as a trap for the Jews (e.g., 1 Cor. 1:23) and the intent of the Pharisees to trap Jesus with something he might say (Mark 12:13; Luke 11:54). WILLIAM R. DOMERIS

SNOW
The mountains of Upper Galilee, the high ground of Edom, and the central hill country may receive snow, while the Lower Galilee, the Coastal Plain, and the Jordan Rift are generally subtropical. Every two or three years, Jerusalem will have a foot of snow on the ground, while Jericho's farms, 24 km. (15 mi.) E but 914 m. (3000 ft.) lower, are growing citrus. The western slopes of the higher ground are, therefore, much more likely to receive snow.

Snowfall was not a significant factor for Israel's agriculture, but melting snow from Mt. Hermon was an important source of water for the Jordan River and the Sea of Galilee. An actual snowfall is mentioned only in 2 Sam. 23:20; 1 Chr. 11:22; 1 Macc. 13:22. Snow is most often mentioned in reference to God as creator of the elements (Isa. 55:10-13).

Figuratively snow represents the whiteness of skin caused by leprosy (Exod. 4:6; 2 Kgs. 5:27) and purity resulting from God's cleansing of sinners (Ps. 51:7[MT 9]; Isa. 1:18). DONALD FOWLER

SNUFFERS
Golden instruments made by the Hebrews used in the service of the tabernacle and temple. This particular item was associated specifically with the lampstand in the earlier setting and apparently also in the Solomonic temple (1 Kgs. 7:50; 2 Chr. 4:22; *mězammĕrôt*). Another common rendering of the word for "snuffer" is "tongs" *(melqāḥayim);* the term is used in Isa. 6:6 to describe an instrument used to take a coal from the altar. Heb. *melqāḥêhâ*, an apparent synonym glossed as "snuffers" (Exod. 25:38; 37:23), is most closely associated with "trimming" or "pruning" (2 Kgs. 12:13[MT 14]; 25:14; cf. "wick-removers," NIV "wick trimmers"). WALTER E. BROWN

SO (Heb. *sô'*)
A "king of Egypt" to whom Hoshea, the last king of Israel, sent messengers before rebelling against Shalmaneser V of Assyria (2 Kgs. 17:4). What sort of help he received from So, if any, is unknown, as is the identity of the Egyptian. So may refer to the city of Sais in the western Nile Delta, since this city became strong under Tefnakht during the late 8th century B.C.E. The name may be an abbreviation of Egyp. *nswt*, "king," or an abridgment of Osorkon (IV) of the 22nd Dynasty who ruled the eastern Nile Delta at the time of Hoshea. This last suggestion is the best, since the Bible indicates that Israel's contact with Egypt during the late 8th century was with Tanis (Zoam) in the eastern Delta (Isa. 19:11-13; 30:4). Because Osorkon ruled in the eastern Delta, he would have been contacted by Hoshea for help.

Bibliography. G. W. Ahlström, *The History of Ancient Palestine* (Minneapolis, 1993); K. Kitchen, *The Third Intermediate Period in Egypt (1100-650 B.C.)*, 2nd ed. (Warminster, 1986); D. F. Redford, *Egypt, Canaan, and Israel in Ancient Times* (Princeton, 1992). PAUL S. ASH

SOAP
See LYE, SOAP.

SOCO (Heb. *śôḵô*) **(PERSON)**
The son of Heber, a Judahite and probably the founder of Socoh **2** (1 Chr. 4:18).

SOCO (Heb. *śôḵô*), **SOCOH** *(śôḵōh)* **(PLACE)**
1. A city of the Shephelah within the second district of the tribal territory of Judah (Josh. 15:35). Just prior to the David-Goliath clash the Philistine army was encamped between Azekah and Socoh (1 Sam. 17:1), illustrating the strategic importance of the region as the buffer between Judah and Philistia. This is likely the Socoh fortified by Rehoboam (2 Chr. 11:7) after the division of the kingdom. As part of the border zone, the city was

temporarily taken from Judah by the Philistines in the time of Ahaz (2 Chr. 28:18).

Socoh is one of four city names which appear (spelled *śwkh*) stamped following the word *lmlk* ("for the king") on the handles of royal storejars found in late 8th-century B.C.E. contexts in Judah. These *lmlk* jars are generally related to the reign of Hezekiah, specifically to his preparations for the invasion of the Assyrian king Sennacherib in 701. Thus, Socoh may have figured in Hezekiah's reorganization of Judah's administrative districts (2 Chr. 32:27-29). Socoh is identified confidently with Khirbet ʿAbbâd/Ḥorvat Socoh (147121) in the Elah Valley E of Azekah. The site remains unexcavated, but has yielded a number of *lmlk* jar handles and other pottery of the expected periods.

2. A town of the hill country of Judah's fifth district (Josh. 15:48), perhaps named for Soco, a descendant of Judah (1 Chr. 4:18). It is generally identified with the unexcavated Khirbet Shuweikeh (150090).

3. A town listed as the center of Solomon's third administrative district (1 Kgs. 4:10), identified with Shuweiket er-Râs (153194), just N of modern Tūlkarm. This is probably the Socoh appearing in several Egyptian lists of conquered cities, including those of Thutmose III and Shishak.

Bibliography. Y. Aharoni, *The Land of the Bible,* 2nd ed. (Philadelphia, 1979); S. Aḥituv, *Canaanite Toponyms in Ancient Egyptian Documents* (Jerusalem, 1984).

DANIEL C. BROWNING, JR.

SODI (Heb. *sôḏî*)
The father of Gaddiel of the tribe of Zebulun, one of the 12 spies sent into the land of Canaan (Num. 13:10).

SODOM (Heb. *sĕḏōm*)
A legendary city in the vicinity of the Dead Sea. The term may have arisen from the word "field," or "burning," or "enclosed space," though there is little scholarly agreement on this point.

According to an ancient tradition for which there is little archaeological evidence, Sodom was one of five cities of the plain (Gen. 14:2) forming a so-called Pentapolis. The other cities were Gomorrah, Admah, Zeboiim, and Zoar. This tradition is based upon the single reference in Genesis, though there are other references to some of the cities. Sodom's inhabitants joined with various other neighbors in fighting the marauding Chedorlaomer, king of Elam (Gen. 14:1). Lot, Abraham's nephew, chose Sodom for his residence (Gen. 13:8-13).

Of the 44 references to Sodom in the Bible, 23 include a reference to Gomorrah; however, of the two, Sodom is the more significant. Sodom is remembered as such an excessively evil city that the wrath of God came upon it. Genesis reflects both sexual perversity and gross inhospitality (Gen. 19:1-11) at Sodom. Some writers equate Sodom with a warning (Deut. 29:17-29[MT 16-28]) and sometimes as an accusation against the covenant people (Amos 4:11; Isa. 1:9-11). The same idea is found in the NT (Matt. 10:15 = Luke 10:12; Rom. 9:29; 2 Pet. 2:6; Jude 7).

The precise location for the ancient city is not known, though most conjecture centers around the Dead Sea. Although there is no creditable evidence, some early 20th-century researchers suggested that Sodom together with other cities of the valley was situated under what is now the southern end of the Dead Sea. These theories pointed to settlement within the 2nd millennium B.C.E. More recent archaeological discoveries have pointed to urban areas just east and south of the Dead Sea during the 3rd and early 2nd millennium. On the basis of excavations at Bab ed-Dhra (located on the tongue of land extending into the Dead Sea from its eastern shore) and at Numeira (further south on the eastern shore), some have proposed that to these two sites belong the valley cities mentioned in the Genesis narrative.

WATSON E. MILLS

SOJOURNER
A "foreigner" or "resident alien" residing among a people or in a land not his or her own (Heb. *gēr,* usually translated "stranger" or "alien").

The sojourner prototype was Abraham (Gen. 12:10; 23:4; cf. Heb. 11:9). The continuing sojourner/alien status of Abraham's progeny is recalled for perpetuity in the credo of Deut. 26:5-10. When Israel became established as a nation and a people, remembrance of Israel's past alien status justified laws regarding fair treatment of the alien among them (Exod. 22:21[MT 20]; 23:9; Lev. 19:34; Deut. 10:19). Officially aliens in Israel enjoyed equal status with regard to worship (Num. 9:14; 15:15-16), sabbath rest (Exod. 23:12; Deut. 5:14), and, with widows and orphans, protective care (Exod. 22:21-24[20-23]; Deut. 24:17, 19-20; cf. Mal. 3:5). This may have been especially or only true for the circumcised alien (Exod. 12:48-49). Alien legislation includes an early example of the so-called great commandment: "You shall love the alien as yourself, for you were aliens in the land of Egypt" (Lev. 19:34).

Of course, in everyday life the alien in Israel did not always enjoy equal or even fair treatment. In fact, Heb. *gēr* may stem from Akk. *gārû,* "enemy" or "opponent." As still today, in ancient times to be a "stranger" was to be considered hostile. Hostility toward aliens was apparent especially in the extreme measures taken by Ezra and Nehemiah following the Exile to segregate the alien wives and their children and those Israelites who had "mixed" with them (1 Esdr. 8:69-70; Ezra 10:44; Neh. 13:3) — the despised Samaritans.

The LXX renders *gēr* as *prosēlytos,* "proselyte." By NT times *gēr,* "sojourner/alien," came to have a more religious than ethnic meaning. There is a blurring of distinctions between the sojourners/aliens, the proselytes proper, and the so-called God-fearers who were attracted first to Judaism and then to Christianity. Eph. 2:19 refers to the gentile "God-fearer" converts as "no longer strangers and aliens, but . . . citizens . . . [and] members of the household of God."

In the final analysis, pious Jews viewed themselves as aliens sojourning in God's world (Lev. 25:23; 1 Chr. 29:15; Ps. 39:12[13]), i.e., as utterly dependent on God's grace as the resident alien was dependent on those among whom he or she lived.

EDMON L. ROWELL, JR.

SOLOMON (Heb. *šĕlōmōh*)

The third king of Israel, son of David and Bathsheba. He was one of the major figures of biblical history and tradition, renowned for his wisdom, wealth, and construction of the First Temple. Understanding his legacy involves coming to grips with how biblical writers, early interpreters, and modern scholars have construed his reign.

Kings

That the authors of both Kings and Chronicles devote considerable attention to Solomon is not accidental. The portrayal of Solomon in both histories is critical to understanding the attitude of each work to the monarchy in general and to the division in particular. In Kings Solomon's reign falls into two distinct periods: one glorious (1 Kgs. 1–10), the other ruinous (ch. 11). Solomon's ascent to power occurs during David's decline. Following David's affair with Bathsheba, the prophet Nathan declares that the sword will never leave David's house (2 Sam. 12:7-12); David spends the rest of his years battling domestic and foreign foes (2 Sam. 13–20) and faces a state of near anarchy in his last years (1 Kgs. 1:1ff.). Ironically, as one of David's youngest sons, Solomon benefits from this turmoil. He does not actively seek the throne, yet is blessed with it. Bathsheba and Nathan convince David to ignore primogeniture and appoint Solomon as his successor (1 Kgs. 1:15-35). Having been instructed by his father (1 Kgs. 2:2-9) and anointed by Zadok and Nathan (1:39-40), Solomon moves quickly to suppress all dissent (2:12-46). Solomon is then able to focus his talents on trading ventures, administrative reorganization, military fortifications, and construction of the temple (1 Kgs. 3–10).

The Deuteronomist depicts the first period of Solomon's reign as a progression: accession and consolidation, efficient administration and judicious diplomacy, temple and palace construction, international commendation and untrammeled prosperity. Solomon's dream at Gibeon introduces these themes. When asked by the Lord what he desires, Solomon humbly requests "an understanding mind to govern your people, able to discern between good and evil" (1 Kgs. 3:8-9). Not only does God fulfill Solomon's wish, he decrees that Solomon's "wise and discerning mind" will be unique among his predecessors and successors (1 Kgs. 3:12). Moreover, God is so pleased that Solomon did not ask for long life, riches, or the life of his enemies, that he decrees to Solomon unprecedented riches and glory as well (1 Kgs. 3:13).

In Kings, Solomon's wisdom takes many forms. The tale of the two prostitutes confirms Solomon's juridical talent (1 Kgs. 3:28), while his national reorganization (ch. 4) reveals his administrative talents. Other statements depict Solomon's wisdom as encyclopedic or natural (1 Kgs. 4:29-34[MT 5:9-14]). However many dimensions Solomon's wisdom has, they cumulatively enhance his unique reputation both within Israel and beyond (1 Kgs. 4:30, 34[5:10, 14]). Royal wisdom also contributes to the well-being of society. 1 Kgs. 4:20-25(5:5) pictures Israel in idyllic terms. Solomon rules over a vast empire, while his people live in security and prosperity (1 Kgs. 4:20; cf. v. 25[5:5]). The peace Israel experiences under Solomon fulfills one of the divine promises made to David, namely that Israel will enjoy "rest from all your enemies" (2 Sam. 7:10-11; 1 Kgs. 5:3-4[17-18]).

The rest God gives Israel, in turn, creates the requisite conditions for the fulfillment of another Davidic promise: the building of the temple. Solomon, like many other ancient Near Eastern kings, capitalizes on the fortunate conditions of his reign by embarking on major building projects. Because the author considers temple building as a major achievement in Israelite history, he devotes much attention to its construction, furnishings, and dedication (1 Kgs. 6:1–9:9). In Deuteronomistic perspective, the temple is the final resting place for the venerable ark (1 Kgs. 8:1-13). Solomon's prayer at the dedication, one of the major speeches in the Deuteronomistic history, presents the temple as a unifying symbol in Israelite life, a place to which people can turn to God in all kinds of predicaments (1 Kgs. 8:22-53). Not only does the author link the temple's completion to the Davidic promises, but also to the law of Moses. As an inducement to piety, the temple is also an inducement toward obedience to torah (1 Kgs. 8:58-60). Considering the ancient Near Eastern association of temples with the kings who built them, it is not surprising that the completion of the Jerusalem temple elicits heightened international admiration of Solomon (1 Kgs. 10:1-10). The summary of Solomon's accomplishments in 1 Kgs. 10:23-24 explicitly confirms his incomparability. As the Gibeon dream promises Solomon unparalleled wisdom, wealth, and glory, so this promise became reality.

The author's depiction of a new and negative phase in Solomon's rule sets the stage for his entire history of the dual monarchies. Solomon abandons the good precedent set by his father by building high places for his many wives, worshipping at these high places, and worshipping other gods (1 Kgs. 11:1-8). Solomon's misdeeds infuriate Yahweh, who ends Solomon's peace by raising up a series of foreign adversaries against him (1 Kgs. 11:14-25). More important, Yahweh decrees the secession of the northern tribes and commends the formation of a (northern) Israelite kingdom under Solomon's servant Jeroboam (1 Kgs. 11:11-13, 29-38; 12:15). The disaster is, however, not total. Because of the promises he made to David (2 Sam. 7:1-16), Yahweh restrains his wrath and leaves Judah under Davidic rule (1 Kgs. 12:1-24). The negative course set in play by Solomon's sins remains unresolved for centu-

Six-chambered gate and casement wall at Gezer, representative of Solomon's extensive building activity. The pillared storehouse in the background dates to the Omride dynasty (L. T. Geraty)

ries. Only with the reforms of King Josiah (2 Kgs. 23:4-20) are Solomon's sins finally reversed.

Chronicles

The Chronicler draws heavily upon the portrayal of Solomon in Kings. Nevertheless, he creates his own distinctive presentation by means of omissions, rewriting, and additions. First, he depicts the transition from David to Solomon as completely smooth and well planned. There is no turmoil in David's latter years. Solomon is not only elect by David, but also by God (1 Chr. 28:6). David grooms his son for succession, furnishes him with a national administration, and provides him with a plan for the temple (1 Chr. 22–29). Second, the Chronicler does not emphasize Solomon's wisdom as much as the Deuteronomist does. Third, he does not depict a second, regressive phase in Solomon's reign. This means that Solomon enjoys a uniformly productive and unblemished reign.

In Chronicles the consolidation of Israel's major institutions occurs during the United Monarchy. Solomon is the perfect complement to David. David unites Israel, consolidates the kingdom, organizes a national administration of Solomon's use, and plans for the construction of the temple. As David's designated successor, Solomon brings these hopes and designs to fruition. He focuses much of his energy on building, equipping, and staffing the temple (2 Chr. 2–4). As in Kings, the temple becomes the focal point of national life. Like the Deuteronomist, the Chronicler affirms centralization of the Yahwistic cultus and the abolition of all other cults (Deut. 12). Sacrifices are to be carried out only at the Jerusalem temple and prayers are to be offered at or toward this site (2 Chr. 5:5–6:42). For his part, God pledges that his eyes will be open and his ears attentive to the prayers offered at the temple (2 Chr. 7:15).

Following the temple's dedication, Solomon's reign is all glorious. Any information that would potentially tarnish his reputation is omitted (e.g., 1 Kgs. 9:11-16; 11:1-38). Solomon ends his reign presiding over a unified, prosperous people, accepting tribute from the nations, and receiving veneration from foreign kings (2 Chr. 8–9). Solomon's tenure is untainted by sin or misadventure. He succeeds in all of the tasks that his father assigned to him (1 Chr. 22:7-16; 28:6-10, 20-21). By idealizing Solomon's reign, the Chronicler heightens the great benefit Davidic leadership and the temple can have for the people. Conversely, because all Israelites flourish under David and Solomon, those who might deviate from this norm will be suspect. Hence, the secession of the north is viewed by the Chronicler as rebellious from the outset. The Chronicler exonerates Solomon and blames Jeroboam (largely) and Rehoboam (somewhat) for the secession (2 Chr. 10–13). The Davidic promises continue to pertain to all 12 tribes (2 Chr. 13:4-12; cf. 1 Kgs. 11:11-13, 29-38). Although he still regards the northern kingdom as Israelite, the Chronicler does not record its independent history. The normative institutions established or confirmed in Solomon's reign — the temple, the priests and Levites, and the Davidic dynasty — find their continuity in Judah and Benjamin (2 Chr. 11:1-4).

Early Interpreters

Just as David, "the sweet singer of Israel," is already associated in antiquity with the composition of the psalms, so Solomon, the incomparable sage, is associated with the composition of wisdom literature. This image is already found in the Hebrew Scriptures. Diverse wisdom works such as Proverbs (Prov. 1:1), Song of Songs (Cant. 1:1), and Ecclesiastes (Eccl. 1:1) are all associated with Solomon. Solomon's wisdom is advanced by early Jewish, Christian, and Muslim interpreters (Sir. 47:14-17; Tg. Eccl. 2:4-6; Matt. 12:42; Luke 11:31; Qur'an 27:15, 16, 81, 82; 31:11), although some also acclaimed the splendor of Solomon's reign (1 Esdr. 1:15; Matt. 6:29; Luke 12:27). In at least one source, prophetic activity is ascribed to Solomon. Solomon prophesied both about the house of David and about the natural world, the beasts and the birds (Tg. 1 Kgs. 5:13). Early commentators took a deep interest in the Solomonic temple — its dimensions, construction, and symbolic importance (Sir. 47:13; *Sanh.* 104b). Some also took note of Solomon's fall in Kings, ascribing it to the influence of his foreign wives (Neh. 13:25-27; Sir. 47:19-21; *Sanh.* 2b, 20c, 21a; Tg. 1 Kgs. 11:4). Solomon's decline thus became an argument against intermarriage. But the dominant image of Solomon's legacy among early interpreters is that of a preeminent sage and a worthy successor to David.

History

Until quite recently, most modern scholars viewed Solomon's reign as one of the most secure periods in Israelite history for historical reconstruction. They associated the kingdom of Solomon with a number of developments in the material culture of ancient Canaan. Historians also made a series of correlations between passages in Samuel-Kings and international developments known from other ancient Near Eastern sources. Neither Saul nor David is depicted as embarking on many building projects, but Solomon is. Public works, most notably the temple and its furnishings, comprise a sizeable portion of Solomon's reign (1 Kgs. 5:13[27]–7:51; 9:15-19, 24; 11:27; cf. 2 Chr. 3:1-17; 4:1–5:1; 8:1, 4, 6, 11). But, according to 1 Kgs. 9:15-19, Solomon also initiated a number of other public works — the *millô'*, the wall of Jerusalem, Hazor, Megiddo, and Gezer. He also (re)built Lower Beth-horon, Baalath, and Ta(d)mor (1 Kgs. 9:18; 2 Chr. 8:4). Other public works included garrison cities, chariot cities, cavalry cities, and sites in Jerusalem, the Lebanon, and throughout his domain (1 Kgs. 9:17-19).

Archaeologists associated such building activities with the rise of monumental architecture in the 10th century B.C.E. Excavations at three of the cities rebuilt by Solomon — Hazor, Megiddo, and Gezer (1 Kgs. 9:15-17) — revealed that the defense systems at these sites seemed to exhibit nearly identical fortification patterns. Scholars also pointed to a general pattern of urbanization in the Iron Age — the rebuilding and expansion of old towns and the establishment of new ones. Whereas Iron I is characterized by a low level of planning and a general absence of public buildings and fortifications, the construction of numerous walled cities, public buildings, and fortifications is considered to be a characteristic feature of Iron II material culture.

If descriptions of Solomon's building activity in Kings seemed to correlate to material evidence, the same can be said for descriptions of Solomon's diplomatic relations in Kings and epigraphic remains from this period. One such correlation was the possibility of a strong regional Davidic-Solomonic state itself. The decline of major states, such as Egypt and Ḫatti, made it possible for minor states to emerge or assert themselves. Studies attempting to situate Solomon's reign more specifically in context of international events centered on Egypt, a state that figures prominently in Solomon's reign (1 Kgs. 4:21, 30[5:1, 10]; 8:51, 53, 65; 11:17-22, 40). Some attempted to corroborate the description of Solomon's marriage to a daughter of the pharaoh (1 Kgs. 3:1; 7:8; 9:16, 24; 11:1) with evidence from epigraphy that diplomatic marriages between members of the Egyptian royal family and the royal families of other states were more common than scholars had recognized. By no means least important of all the comparisons made with Egyptian history is the evidence pertaining to the invasion of Shishak provided by epigraphic sources and archaeological excavations. The fragmentary stela at Megiddo, the fragmentary temple inscription at Karnak, and the destruction of various sites near the end of the 10th century were thought to dovetail with the notices of Shishak's invasion in 1 Kgs. 14:25-26; 2 Chr. 12:1-12. The success of Shishak's invasion was thought to confirm a decline in the fortunes of Israel and Judah.

In recent years, however, some commentators have challenged the tenability of this general reconstruction by questioning the 10th-century date of some of the relevant fortifications at Gezer, Hazor, and Megiddo. Others have challenged the links made between epigraphy and the Bible. For instance, the lack of mention of Jerusalem and a number of other Judahite sites in the Karnak relief is cited as proof that Judah was not a state in the 10th century. It is uncertain what long-term effect this new discussion will have on historical reconstruction. At the very least, it indicates that Solomon's legacy will continue to elicit a lively debate.

Bibliography. L. K. Handy, ed., *The Age of Solomon.* SHANE 11 (Leiden, 1997).

GARY N. KNOPPERS

SOLOMON, BOOK OF THE ACTS OF

A book referred to at 1 Kgs. 11:41, thought to be a major source for 3:1–11:40. What was included in this book and what was derived from other sources cannot be determined with certainty, but the reference to both deeds and wisdom suggests a variety of materials.

SOLOMON, ODES OF

An apocryphal collection of 42 odes or hymns, dating to the end of the 1st century C.E. While the text reflects an expectedly strong relationship to Jewish theology of the 1st century, the Odes of Solomon is most certainly a Christian collection, possibly of early Christian hymns. If so, this book is the oldest collection of Christian hymns preserved.

The texts available are few, and there is no complete text in any one language. The Syriac manuscript H is the most complete with 3:1b–42:20, but the manuscript dates to the 15th century. Portions of Odes survive also in Greek and Coptic. Since the original language is indiscernible, although probably either Greek or Hebrew/Aramaic, the provenance is equally difficult to determine. The date of 100 C.E. suggests, however, that a major center of Christianity be considered, i.e., Antioch or Alexandria.

Historically, the Odes offer significant information on topics such as the coming of the Messiah, their connection to the psalms of the Dead Sea Scrolls, a relationship with the Gospel of John, and early Christian worship. The Odes, as an early Christian hymnbook, reveals much theology of the earliest believers, not through narrative or epistle, but through worship and song.

Bibliography. J. Charlesworth, "Odes of Solomon," *OTP* 2:725-71. MARC A. JOLLEY

SOLOMON, PSALMS OF

The most important noncanonical psalter. Reflecting the turmoil of political and religious events in the immediate pre-Christian century when Roman armies first occupied Palestine, it provides the most detailed expectation of the Jewish messiah before the NT.

The period between 65 and 30 B.C.E. is the most likely time of its original composition in Hebrew. A translation into Greek followed, perhaps in Egypt about the turn of the era, and a later translation appeared in Syriac, apparently based on both the Hebrew and Greek texts. Psalms of Solomon survives in 11 Greek and four fragmentary Syriac manuscripts, from the 10th to the 16th centuries. No known Hebrew text exists. It appears in several canon lists of Scripture, including the 5th-century catalogue in the Codex Alexandrinus, and in canon lists from the early 6th to the 10th century. More than 30 editions and translations have been published from 1626 to the present.

Several psalms (1, 2, 8, 15) are vivid, apparently eyewitness, reactions to the events in the decades surrounding the Roman occupation of Palestine from the invasion of Pompey in 63 B.C.E. to the rule of Herod the Great in 37 B.C.E. Other psalms are more generic, with themes much like the biblical Psalter. Pss. Sol. 17 is an extended messianic hymn describing the anticipated victory and reign of the expected redeeming king, the anointed Son of David. This "Lord Messiah" is to lead the pious in a rebellion against the occupying forces, expulsion of foreign influences, and displacement of the corrupt administrations of state and temple. He is to establish an independent and holy Jewish state to which foreign nations would pay allegiance. Most seditious writings, such as Daniel and Revelation, are veiled in cryptic vocabulary innocuous to the eyes of outsiders. However, Psalms of Solomon is an open call for rebellion against both foreign domination and internal corruption, albeit with divine intervention. Unless the Psalms were assured of a strictly controlled circulation, the community was either reckless or emboldened by their belief in an imminent divine intervention.

By superscriptions and tradition, the psalter is ascribed or dedicated to Solomon, although no references to him appear within the poems themselves. The similarity between the most prominent psalm (Pss. Sol. 17) and the canonical Ps. 72, already known as a "Psalm of Solomon," may have prompted the editorial ascription to the one who, next to David, enjoyed a reputation as a poet (1 Kgs. 4:32-34[MT 5:12-14]). Like most late Hebrew poetry, the psalms are of mixed types. Because of the unusual prominence of Jerusalem in Psalms of Solomon, there is little doubt of its provenance. Several authors and an editor/collator appear to have been involved in the composition.

The Pharisees have been most often linked with the psalter, but that identification must now be abandoned. Other scholars have linked it to the Hasidim, Sadducees, Essenes, or even Christians. While few have suggested Qumran itself as a venue for the psalter, many have pointed to similarities to several of the Dead Sea Scrolls. Within the complex of religious coalitions active during this period, the most precision we can have is to say that a separatist group of Jewish messianic protesters in the 1st century B.C.E. is responsible for the psalter.

There are some indications of a synagogue venue for the Psalms of Solomon. The community apparently worshipped apart from the corrupt temple, and abstained from the despoiled sacrifices. Piety had become a substitute for sacrifice, so that sins were now cleansed through confession and penance in the "synagogues of the pious" (17:16; 10:7), where they gave thanks to God (10:6).

As in the biblical prophets and Qumran, the psalter sees God as using foreign powers to discipline Israel. There is a tension between God's sovereignty and human choice: humans can do nothing outside the scope of God's control, but themselves have the power to choose right over wrong.

Composed within a century of the beginnings of Christianity, Psalms of Solomon illuminates the background setting of the Gospels. Especially in Pss. Sol. 17, 18 these poems show how disillusionment with state and temple has increased and hopes for divine intervention have risen. The term "messiah," often used for past and present individuals, now is to be specifically a descendant of David (a rebuke to the Hasmonean rulers), a future ideal king who will restore Israel to a glorious future.

This Lord Messiah is not a supernatural being. However, he will be sinless and have a "holy people" whom he will "lead in righteousness." Using what may have been increasingly common terminology of the time, the righteous person is a "beloved offspring" (13:9) and a "firstborn child" (18:4). These holy ones are "innocent lambs" (8:23), among sinners. The Messiah will bring the "salvation of the Lord" upon Israel forever (12:6).

With the title Lord Messiah, these psalms link for the first time the concepts of "Messiah" and "Lordship" into a new construct available in the contemporary religious environment for Luke to use as a title for Jesus (Luke 2:11), and which the NT develops into the image of "Christ the Lord," a theme central in the development of NT Christology.

Bibliography. K. Atkinson, "Herod the Great, Sosius, and the Siege of Jerusalem (37 B.C.E.) in Psalm of Solomon 17," *NovT* 38 (1996): 313-22; G. Ward, *A Philological Analysis of the Greek and the Syriac Texts of the Psalms of Solomon* (diss., Temple University, 1996); R. B. Wright, "The Psalms of Solomon," *OTP* 2:639-70; *The Psalms of Solomon: A Critical Edition of the Greek Text* (forthcoming); "The Psalms of Solomon, the Pharisees and the Essenes," *1972 Proceedings*, ed. R. A. Kraft. SBLSCS 2 (Missoula, 1972): 136-54. ROBERT B. WRIGHT

SOLOMON, TESTAMENT OF

A pseudepigraphal account, in haggadic style, of King Solomon building the Jerusalem temple. Written originally in koine Greek between 100-300 C.E., the purpose of the story is not easy to discern. It is complete with stories of demons, angels, magical spells, and astrology. While the narrative seems overburdened with such stories, the purpose of the Testament seems unclear. That by the 3rd century the temple was of no importance to Christians begs the question of importance.

Perhaps the text is designed to be "narrative therapy" for human problems (human frailty, sickness, death). Also, in keeping with the long tradition of Solomonic texts (Proverbs, Song of Songs, Ecclesiastes, Wisdom of Solomon, Odes of Solomon, Psalms of Solomon), this text may testify more against the individual who, like Solomon, puts physical pleasures and desires before God. Whoever places God first will find "grace forever" (T. Sol. 26:8).

Historically, the text is a mine of antique information regarding demonology, angelology, magic, dualism, and cosmology. Yet, for all this, there exists the curious fact that not only is belief in the afterlife not referred to, it is not even hinted at. There is only *now*. The text is, however, an invaluable resource for understanding religion in the beginning of Christianity.

Bibliography. D. C. Duling, "Testament of Solomon," *OTP* 1:935-87. MARC A. JOLLEY

SOLOMON'S OFFICIALS

Solomon's officials included a priest, two scribes, a herald, a general, the friend of the king, the officer over the royal estate, and the administrator of corvée labor (1 Kgs. 4:2-6). The list has some continuity with two other royal administration lists under David's reign (2 Sam. 8:16-18; 20:23-26). These officials governed 12 or 13 administrative districts (1 Kgs. 4:7-20), depending on whether Judah is included. Judah could possibly have been a separate administrative district since the administrative structure was set up in the south when David reigned from Hebron. BRUCE W. GENTRY

SOLOMON'S PORTICO

The public meeting place on the eastern side of the temple mount platform which was surrounded by rows of pillars forming a portico (Gk. *stoá toú Solomṓntos*). According to Josephus, who regarded this area as a remnant of Solomon's temple, its Herodian expansion during the end of the Second Temple period is said to have included a span of 15 m. (49 ft.) of double monolithic columns some 11.5 m. (38 ft.) tall, fashioned of white marble supporting an impressive roof paneled with cedar. This colonnaded area of the temple precinct served as a gathering place for Jesus and his disciples (John 10:23) as well as the early Jerusalem Church (Acts 2:46; 5:12). Because people customarily assembled in this place to discuss religious matters when going to the temple for ceremonial rituals, it was an ideal location for Jesus' teaching and the apostles' confirmatory performance of miracles (Acts 3:11; 5:12). No remains exist today, but some have suggested, based on a report by the 6th-century Byzantine historian Procopius of Caesarea, that the Nea Church, whose remains have been discovered, was constructed of pillars from this area.

J. RANDALL PRICE

SOLOMON'S SERVANTS

In a general sense, all who were in the employ of Solomon's household and officials of the kingdom (1 Kgs. 4:1-19; cf. 3:15; 5:6[MT 20]). Among those who returned to Judah following the Exile were a group designated "the sons of Solomon's servants" (Ezra 2:55-58 = Neh. 7:57-60), probably the descendants of non-Israelites enslaved by Solomon who came to represent a distinct class in Judah and Israel (1 Kgs. 9:20-21). They apparently constituted a class of postexilic temple personnel similar in function to the Nethinim (Ezra 7:24).

SON

A male descendant (Heb. *bēn;* Gk. *huiós*), including one beyond the first generation (e.g., Gen. 31:28; Exod. 12:24). The term is also a generic name for children, sometimes used to categorize groups: an entire nation, male and female ("sons of Israel," Gen. 32:32[MT 33]); a geographical designation ("sons of Zion," Ps. 149:2; "sons of the east," 29:1); a class or profession ("descendants of Aaron" or "Asaph," 2 Chr. 35:14-15; "sons of the perfumers," Neh. 3:8; "sons of prophets," 2 Kgs. 2:3; cf. Amos 7:14). It can also designate a person displaying a certain quality: "son of virtue" (1 Kgs. 1:52); "Sons of Thunder" (Mark 3:17).

The role of the son was of great importance in the ancient social order. Throughout the ancient Near East the standard inheritance pattern for transference of property was from father to son, with particular significance given to the firstborn (e.g., Gen. 27:19; Deut. 21:15-17). If a man died without issue, his widow married his brother; the union's first son upheld the dead man's name, so that it would "not be blotted out in Israel" (Deut. 25:5-6). Firstborn sons must be redeemed (Exod. 34:20). A frequent OT story concerns the childless couple. Abram and Sarai longed for a son; Isaac's miraculous birth came when his parents were elderly (Gen. 21). Often such a son becomes a deliverer like Samson (Judg. 13) or fulfills a special mission like Samuel (1 Sam. 1–2).

Along with privilege came responsibility for the son. Sons must honor their parents (Exod 20:12), and must be instructed and disciplined (13:14; Deut. 8:5; 11:19; Josh. 4:6). A son is his father's delight, but must heed his father's commands and not abandon his mother's teachings (Prov. 3:12; 6:20). Sexual relations are prohibited between a son and his mother, father's wife, sister, son's daughter, daughter's daughter, father's sister, mother's sister, and daughter-in-law (Lev. 18:6-30).

"Sons of God" or "sons of gods" refer to divine or semi-divine beings related to the heavenly assembly (Job 1:6; Ps. 89:5-6[6-8]), angels (Dan. 3:25), or primordial beings (Gen. 6:2, 4). God calls Israel his firstborn son (Exod. 4:22), as is also its king (2 Sam. 7:14; Ps. 2:7). In the NT Jesus is called the Son of God (Matt. 14:33; 16:16; Mark 1:1; 3:11; Luke 1:35; cf. Mark 14:61).

Jesus is called the son of Abraham and the son of David (Matt. 1:1; Luke 20:41). Jesus' favorite messianic definition of himself was Son of Man, a clear reference to Daniel's vision of "one like a son of man" (Dan. 7:13; Mark 14:62).

Robin Gallaher Branch/Lee E. Klosinski

SON OF GOD

A person or people having a close relationship with God; in the NT a designation of Jesus. The Lord promised through Nathan that David's ancestor would be "a son to me" (2 Sam. 7:14; 1 Chr. 17:13; 22:10; 28:6), and other texts call the king the Lord's son (Ps. 2:7; cf. Isa. 9:6-7[MT 5-6]) and firstborn (Ps. 89:27-29[28-30]). Several passages call the Lord the "father" of Israel (Deut. 32:6; Isa. 64:8[7]; Jer. 31:9), and others refer to Israel or Ephraim as the Lord's "son" (Exod. 4:22-23; Jer. 31:9; Hos. 11:1). The people can be called the Lord's sons and daughters (Deut. 32:19; Isa. 43:6; Hos. 1:10[2:1]).

Intertestamental Jewish sources call the angels sons of God (Wis. 5:5) and identify the suffering righteous man as God's son (Wis. 2:16-18; Sir. 4:10), and several texts from Qumran, especially the hotly debated Aramaic text 4Q246, provide enigmatic evidence concerning the term "son of God" (cf. also 4QFlor 1:11-13; 1QSa 2:11). The Greco-Roman world bestowed the title Son of God on Caesar.

Although Paul speaks of the Son 15 times, he uses the full title Son of God only three times (Rom. 1:4; 2 Cor. 1:19; Gal. 2:20). One of these three is in the early Christian confession that Jesus was "declared to be Son of God with power" at his resurrection (Rom. 1:3-4). Other Pauline references to the Son are in assertions that God did not spare his own Son (Rom. 8:32), sent him to condemn sin (v. 3) and to redeem those under the law (Gal. 4:4), predestined believers to be conformed to the image of his Son (Rom. 8:29), revealed his Son to Paul (Gal. 1:16), and sent the Spirit of his Son (4:6). Other references to the Son are in statements with divine passives (Rom. 1:4; 5:10; 1 Cor. 15:28; cf. 1:9), though Paul once says that the Son of God gave himself for him (Gal. 2:20). Most of these references to the Son are in two locations, Rom. 1–8 and Galatians. The Deutero-Pauline letters seldom refer to the Son (Eph. 4:13; Col. 1:13).

The Q material claims that the devil tempted Jesus as the Son of God (Luke 4:3, 9) and that Jesus once spoke absolutely of both "the Father" and "the Son" (10:22). Mark repeatedly proclaims that Jesus is God's Son. A heavenly voice calls Jesus "my Son, the Beloved" at his baptism (Mark 1:11; cf. v. 1) and transfiguration (9:7); the unclean spirits recognize him (3:11; 5:7); Jesus refers to a beloved son in a parable (12:6) and speaks of the Son in a saying (13:32); and the high priest asks if Jesus is the Christ the son of the Blessed One (14:61). But a gentile centurion is the only human who confesses Jesus as Son of God in Mark's Gospel (Mark 15:39).

Matthew claims that the disciples confessed Jesus as Son of God (Matt. 14:33) and that Peter confessed him as the Christ the Son of the living God (16:16); however, Matthew also notes that opponents twice use this title when mocking the dying Jesus (27:40, 43). Although the Lukan Infancy narrative promises that Jesus will be called the Son of the Most High (Luke 1:32) and Son of God (v. 35), the disciples do not voice either confession in this Gospel. Paul twice stresses Jesus' identity as God's Son in Acts (9:20; 13:33).

The Gospel of John frequently refers to the Son and the Son of God. The Father sent the Son into the world he had created (John 3:17; 5:23; 10:36) and gave him all things (3:35; 5:22, 26); whoever believes in the Son is not judged (3:17-18) but will have eternal life (3:16, 36; 5:21; 6:40). The Son does what he sees the Father doing (John 5:19-21); indeed, the Father and the Son are one (10:30). Several of the Son of God references are in confessions (John 1:34, 49; 11:27), including the author's statement of purpose (20:31). Many references to the Son and the Son of God also occur in 1-2 John, especially 1 John 4:9–5:20.

Hebrews announces that God recently spoke to us by a Son (Heb. 1:2), who ranks above the angels (vv. 4-13). Designated by God as a high priest according to the order of Melchizedek (Heb. 4:14; 5:6, 10), the Son secured eternal redemption through his own blood for believers (1:3; 9:12), whom God is treating as sons (12:5-8). Having learned obedience through suffering and having been made perfect, the Son became the source of salvation (Heb. 5:8-9; 7:28); however, punishment awaits those who spurn the Son after once believing (6:6; 10:29). Other references to the Son occur in 2 Pet. 1:17; Rev. 2:18.

Bibliography. J. A. Fitzmyer, "4Q246: The 'Son of God' Document from Qumran," *Bibl* 74 (1993): 153-74; R. H. Fuller, *The Foundations of New Testament Christology* (New York, 1965); F. Hahn, *The Titles of Jesus in Christology* (New York, 1969); M. Hengel, *The Son of God* (Philadelphia, 1976); J. D. Kingsbury, *Matthew: Structure, Christology, Kingdom,* rev. ed. (Minneapolis, 1989), 40-83; W. Kramer, *Christ, Lord, Son of God.* SBT 50 (Naperville, 1966).

ROBERT L. MOWERY

SON OF MAN

A title derived from a Hebrew *(ben 'āḏām)* and Aramaic *(bar 'ĕnāš)* idiom which designates a collective (humanity) or an individual within the collective (human being). Its use as a self-designation for Jesus in the four Gospels and uncertainty about whether it is a christological title have led to widespread and still inconclusive debate about its precise meaning.

In the OT the phrase occurs often as a designation for "humanity" or a "human being" in contrast with divine prerogatives (Ps. 8:4[MT 5]; cf. also Num. 23:19). The phrase is used 93 times in Ezekiel as a designation for the prophet, perhaps here too emphasizing the mere mortal nature of the prophet in contrast to the majesty of God who speaks to him (e.g., Ezek. 2:1).

The occurrence of "son of man" in Dan. 7:13-14, a text of enormous influence in later Jewish and NT traditions, raises the question of whether or not at this pre-Christian stage "son of man" had taken on a titular meaning. In his apocalyptic vision which proclaims the ultimate triumph of Israel over the Seleucid tryant Antiochus IV, Daniel sees "one like a son of man" presented in triumph before the throne of God. This "son of man" represents the eschatologically triumphant Israel or perhaps Israel's angelic representative before the throne of God. This one "like a son of man" is exalted, in contrast to the last of the four terrifying beasts (probably representing Antiochus) whom God destroys. In Daniel the royal function of the "son of man" is emphasized as he receives from God dominion over all the peoples of the earth and the promise of an everlasting kingship (Dan. 7:14-18). Whether at this stage the term is used in a titular sense or simply as a designation for a human being is uncertain.

The term is also used in the so-called parables of Enoch (1 En. 37–71). Here a titular and messianic content to "Son of Man" is more evident. Enoch has merged several traditions — wisdom mythology about the preexistence and descent to earth of God's redeeming word, the servant imagery of the latter part of Isaiah, the notion of the just Israelite who suffers and is vindicated by God as found in the Wisdom of Solomon, and the apocalyptic vision of Daniel — to give "son of man" definition as an eschatological redeemer figure. To what extent the parables of Enoch influenced NT use of the title is impossible to determine. Some authors consider 1 En. 37–71 to be later than the Gospel materials and, in the view of some, may even be of Christian origin. At least these Jewish texts provide a parallel to the kind of development that seems to have taken place in the Gospel tradition where Son of Man takes on greater theological weight.

The term "Son of Man" issued almost exclusively in the NT as a self-designation for Jesus (Gk. *huiós toú anthrṓpou*). The only exceptions are passages where Dan. 7:13-14 (Acts 7:56; Rev. 1:13; 14:14) or Ps. 8:4(5) are cited (Heb. 2:6). Interpreters have generally sorted the various uses of the title into three major categories:

a. Jesus within the context of his earthly ministry: e.g., Mark 2:10 (authority to forgive sins); 2:28 (lord of the sabbath); Matt. 8:20 (nowhere to lay his head); 13:37 (sows the good seed); 12:32 (a word spoken against); 16:13 (who do people say he is); 18:11 (come to save the lost); Luke 7:34 (comes eating and drinking); 11:30 (a sign to this generation).
b. Humiliation and sufferings of the Son of Man: Mark 8:31; 9:31; 10:33 par. (passion predictions); Mark 9:12; 10:45 (gives his life in ransom for the many); Matt. 12:40 (sign of Jonah).
c. Future coming in judgment: e.g., Mark 8:38; 14:62; Matt. 16:27-28; 19:28; 24; Luke 17:22, 24, 26, 30; 21:36.

In John's Gospel Son of Man is applied to Jesus as the one sent by God who descends from heaven and returns in exaltation (John 1:51; 3:13; 6:62). The title is also used in connection with the death of Jesus which John describes as the hour of Jesus' glorification or exaltation (John 3:14; 12:23, 34; 13:31).

A much debated point is whether this title was used by the historical Jesus. Some suggest that Jesus used it simply as a self-designation in the mode of the Aramaic and Hebrew idiom (i.e., this human being) or as an expression of humility. Others contend that Jesus referred to an apocalyptic son of man figure in the mode of Dan. 7:13-14 but did not identify himself with this triumphant figure (e.g., Mark 8:38; Luke 12:8). Still others argue that son of man had already taken on a titular sense in the mode of Dan. 7:13-14; 1 Enoch but was given a distinctive set of meanings by the developing Gospel tradition in its application to Jesus. In the manner of Dan. 7:13-14, the title was applied to the glorified Christ but with emphasis on his role as judge at the Parousia rather than king. By extension the title was applied to the earthly ministry of Jesus and to his sufferings, uses that are analogous to the kind of merging of traditions found in 1 Enoch.

Consensus about the tradition history and precise meaning of the son of man designation remains elusive. Interpretation of any given passage must depend on an appreciation of its immediate context and the nuances given the designation by a particular NT author.

DONALD SENIOR

SONG OF SOLOMON

"The Song of Songs, which is Solomon's" (1:1), also called the Canticle of Canticles. One of the Five Scrolls read liturgically by Jews at various times in the ritual year, it is associated with the spring Festival of Passover. In Christian Bibles it is grouped with the other Solomonic writings, immediately preceding the prophets. As love poetry, seemingly devoid of religious content, it has always appeared anomalous; hence a long tradition of allegorical and mystical interpretation developed. The hyperbolic anxiety attached to it may be exemplified by Rabbi Akiba, who is reported to have declared that "the Song of Songs is the Holy of Holies" (*m. Yad.* 3:5) and also that one "who trills it in the banqueting-house loses his share in the world to come" (*Sanh.* 102b). Nevertheless, its influence both on secular Western erotic poetry and on Jewish and Christian mystical traditions is unfathomable.

It is not known when the Song was written. Estimates range from the 10th to the 3rd century B.C.E., with the majority of recent commentators favoring the latter. Its early adoption as a proto-canonical text is proved by the presence of fragments among the Dead Sea Scrolls. Jerusalem is the center of its symbolic world, which induces most critics to regard it as the place of composition. Some scholars, however, see evidence of northern Israelite influence, both in geographical allusions and linguistic dialect. There is no unanimity, either, on the literary unity of the Song. Many critics argue from the lack of any coherent sequence in the Song that it is an anthology of love poems; this would allow for a diversity of dates and origins. Others hold that it was a highly articulated literary structure. A compromise position has been promoted by a number of authors, that it is an artful composition using preexistent and traditional materials.

Most of the Song consists of monologues or dialogues between a pair of lovers, with the female voice dominant. At times a third, impersonal voice, which may be identified with that of the narrator or poet, seems to intervene, and at two points at least (5:9; 6:1) there is a chorus of daughters of Jerusalem. Many critics, however, assign much more material to the chorus, sometimes introducing a male chorus as well (e.g., 8:8-9).

It is not clear what, if anything, happens in the Song. Much effort has been devoted to reconstructing a story. Reconstructions, however, generally necessitate considerable conjecture, and risk imposing a narrative structure on a nonnarrative, lyric discourse. The lovers speak to and about each other, in memory, anticipation, and desire; the boundary between reality and imagination is always ambiguous. For instance, at the center of the Song the man asserts that he has entered "his garden" (5:1), which, in context, is a metaphor for the woman; in the following verse, however, half-asleep she hears him outside her door, pleading to be admitted. We do not know if the lovers ever have intercourse; they are in any case figments of the poet's imagination, and the task of the lyric is to communicate the sensations of love in language. It is less concerned with the adventures of a particular pair of lovers than with making them representative of all lovers. The different roles they play — king and shepherd, country and city girl — are evidence not so much of diverse origins as the intersection of different traditional paradigms of love. One persona particularly associated with the man is that of King Solomon, not only as supreme lover and poet (cf. 1 Kgs. 4:32[MT 5:12]), but as a symbol of human perfection.

The Song is composed of numerous units of various length, usually clearly demarcated from each other and without obvious continuity. These are either separate poems or, for those who think that the Song has literary unity, they juxtapose contrasting perspectives and genres. Various units match each other across the text, often with significant variations or inversions; proponents of unity regard this as the main principle of composition. Among matching units are formal portraits of the lovers, technically called *wasfs* (4:1-7; 5:10-16; 6:5-7; 7:2-7[1-6]), in which parts of the body are metaphorically elaborated; two dream sequences (3:1-4; 5:2-7), in which the woman searches for her lover through the nocturnal city; two descriptions of the spring (2:10-13; 7:11-13[12-14]). The climax of the book, corresponding to the description of the garden of love at its center (4:12–5:1), is a set of equivalences, in which love is said to be as strong as death and unquenchable (8:6-7).

The poetic quality of the book fully justifies the superlative asserted by the title, "The Song of Songs." Like all great poetry, it is both sensually rich, a literary analogue of the sensory world of the lovers, and dense with significance. In particular, it is remarkable for its intense, sometimes bizarre, imagery, the richness of its vocabulary, and its pervasive alliteration and wordplay. The metaphors often attain a life of their own, subverting the difference between figure and referent. The distance between the image and its subject is a source of aesthetic tension and hermeneutic richness, and allows the openness of interpretation. Some scholars have noted the phonological patterning and the connections between alliteration and metaphor throughout the Song, and intertextually elsewhere in the OT, so that sounds and meanings are mutually generative.

Through metaphor, the experience of the lovers is transferred onto the world and language. The lovers are compared with animals and flowers; they thus become representative of the land of Israel in springtime. In one of the formal portraits or *wasfs* there is an extended comparison between the woman and the land (7:1-6[2-7]). This has led some to argue that the Song is concerned with an erotic vision of the world. The metaphors culminate in the opposition of love and death; love is of ultimate value, because it alone is immortal. The Song may be compared to Ecclesiastes, seeing in both a reaction to the anomie of the Hellenistic age. Furthermore, the Song may be associated with the Wisdom tradition, with its search for value and its humanism.

A large number of recent scholars have discussed the feminist implications of the Song. Some have postulated female authorship, pointing to the dominance of the female voice in the Song, and its inversion of patriarchal values. Others find female authorship improbable, given the conditions of literary production in the ancient world, suggesting that the Song is a male erotic fantasy, and that the centrality of the woman expresses male desire.

Some critics hold that the Song has an element of self-parody, subverting its own ideal of beauty; thereby it promotes love as that which transpires between real, imperfect human beings. Others see it as infused with a comic vision, of the integration of the world through love.

Various scholars have investigated parallels between the Song and other ancient Near Eastern erotic literature. Correlations are especially close with the love poetry of ancient Egypt. Other critics have explored intertextual connections between the Song and the rest of the OT, including Ecclesiastes and the garden of Eden, which they see reconstituted and questioned in the Song. Those who read the Song as a political or religious allegory find in it numerous allusions to the prophetic or historical literature.

The spiritual significance of the Song, and the reason for its incorporation in the canon, have been subject to much discussion. Some hold it to be a purely secular work; others find references in it to mortuary or other cults. At the climax of the book (8:6) the name of God appears albeit as a suffix to the noun *šalheḇeṯ*, "flame." Frequently interpreted as a conventional superlative ("mighty flame"), it might also mean that love is the flame of God, which burns on the altar. The frequent references to the geography of the land of Israel and to King Solomon, as well as one to David, suggest that Israel's history and landscape are drawn into the network of comparisons and allusions. If Solomon represents Israel at the height of its glory, that glory is nostalgically evoked and critiqued, in the context of its passing.

Bibliography. A. Bloch and C. Bloch, *The Song of Songs* (1995, repr. Berkeley, 1998); A. Brenner, ed., *A Feminist Companion to the Song of Songs* (Sheffield, 1993); M. V. Fox, *The Song of Songs and the Ancient Egyptian Love Songs* (Madison, 1985); M. D. Goulder, *The Song of Fourteen Songs.* JSOTSup 36 (Sheffield, 1986); F. Landy, *Paradoxes of Paradise: Identity and Difference in the Song of Songs* (Sheffield, 1983); R. E. Murphy, *The Song of Songs.* Herm (Minneapolis, 1990); M. H. Pope, *Song of Songs.* AB 7C (Garden City, 1977).

FRANCIS LANDY

SONG OF THE THREE YOUNG MEN

See DANIEL, ADDITIONS TO.

SOPATER (Gk. *Sṓpatros*)

A companion of Paul on the latter's final journey to Jerusalem to deliver an offering from the gentile churches to the church at Jerusalem (Acts 20:4). He is mentioned as being from Beroea. The name (Gk. "of sound parentage") may be a variant of Sosipater (Rom. 16:21).

JOE E. LUNCEFORD

SOPHERETH (Heb. *sôp̄ereṯ*)
(also HASSOPHERETH)

One of "Solomon's servants" whose descendants returned with Zerubbabel from exile in Babylon (Neh. 7:57). At Ezra 2:55 he is called Hassophereth.

SOPHIA (Gk. *sophía*)

Greek name for "Wisdom" (Heb. *ḥoḵmâ*), also referred to as "Woman Wisdom." This female figure appears in Prov. 1–9; Job 28; and in the apocryphal books of Sirach, Baruch, and Wisdom of Solomon.

Portrayed as crying out from the city gates to those "simple ones" who might listen, Woman Wisdom in Prov. 1–9 is a teacher who, unlike the smooth-talking "strange woman" *(ʾiššâ zārâ),* offers truth and justice, wise counsel, prosperity, and long life. In existence since before creation, she is an *ʾāmôn* ("master craftsworker" or "little child") at the side of God (Prov. 8:30), playing on earth, perhaps participating in creation, and finding her delight in humanity. In Job 28, however, Wisdom is inaccessible to humanity, a mystery more precious than the finest of metals; God alone knows the "way" to her, having seen and established her at the time of creation (v. 27). Ben Sira and Baruch identify Woman Wisdom directly with the Torah (Sir. 24:23; Bar. 4:1), while in the Wisdom of Solomon she orders the cosmos as the emanation of God's glory and a reflection of the divine image (Wis. 7:25-26; 8:1).

Certainly a figure whose description was expanded over time, the "identity" of Woman Wisdom remains complex: she is a gift from God yet one to be sought with discipline, a transcendent figure who fashions the world yet is immanently present with, and concerned for, humanity. Some scholars addressing the origin and development of Woman Wisdom have posited that she emerged as an Israelite parallel to such ancient Near Eastern goddesses as Ishtar, Maat, or Isis, or that she is a hypostasis of God's wisdom. Others argue that she is the personification of a "concept" such as school wisdom or the mysterious order of creation itself. Attention has also been given to the literary function of Woman Wisdom as a metaphor and the apparent appropriation of Sophia imagery in early Christian attempts to define the nature and role of Christ (1 Cor. 1:24; cf. 2:7; Col. 2:3).

Bibliography. C. V. Camp, *Wisdom and the Feminine in the Book of Proverbs* (Sheffield, 1985); B. Lang, *Wisdom and the Book of Proverbs: A Hebrew Goddess Redefined* (New York, 1986).

CHRISTINE ROY YODER

SOREK (Heb. *śōrēq*), **VALLEY OF**

Wadi eṣ-Ṣarâr/Naḥal Sorek/Nahr Rubin, which forms a natural passage into the Judean hill country for travelers beginning in the coastal area of Jaffa. The valley follows the wide meanders of the Sorek streambed across the fertile alluvial soil. At the base of the hill country, the valley widens at its juncture with the Wadi Ghurab descending from the north and the Wadi en-Najil from the south. Overlooking the confluence of the three wadis, the towns of Zorah and Eshtaol sat on the northern side, Beth-shemesh on the south. The settlements of the Sorek (Timnah, Beth-shemesh) maintained vigilance over trade passing through the valley destined for Jerusalem or Bethlehem in the interior or turning south toward the other valleys and settlements within the Shephelah. Delilah's home was in the Sorek Valley (Judg. 16:4).

Bibliography. Y. Aharoni, *The Land of the Bible,* 2nd ed. (Philadelphia, 1979); G. A. Smith, *The Historical Geography of the Holy Land,* 25th ed. (New York, 1966). DAVID C. MALTSBERGER

SOSIPATER (Gk. *Sōsípatros*)

1. A captain under Judas Maccabeus who destroyed the garrison at Charax. He subsequently captured the governor Timothy, who coaxed Sosipater into releasing him (2 Macc. 12:19-25).

2. A Jewish Christian who was with Paul at the time of the writing of the Epistle to the Romans (probably at Corinth shortly before Paul's final journey to Jerusalem) and whose greetings are conveyed to the church at Rome (Rom. 16:21). He is identified as one of Paul's "relatives" (NRSV; cf. mg "compatriots"). He may be the same person as Sopater (Acts 20:4). JOE E. LUNCEFORD

SOSTHENES (Gk. *Sōsthénēs*)

1. The "ruler" of a synagogue at Corinth who was beaten by a mob because the proconsul Gallio refused to entertain "the Jews'" charges against Paul (Acts 18:17).

2. One whom Paul refers to as "our brother" (1 Cor. 1:1). If he is the same as **1** above, he has now become a Christian and a co-worker with Paul.

JOE E. LUNCEFORD

SOTAI (Heb. *sōṭay, sôṭay*)

The head of a family of "Solomon's servants" who returned with Zerubbabel from exile (Ezra 2:55; Neh. 7:57).

SOUL

Although Heb. *nep̱eš* has a wide range of usage, it most frequently designates the life force of living creatures. Thus, all the earth is full of "living creatures" that have the "breath of life" (Gen. 1:20-21, 24, 30). When God creates Adam, God breathes the breath of life into Adam's nostrils, and Adam becomes a "living being" (Gen. 2:7). Far from referring simply to one aspect of a person, "soul" refers to the whole person. Thus, a corpse is referred to as a "dead soul," even though the word is usually translated "dead body" (Lev. 21:11; Num. 6:6). "Soul" can also refer to a person's very life itself 1 Kgs. 19:4; Ezek. 32:10).

"Soul" often refers by extension to the whole person. Thus, Leah bears Jacob 16 souls (Gen. 46:18), and when Jacob moves into Egypt, there were "70 persons ('souls') in his house" (v. 27). In the Shema (Deut. 6:4-9) Israelites are commanded to love their God with all their heart, soul, and strength. Although "soul" appears in the translation to be a separate faculty of the body, the verse is an exhortation to love God with one's entire self.

The soul is also the seat of the emotions. It is both the center of joy in God (Ps. 86:4; cf. 62:1[MT 2]) and the seat of the desire of evil in the wicked (Prov. 21:10).

In the NT "soul" (Gk. *psychḗ*) refers to the living being of the whole person (Acts 2:41; 3:23) and to a person's life. After Herod's death, the angel commands Joseph to take his wife and child (Jesus) back to Israel, for "those who were seeking the child's life (soul) are dead" (Matt. 2:20). Before he heals the man with the withered hand, Jesus asks the synagogue authorities whether it is lawful on the sabbath to "save life (soul) or to kill" (Mark 3:4). In the parable of the rich young fool (Luke 12:13-20), the young man says to his soul that he has ample goods laid up for many years; Jesus then tells him, "This very night your soul ('life force') is being demanded of you."

Although the NT contains little evidence of the body-soul dualism that is apparent in Hellenistic philosophy, some passages indicate that the soul lives on after death (Luke 9:25; 12:4; 21:19). While Plato, in the myth of Er in *The Republic,* seems to argue for the preexistence of souls, the Bible offers evidence of no such belief. Some early Christian thinkers like Origen apparently believed that the earthly body was a prison in which the soul was bound for some evil it had committed in the heavenly realm. As to the immortality of souls, the clearest biblical example may be found in Revelation, where the "souls of those who had been beheaded for their testimony to Jesus and for the word of God" are asked to rest a "little longer" until the final judgment (Rev. 20:4). HENRY L. CARRIGAN, JR.

SOUTH

Because the Israelites thought of the compass points in relation to a person facing eastward, their words for "south" included Heb. *yāmîn,* "on the right, right hand, south," and the related word *têmān.* Other Hebrew terms are *negeḇ,* which is also the name of the southern region of Judah, "the Negeb," and *dārôm.* "The king of the south" designates various Ptolemaic rulers of Egypt at Dan. 11. NT terms include Gk. *nótos* and *mesēmbría* (Acts 8:26), which might also be translated "midday" (NRSV mg "noon"). "The queen of the South" (Matt. 12:42; Luke 11:31) is the queen of Sheba (cf. 1 Kgs. 10:1-10).

SPAIN (Gk. *Spanía*)

In biblical usage all of the Iberian Peninsula, i.e., both Spain and Portugal. It has been argued that Tarshish, a land containing an abundance of minerals (Ezek. 27:12; 1 Macc. 8:3) and situated far away, "out of reach of the Lord" (Jonah 1:3), could possibly refer to Spain.

At least the southeastern portion of the land was populated by the rugged Iberians from ca. 3000 B.C. The Phoenicians established scattered trading outposts, and in the 6th century the Phocaean Greeks colonized the eastern and southern coasts. At the same time the Celts were occupying large portions of the peninsula. During the 3rd century the Carthaginians invaded Spain and established Carthago Nova (modern Carthage) as their capital. From Spain the general Hannibal mounted the Second Punic War against Rome. Following their victory in 201 the

Romans formed two provinces in Spain (Hispania Citerior along the eastern coast and the Ebro River Valley and Hispania Ulterior along the southern coast and the Baetis [Guadalquivir] Valley), but native resistance continued until 133. The Roman emperors Trajan, Hadrian, and Theodosius I were of Spanish origin.

Paul intended to stop in Rome on his way to Spain (Rom. 15:24, 28), but nothing in the NT suggests that he ever went there. However, 1 Clem. 5:6-7 (probably A.D. 97) calls Paul a herald both in the east and the west and says that he reached "the limits of the west," which, from the perspective of a writer in Rome, most likely refers to the Iberian peninsula of Gibraltar. It has been suggested that Paul's travel plans to Spain should be understood in light of his writings on "the full number of the Gentiles" (Rom. 11:25). Irenaeus is probably the first to mention the existence of Christian communities in Spain (*Adv. haer.* 1.10.2; ca. A.D. 180).

Bibliography. A. J. Dewey, "Εἰς τὴν Σπανίαν: The Future and Paul," in *Religious Propaganda and Missionary Competition in the New Testament World,* ed. L. Bormann, K. Del Tredici, and A. Standhartinger. NovTSup 74 (Leiden, 1994), 321-49; O. F. A. Meinardus, "Paul's Missionary Journey to Spain," *BA* 41 (1978): 61-63. JESPER SVARTVIK

SPAN

A unit of length (Heb. *zereṯ*) based on the distance from the thumb to the fifth finger of a spread hand and equivalent to ca. 22.2 cm. (8.75 in.; Exod. 28:16; 39:9; Ezek. 43:13). In a rhetorical question Isa. 40:12 refers to God's span as that which "marked off the heavens."

SPARROW

A general designation for many types of small birds that inhabited the areas around houses and gardens (Deut. 4:17; Ps. 84:3[MT 4]; 104:17; Eccl. 9:12). Sparrows (Heb. *ṣippôr;* Gk. *strouthíon*) are small brown and gray birds that swarm in groups throughout Palestine. They build their nests in many places such as walls, gardens, vineyards, houses, and bushes, and feed on seeds, worms, and small insects. They were considered a clean bird (Deut. 14:11). The sparrow was used in sacrifices but was too small to be cut in half and placed on the altar (Gen. 15:10). A leper was commanded to offer two live, clean birds as a testimony to his or her cleansing (Lev. 14:4). The poor were allowed to offer a small bird for the sin offering if they could not afford a lamb (Lev. 5:7). The sparrow was hunted and snared but provided little meat for consumption (Ps. 124:7; Prov. 6:5). Sparrows were plentiful in NT times, and two could be purchased for a penny (Matt. 10:29; cf. Luke 12:6).

A man who pursued a prostitute or fell into great debt was compared to a bird that was captured in the snare of a hunter (Prov. 6:5; 7:23; 27:8). Jesus taught that God's care for the sparrow was an indication of God's greater care and value of human beings (Matt. 10:31; Luke 12:6).

Bibliography. G. R. Driver, "Birds in the Old Testament — Part 1: Birds in Law," *PEQ* 87 (1955): 5-20; "Part 2: Birds in Life," *PEQ* 87 (1955): 129-40.

JOHN A. MCLEAN

SPARTA (Gk. *Spartē*)

The capital city of Laconia in the Peloponnese of Greece. Founded ca. 1000 B.C.E. by Dorians, it was first known as Lacedaemon. At first a number of independent villages, the Spartans united under two kings and eventually came to supreme power in Greece. They detested luxury and prized service to the state and constant preparation for war. Spartans emphasized courage, selflessness, and rigor (weak newborns being exposed to die, boys being reared severely by the state from seven to 20 years, married men living in military barracks). Sparta bravely supported Athens in the Persian Wars but defeated her as an enemy in the Peloponnesian Wars (431-404). Correspondence between the Jews and Spartans indicates attempts at diplomatic relations (cf. 1 Macc. 12:2-23; 14:16-23; 15:16-22). In 168 the Oniad priest Jason sought asylum in the Jewish community at Sparta following his failed coup (2 Macc. 5:9).

Bibliography. C. B. Avery, ed., *The New Century Handbook of Classical Geography* (New York, 1972), 314-17; R. J. A. Talbert, ed., *Atlas of Classical History* (New York, 1985), *s.v.* RICHARD A. SPENCER

SPEAR

Originally a blade with a thin tail inserted in a wooden shaft and held with binding. In the 2nd millennium the socketed head was introduced. At this time metal butts also appeared, which enabled the end of the spear to be used as a club or stuck in the ground when not in use (1 Sam. 26:7; 2 Sam. 2:23). The average spear was 2-3 m. (6.5-10 ft.) long. It was a basic weapon of the infantry, and later the chariotry. Spears were used to defend against cavalry attack, in hand-to-hand combat, and in defense of a city under siege. Used in a thrusting motion, the spear was capable of producing a lethal wound. It remained in the hands of the warrior throughout the battle and is therefore classified as a short-range weapon. In comparison, the javelin, which was both shorter and lighter, was designed primarily for throwing (1 Sam. 17:6-7, 45). The major improvement in these weapons involved the material from which the blade was constructed (first stone, then copper, bronze, and iron).

Originating in prehistoric times as a device for hunting, the spear was adapted for use in war at least as early as the 4th millennium. It made its appearance in Israel at the end of the 3rd millennium by means of nomadic wanderers from the north. The metal-bladed spear and other technologically advanced weapons were in short supply in the early history of Israel (1 Sam. 13:19-20). From the United Monarchy onward, however, the spear appeared with greater frequency. Initially it was found only in the hands of the elite (1 Sam. 13:22). In the later monarchial period it became a primary armament of the military forces (1 Chr. 12:8, 24, 34; 2 Chr. 11:12; 14:8; 26:14).

Bibliography. T. R. Hobbs, *A Time for War.* OTS 3 (Wilmington, 1989); Y. Yadin, *The Art of Warfare in Biblical Lands,* 2 vols. (Jerusalem, 1963).

W. E. NUNNALLY

SPELT

A form of wheat (Heb. *kussemet*), probably either spelt (*Triticum spelta* L.) or emmer wheat (*Triticum dicoccum* Schrank). It survived the plague of hail in Egypt (Exod. 9:32), was used to border fields in Palestine (Isa. 28:25), and was made into bread in Babylonia (Ezek. 4:9).

SPICES

A generic term for any expensive perfume that was highly valued as a precious commodity (Heb. *bōśem*). The high monetary value of spice is indicated by its repeated association with precious metals and stones (Ezek. 27:22), and they were a significant part of trade in luxury items (cf. Rev. 18:13; Gk. *ámōmon*). The queen of Sheba brought some exclusive spices from her land to Solomon (1 Kgs. 10:2, 10 = 2 Chr. 9:1, 9; cf. Ezek. 27:22), as did all foreign dignitaries who visited Solomon (1 Kgs. 10:25). Hezekiah built special treasuries just for his spices (2 Kgs. 20:13 = 2 Chr. 32:27). Asa's bier contained spice at his funeral (2 Chr. 16:14); spices (Gk. *árōma*) were used to embalm Jesus (Mark 16:1; Luke 23:56; 24:1), in accordance with Jewish burial custom (John 19:40).

Spices also had an aromatic use, and are mentioned frequently in the Song of Solomon. Here they appear to be used as an aphrodisiac as the lover is obsessed with the scent (Cant. 5:13). They are used along with myrrh (Cant. 5:1). The lover is personified as a "bed of spices" (Cant. 6:2), yet her fragrance is better than spice (4:10, 14). The sexual energy of the lover is compared to that of a stag and a gazelle on a "mountain of spices" (Cant. 8:14).

Further, spices had a cultic use and were a major ingredient in the oil used for anointing (Exod. 35:8, 28). The ingredients for this special spice were liquid myrrh, cinnamon, aromatic cane, and cassia (Exod. 30:22-24). Certain Levites were especially assigned to take care of the temple spices (1 Chr. 9:29), and others were responsible for preparing the mixture (v. 30). "Sweet spices" (Heb. *sam*) used in anointing were noted for their fragrance (Exod. 30:34; 37:29; cf. NRSV).

Heb. *nĕḵôṯ*, sometimes translated "gum," appears to be a condiment (Gen. 43:11). It has been identified as the *Astragalus tragacantha* plant.

KEITH A. BURTON

SPIDER

An Arachnid of the order Araneida, of which numerous species exist in Palestine (Heb. *'akkāḇîš*). Distinguished from insects by the division of their bodies into two portions, the cephalothorax and abdomen, spiders are unique among animals because of their spinnerets, appendages to their abdomen which emit through spinning tubers a silky fluid. The manner in which a spider's web is woven is a metaphor for the deliberate sinful actions of the wicked (Isa. 59:5). The web itself typifies the fragile existence of the ungodly (Job 8:14).

SPINNING, WEAVING, LOOM

Spinning and weaving are the major processes in the production of cloth and were familiar in biblical times. While these activities were traditionally the work of women in the home (Prov. 31:13, 19, 22, 24), there is evidence that men became involved in cloth production as an economic enterprise.

Threads were produced from raw fibers by spinning (Matt. 6:28 = Luke 12:27). Flax, or linen (Heb. *pēšeṯ, pištâ;* Lev. 13:47-48; Prov. 31:13; Jer. 13:1; Ezek. 40:3; 44:17; Hos. 2:5[MT 7]), and wool (*ṣemer;* Lev. 13:47) were the major fibers used in the biblical world. In spinning *(ṭāwâ),* raw fibers were pulled into a loose strand, often held by a distaff (*kîšôr;* Prov. 31:19), and twisted to form a continuous thread. A spindle (*pelek;* 2 Sam. 3:29; Prov. 31:19) was a slender stick which could be twirled to twist a strand of fibers caught in a hook or slot at the top. A disklike weight, or spindle whorl, was fitted to the spindle as a flywheel for more efficient twisting. Spun thread was wound onto the stick.

Sometimes thread, especially linen, was twined *(šāzar),* two or three threads being twisted together (Exod. 26:1; 36:8, 35). Finished thread, whether wool or linen, could be used for weaving (Exod. 35:25).

Weaving is the interlacing of threads to form fabric. While weaving was conducted in homes, some weavers apparently were professionals who specialized in particular types of work. The OT differentiates between ordinary weavers (*'ōrēḡ;* Exod. 39:22, 27), "designers" (*ḥōšēḇ;* 26:1; 28:6; 36:8), and "embroiderers" (*rōqēm;* 26:36; 28:39; 36:37).

Weaving was generally conducted on looms, devices designed to create openings (sheds) between alternating vertical warp threads through which the horizontal weft threads were passed. After each weft thread was placed, it was beaten against the previous one with a flat stick, thus firming up the fabric. Three main loom designs were used in the biblical world. On a horizontal ground loom, the warp threads were stretched between beams pegged to the ground. This type is apparently referred to in the Samson story (Judg. 16:13-14), as it would have enabled Delilah to weave his locks while he slept; when Samson jumped up, he pulled away the pins of the loom (*'ereḡ;* v. 14b) which secured the beams to the ground.

In some vertical looms the warp was stretched between two beams fixed in a rectangular frame. Work proceeded from the bottom of the loom and the woven cloth could be rolled onto the bottom beam (Isa. 38:12). This permitted the weaver to remain seated and produce much longer finished products. The metaphor by which the shaft of a mighty man's spear is likened to a "weaver's beam" (1 Sam. 17:7; 2 Sam. 21:19) may derive from the size of the bottom beams of upright looms. It is also possible that the image indicated the spear was attached to a thong by a ring, like the shuttle used by the weaver to throw the weft through the shed of large looms.

Warp-weighted looms had the warp threads attached to an upper beam and held taut in groups by a series of stone or clay weights. Weaving was done from the top to the bottom and the weft beaten upward. Large numbers of excavated loom weights testify to the popularity of warp-weighted looms in ancient Israel. Stripes or bands of color were made by using dyed threads for portions of the warp or weft threads. Warp-weighted looms allowed portions of the shed to be opened at a time, so intricate patterns could be made in the weft by covering small areas with different colors. This type of weaving was most easily and effectively done by using linen warps and wool wefts. The work of "embroiderers" and "designers" in producing curtains for the tabernacle and the high priestly garments (Exod. 26:1, 36; 39:29) may have involved such mixing. The prohibition of wearing clothes made of linen and wool woven together (Deut. 22:11) may lie in a taboo against using "sacred" techniques for profane purposes.

Bibliography. E. J. W. Barber, *Prehistoric Textiles* (Princeton, 1991); *Women's Work: The First 20,000 Years* (New York, 1994); C. Bier, "Textile Arts in Ancient Western Asia," *CANE* 3: 1567-88.

DANIEL C. BROWNING, JR.

SPIRIT

In the OT, Heb. *rûaḥ* means first of all wind and breath, but also the human spirit in the sense of life force and even personal energy. In 1 Kgs. 18:45; Ps. 103:16; Jer. 4:11 it means wind, a phenomenon of nature. In some cases, however, wind is seen as God's instrument (e.g., Gen. 8:1; Num. 11:31; Isa. 11:15). The term occurs with the meaning of breath in Gen. 6:17; Job 34:14-15. In the latter passage, it is explicit that God is the source of human breath. In Judg. 15:19; 1 Kgs. 10:5 "breath" stands for human energy. Sometimes the term becomes virtually a synonym for *nep̄eš*, "soul" or "life force," and *lēḇ*, "heart" (not in the modern sense of the seat of love, but in the ancient meaning of the center of the personality, including intelligence and will); cf. Job 20:3; 32:18; Isa. 54:6; 57:15; 66:2; Dan. 5:20.

Heb. *rûaḥ* refers not simply to the life given to humanity by God. God also is spirit. God's spirit came upon people and empowered them for special service (Judg. 3:10). God could also trouble people with an evil spirit (Judg. 9:23; 1 Sam. 16:14-23). Prophecy was understood as a sign of the presence of God's spirit (Num. 11:25-26; Isa. 41:1; 61:1; Mic. 3:8). God's spirit was expected to be poured out in abundance in the future (Joel 2:28-29[MT 3:1-2]). The ancient Hebrews understood God's power to be everywhere (Ps. 139:7), to be personal (Isa. 34:16; 48:16), and yet to be awesome and transcendent.

Sometimes it is not clear which nuance of *rûaḥ* is intended. Gen. 1:2 may be translated "a wind from God," "a mighty wind," or "the spirit of God."

A notion of spirits as supernatural beings is found in certain Hebrew writings (e.g., 1 Kgs. 22:21).

In the NT Gk. *pneúma* can mean wind (John 3:8; Heb. 1:7, quoting Ps. 104:4). It can also have the meaning breath (2 Thess. 2:8; Jas. 2:26; Rev. 11:1; 13:15). The term is found with the meaning of inner self in Mark 2:8; 8:12; Luke 1:80; John 11:33; 13:21. The plural is used for the concept of (evil) spirit in numerous passages (e.g., 2 Cor. 11:4; 1 Tim. 4:1; Rev. 16:13-14). The plural may also refer to the dead, i.e., to ghosts (Matt. 14:26; Mark 6:49; Luke 24:39; Heb. 12:23; 1 Pet 3:19).

Jesus refers to the spirit when he quotes from Isa. 61:1 (Luke 4:18). What is referred to as God's spirit in the OT often is described as the Holy Spirit in the NT. For example, when Jesus is baptized Matthew, Mark, and John say that the Spirit descended on Jesus like a dove (Matt. 3:16 = Mark 1:10 = John 1:32). However, Luke 3:22 indicates that it was the Holy Spirit that descended upon Jesus. At Pentecost likewise the outpouring of God's spirit prophesied in Joel 2:28-29 is fulfilled as people are filled with the Holy Spirit (Acts 2:4). Sometimes the spirit received by Christians is identified as Jesus' spirit (Gal. 4:6). In 1 Cor. 12:4-6 the Spirit, God, and the Lord are identified.

God's spirit is envisioned in the NT as having been given to the people in a new way (John 7:38-39; Acts 2:1-21; Gal. 3:2, 14; Titus 3:6). People worship God "in spirit" (John 4:24; Phil. 3:3), they are born of the spirit (Gal. 4:29), but the conflict between the spirit and the flesh continues (Rom. 8:2-17; 1 Cor. 3:1; Gal. 3:3; 5:16-18). Although this suggests that the NT authors had bought into a Hellenistic body/spirit dualism, probably they used the Greek terminology, but understood it in a more Semitic, i.e., more holistic, way (Rom. 8:10; 1 Cor. 5:5; 2 Cor. 4:16; Eph. 2:2-3; 1 Thess. 5:23; Heb 4:12).

Living in the Spirit is contrasted with slavery to the law (Rom. 7:6). Its fruits are love, joy, peace, patience, kindness, generosity, faithfulness, gentleness, and self-control (Gal. 5:22-23). Those who live by the Spirit are counseled to be guided by it as well (Gal. 5:25).

During the Hellenistic period, the concept of hierarchy of spiritual powers had also developed, and this conception probably colored the NT writers' understanding of the spiritual forces with which Christians were thought to do battle (Acts 23:8; 1 Cor. 12:10; Eph. 6:12).

Finally, "spirit" can mean an immediate or direct contact with divine realities in contrast with the more cerebral approach associated with the term "mind" (1 Cor. 14:14-15), but both "spirit" and "mind" are used of the whole person and not simply of component parts. ALICE OGDEN BELLISB

SPIRIT, EVIL/UNCLEAN

A spiritual being under the authority of Yahweh who carries out the more negative aspects of his will (Heb. *rûaḥ ra'â;* Judg. 9:23; 1 Sam. 16:14-23; 18:10; 19:9; cf. 1 Kgs. 22:19-23, "lying spirit"; Zech. 13:2, *rûaḥ ṭum'â,* "unclean spirit"). Postbiblical Jewish texts refer to "evil spirits" (T. Sim. 4:9; 6:6; Jub. 10:3, 13; 11:4; 12:20; 4Q511 15 1:7; 81 1:3) and "unclean spirits" (cf. T. Benj. 5:2; 11QPs 19:15; 1 En.

99:7). There are synonymous designations for these beings, which, unlike the evil spirits in the OT, operate independently of God, seeking to lead human beings away from obedience to God. Often they are under the authority of a single evil spiritual being who is variously named, e.g., Satan, Mastema, Belial.

In the Gospels Jesus is said to exorcise "evil spirits" (Gk. *pneúmata akártharta;* Mark 3:11; Luke 8:2; cf. 11:26) or "unclean spirits" (Mark 1:23-28 par.; 5:2-13 [cf. Luke 8:29]; Mark 6:7 par.; 7:25; 9:25 par.). The early Church is also said to have cast out unclean spirits (Acts 5:16; 8:7) and evil spirits (19:11-12; cf. vv. 13-16). Eph. 6:12 refers to "spiritual forces of evil in the heavenly places" against which believers are to defend themselves.

Bibliography. J. M. Hull, *Hellenistic Magic and the Synoptic Tradition.* SBT, 2nd ser. 28 (Naperville, 1974); G. H. Twelftree, *Jesus the Exorcist* (Peabody, 1994).

Barry D. Smith

SPIRITUAL GIFTS

Affirmations of the power of the Spirit of God present in the world abound in both the OT and NT. God's Spirit empowers individuals from the time of Moses and the wilderness wanderings (Num. 11:25, 29) and is often linked especially with the gift of prophecy (Isa. 42:1; 61:1-2; Joel 2:28-29[MT 3:1-2]; Zech. 12:10). The Israelite judges (e.g., Othniel, Judg. 3:10) received confirmation for their leadership through the gift of the Spirit of the Lord, and Isaiah prophesies that the "shoot from the stump of Jesse" will be the one on whom the Spirit of the Lord shall rest (Isa. 11:1-2). This text, moreover, specifies what the signs (traditionally, "gifts") of this Spirit will be: "wisdom, understanding, counsel, might, knowledge, and fear of the Lord." To this list, the LXX adds "piety," rounding out the number to seven. These OT references constitute at best implicit gifts of the Spirit; only in the Christian texts do we find a more precise vocabulary referring to spiritual gifts.

Paul speaks often of the Spirit's presence and empowerment within the Christian community. In Gal. 5:22 he lists the "fruits" of the Spirit as "love, joy, peace, patience, kindness, generosity, faithfulness, gentleness, and self-control." These fruits are common to all spiritual manifestation and are given equally to every person. In contrast to the spiritual fruits, Paul uses two different Greek terms to identify the gifts of the Spirit: *tá pneumatiká* ("spiritual gifts"; e.g., 1 Cor. 14:1) or simply *tá charísmata* ("gifts, charisms"; e.g., Rom. 12:6). Gk. *pneumatiká* stresses that these gifts derive solely from the Spirit *(pneúma); charísmata* highlights the fact that they are entirely gratuitous, the effect of God's grace *(cháris).* For Paul, there are two essential characteristics of these spiritual gifts. First, there is *one* Spirit who is the source of all gifts and empowerment (1 Cor. 12:4); therefore any manifestation of the Spirit ought to be a sign and source of unity. Second, the gifts of the Spirit differ and are bestowed on individuals in different forms but always for the common good (1 Cor. 12:7) and not for the individual's benefit alone. It was a fundamental misunderstanding of these principles at Corinth that caused Paul to clarify his position so vehemently in 1 Cor. 12–14.

Three times in 1 Cor. 12 Paul lists the gifts of the Spirit (vv. 8-10, 28, 29-30), and gives a fourth list again in Rom. 12:6-8. No two lists are exactly alike, and each mixes both technically "spiritual" gifts with ordinary gifts of practical ministry. The lists are meant to be representative and not exhaustive, and their variety attests to their ad hoc nature. The various gifts enumerated fall into three general categories. First, there are gifts of "utterance" like "utterance of wisdom, utterance of knowledge" (1 Cor. 12:8), prophecy (vv. 10, 28, 29; Rom. 12:6), discernment of spirits (1 Cor. 12:10), teaching (v. 28; Rom. 12:7; cf. 1 Cor. 14:6), speaking or interpreting tongues (1 Cor. 12:10, 28, 30; cf. 14:5, 13). Second, there are gifts of practical ministry like helping, administration (1 Cor. 12:28), serving, comforting, contributing, giving aid, and working acts of mercy (Rom. 12:7-8). Finally, there are gifts of wonder-working like healing, miracles, acts of powerful faith (1 Cor. 12:9-10, 28-30).

One list seems to designate a hierarchy of gifts by its ordinal counting of "first apostles, second prophets, third teachers" (1 Cor. 12:28), but the ordinal references do not continue in the list. Surely, for Paul, the gift of apostleship is prior to any other, and in a sense encompasses the rest. It is the primary category Paul uses in his letters to identify himself and the one gift he prizes most of all. Whatever the gift, however, its value is measured by the degree to which the gift builds up the one body of Christ.

Barbara E. Bowe

SPIT

In both the OT and NT spitting is regarded as a sign of contempt (Job 17:6; 30:10; Isa. 50:6; Mark 10:34; 14:65; 15:19). At Deut. 25:9 (and perhaps Num. 12:14) it is part of a legal ritual of humiliation. Ritual uncleanness was conveyed by spitting (Lev. 15:8). "Until I swallow my spittle" (Job 7:19) was an expression meaning "for just a brief moment." Saliva running down from a person's mouth was taken as a sign of insanity (1 Sam. 21:13[MT 14]). Jesus' use of his saliva in healings (Mark 7:33; 8:23; John 9:6) reflects the understanding of saliva as a curative substance.

SPRING, FOUNTAIN

In Israel where perennial rivers and streams are few and little if any rain falls for over half of the year, most settlements had to rely on springs or fountains (Heb. *'ayin,* "bubble up, flow") for their fresh water supply. The key consideration in establishing a settlement was a reliable and secure water supply. Absent a perennial river, towns would normally be built around a spring. During the Jewish Revolt of A.D. 70, one of the reasons the Jews at Masada were able to withstand the Roman legions for an extended period was because a spring was located with the fortress. Often town names indicate the presence of a spring: e.g., En-gedi (1 Sam. 24:1), En-rogel (1 Kgs. 1:9), and En-rimmon (Neh. 11:29).

Springs are formed when underground water runs along hard, impenetrable rock and then percolates to the surface where a rock outcropping appears. Springs and fountains occur with some frequency in Syro-Palestine, mostly in the valleys. Most of the region has substantial formations of karstic limestone below the surface which allows rain water to be absorbed until it reaches the underlying granite bedrock. The underground water then flows into the adjoining valleys, occasionally coming to the surface.

Not all springs produce potable water; mineral deposits, particularly lead, could contaminate water. The elders of Jericho told Elisha that the spring water was bad and the land unfruitful, both in terms of agriculture and miscarriages of both animals and human residents of the area; Elisha threw a handful of salt into the spring and God purified the spring (2 Kgs. 2:19-22).

Spring water was considered the "best" source of water, and springs were considered a sign of God's blessing (Ps. 104:10-13; Isa. 41:18; 58:11; Rev. 21:6). "Spring" is also used symbolically as the source of wisdom (Prov. 18:4) and of God as the source of salvation (Jer. 17:13-14).

Bibliography. R. Miller, "Water Use in Syria and Palestine from the Neolithic to Bronze Age," *World Archaeology* 11 (1980): 331-41; J. Wilkinson, "Ancient Jerusalem: Its Water Supply and Population," *PEQ* 106 (1974): 33-51. DENNIS M. SWANSON

SQUAD

A detachment of four soldiers (Gk. *tetrádion*). Probably because Peter had escaped from prison once before (Acts 5:19), Herod Agrippa I placed the apostle under a heavy guard consisting of four such contingents (12:4).

SQUARE

A broad open public place in towns or cities. The square (Heb. *rĕḥôḇ*) could be a place of public assembly (2 Chr. 29:4; 32:6; Ezra 10:9; Neh. 8:1) or a place where public displays or performances are held (Deut. 13:16[MT 17]; 2 Sam. 21:12; Esth. 6:9-11; Prov. 1:20; Isa. 15:3; Ezek. 16:24, 31). There the elders gather (Job 29:7), the children play (Zech. 8:4-5), and people exchange information (Esth. 4:6; cf. Jer. 5:1) or conduct business (Ps. 55:11[12]; cf. Isa. 59:14). Passersby without lodging might sleep at the square (Gen. 19:2; Judg. 19:15, 17, 20). In some occurrences, the term is specifically distinguished from "roofs" or "housetops," "streets," or "cities" (Neh. 8:16; Prov. 7:12; Cant. 3:2; Isa. 15:3; Jer. 48:38). HYUN CHUL PAUL KIM

STACHYS (Gk. *Stáchys*)

A Christian in Rome greeted by Paul as "my beloved" (Rom. 16:9).

STACTE

One of the "sweet spices" (Heb. *nāṭāp*) used in making the incense of the tabernacle (Exod. 30:34), probably a resin from the storax tree (*Styrax officinalis* L.).

STADION (Gk. *stádion*)

Unit of distance equivalent to 170-190 m. (189-215 yds.). The NRSV represents stadia by the equivalent in miles (Luke 24:13; John 6:19; 11:18; Rev. 14:20; 21:16).

STAFF

Any substantial stick used as a walking stick (Gen. 32:10[MT 11]; Matt. 10:10), by shepherds as a defense against predators (Zech. 11:7; cf. Ps. 23:4), as a ceremonial object like a scepter (Gen. 49:10; Isa. 14:5), for punishment (30:32), or as a goad (Num. 22:27), a divining stick (Hos. 4:12), or weapon of war (Isa. 10:24). The use of a staff to support the body is the basis for the expression "the staff of bread" for food sufficient to support a given society (Lev. 26:26; Ps. 105:16; Ezek. 4:16; 5:16; 14:13; cf. Isa. 3:1).

STAR

Though the ancient Hebrews believed that God made all the heavenly bodies, including the stars (Heb. *kôḵāḇ*; Gen. 1:16; Amos 5:8), it was widely believed by many ancient people that the stars were cosmic deities (Isa. 47:13). Belief in the animation of the stars was never a major tenet among the Hebrew people, though such beliefs were sometimes echoed in periods of monotheistic apostasy (Amos 5:26). The Torah prohibited the worship of the stars (Deut. 4:19; 17:2-5). Nevertheless, the people of Israel were familiar with astronomical observations and constellations (Job 38:31-32; Isa. 13:10; Amos 5:8).

Stars are sometimes used as symbols for angels. Job 38:7 alludes to the sons of God (angels) as morning stars. Similarly, in Rev. 1:20 the seven stars of the vision are identified as angels of the seven churches. This is probably also the sense of Dan. 8:10, where the little horn caused some of the "host of heaven" and the stars to fall to the earth (cf. Isa. 14:12-13; Rev. 12:4). Jude 13 calls certain apostates in the Church "wandering stars" (cf. the unfaithful angels in 1 Enoch).

The ancients frequently looked to the stars and celestial bodies for signs of the end (e.g., Luke 21:25; Mark 13:25 par.), as reflected in apocalyptic literature (Rev. 6:12-13; 8:10, 12; 12:1, 4). The belief that stars offered signs also brought the Magi from the east to witness the birth of Christ (Matt. 2:1-10). MARK R. FAIRCHILD

STATUE

An object preserved in the temple of Artemis in Ephesus (Acts 19:35). The "statue" (NRSV) or "sacred stone that fell from heaven" (RSV) are paraphrases for Gk. *diopetḗs,* which occurs only here in the NT. Most scholars interpret this as a meteorite phenomenon, considered supernatural by the ancients. Livy spoke of such a stone in the *Magna Mater* brought from Pessinus to Rome ca. 204 B.C.E. (*Urb. cond.* 29.11.7). Such rocks became sacred cult objects: the image of Tauric Artemis (Euripides *Iph. A.* 91, 1395); Ceres at Enna, Sicily (Cicero *Verr.*

2.7.72.187); El Gabal of Emesa (Herodotus *Hist.* 5.3, 5); Athene (Pausanias *Descr. Gr.* 1.8.4; 1.26.4).

GERALD L. STEVENS

STEPHANAS (Gk. *Stephanás*)
A prominent Corinthian Christian and Paul's first convert in Achaia (1 Cor. 16:15; cf. Acts 17:34), whom he personally baptized (1 Cor. 1:16). Along with Fortunatus and Achaicus (members of his household?), Stephanas visited Paul in Ephesus as he wrote 1 Corinthians. Perhaps they provided Paul with news of the Corinthian problems or brought him the church's letter, to which he responded (1 Cor. 7:1; cf. v. 25; 8:1; 12:1; 16:1). They may have brought all or some portion of 1 Corinthians back to that congregation. Their visit seems to have helped Paul at the outset of a difficult period with the Corinthian church (1 Cor. 16:17-18). Paul endorsed Stephanas' authority in the congregation, because he and his household "devoted themselves to the service of the saints" (1 Cor. 16:15-16). This service, though not a formalized function, may have included teaching, preaching, or some form of patronage for the church.

CHRISTOPHER SCOTT LANGTON

STEPHEN (Gk. *Stéphanos*)
A leader in the Jerusalem church and the first Christian martyr. He was one of seven men chosen and approved, by both the Twelve and the community, for the daily distribution of food.

The story of Stephen (Acts 6:1–8:2) relates to Jewish-Gentile conflicts in Jerusalem as well as to official Jewish opposition to the Christian mission within the city. Set in the context of a dispute between Christians who are Hebrew- (or Aramaic-) speaking and Greek-accultured Jews (Hebrews and Hellenists, respectively), the account has direct bearing, according to the author of Acts, on the spread of the Jesus movement beyond the Holy City into the Diaspora and the Greek world.

Stephen confronts and confounds the Diaspora Jews, who bring suborned charges before the Jewish council against him relating to the temple, the Law, and the customs of Moses (Acts 6:8-15). In a lengthy address before the Sanhedrin (Acts 7:1-53), Stephen speaks of Israel's relation to the God of Abraham, Isaac, and Jacob. After a caustic retelling of Jewish history, he concludes by accusing the listeners of being worthy descendants of rebellious ancestors. The reaction of the audience is predictable, especially in light of Stephen's statement that he sees the risen Jesus at God's right hand. Stephen is stoned (in the presence of the young persecutor Saul), the Christian community is scattered, and the body of the Christian preacher is buried (Acts 7:54–8:4).

The episode raises a host of historical and theological issues. The narrative introduction depicts an ecclesial problem which is resolved by the choice of seven men routinely assumed to be Hellenists. They are chosen to address the food distribution problem and thereby free the disciples for their ministry, but Stephen and Philip are later reported as fully engaged in preaching or missionary work rather than food distribution. Another issue is the relationship, culturally, of Stephen to the opponents he encounters (Acts 6:9): Is he a Greek-speaking Christian and thus the connecting link or impetus for the spread of the good news among the Greeks (Acts 11:19-20)? Further, the accusations brought against Stephen are clearly reminiscent of those brought against Jesus and Paul at their respective trials.

The speech itself is rarely seen as a response to the accusations noted earlier. Instead, scholars view it as the product of the author, who seemingly pays little attention to the accusations and considerably more to the history of Israel and its relation to its God. Despite some hesitation, scholars readily view the speech as a unified whole, addressing the new movement's turning away from Judaism and Jerusalem as it moves out into the Greek world (cf. Acts 1:8b).

The narrative conclusion presents other problems. Does the death scene presume a formal, legal trial or mob action that ends in a lynching? Why is there such a sharp change of tone at the end of the speech (Acts 7:51-52) and why the mixing of legal, mob, and visionary elements in the death scene? Which of these, as well as earlier elements of the narrative and speech, are historical? Which are the product of the author's activity?

Employing the early community's tradition and lore about the early days, Luke accepts the pivotal role of Stephen as first martyr (Acts 22:20) and impetus for the Christian mission out of Jerusalem into the Greek world. The Stephen episode and figure, drawn from tradition, become for Luke the means to review Jewish history (use of the LXX to formulate an appropriate speech) and to prepare for a wider expansion of the movement.

Within the book of Acts, this episode constitutes the last Jerusalem scene and provides the third climactic confrontation with the populace of the Holy City: warning, flogging, and death (Acts 2-7). Stephen's speech, like earlier discourses, is a response to an official question (cf. Acts 4:7-12; 5:27-32), and provides the episode its turning point for the movement's departure from Jerusalem into the Greek world. The references to Saul (Acts 7:58; 8:1) point to the work's principal character and activity.

The episode also pays particular attention to a series of accusations against the early community, namely, its blasphemous treatment of Moses and God and disregard of the Law and Mosaic customs. Principally, it offers a negative and positive treatment of Judaism, its history, and its relation to the Jesus movement. While the Jewish leaders are castigated (Acts 7:51-53), large numbers of priests are said to have joined the community (6:7). Rather than speak against Moses (as accused), Stephen underscores his important role in God's dealings with Israel. There is, however, a movement away from "this place" or temple to a more universal view of God's dwelling (Acts 6:13-14; 7:49-50). The Jesus movement spreads from Jerusalem and cannot be limited to that place; at the same time, it takes its origin and finds its roots in this Jewish center and milieu.

From the outset Stephen, along with others in Acts (e.g., Cornelius, Timothy), is identified as a distinguished or reputable member of the community; he is also full of the Spirit, faith, grace, and power (Acts 6:3, 8). He is an orthodox member of the community who speaks in its name. He is an OT-like figure who performs signs and wonders, and he is a man of wisdom, like Joseph and Moses (Acts 7:10, 22), who understands God's purpose (6:3, 10), seeks to clarify God's plan for the audience, and dies a Christlike death as the community is scattered beyond Jerusalem.

Bibliography. C. K. Barrett, *The Acts of the Apostles,* 1. ICC (Edinburgh, 1994); E. Haenchen, *The Acts of the Apostles* (Philadelphia, 1971); L. T. Johnson, *The Acts of the Apostles.* Sacra Pagina 5 (Collegeville, 1992); J. J. Kilgallen, "The Function of Stephen's Speech (Acts 7, 2-53)," *Bibl* 70 (1989): 173-93; E. J. Richard, *Acts 6:1–8:4: The Author's Method of Composition.* SBLDS 41 (Missoula, 1978).

EARL J. RICHARD

STEPHEN, APOCALYPSE OF

An apocryphal book, no longer extant, listed by the 6th-century Decretum Gelasianum among works to be rejected by the Church. Some scholars contend that this is a mistaken reference to a document composed in 415 C.E. which tells of Lucian's discovery of the relics of Stephen. While the title *Revelatio Sancti Stephani* could be taken to be an apocalypse, it is still possible, given the experience of Stephen recorded in Acts 7:55-56, that this is a pseudepigraphical apocalypse written in the name of Stephen.

TIMOTHY W. SEID

STEWARD

One designated by a master to oversee family, household, or state matters. Responsibilities might include the palace (1 Kgs. 16:9; 2 Kgs. 10:5), business affairs (Matt. 20:8), or the city treasury (Rom. 16:23). The steward might also be responsible for the entire household, as with Joseph's steward. It is with the steward that Joseph's brothers cast their fears and in turn receive assurance (Gen. 43:19-25; cf. 44:1; Isa. 22:15). At the wedding feast at Cana, it is the steward who tastes the water turned into wine by Jesus (John 2:8-9).

The Apostle Paul refer to bishops and elders as stewards of God. They are responsible to live lives that reflect this relationship with God. An elder or bishop is not to be arrogant, quick-tempered, violent, greedy, or an alcoholic, but rather must be hospitable, a lover of goodness, be prudent, upright, have self-control, and be devout (Titus 1:5-9). In general, every Christian is a steward, entrusted with gifts from God (1 Pet. 4:10). The parable of the talents spells out in detail the importance of investing well the gifts received from God; those who do not invest their gifts well, will lose them (Matt. 25:14-30).

Metaphorically, the steward is responsible for the mysteries of God (1 Cor. 4:1). It is expected that every steward will be trustworthy (1 Cor. 4:2). One is blessed for being a faithful steward, while unfaithfulness results in judgment (Luke 12:42-44).

HEMCHAND GOSSAI

STOCKS

Instruments for confining and restraining prisoners. Stocks were probably made of wood and were bulky enough to be a real impediment and discomfort to those held in them. Stocks included burdensome neck collars (Jer. 29:36) or blocks into which the feet were inserted to prevent movement (Job 13:27; 33:11), such as those into which Passhur put Jeremiah when he became angered over the prophet's temple sermon (Jer. 20:2-3; cf. 29:26). A variation of stocks was a kind of tinkling ornament placed on fools to correct them (Prov. 7:22; cf. KJV). The purpose of the device was to give discomfort to the victim by distorting or twisting the body unnaturally. Some English Bibles translate Heb. *ʿēṣ* ("wood") as "stocks," when it really is part of a technical phrase, "stones and trees," connected with fertility cults (e.g., Jer. 2:27; 3:9; Hab. 2:19). In Philippi, Paul and Silas were put into stocks (Acts 16:24), which may have been made of a wooden beam with five sets of holes for spreading the legs and causing variable degrees of pain.

RICHARD A. SPENCER

STOICS (Gk. *Stōikoi*)

Stoicism, a philosophical school founded at Athens by Zeno (ca. 336-263 B.C.E.). Zeno was greatly influenced by Socrates. His teaching was a reaction against Epicurus, who taught that everything that exists is the result of the random or accidental collision of atoms. Zeno, quite the contrary, saw all the universe as governed by Reason and the purpose of life as more social, religious, and moral. The name of the school of thought comes from Gk. *Stoa Poikilē,* the "painted porch" or colonnaded structure in Athens where Zeno taught. Followers of this school, which appealed most to an intellectual elite, include Cicero, Epictetus, Seneca, and Marcus Aurelius, though the teaching of Zeno was for women and men alike. Stoicism offered to its followers a community of intellectualism, freedom from the fear of death, a philosophical outlook that involved more than personal salvation, a world in which the material order was permeated with God, a consistent and respectable ethical platform, and a philosophy with a lively mix of religion and morality.

Stoics sought happiness through wisdom and the recognition of Reason behind the universe, which supplied life with moral purpose and made the world understandable. They held that the entire material world is permeated with God, with Reason. This means that throughout all the universe is a divine and rational harmony. The Stoics called this cosmic reason Logos and saw the human soul as a spark of the universal mind. Though Logos gave order to the universe, it was subordinate to Fate. Their belief that Logos was subordinate to Fate created a tension in the Stoics' philosophical system, for if Reason were a binding and universal Law and Fate were unalterable, how could humans have any real freedom and why should one bother to try to bring about change for good in the world? They answered that it was not the results of one's acts and behavior but the attempt itself to live a good life and to achieve virtue that mattered finally. They saw that even if one could not choose for life to bring different circumstances to them, at least they could choose the attitudes with which they would accept the inevitable circumstances. Consequently, they sought to control what was within their power and to accept with dignity what life brought to them. They held that it is the task of humans to perceive and fit in with the universal order, to play one's part in the human experience, and to choose how one handles events in life. The happy person, they taught, does not fight against life but accepts it with tranquility and dignity, and endures both favorable and tragic experiences with unperturbed equanimity. By self-control and stability, one attains happiness. Stoics believed that one should not fear death because the immortal soul, a part of the fiery universal principle, will live again many times. If people cannot escape death, at least they can escape the fear of death.

Stoics were in Paul's audience when he spoke in Athens (Acts 17:18).

Bibliography. F. H. Sandbach, *The Stoics* (New York, 1971). RICHARD A. SPENCER

STOMACH

Various Hebrew words refer in a general way to the human abdomen. Heb. *beṭen* is used most often for the womb (Gen. 25:23; Ps. 139:13), but can indicate the abdomen in general (Judg. 3:21-22) and the actual stomach (Job 20:15; Ezek. 3:3). Heb. *mēʿîm* is used generally for "internal organs, inward parts" (e.g., "bowels"; Num. 5:22; 2 Chr. 21:15, 18-19), but can also mean the stomach specifically (Job 20:14; Ezek. 3:3). Gk. *koilía* most frequently refers to the womb, but can also be translated "stomach" (Matt. 15:17; 1 Cor. 6:13); the usage is primarily figurative. Gk. *stómachos* is found only in 1 Tim. 5:23, where Paul advises Timothy to "use a little wine for the sake of your stomach."

The Hebrews viewed the intestines as the seat of deep emotions, and thus *beṭen* and *mēʿîm* are occasionally translated "heart" (Job 15:35; Isa. 63:15; Jer. 4:19). Similarly, while Gk. *splánchna* originally meant "bowels" or "intestines" (cf. Acts 1:18), by NT times it came to designate the seat of love or mercy (Col. 3:12; 1 John 3:17). The verbal form was used often to describe the compassion of Christ (Matt. 9:36; 14:14; 15:32 par.; Mark 1:41; Luke 7:13).

Of course, the bowels can also be the seat of negative emotions (avarice, Job 20:20; distress, 30:27; Lam. 1:20; greed or desire, Rom. 16:18; Phil. 3:19).

Bibliography. H. W. Wolff, *Anthropology of the Old Testament* (Philadelphia, 1974).

JOHN S. HAMMETT

STONING

Execution by stoning in the OT (Heb. *sāqal* or *rāgam*) often meant pelting the criminal to death with stones (1 Sam. 30:6; 1 Kgs. 12:18), an action conveying a corporate obligation for removing sin from the community. The location of the stoning was outside the camp or city (Lev. 24:14; Num. 15:35; Deut. 17:5; 22:24; 1 Kgs. 21:13). The victim was stripped and then struck with stones (Ezek. 16:39-40), first by the witnesses and then by all the people (Deut. 17:7). NT examples of this form of stoning *(litházō* or *lithoboléō)* included the punishment for the woman caught in adultery (John 8:7) and the reaction to Jesus' and the apostles' controversial claims (John 10:31; Acts 14:5). The mob threw stones at Stephen until he died (Acts 7:58).

Later Jewish literature (*m. Sanh.* 6:1-4) describes a very deliberate process for stoning criminals, which allowed for last-minute testimony that might interrupt the execution. The victim was pushed from a 3 m. (10 ft.) height by a witness, sometimes causing death. If not, a large stone was rolled over the edge and onto his chest. If this still did not cause death, participants threw stones until he died.

Offenses punishable by stoning included idolatry (Deut. 17:2-7; 13:6-10[MT 7-11]), sacrificing children to Molech (Lev. 20:2-5), prophesying in the name of a foreign god (Deut. 13:1-5[2-6]), divination (Lev. 20:27), blasphemy (24:15-16), sabbathbreaking (Num. 15:32-36), death caused by an ox (Exod. 21:28-32), adultery (Deut. 22:22-24), and rebellion by children (21:18-21).

DENNIS GAERTNER

STRAIGHT, STREET CALLED

A street in Damascus which Saul of Tarsus (Paul) was instructed to enter after his encounter with the resurrected Jesus, the home of one Judas (Acts 9:11). Like many cities of the classical period (e.g., Caesarea, Gerasa), Damascus was bisected by a long, broad colonnaded street *(cardo maximus)* that ran westward from the East Gate of the city. In Paul's day the street was lined with shops and monumental architecture including a Roman arch, theater, and perhaps a palace. The remains of this street (Arab. Darb al-Mustaqim) can still be seen in column fragments and bases. D. LARRY GREGG

STRANGER

See SOJOURNER.

STRANGLING

Job mentions strangling in connection with Ahithophel's suicide (2 Sam. 17:23; Heb. *ḥānaq*, generally translated "hanged"), remarking that he himself would prefer death by strangling than continuation of his suffering (Job 7:15). Nahum speaks of strangling as a lion's method of killing prey (Nah. 2:12[MT 13]). The Mosaic prohibition of eating blood (Gen. 9:4; Lev. 3:17; Deut. 12:23-25) led to specific methods of slaughtering in such a way that blood was drained off. Thus strangling was excluded, and what was not slaughtered in the prescribed swift fashion was considered "strangled" (*m. Ḥul.* 1:2). The prohibition of "blood" and "what is strangled" was passed on to the Gentile Christians of Syria and Asia Minor as an accommodation to the scruples of Jews (Gk. *pniktós;* Acts 15:20, 29; 21:25).

STREET
Generally an urban road, usually of dirt, but the Greek and Hebrew words normally translated as "street" can also mean "market" or "bazaar." The OT era saw the emergence of streets as we know them. Prior to that time, ancient Near Eastern cities simply had open spaces between buildings. In NT times newer cities were planned and had a fairly organized system of streets. Old established cities, however, had an unplanned collection of streets that emerged according to traffic patterns.

Used metaphorically, "street" often connotes a filthy or disgraceful place (Mic. 7:10; Zech. 10:5). Since streets were not paved and sewer systems were primitive (at least in the OT period), it is easy to see how these connotations came to exist. Phrases such as "in the streets" are common biblical ways of describing the arena where a message is proclaimed to the public (e.g., Amos 5:16). Jesus decries hypocrites who make a public display of their almsgiving "in the streets" (Matt. 6:2).

CHRIS CALDWELL

SUAH (Heb. *sûaḥ*)
An Asherite, the firstborn son of Zophah (1 Chr. 7:36).

SUCATHITES (Heb. *śûḵāṯîm*)
One of the families of "the scribes that lived at Jabez," listed among the descendants of Caleb and perhaps a Kenite or Rechabite group (1 Chr. 2:55).

SUCCOTH (Heb. *sukkôṯ*)

1. The first encampment of the Israelites during the exodus from Egypt, after leaving Rameses (Exod. 12:37; Num. 33:5-6). Many scholars have suggested that Succoth is an adaption of Egyptian Tjeku (Egyp. *tkw*), located near Egypt's western border, although there is some debate about whether Tjeku referred to a border town, an administrative district, or both. Those who believe Tjeku was a town have proposed Tell el-Maskhûṭa in the Wadi Ṭumilat as the most likely candidate. Excavations at Tell el-Maskhûṭa have revealed structures from the Roman period and earlier building foundations that appear to be part of a typical Egyptian frontier fortress from the time of Pharaoh Neco II. However, excavations reveal an occupational gap at the site between ca. 1650 and 610 B.C.E.

2. A place on the east side of the Jordan Valley near the confluence of the Jabbok and Jordan rivers where, according to Gen. 33:17, Jacob built booths (Heb. *sukkôṯ*) for his cattle upon his return from Paddan-aram to Canaan. By the time of the Conquest, Succoth had become a Canaanite city within the territory of Sihon of Heshbon. Subsequently it was allotted to the tribe of Gad (Josh. 13:27). Gideon asked the people of Succoth (and Penuel) to provide food for his army while he was pursuing the Midianites. Gideon later punished them for their refusal to grant this request (Judg. 8:5-17). During the time of Solomon, foundries were established near Succoth to cast various bronze implements for the temple (1 Kgs. 7:45-46 = 2 Chr. 4:16-17). Succoth is one of six sites in the valley of Succoth mentioned by Shishak (cf. Ps. 60:6[MT 8]).

At least two candidates have been proposed for Succoth. One is Tell el-Ekjsas (Arab. "booths"), ca. 2.5 km. (1.5 mi.) W of Deir ʿAllā. The second is Deir ʿAllā (208178) itself, where excavation has revealed occupation and/or activity during early biblical periods. The Late Bronze Age settlement appears to have been destroyed early in the 12th century B.C.E., possibly by conflagration. Yohanan Aharoni has suggested that this might reflect Gideon's vengeance, although such a claim must remain purely speculative. Also of interest are the subsequent Iron I remains, including remnants of furnaces for smelting bronze and post-holes for tents (of metalworkers?), perhaps anticipating the activity of Solomon's workers in the same area at a slightly later time. The material culture of Deir ʿAllā is as eclectic in nature as might be expected for a border site.

RANDALL W. YOUNKER

SUCCOTH-BENOTH (Heb. *sukkôṯ bĕnôṯ*)
A Babylonian deity mentioned only once in the Bible (2 Kgs. 17:30) and never in cuneiform sources. Following the Assyrian king Shalmaneser V's destruction of the northern kingdom of Israel in 722 B.C.E. and subsequent deportation of its inhabitants (2 Kgs. 17:1-6; 18:9-12), he and his successor Sargon II resettled in their place conquered peoples from other regions (17:24). Remaining Israelites attempted to teach the new inhabitants about Yahwism (2 Kgs. 17:27, 28), but "every nation still made gods of its own" (v. 29), with the Babylonians worshipping Succoth-benoth. The precise meaning of the name is uncertain (cf. Heb. "booths of/for girls"); "The Image of the Creatress (Banitu)" has been suggested.

Bibliography. M. Cogan, "Sukkoth-Benoth," *DDD*, 821-22. CHRIS A. ROLLSTON

SUKKIIM (Heb. *sukkîîm*)
One of the groups of mercenaries that fought against Judah for Pharaoh Shishak of Egypt (2 Chr. 12:3). The name is probably the equivalent of Egyp. *ṯktn*, a technical term for a class of soldiers from the Libyan oases.

SUKKOTH (Heb. *sukkôṯ*)
The Feast of Booths (also called Tabernacles and Ingathering), one of the three great pilgrimage feasts.

See TABERNACLES, FEAST OF.

SUMERIAN
Language spoken by the inhabitants of southern Mesopotamia until sometime in the late 3rd or

early 2nd millennium B.C.E., when it gave way to the Semitic Akkadian. Thereafter, scribes continued to employ Sumerian as a religious, learned language until the beginning of the present era. The world's oldest written documents known thus far date from ca. 3100 and were found at ancient Uruk in southern Mesopotamia; although for the most part undeciphered, indications are that their language was Sumerian.

Progress in the analysis of the Sumerian language has been slow due to several factors. It is linguistically unrelated to any other known language, so comparative data are nonexistent. Early texts were extremely selective in their representation of the morphemes of the spoken language, being apparently composed primarily as aids to memory. Later texts, while more explicitly written, were produced by Akkadian-speaking scribes who had learned Sumerian in the schools and whose usage is, consequently, less trustworthy. Nevertheless, monolingual Sumerian texts can now be read with considerable understanding; and reliable editions of literary texts are being produced.

Linguistic investigation has been facilitated by several kinds of texts. Lexicography has benefited from lexical lists which provide Akkadian translations of many Sumerian words, and pronunciations are sometimes included, to the aid of phonology. Phonology has also profited, as well as morphology, from Sumerian texts written wholly in syllabic script (in contrast to the customary continuation of syllabic and logographic signs), although these texts are limited in number, relatively late, or not from Sumer proper. Initial decipherment of the language and subsequent study of syntax have been aided by bilinguals that contain Akkadian translations of connected Sumerian compositions. Both morphology and syntax have been assisted by grammatical texts with their elaborate principles of organization.

Nominal and verbal chains were formed in Sumerian by placing morphemes and words in a determined sequential order with limited internal modification. The main verbal chain occupied the final position in a clause. Some access to the ways in which Akkadian scribes understood and translated Sumerian verbal forms comes from two Akkadian terms employed in the Sumerian grammatical texts they produced, although these texts derive from the later Neo-Babylonian period. Sum. *ḫamṭu* (or *ḫanṭu*) means "quick" and indicates something like punctual *Aktionsart; marû* means "fat" or, by derivation, "slow" and indicates something like durative *Aktionsart*. Subjects of some *ḫamṭu* verbs were marked, whereas others and all subjects of *marû* verbs were not. There were likely dialectal differences in southern Mesopotamia during the period while Sumerian was in living use, but only two can thus far be certainly identified, a main dialect *(eme-gir$_{15}$)* and a specialized dialect used in literary texts by women and lamentation priests, and possibly in other contexts *(eme-sal)*. WALTER R. BODINE

SUMERIANS

The first major civilization in Mesopotamia. The Sumerians first emerge into history in southern Mesopotamia ca. 3100 The first explicit evidence of their presence appears in texts found at the site of Uruk and composed in what can arguably be identified as the Sumerian language. They were settled in the lower part of the alluvial plain extending northward from the Arabo/Persian Gulf at least as far as ancient Shuruppak, and at an early date their settlement extended further north to somewhere above Nippur, which became their religious capital. This plain was to be their homeland, known to them as Kiengi and to the Semitic Akkadians as Shumeru (from which comes Eng. Sumer). It is the general area identified as the setting of the Garden of Eden in Gen. 2–3. The Sumerians remembered their first city to have been just above what was then the head of the gulf, at Eridu, ever thereafter regarded as sacred to Enki, the god of wisdom and the watery deep (the Apsu).

Sumerian civilization developed its characteristic features between ca. 3400-2900. Writing emerged first in brief administrative documents and can only in the following period be employed for historical reconstruction. Nevertheless, this was likely already the creative period of Sumerian mythology, and a rich literature was to follow. Cities also emerged, as well as the accumulation of capital and a primitive form of democracy, later to give way to monarchy. The story of Ziusudra surviving a divinely ordained, catastrophic flood in a boat, located in Sumerian tradition at the end of this period, has clear connections with Gen. 6–9.

In the following period (Early Dynastic, ca. 2900-2334) city walls appeared, and the political leadership that had earlier been temporary became institutionalized in the office of the king, indicating increased warfare. The first seat of kingship following the flood was at Kish according to the Sumerian King List, reflected in the later usage of the title "King of Kish" by Mesopotamian monarchs as a claim to universal dominion. Heroic tales of legendary kings such as Etana, Enmerkar, Lugalbanda, Dumuzi (Babylonian Tammuz; Ezek. 8:14), and Gilgamesh, all but the first ruling at Uruk, have their setting in this time. Sumerian culture was disseminated across the Near East, as witnessed by the extensive use of the Sumerian language and cuneiform script at the North Syrian site of Ebla in the mid-3rd millennium.

The royal tombs excavated at Ur, deriving from the latter part of the Early Dynastic period, have yielded important examples of art and craftsmanship as well as evidence of the mass burial of an entire court with the deceased king, a practice that cannot otherwise be traced thus far. Urukagina/Uruinimgina of Lagash promulgated a reform limiting royal prerogatives and righting social grievances. Lugalzagesi of Umma conquered Lagash, Uruk, and the rest of Sumer according to his claims; but such imperial aspirations can assuredly be recognized as reality only in the following period of Semitic dominance.

Statue of a male figure, possibly a priest, from the Early Dynastic II (early 3rd millennium B.C.E.) Square Temple of Abu, Tell Asmar (Courtesy of the Oriental Institute of the University of Chicago)

A Semitic presence in Mesopotamia can be documented by the middle of the Early Dynastic period, and the symbiosis between their culture and that of the Sumerians progressed until the latter were absorbed by the early 2nd millennium, but not without leaving their pervasive and lasting imprint. From ca. 2334-2154 the Akkadians ruled from Akkad, the new capital established by the founder of the dynasty, Sargon. Akkadians were appointed to administrative posts; the Akkadian language was employed in official documents alongside Sumerian; and Sargon gained supremacy over all of lower and middle Mesopotamia. At the same time, Sargon honored his Sumerian subjects by installing his own daughter Enheduanna as high priestess of the moon-god Nanna of Ur. This gifted woman, the first identifiable author in world literature, composed Sumerian hymns honoring the goddess Inanna and the temples of Sumer and Akkad. Palace revolts recurred throughout the dynasty, and it finally collapsed under pressure from several outside peoples, conventionally understood as including, in particular, the Gutians.

During the following brief period the foreign Gutians exercised power primarily in the Diyala region, while a Sumerian dynasty at Lagash maintained considerable influence in the south. Gudea, the best known of its rulers, rebuilt the Eninnu temple of Ningirsu at Girsu. The two cylinders recounting this project preserve the most extensive Sumerian literary composition recovered to date.

Centralized Sumerian rule over southern and central Mesopotamia and beyond was restored by the 3rd dynasty of Ur (Ur III; ca. 2112-2004). The first known collection of precedent law is credited to the founder of the dynasty, Ur-nammu, or to his son, Šulgi. By the reign of Ur-nammu, if not earlier, the ziggurat, a layered tower with a shrine at its top, appeared, likely the sort of structure pictured in Gen. 11:1-9. Following Ur-nammu, Šulgi ruled over a thriving kingdom whose military operations were largely successful and whose trade was extensive. It was a period in which scribal education and Sumerian literature flourished, though our copies of Sumerian literary texts come largely from the later Old Babylonian period. More royal hymns written in Šulgi's honor are known than for any other Mesopotamian monarch, and he claimed divinity, as had the Akkadian rulers Naram-sin and Shar-kali-šarri before him. Šulgi's three successors unsuccessfully attempted to hold at bay the incoming Amorites from the northwest, who finally, along with forces from the east, overran the empire.

A period of shifting power ensued in which the city-states of Isin and Larsa played dominant roles in keeping Sumerian culture alive in the south. Their culture, however, with the subjugation of southern and central Mesopotamia to the Old Babylonian king Hammurabi, was finally absorbed into that of the Semites. Yet the Sumerian way of life was revered by the Babylonians and lived on in the amalgam that resulted. Enlil, the active head of the Sumerian pantheon, gave place to the gods Marduk of Babylon and, at a later time, to Assur of Assyria.

Main stairway of the ziggurat at Ur (Jack Finegan)

Other Sumerian gods continued to be worshipped in their Semitic counterparts, e.g., Inanna in Ishtar, Enki in Ea, Utu in Šamaš, and Nanna in Sin. Scribal schools preserved the Sumerian language in written form after it disappeared from living usage and transmitted Sumerian literature until their demise following the Old Babylonian period, after which the tradition was kept alive by scribal guilds and families.

Many fundamental elements of modern civilizations appeared first among the Sumerians. Their attainments and outlook deeply influenced the entire ancient Near East in their time, in particular the Babylonians who followed them in southern Mesopotamia. Especially through the Babylonians, that influence extended to ancient Israel and the Hebrew Bible. Through the latter medium, as well as through the underlying ancient Near Eastern impact on Greek civilization, their legacy reached the Western world. An informed approach to the history of Western civilization, as well as that of the Bible, must not stop short of the search for the ancient Sumerians. WALTER R. BODINE

SUN

The physical reality of the sun was a constant presence for those in Palestine. It could be oppressively hot (1 Sam. 11:9; Neh. 7:3) and could tan the skin (Cant. 1:6) or burn crops (Matt. 13:6). The darkening of the sun was viewed as a sign of judgment (Ezek. 32:7; Isa. 13:10; Matt. 24:29) and its radiance a symbol of inspiration and divine favor (Exod. 34:29; Matt. 17:2; Acts 26:13).

Within the ancient Mediterranean world the sun was regularly embued with divine powers. In Egypt the sun, under a variety of names, was the chief god and the creator. Mesopotamians also worshipped the sun (Šamaš) and, like Egyptians, regarded him as the omniscient protector of justice. In such a context it is perhaps surprising that the Bible only speaks of worshipping the sun in terms of prohibition. This is explicit in Deut. 4:19 and implicit in Gen. 1:14-19, where Heb. *šemeš* does not even occur in the account of the creation of the sun. This did not, however, mean that there were none who worshipped the sun within Israel. Quite the opposite was the case, as evidenced by Josiah's removing the horses and chariots dedicated to the sun (2 Kgs. 23:11), and Ezekiel's vision of 25 men worshipping the sun within the temple court (Ezek. 8:16).

The Lord is frequently described in terms related to the sun (e.g., Deut. 33:2: "shining forth"; Ps. 19:8[MT 9]: his commandments "enlighten the eyes"; Rev. 1:16: face "like the sun"). God is also empowered with roles usually assigned to the sun-god, such as judge and creator, and the Jerusalem temple was built along an east-west axis. But in spite of these similarities the Bible conveys a consistent picture of the Lord as the creator of the sun (Deut. 4:19) and its master (Matt. 5:45).

Bibliography. H. G. May, "Some Aspects of Solar Worship in Jerusalem," *ZAW* 55 (1937): 269-81; J. Morgenstern, "The Gates of Righteousness," *HUCA* 6 (1929): 1-37; M. S. Smith, "The Near Eastern Background of Solar Language of Yahweh," *JBL* 109 (1990): 29-39. CHRISTIAN M. M. BRADY

SUPERSCRIPTION

In the MT Psalter, 117 of the 150 psalms are preceded by a superscription or heading. These contain four possible types of information: (1) Personal names (with the prep. *lĕ*). Seventy-three psalms mention David; other have Asaph (Pss. 50,

73–83), the sons of Korah (42, 44–49, 84–85, 87–88), Solomon (72, 127), Ethan (89), Heman (88), Moses (90), and possibly Jeduthun (39, 62, 77). (2) "Genre" classifications (not form-critical genres), including nontechnical (e.g., Heb. *mizmôr,* "psalm"; *šîr,* "song") and technical terms (e.g., *miktām, maśkîl*). (3) Liturgical directions, including the phrase *lamnaṣṣēaḥ,* "to the leader"; and other obscure terms denoting melodies, musical instruments, and/or cultic procedures. (4) Situational ascriptions relating individual psalms to David's life (Pss. 3, 7, 18, 34, 51–52, 54, 56–57, 59–60, 63, 142).

The superscriptions are most likely not original to the psalms, but were added piecemeal before the compilation of the book. The liturgical instructions may also have been originally subscripts (cf. Hab. 3:1, 19). The personal names in the superscripts reflect an ancient tradition, though some may denote authorship (or patronage). For example, David's association with the origin of psalmody in Israel is clearly ancient (2 Sam. 22:1-51; 1 Chr. 16:7-36), though it also grew with time (the cross-references to David's life in some superscripts are likely midrashic comments based upon this growing tradition). The primary significance of the superscriptions is the light they shed on the composition and use of the book of Psalms in ancient Israel.

Bibliography. B. Bayer, "The Titles of the Psalms: A Renewed Investigation of an Old Problem," *Yuval* 4 (1982): 29-123; J. F. A. Sawyer, "An Analysis of the Context and Meaning of the Psalm Headings," *TGUOS* 22 (1970): 26-38; B. K. Waltke, "Superscripts, Postscripts, or Both," *JBL* 110 (1991): 583-96. TYLER F. WILLIAMS

SUPH (Heb. *sûp̱*)
The place from which Moses gave his final addresses, in the land of Moab E of the Jordan River (Deut. 1:5), where Israel was still "in the wilderness" (v. 1) and soon to enter the Promised Land. The geographical data given here is difficult. Suph (Heb. "sea weed") has been identified with Khirbet Sufah, 7 km. (4.3 mi.) SE of Madeba, or with a Greek town called Papyron, mentioned by Josephus (*Ant.* 14.33). Some scholars emend the phrase "opposite Suph" to "from the Re(e)d Sea," a reading supported by LXX and Vulg.

Bibliography. E. G. Kraeling, "Two Place Names of Hellenistic Palestine," *JNES* 7 (1948): 199-201. ROBERT DELSNYDER

SUPHAH (Heb. *sûp̱â*)
A region in Moab, probably near the valley of the Arnon River (Num. 21:14; cf. Samaritan Pentateuch and Vulg. "Red Sea," from Heb. *[yam]-sûp̱*). Suphah may bear some relation to Khirbet Sufah, ca. 6 km. (15 mi.) N of the Arnon, and to Suph (Deut. 1:1), but this is not certain.

SUR (Heb. *sûr;* Gk. *Soúr*)
1. An inner gate at the northwestern enclosure of Solomon's temple which led from the royal quarters to the temple area (2 Kgs. 11:6). Called the Sur Gate or the Foundation Gate (2 Chr. 23:5; Heb. *yĕsôḏ*), this was where Jehoiada the priest posted a guard to protect the coronation of Josiah from Athaliah the wicked queen.

2. A town on the Mediterranean coast, otherwise unattested, which sent envoys to seek peace with Holofernes (Jdt. 2:28). Sur may be a corruption of the name Dor (a seacoast town 24 km. [15 mi.] S of Mt. Carmel), but this would not coincide with the order of the towns as listed in Judith. The reference may be fictitious or simply incorrect.

Bibliography. N. Avigad, *Discovering Jerusalem* (Nashville, 1980); J. J. Simon, *Jerusalem in the Old Testament* (Leiden, 1952). DENNIS M. SWANSON

SUSA (Heb. *šûšan;* Akk. *šušān*)
Ancient Elamite Šušun (modern Shūsh), located in the Susiana Plain in southwestern Iran. The site, comprising five mounds scattered over 250 ha. (615 a.), was noted by many early travelers and excavated by William K. Loftus in 1851-52 and Marcel and Jane Dieulafoy in 1884-86. French excavations worked each year at the site from 1897-1979, except during the wars.

The site was founded in the early 5th millennium as one of the dominant sites in Susiana. The settlement of this period was dominated by a large platform, upon which stood a temple or elite residence. A cemetery containing more than 1000 burials, possibly the result of some catastrophe, dates to this period.

Little architecture from the periods between the 5th and 1st millennium has been successfully excavated at Susa, although its historical role is better known. Beginning in the 3rd millennium Susa, along with Anshan, was a capital of Elam. Susa was in constant conflict with states in Sumer and Akkad, ultimately being incorporated into the Akkadian and Ur III empires. During the early 2nd millennium Susa and Anshan again ruled Elam (one of the major powers in the Near East at that time), negotiating alliances with Šamši-adad of Assur, Hammurabi of Babylon, and Zimri-lim of Mari. In the late 2nd millennium, the Elamite ruler Šutruk-nahhunte briefly conquered Babylonia and brought back as spoils of war such relics as the stela of Hammurabi. After a period of collapse, Susa became a capital in a Neo-Elamite state, which was to be conquered by Assurbanipal in 646.

Susa was next conquered by Cyrus II in 539 and used as a capital the Achaemenid Empire. Darius I (521-486) rebuilt the city, constructing a palace and audience hall *(apadana)* as well as a city wall. His successor Artaxerxes II (404-359) built a palace to the west of the mounds. These Achaemenid palaces are notable for their friezes of glazed bricks depicting archers.

Susa was conquered again in 331 by Alexander the Great, who used the city as the site of a mass marriage between Macedonian soldiers and Persian women. The city never again functioned as a capital, but continued to be occupied under Seleucid, Parthian, Sassanian, and Islamic rule. A medieval tomb on the top of the site — apocryphally the tomb of Daniel — remains a modern pilgrimage center.

Biblical references to Susa (Neh. 1:1; Esther; Dan. 8:2) concern the Jewish community living in the city during the Achaemenid period.

Bibliography. P. O. Harper, J. Aruz, and F. Tallon, ed., *The Royal City of Susa* (New York, 1992).

GEOFF EMBERLING

SUSANNA (Gk. *Sousanna*)

1. The major figure of the apocryphal work bearing her name.

See DANIEL, ADDITIONS TO.

2. One of the women who provided financial and other support for Jesus and his disciples (Luke 8:3).

SUSANNA, BOOK OF

See DANIEL, ADDITIONS TO.

SUSI (Heb. *sûsî*)

The father of Gaddi of the tribe of Manasseh, one of the 12 Israelite spies sent into Canaan (Num. 13:11).

SWADDLING CLOTHS

Bands of cloth used to wrap an infant (Ezek. 16:4; Wis. 7:4; cf. Job 38:9) or to set a broken limb (Ezek. 30:21). After a cloth was folded around the infant, strips of cloth were wound around the child from the navel to the feet. The custom assumed that the restricted movement of the child's legs would strengthen them. In Luke 2:7, 12 Mary's swaddling of the infant Jesus is part of the sign that the angels provide the shepherds to identify Jesus as the Messiah. The cloths also signify that Jesus had received proper parental care (cf. Wis. 7:4). EMILY CHENEY

SWALLOW

Any number of small birds of the family Hirundinidae, with long, pointed wings, a round head, and small legs and feet. They are noted for their graceful flight. Although it is uncertain what species is designated by Heb. *dĕrôr,* the swallow seems likely. The bird's nesting instinct is used to depict the worshipper's desire to rest in God's temple and presence (Ps. 84:3[MT 4]), and its ceaseless flitting from place to place illustrates an undeserved curse (Prov. 26:2; LXX "sparrow"). The evidence remains inconclusive as to what bird is meant by Heb. *sîs* in Isa. 38:14 (LXX "swallow"); Jer. 8:7.

T. J. JENNEY

SWEET CANE

A variety of aromatic cane or grass (Heb. *qāneh,* "reed, branch, stick"; Ezek. 27:19). At Cant. 4:14 the term is rendered "calamus." Among the plants thus referred to might be sweet flag (*Acorus calamus,* also called calamus), Indian lemon-grass *(Andropogon citratus),* and other grasses and reeds. These plants were used in perfumes (Cant. 4:14) and in the incense made for the tabernacle and temple worship (Exod. 30:23; Isa. 43:24; Jer. 6:20; cf. Exod. 30:23, "aromatic cane").

SWINE

Even though the pig is the best known of the biblically "unclean" animals, it is comparatively uncommon in the Bible (in the NT 8 of the 12 references occur in the Gadarene demoniac story). It is specifically forbidden as food in Lev. 11:7; Deut. 14:8, even though its hoof is cloven. Apparently it was the only cloven-hoofed animal not to ruminate, which was considered abnormal or unclean. Further, its omnivorous nature and scavenging habits certainly would have been considered to be unclean. By the intertestamental period, the pig seems to have become the paradigm example of uncleanness, for Antiochus used it to expose religious Jews (2 Macc. 6:18) and to defile the temple altar (1 Macc. 1:47).

The pig is used in both the OT and NT as a metaphor for incongruity. An indiscreet woman is like a gold ring in a pig's snout (Prov. 11:22). Jesus commands his disciples not to cast their pearls before swine (Matt. 7:6).

The pig is unclean to Jews and Muslims, although ancient Israel's neighbors did not share this view. Today the wild boar prospers on either side of the Jordan River's banks as well as the more remote areas of the Golan and the upper Galilee.

DONALD FOWLER

SWORD

An offensive weapon of war and conflict designed to inflict the greatest injury on one's opponent. Unlike the arrow, sling, spear, and possibly the javelin, the sword (Heb. *ḥereḇ;* Gk. *máchaira, rhomphaía*) is a close-order weapon, used when lines of infantry clashed in battle. It is the most frequently mentioned weapon of war in the Bible, in accounts of real warfare and also as a metaphor of the activity of God and his people.

Archaeological excavations have unearthed several types of bronze and iron swords which were used in battle and for ceremonial purposes. The bronze "sickle sword," frequently depicted on Egyptian reliefs, was used as a badge of rank in the Egyptian army and as a "slashing" weapon with its edge on the outer curve of the blade.

The straight sword is a later design and is associated with the arrival of the "Sea Peoples," possibly from the Aegean. Egyptian pictures of battles between their forces and the Sea Peoples depict the latter bearing the straight, stabbing sword. Examples, often made of iron, have been found in burial sites of the Philistine region.

The "double edged" sword *(rhomphaía)* is not necessarily a slashing weapon, but rather designed with a sharp point, honed on either side for deeper penetration of an opponent. The ultimate stage of the development of this weaponry during the biblical period was the steeled Roman gladius. A penetrating wound on an enemy is far more likely to do greater damage than a slash or cut, which might more easily be deflected away by armor or a shield. However, in OT times both cutting (Josh. 8:24; 10:30) and stabbing (Ps. 37:15) were common in the use of the sword.

The Bible, especially the OT, knew the horrors of ancient warfare in which the sword was a main weapon. But this was a terror which Israel and Judah themselves manipulated and exploited (Deut. 13:15; 20:13; Josh. 6:21; 8:26). The preexilic and exilic prophets often mention the terror the sword inspired; Jeremiah and Ezekiel, especially, depict the physical and psychological damage that attacks with the sword can inflict on a population (Jer. 6:25; Ezek. 5:12; 11:8). The sword became a symbol of warfare throughout the OT (Lev. 26:7; Deut 32:42) and was an ideal symbol of judgment (e.g., Lev. 26:25, 33).

The sword is associated metaphorically with the mouth. It devours its victims (Isa. 1:20; Jer. 2:30) and becomes sated with blood (Isa. 34:6). Liars have teeth as sharp as swords (Ps. 57:4[MT 5]), and tongues which do similar damage (64:3[4]). Thus the sword becomes a synonym and metaphor for the powerful word of God (Eph. 6:17; Heb. 4:12; Rev. 1:16).

While the hope for peace without the sword is expressed many times in the Bible (Lev. 26:6; Isa. 2:4; Mic. 4:3), the weapon is far too common a feature of ancient life to be so dismissed. The opening chapters of Genesis present the enigmatic "flaming and turning sword" as the weapon by which humans are barred from Paradise (Gen. 3:24), and Revelation depicts the sword as the weapon by which the apocalyptic horsemen destroy their victims in judgment (Rev. 6:4, 8). Jesus' comment that those who live by the sword shall also perish by it (Matt. 26:52) is less an ethical pronouncement than an unfortunate statement of fact.

Bibliography. R. Maxwell-Hyslop, "Daggers and Swords in Western Asia," *Iraq* 8 (1946): 1-65.

T. R. Hobbs

SYCAMORE

Ficus sycomorus L., the sycamore fig, a hardy tree that grows up to 14 m. (45 ft.) tall. This tropical tree grew abundantly in the Shephelah (1 Kgs. 10:27; 2 Chr. 1:15; 9:27). It is not the American sycamore *(Platanus occidentalis),* the Old World sycamore *(Platanus orientalis),* or the sycamine (mulberry, *Morus Nigra* L.), as earlier thought. Perhaps the most famous sycamore tree is the one Zacchaeus climbed in order to see Jesus (Luke 19:4; Gk. *sykomoréa*).

Both the wood and the fruit of the sycamore tree are valuable. The soft, porous wood was used in construction of Egyptian tombs and coffins. The sycamore fig is inferior to the common fig, *Ficus carica* L., but was cultivated and eaten in ancient times. About three days before the sycamore fig harvest, a gash was made in the fruit to hasten ripening. Amos was, by profession, a dresser of sycamore figs (Amos 7:14; Heb. *šiqmâ*).

The sycamore fig of biblical times was fertilized by wasps. Modern sycamores produce seedless figs and grow only in cultivated form.

Megan Bishop Moore

SYCHAR (Gk. *Sychár*)

The city in Samaria at which Jesus spoke with a Samaritan woman (John 4:5). The Gospel situates Sychar near the field which Jacob gave to his son Joseph (Gen. 33:18-19; Josh. 24:32 mention the field, but not Sychar), and notes that Jacob's Well was there (John 4:6). Despite the fact that the NT connects Sychar with Jacob's Well, the actual site of Sychar is disputed. Some identify Sychar with the similarly named modern town of Askar, located near Shechem, while others associate the city with Shechem itself, with Sychar being corrupted to the more familiar Shechem (Lat., Gk. "Sychem"; cf. Acts 7:16). Although the exact location of Sychar remains unclear, Jacob's Well more confidently has been identified with Bir Ya'aqûb (177179) in modern Balâṭah, ca. 1.7 km. (1 mi.) SE of Nablus, near a pass between Mt. Gerizim and Mt. Ebal.

Monica L. W. Brady

SYENE (Heb. *sĕwēnēh, sînîm;* Gk. *Syḗnē*)

A city in Upper Egypt, located on the east bank of the Nile, just N of the First Cataract, at the southern border of ancient Egypt. The name appears twice in the context of oracles against Egypt, expressing the geographical extent of the coming devastation ("from Migdol to Syene"; Ezek. 29:10; 30:6) and once in an oracle of salvation in which the scattered people of Israel are gathered together (Isa. 49:12). Most information concerning Syene comes from the Aramaic Elephantine Papyri, which describe Syene as supplementary to Elephantine (a Jewish military colony and Persian period religious, commercial, and administrative center for Upper Egypt, located on an island opposite Syene) but significant for its role in commerce and its abundant granite quarries (whose stones were called "syenite"). Remains of Syene lie under modern Aswan, which is best known as the site of a dam completed in 1970.

Monica L. W. Brady

SYMEON (Gk. *Symeṓn*)

1. A prophet and teacher in the church at Antioch who was surnamed Niger and may have been, therefore, black (Lat. *niger;* Acts 13:1 RSV; NRSV "Simeon" [**6**]).

2. Another name for Simon Peter (Acts 15:14; 2 Pet. 1:1 RSV).

SYNAGOGUE

The place of assembly used primarily for worship by Jewish communities. Gk. *synagōgḗ* is originally a secular term denoting a "group of people" or a "collection of things." There is no clear reference to the synagogue in the OT. The word is commonplace in the NT, where it refers to an actual building.

The exact origin of the synagogue is unknown, and scholars continue to debate whether it emerged during the Babylonian Exile or in the Hellenistic period. Those who argue for an exilic date believe that the synagogue arose as a place where Jews, removed from the Jerusalem temple, could worship. Many believe that Ezekiel played a central role in establishing the synagogue (Ezek. 11:16), although

Synagogue at Gamla in the southern Golan, built at the time of Alexander Janneus (1st century B.C.E.) and destroyed by Vespasian and Titus (67 C.E.). Benches line the unpaved hall on all four sides
(Phoenix Data Systems, Neal and Joel Bierling)

others cite Jer. 39:8 as evidence for such houses of worship prior to the Exile. While it is probable that the synagogue existed prior to the Hellenistic period, its absence in Ezra and Nehemiah suggests that the Jews who returned from the Exile were unfamiliar with the institution. At present there is no direct textual or archaeological evidence for the existence of pre-Hellenistic synagogues.

The earliest unambiguous documentary evidence for the synagogue is an inscription from Egypt, which records the construction of a synagogue building during the reign of Ptolemy III Euergetes (247-221 B.C.E.). 1st-century B.C.E. Egyptian synagogue inscriptions have led some scholars to propose the origin of the synagogue in the diaspora of the Hellenistic period, possibly within Egypt itself. However, the exact date and locale of the synagogue's origin remains a mystery. Although no clear literary evidence for Palestinian synagogues exists prior to the Maccabean period, numerous references to Galilean and Jerusalem synagogues in the NT and Josephus suggest that sabbath worship within synagogue buildings is already an established institution prior to the 1st century C.E. (e.g., Matt. 4:23; Mark 1:21; Luke 4:16-30; 7:5; Acts 13:5, 14-15, 43; 14:1; 15:21; Josephus *BJ* 2.285-91; *Vita* 280).

During the Second Temple period *synagōgḗ*, "house of assembly," is the most frequently used term to refer to the synagogue building. In diaspora localities, however, Gk. *proseuchḗ*, "house of prayer," is the common designation for the synagogue edifice. Some scholars suggest that the older term *proseuchḗ*, dating to the 3rd century B.C.E., is later replaced by *synagōgḗ*, which becomes the predominant designation for the synagogue building by the 2nd century C.E. Gk. *synagōgḗ* corresponds to Heb. *bêṯ kĕnesseṯ*, while *proseuchḗ* is equivalent to Heb. *bêṯ tĕpillâ*. These latter two terms, however, stem from post-70 C.E. literature, and are not used in the Bible in reference to the synagogue building.

Archaeology has provided physical evidence of 1st-century B.C.E.–1st-century C.E. synagogues in Palestine and the Diaspora. The earliest known synagogue is preserved on the Aegean island of Delos, whose Jewish community is mentioned both by Josephus and in inscriptions. This synagogue, built in the 1st century B.C.E., continued in use throughout the 1st and 2nd centuries C.E. A 1st-century C.E. synagogue was also discovered in the Roman part of Ostia, which remained in use until the 4th century. Although other early diaspora synagogues have been excavated, they postdate the NT period.

Our best evidence for the appearance of the NT synagogue comes from Palestine, where three pre-70 C.E. synagogues have been excavated, at Gamla, Masada, and Herodium. Although some scholars suggest the existence of 1st-century C.E. Palestinian synagogues at other sites, such as Migdal and Capernaum, the evidence is inconclusive. Of the known pre-70 C.E. synagogues, only the one at Gamla was originally designed and constructed for Jewish worship. Those at Masada and Herodium were secular meeting halls only later converted into synagogues. These three synagogue buildings closely resemble one another, and may have derived their design from secular assembly halls of the Hellenistic period.

The Gamla synagogue, constructed between

the latter part of the 1st century B.C.E. and the first half of the 1st century C.E., was destroyed by the Romans in 67 C.E. It is the oldest known synagogue found in Israel, and best illustrates the appearance of the NT era synagogue building. The Gamla synagogue was an elongated hall (20 × 16 m. [66 × 52 ft.]) with its principal entrance to the west, facing toward Jerusalem. A small rear entrance also led to an adjacent street. The main hall was divided by four rows of columns into a central nave (9.3 × 13.4 m. [30 × 44 ft.]) surrounded by four aisles, one on each side. The columns supported a wooden roof, and the synagogue lacked an upper story. Four rows of basalt benches, sufficient to hold ca. 300 people, surrounded all four sides of the main hall. A *mikveh* (3 × 13 m. [10 × 43 ft.]), or ritual bath, situated directly in front of the main entrance was used for purification prior to worship. A small room with benches, attached to the rear of the main hall, served possibly as a school or study room. The synagogue itself was adorned by an ornamented lintel, decorated by a six-petalled rosette flanked by date palms, and doric columns. A raised recess in the rear of the northwest corner of the main hall may have held the Torah scrolls used during worship services.

The synagogue's most important functions were as a place for worship, prayer, and religious study. The Theodotus inscription, discovered in Jerusalem and believed to date to the early 1st century C.E., describes a Jerusalem synagogue founded as a place for "the reading of the law and the teaching of the precepts" (cf. Luke 4:16-20). The very design of the Palestinian synagogue, with benches along all four walls, facilitated worship by focusing the congregation's attention toward the speaker, as reflected in NT accounts of synagogue services (Mark 6:1-5; Luke 4:16-30; Acts 13:13-16). By NT times, synagogue worship was already highly structured, and consisted of readings from the Torah and Prophets followed by an address or sermon (e.g., Luke 4:15-30; John 18:20; Acts 13:15). The seating within the synagogue was arranged in a certain order, with prominent places reserved for distinguished members (Mark 12:39 par.; Luke 20:46). Additional synagogue functions included its use as a general assembly hall for secular meetings and correction (Matt. 10:17; 23:34; Mark 13:9; Acts 22:19; 26:11; Josephus *Vita* 280). Epigraphic evidence, describing pre-70 C.E. diaspora synagogues, also documents communal means and slave manumissions conducted within the synagogue building.

Bibliography. K. Atkinson, "On Further Defining the First-Century CE Synagogue: Fact or Fiction?" *NTS* 43 (1997): 491-502; J. Gutmann, ed., *The Synagogue* (New York, 1975); H. C. Kee, "The Transformation of the Synagogue after 760 C.E.," *NTS* 36 (1990): 1-24; "Defining the First-Century C.E. Synagogue," *NTS* 41 (1995): 481-500; L. I. Levine, ed., *Ancient Synagogues Revealed* (Jerusalem, 1981); D. Urman and P. V. Flesher, eds., *Ancient Synagogues.* Studia postbiblica 47 (Leiden, 1995).

KENNETH ATKINSON

SYNOPTIC GOSPELS

Three Gospels — Matthew, Mark, and Luke — so called because of the very close relationship they bear to each other, so close that one can usefully place them alongside each other and compare them (Gk. *syn*, "with" + *optikóss*, which refers to "looking"). All three agree extensively in the order of the events they describe, and there is also a high measure of verbal agreement in the stories and traditions they share in common. This wide-ranging agreement has led to the almost universal view that the three Gospels are related to each other through a literary relationship: the work of one Evangelist has been used by one or more of the others, and/or the Evangelists had access to (a) common source(s). The problem of determining the precise nature of this relationship is known as the Synoptic Problem.

The most widely held solution to the Synoptic Problem today is the so-called Two Source theory. This theory claims that Mark's Gospel was used as a source by Matthew and Luke. In addition, Matthew and Luke had access to another body of source material, usually known as Q. (There is, however, much more disagreement about the precise nature of Q.)

Such a solution has in broad terms commanded widespread support. However, it is by no means universally accepted. A strong minority view has continued to defend the theory (associated above all with the 18th-century scholar J. J. Griesbach) that Mark's Gospel was written last, not first, using both Matthew and Luke as sources. (This "Griesbach hypothesis" is staunchly advocated today by William R. Farmer and others.) Others too, while accepting the theory that Mark's Gospel was a source for Matthew and Luke (the theory of "Markan priority"), have questioned the existence of the hypothetical Q, and have argued that direct dependence of Luke on Matthew can best explain the agreements between these Gospels (cf. Michael D. Goulder).

The current debate about the Synoptic Problem has highlighted the weaknesses of some arguments used in the past to establish and defend the Two Source theory. For example, simply appealing to the fact that virtually all of Mark's Gospel is paralleled in Matthew or Luke or both, as some have done to argue for Markan priority, is now seen to be inconclusive. Of itself it shows nothing. Defenders of the Two Source theory would, however, seek to argue further that the theory of Markan priority can be made more plausible when one considers the nature of the contents shared by all three Gospels within each Gospel. Matthew's and Luke's parallels to Mark are often shorter, and Matthew and Luke both have a lot more material than Mark. If Mark's Gospel were first, Matthew and Luke would have abbreviated Mark's stories to make space for other traditions they had available. This seems to be a plausible general editorial procedure. The Griesbach hypothesis has to presume that Mark omitted large parts of Matthew and Luke, but also expanded the material he did retain quite considerably. Such a redactional procedure seems rather less plausible.

Detailed comparison of the wording of individual traditions also seems to many to be most easily explained if Mark's Gospel came first. Mark's version of Peter's confession at Caesarea Philippi in Mark 8:29 is "You are the Christ." This is paralleled in Matt. 16:16 by the longer "You are the Christ, the Son of the living God." If Matthew used Mark as a source, he must have added the extra reference to Jesus as Son of God, and such a note is thoroughly characteristic of Matthew's Christology. If Matthew came first, and Mark used Matthew, Mark must have omitted this reference to Jesus as Son of God. Given Mark's clear interest in Jesus' divine sonship elsewhere (cf. Mark 1:1; 15:39) this seems very difficult to envisage. It is on the basis of arguments such as these that a progressive and plausible case for the theory of Markan priority can be built up.

The case for the existence of Q is clearly more complex, if only because the alleged Q source is no longer extant. Most scholars would base the case for such a source on the implausibility of either Matthew or Luke (usually Luke) using the other as a direct source. If, e.g., Luke used Matthew, he must have changed Matthew's order drastically: yet he seems to have kept closely to the Markan order. Further, Luke seems to know none of Matthew's substantial additions to Mark in Markan passages (cf. Matt. 16:17-19). In addition, many would argue that, in the material they share in common which is not derived from Mark, neither Matthew nor Luke consistently gives the more original form of the tradition: sometimes Matthew is more original, sometimes Luke (e.g., Luke's shorter versions of the Beatitudes in 6:20-23, or the Lord's Prayer in 11:2-4, are both widely regarded as more original than Matthew's expanded versions). Hence, it is argued, direct dependence of one Gospel writer on the other is unlikely and the close verbal agreement between the Gospels is to be explained by common dependence on prior source material(s) Q. Whether Q was a single source or a more general set of unrelated materials is a further question, though there has been a strong movement in recent years to analyze Q from the point of view of redaction criticism and to try to determine characteristic theological features of Q.

The Synoptic Problem is important for study of the Synoptic Gospels at a number of levels. If one's interest in the Gospels is in discovering information about Jesus, then it is important to be able to identify the earliest strands of the tradition, and to be able to recognize which of the parallel versions in the Gospels is likely to be the earlier and which secondary. This does not of course mean that by isolating the earliest strands of the Gospels we have necessarily reached a pure, unvarnished Jesus. Redaction criticism has taught that all our Gospels are influenced by the outlook and situation of their authors, and this applies as much to Mark (and probably to Q for those who believe in its existence) as to Matthew and Luke.

Our understanding of the Evangelists themselves is also significantly dependent on the Synoptic Problem. One way of determining the Evangelists' concerns is to see the way they use their sources: and hence an accurate delineation of the source relationships between the Gospels is vital to enable that work to be undertaken. Certainly different solutions to the Synoptic Problem would lead to rather different conclusions about the concerns and interests of the Evangelists.

In one sense, treating "the" Synoptic Gospels as a whole is an anachronism. Each Gospel deserves to be treated on its own merits. But a study of all three together does throw fascinating light on the ways in which traditions about Jesus were circulating, and the freedom which the Evangelists evidently felt in relation to those traditions, in a period prior to the canonizing and fixing of these books as "scriptural."

Bibliography. A. J. Bellinzoin, Jr., ed., *The Two-Source Hypothesis* (Macon, 1985); W. R. Farmer, *The Synoptic Problem* (1964, repr. Macon, 1981); J. A. Fitzmyer, "The Priority of Mark and the 'Q' Source in Luke," in *Jesus and Man's Hope* (Pittsburgh, 1970), 1:131-70 (repr. in *To Advance the Gospel,* 2nd ed. [Grand Rapids, 1998], 3-40); M. D. Goulder, *Luke: A New Paradigm.* JSNTSup 20 (Sheffield, 1989); C. M. Tuckett, "The Existence of Q," in *The Gospel Behind the Gospels,* ed. R. A. Piper. NovTSup 75 (Leiden, 1995), 19-47 (repr. in Tuckett, *Q and the History of Early Christianity* [Peabody, 1996], 1-39). CHRISTOPHER TUCKETT

SYNTYCHE (Gk. *Syntýchē*)

A woman in the church of Philippi whom Paul urged to settle some sort of dispute with another member, Euodia (Phil. 4:2-3).

SYRACUSE (Gk. *Syrákousai*)

A large maritime city on the southeastern corner of the island of Sicily, founded by Archias of Corinth in the 8th century B.C. Particularly in the 5th and 4th centuries, Syracuse was the most prosperous Greek colony in the western Mediterranean. It was connected by a mole with the mainland, where the city established outposts. Under the Romans it served as capital of the eastern half of Sicily. A temple of the Greek goddess Athena was located there, as well as a magnificent rock-hewn theater. Cicero called it the greatest of Greek cities, and the most beautiful.

This was the first stopping place on Paul's voyage to Rome after he and his party wintered at Malta. They spent three days at Syracuse (Acts 28:12), but no record of any preaching or ministry is given. Apparently the party waited on ship for a favorable wind to direct their way to Rome.

DALE ELLENBURG

SYRIA

In ancient times, the region bordering the eastern Mediterranean and extending northward from (and sometimes including) Palestine and Phoenicia to the Euphrates in the northeast and the Taurus Mountains in the northwest.

Syria's cultural heritage begins with Stone Age

hunters who pursued migrating animal herds that moved northward through the Orontes River valley until they reached the valley of Nahr el-Kabir. At that point, the game trail must have turned westward toward the Mediterranean Sea. Analysis of the stone tools, and the geomorphological setting at sites such as Sitt Marko and Latamne, date them from 500 thousand to 1 million years old. The most ancient archaeological sites in Syria are associated with Homo erectus populations that were replaced ca. 100 to 200 thousand years ago by both modern Homo sapien and Homo sapien var. Neandertal populations.

Ten thousand years ago, the hunting and gathering bands scattered across wide sections of Syria began to establish more settled villages such as Mureybet and Abu Hureyra. Animal bones and carbonized seeds recovered from these Neolithic villages demonstrate that domesticated wheat, barley, sheep, goats, and cattle would replace a diet of wild gazelle and gathered wild seeds. The change from hunting and gathering to food production by cultivation went hand in hand with population increases, advances in domestic architecture, and the rise of complex burial rituals designed to honor the dead.

The need to control economic surplus in the Neolithic settlements would eventually give rise to a system of fingersize clay tokens designed to keep track of commodities such as bread, oil, meat, beer, and garments. Tokens, a precursor to writing, would remain in use in urban settings until the advent of cuneiform script written on clay tablets. In some rural contexts, even after 3rd-millennium urban populations had shifted to the cuneiform script, tokens would continue in use as a recording technique.

Rich economies developed in Syria during the 3rd millennium when the western arc of the Fertile Crescent was formed by Syria. The modern cities of Damascus and Aleppo trace their origins to this period. Large urban centers, surrounded by circular walls, develop during the 3rd millennium in northern Syria at sites such as Tell Leilan, Tell Chuera, and Tell Mozan. Discoveries at Tell Mozan have demonstrated that it was the ancient city of Urkesh ruled by people speaking Hurrian.

Unquestionably the most remarkable of Syria's first cities was ancient Ebla (Tell Mardikh). Extensive research at Ebla has demonstrated that the city thrived for 800 years and that the urban center included extensive palaces, temples, workshops, and royal tombs. A major archive of cuneiform tablets, discovered during 1975, continues to expand our understanding of the city's political, economic, and religious traditions. Ebla's economy was fueled by its agricultural surpluses and textile industries, while trade brought objects to the kingdom including lapis lazuli from Afghanistan and carved stone vessels from Egypt. Cuneiform texts from Ebla provide clues to its pantheon of ca. 40 principal deities including Kura (principal god of the city), Hadad (storm-god), Dagan (lord of the region), Rashap (god of the underworld), Adamma (underworld goddess and spouse of Rashap), Ishara (principal goddess of the city), Ishtar (goddess of love and war), and Idabal (god associated with the Orontes Valley).

Complex patterns of urban growth and abandonment at the end of the 3rd millennium would coincide with the expansion and political ascension of West Semitic nomadic and seminomadic tribes often called Amorites. An Amorite king named Yaggid-lim established a powerful lineage at Mari (modern Tell Hariri) which would eventually be displaced by Šamši-adad, progenitor of the subsequent Assyrian Empire. The story of Mari began in the 3rd millennium and ended when the palace of Zimri-lim was destroyed (ca. 1759 B.C.) by Hammurabi of Babylon. Mari is of particular importance because of the ca. 15 thousand cuneiform documents discovered during the decades of excavation by French archaeologists. Physical remains of three temples have been identified near the palace; the temples were dedicated to the goddesses Ishtar, Ninizaza, and Ishtarat. Cuneiform texts attest to the importance of several deities including Itur-mer (lord of the land of Mari), Šamaš (sun-god), Dagan, and a principal pantheon of ca. 40 gods and goddesses.

Heavy defensive walls are a hallmark of the cities of Syria during the 2nd and 3rd millennia. The walls were meant to defend against the armies from southern Mesopotamia, Turkey, Egypt, and the islands of the Mediterranean Sea. One such invasion was led by the Egyptian king Thutmose I (1504-1492), who invaded the Mitannian kingdom situated within Syria and north of the Euphrates River. Thutmose I's invasion was in retribution for the invasion of the Egyptian delta by Syro-Palestinians, but it also brought rich tribute into the Egyptian Empire. The rich agricultural resources of Syria made it a target for expansionist empires. In 1285, at Qadesh on the Orontes River, Egyptian troops under Rameses II clashed with the infantry and chariots of the Hittite king Muwatallis. Rameses claimed victory in his monumental reliefs, but the extension of Hittite influence southward to Damascus suggests greater reliability in the Hittite version.

Ancient cities were established in both the interior of Syria and along its Mediterranean coastline. Ancient Ugarit (Ras Shamra) is the best investigated site along the Syrian coast. The builders of Ugarit were able to take advantage of stone suitable for palaces, temples, houses, and a defensive wall. Artifacts point to trade routes reaching south to Egypt and west to the Mycenean culture in Greece. The kingdom of Ugarit would fall victim to the Sea Peoples between 1180 and 1175. Among the significant discoveries of Ugarit is a small tablet dated to the 14th century bearing an abecedary. The two main temples in the city of Ugarit were dedicated to Dagan (god of the underworld) and Baal (god of strength and fertility). Cuneiform texts refer to a pantheon including El (father of the gods), Athirat (goddess of the sea and spouse of El), ʿAnat, Mot (death), Rashap, Nikkal, and Kotarot.

Aramean and Neo-Hittite principalities rose in power after 1200, but their autonomy was curtailed as the Assyrian Empire annexed the cities of Syria. An exceptional temple from this period is situated at Ain Dara, in the Afrin Valley near Aleppo. The iconography of the Ain Dara temple links it with Ishtar, goddess of fertility. The exterior of the temple is decorated with carved designs of mountain gods, sphinxes, and lions.

In 612 the Babylonians and Iranian Medes toppled the Neo-Assyrian Empire and Syria came under Babylonian control. The Achaemenid Persians annexed Syria into their empire during the 6th century, but lost it to the Greeks during the 4th century. The mixture of the Greek and Syrian traditions resulted in artistic and architectural achievements that would continue even after the Romans dislodged Greek control from Syria. The Greek and Roman period produced many of Syria's greatest monuments, still preserved at sites such as Dura Europos, Palmyra, Bosra, and Apamea. Of great significance is the fact that two Syrians, Elagabalus (A.D. 213-222) and Philippus (244-249), achieved the rank of emperor.

Roman period cities like Dura Europos supported thriving multi-ethnic/multi-religious communities. Several temples to traditional Syrian and Roman deities, a house church, and an elaborately decorated synagogue were all found at Dura Europos. This mixture changed as the Christian communities steadily grew and as the traditional temples dwindled in power and influence.

Bibliography. H. Weiss, ed., *Ebla to Damascus: Art and Archaeology of Ancient Syria* (Washington, 1985).

MICHAEL J. FULLER

SYRIAC

A form of late Eastern Aramaic; a member of the Aramaic subfamily of Northwest Semitic languages. The Syriac alphabet comprising 22 consonants is written in three forms: Estrangela, found in the oldest inscriptions and manuscripts; Nestorian, used primarily by the Syrian Christians in the Persian Empire; and Serta, or Jacobite, used by Syrian Christians in the Roman Empire. Individual consonants are written in slightly modified form depending on their initial, medial, or final position in a word and whether they stand alone or are joined to others. Syriac is written from right to left. Lexical roots are predominantly triliteral. Derived forms are generated by prefixing or suffixing consonants to a triliteral (or biliteral) root and by vocalization modifications.

Originally the dialect of Edessa (a 2nd-century center of Christianity), Syriac superseded other forms of Aramaic in the region and maintained prominence as a spoken and literary language of western Asia until the 8th century. A vast corpus of religious and nonreligious writing, both poetry and prose, was produced during this time. From the 8th century onward, Syriac was superseded by Arabic as the common language, although Syriac remained widespread as the liturgical language of Eastern Christianity until the 13th century. In 489 theological controversy and ecclesiastical disputes produced a linguistic split. The Nestorian East Syrians (Nisibis) separated themselves from the Jacobite West Syrians (Edessa), giving rise to the development of two distinct dialects and orthographies.

Syrian authors have produced a vast and rich body of literature, making Syriac the most extensively documented Aramaic dialect. Although religious texts are most abundant, the translations of the OT and NT into Syriac and the theological treatises, biblical expositions, hymns, and homilies of the early church fathers should not be allowed to overshadow Syrian literary contributions in the areas of science, philosophy, mathematics, and medicine.

Bibliography. G. Bergsträsser, *Introduction to the Semitic Languages* (Winona Lake, 1983); K. Beyer, *The Aramaic Language: Its Distribution and Subdivisions* (Göttingen, 1986).

DENNIS R. MAGARY

SYRIAC VERSIONS

Translations of the Bible into Syriac are numerous compared to the number of versions produced by other early Christian communities. The earliest Syriac translation of the OT is the Vetus Syra, the Old Syriac version. It remains a matter of debate as to whether the origin for this translation lies in the conversion of the kingdom of Adiabene to Judaism, or coincides with the introduction of Christianity into Mesopotamia. In either case, this early Syriac translation of the OT dates to about the middle of the 1st century C.E. and was an adaptation or translation of some form of Aramaic Targum (either West Aramaic or Palestinian).

The Old Syriac version of the NT, which had its origin in the 3rd century, is attested to by two incomplete texts of the four Gospels, both belonging to the first part of the 5th century. The Syriac designation of this version, *Evangelion da-mepharreshe* ("the Gospel of the Separated"), establishes a relationship to Tatian's Diatessaron which was constituted *Evangelion de-mehallete* ("the Gospel of the Mixed"). The consensus is that Codex Syrus Curetonianus and Codex Syrus Sinaiticus, the two major manuscripts of the Old Syriac, represent two independent textual traditions of the same version. Differences between the two manuscripts include the order of the Gospels in Curetonianus (Matthew, Mark, John, and Luke, with most of Mark and much of John missing) and the longer ending of Mark attested in Curetonianus but not found in Sinaiticus. Extant for the Old Syriac NT are the Gospels. Although citations from Acts and the Pauline Letters can be found in early commentaries of the church fathers, no Old Syriac text of Acts or the Epistles survives.

Syrian convert to Christianity and student of Justin Martyr, Tatian (ca. 110-72) produced his *Evangelion da-mehallete* ca. 170 C.E. This early Syriac version, better known by its Greek name Diatessaron ("through the four"), is Tatian's harmony of the four Gospels. Unfortunately, no manuscript of the Diatessaron survives. Our knowledge of this version derives entirely from citations and secondary sources. The original language of the Diatessaron has been a matter of dispute. Although the evidence would suggest that Tatian composed his harmony in Syriac, it has been argued that this version was originally composed in Greek and then translated into Syriac. The Diatessaron was Tatian's effort to weave together the disparate and detailed material of all four NT Gospels, along with selected readings from apocryphal sources, into one continuous narrative of the life of Jesus. For more than a century Tatian's Syriac Gospel narrative was regarded as authoritative within the Syrian Church. Its broad acceptance and popularity outside the Syrian-speaking community is attested to by the widespread translation of the Diatessaron into a number of other languages. Uncertainty regarding the relationship between the Diatessaron and the Old Syriac version remains. Arguments have been advanced in favor of the Diatessaron being the earlier work, thus influencing the composition of the Old Syriac Gospels. Others have espoused the priority of the Old Syriac Gospels, which served in some ways as the source for the Diatessaron.

From the 5th century on, the Syriac Peshiṭta was the standard version of the Syrian Church. This late Eastern Aramaic translation of the OT and NT is the second oldest of the primary versions and one of the earliest documents of Syrian literature. Its name, *Peshiṭta,* the "simple" or "common version," is most likely intended to distinguish it from the more sophisticated, annotated Syro-Hexapla. When and where the translation originated and why the translation was made and by whom remain uncertain. Arguments have been advanced for origin of the translation as early as the 1st or 2nd century C.E., and debate continues as to whether the Peshiṭta was a Jewish or Christian translation. The evidence continues to suggest that biblical books were translated individually over an extended period of time, that the translation represents the work of more than one translator and goes back to a Hebrew original which is very close to the MT. Some books exhibit a connection with Jewish targumic traditions. Other books give evidence of influence from the LXX, but the influence of Targum and Greek text varies from book to book.

The Peshiṭta version of the NT (completed in the early 5th century) was not a new translation, but rather a revision of the Old Syriac, bringing it more closely into line with the Greek. Among the distinctives of the NT Peshiṭta are the omission of several verses in Matthew, Luke, John, and Acts and the absence of five canonical books (2 Peter, 2 John, 3 John, Jude, Revelation).

At the beginning of the 6th century Philoxenus, bishop of Mabbug, expressed dissatisfaction with the Peshiṭta version because the translators had made so many mistakes, and because the rendering into Syriac was not close enough to the original Greek. To remedy these deficiencies, Philoxenus appointed Polycarp to prepare a thorough and comprehensive revision of the Peshiṭta version of the NT. Polycarp's revision, a thoroughgoing correction of variant readings, particles, syntax, and style, was completed in 508.

A century later another version appeared that gave evidence of the ongoing effort to bring the Syriac NT into exacting conformity with the underlying Greek. In 616 Thomas of Herakleia (Harkel) produced a Syriac version of the NT, believed to be a revision of the Philoxenian version, complete with marginal notes of variant readings found in Greek manuscripts.

Fragments of a Palestinian Syriac text preserve a dialect that is more accurately classified as Western (Palestinian) Aramaic. The script is Syriac, but an archaic form of Estrangela. The translation was made from the LXX. Influence from the Peshiṭta and Targums has been claimed by some. The date of the version is a matter of conjecture (probably 4th or 5th century).

At the request of Athanasius I, Bishop Paul of Tella, along with a contingent of coworkers, made a Syriac translation of the LXX text found in the fifth column of Origen's Hexapla. The translation technique employed and the great care exercised by the translators have rendered the Syro-Hexaplar invaluable in restoring the lost Hexapla of the LXX.

Finally, Jacob of Edessa (640-708) produced a revision of both the Peshiṭta and Syro-Hexaplar. Jacob's work on the Peshiṭta was yet another attempt to improve on the Syriac translation. His labor on the Syro-Hexaplar was devoted to bringing it back into conformity with the style and idiom of the Syriac language. These recensions, which survive only in part, marked the end of almost eight centuries of Bible translation among the Syrians.

See PESHIṬTA.

Bibliography. K. Luke, "The Old Syriac Version of the Bible," *Bible Bhashyam* 18 (1992): 105-23; "The Syriac Versions of the New Testament," *Bible Bhashyam* 19 (1993): 300-314; 20 (1994): 124-38; "The Syriac Versions of the Old Testament," *Bible Bhashyam* 18 (1992): 163-77; B. M. Metzger, *The Early Versions of the New Testament* (Oxford, 1977); A. Vööbus, *Early Versions of the New Testament* (Stockholm, 1954); W. Wright, *A Short History of Syriac Literature* (1894, repr. Amsterdam, 1966).

DENNIS R. MAGARY

SYROPHOENICIAN (Gk. *Syrophoiníkissa*)
The gentile ("Greek") woman who begs Jesus to remove the evil spirit from her daughter (Mark 7:24-30). The parallel passage in Matt. 15 refers to the woman as a Canaanite. Her "Syrophoenician origin" indicates that she came from the region of Tyre and Sidon in the Roman province of Syria. At first Jesus refuses to heal the daughter on the grounds that he has come only for Jewish people. Jesus tells the woman that children must be fed before dogs, with readers understanding that the children were Jews and dogs were Gentiles. When the woman reminds Jesus that dogs eat the crumbs from the children's table, Jesus rewards her persistence and heals her daughter. MICHELLE TOOLEY

SYRTIS, THE (Gk. *hē Sýrtis*)
The two shallow bays that form a broad gulf on the coast of modern Libya and Tunisia, Syrtis Major (now called the Gulf of Sidra or Sirte) to the southeast and Syrtis Minor to the northwest, south, and southwest of Sicily. The sailors of the ship Paul boarded in Myra of Lycia feared that the wind from the northeast they encountered off Crete would drive the ship "on the Syrtis" (Acts 27:17).

SYZYGOS
See YOKEFELLOW.

T

TAANACH (Heb. *ta'ănāḵ*)
A city in the southern corner of the Jezreel Valley in the foothills of the Samarian hill country. Its identification with modern Tell Ta'annek (171214) is undisputed because of the continuity in the name and because of its location on the southern branch of the Via Maris, next to the pass of Megiddo. Taanach is 8 km. (5 mi.) SE of Megiddo and ca. 40 km. (25 mi.) from the coast. The pear-shaped mound measures 340 m. (1115 ft.) from north to south, and up to 140 m. (460 ft.) from east to west. It rises ca. 40 m. (130 ft.) above the surrounding plain and 180 m. (590 ft.) above sea level.

Taanach is mentioned in Pharaoh Thutmose III's account of the battle of Megiddo (ca. 1468 B.C.) as a southern bypass to Megiddo and a place where Egyptian troops were mustered, and occurs in the Palestine list in the Amon temple at Karnak. Its prince Yašdata fled to Megiddo because of a conflict with Shechem (EA 248:14). Taanach was one of the Israelite cities destroyed in Shishak's campaign ca. 918. Its king was one of the 31 kings defeated by Joshua (Josh. 12:21), and it is named among the levitical cities (21:25). The city was assigned to Manasseh, but it was not immediately conquered (Judg. 1:27; Josh. 17:11-12). Taanach finally came under Israelite control at the time of Solomon and was one of his administrative centers (1 Kgs. 4:12).

The site was first excavated by Ernst Sellin in three campaigns, 1902-4. This was one of the first excavations in Palestine and the first in the north of Israel, and excavation techniques and recording systems were still in their infancy. A keen observer and careful in his conclusions, Sellin was reluctant to interpret the many child burials as remains of child sacrifices. Besides the small cuneiform archive, the most important findings were fragments of two cult-stands and the bronze figurine of a goddess of Hurrian type. Sellin emphasized the traces of influence from Cyprus (later to be identified as Mycenean) during the Canaanite period (ca. 1400). In 1963-68 Paul W. Lapp excavated the west and southwest of the tell, demonstrating that the town was protected by city walls in all major periods. Ceramics differentiated several phases of the Bronze Age city and identified a gap in occupation of about half a millennium between Early Bronze II and III and Middle Bronze II (down to ca. 1700).

The oldest archaeological evidence shows Taanach as a prestigious center for EB (ca. 2700-2300). In later phases retaining walls and a large glacis were added. After the 500-year gap, Taanach revived as an impressive MB city (ca. 1700-1350), with extensive building activity. The city had far-reaching trade relations, but it was always dependent on the still larger Megiddo. Personal names in letters and lists show a mixed population (ca. 60 percent Semitic, the rest Hurrite, Hittite, and Indo-Aryan). As did Megiddo, Taanach sided with the Syrian powers against Egypt and was consequently seriously affected by the victory of Thutmose III at Megiddo in 1468. Its culture and population declined during LB. The archive from ca. 1450 mentions the Egyptian governor at Gaza and shows Egyptian dominance in the local affairs of the Jezreel Valley. During the Amarna period Taanach was affected by the local conflict between Megiddo and Shechem.

During the 12th century Taanach seems to have suffered two (at least partial) destructions, but its population increased again in the 10th century. It was now under the domination of the newly formed Israelite state. A large building found by Sellin may have been the residence of the Israelite governor. Destroyed by Shishak ca. 918, it recovered under the Omrides in the 9th century; the so-called northeast-outwork belongs to the extensive building activities of Omri and Ahab.

Taanach may have suffered as a consequence of the Aramean wars in the late 9th century and the Assyrian war in 733. Its final destruction ca. 600 may have been at the hand of the Egyptians (Neco) or the Babylonians. In Hellenistic and Roman times the village was located E of the tell. Jerome indicates that it had become quite large during the Byzantine period.

The 12 texts discovered by Sellin were the first and to date only cuneiform archive found in Palestine. Included are four letters (ca. 100 readable lines) and nine name lists (ca. 80 personal names). The letters bear witness to the domination of the Egyptian governor Amanhatpa, who resided at Gaza and visited Meggido. Evidently, the Akkadian language and script were used not only for international diplomacy, but also for local and even private affairs in the region.

Bibliography. A. E. Glock, "Taanach," *NEAEHL* 4 (New York, 1993); "Texts and Archaeology at Tell Ta'annek," *Berytus* 31 (1983): 57-66; 1428-33; P. W. Lapp, "The 1963 Excavation at Ta'annek," *BASOR* 173 (1964): 4-44; "The 1966 Excavation at Tell Ta'annek," *BASOR* 185 (1967): 2-39; "The 1968 Excavation at Tell Ta'annek," *BASOR* 195 (1969): 2-49; L. Nigro, "The 'Nordostburg' at Tell Ta'annek," *ZDPV* 110 (1994): 168-80; W. E. Rast, *Taanach I: Studies in the Iron Age Pottery* (Cambridge, Mass., 1978). SIEGFRIED KREUZER

TAANATH-SHILOH (Heb. *ta'ănaṯ šilōh*)
A border city in the tribal territory of Ephraim (Josh. 16:6). It is perhaps to be identified with Khirbet Ta'na el-Fôqā (185175), ca. 11 km. (7 mi.) SE of Nablus.

TABBAOTH (Heb. *ṭabbā'ôṯ*)
The ancestor (or head) of a group of temple servants who returned with Zerubbabel from the Babylonian Exile (Ezra 2:43; Neh. 7:46).

TABBATH (Heb. *ṭabbāṯ*)
A place where the Midianites fled after Gideon's surprise attack (Judg. 7:22). Its precise location depends on the placement of other sites which have not been identified. Suggestions include Râs Abū Ṭâbât on Wadi Kufrinjeh E of Beth-shean and the Jordan. It has also been placed S of Jabesh-gilead and Abel-meholah and N of Zarethan and Succoth as well as near Karkor and Heres. PHILIP R. DREY

TABEEL (Heb. *ṭāḇĕ'ēl, ṭāḇĕ'al*)
1. A Samaritan official who petitioned Artaxerxes to halt the rebuilding of Jerusalem (Ezra 4:7).

2. The otherwise unknown father of the person whom the Syro-Ephraimite coalition (ca. 735 B.C.E.) planned to place on the throne of Judah (Isa. 7:6). The change from the original form of the name, Heb. *ṭāḇĕ'ēl*, to *ṭāḇĕ'al* might be a Hebrew wordplay making "God is good" into "no-good" (or "good-for-nothing").

If the name is personal, Tabeel was likely a Syrian officer and confidant of Rezin. An 8th-century Assyrian letter refers to a "Tabeelite," implying that Tabeel was a tribal name, possibly ancestor to the Tobiad family in postexilic Judah. Tabeel could also be a regional or geographic name, connected to the "land of Tob" (Judg. 11:3, 5; 2 Sam. 10:6, 8).

Bibliography. W. F. Albright, "The Son of Tabeel (Isaiah 7:6)," *BASOR* 140 (1955): 34-35; J. A. Dearman, "The Son of Tabeel (Isaiah 7.6)," in *Prophets and Paradigms*, ed. S. B. Reid. JSOTSup 229 (Sheffield, 1996); B. Mazar, "The Tobiads," *IEJ* 7 (1957): 137-45, 229-38. ANDREW H. BARTELT

TABERAH (Heb. *taḇ'ērâ*)
A site (Heb. "burning") along the Exodus route, in the southeastern Sinai Peninsula three days N of Mt. Sinai (Num. 11:3). Here the Lord set fire to the outer edges of the camp as punishment for the people's complaining (Num. 11:1-3; cf. Deut. 9:22).
PETE F. WILBANKS

TABERNACLE
The portable sanctuary said to have been built at Mt. Sinai in the time of Moses and used until Solomon built the First Temple. The term (Heb. *miškān*) means "dwelling." Other names are the "tent of meeting" *('ōhel mô'ēḏ)* and the "sanctuary" *(miqdāš)*.

The story of the tabernacle's construction dominates Exod. 25–40. God showed Moses the heavenly pattern for the tabernacle on Mt. Sinai (Exod. 25:9, 40), but before construction could begin the people committed apostasy by making a golden calf. God threatened to withdraw his presence from Israel, but Moses interceded and afterward the people furnished material for the tabernacle. Construction was supervised by the craftsman Bezalel, and when the work was completed, the glory of God filled the tabernacle (Exod. 40:34-38).

The design given in the final form of the Pentateuch locates the tabernacle in a courtyard in the center of the Israelite camp. The courtyard was 46 m. (150 ft.) long, 23 m. (75 ft.) wide, and enclosed by curtains that were 2.3 m. (7.5 ft.) high. Within the courtyard was a bronze wash basin in which the priests purified themselves as well as a bronze altar for burnt offerings. The tabernacle itself was a kind of tent made of wooden frames covered with goat hair and leather; it was 4.6 m. (15 ft.) high, 4.6 m. (15 ft.) wide, and 14 m. (45 ft.) long. The interior was divided into two parts. The forecourt, which had a multicolored screen at its entrance, was furnished with a seven-branched lampstand; a table; 12 loaves of bread, known as the bread of the presence; and a golden incense altar. A multicolored curtain covered the entry into the second part of the sanctuary or "holy of holies." In this inner sanctuary was the ark of the covenant, a box made of acacia wood overlaid with gold, in which the tablets inscribed with the Ten Commandments were kept. The ark had a golden cover known as the mercy seat, which was adorned with two cherubim. Items that were later placed in the holy of holies included a jar of manna (Exod. 16:33-34) and Aaron's staff, which had miraculously borne almonds (Num. 17:1-11[MT 16-26]).

The tabernacle was the place where offerings were made to God and revelations received from God. Offerings were made daily on the bronze altar in the courtyard and the incense altar in the forecourt, but the most solemn rite took place once a year on the Day of Atonement, when the high priest sprinkled the blood of a bull and a goat before the mercy seat to make atonement for Israel's sins. Revelations of God's will were sometimes said to have been given at the mercy seat in the holy of holies (Exod. 25:22) and sometimes at the door of the tent (Num. 12:5; Deut. 31:14-15).

The Israelites took the tabernacle with them as they traveled through the desert toward Canaan. Responsibilities for transporting and assembling it at each new encampment were entrusted to the Levites. When the people reached the Promised Land, the tabernacle was placed at Shiloh (Josh. 18:1; 19:51; Ps. 78:60); later sources say that it was also at Gibeon for a time (1 Chr. 16:39; 21:29; 2 Chr. 1:3-6, 13). When David brought the ark to Jerusalem, he placed it in a tent following the pattern of earlier sanctuaries (2 Sam. 6:17; 7:5-7). Solomon built a permanent temple, and at the time of the dedication he had the tent of meeting, the ark, and the holy vessels placed in the temple so that the temple became the successor to Israel's earlier tent sanctuaries (1 Kgs. 8:4).

The depiction of the tabernacle in the final form of the Pentateuch is based on multiple traditions which can be discerned on the basis of incongruities in the text. An early tradition tells of the simple tent that was set up outside the Israelite camp before the tabernacle was built. This tent was attended by one man, Joshua the son of Nun, rather than by Aaron and the levitical priests (Exod. 33:7-11). It was apparently not used for sacrifice and did not house the ark of the covenant. God spoke with Moses at the door of this tent rather than in the holy of holies. The name "tent of meeting" was suitable for such a tent since God occasionally met people there, while the name "tabernacle" or "dwelling" was more suitable for a shrine in which God dwelt continually.

The elaborate plans for the tabernacle are generally regarded as the literary creation of the Priestly writer (P), whose design incorporates features from various Israelite sanctuaries. The covering of goat hair and leather recalls the simple tent sanctuary mentioned in the earliest sources; the extensive wooden framework and the name "tabernacle" or "dwelling" is reminiscent of semi-permanent sanctuaries located in Canaan; and the sanctuary's furnishings correspond closely to those of Solomon's temple. Some have argued that the Priestly writer sought to legitimate the cult of his own time by projecting it back into the wilderness period, but others dispute this since the tabernacle's design draws on premonarchical traditions and differs from Solomon's temple in numerous respects. The description of the tabernacle may correct certain ideas associated with the temple since the tabernacle was a sanctuary designed by God and made with freewill offerings, while the temple was a royal project that depended on forced labor. Moreover, God sometimes "met" with Israel in the tent sanctuary but was not confined there.

NT references to the tabernacle (Gk. *skēnḗ*) appear in the speech ascribed to Stephen, which considers the tabernacle to represent worship that was acceptable to God but criticizes the temple as an attempt to usurp God's prerogatives (Acts 7:44-50). Hebrews interprets the forecourt of the tabernacle as a symbol for the realm of the flesh and the present time, and identifies the holy of holies where Jesus carries out his high priestly ministry with the purified conscience and the new age of salvation (Heb. 8:1-6; 9:1-14). John's Gospel announces the Incarnation by saying that "the Word became flesh and tabernacled among us," as the locus of God's glory (John 1:14), and Revelation speaks of heaven and the New Jerusalem as God's "tabernacle" (Rev. 13:6; 15:5; 21:3).

Bibliography. J. I. Durham, *Exodus.* WBC 3 (Waco, 1987), esp. 349-501; M. Haran, *Temples and Temple-Service in Ancient Israel* (Oxford, 1978); C. R. Koester, *The Dwelling of God.* CBQMS 22 (Washington, 1989). CRAIG R. KOESTER

TABERNACLES, FEAST OF

The final and greatest feast of the Israelite agricultural year, one of three annual pilgrimage festivals (Exod. 23:14-19; 34:22-24; Lev. 23:33-36, 39-43; Num. 29:12-38; Deut. 16:16-17; 31:9-13). It specifically celebrated the harvest of grapes and olives and the end of the harvest season in general. The Feast of Tabernacles (or Booths) is called Sukkot(h) (or Succoth) in Hebrew (2 Chr. 8:13). The OT also refers to it as the Festival of Ingathering (Exod. 23:16; 34:22), the Feast of the Lord (Lev. 23:39, 41), or the "appointed feast" (Lam. 2:6, 7; Hos. 12:9) or even simply "the feast" (1 Kgs. 8:2, 65; 12:32).

Tabernacles shared a number of elements with other vintage feasts of the region. The Greeks and Romans of the 1st century C.E. saw similarities to their own feast for Dionysus/Bacchus (Tacitus *Hist.* 5.5; Plutarch *Quaest. Cov.* 4.6.671 D-E), and scholars have speculated on this feast's relationship to the Babylonian New Year celebration.

The Feast of Tabernacles was to be held after the harvest (Deut. 16:13; Lev. 23:39), on the 15th through the 22nd of Nissan, the seventh month (Sept.-Oct.; Lev. 23:34; Num. 29:12-38). It followed two other celebrations, the New Year (1st of Nissan) and the Day of Atonement (10th of Nissan).

The Feast of Tabernacles was a time of celebration. The seven-day feast began and ended with a special sabbath. The work of harvest completed, the people were to rest, rejoice (Lev. 23:39-40), and to eat and drink (cf. Deut. 14:22-26, a tithe of their annual crops). Celebrants were to construct temporary shelters, the "tabernacles" or "booths," in which to eat and sleep during the feast (Neh. 8:14-17), reminding them of Yahweh's protection during the wilderness wanderings (Lev. 23:42, 43). The priests offered special sacrifices, including a unique one of a descending number of bulls each day (beginning with 13 the first day and concluding with seven the final day, a total of 71) (Num. 29:13-38). Every seventh year during Tabernacles the entire Law was to be read (Deut. 31:10-11).

Postexilic observances included the lighting of giant menorahs in the temple courtyard, all-night dancing to flutes by torchlight, dawn processions ending with libations of water and wine at the bronze altar, prayers for rain and resurrection of the dead, the priests marching around the altar and the people carrying fruit and waving palm branches *(m. Sukk.)*. When the high priest Alexander Jannaeus (ca. 100 B.C.E.) refused to offer the libations properly, troops called to quell the ensuing riot left 6000 people dead (Josephus *Ant.* 13.372-73).

Tabernacles came to be tied to Jewish hopes for a Davidic messiah and national independence. Judas Maccabees used the feast as a model for his celebration of the rededication of the Jerusalem altar in 164 B.C.E. (1 Macc. 4:54-59), the first celebration of Hannukah (2 Macc. 1:1-36). Elements of the Tabernacles celebration figure in Jesus' triumphal entry and crucifixion (Mark 11:1-11 par.), reflecting the people's longing for Jewish independence (cf. quotation from the Great Hallel, Ps. 118:25-26; the title Son of David, Matt. 21:9). The leaders of both Jewish revolts against Rome (66-70 and 132-135 C.E.) also used symbols and slogans from the feast.

Only the Fourth Gospel mentions a celebration of the Feast of Tabernacles itself (John 7:2), with Jesus referring to himself as the living water, perhaps a reference to the high priest performing the dawn water libation.

Some scholars have argued that this "Feast of the Lord" was the origin of the concept of the "Day of the Lord," a major theme in the Hebrew prophets and the NT (note extensive use of harvest as an image of the end of time; e.g., Matt. 9:37-38; 13:39; John 4:35; Rom. 1:13; Rev. 14:15).

Bibliography. J. A. Draper, "The Heavenly Feast of Tabernacles: Revelation 7.1-17," *JSNT 19* (1983): 133-47; W. Harrelson, "The Celebration of the Feast of Booths according to Zech xiv,16-21," in *Religions in Antiquity*, ed. J. Neusner. NumenSup 14 (Leiden, 1968), 88-96; N. Hillyer, "First Peter and the Feast of Tabernacles," *TynBul* 21 (1970); 39-70; G. H. MacRae, "The Meaning and Evolution of the Feast of Tabernacles," *CBQ 22* (1960): 251-76; J. C. de Moor, *New Year with Canaanites and Israelites*, 2 vols. (Kampen, 1972); H. N. Richardson, "*Skt* (Amos 9:11): 'Booth' or 'Succoth'?" *JBL* 92 (1973): 375-81; H. Ulfgard, *Feast and Future: Revelation 7:9-17 and the Feast of Tabernacles.* ConBNT 22 (Lund, 1989).

TIMOTHY P. JENNEY

TABITHA (Gk. *Tabithá;* Aram. *ṭĕḇîṯāʾ*)
Aramaic name of Dorcas ("gazelle"), a Christian at Joppa noted for her good works who was raised from the dead by Peter (Acts 9:36).

TABLE OF NATIONS
Following the narrative of the Flood in Gen. 6–9, a schematic representation describing the expansion of humankind from the family of Noah to many families and their dispersion into many lands (10:1-32). In its present setting, it depicts the outworking of the divine blessing pronounced at creation and repeated after the Flood, "Be fruitful and multiply, and fill the earth" (Gen. 1:28; 9:1, 7). In contrast to the incident at Babel in Gen. 11, the Table of Nations accounts for the diversification of human language and the spreading out of peoples on the earth as a process of genealogical expansion rather than as the result of divine intervention and judgment.

The Table takes the form of a segmented genealogy in which descendants branch out in each successive generation (compare the linear genealogy of Shem in Gen. 11:10-26, where one featured individual is named in each generation). It is organized with summarizing statements at the end of each of the lines of descent from Noah's three sons, Japheth, Ham, and Shem ("These are the descendants of PN in their lands, with their own language, by their families, in their nations"; Gen. 10:5, 20, 31). It concludes with a comprehensive summary in Gen. 10:32. The emphasis in these summaries on "lands, languages, and nations" is an important clue to the nature of this genealogy, which engages in ethnography by political geography rather than by ethnic origins. The geographical range reaches from northern Africa and Ethiopia in the south to the Caucasus Mountains in the north, and from Iran in the east to the Aegean in the west (and perhaps as far as Spain).

The descendants of Japheth (Gen. 10:2-4) extend above the northern reaches of the entire Fertile Crescent and westward above the Mediterranean Sea. The line of Ham (Gen. 10:6-20) extends from the south and west (North Africa and Ethiopia) to the north and east (Mesopotamia). The descendants of Shem (from which "Semite" is derived; Gen. 10:21-31) stand roughly between the other two, stretching from Anatolia in the west toward the south into Arabia and east to Elam.

Although portions of the Table may derive from as early as the 10th century B.C.E. (the time of Solomon), other parts seem to reflect familiarity with geo-political circumstances in the 7th century and priestly redaction in the 5th century.

JEFFREY S. ROGERS

TABLELAND
That part of the Transjordanian plateau N of the Arnon River and E of the Dead Sea around the cities of Bezer and Medeba (Deut. 3:10; 4:43; Josh. 13:9, 16-17, 21; 20:8; Jer. 48:21). In its basic sense Heb. *mîšôr* designates any level ground (cf. 1 Kgs. 20:23, "plain").

TABOR (Heb. *tāḇôr*)
1. Mt. Tabor, an isolated mountain with distinctive steep slopes rising to a height of 562 m. (1843 ft.) in the northeast portion of the plain of Esdraelon (187232). In the past its slopes were densely forested. Its eastern slope is a watershed for the Jordan River. The prominence of Mt. Tabor is determined in part by the excellent view it affords of the valley, giving it control of important crossroads. One of the main routes from Hazor and Damascus in the north to the pass of Megiddo and the coastal plain goes along the northwest side of the mountain. The three tribal lands of Issachar (Josh. 19:22), Zebulun (cf. v. 12), and Naphtali (cf. v. 34) meet at Mt. Tabor. This mountain is where Barak was instructed to assemble a force of 10 thousand men (Judg. 4:14).

Apparently not integrally affiliated with any one of the tribal lands, Mt. Tabor was probably a cultic center shared by the northern tribes. Deut. 33:18-19 refers to a mountain of Zebulun and Issachar where sacrifices are offered. Hos. 5:1 mentions "a net spread upon Tabor," an expression indicating some sort of cultic practice.

Even though Tabor is not very high in absolute terms, its prominence in the plain led the psalmist (Ps. 89:12[13]) and the prophet Jeremiah (Jer. 46:18) to compare it with Mt. Carmel and Mt. Hermon, two lofty peaks which can be seen from its summit.

Although Tabor is not mentioned in the NT, since the 4th century C.E. it has been regarded by Christian tradition as the site of the transfiguration of Jesus, described as having taken place on a "high mountain" (Matt. 17:1; Mark 9:2, cf. Luke 9:28).

2. The Oak of Tabor, which marked a place in the territory of Benjamin where Samuel instructed Saul to go to after he had anointed him (1 Sam. 10:3). Located near Bethel and evidently a prominent landmark, the oak's exact site is uncertain.

3. A levitical city assigned to the Merarites (1 Chr. 6:77[MT 62]). Located on the border of Zebulun, it may be the same as Chisloth-tabor (Josh. 19:12).

JOHN GILLMAN

TABRIMMON (Heb. *ṭaḇrimmōn*)
The son of Hezion and father of King Ben-hadad I of Damascus (1 Kgs. 15:18; cf. *ANET*, 655).

TADMOR (Heb. *tadmōr;* Akk. *tadmar*)
An oasis city in the Syrian Desert, midway between Mari and Damascus, which served as an important stop along the desert trade routes between Syria-Palestine and Mesopotamia. 2 Chr. 8:4 credits Solomon with fortifying the city as part of his trading empire. The issue of whether the Tamar of 1 Kgs. 9:18 should be read as Tadmor (so **Q**, LXX Lucian) is still uncertain. Tadmor was renamed Palmyra during the Hellenistic period and destroyed by the Romans in 273 C.E.

See PALMYRA.

GARY P. ARBINO

TAHAN (Heb. *taḥan*)
A descendant of Ephraim; ancestor of the Tahanites (Num. 26:35; 1 Chr. 7:25; cf. "Tahath" at v. 20).

TAHASH (Heb. *taḥaš*)
The third son of Nahor and his concubine Reumah (Gen. 22:24).

TAHATH (Heb. *taḥaṯ*) **(PERSON)**

1. An ancestor of the prophet Samuel (1 Chr. 6:24, 37[MT 9, 22]; at v. 33[18] also Heman the temple musician). Although the genealogies of 1 Chr. 6:22-28, 33-38(7-13, 18-23) are somewhat confused, they are intended to identify Samuel as a Levite, of the family of Kohath.

2. An Ephraimite, the son of Bered (1 Chr. 7:20).

3. An Ephraimite, son of Eleadah and grandson of Tahath **2** (1 Chr. 7:20).

TAHATH (Heb. *taḥaṯ*) **(PLACE)**
A place where the Israelites camped during the wilderness wanderings (Num. 33:26-27). Its exact location is unknown.

TAHCHEMONITE (Heb. *taḥkĕmōnî*)
A gentilic ascribed to Josheb-basshebeth, one of David's warriors (2 Sam. 23:8). The name may be a scribal error for "the Hachmonite" *(haḥaḵmōnî* or *ben-ḥaḵĕmônî)*, in which case Josheb-basshebeth may be the same person as "Jashobeam, a Hachmonite" (1 Chr. 11:11).

TAHPANHES (Heb. *taḥpanḥēs;* Egyp. *t3-ḥ[t]-[n.t]-p3-nḥsy*)
An Egyptian outpost bordering Sinai, identified with classical Daphnae (Herodotus *Hist.* 2.30), modern Tell Defneh near Lake Manzaleh in the northeast Delta. The Hebrew form transcribes the Egyptian, which means "the fortress of Penhase." (Penhase was a Theban general in the 11th century B.C.E. who suppressed a rebellion in the Delta.) According to the biblical narrative Tahpanhes was a city of refuge for the Jews escaping from Palestine. It was also the place where Jeremiah ended his career (Jer. 43:7; cf. 42:19). The city is mentioned in Ezekiel's condemnation of Egypt (Ezek. 30:18, "Tehaphnehes").

William F. Albright suggested that Tell Defneh was the site of Baal-zephon, one of the places mentioned in the route of the Exodus. W. M. Flinders Petrie, who excavated the site in the 1880s, was incorrect in his interpretation of the strata. He dated the mud-brick walls beneath the 7th-century buildings to the period of Rameses II; later it was determined that they were actually foundations for the 7th-century buildings. There was no evidence of earlier occupation at the site.

LAWRENCE A. SINCLAIR

TAHPENES (Heb. *taḥpĕnês*)
An Egyptian queen whose sister became the wife of the Edomite Hadad (cf. Egyp. *t.ḥmt.nsw,* "wife of the king"), Solomon's adversary (1 Kgs. 11:19). According to 1 Kgs. 11:20 Tahpenes helped rear Hadad's son Genubath in the Egyptian court.

TAHREA (Heb. *taḥrēaʿ*) (also TAREA)
A son of Micah, and descendant of King Saul (1 Chr. 9:41); called Tarea at 8:35.

TALENT
In the OT, a unit of weight equivalent to ca. 34.27 kg. (75.6 lb.; Heb. *kikkār*); in the NT, a unit of money (not actually minted) equivalent to ca. 6000 drachmas (Gk. *tálanton*).

TALITHA CUM (Gk. *talithá koúm*)
Mark's Greek transliteration of the Aramaic phrase *ṭalyĕṯāʾ qûmî,* "little girl, arise," spoken by Jesus to Jairus' daughter as he raised her from the dead (Mark 5:41).

TALMAI (Heb. *talmay*)

1. One of the Anakim who, along with his brothers, was expelled by Caleb from Hebron (Num. 13:22; Josh. 15:14; Judg. 1:10).

2. The king of Geshur and father of Maacah, one of David's wives (2 Sam. 3:3; 13:37; 1 Chr. 3:2).

TALMON (Heb. *ṭalmōn, ṭalmôn*)
The ancestor of a family of postexilic Levite gatekeepers (1 Chr. 9:17; Ezra 2:42; Neh. 7:45; 11:19; 12:25).

TALMUD
The masterwork of rabbinic Judaism, the book that distinguishes Judaism from other faith traditions that lay claim to Hebrew Scripture and/or its tradition of prophetic revelation. The Talmud (lit., "the study") is based upon and includes the Mishnah in its entirety, but grafts to it the Gemara (lit., "the completion"), a far lengthier work woven from the discussions in the academies of Babylonia and the Galilee in the 3rd through 6th centuries C.E. Since the great bulk of the Talmud is the Gemara, the two names are often used interchangeably, except when a distinction must be made between the two parts of the talmudic text.

The Talmud follows the topical structure of the Mishnah, but differs in many other ways. It departs from the Hebrew of the Mishnah, being written in the Aramaic vernacular of most of the Middle East of that time. Where the Mishnah is concise and focused, the Gemara is expansive; where the Mishnah summarizes and codifies the law, the Gemara analyzes and debates, exposing the process of thought behind the surface, and actively engaging its readership in that process.

The authors of the Talmud and its readership understood the work as the authoritative transmission of the Torah's oral tradition. As such, it continually refers beyond its written page to the concrete realities of Jewish life, of which the Written Law is foremost. It extends itself in this way through two basic modes, *halakhah* and *haggadah.* Halakhah (lit., "walking" or "going") is law, the determination of divine instruction in precise and concrete terms; *haggadah* (lit., "telling") is the recasting of those concrete terms in light of their deeper significance. The halakhic material strives to define the divine in practical norms of behavior; the haggadic, to uncover the divinity hidden in the everyday realities and reveal the living core which animates the life defined by the law.

There are actually two Talmuds, the *Bavli* or Babylonian Talmud, produced in the academies of Sassonid Iraq and redacted primarily by R. Ashi and Ravina, and the *Yerushalmi* or Palestinian Talmud, coming from the schools in the north of the land of Israel. The Palestinian Talmud is a shorter, more difficult, and less-studied work. Political instability and religious persecution closed the academies there a full hundred years before the redaction of the Babylonian Talmud was completed, both hurrying the work of redaction and denying the environment in which an interpretive tradition could arise. By contrast, the yeshiva of Sura, the greatest of the Babylonian academies, remained a center of teaching for nearly five centuries after the Bavli's completion, ensuring a continuous interpretive tradition for the text in part produced within its doors. Accordingly, the Babylonian Talmud has been the center of religious study, and it is of greater legal authority, whereas it is usually only the accomplished scholar who ventures into the Palestinian Talmud.

The Talmud was first set in print during the late 15th century. Despite being variously banned, burned, and altered by censorship in Christian Europe, it has continuously served as the center of traditional Jewish study. In the nearly 1500 years since its redaction, it has inspired countless exegetical, homiletical, legal, and even poetic and mystical works. Its study today remains fundamental to Jewish scholarship.

Bibliography. A. Guttmann, *Rabbinic Judaism in the Making* (Detroit, 1970); A. Steinsalts, *The Essential Talmud* (1976, repr. Northvale, N.J., 1992).

SHMUEL KLATZKIN

TAMAR (Heb. *tāmār*) **(PERSON)**

1. Daughter-in-law of Judah (Gen. 38). Tamar, possibly a Canaanite woman, is given in marriage to Judah's firstborn son, Er. Because he "was wicked in the sight of the Lord," Er is killed by the Lord, before he can sire a son (Gen. 38:7). Judah's next son Onan is given to Tamar to perform the duties of levirate marriage (Deut. 25:5-10), but withdraws before climax, spilling his semen upon the ground, and so is killed by the Lord. Judah, having but one son left, refuses to give him to Tamar.

Tamar then sees to it herself that an offspring be raised up for her dead husband. Dressing as a harlot, she sits by the city gate, enticing Judah to have intercourse with her. She becomes pregnant, and when her pregnancy can no longer be hidden, Judah seeks to burn her as a harlot. When Tamar produces Judah's signet, staff, and cord, convincing evidence that Judah is the father, he acknowledges that she is more righteous than he, since he himself had violated the levirate requirements by refusing to give her his son Shelah. She gives birth to twins, Perez and Zerah, the former being a key ancestor of David (Ruth 4:12, 18). Tamar is one of four women included in Matthew's genealogy of Jesus (Matt. 1:3).

2. Daughter of David and Maacah. She was the half sister of Amnon, David's oldest and the heir apparent, and full sister of Absalom, the second in line for the throne. Amnon falls madly in love with Tamar, and is desperate to have relations with her (2 Sam. 13). He finally gets her into his chambers through the ruse of being sick and needing Tamar to nurse him, but Tamar stoutly resists his advances, asking that they be married first (2 Sam. 13:12-13). After he forces himself on Tamar, Amnon's love turns to hate and he orders her to leave. Tamar protests that this is worse than the rape itself (2 Sam. 13:16), so Amnon thrusts her out of his chambers. Absalom comforts her and, biding his time, takes advantage of the opportunity to kill his brother, thereby avenging Tamar (2 Sam. 13:23-39). There is more to this story than vengeance, however, since by having Amnon killed Absalom becomes David's oldest living son, and therefore the presumed heir to the throne.

3. Absalom's only daughter (2 Sam. 14:27), most likely named after Absalom's sister. Some ancient manuscripts list Maacah rather than Tamar as Absalom's daughter (LXX, OL), but it seems probable that Tamar is the original reading and that Maacah perhaps appeared through a scribal change based on 1 Kgs. 15:2.

Bibliography. G. W. Coats, Jr., "Widow's Rights: A Crux in the Structure of Genesis 38," *CBQ* 34 (1972): 461-66; C. Conroy, *Absalom Absalom! Narrative and Language in 2 Samuel 13–20.* AnBib 81 (Rome, 1978); J. A. Emerton, "Judah and Tamar," *VT* 29 (1979): 403-15; S. Niditch, "The Wronged Woman Righted: An Analysis of Genesis 38," *HTR* 72 (1979): 143-49. ALAN J. HAUSER

TAMAR (Heb. *tāmār*) **(PLACE)**

1. A city "in the wilderness" fortified by Solomon (1 Kgs. 9:18 **K**), along with Hazor, Megiddo, and Gezer (**Q** "Tadmor").

2. A site marking the southeastern border of the restored, ideal Israel (Ezek. 47:18-19; 48:28). This would place Tamar in the Arabah on the eastern fringes of the Negeb. The Madeba Map locates a Thamara in the Arabah, which many scholars have identified with Roman remains at Qaṣr el-Juheiniyeh (173048), 21 km. (13 mi.) WSW of the Dead Sea. There is stronger evidence, however, to associate Tamar with Iron Age remains at ʿEn Ḥaṣeva/ʿAin Ḥuṣb (173024), 40 km. (25 mi.) SW of the Dead Sea. The latter site coalesces well with the Madeba Map and satisfies the place name connection between Iron Age, Roman, and Byzantine periods. The stratum VI fortress at ʿEn Ḥaṣeva holds the potential for a 10th-century B.C.E. date, placing it theoretically within an acceptable Solomonic time frame. It is identified with Hazazon-tamar at 2 Chr. 20:2.

Bibliography. R. Cohen and Y. Yisrael, "The Iron Age Fortresses at ʿEn Ḥaṣeva," *BA* 58 (1995): 223-35. RYAN BYRNE

TAMARISK

Twelve species of the tamarisk (genus *Tamarix;* Heb. *ʾēšel*) are found in or near Palestine. They are found in the thickets of Jordan, in the swamps of the Dead Sea, and along the coastal plains of the Negeb and Sinai. One species can grow to a height of 60 m. (20 ft.); it has small leaves and requires a high intake of water and was large enough to provide shade from the sun (1 Sam. 22:6).

According to Gen. 21:33 Abraham planted a tamarisk tree in Beer-sheba to identify the place where he called upon the name of the Lord. The tree was significant enough as an identification marker that the men of Jabesh-gilead buried the bones of Saul and his sons under a tamarisk tree (1 Sam. 31:13). Christian tradition from as early as St. Anthony (A.D. 250-355) suggests that the biblical manna came from the secretion of insects on the branches of tamarisk trees. JOHN A. MCLEAN

TAMBOURINE

See TIMBREL.

TAMMUZ (Heb. *tammûz;* Sum. *Dumuzi*)

A Mesopotamian deity attested from the 3rd–1st millennia B.C.E. While the variety of traditions portraying Tammuz almost defies a singular and coherent characterization of the deity, he is represented consistently as a young man who dies too young, the object of women's grief. The literature focuses on his marriage to Inanna/Ishtar and his premature death. Sumerian myth relates how the young shepherd-god Dumuzi, murdered while tending his flock in the desert, was mourned by his mother, sister, and wife. Lamentation for Dumuzi, the subject of songs and liturgical compositions in Sumerian and Akkadian, was observed annually in ritual form, probably during the fourth month, which in the Babylonian calendar bears his name (*Du'uzu,* June-July; cf. Ezek. 8:1, 14). Mesopotamian worship of Dumuzi, who was not among the chief gods, was popular in nature and mostly distinct from the official religion of festivals and temple cult. Ezekiel's portrayal of the predominantly female worship of Dumuzi (Ezek. 8:14) is consistent with the following: a reference to large numbers of women mourning (apparently) for Dumuzi at Mari (ARM 9:175); the preponderance of *emesal* (a literary dialect of Sumerian employed for women's speech) in 1st-millennium texts about Dumuzi; and the persistence of ritual mourning for Ta'uz (Tammuz) into the 10th century C.E. among Sabean women in Harran.

The influential view of James G. Frazer and S. H. Langdon, that Tammuz was a "dying and rising" vegetation deity corresponding to Egyptian Osiris and Phoenician/Greek Adonis, is no longer viable. It is only in Dumuzi's identification with other minor gods that he takes on the attributes of a seasonal vegetation deity. The only evidence for Tammuz' return from the dead (a fragmentary passage in the Akkadian myth, The Descent of Ishtar to the Netherworld) is disputed. The Vulg. of Ezek. 8:14 substitutes the name Adonis for Tammuz, implying an equation of the two gods that is otherwise first attested in Origen. There is no evidence either to support or deny that "the beloved of women" (Heb. *ḥemdaṯ nāšîm*) in Dan. 11:37 is Tammuz or Adonis.

Bibliography. B. Alster, "Tammuz," *DDD,* 828-34; O. R. Gurney, "Tammuz Reconsidered: Some Recent Developments," *JSS* 7 (1962): 147-60; T. Jacobsen, "Toward the Image of Tammuz," *HR* 1 (1961): 189-213; repr. in *Toward the Image of Tammuz,* ed. W. L. Moran (Cambridge, Mass., 1979), 73-101; R. Kutscher, "The Cult of Dumuzi/Tammuz," in *Bar-Ilan Studies in Assyriology Dedicated to Pinhas Artzi,* ed. J. Klein and A. Skaist (Ramat Gan, 1990), 29-44. JOEL BURNETT

TANHUMETH (Heb. *tanḥumeṯ*)
A Netophathite and the father of Seraiah, a general in Judah when Gedaliah was governor (2 Kgs. 25:23; Jer. 40:8).

TANIS (Gk. *Tanís*)
Greek name of Zoan, a major Egyptian city on the Tanitic branch of the Nile in the eastern Delta (Jdt. 1:10).

TANNING
A process employing a variety of materials and solutions to transform tough animal hides into a soft and pliable product. Evidence from texts and paintings indicates the ancient technology can be traced to Egypt, and required the scraping away of animal hair and flesh from the skin, after which application of lime, juice from certain plants, and the bark or leaves of certain trees produced the desired effect. A form of Heb. *'āḏōm* (used for animal skins dyed red) carried with it a reflection of this process (Exod. 25:5; 26:14; 35:7, 23; 36:19; 39:34), since tanning a skin tended to produce a reddish appearance. The LXX uses Gk. *ēruthrodanōména,* "to dye red."

Tanned skins served a variety of uses, functioning as hangings in the tabernacle (Exod. 25:5; 26:14), as well as in the production of clothing, leather buckets, waterskins, wineskins, and butter churns (Gen. 21:14; Judg. 4:19; Matt. 9:17). Whole hides of animals with the holes sewn up served as household containers, storing such items as oil for cooking, toiletry items, medicine, and fuel for lamps. Leather was used for furniture, as well as the production of weapons such as shields, helmets, slings, and quivers. John the Baptist was known for his leather belt (Matt. 3:4; Mark 1:6), as was Elijah, his predecessor (2 Kgs. 1:8).

Living near a tanner was not considered a pleasant experience due to the odor produced in the process of working with animal hides. Simon the tanner (Gk. *byrseús*) lived outside of the city of Joppa (Acts 9:43; 10:6, 32). Talmudic literature frequently confirms this negative attitude toward tanners. Peter's decision to stay with Simon the tanner highlights the apostle's receptivity to the accessibility of the gospel to those once considered unclean.

Bibliography. R. J. Forbes, "Leather in Antiquity," *Studies in Ancient Technology* 5, rev. ed. (Leiden, 1966): 1-79.
Dennis Gaertner

TAPHATH (Heb. *ṭāpaṯ*)
The daughter of King Solomon and wife of Ben-abinadab, administrator of the district of Naphath-dor (1 Kgs. 4:11).

TAPPUAH (Heb. *tappûaḥ*) (also EN-TAPPUAH)
1. A town in the northern Shephelah, the second district of Judah (Josh. 15:34). This town should not be confused with Beth-tappuah, which is listed in the eighth district (Josh. 15:53). The modern identification of the town is unknown, although the village of Beit Natif (149122), ca. 19 km. (12 mi.) W of Bethlehem, has been suggested.

2. A town (also called En-tappuah) that forms the northern border of Ephraim (Josh. 16:8). Although the town belonged to Ephraim, the land of Tappuah belonged to Manasseh (Josh. 17:8). It is commonly identified with the modern Sheikh Abû Zarad (172168), ca. 19 km. (12 mi.) S of Shechem.

3. A town in the territory of Tirzah that King Menahem destroyed (2 Kgs. 15:16). The MT reads *tip̱saḥ* (NRSV "Tiphsah"), which is located on the Euphrates and unlikely to have been sacked by Menahem. Many versions and commentators emend the text to Tappuah following the LXX, which reads *Taphōe.* This town is not likely to be identified with the Tappuah of Ephraim, since the latter is located too far from Tirzah (Tell el-Fâr'ah) — ca. 22 km. (14 mi.) — to be considered within its territory.
Ronald A. Simkins

TARALAH (Heb. *tar'ălâ*)
A town in the tribal territory of Benjamin (Josh. 18:27), in the district NW of Jerusalem. A suggested site is Khirbet Irha, located near Tell el-Fûl (Gibeah).

TAREA (Heb. *ta'rēa'*) (also TAHREA)
A descendant of King Saul (1 Chr. 8:35). At 1 Chr. 8:41 he is called Tahrea.

TARGUM
A written translation or paraphrase of a biblical text. The need for rendering the Bible into Aramaic or Greek arose in the Second Temple period, when for many Jews the Hebrew of ancient Scriptures ceased to be the spoken language. The Greek LXX and Aramaic Targum of Job discovered at Qumran (11QTJob) are evidence that in prerabbinic Judaism translating had already developed into a complex process, through which the original text was expanded with interpolated exegetical interpretations. By establishing rules and limitations, the Mishnah testified to the struggle of the rising rabbinic movement to control this phenomenon after the 1st century C.E. These rules first applied to both Aramaic and Greek translations. The need for setting clear boundaries between rabbinic Judaism and Christianity, however, gradually led the rabbis to abandon Greek as a legitimate language of theological discourse and to concentrate exclusively on Aramaic. So, while "Targum" could designate a translation of a biblical text into any language, it is to the corpus of Aramaic versions composed in rabbinic times that the term more specifically applies. The rabbis realized the importance of Targum as a highly effective means of religious education in schools, as well as in the liturgical setting of the synagogue. The Targum was understood as part of the Oral Torah. Its haggadah was tendentially harmonized to the rabbinic theological and halakhic principles. The culmination of this process was the composition in Babylon of official rabbinic Targums (Onkelos to the Pentateuch and Jonathan to the Prophets).

Rabbinic authorities found it very difficult to control these autonomous and creative techniques of translation on which the Targums were based. In many cases, the antiquity of targumic tradition demonstrated an amazing power of resistance, stronger than any attempt to censorship. Its captivating exegesis never ceased to attract the curiosity, if not the religious consensus, of readers and scholars who, as late as the Middle Ages, continued to write in this tradition and took pleasure in making copies of earlier Targums.

A chronology of extant rabbinic Targums can be only tentatively reconstructed. The presence of premishnaic traits suggests that the composition of the Targum Neofiti might go back to the 2nd century C.E. Closely related to Neofiti but certainly later is the Fragmentary Targum, which owes its name to its survival only in scholarly excerpts. The redaction of the Targum Onkelos probably took place in the 4th or 5th century and marked the most consistent attempt to rabbinize the Targum and produce an official standard text. From talmudic times (7th-8th century) comes finally the most expansive of the Targums of the Pentateuch, the Targum Pseudo-Jonathan, which represents a sort of summa of centuries of exegetical creativity and rabbinic ingenuity (and censorship), in a uniquely free combination of early and late traditions. The composition of the Targums to the Prophets and the Writings (only Ezra-Nehemiah and Daniel are without Targums) is generally dated to talmudic and posttalmudic times, even though it is apparent that some of them also contain pieces of ancient exegesis.

Bibliography. P. V. M. Flesher, "The Targumim in the Context of Rabbinic Literature," in J. Neusner, *Introduction to Rabbinic Literature* (New York, 1994), 611-29; M. McNamara, *The New Testament and the Palestinian Targums to the Pentateuch.* AnBib 27A (1966, repr. Rome, 1978); McNamara and D. R. G. Beattie, eds., *The Aramaic Bible: Targums in Their Historical Context.* JSOTSup 166 (Sheffield, 1994). GABRIELE BOCCACCINI

TARSHISH (Heb. *taršîš*) **(PERSON)**

1. One of the descendants of Javan (Greece) named in the Table of Nations (Gen. 10:4 = 1 Chr. 1:7).

2. A Benjaminite, the son of Bilhan (1 Chr. 7:10).

3. One of the officials of Persia and Media, who had access to the king (Esth. 1:14). As yet the name has not been found in extrabiblical sources.

Bibliography. A. R. Millard, "The Persian Names in Esther and the Reliability of the Hebrew Text," *JBL* 96 (1977): 481-88. ISAAC KALIMI

TARSHISH (Heb. *taršîš*) **(PLACE)**

A seaport which exported silver, iron, tin, and lead to Tyre (Ezek. 27:12). Tarshish was located far away from Phoenicia and the land of Israel (Isa. 66:19; Jonah 1:3; Ps. 72:10), but its exact location is vague.

Some scholars place Tarshish in Africa, somewhere on the coast of the Red Sea, which is rich with the precious stone by the same name in Hebrew (Exod. 28:20; 39:13; Ezek. 28:13; cf. Cant. 5:14; Ezek 10:9; Dan. 10:6). According to this view, the designation "ships of Tarshish" refers to their cargo: "stone of Tarshish." This unique type of ships was distinguished by its strength, large size, and peculiar shape, which allowed the ships to sail long distances in the open sea. Such ships were in the service of Tyre as well as Israel (1 Kgs. 10:22; 22:49; Isa. 2:16; 23:1, 14; Ezek. 27:25; Ps. 48:7[MT 8]). However, there is no evidence that King Solomon and Hiram king of Tyre (cf. 1 Kgs. 10:22) imported this stone from Tarshish. Likewise, 2 Chr. 9:21; 20:36-37, which place Tarshish on the Red Sea coast, to which one sailed from Ezion-geber, are misinterpretations of this expression.

That Tarshish is located on the Mediterranean coast emerges clearly from the inscription of King Esarhaddon of Assyria: "All the kings from (the islands) amidst the sea — from the country Iadanana (Cyprus), as far as Tarsisi, bowed to my feet and I received heavy tribute (from them)" (*ANET,* 290). This is also the background of the story in Jonah 1:3 which relates that the prophet Jonah fled from God's mission by a ship which sailed from the port of Joppa to Tarshish, W of the Mediterranean Sea. The Table of Nations in Gen. 10:4-5 (= 1 Chr. 1:7) reckons Tarshish among other "descendants" of Javan (Greece): Elishah (Cyprus), Kittim, and Rodanim are all located in the Mediterranean Sea.

It is reasonable to identify Tarshish with Tharsis in southwestern Spain, in the Guadalquivir Valley. This place, which was colonized by the Phoenicians, is well known for its metals and precious stones. It is called Tartessus in the classical sources (Strabo *Geog.* 3.2.11; Pliny *Nat. hist.* 37.43). According to Herodotus (*Hist.* 4.152) it is placed "beyond the Pillars of Heracles." The LXX reading of Ezek. 27:12 (Gk. *Karchedónioi,* "Carthage") does not necessarily indicate identification with Carthage in North Africa, since there is a "Carthage" also on the west coast of Spain (Strabo *Geog.* 3.2.10).

The name Tarshish may be derived from Akk. *rašašu,* "to be smelted," as suggested by William F. Albright.

Bibliography. W. F. Albright, "The Role of the Canaanites in the History of Civilization," in *The Bible and the Ancient Near East,* ed. G. E. Wright (1961, repr. Garden City, 1965), 438-87; M. Elat, "Tarshish and the Problem of Phoenician Colonisation in the Western Mediterranean," *Orientalia lovaniensia periodica* 13 (1982): 56-69.

ISAAC KALIMI

TARSUS (Gk. *Tarsós*)

The capital of Cilicia in Asia Minor, located on both sides of the Cydnus River ca. 19 km. (12 mi.) inland from the Mediterranean and 40 km. (25 mi.) S of the Cilician Gates, which for three millennia have been the only major pass through the Taurus mountain range between Cilicia and Syria. Because of its strategic location (the Cydnus River was navigable only to the port of Rhegma at Tarsus, where several of the most important roads of Cilicia converged), it became one of the most prominent places in Asia Minor, developing important commercial and social relations with other cities and countries. Archaeological excavations show that it was inhabited from the Neolithic Age until the Islamic invasions.

While the people of Tarsus claimed that their city was founded by Perseus and Hercules, it was settled by Greeks after the Trojan War and developed during the period of Greek colonization. First mentioned in historical record as being rebuilt under the Assyrians by Sennacherib (704-681 B.C.E.), it had a long history as a Semitic town. Xenophon described it during the 5th century as a great and prosperous place (*Anab.* 1.2). During the Persian period it was ruled by satraps (provincial governors). Alexander the Great prevented the Persians from burning the city (333). It was fought over by his successors, submitting for a while to the Ptolemaic Dynasty but dominated mostly by the Seleucid Dynasty. As a result it was renamed Antioch on the Cydnus (after Antiochus Epiphanes, the Syrian king).

Pompey made Tarsus part of the Roman province of Cilicia in 67 B.C.E., during his attempt to exterminate the pirates from the rugged western coastlands of the country. Cicero served as proconsul in Tarsus during the year 51-50 B.C.E. In the civil war between Caesar and Pompey (47 B.C.E.) the people of Tarsus sided with Caesar, and to honor him changed the name of the city to Juliopolis. Mark Antony declared it a free city and made it exempt from taxes. It was here in 41 B.C.E. that Mark Antony first met Cleopatra, who sailed up the Cydnus disguised as Aphrodite. During the reign of Augustus Paul was born in Tarsus, the population grew to about one half million, and the city reached its peak. It was a strategic location for the Romans during their campaigns against the Parthians and the Persians.

Strabo describes the city during the 1st century C.E. as surpassing Athens and Alexandria in culture and learning (*Geog.* 14.5.131). The city had a long history as a seat of learning and a school of philosophy.

Perhaps Tarsus' greatest claim to fame is as the birthplace of the Apostle Paul (Acts 9:11, 30; 11:25; 21:39; 22:3). Whether Paul acquired his Greek and Roman education in Tarsus or as a youth in Jerusalem (Acts 22:3) is debatable.

Bibliography. M. Gough, "Tarsus," in *The Princeton Encyclopedia of Classical Sites,* ed. R. Stilwell (Princeton, 1976), 883-84; W. Smith, *A Dictionary of Greek and Roman Geography* (1873, repr. New York, 1966) 2:1105-6.

RICHARD A. SPENCER

TARTAK (Heb. *tartāq*)
A deity worshipped by the Avvites (2 Kgs. 17:31). Tartak is probably to be identified with Atargatis, the Syrian fish-goddess and consort of Dagon; she was worshipped in Babylonia as Derketo, mother of the city's legendary founder, Semiramis.

TARTAN (Heb. *tartān;* Akk. *turtānu, tartanu*)
A high functionary in the Assyrian army, possibly commander in chief (so NRSV at Isa. 20:1); the NJB rendering "cupbearer in chief" suggests an even more significant rank. The OT alludes to two such officials without giving their names: one sent by Sargon II to destroy Ashdod (Isa. 20:1; 711 B.C.E.) and the other dispatched by Sennacherib to King Hezekiah of Judah (2 Kgs. 18:17; 701).

TASSEL
A pendant ornament for clothing and other articles made by fastening a bunch of cords or threads of even length at one end. The Israelites were to make tassels (Heb. *gĕḏilîm*) for the four corners of their cloaks (Deut. 22:12; cf. Num. 15:37-39, *ṣiṣiṯ*). Heb. *gĕḏilîm* occurs elsewhere in the OT only at 1 Kgs. 7:17, where it describes a lattice-work construction giving a chainlike or wreathlike effect to the capitals at the tops of the two bronze pillars at the vestibule of Solomon's temple. This use is similar to the use of *ṣiṣiṯ,* "fringe," in Ezek. 8:3 (NRSV "lock [of hair]"), in that it is suggestive of the appearance of tassels but does little to elucidate their purpose. If "fringe" and "tassel" are synonymous, then the Deuteronomic law is an abridged reference to a dress custom that is designed to remind individuals of their covenant obligations. KEVIN D. HALL

TATIAN
Second-century C.E. Christian apologist who composed the Diatessaron.

See DIATESSARON; SYRIAC VERSIONS.

TATTENAI (Aram. *tattĕnay*)
The Persian governor of the province Beyond the River (Ezra 5:3, 6; 6:6, 13). He informed King Darius I Hystaspes concerning the reconstruction of Jerusalem (ca. 520 B.C.E.) and was instructed not to hamper this work.

TAX
Wide variations existed in the ways that governments secured revenues for their operation in ancient times, including fees, fines, rents, and property, personal, and travel taxes. The most direct form of governmental acquisition of resources was forced labor (Heb. *mas*), the conscription of laborers to complete tasks assigned by the rulers (e.g., Josh. 16:10; 2 Sam. 20:24; 1 Kgs. 12:18). Most taxes, however, were of two sorts, direct and indirect. A regular system of taxation is prescribed in Lev. 27:1-8. David's census appears to have been part of a systematic taxation of Israel (2 Sam. 24). Occasional taxations are also mentioned: Jehoash's tax for repairs to the temple (2 Kgs. 12:4-18); Menahem's tax on the wealthy to bribe the king of Assyria (15:20); Jehoiakim's tax which he gave to Pharaoh Neco (23:35).

During the early period of the Roman Republic the rent of public lands brought in governmental revenues. From the 2nd century B.C.E., however, Rome's wealth was increased enormously by the conquest of foreign peoples and the confiscation of their resources. Later, a system of taxes was introduced. Paul advised his readers to pay the Romans both direct and indirect taxes (Rom. 13:6-7). The direct tax, known as the "tribute" (Gk. *phóros;* Lat.

tributum), was a tax on land *(tributum soli)* or a personal tax on everyone of taxable age *(tributum capitis),* used to support the Roman military presence, to foster building programs, and for general maintenance of the empire. It was collected by Roman procurators. When natural disasters occurred, emperors often lifted the burden of this tax from the affected town or province. The indirect taxes (Gk. *télos;* Lat. *vectigal*) were taxes levied in self-governing townships. They included taxes on imports and exports *(portorium),* a 5 percent inheritance tax *(vicesima hereditatium),* a 5 percent emancipation tax *(vicesima libertatis),* a 1 percent tax on public auctions (which went to the military pension fund), a 4 percent tax on the sale of slaves (to support the local police), and other local taxes such as tolls at bridges and ferries and taxes on houses and builders.

For collecting some of these taxes, a system of "tax farming" was used by the Romans, whereby the government auctioned off contracts to publicans (wealthy tax collectors) who would pay the Romans out of their own pockets and then collect from the public as much as they wanted to recover their investment. These greedy and cruel profiteers made their profit by collecting much more than they spent for their contracts (cf. Luke 19:2-8). The system allowed constant abuses of the public. We have evidence from Egypt that occasionally the publicans were accompanied by the military or police to extort money from the public.

Another kind of tax mentioned in the NT is the temple tax, a tax of one half shekel paid annually in March by Jewish men to help with the upkeep of the Jerusalem temple (Matt. 17:24-27).

RICHARD A. SPENCER

TEACHING

Jesus is presented in the NT Gospels as a teacher (Gk. *didáskalos*) or "rabbi" (Mark 4:38; 9:5; John 1:38), teaching *(didaskeín)* "with authority" (Mark 1:22; Luke 4:32). In Matthew Jesus gives the disciples authority to continue this teaching (Matt. 28:19-20). For John, Jesus' teaching authority is from the Father (John 8:28); the Holy Spirit will teach the disciples when Jesus departs (14:26; cf. Luke 12:12 par.).

The NT distinguishes between teaching and proclaiming or preaching (Acts 4:2; 1 Tim. 5:17). The subject matter of teaching is vague; it included but went beyond the basic *kḗrygma* of preaching. Jas. 3:1 emphasizes the serious burden of the teacher's task.

Paul understands teaching as one of the individual spiritual gifts to be used for the benefit of the whole body of Christ (Rom. 12:7). In 1 Cor. 12:28 the office of teacher is listed third (after apostles and prophets; cf. Eph. 4:11). Paul himself is occasionally presented as a teacher (of traditions, 2 Thess. 2:15; of "my ways in Christ Jesus," 1 Cor. 4;17; cf. Col. 1:28; 1 Tim. 2:7).

Gk. *didaskalía* occurs 15 times in the Pastoral Letters as a term for authoritative Christian doctrine (cf. *didachḗ* in Acts 2:42; Rom. 6:17; 16:17; 2 John 9-10). The teaching of "sound doctrine" (1 Tim. 1:10; Titus 1:9) is opposed to false teachings (1 Tim. 1:3-7; Titus 1:10-16), and is linked to proper interpretation of Scripture (1 Tim. 1:8-11; 2 Tim. 3:16). The Pastorals emphasize the teaching office of the bishop (1 Tim. 3:2; Titus 1:9); women are not to teach men (1 Tim. 2:12; but cf. Titus 2:3).

Bibliography. J. A. Fitzmyer, "The Office of Teaching in the Christian Church According to the New Testament," in *Teaching Authority and Infallibility in the Church,* ed. P. C. Empie, T. A. Murphy, and J. A. Burgess (Minneapolis, 1980), 186-212; response by J. Reumann, 213-31. MARTIN C. ALBL

TEACHING OF THE TWELVE APOSTLES

See DIDACHE.

TEBAH (Heb. *ṭeḇaḥ*)

The eldest son of Nahor and his concubine Reumah (Gen. 22:24). His name is associated with the city Tibhath (1 Chr. 18:8), which he may have founded (cf. Betah, 2 Sam. 8:8).

TEBALIAH (Heb. *ṭĕḇalyāhû*)

A levitical gatekeeper, the third son of Hosah, and a descendant of Merari (1 Chr. 26:11).

TEBETH (Heb. *ṭēḇēṯ;* Akk. *ṭebītu*)

The tenth month of the Hebrew year (Dec.-Jan.).

TEHAPHNEHES (Heb. *tĕḥapnĕḥēs*)

Alternate name of the Egyptian outpost Tahpanhes (Ezek. 30:18).

TEHINNAH (Heb. *tĕḥinnâ*)

A Judahite, son of Eshton and "father" (founder) of Irnahash (1 Chr. 4:12).

TEKOA (Heb. *tĕqôaʿ*)

A town in the hill country of Judah, fortified by Rehoboam (2 Chr. 11:6). Tekoa also refers to the wilderness region E of the town (2 Chr. 20:20; cf. 1 Macc. 9:33, where the wilderness was Jonathan's theater of operations during the Maccabean Revolt). The ancient town, which apparently flourished up to the time of the Crusades, is almost certainly to be located at modem Khirbet Tequʿa (170115), ca. 10 km. (6 mi.) S of Bethlehem (cf. Josh. 15:59a LXX).

One of David's Mighty Men, Ira son of Ikkesh, came from Tekoa (2 Sam. 23:26; 1 Chr. 27:9), as did the prophet Amos (Amos 1:1). Joab sought the assistance of a wise woman from Tekoa in his attempt to reconcile David with his son Absalom (2 Sam. 14:2), and the inhabitants of Tekoa were among those who rebuilt the wall of Jerusalem after their return from Babylonian exile (Neh. 3:5, 27).

WADE R. KOTTER

TEL-ABIB (Heb. *tēl ʾāḇîḇ*)

A mound of ruins in Babylon (Akk. *Til-abûbi,* "mound of the flood") where a group of Jewish exiles lived (Ezek. 3:15). It was located by the Chebar River, a canal near Babylon.

TELAH (Heb. *telaḥ*)
An Ephraimite, son of Resheph and ancestor of Joshua (1 Chr. 7:25).

TELAIM
The place where Saul mustered and numbered his troops before attacking the Amalekites (1 Sam. 15:4). *BDB* derives the name from a verb meaning "spotted" or "variegated," typically concerning the markings on sheep and goats. A second plural noun *tĕlāʾîm* means "lambs" or "kids," leading to the suggestion that Telaim was associated with sheep. Its location is unknown, though it probably was in southern Judah, not far from Edom, where the Amalekites lived. The LXX reads "at Gilgal," but that is likely an example of a tradition moving to a better-known location with which the hero of a story is often associated. PAUL L. REDDITT

TEL-ASSAR (Heb. *tĕlaʾśśār, tĕlaśśār*)
A place inhabited by the "people of Eden," named in a message of an Assyrian official to King Hezekiah of Judah as one of the places destroyed by Assyrian forces (2 Kgs. 19:12; Isa. 37:12). It is perhaps to be identified with Til Aššuri, a site on the middle Euphrates, or with Til Barsip (Tell Aḥmar) on the eastern bank of the Euphrates.

TELEM (Heb. *ṭelem*) **(PERSON)**
A postexilic levitical gatekeeper among those who divorced their foreign wives (Ezra 10:24).

TELEM (Heb. *ṭelem*) **(PLACE)**
A city in the Negeb region of Judah (Josh. 15:24). It is generally identified with Telaim.

TEL-HARSHA (Heb. *tēl ḥaršāʾ*)
A Babylonian town of unknown location, mentioned in the census of the first return from exile to Jerusalem in 537 B.C.E. (Ezra 2:59; Neh. 7:61; cf. 1 Esdr. 5:36). It is listed among other cities whose citizens were not able to prove their Jewish lineage by appropriate genealogies. C. MACK ROARK

TELL (also TEL)
A settlement in the form of a mound, often found in otherwise level countryside. Related words are *tepe, huyuk,* and *khirbet,* and all have been used as elements of modern names and in ancient site identifications made from them. Biblical references are made to both the location of ruins and to existing cities built on mounds.

Tells are the result of a specific type of architecture — mudbrick. They are most characteristic of areas without access to large quantities of alternative building materials such as stone or timber, as is the case in most of Syria-Palestine and Mesopotamia. Mud-brick architecture, though fairly durable when properly maintained, must often be torn down and rebuilt. The tell is formed when this happens, and when abandoned structures disintegrate and new ones are constructed directly on top of their remains. Thus each successive building phase is on a raised surface, and the result is the formation of a mound or tell.

In an environment with scant water supplies, ancient inhabitants often preferred to stay in one place rather than move to another. Tells consequently appear along waterways and close to springs or are placed in other strategic locations such as the center of an area capable of supporting a large population or with good access to raw materials. Others are situated in strategic political positions in naturally defensive areas or on boundaries between political or ethnic entities. Most tell definitions cite the availability of water as the major deciding feature, but this may be overridden by the significance of religion as at, e.g., Jerusalem (though it originally was chosen as a settlement for its neutrality at the time of the Israelite monarchy).

Tells have often been lumped together and referred to in generalities. William G. Dever, however, stresses the uniqueness of each tell and its reflection of individual settlement history. The recognition of these histories is hindered by the complexity of stratigraphy at these sites, making them difficult to excavate. Though easy to identify, the chances of the entire settlement area being delineated are very slim since buildings on the edge are much more vulnerable to wind and rain and the outer limits are likely to be eroded away. Thus the maximum extent of occupation is often obliterated. Additionally, the history of the tell is further obscured since earlier periods may be many meters below the tell surface.

Bibliography. W. G. Dever, "The Tell: Microcosm of the Cultural Process," in *Retrieving the Past,* ed. J. D. Seger (Winona Lake, 1996), 37-45.
KATHARINE A. MACKAY

TELL EL-AMARNA
See AMARNA.

TEL-MELAH (Heb. *tēl melaḥ*)
A site, probably in Babylonia, from which Jewish exiles returned to Judah (Ezra 2:59; Neh. 7:61; 1 Esdr. 5:36). These returnees were among those who could not prove their Israelite ancestry and thus were excluded from the priesthood.
STEPHEN J. ANDREWS

TEMA (Heb. *têmāʾ*) **(PERSON)**
A son of Ishmael (Gen. 25:15; 1 Chr. 1:30), eponymous ancestor of an Arabian tribe and associated with an oasis city in northwest Arabia (Isa. 21:14; Jer. 25:23).

TEMA (Heb. *têmāʾ*) **(PLACE)**
A city in north Arabia (Isa. 21:14; Jer. 25:23) associated with a son of Ishmael (Gen. 25:15; 1 Chr. 1:30). Tema (Taymâʾ; modern Teimā, 360 km. [220 mi.] ESE of Aqaba) was an important commercial center located at the convergence of three important trade routes (Job 6:19). In 553/552 it became the headquarters for Nabonidus, the last Neo-Babylonian (or Chaldean) king. Nabonidus' son Belshazzar ruled in his place in Babylon while the king resided in Tema. The city was probably a center for

Persian power in north Arabia during the 5th century B.C.E.

Bibliography. C. Edens and G. Bawden, "History of Taymā' and Hejazi Trade during the First Millennium B.C.," *JESHO* 32 (1989): 48-103.

C. Shaun Longstreet

TEMAH (Heb. *temaḥ*)
A temple servant whose descendants returned with Zerubbabel from captivity in Babylon (Ezra 2:53; Neh. 7:55).

TEMAN (Heb. *têmān*), **TEMANITE** *(têmānî)*
A grandson of Esau and son of Eliphaz (Gen. 36:9-11); eponymous ancestor of an Edomite clan.

Teman appears as a parallel expression for the Edomite nation in several instances (Jer. 49:20; Amos 1:12; Gen. 36:34; 1 Chr. 1:45). As a result of Teman's genealogical connection to Esau and the linguistic synonymity with Edom, the location of Teman is generally placed within Edom. (The Hebrew term means "on the right side" or "southern.") The traditional locale is Tawīlân (197971), NE of Elji. Archaeological evidence suggests a site of significant size, while vast pottery finds imply the traffic of busy trade routes within a central Edomite location.

"Temanite" (Heb. *têmānî*) refers to one from the clan of Teman or the land of Teman (Gen. 36:34; 1 Chr. 1:45). One of the monarchs of Edom was a Temanite named Husham (Gen. 36:31-34). In Job 2:11 "Eliphaz the Temanite" may refer to one from Tema in Arabia (Job 6:19). J. Randall O'Brien

TEMENI (Heb. *têmĕnî*)
A son of Ashhur and Naarah of the tribe of Judah (1 Chr. 4:6). The name appears to be a gentilic (NJB "Timnites"), meaning "the people of the south."

TEMPLE
A sacred, demarcated place. The English term derives from Lat. *templum,* a place set aside for the purpose of augury (Varro *De ling. lat.*; cf. "contemplate"). A Greek cognate, *témenos,* was a precinct, a piece of land marked off from common uses and dedicated to a god; the term now means the platform on which the temple building stands — an architectural structure that separated the building off from common, everyday activities (cf. Sum. *temen,* a heaped-up pile of earth, as in *É-temen-an-ki,* the "House of the Foundation of Heaven and Earth," the Neo-Babylonian ziggurat and traditional tower of Babel).

The Babylonian temple unites the three primary world regions in the cosmos — sky, earth, and underworld — with a central pillar connecting the three zones (cf. *temen-abzu,* "Foundation of the Abyss"). Egyp. *ḥwt nṯr* signified the manor or mansion where the god lived and where his ritual worship took place. Inscriptions call the Ptolemaic period temple of Edfu the "Foundation Ground of the Gods of the Beginnings"; the inner sanctum itself was called the "High Seat," the mythical mound of primordial creation, the most powerful and sacred earthly place imaginable.

Several Hebrew words designate the temple in the Bible. Heb. *hêḵāl* (Akk. *ekallu,* from Sum. *é-gal,* "great house," thus "palace"). Heb. *hêḵāl* is frequently used for shrines, high places, etc. prior to the temple of Solomon, but also for the heavenly sanctuary (Isa. 6:1). Most common in the OT are *bêṯ YHWH,* "house of Yahweh," and *bêṯ 'ĕlōhîm,* "house of God." Heb. *miqdāš* is used for the Jerusalem temple (cf. 2 Chr. 36:17, *bêṯ miqdāš,* "house of holiness").

Sacred space became so regarded because it is where the primordial acts of creation occurred, and where a prophet or king met with deity. Because the earthly temple is built on the pattern of a heavenly model, it represents the heavenly prototype established on earth. The earthly temple incorporates, encompasses, encloses this space, and passes on its power to humankind through their contact with the temple. In general this occurs through ritual, a highly prescribed, detailed set of instructions and actions, controlled by priestly functionaries, possessed of the authority of deep antiquity, and requiring exactitude and care in its performance. The temple cannot be approached or entered casually, without proper authority and without extensive ritual preparations (e.g., washing, anointing, donning of clean, ritual clothes).

Symbolism

"Temple" thus means an association of symbols and practices connected in the ancient world with both natural mountains or high places and built structures. These symbols include the cosmic mountain, the primordial mound, waters of life, the tree of life, sacral space, and the celestial prototype of the earthly sanctuary. These practices, which can be called the temple ideology, emphasize spatial orientation and the ritual calendar; the height of the mountain/building; revelation of the divine prototype to the king or prophet by deity; the concept of "center," according to which the temple is the ideological, and in many cases the geographical, center of the community; the dependency of the well-being of the community on proper attention to the temple and its rituals; initiation, including dramatic portrayal within the temple of the cosmogonic myth as the primary vehicle of ritual; extensive concern for death and the afterlife, including burial within the temple precincts; sacral (covenant-associated) meals; revelation in the inner sanctum to the king or prophet by means of the Tablets of Destiny; formal covenant ceremonies in connection with the promulgation of law; animal sacrifice; secrecy; and the extensive economic and political impact of the temple on society.

The two most important features of temples are the mountain and heaven. In the Babylonian creation account, *Enuma Elish,* when the waters of chaos subsided following their defeat by the forces of cosmos (Marduk), there appeared a mound of earth, the primary and primordial mound of creation, where the deity first appeared. This mound became transformed into the sacred mountain, the most holy place on earth, the archetype of the tem-

Temple of Baalat Gebal, Byblos (4th millennium B.C.E.) (Phoenix Data Systems, Neal and Joel Bierling)

ple. In virtually all cultures, temples are either the architectural representation of the primordial mound, or of a world mountain, or some combination of the two.

The mountain and the temple are inseparable (Isa. 2:2-3). All of those features which cause/create/determine the sacredness of the mountain are attached to the temple, and determine its architecture, symbolism, and ritual. The Egyptian Step Pyramid of Zoser was an architectural realization of the primordial hill, later modified into the true pyramid. The canonical foundation ceremonies for temples in ancient Egypt included the ritual of "hoeing the earth" which is directly related to the concept that the temple is the upward architectural extension out of the primeval waters of creation leading up into the sky above the primordial mound.

In ancient Judaism a foundation stone appears in the place of the primeval mound. According to Midrash Tanḥuma (*Ked.* 10) the foundation stone is in front of the ark, which spot is the foundation of the world. This foundation stone played the same role as the primordial mound in Egypt: it was the first solid material to emerge from the waters of creation, and it was upon this stone that the deity effected creation. According to Jewish legend, it was this primordial rock on which Jacob slept, at the place he subsequently named Bethel (Gen. 28). This same rock then came to be placed in the inner sanctum *(dĕḇîr)* of Solomon's temple. According to Islamic tradition, it is this same rock from which the Prophet Mohammed ascended into heaven, over which the Dome of the Rock is built.

The mountain, a powerful earthly center and point of contact with the heavens, became a gathering place for the celebration of seasonal rituals and for renewal ceremonies at the New Year. A main purpose of the New Year festivals was to rededicate the temple, to reestablish and reaffirm the people's connection with the gods in the heavens. Numerous reliefs depict the processions of kings and nobles, approaching the city in order to attend the New Year festivals, where rededication of the temple would signal the resumption of cosmic union and harmony.

The vegetation that the creative waters produced, which can be equated with the "trees of life," was luxurious, pristine, and life-giving. This symbolism is exceptionally vivid in OT references to the messianic temple of the end time (e.g., Ezek. 47:1, 12). Other sources indicate that these waters flowed out from under the inner sanctum, and were in fact held or capped in place by the foundation stone. Temple architecture, paintings, and reliefs depict the "primordial landscape," the world as it was in the beginning — mound, water, and trees of life (or other vegetation) in or near the inner sanctum.

Not only do creation and life come up out of the depth; they come down from the sky, from the heavens, the classic dwelling place of the gods. The basic idea is that there exists in the sky a perfect place, the "city" of the gods. The goal of human life is both to establish contact with this place and to return to it after death, thus to share in the life of the gods. The primary way by which the gods share with humans the knowledge of this place, and information on how one gets there, is through the temple.

The god reveals to a king or prophet the architectural plan for the earthly temple, which is a replica of the heavenly temple. Exod. 19, 25 provide the classic pattern: the prophet ascends the holy mountain, where he is shown a "pattern" (Heb. *tabnîṯ*) of the heavenly temple to examine (25:9) in order to transfer its architecture to the earth. The Apostle John is transported to the mountain to view the heavenly city of Jerusalem, which in the context of the book of Revelation is one vast temple (Rev. 21:10, 15), prior to its restoration to the earth at the end of time (cf. Ezek. 40:2-3).

The innermost sanctuary of the temple, the most holy place, is a model on earth of the place where God lives. He does not live in the earthly temple's most holy places; this is clear from Exod. 19:18, 20, where the Lord descends out of heaven onto the mountaintop. The deity offers a glimpse into this heavenly place through the inner sanctum of the temple, where his presence is experienced by the prophet or the king on special occasions.

But how does one reach heaven? The answer is to be found in the mountain — the archetype and prototype of the built temple. Exod. 19 points conveniently and profoundly in the right direction. The way up the mountain involves ritual, or rites of passage, through which the prophet mediates knowledge of God to the people who have been prepared by this ritual to approach the holy place. In many of the great religious traditions, the gods were thought to live on a mountain, or to descend from heaven to a mountain, there to meet with those who have made the arduous journey to the center to be instructed. The mountain is the center because it is the first place of creation. It is the vertical pole connecting the heavens with the earth, the navel of the earth. To become one with God, one must join God at the mountain. The journey to the mountain and the ascent once one has reached its base are arduous, fraught with dangers and obstacles (cf. the labyrinthine nature of ritual initiation). This is the symbolism of Exod. 19–24.

The mountain (the temple) is "the meeting place of heaven and earth." Through its origins in the underworld, as symbolized in the primordial mound of creation, it also unites the three world regions: underworld, earth, heaven. A central axis or pillar uniting these three zones provides a means of access to and through them by prophets (cf. Gen. 28:10-12, 18-19, 22; esp. v. 17).

Jerusalem Temple

All of this symbolism is applied in some way in the Bible, the intertestamental literature, and postbiblical Jewish literature to pre-Solomonic high places and shrines (including the tabernacle), and to the temple of Solomon itself in its three manifestations: the original structure, the Zerubbabel postexilic reconstruction, and the Herodian expansion. Basic to temple ideology is the act of appearing, "before the Lord" (e.g., 1 Sam. 7:6); the phrase (Heb. *lip̄nê YHWH*) is a technical formula stemming from the basic conception of temple as dwelling place, and related cultic activity can be considered an indication of a temple at the site.

The primary difference between the pre-Solomonic temple shrines and sanctuaries and the temple of Solomon itself is that, with the advent of dynastic kingship in Israel, the people of Israel had to build an appropriate national, dynastic temple, "like all the nations" (1 Sam. 8:5), to give divine legitimacy to the dynasty. Israel had made the transition from a chiefdom to the state, in political terms, and needed all the accoutrements of state polity. Chief among these was a great national temple, to be built in the national, holy city.

The temple of Solomon was completed in 953 B.C.E., destroyed by Nebuchadnezzar in 587, rededicated by Zerubbabel in 516, dramatically expanded during the reign of Herod the Great, beginning in 20 B.C.E., and destroyed by the Romans under Titus in 70 C.E.

No architect is named, but in the ancient Near East gods and kings were regarded as architects and builders. Kings received architectual plans from gods through vision, often while spending the night in a sanctuary. The plan of his temple was revealed to Solomon during a night in the sanctuary at Gibeon (2 Chr. 1:7-13). According to the ancient pattern, the king went to the Lebanon for building materials, chiefly the precious cedar (2 Chr. 2:3-10[MT 1-9]). He also received technical assistance from Phoenician craftsmen there (1 Kgs. 7:13-14, 45), which justifies the assumption that the final product was architecturally and, in terms of decoration, Phoenician, or perhaps Phoenico-Egyptian, or Syrian (parallels have been drawn to Temple D in Middle Bronze Age Ebla, to the 9th-century Neo-Hittite temple at Tell Taʿyinat, and Late Bronze temples excavated at Emar). Nothing remains today of the temple of Solomon, or of any of its successors, with the exception of the Herodian platform, most famously the Western Wall.

The primary building material was finely dressed ashlars, prepared in an off-site quarry. The entire inner building was lined with cedar, then gilded. Gilded olive-wood doors formed the entrances to both *hêḵāl* and *dĕḇîr*. According to the Chronicler, a veil of blue, purple, and crimson linen, with cherubim embroidered on it, was hung immediately before the ark of the covenant, separating the *dĕḇîr* from the *hêḵāl* (2 Chr. 3:14).

The temple was a tripartite structure, on a straight axis; it consisted of three distinct architectural units, and the worshipper would enter at the front door and proceed on the same line to the rear sanctuary. The three units were the *ʾûlām*, "porch" or "vestibule"; the *hêḵāl*, "cella" or "nave" (this word came to be used for the entire building); and the *dĕḇîr*, the inner sanctuary or most holy place. The length of the temple was 60 cubits, its width 20 cubits, its height 25 cubits. The *ʾûlām* was 20 cubits wide and 10 cubits long, the *hêḵāl* was 40 cubits long, and the *dĕḇîr* was a cube, 20 cubits on each side. The inner sanctuary was thus 5 cubits shorter than the rest of the building, presumably because the inner sanctuary stood over the rock of foundation, the original place of creation in the cosmogony. The *dĕḇîr* housed the ark of the covenant, with typical Near Eastern protective cherubim standing over it, thus forming the cosmic throne of the deity. The *hêḵāl* housed the

Western Wall, lower levels of which contain the sole surviving portions of the Herodian expansion of the Second Temple at Jerusalem (Phoenix Data Systems, Neal and Joel Bierling)

lampstand, the table of showbread, and other ritual objects described for the tabernacle. A three-story annex surrounded the *hêḵāl* and the *dĕḇîr,* but not the *'ûlām.*

Two hollow, cast-bronze pillars stood in front of the *'ûlām,* named Jachin (the southernmost) and Boaz (the northernmost); the temple was oriented toward the east (cf. Ezek. 8:14-16). The pillars carried cosmic connotations, founding the temple in the underworld while uniting it with the heavenly sphere. The names of the pillars symbolized the cosmic, universal rule of Yahweh and of the Davidic dynasty that the building of the temple founded and legitimized: Jachin meant that Yahweh founded the dynasty and the temple, while Boaz meant that Yahweh's power emanates from the temple. It was in front of these pillars that King Josiah recovenanted the people of Judah following the cleansing and restoration of the temple (2 Kgs. 23:2-3; cf. Joshua at Shechem, Josh. 24:25-27).

The overall impression of the temple precinct in Jerusalem in the time of Solomon is that of a Near Eastern cosmic temple, sitting on top of the sacred mountain — the ultimate architectural expression of the heavenly temple revealed on the mountain of God and built after the pattern revealed there (Exod. 25:8-9). The primordial waters of the abyss from the time of creation were harnessed, present in the symbolism of the bronze sea. Everywhere were sacred trees and life-giving vegetation, both real-life and decorative (the walls of the nave and inner sanctum were carved with cherubim, palm trees, and flowers, then gilded), representing the "primordial landscape," the state of the world at the creation.

That phase of Solomon's temple that was rebuilt by the Jewish people returning from Babylonian Exile (known as the Second Temple) was much less grand than the original had been, due to the poverty of the people (Hag. 2:1-3). It was the decree of the farsighted Persian king (Ezra 6:1-5) that initiated the process of rebuilding. The temple was to be a 60 cubit wide by 60 cubit high house of God, constructed of ashlars and timber. Here sacrifices and burnt offerings were to be brought, and the gold and silver vessels taken to Babylon by Nebuchadnezzar returned.

The Herodian phase of the Second Temple consisted primarily of the extension of the temple platform to vast proportions (144,000 sq. m. [172,000 sq. yd.] — the largest sacred temenos in ancient times), the additions of several courtyards, and the use of enormous quantities of luxury building materials, primarily gold, in the decoration of the edifice. Knowledge of the Herodian temple comes from the NT, several intertestamental writers, Josephus, and the Mishnah.

The destruction of the temple in 70 C.E. was a catastrophe which still hangs over the Judeo-Christian world and, from the perspective of that tradition, over all humankind. The great European cathedrals of the Gothic Age were thoroughgoing attempts to replicate the ideology of the temple in all its details, but, for a variety of reasons, could not be successful in that enterprise. The same can be said for the Jewish synagogue and the primary mosque/shrines of Islam, the architecture and symbolism of which are pervaded by temple symbolism. The catastrophic nature of the destruction of the temple is easy to understand in terms of the fundamental religious assumptions that underlie the building of temples.

Bibliography. J. Gutman, ed., *The Temple of Solomon* (Missoula, 1976); M. Haran, *Temples and Temple-Service in Ancient Israel* (1978, repr. Winona Lake, 1985); C. T. R. Hayward, ed., *The Jewish Temple* (London, 1996); V. Hurowitz, *I Have Built You an Exalted House: Temple Building in the Bible in Light of Mesopotamian and North-west Semitic Writings.* JSOTSup 115 (Sheffield, 1992); J. M. Lundquist, "Biblical Temple," *OEANE* 1:324-30; *The Temple: Meeting Place of Heaven and Earth* (London, 1993); J. Maier, "The Architectural History of the Temple in Jerusalem in the Light of the Temple Scroll," in *Temple Scroll Studies,* ed. G. J. Brook (Sheffield, 1989), 23-62; R. Patai, *Man and Temple in Ancient Jewish Myth and Ritual,* 2nd ed. (New York, 1967).

John M. Lundquist

TEMPLE SERVANTS

A group of temple personnel, often simply transliterated "Nethinim" (lit., "the ones given," presumably to the service of the sanctuary). These servants are distinct from the *nĕṯûnîm* of Num. 3:9; 8:19, taken as referring to the Levites. Except for one reference (1 Chr. 9:2), all references to the temple servants are included in Ezra and Nehemiah. Ezra 2:43-58; Neh. 7:46-60 list 392 temple servants among the exiles who returned to Jerusalem with Zerubbabel. A second group of 220 temple servants and 38 Levites returned with Ezra (Ezra 8:16-20).

According to Ezra 8:20 the temple servants served the Levites. They may have been dependent upon the income of the temple, but they were not slaves (e.g., they owned property; 1 Chr. 9:2). Most likely the temple servants were a group of family guilds that served priests and Levites and worked alongside cultic personnel.

Most of the personal names are Northwest Semitic, suggesting that the temple servant families originated from neighboring peoples, possibly as prisoners of war. However, these people would have long been assimilated into Israelite culture and thus not the reference of Ezekiel's condemnation of turning the temple over to foreigners (Ezek. 44:6-7). There is no other evidence of cultural distinction.

Bibliography. A. Cody, *A History of the Old Testament Priesthood.* AnBib 35 (Rome, 1969).

Bruce W. Gentry

TEMPTATION, TESTING

"Temptation" and "testing" (both Heb. *nsh;* Gk. *peirázō*) denote one of the important aspects of the relation between God and human beings in the Bible. Whereas human beings are not supposed to test God (Deut. 6:16), God tests human beings' faithfulness with various tools such as hardship or difficult commands. If they overcome the temptation to turn back against God in the face of these difficulties, they will prove their steadfastness and pass the divine testing.

In the Exodus tradition, God is frequently portrayed as testing the Israelites (e.g., Exod. 15:22-26; 16:1-5; 20:18-21). According to Deuteronomistic interpretation, these divine testings have pedagogical purpose: God tests people to discipline and benefit them (e.g., Deut. 8:2-6). This interpretation became popular in later biblical traditions (e.g., Sir. 4:11-19; Wis. 3:1-9; Jdt. 8:25-27). The most famous testing stories in the OT, however, are those of Abraham and Job. God tests Abraham by telling him to sacrifice his son Isaac (Gen. 22:1-2). God gives permission to the Adversary (Heb. *śāṭān*), one of God's court ministers ("sons of God," Job 1:6; 2:1), to test Job with the severest afflictions (1:12; 2:6). Both Abraham and Job prove themselves faithful to God and are rewarded (Gen. 22:15-18; Job 42:11-17).

All of the Synoptic Gospels record that immediately after his baptism and just before beginning his public ministry Jesus is tested by the devil, also called Satan or the tempter (Mark 1:12-13; Matt. 4:1-11; Luke 4:1-13). In the longer version of the story (i.e., in Matthew and Luke) the devil tests Jesus with three temptations, all of which Jesus resolutely succeeds in overcoming. It is noteworthy that God is involved in Jesus' temptations by the devil, as Matt. 4:1 explicitly states that the Spirit took Jesus to the desert so that the devil might tempt him.

According to the Synoptics, Jesus confronted and overcame temptations not only at the beginning but throughout his ministry. In these later temptations, God's involvement is no longer clear and human beings, not the devil, appear as the tempters. Jesus' compatriots test him by asking him for a sign from heaven (Mark 8:11; Matt. 16:1; Luke 11:16) or by asking difficult legal questions (e.g., Matt. 19:3; 22:35). Although "temptation" or related words are not explicitly used, two important events strongly suggest that they meant to be understood as temptations Jesus suffered. When Peter rebukes Jesus, who has just foretold his passion, death, and resurrection, Jesus rebukes Peter with the same words that he used when the devil tempted him (Matt. 4:10): "Get behind me, Satan!" (Mark 8:33; Matt. 16:23). Similarly, while Jesus is on the cross, Jewish leaders mock him with words reminiscent of the devil's temptation (Matt. 4:6; Luke 4:9), saying that if Jesus is the Christ he can come down from the cross (Mark 15:32; Matt. 27:42-43; Luke 23:35).

In the OT it is always by the directive of God's own will that humans are tested, but God's purpose in testing is positive, never meant to seduce humans to do evil. This is not always true in postbiblical Jewish literature and the NT. In several documents from postbiblical Judaism (e.g., 1-2 Enoch, 2 Baruch, Apocalypse of Abraham, Martyrdom of Isaiah, and esp. Qumran), a personified evil figure, identified with various names such as Beliar, Belial, Satan, Azazel, or Mastema, appears as the tempter in the eschatological tribulations. As the ruler of the present age, the personified evil aims to seduce God's people to do evil against God's own will. The concept of temptation here becomes almost synonymous with "sin" or "evil." Early Christians interpreted their persecutions in the same perspective, while eagerly awaiting the return of Christ which would consummate the eschatological reign of God (e.g., Matt. 6:13; Luke 22:40; 1 Pet. 1:6-

7). Christians believed that Christ, who himself experienced temptations in every aspect (Heb. 4:15; cf. Luke 22:28), would help them to overcome the testings (Heb. 2:18).

Bibliography. J. B. Gibson, *The Temptations of Jesus in Early Christianity.* JSNTSup 112 (Sheffield, 1995).

Seung Ai Yang

TEN COMMANDMENTS

A series of commands given by God to his covenant people through Moses. The Bible records the Ten Commandments twice. In Exod. 20:1-17 they are the words that God speaks to Israel at Mt. Sinai. In Deut. 5:6-21 they are the words of Moses, who recounts what God revealed to him on Mt. Horeb. Both versions are embedded in the story of Israel's liberation from slavery in Egypt. To detach the commandments from this narrative framework risks misunderstanding the significance of the commandments themselves. The commandments, then, are not arbitrary stipulations but the revelation of the God who freed the Hebrew slaves.

The biblical tradition presents the commandments as the basis upon which Israel's continuing relationship with God becomes possible. God's deliverance of Israel from slavery in Egypt established that relationship. The Ten Commandments provide Israel with the moral framework for maintaining it. The metaphor that the Bible uses to express this relationship is covenant. While the metaphor comes from the sphere of international law, it is wrong to understand the commandments merely as a summary of Israel's legal obligations toward God. They were not contraints on Israel's freedom but the way that was to lead Israel to the fullness of life in the land that God was to give them. Also, Israel's obedience to the commandments was not a matter of submission to the divine will as much as it was a response of love. God's goodness and love, experienced by Israel in its liberation from slavery, elicited a response of love from a grateful Israel.

The Bible does not suggest how the commandments are to be divided or numbered. References to the "ten commandments" (Heb. "ten words," hence "Decalogue") do not appear in either Exod. 20 or Deut. 5 but in Exod. 34:28; Deut. 4:13; 10:4. The Roman Catholic and Lutheran traditions follow Origen, Clement of Alexandria, and Augustine, who considered the prohibition of worshipping other gods and the making of images as one commandment and who separated the prohibition of coveting the wife and possessions of one's neighbor into two commandments. The rabbinic and Reformed traditions join the two commandments prohibiting covetousness and separate the prohibition of false worship and the making of images into two commandments.

There does not appear to be a logical order to the commandments, though the series begins with obligations Israel has toward God and then continues with the obligations that the Israelites have toward each other. The content of the commandments is not unique in the Israelite tradition. What is unique is their association in this group of 10. The simplicity of the commandments is also striking. They are straightforward and require no expert legal interpretation. The Deuteronomic tradition underscores the comprehensiveness of the Decalogue when it notes that after giving the commandments God "added no more" (Deut. 5:22).

The understanding of divinity in the ancient Near East set the parameters of the commandments dealing with Israel's obligations toward God. The commandments forbid any activity that implies human control over the divine. People set up images of their gods in their temples to assure the divine presence in their midst, but no image could compel the divine presence in Israel. The mythological worldview in the ancient Near East imagined the heavens to be populated by many gods, while the commandments require Israel to serve its God exclusively. The God of Israel was not to serve as a guarantor of unnecessary oaths. The prohibition of working on the sabbath shows that Israel's God was going to determine the pattern of its life.

The commandments that deal with the Israelites' obligations toward each other have parallels in the law codes of other ancient Near Eastern peoples, and reflect a time when people begin to live together in groups. To maintain group solidarity members need to trust each other, to respect each other's life, marital relationships, and property. What society could last very long if people regularly lied to each other, stole from each other, did not respect marital bonds, and condoned murder? What made ancient Israel's approach to these common obligations unique was its belief that people's relationship with God was dependent upon the creation and maintenance of just intrasocietal relationships. Any breech in these relationships compromised Israel's relationship with God. The Ten Commandments have no penalties attached to them because the ultimate penalty for stealing, lying, murder, and adultery is not a penalty that the community can impose but one that only God can impose.

The commandment that requires the Israelites to honor their parents (Exod. 20:12; Deut. 5:16) is atypical because it carries with it the implied threat that a lack of respect for one's parents may lead to an abrupt end to one's days in the land that God is giving to Israel. The commandment that forbids murder (Exod. 20:13; Deut. 5:17) sees the killing of another human being as an act incompatible with the covenantal relationship that binds Israelites to God and each other. It does not forbid capital punishment (Deut. 17:2-7; 19:12) or war (chs. 20–21); other legislation deals with accidental killing (19:1-13). The Ten Commandments forbid adultery (Exod. 20:14; Deut. 5:18) but not other forms of illicit sexual activity; other laws deal with these (chs. 22–25). The biblical tradition views the violation of marital fidelity as a threat to the integrity of Israel's relationship with God (Job 24:13-17; Jer. 5:7; Hos. 4:2).

There is a question about what the commandment against theft (Exod. 20:15; Deut. 5:19) prohibits: simple theft or the taking of a person by force for sale as a slave. Both crimes undermine social relations. The commandment forbidding lying (Exod.

20:16; Deut. 5:20) is designed to uphold the integrity of the legal system by insuring truthfulness in testimony. Still, such truthfulness is not a legal necessity but a requirement from God. The commandments that forbid covetousness (Exod. 20:17; Deut. 5:21) deal with motivation rather than overt actions. They form a fitting conclusion to the Decalogue, since they forbid fostering the desire that leads to overt actions against the other commandments.

The Ten Commandments reflect the insight that the God of Israel is a God who governs all spheres of human life and that this God requires obedience. Still, it is essential to see the commandments in context of Israel's covenant with God. The obedience that God requires of Israel flows from God's liberating action on Israel's behalf. Freeing the Hebrew slaves from Egyptian bondage established a relationship between them and their God. The Ten Commandments are the means by which ancient Israel was to maintain that relationship. Finally, the individual stipulations that make up the Ten Commandments show that the status of Israel's relationship with God was a by-product of harmony within the Israelite community.

Bibliography. C. M. Carmichael, *Law and Narrative in the Bible* (Ithaca, 1985); W. Harrelson, *The Ten Commandments and Human Rights* (Philadelphia, 1980); A. Phillips, "The Decalogue — Ancient Israel's Criminal Law," *JJS* 34 (1983): 1-20; E. Nielsen, *The Ten Commandments in New Perspective*. SBT, 2nd ser. 7 (Naperville, 1968). LESLIE J. HOPPE

TEPHON (Gk. *Tephōn*)
A city in Judah fortified by Bacchides (1 Macc. 9:50). Although Josephus suggests that the site is Tekoa (*Ant.* 13.1.3. [15]), it is more likely to be identified with Tappuah (Vulg.; cf. Josh. 17:8).

TERAH (Heb. *teraḥ*) **(PERSON)**
A descendant of Shem and father of Abram, Nahor, and Haran (Gen. 11:24, 26). Terah was the last connecting link between the primeval history and his son, Abram, through whom God began a new kind of covenant work, a significance apparently reflected in the fact that the Abram story is subsumed under the structural heading "these are the generations of Terah" (Gen. 11:27). However, after the brief reference to his move from Ur and his settlement in Haran (Gen. 11:31), the only reference to Terah is the notice of his death (v. 32). The fact that this death report appears narratively before Abram's independent movement to Canaan, although Terah apparently was alive through most of the period, seems to reflect negatively on him. Clearly, he had no part in the continuing covenant story. The name Terah may reflect moon worship, which was popular in both Haran and Ur (cf. the reference to Terah in Josh. 24:2 as one who served other gods). WALTER E. BROWN

TERAH (Heb. *tāraḥ*) **(PLACE)**
A place where the Israelites encamped during their wilderness wanderings (Num. 33:27-28). Its location is unknown.

TERAPHIM (Heb. *tĕrāpîm*)
A technical term usually translated "household gods," "gods," "idol," or transliterated. At 1 Sam. 15:23 the term is generalized to encompass all idolatry. The etymology of the Hebrew term is uncertain. Some scholars connect it with Hittite *tarpiš*, denoting a spirit that can be either protective or malevolent. Others connect it with Heb. *rāpâ*, meaning "to sink down" as the heavenly bodies sink into the underworld, or as a pejorative term meaning "to be weak." By comparing Nuzi texts with Rachel's theft (Gen. 31:34), some scholars suggest that teraphim are connected with inheritance rights, perhaps representing ancestors. Most likely, teraphim served as a link (a channel) with a deity and represented a deity's presence.

Teraphim are usually small. Rachel hid Laban's teraphim in saddlebags (Gen. 31:34); however, Michal dressed up a large teraphim to resemble David sick in bed (1 Sam. 19:13). As objects of worship, teraphim are found in both shrines and homes. Laban called his teraphim "gods" (Gen. 31:30). Teraphim may be associated with Yahweh. Micah set up a house shrine dedicated to Yahweh containing teraphim, a graven image, a molten image, an ephod, and a Levite priest, which the Danites later carried off and set up in the city of Dan (Judg. 17–18). Hosea relates teraphim with the ephod, pillar, and sacrifice, suggesting a legitimate use in Yahweh worship (Hos. 3:4). Along with idols, Josiah removed teraphim from Jerusalem during his reform (2 Kgs. 23:24). Ezekiel says the king of Babylon consulted teraphim before marching on Jerusalem (Ezek. 21:21[MT 26]).

Teraphim may be among the small terra-cotta figurines so abundantly found at Near Eastern sites, especially from the time of the Divided Monarchy through the Persian period. TERRY W. EDDINGER

TEREBINTH
Heb. *'ēlâ, 'allâ*, often translated "terebinth," are also inconsistently translated "oak"; it is unclear whether these words refer to large trees in general or if nuances in meaning have been lost. Of the several species of terebinth that inhabit Israel, *Pistacia. Atlantica* Desf. is large and long-lived like the oak. It is deciduous, and grows in relatively dry climates. Other species common to the area include *P. lintiscus* and *P. terebinthus palaestina*. The pistachio nut (Heb. *boṭnâ;* Gen. 43:11), smaller than those sold in the West, has been found in excavations at Beersheba and Arad.

The prophets berate the populace for sacrificing to other gods under large trees such as the terebinth (e.g., Hos. 4:13). The association of large trees, both the oak and the terebinth, with ritual activity and the appearance of divine beings may occur because of the impressive stature and longevity of these trees. Jacob buries Laban's household idols under a terebinth (Gen. 35:4). The bones of Saul and his sons were also buried under a terebinth (1 Chr. 10:12).

MEGAN BISHOP MOORE/RANDALL W. YOUNKER

TERESH (Heb. *tereš*)
One of the two eunuchs who guarded the royal threshold of King Ahasuerus and planned to kill the king. Mordecai discovered their plot and had Esther report it to the king (Esth. 2:21-22; 6:2).

TERROR ON EVERY SIDE
The new name (Heb. *māḡôr missāḇîḇ*) which Jeremiah gives to the priest Pashhur to indicate that he would become fearful to his friends and to himself (Jer. 20:3; NRSV "Terror-all-around"). Magor, however, may also mean,"sojourning, dwelling place," and perhaps even "enmity, attack." Therefore, it has been suggested that Jeremiah may have been engaging in a multi-faceted play on words, sounds, and ideas when he renamed Pashhur. The phrase occurs elsewhere, expressing a state of extreme danger as personified in one's enemies (Ps. 31:13[MT 14]; Jer. 6:25; 20:10; 46:5; 49:29; cf. Lam. 2:22).

Bibliography. W. L. Holladay, "The Covenant with the Patriarchs Overturned: Jeremiah's Intention in 'Terror on Every Side' (Jer. 10:1-6)," *JBL* 91 (1972): 305-20; *Jeremiah 1.* Herm (Philadelphia, 1986). DAVID CLEAVER-BARTHOLOMEW

TERTIUS (Gk. *Tértios;* Lat. *Tertius*)
Paul's secretary who at the apostle's dictation wrote the Letter to the Romans, adding his own greetings (Rom. 16:22).

TERTULLUS (Gk. *Tértyllos*)
A professional orator brought to Caesarea by the Jewish high priest Ananias and elders to appeal their case against Paul before the Roman governor Felix (Acts 24:1-8). It is unclear whether Tertullus himself was Jewish or Roman or, perhaps, both a Hellenistic Jew and Roman citizen — like Paul. His references to "this nation (Gk. *éthnos*)" and "all the Jews" intimate a certain distance from the Jewish people; but mostly Tertullus employs "we"-language, effectively arguing the opinion of the Jewish authorities as his own (the Western addition in Acts 24:6b reinforces this stance: "*We* would have judged him according to *our* law").

In any case, Tertullus functions as an advocate skilled in standard forensic rhetoric. His opening gambit *(exordium)* appeals to the magistrate's penchant for brevity and flattery, particularly extolling Felix's noble commitment to Jewish peace and welfare. This sets up the statement of charges *(narratio),* in which Tertullus accuses the "pestilent" Paul of threatening the peace not only in Judea but throughout the empire. Finally, he offers as corroborating evidence *(probatio)* Paul's recent attempt to defile the temple, leading to his arrest (cf. Acts 21:27-36). According to Acts, such charges are groundless, as Paul's subsequent defense makes clear (Acts 24:10-21).

Bibliography. B. Rapske, *Paul in Roman Custody,* vol. 3 of *The Book of Acts in Its First Century Setting,* ed. B. W. Winter (Grand Rapids, 1994), 158-72; Winter, "The Importance of the *Captatio Beneuolentiae* in the Speeches of Tertullus and Paul in Acts 24:1-21," *JTS* N.S. 42 (1991): 505-31. F. SCOTT SPENCER

TESTAMENT
A literary genre containing the last words of a famous or ideal figure, often in the form of blessings or moral exhortations (e.g., Gen. 49; Deut. 33). Particularly common in the Second Temple period, such works may convey apocalyptic visions of the future (e.g., Testaments of the Twelve Patriarchs, Testament of Moses).

TESTAMENTS OF THE TWELVE PATRIARCHS
A collection of documents purporting to be the last will and testaments of major figures in ancient Israel, modelled after Jacob's farewell address to his 12 sons in Gen. 49 and Moses' final blessing of Israel in Deut. 33. These works point up the strengths and weaknesses of the patriarchs and predict the divine blessing and punishment that will take place in the future. In the Greco-Roman period similar testaments were produced in the name of Moses, Solomon, Adam, and Job. Among the Dead Sea Scrolls were found fragments of writings somewhat similar to the testaments, attributed to Levi, Joseph, and Naphtali. Written in Aramaic, those writings attributed to Levi may have been sources used by the author of the Testaments of the Twelve Patriarchs, but there are no direct literary correspondences.

A major aim of the Testaments of the Twelve is to convey the messianic hope for an anointed king and anointed priest who will bring about the renewal of God's people and the world order. The model for the renewed world is based on two sources: the law of Moses and the theory of moral and cosmic order which dominated the Greco-Roman world among both Jews and Gentiles. Its basic perception of a universe ordered by natural law, to which humans could respond by means of the conscience which each possessed, would result in individual and social renewal. The ethical system and terminology set forth in this writing have been shaped by Hellenistic philosophy, and specifically by Stoic thought. The detailed description of the human body and its capacities is based on Greek terminology, as in T. Naph. 2, where the human organs and their psychological functions are depicted. The abstract terminology used in defining religious understanding and human moral structure is likewise derived from Hellenistic philosophy. The highest aspiration of the moral person is to achieve "self control" *(sophrosýmē)* and "simplicity" *(haplosteía),* which can be attained only by those who are "single-minded" *(monoprósopos).* These terms are found only in the latest parts of the LXX, and especially in the non-Hebrew wisdom literature, which confirms the inference that the Testaments are Greek in origin and from a strongly Hellenistic environment.

The basically Jewish nature of this document is apparent from the frequency of messianic passages, in which the crucial roles are linked with Levi (the priest) and Judah (the king). Levi is the superior figure in God's redemptive program (T. Levi 18:1; T. Jos. 19:4), and will overcome the power of evil (T. Levi 18:12). The temple will be destroyed as an act of divine judgment (T. Levi 10:3; 15:1; 16:4-5), but will ultimately be restored (T. Benj. 9:2). God will be revealed to all the nations (T. Levi 4:4), for whom Israel as the people of God will be the divinely enabled light (14:34; T. Sim. 7:2; T. Jud. 22:3; 25:5; T. Benj. 9:5).

The ethical requirements for the community are drawn in part from the law of Moses, but the dominant emphasis is on the universal moral qualities, which can be recognized as the Stoic origin: piety (T. Reu. 6:4; T. Iss. 7:5; T. Levi 16:2); uprightness (T. Iss. 13:1; 4:6; T. Gad 7:7; T. Sim. 5:2); honesty (T. Dan 1:3); generosity (T. Iss. 3:8; 4:2; 7:3), and hard work (5:3-5). The resources on which one must draw to achieve this moral life are not only direct divine factors — God's spirit (T. Sim. 4:4) and fidelity (T. Jos. 9:2) — but also the internal force of the conscience (T. Reu. 4:3; T. Jos. 20:2) and in universally inherent power of good to overcome evil (T. Benj. 5). The law of Moses is treated according to the Jewish wisdom tradition of the Hellenistic period: as the embodiment of wisdom (T. Levi 13:1-9). It is binding upon all humanity (T. Levi 14:4) and is as much a part of the laws of nature as are the physical laws which determine the course of sun, moon, and stars. Gentiles and wicked people throughout history, such as the inhabitants of Sodom (Gen. 19), are guilty before God for having violated the laws of nature, having failed to discern the principles which are inherent in the creation (T. Naph. 3).

Since the Testaments of the Twelve relies on the LXX, it must have been written after the mid-3rd century B.C.E. The major use of Stoic terminology can be plausibly dated to the same time. Its view of the dual messianic roles — king and priest — matches that of the Maccabean period (165-63), as well as that of the Qumran community, so the work may well date from that period. It manifests three important factors: the earnest hope for a divine agent(s) of renewal; the need to redefine the covenant community; and the conviction that God provides special insights to the faithful. Later versions of the original Greek Testaments have been found in Armenian, Slavonic, Hebrew, and Aramaic, but the latter two are clearly dependent on a Greek original.

HOWARD CLARK KEE

TESTIMONIA

A technical term referring to NT citations of OT texts, particularly with reference to the identification of Jesus as the Messiah. Examples include the use of Hab. 2:4 by Paul in Rom. 1:17; Gal. 3:11 to prove his contention that salvation comes by faith (cf. Phil. 3:9). The combining of certain OT texts by different NT writers gives evidence that such combinations were already a part of the Christian tradition. For instance, both Rom. 9:32-33; 1 Pet. 2:6-8 tie together Isa. 8:14; 28:16 in speaking of salvation. Some scholars contend that the OT references in the speeches in Acts originated from a written testimonia. It is much more likely that testimonia, like the sayings of Jesus, circulated in oral form prior to the writing of NT materials.

CASEY W. DAVIS

TESTIMONY

Gk. *mártys* ("testimony" or "witness") was originally used of a witness in a court of law. The term and its cognates appear mainly in support of Christian beliefs about Jesus.

Much of the Gospel of John is structured as a juridical debate on whether Jesus is the Messiah, the Son of God (John 20:31). Many witnesses testify about Jesus: the Baptist (John 1:7-8), the Samaritan woman (4:39), Scripture (5:39), the Father (5:37; 8:18), Jesus himself (8:18), and Jesus' works (10:25). The disciples and the Paraclete will continue as witnesses (John 15:26-27; cf. 1 John 5:7) after Jesus departs. The credibility of the Gospel itself depends on the author's witness (John 19:35; 21:24).

Eyewitness testimony is key in the Acts of the Apostles. The apostles witness to Jesus' life (Acts 10:39), death (3:15), and, most importantly, his resurrection (1:22; cf. 1 Cor. 15:5-8 and the Gospel accounts of resurrection witnesses, including women). The Holy Spirit (Acts 5:32) and Scripture also witness to Jesus (28:23).

The book of Revelation presents several witnesses who are faithful to Jesus until death (Rev. 2:13; 20:4) and thus anticipates the later technical meaning of "martyr." Testimony in a strictly legal sense is found in the Synoptic accounts of the trial of Jesus (Mark 14:55-56 par.) and as a rule of order in Matthew's church (Matt. 18:16; cf. Deut. 19:15).

See WITNESS.

Bibliography. A. A. Trites, *The New Testament Concept of Witness*. SNTSMS 31 (Cambridge, 1977).

MARTIN C. ALBL

TETRAGRAMMATON

The sacred name of Israel's God. The term (Gk. "four letters") came into use partly because of the uncertainty concerning which vowel sounds were used in the pronunciation of the four-consonant name *(YHWH)* and partly because in the MT the ineffable name was written with the vowel points for Heb. *'ăḏōnāy*, "my Lord," signaling the reader to pronounce aloud only the Kethib form.

See YAHWEH.

TETRARCH

Originating in 5th-century Greece, a title used as far away as Thessaly and Galatia. Although Gk. *tetrárchēs* originally meant "ruler of a fourth" part of a tribe or country, by Roman times it had become a favorite designation for provincial rulers in Palestine. "Tetrarch" referred to emperor-appointed vassals who retained local sovereignty but whose income was fixed and who had no autonomy concerning foreign affairs. The title is used of three NT figures: Antipas (always called Herod; Matt. 14:1; Luke 3:1, 19; 9:7; Acts 13:1) and Philip (Luke 3:1), who were appointed at the death of their father, Herod the Great; and Lysanias of Abilene (3:1).

W. E. NUNNALLY

TEXT OF THE OLD TESTAMENT

The text of the OT or Hebrew Bible has a history of more than 2200 years of repeated copying and editing. Scholars differ over whether the transmission history of the text actually began when the text was fully completed and fixed or with the earliest written forms of the text. Clearly, older compositions such as the Pentateuch reached their final form much earlier and therefore have a longer transmission history than younger compositions such as the book of Daniel (perhaps 2nd century B.C.E.). Each composition in the biblical collection comes from a different period and has its own history of editing and copying. At different points in time, depending on the material in question, compositions were associated with each other (e.g., the "books" of the Pentateuch), and the transmission history of each individual composition becomes identical with that of the collection. The same is true of other collections, such as the 12 Minor Prophets which were probably transmitted as a single collection on a single scroll perhaps as early as the 5th century.

Copying and Transmission

Texts were copied on scrolls usually made from the skins of animals such as goats or gazelles. Usually only one side was smoothed and prepared to receive writing. If a composition was too long for a single piece of leather, the copyist or scribe would sew pieces of leather together to make a scroll long enough. The scribe might also impress onto the leather dry lines to guide the writing and to delineate the edges of columns. Various scribal signs were sometimes used to indicate corrections or passages of special interest. The biblical manuscripts from Qumran provide excellent examples of scribal practices from as early as 275 B.C.E. to ca. 68 C.E. Biblical manuscripts were usually prepared carefully, although apparently no established standards were applied in the copying until perhaps the end of the 1st century C.E. Usually semiformal or formal scripts were used for biblical manuscripts, although several from Qumran were copied in semicursive scripts. The biblical manuscripts from Qumran and elsewhere in the Judean desert show widespread variation in scribal practices in the last three centuries B.C.E. By the 1st century C.E. scribal practice in copying biblical manuscripts became standardized. Those rules are preserved in the Babylonian Talmud and the treatises Masseket Sefer Torah and Masseket Soferim, the latter compiled in the 9th century C.E.

Compositions which were thought to belong together such as the "books" of the Pentateuch could be copied on a single long scroll. The scroll format was dominant until after the adoption of the codex or book format by Christians for the NT. Thereafter, Christians used the codex format for the text of the OT as well. Within Judaism, the codex was only slowly adopted for texts not used in the liturgy. Liturgical texts, especially the Torah, continued in scroll format. The Torah continues in unvocalized and unaccented scroll format still today. The first Jewish codices appear between 600-700.

The form of the Hebrew alphabet used to copy the text has also changed over the centuries. The most ancient form of the Hebrew alphabet, derived from the Phoenician script, is attested in only a few documents (e.g., silver scrolls). In the Persian period (538-36) a form of the alphabet derived from the Aramaic script used by the Persians was generally used and developed different styles. Only between 500-700 were new graphic symbols developed and added to nonliturgical texts to indicate vowels and syntax (punctuation). More than one such vocalization system developed, but two dominated: the Tiberian (named after the city of Tiberias) and the Babylonian. Eventually, the Tiberian system was accepted by most communities, but only slowly.

Ancient Manuscripts

Qumran and Judean Desert

From the Judean desert and especially Qumran, a treasure trove of biblical manuscripts and commentaries *(pesharim)* have survived. Also, numerous paraphrases or rewritten biblical texts which are not strictly categorized as biblical manuscripts provide important evidence for the centrality of biblical material for Palestinian Judaism in the Greco-Roman period; the history of the interpretation of biblical compositions; and, occasionally, variant forms of the Hebrew textual tradition.

Qumran. The biblical manuscripts from Qumran range from the middle of the 3rd century B.C.E. until ca. 68 C.E. Every book of the Hebrew Bible has been found with the exception of Esther. An enormous amount of secondary literature exists on the biblical manuscripts. Of the 11 caves at Qumran, the most extensive group of manuscripts, biblical and nonbiblical, come from Cave 4. Some of the more significant manuscripts, such as 4QSam^{a} and 4QJer^{b}, have established that variant forms of the Hebrew text were known and used in Palestine and Qumran from the 3rd century B.C.E. to the 1st century C.E.; and many of these Hebrew manuscripts which vary from the received Hebrew text (the MT, medieval in date) are identical to or at least closely related to the Hebrew Vorlage of the Greek LXX and/or the Samaritan Pentateuch. The biblical manuscripts from Qumran seem to indicate a greater textual diversity than had been suspected prior to the first discoveries of these manuscripts beginning in 1947. Emmanuel Tov has argued that although textual diversity existed, the majority of the biblical manuscripts from Qumran are proto-Masoretic in textual type and thus closely related to the consonantal text of the MT. He has also argued that the proto-Masoretic manuscripts found at Qumran were usually more carefully copied with fewer scribal corrections than manuscripts of other textual types. There is not yet consensus on these two points. The Qumran biblical manuscripts are enormously important for understanding the development of the Hebrew textual traditions and the relationship to the Greek textual traditions and the transmission of the text in both languages in the

Greco-Roman period. Thanks to the Dead Sea Scrolls, we have verified the antiquity of the consonantal component of the MT, now understood to have been only one of many textual traditions during this period. The proto-Masoretic text (the consonantal text without vocalization, accents, or masora) is the Hebrew text of the OT which survived to the end of the period and became, eventually, the canonical text.

Judean Desert. Among biblical texts from the Judean desert (excluding Qumran) are those from Masada, the Naḥal Ḥever, and the Wadi Murabba'āt. Their importance for knowledge of the OT text and its history goes beyond their obvious antiquity. With one possible exception, the text of the Hebrew manuscripts from these sites corresponds almost exactly to the text of the proto-MT. The data seem to indicate that the textual diversity attested at Qumran, and presumably also throughout Palestine, disappears from the evidence by the time of the Second Jewish Revolt against Rome (132-135 C.E.). The evidence from Masada is not as clear, but all of the biblical fragments from Murabba'āt agree with proto-MT including the Minor Prophets scroll dating to the second half of the 1st century C.E. (i.e., between the two Jewish wars, ca. 70-132). Finally, the great manuscript of the Minor Prophets in Greek from Naḥal Ḥever reflects a recension (a conscious revision) of the older Greek translation (the LXX) to bring it closer to a Hebrew text of the Twelve which is usually described as not quite identical to proto-MT. 8 Ḥev XIIgr is clear evidence of recensional activity in the 1st century B.C.E., which may be taken as evidence of an awareness of obvious differences between the Greek and Hebrew textual traditions and of the preference for the Hebrew text as authoritative in form. It may reflect the abandonment of the older LXX translation at an earlier period than its adoption by Christian communities in the 1st century.

Printed Bibles

Between the Jewish wars with Rome, and probably by the beginning of the Second War (132 C.E.), the text of the Hebrew Bible seems to have been stabilized. This is indicated in particular by the evidence from the Judean desert, especially Wadi Murabba'āt. The Hebrew Minor Prophets scroll (second half of the 1st century C.E.) shows hardly any disagreement from the proto-MT. Attested at Qumran as one of many forms of the Hebrew text, the proto-MT is by the time of the Second War virtually the only form of the Hebrew text which survives. It is unclear how this particular textual tradition became the dominant text form. Usually it is conjectured that this was somehow due to the activity of the Pharisees and later rabbis, but there is no conclusive evidence. From the 2nd century C.E. until the early Middle Ages (ca. 896 for the Cairo Codex of the Prophets), we have no manuscript evidence. From the 9th century to the first printed Hebrew Bible is less than 500 years.

The first complete printed Hebrew Bible was produced by the Soncino brothers in 1488. This was followed in 1491-93 by the Naples Bible, also produced by Soncino. In 1495 Gershom Soncino produced an improved version of the 1488 Bible, printed in a small octavo ("pocket") format, easier for Jews to transport when fleeing persecution than the folio size. This edition was used by Martin Luther for his translation of the OT. In 1514-17 the first Polyglot Bible was printed at Alcala de Henares (Lat. Complutum) under the patronage of Cardinal Ximenes de Cisneros. The first printed Bible produced in Spain, it was authorized by Pope Leo X only in 1520, three years after the death of Cardinal Cisneros. This first Polyglot Bible was issued in a facsimile edition beginning in 1983. Slightly later (1516-17) Daniel Bomberg, a Christian merchant who settled in Venice, hired Felix Pratensis to edit the first Great Rabbinic Bible. This was published in four volumes and included the Targums and commentaries. In 1524-25 Bomberg produced the Second Great Rabbinic Bible. Edited by Jacob ben Hayyim ibn Adonijah, it became the standard text of printed forms of the Hebrew Bible for nearly 400 years. It was issued in four volumes and included the Targums and the commentaries of Rashi, Ibn Ezra, David and Moses Kimhi, and Levi ben Gershom. The first break from this tradition came in 1611 when Johan Buxtorf produced a small format edition which, unlike previous editions, was based partially on Sephardic manuscripts. This served as the basis of the first critical edition of Johann Heinrich Michaelis in 1720, using 19 printed editions as well as five manuscripts from Erfurt.

From 1905-1906 the first edition of Rudolf Kittel's *Biblia Hebraica* was produced. The basis of the first and second editions was the 1524-25 edition of Bomberg with certain variations and additions. In 1937 for the third edition the Firkowitch I. B19a (Leningradensis [L]) manuscript was used because it represented the oldest complete Ben Asher Masoretic manuscript known at that time. Beginning in 1967 the next edition of *BH (Stuttgartensia)* began to appear (1967-77) which also included the masora of L. Another revision, *Biblia Hebraica Quinta,* is in process, with the assistance of the United Bible Societies.

The Hebrew University Bible Project uses the Aleppo Codex (ca. 925) where it is extant as the basis for a diplomatic critical edition. Isaiah and Jeremiah have appeared, and Ezekiel is in an advanced state of preparation. Both the Hebrew University Bible Project and the Biblia Hebraica Quinta continue the tradition of diplomatic critical editions. The text which is offered as the base text is that of a single manuscript. *BHQ,* as did the earlier editions, will offer suggested emendations in the apparatus. Currently there is interest for an edition which would offer as the base text an emended, eclectic text with discussion of the basis for the emendations in the apparatus.

Ancient Versions

Greek Versions

The oldest translation of the Hebrew Bible is the Greek Septuagint (LXX), "the translation of the Seventy." The name was originally applied only to a translation of the Pentateuch which was begun in Alexandria, Egypt, probably during the reign of the Greek ruler Ptolemy II Philadelphus (285-247 B.C.E.). Gradually, the name was extended to the Greek translation of the Prophets and Writings as well. The LXX was probably complete by the time of Ben Sira (ca. 190). Since it was done over more than half a century, the translation was the work of many translators, and thus the style and quality of the translation varies from book to book. Some sections were certainly the work of a single translator (e.g., the Minor Prophets), others the work of several. This translation was probably undertaken by the Jewish community of Alexandria because of the need for the Scriptures in what had become the everyday language. In addition to the books of the Hebrew Bible, the LXX contains the Apocrypha. Although made by the Greek-speaking Jewish community in Egypt, eventually it fell out of use within Judaism, probably for two major reasons. First, there was an awareness of differences between the text of the LXX and that of the contemporary Hebrew Bible. It was probably assumed that the translation was inaccurate, not that the text of the Hebrew Bible had continued to evolve after the time of the translation. This dissatisfaction is reflected in early recensions of the LXX to produce Greek versions corresponding closely to the contemporary Hebrew text (e.g., the Greek Minor Prophets scroll from Naḥal Ḥever, second half of the 1st century B.C.E.). Second, Jewish communities abandoned the LXX because of its early adoption by Greek-speaking Christians. This probably motivated in part the production of the later Jewish revisions of the LXX, those of Aquila, Symmachus, and Theodotion in the 2nd century C.E. In the 3rd century Origen created a revision of the LXX as column five in his Hexapla. This revision, based on comparison to the proto-Masoretic Hebrew text extant at this time, was recopied, frequently without the accompanying diacritical marks which Origen used in the Hexapla to indicate places where the Greek and Hebrew texts differed and where he had changed the LXX to bring it into conformance with the Hebrew text.

Latin Versions

In the West, Latin-speaking Christians probably began translations of the LXX into Latin as early as the 2nd century C.E. There was apparently no single "Old Latin" translation of the entire OT. In the 4th century Pope Damasus commissioned Jerome to produce a single Latin version of the Bible for common use — the Vulgate. He began ca. 392 with Psalms, initially using Origen's revised LXX text as the basis for his work. Jerome's first version of the Psalter, known as the Gallican Psalter, became quite popular. For the rest of the OT he became convinced that it was necessary to create a new translation directly from the Hebrew. This process took ca. 15 years. Jerome's work was not widely accepted until ca. the 6th century, first being mixed with the older Latin translations which were circulating.

Targums

Targums (translations of a composition or compositions in the Hebrew Bible into Aramaic) exist for every book in the Hebrew Bible except Ezra, Nehemiah, and Daniel. Targums became important perhaps as early as the late Persian period, when Biblical Hebrew was not easily understood by most of the people. There are official rabbinic targums for the Pentateuch (Targum Onkelos) and the Prophets (Targum Pseudo-Jonathan). There is no official targum for the Writings, although numerous targums do exist. Recently discovered targums include Targum Neofiti, a Palestinian targum to the Pentateuch discovered in 1957 in the Vatican Library, and the Fragment Targum.

Samaritan Pentateuch

Although not strictly speaking one of the ancient versions, the Samaritan Pentateuch is usually discussed along with them. The canonical scripture of the Samaritan community which survives to this day, it was "discovered" by scholars in the 19th century and immediately engendered discussions concerning its antiquity and relationship to the proto-MT and the LXX. Since the discovery of the Dead Sea Scrolls it has become clear that there existed a "proto-Samaritan" text type with similar sorts of expansions which exist in the Samaritan Pentateuch. Apparently the biblical manuscripts from Qumran which are proto-Samaritan texts (e.g., 4QNum) provide evidence for the early history of the text type which the Samaritans chose for their Pentateuch and to which they added unique expansions which do not exist in the proto-Samaritan manuscripts from Qumran.

Textual Criticism

Any text, ancient or modern, suffers corruption in its transmission. This has always been true, although with electronic transmission of texts it is less likely to occur. The removal of errors, either accidental or deliberate, which were introduced into the text during the period of its transmission is the focus of the textual criticism of the Hebrew Bible. In this task the ancient versions and the Qumran biblical manuscripts may offer an incorrupt reading which would allow correction of an error in the Hebrew text. The versions, of course, do not exist simply to be mined for incorrupt or variant readings, but are important and independent forms of the text in their own right. But if the focus is the Hebrew text, they may provide the means to correct errors that have developed during the transmission of the Hebrew text.

Some scholars hold that the proper goal of the textual critic should be the recovery or reconstruction of the oldest form of the text it is possible to reconstruct on the basis of the evidence. This is similar to the view of textual criticism in other disciplines, such as the study of Greek or Latin literature. With the availability of biblical manuscripts from Qumran, it may be possible to reconstruct a form of the Hebrew text far earlier than what we now have. Other textual critics feel that the proper goal of the textual criticism is to produce as error-free an edition of the MT as possible. Yet others think that the proper goal is to reconstruct the proto-MT, the consonantal form of the text when it became canonical for Judaism at the end of the 1st century C.E. and subsequently for many Protestants.

Bibliography. F. M. Cross, *The Ancient Library of Qumran,* 3rd ed. (Minneapolis, 1995); M. J. Mulder, "The Transmission of the Biblical Text," in *Mikra.* CRINT 2/1 (Philadelphia, 1988), 87-135; L. H. Schiffman, *Reclaiming the Dead Sea Scrolls* (Philadelphia, 1994); N. H. Snaith, "Printed Editions (Hebrew)" in "Bible," *EncJud* 4:835-41; E. Tov, *Textual Criticism of the Hebrew Bible* (Minneapolis, 1992); E. Ulrich, "Multiple Literary Editions: Reflections Toward a Theory of the History of the Biblical Text," in *Current Research and Technological Developments on the Dead Sea Scrolls,* ed. D. W. Parry and S. D. Ricks. STDJ 20 (Leiden, 1996), 78-105; repr. in *The Dead Sea Scrolls and the Origins of the Bible* (Grand Rapids, 1999), 99-120; I. Yeivin, *Introduction to the Tiberian Masorah.* SBLMasS 5 (Missoula, 1980).

RUSSELL T. FULLER

TEXT OF THE NEW TESTAMENT

None of the autographs of the NT writings survives. The texts of these works must therefore be reconstructed on the basis of surviving evidence, which comprises (a) Greek manuscripts produced in later centuries, (b) copies of ancient translations into other languages (i.e., the Versions), such as Latin and Syriac, and (c) NT quotations found in Christian authors, especially Greek and Latin. The discipline of textual criticism works to establish the wording of the text as originally produced and to determine where, when, how, and why the text came to be changed over the course of its transmission.

History of the Discipline

The roots of the discipline lay in an important confluence of events at the beginning of the 16th century. Key figures of the Protestant Reformation insisted that the words of Scripture, interpreted literally, be the sole authority for Christian faith and practice; at the same time, a resurgence of interest in ancient texts emerged among Renaissance humanists, such as Desiderius Erasmus, who in 1516 published the first printed edition of the Greek NT, just a year before Martin Luther posted his 95 theses. The Greek Testament that Erasmus produced, however, was reconstructed from late manuscripts that were incomplete (his text of Revelation lacked the final six verses, which he himself had to translate from the Latin Vulgate into Greek) and did not always agree with one another. The Reformation's insistence on the importance of the words of Scripture and the concomitant recognition that these words do not survive intact eventually drove scholars to devise methods of establishing the original text of the NT.

Only scant progress was made along these lines through the 16th and 17th centuries, which saw little more than the republication of Erasmus' edition of the text in slightly altered form. Since this basic form of the text became so widely used, it was eventually dubbed the Textus Receptus (TR), or Received Text. The end of the 17th century and beginning of the 18th, however, marked a significant shift, as scholars began assiduously to collect and compare manuscript copies of the NT. A milestone came in 1707, when John Mill published his *Novum Testamentum Graece,* which printed the TR but included an apparatus indicating some 30 thousand places of variation among the hundred or so Greek manuscripts, early Versions, and Patristic quotations that he had examined. The publication sparked immediate and widespread controversy, especially among those concerned about divine authority residing in a text which was evidently no longer available.

The debates that ensued brought some of the most brilliant minds and assiduous workers of the 18th and 19th centuries to bear on the problems of the text (principally in England and Germany), including such eminent names as Richard Bentley, J. A. Bengel, J. J. Wettstein, J. J. Griesbach, Karl Lachmann, Constantin von Tischendorf, B. F. Westcott, and F. J. A. Hort. Some of these scholars worked principally on collecting, analyzing, and compiling manuscript evidence for the original text (e.g., Wettstein and Tischendorf); others focused on devising methods for reconstructing the text on the basis of the surviving witnesses (Bengel, Griesbach, and esp. Westcott and Hort). Their labors have informed the discipline to this day, as evident both in methods of evaluating variant readings and in the most widely accepted form of the Greek text.

The State of the Text

Due to extensive manuscript discoveries of the 20th century, the amount of evidence available today completely dwarfs what was available to John Mill in the early 18th century, and even that known to Westcott and Hort at the end of the 19th. The official tabulation of Greek manuscripts is maintained by the Institute for New Testament Textual Research in Münster, Germany, founded by Kurt Aland and now headed by Barbara Aland. As of 1994, the Institute recorded a total of 5664 known Greek manuscripts, ranging in date from the 2nd to the 16th centuries and in size from credit-card sized fragments discovered in trash heaps in Egypt to massive tomes housed in the libraries of Europe. These are normally categorized under four rubrics: (1) papyri manuscripts, written on papyrus in "uncial" letters (somewhat like our "capitals"); these are the oldest available witnesses, dating from the 2nd-8th centuries (99 are known at present); (2) majuscule manuscripts, also written in uncial, but on parchment or vellum; these date from 3rd-

10th centuries (306 known); (3) minuscule manuscripts, written in a kind of "cursive" script, which became popular in the Middle Ages, possibly because it was faster and more convenient to write; these date from the 9th-16th centuries (2856 known); and (4) lectionary manuscripts, selections from the NT compiled for liturgical reading, whether written in uncial or minuscule script; these date from the 4th to the 16th centuries (2403 known).

In addition to these Greek witnesses are manuscripts of the early Versions of the NT; by the end of the 2nd century, the NT had already been translated into Latin (of which we have thousands of copies through the Middle Ages) and Syriac, somewhat later into Coptic, and eventually into Ethiopic, Armenian, Georgian, and other languages. These versions can indicate the form of the text in the time and place the translations were originally made. So too, the quotations of the church fathers can be used to reconstruct the forms of the text available to them. Such Patristic sources are particularly useful for understanding how the text was transmitted regionally, since in many instances we know exactly when and where the fathers were living.

From this mass of evidence scholars work to determine both the original form of the text and the alterations made in the course of its transmission. The difficulty of the task, in part, is that none of our primary witnesses, the Greek manuscripts, are in complete agreement with one another. Sometimes the disagreements are extremely minor and of very little moment, involving such things as differences of spelling. But at times they are of supreme importance: today there is widespread agreement, e.g., that the story of the woman taken in adultery (John 7:52–8:11) was not originally part of the Fourth Gospel but was added by later scribes; the same can be said of the final 12 verses of the Gospel of Mark (Mark 16:9-20). In many instances, however, the surviving witnesses are so significantly divided that scholars cannot agree concerning the original form of the text. Did the voice at Jesus' baptism in Luke originally say "You are my beloved son in whom I am well pleased," or did it say "You are my son; today I have begotten you" (Luke 3:22)? In Luke, did Jesus pray for his enemies' forgiveness during his crucifixion (Luke 23:34) or not? Did the Prologue of John's Gospel end by calling Jesus the "unique Son who is in the bosom of the Father" or the "unique God who is in the bosom of the Father" (John 1:18)? Scholars continue to debate scores of such differences among our manuscripts.

Methods of Textual Criticism

In deciding which form of the text is original, most scholars apply an "eclectic" method, which appeals, on a case-by-case basis, to a number of different criteria that are traditionally categorized either as "external" (those based on the kinds of manuscripts that support one reading or another) or "internal" (those based on the likelihood that a reading goes back either to the original author or to an error introduced by a scribe). To be sure, there continue to be proponents of the "Majority text," who claim that the form of text found in the majority of surviving witnesses is always, or nearly always, to be preferred (an emphasis almost exclusively on one kind of external evidence); and there are others who maintain that since all of the manuscripts contain mistakes, it is wrong to consider the manuscripts *at all* when deciding what the authors originally wrote (emphasizing "internal" evidence). The majority of scholars, however, continue to adjudicate the differences among manuscripts by considering the whole range of surviving evidence.

External Evidence

The following are among the most important "external" principles that are sometimes invoked in deciding one textual reading over another.

Number of Supporting Witnesses. A reading found more frequently among our manuscripts may, theoretically, have a superior claim to being the original. Although widely favored by advocates of the "Majority text," this principle is nonetheless discounted by most other scholars, and for fairly compelling reasons. For if, hypothetically, one manuscript of the 2nd century was copied three times, and another was copied 300 times, this would not mean that the latter was more *accurate* (and its copyists would have no way of knowing); it would simply mean that it was copied more often. The number of surviving witnesses, therefore, actually tells us little about the original text.

Chester Beatty papyrus II (𝔭46), ca. 200 C.E., containing Rom. 15:29-33; 16:25-27, 1-3 (Institute for New Testament Textual Research, Münster/Westphalia)

TEXT OF THE NEW TESTAMENT

Age of Supporting Witnesses. More important, obviously, than the number of surviving witnesses for any particular reading is the *age* of its supporting manuscripts. In general, earlier manuscripts will be less likely to contain errors, since they have not passed through as many hands. This criterion is not foolproof either, however, since a 7th-century manuscript could, conceivably, have been copied from an exemplar of the 2nd century, whereas a 6th-century manuscript (which is therefore older) could have been copied from one of the 5th century.

Geographical Diversity of the Witnesses. Less problematic is an appeal to the widespread distribution of a reading: any form of the text that is found in witnesses scattered over a wide geographical range, as opposed to one found in manuscripts located, e.g., in only one city or region, has a greater chance of being ancient.

"Quality" of the Supporting Witnesses. As in a court of law, some textual witnesses are more reliable than others. Witnesses *known* to produce an inferior text when the case can be decided with a high degree of certainty (on the "internal" grounds discussed below), are also more likely to produce an inferior text where the internal evidence is more ambiguous.

Quality of the Supporting "Groups" of Witnesses. Since the 17th century, scholars have recognized that some manuscripts are closely related to one another, in the sense that they typically support the same wording of the text in a large number of passages. Witnesses can thus be "grouped" together in light of their resemblances. Today there are three major groups that are widely accepted: (1) "Alexandrian" witnesses, which include most of the earliest and "best" manuscripts, as judged by their overall quality (e.g., Codex Vaticanus); these may ultimately go back to the form of text preserved among scholars in Alexandria, Egypt; (2) "Western" witnesses (a misnomer, since some of these witnesses were produced in Eastern Christendom), which include manuscripts associated with the famous Codex Bezae in the Gospels and Acts; these appear to preserve an early but generally unreliable form of the text; and (3) "Byzantine" witnesses, which include the vast majority of later manuscripts, and are judged by a preponderance of scholars to preserve an inferior form of the text. The general rule of thumb for most critics is that readings attested only in Byzantine or only in Western witnesses are highly suspect; readings found among the Alexandrian witnesses, on the other hand, are more likely to be given the benefit of the doubt, especially when these are also attested by witnesses of the other two groups.

By way of summary, most scholars maintain that the sheer number of witnesses supporting one reading or another rarely matters for determining the original text. More significant are the age, geographical diversity, general quality, and textual grouping of external support; that is, readings found in the oldest, most widespread, and "best" manuscripts are most likely to be original.

Internal Evidence

Internal evidence is concerned not with the witnesses that support one reading or another, but with the competing merits of the variant readings in and of themselves. Two kinds of issues are involved: "transcriptional probabilities," i.e., arguments concerned with readings that would have most appealed to the interests and concerns of scribes, and thus are likely to have been created by them in their transcriptions (and occasional alterations) of the text; and "intrinsic probabilities," i.e., arguments concerned with readings that conform most closely with the language, style, and theology of the author in question, and are thus intrinsically most likely to be original.

Transcriptional Probabilities. A study of our earliest manuscripts confirms several commonsense assumptions about the kinds of readings scribes would create when they altered the text they copied. For example, scribes appear to have been more likely to harmonize two passages that stood at apparent odds with one another than to make them differ; they were more likely to improve the grammar of a passage than to make it worse; they were more likely to bring a passage into conformity with their own theological views than to make it "unorthodox." As a result, the critic can employ a general rule of thumb when considering transcriptional probabilities, a rule that may at first sound backwards, even though it is established on sound principles: the more difficult reading — i.e., the reading that is less harmonized, grammatical, and theologically "correct" — is more likely to be original.

Intrinsic Probabilities

Whereas transcriptional probabilities look for readings that were most likely to have been created by scribes in the process of transcription, intrinsic probabilities look for the reading that is most likely to have been created by the author of the NT book himself. At issue here is the language, style, and theology of the author who originally produced the text. Readings that conform most closely with the author's own thought and way of expressing it are most likely to be his own. Making this determination, of course, requires a sophisticated application of traditional forms of exegesis and a substantial knowlege of the author in question.

The Text at the End of the Twentieth Century

Significant progress has been made in the study of the NT text over the past two centuries. Instead of poorly edited Greek texts, scholars and students now have ready access to carefully edited versions filled with textual information (e.g., apparatuses that indicate differences among the surviving witnesses), the two most popular of which are the United Bible Societies' *Greek New Testament* (principally for Bible translators and beginning students; now in its 4th edition) and the 26th edition of the "Nestle-Aland" *Novum Testamentum Graece*, which contains exactly the same Greek text as the UBS edition, but with a far more extensive apparatus.

Moreover, the industrious labors of present-day scholars and the momentous opportunities opened up by the computer have led to a burst of productivity in this field, including a spate of invaluable publications from the Institute of New Testament Textual Research, probably the most important of which is the much-anticipated *Editio Critica Maior,* an edition that will include an impressive apparatus of textual evidence which should eclipse any now available (presently at work on the General Epistles). Significant projects are under way outside of the Institute as well, such as the International Greek New Testament Project, whose British and American committees have already published an extensive apparatus of the Gospel of Luke and are now at work on one for John.

Probably the single greatest desideratum in the field at present is a viable history of the text — i.e., an account of where, when, how, and why the text came to be changed over the course of its long and varied transmission. This history is of crucial importance both for reconstructing the text's earliest stage (i.e., its "original" form) and for establishing the close relationship between the text and the social world within which it was transcribed. This latter issue — the socio-historical context of scribal transmission — has become particularly significant for scholars in recent years, as they have come to recognize that the alterations of the text may reflect the theological concerns and social worlds of the scribes who changed it. A full history of the text, however, will require substantial preliminary work to be done on the early Versions and, especially, individual church fathers, a significant beginning on which can be found in the series, The New Testament in the Greek Fathers (Atlanta, 1991–).

Bibliography. K. Aland and B. Aland, *The Text of the New Testament,* 2nd ed. (Grand Rapids, 1989); B. D. Ehrman, *The Orthodox Corruption of Scripture* (Oxford, 1993); Ehrman and M. W. Holmes, *The Text of the New Testament in Contemporary Research.* Studies and Documents 46 (Grand Rapids, 1995); E. J. Epp, "Textual Criticism," in *The New Testament and Its Modern Interpreters,* ed. Epp and G. W. MacRae (Philadelphia, 1989), 75-126; B. M. Metzger, *The Text of the New Testament,* 3rd ed. (Oxford, 1992); *The Early Versions of the New Testament* (Oxford, 1977); *Manuscripts of the Greek Bible* (Oxford, 1981); *A Textual Commentary on the Greek New Testament* (Stuttgart, 1971).

BART D. EHRMAN

TEXTUS RECEPTUS

The form of NT text that became standard in the 16th-17th centuries. Johann Froben, a Swiss printer, learning of the intent of Cardinal Ximines to produce a Greek NT, asked Desiderius Erasmus in April 1515 to prepare an edition of the NT as quickly as possible. Using six manuscripts at hand, only one of which (Cod. 1) was of any relative antiquity, Erasmus' edition was begun in September and published in March 1516. Ximines' edition, the Complutensian Polyglott, was printed in 1522, although it had actually been completed in 1514.

Robert Stephanus published four editions of the Greek NT between 1546 and 1551, using the texts of Erasmus and Ximines. His 3rd edition (1550), which gave variant readings from 15 manuscripts, became the standard text in Great Britain and the U.S. Theodore Beza, Calvin's successor in Switzerland, published nine editions of the Greek NT from 1565 to 1604, essentially presenting the text printed by Erasmus and Stephanus; his reputation helped establish the form of the printed Greek text.

The two Elzevir brothers published in Holland seven editions of the Greek NT between 1624 and 1678, all based upon the text presented by Erasmus, Stephanus, and Beza. In the preface of their 2nd edition (1633), which became the standard text printed in Europe, they wrote: "You have therefore the text now received by all: in which we give nothing altered or corrupt." The term *textus receptus,* then, refers to a "commonly published" text.

This text, based upon the text form of the Byzantine era, became the accepted printed form by mere chance. It is not a "bad" or misleading text, but it is a later form of text. Three centuries were to pass before scholars would succeed in replacing this hastily prepared text with one having evidence of being closer to the NT autographs.

CARROLL D. OSBURN

THADDAEUS (Gk. *Thaddaíos*)

One of Jesus' 12 disciples, according to the lists of Matthew (Matt. 10:3) and Mark (Mark 3:18). Luke and Acts read "Judas son (brother?) of James" (Luke 6:16; Acts 1:13).

Lebbaeus, a textual variation for the name Thaddaeus, appears in some manuscripts of Matthew and Mark. Thaddaeus may be connected to Aram. *taddāʾ,* "breast, nipple," while Lebbaeus could be derived from *lēḇ,* "heart." Lebbaeus could also be a term of endearment. Which name is original is unknown.

In the extracanonical Acts of Thaddaeus, Thaddaeus was active in the church in Edessa in Mesopotamia and was one of the Seventy (cf. Eusebius *HE* 1.13; 2.1.5-7).

BENNIE R. CROCKETT, JR.

THADDEUS, ACTS OF

A 5th-century Greek writing developed on the basis of the legend that the disciple Thaddeus was to evangelize Edessa as the fulfillment of a promise made by Jesus to King Agbar. The legend may be found in Eusebius (*HE* 1.13.11-22; 2.1.5-7).

WATSON E. MILLS

THANKSGIVING (also THANK OFFERING)

The response a loving God expects from his people (Heb. *tōdâ;* Gk. *eucharistía*). Thanksgiving is an activity which involves the community of faith in both the OT and NT (e.g., 1 Chr. 16:35; Ezra 3:11; Ps. 44:8[MT 9]; 75:1[2]; 79:13; 2 Cor. 1:11; 4:15; Eph. 1:16).

In the OT thank offerings were expressions of thanksgiving (Lev. 7:12-15; 22:29), showing gratitude for release from trouble, affliction, or death (Ps. 56:12[13]; 107:17-22; 116:17). In Jerusalem, temple musicians played the lyre and provided leadership "in thanksgiving and praise" (1 Chr. 25:3; 2 Chr. 5:13). In David's day trained leaders conducted the "songs of praise and thanksgiving" (Neh. 12:46). When Manasseh was restored, he offered "sacrifices of thanksgiving" in gratitude for deliverance (2 Chr. 33:16; cf. Ps. 50:14; Amos 4:5). In Nehemiah's time Mattaniah and other Levites led the public thanksgiving and "the songs of thanksgiving" (Neh. 12:8; cf. 11:17).

Thanksgiving featured prominently in the Psalms (Ps. 7:17[18]; 28:7; 30:4[5]; 50:23; 69:30[31]; 86:12; 111:1). The psalmist thanked God for deliverance from enemies (Ps. 35:11-18), hostile accusers (109:29-30), and death (86:12-13). Included are songs of thanksgiving (Ps. 26:7; 42:4[5]; cf. Isa. 51:3; Jer. 30:19), exhortations to enter God's presence with thanksgiving (Ps. 95:2; 100:4), and calls to "give thanks" (97:12; 105:1; 107:1; 118:1; 136:1-3; cf. 1 Chr. 16:8, 34; 2 Chr. 20:21; Isa. 12:4; Jer. 33:11).

Jesus gave thanks (Mark 8:6 par.; 14:23 par.; Luke 22:17, 19; John 6:11, 23; 1 Cor. 11:24; cf. Matt. 11:25 par.), and the Lord's Supper is the Church's great thanksgiving meal (the eucharist). The healed leper thanked Jesus (Luke 17:16), but the self-righteous Pharisee mistakenly thanked God that he was unlike others (18:11).

Paul stressed thanksgiving (1 Cor. 14:16; 2 Cor. 9:11-12; Phil. 4:6; 1 Thess. 3:9; cf. Eph. 5:4, 20; Col. 2:7; 4:2; 1 Tim. 2:1), especially for Christ (2 Cor. 2:14; 9:15); unthankfulness signified depravity (Rom. 1:21). Food is acceptable if it is "received with thanksgiving" (1 Tim. 4:3-4). Thanksgiving is an aspect of heavenly worship (Rev. 4:9; 7:12).

ALLISON A. TRITES

THASSI (Gk. *Thássi*)
Nickname of the Hasmonean Simon (**4**), second son of Matthias (1 Macc. 2:3).

THEATER
An outdoor structure for dramatic performances or spectacles (Gk. *théatron*, a "place for seeing"). Although theaters are not prominent in the Bible, the word occurs twice in connection with a mob riot in Ephesus, where people rushed into the theater, dragging Paul's companions with them (Acts 19:29-31). The word is also used metaphorically to describe a spectacle; thus Paul sees the apostles becoming "a spectacle to the world, to angels and to mortals" (1 Cor. 4:9; cf. Heb. 10:33). Similarly the Stoics made metaphorical use of the spectacle (Epictetus *Discourses* 2.19, 25; 3.22, 59).

While its origins are obscure, theater can be traced back at least to 600 B.C., when the Greeks offered choral performances of singing and dancing in honor of the god Dionysus. Later they held annual dramatic contests in Athens which included choric readings and spoken exchanges between the chorus leader and an answering partner. Gradually drama developed into two well-defined forms, tragedies and comedies. The 5th century was the most creative period in ancient drama, producing works of enduring artistic influence such as Sophocles' tragedy *Oedipus Rex* and Aristophanes' comedy *The Clouds*. In the Hellenistic age both types of drama were widely produced and performed before large audiences. Eventually "new comedy" evolved as a form of social satire without the use of the chorus. Menander (d. 292) was probably the best-known comic dramatist of the time. His comedy *Thais* is quoted by Paul in 1 Cor. 15:33.

Hellenistic theaters were generally constructed on natural slopes. The auditorium usually consisted of a semicircular cavity cut in the side of a hill. The seats were arranged concentrically in an ascending pattern, divided into several sections by gangways, and cut from rock, stone, marble, or wood. The chorus was located in the orchestra, the circular space in front of the stage at ground level. The stage and scene were built on the diameter, and often appeared like the face of a temple. Several rows of specially carved, ornamented seats in the front were kept for priests and public officials.

Roman theaters frequently were complete buildings, and often had roofed stages and partially roofed auditoriums. Theaters were recognized centers for public meetings (Acts 19:24-41); here decrees were recorded, benefactors crowned, and edicts proclaimed. The theater at Ephesus accommodated more than 24 thousand people.

Drama held an important place in the cultural life of the Hellenistic world, and every city has its own theater. There are impressive ruins of Greek and Roman theaters in such Pauline cities as Athens, Corinth, Ephesus, Miletus, and Philippi. Similarly, archaeology has unearthed theaters in Caesarea, Damascus, Gadara, Jerusalem, Philadelphia, and Scythopolis. Several theaters built by Herod the Great are mentioned in Josephus (*Ant.* 15.8.1; 9.6; 17.8.2; *BJ* 1.21.8). Some have suggested that the book of Revelation is to be understood against the background of Hellenistic drama.

ALLISON A. TRITES

THEBES (Gk. *Thebes*)
The second most populous and important city in Egypt after Memphis. Heb. *nōʾ* corresponds to Egyp. *nỉw(t)*, "the City," and No-Amon corresponds to Egyp. *nỉw(t)-ʾImn*, "the City of (the god) Amun." Thebes is its Greek name.

Thebes is located ca. 483 km. (300 mi.) S of Cairo. The site spans the two banks of the Nile, and is surrounded by an unrivaled combination of sacred precincts and temples, attesting the religious importance of the city. The ruins of the ancient city cover an area of ca. 41-47 sq. km. (16-18 sq. mi.); because of the sparse occupation of the site over the last 1500 years many ancient buildings have survived. The east side of the Nile is marked by the two vast temple precincts of the god Amon, now known by the Arab names Karnak and Luxor; the west side is marked by a row of royal funerary temples behind which extends a vast necropolis of rock-cut tombs. Thebes straddles the Nile at a point where the alluvial plain broadens to a width of ca.

15 km. (9 mi.) providing the region with moderate productivity in crops.

Thebes was capital of Egypt during most of the nation's periods of political unity from the Middle Kingdom to the Assyrian invasion under Assurbanipal (ca. 661 B.C.). During the imperial 18th-20th Dynasties the treasures of Asia and Africa poured into the coffers of Amon of Thebes. All this wealth plus the continuing gifts of Late Period pharaohs such as Shishak fell as spoil to the conquering Assyrians under Assurbanipal.

It was during the 11th Dynasty that Thebes rose from relative obscurity to become the capital of Egypt. The city lost this prominent position with the coming of the Hyksos at the close of the Middle Kingdom but regained its supremacy at the beginning of the New Kingdom.

The 7th-century prophet Nahum compares the imminent fall of Assyria with the conquest of Thebes that has already happened (Nah. 3:8, 10). In the early 6th century both Jeremiah (Jer. 46:25-26) and Ezekiel (Ezek. 30:14-16) spoke against Thebes.

LARRY L. WALKER

THEBEZ (Heb. *tēḇēṣ*)
A city in Ephraim that Abimelech the son of Gideon besieged and conquered, except for the "strong tower," from which a woman dropped a millstone, crushing his skull (Judg. 9:50-54; 2 Sam. 11:21). The city is usually identified with modern Ṭūbâṣ (185192), ca. 16 km. (10 mi.) NE of Nablus.

THEFT
The felonious appropriation of another's property. When accompanied by violence or the threat thereof, theft is normally designated "robbery." In the biblical legal codes, the punishment stipulated for theft is restitution with compensation (Exod. 22:1-4[MT 1b-5]; Lev. 6:1-7[5:20-26]). The command against stealing in the Decalogue (Exod. 20:15; Deut. 5:19) has been understood as referring first to kidnapping, the seizure of persons. In a society in which slavery was practiced, the abduction of persons would of course be addressed in legal codes. Capital punishment is prescribed for the crime of kidnapping (Exod. 21:16; Deut. 24:7). It is likely, however, that the Decalogue command against theft also extended beyond kidnapping. The legal codes address property damage (Exod. 22:5-6[4-5]), dishonest business practices (Lev. 19:35-36; Deut. 25:13-16), and even negligence to prevent another's property from suffering damage (Exod. 23:4-5; Deut. 22:1-4). Interest on loans was prohibited (Exod. 22:25[24]; Deut. 23:19-20; Lev. 25:35-38), and the practice of pledges was regulated (Exod. 22:26-27[25-26]; Deut. 24:6, 10-13). The periodic cancellation of debts (Deut. 15:1-3) and release of slaves (Exod. 21:2-6; Deut. 15:12-18; Lev. 25:39-55) was legislated. It was stipulated that fair wages be paid without deferral to poor laborers (Deut. 24:14-15; Lev. 19:13).

The concern for just and regulated property dealings was taken up by the prophets. The designations "theft" and "robbery" are employed for economic oppression (e.g., Isa. 10:2; Jer. 21:12; Ezek. 18:7). There is the recurring protest against illegal territorial expansion (Jer. 22:13-14; Hab. 2:9; cf. Job 24:2-12; Matt. 23:14). In the postexilic era, Nehemiah made efforts to curtail such economic oppression (cf. Neh. 5). The Wisdom writings continue the prophetic critiques of economic oppression (Prov. 22:22-23; Sir. 4:1-6; 7:3, 20). The NT assumes a similar stance (Luke 3:14; Eph. 4:28; 1 Thess. 4:6; Jas. 5:4-6).

Finally, the Bible speaks of the reality of stealing people's hearts through deceit and demagoguery (Gen. 31:20, 26; 2 Sam. 15:6).

Bibliography. R. Gnuse, *You Shall Not Steal: Community and Property in the Biblical Tradition* (Maryknoll, 1985).

GERALD M. BILKES

THEODOTION
Theodotion of Ephesus, according to early testimony the mid-2nd century scholar responsible for the sixth column of Origen's Hexapla. Theodotion's version appears to be a faithful and literal translation (or in some books a revision of the LXX) of a Semitic text that was very similar to that now known as the MT.

Despite early references to Theodotion, there are difficulties in determining the exact nature and extent of his work. For example, quotations of Theodotion's version, particularly from Daniel, are found in the NT. This led some to conclude that Theodotion added to the work of an earlier writer whom scholars designate Ur-Theodotion, but this notion is increasingly being abandoned. J.-D. Barthélemy argued that Ur-Theodotion, whom he identified as Jonathan ben Uzziel, was the real author and that there were identifying traits of his work, now known as the *kaige* (Palestinian) recension. Some have attempted to propose more characteristics, and, in this approach, *kaige*-Theodotion is still conceived as a unified work. However, it has been shown that books such as Daniel and Job cannot be connected with *kaige*. Thus, the nature and extent of *kaige*-Theodotion remain in question.

Bibliography. T. McLay, *The OG and Theodotion Versions of Daniel.* SBLSCS 43 (Atlanta, 1996); J. W. Wevers, "Barthélemy and Proto-Septuagint Studies," *BIOSCS* 21 (1988): 23-34.

TIM MCLAY

THEODOTUS (Gk. *Theódotos*)
One of the ambassadors sent by Nicanor to Judas Maccabeus to establish peace (2 Macc. 14:19).

THEOPHANY
Technical term for the appearance of God in the OT. The term, which is Greek in origin (from the festival at Delphi; Herodotus *Hist.* 1.51), is a compound of *théos* ("God") and *phaínein* ("to appear"). Although there is no exact Hebrew equivalent for Gk. *theopháнia,* a niphal form of the common Hebrew root *r'h* comes closest. "Theophany" may be translated as the "appearing," "revealing," "shining forth," or simply "vision" of God.

Theophanies take many forms in the OT and function within different contexts in distinct ways. Pentateuchal narratives contain numerous stories of God, or God's manifestation ("glory," "messenger," or "face"), appearing to individuals at moments of narrative tension when the divine promises of land, progeny, and relationship are in doubt (cf. Gen. 12:7; 17:1; 18:1; 26:2, 24; 32:24-32; 35:9; Exod. 3:2; Num. 12:5). In Gen. 12:4-9, e.g., Abram departs Haran under the care of the divine promises, only to discover that the Promised Land is inhabited by Canaanites; at that moment (v. 7) Yahweh appears to reassure the promise of land.

On rarer occasions Yahweh appears to groups as at Sinai (Exod. 19:16-25; cf. 16:10), or when the 70 elders of Israel are vouchsafed a vision of God that is described in uncharacteristically direct terms (24:9-18).

Theophanies in narrative traditions ordinarily bring divine communication and only rarely describe what is seen (cf. Exod. 33:21-23; Ezek. 1). Many texts include language that symbolizes God's nearness, yet emphasizes that direct access to God's presence is limited if not impossible. Earthquake, thunder, lightning, storm wind, shofar blasts, brightness, and darkness suggest God's nearness (Exod. 19:16, 18-19). God tells Moses, "You cannot see my face; for no one shall see me and live" (Exod. 33:20; but cf. Num. 12:8). The extraordinary nature of theophanies is often stressed by the awe or fear of those vouchsafed divine encounters (cf. Gen. 16:13; 32:30; Exod. 3:6; 24:11; Judg. 13:20).

Other contexts for theophanies include prophetic call experiences (cf. 1 Kgs. 22:19; Isa. 6:1, 5; Ezek. 1:1, 27-28; Amos 9:1) and later visions including the hope that Yahweh will appear at a future time to restore Israel (Isa. 35:2; 40:5; 60:2; Zech. 9:14) or to judge (Mal. 3:2-5). Yahweh's appearing is sometimes specifically related to the cult or worship (Lev. 9:4, 6, 23-24; 16:2; Ps. 63:2[MT 3]; 84:7[8]).

Some scholars find the original life-setting of OT theophany in the Song of Deborah (Judg. 5:4-5), a victory hymn following the "Yahweh war." Although the hymn includes the response of nature to Yahweh's presence, it does not include direct divine communication to humans as in other contexts. Perhaps the literary type became dissociated from its original setting with the end of the Yahweh wars during the Monarchy and was freed to move into narrative compositions and be adapted into prophetic oracles.

The theological language of theophany is taken over in certain NT texts that suggest the divine presence in Jesus including the announcement to Joseph (Matt. 1:18-25), baptism (Mark 1:9-11), Transfiguration (9:2-8), and Ascension (Acts 1:6-11; cf. 9:1-9) narratives.

Bibliography. J. K. Kuntz, *The Self-Revelation of God* (Philadelphia, 1967); C. P. Staton, *"And Yahweh Appeared": A Study of the Motifs of "Seeing God" and of "God's Appearing" in Old Testament Narratives* (diss., Oxford, 1988). Cecil P. Staton, Jr.

THEOPHILUS (Gk. *Theóphilos*)
The person to whom Luke's Gospel and Acts are addressed (Luke 1:3; Acts 1:1). Gk. *krátistos,* the adjective translated "most excellent" in Luke 1:3, favors the view that Theophilus ("loved of God" or "friend of God") is the name of a real individual and not merely a symbol for Christian or God-fearing readers. Furthermore, this honorific form of address suggests that Theophilus is highly respected in society, possibly a man of considerable financial means who helped fund the publication of Luke's writings. It is also possible that "most excellent" alludes to an official position he holds within the Roman government (cf. Acts 23:26; 24:2; 26:25).

The author of Luke-Acts wants to make sure that Theophilus has an accurate and orderly historical account of the events surrounding the ministry of Jesus and the emerging Church (Luke 1:2-3) in order that Theophilus might be fully assured of the truth about such matters (v. 4). Whether Theophilus has embraced the Christian faith or not is difficult to determine, for the preface of Luke (1:1-4) and the content of Luke-Acts in general seem appropriate for the interests of evangelism as well as Christian training. Peter K. Nelson

THESSALONIANS, FIRST LETTER TO THE
A letter composed by the Apostle Paul for Christians living in the Macedonian city of Thessalonica. Probably written ca. 51 C.E., 1 Thessalonians is widely regarded as the earliest of Paul's letters and thus the earliest evidence of the Christian movement.

Historical Context

Paul, Silvanus, and Timothy had preached in Thessalonica, following which they left the city and were unable to return (1 Thess. 2:17-19; cf. Acts 17:1-9). Timothy subsequently returned to Thessalonica alone, and his report to Paul about the continued faithfulness of the Thessalonians prompts Paul's letter.

The letter provides little information about the addressees. The assertion in 1:9 that they "turned to God from idols" means that they are Gentiles (cf. 4:5), since Jews already believed in God and are not referred to in this way. Although Acts 17:4 indicates that Jews were among those converted in Thessalonica, the letter does not corroborate that report. Scholars have explored a variety of additional factors in Thessalonica that might shed light on the expectations and experience of the addressees, such as the imperial cult, the predominance in Thessalonica of the worship of Dionysus and Cabirus, and the widespread activity of philosophical teachers.

Epistolary Structure and Function

1 Thessalonians conforms to the structure common in Greco-Roman letters. Following the salutation (1:1), the thanksgiving extends from 1:2 at least through 1:10. Because elements of thanksgiving also appear in 2:13-16; 3:9, however, it is difficult to demarcate the thanksgiving in this letter with any con-

fidence. The main body of the letter consists of two major sections. The first (2:1–3:13) recalls the behavior of the apostles in Thessalonica and the anxiety created by the extended absence of the apostles. The second section (4:1–5:24) addresses issues regarding sexual behavior (4:1-8), the expectation of Jesus' return and its implications both for believers who have died and for those who remain alive (4:13–5:11), and a variety of concerns about life within the community (4:9-12; 5:12-24). Conventional greetings conclude the letter (5:25-28).

Extensive debate focuses on the function of the letter. The study of ancient epistolary theory prompts some to argue that 1 Thessalonians is epideictic (i.e., a letter of praise), while others see it as deliberative rhetoric (i.e., a letter persuading the addressees to follow a particular course of action). Debate on this topic continues, but agreement is emerging that 1 Thessalonians has generally to do with consolidating and correcting the Thessalonians rather than with defending Paul and his colleagues against charges made concerning their behavior.

Significant Features

Eschatology

Eschatological expectations pervade this letter. As early as 1:9 Paul summarizes the Thessalonians' faith as faith in Jesus who is to return "from heaven" and who saves believers from impending wrath (cf. 2:16; 3:13; 5:23). 1 Thess. 4:13–5:11 contains an extended discussion of this topic, apparently provoked by the deaths of some among this group of believers. Drawing on conventional apocalyptic language, Paul assures the Thessalonians that Jesus' triumphant return will mean that both those who have already died and those who remain alive will be with Jesus (4:13-18). That return will come suddenly and requires believers to remain ever vigilant (5:1-11).

Familial Language

1 Thessalonians draws heavily on familial terminology to describe relationships within the church, perhaps as a way of reinforcing the close connections. Believers are siblings of one another (e.g., 2:1; 3:7; 4:1; 5:12). Paul describes the apostles in relationship to the Thessalonians as nursing mothers (2:7), fathers (2:11), and even as orphans (2:17; cf. also 2:7, where several important early manuscripts read "babes" rather than "gentle").

Ethical Instruction

Paul's desire to strengthen the fledgling community at Thessalonica also emerges in the letter's ethical teaching. He warns against sexual immorality (4:1-8) and advocates a quiet, self-sufficient life-style (4:9-12). Neither of these admonitions is unique to Christian teaching, as the philosophical teachers of the day offered similar instructions. What distinguishes Paul's teaching appears to be the goal of pleasing God (4:1) and strengthening the life of the community.

Wrath against "the Jews"

The highly polemical statement in 2:14-16 about Jewish persecution has no parallel in Paul's other letters. Paul seldom speaks of the agents involved in Jesus' death, and nowhere else does he blame Jews for Jesus' death. Moreover, the end of this passage ("God's wrath has overtaken them at last") has no counterpart in other letters. Some scholars suggest that a later editor has inserted these verses, but no manuscript evidence supports that hypothesis. More persuasive is the observation that the sharp wording Paul employs here was a convention of 1st-century writers. In addition, the passage refers to a limited number of Jews or Judeans (residents of the province of Judea), not to all Jews.

Bibliography. F. F. Bruce, *1 and 2 Thessalonians.* WBC 45 (Waco, 1982); R. F. Collins, *The Birth of the New Testament* (New York, 1993); K. P. Donfried and I. H. Marshall, *The Theology of the Shorter Pauline Letters.* New Testament Theology (Cambridge, 1993); E. J. Richard, *First and Second Thessalonians.* Sacra Pagina 11 (Collegeville, 1995).

BEVERLY ROBERTS GAVENTA

THESSALONIANS, SECOND LETTER TO THE

A letter addressed to the church in Thessalonica and attributed to Paul, Silvanus, and Timothy. Despite this attribution, several features of the letter have given rise to a debate about its relationship to 1 Thessalonians. First, 2 Thessalonians closely follows both the form and the wording of 1 Thessalonians (e.g., compare 2 Thess. 1:1-2 and 1 Thess. 1:1; 2 Thess. 2:17 and 1 Thess. 3:13). Second, alongside the similarities are significant differences from 1 Thessalonians and other Pauline letters such as the impersonal, even distant tone of 2 Thessalonians; the absence of reference to the cross or resurrection of Jesus Christ; the expectation of a delayed Parousia (2:1-4) coupled with the striking language anticipating divine vengeance against nonbelievers (e.g., 1:6-10).

Those who contend that Paul wrote 2 Thessalonians point out that the letter is attested in other Christian writings as early as the 2nd century C.E. and that it appears in early canonical lists. According to this view, a persecution at Thessalonica grew more intense within just a few months of Paul's first letter, and that persecution has yielded both unbridled speculation about the return of Jesus and an unwillingness to work. Paul writes to calm this frenzy; the similarities in form and language to 1 Thessalonians occur because this letter follows so quickly on the first.

Those who argue that 2 Thessalonians was not written by Paul find it unlikely that Paul's tone and instruction on the eschaton would have shifted so substantially in a brief period of time. The reference to forgery in 2:2 creates difficulties, since presumably some substantial period of time would be required in which spurious letters could be written and circulated. In addition, the claim in 3:17 that "every letter" of Paul's bears his greeting seems odd if 2 Thessalonians is among Paul's earliest letters. If not written by Paul, 2 Thessalonians may have been written by someone among his co-workers or disciples who employed the authority of Paul to address a situation in which Christians were undergoing intense persecution. Given the early citation of the letter and the sporadic persecutions toward the end of the 1st century, a composition date of the late 1st century is probable. On this view, the identity of the author and audience remain unknown.

Structure and Purpose

In conformity with Greco-Roman letter writing practice, 2 Thessalonians opens with a salutation (1:1-2) and a thanksgiving (1:3-12). The thanksgiving is unusual because of its length and because it introduces a lengthy discussion of Jesus' return (vv. 5-12). The body of the letter (2:1–3:15) concerns the events that surround the "day of the Lord" (2:1-12) and includes a section of ethical instruction (3:1-15). The conventional greetings conclude the letter (3:16-18).

According to rhetorical analysis, the letter is deliberative in that it seeks to persuade the audience to take a certain action. In this case, the author urgently desires that the audience continue in their Christian faith and that they not be troubled by wild apocalyptic speculation.

Significant Features

Divine Justice

2 Thessalonians promises that the future return of Jesus will bring with it judgment against those who have persecuted believers. The writer not only anticipates punishment for those who have afflicted the faithful, but extends that punishment to include "those who do not know God" and "those who do not obey the gospel" (1:8). Such persons will receive "eternal destruction," separated from the presence of the Lord Jesus (1:9). Because the letter does not address the persecutors themselves, as might be expected if its purpose were to warn them about their behavior and urge a conversion in practice and thought, this insistence on the future judgment appears to be aimed at comforting Christians themselves. 2 Thessalonians assures believers that those who currently persecute them will themselves receive justice.

The "Day of the Lord"

In an effort to assure the audience that the "day of the Lord" has not already come, 2 Thessalonians explains that the day itself cannot arrive unless preceded by "the rebellion" and "the lawless one." Other NT writers also expect a time of rebellion against God and a blasphemous antichrist (e.g., Matt. 24:4-28; 1 Tim. 4:1; 1 John 2:18). Discerning exactly who or what the author understands by "the lawless one," if indeed the author had a specific reference in mind, is now impossible. Whatever the nature of the rebellion, the author is confident that God will triumph over it.

Bibliography. F. F. Bruce, *1 and 2 Thessalonians.* WBC 45 (Waco, 1982); K. P. Donfried and I. H. Marshall, *The Theology of the Shorter Pauline Letters.* New Testament Theology (Cambridge, 1993); E. Krentz, "Through a Lens: Theology and Fidelity in 2 Thessalonians," in *Pauline Theology,* ed. J. M. Bassler (Minneapolis, 1991) 1:52-62; E. J. Richard, *First and Second Thessalonians.* Sacra Pagina 11 (Collegeville, 1995). BEVERLY ROBERTS GAVENTA

THESSALONICA (Gk. *Thessaloníkē*)
A city located on the Thermaic Gulf to the west of the Chalcidice Peninsula. The Axios River lies to the west and the Strymon River to the east. The city was probably built near, but not on, the original site of Therme.

Thessalonica was founded in 316 B.C.E. by Cassander, one of Alexander the Great's generals, and named after his wife, a stepsister of Alexander. It became the main port of the Macedonian capital of Pella. The city was surrendered to Rome after the defeat of Perseus at the battle of Pydna (168). When Macedonia was divided into four districts, Thessalonica was made the capital of the second. However, it retained the right to be governed according to its ancestral laws and to have its own officials. As a result of its support for Augustus, Thessalonica was made a free city in 42 B.C.E. It retained its Greek character and language throughout the Roman period.

Thessalonica had always been a prominent center of trade, but by the Roman period it was at the junction of two important transportation routes. The primary east-west land route, the Via Egnatia, ran through the center of Thessalonica while its port was the beginning of the primary route from the Aegean Sea to the Danube River. The Sea itself made Thessalonica accessible from all points in the circum-Mediterranean.

Unfortunately, little of Thessalonica has been excavated as the modern city is built upon the ancient site. Significant finds from the Roman period or earlier include the forum and a Serapeum. A 4th-century C.E. inscription attests the presence of a Samaritan community at Thessalonica.

During the 1st century C.E. mystery cults were thriving at Thessalonica, particularly that of Sarapis and Isis, Dionysos, Asclepius, Demeter, and the Cabiri/Dioscuri. The worship of the Egyptian gods may even date to as early as the 3rd century B.C.E. Emperor worship was also particularly strong at Thessalonica, and there is some evidence for the worship of the goddess Roma. Many inscriptions were also set up by the Thessalonians honoring Roman patrons and Roman client rulers who had been benefactors of the city. A number of voluntary associations are attested at Thessalonica, including the *mystai* of Dionysos and various professional associations.

The primary source of information for the church at Thessalonica comes from the two Pauline epistles addressed there (1 and 2 Thessalonians) and from Acts. Thessalonica was the second European city visited by Paul (Acts 17:1-9; 1 Thess. 2:2). According to Luke's account Paul first preached in a synagogue with limited results among Jews and God-fearers, including some wealthy women.

When the Jewish leaders incited a mob to attack the house of Jason, Paul's host, Paul and Silas fled to Beroea. The remaining Christian community was predominantly Gentile and served as an example to other churches in Macedonia and Achaia (1 Thess. 1:8-9). The term *politárchēs,* used for the civic magistrates of Thessalonica in Acts 17:6-8, has now been found in a number of 1st-century C.E. inscriptions from Thessalonica.

Bibliography. K. P. Donfried, "The Cults of Thessalonica and the Thessalonian Correspondence," *NTS* 31 (1985): 336-56; H. L. Hendrix, *Thessalonians Honor Romans* (diss., Harvard, 1984); A. E. Vacalopoulos, *A History of Thessaloniki* (Thessalonica, 1963), 3-18. RICHARD S. ASCOUGH

THEUDAS (Gk. *Theudás*)

Leader of a popular Jewish resistance movement put down by the Romans. In Acts 5:36 Gamaliel reports before the Jerusalem council that Theudas, purporting "to be somebody," had rallied some 400 supporters for his cause; in the end, however, he was executed and his followers were scattered. In Gamaliel's view this outcome justified a "wait-and-see" policy toward Peter and fellow witnesses: if they were not authorized by God, they would ultimately fail — like Theudas and Judas the Galilean (another frustrated rebel mentioned in Acts 5:37).

Josephus identifies Theudas as a prophetic pretender who incited a majority of Judean peasants to take up their possessions and follow him to the Jordan River (*Ant.* 20.97-98). Here he planned to part the waters by fiat and lead his people across, effecting either a Moses-style "exodus" from oppressive rule or a wilderness "exile" in preparation for a new Joshua-type "conquest" of the Promised Land. In any case, his seditious scheme was thwarted by an ambush from a Roman cavalry unit dispatched by the governor Fadus (44-46 C.E.). Theudas' head was cut off and put on display in Jerusalem.

Bibliography. R. A. Horsley and J. S. Hanson, *Bandits, Prophets, and Messiahs: Popular Movements at the Time of Jesus* (1985, repr. Harrisburg, 1999), 160-67. F. SCOTT SPENCER

THIGH

The upper part of the leg. The term (Heb. *yārēḵ*) has sexual connotations and probably refers to genitals. When used in conjunction with the verb *yāzāʾ,* "to come from," the expression is understood as a reference to "offspring" (those who "come from" the thigh; Gen. 46:26; Exod. 1:5; Judg. 8:30). Sometimes the term is translated "hip" or "hip socket." The related Hebrew word *yarkâ* also has cultic connotations, meaning "side" (of the altar; Exod. 40:22, 24; Lev. 1:11; Num. 3:29, 35; 2 Kgs. 16:14) or "base" (of the golden lampstand; Exod. 25:31; 37:17; Num. 8:4).

Swords were worn on the thigh (sometimes rendered "side"; Exod. 32:27; Judg. 3:16, 21; Ps. 45:3[MT 4]; Cant. 3:8). One might be hit or "smote" there in battle or to express remorse (Judg. 15:8; Jer. 31:19; Ezek. 21:12[17]). The priests wore linen breeches from the loins to the thigh (Exod. 28:42). When a woman has been unfaithful to her husband, and a priest makes her drink the "water of bitterness" (Num. 5:16-28), her thigh will "fall away" (vv. 21, 22, 27), perhaps meaning to suffer a miscarriage. The thigh is part of the stew in the cookingpot in Ezekiel's vision of the rebellious house (Ezek. 24:4). Finally, the author of Canticles describes his lover's thighs as jewels (Cant. 7:1[2]).

Abraham's servant swears that he will carry out Abraham's dying wish (Gen. 24:2, 9), placing his hand under the "thigh" of Abraham. This is clearly a serious oath, sworn on the genitals, the source of life, and thus under threat of the loss of fertility. When Jacob struggles with God at Penuel, God hits Jacob in the genitals/thigh (Gen. 32:25-26[26-27]), causing Jacob to limp (v. 31[32]); the account becomes an etiological story about a ban on consuming that portion of an animal (v. 32[33]). Like Abraham's servant, Joseph places his hand under the thigh of his dying father Jacob and swears an oath (Gen. 47:29).

In the NT Gk. *mērós* occurs only in Rev. 19:16, where the phrase "King of kings and Lord of lords" is written upon the "thigh" and robe of Christ.

Bibliography. S. Gevirtz, "Of Patriarchs and Puns: Joseph at the Fountain, Jacob at the Ford," *HUCA* 46 (1975): 33-54; M. Malul, "More on *paḥad yiṣḥāq* (Genesis XXXI 42, 53) and the Oath by the Thigh," *VT* 35 (1985): 192-200; S. H. Smith, "'Heel' and 'Thigh': The Concept of Sexuality in the Jacob-Esau Narratives," *VT* (1990): 464-73.

JOHN R. SPENCER

THIRTY, THE

The standard designation of David's special cadre of elite warriors, also called "Mighty Men" (Heb. *gibbôrîm,* "heroes, champions, heroic warriors"). The OT contains two similar — though hardly identical — lists of these warriors: 2 Sam. 23:24-39; 1 Chr. 11:26-47, neither of which contains 30 names. 2 Samuel lists 32, not mentioning the named (and unnumbered) "sons of Jashen," while 1 Chr. 11 gives 46, omitting the various groups whose members are also unnamed and unnumbered.

Despite the dominance of the traditional reading "the Thirty" *(haššĕlôšîm),* variant Hebrew manuscripts, and certain readings of the MT itself, attest a muted tradition in which Heb. *šālîšîm,* "third" (pl.), was read. Heb. *šālîš* may originally have referred to the third man in the chariot, hence its presence in Exod. 15:4. From the time of David onward the *šālîšîm* have nothing to do with chariotry, but appear as elite infantry alongside other obscure special units, such as the *rāṣîm,* "runners" (cf. 2 Kgs. 10:25). A possible explanation of the term in this context is that the *šālîšîm* were organized into squads of three, as special commandos, fighting in support of one another. Thus the stories prefixed to the two lists count the exploits of "the three," then proceed to the story of the anonymous three who broke through the Philistine line at Bethlehem to draw water from the well there for David. When these *šālîšîm* became a separate cadre within David's army is unclear, but the inclusion of this incident from the Philistine wars, and the name of Asahel, brother to Joab and Abishai, suggests an early date.

Scant evidence exists that there were ever 30 of these. The inclusion of men such as Asahel, who was killed early on in the war with the house of Saul, and Uriah the Hittite, sent to his death by David during the Ammonite wars (2 Sam. 11-12), as well as the latecomer Benaiah ben Jehoiada, who served as commander of the army throughout Solomon's reign, indicates that the lists contain no set number of men, but rather the names and groups who attained this elite status throughout David's reign.

Both Hebrew terms refer to the same body of elite retainers, attached directly to the person of the king, and chosen for this service by special acts of valor. They were by profession heavily armed infantrymen, "champions." As such, either singly or in their three-man groups, they could be stationed along a battle line to strengthen the levies, or massed as a group at a single point to break the enemy line, a tactic employed by Joab and Abishai against the Syrians and Ammonites (2 Sam. 10). Certain of these warriors were appointed to positions as high-ranking officers in David's military (e.g., Abishai, Benaiah).

Bibliography. D. G. Schley, "The *Šālîšîm:* Officers or Special Three-man Squads?" *VT* 40 (1990): 321-26.

DONALD G. SCHLEY

THISTLE

Various Hebrew words have been translated "thistle," "thorn," "brier," "bramble," and "nettle," and one translation may use various English terms for the same Hebrew word. However, translations have rendered Heb. *dārdar,* "thistle," quite consistently. This word occurs only twice in the Bible, once as part of God's curse on the land (Gen. 3:18) and once as a symbol of Israel's destruction (Hos. 10:8). Both times, *dārdar* is coupled with *qôṣ,* usually translated "thorn." Heb. *ḥôaḥ* is also sometimes rendered "thistle." In the NT thistles (Gk. *tríbolos,* "three pronged") are also paired with thorns (Gk. *ákantha*).

Thistles are widespread in Israel. Some species include the Spanish thistle *(Centaurea iberica Spreng),* which has whorl-like leaves, the Globe thistle (*Echinops viscosus* DC), which bears round purple flowers, the Syrian thistle (*Notobasis syriaca* [L.] Coss.), and the Holy thistle, or "Mary's thistle," (*Silybum marianum* [L.] Gaertn).

Thistles and thorns quickly take over uncultivated land, and thus they represent uselessness (cf. Matt. 7:16; Heb. 6:8). Thistles burn easily, and fire is the most common and effective form of clearing.

MEGAN BISHOP MOORE

THOMAS (Gk. *Thōmás*)

One of Jesus' original 12 disciples. He is named in all the Synoptic Gospels and Acts (Matt. 10:3; Mark 3:18; Luke 6:15; Acts 1:13), but plays no further role in those writings. The name is a Greek transliteration of Aram. *tĕ'ômā',* "twin," translated as Didymus (Gk. *Dídymos,* "double") in John 11:16; 20:24; 21:2.

Thomas appears prominently in John, during the final stages of Jesus' earthly life. When Jesus indicates that he is going back into Judea where "the Jews" had recently tried to stone him to death, Thomas courageously urges the disciples to accompany Jesus, "that we may die with him" (John 11:16). In John 14:5 he appears to lack a deeper understanding of Jesus, questioning how they can follow Jesus when they do not even know his destination; Jesus responds that he is that "way." When the other disciples report that Jesus has appeared to them, Thomas adamantly says that he will not believe Jesus is alive unless he can put his finger into the print of the nails in Jesus' hands and put his hand into Jesus' side (John 20:24-25). Jesus appears to the disciples eight days later when Thomas is present and invites him to satisfy his conditions for belief; Thomas responds, "My Lord and my God!" (John 20:26-28). Thomas is last mentioned among a group of disciples to whom the risen Jesus appears beside the Sea of Tiberius/Galilee (John 21:2).

JOE E. LUNCEFORD

THOMAS, ACTS OF

The only one of the apocryphal acts to survive in its entirety. The Acts of Thomas relates the evangelical work of the apostle during his journey to India. As with most of other acts, the apostle is depicted as working numerous miracles, including casting out demons and reviving the dead. In several of the episodes those who return from the dead give explicit descriptions of hell and heaven. Also included are animals that speak, including one wild ass that exorcizes a demon and then preaches to the assembled multitude. Thomas is martyred by a powerful Indian official because the apostle had converted his wife to a celibate and ascetic life-style.

Two extended poetic sections, the Hymn of the Bride and the Hymn of the Pearl, which display clearly identifiable gnostic elements, have led many to characterize the whole of the Acts of Thomas as gnostic. For example, in the Hymn of the Pearl the story of an eastern prince's recovery of a pearl and his receiving a special garment as a reward for its retrieval is often interpreted as an allegory of the soul's journey through the material world and its eventual reunion with the heavenly realms. However, the majority of the legendary tales involve little that can be clearly reckoned as gnostic. Instead, like most of the other apocryphal acts, the Acts of Thomas seems to reflect popular early Christian themes of ascetic piety and unworldliness.

Preserved in several languages, the primary witnesses to the Acts of Thomas are Syriac and Greek. Syriac is the most likely candidate for its original language, as the Greek displays several errors which resulted from misunderstanding of the Syriac. However, the surviving Syriac versions clearly have undergone some emendations to make them more palatable to later "orthodox" Christians. The work most likely originated in Syria, probably in Edessa, in the first half of the 3rd century. Although the text claims that Judas Thomas, the twin of Jesus, is the author, the dating of the text makes such a claim improbable. As such, the Acts are generally regarded as an anonymous composition.

Bibliography. J. K. Elliott, *The Apocryphal New Testament*, rev. ed. (Oxford, 1993), 439-511; A. F. J. Klijn, *The Acts of Thomas*. NovTSup 5 (Leiden, 1962).

JAMES R. MUELLER

THOMAS, GOSPEL OF (II, 2)

A Coptic document buried near Nag Hammadi, Egypt, ca. A.D. 340, containing "the secret sayings that the living Jesus spoke and Didymos Judas Thomas recorded." Like most of the early Christian Coptic texts in the Nag Hammadi library, it is a translation of what originally was a Greek text. Less than 10 percent of the material in the Coptic manuscript exists in the fragmentary Greek manuscripts written ca. A.D. 140 and found earlier in the remains of Oxyrhynchus, Egypt. Both Didymos (Greek) and Thomas (Aramaic) mean "the twin," so Judas, the supposed author of the text, had a bilingual nickname. Who this man was is unknown, but it is highly unlikely that he was Jesus' disciple Thomas.

A list of at least 150 separate sayings attributed to Jesus, the Gospel of Thomas is the most important noncanonical Christian text for inquiry into the teachings of the historical Jesus. Scholars divide those sayings into units (some containing several sayings) separated by the very common introductory phrase "Jesus said." This manner of division results in a set of 114 sayings, the basis of the numbering system used by all scholars today. The structure of the Gospel is an almost random list of separate sayings connected sometimes by "catchwords" (words which appear in several sayings in a row). This is evidence that Thomas may indeed be what it says it is, a list put together from memory by an individual. There are few glosses and little commentary in the text itself. What little there is emphasizes a theme of unity, e.g., making the two one, becoming a single one, but the question "two what into one what?" is never clearly answered.

Both Q and Thomas are lists of sayings, having about one third of their sayings in common, but they are not otherwise connected. Thomas is not Q, nor a source for Q, nor is Q a source for Thomas. The Q hypothesis does, however, gain strength from the fact that Thomas proves that lists of sayings did circulate in the early churches.

More than half of the sayings of Jesus in the Gospel of Thomas also appear in the Gospels of Matthew, Mark, and Luke (very few also appear in John). Most of the remainder are otherwise unknown. Many of those hitherto unknown sayings indicate that the kingdom of the Father is to be found now, within people and spread out upon the earth. Discovery of the kingdom of the Father requires, in the Thomasine view, discovery of the light within oneself and realization that the kingdom has been present, although invisibly, since the beginning of time. From the Thomasine perspective, Jesus came to earth to reveal the hidden presence of the kingdom. Some call these perspectives "gnostic," others "proto-gnostic"; still others simply find them to reflect ideas common in 1st-century Platonism and see no need to apply the loaded term "gnostic" to Thomas.

Although Thomas contains sayings parallel to material unique to the Synoptic Gospels and a considerable number of sayings that are also found in Q, the additions and contextualizations and elaborations of sayings that characterize the efforts of Matthew, Mark, and Luke as they worked to include Jesus' sayings into their Gospels are almost completely lacking here. It is highly unlikely that Thomas went through the three Synoptic Gospels, carefully cutting sayings from their narrative contexts and eliminating in detail the additions to sayings that we have reason to believe were put there by the Synoptic authors. The versions of the sayings in Thomas that are also found in the Synoptic Gospels often form critically less elaborated versions lacking allegorical commentary and narrative context, and so they appear to be in more primitive forms. Such considerations allow scholars to conclude that the Gospel of Thomas came into being as an independent document, deriving its sayings from oral tradition and not from the canonical Gospels. Because it was repeatedly copied by Christian scribes, who at any point may have inserted elements they knew from other Gospels into the Thomas text they were copying (a process called "scribal harmonization" that is well known to text critical scholarship of the NT), Thomas in some places shows knowledge of details found in canonical Gospels. While some scholars believe that these details prove Thomas' dependence upon the canonical texts, that perspective is less frequently adopted today than it was decades ago.

The date of the Gospel of Thomas is unknown. Because it is simply a list of sayings, and because it made use of material circulating in early oral tradition, Thomas may derive from the same time as Q, ca. 50-80. Indeed, recent scholarship has shown that Q was a more organized sayings list than Thomas, a fact that hints at a somewhat later date for Q. However, scholars who take the view that Thomas is a gnostic text tend to date its origin to the early to mid-2nd century. Similarly, the place of Thomas' origin is unknown. Various documents having to do with the Apostle Thomas seem to have originated in Syria, although at a considerably later date than the Gospel of Thomas, and so some argue that Thomas also probably originated there. Alternatively, because it was well known in Oxyrhynchus at an early date, it is possible that Thomas is an early example of Egyptian Christianity.

Two parables found in the Gospel of Thomas are particularly interesting because they show every sign of having been spoken by Jesus himself, and yet they are not to be found in the canonical Gospels. They are:

97. Jesus said, "The Kingdom of the [Father] is like a certain woman who was carrying a jar full of meal. While she was walking [on] a road, still some distance from home, the handle of the jar broke and the meal emp-

tied out behind her on the road. She did not realize it; she had noticed no accident. When she reached her house, she set the jar down and found it empty."

98. Jesus said, "The Kingdom of the Father is like a certain man who wanted to kill a powerful man. In his own house he drew his sword and stuck it into the wall to order to find out whether his hand could carry through. Then he slew the powerful man."

The following two sayings seem to express a particularly Thomasine view of the teachings of Jesus:

3. Jesus said, "If those who lead you say, 'See, the kingdom is in the sky,' then the birds of the sky will precede you. Rather, the kingdom is inside of you, and it is outside of you. When you come to know yourselves, then you will become known, and you will realize that it is you who are the sons of the living Father. But if you will not know yourselves, you dwell in poverty and it is you who are that poverty."

113. His disciples said to him, "When will the kingdom come?" <Jesus said,> "It will not come by waiting for it. It will not be a matter of saying 'Here it is' or 'There it is.' Rather, the kingdom of the Father is spread out upon the earth, and men do not see it."

Bibliography. S. Davies, *The Gospel of Thomas and Christian Wisdom* (New York, 1983); A. D. DeConick, *Seek to See Him: Ascent and Vision Mysticism in the Gospel of Thomas.* VCSup 33 (Leiden, 1996); M. W. Meyer, *The Gospel of Thomas* (San Francisco, 1992); S. J. Patterson, *The Gospel of Thomas and Jesus* (Sonoma, 1993). STEVAN DAVIES

THOMAS, INFANCY GOSPEL OF

A collection of folkloric tales of Jesus' childhood, from the age of five to 12 years, which exists in numerous translations and textual recensions, some of which do not attribute the text to Thomas. The best-known version of the tales was edited by Constantin von Tischendorf in the 19th century (Greek A), based on two Greek manuscripts dating from the 15th century; he also edited a shorter Greek version (Greek B), based also on a medieval manuscript which appears to be a deliberate abridgment of a longer recension, and a Latin version. Though Greek A has virtually become the *textus receptus* of the Infancy Gospel, it should not be assumed that it represents the earliest textual version. Many are skeptical that we can ever reconstruct an "autograph," since the traditions contained in the various manuscripts were free-floating and apparently whole tales were added and deleted after the traditions were first written down. Irenaeus is familiar with a written form of some of these traditions, leading most to date the earliest written version of these stories to the later part of the 2nd century. There is debate whether the original language of the first written text was Syriac or Greek. There is also debate as to whether one should label the tales as gnostic.

Some of the more intriguing stories include those of the young Jesus bringing to life clay sparrows which he had fashioned (2:1-5 [Greek A, as are all references]), encountering the Jewish teacher Zacchaeus (6:1–7:4), raising from the dead a child who fell from a roof (9:1-3), and lengthening a board which Joseph had cut too short (13:1-2). It ends with a version of Jesus' trip to the Jerusalem temple (cf. Luke 2:41-51).

Bibliography. J. K. Elliot, *The Apocryphal New Testament* (Oxford, 1993), 68-83; O. Cullmann, "The Infancy Story of Thomas," in *New Testament Apocrypha,* ed. W. Schneemelcher and R. McL. Wilson, rev. ed. (Louisville, 1991) 1:439-51.

J. BRADLEY CHANCE

THORN

The thorn of the Bible is not one particular plant. Like the English word "thorn," it is a general designation for several species. More than 20 Hebrew words have been rendered "thorn," "thistle," "brier," "bramble," and "nettle" by various translations, often inconsistently. Of these, Heb. *qôṣ, šayiṯ, 'āṭāḏ,* and *ḥôaḥ* appear frequently in pairs. Gk. *ákantha* also means "thorn."

Thorns grew profusely and easily in ancient Israel. *Ziziphus spina-christi* (L.) Desf. and *Paliurus spina-christi* Mill. are two common thorns that have been identified with Christ's crown of thorns (Matt. 27:29 par.). However, it is impossible to discern which plant was used to make the crown, as there are more than 70 species of thornlike plants in the Holy Land. *Ziziphus spina-christi* may grow more than 9 m. (30 ft.) in height and bears a small, low-quality fruit. It may be the thorn of Jotham's parable in Judg. 9:8-15 (NRSV "bramble"). Jesus alludes to the low-quality fruit of the thorn when he asks, "Are grapes gathered from thorns, or figs from thistles?" (Matt. 7:16; cf. Luke 6:44).

In Gen. 3:17-18 God curses the ground, declaring that it would bear thorns and thistles. Indeed, farmers must constantly battle thorns which grow readily on untended land (Prov. 15:19). Jesus uses this image in the parable of the Sower (Mark 4:1-9 par.). The prophets use thorns and briers as symbols of the desolation of the land and the people (e.g., Isa. 5:6; Jer. 12:13).

Thorns were used as hedges (Sir. 28:24) and instruments of torture (Judg. 8:16). They are highly flammable (Exod. 22:6[MT 5]), cleared by burning (Isa. 33:12), and were used in hearth fires (Ps. 58:9; Eccl. 7:6).

At 2 Cor. 12:7 Gk. *skólops* refers to a physical affliction ("a thorn . . . in the flesh").

MEGAN BISHOP MOORE

THOUSAND

In its earliest meaning, a subdivision among the tribes, with varying breadth (Heb. *'elep*). The term stands in parallel to *mišpāḥâ,* "family," in 1 Sam. 10:19, but in Num. 1:16; 10:4, 36; Josh. 22:21 it appears to be the equivalent of *šēḇeṭ,* "tribe." In a general sense, however, this subdivision is usually different from, and smaller than, the tribe. A similar subdivision existed among the early Arab tribes.

Later, as first Saul, then later David, moved to organize the infantry along more regular lines, the subdivision "thousand," which roughly corresponds to a modern battalion, became the largest of the various military units. As such, it probably continued in use down to the end of the monarchy.

DONALD G. SCHLEY

THRACE (Gk. *Thrakē*)

The mountainous northernmost region of Greece, lying between the Danube River on the north and the Strymon River and Illyria on the west, and N of Macedonia. Thracians were considered primitive (dyeing their hair and tattooing their skin) and warlike (often hiring out as mercenaries; 2 Macc. 12:35), living by plunder rather than by agriculture, but skilled at making tools and weapons. In Greek poetry Thrace symbolizes isolation, desolation, and inhospitable frigidity. Urbanization of their villages came only with the conquest of Thrace by the Romans. Claudius made it a province in 46 C.E., dividing it in two, with the region N of Mt. Haemus becoming Moesia and that to the south becoming Thrace proper. The Thracians influenced Greek religion greatly, particularly in the worship of the god of war Ares and the god of wine Dionysus (whose wild, orgiastic nighttime worship was outlawed by the Roman Senate in 186 B.C.E.).

Bibliography. J. J. Wilkes, "Thrace," in *The Oxford Classical Dictionary,* ed. S. Hornblower and A. Spawforth, 3rd ed. (Oxford, 1996), 1514-15.

RICHARD A. SPENCER

THREE TAVERNS

A station ca. 48 km. (30 mi.) S of Rome on the great Roman highway, the Appian Way. The Christians of the church at Rome met Paul here to encourage him as he came to stand trial in the imperial capital (Acts 28:15).

THRESHING FLOOR

The site where harvested grain (barley or wheat) is spread out to dry so the seed kernels can be separated from the chaff. This separation can be accomplished by beating the stalks of grain with a flail, but it most typically involves the use of a threshing sledge. This sledge, made of a heavy board or boards into which stones have been embedded, is dragged repeatedly by an ox or donkey across the grain, separating husk from seed.

Threshing floors seem to have been located at the edge or gate of a village or town (1 Kgs. 22:10 = 2 Chr. 18:9), and, perhaps because of this proximity, they can be sites of activities other than agricultural: e.g., Ruth's seduction of Boaz (Ruth 3:1-18). These nonagricultural activities are often cultic in nature. In Gen. 50:10-11, when Joseph and his brothers return the bones of their father Jacob to Canaan, their mourning rituals are held at the threshing floor of Atad, somewhere on the east bank of the Jordan. According to Judg. 6:37 Gideon, desiring a sign that he will indeed serve as God's deliverer in Israel's war against Moab, receives the assurance he seeks at a threshing floor. 1 Kgs. 22:10 par. report that prophets prophesy before the kings of Israel and Judah at the threshing floor of Samaria. Most significant, though, are the traditions found in 2 Sam. 24 (= 1 Chr. 21), where David sees an angel of Yahweh at the threshing floor of Araunah the Jebusite (vv. 16-17) and subsequently buys the property and erects an altar there (vv. 18-25). 2 Chr. 3:1 associates this location with the site in Jerusalem where Solomon eventually built his great temple.

SUSAN ACKERMAN

THRESHOLD

The base or sill of the doorway, usually made of stone, that contains the sockets on which the door pivot turns (Heb. *sap̱*).

In Judg. 19:27 the concubine of a Levite is killed and the body is left lying at the entrance to his home with her hands on the threshold. Dagon lies fallen across the threshold of his temple at Ashdod where his head and hands have been broken off, causing the Philistines not to tread on the threshold from that day forward (1 Sam. 5:4-5). When the queen crosses the threshold of the house, Jeroboam's son dies, fulfilling the oracle of the Lord spoken by the prophet Ahijah (1 Kgs. 14:17).

Numerous references indicate that guards protected the thresholds of cities. Esth. 2:21 (cf. 6:2) describes the plot against Ahasuerus by two eunuchs who guarded the threshold of the palace. Gatekeepers who stood at the king's gate and at the thresholds to the camp of the Levites and the sanctuary number 212 (1 Chr. 9:17-22). The threshold of Solomon's temple is lined with gold (2 Chr. 3:7). During the Divided Monarchy the threshold of the temple is guarded by selected individuals (2 Kgs. 12:9; 22:4; 23:4; 2 Chr. 34:9; Jer. 35:4), at times three in number (2 Kgs. 25:18 = Jer. 52:24).

In OT apocalyptic the threshold has religious and spiritual significance. It is to the threshold of the temple that Yahweh goes to deliver a message (Ezek. 9:3; 10:4). During Ezekiel's oracle the threshold of the new temple of Yahweh is measured (Ezek. 40:6-7). Worship is associated with the threshold of the gate (Ezek. 46:2), and the temple threshold area is to have sufficient space from the common homes of the people (43:8). The practice of leaping over the threshold is denounced (Zeph. 1:9) and may refer to a pagan custom (cf. 1 Sam. 5:5). The theophany of God is often accompanied by earthquakes that shake the thresholds (Isa. 6:4; Amos 9:1).

Threshold stones have been found throughout Syria-Palestine. Often made of a solid piece of limestone, they are found in the gates of major cities of various periods (Gezer, Hazor, Lachish, Megiddo, Shechem). Temples also exhibit the same type of threshold at their entrances (Ashdod, Tel Miqne-Ekron, Lachish, Hazor). At Tel Miqne-Ekron three massive threshold stones mark the entrance to an Assyrian-type temple dedicated to the god *ptgyh*. The religious significance of the threshold is evident in numerous archaeological contexts where "lamp-and-bowl" foundation deposits or child burials have been found beneath the area where thresholds were located.

Bibliography. S. Bunimovitz and O. Zimhoni, "'Lamp-and-Bowl' Foundation Deposits in Canaan," *IEJ* 43 (1993): 99-125; S. Gitin, T. Dothan, and J. Naveh, "A Royal Dedicatory Inscription from Ekron," *IEJ* 47 (1997): 1-16; A. Kempinski and R. Reich, eds., *The Architecture of Ancient Israel* (Jerusalem, 1992). MICHAEL G. HASEL

THRONE

A seat that symbolizes authority and majesty, particularly that of a king (Gen. 41:40; 2 Sam. 3:10). The king is God's representative, and the king's throne typifies the heavenly divine throne (1 Chr. 28:5-7; 1 Kgs. 22:10, 19; Isa. 6:1). As such the throne and its occupant are to emulate God's character and commandments (Prov. 16:12; 20:28). David is promised that his descendants on the throne will be as God's sons, disciplined for sin but perpetually receiving God's loyal love on an eternal throne (2 Sam. 7:13-16; cf. Ps. 89:4[MT 5]).

Mary is promised that Jesus will occupy David's throne forever (Luke 1:32; cf. Isa. 9:7[6]; 16:5; Acts 2:30; Heb. 1:8; 8:1; 12:2). The 12 apostles who have followed Jesus in this world will reign with him on 12 thrones in the coming world (Matt. 19:28; Luke 22:30). Angelic powers, both good and evil, are also described as thrones (Col. 1:16; cf. Eph. 1:21; Rev. 2:13).

The book of Revelation focuses upon God, who alone sits upon the throne (Rev. 4:2–5:1). Yet Jesus, envisioned as the Lamb, is worthy of the same praise as God and will reign with God forever (Rev. 5:6-13). Perhaps the enigmatic 24 elders (e.g., Rev. 4:4) who sit on 24 thrones symbolize the ultimate people of God, comprised of Israel (12 tribes) and the Church (12 apostles). The final judgment issues from the One who sits upon a great white throne (Rev. 20:11-15). DAVID L. TURNER

THUMB

The inner, opposable digit of the human hand (Heb. *bōhen*). The priestly ordination of Aaron and his sons involves applying sacrificial blood on each one's right thumb, right big toe, and right ear lobe (Exod. 29:20; Lev. 8:23-24). The same activity is part of the ritual of cleansing a leper (Lev. 14:14, 17, 25, 28). King Adoni-bezek, after being captured by Judah and having his thumbs and big toes cut off, boasts that he himself severed the thumbs and big toes of 70 other rulers (Judg. 1:6-7). In all of these passages, the Hebrew word for thumb and big toe is the same. JOHN KALTNER

THUMMIM

See URIM AND THUMMIM.

THUNDER

Thunder was believed by peoples of the ancient Near East to be the manifestation of God's voice (Heb. *qôl*), an aspect of divine self-revelation in storms (Exod. 19:19; 20:18; 2 Sam. 22:14 = Ps. 18:13[MT 14]). Lightning and thunder might signify God's power and majesty (Job 37:2-5; Ps. 29:3-9) or might be part of the exercise of his anger against his people when they sinned (1 Sam. 12:17-18; Isa. 29:6) or against the enemies of his people (Exod. 9:23; 1 Sam. 2:10; 7:10). John 12:29 notes that some of the crowd interpreted the voice from heaven responding to Jesus at the end of his public ministry as thunder. In Revelation thunder is associated with the divine majesty (Rev. 4:5, possibly an allusion to Exod. 19:16) and with judgment (e.g., Rev. 10:3-4).

THUNDER, SONS OF

See BOANERGES.

THUTMOSE (Egyp. *ḏḥwty-ms;* Gk. *Tythmósis*)

The name of four kings of Egypt's 18th Dynasty. Following the expulsion of the Hyksos by Ahmose and the subsequent unification of Egypt, the early kings of the 18th Dynasty carved out an Egyptian Empire from Nubia (Cush) to northern Syria. The Thutmosids played an integral part in the expansion, especially in Palestine and Syria, through a series of campaigns against pressure from the kingdom of Mitanni located E of the Euphrates River. The military victories and building projects of these kings propelled Thebes and Amon (Amon-Re), the local Theban deity, into national prominence.

1. Thutmose I (1525-1512 B.C.), son-in-law of Amenhotep I. He campaigned deep into Nubia, extending Egyptian control beyond the Third Cataract. More importantly, he led a military expedition northward crossing the Euphrates and engaged the army of Mitanni, an event commemorated by a stela erected on the east bank of the river. This raid was the harbinger of more concentrated efforts to bring the Levant under Egyptian control.

2. Thutmose II (1512-1504), married to his half sister Hatshepsut. He crushed a revolt in Nubia and led a razzia into southern Palestine, but poor health led to a premature death. The heir apparent, Thutmose III, was too young to assume his kingly duties; Hatshepsut assumed the role of coregent at first, but ruled independently for 20 years (1502-1482).

3. Thutmose III (1504-1450). He emerged from Hatshepsut's shadow to become one of the most capable kings of ancient Egypt. An unusually gifted military leader, he launched a campaign (ca. 1482/1481) against a coalition of rebellious Levantine kings headed by the king of Kadesh, a coalition no doubt inspired by the king of Mitanni. Thutmose III defeated the coalition, said to include 330 kings of various cities, at Megiddo. Detailed accounts of the victory, including a lengthy text in the temple of Amon-Re at Thebes, describe the Egyptian battle tactics and booty recovered from the region. Three lists of conquered cities also inscribed on the temple's walls contain the names of 119 cities and villages in Palestine and southern Syria, an invaluable source for Late Bronze Age Palestine. Subsequently, Thutmose III made at least 15 more campaigns into the Levant, establishing an Egyptian Asiatic empire that extended at least to southern Syria. On his eighth campaign, Thutmose III crossed the Euphrates and defeated Mitannian forces, setting up a victory stela as had his grandfather decades earlier.

4. Thutmose IV (1425-1417), successor to Amenhotep II (1450-1425). He followed his father in continuing the Egyptian hegemony of the kings of the Levant established by Thutmose III. Recent studies suggest that Thutmose IV, although he did not campaign as vigorously as had his father, lost none of the hard-won Egyptian control or prestige in Asia. A growing detente between Egypt and Mitanni during the late 15th century was consummated by the marriage of a Mitannian to Thutmose IV.

Bibliography. B. M. Bryan, *The Reign of Thutmose IV* (Baltimore, 1991); M. S. Drower, "Syria *c.* 1550-1400 B.C.," *CAH*³ 2/1:417-525; W. C. Hayes, "Egypt: Internal Affairs from Tuthmosis I to the Death of Amenophis III," *CAH*³ 2/1:313-416.

THOMAS V. BRISCO

THYATIRA (Gk. *Thyátira*)

A city (modern Akhisar) just E of the Pergamum/Sardis highway on the plain of the river Lycus. Little is known of its earliest years, but evidence suggests that it was founded in the 2nd century B.C. Following the Greek conquests of the 4th century and the subsequent kingdoms of the Hellenistic period, Thyatira became a garrison town between western regional empires (Pergamum) and the eastern powers in Syria. By 190 it was subject to Pergamum and in 133 fell subject to Rome. It was one of the seven churches of Asia mentioned in Rev. 1:11.

As a city of commerce and manufacturing Thyatira became well known for many of its trades. Inscriptions and literary references mention trade guilds working in wool, linen, leather, bronze, armor, dye, tanning, pottery, and baking. In addition artisans from Thyatira discovered how to make purple dye from the madder root without using the expensive shellfish murex. Lydia, a prominent Christian in Philippi, was from Thyatira and sold purple textiles, a vocation that fits perfectly the archaeological evidence.

Paul likely evangelized the city during his two-year ministry in Ephesus (Acts 19:10). It is reasonable to assume that Thyatira had a Jewish population like so many other Asian cities. The greatest hurdle for Christian discipleship in Thyatira was posed by the trade guilds; these were not merely business associations, but also religious and civic groups which devoted themselves to patron divinities and indulged in sexual revelry (cf. Rev. 2:18-29). By A.D. 200 Thyatira enjoyed a strong Christian presence and continued to flourish. But because of its geographical vulnerability (crossroads, no natural defenses), it was sacked repeatedly.

Bibliography. E. M. Blaiklock, *Cities of the New Testament* (London, 1965), 107-11; T. R. S. Broughton, *Roman Asia,* in *An Economic Survey of Ancient Rome,* ed. T. Frank (1938, repr. Paterson, N.J., 1959) 4:499-916; C. Foss, "Archaeology and the 'Twenty Cities' of Byzantine Asia," *AJA* 81 (1977): 469-86; C. J. Hemer, *The Letters to the Seven Churches of Asia in Their Local Setting* (1986, repr. Grand Rapids, 2000); J. McRay, *Archaeology and the New Testament* (Grand Rapids, 1991).

GARY M. BURGE

TIBERIAS (Gk. *Tiberiás*)

Located on the western shore of the Sea of Galilee (201242), a city founded by Herod Antipas between 18 and 20 C.E. as his new Galilean capital and named in honor of his patron and then emperor Tiberias.

Since it was built atop an ancient cemetery, many Jews refused to settle there; only financial inducement or compulsion on the part of Antipas filled the city with Jewish and Greek inhabitants (Josephus *Ant.* 18.36-38). Josephus also tells of a sumptuous palace in Tiberias, with gilded ceilings and representations of animals that broke aniconic Jewish traditions (*Vita* 65-66). Coinage minted at Tiberias, however, contained neither Antipas' nor human or pagan images; instead coins were often imprinted with a reed, a local plant that grew along the Sea of Galilee. After the two Jewish-Roman wars, Tiberias became one of the most important centers of Jewish learning, and hence holds a prominent place in rabbinic literature. Rabbi Yohanan led one of the largest study houses in 2nd-century Tiberias. In the Middle Ages the Masoretes developed the Tiberian vowel pointing of the Hebrew Bible there.

Archaeological excavations have been restricted to isolated probes and salvage operations since the ancient site stands beneath a modern city. A city gate, protected by two massive circular towers, was uncovered, which might date to Antipas' founding of the city. This gate, coupled with evidence for a cardo, or north-south axis road (whose remains date best to the Byzantine period), indicates that the original city was likely laid out in an orthogonal grid pattern. The Byzantine wall of the city encompasses an area of 185 ha. (457 a.) and encircles Mt. Bernice to the west and the hot springs of Tiberias to the south. Excavations at the latter site of Hammat (Heb. "hot springs") Tiberias, where travelers since the Roman period have enjoyed its curative powers, have unveiled a 4th-century synagogue mosaic depicting a spectacular zodiac.

In the NT only the Gospel of John mentions Tiberias, in reference to "the sea of Tiberias" (John 6:1; 21:1) and indicating the city as the locale from which many come on boats to see Jesus (6:23). Like Herod Antipas' other major city Sepphoris, no activity of Jesus is recorded or associated with Tiberias. Perhaps Jesus avoided Tiberias as the seat of Antipas' political power.

Bibliography. Y. Hirschfeld, G. Foerster, and F. Vitto, "Tiberias," *NEAEHL* 4:1464-73; G. Theissen, *The Gospels in Context* (Minneapolis, 1991).

JONATHAN REED

TIBERIAS, SEA OF

See GALILEE, SEA OF.

TIBERIUS (Gk. *Tiberios;* Lat. *Tiberius*)
Tiberius Caesar, both stepson and adopted son of Augustus Caesar; the second emperor of Rome upon Augustus' death in 14 C.E. Tiberius' reign continued until his own death in 37, and while founded upon adherence to the policies of Augustus, was nevertheless marked by political discontent among a Roman senatorial aristocracy far less confident in the abilities of Tiberius as compared with those of the much admired Augustus.

Born Tiberius Claudius Nero, Tiberius was raised in the household of his mother Livia and his stepfather Augustus. Much of his life was marked by service to Rome since Tiberius, along with other members of the imperial family, filled important military and administrative posts. Tiberius was a successful general, bringing into the empire through conquest Pannonia and other areas along the Danube. Following the death of Augustus' friend Marcus Agrippa, Tiberius was forced to marry Julia, Agrippa's widow and the daughter of Augustus, so that he could become protector to Augustus' grandsons and heirs. After their deaths, Augustus had no one whom he could elevate as successor except Tiberius. However, Augustus insisted that Tiberius' nephew Germanicus, husband of Augustus' granddaughter Agrippina, be placed in the succession over Tiberius' own son, Drusus. The strange circumstances of Germanicus' death several years after Tiberius' succession aroused suspicions about Tiberius' possible involvement in the death and provided a rallying point for Tiberius' opponents. Finally, tired of politics, Tiberius retired to Capri, leaving Rome in the charge of his praetorian prefect Sejanus. The slow annihilation of opponents in the senate, including members of the imperial family, secured Sejanus an infamous place in Rome's history. The primary historical source for these events, Tacitus' *Annals*, written a century later, offers an indicting account of Tiberius' reign.

Tiberius was emperor during the events described in the Gospels. Allusion to his reign (Luke 3:1) provides the only firm NT reference for dating events. Pontius Pilate was appointed procurator of Judea by Tiberius and served the emperor in that capacity from 26-36. In 18 C.E. Tiberius' client, Galilean tetrarch Herod Antipas, founded in honor of the emperor the city of Tiberias.

Bibliography. B. Levick, *Tiberius the Politician* (1976, repr. London, 1986); F. B. Marsh, *The Reign of Tiberius* (London, 1931). JOHN F. HALL

TIBHATH (Heb. *ṭiḇḥaṯ*) (also BETAH)
A place in Syria from which David took much spoil after a victory (1 Chr. 18:8). Called Betah in the parallel passage (2 Sam. 8:8), it is possibly to be associated with Tebah (Gen. 22:24). Tibhath is thought to be situated in the Beqaʿ region, but its precise location is unknown.

TIBNI (Heb. *tiḇnî*)
The son of Ginath; favored to be king by half of the northern kingdom of Israel after the death of King Zimri (ca. 882 B.C.E.; 1 Kgs. 16:21). But in the three-year civil war that followed Zimri's suicide, those following his rival Omri soon gained the upper hand, and Tibni lost his life (1 Kgs. 16:22).

TIDAL (Heb. *tiḏʿāl;* cf. Hitt. *Tudḫaliya*)
The king of Goiim; one of Chedorlaomer's allies who helped subdue the rebellious kings of the plain (Gen. 14:1, 9). Neither Tidal nor his subjects have been identified.

TIGLATH-PILESER (Heb. *tiglaṯ pilʾeser;* Akk. *Tukultī-apil-ešarra*)
(also PUL, TILGATH-PILNESER)

1. Tiglath-pileser I, king of Assyria (1115-1077 B.C.E.); son of Assur-reša-išši I. Successful campaigns against the powerful Muški and Aramean coalitions to the west and the Babylonians to the south brought prosperity and greatly expanded Assyrian territory.

2. Tiglath-pileser II, king of Assyria, 966-935; son of Assur-reša-išši II and father of Assur-dan II.

3. Tiglath-pileser III (744-727), also referred to as Tilgath-pilneser (1 Chr. 5:6, 26; 2 Chr. 28:20) and Pul (2 Kgs. 15:19; 1 Chr. 5:26) in the OT and Pulu in the Babylonian King List (*ANET,* 272); a usurper who seized the throne of Assyria during a revolt in the city of Calah in 745. His reign was marked by renewed incursions into the north, where he had to confront the formidable Urartu; the west, where he conquered territories up to the Egyptian border; the east, where he expanded Assyrian sovereignty into Namri and Media; and the south, where he eventually was crowned king of Babylon in 729. Thus, by the time of his death in 727 the Assyrian Empire was at the zenith of its expansion. The Assyrian source material from his reign is impressive (*ANET,* 282-84) and includes his annals, summary inscriptions, a stela, and a rock relief inscription.

Two events are of significance to the history of Israel and Judah during the reign of Tiglath-pileser III. The first, recorded in 2 Kgs. 15:19-20, occurred during the reign of Menahem of Israel (745-736). Scholars generally interpret this text as referring to an invasion of Israel by Tiglath-pileser, during which Menahem taxed the wealthy classes to pay off the Assyrian king. However, T. R. Hobbs suggests instead that Tiglath-pileser (identified as Pul) went to Israel, presumably at Menahem's request, to provide Menahem with military assistance at a time when his hold on the kingdom was threatened. In exchange for Tiglath-pileser's assistance, Menahem gave him "a thousand talents of silver" as payment for the military personnel that the Assyrian king supplied. This event is probably to be located in the context of a major Assyrian campaign in the west during the period of 743-740, where Tiglath-pileser had to deal with an anti-Assyrian movement of Anatolian and northern Syrian states. It is likely that as a result of this aid Menahem remained a loyal subject of Assyria, since the Assyrian king notes in two of his inscriptions that he received the payment of tribute from Menahem (*ANET,* 283).

The second event is related to the so-called

Syro-Ephraimitic crisis (2 Kgs. 16:5-9; cf. Isa. 7:1-9). The inscriptions of Tiglath-pileser III reveal that the Assyrian king was involved in an effort to suppress a widespread anti-Assyrian rebellion in Syria-Palestine in 734-731 (*ANET,* 283-84). Members of the coalition included Rezin of Aram-Damascus (the leader of the coalition), Hiram of Tyre, Pekah of Israel, Samsi of Arabia, Mitinti of Ashkelon, and Hanun of Gaza. The attack on Ahaz of Judah — who decided to remain loyal to Assyria (cf. 2 Chr. 28:16-21) — by Rezin and Pekah was an effort to force Judah to join the coalition. As a result of the Assyrian invasion of the region, the attack by Rezin and Pekah was aborted. During this campaign, Tiglath-pileser dealt with the rebels one after another. In particular, Rezin was soundly defeated and Aram-Damascus turned into an Assyrian province. Israel, however, lost some territories to Tiglath-pileser (2 Kgs. 15:29) but Samaria was spared. In the process, Tiglath-pileser also appointed Hoshea as king over Israel (*ANET,* 284). The biblical text notes that Hoshea eventually led a conspiracy against Pekah and assassinated him (2 Kgs. 15:30).

Bibliography. T. R. Hobbs, *2 Kings.* WBC 13 (Waco, 1985); H. Tadmor, *The Inscriptions of Tiglath-pileser III, King of Assyria* (Jerusalem, 1994).

JEFFREY K. KUAN

TIGRIS (Gk. *Tígris*)
The easternmost of the two rivers which give the region of Mesopotamia its name (Gk. *mesopotamos,* lit., "beween the rivers"). The Tigris (Heb. *ḥiddeqel;* Akk. *idiglat*) may have at one time emptied into the Persian Gulf, though today it and the Euphrates share a common mouth for some 64 km. (40 mi.), the Shaṭṭ al-ʿArab.

Though the two rivers are intertwined both physically and historically, riverine life is sharply contrasted between the Tigris and the Euphrates. The Tigris was not utilized for irrigation until Islamic times, and then only in the region S of Samarra (ca. 644 km. [400 mi.] from the Persian Gulf). The Euphrates was employed in irrigation agriculture for ca. 2092 km. (1300 mi.) of its length, from Syria to the Persian Gulf. The Tigris has a much narrower channel, and descends at a much sharper grade than the Euphrates. Further, the region drained by the Tigris (e.g., the Zagros Mountains) includes more snowmelt (cf. Sir. 24:25). Finally, the river is affected throughout its length by winter rains, occurring from March through May, just prior to the highest snowmelt period. These factors make the Tigris prone to flooding, thus rendering life along the river precarious.

The Tigris Valley, for the most part, is within the range of dry farming, above the 200 mm. (7.8 in.) isohyet. Thus the area is agriculturally productive despite its lack of river water. The river is at its low point during planting, and the flood comes just prior to maturation of the crops, often negating the positive effects of the rainy season. Animal husbandry flourishes in the more marginal regions. The river was navigable by most riverine craft of antiquity. Its primary tributaries are the Greater Zab, the Lesser Zab, and the Diyala (the latter was the terminus of the silk road to China).

The entirety of the system fell within the cultural realm of southern Mesopotamia. Sargon conquered the region, with inscriptions discovered in the Diyala Valley (ca. 2300 B.C.E.). The region was the homeland of Assyria, which was never completely subsumed by southern Mesopotamian culture. Nineveh, Calah, Kar-shalmanezer, and Assur are all located on the Tigris. The Hurrian Empire reached the north bank of the Tigris (16th-15th centuries).

The Tigris is mentioned as one of the rivers flowing from the garden of Eden (Gen. 2:14). The significance of this identification is that it is one of the rivers which Yahweh created in order to bring life to the world, in his role of creator and sustainer of all. The river is mentioned elsewhere in the OT only in Dan. 10:4, likely as a mistaken gloss for "the great river," an epithet normally applied to the Euphrates (the gloss preserved in the Peshiṭta).

MARK ANTHONY PHELPS

TIKVAH (Heb. *tiqwâ*) (also TOKHATH)
1. The father of Shallum (**2**), husband of the prophetess Huldah (2 Kgs. 22:14). He is called Tokhath at 2 Chr. 34:22.

2. The father of Jahzeiah, who opposed Ezra's plan to dissolve the marriages with foreign women (Ezra 10:15).

TILGATH-PILNESER (Heb. *tillĕg̱laṯ pilnʾeser*)
See TIGLATH-PILESER.

TILON (Heb. *tîlôn*)
A son of Shimon of the tribe of Judah (1 Chr. 4:20).

TIMAEUS (Gk. *Timaíos*)
The father of the blind beggar Bartimaeus, whom Jesus cured at Jericho (Mark 10:46).

TIMBREL
A musical instrument, probably a small hand drum, perhaps with bells or small pieces of metal around its periphery (Heb. *tōp;* e.g., Exod. 15:20; Ps. 68:25[MT 26]; Jer. 31:4; NRSV "tambourine").

TIME
As Gen. 1 makes clear, the creation of time is part of the creation of the universe. The measurements and divisions of time come about as God separates day from night (Gen. 1:3-5) and creates the sun, moon, and stars which "mark the fixed times, the days and the years, and serve as lights in the firmament of the sky" (vv. 14-15). Israel recognized that its God not only had created but also continued to sustain this temporal rhythm along with the meteorological cycle of winter rains and summer drought which made possible its agricultural cycles of plowing and planting, ripening and harvesting. The liberating actions of this God defined Israel's past and offered renewed possibilities for its future.

Vocabulary

While Biblical Hebrew uses several words to identify specific moments, it lacks a general term for time as a category. Many scholars argue that the Hebrew verb system itself does not have "tenses," that it indicates whether an action has been completed but not whether that completion took place, has taken place, or will have taken place. The storytellers and poets of ancient Israel must have, nonetheless, been familiar with some notion of time, even if it was not mathematical and linear; they wrote passages filled with references to past, present, and future events.

Spatial terms, e.g., *qeḏem* ("in front of" the present moment) and *'aḥărîṯ* ("behind" the present moment), convey temporal notions of "past" and "future." The phrase *bĕ'aḥărîṯ hayyāmîm* ("in the days to come") indicates a remote time in the future, while *hāri'šônîm* ("the former things") designates past events (e.g., Isa. 41:22). To express duration, Biblical Hebrew offers several combinations of *'ôlām* (e.g., "forever, lifelong") and of *dôr* (e.g., "generation after generation," "generation to generation"). In contrast, *rega'*, "moment," is a very short interval of time.

Heb. *'ēṯ* is generally translated "time." It specifies a particular event or the duration of an event, rather than a moment or measure of time. In Ps. 10:1 *'ittôṯ baṣṣārâ* characterizes the duration of the speaker's troubles; in Josh. 5:2 *'ēṯ* is the occasion of the re-circumcision of the Israelites after they have crossed the dried-up Jordan river bed into the land of Canaan; in Esth. 1:13 "those who know the times" (i.e., future events) are astrologers; in Amos 5:13 the evil time is synonymous with the performance of unjust deeds. In 2 Sam. 11:1 *'ēṯ* means the "usual time," the spring of the year when kings go out to battle.

For the author of Eccl. 3:1-8, time is ordered by a succession of events occurring in fixed succession. There is a time for everything, according to this pessimistic reflection, and "nothing new under the sun." Such temporal rigidity supports the Preacher's view that an unbridgeable gulf separates human life and divine activity; the locked-step nature of time precludes any intervention from outside.

Often the phrase *be'ittô* ("in his/its time") carries the nuance of "proper time," "appropriate season." In Deut. 11:14 it refers to the expected time of the winter rains. In 1 Sam. 18:19 it indicates the time appointed for the handing over of Saul's daughter Merab in marriage. Sometimes the plural of *'ēṯ* carries the sense of "fate" or "destiny" (e.g., 1 Chr. 29:30).

The Hebrew word for "day," *yôm,* often functions as a synonym for *'ēṯ.* Expressions like "the day of Moab" or "the day of Jerusalem" (Ps. 137:7) are generally negative; they indicate the events, past or future, that mark the destruction of the nation or city whose day it is. Similarly, the "Day of the Lord" *(yôm YHWH;* Amos 5:18-20; Isa. 2:12; 13:6, 9; Joel 1:15) is both the event through which the Lord executes judgment on Israel or on its enemies and the time in which that judgment occurs. In Jer. 50:31 the prophet uses the phrase "your day has come" in order to announce disaster and death. The plural of *yôm (yāmîn)* indicates a distinctive period of time with a beginning and an end; e.g., 2 Sam. 21:1 reports a famine that occurs during the reign of David (*yĕmê dawîḏ,* "in the days of David").

Past and future are expressed spatially, with the present as the point of orientation. While Westerners may conceptualize the future ahead of them, biblical Israelites situated the future behind *('aḥărîṯ)* them as events yet to appear; it approaches, unfolding slowly to move past the present. In Isa. 30:8 the Lord commands the prophet to write the divine message on a tablet, so it could be an eternal witness in the "future days." Similarly, a valuable wife laughs at "the days to come" (Prov. 31:25). Similarly, while some readers think of the past as something they can put behind them, for biblical Israelites the past is in front *(qeḏem)* of them, visible, known, its events moving farther and farther into the distance. In Isa. 23:7 Tyre is the city whose origins were "of old." Jerusalem remembers the past days when her people were driven into exile (Lam. 1:7).

While *'ēṯ* generally identifies political, military, or personal events that may occur randomly, *mô'ēḏ,* from a verb meaning "to appoint," refers to events that are fixed or determined ahead of time, such as meetings, events, or assemblies. In Dan. 8:19 *mô'ēḏ* points to the appointed, eschatological ending of history; in 1 Sam. 20:35 it designates Jonathan's prearranged meeting with David; in Deut. 31:10 it announces the Jubilee Year as "the scheduled year of remission" of debt. The word also conveys that there are appropriate moments in nature at which an event should occur (e.g., Jer. 8:7).

Biblical writers also used *mô'ēḏ* to distinguish religious time, set apart for remembering Israel's past and its relationship to the Lord, devoted to celebrating saving deeds and successful harvests. The prophet Isaiah calls Jerusalem the "city of appointed festivals" (Isa. 33:20). During these liturgical celebrations (Lev. 23), lasting for days, people retold the stories of the events the festivals commemorated, victorious occurrences that marked their relationship with the Lord. These retellings allowed them to experience the very events they were hearing about, as if they were happening to them, in their own time (e.g., Exod. 13:8). Within this context of remembered blessings, each generation affirmed for itself its covenant relationship with Israel's Lord, in gratitude for a saving power that acted in time but was beyond it.

Measures of Time

The OT also uses vocabulary that corresponds to the more universal divisions of time: day, week, month, and year. "Day" *(yôm)* extends from morning to evening or from sunset to sunset (Gen. 1:5). In Ps. 55:17(MT 18) "day" has three divisions of "evening, morning, and noon"; elsewhere it has four (e.g., Neh. 9:3). "Night" *(laylâ)* has three sections or watches (Exod. 14:24; Lam. 2:19).

Heb. *šāḇûaʿ* (lit., "seven") means "week." The days of the week are not named; they are numbered one through six. The final and seventh day alone has a special designation, "sabbath," in reference to God's rest after creation (Gen. 2:2-3; Exod. 20:10-11). According to the Gen. 1 Creation story, just as "divine images" maintain order within the universe, the Israelites follow divine example, resting on this day. Another writer cites the Lord's liberation of the Hebrew slaves from Egyptian bondage as an additional reason for faithful Israelites, their slaves, and their farm animals to refrain from physical labor on the last day of the week (Deut. 5:14-15).

Heb. *yārēaḥ* and *ḥōḏeš,* "moon," also mean "month." Israel's lunar calendar measured the duration of a month from new moon to new moon. Some of the names of the months mentioned in the OT reflect Israel's Canaanite origins, e.g., Abib (Exod. 13:4), Ziv (1 Kgs. 6:1, 37), Ethanim (8:2), Bul (6:38). Later texts use the Babylonian names, e.g., Nisan (Neh. 2:1), Sivan (Esth. 8:9), Elul (Neh. 6:15), Chislev (1:1), Adar (Ezra 6:15).

The beginning of a new month was a day of rest; the priests offered special sacrifices (Num. 28:11-15) and blew the ceremonial shophar in the hope that the Lord would remember Israel (10:10; Ps. 81:3[4]; cf. Hos. 5:7; Amos 8:5). Major feasts like Passover and Sukkoth fell at full moon.

The Days to Come

The postexilic Judahite community was positioned between a disastrous past and an uncertain future. In front of it were the gracious and liberating acts, the mighty deeds, which its God had performed on its behalf: liberation from Egypt, covenant, settlement in the land, kingship (in at least one tradition). At the same time, its own infidelities and forgetfulness of this divine goodness littered that past. Over and over again, the Lord had to apply the rod, often under the guise of defeat at the hands of other nations, to teach Israel a more productive way of life.

In back of Judah and Jerusalem was hidden its future, "the days to come." While no one text gives a systematic unfolding of this future, some characteristics are clear. Some "day of the Lord" inaugurates this new epoch in Israel's history. A divine army slaughters the enemies of the Lord's people (Joel 3:9-14[4:9-14]) and, in some cases, destroys their very lands (v. 19). Foreigners flock to Jerusalem to learn torah from faithful Judahites (Mic. 4:1-2) or to serve them as their slaves (Isa. 60:10-12). Judah enjoys agricultural prosperity and political autonomy (Joel 3:18-21[4:18-21]). This is the time of Jeremiah's new covenant (Jer. 31:31). Using powerful images, Israel's poets express a conviction that at some unknown point in the future, Judah's political, religious, and economic circumstances will undergo a lasting change.

New Testament

The NT writers build on the OT notions of time. In the Gospels a day continues to run from sundown to sundown; thus, the Last Supper and Crucifixion occur on the same day. There are also important differences. Because the Evangelists believe that past promises and future hopes coalesce in the gospel Jesus, they sometimes make no clear distinctions between past, present, and future.

NT use of Gk. *aiṓn,* "age" or "eternity," probably reflects Christianity's Jewish roots. Intertestamental Jewish literature often distinguished between the present world controlled by the powers of evil and the world to come already under the dominion of God and the powers of good (cf. Matt. 12:32; Mark 10:30; Eph. 1:21; 2:7). One way to understand the plot of Mark's Gospel is to see it as a struggle in which Jesus of Nazareth breaks the hold of the devil on this world in order to establish the kingdom of God in history. The adjective *aiṓnios,* "eternal" or "everlasting," describes the covenant which Christ mediates (Heb. 13:20), the abode which Christians enter when they die (Luke 16:9; 2 Cor. 5:1; 2 Tim. 2:10), everlasting good news (Rev. 14:6), hope of unending life (Titus 3:7), the perpetual flames of punishment (Matt. 18:8), eternal judgment (Heb. 6:2), the quality of sin which separates one permanently from God (Mark 3:29).

In the NT "everlasting" or "eternal" properly belongs to God since God alone has no end of days. Applied to Christians, the adjective suggests that even in "this world" Christians participate in divine life. The believer is safe from the evils of the present time (Gal. 1:4) and already experiences future salvation (Heb. 6:5). The present age is the decisive moment, the "now" of salvation (Luke 19:9; 23:43). In the Gospel of John, eternal life begins "now," once people begin to believe in Jesus; this coming to faith is the central moment in an individual's life. Because Jesus is resurrection and life, here and now, he raises believers from death and bestows the fullness of life here and now.

Gk. *chrónos* designates a length of time, usually described by adjectives like "brief" or "long." Occasionally it is a specific period of time (e.g., Luke 1:57; Acts 7:17; Gal. 4:4). The word can be translated "span of time," "set time," "term."

The most important word related to "time" in the NT is *kairós,* "opportune" or "appointed time." Sometimes it occurs simply as a synonym for *chrónos* (Luke 4:13; 21:36; Matt. 11:25). It can also describe fixed, regularly occurring times: the harvest season (Matt. 13:30), the season in which figs ripen (Mark 11:13), or liturgical feasts (Gal. 4:10). The word's significance, however, derives from those Gospel passages in which it refers to critical moments in the life of Jesus of Nazareth: his advent; the beginning of the reign of God; his passion, death, and resurrection; and his return. Mark identifies the beginning of Jesus' public ministry, the proximity of the reign of God, and the invitation to repentance and faith (Mark 1:15) as a critical moment of fulfillment. Mark emphasizes the urgency implicit in *kairós* with repeated use of the adverb *euthýs,* "immediately." Both Matthew (Matt. 26:18) and Paul (Rom. 5:6) designate the time of Jesus' passion and death as *kairós.* 1 Tim. 6:15 observes that Jesus will return again "at the right time."

In the Gospel of John Gk. *hṓrā,* "hour," takes the

place of the Synoptics' *kairós*. The Synoptics generally use *hṓrā* to refer to the hour of a day (Luke 13:31); a time of persecution for the disciples (Mark 13:11; Luke 12:12); and, in some instances, Jesus' passion (Matt. 26:18, 45; Mark 14:35) or return (Luke 12:40; Matt. 24:36; Mark 13:32). In John's Gospel, "the hour" or "my hour" no longer refers to a temporal category. Rather, the expression means the time of Jesus' passing from "this world . . . to the Father" (John 13:1) and encompasses his passion, death, resurrection, and glorification at God's right hand. In John 2:4; 7:30; 8:20 Jesus' "hour" has not yet come, but in 12:23 it has. Jesus' hour brings persecution to believers (John 16:2); it also promises resurrection (5:25, 28-29) and teaches true worship (4:21, 23).

For the believer the *kairós* that Jesus originates is a time to use wisely (Eph. 5:16; Col. 4:5), the time to wake from sleep for salvation draws near, a time to conduct oneself properly (Rom. 13:11-14). Because the length of time until Christ's return is unknown, Christians should fill this time of *kairós* with watching, waiting, praying for Christ's return. God may delay that return in order to help Christians prepare better for it. While God has established the times of salvation and has chosen not to disclose any detailed information about them, Christians must learn to interpret the signs of the times to be ready for the final *kairós* of the last days (1 Pet. 5:6). This event to which the NT looks is a time of judgment (Mark 13:33; 1 Pet. 4:17).

In the NT all categories of time begin and end with Jesus of Nazareth. The genealogies of Matthew and Luke read the story of creation onward as a history that prepares for and finds its significance in his life and death. John portrays the Christian living betwixt and between the "now" and the "not yet"; the center of history and its end point are one and the same, the presence of Jesus Christ. The resurrected Christ offers the Spirit to the believing community so it can follow his example; at the same time, that community must continually resist the powers of this world, living justly and devoutly until the Lord's return.

Once Christianity became the state religion of the Roman Empire, Christian theologians interpreted the birth of Jesus of Nazareth as a *kairós*, an "appointed time," for the world, making that event the center of the calendar. The Venerable Bede (d. 735) popularized the notion of *anno domino*, A.D. or "Christian era." The emperor Charlemagne promulgated that terminology throughout Europe. Only in the 17th century did Jacques Benigne Bosseut begin the custom of counting time before the birth of Jesus of Nazareth as if its fulfillment and meaning derived from that birth.

KATHLEEN S. NASH

TIMNA (Heb. *timnaʿ, timnāʿ*)

1. The concubine of Esau's son Eliphaz, mother of Amalek, and sister of the Horite chief Lotan (Gen. 36:12, 22; 1 Chr. 1:39).

2. A chief of Edom (Gen. 36:40; 1 Chr. 1:51).

3. A son of Eliphaz and descendant of Esau (1 Chr. 1:36). He may be the same as **2.** If the names are taken as eponymous ancestors of social groups, this Timna may represent a different sociopolitical alignment of the same or related people as **1.**

TIMNAH (Heb. *timnâ*)

1. A city on the northern border of Judah (Josh. 15:10), originally assigned to the tribe of Dan (19:43). Timnah, however, was occupied by Philistines and was the scene for Samson's conflict after having taken a Philistine wife (Judg. 14–15). Timnah probably came under Israelite or Judean control with the conquests of Uzziah (2 Chr. 26:6), but the Philistines are said to have taken it from Judah during the reign of Ahaz (2 Chr. 28:18). The city apparently reverted to Judean control under Hezekiah, as it is named in the inscriptions of the Assyrian Sennacherib in connection with his campaign against Hezekiah in 701 B.C.E. (cf. 2 Kgs. 18:13).

Timnah is convincingly identified with Tell el-Baṭâshī/Tel Baṭash (141132) in the Sorek Valley (cf. Judg. 16:4). Excavations have produced finds paralleling biblical and historical data. A massive earthen rampart, constructed in the Middle Bronze Age, determined the mound's distinctive square concave shape and marks the beginning of continuous occupation lasting through the Late Bronze Age. This occupation makes the site a likely candidate for the Timnah to which Judah took his sheep to be sheared (Gen. 38:12-14). An extensive Philistine occupation in Iron I was followed by a 10th-century city with distinctive Israelite pottery. A destruction, perhaps the work of Shishak (1 Kgs. 14:25-28), initiated a period of abandonment until the 8th century, when the city was rebuilt. This level contained extensive fortification, as well as storejars having handles impressed with seals of winged scarabs and Heb. *lmlk* ("belonging to the king"), known to date to the period of Hezekiah. The destruction of this city almost certainly took place during the campaign of Sennacherib in 701. Timnah reemerged as a flourishing town in the 7th century, only to suffer another destruction, probably by the Babylonians ca. 603.

Bibliography. G. L. Kelm and A. Mazar, *Timnah: A Biblical City in the Sorek Valley* (Winona Lake, 1995).

2. A town of the hill country of Judah (Josh. 15:57). Although not identified, it is presumably near Maon, with which it is listed, ca. 16-24 km. (10-15 mi.) S of Hebron.

DANIEL C. BROWNING, JR.

TIMNATH (Gk. *Thamnatha*)

A town in Judea fortified in 160 B.C.E. by the Seleucid general Bacchides (1 Macc. 9:50). Situated in the hill country of Ephraim, it is probably to be identified with Khirbet Tibnah (160157), ca. 14 km. (9 mi.) NW of Bethel.

TIMNATH-HERES (Heb. *timnaṯ-ḥeres*), **TIMNATH-SERAH** (*timnaṯ-seraḥ*)

The town given to Joshua as his private inheritance (Timnath-heres, Judg. 2:9; Timnath-serah, Josh.

19:50; 24:30). Most scholars accept Timnath-heres as the original name, although there is debate over the difference between the two variants. Since Timnath-heres may mean "Portion of the Sun," some have suggested that it was the location of a sanctuary dedicated to the sun-deity. The change to Timnath-serah may have been an attempt by later editors to remove any hint of a connection between Joshua and solar worship. More likely, *seraḥ* represents a deliberate metathesis of *ḥeres,* based on a folk etymology, with Timnath-serah meaning "left-over portion" because Joshua was given his private inheritance only after land was allotted to all the other tribes. Khirbet Tibnah (160157), ca. 24 km. (15 mi.) SW of Shechem on the southern slopes of Ephraim, is the most likely modern candidate for its location (cf. Timnath, 1 Macc. 9:50).

WADE R. KOTTER

TIMNITE (Heb. *timnî*)
A gentilic designating an inhabitant of Timnah (**1;** Judg. 15:6).

TIMON (Gk. *Tímōn*)
One of the seven chosen to aid in the distribution to the widows of the Church (Acts 6:5).

TIMOTHY (Gk. *Timótheos*)

1. Commander of the Ammonite forces. He was repeatedly defeated in a series of battles against Judas Maccabeus and his brothers (1 Macc. 5:6-7, 11, 34, 37-39; 2 Macc. 8:30-33; 9:3; 12:2-25).

2. A close coworker and emissary of Paul. The first recorded encounter between the two occurs when Paul enters the Lycaonian town of Lystra (Acts 16:1-5) during his second missionary journey. Timothy, the son of a Greek father and a Jewish-Christian mother, is already a respected member of the Christian community. Paul wishes Timothy to accompany him on his mission to the churches, but is said to have had Timothy circumcised first, for the sake of the Jews, who knew that Timothy's father was a Gentile (and also, presumably, that his mother was a Jew). The reason for Timothy's circumcision is difficult to understand in view of Paul's stance regarding the Judaizers' insistence that Titus be circumcised (Gal. 2:3). The question is partly one of identity: was Timothy considered primarily a Jew or a Gentile? Timothy's Jewish mother and grandmother, Eunice and Lois (2 Tim. 1:5), are said to have been faithful Christians and influential in his spiritual development, bringing him up in the knowledge of the Jewish Scriptures (2 Tim. 3:15). And yet the family was evidently not so observant of its Jewish heritage as to have had Timothy circumcised as an infant. The role of Timothy's gentile father in his upbringing, and his response to Timothy's circumcision, are not mentioned, perhaps indicating that the man was deceased by the time of the events described in Acts. The author of Acts at least seems to have held that Timothy would have been considered a Jew on account of his mother, and that his lack of circumcision would have suggested, wrongly, that Paul showed no respect for Jewish custom (Acts 21:21).

From Lystra, Timothy accompanies Paul and Silas (Silvanus), first throughout the neighboring towns, and then further west into Macedonia, circulating to the churches the decisions rendered by the elders of the church in Jerusalem, and evangelizing new territories. Apparently Timothy's role increases in authority as he and Silas become Paul's emissaries in Beroea (Acts 17:14) and elsewhere in Macedonia (19:22).

Timothy's legitimacy and trustworthiness as Paul's authoritative representative are underscored in the Pauline Epistles (1 Cor. 4:17; 16:10-11; Phil. 2:19-22; 1 Thess. 3:1-6). Timothy is sent by Paul to the churches not only to gather information concerning their welfare, but to further the work of the gospel among them, to remind them of Paul's teaching, to encourage them to endure in the face of persecution, and in many ways to serve as Paul's selfless emissary. In addition, Timothy is described as the co-sender of Philippians, 2 Corinthians, 1 Thessalonias, and Philemon, as well as Colossians and 2 Thessalonians. Paul's language in describing Timothy emphasizes the special relationship of trust which developed between the two over the course of their association (1 Cor. 4:17; Phil. 2:22; 1 Thess. 3:2).

That Timothy is the named recipient of the Pastoral Letters that bear his name (1-2 Timothy) attests to his reputation during the 1st century as an important follower and close coworker of Paul, although he is characterized in the letters as somewhat inexperienced and in need of encouragement. In the first letter, Paul urges Timothy to remain in Ephesus to deal with false teachers and to establish proper patterns of worship and of community order. The second letter, written ostensibly during Paul's imprisonment (possibly in Rome), is primarily a letter of exhortation and encouragement, in the style of a final testament. Paul warns Timothy to avoid becoming entangled in controversies, but to continue to be bold in opposing false teaching and to uphold the traditions handed on to him. In contrast to the first letter, Timothy is here urged not to remain in Ephesus, but to return to Paul as soon as possible. A reference to Timothy in Heb. 13:23 suggests that he was at one time imprisoned, but later released.

Bibliography. F. F. Bruce, *The Pauline Circle* (Grand Rapids, 1985); C. Bryan, "A Further Look at Acts 16:1-3," *JBL* 107 (1988): 292-94; S. J. D. Cohen, "Was Timothy Jewish (Acts 16:1-3)?" *JBL* 105 (1986): 251-68; M. M. Mitchell, "New Testament Envoys in the Context of Greco-Roman Diplomatic and Epistolary Conventions: The Example of Timothy and Titus," *JBL* 111 (1992): 641-62; W. D. Walker, "The Timothy-Titus Problem Reconsidered," *ExpTim* 92 (1980-81): 231-35.

See PASTORAL EPISTLES. JANE S. LANCASTER

TIMOTHY, LETTERS TO
Two letters from the Apostle Paul to his coworker Timothy. They are generally considered together

with the letter of Paul to Titus because of the similarities in the three letters.

See PASTORAL EPISTLES.

TIN

A metal that, when mixed with copper in a ratio of 10 percent tin to 90 percent copper, produces a harder alloy, bronze. The existence of bronze led to the creation of stronger weapons and tools, as well as coins and mirrors.

Tin ore occurs in rock veins or in the form of gravel or sand in alluvium. Early smelting was carried out using pit fires. The ore was thrown onto the fire and the metal was gathered from the sand and ashes. Advances in smelting eventually created blocks of tin from furnaces that could direct the flow of the metal (Ezek. 22:20; Diodorus Siculus *Hist.* 5.21-22).

The Phoenicians imported tin to the Near East by ship from Tarshish (Ezek. 27:12). The Romans used tin in the production of pewter plates, brooches, and flagons.

Bibliography. E. S. Hedges, *Tin in Social and Economic History* (New York, 1964).

JAMES V. SMITH

TIPHSAH (Heb. *tip̱saḥ*)

1. A city on the west shore of the Euphrates River, ca. 110 km. (68 mi.) S of Carchemish. An important river crossing, Tiphsah was the northern frontier of Solomon's empire (1 Kgs. 4:24[MT 5:4]). During the Persian period the city was known as Thapsacus and later as Amphipolis.

2. The site of a brutal slaughter by King Menahem of Israel (2 Kgs. 15:16). Although 2 Kgs. 14:28 indicates that Jeroboam II's kingdom extended into Hamath, raids by Menahem to the Euphrates are problematic. The name should probably be read "Tappuah" (so LXX), placing the city on the Ephraim-Manasseh border (Josh. 17:7-8).

GARY P. ARBINO

TIRAS (Heb. *tîrās*)

According to the Table of Nations, a son of Japheth (Gen. 10:2; 1 Chr. 1:5). His descendants are assumed to have been a component of the Sea Peoples (called Turusa in Egyptian inscriptions and the Tyrsenoi by the Greeks) of the Aegean and eastern Mediterranean.

TIRATHITES (Heb. *tir'āṯîm*)

One of the "families of scribes" (or "Sopherites"; cf. NJB "Sophrite") at Jabez, reckoned among the Kenites (1 Chr. 2:55).

TIRHAKAH (Heb. *tirhāqâ;* Egyp. *Thrk;* Akk. *Tarqū*)

King of Egypt (690-664 B.C.E.) who came to the aid of King Hezekiah during Sennacherib's military campaign in Judah (2 Kgs. 19:9 = Isa. 37:9). 2 Kgs. 19:9 describes Tirhakah as "king of Ethiopia (= Cush)," reflecting his Nubian (Sudanese) origins (cf. the Nubian form of his name, Taharqa). Tirhakah's father, Piankhi (Piye) of Napata, founded the Ethiopian or 25th Dynasty after conquering and unifying a then splintered Egypt. Piankhi's son Shebitku (Shabataka), upon becoming king, summoned Tirhakah to the royal court at Thebes, and it was probably Shebitku who dispatched Tirhakah to Judah to assist Hezekiah during the Assyrian invasion of 701.

During Tirhakah's rule, Egypt experienced a time of prosperity and renewal as he initiated extensive building projects throughout the country. In the sixth year of this reign the Nile had an exceptionally large inundation, resulting in abnormally abundant crops, a phenomenon understood as a sign of divine favor from the god Amon, whose temples at Thebes and Napata greatly benefited from Tirhakah's domestic policies. Despite these favorable beginnings, Tirhakah's reign saw the Assyrian Empire's greatest expansion, first under Esarhaddon, who conquered Memphis, Egypt's capital, in 671, and again under Assurbanipal, who reasserted Assyrian control over Egypt in 667. Tirhakah died at Napata in 664.

Bibliography. K. A. Kitchen, *The Third Intermediate Period in Egypt (1100-650 B.C.),* 2nd ed. (Warminster, 1986).

JEFFREY C. GEOGHEGAN

TIRHANAH (Heb. *tirḥănâ*)

A child of Caleb and his concubine Maacah (1 Chr. 2:48), perhaps the name of a clan.

TIRIA (Heb. *tîryā'*)

A Judahite, son of Jehallelel (1 Chr. 4:16).

TIRZAH (Heb. *tirṣâ*) **(PERSON)**

One of the daughters of the Manassite Zelophehad for whom special provision was made that they might inherit their family's land (Num. 26:33; 27:1; 36:11; Josh. 17:3).

TIRZAH (Heb. *ṭirṣâ*) **(PLACE)**

A city in the hill country of Samaria whose Canaanite king was defeated by Joshua (Josh. 12:24). Tirzah later served as capital of the northern kingdom under Jeroboam I (1 Kgs. 14:17), Baasha (15:21, 33), and Elah, who was assassinated there by Zimri (16:6, 8-10), who in turn was besieged by Omri and died in the destruction of the palace after a seven-day reign (vv. 15-18). Omri ruled from Tirzah for six years before moving the capital to Samaria (1 Kgs. 16:21-24). Later, Menahem usurped the throne of Israel (ca. 752 B.C.E.) from Tirzah (2 Kgs. 15:14).

Tirzah is generally identified with the northern Tell el-Fâr'ah (1823.1822), ca. 11 km. (7 mi.) NE of Shechem. The town's name ("pleasure" or "beauty") may have resulted from its location amid one of the most beautiful landscapes in the Holy Land (Cant. 6:4). Excavations at the site between 1946 and 1960 by Roland de Vaux discovered occupation in the Early, Middle, and Late Bronze Ages. It is not clear from the Bible (Josh. 12:24) or archaeology if the Israelites brought an end to Canaanite Tirzah. Israelite Tirzah of the late 10th and early 9th centuries featured well-planned houses, each of a similar size and plan, reflecting little social inequality. This city was violently destroyed near the beginning of the 9th century, possibly in the invasion of Egyptian pharaoh Shishak. But the date of the destruction also accords well with the biblical account of Omri's siege and Zimri's suicidal fire of his own palace (1 Kgs. 16:17-18). Over the burned debris at the site, foundations of unfinished structures were found. The abandoned work may be related to Omri's decision to move the capital to Samaria.

In the 8th century Tirzah became a vibrant city again. The remains of this period include a group of large private homes which testify to the prosperity of their inhabitants. But this quarter was separated by a long straight wall from the miserable houses of the poor, huddled together in stark contrast to the comfortable villas of the rich. Tirzah and its fine houses were completely destroyed by fire, probably by the Assyrians in 723. Following a poor occupation, the site was finally abandoned ca. 600.

Bibliography. R. de Vaux, "Tirzah," in *Archaeology and Old Testament Study,* ed. D. W. Thomas (1967, repr. London, 1978), 371-83; de Vaux, P. de Miroschedji, and A. Chambon, "Far'ah, Tell el- (North)," *NEAEHL* 2:433-40.

DANIEL C. BROWNING, JR.

TISHBE (Heb. *tišbê*), **TISHBITE** *(hattišbî)*
The place of origin for Elijah the prophet (1 Kgs. 17:1). Early witnesses (LXX, Josephus *Ant.* 8.13.2) and most modern translations render Heb. *mittōšāḇê gil'āḏ* similarly to NRSV "of Tishbe in Gilead." In support of this reading is the preceding gentilic, *hattišbî,* "the Tishbite." However, there is no reference to a Tishbe in Gilead elsewhere in either biblical or nonbiblical literature. Nelson Glueck suggested that the text originally read "Elijah the Jabeshite from Jabesh-gilead." A more popular emendation is "one of the settlers of Gilead." Elijah, then, would be a permanent settler of Gilead, though not a native from there.

Tishbe probably was a place name that is not otherwise mentioned because it was a tiny, insignificant village with only one claim to fame, the great prophet Elijah who lived there. The location is uncertain, but Tishbe has traditionally been identified with modern Listib (el-Istib), ca. 13 km. (8 mi.) N of the Jabbok in Transjordan. STEPHEN R. MILLER

TISHRI (Heb. *tišrî*)
The postexilic Babylonian name for the seventh month of the Jewish civil or economic calendar and the first month of the religious year (Sept./Oct.). The earlier Hebrew name of the month was Ethanim.

TITHE
A tenth of one's annual income set aside for sacral purposes. Tithing was common not only in ancient Israel but throughout the ancient Near East, and while the primary function was sacral, it was also utilized for state income (1 Macc. 3:49; 10:31). Most biblical texts indicate that the believer was obliged to tithe, though the manner in which this was practiced seems to vary from era to era.

The nature of the sacral tithe is most clearly and consistently outlined in the pentateuchal traditions. Lev. 27:30-33 establishes that all the seeds from the land and fruits from trees belong to God, and a tenth of all herd and flock are holy to the Lord. The people were expected to tithe their grain, wine, oil, and firstlings from the herd and flock (Deut. 14:22-24). An important component of the tithe involved the bringing of the yield to the designated sanctuary, where the people would participate together in a meal. If it was not possible to transport the yield because of distance, then the yield could be redeemed for cash and the money used for whatever the person desired. However, if one's yield was redeemed for cash, then a further fifth of the yield must be added to the sum (Lev. 27:31).

The tithe also included a social component to care for the poor within the society, and every third year the tithe must be set aside for the Levite, the resident alien, the orphan, and the widow. Blessings from God are directly connected to this mandate (Deut. 14:28-29). The worshipper is to make all offerings, including the tithe, with joy and happiness (Sir. 35:8-12). Amos was critical of the people for fulfilling all their sacral duties, including the giving of tithes, yet not living just lives (Amos 4:4-5).

The Levite, unlike other residents, does not have an inheritance, and since what the people have is considered the allotment of the Levite's inheritance, then a tenth must be given to the Levite (Num. 18:21-32). Part of Ezra and Nehemiah's widespread reform included a tithe (tax) collected at the temple, to support the priests and the Levites (Neh. 10:37-38). Like some other mandatory laws, the tithe was not always kept (Mal. 3:8, 10).

The distinction between sacral and nonsacral purposes of the tithe is sometimes blurred, particularly when the tithe is given to a royal sanctuary (2 Sam. 6; 1 Kgs. 12:25-33). King Hezekiah is said to have collected tithes and stored them for the temple (2 Chr. 31:5-6). When the people seek to establish a monarchy, Samuel warns them that the king would require a tithe of grain, vineyards, and flocks of all the citizens for his officers (1 Sam. 8:14-15).

HEMCHAND GOSSAI

TITIUS JUSTUS
See JUSTUS **2.**

TITTLE
KJV rendering of Gk. *keraía,* a small stroke or hook that probably served to distinguish otherwise similar Hebrew letters (Matt. 5:18; Luke 16:17).
See DOT.

TITUS (Gk. *Títos*)

1. Titus Manius, one of two Roman envoys sent to the Jews following the defeat of Lysias in 165 B.C.E., to bear the notice of Roman consent to the agreement worked out by Maccabeus with Lysias and King Antiochus with regard to the restoration of the Jewish temple and noninterference with Jewish custom (2 Macc. 11:34).

2. A coworker and emissary of Paul. For Paul's important second visit to the Jerusalem church, seeking validation of his mission to the Gentiles, he took Barnabas and Titus as companions (Gal. 2:1). Titus' role was to prove especially significant, as he (an uncircumcised Gentile) was not compelled by the Jerusalem leaders to be circumcised as a requirement of his conversion to Christianity (Gal. 2:3). Thus, Paul's mission "to the uncircumcised" was respected as a legitimate counterpart to Peter's mission "to the circumcised" (Gal. 2:7-9).

Titus' subsequent role as Paul's coworker and trusted emissary is revealed most clearly in the correspondence with the Corinthian church. Because Titus' name does not appear in 1 Corinthians, it is assumed that he did not enter into this work until some time after the events of that letter, perhaps only as relations between Paul and the Christians at Corinth began to deteriorate further. His name does, however, appear in both 2 Cor. 1–9 and 10–13, thought by most scholars to represent two distinct letters. Titus seems to have been valued by Paul as a skillful mediator in his dealings with that fractious community. It appears that Titus was either the bearer of the "tearful letter" (2 Cor. 2:4) sent by Paul to the Corinthians, or that he arrived shortly thereafter and was instrumental in bringing about the repentance of the community with regard to their chastisement of a member and their respect for Paul. Paul describes his distress and anxiety as he awaited news of the Corinthians from Titus, who did not rejoin him as soon as Paul had hoped (2 Cor. 2:13; 7:6). From Paul's description of Titus' report, we may gather that Titus was skilled not only in bringing about the desired change of heart among the Corinthians, but also in conveying that change convincingly to Paul (2 Cor. 7:7).

Paul himself stresses the stature of Titus as his emissary, assuring the Corinthians that Titus has in his heart "the same eagerness for you that I myself have" (2 Cor. 8:16), and that he is Paul's "partner and coworker" (v. 23) in service to them. In fact, Titus' exemplary behavior among the Corinthians is a part of Paul's defense of his own conduct among them (2 Cor. 12:18). In addition, Paul largely entrusts to Titus the gathering of the collection for Jerusalem among the Corinthians, a significant part of the ongoing validation of Paul's mission in the eyes of the Jerusalem church (2 Cor. 8:6).

It is a testimony to Titus' continuing reputation as a trusted coworker of Paul that a letter should bear his name as recipient. The letter situates Titus in Crete, where he has been left by Paul to establish order in the churches there (Titus 1:5), and it is assumed that the instructions contained in the letter were intended to carry on the traditions of Paul into the lives of a new generation of churches. Given such evidence for Titus' reputation, it is remarkable that he is not mentioned in the book of Acts, although perhaps this omission is evidence of lingering controversy surrounding the issues of circumcision and the collection for Jerusalem.

See Pastoral Epistles.

Bibliography. C. K. Barrett, "Titus," in *Neotestamentica et Semitica,* ed. E. E. Ellis and M. Wilcox (Edinburgh, 1969), 1-14; F. F. Bruce, *The Pauline Circle* (Grand Rapids, 1985); M. M. Mitchell, "New Testament Envoys in the Context of Greco-Roman Diplomatic and Epistolary Conventions: The Example of Timothy and Titus," *JBL* 111 (1992): 641-62; W. D. Walker, "The Timothy-Titus Problem Reconsidered," *ExpTim* 92 (1980-81): 231-35.

Jane S. Lancaster

TITUS, EPISTLE OF

A pseudepigraphal text, attested in a single manuscript, composed in unrefined Latin and dating to the 8th century C.E. The author, purporting to be the Titus to whom the third of the Pastoral Epistles was addressed, composed a vehemently pro-ascetic address to a celibate Christian congregation, a theme ironically opposing the antiascetic tone of the Pastoral Epistles. The Epistle of Titus demands a chaste life-style from a group of male and female ascetics, some of whom have strayed from the ascetic ideal. To rectify the situation, the author adduces exemplars and allegorizing references to spiritual marriage from the OT, NT, and most notably, the apocryphal acts. The presumed authority of the apocryphal acts suggests that the Epistle of Titus functioned in a setting where asceticism was common and the apocryphal acts enjoyed popularity, perhaps the Priscillianist movement in 5th-century Spain.

Bibliography. J. H. Charlesworth, ed., *The New Testament Apocrypha and Pseudepigrapha* (Chicago, 1987), 410-11.

Melissa M. Aubin

TITUS, LETTER TO

A letter attributed to the Apostle Paul, written to his coworker Titus. Because of their similarities, it is generally treated together with the two letters of Paul to Timothy.

See Pastoral Epistles.

TIZITE (Heb. *tîṣî*)

A gentilic applied to Joha, one of David's Mighty Men (1 Chr. 11:45), probably designating an otherwise unknown place of origin in Transjordan.

TOAH (Heb. *tôaḥ*) (also NAHATH, TOHU)

A Levite of the Kohathite clan, the son of Zuph and an ancestor of Samuel (1 Chr. 6:34[MT 19]). Elsewhere he is called Nahath (**2;** 1 Chr. 6:26[11]) and Tohu (1 Sam. 1:1).

TOB (Heb. *ṭôḇ*)

An Aramean city located in southern Hauran, perhaps capital of a larger region. In this area the elders of Gilead found Jephthah (Judg. 11:3, 5). Later, when the Ammonite king Haunan raised rebellion against David, Tob dispatched 12 thousand warriors to support Haunan (2 Sam. 10:6-8). In Hellenistic times Jews resettled the area, but their gentile neighbors attacked them, slaying thousands of Jews and taking captive their wives and children. The city was recaptured by Judas Maccabeus (1 Macc. 5:9-17).

Some scholars identify this city with *t-b* (no. 22) on Thutmose III's list of captured cities, *dubu* in the Amarna Letters, and modern eṭ-Ṭayibeh (266218), located 19 km. (12 mi.) E of Ramoth-gilead, between Bozrah and Edrei.

Bibliography. B. Mazar, "The Tobiads," *IEJ* 7 (1957): 137-45, 229-38. ZELJKO GREGOR

TOB-ADONIJAH (Heb. *ṭôḇ 'ădônîyâ*)
A Levite who instructed the people in the law under King Jehoshaphat (2 Chr. 17:8). The name may be a scribal dittograph after "Adonijah, Tobijah."

TOBIAD(S)
See TOBIAH **2.**

TOBIAH (Heb. *ṭôḇîyâ*)
1. The head of a family that returned to Judah with Zerubbabel and Jeshua, and whose Israelite ancestry was not recorded in the genealogies acceptable to the scribes responsible for the list in Ezra 2:60; Neh. 7:62; 1 Esdr. 5:37.

2. One who, with Sanballat the Horonite and Geshem the Arab, opposed Nehemiah's journey to Jerusalem (Neh. 2:10, 19) and his plans for the city. The three are vilified in the book of Nehemiah, but seem to have considered themselves loyal servants of the Persian king Artaxerxes I and to have regarded Nehemiah a traitor for desiring to re-establish Jerusalem as a center of government with a king (Neh. 2:19; cf. 6:6-7). The three were prepared to use force, if necessary, to stifle Nehemiah's ambitions (Neh. 4:1-8[MT 3:33–4:2]), which probably threatened their own interests in Judah. When they requested a meeting with Nehemiah to discuss his actions, he rejected their overture (Neh. 6:1-9).

Tobiah is identified as "the Ammonite," which suggests he exercised political control over that area. He was allied with nobles in Judah (Neh. 6:17), who may well have opposed Nehemiah's reforms for economic, political, and/or religious reasons. Further, he was related by marriage to the high priest Eliashib, who prepared a living space for him within the temple precincts while Nehemiah was out of the city (Neh. 13:4-9). If he was descended from Tobiah **1,** he may have felt entitled to a place in the temple; Nehemiah nevertheless had him ousted. Even so, he was the head of the later Tobiad family that rivaled the Oniads for control of Jerusalem during the Hellenistic period. PAUL L. REDDITT

TOBIAS (Gk. *Tōbías*)
1. The son of Tobit and Anna (Tob. 1:9) who, guided by the angel Raphael, healed his father's blindness and drove out a demon from Sarah, the daughter of Raguel.

2. A prominent and wealthy landowner of the Maccabean period; ancestor (Gk. "son") of Hyrcanus (**1;** 2 Macc. 3:11; cf. Josephus *Ant.* 12.160, 186).

TOBIJAH (Heb. *ṭôḇîyāhû*)
1. One of the Levites sent out by King Jehoshaphat to teach in the cities of Judah (2 Chr. 17:8).

2. A descendant of Tobiah (**1**) who was unable to authenticate his Israelite origin (Ezra 2:60; Neh. 7:62).

3. One of three repatriates (Zech. 6:10) from whom Zechariah was to collect silver and gold to take to Josiah, the son of Zephaniah, to fashion crowns either to place on the head of Jeshua (or Zerubbabel; v. 11) or to be kept in the temple by the three as a memorial (v. 14). PAUL L. REDDITT

TOBIT (Gk. *Tōbeit, Tōbeit*)
A Naphtalite, son of Tobiel of the line of Asiel, exiled from his home at Thisbe in Galilee to Nineveh (Tob. 1:1-2); the central figure of the book of Tobit. Characterized as a pious Jew, he is blinded (Tob. 2) and eventually cured by the angel Raphael working through Tobias, the son of Tobit and Anna (11:1-15).

TOBIT (Gk. *Tōbeit*), **BOOK OF**
A postexilic Jewish book with clear folktale antecedents yet modeled on Jewish sacred literature, found in the Apocrypha.

Story

Exiled in Nineveh in the days of the Assyrian Empire, the Jewish household of Tobit, his wife Anna, and their son Tobias combine piety with success in the gentile world, until a wicked king, Sennacherib, ascends the throne and persecutes the Jews (1:1-18). As a result of providing a decent burial for his kinsmen, Tobit loses first his wealth and then his eyesight (1:19–2:10).

Tobit prays for death (2:11–3:6), but he also recalls some money he left in trust with Gabael, a relative in Media. Should he not tell Tobias about this money before God grants his prayer (3:7–4:4)? So Tobit dispatches his son to Media, provided with much good advice (4:5-21) and a guide. The guide gives himself out as Azariah, a relative from Tobit's tribe, but he is in reality the angel Raphael ("God heals"; 5:1-21).

Along the way, Raphael instructs Tobias to catch a large fish and preserve its liver, heart, and gall for use in healing and exorcism (6:1-9). Then Raphael leads Tobias to the home of Raguel and Edna (6:10–7:18). Their daughter Sarah is beautiful, virtuous, and an ideal match for Tobias, but she is also bewitched: the demon Asmodeus has killed her previous seven husbands on their wedding night. But by heeding Raphael's exhortation to piety and his instructions about the use of the fish's heart and liver, Tobias is able to marry Sarah and live till the next morning (8:1-9).

Raguel holds a two-week feast for the newlyweds, during which time Raphael retrieves the money from Gabael (8:10–10:12). At the end of two weeks, Tobias returns with Sarah to Nineveh. At this point, the healing property of the fish gall become evident, as Tobias uses it to cure Tobit's blindness (11:1-18).

When the time comes to pay "Azariah," the guide reveals himself as Raphael, an angel sent in answer to their prayers, who exhorts them to continue in their piety (12:1-22). Tobit praises God and predicts a glorious future for restored Israel (13:1–14:15).

Literary Antecedents

Tobit is rife with motifs from folktales to which scholars have given colorful names: e.g., The Grateful Dead Man, The Monster in the Bridal Chamber. Beneath these motifs lies a classic fairy-tale plot which begins when a hero leaves his family to go on a journey to remedy some misfortune that has befallen them. In the course of his journey, he finds a young woman in distress. Having obtained some special agent that helps him deal with this distress where others have failed, he marries her, finds a remedy for his family's initial misfortune, and returns home with his bride.

In Tobit this fairy-tale plot is placed in a context that makes it a vehicle for Jewish edification and encouragement. Unlike the fairy tale, Tobit unfolds in a specific time and place: the (Assyrian) Exile. Just as the troubles of Tobit and Sarah are brought on ultimately by their condition of exile, so the healing of their troubles points toward the end of their exile. This message is reinforced by a wealth of references to stories, laws, ethical teachings, and prophecies from the Law, the Prophets, and other Jewish sacred literature. There is also reference to the story of Ahikar, who is introduced into the story as Tobit's nephew.

Tobit's fairy-tale source(s) and numerous anachronisms explain the present scholarly consensus that Tobit is fictional. This view goes back at least as far as Luther, who described Tobit as "useful fiction" and a "delightful, pious comedy."

Date, Language, and Versions

Tobit has been reasonably dated as early as the 5th century B.C.E. and as late as the 2nd century. Fragments of the book (four in Aramaic, one in Hebrew) were found at Qumran. Assuming Joseph Fitzmyer is correct in dating the oldest of these to 100 B.C.E., a later date for Tobit is not possible.

The Qumran fragments have buttressed the prevailing critical opinion that Tobit was originally written in Aramaic. The full text of the book has come down to us in two Greek recensions that are markedly different: Sinaiticus and Vaticanus. Earlier translations, as recently as the RSV and Goodspeed, relied heavily on Vaticanus. However, for several decades, Sinaiticus has been generally regarded as the earlier of the two recensions, and this conclusion is now supported by the Qumran material. Most recent translations make some use of Vaticanus as well, if only to fill in the lacunae that occur in Sinaiticus at 4:7-19; 13:6-10. Names in Tobit are often rendered according to their Greek transliterations (e.g., "Tobias") rather than their Aramaic antecedents ("Tobiah").

Themes

Tobit incorporates a wealth of Jewish attitudes and beliefs. Prominent among them are those related to the Jewish family, almsgiving, and angels. Concern for family lineage is shown when Tobit seeks to determine whether "Azariah" is a fit guide for his son, and also in the proposed marriage of Tobias and Sarah. Unlike other postexilic books, Tobit advocates marriage between cousins (perhaps partly as a way of consolidating a family's wealth). Filial duty is prescribed by the parents and embodied in the children. Yet family life is not always ideal. The friction that exists between Tobit and Anna when she becomes the "breadwinner," or when they fear for Tobias' safety, is tellingly depicted. There are many other vignettes of family life: weddings, burials, meals, sleeping arrangements, farewells, and reunions.

In a larger sense, the entire Jewish community is Tobit's "family." The duty Tobit has to them, and which he enjoins on his son, is summed up in the word *eleēmosýnē,* traditionally translated "almsgiving." The primary acts of charity described as almsgiving in Tobit are feeding the hungry, clothing the naked, and giving the dead a proper burial. Such conduct will ultimately be rewarded by God, which is why Tobit can say "almsgiving delivers from death" (4:10).

These words are repeated verbatim by Raphael when he explains that it was in response to Tobit's almsgiving and prayer that he was sent by God to aid them. Raphael describes himself as one of seven angels who "stand ready and enter before the glory of the Lord" (12:15). He fights demons and assists mortals, but his sphere is uniquely heavenly, and he reminds Tobit and Tobias that he did not really eat and drink, but only appeared to. All this reflects the developed angelology of the postexilic period.

Later Use of Tobit

Tobit contains perhaps the earliest statement of the "Golden Rule" (in its "negative" form, 4:15) which has proved a fountainhead of Jewish and Christian moral teaching. The presence of Tobit at Qumran attests to the esteem in which it was held in ancient Judaism, but despite its popularity and piety it was not included in the Jewish Bible. *Midrash Tanḥuma* (ca. 500 C.E.) contains a folktale similar to Tobit, although there is probably no direct dependence either way.

While many Eastern Church fathers did not regard Tobit as canonical, in the Western Church its canonicity received either qualified or (more often) unqualified endorsement. Readings from Tobit have been used in the Roman Church to celebrate holy days in honor of angels; other readings (e.g., Tobias' prayer, 8:5-8) have been used for marriage ceremonies.

Bibliography. J. C. Dancy, *The Shorter Books of the Apocrypha.* Cambridge Bible Commentary (Cambridge, 1972), 1-66; G. Nickelsburg, "Stories of Biblical and Early Post-Biblical Times: Tobit," in *Jewish Writings of the Second Temple Period,* ed.

M. E. Stone. CRINT 2/2 (Philadelphia, 1984), 40-46; W. Soll, "Misfortune and Exile in Tobit," *CBQ* 51 (1989): 209-31; F. Zimmermann, *The Book of Tobit* (New York, 1958). WILL SOLL

TOCHEN (Heb. *tōḵen*)
A Simeonite village, the site of which is unknown (1 Chr. 4:32).

TOGARMAH (Heb. *tōgarmâ, tôgarmâ*)
A son of Gomer and descendant of Japheth (Gen. 10:3 = 1 Chr. 1:6). The name is related to the city and region of Beth-togarmah.

TOHU (Heb. *tōhû*) (also NAHATH, TOAH)
The son of Zuph and an ancestor of Samuel (1 Sam. 1:1). Elsewhere he is called Nahath (**2;** 1 Chr. 6:26[MT 11]) and Toah (v. 34[19]).

TOI (Heb. *tōʿî*) (also TOU)
A king of Hamath who sent his son Joram with lavish gifts to congratulate David for defeating Hadadezer, the king of neighboring Zobah (2 Sam. 8:9-10). At 1 Chr. 18:9-10 he is called Tou and his son Hadoram.

TOKHATH (Heb. *toqhaṯ*) (also TIKVAH)
The father-in-law of the prophetess Huldah (2 Chr. 34:22). He is called Tikvah (**1**) at 2 Kgs. 22:14.

TOLA (Heb. *tôlāʿ*)

1. The eldest son of Issachar (Gen. 46:13; 1 Chr. 7:1), whose descendants — heads of fathers' houses and warriors during the reign of King David (v. 2) — were called Tolaites (Heb. *tôlāʿî;* Num. 26:23).

2. The son of Puah from the tribe of Issachar. A resident of the Ephraimite hill country town of Shamir, he was a judge of Israel for 23 years (Judg. 10:1).

TOLAD (Heb. *tôlaḏ*)
A Simeonite town (1 Chr. 4:29); alternate name for Eltolad.

TOMB
Tombs and cemeteries are frequently found in proximity to archaeological ruins. While grave robbing has destroyed much evidence about ancient burials, the legal excavation of tombs in the biblical world has revealed much information about ancient life. Naturally, burials — along with ancient literature — supply much information on mortuary practices, but the artifacts found in tombs also reveal much about how ancient people lived. Burial practices and tomb construction went through many changes in the Near East during the biblical period; there is much diversity among types and contents of tombs, but there were also common practices and rituals.

In the Greco-Roman world, the dead were often cremated, but the Israelites and Jews, along with most ancient peoples, normally dug graves or constructed tombs for deceased members of their societies. Indeed, the Hebrews held strong beliefs about the importance of proper burial and fear of exhumation (1 Kgs. 14:11; 16:4; 2 Kgs. 9:37; Ps. 79:3; Ezek. 29:5; Rev. 11:9); in horrifying terms Jeremiah preached about the exposure of corpses (Jer. 7:33; 8:1-2; 16:4-6; 22:19). Burial took place quickly, often within 24 hours of death (Num. 19:11-19; Deut. 21:22-23; Ezek. 43:6-9; Hag. 2:13; cf. Matt. 27:57-61).

As in modern times, ancient mortuary procedure consisted of three stages: preparation of the tomb, preparation of the corpse for burial, and performance of rites that accompanied burial. Throughout their history, most Israelites were buried in simple shallow graves, which were often covered with heaps of stones. Such simple graves were sometimes lined with reed mats or stones, but coffins were not used in ancient Israel, except in the case of Joseph (Gen. 50:26).

In prehistoric times the dead were sometimes buried beneath the floors of houses or they were placed in shallow pits; infants were sometimes buried in ceramic jars. In the Early Bronze Age the dead were entombed in caves or in rock-cut tombs, while megalithic monuments called dolmens continued in use from the Chalcolithic period. At the same time, the Egyptians and Sumerians constructed elaborate tombs for their nobility; the Great Pyramids and Royal Cemetery of Ur are among the most elaborate tombs of antiquity. Burials with small domed chambers at the bottom of vertical shafts were also common in this period, as illustrated in the thousands of "shaft tombs" discovered at Bab edh-Dhra', near the Dead Sea. Gen. 23 describes Abraham's purchase of the cave of Machpelah for the burial of Sarah; this cave was also used as the burial plot for other members of Abraham's family (25:8-9; 49:31; 50:13). During much of the 2nd millennium B.C. and on into the period of the Israelite monarchy, families hired craftsmen to prepare small, rock-cut chambers in the limestone hills of Palestine (Isa. 22:16). These tombs included outer courtyards and low entrances, and the corpses were placed on stone benches carved inside the tombs. When a tomb was reused, the skeletal remains from earlier burials were pushed aside or placed in repository pits inside the same tomb. Family tombs were common in Israel (Judg. 8:32; 2 Sam. 2:32; 17:23), and community cemeteries were located outside of towns and villages (2 Kgs. 23:6), at Beth-shan and Tell es-Saʿidiyeh.

In Hellenistic and Roman times elaborate tombs in Palestine were similar to those constructed elsewhere in the Mediterranean world (e.g., tombs of the Sanhedrin in Jerusalem). Hundreds of funerary monuments carved from sandstone at Petra reflect the influence of Greek and Roman architecture in the Near East. Niches radiated off the main tomb chamber and made it possible for many bodies to be buried in a single tomb complex. Sometimes ossuaries or "bone boxes" were used for secondary burial; this concern for the careful preservation of skeletons probably reflects the Jewish belief in resurrection. Rock-cut tombs, which included stones that rolled into place to block doorways, were used at the time of Jesus' burial (Matt. 27:60, 66; 28:2).

Preparation of the body for burial was carried out by relatives and friends of the deceased, usually by women (Luke 23:54–24:1; cf. John 19:39). The corpse was often carried on a litter to the burial site, as in the funerary procession of Herod the Great (whose tomb has not been found), and interment was accompanied by a variety of funerary rites — e.g., weeping, fasting, music. The Canaanites placed jewelry, weapons, pottery, containers of food, and even furniture in tombs (as illustrated in the famous cemetery at Jericho); Hebrew tombs often contain grave goods that reflect the status held by the deceased and the respect in which he/she was held in life and death. The Hebrews were not permitted to make offerings for the dead (Deut. 26:14).

See BURIAL.

Bibliography. R. Gonen, *Burial Patterns and Cultural Diversity in Late Bronze Age Canaan.* ASORDS 7 (Winona Lake, 1992); S. Loffreda, "Typological Sequence of Iron Age Rock-Cut Tombs in Palestine," *Liber Annuus* 18 (1968): 244-87; D. Ussishkin, *The Village of Silwan: The Necropolis from the Period of the Judean Kingdom* (Jerusalem, 1993). GERALD L. MATTINGLY

TONGS

See SNUFFERS.

TONGUES

Unlearned languages spoken under the influence of the Holy Spirit. Apart from the reference to "new tongues" in the longer ending of Mark (Mark 16:17), tongues appear in the NT only in Acts and 1 Corinthians. In Acts the writer tells of various groups of believers who spoke in tongues, and in 1 Corinthians Paul discusses the meaning and importance of tongues as he writes to a congregation that makes use of them. The word "glossolalia," which does not appear in the NT, comes from the NT description of the phenomenon, *laleín (en) glṓssē* or *laleín (en) glṓssais,* "to speak in/with a tongue" or "to speak in/with tongues."

On the Pentecost after Jesus' death and resurrection, the Twelve (or possibly the 120) "began to speak in other languages, as the Spirit gave them ability" (Acts 2:4). Their hearers hear them "each in his/her own language *(diálektos)*" proclaiming "God's deeds of power" (Acts 2:11). Later in Acts two other groups speak in tongues: the household of Cornelius when they hear Peter's message about Jesus (Acts 10:46) and the 12 men of Ephesus after Paul baptizes them and lays hands on them (19:6).

In 1 Cor. 12–14 Paul deals with *tá pneumatiká,* "spiritual gifts," and *hoí pneumatikoí,* the "spiritual persons" who may use those gifts (1 Cor. 12:1; 14:1, 37; cf. 2:12-15; 3:1; Gal. 6:1). He makes several points which apply to spiritual gifts in general and to tongues specifically. The content of a speech carries more weight than its manner of delivery, even including ecstatic speech (1 Cor. 12:1-3). The Holy Spirit decides which believer receives which gifts (12:4-11). The gifts should benefit the body of believers, not any individual (14:1-5). Less spectacular gifts can mean as much as the more dramatic ones (12:14-26). Not all believers receive all gifts (12:29-31). Communicating God's truth in plain language (i.e., prophecy) means more than obscure communication in tongues (14:13-25). The Church should restrict tongues speaking to those occasions when someone can interpret (14:26-33). The most spectacular gifts mean nothing without love (13:1-13).

Scholars differ on the nature of NT tongues speaking and the historicity of the accounts. The main schools of thought are these: (1) The tongues speaking in Acts 2 is unhistorical, and the Corinthian experience involved "ecstatic utterance" (1 Cor. 12:10 NEB) not to be identified with any human language. This view largely excludes any idea of miraculous speech. (2) The tongues speaking in Acts 2 is historical, and the tongues of 1 Corinthians are human languages. This represents an attempt to see all NT tongues speaking as the same phenomenon. (3) The tongues speaking in Acts 2 is historical, but the tongues of 1 Corinthians are not real human languages. This would account for the fact that Paul does not seem to envision a situation like that of Acts 2, where ordinary speakers heard their own languages miraculously spoken.

The idea that the "baptism of the Spirit," a postconversion experience, always involves speaking in tongues finds scant support in the NT. Acts 11:15-17 suggests that its author regarded the "gift" *(dōreá)* and the "baptism" of the Spirit as two words describing the same phenomenon. However, the idea that miraculous gifts would cease upon the completion of the NT canon, or the books of the canon, is a theological construct uncomfortably imposed on Paul's words in 1 Cor. 13:9-10.

Bibliography. W. E. Mills, *A Theological/Exegetical Approach to Glossolalia* (Lanham, 1985); Mills, ed., *Speaking in Tongues* (Grand Rapids, 1986); V. S. Poythress, "The Nature of Corinthian Glossolalia: Possible Options," *WTJ* 40 (1977): 130-35. CARL BRIDGES

TOPAZ

A mineral (a silicate of aluminum) that occurs in translucent or transparent prismatic, orthorhombic crystals of various colors, valued as a gemstone (Gk. *topázion*). Topaz is named at Rev. 21:20 as the ninth foundation stone of the heavenly Jerusalem. In 1900 topaz was discovered in great quantities on an island in the Red Sea near the Egyptian coast.

See CHRYSOLITE.

TOPHEL (Heb. *tōp̱el;* Gk. *Tophol*)

A place in the desert east of the Jordan River, in the vicinity of which Moses recollected the law to the Israelites (Deut. 1:1; cf. LXX). Deut. 1:5 places the event in the territory of Moab. Although the precise location is unknown, it may be identified with eṭ-Ṭafîleh (208027) based on a phonological similar-

ity. Yohanon Aharoni located Tophel on the King's Highway between Punon and Wadi Zered but S of Moab.
PHILIP R. DREY

TOPHETH (Heb. *tōpeṯ*)
A location in the Hinnom Valley in Jerusalem where children were burned in sacrifice to Molech (2 Kgs. 23:10). Jeremiah condemns the site and proclaims that one day it will become a mass grave where the slain inhabitants of Jerusalem will be buried (Jer. 7:32; 19:4-14). In the late 7th century the place was destroyed as part of Josiah's reform program (2 Kgs. 23:10). A variant reading in Isa. 30:33 refers to the immolation of the king of Assyria (Heb. *topteh,* "burning place").

The etymology of the word is uncertain, although most scholars assume that it derives from Aram. *tēpaṯ* ("fireplace," "hearth") pointed with the consonants of Heb. *bōšeṯ* ("shame"). This may represent a homonym with Heb. *tōpeṯ,* "spitting" (Job 17:6), introduced by the Masoretes. Another suggestion is an original Egyptian form meaning "city of Ptah."

The exact location of Topheth is as yet unknown, but it was likely at the lower end of the Hinnom Valley close to the southern tip of the City of David.

Bibliography. G. C. Heider, *The Cult of Molek.* JSOTSup 43 (Sheffield, 1985), 347-65, 383-408.
BRIAN P. IRWIN

TORAH (Heb. *tôrâ*)
A name (Heb. "instruction, guidance, law") ascribed to the first division of the Hebrew canon, the five books of Moses or the Pentateuch. In a more general sense, torah indicates the divine law or instruction according to which Israel was to live as stipulated in the covenant.

TORCH
A light carried in the hand consisting of combustible substance such as a stick of resinous wood or bundle of tow. As a source of light which provides vision in the darkness, it is often used poetically to speak of new vision gained.

In the covenant ritual between Abram and Yahweh (Gen. 15:17), a torch passes between the pieces of the sacrificial animals. Placing their torches under jars allows Gideon's 300 men to surprise the Midianite camp (Judg. 7:16, 20), and Samson ties a torch to the tails of many foxes to burn the Philistine's food supply (15:4-5). Judas brings soldiers and guards with torches to find Jesus in the garden.

Used poetically, the torch may represent enlightenment and power. Salvation for Jerusalem is like "a burning torch" (Isa. 62:1). In his vision of God's presence Ezekiel views something from the four creatures that seemed like "torches moving to and fro" (Ezek. 1:13). Zechariah speaks of Jerusalem as God's instrument, which "like a torch" will devour surrounding peoples (Zech. 12:6). In Daniel's revelation about the great war an angel-warrior has eyes "like fiery torches" (Dan. 10:6). From the one seated on the heavenly throne come "seven flaming torches," which are seen as the seven spirits of God (Rev. 4:5). When the third angel opens the seal, he blows his trumpet and a large star "burning like a torch" falls from the sky (Rev. 8:10).
C. GILBERT ROMERO

TOU (Heb. *tōʿû*)
Alternate form of Toi (1 Chr. 18:9-10).

TOWER
A defensive structure either built into a city wall or located on a hill as a watchtower. Towers (Heb. *migdāl*) were built into city walls at strategic positions such as corners, city gates, and vulnerable locations. Massive towers built as part of the city gate structure (e.g., Megiddo, Samaria, Hazor, Dan, Beer-sheba, Timnah) increased defense capabilities at a city's most vulnerable location.

Towers, built into the walls at intervals to increase defense capabilities, usually jutted out beyond the city wall giving defenders a clear view of the wall's foundation and anyone attempting to breech the wall. This type of tower is typically taller than the adjoining city wall. Defense towers built into walls can be rectangular (Late Bronze Tell Beit Mirsim and Megiddo), semicircular (Early Bronze Arad), or round (Khirbet eš-Šaqq), but are usually square. Two square towers in Jerusalem, dating to the second temple period, extended several meters from the city wall. They were built of roughly hewn stones and spaced ca. 20 m. (66 ft.) apart. These towers are three-sided, being open to the inner city. Three massive 1st-century towers built by Herod into the western city walls in Jerusalem were large, fully enclosed, and contained several rooms; these towers, named after Herod's relatives, also served as small fortresses. Reliefs from Sennacherib's palace in Nineveh depict square towers projecting out from the city walls of Lachish. Nehemiah gives the names of several towers built into the Jerusalem walls: Tower of the Hundred, Hananel (Neh. 3:1), the Ovens (v. 11), and Furnaces (12:38). Jer. 31:38; Zech. 14:10 also name a Jerusalem tower, Hananel. Ezekiel predicted the destruction of the towers of Tyre (Ezek. 26:4, 9) and describes the defenders as placing their shields on the walls (27:11). Isaiah refers to a Babylonian guard standing watch on a watchtower (*miṣpeh;* Isa. 21:8).

Independent watchtowers on hilltops served as observation posts and forward defense stations. These small self-contained structures look more like small fortresses than towers. Small fortresses (towers) in the Negeb usually were built with casemate walls (two parallel walls intervally connected by transverse walls), gates, and internal structures. The smaller fortresses are generally square, ca. 20 m. (66 ft.) on a side. The larger fortresses have towers built into the walls and are shaped to conform to the terrain. Archaeologists have discovered three Iron Age circular towers in the desert of Samaria, measuring 19-19.5 m. (62-64 ft.) and built of three concentric stone walls. A rectangular building (guard quarters?) and a casemate parameter wall accompanies each tower. These towers guarded major Transjordanian roads. Watchtowers are also connected to agricul-

Central tower at ar-Rumayl, SE of Madaba, one of several strategically located Iron Age watchtowers in the region (M. P. Michèle Daviau)

ture, especially vineyards. Such towers functioned as lookout stations to protect crops (Isa. 5:2; Matt. 21:33 = Mark 12:1; Gk. *pýrgos*).

Uzziah built towers in the wilderness (2 Chr. 26:10), and Jotham on wooded hills (27:4). Evidently villages sprang up around some watchtowers, as reflected in names such as Migdal-gad (Josh. 15:37) and Migdal-el (19:38).

A *miḡdāl* can also be an inner citadel or a temple built as a fortress. A woman on a tower in the center of Thebez killed Abimelech by throwing down a millstone (Judg. 9:50-53). A thousand people in the Tower of Shechem died in the inner chamber of a temple-fortress (Judg. 9:46-49). Gideon tore down the tower of Penuel (Judg. 8:9, 17), an inner city fortress. Israel sinned by building high places in its watchtowers (2 Kgs. 17:9). Although not a defensive structure, the Tower of Babel is a *migdāl* (Gen. 11:4-5).

Temporary towers, constructed for offensive besieging of cities, allowed observers to see into a city and gave archers better angles for shooting at defenders. The Babylonians built such towers at Tyre (Isa. 23:13), and Joab set up similar siege works against Abel-beth-maacah (2 Sam. 20:15). The Lachish reliefs depict Assyrian mobile towers containing archers on the upper level and a battering ram with operators on the lower level.

Metaphorically, towers illustrate the beauty of human body parts: the neck (Cant. 4:4; 7:4), nose (7:4), and breasts (8:10). God is described as a strong tower (Ps. 61:3[MT 4]; Prov. 18:10).

Bibliography. A. Zertal, "Three Iron Age Fortresses in the Jordan Valley and the Origin of the Ammonite Circular Towers," *IEJ* 45 (1995): 253-73.

TERRY W. EDDINGER

TOWN

A relatively small settlement, presumably larger than the village but smaller than the city. Although towns are occasionally distinguished from villages (Josh. 15:45; Matt. 10:11; Luke 13:22; cf. 8:1; Matt. 9:35), precise classification is made difficult because of the town's designation by the same terms elsewhere used for "village" or "city" (e.g., Heb. *ʿîr*, Judg. 17:8; Gk. *pólis*, Luke 2:4; *kṓmē*, John 7:42). In some cases the term may simply indicate a settlement of any size (cf. Matt. 10:5).

Archaeological evidence suggests that the early Israelites were heavily concentrated in towns throughout the central Palestinian hill country. Unlike villages, towns might be fortified, usually by ramparts or walls with gates and occasionally a moat (1 Sam. 23:7; Prov. 8:3; cf. Tell el-ʿUmeiri). Towns were administered by elders; larger settlements also controlled the economic affairs of surrounding hinterland tribes. Even during the Early Iron Age (12th-10th centuries B.C.E.) the inhabitants remained primarily transhumants. When dependent on larger fortified cities, towns are referred to by the kinship term Heb. *baṯ*, "daughter" (e.g., Josh. 15:45, 47; NRSV "dependencies"; 1 Chr. 2:49; 7:28), which may also reflect the social and political history of their relationships. ALLEN C. MYERS

TOWN CLERK

A high-ranking civic official who led city politics and often acted as spokesperson for the city assembly. In addition, the town clerk (Gk. *grammateús*, usually "scribe") was responsible for drafting decrees in conjunction with the local magistrates and for many of the details of city administration, including maintaining order (cf. Acts 19:35). Little more is known about this position in the city government.

The title applied to the official in Ephesus was "temple-warden *(neōkóros)* of the great Artemis." The term, used in Acts and by Philostratus in the 32nd letter of Apollonius of Tyana (1.352.7), refers lit., at least in Ephesus, to a secretary or clerk. Among Jews of the 1st century C.E. the term also refers to an expert in the law who is often connected with the scribes and high priests (Acts 23:9).

JOSEPH CORAY

TRACHONITIS (Gk. *Trachōnítis*)

The region in northern Transjordan which was the northeastern extent of the kingdom of Herod the Great. Trachonitis, also called the Hauran, was located SE of Damascus and NE of the Sea of Galilee. In pre-Hellenistic times, the territory encompassed the northern limits of Bashan and was always sparsely populated. The name Trachonitis refers to the "rough, rocky" topography of the basalt plateau. Following Herod's death in 4 B.C.E., Trachonitis was passed on to Herod Philip (Luke 3:1). Administration of the region vacillated between the governors of Syria and Philip's heirs until 98 C.E. when it became part of the Roman province of Syria.

GARY P. ARBINO

TRADE AND COMMERCE

Trade represents the institutionalized exchange of material goods. Commerce is the sale and purchase of material goods (commodities) in a monetary economy. All commerce involves trade, but not all trade is commercial.

Antiquity and Varieties of Trade

Thousands of years before the Iron Age emergence of the biblical peoples, trade relations brought obsidian (volcanic glass used for blades) to the Levant from sources in the Anatolian highlands. Seashells from distant shores found their way into the remains of pre-Neolithic villages. Even for prehistoric times, archaeologists and Near Eastern historians can paint fairly detailed portraits of trade since trade goods stand out in the archaeological record and often possess chemical or other "fingerprints" that permit their sources to be ascertained. The historic periods offer up documentary evidence of trade. The most extensive documentation derives from Kültepe in northern Iraq (ancient Kārum Kanesh) where an archive containing thousands of tablets details the transactions of an Old Assyrian (20th-18th centuries B.C.E.) merchant colony. The merchants moved tin and textiles from the south and traded these for gold and silver mined in Anatolia. The 14th-century Amarna Letters from Egypt's New Kingdom depict exchanges between various "heads of state" such as Pharaoh and the king of Cyprus (Alashiya). The OT also makes reference to such diplomatic trade relations — e.g., the relations between Hiram of Tyre and Solomon — as well as displaying the vigorous nature of trade carried on by the cities of Phoenicia, especially Tyre, labeled the "merchant to the peoples" (Heb. *rōḵeleṯ hā'ammîm,* Ezek. 27:3).

Participants in Western, market-oriented capitalism tend to view trade in purely utilitarian terms, the product of national economic choices made by the exchange participants based upon their own cost-benefit calculus. Trade decisions in the ancient economy, however, included a range of noneconomic parameters. While modern trading relationships are by no means devoid of noneconomic motivations, such parameters had a greater weight in the preindustrial world. Because of this "substantive" understanding of the economy, some ancient historians deny the existence of a price-setting market shaped by supply and demand of trade carried on by private entrepreneurs independent of the dictates of their royal palace. Yet most researchers have concluded that a variety of economic mechanisms promoted ancient trade. For example, literary traditions of Solomon's trading activities — especially with Sheba — may be taken to represent the gift-giving and sanctions of reciprocal exchange; i.e., trade that is not commercial in nature. Such trade would be typical of palace-oriented exchange in which "gifts" pass between the trading parties at the highest political level. The queen gave *(ntn)* the king gold, spices, and precious stones. The king reciprocated: he gave *(htn)* her whatever she desired *(ḥpṣ).* Here as elsewhere, the verb *ḥpṣ* appears to be a component of the technical vocabulary of royal trade negotiations (e.g., 1 Kgs. 5:8-10[MT 22-24]). Solomonic importation of horses and chariots may represent the "economizing" exchange of goods in a price-producing market arena, i.e., commercial trade. Unfortunately, the textual tradition locates this hint of enterpreneurial trade within royal initiative — it is the work of "the king's traders" (1 Kgs. 10:28), and there is no reference to any independent merchants who may have initiated and carried out the horse trade. Here, as elsewhere, the Bible records nothing about the operation of private ventures. This may well be due to its focus on the monarchy rather than the dearth of nonroyal trading operations. All efforts to understand trade in the ancient world encounter the potential bias of documentation.

In an age in which issues of international trade dominate economic forums and the news pulses with reports on tariff negotiations, favored-nation status decisions, and the ebb and flow of the balance of trade, it is well to remember that trade still accounts for but a small percentage of the gross production of an industrial or postindustrial democracy. The fraction of the total economy that produced and consumed trade goods was all the smaller in the ancient agrarian economies of Israel, Judah, and their neighbors. Moreover, ancient trade networks did not encompass huge volumes of everyday goods. Most people remained subsistence farmers and pastoralists: they produced mostly what they consumed and consumed mostly what they produced.

Trade goods consisted predominantly of special goods, "preciosities" consumed by the elite segment of the society, and strategic goods valued by the military and manufacturing interests. In contrast to most everyday commodities, these special goods possessed high value to weight and volume ratios — like computer chips and pharmaceuticals, unlike cement and plastic goods. With its reliance on animal power — donkeys, camels, and ox carts — ancient transportation technology forced severe limits on the range of heavy and/or bulky goods such as ordinary pottery, grain, and building materials. These could only be moved great distance by sea; overland trade in such items was infrequent and costly.

The regular wares of international trade constitute a concise list of goods evidenced by inscriptional, archaeological, and literary data. The reports of Solomon's international income cite gold, silver, ivory, curious animals (1 Kgs. 10:22), garments, weapons, spices, horses, mules (19:25), almug wood (red sandalwood?; 10:11), chariots (v. 28), and cedar and cypress timber (5:10[24]) as imports to the royal household and building projects. Analogous inventories of precious and strategic goods show up as Assyrian tribute demands such as that imposed upon Hezekiah: gold, silver, gems, ivory-inlaid couches, elephant hides, African blackwood, boxwood, and human beings. From the end of the Iron Age, Neo-Babylonian tablets document commodities imported from the west: copper, iron, tin, dye, blue-purple wool and other fibers, lapis lazuli, alum, assorted honey, white swine, spice, and juniper resin. The Late Bronze Age Amarna Letters discuss the exchange of gold, silver, copper, lapis lazuli, ivory, chariots and horses, linen garments, "sweet oil," timber for ship construction, and various categories of human beings. Within a few decades of this correspondence, the Mediterranean Sea claimed a transport vessel off the coast of Turkey. The Ulu Burunm shipwreck has offered archaeologists just this kind of cargo: copper and tin ingots, African blackwood, cobalt-blue glass ingots, unworked ivory, amphoras filled with terebinth resin, and storejars stacked with Cypriot pottery.

The role of long-distance trade in the small kingdoms of Israel and Judah began and ended with an urban elite sector, outside of which few items secured by long-distance trade circulated. As the citations above show, trade provided this sector with some necessities, e.g., timber for monumental construction, metals for military hardware. It procured status markers for the elite segment of society, e.g., ivory inlays for furniture (Amos 6:4), jewelry and choice apparel (Isa. 3:18-23), and fine tableware. Perhaps more significantly, trade represented the means by which the small kingdoms on the periphery of Assyrian imperial power could acquire the tribute goods demanded by their suzerain. Long-distance trade also spawned a coterie of trading specialists, e.g., people whom texts of the OT designated as "traders" *(ʾanšê hattārîm),* "merchants" *(rōḵᵉlîm),* and "the king's traders" *(sōḥărê hammeleḵ).* A variety of texts also employed the term "Canaanite" as a designation for these specialists in international exchange (e.g., Isa. 23:84; Ezek. 17:4; Hos. 12:7[8]; Prov. 31:24; Zeph. 1:11), though apparently without any connotation of trading as a foreign specialty.

Though trade goods played a limited role outside of the elite social sector, the effects of trading ventures did extend beyond the palace compound. The cost of entering the trading network to garner specialized goods was borne by the primary producers of the ancient economy. Trading possibilities engendered both economic pressures and direct royal initiatives to increase the production of commodities which could most easily be traded. In a land of few natural resources (e.g., no significant deposits of ore), the agricultural sector bore the weight of this demand. Trade "policy" stimulated the production of the most tradable goods, namely olive oil and wine, the products of the field with the greatest value to weight ratios. Perfume (balsam) was another commodity developed, as excavations of the Dead Sea oasis of En-gedi (Tel Goren) have suggested, but its production was limited. During the Late Iron Age, widespread agricultural intensification and specialization converted arable land to orchards and hillsides to terraced slopes. Farming families increasingly produced for market rather than for subsistence, creating an increased state of interdependence. Rising land values and ownership defenses constricted the pastoral segment of the village economy — a family's "food bank on the hoof" — further escalating the vulnerability of a farming family to economic disaster. Loss of ancestral property and its agglomeration in smaller numbers of hands resulted (Isa. 5:8; Mic. 2:2, 9).

Trends toward increased royal interference with the structure of rural life may have been dampened by income from tolls imposed on the movement of trade across Israel and Judah's strategically positioned territories. Tolls imposed on caravans bringing the incense, spices, and gold of south Arabia across the desert toward the Mediterranean may have subsidized royal building projects and elite life-styles to a degree. This source of income from trade would have been especially significant during periods when Egypt's reach into southern Palestine was reduced. The ebb and flow of settlement in the southern Negeb provides a barometer of Judean resources committed to controlling, protecting, and provisioning this trade for a portion of its profits. Transit tolls may have reached 25 percent of the value of this commercial traffic.

Commercialization

Long-distance trade promoted the commercialization of the Israelite and Judean economies, economies in which the products as well as the forces of production — land and labor — themselves were increasingly available for sale and purchase. Instead of producing a diverse repertoire of foodstuffs for their own subsistence and for bartering for needed craft specialties, farming families experienced pressures and incentives to produce commodities for market and for cash sale. Biblical literature and archaeological finds have both manifested the existence of commercial exchange and its growth to prominence in the Late Iron II period. Urban marketplace scenes animated the prophetic collection of Amos (e.g., 8:4-6). Jeremiah refers to the specialized production required in a commercial economy: the prophet acted out destruction at the Potters' Gate with a purchased jar (Jer. 19:2) and ate bread bought at the bakers' court (37:21).

Silver was the means of payment for transactions. Omri paid in silver for the property of Shemer (1 Kgs. 16:24), and shekels of silver measured the wild variation of the prices of foodstuffs during times of famine and feast (2 Kgs. 6:25; 7:1).

Silver functioned more as a standard of value than a form of payment. Yet the precious metal did change hands during commercial exchanges. Since coins played no part in the economy until the Persian period (late 6th century), silver bits were weighed out on scales. Jer. 32:10 offers a succinct description of a real estate transaction: "I wrote a deed, sealed it, and had it witnessed; and I weighed out the silver on a balance." Crooked scales and false weight are castigated occasionally in legal (e.g., Lev. 19:36), proverbial (e.g., Prov. 20:23), and prophetic literature (e.g., Hos. 12:7).

Archaeological discoveries have also portrayed a developed commercial economy. Excavators have unearthed standardized weights at numerous Judean sites beginning in the Late Iron II (ca. 700). These dome-shaped limestone weights (merely called "stones" in the Bible) have also been found at Philistine sites, suggesting their regional adoption as weight standards. Many of these weights are inscribed with their values: up to 40 shekels (by weight, with each shekel possessing a mass of 11.33 gm.), with the shekel divided into 24 gerahs. Such weights were used with balances, and bronze scale pans have been discovered at En-gedi and Megiddo. Balances of this type, with pans suspended from a beam supported freely at its center, are widely depicted: from an 18th-Dynasty Egyptian tomb painting — in which merchants in booths hung with a set of scales received wares from the cargoes of ships — to the 9th-century obelisk of Assurnasirpal II — where the scales serve in the reception of tribute. Silver bits — scrap, pieces of jewelry, and free-form ingots — emerge from several hoards such as those found at LB (20th Dynasty) Beth-shean, Iron Age Eshtemoa, and Late Iron En-gedi.

Late Iron Judah offers an abundance of stamp seals. Judeans pressed their seals into soft clay for a variety of administrative and undoubtedly commercial purposes, as Jeremiah's real estate transaction shows. Dozens of recovered seals clearly disclose their use by royal officials in the administrative bureaucracy: along with personal names, they bear titles such as "minister of the king." Private seals — seals containing personal or place names and without mention of a particular title — are even more abundant.

Stamp seals served most frequently to seal and certify rolled-up papyrus documents. Archaeologists recover the bullae, lumps of clay with seal impressions on one side and often the impression of the papyrus on the other, signals of the vanished deed or contract itself. Lachish and Jerusalem have produced hoards of bullae which hint at locations serving as repositories for now-vanished records. In the absence of the documents themselves, it is impossible to know what commercial transactions were included in their number. Yet the abundance of personal seals can probably be taken as indicative of the prevalence of commerce or at least the hands-on administration of some sort of commodity-producing economy.

Stamped into the handles of still-wet pottery, seals could also indicate the ownership of a vessel and/or the provenance of its contents. The most prevalent stamp of this type is the *lmlk* ("belonging to the king" or "royal") stamp used on the handles of a ca. 45 l. (12 gal.) wine transport jar most likely associated with the royal production and distribution of wine during Hezekiah's administration of a wartime economy. The jar represents royal involvement in wine production, but monarchical vineyards were not alone in producing wine at this time. Excavators of Gibeon uncovered a massive winery. Inscribed handles were among the artifacts — ca. two dozen inscriptions included the name Gibeon as well as one of several personal names, perhaps vineyard proprietors or managers. These small capacity jugs (ca. 10-15 l. [2.6-4 gal.]) made Gibeon's wine available for commercial exchange. Operating simultaneously, the vineyards of Gibeon and those of the royal house indicate the complex interaction between entrepreneurial and royal enterprise in Late Iron Judah.

Against these indicators, it is worth noting that archaeological data for commerce are not particularly extensive. The artifacts of commerce are thinly distributed. It is telling that Iron Age city layouts generally did not include an open "square," like the Greek agora, for the gathering of a regular market (though some scholars have sought to understand the common tripartite building as a marketplace). While a small constellation of biblical texts signals the presence of a multifarious commerce, their number also betrays its relative unimportance, especially, e.g., when biblical legislation is compared to other ancient Near Eastern legal collections. These deficiencies help to gauge the relatively low degree of Israelite and Judean societies' commercial orientation. Only a very small portion of the total agricultural product moved by means of commercial exchange. Most produce stayed at home or was taken as taxes. The rural zone itself required few products, and thus there was no massive demand emanating from the hinterlands to drive the commercialization of the economy. However far and by whatever agency, royal or private, the commercialization of the ancient Israelite and Judean economies advanced, the ultimate use of commodities stayed within the framework of elite control and consumption.

Bibliography. M. Elat, "The Monarchy and the Development of Trade in Ancient Israel," in *State and Temple Economy in the Ancient Near East,* ed. E. Lipinsky (Leuven, 1979), 527-46; J. Holliday, "The Kingdoms of Israel and Judah: Political and Economic Centralization in the Iron IIA-B (ca. 1000-750 B.C.E.)," in *The Archaeology of Society in the Holy Land,* ed. T. E. Levy (New York, 1995), 369-98; M. Liverani, "The Collapse of the Near Eastern Regional System at the End of the Bronze Age: The Case of Syria," in *Centre and Periphery in the Ancient World,* ed. M. Rowlands, M. Larsen, and K. Kristiansen (Cambridge, 1987), 66-73; D. C. Snell, *Life in the Ancient Near East, 3100-332 B.C.E.* (New Haven, 1996); N. Yoffee, "The Economy of Ancient Western Asia," *CANE* 3:1387-99.

David C. Hopkins

TRADITION

Teaching regarding belief, practice, and parenesis which has been passed on orally or later in written form, often parallel to canonical or other authoritative texts. The term originally referred to the handing over or transmitting of such teaching. It was also used as handing over in the sense of betrayal. In the NT the term "tradition" (Gk. *parádosis*) itself refers to rabbinic usage, Christian traditions, and classical tradition.

In the Gospels references to the "traditions of the elders," to dietary and purification laws, occur in accounts of conflicts between Jesus and religious leaders as to the intent of the law (Mark 7:1-13; Matt. 15:1-9). Such traditions are portrayed in contrast to the message of Jesus, as being of merely human origin. This is starkly demonstrated in the "you heard it was said, but I say to you" formula used by Jesus in the Sermon on the Mount (Matt. 5–7).

In the letters of Paul by contrast, "tradition" is viewed positively as that which Paul had received, passed on and taught concerning the resurrection of Jesus (1 Cor. 15:3-4), liturgical practice at the eucharist (11:23-24), and ethical precepts (vv. 2-16; cf. 2 Thess. 3:6). Paul claimed the authority both to pass on dominical and apostolic instructions which he had received, as well as to exercise his apostolic authority in specific situations (1 Cor. 11:23; 15:1-4).

Modern scholarship employs the term "tradition" in a differing sense, as the recognition that elements of the biblical text existed prior to the final canonical form. These elements, in oral or even written form, formed part of a process which resulted in the text as it exists today. Such traditions have been most fully studied in the OT. In NT studies form and redaction criticism have examined the reworking of traditions in the Gospels, while in the Pauline (and deutero-Pauline) letters the isolation of earlier traditional materials becomes critical for understanding the significance of the community and for comprehending Paul's interpretative method.

Though debate surrounds the definition and extent of such traditions, the following kerygmatic, parenetic, catechetical, liturgical, and persecution traditions have been discerned. Based on the early work of C. H. Dodd on the typical composition of the apostolic preaching in Acts (the kerygma), such traditional material is recognized in the Pauline corpus (1 Cor. 15:3) and in the Markan summary of Jesus' message. Hortatory traditions are those comprising moral regulations for believers (Rom. 6:17; 1 Cor. 11:2; Col. 2:6; 2 Thess. 3:6), while catechetical traditions focus on the death of Jesus and brief confessional declarations (Rom. 10:9; 1 Cor. 15:3; 1 Tim. 2:5-6; 1 Pet. 3:18). Liturgical traditions include material whose context or content reflect baptismal or eucharistic practices as well as fragments of early hymns (Phil. 2:6-11; Col. 1:15-20; 2 Tim. 2:11-13). Finally, some scholars isolate material which reflects situations of conflict, persecution, and confession, modeled ultimately upon the example of Jesus, the persecuted prophet.

Bibliography. M. Dibelius, *From Tradition to Gospel* (New York, 1965); R. P. C. Hanson, *Tradition in the Early Church* (Philadelphia, 1963); A. M. Hunter, *Paul and His Predecessors,* rev. ed. (Philadelphia, 1961).

IAIN S. MACLEAN

TRAJAN

Marcus Ulpius Traianus, Roman emperor (98-117 C.E.). His reign is sometimes described as a golden era similar to that during the reign of the great Augustus. The first Roman emperor to have come from the provinces, he was born in Spain in 53, his father the first member of the provincial Ulpii Traiani to have been granted senatorial status at Rome. Trajan rose to power through his success as a military commander, receiving senatorial rank and honors appropriate to his military position. The aged emperor Nerva chose Trajan, then governor of Upper Germany, to be his heir and successor on grounds of merit, adopting Trajan in 97. Upon Nerva's death a year later a smooth transition saw Trajan elevated to the imperial purple.

Trajan pursued an expansionist foreign policy, adding Dacia (Romania), Armenia, and Mesopotamia to the empire. Under Trajan the Roman Empire reached its greatest territorial extent, and Roman arms achieved a reputation that did more to discourage Rome's enemies than the fortifications of Trajan's predecessors and successors. Excellent relations with the senate and a high level of internal harmony further marked Trajan's administration. The historian Tacitus, also one of the leading senators of the era, was effusive in his praise of Trajan as *optimus princeps,* "the best of emperors."

Provincial administration was similarly important to Trajan. The correspondence between the emperor and the governor of the province of Bithynia Pontus in Asia Minor, the well-known literary figure Pliny the Younger, establishes Trajan's thorough involvement in the administration of the empire and its provinces. The correspondence is illuminating as it reveals the kinds of issues and concerns a provincial governor and the emperor faced.

Two of the Pliny-Trajan letters (*Ep.* 10.96, 97) provide information about the Roman perception of the early Christians and their rituals, as well as treating the issue of the legal status of Christians and their religion. Due to increasing accusations against Christians in his province, some of them anonymously made, Pliny writes Trajan to ascertain whether being a Christian is a crime in and of itself, or whether guilt on a specific charge must be proved. Trajan's reply provides the official position of the imperial government on the question of the Christians. He instructs Pliny that there is to be no general prosecution; each case is to be tried on its own merit. Guilt must be proven through normal legal procedure. Being a Christian is not by itself cause for prosecution; a crime must be proven. Yet, Trajan continues, if a person so charged and convicted repents of his Christianity, he may be pardoned. While it is not a crime to be a Christian, and no persecution of Christians is to be conducted, clearly being a Christian would explain a person's involvement in crime.

Bibliography. H. Mattingly, *Christianity in the Roman Empire* (New York, 1967). JOHN F. HALL

TRANSFIGURATION, THE

An event in Jesus' life attested in all three Synoptic Gospels (Matt. 17:1-8; Mark 9:2-8; Luke 9:28-36). Another possible reference is 2 Pet. 1:16-18. In all three Gospel accounts, the disciples Peter, James, and John accompany Jesus to the top of a mountain and witness his transformation (Gk. *metamorphóomai,* "to undergo a metamorphosis"). Jesus' clothes become an intensely brilliant white and the prophets Elijah and Moses converse with him. Peter responds by suggesting they set up three tents, one each for Jesus, Moses, and Elijah. Before Peter can be verbally rebuked (cf. Mark 8:33 par.), a cloud moves in, casting a shadow over them and a voice says, "This is my favored son, listen to him!" As the disciples look around, they see no one, and are alone with Jesus. This is symbolic of Jesus' superiority over Elijah and Moses from the Gospel writers' perspective.

Details of the accounts vary, but one of the purposes for each Gospel writer is to link Jesus with personalities and prophecy from Hebrew Scripture. Not only did Moses and Elijah suffer as great prophets and lawgivers, but each had a vision of the glory of God on a mountain (Moses on Mt. Sinai, Exod. 24:15; Elijah on Mt. Horeb, 1 Kgs. 19:8) and both seem to have escaped natural deaths. Elijah was taken up into heaven (2 Kgs. 2:11), and since Moses' burial place was not known (Deut. 34:5-8), the legend arose that he ascended directly into heaven (pseudepigraphical Assumption of Moses). According to some traditions, both were also expected to return. The very last verses in the Hebrew Bible include the figures Moses and Elijah (Mal. 4:4-6[MT 3:22-24]). In addition, there are several connections between the story of Jesus' transfiguration on a mountaintop and the story of Moses on Mt. Sinai: e.g., three men accompanied Moses (Exod. 24:1); the cloud covered the mountain for six days and God called to Moses out of the cloud (24:15-18); and later when Moses came down from Mt. Sinai, the skin of his face shone because he had been talking with God (34:29). Peter's desire to set up tents may suggest a reminiscence of the Judean Feast of Tabernacles or Booths, the annual harvest festival commemorating the tents used during the Exodus, or of the tent over the tabernacle described during Moses' Sinai encounter (Exod. 26:7-14). The Mosaic theme is unmistakable. Other themes include an echo of Jesus' baptism, a reminder of Peter's confession just preceding this story, a foreshadowing of the Resurrection and an anticipation of the Parousia, the disciples' fear and subsequent silence. Matthew follows Mark's account more closely than does Luke. Luke uniquely includes a premonition about the events that would happen in Jerusalem as an additional theme.

Traditional interpretation differs. Some scholars suggest that the historical basis of the story was originally the account of a resurrection appearance which was later transferred into the earthly life of Jesus; others propose that it is an epiphany describing Jesus' divinity or an enthronement tradition shaped in light of the suffering Son of Man being proclaimed as the Son of God. Other suggestions include the story as a theophany, a Hellenistic mystery legend, or a tale from the world of magic; still others maintain that the story reflects an actual experience on the part of the disciples.

Later Christian tradition identified the mountain on which the Transfiguration took place with Mt. Tabor. If the sequence of events is taken literally in the Synoptic accounts, that choice would be unlikely since Mt. Tabor is 72 km. (45 mi.) from Caesarea Philippi, where Jesus and his disciples were just six days (eight days in Luke) earlier. A better possibility is Mt. Hermon, a high mountain just N of Caesarea Philippi. Whatever the location, the event was a peak experience in relaying God's relationship to and purpose for Jesus.

Bibliography. W. D. Davies and D. C. Allison, *The Gospel according to Saint Matthew* 2. ICC (Edinburgh, 1991); M. D. Hooker, *A Commentary on the Gospel according to St. Mark* (London, 1991).

GLENNA S. JACKSON

TRANSGRESSION

See SIN.

TRANSJORDAN

An expression derived from Heb. *ʿbr hyrdn* (e.g., Josh. 12:1; Num. 34:14-15), variously translated "beyond the Jordan," "the other side of the Jordan." While technically it simply refers to the opposite side of the Jordan River from the perspective of the observer, it came to be associated almost exclusively with the region E of the Jordan Rift Valley from Mt. Hermon in the north to the Gulf of Aqabah/Elath in the south.

Geophysically, most of Transjordan is a high plateau that, although punctuated by marked undulations, gradually increases in height from north to south — from a low point of 400 m. (1310 ft.) in Bashan to the Moabite plateau which reaches above 1200 m. (3940 ft.). This plateau is anchored on the north by Mt. Hermon, whose elevation exceeds 2100 m. (6890 ft.), and in the south by the heights of Edom which exceed 1500 m. (4921 ft.). This central high plateau is bordered by the Sea of Galilee, the Jordan Rift Valley, the Dead Sea, and the Arabah to the west and the desert to the east. It is also bisected east to west by four important rivers (from north to south): Wadi Yarmuk, Wadi Zerqa (biblical Jabbok), Wadi Môjib (Arnon), and Wadi el-Ḥesa (Zered). While the highlands of Cisjordan create a "rainshadow" over the Jordan Rift Valley (meaning that little rain falls there), the mountains and high plateaus of Transjordan's central ridge are elevated enough to induce precipitation. Rainfall generally decreases from north to south, although the increasing elevation of the mountains in Edom does attract a modest rainfall in the southern part of the country.

Occupation in Transjordan has been traced back to prehistoric cultures including the Old Stone Age, Middle Stone Age (Natufian), Neolithic, Chalcolithic, as well as Early Bronze. Some scholars believe that the famous "King's Highway" (Heb. *derek hammelek*) that transected Transjordan's north-south axis from Damascus to Aqaba (Num. 20:14-21) dates as early as this latter period (Gen. 14:1-16). For many years it was thought that there was a settlement hiatus between the end of EB IV and Iron I. However, extensive surveys in recent years have shown that, although settlement size and frequency do diminish during the MB and LB periods, the land was by no means unoccupied. Rather, there seems to have been a shift from sedentary modes of occupation to seminomadism and nomadism.

Ca. 1200 B.C.E. (the LB IIB–Iron IA transition) the archaeological evidence testifies to a dramatic resedentarization phase in Transjordan similar to what has been noted in western Palestine during this same time. Several villages and walled towns were established at this time. Recent work at Tell el-ʿUmeiri, S of Amman, has revealed perhaps one of the earliest of these Iron I highland settlements in either Cisjordan or Transjordan. The site was surrounded by a casemate wall. Within the casemates were numerous collar rim jars — well-known markers of the early settlement period in the highlands. At this same time, a number of regions and/or territories came to be identified within Transjordan. These included (from north to south) the regions of Bashan and Gilead (where the tribes of Reuben, Gad, and half Manasseh settled; cf. Num. 34:14-15; Josh. 12:6), and the lands of Ammon (within the upper tributaries of the Jabbok/Zerqa), Moab (N of Wadi Môjib to Wadi el-Ḥesa — the area between the Wadi Môjib and Wadi el-Ḥesa is sometimes referred to as the southern Moabite plateau or Kerak plateau), and Edom (S of the Wadi el-Ḥesa).

There also appears to have been an Israelite enclave consisting mostly of the tribe of Reuben, sandwiched between Ammon and Moab, during much of the early part of the Iron Age. Israel also occupied for a time a stretch of the east side of the Jordan Valley, N of the Dead Sea, known as the plain of Moab. While the political boundaries of Ammon, Moab, and Edom generally coincided with the natural boundaries, varying political circumstances (which often included interaction with the kingdoms of Israel and Judah) did result in the movement of the political boundaries of these three Transjordanian kingdoms from time to time throughout the Iron Age (ca. 1200-550).

Toward the end of the Iron Age (8th-6th centuries), Transjordan's local polities experienced a sequence of subjugation by powerful, nonlocal polities, beginning with the Assyrians (ca. 735-605), Babylonians (ca. 605-539), and Persians (ca. 539-333). After the Greek conquest of the Persians, Transjordan continued to be controlled by external powers, first the Ptolemies (ca. 333-198), then the Seleucids (ca. 198-153), Hasmoneans (153-63), and Romans (ca. 63). During the Roman period, the Nabateans were dominant in the former heartland of Edom with Petra as their capital. However, they were eventually incorporated into the Roman Empire ca. 106 C.E. After the Byzantine period (ca. 325-632), the Muslims conquered the region.

Important excavations have been undertaken at many sites in Transjordan which are associated with biblical history. These include Abila, Umm el-Qais, Jerash, Pella, the Amman citadel, ʿIraq el-Emir, Hisban/Heshbon, Mt. Nebo, Mukawir/Mechaerus, Dhībān/Dibon, ʿAraʿir/Aroer, Kerak/Kir Moab, Buseira/Bozrah, and Petra/Umm el-Biyarah. Many other major excavations of sites that date to the biblical period but are of uncertain identification have also been conducted. These include Umm ad-Dananir, Tell Safut, Rujm Malfuf, Tell Deir ʿAlla, Tell Iktanu, Tell Jawa, Tell Mazar, Tell Nimrin, Tell Siran, Tell Sahab, Tell el-ʾUmeiri, Tell Jalul, Ader, Baluʾa, Khirbet al-Medeineh, Lehun, Bab edh-Dhra, Feifa, Ghrareh, Khirbet Khanazir, Tawilan, and Tell el-Kheleifeh.

Important and interesting archaeological finds from the biblical periods include a number of Ammonite statues and crowned busts found at or near Amman, the anthropomorphic sarcophagi in tombs at and near Amman, and a number of important inscriptions. The more important inscriptions include the Amman citadel inscription, the Tell Siran bottle inscription (which included the names of two kings named Amminadab), the Balaam inscription from Deir ʿAlla in the Jordan Valley, and the Mesha inscription (also known as the Moabite Stone) from Dhībān.

Two important stela from Transjordan are the Baluʿa stela (ca. 1200) from north of Kerak, and the Shihan Warrior stela from Rujm el-Abd. The Baluʾa stela depicts three figures in a local, imitation Egyptian style, apparently representing some formal inauguration ceremony. The upper part of the stela contained an inscription that is no longer legible. The Shihan Warrior stela appears to depict a warrior god holding a spear. The figure is similar to depictions of the Canaanite god Baal.

Transjordan has also yielded a considerable number of seals from Ammon, Moab, and Edom. The corpus is now large enough that it is usually possible to identify seals as Ammonite, Moabite, or Edomite by both linguistic and paleographic characteristics. The gods of these three kingdoms are often represented on the seals as theophoric elements of people's names: Milcom for Ammon, Chemosh for Moab, and Qos for Edom. The vast majority of these seals and seal impressions date to Iron II (8th to 6th centuries).

RANDALL W. YOUNKER

TRAVEL, TRANSPORTATION

Individuals in biblical times traveled for the same reasons people have always traveled: searching for employment (Judg. 17:8), procuring goods (Prov. 31:14), moving (1 Kgs. 2:36), courting (Judg. 14:5-7), attending weddings and funerals (Gen. 50:1-14; Judg. 14:8-10; John 2:1), visiting relatives and friends (Luke 1:39; 2 Kgs. 8:29), and attending banquets (2 Sam. 13:27). Merchants thronged the highways, and messengers traveled everywhere, serving as the postal service of the biblical world. Royal officials moved back and forth on behalf of their governments, visiting foreign dignitaries (2 Sam. 10), serving as ambassadors (Isa. 30, 39; Jer. 27), collecting taxes (2 Kgs. 15:20), procuring provisions for the palace (1 Kgs. 4:27-28), and overseeing the labor gangs (1 Kgs. 5:13-17; 11:28-29). People traveled for various religious occasions (cf. 1 Sam. 1; 1 Kgs. 12; 2 Kgs. 10; Amos 5:4-5; Luke 2:41; John 2:13). Armies constantly moved about for military purposes.

Modes of Travel

Travel by land was confined to only a few modes: foot, donkey, mule, horse, camel, palanquin (rarely attested), and chariot. People in both the OT and NT periods normally traveled by foot (Num. 13:23; Deut. 11:24-25; 29:5; Josh. 1:3; 3:13, 15; Matt. 10:10-14). Travel by donkey-back was also common, by women and children (Josh. 15:18; Judg. 1:14; 1 Sam. 25:20, 23, 42; 2 Sam. 16:1-2) or men who were old or infirm (2 Sam. 19:26).

Occasional travel by mule-back is mentioned from David's time on (2 Sam. 13:29; 18:9; 1 Kgs. 1:33-44), becoming much more common by the Roman period. Travel by horseback also seems to have been a rarity in ancient Israel, at least as a mode of everyday travel. Nearly all references to riding horseback are in military settings (cf. 1 Kgs. 20:20; 2 Kgs. 7:13-15; Isa. 30:16; Jer. 6:23; 50:42; 51:21). Allusions to traveling by horseback in times of peace include 2 Kgs. 9:18-19; Esth. 6:8-11; 8:10; Job 39:18; and possibly Eccl. 10:7. During the Roman period higher government officials often traveled by horseback (although the stirrup had still not been introduced). Travel by camel is only occasionally mentioned in the biblical period (Gen. 24:10, 64; Judg. 6:5; 7:12; 1 Sam. 30:17; Isa. 66:20).

Palanquins (sedan chairs) may have been used occasionally as a means of travel in Israel, since their use is attested elsewhere in the ancient world (cf. Cant. 3:7-10). During the NT period the sedan chair became more common, particularly among the well-to-do.

The light, horse-drawn chariot first appeared early in the 2nd millennium B.C.E., having developed from the heavier riding carts of the 3rd millennium. With its two spoked wheels and light body, pulled by two horses, the chariot had far greater mobility than its predecessors, making it an important vehicle for armies. At first, chariots were only owned by Canaanites (Josh. 11:4, 6, 9; 17:16, 18; Judg. 1:19; 4:3, 7, 13, 15-16). Eventually David began to develop Israel's own chariotry (2 Sam. 8:4; 1 Chr. 18:4). Solomon had 1400 chariots, which he garrisoned in chariot cities (1 Kgs. 4:26; 10:26). The Israelite chariot was pulled by two horses (cf. Zech. 6:1-3) and was probably ridden into battle by at least two men, a driver and an archer (1 Kgs. 22:34-35; 2 Kgs. 9:24-25). Individuals also traveled about in chariots during times of peace (cf. 2 Sam. 15:1; cf. 1 Sam. 8:11). Peacetime travel by chariot continued into the NT period, although the NT mentions only that of the Ethiopian eunuch (Acts 8; cf. Rev. 9:9; 18:13). More common was travel by carriage, a riding vehicle used throughout the Roman world, particularly by more well-to-do citizens. The *verreda* was drawn by four mules and could transport two to three persons, while the two-wheeled *birota* had three mules and carried one or two passengers.

Rate of Travel

A typical day's journey by foot was ca. 32 km. (20 mi.), depending on terrain and road conditions. During the Persian period ordinary travelers averaged ca. 29 km. (18 mi.) a day on the Royal Road, and could cross the entire empire from Persepolis to the Aegean Sea in about three months. Josephus states that the journey from the southern edge of Galilee to Jerusalem, a distance of ca. 105 km. (65 mi.), was generally done in three days by foot, in two by horseback. The journey of Mary and Joseph from Nazareth to Bethlehem, therefore, was probably a three-day trip, if they took the shortest and most commonly used route through Samaria.

Travel by horse or mule was somewhat faster (and less tiring), averaging ca. 5 km. (3 mi.) per hour in normal terrain. A person could travel 40-48 km. (25-30 mi.) in a day on horseback without too much difficulty, and the couriers of the ancient world covered far greater distances. Camels could travel 40 km. (25 mi.) a day, even carrying loads of 225-450 g. (500-1000 lb.), and could continue three days without water. When necessary, distances of up to 96 km. (60 mi.) in a single day were possible. By chariot or carriage 40-48 km. (25-30 mi.) could easily be covered in a day, 64-72 km. (40-45 mi.) if one were in a hurry — although such distances would be tiring.

Messengers and couriers traveled more quickly. Hammurabi of Babylon (18th century) expected an official at Larsa (195 km. [120 mi.] away) to travel day and night and to arrive at Babylon within two days (i.e., 95 km. [60 mi.] a day). Imperial Persian messengers covered the Royal Road from Persepolis to Sardis (a distance of ca. 2510 km. [1560 mi.]) in nine days, averaging ca. 275 km. (170 mi.) a day. This efficient postal service was set up somewhat like the Pony Express in early America, with regular posting stations ca. 24 km. (15 mi.) apart, with fresh horses and riders. Roman government couriers averaged 8 km. (5 mi.) per hour (by horse or carriage), 80 km. (50 mi.) per day.

Armies generally moved at speeds of up to 22-24 km. (14-15 mi.) a day. Thutmose III crossed Sinai from Egypt to Gaza, a distance of ca. 240 km. (150 mi.), in nine or 10 days (ca. 8 km. [5 mi.] per day). Alexander the Great's army, famous for its speed, could average 29-32 km. (18-20 mi.) a day, but on certain occasions even marched ca. 72 km. (45 mi.) in a single day.

Traveling Conditions

Throughout the biblical period travel was generally not as difficult as some have suggested. The Persian royal road had inns and way stations spaced at intervals of 17-24 km. (10-15 mi.), depending upon the terrain. Evidence suggests that inns and way stations existed in Israel during the OT period (cf. Josh. 4:3, 8; Isa. 10:29; Gen. 42:27; 43:21; Exod. 4:24). During the Roman period a fairly adequate network of inns and hostels existed throughout the empire. These serviced the traveler with food, a place to sleep, and care for his animals. Along the Appian Way inns were available at Bobillae, 19 km. (12 mi.) from Rome, then 6.5 km. (4 mi.) farther at Aricia, and then another 27 km. (17 mi.) along at Tres Tabernae, where some Christians met Paul on his way to Rome (Acts 28:15). Normally, larger inns were established at intervals of 40-48 km. (25-30 mi.) in desert and unpopulated areas, much closer in densely settled areas. Usually there was an inn *(mansiones),* followed by one or two more simple hostels *(mutationes),* then another larger inn, and so forth.

Transportation

Goods and materials of considerable size and weight often had to be transported by farmers, taxpayers, merchants, and the like. By far the most common means of transport was the donkey, whose superiority in transportation was due to the fact that it can travel easily along steep and stony mountain paths which could not be used for wheeled vehicles and which would be uncomfortable or dangerous for camels (cf. Gen. 22:3; 42:26, 27; 44:13; 45:23; Josh. 9:4; Neh. 13:15).

Other beasts of burden include the mule, the camel, and the ox (cf. 1 Chr. 12:40). Use of the camel for transportation in Israel during the biblical period was limited. The camel, or more accurately the dromedary (the one-humped *Camelus dramedarius,* or Arabian camel), began to be more frequently used toward the end of the 2nd millennium. This animal could carry much greater loads than the donkey, having perhaps five times the capacity of the later, and was able to travel for extended periods of time without water, which made it especially valuable in desert transportation. Its disadvantage was that its physical makeup, especially its wide, tender hooves, prevented it from being a useful beast of burden in hilly regions and on rugged or rocky mountain paths.

In addition to pack animals, the Israelites used wagons (four-wheeled) and carts (two-wheeled) to transport goods (Gen. 45:19, 21, 27; 46:5; 2 Sam. 6:3-6; Isa. 5:18; 28:27, 28; Amos 2:13). A two-wheeled cart appears in Sennacherib's relief of the siege of Lachish, drawn by two oxen, carrying two women and two children who are sitting atop some bundles. During the Roman period the most common means of land transportation was the ox-drawn wagon, normally drawn by eight oxen or horses in the summer, 10 in the winter. Heavy goods, army supplies, products from the imperial estates, lower officials, soldiers traveling great distances, and sick people were all transported by these heavy *clabulariae,* which could carry as much as 1500 Roman pounds. Express goods, precious metals, etc., were carried by the swifter *cursus velox,* which employed several types of lighter carriages.

Bibliography. L. Casson, *Travel in the Ancient World* (1974, repr. Baltimore, 1994), 163-75; V. G. Childe, "Wheeled Vehicles," in C. Singer et al., eds., *A History of Technology* (London, 1954) 1:716-29; S. M. Cole, "Land Transport Without Wheels," in Singer, *A History of Technology* 1:704-12; D. A. Dorsey, *The Roads and Highways of Ancient Israel* (Baltimore, 1991); R. G. Goodchild and R. J. Forbes, "Roads and Land Travel," in Singer, *A History of Technology* 2:493-536; Forbes, "Land Transport and Road-Building," in *Studies in Ancient Technology,* 3rd ed. (Leiden, 1993) 2:131-92; M. A. Littauer and J. H. Crouwel, *Wheeled Vehicles and Ridden Animals in the Ancient Near East.* HO 7/1, 2/B/1 (Leiden, 1979).

DAVID A. DORSEY

TRAVELERS, VALLEY OF THE

The end-times burial place of the defeated armies of Gog, and one subsequently to be renamed the valley of "Hamon-gog" ("hordes of Gog"; Ezek. 39:11; Heb. *gê hāʿōḇĕrîm*). Although the MT points *hʿbrym* as a participle ("the Travelers," "the Ones Passing Through"), most scholars follow the Coptic version and read *hāʿăḇārîm* (Abarim), a mountainous region in Moab, E of the Dead Sea (Num. 27:12; 33:47-48; Deut. 32:49; Jer. 22:20). However, Abarim does not fit the requirement that the valley be "in Israel," and the specification "east of the Sea" better describes the Mediterranean than the Dead Sea.

Identification of the valley is uncertain. Some scholars suggest the Jezreel Valley, a major east-west thoroughfare with a long military history and a region suiting the text's symbolic requirement for a burial place of vast size. Others propose the Hinnom Valley in Jerusalem. Recently, scholars have suggested that *hāʿōḇĕrîm* alludes to passage into the underworld. The name of the valley then emphasizes the fact that it will be a place where the armies of Gog will pass over to the underworld.

Bibliography. B. P. Irwin, "Molek Imagery and the Slaughter of Gog in Ezekiel 38 and 39," *JSOT* 65 (1995): 93-112; M. S. Odell, "The City of Hamonah in Ezekiel 39:11-16: The Tumultuous City of Jerusalem," *CBQ* 56 (1994): 479-89.

BRIAN P. IRWIN

TREASURER, TREASURY

Though offerings to the Lord are noted in the account of Cain and Abel (Gen. 4:3-4), and gifts of money and firstfruits are commanded in Exod. 23:16; 30:13, there is no explicit description of a treasury in the tabernacle. According to Josh. 6:19, 24 all the silver, gold, bronze, and iron from the capture of Jericho must be devoted to God and placed in "the treasury (Heb. *ʾôṣār*) of (the house of) the Lord."

David's plans for the Jerusalem temple included the treasuries of the house (= temple) of God and the treasuries for dedicated gifts, meaning booty won in battle (1 Chr. 26:20; 28:11-12). These treasuries could contain a wide variety of materials: money, gold objects, temple vessels and furniture, and precious stones (cf. 1 Chr. 29:2-8). 2 Kgs. 12:4 mentions census money, personal vow money, and voluntary offerings which were brought to the temple treasury.

Royal treasuries are also mentioned. The treasure Solomon received from taxes, trade, and gifts was staggering (1 Kgs. 10:14-29), and Hezekiah later built additional treasuries for his silver, gold, and precious stones, spices, shields, and "all kinds of costly objects" (2 Chr. 32:27).

Treasurers (Heb. *gizbār*) are mostly described as those who are "over" or "in charge of" treasuries (1 Chr. 26:20). While David had placed Levites in such positions in the temple treasuries, in reality both royal and temple treasuries were under the control of the king. In times of political or military crisis, kings did not hesitate to use the resources of both treasuries to buy military alliances (e.g., Asa, 1 Kgs. 15:18; Ahaz, 2 Kgs. 16:8; Hezekiah, 18:14-16). Conquering kings pillaged both temple and royal treasuries alike (Shishak, 1 Kgs. 14:26; Jehoash, 2 Kgs. 14:14; Nebuchadnezzar, 24:13).

The temple treasury appears rarely in the NT. The widow who gave all she had (Mark 12:41-44 par.) put her money into the *gazophylakeíon*, meaning "contribution boxes or receptacles," here apparently in or near the Court of the Women (cf. John 8:20). According to the Mishnah, there were 13 such trumpet-shaped receptacles, seven for various required offerings and six for freewill offerings (*m. Šeqal.* 6.5). The administration of the treasury by this time had passed to the chief priest (Matt. 27:6), a fact confirmed by Josephus (*Ant.* 11.5.2). The Ethiopian eunuch is described as being "in charge of" his queen's treasures (Acts 8:27). Erastus, the city treasurer (Gk. *oikonómos*) of Corinth, sends his greetings to Rome (Rom. 16:23).

Bibliography. R. de Vaux, *Ancient Israel: Its Life and Institutions* (1961, repr. Grand Rapids, 1997).

JOHN S. HAMMETT

TREES

Botanically speaking, any woody perennial plant with one main stem or trunk and at least 3 m. (10 ft.) tall. Woody plants less than 3 m. tall are shrubs. At least 51 Hebrew and 12 Greek terms have been identified in the Bible as referring to specific types of woody plants or trees. This number can be contrasted with the contemporary flora of modern Israel, which feature more than 850 genera and 3500 species of plants; however, the ancient biblical writers certainly did not use our modern classification scheme, and some of their terms probably encompassed several modern species. Beyond references to specific types of trees, the Bible contains more than 300 general references to forests, groves, or trees in a general or generic sense.

Trees were important during biblical times in many different ways. Trees provided wood for building houses, furniture, tool and weapon handles, musical instruments, boats, ships, chariots, carts, wagons, and yokes. Trees provided fuel for domestic, cultic, and industrial purposes. Some species, of course, provided food in the form of fruits and nuts. By-products from various species of trees included ointments and perfumes, oil for lamps, spices, rope, tannins for leather, and chemicals for ink. Indeed, trees played such an important part in the day-to-day lives of people of antiquity that they (trees or their wood) were even turned into objects of worship by many.

Trees were also important environmentally. They provided homes and shelters for birds and beasts, their leafy branches providing shade from the sun or cover from the rain. Their root systems prevented soil erosion. Indeed, the removal of forests during the Roman and Ottoman periods had a devastating impact on the environment, turning the land into a virtual wilderness. Fortunately, recent aggressive reforestation projects in both Israel and Jordan are gradually reversing those negative effects and forests are being reestablished in the highlands of what was ancient Palestine.

The various trees and woody plants mentioned in the Bible can be roughly divided into four categories: cultivated nut and fruit trees; trees and shrubs of the forest; waterway trees; and wilderness trees. Cultivated nut trees include the almond, pistachio, and walnut. Cultivated fruit trees include the pomegranate, fig, olive, date palm, black mulberry, carob, citrus, apple, and the vine. Forest trees include the cedar, cypress, fir, juniper, pine, oak, terebinth, sycamore, tamarisk, acacia, storax, myrtle, laurel, ebony, and red saunders. Trees of desert or wilderness regions include the leafless tamarisk, common acacia, mudar (apple of Sodom), and the Phoenician juniper.

It should be added that many tree products that are mentioned in the Bible, including lumber and such valued items as frankincense, myrrh, cinnamon, and ebony, did not come from native trees but were imported from other lands. Palestine's unique location astride so many important crossroads of the Middle East made it easy for its peoples to acquire such exotic tree products.

The following are trees and woody plants believed to be referred to in the Bible but not designated by their common names in English translations. For other trees, consult the individual entries.

Heb. *'ōren* (Isa. 44:14) has been variously translated "ash," "fir," "cedar," "pine." However, the word for laurel in Targum Jonathan is Aram. *'ûrnā'* and in Arabic it is *ġār*, suggesting that Heb. *'ōren* probably refers to the same tree, the bay laurel (*Laurus nobilis* L.).

It is not certain which tree Heb. *tĕ'aššûr* (Isa. 41:19; 60:13; cf. Ezek. 27:6) represents, but several commentators suggest the box tree *(Buxus longifolia),* which does grow in the mountainous regions of Palestine. Other botanists have suggested the cypress or cedar.

It has been suggested that the broom tree *(Retama raetam)* should be identified with Heb. *rōṯem,* the bush under which Elijah slept (1 Kgs. 19:4-5; Job 30:4).

Some authorities think that the "godly tree" of Lev. 23:40 *(ayēṣ hāḏār)* is the citron *(Citrus medica),* although its appearance in Palestine is rather late.

Heb. *'ahāl* (Num. 24:6; Ps. 45:8[9]; Prov. 7:17; Cant. 4:14) has also often been translated "aloe," but is probably best identified with the eaglewood *(Aquilaria agallocha),* a tall tree with aromatic

Trees of the Bible

Common Name	Hebrew/Greek	Principal References	Scientific Name
acacia	*šiṭṭîm*	Exod. 26:15	*Acacia raddiana*
algum (see almug)	*'algûmmîm = 'almuggîm?*	2 Chr. 2:8(7); 9:10-11	*Juniperus phoenicia excelsa?*
almond	*šāqēḏ, lûz*	Gen. 43:11; Num. 17:8(23); Eccl. 12:5; Jer. 1:11; Gen. 28:19; 30:37	*Prunus amygdalus; Prunus dulcis; Amygdalus communis*
almug	*'almuggîm = algûmmîm?*	1 Kgs. 10:11-12	*Pterocarpus santolinus*
aloe (see eaglewood)	*alóē*	John 19: 39	*Aloe vera; A. succotrina*
apple	*tappûaḥ*	Prov. 25:11; Cant. 2:3, 5; 7:8(9); 8:5; Joel 1:12	*Malus sylvestris*
apricot (see apple)			
ash (see bay laurel)			
bay laurel	*'ōren*	Isa. 44:14	*Laurus nobilis* L.
bay tree, cedar, [native] tree	*'ezrāḥ*	Ps. 37:35	
box tree	*tě'aššûr*	Isa. 41:19; 60:13; Ezek. 27:6	*Buxus longifolia*
broom	*rōṯem*	1 Kgs. 19:4-5; Job 30:3-4	*Retama raetam*
carob	*kerátion*	Luke 15:16	*Ceratonia siliquia*
cassia	*qiddâ, qěṣî'â*	Exod. 30:24; Ezek. 27:19; Ps. 45:8(9)	*Cinnamomum cassia*
cedar	*'erez*	see concordance	*Cedrus libani*
cinnamon	*qinnāmôn*	Exod. 30:23; Prov. 7:17; Cant. 4:14	*Cinnamomum verum* (formerly *C. Zeylanicum*)
citron	*'ēṣ hāḏār*	Lev. 23:40	*Citrus medica*
cypress (see evergreen)			
date palm	*tāmār*	Exod. 15:27; Num. 33:9; Judg. 1:16; Ps. 92:13(14); Cant. 7:8	*Phoenix dactylifera*
eaglewood or aloe	*'ahāl, 'ăhālîm, 'ăhālôṯ 'ăhālôṯ*	Num. 24:6; Ps. 45:8(9); Prov. 7:17	*Aquilaria agallocha* Roxb.
ebony	*hoḇnîm*	Ezek. 27:15	*Dalbergia melanoxylon* or *Diospyros ebenum*
evergreen	*běrôš*	see concordance	*Abies cilicica; Cupressus sempervirens; J. excelsa*
fig	*tě'ēnâ, pag, bikkûrâ, bikkûrâ, děḇēlâ*	see concordance	*Ficus carica*
fir (see evergreen)			
frankincense	*lěḇônâ; líbanos*	Exod. 30:34; Lev. 2:1; Cant. 3:6; Matt. 2:11; Rev. 18:13	*Boswellia sacra, B. papyrifera*
gopher (cypress?)	*gōp̄er*	Gen. 6:14	*Cupressus sempervirens?*
henna (Egyptian privet)	*kōp̄er*	Cant. 1:14; 4:13; (7:11)	*Lawsonia inermis*
holm oak (see pine)	*tirzâ*	Isa. 44:14	*Quercus ilex*
Judas tree		Matt. 27:5	*Cercis siliquastrum*
juniper (see evergreen)	*'aro'ār*	Jer. 17:6; 48:6	*Juniperus phoenicia*
mulberry	*bāḵā'; sykáminos*	2 Sam. 5:23-24; 1 Chr. 14:14; Luke 17:6	*Morus nigra*
myrtle	*hăḏas*	Neh. 8:15; Isa. 41:19; 55:13; Zech. 1:8, 10-11	*Myrtas communis*
nut (see walnut)			
oak	*'allôn, 'ēlôn*	see concordance	*Quercus ithaburensis, Q. calliprinos*
olive	*zayiṯ; elaía*	Deut. 6:11; 8:8	*Olea europeae*
olive (wild)	*agriélaios*	Rom. 11:17, 24	*Elaeagnus angustifolia*
pine (stone); (see evergreen)	*'ēṣ šemen*	Neh. 8:15; Isa. 41:19	*Pinus pinea*
plane tree	*'ermôn*	Gen. 30:37; Ezek. 31:8	*Platanus orientalis*
pomegranate	*rimmôn*	Exod. 28:33; 1 Sam. 14:2; 2 Chr. 3:16; Cant. 4:3; Joel 1:12; Hag. 2:19	*Punica granatum*
poplar	*liḇneh*	Gen. 30:37	*Pupulus alba*
red saunders (see almug)			
storax	*ṣŏrî*	Gen. 37:25; Jer. 8:22	*Liquidambar orientalis*
stryax	*liḇneh*	Hos. 4:13	*Stryax officinalis*
sycamore fig	*šiqmâ*	1 Chr. 27:28; 2 Chr. 9:27; Ps. 78:47; Isa. 9:10	*Ficus sycomorus*
tamarisk	*'ēšel*	Gen. 21:33; 1 Sam. 22:6; 31:13	*Tamarix aphylla; T. Pentandra*
terebinth (pistachio tree)	*'ēlâ, 'allâ*	Hos. 4:13	*Pistacia atlantica, P. palaestina*
vine	*gep̄en*	Gen. 40:9-10; Deut. 8:8	*Vitis vinifera*
walnut	*'ěḡôz*	Cant. 6:11	*Juglans regia*
willow	*'ărāḇâ*	Lev. 23:40; Job 40:22; Ps. 137:2; Isa. 15:7	*Salix alba/Populus euphratica*

leaves and wood. Gk. *alóē* (John 19:39), however, is properly identified with one of a couple of species of the aloe *(Aloe vera, A. succotrina)*, a spiny, succulent plant.

Most likely Heb. *bĕrôš* refers to several species of evergreen, including the Cilician fir *(Abies cilicica)* which grows in Lebanon. It likely also includes the cypress *(Cupressus sempervirens)*, which is fairly widespread in Palestine.

Cercis siliquastrum has been identified as the Judas tree, the type of tree upon which it is thought that Judas hung himself (Matt. 27:5).

Heb. *ʾarʿār* (Jer. 17:6; cf. 48:6 MT) probably refers to the juniper *(Juniperus phoenicia;* cf. Arab. *ʾarʾar)*.

Heb. *ʿermôn* (Gen. 30:37; Ezek. 31:8) is usually identified with the plane tree *(Platanus orientalis)*.

The storax or liquidambar *(Liquidambar orientalis)* is most likely to be identified with Heb. *ṣŏrî* (Gen. 37:25; Jer. 8:22), from which Gk. *stórax* seems to derive.

The walnut *(Juglans regia)*, a native tree of western Asia, is generally identified with Heb. *ʾĕḡôz* (Cant. 6:11).

RANDALL W. YOUNKER

TRIBE

Throughout Bible times, from the Hebrew patriarchs (Gen. 49:28) to the early Christian apostles (Phil. 3:5), to belong to a tribe meant being a part of a named group whose members were obliged to cooperate for a variety of practical and ideological purposes and who, in turn, enjoyed certain rights and privileges important to daily existence. Typically, tribes employ the idea of descent from a common-named ancestor as a means to link together for political and other purposes clans and families as subunits within the larger tribe (Josh. 7:16-18). To be able to claim such membership has been absolutely essential for the average person's identity as an individual and for his or her physical survival (Num. 27:1-11) on a daily basis from ancient until modern times in the Middle East.

The Bible is replete with examples of what it meant to belong to a tribe. To be a descendant of Abraham meant being linked to the father of all humans, Adam (Gen. 5:1-32). It meant belonging to a federation of 12 tribes who shared certain historical fortunes and destinies (Gen. 49:1-33), and knowing where to go to find an acceptable spouse for one's sons and daughters (Gen. 24:1-67). It meant having use rights to certain specific pastures, watering sources, ritual centers, and burial grounds (Gen. 13:1-8; 23:1-20; 1 Kgs. 21:1-3). It meant joining together as "sons of Jacob" to escape bondage in Egypt (Exod. 6:28–7:13; Num. 1:1–4:49); attaining a distinctive system of beliefs and ritual practices as "God's covenant people" while wandering in the Sinai desert (Exod. 19:1–24:18); and taking possession of the Promised Land as "the tribes of Yahweh" (Deut. 3:12-22; Josh. 2:1–11:23). Most important of all, perhaps, it meant being allotted a specific plot of land within a larger tribal territory whereon to make a living in the newly conquered land (Josh. 13:1–21:45). Once allotted, such lands were to remain in the possession of clans and families in perpetuity, as illustrated in the story of Ruth.

While tribal social organization was obviously central to this early experience of the Israelites, and no doubt also to that of their neighbors, scholars have tended to see the rise of the monarchies in the southern Levant during the Early Iron Age as somehow replacing the tribe as a source of identity and economic empowerment under the reign of kings. With so many of the prophets railing against the abuses not only of the kings of Israel and Judah, but also against the kings of their neighbors — the Philistines, the Ammonites, the Moabites, and the Edomites — the continuing importance of tribal sentiments and loyalties is less obvious, at least as far as the biblical text is concerned. There are good reasons to suppose, however, that despite the rise of these Iron Age "supratribal polities" or "kingdoms," the tribe continued almost unabated as a source of identity and economic empowerment among the vast majority of the populations of these kingdoms. In other words, despite the emergence of "kings" in these societies, and the reference to them as "kingdoms," these were fundamentally tribal societies or "tribal kingdoms." The salient features of these polities can be summarized as follows:

The peoples who founded the kingdoms of Israel, Ammon, Moab, and Edom were, by and large, range-tied shepherds (Num. 32:1; 2 Kgs. 3:4; Jer. 49:20) and land-tied farmers (Gen. 36:7; Num. 20:17; Ruth 2–3). Throughout their histories, the extent to which one or the other of these two pursuits was emphasized by a given household or cluster of families was determined by local climatic and landscape conditions and by changing opportunities for involvement in local and regional trade. The organizational principle which facilitated adaptive shifts in either the direction of pastoral or agricultural pursuits was tribalism — an ideology based on the idea of claimed descent from a common ancestor with possibilities for manipulation to accommodate shifts back and forth between land-tied and range-tied pursuits at the level of either individual households, groups of households, or whole communities.

The economic pursuits of most people were either centered on land-tied production of cereals and tree fruits, or on the production of meat and milk on the hoof by means of range-tied husbandry of sheep and goats. Depending on which of these pursuits were emphasized, the particulars of tribal social organization would vary. A shift in emphasis toward land-tied production through sedentarization involved ascent of village-based clans linking people to particular plots of agricultural lands. A shift in the opposite direction through nomadization typically led to greater emphasis on creation of tribal networks extending over wider regions. While households specializing more in one or the other of these pursuits coexisted in the same villages and hamlets, the proportion represented by one or the other pursuit would vary considerably from one village to the next. This proportion might also vary considerably over time within a particular household, hamlet, village, or region.

By means of manipulation of claimed ancestors, individuals and households were able to affiliate with named groups and sections within the larger tribes (Num. 13:6; 32:12). Such generative genealogy permitted individuals and households, as well as larger social units, to split, subdivide, or coalesce, depending on economic opportunities or conflicts arising within a given social unit (Gen. 36). Given sufficient external threat, it also permitted coalescing of tribes into supratribal entities to form kingdoms.

While the rise of kings involved introduction of a transient, supratribal layer of bureaucratic organization, it did not extinguish the premonarchical tribal social order (1 Kgs. 4:7-19). Instead, this order accommodated itself to the new supratribal monarchical order. Such accommodation was facilitated in part by the mechanism of generative genealogy. The persistence of the tribal order is reflected, in part, in the continued association of particular tribes with their traditional tribal territories throughout the monarchical period. It was also reflected in residential proximity of kindred and patterns of cooperation and conflict throughout the period.

Whereas in Egypt and Mesopotamia, the rise of supratribal polities in the form of centralized states led to a division of society into two realms — urban elite and rural tribesmen — no such pronounced division of society occurred in the Iron Age kingdoms of the southern Levant. While a nascent form of such division may have emerged in certain major urban centers, it was by no means on par with that found in Egypt and Mesopotamia. To the extent that it did occur, it would have been in Cisjordan more than in Transjordan during the Iron II period. This is because predation on rural tribesmen by urban elites could be done with less risk of resistance in Cisjordan due to its more favorable agricultural conditions.

During Iron II, administration of hinterland tribal territories was centered in fortified "towns" usually consisting of a cluster of administrative buildings located on the top of a hill of some sort and surrounded by ramparts and/or walls and sometimes protected by a moat and entered by gates. To varying degrees, each major town had an administrative bureaucracy consisting of a cadre of bureaucrats whose role it was to administer the economic affairs of the surrounding hinterland tribes. The existence and extent of power of such bureaucrats can be ascertained from the study of instruments of delegated power, such as stamp seals and related artifacts.

The daily lives of most members of these ancient kingdoms were caught up in activities related to the quest for food. People lived in small villages and hamlets surrounded by agricultural lands and pastures. Villages and hamlets consisted of various configurations of houses, caves, and tents, depending on the conditions of production in various geographical regions. As a general rule, the more "risky" these food production conditions were, whether due to the vicissitudes of climate, trade, or politics, the greater the fluidity of the tribal social networks and the greater the shifts in rural settlement patterns. Cycles of sedentarization and nomadization appear generally to have been more pronounced in Transjordan than in Cisjordan. In Transjordan such cycles become more pronounced as one moves southward from Ammon, to Moab, into Edom.

Power relations within each of these Iron Age tribal kingdoms are best described as being counterpoised rather than ranked within some scalar hierarchy. Thus it was possible for there to be several political centers of gravity within each kingdom, each center basing its power on a different political resource. For example, one center may be politically powerful because of its location on the junction of two or more intersecting highways (Gezer, Heshbon). Another may base its power on being a processing and distribution center for certain agricultural products (Beer-sheba?). A third may base its power on its being the home of an important religious service or shrine (Jerusalem). Such structures stand in sharp contrast to the scalar hierarchies associated with the hydraulic societies of Egypt and Mesopotamia. They also are more consonant with the egalitarian ideals of tribal societies.

Consistent with the existence of hierarchical power structures would be overlapping territorial units. The boundaries separating different local-level political units would best be described as fuzzy and fluid rather than clear and fixed (Josh. 15; 19:1-9). This is because the economic activities engaged in by one group may be such that they can easily co-occur with those carried out by another. For example, one tribal segment may be primarily pastoral, another primarily agricultural. Thus both would stand to benefit from the one overlapping the other, as pasture animals belonging to one group would be allowed to graze on the stubble fields claimed by another.

While the biblical evidence could be interpreted to suggest that kings emerged already at the end of Iron I, the archaeological evidence points to Iron IIB-C as being the period when land-tied food production, sedentarization, bureaucratic control, and regional integration reached its highest peak. Iron IIA appears to have been a transitional period. The initial impetus for the coalescence of these tribal kingdoms surely includes the arrival of the Philistines in Iron IA, which forced the Israelite tribes to coalesce under a "king." The rise of the monarchy in Israel, in turn, very likely was one of the factors which compelled first the Ammonite tribes, then the Moabite tribes, and last the Edomite tribes to coalesce under a "king."

Bibliography. P. Bienkowski, "The Date of Sedentary Occupation in Edom," in *Early Edom and Moab* (Sheffield, 1992), 92-112; I. Finkelstein, "The Great Transformation: The 'Conquest' of the Highlands Frontiers and the Rise of the Territorial States," in *The Archaeology of Society in the Holy Land*, ed. T. E. Levy (Sheffield, 1994), 349-65; N. K.

Gottwald, *The Tribes of Yahweh* (Maryknoll, 1979); L. G. Herr, "Tell el-'Umayri and the Madaba Plains Region during the Late Bronze–Iron Age I Transition," in *Mediterranean Peoples in Transition*, ed. S. Gitin, A. Mazar, and E. Stern (Jerusalem, 1998), 251-64; Ø. S. LaBianca, *Sedentarization and Nomadization: Food System Cycles at Hesban and Vicinity in Transjordan*. Hesban 1 (Berrien Springs, 1990); LaBianca and R. W. Younker, "The Kingdoms of Ammon, Moab and Edom," in *The Archaeology of Society in the Holy Land*, ed. Levy (Sheffield, 1994), 399-445; J. M. Miller, "Early Monarchy in Moab?" in *Early Edom and Moab*, ed. Bienkowski (Sheffield, 1992), 77-91; R. W. Younker, "Moabite Social Structure," *BA* 60 (1997): 237-48.

ØYSTEIN S. LABIANCA

TRIBULATION

A term designating affliction of various kinds (Heb. *ṣar, ṣārâ;* Gk. *thlípsis*). In the OT it is the expected fate of the righteous (Ps. 34:19[MT 20]; 71:20) and often came upon Israel from political enemies (1 Sam. 10:18-19). It was regarded as an integral part of the salvation history of Israel and something from which God was to deliver the people, even if it originated with God as a punishment for disobedience (Exod. 3:9-10; Deut. 4:30-31). In the intertestamental literature tribulation refers to the suffering of the righteous (2 Apoc. Bar. 15:8; 1QH 2:6-12; 5:12) as well as the last Great Tribulation before the day of the Lord (1QM 1:12; 15:1). In the NT the tribulation that belonged to Christ is the lot of those who follow him (John 16:33; Col. 1:24; 1 Thess. 3:3; 2 Tim. 3:12). It produces endurance (Rom. 5:3) and glorification in the Christian (8:17; 2 Cor. 4:7-8, 17). Tribulation is the fate of the wicked both on earth (Rev. 2:22) and in the judgment (Rom. 2:9).

The persecution of the Jews by the Seleucid king Antiochus IV Epiphanes (167 B.C.E.) established the pattern of the tribulation of the faithful by evil forces (Dan. 12:1) which was repeated in the fall of Jerusalem. This persecution will be fully manifested in the Great Tribulation of the last days prior to Christ's return (Mark 13:14-27 = Matt. 24:15-31). The Tribulation is an intensification of the battle between good and evil in the last days (2 Thess. 2:1-12; Rev. 3:10, 7:14). It is a period of intense persecution of the Church by evil forces epitomized by the antichrist, and the judgment of those forces by God.

Bibliography. S. Harding, "Imagining the Last Days: The Politics of Apocalyptic Language," in *Accounting for Fundamentalisms*, ed. M. E. Marty and R. S. Appleby (Chicago, 1994), 57-78; L. Thompson, "A Sociological Analysis of Tribulation in the Apocalypse of John," in *Early Christian Apocalypticism*, ed. A. Y. Collins. Semeia 36 (Atlanta, 1986), 147-74.

DUANE F. WATSON

TRIBUNAL

A raised platform on which a judge sat, or, by extension, the court itself (Gk. *bḗma, kritḗrion;* Lat. *rostrum*). When Pilate addressed the crowd, he sat on his judgment seat (Matt. 27:19; John 19:13). Paul appeared before Gallio at his *bḗma* (Acts 18:12-17), an ornate platform such as one among the remains of Corinth. Paul also stood before the tribunal of Festus in Caesarea (Acts 25:6-21).

GARY S. SHOGREN

TRIBUTE

A tax or levy imposed by a sovereign, usually upon a conquered people. It involved monetary tax or servitude, or both. Tribute (Heb. *mas;* Gk. *phóros, kḗnsos*) might be paid to foreign kings, kings of Israel, or to the ultimate king, Yahweh.

Issachar is said to be a tribe under tribute (Gen. 49:15; Heb. *'ōḇēḏ;* NRSV "forced labor"). There is no indication that Issachar's "tribute" involved a monetary obligation; in this instance servitude is probably intended, either to a foreign power or their own countrymen. Although Solomon seems to have used primarily foreigners for his building projects (1 Kgs. 9:20-21 = 2 Chr. 8:7-8), at one point he was using 30 thousand Israelites (1 Kgs. 5:13-14).

The Israelites paid monetary tribute to Moab (Judg. 3:15-18), but later David extracted tribute from Moab (2 Sam. 8:2) and Syria (v. 6). Solomon received tribute and service from "all the kingdoms from the Euphrates to the land of the Philistines, even to the border of Egypt" (1 Kgs. 4:21[MT 5:1]). The Philistines brought silver as tribute to Jehoshaphat (2 Chr. 17:11), but Jehoahaz was forced to pay tribute to Egypt (2 Kgs. 23:33). The tribute the postexilic Jews were required to pay to the Persian Empire was an issue in opposition to the rebuilding of Jerusalem (Ezra 4:13, 20; 6:8; cf. Neh. 5:4); temple personnel were exempt (7:24). Tribute to Yahweh included spoils of war (Num. 31:28, 37-38, 40) and freewill offerings of whatever Yahweh had given (Deut. 16:10).

Most references to tribute in the NT regard the propriety of paying monetary tribute to Caesar (Matt. 22:17, 19; Mark 12:14; Luke 20:22; cf. 23:2; Rom. 13:6-7). Jesus paid tribute in the form of the temple tax (Matt. 17:24-25). JOE E. LUNCEFORD

TRICKSTER

A symbolic figure of myths, fairy tales, folktales, and legends whose aberrant behavior is customarily embraced and celebrated by a given society or culture. He is characteristically liminal, existing betwixt and between the confines of social convention and the unlimited expanse of nature; his conduct is scatological and deconstructive, yet simultaneously creative of those values which establish social harmony. The trickster is a master of deception, noted for feats of trickery, survival, irreverence, humor, and creativity, who outsmarts his opponents with disguise and rhetorical skill, yet often succumbs to his own conceit and recklessness. He is frequently portrayed as both deceiver and deceived, wise and foolish, powerful and weak, moral and immoral, creator and destroyer. The trickster figure is paradigmatic of human behavior in its extremes, and thus a means by which humans come to understand the fundamental ambiguity of their own existence. The trickster is central to many tales narrated in Africa, China, Japan, India, the ancient Near East, ancient Greece, as well as the folklore of the Indo-europeans.

Tales about tricksters and countertricksters suggest not only the ambiguity of the trickster, but also a socioeconomic context wherein normal structures of power are reversed in favor of the weaker. The trickster figure has been seen as a universal or archetypal image, whose ambiguous actions can not only wreak havoc with culture, but also account for the creation of natural phenomena. The trickster figure is frequently made responsible for the ambiguity which exists in the world and, as such, the symbolic representation of the fundamental ambiguity of humanity. The trickster also represents a "transforming archetype," suggesting movement and change from shadow (the dark side of the self as source of foolishness, pain, and harm) to anima (the soul as creative principle of life). Trickster-hero tales may function, in part, as a means to resist the status quo. In this context, the trickster disrupts or overturns prevailing structures and relations of power: the weak become strong and the strong become weak. The trickster may be a clown (or court jester) whose scatological humor and wild antics not only make us laugh, but customarily do so at the expense of the prevailing authorities and their social conventions.

Formal trickster tales do not occur in the biblical material with the same clarity or frequency as in the mythologies of the North American Indians and elsewhere; nor does the Judeo-Christian tradition testify to an established practice of celebration on behalf of the trickster. Perhaps this explains, in part, why biblical scholarship has not customarily focused upon the trickster figure in the Hebrew and Christian literature, though the scholarship is clearly aware that characteristics of the trickster are present. Certainly the image of Satan — whether that of the Accuser in the book of Job or Deceiver and enemy of God in later manifestations — is frequently associated with various offensive images of the trickster. Yet, at the same time, the Hebrew God frequently exhibits the unpredictable and playful behavior that is also characteristic of a trickster. Moreover, such stories as Jacob's successful ruse against his brother Esau, or David's encounter with Goliath, clearly demonstrate trickster motifs. Some early Christian representations of Jesus likewise appear to illustrate aspects of the trickster figure, especially in the context of those controversy dialogues wherein Jesus confounds his opponents with his quick wit and rhetorical skill (e.g., when dealing with the question of the tax money or engaging the Pharisees' charge of collusion with Beelzebul). In the context of the social and cultural oppression enacted by the Romans, and in accordance with the many and diverse Jewish organizations fighting for cultural recognition, it is not surprising that the early Jewish Christians should embrace a story which represents the poor and the weak over against the rich and the powerful, and that this strength to resist is manifest frequently in Jesus' ability to confound his opponents with his tricksterlike mastery of language.

Bibliography. C. G. Jung, *Four Archetypes: Mother, Rebirth, Spirit, Trickster* (1959, repr. London, 1972); R. D. Pelton, *The Trickster in West Africa* (Berkeley, 1980); P. Radin, *The Trickster* (1956, repr. New York, 1972); S. Thompson, *The Folktale* (1946, repr. Berkeley, 1977); J. D. Zipes, *Fairy Tales and the Art of Subversion* (New York, 1983).

MICHAEL L. HUMPHRIES

TRINITY

The distinctive Christian understanding that the creator God disclosed in history as the God of Israel and the God and Father of Jesus Christ is tripersonal. This distinctive trinitarian understanding has been maintained, on the one hand, against modalism which asserts that the one God has disclosed the divine self in three successive manifestations or forms and, on the other hand, against tritheism which asserts that there are essentially three gods, the Father, Son, and Holy Spirit. The term "trinity" emerged in early Christian history as the designation for the uniquely Christian monotheistic understanding of God the Father, God the Son, and God the Holy Spirit as tri-unity.

The term may be traced to Tertullian, the 3rd-century C.E. Latin father, who coined the word *trinitas* to express this unique intradivine relationship. While the term "trinity" itself is not a biblical word, the doctrine of the trinity is clearly founded upon both the OT and NT. The OT frequently uses such terms as "Spirit of God" (e.g., Gen. 1:2) and "angel of the Lord" (Exod. 23:23) which suggest plurality in the personal nature of God. Further, the frequent use of the divine name in its plural form (Gen. 1:26; 11:7) and the intimations of divine personhood in references to the Word of God (Ps. 33:6) and the Wisdom of God (Prov. 8:12) all imply OT roots for a doctrine of the trinity.

While there is no explicit doctrine of the trinity in the NT, one can more easily trace its trinitarian reflection. The divinity of Jesus is clearly set forth (Matt. 16:16; John 20:28), and the divine nature of the Spirit or Comforter is equally well attested (14:16-26; 15:26; 16:5). Most compelling are the trinitarian formulas found throughout the NT literature. 2 Cor. 13:13 probably represents the earliest known trinitarian formula, which Paul uses to bless the community of faith, and the doctrine of the trinity is clearly articulated in the baptismal formula of Matt. 28:19. All three persons of the trinity are brought together at the baptism of Jesus (Matt. 3:16). The salvation of the believer is intimately associated with Father, Spirit, and Jesus Christ in 1 Pet. 1:2. Thus trinitarian doctrine is intimately integrated into the central doctrines of the Christian faith in its earliest confessional literature.

In the earliest centuries of the Christian era, the doctrine of the trinity was developed in the context of the pre- and post-Nicene christological debates. In the early centuries, particularly under the leadership of the Cappadocian fathers, attention was focused upon *oikonomia* or the economic trinity with its soteriological focus. The Middle Ages saw a shift of attention toward *theologia*, or the question of the trinitarian nature of God *in se*, the immanent trinity. Many contemporary theologians, within both Catholic and Protestant traditions, argue that any distinction between how God has disclosed God's self in salvation history and how God is in God's own self is an artificial distinction. The doctrine of the trinity lies at the center of contemporary Christian dialogue with other world religions.

D. LARRY GREGG

TRIPOLIS (Gk. *Trípolis*)
A Phoenician port ca. 70 km. (43 mi.) N of Beirut. It was founded on a prominent peninsula by the Phoenician cities of Tyre, Sidon, and Byblos, each of which controlled a walled sector of the city (hence its name, lit., "three cities"). During the Persian period, this city became the administrative center of Phoenicia. The city did not resist Alexander, and later was a Seleucid stronghold. It was the scene of the first battle (161 B.C.E.) for the Seleucid throne between Demetrius I Soter (the eventual winner), recently escaped from detention in Rome, and his cousin Antiochus V Eupator (1 Macc. 7:1-4; 2 Macc. 14:1). Tripolis became independent in 111 B.C.E., in the wake of the collapse of Seleucid power in the region. It was organized as a Roman province in 65 B.C.E. The Apostle Peter is credited with founding a Christian community in the city. A roster of bishops of Tripolis beginning in 325 C.E. survives. MARK ANTHONY PHELPS

TROAS (Gk. *Trōás*)
A principal seaport on the Aegean Sea located in northwest Asia Minor ca. 20 km. (12 mi.) SSW of ancient Troy (Ilium). The city was founded as Antigonia ca. 310 by Antigonus, the successor of Alexander the Great. After defeating Antigonus, Lysimachus renamed it Alexandria Troas after Alexander the Great (301). One of the more important cities of the Roman Empire, Troas came into Roman possession in 133 and became a Roman colony under Augustus.

Luke places Paul in Troas twice. From Troas Paul sailed to Macedonia in response to a vision (Acts 16:8-11). The first "we" passage occurs here, suggesting that Luke joined Paul at Troas. Paul also spent a week at Troas on his way to Jerusalem after his third journey (Acts 20:5-12). There Paul revived Eutychus after he tumbled from a window during Paul's sermon.

Paul mentions one visit to Troas (2 Cor. 2:12-13) which is thought to be a separate visit made between those recorded in Acts. According to 2 Tim. 4:13 Paul left a cloak, books, and parchments at Troas. Neither Paul nor Luke discuss the founding of the church at Troas.

Bibliography. J. H. M. Cook, *The Troad: An Archaeological and Topographical Study* (Oxford, 1973), esp. 198-204; C. J. Hemer, "Alexandria Troas," *TynBul* 26 (1975): 79-112. RICHARD S. ASCOUGH

TROGYLLIUM (Gk. *Trōgýllion*)
A promontory of Mt. Mycale, a peninsula on the coast of Asia Minor extending toward the island of Samos. According to the Western text of Acts 20:15, the ship carrying Paul's party reached the island of Samos, where navigational problems in the narrow strait between the island and the promontory compelled the crew to remain at Trogyllium before leaving for Miletus the next day (so NRSV mg).

TROPHIMUS (Gk. *Tróphimos*)
Based on Gk. *tróphos*, "nursemaid" (1 Thess. 2:7), Trophimos either means "foster child" or is a proper name. In the NT Trophimus is an Ephesian, probably an uncircumcised gentile convert to Christianity who, along with Tychicus, represented the province of Asia on Paul's last trip to Jerusalem (Acts 20:4). His alleged presence in the temple's court of Israel was prohibited by Jewish law (sanctioned by the Roman government) and led to Paul's being arrested (Acts 21:29; cf. the reference to the dividing wall in Eph. 2:14).

2 Tim. 4:20 indicates that Paul left Trophimus ill in Miletus, a town near Ephesus. According to Acts, however, Paul did not return to the province of Asia after his arrest in the temple. Some scholars use this passage to support the early Church tradition for a second Roman imprisonment. CHARLES A. RAY, JR.

TRUMPET
English "trumpet" or "horn" translates Gk. *sálpinx*, which encompasses both Heb. *šôp̄ār* ("ram's horn") and *ḥăṣōṣĕrôṯ* ("metal trumpet"). Trumpets and horns were multifunctional. They were used in war (Num. 10:9; Josh. 6:4-20, Judg. 3:27; 6:34) for issuing signals (1 Sam. 13:3; Isa. 18:3; 27:13; 58:1), assembling in battle (Judg. 7:19), and making or breaking camp (Num. 10:2). They were also used by the watchman (Jer. 6:1, 17; Ezek. 33:3-6). In worship, the trumpet or shophar was blown to signal the Day of Atonement as well as other appointed feasts and festivals (Lev. 25:9). Burnt offerings and fellowship offerings were also accompanied by the blowing of the trumpet (Num. 10:2, 10). In later traditions, the trumpet apparently was blown by the priests rather than the Levites (2 Chr. 5:12; 29:26); however, other accounts ascribe trumpet playing to the Levites as well (1 Chr. 16:42).

Gk. *sálpinx* refers to a variety of musical instruments, and is significant for military, cultural, and religious contexts. It was the sounding of the *sálpinx* that would herald the messianic times (1 Thess. 4:16) or the resurrection of the saints (Ques. Ezra B12; 1 Cor. 15:52). It was also associated with judgment and fire (Apoc. Zeph. 9-12; Matt. 24:31; T. Abr. 12:10). The *sálpinx* plays a key role in Revelation, where the themes of judgment, devastation, and the announcement of the day of the Lord come together in the trumpet scenes (Rev. 8:6–9:21; 11:15-20). MELISSA L. ARCHER

TRUMPETS, FEAST OF
"A day to blow trumpets," a feast on the first day of the seventh month, Tishri (Sept.-Oct.), beginning

Israel's most sacred month which also included the Feast of Booths and the Day of Atonement. The feast was inaugurated with trumpet blasts (Num. 29:1). All work was to cease and the people gather together to hear a public reading of the Law (Neh. 7:73b–8:12). Sacrifices included one young bull, one ram, and seven male lambs all one year old, accompanied by grain offerings (Num. 29:2-6). In addition to this and the daily and monthly burnt offerings and grain offerings, a male goat was to be sacrificed as a sin offering to make atonement for the people. Perhaps this was in anticipation of the Day of Atonement that would occur nine days later.

Although the biblical texts prescribe the necessary details for the feast, there is no mention of the original purpose or function of the feast. Since the advent of postbiblical Judaism, the Feast of Trumpets has been celebrated as a New Year's Day celebration. There is no mention of a New Year's Day celebration in the OT, Josephus, or Philo (cf. Ezek. 40:1, which refers only to the time of year). Some speculate that the significance of a New Year's celebration would have been downplayed because of its prominence among the polytheistic religions of Israel's neighbors, but if such an event were indeed celebrated, it would have been on this day.

MELISSA L. ARCHER

TRUTH

The most common term for truth in the OT is Heb. *'ĕmeṯ,* meaning a reality which is "firm" or "certain." It contains the idea of solidity, validity, faithfulness, and steadfastness. When referring to an individual's speech, action, or thought, truth denotes a quality of integrity in line with what is "true." In the LXX this is most often translated by Gk. *alḗtheia,* "truth," or one of its forms.

As a legal term *'ĕmeṯ* denotes authentic facts which can be verified. If charges brought against a bride by the husband are not false but "true," then legal action is justified based on evidence (Deut. 22:20). A charge of idolatry may be punishable by a sentence of death if the "charge is proved true" (Deut. 17:4). The queen of Sheba verifies that the report of Solomon's accomplishments and wisdom was "true" by visiting to see for herself (1 Kgs. 10:6-7). In Daniel's vision of the last days the word revealed to him was "true" and indisputable (Dan. 10:1).

Truth proceeds from the nature of God, as seen in the words of a prophet. Elijah's raising of the widow's son from the dead was proof to her that "the word of the Lord" in his mouth is truth (1 Kgs. 17:24). Zechariah sets forth the essence of prophetic moral teachings as rendering "true judgments" along with showing kindness and mercy (Zech. 7:9). The judicial aspect of *'ĕmeṯ* is also present in Zechariah's instruction to "speak the truth to one another, render in your gates judgments that are true" (Zech. 8:16-17).

The concept of truth in the OT appears most frequently in the religious sense, denoting an experiential reality or feeling apart from any essential forensic meaning. God desires "truth in the inward being" (Ps. 51:6[MT 8]). One who speaks "truth from the heart" has the moral qualification for a cultic position in the congregation; he has a mind fixed on truth, "walking blamelessly" and "doing what is right" (Ps. 15:2). God's judgments are called *'ĕmeṯ* by the psalmist, who seems to equate truth with Scripture (cf. Dan. 10:21). "Truth" may also denote the Jewish religion (Dan. 8:12; cf. 1 Esdr. 4:36-40).

In rabbinic literature "truth" denotes a human attitude which reflects the divine reality. Rabbi Simeon stated that "The world rests on three things; on righteousness, on truth, and on peace" (*'Abot.* 1.18). In the legal sphere the execution of law by humans has a religious dimension. God is the divine Judge who judges all things according to *'ĕmeṯ.* The Torah itself is "truth" as an expression of the divine Word. The essence of God is *'ĕmeṯ.*

In the hymn of praise to "truth" (1 Esdr. 4:36-40), truth (Gk. *alḗtheia*) is personified as a powerful actor in nature and society whose righteousness stands in stark contrast to the unrighteousness of wine, the king, women, and all human beings (4:37). She endures and is strong forever. While this hymn in praise of truth, "the strongest thing in the world," comes out of the general wisdom literature of the ancient Near East, it has been adapted to fit the character of God as Lord of nature and society as found in the OT.

In the NT the meaning of *alḗtheia* is determined partly by the Semitic use of *'ĕmeṯ* and partly by the Greek and Hellenistic use of *alḗtheia.* In the original Greek usage, *alḗtheia* has the basic meaning of disclosing that which has been concealed. The historian would use it to indicate a real state of affairs as contrasted with a myth or legend in which reality has been concealed or hidden. Philosophers would use the term to distinguish a real state of existence from one which had only the appearance of reality. In Plato the real world was the world of ideas which could only be comprehended through thinking, not through the senses. In certain Hellenistic quarters, however, "truth" takes on an "eschatological" meaning with comprehension of this reality available to mortals only through ecstasy or revelation from the divine realm. This understanding of "truth" is developed in the gnostic writings as well as in Philo and Plotinus.

Early Christian use of *alḗtheia* reflects the diversity of meanings which *'ĕmeṯ* has in the OT and rabbinic sources as well as Greek and Hellenistic usage. The author of Ephesians uses *alḗtheia* in the sense of that which "has certainty and force" in contrast to pagan ways and of the "truth" that was in Jesus (Eph. 4:21). Likewise, for Paul "truth" means a legitimate standard, that which is "genuine" or "proper," which could be used to measure the claims of his opponents against him (Gal. 2:5). It is also used in the sense of "uprightness" (e.g., "do the right thing"; John 3:21; 1 John 1:6). "Truth" is the opposite of wrongdoing (1 Cor. 13:6). It can also designate that which is reliable or trustworthy, as opposed to human falsehood; likewise, it can refer to God's justice in contrast to mankind's injustice (Rom. 3:3-7). "Truth" can also simply mean "sincerity or honesty" (2 Cor. 7:14).

Truth can also indicate "the real state of affairs" in the Greek philosophical sense, as when Paul speaks of people giving up the "truth about God for a lie," serving the creature rather than the Creator (Rom. 1:25). This is reflected in 1 John 3:18, which exhorts the reader to love "not in word or speech, but in truth and action." "Doing the truth" may also have this meaning, but seems to allow also the interpretation of truth with the divine revelation (John 8:40, 45; 5:33).

Sometimes "truth" simply means the "sober truth" or a "statement of fact," as in Paul's response to Festus' judgment that Paul's defense reflected his insanity (Acts 26:25) and in Jesus' statement of fact about the widows in Israel during Elijah's time (4:25). Paul calls the gospel "truth" (2 Cor. 4:2); Col. 1:5 speaks of the preaching of the gospel as the "word of truth."

For John "truth" could mean a saving knowledge, not simple knowledge in general. It could free one from sin and slavery (John 8:32). Although some see gnostic overtones in the antithesis between divine and antidivine reality which John draws in his Gospel, it is more likely that John understood "truth" and "falsehood" as real possibilities for human life rather than permanently opposed cosmological "substances" (John 8:44). The Holy Spirit promised by Jesus is the "Spirit of truth" (John 14:17; 15:26; 16:13; cf. Mark 13:11; Acts 1:8). This "truth" functions as a part of revelation, a witnessing spirit in the community (1 John 5:6).

Bibliography. R. E. Brown, *The Gospel According to John I–XII.* AB 29 (Garden City, 1966); R. Bultmann, G. Quell, and G. Kittel, "alḗtheia," *TDNT* 1:232-51.

WILLIAM R. GOODMAN, JR.

TRUTH, GOSPEL OF (I, 3; XII, 2)
A gnostic sermon or reflection upon the gospel, discovered at Nag Hammadi. This tractate is a rhetorical masterpiece and can be described as both gnostic and Valentinian. It exists in two Coptic recensions found in Codices I, 3 (Subakhimic) and XII, 2 (Sahidic). Since the latter exists in an extremely fragmentary form, the former has, of necessity, become the focus of scholarly analysis.

Since its discovery this text has provoked scholarly speculation regarding its authorship. The debate is sparked by Irenaeus' comment ca. 180 that "reckless" Valentians claimed to possess numerous gospels, including a "Gospel of Truth" which "they themselves only recently wrote" and which "agrees at no point with the gospels by the apostles" (*Adv. haer.* 3.11.9). From this statement, many scholars have attributed this work to the gnostic teacher Valentinus (A.D. ca. 100-ca. 175). As support commentators have pointed to stylistic similarities between the Gospel of Truth and the extant fragments which are attributed to Valentinus, the Valentinian conceptual character of the text, and the opening line of the tractate itself which refers to the "gospel of truth." However, Irenaeus does not directly attribute the Gospel of Truth to Valentinus himself, but rather to his followers. The stylistic similarities are dubious due to the brevity of the comparative fragments and a lack of a Greek original; they may merely reflect similar rhetorical training. Realistically, the eagerness of commentators to attribute this work to Valentinus may be more fancy than fact.

Bibliography. H. W. Attridge and G. W. MacRae, "The Gospel of Truth (I,3 and XII,2)," in *Naq Hammadi Codex I,* ed. Attridge. NHS 22 (Leiden, 1985); J. A. Williams, *Biblical Interpretation in the Gnostic Gospel of Truth from Nag Hammadi.* SBLDS 79 (Atlanta, 1988).

ANDREA LORENZO MOLINARI

TRYPHAENA (Gk. *Trýphaina*)
A Christian woman in Rome to whom, along with Tryphosa, Paul sends his greetings (Rom. 16:12).

TRYPHO (Gk. *Tryphṓn*)
Epithet ("magnificent, luxurious") of Diodotus, general and later king in the tumultuous latter years of Seleucid rule in Syria, which included Palestine. The consequences of his deeds for policies and events in Judea are recorded in 1 Macc. 11–15.

Trypho first appears in historical sources as a general under Alexander Balas, who wrested the Seleucid throne from Demetrius I Soter in battle (150 B.C.E.). Balas in turn was defeated by supporters of Demetrius' son, Demetrius II Nicator (145). Trypho used this situation to advance his own power; making Balas' young son Antiochus VI his ward and claiming the throne in his name. In 142 Trypho had Antiochus VI murdered and claimed the throne for himself. Trypho committed suicide after his defeat in 138 by Antiochus VII Sidetes, brother of Demetrius II.

At the time of these events, the Hasmoneans were increasing their power in Judea. Under Jonathan's leadership, they attempted to play the rival claimants off against each other, generally with success. Jonathan sided with Antiochus VI and Trypho shortly after they claimed the throne (1 Macc. 11:54-59). However, in 143 Trypho, apparently fearing that the rise of Jewish power would lead to an independent kingdom, became hostile toward the Hasmoneans. He encountered Jonathan's army at Beth-shan, but he claimed peaceful intentions and showered Jonathan with honors. He persuaded Jonathan to disband his army, keeping only a guard of 1000 men, and to go with him to Ptolemais. Upon their arrival, Jonathan's guard was massacred (1 Macc. 12:29-48). Jonathan himself was taken hostage and subsequently killed in 142 (1 Macc. 13:12-30).

Leadership of the Hasmoneans now fell upon Jonathan's brother, Simon, who of course allied himself with Demetrius II. Simon took advantage of Demetrius' relatively weak position with respect to Trypho to obtain promises of Jewish independence. While Demetrius (and subsequently Antiochus VII) later attempted to revoke these privileges, the Hasmoneans saw the year 142 as the beginning of a new era, when "the yoke of the Gentiles was removed from Israel" (1 Macc. 13:41-42). WILL SOLL

TRYPHOSA (Gk. *Tryphṓsa*)
A Christian in Rome to whom Paul sends his greetings (Rom. 16:12). She and Tryphaena "worked hard in the Lord," and were perhaps sisters.

TUBAL (Heb. *tuḇal*)
A son of Japheth listed in the Table of Nations (Gen. 10:2; 1 Chr. 1:5) and the nation purportedly descended from him. Tubal was located somewhere in eastern Asia Minor, perhaps Cilicia. It is linked with Javan (Ionia; Isa. 66:19; Ezek. 27:13) and Meshech (Phrygia; Isa. 66:19 LXX; Ezek. 27:13; 32:26; 38:2-3; 39:1). Herodotus (*Hist.* 3.94) links Meshech and Tubal (Gk. *Tibarānoi*) in the 19th satrapy of Darius I. The three traded slaves and bronze vessels with Tyre (Ezek. 27:13). Sargon II, who finally subjugated Tubal, claimed bowls of the land of *Tabal* with gold handles as booty. In Ezek. 32:26 Meshech-tubal (no conjunction) is an example for Egypt of a nation now dead, judged for spreading terror. According to Ezek. 38:2-3; 39:1 Gog will be the chief prince of (a rejuvenated?) Meshech and Tubal. PAUL J. KISSLING

TUBAL-CAIN (Heb. *tûḇal qayin*)
A son of Lamech and Zillah, and a descendant of Cain (Gen. 4:22). Tubal-cain is called the (first) forger of all instruments of bronze and iron, and apparently lived in a period of cultural expansion (cf. Gen. 4:20-21).

TUMORS
A punishment inflicted by God on the inhabitants of Ashdod (1 Sam. 5:6–6:17) and mentioned among the curses of Deut. 28:27 (NRSV "ulcers"), probably to be identified as hemorrhoids. The Philistines included five golden tumors as part of a guilt offering when they returned the ark of the covenant to Israel (1 Sam. 6:4-18).

TUNIC
An undergarment made from two pieces of linen or wool, sewn on the sides and shoulders, with holes for the head and the arms (Heb. *kuttōneṯ;* Gk. *chitṓn*). It was often monochrome but at times decorated. With or without sleeves and with a hem extending to the knees or the ankles, it was worn occasionally with a belt. A tunic was the garment that God made for Adam and Eve (Gen. 3:21) and that Joseph wore (37:3-33). It was part of the priest's clothing (Exod. 28:4; Josephus *Ant.* 3.7.2).

John the Baptist says giving away one of two tunics proves repentance (Luke 3:11). Jesus tells his disciples to carry only one tunic (Luke 9:3) and to surrender the outer garment *(himátion)* if sued for one's tunic (Matt. 5:40; cf. Luke 6:29). Jesus' tunic was uniquely seamless (John 19:23). White Roman tunics (Lat. *tunica*), over which were worn formal togas, had broad, vertical purple stripes for senators and narrow stripes for military tribunes of the equestrian order and the sons of distinguished families. RICHARD A. SPENCER

TURBAN
A headdress made of cloth and wound around the head. Heb. *pe'ēr* is a term for headgear in general, including ceremonial garlands (Isa. 3:20; 61:3, 10); it is used once for the high priest's linen turban (Ezek. 44:18). Removal of one's head covering was a normal part of mourning practices (cf. Ezek. 24:17, 23).

Another general word for headgear is Heb. *ṣānîp,* which is used for the turban of the ordinary free male (Job. 29:14; Isa. 3:23), the high priest's turban (Zech. 3:5), and a royal crown (Isa. 62:3).

A linen turban (Heb. *miṣnep̱eṯ)* was worn by Israel's high priest (Exod. 28:4, 39). Attached to this turban was a gold pendant or diadem inscribed "Holy to the Lord" (Exod. 28:36-38; 29:6; 39:30; Lev. 8:9; Sir. 45:12). Priests other than the high priest wore "caps" of fine linen (*[pa'ărê ham]migba'ōṯ;* Exod. 28:40; 29:9; 39:28; Lev. 8:13), perhaps similar to fezzes. At a later time all the priests apparently wore turbans (Gk. *kídaris;* Jdt. 4:15).
RICHARD E. MENNINGER

TURTLEDOVE
A designation for the various species of the genus *Streptopelia,* small gray- and buff-colored pigeons with various kinds of ring-coloring around their necks (Heb. *tôr, tōr;* Gk. *trygṓn*). In Palestine the turtledove is one of the earliest harbingers of spring (Cant. 2:12; Jer. 8:7). The Hebrew term derives from the sound of their call. Turtledoves were considered clean for sacrifice and consumption (Gen. 15:9; Lev. 1:14; 5:7; Luke 2:24). The defenseless people of God are represented as a turtledove at Ps. 74:19 (NRSV "dove").

TWELVE, THE
The central circle of Jesus' disciples, whom he called to be apostles. The term "the Twelve" appears in all four Gospels (even after the death of Judas at John 20:24; cf. Luke 24:9). Lists of the Twelve in the Synoptic Gospels and Acts agree on the number but not entirely on their names (Matt. 10:2-4; Mark 3:16-19; Luke 6:14-16; Acts 1:13). "The Twelve" also appears as a designation for the apostles at Acts 6:2; 1 Cor. 15:5; Rev. 21:14. The uses of the term suggest that a particular significance was attached to the number itself. Jesus related the number of this group to the 12 tribes of Israel in such a way that the apostles become the core of an eschatological Israel (Matt. 19:28 = Luke 22:30); a similar idea is expressed at Rev. 21:14 (cf. Eph. 2:20). The choosing of Matthias after the death of Judas was an attempt to restore the number of the Twelve (Acts 1:15-26).

TWIN, THE
See THOMAS

TWIN BROTHERS
In Greek mythology, the twin sons (Gk. *Dióskouroi*) of Zeus and the moon-god Leda, named Castor and Pollux (Polydeuces). They were regarded as heroes

worthy of the honors given to gods. A number of their exploits were recounted, and they were sometimes connected with the constellation Gemini. They were revered as saviors in all kinds of distress and particularly as protectors of mariners. Many Roman ships bore images of Castor and Pollux, as did the grain ship that carried Paul from Malta to Puteoli (Acts 28:11).

TYCHICUS (Gk. *Tychikós*)
A Christian from Asia Minor, described as a beloved brother, faithful minister, and fellow servant (Col. 4:7; 2 Tim. 4:12; Titus 3:12) who served as a messenger and letter carrier for Paul (Col. 4:7, 16; Eph. 6:21-22). Tychicus (Gk. "fortunate") accompanied Paul and delegates from the gentile churches in delivering gifts to the Jerusalem church (Acts 20:4). The name is attested in nine inscriptions from his native region of Magnesia. Late Greek tradition holds that Tychicus was one of the first bishops of Chalcedon.

Bibliography. S. L. Cox, "Tychicus: A Profile," *Biblical Illustrator* 21 (1995): 79-80.

STEVEN L. COX

TYPOLOGY
A method of biblical interpretation by which a person, event, or institution ("type") in the OT corresponds to another one ("antitype") in the NT within the framework of salvation history. It was frequently employed by the church fathers and favored by the Reformers. It was rejected by the "enlightened" theologians but reanimated in the wake of the Biblical Theology movement. After losing ground it again is experiencing a renaissance, especially among evangelical circles in North America.

The traditional understanding of biblical typology views the OT type as divinely ordained and a detailed predictive prefiguration of Jesus and the gospel realities brought about by him. "Postcritical neotypology" discovers typological relations in retrospective, often leaving room for an unlimited number of types. Others try to interpret typology in terms of 1st-century hermeneutical methods, leaving it without proper controls. The question has been raised whether typology is a hermeneutical method at all. The key issue appears to be whether a type is prophetic or not.

From the passages in the NT that employ Gk. *týpos* ("example") hermeneutically (1 Cor. 10:1-13; Rom. 5:12-21; 1 Pet. 2:18-22; Heb. 8:5; 9:24), the following elements of biblical typology emerge: The historical element emphasizes that type and antitype are historical realities whose historicity is assumed and is essential to the typological argument. There is an intensification from type to antitype. The prophetic element considers the type as an advance presentation of the corresponding antitype. It is divinely designed and has a necessary quality giving it the force of a predictive foreshadowing (e.g., Rom. 5:14). The eschatological element links the type either with the first advent of Christ, or focuses on the dispensation of the Church, or links it with the second coming of Christ. The christological-soteriological element points out the essential focus and thrust of OT types. The ecclesiological element designates the possible aspects of the Church that may be involved: the individual worshipper, the corporate community, and the sacraments. These elements provide a proper hermeneutical control for defining biblical types.

Bibliography. D. L. Baker, *Two Testaments, One Bible,* rev. ed. (Downers Grove, 1991); R. M. Davidson, *Typology in Scripture.* Andrews University Seminary Doctoral Dissertation Series 2 (Berrien Springs, 1981); F. Foulkes, *The Acts of God: A Study of the Basis of Typology in the Old Testament* (London, 1958); L. Goppelt, *Typos* (Grand Rapids, 1982); G. W. H. Lampe and K. J. Woollcombe, *Essays on Typology.* SBT 22 (Naperville, 1957).

FRIEDBERT NINOW

TYRANNUS (Gk. *Týrannos*)
A teacher at Ephesus in whose lecture hall Paul taught daily for two years, having ceased preaching in the synagogue because of opposition (Acts 19:9).

TYRE
Phoenician port and kingdom located on an island originally situated some 700 m. (1300 ft.) offshore and ca. 35 km. (22 mi.) S of Sidon. The modern town of aṣ-Ṣûr covers the ancient city and little is known about the city from archaeology. The ancient city had two havens: the northern harbor and the southern (Egyptian) harbor. The Canaanite name of the island was *Ṣurru,* "The Rock" (Phoen., Heb. *Ṣôr*). The Greek name *Týros* is first attested in Classical sources.

Tyre is mentioned in Egyptian *(Ḏr),* Hittite, and Ugaritic *(Ṣr)* texts of the 2nd millennium B.C.E. It was a loyal ally of Egypt in the troublesome period of the Amarna Age (14th century), as is known from the contemporary letters of its king Abi-milki, found in the el-Amarna archive in Egypt. Other documents mention that Tyre had a settlement on the mainland opposite the island, known as *Usu,* Egyp. *iṯ,* and later called *Palaityros,* "Old Tyre," by the Greeks. The island was originally supplied with water by boats from the mainland, until the advent of lime plastered cisterns at the beginning of the Iron Age.

Shortly after 1200 Tyre was destroyed, evidently by the Sea Peoples, but was rebuilt by refugees from Sidon and recovered very rapidly. Unlike other Phoenician kingdoms, Tyre seems not to have capitulated to the Assyrian king Tiglath-pileser I (1114-1076), who conquered the Levantine littoral. By the 10th century, under a dynasty founded by Abi-baal (ca. 1020-980) the father of Hiram I, Tyre was the principal Phoenician port, having eclipsed Sidon, and retained its prominent role under the Assyrian domination and the subsequent centuries. During his siege of Tyre in 332, Alexander the Great was able to capture the city by constructing a mole to connect the island to the mainland. Due to sediments borne by sea currents and winds, the island later became a peninsula.

The earliest biblical references to the city appear in Pss. 83, 87, which link Tyre to Philistia, perhaps because of their trade in the era of the judges. According to 2 Sam. 5:11 = 1 Chr. 14:1 the king of Tyre, Hiram I (980-947), initiated an alliance with King David, and this partnership was greatly expanded in the reign of Solomon (971-932). The Tyrians supplied various timbers and masons for the construction of the Solomonic temple in Jerusalem (1 Kgs. 5:10, 18[MT 24, 32]), and a Tyrian coppersmith also named Hiram (also Huran, Hirom) executed all the bronzework for the building (7:13). It is noteworthy that the palace of Solomon, known for its rows of imported cedar columns, was named the Lebanon Forest House. Tyrian masons also participated in building the Second Temple in Jerusalem in the 6th century (1 Chr. 22:4).

Beginning in the 10th century, Israel supplied Tyre with large quantities of grain and oil (1 Kgs. 5:11[25]), to which the parallel account in 2 Chr. 2:10 (9) adds wine. Solomon ceded the land of Cabul in the Galilee to Tyre (1 Kgs 9:11; but cf. 2 Chr. 8:2). As part of his treaty with Hiram I, he also imposed a forced labor on the Israelites which required three groups of 10 thousand men each to work in the Lebanon in shifts (1 Kgs. 5:13-14[27-28]).

The primary pursuit of the Tyrian-Israelite pact was to secure large quantities of luxury goods by means of joint maritime ventures on both the Mediterranean and the Red Sea. One such allied fleet sailed to Tarshish (south Spain) to secure precious metals, ivory, and exotic animals (1 Kgs. 10:22 = 2 Chr. 9:21), while the Red Sea fleet journeyed to Ophir (location uncertain) to acquire gold, timber, and precious stone (1 Kgs. 9:26-28; 10:11; 2 Chr. 8:17-18).

The Tyrian-Israelite alliance was perpetuated by King Ahab of Israel (873-852), who married Jezebel the daughter of Ethbaal king of Tyre (878-847). The royal wedding song in Ps. 45, celebrating the arrival of a Tyrian princess in Israel, was perhaps composed on this occasion. Another Tyrian princess named Elissa, also known as Dido, founded the city of Carthage in North Africa ca. 825 (other sources: 814). In the 8th century, the Judean prophet Amos could still call the pact between Tyre and Israel a "covenant of brothers" (Amos 1:9-10), namely, of equal partners. Extensive agricultural trade with Tyre, conducted by both Israel and Judah, is still mentioned in Ezek. 27:17.

The celebrated maritime empire of Tyre, her far-flung commercial networks on land and sea, and her great wealth, are the subject of pronouncements by several other biblical prophets (Isa. 23; Jer. 25, 47; Zech. 9). A very concise poetic account of the nature and scope of the Tyrian trade is found in Ezek. 27. Tyre prospered throughout the Persian and Hellenistic eras and even established settlements on the coast of Palestine between Dor and Jaffa. The continuing importance of the area between Tyre and Sidon in NT times is indicated by the account of Jesus' activity in that region (Matt. 15:21-28 = Mark 7:24-31).

Bibliography. H. J. van Dijk, *Ezekiel's Prophecy on Tyre.* BibOr 20 (Rome, 1968); H. J. Katzenstein, *The History of Tyre* (Jerusalem, 1973); B. Mazar, "The Philistines and the Rise of Israel and Tyre," *Proceedings of the Israel Academy of Sciences and Humanities* 1/7 (Jerusalem, 1964): 1-22; R. R. Stieglitz, "The Geopolitics of the Phoenician Littoral in the Early Iron Age," *BASOR* 279 (1990): 9-12.

ROBERT R. STIEGLITZ

TYROPOEON VALLEY

One of the principal valleys that defined the topography of ancient Jerusalem. Jerusalem developed upon two roughly parallel ridges or hills that extend north to south. Deep valleys protect the ridges on the east (the Kidron Valley), west, and south (the Hinnom Valley). The Tyropoeon Valley (modern el-Wad) ran between the two ridges dividing the city into two sections. The temple mount, Ophel, and City of David or "Lower City" occupied the eastern ridge, while the higher southwestern ridge was known as the "Upper City" in NT times. Unnamed in biblical sources, the Greek name Tyropoeon Valley derives from a single reference in Josephus (*BJ* 5.140) and means "Valley of the Cheesemakers" (Gk. *hē tṓn tyropoiṓn phā́ranx*). Modern topographical descriptions of Jerusalem often use the term "Central Valley" as a synonym of this valley.

The true course and depth of the Tyropoeon Valley have been obscured by accumulations of debris, at times reaching 20-30 m. (65-98 ft.) thick. The valley began just N of the Damascus Gate, its upper course following a southeasterly direction to the southwestern corner of the temple mount. The valley then descended more precipitously on the west side of the City of David down to the pool of Siloam and a junction with the Kidron Valley. Excavations have revealed sections of a Herodian road, in places 10 m. (33 ft.) wide, that followed the length of the valley. A large drainage system under the road funneled runoff water to the pool of Siloam, which also was supplied by the Gihon Spring. A bridge built on a series of great vaults spanned the Tyropoeon Valley linking the Upper City with the temple mount. Wilson's Arch, though partially rebuilt in Arab times, preserves one of the vaults sustaining the bridge that carried foot traffic and water, along an aqueduct, across the valley. At the southeast corner of the temple mount a monumental flight of stairs ascended from the Herodian road in the valley upward to an entrance into the temple precincts. Robinson's Arch, protruding from the southern end of the western wall, was a part of this staircase. Two other gates (today known as Barclay's Gate and Warren's Gate) led into the temple mount at a lower level from a branch of the Herodian road flush with the western wall. Numerous shops along the valley coupled with access to the temple mount made the Tyropoeon Valley a busy thoroughfare of Herodian Jerusalem.

THOMAS V. BRISCO

U

UCAL (Heb. *'ukāl*)
If a proper name, one of two people whom Agur addressed in his oracle, perhaps his son or nephew (Prov. 30:1). However, the Hebrew in the verse is obscure and some scholars, as do LXX and Vulg., find not names but an expression such as "I am weary" (NSRV).

See Ithiel **2.**

UEL (Heb. *'û'ēl*) (also JOEL)
A postexilic Israelite who had taken a foreign wife (Ezra 10:34). At 1 Esdr. 9:34 he is called Joel.

UGARIT
An ancient city on the north coast of the eastern Mediterranean, located under a mound now known in Arabic as *Ras (esh-)Shamra* ("Fennel Cape"). It flourished in the 2nd millennium B.C.E. until its destruction ca. 1200. The mound is located ca. 1 km. (.6 mi.) from the Mediterranean Sea and ca. 10 km. (6 mi.) N of modern Lādiqīye (ancient Greek Laodikeia). Excavations at Tell Ras Shamra began in 1929 after the chance discovery of a funerary vault at the tiny port of Minet el-Beida. Attention quickly shifted to the large mound, Ras Shamra, 1 km. to the east. Excavations have continued year by year since then except for a decade hiatus around World War II (1939-1948). The present mound covers ca. 20 ha. (50 a.); however, the Late Bronze city was somewhat larger.

The ancient city was shaped by its location on the Mediterranean Sea. It was surrounded to the north, east, and south by mountains. Ancient Mt. Sapanu (1780 m. [5840 ft.]) on the northern horizon (also known as Mt. Zaphon in biblical literature, Mons Casius in Latin literature, today known as Jebel el-Aqra') was the dwelling place of the storm-god Baal. A valley to the northeast of the city was the gateway to the ancient kingdoms in Mesopotamia. The plain around Ugarit was fertile, producing abundant wheat and barley. Foothills and mountains that surrounded Ugarit were cultivated for vineyards and olives. The mountains provided a ready source of the famed "cedars of Lebanon" for construction and trade. As an international harbor, Ugarit's economy was naturally engaged in export and import. Ugarit also developed industries which were shaped by its maritime location, such as purple dye manufacturing (from the murex snails) and shipbuilding. In addition, the city developed craft industries related to its trade in raw materials such as copper. The fertile hinterland was also exploited for trade in grains and oil. In the internationalism that shaped the late 2nd millennium (15th-13th centuries), a certain uneasy equilibrium developed between the conflicting interests of the major powers of Egypt, the Hittites, Mitanni, Kassite Babylonia, and Assyria. Ugarit was well situated to serve as an intermediary of the commercial interests of these major states. The rise of Ugarit at this juncture reflects a skillful exploitation of the city's geographical advantages.

Tell Ras Shamra has a long history. The earliest settlement of the site dates back to ca. the 6th millennium and continues almost uninterrupted through the 2nd millennium when it became a major commercial center. Even before the discovery of the ancient site, scholars had known of Ugarit's existence and significance from other texts. It is mentioned in a number of the Amarna Letters, including one which belies its grandeur: "Look, there is no mayor's residence like that of the residence in Tyre. It is like the residence in Ugarit. Exceedingly [gr]eat is the wealth [i]n it" (EA 89:48-53; W. L. Moran, ed., *The Amarna Letters* [Baltimore, 1992], 162). The importance of Ugarit as a commercial hub derives from its geographical location. Standing on the coastal highway of Syria with all the advantages of the Mediterranean trade, Ugarit connected the Mediterranean with the interior of northern Syria. Although Ugarit never became a major power, it did become a major commercial center as well as a medium-sized kingdom covering more than 3212 sq. km. (1240 sq. mi.). An important phase of Ugarit's history began ca. 2000. Both the Ugaritic king list and the epic literature discovered at Ugarit point to the arrival of seminomadic

Main street of the city of Ugarit (Ras Shamra). At right are the West Archives of the royal palace, which contained Ugaritic and Akkadian administrative documents and correspondence (David Toshio Tsumura)

pastoral tribes known as the Amorites, who settled ancient Ugarit and initiated a new urban phase of its history. The history of the kingdom was closely tied to the larger kingdoms of the Near East, first Mari in the early 2nd millennium, then Egypt, and finally the Hittite kingdom. The final destruction of Ugarit is usually attributed to the Sea Peoples in the early 12th century, although the disintegration of Ugarit's palace-temple economy had already begun well before the Sea Peoples' migrations. The end of the Late Bronze Age was marked by a general process of ruralization in the countryside that undermined the support of the urban economy and ultimately exacerbated the ultimate demise of Ugarit as well as other Late Bronze kingdoms.

The culture of Ugarit was composite. It was all at the same time: a Syrian port with Mediterranean trade, a West Semitic city-state which was a vassal of the Hittite kingdom, and a West Semitic population in a cuneiform world. By whatever measure we use — personal names, language, religion, or material culture — Ugarit appears to be an eclectic admixture of Canaanite, Syrian, Anatolian, Mesopotamian, Egyptian, and Mediterranean cultures. Given that Ugarit was situated on the coastal route that united Asia Minor with Syria-Palestine as well as being the closest harbor on the eastern Mediterranean to Cyprus, it is hardly surprising that Ugarit was a multilingual society. This cosmopolitan character is reflected in the many languages and scripts discovered in the excavations at Ras Shamra. Clay tablets were found inscribed in a variety of scripts (cuneiform, alphabetic cuneiform, hieroglyphic) and languages (Ugaritic, Akkadian, Sumerian, Hurrian, Hittite, Egyptian, Cypro-Minonan), although the primary languages were Ugaritic and Akkadian. Nearly all the remains of the Ugaritic language have been discovered during excavations by Claude Schaeffer and his successors carried out at this site since 1929. A small number of Ugaritic texts have been found at the small port site of Ras Ibn Hani, 5 km. (3 mi.) S of Ras Shamra. A few short texts using the Ugaritic alphabet have been found elsewhere in the western Mediterranean area on Cyprus (Hala Sultan Tekke near Larnaca), in Syria (Tell Sukas, Tell Nebi Mend [Kedesh]), Lebanon (Kamid el-Loz, Sarepta), and Israel (Mt. Tabor, Taanach, Beth-shemesh). Archives were found primarily in the palace and temple areas of Ras Shamra, although texts were also found in the homes of apparently important individuals. The library of ancient Ugarit shows evidence of a multilingual and highly cultured society. Scribes were evidently persons of great standing in Ugaritic society with broad education. The library at Ugarit includes literary texts (myths), economic texts, letters, and school texts (e.g., exercises, lexicons, syllabaries). A most distinguished scribe was Ilimilku, who was responsible for the transcription and collation of many of the literary works found at Ugarit. The best preserved of these are the Legend of King Keret (or Kirtu), the Legend of Aqhat, and the Baal cycle. This literature has opened a window into Canaanite culture of the late 2nd millennium and has supplied a surprising treasure of cultural, religious, and linguistic insight into ancient Israel.

The head of state in ancient Ugarit was the king, whose line had divine sanction and whose authority was considered a religious obligation. There is some evidence to suggest that the king may have been given divine status in Ugarit (perhaps in contrast with ancient Israel). The good king defends the widow, the orphan, the poor, and the downhearted (cf. Aqhat 1.21-25; 2.V.6-8; 127.33-34, 45-48). Members of the king's clan exercised control in the secular and religious institutions, particularly the high priesthood. The Kirtu Epic associates the king with the clan of *ṯa'* and also glorifies the clan of *ditana.* King Niqmad is called a *ṯa'i-ite (ṯ'y).* The chariot-warriors *(maryanûma)* include a group of priests called "sons of the *ta'ites*" and "sons of the *ditanites,*" who are among the well-paid members of the army. Their family members are also listed on the military payroll.

Military manpower was derived from draft quotas taken from communities and guilds (cf. Solomon's corvée, 1 Kgs. 9:15-21). There were two branches of military service: the army (including charioteers and infantry) and the navy. The professional military were paid in silver. Land grants including grants of livestock may have been made to professional soldiers. Based on the Code of Hammurabi (§§27-29, 31-32, 35-37, 41), we may assume that special legal protection over land and property was probably extended to these soldiers.

The religion of Ugarit is known mostly through the epic literary myths: Keret, Aqhat, and the Baal cycle. The latter are stories known from tablets of the high priest's library. It probably formed a six-volume "set" produced by the scribe Ilimilku. From what remains of the tablets we can reconstruct three stories concerning (1) the storm-god Baal and the sea-god Yamm, (2) the building of Baal's palace, and (3) Baal and his brother Mot, the god of death. Because the tablets are not complete, it is difficult to know with certainty the precise order of the cycle of stories. The story concerning Baal and Yamm is in many ways typical of Near Eastern cosmological stories (e.g., Enuma Elish; cf. Exod. 15) and marks Baal's rise to power with his defeat of Yamm (cf. Marduk's victory over Tiamat). The last story describes Mot (i.e., "Death") killing Baal and confining him to the underworld, which results in a disruption of the fertility cycle. The goddess Anat kills Mot and rescues her brother Baal, who is returned to his throne. But Death (Mot) will not die, and only through the intervention of El, the head of the Ugaritic pantheon, is a kind of order restored. The Baal cycle, though incomplete, was apparently central to Ugaritic religious beliefs; indeed, since Baal was worshipped throughout Syria-Palestine, the Baal cycle necessarily forms one of the main sources for our understanding of the religious beliefs of the entire ancient Near East.

Bibliography. P. C. Craigie, *Ugarit and the Old Testament* (Grand Rapids, 1983); M. Heltzer, *The Internal Organization of the Kingdom of Ugarit* (Wiesbaden, 1982); G. del Olmo Lete, *Canaanite Religion: According to the Liturgical Texts of Ugarit* (Bethesda, 1999); M. S. Smith, ed., *The Ugaritic Baal Cycle.* VTSup 55 (Leiden, 1994); Smith et al., *Ugaritic Narrative Poetry* (Atlanta, 1997); M. Yon, *The City of Ugarit at Tell Ras Shamra* (Winona Lake, 1999).

WILLIAM M. SCHNIEDEWIND

ULAI (Heb. *'ûlay*)
A river in the province of Elam, near the Persian capital of Susa, where Daniel saw himself in his vision of the ram and the he-goat (Dan. 8:2, 16). Mentioned in an Assyrian inscription ca. 640 B.C.E. (Akk. *U-la-a*) and called Eulaeus by classical writers, the Ulai was actually a canal connecting the rivers Choaspes (modern Kerkha) and Coprates (modern Abdizful).

ULAM (Heb. *'ûlām*)

1. A Manassite, son of Sheresh and descendant of Maacah and Machir (1 Chr. 7:16-17).

2. The oldest son of Eshek, a descendant of Saul, and head of a Benjaminite family of archers (1 Chr. 8:39-40; cf. 2 Chr. 14:8b[MT 7b]).

ULLA (Heb. *'ullā'*)
The head of an Asherite clan (1 Chr. 7:39).

UMMAH (Heb. *'ummâ*)
A city in the tribal territory of Asher (Josh. 19:30). Ummah may be a scribal error for "Acco" (Heb. *'akkô;* the consonants *kaph* and *mem* were written similarly and thus easily confused), a significant Canaanite town missing from Joshua's list (Josh. 19:24-31; cf. Judg. 1:31).

UNCIAL
A rounded form of Greek or Roman majuscule (capital) letters. Although some scholars derive the word "uncial" from Lat. *uncus,* "hook" (a reference to their form as hooked or bent capitals), most trace it to *uncia,* "a twelfth part," a term used by Jerome in the introduction to his translation of Job to refer disparagingly to Greek manuscripts that used ostentatious letters "an inch wide." Both Greek and Latin texts from the 3rd through 9th centuries C.E. were written in uncial script; after this time, the smaller, connected minuscule characters almost completely replaced uncials.

Uncial letters were used to write early lectionaries and papyrus manuscripts, but the term "uncial" often refers to those manuscripts of the OT and NT written in uncial characters on parchment. More than 300 uncial manuscripts, mostly fragmentary, are extant. Among the more important are the codices Alexandrinus, Vaticanus, and Sinaiticus.

JAMES R. ADAIR, JR.

UNCLEAN
See CLEAN AND UNCLEAN.

UNFORGIVABLE SIN
A phenomenon also called the "unpardonable sin." Specific references include the Beelzebul controversy (Mark 3:20-30 par.), an "eternal sin" identified as a "blasphemy against the Holy Spirit"; the Lukan prophetic warning of future persecution and Holy Spirit assistance (Luke 12:4-12); 1 John 5:13-21, a "mortal sin." Other references include lying to the Holy Spirit (Acts 5:3); the warning against those enlightened but now unrepentant (Heb. 6:4-6; cf. 10:26-30); and the condemnation of those who

slander (blaspheme) angelic beings (Jude 8). References are also found in Did. 11:7b; Gos. Thom. 44.

Theological interpretation of this concept has been varied. Some have seen this as an extreme form of rejection of the gospel. The rejecters are not candidates for God's forgiveness because their refusal to believe the gospel necessarily includes a refusal to repent of sin. This view is that it does little more than equate the unforgivable sin with the unsaved condition. Others see this as a definite action from which there is no turning back. In this interpretation, if a person willingly commits a certain forbidden act, it is the deliberate commission of a sin for which there is no hope of forgiveness. This is in keeping with the warning of Mark 3:30, that the sin is to attribute the supernatural activity of the Holy Spirit to an "unclean spirit." It is the ultimate demonstration of the mind-set of Isaiah's opponents who "call evil good and good evil, who put darkness for light and light for darkness, who put bitter for sweet and sweet for bitter" (Isa. 5:20).

Bibliography. J. G. Williams, "A Note on the 'Unforgivable Sin' Logion," *NTS* 12 (1965): 75-77.

MARK S. KRAUSE

UNKNOWN GOD, THE

Designation in an Athenian altar inscription "to the (or 'an') unknown god," used by Paul as the text for his "Areopagus sermon" (Acts 17:22-31). Paul took this inscription as indication of Athenian religiosity, and on that basis preached the Christian gospel to them, refuting their earlier charge that he was introducing new deities (Acts 17:18). While ancient writers (Pausanias, Philostratus, Tertullian, Jerome) attest to the Athenian concern over omission of any unknown gods from their religious devotions, there is no evidence outside Acts for any altar to an unknown god. The historicity of the inscription and sermon is therefore subject to scholarly debate. Scholars agree, however, that both accurately reflect the religious climate of the 1st-century C.E. Hellenistic world. The inscription should not suggest any nascent gnostic or monotheistic notions.

Bibliography. H. Conzelmann, "The Address of Paul on the Areopagus," in *Studies in Luke-Acts,* ed. L. E. Keck and J. L. Martyn (1966, repr. Philadelphia, 1980), 217-30.

CHRISTOPHER SCOTT LANGTON

UNLEAVENED BREAD

Flat, rounded bread (Heb. *maṣṣâ;* Gk. *ázymos*) baked entirely of flour and water without any fermentation (e.g., hops or yeast), an integral part of the daily Middle Eastern diet (Gen. 19:3; Judg. 6:19; 1 Sam. 28:24). In ancient times a piece of dough was exposed to the air in order to ferment and develop an acidic composition. This process, in combination with new dough, caused the bread to rise. The Israelites viewed this leavening process, the mixing of what is essentially a decayed product, as symbolic of moral decay and corruption. Therefore, unleavened bread became an emblem of purity, and the most important religious festivals, such as Passover, required its use. The weeklong Feast of Unleavened Bread formed the greater part of the Passover ritual. During such festivals leaven and any foods contains leaven were not permitted in homes let alone consumed. On the eve of Passover, the home is thoroughly searched for traces of leaven and then burned, symbolic of one searching their very soul for moral decay and sin and then casting it out. Of the sacrificial offerings brought to the altar, the cereal offerings were always unleavened bread (Lev. 2:5), except for the thanksgiving offering of well-being, which could include leavened bread (7:13).

NT texts make symbolic reference to leaven for purposes of instruction. Jesus warns his disciples to "beware of the leaven of the Pharisees and Sadducees" (Matt. 16:6). In a statement that many scholars view as ironic, if not sarcastic, Jesus likens the kingdom of heaven to leaven (Matt. 13:33). Paul emphatically admonishes his readers to celebrate a festival "with the unleavened bread of sincerity and truth" (1 Cor. 5:6-8). Perhaps the most significant symbolic use of unleavened bread for Christians comes from the traditional words and actions of Jesus at the Last Supper (Matt. 26:26).

Bibliography. J. Neusner, *The Idea of Purity in Ancient Judaism.* SJLA 1 (Leiden, 1973); G. J. Wenham, "The Theology of Unclean Food," *EvQ* 53 (1981): 6-15.

TONY S. L. MICHAEL

UNLEAVENED BREAD, FEAST OF

The first of three festivals mentioned in the earliest festival prescriptions in Exod. 23:14-17; 34:18-24. It has generally been argued that the Pilgrimage of Unleavened Bread *(ḥag hammaṣṣôṯ)* was initially an agricultural observance of the Canaanites associated with the barley harvest and adapted by the Israelites. In the early biblical texts, however, the pilgrimage is associated specifically with the Exodus from Egypt. The Israelites are to avoid eating leaven for seven days. The seven-day festival takes place in the first month, Abib (Apr.-May) in the older calendars, and is observed from the 15th day through the 21st day (cf. Exod. 12:18; Lev. 23:6). Lev. 23:9-16 envisions the Feast of Unleavened Bread as the occasion for the presentation of the first sheaf of the harvest and dates the Feast of Weeks 50 days after this presentation. Unleavened Bread eventually became associated with Passover in such a way that the two originally distinct observances were viewed as one ritual observance with two movements (Exod. 12–13; Deut. 16:1-8; Lev. 23:4-8).

See PASSOVER, FEAST OF.

FRANK H. GORMAN, JR.

UNNI (Heb. *ʿunnî*)

1. A levitical musician appointed to accompany the ark of the covenant when David brought it to Jerusalem (1 Chr. 15:18, 20).

2. A Levite who returned with Zerubbabel from the Babylonian Captivity (Neh. 12:9 **Q**; NRSV "Unno"). The name is omitted in the LXX.

UNNO (Heb. *ʿunnô*)
A levitical musician who returned from the Exile with Zerubbabel (NRSV Neh. 12:9, following **K**); alternate reading of Unni **2.**

UPHAZ (Heb. *ʾûpāz*)
A place known for its gold (Jer. 10:9; Dan. 10:5). Some interpreters read Uphaz as Ophir (following Peshitta, Targ., and some Hebrew manuscripts), a well-known source for gold (cf. 1 Kgs. 9:28). Others emend the text to read Heb. *mûpāz,* "refined, pure" (following LXX). R. DAVID MOSEMAN

UPPER ROOM
A room in the upper story or one built onto the flat roof of a large Palestinian house. It was in such an upper guest chamber (Gk. *anágaion*) in Jerusalem that Jesus gathered with his disciples for the Last Supper (Mark 14:15 = Luke 22:12; cf. Matt. 26:18). The upper room is described as being both "large" and "furnished," the latter indicating the provision of cushions for dining. Later tradition (10th century C.E.) identified the room as a vaulted chamber (the Coenaculum or Cenacle) on the second floor of the mosque en-Nebi Daud, which also contains on the first floor the reputed tomb of David.

Gk. *hyperṓon* designates the place in Jerusalem where the disciples stayed following the ascension of Jesus (Acts 1:12-14). The use of the definite article ("the" upper room) has led to the suggestion that it is identical with the well-known location of the Last Supper. It could also possibly be in the home of Mary, the mother of John Mark (Acts 12:12).

Other references to upper rooms include the place in Joppa where Tabitha/Dorcas was taken after her death and subsequently resuscitated by Peter (Acts 9:36-43) and the place in Troas where Paul preached at length and the drowsy Eutychus fell out of a third-story window (20:7-12).

B. KEITH BREWER

UR (Heb. *ʾûr*) **(PERSON)**
The father of Eliphal, one of David's warriors (1 Chr. 11:35).

UR (Heb. *ʾûr;* Sum. *Urim*) **(PLACE)**
A major city of ancient Mesopotamia. Tell al-Muqayyar, discovered in the early 17th century by the explorer Pietro della Valle, is a large imposing site, oval in shape, and rising some 18 m. (60 ft.) above the flood plain. It was first excavated in 1849 by William Kennett Loftus, followed in 1855 by the British consul at Basra, J. E. Taylor, who found the first cuneiform inscriptions. Henry Rawlinson identified the site based on an inscription excavated by Taylor, but it was not until the joint British Museum–University of Pennsylvania excavations from 1922 to 1924 under the direction of C. Leonard Woolley that the site was substantially explored. Since that time only restorations but not significant excavations have been conducted at the site.

The city was established sometime during the Ubaid period in the middle of the 5th millennium B.C.E. and was occupied until its abandonment in the Achaemenid period. At the rise of widespread urbanization in the late 4th millennium Ur appears to have become a significant settlement, although the excavated areas from that period are limited. The city continued to prosper through the Uruk and Jemdet Nasr periods (3900-2900), from which come a large temple platform with thousands of associated decorative clay cones used to decorate the facades of the public buildings. An extensive cemetery, in use from the Uruk through Early Dynastic II periods but originally dated to the Jemdet Nasr period, was also partially excavated. In the Early Dynastic period (ca. 2900-2350), extensive renovations of the temple precinct were undertaken and in the nearby rubbish dump area the so-called royal cemetery was found. The approximately 2000 graves in this cemetery were dug throughout the Early Dynastic III, Akkadian, and post-Akkadian periods (ca. 2600-2100), although the 16 famous alleged royal burials date to the earliest use. These tombs, with their numerous precious objects (jewelry, ceremonial weapons of gold, the war and peace standards, musical instruments) and accompanying human and animal sacrifices, remain among the most vivid remnants of this age. There is little excavated evidence for the city during the Akkadian period, although contemporary written sources indicate that it remained an important center. An inscribed alabaster disk found at Ur was dedicated by Enheduanna, the high priestess of Nanna, the patron (moon-) god of Ur, and daughter of Sargon, founder of the Akkadian dynasty.

However, it was in the 21st century, during the Third Dynasty of Ur (ca. 2100-2000), that the city became the capital of an empire that extended from the Persian Gulf to north Syria. Ur-namma, the founder of the dynasty, began an ambitious building program. It was concentrated on the religious center of Ur that was dominated by a huge ziggurat and temple complex dedicated to Nanna and called the temenos area by its excavator, Woolley. The city grew to at least 50 ha. (124 a.). This period is characterized by tens of thousands of archival tablets found in the excavations and from the literary sources from later periods attributed to the kings of this dynasty. Among the contemporary monuments is the stela of Ur-namma found in the ziggurat area and which depicts Ur-namma receiving the directive to construct the temple and the celebrations associated with its completion. The city was plundered by the Elamite invaders who put an end to the dynasty. The demise of the city is poignantly related in the Lament over the Destruction of Ur, written in Sumerian and preserved in an Old Babylonian copy. Shortly after its destruction, the region was incorporated by the kings of the nearby city of Isin and the city was extensively rebuilt and many older structures restored. Ur was expanded to it largest extent, ca. 60 ha. (148 a.), and continued to be an important commercial and religious center. Substantial remains from this period have been recovered along with numerous texts found in the public and private buildings. The texts provide vivid details of official functions and private lives of those who worked and lived in the city.

In the 18th century the political control of the Hammurabi dynasty in Babylon and other factors caused a decline in the prosperity of Ur along with other cities in southern Babylonia. The city underwent a number of rebuilding phases and was continuously occupied through the end of the Old Babylonian period and into the following Kassite/Middle Babylonian age. During the reign of Kurigalzu (ca. 1400) the temenos area was restored once again and the city and its surrounding countryside appear to have prospered. However, Ur never again achieved the importance it held in earlier periods. In the 1st millennium the temenos area continued to receive the attention of various rulers. In the 7th century one of its governors renovated some of the structures. Under the Neo-Babylonian kings Nebuchadnezzar (604-562) and Nabonidus (555-539) the ziggurat, temenos wall, and some of the residential areas were restored. Nabonidus favored the cult of the moon-god Sîn at Ur and appointed his mother high priestess and built a palace for her there. The city diminished in importance after that time and shortly after 400, in the Achaemenid period, it fell into obscurity and was abandoned.

Bibliography. P. R. S. Moorey and C. L. Woolley, *Ur of the Chaldees,* rev. ed. (Ithaca, 1982); S. Pollock, "Chronology of the Royal Cemetery of Ur," *Iraq* 47 (1985): 129-47; "Ur," *OEANE* 5:288-91; J. M. Sasson, ed., *CANE,* 4 vols. (New York, 1995); C. L. Woolley, *Ur Excavations,* 2-10 (London, 1934-1974).

David I. Owen

URBANUS (Gk. *Ourbanós*)

A Christian believer at Rome to whom the Apostle Paul sent his greetings (Rom. 16:9). Because the name was common among Roman slaves listed in inscriptions of the Roman imperial household (cf. Lat. *Urbanus,* "belonging to a city"), Urbanus may be one of the members of Caesar's household (cf. Phil. 4:22). He is called a "coworker" (Gk. *synergós*) of Paul (cf. Prisca and Aquila, Rom. 16:3; Timothy, v. 21).

URI (Heb. *'ûrî*)

1. A Judahite, father of Bezalel, the supervising craftsman employed in building the tabernacle (Exod. 31:2; 35:30; 38:22; 1 Chr. 2:20; 2 Chr. 1:5).

2. The father of Geber, Solomon's officer in Gilead (1 Kgs. 4:19).

3. A postexilic gatekeeper who had taken a foreign wife (Ezra 10:24).

URIAH (Heb. *'ûrîyâ, 'ûrîyāhû*)

1. Uriah the Hittite, husband of Bathsheba (2 Sam. 11:1-26) and one of David's elite 30 warriors (23:39; 1 Chr. 11:41). The Hittites of Palestine were an ethnic group of uncertain relatonship to the Neo-Hittite states to the north. Ethnic Hittites could be assimilated into Israelite society, as shown by Uriah's Yahwistic name and high rank in David's army (cf. Ahimelech the Hittite, 1 Sam. 26:6). If Eliam the father of Bathsheba (2 Sam. 11:3) was Eliam the son of Ahitophel the Gilonite (23:34), then Uriah also made a good marriage. His father-in-law was both an elite warrior and the son of David's esteemed counselor (2 Sam. 15:12; 16:23). Uriah's marriage may explain the proximity of his house to the palace (2 Sam. 11:2-3).

The story of David and Bathsheba condemns David for adultery and murder (2 Sam. 11:1–12:25). Having impregnated Bathsheba, David brings Uriah home from the front, assuming that a visit with his wife will make it look as though he is the father (2 Sam. 11:1-8). However, Uriah does not go home, but instead spends the night with the royal servants (2 Sam. 11:9). When David questions him, he professes solidarity with his fellow soldiers, whose engagement in holy war requires sexual abstinence (2 Sam. 11:10-11; cf. 1 Sam. 21:5[MT 6]). Also, Uriah may have learned of the adultery from David's servants, who had fetched Bathsheba for David (cf. 2 Sam. 11:4). Knowledgeably or innocently, Uriah still refuses to visit his wife, even when made drunk by David (2 Sam. 11:12-13). Foiled by his subordinate, David then directs Joab to have Uriah killed in battle so that he can marry Bathsheba and the baby will appear legitimate (2 Sam. 11:14-27). The contrast between Uriah's staunch loyalty to the most stringent of Yahwistic demands, though a foreigner, and the king's shameless transgression of its most basic commandments is starkly drawn.

2. High priest under Ahaz (735-715), who built a Syrian altar for the king and performed Yahweh's sacrifices and offerings on it (2 Kgs. 16:10-16). He also was called by Isaiah to witness to the name Maher-shalal-hash-baz ("Pillage hastens, looting speeds"), signifying the imminent Assyrian despoliation of Damascus and Samaria (Isa. 8:2).

3. Prophet at the time of Jeremiah, killed by Jehoiakim for prophesying against Jerusalem and Judah (Jer. 26:20-23).

4. Father of Meremoth the priest, at the time of Ezra and Nehemiah (Ezra 8:33; Neh. 3:4, 21).

5. One who stood with Ezra at the reading of the Torah (Neh. 8:4), possibly the same as **4.**

Bibliography. P. K. McCarter, Jr., *II Samuel.* AB 9 (Garden City, 1984); M. Garsiel, "The Story of David and Bathsheba," *CBQ* 55 (1993): 244-62.

Marsha White

URIEL (Heb. *'ûrî'ēl;* Gk. *Ouriḗl*)

1. The chief of the Kohathite Levites (1 Chr. 15:5) who assisted King David in bringing the ark of the covenant to Jerusalem (vv. 11-12); the son of Tahath and father of Uzziah (6:24[MT 9]).

2. A resident of Gibeah; maternal grandfather of King Abijah of Judah (2 Chr. 13:2).

3. An archangel, one of the holy angels who led Enoch on his visionary journeys through the heavens (e.g., 1 En. 21:5; 80:1). According to some manuscripts, he is also named among the four angels of the Presence (1 En. 9:1). In 2 Esdras, Uriel was the angel sent to Ezra to respond to his complaint against God and his ways (2 Esdr. 4:1; 5:20; 10:28).

URIM (Heb. *'ûrîm*)
AND THUMMIM (*tûmmîm*)
Most likely divining stones used by priests to inquire judgments from God. They are first mentioned in Deut. 33:8 as belonging to the Levites in general, arising from their zealous devotion to God above family. As a consequence the Levites acquire three functions: they transmit divine law to Israel, burn incense, and sacrifice on the altar. The function of conveying divine judgments through teaching may be associated with the Urim and Thummim.

Priestly writers limit the use of the Urim and Thummim to the high priest. In Exod. 28:30 the Urim and Thummim are part of the special garments of the high priest, attached to the breastplate in a pouch. When the high priest wore the Urim and the Thummim in the inner sanctuary before God, he was not only representing the people before the deity, but actually seeking a divine judgment on their behalf. The details of the inquiry are not provided. If the Urim and Thummim were stones, then the ritual may have resembled the casting of lots, in which questions were posed to God requiring a "yes" or "no" answer.

The story of the choice of Joshua to succeed Moses in Num. 27:12-23 provides an illustration of how the Urim and Thummim functioned in relationship to the high priest. Here God informs Moses of his impending death and Moses requests a successor. God selects Joshua. But for this selection to be official, Joshua must be presented before Eleazar, the high priest, who must "inquire for him [Joshua] by the decision of the Urim before the Lord" (Num. 27:21). The brief statement by Saul in 1 Sam. 14:41 provides a glimpse into how the Urim and Thummim functioned as a casting of lots. In this story Saul requests Urim to designate guilt in himself and Jonathan and Thummim to designate guilt in the people of Israel. The Urim and Thummim are also mentioned in Ezra 2:63 = Neh. 7:65 without explanation or comment.

Bibliography. M. Haran, *Temples and Temple-Service in Ancient Israel* (1978, repr. Winona Lake, 1985).

THOMAS B. DOZEMAN

UTHAI (Heb. *'ûṯay*)

1. The son of Ammihud, a Judahite of the family of Perez. He was among the first to return from exile to resettle on his own property in Jerusalem (1 Chr. 9:4).

2. A head of the family of Bigvai who returned with Ezra from the Babylonian Captivity (Ezra 8:14).

UZ (Heb. *'ûṣ*) **(PERSON)**

1. A son of Aram and grandson of Shem (Gen. 10:23). At 1 Chr. 1:17 he is called a son of Shem.

2. A son of Milcah and Nahor, Abraham's brother (Gen. 22:21).

3. A son (or descendant) of the Horite chief Dishan (Gen. 36:28 = 1 Chr. 1:42). The name may represent a clan or similar social group.

UZ (Heb. *'ûṣ*) **(PLACE)**
The homeland of Job (Job 1:1). Two traditions exist concerning the location of Uz: Edom in the southeast and Syria in the northeast. Neither tradition is completely persuasive, and the evidence concerning the location cannot be reconciled.

Among the arguments for the Edomite location, the personal name Uz appears in Edomite genealogies (Gen. 36:28 = 1 Chr. 1:42), and personal names in the book of Job probably are Edomite in origin (cf. Job 2:11). The personal name Uz is linked with Buz (Gen. 22:21), which also appears as a place name associated with Edom (Jer. 25:23). The LXX appendix to Job describes Uz as bordering on Idumea and Arabia (Jer. 42:17b). Also, Uz is poetically parallel to "daughter Edom" at Lam. 4:21.

Other arguments place Uz in Aram (Syria), near Damascus or S of Damascus in the Hauran. The person Uz is a descendant of Aram (Gen. 10:23; 1 Chr. 1:17) and the oldest son of Abraham's Aramean brother, Nahor (Gen. 22:21). According to Josephus Ouses (Uz), the son of Aram, founded Damascus and Trachonitis. Byzantine and Arab traditions place Job's homeland in the Hauran.

PATRICIA A. MACNICOLL

UZAI (Heb. *'ûzay*)
The father of Palal, one who helped build the wall of Jerusalem (Neh. 3:25).

UZAL (Heb. *'ûzāl*)
A son of Joktan and descendant of Shem (Gen. 10:27 = 1 Chr. 1:21). His descendants constituted an Arabian tribe traditionally located at 'Azal (modern Ṣan'ā', the capital of Yemen). According to Ezek. 27:19 Uzal was a source of wine.

UZZA (Heb. *'uzzā'*) **(PERSON)**

1. A Benjaminite; son of Gera (Heglam; cf. NRSV) and descendant of Ehud (1 Chr. 8:7).

2. An ancestor of temple servants among the first to return with Zerubbabel from exile in Babylon (Ezra 2:49 = Neh. 7:51).

UZZA (Heb. *'uzzā'*) **(PLACE)**
A palace garden where the Judahite kings Manasseh and Amon were buried (2 Kgs. 21:18, 26). Why the garden was so named is disputed. The parallel account (2 Chr. 33:20, 25) omits the name.

UZZAH (Heb. *'uzzā', 'uzzâ*)

1. A son of Abinadab, in whose house at Kiriath-jearim the ark of the covenant had remained 20 years. Uzzah and his brother Ahio guided the ox-cart carrying the ark as it was transported to Jerusalem. When the oxen stumbled, Uzzah touched the ark to steady it, an act of irreverence for which he was smitten by God and died (2 Sam. 6:3-7; 1 Chr. 13:7-11).

2. A Levite of the family of Merari (1 Chr. 6:29[MT 14]).

UZZEN-SHEERAH (Heb. *'uzzēn še'ĕrâ*)
One of three villages built by Sheerah, the daughter of Beriah and descendant of Ephraim (1 Chr. 7:24). It is presumably located in the vicinity of Upper and Lower Beth-horon.

UZZI (Heb. *'uzzî*)

1. An Aaronite priest descended from Eleasar; son of Bukki and father of Zerahiah (1 Chr. 6:5-6, 51[MT 5:31-32; 6:36), and an ancestor of Ezra (Ezra 7:4).

2. A clan chief of Issachar, son of Tola (1 Chr. 7:2-3).

3. A son of Bela of the tribe of Benjamin (1 Chr. 7:7).

4. The father of Elah, one of the first Benjaminites to resettle on their own property in Jerusalem after the Babylonian Exile (1 Chr. 9:8).

5. The son of Bani, descendant of Asaph; overseer of the postexilic Levites in Jerusalem (Neh. 11:22).

6. The head of Jedaiah's priestly lineage at the time of the high priest Joiakim (Neh. 12:19).

7. A priest who participated in the dedication of the repaired walls of Jerusalem (Neh. 12:42).

UZZIA (Heb. *'uzzîyā'*)
One of David's warriors; "the Ashterathite," from Ashtaroth in Bashan (1 Chr. 11:44). He is absent from the list in 2 Sam. 23:24-39.

UZZIAH (Heb. *'uzzîyâ, 'uzzîyāhû*; Gk. *Ōzias*) (also AZARIAH)

1. King of Judah during the 8th century. His exact dates are debated, both as a part of the larger problem of dating the kings of Israel and Judah and because 2 Kgs. 15:2; 2 Chr. 26:3 assign him the lengthy reign of 52 years. William F. Albright allocated him a shorter reign from 783 to 742, positing a co-regency from 750 with his son Jotham. More recently scholars have supported a 52-year reign, including an early co-regency with his father Amaziah from 791/790, sole regency from 768/767, and a later co-regency with his son Jotham from 750 until Uzziah's death in 740/739. Whatever his precise dates, Uzziah's reign coincided approximately with a temporary waning of Assyrian influence in Israel and a lengthy reign by the formidable Jeroboam II in Israel. As a consequence, Uzziah's years were marked with relative peace and prosperity.

The name Uzziah is used of the king in the narratives about his reign in 2 Chr. 26:1-23, while the name Azariah (**3**) is used in 2 Kgs. 15:1-7. The presence or absence of the letter *r* is the main difference in the names. It is probably not a consequence of textual corruption, as some scholars have suggested. Rather, Uzziah may have been his throne name and Azariah his given name. (See similarly the names Jehoahaz/Shallum and Jehoiachin/[Je]coniah, sons of Josiah who succeeded him as king.)

According to 2 Kgs. 14:21 he ascended to the throne at the age of 16, upon the death of his father Amaziah at the hands of rebels. If the newer dating system mentioned above is correct, his age of 16 must have applied instead to the beginning of his earlier co-regency some 23 years previous. He received a mixed review in 2 Kgs. 15:1-7. On the one hand, he is said to have "done right" in the eyes of the Lord, as his father had done before him. On the other hand, he did not remove all other sanctuaries than the temple. That is perhaps the explanation for his contracting leprosy and completing his life with his son Jotham as his co-regent.

2 Chr. 26 adds to this sparse narrative in two ways. First, it amplifies the good that Uzziah did by describing successful military campaigns against the Philistines and others, the exacting of tribute from the Ammonites, and the improvement of Judah's military capabilities. Second, it explains why such a good king would contract leprosy. He became proud and sinned by entering the temple and usurping the priests' role of offering sacrifices. When the priests called him to account, he became angry with them and was stricken with leprosy. Finally, 2 Chr. 26:21 carefully explains that Uzziah was not buried with the other kings, as 2 Kgs. 15:7 had said, but in a separate, nearby field that belonged to the monarchy.

2. A levitical priest descended from Kohath (1 Chr. 6:24).

3. The father of a man named Jonathan, an overseer in charge of outlying towns and villages within David's treasury office (1 Chr. 27:25).

4. A levitical priest, descended from Harim, who returned with the exiles from Babylon. He was one of the priests who married foreign wives and was required by Ezra to get a divorce (Ezra 10:21).

5. One of the 468 descendants of Perez who moved to Jerusalem upon completion of the repair of the wall of Jerusalem under Nehemiah (Neh. 11:4).

6. A chief elder in the city of Bethulia, home town of Judith (Jth. 6:15-16, 21), who urged the people to hold out against the Assyrians for five days to allow God to rescue them (7:30-31).

PAUL L. REDDITT

UZZIEL (Heb. *'uzzî'ēl*)

1. The grandson of Levi and fourth son of Kohath; the presumed founder of the levitical guild of Uzzielites (Exod. 6:18; Num. 3:19, 27; 1 Chr. 6:2, 18[MT 5:28; 6:3]; 23:12). He is the father of Mishael, Elzaphan, and Sithri (Exod. 6:22). This genealogy reflects the political structure of the levitical guilds late in the Monarchy. Some references to the Uzzielites (Heb. *'āzzî'ēlî*) suggest that during the early history of Israel they were a powerful guild (1 Chr. 15:10). Later as the Uzzielites' levitical role became less prominent, Uzziel was subordinated to Kohath and Elzaphan to Uzziel. Uzziel's son Elzaphan is listed as head of all the Kohathites, and given responsibility for the service of the ark, table, lampstand, altars, screen, and vessels of the sanctuary (Num. 3:30-31). Micah and Isshiah are also listed as sons of Uzziel (1 Chr. 23:20; 24:24), i.e., heads of the Uzzielites during the time of David's organization of the levitical guilds. The Uzzielites, along with the other Kohathites, were given charge of the treasuries (1 Chr. 26:23).

2. One of four sons of Ishi who during the time of King Hezekiah led 500 Simeonites against the Amalekites who had sought refuge on Mt. Seir (1 Chr. 4:42). After destroying the Amalekites, Uzziel and the Simeonites settled in Edom.

3. The third son of Bela, the son of Benjamin (1 Chr. 7:7). Uzziel is absent from the genealogy of Bela at 1 Chr. 8:3, but the Benjaminite genealogies have numerous inconsistencies.

4. The son of Heman, the presumed founder of postexilic levitical guild of singers (1 Chr. 25:4).

5. A Levite, the son of Jeduthun, who joined other Levites in cleansing the temple under Hezekiah (2 Chr. 29:14).

6. The son of Harhaiah, a goldsmith, who helped to rebuild the wall of Jerusalem (Neh. 3:8).

Ronald A. Simkins

V

VAIZATHA (Heb. *wayzāṯāʾ*)
One of the 10 sons of Haman killed in Susa by the Jews on their day of reprisal against their enemies (Esth. 9:9).

VALE, VALLEY
Valleys of various sizes and shapes are located throughout the land of Palestine. Some are deep and precipitous narrow gorges, such as those located between Bethlehem and the Dead Sea area. Others are wide fertile plains, such as the valley of Jezreel.

Several Hebrew words, translated variously in different versions, indicate a valley or plain. Heb. *biqʿâ* denotes a cleaving or separation of mountains. The term most often indicates a widely extended plain, such as Babylon (Gen. 11:2; Ezek. 3:23; 37:1), Lebanon at the foot of Mt. Hermon (Josh. 11:17), and Megiddo (Zech. 12:11).

Heb. *gayĕʾ* indicates a valley or low, flat region. The term specifically designates the valley of the craftsmen in the plain of Philistia (Neh. 11:35); the valley of the Sons of Hinnom (Ben-hinnom) outside Jerusalem, where sacrifices were offered to Molech (2 Kgs. 23:10); and the valley of vision (Isa. 22:1).

Another term, *ʿēmeq*, derives from the verb "to be deep." This can indicate a valley of wide extent fit for agriculture (Job 39:10; Ps. 65:13[MT 14]) or warfare (Job 39:21). The Jordan Valley is indicated in Josh. 13:19, 27.

The word *nāḥal* can indicate a stream or torrent, or the valley which contains the torrent. Among the particular wadis so designated are Eshcol (Num. 32:9), Sorek (Judg. 16:4), Shittim (Joel 3:18[4:18]), and the Wadi of Egypt, or Wadi el-ʿArish (Josh. 15:4).

A final word indicating a lowland region is *šĕp̄ēlâ* ("Shephelah"). Though translated variously, all references (except Josh. 11:2, 16b) are to the foothills W of the Judean highlands. The designation is a technical term for the low region near the Mediterranean Sea extending from Joppa to Gaza.

Bibliography. D. Baly, *The Geography of the Bible,* rev. ed. (New York, 1974). Harold R. Mosley

VANIAH (Heb. *wanyâ*)
An Israelite in the time of Ezra who had taken a foreign wife (Ezra 10:36).

VANITY
The traditional translation of Heb. *heḇel,* lit., "a puff of air," "a breath," or "vapor," and Gk. *mataiótēs,* which ranges in meaning from "nothingness" or "emptiness" to "useless" or "futile" (cf. Acts 14:15; Rom. 8:20; Eph. 4:17; 2 Pet. 2:18).

In modern English usage, vanity often refers to false pride or arrogance and has overtones meaning "lacking in value." But the foundational sense of the word as used in biblical texts is tied to the concept of brevity (e.g., Prov. 21:6, where treasures gained by deceit are compared to a "vapor" which quickly vanishes). Vanity is frequently paired or equated with words such as "wind" (Isa. 57:13), "nothing" (41:29), or "empty" (30:7).

In a number of poetic passages vanity is used to describe the brevity of human life and the transitory nature of human concerns compared to the eternity of God and the durability of God's concerns (cf. Job 7:16; Ps. 39:5, 11[MT 6, 12]; 62:9[10]; 78:33; 94:11; 144:4). "Vanity" occurs most frequently in the book of Ecclesiastes (where it is used 38 times compared to only 35 other uses in the rest of the OT). No single English term can adequately represent the range of meaning this word takes on as it is used in various contexts that imply connotations ranging from "evil" to merely "temporary."

The KJV's use of the English word "vanity" may have been influenced by Jerome's Latin translation (Vulgate). The abstract Latin noun *vanitas* can mean "unsubstantial" and "lacking in permanence" as well as "useless, futile or illusory." The negative connotations associated with "vanity" fit well with the Bible's use of the plural of *heḇel* to refer to "idols" (e.g., Jonah 2:8; Jer. 8:19; 10:8; Ps. 31:6[7]). The prophets use *heḇel* to imply that idols are "airlike" (transitory and lacking in substance), and they warn their people that those who worship *heḇel* (entities that are airlike) will themselves "become *hebel*" (Jer. 2:5; 2 Kgs. 17:15). However, when modern translations replace the KJV's "vanity" with words such as "futility" (e.g., Job 7:3 NIV), "what is worthless" (15:31 NIV), or "meaningless" (Ecclesiastes NIV), they obscure the fact that in Hebrew the essential quality to which *hebel* refers is lack of permanence rather than lack of worth or value.

The KJV also occasionally uses vanity to translate Heb. *ʿāwen,* which more properly means "misfortune," "trouble," or "evil" (cf. Prov. 22:8; Job 15:35; Ps. 10:7).

Bibliography. K. Farmer, *Who Knows What Is Good?* ITC (Grand Rapids, 1991); K. Seybold, "hebel [hebhel]," *TDOT* 3:313-20.

Kathleen A. Farmer

VASHNI (Heb. *wašnî*)

According to the MT, a son of Samuel (1 Chr. 6:28[MT 13]; NRSV mg). The Hebrew may better be translated "and the second" (so NRSV).

VASHTI (Heb. *waštî*)

The queen of Persian king Ahasuerus (Xerxes I, 486/485-465 B.C.E.). At the culmination of a great display of his wealth before his satraps, Ahasuerus orders Vashti (cf. Pers. *vahišta,* "the best"; *uas,* "the beloved" or "desired one") to display her beauty before the assembly (Esth. 1:11). Her refusal (Esth. 1:12) enrages Xerxes, who banishes her and proclaims that all women show obeisance to their husbands (vv. 16-22). The king's aides search the kingdom for young beauties to replace Vashti, and young Jewish virgin Esther succeeds her as queen (Esth. 2:2-17).

Scholarly attempts to identify Vashti as a historical figure (e.g., Amestris, Herodotus *Hist.* 7.61; 9.108-12; Stateira, the queen of Artaxerxes II) have been unconvincing.

Jewish tradition depicts her as granddaughter of Nebuchadnezzar and daughter of Belshazzar, neither favorably disposed toward the Jews. Jewish lore further views Vashti's own banquet (Esth. 1:9) as laden with political intrigue; the nobles' wives are in fact captives, used as insurance that their husbands not rebel against Xerxes. One account portrays Vashti as both immodest and immoral, fully intending to parade nude before the royal guests but soon found to have leprosy. Another version says she thinks the king would be killed if his nobles see her beauty, for "they will want to enjoy me themselves, and will kill you" (*Esth. Rab.* 3:14); when Xerxes repeats his request, she insults him by reminding him he once had been a stable boy in her father Belshazzar's stable. Jewish lore maintains that Vashti was put to death on the sabbath because during her queenship she forced Jewish maidens to disrobe and work in the nude on the sabbath.

Robin Gallaher Branch

VEGETABLES

Vegetables (Heb. *yārāq, ʾōrōt*) were a dietary mainstay of the ancient world, alongside oil and wine (Pliny *Nat. hist.* 19.52-189). Ancient Near Eastern varieties include cucumber, endive, garlic, leeks, and onions, for which Egypt was especially well known (cf. Deut. 11:10). Heb. *zērūʿîm* ("things sown") includes legumes (2 Sam. 17:28; Dan. 1:12, 16).

The Greeks prized vegetables as healthy, simple food (Plato *Republic* 2.372; cf. Prov. 15:17). Generally "vegetables" (Gk. *láchana*) were leafy plants, as distinct from legumes. Included in the term were artichokes, asparagus, endive, watercress, lettuce, cucumbers, various cabbages, and some root vegetables such as radishes, carrots, onions, and occasionally herbs. Wild vegetables may also be *láchana* (Josephus *BJ* 5.437).

In the NT *láchana* includes vegetables and herbs (cf. the mustard seed that becomes the greatest of all garden plants, Mark 4:30-34 par.; and the Pharisees' tithe of herbs, Luke 11:42). According to Rom. 14:2 the weak eat only vegetables. Since consistent vegetarianism (as opposed to occasional fasting) was alien to official Judaism, scholars debate the meaning of this passage. Some scholars maintain that "eating vegetables" stands for any abstinence from certain foods, and others argue that the phrase is evidence that observant Jewish Christians in Rome ate "only vegetables" because of the impossibility of obtaining ritually clean meat and wine in the aftermath of the rescinding of the edict of Claudius (cf. Dan. 1:12, 16; 2 Macc. 5:27).

Bibliography. G. Bornkamm, "láchanon," *TDNT* 4:65-67; F. Watson, "The Two Roman Congregations: Romans 14:1–15:13," in *The Romans Debate,* ed. K. Donfried, rev. ed. (Peabody, 1991), 203-15.

Thomas Scott Caulley

VEIL

A cloth covering used to conceal the face or head (Heb. *ṣāʿîp*). It is usually a separate garment, but could also be part of the outer garments drawn up and over the head (1 Kgs. 19:13). The male version of the veil is the turban made of linen or other fabric that was worn by priests (Exod. 29:6; Zech. 3:5) and royalty (Ezek. 21:26[MT 31]).

Although women were not covered at all times, in biblical references the veil is associated with them more often than with men. The veil identifies a woman as a prostitute (Gen. 38:14-15, 19), though it was apparently also part of the finery worn by royal (Isa. 47:2) and haughty (3:23) women. An air of mystery could also be added by this garment, enabling it to contribute to the beauty of a woman (Cant. 4:1, 3; 6:7). Rebekah wore a veil when she met Isaac on her wedding day (Gen. 24:65); this may be indicative of her status as a single woman (though single women elsewhere do not always go veiled) or may be part of a woman's bridal attire. The presence of a bridal veil could explain why Jacob did not realize that he had been deceived into marriage with Leah instead of Rachel (Gen. 29:18-25).

Moses used a veil to hide his shining face after he had spoken to the Lord on Mt. Sinai (Exod. 34:33-35) so that he would no longer induce fear among his people. Paul explains this veil as a means by which the temporary nature of the old covenant could be disguised (2 Cor. 3:13) and uses it metaphorically to explain Jewish misunderstanding of the Scriptures (2 Cor. 3:14-18).

Katharine A. Mackay

VEIL OF THE TEMPLE

Of the curtains of the tabernacle (Exod. 26) and temple (cf. *Yoma* 5.1), two were of particular importance. The "inner veil" (Heb. *pārōḵeṯ*) screened the holy of holies *(dĕḇîr),* separating it from the holy place sanctuary *(hêḵāl);* within this space the high priest officiated once a year on the Day of Atonement (Exod. 26:31-33; Lev. 16:12-15; Josephus *BJ* 5.219; Philo *Life of Moses* 2.101: Heb. 9:3). The "outer veil" *(māsāḵ)* hung at the entrance to the tabernacle sanctuary; inside the priests offered the daily incense offering (Exod. 26:36; Josephus *BJ* 5.212; Philo *Spec. leg.* 1.171, 274; Ep. Arist. 86). The linguistic distinction between the terms is usually maintained in Hebrew, but not in the LXX which uses Gk. *katapétasma* for both, nor in the writings of Josephus or Philo. The "house of the veil" (most likely the inner curtain) designates the sanctuary of the temple in Sir. 50:5.

The rendering (by God) of the veil *(katapétasma)* of the temple sanctuary, in response to (Matt. 27:51; Mark 15:38) or preceding (Luke 23:45) the death of Jesus could refer to either curtain, though most take it to refer to the inner because of its particular significance. In all three it seems primarily an ominous sign for the temple and its cult, though less emphatic in Luke. It probably also conveys the positive sense of a new beginning. In Hebrews (cf. Heb. 10:19-20) Jesus' passing through the inner veil opens a new way to God for believers.

Bibliography. H. W. Attridge, *The Epistle to the Hebrews.* Herm (Philadelphia, 1989); R. E. Brown, *The Death of the Messiah* (New York, 1994) 2:1097-1113; F. Ó. Fearghail, "Sir 50, 5-21: Yom Kippur or the Daily Whole-Offering?" *Bibl* 59 (1978): 301-16; O. Hofius, "Katapétasma, -atos," *EDNT* 2:266; D. D. Sylva, "The Temple Curtain and Jesus' Death in the Gospel of Luke," *JBL* 105 (1986): 239-50.

Fearghus Ó. Fearghail

VENGEANCE

Punishment as retribution for harm against persons. It seems quite clear that the OT endorses the notion of both human and divine vengeance (from Heb. *nqm*) at least under certain circumstances. The OT records specific instances where God declares war against an enemy of the Israelites as an act of vengeance for a previous atrocity (Num. 31; Deut. 25:17-19). In fact, at least one prophet apparently considered vengeance to be an attribute of God (Nah. 1:2). A similar view of God can be found in the NT (Rom. 12:19; 2 Thess. 1:5-10).

The question of human vengeance is somewhat more complicated. The OT does recognize the right of relatives of an accidental homicide victim to take direct vengeance against the perpetrator. However the OT also seeks to limit this right by allowing the perpetrator to flee to one of the cities of refuge (Exod. 21:13; Num. 35; Deut. 19:1-13). While some biblical characters do take vengeance (1 Kgs. 2:5-9), it is also true that the OT condemns vengeance when it is directed at another Israelite (Lev. 19:18). This attempt to discourage human vengeance becomes an important part of Jesus' message (Matt. 5:38-48).

Bibliography. K. Koch, "Is There a Doctrine of Retribution in the Old Testament?" in *Theodicy in the Old Testament,* ed. J. L. Crenshaw. IRT 4 (Philadelphia, 1983), 57-87; G. E. Mendenhall, *The Tenth Generation* (Baltimore, 1973).

Joel S. Kaminsky

VERMILION

A bright red mineral pigment used in painting, routinely applied by the Assyrians and the Babylonians to their bas-reliefs (Heb. *šāšēr;* Gk. *míltos*). Jeremiah condemns King Jehoiakim of Judah for his attention to the furnishing of his own palace, painted in vermilion (Jer. 22:14), rather than to the cause of the poor and needy (vv. 16-17). Ezekiel, in his allegorical condemnation of the idolatry of Samaria and Jerusalem, refers to the latter's lusting after Chaldean soldiers "portrayed in vermilion" (Ezek. 23:14). According to Wis. 13:14 wooden idols were painted with vermilion (NRSV "red paint").

VERSE

The division of the biblical books into numbered chapters and verses is not a part of the original texts. There are, however, precursors to this step.

The primary evidence for early division of the Hebrew text into smaller units is Masoretic, but there is pre-Masoretic evidence for similar activity, as early as Qumran and the Mishnah. The Masoretes divided the text into what may be termed "chapters" *(parashoth)* and "verses" *(pasuq).* Furthermore, the Masoretes marked off sections by leaving a line blank (thus an "open" section) or by skipping some spaces within a line (a "closed" section). That the Masoretes were dividing the text into what amounted to verses is seen in their use of the accent *silluq* to mark the end of a sense unit. The division of the Hebrew text into numbered chapters and verses as we now have them was accomplished under the influence of the Vulgate tradition after the 13th century.

Chapter divisions in the NT go back at least as far as the 4th-century Codex Vaticanus, and other divisions of the texts are traceable through lectionary development. The division of the NT into verses occurs for the first time in the edition published by Robert Stephanus (Estienne) in Paris in 1551.

Bibliography. B. M. Metzger, *The Text of the New Testament,* 3rd ed. (Oxford, 1992); E. Tov, *The Textual Criticism of the Hebrew Bible* (Minneapolis, 1992).

Michael L. Ruffin

VERSIONS

See Bible Translations; Text of the Old Testament; Text of the New Testament.

VESPASIAN

Titus Flavius Vespasianus, Roman emperor, 69-79 C.E. He was born into a middle-class Roman family on 17 November 9 C.E. at Falacrinae NE of Rome. His impressive career included a tribunate in Thrace, a questorship in Crete and Cyrene, a praetorship under Caligula, command of the Second Legion "Augusta" in Britain, and governorship of Africa. In 67 Nero appointed him governor of Judea in charge of suppressing the Jewish rebellion. His efforts were successful, with Galilee quickly coming under Roman control. At Nero's death in 68, a period of imperial instability ensued. Vitellius, who was supported by western legions, emerged from the civil strife in Rome as emperor in early 69. Vespasian's own legions soon proclaimed him emperor. Vespasian left his son Titus in charge of closing the Jewish War, including the siege and destruction of Jerusalem. From his base in Alexandria, which controlled the grain trade, Vespasian won support from other legions and replaced Vitellius in July.

Although a military person, Vespasian's rule was mostly peaceful. He established the Flavians as legitimate successors to the Julio-Claudian dynasty and engineered the succession of his sons Titus and Domitian in turn. His building accomplishments included the Colosseum and the temple of the Deified Claudius. He also replenished the state treasury that had been depleted by the civil strife following Nero's death and the Jewish War, but his methods were ruthless and included exorbitant taxation. He was noted for being just, fair, and lenient in legal and political matters and for cooperation with the senate. He died 23 June 79.

Bibliography. F. Millar, *The Roman Near East: 31 B.C–A.D. 337* (Cambridge, Mass., 1993); C. Scarre, *Chronicle of the Roman Emperors* (London, 1995).

SCOTT NASH

VIA DOLOROSA

The traditional path walked by Jesus from Pilate's praetorium through the Old City of Jerusalem to the Church of the Holy Sepulchre (Lat. "the Sorrowful Way").

As early as the 4th century A.D. pilgrims visited Jerusalem with a desire to pray at the places hallowed by Jesus' last hours. Egeria (ca. 380) reports an annual (not weekly) procession: after spending the night of Holy Thursday on the Mount of Olives, worshippers descended at cockcrow to Gethsemane for readings commemorating Jesus' agony and betrayal. Then they mounted up to the city, entering with singing through the eastern gate at first light. They passed through the city on approximately the same route as the present Via Dolorosa and moved without stopping to the Church of the Holy Sepulchre.

The present Way grew out of the new devotion to the humanity and wounds of Jesus, central to the piety of Bernard of Clairvaux (1090-1153), Francis of Assisi (1182-1226), Bonaventure (1221-1274), and St. Gertrude (1256-1301).

The route has not changed much since the 13th century, but the number and order of stations has developed. The present Way with exactly 14 stations was definitively fixed only in 1914. The stations commemorate in succession (1) Jesus' condemnation, (2) the imposition of the cross, (3) his fall under the weight of the cross, (4) meeting his mother, (5) placing of the cross on Simon of Cyrene, (6) Veronica's wiping of his face, (7) falling a second time, (8) his words to the daughters of Jerusalem, (9) falling a third time, (10) removal of his garments, (11) nailing to the cross, (12) death on the cross, (13) his body taken from the cross, (14) his burial. Jesus' falling three times, meeting his mother, and encountering Veronica are not attested in the NT but have become fixed features of the Way.

The route was established at a time when Jesus' condemnation was believed to have taken place at the Fortress Antonia, serving as Pilate's praetorium. It is now thought that the praetorium is to be identified with Herod's palace to the west of the Church of the Holy Sepulchre and not with the Antonia to the east. Thus pilgrims walking the Via Dolorosa are probably traveling in the opposite direction from the historical path.

Bibliography. A. Storme, *The Way of the Cross* (Jerusalem, 1976); H. Thurston, *The Stations of the Cross* (London, 1906); J. Wilkinson, *Egeria's Travels in the Holy Land,* rev. ed. (Jerusalem, 1981).

ROBERT HARRY SMITH

VIAL

A container or flask used for holding oil and normally associated with the practice of anointing (Heb. *pak̠;* 1 Sam. 10:1; 2 Kgs. 9:1, 3, 6). Gk. *phiálē,* "vial," is found in the NT only in Revelation, where it refers to a broad, shallow bowl (so NRSV) where incense or a drink offering could be poured out. Some bowls were full of incense, which were the prayers of the saints (Rev. 5:8). The seven golden bowls contained God's wrath and judgment upon the earth (Rev. 15:7; 16:1-17; 21:9).

J. GREGORY LAWSON

VILLAGE

A small, usually unfortified settlement (Deut. 3:5; 1 Sam. 6:18; Esth. 9:19; Heb. *ḥāṣēr,* "enclosure"), in biblical usage often difficult to distinguish from the town (cf. Luke 13:22). Although urban life may have developed from the agricultural village, such settlements do not necessarily represent a direct evolutionary stage of urbanization. Generally the home base for ancient Palestinian (and ancient Near Eastern) transhumants (cf. Gen. 13:2, 12; 26:12-14), the village might be little more than a hamlet, scarcely distinguishable from the open field (Ezek. 38:11; cf. Lev. 25:31, 34).

Villages might be founded by a city (cf. Heb. *bat̠ X,* "daughter of X," especially common in genealogical material; e.g., 1 Chr. 2:3, 21, 35, 49; cf. Ps. 48:11[MT 12]). A number of villages might be associated with a city, thus references to a city "and its villages" (e.g., Josh. 15:21-62; cf. Neh. 12:29; Jer. 49:2-3). Villages generally were dependent on the larger walled settlement for protection and might in turn provide military service (Judg. 5:7, 11; cf. Hab. 3:14).

Archaeological evidence indicates a significant increase in the number of such settlements in the Iron I period, particularly in the central Palestinian hill country. It is estimated that in Iron I some 250 thousand people lived in villages; by Iron II (ca. 1200 B.C.E.) that number had increased to 750 thousand. Often clustered within sight of one another, villages ranged in size from .3–1 ha. (.75–2.5 a.) and consisted of various configurations of houses, caves, and tents. Traditional law prevailed in village society.

See PEASANTRY. ALLEN C. MYERS

VINE, VINEYARD

The origin of viticulture in the southern Levant is dated to the Chalcolithic period (4000-3500 B.C.), based on the discovery of wine-treading installations in the region. The geography, soil, and climate of the eastern Mediterranean steppe and hill country were favorable for vineyard cultivation. Upper Mediterranean basin finds of the two strains of grapes, *Vitis silvestris* (a wild grape species common to parts of Europe and North Africa) and *Vitis vinifera* (domesticated grapes), have been dated to the Neolithic period (8000-3500), but no examples of *Vitis silvestris* have been uncovered in Israel.

The first example of viticulture in the Bible is the account of Noah's planting of a vineyard, which presumes an earlier knowledge of the practice by this "man of the soil" (Gen. 9:20). Examples of *Vitis vinifera* were found in the Early Bronze strata at Lachish, and the region remains a prominent producer of grapes today. The region of modern Israel, Palestine, and Lebanon produced an abundance of wine in the Middle Bronze Age, where according to the annals of Sinuhe, "Figs were in it and grapes, and it had more wine than water" (*ANET,* 19). During the Late Bronze Age, viticulture was a vital element of the economy of Canaan. Thutmose III brought back grapevines and other botanical varieties from Canaan to Egypt. Solomon traded wine along with wheat, barley, and olive oil in securing lumber and other products and services for the building of the Jerusalem temple (2 Chr. 2:8-10).

Vineyard horticulture is described variously in the Bible and ancient texts. In the rocky terrain of ancient Israel extensive ground preparation was necessary (Isa. 5:1-8). Clearing stones and hoeing preceded the selection and planting of choice grape vine stock. Apparently red grapes were preferred, as Heb. *śōrēq* suggests (Jer. 2:21; Isa. 5:2). Other varieties, such as the *gepen sĕmāḏar* (Cant. 7:12[MT 13]) and *gepen bôqēq* (Hos. 10:1), some of which produced green or white grapes, are recounted. The vinedresser would build a wall of gathered stones or heavy brush and briers around the vineyard for protection from people and animals and for defining of boundaries, and then a stone watchtower was erected within the enclosure. Ancient law permitted the eating of grapes while within a neighbor's vineyard, but removal of grapes using any kind of vessel was prohibited (Deut. 23:24). Pathways between neighboring walled vineyards were common, as where the angel wielding a sword stood before Balaam and his donkey (Num. 22:24-33).

Vines could be oriented to spread along the contours of the ground in very small hill country plots or trained to grow on supporting poles and trellises, creating linear rows or canopies (*ANEP,* 156). Pruning was necessary to maximize the grape production and ensure the ripening of the fruit (Isa. 18:5; John 15:2). The pruning knife *(mazmerâ)* was a small curved knife, like a small sickle. No pruning or other form of viticulture was to be done during the Sabbatical Year for the land (Lev. 25:4-5).

The joyous time of harvesting occurred from late summer through the fall, according to the region and elevation (Judg. 9:27; cf. Isa. 16:9-10). The grape clusters were removed with a knife from vines which were at least four years old. The produce of the fourth year was dedicated to the Lord as an offering of praise, and then the year following the vineyard owner could reap the benefits of the produce (Lev. 19:23-25). One who was called into military service could be released at the time of harvest to enjoy the fruit of the vine if he had not yet done so (Deut. 20:6). Gleaning of the grape harvest was a special provision for the poor, aliens, widows, and orphans who otherwise might not be able to enjoy the plentiful produce of the land (Lev. 19:10; Deut. 24:21).

Though some grapes were consumed right from the vine, most were brought to the winepresses for the family activity of treading the grapes. Winepresses of the OT and NT periods have been discovered throughout the hill country and valleys of modern Israel and Palestine. Most of the Iron Age installations are of the hewn stone type *(yeqeḇ)* and found in proximity to the vineyards; others built of stone and mortar *(gaṯ)* occur in town and city environs, more common in the Roman and Byzantine eras.

Throughout Israelite history the vineyard played an important role in the agricultural and literary aspects of her religious development. A fruitful vineyard was a symbol of God's faithful beneficence. A large grape cluster from the vineyards of the Eshcol Valley was brought back to the Israelite camp at Kadesh as evidence of the great productivity of the Promised Land (Num. 13:23-24; Deut. 6:11). The vineyards would continue to be fruitful if the people observed the Lord's commandments (Deut. 8:6-10). Jesus used similar imagery of the vine and vine dressing to describe the nature of discipleship, by which the branches of his disciples bear abundant fruit as they are sustained and nurtured by the central vine in keeping his commandments (John 15:1-17). The wise psalmist stated that one who fears God will be blessed with a wonderful wife who is like a fruitful vine (Ps. 128:1-3).

The vineyard could also be a symbol of judgment upon the nation. Isaiah's "Song of the Vineyard" portrays Israel as the choicest of vines planted and nurtured by the Lord, but which yielded sour fruit. The result would be the devastation of the vineyard and its protection because of Israel's injustice and unrighteousness (Isa. 5:1-7; cf. Ps. 80:8-16[9-17]; Hos. 10:1-2; Jer. 8:13). The vines would dry up and be stripped bare by their ravaging enemies (Joel 1:6-12). Judgment upon the nations surrounding Israel can also be contextualized in vineyard imagery (Jer. 48:32-33).

Abstention from the vineyard and its produce carried a special connotation of consecration in the Bible. Nazirites were prohibited from contact with or consumption of anything originating in the vineyard, whether vines, grapes, or juice and wine produced from them (Num. 6:1-4). The faithful Rechabites also abstained from consumption of wine and cultivation of vineyards (Jer. 35:1-11). Priests were to refrain from wine consumption during their time of cultic service (Lev. 10:8).

Israel's restoration after exile and captivity was to be evidenced in the productivity of the vineyards, with wine dripping from the mountains as the people plant vineyards and drink their wine (Amos 9:13-15; cf. Hos. 2:15[17]; 14:7[8]). The Lord will water and watch over his vineyard continually so that it bears abundant fruit (Isa. 27:2-4; Jer. 31:1-14).

Bibliography. O. Borowski, *Agriculture in Iron Age Israel* (Winona Lake, 1987); R. Frankel, *The History of the Processing of Wine and Oil in Galilee in the Period of the Bible, the Mishnah, and the Talmud* (diss., Tel Aviv, 1984); J. M. Renfrew, *Palaeoethnobotany* (New York, 1973); *Wine and Oil Production in Antiquity in Israel and Other Mediterranean Countries.* JSOT/ASORMS 10 (Sheffield, 1999).

R. Dennis Cole

VINEGAR

The product of soured or over-fermented wine. Boaz invites Ruth to dip her food in vinegar to season it (Heb. *ḥōmeṣ;* Ruth 6:21; NRSV "sour wine"). Diluted vinegar was commonly served to quench laborers' thirsts, although Nazirites were forbidden to drink vinegar (Num. 6:3). The psalmist feels mocked by enemies who serve him vinegar to quench his thirst (Ps. 69:21[MT 22]), perhaps because undiluted vinegar induced thirst. Proverbs refers to vinegar as an irritant to the teeth (Prov. 10:26) and to a wound (25:20).

The Gospels report that on the cross Jesus was offered wine (Gk. *oínos*) and vinegar, or "sour wine" (*oxós;* Matt. 27:34 par.). Roman soldiers commonly kept vinegary wine on hand to quench their thirst, and this could be an act of kindness or an attempt to revive Jesus. Other elements of mockery in this scene, however, make the offering of vinegar much more likely an act of derision.

Bibliography. R. E. Brown, *The Death of the Messiah* (New York, 1994) 2:1058-66.

Chris Caldwell

VIOLENCE

The Hebrew concept of violence (from Heb. *ḥāmās,* "treat or act violently") concerns ethical, physical wrong; extreme wickedness, malicious witness; institutional injustice; injurious language, violent mechanisms. It designates innocent suffering, with human subjects and objects, resulting from greed or hatred, but not natural catastrophes. Another term, *gāzal,* means "to take by force; steal; tear away" or "robbery; a thing plundered or spoiled; extorting justice." Greek words include *bíā,* "hostile force"; *biastḗs,* "a violent person"; and *biázō,* "to enter violently" or "to destroy, murder."

In the Pentateuch violence impedes creation, curses humanity, and problematizes cosmos. Human violence often requires violent divine response, to affect a new creation (Gen. 3). In *milḥāmâ* ("battle"), Yahweh — a "warrior" (Exod. 15:3) — uses violence to rescue Israel. God, perceived as Israel's sovereign patron, is always with them, even in violence. God wages war *(lāḥam)* on Israel's behalf and calls Israel to war against the enemy, their mutual opponents. While only God affects the outcome, God may attack Israel for disobedience. God condones domestic violence in Deuteronomy, sanctions violence in the land conquest, and supports the demise of kingship. David's saga reflects human collective violence, desire for power, rivalry, and scapegoating.

Prophetic literature lauds the day of the Lord and critiques the profane and religious understanding of violence, especially selfish gain that devastates society and the land. Some prophets protest their powerlessness. Others use battering imagery and misogynistic metaphors of marriage against women to deliver divine communication. In Job chaos meets gratuitous violence, and human suffering remains unanswered amid a divine litany on creation.

The practice of *ḥāram,* "ban, devote, destroy utterly," requires one to "dedicate" something that resists God's work. OT war texts contain complex war justifications, human violence, and sacrifice, glorification of warriors, and war-related deception. Humans attempt to make sense of killing amid compassion and malice.

Ancient peoples desired stability, intimately related to Yahweh, which grounded the sacrificial system. The covenants provided divine assurance that life could continue. Disturbances to such order involved evil, suffering, and death. Though God chose Israel, the Deuteronomistic history defends God's retribution against Israel. Sometimes psalmists deny evil exists. In saving God's honor, the Hebrew text sacrifices human integrity and dignity.

The OT distinguishes between legitimate force and violence, and talks about the Messiah ending violence and establishing justice (suffering servant). The NT sets out normative nonviolent intervention and resistance. Violence, the abuse of power, spirals from structural revolt, rebellion, repression. Such violence produced institutional vigilantism, which caused Jesus' death.

The Synoptic Gospels depict divine and human violence: Jesus drives out unclean spirits; a spirit forces Jesus into the wilderness; establishment and mob crowds want to destroy Jesus. Such violence preserves the status quo. The NT exposes violence though is ambiguous regarding whether Jesus is a pacifist or a zealot (cf. Luke 22:35-38, 49-51). Jesus' attitude toward the state results from his belief that soon God will judge, vindicate, and empower people (cf. Mark 12:14-17; cf. Rom. 13).

Within Jesus' ministry and 1st-century Jewish Palestine, some social unrest existed. Within this communal cosmology of the religious and secular, Jesus is a catalyst of nonviolent social revolution. Jesus opposed all repressive and oppressive violence — but was probably not a pacifist. Jesus and his disciples sensed an imminent fulfillment of God's rule, and their vindication by God (Mark 8:35-38; Luke 17:33). Jesus was a dangerous, revolutionary, popular leader, who viewed his work within God's historical salvific acts, ongoing renewal, and fulfillment. Jesus preached God's liberation, where "Love your enemies" indirectly caused political change and directly changed socioeconomic realities.

The Bible exposes societal violence in a cosmology that instigates violence. More than 600 passages of human violence and some 1000 passages of divine violence occur in the OT. A violent God emerges as an irrational killer, a vengeance seeker, one who sanctions through human beings, and a retributive consequentialist, toward new communal peace and love.

God uses violence to liberate in the Exodus; God experiences violence at the Cross. Divine violence exists dialectically opposite grace. Biblical texts disclose a Promised Land, an elect, patriarchal society with a gospel that discards these ideas by revealing scapegoat violence. Violence generated within institutionalized religion that orders societal powers is itself sacred violence. Jesus challenges the authority of sacred violence represented by the temple (Mark 11). Violence deflected on the victim is sacrifice; faith and prayer renounce vengeance and replace the sacrificial system. Violence is multifaceted injury and coercion. It destroys, describes, is personal and systemic, and shapes values, symbols, and habits.

Bibliography. R. Girard, *Violence and the Sacred* (Baltimore, 1977); R. G. Hammerton-Kelly, *The Gospel and the Sacred: Poetics of Violence in Mark* (Minneapolis, 1994); R. Horsley, *Jesus and the Spiral of Violence* (1987, repr. Minneapolis, 1993); B. J. Malina, "Establishment Violence in the New Testament World," *Scriptura* 51 (1994): 51-78; S. Niditch, *War in the Hebrew Bible* (Oxford, 1993); R. Schwager, *Must There Be Scapegoats? Violence and Redemption in the Bible* (San Francisco, 1987); A. F. Venter, "Biblical Ethics and Christian Response to Violence," *Theologia Evangelica* 24/2 (1991): 25-39; R. J. Weems, *Battered Love: Marriage, Sex, and Violence in the Hebrew Prophets*. OBT (Minneapolis, 1995); J. G. Williams, *The Bible, Violence, and the Sacred* (Valley Forge, 1995).

CHERYL A. KIRK-DUGGAN

VIPER

Among the approximately 35 species of snakes in Israel, seven are venomous and can inflict a fatal bite. Six of these venomous snakes are vipers: the Palestinian viper, Burton's carpet viper, Field's horned viper, the lesser cerastes viper, the greater cerastes viper, and the Engedi mole viper. The Palestinian viper inhabits the Huleh Basin, Galilee, the Jezreel Plain, the Coastal Plain, the central mountains, and the Shephelah. The others live in the desert and semi-arid regions.

Zophar speaks of wicked persons figuratively as "the tongue of a viper" (Job 20:16). In his warning to Judah concerning an Egyptian alliance, Isaiah mentions the viper as one of several dangerous animals which inhabit the Negeb, a land of "distress and anguish" (Isa. 30:6). Isaiah also depicts the iniquity of God's people, who "hatch out vipers" (Isa. 59:5). Heb. *ʿaḵšûḇ* may be translated "adder," "viper," or possibly "spider" (Ps. 140:3[MT 4]).

John the Baptist calls the Pharisees and Sadducees who came to watch him a "brood of vipers" (Gk. *échidna;* Matt. 3:7; at Luke 3:7 he addresses the multitudes). Jesus likewise condemns the Pharisees as a "brood of vipers" (Matt. 12:34; 23:33), indicating their hypocrisy and wickedness. Only in Acts 28:3, where a viper latches onto Paul's hand, is the viper mentioned literally.

Bibliography. *Atlas of Israel,* 3rd ed. (Tel Aviv, 1985); E. Orni and E. Elisha, *Geography of Israel,* 4th rev. ed. (Jerusalem, 1980).

ALAN RAY BUESCHER

VIRGIN

Heb. *bĕṯûlâ,* typically translated "virgin," is more accurately understood as designating a female who had reached puberty and who therefore was potentially able to bear children. This potential fertility meant that the young woman was, according to the customs and values of her culture, of marriageable age.

In Gen. 24 Abraham's servant is on a quest for a bride for Isaac when he encounters Rebekah, described as "a very attractive girl, a *bĕṯûlâ* whom no man had known" (v. 16). Similarly, in the context of finding marriage partners for the survivors of the defeated Benjaminites, 400 young women of Jabesh-gilead are depicted as *bĕṯûlâ,* again with the qualification "whom no man had carnally known" (Judg. 21:12). In both passages either the qualification is redundant or *bĕṯûlâ* does not mean virgin. As well, both passages are concerned with procuring brides. The book of Esther provides additional evidence. In ch. 2, the young women whom King Ahasuerus has already bedded in his search of a new wife and who, therefore, clearly are not virgins, are nevertheless referred to as *bĕṯûlôṯ.* While these texts make it clear that *bĕṯûlâ* and "virgin" are not synonymous terms, a related term, *bĕṯûlîm,* may have had the specialized meaning "virginity" in a strictly legal context (Deut. 22:13-19).

Ancient Israel's patriarchal culture closely regulated female sexuality. The patrilineal system of reckoning descent and the concomitant transfer of property was premised on controlling female sexuality so that paternity could be reliably determined. Thus, once a young woman's family had formally committed her to a future marriage partner in exchange for a bride-price *(mōhar),* she was expected to remain sexually continent. Willing transgression of this restriction was punishable by death, both for herself and for her illicit sexual partner (Deut. 22:13-21, 23-27). Males who had sexual intercourse with potentially fertile young women who had not been formally pledged for marriage were obliged to marry them. According to Exod. 22:16-17(MT 15-16) the young woman's father had to consent to the marriage, but a bride-price was to be paid in any event. Deut. 22:28-29 does not specify paternal consent, and the wording strongly implies that the male in this case had forced the young woman to comply. Chillingly, this law prescribes that a woman thus sexually violated was to marry her assailant, who was not permitted to divorce her. Desirable virgins captured on the battlefield could be forced to marry their captors. Should the man subsequently deem such a wife unsatisfactory he could divorce her, but could not sell her as a slave (Deut. 21:10-14). Fathers could sell their (virgin) daughters as debt slaves to other Israelites. Unlike male debt slaves, females were not released from servitude after six years of service. Rather, because the servitude included sexual access, and presuming that the owner wanted to maintain the arrangement, female debt slaves were not freed after a specified length of service. They could be "redeemed" (i.e., their freedom could be purchased by payment of the debt) if the owner agreed to terminate the arrangement, and were to be released without payment should the owner fail to meet prescribed obligations (Exod. 21:2-11).

Bibliography. J. Bergman, H. Ringgren, and M. Tsevat, "b^{e}ṯûlâ (b^{e}thûlāh)," *TDOT* 2:338-43; P. L. Day, "From the Child Is Born the Woman: The Story of Jephthah's Daughter," in *Gender and Difference in Ancient Israel* (Minneapolis, 1989), 58-74; G. J. Wenham, "*b^{e}tûlāh* 'A Girl of Marriageable Age,'" *VT* 22 (1972): 326-48. PEGGY L. DAY

VIRGIN, APOCALYPSE OF THE

Two early Christian apocalypses, properly distinguished as the Apocalypse of the Virgin Mary and the Apocalypse of the Holy Mother of God Concerning the Punishments. Both narrate otherworldly journeys by Mary, emphasizing her vision of specific punishments assigned to particular classes of sinners. These accounts depend upon the Apocalypse of Paul, indicating composition after 388 C.E. In both apocalypses Mary intercedes for Christian sinners, winning temporary relief for them during Pentecost in the Apocalypse of the Holy Mother of God and forgiveness for those who repent in the Apocalypse of the Virgin Mary.

Bibliography. M. R. James, *The Apocryphal New Testament* (Oxford, 1924), 563-64.

GREG CAREY

VIRGIN BIRTH

The doctrine drawing on the tradition that, by the power of the Holy Spirit, Mary conceives and bears Jesus apart from sexual intercourse with her husband Joseph.

Only two NT texts refer to a virginal conception and birth. In Matt. 1:18-25 Mary discovers she is pregnant "with the child of the Holy Spirit before they [she and Joseph] came together" (v. 18). Though Joseph decides to divorce Mary quietly, an angel tells him that Mary's child has been conceived by the Holy Spirit and that the child, whom they are to name Jesus, "will save his people from their sins" (Matt. 1:21). Immediately following this story, the writer of the Gospel inserts a passage from Isa. 7:14 — "Behold, the virgin shall conceive and bear a son" — to demonstrate that Jesus' miraculous conception fulfills ancient prophecy. However, since the writer quotes from the LXX, he uses Gk. *parthénos* ("virgin") to translate Heb. *'almâ* ("young woman"); later commentators often demonstrate that the doctrine of the virgin birth is based upon an inexact translation.

In Luke 1:26-38 Gabriel appears to a virgin *(parthénos)* named Mary and tells her that she will conceive and bear a son named Jesus. Since Mary has no husband, she asks Gabriel how this will occur, and the angel says: "The Holy Spirit will come upon you . . . ; therefore the child to be born . . . will be called Son of God" (Luke 1:35). While the Matthean passage attempts to show how Jesus fulfills Isaianic prophecy, the Lukan passage connects Jesus with the Davidic kingship.

No other NT passages mention this miraculous birth, although a number of verses defend Jesus' human paternity and maternity (Matt. 13:55; Mark 6:3; Luke 4:22; Gal. 4:4). Heb. 7:3 describes Melchizedek as "without father, without mother, without genealogy" and resembling the Son of God.

The popularly accepted tradition of Mary as the God-Bearer, or Theotokos, was challenged by Nestorius in the early 5th century as contradictory to Jesus' full humanity. Later theologians challenged the doctrine of the virgin birth on the grounds that it is based on an inexact translation of the Hebrew in the LXX; there are no other NT allusions to the birth; and the emphasis on Christ's humanity would have been better supported by his being born as other humans are born. Many feminist theologians reject the virgin birth on the grounds that Mary was raped by the Holy Spirit, thus demonstrating the power of men over women in the patriarchal society of 1st-century Palestine. While only the Catholic Church holds the doctrine of the virgin birth as authoritative for faith and practice, most Protestant denominations acknowledge the substance of the doctrine as an explanation of the admixture of Jesus' divine and human natures. In any event, the doctrine is more christological than mariological in intent.

HENRY L. CARRIGAN, JR.

VIRTUE

An ability or disposition toward excellence, usually in the moral sense (Heb. *ḥayil;* Ruth 3:11; Prov. 12:4; esp. 31:10); in the NT an excellence of any kind (Gk. *aretḗ;* Phil. 4:8; 1 Pet. 2:9; 2 Pet. 1:3, 5).

In Aristotle virtue is that which allows something to perform its function well (e.g., the virtue of the horse is running). In reference to the person the virtues are those qualities which constitute a person's character (i.e., the excellence of one's character). A virtue is a disposition which makes one good and causes one to do her/his work well.

Virtue lists appear in all of the Pauline Letters except for 1-2 Thessalonians and Philemon. Unlike classical Greek moral reflection, the NT places very little emphasis on virtue. In particular, the four cardinal virtues of prudence, justice, temperance, and fortitude are missing from the NT ethical catalogs (which may reveal a Jewish background to the lists). However, while it is true that virtue language is not present in the way it is in Aristotle, virtue and character are themes present throughout the Bible. Indeed, the Bible's continual storytelling of the great persons of the faith by necessity emphasizes the importance of virtue in the godly life.

What is important here is that virtue not be separated from character. The character of the believer is to be formed after the image of God, and the virtues are the habits which form that character. In the NT the emphasis is further defined as being conformed to the image of Christ (Gal. 4:19; cf. Phil. 3:17; 1 Thess. 1:6; 2:14) who is the incarnate image of God (Col. 1:15).

Therefore, while virtue catalogs can be found only sporadically throughout the NT, the notion of virtue permeates the Bible. The emphasis, however, is not on a formal analysis of virtue, but on discipleship. What virtue then means for the Christian can only be understood in reference to the character of Jesus Christ.

Bibliography. B. W. Farley, *In Praise of Virtue* (Grand Rapids, 1995); E. Schweizer, "Traditional Ethical Patterns in the Pauline and Post-Pauline Letters and Their Development," in *Text and Interpretation,* ed. E. Best and R. McLachlan Wilson (Cambridge, 1979), 195-209. Allan R. Bevere

VISION

A visual or auditory event which reveals something otherwise unknown. Visions and dreams are closely related in the ancient Near East in general, including the biblical tradition. They were an accepted means of communication and revelation throughout the history of Israel and in the early Christian Church. Visions occur throughout the OT, in the Torah, Prophets, and Writings. Though less frequent in the NT, they are important in Acts and Revelation. Visions are related to, yet distinct from, other revelatory phenomena such as theophanies, angelophanies, and heavenly journeys; in these, the emphasis is usually on the message conveyed or the secret revealed rather than on the image as in visions.

Visions may be classified into the following categories: visions of the deity or the divine council (Exod. 24:9-11; 1 Kgs. 22:19-23; Isa. 6; Ezek. 1:1-3, 15; Rev. 4:2-11); visions of other scenes or events which require no interpretation (1 Kgs. 22:17; Jer. 4:23-26; Ezek. 8–11, 40–48; Amos 7:1-3, 4-6; Zech. 2:1-5[MT 5-9]; 3:1-10; Acts 16:9-10); visions based on wordplays (Jer. 1:11-12; Amos 8:1-3); symbolic visions which require interpretation (Jer. 1:13-19; Ezek. 37:1-14; Dan. 7–8; Amos 7:7-9; Zech. 1:7–2:5[9]; 5:1-11; Acts 10:9-16); allegorical visions found primarily in apocalypses (Rev. 12, 17). The first two categories are often further delineated by whether or not the seer participates in the scene.

Certain elements are common to all types of vision accounts. They are usually narrated in the 1st person by the seer. As in dream accounts, there is often an introductory "frame" which provides the information on the date, time, and place where the vision occurred. This is followed by the narration of the contents of the vision and an interpretation, if necessary. The account often concludes by noting the reactions of the visionary.

In the OT visionary experiences are usually identified by nouns derived from the Hebrew roots *r'h* or *ḥzh.* Some visions simply provide an occasion for an accompanying oracle. In these cases, the oracle carries the primary message, with the vision being secondary. In other instances, particularly in symbolic visions, the vision itself is the primary means of communication, often revealing future events.

The NT commonly uses Gk. *hórama* and *optasía* as well as the more general term *eídos* found in the narration of vision experiences. Vision accounts in the NT are found primarily in the books of Acts and Revelation and tend to be of the symbolic type. The apocalyptic books (Daniel and Revelation), in particular, tend toward highly symbolic or allegorical visions with vivid and even bizarre imagery. Jenny Manasco Lowery

VOICE

The same word, Heb. *qôl,* is used in the OT to convey the sound of the human voice (1 Sam. 26:17), a crowd (Exod. 32:18), musical instruments (19:16), animals (Job. 4:10), and natural sounds like thunder (Exod. 9:23). The expression "lift up one's voice and weep" marks times of both joy (Gen. 29:11) and sadness (27:38). Obedience to the commandments of God lies behind the common phrase "to obey (lit., 'to hear') the voice of God" (Deut. 27:10). The phrase for issuing a proclamation is "to give voice" (Neh. 8:15).

Biblical revelation is essentially an oral experience. Accounts of theophany are full of sound (Exod. 9:23-34; Isa. 6:8; Ezek. 1:24; cf. Rev. 7:10). The voices of various messengers of God ring out, from the blood of Abel (Gen. 4:10) to the herald in the wilderness (Isa. 40:3), from the suffering servant who does not open his mouth (53:7), to the voice of the Lamb whose word is like a two-edged sword (Rev. 19:15). God may speak in the silence (1 Kgs. 19:12), or like a mighty storm (Job. 37:2-5; Ps. 29:3-9).

In the NT Gk. *phōnḗ* ("sound") and *phōnéō* ("produce a sound") occur regularly, especially in the Gospels (the voice of Jesus; John 5:25; 10:27) and Acts (proclamation; 2:14). The voice of God marks key moments in the life of Jesus (Mark 1:11).

Bibliography. C. Rowland, *The Open Heaven* (New York, 1982).

WILLIAM R. DOMERIS

·**VOPHSI** (Heb. *wopsî*)
A Naphtalite; the father of Nahbi, one of 12 spies sent to explore the land of Canaan (Num. 13:14).

VOW
A solemn promise made to God either to do or to abstain from some action. Heb. *nāḏar* seems to mean "to separate from profane use; to consecrate to God." As made to God, a vow is an act of worship; it is a conditional promise to give something to God if God first grants some favor. Vows were most often made in situations of need and have a bargaining quality about them (Ps. 132:2 seems to be an exception).

As Jacob leaves Bethel for Haran, he promises that if God protects him on his journey and brings him back safely, he will faithfully return to God a tenth part, a tithe, of what God has granted him (Gen. 28:20-22; 31:13). About to enter the land, Israel must face and fight Arad. Israel promises that if God delivers this people to them, they will "doom" (consecrate completely to God) them and their cities (Num. 21:2-3). In exchange for victory over the Ammonites, Jephthah vows to sacrifice to God whoever first comes from his house to greet him. This turns out to be his daughter; he is grief-stricken but fulfills his vow (Judg. 11:30-39). The childless Hannah vows that if she bears a child, she will consecrate him to the service of God (1 Sam. 1:11). Absalom, while in Aram, makes a vow to worship God in Hebron if God will return him safely to Jerusalem (2 Sam. 15:7-8).

While later Judaism will devote a whole tractate of the Mishnah to vows *(Nedarim)*, the Bible itself, in the legal sections of Leviticus, Numbers, and Deuteronomy, contains only scattered references to vows. These deal particularly with the objects of vows. In addition to tithes, conquered persons and cities, persons, and worship, as noted in the narrative examples, the most frequent vow seems to have involved offering some kind of sacrifice: holocausts (Lev. 22:18-20), peace-offerings (7:16; 22:21-22). Either could be accompanied by secondary cereal offerings and libations (Num. 15:3, 8; summarized in 29:39). Things already belonging or otherwise consecrated to God (Lev. 27:26) or offensive to God's holiness (e.g., revenue from sacred fertility rites; Deut. 23:18) could not be the object of vows. One might vow oneself to God for a determined period of time. This was the vow of a Nazirite *(nazîr)*, as summarized in Num. 6:1-21. Indications are that the *nazir* originally represented a lifelong call (Samson, Judg. 13:3-5; Samuel, 1 Sam. 1:11)) but that later it could be made for a determined length of time (Num. 6:2). Other persons offered to the Lord are to be redeemed for a fixed sum of money (Lev. 27:2), with special accommodation for the poor (v. 8).

The vow of a man cannot be annulled; the vow of a woman can be annulled by her father or husband. If, however, she is independent (divorced or a widow), then her vow too must stand (Num. 30). A vow is a serious commitment and must be fulfilled or "paid." Heb. *šillēm* (piel), from the same root as *šālôm*, indicates that the vow, as it were, hung in the air incomplete until "brought to wholeness" by the performance of the vow (Deut. 23:21-23[MT 22-24]). Deuteronomy further specifies that vows should be fulfilled only in the place which the Lord chooses (i.e., Jerusalem; Deut. 12:6, 11, 17, 26).

Oppressed by Assyria, Judah apparently made vows to God praying for deliverance. With the fall of Assyria, the prophet Nahum tells Israel to celebrate and fulfill its vows (Nah. 1:15[2:1]). Faced with the threat of Babylon, some of the Jerusalemites had made vows to the queen of heaven; Jeremiah denounces their idolatry (Jer. 44:25). The sailors, afraid of the storm, make vows to God (Jonah 1:16), as does Jonah himself from the belly of the fish (2:9[10]). Malachi denounces those who make a vow to God but then cut corners in fulfilling it (Mal. 1:14). On the coming day of the Lord, Egypt will turn to the Lord and make vows, praying for deliverance (Isa. 19:21).

Since vows were most often made in situations of distress, lamentation psalms especially contain references to fulfilling vows with thanksgiving sacrifices (e.g., Ps. 116:14, 18). The act of fulfilling vows in the sacred assembly constituted acknowledgement of what God had done and was itself a public act of praise and thanksgiving (e.g., Ps. 22:25[26]; 50:14; 56:12[13]; 61:5, 8[6, 9]; 66:13-14; 76:11[12]).

In general, the Wisdom texts do not say much about cultic behavior, but references to vows do appear. The seductive woman tempts the fool, "Today I have paid my vows, so now I have come out to meet you" (Prov. 7:14-15). The queen mother of Lemuel begins her words of advice by calling him "son of my vows" (Prov. 31:2), suggesting a situation like that of Hannah praying for a child (1 Sam. 1:11). Eliphaz admonishes Job, in his distress, to return to God so that God will hear him, and Job can then pay his vows (Job 22:27). The seriousness of taking and fulfilling a vow is also stressed (Prov. 20:25; Eccl. 5:4-5[3-4]; Sir. 18:22-23).

A vow (Gk. *euchḗ*) is mentioned only twice in the NT. Both instances involve Paul (Acts 18:18; 21:23-26) and seem to be examples of the temporary Nazirite vow (Num. 6:1-21).

MICHAEL D. GUINAN, O.F.M.

VULGATE
The Latin version of the Bible prepared by Jerome (ca. 347-420). In view of proliferating variations in the Old Latin text, Pope Damasus asked Jerome, the outstanding biblical scholar of the day, to prepare a new Latin text, standardizing it by the "true Greek text." He accepted the assignment reluctantly, anticipating that people in the churches would not like the change — and they did not. Two years later, in 384, Jerome had finished the Gospels, making changes only where he felt necessary. He altered the Western order of the Gospels to that known today and restored texts peculiar to each Evangelist which

had been harmonized in the Old Latin. Whether Jerome or someone else completed the revision is not known.

The Vulgate was adopted in Rome, but even in Pope Gregory's time (6th century) both the Vulgate and Old Latin were widely used. In fact, the supremacy of the Vulgate was not assured until the 9th century, and not until the Council of Trent (1546) did the Vulgate become the standard for the Catholic Church.

Vulgate manuscripts were constantly being corrected to the Old Latin and altered over the centuries. In an effort at standardization, Pope Sixtus V published an edition of the Vulgate in 1590, declaring that it "must be received and held as true, legitimate, authentic, and undoubted, in all public and private disputations, lectures, sermons, and explanations." Unfortunately, it was soon discovered that the edition was flawed and needed to be replaced. A new edition appeared in 1592 under Clement VIII, introducing more than 5000 changes in the text, although the "Sixtine" edition had threatened excommunication for changes. Although more careful than the Sixtine, neither the edition of 1590 or 1592 succeeded in representing Jerome's original text or its Greek base with any accuracy. Ca. 8000 Vulgate manuscripts are extant. The recovery of the original text of the Vulgate is the aim of John Wordsworth, H. J. White, and H. F. D. Sparks, *Novum Testamentum Domini nostri Iesu Christi latine* (3 vols.; Oxford, 1889), and Robert Weber, *Biblia Sacra* (3rd ed., 1975). CARROLL D. OSBURN

VULTURE

Any large bird of prey common to the ancient Near East, including vultures, eagles, falcons, and owls. Several Hebrew words *(nešer, ʿayiṭ, peres, ʿoznîyâ, rāḥām)* are variously translated as "vulture," "eagle," "hawk," "bird of prey," and "ravenous" or "carrion bird," although *nešer* (cf. NT Gk. *aetós*) is the most common. The birds designated by these terms share many of the same characteristics. All are large carrion eaters, have long wing spans and heavy bodies, and soar at great heights.

While the vulture is regarded as a devourer, it portrays several images in the Bible. It is described as swiftly flying over its prey (Deut. 28:49; Job 9:26; Prov. 30:17; Hab. 1:8), unclean (Lev. 11:13; Deut. 14:12), soaring (Prov. 23:5; 30:19), one nurturing its young (Deut. 32:11; cf. Exod. 19:4), and a cherubim in a vision (Ezek. 1:10-14).

Three different large birds are named as being unclean for food, representing three different Hebrew words *(nešer, peres, ʿayiṭ)*. Translations vary for each type of bird, including "eagle," "vulture," "osprey," and "buzzard."

The NT translates Gk. *aetós* as "vulture" when describing a bird flying over a corpse (Matt. 24:28 = Luke 17:37), but "eagle" for all other images.

As a scavenger in the walled cities and villages of Egypt, the vulture's work was so valued that the death penalty was given to anyone guilty of killing the bird. At altars throughout the ancient Near East vultures ate the entrails of cattle, lambs, goats, and birds being prepared for sacrifice.

Bibliography. G. R. Driver, "Birds in the Old Testament," *PEQ* 87 (1955): 5-20, 129-40; "Once Again: Birds in the Bible," *PEQ* 90 (1958): 56-58; Y. Leshem, "Trails in the Sky: Fall Migration of Raptors over Israel," *Israel Land and Nature* 10 (1984-85): 70-77. MICHELLE ELLIS TAYLOR

W

WADI (Arab. *wâdī*)
A river, brook, or stream bed. Many of these streams flow only seasonally, and hence are an undependable water source. Significant wadis include Wadi Murabbaʿāt (about halfway between Qumran and En-gedi) and Wadi Mukhmas (whose source is in the hills of Bethel), two places containing caves where important discoveries have been made. Another example is the Wadi Qelṭ at Jericho, three springs whose waters make this area a flourishing oasis for agriculture. JOHN L. GILLMAN

WAGES
Any form of economic compensation received in exchange for labor or the performance of a service. Such compensation might include shelter and provisions along with additional remuneration either in kind or some object of value. Thus, Jacob was to receive a portion of Laban's flocks in exchange for his shepherding services (Gen. 30:31-33). The use of money, in the form of coinage, did not emerge in the Palestinian economy before the Persian period, and even then was not widespread until the Hellenistic period. Prior to that time wages might be received in weighed amounts of useful or precious metals, such as bronze or silver.

The emergence of wage laborers within an economy requires sufficient agricultural progress to free people from the necessity of directly meeting their own subsistence needs. However, a considerable portion of the wage labor population in biblical times continued to work in the agricultural sector, providing such services as farm labor (Matt. 20:1-6; Luke 15:17) and shepherding (John 10:12). Other wage earners include fishing crews (Mark 1:20), mercenary soldiers (2 Sam. 10:6; Luke 3:14), construction craftsmen (2 Chr. 24:12), priests (Judg. 18:4; Mic. 3:11), prophets and seers (Deut. 23:4[MT 5]; 1 Sam. 9:6-9), wet nurses (Exod. 2:9), and prostitutes (Gen. 38:16-17; Mic. 1:7).

The level of compensation a wage earner received was a matter of negotiation, and was often subject to manipulation by either party to the agreement (Gen. 30:31-43; 31:41; Matt. 20:1-16). A typical wage for a day laborer in Palestine during the 1st century C.E. is generally taken to be about one denarius (Matt. 20:2; cf. Rev. 6:6 where the severity of the famine is illustrated by the exorbitant prices). Since such laborers were dependent upon their wages for their subsistence, the Mosaic law stipulated that laborers were to receive their wages daily (Lev. 19:13; Deut. 24:14-15). The prophets denounced those who paid an insufficient wage or failed to pay their workers in a timely matter — some withholding the wages altogether (Jer. 22:13; Mal. 3:5; cf. Jas. 5:4).

The Hebrew *(śāḵār, pĕʿullâ)* and Greek *(misthós)* words for "wages" are often used metaphorically to refer to both God's positive and negative responses to human conduct, and so translated into English in certain contexts as either "reward" or "recompense" respectively (e.g., Isa. 40:10). God is said to provide wages for those who perform some work on God's behalf (judgment, Ezek. 29:18-19; spreading the gospel, 1 Cor. 3:8-9), and children are sometimes seen as the currency of God's reward (Gen. 30:18; Ps. 127:3; Jer. 31:15-16). The image of wages as divine judgment is perhaps most clearly seen in Paul's assertion that "the wages of sin is death" (Rom. 6:23). The language of "wages" or "reward of unrighteousness" is also used in the NT somewhat more literally of material gain from sinful conduct (Acts 1:18; Titus 1:11; 2 Pet. 2:3).

TIMOTHY B. CARGAL

WAHEB (Heb. *wāhēḇ*)
Possibly a place in the Moabite region of Suphah near the river Arnon (Num. 21:14). It is mentioned in a quotation from the Book of the Wars of the Lord, but the Hebrew is obscure (LXX Gk. *Zōob;* cf. Heb. *zāhāḇ*, "Zahab").

WALLS
Walls provided the primary defense of a city or fortress, along with towers and gate complexes. The height and thickness of a city wall depended upon

the perceived need for the defense of a particular city and its economic capabilities (for labor and materials). Cities important to a monarchial administration for economic or strategic reasons generally have larger walls while less important or nonstrategic cities generally have lighter or no fortifications. Besieging armies also built walls.

Wall Types

Several types of city walls are attested: a peripheral belt of houses, a massive (solid) wall, and a casemate wall. Some villages and small cities built a peripheral belt of houses, i.e., houses abutted in a circular manner facing inward so that the solid back wall of the houses doubled as a defense wall. The roofs of the houses served as observation posts and provided strategic positions for defenders in case of attack. This provided defense for a city or village with minimal economic resources.

The three types of massive walls are regular, a wall with towers, and the offset-inset wall. Regular massive walls are simple solid walls, separate from any other structure, composed of field or dressed stones, mudbrick, or both. Walls with towers are regular massive walls with built-in towers at regular intervals and strategic positions such as at corners and gates. The towers usually extended beyond and were taller than the city walls, creating an enfilade. Offset-inset walls were built in sections that alternately project and recede as the wall stretched around a city. Archaeologists suggest that this type of construction provided greater stability to the wall than a straight massive wall.

Casemate walls, requiring less materials and labor hours than solid walls, are two parallel solid walls connected in intervals by solid transverse walls, thereby creating rooms within the walls. There are also three types of casemate walls: freestanding, integrated, and filled. Freestanding casemate walls are separated from any other structures. Integrated casemate walls are walls whose rooms were used for a secondary purpose, such as a room for a house. Filled casemate walls are freestanding casemate walls whose rooms have been filled with soil or debris, thus creating a thick solid wall. The idea was to strengthen the wall against attack without the economic constraints of building a solid stone or mudbrick wall. Filled casemate walls could be built higher than empty casemate walls. However, the filled casemate wall was no more resistant to a battering ram than an empty wall. Once the solid wall frame was breeched, the fill either split out or could easily be removed by the invaders so that the inner wall could be breeched.

Siege walls, defensive walls built by an invading army, were erected around a city or fortress. These walls provided protection for the invading army and kept the inhabitants from escaping the besieged city. Ezekiel tells that the Babylonians built siege walls at Jerusalem (Ezek. 17:17). Remnants of a Roman siege wall, from the 68 C.E. Jewish Revolt, are still visible around the mountain fortress of Masada.

Evolution of City Walls

The wall and tower at Jericho, dating to ca. 7800 B.C.E., is the earliest known structure of this type. However, the Jericho wall may have been used to prevent flooding rather than for defense. The earliest city walls (for defense) in Palestine are of the massive type and date to the Early Bronze Age I (ca. 3000). Walls found at Tel ʿErani, composed of mudbrick with rectangular towers, were ca. 4.5 m. (15 ft.) thick. City walls at other sites from this time, such as Jericho, were generally thinner (1 m. [3 ft.] or so) and contain semicircular towers. Walls increased in thickness through EB so that they were 5-7 m. (16-23 ft.) thick by EB III (2650-2200). EB II walls surrounded the city of Arad with towers abutted to the walls at intervals of 25-40 m. (82-130 ft.).

City walls disappear at the end of EB III and do not reappear again until MB II. The first MB walls were relatively thin (ca. 2 m. [6.5 ft.] thick) and were of the offset-inset type (with towers), as at Megiddo, or the wall-with-towers type, as at Tell Beit Mirsim. Both types of walls were built of mudbrick on stone foundations. Late in MB II, walls became more complex, with the addition of a glacis (a sloping outer surface, made of beaten earth, stones, and mudbrick, placed against the lower part of a city wall for added strength and protection against attackers attempting to dig underneath the wall's foundation). Casemate walls were introduced in MB and continued into LB, such as at Hazor. City gates began to be constructed of ashlar masonry (cut and dressed stones) and with chambers. An MB variant of a wall is the rampart. First appearing in MB II, a rampart is a mass earthen belt anchored by an inner core of stone or mudbrick. Ramparts measure 25-40 m. (82-130 ft.) wide, 10-15 m. (33-49 ft.) high, and have one or both sides sloped, often with a ditch or trench along the bottom edge. Sites with ramparts include Tel Dan, Akko, Hazor, Yavneh-Yam, and Tel Kabri.

Several sites that had offset-inset walls in the previous period have casemate walls in LB (as at Shechem). Although fortifications continued with little change between MB and LB, the LB walls decline in quality and thickness from MB walls.

Walls generally disappear in Iron I except the peripheral belt of houses; however, most types of walls are found in Iron II. Megiddo, Gezer, Lachish, and Tell en-Naṣbeh began Iron II with a peripheral belt of houses but quickly changed to freestanding walls. Casemate walls predominate in the 10th century, but solid walls quickly replaced them in the 9th century and beyond. Hazor stratum X (10th century) had freestanding casemate walls attributed to Solomon that were filled in stratum VIII (9th century). Beer-sheba stratum III (9th century) had integrated casemate walls. Megiddo stratum IVB (10th century) had casemate walls attributed to Solomon. However, in stratum IVA (9th century) solid offset-inset walls replace the casemate walls, which are attributed to Ahab. Associated with the Megiddo walls is a six-chambered gate complex built of cyclopean ashlar stones; however, a four-chamber gate in stratum IVA replaced this gate complex. Lachish (8th century) had two massive (parallel) walls with towers, according to Assyrian reliefs and on-site excavations (excavators found walls 6 m. [20 ft.] thick, built of mudbrick on a stone foundation). A regular massive wall made of mudbrick was found at Ashdod (10th-9th centuries). Archaeologists discovered a solid massive wall in Jerusalem that measures 7 m. (23 ft.) thick and dates to the early 7th century. City walls were not only large in Iron II but they also typically had glacis. The variety of fortifications from Iron II indicates that location, function, and administrative importance of a city determined the type of wall built instead of a uniform master plan.

Persian period walls basically are a continuation of walls from Iron II; however, many sites in the Persian period were unfortified. Massive walls at Tell Abu Hawan were built with a combination of field stones with ashlar pillars (one stretcher and two headers) every 2-3 m. (6.5-10 ft.), possibly to add strength. Tel Megadim had a casemate wall.

City walls in Greek and Roman times were typically solid, massive walls with towers. Hasmonean rulers built massive walls with towers around Jerusalem. Herod restored and enlarged sections of this wall along with its towers.

Biblical References

Rahab's home was part of the Jericho city wall (Josh. 2:15), and Joshua and his army marched around the walls of Jericho that fell at the trumpets' sound (ch. 6). According to 1 Kgs. 9:15 Solomon built walls around Jerusalem, Hazor, Megiddo, and Gezer. Rehoboam built defenses in several towns of Judah (2 Chr. 11:5-10), and Asa also fortified the towns of Judah (14:7[MT 6]). Jehoshaphat built fortifications in Judah (2 Chr. 17:12). Nehemiah, returning to a city that the Babylonians had decimated in 586, repaired the walls of Jerusalem (Neh. 2:11–4:23). Disciples lowered Saul in a basket from an opening in the Damascus city wall to avoid the Jews who sought to kill him (Acts 9:25). Rev. 21 describes the walls of the New Jerusalem.

Bibliography. A. Ben-Tor, ed., *The Archaeology of Ancient Israel* (New Haven, 1992); A. Kempinski and R. Reich, eds., *The Architecture of Ancient Israel* (Jerusalem, 1992); A. Mazar, *Archaeology of the Land of the Bible, 10,000-586 B.C.E.* (New York, 1990).

TERRY W. EDDINGER

WAR

War (Heb. *milḥāmâ;* Gk. *pólemos*) was a very common feature of life in the periods of both the OT and NT. Generally regarded as something to be feared and avoided if possible (Jer. 4:29; 6:1; Mark 13:14-19), it also provides a most fruitful source of metaphors for the life of the people of God. By no stretch of the imagination can one say that the Bible presents a "pacifist" point of view on violence and war; that would be anachronistic, and a distortion of the text. Like most people, ancient Israelites and Judeans, and the adherents to Jesus and his group in primitive Christianity did not like the effects of war, but for most it was taken for granted as a fact of life. During periods of ancient Israel's history the experience and effect of war was not far from Israelites and Judeans.

Modern conventions of warfare, such as having an internationally recognized cause for fighting and a legally declared state of hostilities, often as a last resort, do not apply in the world of the Bible. There violence was often a first resort. The practice of warfare in the biblical period is limited not so much by international convention, as by the ability of people to wage war. To do so would require large numbers of men to be trained to fight and large amounts of resources, which were not always available during ancient Israel's history, and certainly not available to the early followers of Jesus. Favorable conditions for protracted warfare did not prevail in ancient Israel and Judah until the time of the Monarchy, but even then the resources and manpower were limited.

In the NT period war was a practice of great empires who had the economic and human resources to wage it. The average follower of Jesus in Judea, or even Rome, was not likely to be an active participant in war unless as a victim, or unless he or she was incidentally a member of some part of the army, such as the royal guard (Acts 10; cf. Phil. 4:22). But even then, the likelihood of active participation in acts of warfare was extremely low.

In the OT violent resolution of conflict was common between groups, and such confrontations would fall into the category of "primitive warfare," or skirmish, when compared to later conflicts. Abraham gathered together sufficient men to chase, overtake, and defeat the alliance of kings who had taken his nephew Lot hostage (Gen. 14). During the period of the judges, the period of Israel's early settlement in the hill country of Palestine, armed conflict was common, and defeat in armed conflict became a sign of the displeasure of God at the behavior of his people (Judg. 2:11-15). By the end of the book of Judges, such common resort to armed conflict resulted in a bloody war between tribal groups that almost annihilated one of the tribes, Benjamin (Judg. 19–21).

It is during the time of the Monarchy that we can truly speak of war, in the sense of a regulated, well-equipped force who carried out the political will of a central authority, the king. According to 2 Sam. 11:1 spring was regularly "a time when kings went forth to war." The great deeds of warfare of kings of Israel and Judah are praised as much as is their piety (1 Sam. 18:7). However, neither Israel nor Judah were strong enough to compete for long on the stage of ancient Near Eastern history in such conflicts. Local squabbles, such as those between Israel and her neighbors in the 11th to 9th centuries, and in which Israel and Judah were often, though not always, successful, eventually gave way to the massive imperial campaigns of the Assyrians and Babylonians and their West Semitic allies. Against such power few could stand, as the records inside and outside of the Bible show.

In the period after the Exile (5th century and

later) conducting a war on the part of the renewed Israel was meaningless. The returnees were small in number and deficient in resources, and it was the Persians and later the Greeks who dominated the region. Nevertheless, surprisingly, war imagery does find a place in the literature of this later period, and Israel is even likened to the army of God once more, reviving perhaps the older traditions of holy war (Zech. 9; 10:6-7; 14:1-15).

The conduct of war is generally divided between elements of grand strategy and more confined tactics. To speak of grand strategy of the armies of Israel and Judah is difficult. One can assume that gaining "rest from one's enemies round about" involved a certain amount of conflict in which Israel and Judah were successful. But whether this was a planned strategy, a necessary and perpetually defensive attitude against foreigners, or opportunistic expansion is never clear. The record states that David's territory extended from the border of Egypt to the river Euphrates (1 Kgs. 4:24), an accomplishment repeated during the reign of Jeroboam II (Amos 6:14). This was undoubtedly achieved by the subjugation of enemies along the borders with Israel and Judah, and beyond (2 Sam. 10; 21:15-22).

Tactics on the battlefield were limited. Cavalry was not often used by the armies of ancient Israel and Judah, and chariotry was expensive and limited, so the bulk of the fighting was left to the foot soldier armed with minimal body protection, a shield, spear, possibly a sword, a sling. References to "slingers" (Judg. 20:15-16; 2 Kgs. 3:25) and "archers" (1 Sam 31:3) suggest that such troops were divided into special units on the field of battle. However, once infantry battle was joined it was a matter of forcing the other side to break and turn its back. Then the killing times began (Ps. 18:37-39[38-40]), and estimates of casualty rates in such times of flight are extremely high.

OT "teaching" on warfare is limited. Numerous metaphors from the institution are used as favorable descriptions of both God and the people of God (Zech. 9:13). One of the earliest designations of the Israelite God, Yahweh, is "Man of War" (Exod. 15:3). Victory in warfare is prized as a blessing from God (Ps. 18). As to the conduct of war, the ancient Israelites were often encouraged to destroy without quarter the people and livestock of captured cities, especially if those cities were within their own territory (Deut. 20:10-18). This practice of *ḥērem* was not always applied, but it was a means of maintaining the sacred and social boundaries of the community. Much of the specific teaching on the conduct of war in Deut. 20–21 is concerned more with efficiency than high moral ideals. In the NT period war was never far from the consciousness of most Judeans, including the followers of Jesus, but its practice was now confined mostly to professional soldiers who had their own codes of conduct. The Gospels mention soldiers and war only in passing (Luke 7:8; 23:11; 14:31), but in such a way as to indicate that it was taken for granted. One of the surprising features of the NT is that it contains no overt references to the war which ravaged Judea and Galilee between 66 and 70 C.E., and which resulted in the destruction of Jerusalem and the temple by the Roman army (Josephus *Jewish War*).

It is in the imagery of the letters that war becomes once again a source of metaphors for the self-understanding of the people of God. Suffering, once a sign of identity with Christ in his shameful death (Mark 8:34-38), now becomes a badge of honor for the "good soldier of Christ Jesus" (2 Tim. 2:3). As with the use of athletic metaphor in Philippians, Paul uses the metaphor of the soldier and his life as fitting for the faithful Christian.

The nature of the Christian life is thereby changed. Images of the family and household are replaced with the army as means of informing the Christian of his (not often her) duties. Much of the language of advice to the Christian "soldier" takes on the tone of the soldier's oath, the *sacramentum*, which every Roman soldier had to take. Such an oath meant a radical change of life and a binding dedication to the service of the emperor. Anything short of this was shameful, often punishable by death, and unworthy of an imperial soldier. It is this which finds its way into the NT as an illustration of the way of life for the Christian servant.

Bibliography. P. C. Craigie, *The Problem of War in the Old Testament* (Grand Rapids, 1978); H. Frankenmölle, "Peace and the Sword in the New Testament," in *The Meaning of Peace: Biblical Studies*, ed. P. B. Yoder and W. M. Swartley (Louisville, 1992), 213-33; T. R. Hobbs, "Aspects of Warfare in the First Testament World," *BTB* 25 (1995): 79-90; "The Language of Warfare in the New Testament," in *Modelling Early Christianity*, ed. P. F. Esler (London, 1995), 259-73; *A Time for War: A Study of Warfare in the Old Testament* (Wilmington, 1989); S.-M. Kang, *Divine War in the Old Testament and in the Ancient Near East*. BZAW 177 (Berlin, 1989); S. Niditch, *War in the Hebrew Bible* (Oxford, 1993).

T. R. Hobbs

WARDROBE, KEEPER OF THE

The person in charge of the vestments worn by the king and priests. One such individual, Harhas, is named at 2 Kgs. 22:14 (called Hasrah at 2 Chr. 34:22). At 2 Kgs. 10:22 the worshippers of Baal were supplied with special garments from the keeper of the wardrobe (cf. Jer. 38:11).

John R. Huddlestun

WARS OF THE LORD, BOOK OF THE

A work attested only in Num. 21:14-15, likely containing poems or songs celebrating victories over enemies. The title, which according to targumic tradition probably served as the opening phrase of the first poem, attributes wars, and hence celebrated victories, to the Lord. Num. 21:14-15 quotes this book in describing the boundaries of Moab. Closely following in Num. 21:17-18, 27-30 are two songs which may also have been part of the collection.

This obscure source stands among other unavailable works attested in the OT: the Book of

Jashar (Josh. 10:13; 2 Sam. 1:18), the Book of the Deeds of Solomon (1 Kgs. 11:41), the Book of the Chronicles of the Kings of Israel (14:19) and Judah (14:29), and various annals (Ezra 4:15; Esth. 2:23; 6:1).

ALICE H. HUDIBURG

WASHING

The act of cleansing, for purposes of personal hygiene as well as ritual purification. References to ordinary washing mention specifically only the feet (Gen. 18:4; 19:2; 24:32; 43:24; John 13:3-11), hands (Exod. 30:19, 21; Matt. 15:2), and face (Gen. 43:31; Matt. 6:17). In terms of ritual purification, priests and Levites were required to wash themselves (Exod. 40:12; Lev. 8:6) as well as their clothing (Num. 8:21; 19:7) before performing their assigned tasks (cf. Exod. 30:20, "so that they may not die"). To purify themselves from disease or contact with dead flesh, other members of the community were also required to observe ceremonial washings (Lev. 15:5; 17:15).

Washing also connotes cleansing from sin (Ps. 51:2[MT 4]; Isa. 1:16) and spiritual regeneration (Titus 3:5 NRSV mg; cf. John 3:5).

See BATHING; FOOTWASHING.

WASP

An insect belonging to the order Hymenoptera, particularly the *Vespa orientalis* still found in certain portions of Palestine. Gk. *sphḗx,* which in the LXX translates Heb. *ṣirʿâ,* (RSV, NRSV mg "hornet"), is used figuratively with reference to Yahweh's driving out the pre-Israelite inhabitants of Canaan (Wis. 12:8; cf. Exod. 23:28; Deut. 7:20; Josh. 24:12). Some scholars suggest that the wasp here represents the Egyptian Empire and its repeated military campaigns into Late Bronze Age Canaan, weakening the city-state defenses and allowing the Israelites to enter and conquer. Others render the Hebrew term "depression" or "discouragement," the result of Yahweh's holy "terror" during war (cf. Exod. 15:14-16; 23:27; Josh. 2:24).

JOHN R. HUDDLESTUN

WATCHER

An angel, messenger, or agent of Yahweh (Aram. *ʿîr;* Dan. 4:13, 17, 23 [MT 10, 14, 20]).

WATER

A primary requirement for the support and survival of plant and animal life. With bread, water has long been understood as the minimum sustenance necessary for human life (cf. Gen. 21:14; Exod. 23:25); lack of either spells dire need and eventual death (Isa. 3:1; Ezek. 4:17; cf. Isa. 30:20). Water is also used extensively for bathing, washing, and ceremonial cleansing.

Physical Aspects

Palestine is largely dependent upon rainfall for moisture. Unlike Mesopotamia and Egypt, with their large rivers fed by mountain watersheds, a slight variation in annual rainfall in Palestine can produce a serious drought. Indeed, famine-producing droughts were a particular problem throughout biblical times (Gen. 26:1; 1 Kgs. 17:1).

In normal years, Palestine has a fall and winter rainy season, separated by a summer dry spell (Ps. 32:4). The amount of rain varies widely throughout Palestine, but the coastal plain averages ca. 56 cm. (22 in.) per annum. Generally, northern and western Palestine get the most rain, as do the slopes of mountains that face the sea. Southern Palestine is a virtual desert, especially in the region around the Dead Sea.

Palestine not only lacks large rivers and watersheds, but also adequate natural storage sites for water reserves. Thus historically its inhabitants had to use a variety of human-made storage facilities. Wells (Gen. 21:30; 29:2-8; John 4:11-12) are deep holes which have been dug in the ground to the depth of the water table in order to provide year-round water. Generally the well is surrounded by a stone wall above ground for safety and below ground to keep the well from caving in or needing to be redug. Cisterns (2 Chr. 26:10; Jer. 2:13), also dug in the ground, were fed by conduits that directed the rainwater from the roofs or ground surface. Generally both wells and cisterns were covered in order to prevent evaporation or contamination. Pools (2 Sam. 2:13; Isa. 7:3; John 5:2-7), usually left uncovered, were made by damming springs or constructing a shallow pond of masonry.

Theological Importance

Cosmology

From time immemorial, ancient people must have been aware that water existed above and below the earth. It descended from above in the form of rain and it could be obtained, if one were willing to dig deep enough, from the depths of the earth. In many ancient Near Eastern societies this apparent paradox was explained by the story of the primordial battle between the hero-god and the dragon of chaos. In the Babylonian version, the victorious Marduk splits the body of the female Tiamat. Then he creates the earth from her body, placing the earth in the womb of chaos below the waters of heaven and above the waters of the deep (cf. Heb. *tĕhôm;* Akk. *tiâmtu,* "Tiamat").

The OT acknowledges this basic understanding of the universe, or cosmogony, but modifies it in the light of Israelite monotheism (the Creation account, Gen. 1:1-10; the Flood account, 7:11; cf. Exod. 20:4; Deut. 4:18; 2 Sam. 22:14-17; Job 26:5-13; Ps. 104:3-6; 136:6; 148:4-7; Jer. 10:11-13; Amos 9:5-6; Jonah 2:2-6). So the "waters of heaven," or cosmic waters, are the waters above the earth held back by the firmament. Rain falls when God opens the floodgates in the firmament (Gen. 7:11; 8:2). The sky is blue (the color of the ocean) because the waters can be seen through the transparent crystal firmament (cf. Ezek. 1:26, which pictures God as seated above the firmament on a throne the color of lapis lazuli [blue or turquoise] — the color of deep water and the sky).

Ritual

The Israelites also reflected a common ancient Near Eastern conception by extending in a metaphysical sense the physical property of water as the primary cleansing agent: water also has the power to make one ceremonially clean. The interpretation of Ezek. 16:4, e.g., hinges upon this twofold cleansing property.

The OT ritual for cleansing, in its most basic form, involves bathing, washing one's clothing, and waiting until evening (Lev. 15:5-27; 16:26-28; 17:15; 22:6; Deut. 23:10-11). Thus Aaron and his sons are required to wash with water before they put on the priestly garments (Exod. 29:4-9; cf. 30:17-21; 40:12-15, 30-32). Water is also used for purification in other types of rituals: cleansing the entrails and the legs of a calf or sheep before sacrificing it as a burnt offering (Lev. 1:9, 13), or cleansing a garment or metal vessel from the blood of a sin offering (6:27-28[MT 20-21]).

Because the water itself could become contaminated (Lev. 11:32-36), later rabbis established the minimum amount of water needed for a ceremonial cleansing bath as forty seahs (264 l. [280 qts.; *m. Miqw.* 1:1-8; cf. John 2:6). This amount of water, they felt, guaranteed that the water's natural cleansing power would not become nullified through an inordinate amount of uncleanness.

The most serious cases of uncleanness were cleansed by using "living water" (or running water) — water that flowed in such a manner that it was continually renewed and therefore could not be made unclean (Lev. 11:32-36; cf. *m. Miqw.* 1). "Living water" was used for the cleansing of a leper or a house contaminated by leprosy. The priest took two birds, slaying the first over running water. Then he dipped hyssop, cedarwood, scarlet cloth, and the other, living bird into the mixture of blood and water, and sprinkled the fluid seven times on the house or individual. Afterwards, he released the living bird into a nearby field (Lev. 14:1-7, 48-53).

"Living water" is also an element of the "water of bitterness" and the "water for impurity." The "water of bitterness (Heb. *mê hammārîm ham-'ārărîm;* Num. 5:18-19) was administered by the priest to a woman suspected of adultery (vv. 16-29; cf. Exod. 32:19-20). The priest wrote curses on a slate to which the woman responded, "Amen, Amen" (cf. John 1:51; 3:3, 5). He then washed the slate and mixed the dirty water with dust from the tabernacle and this "holy" water (*mayim qĕḏōšîm,* probably running water). The woman was then forced to drink the water. If she was innocent there would be no damage, but if she were guilty the water would cause her abdomen to swell and her thigh to waste away.

The "water for impurity" (Heb. *mê niddâ;* Num. 19:9) was also water combined with several other ingredients to make its cleansing power more efficacious. A priest offered a red heifer as a burnt offering outside the camp together with cedarwood, hyssop, and scarlet cloth according to proper ceremony (Num. 19:1-22). He then mixed the ashes from the fire with running water and sprinkled this "water for impurity" over anyone or anything that had touched a dead body. This was done on the third and the seventh day. After bathing on the seventh day, the offending party was considered ceremonially clean. The Israelites also used the "water of impurity" to purify the Midianite booty they had captured (Num. 31:23). The "water of expiation" used to purify the Levites (*mê haṭṭāṯ;* Num. 8:7) is probably identical with the water of impurity.

References to water in the NT occur frequently in connection with both Christian baptism (Acts 8:36-39; Heb. 10:22; 1 Pet. 3:20) and John's baptism of repentance (Matt. 3:11; Mark 1:8; Acts 1:5; 11:16). Baptism is a rite of passage that initiates the convert from the world into the community of the regenerate, and hence, in its primary association, an initiatory cleansing ritual. The symbolism of water is particularly appropriate in this ritual. Here the initiate is submerged in the water (reminiscent of the waters of the underworld, and thus symbolic of death). Then he rises to new life (perhaps like the newborn baby emerges from the womb with a burst of water [cf. John 3:5] or reminiscent of the creation of the world "out of water" [Rom. 6:3-4; Col. 2:12]). Baptism is also a cleansing ritual; the initiate emerges with his body "washed with clean water," a symbol of an inner cleansing (Heb. 10:22).

Holy Spirit

Several OT passages figuratively use water for the spirit of God (Isa. 44:3-4; cf. Ezek. 36:25-26; Joel 2:23, 28[3:1]) or for God himself (Jer. 2:13; 17:13). Even more passages refer to the Spirit in terms normally used of a fluid (*šāp̱aḵ*, "pour out," Ezek. 39:29; Joel 2:28-29[3:1-2]; *yāṣaq,* Isa. 44:3; *nāḇaʿ,* Prov. 1:23; *ʿārâ,* Isa. 32:15; *mālēʾ,* "be filled," Exod. 31:3; 35:31; Deut. 34:9). Also the Spirit is active in creation, where it is found hovering over the face of the waters (Gen. 1:2).

The spirit of God may have come to be associated with the water that gives life or with cleansing (cf. *m. Soṭa* 9:15). Or there may be a deeper, more mythological association between the spirit of God and the cosmic waters (cf. Gen. 1:2; Ezek. 1:26).

The NT uses the water for spirit in all of these connections. Luke-Acts, especially, continues the "fluid-oriented" vocabulary of the Spirit ("pour out," Acts 2:17-18; 10:45; "filled," Luke 1:15, 41, 67; Acts 2:4; 4:8; Eph. 5:18).

The most complex water symbolism in the NT may be that of the Gospel of John, where water occurs as a focal point of several incidents. In addition to the baptism of Jesus (John 1:26-33), seven of these "water" pericopes are unique to John: the transformation of water to wine (2:7-9; 4:46), Jesus' conversations with Nicodemus (3:5) and the Samaritan woman (4:7-15), the healing of the man at the pool of Bethzatha (5:3-7), Jesus' proclamation at the Feast of Tabernacles (7:38), the washing of the disciples' feet (13:5), and the blood and water that flowed from the crucified Jesus' side (19:34). John uses water almost exclusively to express his theology of the Spirit, which is closely linked to the activity of the Spirit (John 1:32-33; 3:5-8; 7:38-39; cf. 19:30) or to the ceremonial cleansings that it displaces (2:6; 13:10-11). The key to this understanding lies in the water libation ritual of the Feast of Booths, which was accompanied by a prayer of the "latter rain" of fall — which the early Church believed to be the outpouring of the Holy Spirit (Acts 2:4, 16-21; cf. Joel 2:28-32[3:1-5]). Jesus announces that he is the source of such "living water" at this very ceremony (John 7:38-39; cf. in this light the water that flows from the side of the crucified Lord; 19:34; cf. Zech. 12:10; 13:1).

"Water of life" (Rev. 21:6; 22:1, 17; cf. 7:17, "living water") denotes genuine, everlasting life, life eternal, for which those in this earthly life thirst. The image points not only to an ever-flowing source of water but also to its quality, which contains, creates, and communicates life.

TIMOTHY P. JENNEY

WATER CITY

See CITY OF WATERS.

WATER OF PURIFICATION

Water used to "cleanse" or remove various forms of ritual impurity (Heb. *mê niddâ,* "waters of impurity"). It consisted of the ashes of the red heifer, cedar wood, hyssop, and scarlet material mixed with water from a running stream (Lev. 14:4-8, 49-52; Num. 19:2-19).

The water was applied in three ways: immersion, sprinkling, and hand-washing. Immersion was required of the priest who sacrificed the red heifer (Num. 19:7), booty (31:21-23), the cleansed leper (Lev. 14:8-9), one who had an emission of semen (Lev. 15:16-18), a menstruant or one who had contact with a menstruant (vv. 19-24), anyone who had a discharge or contact with anyone who did (vv. 2-15, 25-28), and anyone who had contact with a corpse or certain carcasses (5:2; 11:8-40; Num. 19:11-13; Deut. 14:8; Hag. 2:13).

Sprinkling preceded immersion in the case of the leper (Lev. 14:1-7) and the one who had contracted corpse uncleanness (Num. 19:14-19). Sprinkling alone was used in the consecration of Levites (Num. 8:7) and in the cleansing of houses affected by leprosy (Lev. 14:49-52). Evidently hyssop was dipped in water to accomplish this rite (Num. 19:18). Hand-washing to remove ritual impurity was practiced almost exclusively by the priesthood (Exod. 30:17-21; 40:31; 2 Chr. 4:2-6).

The cleansing accomplished by these methods involved ritual impurity, and not moral impurity (sin). Later authors, however, used such language figuratively to refer to moral/ethical cleansing (Ps. 26:6; 51:2, 7[MT 4, 9]; Isa. 1:16-18; Jer. 4:14; Ezek. 36:25).

In the NT immersion (baptism) is referred to as "purification" (Luke 2:22; John 3:25; Acts 21:24, 26). In addition to the situations requiring immersion in the OT, tradition had added entrance into the temple (Josephus *Ant.* 12.145; *m. Yoma* 3:3; *y. Yoma* 40b) and grave uncleanness (*Para* 3:7; cf. Heb. 6:2; 9:10). Proselytes (gentile converts to Judaism) had to undergo immersion (*y. Qidd.* 64d; *Yebam.* 46a-47b; 71a; *Ker.* 9a; cf. also 1QS 3:1-9; 4:20-23), which is probably the antecedent to Christian baptism. Sprinkling appears only in the metaphorical sense (Heb. 9:13; 10:22; cf. 1QS 4:20-23).

Hand-washing enjoyed a marked increase in popularity in intertestamental Judaism. Evidently the sages expanded this requirement of priestly purity to apply to common people on the basis of Lev. 15:11 (*Ḥul.* 106a; cf. *t. Ḥag.* 3:2-3; *Dem.* 2:2). A more stringent position on hand-washing was taken by the school of Shammai, which required hand-washing before and after meals (*y. Šabb.* 1:7 [3c]; cf. *BJ* 2.129-30). The more lenient initially resisted it (*'Ed.* 5:6; *'Erub.* 21b), a development directly reflected in the NT (cf. Mark 7:1-16 par.; Luke 11:37-41). Such ceremonial cleansing provides the background against which to understand the presence of the large jars of water at the wedding of Cana (John 2:6). Hand-washing is mentioned metaphorically in Jas. 4:8.

W. E. NUNNALLY

WATER WORKS

The inhabitants of ancient Palestine developed ingenious techniques to manage seasonal and scarce water resources. Stone terrace walls were constructed along the contours of the steep hillsides, providing new land for cultivation, controlling erosion, and impeding the flow of water down the slopes so it would have time to infiltrate the soil. In the Negeb and Transjordan, wall complexes dating as early as the beginning of the 4th millennium B.C.E. were constructed across streambeds, creating a series of dams to control the seasonal floods and irrigate low-lying fields of desert "runoff farms." The Nabateans, masters of water management during Hellenistic and Roman times, made the deserts of southern Israel and Jordan bloom.

Cisterns were excavated to catch and store rainwater in areas where the water table could not be reached or perennial springs were absent. Caves and natural rock basins were easily adapted for this purpose. However, developing technology permitted structures to be hewn in stone that were distinctly bottle-shaped with a narrow neck leading to the surface. Slaked lime plaster made cisterns watertight when geological circumstances demanded, and openings were protected with circular stone collars and heavy stone covers. Cisterns served both public and private purposes, and the Israelites considered them an amenity ranking with the vine, fig, and olive in idealistic descriptions of their land (Deut. 6:10-12; 2 Kgs. 18:31 = Isa. 36:16; Neh. 9:25; cf. 2 Chr. 26:10).

Springs and wells permitted the easiest access to fresh water, but they were often located inconveniently outside the city walls or deep beneath the mounds on which cities were built, requiring extensive ingenuity to reach them. Shafts and tunnels leading to aquifers or springs were excavated at Hazor, Yoqneam, Gezer, Beer-sheba, Arad, Kadesh-barnea, Gibeon, Megiddo, Ibleam, and Jerusalem. At Tell es-Say'idyeh a roofed stairway was constructed along the slope of the mound to the spring.

One of three "pools of Solomon" S of Bethlehem that supplied water for Jerusalem; Hasmonean period, 2nd century B.C.E. (Phoenix Data Systems, Neal and Joel Bierling)

Jerusalem's Gihon Spring was diverted underneath the Ophel hill, where it could be reached by a vertical shaft ("Warren's Shaft") from inside the city. Later, perhaps in the 8th century, although the date is not certain, a tunnel 533 m. (1750 ft.) long ("Hezekiah's Tunnel") was hewn connecting the Gihon with the pool of Siloam.

Pools were designed to store water from runoff and springs. The most famous ones mentioned in the Bible were at Gibeon (2 Sam. 2:13), Hebron (4:12), Samaria (1 Kgs. 22:38), Heshbon (Cant. 7:4), and Jerusalem (2 Kgs. 18:17 = Isa. 36:2; Neh. 2:14; 3:15-16; Eccl. 2:6; Isa. 7:3; 22:9; John 9:7). The growing population of Jerusalem in postexilic times led to the need for numerous reservoirs there. Josephus refers to the pool of the Serpent, Tower Pool, and Struthion Pool. Another, the pool of Israel, was located along the northern wall of the temple enclosure. Water was brought to Jerusalem from the pools of Solomon and springs south of Bethlehem by a complex aqueduct system. The ruins of an aqueduct constructed by Herod the Great to bring water to Caesarea from the heights to the north can be seen today.

Bibliography. R. Amiran, "The Water Supply of Israelite Jerusalem," in *Jerusalem Revealed,* ed. Y. Yadin (New Haven, 1976), 75-78; D. Cole, "How Water Tunnels Worked," *BARev* 6/2 (1980): 8-29; W. G. Dever, "The Water Systems at Hazor and Gezer," *BA* 32 (1969): 71-78; R. J. Forbes, "Irrigation and Drainage," in *Studies in Ancient Technology,* rev. ed., 2 (Leiden, 1965): 1-79; "Water Supply," in *Studies in Ancient Technology* 1, 3rd ed. (Leiden, 1993): 149-94; T. E. Levy, "How Ancient Man First Utilized the Rivers in the Desert," *BARev* 16/6 (1990): 20-31; A. Mazar, "The Aqueducts of Jerusalem," in *Jerusalem Revealed,* ed. Yadin, 79-84; Y. Olami and Y. Peleg, "The Water Supply of Caesarea Maritima," *IEJ* 27 (1977): 127-37; J. P. Oleson, "The Origins and Design of Nabataean Water-Supply Systems," in *Studies in the History and Archaeology of Jordan V,* ed. K. ʿAmr, F. Zayadine, and M. Zaghloul (Amman, 1995), 707-19; J. B. Pritchard, *The Water System of Gibeon* (Philadelphia, 1961); Y. Shiloh, "Underground Water Systems in Eretz-Israel in the Iron Age," in *Archaeology and Biblical Interpretation,* ed. L. G. Purdue, L. E. Toombs, and G. L. Johnson (Atlanta, 1987), 203-44; T. Tsuk, "Reservoirs," *OEANE* 4:422-23; J. Wilkinson, "Ancient Jerusalem: Its Water Supply and Population," *PEQ* 106 (1974): 33-51.

JAMES H. PACE

WAVE OFFERING

See ELEVATION OFFERING.

WAY

In the concrete sense, a road (Deut. 1:2; Ruth 1:7) or a movement along a particular path, i.e., a journey (Exod. 13:21; 1 Kgs. 19:4). However, Heb. *derek̲* was also employed more broadly. To walk in the ways of God meant to live according to his will and commandments (Deut. 10:12-13; 1 Kgs. 3:14). In Isaiah "the way of the Lord" can refer to God's provision of deliverance from enslavement or exile (Isa. 40:3; 43:16-19). The word was often used to identify the overall direction of a person's life, whether righteous or wicked (Judg. 2:17-19; Ps. 1:6; cf. Matt 7:13-14), wise or foolish (Prov. 4:11; 12:15).

In the NT Gk. *hodós* has a similar range of

meanings. In Mark's Gospel it is used repeatedly to present Jesus as "on the way," i.e., on his journey to Jerusalem (Mark 8:27; 9:33-34; 10:32). The broader context adds a deeper significance to these more literal references, since Jesus' willingness to go the way of suffering provides an example for his followers who must also prepare to suffer (Mark 8:31-34). In John 14:6 Jesus claims to be "the way," i.e., the only means of access to God (cf. Heb. 9:8; 10:19-20). In Acts "the Way" functions as a title for the Christian message (Acts 19:9, 23; 22:4; 24:22) or the Christian community (9:2; 24:14).

JOEL F. WILLIAMS

WEALTH

The abundance of material possessions (land, livestock, agriculture); also synonymous with "greed."

The OT view of wealth (or "riches") is determined by a religious understanding. Yahweh is the creator and ruler over all creation; all things belong to him (Ps. 24:1). Wealth and riches may be a sign of God's blessing or the cause of God's wrath. Stern warnings are directed against those who strive for wealth through greed, trickery, and treachery (2 Sam. 12:1-14; Isa. 10:3; Jer. 5:27; 17:3; Ezek. 7:11; Hos. 12:8[MT 9]; Mic. 6:12). On the other hand, to those who are faithful, Yahweh promises the wealth of the nations (Isa. 45:14; 60:5, 11). A growing refrain of charges against the wealthy emerges. The main charge is that they oppress the poor (Isa. 10:1-2; Ezek. 22:25-29; Amos 2:6; 5:11). They reflect a small group of greedy people who acquire wealth at the expense of the poor, the powerless, and those whose rights are not respected.

Most of the OT statements about wealth occur in the Wisdom Literature. Sometimes wealth is praised as the fruit of wisdom (Prov. 3:16) and humility (10:22). More often it is criticized: Job protests the view that goodness brings wealth and wickedness brings poverty. In a number of Psalms (Pss. 10, 12, 37, 41, 52, 72) "rich" is practically identical with "wicked," while "poor" is synonymous with "righteous."

The NT continues the growing critique of wealth. Here the terms "rich or wealthy" are synonymous with "greedy." Morally the wealthy were evil because they opted to devote their lives to greed, rather than to God. In a sense, wealth is a force that competes with God, drawing loyalty away from God (Matt. 6:21, 24). This is illustrated in the classic example of the rich young man who rejects Jesus' invitation to follow him (Mark 10:17-31 par.). This story prompts Jesus' sayings on the difficulty the rich have in entering the kingdom of God as compared to a camel passing through a needle's eye (Mark 10:25 par.). Again the perspective is that of the greedy who erect obstacles, making it impossible to enter God's kingdom (Luke 6:24). The same incompatibility is illustrated in the parable of the rich man and Lazarus (Luke 16:19-31). While the passages where Jesus speaks about wealth are few, they are nevertheless forceful.

The Epistle of James also depicts the wealthy as those who are godless and greedy. Jas. 5:1-6 provides the fullest critique of the wealthy: they place their trust in themselves and in the fortunes that they have amassed at the expense of the harvesters whom they have defrauded. A day of judgment awaits these greedy rich. A study of the anthropology and sociology of the world of the NT has demonstrated that the condemnation of the greed of the rich arises from a basic worldview that the supply of wealth was actually limited — the amassing of a fortune by one person occurred at the expense of someone else.

Other NT writings also pay attention to the dangers of wealth. 1 Tim. 6:9-10 describes "the love of money" (avarice) as "a root of all kinds of evil." The book of Revelation condemns the church at Laodicea; her greed is demonstrated in her total reliance upon herself (Rev. 3:17). The greed of the Roman world is also graphically denounced in Rev. 18:17.

Bibliography. D. E. Gowan, "Wealth and Poverty in the Old Testament," *Int* 41 (1987): 341-53; B. J. Malina, "Wealth and Poverty in the New Testament and Its World," *Int* 41 (1987): 354-67.

PATRICK J. MARTIN

WEAPONS

From as far back as we can determine, human beings have needed weapons to hunt and to protect themselves. As early as 7000 B.C. Jericho had a wall around the center part of the town with a tower inside the wall. This method of protecting towns with walls continued throughout the biblical period. Any sizable city had to expend the labor and money to build such a protective wall. Because of the expense, these walls covered only a small area of the city and contained primarily palace, temple, and government buildings plus some living areas. The majority of the population lived and farmed outside the walls, and rushed inside the city walls in time of an attack. The complex gate system was designed to prevent easy access into the city, and the walls were made high enough and thick enough that they could not be scaled or broken through. Inside the city there had to be great supplies of food and water to withstand sieges that might last three or more years (Samaria, 2 Kgs. 17:5-6; Jerusalem, 25:1-12). The enemy sought to penetrate the gate or city walls by undermining the foundations, weakening the walls and smashing through them, or scaling them with ladders. Battering rams with wheels brought enemy soldiers close to the walls where the long beam with a metal tip could be used to loosen and dislodge the wall material and break through. Of course, the soldiers inside the city sought to prevent this from happening. In many cases the siege was a standoff until food or water ran out and the city surrendered.

Offensive weapons can be divided into hand-held or short-range, medium-range, and long-range weapons. Among short-range weapons, the club was usually larger at the striking end (Prov. 25:18). The mace was a variation of the club with a stone or metal head (possibly implied in Ps. 68:21[MT 22]; Hab. 3:13). The battle-ax came from axes used for cutting wood (possibly Jer. 51:20). The spear had a sharp blade affixed to the end of a long stick. It was a stabbing or thrusting weapon (John 19:34). The sword was very common (more than 400 occurrences in the OT), used for stabbing in hand-to-hand combat. It was short or longer, straight, and generally kept in a sheath (1 Sam. 17:51). The sickle sword was curved like a sickle and sharp on only one side. It was used for slashing rather than stabbing, and is implied in "smiting someone with the edge of a sword" (Josh. 8:24; Judg. 21:10).

Medium-range weapons included a spear that was light enough to be thrown (1 Sam. 18:11). Most common in this category was the javelin, which was generally smaller than the spear (1 Sam. 17:6-7). It was essentially a long arrow with a string looped around the shaft. This increased the distance and accuracy because of the spin the string produced.

The two long-range weapons were the sling and stone and the bow and arrow. The sling was a long string made of woven materials on either end with a pouch to hold the stone in the middle. After circling over the head of the slinger several times, one string was released; the stone then ejected from the pouch and traveled well over 100 mph. The stones were 5-8 cm. (2-3 in.) in diameter, having been roughly rounded in wadi beds. Often the slingers worked to round them off even more so they would fly accurately (Judg. 20:16). David's sling and stones put Goliath in range, but even Goliath's javelin could not reach David, which explains why Goliath was trying to move closer to David (1 Sam. 17:41, 48).

The bow and arrow was the longest range weapon, effective up to 160-180 m. (175-200 yds.). Composite bows in classical times could reach up to 155 m. (500 yds.) in exceptional cases. The bow was 1-2 m. (3-6 ft.) in length, and could be made of wood or glued layers of wood, horn and sinew, or even bronze (2 Sam. 22:35). Arrows were made of wood shafts or reeds with an arrowhead of stone or metal and guiding feathers. Light weight and straightness was the key to accuracy and distance. A leather quiver holding 20-30 arrows was strapped to the back or slung over the shoulder. Quivers on chariots could hold up to 50 arrows. Jonathan used a bow in war (2 Sam. 1:22), but also to signal David (20:18-23). The Benjaminites (2 Chr. 17:17) as well as the Reubenites, Gadites, and the half-tribe of Manasseh had expert archers (1 Chr. 5:18). Four Israelite or Judean kings were wounded or killed by enemy arrows: Saul (1 Sam. 31:3), Ahab (1 Kgs. 22:34), Joram (2 Kgs. 9:24), and Josiah (2 Chr. 35:23).

The iron chariot was the ultimate offensive weapon. Pulled by two horses, it was a mobile fighting platform for two or three soldiers. The chariot was valuable when the land was flat and open, but useless in heavily wooded hill country. This is why Israel, who had no chariots until Solomon's time, could take the hill country but were not able to drive out the people of the coastal plain (Judg. 1:19).

Defense against offensive weapons included a shield carried to protect the body and various pieces of armor worn on the body. Though shields came in a variety of shapes, they can be divided into two groups by size (2 Chr. 23:9). The smaller shield was round and covered about half the body. It could be held in one hand and a lighter weapon in the other hand for hand-to-hand combat. Nehemiah and the tribe of Benjamin preferred these smaller shields (Neh. 4:16; 2 Chr. 14:8). The buckler was also small and round, but worn on the arm rather than carried in the hand (Jer. 46:3). The larger shield was more rectangular and covered most, if not all, of the body. Often it required a shield-bearer to hold it in front of the warrior (1 Sam. 17:41). The tribes of Judah (2 Chr. 14:8[7]), Gad (1 Chr. 12:8) and Nephtali (12:34) used this type of shield with spears. The long shield was typically used in sieges. Leather, wood, and metal were typically used to make both types of shields.

Armor protected the body while allowing some mobility for hands and legs. The helmet, often made of metal but also of leather, came in a variety of shapes and was often decorated differently to distinguish enemy from comrade. Goliath (1 Sam. 17:5) and Saul (v. 38) wore bronze helmets. Though helmets were rare this early, they seem to be common later (2 Chr. 26:14; Jer. 46:4). Roman helmets were made of iron with plume or hair for decoration.

The coat of mail was necessary to protect against the arrow. It was made of small metal plates tied or sewn together in fishlike scales. They could number 700-1000 per "coat," making the "coat" heavy and expensive. David found Saul's armor heavy and awkward and did not use it (1 Sam. 17:38-39). The breastplate was a piece of metal armor worn by Greek and Roman soldiers that covered the neck and torso with a second piece protecting the back (Eph. 6:14). Leg armor or greaves covered the shins and were rare (cf. 1 Sam. 17:6).

Since warfare was common in the ancient world, the symbolic reference to weapons is frequent in the Bible. The sword is often a symbol of destruction and judgment (Exod. 5:3) and is also associated with justice (Rom. 13:4). The bow symbolized a nation's power; God breaks the bow to defeat a nation (Jer. 49:35). The power and might of God are often depicted in shattering the weapons of war (Ps. 76:3[4]). God's protection can be depicted by the shield (Gen. 15:1; Prov. 30:5). In Eph. 6:10-17 Paul exhorts the Christian to put on the whole armor of God in order to stand against the devil; the Roman soldier is his inspiration along with Isa. 59:17.

Bibliography. R. Gonen, *Weapons of the Ancient World* (Minneapolis, 1976); Y. Yadin, *The Art of Warfare in Biblical Lands in the Light of Archaeological Study,* 2 vols. (New York, 1963).

JAMES C. MOYER

WEASEL

A small carnivorous mammal of the genus Mustela, some species of which the Israelites considered unclean (Lev. 11:29). Heb. *ḥōleḏ* may derive from the common Semitic root *ḥld,* "dig, creep." Although the translation "weasel" *(Mustela nivalis)* is supported by the LXX and other versions, more recent translators have preferred the related species "mole" *(Spalax Ehrenbergi)* or "mole-rat" *(Spalax typhlus).* JOHN R. HUDDLESTUN

WEAVING

See SPINNING, WEAVING, LOOM.

WEEDS

Uncultivated nuisance plants, found in the OT at Job 31:40 (Heb. *bā'ăšâ;* NRSV "foul weeds"); Hos. 10:4 (*rōš;* NRSV "poisonous weeds"). The reference at Jonah 2:5(MT 6) probably indicates seaweed *(sûp).*

In the NT all instances of Gk. *zizánion* are found in the parable of the weeds of the field and its interpretation (Matt. 13:24-30, 36-43; KJV "tares"). This particular weed was probably darnel *(Lolium tremulentum),* a poisonous weed that as a seedling closely resembles the young wheat plants, thus making early separation of the two almost impossible (cf. Matt. 13:29). In the parable these weeds represent the children of the evil one who dwell in the world alongside the children of the kingdom. As with the weeds and the wheat, the separation of good from bad people will not take place until the judgment at the end of the age, represented in the parable by the harvest and the burning of the weeds.

WEEKS, FEAST OF

A spring agricultural festival (*ḥag šāḇu'ōṯ;* Deut. 16:10) that required a pilgrimage to a sacred site; also termed "the feast of harvest" (*ḥag haqqāṣîr;* Exod. 23:16) and "the day of the first fruits" (*yôm habbikkûrîm;* Num. 28:26). After the Babylonian Exile, the festival became associated with the making of the Sinai covenant. In Greek, the feast was termed Pentecost because it was observed 50 days after Passover and Unleavened Bread.

Originally, the pilgrimage was made to a local shrine where the farmer presented the firstfruits of the barley harvest in the early spring (generally, the month of May). Neither Exod. 23:14-17 nor 34:18-24 attempts to fix the date of this observance. Both associate it with the presentation of the firstfruits of the harvest.

Deuteronomy seeks to establish a more precise date for the observance. The pilgrimage was to be observed seven weeks (hence, the Feast of Weeks) after the sickle was first put to the grain (Deut. 16:9). Deuteronomy's emphasis on cult centralization (ch. 12) required that the pilgrimage be made to the central sanctuary. Such a lengthy absence from the field at the beginning of the harvest, however, would have been impractical. Thus, it appears that Deuteronomy turned what was initially an individual offering of "firstfruits" into a national pilgrimage that concluded the spring harvest season.

Lev. 23:15-16 also seeks to provide a more precise date for this observance. It was to be observed seven weeks from the day after the sabbath on which the sheaf of the elevation offering was presented. It is not termed a "pilgrimage" in this text. The "sheaf of elevation" is discussed in Lev. 23:9-14 and, as the chapter now stands, is associated with the seven-day observance of Unleavened Bread. The precise meaning of the phrase "on the day after the sabbath," however, is unclear, and controversy concerning its meaning continued into 1st-century Judaism. Three basic positions developed: the day immediately following Passover; the day following the sabbath that fell during the Festival of Unleavened Bread; the day following the sabbath that came after the conclusion of Unleavened Bread. The text clearly seeks to relate the Festival of Unleavened Bread and the Festival of Weeks in terms of festal observance and harvest practice. Lev. 23:15-21 lists in detail the sacrifices and offerings that are to be presented in conjunction with the observance of Weeks (cf. Num. 28:26-31).

After the Babylonian Exile, the festival became associated with the making of the Sinai covenant. This connection is in all probability based on the combination of two texts from the OT. Exod. 19:1 reports that the Israelites entered into the wilderness of Sinai in the third month. 2 Chr. 15:8-15 describes a national ritual that was observed by Asa in the third month in which the people entered into a covenant with Yahweh. Thus, the third month, the month in which the Festival of Weeks was observed, became the occasion for making covenants and oaths. The book of Jubilees (ca. 150 B.C.E.) locates a number of important covenants and oaths in the third month, e.g., Sinai (Jub. 1:1), Noah (6:10), and Abraham (14:1-20). It is probable that Jubilees understands the festival to fall on the 15th day of the third month. This also appears to be the position of the Qumran community.

Bibliography. J. van Goudoever, *Biblical Calendars,* 2nd ed. (Leiden, 1961); H. J. Kraus, *Worship in Israel* (Richmond, 1966). FRANK H. GORMAN, JR.

WEIGHTS AND MEASURES

The ascertainment of mass, distance, and capacity. While fixing exact standards to biblical weights and measures is quite tentative, approximations can be derived from three sources: the OT and NT; other ancient Near Eastern sources (notably Egyptian and Mesopotamian metrologies); and archaeology.

Linear

The cubit represents the average length of a person's forearm, from the elbow to the tip of the finger, and serves as the prevalent form of linear measurement in the ancient Near East. While this length varies considerably, evidence from both archaeology and literature suggests an average length for the common cubit of 44.5 cm. (17.5 in.). For smaller linear measurements, the cubit is divided into 2 spans, which represent the maximum distance between the thumb and the little finger as in an outstretched hand (Exod. 28:16). Thus, when Goliath is described as 6 cubits and a span tall, this converts to 2.9 m. (9.5 ft.; 1 Sam. 17:4). The cubit is further divided into 6 handbreadths (Exod. 25:25;

Units of Weight and Measure with approximate metric and English equivalents

Biblical Name[1]	Biblical Weight or Measure	Metric Weight or Measure	English Equivalent
	WEIGHT		
Old Testament:			
gerah	—	0.57 g.	0.02 oz.
beka	10 gerahs	5.7 g.	0.2 oz.
pim	1.33 bekas	7.8 g.	0.27 oz.
shekel	2 bekas	11.4 g.	0.4 oz.
New Testament:			
mina	50 shekels	571.2 g.	1.26 lb.
talent	60 minas	34.27 kg.	75.6 lb.
pound[2]	—	340 g.	12 oz.
	LINEAR		
Old Testament:			
finger	—	1.85 cm.	0.73 in.
handbreath	4 fingers	7.4 cm.	2.92 in.
span	3 handbreaths	22.2 cm.	8.75 in.
cubit	2 spans	44.5 cm.	17.5 in.
long cubit	7 handbreaths	51.9 cm.	20.4 in.
reed	6 cubits	2.7 m.	8.75 ft.
New Testament:[3]			
cubit	—	42-48 cm.	17-19 in.
fathom	4 cubits	1.8 m.	6 ft.
stadion	400 cubits	183 m.	200 yds.
mile	8 stadia	1480 m.	1618 yds.
	CAPACITY (Dry and Liquid)		
Old Testament:			
kab	4 logs	1.2 l.	1.3 qt.
omer	0.1 ephah	2.2 l.	2.3 qt.
seah[4]	2 hins	7.3 l.	2 gal.
ephah	3 seahs	22 l.	5.8 gal.
lethech	5 ephahs	110 l.	29 gal.
cor/homer	10 ephahs	220 l.	6.25 U.S. bu.
New Testament:			
modios	—	7.4 l.	.5 U.S. bu.
Old Testament:			
log	—	0.3 l.	0.63 pt.[5]
hin	12 logs	3.6 l.	1 gal.
bath	3 seahs	22 l.	5.8 gal.
homer	10 baths	220 l.	58 gal.
New Testament:			
choinix	—	.95 l.	1 qt.
modios[6]	—	38-115 l.	10-30 gal.

[1] NRSV terminology except where NRSV transposes into modern units.
[2] Gk. *lítra* also represents a unit of capacity equivalent to ca. 0.5 l. (1.13 gal.).
[3] NT linear measures differ according to whether Roman, Greek, or Palestinian units are used.
[4] Also referred to as a "tenth" (i.e., of an ephah).
[5] English units of capacity are U.S. liquid units.
[6] NRSV transposes into gallons.

2 Chr. 4:5), and 1 handbreadth consists of 4 fingers (Jer. 52:21).

For linear measurements larger than the cubit, a fathom represents the distance covered by outstretched arms (Acts 27:28), ca. 4 cubits, while a reed consists of 6 cubits (Ezek. 40:3, 5-7; 42:16-19). Consequently, the common cubit yields the following conversions: ⅙ reed = ¼ fathom = 1 cubit = 2 spans = 6 handbreadths = 24 fingers. The picture is complicated by the fact that just as there were two cubits in Egypt and Mesopotamia, we learn from Ezek. 40:5; 43:13 that a longer cubit existed which measures 7 handbreadths as opposed to 6. This longer measurement is frequently referred to as a royal cubit.

Longer distances in the OT are approximated by bowshot (Gen. 21:16), a furrow's length (1 Sam. 14:14), a day's journey (1 Kgs. 19:4; Jonah 3:4; Luke 2:44), and three days' journey (Gen. 30:36; Jonah 3:3). In the NT the stadion represents 400 cubits, ca. 183 m. (200 yds.) (Luke 24:13; John 6:19; 11:18; Rev. 14:20; 21:16). The Roman mile in Matt. 5:41 represents 1481 m. (1620 yds.).

Weights

The weight of smaller objects was ascertained most often in the ancient Near East through the use of hand-held balances. Such devices apparently consisted of a beam supporting two pans. Balances are referred to in several OT passages (Lev. 19:36; Job 6:2; 31:6; Ps. 62:9[10]; Prov. 11:1; 16:11; 20:23; Isa. 40:12; Ezek. 5:1; 45:10; Dan. 5:27; Hos. 12:7[8]; Amos 8:5; Mic. 6:11). The Israelite system of weights was largely borrowed from their Mesopotamian neighbors, as the benefits created by a standard metrology greatly enhanced commerce for all participants. Nevertheless, while the Israelites maintained the Mesopotamian terminology for their weights, they seem to have reassigned their values. The Mesopotamian system was sexagesimal, i.e., the number 60 served as their base. The Israelites seem to have incorporated a quinquagesimal system, where the base was now 50. Thus, in the Mesopotamian system one talent consists of 60 shekels, whereas in ancient Israel the talent consists of only 50.

The shekel was by far the most common weight in the Bible, and shekels of silver the most common method of payment. The Hebrew word is derived from a root meaning "to weigh." Yet, just as there were two cubits employed for linear measurements, there were at times two separate weights assigned to the shekel. The sanctuary shekel is referred to in Exod. 30:24; 38:25-26, as is the "shekel by the king's weight" in 2 Sam. 14:26. These weights seem to be slightly larger than the average weight for the common shekel of 11.405 g. (.4 oz.).

The largest weight in the Bible is the talent, consisting of 50 shekels. The word "talent" is derived from Gk. *tálanton,* "weight." The Hebrew term is *kikkār,* lit., a "round object," in reference to the frequent circular shape of the weight. For smaller weights, there is one reference to a pim as the price for sharpening iron (1 Sam. 13:19-21). A pim averages 7.8 g. (.27 oz.), roughly ⅔ of a shekel. The shekel is further divided into 2 beka, a word meaning "to split" (Gen. 24:22; Exod. 30:13-15; 38:26). Finally, 20 gerahs compose a shekel according to Exod. 30:13; nevertheless, archaeology provides evidence that throughout most of the OT period, there were 24 gerahs in the average shekel.

Far fewer references to weight exist in the NT. The Greek talent equaled 6000 drachmas (Matt. 18:24; 25:15-28). The exact weight of the mina (Luke 19:13-25) is uncertain. The pound (Gk. *lítra*) of ointment was equal to 340 g. (12 oz.; John 12:3; 19:39).

Area

The measurement of surface area is poorly attested to in the OT, and completely absent in the NT. In the OT, two references approximate land area by a yoke (1 Sam. 14:14; Isa. 5:10; cf. Ps. 129:3). The yoke probably represents the amount of land that a team of oxen might plow in a day, or just under an acre. The only other method of determining land area in the OT is by estimating the amount of seed necessary to sow it (1 Kgs. 18:32; Isa. 5:10).

Dry Capacity

The homer serves as the standard expression of dry capacity in the OT. The word "homer" is cognate to "ass," and serves as an approximation to the normal load carried by this animal. The cor is of equal value to the homer, both measuring ca. 220 l. (6.25 U.S. bu.; Ezek. 45:14). The homer/cor standard is divided into 2 lethechs (Hos. 3:2), 10 ephahs (Ezek. 45:11-14), and 30 seahs (Gen. 18:6). The omer represents a day's ration of grain, or $\frac{1}{100}$ of a homer (Exod. 16:16-18). The smallest unit seems to be the kab, referred to only once in the OT (2 Kgs. 6:25). The kab measures only $\frac{1}{180}$ of a homer. Thus we arrive at the following conversions for OT measures of dry capacity: 1 homer = 2 lethechs = 10 ephahs = 30 seahs = 100 omers = 180 kabs.

In the NT, Gk. *módios* is employed for the bushel (Matt. 5:15; Mark 4:21; cf. Luke 11:33). The modios converts to ca. 7.4 l. (.5 U.S. bu.).

Liquid Capacity

The standard measure of liquid capacity in the OT is the bath, converting to ca. 22 l. (5.8 U.S. gal.; 1 Kgs. 7:26, 38; 2 Chr. 2:10[9]; 4:5; Isa. 5:10). The word "bath" derives from the Hebrew word for "daughter," and presumably represents the capacity of water jars carried from the well (cf. Gen. 24:15, where a young Rebekah carries out this task). Larger measurements are again expressed by the homer, the same term used for dry capacity (Ezek. 45:11, 14). The liquid homer is composed of 10 baths. Units smaller than a bath include hin, measuring ⅙ of a bath (Exod. 29:40; 30:24; Lev. 19:36; 23:13; Num. 15:4-7, 9-10; 28:5, 7, 14). The hin is further divided into 12 logs (Lev. 14:10, 12, 15, 21, 24). Thus, for the OT we arrive at the following conversions for liquid capacity: $\frac{1}{10}$ liquid homer = 1 bath = 6 hins = 48 logs.

In the NT the *metrētḗs* has been estimated to contain anywhere from 38-115 l. (10-30 gal.; John 2:6). A less tentative value may be ascribed to the *choínix* (NRSV "quart"), which equals .95 l. (1 qt.; Rev. 6:6).

Bibliography. G. Barkay, "Iron Age Gerah Weights," *ErIsr* 15 (1981): 288-96, 85*; W. G. Dever, "Iron Age Epigraphic Material from the Area of Khirbet El-Kôm," *HUCA* 40-41 (1969-70): 139-204; R. B. Y. Scott, "Weights and Measures of the Bible," *BA* 22 (1959): 22-40. MICHAEL M. HOMAN

WELL

A shaft excavated to collect seepage from a water-bearing stratum beneath the ground (Heb. *bĕ'ēr, bôr;* Gk. *pēgḗ, phréar*). Unlike a spring, its water is not visible on the surface.

The idea of digging for water must have occurred upon observation of springs coming from the ground or from seeing animals scratching the surface of dry streambeds to reach water 10-20 cm. (4-8 in.) below. Today, Bedouin of the Negeb dig these shallow wells, and in some areas chains of wells *(qanats),* tapping the same aquifer in a line as long as 3-4 km. (2-2.5 mi). Wells were lined with wood, stone, or baked brick for stability, capped with stone wellheads, and protected by a stone covering the openings. Large wells, such as the one 21 m. (69 ft.) deep at Arad, served the needs of entire communities.

The prominence of wells led to the incorporation of the term in many place names (e.g., Beer-sheba), and wells themselves were given names (Gen. 26:20-22). The Song of the Well in Num. 21:16-18 reflects not only the joy of successfully digging a well, but also the leadership required to support such an undertaking. Wells were the object of strife among local inhabitants (Gen. 21:25-30; 26:18-22) and were sometimes filled in by enemies (26:18). They were located inside cities (2 Sam. 17:18-19) as well as outside (Gen. 16:7, 14; 24:11; 29:2; 2 Sam. 23:15; John 4:6-8), where they also served livestock (Gen. 29:1-10; Exod. 2:15-17). Some wells were open to strangers and a location for conversation and information (Gen. 24:10-27; 29:1-14; John 4:6-8).

"Well" is used figuratively to refer to an adulteress (Prov. 23:27), a lover (Cant. 4:15), a city (Jer. 6:7), and a source of eternal life (John 4:14).

Bibliography. R. Amiran, R. Goethert, and O. Ilan, "The Well at Arad," *BARev* 13/2 (1987): 40-44; I. Carmi et al., "The Dating of Ancient Water-Wells by Archaeological and 14C Methods," *IEJ* 44 (1944): 184-200; M. Evenari, L. Shanan, and N. Tadmor, *The Negev: The Challenge of a Desert,* 2nd ed. (Cambridge, Mass., 1982); R. J. Forbes, "Water Supply," in *Studies in Ancient Technology,* 3rd ed. (Leiden, 1993) 1:149-94; D. Hillel, *Rivers of Eden: The Struggle for Water and the Quest for Peace in the Middle East* (Oxford, 1994); V. R. Matthews, "The Wells of Gerar," *BA* 49 (1986): 118-26. JAMES H. PACE

WEST

Although the Hebrews recognized the four points of the compass (Gen. 13:14; 28:14; Deut. 3:27; Luke 13:29; cf. Isa. 11:12; Ezek. 37:9), east held the preeminent place and the other directions were often reckoned and described according to their relationship to that point. Thus west was considered the rear (Heb. *hayyām hā'aḥărôn,* the Mediterranean Sea, Palestine's western border; Joel 2:20; cf. Deut. 11:24; Josh. 15:12) and was opposite to the rising of the sun (*ma'ărāḇ;* Isa. 45:6; 59:19).

In Matthew's Gospel west and east are set opposite to one another to represent the ends of the earth from which the righteous will gather (Matt. 8:11; cf. Ps. 107:3; Isa. 43:5-6) and the universal visibility of the coming of the Messiah (Matt. 24:27).

WESTERN SEA

Another name for the Mediterranean Sea (Heb. *hayyām hā'aḥărôn;* Deut. 11:24; 34:2; Joel 2:20; Zech. 14:8).

WHEAT

The preferable cereal in food preparation and for baking. One of the crops and fruit trees with which the land of Israel was blessed (Deut. 8:8), it was domesticated early in the Neolithic period. Wheat *(Triticum;* Heb. *ḥiṭṭâ)* is a winter crop and succeeds best in high mean winter temperature and an annual rainfall of 500-700 mm. (19.7-27.5 in.). Its planting starts in late October and continues into November; wheat is ready for harvest, depending on the region, between the end of April and late May, ending with the Festival of Weeks *(šāḇu'ôṯ).*

There are several species of wheat, including einkorn (*T. monococcum* L.), emmer *(kussemet;* Exod. 9:32; *T. dicoccum Schübl.),* hard wheat (*T. durum* Desf.), spelt (*T. spelta* L.), and bread wheat (*T. Aestivum* L.). Wheat depletes the soil, thus it needs to be integrated within a crop rotation cycle, and other measures for restoration of soil fertility, such as fertilizing the soil with manure or ash, must be employed.

Wheat can be eaten raw, parched *(qālî),* or ground into flour *(qemaḥ)* for baked goods (Exod. 29:2). It can also be crushed *(gereś)* and used also in other foods such as gruel.

Bibliography. O. Borowski, *Agriculture in Iron Age Israel* (Winona Lake, 1987); J. M. Renfrew, *Palaeoethnobotany: The Prehistoric Food Plants of the Near East and Europe* (New York, 1973). ODED BOROWSKI

WHEEL

The chariot wheels (Heb. *'ôpan*) described in the Bible are of a fully developed form made from cast axles, rims, spokes, and hubs (1 Kgs. 7:33). Other types also existed, and archaeological evidence shows a degree of experimentation in Near Eastern countries indicating a local development from the bulky, solid wooden disc-wheel that was attached to the axle with the whole contraption turning as one, to the crossbar wheel which then developed into the spoked wheel able to turn on its axle. This development created a lighter wheel enabling greater vehicular maneuverability. The manufacture of these items required a large number of craftsmen with many skills: leatherworkers, metalworkers, chariot-makers, carpenters, and wheelwrights.

The wheel, however, was not used only in vehicles. Biblical references indicate that it was part of a mechanical device employed to move the 10 laver stands in Solomon's temple (1 Kgs. 7:30, 32-33), as a potter's wheel (Jer. 18:3), in the pulley system used to draw water from cisterns (*galgal;* Eccl. 12:6), and in threshing grain (Isa. 28:27-28). The wheel is also used symbolically. Rumbling chariot wheels represent images of battle (Nah. 3:2) and of God's judgment over the Philistines (Jer. 47:3), wheels of burning fire carry the throne of the Ancient One (Dan. 7:9), and Ezekiel's vision of God's throne features four crystalline-eyed wheels (Ezek. 1:15-21).

KATHARINE A. MACKAY

WHIRLWIND

Literally a twisting, swirling wind that leaves destruction in its path. Its predominant use in Scripture is symbolic or metaphoric. The word may be understood in a literal sense (2 Kgs. 2:1; Job 37:9; 38:1; Nah. 1:3), but even among these, the whirlwind is the vehicle of God's appearance in theophany (Job 38:1; Ezek. 1:4).

In most biblical citations the whirlwind is symbolic of God's swift and thorough judgment (e.g., Prov. 1:27; Isa. 21:1; Hos. 8:7; Zech. 9:14). God will scatter his foes by whirlwind (Isa. 41:16) and come like a whirlwind to bring wrath (66:15). The whirlwind of the Lord will fall grievously upon the head of the wicked (Jer. 23:19; 30:23), and a great whirlwind will be raised up against the "false shepherds" of Israel (25:32). The Lord scattered Israel among the nations by whirlwind (Zech. 7:14). In Isa. 5:28; Dan. 11:40 the symbolism is that of a clash between opposing armies.

JOE E. LUNCEFORD

WHITE

The OT does not have a well-developed vocabulary for different colors. Many words used for colors were originally descriptive rather than a name for a specific color. Heb. *lāḇān* is normally translated "white," but can also carry the meanings "light," "bright." In Lev. 13 it applies to skin diseases (cf. Exod. 4:6; 2 Kgs. 5:27, where diseased skin is likened to snow).

In both the OT and NT "white" usually conveys ritualistic purity. In the NT it occurs with christological images as a sign of purity (Gk. *leukós;* Rev. 3:4-5, 18; 7:9, 12-14) and also as a symbol of salvation and/or purity (4:4; 6:11; 19:14). However, in Rev. 6:2 the first horse, a white horse, symbolizes the suffering that any war brings; it also constitutes an eschatological punishment upon sinful humanity (cf. 19:11, 14). In general, in the book of Revelation "white" symbolizes a positive association with God Almighty, Christ, or the righteousness of Christian believers who have conquered as Christ conquered (e.g., Rev. 1:14; cf. 2:17, the white stone given to persevering Christians as token of their reception into eternal life).

THOMAS B. SLATER

WHITEWASH

A liquid plaster colored with lime and used to whiten walls. Metaphorically, "whitewash" implies hypocrisy, the concealment of inner corruption. All biblical references to whitewash (except Prov. 21:9 LXX) carry this force.

Ezekiel likens promises of peace made by false prophets to a whitewashed wall of loose stones (Ezek. 13:10-16), and Paul employs similar imagery in referring to Ananias (Acts 23:3). Jesus calls the Pharisees "whitewashed tombs" (Matt. 23:27), but the Jewish practice of chalking graves in order to avoid accidental defilement may have suggested this rich metaphor.

PERRY L. STEPP

WIDOW

Heb. *'almānâ,* generally translated "widow," means something more nuanced than simply a woman whose husband has died. Primarily on the basis of the Akkadian cognate *almattu* in Middle Assyrian Law 33, some scholars have argued that an *'almānâ* in ancient Israel was a woman whose husband and father-in-law were both dead, and who had no son. In order to accommodate this definition to biblical texts that speak of an *'almānâ* having a son or sons (e.g., 2 Sam. 14:4-8; 1 Kgs. 17:8-24), the lack of a son has been qualified as referring to the lack of an adult son with the economic means to support his mother. However, in 1 Kgs. 11:26 the mother of Jeroboam, clearly an adult man of means, is nevertheless called an *'almānâ* (cf. 7:13-14). Also, in Gen. 38 the *'almānâ,* Tamar's father-in-law Judah, is very much alive. Here Tamar is not called an *'almānâ* until Judah instructs her to return to her father's household (Gen. 38:11), so only when Tamar is deprived of her father-in-law's support is she termed an *'almānâ.* This presumes that withdrawal of the father-in-law's material support is the functional equivalent of his death.

Given that landed property in ancient Israel was normally passed down from father to son(s), a widow who had no son to inherit patrilineal property was in an economically precarious and socially vulnerable situation. Though explicitly concerned with perpetuating a dead husband's name, levirate law, which encouraged a man's kin to sire a son with his widow, benefited the widow by securing her access to landed property and hence a means of support (Deut. 25:5-10; Ruth 4; cf. 2 Sam. 14:5-7). A kinsman could, however, refuse to perform his duty (Deut. 25:7-10; Ruth 4:1-6). In the absence of levirate or another form of remarriage the biblical texts present widows as stereotypically vulnerable and thus in need of special legal protection (e.g., Deut. 10:18; 24:17; 27:19; 2 Sam. 14:4-11; Job 24:3; Ps. 94:4-7; 146:9; Isa. 10:2). While certain widows might have been able to return to their natal households for support (Gen. 38:11; Lev. 22:13), widows' access to gleaned and tithed produce provided a legislated form of social assistance (Deut. 14:28-29; 24:19-21). A widow's pledge or vow was immediately binding, without recourse to male approval (Num. 30:10).

Personified cities could be described as widows (Isa. 47:8-9; Lam. 1:1; cf. Isa. 54:4). Widowhood in these contexts may metaphorically express the vassaldom of previously independent cities. This metaphorical correspondence of widow and vassal is premised on the dubious typification of marriage as a status or condition of female independence. Rather, the widowed city (or nation) metaphor draws upon an analogy between a wife bereft of her husband and a geopolitical entity bereft of its male citizenry and/or abandoned by its male deity.

Bibliography. C. Cohen, "The 'Widowed' City," *JANES* 5 (1973): 75-81; F. S. Frick, "Widows in the Hebrew Bible," in *A Feminist Companion to Exodus to Deuteronomy,* ed. A. Brenner (Sheffield, 1994), 139-51; P. S. Hiebert, "'Whence Shall Help Come to Me?': The Biblical Widow," in *Gender and Difference in Ancient Israel,* ed. P. L. Day (Minneapolis, 1989), 125-41; R. Westbrook, "The Law of the Biblical Levirate," *Property and the Family in Biblical Law.* JSOTSup 113 (Sheffield, 1991), ch. 4; F. Yurco, "Merenptah's Canaanite Campaign," *Journal of the American Research Center in Egypt* 23 (1986): 189-215, esp. 189. PEGGY L. DAY

In the NT Luke associates Jesus of Nazareth with the prophet Elijah and with the Lord's care for widows, by having him restore to life a widow's only son (Luke 7:11-17). Widows also appear in the parables as embodiments of generosity (Mark 12:41-44) and persistence (Luke 18:1-8). The Jerusalem community provided food for widows (Acts 6:1), and the Greek Dorcas wins praise for having made clothing for them (9:39). Care of widows and orphans is a mark of religious commitment (Jas. 1:27). By the 2nd century C.E. care of widows had become an institutionalized ministry. In order to receive aid, a widow had to meet certain criteria: she had to be 60 years old, childless, with a good reputation and no relatives to support her, and willing to live a life of prayer and good works (1 Tim. 5:3-16). Community leaders thus assumed the responsibility of male relatives to regulate the sexuality of female family members and to determine the ministerial roles open to women.

KATHLEEN S. NASH

WIFE OF POTIPHAR

The wife of Joseph's Egyptian master, unnamed in the biblical account (cf. Mut-em-enet [Thomas Mann, *Joseph in Egypt*]; Zuleika [Midrash, Qur'an *Sura* 12]). Enamored with the handsome Joseph, she repeatedly tempts the virtuous hero with all the wiles of the stereotypical "foreign woman," falsely accusing him of rape (Gen. 39:6-20). Driven by sexual desire, her actions sharply contrast with the customary passivity expected of wives (cf. also Tamar, Gen. 38). Potiphar displays loyalty to his wife by having Joseph jailed rather than executed, the penalty for adultery.

Her efforts are intensified in the version of the narrative found in the Testament of Joseph (cf. T. Jos. 6:1-8; 9:1). After vowing to have her husband (Pentephres) killed so she and Joseph can marry (T. Jos. 5:1), she persuades him to rescue Joseph from the Ishmaelite merchant (14:1) and pressures him to purchase the enslaved Hebrew (16:4).

Bibliography. A. Bach, *Women, Seduction, and Betrayal in Biblical Narrative* (Cambridge, 1997).

WILDERNESS

Literally, a place not inhabited by human beings. As such, it came to be considered the natural habitation of demons (Matt. 12:43; Luke 8:29). The word does not necessarily imply a bleak, desert area, only one not inhabited by human beings.

By far the majority of biblical references are to the wilderness of Sinai in which the Israelites wandered for 40 years. At least three significant theological ideas became associated with that wilderness: covenant, miraculous provision, and judgment. It was in the wilderness at Mt. Sinai that Israel was given the law and became the covenant people of God. This apparently became idealized as a time of covenant faithfulness (Jer. 2:2). Hosea and Ezekiel predicted that God would lead Israel again into the wilderness to renew the covenant (Hos. 2:14[MT 16]; Ezek. 34:25). Concerning miraculous provision, God is said to have found "Jacob" in a howling waste of a wilderness and to have cared for him (Deut. 32:10; cf. Hos. 9:10). Israel is repeatedly exhorted to remember how God led her in the wilderness (Deut. 8:2; 29:5; cf. Amos 2:10). The provision of manna in the wilderness is referred to in Deut. 8:16 and is implied in Neh. 9:21; Hos. 13:5-6 (cf. Jer. 31:2; Rev. 12:6).

More common than references to God's covenant or provision in the wilderness are passages referring to God's judgment. Most frequently mentioned is the death of the original generation that came out of Egypt (except Joshua and Caleb) because of their lack of faith (Num. 14:22-23, 29, 32, 35; Josh. 5:6; Ps. 95:8-11; Ezek. 20:15). Additional references detail God's judgment in the wilderness during the period of the Hebrew Kingdoms and later. God threatens to make the rivers like a wilderness (Isa. 50:2). Isaiah laments that Zion has become a wilderness (Isa. 64:10). Ezekiel and Jeremiah convey a threat that God will make Israel like a wilderness (Jer. 22:6; Ezek. 6:14), and Jeremiah laments this judgment as already being realized (Jer. 4:26; 12:10). Biblical writers also spoke of God's judging foreign nations in the wilderness, or predicted that the judgment would be like a wilderness. Edom is predicted to become a desolate wilderness because of violence done to Jacob (Joel 3:19[4:19]). God promises to make Nineveh "dry like a wilderness" (Zeph. 2:13) and to abandon Pharaoh in the wilderness (Ezek. 29:5). Isaiah in particular employs the theme of judgment reversal, of making the wilderness fruitful (Isa. 35:1, 6; 41:18-19; 43:19-20; 51:3).

NT writers refer to wilderness only sparingly. Jesus' disciples question where they are to get food in the wilderness (Matt. 15:33). Paul mentions being in danger in the wilderness (2 Cor. 11:26). Most prominently, the wilderness is the locus of the ministry of John the Baptist (Matt. 11:7; cf. 3:1; Mark 1:4; Luke 7:24).

See DESERT. JOE E. LUNCEFORD

WILD GOATS, ROCKS OF THE

A rocky wilderness region near En-gedi (Heb. *ṣûrê hayyĕʿēlîm*), not far from the western shore of the Dead Sea, where wild goats have long been plentiful

(1 Sam. 24:2[MT 3]). In one of the caves in the area David had an opportunity to kill King Saul, but refused to raise his hand against the Lord's anointed.

WILLOWS, WADI OF THE

A brook (Heb. *naḥal hā'ărāḇîm*) on the Moab-Edom border, crossed by Moabite refugees carrying their belongings (Isa. 15:7). It has been identified with the Seil el-Qurahi, the lower course of the Wadi el-Ḥesā, the biblical Brook Zered. It may be the same as the "Brook of the Arabah" (*naḥal hā'ărāḇâ;* Amos 6:14).

WILLOW TREE

A plant of the genus *Salix,* generally found growing along streams and rivers. Heb. *ṣapṣāpâ* occurs only in Ezekiel's allegory of the two eagles (Ezek. 17:5), designating a willow, the twigs of which quite readily take root. Heb. *'ărāḇâ* may indicate either the willow or the similar Euphrates poplar *(Populus euphratica).* The latter is most likely intended at Ps. 137:2, for it grew commonly by the waters of Babylon. Particular species are uncertain in the other references, e.g., Lev. 23:40, where branches are used in constructing booths (Neh. 8:15) and waved to celebrate the Feast of Tabernacles (Job 40:22; Isa. 44:4).

WIND

The horizontal movement of air (Heb. *rûaḥ;* Gk. *ánemos*). Certain winds were known by reputation, such as the powerful and blighting east wind (Gen. 41:6, 23, 27; Ezek. 19:12). The west wind, generally the prevailing wind in Palestine, moderated the summer heat and brought needed rain (1 Kgs. 18:45). Likewise, the north wind supplied rain (Prov. 25:23), and the south wind conveyed scorching heat (Job 37:17; Luke 12:55).

It was believed that God controlled the wind (Gen. 8:1; Ps. 78:26). The parting of the Red Sea occurred by the wind of God's nostrils (Exod. 15:8-10). Likewise, Jesus demonstrated his power over the wind in the stilling of the storm on the Sea of Galilee (Mark 4:37-41).

Wind was a welcome partner in the threshing process, carrying away the chaff; nevertheless, both were used as a figure for the wicked, scattered by the Lord (Job 21:18; Isa. 41:16). Wind represents the emptiness of vain speech (Eccl. 1:14, 21) and the transitory nature of human existence (Ps. 78:39; 103:15-16).

Heb. *rûaḥ* is also often translated "breath," understood as the animating force of life, the breath of life, and thus "spirit." This interconnection is clear in Ezekiel's vision of the valley of dry bones (Ezek. 37:1-14). Similarly, Gk. *pneúma,* from the verb "to blow," is mostly translated "spirit." Jesus claims that all who are born of the spirit are like the wind, which blows wherever it wishes (John 3:8). Similarly, the coming of the Holy Spirit on the day of Pentecost (Acts 2:2) is described as a violent wind *(pnoḗ).*

MARK R. FAIRCHILD

WINDOW

A rectangular opening in the wall of a house. It could be opened as needed (2 Kgs. 13:17), and was often covered with a lattice through which one could look out (Judg. 5:28; 2 Sam. 6:16 = 1 Chr. 15:29; Prov. 7:6) or in (Cant. 2:9). Windows were usually small and few in number, in order to keep temperatures inside the house warm in winter and cool in summer. Some were still large enough to permit an intruder (Joel 2:9; cf. Jer. 9:21[MT 20) or a fugitive (Josh. 2:15; 1 Sam. 19:21; 2 Cor. 11:33; cf. 2 Kgs. 1:2; 9:2) to pass easily through, and so would usually be placed on upper floors if the building had more than one story (Dan. 6:10[11]; the ground floor would be suitably illuminated through the doorway). References to the "windows with recessed frames" of Solomon's temple (1 Kgs. 6:4) and Ezekiel's eschatological temple (Ezek. 40:16, 22, 25, 29; 41:16), as well as to the elaborately planned windows in Jehoiakim's house (Jer. 22:14), imply the contrasting simplicity of general window design. It has been suggested also that these latter windows, and Jezebel's window at 2 Kgs. 9:32, included balconies for public appearances, imitating Egyptian royal architecture.

Heb. *'ărubbâ* denotes an opening rather than an architectural feature per se. The image "windows of heaven" thus appears to depict wide openings through which blessing or judgment can cascade to earth (Gen. 7:11; 8:2; 2 Kgs. 7:2, 19; Isa. 24:18; Mal. 3:10).

WINE

Several types of wine and other fruit beverages were consumed regularly in the ancient Near Eastern world. These included Heb. *yayin,* the most common term for wine; *tîrôš,* "new or sweet wine"; *šēḵār,* "strong drink"; *ḥemer,* "wine (red?)"; *'āsîs,* "sweet wine"; and Gk. *oínos,* a generic word for wine. Study of the philology and etymology of Heb. *yayin* and Gk. *oínos* suggests common origin with cuneiform *uiian,* hieroglyphic *uianas,* and Mycenaean Gk. *woi-ne-wei.* All biblical forms were capable of producing intoxication (Hos. 4:11; Joel 1:5).

The origins of wine production are to be dated to the Neolithic period in the upper Mediterranean basin. The earliest wine-treading installations discovered in Israel date to the Chalcolithic period (4000-3500 B.C.). The Levant was known for its abundance of wine during the Middle Bronze Age, where according to the annals of Sinuhe, "Figs were in it, and grapes. It had more wine than water" (*ANET,* 19). Wine was traded by Solomon along with wheat, barley, and olive oil in securing lumber and other products and services for building the Jerusalem temple (2 Chr. 2:8-10).

Wine was processed from the vineyards in late summer and early fall as the grapes ripened. The production took place in eight stages: (1) producing a first must, (2) treading the grapes by foot in hewn stone vats, (3) pressing the remaining grape skins and stalks, (4) straining the must, (5) adding water to the pressed skins to make inferior wine, (6) producing concentrated must by boiling, (7) first fermentation, (8) second fermentation. Painted murals from Egypt depict the ancient process of treading, fermenting, and pouring wine into storage jars (*ANEP,* 345). Excavations at Gibeon and nearby el-Burj have evidenced hewn bell-shaped subterranean vaults used for the storage of wine during its various stages of production. A year-round temperature was maintained between 17-19° C. (63-67° F.) for quality control. Storage jars capable of holding 2-10 l. (.5-2.6 gal.) were used in the fermentation and long-term storage stages.

The produce of the vineyard was viewed by ancient peoples as a special gift from their deities (*ANET,* 48, 214). In the Bible wine was viewed as a gift from God (Deut. 7:13; 11:14) that was to be used in celebration of his goodness accompanying various sacrifices in the cult (Num. 15:5, 7), as well in communal ceremonies of marriage and the Feast of Passover (John 2:1-11; Luke 22:14-20). The drink offering of wine accompanied the various daily, monthly, and annual sacrifices of the festival calendar (Num. 28–29). New wine was among the agricultural products brought as firstfruit offerings for the priest and Levites (Num. 18:12). But the priests were not to consume wine or strong drink in the service of the cult, lest they discharge their service improperly (Lev. 10:9; Isa. 28:7). Likewise the Nazirite was to abstain from all produce of the vineyard during the period of consecration (Num. 6:1-4). The tithe of new wine was to be consumed in the central worship place in a rite of communal celebration by the people (Deut. 12:15-18).

Numerous metaphors using wine reflect upon the goodness of life. One who fears the Lord will have a wife like a fruitful vine (Ps. 128:3). God provides the wine that gladdens the heart (Ps. 104:15), but he withholds it as a form of judgment (Isa. 16:10; 24:7-13). Drinking wine and eating bread were symbols of peace and prosperity (2 Kgs. 18:31-32; Prov. 3:10). Israel's restoration from judgment and captivity is envisioned as a time of abundant produce from the vineyards (Jer. 31:12; Joel 2:19, 24; Amos 9:13-14).

Excess consumption of wine leading to drunkenness is condemned summarily in the Bible. Abuse of wine evidences a lack of wisdom (Prov. 20:1), which can lead to mindless confusion (23:30-35), violence (4:17), or poverty (21:17; 23:20-21). Drunkenness leads to dissipation (Eph. 5:18), arrogance (Hab. 2:5), and abuse of the poor (Amos 6:6). The devastating effects of drunkenness from wine are a common metaphor for God's judgment (Jer. 25:15; Rev. 18:3). Hence, leaders in the Church are to be those who do not indulge in much wine (1 Tim. 3:3, 8; Titus 1:7; 2:3).

Bibliography. O. Borowski, *Agriculture in Iron Age Israel* (Winona Lake, 1987); R. Frankel, *The History of the Processing of Wine and Oil in Galilee in the Period of the Bible, the Mishnah, and the Talmud* (diss., Tel Aviv, 1984); *Wine and Oil Production in Antiquity in Israel and Other Mediterranean Countries.* JSOT/ASORMS 10 (Sheffield, 1999); J. B. Pritchard, *Gibeon, Where the Sun Stood Still* (Princeton, 1962); A. F. Rainey, "Wine from the Royal Vineyards," *BASOR* 245 (1982): 57-62; J. M. Renfrew, *Palaeoethnobotany: The Prehistoric Food Plants of the Near East and Europe* (New York, 1973).

R. Dennis Cole

WISDOM, WISDOM LITERATURE

Dictionaries define wisdom as the ability to make sound judgments on what we know, especially as it relates to life and conduct. The wise do not value the quantity of knowledge by itself, but the ethical and moral dimensions of how we evaluate human experience and act on it. The sages of Israel lived in a time of much less scientific knowledge of the universe and its operations, and depended more heavily on traditional understandings and ways of acting than modern society does, so that they worked from a somewhat broader concept of wisdom. On the one hand, they saw wisdom as a serious intellectual pursuit of knowledge about the world and its rules of order and the dynamics behind its mysterious operations; on the other, they sought the proper human response to all dimensions of this world, especially in terms of understanding themselves in relation to their human nature and to God the Creator. To the ancient mind, the universe was profoundly interpersonal, and all things were the product of either the personal will of the deity or of human decisions.

Wisdom Books

Three biblical books are clearly identified as the product of wisdom thinking: Proverbs, Job, and Ecclesiastes (Qoheleth). Two books that occur among the deuterocanonical books of the Roman Catholic and Orthodox canons should also be included: Sirach (Ecclesiasticus) and the Wisdom of Solomon. Scholars note close connections to many elements of these books in other parts of Scripture as well. The following have been generally recognized as showing wisdom similarities: Gen. 2–3, the story of sin in creation; Gen. 37–46, the tale of Joseph; Deut. 1–4, the general introduction to the book; Deut. 32, the Song of Moses; 2 Sam. 9–20, the Succession Narrative of David; 1 Kgs. 3–11, the model story of Solomon; Amos, considered as a prophet from wisdom circles; Ezek. 28, metaphors of the king of Tyre; the Song of Songs, an extended meditation on creation and covenant based on old wedding songs; certain Psalms, namely Pss. 1, 19, 49, 73, 111, 112, 119, and others that contain expressions and themes similar to Proverbs; and the book of Daniel, in which the first six chapters describe the hero as a sage. Scholars have noted wisdom echoes here and there in most of the prophetic books, esp. Jeremiah and Isa. 1–39.

Much of the language found in the secondary examples may be merely a part of the general intellectual culture, so defining wisdom characteristics should be based on information taken from the five full wisdom books. However, two texts in the prophets strongly suggest that wisdom was identified with a definite body of learned scholars who performed a role that corresponded to the roles of priests and prophets in seeking the divine will: "Come let us make plots against Jeremiah — for *torah* shall not perish from the priest, nor *counsel* from the wise, nor the *word* from the prophet" (Jer. 18:18; cf. Ezek. 7:26). Certainly, in the talmudic period, rabbis were considered successors to the sages

WISDOM, WISDOM LITERATURE

of the Bible. Even Jesus is treated in part as a wisdom teacher (Matt. 11:19; 13:54; Luke 2:40, 52; Acts 6:3).

Characteristics

Although the books of wisdom are quite different in form and style, they possess certain elements in common:

1. Little interest in the history of Israel and its specific tradition of revelation: the torah as a body of laws, the covenant, the possession of the land, and the temple or cult.
2. Strong interest in the order of the universe and its rules of cause and effect, the nature of time, the limits to human mastery of the world, and the ability to find God revealed in creation.
3. A willingness to explore the difficult and painful mysteries of life experience: death and afterlife, divine reward and punishment, the inequality of fate and destiny in people's lives, the apparent arbitrariness of divine blessing.
4. The inscrutability of God's intentions and plans.
5. The education of the young in the tried and true ways of tradition.
6. An interest in developing skilled administrators, leaders, and good citizens.
7. Cultivation of a life of prudent behavior and virtue.

Wisdom books feature certain literary genres in order to express their concerns:

1. The proverb, found prevalently in Proverbs and Sirach, and to a lesser degree in Qoheleth.
2. The dialogue or disputation, the major genre of Job, and prominent in the Wisdom of Solomon.
3. The didactic lesson, often directed to the student, as in Prov. 1–9 and Ecclesiastes.
4. The metaphor or allegory, often in the form of hymns or poems (e.g., Ezek. 28; Prov. 8, 9; Wis. 7; Sir. 24). Also common and scattered throughout Wisdom Literature are rhetorical questions, numerical sayings, torah psalms, and a teacher's summons to heed wisdom lessons.

Ancient Setting

Two settings need to be distinguished: the ancient Near Eastern context, and the specific role of wisdom in Israel's faith. Wisdom was not a unique possession of Israelite religion. Both Egyptian and Mesopotamian societies cherished wisdom and left a considerable body of wisdom works that often show remarkable similarities to biblical texts. Included are Mesopotamian dialogues on suffering and theodicy similar to Job and Qoheleth, collections of proverbs that appear among the earliest known writings in the world (between 3000 and 2000 B.C.E.), as well as fables, treatises on the value of sages and scribes, and didactic instructions to the young. Passages are often very close to Israelite thought. For example, the Words of Ahiqar advises, "Withhold not thy son from the rod, else thou will not be able to save [him from wickedness]" (*ANET*, 428), which is close to Prov. 13:24. Indeed, the same thought appears in Prov. 23:13, which seems to come from imitation of an Egyptian collection of Proverbs, the Wisdom of Amenemope. Since Egyptian literature is even richer than Mesopotamian in wisdom books, it seems highly likely that Israel, like many other smaller nations in the Near East, was influenced by the international intellectual currents that moved freely from the Nile to the Tigris rivers and incorporated the treasures of wisdom into their own thinking in a way that they could not with the specific religious cultic texts of these peoples. Scholars have long pointed to clear parallels between the Wisdom of Amenemope and Prov. 22:17–24:2. The translators of the NAB have even rediscovered a reference to Amenemope by name in Prov. 22:19. If so, it illustrates that Israel was not isolated in its cultural exposure and understanding but participated willingly in the thought world of the Near East except where specific polytheistic claims had to be refuted and rejected in light of its monotheistic faith development.

Almost all of the important wisdom themes in Israel's writings are also known in Egyptian or Mesopotamian works. This suggests that international or universal wisdom played a role in Israel's faith that served understanding of God's ways but did not directly challenge the central tenets of Israel's religious institutions represented by torah and prophecy. Scholars usually point to two separate social settings for Israelite wisdom: the home and the royal administration. Many proverbs probably originated before the dawn of writing, and seem to reflect the typical advice of parents to children in preparing them for life (e.g., the lesson on laziness in Prov. 6:6-11). Others are directed at parents about educating children (cf. Prov. 10:1). Perhaps many of the proverbial sayings of the prophets (e.g., Isa. 28:23-28) come from daily life.

The vast majority of our current wisdom texts seem to be cultivated in schools. Kings in ancient societies were considered to be especially endowed with divine wisdom to rule, and this is prominent in the story of Joseph in Gen. 37–46 and the portrait of Solomon. The necessity of a fully literate court and government apparatus able to deal on the international scene gave impetus to the new kingdom of David to foster special training modeled on typical Near Eastern patterns for its governors, ambassadors, accountants, and scribes. Although schools are rarely if ever even hinted at in the Bible, writing and mastering traditional literature, esp. proverbial maxims, seems to have formed the core of most ancient education for the elite. The close links of biblical wisdom to that of other nations stems from the need for a common ground of discourse and cultural understanding between peoples. Wisdom is often associated with courtiers and royal counselors (cf. esp. 2 Sam. 15–17; Dan. 1–6). The term "counsel" associated with the wise in Jer. 18:18; Ezek. 7:26 is most easily identified as political advice for decision makers. But wisdom is also associated with teachers (Prov. 9:9-12; Jer. 8:8-9), insightful women (2 Sam. 14:1-20, 20:16-22), skilled craftspersons (Exod. 31:2-6), and even magicians (Exod. 7:11, 22). Thus it seems to be a wider category than merely political wisdom. It stands for skill learned from others, and is associated above all with training and schools. Sirach is identified as a teacher in the later wisdom tradition of the 2nd century, and the speaker of Proverbs assumes the role of teacher throughout.

Religious Values

Although wisdom is commonly associated with the noncultic side of Israel's life, this does not mean it is simply pragmatic and a-religious. All ancient religion is about a personal god or gods who make decisions about the world of humans. This translates into wisdom's concern with the mystery of the universe: certain questions reflect a problem about God, whether one is a member of Israel's covenant or a foreign polytheist. How do the rules of creation work? How is divine providence manifested for people to understand? Why does suffering and death not respect piety and moral uprightness? The search for order, and determining the proper role of human ambition, and coping with the limits of knowledge consume wisdom teachers. These are all part of the conviction that God guides the universe and that discovering God's will is crucial to human welfare. Because of this, wisdom can be described variously as a "tree of life" (Prov. 3:18) or the first created being in God's plan for the world (8:22; Sir. 24). Qoheleth can affirm that God gives us what we have in order to enjoy it and do God's will (Eccl. 7:15-19); Proverbs tells us to trust God with all our heart (Prov. 3:5), and Job rejoices that God can be found and seen even if beyond human understanding (Job 42:2-6). Prov. 1–9, 31 also develop an elaborate metaphor of wisdom as a woman whom a young scholar is to love and embrace. From there it was a small step to identify Lady Wisdom with the Torah itself in the postexilic period (Sir. 24:23).

Two themes stand out for the religious role of wisdom. The first is the choice between the way of evil and the way of uprightness. The idea of two ways for us to choose permeates Proverbs and stands as the theme statement for the book of Psalms in Ps. 1. It offers human freedom the option of moral adherence to God's will as manifested in the goodness of creation and in Israel's revelation. References, sometimes indirect, to blessings received from choosing faithful and trusting obedience to the God of the covenant and torah are woven throughout the wisdom books. Second, one regularly encounters the expression "fear of the Lord (is the beginning of wisdom)" (e.g., Prov. 1:7, 29; 9:10; 14:27; 15:16; 19:23; Eccl. 12:13). Like the NT "God-fearers" (Acts 13:26), it describes faithful believers who possess a fundamental orientation to God's will. But the concept also includes cultic practice, an awareness of God's presence, proper moral behavior, observance of torah, and just plain humbling oneself before the Almighty. Like the way of uprightness, an attitude of fear of the Lord encompasses one's entire life and focuses a person's behavior on doing God's will.

"Wisdom" as a major category gave way to Torah study in postbiblical Jewish reflection, but it was never excluded from the canon of the Hebrew Scriptures because it is identified with the restless human search for God, respect for the mystery of God's freedom, and awareness of the vast moral sphere of decision making beyond formal cultic worship. Even Qoheleth the sceptic could be brought into this vision by adding a final editorial note (Eccl. 12:13-14).

Bibliography. J. Crenshaw, *Old Testament Wisdom* (Atlanta, 1981); J. Gammie and L. G. Perdue, eds., *The Sage in Israel and the Ancient Near East* (Winona Lake, 1990); R. Murphy, *The Tree of Life*, 2nd ed. (Grand Rapids, 1996); K. M. O'Connor, *The Wisdom Literature*. Message of Biblical Spirituality 5 (Wilmington, 1988). LAWRENCE BOADT

WISDOM OF SOLOMON

One of the most important deuterocanonical wisdom writings. The Greek (LXX) tradition attributed this work to Solomon: "the Wisdom of Solomon." Although Solomon is not mentioned by name in this book, it is obvious that the author is speaking in the persona of that famous king. The prayer in ch. 9 is an expansion of the devout portrayal of Solomon in 1 Kgs. 3:6-9. The work is also known by the title it received in the Latin tradition, "The Book of Wisdom." Thus, it is a pseudepigraph, and its canonicity was questioned in antiquity. Again, Jerome and Augustine were divided on the point; it was a favorite book of Augustine, and eventually was considered as part of the Bible in the Roman Catholic and Orthodox churches.

The date of the book cannot be fixed exactly. The evidence depends on judgments concerning the influences that can be detected in it (Philo?). The range of dating goes from late in the 1st century B.C.E. to the first half of the 1st century C.E. From the internal evidence of the book itself we know that the author was a Jew who was well acquainted with the traditions of his people. He worked with the LXX translation of the OT, in many cases carrying over its terminology. The passion with which the Jewish tradition is presented (e.g., chs. 10–19) is another indication of Jewish origins. This suggests that the author should probably be sought among the large and prosperous Jewish community of Alexandria in Egypt. It is therefore a work from the Jewish Diaspora. At the same time, the author displays a remarkable knowledge of the Greek language and culture. Despite the efforts of some scholars in the past to claim a plurality of authors (or even that it is a translation from an Aramaic original!), there is general agreement that it is the work of one person.

As will be evident, wisdom (Gk. *sophía*) is a key notion in the work; it occurs more than 50 times. But it shows striking differences from the accepted "wisdom" books (Proverbs, Job, Ecclesiastes, and Sirach). It has no collections of proverbial sayings or wisdom poems. There is nothing of the impassioned speeches of Job or the lectures of his three friends. The acerbity of Qoheleth's thought is absent (although some have erroneously thought to see Qoheleth's reflection in the presentation of the views of the wicked in ch. 2). A very distant similarity to Sirach might be found in the fact that both include the history of Israel within their ambit. And yet no one would deny that this is a "wisdom" book, even if of an unusual sort.

Literary Genre

Recent scholarship has intensified efforts to discover the literary form, particularly by similarities to Hellenistic literature. Some scholars have described it as an exhortation, or protreptic. This designation is somewhat loose in that it allows for the employment of other forms such as the diatribe, the problem *(aporia)*, and *syncrisis* or comparison. Others have looked to the epideictic genre described by Aristotle, which includes the encomium or praise. These studies describe the book in its relation to Hellenistic culture. But these theoretical determinations do not contribute much to the actual understanding of the text of Wisdom. More important is the recognition of the *inclusio* (the repetition of a word or group of words to mark off a unit within the work). More helpful, too, is the fairly obvious partition of the book in three sections, based upon content. However, this rough division passes over details; e.g., 6:22 is clearly the introduction to chs. 7–9. The divisions can be summed up as Wisdom's gift of immortality (chs. 1–6); Solomon's description of Wisdom (chs. 7–9); the work of Wisdom in history, especially the Lord's dealing with the people during the Egyptian plagues (chs. 10–19). Ch. 10, describing Wisdom's saving activity through the ages, serves as an introduction to the specific events of the Exodus.

Contents

The first part (chs. 1–6) opens with an address to kings, "rulers of the earth," who also will appear again in 6:1. Such an address is not easy to understand (Solomon addressing earthly kings?). The entire thrust of the book is Jewish and rests upon Jewish traditions, so it must be aimed at a Jewish audience since only they could absorb it. Some insist that a gentile audience is also targeted, at least in the sense that the work is a sort of propaganda (but the treatment of Gentiles hardly favors that view). Rather, it seems to be a simple literary fiction, prompted by the royal dignity of the putative Solomon. Such a move has a precedent in the role of Qoheleth (cf. Eccl. 1:1, 12), and perhaps in Egypt it provided some status for the Jewish minority.

From the outset it is clear that we are dealing with Jewish wisdom and the ethical ideals associated with it. One is to live the virtuous life that is associated with wisdom, that "kindly spirit" (1:6; lit., "philanthropic"), a spirit that fills the world (a Stoic idea) and thus has knowledge of human conduct. *Parallelismus membrorum,* a familiar feature of Hebrew poetry which aligns two similar or contrasting ideas, marks the opening lines and continues throughout the work. Almost immediately the author confronts the issue of death and offers his own view of it. It is not of God's making, but is the "friend" of the wicked who covenant with it. This is clearly spiritual or eschatological death (1:13-16). The same idea is found in 2:23, where it is said that God made humans for *aphtharsía,* or incorruptibility, in his image, but death entered the world through the devil, and those who belong to his "company" *(merís)* experience it (2:24; 1:16). The author is aware of physical death, which afflicts everyone, but his interest is in the death that "destroys the soul" (1:11). "Righteousness is undying" (1:15). Here is the essence of immortality: a right relationship to God. It can be destroyed, and the wicked, so vividly described in ch. 2, are the living proof of that. But of itself, this relationship to God is undying. Thus the author seems clearly to explain immortality from what may be called a biblical point of view — not from the (Greek) point of view of the human constitution or composite (body/soul). He could have easily been inspired by the typically Greek idea of the natural immortality of the soul, of which he was surely aware, but he never reasons from the intrinsic nature of the soul to its immortality. For him immortality was far more than prolongation in time; it was a gift to the righteous. He is almost disinterested in the fate of the wicked. They are destined for suffering (4:19), but their real fate is revealed in their cry, "fools that we were!" (5:4), when they see the just man whom they persecuted accepted among the sons of God, the divine family (v. 5).

Woman Wisdom is the subject of the second part of the work (chs. 7–9), but the author does not lose sight of his supposed royal audience (1:1). It is precisely to kings that "he will tell what wisdom is and how she came to be" (6:22; cf. v. 9). In a typical Greek sorites he shows how wisdom leads to a kingdom (6:17-20). Wisdom must be prayed for (7:7), but she is more priceless than any human possession. With her come lessons in all the mysteries of the physical works, for she is the "fashioner of all things" (7:22; cf. Prov. 8:30). She also teaches the four Greek cardinal virtues: temperance, justice, prudence, and fortitude (8:7). She is to be wooed, loved, taken as one's bride. Hence Solomon prayed to the Lord for the gift of wisdom — the only way of acquiring her: "Who has learned your counsel, unless you have given Wisdom and sent your holy spirit from on high?" (9:17).

The story of the plagues (chs. 10–19) is prefaced by an unusual presentation of Wisdom as savior in history, from Adam to Moses (ch. 10). Then begins a series of comparisons (Gk. *sýnkrisis*) between the experience of Israel and the plagues that afflicted the Egyptians. Certain principles guide the presentation: Israel benefits "through the very things by which their enemies were punished" (11:5, 16). This point is then illustrated by several antithetical diptychs; e.g., Israel receives water from the rock, in contrast to the Egyptians who suffer from the Nile being changed into blood. There are also some deliberate digressions, such as the worship of nature and idolatry (13:1–15:17). The final comparison deals with the fate of the Egyptian firstborn and the freeing of Israel (18:5–19:22). The ending is somewhat abrupt, but the author followed his plan.

Bibliography. J. M. Reese, *Hellenistic Influence on the Book of Wisdom and Its Consequences.* AnBib 41 (Rome, 1970); D. Winston, *The Wisdom of Solomon.* AB 43 (Garden City, 1979); A. G. Wright, "Wisdom," *NJBC,* 512-22.

ROLAND E. MURPHY, O.CARM.

WISE MEN

Figures from Matthew's Infancy narrative who visit the infant Jesus in Bethlehem (Matt. 2:1-12). These wise men (Gk. *mágoi*) from "the East" are led to Judea sometime after Jesus' birth in order to "pay him homage." Having been led by a star "at its rising," they inquire of Herod the Great the exact location of the "king of the Jews." Herod, fearful of a rival king, consults the chief priests and scribes regarding the location of the birth of the Messiah. Herod responds by calling for the wise men "secretly," inquires of them the time of the star's appearance, and requests them to find the child Jesus and report back to him so that Herod, under a ruse, might himself pay homage. The wise men in turn set out to find Jesus in Bethlehem, being led by the star. They pay homage to the child and offer gifts of gold, frankincense, and myrrh. The story concludes with their departure for their "own country by another road," since they are warned in a dream not to return to Herod. This infuriates Herod, who responds by slaughtering young male children in and around Bethlehem in an attempt to kill the child Jesus (Matt. 2:16-18).

In Matthew's overall narrative, the pericope (Matt. 2:1-12) functions as the first of two acts that depict the recognition of Jesus as "king of the Jews" and Herod's sinister response to it (vv. 13-23). The story of the wise men is a necessary component to Matthew's narrative since their visit results in Jesus and his family fleeing to Egypt to avoid Herod's wrath. It is likely, too, that Matt. 2:1-12 anticipates the passion of Jesus where he is again identified as "King of the Jews" (27:11, 29, 37) and is not recognized as such by his own people. The visit of the wise men also demonstrates Matthew's continued interest in the OT, alluding to Ps. 72:10-11, 15; Isa. 60:5-6.

It is no accident that the wise men are portrayed as Gentiles. As such, they are the first to worship Jesus, who is both the son of David and the son of Abraham, according to Matthew's genealogy (Matt. 1:1). While Gentiles are the first to pay homage to Jesus, his own people are the first to seek to destroy him, which is seen on various subsequent occasions in Matthew's Gospel. Both narratively and theologically, the story is significant in that, as royal delegates from a foreign land, the wise men are the ones who worship the child Jesus, while Herod, the royal representative of Jesus' land and people, attempts to destroy this rival king.

Various efforts have been made to identify the "wise men" as astrologers, interpreters of dreams, or magicians. Most scholars identify them as astrologers since their visit is in response to the appearance of a star, whose "eastern" home is possibly Parthia or Persia, Babylon, or the Arabian or Syrian deserts.

Bibliography. R. E. Brown, *The Birth of the Messiah,* rev. ed. (New York, 1993), 165-201, 608-10; W. D. Davies and D. C. Allison, *The Gospel according to Saint Matthew* 1. ICC (Edinburgh, 1988), 224-56.

ROBERT A. DERRENBACKER, JR.

WITCHCRAFT

The practice of sorcery (cf. Exod. 22:18) or necromancy (1 Sam. 28) for divination or the manipulation of (generally evil) spirits (cf. Deut. 18:10-11).

See MAGIC; MEDIUM, WIZARD.

WITNESS

One who helps establish the truthfulness of a matter by testifying firsthand about what was seen or heard. The necessity of recollecting and reiterating what happened implies that witness bearing includes a historical dimension. Although this activity originated in legal contexts, its vocabulary (Heb. *ʿēḏ;* Gk.*mártys*) quickly expanded to other social and religious settings.

The Mosaic law ensured truthfulness by requiring two or three witnesses to convict a person of a criminal offense and obligating them to lead in the execution of capital sentences (Deut. 17:6-7). Furthermore, it made bearing false witness punishable by *lex talionis* (Deut. 19:15-19).

Important transactions could be certified orally before the elders at the city gate or in writing by the signatures of witnesses. Even an inanimate heap of stones or an altar might serve as commemorative witnesses to a covenant (Josh. 22:26-27; 24:27). The tablets of the Law were preserved in the ark of testimony as a perpetual witness to the Israelites' covenant with Yahweh; the nation, in turn, was a witness to the Gentiles of Yahweh's saving activity. Since all actions are seen by God along with heaven and earth, which are personified as ever-present observers, they can be called to witness even hidden deeds.

The NT speaks of witnesses in a legal sense with reference to the trial of Jesus (Mark 14:63) and of Stephen (Acts 7:58), and it carries over the requirement of multiple witnesses to cases of church discipline and the claims of Jesus, whose witness was confirmed both by his Father and his works. Of special importance is the testimony of the apostles and other eyewitnesses who had seen the risen Jesus (Acts 1:22). Driven by deep conviction and missionary zeal, they thrust their lives into persuading the world of not only the historical events of the gospel but also their theological significance, which they regarded as no less factual: it was God who raised Jesus from the dead, and by believing in his name one could receive forgiveness of sins. Some of them witnessed unto death and in this way prepared the word *mártys* to become a technical term for a martyr (cf. Heb. 12:1). In addition to their human witness, the Holy Spirit confirms that believers are God's children (Rom. 8:16).

Bibliography. A. A. Trites, *The New Testament Concept of Witness.* SNTSMS 31 (Cambridge, 1971).

DALE F. LESCHERT

WIZARD

See Medium, Wizard.

WOE

An onomatopoeic exclamation (Heb. *hôy;* Gk. *ouaí*), generally of lamentation, expressing an outburst of emotion. In the OT *hôy* is used to describe funeral laments (1 Kgs. 13:30) and to attract attention (Isa. 55:1). It predominately occurs in prophetic speeches, usually in a series of such utterances, and signals an announcement of impending destruction. The distinguishing feature of the woe oracle is the opening interjection, "Woe to . . . ," which is followed by the description of evil deeds and a prediction of divine judgment (Isa. 5:8-10; Mic. 2:1-5). Some scholars attribute the origin of the woe oracle to the cultic practice of curses (Deut. 27:15-26); others, to the funerary lament. In the NT "woe" functions as prophetic denunciation (Matt. 11:21; Jude 11) or lamentation. It appears predominately in the Synoptic Gospels.

Kenneth J. Archer

WOLF

A large member of the canine family, *Canis lupus.* The Bible refers to several canine species, including dogs, foxes, jackals, hyenas, as well as wolves. Most biblical references to wolves (Heb. *zĕ'ēḇ;* Gk. *lýkos*) are symbolic and allude to their savage nature. Thus, the tribe of Benjamin is described as a ravenous wolf (Gen. 49:27), and Israel's princes are likened to wolves tearing their prey (Ezek. 22:27; cf. Zeph. 3:3).

In the NT wolves exclusively symbolize people who are a threat to the Christian community. The followers of Christ are portrayed as sheep in the midst of wolves (Matt. 10:16; Luke 10:3). In Jesus' discourse on the good shepherd, the wolf is one who snatches sheep from the fold (John 10:12). False prophets are concealed in sheep's clothing, but they are really ravenous wolves (Matt. 7:15). Paul's parting fear and warning to the Ephesians was that, after his departure, savage wolves would come in among them, not sparing the flock (Acts 20:29)

Mark R. Fairchild

WOMEN IN THE ISRAELITE CULT

The primary term for priest in the Hebrew Bible is *kōhēn,* which appears only in the masculine. The feminine *khnt* occurs in cognate languages and even Rabbinic Hebrew, but not with the Bible's meaning, and each reference must be judged on its own merits.

A distinctively cultic role, though without a title, was enacted by Miriam, sister of Moses and Aaron. In a controversy with Moses (Num. 12), she acted together with Aaron, the eponymous priest, so one could assume that she was acting in a priestly role also. The fact that she was punished with leprosy shows the significance of her actions. Exod. 15:20 shows Miriam, here entitled "prophetess," leading women in music and dancing, a cultic role. Here it is emphasized that she was the sister of Aaron, and, indeed, sang a psalmlike utterance that was the first verse of the psalm in Exod. 15:1b-18, a psalm of praise for deliverance as often found in the Psalter.

No women had a worship role inside the temple, but immediately outside were some whose description as perhaps the "ministering women" or "serving women" may not be a title. (The root *ṣb'* is a general term meaning simply "work, serve.") In Exod. 38:8 they have bronze mirrors, and in 1 Sam. 2:22 (if the same persons) they sinfully lay with the sons of the priest Eli. No details of their practices are given; in Exod. 38:8 their mirrors may indicate beauty, but whether for seduction or not one should not say.

The *gĕḇîrâ,* "queen mother," had a high place in court, at times equaling the authority of the king, at least ceremonially (1 Kgs. 2:19; Jer. 13:18), even crowning the figure called King Solomon in Cant. 3:11. 1 Kgs. 15:13 indicates a cultic milieu, for among other suppressions of foreign cult practices, King Asa had his mother removed from the *gĕḇîrâ*-ship because she had an abominable image made for Asherah.

Women often appear in the roles of singer, musician, and dancer, and most of these are cultic. The female participants were probably among the lesser offices. The OT mentions at least 25 different types of musical instruments of the horn, lyre, and percussion types, some of which were played by women. In Exod. 15:20 Miriam plays a *tōp̄,* "drum" or "tambourine," and Jephthah's daughter also plays this instrument (Judg. 11:34) in a story that may be the etiology of a lost cult; both women also dance. Male and female singers are mentioned together in postexilic sources (Ezra 2:65; Neh. 7:67).

Deborah sings her magnificent poetry (Judg. 5:2-31), and Hannah prays (1 Sam. 1:10). Tradition calls the beautiful psalm of praise attributed to Hannah (1 Sam. 2:1-10) a prayer, but the verse form shows that it is poetry and therefore sung. Women appear in temple processions (Ps. 68:25[MT 26]), which continue into the "sanctuary." Those who give the joyful tidings that the enemy has been overcome are also women (Ps. 68:11-12[12-13]).

Cultic weeping and mourning also took place. A woman is to teach her daughter and neighbors a lament over the fall of Jerusalem (Jer. 9:20[19]), and an earlier verse (v. 17[16]) indicates a group of mourning women. This same *qînâ* ("lamentation") form is found in the book of Lamentations. There the weeping is done by someone who sings of women's concerns, for Jerusalem the "daughter of Zion," and this may indicate that the book, or a large part of it, was chanted by women. Though the temple as a worship place does not appear in the book, spiritual elements are found all through.

Women also had roles in foreign and forbidden cult practices. Though their sitting and weeping for Tammuz (Ezek. 8:14-15) is described as "an abomination," it was done at one of the gates of the temple. This was a late variant of a 2nd- or even 3rd-millennium rite borrowed from the Babylonians, reflecting the yearly return of Tammuz/Dumuzi to the netherworld. Women also made a special recipe of cakes for the queen of heaven (Jer. 7:18). Her identity has been much discussed, but she probably was one of the Canaanite goddesses of the Asherah, Ashtoreth, or Anat family, ultimately reflecting a Babylonian Ishtar cult. Women also wove *battim* (RSV "hangings," but lit., "houses" or "vestments") for the Asherah (2 Kgs. 23:7). This weaving was done in the house of the *qědēšîm,* a controversial cultic figure; this apparently foreign title occurs in both masculine and feminine forms.

The picture of Palestinian and Israelite women would not be complete without mention of the prolific clay figurines, usually female and usually naked. These have been found from the 8th millennium on, but increasingly in Middle Bronze–Early Iron levels. The figures usually hold the breast area, and the pubic region is emphasized by an incised triangle. Later they come to be stylized in pillar form. Scholars disagree about whether these figurines represent a goddess or her votary, and both are possible. Early attempts to identify these with a known goddess have largely been abandoned. Because the figurines are usually found in houses, this may reflect a "people's religion," not recorded in the Bible. They may also represent the "images" so frequently denounced (e.g., Exod. 20:4).

The forbidden area of divination was rejected out of hand by Hebrew orthodoxy, yet all the evidence points to its prevalence throughout history. Both men and women appear in these roles, usually vaguely translated "witch" or "sorcerer/ess" (Deut. 18:10-11; 2 Kgs. 21:6; Jer. 27:9; Lev. 19:26, 31). A few titles provide a general idea of their practices: necromancy, dream interpretation, divination by arrows, whispering, and serpent handling.

Bibliography. P. A. Bird, "The Place of Women in the Israelite Cultus," ed. P. D. Miller, P. D. Hanson, and S. D. McBride, *Ancient Israelite Religion* (Philadelphia, 1987), 397-419; R. A. Henshaw, *Female and Male: The Cultic Personnel: The Bible and the Rest of the Ancient Near East.* PTSMS 31 (Allison Park, 1994): K. van der Toorn, *From Her Cradle to Her Grave: The Role of Religion in the Life of the Israelite and the Babylonian Woman.* Biblical Seminar 23 (Sheffield, 1994); C. J. Vos, *Woman in Old Testament Worship* (Delft, 1968).

Richard A. Henshaw

WOOD

Wood (Heb. *ʿēṣ;* Gk. *xýlon*) was an important commodity in biblical times. Timber was used in the construction of buildings such as Solomon's temple, which contained a variety of woods including cedar, algum, cypress, and olive wood (1 Kgs. 6:14-36). To acquire cedar, cypress, and algum timber, Solomon contracted with King Hiram of Tyre (2 Chr. 2:8[MT 7]). Ezekiel provides further evidence of active trading in wood products, including the luxurious ebony (Ezek. 27:15). Wood was also an important construction item for houses of the common people. Branches could be used for huts, and lumber provided supports for the walls, roof, doors, and windows. Carts and litters were also made of wood (1 Sam. 6:14; Cant. 3:9), as were seafaring vessels. Noah constructed his ark of gopher wood (probably cypress; Gen. 6:14).

Wood is mentioned in many cultic contexts. *Šiṭṭîm* wood (probably acacia) figures heavily in Exodus, where it is the material for the ark of the covenant (Exod. 25:10), the supports for the tabernacle (26:18), and the altar (27:1). Wood is prescribed for sacrifices (Lev. 1:8), and cedar for cleansing (14:4). Isaiah condemns worshippers of wooden idols (Isa. 44:14-20).

In ancient times Israel had more forest land than today. Cooking fires were one of many everyday uses for wood, although deforestation may have required people to search out alternative, cheaper kindling such as dung and thorns. Wood was also material for agricultural implements (2 Sam. 24:22), household vessels (Lev. 15:12), and musical instruments (1 Kgs. 10:12).

Megan Bishop Moore

WORD

In the OT the main term for "word," Heb. *dāḇār,* means an articulate and intelligible utterance. It is used more frequently in such phrases as "the word of the Lord" or "the word of God" than in other technical senses, though it also appears in reference to human speech (Ps. 19:14[MT 15]). When not literally referring to human verbal expression the term has mainly a metaphoric meaning, implying that God, e.g., sets forth a message, command, instruction, or announcement. Sometimes this word comes as an hypostasis of God, i.e., as a divine agent acting as an emission of God's power. At other times it is described as a personalization of God's power in the speech of a human agent such as a prophet. It was a short step from such usage to identification of the spoken or written word of the prophets and apostles as the word of God.

The NT generally uses Gk. *lógos,* which means essentially the same as *dāḇār* in the OT. The term normally implies a dialogue between the sender and receiver of the word. In Scripture the dialogue is between humans, or in the case of the word of God it is usually between God and a person or persons. As in all communication, the sender may intend something different than the receiver hears or perceives. Words carry meaning freight which is varied with the contexts and constructs in which they are used. The Bible frequently notes that when the word of God is sent forth humans do not always "have ears to hear" or "hearts to receive" the word. This is a problematic factor in the divine-human dialogue, often associated in Scripture with human failure or disfunction. This often becomes the virtual definition of sin in the Bible, namely, broken communication and hence alienated covenant relationship. When God's word is heard and heeded it has the power to save. The word in both testaments, particularly when associated with divine expression, is powerful to create, redeem, or judge. In the prologue to the Fourth Gospel the Word is personalized as the agent of God in creating the world, sustaining it in divine providence and illumination, and redeeming it through incarnation in Jesus

Christ, who is therefore described as the transcendent and preexistent Logos.

See Logos. J. Harold Ellens

WORKS

Acts of God and deeds of humankind in keeping God's commandments.

Works of God

In the OT the "work(s)" (Heb. *ma'ăśeh, mĕlāḵâ*) of God are his deeds in creation, salvation, and judgment. The Genesis narrative describes God's work in creation (Gen. 2:2, 3). Writers occasionally employ anthropomorphic language to describe "the work(s) of his (your) hands" (Job 14:15; 24:19; Ps. 8:6[MT 7]) and "the work of your fingers" (Ps. 8:3[4]) with reference to the creation. In other instances (cf. Ps. 145:4, 9-10, 17; Isa. 5:12), writers speak of God's works in creation and deliverance. Godly people are to "meditate" on God's good works (Ps. 77:12[13]; 143:5) and to "remember" them (77:11[12]).

In the NT the works of God become a major topic in the Gospel of John. In keeping with John's consistent depiction of the Son as the one who encountered a hostile world that did not "receive" him (John 1:10-11), the writer portrays a world that is divided between those whose "works are evil" (7:7; cf. 3:19) and the One who does the works of the Father (8:41). Jesus declares, "My Father is still working, and I also am working" (John 5:17; cf. v. 36), and further, "The works that I do in my Father's name testify to me" (10:25; cf. 4:34; 10:32). The Father gave Jesus this work (John 5:36; 17:4), and now the Father dwells in him as he performs these works (14:10). As a result of the work of Jesus, those who believe in him will do even greater works (John 14:12). This view, therefore, is fully integrated within John's understanding of the believing community as the people who have "beheld his glory" (John 1:14) in the works which the Son performed.

Although Paul employs Gk. *érgon/érga* primarily for human activity, he also refers to the drama of salvation as God's unfinished work. The Christian brother is the work of God: "Do not, for the sake of food, destroy the work of God" (Rom. 14:20). The spiritual and ethical transformation of the community is the work of God (Phil. 1:6). His demand to "work out your own salvation" is accompanied by the assurance that "it is God who is at work in you" (Phil. 2:13).

Human Works

Acts of obedience to God are commonly described as works. Paul shares the Jewish tradition's positive evaluation of good works (cf. Neh. 13:14; Matt 5:16; 11:19) in his comments about moral conduct. God will judge each one according to his works (Rom. 2:6, 7; cf. 1 Cor. 3:13, 15; 2 Cor. 11:15). Consequently Paul challenges his readers to abound "in every good work" (2 Cor. 9:8; Col. 1:10; 2 Thess. 2:17). Indeed, he describes Christian service as "the work of the Lord" (1 Cor. 15:58; 16:10) or "the work of faith" (1 Thess. 1:3; cf. 5:13).

Although Paul challenges his communities to be engaged in good works, he speaks negatively of "works of the law" (sometimes abbreviated to "works"; e.g., Rom. 3:27; 4:2, 6; 9:12, 32; 11:6), especially in the polemical situation of Galatians and Romans, where he argues for the admission of Gentiles into community without the entrance requirement for circumcision. To make circumcision an entrance requirement for salvation is to insist on works of the law. The phrase "works of the law," which is only rarely attested in the Judaism contemporary with Paul, is apparently the equivalent of the "deeds of Torah" that are mentioned in the Dead Sea Scrolls. These "deeds of Torah" consist of the fulfillment of the covenantal obligations that are required by the law. Because of the threat of assimilation among Jews who lived among Gentiles in the two centuries immediately prior to Paul, the boundary markers that most clearly distinguished Jews from their neighbors — circumcision, the sabbath, and the purity laws — took on special significance in Jewish polemics. In Galatians and Romans Paul argues from the experience of his converts (Gal. 3:1-5) and from Scripture (cf. 3:6-29; Rom. 4:1-25) that one is justified, not by works of the law, but by faith (Rom. 3:28; 4:3-4; Gal. 2:16; 3:2, 5-9). Thus in this polemical context faith is the normal corollary to works. In most instances the object of faith is Jesus Christ (Gal. 2:16b, 20; 3:26; cf. Rom. 10:9-10). However, the Greek phrase *pístis Iesoú Christoú,* which most translations render as "faith in Jesus Christ," may refer instead to the faithfulness *of* Jesus Christ as the corollary to human works. In either case, Paul insists that no one is saved by those boundary markers that he describes as works of the law.

In the Epistle of James faith and works are again set in contrast. James insists that "faith without works is dead" (Jas. 2:17) and that one's faith is demonstrated by one's works (v. 18). In contrast to Paul (Rom. 4:3-5; Gal. 3:6-10), James insists that Abraham was justified by his works (Jas. 2:21-23). James refers to works of mercy, not the "works of the law" described by Paul. He challenges his community to be engaged in the "pure religion" (Jas. 1:27) that consists of adherence to the love command (2:8).

Bibliography. J. D. G. Dunn, "The Theology of Galatians," in *Pauline Theology,* ed. J. M. Bassler (Minneapolis, 1991) 1:125-46; E. P. Sanders, *Paul and Palestinian Judaism* (Minneapolis, 1977).

James W. Thompson

WORLDVIEW

A way of looking at reality; the basic assumptions a people have about the world. A worldview is derived from people's experience of their social and physical environments, and provides a more or less coherent way of thinking about the world. It serves in turn as the cognitive basis for the people's interaction with their social and physical environments. The worldview of the Israelites included assumptions about the self and its relation to other selves, gender, causality, space, and time.

The distinction between the self and one's environment is fundamental to all worldviews, yet how the self is understood is culturally specific. The majority of people in the United States, e.g., define the self in individual terms; the self is coterminous with the body and the individual's behavior is largely determined by personal goals. Although pervasive throughout Western culture, individualism is rare in the history of humankind. The Israelites in contrast defined the self in collective terms. The self belongs to a group and self-identity is embedded in the group. The person's social behavior is largely determined by the goals of the group. Individual desires and values are subordinated to the desires and values of the group.

In collectivist societies such as Israel, other selves (including their resources such as land and animals) are classified according to what group they belong. All in-group members share similar goals and values, whereas the goals of the out-group will be unrelated, inconsistent, or even hostile to those of the in-group. An Israelite's self-identity was embedded foremost in his or her kin group. Other in-groups in which an Israelite was embedded include professional (priests, prophets, sages), class (administrators, landowners, elders, "people of the land"), geographical (clans, tribes), and political groups (Israelite, Judahite).

The Israelites' assumptions about gender were rooted in their understanding of procreation and the contribution that males and females each make to the process. Although the biological differences between males and females in sexual reproduction have no meaning in and of themselves, the Israelites defined these differences in terms of agriculture. The man is like a farmer and the woman arable land. Just as a man sows seeds into the soil and thereby causes the earth to produce vegetation, a man can sow his seed (semen) into a woman causing her to give birth to a child. In both cases, the man provides what is essential for life: seed and semen. The man's semen, like seed, determines the character or quality of what will be produced; it contains all the essential characteristics of the child that will be born. The woman, who is like the soil, nurtures to full development the seed planted within her. She contributes nothing essential to the makeup of the newborn child. Her role in procreation is dependent upon the man's seed.

This metaphorical relationship is presented in the Yahwist Creation myth which, among other purposes, served to symbolize and thereby reinforce the Israelite construction of gender. The man (Heb. *hā'āḏām*) is born from the arable land *(hā'ăḏāmâ),* anticipating human births from Eve, the mother of all living. Yet the arable land is dependent upon the man to till and sow it; the land remains barren without the man's contribution, and for this reason he was created (Gen. 2:4-7). Similarly, the woman *('iššâ)* is taken from the man *('îš),* constructing a metaphor between the woman and the land (Gen. 2:21-23). Like the arable land, the woman will give birth to new life, and with the acquisition of knowledge the woman knows to bear children. However, she is also dependent upon her husband to sow seed in her, just as he plows and sows the field (Gen. 3:16-19). This understanding of gender is also articulated in the numerous references identifying a man's "seed" with his descendants. The Israelites' assumptions of gender were expressed through their social values of honor and shame.

The Israelites' assumptions about causality are best described in contrast to the assumptions made by most Westerners, which include both personal and natural causality. The Israelites, in contrast, perceived only personal causality. All change in the world was attributed to personal agents — to either humans (and animals by personification) or the gods. Natural events were manifestations of divine activity. One common example is that the Israelites attributed childbirth and infertility to God's agency rather than natural causes; God opened and closed the wombs of women (cf. Gen. 29:31; 30:2).

The Israelites' assumptions about space were shaped by their experience of theophany. God's appearance gave orientation to space and introduced qualitative distinctions within space. Two complementary orientations to space can be detected. According to a horizontal orientation, God's life-sustaining activity in creation is located at the center of the world and diminishes in its significance and effect as one moves to the periphery. God's theophany makes the land at the center holy in a cosmological sense. The land is characterized by divine order; it is the point from which the creation originated. The divine sacredness of the center stands in contrast to the periphery which is experienced as demonic and diabolical. The periphery is chaotic, hostile to life. It is symbolized by both the desert and the sea which form the boundary between the land of the living and the netherworld. The periphery is a sterile region inhabited by demons, wild animals, and sea monsters. Humans are unable to dwell there apart from divine assistance.

According to a vertical orientation, the world is oriented around a cosmic mountain. The base of the mountain is the ordinary world of human beings. As one ascends to the summit, one reaches heaven, the dwelling of God. Thus, the Israelites built their temples and shrines on mountain peaks. Beneath the mountain lies the underworld, the realm of the dead. Often a spring issues from the base of the mountain, originating from a source of water in the underworld. The mountain serves to unite heaven, the earth, and the underworld, making communication between the three realms of the world possible.

The Israelites' assumptions about time can best be described as a present orientation. In contrast to most Westerners who look toward the future to achieve goals and solve problems, the Israelites focused on the present. Rather than simply a moment in time, the present encompasses a range of human experiences: all that one has experienced in the past relative to what one is currently experiencing and what one is about to experience as a result of the past and the present. The present is repetitive, marked by regular intervals, during which the tasks of life — working, eating, sleeping, playing — are carried out. As a result, the present is subject to environmental constraints. The times of planting and harvesting, e.g., are determined by the ecological conditions of a region. Times of eating and defecating are necessitated by the biological demands of the human body. The rainy winter months were typically a period of reduced outside activity.

Beyond the present is an imaginary time. It is outside the scope of current human experience, and as such, is not subject to the constraints of human experience. Imaginary time is the time of monsters and mythological creatures, heroes and heroic exploits, miracles and disruptions of the rhythms of nature. From the perspective of the Israelites, imaginary time was the exclusive domain of God. The possible worlds of the past and the future are made possible by God; they are outside of human control. As the time of God, the past and the future give warrant to Israelite society in the present. Present concerns and aspirations are projected onto the past and the future. The Israelites turned to the past in order to explain certain customs, such as the redemption of the firstborn child from sacrifice (Gen. 22:1-18; Exod. 13:11-16), or to justify social demands, such as the laws of the covenant. Israel also enforced the demands of the laws by turning to the future with prophetic warnings of God's coming judgment.

Bibliography. R. J. Clifford, *The Cosmic Mountain in Canaan and the Old Testament.* HSM 4 (Cambridge, Mass., 1972); M. Kearney, *World View* (Novato, Calif., 1984); B. J. Malina, "Christ and Time: Swiss or Mediterranean?" *CBQ* 51 (1986): 1-31; R. A. Simkins, *Creator and Creation: Nature in the Worldview of Ancient Israel* (Peabody, 1994); H. C. Triandis, "Cross-Cultural Studies of Individualism and Collectivism," in *Cross-Cultural Perspectives,* ed. J. J. Berman (Lincoln, 1990), 41-133.

RONALD A. SIMKINS

WORM

Small, creeping creatures such as larva worms (Heb. *tôla'aṯ, tôlē'â*). The most common types represented in the Bible are those larvae or maggots active in the decomposition process. Worms ate the manna that the Israelites left until morning (Exod. 16:20), as well as the plant that made shade over the head of Jonah (Jonah 4:7). In a list of curses, vineyards will be devoured by worms (Deut. 28:39).

Biblical authors used the worm as a symbol of something humble, worthless, and useless (Ps. 22:6[MT 7]; cf. Isa. 41:14). It also represented death: the end of every human being is worms and maggots (Job 21:26; 25:6; Isa. 14:11). In postbiblical literature some authors used the literary topos "eating by worms" as a proper punishment for those who defiled God, his temple, and other sacred objects and places (e.g., 2 Macc. 9:9). ISAAC KALIMI

WORMWOOD

Any of several species of a shrublike plant of the genus *Artemisia,* known for its bitter taste (LXX "bitterness"). Biblical references to the plant (Heb. *la'ănâ;* Gk. *ápsinthos*) are metaphors for bitterness and sorrow, evoking the unfortunate circumstances including warning against an illicit affair with an unprincipled woman (Prov. 5:4), the bitterness of God's judgment on sin (Jer. 9:15[MT 14]), judgment, subjugation, and homelessness (Lam. 3:15, 19), and injustice (Amos 5:7; 6:12). Wormwood is sometimes used with "gall" (Lam. 3:1; cf. Deut. 29:18[17]; Jer. 9:15; 23:15; NRSV "poisonous water"). In the book of Revelation a star named Wormwood falls from the heavens and turns one third of the inland waters bitter and poisonous, causing many to die (Rev. 8:10-11). T. J. JENNEY

WORSHIP, ISRAELITE

The liturgical life of ancient Israel can be broken down into three main rubrics:

1. Fixed calendrical moments of worship. These include the three great pilgrimage festivals (Exod. 23:14-17; Deut. 16) and other minor and major festivals tied to the calendar (Lev. 23; Num. 28–29).
2. Moments of worship that celebrate great foundational moments in the history of Israel. These include the inauguration of a high priest (Lev. 8) or a king (1 Kgs. 1:32-37), the celebration of the covenant (cf. Josh. 24), and the procession of the ark into the temple (Ps. 24:7-10; Ps. 132).
3. Irregular occasions for worship that pertain to the individual or small clan. These include episodic moments of lamentation (2 Sam. 3:31-35) or celebration (1 Sam. 20:28) as they related to smaller sodalities; and similar irregular occasions for the entire community such as defeat (lamentation, Josh. 7:6) or victory (celebration, 1 Sam. 18:6-8) in battle.

Seasonal Festivals

The seasonal festivals can be further subdivided into two groups: the three major pilgrimage feasts (Exod. 23:14-17; Deut. 16): Unleavened Bread/Passover, Weeks (or as it is sometimes known, Pentecost), and Booths; and the minor calendrical feasts that did not involve such pilgrimage (Lev. 23; Num. 28–29): sabbath, new moon, New Year, and perhaps the Day of Atonement.

Though the Bible fixes quite specifically in which season and month these festivals are to occur, it provides no explicit guide as to how the Israelite months coincided each year with the same season. Clearly, the preexilic calendar, which seemed to function on a lunar basis, had some method of intercalation that prevented these feasts from straying too widely from their seasonal rubrics. Unlike Islam, where festivals can swing across the seasons, in Israel they were stable. This is important to grasp, for already in the early Second Temple period the manner by which one fixed these seasons was hotly contested with two options available: a precise solar calendar or a lunar calendar with periodic yet fixed intercalations of the months so as to achieve calendrical stability.

The three major pilgrimage feasts were linked

to key moments in the Israelite agricultural calendar. Unleavened Bread (Deut. 16:1-8) marked the harvest of the first new grain. Nothing leavened was permitted during this feast. The feast lasted seven days and was intimately associated with the festival of Passover. Because of this close association, the Feast of Unleavened Bread was frequently "historicized," meaning that its agricultural origins were displaced in favor of a symbolic association with the Exodus from Egypt (Deut. 16:3). The Feast of Weeks (Deut. 16:9-12) occurred some seven weeks (50 days, so the term "Pentecost") afterwards. This festival lasted only a day and received no historical association for most of the biblical period. Its significance was, at origin, purely agricultural. It was a festival honoring the firstfruits, most importantly those of the summer wheat harvest. Over time this festival became associated with the giving of the Torah at Mt. Sinai. This had already taken place in the Priestly source (cf. date given in Exod. 19:1), and the associations grow richer and deeper in the Second Temple period. The Feast of Booths (Deut. 16:13-15) is a seven-day festival like Unleavened Bread and marks the end of the agricultural cycle and the (hoped for) onset of the winter rains. This festival is certainly the most complex of the three. At one level the dwelling in booths represents an agricultural practice of setting up temporary dwellings in the field as the harvest was brought in (cf. Deut. 16:13). Yet because Israel herself lived in such "booths" during her trek from Egypt to Canaan, the festival also sought to re-create that moment (cf. Lev. 23:42-43).

Other Seasonal Celebrations

The moments of sabbath and new moon were known to be occasions of liturgical celebration, though they did not have the force of an all-Israelite pilgrimage festival. Biblical texts which describe sabbath observance are rare, though the laws prescribing its existence are early and widespread. The "rest" experienced on the sabbath day (Gen. 2:2) was often compared to the rest experienced in the temple (Ps. 132:14). In the Holiness code, sabbath observance and respect for temple law are often paired (Lev. 19:30). One can aver that at some deeper level sabbath observance in the private home stood in some sort of analogical relationship to public festivities within the temple. Festivals on the day of the new moon are attested but very briefly.

The celebration of the New Year — known in the Priestly source as "the first day of the seventh month" (Lev. 23:24) — was a major event. Yet our sources are also meager in terms of what exactly happened on that day. Part of the problem concerns just which month was considered the first. The Bible contains conflicting evidence for a spring and fall New Year. The Priestly source favors the fall, yet the calendar of ancient Israel suggests that the "first day of the first month" came in the spring (Nisan). Some scholars have suggested that our knowledge of this festival can be expanded by presuming that the New Year was the occasion for celebrating the institution of kingship, both divine and human. For these scholars, many of the Royal Psalms have their origins in this festival and provide some degree of detail about the liturgical practices on this day.

The Day of Atonement, according to P (Lev. 16), is the most solemn holy day of ancient Israel. Only on this day could the high priest enter the holy of holies and offer incense. It was also the day on which the sins of the entire community were transferred to a goat which was then driven out into the desert, bearing away the sin of the people. According to the final form of P, the date was fixed in the fall and it fell between New Year's day (or the first day in the seventh month) and Booths. Some have argued that, in origin, this holy day was an occasional rite that was enacted whenever the community believed the temple complex required cleansing from its various impurities. At some latter date this rite of temple cleansing was combined with the practice of personal penance and the day became a fixed rite of general purgation, both of persons and the temple. This fixed day of temple cleansing became known as the Day of Atonement. Our entire knowledge of the rite comes from the very terse laws about the rite in the Pentateuch; the holy day itself was passed over in silence in the books of Samuel and Kings.

Foundational Moments

Some of the most poignant liturgical moments in the Bible are associated with the foundational moments of great institutions (the building of the temple, establishment of the covenant) and with their close relatives: moments when important figures are installed into office (coronation of kings, installation of the high priest).

Priesthood

The rites associated with the priests in general and the high priest in particular revolve around the graded sanctity of the temple environs. One of the major reasons for the institution of the priesthood in Israel is the belief that the presence of the deity in the temple can be the source of both security and danger. Because of the high moral and cultic purity required of those who would draw near to the deity (cf. Pss. 15, 24), Israelite culture took great care in maintaining rigorous control over who was allowed access to the inner localities of the temple. The rites associated with these moments of ordination included anointment with oil, sacrificial cleansing, and adornment with special garments (Lev. 8). The anointment with oil served to mark the high priest as especially holy and entirely given over to the deity. The garments of the priests matched those places within the temple that they were allowed access. The most glorious of the priestly vestments, those put upon the high priest, matched very closely the draperies that adorned the inside of the temple (the holy place and the holy of holies). For it was only the high priest, on the Day of Atonement, who was allowed access to the most sacred room in the entire temple, a moment of great opportunity for the priest and the people he represented, but also a moment of great foreboding if the individual who so entered was not properly prepared. The other priests were vested with garments during a ceremony of installation; these garments matched the fabrics found in those parts of the temple to which they were allowed entry.

Kingship

For kings, the ceremony of installation or coronation was quite different. On this day they too were anointed with oil and vested in ceremonial garb. But in addition, they were frequently renamed and "adopted" by the deity as "a son of God" (cf. Ps. 2:7). This high mythic status was thought to be conferred by the act of anointing with oil on the day of coronation. Some have argued that this moment of coronation, though formally limited to the inauguration of a king to office, was celebrated in a yearly festival devoted to God's kingship. The evidence for such a celebration comes mainly from other ancient Near Eastern sources and the belief that just such a festival stands behind numerous Psalms which praise the deity as king.

Covenant Renewal

The theme of covenant establishment and covenant renewal no doubt had deep liturgical resonances in ancient Israel. This theme, however, has occasioned considerable debate among scholars as to when such a festival would have had its inception. Some scholars believe that the modeling of Israelite religious identity according to a covenant charter began in the earliest period of Israelite history under Hittite influence, whereas others believe that this influence began much latter, during the Neo-Assyrian period. In any event, it is clear that the book of Deuteronomy in particular, and the Deuteronomic history in general, has imagined that Israel's worship life was characterized by periodic reflection on her covenantal charter. This is very evident in the words of Moses himself when he charged the Israelites to renew the covenant in Shechem after they had crossed into the Promised Land (Deut. 27). This charge of Moses is not only fulfilled at Shechem, but becomes the subject of a rather long narrative (Josh. 24). This particular episode has given numerous scholars evidence for positing other such covenant renewal ceremonies during the reigns of Israel's various kings. Perhaps it was a festival similar to this that eventually precipitated into the Feast of Weeks and gave to this festival the Sinaitic identity it came to have in the Second Temple period.

See RITUAL.

Bibliography. M. Haran, *Temples and Temple-Service in Ancient Israel* (Oxford, 1978); I. Knohl, *The Sanctuary of Silence* (Minneapolis, 1995); H.-J. Kraus, *Worship in Ancient Israel* (Richmond, 1966); G. E. Mendenhall, *Law and Covenant in Ancient Israel and the Ancient Near East* (Pittsburgh, 1955); S. Mowinckel, *The Psalms in Israel's Worship* (Nashville, 1967).

GARY A. ANDERSON

WORSHIP, NEW TESTAMENT

Worship in the NT usually means expression of praise or thanksgiving (Luke 17:15-16). Sometimes it implies obeisance as an attitude for supplication (Matt. 8:2). In any case, it is the appropriate human response to the magnificent glory of God.

Summons and encouragement to worship abound (Col. 4:2; Heb. 13:15). The centrality of worship of Christians is evident in a book such as the Gospel of Luke, which opens and closes with scenes depicting worshippers (Luke 1:8; 24:52-53) and contains 21 specific references to people glorifying, praising, or giving thanks to God. Likewise, the book of Revelation is inundated with images of worship.

Origins

Christian worship seems to have developed as an adaptation of what had come to be practiced in the diaspora synagogues during the intertestamental period. This is not surprising since the first Christians were Jewish and probably continued for a time to worship in the synagogues themselves until this became impossible (John 9:22; 16:2). Even though Acts portrays the earliest disciples of Jesus continuing to worship in the Jerusalem temple (Acts 2:46), the sacrificial cult associated with that institution came to be viewed as obsolete in NT writings. This is due not only to the historical fact that the temple was destroyed in 70 C.E. before much of the NT was written, but also to the theological proposition that Jesus' death on the Cross had a redemptive effect making subsequent sacrifices unnecessary (Heb. 9:11-12, 24-26).

Synagogue worship, however, was primarily verbal (a "Service of the Word"), and the NT depicts Christian worship from the first as also involving participatory action in a sacred meal. Indeed, Acts 2:46 depicts even those believers who continued to worship in the temple as also gathering regularly for "the breaking of bread." This meal appears to have had features in common with both Jewish festivals (such as Passover) and Hellenistic symposia (social banquets). Paul contrasts the Christian celebration with pagan meals in 1 Cor. 10:14-22.

Description

The book of Acts describes Christians gathering to worship daily (Acts 2:46) but also notes a preference for "the first day of the week" (20:7; cf. 1 Cor. 16:2). Locations for worship appear to be deemed irrelevant by some NT texts (Matt. 18:20); when locations are designated, the most typical gathering places are homes of community members (Acts 2:46; 1 Cor. 16:19). As for content, the NT never describes a Christian worship service in any detail. Reconstruction of such services or reflection on their general nature employs three sources.

First, the NT writings incorporate materials that were no doubt used in early Christian worship. These include hymns (Luke 1:46-55), doxologies (Rom. 16:25-27), prayers (Matt. 6:1-13), and credal or confessional statements (1 Cor. 15:3-5). The existence of such materials indicates a fairly high degree of liturgical development.

Second, although no liturgy for Christian worship is ever prescribed, elements of worship are often mentioned. These include characteristic features of the Jewish synagogue service: prayer (1 Tim. 2:1-2, 8), singing (Eph. 5:19), teaching (Acts 2:42), preaching (Phil. 1:15-18), collection of offerings (1 Cor. 16:2), and public reading (1 Tim. 4:13). The latter was transformed early in that new writings came to be read alongside the Scriptures, including works that eventually became part of the NT (1 Thess. 5:27; Rev. 1:3). In some locations, these standard elements of worship were supplemented by the practice of such spiritual gifts as speaking in tongues and prophesying (1 Cor. 14:24-33). Also mentioned frequently are two chief rituals of Christian worship, baptism (Matt. 28:19; Rom. 6:1-11) and the eucharistic meal (Mark 14:16-26; 1 Cor. 11:23-26). Other rituals include foot washing (John 13:3-15), anointing with oil (Mark 6:13; Jas. 5:14), exchanging a kiss of peace (1 Pet. 5:14), and the laying on of hands, which may have been associated with prayer (Acts 28:8), reception of the Spirit (8:17), or ordination (13:3; 1 Tim. 5:22).

Third, more explicit descriptions of worship services are found in writings shortly after the NT period, such as the Didache (ca. 100) and the first Apology of Justin Martyr (ca. 155). These documents list several of the features mentioned above in what appear to be fixed chronological orders. Justin's Apology is merely descriptive, but the Didache attempts to define or regulate what it regards as normative procedure.

Theology

The NT takes over the concern of OT prophets that worship be integrated into the life of faith. Thus, passages that prioritize mercy over sacrifice (Hos. 6:6) or decry worship with lips but not heart (Isa. 29:13) are quoted in new contexts (Matt. 9:13; Mark 7:6-7). Genuine worship is not merely for show (Matt. 6:1-18) but involves surrender of the self to God in faithful obedience (Rom. 12:1).

The most distinctive theological characteristic of NT worship is the centrality of Christ as its rationale, mediator, and ultimate object. First, what Christ has done becomes the greatest of all reasons for praising God (1 Cor. 1:4). This perspective colors Luke's narrative of the Crucifixion, where the death of Jesus itself becomes an occasion for glorifying God (Luke 23:47).

Next, we read that thanks is given to God not only "for" Jesus Christ but "through" Jesus Christ (Rom. 1:8; Heb. 13:15). A common theme in John's Gospel is that the Father is glorified through the Son (John 17:4). Since God is unseen Spirit, those who would worship in Spirit and in truth must worship the God made known through the Son (John 1:18; 4:24).

Finally, Christ is depicted as one who is himself worthy of receiving worship (Phil. 2:9-11; Rev. 5:11-14). The Gospel of Matthew relates its story of Jesus from this perspective, presenting Jesus as a recipient of worship nine times during his life on earth (e.g., Matt. 2:11; 14:33; 28:9). In light of Matt. 4:10, such worship is not merely homage or respect but, in the mind of this Evangelist, evidence that Christ is now accorded what is normally the exclusive prerogative of God.

Christ-centered worship is definitively historical and eschatological in orientation. It simultaneously reflects upon the revelation of God in the life and ministry of the earthly Jesus and anticipates the consummation of all things. This dual focus is evident in much of the worship material preserved in NT writings, including hymns (Phil. 2:6-11) and the eucharistic liturgy (1 Cor. 11:23-26).

See RITUAL.

Bibliography. F. Hahn, *The Worship of the Early Church* (Philadelphia, 1973); D. P. Peterson, *Engaging with God: A Biblical Theology of Worship* (Grand Rapids, 1992). MARK ALLAN POWELL

WRATH

Of the four words for anger in the OT, the most common is *'ap̱*. While it may be etymologically related to the word for "snorting," an anthropomorphism of God snorting in anger is not indicated by usage. In the LXX and NT the major word groups are related to Gk. *thymós* and *orgḗ*. The former may have had the sense of an outburst of anger (2 Cor. 12:20), but this distinction is not consistent in biblical usage, and usually the words are used interchangeably.

In the ancient world there were competing theories as to how the deity should act. The Greco-Roman myths frequently portrayed the gods as angry and vengeful. While performing the proper sacrifices might turn away divine anger, the gods were unpredictable and hard to appease. Divine wrath is a driving theme in Virgil's *Aeneid*, Aeschylus' *Prometheus Bound*, and Ovid's *Metamorphoses*. Meanwhile, the deity of the Greek philosophers was perfection itself, and perfection was thought by many to exclude the vice of anger. The hellenized Jewish thinker Philo believed that anger was inappropriate for God, and that statements about God's wrath were merely an accommodation to the readers. Similarly, some modern readers have taken the wrath of God as a carryover from a mythological worldview, or a metaphor of the automatic consequences of sin.

The God of the Bible, however, is unlike both the pagan gods and the impassible God of the philosophers. He experiences real anger against the wicked. In fact, the vast majority of the references to wrath in the OT (save in Proverbs and Ecclesiastes) concern God's anger against Israel for its sin, especially for idolatry. Warnings abound not to "provoke Yahweh to wrath." During the Exodus, Israel habitually drew God's anger, e.g., at Meribah (Ps. 106:32) and Kadesh (29:8). Other nations too may feel the heat of God's wrath (Ps. 2:5; Jer. 50:13).

Still, God is unlike the pagan gods. Since he becomes provoked by offenses against his revealed will, God's anger is neither capricious nor unforeseeable (contra human anger in Prov. 14:17a). Unlike the impotent idols, God is capable of following up his wrath with punishing deeds (Hos. 13:9-11). Nevertheless, he also reveals himself as "merciful and gracious, slow to anger and abounding in steadfast love. He will not always accuse, nor will he keep his anger forever . . ." (Ps. 103:8-9; cf. Isa. 57:15-17; Jer. 3:12). God is swift to forgive and to show mercy (Jonah 4:2; Mic. 7:18). By the same token, he transcends mere human emotion, never neglecting justice or forgetting offenses (e.g., Mal. 1:4). When Jesus displayed his anger in the clearing of the temple, it was an incarnate display of the wrath of Yahweh in Isa. 56:7: "My house shall be called a house of prayer."

By definition, God's anger is always righteous anger. Human beings may experience righteous anger too if they view sin from God's viewpoint (cf. Exod. 16:20b) while leaving ultimate justice in God's hands (Rom. 12:19). God instituted human government to execute, albeit provisionally, the divine wrath against evildoers (Rom. 13:4-5).

The wrath of God may be represented by metaphors: the pouring out of anger from a bowl (cf. Ezek. 7:8; Rev. 16:1), or the trampling of the wicked as if they were grapes in a wine press (Isa. 63:1-6; Rev. 19:15). But the most common symbol is heat (Zeph. 3:8) or a consuming, burning fire (2 Thess. 1:8), the fire that culminates in the lake fire.

The wrath of God is delayed until the last times. John the Baptist warned his hearers to escape the eschatological wrath of God (Matt. 3:7 = Luke 3:7). At the end of human history will come the "day of his wrath" (Lam. 1:12; Zeph. 1:18). This may be synonymous with the day of the Lord, which brings darkness and judgment on the rebellious (Joel 1:15).

The "wrath of God" comes to the fore in the gospel as the equivalent to God's judgment and the antithesis of salvation and life (John 3:36). Rom. 1:18 even states that God's wrath is revealed in the present (cf. Eph. 2:3), but the outpouring of his anger will take place in the future (Rom. 2:5). The death of Christ provides a "propitiation," a sacrifice that turns away God's wrath both presently (Rom. 3:25; 5:9; cf. 1 John 2:2; 4:10) and in the eschaton (cf. 1 Thess. 1:10). Revelation in particular focuses on God's anger against rebellious humanity (e.g., Rev. 14:10).

Bibliography. G. C. Berkouwer, *Sin* (Grand Rapids, 1971), 354-423; F. Büchsel, "thymós," *TDNT* 3:167-68; H.-C. Hahn, "Anger, wrath," *NIDNTT* 1:105-13; H. Kleinknecht et al., "orgḗ," *TDNT* 5:382-447.

Gary S. Shogren

WREATH

A garland of leaves or flowers worn around the head. In the OT the term appears for certain only in Isa. 28:1, 3, 5 (Heb. *ʿăṭārâ*), where the wreath worn by the drunkards of Ephraim will be trampled underfoot when God judges Israel. Otherwise, various English versions translate several Hebrew words as "wreath" or "wreathen (work)," referring to decorative features of the high priest's regalia (*ʿăḇōṯ*; Exod. 28:14-25; 39:15-18; NRSV "chains," "cords") or the Jerusalem temple (*gĕḏilîm;* 1 Kgs. 7:17, 29-30, 37).

A wreath appears on the head of a successful master of a feast (Sir. 32:2) and, figuratively, on the heads of martyrs (4 Macc. 17:15). Jesus wears a wreath, or crown, of thorns (Matt. 27:29 par.). Winners in Greek games received a wreath of laurel, pine, or celery (Plutarch *Quaest. conv.* 5.3.1-3), an image used in the Epistles to describe the honor due one who successfully completes the Christian life (1 Cor. 9:25; 2 Tim. 4:8; Jas. 1:12; 1 Pet. 5:4; Rev. 2:10).

Carl Bridges

WRITING

The three biblical languages are written with two scripts: Hebrew and Aramaic with Square Hebrew script, and Greek with Greek script. The language of each of the ancient versions is written with its own distinctive script: Syriac, Arabic; Ethiopic; Latin, Coptic, Gothic; Armenian, Georgian, Old Church Slavonic. Languages of the ancient Near East that are often consulted by biblical scholars add several additional scripts: Mesopotamian cuneiform, Egyptian hieroglyphics, and numerous varieties of the West Semitic script, including Ugaritic, Old South Arabian, Phoenician, and Aramaic.

Biblical Scripts

Hebrew

Square Hebrew (col. 3 in the table) is itself a form of Aramaic script that had arrived at virtually its modern appearance by the time of the Dead Sea Scrolls (ca. 200 B.C.E.). Like all the West Semitic scripts, it is a consonantary, explicitly denoting only consonant segments (phonemes): the term "abjad" is recommended for this type of script, with "alphabet" reserved for those scripts that explicitly and necessarily denote both consonant and vowel segments. The consonants are recorded one by one, with linear order (right to left) corresponding to the time-sequence in which the sounds are uttered. Every word includes vowels as well as consonants, but the vowels are not written: they emerge from the context or from the reader's previous familiarity with the text; it was not impossible for readers to mistake the intended sense by choosing an alternative interpretation of the consonantal text. This problem could at times be exacerbated by lack of division between words (by space or a mark), though such *scriptio continua* was not the rule whenever or wherever abjads were used. Distinctive forms of some letters for the ends of words in Hebrew (and Greek) seem to result from prolongation of pen strokes anticipatory of spacing between words (so while they mark word ends, they were not deliberately introduced for that purpose).

The 22 Hebrew letters denote 23 different consonants (*š* and *ś* were similar but distinct sounds when Hebrew spelling was established), including the glides *w* and *y*. Sound changes operating in Northwest Semitic languages included diphthongs becoming long vowels: *ay*>*ē* and *aw*>*ō*. The letters

Val.ᵃ	I	2a	2b	3ᵇ	4	5a	5b	5c	Num.	Val.	6a	6b	6c	6d	Num.	Val.	7	Val.	8ä	8u
ʾ (ā)									1	a					1	h		h		
b									2	b					2	l		l		
g									3	t					400	ḥ		ḥ		
(ḫ)										ṯ					500	m		m		
d									4	ǰ					3	q		š		
h {-ī}									5	ḥ					8	w		r		
w									6	ḫ					600	s²		s		
z									7	d					4	r		q		
ḥ {h}									8	ḏ					700	b		qʷ		
ṭ									9	r					200	t		b		
y									10	z					7	s¹		t		
k									20	s					60	k		ḫ		
(š)										š					300	n		ḥʷ		
l									30	ṣ					90	ḫ		n		
m									40	ḍ					800	ṣ		ʾ		
(d)										ṭ					9	s³		k		
n									50	ẓ					900	f		kʷ		
ẓ										ʿ					70	ʾ		w		
s									60	ġ					1000	ʿ		ʿ		
ʿ									70	f					80	d		z		
p									80	q					100	g		y		
ṣ									90	k					20	ġ		d		
q									100	l					30	ṭ		g		
r									200	m					40	z		gʷ		
ś										n					50	ḏ		ṭ		
š (t)									300	h					5	ġ		p̣		
ġ										w					6	ẓ		ṣ		
t									400	y					10	f		ḍ		
(i)										lā					—			f		
(u)																		p		
(s)																				
{dī}																				

Vowel symbols:

Val.	3ᵇ	5a/5b	5c	6	7
i[c]					–ِبٌ (– -in)
e					
ε					–َبٌ (– -an)
a					ٓا (ʾā)
ɔ			(ā)		
o					
u					–ُبٌ (– -un)
Ø					–ْب
ə					
ě					
ă					
ŏ					

a. The transliterations are those most often used by the respective specialists. Cols. **1-8** display the most usual attested orders. The horizontal alignment of cols. **9-16** demonstrates the correspondences between the Greek and the later alphabets, also shown in their standard orders.
Val.: Phonetic value; (Ugaritic values); {Mandaic values}; <Gothic values>; <not used in modern Georgian>.
Num.: Arithmetic value when the letter is used as a numeral.
b. **3, 5, 9**: Where two forms are given, the one on the right occurs at the end of a word.
c. **3, 5a-b, 5c, 6**: Vowel symbols shown alone with b. West Syriac (Serto) vowel symbols may be placed above or below the consonant symbol.

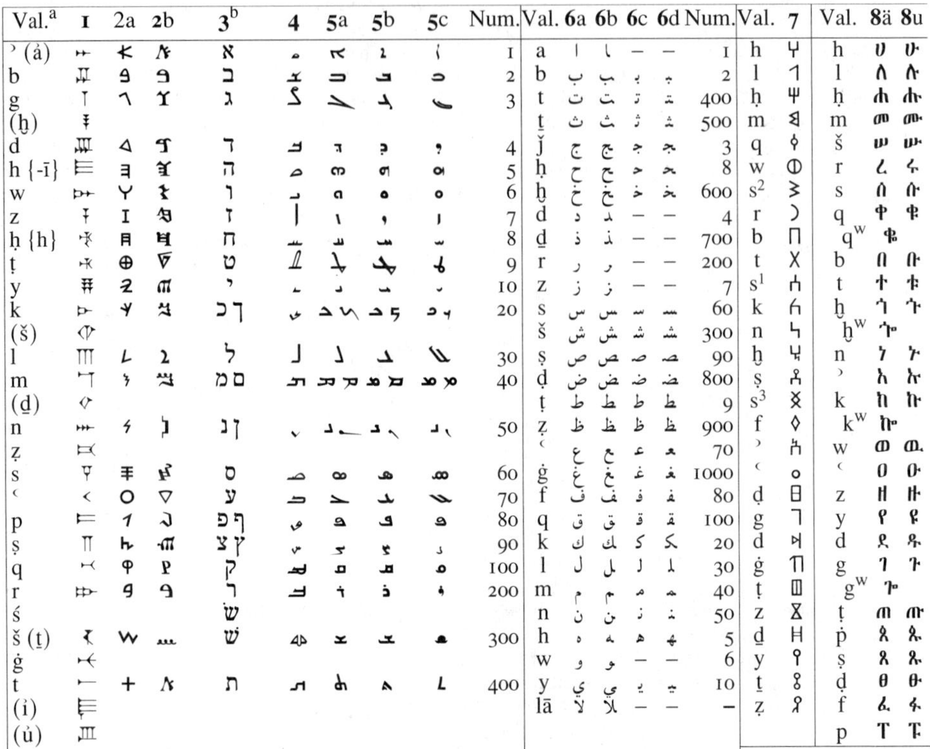

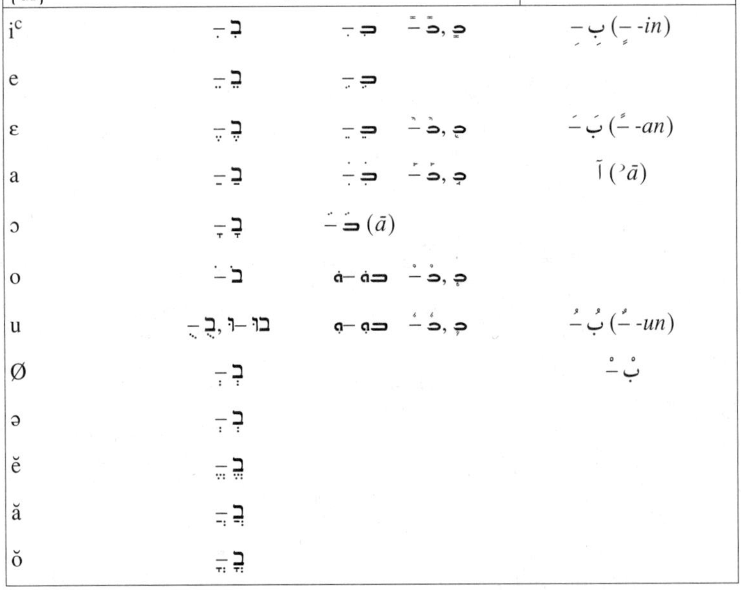

Scripts of the Bible and of the ancient versions, and some of their antecedents

8i	8a	8e	8ə	8o
ሂ	ሃ	ሄ	ህ	ሆ
ሊ	ላ	ሌ	ል	ሎ
ሒ	ሓ	ሔ	ሕ	ሖ
ሚ	ማ	ሜ	ም	ሞ
ሢ	ሣ	ሤ	ሥ	ሦ
ሪ	ራ	ሬ	ር	ሮ
ሲ	ሳ	ሴ	ስ	ሶ
ቂ	ቃ	ቄ	ቅ	ቆ
ቊ	ቋ	ቌ	ቍ	
ቢ	ባ	ቤ	ብ	ቦ
ቲ	ታ	ቴ	ት	ቶ
ኂ	ኃ	ኄ	ኅ	ኆ
ኊ	ኋ	ኌ	ኍ	
ኒ	ና	ኔ	ን	ኖ
ኢ	ኣ	ኤ	እ	ኦ
ኪ	ካ	ኬ	ክ	ኮ
ኲ	ኳ	ኴ	ኵ	
ዊ	ዋ	ዌ	ው	ዎ
ዒ	ዓ	ዔ	ዕ	ዖ
ዚ	ዛ	ዜ	ዝ	ዞ
ዪ	ያ	ዬ	ይ	ዮ
ዲ	ዳ	ዴ	ድ	ዶ
ጊ	ጋ	ጌ	ግ	ጎ
ጒ	ጓ	ጔ	ጕ	
ጢ	ጣ	ጤ	ጥ	ጦ
ጲ	ጳ	ጴ	ጵ	ጶ
ጺ	ጻ	ጼ	ጽ	ጾ
ፂ	ፃ	ፄ	ፅ	ፆ
ፊ	ፋ	ፌ	ፍ	ፎ
ፒ	ፓ	ፔ	ፕ	ፖ

Val.	9a	9b	10	11	Num.
a	Α	α	ⲁ	𐌰	1
b	Β	β	ⲃ	𐌱	2
g	Γ	γ	ⲅ	𐌲	3
d	Δ	δ	ⲇ	𐌳	4
e	Ε	ε	ⲉ	𐌴	5
– ⟨kʷ⟩	Ϝ			𐌵	6
z	Ζ	ζ	ⲍ	𐌶	7
ē ⟨h⟩	Η	η	ⲏ	𐌷	8
th	Θ	θ	ⲑ	𐌸	9
i	Ι	ι	ⲓ	ı ï	10
k	Κ	κ	ⲕ	𐌺	20
l	Λ	λ	ⲗ	𐌻	30
m	Μ	μ	ⲙ	𐌼	40
n	Ν	ν	ⲛ	𐌽	50
ks ⟨j⟩	Ξ	ξ	ⲝ	𐌾	60
o	Ο	ο	ⲟ	𐌿	70
p	Π	π	ⲡ	𐍀	80
–		Ϙ		𐍁	90
r	Ρ	ρ	ⲣ	𐍂	100
s	Σ	σ ς	ⲥ	𐍃	200
t	Τ	τ	ⲧ	𐍄	300
u ⟨w⟩	Υ	υ	ⲩ	𐍅	400
ph	Φ	φ	ⲫ	𐍆	500
kh	Χ	χ	ⲭ	𐍇	600
ps ⟨hʷ⟩	Ψ	ψ	ⲯ	𐍈	700
ō	Ω	ω	ⲱ	𐍉	800
–	ϡ			𐍊	900
š			ϣ		
f			ϥ		
h			ϩ		
ḏ			ϫ		
q			ϭ		
ti			ϯ		
smooth	ἀ				
rough	ἁ				
acute	ά				
grave	ὰ				
circumflex	ᾶ				

Val.	12	Num.
a	ա	1
b	բ	2
g	գ	3
d	դ	4
e	ե	5
z	զ	6
ē	է	7
ə	ը	8
t‘	թ	9
ž	ժ	10
i	ի	20
l	լ	30
x	խ	40
c	ծ	50
k	կ	60
h	հ	70
j	ձ	80
ł	ղ	90
č	ճ	100
m	մ	200
y	յ	300
n	ն	400
š	շ	500
o	ո	600
č‘	չ	700
p	պ	800
ǰ	ջ	900
ṙ	ռ	1000
s	ս	2000
v	վ	3000
t	տ	4000
r	ր	5000
c‘	ց	6000
w	ւ	7000
p‘	փ	8000
k‘	ք	9000
u	ու	–
ō	օ	–
f	ֆ	–

Val.	13	Num.
a	ა	1
b	ბ	2
g	გ	3
d	დ	4
e	ე	5
v	ვ	6
z	ზ	7
ey/ē	⟨ჱ⟩	8
t	თ	9
i	ი	10
ḳ	კ	20
l	ლ	30
m	მ	40
n	ნ	50
y	⟨ჲ⟩	60
o	ო	70
ṗ	პ	80
ž	ჟ	90
r	რ	100
s	ს	200
ṭ	ტ	300
wi/ü	⟨ჳ⟩	400
u	უ	400
p	ფ	500
k	ქ	600
ğ	ღ	700
q/q̇	ყ	800
š	შ	900
č	ჩ	1000
c	ც	2000
j	ძ	3000
ċ	წ	4000
č̣	ჭ	5000
x	ხ	6000
q	⟨ჴ⟩	7000
ǰ	ჯ	8000
h	ჰ	9000
ow/ō	⟨ჵ⟩	10000

Val.	14	15	16	
a	Ⰰ	а	А	а
b	Ⰱ	б	Б	б
v	Ⰲ	в	В	в
g	Ⰳ	г	Г	г
d	Ⰴ	д	Д	д
e	Ⰵ	є	Е	е
ž	Ⰶ	ж	Ж	ж
dz	Ⰷ	ѕ		
z	Ⰸ	ꙁ	З	з
i	Ⰹ	и	И	и
i	Ⰺ / Ⰻ	ї/ı	Й	й
ǵ	Ⰼ	ђ		
k	Ⰽ	к	К	к
l	Ⰾ	л	Л	л
m	Ⰿ	м	М	м
n	Ⱀ	н	Н	н
o	Ⱁ	о	О	о
p	Ⱂ	п	П	п
r	Ⱃ	р	Р	р
s	Ⱄ	с	С	с
t	Ⱅ	т	Т	т
u	Ⱆ	оу/ꙋ	У	у
f	Ⱇ	ф	Ф	ф
x	Ⱈ	х	Х	х
o	Ⱉ	ѡ/ѿ		
c	Ⱌ	ц	Ц	ц
č	Ⱍ	ч	Ч	ч
š	Ⱎ	ш	Ш	ш
št	Ⱋ	щ	Щ	щ
″/ъ	Ⱏ / Ⱏ	ъ	Ъ	ъ
y	ⰟⰊ / ⰟⰉ	ы/ъи	Ы	ы
′/ь	Ⱐ	ь	Ь	ь
ě	Ⱑ	ѣ	Э	э
ju	Ⱓ	ю	Ю	ю
ja		ꙗ	Я	я
je		ѥ		
ę	Ⱔ	ѧ		
ję	ⰅⰔ	ѩ		
ǫ	Ⱘ	ѫ		
jǫ	Ⱙ	ѭ		
ks		ѯ		
ps		ѱ		
f	Ⱚ	ѳ		
i/v	Ⱛ	ѵ		

Column identifications

1. Ugaritic
2a. Phoenician
2b. Samaritan
3. Square Hebrew
4. Mandaic
5. Syriac
a. Estrangelo
b. Nestorian
c. Serto

6. Arabic
a. isolated
b. final
c. initial
d. medial
7. South Arabian (Sabaean)
8. Ethiopic (Geʿez): consonant followed by each of the seven vowels (6th order, ə or no vowel)

9. Greek
a. Majuscule
b. Minuscule
10. Coptic
11. Gothic
12. Armenian
13. Georgian
14. Glagolitic
15. Old Cyrillic
16. Russian.

y and *w* were still written in the text (spelling is quite resistant to change through time), so in some circumstances they ended up representing *ē* and *ō*, respectively. Over time, they came to be used for *ī* and *ū* as well, and at the ends of words *h* and sometimes ' could represent *ā*. Letters that thus represent vowels are called *matres lectionis* ("mothers of reading"). Eventually they could be inserted where they were not historically justified (i.e., for vowels that had not earlier been diphthongs); and by the rabbinic stages of Hebrew and Aramaic the script functioned nearly alphabetically, with most vowels, even short ones, indicated by *matres lectionis.*

By the middle of the 1st millennium C.E., with Hebrew no longer spoken, Jewish scholars called Masoretes recognized the danger that oral transmission of the exact pronunciation of the text of the Bible might be corrupted or interrupted, and over several centuries and in several academies (in Nisibis[?], Mesopotamia, called the Babylonian; southern Palestine; and Tiberias, Galilee — the last emerging as definitive) devised supplemental marks to record the vowels, consonantal nuances, accentuation, parsing, and changing of the biblical text. Because the form, the very orthography, of the text is itself sacred, the inherited consonantal text is preserved unaltered, with these marks — called pointing (Heb. *niqqud*) or vocalization (but not *matres lectionis*) — written above, below, or even within the letters; indeed they are not included in the most holy Torah scrolls, those used during public Scripture reading in the synagogue (where a learnèd scholar, a *gabbai,* assists lay readers with accurate pronunciation).

Torah scrolls represent the survival of the earliest format of long books: papyrus or leather scrolls. These were inscribed in an ink made of soot (lampblack) mixed with water and a little gum arabic, using a pen cut from a hollow reed. Temporary memoranda could be jotted on a potsherd (in this function called an ostracon) using pen and ink, or on a pair of wooden boards hinged together, the inner faces coated with wax, using a stylus to scratch in the soft, reusable surface. Around the turn of the era, the codex began to come into fashion, a group of nested folded sheets like a modern book; this format came to be associated with Christian writings.

Greek

Manuscripts of the NT, the church fathers, and other Greek literature were written with a full alphabet of 24 letters (col. 9), in uncial forms similar to those now used as capitals (majuscules; the minuscule or lowercase letters developed during medieval times). The linear sequence is left to right for vowels and consonants; atop the letters appear the two breathings — which mark vowel- and *r*-initial words as beginning with ("rough") or without ("smooth") *h* — as well as the three accents, whose exact interpretation is uncertain. These marks were available from at least the 2nd century B.C.E. but were not used consistently until ca. 800 C.E. *Scriptio continua* is more characteristic of Greek texts than of West Semitic — in many Classical Greek inscriptions, the letters are equidistant both vertically and horizontally — but is less problematic, because Greek words can end with only a limited set of letters.

Postbiblical Scripts

The historical context of the Square Hebrew and Greek scripts can begin to be appreciated with consideration of other scripts in use in late antiquity. The Syriac (col. 5) and Arabic (col. 6) scripts are the principal survivors (another is Mandaic, col. 4) of a complex of Aramaic abjads that flourished throughout southwestern Asia around the turn of the Common Era, emerging respectively in the Palmyran and Nabatean areas. These Aramaic scripts were usually pen-written (always from right to left) on papyrus, leather, or parchment, or potsherds, rather than incised on hard surfaces — cursive rather than monumental — in utilitarian rather than artistic functions. Their ordinariness and ephemerality, and the convenience of their users, meant that the sometimes conflicting requirements of speed and legibility were the paramount factors in their evolution. A frequent outcome was the connection of adjacent letters within a word — avoidance of time-consuming pen lifts; this meant that some letters could take on rather different appearances according to their position within a word, and some letters could become uncomfortably similar — inhibiting legibility. This difficulty was alleviated by the introduction of dots to distinguish letters whose basic forms had converged — *d* and *r* in Syriac (those letters were very similar in almost all Aramaic hands), several sets in Arabic.

These Aramaic scripts inherited the use of *matres lectionis,* and systematized their use for all long vowels (in Mandaic, almost all vowels), but for reasons similar to those that were to prevail in the Hebrew domain, it became necessary to indicate (optionally) the short vowels as well. Classical Syriac was no longer spoken at least by the time of the Arab Conquest in the early 7th century, so the pronunciation of the biblical text needed to be preserved; well before then, the influx of Persian and Greek words in scientific and theological works had made the recording of vowels desirable. The earliest extant dated Syriac manuscript (411 C.E.) bears vowel pointing (literally; only dots are used) in the system that developed in the eastern portion of Syrian Christianity. Somewhat later, in the western sector, tiny Greek vowel letters came to be added alongside the consonantal text. (A scheme for inserting Greek-like vowel characters directly into the lines of writing was rejected both because it would tamper with the sacred text and because it would render all existing manuscripts unreadable within a generation.) The practices of Syriac scribes were probably known to both Hebrew and Arab scholars when they developed their vocalization techniques.

For Arabic, the problem was the preservation of the text of the Qur'an in the face of a multiplicity of Arabic dialects. The solution involved symbols not

Barrel cylinders commemorating construction of the city wall at Maškan-šapir by Sin-iddinam of Larsa (1849-1843 B.C.E.) (Elizabeth C. Stone Zimansky)

just for the three short vowels of Arabic, but also for various grammatical (morphophonemic) processes that operated in the dialect that became Classical Arabic but perhaps not in that spoken by those who first recorded the consonants of the Qur'an as it came from the mouth of the Prophet Mohammed. Both consonant dotting and vowel indications occur in the earliest secular papyri, from early in the 1st century of Islam, found in the Cairo Geniza.

The earliest West Semitic script to denote vowels, however, was none of the above — it was the Ethiopic (col. 8). Ethiopic script is usually said to have been imported from south Arabia around or before the turn of the era. A number of Sabean inscriptions have been found in the ancient kingdom of Aksum, which straddled the modern Eritrea-Ethiopia border; a dozen monuments in the Geʿez language and Ethiopic script survive from the mid-4th century C.E. At first the script was very similar to the Sabean (col. 7), save that it now read left to right; but from the midst of the reign of King Ezana, and coinciding with his conversion to Christianity, the inscriptions are fully vocalized. The vocalization is applied not with letters as in Greek or Coptic (most likely the languages of the missionaries involved), nor as in Syriac (not known to have had any vocalization at the time), but by attaching appendages to the consonant letters (the letters sometimes are quite deformed in the process) — except a letter with no appendage represents its consonant plus *a,* rather than its consonant alone. (Thus each of the 182 Ethiopic letters denotes a consonant-vowel [CV] syllable; this type of script can be called "abugida," and must be distinguished from a syllabary, where there is no similarity between the characters including a particular consonant or a particular vowel.) Such a pattern is found elsewhere only in the scripts of India (where, some 500 years before, when they are first attested, phonetic science flourished). Were these independent developments? Or is it possible that the missionaries who brought Christianity to Aksum had crossed the Arabian Sea and also brought their own notion of how writing should work?

The language that became the vehicle for Western Christianity, Latin, had been written with an offshoot of the Greek alphabet — mediated through Etruscan — since the 7th century B.C.E. Though the voiced stops *b, d, g* and the vowel *o* did not occur in the Etruscan language (and do not appear in Etruscan inscriptions), their letters were preserved in the alphabet (the ancestors of *B, D, C,* and *O*), and were used for Latin. Conversely, Etruscan distinguished three varieties of *k,* written with *C* before *e/i, K* before *a,* and *Q* before *u;* this unneeded distinction persists in Latin and the Romance languages today. Since Latin did need to distinguish *g* from *k, G* was distinguished from *C* in the 4th century B.C.E. (*I/J* and *U/V* did not become fully independent until modern times.) The capital letters reached their final forms in imperial Rome; the generalization that rustic hands serve pagan works and uncial (Greek-like) and half-uncial (associated with Celtic scribes) serve Christian writings is overly broad but workable. The minuscules are the result of gradual development and were codified in the time of Charlemagne (early 9th century); the italic forms were perfected during the Italian Renaissance. The distinctive German forms used until the mid-20th century represented parallel developments of the North European Renaissance.

It is noteworthy that wherever Western Christianity reached, and Latin remained the liturgical language, local languages came to be written in the roman alphabet, generally with very little modification; but in the realm of Eastern (Orthodox, or Greek-speaking) Christianity, where the vernacular was adopted for sacred use, the local languages received their own scripts, derived from or inspired by the Greek alphabet. (Iranian forms of Aramaic script were carried through Central Asia by both Christian missionaries and secular administrations. Some form of Aramaic was the likely inspiration of the scripts of India; their sophistication may indicate that they were devised after the flowering of the Indian grammatical tradition.)

Coptic Christians added several letters borrowed from Demotic to the Greek alphabet for sounds found in Egyptian but not Greek; in typical fashion, the added letters are not interspersed within the standard order among similar-looking or sounding letters but appear at the end. Coptic (col. 10) has been used since the 4th century C.E. The Gothic alphabet (col. 11), recording the earliest Germanic language to have survived in any quantity, was devised by Bishop Wulfila (also 4th century) to record his Bible translation.

The histories of the two surviving indigenous scripts of the Caucasus, Armenian and Georgian, are intertwined more in legend than perhaps is warranted by history. Both are attributed (in Armenian tradition) to St. Mesrop, whose Armenian alphabet (col. 12) dates to 406/7 C.E.; its related order but dissimilar appearance indicate that its structure but not its form derives from the Greek. Georgian scholars argue that Mesrop was unfamiliar with the Georgian language, and that its alphabet (col. 13) — first attested (in a church in Palestine!) in 430 C.E. — dates from some time after the introduction of Christianity to the country ca. 337. Its adherence to the order of the Greek alphabet, with new letters appended, demonstrates its dependence thereon.

The two scripts of Old Church Slavonic (Old Bulgarian) are also attributed to saints, Constantine (Cyril) and Methodius of the mid-9th century. Glagolitic (col. 14) appears to have developed out of cursive Greek during the 7th-9th centuries and to have been formalized by Cyril during the early 860s; Cyrillic (col. 15) seems to have been modeled on the more dignified Greek uncials by disciples of Cyril's in the 890s, with the added letters modeled on Glagolitic. (Glagolitic drifted slowly out of use, especially in secular functions, beginning in the 12th century; Cyrillic remains widespread, col. 16.)

Prebiblical Writing

For over 2000 years, the principal, and for more than half that time the only, script used internationally throughout the ancient Near East was Mesopotamian cuneiform. The latest indications are that this script was devised in Uruk, ca. 3200 B.C.E., for Sumerian — i.e., very near in time and space to the earliest examples that have been found by archaeologists. Its earliest uses were economic and scholarly: for keeping records of commodities involved in the temple economy, and for maintaining lists of all sorts of items relevant to the society. At first the script recorded only root words (names of things and actions; the characters at first were recognizable images, but quickly became abstract), but it soon came to notate grammatical affixes as well, and with the flexibility thus provided, it could record connected prose — interpersonal communications, annals, decrees, belles lettres. The subtleties of Sumerian phonology are not yet well understood, but the writing system was subtle enough to be adaptable to unrelated languages with sufficient efficiency to serve for millennia.

Probably the first and the most important such language was the Semitic Akkadian, the decipherment of which opened a universe of materials from Mesopotamian civilization with direct relevance to the Bible. Hence Akkadian cuneiform is characterized here. Its script is a logosyllabary — a syllabary (characters — known as signs — representing syllables of the form CV, V, VC, or CVC) whose signs (logograms) also stand for entire words. The phonetic values of the signs are related to the words the signs originally represented (and because the signs can be read as words in Sumerian or Akkadian, and because signs can represent more than one word in either language, and because there are more sounds in Akkadian than in Sumerian, signs can have quite a few different phonetic and word readings). When words are written entirely with signs used phonetically (and this is the most common way of using the script), reading them is quite straightforward. A number of frequent words are usually written logographically; in these cases, grammatical affixes are added with phonetic signs. If a logogram might be unfamiliar or ambiguous, it may be provided with a semantic determinative sign marking a classification of the intended sense (e.g., divine name, wooden object, place); or portions of the reading of the intended word may be added with phonetic complement signs before and/or after the logogram in question. It must be kept in mind that even though transliterations into the roman alphabet use a varied panoply of italic and roman type, vertical displacement, accents, and numerical indices, the original texts include no indication of whether any particular sign is used as a logogram, a phonogram, or an auxiliary.

The name cuneiform means "wedge-shaped." It refers to the indentations made in the surface of the small mass of clay that was the usual material for writing. The indentations were made by touching the corner of a reed stylus to the surface; from one to a dozen or so wedges make up each sign. (The wedges could also be imitated by chiseling into a hard surface, or by outlining on a metal ground.) The typical clay object, a tablet, was usually a rectangle with a flat front and a gently convex back and could conveniently be held in one hand, its size depending on the length of the text to be recorded; there were also numerous standard shapes used for particular purposes. Signs were written from left to right employing *scriptio continua*, but a word is virtually never broken between lines, and often the last sign on a line is spaced over to the right margin.

Straight lines could be ruled on a tablet by impressing a taut string, to divide a text into sections (in earlier times, individual entries in a list or lines of a literary composition could be set off in ruled boxes).

Cuneiform script was adapted for numerous languages around Mesopotamia, including Elamite, Hittite, Hurrian, Urartian, and Canaanite, the last known almost exclusively from the Amarna archives that accidentally preserved the diplomatic correspondence of Akhenaten's court. The Egyptian language itself, though, was not adapted to cuneiform, even for international purposes.

Egyptian hieroglyphics remains unique among the world's scripts in denoting only consonants, during its entire history of more than three millennia. It is a logoconsonantary, comprising signs of one, two, or three consonants; logograms; and determinatives (phonetic and semantic) that are used more consistently than those in cuneiform — to such an extent that the semantic determinatives serve dependably as word-end markers. Note that although 24 monoconsonantal signs can be listed, at no time did this set serve as an "alphabet" used to the exclusion of other phonetic signs in composing words. Nor do the signs represent syllables with indeterminate vowels, for one and the same polyconsonantal sign can mark a consonant cluster, the beginning and end of a syllable, or the end of one syllable and the beginning of the next.

Egyptian hieroglyphs, like cuneiform signs, originated as recognizable images, but all through their use they retained their pictorial quality. Nonsymmetrical signs — particularly, those representing people and animals — always face toward the beginning of the writing line. Usually writing is from right to left, but design considerations, such as symmetry on a wall, can call for inscriptions to read left to right. Alongside hieroglyphic, which continued to be used in formal situations until the end of Egyptian civilization, there developed a cursive style of writing the same characters, known as Hieratic, as well as a quicker hand, Demotic, in which many ligatures represent combinations of hieroglyphs; Hieratic can, but Demotic cannot, be transposed directly into hieroglyphs.

It is generally agreed that Egyptian hieroglyphs had some sort of influence on the development of the West Semitic abjad, but in what that influence consisted is difficult to imagine. The earliest inscriptions that have been placed in that lineage, the handful of Proto-Sinaitic texts, comprise characters that bear some resemblance to hieroglyphs; but even if their interpretation as Semitic is correct (and the argument to that effect is circular), the sound values of the letters do not agree with their values in Egyptian. Usually when a script is borrowed, its values as well as its forms are taken over. Moreover, there was no precedent within Egyptian for using nothing but monoconsonantal characters. Perhaps all that can be said is that a Semitic speaker knew just a little bit about how Egyptian was written, but not enough to directly imitate the writing system.

The earliest abjadic texts that clearly belong in the West Semitic line of development are the Proto-Canaanite inscriptions on small objects, none more than a few letters long; when they can be interpreted, they appear to be owners' names. The first large corpus is the Ugaritic texts from Ras Shamra and environs, dating to the 14th century B.C.E. The script (col. 1) is impressed on clay like cuneiform, but is otherwise not related; the letter shapes can be related to contemporary West Semitic forms. We are fortunate to have several abecedaries demonstrating that the familiar alphabetical order has been in use since near the beginning of segmental writing. Added to the Ugaritic abjad are three additional letters — the last was a sibilant, needed for Hurrian or perhaps Indo-european texts; the others were extra forms of *aleph:* each of the three *aleph* letters denotes a different following vowel. Again, these may have been prompted by the need to record foreign texts or names, but many centuries older.

Like the Ugaritic, the South Arabian script group (most prominently, Sabean, col. 7) preserves several consonant distinctions that were lost in most Semitic scripts; also now known is the letter order, which is fully independent from the familiar one but similar to the Ethiopic. The reduced inventory of 22 consonants prevailed in the most widespread family of Semitic abjads, the Phoenician (col. 2a); it gave rise to an Old Hebrew/Phoenician group (surviving only in Samaritan, col. 2b) and an Aramaic group, scions of which remain important to this day (the Hebrew language took up the Aramaic script perhaps during the Babylonian Exile and revived the Old Hebrew script, called Paleo-Hebrew, only in sacred and archaizing contexts, such as to write the tetragrammaton in some Dead Sea Scrolls texts).

One offshoot of Phoenician script did prove important. Via a process that remains ill understood and deeply controversial, the Phoenician abjad became the Greek alphabet. A likely scenario is that this was an essentially accidental event (and not a discovery or invention), perhaps ca. 800 B.C.E. A Greek scholar or merchant, admiring a Phoenician's ability to record transactions, sought to do the same; since Semitic includes various guttural consonants that are not part of Greek, and thus would be difficult for a Greek speaker to perceive, the values of some of the letters could have been interpreted as (what seemed to be) the initial vowels of their names (or of relevant words) — thus the glides *y* and *w* could be used as *i* and *u,* and the gutturals ʾ, ʿ, and *h* as *a, o,* and *e,* respectively. This need have happened once only, and been communicated around the Greek world fairly rapidly, with various communities supplementing the alphabet in varying ways to account for Greek sounds not found in Phoenician. The Greek alphabet was standardized by Athens in 402 B.C.E., preparing the way for its and its descendants' use around the world; but it must not be supposed that "the alphabet" is responsible for "literacy" and "civilization" — which predate it by millennia; the sword and the icon, both, mightily prepare the way for the pen.

Bibliography. British Museum, *Reading the Past* (Berkeley, 1990) (also a series of pamphlets, 1987-1991); P. T. Daniels and W. Bright, eds., *The World's Writing Systems* (Oxford, 1996); G. R. Driver, *Semitic Writing from Pictograph to Alphabet,* rev. ed. (Oxford, 1976); J. Naveh, *Early History of the Hebrew Alphabet,* 2nd ed. (Leiden, 1987); S. Segert, "Writing" *ISBE* 4 (Grand Rapids, 1988): 1136-60.

PETER T. DANIELS

WRITINGS

The last of the three sections of the Hebrew canon (Heb. *kĕṯûḇîm*). Included are the books of Psalms, Job, Proverbs, Ruth, Song of Solomon, Ecclesiastes, Lamentations Esther, Daniel, Ezra, Nehemiah, and 1-2 Chronicles. This sequence, found in modern versions of the OT, is probably no older than the 12th century C.E.; in fact, the order varied greatly at different times and was never officially set by the synagogue. The books were probably grouped together between 300 B.C.E. and 100 C.E.

X

XANTHICUS (Gk. *Xanthikos*)
A month of the Macedonian calendar corresponding to the Jewish month Nisan (Mar.-Apr.). The name occurs in two letters written to the Jews in 164 B.C.E by Antiochus V and the Romans (2 Macc. 11:30, 33, 38).

XERXES (Gk. *Xerxēs*)
Xerxes I, Achaemenid king of Persia, 486-465 B.C.E., who ascended the throne upon the death of Darius I. There is inscriptional evidence to suggest that Xerxes I was the crown prince for some time, and held a coregency with his father (he is noted on the south doorway of Darius I's private palace). This is notable because there is evidence that Darius had earlier indicated that his eldest son, Artobazanes, would succeed him. However, Darius fathered Xerxes by Atossa, daughter of Cyrus the Great and wife of Cambyses. Among the Persepolis inscriptions, Xerxes himself notes that although he had brothers, he was himself selected by the will of Ahura Mazda (the Zoroastrian patron god of the Achaemenid line) to be the new king. From 498 until his accession 12 years later, Xerxes served as satrap of Babylonia, the second most powerful position in the Persian Empire.

Xerxes is noted for a campaign in Egypt, which may have also involved an invasion of Judah along the way. The revolt in Egypt was finally crushed in January 484. The Greek sources narrate his military preparations for an invasion of Greece, but he was preoccupied with rebellion within his own empire — notably in Babylon. There is some controversy as to Xerxes' policies toward Babylon. It seems certain that his general, Megabyzus, actually melted down the statue of Marduk as part of the policy of reducing Babylon to compliance. This may have been an example of wider policy, as there is indication that Xerxes treated local temples (often the centers of revolt) severely in his responses to insurrection (and in contrast to the more liberal policies of Darius). His burning of Athens was the celebrated cause of Greek hatred of Xerxes, who passed into Greek lore as a despotic monster. He was defeated by the Hellenic fleet at Salamis in September 480, and again suffered defeat of his army at Plataia in 479. It was undoubtedly as a result of his many failures that he was eventually open to receive a peace delegation led by Kallias, who was sent by the Athenians. The peace negotiations carried on, despite palace intrigues that led to the assassination of Xerxes and the eventual succession of Artaxerxes I to the throne; the latter continued to abide by the short-lived peace agreement as well.

Xerxes, in his later reign, is noted in classical literature for many palace and harem intrigues — some of which may provide the historical "background color" behind the popularity of Hebrew stories such as Esther. Jon L. Berquist, however, suggests that only Malachi may come from the time of Xerxes, and Malachi's concern with temple offerings may reflect Xerxes' policy of cutting off funds for local shrines — funds that were generous under his father Darius. Such a financial crisis may be reflected in the concern for "tithes," temple personnel, and temple power in Malachi.

Bibliography. J. M. Balcer, *A Prosopographical Study of the Ancient Persians Royal and Noble c. 550-450 B.C.* (Lewiston, 1993); J. L. Berquist, *Judaism in Persia's Shadow* (Minneapolis, 1996); J. M. Cook, *The Persian Empire* (New York, 1983).

DANIEL L. SMITH-CHRISTOPHER

Y

YAHWEH

The God of Israel. Shortened forms occur in Israelite names (*yĕhô* and *yô* at the beginning and *yāhû* and *yâ* at the end), and in "Hallelujah" ("Praise Yah"). The precise pronunciation is uncertain, since from the Persian period onward the sacred name was replaced by various titles and epithets. The most common alternative was *'ăḏōnāy* ("my Lord"); its vowels were eventually added to the consonantal text (allowing for a shift in the initial vowel because of the *yodh* rather than an *aleph*) and the resultant hybrid was transliterated by Christians as Jehovah. The pronunciation *yahwēh* is based upon Hebrew grammatical rules and supported by the suffixed forms in names and Greek renderings such as *iaō, iaou,* and especially *iaē.*

The initial *yodh* suggests a 3rd masculine singular verbal form, and the vocalization *yahwēh* points to the causative form, but of what verb? Despite appeals to the Arabic root *hwy,* meaning "to fall," "to blow," or "to love/be passionate," the scholarly consensus still favors derivation from the Hebrew root *hwh* (later *hyh*), "to be." Thus, *yahwēh* alludes to the deity's creative activity.

Yahweh is linked with *ṣĕḇā'ôṯ* ("armies/hosts") 284 times in the Hebrew Bible. Frank M. Cross sees this as a shortened title of El, the head of the Canaanite pantheon (originally, *il ḏu yahwî ṣĕbāôt,* "El who creates the [heavenly] armies") and equates Yahweh and El. The two do share many characteristics (wisdom, kindness, great age, a cherubim throne, rule over the divine council), but there are important differences. First, Yahweh is a divine warrior (e.g., Exod. 15:3) whereas El is not; in the Ugaritic corpus it is Baal, the storm-god, who does battle. Second, unlike El, Yahweh originates in the far south. In various war theophanies he marches forth from southern locations: Sinai (Deut. 33:2; cf. "the one of Sinai," Judg. 5:5; Ps. 68:8[MT 9]), Seir (Deut. 33:2; Judg. 5:4), Paran (Deut. 33:2; Hab. 3:3), Edom (Judg. 5:4), and Teman (Hab. 3:3). The invocation of "Yahweh of Teman" alongside "Yahweh of Samaria" in an 8th-century inscription from Kuntillet 'Ajrûd/Ḥorvat Teman shows Yahweh's southern associations survived well after the settlement in the north. Finally, Yahweh and El are distinguished in Deut. 32:8-9; since "the Most High" *('elyôn)* is an epithet of El, Yahweh must be one of the "sons of God" (thus LXX, Qumran, Symmachus, and Old Latin) to whom El gives Israel. Any common characteristics should be explained as assimilation, not identification.

Yahweh's southern origin leads to the hypothesis that he was the god of the Kenites, a Midianite clan, and was mediated to Moses by his father-in-law, a Midianite priest. He was brought to Canaan by Moses' group of escaped Egyptian slaves, and eventually took on most of El's characteristics.

Bibliography. F. M. Cross, *Canaanite Myth and Hebrew Epic* (Cambridge, Mass., 1973), 44-75; H. H. Rowley, *From Joseph to Joshua* (Oxford, 1950), 149-63; K. van der Toorn, "Yahweh יהוה," *DDD,* 910-19.

John L. McLaughlin

YAHWIST

One of the literary sources which many scholars discern as comprising the Pentateuch or Torah. Though the hypothesis of a composite text has dominated the last 200 years of scholarly pentateuchal study, substantial disagreement remains about virtually every facet of any Yahwist hypothesis. Still, a heuristic sketch may be offered.

The Yahwist, abbreviated by the siglum "J" (from Ger. *Jahweh*), is typically recognized as the most brilliant of the pentateuchal storytellers, responsible for much of the material in Genesis and substantial portions of narrative in Exodus and Numbers. Hence J carries the story line from the origins of human existence to the eve of entrance into the Promised Land, a span composed of 22 generations: primeval episodes, adventures of the founding ancestors of Israel, journeys of Moses and the Exodus-wilderness group. The Yahwist may be presumed to have been active in the Davidic court, hence writing ca. the 10th century B.C.E. Since the interest of the materials is southern, the presumed location of the writer is Judah, specifically Jerusalem. The Jerusalem location and early date suggest to some that the Yahwist is an apologist for the Davidic monarchy and enterprise, the epic recounting the tribal roots of the emergent state.

Though it is not clear whether the Yahwist is best seen as a composer, a collector, or a compiler, some persistent characteristics of both style and content mark texts commonly attributed to J. Early noted was a tendency to name the deity as Yahweh, a fondness for puns and etiologies, a set of vivid characters who act boldly, dialogue pungently, and soliloquize revealingly; J uses a technique of singling an individual out from a larger group, providing a matrix of minor players while giving one primary focus. The Yahwist stories are rich in imagery. The deity in the J narrative is not quite so omnipotent and competent as in other sources, and the humans that emerge from J are often very flawed but highly memorable. The key opponent in the Yahwist story is Egypt, with its oppressive ways. Some major longitudinal themes seen in J include furtherance of blessing, the accomplishment of divine purposes, and the establishment of key cultural institutions. There is substantial resonance between extrabiblical material (e.g., Sumerian, Akkadian, and Ugaritic epic material that features the entanglements of deities and human beings) and many structural elements and smaller motifs in J.

Major dissent to the position sketched here includes the likely identity of J (a woman has been suggested, or a popular bard), the genre (history or theology rather than apology), the date (ranging from Solomonic to exilic), and the purposes (often described more theologically and generally than socially). Since any discussion of the Yahwist is embedded in conversations about pentateuchal studies, those who doubt the usefulness of the standard strata or source hypothesis will view the "Yahwist" texts very differently than those for whom it remains a viable model of authorship.

Bibliography. R. B. Coote and D. R. Ord, *The Bible's First History* (Philadelphia, 1989); R. Rendtorff, "The Yahwist as Theologian? The Dilemma of Pentateuchal Criticism," *JSOT* 3 (1977): 2-10 and responses, 11-32; J. Van Seters, *Prologue to History: The Yahwist as Historian in Genesis* (Louisville, 1992); H. W. Wolff, "The Kerygma of the Yahwist," in *The Vitality of Old Testament Traditions,* ed. W. Brueggemenn and Wolff, 2nd ed. (Atlanta, 1982), 41-66.

BARBARA GREEN, O.P.

YARMUK

Šerīʿat el-Menādireh, the northernmost of the major perennial rivers in Transjordan. Separating Bashan from northern Gilead, the river and its tributaries drain both Bashan and Hauran. From the confluence of three of its major tributaries (Wadi el-Meddān, Wadi el-Ehreir, and Wadi eš-Šallāla) at Maqarin to the Jordan River, the Yarmuk is ca. 35 km. (22 mi.) long. The Yarmuk joins the Jordan ca. 6.5 km. (4 mi.) S of the Sea of Galilee where both are at this point ca. 9 m. (29.5 ft.) wide. At this junction the Yarmuk is deeper and carries almost as much water as the Jordan itself.

While the north side of the river and its tributaries have spacious terraces descending from the upper slopes, the southern side is for the most part very steep with considerable overgrowth. Thus, there is more usable land on the northern side of the Yarmuk Valley.

The Yarmuk is not mentioned in the Bible, though it is possibly the "brook" of 1 Macc. 5:40. It is first mentioned by Pliny *(Nat. hist.)* in the 1st century A.D.

Bibliography. K. Yassine, T. M. Kerestes, B. G. Wood, and J. M. Lundquist, "An Archaeological Survey of Three Reservoir Areas in Northern Jordan, 1978," *ADAJ* 22 (1978): 108-35.

PAUL J. RAY, JR.

YEAR

The basic unit of the calendar for the ancient Israelites and other ancient Near Eastern peoples. It was based on the annual cycle of the movement of the sun, moon, and stars, and on the cycle of planting and harvesting crops. The OT does not contain a full calendar for ancient Israel, so one must be constructed from the references in various passages to days, dates, months, seasons, and years.

The OT is unclear about whether the ancient Israelite year began in the spring or in the fall. Exod. 23:16; 34:22 state that the fall festival, the Feast of the Ingathering, is to be celebrated at "the end of the year" (23:16) or "the turn of the year" (34:22). Lev. 23:5; Num. 28:16 assert, however, that the Passover, the major spring festival, is to be celebrated on the fourteenth day of the first month. The Gezer Calendar (ca. 925 B.C.E.) indicates that the year began in the autumn. The autumn may have marked the end/beginning of the agricultural calendar, while the spring marked the commencement of the cultic calendar. Regardless of when the year began, the month names, borrowed from the Babylonian, were fixed:

Hebrew	Babylonian	Equivalent
Nisan (Abib)	Nisanu	Mar./Apr.
Iyyar	Ayaru	Apr./May
Sivan	Siwanu/Simanu	May/June
Tammuz	Du'uzu	June/July
Ab	Abu	July/Aug.
Elul	Elulu/Ululu	Aug./Sept.
Tishri	Tisritu	Sept./Oct.
(Mar)hesvan	(W)arah-sammu	Oct./Nov.
Kislev	Kisliwu/Kislimu	Nov./Dec.
Tebet	Tebitu	Dec./Jan.
Shĕbat	Sabatu	Jan./Feb.
Adar	Addaru	Feb./Mar.

In the Bible, only four month-names are given: the spring months of Abib (Nisan) and Ziv (Iyyar) and the fall months of Ethanim (Tishri) and Bul (Marhesvan). These were the most important months of the year, since significant events in the agricultural life of Palestine and the solar equinoxes occurred in them.

Major festivals divided the year in ancient Israel. The biblical descriptions of the festivals emphasize, for the most part, their cultic significance, but most of the festivals were incorporated into already existing agricultural celebrations. The ancient Israelite cultic celebrations began with Passover, the Feast of Unleavened Bread, and the Festival of the Wave Offering, which were observed beginning on the fourteenth day of Abib (Nisan; Exod. 12; Lev. 23:5-14). The celebration coincided with the early barley harvest in Palestine.

Pentecost, or the Feast of Weeks, observed 50 days after Passover, marked the giving of the law at Sinai and the end of the grain harvest (Lev. 23:15-22). Lev. 23:24-25 states that a sabbath rest is to be observed on the first day of Tishri. Later Judaism celebrated this day as the New Year *(rô'š haššānâ)*. The OT, however, contains no reference to the celebration of a New Year.

On the tenth day of the seventh month (Tishri), the Israelites observed the Day of Atonement (*yôm kippur;* Lev. 23:26-32). On the fifteenth day of the same month, the Feast of Booths or Tabernacles, also called the Feast of Ingathering, was celebrated (Lev. 23:33-44). The feast commemorated the Israelites' wandering in the wilderness and living in tents, and it coincided with the fall harvest. In addition, ancient Israel celebrated a sabbatical year every seven years, in which the agricultural land lay fallow, and a year of jubilees every 50 years, in which a general rest and release of held property took place.

The 364-day calendar existed from at least the 3rd century B.C.E., but it is not clear whether this calendar was ever used by mainstream Jewish communities. The present-day Jewish calendar evolved over several centuries after the close of the biblical period. Some maintain that the problem of dating the Last Supper in the NT can be solved by positing the use of the 364-day calendar by the Jewish community. The Synoptic Gospels indicate that Jesus and the disciples ate the Last Supper near sundown as the 15th of Nisan began (Matt. 26:17-19; Mark 14:12-21; Luke 22:7-13). John implies, however, that the meal was eaten as the 14th of Nisan began (John 18:28; 19:14, 31, 42). If the Synoptic writers used the 364-day calendar and John used the lunisolar calendar, then the discrepancy in the dates could be explained. There is no evidence, however, that Jesus or his disciples used the 364-day calendar, and many suggest that John shaped his account from a theological motivation to present Jesus as the Passover lamb.

Bibliography. D. J. A. Clines, "The Evidence for an Autumnal New Year in Pre-exilic Israel Reconsidered," *JBL* 93 (1974): 22-40; J. Finegan, *Light from the Ancient Past,* 2nd ed. (Princeton, 1959) 2:552-98; W. S. LaSor, D. A. Hubbard, and F. W. Bush, *Old Testament Survey,* 2nd ed. (Grand Rapids, 1996), 632-36.

NANCY L. DE CLAISSÉ-WALFORD

YELLOW

One of the indications of "leprosy" mentioned in the legal provisions for diagnosis of skin diseases is hair that is "yellow [and] thin" (Heb. *ṣāhōḇ dāq;* Lev. 13:30; cf. vv. 32, 36). Favus, a fungal disease, is characterized by yellowing of the hair, and so may be a part of the complex of skin conditions spoken of at Lev. 13.

YIRON (Heb. *yir'ôn)*

A fortified city in the tribal territory of Naphtali (Josh. 19:38), probably modern Yārûn (189276), the Irruna in Upper Galilee conquered by Tiglath-pileser III.

YOKE

A mechanism for harnessing the power of domesticated animals (Heb. *'ōl, ṣemeḏ, môṭâ;* Gk. *zugós*). Most often the ox and donkey (1 Sam. 11:7; 1 Kgs. 19:19, 21; Job 1:3; Luke 14:19), but also cattle (Num. 19:2; Deut. 21:3; 1 Sam. 6:7), were yoked plowing (Deut. 22:10 forbids yoking an ox and a donkey together).

Because the yoke was such a common agricultural implement, it became a vivid symbol with many nuances. Sometimes it was used to describe oppression and servitude, politically (Gen. 27:40; Lev. 26:13; 1 Kgs. 12:4-14 = 2 Chr. 10:4-14; Isa. 58:6, 9; Jer. 28:1-14) and religiously (Acts 15:10; Gal. 5:1; 1 Tim. 6:1). Lam. 1:14 employs the figure to describe the negative results of sin. The figure of humans yoked usually represents an unhealthy relationship (2 Cor. 6:14; cf. Ps. 106:28).

Elsewhere the metaphor of yoke is used in a very positive way. Lam. 3:27 refers to the yoke as correction administered by God. Even more striking is Jeremiah's use of the term as a metaphor for God's authority, probably as expressed in the covenant and the word of God (Jer. 2:20; 5:5). Jesus' shorthand use of the term in Matt. 11:28-30 refers to the rabbinic concepts of "the yoke of the kingdom of heaven/Torah/commandments" (cf. *m. Ber.* 2:2, 5; *b. Sanh.* 94b; Sir. 6:24-30; Pss. Sol. 7:9).

W. E. NUNNALLY

YOKEFELLOW

A term for a partner in some enterprise (Gk. *sýzygos*). It is used to mean "comrade, companion" (Euripides *Iph. T.* 250; Aristophanes *Plut.* 945), and "brother" (Euripides *Tro.* 1001). Used as a feminine form, the term can mean "wife" (Euripides *Alc.* 314, 34).

Paul asks the "true yokefellow" to help Euodia and Syntyche settle their disagreement (Phil. 4:3), and he may be referring to either Timothy, Epaphroditus, Silas, Luke, the husband or brother of Euodia or Syntyche, Paul's wife, a church official at Philippi, a man named Syzygos ("Yokefellow"), a fellow prisoner with Paul, any volunteer in the Church who might help, the whole Philippian church, or even Christ. The identity of the person remains a mystery.

Bibliography. M. Hájek, "Comments on Philippians 4:3 — Who Was 'Gnésios Syzygos'?" *Communio Viatorum* 7 (1964): 261-62.

DOUGLAS S. HUFFMAN

YOM KIPPUR (Heb. *yôm kippûr*)

The holiest of Jewish holy days from the biblical period on.

See ATONEMENT, DAY OF.

Z

ZAANAN (Heb. *ṣaʼănān*)
An unidentified site in the Shephelah of Judah (Mic. 1:11). It may be the same as Zenan at Josh. 15:37, which also appears in context with Lachish.

ZAANANNIM (Heb. *ṣaʻănannîm*)
A location on the southern border of Naphtali's tribal inheritance (Josh. 19:33) and site of Heber the Kenite's encampment (Judg. 4:11). The complete name is "oak of Zaanannim" (Heb. *ʼēlôn bĕṣaʻănannîm*), and likely refers to a familiar landmark rather than a town. The location of Zaanannim is unknown, and it is unclear whether both accounts refer to the same locale. KENNETH ATKINSON

ZAAVAN (Heb. *zaʻăwān*)
The second son of Ezer the Horite, ancestor of an Edomite clan (Gen. 36:27; 1 Chr. 1:42).

ZABAD (Heb. *zāḇāḏ*) (also JOZACAR)
1. A descendant of Jerahmeel of the tribe of Judah; son of Nathan and father of Ephlal (1 Chr. 2:36-37).
2. The son of Tahath, and a descendant of Ephraim (1 Chr. 7:21).
3. One of David's Mighty Men, the son of Ahlai (1 Chr. 11:41).
4. The son of Shimeath the Ammonite woman who conspired with Jehozabad to murder King Joash of Judah (2 Chr. 24:26). At 2 Kgs. 12:21(MT 22) he is called Jozacar.
5. An Israelite of the sons of Zattu who had taken a foreign wife (Ezra 10:27).
6. An Israelite of the sons of Hattum required to divorce his foreign wife (Ezra 10:33).
7. A man among the sons of Nebo who had married a non-Israelite wife (Ezra 10:43).
GARY M. BURGE

ZABADEANS (Gk. *Zabadaíoi*)
An Arab people, apparently named for their village of Zabad, attacked and crushed by the Hasmonean Jonathan when the Seleucid opponents he had been pursuing eluded him across the Eleutherus River (probably the Nahr el-Kebir in central Lebanon; 1 Macc. 12:31). Since Jonathan promptly returned to the region of Damascus (1 Macc. 12:32), the village was apparently NW of that city, possibly at modern Zebdani, ca. 28 km. (17 mi.) from Damascus (cf. Kepherzabad, "town of Zabad," NW of Hamath).

ZABBAI (Heb. *zabbay*)
1. An Israelite who had taken a foreign wife (Ezra 10:28).
2. The father of Baruch, who helped repair a section of the wall (Neh. 3:20 **K; Q** "Zaccai"). He may be the same as **1** above.

ZABDI (Heb. *zaḇdî*) (also ZICHRI, ZIMRI)
1. A Judahite, ancestor of Achan (Josh. 7:1, 17-18). He is called Zimri (**3**) at 1 Chr. 2:6.
2. A son of Shimei of the tribe of Benjamin (1 Chr. 8:19).
3. A Shiphmite; steward of David's wine cellar (1 Chr. 27:27).
4. A Levite and son of Asaph (Neh. 11:17). He is called Zichri (**5**) at 1 Chr. 9:15.

ZABDIEL (Heb. *zaḇdîʼēl;* Gk. *Sabdiḗl*)
1. A Judahite; the father of Jashobeam, commander of David's first army division (1 Chr. 27:2).
2. The son of Haggedolim; overseer of Jerusalem priests after the Exile (Neh. 11:14).
3. An Arab who decapitated Alexander Balas when he sought refuge in Arabia from the Egyptian king Ptolemy VI Philometor. Zabdiel then sent the head to Ptolemy (1 Macc. 11:17).

ZABUD (Heb. *zāḇûḏ*)
A son of Nathan; a priest at the time of Solomon who held the office of "king's friend" (1 Kgs. 4:5).

ZACCAI (Heb. *zakkay*)
An Israelite whose descendants returned with Zerubbabel from captivity in Babylon (Ezra 2:9 = Neh. 7:14; cf. 3:20 **Q**).

ZACCHAEUS (Gk. *Zakchaíos*)

1. An officer in the Maccabean army (2 Macc. 10:19).

2. The diminutive tax official who climbs a tree to catch a glimpse of the wayfaring Jesus, a story unique to Luke (Luke 19:1-10) and containing many of his important themes. The designation "chief tax collector" (Gk. *architelṓnēs*), a term found only here in the extant Greek literature, identifies Zacchaeus as a marginal Jew (a "sinner," Luke 19:7), a member of the "lost" (v. 10) whom Jesus comes to save. The hospitality extended by Zacchaeus underscores the inclusive nature of Jesus' table-fellowship practice; that the "rich" Zacchaeus (Luke 19:2) is willing to recompense his victims fourfold demonstrates a proper stance toward wealth that finds particular emphasis in the journey section of Luke's Gospel (16:13-14, 19-31; 18:18-30). As to whether Zacchaeus is defending himself against charges of extortion or expressing resolve to right past wrongs, the present tense of the Greek verbs in Luke 19:8 permits either interpretation. In the case of the latter, the story focuses on the conversion of a "son of Abraham" (Luke 19:9) who brings forth the righteous fruits of repentance (3:8). That the entire household of Zacchaeus experiences the salvation that Jesus brings places this story squarely within the "household salvation" matrix of Luke and Acts (Acts 10:2; 11:14; 16:14-15, 31-34; 18:8) and invests the pattern with dominical significance. An unfortunate consequence of the descriptive powers of the Third Evangelist is the fact that for many readers the most notable characteristic about Zacchaeus is that he was short.

Bibliography. D. L. Bock, *Luke* (Grand Rapids, 1996) 2:1513-24; A. A. Just, Jr., *The Ongoing Feast: Table Fellowship and Eschatology at Emmaus* (Collegeville, 1993), 184-93; D. L. Matson, *Household Conversion Narratives in Acts.* JSNTSup 123 (Sheffield, 1996), 70-75. DAVID LERTIS MATSON

ZACCUR (Heb. *zakkûr*)

1. The father of the spy Shammua of the tribe of Reuben (Num. 13:4).

2. A Simeonite; the son of Hammuel, and a descendant of Mishma (1 Chr. 4:26).

3. A Levite of the Merarite line (1 Chr. 24:27).

4. A Levite and son of Asaph who was leader of the third division of temple musicians during the reign of David (1 Chr. 25:2, 10; Neh. 12:35).

5. A descendant of Bigvai who returned from exile with Ezra (Ezra 8:14).

6. A son of Imri who was among those who rebuilt the walls of Jerusalem (Neh. 3:2).

7. A Levite who set his seal to the new covenant under Nehemiah (Neh. 10:12[MT 13]).

8. The father of Hanan, a Levite who lived during the governorship of Nehemiah (Neh. 13:13).

GREGORY D. JORDAN

ZADOK (Heb. *ṣāḏôq*; Gk. *Sadṓk*)

1. A man of obscure genealogy who served first as high priest under David alongside Abiathar (2 Sam. 8:17), and later as sole high priest during Solomon's long reign. That Zadok served both David and Solomon suggests that he was considerably younger than Abiathar and, like Benaiah ben Jehoiada, may have been a latecomer to David's entourage. After Solomon had expelled Abiathar over his support for Adonijah, Zadok became sole holder of the high priestly office under Solomon and the progenitor of the Jerusalemite priesthood. This sinecure was Zadok's reward for his support of Bathsheba and Solomon in the intrigue surrounding the succession to David's throne (1 Kgs. 1:8, 34, 38-39). Zadok's son Ahimaaz appears to have been one of David's professional soldiers (2 Sam. 18:19, 22).

Although the genealogies in 1 Chr. 5:24–6:3(MT 5:29); 24:3 make Zadok a descendant of Aaron, the best evidence is that Zadok was the founder of a new priestly line, intended to replace the northern priesthood represented by the Aaronites at Shiloh and Bethel, and perhaps by Abiathar and his descendants as well. The Davidic language of the prophecy against the Aaronite Eli and his sons in 1 Sam. 2:27-36, reminiscent of the prophecy of Nathan in 2 Sam. 7, can only apply to Zadok, and like Ps. 78:56-72 looks to replacing the northern tradition with a new one (based in Jerusalem). Many scholars look for Zadok's origins in pre-Israelite Jerusalem, perhaps as the pre-Davidic priest-king of Jerusalem, placed into the high priesthood of Israel as a conciliatory gesture toward the conquered Jebusite majority. Thus, the Aaronite genealogies of Zadok would simply be later attempts, probably postexilic, to incorporate Zadok into the more orthodox traditions of Israel. This interpretation implies that the Zadokites' attempt to establish themselves as a new line, replacing the old Aaronite priestly houses of the north, failed. Unable to overcome the weight of tradition, the Zadokites had to have themselves grafted onto the despised Aaronite heritage in place of Eli and his sons in order to establish their full legitimacy within the Israelite religion.

Nevertheless, during the postexilic age the Zadokites eventually did prevail in their claim to be the chosen priesthood, and they may have held the high-priestly office until the reign of Antiochus IV Epiphanes. The NT Sadducees are probably the descendants of this extremely old and conservative sect, whose members transcended their Canaanite origins to become the guarantors of the Yahwistic cultus.

2. The father of Jerusha, the mother of King Jotham of Judah (2 Kgs. 15:33 = 2 Chr. 27:1).

3. One who took part in the postexilic rebuilding of the walls of Jerusalem; the son of Baana (Neh. 3:4).

4. The son of Immer who repaired the Jerusalem wall "opposite his own house" (Neh. 3:29).

5. One of the "leaders of the people" who set their seals to the covenant in the time of Nehemiah (Neh. 10:21[22]).

6. A scribe appointed by Nehemiah as one of the treasurers over the Levites' storehouses (Neh. 13:13).

7. The father of Achim and son of Azor (Matt. 1:14) according to the Matthean genealogy of Jesus, which traces Jesus' descent through Joseph back to the house of David. The name is not found in the Lukan genealogy, except in a single obscure manuscript (D).

DONALD G. SCHLEY/MICHAEL S. SPENCE

ZADOKITE FRAGMENTS (CD)

See DAMASCUS DOCUMENT.

ZAHAM (Heb. *zāham*)
A son of King Rehoboam and Mahalath (2 Chr. 11:19).

ZAIR (Heb. *ṣā'îr*)
The site of King Joram's unsuccessful battle to maintain Judean sovereignty over the Edomites (2 Kgs. 8:21). Zair was probably in or near Edom (Seir; cf. Zoar, Gen. 19:20-22); the identification with Zior, a town in the Judean hill country (Josh. 15:54) as suggested by some LXX manuscripts, is less likely.

ZALAPH (Heb. *ṣālāp̱*)
The father of Hanun, one who worked with Nehemiah to repair the Jerusalem walls (Neh. 3:30).

ZALMON (Heb. *ṣalmôn*) **(PERSON)** (also ILAI)
An Ahohite, and one of David's Champions (2 Sam. 23:28). At 1 Chr. 11:29 he is called Ilai.

ZALMON (Heb. *ṣalmôn*) **(PLACE)**

1. A mountain in the vicinity of Shechem where Abimelech and his men cut wood to use in burning out the people who had barricaded themselves in the "tower of Shechem" (Judg 9:48-49). It is most often identified with the slopes of either Mt. Gerazim or Mt. Ebal, although it could simply be an alternative name for one or the other of these famous peaks.

2. A mountain mentioned in Ps 68:14(MT 15). The poetic context seems to place it parallel to the "mountain of Bashan," which to most scholars implies a location E of the Jordan River, perhaps in the vicinity of Mt. Hermon. Even so, this passage may refer to the mountain near Shechem (**1** above).

WADE R. KOTTER

ZALMONAH (Heb. *ṣalmōnâ*)
An Israelite campsite during the wilderness wanderings, located between Mt. Hor and Punon (Num. 33:41-42).

ZALMUNNA (Heb. *ṣalmunnā'*)
One of a pair of Midianite kings whom Gideon captured and slew because they had murdered his brothers (Judg. 8:4-21; Ps. 83:11[MT 12]).

ZAMZUMMIM (Heb. *zamzummîm*)
The name given by the Ammonites to a group of Rephaim who had dwelt in Canaan. The Ammonites displaced them, in spite of their great number, strength, and size (Deut. 2:20-21; cf. Gen. 14:5; Deut. 3:11).

ZANOAH (Heb. *zānôaḥ*) **(PERSON)**
The son of Jekuthiel, and a descendant of Mered and his Jewish wife (1 Chr. 4:18); perhaps the founder of the Calebite town Zanoah **2.**

ZANOAH (Heb. *zānôaḥ*) **(PLACE)**

1. A town in the northeastern Shephelah of Judah and part of that tribe's inheritance (Josh. 15:34). It may have served as a subdistrict in the district of Keilah after the exiles returned from Babylon (Neh. 11:30); its inhabitants helped repair the Valley Gate (3:13). The site is commonly identified with Khirbet Zānû'/Ḥorvat Zānôaḥ (150125), situated on the ridge S of the Sorek Valley, overlooking the north-south valley that separates the Shephelah from the hill country, ca. 3.5 km. (2 mi.) S of Beth-shemesh. Remains of a Late Roman/Byzantine public building have been identified.

2. A town in the eastern hill country of Judah, within the same district as Maon and Ziph (Josh. 15:56). It is listed among the descendants of Judah (1 Chr. 4:18), apparently founded by Jekuthiel and thus linked by a possible Calebite kinship connection (1 Chr. 2, 4). The other sites mentioned in close proximity (Socoh, Jekuthiel, Keilah, and Eshtemoa) are not necessarily hill country sites. The location of Zanoah is uncertain, but it may be in the vicinity of Wadi Abu Zennakh.

Bibliography. Y. Aharoni, *The Land of the Bible,* 2nd ed. (Philadelphia, 1979); Z. Ilan, "Ancient Synagogues Survey: Judean Shephelah," *Excavations and Surveys in Israel* 7-8 (1988/89): 5-6; A. F. Rainey, "The Biblical Shephelah of Judah," *BASOR* 251 (1983): 1-22.

JENNIFER L. GROVES

ZAPHENATH-PANEAH (Heb. *ṣāp̱ĕnaṯ pa'nēaḥ*)
The Egyptian name given to Joseph when Pharaoh set him "over all the land of Egypt" (Gen. 41:45). The meaning of the name is not certain; its derivation from Egyp. *ḏd-pꜣ-ntr-w.f-'nh* ("the deity speaks and [the bearer of the name] lives") is commonly accepted, but would have to be dated later than Joseph.

GARY M. BURGE

ZAPHON (Heb. *ṣāp̱ôn*) **(CITY)**
A city on the eastern side of the Jordan River, taken from Sihon and given to the tribe of Gad (Josh. 13:27). Later it became a battleground between the forces of Jephthah and Ephraimites who assailed Jephthah for not inviting them to pursue the Ammonites (Judg. 12:1). Zaphon probably appears in the Egyptian records of 18th Dynasty as Dapuna, and in the Amarna Letters as Sapuna. It is generally identified as modern Tell el-Qôs (208182), 5 km. (3 mi.) N of Deir 'Alla on the N side of the Wadi Raġib.

Bibliography. N. Glueck, "Three Israelite Towns in the Jordan Valley: Zarethan, Succoth, Zaphon," *BASOR* 90 (1943): 2-23.

ZELJKO GREGOR

ZAPHON (Heb. *ṣāpôn*) **(MOUNTAIN)**
A high mountain (ca. 1770 m. [5807 ft.]) on the coastal border between Syria and Turkey (W. Sem. *ṣpn/ṣpwn* [**ṣapūnu*], classical Mons Casius, modern Jebel el-Aqraʿ). It is the divine abode of the weather-god Hadad/Haddu, Lord of Zaphon (Baal-zaphon). The mountain plays a central role in Ugaritic/Canaanite mythological tradition and as such underlies the biblical accounts (Ps. 48:2[MT 3]; Isa. 14:13; cf. Ps. 89:12[13]; Ezek. 1:4). Heb. *ṣāpôn*, "north" (regarding wind direction), and place names such as Baal-zephon (Exod. 14:2) and Zaphon (Josh. 13:27) may derive from Baal's mythical abode.

Bibliography. H. Niehr, "Zaphon," *DDD*, 927-29.

MEINDERT DIJKSTRA

ZARATHUSTRA (O. Pers. *zrdrwšt*),
ZOROASTER (Gk. *Zōroástrēs*)
The founder of Zoroastrianism, the major pre-Islamic religion of Iran. He is typically dated ca. 628-551 B.C.E., but some authorities argue for a date between 1500 and 1200, and some devotees even claim he lived several thousand years earlier. The claim for the earlier periods revolves around the date of 17 hymns, the Gāthās, which are the primary written evidence for his existence and which contain archaic linguistic forms as old as the Rig Veda in Hinduism.

Zoroaster was born in central Iran into a well-to-do family, who provided him with a formal education at the hands of a tutor. At age 20 he left his parents to wander about, seeking answers to the meaning of life. At 30 he had a call vision, which included the visit of an archangel. He spent 10 years teaching before registering his first convert, a cousin. Zoroaster's career reached a turning point when he traveled to eastern Iran to the court of the Aryan king Vishtāspa. The priests of Vishtāspa resisted his ideas and managed to have him thrown into prison, but Zoroaster healed one of the king's favorite horses. In exchange the king and queen accepted his teachings, their son agreed to fight for Zoroaster, and the priests who had imprisoned him were punished. The last 20 years of Zoroaster's life were spent promoting and defending his new religion. He died at the age of 77 in a battle against the Turanians (marauding nomads from north of Persia).

See ZOROASTRIANISM. PAUL L. REDDITT

Mede carrying a barsom or bundle of rods used in Zoroastrian ritual. Gold plaquette from the Oxus treasure (Copyright British Museum)

ZAREPHATH (Heb. *ṣārĕp̱aṯ*; Gk. *Sárepta*)
A Phoenician port city (176316; modern Ṣarafand) located on the Mediterranean coast between Tyre and Sidon. Captured by Sennacherib in 701 B.C.E. (Akk. *Zaribtu*), it was a thriving commercial center in the Roman period.

During a time of severe famine God commanded Elijah to go to Zarephath, where a widow would take care of him (1 Kgs. 17:8-24). As reward for her hospitality, Elijah miraculously replenished her supply of oil and flour and healed her dying son (cf. Luke 4:25-26). Obad. 20 promises that the restored exiles would possess the land from Edom to Zarephath.

JOE E. LUNCEFORD

ZARETHAN (Heb. *ṣārĕṯān*)
A city or region on the east side of the Jordan Valley near the town of Adam (modern Tell ed-Dâmiya), and near which the waters of the Jordan heaped up when the Israelites crossed the river en route to Canaan (Josh. 3:16). King Solomon's foundry was later located near Zarethan (1 Kgs. 7:46). Many scholars equate the Zeredah of 2 Chr. 4:17 and Zereath of Judg. 7:22 with Zarethan.

Identifying the site of Zarethan has been exacerbated by the fact that the locations of the other sites associated with Zarethan in the biblical text are also, for the most part, uncertain. The fact that a Zarethan appears within a list of northern Jordan Valley towns which were located within Solomon's fifth administrative district (1 Kgs. 4:12) has led scholars to place Zarethan more to the north in the Jordan Valley. These scholars maintain that rather than translating Adam's location in Josh. 3:16 as "beside" or "near" Zarethan, the text should read, "from Adam as far as Zarethan," which would allow a more northerly location and make the event appear all the more miraculous.

The favored candidate for Zarethan has been Tell es-Sa'idiyeh (204186; 18 km. [11 mi.] N of Tell ed-Dâmiya), although Tell Umm Ḥamâd (205172; ca. 6 km. [4 mi.] NE of ed-Dâmiya), Tell Qos (5 km. [3 mi.] ESE of Tell es-Sa'idiyeh), Qarn Sartabeh (193167; west bank, opposite of Dâmiya), and Tell Sleihat (16 km. [10 mi.] N of Deir 'Alla) have also been suggested. Unfortunately, currently available textual and archaeological data are insufficient to resolve conclusively the question of Zarethan's location and identity. RANDALL W. YOUNKER

ZARIUS (Gk. *Zários*)
The brother of King Jehoiakim whom Jehoiakim brought back from (or exiled to) Egypt (1 Esdr. 1:38). However, the author of 1 Esdras apparently confused 2 Chr. 36 and 2 Kgs. 23:30-35 and Jehoiakim with Jehoiakin, thus associating this Zarius with Jehoahaz (also called Jeconiah in 1 Esdr. 1:34), who was made king upon the death of Josiah in 609 but later exiled to Egypt (where, according to 2 Kgs. 23, he died). The name Zarius may also derive from a corruption of Zedekiah, one of the three brothers of Jehoiakim (1 Chr. 3:16).
DANIEL L. SMITH-CHRISTOPHER

ZATTU (Heb. *zattû'*)
An Israelite whose descendants returned with Zerubbabel from the Babylonian Exile (Ezra 2:8; Neh. 7:13; cf. NRSV Ezra 8:5, following LXX, 1 Esdr. 8:32). Six members of the clan are named as having taken foreign wives (Ezra 10:27), and the current leader set his seal to the renewed covenant under Nehemiah (Neh. 10:14[MT 15]).

ZAZA (Heb. *zāzā'*)
A Judahite, son of Jonathan (**18**) and descendant of Jerahmeel (1 Chr. 2:33).

ZEAL, ZEALOT
The display of fervent devotion or jealousy on behalf of valued possessions (including persons) perceived to be under threat from rival claimants. Righteous zeal (Heb. *qin'â;* Gk. *zēlos*) is manifested chiefly in the interest of maintaining the covenantal bond between Yahweh and Israel. The Lord himself is "a jealous God" (Exod. 20:5; Deut. 5:9; Josh. 24:19), fiercely protecting his people and demanding their exclusive loyalty. When "provoked to jealousy" by their apostasy, the Lord retaliates in judgment, typically abandoning them to oppressive foreign powers (Deut. 29:14-29; 32:16-27; 1 Kgs. 14:22-26). Ultimately, however, the Lord's zeal for his own honor (or "holy name," Ezek. 39:25) will incite him to rise up against Israel's enemies in fiery wrath (Isa. 26:11-15; Ps. 79:5-13) and restore her to the Promised Land and holy city of Jerusalem (also objects of the Lord's zeal; cf. Ezek. 36:5-7; Joel 2:18-20; Zech. 1:14-17).

In reciprocal response to Yahweh's faithful passion, Israel is expected to be "consumed" with zeal for the Lord, his law, and his sanctuary (Ps. 69:9[MT 10]; 119:139). Classic models include Phinehas the priest, who speared to death an Israelite man and his foreign (Midianite) wife, thus staving off the devouring "jealousy" of the Lord (presumably regarding Israel's consorting with idolaters; Num. 25:6-18), and Elijah the prophet and Jehu the king, both of whom demonstrated exceptional zeal for the Lord by brutally eradicating, through fire and sword, the worship of Baal in 9th-century Israel (1 Kgs. 19:10, 14; cf. 18:20-46; 2 Kgs. 10:16-28).

In the Second Temple era, Phinehas and Elijah are both memorialized as heroic zealots (Sir. 45:23-26; 48:1-11; 1 Macc. 2:26, 54, 58). These two figures became the prototypes for Mattathias and the Maccabean rebels against Hellenistic assimilation; like his forebears, Mattathias "burned with zeal" for the covenant (1 Macc. 2:24), prompting vicious action against both Judean quislings and Greek overlords.

In the NT, the Fourth Gospel refers to Jesus' zeal, associating his disruptive demonstration in the temple with the psalmist's consuming "zeal for your house" (John 2:17; Ps. 69:9[10]). The mention of Simon dubbed *Zēlōtēs* among the 12 apostles marks the only other link between zeal and the Jesus movement (Luke 6:15; Acts 1:13; the "Cananaean" in Matt. 10:4; Mark 3:18 probably stems from an Aramaic equivalent for "zealot"). Nothing, however, is known concerning Simon's particular expression of zeal. Any connection with the Zealot party described by Josephus — a guerilla band of Jewish peasants who overran Jerusalem in 67-68 C.E. in opposition to Herodian and Roman rule (*BJ* 4.128-584) — remains speculative.

Both his letters and the book of Acts attest to Paul's intense zeal for God and ancestral Jewish law, which spurred him to carry out violent reprisals — not against Rome or any other foreign foes, but against the followers of Jesus Messiah whom he regarded in some sense as blasphemous covenant-breakers (Gal. 1:14; Phil. 3:6; Acts 22:3). Acts also depicts other Jewish leaders as zealous attackers of the Church (Acts 5:17; 13:45; 17:5); here, however, they appear zealous (jealous) not primarily for God's honor but for their own position which they perceive being undermined by popular Christian evangelists.

In the wake of his shattering conversion, Paul's zeal was redirected toward promoting the Way which he had persecuted. He continued to affirm his fellow Jews' basic "zeal for God" but insisted they become more "enlightened" concerning the righteousness which God established through faith in Christ, apart from the law (Rom. 10:1-4). Paul aimed to provoke his people to such renewed zeal by making them jealous of his salvific ministry to the Gentiles (Rom. 10:19; 11:11, 14). Alternatively, Acts stresses that Paul's law-free gentile mission in no way compromised his affinity with Jewish believers who remained "zealous for the law" (Acts 21:20-26).

Bibliography. R. H. Bell, *Provoked to Jealousy: The Origin and Purpose of the Jealousy Motif in Romans 9–11.* WUNT 63 (Tübingen, 1994); R. A.

Horsley, *Jesus and the Spiral of Violence: Popular Jewish Resistance in Roman Palestine* (1987, repr. Minneapolis, 1993); C. Seeman, "Zeal/Jealousy," in *Biblical Social Values and Their Meaning*, ed. J. J. Pilch and B. J. Malina (Peabody, 1993), 185-88; N. T. Wright, "Paul, Arabia, and Elijah (Gal. 1:17)," *JBL* 115 (1996): 683-92. F. SCOTT SPENCER

ZEBADIAH (Heb. *zĕḇadyâ, zĕḇaḏyāhû*)

1. A Benjaminite, one of the nine sons of Beriah (1 Chr. 8:15).

2. A Benjaminite, one of the seven sons of Elpaal (1 Chr. 8:17).

3. One of the two sons of Jeroham from Gedor who came to David at Ziklag (1 Chr. 12:7[MT 8]). A Benjaminite warrior and kinsman of Saul, he could sling stones with either hand (1 Chr. 12:2[3]).

4. A temple gatekeeper, the third of seven sons of Meshelemiah; according to the MT a Korahite and one of the sons of Asaph (1 Chr. 26:2).

5. The son of Joab's brother Asahel. He succeeded Asahel in commanding the fourth division of David's army (1 Chr. 27:7).

6. A Levite sent by King Jehoshaphat to teach the book of the law in the cities (2 Chr. 17:8).

7. The son of Ishmael and leader of the tribe of Judah during the reign of Jehoshaphat (2 Chr. 19:11). He supervised the judges responsible for royal law.

8. Son of Michael, head of the descendants of Shephatiah, and leader of a group who returned with Ezra to Jerusalem during the reign of Artaxerxes (Ezra 8:8).

9. A descendant of the priestly family of Immer. Zebadiah had married a foreign woman and divorced her at Ezra's urging (Ezra 10:20).

ROBIN GALLAHER BRANCH

ZEBAH (Heb. *zeḇaḥ*)

A Midianite king whom Gideon captured and slew in retaliation for the murder of his brothers (Judg. 8:4-21; Ps. 83:11[MT 12]).

ZEBEDEE (Gk. *Zebedaíos*)

A Galilean fisherman and father of the apostles James and John. Zebedee may have been wealthy since he employed fishermen and owned a boat (Mark 1:19-20). The departure of his two sons exemplifies the breaking of familial ties found in Jesus' teachings (Mark 10:29 par.; Matt. 10:37; Luke 14:26). Zebedee reappears only in references to his sons and to their mother, Salome (Matt. 27:56; cf. Mark 15:40), who requested that Jesus allow James and John to sit at his right and left in his kingdom (Matt. 20:20-21). EMILY CHENEY

ZEBIDAH (Heb. *zĕḇîḏâ*)

The daughter of Pedaiah of Rumah; mother of King Jehoiakim of Judah (**K** 2 Kgs. 23:36; **Q** *zĕḇûḏâ*).

ZEBINA (Heb. *zĕḇînā'*)

A postexilic descendant of Nebo who divorced his foreign wife (Ezra 10:43).

ZEBOIIM (Heb. *ṣĕḇō'îm, ṣĕḇōyîm*)

One of five "cities of the plain" destroyed by the Lord, along with Sodom and Gomorrah, because of their wickedness (Gen. 19:24-29). Although the account of God's overthrow of Sodom and Gomorrah does not mention Zeboiim, its destruction is assumed in Deut. 29:23(MT 22); Hos. 11:8. Zeboiim marked the Canaanites' southern border (Gen. 10:19), and was one of the five cities attacked by Chedorlaomer and three other kings; Shemeber, king of Zeboiim, with his four allies, opposed Chedorlaomer and was defeated in the valley of Siddim (Gen. 14:1-10). KENNETH ATKINSON

ZEBOIM (Heb. *ṣĕḇōʿîm*)

1. A valley in Benjamin, located SE of Michmash, possibly identified with modern Wadi Abū Ḍabāʿ, toward which a reconnaissance party of Philistine soldiers from Michmash was sent during the reign of Saul (1 Sam. 13:18).

2. A town occupied by the Benjaminites following the Exile (Neh. 11:34). Its location is unknown. KENNETH ATKINSON

ZEBUL (Heb. *zĕḇul*)

The ruler of the city of Shechem who informed the judge Abimelech of Gaal's plans to lead the Shechemites in revolt against Israel. After Gaal was defeated, Zebul drove him and his kinsfolk from Shechem (Judg. 9:30-41).

ZEBULUN (Heb. *zĕḇûlûn;* Gk. *Zaboulṓn*)

Jacob's tenth son and Leah's sixth and last (Gen. 30:19-20); the eponymous ancestor of the tribe inhabiting territory in the Galilee region. The name is related by folk etymology at Gen. 30:20 to Heb. *zbl*, "to exalt, honor," also a play on the related root *zbd*, "give" or "gift." Moreover, the meaning "to exalt" may have topographical significance, since the tribal allotment of Zebulun includes the mountainous (exalted, raised up) region north of Jezreel.

The tribal territory of Zebulun shared borders with Asher to the west, Naphtali to the east, Manasseh to the southwest, and Issachar to the southeast. Although this territory may have included part of the plain of Jezreel or the plain of Acco, it was mainly confined to the mountain rim N of Jezreel. Thus Zebulun was situated in a richly forested region, landlocked and removed from the main centers of Canaanite settlement. References to Zebulun living by the sea (Gen. 49:13) and feasting on the abundance of the seas (Deut. 33:19) suggest that the tribe did extend at some time to the Mediterranean (Josephus *Ant.* 5.1.22).

Although Zebulun is listed among those tribes that failed to drive out the Canaanites from their territory (Judg. 1:30), other reports suggest that they were loyal members of the Israelite tribal league. The Song of Deborah praises the Zebulunites for their exceptional courage in defeating Sisera's forces (Judg. 4:6, 10; 5:14, 18). Gideon summons Zebulunites to accompany him in his victory against the Midianites and Amalekites (Judg. 6:35). The Zebulunite Elon led Israel for 10 years as judge

(Judg. 12:11-12). Furthermore, the tribe of Zebulun provides David with a large contingent of troops (1 Chr. 12:33), and Zebulunites participate in Hezekiah's Passover (2 Chr. 30:11). Finally, the prophet Jonah came from Gath-hepher, a city located within Zebulun (2 Kgs. 14:25).

The tribes of Zebulun and Issachar are closely connected in several passages, including Moses' blessing (Deut. 33:18; cf. Judg. 5:14; Ezek. 48:26, 33), reflecting their proximity in birth and in location (Gen. 30:17-20; Josh. 19:10-23). Similarly, Zebulun is paired with Naphtali (Judg. 4:6; 5:18; 6:35; Ps. 68:27[MT 28]). Noteworthy is Isaiah's prophecy of Zebulun's glorious future (Isa. 9:1-2[8:23–9:1]), which Matt. 4:13-16 connects with Jesus' ministry in the Galilee region.

Bibliography. Z. Kallai, *Historical Geography of the Bible: The Tribal Territories of Israel* (Leiden, 1986). JEFFREY C. GEOGHEGAN/DANIEL L. HAWK

ZECHARIAH (Heb. *zĕḵaryâ, zĕḵaryāhû;* Gk. *Zacharías*) (also ZECHER)

The name means "Yahweh remembers," evidently a plea for God to remember his covenant with Israel and extend divine aid, which probably explains its popularity during the exilic and postexilic periods.

1. A king of the northern kingdom (746 B.C.), the son of Jeroboam II (2 Kgs. 14:29; 15:8-12). Zechariah reigned only six months before he was assassinated by Shallum. With Zechariah's death the dynasty of Jehu came to an end, a fulfillment of the prophecy that this dynasty would rule for four generations (2 Kgs. 10:30; 15:12).

2. The father of Abi (Abijah), the mother of King Hezekiah (2 Kgs. 18:2 = 2 Chr. 29:1). Probably, the same person as **28** below.

3. The head of a family of Reubenites (1 Chr. 5:7).

4. A wise and prominent levitical gatekeeper during the reign of David (1 Chr. 9:21-22; 26:2, 14).

5. A Benjamite of Gibeon (1 Chr. 9:37). His brother Ner was the father of Kish, the father of King Saul (1 Chr. 9:36, 39). At 1 Chr. 8:31 he is called Zecher, an abbreviation of the name without the theophoric ending.

6. A levitical musician who played the harp as the ark was brought into Jerusalem during the reign of David (1 Chr. 15:18, 20; 16:5).

7. One of the priestly trumpeters who led the procession as the ark was brought into Jerusalem (1 Chr. 15:24).

8. A Levite and son of Isshiah, a contemporary of David (1 Chr. 24:25).

9. A levitical gatekeeper at the time of David; son of Hosah the Merarite (1 Chr. 26:11).

10. The father of Iddo, one of David's officers who ruled over the half-tribe of Manasseh in Gilead (1 Chr. 27:21).

11. An official of King Jehoshaphat assigned to teach the book of the law in the cities of Judah (2 Chr. 17:7-9).

12. A Levite and father of Jahaziel (2 Chr. 20:14), who prophesied that Jehoshaphat would be victorious over the Moabites, Ammonites, and Meunites (vv. 15-17).

13. A son of Jehoshaphat slain by his brother Jehoram (2 Chr. 21:2, 4).

14. A son of Jehoiada the priest. Zechariah publicly denounced Joash for his sin and was subsequently stoned to death by order of the king (2 Chr. 24:20-22). The murder was particularly heinous in light of the place where it occurred — the temple courtyard — and the kindness that Zechariah's father Jehoiada had shown to Joash. Because of this repulsive deed some of Joash's officials put the king to death (2 Chr. 24:25). Jesus alluded to Zechariah's martyrdom when condemning the hypocritical religious leaders of his day (Matt. 23:35; Luke 11:51).

15. An instructor of Uzziah (2 Chr. 26:5). Zechariah taught Uzziah "the fear of God," evidently an allusion to the Hebrew Scriptures (cf. Ps. 19:9[MT 10]). He has been variously identified as the Zechariah of Isa. 8:2 (**28**), the son of Jehoiada (**14**), or some other individual.

16. A levitical descendant of Asaph who participated in the purification of the temple during Hezekiah's religious reforms (2 Chr. 29:13).

17. A levitical descendant of Kohath who supervised the repairs of the temple during the reign of Josiah (2 Chr. 34:12).

18. One of three high-ranking priests who liberally contributed animals for Passover offerings during Josiah's reign (2 Chr. 35:8 = 1 Esdr. 1:8).

19. Head of the family of Parosh who with 150 kinsmen returned from Babylonia to Jerusalem with Ezra in the mid-5th century (Ezra 8:3).

20. Head of the family of Bebai who with 28 relatives returned to Jerusalem with Ezra (Ezra 8:11).

21. A leader of the Jewish exiles, sent to obtain ministers at Casiphia (Ezra 8:16); possibly the same as **19** or **20.**

22. A 5th-century Judean who had married a foreign wife (Ezra 10:26).

23. A leader who stood on the platform with Ezra during the public reading of the law (Neh. 8:4); likely the same as **21.**

24. An Judahite descendant of Perez, an inhabitant of Jerusalem in the Persian period (Neh. 11:4).

25. An ancestor of the Judahite Maaseiah, a resident of Jerusalem in the Persian period (Neh. 11:5).

26. An ancestor of Adaiah the priest, a postexilic inhabitant of Jerusalem (Neh. 11:12).

27. A priestly trumpeter who participated in Nehemiah's dedication of the walls of Jerusalem (Neh. 12:35, 41).

28. One of two prominent and trusted leaders in Jerusalem whom Isaiah called to be witnesses to the prophecy of the Assyrian destruction of Samaria and Damascus (Isa. 8:1-4). The son of Jeberechiah, he was probably the same Zechariah as the father of Abi mentioned in 2 Kgs. 18:2 = 2 Chr. 29:1.

29. The late 6th-century prophet to whom the book of Zechariah is attributed (Zech. 1:1, 7; 7:1, 8;

Neh. 12:16; Ezra 5:1; 6:14). Zechariah was also a priest and a contemporary of the prophet Haggai.

30. The father of Joseph, a Jewish general during the Maccabean War (1 Macc. 5:18, 56).

31. A representative of Josiah at the Passover festival (1 Esdr. 1:15); an alternate name for Heman (cf. 2 Chr. 35:15).

32. The father of John the Baptist, a member of the priestly division of Abijah (Luke 1:5-25, 57-80). The angel Gabriel appeared to Zechariah in the temple and informed him that his wife Elizabeth would bear an extraordinary child. Because of his unbelief, Zechariah was unable to speak until after the child was born. On the day the child was named, Zechariah's voice returned. He then uttered a beautiful prophecy concerning Israel's messianic hope, commonly known as the Benedictus (Luke 1:68-79). STEPHEN R. MILLER

ZECHARIAH, BOOK OF

The 11th book among the Minor Prophets. Zechariah is typically divided into two or three sections. Chs. 1–8 contain the preaching of the prophet Zechariah from the late 6th century B.C.E. Chs. 9–14 taken together may be called Second or Deutero-Zechariah. The fact that 9:1; 12:1 bear nearly identical superscriptions, however, has led many scholars to divide chs. 9–14 into Deutero-Zechariah (chs. 9–11) and Trito-Zechariah (chs. 12–14).

The view that Zech. 9–14 arose separately from Zech. 1–8 goes back at least to the 16th-century scholar Joseph Mede, who observed that Zech. 11:12-13 is attributed to Jeremiah in Matt. 27:9-10. Further, Zech. 12–14 exhibits stylistic features very different from Zech. 1–8, and nothing in Zech. 9–14 addresses the 6th-century conditions or persons prominent in Zech. 1–8.

Zechariah 1–8

Author and Date

Three superscriptions (1:1, 7; 7:1) attribute chs. 1–8 to Zechariah. He was a contemporary of Haggai, whose preaching seems to have undergone editing by the same hand as Zech. 1–8. The superscriptions all date between 520 and 518. Since these dates are redactional, a few scholars have questioned them, arguing that some of the visions between 1:7 and 6:15 actually arose a few years earlier.

Historical Setting

When in 538 Cyrus the Great issued his edict allowing exiles to return to Judah, few accepted the offer. According to Ezra 1:11 Sheshbazzar led a group back (Ezra 1:11) and began to rebuild the temple (5:16). That work ceased before the death of Cyrus in 530 and did not resume until 520, under the urging of Haggai and Zechariah upon the arrival in Jerusalem of Zerubbabel, the grandson of King Jehoiachin. Haggai called him God's signet right (Hag. 2:23), a title clearly reversing Jer. 22:24, where Jehoiachin is compared to a signet ring that God tore from his finger and threw away. Haggai apparently considered Zerubbabel to be the new Davidic king. Likewise, Zech. 4:9 attributes to Zerubbabel the kingly task of founding the new temple.

Message

Proto-Zechariah falls into three sections, each with its own superscription.

1:1-6. The first section, dated mid-October to mid-November 520, was probably a composition of the redactor. It contains a general admonition for the readers to avoid the mistakes of their preexilic forebears.

1:7–6:15. The second section, dated in early 519, contains eight visions, interspersed with two exhortations.

1:7-17. In the first vision Zechariah reports that God would become merciful toward Jerusalem. This vision might presuppose a Babylonian audience prior to their return to Jerusalem, just before 539 or, more likely, close to 520.

1:18-21(MT 2:1-4). The second vision reports the appearance of four horns and four blacksmiths. The horns represent the nations that had oppressed Israel, and the smiths represent God's agents who would strike them down.

2:1-5(2:5-9). In the third vision Zechariah sees a young man (angel?) measuring Jerusalem to see how many inhabitants it would hold. He is told not to worry. Since God would be its wall, there would be no limit to its growth.

2:6-13(2:10-17). The first exhortation calls the exiles in Babylon to return home. That exhortation suggests a date after 539, when such a journey was possible.

3:1-10. The fourth vision is sufficiently different from the others that some scholars think it is secondary, though written by Zechariah nonetheless. It shows God ordaining or installing Joshua as high priest for Jerusalem. The reference to the Branch in 3:8 and the picture of messianic peace in 3:10 perhaps referred to Zerubbabel originally.

4:1-14. The next vision depicts God's presence among his people. It is interrupted in 4:6b-10a with two short prophetic announcements about the role of Zerubbabel in rebuilding the temple where God would be present.

5:1-4. The sixth vision is of a huge, flying scroll that would purge the land of thieves and liars.

5:5-11. The seventh vision portrays wickedness being bottled up and sent to Babylon, where it would be worshipped.

6:1-8. The last vision depicts the future Jerusalem, where life would be good again and God could take a sabbath rest.

6:9-15. In view of what God was about to do among his people, a second exhortation also calls for the exiles to return to Jerusalem. An original injunction for Zechariah to have (four?) crowns made and placed in the temple as a memorial was changed into an injunction to set "crowns" on Joshua (6:11). The name Joshua is so unexpected here that many scholars suggest his name replaced that of Zerubbabel.

7:1–8:23. The third section of Proto-Zechariah is a collection of injunctions, not all perhaps authentic to Zechariah, within the framework of a question asked of him by emissaries from Bethel in 7:1-7 and answered in 8:18-19.

Zechariah 9–14

Date and Historical Setting

Various dates have been assigned to Zech. 9–14. The mention of Hadrach in 9:1 is said to require a date before 738, when that city lost its independent status. Also, the mention of Gaza is said to point to the defeat of that city by Sargon II in 720, and 10:10 is said to presuppose the Assyrian period after 660, probably in the time of Josiah. The majority thinks the campaign of Alexander the Great is reflected in 9:1-8, and the mention of "Greece" in 9:13 is said to clinch a date during the Greek period. Actually, the cities mentioned do not, in fact, represent Alexander's path to or from Egypt, and Judah had contact with Greece long before the 4th century. Dates as late as the Hasmoneans have been adduced from the reference to three deposed shepherds in 11:8 and the one who had been "pierced" mentioned in 12:10.

The Persian period seems a better date than any of these suggestions for several reasons. First, Zech. 9:8 presupposes both the destruction and the rebuilding of the temple, so both ch. 9 and the redaction of chs. 9–14 date after 515. Further, Zech. 14 is widely held to be the latest part of Deutero-Zechariah, and 14:10 describes the boundaries of the future Jerusalem. In doing so, it mentions gates known from preexilic times (the Benjamin Gate and the Corner Gate), but not repaired by Nehemiah. That might suggest that the redactor worked before Nehemiah's mission to repair the walls and used the only boundaries known to him and his contemporaries. If so, Zech. 14 was written before 445, and the redaction of Zech. 9–14 could have occurred any time after that.

Life in the tiny subprovince of Judah in the first half of the 5th century would have been characterized by several tensions that Deutero-Zechariah addresses. The first was the division between those people who had experienced the Exile and those who had not. The most obvious areas of competition were over land ownership and control of offices, especially the priesthood. Even the repatriated exiles, coming in waves for different reasons, may well have competed among each other for the perquisites of the postexilic community. A second division that shows itself in Neh. 13 is the struggle between the inhabitants of Jerusalem and some of those who lived elsewhere, particularly landed nobles in Judah. The third division was geographic, north versus south, over control of Judah and Jerusalem, as Nehemiah's troubles with Sanballat and Tobiah make clear.

Author

Deutero-Zechariah was anonymous. It was attached to Proto-Zechariah, perhaps because it seems to explain why the joyful feasts and contagious spirituality and prosperity envisioned in 8:18-23 had not yet come about. Two schools of thought have emerged to locate the social setting of the author and his group. One suggestion is that Zech. 9–14 is the product of nonpriestly, disenfranchised persons, more or less apocalyptic. The opposing view is that the chapters are the product of priests, who nevertheless were no longer in power. Either way, the group and its spokesperson perceived themselves as outside the real power structure in postexilic Judah and having written a program for a better future.

Message

In that program, Deutero-Zechariah dealt with the problem of unfulfilled expectations in postexilic Israel by using, with modifications, traditional hopes of the community.

9:1-17. Deutero-Zechariah envisioned the future restoration of the monarchy over the old Davidic Empire.

10:1-12. In the process Israel and Judah would be reunited.

11:1-17. Unfortunately, these hopes were nowhere near fruition, because the shepherds, the leaders of the people, were more interested in personal gain than in being good shepherds.

12:1-9. The redactor used the image of a future attack against Jerusalem to warn that the city would not outrank Judah when God set things right.

12:10-13:9. Indeed, what was needed before God could bring about full restoration was for him to send compassion and contrition on the haughty leading families in Jerusalem and to make false prophets ashamed of what they were doing.

14:1-21. When the city was purged of its sin, God could turn it into the place of blessing God intended it to be.

Bibliography. C. L. Meyers and E. M. Meyers, *Haggai, Zechariah 1-8.* AB 25B (Garden City, 1987); *Zechariah 9-14.* AB 25C (Garden City, 1993); R. F. Person, Jr., *Second Zechariah and the Deuteronomic School.* JSOTSup 167 (Sheffield, 1993); D. L. Petersen, *Haggai and Zechariah 1-8.* OTL (Philadelphia, 1984); *Zechariah 9-14 and Malachi.* OTL (Louisville, 1995); P. L. Redditt, *Haggai, Zechariah, Malachi.* NCBC (Grand Rapids, 1995); J. E. Tollington, *Tradition and Innovation in Haggai and Zechariah 1-8.* JSOTSup 150 (Sheffield, 1993).

PAUL L. REDDITT

ZECHER (Heb. *zeḵer*) (also ZECHARIAH)
A Benjaminite of the line of Gibeon (1 Chr. 8:31). The name is a shortened form of Zechariah (**5**) at 1 Chr. 9:37.

ZEDAD (Heb. *ṣĕḏāḏâ*)
A place on the northern border of Israel (Num. 34:8; Ezek. 47:15), probably to be identified with modern Ṣadâd (330430), ca. 105 km. (65 mi.) NE of Damascus in the vicinity of Riblah.

ZEDEKIAH (Heb. *ṣiḏqîyâ, ṣiḏqîyāhû*)
1. A (false) prophet at the court of Ahab of Israel who led the 400 prophets associated with

Samaria in their oracular support of a military campaign against Aram (1 Kgs. 22:1-36 = 2 Chr. 18:1-27); son of Chenaanah. In contrast to the corroborative message of Zedekiah, Micaiah the son of Imlah, summoned subsequently by Ahab at Jehoshaphat's request, opposed the military campaign and predicted Israel's defeat at Ramoth-gilead.

2. The last king of Judah (ca. 597-586 B.C.E.), uncle and successor of Jehoiachin (cf. 2 Chr. 36:10, "brother"). His given name, Mattaniah, was changed to Zedekiah by Nebuchadnezzar when the king of Babylon chose him to succeed Jehoiachin (2 Kgs. 24:17). Zedekiah reigned over Judah during the most tumultuous and tragic time in its history. He was 21 years old on his accession, and reigned 11 years in Jerusalem; his mother was Hamutal, daughter of Jeremiah of Libnah (2 Kgs. 24:18-19). According to the Deuteronomist Zedekiah was one of a long line of kings who did "evil in the sight of the Lord" (2 Kgs. 24:19). The Chronicler adds only that Zedekiah "did not humble himself before the prophet Jeremiah who spoke from the mouth of the Lord" (2 Chr. 36:12).

Little direct knowledge of Zedekiah or his kingdom survives outside the biblical materials. According to the biblical sources Zedekiah rebelled against Nebuchadnezzar and Babylonian sovereignty over Judah and appealed to Egypt for military support. This event receives considerable attention in 2 Chr. 36:13-14 (cf. Ezek. 17:11-21), the Deuteronomic history (2 Kgs. 24:20–25:21), and especially in the book of Jeremiah. The latter two sources view Zedekiah's rebellion as one of the determinate factors that led to the destruction of Jerusalem in 587 (cf. 1 Esdr. 1:46-58). In Jeremiah the prophet is depicted as counselor and confidant of Zedekiah who insisted that the king submit to Nebuchadnezzar as to the will of Yahweh. Although the demand for submission is accompanied by promises of well-being (e.g., Jer. 38:17-23), Zedekiah refuses to heed Jeremiah. Zedekiah, who is portrayed throughout the book of Jeremiah as a weak and tragic figure (in contrast to Jehoiakim, who is viewed as an evil ruler who controls his own destiny and that of the nation for ill; Jer. 36), cannot muster the faith and courage to prevent the collapse of Judah.

Although not mentioned directly in Ezekiel, Zedekiah is alluded to as one who wrongfully reneged on his oath to the king of Babylon (Ezek. 17:11-21).

3. A son of Josiah, included in the Chronicler's genealogy of Solomon (1 Chr. 3:15-16). He is associated with the construction of temple vessels that were eventually returned to the land of Judah by Baruch (Bar. 1:8).

4. An otherwise unknown leader of the Judah who signed the document that pledged obedience to the covenant of Nehemiah (Neh. 10:1[MT 9:38]).

5. A prophet whom Jeremiah accused of immoral conduct and of "prophesying a lie" in the name of Yahweh to the exiles residing in Babylon; son of Maaseiah (Jer. 29:21-23). Jeremiah predicted his execution at the hands of the Babylonian king on account of Zedekiah's deceptive words. Along with Ahab son of Kolaiayh and Hananiah son of Azzur, Zedekiah apparently represented a royal-temple ideology that affirms the invincibility of the premonarchic institutions. In contrast, Jeremiah insisted that such institutions and their belief systems were to be overthrown and nullified for new social and symbolic meanings during the exilic period.

6. The son of Hananiah; one of the officials of Judah, with whom Micaiah conversed after hearing Jeremiah's scroll read by Baruch. As one of the court officials of Jehoiakim, Zedekiah is "alarmed" when he hears the contents of the scroll and in response demands that it be read to the king (Jer. 36:11-19).

7. An ancestor of Baruch (Bar 1:1).

LOUIS STULMAN

ZEEB (Heb. *zĕʾēḇ*)
A Midianite prince who, together with Oreb, was captured by the Ephraimites, who beheaded him at his wine press (or a place so named because of this incident; Judg. 7:25; 8:3). The defeat of Midian and particularly of Oreb and Zeeb was long remembered in Israel (Ps. 83:11[MT 12]; cf. Isa. 10:26).

ZELA (Heb. *ṣēlaʿ*)
A site in the territory of Benjamin (Josh. 18:28), the burial place of Saul and Jonathan and of Saul's father Kish (2 Sam. 21:14) and so apparently the ancestral home of Saul's family. Some have suggested the name may have originally read *ṣēla haʾelep̱*, "rib of the ʾeleph," referring to the basic military unit (the "thousand") of the village. The location is unknown.

JOHN R. SPENCER

ZELEK (Heb. *ṣeleq*)
An Ammonite, perhaps a mercenary, among David's Thirty (2 Sam. 23:37; 1 Chr. 11:39).

ZELOPHEHAD (Heb. *ṣĕlop̱ĕḥāḏ*)
A descendant of Joseph through Manasseh (Num. 26:28-33) who died in the wilderness without a male heir and, presumably, without a widow who could benefit from invocation of the levirate custom. The significance of Zelophehad's plight is emphasized literally by a break in the pattern of the census report which stresses sons, clans, and descendants (Num. 26:33), by an inclusion of "daughters" enclosing the repetition of the phrase "the son of" (27:1), and by contrast of the repeated phrase "the son of" with the statement "had no sons, but daughters" (26:33; cf. Josh. 17:3). The prospect that Zelophehad's family would have no inheritance in Canaan seemed severe; accordingly, his daughters pleaded that he was not among those who rebelled with Korah and his personal sin no more severe than other ancestors who had died in the wilderness (Num. 27:1-4).

WALTER E. BROWN

ZELOPHEHAD'S DAUGHTERS (Heb. *ṣĕlop̱ĕḥāḏ*)
The daughters of Zelophehad, of the tribe of Manasseh, who petition Moses for inheritance of their father's property (Num. 27:1-11). The petition is notable because elsewhere in the Bible property

went to surviving male relatives (Deut. 21:15-17; Ruth 4:3; Jer. 32:6-15), and Zelophehad "had no sons, but daughters" (Num. 26:33). The daughters do inherit along with their father's brothers, and a new law is established for daughters to inherit land when there are no sons (Num. 27:6-11). The legal precedent implies that women were able to work and live off the land (Prov. 31:16; Cant. 8:12). In Num. 36:2-12 a further provision adds that the daughters must marry within their own tribe in order to retain the property within the tribe. This too becomes the occasion for a general law, that any daughter inheriting land from her father must marry within her father's tribe. The daughters retain their father's name by inheriting his land, and are themselves remembered by name in biblical texts: Mahlah, Noah, Hoglah, Milcah, Tirzah (Num. 26:33; 27:1; 36:11; Josh. 17:3). Two of those names, Hoglah and Noah, are mentioned in the Samaria ostraca in the region of Manasseh. Job, perhaps in extension from this law, generously gives his daughters an inheritance along with his sons, and they too are named in the text (Job. 42:13-15).

Bibliography. J. Weingreen, "The Case of the Daughters of Zelophchad," *VT* 16 (1966): 518-22.

CAREY WALSH

ZELZAH (Heb. *ṣelṣaḥ*)
A place where Samuel tells Saul he is to find the first of three signs confirming his anointing as king (1 Sam. 10:2). No such location "in the territory of Benjamin" is known, and the four consonants suggest a non-Semitic place name. The LXX renders the word "leaping greatly," and the Vulg. takes it as a temporal noun, "at noon." Numerous other suggestions have been made, including emending the word to read *bĕṣelṣĕlîm,* "with music," which would fit well the context of 1 Sam. 9–10.

PAUL L. REDDITT

ZEMARAIM (Heb. *ṣĕmārayim*)

1. A town in the tribal territory of Benjamin (Josh. 18:22). It is often identified with Râs eṭ-Ṭāḥûneh (170147), in the vicinity of Ramallah and el-Bireh.

2. A mountain in the hill country of Ephraim (2 Chr. 13:4), from which King Abijah of Judah addressed Jeroboam and the armies of Israel before defeating them in battle (vv. 4-18).

ZEMARITES (Heb. *ṣĕmārî*)
A people related to the Canaanites (Gen. 10:18; 1 Chr. 1:16). They are probably to be associated with Sumra, a city on the Phoenician coast between Tripoli and Arvad, called Ṣimirra in Assyrian texts and Ṣumur in the Amarna Letters.

ZEMER (Heb. *ṣemer*)
A city on the Phoenician coast, from which came skilled pilots who served on the Tyrian ships (Ezek. 27:8; MT "O Tyre"). The site may be modern Sumra, related to the Zemarites.

ZEMIRAH (Heb. *zĕmîrâ*)
A son of Becher of the tribe of Benjamin (1 Chr. 7:8).

ZENAN (Heb. *ṣĕnān*) (also ZAANAN)
A town in the Shephelah, or lowland, of Judah and part of that tribe's inheritance (Josh. 15:37). The location of the site is unknown, but it is listed within the district of Lachish and Eglon. Zenan is also included in Micah's lamentation over the Judean cities with the variant spelling *ṣa'ănān* (Zaanan; Mic. 1:11).

JENNIFER L. GROVES

ZENAS (Gk. *Zēnás*)
The apparent bearer, together with Apollos, of the Epistle to Titus, who is instructed to help them (materially) on their further travels (Titus 3:13). The designation of Zenas as a "lawyer" (Gk. *nomikós*), which in the Synoptic Gospels signifies a scribe versed in the Torah, may indicate here an expert in Roman or Greek law.

ZEPHANIAH (Heb. *ṣĕp̱anyâ, ṣĕp̱anyāhû*)

1. A Kohathite Levite, ancestor of the levitical singer Heman, to whom David gave responsibility for the ministry of music in the temple (1 Chr. 6:36[MT 21]).

2. The son of Cushi and a prophet during the reign of Josiah. He may have actively advanced the king's reforms. Unique in the prophetic corpus, the superscription to the book traces his ancestry back four generations (Zeph. 1:1), perhaps because he was a descendant of King Hezekiah. If so, Zephaniah was related to the royal family he was criticizing.

3. The son of Maaseiah, the "second priest" (next in rank to the high priest Seraiah) of Jerusalem (Jer. 21:1; 52:54) who on two occasions came as an emissary from King Zedekiah to the prophet Jeremiah (21:1; 37:3). Shemaiah, a false prophet exiled to Babylon, wrote Zephaniah a letter rebuking him for not having reprimanded or imprisoned Jeremiah (Jer. 29:24-28); instead, Zephaniah simply read this letter to the prophet (24:29). After the destruction of Jerusalem he was among the leaders of the city taken captive by Nebuzaradan, the captain of Nebuchadnezzar's guard, and brought before the Babylonian king at Riblah and put to death (2 Kgs. 25:18-21; Jer. 52:24-27).

4. The father of Josiah, to whose house the prophet Zechariah was directed to take the gold and silver collected from returned exiles to make a crown for the high priest Joshua (Zech. 6:10, 14).

GREG A. KING/MICHAEL A. GRISANTI

ZEPHANIAH, APOCALYPSE OF
A Jewish text bearing the pseudonym of the biblical prophet Zephaniah. Typical of the genre apocalypse, it consists of a 1st person report of the seer's cosmic journeys and visions in the presence of an interpreting angel. Zephaniah sees how angels record the deeds of humankind and he beholds the punishment of wicked souls in Hades. He soon finds himself in Hades, where he undergoes an or-

deal before the accusing angel who holds the manuscript of his sins. After praying for God's mercy, Zephaniah is declared triumphant by the good angel Eremiel, who possesses the manuscript of his righteous needs. Zephaniah then witnesses a series of angelic trumpet blasts and learns that the righteous patriarchs intercede for those in torment that sinners might repent and receive mercy before the final day of God's coming wrath.

Only about one fourth of the text has been preserved in two Coptic manuscripts and a Greek citation by Clement of Alexandria. It was probably composed in Greek in Egypt sometime between 100 B.C. and A.D. 175.

Bibliography. O. S. Wintermute, "Apocalypse of Zephaniah," *OTP* 1:497-515. RANDAL A. ARGALL

ZEPHANIAH, BOOK OF

One of the Minor Prophets, attributed to the prophet Zephaniah who ministered during the latter decades of the 7th century. This brief book of three chapters is notable for its single-minded focus on the day of the Lord and for parallels to other OT prophetic books, particularly the earlier prophets Amos, Isaiah, and Micah.

Historical Background

There seems little reason to doubt the information found in the book's superscription (1:1), locating the prophecy of Zephaniah during the reign of Josiah (640-609). The condemnation of idolatry (1:4-5), identity of foreign enemies (2:4-15), use of phraseology from Deuteronomy (e.g., compare 1:13 with Deut. 28:30; 3:19-20 with Deut. 30:3), as well as other features of the book, are consistent with the time of Josiah which witnessed the discovery of "the book of the law" (possibly including part or all of Deuteronomy) and vigorous religious reformation, including a purge of syncretistic worship practices.

Because the book refers to idolatrous worship (1:4-5) and lacks any explicit mention of Josiah's reforms, it is often maintained that Zephaniah prophesied before 622, Josiah's 18th year, when the law book was discovered in the temple (2 Kgs. 22:3, 8). However, the issue is probably not so clear-cut. It is likely that some idolatry either survived the reforms or quickly reappeared after them. Also, the similarities of phraseology and thought between Zephaniah and Deuteronomy may suggest that the prophet had access to the law book, thus arguing for a date after its discovery. Additionally, 2 Chr. 34:3-7 indicates that Josiah's reforms began several years prior to the discovery of the law book and were spread over a period of time. Zephaniah may well have been active among those who helped to further the reformation, but it is difficult to pinpoint with certainty the exact time of his ministry during the reign of Josiah.

Unity

While nearly all scholars accept a context during Josiah's reign, some, particularly those from an earlier generation, have regarded certain verses and/or units in the book as secondary and attributed them to a later exilic or postexilic editor. This is especially true of the sections of chs. 2 and 3 that express hope and salvation (2:7, 9b; 3:9-20 or portions thereof), because these motifs are deemed incongruent with the strong emphasis on judgment found in the book. However, several factors urge caution. The judgment and hope announced in Zephaniah are not antithetical to one another, but complementary, two sides of the same coin. The book proclaims purification through punishment, a purging judgment which issues in salvation. Moreover striking literary features serve to integrate the entire book, including the verses speaking of salvation. Additionally, there is good evidence that the various units composing the book are structured and ordered so as to proclaim a larger message, one that exceeds the sum of its parts. This purposeful literary arrangement suggests that the book is intended to be taken as a unity. Most recent interpreters, of Zephaniah and of other prophetic books as well, tend to follow a holistic approach.

Contents and Message

The entire book is dominated by one theme — the day of the Lord. Both judgment and salvation are aspects of this Day. Ch. 1 immediately launches into a description of the judgment aspect of this Day. It is coming soon (1:7, 14) and will result in a cataclysmic, divine punishment that threatens to sweep away every living creature (1:2-3). It is a judgment without parallel, surpassing even the Genesis Flood in its totality. This worldwide judgment serves to demonstrate Yahweh's universal sovereignty.

The consequences of this judgment for the inhabitants of Judah and Jerusalem are spelled out in chilling and vivid detail (1:4-13). Because of evils such as idolatry, violence and oppression (cf. 3:1-2), and spiritual apathy and complacency, Yahweh will pay an unwelcome personal "visit" (Heb. *pāqaḏ*, often translated "punish"; 1:8-9, 12) to his covenant people. In one of Zephaniah's best-known images, Yahweh will give the lie to those who consider him an inactive, absentee deity, an attitude tantamount to practical atheism, searching Jerusalem's dark areas with lamps to ensure that evildoers do not escape (v. 12). No human resource or skill can avail at that time (v. 18), implying that the only hope for deliverance is found in Yahweh himself. Yahweh's sacrificial banquet is prepared, but instead of being honored guests, the people of Judah are the sacrificial victim (vv. 7-8). Although military defeat by a foreign power (vv. 13, 16) may be included in this judgment, it is clear that the scope of the judgment transcends any military setback. Yahweh is the driving force behind his punishment and it will sweep over the entire world (v. 18).

Ch. 2 begins by sounding an appeal in light of this impending punishment. Judah is urgently summoned to assemble in repentance and humility, to seek Yahweh and to follow his commands (2:1-3). Such a dramatic change on their part might offer a glimmer of hope, but at this point it is only a glimmer (v. 3b). Then the emphasis on judgment is resumed, with several of Judah's traditional enemies targeted for punishment. The Philistines, Moabites and Ammonites, Cushites, and Assyria (esp. Nineveh) — nationalities representing the four points of the compass — will all experience destruction at the hand of Yahweh. This destruction is brought on by their arrogance and their treatment of the covenant people (vv. 8, 10, 15). In the process foreign gods are judged as well, by having their impotence exposed, thus manifesting Yahweh's supremacy and superiority over every other claimant to deity (v. 11).

However, this judgment is not an end in itself. Rather, in a foreshadowing of the note of hope on which the entire book concludes, it becomes a source of blessing for the remnant of Judah because it enables them to spread out from their own land and occupy territory formerly held by their enemies (2:7, 9b). The existence of this band of survivors is another important theme, guaranteeing that there will be those who emerge from the judgment and live under the blessing of Yahweh. The possibility of survival in 2:3 becomes a promise for the future in v. 7! Also, upon the downfall of their gods, some from the nations also outlast the judgment and bow down to Yahweh (2:11).

Ch. 3 connects with the last part of ch. 2 by continuing its focus on a wicked city destined for punishment, but the city is now Jerusalem (3:1-7). The Jerusalemites' knowledge of the punishment suffered by others does nothing to bring them back to God (vv. 6-7). Misled by their civil and religious leaders and following their example of oppression (v. 1), they obstinately refuse to repent and are in fact eager to engage in deeper corruption (v. 7b). Such rebellion can result in nothing other than the people of Jerusalem being summoned before the bar of God's judgment along with other wicked nations to receive their just deserts (v. 8).

But judgment does not have the final word. According to Zephaniah, worldwide judgment (3:8) does not mean complete annihilation. Rather, as in the Genesis Flood story, it connotes purification. As already implied in ch. 2, Yahweh will save and transform some people from the nations, engendering their worship of him (3:9-10). He will also deliver a remnant from the covenant people, humble and truthful people who seek him and follow his ways (vv. 11-13). They are promised the blessings of restoration, complete security, and worldwide renown due to Yahweh's love for them and presence in their midst (vv. 15-20). Yet although the book reaches its climax in this portrayal of deliverance and hope, the salvific aspect of the day of the Lord should not be overlooked or ignored.

In various aspects and nuances of his message, Zephaniah not only echoes his great prophetic predecessors, but also anticipates the final intervention and great consummation later proclaimed by the NT, particularly the book of Revelation.

See Day of the Lord.

Bibliography. I. J. Ball, *A Rhetorical Study of Zephaniah* (Berkeley, 1988); E. Ben Zvi, *A Historical-Critical Study of the Book of Zephaniah.* BZAW 198 (Berlin, 1991); A. Berlin, *Zephaniah.* AB 25A (New York, 1994); G. A. King, "The Message of Zephaniah: An Urgent Echo," *AUSS* 34 (1996): 211-22; J. J. M. Roberts, *Nahum, Habakkuk, and Zephaniah.* OTL (Louisville, 1991); O. P. Robertson, *The Books of Nahum, Habakkuk, and Zephaniah.* NICOT (Grand Rapids, 1990). Greg A. King

ZEPHATH (Heb. *ṣĕp̄aṯ*)
A Canaanite city in the Negeb, not far from Arad. It was not taken in the original Israelite conquest, but later the Judahites and Simeonites destroyed the city and renamed it Hormah (Judg. 1:17).

ZEPHATHAH (Heb. *ṣĕp̄aṯâ*)
A valley in Judah near Mareshah (Tell Sandaḥannah) where King Asa met and defeated the Ethiopian Zerah and his forces (2 Chr. 14:10[MT 9]). It may be identified with Wadi eṣ-Ṣāfiyeh.

ZEPHI (Heb. *ṣĕp̄î*), **ZEPHO** (*ṣĕp̄ô*)
The third son of Eliphaz and grandson of Esau (Zepho, Gen. 36:11; Zephi, 1 Chr. 1:36). Named among "the clans of the sons of Esau" (Gen. 36:15; MT "chiefs"), he was apparently the eponymous ancestor of an Edomite subgroup.

ZEPHON (Heb. *ṣĕp̄ôn*) (also ZIPHION)
The eldest son of Gad; ancestor of the Zephonites (Num. 26:15). At Gen. 46:16 his name is given as Ziphion.

ZER (Heb. *ṣēr*)
A fortified city in the tribal territory of Naphtali (Josh. 19:35). The otherwise unattested name may reflect a repetition of the preceding Heb. *wĕʿārê miḇṣār,* "fortified cities" (cf. LXX Gk. *Týros,* "Tyre").

ZERAH (Heb. *zeraḥ*) (also ZOHAR)

1. An Edomite, son of Reuel and grandson of Esau. His descendants became a subtribe of Edom (Gen. 36:13, 17; 1 Chr. 1:37).

2. An Edomite king, father of Jobab (Gen. 36:33; 1 Chr. 1:44).

3. A twin son of Judah and Tamar (Gen. 38:30; 46:12); founder of one of the subtribes of Judah (Num. 26:20; 1 Chr. 9:6; Neh. 11:24), and the ancestor of Achan (Josh. 7).

4. A son of Simeon, who founded one of the subtribes of Simeon (Num. 26:13; 1 Chr. 4:24). At Gen. 46:10; Exod. 6:15 he is called Zohar.

5.-6. Two Levites, a descendant of Gershom (1 Chr. 6:21[MT 6]) and a Kohathite (v. 41[26]).

7. "Zerah the Cushite" (MT), who attacked Judah with a large army but was routed by King Asa of Judah (2 Chr. 14:9-15[8-14]). Cush (also referred to as Nubia or Ethiopia) was a black African nation to the south of Egypt, and Cushite soldiers frequently served in the Egyptian army. This individual was probably a commander under Pharaoh Osorkon. Some scholars, however, argue that this Zerah was a Midianite, an Arab, or a Bedouin, noting the mention of camels and citing Hab. 3:7 as a Cushite/Midianite connection. However, the army of Zerah does not come riding on camels, like Bedouins, Arabs, or Midianites, but rather on chariots, like Egyptians and Cushites (cf. 2 Chr. 12:3); also, the camels of Zerah's forces are not listed with the army, but with the booty, apparently captured by Zerah as he advanced through Arabia and recaptured by Asa after Zerah's defeat.

Bibliography. J. D. Hays, "The Cushites: A Black Nation in the Bible," *BSac* 153 (1996): 396-409. J. DANIEL HAYS

ZERAHIAH (Heb. *zĕraḥyâ*)

1. The son of Uzzi and father of Meraioth, a descendant of Aaron (1 Chr. 6:6, 51[MT 5:32; 6:36]) and ancestor of Ezra (Ezra 7:4).

2. A man of the lineage of Pahath-moab, whose son Eliehoenai returned with Ezra from the Exile (Ezra 8:4).

ZERAHITES (Heb. *zarḥî*)

A name referring to several groups mentioned in the OT. Most prominent are a Judahite clan, descended from Zerah, son of Judah by his daughter-in-law Tamar (Gen. 38:30; 1 Chr. 9:6; 27:11, 13; Neh. 11:24), and a Simeonite clan (Num. 26:13; 1 Chr. 4:24). The relationship between the two may reflect the social history of early Israel; Simeon was subsequently absorbed into the tribe of Judah (cf. Gen. 49:7; Josh. 19:1). Other Zerahite groups include the offspring of Zerah, son of the Edomite Reuel (Gen. 36:13, 17; 1 Chr. 1:37), and the levitical clan of Zerahiah of Meraioth (1 Chr. 6:6[5:32]).

JOHN KALTNER

ZERED, BROOK (Heb. *naḥal zereḏ*)

A wadi marking the end of the wilderness wanderings of the children of Israel (Num. 21:12; Deut. 2:13-14) and forming the traditional border between Moab and Edom. Earlier scholars connected it with a tributary of Wadi Kerak or Wadi Môjib, but it is currently identified with Wadi el-Ḥesa. Other references often associated with this wadi are the "brook of the willows" (Isa. 15:7), the "brook of the Arabah" (Amos 6:14), or simply "this dry stream bed" (2 Kgs. 3:16).

Beginning in the Arabian desert of eastern Transjordan, the Wadi el-Ḥesa is 56 km. (35 mi.) long and flows in a northwesterly direction, emptying into the southern Ghor (southeastern plain) of the Dead Sea at eṣ-Ṣafi. The area is marginal for dryland agriculture, and recent survey information on 1074 sites found to the south of the wadi has shown that it has been inhabited from Palaeolithic to modern times with the exception of only a few periods.

Bibliography. B. MacDonald, *The Wadi el-Hasa Archaeological Survey, 1979-1983, West-Central Jordan* (Waterloo, Ont., 1988). PAUL J. RAY, JR.

ZEREDAH (Heb. *ṣĕrēḏâ*)

1. Probably the birthplace and certainly the place of residence of Jeroboam, the son of Nebat, who revolted against Solomon (1 Kgs. 11:26) and ultimately established his capital in Shechem (12:25). Jeroboam's identification as an Ephraimite indicates that Zeredah was located in the hill country of Ephraim. It may be Deir Ghassâneh (159161; ca. 24 km. [15 mi.] SW of Shechem) or the nearby 'Ain Ṣeridah. Zeredah is probably an alternate form for Zererah (Judg. 7:22).

2. A place in the Jordan Valley (2 Chr. 4:17). The name is a variant spelling of Zarethan (1 Kgs. 7:46). PAUL L. REDDITT

ZERERAH (Heb. *ṣĕrērâ*)

A place through which the Midianites fled following their ambush by Gideon (Judg. 7:22). The name may be a variant of Zeredah (NRSV mg) or Zarethan.

ZERESH (Heb. *ṣereš*)

The wife of Haman, Mordecai's antagonist (Esth. 5:10). At first she counseled Haman to build a gallows for Mordecai (Esth. 5:14), but soon predicted her husband's fall before his Jewish enemy (6:13).

ZERETH (Heb. *ṣereṯ*)

A Judahite; the first son of Ashhur and Helah (1 Chr. 4:7).

ZERETH-SHAHAR (Heb. *ṣereṯ haššaḥar*)

A Moabite city E of the Jordan River, given to the tribe of Reuben (Josh. 13:19). The LXX lists two towns, Serada and Sior on top of Mt. Emak (a transliteration of Heb. *'emeḵ*, "valley"). The location of the site is unconfirmed, although 'ez-Zārât (203111), near 'Attarus E of the Dead Sea, is a possibility. The traditional identification is ez-Zārâ, near Wadi Zerqā Ma'în, but only Roman ruins have been found there. PHILIP R. DREY

ZERI (Heb. *ṣĕrî*) (also IZRI)

One of the sons of the levitical family of Jeduthun, set apart by David for musical service in the temple (1 Chr. 25:3). At 1 Chr. 25:11 his name is given as Izri (Heb. *yiṣrî*).

ZEROR (Heb. *ṣĕrôr*)

A Benjaminite and ancestor of King Saul (1 Sam. 9:1).

ZERUAH (Heb. *ṣĕrû'â*)

An Ephraimite, the widow of Nebat and mother of King Jeroboam I (1 Kgs. 11:26).

ZERUBBABEL (Heb. *zĕrubbāḇel*)

The somewhat enigmatic postexilic figure with whom messianic language is associated in the books of Zechariah and Haggai. Identified frequently as "son of Shealtiel" (Ezra, Haggai), Zerubbabel was clearly a co-leader of the second major group of exiles with the priest Joshua. Under their leadership, a Jewish group was permitted to travel from the eastern Diaspora to Palestine (note the continued legacy of this co-leadership in Sir. 49:11-12).

The name itself is difficult (lit., "born/sown in Babylon"? "seed of Babylon"?), although it was not unprecedented for major figures among postexilic

Jews to carry non-Hebrew names (cf. Sheshbazzar and Mordecai, the latter built on the Babylonian patron god, Marduk; note also that some names were intentionally changed, as indicated in Dan. 1). If, however, Zerubbabel was a Davidide, then a diaspora name is all the more interesting. The royal lineage of Zerubbabel is suggested by the late source (1 Chr. 3:16-19), which lists Shealtiel as among the seven sons of Jehoiachin ("Jeconiah"). But the Chronicler lists Zerubbabel as the son of Pediah, Shealtiel's brother, against the witness of Zerubbabel as "son of Shealtiel" in Ezra and Haggai. The NT, in listing Zerubbabel in the genealogy of Jesus, clearly establishes the late Hellenistic belief that Zerubbabel was, in fact, in the royal line (Matt. 1:12, 13; Luke 3:27). Some scholars deny this royal lineage, preferring to see Zerubbabel as a court-appointed official who originally served in the court of Cambyses or possibly Cyrus. This view would suggest at least some historical background to the otherwise fanciful court legend in 1 Esdr. 3–4, where a counselor to King Darius proves his wisdom by proving that women are stronger than kings, wine, gold, and power, but truth is the greatest power of all. The delightful story — very much along the lines of the court tales of Dan. 1–6, Joseph, and Esther — is about three advisors to Darius, although the identification of the third as Zerubbabel may not be original to the folktale, and is somewhat awkwardly based on a single reference in 1 Esdr. 4:13.

Zerubbabel appears in Ezra as one of the two leaders (with the priest, Joshua) of a group of Hebrews who carry the permission of the Persian emperor to return to Palestine and begin rebuilding the temple (Ezra 2:2; 3:2, 8; 4:2, 3; 5:2). He is referred to as "governor" (Heb. *peḥâ*) in Hag. 1:1; 2:21, although also paired with Joshua, presumably sharing authority with the head of the temple (1:12).

Part of the mystery surrounding Zerubbabel is the strong messianic language of Zech. 4:6-10. Despite this initial presentation of Zerubbabel, it is Joshua who receives the crown in Zech. 6:9-14 and is called "Branch" — a term that may previously have referred to Zerubbabel, since 3:8 appears to refer to someone other than Joshua. Leroy Waterman, in a widely cited study, proposed that the biblical text has suppressed evidence of a rebellion led by Zerubbabel, instigated at the death of the Persian monarch Cambyses, which was then put down by Darius I when his reign was clearly established. Jon L. Berquist, however, points out that the chronology of such a proposed revolt does not work, since Zerubbabel's temple construction begins in 520 B.C.E., fully two years after the revolts break out in 522, and also after Darius' successful quelling of these revolts in 521.

Bibliography. J. L. Berquist, *Judaism in Persia's Shadow* (Minneapolis, 1996); L. Waterman, "The Camouflaged Purge of Three Messianic Conspirators," *JNES* 13 (1954): 73-78.

DANIEL L. SMITH-CHRISTOPHER

ZERUIAH (Heb. *ṣĕrûyâ*)
The mother of Abishai, Joab, and Asahel, the notorious "sons of Zeruiah" (2 Sam. 2:18; 1 Chr. 2:16). Abishai was the chief of David's Three (2 Sam. 23:18), Joab the commander of David's army (8:16), and Asahel one of David's Thirty (23:24). It is uncertain why these men are always identified by the name of their mother. Zeruiah may have been a prominent woman, eclipsing her husband, or possibly was named in order to connect her sons to David's family. Zeruiah and Abigail are listed only as the sisters of David (1 Chr. 2:16). 2 Sam. 17:25 identifies Abigail as the daughter of Nahash, perhaps an earlier, deceased husband of Jesse's wife, in which case Zeruiah might have been the half sister of David.

RONALD A. SIMKINS

ZETHAM (Heb. *zēṯām*)
A Gershonite Levite descended from Ladan (1 Chr. 23:8; 26:22).

ZETHAN (Heb. *zêṯān*)
A Benjaminite, son of Bilhan and descendant of Jediael (1 Chr. 7:10).

ZETHAR (Heb. *zēṯar*)
One of the seven eunuchs who served the Persian king Ahasuerus as chamberlains (Esth. 1:10).

ZEUS (Gk. *Zeús*)
The Greek deity considered to be the greatest of the Olympian gods. Zeus was clearly of Indo-european origin, and the genitive of Zeus (Gk. *Diós*) was the word for god in various Indo-european languages. Zeus was portrayed as the god of the sky and weather (esp. thunderbolts). Homer often called him "the father of gods and men," the ruler and protector of all. The Romans associated him with their Jupiter. According to Hesiod's *Theogony*, at birth Zeus' mother Rhea hid him in a cave from his father Kronos. When Kronos wished to devour his son, Rhea conned him into swallowing a large stone instead. Later, Zeus, along with the other Olympian gods, overthrew the older Titans, including Kronos (*Theog.* 472-508; 621-825). In much mythology, Zeus was the legitimate spouse of Hera (though sometimes paired with Dione), but he engaged in a series of unfaithful associations with other goddesses and women. Through such relations, he became the father of Athena, Persephone, Apollo, Artemis, Ares, Hephaestus, Hermes, the Muses, and Dionysius, among others. Zeus was described as the source of universal laws, defender of justice, benefactor of victory, guardian of hospitality, revealer of the future, dispenser of good and evil destinies, and savior of mankind (Zeus Soter). Although supreme among gods, he appears to have been limited by the power of Fate. The personality of Zeus inspired much art and literature, including Phidias' famous gold and ivory colossus at Olympia and Cleanthes' hymns to Zeus.

According to Acts 14:8-18 the inhabitants of Lystra identified the miracle-working Paul and Barnabas with Hermes and Zeus respectively. An earlier legend had described Hermes and Zeus as earthly visitors in human form in the "Phrygian hills" near Lystra (Ovid *Metam.* 8.616-724). Inscriptional remains (3rd century A.D.) also exhibit the association of these gods in the indigenous worship of the surrounding region. The Codex Beza version of Acts 14:13 speaks of "the local Zeus-before-the-city," implying a native cult.

2 Macc. 6:2 reports that Antiochus IV Epiphanes planned to name the Jerusalem temple the "temple of Olympian Zeus" and the Gerizim temple the "temple of Zeus-the-Friend-of-Strangers" (cf. "Abomination of Desolation," 1 Macc. 1:54; Dan. 11:31; 12:11).

Bibliography. K. W. Arafat, *Classical Zeus* (Oxford, 1990); H. Lloyd-Jones, *The Justice of Zeus,* 2nd ed. (Berkeley, 1983); C. R. Long, *The Twelve Gods of Greece and Rome.* EPRO 107 (Leiden, 1987).

PAUL ANTHONY HARTOG

ZIA (Heb. *zîaʿ*)
A Gadite who lived in Bashan (1 Chr. 5:13).

ZIBA (Heb. *ṣîḇāʾ*)
A steward of the household of Saul. Out of David's desire to do kindness to the house of Saul for Jonathan's sake (1 Sam. 20:14-17, 42), David queries Ziba, who brings Jonathan's son Mephibosheth to the king's attention (2 Sam. 9:1-4). After elevating Mephibosheth to the king's dole, David bestows upon him a royal grant of all Saul's former land holdings. David then places Ziba, his 15 sons, and his 20 servants (2 Sam. 19:17[MT 18]) at the disposal of Mephibosheth to manage and work this estate (9:9-10).

When David evacuates Jerusalem during the attempted coup of Absalom, Ziba arrives with transport for David and provisions for his entourage. Ziba's actions raise questions in David's mind regarding the whereabouts and motives of Mephibosheth. When Ziba implicates Mephibosheth in a treasonous effort to restore the house of Saul to the throne, David transfers all Mephibosheth's land holdings to Ziba (2 Sam. 16:1-4).

Following the death of Absalom, Ziba with his sons and servants assist the king in crossing the Jordan on his return to Jerusalem. When Mephibosheth also arrives, an impromptu legal hearing is held at which he charges Ziba with deceit and slander. David divides the former land holdings of Saul between Ziba and Mephibosheth (2 Sam. 19:24-30[25-31]). JOHN D. FORTNER

ZIBEON (Heb. *ṣiḇʿôn*)
1. The father of Anah and the grandfather of Oholibamah, Esau's wife (Gen. 36:14; called a Hivite at v. 2).

2. A Horite clan chief, the third son of Seir (Gen. 36:20, 24, 29; 1 Chr. 2:38, 40).

ZIBIA (Heb. *ṣiḇyāʾ*)
One of the seven sons of Shaharaim and Hodesh; head of a Benjaminite father's house in postexilic Jerusalem (1 Chr. 8:9, 28).

ZIBIAH (Heb. *ṣiḇyâ*)
The mother of King Joash (Jehoash) of Judah, from Beer-sheba (2 Kgs. 12:1[MT 2] = 2 Chr. 24:1).

ZICHRI (Heb. *ziḵrî*) (also ZABDI)
The name is possibly a short version of Zechariah.

1. A Levite, son of Izhar and brother of Korah (Exod. 6:21).

2. A Benjaminite, son of Shimei (1 Chr. 8:19).

3. A Benjaminite, son of Shashak (1 Chr. 8:23).

4. A Benjaminite, son of Jeroham (1 Chr. 8:27).

5. A Levite, the son of Asaph and ancestor of Mattaniah (1 Chr. 9:15). At Neh. 11:17 he is called Zabdi.

6. Eliezer's descendant who was in charge of the treasuries of gifts dedicated to the Lord (1 Chr. 26:25). He was the father of Shelomith and son of Joram.

7. A Reubenite and father of Eliezer; an officer in David's court (1 Chr. 27:16).

8. A Judahite and father of Amasiah (2 Chr. 17:16).

9. The father of Elishaphat, one of five commanders who helped to overthrow Queen Athaliah (2 Chr. 23:1).

10. A warrior and Ephraimite who killed three men, including Maaseiah, son of King Ahaz (2 Chr. 28:7).

11. A Benjaminite, the father of Joel; an overseer during the time of Nehemiah (Neh. 11:9).

12. The head of the priestly family of Abijah in the days of the high priest Joiakim (Neh. 12:17).

ROBIN GALLAHER BRANCH

ZIDDIM (Heb. *ṣiddîm*)
An otherwise unknown fortified city assigned to the tribe of Naphtali (Josh. 19:35 NRSV). The Hebrew text is unclear and may not indicate a place name.

ZIHA (Heb. *ṣîḥāʾ*, *ṣiḥāʾ*)
1. The head of a line of temple servants (Nethinim) who returned from exile with Zerubbabel (Ezra 2:43; Neh. 7:46).

2. An overseer of the postexilic temple servants (Neh. 11:21).

ZIKLAG (Heb. *ṣiqlag*)
A town in southwest Palestine, at the southern edge of the Shephelah. It was an ancestral holding of Simeon (Josh. 19:5) and then Judah (15:31). According to 1 Chr. 4:30-31 when David became king of Judah, Ziklag and several other towns in its vicinity became part of Judah. Apparently Josh. 15:31 reflects the time of the Monarchy.

While Saul ruled Israel, Ziklag was in Philistine hands, and Achish, king of Gath, gave Ziklag to David as a fief (1 Sam. 27:1-6). After David had lived there for a year and four months, the Amalekites attacked the town and destroyed it while David was away (1 Sam. 30:1-3). The Amalekites plundered Ziklag, but David and his band pursued and defeated them somewhere south of Gaza. David then returned to Ziklag's remains. Shortly afterward, David left Ziklag for Hebron, where the Judahites anointed him king of Judah.

The exact location of Ziklag is unknown. Two modern sites are possible candidates: Tel Ḥalif (Lahav)/Tell el-Khuweilefeh (137087), ca. 16 km. (10 mi.) NE of Beer-sheba, and Tell esh-Shariʿa/Tel Seraʿ (119088), midway between Beer-sheba and Gaza. Excavations at Tel Ḥalif show it also was under Philistine influence ca. 1000 B.C.E., and it flourished during the following centuries as well. Tell esh-Shariʿa is a more likely location since it is closer to Philistia. Excavations there have revealed several phases of occupation in the Iron Age, all with a strong Philistine presence. The most intense building activity occurred during the 10th-9th centuries. Typical Israelite four-room houses and impressive buildings of ashlar masonry have been found. If this is the correct site for Ziklag, it was rebuilt after David's departure and remained part of Judah.

PAUL S. ASH

ZILLAH (Heb. *ṣillâ*)
One of Lamech's two wives, and the mother of Tubal-cain and Naamah (Gen. 4:19, 22-23).

ZILLETHAI (Heb. *ṣillĕṯay*)

1. A son of Shimei; head of a Benjaminite family house in postexilic Jerusalem (1 Chr. 8:20).

2. A Manassite military leader who deserted to David at Ziklag and became a commander in his army (1 Chr. 12:20[MT 21]).

ZILPAH (Heb. *zilpâ*)
The maid of Laban, whom he gave to his daughter Leah when she married Jacob (Gen. 29:24). Subsequently Leah, who had become barren, gave Zilpah to Jacob "as a wife"; she bore him Gad and Asher (Gen. 30:9-13; cf. 35:26; 37:2; 46:18).

ZIMMAH (Heb. *zimmâ*)
A Gershonite Levite, the father of Joah (1 Chr. 6:20, 42[MT 5, 27]; 2 Chr. 29:12).

ZIMRAN (Heb. *zimrān*)
The first son of Abraham and Keturah (Gen. 25:2; 1 Chr. 1:32); ancestor of an Arabian clan.

ZIMRI (Heb. *zimrî*) **(PERSON)** (also ZABDI)

1. A leader among the Simeonites; the son of Salu (Num. 25:6-18). He brought the Midianite princess Cozbi into his tent, for which both were executed by Phinehas. The event is presented as part of Israel's apostasy at Peor and the legitimization of the Zadokite priesthood.

2. King of Israel in the early 9th century B.C.E. Zimri was commander of half of Israel's chariotry when he began his coup and assassinated King Elah; he then orchestrated the death of all males in the house of Baasha (1 Kgs. 16:8-14). However, support fell to Omri, commander of Israel's army, and Zimri's reign lasted but one week. When Omri was about to capture the capital Tirzah, Zimri committed suicide by setting the royal palace on fire (1 Kgs. 16:15-20). Later, "Zimri" became an insulting epithet for one who murders his master under the guise of peace (2 Kgs. 9:31).

3. The son of Zerah and grandson of Judah and Tamar (1 Chr. 2:6). He is called Zabdi at Josh. 7:1.

4. A descendant of Saul; father of Moza and son of Jehoaddah/Jarah (1 Chr. 8:36; 9:42).

GARY W. LIGHT

ZIMRI (Heb. *zimrî*) **(PLACE)**
A kingdom that is to suffer Yahweh's wrath (Jer. 25:25, "cup of wrath"). Such a place in unknown. It may be that the name Zimri should be read as Zimki and understood in the Hebrew athbash code as Elam (listed next in Jer. 25:25). This is suggested by MT's use of an athbash for Babylon, Sheshach (Jer. 25:26) and the fact that the LXX omits both references in its translation. GARY W. LIGHT

ZIN (Heb. *ṣin*), **WILDERNESS OF**
A desert area in northeast Sinai which included Kadesh-barnea. The Negeb is to the north, the Arabah and Edom to the east, and the wilderness of Paran to the south. The wilderness of Zin constituted part of the southern border of Canaan (Num. 34:3; Josh. 15:1) and was the southern extent of the land spied out by the Israelites during the Exodus wandering (Num. 13:21). Miriam died while the Israelites were camped in the wilderness of Zin at Kadesh-barnea, and Moses sinned at the waters of Meribah, forfeiting his right to enter the Promised Land (Num. 27:14; Deut. 32:51). The wilderness of Zin should be distinguished from the wilderness of Sin (Heb. *sin;* not differentiated in LXX or Vulg.).

BRADFORD SCOTT HUMMEL

ZINA (Heb. *zînāʾ*)
A Levite, the son of Shimei of the family of Gershon/Gershom (1 Chr. 23:10); probably a scribal error for Zizah in v. 11.

ZION (Heb. *ṣîyôn;* Gk. *Siṓn*)
An ancient name for various aspects of Jerusalem, Judah, and the whole country, and also a metaphor for the people of Yahweh. The original meaning of the term is uncertain. Possible suggestions include a rock, stronghold, a dry place, or running water.

The name Zion was first mentioned for the Jebusite fortress ("the stronghold of Zion") in 2 Sam. 5:6-10. David took Jerusalem from the Jebusites, and Zion was subsequently equated with the name Jerusalem, the city of David (1 Kgs. 8:1 = 2 Chr. 5:2). Associated with this is an understanding that the temple mount, Mt. Zion, is a dwelling place of Yahweh, the divine King of Israel (Ps. 9:11[MT 12]; 76:2[3]; Isa. 8:18; 18:7; 24:23; Joel 3:17[4:17]). With the transfer of the ark from the city of David to the temple built by Solomon, Yahweh was said to dwell in the Zion-temple compound.

The term is also frequently used for the whole of Jerusalem (Isa. 2:3; 33:14; Joel 2:32[3:5]). One apparent exception is its parallel use with Samaria (Amos 6:1).

Zion also refers to the inhabitants of Jerusalem or the whole people of Israel. This includes such expressions as "sons of Zion" (Lam. 4:2), "daughter(s) of Zion" (Cant. 3:11; Isa. 3:16; 4:4; also Matt. 21:5; John 12:15), "daughter Zion" (Jer. 4:31; 6:2; Zech. 9:9), and "virgin daughter Zion" (Isa. 37:22; Lam. 2:13; 2 Kgs. 19:21). This metaphorical usage continues in the NT, in reference to the Church, "heavenly Jerusalem" (Heb. 12:22), or in the eschatological battle (Rev. 14:1).

At present the hill S of the southwestern portion of the Old City of Jerusalem, where the traditional site of David's tomb and the upper room of the Last Supper are located, is called "Mt. Zion." Evidently by the Byzantine period the name had been transferred to the southwestern hill (cf. Josephus *BJ* 5.4.1 [137]). AARON W. PARK

ZIOR (Heb. *ṣîʿōr*)
A town in the hill country of Judah SSW of Hebron (Josh. 15:54).

ZIPH (Heb. *zîp̱*) **(PERSON)**

1. A descendant of Caleb (1 Chr. 2:42); ancestor of a clan or region in Judah.

2. A Judahite from the line of Caleb; the eldest son of Jehallelel (1 Chr. 4:16).

ZIPH (Heb. *zîp̱*) **(PLACE)**

1. A town in the hill country of Judah S of Hebron (Josh. 15:55), said to have been fortified at a later time by Rehoboam (2 Chr. 11:8). The town shared its name with the desert region to the east (the wilderness of Ziph) where David and his men fled after breaking away from Saul (1 Sam. 23:14-15). Following a visit from Jonathan, the people of Ziph betrayed David to Saul (1 Sam. 23:16-24; 26:1). During the resulting campaign David and Abishai entered Saul's camp and stole his spear and water jar, but refused to kill him (1 Sam. 26:6-25; cf. Ps. 54 superscript[MT 1-2]). Most scholars identify the ancient town with modern Tell Zîf (162098), ca. 5 km. (3 mi.) SW of Hebron, although the history of occupation at this site is unknown.

2. A town in the southern Negeb close to the border with Edom (Josh. 15:24). A site named Khirbet ez-Zeifeh (156048) is located in the appropriate region, but it has not yet been examined by archaeologists. Some scholars question the very existence of this town, since in the various LXX versions the name Ziph is either corrupt or omitted entirely. WADE R. KOTTER

ZIPHAH (Heb. *zîp̱â*)
The second son of Jehallelel of the tribe of Judah (1 Chr. 4:16).

ZIPHION (Heb. *ṣip̱yôn*) (also ZEPHON)
The firstborn son of Gad, grandson of Jacob and Zilpah (Gen. 46:16); called Zephon at Num. 26:15.

ZIPHRON (Heb. *zip̱rôn*)
A city along the northern border of the land of Canaan between Zedad and Hazar-enan (Num. 34:9). The exact location is unknown. PETE F. WILBANKS

ZIPPOR (Heb. *ṣippôr, ṣippōr*)
The father of the Moabite king Balak, who sought to hire Balaam to curse Israel (Num. 22:2, 4, 10, 16; 23:18; Josh. 24:9; Judg. 11:25).

ZIPPORAH (Heb. *ṣippōrâ*)
Wife of Moses and daughter of a Midianite priest, Reuel/Jethro (Exod. 2:16-22). Zipporah gave birth to two sons, Gershom and Eliezer.

Zipporah's most important role comes in the mysterious account of a threat to Moses' life in Exod. 4:24-26, in which she is responsible for saving Moses from a divine attack on his life. The reason for the attempt to kill Moses is not given, but Zipporah's quick thinking and acting ward off the divine menace. According to the narrative, she performs a threefold act: cutting off her son's foreskin, touching his feet (perhaps a euphemism for his genitals), and saying the words, "Surely you are a bridegroom of blood (Heb. *ḥăṯan dāmîm*) to me!" (Exod. 4:25). This has been compared to some kind of a ritual or priestly function, but there several problems of interpretation. To whom does the pronoun "he" refer in the second step, Moses or the son? The narrative leaves it unclear as to whom Zipporah spoke the words in Exod. 4:25. Also, there is considerable debate about the interpretation of *ḥăṯan dāmîm*. In addition, there is no information about how Zipporah knew what to do to save her husband.

According to the tradition found in Exod. 18:1-9, Zipporah and her sons remained with Jethro during Moses' involvement in the Exodus. Jethro brought Zipporah and the children with him when he met the Israelites in the wilderness.
LISA W. DAVISON

ZIV (Heb. *ziw*)
An early Canaanite name for the second month of the Hebrew religious year (Apr./May). Its postexilic Babylonian name was Iyyar.

ZIZ (Heb. *ṣîṣ*)
An ascent from En-gedi to near Tekoa through which the Moabites and their allies attempted to attack King Jehoshaphat of Judah (2 Chr. 20:16; ca. 850 B.C.E.). While this steep road was difficult, it was the shortest route from Moab to Judah. Possibly as a result of the invasion, Judean forts were built on the summits of Masada and En-gedi. The ascent is identified with Wadi Ḥaṣâṣah/Naḥal Ḥaṣeṣôn. BRADFORD SCOTT HUMMEL

ZIZA (Heb. *zîzāʾ*)

1. The son of Shiphi who with other Simeonite family heads led an expansion of their tribe toward Gedor (1 Chr. 4:37-40).

2. A son of King Rehoboam of Judah and his favorite wife, Maacah (2 Chr. 11:20).

ZIZAH (Heb. *zîzâ*) (also ZINA)
A Gershonite Levite, the second son of Shimei (1 Chr. 23:11). The name occurs as Zina in 1 Chr. 23:11.

ZOAN (Heb. *ṣōʿan*)
The biblical name of the Egyptian capital of the 21st and 22nd Dynasties, Djaʿnet (Gk. Tanis; Isa. 19:11, 13). The city is located on a branch of the Nile in the eastern Delta, at modern San el-Hagar, ca. 47 km. (29 mi.) S of the Mediterranean. The city was excavated by Auguste Mariette (1850s), W. M. Flinders Petrie (1883-86), and extensively by Pierre Montet (1929-1951). The city was initially identified with the Hyksos capital, Avaris, and the Ramesside capital, Pi-Ramesses, because of the numerous blocks and monuments bearing Ramesside and Hyksos names. However, it is now certain that Avaris is to be identified with Tell ed-Dabʿa and Pi-Ramesses with a site just N of Avaris near modern Qantir, ca. 48 km. (30 mi.) S of Zoan. Blocks and monuments from these cities were salvaged by the later builders of Zoan.

Zoan came to prominence in Egypt when Smendes (1070-1044 B.C.E.), a resident of Zoan and governor of Lower Egypt under Rameses XI, established the 21st Dynasty upon Rameses' death. Zoan became the administrative center of Lower Egypt. The prominent feature of Zoan is the great temple of Amon built by Psusennes I (1040-992), with additions by Siamun (978-59), Osorkon III (883-55), and Shoshenq III (835-783). The tombs of Psusennes I, Amenemope (993-84), Osorkon III, and Shoshenq III, along with two anonymous tombs, were found intact within the temple complex, just below ground level. Although the administrative center shifted to Sais in the Late Period, Zoan continued to serve as the capital of the 19th nome and to be subject to royal building projects into the Ptolemaic period.

The biblical phrase "fields of Zoan" (Ps. 78:12, 43) is an accurate Hebrew translation of the Egyptian phrase ("Field of the Storm") which refers to the district of Djaʿnet. RONALD A. SIMKINS

ZOAR (Heb. *ṣōʿar*)
The southernmost city in the "valley of Jericho" (Deut. 34:3; Gen. 13:10). One of the five "cities of the valley" in a coalition (with Sodom, Gomorrah, Admah, and Zeboiim) that rebelled against King Chedorlaomer of Elam (Gen. 14:2, 8). Because the kings of the other cities are called by name, scholars have suggested that Bela was the original name of the king of Zoar; however, Bela could simply be the earlier name of Zoar, as all versions attest. Zoar escaped the fate of the other cities of the valley, and provided a temporary refuge for Lot and his daughters (Gen. 19:22-23, 30). Later prophetic texts mention Zoar in the context of God's judgment on Moab. Fugitives from Moab will flee as far as Zoar (Isa. 15:5), and the sound of their cry will be heard in Zoar (Jer. 48:34).

Zoar continues to be attested in records until the Middle Ages. All the references to Zoar, including its identification on the Madeba Map, suggest that it was located on the south bank of the Brook Zered (Wadi el-Ḥesa) in the area of eṣ-Ṣâfî (194049), the territory of Edom.

RONALD A. SIMKINS

ZOBAH (Heb. *ṣôḇâ;* Aram. *ṣôḇāʾ*)
Aram-zobah, a powerful Aramean state along the upper Orontes River in the Beqaʿ Valley of Lebanon. It was mentioned among the enemies of Saul of Israel (1 Sam. 14:47). During the reign of David Hadad-ezer was the king of Aram-zobah by way of a dynastic union with another Aramean state, Beth-rehob. This Aramean king ruled over a vast territory in the Damascus area, had vassals in northern Transjordan (2 Sam. 10:6; 1 Chr. 19:6), was influential as far as Ammon in the south and Hamath in the north (2 Sam. 8:9-10), and expanded beyond the Euphrates (8:3; 10:16; 1 Chr. 19:16). Hadad-ezer was ultimately defeated by David. Soon thereafter, Aram-zobah was replaced by another Aramean dynasty from Damascus (2 Sam. 8:5; 10:16-19).

The "king of Aram" who seized two Euphrates cities from Assyria at the beginning of the 10th century B.C. may have been Hadad-ezer of Aram.

Bibliography. A. Malamat, "Aspects of the Foreign Policies of David and Solomon," *JNES* 22 (1963): 1-17; "The Kingdom of David and Solomon in Its Contact with Egypt and Aram Naharaim," *BA* 21 (1958): 96-102, repr. in *BAR* 2, ed. D. N. Freedman and E. F. Campbell (Garden City, 1964), 89-98; B. Mazar, "The Aramean Empire and Its Relations with Israel," *BA* 25 (1962): 97-120, repr. in *BAR* 2, ed. Freedman and Campbell (Garden City, 1964), 127-51; W. T. Pitard, *Ancient Damascus* (Winona Lake, 1987). MARK W. CHAVALAS

ZOBEBAH (Heb. *ṣōḇēḇâ*)
A son (or subgroup) of Koz of the tribe of Judah (1 Chr. 4:8).

ZOHAR (Heb. *ṣōḥar*)

1. The father of Ephron the Hittite (Gen. 23:8; 25:9), from whom Abraham purchased the cave of Machpelah.

2. An alternate name for Simeon's son Zerah (**4;** Gen. 46:10; Exod. 6:15).

3. Alternate reading for the Judahite Izhar (**2**), son of Helah (1 Chr. 4:7; NRSV mg).

ZOHETH (Heb. *zôḥēṯ*)
The elder son of Ishi of the tribe of Judah (1 Chr. 4:20).

ZOPHAH (Heb. *ṣôpaḥ*)
A select warrior and family head of the tribe of Asher; son of Helam/Hotham (1 Chr. 7:35-36).

ZOPHAI (Heb. *ṣôpay*) (also ZUPH)
The son of Elkanah, a Levite of the family of Kohath and an ancestor of Samuel (1 Chr. 6:26[MT 11]). He is called Zuph at 1 Chr. 6:35(20); cf. 1 Sam. 1:1.

ZOPHAR (Heb. *ṣôp̱ar*)
The Naamathite, one of Job's three friends who intends to commiserate with Job (Job 2:11) but ends up arguing with him (16:2). Zophar's name appears nowhere else in the OT; he does not come from Naamah in Judah (Josh. 15:41). Edomite connections are argued.

In the first two dialogue cycles in the book of Job, each friend offers a speech of approximately the same length; Zophar speaks last. The third cycle contains no speech from Zophar, and various explanations have been offered for accidental and deliberate dislocation.

Zophar's first speech (Job 11:1-20) reproaches Job for his claims of innocence (vv. 2-6), emphasizes God's inscrutability (vv. 7-12), and counsels repentance (vv. 13-20). He argues that God has not punished Job to the extent he deserves (Job 11:6). Zophar's second speech (Job 20:1-29) stresses the inescapable fate of the wicked. Locked in retributive theology, his tone is aggressive and contemptuous. Ultimately, Zophar is rebuked by God (Job 42:7-9). PATRICIA A. MACNICOLL

ZOPHIM (Heb. *ṣōp̱îm*)
A place to which Balak took Balaam so he could look out over the Hebrews and curse them (Num. 23:14). The "field of Zophim" (or possibly "field of watchers") was located near or on top of Mt. Pisgah in the northern plains of Moab.

ZORAH (Heb. *ṣorʿâ*)
A small village in the tribal inheritance of Dan (Josh. 19:41), later annexed to Judah (15:33). The site is identified with Ṣarʿah/Tel Zorʿa (148131), ca. 21 km. (13 mi.) W of Jerusalem. High upon a hill, the settlement controlled the highway through the "great fosse" passing along the western base of the hill country connecting the Judean Shephelah and the road to Jerusalem. Zorah may have had limited access to fields in the valley, but nearby Beth-shemesh maintained strict control over the area. The Amarna Letters call Zorah *Sia-ar-ha.*

Samson's Danite father, Manoah, was a Zorahite (Judg. 13:2). The village was fortified by Rehoboam prior to the invasion by Shishak of Egypt (2 Chr. 11:10) and was resettled in the postexilic period (Neh. 11:29).

Bibliography. G. A. Smith, *The Historical Geography of the Holy Land,* 25th rev. ed. (New York, 1966). DAVID C. MALTSBERGER

ZOROASTRIANISM
The religious tradition that bears the name of its prophetic founder Zoroaster (Gk. *Zōroastrēs;* O. Pers. *Zarathustra*). It survives today primarily in Iran and India. Zoroastrianism arose as a result of a dual migration of Aryans, one into Iran ("the land of the Aryans"), the other into India, some time before 1000 B.C.E. The western Aryans were polytheistic, their most important gods being the sun, moon, stars, earth, fire, water, and wind. Their chief god was Mithra, god of war, light, and loyalty. Religious rituals included lighting a fire, pouring out *haoma* juice as a libation, and cereal or animal sacrifice.

Zoroaster apparently revised this religion along somewhat dualistic lines. In his worldview, two basic forces struggled for control of the world: Spenta Mainyu, the good spirit, and Angra Mainyu, the evil spirit. The origin of the two spirits is not clear, but Angra Mainyu seems to have come into being only with the creation of the world. Zoroaster avoided the moral dilemma of dualism (i.e., which spirit to follow) by postulating the existence of one supreme god, Ahura Mazda, who is symbolized by fire and to whom alone worship is due. Ahura Mazda makes his will known through Spenta Mainyu.

This belief in two spirits reflects the existential perception that humans are pulled morally in two different directions. Apparently, flesh is bad and pulls one toward Angra Mainyu, while spirit is good and pulls one toward Spenta Mainyu. Hence, humans often make the wrong moral choice and commit evil. The solution to human ills is to follow prescribed works, including worship, prayer, and moral purity, though not celibacy. Rites of passage include an initiation of all children before puberty, weddings, and funerals, in which the body is wrapped in white cloth and then placed atop a Tower of Silence for disposal through exposure; it is never cremated, since dead flesh would contaminate the holy fire.

Some scholars see Zoroastrianism as the source of dualistic thinking in Judaism. Cyrus the Great presumably was a Zoroastrian, though Achaemenid texts only mention Ahura Mazda, not Zoroaster. Any direct influence on the NT is dubious.

PAUL L. REDDITT

ZUAR (Heb. *ṣûʿār*)
The father of Nethanel, the leader of the tribe of Issachar during the wilderness wanderings (Num. 1:8; 2:5; 7:18, 23; 10:15).

ZUPH (Heb. *ṣûp̱*) **(PERSON)** (also ZOPHAI)
An ancestor of Samuel, designated an Ephraimite at 1 Sam. 1:1 and a Levite at 1 Chr. 6:35(MT 20; **K** "Ziph"). He is called Zophai (a Levite) at 1 Chr. 6:26(11).

ZUPH (Heb. *ṣûp̱*) **(PLACE)**
The district where Saul searched for his father's lost asses (1 Sam. 9:5). Presumably the "land of Zuph" was in Ephraim and received its name from the family of Zuph (cf. Ramathaim-zophim, 1 Sam. 1:1 MT).

ZUR (Heb. *ṣûr*)

1. One of the five kings of Midian slain in battle against Israel (Num. 31:8) and the Amorites (Josh. 13:21). His daughter Cozbi and her Israelite husband Zimri were killed by Phinehas (Num. 25:15).

2. A Benjaminite, the second son of Jeiel and Maacah (1 Chr. 8:30; 9:36).

ZURIEL (Heb. *ṣûrî'ēl*)
A Levite; son of Abihail, and head of the Merarites during the wilderness wanderings (Num. 3:35).

ZURISHADDAI (Heb. *ṣûrîšadday*)
The father of Shelumiel, the leader of the tribe of Simeon during the wilderness wanderings (Num. 1:6; 2:12; 7:36, 41; 10:19).

ZUZIM (Heb. *zûzim*)
A people destroyed by Chedorlaomer and his alliance (Gen. 14:5). Their territory lay E of the Jordan, and Ham was their principal city. The Zuzim are likely to be the same as the Zamzummim (Heb. "strong peoples"; cf. LXX Gk. *éthnē ischyrá*) mentioned in Deut. 2:20. In Genesis they are listed alongside the Rephaim and the Emim, but in Deuteronomy both the Zamzummim and the Emim are equated with the Rephaim.

Christian M. M. Brady